CONGRESSIONAL QUARTERLY

Almanac

97th CONGRESS

2nd SESSION 1982

VOLUME XXXVIII

Congressional Quarterly Inc.

Washington, D.C.

CQ 1982 Almanac

Editor and President
Eugene Patterson

Publisher
Wayne P. Kelley

Executive Editor
Peter A. Harkness

General Manager
Robert C. Hur

Director, Research and Development
Robert E. Cuthriell

EDITORIAL DEPARTMENT
Charles W. Hucker *(Managing Editor)*
Kathryn Waters Gest *(Asst. Managing Editor)*
Alan Ehrenhalt *(Political Editor)*

News Editors: Martha Angle, Marsha Canfield, Mary Cohn, Peg O'Hara

Assistant Political Editor: Michael Glennon

Reporters: Nadine Cohodas, Rhodes Cook, Joseph A. Davis, Harrison Donnelly, Phil Duncan, John Felton, Pamela Fessler, Diane Granat, Rob Gurwitt, Alan Murray, Brian Nutting, Andy Plattner, Judy Sarasohn, Susan Smith, Dale Tate, Pat Towell, Tom Watson, Elizabeth Wehr, Laura B. Weiss, Elder Witt

Production Editor: William L. Bonn

Editorial Coordinator: Colleen McGuiness

Proofreaders: Eugene J. Gabler, Gina L. Henderson

Editorial Assistants: Renee Amrine, Lynnemarie Hofman, Leah Fackos Klumph, Frank V. Ortiz

RESEARCH DEPARTMENT: Michael L. Koempel *(Director)*, Wayne Walker *(Asst. Director)*, Edna Frazier-Cromwell *(Librarian)*, Diane Huffman *(Indexer)*, Julia McCue *(Seminar Manager)*, Walter E. Eling, Diane R. Galligan, Joan Levit, James M. McCarthy, Sandra McDermin, Barbara L. Miracle, Florence A. Mosebach, John Noukas, Ben Z. Rose, Mary Anne Rothwell, T. Siafa Sherman Jr.

ART DEPARTMENT: Richard A. Pottern *(Director)*, Robert O. Redding, Belle T. Burkhart

PRODUCTION: I. D. Fuller *(Manager)*, Maceo Mayo *(Asst. Manager)*, Sydney E. Garriss *(Computer Services)*

SALES AND PROMOTION: James V. Bullard *(Manager)*

CONTROLLER: Jonathan C. Angier

BOOK DEPARTMENT: David R. Tarr *(Director)*, Joanne D. Daniels *(Director, CQ Press)*

NEWSLETTERS: Kenneth B. Dalecki *(Editor)*

CONGRESSIONAL MONITOR: Michaela Buhler *(Editor)*, Robert Healy *(Managing Editor)*

EDITORIAL RESEARCH REPORTS: Hoyt Gimlin *(Editor)*, Sandra Stencel *(Managing Editor)*

WASHINGTON ALERT SERVICE: Ross Evans *(Manager)*, Steve Newman *(Editor)*

Chairman of the Board: Nelson Poynter (1903-1978)

Library of Congress No. 47-41081
International Standard Book No. 0-87187-269-2

Copyright 1983 by Congressional Quarterly Inc.
1414 22nd Street, N.W., Washington, D.C. 20037

Congressional Quarterly Inc.

Congressional Quarterly Inc. is an editorial research service and publishing company serving clients in the fields of news, education, business and government. Congressional Quarterly, in its basic publication, the CQ Weekly Report, covers Congress, government and politics. Congressional Quarterly also publishes hardbound reference books and paperback books on public affairs. The service was founded in 1945 by Henrietta and Nelson Poynter.

An affiliated service, Editorial Research Reports, publishes reports each week on a wide range of subjects. Editorial Research Reports also publishes hardbound and paperback books.

CS
Ref.
328.73
C749a
1982

Almanac Editor: Mary Cohn
Editorial Coordinator: Renee Amrine
Assistant Editors: Martha Angle, Marsha Canfield, John Felton, Kathryn Waters Gest, Michael Glennon, Peg O'Hara, Elder Witt
Editorial Assistants: William L. Bonn, Eugene J. Gabler, Gina L. Henderson, Colleen McGuiness, Evelyn Russell
Other Contributors: Irwin B. Arieff, Nadine Cohodas, Rhodes Cook, Joseph A. Davis, Harrison Donnelly, Phil Duncan, Alan Ehrenhalt, Ross Evans, Pamela Fessler, Diane Granat, Rob Gurwitt, Bill Keller, Michael L. Koempel, Larry Light, James M. McCarthy, Julia McCue, Sandra McDermin, Florence A. Mosebach, Alan Murray, Andy Plattner, Ben Z. Rose, Judy Sarasohn, T. Siafra Sherman Jr., Dale Tate, Pat Towell, Tom Watson, Elizabeth Wehr, Laura B. Weiss, Richard Whittle, Michael D. Wormser
Roll-Call Charts: Barbara L. Miracle; **Vote Studies:** Wayne Walker
Indexers: Nancy Blanpied, Diane Huffman
Production: I.D. Fuller (manager), Maceo Mayo (assistant manager)

"By providing a link between the local news-paper and Capitol Hill we hope Congressional Quarterly can help to make public opinion the only effective pressure group in the country. Since many citizens other than editors are also interested in Congress, we hope that they too will find Congressional Quarterly an aid to a better under-standing of their government.

"Congressional Quarterly presents the facts in as complete, concise and unbiased form as we know how. The editorial comment on the acts and votes of Congress, we leave to our subscribers." Foreword, Congressional Quarterly, Vol. I, 1945.

Henrietta Poynter, 1901-1968
Nelson Poynter, 1903-1978

C Q

SUMMARY TABLE OF CONTENTS

TABLE OF CONTENTS

Chapter 1 — 97th Congress, Second Session

Chapter 2 — Economic Policy

Chapter 3 — Defense

Chapter 4 — Foreign Policy

Chapter 5 — Budget and Appropriations

Chapter 6 — Energy

Chapter 7 — Transportation/Commerce/Consumers

Chapter 8 — Agriculture

Chapter 9 — Law Enforcement/Judiciary

Chapter 10 — Environment

Chapter 11 — Health/Education/Welfare

Chapter 12 — Congress and Government

APPENDICES

Special Reports

Political Report

Voting Studies

Lobby Registrations

Presidential Messages

Public Laws

Roll-Call Charts

Index

ERRATA

1981 Almanac: P. 355, col. 2, Treasury/Post Office Funds: Fiscal 1982 appropriations for Treasury, Post Office and other agencies were included in a continuing appropriations resolution (H J Res 370 — PL 97-92), not PL 95-92. **P. 356,** col. 1, Treasury/Post Office Funds: The Senate approved an amendment to bar the Reagan administration from reorganizing or eliminating the Bureau of Alcohol, Tobacco and Firearms before March 31, 1982, not 1981. **P. 404,** col. 2, Regulatory Reform: The Senate Judiciary Committee report on the bill was S Rept 97-284; the Governmental Affairs Committee report was S Rept 97-305. The report numbers were transposed in the story.

1977 Almanac: P. 72-S, vote 501, Temporary Debt Increase: The bill provided a temporary debt limit to $752 billion through March 31, 1978, not March 21.

Glossary of Congressional Terms

Act—The term for legislation once it has passed both houses of Congress and has been signed by the president or passed over his veto, thus becoming law. Also used in parliamentary terminology for a bill that has been passed by one house and engrossed. (See Engrossed Bill.)

Adjournment Sine Die—Adjournment without definitely fixing a day for reconvening; literally "adjournment without a day." Usually used to connote the final adjournment of a session of Congress. A session can continue until noon, Jan. 3, of the following year, when, under the 20th Amendment to the Constitution, it automatically terminates.

Adjournment to a Day Certain—Adjournment under a motion or resolution that fixes the next time of meeting. Under the Constitution, neither house can adjourn for more than three days without the concurrence of the other. A session of Congress is not ended by adjournment to a day certain.

Amendment—A proposal of a member of Congress to alter the language, provisions or stipulations in a bill or in another amendment. It usually is printed, debated, and voted upon in the same manner as a bill.

Appeal—A member's challenge of a ruling or decision made by the presiding officer of the chamber. In the Senate, the senator appeals to members of the chamber to override the decision. If carried by a majority vote, the appeal nullifies the chair's ruling. In the House, the decision of the Speaker traditionally has been final; seldom are there appeals to the members to reverse the Speaker's stand. To appeal a ruling would be considered an attack on the Speaker.

Appropriations Bill—Provides the actual monies approved by authorization bills, but not necessarily the full amount permissible under the authorization measure. By congressional custom, an appropriations bill originates in the House, and normally it is not considered by the full House or Senate until the related authorization measure is enacted. Under the 1974 Congressional Budget and Impoundment Control Act, general appropriations bills are supposed to be enacted by the seventh day after Labor Day before the start of the fiscal year to which they apply, but in recent years this deadline rarely has been met. In addition to a general appropriations bill, there are two specialized types. (See Backdoor Spending, Supplemental Appropriations Bill.)

Authorization -Basic, substantive legislation that establishes or continues the legal operation of a federal program or agency, either indefinitely or for a specific period of time, or which sanctions a particular type of obligation or expenditure. An authorization normally is a prerequisite for an appropriation or other kind of budget authority. An authorization may limit the amount of budget authority to be provided or may authorize the appropri-

ation of "such sums as may be necessary." (See Contract Authorizations.)

Backdoor Spending—Spending authority provided in legislation outside the normal appropriations process. The most common forms of backdoor spending are borrowing authority, contract authority and entitlements. In some cases, such as interest on the public debt, a permanent appropriation is provided that becomes available without further action by Congress. The 1974 budget act places limits on the use of backdoor spending.

Bills—Most legislative proposals before Congress are in the form of bills and are designated as HR (House of Representatives) or S (Senate), according to the house in which they originate, and by a number assigned in the order in which they are introduced during the two-year period of a congressional term. "Public bills" deal with general questions and become public laws if approved by Congress and signed by the president. "Private bills" deal with individual matters such as claims against the government, immigration and naturalization cases, land titles, etc., and become private laws if approved and signed. (See also Concurrent Resolution, Joint Resolution, Resolution.)

Bills Introduced—In the Senate any number of senators may join in introducing a single bill. In the House until 1967 only one member's name could appear on a single bill. Between 1967 and 1978 there was a limit of 25 cosponsors on any one bill. A resolution adopted in 1978 eliminated the ceiling on the number of cosponsors, beginning at the start of the 96th Congress.

Many bills in reality are committee bills and are introduced under the name of the chairman of the committee or subcommittee as a formality. All appropriations bills fall in this category, as do many other bills, particularly those dealing with complicated, technical subjects. A committee frequently holds hearings on a number of related bills and may agree on one of them or on an entirely new bill. (See Clean Bill and By Request.)

Bills Referred—When introduced, a bill is referred to the committee (or committees) that has jurisdiction over the subject with which the bill is concerned. Under the Standing Rules of the House and Senate, bills are referred by the Speaker in the House and by the presiding officer in the Senate. In practice, the House and Senate parliamentarians refer the vast majority of bills.

Borrowing Authority—Statutory authority that permits a federal agency to incur obligations and make payments for specified purposes with borrowed money. The 1974 budget act sets limits on new borrowing authority, except in certain instances, to the extent or amount provided in appropriations acts.

Budget—The document sent to Congress by the president early each year estimating government revenue and expenditures for the ensuing fiscal year and recom-

mending appropriations in detail.

Budget Authority—Authority to enter into obligations that will result in immediate or future outlays involving federal funds. This term does not include authority to insure or guarantee the repayment of indebtedness incurred by another person or government. The basic forms of budget authority are appropriations, contract authority and borrowing authority. Budget authority may be classified by 1) the period of availability (one-year, multiple-year or without a time limitation), 2) the timing of congressional action (current or permanent), or 3) the manner of determining the amount available (definite or indefinite).

Budget Process—The congressional budget process is organized around two concurrent resolutions. The deadline for approval of the first resolution is May 15. The resolution must be passed before the House and Senate consider appropriations, revenue and entitlement legislation. The deadline for the second budget resolution is Sept. 15, two weeks before the Oct. 1 start of the next fiscal year. (Congress has failed to meet these deadlines in recent years.) Concurrent resolutions do not have the force of law. Consequently, Congress cannot appropriate money or impose taxes or directly limit federal expenditures by means of a budget resolution. The sole purpose of the budget resolutions is to guide and restrain Congress in its actions on the separate annual appropriations, revenue raising and debt bills. Unless it otherwise stipulates, Congress is not bound by the targets in the first budget resolution when it acts on appropriations and tax legislation. The second resolution sets a ceiling on new budget authority and outlays and a floor on revenues for the coming year. After its adoption, a point of order can be raised against any legislation that would cause expenditures to exceed or revenues to drop below budgeted amounts. Congress can revise its budget decisions at any time during the fiscal year by adopting supplementary budget resolutions.

Budget Reconciliation—The 1974 budget act provides for a "reconciliation" procedure for bringing existing spending by the federal government into conformity with the congressional budget resolutions. Under the procedure, Congress instructs designated legislative committees to approve measures adjusting revenues and expenditures by a certain amount. The committees have a deadline by which they must report the legislation, but they have the discretion of deciding what changes are to be made. The recommendations of the various committees are consolidated without change by the Budget committees into an omnibus reconciliation bill, which then must be considered and approved by both houses of Congress.

Budget Waivers—When Senate authorizing committees fail to meet the May 15 deadline in the 1974 budget act for reporting legislation, they can introduce budget waiver resolutions, allowing them to report legislation after that date. Such resolutions are referred to the Senate Budget Committee, which decides whether to grant the waiver. In doing so it may consider the effect of the waiver on the budget priorities established by the congressional budget resolution as well as other factors affecting the appropriations process. In the House, waivers are written into the "special rules" issued by the Rules Committee that set the terms and conditions under which legislation is considered on the floor.

By Request—A phrase used when a senator or representative introduces a bill at the request of an executive agency or private organization but does not necessarily endorse the legislation.

Calendar—An agenda or list of pending business before either chamber. The House uses five legislative calendars. *(See Consent, Discharge, House, Private and Union Calendar.)*

In the Senate, all legislative matters reported from committee go on a calendar. They are listed there in order, but may be called up irregularly by the majority leader either by a motion to do so or by obtaining the unanimous consent of the Senate. The minority leader and other senators are consulted to assure unanimous consent. Only through successful cloture votes can debate be limited on bills thus called up. *(See Call of the Calendar.)*

The Senate also uses one non-legislative calendar; this is used for treaties and nominations. *(See Executive Calendar.)*

Calendar Wednesday—In the House, committees, on Wednesdays, may be called in the order in which they appear in Rule X of the House *Manual*, for the purpose of bringing up any of their bills from either the House or the Union Calendar, except bills that are privileged. General debate is limited to two hours. Bills called up from the Union Calendar are considered in Committee of the Whole. Calendar Wednesday is not observed during the last two weeks of a session and may be dispensed with at other times by a two-thirds vote. This procedure is rarely used and routinely is dispensed with by unanimous consent.

Call of the Calendar—Senate bills that are not brought up for debate by a motion or a unanimous consent agreement are brought before the Senate for action when the calendar listing them is "called." Bills must be called in the order listed. Measures considered by this method usually are non-controversial, and debate is limited to a total of five minutes for each senator on the bill and any amendments proposed to it.

Chamber—The meeting place for the membership of either the House or the Senate.

Clean Bill—Frequently after a committee has finished a major revision of a bill, one of the committee members, usually the chairman, will assemble the changes and what is left of the original bill into a new measure and introduce it as a "clean bill." The revised measure, which is given a new number by the House clerk or the secretary of the Senate, then is sent to the floor for consideration. This often is a timesaver, as committee-recommended changes in a clean bill do not have to be considered and voted on one at a time by the chamber.

Clerk of the House—Chief administrative officer of the House of Representatives, with duties corresponding to those of the secretary of the Senate. *(See Secretary of the Senate.)*

Cloture—The process by which a filibuster can be ended in the Senate, other than by unanimous consent. A motion for cloture can apply to any measure before the Senate, including a proposal to change the chamber's rules. A cloture motion requires the signatures of 16 senators to be introduced, and to end a filibuster the cloture motion must obtain the votes of three-fifths of the entire Senate membership (60 if there are no vacancies), except that to end a filibuster against a proposal to amend the Standing Rules of the Senate a two-thirds vote of senators present and voting is required. The cloture request is put to a roll-

call vote one hour after the Senate meets on the second day following introduction of the motion. If approved, cloture limits each senator to one hour of debate. The bill or amendment in question comes to a final vote after 100 hours of consideration (including debate time and the time it takes to conduct roll calls, quorum calls and other procedural motions).

Committee—A subdivision of the House or Senate that prepares legislation for action by the parent chamber, or makes investigations as directed by the parent chamber. There are several types of committees. *(See Standing, Select or Special.)* Most standing committees are divided into subcommittees, which study legislation, hold hearings and submit bills, with or without amendments, to the full committee. Only the full committee can report legislation for action by the House or Senate.

Committee of the Whole—The working title of what is formally "The Committee of the Whole House [of Representatives] on the State of the Union." Unlike other committees, it has no fixed membership. It is comprised of any 100 or more House members who are present on the floor of the chamber to consider legislation before the body. Such measures, however, must first have passed through the regular legislative or appropriation committees and be placed on the calendar.

Technically, the Committee of the Whole considers only bills directly or indirectly appropriating money, authorizing appropriations or involving taxes or charges on the public. Actually, the Committee of the Whole often considers other types of legislation. Because the Committee of the Whole need number only 100 representatives, a quorum is more readily attained, and legislative business is expedited. Before 1971 members' positions were not individually recorded on votes taken in Committee of the Whole, except for automatic roll calls conducted in the absence of a quorum. *(See Teller Vote.)*

When the full House resolves itself into the Committee of the Whole, it supplants the Speaker with a "chairman." The measure is debated and amendments may be proposed, with votes on amendments as needed. When the committee completes its work on the measure, it dissolves itself by "rising." The Speaker returns, and the chairman of the Committee of the Whole reports to the House that the committee's work has been completed and recommends that the bill in question be passed.

At this time members may demand a roll-call vote on any amendment *adopted* in the Committee of the Whole. The final vote is on passage of the legislation.

Committee Veto—A requirement added to a few statutes directing that certain policy directives by an executive department or agency be reviewed by certain congressional committees before they are implemented. Under common practice, the government department or agency and the committees involved are expected to reach a consensus before the directives are carried out. *(See also Legislative Veto.)*

Concurrent Resolution—A concurrent resolution, designated H Con Res or S Con Res, must be adopted by both houses, but they are not sent to the president for his signature and therefore do not have the force of law. A concurrent resolution, for example, is used to fix the time for adjournment of a Congress. It also is used as the vehicle for expressing the sense of Congress on various foreign policy and domestic issues.

Conference—A meeting between the representatives of the House and the Senate to reconcile differences between the two houses on provisions of a bill passed by both chambers. Members of the conference committee are appointed by the Speaker and the president of the Senate and are called "managers" for their respective chambers. A majority of the managers for each house must reach agreement on the provisions of the bill (often a compromise between the versions of the two chambers) before it can be considered by either chamber in the form of a "conference report." When it goes to the floor it cannot be amended, and if it is not approved by both chambers the bill may go back to conference under certain situations, or a new conference must be convened. Many rules and informal practices govern the conduct of conference committees. Bills that are passed by both houses with only minor differences need not be sent to conference. Either chamber may "concur" in the other's amendments, completing action on the legislation. Also, sometimes leaders of both committees (or staff) work out an informal compromise instead of having a formal conference. *(See Custody of the Papers.)*

Congressional Record—The daily, printed account of proceedings in both the House and Senate chambers, with substantially verbatim debate, statements and the like incorporated in it. Committee activities generally are not covered, except that their reports to the parent body are noted. Highlights of legislative and committee action are embodied in a Daily Digest section of the Record, and members are entitled to have their extraneous remarks printed in an appendix known as "Extension of Remarks." They may edit and revise remarks made on the floor during debate, and quotations from debate reported by the press are not always found in the Record.

Beginning on March 1, 1978, the Record incorporated a procedure to distinguish remarks spoken on the floor of the House and Senate from undelivered speeches. Congress directed that all speeches, articles and other matter that members inserted in the Record without actually reading them on the floor were to be set off by large black dots, or bullets. However, a loophole allows a member to avoid the dots if he delivers any portion of the speech in person.

Congressional Terms of Office—Begin on Jan. 3 of the year following a general election and are for two years for representatives and six years for senators.

Consent Calendar—Members of the House may place on this calendar any bill on the Union or House Calendar that is considered to be non-controversial. Bills on the Consent Calendar normally are called on the first and third Mondays of each month. On the first occasion that a bill is called in this manner, consideration may be blocked by the objection of any member. The second time, if there are three objections, the bill is stricken from the Consent Calendar. If less than three members object, the bill is given immediate consideration.

A bill on the Consent Calendar may be postponed in another way. A member may ask that the measure be passed over "without prejudice." In that case, no objection is recorded against the bill, and its status on the Consent Calendar remains unchanged.

A bill stricken from the Consent Calendar remains on the Union or House Calendar.

Continuing Resolution—A joint resolution drafted by Congress "continuing appropriations" for specific ongoing activities of a government department or depart-

ments when a fiscal year begins and Congress has not yet enacted all of the regular appropriations bills for that year. The continuing resolution usually specifies a maximum rate at which the agency may incur obligations. This is based usually on the rate for the previous year, or the lower amount in the appropriations bill(s) for that year if the legislation has been passed by the House and Senate, but not cleared.

Contract Authorizations—Found in both authorization and appropriations bills, these provisions permit the federal government to let contracts or to obligate itself for future payments from funds not yet appropriated by Congress. The assumption is that funds will be available for payment when the contracted debts come due.

Controllable Budget Items—In the federal budget this refers to programs over which the federal government can control budget authority or outlays during a fiscal year without changing existing substantive law. The concept "relatively uncontrollable under current law" includes outlays for open-ended programs and fixed costs such as interest on the federal debt, Social Security benefits, veterans' benefits and outlays to liquidate prior-year obligations.

Correcting Recorded Votes—Rules prohibit members from changing their votes after the result has been announced. But occasionally, hours, days, or months after a vote has been taken a member may announce that he was "incorrectly recorded." In the Senate, a request to change one's vote almost always receives unanimous consent. In the House, members are prohibited from changing their votes if tallied by the electronic voting system installed in 1973. If taken by roll call, it is permissible if consent is granted. Errors in the text of the Record may be corrected by unanimous consent.

Current Services Estimates—Estimated budget authority and outlays for the forthcoming fiscal year based on continuation of existing levels of funding for programs without policy changes. These estimates of budget authority and outlays, accompanied by the underlying economic and policy assumptions upon which they are based, are transmitted by the president to Congress when the budget is submitted.

Custody of the Papers—To reconcile differences between the House and Senate versions of a bill, a conference may be arranged. The chamber with "custody of the papers" — the engrossed bill, engrossed amendments, messages of transmittal — is the only body empowered to request the conference. By custom, the chamber that asks for a conference is the last to act on the conference report once agreement has been reached on the bill by the conferees. Custody of the papers sometimes is manipulated to ensure that a particular chamber acts either first or last on the conference report.

Deferrals of Budget Authority—Any action taken by U.S. government officials that withholds, delays or precludes the obligation or expenditure of budget authority. The 1974 budget act requires a special message from the president to Congress reporting a proposed deferral. Deferrals may not extend beyond the end of the fiscal year in which the message reporting the deferral is transmitted. They may be overturned by adoption of a disapproval resolution by either house of Congress.

Dilatory Motion—A motion made for the purpose of killing time and preventing action on a bill. The rules outlaw dilatory motions, but enforcement is largely within the discretion of the presiding officer.

Discharge a Committee—Occasionally, attempts are made to relieve a committee from jurisdiction over a measure before it. This is attempted more often in the House than in the Senate, but the procedure rarely is successful.

In the House, if a committee does not report a bill within 30 days after the measure is referred to it, any member may file a discharge motion. This motion, treated as a petition, needs the signatures of 218 members (a majority of the House). After the required signatures have been obtained, there is a delay of seven days. Then, on the second and fourth Mondays of each month, except during the last six days of a session, any member who has signed the petition may be recognized to move that the committee be discharged. Debate on the motion to discharge is limited to 20 minutes, and, if the motion is carried, consideration of the bill becomes a matter of high privilege.

If a resolution to consider a bill is held up in the Rules Committee for more than seven legislative days *(see Rules)*, any member may enter a motion to discharge the committee. The motion is handled like any other discharge petition in the House.

Occasionally, to expedite non-controversial legislative business, a committee is discharged upon unanimous consent of the House, and a petition is not required. *(Senate procedure, see Discharge Resolution.)*

Discharge Calendar—The House calendar to which motions to discharge committees are referred when they have the required number of signatures (218) and are awaiting floor action.

Discharge Petition—In the House, a motion to discharge a committee from further consideration of a bill. The motion, or petition, requires the signatures of 218 House members.

Discharge Resolution—In the Senate, a special motion that any senator may introduce to relieve a committee from consideration of a bill before it. The resolution can be called up for Senate approval or disapproval in the same manner as any other Senate business. *(House procedure, see Discharge a Committee.)*

Division Vote—Same as Standing Vote.

Enacting Clause—Key phrase in bills beginning, "Be it enacted by the Senate and House of Representatives. . . ." A successful motion to strike it from legislation kills the measure.

Engrossed Bill—The final copy of a bill as passed by one chamber, with the text as amended by floor action and certified to by the clerk of the House or the secretary of the Senate.

Enrolled Bill—The final copy of a bill that has been passed in identical form by both chambers. It is certified to by an officer of the house of origin (House clerk or Senate secretary) and then sent on for the signatures of the House Speaker, the Senate president and the president of the United States. An enrolled bill is printed on parchment.

Entitlement Program—A federal program that guarantees a certain level of benefits to persons who meet the requirements set by law, such as Social Security or unemployment benefits. It thus leaves no discretion to Congress on how much money to appropriate.

Executive Calendar—This is a non-legislative calendar in the Senate on which presidential documents such as treaties and nominations are listed.

Executive Document—A document, usually a treaty, sent to the Senate by the president for members' consideration or approval. These are identified for each session of Congress as Executive A, 97th Congress, 1st Session; Executive B, etc. They are referred to committee in the same manner as other measures. Unlike legislative documents, however, treaties do not die at the end of a Congress but remain "live" proposals until acted on by the Senate or withdrawn by the president.

Executive Session—A meeting of a Senate or House committee (or, occasionally, of either chamber) in which only the group's members are privileged to attend. Frequently, witnesses appear at committee meetings in executive session — for example, Defense Department officials during presentations of classified defense information. Other members of Congress may be invited, but the public and press are not allowed to attend.

Expenditures—The actual spending of money as distinguished from the appropriation of funds. Expenditures are made by the disbursing officers of the administration; appropriations are made only by Congress. The two are rarely identical in any fiscal year. Expenditures may represent money appropriated one, two or more years previously.

Filibuster—A time-delaying tactic used by a minority in an effort to prevent a vote on a bill that probably would pass if voted upon directly. The most common method is to take advantage of the Senate's rules permitting unlimited debate, but other forms of parliamentary maneuvering may be used. The stricter rules used by the House make filibusters more difficult, but delaying tactics are employed occasionally through various procedural devices allowed by House rules. (Senate filibusters, see Cloture.)

Fiscal Year—Financial operations of the government are carried out in a 12-month fiscal year, beginning on Oct. 1 and ending on Sept. 30. The fiscal year carries the date of the calendar year in which it ends. (From fiscal year 1844 to fiscal year 1976, the fiscal year began July 1 and ended the following June 30.)

Floor Manager—A member who has the task of steering legislation through floor debate and the amendment process to a final vote in the House or the Senate. Floor managers are frequently chairmen or ranking members of the committee that reported the bill. Managers are responsible for apportioning the debate time granted supporters of the bill. The ranking minority member of the committee often apportions time for the minority party's participation in the debate.

Frank—A member's facsimile signature on envelopes, which is used in lieu of stamps and thus is postage-free, for his official outgoing mail. Also the privilege of sending mail postage-free.

Germane—Pertaining to the subject matter of the measure at hand. All House amendments must be germane to the bill being considered. The Senate requires that amendments be germane when they are proposed to general appropriations bills, bills being considered once cloture has been adopted, or, frequently, when proceeding under a unanimous consent agreement placing a time limit on consideration of a bill.

Grandfather Clause—A provision exempting persons already engaged in an activity from rules or legislation restricting or prohibiting that activity.

Grandfather clauses are sometimes added to legislation in order to avoid antagonizing groups with established interests in the activities being restricted.

Grants-in-Aid—Payments by the federal government that aid the recipient state, local government or individual in administering specified programs, services or activities.

Guaranteed Loans—Loans for which the federal government guarantees, in whole or in part, the repayment of principal and/or interest.

Hearings—Committee sessions for hearing witnesses. At hearings on legislation, witnesses usually include specialists, government officials and spokesmen for persons affected by the bill or bills under study. Hearings related to special investigations bring forth a variety of witnesses. Committees sometimes use their subpoena power to summon reluctant witnesses. The public and press may attend open hearings, but are barred from closed, or "executive" hearings. The vast majority of hearings are open to the public.

Hold-Harmless Clause—A provision added to legislation to ensure that recipients of federal funds do not receive less in a future year than they did the previous year if a new formula for allocating such funds would result in a reduction in the amount. To hold a state or city government "harmless" means that neither would be responsible for providing the additional funds or services to make up the difference between the level of benefits previously received and that which would be allowed under the new formula. The federal government would be obliged to provide the additional funds or benefits. This clause has been used most frequently to soften the impact of sudden reductions in federal grants.

Hopper—Box on House clerk's desk where bills are deposited when they are introduced.

House—The House of Representatives, as distinct from the Senate, although each body is a "house" of Congress.

House Calendar—A listing for action by the House of public bills that do not directly or indirectly appropriate money or raise revenue.

Immunity—The constitutional privilege of members of Congress to make verbal statements on the floor and in committee for which they cannot be sued or arrested for slander or libel. Also, freedom from arrest while traveling to or from sessions of Congress or on official business. Members in this status may be arrested only for treason, felonies or a breach of the peace, as defined by congressional manuals.

Impoundments—Any action taken by the executive branch that precludes the obligation or expenditure of budget authority previously approved by Congress. (See also Deferrals of Budget Authority.)

Joint Committee—A committee composed of a specified number of members of both the House and Sen-

ate. A joint committee may be investigative or research oriented, such as the Joint Economic Committee. Others have housekeeping duties such as the joint committees on Printing and on the Library of Congress.

Joint Resolution—A joint resolution, designated H J Res or S J Res, requires the approval of both houses and the signature of the president, just as a bill does, and has the force of law if approved. There is no practical difference between a bill and a joint resolution. The latter is generally used in dealing with limited matters, such as a single appropriation for a special purpose.

Joint resolutions also are used to propose amendments to the Constitution. They do not require a presidential signature, but become a part of the Constitution when three-fourths of the states have ratified them.

Journal—The official record of the proceedings of the House and Senate. The Journal records the actions taken in each chamber, but, unlike the *Congressional Record,* it does not include the substantially verbatim report of speeches, debates, etc.

Law—An act of Congress that has been signed by the president, or passed over his veto by Congress; for example, the 1980 public debt bill (HR 7428) that contained a section killing President Carter's proposed 10-cent-a-gallon surcharge on gasoline became Public Law 96-265 during the second session of the 96th Congress.

Legislative Day—The "day" extending from the time either house meets after an adjournment until the time it next adjourns. Because the House normally adjourns from day to day, legislative days and calendar days usually coincide. But in the Senate, a legislative day may, and frequently does, extend over several calendar days. *(See Recess.)*

Legislative Veto—A procedure permitting either the House or Senate, or both chambers, to review proposed executive branch regulations or actions and to block or modify those with which they disagree. The specifics of the procedure may vary, but Congress generally provides for a legislative veto by including in a bill a provision that administrative rules or actions taken to implement the law are to go into effect at the end of a designated period of time unless blocked by either or both houses of Congress. Another version of the veto provides for congressional reconsideration and rejection of regulations already in effect.

Lobby—A group seeking to influence the passage or defeat of legislation. Originally the term referred to persons frequenting the lobbies or corridors of legislative chambers in order to speak to lawmakers.

The definition of a lobby and the activity of lobbying is a matter of differing interpretation. By some definitions, lobbying is limited to direct attempts to influence lawmakers through personal interviews and persuasion. Under other definitions, lobbying includes attempts at indirect, or "grass-roots" influence, such as persuading members of a group to write or visit their representatives and senators or attempting to create a climate of opinion favorable to a desired legislative goal.

The right to attempt to influence legislation is based on the First Amendment to the Constitution, which says Congress shall make no law abridging the right of the people "to petition the government for a redress of grievances."

Majority Leader—Chief strategist and floor spokesman for the party in nominal control in either chamber. He is elected by his party colleagues and is in essence the program director for his chamber.

Majority Whip—In effect, the assistant majority leader, in either the House or Senate. His job is to help marshal majority forces in support of party strategy and legislation.

Manual—The official handbook in each house prescribing its organization, procedures and operations in detail. The Senate manual contains standing rules, orders, laws and resolutions affecting Senate business; the House manual is for operations affecting that chamber. Both volumes contain previous codes under which Congress has functioned and from which it continues to derive precedents. Committee powers are outlined. The rules set forth in the manuals may be changed by the chamber, as spelled out in the manuals.

Marking Up a Bill—Going through the contents of a piece of legislation in committee or subcommittee, considering it section by section, acting on amendments to provisions and proposed revisions to the language, penciling in new sections and phraseology, etc. If the bill is extensively amended, the committee's version may be introduced as a separate bill, with a new number, before being considered by the full House or Senate. *(See Clean Bill.)*

Minority Leader—Floor leader for the minority party. *(See Majority Leader.)*

Minority Whip—Performs duties of whip for the minority party. *(See Majority Whip.)*

Morning Hour—The time set aside at the beginning of each legislative day for the consideration of regular routine business. The "hour" is of indefinite duration in the House, where it is rarely used. In the Senate it is the first two hours of a session following an adjournment, as distinguished from a recess. The morning hour can be terminated earlier if the morning business has been completed. The business includes such matters as messages from the president, communications from the heads of departments, messages from the House, the presentation of petitions, reports of standing and select committees and the introduction of bills and resolutions.

During the first hour of the morning hour in the Senate, no motion to proceed to the consideration of any bill on the calendar is in order except by unanimous consent. During the second hour, motions can be made but must be decided without debate. Senate committees may meet while the Senate is in its morning hour.

Motion—In the House or Senate chamber, the request by a member to institute any one of a wide array of parliamentary actions. He "moves" for a certain procedure or the consideration of a measure or to suspend the rules and pass a bill, etc. The precedence of motions, and whether they are debatable, is set forth in the House and Senate manuals.

Nominations—Appointments to office by the executive branch of government subject to Senate confirmation. Although most nominations win quick Senate approval, some are controversial and become the topic of hearings and debate. Sometimes senators object to appointees for

patronage reasons — for example, when a nomination to a local federal job is made without consulting the senators of the state concerned. In such situations a senator may object that the nominee is "personally obnoxious" to him. Usually other senators join in blocking such an appointment out of courtesy to their colleague. *(See Senatorial Courtesy.)*

One Minute Speeches—Addresses by House members at the beginning of a legislative day. The speeches may cover any subject, but are limited to one minute's duration. By unanimous consent, members also may be recognized to address the House for longer periods after completing the day's legislative business. Senators, by unanimous consent, are permitted to make speeches of a predetermined length during the "Morning Hour."

Override a Veto—If the president disapproves a bill and sends it back to Congress with his objections, Congress may try to override his veto and enact the bill into law. An override of a veto requires a two-thirds majority vote in each chamber, and the Constitution requires a recorded vote. The question put to each house is: "Shall the bill pass, the objections of the president to the contrary notwithstanding?" *(See also Pocket Veto and Veto.)*

Oversight Committee—A congressional committee, or in some cases a designated subcommittee of an authorizing committee, that is charged with general oversight of a federal agency's programs and activities. Usually, the oversight panel for a particular agency also is the authorizing committee for that agency's programs and operations.

Pair—An arrangement between two lawmakers, usually on the opposite sides of an issue, who agree to withhold their votes on certain questions so that the absence of one of them will not affect the outcome of the vote. If passage of the measure requires a two-thirds majority vote, a pair would require two members favoring the action to one opposed to it.

Pairs can take one of three forms — special, general and live. The names of lawmakers pairing on a given vote and their stands, if known, are printed in the *Congressional Record*.

The special pair applies to one or more votes on the same subject. On special pairs, lawmakers usually specify how they would have voted.

A general pair in the Senate, now rarely used in that chamber, applies to all votes on which the members pairing are on opposite sides. It usually does not specify the positions of the senators pairing.

In a general pair in the House, no agreement is involved and the pair does not tie up votes. A representative expecting to be absent may notify the House clerk he wishes to make a "general" pair. His name then is paired arbitrarily with that of another member desiring a pair, and the list is printed in the *Congressional Record*. He may or may not be paired with a member taking the opposite position. General pairs in the House give no indication of how a member would have voted. *(See also Recorded Vote.)*

In a live pair involving two members, one is present for the vote, the other is absent. The member present casts his vote and then withdraws it and votes "present." He then announces that he has a live pair with a colleague, identifying how each would have voted on the question. A live pair subtracts the vote of the member in attendance from the final vote tabulation.

Petition—A request or plea sent to one or both chambers from an organization or private citizens' group asking support of particular legislation or favorable consideration of a matter not yet receiving congressional attention. They are referred to appropriate committees and considered or not considered, according to committee decisions.

Pocket Veto—The act of the president in withholding his approval of a bill after Congress has adjourned. When Congress is in session, a bill becomes law without the president's signature if he does not act upon it within 10 days, excluding Sundays, from the time he gets it. But if Congress adjourns within that 10-day period, the bill is killed even if the president does not formally veto it. The U.S. Court of Appeals for the District of Columbia Circuit on Aug. 14, 1974, upheld a congressional challenge to a pocket veto used by former President Richard M. Nixon during a six-day congressional recess in 1970. The court declared that it was an improper use of the pocket veto power. After the 1974 court case the White House and Congress reached an informal agreement that the pocket veto would be employed only when Congress adjourns *sine die*.

Point of Order—An objection raised by a member that the chamber is departing from rules governing its conduct of business. The objector cites the rule violated, the chair sustaining his objection if correctly made. Order is restored by the chair's suspending proceedings of the chamber until it conforms to the prescribed "order of business." Members sometimes raise a "point of order" — when there is noise and disorderly conduct in the chamber.

President of the Senate—Under the Constitution, the vice president of the United States presides over the Senate. In his absence, a president pro tempore (president for the time being) presides.

President Pro Tempore—The chief officer of the Senate in the absence of the vice president. He is elected by his fellow senators. The recent practice has been to elect to the office the senator of the majority party with the longest period of continuous service.

Previous Question—A motion for the previous question, when carried, has the effect of cutting off all debate and forcing a vote on the subject originally at hand. In the House, the previous question sometimes is moved in order to prevent amendments from being introduced and voted on. The motion for the previous question is a debate-limiting device and is not in order in the Senate.

Private Calendar—In the House, private bills dealing with individual matters such as claims against the government, immigration, land titles, etc., are put on this calendar. When it is before the chamber, two members may block a private bill, which then is recommitted to committee.

Backers of a private bill thus recommitted have another recourse. The measure can be put into an "omnibus claims bill" — several private bills rolled into one. As with any bill, no part of an omnibus claims bill may be deleted without a vote. When a private bill goes back to the House floor in this form, it can be defeated only by majority vote. The private calendar can be called on the first and third Tuesdays of each month.

Privilege—Privilege relates to the rights of members of Congress and to the relative priority of the motions and

actions they may make in their respective chambers. The two are distinct. "Privileged questions" deal with legislative business. "Questions of privilege" concern legislators themselves. *(See next entry.)*

Privileged Questions—The order in which bills, motions and other legislative measures are considered by Congress is governed by strict priorities. A motion to table, for instance, is more privileged than a motion to recommit. Thus, a motion to recommit can be superseded by a motion to table, and a vote would be forced on the latter motion only. A motion to adjourn, however, takes precedence over a tabling motion and thus is considered of the "highest privilege."

Pro Forma Amendment—*(See Strike Out the Last Word.)*

Questions of Privilege—These are matters affecting members of Congress individually or collectively.

Matters affecting the rights, safety, dignity and integrity of proceedings of the House or Senate as a whole are questions of privilege in both chambers.

Questions involving individual members are called questions of "personal privilege." A member rising to ask a question of personal privilege is given precedence over almost all other proceedings. An annotation in the House rules points out that the privilege rests primarily on the Constitution, which gives him a conditional immunity from arrest and an unconditional freedom to speak in the House.

Quorum—The number of members whose presence is necessary for the transaction of business. In the Senate and House, it is a majority of the membership (when there are no vacancies, this is 51 in the Senate and 218 in the House). A quorum is 100 in the Committee of the Whole House. If a point of order is made that a quorum is not present, the only business that is in order is either a motion to adjourn or a motion to direct the sergeant-at-arms to request the attendance of absentees.

Readings of Bills—Traditional parliamentary law required bills to be read three times before they were passed. This custom is of little modern significance except in rare instances. Normally a bill is considered to have its first reading when it is introduced and printed, by title, in the *Congressional Record*. Its second reading comes when floor consideration begins. (This is the most likely point at which there is an actual reading of the bill, if there is any.) The third reading (again, usually by title) takes place when floor action has been completed on amendments.

Recess—Distinguished from adjournment in that a recess does not end a legislative day and, therefore, does not interfere with unfinished business. The rules in each house set forth certain matters to be taken up and disposed of at the beginning of each legislative day. The House, which operates under much stricter rules than the Senate, usually adjourns from day to day. The Senate often recesses, thus meeting on the same legislative day for days or even weeks at a time.

Recommit to Committee—A simple motion, made on the floor after a bill has been debated, to return it to the committee that reported it. If approved, recommittal usually is considered a death blow to the bill. In the House, a motion to recommit can be made only by a member opposed to the bill, and in recognizing a member to make the motion the Speaker gives preference to the minority party over the majority.

A motion to recommit may include instructions to the committee to report the bill again with specific amendments or by a certain date. Or the instructions may direct that a particular study be made, with no definite deadline for further action. If the recommittal motion includes instructions to "report the bill back forthwith," and the motion is adopted, floor action on the bill continues immediately; the committee does not actually reconsider the legislation.

Reconciliation—*(See Budget Reconciliation.)*

Reconsider a Vote—A motion to reconsider the vote by which an action was taken has, until it is disposed of, the effect of suspending the action. In the Senate the motion can be made only by a member who voted on the prevailing side of the original question or by a member who did not vote at all. In the House it can be made only by a member on the prevailing side.

A common practice in the Senate after close votes on an issue is a motion to reconsider, followed by a motion to table the motion to reconsider. On this motion to table, senators vote as they voted on the original question, which allows the motion to table to prevail, assuming there are no switches. The matter then is finally closed and further motions to reconsider are not entertained. In the House, as a routine precaution, a motion to reconsider usually is made every time a measure is passed. Such a motion almost always is tabled immediately, thus shutting off the possibility of future reconsideration, except by unanimous consent.

Motions to reconsider must be entered in the Senate within the next two days of actual session after the original vote has been taken. In the House they must be entered either on the same day or on the next succeeding day the House is in session.

Recorded Vote—A vote upon which each member's stand is individually made known. In the Senate, this is accomplished through a roll call of the entire membership, to which each senator on the floor must answer "yea," "nay" or, if he does not wish to vote, "present." Since January 1973 the House has used an electronic voting system for recorded votes, including year-and-nay votes formerly taken by roll calls. *(See also Teller Vote.)*

The Constitution requires yea-and-nay votes on the question of overriding a veto.

A recorded vote can be obtained on other questions in the House on the demand of one-fifth (44 members) of a quorum or one-fourth (25) of a quorum in the Committee of the Whole.

Report—Both a verb and a noun, as a congressional term. A committee that has been examining a bill referred to it by the parent chamber "reports" its findings and recommendations to the chamber when the committee completes its consideration and returns the measure. The process is called "reporting" a bill.

A "report" is the document setting forth the committee's explanation of its action. House and Senate reports are numbered separately and are designated S Rept or H Rept. Conference reports embody the compromise bill agreed to by the conferees from each chamber.

Adverse reports occasionally are submitted by legislative committees when a committee is opposed to a bill it simply fails to report it at all. Some laws require that committee reports (favorable or adverse) be made. When a

committee report is not unanimous, the dissenting committee members may file a statement of their views, called minority views and referred to as a minority report. Members in disagreement with some provisions of a bill may file additional or supplementary views. Sometimes a bill is reported without a committee recommendation.

Rescission Bill—An item in an appropriations bill rescinding or canceling funds previously appropriated by Congress but not spent. The president may request repeal of a previous appropriation to reduce spending. Under the 1974 budget act, unless Congress approves a rescission within 45 days of continuous session after receipt of the proposal the funds must be made available for obligation. *(See also Deferrals of Budget Authority.)*

Resolution—A simple resolution, designated H Res or S Res, deals with matters entirely within the prerogatives of one house or the other. It requires neither passage by the other chamber nor approval by the president, and it does not have the force of law. Most resolutions deal with the rules or procedures of one house. They also are used to express the sentiments of a single house, as condolences to the family of a deceased member or to give "advice" on foreign policy or other executive business. *(See also Concurrent and Joint Resolution.)*

Rider—An amendment, usually not germane, which its sponsor hopes to get through more easily by including it in other legislation. Riders become law if the bills embodying them are enacted. Riders providing legislative directives in appropriations bills are outstanding examples, though technically they are banned. The House, unlike the Senate, has a strict germaneness rule; thus riders usually are Senate devices to get legislation enacted quickly or to bypass lengthy House consideration and, possibly, opposition.

Rules—The term has two specific congressional meanings. A rule may be a standing order governing the conduct of House or Senate business and listed among the permanent rules of either chamber. The rules deal with duties of officers, the order of business, admission to the floor, parliamentary procedures dealing with amendments and voting, jurisdictions of committees, etc.

In the House, a rule also may be a decision made by its Rules Committee about the handling of a particular bill on the floor. The committee may report a "special rule" in the form of a resolution. If the resolution is adopted by the House, the temporary rule becomes as valid as any standing rule and lapses only after action has been completed on the measure to which it pertains.

A special rule sets the time limit on general debate. It also may waive points of order against provisions of the bill in question, such as non-germane language, or against certain amendments intended to be proposed to the bill from the floor. It may even forbid all amendments or all amendments except, in some cases, those proposed by the legislative committee that handled the bill. In this instance, it is known as a "closed" or "gag" rule as opposed to an "open" rule, which puts no limitation on floor amendments, thus leaving the bill completely open to alteration. *(See Suspend the Rules.)*

Secretary of the Senate—Chief administrative officer of the Senate, responsible for overseeing the duties of Senate employees, educating Senate pages, administering oaths, handling the registration of lobbyists, assigning bill numbers and handling other tasks necessary for the continuing operation of the Senate.

Select or Special Committee—A committee set up for a special purpose and, generally, for a limited time by resolution of either the House or Senate. Most special committees are investigative, rather than legislative, in nature.

Senatorial Courtesy—Sometimes referred to as "the courtesy of the Senate," it is a general practice — with no written rule — applied to consideration of executive nominations. Generally, it means that nominations from a state are not to be confirmed unless they have been approved by the senators of the president's party of that state, with other senators following their lead in the attitude they take toward consideration of such nominations. *(See Nominations.)*

Sine Die—See Adjournment *sine die.*

Slip Laws—The first official publication of a bill that has been enacted into law. Each is published separately in unbound single-sheet or pamphlet form. It usually takes two to three days from the date of presidential approval of a bill to the time when the slip law becomes available.

Speaker—The presiding officer of the House of Representatives, selected by the caucus of the party to which he belongs and formally elected by the whole House.

Special Session—A session of Congress after it has adjourned *sine die*, completing its regular session. Special sessions are convened by the president of the United States under his constitutional powers.

Standing Committees—Committees permanently authorized by House and Senate rules. The standing committees of the House were last reorganized by the committee reorganization act of 1974. The last major alignment of Senate committees was in the committee system reorganization of 1977.

Standing Vote—A non-recorded vote used in both the House and Senate. A standing vote, also called a division vote, is taken as follows: Members in favor of a proposal stand and are counted by the presiding officer. Then members opposed stand and are counted. There is no record of how individual members voted.

Statutes-at-Large—A chronological arrangement of the laws enacted in each session of Congress. Though indexed, the laws are not arranged by subject matter nor is there an indication of how they affect previously enacted laws. *(See U.S. Code.)*

Strike from the Record—Remarks made on the House floor may offend some member, who moves that the offending words be "taken down" for the Speaker's cognizance, and then expunged from the debate as published in the *Congressional Record.*

Strike Out the Last Word—A move whereby House members are entitled to speak for a fixed time on a measure then being debated by the chamber. A member gains recognition from the chair by moving to "strike out the last word" of the amendment or section of the bill under consideration. The motion is pro forma and requires no vote.

Substitute—A motion, an amendment, or an entire bill introduced in place of the pending legislative business. Passage of a substitute measure kills the original measure by supplanting it. The substitute also may be amended.

Supplemental Appropriations Bill—Legislation appropriating funds after the regular (annual) appropriations bill for a federal department or agency has been enacted. A supplemental appropriation provides additional budget authority beyond original estimates for programs or activities (including new programs authorized after the enactment of the regular appropriations act) for which the need for funds is too urgent to be postponed until enactment of the next year's regular appropriations bill.

Suspend the Rules—Often a time-saving procedure for passing bills in the House. The wording of the motion, which may be made by any member recognized by the Speaker, is: "I move to suspend the rules and pass the bill...." A favorable vote by two-thirds of those present is required for passage. Debate is limited to 40 minutes and no amendments from the floor are permitted. If a two-thirds favorable vote is not attained, the bill may be considered later under regular procedures. The suspension procedure is in order every Monday and Tuesday and is intended to be reserved for non-controversial bills.

Table a Bill—A motion to "lay on the table" is not debatable in either house, and usually it is a method of making a final, adverse disposition of a matter. In the Senate, however, different language sometimes is used. The motion is worded to let a bill "lie on the table," perhaps for subsequent "picking up." This motion is more flexible, merely keeping the bill pending for later action, if desired. Tabling motions on amendments are effective debate-ending devices in the Senate.

Teller Vote—In the House, members file past tellers and are counted as for or against a measure, but they are not recorded individually. The teller vote is not used in the Senate. In the House, tellers are ordered upon demand of one-fifth of a quorum. This is 44 in the House, 20 in the Committee of the Whole.

The House also has a recorded teller vote, now largely supplanted by the electronic voting procedure, under which the votes of each member are made public just as they would be on a recorded vote. *(See also Recorded Vote.)*

Treaties—Executive proposals — in the form of resolutions of ratification — which must be submitted to the Senate for approval by two-thirds of the senators present. Treaties today are normally sent to the Foreign Relations Committee for scrutiny before the Senate takes action. Foreign Relations has jurisdiction over all treaties, regardless of the subject matter. Treaties are read three times and debated on the floor in much the same manner as are legislative proposals. After approval by the Senate, treaties are formally ratified by the president.

Trust Funds—Funds collected and used by the federal government for carrying out specific purposes and programs according to terms of a trust agreement or statute, such as the Social Security and unemployment compensation trust funds. Such funds are administered by the government in a fiduciary capacity and are not available for the general expenses of the government.

Unanimous Consent Agreement—A device used in the Senate to expedite legislation. Much of the Senate's legislative business, dealing both with minor and with controversial issues, is conducted through unanimous consent agreements. On major legislation, such agreements usually are printed and transmitted to all senators in advance of floor debate. Once agreed to, they are binding on all members unless the Senate, by unanimous consent, agrees to modify them. An agreement may list the order in which various bills are to be considered, specify the length of time bills and contested amendments are to be debated and when they are to be voted upon and, frequently, require that all amendments introduced be germane to the bill under consideration. In this regard, unanimous consent agreements are similar to the special rules issued by the House Rules Committee for bills pending in the House. *(See Rules.)*

Union Calendar—Bills that directly or indirectly appropriate money or raise revenue are placed on this House calendar according to the date reported from committee.

U.S. Code—A consolidation and codification of the general and permanent laws of the United States arranged by subject under 50 titles, the first six dealing with general or political subjects, and the other 44 alphabetically arranged from agriculture to war and national defense. The code is revised every six years, and a supplement is published after each session of Congress.

Veto—Disapproval by the president of a bill or joint resolution, other than one proposing an amendment to the Constitution. When Congress is in session, the president must veto a bill within 10 days, excluding Sundays, after he has received it; otherwise it becomes law with or without his signature. When the president vetoes a bill, he returns it to the house of origin along with a message stating his objections. The veto then becomes a question of high privilege. *(See Override a Veto.)*

When Congress has adjourned at the end of a session, the president may veto a bill merely by not signing it (since it cannot be returned to Congress for further consideration). *(See Pocket Veto.)*

Voice Vote—In either the House or Senate, members answer "aye" or "no" in chorus, and the presiding officer decides the result. The term also is used loosely to indicate action by unanimous consent or without objection.

Whip—See Majority Whip.

Without Objection — Used in lieu of a vote on non-controversial motions, amendments or bills that may be passed in either the House or Senate if no member voices an objection.

How a Bill Becomes Law

Note: Parliamentary terms used below are defined in the Glossary.

Introduction of Bills

A House member (including the resident commissioner of Puerto Rico and non-voting delegates of the District of Columbia, Guam, the Virgin Islands, and American Samoa) may introduce any one of several types of bills and resolutions by handing it to the clerk of the House or placing it in a box called the hopper. A senator first gains recognition of the presiding officer to announce the introduction of a bill. If objection is offered by any senator the introduction of the bill is postponed until the following day.

As the next step in either the House or Senate, the bill is numbered, referred to the appropriate committee, labeled with the sponsor's name, and sent to the Government Printing Office so that copies can be made for subsequent study and action. Senate bills may be jointly sponsored and carry several senators' names. Until 1978, the House limited the number of members who could co-sponsor any one bill; the ceiling was eliminated at the beginning of the 96th Congress. A bill written in the Executive Branch and proposed as an administration measure usually is introduced by the chairman of the congressional committee which has jurisdiction.

Bills—Prefixed with "HR" in the House, "S" in the Senate, followed by a number. Used as the form for most legislation, whether general or special, public or private.

Joint Resolutions—Designated H J Res or S J Res. Subject to the same procedure as bills, with the exception of a joint resolution proposing an amendment to the Constitution. The latter must be approved by two-thirds of both houses and is thereupon sent directly to the administrator of general services for submission to the states for ratification rather than being presented to the president for his approval.

Concurrent Resolutions—Designated H Con Res or S Con Res. Used for matters affecting the operations of both houses. These resolutions do not become law.

Resolutions—Designated H Res or S Res. Used for a matter concerning the operation of either house alone and adopted only by the chamber in which it originates.

Committee Action

A bill is referred to the appropriate committee by a House parliamentarian on the Speaker's order, or by the Senate president. Sponsors may indicate their preferences for referral, although custom and chamber rule generally govern. An exception is the referral of private bills, which are sent to whatever group is designated by their sponsors. Bills are technically considered "read for the first time" when referred to House committees.

When a bill reaches a committee it is placed upon the group's calendar. At that time it comes under the sharpest congressional focus. Its chances for passage are quickly determined — and the great majority of bills fall by the legislative roadside. Failure of a committee to act on a bill is equivalent to killing it; the measure can be withdrawn from the group's purview only by a discharge petition signed by a majority of the House membership on House bills, or by adoption of a special resolution in the Senate. Discharge attempts rarely succeed.

The first committee action taken on a bill usually is a request for comment on it by interested agencies of the government. The committee chairman may assign the bill to a subcommittee for study and hearings, or it may be considered by the full committee. Hearings may be public, closed (executive session), or both. A subcommittee, after considering a bill, reports to the full committee its recommendations for action and any proposed amendments.

The full committee then votes on its recommendation to the House or Senate. This procedure is called "ordering a bill reported." Occasionally a committee may order a bill reported unfavorably; most of the time a report, submitted by the chairman of the committee to the House or Senate, calls for favorable action on the measure since the committee can effectively "kill" a bill by simply failing to take any action.

When a committee sends a bill to the chamber floor, it explains its reasons in a written statement, called a report, which accompanies the bill. Often committee members opposing a measure issue dissenting minority statements which are included in the report.

Usually, the committee "marks up" or proposes amendments to the bill. If they are substantial and the measure is complicated, the committee may order a "clean bill" introduced, which will embody the proposed amendments. The original bill then is put aside and the "clean bill," with a new number, is reported to the floor.

The chamber must approve, alter, or reject the committee amendments before the bill itself can be put to a vote.

Floor Action

After a bill is reported back to the house where it originated, it is placed on the calendar.

There are five legislative calendars in the House, issued in one cumulative calendar titled *Calendars of the United States House of Representatives and History of Legislation.* The House calendars are:

The Union Calendar to which are referred bills raising revenues, general appropriation bills and any measures directly or indirectly appropriating money or property. It is the Calendar of the Committee of the Whole House on the State of the Union.

The House Calendar to which are referred bills of a public character not raising revenue or appropriating money or property.

The Consent Calendar to which are referred bills of a non-controversial nature that are passed without debate when the Consent Calendar is called on the first and third Mondays of each month.

The Private Calendar to which are referred bills for relief in the nature of claims against the United States or private immigration bills that are passed without debate when the Private Calendar is called the first and third Tuesdays of each month.

The Discharge Calendar to which are referred motions to discharge committees when the necessary signatures are signed to a discharge petition.

There is only one legislative calendar in the Senate and one "executive calendar" for treaties and nominations

Progress of Legislation

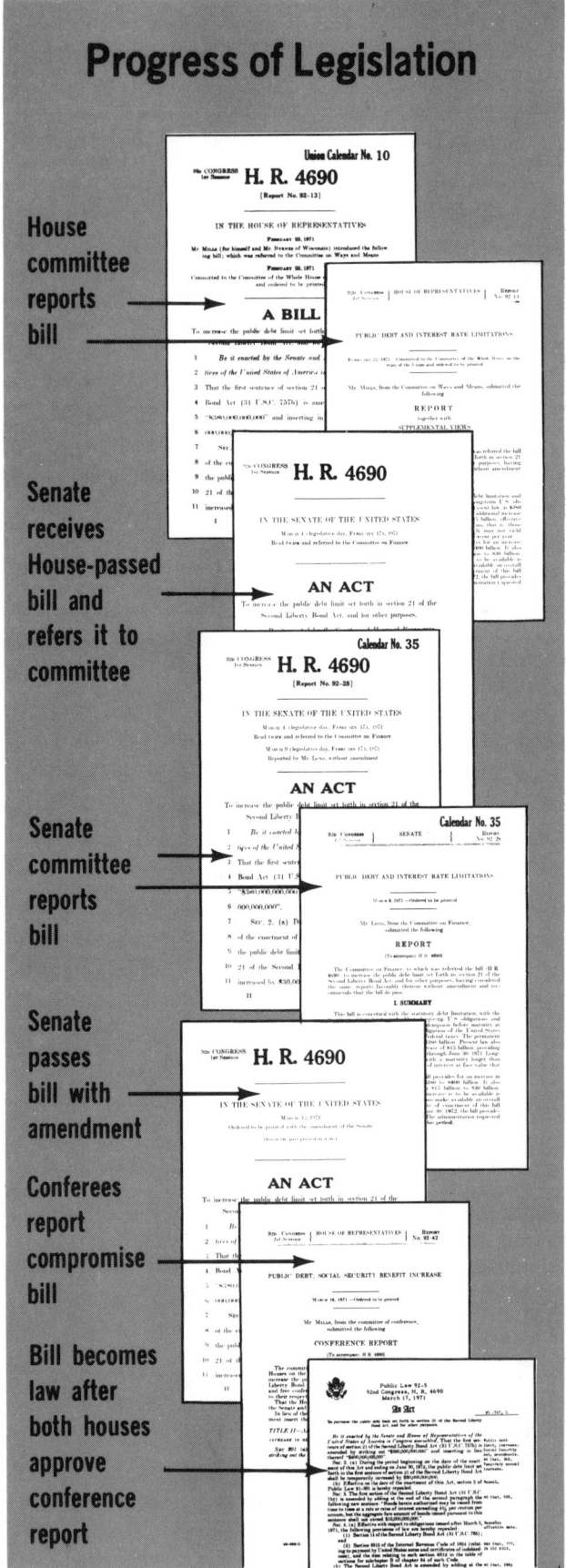

House committee reports bill

Senate receives House-passed bill and refers it to committee

Senate committee reports bill

Senate passes bill with amendment

Conferees report compromise bill

Bill becomes law after both houses approve conference report

submitted to the Senate. When the Senate Calendar is called, each senator is limited to five minutes' debate on each bill.

DEBATE. A bill is brought to debate by varying procedures. If a routine measure, it may await the call of the calendar. If it is urgent or important, it can be taken up in the Senate either by unanimous consent or by a majority vote. The policy committee of the majority party in the Senate schedules the bills that it wants taken up for debate.

In the House, precedence is granted if a special rule is obtained from the Rules Committee. A request for a special rule is usually made by the chairman of the committee that favorably reported the bill, supported by the bill's sponsor and other committee members. The request, considered by the Rules Committee in the same fashion that other committees consider legislative measures, is in the form of a resolution providing for immediate consideration of the bill. The Rules Committee reports the resolution to the House where it is debated and voted upon in the same fashion as regular bills. If the Rules Committee should fail to report a rule requested by a committee, there are several ways to bring the bill to the House floor — under suspension of the rules, on Calendar Wednesday or by a discharge motion.

The resolutions providing special rules are important because they specify how long the bill may be debated and whether it may be amended from the floor. If floor amendments are banned, the bill is considered under a "closed rule," which permits only members of the committee that first reported the measure to the House to alter its language, subject to chamber acceptance.

When a bill is debated under an "open rule," amendments may be offered from the floor. Committee amendments are always taken up first, but may be changed, as may all amendments up to the second degree, i.e., an amendment to an amendment to an amendment is not in order.

Duration of debate in the House depends on whether the bill is under discussion by the House proper or before the House when it is sitting as the Committee of the Whole House on the State of the Union. In the former, the amount of time for debate is determined either by special rule or is allocated with an hour for each member if the measure is under consideration without a rule. In the Committee of the Whole the amount of time agreed on for general debate is equally divided between proponents and opponents. At the end of general discussion, the bill is read section by section for amendment. Debate on an amendment is limited to five minutes for each side.

Senate debate is usually unlimited. It can be halted only by unanimous consent by "cloture," which requires a three-fifths majority of the entire Senate except for proposed changes in the Senate rules. The latter requires a two-thirds vote.

The House sits as the Committee of the Whole when it considers any tax measure or bill dealing with public appropriations. It can also resolve itself into the Committee of the Whole if a member moves to do so and the motion is carried. The Speaker appoints a member to serve as the chairman. The rules of the House permit the Committee of the Whole to meet with any 100 members on the floor, and to amend and act on bills with a quorum of the 100, within the time limitations mentioned previously. When the Committee of the Whole has acted, it "rises," the Speaker returns as the presiding officer of the House and the mem-

ber appointed chairman of the Committee of the Whole reports the action of the committee and its recommendations (amendments adopted).

VOTES. Voting on bills may occur repeatedly before they are finally approved or rejected. The House votes on the rule for the bill and on various amendments to the bill. Voting on amendments often is a more illuminating test of a bill's support than is the final tally. Sometimes members approve final passage of bills after vigorously supporting amendments which, if adopted, would have scuttled the legislation.

The Senate has three different methods of voting: an untabulated voice vote, a standing vote (called a division) and a recorded roll call to which members answer "yea" or "nay" when their names are called. The House also employs voice and standing votes, but since January 1973 yeas and nays have been recorded by an electronic voting device, eliminating the need for time-consuming roll calls.

Another method of voting, used in the House only, is the teller vote. Traditionally, members filed up the center aisle past counters; only vote totals were announced. Since 1971, one-fifth of a quorum can demand that the votes of individual members be recorded, thereby forcing them to take a public position on amendments to key bills. Electronic voting now is commonly used for this purpose.

After amendments to a bill have been voted upon, a vote may be taken on a motion to recommit the bill to committee. If carried, this vote removes the bill from the chamber's calendar. If the motion is unsuccessful, the bill then is "read for the third time." An actual reading usually is dispensed with. Until 1965, an opponent of a bill could delay this move by objecting and asking for a full reading of an engrossed (certified in final form) copy of the bill. After the "third reading," the vote on final passage is taken.

The final vote may be followed by a motion to reconsider, and this motion itself may be followed by a move to lay the motion on the table. Usually, those voting for the bill's passage vote for the tabling motion, thus safeguarding the final passage action. With that, the bill has been formally passed by the chamber. While a motion to reconsider a Senate vote is pending on a bill, the measure cannot be sent to the House.

Action in Second House

After a bill is passed it is sent to the other chamber. This body may then take one of several steps. It may pass the bill as is — accepting the other chamber's language. It may send the bill to committee for scrutiny or alteration, or reject the entire bill, advising the other house of its actions. Or it may simply ignore the bill submitted while it continues work on its own version of the proposed legislation. Frequently, one chamber may approve a version of a bill that is greatly at variance with the version already passed by the other house, and then substitute its amendments for the language of the other, retaining only the latter's bill designation.

A provision of the Legislative Reorganization Act of 1970 permits a separate House vote on any non-germane amendment added by the Senate to a House-passed bill and requires a majority vote to retain the amendment. Previously the House was forced to act on the bill as a whole; the only way to defeat the non-germane amendment was to reject the entire bill.

Often the second chamber makes only minor changes.

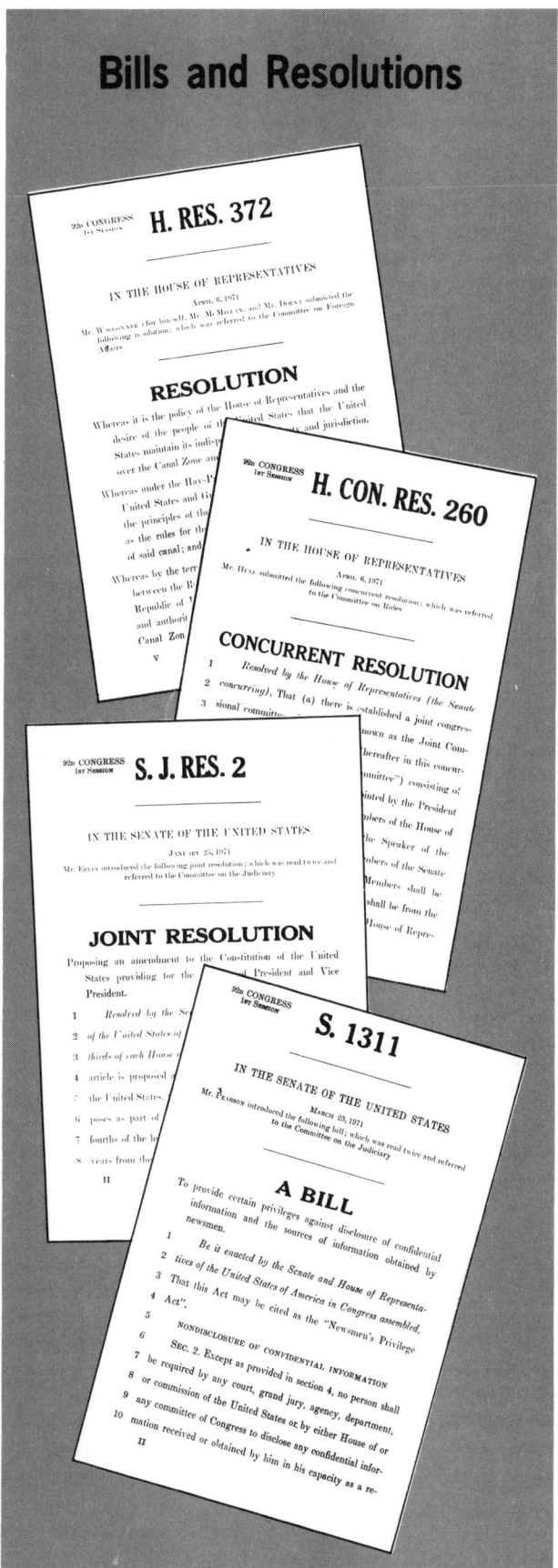

Bills and Resolutions

If these are readily agreed to by the other house, the bill then is routed to the White House for signing. However, if the opposite chamber basically alters the bill submitted to it, the measure usually is "sent to conference." The chamber that has possession of the "papers" (engrossed bill, engrossed amendments, messages of transmittal) requests a conference and the other chamber must agree to it. If the second house does not agree, the bill dies.

Conference, Final Action

CONFERENCE. A conference undertakes to harmonize conflicting House and Senate versions of a legislative bill. The conference is usually staffed by senior members (conferees), appointed by the presiding officers of the two houses, from the committees that managed the bills. Under this arrangement the conferees of one house have the duty of trying to maintain their chamber's position in the face of amending actions by the conferees (also referred to as "managers") of the other house.

The number of conferees from each chamber may vary, the range usually being from three to nine members in each group, depending upon the length or complexity of the bill involved. There may be five representatives and three senators on the conference committee, or the reverse. But a majority vote controls the action of each group so that a larger representation does not give one chamber a voting advantage over the other chamber's conferees.

Theoretically, conferees are not allowed to write new legislation in reconciling the two versions before them, but this curb sometimes is bypassed. Many bills have been put into acceptable compromise form only after new language was provided by the conferees. The 1970 Reorganization Act attempted to tighten restrictions on conferees by forbidding them to introduce any language on a topic that neither chamber sent to conference or to modify any topic beyond the scope of the different House and Senate versions.

Frequently the ironing out of difficulties takes days or even weeks. Conferences on involved appropriation bills sometimes are particularly drawn out.

As a conference proceeds, conferees reconcile differences between the versions, but generally they grant concessions only insofar as they remain sure that the chamber they represent will accept the compromises. Occasionally, uncertainty over how either house will react, or the positive refusal of a chamber to back down on a disputed amendment, results in an impasse, and the bills die in conference even though each was approved by its sponsoring chamber.

Conferees sometimes go back to their respective chambers for further instructions, when they report certain portions in disagreement. Then the chamber concerned can either "recede and concur" in the amendment of the other house, or "insist on its amendment."

When the conferees have reached agreement, they prepare a conference report embodying their recommendations (compromises). The reports, in document form, must be submitted to each house.

The conference report must be approved by each house. Consequently, approval of the report is approval of the compromise bill. In the order of voting on conference reports, the chamber which asked for a conference yields to the other chamber the opportunity to vote first.

FINAL STEPS. After a bill has been passed by both the House and Senate in identical form, all of the original papers are sent to the enrolling clerk of the chamber in which the bill originated. He then prepares an enrolled bill which is printed on parchment paper. When this bill has been certified as correct by the secretary of the Senate or the clerk of the House, depending on which chamber originated the bill, it is signed first (no matter whether it originated in the Senate or House) by the Speaker of the House and then by the president of the Senate. It is next sent to the White House to await action.

If the president approves the bill he signs it, dates it and usually writes the word "approved" on the document. If he does not sign it within 10 days (Sundays excepted) and Congress is in session, the bill becomes law without his signature.

However, should Congress adjourn before the 10 days expire, and the president has failed to sign the measure, it does not become law. This procedure is called the pocket veto.

A president vetoes a bill by refusing to sign it and before the 10-day period expires, returning it to Congress with a message stating his reasons. The message is sent to the chamber which originated the bill. If no action is taken there on the message, the bill dies. Congress, however, can attempt to override the president's veto and enact the bill, "the objections of the president to the contrary notwithstanding." Overriding of a veto requires a two-thirds vote of those present, who must number a quorum and vote by roll call.

Debate can precede this vote, with motions permitted to lay the message on the table, postpone action on it, or refer it to committee. If the president's veto is overridden by a two-thirds vote in both houses, the bill becomes law. Otherwise it is dead.

When bills are passed finally and signed, or passed over a veto, they are given law numbers in numerical order as they become law. There are two series of numbers, one for public and one for private laws, starting at the number "1" for each two-year term of Congress. They are then identified by law number and by Congress — i.e., Private Law 21, 97th Congress; Public Law 250, 97th Congress (or PL 97-250).

How a Bill Becomes Law

This graphic shows the most typical way in which proposed legislation is enacted into law. There are more complicated, as well as simpler, routes, and most bills never become law. The process is illustrated with two hypothetical bills, House bill No. 1 (HR 1) and Senate bill No. 2 (S 2). Bills must be passed by both houses in identical form before they can be sent to the president. The path of HR 1 is traced by a solid line, that of S 2 by a broken line. In practice most bills begin as similar proposals in both houses.

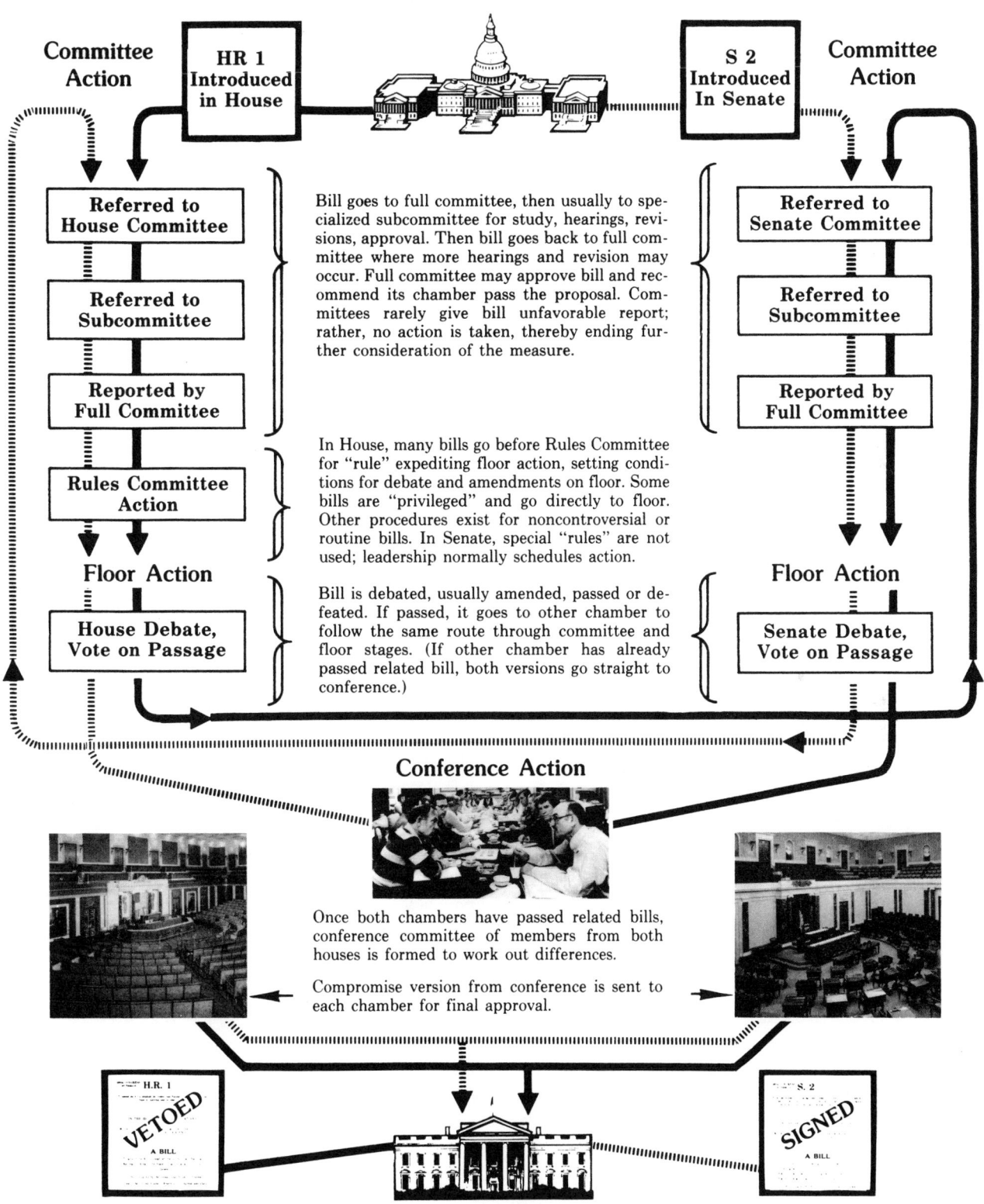

Committee Action

HR 1 Introduced in House

S 2 Introduced In Senate

Committee Action

Referred to House Committee

Referred to Subcommittee

Reported by Full Committee

Rules Committee Action

Bill goes to full committee, then usually to specialized subcommittee for study, hearings, revisions, approval. Then bill goes back to full committee where more hearings and revision may occur. Full committee may approve bill and recommend its chamber pass the proposal. Committees rarely give bill unfavorable report; rather, no action is taken, thereby ending further consideration of the measure.

In House, many bills go before Rules Committee for "rule" expediting floor action, setting conditions for debate and amendments on floor. Some bills are "privileged" and go directly to floor. Other procedures exist for noncontroversial or routine bills. In Senate, special "rules" are not used; leadership normally schedules action.

Referred to Senate Committee

Referred to Subcommittee

Reported by Full Committee

Floor Action

House Debate, Vote on Passage

Bill is debated, usually amended, passed or defeated. If passed, it goes to other chamber to follow the same route through committee and floor stages. (If other chamber has already passed related bill, both versions go straight to conference.)

Floor Action

Senate Debate, Vote on Passage

Conference Action

Once both chambers have passed related bills, conference committee of members from both houses is formed to work out differences.

Compromise version from conference is sent to each chamber for final approval.

H.R. 1 VETOED A BILL

S. 2 SIGNED A BILL

Compromise bill approved by both houses is sent to the president, who can sign it into law or veto it and return it to Congress. Congress may override veto by a two-thirds majority vote in both houses; bill then becomes law without president's signature.

97TH CONGRESS, SECOND SESSION

The 97th Congress Trudged to a Bitter End

When the 97th Congress trudged to an end Dec. 23, few members went home happy.

Senators, particularly, left at Christmastime with a bitter taste, feeling their institution had changed to the point where filibusters were the order of the day and courtesy was a thing of the past.

House Speaker Thomas P. O'Neill Jr., D-Mass., frustrated by President Reagan's unwillingness to compromise, swore he would never agree to another lame-duck session except in a national emergency.

Neither chamber operated smoothly during the 97th Congress and the wheels nearly came entirely off the cart by the end of the post-election session.

In 1982, Congress was absorbed primarily in economic decisions from the time Reagan sent Congress his fiscal 1983 budget in February until it passed a stopgap funding bill and went home in December.

Many legislative decisions were collected into omnibus budget and reconciliation bills. Then, when Congress could not pass appropriations bills following these budget dictates, it wrapped most of its appropriations decisions into a series of massive continuing resolutions.

The budget almost totally dominated the congressional schedule and, as the year ended, members of both parties were considering changes in the budget process.

Filibusters in the Senate were a regular occurrence throughout 1982, not just in the lame-duck session. In late summer, for example, the Senate spent weeks bogged down in protracted debate over amendments on abortion and school busing as part of a bill increasing the national debt limit. The bill passed, the amendments failed.

If these filibusters were not enough to make civility difficult in the Senate, senators also had to debate the expulsion of one of their colleagues, Harrison A. Williams Jr., D-N.J. (1959-82), who resigned before a vote was taken to oust him over his Abscam conviction. Senators, a handful of whom unofficially began running for president, also fought institutional battles over whether Senate proceedings would be televised and whether senators should get a gymnasium in the new Hart office building, which opened in November.

Both television and the gym were defeated, to the displeasure of many senators. The new office building, which had been politically ridiculed as a costly palace, was so unpopular that the most junior senators had to be ordered into offices there.

Going Home

Adjournment of the 97th Congress finally came on Dec. 23 as a bone-tired Senate turned off the lights and went home.

The House had called it quits Dec. 21, although by then many of its members had already left the Capitol.

The lame-duck session, which President Reagan had

insisted upon, had begun Nov. 29. Although the president had requested that Congress pass a long list of bills, the lame-duck session produced far more anguish than legislation.

It did manage to enact a long-sought nuclear waste disposal bill and a measure to repair the nation's roads and bridges through a nickel increase in the federal gasoline tax.

And, although the lame-duck session was called primarily to pass appropriations bills, Congress was unable to pass half of the annual money bills and had to enact a massive, stopgap funding bill to keep the government running.

House Democrats added a $5.4 billion jobs program to this stopgap funding bill but agreed to strip it out when Reagan made clear he would slap a veto on a bill containing a jobs program.

The inability to find common ground with the White House caused O'Neill to say, "The president doesn't know what compromise is. He thinks compromise is when we give

---

97th Congress Leadership

SENATE

President Pro Tempore — Strom Thurmond, R-S.C

Majority Leader — Howard H. Baker Jr., R-Tenn..

Majority Whip — Ted Stevens, R-Alaska

Republican Conference Chairman — James A. McClure, R-Idaho

Republican Conference Secretary — Jake Garn, R-Utah

Minority Leader — Robert C. Byrd, D-W.Va.

Minority Whip — Alan Cranston, D-Calif.

Democratic Conference Secretary — Daniel K. Inouye, D-Hawaii

HOUSE

Speaker — Thomas P. O'Neill Jr., D-Mass.

Majority Leader — Jim Wright, D-Texas

Majority Whip — Thomas S. Foley, D-Wash.

Minority Leader — Robert H. Michel, R-Ill.

Minority Whip — Trent Lott, R-Miss.

Chairman of the Conference — Jack F. Kemp, R-N.Y.

Republican Policy Committee Chairman — Dick Cheney, R- Wyo.

Public Laws

A total of 328 bills cleared by Congress in 1982 became public laws. Following is a list of the number of public laws enacted since 1967:

Year	Public Laws	Year	Public Laws
1982	328	1974	402
1981	145	1973	247
1980	426	1972	483
1979	187	1971	224
1978	410	1970	505
1977	223	1969	190
1976	383	1968	391
1975	205	1967	249

him 80 percent of what he asks for and he gives us nothing.

"Cooperation is a two-way street. For two years, we have cooperated with the president and waited for him to cooperate with the congressional agenda. We are still waiting."

Filibusters in the Senate

The lame-duck Senate grew increasingly irritable as it bogged down in a series of filibusters over a variety of bills. Gentlemanly manners, long a tradition in the Senate, were often discarded as senators shouted at one another, saying things about colleagues they later regretted and had removed from the *Congressional Record.*

The filibusters necessitated marathon sessions in the Senate. At one point, the Senate was in session for just shy of 38 straight hours. One senator called the delay tactic a "verbal sit-in."

Major policy issues, including defense, unemployment benefits and jobs programs, were debated as amendments to either the gasoline tax bill or the stopgap funding bill. In some cases, these amendments were discussed by groggy senators in the wee hours of the morning.

For example, at 3:15 a.m. on Dec. 17, the Senate decided a crucial amendment on the MX missile.

Senators grew increasingly tired and cranky as the sessions stretched out. A few senators slept in the cloakrooms, coming out for votes. Some just dozed on the Senate floor. Jennings Randolph, D-W.Va., and an aide slept side by side in their chairs. An aide to John H. Chafee, R-R.I., whispered in Chafee's ear at one point, but Chafee appeared to be asleep.

The most contentious filibuster came over the increase in the gasoline tax, a bill a handful of conservatives wanted to block. For the most part, Republicans battled among themselves. Majority Leader Howard H. Baker Jr., R-Tenn., was repeatedly unable to control North Carolina's two Republican senators, Jesse Helms and John P. East.

When East was refusing to yield the floor, S.I. "Sam" Hayakawa, R-Calif., sarcastically asked whether East believed that the opinions of other senators did not matter. "If such is the case ... why does he demean himself by associating himself with clods and peasants like us?"

Helms' refusal to let the Senate vote on the gas tax and go home Dec. 21 prompted Alan K. Simpson, R-Wyo., to say, "Seldom have I seen a more obdurate, more obnoxious performance."

Wendell H. Ford, D-Ky., said Helms and East did not understand the difference "between expressing your opin-

Membership Changes, 97th Congress

HOUSE

Party	Member	Died	Resigned	Successor	Party	Elected	Sworn In
R	Dave Stockman - Mich.		1/27/81	Mark Siljander	R	4/21/81	4/28/81
D	Gladys Noon Spellman - Md.		2/24/81*	Steny Hoyer	D	5/19/81	6/3/81
R	Tennyson Guyer - Ohio	4/12/81		Michael G. Oxley	R	6/25/81	7/21/81
R	Jon Hinson - Miss.		4/13/81	Wayne Dowdy	D	7/7/81	7/9/81
D	Raymond F. Lederer - Pa.		5/5/81	Joseph F. Smith	D	7/21/81	7/28/81
D	William R. Cotter - Conn.	9/8/81		Barbara B. Kennelly	D	1/12/82	1/25/82
D	Eugene V. Atkinson - Pa.			Atkinson switched to the Republican Party on Oct. 14, 1981.			
D	George E. Danielson - Calif.		3/9/82	Matthew G. Martinez	D	7/13/82	7/15/82
R	John M. Ashbrook - Ohio	4/24/82		Jean S. Ashbrook	R	6/29/82	7/12/82
D	Fred Richmond - N.Y.		8/25/82				
D	Adam Benjamin Jr. - Ind.	9/7/82		Katie Hall	D	11/2/82	11/29/82

SENATE

Party	Member	Died	Resigned	Successor	Party	Appointed	Sworn In
D	Harrison A. Williams Jr.		3/11/82	Nicholas F. Brady	R	4/12/82	4/20/82
R	Nicholas F. Brady		12/27/82	Frank Lautenberg	D	12/27/82	12/27/82

*Rep. Spellman suffered cardiac arrest four days before the November 1980 general election and remained in a trance-like state of consciousness from that time. Although she was elected to the 97th Congress, she was never sworn in as a member. On Feb. 24, 1981, the House voted to declare her seat vacant.

ion and thwarting the will of the majority."

Helms was unfazed by the criticism. He said of his colleagues, "their top priority is getting home and their convenience."

Two days later, the Senate broke the Helms filibuster, passed the gasoline tax and went home. Several senators left suggesting the need for changes in the Senate rules to prevent a small minority from tying up the chamber.

Baker said he wanted "to let it cool off a bit" before considering any changes. Baker had earlier appointed two former senators — James B. Pearson, R-Kan., (1962-78) and Abraham A. Ribicoff, D-Conn. (1963-81) — to spend a year studying the operation of the Senate. Their report was due in mid-1983.

The inability of the Senate to finish its work because of obstruction by a few senators gave credence to the observation of academics, journalists and former senators that the Senate had turned from a club-like institution into a loose collection of 100 individuals.

Pay Raise in the House

By comparison, the House had little acrimony in the final days of the lame-duck session.

It was not without controversy and frustration, however. For several years, the House had voted down every pay raise for members on which it had an opportunity to cast a recorded vote. But, with substantial and disproportional help from lame-duck members, the House approved a 15 percent pay raise for itself. An amendment to knock out the raise failed on a 208-208 tie.

The House leadership, too, was faced with a type of filibuster, even though House rules did not allow the unlimited debate that sometimes occurred in the Senate. When the leadership tried to move an immigration reform bill that had been passed by the Senate and pushed by the administration, members opposing the measure filed hundreds of amendments, which could have taken weeks to consider. The leadership was forced to simply pull the bill off the floor.

By the end of the lame-duck session, members, particularly senators, staff, reporters and lobbyists had taken to wearing bright yellow lapel pins in the shape of a duck. Some of the pins showed an entire duck, but the most popular versions were those that just presented the rear end.

Appropriations Squeeze

Because Congress spent so much time on the budget process, following the practice of recent years, there was little time left for passing appropriations bills that actually funded the budget decisions. It was this lack of time that caused President Reagan to insist on a lame-duck session to work on appropriations bills.

In 1982, the first six months of the session were spent on lengthy budget negotiations, drafting sessions and floor consideration of the first fiscal 1983 budget resolution — twice by the House and once by the Senate. The exercise proved so painful that members decided to sidestep action on a second budget resolution.

Following adoption of the budget resolution, Congress became tied up with reconciliation measures to carry out the spending cuts and revenue increases mandated by the budget resolution. Action on the reconciliation legislation was not completed until mid-August, less than two months before the Oct. 1 beginning of the new fiscal year.

As a result of the budget process, the Appropriations

Senate Cloture Votes, 1982

Following is a list of all cloture votes taken by the Senate during 1982. Cloture motions required a majority of three-fifths of the total Senate (60 members) for adoption, under a rule adopted in 1975. Previously cloture could be invoked by a two-thirds majority vote of those senators present and voting, except between 1949 and 1959, when the rule required a two-thirds majority of the entire Senate.

Since 1979, Senate rules had required, after no more than 100 hours of post-cloture debate, a final vote on a measure on which cloture had been invoked.

The 19 cloture votes in 1982 brought to 187 the total number of cloture votes taken since the adoption of Rule 22 first allowed them in 1917, four short of the record 23 taken in 1975. However, the 15 cloture votes between September and December of 1982 were the most in any four-month period since the rule was adopted. It took the Senate 28 years, until 1944, to cast its 15th cloture vote. *(Cloture votes, 1919-81, 1981 Almanac p. 10; 1977 Almanac p. 813)*

Issue	Date	Vote
Broadcast Senate Proceedings	April 20, 1982	47-51
Criminal Code Reform Act	April 27, 1982	45-46
Urgent Supplemental Appropriations, Fiscal 1982	May 27, 1982	95-2
Voting Rights Act	June 15, 1982	86-8
Debt Limit Increase	Sept. 9, 1982	41-47
Debt Limit Increase	Sept. 13, 1982	45-35
Debt Limit Increase	Sept. 15, 1982	50-44
Debt Limit Increase	Sept. 20, 1982	50-39
Debt Limit Increase	Sept. 21, 1982	53-47
Debt Limit Increase	Sept. 22, 1982	54-46
Debt Limit Increase	Sept. 23, 1982	53-45
Antitrust Equal Enforcement Act	Dec. 2, 1982	38-58
Antitrust Equal Enforcement Act	Dec. 2, 1982	44-51
Transportation Assistance Act	Dec. 13, 1982	75-13
Transportation Assistance Act	Dec. 16, 1982	48-50
Transportation Assistance Act	Dec. 16, 1982	5-93
Transportation Assistance Act	Dec. 19, 1982	89-5
Transportation Assistance Act	Dec. 20, 1982	87-8
Transportation Assistance Act	Dec. 23, 1982	81-5

committees, once the most powerful of congressional committees, were relegated to a secondary role — following up on what the budget resolutions instructed them to do.

The budget process also compressed the time Congress had to consider appropriations bills. A consequence of this compression was massive continuing appropriations resolutions, since regular appropriations for many agencies did not clear Congress before the fiscal year began.

In 1981, Congress had to approve four continuing resolutions. At one point, the entire government except for the legislative branch, was operating under stopgap funding and many agencies operated all of fiscal 1982 under temporary funding.

In 1982, Congress was able to clear only three of the 13 annual appropriations bills before it adjourned Oct. 2 for the election recess. During the lame-duck session, four more of the bills were cleared, leaving six bills, including the defense and energy bills, unfinished.

Recent Lame-Duck Sessions

Congress has held seven post-election sessions since 1945.

Year	Congress	Chamber	Dates
1948	80th	Senate House	Dec. 31, 1948 (2-hour session)
1950	81st	Senate House	Nov. 27, 1950-Jan. 2, 1951
1954	83rd	Senate	Nov. 8, 1954-Dec. 2, 1954
1970	91st	Senate House	Nov. 16, 1970-Jan. 2, 1971
1974	93rd	Senate House	Nov. 18, 1974-Dec. 20, 1974
1980	96th	Senate House	Nov. 12, 1980-Dec. 16, 1980
1982	97th	Senate House	Nov. 29, 1982-Dec. 23, 1982 Nov. 29, 1982-Dec. 21, 1982

1948. The 1948 post-election session of the 80th Congress lasted only two hours. Both chambers swore in new members, approved several minor resolutions and received last-minute reports from committees.

In addition to final floor action, several committees resumed work. The most active was the House Un-American Activities Committee, which continued its investigation of alleged communist espionage in the federal government. *(1948 Almanac p. 419)*

1950. Following the 1950 elections, President Harry S Truman sent a "must" agenda to the lame-duck session of the 81st Congress. The president's list included supplemental defense appropriations, an excess profits tax, aid to Yugoslavia, a three-month extension of federal rent controls and statehood for Hawaii and Alaska. During a marathon session that lasted until only a few hours before its successor took over, the 81st Congress acted on all of the president's legislative items except the statehood bills, which were blocked by a Senate filibuster. *(1950 Almanac pp. 28, 33)*

1954. Only one chamber of the 83rd Congress convened after the 1954 elections. The Senate returned Nov. 8 to hold what has been called a "censure session," a continuing investigation into the conduct of Sen. Joseph R. McCarthy, R-Wis. (1947-57). By a 67-22 roll call the Senate voted Dec. 2 to "condemn" McCarthy for his behavior.

In other post-election floor action, the Senate passed a series of miscellaneous and administrative resolutions and swore in new members. *(1954 Almanac p. 471)*

1970. President Richard M. Nixon criticized the lame-duck Congress as one that had "seemingly lost the capacity to decide and the will to act." Filibusters and intense controversy contributed to inaction on the president's request for trade legislation and welfare reform.

Congress nevertheless claimed some substantive results during the post-election session, which ended Jan. 2, 1971. Several major appropriations bills were cleared for presidential signature. Congress also approved for-

eign aid to Cambodia, provided interim funding for the supersonic transport plane (SST) and repealed the Tonkin Gulf Resolution. *(1970 Almanac p. 22)*

1974. In a session that ran from Nov. 18-Dec. 20, 1974, the 93rd Congress cleared several important bills for presidential signature, including a mass transit bill, the Labor-HEW appropriations bill and the foreign aid package. A House-Senate conference committee reached agreement on a major strip-mining bill, but President Gerald R. Ford vetoed it.

Congress approved the nomination of Nelson A. Rockefeller as vice president. It also overrode presidential vetoes of two bills — one broadening the Freedom of Information Act, a second authorizing educational benefits for Korean War and Vietnam-era veterans. *(1974 Almanac p. 3)*

1980. The lame-duck session of the 97th Congress was productive, at least until Dec. 5, the original adjournment date set by congressional leaders. By that date a budget had been approved, along with a budget reconciliation measure. Ten regular appropriations bills had cleared, though one subsequently was vetoed. Congress had approved two major environmental measures — an Alaskan lands bill and toxic waste "superfund" legislation — as well as a three-year extension of general revenue sharing.

After Dec. 5, however, the legislative pace slowed noticeably. Action on a continuing appropriations resolution for those departments and agencies whose regular funding had not been cleared was delayed, first by a filibuster on a fair housing bill and later by more than 100 "Christmas tree" amendments, including a $10,000-a-year pay raise for members. After the conference report failed in the Senate and twice was rewritten, the bill was shorn of virtually all its "ornaments," and finally cleared both chambers on Dec. 16. *(1980 Almanac p. 16)*

1982. Despite the reluctance of congressional leaders, President Reagan urged the convening of a post-election session, principally to pass remaining appropriations bills.

Rising unemployment — and Democratic election gains in the House — made job creation efforts the focus of the lame-duck Congress, however. Overriding the objections of Republican conservatives, Congress passed Reagan-backed legislation raising the federal gasoline tax from 4 cents to 9 cents a gallon to pay for highway repairs and mass transit. Supporters said the legislation would help alleviate unemployment by creating 300,000 jobs.

Congress eventually cleared four additional appropriations bills, packaging the remaining six in a continuing appropriations resolution that also included a pay raise for House members. Conferees dropped funding for emergency jobs programs to avert a threatened veto of the resolution.

The lame-duck session also was highlighted by Congress' refusal to fund production and procurement of the first five MX intercontinental missiles, the first time in recent history that either house of Congress had denied a president's request to fund production of a strategic weapon. *(Session summary, p. 10)*

Two continuing resolutions were needed; one in October and one in December. Both became the vehicles for other legislation to be attached.

"It's a sad way to do business," lamented House Appropriations Committee Chairman Jamie L. Whitten, D-Miss. "We've been forced to do it — it's not because we want it that way.

"The last three or four years," Whitten said, "the delay in arriving at a budget ceiling has brought us to where we've about 70 days to act. It's a poor way to run a railroad."

The antipathy toward the budget process on the House Appropriations Committee was overwhelming.

"We're in this position because of the budget process," complained Rep. David R. Obey, D-Wis., in mid-September when the Appropriations Committee had to mark up another stopgap funding bill. Obey was a member of the Budget Committee as well as the Appropriations Committee.

"The appropriations process and the authorization process and all the other damned committees — there ain't nothing left for us to do."

But Senate Budget Committee Chairman Pete V. Domenici, R-N.M., defended the budget process. "If you genuinely look at how much time the Appropriations committees have, you'll see that the budget resolution was passed two and one-half months ago. And yet not one appropriations bill has been enacted."

Domenici agreed that funding by continuing resolution was bad. "The more government a continuing resolution covers, the worse it is," he said. "It becomes very difficult to know where things are."

—By Andy Plattner

Vetoes Cast by President Reagan

President Reagan vetoed 12 public and one private bill in his second year in office, bringing his total to 15.

Congress was successful in overriding two of the five vetoes on which an override attempt was made. The first to be overridden was a measure to extend until 1986 a clause in the copyright law requiring most books and periodicals written in English by American authors to be printed and bound in the United States or Canada in order to receive full copyright protection. *(Story, p. 380)*

The second override came on a $14.2 billion supplemental appropriations bill, which the president described as a "budget buster," that cut his defense spending request while providing an additional $900 million for social programs. *(Story, p. 219)*

The two overrides matched Jimmy Carter's four-year total. Gerald R. Ford had 12 vetoes overridden, the most since Andrew Johnson.

When Congress is in session, a bill becomes law without the president's signature if he does not act upon it within 10 days, excluding Sundays, from the time he receives it. But if Congress adjourns within that 10-day period, the bill is killed, or pocket vetoed, without the president's signature. Five of the 13 vetoes in 1982 were pocket vetoes. There was one pocket veto in 1981.

Reagan's 15 vetoes exceeded by five the number cast by the first six presidents in the 40 years from 1789 to 1829. Seven presidents vetoed no bills during their tenures. The greatest number of vetoes, 635, was cast by Franklin D. Roosevelt. More recently, Carter vetoed 31 bills during his term; Ford vetoed 66; Richard M. Nixon, 43; Lyndon B. Johnson, 30; and John F. Kennedy, 21.

1981
1. H J Res 357 (Continuing Appropriations)
   Vetoed: Nov. 23
   No override attempt
2. HR 4353 (Bankruptcy Fees on Lifetime Communities Inc.)
   Pocket vetoed: Dec. 29

1982
3. S 1503 (Standby Petroleum Allocation Act)
   Vetoed: March 20
   Senate sustained March 24: 58-36*
4. HR 5118 (Southern Arizona Water Rights Settlement Act)
   Vetoed: June 1
   No override attempt
5. HR 5922 (Urgent Supplemental Appropriations, Fiscal 1982)
   Vetoed: June 24
   House sustained June 24: 253-151*
6. HR 6682 (Urgent Supplemental Appropriations, Fiscal 1982)
   Vetoed: June 25
   House sustained July 13: 242-169*
7. HR 6198 (Manufacturers Copyright Bill)
   Vetoed: July 8
   Veto overridden July 13*
   House: 324-86, July 13

Senate: 84-9, July 13
8. HR 6863 (Supplemental Appropriations, Fiscal 1982)
   Vetoed: August 28
   Veto overridden Sept. 10*
   House: 301-117, Sept. 9
   Senate: 60-30, Sept. 10
9. HR 1371 (Contract Disputes)
   Vetoed: Oct. 15
   No override attempt
10. S 2577 (Environmental Research and Development)
    Vetoed: Oct. 22
    No override attempt
11. S 2623 (Indian Controlled Community Colleges)
    Pocket vetoed: Jan. 3, 1983
12. HR 5858 (Private bill for relief of certain silver dealers)
    Pocket vetoed: Jan. 4, 1983
13. HR 7336 (Education Consolidation and Improvement Act)
    Pocket vetoed: Jan. 12, 1983
14. HR 9 (Florida Wilderness Act)
    Pocket vetoed: Jan. 14, 1983
15. HR 3963 (Anti-Crime Bill)
    Pocket vetoed: Jan. 14, 1983

Veto overrides require a two-thirds majority vote of both houses.

Members of the 97th Congress, Second Session . . .

As of Dec. 31, 1982

Representatives
D 242; R 192
1 Vacancy[1]

A

Addabbo, Joseph P., D-N.Y. (7)
Akaka, Daniel K., D-Hawaii (2)
Alexander, Bill, D-Ark. (1)
Anderson, Glenn M., D-Calif. (32)
Andrews, Ike, D-N.C. (4)
Annunzio, Frank, D-Ill. (11)
Anthony, Beryl Jr., D-Ark. (4)
Applegate, Douglas, D-Ohio (18)
Archer, Bill, R-Texas (7)
Ashbrook, Jean S., R-Ohio (17)
Aspin, Les, D-Wis. (1)
Atkinson, Eugene V., R-Pa. (25)
AuCoin, Les, D-Ore. (1)

B

Badham, Robert E., R-Calif. (40)
Bafalis, L. A. "Skip", R-Fla. (10)
Bailey, Don, D-Pa. (21)
Bailey, Wendell, R-Mo. (8)
Barnard, Doug Jr., D-Ga. (10)
Barnes, Michael D., D-Md. (8)
Beard, Robin L., R-Tenn. (6)
Bedell, Berkley, D-Iowa (6)
Beilenson, Anthony C., D-Calif. (23)
Benedict, Cleve, R-W.Va. (2)
Bennett, Charles E., D-Fla. (3)
Bereuter, Douglas K., R-Neb. (1)
Bethune, Ed, R-Ark. (2)
Bevill, Tom, D-Ala. (4)
Biaggi, Mario, D-N.Y. (10)
Bingham, Jonathan B., D-N.Y. (22)
Blanchard, James J., D-Mich. (18)
Bliley, Thomas J. Jr., R-Va. (3)
Boggs, Lindy (Mrs. Hale), D-La. (2)
Boland, Edward P., D-Mass. (2)
Bolling, Richard, D-Mo. (5)
Boner, Bill, D-Tenn. (5)
Bonior, David E., D-Mich. (12)
Bonker, Don, D-Wash. (3)
Bouquard, Marilyn Lloyd, D-Tenn. (3)
Bowen, David R., D-Miss. (2)
Breaux, John B., D-La. (7)
Brinkley, Jack, D-Ga. (3)
Brodhead, William M., D-Mich. (17)
Brooks, Jack, D-Texas (9)
Broomfield, William S., R-Mich. (19)
Brown, Clarence J., R-Ohio (7)
Brown, George E. Jr., D-Calif. (36)
Brown, Hank, R-Colo. (4)
Broyhill, James T., R-N.C. (10)
Burgener, Clair W., R-Calif. (43)
Burton, John L., D-Calif. (5)
Burton, Phillip, D-Calif. (6)
Butler, M. Caldwell, R-Va. (6)
Byron, Beverly B., D-Md. (6)

C

Campbell, Carroll A. Jr., R-S.C. (4)
Carman, Gregory W., R-N.Y. (3)
Carney, William, R-N.Y. (1)
Chappell, Bill Jr., D-Fla. (4)
Chappie, Gene, R-Calif. (1)
Cheney, Dick, R-Wyo. (AL)
Chisholm, Shirley, D-N.Y. (12)
Clausen, Don H., R-Calif. (2)
Clay, William, D-Mo. (1)
Clinger, William F. Jr., R-Pa. (23)
Coats, Dan, R-Ind. (4)
Coelho, Tony, D-Calif. (15)
Coleman, E. Thomas, R-Mo. (6)
Collins, Cardiss, D-Ill. (7)
Collins, James M., R-Texas (3)
Conable, Barber B. Jr., R-N.Y. (35)
Conte, Silvio O., R-Mass. (1)
Conyers, John Jr., D-Mich. (1)
Corcoran, Tom, R-Ill. (15)
Coughlin, Lawrence, R-Pa. (13)
Courter, Jim, R-N.J. (13)
Coyne, Jim, R-Pa. (8)
Coyne, William J., D-Pa. (14)
Craig, Larry E., R-Idaho (1)
Crane, Daniel B., R-Ill. (22)
Crane, Philip M., R-Ill. (12)
Crockett, George W. Jr., D-Mich. (13)

D

D'Amours, Norman E., D-N.H. (1)
Daniel, Dan, D-Va. (5)
Daniel, Robert W. Jr., R-Va. (4)
Dannemeyer, William E., R-Calif. (39)
Daschle, Thomas A., D-S.D. (1)
Daub, Hal, R-Neb. (2)
Davis, Robert W., R-Mich. (11)
Deckard, H. Joel, R-Ind. (8)
de la Garza, E. "Kika", D-Texas (15)
Dellums, Ronald V., D-Calif. (8)
DeNardis, Lawrence J., R-Conn. (3)
Derrick, Butler, D-S.C. (3)
Derwinski, Edward J., R-Ill. (4)
Dickinson, William L., R-Ala. (2)
Dicks, Norman D., D-Wash. (6)
Dingell, John D., D-Mich. (16)
Dixon, Julian C., D-Calif. (28)
Donnelly, Brian J., D-Mass. (11)
Dorgan, Byron L., D-N.D. (AL)
Dornan, Robert K., R-Calif. (27)
Dougherty, Charles F., R-Pa. (4)
Dowdy, Wayne, D-Miss. (4)
Downey, Thomas J., D-N.Y. (2)
Dreier, David, R-Calif. (35)
Duncan, John J., R-Tenn. (2)
Dunn, Jim, R-Mich. (6)
Dwyer, Bernard J., D-N.J. (15)
Dymally, Mervyn M., D-Calif. (31)
Dyson, Roy, D-Md. (1)

E

Early, Joseph D., D-Mass. (3)
Eckart, Dennis E., D-Ohio (22)
Edgar, Robert W., D-Pa. (7)
Edwards, Don, D-Calif. (10)
Edwards, Jack, R-Ala. (1)
Edwards, Mickey, R-Okla. (5)
Emerson, Bill, R-Mo. (10)
Emery, David F., R-Maine (1)
English, Glenn, D-Okla. (6)
Erdahl, Arlen, R-Minn. (1)
Erlenborn, John N., R-Ill. (14)
Ertel, Allen E., D-Pa. (17)
Evans, Billy Lee, D-Ga. (8)
Evans, Cooper, R-Iowa (3)
Evans, David W., D-Ind. (6)
Evans, Thomas B. Jr., R-Del. (AL)

F

Fary, John G., D-Ill. (5)
Fascell, Dante B., D-Fla. (15)
Fazio, Vic, D-Calif. (4)
Fenwick, Millicent, R-N.J. (5)
Ferraro, Geraldine A., D-N.Y. (9)
Fiedler, Bobbi, R-Calif. (21)
Fields, Jack, R-Texas (8)
Findley, Paul, R-Ill. (20)
Fish, Hamilton Jr., R-N.Y. (25)
Fithian, Floyd, D-Ind. (2)
Flippo, Ronnie G., D-Ala. (5)
Florio, James J., D-N.J. (1)
Foglietta, Thomas M., D-Pa. (1)
Foley, Thomas S., D-Wash. (5)
Ford, Harold E., D-Tenn. (8)
Ford, William D., D-Mich. (15)
Forsythe, Edwin B., R-N.J. (6)
Fountain, L. H., D-N.C. (2)
Fowler, Wyche Jr., D-Ga. (5)
Frank, Barney, D-Mass. (4)
Frenzel, Bill, R-Minn. (3)
Frost, Martin, D-Texas (24)
Fuqua, Don, D-Fla. (2)

G

Garcia, Robert, D-N.Y. (21)
Gaydos, Joseph M., D-Pa. (20)
Gejdenson, Sam, D-Conn. (2)
Gephardt, Richard A., D-Mo. (3)
Gibbons, Sam, D-Fla. (7)
Gilman, Benjamin A., R-N.Y. (26)
Gingrich, Newt, R-Ga. (6)
Ginn, Bo, D-Ga. (1)
Glickman, Dan, D-Kan. (4)
Goldwater, Barry M. Jr., R-Calif. (20)
Gonzalez, Henry B., D-Texas (20)
Goodling, Bill, R-Pa. (19)
Gore, Albert Jr., D-Tenn. (4)
Gradison, Bill, R-Ohio (1)
Gramm, Phil, D-Texas (6)
Gray, William H. III, D-Pa. (2)
Green, S. William, R-N.Y. (18)
Gregg, Judd, R-N.H. (2)
Grisham, Wayne, R-Calif. (33)
Guarini, Frank J., D-N.J. (14)
Gunderson, Steve, R-Wis. (3)

H

Hagedorn, Tom, R-Minn. (2)
Hall, Katie, D-Ind. (1)
Hall, Ralph M., D-Texas (4)
Hall, Sam B. Jr., D-Texas (1)
Hall, Tony P., D-Ohio (3)
Hamilton, Lee H., D-Ind. (9)
Hammerschmidt, John Paul, R-Ark. (3)
Hance, Kent, D-Texas (19)
Hansen, George, R-Idaho (2)
Hansen, James V., R-Utah (1)
Harkin, Tom, D-Iowa (5)
Hartnett, Thomas F., R-S.C. (1)
Hatcher, Charles, D-Ga. (2)
Hawkins, Augustus F., D-Calif. (29)
Heckler, Margaret M., R-Mass. (10)
Hefner, W. G. "Bill", D-N.C. (8)
Hendon, Bill, R-N.C. (11)
Hertel, Dennis M., D-Mich. (14)
Hightower, Jack, D-Texas (13)
Hiler, John, R-Ind. (3)
Hillis, Elwood, R-Ind. (5)
Holland, Ken, D-S.C. (5)
Hollenbeck, Harold C., R-N.J. (9)
Holt, Marjorie S., R-Md. (4)
Hopkins, Larry J., R-Ky. (6)
Horton, Frank, R-N.Y. (34)
Howard, James J., D-N.J. (3)
Hoyer, Steny H., D-Md. (5)
Hubbard, Carroll Jr., D-Ky. (1)
Huckaby, Jerry, D-La. (5)
Hughes, William J., D-N.J. (2)
Hunter, Duncan L., R-Calif. (42)
Hutto, Earl, D-Fla. (1)
Hyde, Henry J., R-Ill. (6)

I, J

Ireland, Andy, D-Fla. (8)
Jacobs, Andrew Jr., D-Ind. (11)
Jeffords, James M., R-Vt. (AL)
Jeffries, Jim, R-Kan. (2)
Jenkins, Ed, D-Ga. (9)
Johnston, Eugene, R-N.C. (6)
Jones, Ed, D-Tenn. (7)
Jones, James R., D-Okla. (1)
Jones, Walter B., D-N.C. (1)

K

Kastenmeier, Robert W., D-Wis. (2)
Kazen, Abraham Jr., D-Texas (23)
Kemp, Jack F., R-N.Y. (38)
Kennelly, Barbara B., D-Conn. (1)
Kildee, Dale E., D-Mich. (7)
Kindness, Thomas N., R-Ohio (8)
Kogovsek, Ray, D-Colo. (3)
Kramer, Ken, R-Colo. (5)

L

LaFalce, John J., D-N.Y. (36)
Lagomarsino, Robert J., R-Calif. (19)
Lantos, Tom, D-Calif. (11)
Latta, Delbert L., R-Ohio (5)
Leach, Jim, R-Iowa (1)
Leath, Marvin, D-Texas (11)
LeBoutillier, John, R-N.Y. (6)
Lee, Gary A., R-N.Y. (33)
Lehman, William, D-Fla. (13)
Leland, Mickey, D-Texas (18)
Lent, Norman F., R-N.Y. (4)
Levitas, Elliott H., D-Ga. (4)
Lewis, Jerry, R-Calif. (37)
Livingston, Bob, R-La. (1)
Loeffler, Tom, R-Texas (21)
Long, Clarence D., D-Md. (2)
Long, Gillis W., D-La. (8)
Lott, Trent, R-Miss. (5)
Lowery, Bill, R-Calif. (41)
Lowry, Mike, D-Wash. (7)
Lujan, Manuel Jr., R-N.M. (1)
Luken, Thomas A., D-Ohio (2)
Lundine, Stanley N., D-N.Y. (39)
Lungren, Dan, R-Calif. (34)

M

Madigan, Edward R., R-Ill. (21)
Markey, Edward J., D-Mass. (7)
Marks, Marc L., R-Pa. (24)
Marlenee, Ron, R-Mont. (2)
Marriott, Dan, R-Utah (2)
Martin, David O'B., R-N.Y. (30)
Martin, James G., R-N.C. (9)
Martin, Lynn, R-Ill. (16)
Martinez, Matthew G., D-Calif. (30)
Matsui, Robert T., D-Calif. (3)
Mattox, Jim, D-Texas (5)
Mavroules, Nicholas, D-Mass. (6)
Mazzoli, Romano L., D-Ky. (3)
McClory, Robert, R-Ill. (13)
McCloskey, Paul N. Jr., R-Calif. (12)
McCollum, Bill, R-Fla. (5)
McCurdy, Dave, D-Okla. (4)
McDade, Joseph M., R-Pa. (10)
McDonald, Larry P., D-Ga. (7)
McEwen, Bob, R-Ohio (6)
McGrath, Raymond J., R-N.Y. (5)
McHugh, Matthew F., D-N.Y. (27)
McKinney, Stewart B., R-Conn. (4)
Mica, Daniel A., D-Fla. (11)
Michel, Robert H., R-Ill. (18)
Mikulski, Barbara A., D-Md. (3)
Miller, Clarence E., R-Ohio 10)
Miller, George, D-Calif. (7)
Mineta, Norman Y., D-Calif. (13)
Minish, Joseph G., D-N.J. (11)
Mitchell, Donald J., R-N.Y. (31)
Mitchell, Parren J., D-Md. (7)
Moakley, Joe, D-Mass. (9)
Moffett, Toby, D-Conn. (6)
Molinari, Guy V., R-N.Y. (17)
Mollohan, Robert H., D-W.Va. (1)
Montgomery, G. V. "Sonny", D-Miss. (3)
Moore, Henson, R-La. (6)
Moorhead, Carlos J., R-Calif. (22)
Morrison, Sid, R-Wash. (4)
Mottl, Ronald M., D-Ohio (23)
Murphy, Austin J., D-Pa. (22)
Murtha, John P., D-Pa. (12)
Myers, John T., R-Ind. (7)

N

Napier, John L., R-S.C. (6)
Natcher, William H., D-Ky. (2)
Neal, Stephen L., D-N.C. (5)
Nelligan, James L., R-Pa. (11)
Nelson, Bill, D-Fla. (9)
Nichols, Bill, D-Ala. (3)
Nowak, Henry J., D-N.Y. (37)

O

Oakar, Mary Rose, D-Ohio (20)
Oberstar, James L., D-Minn. (8)
Obey, David R., D-Wis. (7)
O'Brien, George M., R-Ill. (17)
O'Neill, Thomas P. Jr., D-Mass. (8)
Ottinger, Richard L., D-N.Y. (24)
Oxley, Michael G., R-Ohio (4)

P

Panetta, Leon E., D-Calif. (16)
Parris, Stan, R-Va. (8)
Pashayan, Charles Jr., R-Calif. (17)
Patman, Bill, D-Texas (14)
Patterson, Jerry M., D-Calif. (38)
Paul, Ron, R-Texas (22)
Pease, Don J., D-Ohio (13)

... Governors, Supreme Court, Cabinet-rank Officers

Pepper, Claude, D-Fla. (14)
Perkins, Carl D., D-Ky. (7)
Petri, Thomas E., R-Wis. (6)
Peyser, Peter A., D-N.Y. (23)
Pickle, J. J., D-Texas (10)
Porter, John Edward, R-Ill. (10)
Price, Melvin, D-Ill. (23)
Pritchard, Joel, R-Wash. (1)
Pursell, Carl D., R-Mich. (2)

Q, R

Quillen, James H., R-Tenn. (1)
Rahall, Nick J. II, D-W.Va. (4)
Railsback, Tom, R-Ill. (19)
Rangel, Charles B., D-N.Y. (19)
Ratchford, William R., D-Conn. (5)
Regula, Ralph, R-Ohio (16)
Reuss, Henry S., D-Wis. (5)
Rhodes, John J., R-Ariz. (1)
Rinaldo, Matthew J., R-N.J. (12)
Ritter, Don, R-Pa. (15)
Roberts, Clint, R-S.D. (2)
Roberts, Pat, R-Kan. (1)
Robinson, J. Kenneth, R-Va. (7)
Rodino, Peter W. Jr., D-N.J. (10)
Roe, Robert A., D-N.J. (8)
Roemer, Buddy, D-La. (4)
Rogers, Harold, R-Ky. (5)
Rose, Charlie, D-N.C. (7)
Rosenthal, Benjamin S., D-N.Y. (8)
Rostenkowski, Dan, D-Ill. (8)
Roth, Toby, R-Wis. (8)
Roukema, Marge, R-N.J. (7)
Rousselot, John H., R-Calif. (26)
Roybal, Edward R., D-Calif. (25)
Rudd, Eldon, R-Ariz. (4)
Russo, Marty, D-Ill. (3)

S

Sabo, Martin Olav, D-Minn. (5)
St Germain, Fernand J., D-R.I. (1)
Santini, James D., D-Nev. (AL)
Savage, Gus, D-Ill. (2)
Sawyer, Harold S., R-Mich. (5)
Scheuer, James H., D-N.Y. (11)
Schneider, Claudine, R-R.I. (2)
Schroeder, Patricia, D-Colo. (1)
Schulze, Richard T., R-Pa. (5)
Schumer, Charles E., D-N.Y. (16)
Seiberling, John F., D-Ohio (14)
Sensenbrenner, F. James Jr., R-Wis. (9)
Shamansky, Bob, D-Ohio (12)
Shannon, James M., D-Mass. (5)
Sharp, Philip R., D-Ind. (10)
Shaw, E. Clay Jr., R-Fla. (12)
Shelby, Richard C., D-Ala. (7)
Shumway, Norman D., R-Calif. (14)
Shuster, Bud, R-Pa. (9)
Siljander, Mark D., R-Mich. (4)
Simon, Paul, D-Ill. (24)
Skeen, Joe, R-N.M. (2)
Skelton, Ike, D-Mo. (4)
Smith, Albert Lee Jr., R-Ala. (6)
Smith, Christopher H., R-N.J. (4)
Smith, Denny, R-Ore. (2)
Smith, Joseph F., D-Pa. (3)
Smith, Neal, D-Iowa (4)
Smith, Virginia, R-Neb. (3)
Snowe, Olympia J., R-Maine (2)
Snyder, Gene, R-Ky. (4)
Solarz, Stephen J., D-N.Y. (13)
Solomon, Gerald B. H., R-N.Y. (29)
Spence, Floyd, R-S.C. (2)
Stangeland, Arlan, R-Minn. (7)
Stanton, J. William, R-Ohio (11)
Stark, Fortney H. "Pete", D-Calif. (9)
Staton, David Michael, R-W.Va. (3)
Stenholm, Charles W., D-Texas (17)
Stokes, Louis, D-Ohio (21)
Stratton, Samuel S., D-N.Y. (28)
Studds, Gerry E., D-Mass. (12)
Stump, Bob, D-Ariz. (3)
Swift, Al, D-Wash. (2)
Synar, Mike, D-Okla. (2)

T

Tauke, Tom, R-Iowa (2)
Tauzin, W. J. "Billy", D-La. (3)

Taylor, Gene, R-Mo. (7)
Thomas, William M., R-Calif. (18)
Traxler, Bob, D-Mich. (8)
Trible, Paul S. Jr., R-Va. (1)

U, V

Udall, Morris K., D-Ariz. (2)
Vander Jagt, Guy, R-Mich. (9)
Vento, Bruce F., D-Minn. (4)
Volkmer, Harold L., D-Mo. (9)

W

Walgren, Doug, D-Pa. (18)
Walker, Robert S., R-Pa. (16)
Wampler, William C., R-Va. (9)
Washington, Harold, D-Ill. (1)
Watkins, Wes, D-Okla. (3)
Waxman, Henry A., D-Calif. (24)
Weaver, James, D-Ore. (4)
Weber, Ed, R-Ohio (9)
Weber, Vin, R-Minn. (6)
Weiss, Ted, D-N.Y. (20)
White, Richard C., D-Texas (16)
Whitehurst, G. William, R-Va. (2)
Whitley, Charles, D-N.C. (3)
Whittaker, Bob, R-Kan. (5)
Whitten, Jamie L., D-Miss. (1)
Williams, Lyle, R-Ohio (19)
Williams, Pat, D-Mont. (1)
Wilson, Charles, D-Texas (2)
Winn, Larry Jr., R-Kan. (3)
Wirth, Timothy E., D-Colo. (2)
Wolf, Frank R., R-Va. (10)
Wolpe, Howard, D-Mich. (3)
Wortley, George C., R-N.Y. (32)
Wright, Jim, D-Texas (12)
Wyden, Ron, D-Ore. (3)
Wylie, Chalmers P., R-Ohio (15)

X, Y, Z

Yates, Sidney R., D-Ill. (9)
Yatron, Gus, D-Pa. (6)
Young, C. W. Bill, R-Fla. (6)
Young, Don, R-Alaska (AL)
Young, Robert A., D-Mo. (2)
Zablocki, Clement J., D-Wis. (4)
Zeferetti, Leo C., D-N.Y. (15)

Delegates

de Lugo, Ron, D-Virgin Islands
Fauntroy, Walter E., D-D.C.
Sunia, Fofó I. F., D-American Samoa
Won Pat, Antonio Borja, D-Guam

Resident Commissioner

Corrada, Baltasar, New Prog.-Puerto Rico

Senators
R 53; D 47 [2]

Abdnor, James, R-S.D.
Andrews, Mark, R-N.D.
Armstrong, William L., R-Colo.
Baker, Howard H. Jr., R-Tenn.
Baucus, Max, D-Mont.
Bentsen, Lloyd, D-Texas
Biden, Joseph R. Jr., D-Del.
Boren, David L., D-Okla.
Boschwitz, Rudy, R-Minn.
Bradley, Bill, D-N.J.
Bumpers, Dale, D-Ark.
Burdick, Quentin N., D-N.D.
Byrd, Harry F. Jr., Ind.-Va.
Byrd, Robert C., D-W.Va.
Cannon, Howard W., D.-Nev.
Chafee, John H., R-R.I.
Chiles, Lawton, D-Fla.
Cochran, Thad, R-Miss.
Cohen, William S., R-Maine
Cranston, Alan, D-Calif.
D'Amato, Alfonse, R-N.Y.
Danforth, John C., R-Mo.
DeConcini, Dennis, D-Ariz.

Denton, Jeremiah, R-Ala.
Dixon, Alan J., D-Ill.
Dodd, Christopher J., D-Conn.
Dole, Robert, R-Kan.
Domenici, Pete V., R-N.M.
Durenberger, David, R-Minn.
Eagleton, Thomas F., D-Mo.
East, John P., R-N.C.
Exon, J. James, D-Neb.
Ford, Wendell H., D-Ky.
Garn, Jake, R-Utah
Glenn, John, D-Ohio
Goldwater, Barry, R-Ariz.
Gorton, Slade, R-Wash.
Grassley, Charles E., R-Iowa
Hart, Gary, D-Colo.
Hatch, Orrin G., R-Utah
Hatfield, Mark O., R-Ore.
Hawkins, Paula, R-Fla.
Hayakawa, S. I. "Sam", R-Calif.
Heflin, Howell, D-Ala.
Heinz, John, R-Pa.
Helms, Jesse, R-N.C.
Hollings, Ernest F., D-S.C.
Huddleston, Walter D., D-Ky.
Humphrey, Gordon J., R-N.H.
Inouye, Daniel K., D-Hawaii
Jackson, Henry M., D-Wash.
Jepsen, Roger W., R-Iowa
Johnston, J. Bennett, D-La.
Kassebaum, Nancy Landon, R-Kan.
Kasten, Robert W. Jr., R-Wis.
Kennedy, Edward M., D-Mass.
Lautenberg, Frank R., D-N.J.
Laxalt, Paul, R-Nev.
Leahy, Patrick J., D-Vt.
Levin, Carl, D-Mich.
Long, Russell B., D-La.
Lugar, Richard G., R-Ind.
Mathias, Charles McC. Jr., R-Md.
Matsunaga, Spark M., D-Hawaii
Mattingly, Mack, R-Ga.
McClure, James A., R-Idaho
Melcher, John, D-Mont.
Metzenbaum, Howard M., D-Ohio
Mitchell, George J., D-Maine
Moynihan, Daniel Patrick, D-N.Y.
Murkowski, Frank H., R-Alaska
Nickles, Don, R-Okla.
Nunn, Sam, D-Ga.
Packwood, Bob, R-Ore.
Pell, Claiborne, D-R.I.
Percy, Charles H., R-Ill.
Pressler, Larry, R-S.D.
Proxmire, William, D-Wis.
Pryor, David, D-Ark.
Quayle, Dan, R-Ind.
Randolph, Jennings, D-W.Va.
Riegle, Donald W. Jr., D-Mich.
Roth, William V. Jr., R-Del.
Rudman, Warren B., R-N.H.
Sarbanes, Paul S., D-Md.
Sasser, Jim, D-Tenn.
Schmitt, Harrison "Jack", R-N.M.
Simpson, Alan K., R-Wyo.
Specter, Arlen, R-Pa.
Stafford, Robert T., R-Vt.
Stennis, John C., D-Miss.
Stevens, Ted, R-Alaska
Symms, Steven D., R-Idaho
Thurmond, Strom, R-S.C.
Tower, John, R-Texas
Tsongas, Paul E., D-Mass.
Wallop, Malcolm, R-Wyo.
Warner, John W., R-Va.
Weicker, Lowell P. Jr., R-Conn.
Zorinsky, Edward, D-Neb.

Governors
D 26; R 24

Ala.—Fob James, D
Alaska—Jay S. Hammond, R
Ariz.—Bruce Babbitt, D
Ark.—Frank D. White, R
Calif.—Edmund G. Brown Jr., D
Colo.—Richard D. Lamm, D
Conn.—William A. O'Neill, D
Del.—Pierre S. "Pete" du Pont IV, R

Fla.—Robert Graham, D
Ga.—George Busbee, D
Hawaii—George Ariyoshi, D
Idaho—John V. Evans, D
Ill.—James R. Thompson, R
Ind.—Robert D. Orr, R
Iowa—Robert Ray, R
Kan.—John Carlin, D
Ky.—John Y. Brown, D
La.—David C. Treen, R
Maine—Joseph E. Brennan, D
Md.—Harry R. Hughes, D
Mass.—Edward J. King, D
Mich.—William G. Milliken, R
Minn.—Albert H. Quie, R
Miss.—William Winter, D
Mo.—Christopher S. "Kit" Bond, R
Mont.—Ted Schwinden, D
Neb.—Charles Thone, R
Nev.—Robert F. List, R
N.H.—Robert B. Monier, R
N.J.—Thomas Kean, R
N.M.—Bruce King, D
N.Y.—Hugh L. Carey, D
N.C.—James B. Hunt Jr., D
N.D.—Allen I. Olson, R
Ohio—James A. Rhodes, R
Okla.—George Nigh, D
Ore.—Victor G. Atiyeh, R
Pa.—Richard L. Thornburgh, R
R.I.—J. Joseph Garrahy, D
S.C.—Richard Riley, D
S.D.—William J. Janklow, R
Tenn.—Lamar Alexander, R
Texas—William Clements, R
Utah—Scott M. Matheson, D
Vt.—Richard A. Snelling, R
Va.—Charles S. Robb, D
Wash.—John Spellman, R
W.Va.—John D. "Jay" Rockefeller IV, D
Wis.—Lee Sherman Dreyfus, R
Wyo.—Ed Herschler, D

Supreme Court

Burger, Warren E.—Minn., Chief Justice
Blackmun, Harry A.—Minn.
Brennan, William J. Jr.—N.J.
Marshall, Thurgood—N.Y.
O'Connor, Sandra Day—Ariz.
Powell, Lewis F. Jr.—Va.
Rehnquist, William H.—Ariz.
Stevens, John Paul—Ill.
White, Byron R.—Colo.

Cabinet

Baldrige, Malcolm—Commerce
Bell, T. H.—Education
Block, John R.—Agriculture
Donovan, Raymond J.—Labor (Designate)
Hodel, Donald P.—Energy
Lewis, Drew—Transportation
Pierce, Samuel R. Jr.—HUD
Regan, Donald T.—Treasury
Schweiker, Richard S.—HHS
Shultz, George P.—State
Smith, William French—Attorney General
Watt, James G.—Interior
Weinberger, Caspar W.—Defense

Other Officers with Cabinet Rank

Brock, William E. III—U.S. Trade Representative
Bush, George—Vice President
Casey, William J.—CIA Director
Kirkpatrick, Jeane J.—U.N. Representative
Meese, Edwin III—Counselor to the President
Stockman, David A.—OMB Director

---

[1] N.Y. 14th Dist.
[2] Includes Harry F. Byrd Jr. (Va.) elected as an independent.

 Legislative Summary

Congress in 1982: Stirrings of Independence

Congress grew increasingly independent of the White House in 1982, creating a breach that could intensify in the 98th Congress.

The legislators adhered to President Reagan's general course of restraining domestic programs while increasing military spending, but they rejected many of the president's specific proposals.

They substantially rewrote Reagan's fiscal 1983 budget and convinced the president to support a large tax increase only a year after passing his plan to cut taxes. For the first time, in September, Congress overrode Reagan's veto of an appropriations bill, a measure the president had labeled a "budget-buster."

Reagan's problems with the 97th Congress seemed to increase after the Nov. 2 elections, when 26 incumbent House Republicans were defeated and some GOP senators found themselves in much tighter races than they had anticipated.

Those difficulties were likely to become more pronounced in the 98th, which would have 57 new House Democrats and a Senate still controlled by the GOP but perhaps less inclined to take direction from the White House.

Unfinished Business

Bills that were not enacted included Reagan-backed measures to limit court-ordered school busing, to allow prayer in public schools and to limit abortions.

Congress turned down most of Reagan's ambitious efforts at reducing the scope of the federal government, and failed to pass his proposals to reform the regulatory process, to revamp clean air and water laws, to abolish the departments of Energy and Education and to establish new financial relationships with the 50 states.

The president's call for a constitutional amendment requiring a balanced federal budget was rejected.

The major foreign policy initiatives Reagan had sought from Congress both died in the Senate. A bill to create Radio Marti, which would beam American propaganda to Cuba, was buried in a filibuster. And a bill containing the trade portions of Reagan's Caribbean Basin Initiative also died in the Senate, stalled behind other bills that were being filibustered.

A late-session presidential request to set up a new farm program, paying farmers in grain as well as cash for keeping land out of production, died in the Senate.

An immigration reform bill sought by the administration passed the Senate but died under a fusillade of amendments from House opponents.

Congress agreed to much of the defense spending increase Reagan sought but rejected his request to begin procurement of two major nuclear weapons — the MX and Pershing missiles.

Other important bills that did not make it through included measures rewriting federal pesticide laws, reauthorizing hazardous waste disposal

Second Session Summary

By using all-night sessions, holding a rare Sunday meeting and finally breaking a filibuster against the president's gasoline tax increase proposal, the second session of the 97th Congress was able to complete its business on Dec. 23, 1982. The Senate adjourned *sine die* at 1:13 p.m. that day. The House had adjourned on Dec. 21 at 9:56 p.m.

The session, which convened at noon on Jan. 25, 1982, lasted 333 days. It was the shortest since the second session of the 95th Congress (1978), but still ranked as the 23rd longest in history. The third session of the 76th Congress, from Jan. 3, 1940, to Jan. 3, 1941, is the longest on record. *(CQ Guide to Congress, 3rd Edition, p. 410)*

The Senate met for 147 days during the year, the House for 140 days. There were 4,520 bills and resolutions introduced during the session, compared to 8,719 in 1981.

President Reagan signed into law 328 public bills that were cleared by Congress, bringing his total for the 97th Congress to 473. Reagan vetoed 12 public bills in 1982. Two of those vetoes were overridden and the bills enacted into law without his signature. The total of 473 public laws enacted during the 97th Congress was the smallest since the 470 enacted during the 66th Congress (1919-21).

During 1982, the House took 459 recorded votes, substantially fewer than the record-setting 834 votes taken in 1978, but 106 more than in 1981. The Senate took 465 recorded votes, well below that chamber's record of 688 taken in 1976, and 18 fewer than in 1981.

Following are the recorded congressional vote totals between 1971 and 1982:

Year	House	Senate	Total
1982	459	465	924
1981	353	483	836
1980	604	531	1,135
1979	672	497	1,169
1978	834	516	1,350
1977	706	635	1,341
1976	661	688	1,349
1975	612	602	1,214
1974	537	544	1,081
1973	541	594	1,135
1972	329	532	861
1971	320	423	743

laws, setting up the urban "enterprise zones" sought by the president and strengthening federal health warnings on cigarette packages.

A nuclear weapons freeze resolution also failed.

Congress did not meet a Supreme Court deadline for legislation to straighten out the federal bankruptcy court system, and it did not take any action on regulation of natural gas prices and supplies or on restructuring the American telecommunications industry.

Congress also failed to deal with the financial woes of the ailing Social Security system.

The 97th's Record

While modifying or rejecting many of Reagan's requests, Congress did not originate too much of its own legislation. A total of 328 bills enacted in 1982 became law, bringing the total number enacted by the 97th Congress to 473. This was far fewer than any Congress in the past 20 years. The 96th Congress in 1979-80 created 613 public laws.

Part of the decrease was explained by the president's belief that the scope of government should be contracted, not expanded. Members spent a lot of their time defending existing programs from budget cuts rather than trying to create new ones.

In addition, Congress packaged many bills into a few omnibus measures. As in 1981, the legislators devoted much of their time to three massive bills: a budget resolution, a bill to reconcile the cuts required by the budget resolution with existing laws and an omnibus, stopgap appropriations bill, made necessary by Congress' inability to pass many of the regular appropriations bills.

The 97th Congress finally adjourned Dec. 23, when the Senate cleared legislation increasing the gasoline tax to pay for highway repairs and mass transit. Senators left town feeling bitter toward a handful of their colleagues who had staged a last-ditch filibuster on the gas tax bill. The normally gentlemanly Senate turned into a collection of 100 tired men and women complaining about each others' bad behavior.

The House adjourned Dec. 21, but many representatives had departed several days before. When the House approved the conference agreement on the gasoline tax bill Dec. 21, only 267 members remained to vote.

Against the wishes of the Senate

and House leadership, Reagan in September had called the lame-duck session, which began Nov. 29. It was requested primarily to deal with the 10 fiscal 1983 appropriations bills Congress had not finished before recessing Oct. 1 for the midterm elections.

Congress eventually cleared four additional appropriations bills during the lame-duck session, packaging the remaining six into the stopgap, continuing appropriations resolution. It added a host of special interest amendments to the continuing resolution, including a pay raise for House members. Breaking with tradition, senators did not take the raise, but the Senate eliminated strict ceilings on outside income that would have gone into effect in 1983.

Voting Rights, Tax Hike Passed

One measure Congress did enact in 1982 was a 25-year extension of the 1965 Voting Rights Act.

Another was the tax increase bill, a measure that would raise $98 billion over the following three years. To it Congress added several other measures ranging from authorizing money for airport development to limiting Medicare and Medicaid payments to hospitals and doctors. Also in the tax bill, Congress extended unemployment benefits for six to 10 weeks.

Another major accomplishment was passage of a nuclear waste disposal bill.

Congress also passed bills deregulating the intercity bus industry, blocking a strike by railroad workers and updating antiquated laws governing the use of federal irrigation water in the West.

Following is a summary of legislation that passed or failed in 1982:

Agriculture

Agriculture Funding, Farm Credit. Congress cleared $34 billion in fiscal 1983 agriculture appropriations when the Senate adopted the conference agreement on the bill (HR 7072 — PL 97-370) Dec. 15, hours after the House had approved it. Conferees averted a veto by dropping or changing controversial dairy, conservation and credit sections. They funded food stamps and other feeding programs at substantially higher levels than the president originally requested, but only after extracting new

budget requests from the administration.

When conferees finished work Dec. 10, the bill totaled $32 billion, compared with an original budget request of $23.1 billion. (An additional $2.3 billion was provided from a special customs receipt fund.)

The higher total also reflected an emergency budget request for $6.7 billion for the Commodity Credit Corporation (CCC), the Agriculture Department (USDA) agency that manages price support programs. The deepening farm recession had greatly increased farmers' use of CCC programs.

Conferees eliminated a deferral on farmers' repayments of Farmers Home Administration (FmHA) loans that the administration opposed. The deferral authority also appeared in a separate House-passed bill (HR 5831) that authorized new FmHA lending ceilings; the Senate did not act on a companion measure (S 2314).

Reconciliation Bill Changes. The budget reconciliation bill cleared Aug. 18 (HR 6955 — PL 97-253) froze dairy price supports at the existing level of $13.10 per hundred pounds for fiscal 1983 and 1984 in an effort to reduce program costs. It also authorized the secretary of agriculture to deduct as much as a dollar from that amount if federal dairy purchases did not drop below specified levels.

The bill also mandated federal payments to farmers for not planting part of their customary wheat and feed grain acreage. Food stamp provisions delayed scheduled benefit adjustments for inflation, tightened eligibility standards and authorized pilot projects in which recipients would lose their food stamps if they did not work at least 20 hours a week.

Commodity Futures, Contract Sanctity. Defying State Department objections, Congress sent to the president a sweeping ban on presidential embargoes on farm exports. The "contract sanctity" guarantee appeared in a four-year reauthorization (HR 5447 — PL 97-444) of the Commodity Futures Trading Commission (CFTC), completed Dec. 9 by conferees. The Senate adopted the conference agreement on Dec. 15 and the House cleared it for the president the next day.

The disputed language generally guaranteed delivery on farm export contracts in existence at the time of an embargo, with exceptions for war or

national emergencies.

The bill had been threatened with a presidential veto for failing to authorize administration-backed fees on commodities transactions. But conferees eliminated that objection when they approved fees for CFTC services, a compromise negotiated between the futures industry and the Office of Management and Budget.

Other sections of the final bill expanded the power of states and individuals to combat futures frauds and ratified a jurisdictional agreement between the CFTC and the Securities and Exchange Commission.

Grain Giveaway. Faced with massive surpluses, chronically depressed farm prices and mounting price-support expenditures, Agriculture Secretary John R. Block asked Congress Dec. 9 to clear the way for a major reversal of administration farm policy. Congress failed to ratify Block's "payment-in-kind" (PIK) plan, despite general acceptance of the concept.

Block proposed to retire up to half the nation's crop land in 1983, paying farmers in surplus crops, as well as cash, for not planting. The Senate Agriculture Committee approved a PIK bill (S 3074) on Dec. 13. But it became snagged when a half-dozen senators announced plans to add controversial amendments.

The House abruptly passed a simpler version Dec. 18. In the final days of the lame-duck session most of the troublesome amendments had been deflected, but Senate Agriculture Committee Chairman Jesse Helms, R-N.C., was blocked in attempts to bring the bill to the floor. Members cited their disapproval of Helms' filibuster of gasoline tax legislation.

The administration Jan. 11, 1983, announced it would implement the program administratively.

Pesticide Law. Conflicting demands of environmental, labor and state government groups, the American Farm Bureau Federation and manufacturers stalemated a revision of federal pesticide law.

The House passed a two-year reauthorization (HR 5203) of the Federal Insecticide, Fungicide and Rodenticide Act (FIFRA) Aug. 11 after dropping industry-backed restrictions on state regulation of pesticides. The bill also allowed private lawsuits to stop FIFRA violations — a provision that brought strong objections from

the powerful farm bureau.

The Senate Agriculture Committee reported an industry-backed version of the bill Sept. 20, but the measure angered environmentalists because it omitted lawsuit authority and placed some new limits on state regulatory programs.

Tobacco. A bill requiring tobacco growers to repay the government for any losses in their price-support loan program was cleared by Congress in July (HR 6590 — PL 97-218). Critics had come close to ending the program or forcing major changes in it during deliberation on the 1981 omnibus farm bill, and that measure (PL 97-98) included a mandate that the program be run at "no net cost" to the federal government.

Western Water. A bill sent to the president Sept. 29 (S 1409 — PL 97-293) settled for a time a long-running battle between environmentalists and Western farmers over the use of federal reclamation water.

Environmental groups wanted strict enforcement of a 1902 law that limited the amount of federally irrigated acreage available to 160 acres for an individual. But the bill instead increased the old limit to 960 acres, with unlimited leasing of additional acreage. It also mandated higher prices for some water used by Western farmers and repealed the old requirement that farmers live on or near their federally irrigated farms.

Appropriations

Continuing Resolution. After four days during which much of the government was technically out of funds, President Reagan Dec. 21 signed a massive $379 billion emergency appropriations bill.

The continuing appropriations resolution (H J Res 631 — PL 97-377) was required because only three of the 13 regular fiscal 1983 funding bills had been signed into law by midnight Dec. 17 when a prior continuing resolution (PL 97-276) expired. Congress cleared four additional appropriations bills before it adjourned Dec. 23.

Lawmakers completed action on the Agriculture (HR 7072), District of Columbia (HR 7144), Housing and Urban Development-Independent Agencies (HR 6956), Interior (HR 7356), Military Construction (HR

6968) and Transportation (HR 7019) bills. Full-year Legislative Branch funding (HR 7073, S 2939) was incorporated in PL 97-276.

H J Res 631 provided funding through the end of fiscal 1983 for the two largest federal departments, Defense and Health and Human Services, as well as the Labor, Education, Commerce, State, Justice, Treasury and Energy departments, the White House, the federal judiciary and the Postal Service. It also provided full-year funding for U.S. foreign aid programs.

Congress completed action on the resolution Dec. 20, after Senate-House conferees bowed to Reagan's veto threats by dropping money for emergency jobs programs.

Fiscal 1982 Supplementals. Congress handed President Reagan his first big budget defeat Sept. 10 when it overrode his veto of a $14.2 billion fiscal 1982 supplemental appropriations bill (HR 6863 — PL 97-257).

The president wanted more spending for defense and less for social programs than the bill provided. But his attempts to portray the measure as a "budget-buster" backfired as Congress insisted on its right to help set spending priorities.

Earlier in the year, Congress spent 16 weeks fashioning an "urgent" supplemental that Reagan would sign. After vetoing two versions as too costly, on July 18 he signed a third measure (HR 6685 — PL 97-216) containing $5.4 billion in new spending and rescinding $5.8 billion of previously appropriated funds. The House failed to override the two vetoes.

Commerce

FTC Authorization. Efforts by the American Medical Association to bar the Federal Trade Commission (FTC) from regulating doctors and other professionals failed during the lame-duck session.

As cleared by Congress Dec. 20, the continuing appropriations resolution (H J Res 631 — PL 97-377) included funds for the FTC with no restrictions on agency efforts to prevent anti-competitive business practices by professionals. The doctors group had lobbied extensively for the exemption.

The House Dec. 1 passed a bill (HR 6995) that authorized FTC fund-

ing for fiscal 1983-85 but exempted doctors, lawyers and other professionals from FTC antitrust jurisdiction and allowed Congress to veto agency rules. The Senate did not act on an FTC authorization bill.

A bitter House fight over FTC restrictions was averted Dec. 9 during debate over the State, Justice, Commerce appropriations bill (HR 6957) when James J. Florio, D-N.J., a supporter of the agency, raised a point of order against including the FTC's $63.64 million appropriation for fiscal 1983 because no authorization had been approved. The funds were eliminated, and no FTC amendments were allowed.

Members assumed that the Senate would include funds for the agency in the continuing appropriations resolution, which it did. Conferees on H J Res 631 agreed to the funding and prevented efforts to add the exemption for professionals. The measure did extend the legislative veto provision and other restrictions that had been contained in the FTC's 1980 authorization (PL 96-252).

Used-Car Veto. Congress in May for the first time used its FTC legislative veto authority to kill the FTC's proposed rule requiring used-car dealers to disclose information about auto defects. The 1980 FTC authorization gave Congress veto authority over the agency.

The rule was blocked when the Senate adopted a resolution of disapproval (S Con Res 60) May 18, and the House followed suit May 26. On Oct. 26, the U.S. Court of Appeals for the District of Columbia overturned the veto because it violated the constitutional principle of separation of powers. The Senate appealed that ruling to the U.S. Supreme Court.

Telecommunications. A settlement by the Justice Department of an antitrust suit against the American Telephone & Telegraph Co. (AT&T) undercut congressional efforts to deregulate the telecommunications industry and to reorganize AT&T.

U.S. District Judge Harold H. Greene of the District of Columbia approved the settlement Aug. 24 after the Justice Department and AT&T accepted some changes he had proposed.

Although some members believed legislation was necessary to supplement the settlement and prevent undue increases in telephone rates, Rep.

Timothy E. Wirth, D-Colo., chairman of the Energy and Commerce Subcommittee on Telecommunications, withdrew his telecommunications bill (HR 5158) because of AT&T's opposition to the bill. The Senate had passed its bill (S 898) in 1981 before the settlement was reached.

Cable, Broadcasting Deregulation. Neither chamber considered a bill (S 2172) that would restrict local control over cable television. Despite interest in the Senate, there was little support in the House because of the cities' opposition.

Another measure (S 1629) that would significantly reduce federal regulation of radio and television was passed March 31 by the Senate. However, some key House members contended that there was not enough competition in broadcasting to warrant lifting federal regulation.

Product Liability. Supporters of legislation (S 2631) to limit business liability for damages caused by defective products were cheered by the Oct. 1 approval of the measure by the Senate Commerce Committee. However, no action was taken by House committees, and the measure never reached the Senate floor.

Congress

Senate TV. Majority Leader Howard H. Baker Jr., R-Tenn., made television and radio coverage of the Senate his first legislative priority when he assumed the post in January 1981, but he was unable to persuade his colleagues to go along.

The Senate Rules Committee voted 7-5 along party lines in July for a detailed plan for TV and radio coverage (S Res 436). But floor action was not scheduled because of strong opposition. Baker had hoped a compromise could be reached in the lame-duck session.

Members' Pay. In late 1981, Congress removed the $3,000-a-year limit on the business-related tax deduction that members could take for Washington, D.C., living expenses. But the action created such a political outcry that Congress reimposed the limit in 1982 in a supplemental appropriations bill (HR 6685 — PL 97-216).

In August, the Senate added a provision to another supplemental

funding bill (HR 6863 — PL 97-257) that could have resulted in a raise for members right after the Nov. 2 elections. But the House rejected the plan.

Before the elections, Congress used the first fiscal 1983 continuing appropriations resolution (H J Res 599 — PL 97-276), which cleared Oct. 1, to block a pay raise for members. But in the second such resolution (H J Res 631 — PL 97-377), cleared in the lame-duck session, Congress voted a 15 percent pay raise for House members but not senators, breaking a long tradition of paying members of both chambers the same salaries. Representatives began getting $69,800 a year, effective Dec. 18, while senators remained at $60,662.50. The Senate, however, did vote Dec. 14 to remove a provision from its rules that would have limited senators to about $9,100 in outside earnings beginning in 1983. Some House members suggested that the Senate got the better deal, because senators could command thousands of dollars in speaking fees.

Defense

Nuclear Freeze. The Senate did not act on widespread calls for a "freeze" in U.S. and Soviet nuclear weapons, a proposal bitterly opposed by the administration.

By a hair-thin margin (204-202), the House Aug. 5 approved an administration-backed substitute nuclear arms resolution (H J Res 521). The original resolution, sponsored by Clement J. Zablocki, D-Wis., called for a "mutual and verifiable freeze."

The Senate Foreign Relations Committee in June approved a nuclear arms control resolution (S J Res 212 — S Rept 97-493) that did not call for a nuclear freeze. The full Senate did not act on the resolution.

Defense Appropriations. Congress included in the second continuing appropriations resolution (H J Res 631 — PL 97-377) the fiscal 1983 Defense appropriations bill providing just over $232 billion (not counting funds for the annual pay raise). The total was $17.6 billion less than what President Reagan had sought.

This was the largest congressional reduction in a president's defense request in decades. But the spending bill left the shape of Reagan's planned weapons buildup nearly unchanged, except for two nuclear missiles for

which production funds were denied: the Pershing II and the MX.

Large parts of the resolution's reductions amounted to no more than bookkeeping changes and demands for tighter contract management.

MX Missile. Conferees on the second continuing resolution (H J Res 631 — PL 97-377) denied $988 million requested to begin procurement of the MX intercontinental missile. This followed an unexpectedly large House vote (245-176) Dec. 7 to drop the funds from the defense appropriations bill (HR 7355). The conference action marked the first time that Congress denied production funds for a strategic weapon sought by a president, and the vote came after a strong pitch by the administration to retain the funds.

But the action appeared in large part to have been a symbolic vote for restraint in defense spending and a rejection of the complex and controversial "dense pack" deployment method, proposed by Reagan Nov. 23, rather than on the missile itself.

The continuing appropriations resolution retained $2.5 billion in funds to continue development of the MX and its basing method, though $560 million of that amount could not be spent before Congress approved a specific MX basing method. The resolution directed the president to recommend a basing method after March 1, 1983. After the report was filed, both houses of Congress would have to pass a concurrent resolution in order for the basing plan to be approved.

Nuclear Carrier, B-1 Bomber. Two other costly and controversial weapons programs were given approval (H J Res 631 — PL 97-377) without significant change in fiscal 1983.

Reagan had requested $6.8 billion to begin work on two giant *Nimitz*-class carriers. Critics tried and failed twice in the Senate to delete one of the two carriers: once during action on the continuing resolution and earlier during action on the defense authorization bill (S 2248) in May. Proponents argued that the Falkland Islands war demonstrated the value of the big ships, and the administration also asserted that a package deal for the two ships would save $750 million compared to the cost of buying the second ship a few years later.

Although long a target of Pentagon critics, the B-1 bomber also survived repeated attacks in both houses in 1982. Reagan's full request for $4.6 billion to buy the first bombers and to continue B-1 research was included in the second continuing resolution.

Critics said the administration's promise to field a fleet of 100 B-1s for a total price tag of $20.5 billion was overly optimistic; they cited higher cost estimates made within the Pentagon. But Republicans embraced the plane as a symbol of what they called the inadequate defense policies of the previous Democratic administration. President Carter terminated production of the B-1 in 1977.

Troops in Europe. The second continuing resolution (H J Res 631 — PL 97-377) set a cap on U.S. troop strength in Europe at 315,600, the number authorized to be on the continent at the end of fiscal 1982. The Senate Defense Apppropriations Subcommittee earlier had approved a lower ceiling that would have forced the removal of 18,900 troops currently in Europe.

Although the administration and its allies, such as Senate Armed Services Committee member Sam Nunn, D-Ga., agreed that the NATO allies were contributing too little to the common defense, they warned that the more restrictive troop cap, proposed by subcommittee Chairman Ted Stevens, R-Alaska, would provoke less cooperation rather than more from the allies and reduce U.S. combat strength in the meantime.

Relations with NATO. Over administration opposition, Congress included in the second continuing resolution (H J Res 631 — PL 97-377) several provisions that made only small defense spending cuts but were bound to cause friction with U.S. allies in Europe. The provisions, designed to signal congressional dissatisfaction with the level of European defense spending, reduced U.S. funding for NATO-related programs, thus implying that European nations would have to make up the difference.

The provisions kept an existing ban on storing equipment in Europe for more than four U.S. Army divisions; rejected a $44.3 million request for equipment to be used in wartime by West German reservists assigned to assist U.S. combat units; and retained tight controls on Pentagon purchases of specialty metals used in jet engines and other weapons that were made by several European countries.

Economic Affairs

Budget Resolution. Beset by election-year pressures stemming from a lingering recession and soaring federal deficits, Congress made no effort to adopt a second, binding budget resolution for fiscal 1983.

Instead, lawmakers included in the first resolution (S Con Res 92) a provision stipulating that the budget targets set in that measure automatically would become binding if Congress did not approve a second resolution by the Oct. 1 beginning of the fiscal year.

Although the validity of the figures in S Con Res 92 was widely questioned, the House and Senate Budget committees put off until the 98th Congress any effort to revise or update them. Thus, the preliminary targets set in S Con Res 92 became binding limits on fiscal 1983 spending decisions.

Congress completed action on S Con Res 92 June 23, nearly six weeks after the statutory May 15 deadline. It had taken five frustrating months to win approval of the measure, which projected deficits above the politically critical $100 billion mark.

The resolution, which did not require the president's signature, provided for $769.8 billion in outlays, $665.9 billion in revenues and a $103.9 billion deficit in fiscal 1983.

To hold the deficit to that level, the resolution included "reconciliation" instructions that required committees to come up with $6.57 billion in spending cuts and $20.9 billion in revenue increases for the fiscal year.

Reconciliation Savings. Congress completed action in August on two massive reconciliation bills designed to achieve the budget savings required by the fiscal 1983 budget resolution (S Con Res 92).

The Omnibus Reconciliation Act of 1982 (HR 6955 — PL 97-253), cleared Aug. 18, cut anticipated federal spending by $13.3 billion over fiscal 1983-85. The measure tightened spending on government pensions, farm programs, food stamps, federal home loans and veterans' benefits.

The Tax Equity and Fiscal Responsibility Act of 1982 (HR 4961 — PL 97-248), cleared Aug. 19, was expected to provide $98.3 billion in increased revenues and cut $17.5 billion

from projected spending for Medicare, Medicaid, welfare and savings bond programs over fiscal 1983-85.

When combined, the measures were expected to reduce the federal deficit by about $130 billion by fiscal 1985.

Taxes. President Reagan reluctantly gave his support to legislation to raise taxes $98.3 billion over the next three years. The tax increase bill (HR 4961 — PL 97-248), cleared Aug. 19, was part of congressional efforts to cap record-high federal deficits through the budget reconciliation process.

Although much of the revenue was to be raised by closing loopholes and clamping down on tax evasion, the vote was a tough one for members facing re-election.

In the House, mainstream Democrats and Republicans joined to win approval of the bill, after conservative Republicans balked at the party line. They charged the measure ran counter to Reagan's own supply-side belief that high taxes would hurt economic growth.

The legislation originated in the Senate Finance Committee, which circumvented a constitutional requirement that the House take the lead on tax measures. The House sent the Senate-passed bill directly to conference without a separate vote on passage.

Savings and Loan Aid, Banking Reform. Congress gave final approval Oct. 1 to legislation to aid commercial banks and savings and loan institutions (S&Ls).

The bill (HR 6267 — PL 97-320) was largely intended to stem the tide of mergers of financially troubled institutions. It permitted federal regulators to aid ailing institutions through a series of paper transactions that were not expected to cost the federal government any money if the institutions pulled through. It also authorized federal regulators to set up a new type of federally insured financial account for banks and S&Ls that would be competitive with popular money market funds.

In addition, the measure expanded the lending and investment powers of savings and loans and eliminated the interest rate differential that had existed between S&Ls and commercial banks.

The final bill was a compromise developed following a year and a half

Budget Totals, Fiscal 1982-85

In its fiscal 1983 budget resolution (S Con Res 92), approved June 23, Congress set the following budget totals for fiscal 1982-85 *(in billions of dollars)*:

	Senate	House	Conference
Fiscal 1982			
Budget authority	$ 777.6	$ 779.30	$ 777.67
Outlays	740.8	729.20	734.10
Revenues	623.0	628.40	628.40
Deficit	−117.8	−100.80	−105.70
Fiscal 1983			
Budget authority	835.7	800.38	822.39
Outlays	784.3	765.17	769.82
Revenues	668.4	665.90	665.90
Deficit	−115.9	−99.27	−103.92
Fiscal 1984			
Budget authority	897.5	862.60	878.47
Outlays	833.3	815.98	821.93
Revenues	741.4	738.00	738.00
Deficit	−91.9	−77.98	−83.93
Fiscal 1985			
Budget authority	973.3	948.50	960.61
Outlays	890.7	874.96	881.36
Revenues	825.5	821.40	821.40
Deficit	−65.2	−53.56	−59.96

of complex negotiations between Congress and divergent elements of the financial community.

Debt Ceiling. Congress completed action Sept. 23 on legislation (H J Res 520 — PL 97-270) increasing the public debt limit to $1.29 trillion through Sept. 30, 1983. After five weeks of debate on extraneous issues such as abortion and school prayer, the Senate passed the bill amendment-free, thus completing congressional action.

The House had approved the debt limit increase as part of the fiscal 1983 budget resolution. H J Res 520 was the second debt limit increase of the year.

Education

Tuition Tax Credit. President Reagan's tuition tax credit proposal was approved by the Senate Finance Committee Sept. 16, but the legislation went no further. The bill (HR 1635) would have provided parents with an income tax credit of up to $300 a year for each child in private elementary and secondary schools.

The bill stirred controversy for a number of reasons, including questions it raised about relations between church and state and the future of public education. It almost died in committee because of a fight over protections against use of the credits by students in racially segregated schools.

College Student Aid. President Reagan's proposals for reducing the costs of college student-aid programs received little support in Congress during 1982.

Under heavy lobbying pressure from colleges, students and their parents, Congress declined to seek cutbacks in the fast-growing guaranteed student loan program. Legislation cleared Sept. 29 (S 2852 — PL 97-301) also reaffirmed Congress' opposition to the administration's proposed reductions in the Pell grant program, the chief form of help to low-income students. The bill specified the rules governing distribution of grants during the 1983-84 school year — in effect overturning Education Department rules aimed at cutting the program.

Education Department. Congress took no action in 1982 on a Reagan administration proposal to replace

the Education Department (ED) with an independent government foundation. Opposition was so strong that the administration did not even send Congress formal legislation to implement the plan, which was outlined in the fiscal 1983 budget.

The proposal would have established a Foundation for Educational Assistance to administer federal education programs. ED had been under attack by some conservative groups ever since it was set up by Congress in 1979.

Science Education. Two House committees reported differing versions of a bill (HR 7130) increasing federal aid to science and math education, but no further action was taken on the measure. Concern over the deteriorating quality of science and math instruction could lead to similar legislation in 1983, however.

The Science Committee's version of the measure would have distributed funds through the National Science Foundation. The Education Committee wanted to hand out funds to improve science and math teaching by formula grants to schools, through the Education Department.

Energy

Nuclear Waste. After more than four years of debate, Congress Dec. 20 finally cleared a bill (HR 3809 — PL 97-425) establishing a national plan for the disposal of highly radioactive nuclear waste.

As in 1980, the fate of nuclear waste legislation was still in doubt in the last days of the lame-duck session. Both House and Senate had passed waste disposal bills, but there were substantial differences between them.

The Senate brought a compromise version to the floor Dec. 20, working through more than 20 amendments in as many minutes. The House agreed to the compromise and accepted the Senate amendments later the same day.

By threatening a filibuster, Sen. William Proxmire, D-Wis., was able to tack an amendment to the bill giving states considerably more power to veto plans to locate a nuclear waste dump within their borders. Both houses had rejected the provision in previous votes, but by taking advantage of the need for consensus in the

closing hours of the lame-duck session, Proxmire managed to overrule the majority.

The Senate passed a waste bill (S 1662) in April, 69-9. But in the House, seven committees staked jurisdictional claims and the House did not pass its bill (HR 3809) until Dec. 2.

The bill set a schedule for picking a location and constructing a permanent facility for storing nuclear waste, to be completed by the end of the century. In the meantime, it provided for the temporary storage of radioactive waste, including spent fuel from private utilities' nuclear reactors.

NRC Authorization. A controversial two-year authorization bill for the Nuclear Regulatory Commission (NRC), first reported from committee early in 1981, was cleared Dec. 16.

The legislation (HR 2330 — PL 97-415) had moved through Congress so slowly that one of the years it covered (fiscal 1982) was already past.

The House approved the conference report on the bill Dec. 2. But it dropped a protectionist provision restricting uranium imports if they reached 37.5 percent of U.S. demand.

That provision had been added at the insistence of Sen. Pete V. Domenici, R-N.M., who wanted to protect the uranium mining industry in his home state. During the lame-duck session, Domenici agreed to a compromise uranium import provision, that triggered investigation, but not necessarily restriction, of imports if they reached the 37.5 percent level. The Senate approved the compromise (S Con Res 135) Dec. 16, and the House on Dec. 20.

Besides authorizing funding for NRC programs, the bill allowed the commission to issue operating licenses to new nuclear reactors before the completion of public hearings. It also prohibited the government from using burned fuel from civilian nuclear reactors to make nuclear weapons.

Energy Preparedness. Congress and President Reagan sparred for months over how to deal with future energy shortages before they finally agreed on energy preparedness legislation.

Reagan Aug. 3 signed into law a bill (S 2332 — PL 97-229) requiring him to speed up the flow of oil into the nation's Strategic Petroleum Reserve and to draw up plans for distributing the oil in times of severe shortage. The legislation also extended an antitrust

exemption for the major U.S. oil companies, allowing them to share petroleum supply information with the International Energy Agency (IEA).

An earlier bill cleared by Congress (S 1503) would have given Reagan power to allocate petroleum supplies and set prices in times of severe shortage — powers he said he did not want. He vetoed that bill, and the Senate upheld the veto. S 2332 generally conformed to Reagan's desire that the market be allowed to allocate supplies in a crisis.

Clinch River Breeder Reactor. The controversial Clinch River project lost a key vote in the House Dec. 14. But strong lobbying by Senate Majority Leader Howard H. Baker Jr., R-Tenn., kept the project alive for another year.

The second continuing appropriations resolution (HJ Res 631 — PL 97-377) approved by Congress provided $181 million for the project, less than the $252 million requested by the administration but enough to continue site preparation and engineering activities for the Tennessee breeder reactor. The resolution, however, prohibited the construction of any major facilities or the initiation of any new construction contracts during fiscal 1983.

The House Dec. 14 voted 217-196 for an amendment to prohibit the use of funds in the continuing resolution for the research, development, design or construction of Clinch River. The amendment allowed spending only for termination and close-out costs.

The Senate Dec. 17 reinstated funds for the reactor by a 49-48 vote, and the final compromise was worked out in conference.

The breeder reactor project — so called because it would produce more plutonium fuel than it consumed while also making electricity — had been opposed by environmentalists since its inception more than a decade earlier. But in recent years opponents were joined by fiscal conservatives, who feared the eventual effects on the federal budget of the $4 billion project.

Natural Gas. Rapidly rising natural gas prices spawned a litter of legislative proposals late in the session. But there was no agreement on what should be done; proposed solutions ranged from immediate deregulation of gas prices to re-regulation. Several members attempted to attach

amendments to the highway/jobs bill (HR 6211). But unable to agree even on why gas prices were rising, Congress took no action on the measures.

The Senate did pass a resolution directing the Federal Energy Regulatory Commission to look at ways to alleviate private contract arrangements that were forcing gas pipelines to buy high-cost gas when cheaper gas was available. The resolution also encouraged the use of all available federal aid for the assistance of low-income natural gas consumers.

DOE Dismantlement. Congress took no action on President Reagan's plan to abolish the Energy Department and shift most of its responsibilities to the Commerce Department. Influential members from both parties gave the proposal a chilly reception, and the administration was forced to retreat. Reagan's new energy secretary, Donald P. Hodel, told the Senate Energy Committee in December the administration realized there was little support for the proposal in Congress and that dismantlement was no longer a top priority of his department.

Three Mile Island Cleanup. Congress failed to act on legislation to finance the cleanup of the Three Mile Island (Pa.) nuclear power plant, damaged in a 1979 accident, with fees collected from all U.S. nuclear utilities.

The Senate Energy Committee approved the measure (S 1606) by a vote of 12-7 March 31, and the Senate Environment Committee reported it without recommendation on July 27. The bill would have left it up to state utility commissions to decide whether utilities could pass the cost of the fee on to ratepayers.

The House took no action on the issue, and the bill died without reaching the floor of either chamber.

However, a provision included in an authorization bill (HR 2330 — PL 97-415) for the Nuclear Regulatory Commission prohibited the use of federal funds for the Three Mile Island cleanup.

Environment

Clean Air Act. Despite two years of intensive work, the 97th Congress failed to pass a reauthorization of the landmark Clean Air Act. The

law's anti-pollution regulations remained on the books, and funds to enforce them were provided in appropriations measures.

However, the congressional inaction meant the Environmental Protection Agency had to enforce provisions of existing law requiring it to impose sanctions on jurisdictions that failed to meet a Dec. 31 deadline for compliance with national air quality standards. Hundreds of counties were potentially subject to the sanctions, which included limited construction bans and a cutoff of federal grants for highways and clean air programs.

The Senate Environment and Public Works Committee Aug. 19 approved a bill (S 3041) that made only modest changes in the existing clean air law and added new provisions aimed at controlling acid rain.

But the House Energy and Commerce Committee deadlocked the same day over a far more sweeping rewrite (HR 5252) that would have loosened auto emission standards and other parts of the present law. The panel never resumed its markup.

Endangered Species. A three-year reauthorization of the 1973 Endangered Species Act was cleared by Congress Sept. 30 (HR 6133 — PL 97-304). The legislation streamlined the law but did not significantly relax it.

The bill shortened from two years to one year the period for the Interior Department to decide whether to list a species as endangered, once it had received a petition to do so. It also required that listing determinations be made solely on biological grounds. The Reagan administration had sought to weigh economic costs in making such decisions.

Barrier Islands. A bill (S 1018 — PL 97-348) banning federal subsidies for development of undeveloped coastal barrier islands was cleared by Congress Oct. 2. It was the only significant new environmental legislation to clear the 97th Congress.

Coastal barriers are subject to floods, storms and erosion. S 1018 prohibited new federal flood insurance for such properties and also barred federal funding for sewers, highways, bridges and other projects supporting commercial or residential development on coastal barriers.

Hazardous Wastes. The House Sept. 8 passed a bill (HR 6307) to reauthorize and strengthen the Re-

source Conservation and Recovery Act, the principal law governing the management and disposal of hazardous wastes.

However, a companion measure (S 2432) died when the Senate Environment and Public Works Committee could not reach a consensus on key issues, such as the regulation of businesses that generated only small quantities of hazardous wastes.

Wilderness Oil and Gas Leasing. Congress extended until Sept. 30, 1983, an existing ban on oil and gas leasing in federal wilderness areas and lands being considered for inclusion in the wilderness system. Conservationists had sought to enact the ban in several forms during the year to check efforts by Interior Secretary James G. Watt to issue leases on pending applications.

The ban was included in the fiscal 1983 Interior appropriations bill (HR 7356 — PL 97-394) cleared Dec. 19. Such a ban had been part of the continuing resolution that expired Dec. 17 (H J Res 599 — PL 97-276).

The House Aug. 12 passed a bill (HR 6542) to ban such leasing, but neither it nor a companion Senate bill (S 2801) ever emerged from the Senate Energy and Natural Resources Committee.

Clean Water Act. Congress failed to approve a reauthorization of major provisions of the Clean Water Act, the nation's principal law for controlling water pollution. The inaction left in place existing law, and programs continued to be funded under appropriations measures.

House and Senate committees held hearings in July on a Clean Water Act reauthorization, but there was no further action. The Reagan administration unveiled its clean water proposals (HR 6670, S 2652) May 25.

EPA Research and Development. President Reagan Oct. 22 vetoed a bill (S 2577) authorizing research and development programs for the Environmental Protection Agency (EPA). The bill required EPA to conduct research on energy-related pollution and indoor air pollution, and it earmarked 20 percent of all EPA research funds for long-term research — all programs the administration wanted to cut. The Senate made no attempt to override the veto, laying it aside indefinitely Nov. 30. Congress had cleared the bill Oct. 1.

The veto did not mean an end to EPA research programs, since Congress Sept. 29 appropriated money for them in the fiscal 1983 funding bill (HR 6956 — PL 97-272) for the Department of Housing and Urban Development and independent agencies.

Federalism

New Federalism. President Reagan's call for a "new federalism," made in his State of the Union speech, received virtually no congressional attention in 1982. Under the proposal, which called for a thorough restructuring of federal, state and local government responsibilities, many existing federal social programs would have been turned over to the states.

Administration officials were unable to work out a satisfactory compromise with the National Governors' Association and similar groups, which were wary of receiving new responsibilities without adequate funds to pay for them. No legislative proposal was transmitted to Congress during the year.

Foreign Policy

Radio Marti. A bill (HR 5427) authorizing the creation of Radio Marti to broadcast news, opinion and entertainment to Cuba became snagged in a Senate filibuster Dec. 6, and was doomed for the year. In its only formal action on the issue, the Senate on Dec. 17 rejected an administration-backed effort to attach Radio Marti funding to the second continuing resolution.

The House passed HR 5427 in August. The legislation faced opposition from two quarters: liberals who said it was a gratuitous attempt to provoke Cuba's Fidel Castro, and owners of U.S. radio stations who feared Cuba would jam Radio Marti, thus causing interference with their broadcasts.

Caribbean Basin Initiative. The second part of President Reagan's three-part Caribbean Basin Initiative, announced in February with much fanfare, finally began moving during the lame-duck session but fell short of final passage.

The House on Dec. 17 passed a watered-down version (HR 7397) of Reagan's program of trade benefits for Caribbean and Central American nations. The Senate Finance Committee hurriedly approved a slightly amended version three days later. However, the full Senate never took up the bill.

Congress approved the first part of the plan in the fiscal 1982 supplemental appropriations bill (HR 6863 — PL 97-257) — $350 million in emergency economic aid to nations in the region.

But the request for special trade and tax benefits encountered widespread opposition in Congress, largely because of complaints from labor unions and businesses who feared those benefits would be at the expense of business and workers in the United States. In fact, the third part of the plan, a proposal to give tax benefits to U.S. firms investing in Caribbean and Central American nations, never was taken seriously by Congress.

Foreign Aid. Congress attached $11.2 billion in funding for most foreign aid programs to the second continuing appropriations resolution (H J Res 631 — PL 97-377), but failed to act on legislation making supplemental foreign aid authorizations for 1983.

The authorization bills (HR 6370, S 2608), pending in both houses since May, included additional military and economic aid, especially for countries in the Middle East and Central America. Aid to Israel was to have been increased substantially by both bills.

The continuing resolution gave Reagan about $1.2 billion of the $2.3 billion in additional military aid he had wanted in fiscal 1983, much of it for nations hosting U.S. military bases. Included in the extra money, however, was increased aid for Israel that Reagan opposed. Reagan had wanted to hold the line on aid to Israel, fearing that Israeli leaders might see an increase as a softening of U.S. disapproval of policies he had condemned. The continuing resolution boosted military grants to Israel by $200 million, but it did not make even larger increases that the Senate had approved.

El Salvador. Congress in 1982 seemed increasingly impatient with the methods and results of Reagan's policies in Central America, especially El Salvador. But aside from refusing to increase military aid to El Salvador, Congress took no action to force a dramatic change in administration policies, which had rested on economic, political and military aid for right-wing regimes that were fighting leftist insurgencies.

Reagan in 1982 twice certified to Congress that El Salvador was making progress in promoting human rights and implementing various reforms. On both occasions, critics said Reagan overstated the amount of progress. Reagan's request for sharp increases in military and economic aid to El Salvador was scuttled by the lack of action on regular foreign aid authorization and appropriations bills for fiscal 1983.

Covert Action. Both houses of Congress blunted efforts by liberals to block reported aid by U.S. intelligence agencies to rightist rebels who were seeking to overthrow the government of Nicaragua. The second continuing appropriations resolution left the administration free to continue supporting the rebels, as long as the stated purpose was not to overthrow the government or to provoke a war between Nicaragua and neighboring Honduras.

Government

Regulatory Reform. The Senate March 24 unanimously approved a sweeping regulatory reform bill (S 1080) giving Congress, the president and the courts more control over the way federal rules were made. But the House Rules Committee bottled up a similar House bill (HR 746).

The legislation, which required cost-benefit analysis of major proposed rules and provided a legislative veto mechanism for many regulations, was supported by business lobbyists and the Reagan administration.

Public interest groups and several House committee chairmen opposed the legislation, arguing that it would undermine health, safety and other consumer protection laws.

Federal Retiree Pensions. Congress in August moved to curb spending on government pensions as part of its budget reconciliation process. The reconciliation bill (HR 6955 — PL 97-253) cut in half, for the next three fiscal years, the annual cost-of-living adjustment (COLA) for federal retirees under age 62. COLAs for all federal retirees were to be delayed one month in each of those years.

The measure also eliminated "double-dipping" by military retirees who collected both military and civil service benefits. The various changes made by the bill added up to a three-year savings of about $4.1 billion.

Freedom of Information Act. Efforts to place new restraints on the Freedom of Information Act (FOIA) never moved beyond the Senate Judiciary Committee. The committee May 20 unanimously approved a bill (S 1730) to limit public access to certain government files. But the bill, which faced news media opposition, never reached the Senate floor.

No action was taken in the House, where Rep. Glenn English, D-Okla., chairman of the Government Operations information subcommittee, refused to hold hearings on FOIA unless the Senate completed deliberations on the subject.

Small Business. The Senate June 29 cleared the Small Business Innovation Research Act (S 881 — PL 97-219) earmarking 1.25 percent of the government's research budget for small businesses. The set-aside was designed to reverse a perceived decline in technological innovation by funneling more research money to small, inventive entrepreneurs.

Debt Collection. The Senate Oct. 2 cleared a bill (HR 4613 — PL 97-365) designed to help the federal government collect billions of dollars in unpaid federal debts. The bill authorized the federal government to use credit bureaus and collection agencies to track down delinquent borrowers.

Health

Medicare/Medicaid. New ceilings on Medicare payments to hospitals and doctors were among spending cuts in the 1982 tax bill cleared Aug. 19 (HR 4961 — PL 97-248).

The bill also required employers to offer Medicare-eligible workers comparable coverage under private employee health plans and authorized grants for peer review of Medicare and Medicaid claims by groups of doctors. The grants replaced the expiring Professional Standards Review Organization (PSRO) program.

Other provisions authorized Medicare coverage for hospice services and revised payment methods to facilitate

Medicare enrollments in prepaid health plans known as health maintenance organizations.

Health Research. Congress did not complete reauthorizations for federal research institutes on cancer, heart, lung and blood diseases. The House Sept. 30 passed a three-year reauthorization bill (H 6457), but the less costly Senate version (S 2311), reported in May, was not brought to the Senate floor. Key senators were reluctant to debate a House-passed amendment barring most medical research on live human fetuses.

The legislation would have established a new research institute on arthritis, a step the administration opposed as too costly. A last-ditch effort to pass a separate arthritis institute bill (S 1939) failed Dec. 21 when Rep. William E. Dannemeyer, R-Calif., objected to bringing it up in the House. The Senate had discharged the bill from committee and passed it Dec. 20. The research institutes, except for the proposed arthritis institute, were funded by the second continuing appropriations resolution (H J Res 631).

Orphan Drugs. Congress sent the president a bill (HR 5238 — PL 97-414) to promote the development of "orphan drugs" — drugs for diseases affecting so few people that costs of development appeared to exceed potential profits.

The president signed the measure Jan. 4, despite an earlier threat to veto the bill because of the cost of its tax credits for drug makers.

Differences between House- and Senate-passed versions had been settled informally without a conference, and the House approved the final compromise Dec. 14. The Senate cleared the bill Dec. 17.

The final version also included a Senate-passed $14 million, two-year authorization for home health-care services.

Health Planning. A controversial type of medical regulation, health planning, was kept alive by the second continuing appropriations resolution (H J Res 631 — PL 97-377) after the failure of efforts to reauthorize the program as optional block grants to states.

The House passed a health planning bill (HR 6173) on Sept. 24, and again endorsed a modified version Dec. 16, as part of a reauthorization (HR 6458) of federal research insti-

tutes on alcoholism and drug abuse. The Senate did not act on that bill.

Housing/ Urban Development

Housing. Congress failed to pass a fiscal 1983 housing authorization bill when efforts to remodel federal housing programs collapsed.

Authorizing legislation (S 2607, HR 6296) was approved by Senate and House Banking committees in May. The bills were different, although both would have replaced Section 8 low-income housing construction aid with a new rental production program, despite the Reagan administration's request to end federal aid for subsidized housing construction.

The House bill was stalled for months because its price tag exceeded the amount allowed by the fiscal 1983 budget resolution. The Senate bill faced opposition because of a provision converting rural housing programs to block grants.

Mortgage Subsidies. A $3 billion emergency mortgage subsidy plan (HR 5922) to revive the depressed housing industry swept through Congress during the spring but was vetoed by President Reagan, who called it a "budget-busting bailout." Congress failed to override the veto.

By subsidizing mortgage interest rates for new home buyers, the measure was designed to spur home construction and provide building trades jobs.

Assumable Mortgages. As part of a measure (HR 6267 — PL 97-320) to help financially ailing savings and loans, Congress limited the assumption of home mortgages.

In a compromise worked out between lenders and real estate brokers, the bill overrode state laws that prohibited the enforcement of due-on-sale clauses in mortgage contracts. The clauses required homeowners to pay off a mortgage when they sold their homes, denying new buyers the ability to take over an old, low-interest loan.

Enterprise Zones. President Reagan's plan to help depressed cities and rural towns by creating enterprise zones remained stuck at the committee level in the 97th Congress.

The Senate Finance Committee approved the proposal Sept. 28 as part of an unrelated tax bill (HR 7094). The plan, which was Reagan's major urban initiative, would have provided tax breaks and regulatory relief to businesses that provided new jobs in blighted areas.

No hearings were held by the House Ways and Means Committee.

Labor/Social Security

Job Creation. Rising unemployment made Congress increasingly sympathetic to direct federal jobs programs in the post-election session.

But the only putative job-creation measure it approved was administration-backed legislation (HR 6211 — PL 97-424) raising the gasoline tax to pay for repairs to the nation's deteriorating roads and mass transit systems. Although President Reagan insisted the measure was not a jobs bill, supporters maintained it would create more than 300,000 jobs.

Both the House and Senate versions of the second fiscal 1983 continuing appropriations resolution (H J Res 631 — PL 97-377), cleared Dec. 20, contained funds for public works and other job-creating projects. The House-passed measure provided $5.4 billion, while the Senate version included $1.2 billion.

However, President Reagan strongly opposed inclusion of the job-creation funds. Facing a likely veto of the resolution, conferees on the continuing resolution agreed to drop both House and Senate proposals.

Job Training. A new job training program was established by Congress in 1982. The legislation (S 2036 — PL 97-300), replacing the expiring Comprehensive Employment and Training Act (CETA), cleared Oct. 1. The new program did not provide public service jobs, as CETA did. Instead, it concentrated on providing skills instruction and other employment-related assistance to low-income people with severe problems in the job market. State governments and businesses were to play a larger role in the program than they had under CETA.

Unemployment Benefits. As part of a major tax and spending bill (HR 4961 — PL 97-248) cleared Aug. 19, Congress agreed to extend jobless benefits an additional six to 10 weeks, for up to 49 weeks of benefits in some states.

The extra payments resulted largely from election-year fears that growing unemployment lines would mean trouble at the polls in November. The new supplemental benefit program was to run from Sept. 12 through March 1983, and help about two million jobless workers who had exhausted existing benefits.

Then, in the final days before adjournment, Congress agreed to add up to six additional weeks to this supplemental benefit program as part of the highway authorization and gas tax increase bill (HR 6211 — PL 97-424). The price tag for the two packages together was expected to be about $2.7 billion.

Social Security. Apart from a spate of partisan rhetoric at election time, Congress managed to skirt this controversial issue throughout the year. It waited instead for recommendations from the president's bipartisan National Commission on Social Security Reform.

Early in 1983, the commission reached agreement on a compromise reform plan, thus paving the way for quick congressional consideration of legislation to keep the retirement system afloat. Major elements of the package called for delaying future cost-of-living adjustments (COLAs), advancing scheduled payroll tax increases and covering federal employees under Social Security.

Without some infusion of new funds, the Social Security system was expected to be unable to pay retirement benefits as early as July 1983.

Disability Benefits. Cleared in the final hours of the 97th Congress was stopgap legislation (HR 7093 — PL 97-455) to allow those thrown off the Social Security Disability Insurance rolls to collect benefits while they appealed. Under existing law, such individuals did not receive benefits, even though about two-thirds of those who appealed before an administrative law judge were eventually reinstated in the program.

Demands for corrective legislation followed a firestorm of complaints from constituents that many still-disabled individuals were being thrown off the rolls. The Reagan administration was attempting to follow a congressional mandate to rid the program of ineligible recipients.

More comprehensive legislation (HR 6181) to overhaul the disability system was approved by the House Ways and Means Committee in May but was stalled by heavy lobby group opposition. Committee members vowed to bring up the issue again in 1983.

Law Enforcement/Judiciary

Voting Rights. A bill (HR 3112 — PL 97-205) extending the enforcement section of the 1965 Voting Rights Act for 25 years was cleared by Congress June 23. The measure also modified a 1980 Supreme Court decision to make it easier to prove certain types of voting rights violations.

The House passed its version of HR 3112 in October 1981 by a 389-24 vote. But the bill ran into trouble in the Senate Judiciary Committee, where a faction led by Orrin G. Hatch, R-Utah, wanted to require proof of intent to discriminate before voting rights violations could be established in cases principally involving at-large election systems.

Civil rights groups vigorously opposed the "intent" standard, contending it was virtually impossible to prove. Robert Dole, R-Kan., finally put together a compromise acceptable to those groups and to a majority of the committee. The Senate passed the bill 85-8 June 18, one day after Jesse Helms, R-N.C., gave up a filibuster against the compromise version. The House accepted the Senate bill June 23 by unanimous consent.

Balanced Budget Amendment. The House Oct. 1 decisively rejected a proposed constitutional amendment (H J Res 350) that would have required Congress to adopt a balanced federal budget each year except in times of war or when three-fifths of the entire Congress voted to allow a deficit. The vote was 236-187 — 46 short of the two-thirds required.

Just two days earlier, supporters of the measure had gathered the discharge petition signatures necessary to pry it out of the House Judiciary Committee, where it had been bottled up for months. The Senate adopted a similar but not identical measure (S J Res 58) Aug. 4.

Abortion and School Prayer. The Senate Sept. 15 killed a proposal

designed to ban most abortions, and with three procedural votes Sept. 23, it also laid aside a measure intended to return prayer to the public schools.

Both proposals had been offered by Jesse Helms, R-N.C., as amendments to legislation raising the public debt ceiling (H J Res 520). The amendments were derailed after opponents led by Lowell P. Weicker Jr., R-Conn., Max Baucus, D-Mont., and Bob Packwood, R-Ore., waged a six-week filibuster against them. Instead of debating the merits of school prayer and abortion, opponents of Helms' proposals argued they would strip the courts of their ability to handle constitutional issues and would erode the independence of the judiciary.

Busing. A sweeping amendment that would virtually end court-ordered school busing for racial balance was adopted by the Senate as part of the fiscal 1983 Justice Department authorization bill (S 951) passed March 2. But when the bill was sent to the House, it was quickly buried in the Judiciary Committee.

Although House proponents of the anti-busing legislation circulated a petition to discharge the committee and bring the measure directly to the House floor, they were unable to gather the necessary 218 signatures.

On Dec. 9, the House by a 243-153 vote attached an anti-busing rider to the fiscal 1983 State, Justice, Commerce appropriations bill (HR 6957). The rider, like those in past years, would bar Justice Department involvement in lawsuits that could lead to busing for racial balance. However, the appropriations bill never cleared, and the anti-busing rider was deleted from the second continuing appropriations resolution (H J Res 631 — PL 97-377) that funded the State, Justice and Commerce departments for fiscal 1983.

Immigration Reform. Despite a last-ditch effort, a wide-ranging immigration reform bill (HR 7357) died in the House Dec. 18. A combination of ailments derailed the measure — opposition from Hispanics, organized labor, business and civil rights groups; an unenthusiastic House leadership; and lack of time.

The bill was aimed at curbing illegal immigration, controlling legal immigration and providing amnesty for millions of illegal aliens already in the United States. The Senate passed a similar measure (S 2222) Aug. 17.

The House Judiciary Committee approved HR 6514, the predecessor bill to HR 7357, on Sept. 22. The Education and Labor Committee, to which the bill had been referred, approved the measure Dec. 1 after changing the temporary worker program to give the Labor Department more control over its operation.

Crime Legislation. Congress Dec. 20 cleared an anti-crime package (HR 3963) that was a potpourri of legislation that had passed one chamber or the other. But President Reagan vetoed the bill Jan. 14.

Reagan objected to provisions that would have established a Cabinet-level office with authority over all federal drug enforcement activities. Attorney General William French Smith and other current Cabinet officers had opposed creation of such a "drug czar."

While HR 3963 included a number of anti-crime initiatives, it did not cover two major areas — bail and sentencing reform. Both were part of a complete revision of the federal criminal code (S 1630) that died in April when the Senate failed to cut off debate on a motion to consider the bill.

HR 3963 increased fines for trafficking in drugs and gave the government new authority to require forfeiture of property related to an illegal drug enterprise; authorized a crime assistance program for states to replace the defunct Law Enforcement Assistance Administration; created a new federal crime of tampering with drugs, cosmetics or other consumer goods; authorized federal prosecutions of so-called "career criminals" who repeatedly committed state crimes with a firearm; and created a Cabinet-level office to oversee drug enforcement.

In other action, Congress in October cleared a bill (S 2420 — PL 97-291) designed to make federal courts more sensitive to victims and witnesses of crime and to provide restitution to victims where possible.

Trade

Auto 'Domestic Content.' The United Auto Workers (UAW) union won a major victory Dec. 15 when the House passed, 215-188, a bill (HR 5133) to require foreign auto companies either to build more of their cars in the United States or to reduce sales here. The House substantially weak-

ened the "domestic content" measure, however, by accepting an amendment that would nullify the bill if it were found to violate the General Agreement on Tariffs and Trade (GATT).

The House vote was largely symbolic, since there was little chance for Senate action on the bill. But supporters said the vote would "send a signal to Japan" to reduce its trade barriers.

The Senate Finance Committee held hearings Dec. 17 and 18 but did not report a bill.

The Reagan administration opposed domestic content legislation, which U.S. Trade Representative William E. Brock III called "the worst piece of economic legislation since the 1930s." But in spite of the severe criticism, the bill was expected to resurface in the 98th Congress.

Trade Reciprocity. Watered-down versions of bills seeking "reciprocity" in trade relations were reported by congressional committees but did not reach the Senate or House floor in 1982. The bills, designed to stiffen the U.S. response to trade barriers imposed by foreign countries, gathered substantial support, particularly in the Senate, and sponsors promised to revive them in 1983.

A bill (S 2094) reported by the Senate Finance Committee June 30 and added to a separate House-passed tariff bill (HR 4566) in September was endorsed by administration trade negotiators. The bill would have strengthened procedures for enforcing violations of existing trade law, and required the government to seek international agreements on services, high-technology and investment trade.

However, the controversial reciprocity provisions were dropped from HR 4566 in the final days of the lame-duck session. Senate supporters of the reciprocity bill, led by John C. Danforth, R-Mo., promised to reintroduce the measure in the 98th Congress.

A bill (HR 5519) reported Aug. 19 by the House Commerce Committee also would have provided negotiating authority for agreements covering trade in services, and set procedures for retaliating against service firms of foreign nations that unfairly restricted access of U.S. companies to their markets.

Export Trading Companies. Before leaving for its election recess, Congress completed action on legislation (S 734 — PL 97-290) designed to encourage the formation of export

trading companies to help small- and medium-sized firms market their goods abroad. The measure eased antitrust barriers that had inhibited joint export activities and allowed banking institutions for the first time to be active partners in the trading companies.

President Reagan and other supporters viewed the legislation as a "jobs bill," contending that it would result in the creation of several hundred thousands of jobs.

Transportation

Highways, Mass Transit. After a bitter and tiring fight, the Senate cleared legislation Dec. 23 authorizing more than $71 billion over four years for highway construction, road repairs and mass transit, and increasing the gasoline tax by a nickel a gallon. The measure also allowed bigger and heavier trucks on the highways, but increased the highway taxes that heavy trucks must pay.

The House adopted the conference report on the bill (HR 6211 — PL 97-424) Dec. 21 and adjourned. The compromise had been approved by House and Senate conferees earlier that day. But Senate action was delayed by filibusters by conservative Republicans who opposed the tax increase. The Senate invoked cloture for a final time Dec. 23 and then adopted the conference report.

The measure also created a new block grant program for mass transit aid. Transit operating subsidies were cut by 20 percent of the fiscal 1982 level for the largest cities. President Reagan originally sought to end operating subsidies after fiscal 1984.

Most mass transit authorizations expired Sept. 30. Although money was included in the first continuing appropriations resolution (H J Res 599 — PL 97-276), which expired Dec. 17, transit backers said program changes were needed to soften the impact of funding cuts.

Maritime Regulation. Maritime interests were unable to obtain a Senate vote on legislation (S 1593) that would broaden antitrust immunity for ocean liner cartels. Sen. Howard M. Metzenbaum, D-Ohio, maintained that he would block consideration of the bill, which he called "atrocious."

The House overwhelmingly approved a similar bill (HR 4374) Sept. 15.

Airports. Congressional disputes over the direction and scope of the airport development program and aviation taxes were resolved, and the program was reauthorized by a general tax increase bill (HR 4961 — PL 97-248). The airport development act (PL 91-258) expired two years before, although it was reprieved briefly in 1981.

The tax bill authorized $4.8 billion for airport development projects in fiscal 1982-87 and about $7.4 billion from the Airport and Airway Trust Fund for Federal Aviation Administration operation of the air traffic control system.

The measure also increased the airline passenger ticket tax to 8 percent, from 5 percent; increased the general aviation fuel tax to 12 cents a gallon, from 4 cents; and imposed a jet fuel tax of 14 cents a gallon.

Railroad Strike. A four-day national railroad strike ended when Congress Sept. 22 passed legislation (S J Res 250 — PL 97-262) requested by President Reagan. The measure ordered the 26,000 striking members of the Brotherhood of Locomotive Engineers back to work and imposed the settlement recommended earlier by a presidential Emergency Board. The settlement barred the union from striking through June 30, 1984.

Some members of Congress had misgivings about passing legislation that imposed a settlement containing a no-strike provision. But those misgivings were outweighed by concerns that the strike eventually might throw a million people out of work and cost the economy $1 billion a day.

Bus Deregulation. The intercity bus industry became the fourth industry to undergo significant deregulation in as many years as a result of legislation (HR 3663 — PL 97-261) cleared by Congress in August. The bill was designed to relax federal and state regulation of buses.

The bill made it easier for new bus companies to start service and for existing carriers to expand operations. Unprofitable routes could be dropped more easily and companies would be able to change their rates with less government involvement. The bus bill followed on the heels of previously enacted laws that eased regulation of airlines, railroads and trucks.

Coal Slurry. Proponents of coal slurry pipelines failed to obtain floor action during the lame-duck session on legislation (HR 4230, S 1844) making it easier to secure rights of way through railroad properties for the construction of the pipelines.

Coal slurry is pulverized coal mixed with water that is then carried by underground pipes. Railroads, the major haulers of coal, lobbied against the legislation, contending that the pipelines would skim off the best coal business. House and Senate committees approved the measures.

Coast Guard, Ports, Waterways. Congress did not adopt the user fees that President Reagan wanted to charge for Coast Guard services, port development and inland waterways.

Critics had staved off the proposals since the administration first offered them in 1981. They contended the Coast Guard plan did not adequately account for the public benefits of the Coast Guard. Also, many members of Congress feared that port fees might hurt the shipping industry, and they could not resolve differences between large and small ports.

Reagan argued that individuals and groups that specially benefited from government services should pay fees for those services.

Veterans

Budget Cuts, COLAs. Veterans' programs, long considered one of Congress' "sacred cows," finally suffered some budget cuts in 1982, although disabled veterans managed to recoup some of their losses with a 7.4 percent cost-of-living increase.

The cost-of-living adjustment (COLA), effective Oct. 1, went to veterans with service-connected disabilities, and their survivors. It was part of legislation (HR 6782 — PL 97-306) that also realigned veterans' job programs run by the Labor Department and limited the Veterans Administration's ability to deny Vietnam-era veterans vocational education benefits.

But what Congress gave with one hand it took away with the other. Instead of making $387 million in cuts as ordered by the budget resolution, Congress voted as part of the reconciliation bill (HR 6955 — PL 97-253) to reduce spending for veterans' programs by about $552 million in fiscal

1983-85. Congress delayed payment of certain compensation and pension benefits and rounded benefit checks down to the next lowest dollar.

Welfare

Food Stamps, AFDC, SSI. The three major income-support programs for the poor — food stamps, Aid to Families with Dependent Children (AFDC) and Supplemental Security Income (SSI) — were the targets of spending reductions ordered by Congress in 1982. But concern about the effects of cuts on the poor during a recession held the reductions to levels below those sought by the administration or by Senate Agriculture Committee Chairman Jesse Helms, R-N.C. The programs already had undergone substantial cutbacks in 1981.

The budget reconciliation bill cleared by Congress Aug. 18 (HR 6955 — PL 97-253) made cuts estimated at $548 million in the projected spending level for food stamps in fiscal 1983. Combined with reductions in dairy price supports mandated by the bill, the cuts were expected to save $6.6 billion over three years. Among other things, the bill held down inflation adjustments in food stamp benefit levels and penalized states that poorly administered the program.

The tax increase/spending cuts bill cleared Aug. 19 (HR 4961 — PL 97-248) included AFDC spending cuts totaling $343 million over three years, and SSI reductions of $386 million. ∎

MAJOR
CONGRESSIONAL
ACTION

Economic Policy

The economic picture became increasingly bleak during 1982 as hopes that the administration's unconventional economic theories might pull the country from recession were quickly dashed.

While interest rates and inflation dropped during the course of the year, they did so at a bitter price. By year's end, unemployment had reached a record post-World War II high of 10.8 percent. With more than 12 million individuals out of work and industrial production on the decline, little comfort was taken from the positive economic signs.

The Reagan administration, confronted by the continued recession, appeared to flounder in its economic policies. While the White House continued to push for cuts in domestic spending, it retreated from its "supply-side" tax reduction policies of the year before.

By summer, the administration reluctantly backed legislation to raise taxes $98.3 billion over the following three years in an effort to close the budget deficit gap. That gap was growing out of control and, although it sometimes seemed impossible, the projected deficit figures grew increasingly more alarming.

Reagan's fiscal 1983 budget proposal to Congress called for a $91.5 billion deficit. But it was expected by the end of 1982 that the real figure would be closer to $180 billion and the annual deficit might grow to $300 billion by fiscal 1988 if nothing was done.

In addition, the international economic picture continued to deteriorate. High interest rates meant a strong U.S. dollar on international markets leading to a record-high trade deficit for 1982. Shaky loans by hundreds of U.S banks to several developing nations spread fears of possibly severe repercussions throughout the U.S. economy.

Congress reacted to the deteriorating economy by splitting with the administration on a number of important economic votes. Not only did members have a November election to worry about, but as conditions worsened fewer and fewer were willing to "give the president a chance" as they had the year before.

The Economy

Economists spent much of the year revising their projections of economic recovery, pushing the expected date further and further into the future. By year's end, it was thought that a modest recovery likely would come during 1983.

Interest rates and inflation were among the two hopeful signs. The prime lending rate, which hovered around 16 percent for the first half of the year, dropped in December to 11.5 percent. The Consumer Price Index also declined dramatically, rising only 3.9 percent in 1982, compared with 8.9 percent in 1981.

While these signs promised better times, most notably in the housing and auto industries, there were more than enough negatives to counteract them. Unemployment not only hit record highs for most of the year, but with factories shutting down across the country there were widespread fears that many jobs would never return.

The nation's "real" gross national product (GNP) — the total output of goods and services, adjusted for inflation — declined at an annual rate of 5.1 percent in the first quarter of the year. After a slight increase during the year, the GNP was declining at an annual rate of 2.5 percent by the final quarter of 1982.

Budget and Taxes

Aggravating the bleak economic scene were signs that federal fiscal policy was in a state of serious disarray. No sooner had Reagan submitted his fiscal 1983 budget request to Congress than Budget committees in both houses rejected the plan as unrealistic and began to work on their own.

Members complained that revised deficit projections of close to $120 billion were far too high and called instead for more cuts in defense spending and higher taxes to close the gap.

After months of haggling, and House rejection of a series of budget alternatives, a budget resolution finally was agreed to in June that called for a $103.9 billion fiscal 1983 deficit. It also required congressional committees to come up with $27.2 billion in spending cuts and $98.3 billion in tax increases for the next three years.

Reflecting congressional frustration, Rep. Bill Frenzel, R-Minn., remarked after the resolution was adopted: "Even though this budget resolution is no one's cup of tea, it is the only one we have."

The required spending cuts were made with surprising ease in comparison with previous years, but the tax increases — euphemistically called "revenue raisers" — proved painful. Not only did the package come before Congress shortly before the election, but support of the measure was difficult for members who had espoused large tax cuts in 1981. In addition, the White House only reluctantly supported the measure.

As it emerged from Congress, the tax-increase measure met its $98.3 billion target, in large part by closing tax loopholes and instituting measures to beef up taxpayer compliance. Untouched was Reagan's 1981 individual income tax-cut initiative that he considered the centerpiece of his economic program. Democrats pushed hard for repeal or delay of the July 1983 installment of that cut, but Republicans and the administration refused to budge.

Unemployment and Jobs

One of the major legislative themes of the year was job creation, but Reagan held firm and opposed all such spending initiatives until he finally backed a gas tax and highway jobs bill that passed in the final days of the session.

Democrats charged throughout the year that high unemployment, one of the most apparent fallouts of the recession, was a clear sign that Reagan's economic policies

had failed.

In part capitalizing on the issue before the election, Democrats made several attempts to push large, new jobs programs. But the administration charged that such plans involved massive government expenditures for "make-work, dead-end" jobs.

Reagan's theory was that more jobs could be created by getting government spending under control and restoring economic growth.

The House — which earlier in the year had unsuccessfuly backed a $1 billion mortgage subsidy plan — in December passed a $5.4 billion jobs program as part of the second fiscal 1983 continuing appropriations bill. With unemployment rising, Senate Republicans followed suit, and the Senate approved a $1.2 billion public works program. Both House and Senate plans eventually fell victim to White House opposition.

Instead, the Reagan administration proposed legislation to raise gasoline taxes and to use the revenue for highway and mass transit improvements. Although Reagan denied the measure was a "jobs" program, it was expected to help create over 300,000 new positions.

Both houses went along with the plan and the measure passed in the final days of the session, the only jobs initiative of the year.

Monetary Policy

As a backdrop to the year's fiscal problems, controversy continued over the policies of the Federal Reserve Board. Some critics charged that the board's tight money policies were preventing economic recovery by keeping interest rates high. Others feared that if the board loosened the money supply inflation would go up once again.

In February, the board set a target growth range for M1, the sum of all currency and checking deposits, of between 2.5 percent and 5.5 percent. It stuck by that range for much of the year. But the board, under great pressure to keep interest rates going down, began in October to pay more attention to interest rates and other money measures, and the money supply loosened.

Disturbed by continued high interest rates, congressional Democrats tried unsuccessfully to push legislation reshaping Federal Reserve policy and calling for presidential authority to have the Fed impose sweeping credit controls. But as interest rates dropped during the latter half of the year, the issue lost much of its steam.

Congress did include in the fiscal 1983 budget resolution a non-binding declaration that the Federal Reserve should re-evaluate its monetary targets if Congress was successful at reducing the federal budget deficit.

—By Pamela Fessler

Tax Increases Meet Deficit Reduction Target

President Reagan continued his unbroken winning streak on budget issues when Congress gave final approval Aug. 19 to a \$98.3 billion tax increase and \$17.5 billion spending reduction package over three years.

But the victory came at a price. Faced with large budget deficits, Reagan was forced to abandon his tax-cutting philosophy of the previous year in an effort to raise the much-needed revenue.

Yet the final package (HR 4961 — PL 97-248) left untouched the heart of his 1981 tax-cut program — a three-year across-the-board reduction in individual income taxes. Instead, the new "revenue-enhancing" bill was labeled a reform and focused on closing tax loopholes and increasing taxpayer compliance with laws already on the books. It did, however, repeal some business tax breaks enacted in 1981 and imposed new excise taxes on individuals.

Election-year politics required the president's strong — albeit reluctant — support for the legislation. Members of both parties who found themselves in close re-election battles feared the wrath of the electorate if they voted for the tax increase without the backing of the popular president.

Besides, Democrats were reluctant to hand Republicans a legislative victory without forcing Reagan to share in the blame. House Speaker Thomas P. O'Neill Jr., D-Mass., and his Democratic lieutenants were critical to the 226-207 House vote to approve the tax increase. Without the support of 123 Democrats, the conference report on the tax/spending bill would have gone down in defeat. *(Vote 289, p. 84-H; defectors from Reagan, box, p. 38)*

But House Republican unity — the hallmark of the president's earlier successes — was broken by the tax bill fight. Conservative Republicans, led by staunch supply-sider Jack F. Kemp, R-N.Y., bolted from the party line. They argued that the middle of a recession was not the time to repudiate the 1980 election mandate to cut taxes and spending. Only 103 Republicans voted for the measure; 89 voted against it.

In the GOP-controlled Senate the vote was more clear-cut. Although 11 Republicans defected, for ideological or parochial reasons, nine Democrats voted for the measure on the final 52-47 tally that cleared the bill for the president's signature. *(Vote 337, p. 55-S)*

The bill was the last piece of the deficit reduction plan mandated by reconciliation instructions included in the fiscal 1983 budget resolution (S Con Res 92). In addition to its tax provisions, the measure revised Medicare, Medicaid and welfare programs to cut projected spending by \$17.5 billion in fiscal 1983-85. Other provisions provided additional unemployment benefits for workers who had exhausted their benefits under existing law and extended authorizations for airport development and air traffic control programs. *(Reconciliation details, p. 199; Medicare, Medicaid, p. 471; welfare, p. 476; unemployment benefits, p. 43; airport programs, p. 333)*

Final Provisions

As signed into law Sept. 3, the Tax Equity and Fiscal Responsibility Act of 1982 (HR 4961 — PL 97-248) included the following revenue-raising provisions (effective Jan. 1, 1983, unless otherwise noted):

Business Taxes

Accelerated Depreciation, Investment Tax Credit. Required that taxpayers subtract half the value of any tax credits — for regular investment, historic rehabilitation or energy — before computing depreciation deductions for a new asset. Previously, taxpayers could depreciate the full value of the asset, even if they had received a 10 percent investment tax credit.

• Limited regular and rehabilitation tax credits to 85 percent of the liability in excess of \$25,000 instead of the current 90 percent.

• Repealed provisions in the Economic Recovery Tax Act of 1981 (PL 97-34) that would have increased the benefits from accelerated depreciation in 1985 and again in 1986 by allowing greater deductions in the early years of an investment.

Corporate Tax Payments. Speeded up collection of corporate tax payments by raising from 80 percent to 90 percent the amount of estimated tax liability a firm must pay during its tax year to avoid penalty. However, any company whose tax payments through the year ended up between 80 and 90 percent of actual tax liability would be assessed only 75 percent of the penalty. The bill also moved up the deadline for final tax payments and increased the amount of estimated tax payment required of certain large corporations.

Possessions Tax Break. Limited a tax break for certain corporations earning income in Puerto Rico and U.S. possessions — mostly pharmaceutical firms — by disallowing credits for income from intangibles such as patents, copyrights and trade names. In general, companies would still be allowed to shelter investment income earned in Puerto Rico.

Foreign Oil and Gas Income. Repealed a tax break allowing oil and gas companies to shelter income through the use of credits and losses from foreign oil and gas extraction.

Corporate Tax Preferences. Reduced several business tax breaks by 15 percent, including special deductions for mining exploration and development, interest on debt used to purchase or carry tax-exempt securities, tax breaks for depletion of coal and iron ore, excess bad debt reserves, rapid write-off of pollution control facilities, certain tax breaks for selling structures, and subsidies for U.S. exporting firms.

• Reduced from 90 percent to 85 percent the amount of tax liability that could be offset by the 10 percent investment tax credit. Full tax breaks for intangible drilling costs could be taken, but would have to be spread over a five-year period for major oil producers, with most of the benefits in the first year.

These changes, imposed in addition to existing corporate minimum taxes, were an alternative to the administration's plan for a new minimum corporate tax.

Construction Deductions. Required corporations to amortize over 10 years interest and property taxes incurred during construction of non-residential real property.

Insurance Tax Breaks. Repealed an existing law allowing life insurance companies to shelter much of their income through a process called "modco," through which firms transferred some of their policyholder risks to other insurance companies and thus paid lower taxes. But in a

Tax Bill's Estimated Revenue Impact

(Fiscal years, in millions of dollars)

Provision	1983	1984	1985	1986	1987
Individual Income Tax provisions:					
Alternative minimum tax	$ (¹)	$ 659	$ 701	$ 741	$ 729
Medical deduction	272	1,788	1,671	1,795	1,947
Ten percent casualty deduction floor	—	666	734	800	880
Total, individual tax provisions	272	3,113	3,106	3,336	3,556
Business Tax Provisions:					
Reduction in corporate preference items	515	936	948	918	995
Investment tax credit basis adjustment	362	1,374	2,658	4,109	5,579
Limit ITC to 85 percent of tax liability	152	259	213	178	164
1985-1986 ACRS changes	—	—	1,541	9,907	18,442
Construction period interest and taxes	555	1,179	1,206	1,084	819
Modifications to pre-ERTA and safe harbor leasing rules	1,036	2,649	4,252	5,496	7,000
Changes in taxation of foreign oil extraction income	200	438.	508	569	621
Limit on possessions credit	201	428	473	516	559
Private purpose tax-exempt bonds	63	261	539	748	1,076
Mergers and acquisitions	427	749	959	1,014	1,064
Accounting for completed contracts	882	2,235	2,535	2,390	2,559
Original issue discount and coupon stripping	163	310	465	629	808
Targeted jobs credit	−182	−551	−591	−271	−54
Accelerate corporate tax payments	1,048	3,025	791	755	484
Total, business tax provisions	5,422	13,292	16,497	28,042	40,116
Compliance Provisions:					
Withholding on interest and dividends	1,344	5,246	3,975	4,605	5,181
Other compliance provisions	2,021	3,623	4,685	5,569	6,036
Total, compliance provisions	3,365	8,869	8,660	10,174	11,217
Pension Provisions	194	780	870	970	1,058
Life Insurance and Annuities	1,942	2,155	2,920	3,138	3,370
Employment Tax Provisions:					
Independent contractors	−117	−107	−79	−85	−92
FUTA tax	1,404	2,353	2,729	1,872	1,501
Federal employees Medicare tax	617	837	927	1,066	1,163
Total, employment tax provisions	1,904	3,083	3,577	2,853	2,572
Excise Tax Provisions:					
Airport and airway taxes	817	962	1,089	1,216	1,357
Telephone tax	616	1,073	1,600	730	—
Cigarette tax	1,275	1,829	1,859	−34	−13
Repeal of Trans Alaska Pipeline System adjustment	90	145	154	142	128
Total, excise tax provisions (net increase)	2,798	4,009	4,702	2,054	1,472
Miscellaneous Provisions:	−38	−37	−34	−32	−30
Total, tax provisions	15,859	35,264	40,298	50,535	63,331
Revenue gain resulting from additional IRS enforcement personnel	2,100	2,400	2,400	1,300	600
Grand Total, all tax provisions	**$17,959**	**$37,664**	**$42,698**	**$51,835**	**$63,931**

¹ *Negligible.*   Source: Joint Committee on Taxation

concession to the life insurance industry — which had complained that, without modco, tax burdens would grow too large — the bill made other changes reducing industry taxes.

Multi-Year Contracts. Instructed the Treasury Department to tighten up regulations governing firms involved in long-term contracts — such as those in the construction and aerospace industries — that could defer tax payments through special accounting procedures. Contractors with annual gross receipts below $25 million for the three preceding years and contracts expected to be completed in less than three years were exempt.

Leasing. Restricted, and eliminated as of Jan. 1, 1984, the use of so-called "safe-harbor leasing" provisions in the 1981 tax bill that allowed firms to sell unused tax breaks. The new provision attempted to eliminate many of the "abuses" of the controversial 1981 provision by limiting to 50 percent the amount of tax liability that could be offset through purchase of such tax breaks and by not allowing leasing to be used to offset tax payments from previous years. In addition, the amount of property that could be leased and the length of the lease term were restricted.

The measure allowed companies to use 150 percent declining balance depreciation for lease transactions. But companies were required to take the investment tax credit over a five-year period compared with three years in the Senate bill.

As of 1984, the bill also would liberalize the use of traditional "leverage" leasing — transactions in which a company transfers tax breaks in reduced lease payments. This type of leasing transaction, however, would have to comply with restrictions that applied to safe-harbor leasing.

Corporate Mergers. Changed current law governing corporate mergers and acquisitions to prevent such actions from being taken only for tax advantages and to limit certain tax abuses. Most of the changes went into effect Sept. 1, 1982.

Payments to Foreign Officials. Allowed a business expense deduction for any payments to foreign officials or agents of a foreign government as long as the payment was legal under the Foreign Corrupt Practices Act.

Restaurant Tips. Required restaurants with more than 10 employees to take 8 percent of their gross income and allocate a share to each employee. The restaurant was required to report that amount under the employee's name to the Internal Revenue Service (IRS) each year. IRS would use the amount reported as a bench mark to measure the accuracy of the amount of tip income reported by the employee. This provision was to take effect April 1, 1983.

Individual Taxes

Medical and Casualty Deductions. Repealed the current deduction for one-half of health insurance premiums up to $150. The bill also allowed deductions for medical expenses exceeding 5 percent of a taxpayer's adjusted gross income, compared to the current 3 percent. After 1983, the provision allowing deductions for prescription drug costs greater than 1 percent of income was to be repealed. Casualty losses were to be deductible only if they exceeded 10 percent of adjusted gross income.

Pension Contributions. Restricted deductions for contributions to corporate pension plans, many of which had been used as tax shelters for wealthy individuals.

The bill lowered the limits on tax-deductible contributions to such plans and increased the allowable annual contribution for self-employed, or Keogh, retirement plans. For corporate, defined contribution benefit plans the maximum dollar limit on contributions was dropped to $30,000 a year from $45,475. For defined benefit plans, or those that allowed contributions necessary to produce a specified benefit level at retirement, the maximum benefit was cut from $136,425 to $90,000. The maximum tax-deferred pension contribution for the self-employed was doubled to $30,000 after 1983.

Federal Employees. Required federal employees to pay the 1.3 percent Federal Insurance Contributions Act (FICA) tax for Medicare coverage. Even though federal workers had not paid the tax previously, about 80 percent of retired federal employees over age 65 had been covered by Medicare because of previous non-government employment or through their spouses.

Individual Minimum Tax. Replaced existing minimum taxes on wealthy individuals with a more comprehensive "alternative" minimum tax that would prevent taxpayers from wiping out their tax liability with large deductions. Such taxpayers were required to increase their taxable income by the amount of certain tax breaks, called preference items, and pay a 20 percent tax on income above $30,000 for individuals, or 20 percent on income above $40,000 for couples filing joint returns.

The minimum tax was to be payable only to the extent that it exceeded regular taxes.

Tax Collection

Compliance. Beefed up compliance with existing tax law by requiring additional reporting of income, by increasing penalties for non-compliance and by strengthening IRS enforcement powers.

● Required the withholding of taxes from pension payments unless taxpayers requested otherwise and increased requirements for reporting tip income.

● Assumed Congress would appropriate funds for additional IRS agents and additional data processing equipment.

● Included provisions to improve tax compliance by so-called independent contractors and extended a congressional moratorium on IRS regulations dealing with independent contractors — which expired June 30 — to Jan. 1, 1983.

Interest and Dividend Withholding. Required withholding of 10 percent of interest and dividend payments, with exceptions for payments to certain low-income and elderly individuals, to tax-exempt institutions and to corporations. This provision would not become effective until July 1, 1983.

● Allowed Treasury to issue regulations giving financial institutions a chance to earn income on the withheld funds to cover administrative costs and to exempt certain small institutions from the requirements.

Other

Airport and Airway Trust Fund. Raised $2.8 billion in various taxes for the Airport and Airway Trust Fund by making changes that included: increasing the passenger ticket tax from 5 percent to 8 percent; raising the general aviation gasoline tax from 4 cents a gallon to 12 cents a gallon; imposing a 14-cent-a-gallon tax on jet fuel; and reinstating the 5 percent air freight waybill and $3 international departure ticket taxes. All the airport and airway

taxes would expire after four years unless extended by Congress. The new taxes would go into effect Sept. 1, 1982.

● Authorized expenditures from the trust fund for airport development and air traffic control modernization.

Unemployment Insurance. Raised net unemployment taxes from .7 percent of the first $6,000 of wages to .8 percent of the first $7,000, for an increase of $6.4 billion for fiscal 1983-85. The increase was expected to cost approximately $1.20 a month for each employee. The federal tax rate was to be increased further in 1985 with the likely effect of pushing up state unemployment taxes.

● Increased the portion of unemployment compensation payments subject to the federal personal income tax in order to finance new supplemental unemployment benefits included in the bill. The income threshold was lowered from $20,000 to $12,000 for single taxpayers and from $25,000 to $18,000 for couples filing joint returns.

Telephone. Raised the current 1 percent telephone excise tax to 3 percent on Jan. 1, 1983. It would stay at that level for three years and then drop to zero after 1985.

Cigarettes. Doubled the excise tax on cigarettes from 8 cents to 16 cents a pack. This provision would expire Oct. 1, 1985.

Industrial Development Bonds. Restricted the use of tax-exempt industrial development bonds (IDBs) issued by state and local governments. The bill required public hearings and official approval of all IDBs, and required private users in most cases to forgo depreciation benefits enacted in 1981. No tax-exempt IDBs could be issued after Dec. 1, 1986. The bill also loosened limits on the use of tax-free mortgage subsidy bonds imposed by Congress in 1980. These changes generally would be effective after July 1, 1982. *(Mortgage subsidy bonds, 1980 Almanac p. 298)*

Other Bonds. Changed the tax treatment of so-called "original issue discount bonds" to limit tax breaks for issuers and tax penalties for those who purchase such bonds. The bill also limited tax advantages of bonds stripped of coupons.

Targeted Jobs Tax Credit. Extended the targeted jobs tax credit program for two more years, through 1985. The credit also was expanded to encourage summer employment of disadvantaged youths. *(1978 Almanac p. 219)*

Debt Management. Allowed the Treasury to offer variable interest rates on U.S. savings bonds and increased the ceiling for long-term bonds from $70 billion to $110 billion.

Studies. Instructed the secretary of the Treasury to study simplification of the tax system. The bill also called for an administration study on alternative ways to set monetary policy.

Windfall Profits. Repealed special windfall profits tax provisions for oil produced at Prudhoe Bay in Alaska.

Background

In 1981, President Reagan scored a legislative coup with the passage of the largest tax reduction bill (PL 97-34) in history. His legislation not only cut individual income taxes 25 percent over three years, but included major tax cuts to encourage new business investment. It was estimated the bill would reduce taxes approximately $749 billion over the following five years. *(1981 Almanac p. 91)*

Reagan promised the measure would bring economic recovery as businesses realized a larger return on investments and individuals were encouraged by lower marginal tax rates to work harder and to save more of their earnings.

But, not long after passage, it appeared that critics of the tax-cut program were more on the mark. As they had predicted, the economy did not improve. Instead, the large tax reductions drained the Treasury of much-needed revenue and, combined with high unemployment and low productivity, led to unprecedented growth in the federal budget deficit.

In September 1981, Reagan proposed additional revenues of $22 billion for fiscal years 1982-84 in an effort to close the deficit gap. But congressional response to raising taxes so soon after cutting them was unenthusiastic. The year ended with no action in Congress and no formal tax increase proposals from the administration.

By the start of 1982, the budget outlook had worsened. It soon became apparent that tax increases, as well as spending cuts, would again be required. The 1983 budget resolution (S Con Res 92) approved June 28 called for the two congressional tax-writing committees — House Ways and Means and Senate Finance — to find $98.3 billion in new taxes over three years and approximately $16 billion in spending cuts.

Despite Democratic calls for repeal or delay of Reagan's individual income tax cut program to meet these large revenue goals, the president held firm. He pushed instead for the closing of tax loopholes and increased taxpayer compliance.

Reagan Proposals

Reagan called for additional tax revenues during his State of the Union address Jan. 26 to help lower large projected budget deficits. Aides later outlined in more detail a package of $86.6 billion in new tax hikes for fiscal 1983-87.

Reagan rejected widespread advice to raise more revenue by increasing federal excise taxes, and reaffirmed his belief that his 1981 individual and business income tax-cut package would stimulate economic recovery. He told the nation he would not retreat from his original plan or "balance the budget on the backs of the American taxpayers."

Instead, Reagan vowed to "plug unwarranted tax loopholes" and strengthen the law requiring corporations to pay a minimum income tax. He also called for improved tax collection, including a requirement for faster corporate tax payments. *(Text of Reagan address, p. 3-E)*

One of Reagan's most controversial proposals was to withhold 5 percent of taxable interest and dividends, comparable to withholding income tax from wages.

A similar request by President Carter in 1980 was overwhelmingly rejected by Congress amid complaints that it would be an administrative nightmare and hurt retirees who relied on dividend payments to cover everyday expenses.

Under Reagan's plan, taxpayers aged 65 and over would be exempt if their total tax liability were less than $500. The administration argued in its favor that 9 percent to 16 percent of interest and dividend income was not reported, and estimated that $8.2 billion could be raised from the provision in fiscal years 1983-87.

More attractive to members of Congress — especially Republicans sensitive to charges that GOP policies favored the rich — was a proposal to strengthen the existing minimum tax on corporations. The new tax was intended to ensure that all profitable corporations would pay at least some income tax, according to Treasury Secretary Donald T. Regan.

The administration also resurrected several "revenue-enhancing" plans it had proposed in September 1981. They included:

● Forbidding use of the so-called completed contract method of accounting, which allowed firms with multi-year contracts to delay payment of taxes until the projects were completed.

● Repealing special 10 percent to 15 percent energy tax credits for businesses. The administration dropped its original plan to seek repeal of energy tax credits for individuals.

● Restricting the use of tax-exempt industrial development bonds. The administration would have required public approval for such bonds and some financial commitment by the government issuer. It also would have prevented businesses benefiting from such bonds from using new accelerated depreciation tax breaks.

● Elimination of a tax code provision that allowed insurance companies to reduce their tax liability by transferring some of their policy risk to another firm.

The administration dropped its September proposal to tighten eligibility requirements for untaxable unemployment compensation benefits.

In addition, Reagan called for:

● A speedup of corporate income tax payments. Corporations had been required to pay at least 80 percent of their taxes in the current taxable year. Reagan would have increased this to 90 percent.

● An increase of 5,000 in the Internal Revenue Service enforcement staff. Regan estimated the Treasury would realize $4 in savings for each $1 spent on additional enforcement.

● Repeal of a provision allowing corporations to immediately write off interest and tax costs incurred during construction.

Lukewarm Reception

Reagan's proposals were met with mixed reaction in Congress. Few members were eager to boost taxes in an election year, but the prospect of record deficits made it difficult to pass up much-needed revenues.

Some members, including Senate Finance Committee Chairman Robert Dole, R-Kan., hinted that even higher tax increases might be necessary to get predicted deficits under control.

Committee aides were already looking at additional tax-hike proposals including ones to strengthen the minimum tax for individuals, as well as corporations, and to revise the controversial "safe-harbor" leasing provisions.

But other members of Congress were reluctant to backpedal on the tax-cutting trend that had been started the previous year by Reagan and his followers.

"We remain very concerned about the deficit numbers we're hearing," said Rep. Charles W. Stenholm, D-Texas, a leader of the Conservative Democratic Forum, a group of conservative House Democrats. "But you don't raise taxes in a recession. I don't think we even ought to be talking about tax increases today."

There were early indications the president's package might have trouble getting off the ground in the Democratic-controlled House Ways and Means Committee, still smarting from Reagan's 1981 tax-cut successes. Aides said committee Chairman Dan Rostenkowski, D-Ill., would have to be convinced of the administration's commitment to the package before the House panel would act.

Democrats were more interested in making an issue of

repealing Reagan's three-year across-the-board cut in individual income taxes, than they were in helping him out of his budget predicament. They argued that the only way to get the budget deficit under control was to repeal or delay the income tax reduction scheduled for July of 1983. "We attempted too much too soon ... and the economy got indigestion," said Sen. Ernest F. Hollings, D-S.C.

Administration Changes

In the months following Reagan's tax increase proposals, economic conditions continued to worsen. The administration soon realized that its "revenue-raising" plans would be insufficient to keep the deficit below $100 billion, an administration goal.

By May, Reagan and Senate Budget Committee Republicans settled on a proposal to raise taxes by $95 billion for fiscal years 1983-1985 to accompany certain spending cuts. But Reagan did not specify how that revenue target would be met, and insisted the money could be raised without altering the personal income tax cuts enacted the previous year.

Heated exchanges between House Ways and Means Committee Democrats and Treasury Secretary Regan May 5 foreshadowed tough days ahead on the tax issue. Regan was called before the House panel to present new revenue-raising options above and beyond those proposed by the president earlier in the year.

While acknowledging that more had to be done to cut the deficit, Regan refused to lay out any new ideas. Instead, he reaffirmed the administration's commitment to its economic program. "We sent our budget up and apparently it was rejected.... Now we'd like to see if the Congress has any suggestions," he said.

But interspersed with the political rhetoric, Regan hinted there were some areas where the administration already had begun to modify its original tax-increase plans.

The Treasury secretary:

● Said the administration would consider changing new "leasing" provisions, the most controversial element of the 1981 tax law. He proposed imposing a cap on the amount of tax liability a firm could offset through leasing, and prohibiting firms from using leasing to get refunds from taxes paid in prior years.

● Said the administration was looking at changes in the 1981 business depreciation benefits to prevent firms from getting what amounted to an investment subsidy. He added, however, that exceptions should be made for some distressed industries.

● Indicated that Treasury was considering allowing firms to use the existing 10 percent investment tax credit to help offset the effects of Reagan's proposed minimum tax on corporations.

● Announced that the president's February budget proposal to withhold taxes from interest and dividend income — which had met with heavy opposition — had been withdrawn.

Tax-Hike Options

Some members of Congress took seriously Regan's challenge to come up with their own suggestions on raising revenues. With the Ways and Means Committee assuming a back-seat role, Dole's Finance Committee staff started to draw up extensive option lists.

Dole originally said that he would prefer to pass one or two "big ticket" revenue-raisers rather than to propose numerous small tax increases that could be shot down by

interest groups. But it soon became apparent that proposals raising the most revenue — an energy tax and changes in Reagan's income-tax cut program — were also the most controversial.

A $5-a-barrel oil import fee — which was pushed by Senate Republican leaders for a three-year savings of $32.4 billion — had little support in the House, and opposition to the fee quickly grew in both houses amid reports that it would hurt Northeastern consumers hardest while aiding domestic oil producers. A proposed gasoline tax was criticized for imposing too great a burden on low- and middle-income taxpayers.

In addition, Reagan remained steadfast in his opposition to any tampering with his income tax cut program — and Dole acceded.

Only one revenue-raising idea gained quick, almost across-the-board acceptance — the beefing up of tax compliance measures. For many members, faced with a mandate to reduce the federal budget deficit, raising revenues by clamping down on those who did not pay their tax bills was politically more palatable than trying to find new taxes to raise. An estimated $95 billion in taxes went uncollected in 1981 alone, according to the IRS.

Both Rostenkowski and Dole introduced similar legislation (HR 6300, S 2198) designed to reduce tax noncompliance by increasing penalties, IRS enforcement powers and the use of tax withholding.

Senate Committee Action

With the House showing little inclination to take its constitutionally required lead on raising taxes, the Senate Finance Committee made the first move. On July 2, the committee approved a package of approximately $98 billion in new taxes and other revenue raisers for fiscal years 1983-85. *(Spending cut package, p. 199)*

The straight party-line vote of 11-9 came at the end of a 15-hour markup session, following several days of closed-door negotiations among committee Republicans and administration officials to come up with a package they all could support.

The final plan, reported July 12 (S Rept 97-494), differed greatly from the tax increases proposed by Reagan earlier in the year. It would raise approximately $21 billion in fiscal 1983, $34 billion in fiscal 1984 and $43 billion in fiscal 1985 — meeting the committee's reconciliation requirements set by the first budget resolution for fiscal 1983.

The proposed tax increases affected both individuals and businesses and included higher taxes on cigarettes and airplane tickets, a minimum tax for high-income individuals and restrictions on deductions for pensions and health costs. Unexpectedly, it included the controversial plan to withhold taxes from interest and dividends.

The bill also cut back some of the business tax breaks approved the previous year, including the controversial leasing provisions, and took steps to improve taxpayer compliance. Left intact was President Reagan's three-year cut in individual income taxes.

The committee circumvented the constitutional requirement that all revenue-raising measures originate in the House by attaching its package to HR 4961, a minor tax bill passed by the House in 1981. *(1981 Almanac p. 116)*

Committee Democrats, who tried unsuccessfully to defeat several provisions in the Republican-crafted legislation, elicited from Dole a tentative agreement to allow one floor vote on repealing the 1983 individual tax cut — which had become a symbol of partisan dispute over economic policy.

An amendment by ranking minority member Russell B. Long, D-La., to defer the 10 percent tax cut indefinitely for all those with high incomes — raising $37 billion over three years — was defeated in committee by a vote of 7-12.

Shaky Coalition

Indicative of the problems awaiting the measure was the shaky GOP coalition in committee in support of the bill.

The Republicans on the panel had tentatively agreed in caucus June 30 to a package of tax increases — most of which were retained in the final bill — that met the committee's revenue targets. But during the course of the markup four Republicans jumped ship and voted to reject the controversial proposal to withhold taxes from interest and dividends. The panel quickly recessed so Republicans could find a way to make up the $12 billion in revenues the measure was expected to raise.

Dole — who had called earlier for total repeal of the troublesome tax leasing provision — hinted that repeal of leasing might be necessary to make up for the committee's rejection of the withholding plan.

But after some back-room bargaining, the committee returned and adopted the withholding provision by a vote of 11-9.

Under the plan, 10 percent withholding was to be applied to all interest and dividend payments, except those made to elderly and low-income individuals, corporations and tax-exempt institutions.

The measure also included several provisions intended to appease banks and other groups who were strongly opposed to withholding. One such provision shortened from one year to six months the time an investor was required to hold on to an investment before profits were taxed at a lower, long-term capital gains rate.

Another provision gave the Treasury Department authority to allow institutions withholding interest and dividends a time lapse in turning the funds over to the Treasury to help pay their administrative costs.

After the withholding vote, the committee went on to approve an amendment by David Durenberger, R-Minn., to restrict the tax leasing provision, raising $7.6 billion for fiscal 1983-85.

Durenberger's plan included several restrictions to prevent some of the most widely publicized "abuses" of the leasing provision, which had allowed some profitable corporations to wipe out their entire tax liability and receive refunds for past tax payments by selling unused tax breaks.

Also included in the Finance measure was retention through 1987 of a leasing tax break for public mass transit facilities with contracts signed before March 31, 1983.

Closing Loopholes

Republicans included in the committee bill other provisions that were designed to counter charges that the party was cutting the budget deficit largely by reducing government spending on programs for the poor.

The largest revenue raiser in the measure was expected to bring in $17.5 billion in revenues over three years by clamping down on tax avoidance and improving IRS enforcement powers.

The bill modified one of the most controversial provisions in Dole's original compliance legislation (S 2198) by

making it easier for employers to report employee tip income.

Also included in the package was a minimum-type tax on both corporations and individuals, expected to raise approximately $3.5 billion over three years. The individual minimum would have required high-income taxpayers who use large deductions to wipe out their tax liability to pay an alternative tax equal to 15-20 percent of certain deductions. It was expected to affect only 200,000 individuals.

Corporations also were required to reduce the value of certain tax breaks by 15 percent. This change, however, would have raised only about one-fourth of the $12 billion for fiscal 1983-85 that had been projected for the administration's corporate minimum tax proposal.

The committee also put restrictions on deductions for contributions to corporate pension plans, which had received widespread publicity as tax shelters for highly paid professionals. The committee bill lowered limits on tax-free contributions to such plans, limited outstanding loans an individual could have from such a plan and froze the indexing of contribution limits for two years.

Other Action

Many of the provisions in the bill, however, were changes directly affecting individual taxpayers. These included an increase in the floor on allowable deductions for unreimbursed medical and casualty expenses to 10 percent of adjusted gross income. The medical expense deduction provision was later changed on the Senate floor and then again in conference.

Other individual tax hikes that remained largely unchanged included an increase in federal unemployment, telephone excise and cigarette taxes.

The committee also agreed to require federal employees to pay a 1.3 percent Social Security tax for Medicare coverage.

The committee made several changes in business tax breaks, including some that were enacted in the 1981 tax bill.

Members voted to:

● Require firms to reduce the value of an asset by half of any investment tax credits they received before depreciating the asset.

● Repeal provisions in the 1981 tax bill that would have permitted additional accelerated depreciation of new assets in 1985 and 1986.

● Accept a compromise stopgap proposal that would limit use of the "modco" insurance tax break.

● Restrict the so-called completed contract method of accounting used by contractors.

● Restrict the use of private purpose tax-exempt industrial development bonds.

● Make a series of complex changes in current law to limit tax-motivated mergers and acquisitions.

● Speed up estimated corporate income tax payments.

The committee also agreed to raise $3.8 billion in revenues for fiscal 1983-85 for the Airport and Airway Trust Fund, as part of a bigger package on airport development. The bill increased the passenger ticket tax from 5 percent to 8 percent, raised taxes on general aviation gasoline and jet fuel and restored the international departure ticket tax of $3 per person.

The committee also extended the targeted jobs tax credit program through 1985 and gave the Treasury authority to offer variable interest rates on U.S. savings bonds. *(Previous extension, 1981 Almanac p. 91)*

Senate Floor Action

The Senate voted early July 23 to accept the Finance Committee bill by a largely party-line vote of 50-47. Despite strong pressure from lobbyists and general unwillingness among members to raise taxes during an election year, the package put together by the Finance Committee was kept largely intact during the lengthy session that began July 22. *(Vote 257, p. 44-S)*

All Democrats voting voted against the measure, and were joined by Republicans Paula Hawkins, Fla., Robert W. Kasten Jr., Wis., and Mack Mattingly, Ga. Independent Harry F. Byrd Jr., Va., voted for the bill.

The Senate action was the first major test of congressional willingness to comply with the reconciliation requirements in the fiscal 1983 budget resolution. As passed, the bill met the committee's spending and revenue mandate.

The bill — which generally had White House backing — raised revenues mainly by closing loopholes and beefing up tax compliance. But it also increased cigarette, telephone and unemployment taxes and required the withholding of some taxes on interest and dividends. Most of the spending cuts affected health programs and increased out-of-pocket costs for recipients.

Finance Committee Chairman Dole was able to fend off most floor challenges, in part because of his thinly veiled threat to impose even tougher tax increases if the bill was sent back to committee. Still, he hit a serious, last-minute snag.

Shortly before the 4:30 a.m. final vote, an amendment by David Pryor, D-Ark., to delete an unpopular provision requiring employers to report employee tip income was adopted by a vote of 70-25. *(Vote 252, p. 44-S)*

The move left the package some $2.8 billion short of the committee's revenue target, threatening final passage. But after some procedural maneuvering, Dole offered an amendment to allow deductions for only half the cost of business — so-called "three-martini" — lunches, covering the entire $2.8 billion shortfall.

Adoption of the amendment, in apparent retaliation for the restaurant industry's strong opposition to the tip provision, paved the way for final passage.

Interest, Dividend Withholding

The most critical vote, however, came earlier over the committee's proposal to withhold 10 percent of interest and dividend income, a plan strongly opposed by banks and other financial institutions.

An amendment by Kasten and Hollings to delete the withholding plan and strengthen interest and dividend reporting instead, was defeated by a vote of 48-49 — but only after some arm-twisting and compromising by Dole. *(Vote 247, p. 43-S)*

Republican leaders considered the provision essential because it raised over $12 billion in fiscal years 1983-85 and there was little prospect for finding another tax increase that large to replace it. It was feared that rejection of the withholding plan could mean collapse of the carefully crafted bill.

To meet some of the objections to withholding, Dole modified the committee plan, exempting individuals with prior-year tax liabilities below $600 ($1,000 for couples). In addition, a proposal by Don Nickles, R-Okla., to require withholding only for those with annual interest and dividends exceeding $100 was adopted 97-0. *(Vote 246, p. 43-S)*

Democratic Challenges

The biggest symbolic challenge to the bill came from Democrats who charged that the large tax-increase package was made necessary by overly generous tax cuts enacted in 1981 and by the failure of the Reagan administration's economic recovery program to work.

They proposed that, instead of cutting spending for health care and raising taxes on individuals, the Senate delay scheduled individual income tax cuts — but only for the wealthy — until the federal budget was balanced.

The Democratic alternative was defeated by a largely party-line vote of 45-54. It would have deferred the 10 percent individual income tax cut scheduled for 1983 for couples earning over $78,700 a year until the federal budget was balanced. Those earning below $46,500 would have received the full tax cut, and those earning in-between would have had their cut reduced. *(Vote 234, p. 41-S)*

In exchange for the $25 billion expected to be raised by reducing the tax cuts, the Democratic plan would have deleted proposals to increase excise taxes on cigarettes and telephone service, to raise federal unemployment taxes and to raise the floor on deductible medical and casualty expenses. It also would have restored some Medicare spending.

Dole warned members, however, that tinkering with the scheduled individual income tax cuts would lead to a presidential veto of the entire package.

Republicans Lowell P. Weicker Jr., Conn., and Mark O. Hatfield, Ore., voted for the Democratic plan. Edward Zorinsky, D-Neb., and Byrd, Va., voted against it.

A later amendment by George J. Mitchell, D-Maine, to redistribute the 1983 tax cut so that it would benefit more of those earning under $50,000 also was defeated, 43-53. *(Vote 245, p. 43-S)*

Spending Changes

Surprisingly little opposition was raised to spending cuts of $4.2 billion for fiscal 1983, $6.0 billion in fiscal 1984 and $7.3 billion for fiscal 1985 that were included in the package.

An amendment by Durenberger to reduce proposed Medicare cuts was the only major change to the spending side of the package. His proposal, adopted by a vote of 99-0, restored approximately $400 million over the next three years. *(Vote 236, p. 42-S)*

The amended measure left the deductible for part B (which pays physicians' fees) at its current level of $75 for 1983, and increased it to approximately $78 in 1984 and $80 in 1985. The committee bill would have raised the deductible each year — up to approximately $89 in 1985 — to reflect increases in the cost of living.

The amendment also would end, or "sunset," after 1985 a provision requiring Medicare premiums to equal approximately 25 percent of program costs. It also revised a committee measure requiring a 5 percent co-payment — estimated at approximately $2 for 1983 — for all home health care visits by making the first 20 visits free.

The Durenberger plan was adopted after an attempt by Max Baucus, D-Mont., to eliminate all three Medicare provisions from the bill for an increase in spending of $1.5 billion over the next three years.

Baucus' proposal was rejected by a vote of 46-53, but eight Republicans voted for it. Durenberger's promise to offer his compromise package following the vote was credited with preventing more GOP defections. *(Vote 235, p. 42-S)*

A proposal by John Heinz, R-Pa., to allow Medicare reimbursement for so-called "hospice" care for the terminally ill also was adopted.

Other Floor Compromises

The GOP concessions on Medicare were among several changes Dole agreed to in an attempt to ensure passage of the package.

When debate began July 19, Dole offered several modifications to the committee bill, in addition to the withholding changes, to dilute much of the opposition to the measure.

The major modification was to lower the floor for medical expense deductions from 10 percent of adjusted gross income — as proposed by the committee — to 7 percent. To pay for the change, the bill was revised to lower from $150 to $100 the maximum deduction for medical insurance premiums.

The Senate also adopted a Dole modification to speed up corporate tax payments and to change the due dates for certain tax penalty payments.

Another compromise was worked out on the committee's plan to double the excise tax on cigarettes from 8 cents to 16 cents a pack, raising almost $5 billion over three years.

After several attempts by tobacco-state senators to defeat or dilute the measure, an amendment by Jesse Helms, R-N.C., to restore the 8-cent rate after three years was approved by a vote of 60-37. *(Vote 240, p. 42-S)*

Other concessions were made in revising provisions to restrict the use of IDBs and to include interest from tax-exempt bonds in an expanded minimum tax on wealthy individuals. Two separate amendments were adopted that would exclude the interest from state and local tax-exempt bonds as a so-called preference item subject to the new minimum tax. Proponents argued that such a tax could be unconstitutional and would hurt the already ailing municipal bond market.

In addition, an amendment by Alfonse D'Amato, R-N.Y., to allow "small issue" IDBs until 1987, instead of 1985 as in the committee bill, was adopted by voice vote.

Additional Changes

One of the major sweeteners added to the package was a proposal by William L. Armstrong, R-Colo., to index the value of some assets subject to capital gains taxes to reflect increases in the cost of living.

The amendment, adopted by a vote of 64-32, would have had a major impact on investments because any gains made on them would have been taxed only to the extent that the profits exceeded inflation. It would have applied only to investments in stock and real property. *(Vote 243, p. 43-S)*

The provision was especially attractive to investors because the committee bill also reduced the time an asset must be held to qualify for lower capital gains taxes from one year to six months. This had been included in part to appease financial firms upset over interest and dividend withholding.

Both provisions were later dropped in conference.

Defeats

Several major challenges to the committee bill were defeated, mostly because of Republican cohesion. They included:

● A move by Lloyd Bentsen, D-Texas, to delete a pro-

posal for increasing unemployment insurance taxes $6.7 billion over the following three years. Bentsen, whose plan was rejected 48-51, argued that the tax would hit small businesses the hardest and hurt economic recovery. *(Vote 237, p. 42-S)*

● An amendment by Howard M. Metzenbaum, D-Ohio, that would have prohibited proposed increases in unemployment taxes unless unemployment benefits were extended for an additional 13 weeks. It was defeated by a vote of 48-49 after Dole announced that his committee would hold hearings on extended jobless benefits July 29. *(Vote 248, p. 43-S)*

● A Baucus amendment to repeal the 1981 tax leasing provisions. The amendment was defeated 31-66. *(Vote 253, p. 44-S)*

● A Mattingly amendment to strike provisions from the bill that would limit business depreciation tax breaks approved in the 1981 tax bill and the use of the investment tax credit. The amendment was defeated, 23-72. *(Vote 242, p. 42-S)*

Airport, Airway Development

Early debate on the bill was bogged down by an amendment to authorize spending for the Airport and Airway Development Program (ADAP).

The proposal, offered by Commerce Committee Chairman Bob Packwood, R-Ore., was adopted by a vote of 93-5 but only after two challenges to its germaneness were defeated. *(Vote 232, p. 41-S)*

The amendment authorized the Airport and Airway Trust Fund to spend approximately $20 billion through fiscal 1987 on airport and airway development programs and to help fund plans for upgrading the nation's air traffic control system. The program was to be funded by increased airline-ticket taxes and other aviation taxes included in the Finance bill.

The spending provisions had been put together by the Commerce Committee but were attached to the Finance bill in committee in an attempt to end a stalemate over ADAP funding.

Democrats made two unsuccessful attempts to defeat the authorization provision. They argued that it was non-germane and that the Finance Committee's procedure could lead to a host of non-germane amendments added to future reconciliation bills.

House Action

Following Senate passage, the Ways and Means Committee — which had been expected to begin markup of a similar tax-increase bill during Senate floor debate — made a surprise move.

Unable to agree in closed-door negotiations what should go into a revenue-raising package, the committee voted July 28 to forgo writing its own tax bill and to go straight to conference on HR 4961. Technically, it could do this because the House had acted already on the minor tax measure amended by the Senate.

Four Republicans — Barber B. Conable Jr., N.Y.; Bill Frenzel, Minn.; Guy Vander Jagt, Mich.; and Bill Archer, Texas — sided with the Democratic majority on the 26-7 vote. Democrat James M. Shannon, Mass., voted against going straight to conference.

Later that day, the full House agreed by a vote of 208-197 to go along with the Ways and Means Committee plan. *(Vote 213, p. 62-H)*

The action meant that the House — including the tax-writing Ways and Means Committee — would have little hand in shaping the legislation. It was a chore many election-minded House members were not sorry to miss, and which Democrats were glad to unload on Republicans.

Republicans charged during floor debate that Democrats were shirking their constitutional duty so that they could blame the GOP for the controversial tax and spending legislation. John H. Rousselot, R-Calif., called the step a "total cop-out," but his resolution challenging its constitutionality was tabled, 229-169. *(Vote 212, p. 62-H)*

Democrats and some Republicans, including ranking Ways and Means minority member Conable, insisted however that the House bypass was the only practical way to get tax increases enacted quickly in an election year.

The House agreed 299-89 to a Conable motion to instruct conferees to meet the revenue-raising and spending-cut targets mandated by the budget resolution. *(Vote 214, p. 62-H)*

Conference Action

The conference agreement, reported Aug. 17 (H Rept 97-760), was crafted over eight grueling days of meetings. Raising taxes in an election year — coupled with cutting benefits and reducing the growth in politically sensitive social programs — proved to be every bit as painful as had been predicted.

Despite the drawn-out conference, made even more complicated than normal by the lack of a House-passed bill, the outlines of the conference report mirrored closely the bill approved by the Finance Committee and passed by the Senate.

Early in the deliberations conferees agreed to one of the most controversial tax increases — the withholding of taxes on income from interest and dividends. Most remaining tax decisions, however, were delayed until conferees resolved major philosophical differences on the spending cut side — principally in the welfare area.

Spending Cuts

The hang-up in the spending portion of HR 4961 involved welfare and Medicaid increases being pushed by House Democrats, who wanted to restore reductions enacted in the 1981 reconciliation bill. By some estimates, these changes would have added $1 billion to the cost of Aid to Families with Dependent Children (AFDC) and Medicaid over fiscal 1983-85.

The House add-ons were adamantly opposed by Long, the ranking Senate Democrat on the conference committee. He argued that the conferees should try "to get the genie back in the bottle as far as spending is concerned."

House conferees finally yielded after senators agreed to go along with several welfare and unemployment provisions the House supported.

As approved by the conferees, the spending package would make legislative savings totaling $15.2 billion over fiscal 1983-85. But under the guidelines governing reconciliation, the conferees were allowed to count as savings non-legislative items, such as debt management, which raised total savings to $17.5 billion over the next three years.

Major elements of the spending cut package included:

● New limits on Medicare reimbursement rates for hospitals for routine operating costs.

● A requirement that the Department of Health and Human Services develop, within a year of enactment, a

procedure for "prospective" payments under which hospitals and nursing facilities would be paid a set amount based on anticipated costs for Medicare patients.

● A prohibition against reimbursements for surgical assistants in teaching hospitals except in unusual medical circumstances.

● A limit on the inflation adjustment used to calculate the reimbursement for physician fees.

● Medicaid co-payment provisions that allow states to specify a maximum nominal fee for hospital, physician, outpatient and clinic services.

● Rounding of AFDC recipients' benefit payments to the next lower dollar.

● An optional program for states to establish employment search programs for welfare recipients.

● Reductions in the portion of a family's AFDC grant for shelter costs if the family shares living quarters with other individuals.

● Reductions in the federal matching rate for state administrative costs under the child support enforcement program.

Tax Increases

Once the welfare problem was worked out, resolution of the spending differences fell into place. Chief among the tax-hike difficulties were the business tax increases contained in the Senate-passed bill.

The Senate bill raised more than $38 billion in business taxes largely by cutting back depreciation tax write-offs and by making major reforms in the "safe harbor" leasing provisions.

House Republicans, led by Conable, tried to convince House Democrats and the Senate conferees to relax some of the business tax increases. Even with the aid of several major business lobbying groups, however, Conable was unable to make major changes in the business tax provisions, although several were softened slightly.

Conferees dropped Senate provisions that liberalized the treatment of capital gains by reducing the holding period that distinguishes long-term from short-term capital gains and losses from one year to six months. They also dropped a Senate floor amendment that would have indexed long-term capital gains taxation to account for inflation after Dec. 31, 1984.

The conferees did an about-face on a provision added on the Senate floor that would have limited deductions for business meals — better known as the 1½-martini lunch. Conferees agreed to go along with a provision requiring restaurants to report employee tip income that had failed on the Senate floor.

Restaurateurs had lobbied heavily and successfully in the Senate against the tip reporting requirement, but found the business lunch provision that was passed in its place even more distasteful.

The conferees went beyond the Senate bill in strengthening the minimum tax on wealthy individuals, nearly tripling the revenue increase to $1.3 billion over the next three years.

Other taxes on individuals included in the Senate bill were accepted with little change. However, conferees agreed to allow deductions for medical costs exceeding 5 percent of adjusted gross income, instead of the 7 percent approved by the Senate. To pay for the change, conferees agreed to eliminate the current $150 deduction for health insurance premiums.

After wrangling over the tax increases and spending

Defections From Reagan

The following representatives voted with President Reagan on three major economic votes in 1981 but voted against him on the 1982 tax increase. The 1981 votes were on Republican substitutes for the first fiscal 1982 budget resolution, the omnibus reconciliation savings bill and the 1981 tax cut bill. *(Vote 289, p. 84-H; votes 30, 102, 166, 1981 Almanac pp. 20-H, 42-H, 58-H)*

Republicans (88) Dickinson, Ala.; Smith, Ala.; Young, Alaska; Bethune, Ark.; Hammerschmidt, Ark.; Clausen, Calif.; Shumway, Calif.; Fiedler, Calif.; Moorhead, Calif.; Rousselot, Calif.; Lungren, Calif.; Dreier, Calif.; Lewis, Calif.; Dannemeyer, Calif.; Lowery, Calif.; Brown Colo.; Kramer, Colo.; Gingrich, Ga.; and

Craig, Idaho; Hansen, Idaho; Crane, P., Ill.; Corcoran, Ill.; Crane, D., Ill.; Hiler, Ind.; Myers, Ind.; Deckard, Ind.; Jeffries, Kan.; Winn, Kan.; Whittaker, Kan.; Snyder, Ky.; Rogers, Ky.; Hopkins, Ky.; Moore, La.; Heckler, Mass.; Siljander, Mich.; Hagedorn, Minn.; Weber, Minn.; Stangeland, Minn.; Taylor, Mo.; Bailey, Mo.; Emerson, Mo.; Daub, Neb.; and

Smith, N.J.; Rinaldo, N.J.; Carney, N.Y.; McGrath, N.Y.; LeBoutillier, N.Y.; Molinari, N.Y.; Gilman, N.Y.; Solomon, N.Y.; Wortley, N.Y.; Lee, N.Y.; Kemp, N.Y.; Johnston, N.C.; Martin, N.C.; Hendon, N.C.; McEwen, Ohio; Kindness, Ohio; Miller, Ohio; Edwards, Okla.; Smith, Ore.; Schulze, Pa.; Coyne, Pa.; Shuster, Pa.; and

Ritter, Pa.; Walker, Pa.; Spence, S.C.; Campbell, S.C.; Napier, S.C.; Roberts, S.D.; Duncan, Tenn.; Beard, Tenn.; Collins, Texas; Archer, Texas; Fields, Texas; Loeffler, Texas; Paul, Texas; Hansen, Utah; Trible, Va.; Bliley, Va.; Daniel, Va.; Robinson, Va.; Parris, Va.; Wampler, Va.; Wolf, Va.; Staton, W.Va.; Roth, Wis.; Sensenbrenner, Wis.;

Democrats (12). Nichols, Ala.; Shelby, Ala.; Stump, Ariz.; Hutto, Fla.; Chappell, Fla.; McDonald, Ga.; Evans, Ga.; Barnard, Ga.; Santini, Nev.; S. Hall, Texas; Stenholm, Texas; Daniel, Va.

reductions, conferees happily agreed to add one "sweetener" to the bill — a provision that would extend unemployment benefits for 6-10 weeks for workers whose current benefits had expired.

Final Action

Lobbying both for and against the final package was as intense as lobbying gets in Washington.

Having been warned by members on both sides of the aisle that passage was impossible without presidential backing, Reagan pulled out all the stops in the final days before the scheduled vote on the conference report. Scores of members visited with him at the White House and Camp David, in groups and individually.

To assuage Democrats' fears that a vote for the tax increase might be used against them in the upcoming election campaign, Reagan promised personal letters to members who supported the bill thanking them for their vote. The Republican National Committee committed $400,000 for advertisements beseeching citizens to urge their representatives to vote for the bill.

Trying to counter the president and the leadership of both parties, the chairman of the American Conservative Union, Rep. Mickey Edwards, R-Okla., sent colleagues a memo warning that the tax vote would be counted on ACU's annual vote rating. A vote for the bill would be a "double negative." A vote against would be a "double plus."

In a sidelong effort to defeat the bill, a number of House members filed a suit in federal court challenging the constitutionality of the legislation, because it was born in the Senate.

Also working against the bill were lobbyists fighting to protect special interests against proposed tax hikes.

But the measure cleared its first hurdle when the House accepted a closed rule barring separate votes on individual provisions in the conference version.

This tight rule was opposed by a sizable number of members — most of whom favored a vote to delete the provision requiring banks, savings and loans and investment firms to withhold taxes from interest and dividend income. But House Minority Whip Trent Lott, R-Miss.,

and others argued that "if we try opening this package of tax and spending cuts at this point, and then succeed in knocking just one provision out on a point of order or a vote, then we risk losing the whole package for good."

The effort to revise the rule failed on a 220-210 procedural vote, and the closed rule was adopted 253-176. *(Votes 287, 288, p. 84-H)*

Within an hour of final House passage, the Senate took up the conference report.

Finance Committee Chairman Dole found that he had picked up some new allies for his cause since the earlier floor debate. Edward M. Kennedy, D-Mass., announced before the final tally that he would vote for the conference report — in large part because it contained tax reforms he had been sponsoring for years.

The Senate dismissed 68-27 a point of order raised by John P. East, R-N.C., who objected that the conference report contained provisions that had not been included in the Senate-passed bill and therefore were non-germane. *(Vote 336, p. 55-S)*

Reagan signed the bill without comment Sept. 3. ∎

New Job Training Program Replaces CETA

Congress completed action Oct. 1 on new job training legislation (S 2036 — PL 97-300) to replace the expiring Comprehensive Employment and Training Act (CETA).

Final action came when the House approved the conference report on the bill by a 339-12 vote. The Senate had approved the conference report by a 95-0 vote Sept. 30. *(House vote 368, p. 110-H; Senate vote 375, p. 63-S)*

President Reagan signed the bill Oct. 13.

The new program authorized by the bill provided training in job skills to the low-income unemployed. Unlike CETA, it did not pay for public service employment for the jobless. *(CETA background, 1981 Almanac p. 108, 1978 Almanac p. 287)*

S 2036 gave more power to state governments in running job training programs. CETA had operated largely through city and county governments. In addition, the legislation provided for a greatly expanded role for private businesses in operating local training programs.

The bill did not set a specific funding level for the new program. But when S 2036 passed the Senate, sponsors estimated annual spending at $3.8 billion.

President Reagan repeatedly had prodded Congress to finish work on the bill, but there was never any real question that it would be enacted. Throughout its legislative history, S 2036 and its House companion (HR 5320) enjoyed overwhelming bipartisan support. The Senate had passed S 2036 by a 95-0 vote July 1; the House approved HR 5320 by a 356-52 vote Aug. 4. *(Vote 207, p. 37-S; vote 233, p. 68-H)*

In the face of rising unemployment and growing concern about its effects on Republican congressional candidates, the White House in the weeks before final approval of the bill had placed major emphasis on the legislation, which had languished in relative obscurity for most of the year.

Public discussion of the legislation in its final stages was marred by some confusion about the relationship between the job training bill and the $1 billion Democratic jobs bill that passed the House Sept. 16. That bill (H J Res

562), based on legislation reported by the Education and Labor Committee earlier in the year, established a new program to provide an estimated 200,000 public works jobs for the unemployed. *(Public works jobs bill, p. 60)*

Reagan several times suggested that the two bills were somehow in conflict, and that House Speaker Thomas P. O'Neill Jr., D-Mass., was holding up the training bill in order to push the Democrats' public works jobs program.

In fact, House Democratic leaders had not opposed the job training bill at any point, although they favored a version that was different in certain important aspects from the one backed by the administration.

Final Provisions

As signed into law, S 2036 (PL 97-300):

● Stated that the purpose of the bill was to aid youths and unskilled adults in entering the job market, and to provide job training to low-income individuals who faced serious problems in finding work.

● Authorized open-ended funding, for fiscal 1983 and thereafter, for the programs established by the bill, with specific requirements of $618 million for the Job Corps in fiscal 1983 and $2 million a year for the National Commission for Employment Policy; also set a maximum funding level for veterans', Indians,' migrant farm workers' and other programs.

Structure of Programs

● Gave the governor of each state the authority to designate, within certain limitations, the "service delivery areas," which would be the units of government within which the job training programs would operate.

● Required a governor to approve a request to be a service delivery area from any unit of local government, or group of local government units, with a population of at least 200,000; the provision also applied to rural areas that had operated job programs under the expired CETA.

● Required each local service delivery area to establish a

Private Industry Council (PIC), composed of business, labor, educational and community representatives; also required that a majority of the members and the chairman of each council be business representatives.

• Gave each PIC the responsibility, along with the local governments, for guiding the training programs. The PIC would provide for development of an overall plan of its training program, and would select either itself, the local government or a non-profit private group to administer the program.

• Established procedures for review and approval by the governor of the plans of each local training program.

• Authorized the Labor Department to develop "performance standards" measuring how successful programs were in increasing the earnings power and reducing the welfare dependency of program participants. A local program that failed to meet the standards after two years would be subject to reorganization or replacement by the governor.

• Limited spending by local programs on administrative and related costs to no more than 30 percent of their funds, thus ensuring that at least 70 percent was spent on direct training. The bill made clear that the 30 percent limitation would cover administration, supportive services and subsistence payments for participants.

• Allowed for waiver of the 30 percent limit on administrative funds in certain circumstances, such as unusually high unemployment in the area.

• Placed certain responsibilities on states, such as coordination of local job training and education programs, establishment of a state job training council, collection of information on labor markets in the state, and for establishment of programs for job training of older workers.

• Established labor protections for participants in training programs, as well as protections for regular employees of businesses or agencies in which training participants might be placed.

• Gave the Labor Department and state governments authority to monitor use of funds by local programs, and impose sanctions in cases of misuse; also provided criminal penalties for persons found to have misused funds.

• Established procedures for transition from CETA to the new training programs.

Training for the Disadvantaged

• Authorized a program of grants to states and local areas for the training of low-income youths and adults.

• Distributed funds to states according to the following formula: one-third on the basis of each state's share of the total low-income population; one-third on the state's share of the total number of unemployed persons living in areas with unemployment rates over 6.5 percent; and one-third according to the ratio between the number of unemployed persons in the state in excess of 4.5 percent of the work force, and the total number of unemployed persons in excess of 4.5 percent of the work force.

• Required states to distribute 78 percent of their allocation to local programs, according to the same formula used to distribute funds to states.

• Limited eligibility for the programs to economically disadvantaged persons, defined as those on welfare or food stamps, foster children, or families with incomes below either the Office of Management and Budget (OMB) poverty level, or 70 percent of the Bureau of Labor Statistics (BLS) lower living standard, whichever was higher.

• Allowed up to 10 percent of local program participants to be not economically disadvantaged, provided that they

had other employment problems such as a physical handicap, alcoholism or limited English proficiency.

• Required local programs to spend at least 40 percent of their funds on persons aged 16-21.

• Authorized use of funds for a wide variety of services, such as job counseling, skill training, remedial education or on-the-job training.

• Authorized funding of summer employment and training programs for youths.

Dislocated Workers

• Established a program of training assistance for workers who had lost their jobs and were unlikely to get them back, for example because of the permanent closing of a factory.

• Distributed funds to states on the basis of the extent of unemployment, and the extent to which the unemployed had been out of work for 15 weeks or more.

• Required states to match federal funds for dislocated worker programs with an equal amount of their own money; allowed states with high unemployment to provide a reduced share.

National Programs

• Authorized funds for national job training for native Americans and migrant and seasonal farm workers.

• Authorized the Job Corps as a national program of residential and non-residential centers for the training and education of disadvantaged young people; established rules and standards for participation, activities, allowances for participants and involvement by states.

• Authorized other national programs including training of veterans, research and demonstration, and labor market information.

• Authorized the National Commission for Employment Policy to review and evaluate national employment policy.

• Authorized training programs aimed at helping federal contractors meet federal affirmative action requirements.

• Extended the authorization of the federal Employment Service, to assist state employment offices.

Senate Committee Action

The Senate Labor and Human Resources Committee reported S 2036 May 28 (S Rept 97-469). A potential split between Republican members of the committee and the Reagan administration was avoided by a compromise that cleared the way for committee approval of the bill.

Dan Quayle, R-Ind., chairman of the Employment Subcommittee, had an agreement with the full committee's ranking Democrat, Edward M. Kennedy, Mass., on the bill as approved by the subcommittee. However, that version was the target of sharp criticism from Labor Department officials.

Administration lobbyists insisted that the bill have a flat ban on payment of wages and allowances to training participants. They also wanted to require local programs to spend at least 70 percent of their funds on training, with no more than 30 percent going for administrative and other costs. In addition, the administration opposed including in the bill a separate authorization for a summer youth jobs program.

The compromise bill, which won a pledge of support from OMB Director David A. Stockman, prohibited use of funds for payment of wages, allowances or stipends to participants. But it allowed local programs to use "support-

ive services" funds — normally spent on things such as transportation and day care — to make cash payments to trainees if needed to support participation in the program.

Under the compromise, there would be a statewide limit of 30 percent on funds spent for administration and support services. But individual programs within a state could use more than 30 percent of their funds for such costs.

Although the bill as reported had an "open-ended" authorization, Quayle said he envisioned spending $3.9 billion on the program in fiscal 1983. The administration had called for a total authorization of $2.4 billion.

The bill contained a separate open-ended authorization for summer programs.

State Control, Wages. The Senate committee accepted the administration's proposal to make job training a basically state-controlled program similar to the block grant programs approved by Congress in 1981. *(1981 Almanac p. 463)*

To a great extent, the CETA program was run by local governments. There were some 475 "prime sponsors," usually cities or counties, who operated employment and training programs under federal supervision. State governments largely were limited to running "balance of state" programs in rural areas.

The Senate bill would replace the prime sponsor structure with a system focused on the states. While state governments in most cases would not actually run programs, the governors would have the power to determine the location and extent of programs within their state.

In a concession to urban areas, the Senate bill guaranteed that units of local government with populations of at least 500,000 would be designed as "service delivery areas." In addition, areas with populations of between 250,000 and 500,000 would get their own programs if sought by the local government and business groups.

While it contained an explicit prohibition on wages and allowances, the Senate bill gave local programs the option of providing some cash to participants if needed for basic necessities. The only exception to the ban on wages in the Senate bill was for summer youth jobs.

Senate Floor Action

The Senate passed S 2036 by a 95-0 vote July 1. *(Vote 207, p. 37-S)*

The Senate made no major changes in the measure as reported by committee.

Perhaps the sharpest criticism of the bill came from Pete V. Domenici, R-N.M., who complained that the legislation would leave state legislatures without any voice in job training policy.

Domenici warned that total control by governors over the programs could lead to abuse. He successfully offered an amendment to make clear that the bill did not preclude a legislature from adopting a plan to implement the program in its state.

Another successful floor amendment placed an upper income limit on participation in the training programs. Under the bill as reported, participation in most cases was limited to persons with incomes below 70 percent of the Bureau of Labor Statistics (BLS) lower living standard. However, the bill allowed 10 percent of training funds to be spent on persons with higher incomes who had other problems, such as a physical handicap, limited English-speaking ability or a criminal record.

The Senate accepted an amendment by Jeremiah Denton, R-Ala., to limit participation by persons with special problems to those with incomes below 250 percent of the poverty level or 175 percent of the BLS lower living standard, whichever was higher.

House Committee Action

The House Education and Labor Committee approved HR 5320 April 27, and reported the measure May 17 (H Rept 97-537).

The bill contained a total fiscal 1983 authorization of $5.4 billion.

The major change made by the Education and Labor Committee in HR 5320 was the jettisoning of a $1 billion "National Economic Adjustment Program" for areas with high unemployment. Funds provided by the proposed program could have been used for public service employment.

Employment Opportunities Subcommittee Chairman Augustus F. Hawkins, D-Calif., said the proposed program would have posed problems for the entire bill when it came to the House floor. So he supported removing the program from the bill in committee.

In contrast to the Senate bill, the House bill retained the prime sponsor structure. It would provide only a modest increase in the coordinating authority of the governors.

At the same time, the House bill would move toward larger prime sponsor areas. Under CETA, a local government had to have a population of at least 100,000 before it could be designated as a prime sponsor. The legislation would increase that minimum to 150,000.

Backers of increasing the minimum population level argued that each prime sponsor area should match up more closely with its "labor market area" — the economic region within which people competed for the same jobs. Job training programs were weakened by competition within the same labor market area, said James M. Jeffords, R-Vt., and other committee members.

Opposing the increase in the minimum were smaller cities and counties who feared they would be neglected if not guaranteed their own programs.

Wages and Allowances. The House bill established three types of allowances that could be paid to participants. A subsistence stipend would be paid to trainees whose other income was less than 70 percent of the BLS lower living standard. The payments would equal the difference between the family's income, including "in-kind" income such as food stamps, and 70 percent of the lower living standard.

Under the House bill, trainees with incomes up to 100 percent of the BLS lower living standard also could receive payments for training-related costs such as transportation, meals and day care. In addition, the bill allowed payment of limited "completion stipends" as incentives for people to finish their training.

The House legislation also provided for payment of wages in certain limited circumstances. Those situations included summer youth jobs and "try-out" employment, under which the prime sponsor paid the wage for a young person working for a private employer.

House Job Creation Bill

Committee Democrats feared that inclusion of the much-criticized public service employment in HR 5320 would cause problems for the bill. But they were unwilling to give up on job creation at a time of severe unemploy-

ment. So they reported HR 6250, the "Community Renewal Employment Act" May 17 (H Rept 97-538). The bill was the precursor of the $1 billion public works jobs plan passed by the House later in the year.

The bill was ordered reported by a 19-10 vote May 5. Committee Republicans opposed the measure.

Arguing that "the direct job creation approach is the most cost effective, timely and efficient means of stimulating employment during a recessionary period," the committee called for a program to provide jobs to the long-term unemployed in areas hit by severe joblessness.

The bill would limit assistance to areas with unemployment rates exceeding the national average. People who had been unemployed for 15 weeks or more would be eligible for jobs funded by the bill.

Examples of jobs that could be funded by the bill were bridge repair, installation of ramps for the handicapped, school security guards and rat control.

House Floor Action

HR 5320 was approved by the House on a 356-52 vote Aug. 4. *(Vote 233, p. 68-H)*

During action on HR 5320, the House removed an important difference with the Senate-passed bill. As reported by the Education and Labor Committee, HR 5320 authorized $5.4 billion in fiscal 1983. The Senate bill did not include a specific funding amount.

Arguing that the $5.4 billion authorization was unrealistically high, House Republicans successfully moved to eliminate it, thus leaving funding levels for the program up to the annual budget and appropriations process. The only program to retain a specific authorization amount was the Job Corps, which would get up to $650 million in fiscal 1983.

The realization that the program probably would not get even $5 billion, compared with the $10 billion provided for CETA during its heyday, angered liberal Democrats such as Paul Simon, D-Ill. "[The bill] is so far from what we ought to be doing in this nation at this time that it is pathetic," he said.

The key amendment adopted by the House would require local programs to spend at least 70 percent of their funds directly on job training. The remainder could be used for administrative costs and living stipends for participants.

James M. Jeffords, R-Vt., the ranking member of the Employment Opportunities Subcommittee, had offered an amendment to set the 70 percent training requirement, which was also found in the Senate bill. Jeffords' amendment specifically excluded spending for supportive services, such as transportation and day care, from being counted as direct training costs.

Simon offered a substitute amendment that included the 70 percent minimum but softened its effect by allowing spending for supportive services to be counted as being spent on training. That allowed local programs considerably more leeway to provide supportive services, which might also include health care, meals and temporary shelter. The amendment was adopted by voice vote.

While it agreed to move toward the Senate bill on the issue of minimum spending for training, the House refused to accept the Senate's position in favor of a greater state role in the new program.

Members rejected an amendment offered by John N. Erlenborn, R-Ill., that would have increased state authority

in two ways. State governments would have chosen which local governments would be authorized to run programs. In addition, the state would review and approve training program plans submitted by local governments and business groups.

Erlenborn's unsuccessful amendment also would have increased the role of business groups, known as private industry councils, in planning and operating local programs. The amendment was rejected 185-219. Subsequently, a motion by Eugene Johnston, R-N.C., to add the Erlenborn amendment was rejected 189-218. *(Votes 230, 232, p. 68-H)*

Amendments adopted by voice vote included those by Robert W. Edgar, D-Pa., to increase minimum funding of training programs for veterans, and Gerald B. H. Solomon, R-N.Y., to exclude violators of the draft registration law from participation in programs under the bill.

An amendment offered by Clint Roberts, R-S.D., to prohibit labor unions from receiving funds for training of migrant farm workers, was rejected 87-308. *(Vote 231, p. 68-H)*

Conference Action

Conferees filed their report Sept. 28 (H Rept 97-889).

Although there was agreement between the House and Senate on basic aspects of the legislation — an end to public service jobs, and an increased role for private businesses in the programs — the two bills conflicted on a couple of key aspects. The conference to resolve those differences was a lengthy one; in the end, the Senate prevailed on most issues.

Efforts to achieve a compromise were complicated by repeated veto threats from the Labor Department if the final version turned out to be too close to the House bill. The deadlock was resolved after conferees negotiated an agreement in a meeting with Reagan Sept. 22.

One key point of dispute concerned the limits imposed on local programs' spending for administration and other services beyond direct job training. Both House and Senate bills had required that local programs spend at least 70 percent of their funds on training.

The House bill, however, had allowed local programs to include within the 70 percent limit costs of supportive services such as day care for the children of program participants. The Senate had required spending for supportive services to be included within the 30 percent limit on administrative costs.

The compromise version limited spending on administration, including supportive services, to 30 percent of a local program's funding. However, it provided for a waiver of the 30 percent limit in certain situations, for example in areas of unusually high unemployment or where day care was particularly expensive.

The other difficult issue resolved by conferees concerned the degree of state and local government control over programs. The House bill in general had retained the local autonomy that characterized CETA. The Senate, by contrast, had given more authority to governors.

Conferees gave primary control over designation of local program areas to the governors. However, they protected the rights of mid-sized cities by permitting local government jurisdictions with populations of 200,000 and over to operate separate programs if they chose.

Conferees accepted the House provision barring draft violators from participation. ∎

Jobless Benefits Extended

Faced with record unemployment and an election less than three months away, Congress agreed Aug. 19 to extend unemployment benefits by six to 10 weeks, for a maximum of 49 weeks in some states.

The supplemental benefit program was adopted as part of a larger revenue-increase and spending-cut package (HR 4961 — PL 97-248) designed to reduce the federal budget deficit. *(Tax/spending bill, p. 29)*

The supplemental jobless benefits went into effect Sept. 12 and were expected to help approximately two million unemployed workers who had exhausted regular and extended benefits from the federal-state program. The extra benefits were scheduled to run through March 31, 1983.

Legislation (HR 6211 — PL 97-424) adding two to six more weeks of jobless payments to the supplemental benefit program was cleared Dec. 23, allowing up to 55 weeks of benefits for some unemployed workers. *(Details, below)*

The initial supplemental jobless aid was tacked onto the tax and spending bill in part because of widespread congressional concern over rising unemployment, which had reached a postwar high of 9.8 percent at the time of the vote. (It climbed to 10.8 percent by December.) Members argued that with a lengthy recession more and more jobless workers were exhausting existing benefits with little chance of finding work.

But in addition, the bill's sponsors anticipated that the measure would attract election-year support for the controversial tax-increase legislation.

Democrats had pushed for the additional benefits for much of the year, but met with little success until the Reagan administration — worried about rising joblessness — indicated it would back the plan.

"This is as large and as timely a benefit package as is going to come our way," House Ways and Means Committee Chairman Dan Rostenkowski, D-Ill., told his colleagues on the House floor Aug. 19. The Ways and Means Committee had approved legislation earlier in the year that called for 13 extra weeks of benefits, but would have targeted them to states with the highest unemployment. That measure never reached the floor.

The full Senate never voted on additional jobless benefits either, but agreed Aug. 5 to a "sense of the Senate" resolution instructing conferees on the tax bill to come up with the supplemental benefit program.

Provisions

Under the new law, jobless workers in every state were to receive the supplemental benefits, but the length of the extra payments was to be determined by the state's unemployment rate.

Most states had offered 26 weeks of regular benefits with up to 13 weeks of extended benefits (EB) when state unemployment was high, for a maximum of 39 weeks.

The supplemental benefit program allowed an additional 10 weeks of payments in the 36 states (plus Puerto Rico and the Virgin Islands) that offered extended benefits on or after June 1, 1982. This meant a maximum of 49 weeks of benefits in states that were still providing extended benefits and up to 36 weeks of payments in those states that had gone, or would go, off the extended benefit program after June 1.

For the remaining states, those with average insured unemployment rates (reflecting those collecting benefits) of 3.5 percent or more were allowed to pay eight more weeks of benefits, for a maximum of 34 weeks. Those with lower unemployment were able to provide six additional weeks, for a total of 32.

To cover the $2.1 billion cost of the new program, Congress agreed in the tax bill to lower the income level at which unemployment benefits would be taxed.

Previously, jobless benefits were not taxed unless an individual had an annual income over $20,000 ($25,000 for couples). The new law lowered these tax thresholds to $12,000 for individuals and $18,000 for married couples.

The provision, effective for benefits paid on or after Jan. 1, 1982, meant that funding for the supplemental program would come from general revenues and not from the financially strained trust funds of the unemployment program.

Impact of 1981 Changes

Ironically, the new supplemental benefits were scheduled to start at just about the same time cutbacks in unemployment compensation approved by Congress in 1981 went into effect.

These changes, included in the 1981 reconciliation bill (PL 96-35), made it more difficult for states to qualify for extended benefits by raising from 4 percent to 5 percent the insured jobless rate needed to offer the 13-week EB program. *(1981 Almanac p. 106)*

As a result, six to 12 of the 25 states offering 13 weeks of extended benefits triggered off the EB program Sept. 25, shortly after the additional 10 weeks became available. Other states were expected to trigger off EB later on.

So while the new change was an improvement over current law, there was a net loss in benefits for many on the unemployment rolls.

In addition, other states had triggered off EB earlier because of two other quirks in the 1981 budget bill that hit hardest on states with high, long-term unemployment.

One change required that states not count those receiving extended benefits when figuring their insured unemployment rate. As a result, some states saw a decline in their insured unemployment rate — upon which benefits are based — although actual unemployment was on the rise. The other change required that a state's insured unemployment rate be 20 percent higher than it was in the two preceding years to qualify for EB.

House and Senate members representing high-unemployment areas tried several times during the year to repeal these changes, with no success.

Senate's Conference Instructions

The Senate, by a vote of 84-13, agreed Aug. 5 to a sense of the Senate amendment instructing conferees on the tax and spending-cut bill to include a provision allowing between 10 and 13 weeks of additional benefits. The amendment was attached to a separate budget reconciliation bill (S 2774). *(Vote 291, p. 49-S)*

Senate Finance Committee Chairman Robert Dole, R-Kan., manager of the tax bill conference, pledged to follow the Senate instructions, including finding some way to finance the extra payments.

While initially opposed to supplemental benefits because of the cost, the White House indicated earlier in the week that it would accept the extra-payment plan.

In addition, Dole, who had been reluctant to provide additional benefits, indicated that he hoped the provision

would prove a sweetener on his controversial tax bill.

The Senate amendment, proposed by Howard M. Metzenbaum, D-Ohio, also instructed conferees to work out some plan to allow states that had provided extended benefits since June 1 to continue to do so after Oct. 1.

Ways and Means Bill

The House Ways and Means Committee voted May 20 to extend unemployment benefits an additional 13 weeks, for a maximum of 52 weeks.

The extension, which would have gone into effect July 1 and ended Sept. 30, 1983, would have been available only in states where the existing 13-week extended benefit program had been "triggered" by a high jobless rate.

The committee approved the bill (HR 6369 — H Rept 97-587) by a vote of 23-5, but only after Republicans complained of the estimated $920 million cost of the package, which also included some welfare program changes, for fiscal 1982-83.

In response to these objections, members agreed by voice vote to pay for the additional jobless benefits by lowering the income level at which such payments would be taxed from $20,000 for individuals and $25,000 for couples to $12,000 and $18,000, respectively. This change was expected to raise almost $2 billion for fiscal 1983-85.

Additional Benefits

The extra two to six weeks of benefits were approved as part of the highway authorization and gas tax bill (HR 6211) cleared by Congress on the final day of the session. *(Story, p. 317)*

Under the new program, states would be eligible for six, four or two extra weeks of benefits depending on their insured jobless rate. Most states — about 30 — were expected to qualify for four more weeks.

The provision, estimated to cost about $560 million on top of the $2.1 billion cost of the program approved during the summer, emerged in the Senate after Democrats balked at voting for cloture on the gas tax bill unless the extra jobless benefits were approved.

Like those benefits passed in the summer, the new supplemental payments were set to expire on March 31, 1983. ∎

Debt Limit Increases

Congress approved two increases in the public debt limit during its 1982 session, ultimately raising the ceiling to $1.29 trillion through Sept. 30, 1983.

The increases were needed to keep the limit from reverting its "permanent" level of $400 billion. Congress in 1981 had set the temporary limit at $1.08 trillion through Sept. 30, 1982. *(1981 Almanac p. 104)*

Both of the 1982 increases were enacted through use of shortcut procedures established in 1979 to depoliticize the debt process. These procedures permitted the House to pass debt limit increases as part of the congressional budget resolutions, which included recommended levels for the public debt.

In approving the final version of the fiscal 1983 budget resolution (S Con Res 92), the House June 22 automatically approved an increase in the debt limit to $1.14 trillion through the remainder of fiscal 1982, and to $1.29 trillion through fiscal 1983. Those increases were incorporated in separate House joint resolutions (H J Res 519 and 520,

respectively) and sent directly to the Senate.

The Senate June 23 approved the fiscal 1982 increase (H J Res 519 — PL 97-204) by a 49-41 vote, thereby clearing the short-term measure for the president's signature. The Senate vote eliminated the need for action on a standby debt bill (HR 6550 — H Rept 97-601) reported by the House Ways and Means Committee June 10. *(Vote 198, p. 34-S)*

The fiscal 1983 debt limit bill (H J Res 520 — PL 97-270) moved less smoothly. A week before the fiscal 1982 ceiling was set to expire, the Senate completed action on the fiscal 1983 measure — finally unencumbered by extraneous amendments and debate over social issues that had burdened the legislation for five weeks.

Senate Action on H J Res 520

Senate passage Sept. 23, by a 50-41 vote, cleared H J Res 520 for the president's signature. The resolution, which increased the ceiling on federal borrowing to $1,290,200,000,000 through Sept. 30, 1983, had been on the Senate floor since Aug. 16. *(Vote 354, p. 60-S)*

Before the bill could be passed, the Senate put an end to efforts by Jesse Helms, R-N.C., to attach curbs on court jurisdiction over abortion and school prayer. *(Story, p. 403)*

But with those social issues dispensed with, the Senate still faced more than 1,400 amendments prepared on other issues. And H J Res 520 had to be stripped of other amendments already adopted on the floor and in the Finance Committee if it was to match the House-passed version and thus be cleared by Congress without further controversy.

Majority Leader Howard H. Baker Jr., R-Tenn., had promised senators for months that they could use the debt limit as a vehicle for their pet legislation. But he told the Senate he was unable to fulfill that commitment because the debate over Helms' efforts already had consumed five weeks. "At some point you have to get on with the country's work," Baker said.

Minority Leader Robert C. Byrd, D-W.Va., was pressing for votes on Democratic proposals to enact a $1 billion jobs program and expand unemployment benefits. In addition, several Republicans wanted the chance to offer riders on issues including presidential rescission power, the Soviet gas pipeline in Eastern Europe and sugar price supports.

Finance Committee Chairman Robert Dole, R-Kan., suggested facetiously that the Senate should simply accept all 1,400-plus amendments in a bloc, then proceed with Baker's plan to excise all amendments.

"Everybody could write home and say, 'They have accepted my amendment, but because of some procedural thing they took it off,' " Dole said. "It would make great copy for a newsletter."

Dole argued that any changes in the House bill, which the House had passed without an explicit vote as part of the budget resolution, would force a House vote and threaten passage.

Baker was able to negotiate a fragile understanding: The bill would be recommitted to the Finance Committee with instructions to strip off all amendments to the House-passed version and return the measure immediately to the Senate floor. Then no further amendments would be accepted, even if they were offered.

The Senate agreed 79-16 to Baker's motion to clean up H J Res 520 in this manner. *(Vote 352, p. 60-S)*

One effect of this cleanup was to strip from the bill an

amendment previously adopted within the Finance Committee to eliminate the $400 billion "permanent" debt ceiling and make the new level of $1.29 trillion the only legal limit. The panel had approved the bill Aug. 11, 10-3.

The recommittal also removed from the bill two amendments previously accepted on the floor: Dole's effort to reduce the holding period investors needed to qualify for long-term capital gains tax rates from one year to six

months; and a provision sponsored by Baker and Byrd to kill plans for a new Senate gym. The Senate later attached a provision to kill the gym onto a housing funds bill (HR 6956). *(Stories, pp. 51, 68)*

When the clean H J Res 520 returned to the Senate floor, Dan Quayle, R-Ind., offered an amendment to reduce sugar price supports, but it was tabled 60-31. *(Vote 353, p. 60-S)* ∎

Savings and Loan Aid, Banking Law Changes

Congress gave final approval late Oct. 1 to major legislation to help bolster the nation's ailing savings and loan industry and to give new powers to both banks and thrift institutions.

The measure (HR 6267 — PL 97-320) was largely intended to stem the tide of mergers of financially troubled institutions. It did not go as far as the overhaul of banking and financial institutions legislation that had been pushed since 1981 by Senate Banking Committee Chairman Jake Garn, R-Utah. *(Background, 1981 Almanac p. 121)*

The legislation permitted federal regulators to aid ailing institutions through a series of paper transactions that were not expected to cost the federal government any money if the institutions pulled through.

It also authorized federal regulators to set up a new type of insured account for commercial banks and savings and loan associations (S&Ls) that would be competitive with popular money market funds. Many ailing institutions had complained that the money market funds, which could offer higher interest rates, had drained regular savings deposits.

The bill required the elimination of all differentials in interest rates between banks and S&Ls by 1984, and gave savings institutions new investment and lending authority.

Commercial banks, however, would not be allowed to sell property and casualty insurance — an authority banks had sought.

As part of a compromise between lenders and real estate brokers, the bill overrode state laws that prohibited enforcement of due-on-sale clauses in mortgage contracts, limiting the assumption of home mortgages. *(Details, box, next page)*

The banking measure followed over a year and a half of complex negotiations between Congress and divergent elements of the financial community. The final compromise largely followed the lines of the Senate version of the bill (S 2879).

As originally passed by the House, HR 6267 was a less comprehensive measure that would have set up a special $8.5 billion Treasury fund to guarantee through paper transactions the net worth of certain financial institutions. The fund would have aided S&Ls, mutual savings banks and credit unions with a net worth — the amount by which assets exceed liabilities — below 2 percent, and commercial banks with net worth below 4 to 5 percent.

The aid program in the final bill, however, would provide partial assistance on a sliding scale to institutions whose net worth fell below 3 percent.

It allowed the Federal Deposit Insurance Corp. (FDIC) and the Federal Savings and Loan Insurance Corp. (FSLIC) to bolster the net worth of these ailing institutions through the exchange of capital notes. Institutions would

not be required to pay off the notes until their condition had improved, but they had to be able to show some ability to recover to qualify for the aid initially.

The conference committee agreed to raise the level of such assistance above the Senate-passed bill, a move the U.S League of Savings Associations said would help 400 more savings associations than would have been helped under the Senate version.

Final Provisions

As signed into law Oct. 15, HR 6267 (PL 97-320):

● Established a program allowing federally insured financial institutions to exchange capital notes with the FDIC and FSLIC to bolster the financial condition of troubled institutions.

● Allowed institutions with net worth of 3 to 2 percent, 2 to 1 percent, and 1 percent and below to receive assistance equal to losses of 50 percent, 60 percent and 70 percent, respectively.

● Required that institutions qualifying for such aid have a net worth of at least .5 percent, have incurred losses during the two previous quarters and have 20 percent of their loans in mortgages.

● Terminated the assistance provisions three years after enactment.

● Gave the Depository Institutions Deregulation Committee (DIDC), an inter-agency regulatory body, two months to create an insured account for thrift institutions and banks that would be "directly equivalent to and competitive with" money market funds. The minimum-account requirement was not to exceed $5,000.

● Required that all interest rate differentials between banks and thrift institutions be phased out no later than Jan. 1, 1984. Under existing law, thrifts could pay a quarter percentage point more interest on certain deposits. *(Background, 1980 Almanac p. 275)*

● Allowed S&Ls to offer checking accounts, but only to those businesses or entities that did loan business with the institution.

● Allowed S&Ls to stabilize their income by putting as much as 10 percent of their assets into commercial loans by 1984. Traditionally, savings institutions had most of their assets invested in low-yield, long-term mortgages — one reason for their current financial predicament.

● Prohibited commercial banks from selling casualty and property insurance. Banks could still sell credit-related insurance.

● Expanded the powers of both the FDIC and the FSLIC to assist troubled banks and thrift institutions through mergers. Such mergers could not be mandated unless the institution had net worth of less than .5 percent and it was determined the institution's net worth would be exhausted

Mortgage Assumption Plan Approved

The savings and loan/banking bill cleared Oct. 1 (HR 6267 — PL 97-320) included provisions overriding state laws and judicial decisions that banned enforcement of due-on-sale clauses in mortgage contracts.

The banking bill provisions amplified a Supreme Court ruling restricting mortgage assumptions, while giving homeowners in certain states a three-year reprieve from the bill's tightened regulations.

The provisions, a compromise worked out with the real estate and thrift industries, were included in the version of the bill reported by the Senate Banking Committee Sept. 3 (S 2879 — S Rept 97-536). The Senate included them in HR 6267, passed Sept. 24, and House conferees accepted the Senate plan with minor changes. *(Action on HR 6267, preceding page)*

Due-on-sale clauses required homeowners to pay off a mortgage when they sold their homes, denying new buyers the right to take over an old, low-cost loan. About 18 states had prohibited financial institutions from enforcing due-on-sale in an effort to help promote home sales through mortgage assumptions during a period of high interest rates.

The Supreme Court June 28 overturned state laws barring due-on-sale enforcement by federally chartered savings and loan associations (S&Ls), in a victory for the thrift industry.

Provisions

HR 6267 took the court decision a step further by extending it to mortgages issued by commercial banks, mortgage banks and state-chartered thrift institutions.

To appease beleaguered home sellers, however, the bill excluded from the new rules mortgages originated or assumed during a "window period." The period began on the date a state restricted due-on-sale enforcement and ended on the bill's enactment date, Oct. 15.

The measure allowed three years for "window period" loans to fall under state laws forbidding financial institutions from calling in mortgages with due-on-sale clauses. After three years, lenders could invoke the due-on-sale clauses unless the state legislature reimposed due-on-sale bans for these loans.

Federal savings and loan associations and federal savings banks were exempt from the "window period" provision because they fell under a 1976 Federal Home Loan Bank Board rule allowing due-on-sale clauses. The June 28 Supreme Court ruling upheld the bank board regulation.

In another concession to the real estate industry, the bill included non-binding language encouraging lenders to negotiate blended rates when mortgages were assumed. With blended rates, lenders would meet borrowers halfway by providing loans at a level between the original interest rate and the current market rate.

The bill also delayed until July 1, 1983, a ban on mortgage assumptions proposed by the Federal Home Loan Mortgage Corp.

The quasi-governmental corporation, known as Freddie Mac, announced in July that it no longer would allow buyers to assume low-interest loans it had purchased. Freddie Mac is a member of the secondary mortgage market, which serves as a link between investors and mortgage lenders.

Background

Due-on-sale clauses in mortgage contracts dated back to the late 1960s. Lenders began writing the clause into contracts to guard against uncreditworthy buyers who might take over a loan. Later, however, banks and S&Ls began to use the clause to hike the interest rates on assumed loans.

By preventing mortgage assumptions without a lender's approval, due-on-sale provisions gave banks and S&Ls more flexibility during a period of volatile interest rates. With the skyrocketing rates of the past few years, lenders said they needed the tool so they could unload old, fixed-rate mortgages and replace them with higher-yielding loans.

"When an S&L or bank makes a mortgage loan for 30 years, it's not really making it for 30 years. They know that a property generally turns over every five to seven years. They know after five to seven years they can bring the loan up to market rate," explained Carol Schatz, a senior vice president of the California Savings and Loan League.

Court Decision

The Supreme Court ruling on due-on-sale clauses came in *Fidelity Federal Savings & Loan Assn. v. de la Cuesta*. The court held, 6-2, that a California law prohibiting enforcement of due-on-sale clauses was preempted by federal rules allowing federal S&Ls to include the clauses in contracts. The regulations were issued in 1976 by the Federal Home Loan Bank Board, which oversees federal S&Ls.

The Supreme Court case arose after Fidelity Federal, a federally chartered S&L in Glendale, Calif., tried to invoke due-on-sale clauses by foreclosing on three homes, each of which had been sold by transferring an old mortgage held by Fidelity to new buyers. The new owners sued to block foreclosure, citing California law banning enforcement of due-on-sale clauses.

A state court decided in favor of Fidelity, but an appellate court reversed it, holding that state law ruled the situation. Fidelity appealed to the Supreme Court.

"Federal regulations have no less pre-emptive effect than federal statutes," Justice Harry A. Blackmun wrote for the Supreme Court majority. "A savings and loan's mortgage lending practices are a critical aspect of its 'operation,' over which the [Federal Home Loan Bank] Board unquestionably has jurisdiction," he wrote.

"Congress delegated power to the Board expressly for the purpose of creating and regulating federal savings and loans so as to ensure that they would remain financially sound institutions able to supply financing for home construction and purchase."

Justices William H. Rehnquist and John Paul Stevens dissented, protesting that the majority view authorized an undesirable federal intrusion into state affairs. Justice Lewis F. Powell Jr. did not take part in the case.

in six months.

● Gave priority for such mergers to in-state acquisitions, followed by acquisitions in contiguous states and other interstate acquisitions.

● Gave the National Credit Union Administration authority to approve mergers between insured credit unions when one faced financial trouble.

● Expanded the authority of bank service corporations, affiliates of two or more banks that provided various clerical services for their parent bank. Under the bill, service corporations would be allowed to perform all the services of a state-chartered bank as well as some of those permitted a bank holding company.

● Overrode state laws barring enforcement of due-on-sale clauses in home mortgage contracts, except for mortgages originated or assumed during a "window period" specified in the bill.

● Prohibited the Federal Home Loan Mortgage Corp. from implementing a ban on mortgage assumptions until July 1, 1983.

● Excluded real estate brokers from provisions of the Truth-in-Lending Act so that they could continue helping with loan arrangements for home sales.

● Amended the Federal Credit Union Act to simplify the organization of credit unions and broaden their mortgage lending powers.

House Committee Action

Legislation to prop up troubled thrift institutions through a paper transaction with the federal government won House Banking Committee approval on a 25-15 vote May 11.

The Net Worth Guarantee Act (HR 6267 — H Rept 97-550), approved in a straight party-line vote, would allow the Treasury to guarantee the net worth of savings and loan associations, mutual savings banks, commercial banks and credit unions if their net worth dropped below 2 percent of assets.

Although the legislation would establish an $8.5 billion fund to back the net worth of these institutions, no money would change hands unless the bank or S&L failed.

"This is a no-cost situation. It's not a bailout," said Committee Chairman Fernand J. St Germain, D-R.I., the bill's sponsor. The Treasury guarantees would restore investors' confidence, he said, adding that wobbly institutions "can indeed survive if they are given this type of assistance."

Because the bill's sponsors viewed HR 6267 as a way to strengthen the housing market, the legislation involved two important conditions: At least 20 percent of a qualifying institution's loan portfolio must be in residential real estate; and a thrift receiving aid must earmark at least 60 percent of its net new deposits for home mortgages.

HR 6267 replaced an earlier proposal by St Germain to channel $7.5 billion in loans to ailing lending institutions. Because of opposition to the large cash outlay involved in the first plan, St Germain offered HR 6267, which used Treasury guarantees instead of direct cash payments.

But St Germain's new version still did not satisfy Reagan administration critics, and Banking Committee Republicans May 11 tried to offer an administration-backed alternative. The substitute, offered by Chalmers P. Wylie, R-Ohio, was tabled without debate in a 21-20 vote.

Wylie's plan would have applied to institutions with a

net worth below 3 percent, compared to HR 6267's 2 percent limit, and it would have guaranteed the institution's net worth for only a portion of its losses. In contrast, HR 6267 would completely make up an institution's losses by bringing its net worth up to 2 percent of assets.

Legislation's Goals

The impetus behind St Germain's legislation was the shaky condition of the thrift industry.

With savers withdrawing money from S&Ls and mutual savings banks and investing instead in higher-yielding Treasury bills and money-market funds, thrifts had suffered huge losses in recent years. In 1981, S&Ls lost $25 billion in savings, the U.S. League of Savings Associations reported, and a record number of S&Ls were merged.

Complicating the problem of withdrawals, thrifts had become saddled with portfolios of low-yield, fixed-rate mortgages. To attract new depositors, the institutions had to pay more for savings than they earned on their mortgage portfolios. Under these conditions, mortgage money had dried up.

The purpose of HR 6267, supporters said, was to ensure the availability of home mortgage loans, stave off further mergers and revive public confidence in thrifts.

To accomplish this, the legislation would work as follows:

● A Net Worth Guarantee Account would be established in the Treasury to back guarantees issued to weakened depository institutions. The fund would be subject to an $8.5 billion limit, and the government would honor any guarantee if an institution were liquidated.

● To qualify for a guarantee an institution must have a net worth below 2 percent of assets; have suffered earnings losses for at least two consecutive quarters, and the losses must not be the result of poor management; have at least 20 percent of its loan portfolio in residential real estate or securities backed by residential real estate; and show prospects of long-term viability. Generally, net worth is an institution's assets, or loans due, minus liabilities, or deposits owed.

● Conditions for receiving assistance included the requirement that an institution retire the net worth guarantees; provide regular reports to the administering agencies on its financial condition and lending practices; and earmark, for as long as the guarantee was outstanding, at least 60 percent of its net new deposits for residential mortgages at or below Federal Housing Administration (FHA) loan ceilings. To partially comply with the last requirement, the thrift could purchase mortgage-backed securities.

● Each institution would receive guarantees to bring its net worth up to 2 percent of assets and maintain that level for not more than two years. Thereafter, an agency could extend the guarantees only if losses resulted from general economic conditions rather than management decisions.

● If an institution were liquidated, the Treasury secretary would pay the institution's receiver the amount of the outstanding guarantees. The government would have a claim on the institution's liquidated assets after all deposits, certificates of deposit and debts were paid.

In considering HR 6267, committee members attempted to restrain bank regulatory agencies from requiring that institutions receiving guarantees sign a merger agreement or make management changes. The requirement could apply, however, to institutions with a net worth level below one-half of 1 percent.

Officials of the U.S. League of Savings Associations, a

major lobbying group supporting HR 6267, praised the limit on the right of regulatory agencies to force mergers when federal guarantees were authorized.

"This has been a demeaning and obnoxious requirement" in an existing government assistance program, said League President William B. O'Connell, "and we are glad to see it eliminated."

House Floor Action

The House passed HR 6267 by a 272-91 vote May 20, nine days after passing legislation to resuscitate the ailing housing industry. *(Vote 86, p. 26-H)*

The two bills, sponsors said, were designed to ward off the collapse of home builders and mortgage lenders who had been hit hard by the recession and high interest rates.

The housing measure (HR 6294), which provided $1 billion in emergency mortgage subsidies for low- and middle-income families buying new homes, passed the House May 11. President Reagan June 24 vetoed a compromise version of the plan, which had been included in supplemental appropriations legislation. *(House housing bill, p. 71; supplemental veto, p. 205)*

The major difference between the two rescue plans was that the mortgage assistance bill involved a direct cash infusion to revive the housing market, while the thrifts bill relied on a paper transaction to shore up troubled financial institutions. Under HR 6267's guarantees, money would change hands only if a bank or S&L failed.

"What we do here is more than help a segment of the financial industry," said Henry B. Gonzalez, D-Texas. "We set the basis for a healthy recovery of housing."

House passage of HR 6267 followed an attempt by Chalmers P. Wylie, R-Ohio, to offer an alternative backed by the Reagan administration. The substitute was defeated 155-209. *(Vote 85, p. 26-H)*

Wylie's proposal, based on a plan suggested by Federal Home Loan Bank Board Chairman Richard T. Pratt, would have offered assistance in the form of interest-bearing promissory notes to institutions with a net worth below 3 percent of assets.

The Wylie plan would use a sliding scale to make up only a portion of a bank or S&L's losses. By contrast, HR 6267 would guarantee a thrift's net worth at 2 percent (or a commercial bank's at 4 to 5 percent), regardless of the size of its losses.

Also, the Wylie substitute would use the Federal Savings and Loan Insurance Corporation's existing insurance funds for any payments if an institution went under. HR 6267 would create a new Treasury account to back the guarantees, with the fund subject to an $8.5 billion limit.

While Wylie claimed his program would be cheaper than HR 6267, Banking Committee Chairman St Germain, the key sponsor of HR 6267, insisted his bill had "no cost, not one red penny."

But the GOP plan, St Germain said, would cost $1.2 billion in cash outlays because the federal government would pay interest on the promissory notes given to banks and S&Ls.

Another criticism raised about the Wylie amendment was that it did not require qualifying institutions to have substantial investments in real estate loans, nor did it require thrifts to earmark funds for new mortgages.

"The role of thrift institutions in this country has always been to provide money for housing. To save those

institutions, and then simply let them make car loans, personal loans, corporate loans, international loans, makes no sense whatsoever," said Charles E. Schumer, D-N.Y.

Two amendments to HR 6267 were adopted by voice vote. An amendment by George C. Wortley, R-N.Y., provided that subordinated creditors at the time guarantees were issued — primarily large banks and investment houses owed money by the covered institutions — would not be paid ahead of the Treasury should an institution fail.

The other amendment, by Schumer, allowed mortgages on apartment buildings to satisfy the requirement that 60 percent of net new deposits be used for home mortgages.

Senate Committee Action

The Senate Banking Committee reported S 2879 Sept. 3 (S Rept 97-536). The committee unanimously approved the measure Aug. 19.

The bill, a stripped-down version of legislation promoted by Banking Chairman Garn, provided help to financially strapped savings and loan institutions and mutual savings banks. The measure also authorized both these thrift institutions and commercial banks to set up new short-term accounts that would be competitive with the popular money market funds.

In late July, after it became apparent that he did not have the votes to push his highly controversial package through the Banking panel, Garn agreed to strip the legislation of its most disputed provisions.

Chief among these were changes backed by the banking industry that would have allowed commercial banks to offer mutual funds and underwrite revenue bonds.

The administration supported Garn's plan to deregulate the banking industry. Treasury Secretary Donald T. Regan said it was "unfortunate" these provisions had to be dropped, although the bill the commitee approved was "a sound package."

The savings and loan industry was buoyed by approval of the measure. William O'Connell, president of the U.S. League of Savings and Loan Associations, called it a "major step forward in preserving and strengthening the savings and loan system."

The American Bankers Association (ABA), which represents commercial banks, called it a "sweetheart savings and loan bill that leaves the commercial banking community at a greater competitive disadvantage than before. Little is left in this legislation which addresses the special needs of the banking industry."

Help for the Thrifts

The bill would establish a program allowing federally insured financial institutions to exchange capital notes with the FDIC and the FSLIC.

If a thrift institution's net worth fell below a certain level, the government would add to the institution's assets by authorizing federal regulators to give it interest-bearing certificates.

In return for the certificate, the thrift would give the insurer a promissory note. The note would be paid off later by returning the certificate to the insurance agency.

In order to qualify for the assistance, the institution would have to meet several tests. It must have incurred losses during the two previous quarters, comply with the

terms established by the insuring agencies, have been solvent for at least six months, and have at least 20 percent of its assets invested in residential mortgages or mortgage-backed securities.

The initial level of aid, which could be modified by the insurance agencies, would be 30 percent of losses if net worth was less than 3 percent, 40 percent of losses if net worth was less than 2 percent, and 50 percent of losses if net worth was less than 1 percent.

Other provisions of the Senate bill would:

• Expand the powers of both the FDIC and the FSLIC to assist troubled banks and thrift institutions through mergers. The emergency merger provisions would expire after five years.

• Expand the investment authority of thrift institutions by permitting them to invest up to 15 percent of assets in commercial loans, up to 30 percent in consumer loans, up to 40 percent in non-residential real estate, and up to 100 percent in state and local obligations.

• Authorize the Depository Institutions Deregulation Committee to phase out all interest rate differentials no later than July 1, 1982.

• Require DIDC, no later than 60 days after enactment, to authorize a new account that effectively competed with money market funds.

• Override state laws and court decisions that barred due-on-sale clauses in home mortgages.

Senate Floor Action

The Senate passed HR 6267 by voice vote Sept. 24 after substituting the provisions of S 2879 as amended on the Senate floor.

Several amendments were added to the Garn-sponsored bill, including a committee amendment designed to win the support of the American Bankers Association, which had opposed the committee bill.

Compromise Plan

The compromise eliminated interest-rate differentials between banks and S&Ls, expanded the authority of bank service corporations and restricted S&L checking accounts to business customers who had borrowed from the institution.

The amendment also eliminated interest-rate ceilings on the proposed new bank and thrift account to compete with the money market funds. It stipulated that the initial minimum balance for such an account was not to exceed $5,000. The amendment was adopted by voice vote.

The ABA later endorsed the bill and called the new account provision "a great victory for the public which has been seeking an insured, convenient market rate account."

Final Action

Working quickly to complete action before the election recess, conferees reached agreement on the complex legislation Sept. 29. They filed their report on the bill Sept. 30 (H Rept 97-899). The final compromise generally followed the Senate bill.

The Senate adopted the conference report by voice vote Sept. 30, and the House followed suit the next day, also by voice vote, completing congressional action.

President Reagan signed the measure into law (PL 97-320) Oct. 15. ∎

Export Trading Companies

Legislation designed to increase U.S. exports was cleared by Congress Oct. 1.

The bill (S 734 — PL 97-290) aimed to encourage the formation of export trading companies to help small- and medium-sized firms sell their goods abroad. The trading companies would provide marketing, transportation, financial and other services.

S 734 eased antitrust barriers that had inhibited joint export activities and permitted banking institutions, for the first time, to be active partners in the ventures.

Export trading companies had been slow to develop in the United States, partly because of the uncertainties caused by antitrust laws and problems in banking regulation. Banking was traditionally separated from commerce to ensure the financial soundness of banking institutions.

President Reagan supported the legislation. During a Sept. 28 press conference, he included it in a list of economic measures that he urged Congress to pass before the election recess. Reagan and other proponents said the bill would result in the creation of several hundred thousand jobs.

Although the legislation had been passed by the Senate early in 1981, action was slow in the House, where three committees had overlapping jurisdiction. The House passed its version July 27. *(Senate action, 1981 Almanac p. 113)*

Provisions

As signed into law Oct. 8, S 734 (PL 97-290):

• Directed the secretary of commerce to establish an office to promote the formation of export trading companies.

• Defined export trading companies as organizations engaged primarily in exporting U.S. goods or services, such as communications, construction, insurance and architecture; or providing export trade services, such as consulting, marketing, trade documentation or processing foreign orders.

• Authorized bank holding companies, banker's banks and Edge Act corporations that were subsidiaries of bank holding companies to invest in trading companies, subject to Federal Reserve Board regulation under the Bank Holding Company Act of 1956. A banker's bank does business solely with other banks and is owned primarily by the banks with which it does business. Edge Act corporations are those formed to aid overseas operations of U.S. banks.

• Provided guidelines for regulations by the Federal Reserve Board to promote the creation of trading companies with broad enough powers to enable them to compete with similar foreign-owned institutions and to foster participation by smaller and regional banking institutions in trading companies. The bill also directed the Federal Reserve Board to facilitate the formation of joint venture export trading companies between eligible banking institutions and exporters.

• Limited a banking institution's investments in a trading company to 5 percent of the institution's capital and surplus. An additional 10 percent could be loaned to the trading company.

• Required a banking institution to provide 60-day prior written notice to the Federal Reserve Board of its intent to invest in a trading company.

• Allowed the Federal Reserve Board to disapprove an investment under certain conditions, such as to prevent

unsound banking practices, unfair competition or conflicts of interest. The board also could disapprove an investment that would have a significantly adverse effect on the financial or managerial resources of the banking institution.

● Prohibited a bank holding company or subsidiary from extending credit to a trading company on terms more favorable than those offered to other borrowers in similar circumstances.

● Barred a trading company from manufacturing, agricultural production, foreign exchange or commodities speculation or securities dealings beyond those currently allowed by law. Some product modification would be allowed to enable the goods or services to conform to foreign requirements.

● Authorized the Export-Import Bank to establish a program to provide loan guarantees to trading companies.

● Made it easier for small- and medium-sized companies to take advantage of special short-term financing, known as "bankers' acceptances," for exports and made it easier for smaller banking institutions to participate in bankers' acceptances.

● Created a certification process that would provide a limited immunity from the antitrust laws to trading companies. The commerce secretary, with the attorney general's concurrence, would approve the certificate.

The certificate could be issued if the company's proposed conduct would not substantially lessen competition within the United States, unreasonably enhance or depress prices within the United States, constitute unfair methods of competition or result in the resale in the United States of goods or services exported by the applicant.

House Action

The House passed its version of the bill by voice vote July 27.

The House version consisted of a bill reported by the Foreign Affairs and Judiciary committees (HR 1799 — H Rept 97-637, Parts I and II) as amended by a separate measure reported by the Banking Committee (HR 6016 — H Rept 97-629). After passing each bill by voice vote under suspension of the rules, the House combined them as a substitute for S 734 and requested a conference with the Senate.

Details of the House legislation:

Banking Committee Bill. As reported by the Banking Committee July 1, HR 6016 authorized investments by bank holding companies and "bankers' banks" in export trading companies.

Proposed investments would have to be disclosed in writing and would be subject to the approval of the Federal Reserve Board, which regulated the activities of bank holding companies under the Bank Holding Company Act. (*Background, 1970 Almanac p. 854; Congress and the Nation Vol. III, p. 139*)

The total investment would be limited. The bill also imposed restrictions on lending to export trading companies by bank entities investing in them.

A bank holding company could be required by the Federal Reserve Board to divest its export trading company holdings or comply with certain conditions if the trading company engaged in certain types of speculation in commodities, securities or foreign exchange.

Export trade services in which trading companies could engage included financing, marketing, advertising and transportation, if those services promoted exports.

Foreign Affairs/Judiciary Bill. As reported by the

Foreign Affairs Committee July 15, HR 1799 authorized bank holding companies, with the approval of the Federal Reserve Board, to invest in export trading companies. It also set limits on investments in and loans to the trading companies.

Unlike the Banking Committee bill, the Foreign Affairs Committee measure allowed banking institutions organized under the Edge Act to invest in export trading companies.

The bill amended the Webb-Pomerene Act of 1918 to clarify antitrust law relating to export trade activities. Export activities of export trading companies would be exempted from antitrust restrictions as long as those activities did not restrain trade within the United States.

The 1918 act permitted the formation of export trade associations with a limited exemption from antitrust laws. But the act was vague, and many companies, fearing antitrust action, had not formed such associations.

The committee bill established a certification procedure allowing the Commerce Department, after consultation with the Justice Department and the Federal Trade Commission, to give export trading companies limited immunity from antitrust laws.

The Judiciary Committee, in reporting the bill July 26, added antitrust certification procedures for the Justice Department.

Conference Action

The compromise legislation, reported by the conferees Oct. 1 (H Rept 97-924), tilted toward the House version, which supporters said provided stronger protections against possible antitrust abuses.

The measure permitted the secretary of commerce to issue a certificate providing limited antitrust immunity for a trading company — but only if the attorney general concurred. The Senate bill had provided a certification process that required the secretary to consult with the attorney general, while the House bill placed the certification process in the Justice Department.

The compromise followed the House measure in excluding commercial banks from investing in trading companies, which the Senate bill would have allowed. But it permitted participation by bank holding companies under Federal Reserve Board regulation.

The Senate adopted the conference report on the bill Oct. 1 by voice vote. The House followed suit later that day, clearing the measure for the president's signature. ∎

Miscellaneous Revenue Bill

Congress completed action Oct. 1 on HR 4717 (PL 97-362), a miscellaneous tax measure that had been in conference for almost 10 months. The House and Senate originally passed the bill in December 1981. (*Previous action, 1981 Almanac p. 116*)

Both chambers adopted the conference report on the legislation (H Rept 97-929) by voice vote Oct. 1. Conferees had reached agreement on the package just hours before final action.

As cleared by Congress, HR 4717 deferred for one year the scheduled Jan. 1, 1982, effective date for regulations governing the taxation of "last in, first out" (LIFO) inventories of liquidating companies. The effective date change applied only to the first $1 million of a company's LIFO

reserves.

The measure also extended from three years to 10 years the period over which the Federal National Mortgage Association could carry back net operating losses to offset taxes, and shortened the period over which such losses could be carried forward. The change gave the association tax advantages already allowed other financial institutions.

Numerous other provisions of HR 4717, added by the Senate in 1981, were deleted from the final package because they had been enacted earlier in 1982 as part of the tax reconciliation bill (PL 97-248). *(Story, p. 29)*

Still included in the legislation were provisions to:

● Allow 13 weeks of unemployment benefits for those who had been honorably discharged from military service and who had generally completed a full term of service. Under the 1981 reconciliation bill (PL 97-35), only those who were not allowed to re-enlist could qualify for jobless payments. The provision was expected to cost $220 million over three years. *(PL 97-35, 1981 Almanac p. 107)*

● Expand the type of oil shale equipment that could qualify for a 10 percent energy investment tax credit, for 1981 and 1982 only.

● Reduce excise taxes on legal betting operations and their employees.

● Liberalize eligibility requirements for the trade adjustment assistance program by repealing a tighter standard enacted in the 1981 reconciliation bill.

Under the 1981 law, benefits were provided to groups of workers only when it was found that foreign import competition was a "substantial cause" for the loss of their jobs. Previous law stipulated that import competition must have "contributed importantly" to the layoffs. *(Background, 1981 Almanac p. 107; 1979 Almanac p. 327; 1974 Almanac p. 553)* ∎

Subchapter S Taxation

Congress Oct. 1 gave final approval to a bill (HR 6055 — PL 97-354) that simplified tax laws governing so-called Subchapter S corporations — firms whose shareholders elected to be taxed as individuals rather than as corporations.

Businesses chose to incorporate under Subchapter S so they could take advantage of certain legal protections allowed corporations, while still enjoying tax advantages similar to those of a partnership.

Shareholders in a Subchapter S firm reported their share of the firm's income, and deducted a share of the losses, on individual tax returns, instead of having a corporate tax imposed directly on the firm's profits and additional taxes placed on shareholder dividends.

HR 6055 increased from 25 to 35 the number of shareholders a firm could have and still elect Subchapter S treatment. In addition, it liberalized requirements that such firms receive not more than 20 percent of their gross receipts from "passive" sources — such as patents — and loosened other eligibility standards for the special tax status. It also made certain changes allowing Subchapter S tax treatment to conform more closely with that of a partnership.

The House originally passed the bill (H Rept 97-826) by voice vote Sept. 20. The Senate passed its version of the measure (S Rept 97-640), which differed little from the House bill, by voice vote Sept. 30. The House accepted the Senate-passed bill Oct. 1, also by voice vote. ∎

Minor Tax Bills

In the closing days of the lame-duck session Congress cleared a variety of minor revenue bills, including a measure to make technical corrections in previously enacted tax legislation.

Lawmakers also approved a measure to allow business tax deductions for conventions on U.S. cruise ships. But an effort to reduce the holding period for special capital gains tax treatment was blocked in the Senate. And a tax break sought by Apple Computer Inc., which had plans to donate computers to thousands of schools, also failed to make it through the legislative mill.

Technical Corrections

Congress completed action Dec. 21 on legislation (HR 6056 — PL 97-448) making technical corrections in the Tax Equity and Fiscal Responsibility Act of 1982 (PL 97-248), the Economic Recovery Tax Act of 1981 (PL 97-34), the Crude Oil Windfall Profit Tax Act of 1980 (PL 96-471) and other tax legislation.

The House passed the measure Sept. 14 and the Senate followed suit Sept. 30, but not without first adding a number of controversial amendments.

House members balked at the excess baggage and blocked final passage before the election recess, claiming that many of the Senate amendments were not purely "technical."

Differences were cleared up during a lame-duck conference (H Rept 97-986). The most controversial provisions — including one to give certain troubled airlines, such as Eastern, a special tax break in the event of bankruptcy — were dropped.

Cruise Ships

A measure to allow certain business tax deductions for conventions aboard U.S. cruise ships was cleared by Congress Dec. 23 as part of a larger gas tax and highway authorization measure (HR 6211 — PL 97-424). *(Story, p. 317)*

The provision, attached on the Senate floor to the highway bill, allowed such deductions as long as the cruise ships stopped at U.S. ports or those of U.S. possessions. The deduction was limited to $2,000 for an individual.

The House passed similar legislation (HR 3191 — H Rept 97-828) Dec. 16 by a vote of 227-172. That bill would have allowed deductions on U.S. cruise ships that stopped anywhere in North America and placed no limit on the amount of the deduction. *(Vote 441, p. 130-H)*

Three days earlier, the measure failed to win passage under suspension of the rules, a shortcut procedure requiring a two-thirds majority for approval. The vote was 219-164. *(Vote 416, p. 124-H)*

Congress voted major restrictions on deductions for all foreign business travel in 1976, because of a proliferation of overseas conventions that many in Congress viewed as thinly veiled vacation trips. But the law was liberalized in 1980 to allow special exemptions for conventions held in Mexico and Canada. *(1976 Almanac p. 44; 1980 Almanac p. 301)*

Periodic Payments, Miscellany

Congress Dec. 21 cleared a bill (HR 5470 — PL 97-473) that put into law current Internal Revenue Service (IRS) rulings that damages paid to individuals for personal

injury or sickness would be tax exempt, whether paid periodically or in a lump sum.

The legislation also included several miscellaneous tax provisions added by the Senate Finance Committee (S Rept 97-646) that:

● Excluded from income all payments made to individuals for care of a foster child, including special payments for handicapped children.

● Gave tax breaks to Indian tribal governments similar to those enjoyed by states.

● Exempted certain multiple employer welfare arrangements and the Hawaii Prepaid Health Care Act from the Employee Retirement Income Security Act (ERISA) of 1974.

Not included in the final measure (H Rept 97-984) was a Senate amendment to allow the Virgin Islands to lower a tax the island government was required to withhold from certain investment income generated there, but paid to U.S individuals or corporations. It was struck in conference because the provision was adopted as part of a separate disability measure (HR 7093). *(Disability, this page)*

The House originally passed the bill (H Rept 97-832) Sept. 20, and the Senate passed its version Oct. 1.

Apple Computer Bill

A proposed tax break for companies that donated computers to primary and secondary schools did not survive the 97th Congress.

A bill (HR 5573) designed primarily to help the Apple computer firm, which had plans to give every school in the country its own computer, was approved by both the House and the Senate Finance Committee.

But by the time the measure was ready for Senate floor action, it had been so changed that even the main beneficiary — Apple — no longer supported the legislation.

Under existing law, firms donating such equipment could deduct only their own costs, not the fair market value of the donated machines.

While the House bill would have allowed Apple — or any other computer company meeting certain restrictions — to deduct up to twice their cost, the Finance version (S Rept 97-647) limited the deduction to 1.5 times the cost.

The change was made because of complaints that the higher deduction would have the effect of almost totally reimbursing the computer firm for the equipment.

The committee also revised the House measure by allowing firms to take the deduction for contributions made in one of any of the following three years, instead of in 1983 only. The change was intended to give more firms a chance to take advantage of the tax break.

In addition, the Senate bill would have allowed the special deduction for donations of computers to libraries and museums that used the equipment for educational purposes. The measure was approved by the committee Sept. 28.

The House passed its version of HR 5573 (H Rept 97-836) Sept. 22 by a vote of 323-62. *(Vote 328, p. 98-H)*

While the bill was promoted as a boost for technological education, some members objected that it was little more than a tax subsidy for Apple. They pointed out that once the donated computer was in place, a school would be constrained to buy more equipment from Apple, rather than another computer company, if it wanted to expand the use of the machine.

It was expected the bill would cost the government $15 million in lost revenues for fiscal 1983 and $21 million in fiscal 1984.

Capital Gains

Despite a lobbying campaign by the securities industry, legislation to shorten the holding period on capital gains failed to clear Congress in 1982.

The proposal would have reduced from one year to six months the required period an investment would have to be held to qualify for special capital gains tax treatment. Capital gains income was taxed at a 20 percent rate, while regular income was taxed at rates as high as 50 percent.

Investors and stockbrokers had pushed for the provision for several years, claiming that the shortened holding period would encourage new investment. But repeated attempts to change the law met with little success. *(Previous action, 1981 Almanac p. 91)*

The capital gains measure passed the Senate July 23 as part of the Finance Committee's tax increase/spending cut bill (HR 4961), but the proposal later was rejected in conference. *(Story, p. 29)*

On Aug. 17, the provision was attached to a public debt ceiling bill (H J Res 520) in the Senate by a 77-17 vote. It was dropped after the debt bill became bogged down in a filibuster on social issues. *(Vote 332, p. 54-S; story, p. 44)*

On Sept. 28, the Finance Committee added the capital gains provision to a House-passed measure (HR 1524) to help out three California public utilities.

In addition, the committee attached an amendment by Max Baucus, D-Mont., allowing artists and writers to deduct the fair market value of their works if given as charitable contributions. Existing law allowed such individuals to deduct only their own cost of materials for such donations.

Both amendments met opposition when Finance Committee Chairman Robert Dole, R-Kan., attempted to bring HR 1524 (S Rept 97-643) to the Senate floor during the lame-duck session, and the Senate never considered the bill.

Eventually, the California utility provision was attached as a separate item to the gas tax/highway bill (HR 6211).

The three utilities were caught in a lengthy legal battle between the California Public Utility Commission and the Internal Revenue Service over passing on tax benefits to utility consumers. The measure tried to resolve the dispute by eliminating a back-tax liability of $2.2 billion for the three utilities — Pacific Telephone and Telegraph Company, General Telephone Company of California and Southern California Gas Company. ∎

Disability Review Eased

After almost a year of legislative haggling, Congress enacted a temporary measure in the final days of the session to help thousands of individuals suddenly cut from the disability benefit rolls.

The bill (HR 7093 — PL 97-455), cleared Dec. 21, allowed individuals dropped from the rolls before Oct. 1, 1983, to continue collecting payments while they appealed their termination. Benefits had to be repaid, however, if the appeal was lost.

The benefit extension was passed after a torrent of complaints that thousands of disabled persons mistakenly were being thrown off the rolls as part of an administration

effort to weed out ineligible recipients.

Even though about two-thirds of those who appealed were eventually reinstated, they did not collect benefits during the appeals process, sometime lasting longer than a year. As a result, many lost homes and savings — and a few died — while pursuing appeals.

"While this is only a temporary measure, it is a significant step in the right direction toward reform of a process in serious disarray," said Sen. John Heinz, R-Pa., chairman of the Senate Special Committee on Aging.

Besides allowing payments until an individual appealed to an administrative law judge, the measure allowed the secretary of health and human services to slow down the department's current review of the disability rolls.

Congress mandated the review in 1980 after reports that as many as 20-30 percent of the approximately four million Disability Insurance recipients were no longer eligible. *(1980 Almanac p. 434)*

Although the three-year review was to have started by 1982, the Reagan administration began nine months early to weed out recipients with what some critics charged was excessive fervor. Some 265,000 recipients had been dropped from the program by the end of 1982.

Provisions

As cleared by Congress, HR 7093:

● Provided disability insurance payments and Medicare coverage to individuals appealing their termination from the disability rolls before Oct. 1, 1983. Benefits would have to be repaid should the appeal be lost.

● Required as of Jan. 1, 1984, that face-to-face hearings be held when individuals initially appealed their termination from the rolls. Previously, some beneficiaries did not have such a meeting until they appeared before an administrative law judge, most often the final stage of appeal.

● Required that no payments to an individual appealing a termination decision be made after June 1984.

● Required the secretary of health and human services to report to Congress semiannually on the operations of the disability review process.

● Extended for seven months — until July 1, 1983 — an exemption from a law requiring that certain spousal Social Security benefits be reduced dollar-for-dollar by any public pension payments. However, the extension applied only to individuals who could prove that they were dependent on their spouse for more than half of their support.

● Allowed the Virgin Islands to reduce taxes on certain investment income earned from sources within the Virgin Islands and paid to individuals in the United States.

Legislative History

The disability bill's passage through Congress proved extremely difficult, despite general agreement among the House, the Senate and the administration that benefits should continue during appeals.

The House Ways and Means Committee reported a measure (HR 6181 — H Rept 97-588) May 26 that allowed payments through an initial appeal. It also provided for four additional months of "adjustment benefits" once it had been decided a recipient was no longer disabled.

However, groups representing the disabled balked at provisions making it more difficult for beneficiaries to introduce additional evidence before an administrative law judge, and the legislation was effectively killed by the time it reached the House Rules Committee.

In the Senate, several Republican and Democratic members worked behind the scenes to fashion a package similar to the one finally included in HR 7093. The Finance Committee approved the measure Sept. 28. To ease enactment, the committee attached its measure (S Rept 97-648) to a minor House-passed bill dealing with Virgin Islands taxation, but Sen. Russell B. Long, D-La., blocked a floor vote before the election recess.

Long objected to a provision that indicated Congress might be willing to accept changes making it more difficult for beneficiaries to be taken off the rolls. The language was modified before Senate passage by a 70-4 vote Dec. 3 and finally deleted in conference. *(Vote 390, p. 66-S)*

The Senate adopted the conference report (H Rept 97-985) by voice vote Dec. 21, and the House went on to clear the bill by a 259-0 vote. *(Vote 458, p. 134-H)*

Long's objections reflected the fear of some members that Congress' mandate to weed the program of ineligible recipients might be weakened under the new bill. Leaders of the Ways and Means and Finance committees assured, however, that the additional benefits would be only temporary until Congress could once again review the disability program in 1983.

"This legislation does not in any way represent a reversal of the 1980 mandate that the Social Security Administration work diligently to remove ineligibles from the benefit rolls," Finance Chairman Robert Dole, R-Kan., told colleagues on the Senate floor.

During the course of congressional debate on the legislation, the administration took some steps on its own to meet the criticisms of its review process. According to officials of the Social Security Administration, which oversees the program, new face-to-face interviews had prevented about 5 percent of those individuals up for review from being mistakenly taken off the rolls.

In addition, the administration slowed down its review of the program in response to charges that overworked state agency employees, who did the actual reviews, did not have time to conduct thorough examinations of an individual's medical record. ∎

Social Security Reform

With the exception of some political rhetoric around election time, Congress managed to skirt the troublesome issue of Social Security during most of 1982.

It waited instead for the report of President Reagan's bipartisan National Commission on Social Security Reform, which had been appointed at the end of 1981 to remove Social Security from the political arena.

The commission originally was scheduled to make its recommendations on saving the financially troubled retirement system by the end of the year but was granted an extension until Jan. 15, 1983. The commission met that deadline, with approval of a last-minute compromise plan.

Under existing law, Social Security's largest trust fund, Old-Age and Survivors Insurance (OASI), was set to run out of funds by July 1983 if nothing was done. Even if Congress allowed the OASI fund to continue to borrow from the system's healthier Disability and Hospital Insurance funds, all three would run out of money in 1984.

In 1980, Congress temporarily reallocated taxes from the disability trust fund to OASI to avert a funding shortfall. In 1981, unable to reach agreement on a more comprehensive package, Congress agreed to allow OASI to borrow from the disability and hospital trust funds until the end of

1982. *(Background, 1981 Almanac p. 117)*

Commission Efforts

The reform commission's 15 members, after repeated attempts, had had little success at reaching an agreement by year's end on just what steps should be taken to keep the Social Security system from going broke. Generally, the commission's eight Republican members leaned toward benefit reductions, while its seven Democratic members favored tax increases, as the best way to save the system.

What most of the commission's members could agree on was that the two principals in the Social Security debate — President Reagan and House Speaker Thomas P. O'Neill Jr., D-Mass. — would have to reach some consensus on saving the system before the commission could make a recommendation.

Ironically, it was the inability of O'Neill and Reagan to reach agreement on the issue in the first place that led to appointment of the commission in 1981. And in 1982, their failure to reach a consensus spelled doom for bipartisan negotiations on the fiscal 1983 budget. *(Budget resolution, p. 186)*

In a three-day marathon session Nov. 11-13, the reform commission did agree on the basic framework of the Social Security debate, which would be one of the first to confront the 98th Congress.

The panel agreed that between $150 billion and $200 billion should be raised betweeen 1983 and 1989 to see the system through its short-term financing problems, caused in large part by high inflation and unemployment.

The commission also agreed that the system would have a long-term financing problem — caused largely by changing demographics — that could require the equivalent of a 1.82 percent rise in payroll taxes over the next 75 years, or $1.6 trillion.

More importantly, the panel made clear that it would not recommend major structural changes in the Social Security system but would call instead for some combination of benefit cuts and tax hikes. Just what the mix would be, however, remained the formidable problem the commission appeared most likely to leave in the lap of the new Congress. ∎

Caribbean Trade Plan

In spite of severe pressure from the White House, the Senate failed at the end of the lame-duck session to act on the trade portion of President Reagan's Caribbean Basin Initiative (CBI).

Nine months after Reagan submitted his plan to Congress, the Senate Finance Committee on Dec. 20 held an impromptu session to act on the trade proposals (HR 7397), which had been passed by the House only two days earlier. But the full Senate did not take up the measure before adjourning Dec. 23.

The president's proposal had received an unexpected boost from the House leadership. Speaker Thomas P. O'Neill Jr., D-Mass., said early in the lame-duck session that the Caribbean trade bill did not have the votes to pass the House. But Ways and Means Chairman Dan Rostenkowski, D-Ill., switched from a skeptic to an ardent supporter of the measure, and bullied it through his committee Dec. 9. Rostenkowski changed his mind while on a trip to the Caribbean during the fall election recess.

The bill would have provided duty-free entry into the United States for products of the nations of the Caribbean basin and Central America. Reagan put heavy emphasis on the measure, saying it would help stabilize the impoverished region and prevent the spread of communism. He pledged on Dec. 22 to push for passage of the bill in 1983. *(Reagan plan, p. 15-E)*

Congress in 1982 approved only one part of Reagan's three-part package of aid for Caribbean and Central American nations: $350 million in emergency economic aid for fiscal 1982. A third part, tax benefits for U.S. companies that invested in the region, never was seriously considered in either house. *(Economic aid, p. 62)*

Little to Offer

Even if it had passed, the trade portion of CBI would have offered little in new benefits to the nations of the Caribbean. More than 80 percent of their non-petroleum products already entered the United States duty-free under the General System of Preferences (GSP), which was established to help underdeveloped countries in 1974. *(1974 Almanac p. 554)*

And many of the products that did not already have free access were excluded from the bill's provisions. Textiles and apparels, petroleum and petroleum products, tuna, footwear, handbags, luggage and other leather goods would have continued to be subject to tariffs, and sugar would have been subject to a quota.

What would have been left for the Caribbean to export? "Not a lot," Trade Representative William E. Brock III told the Senate Finance Committee. "Not much but hope."

Brock said the duty-free provisions would encourage the nations to diversify into new products they did not currently manufacture.

The bill also would have given the region some assurance that it would not suffer if Congress failed to reauthorize the GSP, due to expire at the end of 1984. The provisions of HR 7397 were to last for the next 12 years.

As passed by the House, the bill also would have allowed business expense deductions for conventions in certain Caribbean countries — over the protests of representatives from Alaska and Puerto Rico.

House Committee Action

The Ways and Means Committee reported HR 7397 Dec. 10 (H Rept 97-958). The committee had approved the bill Dec. 9 on a 27-6 vote.

Committee leaders successfully fought back amendments by members who were afraid the duty-free Caribbean imports would harm industries in their districts.

Attempts to exclude various products — including tuna, processed steel and mushrooms — from the tariff exemptions were defeated, as was an amendment by Richard T. Schulze, R-Pa., to exempt for five years all products that had been found to be "import sensitive" by the U.S. International Trade Commission.

Committee members also voted to eliminate a provision restricting the amount of duty-free Caribbean rum entering the country. That amendment had been added by the Trade Subcommittee, which approved its version of the bill (HR 5900) May 5.

As reported, the bill did provide protection to U.S. leather goods, textile and sugar industries by excluding those products from the measure. The textile and sugar exemptions had been recommended by the administration,

and the leather goods exemption was added by the Trade Subcommittee.

The committee also added petroleum and petroleum products to the list of exempted products.

To prevent exports from other nations gaining duty-free access to the U.S. market by simply "passing through" the Caribbean, the bill required that 35 percent of the labor and parts going into duty-free exports come from the Caribbean. That "domestic content" ratio would drop to 20 percent if at least 15 percent of the parts and labor were of U.S. origin.

As proposed by the president, the bill would have required only 25 percent domestic content. But confronted with fears that developed countries would build final assembly plants in the region and flood the U.S. market with tariff-free imports, the committee raised the percentage. The GSP program also required 35 percent domestic content.

The bill permitted the president to exclude a Caribbean nation from the program if it was a communist country, if it had nationalized U.S. property, if it had not acted in good faith in recognizing arbitration awards in favor of U.S. citizens, or if it offered special trade preferences to other nations that it did not offer the United States.

At the request of Marty Russo, D-Ill., the bill also excluded countries whose governments broadcast copyrighted films or television shows without the consent of the owner. And it contained an amendment by Andrew Jacobs Jr., D-Ind., excluding countries that had not signed an extradition treaty with the United States.

A provision added by Thomas J. Downey, D-N.Y., also required that each country submit a "stable food production plan" to ensure that land needed for basic foodstuffs was not being converted to export industries.

To help shelter Puerto Rico and the Virgin Islands from the consequences of the measure, the bill required that all excise taxes collected on foreign rum be transferred to those U.S. islands. That provision would cost the United States an estimated $13 million in revenue in fiscal 1983.

The bill included a provision allowing tax deductions for the expense of attending conventions in the Caribbean.

House Action

When the bill reached the House floor Dec. 17, Majority Leader Jim Wright, D-Texas, gave an impassioned speech supporting the measure that caused his colleagues in the chamber to rise and applaud. "The history of our relations with Latin America has been a history mottled by recurrent broken promises and benign neglect, raising hopes that then were dashed," he said.

Opponents of the bill argued that it would export jobs to the Caribbean. They complained that the president was enacting a jobs program for foreigners but refusing to enact one for U.S. citizens.

But on the final vote, Wright's position prevailed, and the bill passed 260-142. *(Vote 447, p. 130-H)*

The House adopted by voice vote an amendment excluding tuna from duty-free status. The amendment was sponsored by Richard A. Gephardt, D-Mo., whose district included the corporate headquarters of Ralston-Purina, a major tuna processor. It was supported by representatives of Puerto Rico, American Samoa and California, all of which had tuna interests.

The House defeated an amendment, proposed by Delegate Ron de Lugo, D-Virgin Islands, that would have set a quota on duty-free Caribbean rum. De Lugo said unlimited duty-free rum imports from the Caribbean would damage sales of Virgin Islands' rum. The amendment was rejected 171-226. *(Vote 446, p. 130-H)*

An amendment by Larry J. Hopkins, R-Ky., to exclude tobacco and tobacco products from duty-free status also was defeated, by voice vote.

Senate Committee Action

Finance Committee Chairman Robert Dole, R-Kan., in July had promised quick action on CBI, but his panel did not get around to working on the bill until Dec. 20.

Brock urged the panel to hold back all amendments, in order to avoid the need for a conference with the House. But two amendments were adopted.

An amendment by George J. Mitchell, D-Maine, gave protection to the textile industry by changing a provision of the bill designed to assist the Virgin Islands.

That provision said exports from the Virgin Islands could enter the United States duty-free if no more than 70 percent of their labor and parts content came from outside U.S. territory. The existing foreign content limit was 50 percent, but it was raised by the bill to ensure that the Virgin Islanders were given more preferential treatment than the Caribbean nations.

Mitchell's amendment said that those products exempted from the Caribbean trade bill, such as textiles and leather goods, also would have to continue to meet the 50 percent foreign content limit in the Virgin Islands.

Another amendment, by John H. Chafee, R-R.I., struck a House provision that exempted a Virgin Islands rum distillery from U.S. federal water pollution controls.

An amendment by Spark M. Matsunaga, D-Hawaii, to eliminate the Caribbean convention tax deduction was defeated 4-9.

The committee reported the bill by a vote of 11-5, but did not issue a formal report. ∎

Auto Domestic Content Rule

The Senate did not act on controversial House-passed legislation that would have forced major Japanese automakers to purchase from the United States as much as 75 percent of the parts and labor used to make automobiles sold in this country.

In a largely symbolic action, the House Dec. 15 passed the bill (HR 5133) on a 215-188 vote. Neither the sponsors nor the opponents of the measure expected it to be considered by the Senate in the few remaining days of the lame-duck session. But supporters said the House vote would send a "clear signal" to Japan to change its trading practices. *(Vote 435, p. 128-H)*

That signal, however, was made considerably less clear after an unexpected amendment by lame-duck Rep. Millicent Fenwick, R-N.J., seriously weakened the bill. Fenwick's amendment said the measure should not "supersede" any "treaty, international convention or agreement on tariffs and trade." That provision would enable U.S. courts to invalidate the measure for violating the General Agreement on Tariffs and Trade (GATT).

"We just gutted the bill," gloated Phil Gramm, D-Texas, an opponent of the House measure, after the Fenwick amendment was adopted by a narrow 195-194 vote. *(Vote 434, p. 128-H)*

Lobbyists for the United Auto Workers (UAW) union,

who lined the halls outside the House chamber throughout the debate, were clearly surprised and angered when they learned of the Fenwick amendment.

The Reagan administration opposed the domestic content measure, which U.S. Trade Representative William E. Brock III called "the worst piece of economic legislation since the 1930s."

The bill would have set domestic content ratios for automakers based on the number of cars they sold in the United States. Given current levels of sales, Toyota and Nissan (Datsun) would have been required to have 70 to 75 percent domestic content in their cars by 1985, while smaller makers like Toyo Kogyo (Mazda) and Honda would have had to achieve ratios of between 20 and 40 percent.

The major U.S. makers would have faced a domestic content requirement of 90 percent, which would have limited their ability to buy parts from abroad.

Stiff quotas would have been applied to companies that failed to meet the bill's required ratios.

Visions of War

In the weeks leading up to the House action, public debate on the content bill had been framed in extreme language.

Supporters, recalling the World War II attack on Pearl Harbor, suggested the recent influx of Japanese cars was its economic equivalent.

Opponents, on the other hand, conjured up visions of World War III, saying the protectionist measure was similar to the Smoot-Hawley Tariff Act of 1930, which triggered a worldwide trade war, pushed the world economy into depression, sparked economic nationalism and thus set the stage for war.

"This is one little step in the same direction," Rep. Sam Gibbons, D-Fla., chairman of the Ways and Means Trade Subcommittee, told the House Rules Committee Dec. 7. "Inexorably we will be repeating history."

The opponents argued that while the bill would undoubtedly help autoworkers, it would lead to higher automobile prices and could trigger retaliation by U.S. trading partners. The result would be a loss of employment in other industries.

The survival of the bill could be attributed almost solely to the UAW, which had pushed tirelessly for the measure since late 1981. The AFL-CIO also had worked for its passage.

The legislation was endorsed by a number of Democratic presidential aspirants, including Walter F. Mondale and Sens. Alan Cranston, Calif.; Ernest F. Hollings, S.C.; and John Glenn, Ohio, who initially had reservations about the bill.

Opposing the measure was a much longer list of business, agriculture and public interest groups. Those groups became more active in their opposition after the Nov. 2 elections, when it became clear the measure was likely to pass the House.

"I think it is fair to say that the overwhelming majority of members of Congress view the domestic content legislation as a perfectly ridiculous piece of legislation," Sen. John C. Danforth, R-Mo., told a U.S. Chamber of Commerce group gathered in opposition to the bill Dec. 8. "The reason they support it is political."

Danforth dismissed the argument that House passage would "send a message" to Japan. "In my opinion a country begins very quickly to lose its credibility if the signals it chooses to use are asinine on their face," he said.

House Committee Action

The House Energy and Commerce Committee reported HR 5133 Sept. 21 (H Rept 97-842).

Before approving the bill on a 25-16 vote Sept. 15, the committee accepted, 27-14, a substitute offered by Richard L. Ottinger, D-N.Y., chief sponsor of the bill. The substitute was crafted partly to ease the potential impact on Volkswagen, which already built cars in the United States.

The committee narrowly defeated an amendment that would have allowed the president to exempt any manufacturer from a country that had substantially reduced quotas and other trade barriers applied to U.S. exports. The panel voted 20-21 on the proposal, offered by Gramm.

Gramm said the amendment would accomplish what the bill's supporters wanted but failed to do with the legislation: open foreign markets to U.S. goods. Ottinger countered that the amendment amounted "to a nullification of our efforts."

In earlier action, the committee Sept. 9 rejected 12-26 an amendment — offered by Norman F. Lent, R-N.Y., and William E. Dannemeyer, R-Calif. — that would have allowed the president to suspend implementation of the bill if it violated GATT rules.

After it was reported by the Energy and Commerce Committee, the bill was sent to the Ways and Means Committee, which did not act on the measure before its jurisdiction expired Oct. 1.

House Floor Action

House debate on the bill began Dec. 10, and continued Dec. 15.

Opponents prepared dozens of amendments designed to weaken or kill the measure.

Amendments debated and rejected included one by William E. Dannemeyer, R-Calif., to change the name of the bill to "The Smoot-Hawley Trade Barriers Act of 1982." The vote was 92-301. *(Vote 432, p. 128-H)*

An amendment by Dan Coats, R-Ind., requiring the Agriculture Department to study the effects of the bill on agricultural exports was adopted by voice vote.

Adoption of the Fenwick amendment was such an unexpected victory that opponents dropped other amendments and allowed a final vote.   ▮

Trade 'Reciprocity'

Watered-down versions of bills seeking "reciprocity" in trade relations were reported by congressional committees but did not reach the Senate or House floor in 1982.

The controversial concept of reciprocity would require retaliatory action against nations that did not provide American firms with access to markets equal to that afforded foreign firms by the United States.

The Reagan administration opposed any bill that would identify non-reciprocity as an independent cause for trade action against another country or require equal access on a product-by-product basis.

The Senate Finance Committee June 30 reported a bill (S 2094) that won the endorsement of administration trade negotiators. The bill would have strengthened procedures for enforcing violations of existing trade law, and required the government to seek international agreements on services, high technology and investment trade.

The Finance Committee Sept. 21 attached the mea-

sure to an unrelated House-passed tariff bill (HR 4566), but the controversial reciprocity provisions were dropped from HR 4566 in the final days of the lame-duck session. *(HR 4566, p. 58)*

In the House, the Energy and Commerce Committee reported a narrower measure (HR 5519) that would have provided negotiating authority for agreements covering trade in services and set procedures for retaliating against service firms of foreign nations that unfairly restricted access of U.S. companies to their markets. The House did not act on the bill.

The administration was seeking the negotiating authority before the ministerial meeting of the General Agreement on Tariffs and Trade (GATT) Nov. 24-29. GATT was a multilateral treaty that had provided a framework for liberalizing world trade since 1948. *(GATT conference, box, this page; background, 1979 Almanac p. 293)*

The pressure for reciprocity legislation reflected increasing congressional frustration over the nation's mounting trade deficit, especially with Japan, and with foreign practices and policies that had caused difficulties for U.S. businesses.

Senate Committee Action

The Finance Committee June 30 reported a compromise version of reciprocity legislation (S 2094 — S Rept 97-483) that resolved administration concerns over restrictions on foreign trade with the United States.

"This bill accomplishes perhaps not the wildest dreams of all of us, but it is a major step forward which the president supports and would sign," said John C. Danforth, R-Mo., chairman of the International Trade Subcommittee.

The bill, approved June 16, was intended to strengthen the president's hand in dealing with unfair trade practices by requiring the administration to report annually to Congress on all barriers encountered by U.S. exporters and on actions being taken to ease those barriers. Danforth said the measure would provide for the first time a systematic method for identifying and dealing with foreign trade curbs.

In addition, the measure authorized the president to negotiate international agreements on trade in investment and services, such as banking, as well as trade in high technology products, such as computers and semiconductors. Existing international rules applied mainly to merchandise.

The Finance Committee approved the bill by a 16-2 vote. The negative votes were cast by Russell B. Long, D-La., and Max Baucus, D-Mont., who contended that the measure did little to fight against policies and practices by Japan and other countries to limit U.S. trade. Baucus said the "wrong message" was being sent to Japan that the United States was "pulling back from action" on trade.

Although Danforth said his bill was never intended to require product-by-product reciprocity, administration officials believed it might spark retaliatory actions against U.S. trade.

After discussions with the administration, the bill was softened to require the United States to demand "fair and equitable" market opportunities, rather then the stricter formula of "substantially equivalent market access."

Provisions. As reported, S 2094 included provisions to:

● Establish as national policy the achievement of fair and equitable commercial opportunities in foreign markets.

Disappointing GATT Talks

The international trade talks held in Geneva Nov. 24-29 made little progress toward resolving pressing trade issues.

The United States went to Geneva with an ambitious agenda. But the communiqué signed by members of the 88-nation General Agreement on Tariffs and Trade (GATT) contained few of the U.S. proposals.

Congressional members of the U.S. delegation came back disillusioned with the GATT process, and angry with the unwillingness of some major nations to work toward the elimination of trade barriers.

The administration and congressional advocates of free trade originally had hoped they would be able to use a GATT agreement to fight protectionist legislation in Congress. But the flimsy accord signed in Geneva was expected instead to fan protectionist flames.

Highlights of the GATT meeting:

● **Agricultural Subsidies.** The United States failed completely in its attempt to get a freeze and then a gradual rollback of the heavy subsidies that the European Community (EC) was using to gain a growing share of the world's agricultural export markets. The Europeans — particularly France — were intransigent; they fought the U.S. proposals to the end.

● **Dispute Settlement.** The United States' major victory at the conference — an agreement on the dispute settlement process — was a thin one. U.S. trade officials were anxious to improve the way in which disputes between nations were settled under the GATT structure. Existing procedures made obstruction easy, and allowed a nation that lost a dispute to simply veto a GATT finding.

The agreement did not eliminate that veto power, but it did commit members to avoid "obstruction" in the dispute settlement process. "We will see what that means in practice," said U.S. Trade Representative William E. Brock III.

● **GATT Expansion.** The U.S. delegation convinced the GATT conference to take a very preliminary look at the problems of trade in services, such as banking, insurance and data processing. But it could obtain no agreement for a study of high technology trade or of trade-distorting investment requirements.

The services agreement called on member nations "with an interest in services" to study and exchange information on the issue. Brock commented that the communiqué "says about as little about services as it can say while still spelling the word right."

● **Safeguards.** The United States had hoped for an agreement to improve the "safeguard" measures nations could take to protect domestic industry from severe damage caused by import competition. It was hoped this would reduce the proliferation of protective actions taken outside the GATT framework — such as the "voluntary" restraint agreement that restricted Japanese automobile imports to the United States.

● **Other Issues.** The trade ministers failed to agree on an approach for negotiations between the industrial and "developing" nations to reduce tariff and non-tariff barriers. They also failed to make any progress on counterfeit production of trade goods.

● Require the U.S. trade representative to report annually to Congress identifying foreign policies or practices that were barriers to American products, services and foreign direct investment. The report would include an estimate of the impact of the barriers on the U.S. economy, as well as information about presidential actions being taken to eliminate those policies or practices.

● Allow the United States to offset the impact of barriers not removed through negotiation or enforcement of the GATT through withdrawal of prior concessions, imposition of duties and other measures.

● Provide for "fast track" consideration of any bill proposed by the president to authorize retaliatory action against unfair trade practices. No amendments would be allowed on the floor of either house.

● Allow the administration to initiate unfair trade practice investigations either to meet trade policies or in instances where businesses might face foreign retaliation.

● Define commerce to include services and foreign direct investment.

● Define unfair trade practices to include barriers to U.S. investments and violation of industrial property rights, including patents.

● Clarify and expand the list of foreign practices that would be considered unfair — and thus subject to presidential action — under Section 301 of the 1974 and 1979 trade acts (PLs 93-618, 96-39) to include unreasonable or unjustifiable measures that restrict U.S. commerce.

Section 301 provided for resolving complaints of unreasonable trade practices under GATT. Under the section, the president could investigate an allegedly unfair practice and take retaliatory action. *(1979 Almanac p. 293; 1974 Almanac p. 553)*

● Authorize the president to negotiate reductions in barriers to services, including restrictions on data processing, and development of dispute settlement procedures.

● Authorize the president to negotiate agreements that would reduce barriers to investment. The definition of international trade would include foreign investment.

● Authorize the president to negotiate agreements to reduce barriers to and tariffs on U.S. high technology products and related services.

House Committee Action

The House Energy and Commerce Committee Aug. 19 reported a bill (HR 5519 — H Rept 97-766) that authorized the administration to negotiate international agreements covering trade in services, such as insurance and telecommunications.

The bill also set procedures for retaliating against service firms of foreign nations that unfairly restricted access of U.S. companies to their markets.

"Passage of this legislation is absolutely essential if we are to convince other nations that the time has come for trade barriers to be eliminated to our banks, airlines, insurance companies, data processors and other service industries," said James J. Florio, D-N.J., chairman of the subcommittee with jurisdiction over foreign commerce.

Provisions. As reported, HR 5519 included provisions to:

● Authorize the administration to negotiate agreements on reducing or eliminating foreign barriers to U.S. trade in services.

● Direct the U.S. trade representative (USTR) to present to congressional committees a proposed 12-month work program for international negotiations on services

and an analysis of U.S. negotiating interests.

● Direct the commerce secretary to establish a program to make U.S. service firms more competitive, to promote the use of U.S. services abroad, and to collect and analyze information about U.S. service industries' foreign activities and about U.S. purchases of foreign services.

● Direct the secretary to present an annual report to Congress containing an analysis of activities by foreign suppliers of services, government regulation of foreign suppliers, and activities of U.S. suppliers of services in foreign countries.

The report also would cover the impact of any policy or practice of a major trading partner that denied benefits to U.S. service industries under any trade agreement or that denied U.S. service industries commercial opportunities like those offered by the United States.

● Provide that if the USTR determined after a Section 301 investigation that a foreign company's services were being subsidized by a foreign nation or determined that a competing U.S. industry was injured, then the subsidization would be considered an "unreasonable practice" that burdened U.S. commerce and the president would take appropriate action.

● Allow the president to impose fees or other restrictions upon foreign services or foreign suppliers of services.

● Authorize the president, upon recommendation of the commerce secretary, to impose restrictions or deny permits to service firms of foreign nations that limited market access to U.S. companies in an unjustifiable or unreasonable manner. The bill would establish a procedure for opening an investigation and for the secretary's recommendations.

● Authorize $20 million to carry out the activities allowed by the legislation. ∎

Miscellaneous Tariff Bill

Congress Dec. 21 cleared a miscellaneous tariff bill (HR 4566 — PL 97-446) that reduced customs duties on items ranging from toy china tea sets to pipe organ parts.

In its last act of the 97th Congress, the House by voice adopted the conference report on HR 4566 (H Rept 97-989) Dec 21. The bill then moved to the Senate, which also agreed to the report by voice vote.

The measure suspended or reduced duties on a variety of articles; the action was temporary or permanent, depending on the article. It also extended international sugar and coffee agreements, and prevented the illegal import of stolen antiquities.

"Although the duty reductions will reduce customs revenue by less than $14 million on an annual basis, many of the provisions are extremely important to small businesses and independent businessmen," said Senate Finance Chairman Robert Dole, R-Kan.

Dole said one of the duty savings was estimated to be as low as $6,400. The largest savings, of between $1 million and $2 million annually, would go to vending machine operators, he said.

The Senate passed the bill by voice Dec. 19, after dropping a controversial reciprocity provision. The reciprocity section, attached by the Senate Finance Committee in September (S Rept 97-564), would have strengthened the president's hand in dealing with unfair trade practices. *(Reciprocity, p. 56)*

The House had first passed HR 4566 (H Rept 97-257) Oct. 13, 1981.

Duty Changes

The main thrust of HR 4566 was the alteration of customs duties on a wide range of imported articles.

The list of more than 200 items included small toys, spark plug insulators, prayer shawls, scrap metal, seed potatoes, red peppers, carrots, caffeine, clock radios, fur used in making hats, bicycle parts and various chemicals.

One provision relieved the National Aeronautics and Space Administration (NASA) of the need to pay duties on imported materials launched into space and articles recovered from space.

The bill also extended the International Sugar Agreement until Jan. 1, 1985, and the International Coffee Agreement to Oct. 1, 1983. The agreements basically sought to moderate extreme price fluctuations in these commodities, Dole said. *(Sugar agreement, 1980 Almanac p. 98)*

"In order to implement these agreements the United States must be able to restrict the entry of non-certified, non-quota, coffee and sugar," he said. "Since the United States still represents the largest free markets for these products, we must be able to enforce the provisions of these agreements for them to function."

Other Provisions

As signed into law, HR 4566 also:

● Implemented the Nairobi protocol to the Florence agreement on the duty-free entry for educational, scientific and cultural materials, and materials for the handicapped. The protocol's purpose was to contribute "to the cause of peace through freer exchange of ideas and knowledge across national boundaries," according to the bill's language.

Among the duty-free items affected were film or recording catalogs, architectural or engineering drawings, loose illustrations, developed photographic film, slides, motion picture films, sound recordings, scientific tools, and articles for the blind or other handicapped persons, such as Braille or raised print books and music.

● Established guidelines to implement the United Nations Educational, Scientific and Cultural Organization (UNESCO) convention on cultural property.

The convention called for the prohibition and prevention of the illegal import, export and transfer of ownership of cultural property.

The president was authorized to restrict imports of illicitly traded artifacts when the major importing nations were implementing similar controls, Dole said.

The guidelines also allowed the president to impose import controls unilaterally in an emergency, and they barred the importation of certain items identified as having been stolen from museums or similar institutions abroad, he said. Items affected by the bill included archeological finds that were at least 250 years old or of cultural significance, and articles of ethnological value. ∎

Anti-Recession Jobs Plans Fail to Clear

Despite mounting pressure for anti-recession jobs legislation, Congress adjourned Dec. 23 without approving any new direct federal job-creation programs.

Prior to the Nov. 2 elections, demands for jobs measures came mostly from Democrats. But rising unemployment and Democratic election gains in the House spurred GOP leaders to join in calling for jobs action in the postelection session that began Nov. 29.

President Reagan vigorously opposed what he described as "make-work job programs." But he did ultimately back, and Congress before adjournment approved, a 5-cent-a-gallon increase in the federal gasoline tax, to finance repair of the nation's deteriorating roads and transit systems and to provide jobs for some of the 12 million unemployed Americans. Although Reagan insisted that the bipartisan measure (HR 6211 — PL 97-424) was not a jobs bill, others maintained it would create more than 300,000 jobs.

The House passed HR 6211 Dec. 7, but Senate action was delayed by a series of filibusters by conservative Republicans who opposed the tax increase. As a result, Congress did not complete action on HR 6211 until Dec. 23. *(Story, p. 317)*

Meanwhile, Democrats pressed for enactment of additional jobs legislation as part of the second fiscal 1983 continuing appropriations resolution (H J Res 631), which was required to maintain funding for agencies whose regular appropriations bills had not been enacted. *(Story, p. 238)*

The House version of the resolution, passed Dec. 14, included a $5.4 billion jobs program drafted by House

Democratic leaders. A Republican effort to delete the jobs program failed on a 215-191 vote. *(Vote 425, p. 126-H)*

The Senate version, passed Dec. 19, included $1.2 billion for a variety of public works jobs projects. That plan was advanced by Appropriations Committee Chairman Mark O. Hatfield, R-Ore., who called it a "reasonable, responsible approach in constructive activities." An effort to delete the funding failed 46-50. *(Vote 434, p. 73-S)*

Despite the House and Senate action, conferees on the continuing resolution agreed to drop the jobs funding from the measure to avert a threatened presidential veto. But in debate on the conference report Dec. 20, proponents vowed to fight for jobs legislation when the 98th Congress convened in 1983. *(Job creation history, box, p. 61)*

Democratic Anti-Recession Efforts

Action on the gas tax bill and the continuing resolution capped a year of halting Democratic efforts to develop politically viable anti-recession legislation.

Democratic leaders, with an eye to the Nov. 2 elections, won House passage Sept. 16 of a $1 billion jobs package (H J Res 562) that Republicans derided as "economic moonshine." The bill was the centerpiece of a Democratic package aimed at creating jobs and stimulating the economy. *(Action on H J Res 562, below)*

Other components of the package included:

● A five-year Defense Production Act reauthorization (HR 5540) that called for $1 billion a year in new aid to industry, $250 million a year in new government grants for job training and $100 million a year in new aid for colleges — all in the name of industrial defense preparedness and

all taken from the defense budget. The bill was pulled off the House floor Sept. 23 following adoption of a weakening amendment, and a simple six-month extension of the Defense Production Act (S 2375 — PL 97-336) was approved instead. *(Story, p. 63)*

● A bill (HR 5133), supported strongly by the United Auto Workers, that would force reductions in sales of foreign cars unless foreign auto companies produced more of them inside the United States. The House passed the bill Dec. 15, but there was no Senate action. *(Story, p. 55)*

● Twin bills (HR 6967, S 2807) based on the theory that the Federal Reserve Board could and should reduce market interest rates and thus spur economic recovery. The bills were designed to force the Fed to target interest rates as well as the "money supply" in its control and regulation of the banking system. There was no action on the measures. *(Story, p. 64)*

In addition to the central elements of the package, the Democrats sought extension of programs authorized by the Economic Development Administration (EDA), to which congressional Democrats had turned to provide jobs during previous recessions. The House passed a reauthorization bill (HR 6100) Aug. 12, but the extension ran up against a stone wall in the Senate. *(Story, p. 62)*

House Majority Leader Jim Wright, D-Texas, said in mid-September that the Democrats would have liked to include in their agenda a more ambitious program to retrain workers laid off in depressed industries and a federal subsidy to stimulate housing construction and sales. But there was no time left for action on a retraining program, he said, and Reagan vetoed a bipartisan housing stimulus plan (HR 5922) June 24. *(Story, p. 205)*

$1 Billion Jobs Plan

The House Sept. 16 passed by a 223-169 vote, largely along party lines, a Labor Department supplemental appropriations bill (H J Res 562 — H Rept 97-764) that both authorized and appropriated $1 billion to create an estimated 200,000 temporary public works jobs. The funding was for the 1982 fiscal year, which ended Sept. 30. *(Vote 319, p. 96-H)*

There was no further action on the House bill. An attempt by Sen. Edward M. Kennedy, D-Mass. to attach the measure to the first fiscal 1983 continuing resolution (H J Res 599) was blocked on a 60-37 Senate vote Sept. 29. *(Vote 372, p. 63-S)*

Funding in the Democratic bill was set at 5 percent of the estimated cost of unemployment compensation for fiscal 1982, a formula that would call for appropriating $1.035 billion.

The bulk of the funds would be distributed to state and local governments meeting the criteria for public-service jobs funds, and ultimately to workers, under a formula patterned loosely after expiring provisions of the Comprehensive Employment and Training Act (CETA).

Most of this money, 83 percent, would be targeted at governments — or possibly combined jurisdictions — qualifying as "eligible entities" because their unemployment rate was above the national average. The other 17 percent of the funds would be set aside for localities that could not meet this standard but experienced a large loss of jobs or "economic dislocation."

Sponsors stressed that the distribution formula was flexible enough — poorly drafted and vague enough, critics charged — to ensure that most congressional districts

might qualify for at least some aid.

The jobs to be funded by the bill would be limited to six months' duration and would involve work on the repair or maintenance of public facilities such as roads and bridges. Workers hired under the program would have to have been unemployed for at least two weeks but would not have to meet any income tests.

Genesis of Plan

H J Res 562 had its genesis in a press conference held by Majority Leader Wright and Budget Committee Chairman James R. Jones, D-Okla., on May 7, the day that a postwar-high unemployment rate of 9.4 percent was announced. Jones and Wright called for urgent action to help the growing numbers of unemployed. (The unemployment rate continued its upward course through the remainder of the year, hitting 10.4 percent in October and 10.8 percent by year's end.)

The jobs proposal was to be coupled with a $1 billion plan to provide lower mortgage interest rates for buyers of new homes, thus increasing jobs in the construction industry. The housing plan, subsequently increased to $3 billion, was vetoed by Reagan as part of the urgent supplemental appropriations bill (HR 5922). *(Story, p. 71)*

After the press conference, the jobs plan, vaguely outlined by Wright and Jones, disappeared from sight for several months. Wright's task force, working with committee chairmen such as Education and Labor head Carl D. Perkins, D-Ky., sought to mold the general goal of job creation into a specific piece of legislation.

As it turned out, however, there was little legislative authority still on the books, especially after enactment of the 1981 reconciliation budget cuts, that could serve as a vehicle for a new program. *(1981 reconciliation bill, 1981 Almanac p. 256)*

The Education and Labor Committee had reported a new job-creation bill (HR 6250) in May, but a whole new authorization would have taken too long to pass to get the program going in 1982.

Similarly, public works projects, used to combat past recessions, were considered to be ineffective against the immediate unemployment problem because they took so long to get started.

The only remaining choice was CETA. While CETA was a logical choice as an authorization for a jobs program — at one time, it had authorized more than 700,000 public service jobs — it was burdened by one of the worst reputations in Congress of any social program. CETA was dogged by charges of widespread waste and fraud throughout much of its history, and was to be replaced by a much smaller job training program beginning in fiscal 1983. *(Job training bill, p. 39)*

The first bill introduced by the task force (H J Res 514) would have relied on existing CETA authority for a fiscal 1982 jobs appropriation. However, that idea ran into trouble in the Appropriations Committee, where Chairman Jamie L. Whitten, D-Miss., refused to support any more funds for CETA.

Instead, the Appropriations Committee approved a second version, H J Res 562, that contained its own, separate authorization as well as an appropriation. The panel reported the measure Aug. 18 (H Rept 97-764).

Normally, appropriations bills were prohibited by House rules from including authorizing legislation. But because it applied to only one appropriations account, H J Res 562 could contain its own authorization.

Fifty Years of U.S. Job Creation Efforts

Throughout their history, federal job-creating programs have had the conflicting goals of making permanent improvements in the economic backbone of the country, and immediately helping people who need jobs.

Carefully planned, long-range capital improvements are a boon to future generations. But they are slow in helping hungry people in need.

Quick-starting repair and service projects ameliorate present suffering. But they do little lasting good, are open to fraud and waste, and are branded forever as "make-work, leaf-raking" jobs.

From the New Deal. . .

Two programs with similar initials, the Public Works Administration (PWA) and Works Progress Administration (WPA), reflected the contrasting sides of job-creation under the New Deal.

The PWA, established in 1933 with initial funding of $3.3 billion, focused on long-range projects. The program lasted for six years and spent a total of $6 billion.

PWA workers pushed the Skyline Drive through Virginia's Blue Ridge Mountains. They dug tunnels for subways in Chicago, built aircraft carriers and hundreds of schools and flood control projects. During the program's heyday, PWA workers helped build two-thirds of the new schools and sewage plants in the country.

Interior Secretary Harold L. Ickes ran PWA with a tight fist. He reviewed all projects, keeping the program free from any significant charges of waste or fraud.

But Ickes' careful stewardship slowed down the program. He was criticized by other members of the Roosevelt administration who argued that the PWA was failing to provide needed economic stimulus.

Better known than the PWA was the WPA, which stressed rapid employment for the jobless. It was set up by Congress in 1935 with a $5 billion appropriation. By 1943, when it ended, the WPA had cost $11 billion.

Under presidential adviser Harry Hopkins, the WPA provided a bewildering variety of jobs ranging from construction to the arts. Its participants worked on an estimated 600,000 miles of highways, 125,000 public buildings and 8,000 parks.

WPA workers also wrote a classic series of guides to the states, put on plays and circuses, performed symphonies and painted murals in post offices and other public buildings around the country.

All told, an estimated eight million workers received help from the program. During the height of the WPA, from 1935 to 1941, an average of 2.1 million people were on the rolls at any one time.

But the program was run poorly. Much of the money was spent on administration, and construction standards were low. To much of the public, WPA workers seemed forever to be resting on their shovels.

Other New Deal jobs programs included the Civilian Conservation Corps (CCC), which employed young men in environmental projects, and the Civil Works Administration (CWA), a short-lived program in the winter of 1933-34 that was plagued by waste and corruption charges.

. . .To the Eighties

After a hiatus of two decades, the government returned to direct job creation programs in the 1960s.

Congress in 1962 passed a $900 million accelerated public works bill (PL 87-658). It was a scaled-down version of President Kennedy's $2 billion proposal for pump-priming public works spending. *(Congress and the Nation Vol. I, p. 877)*

In the early 1970s, Congress and President Nixon clashed repeatedly over job-creating programs. After two successful vetoes, bills establishing a $2.25 billion public service employment program (PL 92-54) and a $3.9 billion public works program (PL 92-65) were enacted in 1971. *(1971 Almanac p. 187)*

The big program of the decade was the Local Public Works program (LPW) enacted in 1976-77.

Acting against the mid-decade recession, Congress in 1976 passed a $2 billion program (PL 94-369) over President Ford's veto. It was followed in 1977 by a $4 billion addition (PL 95-28), proposed by President Carter as part of his economic stimulus package. *(1976 Almanac, p. 76; 1977 Almanac p. 112)*

LPW funded a total of 10,616 projects. Most of the projects involved work on sewers, streets and bridges, and local government buildings.

A related program, like LPW run by the Economic Development Administration (EDA), continued to fund public works projects in economically depressed areas. *(EDA extension, p. 62)*

The other main federal job-creation programs were under the Comprehensive Employment and Training Act (CETA). Along with job training programs, CETA provided as many as 750,000 public jobs during the early years of the Carter administration.

There was a substantial amount of waste and fraud in CETA's public service employment programs, however, and the jobs generally were of little permanent benefit. Congress abolished public service employment in 1981, and even its most ardent supporters made only a token effort to re-establish it during 1982 congressional consideration of the job training legislation that replaced CETA. *(Job training, p. 39)*

Floor Debate

During floor debate Sept. 16, Republicans derided H J Res 562 as a "bottle of economic moonshine labeled 'Old Budget-Buster,'" a "callous, election-year gimmick," a "billion-dollar ballot-box bailout bill," a "watermelon," a "hoax," and a "phony."

But their opposition was overwhelmed by Democrats who openly challenged the GOP to oppose such a program shortly before the Nov. 2 congressional elections while the nation's unemployment rate had approached double digits.

"I find it amazing that there are actually members of this Congress in September 1982 who are going to go and

campaign on the basis that they voted against this bill," John Conyers Jr., D-Mich., exclaimed with relish on the floor. "Fantastic!"

Speaker Thomas P. O'Neill Jr., D-Mass., chided Minority Leader Robert H. Michel, R-Ill., personally. O'Neill said there were four bridges needing repair in Peoria, Ill., part of Michel's district, and 16 percent unemployment. "You have an opportunity to repair some needed work in your own area," O'Neill declared.

Michel responded, "In my home community of Peoria, I can assure you that Reaganomics is going to play much better than Tip O'Nomics."

Republican Substitute

Before passing the Democratic bill, the House rejected 152-243 a Republican substitute sponsored by Lynn Martin, R-Ill., who was designated by Michel to offer a GOP alternative. *(Vote 318, p. 94-H)*

Her approach called for a $1.5 billion jobs program targeted only at localities with unemployment above the national average.

The $1.5 billion would be transferred from budget authority already approved for the Synthetic Fuels Corporation but not expected to be spent for several years. Jobs created under Martin's plan would involve the same public-works chores as in the Democratic bill. But 75 percent of the hiring would have to be of workers who already received or had exhausted unemployment benefits, or of beneficiaries of Aid to Families with Dependent Children, thus replacing benefits under these programs.

As a result, Martin claimed, the GOP plan "would create twice the jobs at half the cost."

Republican leaders complained that their party had been forced to draft a substitute with less than one day's notice by a surprise rule adopted Sept. 15 by the Rules Committee.

The rule allowed only one amendment, to be offered by Michel or his designee, on the House floor. The committee approved the procedure without notifying Michel that he was expected to have a substitute. ∎

Economic Development

Legislation (HR 6100) to extend the Economic Development Administration (EDA) fell prey to opposition from the administration and Senate Republicans in 1982.

The existing authorization for the economic development program expired Sept. 30, but Congress provided $168.5 million in fiscal 1983 funding for EDA, plus $30 million in transfers of unobligated funds, through a continuing appropriations resolution (H J Res 631) cleared Dec. 20. *(Continuing resolution, p. 238; previous action, 1981 Almanac p. 108)*

While not a large program — spending over the years for its public works development totaled about $5 billion — the Commerce Department's EDA provided a good example of the limbo into which many Great Society programs had fallen under the Reagan administration. From the time of his first budget, Reagan had sought to abolish the EDA.

The idea behind the program was that communities afflicted with poverty or high unemployment lacked the resources to pay for the infrastructure of public facilities needed to support economic growth. Funds had gone for everything from sewer construction to renovation of old market buildings for new stores.

The most telling criticism of the economic development program was that Congress gradually had expanded its jurisdiction until almost all of the country was eligible for assistance that was supposed to be reserved for impoverished communities.

Especially after it became the vehicle for a separate $6-billion public works program pushed by congressional Democrats to combat the 1974-75 recession, EDA was attacked as fostering wasteful pork-barrel projects. The symbol of that criticism was the replica of the Great Pyramid being built with EDA funds in southern Indiana.

Background

In the past, legislative battles over EDA had arisen from two different sources: efforts by Republican presidents to abolish the program, and by congressional Democrats to make it a vehicle for broader anti-recession programs.

The basic legislation (PL 89-136) establishing the EDA was passed by Congress in 1965. Backed by the Johnson administration, the legislation expanded a smaller area redevelopment program set up in 1962. *(Congress and the Nation Vol. II, p. 290)*

Over the years, Congress repeatedly reauthorized the EDA program, as well as those for the Appalachian Regional Commission (ARC), which fostered anti-poverty programs and highways in a 13-state area. Twice during the Nixon administration Congress tried to transform the EDA program into a counter-cyclical program to combat joblessness. President Nixon successfully vetoed both bills. *(Congress and the Nation Vol. III, p. 178)*

Nixon then tried to abolish the EDA in 1973, with its functions distributed to other agencies. Congress did not buy the idea, however, and continued reauthorizing the program at two- or three-year intervals. *(Congress and the Nation Vol. IV, p. 144)*

In 1976 and 1977, Congress approved a total of $6 billion in counter-cyclical public works projects, to be spent by EDA. The first year, the aid was approved over President Ford's veto; the second year, with President Carter's support. *(Congress and the Nation Vol. IV, p. 708; Vol. V, p. 401)*

Carter later sought to expand EDA's lending power, as part of his urban policy. The proposal died in Congress after Reagan's election. *(1980 Almanac p. 306)*

By 1982, EDA was operating a number of different programs for distressed areas. Grants were given to eligible areas that could show that federally funded projects would aid their overall economic development. In addition, the agency provided loans to developing businesses, and financed planning and technical assistance to help areas plan their economic development.

The ARC funded both social-service programs, such as health facilities and vocational training, and construction of highways in the Appalachian region.

Administration Criticisms

In calling for the abolition of EDA, Reagan administration officials attacked its program as being too thinly spread around the country, too costly and too slow to do much good.

When the EDA was established in 1965, about 12 percent of the country was eligible for aid. Projects were

supposed to be limited to areas with particularly severe economic problems.

But the tendency in Congress to let more areas into the program was irresistible.

By 1982, eligibility for the program had expanded to include 80 percent of the population. It would have been even higher if House Democrats had had their way — in 1979, they approved a bill to cover 90 percent.

In addition, argued Assistant Secretary of Commerce Carlos C. Campbell, the aid did not necessarily go to areas with the worst problems. Michigan, for example, had 7 percent of all the unemployed people in 1980, but got only 4 percent of EDA money. New York, with only slightly more unemployed, 7.8 percent of the total, got 13.6 percent of the funds.

Another problem with the program was that it was a fairly expensive way to provide jobs. According to the Commerce Department, each job cost around $40,000 to create. Other estimates were lower: The House Economic Development Subcommittee estimated that it took $22,000 in public works spending for each job.

The administration also attacked the EDA loan program to businesses as inefficient and unreliable. EDA found that of the $1 billion in direct and guaranteed loans, nearly half were delinquent, having fallen at least 30 days late in payment.

Finally, EDA public works jobs were found to be generally ineffective in combating temporary unemployment. The projects took so long to get started that by the time workers were hired, the recession was over. EDA in 1982 was still overseeing projects funded by the anti-recession bills of 1976 and 1977.

House Action

A heavy majority in the House supported extension of EDA, albeit with some changes. By a 281-95 vote, the House Aug. 12 passed HR 6100, which authorized three years of development assistance, at $500 million a year. The bill had been reported by the Public Works and Transportation Committee May 17 (H Rept 97-540). *(House vote 263, p. 78-H)*

Responding to criticisms of the existing EDA program, HR 6100 focused eligibility for aid on areas with severe problems. The bill also extended the authorization for the Appalachian Regional Commission. Funding for ARC programs was to be gradually reduced, until the non-highway programs were terminated by 1987.

James L. Oberstar, D-Minn., chairman of the House Public Works Subcommittee on Economic Development, and other sponsors of HR 6100 argued that their bill answered administration criticisms of the EDA program.

Most importantly, the bill would reduce the scope of the program, so that only 41 percent of the population would be eligible for assistance. The only areas that could get aid would be those that had had unemployment rates one percentage point over the national average for the preceding two years, or had per-capita incomes below 80 percent of the national average or were about to experience a sudden increase in unemployment.

Even those areas that were eligible for aid, however, would have to prove that they could use it effectively before getting any money. The bill would require areas to show how they would use federal funds, as part of an overall economic strategy, to achieve their goals.

The legislation would end direct federal involvement with loan and loan guarantee programs to businesses. Instead, it would allow areas to apply for grants of up to $1 million, to establish revolving funds for loans to small businesses.

Senate Action

In contrast to the House, the Senate Environment and Public Works Committee three times during the 97th Congress voted against recommending funds for EDA.

However, the Senate did not go along with the Reagan administration in its efforts to do away immediately with the non-highway programs of the ARC. The commission had some determined allies in the Senate, especially Jennings Randolph, D-W.Va.

The Senate passed S 2144, to provide a one-year extension of the ARC, by voice vote June 9. The bill had been reported by the Environment and Public Works Committee May 28 (S Rept 97-452).

Although the Senate-passed bill dealt only with the ARC, the House Aug. 12 sought a conference on S 2144 and its own broader measure.

"Senators want to see the ARC continue. The only way they will see that is to go to conference with HR 6100. It's a question of who will blink first," said Rep. William F. Clinger Jr., R-Pa.

But the Senate did not agree to a conference, and the legislation died when Congress adjourned. However, funding for ARC was included in the second fiscal 1983 continuing resolution (H J Res 631). *(Energy/water appropriations, p. 292)* ∎

Production Act/Stimulus

Congress Oct. 2 completed action on a stopgap, six-month extension of the Defense Production Act, after a five-year extension measure became embroiled in an attempt by House Democrats to establish a $6.75 billion economic stimulus program.

Both the House and the Senate, during early-morning sessions that began Oct. 1, gave voice vote approval to a bill (S 2375 — PL 97-336) extending the defense production law through March 31, 1983. Authority for the program had expired after Sept. 30. *(1981 Almanac p. 205)*

The Defense Production Act, first passed in 1950, gave the president various economic powers to ensure defense-related production during times of national emergency.

Action on the reauthorization legislation was slowed by House Democrats' efforts to attach the stimulus program. The way was cleared for final action on S 2375 when Democratic sponsors of the stimulus plan won a promise that their legislation would be considered again on the House floor during the post-election session. The measure was not brought up in the lame-duck session, however.

The House Sept. 23 had considered the Defense Industrial Base Revitalization Act (HR 5540), which would have established a $6.75 billion, five-year program of grants and loans for small-business and job-training aid. But the bill, which also included a five-year extension of the Defense Production Act, was pulled from the schedule after Republicans won a key vote on an amendment to limit loan authority under the new program.

Democratic Stimulus Plan

Unable to defeat a key Republican amendment, House Democratic leaders decided Sept. 23 to postpone further floor action on HR 5540, the $6.75 billion stimulus plan.

The action followed the adoption, by a 173-154 vote, of an amendment offered by Bill McCollum, R-Fla. The amendment gave the Treasury Department the right to block loans and loan guarantees under the bill if it determined that they would lead to higher interest rates. Bill sponsor James J. Blanchard, D-Mich., described the amendment as a "killer" provision. *(Vote 346, p. 102-H)*

HR 5540 sought to help ailing industries by making loans and payments to small businesses struggling against foreign competition and other economic problems. The five-year authorization bill also would have established a new vocational education program, and provided high-technology equipment to colleges and universities for use in professional training.

HR 5540 authorized $1 billion a year in economic aid to small firms. Funds were to be distributed, in the form of direct or guaranteed loans, price guarantees or purchase agreements, to industries that the Defense and Commerce departments decided were essential to national defense and most in need of help.

The $250 million in annual vocational training funds was to be distributed through state governments. The states would have to contribute an increasing share of their own funds to match the money provided by the federal government.

Another $100 million a year was to go to institutions of higher education, to purchase equipment needed to train personnel for key industries.

Blanchard said the aim of the bill was to help small businesses modernize their equipment in order to survive and be ready in case they were needed in time of war. They were unable to take advantage of the investment incentives provided by the 1981 tax cut, he said. Another goal of the legislation was to reduce U.S. dependence on the importation of key materials used in defense production.

In addition, the vocational education sections of the bill sought to fill what some experts predicted would be a growing shortage of highly skilled people to fill jobs such as machinists and tool and die makers.

Critics of the measure, such as Ed Bethune, R-Ark., argued that it was nothing but a massive subsidy to businesses largely unrelated to national defense. The Reagan administration also opposed the bill.

The legislation enjoyed bipartisan support, however. It had backing from a majority of Republicans on the Banking Committee, which along with the Education and Labor Committee reported the measure May 17 (H Rept 97-530, Parts I and II).

Democrats on the Education panel supported the bill, but only if they did not have to pay for it. Education Chairman Carl D. Perkins, D-Ky., successfully offered an amendment during initial House debate Aug. 18 to ensure that any spending for the new programs come out of the budget allocation for defense programs, and not from the education and labor accounts.

Despite complaints from Armed Services Committee members that they had no extra money to give up, the House adopted Perkins' amendment 242-180. *(Vote 279, p. 82-H)*

Defense Production Act Extension

The main issue during the hurried congressional consideration of S 2375 was how long the bill would extend the existing Defense Production Act. Originally reported (S Rept 97-412) by the Banking Committee May 21 with a five-year extension, the bill was brought to the Senate floor on Oct. 1 as a one-year measure.

The fight over the expiration date, not in itself controversial, really was over subtle tactical considerations involving the fate of HR 5540 in the House. The issue was complicated by the fact that unanimous consent was needed to consider the bill, thus giving any member the ability to block final action on the emergency extension.

HR 5540 sponsor Blanchard favored a three-month extension. That would have forced Congress to consider another extension during the post-election session, providing a second opportunity to push the new program contained in HR 5540. House opponents of HR 5540, led by Bethune, wanted a longer expiration date that would eliminate the need for reopening the issue until 1983.

Anxious to pass a Defense Production Act extension that would gain House approval in the final hours of the session, the Senate Oct. 1 first passed S 2375 with a 90-day extension. The amendment to terminate the extension on Dec. 31, 1982, offered by James A. McClure, R-Idaho, was adopted 49-37. *(Vote 383, p. 64-S)*

Before passing S 2375, the Senate adopted amendments to establish a White House Conference on Productivity, and a presidential commission on the stockpiling of strategic materials.

In the House, the dispute between Blanchard and Bethune was resolved by amending S 2375 to provide for a six-month extension of the Defense Production Act. After stripping S 2375 of all its provisions except the six-month extension, the House early Oct. 2 passed the bill by voice vote. The Senate accepted the House version, clearing the measure.

Productivity Conference. Since the White House productivity conference was taken out of S 2375, both House and Senate by voice votes Oct. 2 passed a separate bill (HR 7292 — PL 97-367) to authorize the conference in 1983. The conference was to explore the causes of the recent declines in productivity growth, and ways to increase productivity.　■

Monetary Policy

Congressional Democrats tried to bring the issue of high interest rates to the House and Senate floors in 1982, but rates dropped as the year advanced, robbing the issue of political momentum.

Congress did include in the fiscal 1983 budget resolution (S Con Res 92), cleared June 23, a non-binding declaration that the Federal Reserve should re-evaluate its monetary targets if Congress made substantial progress toward reducing budget deficits. The move reflected an argument advanced by many economists who blamed the debilitating effects of high interest rates on Fed policy. *(Budget resolution, p. 186)*

In addition, Democrats in both houses tried to press two major pieces of credit-related legislation:

One would have restored and expanded the authority of the president and the Federal Reserve Board to control credit; the other would have directed the Fed to emphasize the regulation of interest rates rather than trying to manipulate the "money supply" as it had done since 1979.

Credit Controls

A credit-control bill (HR 6124 — H Rept 97-774) was reported by the House Banking Committee Aug. 19, but there was no further action on the measure.

The bill would have restored presidential authority to have the Fed impose sweeping controls over borrowing and lending throughout the economy. Such authority, which the 96th Congress voted to kill in the wake of President Carter's use of the power, lapsed July 1. The Fed and the Reagan administration opposed restoration of the power. *(1980 Almanac p. 305)*

The House bill also would have expanded the president's powers by bestowing explicit authority to invoke controls during times of recession and high unemployment. In addition, it would have given the Fed authority to collect information on bank loans of $100 million or more granted for the purpose of corporate mergers, and the power to forbid such "non-productive" loans.

A similar bill (S 2526) was introduced in the Senate by Minority Whip Alan Cranston, D-Calif., but the Senate did not act on the measure.

Fed Policy

The other major Democratic thrust was aimed at reshaping Federal Reserve policy.

Democratic leaders in both houses introduced separate versions of legislation (HR 6967, S 2807) entitled the Balanced Monetary Policy Act of 1982, but there was no action on the measures.

The bills shared a common purpose: to force the Fed to abandon its emphasis on controlling the "money supply" — the economy's total cash plus funds in various accounts at banks and other financial institutions.

But efforts to coordinate the work of Senate and House Democrats were not entirely successful. "It was a disaster," said one Democratic aide.

Reflecting theoretical disagreements over monetary economics, the two versions of the bill differed on a key point:

The Senate bill, sponsored by Minority Leader Robert C. Byrd, D-W.Va., and 32 other Democrats, would have directed the Fed to target "positive real short-term interest rates" — keeping short-term rates a few percentage points above the rate of inflation.

The House bill was sponsored by Majority Leader Jim Wright, D-Texas, Banking Chairman Fernand J. St Germain, D-R.I., Joint Economic Chairman Henry S. Reuss, D-Wis., and 63 other members. It would have required the Fed to target long-term interest rates, with no adjustment for inflation. HR 6967 also would have given the central bank more flexibility than the Senate bill in emphasizing interest rates over the money supply, and required the president to take a public position on Fed decisions.

Gold Commission Recommendations. In a related action, the Gold Commission, mandated by Congress in 1980 to study whether the United States should again back the dollar with gold, voted 15-2 Feb. 12 against a return to the gold standard. The standard had long been pushed by supply-side advocates as a necessary step for getting inflation and interest rates under control.

However, the 17-member panel recommended that the Treasury issue new gold coins to be sold at market value, with a slight markup to cover minting costs. The coin would be exempt from capital gains and sales taxes but would not be considered legal tender. ∎

Union Corruption

Two bills aimed at cracking down on alleged union corruption died at the end of the 97th Congress.

After passing the Senate easily, the Labor Racketeering Act (S 1785) and legislation revising the federal workers' compensation law for longshore workers (S 1182) ran into fatal opposition in the House, especially from Labor-Management Subcommittee Chairman Phillip Burton, D-Calif.

The House took no action on either measure.

S 1785, which had AFL-CIO support, was opposed by the Teamsters union. While union management negotiators had settled some disagreements over S 1182, Burton and others worried that the bill would restrict coverage of the longshore act too much.

S 1785, approved by the Senate July 28, would have increased the penalties for illegal practices by union and management officials. It also would have barred union officials who had been convicted of labor crimes from continuing to hold their union offices.

With S 1785 blocked in the House, sponsor Sam Nunn, D-Ga., sought to attach its provisions to other legislation. The Senate Dec. 19 added the text of the measure to an unrelated, minor House bill (HR 1029), but there was no further action on it.

S 1182, which would have limited future increases in benefits paid to disabled dockworkers, passed the Senate by voice vote July 27. Pushed by a coalition of shipping and insurance companies, the bill also would have limited the jurisdiction of the federal program, which provided disability insurance for dockworkers not covered by state workers' compensation laws.

The longshore bill also contained anti-fraud provisions designed to stop alleged abuse of the program by organized crime. According to backers, led by Nunn, the legislation also would prevent unethical physicians from certifying that a worker was disabled, and thus eligible for benefits, even if he was not.

Action on Racketeering Bill

The Senate July 28 passed S 1785 by voice vote.

Nunn, whose investigations of waterfront corruption provided the impetus for the measure, called it "the most significant piece of anti-racketeering legislation that has come through the Congress since the Landrum-Griffin bill" of 1959. *(Congress and the Nation Vol. I, p. 568)*

Supporters of the legislation, including Labor Committee Chairman Orrin G. Hatch, R-Utah, described the existing penalties against labor-management corruption as weak, and enforcement of laws as often lax. Because of those inadequacies, Nunn said, crooked officials with ties to organized crime were able to dominate labor activities in the longshore, restaurant and other industries.

S 1785 increased the monetary fines for the purchase of "labor peace" — bribes to union officials to maintain pro-management policies. It also expanded the list of crimes for which union officials could be barred from holding office if convicted, and lengthened the time during which they would be barred.

In addition, the measure excluded officials from union office upon conviction for labor offenses — thus preventing a recurrence of the situation found by the Senate Permanent Subcommittee on Investigations, in which convicted officials continued serving in office for years, pending out-

come of their appeals.

As an example of the sort of problem the bill was trying to prevent, Hatch cited the case of Landon Williams, a Florida official of the International Longshoreman's Association. Despite a 1979 conviction for accepting bribes, Hatch said, Williams continued to serve as union local president and trustee of union pension plans.

Another provision of the bill expanded the responsibilities of the Labor Department in seeking prosecution of labor law violators. Hearings by both the Labor Committee and the Investigations Subcommittee during the 97th Congress had led to charges of inadequate enforcement by the department, particularly under Employee Retirement and Income Security Act (ERISA) rules against pension fund misuse.

Committee Report. The Labor Committee reported S 1785 July 19 (S Rept 97-497). The bill was approved by voice vote.

Major provisions of the committee-approved bill:

● Increased the maximum penalty for violation of certain anti-racketeering laws by labor or management officials to five years' imprisonment and a $15,000 fine, from one year's imprisonment and a $10,000 fine.

● Expanded the list of offenses for which a convicted person could be disqualified from serving in a union or benefit plan office; also expanded the list of union or benefit plan offices from which convicted persons were barred.

● Increased the maximum period of disqualification from union or benefit plan offices to 10 years from five.

● Required that persons convicted of certain labor-related offenses be excluded from union or benefit plan office upon conviction, rather than upon conclusion of the appeals process, as under existing law.

● Emphasized the Labor Department's responsibility to refer to the Justice Department evidence relating to potential prosecutions under labor and pension statutes.

Action on Longshore Bill

The Senate passed the longshore bill, which limited to 5 percent a year benefit increases in the program for disabled longshoremen, by voice vote July 27.

The product of lengthy negotiations between Republicans and Democrats on the Senate Labor Committee, S 1182 also contained other provisions to scale back jurisdiction and benefits under the longshoremen's program. However, it did not go as far in limiting the program as the Reagan administration or a coalition of insurers and port businesses had sought.

S 1182 was reported by the Labor Committee July 19 (S Rept 97-498). Differences over two key issues — jurisdiction of the program and the bill's anti-fraud provisions — had held the bill up for months.

Congress in 1972 expanded the traditional jurisdiction of the 1927 Longshoremen's and Harbor Workers' Compensation Act, covering only persons actually working over water, to include other workers engaged in maritime activities. The Reagan administration wanted to return to the more restrictive coverage. *(Background, 1972 Almanac p. 134)*

The compromise approved by the committee specifically excluded from coverage certain businesses, such as builders of small vessels, and certain types of jobs, such as clerks in shipping businesses.

The anti-fraud provisions were based on evidence from the Senate Permanent Subcommittee on Investigations,

which found that organized crime was manipulating the program to obtain the high disability benefits provided by insurers. A key element in the abuse of the program was reliance on certain unethical doctors to certify that a worker was disabled, even if he really was not.

The original version of S 1182 had sought to limit the injured worker's previously unrestricted choice of doctor to one whose name appeared on a list approved by the Labor Department. The compromise allowed the department to compile a list of doctors who could not be used to evaluate injuries. ∎

Migrant Farm Worker Relief

Congress Dec. 20 approved a major revision of federal laws governing the treatment of migrant farm workers.

The bill (HR 7102 — PL 97-470) replaced the existing Farm Labor Contractor Registration Act (FLCRA) with a new set of federal protections for migrant and seasonal workers.

Final action came when the House by voice vote accepted the version of the bill passed by the Senate Dec. 19. The House had reported the bill (H Rept 97-885) Sept. 28.

The measure was a compromise that enjoyed support from the Reagan administration, unions and agricultural employers. The only serious obstacle it encountered came in the Senate, where Sam Nunn, D-Ga., temporarily blocked action in hopes of using the bill as a vehicle for anti-racketeering legislation (S 1785) that was stalled in the House. *(Story, p. 65)*

Registration of Contractors

Agricultural groups had pushed for the legislation because farmers resented the burdens imposed on them by FLCRA (PL 88-582), which was passed by Congress in 1963 to prevent abuses by "crew leaders" — independent contractors who recruit and transport migrant workers from farm to farm. Its most important provision required contractors to register with the Labor Department. Congress in 1974 enacted amendments (PL 93-518) that broadened the coverage of the 1963 act and toughened its penalties. *(1963 law, Congress and the Nation Vol. I, p. 760; 1974 amendments, Vol. IV, p. 728)*

The Labor Department in recent years had required many farmers to register under the law as farm labor contractors. HR 7102 would prevent that by exempting "fixed-site" farm employers from the registration requirements imposed on farm labor contractors.

However, farm employers as well as farm labor contractors would have to satisfy other requirements in the bill relating to treatment of workers. The bill required that workers receive adequate housing, safe transportation and correct information about their pay.

Final Provisions

As cleared by Congress, HR 7102:

● Made clear that fixed-site farm employers were not farm labor contractors, and thus were not required to register as such with the Labor Department.

● Defined farm labor contractors as persons who recruited, hired and transported migrant farm workers.

● Required farm labor contractors to register with the Labor Department; allowed the department to refuse to provide registration certificates to persons convicted of

certain crimes.

● Prohibited farm labor contractors from knowingly hiring illegal aliens.

● Established protections for migrant farm workers by requiring farm employers as well as farm labor contractors to meet a series of standards involving payroll records, health, safety and housing.

● Created a separate legal category for seasonal farm workers, who performed temporary farm labor while returning to their homes each night; also established standards governing treatment of such workers.

● Provided for regulations governing the safe transportation of migrant and seasonal farm workers.

● Established criminal and civil penalties for violation of the law.

● Provided exemptions from the provisions of the bill for small and family businesses.   ∎

Donovan Investigation

Concluding a nine-month investigation, federal special prosecutor Leon Silverman announced Sept. 13 that he had uncovered no evidence to warrant bringing charges against Labor Secretary Raymond J. Donovan.

As he had in an earlier report on Donovan released in June, Silverman said there was "insufficient credible evidence" to support allegations of Donovan's ties with organized crime and labor corruption.

But Silverman said he remained troubled by the frequency of reports from witnesses that Donovan was linked with the criminal underworld.

Responding to the report — and particularly to the fact that one witness had recanted earlier allegations against him — Donovan said he was "angry that I have had to endure months and months of relentless press coverage of groundless charges made by nameless accusers."

Interest in the Silverman investigation was heightened after the Aug. 25 murder of Nathan Masselli, the son of an underworld figure with alleged ties to Donovan. However, Silverman said that he had found no evidence to connect Donovan with the case.

The earlier report, released June 28, had focused on a charge that Donovan had participated in an illegal payoff by his New Jersey construction firm to a corrupt labor union official. Silverman found there was "insufficient credible evidence on which to base a prosecution" of Donovan on charges involving labor corruption and links to organized crime.

The prosecutor's report left several loose threads hanging about other allegations involving Donovan and his firm, Schiavone Construction Co. It said there were a "disturbing" number of allegations that Donovan was connected with organized crime figures.

In addition, the special prosecutor turned over certain aspects of the case to other federal agencies for further investigation.

Background

A three-judge federal court panel in Washington, D.C. on Dec. 29, 1981, appointed Silverman, a New York City attorney, to investigate allegations of corruption against Donovan. The appointment of a special prosecutor had been requested by Donovan.

Although President Reagan stood behind his embat-

tled Cabinet secretary throughout the ensuing investigation, the crisis found Donovan with few other strong political allies. Senate Democrats June 15 called for Donovan to step down from his post, at least until Silverman completed his inquiry. And Senate Labor Committee Chairman Orrin G. Hatch, R-Utah, expressed doubt about Donovan's ability to fulfill his duties in the face of widespread criticism. AFL-CIO and other union leaders already had broken relations with Donovan over other issues.

Questions about Donovan's past had surfaced shortly after he was nominated for the labor post in 1981.

The first round of allegations held up Donovan's confirmation for several weeks early in 1981. They ranged from the general observation of one informer that the Schiavone Co. was "mobbed up," to specific accounts of illegal payoffs allegedly made by the company to local union leaders.

Accepting the argument that nothing had been proven against Donovan, who heatedly denied wrongdoing, the Senate approved his nomination 80-17. It was subsequently disclosed that the FBI had damaging information that was provided to the White House but withheld from the Senate Labor Committee hearings on Donovan's confirmation. *(Confirmation, 1981 Almanac p. 17-A)*   ∎

Canadian Port Diversion

Legislation designed to discourage the channeling of U.S. foreign trade through Canadian ports was approved by two House committees, but the House did not act on the measure in 1982.

The bill (HR 3637 — H Rept 97-419, Parts I and II) would have put foreign ocean carriers shipping U.S. goods through Canadian ports on the same regulatory footing as vessels operating out of U.S. ports. It was reported April 6, 1982, by the Energy and Commerce Committee and Dec. 30, 1981, by the Merchant Marine and Fisheries Committee.

East Coast U.S. ports said carriers shipping U.S exports and imports through Canadian ports enjoyed an unfair competitive advantage because they were not bound by the same tariff rules.

On the West Coast, much of the Canadian traffic went through U.S. ports, which were better equipped to handle it.

Foreign carriers operating out of Canadian ports used trucks or rail to haul the goods to and from U.S. cities.

Changes in Existing Law

Under existing law, only vessels operating out of U.S. ports had to file their tariffs with the Federal Maritime Commission (FMC) and were required to make the same rate available to all similarly situated shippers.

As reported, HR 3637 required foreign carriers that solicited traffic and arranged for transportation from points within the United States to file tariffs with the FMC.

Supporters said the bill would not require foreign carriers to raise rates. Opponents, however, argued that it would indeed increase transport costs.

The Canadian government opposed the bill, which it said "would be an attempt to exercise unacceptable extraterritorial jurisdiction."   ∎

Urban Enterprise Zones

President Reagan's only new program to help cities — his proposal to create "enterprise zones" to revive decaying urban areas — made little headway in Congress in 1982.

The plan, disclosed by Reagan March 23, aimed to revitalize blighted areas by providing federal tax and regulatory relief to businesses that invested in economically depressed inner cities and rural towns.

A modified version of the proposal was approved Sept. 28 by the Senate Finance Committee as part of an unrelated tax bill (HR 7094), but there was no further action and the legislation died when Congress adjourned.

Although administration officials described the enterprise zone proposal as a key element in Reagan's urban policy, congressional aides said they gave it low priority. House Democratic leaders staunchly opposed the plan.

Because of the lack of any other offers from the administration, most urban groups endorsed the enterprise zone concept. But they warned that it would not make up for cuts in federal aid cities had suffered under Reagan's policies. "We're a lot worse off than we were two years ago," said John Gunther, executive director of the U.S. Conference of Mayors.

Critics argued that the program would not succeed because the zones would merely lure businesses away from other parts of a city. And special tax treatment, they said, would give an unfair competitive edge to some firms.

Reagan Proposal

Although Reagan had promoted the idea in his 1980 campaign, the administration did not present its plan to Congress until March 23, 1982.

"The enterprise zone concept is based on utilizing the market to solve urban problems, relying primarily on private sector institutions," Reagan said in a message to Congress. He said the approach would reverse a tradition of heavy government subsidies to spur economic growth. *(Text, p. 17-E)*

Reagan's program closely resembled an enterprise zone bill (HR 3824) introduced in 1981 by Reps. Jack F. Kemp, R-N.Y., and Robert Garcia, D-N.Y. Sen. John H. Chafee, R-R.I. sponsored the Kemp-Garcia bill in the Senate (S 1310).

The administration described its plan as "an experimental, free-market initiative" to create jobs and stimulate new economic activity.

Up to 25 zones a year would be selected by the secretary of housing and urban development in the first three years. Cities and states would nominate areas, which must be hard-hit by poverty and unemployment.

Because of the emphasis on tax relief, the Treasury Department estimated each zone would cost the federal government $12.4 million a year in lost tax revenue.

Tax concessions offered to businesses locating in the zones would include a credit for capital investments, a 10 percent income tax credit to employers for payroll paid to qualified zone employees in excess of payroll paid in the previous year, a 50 percent credit to employers on wages paid to disadvantaged employees and the elimination of capital gains taxes.

Federal agencies could relax or eliminate some regulations within the zone upon the request of state and local governments, but health, safety or civil rights rules would not be touched.

The White House suggested that state and local governments could reduce taxes in the zones; loosen zoning, licensing, permit and building code requirements; and fund job-training or other economic development.

Finance Committee Action

After two years in legislative limbo, the enterprise zone plan got a push from the Senate Finance Committee just before Congress departed for the campaign season.

As approved by the committee Sept. 28, the plan would provide tax and regulatory relief to businesses that created new jobs in depressed neighborhoods. The measure was reported (S Rept 97-662) Oct. 18 as an amendment to HR 7094, an unrelated House-passed bill dealing with pension plan taxation.

Under the Finance Committee bill, enterprise zones would be selected on the basis of an area's unemployment, poverty level and population loss; 25 zones would be created annually for three years.

In a concession to farm-state senators, the panel decided that eight zones per year would be in rural areas. Of the 2,000 communities eligible for the program, 1,500 had populations of 50,000 or less, according to officials at the Department of Housing and Urban Development.

The proposal carried a relatively low cost, compared to some of the major urban programs of the past two decades. The Treasury Department estimated a tax loss of about $400 million per year for 25 zones, although the Joint Committee on Taxation said the actual cost could be considerably higher or lower. ∎

Efforts to Revise Housing Programs Collapse

Congress adjourned without enacting a fiscal 1983 housing authorization bill, partly because of the reluctance of House Democrats to tailor their legislation to fit spending constraints set by President Reagan and the congressional budget resolution.

The House Banking, Finance and Urban Affairs Committee rejected Reagan's proposal to slash federal housing programs, and the panel's legislation far exceeded spending ceilings recommended by the president and the budget. It was not until December — too late for adequate floor consideration — that committee Democrats agreed to lower their sights and settle for a smaller housing program.

When Congress recessed Oct. 2 for the elections break, it had not approved authorizations reported by committees in May (HR 6296 — H Rept 97-532, S 2607 — S Rept 97-463), and fiscal 1983 began with no new budget authority for subsidized housing.

Funds for a number of Department of Housing and Urban Development (HUD) programs had been included in a regular appropriations bill (HR 6956 — PL 97-272) cleared in September, but money for most subsidized low-income housing had been excluded pending enactment of an authorization. *(Appropriations, p. 231)*

When it appeared that the lame-duck session would

end without action on authorizing legislation, subsidized housing funds were included in the continuing resolution (H J Res 631 — PL 97-377) cleared Dec. 20. *(Story, p. 238)*

For fiscal 1983, H J Res 631 appropriated $8.65 billion for existing low-income housing programs. Funds also were included for 2,000 units of Indian housing and 14,000 units for the elderly and handicapped. The resolution provided an additional $2.5 billion in new budget authority for public housing modernization.

The resolution largely continued existing programs, in contrast to the plans of House and Senate Banking committees, which would have revamped housing programs through their authorization bills.

The authorizations reported by the Banking panels differed widely, but each included new housing production and rehabilitation initiatives to replace the troubled Section 8 housing program. Section 8, the primary program to provide rental assistance to low-income families, was criticized for its high costs and other shortcomings.

In a fundamental shift in federal housing policies, the administration wanted to end construction aid for low-income housing and instead to provide vouchers that poor families could apply toward rental housing.

The House Banking, Finance and Urban Affairs Committee bill rejected the voucher plan, but the Senate Banking, Housing and Urban Affairs Committee included a modified program in its bill.

Both bills also exceeded the administration's funding request. Nearly all of the money in Reagan's fiscal 1983 housing budget would have come from rescissions of funds previously obligated — including a rescission of $5 billion for subsidized housing — so virtually no new budget authority had been requested.

For fiscal 1983 housing programs, the president in February requested outlays of $7.67 billion, compared to $8.55 billion in 1982. Budget authority — the amount the government could obligate — would have dropped from $33.4 billion in 1981 to $13.02 billion in 1982 and $684 million in 1983.

Congress had authorized $18.09 billion for assisted housing in fiscal 1982, which included about 153,000 new units (PL 97-35). *(1981 Almanac p. 110)*

HR 6296 as reported May 17 totaled $29.1 billion in budget authority for fiscal 1983 for assisted housing, rural housing and other HUD programs, according to the Congressional Budget Office (CBO). The Senate committee bill reported May 28 totaled $14 billion for fiscal 1983, CBO said, while the first budget resolution (S Con Res 92) passed by Congress in June allowed $17 billion. *(Story p. 186)*

In addition, both bills authorized $4.2 billion for the Community Development Block Grants and Urban Development Action Grants, the same level as set by a three-year authorization (PL 96-399) approved in 1980. *(1980 Almanac p. 279)*

Soon after the bills were reported, they ran into opposition. A key point against the House committee bill was its cost. In the Senate, controversy surrounded a proposal to convert Farmers Home Administration (FmHA) rural housing programs into block grants to the states. Senate leaders also were unwilling to bring the measure to the floor unless they were certain the House would act on a housing bill.

Another problem was that some of Congress' energy for housing legislation was sapped by a fight over an emer-

gency mortgage subsidy program considered in the spring of 1982 to help shore up the sagging housing industry. The president vetoed the mortgage aid plan and Congress failed to override the veto. *(Box p. 71)*

Without a HUD authorization, some programs expired Sept. 30. The main program, the Federal Housing Administration (FHA) insurance program, was extended until May 20, 1983, by separate legislation (H J Res 612 — PL 97-289).

Other major programs were not affected either because they had multi-year authorizations, such as the Community Development Block Grants, or because money had been committed in earlier years, such as with Section 8 housing subsidies.

Senate Committee

On May 28, the Senate Banking, Housing and Urban Affairs Committee unanimously reported a bipartisan three-year HUD authorization (S 2607 — S Rept 97-463).

The bill authorized $6.86 billion in fiscal 1983, $1.1 billion in fiscal 1984 and $862 million in fiscal 1985. In addition to the $6.86 billion for 1983, however, the bill authorized $7.2 billion for subsidized housing using already appropriated funds that were expected to be recaptured through deobligations, that is by pulling back money for projects in the process of obtaining approval. Those recaptures never occurred, however, and the actual budget authority required by the bill for 1983 was $14 billion, according to CBO.

The authorization included a rental production and rehabilitation program with funding at $300 million. The program would have awarded grants to cities with rental housing shortages to renovate or build new rental housing. Very-low income tenants of buildings rehabilitated under the program were to receive assistance through the modified Section 8 voucher program.

Funds would have been distributed to states and local communities from the Community Development Block Grant program and would have been primarily for rehabilitation. The bill authorized $4.196 billion for community development grants, up from $4.166 billion for fiscal 1982.

Except for housing for the elderly and handicapped, all Section 8 new construction authority would have been replaced by a modified voucher program. The vouchers would have been for a five-year period and issued to public housing agencies on behalf of very-low income families (at or below 50 percent of the median income).

The recipients would have received cash to shop directly for housing. Under the existing system, developers received subsidies for particular housing units. The voucher program would have covered approximately 137,000 units, according to CBO.

Initially, floor consideration of S 2607 was delayed by negotiations on the rural housing clause. Minority Whip Alan Cranston, D-Calif., opposed plans to cut rural housing funding and turn the programs over to the states to run as they chose.

In addition, S 2607 was attacked by William L. Armstrong, R-Colo., who placed a hold on the bill. Armstrong disliked the bill's plans to provide vouchers to help poor families pay their rents, according to Peter Harkins, staff director of the Senate Housing subcommittee.

The Senate leadership also showed little interest in the measure as hopes dimmed for House action.

"The biggest problem consistently since May was the

House's inability to get anything done," Harkins said. "Given the crush of business and filibusters going on, the Senate was only going to act on bills that had a chance of becoming law."

Rural Housing

The disagreement on the rural housing block grants involved who should run rural housing programs: the federal government, through the 33-year-old Farmers Home Administration (FmHA) program, or the states, using federal block grants.

And a secondary question was: How much money should be spent to improve rural housing conditions in America?

The Banking Committee adopted the proposal of Sen. Harrison "Jack" Schmitt, R-N.M., the chairman of the Senate Banking subcommittee on rural housing, to lump rural housing aid into a block grant to be administered by states as they desired.

In addition, he proposed a sharp cut in federal rural housing spending — from \$4.2 billion in fiscal 1982 to about \$2.5 billion in fiscal 1983 — and suggested that FmHA charge prevailing interest rates on its loans, instead of continuing to subsidize rates to as low as 1 percent.

Thad Cochran, R-Miss., chairman of a Senate Agriculture subcommittee and the Appropriations subcommittee on agriculture, joined Cranston in fighting the measure.

They argued that the block grant concept was still too experimental to replace the time-tested FmHA program. Also, they warned that the spending cuts could seriously harm the supply of housing credit in rural areas. By raising interest rates and the income ceiling needed to qualify for housing loans, Schmitt's proposal would have made it difficult for rural Americans to find home financing, Cochran said.

Although the Reagan administration had officially endorsed the block grant proposal, there were quiet rumblings of dissent within the Agriculture Department.

Officials there said they believed the plan could disrupt a program that they said generally worked well. They also cautioned that unless proposed interest rate increases were phased in carefully, there could be widespread defaults on FmHA loans and enormous losses to the government.

The Reagan administration had proposed slashing FmHA funds for rural housing loans by about two-thirds.

In his Feb. 8 budget message, President Reagan recommended \$1.1 billion in fiscal 1983 for rural housing loan programs, a drop from \$3.7 billion in fiscal 1982. The 1983 budget called for 32,830 housing units, compared to 104,680 units in 1982. *(Budget message, p. 6-E)*

In its first budget resolution (S Con Res 92) adopted in June, Congress rejected Reagan's FmHA housing cuts. Instead, the resolution called for fiscal 1982 funding levels. *(Story, p. 186)*

House Committee

A wide-ranging bill (HR 6296 — H Rept 97-532) rebuffing administration proposals to slash housing aid was reported by the House Banking, Finance and Urban Affairs Committee May 17. The bill, authorizing \$29.1 billion for HUD and rural housing programs in fiscal 1983 and \$200 million for fiscal 1984, was approved in a 24-18 party-line vote and was nearly identical to the version passed May 5 by the Housing Subcommittee.

With a new \$1.3 billion program to produce rental housing, the legislation rejected Reagan's proposal to end federal subsidies for low-income housing construction. The new rental production program would have provided grants to cities and states to use toward the cost of constructing or rehabilitating multifamily housing in areas with a severe shortage of affordable rental housing. The bill required that at least 20 percent of the units in any project had to be affordable to poor families.

The bill included \$3.5 billion to stimulate single-family housing production and \$1.1 billion for the Section 235 program to help lower-income families buy homes.

The \$3.5 billion to help the depressed housing industry was directed at middle-income families who could not afford to buy a home because of high interest rates. The mortgage subsidy plan resembled a bill (S 2226) approved by the Senate Banking Committee April 21. While the Senate panel handled its HUD authorization and mortgage subsidy proposals as separate bills, the House committee insisted that the two issues be considered together.

HR 6296 reversed provisions of the 1981 budget reconciliation act raising the rent of tenants of assisted housing from 25 percent of income to 30 percent. The bill would have returned the rent payment to 25 percent of income. Because the bill never was approved, HUD implemented the rent increase through regulations. *(1981 Almanac p. 111)*

Subcommittee

The Banking Subcommittee on Housing and Community Development worked on the Democratic proposal April 27, April 29, May 4 and May 5.

Before approving the bill by a 23-4 vote May 5, the subcommittee rejected an administration-supported amendment that would have offered direct cash payments to the poor to apply toward rent. The panel also defeated a Republican amendment to ban the use of rental housing production funds in cities with rent control or rent stabilization laws.

The subcommittee preserved two programs the administration wanted to eliminate: Section 312 rehabilitation loans and Section 108 loan guarantees to help communities purchase or improve public properties.

The legislation, as later approved by the full committee, was stymied throughout the summer as members tried to whittle the cost to bring it within the \$17 billion limit on budget authority for all housing imposed by the first budget resolution (S Con Res 92).

In a letter Sept. 2 to Fernand J. St Germain, D-R.I., chairman of the Banking Committee, and to Henry B. Gonzalez, D-Texas, chairman of the Housing Subcommittee, a coalition of interest groups pressed for enactment of an authorization that included a program to produce new rental housing for low- and moderate-income people.

The letter, signed by 30 national groups including Americans for Democratic Action, the AFL-CIO Building and Construction Trades Department, the Mortgage Bankers Association and the U.S. Conference of Mayors, said they would settle for the \$10.4 billion the budget resolution allowed for low-income housing.

The first break in the impasse occurred Dec. 1 when Democrats on the House Banking panel caucused and agreed to cut the \$29.1 billion authorization to about \$17 billion. Their goal was to meet the budget resolution's requirements and to give guidance to the House Appropriations Committee.

Emergency Mortgage Aid Plan Failed

In the midst of the worst housing industry depression since World War II, Congress in 1982 approved an emergency mortgage subsidy program to revive the housing market. But President Reagan refused to sign the measure, and Congress failed to override his veto.

The $3 billion measure was inserted into an urgent supplemental appropriations bill (HR 5922) vetoed by the president June 24. The proposal was designed to stimulate single-family home construction and create jobs in the building trades by subsidizing interest rates for buyers of new homes. *(Story p. 205)*

The plan was crafted by the home building and lumber industries, which were battered by the recession and high interest rates. Home builders called for action by June 1 so that help would come during the 1982 building season.

Reagan opposed the legislation, however, calling it a "budget-busting bailout."

Noting that farmers, small businesses, the thrift industry and automobile manufacturers also were suffering from the recession and high interest rates, Reagan said, "We cannot justify singling out one industry for special relief."

Reagan said, "We will not promote a housing recovery by going even deeper in debt. More red ink spending will only make the housing recession worse."

Genesis of Plan

Although the mortgage aid program was included in HR 5922, the subsidy had its genesis in other bills.

The idea was presented in March by Sen. Richard G. Lugar, R-Ind., and it quickly became identified as the "Lugar bill."

Lugar's measure (S 2226 — S Rept 97-362) was unanimously approved by the Senate Banking Committee April 21. It was a five-year, $5.1 billion program that would have brought down the mortgage interest rate on new homes by as much as 4 percentage points.

At prevailing rates of 15½ percent, for instance, the government would have brought down the rate to 11½ percent, although the rate could not have dropped below 11 percent. Subsidies would have been available to families with an annual income of $30,000 or less who were buying newly constructed homes.

"Housing has led us out of past recessions, and it can do so again," Lugar said. He said the bill could put 700,000 persons back to work in construction-related jobs and spur up to 450,000 new housing starts in 1982.

A similar bill (HR 5834) was introduced in the House by Jerry M. Patterson, D-Calif., and Les AuCoin, D-Ore. The House Banking Committee wrapped elements of the Patterson-AuCoin proposal into the panel's fiscal 1983 authorization for the Department of Housing and Urban Development (HUD) (HR 6296). *(Story p. 68)*

That bill, which was not acted upon by Congress before adjournment, authorized $3.5 billion in fiscal 1983 for subsidies to moderate-income home buyers, but no money for fiscal 1982. Committee leaders said they wanted to include the mortgage aid plan in the HUD bill to ensure support for less-popular low-income housing programs also contained in the bill.

Democratic Counterproposal

In early May, political pressures forced House Democratic leaders to design a separate bill (HR 6294) that would have started the mortgage subsidy in fiscal 1982.

House Democratic leaders made the $1 billion mortgage plan a cornerstone of a $2 billion jobs program announced May 7 to combat a 9.4 percent unemployment rate. Other funds were to be funneled into public works projects to create jobs in the construction trades, where unemployment was 19.4 percent.

"HR 6294 is much more than a housing bill. It is clearly a jobs bill for an industry that has all but been wiped off the books by high interest rates," said House Banking Committee Chairman Fernand J. St Germain, D-R.I.

On May 11 the House voted 349-55 to approve HR 6294, authorizing $1 billion in 1982 to subsidize mortgage rates by as much as 6 percentage points. *(Vote 63, p. 20-H)*

The next day, the House appropriated the $1 billion through the supplemental appropriations bill (HR 5922) and included HR 6294's authorizing language in that legislation.

The Senate went along with the idea of including the mortgage subsidy in the supplemental appropriations bill. By a 69-23 vote May 27, it attached the full $5.1 billion Lugar plan to HR 5922, authorizing the program and appropriating its funds at the same time. *(Vote 167, p. 29-S)*

Compromise Reached

Despite the threat of a presidential veto, House and Senate conferees on HR 5922 June 10 reached agreement on a $3 billion compromise for the mortgage subsidy program — halfway between the $5.1 billion approved by the Senate and the $1 billion backed by the House. Their report, H Rept 97-605, was filed June 10.

Of the $3 billion total for the program, $2.5 billion would have gone for mortgage subsidies for newly built homes. Families with incomes up to $30,000 a year would have been eligible for mortgages 4 percentage points below the market rate, down to an 11 percent rate.

Another $400 million would have been provided for mortgages on homes that had been built but not sold; the remaining funds were for subsidies on homes in "high cost" areas.

Reagan fulfilled his promise and vetoed HR 5922 June 24. *(Veto message, p. 24-E)*

Despite earlier support for the subsidy program, the House failed by 17 votes June 24 to obtain the two-thirds majority needed to override Reagan's veto. The vote was 253-151. *(Vote 165, p. 48-H)*

The panel's Democrats lowered the subsidized housing section of the bill from $16 billion to $10.4 billion, the amount allowed by the budget resolution.

Low-income housing advocates lobbied intensely for a pared-down bill.

In a Nov. 22 letter to House Speaker Thomas P. O'Neill Jr., D-Mass., hundreds of housing groups asked for lame-duck action to end "the de facto congressional moratorium" on low-income housing aid.

"This is a time of housing crisis, epecially for low-income people," the letter said. "New production is at its lowest level in two generations. Rents in the private market are beyond the reach of millions of low-income households. An ever-growing number of people are homeless — unable to find any accommodations whatsoever. Almost 20 percent of all construction workers are unemployed."

But the reduced bill never reached the floor before the 97th Congress adjourned. ∎

Defense

At a minimum, the political momentum of Ronald Reagan's defense buildup was partly checked by Congress in the second half of 1982:

• His original $258 billion Pentagon budget was pared rather than being revised in any basic way. But the chilling prospect of massive budget deficits led Congress to make an unprecedentedly large — though diffuse — reduction of nearly $19 billion in budget authority, a cut of 7.27 percent in the program.

• Congress' refusal to approve initial production funds for the MX intercontinental missile in late December marked the first time the legislature had ever denied funds for a major nuclear weapon requested by a president, though the action was a deferral rather than an outright cancellation of the missile.

• And in early August, the House fell a single vote shy of calling for a nuclear arms freeze that the administration had spent a tremendous amount of political capital to oppose. This followed by only two weeks a House vote against production of a new form of lethal chemical weapons, after a debate in which arms control arguments dominated arguments against the weapons.

In each of those battles some Republicans and conservative Democrats, who typically had been bedrock supporters of a hard line on defense issues, defected from the administration line.

One spur to that political hemorrhage was the contrast between continued defense spending increases and the administration's calls for greater domestic austerity at a time when deficits were reaching record-high levels.

Another contributing factor was the administration's occasional insensitivity to the fine line between "toughness" in the international arena and politically unpalatable bellicosity.

For the most part, Reagan and his aides managed in 1982 to avoid the sort of provocative statements on nuclear war that had created alarm throughout the world in 1981. Those statements — such as Reagan's offhand musings October 16 about the possibility of limiting nuclear war to Europe — created the impression that he was too casual in his willingness to countenance nuclear war as an instrument of policy.

But the political burden of those earlier statements lingered through 1982. And the apprehension was widespread in Washington and among U.S. European allies that the administration would be too rigid to reach any nuclear arms limitation agreement.

Compounding the administration's political problems was an apparently widespread suspicion that neither Reagan nor Defense Secretary Caspar W. Weinberger had a firm personal grip on the details of defense policy. That belief was linked to complaints that there was no underlying purpose to the administration's defense buildup — that the services simply had been allowed to go on uncoordinated buying sprees.

Defense Budget Totals

Shortly after taking office, Reagan proposed a five-year (fiscal 1982-86) defense plan costing $1.47 trillion, and an additional increase of $6.8 billion for a fiscal 1981 supplemental defense appropriation above Carter's planned supplemental request. This initial Reagan plan would have cost about $200.9 billion more than Jimmy Carter had projected for the same period.

Congress at first seemed disposed to give Reagan nearly all of what he asked. And in February 1982, his new five-year plan (covering fiscal years 1983-87) came to a total of $1.7 trillion.

But by the end of 1982, after a faltering economy had forced two years of compromises with congressional budgeteers, Reagan's defense plans had been trimmed by $27 billion.

Reagan's $263 billion fiscal 1983 request for defense programs (including both the Pentagon and nuclear weapons programs run by the Energy Department) came in a key year for several weapons programs that were crucial to the Reagan plan. Funds were requested for the first seven production-line models of a new version of the B-1 bomber ($4 billion), the first nine production versions of the MX missile ($1.5 billion) and the two nuclear-powered aircraft carriers that would be the core of the naval expansion ($6.8 billion).

From the outset, the fiscal 1983 request came under heavy fire both from prominent conservatives — who were alarmed at a prospective fiscal 1983 deficit that was almost universally expected to run far above the projected $91.5 billion — and from liberals who were outraged that the Pentagon budget would grow 13.1 percent in real terms while many domestic programs were being effectively slashed.

Pre-emptive Attack. But the Pentagon went on the offensive, insisting in its earliest presentations to congressional committees that management improvements and cost-reduction initiatives under the leadership of Deputy Defense Secretary Frank C. Carlucci already had wrung the budget dry of unnecessary spending.

Carlucci and other officials claimed these reforms had saved $7.4 billion in the fiscal 1983 budget and would save a total of $51.5 billion through fiscal 1987. Critics, however, immediately pointed out that a governmentwide pay cap on federal employees accounted for more than half of the $51.5 billion savings.

The administration also maintained that its budget would save money over the long run by spending a little more immediately: making more realistic — and thus higher — estimates of the cost of inflation and buying some weapons in larger lots to achieve some economies of scale.

The most dramatic instance of such spending immediately to save later was the decision to buy two *Nimitz*-class nuclear aircraft carriers in a single $6.8 billion package. According to the Navy, this would save $754 million and 21

months compared to the usual pattern of contracting for the ships separately, three or four years apart.

Most galling to some Pentagon critics was the administration argument that defense cuts would offer little help in reducing the projected deficit. Significant reductions in the personnel and operations requests would yield immediate cuts in outlays, but would risk sharp reductions in the number and combat-readiness of units in the field, the Pentagon warned.

On the other hand, reductions in the weapons procurement accounts, which were the target of many liberal critics, would yield only small outlay reductions in fiscal 1983. For instance, Carlucci told reporters Feb. 6, if Congress refused to appropriate the entire $19.5 billion requested for the B-1 bomber, the MX missile, two carriers, two Trident submarines and the cruise missile program, fiscal 1983 outlays would drop by only $5 billion.

Budget Negotiations. Congress and the White House were deadlocked over Reagan's overall budget proposal until early May, when Senate GOP leaders drove a new budget bargain with Reagan that included $95 billion in tax hikes, $40 billion in unspecified savings in Social Security and a $22 billion reduction in defense outlays (other than pay caps) over a three-year period.

Subsequent negotiations with the House yielded further defense cuts in the final version of the first concurrent budget resolution (S Con Res 92) cleared June 23. That left Congress committed — with administration concurrence — to a reduction in fiscal 1983 defense outlays of almost $9 billion below the level projected in Reagan's initial budget.

(Since subsequent battles over the defense budget were dominated by a concern for reducing the projected deficit, most rounds of the battle were fought over the figure for outlays, which represented actual spending, rather than the figure for budget authority, which set the total funding levels for programs.)

With the annual defense authorization bill (S 2248) on the Senate floor during the budget negotiations in May, the Senate Armed Services Committee proposed a $2.8 billion reduction in new budget authority — on top of $3.3 billion the panel already had trimmed from the authorization request.

The House Armed Services Committee, which had trimmed some $3.2 billion from its version of the military authorization bill (HR 6030), cut another $3.2 billion on the House floor to bring the new, lower ceiling within reach. And the House took a symbolic swipe at the Pentagon by approving an additional across-the-board cut of 1 percent, amounting to $1.7 billion in budget authority.

The final version of S 2248, cleared for the president Aug. 18, authorized $177.9 billion in new budget authority, $5.59 billion less than Reagan originally had requested for the portions of his defense budget requiring annual authorization.

According to the Congressional Budget Office, this was expected to trim some $2.6 billion from estimated defense outlays in fiscal 1983. A pay cap and reductions in other defense-related bills brought the total defense outlay reduction to about $4.6 billion by the time the Appropriations committees began to work the problem.

Appropriations Battles. The defense ceiling in the budget resolution was, in effect, slightly reduced when the two Appropriations committees allocated the congressional budget among their subcommittees.

The Senate panel increased the defense outlay reduc-

tion by only a slight amount. But the defense appropriations bill then was stalled because of a disagreement between the Senate Defense Appropriations Subcommittee and Secretary Weinberger over just how deep an outlay reduction the administration had agreed to in June.

At issue was a provision in the budget resolution that was separate from the ceilings allocated to defense and other budget areas. It required each federal agency to absorb from within its budget one half the cost of the 4 percent pay hike granted to all federal workers.

The Defense Appropriations Subcommittee insisted that this required a total reduction in outlays from the defense bill of $8.7 billion below the Reagan request. Weinberger balked at what he insisted was an additional $1.2 billion cut beyond the level to which he had agreed.

After a few days, the impasse was broken simply by deferring the pay absorption question, though the subcommittee declared its determination to make the additional cut.

As reported Sept. 23 by the full Senate Appropriations Committee, the bill (S 2951 — S Rept 97-580) cut $12.1 billion from Reagan's original request for new budget authority, which the panel estimated would reduce outlays by $8.7 billion.

In the post-election session in December, the defense bill was approved by the Senate, essentially as reported by the Appropriations panel, as part of a continuing resolution (H J Res 631).

During debate on the continuing resolution, an amendment that would have reduced budget authority for procurement and research by an additional $5.6 billion was rejected 52-45, with members splitting essentially along liberal-conservative lines.

The House version of the defense appropriations measure (HR 7355), passed Dec. 8, was $17.99 billion below Reagan's request for new budget authority in the bill. That 7.2 percent was the largest congressional swipe at a defense bill in years.

The total new budget authority in the final defense appropriations bill, which was incorporated into the continuing resolution, was closer to the House-passed figure than the Senate total: $232 billion.

By CBO's estimate, this put the politically vital outlay total for all defense activities in fiscal 1983 at $212.4 billion — $8.7 billion lower than the administration's February 1982 request. For the Defense Department alone, the outlay total was projected at $206.6 billion, down from an initial request of $215.9 billion.

Few Casualties. Despite the size of the congressional reduction, most of it came from routine cheeseparing rather than dramatic changes in the shape of Reagan's program.

The bulk of the cut came from various kinds of bureaucratic belt-tightening — most directly, by a $2.3 billion reduction in the size of the annual pay hike, an austerity measure imposed on all federal agencies. A substantial portion of the reduction came from changes in the facts of life since the budget was drafted, such as the $833 million cut in fuel purchase funds, reflecting the continuing decline in the cost of petroleum.

Nearly $9 billion in budget authority was cut from weapons procurement requests. But with few exceptions — the MX and Pershing II missiles and the new chemical weapons — major programs were subjected only to relatively minor slowdowns in the planned rate of production.

For example, predominantly liberal critics of the Pen-

tagon budget had targeted several new Army weapons as too complex and too costly. But none of them — the M-1 tank, the M-2 armored troop carrier, nor the Apache anti-tank helicopter — suffered serious program cuts.

Neither was there any immediate challenge to the Navy buildup, which had become a symbolic totem of the overall Reagan defense plan. With the two additional nuclear carriers fully funded at year's end, John F. Lehman Jr., the administration's aggressive — some would say abrasive — Navy secretary could boast that the "600-ship Navy" was well along to becoming an accomplished fact.

A minor cloud on the Navy's horizon was Congress' refusal to provide a $94 million down payment on the conversion of a third battleship to carry long-range cruise missiles. But the first of the converted ships, the *New Jersey,* was recommissioned on Dec. 28 and the continuing resolution contained $301 million to complete conversion of the second, the *Iowa.*

There were only minor changes in the requests for combat aircraft except for the A-10 tank-hunting bomber. In a wrestling match redolent of the aroma of the pork barrel, funds requested for 20 of the planes were not authorized (at the insistence of Senate Armed Services) but were appropriated. However the A-10 money could be spent only in the unlikely event that both Armed Services panels approved. In both the Senate and House Appropriations committees, members of the New York congressional delegation had insisted on appropriations for the A-10, which was built on Long Island.

The most heated contest of the whole defense funding cycle on Capitol Hill — apart from the MX missile fight — was a viciously lobbied battle among major aircraft manufacturers over long-range transport planes. After an embarrassing loss in the Senate to supporters of the Boeing 747, the administration prevailed on its plan to buy an additional 50 Lockheed C-5 transports. However, a token amount was added to the defense budget to buy a few used 747s and development funds for a new, smaller long-range plane (the McDonnell-Douglas C-17) were increased.

Except for the Navy, Reagan's plans to increase the size of the U.S. combat force were deferred in the course of budget-cutting negotiations with Congress. But most of the proposed increases would not have occurred before mid-decade in any case.

Nuclear Missiles, Arms Control

The administration's most dramatic congressional setbacks came in the fields of nuclear weaponry and arms control. And by nearly all accounts, the damage was largely self-inflicted.

Low confidence in the administration's commitment to arms control was the key factor in the nuclear freeze campaign's near humiliation of the president in the House. A switch of one vote in the Aug. 5 showdown would have given the battle to freeze backers.

In the form nearly approved by the House, the freeze resolution called on the United States and Soviet Union to "decide when and how" to begin a freeze on the testing, production or deployment of nuclear weapons or nuclear delivery vehicles (such as long-range bombers or missiles).

Such an approach was clearly at odds with the Reagan administration's fundamental premise on nuclear arms issues: the belief that the current U.S.-Soviet nuclear balance was dangerously tilted to Moscow's advantage, largely because previous administrations of both parties had placed too much faith in arms control agreements as a way

to deal with Moscow's nuclear buildup.

Widespread public concern over the administration's nuclear arms policies, fostered in part by apparently loose administration talk about the prospect of a "limited" nuclear war, had boosted the freeze movement to national prominence in the first place.

After the scope of the freeze movement had become evident, Reagan unveiled on May 9 a negotiating offer for the Strategic Arms Reduction Talks (START) with Moscow, that would sharply cut both arsenals of land-based ICBMs to the equal levels far lower than the current U.S. force.

In November 1981, Reagan had temporarily regained the political initiative on the nuclear arms issue by a similar move, proposing the abolition of U.S. and Soviet medium-range missiles in Europe. But the freeze movement had gained too much momentum to be deflected by the START proposal. Even later in the month, when Reagan said he would not violate the limits of the unratified SALT II treaty, provided Moscow did likewise, he accomplished little more than frustrating hard-line conservatives who remained profoundly suspicious that the whole arms control process undermined public support for U.S. rearmament.

A fundamental belief of these conservative critics was that the entire U.S.-Soviet strategic arms control process that produced the SALT I and SALT II agreements had worked to Moscow's advantage. According to this view, the pacts favored the Russians to start with, the Soviets cheated on them to boot, and the American policy was so hypnotized by the existence of an arms control agreement that it could not muster the resources to offset the Soviet buildup and did not even challenge the cheating.

Spearheaded by Sen. Jesse Helms, R-N.C., on Capitol Hill and, reputedly, by Assistant Secretary of Defense Richard N. Perle, a former aide to Sen. Henry M. Jackson, D-Wash., these conservatives vigorously opposed any arms control agreements that did not essentially eliminate the large, multiple-warhead ballistic missiles that were the core of the Soviet strategic arsenal. Any half-measures, they warned, would leave a substantial Russian threat in place while sapping the U.S. will to field countervailing weapons.

The administration eventually staved off defeat in the freeze battle by offering moderate Republicans and conservative Democrats an alternative resolution that used the politically potent word "freeze," but redefined it to support the administration insistence that a freeze would occur only after both superpower strategic arsenals had been reduced to lower and equal levels.

And Reagan whipped in the last few votes needed for victory by warning that a vote for the freeze would undermine U.S. SALT negotiators, a contention buttressed by SALT Ambassador Edward L. Rowny in phone calls to wavering members from Geneva.

But even as it was wringing out its narrow win, the administration encountered blunt warnings from some of its supporters that, while they were willing to let the president try arms control talks on its own terms, they wanted results.

And the scope of public concern over the nuclear arms issue was underscored anew in the November elections. Referendums calling for a freeze were adopted by voters in California, Massachusetts, Michigan, Montana, New Jersey, North Dakota and the District of Columbia. The freeze resolution failed only in Arizona.

There were other signs of a widespread congressional

hopefulness for arms control, which stood in stark contrast to the hostility of many defense hard-liners, including some senior officials in the Reagan Pentagon.

During debate on the defense authorization bill in July, the House in effect voted 192-225 against beginning production of so-called "binary munitions," which would have been the first, lethal chemical weapons produced by the United States in 13 years. Arms control and diplomatic arguments dominated the case against the chemical weapons.

On the other hand, the House rejected by hefty margins amendments that would have canceled programs (including the B-1 bomber and the Trident-missile-carrying submarine) that some liberals warned would pose too dangerous a threat to the Soviet Union.

MX Missile. Alarm over the risks of a nuclear arms race also loomed large in the opposition to procurement of the MX missile. But the state of the economy and the Democrats' edge in the November elections also contributed to the unprecedented House vote on Dec. 7 against procurement of a major nuclear weapon requested by a president.

The defense appropriations bill, within which MX procurement was debated, offered members their first post-election opportunity for a symbolic vote to restrain the Pentagon budget. Democratic gains were widely interpreted as reflecting public sentiment to trim Reagan's defense plan. And what singled out MX as the sacrificial goat was another series of Reagan team fumbles.

The question of the MX "basing mode" — the kind of launchers in which the new missiles would be emplaced — had become a running gag as the administration strove to come up with a technique that would be politically acceptable and militarily effective.

The public goal of the MX program long had been deployment of the new missiles in a basing mode that would be proof against a surprise attack by Moscow's ICBMs. The theoretical vulnerability to such attack of the current fleet of Minuteman missiles, deployed in underground silos, was the basic political rationale for the MX program.

During his presidential campaign, Reagan had condemned the basing method endorsed by the Air Force, the Ford administration and, reluctantly, by Jimmy Carter. This would have scattered thousands of underground launch sites across Utah and Nevada among which 200 MXs would be shuttled at random.

In October 1981, Reagan killed the Carter plan, to the glee of liberals who opposed MX in any form and conservatives from Utah and Nevada. But his alternative was to deploy 40 MXs in Minuteman silos while deferring until 1984 a choice among several radically new long-term deployment methods, including launching the missiles from giant airplanes.

That temporary alternative was rejected overwhelmingly by the Senate, led by Armed Services Committee members who remained committed to the Carter approach.

In spring of 1982, Senate Armed Services gave the screw another turn by refusing to approve funds for the initial purchase of production line MXs unless Reagan chose by December a basing mode that would enable the missiles to survive a Soviet attack.

The White House concurred and began to concentrate on a new approach, to which the Air Force and some Senate Armed Services members turned when it appeared that Reagan would not retract his condemnation of the Carter plan. This was "dense pack," which would have deployed 100 MXs in very heavily armored silos close enough together that, according to the Pentagon, attacking Soviet missiles would destroy each other while leaving most of the MXs intact.

But the president committed himself to the dense pack method only in late November. When the House faced an MX decision Dec. 7, only a handful of members had been briefed on the novel and untested approach.

Despite Reagan's strenuous invocation of the previously powerful argument that he needed MX to strengthen his hand at the START table, the House rejected, by a 245-176 vote, funds to produce the first five MX missiles.

Though the Senate approved MX production funds by a vote of 56-42 on Dec. 16, the House position prevailed in the conference committee on defense funding.

—By Pat Towell

Strategic Arms Top List of Defense Cuts

About a third of the congressional reductions in President Reagan's defense authorization request came from strategic war programs, which accounted for only about 9 percent of the original fiscal 1983 defense budget.

The $177.9 billion fiscal 1983 authorization bill (S 2248) was cleared for the president Aug. 18, and signed into law on Sept. 8 (PL 97-252).

Of some $5 billion actually cut from planned programs in the final version of the bill, $1.6 billion came from four large cuts in strategic programs:

● $699 million associated with the approval of only one Trident missile-launching submarine instead of two requested;

● $414 million from the MX intercontinental missile program, partly because procurement of five missiles was authorized instead of the requested nine;

● $350 million of $727 million requested for development of an anti-ballistic missile system;

● $100 million of $254 million requested for civil defense planning.

Though they accounted for a relatively small part of the total defense budget, the strategic programs experienced proportionately rapid growth under Reagan.

The defense bill also reduced Reagan's request by $638 million through essentially bookkeeping changes that did not reduce the size of the defense program funded under the bill. These changes included lower-than-estimated fuel prices and increases in the value of the dollar against some foreign currencies.

Apart from fuel and currency adjustments, the authorization for operations and maintenance activities was cut by only $479 million. This compared with reductions of $3.16 billion in procurement and $1.2 billion in research and development.

Some $230 million of the operations and maintenance reduction came from decisions to mothball 13 ships earlier than had been planned and to defer activation of a new Air Force wing.

In all, S 2248 reduced Reagan's authorization request by $5.6 billion. But the bill made little substantial change in Reagan's program.

The only major weapon denied by Congress was a new class of lethal nerve gas bombs and artillery shells, called binary munitions. By a margin of 3-2, the House had denied the $54 million requested to begin production of the new weapons, and the conferees reluctantly concurred.

The conference report on S 2248 (H Rept 97-749) was filed Aug. 16. It was approved by the Senate Aug. 17 by a vote of 77-21, and by the House Aug. 18 on a 251-148 vote. *(Senate vote 331, p. 54-S; House vote 284, p. 84-S)*

Conference Report

The conferees approved $177.87 billion, which was $5.59 billion less than the president had requested in February. The conference total was almost $20 million higher than the amount authorized by the Senate and $801 million above the House-passed authorization of $177.066 billion. *(Chart, p. 79)*

The conferees dropped a provision added on the House floor that would have held actual expenditures on the authorized programs to $175.3 billion, 1 percent less than the House-passed total.

Senate conferees insisted adamantly that any reductions be made in specific programs, rather than by granting the executive branch discretion to apply a percentage cut within the whole range of authorized programs.

However, House rules required a conference committee to settle disputed amounts within the range bounded by the amounts passed by the Senate and House. When applied to the accounts included in the defense authorization bill, following that rule would have made it impossible to reduce the bill's total amount to $175.3 billion.

Budget Ceiling. The conferees pointed out that there was no direct relationship between the total authorized by the defense authorization bill and the defense ceiling set by the first budget resolution, which limited appropriations.

Nevertheless, the conferees maintained they had been mindful that the budget resolution had set a ceiling $9.8 billion below Reagan's fiscal 1983 request for defense appropriations. The conference report on S 2248 took a big step toward that goal by cutting $5.6 billion from Reagan's request for programs covered by the bill, they said. Additional reductions would come in other bills covering nuclear weapons, military pay and military construction and in the companion appropriations bills.

Fiscal 1982 Supplemental. The conference report also included $182.4 million in supplemental authorizations for fiscal 1982, of which $120 million was to buy KC-10s, tanker versions of the DC-10 airliner.

The administration had requested $1.45 billion in supplemental authorization. The House approved no funds and the Senate $830.5 million.

Strategic Warfare

Both Armed Services committees and the Air Force long had endorsed a proposal to shuttle MX intercontinental ballistic missiles (ICBMs) among more than 20 launch sites to thwart a Soviet attack. President Carter reluctantly agreed to the shuttle system in 1978, but Reagan, who had ridiculed the shuttle during the 1980 presidential campaign, canceled the plan in October 1981.

Reagan proposed deploying the first 40 MXs in existing Minuteman missile silos while studying various alternative basing schemes that, he maintained, would be better able than the shuttle to survive a Soviet attack.

For fiscal 1983, Reagan requested $4.256 billion in MX funds: $1.497 billion to manufacture the first nine missiles, $1.734 billion to continue development of the missile, $715 million for research related to the proposed deployment in Minuteman silos and $310 million for research on long-term basing methods.

The House Armed Services Committee made relatively small reductions in the MX request, and the full House narrowly rejected a move to dent the procurement funds. But the Senate had denied all procurement authorization and had cut $715 million from the development request. The Senate Armed Services Committee had intended those reductions as a signal to the administration that Congress would not fund the proposed interim deployment method.

To begin procurement of the MXs, the conferees authorized $830 million for the first five production-line missiles and $158 million for support equipment, some of which would be related to the basing of the missiles.

The conferees retained a provision, adopted on the

House floor, barring expenditure of the $158 million until Congress had 30 days in session to review the permanent basing method chosen by the president for the MX.

Also authorized was $2.51 billion for MX development, of which $715 million was subject to the same requirement of 30 days' prior congressional notice.

The conferees dropped a Senate-passed requirement that Reagan choose a survivable MX basing method by Dec. 1, a deadline to which the White House had agreed after the Senate passed S 2248. But the conferees asked Reagan to include in his report on the basing decision any additional refinements that the Pentagon might plan to add to whatever basing method was chosen.

Anti-Missile Defense. The conferees approved $377.1 million of the $727.3 million requested to develop an anti-missile missile system, called LoADS, intended to protect MX missiles against Soviet missile attack. Until the MX basing method was chosen, they said, it would be "ill-advised" to accelerate the LoADS program so rapidly.

For research on more exotic anti-missile programs that might use laser-armed satellites or other "directed-energy weapons" to shoot down Soviet missiles, the conferees had to compromise between very different House and Senate positions. The conference report approved $81.7 million of the $122.3 million requested for long-wavelength laser development. The Senate had backed the request, and the House had denied it entirely.

The conference bill also accepted $20 million of the $50 million added by the House for development of short-wavelength laser weapons. And for development of "particle beam" technology, it authorized $33 million as recommended by the House, a $2 million increase over the administration request.

At the insistence of House conferees, the final version of S 2248 also omitted a Senate provision directing the Pentagon to move as quickly as possible to deploy an experimental laser weapon in orbit. The Senate provision had been sponsored by Malcolm Wallop, R-Wyo., leader of a group of predominantly conservative senators who complained that Pentagon scientists were needlessly delaying development of laser weapons that might defend the country against any Soviet attack.

Arms Control. The conferees said that deployment of the MX was consistent with the administration's aim of making the U.S.-Soviet nuclear balance more stable while reducing the size of the two nuclear arsenals.

But they dropped a provision adopted on the House floor that would have limited the use of funds for any program that would violate President Reagan's statement May 31 that he would "not undercut" existing arms control agreements. Administration officials had said that statement included the unratified SALT II nuclear arms treaty. That provision could have affected the proposed "Dense Pack" basing scheme, which some critics had said might violate SALT II.

Noting that strategic arms reduction talks (START) already were in progress, the conferees said the provision "would not add anything to the negotiating position of the United States."

Older ICBMs. The conferees concurred in the administration decision to retire the 52 very large, old Titan II missiles. They did so by dropping the $80 million added by the Senate to continue operating those liquid-fueled ICBMs.

The administration planned to begin retiring the large, old missiles in fiscal 1983. Senate Armed Services had

opposed the retirement, until a final MX basing decision was made, but the House had approved the retirement.

Conferees also approved $35.5 million requested by Reagan and approved by the House to install in existing Minuteman ICBM silos lithium batteries that could keep those missiles operating for days after commercial electric power had been cut off. But the conference report also followed the House in dropping $15 million requested to replace 50 single-warhead Minuteman IIs with multi-warhead Minuteman III missiles currently in storage.

Missile Submarines. For the tenth Trident missile-firing submarine, the conferees authorized $1.5 billion. The tenth Trident was to be equipped to fire the Trident II, a larger version of the missile carried by earlier Tridents. The conference also approved $282 million for components that would be used on the next three missile submarines.

The conference action mirrored the House version of the bill. The House cut of $699 million in the Trident request was one of the largest single cuts either house made in Reagan's defense budget.

The administration had requested $2.24 billion for two submarines equipped to fire the current-model Trident I and $244 million for components of the next two boats. The Senate bill had approved the components request but reduced the authorization for the two submarines to $1.96 billion, deleting all components associated with the Trident I missile.

Bombers, Cruise Missiles. Both houses had approved as requested $3.9 billion to begin procurement of the B-1B bomber, including purchase of the first seven production-line planes, and $753.5 million for B-1B research and development.

An additional, unspecified amount was included for development of the so-called "stealth" bomber, intended to penetrate Soviet defenses in the 1990s.

But the two chambers had differed over their treatment of the existing B-52 bomber fleet.

The conference report approved the full amount requested to modify existing B-52s ($554.6 million) but included $90 million of the $121.8 million requested to develop further B-52 improvements.

And conferees agreed with the administration and the House position to begin retiring the oldest surviving class of B-52s, the "D" model planes. But they ordered the Pentagon to hold in "inviolate storage" one of the three squadrons of B-52Ds that would be retired in fiscal 1983, so it could be reactivated on short notice.

Senate Democrats had seized on Reagan's decision to retire the Titan II missiles and the B-52Ds — after he had criticized Carter for allowing U.S. nuclear power to atrophy — as proof of the contradictions in Reagan's defense program. The Senate version of S 2248 had included $20 million to hold in a state of advanced readiness one of the three B-52D squadrons slated for retirement.

Warning and Command. Insisting that the decision reflected only budgetary limits, not a decision on the merits of the program, the conferees dropped $39.2 million requested and approved by the Senate to improve the DEW Line of bomber detection radars near the Arctic Circle.

The House had denied the funds, questioning the cost-effectiveness of the proposed modifications.

The conferees also greatly loosened a Senate provision that barred the stationing at Andrews Air Force Base, near Washington, D.C., of a 747 jumbo jet equipped as an airborne national command post. The ban would have been waived if the president certified in writing that the national

Defense Authorizations for Fiscal 1983

Following are the authorizations in S 2248 for Defense Department programs in fiscal year 1983:

(in thousands of dollars)

Program	Reagan Request	House Amount	Senate Amount	Final Authorization
PROCUREMENT				
Aircraft				
Army	$ 2,745,900	$ 2,541,600	$ 1,786,900	$ 2,541,600
Navy and Marine Corps	11,582,300	11,424,500	11,167,800	11,304,600
Air Force	17,756,700	17,243,400	17,783,800[1]	17,485,700
Missiles and other weapons				
Army	2,846,600	2,898,500	2,846,600	2,846,600
Navy	3,296,700	3,236,000	3,205,300	3,226,000
Marine Corps	263,900	263,900	263,900	263,900
Air Force	6,827,900	6,333,300	5,269,800	6,038,700
Naval Vessels	18,648,300	18,228,400	18,368,700	17,965,000
Ammunition				
Army	2,639,000	2,410,600	2,733,400	2,486,400
Marine Corps	630,200	470,000	530,200	470,000
Weapons and tracked combat vehicles				
Army	5,030,700	4,707,700	4,705,000	4,707,600
Marine Corps	478,500	386,800	476,500	476,500
Torpedoes, Navy	604,900	624,900	604,900	614,900
Other procurement				
Army	4,567,500	4,509,500	4,364,000	4,391,100
Navy	3,970,200	3,933,300	3,971,800	3,936,500
Marine Corps	928,100	864,200	928,100	921,200
Air Force	5,845,200	5,656,700	5,721,600	5,656,700
Defense agencies	890,300	863,400	859,600	859,600
National Guard and Reserve equipment [2]	0	0	200,000	200,000
TOTAL PROCUREMENT	89,552,900	86,596,700	85,787,800[3]	86,392,600
RESEARCH AND DEVELOPMENT				
Army	4,484,000	3,651,741	4,161,741	3,926,367
Navy and Marine Corps	6,235,316	6,026,208	6,131,698	6,129,115
Air Force	11,220,400	10,409,196	10,760,643	10,720,884
Defense Agencies	2,320,684	2,219,730	2,276,384	2,271,503
TOTAL, RESEARCH AND DEVELOPMENT	24,260,400	22,306,875	23,330,466	23,047,869
OPERATIONS AND MAINTENANCE				
Army	18,638,775	18,554,775	18,675,775	18,622,714
Navy and Marine Corps	24,348,985	23,722,215	24,075,915	23,897,865
Air Force	20,472,800	19,783,900	19,937,300	19,884,800
Defense-wide	5,931,110	5,849,310	5,896,010	5,869,360
TOTAL, OPERATIONS AND MAINTENANCE	69,391,670	67,910,200	68,585,000	68,274,739
CIVIL DEFENSE	252,340	252,340	144,530	152,340
GRAND TOTAL	$183,457,310	$177,066,115	$177,847,796	$177,867,548

1. Includes $450 million for C-5B transport planes. The obligation or expenditure of that amount was prohibited by a Senate floor amendment.
2. In addition to procurement for the National Guard and Reserve included under the service accounts.
3. Numbers do not add due to rounding.

security required stationing of the plane at Andrews.

The Senate Armed Services Committee had argued that the plane should be stationed further inland, where it would be less vulnerable to attack by Soviet missile-firing subs.

The conference report simply required the president to comment on the inland-basing idea by the time he submitted his fiscal 1984 budget to Congress in January 1983.

Civil Defense. For attack-related civil defense programs, the conference report authorized $152.3 million. The Senate had approved $144.5 million. The House approved the full request of $252.3 million, which was to be the first installment of a controversial seven-year, $4.2 billion program to beef up the U.S. civil defense program. The House rejected an effort to cut the civil defense amount to the Senate level. *(Box, p. 87)*

Transports

Unsurprisingly, since both Armed Services committees clearly had favored procurement of the C-5B wide-body cargo plane, the conferees approved the plan to resume production of the planes. They authorized $847.5 million to buy the first plane, procure the necessary facilities and equipment, and purchase an initial stock of spare parts.

They also recommended transferring to the C-5B program $50 million appropriated for other purposes but not spent in fiscal 1982.

After a vigorous lobbying effort by the Boeing Corp., the Senate in May rejected the C-5 plan and instead ordered procurement of Boeing 747 transports. But the House accepted the administration request for C-5s, built by Lockheed Corp.

To buy three used 747s for Air Force cargo hauling, the conferees approved $60 million in new authority and $84.8 million previously appropriated but not spent. No 747s had been requested, and the conference report presented no specific rationale for the addition. But the directive was an obvious political gesture toward the Senate position favoring the Boeing planes. One Senate conferee was Henry M. Jackson, D-Wash., who had led the fight to buy Boeing rather than Lockheed planes. Boeing was headquartered in Seattle.

The conferees urged the Air Force to expedite a long-stalled plan (called CRAF) to modify existing civilian airliners so they could be quickly converted to haul military cargo in case of an emergency. They also approved $1 million to continue development of the C-17 (formerly called CX), a wide-bodied cargo jet that was a likely successor to the Air Force's fleet of C-141s in the early 1990s.

Tanker Planes. For the fiscal 1983 share of a multi-year contract to buy 44 KC-10 tanker planes, the conferees approved $795 million, as approved by the Senate. This was essentially the amount the administration wanted after it had decided to buy the planes under a multi-year contract.

The conferees also followed the Senate's lead — and the administration's belated request — to provide a $120 million supplemental authorization in fiscal 1982 to begin the KC-10 contract.

To continue replacing obsolete engines on some 600 Air Force KC-135 tanker planes, the conferees authorized $435.6 million. Of that amount, $60 million was earmarked for the use of second-hand airliner engines and the rest was for new, fan-jet engines. The administration had requested $490.6 million, all to be used for the new fan-jets.

Tank, Anti-tank Warfare

Conferees approved $1.56 billion to buy 855 M-1 tanks, of which $198.2 million was authorized but not spent in prior years. Originally, the administration had requested $1.48 billion for 776 tanks, but Army contract negotiations had turned out better than expected and the administration revised its request to buy more tanks at less-per-copy.

Also approved was $380.9 million for components to be used to build 900 M-1s in fiscal 1984.

House conferees also dropped their insistence on funding part of the fiscal 1983 Army program with $40.4 million appropriated in fiscal 1982 to buy the first 36 copies of a high-speed, armored bulldozer that, among other missions, could dig defensive emplacements for tanks. The House panel had complained that the Army had no firm production plan for additional purchases of those bulldozers, but conferees said that such a plan had since been approved.

Light Tanks. The Senate-approved request for $89.7 million to buy 147 lightweight tanks for the Marine Corps, which the House had rejected, was included in the conference report.

But conferees approved only $25 million of the $111.3 million requested to buy 175 similar vehicles for the Army. The House had denied all funds for that project as well.

Both services wanted a new, lightweight tank, but they disagreed about several of its important features. The services had been testing four models and were under congressional pressure to agree on one vehicle.

Under the conference agreement, the Army funds could not be spent until 30 days after the secretary of defense had submitted to Congress a report justifying the Army's choice of a vehicle from among several competitors and had certified that future Army budgets would include adequate funding for the program.

The $25 million was to be transferred to the Marine Corps' program if that report was not been submitted by Dec. 31.

Tank Hunters. The Senate prevailed to block further production of the A-10, a small bomber designed to attack tanks. The administration had planned to end A-10 production after buying 20 planes in fiscal 1983, for which it requested $357.3 million. The House, which wanted to keep the plane in production for several more years, had approved $329.3 million for 30 planes in fiscal 1983.

But the conferees approved $710 million for 48 Apache (AH-64) anti-tank helicopters and $115 million for components to be used in fiscal 1984. This was only a few million less than had been approved by the House and slightly less than the request of $760.3 million for procurement and $116.5 million for components.

Unhappy over the escalating price of the helicopter, the Senate had approved only $73 million to keep the Apache production line intact for one year without making a commitment to begin production. But in a press release issued at the end of the conference, Senate Committee Chairman John Tower, R-Texas, praised the Army for ratcheting down the price of the helicopters.

The conference report also took the House position providing only $15 million for the Copperhead, laser-guided anti-tank artillery shell, enough to shut down the production line. The conference report echoed the House committee in pointing to escalating costs and recent test troubles to justify the termination.

The Senate had approved the request for $183.6 million to buy 7,629 of the shells.

Binary Chemical Weapons

According to the conference report, the request for $54 million to begin production of a new class of lethal chemical weapons — the so-called binary munitions — was denied "without prejudice." Binary munitions were bombs and artillery shells containing two chemicals that combined to produce lethal nerve gas when the shell was fired or the bomb dropped. *(Box, p. 83)*

The Senate had narrowly turned back an effort to kill the program. By a 3-2 margin, over the strenuous objection of Armed Services members, the House had dropped the $54 million and had imposed a ban on production of the weapons.

In the conference report, Senate conferees included unusually strong language on the issue, arguing that production of binary weapons was "vital to national security."

One source said the Senate conferees agreed to drop their insistence on binary funding in return for the House conferees' agreement to end procurement of the A-10 airplane.

The conferees accepted a Senate provision expressing the support of Congress for negotiations toward a "complete, effective and verifiable prohibition of the development, production and stockpiling" of chemical weapons.

Aerial Combat

Splitting the difference, the conferees approved the purchase of 39 F-15 fighters ($1.24 billion) instead of the 48 recommended by the Senate ($1.4 billion) and the 30 included in the House bill ($982.2 billion).

The authorization for advance procurement of F-15 components also was a compromise: $162 million instead of $142 million approved by the House and $202.5 million as approved by the Senate.

Both houses had approved the request for 120 F-16s, though the conference report reduced the authorization from $1.735 billion to $1.711 billion. But the final bill increased the authorization for components from $223 million to $323 million, enough to build 150 planes in each of the following two years, instead of the 120 planned. The Senate had approved $391 million for advance components to allow production of 180 planes in each of the next two years.

Conferees also approved the $140.6 million requested for two E-3A (AWACS) radar warning and command planes, along with $25.7 million for AWACS components. The House had cut the procurement authorization to $30.6 million for one plane.

Air Base Defense. Both houses had approved the $98.9 million requested to buy British Rapier anti-aircraft missiles that would be used by British troops to defend U.S. air bases in the United Kingdom.

But the conference report agreed with the House and authorized an additional $50 million to buy Rapiers that other European countries could use to defend U.S. air bases on the European mainland.

Future Fighters. The conference report included $47 million of the $51.3 million requested by the Air Force to test modified versions of the F-15 and F-16 for future procurement. But the report emphasized that no commitment to buy the planes was being made. The Senate had approved the request and the House had denied all funds.

The conferees ordered the Pentagon to cancel development and production of a planned radio system for combat planes, called Seek Talk, designed to thwart enemy efforts to jam it or intercept it. The system was estimated to cost

$3.6 billion to develop and produce, with $77.3 million requested for fiscal 1983.

But to develop a less ambitious and less expensive jam-proof radio system, the conferees added $10 million to the bill and approved for that use an additional $15 million that had been appropriated in fiscal 1982 for Seek Talk.

Conferees also approved $26.5 million to develop an air-launched version of the Tomahawk cruise missile (called MRASM) that would allow U.S. planes to attack ships and land-targets from a distance of several hundred miles. The administration had requested $19.9 million; the Senate approved $4.9 million and the House recommended $39.9 million.

The conferees authorized $100 million of the $103.8 million requested for development of the Lantirn system, a combination of radar and infrared television intended to enable Air Force fighter planes to attack ground targets at night. But they also added $20 million to modify an infrared television system for the Navy's F-18 fighters. They ordered the Air Force to compare it with the infrared television component of Lantirn and procure the better one.

Carrier Aircraft. As requested and approved by the House, the conference report authorized $247.7 million for eight A-6E carrier-borne bombers and $289.9 million for six EA-6Bs, a version of the plane adapted to jam enemy radars. The Senate bill would have canceled production of the bomber and authorized 12 jammer planes ($494.4 million).

Warships

Both Houses had approved without change most of Reagan's request for warships: $6.795 billion for two aircraft carriers, $1.027 billion for two attack submarines, $3.1 billion for three Aegis cruisers and $323 million to modernize and recommission the battleship *Iowa*.

The two *Nimitz*-class nuclear powered carriers were to replace the two smallest carriers, the *Coral Sea* and the *Midway*. Both ships, of World War II vintage, were scheduled for retirement in the late 1980s. The new ships would keep the usable carrier fleet at 14; the administration wanted to increase the fleet to 15.

The conferees accepted $40 million added by the House to the $666.4 million request for two guided missile-armed frigates of the FFG-7 class. The added funds were to ensure that at least one of the two ships had a much more powerful aircraft-detection radar, which Congress had been urging on a reluctant Navy. They also added to the bill $15 million to speed development of the new radar.

Both versions of the bill had approved the request for $138.6 million to continue development of a new class of anti-aircraft destroyers. The first of these ships, the DDG-51, was to be requested in fiscal 1985. But the conference report retained a House provision that would block use of those funds unless the Navy submitted a plan to equip the ships to fire laser-guided cannon shells.

The House Armed Services Committee had been a staunch supporter of guided shells for naval guns, a project the Navy had sidetracked for budgetary reasons. The House panel had added $117 million for the laser artillery to its version of the bill, and the conferees retained $60 million.

Anti-Submarine Warfare

Both Armed Services panels had sharply reduced the purchase of LAMPS III anti-submarine helicopters from

the 48 requested ($858.4 million). The conferees approved the House-passed figure of 27 helicopters ($558.4 million) instead of the 24 authorized by the Senate ($538.4 million).

The conference report also approved $18 million for Project Arapaho, designed to test the stationing of anti-aircraft helicopters and other weapons on cargo ships through use of containerized modules, an approach used by the United Kingdom during the Falkland Islands war in the spring of 1982.

For the Mark 48 torpedo, to be used by U.S. subs against submarines and surface ships, the conferees split the difference between the Senate-passed request ($124.3 million) and the House-passed amount ($144.3 million). But they said the conference amount ($134.3 million) would buy 144 torpedoes, the number for which the House authorized a higher amount.

The House had added to the bill $22 million to let nuclear submarines continue carrying the Subroc missile that could attack another submarine 30 miles distant with a nuclear depth charge. Without the additional funds, Subrocs would have been removed from those submarines as they were equipped with the Tomahawk cruise missile.

The conferees retained $11 million for the Subrocs.

Reserve, Guard Equipment

The conferees retained 11 of the 12 new Cobra helicopters armed with the TOW anti-tank missile ($53.9 million), which the House bill had added to beef up the National Guard.

But they dropped the $55 million the House had added to modernize older Cobras for the Guard.

Also dropped was a House addition of $51.9 million to begin equipping National Guard divisions with Chaparral anti-aircraft missile launchers.

On the issue of C-130 transports added to the bill for use by Guard and Reserve units, the conferees compromised on eight planes ($179 million), compared with the Senate recommendation of four and the House proposal for 12.

The conference bill also approved the $16.2 million recommended for C-9B transport planes flown by the Navy Reserve, instead of the $44.2 million recommended by the House.

But conferees adopted a Senate provision that added to the bill $200 million parceled out among the various National Guard and Reserve forces for equipment purchases. The House bill had added $148.6 million earmarked for various kinds of equipment for Guard and Reserve forces.

The conference report did not include a House provision imposing a one-year moratorium on the transfer of naval vessels to foreign countries, unless specifically authorized by Congress. But the conferees agreed that a ship should not be taken from a Navy Reserve unit for transfer abroad unless a replacement was at hand, which was the specific point at issue.

Operations, Maintenance

The conferees reduced the authorization request by $229.9 million, to be saved by the early retirement of 13 old Navy destroyers and a delay in the formation of an Air Force fighter wing.

The House bill had recommended cutting an additional $74 million by retiring nine other ships and disbanding four Army battalions.

A House reduction of $100 million in the Navy's $6

billion request for ship and aircraft overhauls was incorporated into the conference report. But so was a House-passed addition of $75 million to the $2.9 billion request for fleet steaming time.

Contracting Out. The conferees appeared to split the difference over the issue of contracting out to private firms jobs currently performed by military or civilian federal employees.

The Senate had approved the administration's ambitious plans for contracting out. But the House had barred such actions during fiscal 1983 and had deleted the $33.5 million requested to carry out cost-benefit studies of proposed contracts.

The House also provided that $567.6 million for contract employee salaries and operational expenses connected with proposed new contract jobs be available only if the jobs continued to be performed by federal civilian employees.

The conferees provided a six-month moratorium on contracting-out decisions, from which they exempted laundry, landscaping, refuse collection and food service jobs. And they accepted a House-passed ban for a year on any contracting out of firefighting or security guard positions.

In keeping with a half-year ban, the conference report approved half the amount requested for contracting-out studies ($16.75 million). The conference report also said half of the $567.6 million for pay and operations would be restricted to use while the jobs were performed "in-house."

Alliance Relations

The conferees approved $15 million of the $31 million requested to begin storing in Europe the tanks, trucks and other heavy equipment of two Army divisions based in the United States. In case war threatened in Europe, the divisions could be flown to pick up their equipment in commandeered airliners. Equipment for four divisions already was stored in these so-called POMCUS sites.

Buy America Provisions. The conference report also followed the Senate bill in dropping or watering down provisions that would have virtually mandated the purchase of various goods from U.S. firms. These included:

● Sedans and light trucks. The conference report allowed their purchase from the United States, Canada or — for those covered by existing contracts — Italy, West Germany or the United Kingdom.

● Specialty metals and chemical warfare protective suits. The report would allow their purchase abroad for the purpose of furthering equipment standardization within NATO.

● Coal. The conferees dropped a House provision requiring the purchase of U.S. coal for U.S. bases in Europe.

The conferees modified a House requirement that Congress be given 30 days' advance notice of any contract that would make the United States dependent on a foreign manufacturer as the sole source of a major piece of equipment. The conference report kept the reporting requirement but dropped the requirement for 30 days' notice.

Other Provisions

The following provisions also were included in the conference report on S 2248:

Former Spouses' Rights. The conferees approved the gist of a House provision that would permit state courts, under certain circumstances, to treat military pensions as property to be divided in divorce settlements.

Student Information. Also approved with slight

Reagan Handed Defeat on Nerve Gas Issue

In acting on the defense authorization bill (S 2248 — PL 97-252), Congress handed the Reagan administration only one major outright defeat, rejecting a $54 million request to begin production of a new class of lethal chemical weapons. The new weapons, called binary munitions, were bombs and artillery shells containing two chemicals that combined to produce lethal nerve gas when the shell was fired or the bomb dropped.

The Senate narrowly turned back an effort to kill the program. But by a 3-2 margin, over the strenuous objection of Armed Services members, the House dropped the $54 million and imposed a ban on production of the weapons.

House-Senate conferees on the bill, most of whom supported the binary program, said the $54 million was being denied "without prejudice."

Senate conferees included unusually strong language on the issue, arguing that production of binary weapons was "vital to national security."

Reagan Request

Both Armed Services committees had approved virtually without change the administration's $705 million chemical warfare program, the bulk of which was earmarked for equipment to protect U.S. troops from Soviet chemical attack.

For fiscal 1983, the administration's chemical warfare program included:

● $508 million for chemical defense, including $236 million for research and development and $189 million for procurement of warning devices, protective suits and the like;

● $74 million for dismantling and "de-toxification" of obsolete chemical weapons;

● $18 million to refurbish existing chemical weapons;

● $1 million for construction of storage facilities; and

● $104 million associated with the administration decision to begin producing binary munitions; $54 million was for actual production of the weapons.

In the previous "unitary" nerve gas weapons, the lethal chemical was stored as a liquid that vaporized when the bomb was fired or the shell exploded. In binary munitions, on the other hand, two relatively harmless liquids were stored separately in the weapon and were mixed to produce the lethal agent when the bomb was dropped or the shell fired.

---

modification was a Senate provision authorizing the secretary of defense to request from secondary schools, on a strictly voluntary basis, the names and addresses of students for recruiting purposes.

Draft Registration. Conferees adopted the House version of a provision barring federal education assistance to any male not registering with the Selective Service System as required by law.

Maybank Amendment. The conferees compromised on the terms of continuing a program under which certain contracts could be directed to areas of high unemployment. This partial waiver of the so-called Maybank amendment would apply to a maximum of $4 billion in contracts for non-strategic materials. The price of any contract awarded to a firm in a high-unemployment area could be no more than 2.2 percent above the price that otherwise would be the winning bid.

Weapons Price Increases. The conferees amalgamated features of Senate- and House-passed provisions intended to give increased visibility to unanticipated increases in weapons prices. The final provision resembled in key respects Sen. Sam Nunn's, D-Ga., cost-control amendment to the fiscal 1982 defense appropriations bill (PL 97-86). *(1981 Almanac p. 229)*

Among other things, the provision in S 2248 required a report to Congress by the secretary of defense whenever the price of any major weapons program increased by more than 15 percent above the projected price.

Transport Commands. A Senate provision, slightly modified, was included to bar consolidation of the Navy's Military Sealift Command, the Army's Military Traffic Management Command and the Air Force's Military Airlift Command.

Inspector General. The conference bill created the position of civilian inspector general in the Defense Department, to be filled by a presidential nominee confirmed by the Senate.

The inspector general would be under the "general supervision of" the secretary of defense, who could prohibit any action by the inspector general in certain kinds of cases in which an inspection would jeopardize national security. The secretary would have to justify any such prohibition to appropriate congressional committees.

Both versions of the bill had authorized an inspector general. The Senate bill was generally similar to the final version, but the House bill would not have allowed the secretary of defense to prohibit any activity by the inspector general.

Baltic States. A House provision was retained in the conference report requiring that maps prepared or bought by the Pentagon show Estonia, Latvia and Lithuania as independent states occupied by the Soviet Union.

Committee Reports

The Senate Armed Services Committee bill (S 2248) was reported April 13 (S Rept 97-330), as was the companion House Armed Services Committee bill, HR 6030 (H Rept 97-482).

Of Reagan's total fiscal 1983 defense request of $263 billion — $257.5 billion for the Defense Department and the rest for other agencies — annual authorization was required for $183,457,280,000. The administration submitted supplemental fiscal 1982 authorization requests totaling $1,451,800,000.

The Senate committee cut $3,171,470,000 from the fiscal 1983 request and $621,300,000 from the 1982 request.

The House committee reduced the fiscal 1983 request by $3,168,880,000 and killed the supplemental request. However, the committee added to the fiscal 1983 bill

$263,400,000 that had been requested in the supplemental for the Navy's shipbuilding account.

Both panels agreed that the 1980s promised to be a dangerous decade:

"The West is confronted by: unfavorable trends in the East-West military balance; new threats in distant world areas; less concerted action by allies resulting from competing internal and external demands and pressures; greater obstacles to the protection of interests; more powerful opposing forces — political, military and economic; and scarcer natural resources and less certainty of access to such resources," the Senate committee warned.

They were in similar overall agreement that the Reagan defense buildup, which would cost $1.6 trillion over the next five years, was both affordable and essential.

Expounding on this theme, the House panel said: "[Budget] increases similar to those projected by that plan are necessary to maintain the military forces required to protect United States interests throughout the world and ensure that the United States would not end up second best if it should become involved in armed conflict."

But the Armed Services committees' general support for the Reagan program broke down on some important specifics, nowhere more dramatically than in the area of planned improvements in the U.S. nuclear arsenal.

Nuclear Warfare

The two panels repeated their earlier endorsements of the general thrust of Reagan's strategic force plan announced Oct. 2, 1981. But they were in substantial disagreement over several components of the package, including Reagan's refusal to build the shuttle-based version of the MX intercontinental missile, and the administration proposals for defending the United States against a Soviet nuclear attack. *(Reagan plans, 1981 Almanac p. 195)*

Intercontinental Missiles

The Senate panel was adamantly opposed to Reagan's proposal for interim silo-basing, partly for fear that the administration would gradually become committed to silo-basing for the whole MX fleet. The committee also was concerned that silo-basing might turn many members against the whole MX program. The MX had been sold to Congress as a solution to the vulnerability of current U.S. missiles to Soviet attack, but the new missiles would be no less vulnerable in fixed silos than existing missiles, the committee said.

In hopes of accelerating the selection of a long-term, survivable basing method for MX, the Senate committee denied the $715 million requested for silo-basing and increased funding for development of the long-term basing by $255 million (to a total of $565 million). The committee ordered the secretary of defense to choose a permanent basing technique by Dec. 1.

The committee also ordered a halt to research on the temporary deployment of MXs in fixed silos.

The Senate panel also dropped the $1.497 billion requested to begin MX production, arguing that production would not be needed until fiscal 1984 to meet the new deadline for a survivable basing method.

Overall, the Senate committee cut MX funding to $2.277 billion.

Missile Diplomacy. House Armed Services, though as unhappy as the Senate panel over Reagan's cancellation of the MX shuttle plan, concluded that MX in the silos

sooner was better than a survivable MX later, for international political reasons.

"Nuclear weapons are political weapons and the sovereign-based ICBM, the currency of superpower status, is most often the determinant in the perception of the relative nuclear balance," the committee said. From this perspective, the MX was essential as a political counterweight to the large, Soviet missiles.

"Further delays in the MX program would send to the Soviet Union and the rest of the world a signal totally inconsistent with the current policy of rebuilding our defense capability," according to the House panel. "National security interests are better served, therefore, even if fixed silo-basing with MX were the only present alternative to redress the strategic imbalance."

The committee approved the bulk of the administration MX request — $3.751 billion — after trimming $332.9 million for items related solely to silo-deployment and $22.3 million the panel said could be transferred from funds appropriated for other purposes in fiscal 1982. The funds approved would pay for basing research that would be compatible with both a long-term MX solution and an interim basing system, so that the missile could be deployed as planned by 1986.

But, as it had done in 1981, the House panel moved to squelch one of the long-term basing techniques under review in the Pentagon: the so-called Continuous Patrol Aircraft (CPA), or air-mobile method. CPA would use a fleet of airplanes which could launch an MX in midair, some of which would be on patrol at all times to prevent their destruction by a missile attack on their airfields. *(1981 Almanac p. 199)*

Both Armed Services committees rejected the CPA on grounds that air-launched missiles would not be accurate

---

Multi-Year Contracts

Both Armed Services Committees in 1982 took another look at the practice of "multi-year procurement" of major weapons.

In 1981, both panels had been staunch supporters of multi-year procurement. Under this approach, all the units of a particular weapon planned for purchase over a period of several years would be covered by a single contract. *(1981 Almanac p. 212)*

Pentagon officials and Armed Services members said the practice would reduce weapons costs, since it would allow contractors to plan for a relatively stable production run over several years.

But the Senate committee protested that it had received a detailed justification for only one of the 15 programs the Pentagon proposed to place under multi-year contracts in fiscal 1983. It approved the multi-year plan for the Army's Blackhawk troop-carrying helicopter, but added a provision requiring 30 days prior notice to the committee of any multi-year contract on several of the other programs.

The House committee directed its criticism at the Navy, which, the panel said, had proposed multi-year contracts for four planes that would be bought in such small numbers that no real economies of scale could be achieved. It disapproved the multi-year proposals and denied $70.8 million requested to fund them.

enough to destroy heavily armored military targets and that the planes could too easily be detected and destroyed even in flight. The House panel cut from the fiscal 1983 request the $74 million earmarked for CPA research.

Re-entry Vehicle. The two committees approved an administration decision to develop a new re-entry vehicle to carry the nuclear warheads of the MX. Compared with the current Mark 12A re-entry vehicles, the new Advanced Ballistic Re-entry Vehicle (ABRV) was more accurate and could produce either a larger nuclear blast for the same amount of nuclear fuel, or the same size blast with less fuel.

The administration had requested $57 million in the supplemental and $362 million in fiscal 1983, for ABRV. The House denied the new fiscal 1982 funds but told the Pentagon to use $57 million appropriated in fiscal 1982 for other purposes. It approved the fiscal 1983 request.

But the Senate panel insisted that ABRV development could be slowed because of its proposal to slow MX production. It denied the fiscal 1982 funds and trimmed $22 million from the fiscal 1983 ABRV request, approving a total authorization of $340 million.

Titans. The two committees also differed on the future of the 52 existing Titan II ICBMs, which the administration had planned to begin retiring in fiscal 1983. As it had done in 1981, the Senate panel insisted that the Titans be kept in service until a final MX decision was made, and added to the bill the amounts needed for modifying and operating the missiles.

The House committee approved the Titan retirement.

Nuclear Defense

The panels' disagreements over MX spilled over into their treatment of Reagan's proposals to increase efforts to defend the United States against a Soviet nuclear attack.

The House committee reduced by more than 50 percent (from $871 million to $402.9 million) the Army's request for development of an anti-ballistic missile system. The committee also reduced by $76 million the Air Force request for $109 million to develop an anti-missile defense for the long-term MX bases and criticized the lack of coordination on anti-missile defenses between the Army and the Air Force.

The committee's rationale was that, since the anti-missile system then under development was designed to protect MX, the program should be slowed until Congress could review the final MX basing proposal and the impact of any anti-missile defense on the 1972 U.S.-Soviet treaty limiting such weapons.

The Senate panel approved the administration's anti-ballistic missile defense requests.

Interceptor Planes. The House panel also was more skeptical than the Senate about the administration's proposed modernization of Air Force fighters intended to destroy Soviet bombers attacking the continental United States. Partly to replace the current defense force of 20-year-old F-106s, the Reagan administration planned to greatly increase the number of F-15s that would be bought for the Air Force.

The House committee authorized only 30 F-15s for fiscal 1983 and components for 30 in each of the following two years ($1.278 billion), instead of the request for 42 planes in fiscal 1983 and components for 60 and 96 in the next two years, respectively ($1.682 billion). The House panel cited several reasons for its reduction, one being lack of a detailed plan for U.S. air defense, with cost estimates.

The Senate committee, by contrast, proposed buying an additional six planes in fiscal 1983 (a total of 48), but approved components for only one additional year, for a total authorization of $1.6 billion.

Civil Defense. On the other hand, Senate Armed Services was skeptical of the proposed rapid increase in civil defense spending. The administration announced in March a seven-year, $4.2 billion program, including plans to evacuate major cities in case of a severe international crisis, in which a U.S.-Soviet war appeared imminent. *(Box, p. 87)*

For fiscal 1983, Reagan requested $252 million to begin the program, up from $133 million authorized in fiscal 1982. The House committee approved the request.

The Senate committee approved $145 million for civil defense, commenting that the proposed "massive" increase could not be justified in the face of the overall budget crunch. The panel acknowledged that Moscow's bargaining leverage in a nuclear crisis might be increased if Moscow could protect most of its citizens and Washington could not. But a committee source said many panel members were skeptical that an evacuation plan would be taken seriously by the U.S. public.

Lasers. The two committees also disagreed tactically over the handling of programs to develop powerful lasers, to be based in orbiting satellites, which some specialists hoped eventually could shoot down Soviet ICBMs and bombers. The panels were agreed in their opposition to laser advocates who insisted that a crash program could field an effective anti-missile defense by about 1990.

Senate Armed Services approved the $121.3 million requested for various space-based laser research projects, and urged the Pentagon to explore a laser utilizing shorter wave-length light than the type of laser currently under study, which would be used in the crash program backed by laser proponents.

The House panel, on the other hand, flatly refused to continue development of the current generation of lasers, denying the $121.3 million authorized by the Senate. But the committee added to the bill $50 million earmarked for development of short wave-length space lasers.

Strategic Bombers

Both committees reiterated their enthusiastic support for an improved B-1 bomber, approving the total administration request for $4 billion to buy the first seven bombers and their spare parts, and $753.5 million to continue development of the plane.

But both also warned the Pentagon that it was politically imperative that the project meet its cost projections and production schedule. Reagan in January certified to Congress that 100 bombers could be bought for $20.5 billion, in fiscal 1981 dollars. But Reagan said that cost target could be met only if Congress approved his annual requests for the bomber.

Because of the political pressure to restrain B-1 costs, the Senate committee urged the Pentagon to use "extreme caution" in considering an acceleration of the program that might increase costs or eventually cause delays.

Both committees apparently approved the secret amounts requested to continue development of a new type of bomber that would use a "stealth" design to evade enemy radar. But they both emphasized their opposition to gambling on the new plane as a replacement for the B-1.

The committees approved the administration request of $664.5 million for 440 long-range cruise missiles to be carried by the current fleet of B-52 bombers and the pro-

jected B-1s and an additional $186.8 million to continue development of the missile.

But the House committee denied $50.8 million for a proposed modification to the missiles that the Senate approved. The purpose of the modification (called HAVE RUST) was secret, but apparently it would equip the missiles to jam Soviet detection gear.

B-52 Retirement. The panels broke on one bomber-related issue: Reagan's proposal to retire the 70-odd oldest B-52s — the D-model planes.

Congress rejected the retirement proposal in 1981, and added to the fiscal 1982 Air Force budget $62.1 million for spare parts to keep operating the B-52Ds.

But in its report, House Armed Services opposed further expenditures to continue flying the D-model planes. The committee cut $50 million from the current Air Force request for spare parts, telling the Pentagon to use $50 million from the fiscal 1982 addition to make up for the reduction.

The Senate panel agreed to the proposed retirement of three of five B-52D squadrons, for an anticipated saving of $251 million. But it added $20 million so that one of the three could be kept ready for quick reactivation, and it ordered the Pentagon to study the value of returning that squadron to service for conventional war missions against warships or non-Soviet targets.

Submarine Missiles

The administration proposal for two more Trident missile-launching submarines — the 10th and 11th ships of the class — was approved by both committees ($2.24 billion) and components to be used to build two more Trident ships in the future ($244 million).

The Senate committee approved, but the House committee rejected, a $106.4 million 1982 supplemental request for "cost growth" in the Trident program.

The first Trident submarine, the *Ohio*, was delivered to the Navy Oct. 1, 1981, 2 years and 5 months behind the original schedule. The Senate committee noted that contract disputes between the Navy and Electric Boat Co., the contractor, had "abated somewhat" since 1981.

Also approved as requested were 72 Trident I missiles ($743 million) and $367 million to continue development of a longer-range, more accurate Trident II (or D-5) missile. But the Senate committee warned the Pentagon not to try to accelerate development of the D-5, if so doing would result in higher costs or poorer performance. Both panels also approved the request for $90.6 million to continue development of the Trident I.

Communications. The request for $49.8 million to develop a large, underground radio antenna (called ELF) to communicate with deeply submerged missile submarines was approved by both panels. The controversial antenna would be located at two sites, in Michigan and Wisconsin.

Also authorized as requested was procurement of two Hercules transport planes equipped with a powerful radio that could communicate with missile subs if they were close to the ocean's surface ($36.8 million).

The Navy wanted to replace its fleet of these so-called TACAMO planes with a new plane (called ECX) with more powerful radios.

The Senate added $3 million to the $56.4 million requested for development of TACAMO and ECX, but the House denied the $41.6 million earmarked for ECX, objecting to the program's projected cost of more than $300 million.

Missiles for Europe

Both committees approved the requests to continue production of two nuclear-armed missiles designed to reach Soviet territory from launchers in Western Europe. They authorized $498.3 million to purchase 91 Pershing II ballistic missiles and $111.3 million to continue development of the Pershing.

In addition, they authorized $530.7 million to procure 120 ground-launched cruise missiles (GLCMs) plus spare parts, launchers and components for more to be bought in the future, and $28.6 million to continue development of the GLCM.

Naval Buildup

The Armed Services panels were in much closer agreement with Reagan's budget (and with each other) in their treatment of the naval buildup toward a fleet of 600 ships, a hallmark of the administration non-nuclear war strategy.

Both expressly endorsed the basic premise of the naval emphasis: that the United States was "an island nation... inextricably dependent on overseas sources of energy and minerals to supply its industries and its people," in the words of the Senate report.

Carriers, Battleships

The heart of the administration program — a package deal for two *Nimitz*-class nuclear powered aircraft carriers ($6.795 billion) — was approved by both committees.

The committees endorsed the administration position that $754 million and 44 months in construction time would be saved if the two ships would be bought as a package, instead of being funded one at a time a few years apart.

Also approved was $699.5 million to continue a program of completely rebuilding each of the eight oldest large carriers to give them 15 more years of usable life — the so-called Service Life Extension Program (SLEP). The fiscal 1983 increment included funds for the second ship, the *Forrestal*.

Modernization of the mothballed battleship *Iowa*, to be armed with cruise missiles, also was approved as requested ($323.4 million), as was $94 million for components to modernize the battleship *Missouri*, in fiscal 1984. The *New Jersey*, first of the four battleships scheduled for modernization, was due to rejoin the fleet in January 1983. The fourth ship (*Wisconsin*) was scheduled for modernization in fiscal 1985.

The Navy planned to use the battleships as the core of a combat fleet in areas where a carrier was not needed. *(1981 Almanac p. 204)*

Anti-Aircraft Escorts

The committees also were in agreement on several Navy programs designed to protect the carriers against the large Soviet arsenal of air-launched and submarine-launched cruise missiles.

They approved the request for $3.134 billion to build three cruisers equipped with the Aegis, computer-controlled anti-aircraft system.

The administration had requested $80 million in fiscal 1982 supplemental funds, to prepare a second shipyard to construct some of the Aegis ships, all of which had been built at the Litton Industries yard in Pascagoula, Miss.

Both panels approved the idea, but the House added the money to the fiscal 1983 authorization and the Senate

Bulk of Civil Defense Program Approved

Congress pared back, but essentially approved, the first installment of the Reagan administration's controversial seven-year $4.2 billion program to beef up the U.S. civil defense program.

For nuclear attack-related civil defense programs, the defense authorization bill included $152.3 million. The Senate had approved $144.5 million, and the House had approved the full request of $252.3 million.

The House rejected an effort to cut the civil defense amount to the Senate level.

House Debate

Civil defense was one of the most contentious issues during House consideration of the defense authorization bill.

By a 163-240 vote, the House July 29 rejected an amendment by Edward J. Markey, D-Mass., to cut $108 million from civil defense. *(Vote 215, p. 64-H)*

President Reagan had requested $252 million in fiscal 1983 as the first installment of a program featuring plans to evacuate U.S. cities if a nuclear war seemed imminent. Markey's amendment would have reduced the fiscal 1983 amount to $144 million, a 6 percent increase over the fiscal 1982 appropriation.

As with several other nuclear war-related issues, Markey and his liberal allies opposed the evacuation plan on policy grounds. "It is based on the Strangelovian notion that we can fight, survive and win a nuclear war," Markey said. "Nothing could be further from the truth."

The reasoning paralleled the argument of many liberals against various nuclear weapons designed for precisely limited nuclear attacks in the course of fighting a nuclear war. Any nuclear war inevitably would escalate to a global holocaust, they maintained. But programs that encouraged a belief that nuclear war could be controlled might tempt a country to start unwittingly up the escalator.

"It is not humanitarian to advance the notion that a nuclear war is winnable," argued Jim Leach, R-Iowa. "Let us not delude the American people into thinking that a nuclear war is survivable and therefore more thinkable."

Markey called "a fraud" the administration's estimate that 80 percent of the population could survive a Soviet attack if evacuated from the likely target areas. "It assumes that there will only be death from the blast effects of bombs. It omits all other deaths from bombs, burns, fallout, starvation and disease," he said.

Civil defense plans would be hopelessly inadequate to cope with the widespread devastation of a nuclear attack, Markey insisted, calling them "a Band-Aid over the nuclear holocaust."

And the critics dismissed as equally unworkable the Soviet evacuation plan, which civil defense advocates cited as one reason for a U.S. plan.

"To match a dumb strategy with a dumb strategy is itself dumb," said Leach.

There was a large component of ridicule in the critics' attacks on the civil defense program.

To the laughter of his allies, Markey described one civil defense recommendation for digging a trench under a car to serve as a fallout shelter: "And then you will sit in an area of 28 inches by 40 inches for about 30 days, before you can peek out behind the left rear tire to figure out whether or not the firestorm has ended."

Several House Armed Services Committee members insisted that much of the preparation for nuclear attack also served civil defense operations that assist in local disasters, such as floods, fires and tornadoes.

"Civil defense, in the dual role which it occupies, works, and it works today," said Jack Brinkley, D-Ga., chairman of the Military Installations Subcommittee. "The crisis relocation [plan for evacuating cities] has only $14.3 million. That is all," Brinkley told the House.

To underscore this theme, the committee's senior Republican, William L. Dickinson, R-Ala., had offered an amendment to change the title of the Federal Emergency Management Agency, which had oversight over civil defense activity, to the Civil Disaster Agency. The amendment was agreed to by voice, just before debate began on the Markey amendment.

But some advocates of the evacuation plan met Markey head on, insisting it would prevent Moscow from using nuclear blackmail against the United States.

"What does an American president do if the Soviet Union, in a time of crisis, evacuates its cities in the four days it takes to implement its civil defense plan?" asked Ken Kramer, R-Colo.

He cited estimates that if Soviet cities were evacuated and U.S. cities were not, 150 million Americans and 15 million Russians would die in a nuclear war. "With those ratios," he concluded, "an American president would have no choice but to virtually surrender."

Something was needed to offset the Soviet evacuation plan regardless of U.S. estimates of its effectiveness, Ike Skelton, D-Mo., added. "Whether [the Russian plan] works or not does not make any difference," he said. "If they believe it works, they feel that they have a strategic advantage against us."

---

told the Navy to seek congressional approval to divert the funds from other fiscal 1982 appropriations.

Also approved was the Navy's request for $138.6 million to design a guided missile-armed destroyer (DDG-51, formerly DDGX) that would have a smaller version of the Aegis system and would replace the large number of antiaircraft ships built around 1960 and due for retirement around 1990.

But both committees said the new ship should be equipped to fire laser-guided artillery shells from its 5-inch caliber cannon, particularly to destroy shore defenses during an amphibious landing. Laser-guided naval artillery had long been a program of keen interest to the two Armed Services committees, but the administration killed the program in 1982, as a budget reduction measure, without prior congressional consultation.

The Senate panel ordered the Navy to spend the money appropriated in fiscal 1982 to begin purchasing the laser-shells and guidance equipment. The House committee barred use of any funds for DDG-51 until the Navy showed the committees a plan to equip the ship with the laser-guided artillery.

The request for $664.4 million to buy two escort frigates was approved. But both committees ordered the Navy to begin a major improvement of the anti-aircraft missile guidance radar aboard these ships. The House panel added $40 million for this program, the Senate panel $15 million.

The Navy had resisted this radar upgrade, arguing that the frigates were designed for convoy escort and other second-line jobs, not to accompany the main battle fleets. But the House panel noted that, out of necessity, the frigates had been used to escort battle groups, and would be for years.

Sub Hunting

The committees also agreed with the bulk of the administration program for dealing with Soviet submarines.

They approved the request for two nuclear powered, sub-hunting submarines of the *Los Angeles* class ($1.027 billion) and components to build three subs in each of the two following years ($416 million).

Both approved continued production of the two helicopters that were the principal anti-sub weapons of all of the Navy's surface warships, though the House unit recommended a slowdown in planned production rates. The Senate panel approved the request for 48 LAMPS III helicopters ($858.4 million) and 18 of the smaller LAMPS Is ($169 million).

The House committee approved the LAMPS I request, but called for only 30 LAMPS IIIs ($655 million), arguing that the Navy was planning to build those helicopters faster than it would have ships on which to station them.

Rapid Deployment

The committees were in similar agreement on programs to equip the Rapid Deployment Force (RDF) for action in the Persian Gulf and to shift U.S. troops rapidly elsewhere around the globe.

The Senate panel, in particular, praised the administration for, according to the committee, shifting its emphasis to forces that were designed to cope with local threats to U.S. interests without relying on local basing rights, instead of concentrating on dealing with an overland Soviet invasion. The local threat was far more likely to arise, the panel said.

Cargo Planes

Both committees approved the administration's new airlift package: 50 new versions of the C-5 cargo plane, designed to carry the largest items of Army combat equipment, and 44 KC-10s, versions of the DC-10 airliner, designed to refuel other planes in midair.

They authorized different amounts for the KC-10 account, because the specific details of a multi-year contract for the 44 planes were in flux while the bills were being marked up.

The Senate bill allowed a total of $832 million in fiscal 1983 for eight planes and components for future purchases and $120 million in fiscal 1982 for two planes. The House bill approved a total of $829.1 million for the eight planes in fiscal 1983 and the advance component procurement,

but told the Pentagon to seek congressional approval for diverting the fiscal 1982 amount from funds appropriated for other purposes.

Both panels approved the request in fiscal 1983 for $860 million for the first two new C-5Bs, plus spare parts for those planes and components for planes to be purchased later. The Senate also approved the $99.1 million requested for the C-5 in the fiscal 1982 supplemental, but the House told the Pentagon to reprogram the funds from other fiscal 1982 appropriations.

After marking up the bill, the Senate committee ordered the Air Force to substantiate its claim that its most critical air transport need was for more C-5s because they could carry very large pieces of combat equipment.

RDF Ships

Approval was granted to convert the remaining four of a class of eight fast cargo ships so they could carry the tanks and other combat gear of two Army divisions ($323 million). Conversion of the first four ships was funded in fiscal 1982.

Also approved was the request for $300 million to begin converting one or more commercial ships into a 2,000-bed hospital ship to accompany the RDF.

But both committees rejected for the second year in a row an administration proposal to charter a dozen or more large commercial ships that would be modified to store the combat equipment of three Marine Corps brigades near potential trouble spots. The "pre-positioning" ships were designed for use when a local government invited U.S. units to land.

When this pre-positioning project was begun in 1980, the Pentagon planned to build the storage ships. But the Reagan administration switched to the charter plan in September 1981 as part of its effort to hold down budget outlays.

Both committees expressed their agreement with the pre-positioning concept, but complained that the Navy had not presented a detailed plan; both questioned the long-term cost of chartering the ships rather than building them.

The Senate committee approved $10 million of the $40 million requested for the ships. The House committee, claiming the Navy acknowledged it could not begin the program until fiscal 1984, approved no money.

Amphibious Assault

The committees warmly endorsed the Reagan administration's greater emphasis on assault ships from which Marine units could fight their way ashore under fire.

To build a landing ship dock (LSD) designed to land tanks and other heavy equipment with small boats (and to buy components for another LSD to be funded in fiscal 1984), the panels approved $417 million.

Also approved was $55 million to buy components for a large helicopter carrier (called an LHD) designed to carry 2,000 Marines. An additional $45 million had been appropriated in fiscal 1982 for components of the LHD which would cost another $1.3 billion in fiscal 1984.

Both panels urged the Navy to put more cannons on warships to provide artillery support for Marine landing teams. This had been one factor in their insistence that the new destroyer be equipped to fire laser-guided shells. They urged the Navy to consider equipping ships with a cannon firing the 155mm shells used by the Army and Marine Corps.

Ground Combat

In the main, the committees concurred in administration plans to equip U.S. forces for dealing with the Soviet Union's huge tank fleet and its growing air attack force.

Tank Battles

The M-1 tank, a favorite target of defense critics because of problems in earlier tests, won strong endorsement by the panels, which said the Army had mastered the earlier cost and performance problems.

The Senate unit approved the request of $1.457 billion for 776 M-1s and $432 million for components for future production. The House panel said the request could be trimmed by $80.6 million since the Army decided, after the budget was submitted, to sign a multi-year contract for the tank.

But both committees rejected a supplemental fiscal 1982 request for $126 million to stockpile components that could be used to rapidly accelerate production of the tanks in case of a crisis. "In the event of a conflict, $126 million will be better spent on fuel, ammunition and spare parts rather than on accelerated tank production," said the Senate panel.

The Senate committee cut $10 million from the $793 million request for 600 Bradley fighting vehicles — armored troop carriers equipped with anti-tank missiles. The House panel, on the other hand, approved the request for 600 Bradleys in fiscal 1983 and added $12.4 million to increase the procurement rate in future years.

House Armed Services was the more enthusiastic of the two committees in supporting planes and helicopters designed to hunt tanks.

The Senate panel, citing large cost increases, deferred for one year all but $73 million of the $760 million requested to produce 48 AH-64 helicopters. The committee also cut $116.5 million requested for advance procurement and $88 million for spare sparts. (The $73 million approved by the committee would preserve the option of producing the planes in fiscal 1984.) The panel also froze further spending of the $444 million authorized in fiscal 1982 for the program, pending new congressional authorization.

But the House committee insisted that inflation and other factors not under the control of Hughes Helicopter Industries, which built the plane, accounted for the bulk of the cost increase.

The "real" cost overrun was relatively small and within the normal range for aircraft programs, the panel said. Moreover, the committee insisted that the AH-64 was needed because it would be a much more effective tank-hunter than the current model Cobra helicopter. The House committee cut $47 million from the AH-64 request, citing recent cost reductions. The committee also criticized the Army's decision to buy only 446 of the helicopters, rather than the 536 originally planned.

To beef up the anti-tank firepower of Reserve and National Guard units, the House committee also added to the bill $68 million to build 12 new AH-1S Cobras equipped with TOW anti-tank missiles and $80 million to equip 22 existing Cobras with TOWs.

The panels also differed over the A-10, a small Air Force bomber designed to hunt tanks.

The Senate committee complained repeatedly in its report that the Pentagon was buying too many kinds of planes at inefficiently low production rates. The committee denied the request for $324 million to buy 20 more A-10s and then shut down the production line. It ordered the line closed immediately, at a cost of $33 million.

But the House panel, citing a need for more A-10s to equip Air National Guard units, increased the fiscal 1983 request to $412 million for 30 planes, with some of the additional funds taken from funds requested for A-10 ground equipment and some from fiscal 1982 appropriations for other purposes. And it told the Air Force to use the $28 million earmarked in the budget to close the production line to buy components for 20 more planes that would be funded later.

Light Armored Vehicles

Partly under prodding by Senate Armed Services, the Army and Marine Corps had begun looking for armored vehicles that would weigh much less than conventional tanks — 10 or 15 tons compared with 60 tons of an M-1.

The Senate committee approved the request for 134 Marine Corps LAVs ($90 million) and 175 Army vehicles equipped with a larger cannon ($111 million).

The House panel denied funds for both programs, complaining that the two services were planning to buy too many different versions of the vehicle and that they were losing control of the costs.

After Congress had cleared the authorization bill, the Pentagon selected an eight-wheeled vehicle called the Piranah, built by General Motors of Canada Ltd.

Anti-Aircraft Weapons

Both committees approved the administration program to better protect combat units in the field against Soviet attack planes. The aerial threat increased substantially during the 1970s as Moscow fielded new types of planes with longer ranges and heavier bomb loads.

In several cases, the House panel added funding to further bolster the program.

The request to continue production of the Patriot long-range anti-aircraft missile to defend Army units in the field ($805 million for 376 missiles and their launchers) was approved by both committees.

The House committee added to the bill $15 million to speed development of an improved radar for the Hawk long-range missile currently used by ground units.

Both committees also approved the $61 million request to buy the last of the European-designed short-range Roland anti-aircraft missiles for the RDF. Another $521 million was approved for 96 Divad anti-aircraft tanks.

The House panel added funds to improve Reserve units' anti-aircraft defenses with less expensive weapons: $50 million to improve existing Vulcan anti-aircraft guns and $52 million to buy 16 additional Chaparral missile launchers.

The request for $99 million to continue buying British-made Rapier short-range missiles to defend U.S. airfields in Britain also was approved by both committees. The weapons would be manned and operated by British units.

But the House committee complained that too little was being done to provide similar anti-aircraft protection to air bases in West Germany and the Netherlands, closer to the NATO frontier. Though anti-aircraft defense was an Army mission, the panel said, "air base defense, by its very nature, is inherently a higher priority to the Air Force than it is to the Army."

So the committee added $50 million to the Air Force budget to explore air base protection arrangements with West Germany similar to the Rapier deal with Britain.

Tactical Air Combat

The committees concurred that the Pentagon was buying too many kinds of airplanes and, as a result, was buying many of them at very low production rates that inflated their unit costs. And the committees each acted to slow — or kill — some of those production lines in order to speed up others. But in picking which lines to speed up and which to slow down, they differed over almost every kind of combat plane being purchased by the Navy and Air Force.

Carrier Planes

The administration requested $248 million to buy six A-6Es, the largest bombers aboard aircraft carriers, and $290 million to buy six EA-6Bs, greatly modified versions of the same plane designed to jam enemy radars.

The House committee approved this program. But the Senate panel canceled additional procurement of the bombers but increased procurement of the electronic warfare version to 12 planes ($494 million).

The Senate committee approved the request for 24 F-14 fighters ($915 million). But the House committee complained that this one year drop from the rate of 30 planes in fiscal 1982 and 1984 would increase the cost of each of the 24 planes by $2.1 million. It added $172 million to the request, bringing the authorization to $1.1 billion for 30 F-14s. Both committees approved $202 million for advance procurement of F-14 parts.

The panels reversed roles in dealing with the smaller F-18 carrier fighter. Both approved the request for 84 planes in fiscal 1983 ($2.4 billion); but the Senate panel authorized $319 million for enough components to buy 108 planes in fiscal 1984. The House committee approved the request for $284 million to buy components for 96 planes in fiscal 1984.

Also at issue was the AV-8B, an improved version of the Harrier light bomber, which could take off and land vertically. The new plane for years had been the Marine Corps' highest aviation priority, but Congress had to champion the program against the hostility of the Carter Pentagon and the indifference of the Navy (which bought the Marines' airplanes).

The Senate committee approved the fiscal 1983 request for 18 Harrier Bs ($677 million) and components for 30 planes to be bought in fiscal 1984 ($74 million). But the panel increased the $114 million research and development request by $22 million to develop a trainer version of the plane and an additional $15 million to test a radar that would help it to fight other airplanes.

The House panel increased the procurement request to $808 million so that 30 Harriers could be bought in fiscal 1983. And it raised the advance component procurement to $90 million so that 40 planes could be built in fiscal 1984.

Air Force Planes

For fiscal 1983, the Air Force requested 42 F-15s ($1.3 billion) and 120 smaller F-16s ($1.735 billion). It requested advance component procurement to support the purchase of 60 F-15s in fiscal 1984 and 96 in fiscal 1985 ($305 million). It also requested advance procurement for 120 F-16s in fiscal 1984 ($223 million).

For fiscal 1983, the Senate committee increased the F-15 production to 48 ($1.4 billion), saying this would reduce the price of each plane by $1.6 million, but approved advance procurement only for fiscal 1984 ($202 million). It concurred in the fiscal 1983 request for F-16s, but ordered

more advance procurement ($391 million) so that 180 of the planes could be bought in each of the next two years, partly to equip Reserve and National Guard units.

The House panel, on the other hand, called for a steady F-15 production rate of 30 per year, citing doubts that the Air Force could afford its planned expansion of the F-15 fleet. It approved $1.079 billion for fiscal 1983 procurement and $142 million for advance procurement for fiscal 1984 of F-15s.

But the committee called for an immediate increase of the F-16 production rate to 140 a year, partly so that Air National Guard units could be quickly equipped with the plane. It increased the fiscal 1983 F-16 procurement request to $1.976 billion and the advance procurement authorization to $253 million.

Future Fighters

To help determine what planes it would buy in the late 1980s, the Air Force requested $25 million to test a modified F-15, $21 million to test a modified F-16 — both equipped as ground attack planes — and $27 million to develop a new fighter design.

The Senate committee trimmed the F-15 amount to $13 million and the F-16 allowance to $11 million, explaining that after one of the two was chosen, all funds would go to it. But the House committee turned down all three amounts, insisting that existing designs would be adequate through the 1980s, if equipped with new weapons and electronic devices.

Operations and Maintenance

Because of economic events since the budget request was prepared, both committees said that several hundred million dollars could be cut from the Pentagon's request for operations and maintenance (O&M) funds without reducing the program.

Lower-than-budgeted fuel prices would allow a reduction of $436 million in the $9.3 billion request to cover fuel cost, according to the House committee. The Senate panel more conservatively estimated a $350 million saving.

Because some O&M funds were spent abroad to pay the cost of operating units overseas, the increasing value of the dollar against some foreign currencies would allow a $192 million reduction in O&M, the House committee said. The corresponding Senate reduction was $195 million.

Building Maintenance

Both committees placed a premium on reducing the backlog of military buildings — including family housing — for which maintenance and repair had been deferred due to budget limits. In addition to impairing military operations, they argued, a deteriorating physical plant undermined morale.

To accelerate reduction of the maintenance backlog, the Senate committee added $483 million to the $3.7 billion real property maintenance request. The House panel increased the request by $295 million.

Objecting that it was not sufficiently urgent to justify a supplemental authorization, both committees rejected the administration request for an additional fiscal 1982 authorization of $460 million to reduce the repair backlog.

Navy Readiness

The House committee also added funds to two O&M accounts to increase the combat readiness of the Navy:

• To increase the amount of time fleets could be at sea, it added $100 million to the budget for "steaming days." The Navy was not unhappy with a slight reduction in steaming time in the fiscal 1983 budget, warning that crews needed more time in port after the long deployments that had been necessary since a fleet was deployed to the Indian Ocean.

• It also added $101 million requested by the Navy, but not included in the budget, for additional modifications to aircraft already in service.

The House panel also complained that General Accounting Office (GAO) audits had cast doubt on the necessity of some of scheduled maintenance overhauls of Navy ships and planes.

As a signal to the Navy of its concern, the committee shaved $100 million from the $6.5 billion ship and plane overhaul accounts.

Manpower

Very minor reductions in the request for 2,147,600 active duty military personnel were recommended by the two Armed Services committees: 9,300 by the House panel, 10,500 by the Senate unit. This ensured that the final version of the bill would approve an increase of at least 20,000 in the size of the active duty force compared to the fiscal 1982 level.

The committees extended through fiscal 1983 a limit on the proportion of male Army recruits that could be accepted without a high school diploma: 35 percent. Existing law (enacted in 1980) limited to 20 percent the proportion of its recruits each service could draw from among those who scored below the middle range on the standard recruiting aptitude test.

Reserves

Both committees touted the value of the Reserve and National Guard units as part of the U.S. military posture, and both backed up the praise with additional authorizations earmarked for equipment to modernize those units.

The Senate committee directed the Air Force to consider using Reserve units for some jobs it had planned to fill with a requested expansion of the active duty force. The House went further, telling all the services to use Reserve forces for all future increases in the size of the U.S. combat force "unless some persuasive evidence exists, developed on a case-by-case basis, that active personnel must be used."

The House added to the bill a total of $1.2 billion to more rapidly modernize Reserve equipment. In addition to anti-tank helicopters and anti-aircraft weapons, this included 16 C-130 cargo planes ($324 million), $44 million to lease or buy used DC-9s transports, and $243 million for various other items.

The House committee also earmarked for the Air National Guard, the 20 F-16 fighters it added to the bill and all 30 A-10 tank-hunters authorized in its bill.

The Senate panel increased the authorization request by $75 million for four C-130s and $200 million for trucks, radios and various other pieces of equipment for Reserve units.

Civilians

The budget request for a civilian Pentagon employee ceiling of 1,024,000 would add 11,000 to the fiscal 1982 ceiling.

The Senate committee rejected the proposed increase.

The House panel proposed to increase the civilian ceiling by 14,560, but that was because the House unit objected to administration plans to contract out some 17,000 jobs to civilian firms.

One headline in the House report called contracting-out "A Sensible Program Gone Awry." The committee granted that contracts for certain kinds of housekeeping jobs, such as janitorial and food services, could save money. But it maintained that the Office of Management and Budget placed enormous pressure on the Defense Department to contract jobs out to arbitrarily reduce the number of federal employees.

As a result, according to the committee, some jobs were contracted out despite any promise of real savings and despite possible harm to combat readiness of units.

Promising to report legislation to regulate contracting out, the committee included in the bill a one-year moratorium on additional contracting out.

The Senate committee, by contrast, recommended a provision that would exempt from the requirement for elaborate cost-benefit studies any proposal to contract out a federal activity staffed entirely by military personnel or by fewer than 50 civilians.

Army Civilians. Both committees complained that they may have been misled by the Army, which was granted an increase of 16,800 civilian employees in 1981. The Army had claimed that the new employees were needed to replace military personnel who were being diverted from combat assignments to perform administrative chores, thus degrading the Army's combat readiness.

According to a GAO report on the use of the new civilians, however, many were assigned to jobs in no apparent order of priority, and in some cases to jobs that had not even existed when the Army requested the new positions.

Moreover, the GAO report called into question the basic argument that the use of military personnel for these non-military jobs eroded combat efficiency.

The Senate committee cut the Army's requested manpower ceiling in fiscal 1983 by 8,400 and told the service to justify its use of the 16,800 new civilians or face a loss of the manpower.

The House committee cut the Army civilian request by 1,000.

Other Provisions

Both committees dropped from the bill $10.7 million requested to begin buying 9mm automatic pistols to replace existing sidearms for personnel in all services. The Pentagon had canceled the request and the Senate panel said it would consider any future proposal for a new gun that was chosen on a competitive basis.

But the House committee added to the bill a flat prohibition on use of any authorized funds to even evaluate another 9mm gun proposal. The panel said the move was not justified, and the services all gave it a low priority.

This was the first year that the annual authorizing bill had covered ammunition and small procurement items. The Armed Services committees in 1981 extended the authorization requirement to those items, arguing that they affected the combat readiness of U.S. forces.

House Provisions

The House panel's version of the bill also:

• Directed the secretary of defense to report to Congress by July 8, 1982, on any proposed changes in the organiza-

tion of the Joint Chiefs of Staff, and to comment on an extensive reorganization proposal by Gen. David C. Jones, chairman of the Joint Chiefs.

● Directed the secretary of the Army and the secretary of the Navy to report to Congress by Jan. 1, 1983, on the extent to which the concept of "maneuver warfare" had been incorporated into the policies and training of the Army and Marine Corps (which was a part of the Navy). Maneuver warfare emphasized tactics designed to disrupt an enemy's ability to coordinate his ground forces rather than trying to destroy enemy forces tank-by-tank.

● Ordered the Pentagon to charge prices in its five executive dining rooms that reflected prevailing prices in similar Washington-area restaurants. The committee said the Defense Department should not subsidize the operation of the facilities by absorbing overhead costs.

Senate Provisions

Senate Armed Services' version of the bill included provisions that:

● Required review by the Armed Services committees of any plan to purchase military equipment, to be sold to foreign countries, with money from the Special Defense Acquisition Fund. The fund was established by the fiscal 1982 foreign aid authorization bill and would be capitalized with receipts from foreign military sales and funds appropriated for grant military aid. *(1981 Almanac p. 162)*

● Barred consolidation of the Air Force's Military Airlift Command, the Navy's Military Sealift Command and the Army's Military Traffic Management Command.

● Directed the secretary of defense to provide Congress with a plan to ensure that the children of military personnel would continue to have access to free public schools. The Reagan administration wanted to slash "impact aid" to school districts with huge military installations that diminished the local school revenue base. Accordingly, several local school boards had closed schools near bases or had begun charging tuition for military dependents. The committee ordered the secretary to explain why the Pentagon should not provide impact assistance.

● Required the secretary of defense to submit to Congress two documents on efforts to control the transfer of sensitive technology overseas: a funding request for Pentagon technology control programs; and a report, to be submitted by Dec. 31, 1982, discussing the adequacy of those programs and making recommendations for improvements.

● Temporarily (through Oct. 1, 1983) increased to 17.5 percent the proportion of Navy flag officers who could hold the rank of admiral or vice admiral. The current limit was 15 percent.

● Authorized the Pentagon to compile, for use in recruiting, information on high school students, such as names, addresses, and academic achievements. Academic officials could not be compelled to provide the information. The Pentagon also would be authorized to ask state and local authorities about the criminal records of recruits.

Senate Floor Action

The Senate May 14 passed a $177 billion defense authorization bill after the Armed Services Committee had turned back most proposals to significantly amend the measure (S 2248) on the floor. As passed by the Senate, the bill authorized $177,397,810,000 for defense research and development, procurement, and operations and maintenance in fiscal 1983.

The Senate began debate on the bill May 3, and continued May 4-6 and 11-12. Final passage came after a marathon session that began at 11 a.m. on May 13 and concluded at 5:28 a.m. on May 14.

The vote was 84-8. *(Vote 120, p. 23-S)*

Although Senate debate on S 2248 sprawled over seven days, few major amendments were dealt with until the last two days. Earlier action on the bill had been bogged down in skirmishes over the fiscal 1983 budget resolution (S Con Res 92). *(Budget resolution, p. 186)*

After the White House and Senate Budget Committee Republicans agreed on an overall budget proposal May 5, Armed Services Chairman John Tower, R-Texas, had agreed reluctantly to reduce S 2248 to help meet the targets. He accepted an $8.9 billion reduction in projected defense outlays and $12.9 billion in budget authority — including funds for military pay and other budget accounts in separate legislation.

The Armed Services Committee agreed on a package to make those cuts on the afternoon of May 10, and the bill was altered by a committee amendment to include them.

The defense measure was tied up for hours on the floor while Democrats used it as a vehicle to attack one part of the Budget Committee budget package — unspecified cost reductions of $40 billion in Social Security during fiscal 1983-85.

Economic Pressure

The political effect of a sluggish economy was too powerful for Tower to beat back some amendments that turned essentially on the politics of the pork barrel.

Tower's most dramatic loss of this sort was the Senate's acceptance of amendments by Slade Gorton, R-Wash., and Henry M. Jackson, D-Wash., that would use funds earmarked for C-5 transport planes, built in Georgia by the Lockheed Corp., to buy surplus wide-body jets from U.S. airlines. The key vote was the Senate's rejection, 39-60, of a motion to table the Jackson amendment. *(Vote 109, p. 22-S)*

The Senate also approved, over the committee's objection, amendments:

● By Daniel Patrick Moynihan, D-N.Y., to allow the Pentagon to pay a premium of up to 1.5 percent to purchase commodities (excluding weapons and fuel) from firms in areas of high unemployment. This partial waiver of the so-called "Maybank" amendment long had been favored by congressional delegations from Northeastern and Midwestern states with high unemployment and relatively little defense industry. Adopted 48-45. *(Vote 115, p. 23-S)*

● By George J. Mitchell, D-Maine, to prevent the Pentagon from "contracting-out" to civilian firms firefighting and security jobs on military bases, jobs that were performed by civilian federal employees. Relatively few jobs would be directly affected by the amendment. But the committee, which in general favored contracting out as a cost-reduction tool, feared that the amendment's adoption by a roll-call vote would undermine the panel's bargaining position when the bill went to conference. The House Armed Services Committee's version of the bill included a flat moratorium on additional contracting-out in fiscal 1983. Adopted 50-47. *(Vote 95, p. 20-S)*

The committee won one important jobs-related fight, when the Senate voted 59-36 to table an amendment by John Heinz, R-Pa., that would have barred the purchase of so-called "specialty metals" from non-U.S. sources. This included various metals and steel alloys that were used in

jet engines because of their ability to withstand extremely high temperatures. *(Vote 116, p. 23-S)*

Weapons purchases had been exempted from the "buy American" requirement for specialty metals from fiscal 1977 until December 1982, when the exemption was dropped from the fiscal 1982 defense appropriations bill (HR 4995). This drew strong objections from the governments of several NATO allies that sold military equipment to the Pentagon, a small portion of which incorporated specialty metals.

The Armed Services Committee had included in S 2248 a provision reinstating the exemption for fiscal 1982.

Arms Talks

Tower suffered a minor tactical defeat May 12, when the Senate rejected 32-60 a motion to table an amendment by Arlen Specter, R-Pa., that would have urged the president to call for a U.S.-Soviet summit meeting to discuss nuclear arms control. *(Vote 98, p. 20-S)*

But the concern of Tower and the administration — that the amendment might appear to force Reagan's hand on nuclear arms control policy — already had been accommodated. Although the amendment was introduced May 4, Specter had agreed to defer a vote until after Reagan announced his nuclear arms reduction proposal May 9.

And before the amendment was adopted May 12 by a vote of 92-6, Specter accepted a Tower amendment that cast the measure in terms of commending Reagan's expressed desire for a summit. *(Vote 102, p. 21-S)*

Cargo Planes

The C-5 battle pitted the administration and Sens. Sam Nunn, D-Ga., and Mack Mattingly, R-Ga., against Gorton, Jackson, and several financially strapped airlines with Boeing 747s they could not fly profitably. (Though the amendment did not stipulate the purchase of 747s, that was its effect.) Boeing's corporate headquarters were in Seattle, Wash. Both Kansas Republicans, Robert Dole and Nancy Landon Kassebaum, also backed the amendment. The 747s were to be modified at a Boeing plant in Kansas.

Technically, the choice between the C-5 and the 747 turned on whether the Air Force needed more planes that could carry "outsize" cargo — large pieces of equipment such as tanks and helicopters that could easily be loaded into the C-5 but not the 747. The Pentagon said yes, citing several scenarios for intervention in the Middle East or reinforcement of U.S. troops in Europe, and asked for 50 more C-5s, in addition to 77 already in service.

Jackson and his allies maintained that the existing C-5s were sufficient if they were used only to carry the extra-bulky cargo. The 747 could carry a larger volume of smaller pieces of cargo, which did not require the C-5's very wide fuselage and loading doors. Supporters of the Jackson-Gorton amendments also insisted that surplus 747s could be bought much more cheaply than the new C-5s.

But Jackson won chiefly by a combination of vigorous personal lobbying and a widespread concern over the state of the airline industry, heightened by the collapse of Braniff International Corp. the day before the amendment was debated. Supporters of the 747 purchase emphasized it would provide airlines with a rapid infusion of cash. In addition to Boeing and Lockheed, several airlines, and banks that had financed their purchase of 747s, had been lobbying on the issue.

Nunn protested that the defense bill was being turned into a relief bill for the airline industry. He sarcastically likened the 747 provision to buying farm combines rather than tanks for the Army in order to help the ailing International Harvester Co.

Nunn then offered an amendment to require that any funds for commercial wide-body jets be used only to lease them through the Civil Reserve Air Fleet (CRAF) program, not to purchase them; Mack Mattingly, R-Ga., offered a slightly different substitute for Nunn's language. The Senate tabled the Mattingly substitute (53-44) and Nunn then withdrew his amendment. Lockheed Corp. would produce the C-5 plane in Marietta, Ga. *(Vote 110, p. 22-S)*

Committee Amendment

The committee amendment, which reduced the authorization by $2.379 billion, was incorporated into the bill when it was recommitted briefly May 12. It had been drafted May 10 after a closed committee meeting with Defense Secretary Caspar W. Weinberger.

The committee's original action on S 2248 had pared $3.166 billion from the authorization. So, in all, the committee reduced Reagan's defense authorization request by $5.545 billion in budget authority.

A reduction of 19,900 from the manpower ceilings set in the original committee version of the bill reduced budget authority by an additional $415 million. This was in addition to a $106 million reduction due to manpower cuts in the committee's initial version.

The committee anticipated making a further reduction of $3.9 billion in budget authority (and almost as much in outlays) by raising military pay only 4 percent and including Pentagon civilians in an overall freeze in federal pay for fiscal 1983. Reagan had budgeted routine pay hikes of 8 percent for military personnel and 5 percent for civilians.

Nuclear Warfare. A net reduction of $200 million was recommended in anti-ballistic missile development funds. The LoADS short-range missile program, designed to protect armored military installations such as missile launchers, was reduced by $300 million. But $100 million was added back to the account for development of a longer-range missile defense that might provide a second layer of protection for the MX missile.

A cut of $285.6 million resulted from a decision to equip the ninth Trident submarine and all later Tridents only with the Trident II missile.

Naval Warfare. The largest single reduction, $450 million, came from halving (to 24) production of the LAMPS III anti-submarine helicopter, which was to be stationed aboard most of the Navy's surface combat ships by the end of the 1980s.

An additional $95 million in operating costs was to be saved by mothballing 13 *Forrest Sherman*-class destroyers, built in 1955-59 and due for retirement in the late 1980s. These were the only destroyers in the fleet not equipped with either anti-aircraft missiles or anti-submarine helicopters.

The committee rejected an administration proposal to mothball four other *Sherman*-class ships that had been equipped with anti-aircraft missiles.

Marine Corps Landings. The panel also rejected a Pentagon proposal to mothball five amphibious landing ships of the LSD-28 class, due for retirement starting in 1985. Money for replacement vessels (the LSD-41 class) was authorized beginning in fiscal 1981.

The Senate committee deleted the $10 million it had approved (of $40 million requested) to begin chartering cargo ships to store the tanks and other heavy equipment

of a Marine division near potential trouble spots.

Other Changes. Four other major weapons programs were among those affected by the new committee action:

● Procurement of armored ammunition carriers for Army artillery was to be canceled (a $111 million cut).

● Funds to increase the production capacity for M-1 tanks were deleted ($200.3 million), although there was no change in the $1.89 billion authorization to buy 776 tanks in fiscal 1983.

● Production of the HARM missile, designed to be fired by airplanes against ground-based radar, was slowed ($150 million).

● The committee expected to save $57.7 million by consolidating the management of Air Force and Navy cruise-missile development programs.

The committee also deleted $135 million for real property maintenance. Initially, it had added $460 million to the administration's property maintenance request.

An additional $91 million was cut in anticipation of lower-than-budgeted fuel prices. In its initial version of S 2248, the committee already had cut $350 million from the administration's fuel price estimate on similar grounds.

In addition to mothballing the 13 Navy destroyers, the committee proposed savings by deactivating one Army battalion. During talks on how to make the new cuts, the administration had proposed deactivating four battalions and one Air Force interceptor wing equipped with older fighters.

Nerve Gas

The Senate split basically along liberal-conservative lines to table (49-45) an amendment by Gary Hart, D-Colo., banning production of the so-called "binary munitions" and to use the $54 million earmarked for that program to buy defenses against chemical attack. *(Vote 118, p. 23-S)*

How Many? The Senate adopted an amendment by Mark O. Hatfield, R-Ore., to:

● ban the use of human subjects in tests of the new munitions;

● require the Pentagon to render "permanently useless for military purposes" one existing nerve gas artillery shell for each binary shell manufactured; and

● build only the number of shells needed for U.S. forces, unless another NATO nation agreed to accept the new shells for its own forces.

Hatfield's amendment was adopted 92-0, but only after it had been modified during negotiations with Warner, whose Armed Services subcommittee handled the binary issue. *(Vote 119, p. 23-S)*

As originally proposed by Hatfield, the amendment also would have barred binary production until the United States and the Soviet Union had been engaged for 300 days in negotiations to conclude a verifiable treaty barring production of chemical weapons, and had concluded that agreement was impossible. This requirement would have been waived if negotiations could not take place because of Soviet refusal to talk. Hatfield's final amendment did not mention a requirement for negotiations.

Treaty Negotiations. The Senate did approve two amendments urging U.S. efforts to further limit chemical and biological weapons by treaty. Agreed to by voice vote were amendments:

● By William Proxmire, D-Wis., calling on the U.S. government to propose amendments to a 1972 treaty banning production and stockpiling of biological weapons. The pro-

posed amendments would establish procedures to investigate alleged violations and would set standards to distinguish research on offensive biological weapons, which was prohibited by the treaty, from research on defenses against biological warfare, which was permitted by the treaty.

Proxmire's amendment also called for diplomatic efforts to condemn the use of biological weapons by Soviet or allied forces.

● By Cochran, as amended by Tower, calling on the U.S. government to "continue to promote" U.N.-sponsored negotiations to produce a treaty banning production and stockpiling of chemical weapons; to demand an explanation of allegations that chemical weapons had been used by Soviet forces or their surrogates; and to communicate to Moscow the U.S. desire for a chemical weapons ban, once the U.S. government was satisfied that the Soviet government was not in violation of existing chemical warfare treaties.

Cochran's original amendment simply would have called on the U.S. government to "actively promote" the U.N. negotiations and to communicate to Moscow its willingness to negotiate.

Strategic Warfare

By a vote of 65-29 vote, the Senate tabled an amendment by Glenn to scrap the MX missile and begin development of a new missile that could more easily be protected against Soviet missile attack. *(Vote 113, p. 23-S)*

Glenn argued for building a much smaller missile that could be hauled around on existing highways in a large truck — an idea many defense specialists called politically unsalable.

The Senate also adopted an amendment by Warner to reduce by $300 million the Army request to develop LoADS, a short-range anti-missile missile designed to protect MX launchers. The amendment also added to the bill $100 million to begin developing a longer-range anti-missile system that could be combined with LoADS to defend an MX "dense pack" basing system.

This amendment had been agreed to by the Armed Services Committee as part of its plan to reduce the authorization total to meet the May 5 budget agreement.

Titan II Missiles. The Senate rejected 40-54 an amendment by Robert Dole, R-Kan., to eliminate from the bill $80 million added by the Armed Services panel to retain in service all of the 52 remaining Titan II ICBMs, which were based in Kansas, Arkansas and Arizona. *(Vote 107, p. 21-S)*

Before rejecting the Dole amendment, the Senate rejected a motion by J. James Exon, D-Neb., to table it (32-61). *(Vote 106, p. 21-S)*

Other Nuclear Issues. The Senate also agreed to three other amendments related to nuclear strategy:

● By Sam Nunn, D-Ga., requiring the secretary of defense to study ways to tighten control over nuclear weapons in case of a crisis, including joint U.S.-Soviet actions, such as establishment of a crisis control center to monitor the use of nuclear weapons by third countries or terrorist groups. Adopted by voice vote.

● By Malcolm Wallop, R-Wyo., to direct the secretary of defense to organize the Pentagon's laser research program to deploy anti-missile lasers on orbiting satellites as soon as possible. Adopted by voice vote.

● By Arlen Specter, R-Pa., commending President Reagan's expressed desire for a U.S.-Soviet summit meeting on nuclear arms reduction. Adopted 92-6. *(Vote 102, p. 21-S)*

The Senate had rejected 32-60 a motion by Charles H. Percy, R-Ill., to table an earlier version of the Specter amendment. *(Vote 98, p. 20-S)*

'Military Reform' Amendments

The Senate approved four non-controversial amendments offered by members of the loosely knit "military reform caucus."

The reform amendments, all approved by voice vote, were designed largely to force senior Pentagon managers to focus on issues of concern to the caucus. They were:

• By Hart, requiring the secretaries of the Army and Navy to report to Congress on the extent to which the concept of "maneuver warfare" has been incorporated into the policies and training of the Army and Marine Corps (which was a part of the Navy). Maneuver warfare emphasized tactics designed to disrupt the enemy's ability to coordinate his ground forces, rather than trying to destroy enemy forces tank-by-tank.

• By Slade Gorton, R-Wash., directing the secretary of each military service to report to Congress on the extent to which military history was taught in each school and training program under his jurisdiction.

• By Nunn, requiring the secretary of defense to report on a study of the future of the National Guard entitled *Vista 1999*. The study proposed, among other things, that simpler, less expensive weapons be procured to modernize the National Guard and Air National Guard.

• By Warner, requiring the secretary of defense to report on "unit cohesion initiatives" taken by the armed services or planned for the next five years. These were personnel policies intended to improve morale and discipline by leaving service members in the same unit for the duration of their military service.

National Guard and Reserve

Four non-controversial amendments to support the National Guard and Reserve component forces were approved by voice vote:

• By Jake Garn, R-Utah, expressing the sense of Congress that members of the Guard and Reserve components deserve public recognition for their contribution to national defense;

• By Proxmire, and Strom Thurmond, R-S.C., to extend to nine months (from six months) the period for which an enlistee in the Guard and Reserve components could delay the start of his training. This was the delay already allowed enlistees in the active service components.

• By Proxmire and Thurmond, to provide an open enrollment period in the survivor benefit plan for certain Guard and Reserve members.

• By Proxmire and Thurmond, to extend education loan repayment benefits to certain junior officers in the selected reserve components.

Pork-Barrel Issues

The Senate rejected two amendments intended to limit Pentagon purchases from abroad of so-called "specialty metals": steel alloys and other metals used in jet engines and other military equipment because of special chemical properties, such as a tolerance for very high temperatures.

An amendment by John Heinz, R-Pa., to bar Pentagon purchase of non-U.S.-made specialty metals, was tabled 59-36. *(Vote 116, p. 23-S)*

Also tabled (56-39) was an amendment by Robert C. Byrd, D-W.Va., to bar Pentagon purchase of non-U.S.-produced specialty metals except for material incorporated into finished products. *(Vote 117, p. 23-S)*

A Heinz amendment, adopted by voice vote, barred the procurement of foreign-made naval ships, or of any major component of the hulls or superstructures of naval ships.

Defense Contracts. The Senate adopted two amendments affecting defense contracts:

• By Daniel Patrick Moynihan, D-N.Y., to waive the so-called "Maybank amendment" by allowing the Pentagon to pay premiums of up to 1.5 percent in order to buy commodities (other than weapons and fuel) from firms in high unemployment areas. Adopted 48-45. *(Vote 115, p. 23-S)*

• By George J. Mitchell, D-Maine, to prevent the Pentagon from contracting to civilian firms firefighting and security jobs on military bases currently performed by federal civilian employees. Adopted 50-47. *(Vote 95, p. 20-S)*

Aircraft Carriers

The administration request for $7 billion to build two *Nimitz*-class, nuclear-powered aircraft carriers survived two attacks by Hart, who long had championed construction of smaller carriers. Hart said smaller carriers could be afforded in much larger numbers than the bigger ships, thus allowing U.S. forces to cover more trouble spots at once.

Hart's amendment to defer indefinitely one of the two *Nimitz* carriers on budgetary grounds was tabled 63-32. *(Vote 111, p. 22-S)*

Another amendment to substitute two smaller carriers for one of the two nuclear-powered ships was tabled 72-19. *(Vote 112, p. 22-S)*

Other Amendments

The following other amendments to S 2248 were adopted by the Senate:

• By Roth, expressing the sense of Congress that NATO nations must pool their resources more effectively for the common defense; 87-1. *(Vote 108, p. 22-S)*

• By Carl Levin, D-Mich., directing the secretary of defense to report to Congress on why the administration did not plan to restation U.S. troops in Europe, if efforts to increase the defense contributions of other NATO nations were not successful. Adopted by voice vote.

• By Dan Quayle, R-Ind., to retain within the Defense Department schools operated overseas for U.S. military dependents, instead of transferring control of those schools to the Department of Education. Adopted 59-38. *(Vote 94, p. 20-S)*

• By Robert T. Stafford, R-Vt., deleting a provision added by the Armed Services Committee to retain within the Defense Department administrative control of 18 schools for military dependents on military bases in the United States. The budget reconciliation act passed in 1981 directed transfer of those schools to the Department of Education. Adopted by voice vote.

• By Levin, requiring the General Accounting Office to review Defense Department reports to Congress filed pursuant to the so-called "Nunn amendment." The Nunn amendment, added to the fiscal 1982 defense authorization bill (PL 97-86) required various reports to Congress on major weapons systems whose costs increased by more than a certain amount. Adopted by voice vote.

• By David Pryor, D-Ark., as amended by Roth, to establish an inspector general for the Defense Department.

The amendment was adopted by voice vote after the Senate voted 94-0 to adopt the Roth substitute.

Earlier, the Senate, by voice vote, tabled a Lloyd Bentsen, D-Texas, substitute for the Roth amendment. A motion to table the Bentsen substitute had been rejected 45-46; but the Senate then agreed to reconsider the vote to table, after a motion to table the motion to reconsider was rejected 42-51. *(Votes 103-105, p. 21-S)*

In large part, the issue between the Roth and Bentsen amendments was the balance between assuring the inspector general's independence from the secretary of defense and allowing the secretary to protect secret information from exposure by the audit process.

Bentsen's amendment made the inspector general statutorily independent of the secretary of defense, allowing the secretary to rule out audits only in case of risk to national security interests or intelligence sources and methods.

In Roth's version, which was the result of prolonged negotiations between the Pentagon and Roth's Governmental Affairs Committee, the inspector general was subject to the authority of the secretary of defense; but audits could be blocked only for certain reasons, similar to those specified by Bentsen's amendment.

● By Jackson and Nunn, increasing the ceiling on damage claims payable to certain military personnel seized in Iran during the 1979-81 hostage crisis. Adopted by voice vote.

● By Warner, expressing the sense of Congress that military personnel killed in 1980 during the effort to rescue U.S. hostages in Iran should be honored with a plaque in Arlington (Va.) National Cemetery. Adopted by voice vote.

● By Mattingly and S. I. "Sam" Hayakawa, R-Calif., to make non-registrants for the draft ineligible for certain federal aid for college education. Adopted by voice vote.

House Floor Action

Except for the emotionally charged issue of chemical warfare, Reagan's defense plans were essentially unscathed by House action on the defense bill (HR 6030).

But unhappiness within Reagan's pro-defense coalition was highlighted by a symbolic swipe at the overall authorization total. Though the bill as passed authorized $177.1 billion for defense programs, the House adopted a provision limiting to $175.3 billion the amount that actually could be spent under the bill — in effect, a 1 percent across-the-board reduction.

On the other hand, the majority of the House was unwilling to challenge specific defense programs.

The House passed the bill 290-73 on July 29, after seven days of debate. *(Vote 221, p. 66-H)*

The $177.1 billion authorized by HR 6030 was $6.4 billion less than Reagan's Feb. 8 request.

Signaling Unhappiness

The 1 percent spending reduction, offered by Dan Glickman, D-Kan., was approved 238-136 as a substitute for an amendment by Patricia Schroeder, D-Colo., that would have set a 5 percent spending reduction. The amended Schroeder amendment then was adopted (235-135). *(Votes 219-220, p. 66-H)*

On both votes, the 1 percent cut was backed by a majority of Republicans and two-thirds of the Democrats.

Glickman insisted the vote was symbolically significant. "Members are reacting to the fact that, with the enormous deficits we face, defense can't be sacrosanct," he said.

According to Glickman, several members said they were supporting his reduction in reaction to Reagan's July 28 statement that he did not feel bound by the first budget resolution's defense ceilings for fiscal 1984 and 1985.

Specific Cuts. Disgruntlement over having to vote for defense increases and domestic cuts produced no broad opposition to specific defense programs. For instance, a Schroeder amendment, that would have cut overseas troop deployments from 490,000 to 250,000 over the next four years was rejected 87-314. *(Vote 217, p. 64-H)*

However, the Schroeder proposal was so sweeping that the vote may not have reflected the depth and breadth of congressional conviction that U.S. allies were shirking their fair share of the burden of common defense.

A substitute amendment by Dennis E. Eckart, D-Ohio, would have withdrawn half of U.S. troops from those NATO nations that fail to meet a 1978 alliance agreement to increase defense spending by an annual real rate of 3 percent. It was rejected by voice vote, and Eckart was unable to force a roll-call vote.

Arms Control, Mixed

There appeared to be little support for the argument that the United States should not build weapons so fast and accurate that they could threaten a surprise attack on Soviet command posts and missile launchers.

A July 29 effort by Thomas J. Downey, D-N.Y., to cancel development of the Trident II missile for this reason was rejected 89-312. *(Vote 216, p. 64-H)*

A move to kill the Pershing II missile on the same grounds lost by a similar vote in earlier action.

Reagan's critics who demanded arms control rather than a nuclear buildup did better against his accelerated civil defense program. But they did not stress arms control arguments against the program so much as the contention that it was unworkable. The 163-240 vote on July 29 against an amendment by Edward J. Markey, D-Mass., to cut $108 million from the $254 million civil defense request was the high water mark of the critics' campaign. *(Vote 215, p. 64-H)*

The House apparently was not eager to abandon existing arms control arrangements.

That may have been a factor in its 3-2 vote against resumption of chemical weapons production, the one clear defeat that Reagan and the Armed Services Committee suffered on the House floor.

The committee also accepted and the House approved without debate an amendment by Les Aspin, D-Wis. It barred the use of authorized funds for any defense program that would "contravene" Reagan's May 31 statement that he would "refrain from actions which undercut" existing arms control agreements. The president could not spend such funds unless he gave Congress 30 days' notice that the action was required by "supreme national interests."

But a House Armed Services source said the Aspin provision was seen as a political counter to grass-roots pressure members had been feeling to vote for a nuclear freeze.

The House debated a freeze resolution (H J Res 521) the following month.

"They've all been coming to us and saying, 'you've got to give us something to vote for [in lieu of the freeze],'" the source said. "Every volunteer fire department and city council back home is passing [pro-freeze] resolutions."

MX Procurement

An amendment that would have removed $1.1 billion for production of the first nine MX missiles was killed by the narrow passage of a substitute amendment, 212-209. *(Vote 188, p. 56-H)*

The closeness of a July 21 vote may have reflected the uncertainty about the basing method for the missile more than outright opposition to it.

The amendment, offered by Armed Services members Nicholas Mavroules, D-Mass., and Beverly B. Byron, D-Md., would have deleted $1.14 billion earmarked for purchase of the first nine production-line versions of the MX.

"The MX program as it currently exists now represents a 'build first, justify later' mentality this nation can no longer afford," Mavroules declared.

He dismissed as inadequate Reagan's assurances, contained in a letter to House leaders, that he would select a final basing technique for the missile by December. "We were told that four or five times in the past by the last administration and by this one," he said.

He and Byron emphasized repeatedly that the amendment would not delay the development of the missile itself or the first test flight, which was set for January 1983.

But William L. Dickinson, R-Ala., warned that the amendment was — if not by intent — "nickeling and diming this weapons system to death.... The net effect is going to be to add millions and millions to the already overburdened weapons system, or else kill it."

To deflect some members' resistance to authorizing funds for an undefined project, Samuel S. Stratton, D-N.Y., offered a substitute amendment that retained the full amount recommended by the Armed Services Committee but barred expenditure of the $259.9 million earmarked for basing until 30 days after the president reported to Congress his chosen basing method.

The substitute was adopted on the 212-209 vote; it was strongly supported by Republicans (142-45) and Southern Democrats (52-23) and was overwhelmingly opposed by Northern Democrats (18-141).

Chemical Weapons

Republicans contributed substantially to the margin by which the House rejected an administration request for $54 million to begin production of a new type of lethal chemical weapons, called binary munitions.

An amendment by Clement J. Zablocki, D-Wis., that deleted the funds was approved July 22 by a 251-159 vote. But the key vote on the issue came minutes earlier, when the House rejected, by 192-225, an administration-approved substitute offered by Jim Courter, R-N.J. The Courter substitute would have allowed production of binary weapons if one existing chemical weapon was dismantled for each new weapon produced. *(Votes 194-195, p. 58-H)*

During the June 22 House debate, binary opponents laid heavy emphasis on the argument that the 13-year-old U.S. ban on chemical weapons production provided valuable propaganda leverage, particularly in the face of evidence that the Soviet Union and its clients had used chemical weapons in Afghanistan and Southeast Asia.

Ed Bethune of Arkansas, Zablocki's principal Republican ally in the anti-binary fight, summarized the propaganda argument early in the debate.

"What it boils down to is this: We are not like the Soviets. We do not want to be like the Soviets. And on this issue, at least, we can prove it," he said. "Our refusal to produce or use chemical weapons sets us apart from the Soviets in a way that corroborates our often-declared goal that we really want to reduce arms,"

David R. Obey, D-Wis., warned that the diplomatic cost of the binary program could be particularly high in Western Europe, where domestic opposition to chemical weapons had made allied government chary of supporting the U.S. program. "We need right now, more than anything else, to shore up support from our allies on arms control, on trade positions, on Poland and the like," Obey said. "This is precisely the wrong time to proceed with the development of this system."

Both Obey and Bethune noted that a decision not to produce the weapons could be reversed if the United States and the Soviet Union could not agree on a treaty banning chemical weapons.

"We are making a decision for the moment and for the moment only," Obey said.

And Bethune hinted that Congress might want to reconsider the issue if, for example, President Reagan and Soviet Premier Leonid Brezhnev met but made no progress on the issue.

Armed Services Committee members started from the assumption that existing chemical weapons stocks were inadequate and unsafe. The liquid in existing chemical weapons was corroding the shells and bombs to the point that they would become unsafe to handle and would have to be destroyed, the committee members insisted.

But chemical weapons could not simply be abandoned, they contended, because an enemy armed with such weapons would be deterred from using them only by the prospect of U.S. retaliation in kind.

"If Adolph Hitler and the Nazi war machine had not been convinced that we had the capability as they did," Rep. William L. Dickinson, R-Ala., said by way of example, "they would have used gas on the invading troops at Normandy."

If the United States did not possess adequate chemical weapons, Dickinson warned, Soviet use of chemical weapons could be deterred only by the prospect of a U.S. nuclear retaliation.

"Is that what we want?" he demanded. "Do we want to lower the nuclear threshold?"

Dickinson also argued that the amendment would undercut U.S. leverage to negotiate limitations on chemical weapons. "Why should [the Russians] come in and bargain in good faith with us, when they say, 'Well, your Congress says you can't even build any to start with. Why do we need to talk with you?'"

The alleged propaganda advantage of continued abstinence from chemical weapons production was challenged by G. William Whitehurst, R-Va., who pointed to the use of chemical weapons by Soviet allies in Cambodia and Laos.

"Has world opinion rushed to our side?" he asked. "I barely heard a peep."

Before adopting the Zablocki amendment, the House adopted 232-181 a Bethune amendment to prohibit the use of any funds authorized in the bill for binary weapons production. *(Vote 193, p. 58-H)*

Also adopted by voice vote was an amendment to Zablocki's amendment by Marge Roukema, R-N.J., expressing the sense of Congress that the United States should continue to seek a negotiated comprehensive ban on chemical weaponry and should press for a full explanation of alleged chemical weapons use by the Soviet Union or its proxies.

Cargo Planes

The administration prevailed in the most heavily lobbied pork-barrel issue in any recent defense bill: the choice of a new fleet of long-range transport planes. By a vote of 127-289, the House rejected an amendment that would, in effect, have mandated the purchase of Boeing 747s, rather than Lockheed C-5 cargo jets. *(Vote 190, p. 56-H)*

When the House took up the airlift issue July 21, the Speaker's Lobby had taken on the aspect of a weapons makers' convention, with giant models of ICBMs standing alongside blown-up photographs of the contending cargo planes.

The battle was waged largely by members with direct constituent interests in the award of the contract.

Norman D. Dicks, D-Wash., offered essentially the same amendment Jackson had won in the Senate; it would have deleted the $860 million for the CX and added $350 million for procurement of "the most cost-effective commercial wide-body cargo aircraft."

The two plane makers had weighed in with full-page newspaper ads, touting their respective aircraft. A Lockheed ad that ran in *The Washington Post* the day of the House debate included several photographs of a demonstration staged for members of Congress and the press at Andrews Air Force Base, near Washington: A C-5 landed and disgorged a Cobra anti-tank helicopter, which flew off within 10 minutes of the C-5's landing.

This was the core of the C-5 proponents' case: The plane's unique ability to carry so-called outsize equipment, such as tanks, helicopters and anti-aircraft weapons. "You want to deliver combat-loaded equipment that rolls off and goes into battle," Newt Gingrich, R-Ga., told the House during the debate.

The 747 could not carry some of the largest items of equipment at all, and could carry others only if they were partly disassembled.

Dicks and the other Boeing backers maintained that the existing C-5 fleet was adequate. "If you dedicate your existing 77 C-5s to that outsize equipment," Dicks told the House, "you have enough planes in the near term to handle the outsize equipment ... and you really need additional capability to handle bulk and oversize [cargo]." Oversize equipment is small enough to fit a commercial wide-body jet; bulk cargo includes ammunition and supplies.

On this premise, Dicks and his allies concentrated on the lower cost of the 747, a theme struck in a Boeing newspaper ad appearing the day before the debate.

Over a 20-year lifetime, Boeing estimated that a 747 fleet would cost about $12.1 billion and a C-5 fleet about $20 billion to buy and operate.

The Air Force put the cost difference at only $1 billion, rather than $7.9 billion, insisting that Boeing had omitted several costs. But Dicks defended the Boeing estimate, complaining that the Air Force "will say anything or do anything to sell their proposal up here on Capitol Hill."

The House rejected Dicks' amendment 127-289, after also rejecting, 74-344, a substitute by Robert E. Badham, R-Calif., that would have dropped funds for both planes. Badham maintained the Pentagon should concentrate on developing a new, smaller out-size plane called the C-17 (formerly CX). *(Votes 190, 189, p. 56-H)*

Debating Assumptions

By a vote of 55-348, the House July 20 rejected a substitute authorization bill, offered by Ronald V. Dellums, D-Calif, an Armed Services Committee member.

His substitute set the stage for a two-and-a-half-hour debate over the fundamental premises of U.S. national security policy. *(Vote 186, p. 54-H)*

The substitute, which would have cut $50.9 billion from the committee bill, was based on "a noninterventionist foreign and military policy, [and] a doctrine of sufficiency rather than superiority, which in the nuclear age is a contradiction in terms," Dellums told the House.

The amendment would have pared U.S. troop strength by 5 percent, partly on the grounds that the European allies were doing too little for their own defense and partly on grounds that existing overseas deployments could tempt U.S. intervention in developing countries.

But much of the floor debate concentrated on nuclear arms policy. The amendment would have canceled most nuclear weapons programs, including the MX, Trident II, Pershing and cruise missiles. The one exception was the Trident submarine.

Dellums said the missiles were weapons "that make the world more dangerous, that bring greater insecurity rather than security, and weapons that provide the basis for the Soviet Union to put their weapons in a launch-on-warning capacity because our weapons become so powerful that we thwart the Soviets' capacity to establish a credible deterrence."

Dellums also argued that Reagan's nuclear arms buildup went "far beyond" what was needed to deter a Soviet attack, on the assumption that it was possible to fight and win a nuclear war. "I would suggest that anyone believing that we can fight, survive and win a nuclear war is living in a never-never land," he declared.

Floyd Spence, R-S.C., argued that Dellums' position assumed "that anything we do to defend ourselves is provocative, is destabilizing and could upset our adversaries to the extent that they might want to have some kind of confrontation with us."

Stratton, an Armed Services Committee member, summarized the administration's contention that deterrence requirements could not be arbitrarily distinguished from nuclear war fighting capabilities.

"In order to have a credible deterrent, it is necessary for any potential adversary ... to recognize that if the deterrent does not deter, you have the capability of fighting," Stratton said.

Dellums' support came almost entirely from liberal Democrats, and included all voting members of the Congressional Black Caucus.

Conyers Amendment. On July 22, the House rejected by a vote of 21-355 an amendment by John Conyers Jr., D-Mich., that would have deleted $10.5 billion in authorization for all of the nuclear weapons programs in the bill, including the Trident submarine and the Trident I missile. *(Vote 198, p. 58-H)*

Pershing Missile. The argument against weapons that would threaten Soviet forces with a surprise attack was the heart of Dellums' case against the Pershing II missile, which he called "the single most destabilizing weapon that we are planning to deploy."

His amendment to delete $498.3 million earmarked to buy 91 of the missiles was rejected 74-311 on July 21. *(Vote 191, p. 56-H)*

The next day, the first test model of the Pershing II failed spectacularly in a test launch from Cape Canaveral, Fla. Army officials destroyed the missile shortly after takeoff, when the first-stage engine failed.

MX Development. In contrast to the narrow (212-209) margin by which the House approved MX missile procurement funds on July 21, it easily turned down an effort on July 27 to reduce MX research funds by $715 million.

At issue was an amendment by Paul Simon, D-Ill., and Bill Green, R-N.Y., to delete from the bill the amount earmarked for development of a way to base the first 40 MXs in existing Minuteman missile silos.

Both members insisted their amendment was intended simply to rule out deployment of the missiles in silos that would be vulnerable to Soviet attack. They emphasized that it did not touch $160 million the committee had approved (of $310 million requested) for research on other MX basing methods that would be more survivable in an attack.

Repeating a tactic he had used a week earlier, during the debate over MX procurement, Stratton sidetracked Simon's attack on MX funding with a substitute that authorized the amount requested, but provided that the money could not be spent until 30 legislative days after Congress had been notified of the president's choice of a permanent, survivable basing method for MX.

Under friendly questioning by Aspin, Stratton agreed that the effect of his substitute was to combine the $715 million for interim MX basing and the $160 million approved for permanent MX basing. This paralleled the course taken by the Senate, which approved $565 million for permanent basing research only.

Simon and Green then accepted Stratton's proposal, which was adopted by voice vote.

By a standing vote of 56-140, the House rejected an amendment by David F. Emery, R-Maine, that would have barred any research on the so-called "deep underground" basing method for MX.

B-1 Bomber. Although he had attacked several proposed nuclear weapons on the grounds that they were dangerous from an arms control standpoint, Dellums employed a different argument against the B-1 bomber. Along with others, Dellums argued that the controversial plane would be a militarily ineffective boondoggle.

The only reason Reagan requested the plane, Dellums charged, was that he had canceled the Air Force's preferred version of the MX missile.

"This administration needed to throw some bone to the Air Force," Dellums said.

His amendment, which was rejected 142-257 on July 22, would have deleted from the bill $4.03 billion, the full amount requested to procure seven B-1s, plus spare parts and components for other planes to be ordered later. *(Vote 196, p. 58-H)*

Aircraft Carriers. A Dellums amendment to delete $6.87 billion for two nuclear-powered aircraft carriers was rejected 83-303. This was the sixth House vote since 1978 on whether or not to build large nuclear-powered aircraft carriers. *(Vote 197, p. 58-H)*

During the July 22 debate on his amendment, Dellums appealed for support both from members who opposed building additional big carriers and from members who wanted simply to defer the $6.9 billion item for a year. Dellums clearly embraced the former position.

A carrier "has no use against the Soviet Union in a nuclear confrontation," he insisted. And he said any U.S.-Soviet conflict would escalate to nuclear war.

"There really are only two functions for large nuclear aircraft carriers: political show of force on the high seas and

fighting against lightly armed Third World countries," he said. Making clear that he opposed the Third World role in particular, Dellums argued that the Navy already had enough carriers for that mission.

Emery countered that carriers, like other conventional forces, were essential to avert nuclear showdowns between the superpowers.

"If we do not provide any conventional forces at all," Emery said, "we are left with the option either of immediately becoming engaged in the very nuclear war [Dellums] would like to avoid, or rolling over and watching our national interests and those of our allies being torn asunder."

Trident II Missile

The House voted 89-312 against an amendment that would have killed development of a larger, more accurate version of the Trident submarine-launched missile — the so-called Trident II or D-5. *(Vote 216, p. 64-H)*

Sponsored by Thomas J. Downey, D-N.Y., the amendment would have deleted $336.7 million from the bill for development of the Trident II. Another $26 million to modify a Trident submarine to carry the heavier new missile also would have been cut.

It would also have added to the bill $26 million to begin development of the Axe, a ballistic missile designed to close Warsaw Pact airfields with hundreds of small, non-nuclear warheads designed to blow up runways.

Committee Reductions

On July 20, before getting down to the real slugging on HR 6030, the House approved with little objection three amendments offered on behalf of the House Armed Services Committee that reduced the bill's total authorization from $180.3 billion to $177.1 billion.

The cuts were intended to bring the bill in line with the fiscal 1983 defense ceiling set by the first concurrent budget resolution. The additional reductions doubled the $3.2 billion cut the committee had made in Reagan's February budget request before it reported the bill.

In all, the three amendments, which were strongly influenced by the Pentagon's recommendations, cut the following amounts from the bill as originally reported by committee: Army, $613 million; Navy and Marine Corps, $1.557 billion; Air Force, $978 million; and defense agencies, $20.1 million. The committee adopted the cuts July 15 after meeting privately with Defense Secretary Caspar W. Weinberger.

Trident Submarine. One amendment consisted of the largest single cut made by the panel: $699 million taken from the account for Trident missile submarines. The remaining $1.542 billion would fund only one missile sub in fiscal 1983 instead of the two requested. Left untouched was $244 million for advance procurement of parts for future subs.

Seapower subcommittee Chairman Charles E. Bennett, D-Fla., explained to the House that the original request would not have been sufficient for two ships in any case. This was because on June 1, after the budget was submitted, the administration decided to equip these ships — the 10th and 11th Trident subs — to carry a larger, and costlier version of the Trident missile, the Trident II.

Other Procurement. An additional $2.1 billion was cut from 37 other programs. Among the reductions embodied in the amendment, compared to the amounts originally approved by the committee, were cancellation of 6 F-14 fighter planes ($179.1 million), 20 F-16 fighters ($329.5

million) and 18 LAMPS III helicopters designed to take off from destroyers and hunt submarines ($96.2 million).

Authorization of $55 million to modify existing Minuteman ICBMs was to be dropped by this amendment. This included $35 million for long-life batteries to keep some missile silos operating for days after commercial electric power was cut off. Another $20 million was to replace 50 single-warhead Minuteman IIs with triple-warhead Minuteman IIIs that currently were warehoused.

A large proportion of the procurement reduction covered amounts the committee had added to the administration request. This included nearly half of the $1.2 billion the panel had added for equipment earmarked for National Guard or Reserve units.

Only one major weapons program would be canceled outright by the amendment: an artillery shell called the Copperhead, designed to home in on enemy tanks by following a laser beam. The committee amendment removed from HR 6030 all $183.6 million for Copperhead procurement.

Operations. The third committee amendment reduced operations and maintenance funds by $398.5 million. Nearly two-thirds of this amount ($249 million) would come from decommissioning 22 Navy ships. The amendment also would require inactivation of four Army battalions ($15 million) and one Air Force fighter wing ($40 million).

Some $30.1 million was removed from the authorization for recruiting expenses, including advertising. Readiness Subcommittee Chairman Dan Daniel, D-Va., said these cuts were acceptable in light of the recruiting success being enjoyed by all services.

Pork Barrel Issues

Three amendments reflecting particular economic interests were accepted by the Armed Services leadership and adopted by voice vote:

● By Les Aspin, D-Wis., barring the Navy from leasing ships to replace the aging T-5 oil tankers unless they were powered by U.S.-built engines. The Fairbanks-Morse Engines Division of Colt Industries Inc., located in Beloit, Wis. (in Aspin's district), was bidding for the contract to build diesel engines for the ships, but a low-speed Japanese-made diesel also was in contention.

● Trible and several other coal-state representatives, prohibiting the purchase of coal mined outside the United States for use at U.S. military bases in Europe. The Pentagon claimed that it would save about $2 million annually by buying European coal. But Trible denounced this as a "false economy," saying it would cost the U.S. economy $36 million in revenues lost by coal companies and shipping lines.

● By Vic Fazio, D-Calif., to impose a one-year moratorium on studies to determine whether Defense Department jobs should be contracted-out to private firms.

Other pork barrel amendments dealt with by the House were:

● By Elwood Hillis, R-Ind., limiting the Pentagon's purchase of sedans and light pickup trucks for overseas use. The amendment required that the vehicles be bought only from the lowest bidder from manufacturers in the United States and Canada or the country in which the vehicles would be used. The amendment was intended to block purchase of Japanese pickup trucks for use in Europe. Adopted by voice vote.

● By Barbara A. Mikulski, D-Md., prohibiting the Pentagon from buying motor vehicles made outside the United States for administrative purposes. Mikulski also said her amendment was directed at curtailing purchases of Japanese-made trucks. Rejected by a 44-109 standing vote.

● By Sam Gejdenson, D-Conn, barring the contracting out to private firms of fire protection and security jobs on military bases. Federal employee unions had vigorously opposed the Reagan administration's campaign to turn non-military functions over to private contractors. Adopted by voice vote.

● By Claudine Schneider, R-R.I., barring the purchase abroad of any naval ship or major ship component, unless the president certified that the purchase was in the national interest and Congress had been given 30 days to review the certification. Adopted by voice vote.

● By Cardiss Collins, D-Ill., barring the purchase of combat rations packaged outside of the United States. A former supplier of Army rations, American Pouch Food Co., was located in her district. Rejected by voice vote.

Divorced Spouses' Rights

The House adopted an amendment that would allow state courts to include service members' military pensions and military benefits in the property to be divided by a divorce settlement.

The amendment was sponsored by Patricia Schroeder, D-Colo., a member of House Armed Services, but the committee leadership opposed it.

Armed Services manpower subcommittee Chairman Bill Nichols, D-Ala., offered an amendment to the Schroeder amendment that would have limited the power of state courts to consider the pensions and benefits, but would grant military medical care and PX privileges to divorced spouses who had been married to a service member for at least 20 years.

The House accepted the Nichols amendment by voice vote, but then adopted, 332-74, an amendment by Kent Hance, D-Texas, that removed Nichols' restrictions on the state courts. *(Vote 208, p. 62-H)*

The amended Schroeder amendment was then adopted by voice vote.

Registration Enforcement

By a 303-95 vote, the House July 28 adopted an amendment by Gerald B. H. Solomon, R-N.Y., that would bar federal education assistance to any young man who did not comply with the law requiring registration with the Selective Service System. *(Vote 211, p. 62-H)*

Solomon said the 93 percent of eligible men who had registered "sorely resent the other 7 percent of Americans who have either intentionally or unintentionally chosen not to register."

A Hartnett amendment to the Solomon amendment requiring the Department of Education to transmit to the Selective Service System the information needed to enforce the Solomon provision, was adopted by voice vote.

A substitute amendment by Paul Simon, D-Ill., that would have exempted from the aid ban anyone informing the Selective Service in writing that he had religious or moral objections to registration, was first gutted and then killed. By a standing vote of 50-13, the House adopted a Bennett amendment to the Simon amendment that removed the exemption for religious or moral objectors, thus rendering Simon's amendment very similar to the Solomon language. The House then rejected the amended Simon substitute 161-241. *(Vote 210, p. 62-H)*

Maybank Amendment

By a 237-170 vote, the House adopted a Stratton amendment extending for one year a policy of allowing the Pentagon to pay a premium price in order to purchase certain goods from firms in areas of high unemployment. *(Vote 209, p. 62-H)*

This waiver of the so-called Maybank amendment would apply to contracts with the Defense Logistics Agency for routine commercial supplies, excluding weapons and petroleum, worth a total of $5 billion. The Maybank amendment, traditionally attached to defense appropriations bills, prohibits the Pentagon from paying such a premium.

Other Amendments

The House also agreed to the following amendments to HR 6030 by voice vote:

• By Stratton, authorizing the use of up to $50 million already included in the bill to procure a "wire-tap proof" telephone system for use by all federal agencies.

• By Glenn English, D-Okla., authorizing use of funds already in the bill to place a balloon-mounted airplane detection radar in Florida. The military rationale for this was the improving military capability of Cuba. Since the fiscal 1982 defense authorization bill allowed the armed services to cooperate with drug enforcement agencies, the radar also would be used to detect low-flying airplanes used in drug-smuggling.

• By Dan Daniel, D-Va., requiring $1 million already in the bill to be used for development of the C-17 (formerly the CX) transport plane.

• By Stratton extending through fiscal 1983 a waiver of the requirement that any high school reserve officer training corps (ROTC) unit have at least 100 members.

• By Dave McCurdy, D-Okla., requiring a report to Congress on any major weapon system with a cost increase or a schedule slip of 15 percent or more. Also adopted by voice vote was an Emery amendment to the McCurdy amendment that would increase the cost threshold at which programs would fall under the reporting requirement to $200 million in research and development costs or $1 billion in procurement costs.

• By Robin L. Beard, R-Tenn., requiring a Pentagon report on the number of civilian personnel in various Defense Department audit agencies and the savings produced by those agencies.

• By Charles F. Dougherty, R-Pa., requiring any maps of the Baltic region prepared by the Army Map Service to show Estonia, Latvia and Lithuania as independent countries, rather than as parts of the Soviet Union.

• By Melvin Price, D-Ill., waiving the requirement for authorization of certain defense appropriations in fiscal 1982. This was to deal with the confusion surrounding the late congressional action on the defense authorization and appropriations bills in 1981. The conference report on the appropriations bill inadvertently included some programs that were not included in the conference report on the authorization.

• By Price, limiting the Defense Department funds that could be transferred to the National Aeronautics and Space Administration to pay for defense payloads carried by the Space Shuttle.

• By Abraham Kazen Jr., D-Texas, requiring 30 days' prior notice to Congress of any purchase of major equipment manufactured outside the United States that would make the United States dependent on foreign sources.

• By Jack Brooks, D-Texas, to establish an independent inspector general in the Defense Department. Also adopted by voice vote was a Stratton amendment to the amendment excluding for one year the Defense Contract Audit Agency from coverage of the Brooks amendment.

• By Thomas F. Hartnett, R-S.C., requiring congressional approval for the transfer of any naval vessel to another country during fiscal 1983.

• By Newt Gingrich, R-Ga., requiring the secretary of defense to report to Congress by Feb. 1, 1983, on ways to implement a study of National Guard and Reserve force reorganization, called Vista 1999.

• By Paul Simon, D-Ill., ordering a Pentagon study of whether officer candidates should be required to study a foreign language.

• By John Edward Porter, R-Ill., allowing the U.S. Military Academy at West Point to continue administering a memorial scholarship.

Amendments Rejected. Four other amendments were rejected by voice vote:

• By Henry B. Gonzalez, D-Texas, to re-establish the Renegotiation Board, which from 1951 to 1979 renegotiated defense and space contracts whose profits were deemed excessive. The board was allowed to die in 1979, under lobbying by defense industries. *(1979 Almanac p. 326)*

• By Robert Garcia, D-N.Y., that would bar: the use of Pentagon teletypes for routine messages, subsidies for meals in the secretary of defense's dining room, the assignment of enlisted members of the armed forces as personal aides to generals and admirals, and the provision of free veterinary care to the pets of military personnel.

• By Ted Weiss, D-N.Y., limiting expenditures for military bands to the fiscal 1982 level of $92.8 million.

• By James Weaver, D-Ore., establishing a $2 billion national security grain reserve.

• By Robert S. Walker, R-Pa., barring any expenditures under the bill that would violate existing legislation (PL 95-435) requiring a balanced federal budget. ∎

Military Construction

Congress Sept. 29 cleared for the president a $7 billion military construction authorization bill (S 2586) giving qualified approval to two projects that had been snared in controversy over construction projects in Europe.

The Senate approved the conference report by voice vote Sept. 28 and the House cleared it by voice vote the next day. President Reagan signed the bill into law (PL 97-321) Oct. 15.

Despite festering sentiment that U.S. allies were not bearing their fair share of defense costs, the authorization conferees approved funds for improving European airfields and building facilities in West Germany.

The Pentagon and the Reagan administration — like the Carter administration before it — generally agreed with Congress that U.S. allies in Europe and Japan ought to carry more of the burden of common defense. But the Reagan team resisted congressional efforts to deny all funds to projects that one or another of the congressional defense committees thought should be funded by the allies.

The conference agreement on S 2586 included $28 million for aircraft parking ramps and supply dumps at six European-owned airfields that would harbor U.S. combat

planes flown to the continent as wartime reinforcements.

The Air Force had pleaded strenuously for these so-called "co-located operating bases" (COBs) for years, but Congress had refused to fund them because they were eligible for funding by NATO's common construction fund, the Infrastructure. The conferees warned that future COB projects would have to be paid for by the alliance.

Also included in the conference report was $37.2 million for projects at Vilseck and Wildflecken in West Germany, where the Army planned to move three combat battalions that were stationed about a hundred miles farther back from the East German border.

The House had insisted that West Germany pay for this Master Re-stationing Plan (MRP), since it would be better defended by the relocated U.S. units. But the conferees took basically the same position as the Senate, authorizing the requests but barring any expenditure until the United States and West Germany reached a cost-sharing agreement on MRP.

Conference Agreement

As reported Sept. 28, the conference report (H Rept 97-880) on S 2586 authorized $7 billion for military construction projects, and for operations and maintenance of military family housing units in fiscal 1983. President Reagan had requested $7.8 billion for fiscal 1983 and an additional $52 million as a supplemental appropriation for fiscal 1982, which S 2586 treated as part of the fiscal 1983 request.

The conference report was slightly closer to the House-passed authorization of $7.5 billion (HR 6214) than to the $6.4 billion level in the Senate-passed version of the bill.

Savings. The conference report reduced the total authorization by $331.6 million by applying an 8.5 percent across-the-board cut to the total authorization of each service (excluding their family housing accounts).

Citing the depressed state of the construction industry, the conferees predicted that the Pentagon would receive bids substantially lower than the budgeted amounts for many projects. In fiscal 1982, they said, bids were running 12 to 15 percent under budget.

In addition to accommodating the 8.5 percent cut, these savings were assumed to be large enough to be used to fund 40 projects that were not requested in the budget but were added to the House version of the authorization.

NATO Construction

The NATO "burden-sharing" fight spilled over into the question of building family housing for married personnel stationed in Britain and Germany, for which the Pentagon sought funds for the first time in more than a decade.

As a budget-cutting tactic, the Senate had denied all requests for new family housing construction, including the request for $91.2 million to build 783 housing units in the two countries.

The House had denied $18.9 million for 157 units at Wildflecken in Germany, apparently in the context of its position on the MRP issue. It also denied a request for 170 units ($18.5 million) at a British base that would house ground-launched cruise missiles (GLCMs).

The House action was in keeping with the position of both Armed Services panels that the GLCM bases in Britain and Sicily should be built with minimal amenities because arms control negotiations with the Soviet Union might negate the planned missile deployment.

Military Construction, Fiscal 1983

(Dollar amounts in thousands)

Following are President Reagan's requests for fiscal 1983 military construction authorizations and the amounts included in the conference agreement on S 2586:

	Reagan Request	Conference Agreement
Army	$2,051,593	$1,924,544
Navy	1,909,293	1,811,325
Air Force	2,867,682	2,397,132
Defense Agencies	405,396	282,714
NATO Infrastructure	375,000	375,000
Guard and Reserve	202,200	240,011
Total	$7,811,164[1]	$7,030,726

[1] *The conference committee also considered Reagan's supplemental request for fiscal 1982 of $52.101 million.*

The conferees deferred all family housing requests for Germany and Britain and told the Pentagon to prepare by 1984 a comprehensive policy for meeting its overseas housing needs. But they also suggested that West Germany could meet the capital costs of new family housing as part of an overall package that would satisfy some of the U.S. complaints on burden-sharing.

One of the burden-sharing options proposed by the U.S. government in November 1980 was for the German government to build housing that would be leased by the Pentagon for U.S. personnel stationed in Germany.

The conferees also approved $13 million for an underground wartime command post (at a secret location) for U.S. forces in Europe. The House had denied the request because the host government did not formally approve the project until after the House finished action on the bill.

MX Missile Construction

The conferees approved only the $40 million allowed by the Senate of the $207 million requested for construction related to the controversial MX missile.

The House had approved $103 million of the request.

The authorized $40 million was for test and supply facilities that would be required regardless of the basing method selected for the new missile.

The conferees insisted that they supported early selection of a basing method for the missile, but said: "The lack of design progress and site selection, together with environmental concerns, make it highly improbable that contracts can be awarded in fiscal 1983" for construction.

Honduras Air Bases

Conferees approved $21 million to improve two Honduras air bases to which U.S. forces would have access, under an agreement negotiated in May.

But they urged the administration to proceed "with extreme caution so as not to exacerbate the problems already existing in that sensitive part of the world."

They added: "A careful review of the requirement for the bases should be made before proceeding with construction."

Land Disposal

A Senate provision giving the president much greater leeway to dispose of surplus military property was dropped at the insistence of the House conferees, who had cited the absence of House hearings on the proposal.

The Senate would have put 5 percent of the net proceeds of such sales into a fund for purchasing replacement defense facilities; the remaining net proceeds would have gone toward reducing the national debt.

House Committee Action

The House Armed Services Committee recommended a reduction of less than 5 percent in President Reagan's $7.8 billion military construction request for fiscal 1983.

But in its version of the military construction authorization bill (HR 6214), the panel recommended several program reductions or deferrals that had a common theme: avoiding expenditures on construction that might soon have to be abandoned because of possible policy changes by the United States or its allies.

As reported by the House Armed Services Committee May 17, HR 6214 (H Rept 97-525) authorized $7,508,014,000 for military construction in fiscal 1983.

The president had requested $7,811,164,000 for fiscal 1983 and an additional $52,101,000 as a supplemental authorization for fiscal 1982. The committee treated the supplemental amount as part of the fiscal 1983 request. Compared to Reagan's total $7.86 billion request, the committee reduced the authorization by $355 million.

NATO Programs

The committee approved the request for the $375 million annual U.S. contribution to the NATO Infrastructure — the alliance's fund for constructing facilities of mutual benefit.

But some important requests for U.S.-funded construction in Europe were denied by the panel, partly because of long-festering unhappiness that U.S. allies in Europe were not doing more to pay for the cost of NATO's defense. *(Background, 1981 Almanac pp. 234, 306)*

Re-stationing Plan. In hopes of persuading West Germany to pay for them instead, the panel denied $56 million requested to replace existing facilities used by some U.S. Army units stationed there.

The projects were part of the Master Re-stationing Plan, intended to shift some Germany-based Army units out of dilapidated quarters into modern facilities closer to the East German frontier. The old bases, which U.S. forces had occupied since the end of World War II, were located substantial distances from the frontier.

In their actions in 1981 on the fiscal 1982 military construction request, the Armed Services panels and the Military Construction Appropriations subcommittees all had insisted, with varying degrees of firmness, that West Germany pay for the MRP. In part, this was based on the committees' belief that, in general, the European allies were not bearing a fair share of the cost of the common defense.

But the panels also cited two specific reasons why the West German government ought to pay the cost of the MRP: First, West German territory could be better defended by U.S. units based in the new areas, they said. Moreover, the Bonn government would benefit directly by using the vacated sites for other purposes. The location of

some of the old sites in major industrial centers made them valuable tracts of real estate.

Congress approved the $14.5 million requested in fiscal 1982 for the first major increment of MRP-related construction. But the authorizing and Appropriations committees emphasized this was only because those particular projects were needed by U.S. units whether or not the MRP was carried out.

In 1982, in its report on HR 6214, House Armed Services said there appeared to be some progress in negotiations with West Germany over the MRP, but that the Bonn government had not yet made any commitment to funding the program. Continued unilateral funding of MRP projects by the United States might only encourage German procrastination, the panel warned.

"In the light of the vast sums being spent in other areas of the world to ensure the security of NATO and the uninterrupted flow of oil, the NATO allies and particularly the German government should expand their support of our mutual efforts in the defense of Europe," the committee said.

European Air Bases. The Armed Services Committee approved a request for $28.6 million to build fuel and ammunition storage dumps at European-owned air bases. These co-located operating bases (COBs) would be used by U.S. warplanes flown to Europe in case of war.

Congress had refused to fund the COB project for several years, since it was eligible for funding by the NATO Infrastructure, the common pool for allied construction projects.

The Pentagon insisted that the projects were urgently needed, and it wanted to pay for them to expedite construction, since Infrastructure funds were fully committed for the next several years. The U.S. expenditures eventually would be recouped from the Infrastructure.

The House panel approved the plan, but expressed its displeasure at the delays in U.S. recoupment of similar costs from the Infrastructure.

Cruise Missile Bases. The committee approved $41 million for facilities to be used when ground-launched cruise missiles (GLCMs) were deployed in Europe beginning in late 1983. But it denied $93.4 million for GLCM facilities that might be canceled either because of arms reduction talks with Moscow or if some allied governments decided not to accept the missiles.

In 1979, NATO agreed to deploy 464 GLCMs and 108 Pershing II ballistic missiles that would be able to hit Soviet territory from launchers in Western Europe. The new missiles were intended to counterbalance Soviet SS-20 missiles, which could strike any target in Western Europe from bases in the Soviet Union.

But to accommodate some Europeans' fears of a new nuclear arms race, NATO also agreed to seek an arms control agreement with Moscow that would neutralize the SS-20 threat without deploying the new U.S. missiles.

Those negotiations began in November 1981, with the United States proposing a "zero-option": cancellation of the planned NATO deployment in return for Soviet scrapping of the SS-20s. *(1981 Almanac p. 238)*

The House committee denied $44.4 million requested for GLCM facilities at an unidentified location where the host government had not yet formally approved of the missiles' deployment. Neither the Netherlands nor Belgium had agreed to accept its allotted 48 missiles.

It also deleted from the bill $30.5 million for two schools in Britain and Italy intended for use by dependents

of U.S. GLCM personnel and $18.5 million to build military family housing at the British GLCM site. Given the possibility that an arms control agreement might make the GLCM deployment a short-term one, the committee said, those bases could be manned initially with personnel who were not accompanied by their dependents.

Spanish Bases. A $5.25 million request for various projects at the U.S. Air Force base at Torrejon, Spain was denied because of what the committee called "uncertainty over future base rights in Spain."

Also deferred for the same reason was a $640,000 family services center for the naval base at Rota, Spain.

Rapid Deployment

The committee cut $131.8 million from the $497.4 million requested for construction to support operations of the Rapid Deployment Force (RDF) near the Persian Gulf or naval units in the Indian Ocean.

Minor cuts, principally involving bookkeeping issues, were made in the requests for Ras Banas in southern Egypt on the Red Sea coast ($172.1 million of the $178.6 million request was approved), and for the British-owned island of Diego Garcia, about 1,000 miles south of India ($108.5 million of the $117.2 million request was approved).

More substantial were:

● a $51.1 million cut in the $60.4 million request for construction in Oman, because the Oman government had not yet approved some construction planned for fiscal 1982;

● denial of the entire $64.9 million request for new facilities at the air base at Lajes in the Portuguese-owned Azores Islands. Congress had refused to fund the Lajes project because negotiations with Lisbon over U.S. rights to use the base had not been completed.

Strategic Arms Bases

The committee approved $103 million of a $207 million request for construction associated with the MX intercontinental missile.

Of the funds approved, $16.7 million was for supply and repair facilities and $20 million was for test launch silos at Vandenburg Air Force Base in California, all of which would be needed to develop the MX missile regardless of the basing mode in which it eventually was deployed.

But the remaining $66.3 million was for MX deployment facilities, at least some of which would be used only if Congress approved the administration plan to deploy the first 40 missiles in existing Minuteman missile silos, pending development of a permanent basing method that would more adequately protect the missiles against Soviet attack.

Anti-Missile Missiles. The committee also approved only $1.4 million of the $23 million requested for construction at the anti-ballistic missile test site on Kwajalein Island in the Pacific Ocean. This paralleled the panel's sharp reduction in funds for anti-ballistic missile development in HR 6030.

The panel argued that Reagan's planned acceleration of anti-missile research should await a firm administration commitment to using anti-missile defenses to protect the MX. The administration had treated anti-missile defenses as only one of many options for protecting MX.

Bases in Members' Districts

The committee added $295.973 million for construction projects that President Reagan had not included in his budget.

Of that amount, $171.86 million (58 percent) was for projects in districts represented by members of the Military Installations and Facilities Subcommittee, which drafted the bill. Another $32.4 million (11 percent) was for projects in districts of members who belonged to the full Armed Services committee but not the subcommittee.

Jack Brinkley, D-Ga., chairman of the installations subcommittee, said his panel added only projects that were of "a higher priority" than some that were requested by the administration. Overall, he noted, the subcommittee made a net cut of $355 million from the $7.8 billion request. Most of the cuts ($327 million) were made in overseas projects.

Brinkley said his subcommittee did not add projects the Pentagon did not want, but merely advanced them to an earlier fiscal year.

"The services wanted them," he said. "They were all in the five-year plan projections."

Three of the subcommittee's additions were for projects at Fort Benning, in Brinkley's district: $9.7 million for reception station barracks, $1.02 million for a troop medical clinic and $270,000 for a post office.

Brinkley said the barracks project was needed to complete construction of a reception station for soldiers assigned to Fort Benning for training.

Brinkley said he did not know why the Pentagon had not requested the $9.7 million for the barracks in fiscal 1983, and had not asked for a reason. "I don't know why they did ask for some other things," he added.

Other Provisions

In HR 6214, House Armed Services also:

● Denied $19.5 million for various gymnasiums and other non-combat facilities in Europe, Korea and Diego Garcia. The panel told the Pentagon to use inflatable air-bubble buildings for those purposes, if tests then in progress proved successful. Air bubble buildings would be cheaper and could be relocated if necessary, the committee said.

The panel exempted from this general policy toward non-combat facilities overseas projects in Turkey for which $4.5 million was approved. Authorization of those projects was justified by the urgency of the requirement and the remoteness of the construction site, the committee said.

● Approved only $15 million of $45 million requested for facilities at unidentified overseas locations that would be used by combat planes of the Tactical Air Command in "contingencies." Without identifying the location, the committee said it had reduced the request because the prospective host country had not yet formally agreed to grant U.S. planes access to the facilities in case of a crisis.

Apparently, this project referred to a plan to develop service and storage facilities at airfields in Honduras that could be used by U.S. planes in case of trouble with Cuba or with radical rebels in El Salvador or elsewhere in the Caribbean region. Honduras and the United States signed a base access agreement May 7; it called for $21 million in U.S. construction.

House Floor Action

By a ratio of 5-3, the House Aug. 11 voted not to withhold the U.S. contribution to a NATO military construction program.

But the vote on the proposal by Dennis E. Eckart, D-Ohio, reflected the bipartisan nature of the long-smoldering congressional belief that U.S. allies were not bearing a

large enough share of the burden of the common defense.

Eckart's measure, an amendment to the bill, was rejected 151-245. Republicans opposed the amendment 64-114, Democrats 87-131. *(Vote 254, p. 76-H)*

Nearly twice as many Republican voted "aye" as typically voted to reduce defense money bills. And GOP supporters of the amendment included several party leaders.

After rejecting Eckart's and all other major amendments to the bill, the House passed HR 6214 by a vote of 332-57. The bill as passed authorized $7,515,167,000 for Pentagon construction projects, including $18.3 million for a plant to manufacture a new type of lethal nerve gas weapon, called binary munitions. *(Vote 256, p. 76-H)*

Eckart's proposal would have withheld the $375 million authorized for the annual U.S. contribution to the NATO Infrastructure, the alliance's kitty for constructing facilities for common use. The bar would have taken effect if three or more NATO members did not meet in 1983 the target of a 3 percent annual real increase in defense spending, agreed to by the alliance in 1978. Two weeks earlier, in debate on the defense authorization bill (HR 6030), the House rejected efforts to withdraw U.S. troops from Europe for the same reasons.

"At a time when we spend a grossly disproportionate share of our gross national product on defense," Eckart said, "we find our NATO allies, who enjoy direct beneficiaries of our tremendous defense expenditures, not pulling their fair share of the load."

Brinkley, chairman of the Military Construction Subcommittee, countered that most of the European allies were making an effort to boost their defense budgets, but added that U.S. forces were deployed in Europe primarily to defend the United States.

"We are not actually in Europe defending them," he told the House. "We are in Europe, in NATO, because of the national interest of the United States of America."

5 Percent Cut. The House rejected by voice vote an amendment by Patricia Schroeder, D-Colo., that in effect would have reduced by 5 percent the amount actually spent on programs authorized by the bill. She said the amendment was equal to a $378 million authorization cut.

"This is a public works bill," Schroeder declared. "There are all sorts of things in there that are nice," she said, but were not critical given the government's budgetary straits. She listed as examples several gymnasiums for military personnel.

That argument drew a broadside from Silvio O. Conte, R-Mass. "You go out in those remote places out there ... where these people are camped, and, my God, that [gymnasium] is the only recreation they have," he shouted.

Honduras Airfields. Also rejected, 109-280, was an amendment by Tom Harkin, D-Iowa, that would have barred any funds for airfield construction in Honduras. *(Vote 255, p. 76-H)*

The House bill contained no such funds, but its Senate counterpart included $21 million to improve two Honduran airfields, to which U.S. forces would have access.

Harkin and several other liberals warned that the airfield improvement was part of a Reagan administration campaign to destabilize the leftist government of Honduras' neighbor Nicaragua. They warned that the project might provoke Nicaragua to attack Honduras.

MX Missile Project. A Brinkley amendment, accepted by voice vote, would bar expenditure of funds for facilities to support the MX intercontinental missile until Congress had been given 30 days' prior notice of the president's selection of a basing method for the MX. The bill as reported included $103 million of $207 million requested for MX facilities. This Brinkley amendment covered $66.3 million of the remaining amount.

The amendment was substituted by voice vote for an amendment by Ronald V. Dellums, D-Calif., that would have deleted the $66.3 million.

Other Amendments. Two other Brinkley amendments also were approved by voice vote:

● shifting funds, within the amount authorized for the Army, to build two secure living quarters in Italy for high ranking U.S. officers. This was spurred by the kidnapping in 1981 of Army Brig. Gen. James Dozier from his apartment in Verona, Italy.

● adding $7.2 million to construct new National Guard armories in Boston, Mass., and Gary, Ind.

Senate Committee Action

As part of its effort to cut Reagan's overall defense budget by 5 percent, the Senate Armed Services Committee reduced the Pentagon's construction budget by nearly 20 percent. The panel approved $6.4 billion of Reagan's $7.8 billion construction request in its version of the fiscal 1983 military construction authorization bill (S 2586) reported May 27 (S Rept 97-440).

More than half of the $1.4 billion reduction came from two sweeping decisions to defer whole categories of projects deemed not essential to combat readiness:

● $416 million was saved by cutting from the budget all construction of new military family housing units or modification of existing units; and

● $431.55 million was saved by dropping dozens of administrative, recreational, supply and laboratory facilities.

In an act of unusual forebearance, the committee also added no projects to the bill that had not been requested by the administration.

In addition to those decisions, which were caused by purely budgetary considerations, the committee shaved more than $300 million from the request because of disagreements with major administration policies.

About $70 million of that amount reflected a growing congressional insistence that U.S. allies in Europe and Japan offset more of the U.S. cost of defending alliance interests in Europe and the Persian Gulf region.

Another $167 million was cut from the request for construction related to the MX missile because the committee had rejected an administration plan to put the first 40 MXs in existing missile silos.

In its report, the committee said it had agreed to "defer without prejudice those projects which it felt could safely be deferred without severely impacting readiness."

Following this rule, the panel generally deferred administrative, supply and laboratory buildings, pollution abatement projects and what the Pentagon calls "morale, welfare and recreational" facilities.

The latter category included gymnasiums, bowling alleys, family service centers and the like, which the Pentagon insisted were important to maintaining the morale of military personnel and their dependents in relatively isolated posts in the United States and abroad.

The dozens of projects deferred by the panel reduced the bill's authorization total by $80 million for the Army, $163.75 million for the Navy, $95 million for the Air Force and $92.8 million for other defense agencies.

GLCM Bases. Of the reduction for defense agencies, $72.9 million was accounted for by a total freeze on the construction and expansion of elementary and secondary schools for the children of military personnel stationed abroad. A large chunk of that cut was made by deferring two $15 million schools for the children of Air Force personnel who would be stationed in Italy and Britain to operate ground-launched cruise missiles (GLCMs).

The Senate committee approved $85.4 million requested to construct the actual GLCM bases.

The Senate committee's freeze on the construction of new military family housing cut from the bill $242.2 million that had been requested for 3,237 housing units. An additional $8.7 million was denied for a community center to support a 2,600-unit Army housing complex in Hawaii.

Also denied was $165.1 million for housing unit modifications. But the committee approved $68.4 million for housing modifications related to energy conservation.

NATO Burden-Sharing

Reiterating a theme it had sounded repeatedly in recent years, along with the other congressional defense committees, the panel insisted that the NATO allies increase their direct support of U.S. military construction in Europe.

At least in part, the panel based its position on the fact that "the United States has undertaken security commitments in Southwest Asia which will require a large commitment of U.S. resources and our European allies will benefit from such commitments."

The panel approved the request for $375 million for the annual U.S. contribution to the NATO "Infrastructure." But the committee flatly refused to fund some projects, including a London headquarters for naval operations in Europe ($3.2 million) and armored supply and ammunition depots at various U.S. airfields in Europe ($11.7 million). NATO should pay for all those projects, the committee recommended.

Re-Stationing Plan. The panel approved $26.5 million for facilities at Vilseck, West Germany, which were part of the $1.2 billion plan to shift three Army brigades — about 20,000 men — from bases in western West Germany to new facilities closer to the borders with East Germany and Czechoslovakia. But the committee added a proviso that none of these funds could be spent on the Master Re-stationing Plan until West Germany had formally agreed to pay some of the MRP costs.

The MRP facilities at Vilseck, near the Czechoslovakian border, were to house two battalions — about 900 men — of the 8th Infantry Division, currently stationed more than 150 miles farther west, near Frankfurt.

The Senate committee approved without comment $10.7 million for facilities at Wildflecken (east of Frankfurt, near the East German border) that were not part of the MRP, but that would be located at a future MRP site. New family housing proposed for Wildflecken ($18.9 million) was deferred under the committee's freeze on housing.

The Pentagon told Congress it planned no additional U.S. funding for the MRP, beyond the fiscal 1983 request, until a cost-sharing agreement was reached.

Reinforcement Air Bases. Also denied by the committee was a $28.6 million request for fuel and ammunition storage dumps and aircraft parking ramps at European-owned air bases.

To service the extra planes, the Pentagon wanted to spend $298 million on "minimum essential facilities" (fuel and ammunition storage and airplane parking ramps) at a network of COBs over the next several years.

Congress had insisted in the past on NATO funding for the bases. And in its report on S 2586, the Senate committee said the $28 million requested for fiscal 1983 was unnecessary since NATO already had agreed to spend $32 million on those projects.

Rapid Deployment Force

The request for $497.4 million to construct facilities for the Rapid Deployment Force was cut by $140.25 million.

Consistent with the committee's policy on administrative buildings, it denied $19.3 million for an RDF headquarters building at MacDill Air Force Base in Tampa, Fla. (Of this amount, $17 million had been requested as a supplemental authorization for fiscal 1982.)

The panel cut $65.25 million from the $117.18 million requested to expand air and naval facilities on Diego Garcia, a British-owned island in the Indian Ocean. Of the cut, $33.25 million was for recreation and other facilities, and $32 million was for a runway expansion, which the committee said would not get under way until 1984.

The committee denied $55.7 million requested to expand facilities at Lajes Air Force Base on the Azores, noting that future U.S. access rights to the base were uncertain. The Air Force relied on Lajes as a refueling base for cargo planes bound from the United States to the Middle East.

Ras Banas. But the committee approved $178.6 million for RDF facilities at Ras Banas in southern Egypt, despite the absence of a formal agreement guaranteeing U.S. access to that base. The committee said that the personal assurances of Egyptian Presidents Sadat and Mubarak that U.S. forces could use the base were adequate. Requiring additional written assurances would be "counterproductive," it said.

Other RDF Facilities. The Senate committee also approved $15 million for Air Force facilities at Cairo West airfield, near the Egyptian capital, which was used by U.S. units in annual RDF exercises called "Bright Star."

The $38.3 million approved as requested for projects in Kenya ($8.3 million) and Somalia ($30 million) would complete the planned naval facilities in those countries. The United States was modernizing the port in Mombassa, Kenya, and facilities at Mogadishu and Berbera in Somalia. The Air Force planned to request a small amount in fiscal 1984 for both countries.

Also approved was the request for $60.35 million to continue construction at Masirah Island, Thamarit and Seeb air bases in Oman. To complete current plans for facilities in Oman, an additional $75.5 million was to be requested in fiscal years 1984 and 1985.

Caribbean Facilities

The committee approved $21 million that was earmarked to improve two airfields in Honduras to which U.S. forces would have access in case of trouble in the Caribbean. Among the specific projects under consideration were lengthening of the runways and expansion of the aircraft parking ramps to accommodate larger aircraft, and construction of underground fuel storage tanks at two of the fields: one near La Cieba on the Caribbean coast and one at Comayagua about 40 miles northwest of the capital of Tegucigalpa.

The Honduras request was included in an administra-

tion request for $45 million for unspecified "contingency facilities" in other countries. The agreement with Honduras for $21 million worth of improvements was signed in May.

The Senate panel dropped the remaining $24 million request from the bill, but did not give a reason. The purpose of the request was classified.

Other Issues

Projects totaling $23 million at the Army's anti-ballistic missile test range on Kwajalein Island in the Pacific were denied. The House Armed Services Committee and the Senate had sharply reduced the request for anti-missile research in their respective versions of the fiscal 1983 defense authorization bill. The Senate committee questioned whether the planned construction on Kwajalein was needed if the program was slowed down.

The committee also turned down $35 million requested for a 100-year lease on 18,000 acres of land in the Mariana Islands, a U.S. trust territory in the western Pacific Ocean. The bulk of the property comprised about two-thirds of the island of Tinian, which was extensively used for training exercises by Navy, Marine and Air Force units.

Instead of approving new authority for the project, the panel renewed the authorization that had been included in the fiscal 1982 construction authorization bill. Funds were not included in the fiscal 1982 construction appropriations bill.

Echoing a concern dating to the mid-1970s, the committee said it was "distressed" that the services had not completed projects to improve protection of chemical and nuclear weapons. Saying the projects, especially the installation of electronic sensors to detect intruders, "have been badly mismanaged," the panel asked quarterly progress reports, starting July 1.

The committee had helped initiate the weapons-security projects. *(1976 Almanac p. 314)*

Senate Floor Action

By a comfortable margin, the Senate on June 30 approved an administration plan to improve airfields in Honduras that would be available to U.S. combat planes in case of a Caribbean crisis.

The $6.4 billion fiscal 1983 military construction authorization bill (S 2586) contained $21 million to improve two Honduran airfields. An amendment by Claiborne Pell, D-R.I., to block the project was tabled (and thus killed) by a vote of 65-29. *(Vote 204, p. 36-S)*

The bill was passed later on June 30, by a 93-1 vote, without significant amendment. *(Vote 205, p. 36-S)*

Honduras Facilities

An agreement between the United States and Honduras, completed May 7, allowed U.S. access to three air bases that would be improved by the United States.

Pell objected that the project increased the risk of U.S. military involvement in Central American turmoil, particularly in operations against the Marxist government of Nicaragua, Honduras' neighbor to the south.

"In the context of the administration's hard-line rhetoric and discussion of U.S. options," Pell warned, the airfield project "sends a signal . . . that the United States is indeed preparing for deeper involvement, including direct military intervention."

Edward Zorinsky, D-Neb., like Pell a Foreign Relations Committee member, echoed Pell's complaint that the project had not received adequate congressional scrutiny because of the secrecy that prevailed during the negotiations.

"The potential for deepening U.S. military involvement in Central America is too stark a reality not to have a wider discussion of the issue within Congress," Zorinsky said.

But Pell's amendment was strongly attacked by Armed Services Committee Chairman John Tower, R-Texas, Military Construction Subcommittee Chairman Strom Thurmond, R-S.C., and Foreign Relations Chairman Charles H. Percy, R-Ill. They said the project was needed to bolster Honduras against threats from Nicaragua.

"With the growing Soviet presence in Nicaragua, which now has the largest standing army in Central America and which is upgrading its airfields and training its personnel to receive Soviet MiG fighters, the United States must respond to maintain the regional balance of power," Thurmond said.

Tower declared that if Pell's amendment were accepted, "we might as well cede the control of this hemisphere outside the North American continent to the Soviet Union and its surrogate, Cuba. We might as well send Castro a cable saying, 'Come in. Take over. We are going to do nothing.' "

Liberal Democrats predominated among Pell's allies. Only three Republicans, John H. Chafee, R.I., Mark O. Hatfield, Ore., and William V. Roth Jr., Del., opposed the tabling motion.

Other Amendments

The Senate also adopted an amendment, accepted by Armed Services, that changed a committee-sponsored provision giving the Pentagon more autonomy in disposing of excess real property.

The General Services Administration (GSA) handled the disposal of excess property for all government agencies, including the Pentagon. The committee said the Pentagon often was required to maintain excess property for several years while the GSA disposed of it.

As reported, the bill would have allowed any service to sell excess property or to exchange it for other property in any case in which the "profit" from the deal would at least cover the cost of the transaction, including the purchase of replacement property, if needed. Any additional profit would be credited to the service's construction account, thus providing an incentive to dispose of unneeded property and to shift facilities out of high-cost areas.

The Senate agreed to an amendment by Thurmond that would allow the service only to recover the cost of each transaction. Of the additional profits, 5 percent (up to an annual total for all services of $50 million) would go into a Pentagon fund to capitalize future replacements of defense facilities. The balance would go to the Treasury's general fund to be used solely for reduction of the national debt.

Three minor amendments also were agreed to:

● By S. I. "Sam" Hayakawa, R-Calif., to alter the terms of a land swap between the Army and the city of Bell, Calif.

● By Robert C. Byrd, D-W.Va., to allow a change in the location of a proposed military reserve center in Charleston, W.Va., that was authorized in fiscal 1982.

● By J. James Exon, D-Neb., to restore $6 million cut by the committee, for two recreation facilities on the Indian Ocean island of Diego Garcia. ■

Arms Control Agency Funds

Congress cleared for the president Oct. 1 a bill (HR 3467) authorizing the Arms Control and Disarmament Agency's (ACDA) budgets for fiscal 1982 and 1983. President Reagan signed the bill into law (PL 97-339) on Oct. 15.

The bill authorized appropriations for ACDA of $18,268,000 in fiscal 1982 and $19,893,852 in fiscal 1983. In February 1981, the Reagan administration had requested that Congress authorize $16,768,000 for fiscal 1982 and "such sums as may be necessary" for the following year.

The final version of HR 3467 incorporated a provision requested by the administration allowing the arms control agency to accept security clearances awarded by the departments of State and Defense, for officials of those agencies who were temporarily assigned to ACDA. Current law required the Office of Personnel Management to conduct full-scale security investigations of such persons, regardless of any clearances they already held — a process which could take months.

The bill also incorporated a Senate-passed provision, sponsored by Larry Pressler, R-S.D., adding anti-satellite activities to the list of arms control problems the agency should study. The Soviet Union reportedly already had — and the United States was developing — a limited capability to destroy space satellites on which the other superpower relied for military communication and warning of enemy attack.

A House-passed provision that would have dropped the word "disarmament" from the agency's name was not included in the final version of the bill.

Background

The House passed its version of HR 3467 June 8, 1981, by voice vote. *(1981 Almanac p. 240)*

The Foreign Affairs Committee had added $1.5 billion to Reagan's request for ACDA's fiscal 1982 authorization. The panel said that the increase was intended to allow for the expense of renewed arms control negotiations and to avoid reductions in the agency's staff and in its budget for research on strategic arms control problems.

Instead of the open-ended authorization requested for fiscal 1983, the committee authorized $19,893,852, an 8.9 percent increase over the fiscal 1982 amount that was intended to cover inflation.

The House bill also would have dropped "disarmament" from the agency's name, to remove what the committee called an "inaccurate and unfounded impression that the agency was in some way involved in unilateral disarmament at the expense of our national security."

Senate Action. The Senate Foreign Relations Committee reported an amended version of HR 3467 on May 26, 1982 (S Rept 97-430).

The panel retained the House-passed authorization levels, but dropped the name change and added the Pressler amendment on anti-satellite activities.

In its report, the committee complained that ACDA was the only federal agency dealing with national security policy whose budget was going down under the Reagan administration.

"Many members of the committee are concerned that such budgetary strictures may soon force the agency to the point where it cannot function effectively internally or within the national security sphere," the committee said.

The Senate passed the committee version of HR 3467 by voice vote, without amendment, Oct. 1. A few hours later, the House accepted the Senate amendments by voice vote, thus clearing the bill for the president. ∎

Nuclear Arms Authorization

Congress in 1982 failed to complete action on legislation (HR 6329, S 2812) authorizing funding for nuclear weapons programs carried out by the Department of Energy (DOE) in fiscal 1983.

After waiting for months on the House calendar, the bill was passed by the House early in the lame-duck session, but the Senate did not take it up during the rush to adjourn.

Appropriations for the DOE weapons programs, normally included in the Energy-Water appropriations bill, were put in the fiscal 1983 continuing resolution (PL 97-377). *(Continuing resolution, p. 238)*

House Action

The House Armed Services Committee approved all but $8.3 million of the $5.75 billion President Reagan requested for defense nuclear programs.

But in HR 6329, the committee shuffled funds to add $70 million to two programs that would test beneficial uses of radioactive byproducts from weapons production.

The House passed the bill without amendment on Dec. 1 by voice vote.

One program, called Special Isotope Separation (SIS), was an effort to use lasers to extract high-grade plutonium, which could be used to make nuclear weapons, from the low-grade plutonium left over from the weapons production process. The committee increased the SIS authorization by $40 million, to a total of $63 million.

The panel also added $30 million to a program testing economically beneficial uses of other radioactive byproducts, such as the sterilization of sewage sludge with cesium.

While other congressional committees had worried considerably about the dangers presented by civilian nuclear waste, Armed Services viewed military waste as a problem easily solved with technological answers. Instead of calling it "waste," the committee used the label "byproducts" to describe the highly radioactive leftovers from weapons production.

As reported May 17 (H Rept 97-551), the bill authorized $5,743,981,000 for DOE military programs, including $109 million to produce fuel for nuclear-powered warships. The administration had put the naval fuel funds in the Navy budget, but the committee transferred the amount to the DOE request, where it had been included in the past.

Counting that $109 million, Reagan's authorization request totaled $5,752,281,000. The Reagan request represented a 12.3 percent increase over the $5.1 billion authorized for DOE nuclear weapons programs in fiscal 1982; the committee-approved amount represented a 12.2 percent increase. *(1981 Almanac p. 231)*

To cope with the need for increased nuclear weapons production, which would have been required even under President Carter's last defense plan, DOE planned to resume production of weapons fuel in one reactor at Savannah River, S.C. in October 1983. Three other reactors at Savannah River produced nuclear weapons fuel and a reac-

tor in Hanford, Wash., was being modified to produce fuel for weapons rather than fuel for nuclear reactors.

The committee approved, without comment, the $55 million request for production of MX warheads. The committee in 1981 had sharply reduced funding for MX warheads, saying it would be years before they were produced.

The committee also added $3 million to begin buying "small, strategically located parcels of land" to serve as buffer zones around nuclear weapons plants.

Plutonium Recovery

The committee linked its proposed $40 million increase in the SIS plutonium recovery process to the increase in nuclear weapons production planned by both the Carter and Reagan administrations.

If SIS proved successful, the panel said, it could save billions of dollars by extracting weapons-grade plutonium from 17 tons of low-grade plutonium from spent fuel being stored by DOE.

The committee shifted the $40 million from other nuclear material production accounts, but told the Pentagon not to let those changes interfere with the plan to resume operation of another plutonium recovery plant (called PUREX), in mothballs at Hanford, Wash.

Nuclear Waste Use

The committee also transferred $10 million from other nuclear waste management programs to a separate program intended to develop "beneficial uses" of radioactive byproducts from the weapons production process.

Among the potentially beneficial uses cited for nuclear byproducts were: sterilization of sewage sludge by irradiating it with cesium; use of strontium as a heat source for power supplies and water heaters; and the use of krypton gas in self-illuminating airfield marker lights.

The panel also added $20 million to build plants that would demonstrate the sewage sludge irradiation process. The first plant was to be in Albuquerque, N.M.

Congress had authorized $5 million for this project in fiscal 1982, but no funds were appropriated.

In addition to the direct economic benefit of such byproducts use, the committee said, extracting the useful materials would reduce the heat and radioactivity of the residue and ease the problem of radioactive waste-disposal.

Inertial Confinement Fusion

The committee also shifted $18 million from various weapons activities to the Inertial Confinement Fusion (ICF) project, increasing its funding to $140 million.

ICF produced on a microscopic scale the kind of pressure and temperature created by a nuclear-weapon blast. This permitted some experiments on weapons material to be performed in the laboratory rather than in underground blasts. The fusion reaction was created by focusing powerful lasers or subatomic particle beams on pellets containing deuterium and tritium, two versions of hydrogen.

The committee insisted that ICF research continue at all three national nuclear weapons laboratories — Los Alamos and Sandia in New Mexico and Lawrence Livermore in California — and at the contractors currently working on the project.

The panel also ordered the administration to manage the program to emphasize the most expeditious possible weapons-related research. "The current and previous administrations have tended to view the projected potential of ICF as an energy source, not as a laboratory tool for

weapons research," the committee complained.

The committee also added $10 million to build a laboratory that would use gamma rays and X-rays to simulate nuclear weapons effects on weapons and equipment.

Weapons Slowdown

Among the programs cut back by the committee were two warhead development projects:

● The panel cut $16.3 million for development of a warhead for the LoAD project, a short-range anti-ballistic missile intended to protect MX missile launchers and other armored, military targets. Some proposals to deploy the MX missile would defend the launchers with LoAD, but the committee said development of the weapon should await a firm decision to deploy LoAD. On the same grounds, the House committee had sharply reduced the administration request for LoAD development (covering components other than the warhead) in the fiscal 1983 defense authorization bill (HR 6030).

● Also cut was $6 million of the $7 million requested to develop a nuclear warhead for the Navy's SM-2 anti-aircraft missile. The committee told DOE to come up with a design that would be simpler and could be in service sooner than the one proposed.

Senate Committee Action

The Senate Armed Services Committee trimmed only 3 percent from the administration's $5.75 billion budget for nuclear weapons and naval reactors. And most of that reduction, in S 2812, was for bookkeeping changes that would have no effect on the planned program.

The largest substantial reduction was a $66 million cut in the $1.57 billion operating budget for weapons production and oversight, a cut from which the committee exempted most major weapons production and renovation activities.

The only specific program targeted for cutbacks by the panel was development of a warhead for an anti-ballistic missile system called LoADS that could be used to protect the MX intercontinental missile. This reflected the slowdown in development of the LoADS system that was embodied in the conference report on the fiscal 1983 defense authorization bill (S 2248).

The committee approved the $55 million requested to construct production facilities for the MX warhead.

The Armed Services panel reported S 2812 on Aug. 5 (S Rept 97-517).

Authorization Total

The administration requested $5,643,000,000 in authorizations for defense nuclear programs managed by the Energy Department.

But the committee treated as part of the request $109 million for enrichment of uranium to be used in the reactors of nuclear-powered ships. Like its House counterpart, the committee insisted that that program continue to be funded through the Energy Department, as it had been in the past, rather than being included in the Navy budget, as Reagan proposed. So, from the committee's standpoint, Reagan requested $5,752,000,000.

As reported, S 2812 authorized $5,570,281,000.

The panel recommended gross reductions of $245 million. But $145 million of that amount was covered by so-called excess authorization left over from previous years. Since the past appropriations for some defense nuclear

projects were lower than the amounts previously authorized, the "leftover" authorization amount was to be available to cover part of the appropriations for the same project requested in fiscal 1983.

The committee also refused to provide new authorizations to cover cost overruns in some projects funded in prior years. Authorization for such added expenses already existed in permanent law, they said.

How Many Bombs?

The committee used its report on the bill to challenge the contention of many proponents of a nuclear-weapons "freeze" that the U.S. nuclear arsenal had steadily increased over the years and would increase further under Reagan's weapons program.

Though the specific number of nuclear weapons in the U.S. stockpile at any time was secret, the committee said that it had peaked in the mid-1960s at "a few tens of thousands of weapons." Despite some fluctuations, the overall trend in stockpile size had been downward since then.

The report did not explain the decline, but contributing factors included the phaseout of nuclear armed anti-aircraft missiles at domestic bases and an 80 percent reduction in the number of long-range nuclear bombers.

In terms of overall explosive force, the stockpile was about one-third as powerful in 1982 as it had been in 1965, the committee said. This was largely because, as U.S. weapons became more accurate, smaller warheads could be used to destroy a given target.

The committee pointed out that obsolescent nuclear weapons were dismantled as new ones were built, partly to recycle the costly nuclear material.

But the panel conceded that the fate of current U.S.-Soviet arms control talks would determine whether or not the U.S. nuclear weapons arsenal would increase under Reagan's program.

The committee trimmed $88.7 million from the $1.297 billion requested for nuclear fuel production, but all of the cuts were bookkeeping changes.

Waste Management

The committee increased to $75 million the $30 million request for a nuclear waste processing facility at the Savannah River, S.C., weapons fuel production plant.

The facility was intended to transform radioactive waste from the fuel production process from a liquid into a solid, glasslike form for permanent storage. The funding increase would accelerate the start of construction to allow completion of the facility by 1990.

The panel cut $39.6 million from the request for $110.8 million for the Waste Isolation Pilot Plant in New Mexico. But this was one of the bookkeeping reductions based on the existence of unused authorization left over from prior years. The committee emphasized its continued support of the plant.

Inertial Confinement Fusion

The committee added $18 million to the request for $122.4 million to operate three projects that would test the inertial confinement fusion process.

Noting that $1 billion had been invested in the projects to date, the panel criticized the administration's decision to slow down funding for the program. The House Armed Services Committee had the same complaint about the fiscal 1982 request. ∎

Joint Chiefs Reorganization

Legislation aimed at giving the chairman of the Joint Chiefs of Staff a stronger hand in challenging the parochial interests of the armed services was passed by the House in 1982 but died in the Senate.

Senate Armed Services Committee Chairman John Tower, R-Texas, displayed little enthusiasm for proposals to reorganize the Joint Chiefs. His committee held hearings but took no steps to draft legislation on the issue.

Congressional debate on the question of reorganizing the military hierarchy had been prompted by former Joint Chiefs Chairman Gen. David C. Jones. Jones, who was Air Force chief of staff from 1974 to 1978 and chairman from 1978 until the end of June 1982, had spent most of his last five months in office campaigning for reorganization of the Joint Chiefs.

House Action

The House on Aug. 16 passed a bill (HR 6954) that was intended to strenghthen the role of the Joint Chiefs chairman. But the bill stopped short of Jones' proposal to correspondingly reduce the clout of the individual services in the Joint Chiefs' deliberations on issues of fundamental policy.

Jones' fundamental thesis, warmly supported by several former Army and Air Force brass and civilian Defense officials, was that the current Joint Chiefs organization tended to evolve policy by compromises that accommodated the bureaucratic interests of the individual services. As a result, he said, the chiefs spent too much time in internal bargaining over the budget and other issues.

Jones' proposal encountered intense opposition from some former Army officers and from a wide range of active duty and retired Navy and Marine Corps leaders. They argued that it risked cutting off civilian leaders from military advice that dissented from the dominant view.

The House Armed Services Committee produced HR 6954 as a compromise, sponsored by Investigations Subcommittee Chairman Richard C. White, D-Texas. White, who was retiring in 1982 after nine terms in the House, had become a staunch supporter of Jones' proposal.

When the House took up the measure Aug. 16, White acknowledged the committee's reservations over going as far as Jones had proposed in shifting the balance of bureaucratic power from the services to the Joint Chiefs chairman. But he said the committee intended the bill to stimulate further reforms within the Pentagon not requiring legislation.

The House passed HR 6954 by voice vote under suspension of the rules.

Background

The Joint Chiefs of Staff was a five-member committee consisting of a chairman and the head of each of the four services — the chiefs of staff of the Army and Air Force, the chief of naval operations and the Marine Corps commandant.

Strictly speaking, the committee did not command U.S. forces in the field. All combat units were organized into nine major commands, to which the Joint Chiefs merely transmitted orders from the secretary of defense.

Six of these were "unified" commands, which included components from more than one armed service, such as the European command. The other three major commands,

called "specified" commands, were Air Force units: the Strategic Air Command, the Military Airlift Command and the Aerospace Defense Command.

The Joint Chiefs' incentive to bargain in search of unanimity in their recommendations came from the fact that, by law, they had to report to the secretary of defense any issue on which they could not reach agreement.

The Jones Plan

Beginning in mid-February 1982, Jones critiqued the current Joint Chiefs organization and spelled out his proposed reforms in several articles and interviews.

In the March issue of *Armed Forces Journal*, a privately owned magazine dealing with defense issues, Jones described the current arrangement as a patchwork institution. It was cumbersome and rarely capable of suggesting fundamental innovation, he said, and tended to give each armed service "a de facto veto" over major decisions.

Stronger Chairman. Jones wanted to strengthen the role of the chairman, by giving him more formal authority to act as an independent source of military advice to the secretary of defense and the president, particularly on issues which pitted the services against each other.

"Many areas cannot be effectively addressed by committee action, particularly when four out of five committee members have institutional stakes in the issues, and the pressure is on to achieve unanimity in order to act," he wrote.

One seemingly minor step, which Jones insisted would further his purpose, was the assignment of a senior officer as deputy chairman. The deputy chairman would assist the chairman in overseeing interservice cooperation and would chair meetings of the Joint Chiefs in the chairman's frequent absences from Washington to inspect U.S. units in the field or consult with foreign governments.

Jones also wanted to increase the influence of the commanders of unified commands. He complained that the heads of Army, Navy and Air Force components within unified commands often approached problems from parochial service viewpoints rather than from more broad-gauged inter-service perspectives.

Stronger Staff. Jones also called for changes in personnel policy to make it more attractive for talented officers to serve in "joint" assignments, which involved coordinating the action of units from different services. In particular, Jones proposed changing a law (PL 80-253), which enforced rapid Joint Staff turnover.

The Joint Staff was intended to assist the Joint Chiefs in providing unified strategic direction for U.S. forces and integrating them into unified commands. But it was barred by law from serving as an overall general staff that would direct all military activity. And, it was limited to 400 officers, a far smaller group than the staffs of the service chiefs or the secretary of defense. With few exceptions, officers were allowed to serve on the Joint Staff for only three years. In addition to those constraints on the Joint Staff's organizational efficiency, Jones argued, it was hampered because officers were dependent on their own services for subsequent assignments and promotions.

Limiting the Services. Jones also wanted to limit the role of the service staffs in the Joint Chiefs' deliberations on interservice issues. The service staffs should merely provide information to the Joint Staff on which all members of the Joint Chiefs would rely for advice, he said. Because the service staffs independently analyzed issues that were before the Joint Staff, the process was much too cumbersome and the service chiefs tended to become the captives of their own bureaucracies' points of view.

"When a service chief acts on a service matter, he should receive advice from his service staff and when he acts on a joint matter he should receive his advice from the Joint Staff," Jones declared.

Opposition

During House Armed Services hearings on Joint Chiefs reorganization, which began April 21, the idea of increasing the chairman's power at the expense of the services encountered broadsides of opposition from several active duty and retired Navy and Marine Corps officers.

Adm. Thomas B. Hayward, the chief of naval operations, who retired at the end of June, told the panel he did not agree with a single one of Jones' proposals.

Hayward told the committee he was "deeply offended by the slanderous criticisms which one frequently hears about the Joint Chiefs being an ineffective group of parochial service chiefs who spend most of their time bickering among themselves, horse-trading to preserve their turf and what is best for their service."

Marine Commandant Gen. Robert H. Barrow concurred, warning that Jones' proposal would "do serious harm to the system." An all-powerful chairman and Joint Staff "would prevent the development of legitimate alternatives that should be presented to appropriate civilian authority for decision," he said.

Committee Report

The Armed Services Committee reported HR 6954 on Aug. 12 (H Rept 97-744).

Chairman's Role. The bill expressly authorized the Joint Chiefs chairman to provide military advice "in his own right" to the president and secretary of defense.

It also created the post of deputy chairman, to be filled by a full general or full admiral from a service other than the chairman's. The deputy would chair meetings of the Joint Chiefs and would vote only in the chairman's absence.

Joint Staff. The Joint Staff was charged by the bill with assisting the chairman, as well as the Joint Chiefs as a corporate body. And the measure directed the secretary of defense to organize the Joint Staff to assure its independence and its effectiveness in helping the Joint Chiefs provide unified strategic direction and operation of U.S. forces under unified command.

But the bill left untouched the current ban on the Joint Staff's functioning as a "general staff" in overall direction of the armed forces.

To improve continuity of personnel on the Joint Staff, the bill doubled to six years the time an officer could spend in continuous assignment to that group in peacetime. It also increased from 30 to 100 the number of officers on the Joint Staff — out of a total of 400 — for whom the secretary of defense could waive the requirement that at least three years elapse between two non-continuous assignments to the Joint Staff.

It empowered the Joint Chiefs chairman to select Joint Staff personnel from lists provided by the services. And it ordered the services to propose for Joint Staff assignment officers who were among their most outstanding.

In what the committee said was an effort to make Joint Staff service more attractive to highly qualified officers, the bill directed the secretary of defense to ensure that the services' promotions and assignments give "appro-

priate consideration" to an officer's performance on the Joint Staff.

It also required the Joint Chiefs chairman to give the president an evaluation of the performance in Joint Staff assignments of any officer being recommended to the president for promotion to admiral, general, vice admiral or lieutenant general.

Service Role. The only facet of Jones' plan the committee expressly disregarded was his recommendation to curb the influence of the service staffs in Joint Chiefs' deliberations.

During floor debate on the bill Aug. 16, White said the committee was not prepared to conclude that the Joint Chiefs system was "fatally flawed" because of the dual responsibilities of the service chiefs.

"Decisions concerning such issues as resource allocations, roles and missions, and doctrine would cause intense internal conflicts within the Department of Defense whether it were organized into services, as at present, or in some other way."

Excluding the services from participation in the formulation of military advice at the highest levels, White warned, "would merely lessen the potential influence of individuals representing the collective knowledge and experience of the organizations most qualified to judge land, sea and air warfare issues."

The bill specifically gave service chiefs and unified and specified commanders the right to add comments to any Joint Staff report prior to its consideration by the Joint Chiefs.

Strategy Advisers. Taking a leaf from proposals by Army Chief of Staff Gen. Edward C. Meyers and others, the committee bill would create a Senior Strategy Advisory Board, consisting of 10 retired generals and admirals who had been either members of the Joint Chiefs or commanders of a unified or specified command.

The board would meet at least monthly to provide the president, secretary of defense and Joint Chiefs with advice on strategy and tactics. Members' terms would be five years. ∎

Military Pay Bill

Congress in 1982 failed to pass separate legislation dealing with military pay, but most pay issues were handled in other defense bills or by the administration under terms negotiated with Congress.

By withholding action on separate pay legislation, Congress implicitly renewed the president's authority to limit pay raises for federal military and civilian employees to a level below the average for employees in the private sector.

After proposing raises of 8 percent for military employees and 5 percent for civilian employees in fiscal 1983, Reagan agreed with Congress on across-the-board federal raises of only 4 percent.

Military pay had been raised by 11.4 percent in fiscal 1981 and an average of 14.3 percent in fiscal 1982.

The House considered pay legislation twice:

● On Sept. 22, the House failed to suspend its rules to pass the first version of pay legislation, HR 6317. The vote was 214-186, well short of the two-thirds majority needed to suspend the rules. *(Vote 330, p. 98-H)*

The House Armed Services Committee had filed its

---

report on the bill May 17 (H Rept 97-552).

In addition to regular pay provisions, the bill included strict limitations on the Pentagon's ability to "contract out" non-combatant chores on military bases to civilian firms. Federal employee unions had wanted those restrictions, fearing the loss of jobs under contracting out. The Armed Services Committee complained that the administration was ignoring requirements of combat efficiency in switching jobs to private firms simply to cut the number of employees. But the bill's restrictions were opposed by the Reagan administration and by companies that hoped to win contracts.

Some restrictions on contracting out already had been included in the fiscal 1983 defense authorization bill (S 2248 — PL 97-252), cleared by Congress Aug. 18. *(Defense authorization, p. 77)*

● On Sept. 29 the House approved a redrafted version of the pay bill (HR 7166). The second bill made fewer restrictions on contracting out than did HR 6317. It also took account of a joint administration-congressional decision to hold military and civilian pay raises to 4 percent in fiscal 1983. That decision was made during negotiations over the first budget resolution, S Con Res 92. The earlier bill had authorized the 8 percent raise that President Reagan had originally requested for military members and 5 percent raise for civilians.

Reagan already had the authority to raise military and civilian pay, so legislation on the issue was not absolutely required.

Both bills also would have extended through fiscal 1987 the Pentagon's authority to continue paying enlistment and re-enlistment bonuses. The bonus authority had been scheduled to expire Oct. 1. The fiscal 1983 continuing appropriations resolution (H J Res 631 — PL 97-377) extended the authority only through March 31, 1983.

The Senate Armed Services Committee reported its military pay raise bill (S 2936 — S Rept 97-565) on Sept. 21, but that measure never reached the Senate floor. ∎

Nuclear Freeze Rejected by House

The House of Representatives on Aug. 5 narrowly rejected widespread public calls for an immediate "freeze" on U.S. and Soviet nuclear weapons, a proposal bitterly opposed by the Reagan administration.

By a 204-202 vote, the House discarded a freeze resolution (H J Res 521) and replaced it with administration-backed language that called for a weapons freeze but at "equal and substantially reduced levels."

The Senate Foreign Relations Committee also rejected the freeze proposal, but it did draft an alternative arms control resolution (S J Res 212) that did embarrass the administration. That measure called on the United States to refrain from actions that would "undercut" the unratified SALT II arms control treaty, which Ronald Reagan had bitterly opposed when he was running for president.

S J Res 212 never reached the Senate floor, largely because the Republican leadership did not want to open up a potentially divisive debate in which the administration would come under attack both from liberals who favored the freeze resolutions and hard-line conservatives who argued that the administration was not taking a tough enough stance on strategic arms issues.

In acting on the freeze issue in 1982, Congress was responding to an apparent groundswell of public concern about nuclear weapons. Legislative bodies in several states and hundreds of towns and cities passed resolutions calling for a nuclear freeze. Freeze resolutions also were endorsed in the November elections by voters in dozens of communities and in Massachusetts, California, Rhode Island, North Dakota, Montana, Oregon, Michigan and the District of Columbia. The freeze was rejected by voters in Arizona.

House Committee Action

H J Res 521 was ordered reported by the House Foreign Affairs Committee June 23 by a vote of 28-8.

The key vote, during the June 22-23 markup of the resolution, came on an amendment by Jonathan B. Bingham, D-N.Y., incorporating the call for a nuclear freeze. That amendment was adopted 26-11, with Democrats supporting it 19-2 and Republicans opposing it 7-9.

The resolution was introduced in the House by Foreign Affairs Chairman Clement J. Zablocki, D-Wis.

The committee report (H Rept 97-640) was not filed until July 19 while supporters of the resolution tried to round up cosponsors from among moderate Republicans. Meanwhile, the committee minority and the Reagan administration urged House Republicans to avoid committing themselves to the Zablocki resolution at least until they could examine an administration alternative.

A Republican alternative, sponsored by William S. Broomfield of Michigan, echoed Reagan's call for a freeze "at equal and substantially reduced levels."

Freeze Proposal

As reported, H J Res 521 said the United States and the Soviet Union "should immediately begin the strategic arms reduction talks (START)," having the following objectives:

● "Pursuing a complete halt to the nuclear arms race";
● "Deciding when and how to achieve a mutual verifiable freeze on the testing, production and further deployment of nuclear warheads, missiles and other delivery systems";

● "Giving special attention to destabilizing weapons whose deployment would make such a freeze more difficult to achieve";
● "Proceeding from this mutual and verifiable freeze, pursuing substantial, equitable and verifiable reductions," in the U.S. and Soviet nuclear arsenals.

In its report, the committee majority based its call for a freeze on the assumption that "nuclear parity presently describes the overall nuclear balance between the two superpowers."

The majority rejected the administration position that Moscow had a dangerous margin of superiority in land-based intercontinental ballistic missiles (ICBMs). The larger and more powerful fleet of Soviet ICBMs, they argued, was offset by U.S. advantages in long-range bombers and submarine-launched missiles.

The administration, by contrast, argued that ICBMs had unique advantages that could not be counterbalanced by other strategic weapons.

Specifically, the administration warned that Moscow had enough accurate, multi-warhead ICBMs that it could destroy the entire U.S. ICBM fleet with only a fraction of the Soviet force. U.S. threats to retaliate against such an attack with its submarine missiles and bombers would not be believed, according to this argument, because both governments would know that the remaining Russian ICBMs could destroy U.S. cities.

The committee dismissed this administration scenario as being "divorced from reality." A Soviet first-strike on U.S. missiles would be "a dangerous gamble with unacceptable risks."

In the first place, the committee noted the extreme difficulty of executing an initial Soviet attack on the U.S. missiles with the necessary precision. Moreover, it argued, even if such an attack were technically feasible, 7-15 million U.S. citizens would be killed immediately, and up to 20 million would die from radiation and other long-term effects of the attack.

"To assume that, first, the president would blithely ignore the incoming Soviet missiles and not order U.S. ICBMs launched, and second, not retaliate when faced with 17 [million to] 35 million American deaths, is an incredible scenario, with no basis in reality," the committee concluded.

Destabilizing Weapons. Paradoxically, having discounted the feasibility of a Soviet missile attack on U.S. ICBMs, the committee then warned that if such a threat developed, it would "greatly increas[e] the danger of a crisis or even an accident leading to a full-scale nuclear war."

Accordingly, the resolution stipulated that the freeze-oriented START negotiations should "give special attention to destabilizing weapons, whose deployment would make a freeze more difficult to achieve." In its report, the panel described such destabilizing weapons as "those which have the capability of destroying the other side's strategic nuclear weapons, thereby reducing confidence in their deterrent value."

The most dangerous of these weapons, the panel said, were those combining "high accuracy, multiple warheads, large explosive force, and short flight time ... since they have the potential capability of destroying protected hard targets like ICBM silos and command posts in a disarming

first strike." That was the same scenario the majority had discounted earlier in its report.

The committee also called for efforts to limit development of anti-submarine and anti-aircraft weapons; these weapons could be destabilizing if they were able to prevent bombers and missile submarines from carrying out a retaliatory strike.

It did not discuss the problem of distinguishing such developments from anti-aircraft and anti-submarine weapons designed to protect conventional forces against such attacks.

Verification. The committee declared that "testing and deployment of Soviet systems can be effectively verified by U.S. national technical means." The phrase "national technical means" was a euphemism for reconnaissance satellites and other electronic intelligence equipment that did not require the cooperation of the country being spied on.

However, the committee also implied that Soviet agreement to allow on-site inspection of alleged freeze violations would improve the verifiability of a freeze. The panel said that, during negotiation for a comprehensive ban on nuclear weapons tests, the Soviet Union had agreed to on-site inspection of possible violations and to the emplacement of U.S. seismic detection equipment on Soviet territory.

"Such procedures would prove highly useful" in verifying a freeze, the committee said.

Since a freeze would require a total halt of all activity involving affected weapons, the majority argued, violations would be easy to detect.

Freeze Effects. Like its discussion of "destabilizing weapons," the committee's analysis of how the resolution would affect U.S. weapons plans contained ambiguities. In

---

Text of Zablocki 'Freeze' Resolution

Following is the resolution, as amended on the House floor, sponsored by Clement J. Zablocki, D-Wis. The original resolution was H J Res 521.

Whereas the greatest challenge facing the Earth is to prevent the occurrence of nuclear war by accident or design;

Whereas the increasing stockpiles of nuclear weapons and nuclear delivery systems by both the United States and the Soviet Union have not strengthened international peace and security but in fact enhance the prospect for mutual destruction;

Whereas on May 9, 1982, President Reagan announced that he had written to President Brezhnev to propose negotiations to achieve an agreement that significantly reduces the number of nuclear weapons, enhances stability and opens the way to even more far-reaching steps in the future;

Whereas the SALT II agreement mandates the prompt reduction of Soviet strategic forces by 254 deployable strategic nuclear delivery vehicles; imposes significant restrictions on Soviet multiple-warhead deployable intercontinental ballistic missiles and on warheads for these missiles, in terms of numbers and throw-weight; prohibits equipment for rapid reload of intercontinental ballistic missile silos; and in these and other verifiable respects improves the ability of the United States strategic forces to carry out their deterrent mission;

Whereas the United States and the Soviet Union have observed the SALT II agreement since its signing;

Whereas adequate verification of compliance has always been an indispensable part of any international arms control agreement; and

Whereas a mutual and verifiable freeze followed by reductions in nuclear weapons and nuclear delivery systems would greatly reduce the risk of nuclear war:

Now, therefore, be it resolved by the Senate and House of Representatives of the United States in Congress assembled, that, consistent with the maintenance of essential equivalence in overall nuclear capabilities, the Strategic Arms Reduction Talks (START) between the United States and the Soviet Union should have the following objectives:

(1) Pursuing a complete halt to the nuclear arms race;

(2) Deciding when and how to achieve a mutual verifiable freeze on the testing, production, and further deployment of nuclear warheads, missiles and other delivery systems, not as an end in and of itself but as a logical first step toward achieving nuclear arms reductions.

(3) Giving special attention to destabilizing weapons.

(4) Providing for cooperative measures of verification, including provisions for on-site inspection, to complement National Technical Means of verification and to ensure compliance.

(4) Proceeding from this mutual and verifiable freeze, pursuing substantial, equitable and verifiable reductions through numerical ceilings, annual percentages or any other equally effective and verifiable means of strengthening strategic stability.

(5) Preserving present limitations and controls on current nuclear weapons and nuclear delivery systems.

(6) Incorporating ongoing negotiations in Geneva on land-based intermediate range nuclear missiles into the START negotiations.

In those negotiations the United States shall make every effort to reach a common position with our North Atlantic Treaty Organization allies on any element of an agreement which would be inconsistent with existing United States commitments to those allies.

Sec. 2. The United States shall continue to adhere to the SALT II agreement so long as the Soviet Union adheres to that agreement and so long as it is in the national security interests of the United States to continue to adhere to that agreement.

Sec. 3. Consistent with pursuing the overriding objective of an immediate freeze, nothing in this resolution shall be construed to prevent the United States from taking advantage of concurrent and complementary arms control proposals.

both cases, the discussion reflected the broad range of views among freeze supporters.

On the one hand, most early freeze proponents were liberals who assumed that nuclear parity currently existed between the United States and the Soviet Union. Accordingly, they objected to further development of new U.S. strategic weapons, such as the MX missile and the B-1 bomber.

But by early summer, the freeze idea had won the support of a large number of moderate Democrats, many of whom had not opposed development of the new U.S. weapons. In part, these moderates were influenced by the political potency of the grass-roots freeze campaign; partly they were impressed by the effectiveness of the freeze as a focus for widespread concern over the administration's earlier cavalier attitude toward arms control efforts.

The committee majority said the resolution "will not unilaterally preclude any defense program proposed by the Reagan administration." This was because the details of the freeze, including when it would be implemented and whether modern replacements could be built for existing weapons, would be negotiated later.

But the panel expressly rejected the administration

contention that, unless development continued of new U.S. weapons such as the MX and B-1, Moscow would have no incentive to agree to reduce its nuclear arsenal.

"Arming in order to disarm brings only higher levels of nuclear forces," the committee said. "The history of previous arms control negotiations is replete with examples of weapons programs which began as bargaining chips and became virtually impossible to control, once production began."

The committee majority also argued that a freeze would "blunt" Soviet advantages in nuclear weapons production over the short run. Presumably, this referred to the fact that Moscow had several types of ICBMs in production or under development, while no U.S. ICBMs were in production.

Euro-Missile Talks. The resolution also called for the START talks to incorporate the separate negotiations in Geneva to limit U.S. and Soviet intermediate-range missiles based in Europe.

In the consolidated negotiations, the resolution said, the United States "shall make every effort to reach a common position" with the other NATO allies on any agreement "which would be inconsistent with existing

Text of Broomfield Substitute Resolution

Following is the text, as amended and then adopted by the House Aug. 5, of the substitute strategic arms resolution sponsored by William S. Broomfield, R-Mich. The substitute resolution originally was introduced as H J Res 538.

Whereas the most serious challenges facing the American people, who are a people of peace, are the preservation of freedom and the prevention of war, with particular reference to nuclear war, by accident, miscalculation or design;

Whereas the consequences of a continued arms race and the accompanying increased risk of nuclear war are unacceptable, it is imperative that the highest priority be given to the successful completion of the START negotiations in a timely fashion;

Whereas the American people share the yearning of the world's people for reductions in nuclear armaments;

Whereas the Soviet Union, by its actions in Poland and Afghanistan, and through its refusal to abide by international chemical weapons agreements, has created threats to world peace;

Whereas stable and verifiable mutual reductions of Soviet and United States nuclear forces to an equal and far lower level would enhance stability and the maintenance of peace;

Whereas the Congress has expressed its mandate in Public Law 92-448 that the United States should not enter into a nuclear arms accord that provides for force levels inferior to those of the Soviet Union;

Whereas the stated policy of the United States government is to negotiate verifiable reductions to equal levels in the nuclear arsenals of both the United States and the Soviet Union;

Whereas the United States and the Soviet Union began formal negotiations in November 1981 in Geneva

on the limitation and reduction of intermediate range nuclear forces;

Whereas in May 1982 the Foreign Ministers of the North Atlantic Treaty Organization nations welcomed the president's proposal to cut stockpiles of long range nuclear missiles as a "far reaching but realistic offer" that could lead to "fair and effective agreements";

Whereas the United States and the Soviet Union began formal negotiations on June 29, 1982, in Geneva on the limitation and reduction of strategic nuclear armaments.

Now, therefore, be it resolved by the Senate and House of Representatives of the United States of America in Congress assembled:

(1) That Congress supports the initiation of strategic arms reduction talks and urges the Soviet Union to join with the United States in concluding an equitable and verifiable agreement which freezes strategic nuclear forces at equal and substantially reduced levels.

(2) That Congress reaffirms support for Public Law 92-448 which states that the United States not enter into an arms accord which provides for force levels inferior to the Soviet Union.

(3) To encourage arms restraint and stability, the United States should propose to the Soviet Union and other nations practical measures to:

(A) reduce the danger of nuclear war through accident or miscalculation;

(B) prevent the use of nuclear weapons by third parties, including terrorists; and

(C) halt the worldwide proliferation of nuclear weapons.

(4) The Congress insists that any arms control agreement must be fully verifiable as our national security cannot be based on trust alone.

United States commitments to those allies."

The Soviet Union had some 300 SS-20 missiles able to strike targets anywhere in Western Europe. Except for a handful of French missiles, there were no land-based missiles in Western Europe able to hit Soviet territory.

In December 1979, NATO agreed to deploy 572 U.S.-made Pershing II and ground-launched cruise missiles to offset the SS-20s, unless an agreement to limit such weapons could be reached with Moscow.

The committee report did not discuss how a freeze at existing levels could be reconciled with the NATO decision to deploy the new missiles if the Soviet Union would not give up its SS-20s.

Approving SALT

The committee resolution directed the United States to "promptly approve the SALT II agreement provided adequate verification capabilities are maintained." The committee insisted that the 1979 treaty would impose two important limits on Soviet nuclear forces.

In the first place, it would require an immediate reduction of Soviet long-range bombers and missiles by about 250 — a cut of 10 percent. And it would prevent a continuation of the current Soviet building program. Without the treaty, the majority said, Moscow's fleet of multi-warhead ICBMs, which the pact limits to 820, could reach 920 by 1985.

The panel also stressed that the treaty would ban Soviet development of equipment to rapidly reload a missile silo so that a second missile could be fired within several hours.

The committee also insisted that some provisions of SALT II would make it easier for U.S. intelligence sources to verify Soviet compliance with the treaty's limits. These included bans on interference with "national technical means" of verification and on encryption of missile test data related to verification of the accord.

The committee also rejected the administration contention that approval of SALT II would undermine efforts to negotiate a START treaty imposing much deeper cuts in the Soviet arsenal.

Since START negotiations would take years, the panel argued, ratification of SALT II would establish "the best possible foundation" for the new talks, "by formalizing agreements already adhered to by both sides." The approval of existing agreements is particularly important, the panel said, "in light of an imminent Soviet leadership succession."

Minority Views

Six committee Republicans endorsed Reagan's call for substantial reductions to equal levels through the START process. They warned that Zablocki's resolution "places the United States in a position of further disadvantage with the Soviets," and would undermine the administration effort to negotiate substantial nuclear arms reductions to equal levels.

In addition to Broomfield, signers of the minority views were Edward J. Derwinski, Ill.; Larry Winn Jr., Kan.; Robert J. Lagomarsino and Robert K. Dornan, Calif.; and Henry J. Hyde, Ill.

SALT II Condemned. Pre-eminent among SALT II's "inherent flaws," the minority said, was its acceptance of a continued Soviet monopoly of large, multiple-warhead ICBMs.

"That the Soviets have made compromises in the

treaty is irrelevant to the central reality of their unilateral advantage in heavy ICBMs and the impact of those ICBMs on the nuclear balance," they declared. Moscow's 308 so-called SS-18 missiles would condemn, "for the foreseeable future, substantial elements of our deterrent forces to Soviet destruction," they warned.

The minority also faulted the pact for excluding the Soviet Backfire bomber from its overall numerical ceilings on strategic weapons. They also discounted the significance of the 250 nuclear launchers Moscow would have to dismantle under SALT II, saying that the Russians would meet that obligation by scrapping older systems.

The significance of that reduction was dwarfed, they argued, by the Soviet Union's "unprecedented array of new strategic weapons" and its increased willingness to use military force outside of its borders, both of which occurred in the 1970s while SALT I was in effect and SALT II was being negotiated.

"We would be well-advised to reject the treaty on this basis alone," they said. "The strategic arms limitation process has allowed enormous growth in nuclear arsenals and failed to restrain increasingly aggressive Soviet behavior."

Anti-Freeze. The six Republicans also echoed the administration's attack on the proposed nuclear freeze.

An immediate freeze would "lock the United States and our allies into a position of military disadvantage and vulnerability," they said. "It would prevent us from correcting existing dangerous deficiencies in our strategic nuclear forces caused by the sustained Soviet buildup of the last 10 years."

The Republicans did not address the contention of some freeze proponents that it would take even longer to improve any U.S.-Soviet force ratios if Moscow could continue building new weapons indefinitely at its current rate, instead of having to respect the SALT II ceilings.

The only specific Soviet advantage the Republicans cited was the current balance in land-based, intermediate range missiles in Europe.

The minority complained that a freeze at existing, high levels of weaponry would undercut administration efforts to negotiate much lower levels, since it would remove any Soviet incentive to agree to lower force levels.

They also insisted a freeze would "seriously jeopardize American leadership and credibility" within NATO, by, in effect, unilaterally withdrawing from the December 1979 agreement on intermediate-range missiles.

Verification. The minority laid heavy emphasis on the argument that neither SALT II nor a freeze could be reliably verified.

A freeze, they insisted, would require on-site inspection that, they implied, the Russians would not accept.

"For example," they said, "it would be extremely difficult to verify a prohibition on improved warhead yields, improved throw-weight [the weight of the warheads that could be launched by a missile], or even new missiles." They also cited the contention of several Reagan appointees that SALT II could not be properly verified — a claim rejected by several Carter administration officials.

And the six claimed that some provisions of SALT II were being violated by the Soviet Union's camouflage of some missile launchers and encryption of some missile test data.

Such questions about Soviet compliance long had been raised by conservative opponents of SALT II.

Broomfield Substitute. The original cosponsors of the administration-backed substitute for H J Res 521 in-

cluded Republicans Broomfield, Winn, William Carney of New York and David F. Emery of Maine and several Democrats from the Armed Services Committee and Defense Appropriations Subcommittee. Among the Democrats were Melvin Price of Illinois, Samuel S. Stratton of New York, John P. Murtha of Pennsylvania and Bill Chappell Jr. of Florida.

The substitute was not included in the minority views on H J Res 521. But its operative provisions paralleled several criteria by which the committee minority found the freeze wanting.

Minority Provisions

As announced July 15, the substitute:

● Declared that Congress supported Reagan's START initiative, which was aimed at "an equitable and verifiable agreement which freezes strategic nuclear forces at equal and substantially reduced levels."

During the months of maneuvering on the freeze issue, some GOP conservatives and administration officials had balked at any use of the word "freeze," insisting that it inevitably would imply an administration surrender.

Congressional pragmatists finally carried the day, at least for purposes of the House battle, by arguing that the word had acquired too much political support to resist. Moreover, they insisted that the term could be redefined to conform with the administration's position, by linking it with equality — which the administration insisted did not exist — and with substantial reductions from existing arms levels.

● Reaffirmed PL 92-448, the resolution by which Congress approved the SALT I offensive arms agreement in 1972, particularly the so-called Jackson amendment. This provision, sponsored by Sen. Henry M. Jackson, D-Wash., "urges and requests the president to seek a future treaty that, inter alia, would not limit the United States to levels of intercontinental strategic forces inferior to the limits provided for the Soviet Union." *(SALT I, Congress and the Nation Vol. III, p. 217)*

● Encouraged various U.S.-Soviet measures of practical restraint to reduce the risk of nuclear war by accident or miscalculation, halt nuclear proliferation and prevent the use of nuclear weapons by third parties, including terrorists.

● Insisted that "any arms control agreement be fully verifiable as our national security cannot be based on trust alone."

House Floor Action

Confidence in the Reagan administration's commitment to serious arms control negotiations, more than the merits of any specific U.S. policy, was the central issue in the Aug. 5 House debate over H J Res 521.

Widespread public concern over that question had boosted the freeze movement to national prominence in the first place. And by accounts from both sides of the issue, the administration's most effective argument in winning the last few votes was that the freeze would jeopardize arms reduction talks now under way in Geneva.

From that perspective, the administration's two-vote victory was a slight endorsement, particularly in light of the extraordinary effort the White House invested in the battle.

In the key test, the House voted 204-202 to substitute administration-approved language sponsored by Broomfield for the freeze proposal sponsored by Zablocki. The House rejected, 175-229, a move to recommit H J Res 521 to the Foreign Affairs Committee and passed the amended measure 273-125. *(Votes 237-239, p. 72-H)*

Though both resolutions were ambiguous, the Zablocki measure called for "a mutual [and] verifiable" freeze to be followed by arms reductions; the Broomfield substitute proposed a freeze at "equal and substantially reduced levels" of nuclear arms. *(Texts, pp. 114, 115)*

Vote of Confidence? Les Aspin, D-Wis., who earlier had favored resuscitation of the SALT II arms treaty in preference to the freeze, was one of many members who explained his support of the Zablocki language as an effort to nudge the administration toward faster progress in arms control talks with Moscow.

"If we had a president who was genuinely interested in arms control, perhaps [the freeze resolution] would not be necessary," Aspin said. "If we had a president who would negotiate in good faith, then I think the Broomfield resolution would be enough — or perhaps no resolution would be needed."

But Reagan's record belied his professed commitment to arms control talks, Aspin said. "For 20 years, Ronald Reagan has opposed every step toward arms control by every president of either political party." Because of his record, and that of his administration, Congress needed to "crowd them a little bit, push them a little bit toward arms control," he said.

More ominous for the administration were the warnings during the House debate from several members who backed the Broomfield substitute. While they were willing to give the administration a chance to try arms control talks on its own terms, they wanted results.

Marc L. Marks, a liberal Pennsylvania Republican on whose support freeze supporters had banked, said he voted for Broomfield because Reagan and his aides recently had spoken "rationally and reasonably" about arms control policy. In contrast, the administration's earlier bellicosity had moved him at first to back the freeze.

Marks urged Reagan not to take a defeat of Zablocki as an indication that the House was unconcerned with arms limitation.

J. J. Pickle, D-Texas, who also supported the Broomfield substitute, phrased the warning more pointedly: "The administration should not gloat over any victory, for it will not be an endorsement of the record to date," Pickle declared.

"What all of this debate boils down to is that the days of stalling are at an end. The American people want an end to this nuclear arms race," he said, "and they want it now."

The symbolic character of the vote was underscored by freeze backers' acceptance of changes to win wavering votes for the Zablocki measure.

Regardless of the resolution's final wording, said one administration official prior to the vote, "It's either going to be 'Freeze Wins!' or 'Freeze Loses!' " in the headlines. "If Zablocki wins, it's going to be called a freeze."

The Big Picture

The central fact of the U.S.-Soviet nuclear balance, according to Zablocki partisans, was the sheer, unalterable power of each side to devastate the other, regardless of who struck first. Against that background, they argued, any marginal Soviet advantage conferred no usable power to extract concessions from the United States by nuclear blackmail.

Jim Leach of Iowa, one of the most prominent Republicans in the freeze campaign, drew the proposition in its most general form. "When American armed forces have the capacity to destroy the Soviet Union many times over," he said, "there is no such conceptualization as [nuclear] inferiority. Death is death. A human being cannot die twice."

From that perspective, Reagan's planned nuclear arms buildup was not only superfluous, but — at best — an expensive waste.

It made more sense to freeze nuclear weapons, Stephen J. Solarz, D-N.Y., told the House, "rather than spending billions of dollars . . . in an effort to achieve absolute nuclear equality with the Soviet Union, when we probably will not be able to achieve exact equality and would not be significantly better off if we could."

But the driving force behind the freeze was a fear that a stepped-up arms race not only would be costly, but would dangerously increase the risk of a nuclear conflict.

Charles E. Schumer, D-N.Y., underscored that warning, just before the debate ended.

"If we continue to play this game of we have to have a little more so they have to have a little more so we have to have a little more," Schumer declared, "we are sealing our own fate."

" 'Enough,' is what the American people are saying," Schumer continued. "Forget the numbers, forget the throw-weights, forget the abstract concepts. This is different."

First Strike. Some freeze leaders focused their warnings of a new and more perilous stage in the arms race specifically on the type of missiles Reagan planned to build: the land-based MX, the Trident II submarine missile and the Europe-based Pershing II. The danger of the new weapons was the combination of speed and accuracy that would enable them to destroy enemy weapons and command posts in a surprise attack, the critics maintained.

"If we produce and deploy these dangerous new weapons," Bingham warned, "you know the Soviets are not going to stand still. They are bound to respond with new and more dangerous systems of their own." The United States, in turn, would view the new Soviet arms as "intolerable threats," he predicted.

"As weapons accuracy increases and as warning times shorten," Bingham explained, "both nations may be forced to adopt a launch-on-warning strategy," which would call for firing their missiles at the first sign of an enemy attack. Since missiles could not be recalled once launched, he added, this would greatly increase the risk of nuclear war by accident.

Warning of Russians

Fundamental to the Broomfield tactic was a decision to try to accommodate public concern on the nuclear arms issue, if not the organized freeze movement itself. The basic point was to underscore Reagan's commitment to substantial arms reductions, as outlined in his START proposal.

"I think everyone here is for a nuclear freeze," William L. Dickinson, R-Ala., told the House late in the debate. "They are for an end to the arms race. The only question is, on what terms?"

The Zablocki freeze would end the arms race on the wrong terms, Dickinson warned, "lock[ing] ourselves into a position of inferiority vis-à-vis the Soviet Union."

Minority Leader Robert H. Michel, R-Ill., amplified that judgment, rejecting the whole image of an arms race as a description of the U.S.-Soviet nuclear relationship.

"The United States is not in a nuclear arms race," he said. "We are instead in a desperate, dangerous and deadly nuclear arms predicament brought about by 10 years of a Soviet nuclear arms buildup unanswered by the United States."

Two specific Soviet advantages were especially perilous, Broomfield and his allies said: Moscow's much more powerful force of multi-warhead ICBMs, and its monopoly in medium-range missiles based in Europe.

Since both kinds of Soviet weapons could devastate U.S. forces in a surprise attack, the administration and its backers insisted, they could not be offset by other kinds of U.S. weapons, such as missile submarines and bombers.

Most Broomfield supporters endorsed Reagan's contention that an immediate weapons freeze would remove any Soviet incentive to give up these presumed advantages.

But in the political atmosphere generated by the freeze campaign, Broomfield's allies were careful not to dwell on what would happen if Moscow took up Reagan's implicit dare to an arms-building competition. They proceeded instead from the premise that a demonstrated U.S. willingness to build countervailing weapons would convince the Soviet Union to accept arms parity at much lower levels.

If that assumption was made, Broomfield argued, "the single, clearest, easiest-to-understand difference between the two measures before us [is that] our substitute is for less; their resolution is for more."

On the other hand, an immediate freeze would eliminate any Soviet incentive to reduce its existing arsenal, particularly in those areas where the Soviets enjoyed an advantage, administration backers warned. And passage of the Zablocki measure would have a direct and fatal impact on current U.S.-Soviet arms negotiations in Geneva, they said.

"Is the Soviet Union likely to sit down and negotiate seriously in Geneva with an administration whose position has been repudiated by Congress?" Broomfield demanded. "Do we want the Soviets to think they should hold out for a better deal from the U.S. Congress?"

Taking on the Experts

A prominent theme among many Zablocki proponents was the argument that Congress was obliged to accept the original freeze concept because of its extraordinary grass-roots support.

"We are not here as leaders; we are here as followers," Norman E. D'Amours, D-N.H., told his colleagues, citing 50 towns in conservative parts of his state that had voted "overwhelmingly" in favor of the freeze.

"There is a movement in this land and it is a powerful and broad movement. That is what we are responding to," D'Amours said.

Toby Moffett, D-Conn., among other Zablocki backers, argued that the public outcry was not simply an expression of opinion, but a peremptory demand.

"People are sick and tired of leaving their fate in the hands of a regime of experts, including us, because we have failed," he said. "There are more weapons. There is more tension. There is more likelihood of war, not less, and the people are telling us that."

Granting that it might sound "a little bit hokey," Moffett told the House that he had addressed a massive disarmament rally in New York City's Central Park while holding his two-month-old daughter.

"On behalf of the children and the infants of this world, let us take just a little bit of a risk, let us take a

small step," and support the Zablocki resolution, Moffett concluded.

Vox Populi? Marjorie S. Holt, R-Md., 61 years old and a mother of three, followed Moffett into the well of the House, to declare: "I don't need a baby in my arms to cry out for a nuclear freeze. I think we all want it. We want to end nuclear weapons."

Her quarrel with the Zablocki resolution, she insisted, was over tactics, not over goals.

But most of the administration's troops recognized all too clearly that they had the harder case to make in the public arena, and some of them bristled at having been put on the defensive by the freeze movement.

"In over 30 years in Washington," Michel told the House, "I have yet to see a proposal so clouded by emotion, so fraught with danger, so unexamined in its consequences, so seemingly plausible, so attractive on the surface, yet so surely wrong and so ultimately deadly to our national survival as H J Res 521."

Hyde expressed the same view more pithily. "This is government by bumper sticker, folks," he said of the Zablocki resolution. "Don't throw the dice with freedom."

How Firm a Freeze?

As had been the case during the whole freeze campaign, freeze proponents on the House floor differed as to the specific effect adoption of the Zablocki resolution would have.

The most zealous freeze leaders argued that H J Res 521 would have precisely the effect it implied at first reading: calling for an immediate, absolute freeze of the nuclear arms status-quo.

"It would bring the arms race to a grinding halt," freeze leader Edward J. Markey, D-Mass., told the House.

Markey, Bingham and national freeze organizers repeatedly had argued that a "freeze" was particularly important to preventing the deployment of new weapons that would destabilize the nuclear balance by threatening enemy nuclear forces. This would include the MX ICBM and the Trident II submarine missile.

But, without discussing the issue in any detail, Zablocki steered clear of any firm commitment to a flat halt in nuclear weapons production. In fact, he commented paradoxically that his resolution "permits the procurement of new weapons to preserve and maintain a United States deterrence while contributing to nuclear reductions."

The Foreign Affairs Committee report on H J Res 521 specifically said the resolution left open to negotiation the question of deploying new, modern weapons to replace strategic arms that were becoming obsolete.

A Week's Difference. The ambiguity of the freeze resolution's effect was highlighted by Ronald V. Dellums, D-Calif., who long had fought a lonely battle against most of the specific weapons programs opposed by the freeze movement. Dellums minimized the significance of the Zablocki resolution in contrast to the large margins by which the House had approved the fiscal 1983 defense authorization bill only a week earlier. In considering that bill (HR 6030), the House rejected efforts by Dellums and others to cut funds from nuclear weapons programs. *(Defense authorization, p. 77)*

"How can you vote for a quarter of a trillion-dollar military budget that brings us closer to the brink of nuclear disaster and then vote for a piece of paper and assume that you have saved the planet from destruction?" Dellums demanded.

Freeze organizers conceded that they deliberately eschewed, for tactical purposes, any linkage of the freeze with battles against specific weapons. But Markey and others promised to carry the battle against specific programs in future years.

Amendments

Except for the Broomfield substitute, the major amendments considered during the floor debate were efforts by Zablocki and his allies to broaden the resolution's appeal in search of a majority.

For weeks before the debate, the administration and its congressional allies had seen this tactic as the most serious threat they faced. They had considered trying to fight the "sweeteners" in hopes that wavering members could not swallow the resolution in its original form.

But eventually they decided not to contest the pro-freeze amendments. In large part, this was because the amendments, when considered on their merits, were appealing to pro-administration conservatives.

SALT II. The first amendment attempted to counter the resistance among Republicans and some Southern Democrats to embracing SALT II. Arguments against the unratified treaty had been a prominent feature of Republican attacks on President Carter's foreign policy in 1980.

As reported from the Foreign Affairs panel, H J Res 521 called on the United States to "promptly approve the SALT II agreement provided adequate verification capabilities are maintained." But within days after the committee approved that provision, Zablocki allies found that it put off several Republicans who had cosponsored Zablocki's original resolution, but who later refused to cosponsor the committee measure.

Zablocki's amendment changed the SALT II language to stipulate that the United States should "continue to adhere to" SALT II so long as Moscow did likewise "and so long as it is in the national security interests of the United States" to do so.

The House accepted the amendment by voice vote.

Equivalence. Also by voice vote, the House accepted a three-part amendment by Bingham that, he insisted, merely clarified the resolution's intent. The amendment:

● Changed the resolving clause to stipulate that, "consistent with the maintenance of essential equivalence in overall nuclear capabilities," the START negotiations should pursue the listed objectives. The original language, drafted before the June 29 beginning of the START talks, had directed that the United States and Soviet Union "should immediately begin" START.

● Stated, as one goal of START, giving "special attention to destabilizing weapons." The change deleted a reference to destabilizing weapons "whose deployment would make such a freeze more difficult to obtain."

This change was made to emphasize that the "special attention" should be directed toward destabilizing weapons that already were deployed, such as Soviet ICBMs, in addition to those still on the drawing board, such as the American MX and Trident II.

● Added a section providing that, consistent with the "overriding objective of an immediate freeze," the resolution did not preclude the United States from pursuing other, "complementary" arms control proposals.

Despite Bingham's insistence that the amendment changed nothing in the resolution, it had been hammered out in hard-fought negotiations between freeze backers and several other Democrats, including Aspin, William J.

Hughes, N.J., Albert Gore Jr., Tenn., Elliott H. Levitas, Ga., and Majority Whip Thomas S. Foley, Wash.

Several of those members said the amendment substantively changed the resolution in their minds and made it possible for them to support the measure. Hughes, for one, said the amendment's first provision made the deci-

sion to seek a freeze contingent on the president's finding that essential equivalence with the Soviet Union had been achieved. The amendment, he said, "gives the president the flexibility he needs during this process."

Bingham vigorously objected to that view, insisting that the amendment spoke of the "maintenance" of essen-

Reagan 'Dense Pack' Plan for MX . . .

President Reagan on Nov. 22, 1982, announced his second plan in a year for deployment of the new MX intercontinental ballistic missile. Reagan proposed putting 100 of the missiles close to each other in a "dense pack" at Warren Air Force Base near Cheyenne, Wyo.

The dense pack plan met with widespread scorn on Capitol Hill, and appeared to be dead following Congress' decision to delete funds for MX production from the fiscal 1983 continuing resolution (PL 97-377). That action was widely viewed as a negative response to the complexities of the dense pack scheme.

Reagan's first plan for deployment of the controversial missile was announced Oct. 2, 1981; it called for putting 100 missiles temporarily in existing undergound silos until a permament plan could be selected. *(1981 Almanac p. 195)*

That plan also was widely condemned in Congress and was repudiated in 1982 by the House and Senate Armed Services committees during action on the fiscal 1983 defense authorization bill (PL 97-252). Congress also killed a plan, once considered by Defense Secretary Caspar W. Weinberger, to base the missiles in large transport planes. The Pentagon announced on June 22 that it was no longer considering the airborne MX plan. *(Authorization bill, p. 77)*

Reagan Speech

The president's dense pack announcement was part of a nationally televised speech intended to bolster support in the United States for his nuclear weapons policies and for his approach to arms control negotiations with the Soviet Union.

The speech embodied two fundamental premises of Reagan's strategic arms policy:

● Peace depended on a nearly symmetrical balance of U.S. and Soviet forces — especially land-based intercontinental missiles — and the current balance was intolerably favorable to Moscow.

● The Russians would agree to reduce their nuclear arsenals only if confronted by clear indications that the United States would match Soviet forces in the absence of an arms control agreement.

Reagan hit the second theme hard in his speech: "Unless we demonstrate the will to rebuild our strength and restore the military balance, the Soviets, since they are so far ahead, have little incentive to negotiate with us."

Both of Reagan's assumptions and the programs they implied, such as MX, long had been rejected by liberal arms control advocates. They maintained that, so long as the U.S. nuclear arsenal contained thousands of warheads, their sheer destructive power would deter a Soviet

attack regardless of any apparent Soviet advantage in particular kinds of weapons.

In 1982, Reagan came within a whisker of seeing Congress repudiate his approach to nuclear arms issues in votes on the nuclear weapons freeze and on the MX missile. *(Nuclear freeze, p. 113)*

But the Nov. 22 speech appeared to reflect an administration judgment that Reagan's political problem was not with the substance of his position but with the style in which it was presented.

From that perspective, what the president did not say Nov. 22 was as notable as what he did.

There were none of the seemingly casual references to "limited" nuclear wars that cost the administration so dearly in its first year. The speech steered clear of any discussion of the complex scenarios of nuclear war that were implicit in the power and accuracy built into the new MX missile and in the design of the dense pack basing method. MX was described only in general terms as a counterweight to existing Soviet missiles, as a replacement for aging U.S. weapons and as an incentive for Moscow to accept mutual arms reductions.

Also missing from the speech was the ideological combativeness toward the Soviet Union that had marked some of Reagan's foreign policy addresses.

Sophisticated electronic graphics were used to display Reagan's contention that Moscow was outstripping the United States militarily, but the comparison was linked to no denunciations of Soviet expansionism or internal politics. In fact, one of Reagan's few specific characterizations of Soviet behavior praised as "serious" the Russian counterproposal to his suggestion for deep cuts in the number of nuclear missiles on each side.

The absence of tough talk and gruesome military detail reflected the administration's effort to demonstrate that it was pursuing arms control and tension reduction with the Soviet Union in good faith. That claim was underscored by Reagan's proposal of several relatively modest measures, such as U.S.-Soviet exchanges of military information, to reduce the risk of accidental war.

Reagan summed up in a word the incongruity — or, as he put it, the sad irony — of linking deployment of MX and a reduction of the risk of nuclear war. He announced that the big missiles, each carrying 10 warheads with an explosive force of about a third of a million tons of TNT apiece, would be called "Peacekeepers."

Protecting the MX

Almost from the earliest congressional involvement in the MX saga in 1976, the most difficult technical factor in the system was the design of a basing method that

tial equivalence, thus implicitly underwriting the freeze movement's position that equivalence now existed.

In any event, Bingham's amendment was good enough for most of the Democratic skeptics, who voted against the Broomfield substitute.

But Levitas supported the administration after the

House rejected by voice vote, at the insistence of Bingham and Markey, an amendment of his that would have dropped the goal of a nuclear freeze after two years.

Other Issues. The House approved by voice vote an amendment by Norman F. Lent, R-N.Y., that added to the list of goals for START "providing for cooperative mea-

. . . Suffers Direct Hit From Congress

would protect the new missiles against the increasingly accurate Soviet ICBM warheads.

It was the theoretical ability of these Russian weapons to destroy existing Minuteman missiles in their underground silos that was the most widely accepted rationale for developing the new U.S. ICBM, called "missile experimental," or MX.

Although more than 30 basing techniques for MX had been mentioned before dense pack emerged in the spring of 1982, three basic approaches, with several variations of each, were under serious consideration.

● The missile could be deployed in underground silos and protected by anti-missile defenses.

● The missile could be carried on a continually moving launch platform, like a plane or truck, so that its location at any moment would be unknown and it could not be targeted by Soviet ballistic missiles.

● It could be moved at random among a large number of covered launch sites, with the total number of launch sites made large enough to exhaust the Soviet missile fleet if two warheads were fired at each U.S. launch site.

This third approach was favored by the Air Force, the Ford administration and, with evident reluctance, the Carter administration. But it faced serious political obstacles because of the cost of the thousands of launch sites, the impact of their construction in sparsely populated areas of Utah and Nevada, and the complicated theory of the system's operation.

Reagan's derisive attacks on the Carter plan during his 1980 campaign signaled the ultimate fate of that approach. His first MX proposal in October of 1981 made it clear to MX backers he was reluctant to adopt a Carter-style multiple launch site system.

Dense Pack Theory

The novel approach that entered public debate on the MX in mid-1982 was a theory of nuclear judo that would use the very power of the Soviet missile warheads to protect U.S. missiles against a Soviet attack.

The theory was that if the U.S. missiles were close together — 1,800 feet apart in Reagan's plan — they could not be wiped out in a single attack because incoming Soviet warheads would be so close together that the first few to explode would disable the rest — a phenomenon referred to by nuclear arms experts as "fratricide."

The first few Soviet warheads to explode in an attack would cause some of the nearby Soviet warheads to malfunction, because of intense radiation. Some might also be blown off course.

These radiation and blast effects would fade within a few seconds, but then the mushroom clouds of debris thrown up by the first explosions would deflect late arriving warheads.

Before the dust cloud dissipated enough to allow a second Soviet attack, the surviving MXs could be launched, according to the theory. In the first few minutes of flight, the MXs would be protected by heavy shields and would be traveling slowly enough to escape damage from the impact of debris.

Dense pack — officially referred to as Closely Spaced Basing — was designed to accommodate 100 MXs in launch capsules of unprecedented toughness. The capsules were to be resistant to 5,000 pounds of pressure per square inch from a warhead exploded next to them in the ground, and up to 20 times that much pressure from a warhead burst overhead.

The capsules were intended to be so hard that the Russians could hope to destroy them only with extremely large warheads set to explode in the ground, thus maximizing their fratricide effect against one another.

U.S., Soviet Options

Critics proposed various techniques by which the Soviet Union might evade the fratricide trap and destroy dense pack.

Some specialists insisted that the Russians could design a so-called "spike" attack, with a warhead aimed at each silo, all timed to explode within two-millionths of a second, the time defense officials said would be available before fratricide occurred.

Others argued that huge warheads could be designed that would plunge into the ground near each capsule to be detonated simultaneously, after they all were impervious to fratricide.

But administration officials insisted to reporters that any of the projected countermoves would take the Russians years to design. They could easily be nullified, they said, by such steps as placing anti-missile launchers around the dense pack array or building more silos than there were missiles, and shuttling the missiles around in a small-scale version of the Carter plan.

Arms Control Issues

Critics warned that Reagan's planned construction of 100 new missile emplacements in an array 14 miles long and a mile wide violated the SALT II treaty's ban on new fixed missile launchers. (Though he opposed ratification of SALT II, Reagan had promised to respect its provisions if the Russians did likewise.)

The administration position was that the holes were not missile launchers since the necessary launching equipment was built into a separate canister that was inserted into the hole. Various administration sources conceded that this interpretation was a strained one, and they were unable to suggest any reason for Moscow to accept it.

sures of verification, including provision for on-site inspection."

Bingham and Markey vehemently opposed the amendment after Lent said that, in his opinion, it required that any freeze include provision for on-site inspection. But when the amendment clearly prevailed on a voice vote, they made no effort to demand a roll-call vote.

Lent's amendment played on the most politically vulnerable aspect of the freeze, or any arms control policy: the widespread public suspicion that Russia could not be trusted to observe an agreement. It was widely assumed that Moscow would reject any requirement for widespread, on-site inspection of its strategic arms facilities. The Soviet Union did agree to a modest program of on-site inspection during negotiations for a comprehensive nuclear test ban treaty.

Porter Amendment. An amendment by John Edward Porter, R-Ill., emphasizing that the freeze was intended as a first step toward reductions and "not as an end in and of itself," was adopted by a roll-call vote of 323-84. *(Vote 236, p. 72-H)*

Amending Broomfield. Immediately before the Broomfield vote, the House agreed by voice vote to Benjamin A. Gilman's, R-N.Y., amendment to the substitute, adding a "whereas" clause assigning the "highest priority" to successful and timely completion of the START negotiations.

Senate Committee Report

The Senate Foreign Relations Committee report on S J Res 212 (S Rept 97-493) was filed July 12.

The nuclear freeze fight in the Senate was more a battle of nuance than of substance. In the committee's report, the principal protagonists sparred over symbols while shrouding their precise meaning in purposeful ambiguity.

Splitting essentially along party lines, the panel rejected the freeze and any formal approval of SALT II. But it approved a provision giving force of law to the policy that the United States "shall not ... undercut" the limits embodied in SALT II.

The administration opposed the provision's mandatory character, though it was similar to a policy announced May 31 by Reagan. While insisting that it did not want to be legally bound to every provision of the treaty, the administration refused to specify the provisions from which it desired some relief.

Foreign Relations Chairman Charles H. Percy, R-Ill., maintained that his resolution imposed a real restraint on the executive branch, and that a majority of the Senate would accept no less. But, partly in hopes of preventing a break with the administration, his committee's report laid great stress on how much freedom Reagan would retain.

To hold the support of John Glenn, D-Ohio, and Joseph R. Biden Jr., D-Del., who originally opposed the freeze, the Democrats deliberately eschewed any clear position on the acceptability of the current strategic balance and the relative importance of ICBMs.

In its report, the committee majority praised the nuclear freeze movement "for catalyzing public debate throughout the United States on arms control."

But it then briefly listed various reasons for the majority's rejection of the freeze as a policy. Some members questioned the verifiability of a freeze. Others worried that it would set in concrete the current Soviet monopoly on

long-range, land-based nuclear missiles in Europe.

However, the report did not specifically endorse the administration contention that Moscow currently enjoyed superiority in land-based ballistic missiles.

The report noted the 7-10 vote by which the committee rejected an amendment by Claiborne Pell, D-R.I., and Alan Cranston, D-Calif., that would have added the gist of the freeze resolution to Percy's resolution. But the report did not mention Percy's agreement at the end of the committee's markup of S J Res 212, to drop the word "freeze" as a label for his goal for a START treaty.

Support for START

The resolution applauded Reagan's efforts to negotiate START with the Soviet Union.

In particular, the panel concurred with Reagan that the first priority in the START negotiations was a significant reduction in the most "destabilizing" weapons: long-range ballistic missiles with multiple warheads. Reagan argued that these weapons were the most dangerous because they might enable one country to disarm its opponent by a surprise attack.

The resolution also affirmed as an ultimate goal of arms control policy the global elimination of nuclear weapons.

The specific goals endorsed by the panel for the first phase of START paralleled those announced by Reagan: "sharply reduced and equal levels on the numbers of ICBMs and SLBMs [submarine-launched ballistic missiles] and the aggregate number of warheads deployed on these systems."

How Many Treaties? The committee called for a START agreement to be negotiated and ratified in at least two stages. The first stage would mandate reductions in the number of missiles held by both countries; the second would cover missile "throw-weight," or warhead capacity.

Reagan had not committed the administration on whether or not a "START I" treaty should be signed and ratified before the throw-weight issue was settled.

Administration hard-liners, especially in the Pentagon, insisted that the throw-weight issue was the most important one for the United States. The Soviet Union had an enormous advantage over the United States because most modern Soviet missiles could carry four or five times the weight of their U.S. counterparts, they maintained.

Other officials, including former Secretary of State Alexander M. Haig Jr., had said the throw-weight issue could be held until the second stage of the START negotiations. The issue would be difficult to negotiate, they said, because it would require a more far-reaching change in Moscow's strategic arms inventory than in Washington's.

Meantime, SALT

Pending negotiation of a START treaty, the Senate resolution stipulated that the United States "shall continue to refrain from actions which would undercut the SALT I and SALT II agreements, provided the Soviet Union shows equal restraint."

The purpose of this provision, according to the committee report, was to "formalize the announced policy of the Reagan administration on interim SALT restraint."

The report cited testimony by Defense Secretary Caspar W. Weinberger that no planned U.S. weapons program would exceed the limits of SALT II. And it quoted Gen. David C. Jones, former chairman of the Joint Chiefs of Staff, to the effect that "mutual restraint" toward viola-

tion of the unratified SALT II treaty would reduce the uncertainties with which U.S. planners would have to cope.

But administration officials insisted the committee resolution went far beyond their position on SALT II.

Many administration officials were loathe to have Reagan personally commit himself to any recognition of the SALT agreements, however informally. As part of an effort to defuse the nuclear arms issue, however, the president said May 31 that he would refrain from undercutting "existing strategic arms agreements."

Contrary to the committee report's excerpt from the speech, Reagan did not mention SALT by name.

What Does It Mean? The panel said the "not-undercut" formula covered "actions which would contravene the agreements in a substantial and irreversible manner." By way of illustration, the report cited the same two examples used by the Carter administration in 1980 to describe its version of a "not-undercut" stance: the policy would not allow testing of missiles with more warheads than the treaty allowed nor the testing of more than one "new type" of ICBM.

Hinting at a possible point of contention with the administration, the panel said it interpreted the not-undercut policy to require continued observance of the SALT I and SALT II limits on the total number of submarine missile launchers.

But much of the committee's discussion of the "not-undercut" provision emphasized what it did not mean:

● "The committee has not attempted to define or elaborate in detail all the hypothetical acts by either side which could arguably undercut the SALT agreements," the panel said. It maintained that the president should have "considerable flexibility and discretion" in deciding the limits of allowable action.

● Responding directly to one administration objection to the "not-undercut" provision, the panel said that it was not intended to provide individuals with legal standing to go to court in order to stop any weapons program on the grounds that it violated SALT.

● Specifically, the committee said its "not-undercut" provision was not intended to prejudge the possibility of deploying the new MX missiles in the so-called Dense Pack method. This would deploy 100 missiles in heavily armored silos built close together.

Some arms control liberals had protested that Dense Pack would violate the SALT II ban on the construction of new, fixed ICBM launchers.

● The committee said it did not intend that a not-undercut regime should "necessarily" extend beyond the Dec. 31, 1985, termination date of SALT II. A continued policy of restraint regarding the SALT II limits might be in the U.S. interest after that date, particularly if the START negotiations still were in progress, the committee said.

Other Moves

The resolution also called on the president to propose to Moscow ways to reduce the risk of nuclear war and halt the proliferation of nuclear arms.

In its report, the committee highlighted proposals to:
● establish a multinational center to monitor the use of nuclear weapons by third countries or terrorists;
● improve the U.S.-Soviet "hotline" for rapid communication in a crisis;
● reduce the vulnerability to attack of each power's military command and communications network.

The resolution also urged the president to decide promptly whether or not the Senate should ratify long-pending U.S.-Soviet treaties that would limit nuclear explosions for weapons tests or for "peaceful purposes." The White House said July 20 it was seeking changes in the treaties to make them more verifiable.

THE DEMOCRATS

All committee Democrats except conservative Edward Zorinsky, Neb., concurred in additional views that called for approval of a nuclear freeze and for some commitment to the SALT II limits that was less ambiguous than the committee's "not-undercut" provision.

In general, the Democrats commended Percy's efforts to draft a bipartisan resolution and concentrated their attack on the administration.

"The record of the Reagan administration on arms

Reagan Sets START Plan

On May 9 President Reagan sought to seize the initiative in U.S.-Soviet nuclear arms talks by proposing a "practical, phased reduction" in the two nation's nuclear forces. Reagan called the talks START, for Strategic Arms Reduction Talks.

Reagan said both the United States and the Soviet Union must "reduce significantly the most destabilizing systems — ballistic missiles, the number of warheads they carry and their overall destructive potential."

The president made his arms proposal in a commencement speech at his alma mater, Eureka College in Eureka, Ill.

As an initial step toward reduction of the U.S. and Soviet nuclear arsenals, Reagan's proposal would set the following approximate limits, to be reached over a period of 5-10 years:

● No more than about 5,000 warheads on long-range land-based missiles (ICBMs) and submarine-launched missiles. Administration officials said there were about 7,500 such warheads in each country's arsenal.

● No more than about 850 ICBMs and sub-launched missiles. The administration placed the current inventories at 2,400 for the Soviet Union and 1,700 for the United States.

● A limit of 2,500 on the number of ICBM warheads. Current totals were 5,500 for the Soviet Union and 2,152 for the United States, according to the administration.

Though Reagan did not propose limits on bombers and cruise missiles in this first stage of START, Secretary of State Alexander M. Haig Jr. told the Senate Foreign Relations Committee May 11 these weapons might be included in a first-phase START treaty.

As a second step, Reagan would seek equal limits on the total throw-weight (weapons carrying capacity) of long-range missiles at a lower level than the current U.S. throw-weight total. By most estimates, Soviet missile throw-weight was about three times the U.S. total because of the much larger average size of Soviet ICBMs. Phase two also would seek equal ceilings on strategic weapons not covered by START I.

control is dismal and causes us to doubt both the ability and the willingness of the administration to achieve effective arms control," they said.

In particular, the Democrats condemned Reagan for:

• poor-mouthing the U.S. nuclear deterrent "without factual justification";

• "irresponsible statements on nuclear war and irresponsible actions such as the pointless doubling of civil defense expenditures"; these aroused fears that the administration believed that a nuclear war might be winnable, they said.

• "Draconian" cuts in the manpower and budget of the Arms Control and Disarmament Agency;

• rejection of SALT II, "the work of three presidents, on the basis of simplistic campaign rhetoric."

Faced with this track record, the Democrats said, the Senate should choose between either strengthening the resolution or abandoning it as "an exercise in futility."

What to Freeze, When?

On its face, the minority report by Democrats endorsed an unalloyed freeze. It called on Congress to "recognize the value of a bilateral, mutual and verifiable freeze on the testing, production and deployment of nuclear warheads, missiles and other delivery systems." Such a step would head off "developments which might frustrate any attempt to achieve substantial arms reductions and bring the arms race under control," they said.

But the Democrats skirted the question of whether the current U.S.-Soviet balance, if institutionalized in a freeze, would be acceptable over the long run. The freeze amendment had been proposed "in the context of" other parts of the Percy resolution, they said.

This "context" was described in unusually vague language that referred to "initial steps to achieve sharply reduced and equal levels on the aggregate number" of ICBMs, submarine-launched missiles and warheads.

The language was crafted to allow Glenn and Biden to support the freeze only as part of an assured sequence of rapid steps toward substantially lower and equal force levels. Both senators had attacked the freeze as a policy, while welcoming the freeze movement for having roused public interest in arms control.

Imprecision born of political compromise also was evident in the Democrats' response to several charges laid against the freeze proposal.

For instance, they denied that an immediate freeze would enshrine a Soviet nuclear advantage. But they set no guidelines, for example, for how broad a Soviet advantage in ICBM throw-weight could be offset by U.S. advantages in the number of bomber-launched cruise missiles. Nor did they take the position that the U.S. deterrent would be credible regardless of any conceivable Soviet advantage.

Similarly, the Democrats rejected the administration position that Moscow would negotiate a force reduction only if faced with the alternative of a U.S. buildup — including the new MX missile — that would be barred by a freeze. They called instead for a "step by step" approach to test Soviet good faith in negotiating arms reductions.

But they offered no guidance as to how much of a change in the Soviet arms program would constitute adequate evidence of good faith. Nor did they discuss whether the freeze should be abandoned if it had not elicited an acceptable Soviet response within a certain time.

The Democrats also asserted that a worldwide freeze of all U.S. and Soviet nuclear weaponry would not undercut NATO's decision to deploy 572 long-range U.S. missiles

unless Moscow agreed to destroy similar missiles aimed at Western Europe. The only explanation provided was that the freeze would be "intended as a basis for achieving reductions," some of which, presumably, could cover the Soviet missiles aimed at Europe.

SALT II

For all practical purposes, the Democrats' position on SALT II was a call for ratification of the treaty.

"If the president could move beyond his campaign rhetoric, [which described] SALT II as 'fatally flawed,' to weigh the pros and cons of formal SALT restraints, he might quite well realize that SALT II ratification is in that national interest," they declared.

Monitoring of Soviet strategic forces would be easier if the treaty were in force, the Democrats insisted, because of several provisions that prohibited actions to conceal some weapons. They did not respond directly to the example of unverifiability Haig had cited to the panel: Moscow's insistence that it was free to encode missile test data that it decided the United States did not need to verify Soviet compliance with the treaty.

The Soviet fleet of more than 300 very large missiles, which was allowed by the treaty, and which had no U.S. counterpart, would not be reduced by non-ratification of SALT II, the Democrats argued. On the other hand, the treaty limited the number of warheads on these so-called SS-18s to 10 rather than the possible 25 or 30.

The thrust of their attack was a suspicion that, in opposing any specification or formalization of the "not-undercut" policy, the administration might actually intend to disregard parts of SALT II.

Administration weapons plans could break the SALT II limits on multiple warhead missiles as early as 1984, they warned, and the Dense Pack version of MX might violate the ban on new, fixed ICBM launchers.

The Democrats did not argue against any of these developments, but insisted that the U.S. and Soviet governments explicitly negotiate the details of an interim arms control regime, to cover the duration of the START negotiations.

THE HELMS DISSENT

Jesse Helms, R-N.C., who had voted by proxy to report the Percy resolution, later renounced his support of the measure. In a minority report, he said he had been misled into believing that the resolution supported the president's position, which it did not. He cited the mandatory reference to a policy of not-undercutting SALT II.

But most of Helms' 54 pages of additional views — more than twice the length of the majority and Democratic views combined — were devoted to a sweeping attack on supporters of the freeze, backers of SALT II and the Reagan administration itself.

All three groups, he said, had acquiesced in an arms control process that permitted the growth of Soviet nuclear superiority while hamstringing possible U.S. countermoves.

On the one hand, Helms demanded that the administration charge Moscow with upwards of two dozen alleged violations of the SALT I and SALT II agreements, partly to alert the public to the character of the Soviet menace.

"The American people deserve to be told officially in at least general terms of the serious dangers already posed to U.S. national security by past Soviet SALT deceptions . . . and the extent to which they have been misled on SALT compliance and the negative effects of detente by

past administrations," he said.

A challenge to Moscow's compliance with current and past treaties would set the stage for demanding more equitable agreements in the future and for holding Moscow to scrupulous adherence to them, Helms maintained.

Moreover, it would provide political support for President Reagan's promised buildup of this country's nuclear forces and for improved intelligence efforts to monitor Soviet activity.

But another, profoundly pessimistic theme surfaced occasionally in Helms' statement: a fear that unequal arms agreements might have won public support because the American people lacked the stomach for an all-out psychological mobilization against the Soviet threat.

"Sadly, it appears that — to the American popular masses — the struggle has all but ended .... If the American people are already self-deterred [from defending themselves], then nuclear freeze makes sense and saves a lot of money for tuition loans for anti-nuclear student activists," he said.

Helms charged Moscow with half a dozen violations of the 1972 treaty limiting anti-ballistic missile (ABM) defenses. Among these was development of a mobile ABM that could allow Moscow to very rapidly exceed the treaty limit of 100 missiles at one site.

He also accused the Russians of exceeding, at least for a time, several of the limits on various kinds of offensive weapons that were set in the 1972 SALT I agreement. The most far-reaching of these charges was that Moscow had stockpiled some 1,300 old ICBMs that were replaced in their armored launch silos by newer missiles but that still could be fired from makeshift launchers.

SALT II Violations. Major provisions of SALT II also had been violated by the Russians, Helms maintained, including encryption of test data from several new types of missiles.

This concealed information needed to verify whether or not the missiles exceeded the treaty's limits.

Moreover, Helms said, the Russians had tested the rapid reuse of some missile silos, after one missile had been fired, to fire another missile.

Either violation, arguably, would "undercut" the treaty because their effects would be irreversible: once taken, those actions would give the Russians capabilities that are barred by the treaty but that could not be "unlearned."

Reagan Failure

Though he steered clear of a direct attack on Reagan personally, Helms lambasted the administration for defecting from strategic arms positions taken by the 1980 Republican platform and subsequently reiterated by Reagan himself. Reagan and the platform had attacked Carter for creating a "window of vulnerability" — a period during which U.S. strategic forces theoretically could be decimated by a Soviet attack. But Helms noted that the Reagan administration brushed aside nearly all of the crash programs that conservative defense specialists had promoted to close the window.

Moreover, the administration's October 1981 strategic arms plan would open the window a little wider by accelerating the retirement of some older B-52s and Titan II ICBMs, Helms said. And because of budgetary limits, that plan contemplated buying fewer new strategic weapons than once had been planned and slowing the rate at which they would be procured.

START and SALT. Helms also condemned the administration's START proposal, though he blamed the "arms control bureaucracy," rather than Reagan.

First, he said, the prospect of a two-stage START treaty continued a fundamental error of the two SALT agreements: limiting the number of missiles and warheads, rather than the gross destructive power of the two nuclear arsenals. Specifically, Helms objected that an initial START agreement would not limit throw-weight of missiles, nor would it necessarily limit Soviet missiles that were stockpiled in other than conventional launchers.

Second, apparently equal limits on U.S. and Soviet forces ignored U.S. military requirements, he said. As a practical matter, the United States would be in a militarily inferior position if U.S. and Soviet offensive forces were equivalent, according to Helms. The Soviet Union had a much larger and more widely dispersed set of military targets than did the United States, and it had ABM defenses to pare down any U.S. attack, he warned.

Finally, and fundamentally, Helms declared, by beginning arms control negotiations with Moscow, the Reagan team would subject its defense programs to political pressures to hold off on needed weapons improvements, lest they damage the arms control process. Moreover, he said, any prospect of an agreement that would rule out a particular weapon would fuel congressional opposition to that weapon. ∎

Foreign Policy

Mutual skepticism characterized the relationship between Congress and the executive branch on foreign policy issues in 1982.

There were no intense foreign policy struggles during the year, such as the highly emotional 1981 battles over the sale of AWACS planes to Saudi Arabia or the unsuccessful appointment of human rights chief Ernest W. Lefever and the policies he represented.

Congress did challenge President Reagan on a few foreign policy items, including economic sanctions against the Soviet Union, aid to El Salvador, covert action against Nicaragua, and foreign aid spending. But none of those challenges produced dramatic fights; instead, the administration and its disparate critics on Capitol Hill tried to outmaneuver each other and wound up making compromises that merely postponed decisions on the basic issues.

The El Salvador issue was a classic example of how Congress influenced foreign policy. By forcing the president to justify in public virtually every step he took in El Salvador, and by giving him some, but not all, the aid resources he asked, Congress limited Reagan's options and forced him to follow a more moderate, cautious approach than he might otherwise have taken.

The administration, of course, saw this as unwarranted interference, or nitpicking, by Congress. There were complaints, for example, that the U.S. embassy in San Salvador was spending so much time collecting information for twice-annual certifications on El Salvador's eligibility for aid that it had little time for routine diplomatic chores.

On many issues, the administration was caught in the middle between two extremes in Congress. On the right, Sen. Jesse Helms, R-N.C., and other conservatives feared Reagan and his aides were adopting too many elements from policies of previous administrations. And on the left, liberals felt the administration was attempting a return to the Cold War.

Both sides extracted some political costs.

The Helms conservatives constantly reminded the foreign policy bureaucracy of the need to respect Ronald Reagan's ideological roots. Whenever the administration seemed to violate the principles that Reagan had espoused throughout his political career, Helms and his colleagues cried "foul." Such was the case in August, when the United States signed a joint communique with the People's Republic of China in which the United States for the first time said it eventually would end arms sales to Taiwan. Helms expressed bitter disappointment that Reagan could betray Taiwan, and the president felt obliged to telephone CBS News anchorman Dan Rather to deny the charge.

Helms and his colleagues also held up Senate action on several foreign policy nominees they judged to be unacceptable. That opposition eventually killed Reagan's nominations of Robert T. Grey Jr. and Norman Terrell to top posts at the Arms Control and Disarmament Agency (ACDA). Left uncertain at the end of 1982 was the fate of former *New York Times* reporter Richard R. Burt, nominated to be assistant secretary of state for European affairs. The conservatives used all three appointments to focus public attention on their criticisms of administration arms control policy.

At the other end of the political spectrum, liberals in Congress helped moderate the extent to which the administration deviated from foreign policy norms that had been established in the 1970s. Among the most important standards were the willingness to negotiate arms control agreements with the Soviet Union and the insistence that countries receiving U.S. military aid adhere to basic standards of human rights. For example, a handful of liberals in the House managed to block for more than a year the administration's plan to resume arms sales to the right-wing government of Guatemala.

Over the longer term, nothing that happened in 1982 seemed likely to alter the balance of power between the executive branch and Congress. The most important congressional foreign policy initiative during Reagan's first two years — the El Salvador certification requirement — was a short-term response to Reagan's policies of the moment. It did not appear to signal a congressional determination to wrest foreign policy powers away from the president.

Toward the end of 1982 leaders of the Senate Foreign Relations and House Foreign Affairs committees expressed concern that Reagan was evading requirements of the War Powers Resolution (PL 93-148) by refusing to seek congressional approval for his decision to station U.S. Marines in Lebanon as part of a multinational peacekeeping force. However, most members of Congress seemed less interested in guarding the sanctity of the War Powers Resolution than in avoiding any action that might upset the chances for a peaceful settlement in Lebanon.

Reagan Foreign Policy

The most significant development in Reagan's foreign policy during the year was the turnover at the top of the foreign policy establishment.

After months of controversy, Reagan on Jan. 4 dumped his National Security Adviser, Richard V. Allen. In his place, Reagan named one of his most trusted deputies, William C. Clark, who had served as deputy secretary of state. Although a novice in foreign policy matters, Clark quickly rejuvenated the National Security Council staff and ended public bickering between the White House and the State Depatment.

Secretary of State Alexander M. Haig Jr., the bellicose former general who had feared a White House conspiracy

to oust him, eventually fell victim to just such a development. Haig resigned June 25, complaining in a statement that the administration was "shifting" from what he described as a "careful course" in foreign policy. Haig later admitted that his resignation was not entirely voluntary and that his disagreement with Reagan's economic sanctions against the Soviet Union and his conflicts with White House aides made his departure inevitable.

George P. Shultz, the former economics professor and Nixon cabinet officer named to replace Haig, changed both the style and substance of U.S. foreign policy.

The change in style was noticeable immediately: Haig's aggressive rhetoric was replaced by Shultz' bland, professorial utterances that nearly put reporters to sleep.

The change in substance was more subtle because Shultz steadfastly refused to take personal credit for the adoption of policy positions, saying he was merely carrying out the wishes of Ronald Reagan. Shultz-watchers inside and outside of government admitted months after he entered the State Department that they had no clear idea of what his views were on many important policy issues.

But shifts of focus and tone were evident in a range of administration policies. Perhaps the most dramatic change was Shultz' quiet work to negotiate an end to the economic sanctions Reagan had imposed on the Soviet Union in retaliation for its pressure on Poland. Shultz had long been on record as opposed to the use of sanctions as a foreign policy tool, and one of his first accomplishments as secretary of state was to reach an agreement with the European allies that enabled Reagan to reverse his policy on the sanctions with only a minimum of embarrassment.

Shultz' hand also was clear in the evolution of administration policy toward the Middle East. Haig had tried to build an anti-Soviet "strategic consensus" by balancing the not-always-compatible interests of the United States, Israel and moderate Arab nations. Meanwhile, the Camp David peace process came to a halt as Israel pursued policies — such as the expansion of Jewish settlements on the West Bank of the Jordan River — that embarrassed the United States and antagonized Egypt.

Shultz shifted the focus of U.S. policy in the Middle East away from the East-West conflict and toward resolution of the Arab-Israeli dispute. He was widely credited with being the principal architect of Reagan's Sept. 1 Middle East "initiative" that reaffirmed U.S. support for Israel but called for Palestinian self-government of the West Bank "in association with" Jordan.

As the year wore on, Shultz became more and more involved in administration deliberations over economic policy, his first love. Some State Department officials began to fear that Shultz would be able to devote less attention to foreign policy issues, possibly costing the administration its most prestigious advocate of a moderate course.

Human Rights. With the exception of nuclear arms control, human rights caused more political trouble for the Reagan administration during its first two years than any other foreign policy issue.

The administration's reluctance to criticize publicly the human rights records of close allies — such as El Salvador, the Philippines and Indonesia — was appreciated by leaders of those nations. But it gave liberals and human rights groups the chance to complain that the administration assigned more importance to the tenure of friendly dictators than to the lives of the people they ruled.

Administration officials said their "quiet diplomacy" on human rights worked. They cited the March elections in El Salvador, a decline in killings by government forces in Guatemala and an improved treatment of East Timor by the Indonesian government as examples of progress that resulted from quiet U.S. persuasion.

Liberals and human rights groups disagreed, saying that Reagan, by keeping quiet about rights abuses, was putting his stamp of approval on the actions of repressive governments that received U.S. military and economic support.

Foreign Aid

Reagan failed in 1982 to match his success the previous year in gaining congressional approval of both foreign aid authorization and appropriations bills. In addition to the usual election-year hurdles, foreign aid faced a variety of political troubles in 1982 that limited its chances to survive a full-scale debate in Congress.

Congress in 1981 had passed a bill (PL 97-113) setting foreign aid authorizations for both fiscal years 1982 and 1983, so there was no absolute need for such legislation to be passed in 1982. But Reagan sought supplemental funding for both fiscal 1982 and 1983, especially for military assistance. Most of the 1982 supplemental request was rejected by the Appropriations committees. Both the House Foreign Affairs and Senate Foreign Relations committees drafted fiscal 1983 supplemental authorizations bills that included some of the president's requests, but neither bill was given floor consideration.

Congress appropriated funds for foreign aid in the fiscal 1983 continuing resolution (H J Res 631 — PL 97-377), marking the third time in four years that it failed to pass a separate aid bill.

As in 1981, the administration and its conservative allies in Congress pressed for more military aid and liberals fought for more development assistance to Third World nations. The administration won. The continuing resolution included substantial increases in military aid (though less than Reagan wanted) but held the line on development assistance, continuing a trend that began the previous year.

There were complaints in Congress from both liberals and conservatives that the administration was promising additional aid to foreign countries and then turning to Congress with a demand that it fulfill the promises. The charge had some validity in the case of countries that hosted U.S. military bases or that faced threats from Soviet-backed insurgencies. The administration did promise substantial military aid increases for countries such as El Salvador, South Korea, Spain, Thailand and Turkey, and it then labeled Congress as irresponsible when the aid bill failed to provide enough money to carry out those promises. The administration said it would return to Congress in 1983 with a renewed request for the military aid that had been cut.

Also left unresolved in 1982 was the longer-term issue of U.S. participation in the World Bank and other international development banks. Ideologically, many administration officials were opposed to those agencies on the grounds that they promoted socialism, wasted money and generally failed to serve U.S. interests.

But after nearly a year's study, the Treasury Department in February issued a report that, in many respects, could have been written by the World Bank's public relations department. Although critical of some policies followed by the development banks, the report generally praised their operations and said they were effectively promoting sound economic development in much of the world.

In spite of those conclusions, the Treasury report called for reduced U.S. contributions to the so-called "soft loan windows" of the banks, which made low-interest loans to the world's poorest nations. Congress already had been following such a policy by sharply cutting the level of funding for the International Development Association (IDA), an arm of the World Bank. The IDA issue threatened to strain relations between the United States and its key allies, many of whom had increased their donations to IDA to make up for reduced U.S. funding.

Latin America

Along with the Middle East, Latin America dominated Reagan administration policy considerations during much of the year.

The administration continued to generate controversy by supporting right-wing regimes in Central America and by launching a not-so-secret war against the government of Nicaragua. If the policy produced no immediate successes during the year, at least it produced no outright disasters.

In El Salvador, the U.S.-backed government held elections in March, with mixed results. The huge turnout was a public relations success both for the government and for the United States. But extreme right-wing figures won key posts in the new Constituent Assembly, severely hampering the U.S. effort to promote a centrist government that could win the loyalty of the population as well as the war against leftist guerrillas.

As required by Congress, Reagan twice certified that El Salvador was making sufficient progress in respecting human rights and implementing various economic and political reforms to justify its receiving U.S. military aid. Both certifications (in January and July) were heavily criticized by liberals and human rights groups. Though Congress made no move to cut off aid to El Salvador, it did sharply reduce that aid below Reagan's request for fiscal 1983.

The Reagan administration also moved during 1982 to restore a military relationship between the United States and Guatemala, which for years had one of the most repressive governments in Latin America. The sale of helicopter spare parts and other military items, announced in January 1983 after months of sparring between the administration and liberals in Congress, seemed certain to provoke a new debate about the extent of U.S. backing for far right regimes.

Another debate that was begun in 1982, with no conclusion, concerned the administration's alleged war against the leftist Sandinista government of Nicaragua.

In December 1981, Reagan reportedly signed an executive order authorizing covert actions by the Central Intelligence Agency to disrupt arms shipments into Nicaragua and to harass what the order called the "Cuban-Sandinista support structure in Nicaragua and elsewhere in Central America."

Reports about the CIA operation, based in neighboring Honduras, began to trickle out early in 1982; by the end of the year the reports had reached flood proportions, as television networks, newspapers, and news magazines featured detailed stories about the "secret" U.S. war against Nicaragua. The House and Senate Intelligence committees, though dominated by members inclined to accept CIA actions, reportedly challenged the breadth of the agency's plans in private.

In December, liberals in Congress proposed legislation to prohibit any CIA paramilitary operations against Nicaragua. Administration lobbying quashed that legislation. Instead, with administration backing, Congress added to the 1983 continuing resolution a provision banning direct CIA efforts to overthrow the government of Nicaragua. But the legislation was expected to have little direct impact, since the stated intent of the CIA operation was to disrupt arms supplies into Nicaragua rather than to overthrow the government.

The administration's policies toward Central America produced mixed reactions in Latin America, but nearly all Latin leaders condemned Reagan's unequivocal support for Great Britain in its war with Argentina over the Falkland Islands. Administration officials and members of Congress saw no choice but to support Britain, the closest ally of the United States. But Latin leaders felt betrayed that the United States would lend support to a European power in what they saw as a battle against colonialism.

At the end of the year Reagan traveled to South and Central America, trying to patch up relations. Although the trip may not have repaired the damage caused by the Falklands dispute, it was an important educational experience for Reagan. Afterwards, the president expressed surprise at the diversity of Latin America and the willingness of Latin leaders to challenge the United States.

The centerpiece of Reagan's policy toward Latin America was supposed to be the Caribbean Basin Initiative (CBI). As proposed by Reagan in February, the CBI was to be a three-pronged approach to the crushing economic troubles of Central American and Caribbean countries: emergency economic aid, trade benefits to encourage exports from the region to the United States and tax benefits to encourage U.S. business investment in those countries.

The CBI ran into fierce opposition from labor unions and small businesses in the United States, who said it would increase foreign competition. Some liberals in Congress also charged that the CBI was an elaborate disguise for increased aid to El Salvador. Most regional leaders praised Reagan's interest but complained that his proposal did too little to address the needs of their countries.

Reagan eventually won passage only of the first shot of economic aid under the CBI: a $350 million supplemental appropriation for fiscal 1982. The House passed a watered-down version of the trade benefits proposal (HR 7397), but the bill died in the Senate during the lame-duck session held after the November elections. Congress never gave serious consideration to the proposed tax incentives for U.S. firms to do business in Central America and the Caribbean.

The Middle East

Events in the Middle East in 1982 demonstrated two seemingly contradictory aspects about the U.S. role in the region. On the one hand, most U.S. actions were merely reactions to occurrences that were beyond American control. Even Israel, the closest U.S. ally in the region and the recipient of massive U.S. aid, seemed to pay little heed to the Reagan administration's advice or requests. On the other hand, there was widespread agreement that the United States was the only nation capable of promoting peaceful change in the Middle East. At the end of the year, it seemed possible that U.S. efforts might lead eventually to historic negotiations between Israel and several of its Arab neighbors.

The dual aspect of the American role was highlighted by the Israeli invasion of Lebanon and subsequent events.

The United States publicly appealed to Israel not to

invade Lebanon, but Israel did so anyway on June 6, with the stated purpose of creating a 25-mile-wide buffer zone in southern Lebanon free of Palestinian guerrillas. Israel kept pushing north, again in spite of U.S. objections, and eventually surrounded thousands of Palestine Liberation Organization (PLO) fighters in West Beirut. At that point, when events seemed beyond anyone's control, U.S. Special Envoy Philip C. Habib negotiated an agreement under which the PLO fighters were shipped out of Lebanon, Israel withdrew its thousands of troops from Beirut and a peacekeeping force composed of American, French and Italian troops temporarily took control.

Events again spun out of U.S. control in mid-September when Lebanon's president-elect, Bashir Gemayel, was assassinated and, in apparent retaliation, hundreds of Palestinian civilians were massacred by Christian militia. Reagan sent Habib back to Lebanon for new negotiations, and once again American, French and Italian troops were dispatched to keep the peace. At year's end, the United States was attempting to shore up the fragile Lebanese government while orchestrating negotiations on the withdrawal from the country of 60,000 Israeli, Syrian and Palestinian troops.

Throughout the course of events in Lebanon, the Reagan administration sought to make the best of the situation. Although opposing Israel's aggression against a neighboring country, the United States reluctantly accepted Israeli Prime Minister Menachem Begin's argument that the eviction of the PLO from southern Lebanon created a new opportunity for peace.

Under Shultz' prodding, Reagan sought on Sept. 1 to seize the opportunity with a speech containing remarkably specific proposals for at least temporary solutions to some of the key Middle East issues. Reagan demanded that Israel halt further construction of Jewish settlements on the West Bank and proposed an association between Palestinians and Jordan to govern the West Bank, but he called for further negotiations to determine the final legal status of the West Bank and of Jerusalem.

The speech came nearly four years after the Camp David meetings among Jimmy Carter, Begin and Egyptian President Anwar Sadat that produced the peace treaty between Israel and Egypt. Although Israel angrily rejected Reagan's initiative, administration officials expressed hope that the key elements of the plan could be put on the negotiating table once all occupying forces had been withdrawn from Lebanon.

Begin's immediate and angry rejection of the initiative was seen at the time as a new low point in relations between the United States and Israel. But an even lower point was reached at the end of the year when the Reagan administration actively opposed a move in Congress to increase aid to Israel beyond the president's request. Administration officials wrote letters to Congress complaining that the aid increase would upset other countries in the Middle East (especially Egypt and Jordan) and would be seen as a reward to Israel for its policies that the United States had opposed.

Congress eventually compromised on the issue, giving Israel an increase in military aid that was substantial but that fell far short of what Israel had sought. However, passage of the aid increase was less a demonstration of congressional support for Israel than a result of unusual legislative circumstances that enabled Israel's staunchest backers in Congress to determine the aid allocations in the fiscal 1983 continuing resolution.

U.S.-Soviet Relations

Like its predecessors, the Reagan administration in 1982 discovered the difficulty of dealing with the Soviet Union on two separate levels: nuclear arms negotiations, and all other bilateral issues. The difficulty was compounded by the death in November of Leonid Brezhnev and his replacement as Communist Party general secretary by Yuri Andropov, a former head of the KGB, the Soviet secret police.

Late in 1981 and early in 1982, Reagan attempted to set the agenda for arms negotiations, first with the November 1981 "zero option" proposal to ban all nuclear weapons from European soil, then with his May 1982 proposal for cuts in both U.S. and Soviet intercontinental missile fleets. The proposals earned some political capital for Reagan, both in the United States (where he faced a growing movement for a nuclear arms "freeze") and in Western Europe (where politicians were increasingly nervous as the December 1983 deadline approached for the installation of U.S. nuclear missiles on their territory).

But Andropov quickly seized the initiative back from Reagan with a series of counter-proposals that were calculated to undermine support in Europe for U.S. negotiating positions.

The Reagan administration continued to insist that arms control negotiations should be linked to all other aspects of Soviet behavior, but it did little to actually enforce such a linkage. Reagan's most important actions directly affecting the Soviet Union — first the imposition then the lifting of economic sanctions — had nothing to do with nuclear arms policy.

The sanctions symbolized Reagan's difficulties in pressuring the Soviet Union while attempting to maintain good relations with U.S. allies in Europe.

In December 1981, shortly after the Polish government imposed martial law, Reagan declared a series of economic sanctions against both the Soviet Union and Poland, the most important of which was a prohibition on U.S. exports of equipment for construction of a natural gas pipeline from Siberia to Western Europe. Reagan expanded the sanctions in June to include pipeline-related exports by foreign subsidiaries of U.S. firms or by foreign firms holding U.S. licenses. The June action infuriated allied leaders, who ordered their firms to fulfill Soviet equipment orders in spite of Reagan's sanctions.

The strain in U.S.-allied relations, plus the damage done to American firms that lost millions of dollars worth of Soviet contracts, led to a move in the House to overturn the sanctions. That effort was rejected Sept. 29 on a 206-203 vote. Six weeks later, Shultz' negotiations with European leaders enabled Reagan to lift the sanctions in the context of a study on future controls on trade with the Soviet Union.

—John Felton

Congress Clears Names-of-Agents Bill

A bill to outlaw what had come to be known as "naming names" — the practice of exposing U.S. intelligence agents to disrupt their work — was signed into law (PL 97-200) on June 23, after a legislative struggle of several years.

A House-Senate conference report (H Rept 97-580) on the bill (HR 4) was filed in each house May 20 after nearly two months of private negotiations.

The House adopted the conference report June 3, on a 315-32 vote. The Senate adopted it June 10, on an 81-4 vote. *(House vote 125, p. 36-H; Senate vote 170, p. 30-S)*

The House passed its original version of the bill Sept. 23, 1981. The Senate passed its version March 18, 1982. *(House committee and floor action and Senate committee action, 1981 Almanac p. 152)*

Provisions

As signed into law, HR 4:

● Provided a fine of up to $50,000 and/or a prison term of up to 10 years for anyone who, having had authorized access to U.S. government secrets identifying covert agents, divulged the identity of an agent to anyone not authorized to receive it.

● Provided a fine of up to $25,000 and/or a prison term of up to five years for anyone who, having had authorized access to any U.S. government secrets, disclosed the identity of a covert agent to anyone not authorized to know it.

● Provided a fine of up to $15,000 and/or a prison term of up to three years for anyone who disclosed the identity of a covert agent after engaging in "a pattern of activities intended to identify and expose covert agents" and "with reason to believe" the disclosure would "impair or impede the foreign intelligence activities of the United States." This provision would apply to persons who had not had authorized access to government secrets.

● Provided that a defendant could escape conviction by proving that, before he disclosed the agent's identity, the government had "publicly acknowledged or revealed" the agent's "intelligence relationship" to the United States.

● Provided that a defendant could be convicted of conspiracy to identify an agent only if he had engaged in a "pattern of activities intended to identify and expose covert agents and with reason to believe" the exposure would harm U.S. intelligence.

A conspiracy conviction also could be obtained against someone who had had authorized access to classified information.

● Exempted from prosecution disclosures made directly to the House and Senate Intelligence committees. The bill did not specify whether the exemption was limited to government officials or extended to private citizens as well.

● Exempted from prosecution an agent's disclosure of his own identity.

● Required the president to submit an annual report to the Intelligence committees on measures taken to protect the identities of covert agents and on any related matters. The first such report was due Feb. 1, 1983.

● Extended the jurisdiction of the law to disclosures made overseas by U.S. citizens or by permanent resident aliens of the United States.

● Provided that nothing in the act was to be construed as justification for withholding information from Congress.

● Defined "covert agent" to mean: any officer or employee of a U.S. intelligence agency, or any member of the armed services assigned to an intelligence agency, whose identity was an official secret and who was serving or within five years had served outside the United States; any U.S. citizen abroad who had a secret "intelligence relationship" with the United States, including work as an agent, informant or "source of operational assistance" to U.S. intelligence; anyone else who had an existing or former secret intelligence relationship with the United States.

● Defined "intelligence agency" to include the CIA, any military intelligence agency or the foreign counterintelligence or foreign counterterrorism arms of the FBI.

● Defined "pattern of activities" as requiring "a series of acts with a common purpose or objective."

The conference report said a pattern of activities "must involve much more than merely restating that which is in the public domain" but could include: efforts to gain unauthorized access to official secrets, physical or electronic surveillance of intelligence agents or "other techniques of espionage," or simply "systematically collecting, collating and analyzing information from documentary sources" in order to divine agent identities.

The report also noted that a pattern of activities did not refer to a pattern of disclosures. It said a "single, first disclosure" was punishable if the other elements of the crime were proven.

Conference Action

The major issue in HR 4 — the standard of proof to be required to convict private citizens of "naming names" — was resolved in identical fashion during House and Senate floor action.

Under HR 4 as passed by both houses, a private citizen without access to official secrets could be convicted of exposing a U.S. intelligence agent if he had engaged in a "pattern of activities intended to identify and expose covert agents" and had "reason to believe" the exposure would harm U.S. intelligence.

But that provision always had been controversial, and it continued to be in conference. Arguments between the House and Senate Intelligence Committee staffs delayed agreement on conference report language for weeks, and several members refused to sign it.

Aides said conferees Peter W. Rodino Jr., D-N.J., and Don Edwards, D-Calif., of the House Judiciary Committee refused to sign because they opposed the bill in principle.

Reps. C. W. Bill Young, R-Fla., and Henry J. Hyde, R-Ill., refused to sign, Hyde said, because no formal meeting of conferees was called, and they were dissatisfied with the conference report negotiated by staff members.

"Yes, we were all confronted with a *fait accompli*, the work of staff," Hyde said. "We take too many leaps in the dark around here we have to take. I just didn't want to take one I *didn't* have to take."

Hyde complained that the report "waters the intent [of the bill] down to a very lukewarm posture that really doesn't accomplish what the legislation intended to do. The way the report ended up, it is less than the sum of all its parts. Staff has just cranked into it some implications and qualifications that have chilled my enthusiasm."

Meanwhile, clashes between Michael J. O'Neill, counsel to the House Intelligence Committee, and Robert R. Simmons, staff director of the Senate Intelligence Committee, were at the heart of the delays and, Simmons said, led to Simmons being removed from the deliberations.

Simmons said John H. Chafee, R-R.I., the principal Senate conferee, asked him to step aside after a House committee staff member wrote a memo attacking Simmons for reluctance to accept report language narrowly defining the scope of the provision affecting private citizens.

O'Neill confirmed that he and Simmons had many disputes and that Simmons was removed from the negotiations, but he said he was surprised that their conflicts were the reason for Simmons dropping out of the bargaining.

"I don't really know why that happened," O'Neill said. "I didn't think he was being personally obnoxious. We reached an impasse several times, but I didn't think it was on personal grounds. I thought it was a disagreement on subject matter. We quibbled about words back and forth, but that's the way these things get worked out. I just thought he was being tough."

A CIA Goal

The CIA and its allies in Congress had pressed for the names-of-agents bill for several years as a way to stop CIA critics such as former agent Philip Agee and the editors of the *Covert Action Information Bulletin* from trying to hamper agency operations by exposing agents.

Intelligence agency advocates claimed the practice had led to the assassination of at least one agent and had endangered the lives of many others.

The American Civil Liberties Union (ACLU) and various press groups fought the measure, saying it would be an unconstitutional abridgment of the First Amendment.

Liberals, press groups and civil libertarians argued that Congress could not constitutionally proscribe publication of agents' names derived from public documents, such as old State Department registers, from which Agee and others said they gleaned the names of agents using diplomatic cover.

However, seeing that Congress was on its way to passing such a law in any event, the American Civil Liberties Union and others argued for a tighter "intent" standard, requiring a prosecutor to show that a defendant had revealed an agent's name with the intent of disrupting intelligence operations.

The ACLU and press groups said such a standard would better protect journalists who might reveal an agent's name incidentally in the course of uncovering intelligence agency abuses. The intent standard failed in both houses.

The bill's critics also feared it would have a "chilling effect" on legitimate reporting of spy agency failures and abuses — especially under the "reason to believe" standard of proof, which the Justice Department had said could cover "negligent" disclosures of agent identities.

It was this central concern that led House conferee Edward P. Boland, D-Mass., and Senate conferee Chafee to agree on report language spelling out what should be considered a crime under the bill.

"A journalist writing stories about the CIA would not be engaged in the requisite 'pattern of activities,' even if the stories he wrote included the names of one or more covert agents, unless the government proved that there was an intent to identify and expose agents," the conference report said.

To be committing a crime, the report said, "a discloser must be engaged in a purposeful enterprise of revealing identities — he must, in short, be in the business of 'naming names.' "

Permitted Activities

The report also listed several specific examples of disclosures that would not be prosecutable, such as:

● Efforts by newspapers, universities or churches to learn if any of their employees had worked for the CIA. "These are activities intended to enforce the internal rules of the organization and not [to] identify and expose CIA agents," the report said.

● A newspaper investigation into possible CIA connections to the 1972 Watergate burglary, which sparked the scandals that led President Richard M. Nixon to resign.

● Newspaper investigations of how mercenary former intelligence agents Frank Terpil and Edmund Wilson had provided explosives and terrorist training to Libya.

Critics of the "reason to believe" standard had cited these examples and others during House and Senate action on the bill as disclosures they feared could be covered by the bill even though they were not the sort Congress wanted to ban.

O'Neill, of the House committee, said the conference report was aimed at making it clear that "this kind of activity that we agree should be proscribed goes beyond mere speech and becomes activity. It's an effort to destroy rather than inform."

The report said the standard of proof affecting private citizens "applies criminal penalties only in very limited circumstances to deter those who make it their business to ferret out and publish the identities of agents."

Added the report: "The conferees expect that the Department of Justice and the federal courts will limit the application of [the provision affecting private citizens] to those engaged in the pernicious business of naming names. . . ."

Peace Corps Policy

One of the few significant differences between the House and Senate versions was a set of House provisions requiring the president to issue an order specifying that government agencies must provide "cover" to U.S. agents.

Sen. Alan Cranston, D-Calif., and other allies of the Peace Corps had opposed that provision for fear it would raise suspicions abroad that the Peace Corps was a haven for CIA agents, so the Senate dropped that section.

Boland, Chafee and Cranston compromised in the conference version by requiring the president to report to Congress annually, beginning no later than Feb. 1, 1983, on measures taken to assure intelligence agents of cover.

In addition, the conference report said nothing in the bill was to be construed as changing the "20-year-old, congressionally-sanctioned executive branch policy of maintaining the total separation of the Peace Corps from intelligence activities."

Senate Floor Action

The Senate March 17 rejected warnings that the First Amendment was at risk and voted to imprison and/or fine journalists or other private persons who expose U.S. spies with "reason to believe" U.S. intelligence might be hurt. The next day, the Senate went on to pass, by a vote of 90-6, its version of the names-of-agents bill. *(Vote 55, p. 12-S)*

The key vote was on an amendment by Chafee to replace a tighter standard the Senate Judiciary Committee had set with the "reason to believe" test. After weeks of intermittent debate, the Senate voted by a surprisingly wide 55-39 margin to accept Chafee's wording. *(Vote 53, p. 12-S)*

The Judiciary Committee had voted by 9-8 on Oct. 6, 1981, to punish agent exposures by a private person only if it was shown a defendant had acted "with intent to impair or impede" U.S. intelligence.

Adoption of Chafee's amendment resolved the key issue in the Senate version of the bill (S 391) and matched its major provisions to the bill (HR 4) the House had passed the previous September.

Both bills already provided jail terms of up to 10 years and fines of up to $50,000 for active or former government employees who expose covert agents, and there was no debate on those provisions.

The Chafee amendment made S 391 match HR 4 in providing up to three years and/or a fine of up to $15,000 for persons never associated with the government who, "in the course of a pattern of activities intended to identify and expose covert agents and with reason to believe that such activities would impair or impede" U.S. intelligence, disclose "any information that identifies an individual as a covert agent to any individual not authorized to receive classified information...."

The House also had substituted the "reason to believe" for an "intent" standard.

Final Senate action was delayed a day when Bill Bradley, D-N.J., tried to tighten the bill's scope with an amendment to more narrowly define "pattern of activities," which some senators said could mean research done by a reporter for a story about intelligence agency abuses.

As reported by the Judiciary Committee (S Rept 97-201), S 391 said a pattern of activities "requires a series of acts with a common purpose or objective."

Bradley sought to specify that "the main direction of said pattern of activities must be to identify and expose covert agents." But the Senate rejected his amendment by a vote of 37-59 before passing the bill. *(Vote 54, p. 12-S)*

Floor Debate

The Senate took up S 391 on Feb. 25 after months of delay and parliamentary maneuvers by Bradley and other foes of the Chafee amendment.

Barry Goldwater, R-Ariz., chairman of the Senate Intelligence Committee, explained as the debate opened why he believed the legislation was needed.

"So far, some 1,200 names have been made public in magazines or newspapers. Another 700 appeared in a book. A bimonthly bulletin exposes CIA, FBI and military intelligence personnel and assignments," Goldwater said. "If someone wants to criticize foreign policy, that is their business. If they want to write about the lousy conduct of some of our citizens, that is okay, too. But they do not have to name names, because that places the lives of human beings in danger. That is not okay."

From that point forward, the debate focused on the Chafee amendment, with Chafee and his foes disputing the merits of the "reason to believe" and "intent" standards and citing various court cases to back up their assertions.

Chafee argued that the Judiciary Committee's "intent" standard would allow persons such as the editors of *Covert Action* — Louis Wolf, William Schaap and Ellen Ray — to escape conviction by persuading a jury that their intent in naming names was not to impair U.S. intelligence but to improve it.

"The difference is," Chafee said, "the committee language depends on the subjective intent of the person engaged in naming names, whereas our language uses an objective standard of proof." His amendment would "place the intent of the defendant ... where it should be in a criminal act — on the intention to perform the harmful act," Chafee said.

"Somebody might be disclosing the names of alleged CIA agents and saying, 'I'm not doing it to impair the intelligence activities of the United States, I am doing it to improve the intelligence activities,' " he said. "The subjective intent standard provides a loophole big enough to drive a truck through."

Joseph R. Biden Jr., D-Del., who led the opposition to the Chafee amendment, responded that the same loophole existed in the "reason to believe" standard.

If someone could plead good intent under the committee language, Biden said, "I submit that under the reason to believe standard, he can say the same thing. He can stand before the jury and say: 'Ladies and gentlemen, I had reason to believe this would help America when I disclosed the name of Joe Doakes.' "

Biden added: "The problem with reason to believe is, it has what we call in the law a 'chilling effect' on that reporter who wants to go out there and expose something that is harming the United States; wants to find the mole in the CIA, if there is one; wants to find out whether that jerk [Frank] Terpil is in fact selling weapons to [Libyan leader Moammar] Qaddafi and aiding terrorism; wants to expose the fact that there may be a CIA agent involved in international drug trafficking."

Biden said newspapers that exposed former CIA employee Terpil's mercenary relationship with Qaddafi might have decided against publishing if Chafee's language were law, for they could have had reason to believe Terpil was in fact a "double agent."

Patrick J. Leahy, D-Vt., also argued strongly against the Chafee amendment on the ground that it would damage the constitutional rights of free speech and press.

But Henry M. Jackson, D-Wash., primary cosponsor of the Chafee amendment, said journalists with good intent would be protected because a prosecutor would have six "burdens of proof" to satisfy in order to convict someone.

Jackson said it would have to be proved a defendant had: 1) engaged in a "pattern of activities intended to identify and expose covert agents;" 2) intentionally disclosed information that indeed exposed a covert agent; 3) revealed the agent to someone unauthorized to know the identity; 4) known that the information did in fact expose the agent; 5) known that the government was "taking affirmative measures" to conceal the agent's identity; and 6) had reason to believe the disclosure would harm U.S. intelligence.

In fact, Jackson argued, the reason to believe standard would better protect constitutional rights.

"Being an objective standard of evidence," he said, "the reason to believe element makes irrelevant an individual's political beliefs, associations and other public activities."

Court Decision Cited

Chafee also cited a summer 1981 Supreme Court decision upholding the State Department's right to revoke former agent Agee's passport for revealing CIA secrets.

"The Supreme Court clearly decided in Agee that disclosures of intelligence operations and names of intelligence personnel which obstruct intelligence operations are not protected by the First Amendment," Chafee said.

The Court said that "Agee's disclosures, among other things, have the declared purpose of obstructing intelligence operations and the recruiting of intelligence personnel. They are clearly not protected by the Constitution. The mere fact that Agee is also engaged in criticism of the government does not render his conduct beyond the reach of the law."

Chafee allies such as John P. East, R-N.C., said the First Amendment was not an absolute right anyway, and the potential damage to it was outweighed by the need to prosecute those who expose agent identities.

"We ought to err on the side of protecting these gentlemen [U.S. agents] and protecting the national security," East said March 1. "Whatever intrusion there may be upon First Amendment rights here, they are modest and gentle and consistent with the overriding need to protect the great national security interests."

After the Senate passed his amendment, Chaffee told reporters: "Don't give the impression, now, that you're being absolutely handcuffed." He added: "You know the type of publication" — *Covert Action Information Bulletin* — the bill was designed to punish.

Senate Provisions

As passed by the Senate, S 391 amended the National Security Act of 1947 (PL 80-253) to ban disclosures of U.S. covert intelligence officers, agents, informants and sources. The bill:

● Made it a crime punishable by a prison term of up to 10 years and/or a fine of up to $50,000 for anyone with authorized access to the identities of U.S. agents to intentionally disclose them to unauthorized persons.

● Made it a crime punishable by a prison term of up to five years and/or a fine of up to $25,000 for anyone who intentionally disclosed agent identities after learning them "as a result of having authorized access" to government secrets of any kind.

● Made it a crime punishable by a prison term of up to three years and/or a fine of up to $15,000 for anyone to disclose agent identities, having learned them from public or secret sources, after having engaged in "a pattern of activities intended to identify and expose covert agents and with reason to believe that such activities would impair or impede" U.S. intelligence.

● Provided that a defendant could not be convicted if the U.S. government had "publicly acknowledged or revealed the intelligence relationship" of the agent whose identity was disclosed.

● Provided that persons with authorized access to U.S. secrets could not be subject to prosecution for conspiracy to disclose agent identities unless they themselves exposed the agent in question, but that persons without authorized access could be prosecuted for conspiracy to expose agents if they met the other tests of guilt for private persons.

● Exempted from the law disclosures of agent identities directly to the House and Senate Intelligence committees.

● Exempted from the law agents who disclosed information identifying only themselves as spies.

● Provided that the law would apply to disclosures made overseas by U.S. citizens or permanent resident aliens.

● Stipulated that the bill was not to be construed as authorizing the withholding of information from Congress. ■

Intelligence Authorization

Congress Sept. 10 cleared a bill (HR 6068) authorizing fiscal 1983 and supplemental fiscal 1982 spending by the CIA and other intelligence agencies.

House-Senate conferees Aug. 19 filed their report on the bill (H Rept 97-779). The House adopted the report by voice vote Sept. 8, and the Senate followed suit Sept. 10.

In addition to setting intelligence agency budgets for fiscal 1983, HR 6068 authorized secret amounts of supplemental spy agency spending in fiscal 1982, which ended Sept. 30. Major agencies included in the bill were the Central Intelligence Agency (CIA), the Defense Intelligence Agency (DIA), the National Security Agency and the Army, Navy and Air Force intelligence branches.

The bill changed the laws on CIA retirement and survivors' benefits to give a share of such benefits to former spouses of CIA employees who had served at least five years overseas.

The measure also barred unauthorized commercial use of the Defense Intelligence Agency's name, initials or insignia.

As signed into law (PL 97-269) Sept. 27, HR 6068 also:

● Authorized $12.1 million for FBI counterterrorism programs in fiscal 1983.

● Authorized $15.4 million to fund a staff of 210 persons for William J. Casey, the director of central intelligence.

President Reagan had requested $18.3 million for a staff of 220. The House bill had authorized $17 million and 220 persons; the Senate bill $15.2 million for a staff of 210.

● Authorized $91.3 million for the CIA Retirement and Disability Fund in fiscal 1983.

● Provided that the CIA director could increase civilian personnel at his agency in fiscal 1982 by up to 2 percent, permitting him to hire persons who otherwise could not be hired until fiscal 1983 began Oct. 1, 1982.

The conference report said the provision was accepted because "an opportunity existed to hire new employees at CIA in several critically important fields" in advance of personnel increases to be authorized in fiscal 1983. The report did not reveal what the fields in question were.

In writing the measure, the House and Senate Intelligence committees stuck by the practice of keeping spy agency spending secret.

Both committees authorized the full administration request of $91.3 million for the Central Intelligence Agency Retirement and Disability Fund in fiscal 1983.

The Senate committee said it had cut the request for the staff of the director of central intelligence (DCI) from $18.3 million down to $15.2 million for fiscal 1983. But that still was an increase from $13.4 million in fiscal 1982. The House committee did not reveal its action on those items.

Both committees approved provisions to protect the initials and insignia of the Defense Intelligence Agency from unauthorized uses, with the attorney general to be authorized to seek a court injunction to halt them. Similar provisions protecting CIA insignia were passed by Congress in 1981. *(1981 Almanac p. 148)*

House Action

The House Intelligence Committee favorably approved HR 6068 on April 5 by voice vote. The House passed the bill May 19, 357-23. *(Vote 75, p. 22-H)*

Although most amounts and programs in the bill were classified, Rep. C. W. Bill Young, R-Fla., a member of the

Intelligence Committee, said in a floor statement that the bill contained special measures in two areas: counterintelligence and controls on transfers of sophisticated technology to American adversaries. Young said the bill contained funds "needed to restore both manpower and resources to the FBI counterintelligence program" in the United States.

The bill also "provides for a stepped-up effort to combat the illegal transfer of plans and equipment." The Soviet Union used "a variety of covert measures" to obtain blueprints for weapons, machinery, communications equipment, and computer hardware and programs, Young said.

The House panel said in a report (H Rept 97-486, Part I) that it had cut the Reagan administration's request.

"The administration requested a major increase for fiscal year 1983 over the amount Congress appropriated for intelligence in fiscal year 1982, a year in which there was substantial growth in intelligence spending," the report said. "The committee was not convinced that the total amount requested for fiscal year 1983 was fully warranted. Therefore, the committee has recommended deferral of certain proposals and the deletion of others, while a few items were increased."

The committee said it had considered again whether intelligence agency budgets should be made public — an issue raised annually in the House — and concluded that they should not be.

"By itself, a single intelligence budget total would probably not harm intelligence activities or capabilities. Such a number, however, would be meaningless in a vacuum," the report said.

Under the circumstances, the committee said it had concluded that "budget disclosure might well mean more to this country's adversaries than to any of its citizens." It noted that a secret annex detailing the intelligence agency budgets was available to all House members.

DIA. The committee approved provisions to protect the Defense Intelligence Agency's initials and other symbols. It said in its report that this "would not prevent legitimate use of these initials by [other] organizations as an abbreviation or logo for their name so long as there is no false representation of DIA endorsement."

The report said members of the public could use the DIA name or initials on "T-shirts and souvenirs" if they did not falsely represent DIA endorsement of the products.

Spouses. The committee extended CIA retirement and survivors' benefits to former spouses of agency employees who have served overseas, saying it was recognizing the disadvantages imposed on CIA spouses by agency work.

Spouses of agency employees assigned overseas seldom were able to develop a career or even work themselves and often had no means of supporting themselves if their marriage ended in divorce, the committee said.

The new provisions would apply to CIA employees who had served at least five years overseas. To qualify for a share of such an employee's benefits, a former spouse would have to have been married to the employee for at least 10 years of the employee's service creditable toward retirement, would have to have spent at least five of those years overseas and could not remarry before the age of 60.

A qualified former spouse would be entitled to 50 percent of the employee's retirement annuity, if married to the employee throughout his or her CIA service, and a pro rata share if married for a lesser period. A former spouse would be entitled to 55 percent of the participant's survivor's annuity if married throughout the employee's creditable service, or a pro rata share if less.

Senate Action

The Senate Intelligence Committee reported S 2487 on May 5. The vote was not reported in S Rept 97-379.

The full Senate passed the bill June 30 by voice vote.

In its report (S Rept 97-379) on the bill, the Senate committee offered no indications as to how it dealt with the administration request for spy agency operations.

The report said amounts recommended for spying, intelligence analysis and covert operations were available to senators in an accompanying secret report.

Implying some dissatisfaction with Casey, who was known for sometimes headstrong dealings with Congress, the panel said the secret report was to "have the full force of any Senate report and ... the intelligence community will comply with the guidelines, directions and limitations contained therein."

The committee said its Budget Authorization Subcommittee had focused during its hearings on the fiscal 1983 request on the condition and capabilities of U.S. intelligence agencies and what their prospects were.

Among the findings, the committee report said, were that "investment in intelligence must grow to ensure the system is able to meet the challenges U.S. policymakers will face in the 1990s." The report said the intelligence community had improved in the past two years "but further enhancements will be necessary."

In the fiscal 1983 budget, the report said, "major investments" would provide for:

● A "new generation" of intelligence collection technology.

● Improvements in agency analysis of information collected.

● Greater capability "to counter foreign espionage and international terrorism."

● Modernizing the "worldwide intelligence support infrastructure."

Reagan had requested a full-time staff of 220 persons for the director of central intelligence office at a cost of $18.3 million in fiscal 1983. The committee cut that to 210 persons and $15.2 million. It said the cut consisted of: $400,000 saved by cutting the staff by 10 persons; $1.2 million by refusing a request for a new computer for the DCI staff; and $1.5 million cut from a request for $4.5 million to pay for "analyses and studies by external contractors." ∎

State Department Authority

The House on Aug. 11 cleared a bill (S 1193) authorizing 1982-83 funds for the State Department and other agencies. The Senate adopted the conference report on the bill Aug. 9. The measure had been stalled in a House-Senate conference committee since October 1981.

President Reagan signed the bill into law (PL 97-241) on Aug. 24.

The normally routine bill was the focus of a revolt in the House on Sept. 17, 1981, when House Republicans shocked the Reagan administration by voting down the first version of the bill. Republicans charged at the time that the bill exceeded the administration request for fiscal 1983, and Democrats refused to vote for the bill because the Republicans were not supporting a bill advocated by their own administration.

The House passed a trimmed version of the bill six

State Department Authorizations, Fiscal 1982-83

The following authorizations were included in S 1193, for the State Department and related agencies in fiscal years 1982 and 1983 *(in thousands of dollars)*:

	Fiscal 1982		Fiscal 1983	
Program	Administration Revised Request	Final Amount	Administration Revised Request	Final Amount
State Department Administration	$1,245,637	$1,245,637	$1,248,059	$1,248,059
International Organizations	503,462	503,462	514,436	514,436
International Commissions	19,808	19,808	22,432	22,432
Science and Technology agreements	3,700	3,700	3,700	3,700
Refugee Assistance	504,100	504,100	460,000	460,000
Asia Foundation	—	4,500	—	4,500
Subtotal	2,276,707	2,281,207	2,248,627	2,253,127
United States Information Agency	494,034	494,034	644,000	559,000 [1]
Board for International Broadcasting	86,519	86,519	98,317	98,317
Inter-American Foundation	12,000	12,000	12,800	12,800
Arms Control and Disarmament Agency [2]	16,768	—	19,942	—
Total	**$2,886,028**	**$2,873,760**	**$3,023,686**	**$2,923,244**

[1] *Included supplementals in separate legislation (HR 5998, S 2581). Also, earmarked the following amounts for fiscal 1983: $84,256,000 for the Fulbright Academic Exchange Program and the International Visitor Program; $3,248,000 for grants for the* Humphrey Fellowship Program; and $8,906,000 for grants to private non-profit organizations.

[2] *Authorizations for the agency were included in separate legislation (HR 3467).*

weeks later, on Oct. 29. *(1981 Almanac p. 157)*

The conference report on the bill (H Rept 97-693) was filed Aug. 3. The bill authorized $2.87 billion in fiscal 1982 and $2.92 billion in 1983 for the State Department, the International Communication Agency (ICA), the Board for International Broadcasting (BIB), and the Inter-American Foundation. The State Department was to receive the bulk of the authorization, $2.28 billion in fiscal 1982 and $2.25 billion in 1983. *(Chart, this page)*

United Nations Funds

The conference committee approved $503.5 million of the State Department funds for international organizations and conferences in fiscal 1982 and $514.4 million in 1983.

Conferees maintained intact previously adopted prohibitions against U.S. contributions to specific U.N. projects. The United States contributed approximately 25 percent of the U.N.'s $1.5 billion annual operating budget.

S 1193 prohibited funding of projects whose primary purpose was to provide political benefits to the Palestine Liberation Organization. The committee said in its report that the prohibition was not a ban on U.S. contributions to projects whose primary purpose was to provide humanitarian, educational, developmental and other non-political benefits to the Palestinian people.

Conferees expressed opposition to efforts by the United Nations Educational, Scientific and Cultural Organization (UNESCO) to "regulate the world press and license journalists," through its call for a New World Information Order. The "order" was an effort by some developing nations to change what they said was a bias against them in the world press.

To back up that opposition, the bill prohibited authorized funds from being used to pay the U.S. assessed contribution to UNESCO if UNESCO "implements any policy which has the effect of licensing journalists or their publications, restricting the free flow of information within or among countries, or imposing mandatory codes of journalistic practice or ethics."

S 1193 required the president to report to Congress on his assessment of the relationship between U.S. contributions to UNESCO and the U.S. national interest.

Refugee Aid

The bill authorized $504.1 million for migration and refugee assistance in 1982 and $460 million in 1983. Conferees earmarked $12.5 million of the 1982 figure and $16.9 million in 1983 for the resettlement in Israel of refugees from the Soviet Union and Eastern Europe.

The measure also extended aid to refugees from Ethiopia and Iran and urged the executive branch to use all appropriate diplomatic means to help Ethiopian Falasha and Iranian Jews to emigrate to Israel.

The conferees said part of the earmarked money, along with contributions from other donors, should go to the 1.5 million ethnic Somali refugees who had fled fighting in the Ogaden region of Ethiopia.

The conference committee instructed the executive branch to implement procedures to ensure that its earmarked funds reach "the needy Somali refugees for whom it is intended and that such assistance is not diverted to other purposes." There had been reports that much of the government and private aid intended for refugees was diverted by the military and other government officials.

In fiscal 1982 and 1983, $1.5 million was earmarked for the "political detainee" program operated by the International Committee of the Red Cross. The program was aimed primarily at helping those held in Poland since the 1981 crisis. Under the program, the Red Cross visited political detainees, provided medical care for them and also monitored conditions under which they were being kept.

S 1193 also requested the president to report to Congress the total cost in fiscal 1981 and 1982 of federal, state and local efforts to assist Cubans and Haitians who came to the United States in boat lifts and who had not been given, or had been denied, refugee status.

Diplomatic Issues

The bill reprogrammed $400,000 in 1982 to reopen and maintain seven U.S. consulates closed by President Carter in an economy move in 1980. Congress ordered the consulates reopened in the fiscal 1980-81 State Department authorization bill (PL 96-60) but neither the Carter nor Reagan administrations had complied. The offices were in Turin, Italy; Salzburg, Austria; Goteborg, Sweden; Bremen, West Germany; Nice, France; Mandalay, Burma; and Brisbane, Australia. *(1981 Almanac p. 160)*

S 1193 blocked a Reagan plan to open three new consulates in the People's Republic of China until the seven closed posts were reopened.

The bill also created an office of foreign missions within the State Department. The office was to oversee the operations of diplomatic posts in the District of Columbia and serve as a liaison between the State Department and local governments over matters of diplomatic privilege and immunities.

The conference agreement was an attempt to settle a longstanding dispute between foreign diplomats and the District of Columbia Zoning Commission over location and expansion of chancery buildings in the district.

Communications Issues

S 1193 renamed the International Communication Agency as the United States Information Agency (USIA). The agency's name was changed to ICA in April 1978. The change back to USIA was to take effect on the date of enactment. Some critics had complained that the acronym ICA was easily confused with that of the Central Intelligence Agency (CIA), reducing the credibility of American communications programs around the world.

The bill authorized $494 million in 1982 and $559 million in 1983 for the agency. The 1983 figure was a compromise amount derived from the original Senate and House authorizations and from the agency's request for supplemental funds, which was included in separate legislation (S 2581, HR 5998). Some items in the supplemental request, approved by committees in both houses, were put in S 1193.

The conference committee approved the $559 million figure in the Senate supplemental bill, but the authorization was still $85 million below the administration's request for fiscal 1983.

The measure required the secretary of state to report to Congress on exchange activities between the United States and the Soviet Union in 1981 and 1982. The report was to include "an assessment of the risk of the transfer to the Soviet Union of militarily significant technology" through scientific exchange programs.

By July 1 of each year the secretary was asked to give Congress the names of Soviet nationals on the list of ex-

change programs for the upcoming academic year. Conferees also requested each person's topic and place of study and a determination by the secretary that the program would not "jeopardize U.S. national security interests."

The United States issued new guidelines and suspended talks to establish additional exchanges with the Soviet Union after its invasion of Afghanistan in December 1979. Three of the 11 science-related exchange programs with the Soviets were discontinued after the Polish crisis.

The bill authorized $86.5 million in 1982 and $98.3 million in 1983 for the Board for International Broadcasting and authorized a merger of the board with the board of Radio Free Europe (RFE) and Radio Liberty (RL).

Previously, BIB was responsible for overseeing the two stations, but it did not direct their operations on a routine basis. The broadcasting board was to be expanded from five to nine voting members, with the station's director to be a non-voting member.

Conferees said the merger was to facilitate efficient management of the stations and was not to be interpreted as "a license to manipulate RFE/RL for the purpose of short-term propaganda or sectarian ideological crusades," the committee said.

Other Provisions

In other provisions, the conference report:

● Stated a concern over the lone U.S. vote on May 21, 1981, against the World Health Organization International Code of Marketing Breastmilk Substitutes. The committee urged the president and the U.S. infant formula manufacturing industry to re-examine their positions regarding support for the code. *(1981 Almanac p. 155)*

● Extended the validity of U.S. passports from five to 10 years. The bill also authorized the secretary of state to set passport and visa fees. The fee for passports for adults was to be increased to $42, from $15.

● Stated that the State Department should expedite the issuance of passports because members of Congress had received complaints from their constituents of long delays.

● Stated that any U.S. government broadcasts directed to Cuba should be called "Radio Marti," after the Cuban patriot José Marti. ∎

Reports on El Salvador

The Reagan administration certified to Congress twice in 1982 that the government of El Salvador was making progress in protecting human and civil rights — a certification required by law for El Salvador to continue getting U.S. military aid.

Both certifications brought cries of protests from critics of President Reagan's policy of providing military arms and advisers to the Salvadoran government. The critics insisted that little progress had been made by either government in power in 1982: the moderate, civilian junta that ruled from Oct. 1979 until May 1982, or the rightist regime that took over after the May 28 elections for a new Constituent Assembly.

The fiscal 1982 foreign aid authorization bill (PL 97-113) established five conditions on further military aid to El Salvador and required the president to certify by Jan. 29 and each 180 days afterward that the conditions had been met. *(1981 Almanac p. 121)*

The bill authorized $26 million in fiscal 1982 for aid to

the Salvadoran junta to buy arms and other defense articles for its security forces, who were battling leftist guerrillas backed by Cuba and other communist nations. The legislation also authorized $75 million in economic aid not subject to the conditions.

January Certification

The strife in El Salvador already had made headlines in the days before the president's January 28 certification when the American Civil Liberties Union charged the junta with continuing repression, including 12,501 murders in 1981, and urged Reagan to decline to make his certification.

On Jan. 27, leftist guerrillas attacked a military base near San Salvador with dynamite, mortars and rockets, inflicting unspecified but heavy damage on helicopters and aircraft in El Salvador's air forces, including some of 14 transport helicopters on loan from the United States.

Also, *The New York Times* and *The Washington Post* published reports from El Salvador quoting witnesses who charged security forces with a massacre of civilians in the Morazan province of El Salvador in December.

In a six-page "Justification" accompanying the formal certification to the Foreign Relations and Foreign Affairs committees, the administration explained how it found that El Salvador had met the conditions on U.S. aid.

PL 97-113 required that the junta be "making a concerted and significant effort to comply with internationally recognized human rights" and be "achieving substantial control over all elements of its own armed forces...."

The administration said the junta had banned a rightist paramilitary organization known as ORDEN, adopted a code of conduct for the military in October 1980 to prohibit armed forces members from violating human rights and removed or reassigned officers sympathetic to the violent right.

It added that one of the "principal missions of our military trainers in El Salvador is to increase the professionalism of the armed forces and improve the system of military discipline and command and control, thus reducing the abuses suffered in the past by the civilian population at the hands of the armed forces."

"These efforts are beginning to have a positive effect," the justification said. "The level of violence — and particularly the number of deaths — is difficult to quantify, but statistics compiled by our embassy in San Salvador indicate a declining level of violence over the past year and a decrease in alleged abuses by security forces." It said there was "a definite trend in this regard."

By contrast, a January report by Amnesty International charged "a systematic and brutal policy of government-sponsored intimidation and repression" in El Salvador in 1981 and "massive" abuses that "constitute a gross and consistent pattern of human rights abuses."

The justification admitted that "ultra-rightist ad hoc groups still operate without official sanction." It warned that "all abuses will not end in the immediate future."

PL 97-113 also required that El Salvador be "making continued progress in implementing essential economic and political reforms, including the land reform program," be "committed to the holding of free elections at an early date" and be ready to "begin discussions with all major factions" that are willing "to find and implement an equitable political solution."

The justification said land reform was progressing despite being "targeted by extremists of the right and left" and disrupted by rightist assassinations of agrarian reform officials and intimidation of the peasants being given the land.

The administration said the junta was committed to "free and fair constituent assembly elections in March 1982 and presidential elections in 1983" and had "invited all parties that renounce violence to participate," offering amnesty to guerrillas and freedom for political parties to campaign. But it said the political-guerrilla coalition had "denounced the elections and rejected the government's standing invitation" to discuss election issues.

Finally, the law required that the junta make "good faith efforts to investigate" the murders of six U.S. citizens in late 1980 and early 1981 — four churchwomen and two American land reform advisers.

The administration said El Salvador had suspects in the cases, with all but one under custody, and had "additional evidence which gives hope of substantial progress" in both cases.

Reaction. Rep. Gerry E. Studds, D-Mass., in a letter to House colleagues, challenged Reagan's claims, saying "the evidence is overwhelming that the president has certified more to what he wishes were the case in El Salvador than to what is actually taking place...."

July Certification

The administration's 51-page report on July 27 acknowledged that violence was continuing in El Salvador but said there were "tangible signs of progress" by the new government in curbing human rights abuses and pursuing land reform and other economic and political changes desired by Congress.

Consequently, the report said, administration officials "believe a firm base has been established for further progress in the months ahead."

It blamed leftist guerrilla attacks for violence that "continues to result in reports of violations of basic human rights committed by leftist guerrillas, right-wing terrorists and members of the government security forces."

It also acknowledged that the land reform program was slowed by changes made by the Constituent Assembly. The changes, the report said, led to "confusion" and illegal evictions of peasants from land already distributed.

But the report said the land reform program had been "relaunched" and the "new government has already undertaken substantial steps to ensure continued progress in human rights" protection.

Those steps, the report said, included orders issued by Defense Minister Jose Guillermo Garcia "that all violations of citizens' rights be stopped immediately" and that military offenders be punished.

"Over the past six months 109 members of the Salvadoran armed forces were disciplined for various offenses, including 56 cases submitted to judicial action," the report said. "In addition, 20 members of the civil defense forces were disciplined...."

But the report said the most promising development since the Jan. 28 certification was the March 28 election of a 60-member Constituent Assembly, which set up the interim government under President Alvaro Magana.

The Constituent Assembly was to write a new constitution and prepare for election of a permanent government. The report said the "development of democratic order in El Salvador is likely to be, over the long term, the best guarantee of human rights...."

Human Rights

The administration said "there has continued to be a downward trend in the monthly total of deaths attributable to political violence during the past six months." The report included graphs and charts to support the assertion.

One chart listed civil war-related deaths for each month since late 1980, as reported by newspapers and human rights agencies in El Salvador. The monthly totals of deaths listed in the chart generally declined in 1982 but still averaged several hundred through May.

The State Department report acknowledged the difficulty of obtaining accurate figures. For example, it noted that press reports were incomplete for areas where armed conflict was most severe, and casualties "resulting from military operations" were not included in the totals.

The report said the U.S. Embassy in San Salvador "has been able to confirm that since Jan. 1, 47 members of the military forces and at least 10 civil defense members have been arrested and confined for violent abuses of authority (murder, assault, rape). Of these, 20 were arrested for murder." The report did not say if any of those arrested had been tried.

At the same time, the report said the civil strife had left El Salvador's court system in a shambles because of "intimidation of judges, witnesses and officials by the right and left," which the report said was continuing.

"The failure of the judicial system is both an effect and a cause of continued human rights abuses and will be a focus of Salvadoran reform efforts and U.S. assistance over the next year," the report pledged.

Armed Forces

There was "no evidence" to support allegations by the guerrillas of large-scale massacres committed by government forces, the report said. But it cited continuing reports, some of them "credible," of "torture and execution of prisoners and the participation of individual members of the security forces in right-wing terrorist activity."

It said human rights abuses had been "exacerbated by guerrilla tactics" because the guerrillas "routinely travel with civilians who provide logistical support" and who have been killed or wounded in battles with government forces.

But it said Garcia's orders, prospective punishment of military offenders and training given Salvadoran forces by the United States and the International Committee of the Red Cross led to the conclusion that "El Salvador is achieving substantial control over all elements of its own armed forces," as required by the law.

Land Reform

The report said the land reform program, aimed at turning over land from large estates to peasants, had suffered setbacks after the March 28 elections. It said foes of the program in the Constituent Assembly "took advantage of an effort to correct some of the program's genuine shortcomings to pass ambiguous legislation which cast doubt on the future of the program and contributed to a surge in illegal evictions."

In addition, it said, "the Minister of Agriculture temporarily and without presidential authorization suspended further taking of [peasants'] title applications" and the ambiguous legislation encouraged 3,822 evictions.

But the report said those setbacks had been reversed.

"The ambiguous legislation was clarified [by the Constituent Assembly]," it said. "The application process was resumed, promotion campaigns began, the first definitive titles were issued and, for the first time, some compensation claims [by owners of land being redistributed to peasants] have been settled."

The report added that Salvadoran armed forces had put 1,900 of the evicted peasants back on their land. It said 11,238 provisional titles had been issued in the previous six months, including 4,865 since the March 28 elections.

Murders of Americans

The report said progress had been made in bringing to trial six National Guardsmen accused of killing four American churchwomen in December 1980. "We expect the date of the trial to be set this fall," it said. It also claimed progress in a case in which two American land reform advisers were killed, saying El Salvador had "moved to reinvigorate the investigation."

Technically, the administration was not required to comment on those cases in its second certification, but members of Congress had demanded that it do so anyway.

On the day the certification was submitted, the Senate passed a House-passed bill (H J Res 494) requiring the president to again certify, as he did in January, that El Salvador was working to bring the perpetrators of those murders to justice.

On Sept. 30, a Salvadoran judge released an army lieutenant who was implicated in the killing of the land reform advisers.

Reaction

The administration's certification drew fire, as expected, from critics in Congress and elsewhere.

Critics charged the administration with "dishonesty" in declaring that respect for human rights and economic and political reforms were advancing in El Salvador.

In a rare foreign policy comment, House Speaker Thomas P. O'Neill Jr., D-Mass., released a statement July 28 calling the certification "simply unbelievable."

Despite the virulence of some critics, officials who defended the report July 29 before the House Foreign Affairs Committee received a mild reception that indicated the certification would stand. It was unclear, though, whether the tone of the hearing indicated a decline in opposition to Reagan's El Salvador policies.

On July 28, a group of House members, led by Studds and Tom Harkin, D-Iowa, introduced a bill (H J Res 552) to declare the certification "null and void" and cut off arms aid. They had 82 cosponsors.

Cosponsor James L. Oberstar, D-Minn., admitted the measure had little chance of passage. And he acknowledged that President Reagan would have to sign the measure for it to become law, which he clearly would not do.

House Hearing

At the House Foreign Affairs hearing, Chairman Clement J. Zablocki, D-Wis., complained that Reagan had tried to separate himself from the certification by failing to sign it and referring to it in a July 28 press conference as the State Department's report. He noted that the law required "the president" to report to Congress.

Zablocki also released a General Accounting Office (GAO) report, done at the request of Sen. Edward Zorinsky, D-Neb., that said the administration should report to Congress that several dozen U.S. military advisers in El Salvador were in danger.

The GAO said the administration should have re-

ported to Congress earlier in the year under the Arms Export Control Act (PL 94-329), which required a report within 48 hours of "significant hostilities" or terrorism in a nation where U.S. military advisers were employed.

The GAO also said the administration should "closely consider" reporting under a section of the War Powers Act (PL 93-148) that would require U.S. military personnel to be withdrawn after no more than 90 days unless Congress extended their stay.

But Zablocki and other members complimented Thomas O. Enders, assistant secretary of state for inter-American affairs, and Elliott Abrams, assistant secretary of state for human rights, on what Zablocki called a "more complete and more balanced" certification than was submitted Jan. 28.

Even committee member Studds, a harsh critic of Reagan's El Salvador policy, said the administration had "done a far more professional job" on the July certification.

Still, Studds and others disputed the findings. Studds called the report "fundamentally a dishonest document" — a comment that drew an indignant protest from Abrams.

Michael D. Barnes, D-Md., chairman of the Inter-American Affairs Subcommittee, said the report was "an improvement over the last one" but "still isn't convincing."

Republicans on the committee, however, generally praised the report as evenhanded and realistic. And while various members asked skeptical questions, the resulting discussion was inconclusive.

The central charge made by the critics was that political violence in El Salvador remained at an alarmingly high level. They also said that, contrary to the administration's assertions, the land reform program was at a standstill.

In essence, Enders rebutted those charges, just as the report did, by saying: "Progress is marred, but real." ∎

U.S.-China Communique

President Reagan infuriated his hard-line conservative backers in Congress Aug. 17 by issuing a joint communiqué with the communist People's Republic of China declaring an accommodation on the issue of U.S. arms sales to Taiwan.

Others, including Sen. John Glenn, D-Ohio, decried the move as an abandonment of Taiwan and discussed whether Congress should act to reaffirm the U.S. commitment to the island nation.

But other reaction in Senate and House hearings Aug. 17 and 18 was comparatively mild, dooming the prospects for legislation to contravene the communiqué.

The nine-paragraph communiqué, produced after 10 months of secret talks, said the United States would hold the quantity and quality of future arms sales to Taiwan below 1979-82 levels and ultimately would halt them.

China claimed Taiwan as a province and had long demanded an end to U.S. arms sales to the anti-communist Republic of China on Taiwan, which said it was the legitimate government of the mainland Chinese.

To soften the blow to Taiwan, the administration Aug. 19 sent Congress formal notice of a decision to extend an agreement permitting Taiwan to co-produce F-5 fighter aircraft. Under the extended agreement, Taiwan could co-produce 30 F-5E and 30 F-5F fighters, at a total price of $622 million over four years. After rejecting Taiwan's request to buy the more advanced F-X fighter, the adminis-

tration in January said the F-5 agreement would be extended. But formal action was delayed during talks with China on the communiqué.

In testimony before the Senate Foreign Relations and House Foreign Affairs committees Aug. 17 and 18, John H. Holdridge, assistant secretary of state for Near East and Pacific affairs, defended the communiqué as a vital move to avoid a "fatal deterioration" in U.S.-PRC relations.

He said Sino-American relations were important because, besides opposing the Soviet Union, the United States and China shared several "strategic" objectives, such as ending the Vietnamese occupation of Cambodia.

The PRC had threatened for months to downgrade diplomatic relations with the United States unless a deadline for an end to U.S. arms sales to Taiwan was set.

But conservatives such as Sen. Barry Goldwater, R-Ariz., declared the communiqué a violation of the Taiwan Relations Act (PL 96-8), a 1979 law governing relations with Taiwan after U.S. relations with China were normalized. Goldwater said the communiqué violated the law by promising cuts in arms sales. PL 96-8 declared that sales would continue at whatever levels the president and Congress decided would meet Taiwan's "legitimate" needs.

The communiqué, Goldwater said in a statement, "is a bad agreement that demonstrates the influence and duplicity" of the State Department bureaucracy. He said it was "full of double talk and false statements."

In an Aug. 17 exchange with reporters at the White House, Reagan said his critics were "not telling the truth" in casting the communiqué as a "sellout" of Taiwan.

Later that day, Reagan telephoned CBS anchorman Dan Rather to complain of the network's coverage of the issue. "There has been no retreat by me" on Taiwan, Reagan told Rather. "We will continue to arm Taiwan."

In the Senate committee hearing, Holdridge noted with pride that the wording of the communiqué was ambiguous in several places, thus allowing the two sides to accommodate irreconcilable views on the Taiwan issue.

For example, the communiqué said the United States "intends to reduce gradually its sales of arms to Taiwan, leading over a period of time to a final resolution." It did not define "final resolution."

Committee Chairman Charles H. Percy, R-Ill., agreed that "a certain amount of ambiguity may be helpful," but he added: "There may be ambiguity in the communiqué, but there can be no ambiguity in the Taiwan Relations Act."

Percy nevertheless seemed to agree with the decision to issue the communiqué; he praised the administration for closely consulting his committee during the negotiations.

Several committee liberals expressed mild support for the communiqué. One, Alan Cranston, D-Calif., said the decision "by both nations to continue on the course of mutual cooperation and understanding" was more important than the communiqué's wording.

Blow to Taiwan

Conservative Jesse Helms, R-N.C., bitterly said Taiwan could only read the communiqué as a defeat.

Holdridge had told the panel: "Quite clearly this has caused some upset in Taiwan [but] it will be taken in stride." Said Helms: "You said there was some upset in Taiwan. You'd better believe it."

A Taiwan government spokesman called the communiqué a "serious mistake" and said Taiwan had "reason to be angry." U.S. press reports from Peking said the communi-

qué was described there as a triumph for Chinese diplomacy but a "minimum" U.S. concession.

Like Goldwater, Helms said the communiqué undercut the Taiwan Relations Act because the act would permit U.S. arms sales to Taiwan to increase if necessary.

In response, Holdridge stressed that the U.S. policy of reducing arms sales was to be "predicated" on China's "strong assurances" that it would pursue its goal of "reunification" with Taiwan by peaceful means only. If China's policies changed, he said, "we would reassess ours."

Holdridge refused to say when U.S. arms sales to Taiwan might end. "We're simply going to let history determine the course of events," he said. Neither would he say to what levels arms sales would be limited, though he said the administration's plan was to "establish some sort of baseline" based on arms sales to Taiwan since U.S.-Chinese relations were normalized.

The United States placed a moratorium on sales to Taiwan in 1979 after breaking relations with the island, but sold Taiwan about $830 million worth of arms in 1980.

Taiwan Arms

The Reagan administration's first blow to Taiwan came on Jan. 11, then the State Department announced that the United States would refuse Taiwan permission to buy advanced U.S. fighter planes. Taiwan would be allowed to continue co-producing and acquiring U.S.-designed F-5E fighters.

The department said the decision — highly important as a reflection of U.S. backing for Taiwan — was reached after a study by U.S. agencies found that Taiwan had "no military need for such [sophisticated] aircraft."

The long-awaited decision, said to have been made Jan. 10 by President Reagan, struck a middle ground between the desires of Taiwan and those of the People's Republic of China — and consequently satisfied neither.

Taiwan had asked permission to buy either of two fighters produced strictly for export by American firms and known by the designation FX: a modified General Dynamics F-16 or the F-5G made by Northrop Corp., which also made the less advanced F-5E.

The Taiwan Relations Act required the United States to "make available to Taiwan such defense articles and defense services in such quantity as may be necessary to enable Taiwan to maintain a sufficient self-defense capability." The act said the United States would decide what weapons were sufficient for Taiwan. *(1979 Almanac p. 99)*

A State Department spokesman described the decision as having been made on purely technical grounds. He said a study by the State and Defense departments and "other national security elements" had found that "no sale of advanced fighter aircraft to Taiwan is required because no military need for such aircraft exists."

The spokesman said: "Taiwan's defense needs can be met as they arise, and for the foreseeable future, by replacing aging aircraft now in the Taiwan inventory with comparable aircraft, and by an extension of the F-5E co-production line in Taiwan."

Taiwan co-produced F-5Es with Northrop under a 10-year agreement — with a mid-1983 expiration — which provided that Taiwan could produce 248 F-5Es.

Reaction in Congress

A move to sell Taiwan the FX probably would have provoked a renewed debate in Congress on the future of

---

Cyprus Resolution

On the eighth anniversary of Turkey's invasion of Cyprus, the House July 20 passed a resolution (H Con Res 310) urging the president to take steps to end Turkey's occupation of the island nation. Turkish troops held 40 percent of Cyprus, where 80 percent of the population was of Greek descent.

The vote on the resolution was 405-6. *(Vote 182, p. 54-H)*

The resolution said the president should consider appointing a personal representative to help solve the dispute. It said the president should call on Turkey to withdraw its military forces from the island, since their presence weakened "the North Atlantic Treaty Organization's southern flank" and caused "ill will toward Turkey throughout" NATO. The resolution also urged the president to "diligently pursue every appropriate avenue" to promote the success of United Nations-sponsored "intercommunal" talks on the dispute.

William S. Broomfield, R-Mich., cosponsor of H Con Res 310, said passage of the measure "will be sending a clear signal to Turkey that the continued occupation of Cyprus is not acceptable and that the rights of the people of Cyprus must be restored."

In a dissent, Paul Findley, R-Ill., said that, contrary to the tone of H Con Res 310, Turkey had supported several initiatives to resolve the Cyprus dispute. He said "it would be far from the truth" to assume that the views of House members "are entirely pro-Greek Cypriot and anti-Turkish Cypriot."

As required by the foreign aid law (PL 95-384), President Reagan in July made a quarterly certification to Congress that Greece and Turkey were continuing to make progress toward a negotiated settlement in Cyprus. The president was required to make such a certification in order to provide military aid to Turkey. Congress imposed an arms embargo on Turkey following the invasion but lifted it in 1978 at the urging of President Carter. *(1978 Almanac p. 416)*

Rep. Lee H. Hamilton, D-Ind., chairman of the House Europe and the Middle East Subcommittee, expressed dissatisfaction with the progress reported by the president. Although Greek and Turkish Cypriots had held some negotiations, Hamilton said, "progress has been insufficient on the critical territorial and constitutional issues which continue to divide the communities on the island."

The law also required the president to make a similar certification when he requested military aid for Greece or Turkey or when he asked Congress to approve major arms sales to either nation.

U.S. relations with the two Chinas.

In taking a middle course, Reagan disappointed not only Taiwan and the PRC but also Helms.

Helms said the decision was "difficult to understand, particularly in light of Reagan's constant assurances [on Taiwan] in the past." He said Reagan had reiterated to him as recently as December his "total support" for Taiwan — a remark made in the course of persuading Helms to withdraw objections to a U.S.-PRC consular convention.

Rep. Stephen J. Solarz, D-N.Y., chairman of the Sub-

committee on Asian and Pacific Affairs, praised Reagan's decision as "wise and statesmanlike."

Spare Parts Sale

The administration announced April 14 that it would sell Taiwan $60 million in military spare parts, and drew a notably mild objection from mainland China. The Chinese formally protested the sale in Peking to U.S. Ambassador Arthur Hummel but did not downgrade diplomatic relations or take other steps that some in the administration had feared.

The sale announced April 14 was for $60 million worth of spare parts for aircraft previously sold to Taiwan. Under a separate contract, the U.S. Air Force agreed to sell Taiwan $37 million worth of aircraft maintenance.

Congress took no action on the sale, thus allowing it to proceed.

Romania Trade Status

Congress in August effectively quashed protests by conservatives against President Reagan's renewal of "most-favored nation" (MFN) status for Romania. The designation was routinely given to all U.S. trading partners, except communist nations, allowing them to export goods to the United States at reduced tariff rates.

The House Ways and Means Committee reported H Res 521 and recommended that it be rejected by the House because it would have denied the renewal. The House killed the measure Aug. 18 by postponing action on it indefinitely.

The Senate Finance Committee rejected a resolution that called for denial of the renewal and wrote its own measure (S Res 445) that, in effect, approved the president's action. The full Senate did not act on the issue before leaving Washington for its Labor Day recess.

Either house could have blocked the one-year extension by passing a resolution before Sept. 1.

Background

On June 2, Reagan waived section 402 of the Trade Act of 1974 (PL 93-618) to allow China, Hungary and Romania access to the tariff benefits. The act withheld the most-favored nation status from communist countries that did not permit citizens to emigrate. The privilege was first extended to Romania in 1975. *(1974 Almanac p. 553)*

Section 402 permitted the president to waive the prohibition for any country if he determined that doing so would promote freedom to emigrate. Section 402 was named after its sponsors, Sen. Henry M. Jackson, D-Wash., and Rep. Charles A. Vanik, D-Ohio (1955-81).

Conservatives in both houses sponsored resolutions disapproving the exemption of Romania. They complained about Romania's refusal to allow free emigration and its alleged human rights violations stemming from harassment and persecution of religious groups and ethnic minorities, including persons of Hungarian extraction.

Opponents of the extension said that Reagan himself expressed reservations in granting the waiver because emigration to Israel of Romanian Jews dropped from a high of 4,000 in 1973 to 1,012 in 1981 and because of reported long procedural delays and official persecution of those who applied for exist visas.

There were no moves in Congress in 1982 to block MFN status for Hungary and China, the only other communist nations to have received it under Jackson-Vanik.

Committee Action

On Aug. 13, S Res 445 was reported (S Rept 97-522) favorably by the Senate Finance Committee. The resolution stated disapproval of Romania's human rights abuses and emigration policies, but it did not overturn Reagan's extension of the trade status for Romania.

The committee said the United States should "seek credible assurances" at meetings with the Romanian government that Romania "will review and take steps with respect to certain emigration procedures."

The committee rejected S Res 428, which would have blocked the waiver. Introducing the measure on July 16, Sen. Jesse Helms, R-N.C., complained: "Year after year we have renewed MFN trade status for Romania, and year after year the Romanian government has promised to improve their emigration policies. We have kept our end of the bargain, but the Romanian government has not."

But in a statement in the Aug. 13 *Congressional Record*, Chairman Robert Dole, R-Kan., said the Finance Committee found that, while Romanian emigration policy remained unsatisfactory, it "would not be beneficial to deny that extension [of MFN to Romania] and, in fact, it could be counterproductive."

H Res 521 was reported unfavorably by the House Ways and Means Committee on Aug. 12 (H Rept 97-743).

Symms Resolution on Cuba

Congress in 1982 adopted a watered-down version of a resolution reaffirming a 1962 threat to use force to stop Cuban subversion or the use of Cuba by the Soviet Union as a base for nuclear weapons.

The original version of the Cuba resolution, sponsored by Steven D. Symms, R-Idaho, was at first rejected by the Senate in April, amidst confusion about the Reagan administration's position on the issue. But, with administration support, it was amended and included in the fiscal 1982 supplemental appropriations bill (HR 6863 — PL 97-257). The supplemental was enacted into law over President Reagan's veto, which concerned the bill's funding levels. *(Supplemental, p. 219)*

Symms Rejected

The Senate foreign policy establishment barely defeated a challenge from anti-communist conservatives April 14 as the Senate narrowly rejected the Symms resolution.

The 41-39 vote came on a motion by Charles H. Percy, R-Ill., chairman of the Foreign Relations Committee, to table — or kill — Symms' amendment restating a 1962 threat to use force against Cuba if necessary. *(Vote 80, p. 17-S)*

Despite its anti-Cuban rhetoric, the administration itself seemed at the time to be divided on the issue. A State Department lobbyist at one point produced a letter saying the measure was not "helpful." But higher State Department officials later retracted that stand and said the administration supported the Symms measure.

The amendment reaffirmed a law (PL 87-733) authorizing the president to use force to stop Cuban subversion in the Western Hemisphere or a buildup of Soviet offensive

weapons in Cuba. *(1962 Almanac p. 334)*

Symms, arguing that the United States must signal to the world its resolve to resist the "communization" of Latin America, offered his proposal as a rider to a resolution (S Res 20) to permit broadcasting of Senate proceedings.

Percy and other Foreign Relations Committee members urged the Senate to table the amendment both so the panel could study it and to avoid sending militaristic signals to nations in the Caribbean and Central America.

The measure said the United States would "prevent by whatever means may be necessary, including the use of arms," Cuban aggression or subversion or an "externally supported" Cuban military buildup endangering the United States. It pledged to "work with the Organization of American States and with freedom-loving Cubans" for Cuban self-determination.

After the Senate action, Percy said his committee would hold hearings on the resolution.

Threat Disputed

Symms and other conservatives said the 1962 policy — adopted during the Cuban missile crisis — had to be reaffirmed to show U.S. resolve in the face of Cuban support for revolution in Central America and evidence of Soviet violations of agreements that ended the 1962 crisis.

They said the measure would respond to Soviet leader Leonid Brezhnev's recent pledge to react in kind to U.S. deployments of nuclear weapons in Europe — read as a veiled threat to reintroduce nuclear weapons into Cuba.

Symms said his amendment would show a will to oppose "Soviet-Cuban subversion and aggression, and it would show the world that the United States was willing to stand up to Soviet nuclear blackmail."

But Percy said there was no emergency requiring the Senate to bypass his committee.

"I know of no threats to this country at present which are in any way comparable to the advanced deployment of Soviet intermediate range nuclear missiles — the danger which prompted congressional action on the original Cuba resolution," he said.

Symms responded that "if the threat was serious in 1962, it is even more serious in 1982, because in 1962 the United States held a superior nuclear, tactical and strategic — any kind of — military" edge over the Soviet Union.

Percy said in the absence of a crisis the amendment would incorrectly signal a belief that Soviet-Cuban subversion is the sole cause of turmoil in Latin America and "armed force is our preferred way of dealing with the region." He said that was "utterly simplistic."

Citing Reagan's Caribbean Basin Initiative of aid and trade concessions for the region, Percy added: "Nothing would more distort our efforts in the Caribbean and Central America than to convey the impression that our orientation is a military one."

Symms said his amendment would reaffirm existing law and policies going back to a 1947 mutual defense treaty among American nations and the 1823 Monroe Doctrine.

To that, Lowell P. Weicker Jr., R-Conn. said: "Locking ourselves into the policies of 1962, and by analogy to those of 1823 and 1947, may be good for public relations or saber-rattling purposes, but it is bad foreign policy."

Weicker said the conservatives were advocating "a policy that 20 years of history have proven to be a failure. I ask the proponents of this amendment: Has this policy we are reaffirming succeeded in keeping the Soviet Union out of Cuba or the Caribbean?"

Spanish Entry into NATO

The Senate, by a standing vote, on March 16 approved a protocol (Treaty Doc 97-22) authorizing the entry of Spain into NATO.

Spain officially became the 16th member of the NATO alliance on May 30, after all other members ratified the treaty. Spain became the first new member since West Germany joined in 1955.

Spain formally requested membership in NATO in November 1981, and the NATO foreign ministers signed the treaty Dec. 10.

The United States maintained two active Air Force bases in Spain (at Torregon and Zaragoza). The two countries ratified a military and economic cooperation treaty in 1976.

Percy cautioned that the amendment might enable a president to evade the 1973 War Powers Act (PL 93-148), which required congressional approval for extended military operations. He compared the amendment to the Tonkin Gulf Resolution (PL 88-408), which President Johnson used to justify escalating U.S. involvement in Vietnam.

"Given the track record of such open-ended resolutions, and the tendency of the executive branch to expand their significance, I think it is a bad precedent," Percy said. "If there is one message that has come from the American people it is, 'Let us not let Central America, El Salvador, become another Vietnam.'" He said the Symms amendment could provide the opening for that to happen.

Symms said his amendment "is a statement of policy and intent" and "if the president were to decide to use military force against the Soviet-Cuban threat, he would still be required to get specific congressional authorization after 60 days."

Foreign Relations Hearing

Symms and his resolution were ridiculed by members of the Senate Foreign Relations Committee in an April 27 hearing on the measure.

The harshest denunciation of Symms' resolution came from Paul E. Tsongas, D-Mass., who called it "a good, old-fashioned, jingoistic resolution that is all talk and no action."

Tsongas also put Symms in an awkward personal position by asking him questions about missiles and other military items in Cuba's arsenal and then chiding him for being unable to discuss the specifics of the threat he saw.

With the exception of S J Res 158 cosponsor Jesse Helms, R-N.C., and Larry Pressler, R-S.D., (who was noncommittal) each of the other members present either derided the resolution's construction, pronounced themselves puzzled by its purpose or warned that it would do more harm than good.

Symms maintained throughout, however, that his resolution was necessary to show congressional resolve to back up Reagan in his pledge to thwart the designs of Cuba's Fidel Castro in Central America and the Caribbean.

"My resolution is an attempt to bring into focus that cancer in our underbelly," Symms said, referring to Cuba, "so that it can be properly diagnosed by Congress, understood by the American people and dealt with through a clear expression of policy."

Symms also said the measure would signal that the United States was prepared to see to its security in the face of Soviet "nuclear blackmail," a reference to a Soviet threat to respond in kind to U.S. deployments of nuclear weapons in Europe, apparently by Cuban deployments.

Supplemental

Because it contained foreign aid funds, HR 6863 emerged in the Senate Aug. 11 as a vehicle for the Symms resolution.

With the administration backing Symms, the Senate adopted the measure as an amendment to the supplemental by a vote of 68-28. *(Vote 306, p. 51-S)*

Several hours later, the Senate adopted, 97-2, an amendment by Dale Bumpers, D-Ark., to clarify that the Symms amendment would not authorize the president to use U.S. armed forces outside the limits of the War Powers Act (PL 93-148). *(Vote 311, p. 52-S)*

But adoption of the Symms amendment nevertheless was reported by newspapers and television as a strong message to Cuba, which Symms had said was its central purpose.

The Symms resolution was included in the final version of the bill. The resolution was worded as a restriction on the use of $350 million in economic aid for Caribbean and Central American nations. The aid was the only portion of Reagan's Caribbean Basin Initiative (CBI) to be passed by Congress in 1982.

The bill stipulated that none of the CBI funds could be spent "in any manner inconsistent" with the 1962 law (PL 87-733), restated in HR 6863, declaring that the United States would use any means, including military force, to stop Cuban subversion in the Western Hemisphere or the use of Cuba by the Soviet Union as a base for nuclear weapons.

The bill provided that nothing in the restatement of PL 87-733 was to be interpreted as authorization for the president to use U.S. troops outside the limitations of the War Powers Act (PL 93-148). ∎

Development Banks Report

The Reagan administration proposed in 1982 to limit future U.S. contributions to the World Bank and pressed the bank to place tighter conditions on its loans to developing nations.

The future cutbacks were proposed in a report to Congress, issued Feb. 18 by the Treasury Department, assessing the U.S. role in the World Bank and other multilateral development banks.

The report was initiated at the urging of several of the banks' critics in Congress, who said the United States should reconsider whether to continue supporting the banks.

Although proposing reduced U.S. contributions to the multilateral banks in the future and demanding several changes, the report generally endorsed the banks' goals and operations. Even with the cutbacks, the report suggested continued large contributions to the International Development Association (IDA), the most controversial arm of the World Bank.

The underlying theme of the report was to play down the development role of official agencies such as the banks

and to emphasize the role of private markets.

Treasury Recommendations

The Treasury report dealt with the World Bank and the three development banks serving Africa, Asia and Latin America, but the bulk of the report concerned the World Bank. The basic thrusts of Treasury's recommendations were to:

● Slow and eventually stop the expansion of lending by the banks.

● Eliminate "paid-in capital" to the banks as soon as possible. Paid-in capital was the money that donor nations paid directly to the banks to back their finances. Donors also subscribed "callable capital," similar to a loan guarantee, which was not directly paid to the banks. Both forms of capital supported the "hard-loan windows," which charged near-market interest rates.

● Limit future U.S. contributions to the "soft-loan windows" of the banks, which made low-cost loans to the world's poorest nations. IDA was the largest soft-loan agency. Although the report did not cite a specific number for IDA, Treasury officials discussed a $750 million annual limit on U.S. donations to IDA starting in fiscal 1985.

● Move aggressively to wean borrowing nations off bank financing.

● Emphasize the role of the private sector in economic development. The administration endorsed "co-financing," under which private banks made joint loans with the development banks. The report also supported plans by World Bank President A. W. Clausen for a major expansion of the International Finance Corporation, the bank agency that lent directly to private businesses in developing countries.

● Exercise U.S. influence in the banks to direct loans to nations willing to change their economic policies to strengthen private enterprise.

Impact on Congress

The Treasury report provided encouragement for both critics and supporters of the development banks.

Critics in Congress were pleased that the report proposed substantial reductions in U.S. contributions to the banks and demanded some changes in bank policies.

Rep. C. W. Bill Young, R-Fla., a vocal critic, said he had sought "positive changes" in the banks; with the report and with Clausen in charge, he said, "I see definite indications that they are coming or have already been made."

Supporters of the banks saw their views vindicated in the report's endorsement of most of the banks' operations and policies.

Congressional aides said members of Congress had suggested numerous changes in a draft of the report circulated in the fall of 1981. Many of the changes were incorporated in the final version.

Bank Response

Before the Treasury report was released, Clausen and World Bank officials had two responses.

First, they said, the bank already was moving to meet U.S. concerns. Spokesman Frank Vogl said the bank had taken steps in line with some U.S. proposals, such as improving efficiency, targeting more aid to the neediest countries (especially in Africa), and helping countries get along without bank loans.

Second, Clausen said the bank needed more, rather than less, support from the United States and other rich nations. The day before the Treasury report was released,

Clausen called on the United States to increase its contributions.

A U.S. delay in making promised IDA contributions was "a heavy blow" to the poorest nations of the world, he said.

U.S. Dilemma

The Treasury report admitted that its recommendations could create a dilemma: The United States was campaigning for changes in the banks at the same time it was cutting back its own contributions.

U.S. influence in the banks "has been directly related" to its contributions and leadership, the report said. "Drastic or precipitous reductions in U.S. financial support for the [banks] could undermine our ability to influence [bank] policies and practices in the future."

But Treasury Under Secretary Beryl W. Sprinkel said the proposed cuts would not reduce U.S. influence because "we will undoubtedly remain the biggest contributor. We do have a lot of influence and we expect to preserve that influence," he said.

"Would you have even more influence if you spent a lot more money? Maybe, but that's not a realistic possibility." ∎

Arms Sale to India

Congress Dec. 13 cleared for the president a bill (HR 6758) lifting legal hurdles facing a Pennsylvania firm that was seeking to make the first major U.S. arms sale to India in nearly 20 years.

The bill was to enable the firm, Bowen-McLaughlin-York Corp., to buy U.S. government-made parts for about 200 howitzers that the firm wanted to sell India. The company would assemble the howitzers at its York, Pa., plant and sell them directly to India. Under previous law, government-made parts could be sold to foreign countries only by the U.S. government. There were estimates that the sale could mean up to $1 billion for the firm, its contractors and the government.

The House first passed the legislation July 19. The Senate passed an amended version Oct. 1, but the Senate bill contained technical errors and had to be withdrawn and repassed on Dec. 8. The House cleared the final version for the president on Dec. 13. President Reagan signed the bill into law (PL 97-392) on Dec. 29.

Provisions

As cleared, the bill authorized the U.S. government to sell military equipment to U.S. companies for the purpose of incorporating it into items to be sold overseas. Military services also could be sold to U.S. companies, but only if they were performed in the United States. Such sales were to be subject to all restrictions of the Arms Export Control Act (PL 90-629).

U.S. government equipment and services could be sold to a U.S. company only if the eventual overseas recipient was a "friendly country" or an international organization. U.S. companies also were required to pay the government the replacement cost of equipment and the actual cost of services.

The president was required to report to Congress on any sale that "could have a significant adverse effect on the combat readiness" of U.S. armed forces.

House Action

The House passed HR 6758 July 19 by voice vote.

In briefly describing HR 6758 to the House, Rep. Bill Goodling, R-Pa., and other backers did not say that a potential sale to India was the main reason for the speedy action on the bill. A House aide said the members were concerned that publicity about the sale could disrupt negotiations with India.

Rep. Clement J. Zablocki, D-Wis., chairman of House Foreign Affairs Committee, described the bill as a noncontroversial measure that "is not designed to stimulate or significantly increase commercial arms sales."

His committee had approved the bill July 15 with no public debate and did not issue a report on it.

Bowen-McLaughlin-York was located in the district represented by Goodling, who sponsored HR 6758 and herded it through the House.

Changing the Law

Goodling's bill repealed a section in the arms sale law that allowed weapons, parts of weapons and other military items manufactured by the U.S. government to be sold overseas only by the government. The law was aimed at placing strict controls on exports of government-made weapons.

The law meant that Bowen-McLaughlin-York could sell India only the tank-like chassis that it made for the cannons. To buy guns and gun mounts for the cannons, a foreign country had to deal with the Pentagon. The cannon's gun — the part that actually fired 155-millimeter shells — was made at the U.S. Army arsenal in Watervliet, N.Y., and the mount for the guns was made at the Army arsenal in Rock Island, Ill.

Under Goodling's bill, the government could sell its weapons parts directly to a private firm, which in turn could sell them overseas — most likely as part of completed weapons. The main restriction would be that the purchaser was a "friendly country" or an international organization.

The bill would not change the requirement that all arms exports be licensed and approved by the government.

The immediate effect would be to allow the Army to sell the cannon guns and gun mounts, at production costs, to Bowen-McLaughlin-York. The firm could then assemble the cannons, called M-109s, and export them.

A division of Harsco Corp., of Camp Hill, Pa., Bowen-McLaughlin-York was competing with a French firm, Groupement Industriel des Armements Terrestres, for the Indian cannon contract.

The six-year contract could be worth $900 million to $1 billion, including cannons, spare parts and ammunition, Goodling said. The Commerce Department had estimated that up to 24,000 jobs could be created or saved at Bowen-McLaughlin-York, the Army arsenals and subcontractors.

In his fiscal 1983 foreign aid request, President Reagan had asked Congress to make the same change in the arms sales law that Goodling's bill made. The House committee approved the request in HR 6370, the 1983 foreign aid authorization bill. *(Authorization bill, p. 156)*

The Senate Foreign Relations Committee deferred the request at the urging of John Glenn, D-Ohio, who asked the General Accounting Office (GAO) to examine how the change would affect the flow of arms overseas.

Goodling told the House that separate legislation on the issue was necessary because the foreign aid bill "may be stalled for some time."

U.S.-Indian Relations

India had not bought major U.S. weapons since 1965, when a war between India and Pakistan led the United States to impose an arms embargo on both countries. The United States lifted the embargo in 1975 but said it would not make a sale to either nation that might disrupt the military balance between the two.

Although it had the world's fourth largest military force, India had bought only about $10 million worth of weapons from the United States in each of the previous five years. Most of the sales involved communications gear, ammunition and other small items.

The Soviet Union had been India's largest weapons supplier since the mid-1960s, but India in the 1970s built up its own armaments industry and bought advanced fighter planes from Britain and France and submarines from West Germany.

In 1980 and 1981, the State Department reported to Congress that India was expected to buy U.S. artillery and anti-tank missiles, in part because India wanted to diversify its sources of arms. But in both years, India backed away from ordering the weapons, reportedly because the terms were not acceptable.

An administration official, who asked not to be identified, said India prefered to buy weapons directly from private firms because that "puts more distance between them and us" than sales made through the government.

He said Indian leaders feared that if they bought weapons from the government, "and conflict should arise in the region, then somehow the U.S. might cut these off, it might cut off spare parts." Although the U.S. government could restrict sales made through commercial channels, the official noted, Indian leaders believed that the government would be quicker to cut off a direct government-to-government sale than one made by a private company.

A Pentagon official said India had sought, but failed to get, "iron-clad assurances" that the United States would not disrupt arms shipments for political or other reasons.

Goodling noted another reason for India and other countries to prefer deals with private companies: They could be negotiated faster than sales made through the U.S. government. "As much as six months can be lost in this whole thing" because of the paperwork involved in government sales, he said.

Senate Action

The Senate Oct. 1 passed HR 6758 by voice vote, after adopting amendments recommended by the GAO.

Sen. William Proxmire, D-Wis., had delayed action on the bill for several days, saying it would lead to an increase in private arms sales overseas.

The GAO had issued similar warnings about the House bill, saying it could open loopholes in existing law and lead to the arms-sales increase that Proxmire feared.

The GAO report was completed Sept. 2, and Sen. John Heinz, R-Pa., immediately sponsored S 2920 including the GAO-recommended changes.

The Foreign Relations Committee approved HR 6758 by voice vote Sept. 21, with little discussion, after substituting the GAO-written provisions of S 2920. The committee report (S Rept 97-586) was filed Sept. 24.

GAO Report

The GAO said the "driving force" behind the bill, was the prospect of the sale of howitzers to India.

The GAO report pointed to several flaws in the original House bill and recommended changes to ensure that arms sales authorized by the legislation would be covered by standard congressional and government restrictions.

The report said federal officials and private contractors "strongly support the objective" of the legislation, but it noted that officials in the State and Defense departments wanted changes to protect their right to review all aspects of arms sales such as the one to India.

The GAO's basic criticism was that HR 6758 as passed by the House did not invoke the 1968 Arms Export Control Act (PL 90-629) in authorizing the transfer of government-supplied equipment to private contractors. The 1968 law gave government agencies and Congress the right to review and approve most overseas arms sales.

Both the GAO and administration officials expressed concern that the House-passed bill would enable arms contractors to expand sales with little government control.

"They were really set to take advantage of this," one Defense Department official said of weapons contractors.

The GAO predicted "a rush of commercial sales" if the provisions of PL 90-629 were not required for sales under HR 6758. Consequently, the GAO flatly opposed the House bill unless the restrictions of PL 90-629 were applied. A GAO official said it would be more profitable for a firm to sell equipment complete with government-made parts than to sell just its own, incomplete equipment.

The House bill, the GAO said, "creates a poor precedent and diminishes the effectiveness of [Arms Export Control Act] controls over military equipment sales."

The GAO cited three other flaws in the original bill:

● By designating the secretary of defense as the chief officer required to review sales under HR 6758, the bill might eliminate the opportunity for the State Department to consider a sale when it was first proposed. The original bill would not require a firm to obtain an export license from the State Department until after it had bought equipment from a Pentagon arsenal. As a result, the firm would have more leverage in pressuring the State Department to approve the export license.

● Each military service would have only a limited chance to review sales of equipment to private contractors.

● The original bill would give wide latitude for contractors to buy the services of U.S. government personnel in connection with the purchase of government equipment.

Under the Arms Export Control Act, sales of defense services (such as training pilots to fly U.S.-supplied planes) were treated the same as equipment sales. But the original House bill would enable the Pentagon to provide any services to private firms for overseas sales without a review by the State Department or the arms control agency.

The GAO said contractors were interpreting the House bill as enabling them to obtain more government services than normally were available, such as assistance in making equipment currently produced only by government arsenals.

The Senate made these changes in HR 6758:

First, as the GAO suggested, the bill put all authorized sales under the Arms Export Control Act, thus subjecting them to the same restrictions as direct government sales overseas. Congress could reject sales to private firms of individual items worth $14 million or more, or sales of several items worth $50 million or more.

Second, the bill incorporated the GAO's suggestion to make the president, rather than the secretary of defense, responsible for delegating reviews of sales. That change

would assure the State Department more of a chance to review sales when they were first proposed.

Third, the bill followed the GAO's recommendation to require the services sold under HR 6758 to be performed in the United States. The Foreign Relations Committee said it intended that services would be performed only in connection with the transfer of parts from the government to the contractor.   ∎

African Development Fund

Congress failed in 1982 to complete action on a bill authorizing money for the African Development Fund, forcing the Reagan administration to default on its commitment of support for the multilateral program. The fund provided low interest loans for development projects in the poorest countries of Africa.

The Senate Foreign Relations Committee approved the legislation (S 2398 — S Rept 97-319) on May 6. The Senate passed S 2398 on May 24, by voice vote with no debate.

The House Banking Committee reported its version (HR 6149 — H Rept 97-513) May 13. But the bill was delayed for months and did not reach the House floor until the last week of the lame-duck session.

Rep. Jerry M. Patterson, D-Calif., chairman of the Banking Committee's International Development Subcommittee, asked the full House to consider the bill Dec. 21. But his request required unanimous consent, and Rep. Hank Brown, R-Colo., objected.

"This certainly is one good cause among many," said Brown, "but we as a country have been unwilling and unable to say 'no' to good causes. . . . It seems to me that to place the priority of the African Development Bank [sic] above the urgent needs of the poor of our country is a mistake."

A group of Republicans and Democrats attempted to convince Brown to withdraw his objection. They argued that the amounts in the bill were small, and constituted only 15 percent of the total funds contributed by donor nations to the institution.

But Brown refused to yield, and the bill died as the session ended.

Money for the African Development Fund was appropriated in the continuing resolution (PL 97-377), which cleared Dec. 21, but that money could not be transferred to the fund until an authorization bill was enacted. *(Continuing resolution, p. 238)*

Background

The fund was established in 1974. Most of its loans had been for agriculture and rural development projects. Major borrowers included Ethiopia, Mali, Tanzania, Somalia, Upper Volta, Mozambique, Malawi and Benin.

The $150 million was for the third international replenishment of resources for the African fund, enabling it to make loans in 1982-84. Under an international agreement reached in February, 1982, the U.S. share of the $1.06 billion replenishment was 14.2 percent.

The replenishment for the African fund was the first such funding agreement for a multilateral development bank to be negotiated by the Reagan administration.

The administration asked Congress to authorize the entire $150 million, with appropriations to be in three installments of $50 million each beginning in fiscal 1983.

The United States had provided $175 million to the fund since 1976. Congress in 1981 appropriated $58.3 million to complete the $125 million U.S. donation to the fund's second replenishment. *(1981 Almanac p. 341)*   ∎

Radio Marti Authorization

A Senate filibuster in the December lame-duck session killed legislation (HR 5427) authorizing the establishment of a U.S. government radio station to broadcast to Cuba.

The House had passed the legislation on Aug. 10.

The station was to be named Radio Marti after José Marti, a Cuban who led the fight for the island's independence from Spain in 1898.

The bill fell victim to complaints by U.S. broadcasters that Cuba would use powerful transmitters to jam the station's broadcasts on the AM band, causing interference with U.S. domestic broadcasts. The National Association of Broadcasters had asked Congress to consider alternatives to putting the station on the AM band, or to at least require that domestic broadcasters be compensated by the government for damages caused by Cuban interference.

Midwest broadcasters were the most active in warning about possible Cuban interference. One important station in the Farm Belt, WHO of Des Moines, Iowa, would have been directly affected by an administration plan to put the station on its frequency, 1040 kHz. Among the opponents of the bill were Iowa's two Republican senators, Charles E. Grassley and Roger W. Jepsen.

Liberals in both houses also complained that the proposed station was merely an effort by the Reagan administration to provoke Cuban leader Fidel Castro.

The White House proposed Radio Marti in 1981 as part of its effort to counter Cuban influence in Central America and the Caribbean. Administration officials said Cubans, insulated from the outside world, needed accurate information about their government and its interference in other nations' affairs.

Advisory Commission Report

The Presidential Commission on Broadcasting to Cuba, established in September 1981 to suggest ways of making Radio Marti a reality, released its report in October.

The report said the station should be designed to provide the Cuban people with information they could not get under their repressive regime, so they could make informed judgments about their government's domestic and international policies and try to hold it more accountable.

In addition to news of Cuba, the station also would carry commentaries, music, cultural programming and sports. F. Clifton White, chairman of the commission, said negotiations already were being conducted with owners of major league baseball teams to rebroadcast games for the Cuban audience.

The commission recommended that the station be operated by Radio Broadcasting to Cuba, Inc., an independent corporation to be similar to the one that operated Radio Free Europe and Radio Liberty.

The proposed 50-kilowatt station would transmit from southern Florida, with the possibility of a second transmitter somewhere in the Caribbean. The station's main studios were to be in Washington, D.C.

It was recommended that Radio Marti broadcast 10 to 14 hours each day on the 1040 kHz frequency.

House Foreign Affairs Action

The House Foreign Affairs Committee reported HR 5427 April 2. As reported (H Rept 97-479, Pt. 1), the bill prohibited Marti from operating on any non-government frequencies or within 10 kHz of those frequencies. That provision would have banned Radio Marti from using either the FM or AM spectrum, and limited the station to shortwave broadcasting.

The bill authorized Marti to use the Voice of America (VOA) facility in Marathon, Fla., 30 miles north of the Navy's Saddlebunch antennas. VOA used frequency 1040 to broadcast from Marathon to Cuba during the Cuban missile crisis in 1962.

The measure authorized $10 million in fiscal 1982 and $7.7 million in 1983. The funds would go for the operation of the proposed station and to provide assistance to domestic stations that might experience interference from Cuban signals.

Democrats Object

In a minority report, seven Democratic members of the committee said they opposed establishment of the station. Radio Marti, they argued, would create more problems than it was intended to solve, since the Cuban government would only "jam" its signal and would regard the station as "an act of political confrontation."

The Democrats' principal objection to creation of the station was that it came at a time when the administration had said it was interested in negotiating with Cuba and Nicaragua to reduce hostilities in Central America. The Democrats said the station would "seem inconsistent and destabilizing" in that context. Instead of helping to bring the Cuban government to the bargaining table, they said, it could invite Cuban retaliation in Central America and against U.S. broadcasters.

'WHO' Was on First

To combat the possibility of increased Cuban interference with U.S. stations, HR 5427 authorized the Board for International Broadcasting (BIB) to compensate domestic broadcasters for expenses incurred in avoiding Cuban interference. BIB would be allowed to make interim payments to the stations while their damage suits were pending against the Cuban government.

According to the Foreign Affairs Committee report, signals from Cuba already were interfering with domestic stations and would affect more than 200 AM stations in 32 states and the District of Columbia if Cuba went ahead with its plan to build two 500-kilowatt transmitters.

The report said that if the Cuban transmitter operated on frequency 1040, it would wipe out Radio Marti signals and interfere with 99 percent of station WHO's nighttime broadcasting.

The committee noted that Cuba's plans to build the transmitters "were announced well in advance of discussions about Radio Marti." It also said that alterations would be made in Radio Marti's operation if its assignment to a particular frequency resulted in significant harm to domestic broadcasters.

The committee also called for the creation of a presidential task force to analyze the interference problem and come up with "practical political and technical solutions."

House Energy-Commerce Report

The House Energy and Commerce Committee ordered HR 5427 reported (H Rept 97-479, Pt. II) on July 13.

The $17.7 million in the Energy and Commerce Committee bill would operate the station in fiscal years 1982-83 and would compensate domestic broadcasters for the costs of avoiding Cuban interference.

As reported, HR 5427 authorized the assistant secretary of commerce for communications and information — who was in charge of the National Telecommunications and Information Administration (NTIA) — to assign Radio Marti an appropriate operating frequency anywhere on the broadcast spectrum. NTIA advised the president on communications policy and allocated frequencies on the part of the radio spectrum assigned to the government.

Committee members Timothy E. Wirth, D-Colo., and Tom Tauke, R-Iowa, had proposed banning Radio Marti from any non-government frequency to protect domestic broadcasters on the AM or FM bands from Cuban interference.

When the full Commerce Committee took up HR 5427 on July 13, Wirth and Tauke dropped their AM/FM prohibition and offered a new amendment allowing the Federal Communications Commission (FCC) to make the frequency assignment. They said their amendment was a compromise reached with the State Department.

But the administration balked on the agreement and on a 24-18 vote, the panel adopted an amendment by Matthew J. Rinaldo, R-N.J., giving the NTIA the assignment power. Rinaldo said the NTIA could act much faster than the FCC to assign a frequency.

Guidelines in the committee-approved bill required the NTIA to identify and analyze the possible losses broadcasters would suffer from the selection of a frequency for Radio Marti and Cuban actions to counter the station. The agency could not assign a frequency to Radio Marti if, as a result, a domestic station would be expected to lose 10 percent of either its audience or its annual revenue.

The panel also adopted an amendment by Al Swift, D-Wash., authorizing the FCC to direct the Board for International Broadcasting to compensate domestic broadcasters for expenses in avoiding Cuban interference. Under HR 5427 the board would supervise Radio Marti. South Florida stations that had previously experienced Cuban interference might be compensated under the bill.

House Floor Action

Sweeping aside foreign policy and domestic political objections, the House Aug. 10 passed HR 5427 by a 250-134 vote, after dispensing with 23 amendments during five and a half hours of debate. *(Vote 250, p. 74-H)*

Most of the amendments were introduced by Rep. Tom Harkin, D-Iowa, in an almost single-handed attempt to defeat or block the bill.

As passed, the bill placed Radio Marti under the supervision of the Board for International Broadcasting. The bill authorized $7.5 million in fiscal 1983 to build facilities and operate the station.

Frequency Amendments

Five amendments were offered in an attempt to keep Radio Marti off the AM spectrum, or at least to confine it to one AM frequency.

In its first day of consideration of HR 5427 on Aug. 3,

the House dealt a blow to critics of the bill by rejecting, 136-244, an amendment by Neal Smith, D-Iowa, to direct the FCC to assign a frequency if the AM spectrum was chosen for Radio Marti. *(Vote 227, p. 68-H)*

Smith's amendment was widely viewed as an effort to block or delay the assignment of an AM frequency for Radio Marti. Before assigning a frequency, the FCC would have to go through lengthy hearings and would have to solicit the views of domestic broadcasters, some of whom opposed putting the station on the AM dial.

On Aug. 10, Harkin offered an amendment in response to statements by Kenneth Giddens, a former director of the Voice of America who helped plan Radio Marti, that station WHO should be glad to sacrifice its frequency for Radio Marti. Harkin's proposal would have made Radio Marti a volunteer effort by authorizing its board to produce programs and rent time from AM commercial stations to broadcast them to Cuba.

The amendment "would allow Mr. Giddens and other broadcasters who agree with him to volunteer to place their idealism, patriotism and stations on the front lines," Harkin said. The amendment also would allow the United States to lease radio time from foreign countries that also broadcast to Cuba.

The amendment was rejected 78-284, in the first indication that Harkin lacked the votes to attach restrictive provisions to the bill. *(Vote 247, p. 74-H)*

Iowa Republican Tauke then introduced an amendment to ban Radio Marti from the AM and FM spectrum in order to protect domestic stations from possible jamming by Cuba in retaliation to Radio Marti.

Tauke quoted UNESCO estimates that there were half a million shortwave receivers in Cuba.

"It makes a great deal more sense to reach that 10, 20, or 25 percent of the Cubans who have shortwave sets with a shortwave broadcast than it does to spend millions of dollars to broadcast on AM with no assurance that any Cuban will hear it," Tauke said.

Harkin said the Cubans built Soviet-designed radio sets that had eight shortwave bands and one AM band.

"It seems like we are going to spend all this money to build this radio transmitter to transmit on the AM band when Cuba is moving in the other direction, and they are going toward the shortwave band," Harkin said.

Opponents of the Tauke amendment argued that shortwave was not an alternative for broadcasting to Cuba because most Cubans listened to AM radio. They noted that the Cuban government translated Radio Moscow shortwave broadcasts into Spanish and rebroadcast them on AM.

Edward J. Derwinski, R-Ill., one of the bill's main supporters, said the Harkin and Tauke amendments were attacks "on the very concept of Radio Marti and broadcasting to the people of Cuba."

The Cubans, Derwinski said, "want to know that the United States is interested in them. They want to know there is an alternative to messages other than those coming out of the Castro-Soviet propaganda machine."

The Tauke amendment was rejected 109-277, with two members voting "present." *(Vote 248, p. 74-H)*

The final effort to knock Radio Marti off the commercial AM band was an amendment offered by Swift, who proposed putting the station just above or below frequencies on the standard AM band. About 80 percent of AM radios in Cuba could pick up signals below 560 kHz and above 1610 kHz, according to studies by the National Asso-

ciation of Broadcasters and the Electronic Industries Association. Swift used the studies to support his amendment.

The House rejected the amendment by voice vote.

Realizing that he did not have the votes to keep Radio Marti off the AM band, Harkin offered another amendment that attempted to restrict Radio Marti to a single frequency in the event the AM band was chosen for the broadcasts.

Harkin's amendment was offered to an amendment by Jim Leach, R-Iowa, which had been pending since the Aug. 3 start of floor action. The Leach amendment would have required Radio Marti to use the Voice of America frequency and broadcasting facility in Marathon, Fla.

Harkin's amendment was rejected by voice vote, and the House then rejected the Leach amendment 109-271. *(Vote 249, p. 74-H)*

The House then accepted by voice vote an Energy and Commerce Committee amendment authorizing the assistant secretary of commerce for communications and information, in consultation with the FCC, to select a frequency for the station from all possible bands.

Funding Amendments

The House agreed to shift fiscal 1982 funds for Radio Marti to fiscal 1983, but cut the $10 million for the station's first year to $7.5 million.

Swift sponsored the cutting amendment, saying the proposed station was "gold-plated" and the three studios requested for it were unnecessary.

Rep. Cecil Heftel, D-Hawaii, who owned radio stations in his home state, said: "I think the gentleman from Washington [Swift] is being generous in suggesting a cut to $7.5 million." A "gold-plated" station could be built for $4 million, he said.

The House rejected by voice an amendment by Rep. Charles E. Schumer, D-N.Y., that would have mandated funding of Radio Marti solely through private contributions to the Board for International Broadcasting.

"The president tells us that there are millions of people in the private sector willing to fund worthy government endeavors," Schumer said. "I am certain that this kind of radio station would attract the kinds of funds that the president is talking about."

Schumer also said the station was not an essential program deserving of a $10 million authorization while "billions of dollars are being cut from other programs."

Navy Construction

Harkin offered an amendment to delay funding for the station until 30 days after Congress received a General Accounting Office study of possible misuse of Pentagon funds to construct a transmitter in Saddlebunch, Fla., for Radio Marti. The Navy's construction of the transmitter, prior to passage of HR 5427, had contributed to opposition to the bill.

The amendment was rejected by voice vote.

Neal Smith said the bill would reimburse the Navy for facilities "they have already illegally built."

Smith asked: "Where can we find $10 million, $17 million, or whatever it is?" The money will not come out "of thin air," he said, but probably would be taken from the Voice of America, Radio Free Europe and Radio Liberty budgets.

Broadcasting Truth

The House adopted an amendment by Leach to pre-

vent Radio Marti from broadcasting propaganda or subversive information to the Cuban audience.

The amendment said Radio Marti broadcasting "shall serve as a consistently reliable and authoritative source of accurate, objective and comprehensive news."

Leach said the amendment was necessary to ensure that the station would broadcast "responsible news rather than propagandistic perspectives for the purpose of subversion or inciting rebellion."

Administration officials had said the station was to broadcast "the truth about Cuba."

At the request of Radio Marti backers, Leach dropped language that would have required the station to operate in the same "objective and accurate" manner as the Voice of America.

Other Harkin Jabs

The House rejected by voice votes several other Harkin jabs at Radio Marti. The amendments would have:

● Banned the hiring of additional federal employees to operate Marti.

● Prevented U.S. military or paramilitary action against Cuba if Cuba jammed Radio Marti.

● Renamed the bill the "John Foster Dulles Cold War Mentality Memorial Radio Broadcasting to Cuba Act."

Opposition to each of Harkin's measures was led by Dante B. Fascell, D-Fla., who called Radio Marti "a small step" to "communicate freely to people about ideas and ideals."

Compensation Amendments

The House adopted, by voice vote, two amendments dealing with compensation for domestic broadcasters who might be harmed by Cuban interference:

● By the Energy and Commerce Committee, authorizing the FCC to direct the Board for International Broadcasting to compensate the broadcasters for the cost of avoiding Cuban interference. Congress had received estimates of the expenses ranging from $10 million to $40 million.

● By Fascell, to include guidelines for the FCC to follow in determining how to make the interference compensations to U.S. broadcasters.

Senate Foreign Relations Action

The Senate Foreign Relations Committee approved an amended version of HR 5427 on Sept. 9, by an 11-5 vote.

Democrats John Glenn of Ohio and Paul S. Sarbanes of Maryland joined the panel's nine Republicans in voting for the bill after it was amended to require the Commerce Department to take into account Cuba's ability to jam U.S. radio programming in retaliation for the establishment of Radio Marti.

The committee filed its report on the bill (S Rept 97-544) on Sept. 15.

The panel had held up consideration of the the measure for several months despite the wishes of its supporters, including committee member Jesse Helms, R-N.C., who professed that Radio Marti "was kind of my idea."

At a hearing on the bill July 1, Helms criticized "a spectacle of senators" for being willing to go to Havana and "smoke cigars and eat ice cream cones" with Castro but unwilling to act on measures like Radio Marti that could counter Soviet and Cuban Caribbean ambitions. (Ranking Foreign Relations Democrat Claiborne Pell, R.I., was one of a number of legislators who had met with Castro in Havana

in recent years.)

Helms warned that "the hour is late" and said action had to be taken to stem a communist takeover in the Western Hemisphere and the 15 million Central American refugees he saw flooding into the United States as a result.

Christopher J. Dodd, D-Conn., attacked the administration's plan as a "juvenile foreign policy proposal." Dodd said he was embarrassed to be in a hearing on a plan to spend "$17 million to make Castro look bigger than life" around the globe.

On Aug. 30, just prior to the committee's action on the bill, the Cuban government blasted the airwaves with simultaneous high-powered broadcasts of the Voice of Cuba on five AM frequencies. The broadcasts drowned out several Midwest stations.

In its Sept. 9 session, the Foreign Relations Committee rejected three attempts by some Democrats to kill or cripple Radio Marti:

● An amendment by Pell to put Radio Marti under the Voice of America was rejected 5-11.

● An amendment by Paul E. Tsongas, D-Mass., to compensate domestic commercial broadcasters for their economic losses suffered as a result of Cuban retaliation was rejected 7-9; and

● An amendment by Dodd to establish a scholarship program for students from the Caribbean, rather than Radio Marti, was rejected 4-12.

In its key action, the committee accepted a compromise worked out between the Reagan administration and senators Grassley and Jepsen, in which the committee stated its opposition to the use of 1040 and 1060 kHz for Radio Marti.

The compromise required the Commerce Department's National Telecommunications and Information Administration (NTIA), in selecting a frequency for Radio Marti, to measure the interference potential of Cuba's proposed AM broadcast operations. The committee said that NTIA should consider FM and shortwave frequencies for Radio Marti, in addition to the AM band.

The committee noted that Cuba had proposed building several very high powered AM stations, some of which would have 10 times the power of Radio Marti or any U.S. commerical stations. Noting that Cuba proposed to put 500,000-watt stations on both 1040 and 1060 kHz, the committee said the NTIA "should not select those frequencies for Radio Marti."

The committee also said "it makes no sense" to assign Radio Marti to 590 kHz, the frequency used by stations WOW in Omaha, Neb., and WGTM in Wilson, N.C., because Cuba planned a 150,000-watt station on that frequency.

Committee member Zorinsky had threatened to delay consideration of HR 5427 because of the potential impact on station WOW.

In addition to determining the potential for Cuban interference with U.S. stations, the NTIA was to determine whether Radio Marti broadcasts could penetrate Cuban interference.

"It would be cruel indeed to raise the hopes of the Cuban people, to provide them with the window on the world, and on their government that they now lack, only to have the project fail because an inappropriate frequency is selected," the committee said.

The compromise also required the NTIA to take into consideration four other criteria, which had been included in the House version of HR 5427:

• Radio Marti's broadcasts could not cause "objectionable interference" with commercial broadcast stations on or near the frequency used by Radio Marti. The FCC already had an established technical standard for determining objectional interference.

• Radio Marti's broadcasts had to result in the least possible interference to commercial stations from any possible countermeasures taken by the Cuban government. The NTIA was to identify possible Cuban countermeasures and assess their impact on U.S. commercial stations.

• The NTIA could not select a frequency for Radio Marti if it determined that Cuban countermeasures on that frequency would cause "objectionable interference" or "substantial economic harm" to any U.S. commercial stations. The committee defined "substantial economic harm" to be the loss of more than 10 percent of a commercial station's gross revenues or audience.

• The NTIA was to select a frequency for Radio Marti that was consistent with the U.S. official positions in international telecommunications conferences. The committee noted that, under international radio regulations, the AM band was intended for domestic use.

As reported, the Senate bill authorized $7.5 million for operation and construction of facilities for Radio Marti in fiscal 1983; $300,000 of that amount was earmarked for administrative expenses of the Board for International Broadcasting, which was to supervise the station.

Radio Marti was to serve "as a consistently reliable and authoritative source of accurate, objective and comprehensive news." Radio Marti was authorized to use Voice of America transmitter facilities at Marathon, Fla., and to use the accompanying Voice of America AM frequency if an AM frequency was selected for Radio Marti by the Commerce Department.

In a minority report, Democrats Pell, Zorinsky, Tsgonas, Dodd and Alan Cranston, D-Calif., said the proposal for Radio Marti was "badly flawed." The $7.5 million authorized by the bill "will buy a radio station of dubious quality and uncertain audience," they said.

"Radio Marti is the absurd conclusion of a bankrupt Cuba policy," the Democrats said. "It is an insult to the American taxpayer."

Senate Floor Action

The Radio Marti proposal ran into a Senate filibuster the week of Dec. 6, led by Zorinsky and J. James Exon, D-Neb. The filibuster prevented the bill from ever reaching the Senate floor.

In its only formal action on the issue, the Senate on Dec. 17 rejected, by voice vote, an attempt by Paula Hawkins, R-Fla., to add $7 million for Radio Marti to the fiscal 1983 continuing resolution (H J Res 631 — PL 97-377).

Zorinsky's filibuster threat had prevented Senate consideration of HR 5427 prior to the Labor Day recess, and most Senate sources had predicted the measure would not be taken up during the lame-duck session.

But Senate Majority Leader Howard H. Baker Jr., R-Tenn., took the bill to the floor Dec. 6 at Reagan's request. On Dec. 7, Baker said the bill could be passed only if the administration was willing to compromise with opponents.

One compromise under consideration at the end of 1982 was to expand Voice of America broadcasts to include programs aimed at Cuba. Zorinksy had expressed interest in that approach, but the administration had insisted that Radio Marti be a separate station, similar to Radio Free Europe.

Senate Debate

Opponents dominated the intermittent debate on the issue during the week of Dec. 6, with Zorinsky and Exon emphasizing the potential cost of Radio Marti and the damage that U.S. broadcasters could suffer if Cuba jammed the station.

Zorinsky said the bill would establish an "entitlement process" that might force the government "to make reparations payments" to broadcasters damaged by transmission interference by Cuba. He cited a Congressional Budget Office estimate that the payments could reach $40 million.

"This is a stupid idea," he said. "We are spending millions of dollars in construction, operation and compensation costs for a radio station whose broadcasts in all probability will never be heard."

Opponents also said Radio Marti was an "anti-Castro" effort that would backfire. Administration officials had said the major purpose of Radio Marti was to tell Cubans the truth about their president, Fidel Castro.

"Radio Marti, in my mind, will probably do Castro more good than ill ... giving Castro something he can point to to evoke empathy among his own people," said Paul E. Tsongas, D-Mass.

Foreign Relations Chairman Percy made no effort to defend the Radio Marti proposal on its merits, merely saying the committee had approved it, and the Senate should follow suit.

Zorinsky and his allies made their filibuster threat clear when debate began Dec. 6. Exon told his colleagues that "we are wasting our time" considering the bill.

Zorinsky spent much of his time reading a report issued in August by the Presidential Commission on Broadcasting to Cuba. The commission report formally proposed establishing Radio Marti, so Zorinsky was, in effect, publicizing views with which he did not agree.

Opponents kept the Radio Marti bill from even reaching the Senate floor by filibustering a motion to consider a waiver from the requirements of the 1974 Budget Act (PL 93-344). S Res 480, waiving the act, was necessary because Foreign Relations did not report the Radio Marti bill before the May 28 deadline for fiscal 1983 authorization bills.

Zorinsky objected to consideration of the budget waiver because it was approved by the committee Sept. 21 during a meeting that was in violation of Senate rules. Under those rules, a committee must get the permission of the Senate to meet later than two hours after the Senate goes into session. Foreign Relations failed to get that permission on Sept. 21, Zorinsky said, and so its approval of the budget waiver was invalid.

Percy admitted Zorinsky was correct but called the issue "a technical point that should not be allowed to hold up" consideration of the bill.   ▮

Caribbean Basin Initiative

Congress in 1982 enacted into law only one of the three parts to President Reagan's Caribbean Basin Initiative (CBI).

In its fiscal 1982 supplemental appropriations bill (HR 6863 — PL 97-257), Congress voted $350 million in emer-

gency economic aid for nations in the Caribbean and Central American region. But Congress did not enact two other legislative portions of the CBI program that would have given trade and tax benefits to those nations. The House passed the trade proposals (HR 7397), but the bill died in the Senate. Reagan's proposal for tax breaks to encourage U.S. businesses to invest in the region was never given serious consideration in either house. *(CBI trade bill, p. 54)*

Reagan Proposal

Reagan Feb. 24 formally unveiled his Caribbean Basin Initiative, which he said was designed to help stabilize an area of "vital interest" to the United States. In an address to the Organization of American States in Washington, he said the plan would help Caribbean and Central American nations "make use of the magic of the market of the Americas to earn their own way toward self-sustaining growth." *(Text, p. 15-E)*

The key elements of the Reagan plan were proposals to:

● Remove for 12 years duties on Caribbean imports to the United States — with the politically important exception of textiles and with limits on duty-free sugar imports.

● Appropriate supplemental fiscal 1982 economic aid of $350 million and supplemental military aid of $60 million for the region. Reagan proposed that about $100 million of the economic aid and $35 million of the military aid would go to El Salvador.

● Enact federal tax credits or other incentives to induce U.S. firms to invest in Caribbean nations.

● Develop a variety of programs using U.S. agencies and businesses and international organizations such as the World Bank to encourage private investment and production in Caribbean nations.

Administration officials said the trade, aid and investment initiatives would complement one another. They said the trade and investment programs would promote long-term recovery while the aid would help nations such as Costa Rica, described as "bankrupt," to service their international debt and survive in the short-term.

The administration's CBI proposal was introduced March 17, as HR 5900 in the House and as S 2237 in the Senate.

TRADE PROPOSALS

Variously described as the "centerpiece," "backbone" and "heart" of Reagan's program was the proposed elimination for 12 years of all duties on imports into the United States from Caribbean basin countries, except for textiles and apparel items. Duty-free treatment of sugar imports also would be limited.

The proposal did not represent a dramatic change in U.S. policy; nearly 90 percent of U.S. imports from Caribbean and Central American countries already were duty-free. But administration officials said the new policy should encourage businesses to expand their operations in the region, thus increasing jobs.

The bill listed 28 countries and territories in the Caribbean and Central America, but the elimination of U.S. duties was not automatic for every country in the region. The bill prohibited the extension of the free-trade features to four categories of countries:

● Communist countries.

● Countries that had nationalized or seized property

belonging to U.S. citizens and had not taken steps to reimburse or negotiate with the property owners.

● Countries that had not acted in "good faith" to recognize binding arbitration awards in favor of U.S. citizens or companies.

● Countries that gave preferential treatment to the products of developed countries other than the United States, if the treatment had "a significant adverse effect" on U.S. commerce. The president would not have to invoke this prohibition if he received assurances that the preferential treatment was being eliminated or reduced so that it had no adverse impact on the United States.

Under the bill, the president could waive any of the first three prohibitions if he certified to Congress that such an action would be in the U.S. national security or economic interest.

The bill also included a long list of criteria the president was to consider when determining whether to make a country eligible for the duty-free imports. Among the criteria were the country's "self-help" measures, its willingness to abide by accepted rules of international trade, and its willingness to provide reasonable access to its markets and basic commodities.

Administration officials said the restrictions were needed to prevent benefits going to countries that were hostile to the United States or that discouraged free enterprise.

A State Department fact sheet on Reagan's proposal excluded Cuba from a list of "potential beneficiaries." However, the legislation included Cuba on the list of countries in the region. In his Feb. 24 speech, Reagan referred to "the tightening grip of the totalitarian left in Grenada and Nicaragua."

Most of the opposition to the duty-free imports proposal came from leather-related industries, which saw themselves as especially vulnerable to competition from Caribbean nations.

The legislation included a "safeguard" mechanism to protect American agriculture and industry that might be harmed by increased Caribbean imports. American businesses claiming such damage could appeal to the U.S. International Trade Commission, which would determine whether the increased imports were a substantial cause of serious harm to the business. The commission could recommend that the president restore duties.

The proposal also would protect U.S. producers of fruit and other perishable items by enabling them to petition the secretary of agriculture for reimposition of import duties to prevent Caribbean producers from flooding the U.S. market.

In order to qualify for duty-free treatment, at least 25 percent of the value of an import would have been required to originate in basin countries. A State Department fact sheet said that requirement was necessary in order to "avoid fostering the type of investment in the region which would result in mere 'pass-through' operations' " in which merchandise from outside the region was merely shipped through a Caribbean country in order to qualify for duty-free treatment.

However, critics said the 25 percent requirement was not high enough to prevent multinational corporations from abusing the duty-free provision.

U.S. business and labor groups also said the process of seeking relief through the trade commission was too time-consuming to offer them meaningful protection. One labor spokesman referred to the trade commission process as

"burial insurance" for industries killed by foreign competition.

Textiles Exempt

The legislation proposed to exempt from the free trade provisions textiles and apparel items that were subject to textile agreements. However, Reagan said he would extend more favorable treatment for textile imports from Caribbean countries on a case-by-case basis under existing bilateral and multilateral trade agreements.

The United States already had bilateral textile trade agreements with Costa Rica, the Dominican Republic, Haiti and Jamaica. Under those agreements, the United States limited the number of imports of specific items, such as women's wool sweaters and men's shirts.

The State Department said only 6 percent of U.S. imports of textiles and apparel items came from the Caribbean in 1981. Most such imports were made by U.S.-owned companies that assembled the items in Caribbean countries using fabric produced in the United States.

Sugar Imports

Duty-free imports of sugar, syrups and molasses were to be limited under the administration plan.

The United States applied a duty of 2.8125 cents per pound to the sugar imports of only the three biggest suppliers: the Dominican Republic, Guatemala and Panama. Sugar imports from other Caribbean countries entered duty-free because of preferential treatment accorded developing countries with small market shares.

Under the Reagan plan, sugar from the three biggest suppliers was to be allowed to enter the United States duty-free, up to specified limits: 780,000 metric tons for the Dominican Republic, 210,000 metric tons for Guatemala and 160,000 metric tons for Panama.

The secretary of agriculture would retain standby authority to limit duty-free sugar imports in order to protect the U.S. sugar industry. Cane sugar was an important crop in Florida, Louisiana, Texas and Hawaii, and beet sugar was produced in 17 states.

Administration officials said the plan would not encourage increased sugar production in the Caribbean.

Puerto Rico, Virgin Islands

Because the free-trade provisions would reduce the preferential advantages that Puerto Rico and the U.S. Virgin Islands enjoyed as U.S. possessions, the administration bill authorized several steps to limit the harm to them. Among those steps:

• The president could remove the duty-free status of rum from other Caribbean countries if it threatened the revenues that Puerto Rico and the U.S. Virgin Islands received from rebates of federal excise taxes on rum. Rum was a major export of both possessions, and the rebate was a major source of revenue for their governments.

• Puerto Rico and the Virgin Islands were to receive rebates on the federal excise taxes on rum from other nations in the region.

• Puerto Rico and the Virgin Islands were to be given the same right as U.S. industries to petition the International Trade Commission for reimposition of duties.

Bilateral Treaties

In addition to the legislative proposals, the administration said it would make other efforts to improve trade with and investment in Caribbean nations.

For example, the administration said it was prepared to negotiate bilateral investment treaties with nations in the region.

Under such treaties, two nations agreed on standards for treating foreign investment and for resolving disputes about such investments. The United States had no such treaties in 1982, but it was negotiating one with Panama.

TAX PROPOSALS

To encourage U.S. investment in the region, the administration proposed extending the domestic investment tax credit to Caribbean nations.

Under the plan, American businesses would receive a credit on their U.S. taxes for up to 10 percent of the value of fixed asset investments used predominantly in qualifying Caribbean nations. To qualify, a Caribbean nation would have to sign an agreement to exchange tax information with the United States.

The credit program would last for five years.

A Treasury Department spokesman said the provision would improve productivity by encouraging "the placement of machinery and equipment" in the region.

The bill also included a "pass-through" mechanism under which U.S. shareholders (either individuals or corporations) owning 5 percent or more of the stock in firms incorporated in Caribbean countries could receive a pro rata share of the investment credit.

J. Gregory Ballentine, deputy assistant secretary of the Treasury for tax analysis, told the House Ways and Means Committee March 17 that the purpose of that provision was to ensure that U.S. companies would not be denied the credit in countries that required all investments to be made by firms incorporated locally.

The bill also would permit American companies investing in Puerto Rico, the Virgin Islands and other U.S. possessions to take advantage of the investment tax credit and the accelerated depreciation system adopted in the 1981 tax cut bill (PL 97-34). The depreciation system, called Accelerated Cost Recovery System (ACRS), enabled a business to write off on its taxes the value of an asset over three, five, 10 or 15 years, depending on the type of asset. *(Tax bill, 1981 Almanac p. 91)*

A pass-through provision would allow Puerto Rican and Virgin Island subsidiaries of U.S. companies to pass their investment tax credits and ACRS benefits on to their parent companies in the United States.

The Treasury Department projected a U.S. revenue loss of $50 million in fiscal 1983 from the tax breaks for Caribbean investments and $55 million from investments in Puerto Rico and the Virgin Islands.

The Bahamas and other "tax haven" nations in the Caribbean were expected to forgo the program rather than agree to exchange tax information with the United States.

Citing those countries, Ballentine said: "We do not believe that it is appropriate for countries to benefit from U.S. tax incentives unless they are willing to cooperate with the United States in matters of tax administration."

The tax provision provoked sharp criticism from members of Congress, labor unions and others who said it would encourage American businesses to flee to low-wage nations of the Caribbean.

The AFL-CIO flatly opposed the tax proposal, saying it would conflict with the administration's policies of encouraging business investment in the United States. The union federation also said such tax breaks could be easily abused, resulting in windfalls for businesses that estab-

lished operations in Caribbean countries to take advantage of the tax breaks without providing jobs in those countries.

AID PROPOSALS

Reagan requested a $350 million fiscal 1982 supplemental appropriation for the Economic Support Fund (ESF), a program of loans and grants that was the primary means of economic and political support for countries friendly to the United States. Administration officials said most of the additional ESF aid would be used to finance imports of U.S. goods by private businesses in recipient nations.

The supplemental would boost fiscal 1982 ESF aid to the region to $490 million. Congress already had approved $211.3 million in traditional development aid to the region.

In his separate foreign aid request, Reagan also asked for $326 million in ESF aid and $217.6 million in development assistance for the region in fiscal 1983.

Reagan's proposed legislation did not specify amounts for individual countries, but the president said in his statement he planned to make the following allocation of the $350 million supplemental:

● $128 million for El Salvador, for a total of $168 million in fiscal 1982. Reagan's message said El Salvador's economy "is in desperate straits."

● $70 million for Costa Rica, for a total of $90 million. Reagan said Costa Rica needed aid to restore the confidence of investors and to provide credit for private business.

● $50 million for Jamaica, for a total of $90 million. The administration considered Jamaica a showcase for democracy and capitalism in the region. Prime Minister Edward Seaga, a conservative who defeated leftist Michael Manley in October 1980 elections, was the first foreign head of state to visit President Reagan.

● $40 million for the Dominican Republic. The statement said the Dominican Republic, like other nations in the region, was suffering from falling prices for sugar, its major export, and heavy dependence on foreign oil.

● $35 million for Honduras. Reagan said Honduras, the poorest nation in Central America, "faces severe balance of payments problems, spawned primarily from falling prices of major exports and rising import costs."

● $10 million for island nations in the Eastern Caribbean, for a total of $30 million in fiscal 1982.

● $10 million for the newly independent nation of Belize (formerly British Honduras).

● $5 million for Haiti.

● $2 million for the American Institute for Free Labor Development, an arm of the AFL-CIO that promoted free labor unions in developing countries.

CONGRESSIONAL OPPOSITION

The CBI proposal encountered congressional opposition on several grounds:

● With unemployment rising in their districts, members were reluctant to support tax provisions that might encourage American businesses to move to the Caribbean, where they could take advantage both of new U.S. tax breaks and low wages.

● U.S. sugar and leather-product industries were concerned about increased competition from duty-free imports from the Caribbean.

● Liberal Democrats criticized the plan because it included no additional money for traditional "development" aid programs such as agriculture, health and education.

Rep. Michael D. Barnes, D-Md., chairman of the House Inter-American Affairs Subcommittee, for example, complained that the administration was "sending conflicting signals" by proposing the Caribbean plan and at the same time saying it would reduce U.S. contributions to the soft-loan window of the Inter-American Development Bank. That agency made low-interest loans for development programs in poor nations of Latin America.

● Although there was broad support in Congress for an economic, rather than military, approach to the problems of the Caribbean and Central America, Reagan's program was widely viewed as an attempt to disguise increased U.S. aid to El Salvador. Both Republicans and Democrats expressed concern that one-third of the "emergency" economic aid would go to El Salvador, where the administration was backing an embattled regime against leftist guerrillas.

Several critics noted that the administration stretched the definition of Caribbean basin to include El Salvador, which fronted on the Pacific Ocean.

● Although the economic aid itself was relatively non-controversial, some members expressed concern about boosting foreign aid when domestic programs were being sharply cut. Rep. Bill Goodling, R-Pa., who generally supported the proposal, told administration officials that "$350 million seems so little . . . but I'm getting letters from my constituents and they think it's outrageous."

● The exceptions to the Reagan program were almost as numerous as the items included.

Two of the most important countries in the region — Cuba and Nicaragua — were to be excluded from any benefits. Also, the duty-free import provisions did not apply to textiles and apparel items, and limits were to be placed on duty-free sugar imports. Tax breaks for American investments were to be allowed only for five years and only in countries that agreed to exchange tax information with the United States. And nearly three-fourths of the supplemental economic aid was to go to just three countries (El Salvador, Costa Rica and Jamaica) with less than one-fourth of the region's population.

In response to congressional complaints about the Caribbean plan, administration officials defended the Reagan proposal as a "balanced" package that did as much as possible at a time when the United States was facing its own economic and budget problems.

"This is an attempt to balance off the needs with the resources available to meet them," said M. Peter McPherson, director of the Agency for International Development.

Foreign Relations Action

The Senate Foreign Relations Committee shocked the Reagan administration and Chairman Charles H. Percy, R-Ill., May 19 by voting 9-8 to transform the CBI aid proposal into a donation to the World Bank.

Sen. Charles McC. Mathias Jr., R-Md., joined eight Democrats to hand the administration an unexpected blow in its quest for the $350 million in bilateral economic aid.

The action came on an amendment by Christopher J. Dodd, D-Conn., to S 2237. The Dodd amendment clearly caught the administration and Percy off guard.

After the committee voted to accept Dodd's amendment, it approved S 2237 by a vote of 16-1. But then Percy announced that "a senator" — clearly Mathias — had "misunderstood" the ramifications of Dodd's plan and the

committee should reconsider Dodd's amendment.

Mathias later denied that he had misunderstood Dodd's amendment, and the committee did not formally reconsider its action until early September. The committee never formally filed a report on S 2237.

Two days after the committee acted, Ernest Stern, World Bank senior vice president for operations, sent Treasury Secretary Donald T. Regan a letter politely rejecting the Dodd plan.

"While we are not fully familiar with all the details, we believe that the proposed trust fund would not be suitable for administration by the World Bank," Stern wrote.

Second Committee Report

Following the World Bank's rejection of the CBI fund proposed by Senate Foreign Relations, Percy and Dodd began work on a compromise. Their efforts produced an entirely new bill, S 2899, which was approved by the committee on Sept. 10 (S Rept 97-541) by a 15-0 vote.

The new bill authorized $350 million and placed various restrictions on the money's use. It did not include the trade and tax portions of the CBI.

The committee said it was reporting the new bill "in order to keep open the possibility of authorizing fiscal 1982 funds before the end of the fiscal year. However, Percy did not attempt to bring the legislation to the Senate floor before the fiscal year expired on Sept. 30.

To take account of Dodd's concerns, the report included a section noting that the $350 million was a short-run, emergency infusion of money for Caribbean and Central American nations and calling for a "major multilateral effort" to attack "the fundamental economic problems facing those nations." Such an effort, the committee said, would provide "multi-year financing for those economic projects and programs which must be undertaken if the appropriate climate is to be created to further the expansion of international investment and trade...."

House Foreign Affairs Action

The House Foreign Affairs Committee July 15 approved by voice vote the $350 million in fiscal 1982 economic aid under the CBI plan. The committee filed its report (HR 5900 — H Rept 97-665, Pt. 1) on July 26.

The vote was the administration's first success on the CBI. Reflecting doubt that other committees would act, Foreign Affairs took the precaution of approving the aid both in an omnibus CBI bill (HR 5900) and as a solitary measure (HR 6755) that the House could consider separately.

But while the action by Foreign Affairs offered the administration a patch of blue among the clouds, even that was a compromise of Reagan's plan, for the panel voted to restrict his use of the aid.

First, the committee limited the amount any one nation could receive to $80 million, so as to block administration plans to give $128 million of the funds to El Salvador.

Then it earmarked $43.8 million for development aid, to prevent the administration from using the entire $350 million to help nations in the region finance imports from the United States.

The panel offered one concession: Waiving a 1962 law banning the use of U.S. aid for property expropriation, it voted to give El Salvador an extra $20 million to pay for property seized under a U.S.-backed land reform program.

Under the deal, arranged by Chairman Clement J.

Zablocki, D-Wis., and Michael D. Barnes, D-Md., chairman of the inter-American affairs subcommittee, the $20 million was subtracted from CBI aid available to other nations.

But the committee's action put the administration in a tight spot. While it provided more money for El Salvador — and in a way some administration officials had urged — it also provoked some of Reagan's conservative allies, who had long opposed aiding in foreign expropriations.

CBI Aid Details

Besides limiting the amount of CBI aid available for any one country, the Foreign Affairs Committee included in HR 5900 and HR 6755 provisions to:

● Require that at least 80 percent of the $350 million be used to "generate local currencies" to be used "to the maximum extent feasible" for development assistance.

● Earmark $7.5 million for scholarships to pay for study in the United States, including training in technical skills, for Caribbean and Central American students.

● Earmark $2 million for the Inter-American Foundation.

● Instruct the president to "seek a reasonable balance" between aid to the public and private sector in CBI nations and between balance-of-payments and development aid.

● Change all references in the bill to read "Caribbean/Central America." The amendment's sponsor, Mervyn M. Dymally, D-Calif., said the term "Caribbean Basin" was misleading.

The committee put in its report on the bills, but not in the texts, the following allocation of the aid funds: El Salvador, $100 million (including the $20 million for land reform); Costa Rica, $70 million; Jamaica, $50 million; Dominican Republic, $40 million; Honduras, $35 million; Haiti, $10 million; Guatemala, $11 million; Belize, $10 million; Eastern Caribbean nations, $20 million; and, as the administration requested, $2 million for the American Institute for Free Labor Development.

Land Reform

The committee also barred any CBI aid for El Salvador unless the president reported to Congress both that the land reform program had not been altered to the detriment of its beneficiaries or potential beneficiaries and that El Salvador had made "substantial progress" in land reform.

The legislation defined "substantial progress" as a "substantial increase" in land titles issued to peasants, a "substantial decline" in peasants being evicted from land they could claim and evidence that the government was continuing to accept peasant applications for titles.

Supplemental Action

Congress finally appropriated the CBI aid package in the fiscal 1982 supplemental — but not until administration critics had used the measure to conduct guerrilla warfare against Reagan's El Salvador policies.

However, the authorization bills that had been reported by the Senate Foreign Relations and House Foreign Affairs committees were never considered by either chamber.

Both the House and Senate Appropriations committees added the CBI economic aid to their versions of the omnibus fiscal 1982 supplemental (HR 6863 — PL 97-257). *(Supplemental, p. 220)*

The House committee approved the full $350 million in economic aid. However, it rejected most of a separate

request for $301.5 million in additional fiscal 1982 military aid, including $52 million for military grants for El Salvador and Honduras. Instead, the committee worked out a compromise providing $52 million in military aid for countries in Latin America, Africa and the Middle East, although none of it for El Salvador.

The Senate committee on Aug. 3 added $5 million for Honduras to the economic aid package, for a total of $355 million. It also approved $253 in military aid, including $67 million in grants and $186 million in loans.

Opponents of Reagan's El Salvador policy were able July 29 to bar a House vote on the aid. George Miller, D-Calif., raised a point of order during action on the fiscal 1982 supplemental appropriations bill (HR 6863) and blocked a vote on an amendment to add the CBI aid. Miller's point, sustained by the chair, was that no legislation authorizing the aid had been passed.

Miller and other critics of Reagan's El Salvador policy complained that a disproportionate share of the CBI aid was to go to El Salvador.

But the aid survived similar attacks in the Senate Aug. 10. Patrick J. Leahy, D-Vt., raised a point of order, saying the aid had not been authorized, but the Senate rejected his point by 53-46. *(Vote 302, p. 51-S)*

Leahy then offered an amendment to delete the CBI aid and the military aid from the bill. That amendment was rejected 42-54. *(Vote 303, p. 51-S).*

Another amendment by Dodd to cut the CBI funds in half was tabled by a 55-409 vote. *(Vote 304, p. 51-S)*

The House-Senate conference committee on the supplemental essentially adopted the House version of the CBI aid, although it added the provisions of a Senate resolution threatening military action against Cuba. *(Cuba resolution, p. 142)*

The supplemental earmarked the $350 million in CBI funds as follows: Not more than $75 million for El Salvador and $10 million for Guatemala, not less than $20 million for eastern Caribbean nations, $41 million for the Dominican Republic, $10 million for Haiti, $50 million for Jamaica, $10 million for Belize, $70 million for Costa Rica, $35 million for Honduras, $2 million for the Inter-American Foundation and $2 million for the American Institute for Free Labor Development; $25 million unallocated.

The supplemental also:

● Barred funds for any of those countries that did not cooperate in preventing the entry of narcotic drugs into the United States from those countries; and

● Provided that the CBI funds could not be spent "in any manner inconsistent" with a 1962 law (PL 87-733), restated in HR 6863, declaring that the United States would use any means, including military force, to stop Cuban subversion in the Western Hemisphere or the use of Cuba by the Soviet Union as a base for nuclear weapons. Also provided that nothing in the restatement of PL 87-733 was to be interpreted as authorization for the president to use U.S. troops outside the limitations of the War Powers Act (PL 93-148).   ■

Foreign Aid Authorization Bill Stalled

Congress failed in 1982 to complete work on legislation authorizing funding for foreign aid programs in fiscal 1983. However, the two foreign aid authorizing committees issued reports that had the effect of sharply altering President Reagan's aid program.

The House Foreign Affairs and Senate Foreign Relations committees reported the legislation (HR 6370, S 2608) in May, but the legislation did not get floor consideration in either chamber. The legislation was doomed by two major factors: a philosophical disagreement over the balance between military and development aid, and the traditional reluctance of Congress to deal with foreign aid issues in an election year.

Appropriations for foreign aid programs were included in the fiscal 1983 continuing resolution (PL 97-377). In writing that legislation, the two Appropriations committees followed the lead of the authorizing committees on such issues as military aid and the levels of aid to El Salvador and Israel. *(Foreign aid funding, p. 238)*

Background

Largely because of an initiative House Foreign Affairs Committee Chairman Clement J. Zablocki, D-Wis., took in 1981, the fiscal 1983 bills were supplementals, authorizing less than $1 billion each rather than the full foreign aid budget of around $7 billion.

Zablocki persuaded his panel and conferees on the fiscal 1982 aid bill to extend the authorizations to fiscal 1983 as well. So President Reagan already was authorized to spend $5.96 billion on aid in fiscal 1983 under existing

law (PL 97-113). *(1981 Almanac p. 161)*

As a result, the House bill (HR 6370 — H Rept 97-547) for fiscal 1983, reported May 17 by the Foreign Affairs Committee, authorized only an additional $778 million. The Senate version (S 2608 — S Rept 97-464), reported May 28 by the Foreign Relations Committee, authorized $786 million.

When Zablocki urged the two-year approach, he explained that he was trying to avoid "having a big bill in an election year that deals with the total amount" of the aid budget.

But the vehemence of the partisan battles provoked by the domestic program cuts and defense spending increases proposed in Reagan's budget overwhelmed any advantage gained by the two-year approach.

Moreover, though the fiscal 1983 bills were comparatively small, they consisted almost entirely of additional authority for military aid — as did Reagan's request. As a result, a fragile coalition that got foreign aid through Congress in 1981 was shattered in 1982, thus dooming the changes for the supplementals.

Democrats who favored development and economic aid over arms assistance grudgingly voted in 1981 for the aid bill, which sharply increased military aid, and they did so only because Republicans who viewed foreign aid as an arm of the defense budget made concessions on humanitarian aid.

In 1982, nine Democrats on the House committee said in the report on HR 6370 that they hoped the emphasis on arms aid was a "temporary aberration" rather than a permanent shift in the ratio between U.S. military and devel-

opment assistance.

"We would like to see our nation identified with providing food and fertilizer, training and technical assistance, not tanks and fighter aircraft, capital goods and budget support," the Democrats said.

Two more liberal Foreign Affairs Committee members, Gerry E. Studds, D-Mass., and George W. Crockett Jr., D-Mich., pledged in minority views to vote against the bill because, as Studds wrote, it lacked "the balance with development assistance struck in last year's legislation."

Senate sentiment was less clear, though attempts in that chamber to slash foreign aid during consideration of the first budget resolution were rejected handily.

However, in the Senate, moderate Foreign Relations member Nancy Landon Kassebaum, R-Kan., voted against reporting S 2608, writing: "I do not believe that major emergencies have arisen during the last five months which justify approval of the funding level authorized in this bill."

Kassebaum also criticized her fellow committee members, adding: "The administration's request for an additional 35 percent in security assistance [military and Economic Support Fund aid] received far too sympathetic consideration" in the committee.

Committee Reports

As reported by the House Foreign Affairs Committee on May 17, HR 6370 (H Rept 97-547) authorized supplemental appropriations of $778 million for fiscal 1983 foreign aid, for a total aid authorization of $6.739 billion.

On May 28 the Senate Foreign Relations Committee reported S 2608 (S Rept 97-464), which authorized extra fiscal 1983 appropriations of $786 million, for a total aid budget of $6.748 billion.

Reagan had requested an increase of $1.221 billion — $975 million of it in military aid. But while both committees pared the request, both did so largely by changing a Reagan plan to subsidize arms loans to selected nations into a mix of grants and off-budget loan guarantees.

Concessional Arms Aid

As was the case in fiscal 1982, both committees claimed major savings from Reagan's budget request by changing an administration formula for giving certain nations a financial break on their arms aid.

Reagan had asked for $1.739 billion to give concessional arms aid to 21 countries: $950 million for grant military aid, including $500 million for Israel, $400 million for Egypt and $50 million for the Sudan; and $789 million to subsidize interest rates on Foreign Military Sales (FMS) credits to 19 nations under a program of "direct credits."

Both committees increased Israel's grants (to $750 million by the House, $850 million by the Senate) and approved the requested grants for Egypt and the Sudan.

But both committees changed the "direct credits" plan to a mix of grants and regular FMS loans — a formula that reduced the appropriations required while providing the recipients the same basic concessions on their arms aid.

For each of the proposed direct credits recipients, the House committee changed the formula to 40 percent MAP (Military Assistance Program) grants and 60 percent FMS loan guarantees. The Senate committee authorized a formula of 50 percent MAP grants and 50 percent FMS loan guarantees. The administration in December sent Congress

a revised request that essentially adopted the Senate committee's formula.

In theory, the new formulas would reduce appropriations required for concessional arms aid by $473 million under the House committee bill and by $394.5 million under the Senate bill.

However, because of changes the committees made in individual accounts, the authorizations approved for MAP grants and FMS loans under the concessional aid program were different.

H Rept 97-547 said $311.8 million of the $349.3 million authorization for MAP grants in HR 6370 was attributable to the committee's 40:60 formula for concessional aid. S Rept 97-464 said $335 million of S 2608's $372.5 million MAP grant total was to satisfy the 50:50 formula.

FMS, MAP Totals

The adoption of the committee formulas for concessional arms aid resulted in cuts in Reagan's requests for direct appropriations; it also produced increases in his requests for regular FMS loan guarantees.

The administration had asked for an increase of $939 million in an existing $800 million authorization for direct spending on FMS grants and low-interest arms loans and no increase in the $238.5 million MAP authorization.

The House committee authorized an increase of $400 million, up to $1.2 billion, in FMS grants and, because of its 40:60 MAP to FMS ratio, added $110.8 million to the MAP authorization, raising it to $349.3 million.

The Senate committee authorized an additional $500 million for FMS grants, up to $1.3 billion, and increased the MAP authorization by $134 million, up to $372.5 million to accommodate its 50:50 MAP to FMS formula.

Both committees also increased the existing $3.27 billion ceiling on FMS loan guarantees beyond Reagan's request for another $659 million. The House committee added $778 million, for a $4.048 billion limit. The Senate committee added $711.3 million, up to $3.981 billion.

ESF Totals

Reagan also had requested an increase of $162.5 million in the existing $2.724 billion authorization for Economic Support Fund (ESF) aid. ESF was a program of loans and grants, designed to help strategic nations ease the economic burden of their defense budgets.

The House committee trimmed the request by only $2.25 million, authorizing $2.884 billion for fiscal 1983, but mandated some changes in administration plans for how to spend it. The Senate committee bill authorized $2.829 billion, reducing Reagan's request by $57 million.

Both panels approved the requested $750 million for Egypt, but the Senate committee added $125 million to the $785 million request for Israel.

The Senate panel also retained other earmarkings in PL 97-113, thus forcing the administration to absorb the increase for Israel by reducing amounts for nations whose ESF aid was not earmarked.

The House panel added $20 million to finance scholarships for Latin American students but cut $25 million from a Reagan request for a $75 million ESF contingency fund, $50 million of which the administration planned to reserve for use in the Caribbean and Central America. In addition, the House panel said $20 million of the fund should be used for development aid in the Caribbean region.

The House committee agreed to delete an earmarking in PL 97-113 requiring that $20 million of the ESF account

be spent only in Nicaragua. The Senate committee retained an earmark of $20 million for Nicaragua's private sector. The Reagan administration cut off aid to the Nicaraguan government in January 1981, but continued direct aid to businesses, cooperatives, labor unions and other groups not involved with the government.

HR 6370 also reduced ESF for African nations by $12.25 million. The committee did not specify what nations should absorb the cuts. It did say, without earmarking the item, that Tunisia should get $36 million. Reagan requested no ESF for Tunisia.

The House committee also added new authority for programs in Southern Africa and said the administration should consider aiding leftist Mozambique with its transportation system if it showed a "desire to improve relations with the United States."

El Salvador

Aid to El Salvador emerged as the most sensitive issue in both committees. *(El Salvador aid certifications, p. 137)*

Reagan requested $61.3 million in regular military aid for El Salvador in fiscal 1983, up from $26 million in 1982; he also asked $105 million in ESF aid, up from $40 million in fiscal 1982.

The fiscal 1983 military aid request envisioned $50 million in FMS credits at low interest rates, $10 million in FMS credits at regular interest rates and $1.3 million in International Military Education and Training (IMET) grants, which paid for U.S. training of foreign soldiers.

In fiscal 1982 Congress authorized $8.5 million in MAP arms grants, $16.5 million in regular FMS credits and $1 million in IMET for El Salvador. Reagan used emergency powers to add another $55 million in military equipment to that total.

The committees faced two essential questions: how much arms aid to give, if any, and whether to condition that aid on "negotiations" between Salvadoran authorities and the guerrillas who were battling the government.

How members answered those questions depended on how they viewed El Salvador's March 28 elections for a Constituent Assembly. The interpretations contrasted sharply, for two central reasons.

First, Salvadorans turned out to vote in large numbers despite leftist attempts to disrupt the balloting, and the elections were generally viewed as free and fair despite predictions they would not be. But critics said they meant little since the left did not participate.

Secondly, rightist parties won control of the Constituent Assembly, disappointing U.S. officials who had hoped for a victory by moderate Christian Democrats under Jose Napoleon Duarte. But under pressure from the United States and the Salvadoran military, the rightists gave a share of power in a new provisional government to the Christian Democrats, who won 40 percent of the vote.

Reagan's critics said that with continued military aid, the rightists would have no incentive to make peace with the left. Some complained that Reagan had been disingenuous when he certified in January that the Salvadoran government had made progress in protecting human rights and was implementing economic and political reforms. Congress voted in 1981 to require the certification before further arms aid was given to El Salvador. *(1981 Almanac p. 161)*

The critics also said human rights abuses by Salvadoran security forces had not decreased, and that the rightists were likely to abrogate land distribution and other economic and political reforms begun by Duarte.

Critics also complained that while moderates had a share in the new government, the Constituent Assembly was headed by Roberto D'Aubuisson, head of the right-wing ARENA party. A former U.S. ambassador to El Salvador had charged d'Aubuisson, a former army major, with complicity in political murders.

Despite those complaints, many in Congress argued that to stop or cut military aid would encourage the left and leave the right feeling cornered. They said the turnout and fairness of the elections had shown that El Salvador's people rejected both violence and the leftists.

Reagan's backers, mostly Republicans, also argued that the new government should be given a chance to keep its pledges to proceed with reforms. They said it would be wrong for Congress to dictate to an elected government what its policy on negotiations should be.

The Senate committee, alarmed by alterations made in a land reform program by the new Constituent Assembly, tentatively rejected the increases, freezing El Salvador's aid at 1982 levels.

The cut was proposed by Christopher J. Dodd, D-Conn., and approved by an 11-0 vote as a warning to El Salvador's new government not to abandon the U.S.-backed land reforms. Dodd offered his amendment on May 26, after meeting privately with Salvadoran peasant leaders worried by the Constituent Assembly's May 18 vote to suspend part of the land reform program.

Thomas O. Enders, assistant secretary of state for inter-American affairs, appealed to the committee to withhold judgment on whether the Assembly's action genuinely put the land reform program in jeopardy.

But Dodd argued that the committee should send a "signal" that Congress would not continue aiding El Salvador if the land reforms were dismantled.

"There should be no doubt about where this [Salvadoran] administration is headed on land reform," Dodd told his colleagues. "They're out to destroy it."

The Senate panel also put a provision in S 2608 declaring that military aid and ESF must be cut off if the Salvadoran government changed or terminated the land reform program in a way that deprived beneficiaries of their rights.

The House committee, acting before the Assembly changed the land reform program, approved Reagan's requests after a heated debate.

But Zablocki later announced that he would offer a floor amendment, similar to the Senate committee's, that would require a cutoff of U.S. aid if the land reform program were undermined or abrogated.

The House committee also approved a new condition on U.S. aid, in addition to conditions existing in PL 97-113, to require the president to certify before continuing military aid that the Salvadoran government was:

● Either "actively engaged in good faith in a dialogue with all major parties willing to participate in the democratic process to bring about an equitable political solution to the hostilities within the context of free and fair elections, including the extension of amnesty, a cease-fire, and international security safeguards if necessary;"

● Or was "unable to proceed with such a dialogue because the opposition is unwilling to participate."

The committee also required that the president to:

● Consult with Congress before certifying that El Salvador was eligible for continued arms aid.

● Declare in his first certification for fiscal 1983 that El Salvador had "made good faith efforts" to bring to justice the murderers of six Americans killed in El Salvador in December 1980 and January 1981.

● Consult with Congress before again using his emergency powers, as he did in fiscal 1982, to give El Salvador U.S. defense equipment beyond levels authorized by Congress.

Defense surveys. On a related matter, the House committee also expanded the legal definition of defense requirements surveys, which were conducted by U.S. military personnel to gauge the needs of nations seeking U.S. military aid.

The provision was inspired by a dispute with the Defense Department over whether House Foreign Affairs and Senate Foreign Relations members could see a survey done for El Salvador.

The Pentagon resisted giving the committees the report, arguing that it was the property of El Salvador, but relented after Senate committee Chairman Charles H. Percy, R-Ill., refused to mark up the aid bill without access to the document.

Israel, Egypt

Continuing what had become a tradition, both foreign aid authorizing committees voted to increase aid to Israel beyond the administration's request, and both approved increases for Egypt proposed by Reagan.

Between them, Israel and Egypt had been receiving more than half of all U.S. foreign aid since Egypt signed a peace treaty with Israel in 1979.

Arms aid. Reagan requested $1.7 billion in Foreign Military Sales credits for Israel, an increase of $300 million over fiscal 1982. He asked that $500 million of the total be grants, down from $550 million Congress mandated for fiscal 1982 and 1983 under PL 97-113.

The administration in 1981 promised Israel FMS increases of $300 million in fiscal 1983 and 1984 as consolation for Reagan's approval of the sale of AWACS radar planes and other weaponry to Saudi Arabia. *(1981 Almanac p. 129)*

The House committee approved the $300 million increase but made grants out of $750 million of Israel's total FMS, leaving $950 million in regular FMS loan guarantees, which had to be repaid at market interest rates.

The Senate committee required that the entire $300 million increase be made grants, for a total of $850 million in grants and $850 million in loan guarantees for Israel in fiscal 1983. The move was sponsored by Rudy Boschwitz, R-Minn.

Both committees approved $1.3 billion in arms aid for Egypt, including a $400 million loan that did not have to be repaid and $900 million in regular FMS loans. Egypt received $900 million in fiscal 1982, including $200 million in grants.

Economic aid. The Senate committee also was more generous on economic assistance for Israel, adding $125 million to the $785 million in Economic Support Fund aid Reagan had requested, for a total of $910 million.

That move was sponsored by Alan Cranston, D-Calif. His original amendment also proposed to put into law that, in the future, Israel's annual payments on its U.S. debt could not exceed Israel's ESF aid. In other words, over time the U.S. government would pay Israel's U.S. debts, which Percy said then amounted to $7.5 billion.

Cranston said Israel's U.S. debt burden exceeded U.S.

aid, and in large measure due to American policies, including the sale of weapons to Arab nations. He noted that Israel had received $785 million a year in ESF since 1978, an annual decrease with inflation.

Charles McC. Mathias Jr., R-Md., questioned the future cost of Cranston's plan, which Cranston said would be about $970 million in fiscal 1984 and $1.02 billion in fiscal 1985.

But Cranston argued that his amendment merely would force the United States to pay for its Middle East policy. "If we don't want that cost to go up, we can stop that policy of arming Israel's enemies," he said.

Mathias and Percy protested that Cranston wanted to offer Israel a financial relationship with the U.S. government preferable to that enjoyed by the American states.

Exclaimed Percy: "It is one of the most astounding proposals I have ever heard."

The committee debated the issue at length on May 25 but delayed action when Dodd questioned the wisdom of putting Cranston's idea in law.

When the committee reconvened on May 26, Cranston modified his amendment to merely increase ESF for Israel to $910 million in fiscal 1983 and say in the committee's report on S 2608 that the president should study whether U.S. aid should cover Israel's annual U.S. debt.

The modified Cranston amendment was adopted on a vote of 9-8, with Boschwitz joining the eight Democrats in favor.

The House committee approved the $785 million request, the same as Israel received in fiscal 1982, without change.

Both committees approved Reagan's request for $750 million in ESF for Egypt, the same as in 1982. Both also earmarked the ESF for Israel and Egypt to prevent its being used elsewhere, and they ordered all of it given in grants. Reagan had proposed making two-thirds of each nation's ESF a grant, and the rest a loan.

Turkey, Greece

Aid to rivals Turkey and Greece re-emerged as a sensitive issue in both committees, in part because the new socialist premier in Greece, Andreas Papandreou, had threatened to end military cooperation with the United States and NATO.

Reagan requested an increase of $65 million in FMS to Turkey, up to $465 million, with $300 million of that to be in direct credits and $165 million regular FMS. He requested an increase of $50 million in ESF for Turkey, up to $350 million, up from $300 million in fiscal 1982.

The administration also asked that Congress delete a provision in PL 97-113 earmarking at least $280 million in regular FMS credits for Greece, which received no ESF aid.

After lengthy debate, the House committee approved the requested aid levels for Turkey, which would come to $186 million in MAP grants and $279 million in FMS credits under the 40:60 formula.

But the House panel also increased the earmarking of FMS for Greece up to $325 million, an increase of $45 million over fiscal 1982, to maintain a traditional ratio of 7:10 in military aid to Greece and Turkey.

The committee also voted to impose conditions that both nations would have to meet to get the increases. Under that provision, the president would have to certify before giving Turkey and Greece their FMS increases that the aid was needed for them to meet their obligations to NATO and that they had taken steps to resolve their

dispute over Cyprus. The president also would have to certify that the military leaders of Turkey had demonstrated plans to return to democratic rule and respect for human rights.

The Senate committee, also after lengthy debate, rejected the requested FMS increase for Turkey. But in a concession to the administration it agreed to make $110 million of Turkey's arms aid MAP grants, up from $57.7 million in fiscal 1982, with the remaining $290 million regular FMS.

China Eligibility

Both committees declined a request to specifically declare mainland China eligible for economic aid and food aid, but both gave the president power to do so himself.

The administration had proposed no aid to China but asked Congress, as a gesture to smooth turbulent U.S.-China relations, to remove China from lists of communist and unfriendly countries prohibited from receiving aid.

Both committees said the president already had the power to declare China eligible for concessional food sales financing under the PL 480 Food for Peace program.

The PL 480 issue was jointly considered by the Senate Agriculture Committee, which concluded that a change in the law requested by the administration was unnecessary. The Agriculture Committee was chaired by Jesse Helms, R-N.C., who was critical of administration attempts to curry favor with China.

S Rept 97-464 said: "It is the Agriculture Committee's judgment that if the president believes that China neither dominates nor is dominated by a world Communist movement, he is free to designate China as a 'friendly country' and, therefore, eligible for PL 480 under existing law."

The report said Foreign Relations agreed with that interpretation but wanted the president to notify the committee 90 days before offering PL 480 aid to China.

Similarly, rather than remove China from a list of communist nations ineligible for economic aid, both panels authorized the president to waive the ban if he decided it was "important to the security of the United States."

Zaire

Angered by continuing reports of corruption and brutality by the regime of President Mobutu Sese Seko in the African nation of Zaire, both committees cut Reagan's requests for that nation.

The administration had requested $20 million in FMS direct credits for Zaire, $1.3 million in IMET and $15 million in ESF. In fiscal 1982 Zaire received $7.5 million in regular FMS, $3 million in MAP grants, $1 million in IMET and no ESF.

The House committee was the more severe of the two, putting a ceiling of $4 million on FMS for Zaire in fiscal 1983 and specifying that it be offered in regular FMS loan guarantees, not concessional aid. The House committee also forbade ESF aid to Zaire.

Howard Wolpe, D-Mich., chairman of the House Africa subcommittee, urged the military aid cutback "to put some political distance between the United States and Zaire." And Stephen J. Solarz, D-N.Y., a former chairman of that subcommittee, urged deletion of the economic aid because much of the past U.S. aid had been pocketed by Zairean officials.

The Senate committee decreased FMS guarantees for Zaire by $500,000 from fiscal 1982, down to $7 million, and froze MAP grants at $3 million, for a cut of $10 million in

the administration's $20 million request.

Foreign Relations did not prohibit ESF but conditioned it on Zaire reaching a new agreement on economic policies with the International Monetary Fund.

Morocco, Pakistan and Tunisia

Both committees also used the aid authorization bill to raise caution flags on U.S. policy in Morocco, where King Hassan II's regime was fighting for the Western Sahara with leftist Polisario guerrillas backed by Libya and Algeria.

Reagan requested authority to more than double arms aid to Morocco, up to $100 million in FMS, with $50 million in direct credits, from $30 million in fiscal 1982.

The House committee recommended, but did not mandate, only $50 million in arms aid for Morocco, with $20 million to be MAP grants and $30 million FMS credits.

It added that, to encourage Hassan to negotiate peace in the Western Sahara, Morocco should not receive military training that would improve its ability to attack the Polisario. It requested a report every six months on what training Morocco was being provided.

While the Senate committee did not cut aid to Morocco, it said in its report that U.S. aid should be conditioned on "Morocco's pursuit of a negotiated, rather than a military, solution to the conflict in the Western Sahara."

Pakistan. The Senate committee approved Reagan's requests for $275 million in FMS credits and $175 million in ESF for Pakistan as part of a six-year, $3.2 billion aid deal negotiated in 1981. But the committee warned that future aid would depend on whether Pakistan moved toward democracy. *(Pakistan aid, 1981 Almanac p. 172)*

The House committee approved the ESF aid, but made no comment on the military aid.

The Senate report praised Pakistan for providing asylum to Afghan refugees fleeing the Soviet invasion of their land, but it said overall respect for human rights had not improved in Pakistan over the past year.

The Senate committee also added a new provision to bar the use of development aid funds for Pakistan. The report said that in fiscal 1982, despite an admonition from Congress not to, the administration substituted $25 million in development aid for $25 million in ESF for Pakistan.

"The development accounts are already hard-pressed by inflation and budgetary restraints and it is the view of the committee that they ought not to be used as a substitute" for ESF, the Senate report said.

Tunisia. The House committee rejected an administration proposal to increase FMS credits to Tunisia by $55 million, to $140 million in fiscal 1983 from $85 million in 1982.

The action was taken on an amendment by Wolpe which offered instead to increase ESF financial aid to Tunisia to $36 million, up from $5 million in fiscal 1982. Reagan had proposed no ESF aid for Tunisia in fiscal 1983.

Military Training

The Senate committee agreed to a Reagan request for an increase of $11.4 million, up from an existing $42 million, in the authorization for IMET, the program providing U.S training for foreign military officers.

The House committee approved only $3.237 million of the requested increase, which H Rept 97-547 said would provide increases the administration wanted for IMET programs in Latin America and Asia.

Guatemala. The House committee's report said no

IMET was to be given Guatemala without the committee's prior approval "because of concern over the widespread abuse of internationally recognized human rights in that country."

The report noted that a coup in Guatemala on March 23 had replaced the regime responsible for past repression with one that had "pledged respect for human rights and political and economic reforms." But the report said it would be "premature for the United States to move immediately to re-establish a military relationship."

Exchange training. On a related issue, both committees approved a Reagan request for authority to send American military students to schools in foreign nations on a one-for-one, cost-free exchange basis.

Peacekeeping

Both committees approved Reagan's request for an increase of $24.474 million, up from $19 million in fiscal 1982, for peacekeeping operations. Both also agreed to a request to give the president authority to draw a total of up to $10 million in commodities and services from any government agency for use in peacekeeping operations.

The funding approved would provide $34.474 million for a U.S.-sponsored peacekeeping force deployed in the Sinai peninsula since April 25, when Israel ceded the territory back to Egypt under their 1979 peace treaty, and $9 million for a contribution to a U.N. force on Cyprus.

Export Controls

A controversial administration decision in February to ease controls on exports to Iraq and South Africa prompted both committees to use the aid authorization bills to amend the Export Administration Act (PL 96-72).

Under the controls, Iraq was listed as a nation that supported international terrorism and could not buy civilian aircraft or military equipment from U.S. firms; exports to South African police agencies were banned because of that nation's racial policies.

The House panel provided in HR 6370 that export controls in effect as of Dec. 31, 1981, must remain in effect until Dec. 31, 1982. But the bill provided that the president could waive the requirement if it was in the "security interests" of the United States to do so and he notified Congress 30 days in advance.

The Senate committee adopted a weaker amendment requiring only that Congress be notified 30 days in advance of any changes in regulations under the Export Administration Act and 60 days in advance of any country being removed from the list of nations supporting international terrorism.

Before removing a country from the terrorism list, the president would have to certify that it had not supported international terrorism or terrorists within the past year.

However, the Senate bill also provided authority for the president to approve on his own an export license for goods going to a nation on the terrorism list. The chairman or ranking minority member of the Foreign Relations or Foreign Affairs committees could demand that the president certify the sale as being in the U.S. national security interest.

Anti-terrorism Aid

In a departure from previous U.S. policy, both committees approved an administration request for new authority to spend $5 million in fiscal 1983 helping foreign police forces train to fight terrorism.

The House committee stipulated that the program would expire in two years, providing a chance to review it. The Senate committee provided authority for three years.

In addition, both committees provided that:

● No military equipment or services could be provided under the program.

● The assistant secretary of state for human rights must be consulted in developing the program and recipients would be governed by human rights and other restrictions on aid.

● Congress must be notified 30 days in advance of what nations were to receive anti-terrorism training.

● Nations prohibited from receiving security assistance under any other program would be barred from receiving anti-terrorism aid, unless the president declared the country threatened by international terrorism and said the aid was in the national interest of the United States.

The House committee bill provided that the training must be provided in the United States and that U.S. advisers could work in recipient nations only 60 days. The Senate committee did not require that the training be conducted in the United States, but it barred U.S. officers from remaining abroad for more than 30 days.

In provisions the House panel's bill did not contain, the Senate committee also authorized the president to sell anti-terrorism training to nations able to pay for it; provided that no State Department employees other than security officers could provide anti-terrorism training; and said no intelligence collection services, equipment, personnel or facilities could be provided under the program.

Arms Aid Administration

The committees made or agreed to a number of changes in the authorities governing U.S. military sales and aid and commercial arms sales as well.

Waiver authority. In a new limitation on the president's power to waive restrictions on foreign aid in emergencies, the House committee put a ceiling of $750 million on the amount of cash arms sales the president could approve using his waiver power for nations otherwise barred from buying U.S. equipment.

Existing law limited FMS financing the president could offer using his waiver power to $250 million worldwide and $50 million to any one nation, unless it was "threatened by Communist aggression." Under the committee provision, the president could offer no more than $500 million overall in cash sales and financing to any one country in any year.

The new provision was inspired by speculation that Reagan might have used his emergency power to thwart the will of Congress if Congress had voted in 1981 to prohibit the sale of AWACS radar planes to Saudi Arabia. A resolution to block the sale passed the House overwhelmingly but narrowly failed in the Senate. *(1981 Almanac p. 129)*

SDAF. Another major House committee provision forbade the Defense Department to use the Special Defense Acquisition Fund (SDAF) to purchase "any aircraft which was designed specifically for export sales" and was not used by U.S. forces for anything other than training. The Senate bill contained no similar provision.

The provision was designed to prevent the Pentagon from using the SDAF to buy FX fighter aircraft — a designation applying to the General Dynamics F-16/79 and the Northrop F-5G. The FX planes were designed for sales abroad but had not found a market.

The SDAF was authorized but not funded in 1981 to

Foreign Aid Authorizations, Fiscal 1983

Following are figures for fiscal 1983 foreign aid authorizations: the existing authorization in PL 97-113, passed by Congress in 1981; President Reagan's requests; and amounts approved by the House Foreign Affairs Committee in HR 6370 and the Senate Foreign Relations Committee in S 2608. The president in December sent Congress a revised request that adopted the Senate committee proposals for Foreign Military Sales credits and loans.

(in thousands of dollars)

Program	Existing Authority	President's Request	House Committee	Senate Committee
FMS Direct Credits[1]	$ 800,000	$1,739,000	$1,200,000	$1,300,000
FMS Guaranteed Loans[2]	(3,269,525)	(3,928,800)	(4,047,560)	(3,980,800)
Military Assistance Program	238,500	238,500	349,340	372,500
International Military Education and Training	42,000	53,700	45,237	53,400
Peacekeeping	19,000	43,474	43,474	43,474
Anti-terrorism	—	5,000	5,000	5,000
Economic Support Fund	2,723,500	2,886,000	2,883,750	2,829,000
Development Assistance	1,607,270	1,643,203	1,664,603	1,610,863
Narcotics Control	37,700	40,000	42,500	40,000
Anti-piracy[3]	—	—	5,000	—
AID operating expenses	335,600	376,000	335,600	335,600
Peace Corps	105,000	105,000	112,000	105,000
Other	52,000	52,000	52,000	52,000
Total	**$5,960,570**	**$7,181,877**	**$6,738,504**	**$6,746,837**

[1]*President Reagan requested a program of low-interest Foreign Military Sales (FMS) loans called "direct credits." The House committee approved forgiven loans of $750 million for Israel, $400 million for Egypt and $50 million for the Sudan. The House committee also set aside $311.84 million in the Military Assistance Program (MAP) for grants to be made in addition to FMS loans to other countries on the* "direct credits" *list. The Senate committee approved grants of $850 million for Israel, $400 million for Egypt and $50 million for the Sudan and provided $335 million for MAP grants to other countries.*

[2]*Guaranteed loans not counted as new budget authority.*

[3]*The House committee established a new program within the migration and refugee account to combat piracy in the Gulf of Thailand.*

allow the Pentagon to buy in advance items commonly requested by FMS recipients so that orders would not have to be filled from U.S. stocks.

Criminal penalty. In action not matched by the House panel, the Senate committee increased the penalty for violating the Arms Export Control Act and the International Traffic in Arms Regulations, which governed arms exports, by raising the maximum fine from $100,000 to $1 million.

FMS abroad. The Senate committee also included a new provision requiring the president to report to Congress 30 days in advance of authorizing the use of FMS funds for weapons procurement overseas.

The report on S 2608 said the provision was intended to offer Congress "an opportunity to review proposed offshore procurements to insure that American FMS guaranteed credits and grants are not used in such a way as to encourage the establishment of an offshore arms production capacity."

The president could waive the notice in an emergency.

Arms sales reports. The Senate committee also added a provision requiring a new annual report listing the value and quantity of military sales to every foreign nation or international organization for the past fiscal year and specifying whether they were cash, credit sales or grants and whether they were government or commercial sales.

Development Assistance

In keeping with its free enterprise philosophy, the administration had tried to shift the emphasis in U.S. development aid programs to assisting the business sectors of developing nations. The reports on HR 6370 and S 2608 signaled resistance to that approach.

The House committee's report noted that U.S. foreign aid laws stated that "a basic and central focus of development assistance . . . is to alleviate the worst manifestations of poverty among the world's poor majority."

The report said the committee wished to reaffirm a "New Directions" mandate Congress issued in the aid law in 1973 (PL 93-189), under which a "substantial amount" of development aid was to be channeled to the poor.

The committee criticized the so-called "private enterprise initiative" within the Agency for International Development (AID). The agency's move to shift funds toward private enterprise and away from anti-poverty projects "remains somewhat lacking in descriptive detail and policy guidance," the committee said in its report.

The committee also complained that AID had not explained how it would fund a new bureau that was coordinating private enterprise programs.

The Senate committee went further, providing in S 2608 that the president must use at least 50 percent of the development aid for "productive facilities, goods and services which will directly benefit those living in absolute and

relative poverty" as defined by the World Bank.

Totals. Reagan asked for an increase of $32.3 million in authorizations for development aid programs run by AID, though the administration planned to spend only $3 million more than the $1.295 billion already authorized under PL 97-113.

The new authority was requested to permit increases in AID's education account, where Reagan wanted to spend $13 million more than the $103 million authorized, and funding for private voluntary organizations and special development programs, under which he planned to spend $19.6 million more than the $147.2 million already authorized.

The House committee approved Reagan's requests but the Senate panel rejected them, noting that the administration proposed to cut the health and population accounts and saying the shift in spending had not been justified.

International organizations. Reagan's budget proposed a cut in U.S. contributions to specialized agencies of the United Nations, down to $173 million, but requested no change in the existing authorization of $218.6 million.

The House committee, opposing the administration's plan, added $21.4 million to the international organizations account, raising it to $240 million.

It also retained earmarkings in PL 97-113 providing minimum percentages of the sum appropriated to the account for each of several U.N. agencies. The Senate committee provided no increase in the authorization, but it also retained the earmarking in PL 97-113.

The earmarkings provided that the U.N. International Children's Emergency Fund (UNICEF) was to receive no less than 19.6 percent of the account or $47 million, whichever was less; the U.N. Development Fund no less than 59.5 percent or $142.8 million; the U.N. Environment Program no less than 4.4 percent or $10.6 million; the U.N. Trust Fund for South Africa no less than .159 percent or $450,000; the U.N. Institute for Training and Research, no less than .196 percent or $500,000.

PLO, SWAPO. The House committee also required that the president must withhold the portion of U.S. contributions to U.N. programs that would go to the Palestine Liberation Organization (PLO) "or entities associated with it," or for the South-West Africa People's Organization (SWAPO), a guerrilla group fighting for power in Namibia.

Peace Corps. The House committee increased by $7 million, up to $112 million, the existing authorization for Peace Corps programs despite administration plans to cut spending by that agency in fiscal 1983 down to $97.5 million. The Senate committee retained the $105 million authorization. ∎

Soviet Economic Sanctions

The House on Sept. 29 narrowly rejected a bipartisan move to force President Reagan to lift economic sanctions against the Soviet Union. A broad range of members complained that the sanctions hurt American workers and businesses more than the Soviets.

On the key vote of 206-203, the House gutted a bill (HR 6838) that would have lifted the sanctions. The weakened measure was never given formal consideration in the Senate.

The sanctions prohibited American companies, their foreign subsidiaries and foreign companies using U.S. licenses from selling to the Soviet Union equipment or technology for the transmission or refining of oil and natural gas. One goal of the sanctions was to prevent the Soviets from using U.S. technology to build a 2,600-mile natural gas pipeline from Siberia to Western Europe.

Reagan himself lifted the pipeline-related sanctions on Nov. 13, saying they had accomplished the purpose of demonstrating U.S. concern with Soviet pressure on Poland. Reagan also said the United States and its western allies had agreed to conduct a study of ways to limit future trade that bolstered the Soviet economy.

Administration critics, however, said Reagan was using the study as a justification for lifting sanctions that had proven politically unpopular in the United States and had irritated the allies.

Reagan in 1982 maintained and even expanded similar economic sanctions he had imposed directly on Poland. On Oct. 28, three weeks after the Polish government disbanded the Solidarity trade union, Reagan suspended indefinitely Poland's "most favored nation" trading status. Poland had held the trade status for 22 years; it guaranteed that tariffs on Polish imports into the United States would be no higher than those levied on the imports of any other nation.

To justify his suspension of the trading status, Reagan declared that Poland had failed since 1978 to meet its obligations under the General Agreement on Tariffs and Trade (GATT) to increase the total value of imports from other GATT member nations by at least 7 percent per year. GATT governed the general terms of trade among most nations.

Background

Reagan issued sanctions on Dec. 29, 1981, and on June 22, 1982, in response to the imposition of martial law in Poland. Reagan blamed the Soviets for the crackdown on Solidarity.

Among other things, the Dec. 29 sanctions required U.S. firms to obtain government licenses for sales to the Soviet Union of equipment or technology for the transmission or refining of oil and natural gas. The sanctions also applied to equipment and technical data for two Soviet truck plants. To put teeth into the sanctions, Reagan ordered the Commerce Department to stop processing all applications for the licenses.

Reagan complained that the natural gas pipeline would make Western Europe overly dependent on the Soviet Union for energy supplies and would provide billions of dollars in hard currency to prop up the ailing Soviet economy.

Reagan raised the international political stakes June 22 by prohibiting foreign subsidiaries of U.S. firms from selling the same equipment and technology and prohibiting overseas firms from selling the Soviets those products made under U.S. licenses.

Administration attempts to enforce the June 22 sanctions brought bitter protests from European leaders, who complained that Reagan was attempting to use American law to force non-American companies to break valid contracts. Great Britain, France and Italy ordered their firms to proceed with their Soviet contracts and West Germany encouraged its firms to do the same.

Reagan's action came only a few weeks after a Western summit meeting at Versailles, France. European leaders reportedly left that meeting with the understanding that the United States would take no further unilateral actions affecting their trade.

House Committee Action

In an unusually bold demonstration of its willingness to challenge the president on foreign policy, the House Foreign Affairs Committee approved HR 6838, to lift the sanctions, on Aug. 10.

The committee action was taken on a 22-12 vote.

Seven Republicans and 15 Democrats supported HR 6838; five Democrats and seven Republicans opposed it. The committee filed its report on the bill (H Rept 97-762) on Aug. 18.

The bill was widely viewed as symbolic because it had almost no chance of taking legal effect. Even Paul Findley, R-Ill., its sponsor, later said "I never dreamed" the bill would become law.

Had it been passed by the House in its original form, the bill would have been bottled up in the Senate Banking Committee by Chairman Jake Garn, R-Utah, who had long waged a personal crusade against the pipeline. Even if it had been passed by the Senate, the bill would have been vetoed by Reagan.

And even if the bill somehow had been enacted over a veto, Reagan would have been free to restore the sanctions under his own authority provided by the 1979 Export Administration Act (PL 96-72).

Nevertheless, backers portrayed the bill as an effort to help Reagan back away from the sanctions. They said the sanctions had irritated the NATO allies and failed either to stop construction of the pipeline or to ease repression in Poland.

"Approving this legislation should help in extricating the president from the corner in which he has painted himself," House Foreign Affairs Committee Chairman Clement J. Zablocki, D-Wis., told the House.

William S. Broomfield, R-Mich., countered that the bill was a futile gesture that would merely "undercut the president."

In the committee debate on the bill, it was evident that two political factors were in conflict: American jobs and the president's right to make foreign policy.

Findley admitted that it "has special meaning for me" because two U.S. firms affected by the sanctions had plants in his district.

Fiat-Allis Construction Machinery Co., in Springfield, had a contract to sell large bulldozers to the Soviet Union. Caterpillar Tractor Co., in Decatur, was to supply pipe-laying equipment for the Soviet pipeline.

The workers at those firms "would gladly bear any burden to bring about progress in Poland," Findley said, but they objected "to being singled out."

The administration lobbied hard against the committee action. Secretary of State George P. Shultz sent all committee members a letter the morning of the vote saying passage of the bill "would severely cripple the president's ability" to carry out foreign policy.

The letter admitted that the sanctions had hurt American firms, but it argued that "unfortunate sacrifice" was needed to continue pressure on the Soviet Union.

House Floor Action

The House essentially gutted Findley's bill Sept. 29.

By a 206-203 vote, the House inserted a clause in the bill saying the sanctions would be repealed only if Reagan certified to Congress that the Soviet Union was not using slave labor on the natural gas pipeline project. Because Reagan realistically could not make such a certification, the sanctions would remain in effect. *(Vote 354, p. 104-H)*

The House then passed the amended bill by a 209-197 vote. *(Vote 355, p. 106-H)*

The slave labor issue had emerged in the previous weeks as a major focus of the congressional debate over the Soviet sanctions. Congressional conservatives had compiled what they said was evidence that the Soviet Union was using thousands of slaves to build the pipeline. That issue was especially compelling to many in the House because the original purpose of the sanctions was to protest the Soviet pressure on Poland that resulted in the crackdown on the independent Solidarity labor union movement.

"No one wants to be for forced labor," Findley said after the vote.

Just five days before the House vote, the Senate, by 80-1, amended a Housing and Urban Development Department funding bill (HR 6956) to ask the State Department to investigate the slave labor charges. The provision was removed in conference. *(Vote 355, p. 61-S)*

The pipeline bill also fell victim to timing: During the week the bill was a hot topic in the House, Secretary of State Shultz was at the United Nations to discuss the sanctions, Poland and other issues with NATO foreign ministers and Soviet Foreign Minister Andrei A. Gromyko.

The bill was to have been considered Sept. 28 under suspension of the House rules, a procedure that would have required its approval by two-thirds of those voting. But House Speaker Thomas P. O'Neill Jr., D-Mass., pulled it at the last minute after a plea from Shultz for a delay.

The bill reached the House floor only because of the efforts of Minority Leader Robert H. Michel, R-Ill., who said he was not contacted by Shultz. Several hours after O'Neill's action, Michel maneuvered to put the bill back on the House calendar for Sept. 29.

Michel broke with Reagan on the issue because his central Illinois district was among those hardest hit by the sanctions. The sanctions overturned a contract that Caterpillar Tractor Co., based in Peoria, had to provide 200 pipe-laying machines to the Soviet Union.

"I have to say, frankly, that it is a matter of parochial interest for me," Michel told the House in opening the one-hour debate on the bill.

The sanctions issue was particularly difficult for House Republicans, many of whom had to choose between supporting their president and voting for a measure that seemed to promise the restoration of jobs for Americans.

Speaking to the House just before the key vote, O'Neill faced the Republicans and alluded to their discomfort: "This appears to be a problem between the party in power in this country at the present time, the secretary of state and the leaders in your party."

But O'Neill also undercut Democratic leaders of the Foreign Affairs Committee, who were strongly supporting the bill. Without openly taking a position on the bill, O'Neill seemed to endorse Shultz' complaint that passage of the measure would be an "embarrassment" for the administration during sensitive negotiations.

House Debate

The basic issue for House members was whether protecting American jobs was more important than supporting the president on a contentious foreign policy issue.

Michel and other supporters of HR 6838 argued that the sanctions did not have their intended effect of pressuring the Soviet Union to loosen its grip on Poland. The

victims of the sanctions, he said, were the American workers who lost their jobs.

Whatever benefit the sanctions had was not worth "the hardship and the frustration" they caused in the United States, he said.

"I represent the needs of workers in Peoria, Decatur and Springfield, but I think my position represents the needs of the workers in Poland as well," Michel added. "In Peoria, they want jobs. In Poland, they want freedom. The sanctions do not accomplish either."

Others noted that the sanctions had strained the ties between the United States and its NATO allies.

Jonathan B. Bingham, D-N.Y., said the outcry caused by Reagan's attempt to enforce the sanctions in Europe was the strongest argument for lifting the sanctions.

The allies had decided to fulfill their contracts with the Soviet Union, Bingham said, "and now we are telling them, as if they were children, that they are wrong, and we are going to try to punish their companies that hold U.S. licenses."

But Broomfield said the House should heed Shultz' plea for support, especially at "the very moment" he was discussing the issue with the allies.

"We are meddling, opposing the president, coming down on the side of Western Europe and the Soviets," Broomfield said. "All we are doing today is undercutting the president and the secretary of state in the conduct of foreign policy."

Broomfield and others did not directly address the criticism that the sanctions had failed to alter Soviet behavior in Poland.

But Edward J. Derwinski, R-Ill., said the sanctions were the only alternative to more direct confrontation. "What we're waging here is logical, economic war, instead of military war," he said.

Broomfield Amendment

With the administration's backing, Broomfield produced his amendment using the slave labor issue to effectively sidetrack the intent of the original legislation.

The amendment said the sanctions would cease to be effective 90 days following the enactment of the bill, provided that within that 90-day period the president certified to Congress "that the Soviet Union is not employing, or encouraging the use of, forced labor in the construction of any project affected by these sanctions."

Broomfield said passage of the original bill "would condone the Soviet use of slave labor" on the pipeline.

Michel protested that Broomfield and the State Department were unfairly using the slave labor issue to retain sanctions on a limited sector of trade with the Soviet Union. Slave labor "is now and always has been a part of the Soviet system."

The United States should trade with the Soviet Union "because it is in our interest, not because we favor slavery," Michel said.

On its 206-203 vote, the House sent the bill to Foreign Affairs with orders to add Broomfield's amendment. Zablocki immediately reported the amended bill, and it was passed.

The Senate never considered the legislation.

Sanctions Lifted

Reagan's Nov. 13 announcement lifting the Soviet sanctions came just three days after the death of Soviet President Leonid Brezhnev and one day after the Polish martial law government announced that it was freeing Lech Walesa, the Solidarity union leader who had been held in detention since December 1981. (Walesa was released Nov. 14.)

But Reagan insisted his action was not related to events in either country. Instead, he linked the lifting of the sanctions directly to the agreement with the allies to conduct the study on trade with the Soviet Union. As a result of the agreement, he said, "there is no further need for these sanctions and I am lifting them today."

Reagan lifted only a narrow range of sanctions that had effectively prohibited U.S. firms from selling the Soviet Union equipment for the transmission or refining of oil or natural gas.

A Commerce Department official said Nov. 13 that the sanctions affected up to $2.2 billion worth of U.S.-related business with the Soviet Union during 1982-84, mostly in equipment for the gas pipeline. That included $600 million in business by U.S. firms and up to $1.6 billion in business by foreign subsidiaries of U.S. firms and foreign firms holding U.S. product licenses.

But another Commerce official said Nov. 17 that some of that $2.2 billion probably would be recouped. He noted that several U.S.-related companies in Europe were ordered by their governments to fulfill their contracts for pipeline equipment, so that business was not lost.

Reagan's decision left in place a 1980 licensing requirement for exports to the Soviet Union of oil and gas exploration and production equipment. Administration officials said those licenses would be processed on a "case-by-case basis." The government also required licenses for exports to the Soviet Union of "high-technology" items, such as computers, that could be used for military purposes.

Also left intact were licensing requirements for exports of parts and equipment for two Soviet truck plants.

Reagan's Nov. 13 action did not affect a companion series of moves that he took during late 1981 to protest Soviet pressure on Poland. Those actions, which were to remain in effect, were: suspension of service to the United States by Aeroflot, the Soviet airline; imposition of a new series of controls on access to U.S. ports by all Soviet ships; closing of the Soviet Purchasing Commission office in New York City, and postponement of negotiations for a new U.S.-Soviet maritime agreement.

A State Department official said those sanctions were kept because they had had "a heavier short-term economic effect on the Soviet Union" than the pipeline sanctions.

Reagan levied similar sanctions against Poland, and they also remained in effect.

Agreement With Allies

Reagan said he was able to lift the sanctions because the United States and its key allies had agreed not to "engage in trade arrangements which contribute to the military or strategic advantage of the U.S.S.R. or serve to preferentially aid the heavily militarized Soviet economy." As examples of such trade, he cited "high-technology products, including those used in oil and gas production."

He also said the allies would conduct an "urgent study" of alternate sources of energy, including the question of Western dependence on Soviet energy supplies. Among the "immediate steps" he said the allies had accepted were:

• No new contracts to buy Soviet natural gas were to be signed or approved while the study was being conducted.

Administration officials said such a study probably could be completed in a matter of months, thus leaving open the possibility that European nations would sign new contracts as early as the first half of 1983.

● Each nation was to strengthen existing controls on the transfer of strategic items to the Soviet Union.

The day after Reagan's speech, the Senate Governmental Affairs Committee released a report calling for tougher U.S. government controls to prevent the Soviet Union from obtaining American technology, either legally or illegally.

● The allies were to create "without delay" procedures to monitor financial relations with the Soviet Union and "will work to harmonize our export credit policies." Reagan had criticized the European practice of providing easy credit for Soviet purchases, saying it enabled the Soviet Union to divert to defense purposes cash that otherwise would be spent overseas. ∎

Japanese Defense Spending

The Senate on Dec. 20 passed by voice vote a resolution (S Con Res 46) saying Japan should "immediately increase" its spending on defense and should "assume a significantly larger share" of the U.S. costs of defending Japan.

The resolution was one of the strongest formal expressions in recent years of congressional dissatisfaction with the Japanese defense efforts.

Carl Levin, D-Mich., was the main sponsor of an earlier version of the resolution. "An America gripped by 10.8 percent unemployment and staggering federal deficits will remain unconvinced when the Japanese government pleads that its own debt-financing situation problems prevent increased defense investments," he said in a statement.

The resolution had been approved on Dec. 14 by the Senate Foreign Relations Committee, whose members warned that Congress would take stronger steps in the future if Japan did not heed the call for increased defense spending.

"There is a wide feeling on Capitol Hill that Japan must do more," committee chairman Charles H. Percy, R-Ill., said. "It is unconscionable for Japan to stand aside" while the United States spent billions of dollars protecting Japan.

And Paul E. Tsongas, D-Mass., said he hoped the Japanese leaders "will see the moderate tone" of the resolution. If Japan did not respond by increasing its defense spending, he said "there will be other initiatives [in Congress] in the future."

Levin's original resolution had issued a specific challenge to Japan to increase its defense spending to at least 1 percent of its gross national product. The United States had spent about 6 percent of its gross national product on defense.

The new version included two key statements:

● That Japan "should immediately increase its annual defense expenditures to the levels required for its forces to deploy fully by 1990 an effective conventional self-defense capability, including the capability to carry out its policy, announced by the prime minister [former Prime Minister Zenko Suzuki] in May 1981 of defending its sea lanes of communication."

● That Japan should assume "a significantly larger share

of the total annual overall operating costs of the U.S. forces in Japan and should contribute to meeting the U.S. costs currently incurred in Japan for operations, maintenance, repair and overhaul of U.S. ships and aircraft operating in Japan's security interests in the Pacific Ocean region."

In his statement, Levin said achieving those goals would require Japan to spend an average of 1.5 to 2 percent of its gross national product on defense each year through the rest of the 1980s.

The House did not take up the measure before adjourning. ∎

BIB Supplemental Funds

A dispute over the salary to be paid to the new head of Radio Free Europe and Radio Liberty helped sidetrack routine legislation (HR 7367, S 3052) making a $13.3 million supplemental fiscal 1983 authorization for the Board for International Broadcasting (BIB), which supervised the stations.

The request itself was non-controversial, but Sen. Edward Zorinsky, D-Neb., used it to launch an attack on the board's recent decision to pay about $200,000 in salary and benefits to its new president, former Sen. James L. Buckley, R-N.Y. (1971-77).

Zorinsky delayed Senate Foreign Relations Committee action on the Senate bill long enough to kill its chances of passage in the lame-duck session.

Zorinsky said Buckley's contract with the broadcasting board called for him to receive a $95,000 salary. Zorinsky estimated that other benefits, such as housing and entertainment allowances, a deferred annuity and household help, would add another $111,000. Buckley's predecessor, Glenn W. Ferguson, was paid $58,000 with fewer side benefits.

"People who are without jobs just can't understand these types of salaries," Zorinsky said.

When the committee took up the BIB bill Dec. 14, he offered an amendment to limit Buckley's salary to the maximum paid to a Foreign Service Officer (about $60,000). The amendment was defeated, 3-5, after board member Ben Wattenberg defended the salary as "comparable to the private sector" and told the committee that Buckley had been hired "to elevate the status" of the radio stations. The committee then approved the bill by voice vote.

The House Foreign Affairs Committee approved its version of the bill the same day. However, neither chamber considered the legislation before the end of the lame duck session. ∎

Aid to Afghan Rebels

The Senate Foreign Relations Committee on Dec. 14 approved a resolution (S Con Res 126) asking the president to aid the rebels who were fighting the Soviet occupation of Afghanistan.

Committee action on the resolution, which was introduced Sept. 30 with 99 Senate sponsors, had been delayed by the 100th senator, Charles McC. Mathias Jr., R-Md., who objected that it might give the Afghan rebels false hope that the United States would enter the protracted war

on their side.

The full Senate did not take up the measure.

The Soviet Union invaded Afghanistan in December 1979; Moslem rebels resisted the occupation by some 100,000 Soviet troops and in late 1982 were reported to control much of the countryside.

Reagan administration officials had refused to confirm or deny reports that the United States had secretly supplied weapons to the rebels, either directly or indirectly through such intermediaries as Egypt.

The resolution's chief sponsor, Paul E. Tsongas, D-Mass., said that if the United States was providing aid, "it is not enough to tip the military scale in the Afghans' favor."

After expressing U.S. encouragement for the rebels, the resolution stated that it should be U.S. policy "to provide the people of Afghanistan, if they so request, with material assistance, as the U.S. considers appropriate, to help them fight effectively for their freedom."

When the Senate committee first considered the issue Dec. 7, Mathias expressed concern that the resolution "may mislead the Afghan people" about the prospect for U.S. aid.

"I don't take this to be an authorization" for such aid, he said, "but the people of Afghanistan might."

When Committee Chairman Charles H. Percy, R-Ill., said the resolution merely expressed congressional sentiment, while leaving an actual decision to the executive branch, Mathias responded: "That is an Indian-giver approach."

A more straightforward approach, Mathias said, would be to authorize a regular military aid program for the Afghanistan rebels. But if the Congress instead wanted the United States to provide covert assistance, he said, "I don't think that's an appropriate subject for a congressional resolution."

Because of Mathias' objections, the committee delayed action on the resolution until its Dec. 14 general business meeting, after Mathias had dropped his active opposition. But Percy said that even though the resolution seemed to promise aid, "we are not by this policy statement making any specific authorization."

The resolution, Percy said, "will be received extremely well by the people of Afghanistan. They will know we have acted."

Tsongas said that "all of the people we have spoken to in the Afghanistan freedom fighters' groups understand what the resolution means." ∎

Reagan Sends Aid, Troops to Lebanon

With Congress watching warily from the sidelines, the Reagan administration in 1982 reacted vigorously to a bewildering series of events in Lebanon following an Israeli invasion of that troubled country. First, the United States shipped millions of dollars in emergency relief aid; then President Reagan dispatched Special Envoy Philip C. Habib to the Middle East for a series of negotiations on the withdrawal of all foreign forces from Lebanon; Reagan twice sent U.S. Marines to join a multinational peacekeeping force in Lebanon; and finally, the United States began a major campaign to train and arm the Lebanese army.

Israel invaded southern Lebanon on June 6, with the stated purpose of creating a 25-mile-wide buffer zone free of Palestinian guerrilla forces. But the Israelis rolled past the 25-mile boundary and by July had surrounded West Beirut, where thousands of Palestine Liberation Organization (PLO) guerrilla fighters were headquartered.

In late August, following negotiations led by Habib, the Palestinians were evacuated and transferred to other Moslem nations. The evacuation was supervised by a three-nation peacekeeping force, including 800 U.S Marines.

But the tragedy of Lebanon was not ended by the departure of the Palestinians. The Lebanese parliament elected a new president, Christian Phalangist leader Bashir Gemayel, on Aug. 23; on Sept. 14, before he could take office, Gemayel was killed in a bomb explosion. Apparently in retaliation, right-wing Christian militiamen on Sept. 16 entered two Palestinian refugee camps and over two days slaughtered at least 300 civilians.

Amin Gemayel, the older, more moderate brother of Bashir Gemayel, was installed as president on Sept. 23. But the authority of his government was effectively limited to Beirut, with thousands of Israeli, Syrian and Palestinian troops dominating the rest of the country. Fighting between armed Christian and Moslem factions continued throughout 1982, resulting in hundreds of deaths.

The events in Lebanon created unprecedented strains in relations between the United States and Israel. The Reagan administration repeatedly condemned the invasion of Lebanon and called for Israel to withdraw its forces.

The strain was especially evident in late June, when Israeli Prime Minister Menachem Begin visited Washington. As Israeli warplanes and gunboats shelled Beirut, Begin appealed both to Reagan and to congressional leaders for support for his policies in Lebanon.

Begin encountered unusually harsh questioning and anger on Capitol Hill — the very center of Israel's political backing in the United States. While insisting that their concern for Israel's security remained undiminished, a wide range of House and Senate members warned Begin that he could no longer count on unswerving support for his military policies.

Several congressional leaders complained to Begin that Israel had used excessive force in Lebanon. Especially irritating to many members was Israel's reported use of U.S.-supplied cluster bombs (which spew dozens of small bombs) on civilian areas.

"They went far beyond where they had to go, and the extent of their attacks on civilian areas [was] excessive," said Lee H. Hamilton, chairman of the Middle East Subcommittee of the House Foreign Affairs Committee.

Nevertheless, a hard core of members — along with key American Jewish leaders — staunchly supported Begin and his policies in Lebanon.

Reagan took two symbolic actions to protest Israel's use of U.S.-supplied weapons in the invasion:

● In June Reagan held up formal notification to Congress of an already-agreed-upon sale to Israel of 75 F-16 warplanes. Reagan had informally notified Congress of the sale in late May, but following the invasion he said he would decide at a later date when to allow the sale to go forward. Notice of the sale still had not been submitted to Congress by the end of 1982.

● Reagan reported to Congress on July 19 that Israel

"may have" violated a 1952 agreement with the United States when it used the cluster bombs in Lebanon. Under the agreement, which was backed by U.S. law, Israel was prohibited from using U.S.-supplied weapons for other than defensive purposes. The administration on July 26 suspended shipments to Israel of 155 mm artillery shells that could have the same effect as cluster bombs. Shipments of those items were still being delayed as of the end of 1982.

Reagan said in November, however, that he would not use the threat of withholding U.S. financial aid as a tool to force changes in Israel's policies. "I don't think to start talking about whether I should or should not make threats of some kind or other is going to be fruitful at all," he said at a Nov. 11 news conference.

The long-term impact in the United States of Israel's actions in Lebanon was less clear than the immediate effect of weapons sanctions. In December, supporters of Israel were able to guide through Congress substantial increases in aid for Israel. They did so in spite of administration objections that an aid boost would be seen in Israel and elsewhere in the Middle East as U.S. approval for Begin's policies, thus angering Arab leaders and jeopardizing peace negotiations then underway. *(Foreign aid appropriations, p. 242)*

U.S. Troops in Lebanon

Reagan in 1982 twice sent armed U.S. Marines to serve as peacekeeping forces in Lebanon. The first deployment was in August, to help oversee the eviction of several thousand Palestinian guerrillas from Beirut; the second deployment began in late September with the goal of stabilizing the situation so that Israel, Syria and the PLO would have enough confidence to withdraw their occupying forces from Lebanon.

In Washington, the deployment of the Marines to Lebanon resulted in a low-key dispute between the president and Congress. The immediate cause of the dispute was Reagan's refusal to invoke the 1973 War Powers Resolution (PL 93-148) in such a way to give Congress a role in reviewing the Marine deployment. Although there were widespread complaints that Reagan had skirted the War Powers Resolution, no member of Congress moved to force Reagan to bring the troops home.

Over the longer term, some congressional leaders feared that the president was making an extensive security commitment to another nation without direct involvement by Congress. At the end of 1982, the Senate Foreign Relations Committee wrote Reagan demanding that he seek congressional approval before embarking on a long-range commitment to bolster the government of Lebanon.

The technical issue in the dispute between Reagan and congressional leaders concerned which section of the War Powers Resolution described the circumstances under which U.S. forces were sent to Lebanon. The answer was important, for had Reagan cited the first of three sections in PL 93-148, the law required him to pull the Marines out within 90 days at most unless Congress extended their stay. Reagan took a simple way out — one taken on two occasions by Ford and once by Carter. He cited no section at all in his report to Congress.

Under PL 93-148, the president was to report to Congress within 48 hours after he introduced U.S. forces:

● "into hostilities or into situations where imminent involvement in hostilities is clearly indicated by the circum-

stances"; or

● "into the territory, airspace or waters of a foreign nation, while equipped for combat, except for deployments which relate solely to supply, replacement, repair or training of such forces"; or

● "in numbers which substantially enlarge United States Armed Forces equipped for combat already located in a foreign nation."

When the use of U.S. troops in Beirut was first discussed in July, administration officials let it be known that, when the time came, they planned to cite the second circumstance, known as the "equipped for combat" section.

But Clement J. Zablocki, D-Wis., chairman of the House Foreign Affairs Committee, complained that an "equipped for combat" report would not accurately describe the circumstances in Beirut and would rob Congress of its rightful role in determining how long the troops stayed. Zablocki argued in a July 6 letter to Reagan that the only proper report would be one under the first section. Senate Foreign Relations Committee Chairman Charles H. Percy, R-Ill., and ranking Democrat Claiborne Pell, R.I.,

U.S. Aid to Lebanon

The United States provided $112 million in emergency-related aid to Lebanon following the June 6, 1982 Israeli invasion. Of that amount, $82 million was made available in fiscal 1982; the remaining $30 million was not made available until after the start of fiscal 1983.

The emergency aid included:

● $2.3 million under the International Disaster Assistance Program.

● $3 million in grants under the PL 480 Food for Peace program.

● $24.5 million under the State Department's regular migration and refugee assistance program.

● $2 million under the State Department's "emergency" migration and refugee fund.

● $50 million appropriated for the migration and refugee program in the fiscal 1982 supplemental appropriations bill (HR 6863 — PL 97-257). The money was authorized in a special bill cleared June 24 (HR 6631 — PL 97-208).

● $30 million in guaranteed loans for housing construction, to be made available starting in fiscal 1983.

In addition, Lebanon in fiscal 1982 received $6 million in previously-planned aid under the Economic Support Fund.

The United States in late 1982 also mounted a major campaign to bolster the Lebanese armed forces, but the actual spending of U.S. military aid dollars was not expected to jump significantly until 1983 and later.

In fiscal 1982, the United States provided $10 million in guaranteed loans to help Lebanon buy U.S. weapons and $575,000 in grants to train Lebanese military officers. Those figures were expected to be substantially higher for fiscal 1983.

In December, Congress approved a $32 million sale to Lebanon of 34 M48-A5 tanks and ammunition — the largest single arms sale to Lebanon in recent years. Lebanon was to pay cash.

made a similar appeal in an Aug. 20 letter to Reagan.

An informed State Department official said debate on the issue within the administration had produced three reasons for not citing any specific section of the act when the Marines were first sent to Lebanon in August.

First, the official noted, the administration planned to withdraw the Marines within 30 days in any event, which would make the War Powers Resolution time limits moot. In his letter, Reagan alluded to this, saying he was sending the Marines "on a limited and temporary basis."

Secondly, the State Department official said, a major part of the settlement arranged by Habib was a series of "assurances" from all parties concerned — Israel, the PLO, Lebanese Christian and Moslem factions and Syria — that the U.S. forces would be in no danger of hostilities.

"There's no point reporting under a paragraph which would indicate that, in a sense, all the assurances that had been received weren't worth very much," the official said, "because if in fact the situation turned out to be the other way, you could always re-report."

Reagan's letter in August said: "I want to emphasize that there is no intention or expectation that U.S. Armed Forces will become involved in hostilities. "Our agreement with the government of Lebanon expressly rules out any combat responsibilities for the U.S. forces."

Reagan gave similar assurances in his September report.

Thirdly, the official said, "Zablocki made clear what his preference was, and his preference was that we not report under the 'equipped for combat' provision." Since the administration was unwilling to report under the first, or "hostilities" provision, the official said, to cite no provision "seemed the eminently sensible thing."

August Deployment

President Reagan Aug. 24 formally notified Congress that 800 U.S. Marines were being sent to Lebanon to help oversee the negotiated eviction of thousands of Palestinian guerrillas.

In reporting to Congress on the Marines' dispatch, Reagan bowed to a pledge he had made when he first offered July 6 to use U.S. troops as part of a Beirut settlement. He said then he would comply with the War Powers Resolution.

Armed with light weapons, the Marines landed in Beirut at dawn Aug. 25. They joined 800 French Legionnaires and 400 Italian soldiers in safeguarding the withdrawal from Beirut of PLO guerrillas under a settlement negotiated by Habib. About 14,000 PLO fighters, who had been held under Israeli siege since June, were evacuated between Aug. 21 and Sept. 1.

The Marines remained until Sept. 10. They left without having fired a shot.

Following precedents established in War Powers Resolution reports submitted by President Ford and one submitted by President Carter, Reagan's report did not admit the constitutionality of PL 93-148.

Reagan's report was submitted in identical letters to House Speaker Thomas P. O'Neill Jr., D-Mass., and Strom Thurmond, R-S.C., president pro tempore of the Senate, as required of reports under PL 93-148.

But the letters said Reagan was reporting on the use of the Marines only "in accordance with my desire that the Congress be fully informed on this matter" and "consistent with" — not pursuant to — PL 93-148.

Implicit was the notion that, rather than "complying"

with the War Powers Resolution, the president merely was submitting a report that met the act's terms, performing more of a courtesy to Congress than an obligation.

The letter said: "This deployment of the United States Armed Forces to Lebanon is being undertaken pursuant to the President's constitutional authority with respect to the conduct of foreign relations and as Commander-in-Chief of the United States Armed Forces."

September Deployment

At the request of the Lebanese government, about 1,200 Marines entered Beirut Sept. 29-30 and took up positions around the airport south of the capital. Earlier on Sept. 29, at U.S. insistence, Israel removed the last of its forces from predominantly Moslem West Beirut, which had been under Israeli control since Sept. 16.

The Marines joined about 2,200 French and Italian troops in reconstituting the multinational peacekeeping force.

The renewed force was made necessary by the sudden deterioration of the situation in Lebanon in mid-September following the assassination of Bashir Gemayel and the massacre in the Palestinian refugee camps.

One Marine was killed Sept. 30 and three others were wounded when a bomb they were trying to defuse exploded. Even before that incident, a senior House Foreign Affairs Committee aide said many members were "apprehensive and uneasy" and were waiting to see what happened to the Marines. "If a few Marines come back in bags, the concern will be a lot greater," he said.

In a Sept. 29 letter notifying Congress of the Marine deployment, Reagan said "isolated acts of violence can never be ruled out." But he gave assurances that "all appropriate precautions have been taken to ensure the safety" of the Marines.

Reagan again skirted the issue of Congress' role in deciding how long the troops would stay. Reagan did not cite any section of the act as authority for his deployment of the troops. Instead, he merely referred to the act as a whole. Reagan said there was "no intention or expectation that U.S. armed forces will become involved in hostilities" in Lebanon.

Percy and Pell had written to Reagan Sept. 22 urging him to cite the War Powers section that would trigger a congressional role. They said "the bitterness and volatility of the situation in Beirut seem only to have increased in the past few weeks...."

On Sept. 30, Percy insisted that Reagan would have to consult with Congress in order to keep the troops in Lebanon past the 90 days. "The clock began to run when the first Marines landed in Lebanon," Percy said. But he did not move to force withdrawal of the Marines once the 90 days were up.

Reagan and his aides were careful not to set a specific timetable for withdrawing the troops. In a news conference Sept. 28, Reagan seemed to set two criteria for pulling out the Marines: One was the removal of all Israeli, Syrian and Palestinian military forces from Lebanon; the other was a determination by Lebanon's leaders "that they have the situation well in hand."

Attempting to amplify those remarks the next day before the House Middle East Subcommittee, Nicholas A. Veliotes, assistant secretary of state for Near Eastern affairs, ran into a storm of questions from members who wanted to know the conditions for removing the Marines.

When Chairman Hamilton characterized the Marine

deployment as "open-ended," Veliotes objected. "This is not an open-ended deployment," he said. "Our troops will be there for a limited period of time."

Veliotes seconded Reagan's statement that the Marines would remain until all other foreign forces had withdrawn, but he said "a mix of factors" could result in the Marines leaving sooner or even remaining longer.

Asked by Hamilton if the Marines would be out of Lebanon by the end of 1982, Veliotes said: "That, certainly, in my view, would be an outer limit."

Hamilton and some other subcommittee members also wanted to know why the administration had not been more vocal in demanding investigations by Lebanon and Israel into the massacre in the Palestinian refugee camps.

The Israeli Cabinet Sept. 28 authorized a full investigation into possible complicity in the massacre by Israeli authorities. The camps were under Israeli control at the time of the slaughter. Begin's initial refusal to allow such an inquiry prompted mass protests in Israel and condemnation worldwide.

Rep. Olympia J. Snowe, R-Maine, said the United States had "guaranteed the safety" of Palestinian civilians under the August agreement for the withdrawal of Palestinian fighters from Beirut. "I think our credibility has been undermined considerably" because of the massacre and Israel's occupation of West Beirut, she said.

Veliotes deplored the incident and said the United States had asked questions about it. But he added: "I'm not sure the massacre is the best place to spend our time and effort."

Foreign Relations Letter

Lebanon on Nov. 29 officially asked the United States, France and Italy to double the number of troops in the

---

President Reagan's Mideast Peace Plan

Hours after the last Palestine Liberation Organization (PLO) guerrillas were evacuated from an Israeli siege of Beirut Sept. 1, Reagan went on national television and set out U.S. proposals for a resolution of the Palestinian issue that were viewed as dramatically specific. *Text, p. 26-E)*

Reagan said the United States would support self-government for Palestinians on the West Bank of the Jordan River and in the Gaza strip in association with Jordan — not in an independent state nor under Israeli sovereignty.

He also called upon Israel to "freeze" further Jewish settlement in the West Bank and Gaza, which Israel had held since the 1967 Arab-Israeli war, as a prelude to resuming negotiations under the 1978 Camp David accords.

The president pledged U.S. fealty to the Camp David plan for an interim agreement to provide self-government for the Palestinians in the West Bank and Gaza for five years while the ultimate status of the territories was negotiated by Israel, Egypt, the United States and Jordan.

But Reagan departed from previous U.S. policy by saying in advance — and strongly — what the United States viewed as the most promising outcome of the negotiations on permanent arrangements for the territories.

"The final status of these lands must, of course, be reached through the give and take of negotiations," Reagan said. "But it is the firm view of the United States that self-government by the Palestinians of the West Bank and Gaza in association with Jordan offers the best chance for a durable, just and lasting peace."

Reagan said the U.S. position was based on the principle "that the Arab-Israeli conflict should be resolved through negotiations involving an exchange of territory for peace" as set out in United Nations Security Council Resolution 242 of 1967. He said the resolution's call for Israel to withdraw from "territories occupied in the recent conflict" clearly applied to the West Bank and Gaza.

The president took pains to reaffirm the U.S. commitment to Israel, and he urged that Israel's enemies recognize Israel's right to exist.

"America's commitment to the security of Israel is ironclad. And, I might add, so is mine," he said. Reagan pledged that the United States would "oppose any proposal — from any party and at any point in the negotiating process — that threatens the security of Israel."

"Finally," Reagan said, "we remain convinced that Jerusalem must remain undivided, but its final status should be decided through negotiations."

Reagan's initiative departed little from various other statements of U.S. views on Palestinian autonomy and related issues, but it was significant for staking out U.S. views firmly and putting forth concrete proposals.

In doing so, Reagan departed from a circumspect posture his administration previously had held on the Palestinian autonomy issue — a posture that had prompted domestic and foreign criticism for more than a year.

Alluding to such criticism, Reagan acknowledged that: "The United States has thus far sought to play the role of mediator; we have avoided public comment on the key issues." But he said Israel's military victory over the PLO in Lebanon had made the time ripe for a "new realism" in the Middle East.

Reagan had transmitted his proposals to Israel in an Aug. 31 letter to Begin.

On Sept. 2, only hours after Reagan spoke, Israeli Prime Minister Menachem Begin's Cabinet unanimously endorsed a statement repudiating the U.S. plan as inconsistent with the Camp David accords and a threat to Israel's security.

The Cabinet statement said the "government of Israel has resolved that, on the basis of these positions, it will not enter into any negotiations with any party." It said Israel instead was "ready to renew" negotiations on Palestinian autonomy in the West Bank and Gaza "in total conformity with the Camp David accords."

By the end of 1982, the United States was centering its efforts on convincing Jordan's King Hussein to enter peace talks with Israel, as a first step toward a broader series of negotiations to expand upon the Camp David accords.

---

peacekeeping force. Deputy Secretary of State Kenneth W. Dam told the Foreign Relations Committee on Dec. 1 that the United States would not agree to send more troops until there was "some progress" in negotiations to withdraw all foreign troops from Lebanon.

Fourteen members of the Foreign Relations Committee on Dec. 15 signed and sent to Reagan a letter insisting that he seek congressional approval before agreeing to send more Marines to Lebanon or to expand the Marines' role in the peacekeeping force.

Committee members said they understood the difficulties the United States faced in reaching agreement on how to expand the peacekeeping force, in conjunction with negotiations on the withdrawal from Lebanon of the foreign occupying forces.

"However," they added, "we would expect Congress to be involved at the earliest possible stage in the development [of proposals to expand the peacekeeping force] and that formal congressional authorization would be sought before undertaking long-term commitments or extending indefinitely the present level of operations."

In describing the letter to the Senate on Dec. 18, Percy said the indefinite presence of U.S. troops in Lebanon "would amount to a major security commitment to that country by the United States, whether or not there is a prospect of actual or imminent hostilities." Since Congress in recent years had demanded a voice in approving such commitments, he said: "I do not think it would be appropriate on constitutional grounds, or wise on political grounds," to keep the troops in Lebanon indefinitely without congressional approval.

The letter also raised the issue of whether the War Powers Resolution should be amended to "clarify the respective roles" of Congress and the president in peacekeeping operations. Committee member Charles McC. Mathias, R-Md., had noted that the resolution made no provision for assigning U.S. troops to peacekeeping roles.

The only committee members who did not sign the letter were Howard H. Baker Jr., R-Tenn.,. who rarely participated in committee actions because of his duties as Senate Majority Leader; Jesse Helms, R-N.C., and Alan Cranston, D-Calif. An aide said Cranston did not sign the letter because it did not make a strong enough demand for a congressional role in the troop deployments.   ∎

U.N. Warned on Israel

Both houses of Congress adopted resolutions warning the United Nations General Assembly against any attempt to expel Israel.

The Senate acted first, on April 14 adopting S Con Res 48. The resolution stated the sense of Congress that if the United Nations General Assembly "illegally" expelled or suspended Israel from either the General Assembly or specialized U.N. agencies, the United States should withhold its assessed contribution to the United Nations or suspend its own participation in the General Assembly or agency in question.

The resolution was a reaction to a Feb. 5 resolution adopted by the U.N. General Assembly, which declared that Israel "is not a peace-loving state." Daniel Patrick Moynihan, D-N.Y., sponsored the Senate resolution, which was adopted by voice vote.

S Con Res 48 noted that a nation could be expelled from the General Assembly, or any U.N. agency, only upon the recommendation of the U.N. Security Council. The United States — Israel's closest ally — had a veto in the Security Council.

The House on May 12 adopted an identical resolution (H Con Res 322) by a 401-3 vote. *(Vote 66, p. 20-H)*

In September the United States suspended its participation in the International Atomic Energy Agency (IAEA) after that U.N.-related body voted to deny Israel's credentials. A similar move in October to expel Israel from the International Telecommunications Union was averted.

The U.N. General Assembly on Oct. 27 rejected an attempt by Iran to expel Israel. The vote on a procedural move to halt debate on Iran's motion was 75 to 9, with 31 abstentions. Earlier, 49 countries, including Iran, had signed a letter criticizing Israel's U.N. membership on the grounds that it was not "a peace-loving state."   ∎

Fiscal 1983
Status of Appropriations
97th Congress, Second Session

Appropriation Bills	House	Senate	Final	Almanac Page
Agriculture and related agencies (HR 7072)	Passed 9/21	Passed 9/28	Signed 12/18 PL 97-370	255
Defense (HR 7355, S 2951)	Passed 12/8	Committee reported 9/23	Funding included in PL 97-276 and PL 97-377	277
District of Columbia (HR 7144)	Passed 9/30	Passed 12/7	Signed 12/22 PL 97-378	266
Energy and Water Development (HR 7145, S 3079)	Committee reported 9/21	Committee reported 12/6	Funding included in PL 97-276 and PL 97-377	292
Foreign Aid (S 3075)		Committee reported 12/3	Funding included in PL 97-276 and PL 97-377	242
Housing and Urban Development, Veterans, NASA (HR 6956)	Passed 9/15	Passed 9/24	Signed 9/30 PL 97-272	231
Interior and related agencies (HR 7356)	Passed 12/3	Passsed 12/14	Congress cleared 12/19	262
Labor, Health and Human Services, Education (HR 7205)	Passed 12/1	Committee reported 12/8	Funding included in PL 97-276 and PL 97-377	250
Legislative Branch (HR 7073, S 2939)	Committee reported 9/9	Committee reported 9/22	Full-year funding included in PL 97-276	236
Military Construction (HR 6968)	Passed 8/19	Passed 9/27	Signed 10/15 PL 97-323	212
State, Justice, Commerce, Judiciary (HR 6957, S 2956)	Passed 12/9	Committee reported 9/24	Funding included in PL 97-276 and PL 97-377	246
Transportation and related agencies (HR 7019)	Passed 9/21	Passed 12/2	Signed 12/18 PL 97-369	267
Treasury, Postal Service, General Government (HR 7158, S 2916)	Passed 11/30	Committee reported 9/16	Funding included in PL 97-276 and PL 97-377	273
First Continuing Resolution (H J Res 599) Expired Dec. 17, 1982	Passed 9/22	Passed 9/29	Signed 10/2 PL 97-276	225
Second Continuing Resolution (H J Res 631) Expires Sept. 30, 1983	Passed 12/14	Passed 12/19	Signed 12/21 PL 97-377	238

Budget and Appropriations

In 1982, Congress wrestled back power from the executive branch and played the major role in setting budget priorities.

Unlike 1981, when the Reagan administration set the boundaries of the budget debate, it was Congress that led and the administration that followed in formulating the fiscal 1983 budget.

The difference — in a word — was deficits. In his first budget submission in 1981, President Reagan promised a balanced budget by fiscal 1984. But by 1982, those rosy economic forecasts had turned sour with the deepening of the recession. And the deficit projections soared.

With the 1982 elections at hand, Congress unequivocally rejected the $91.5 billion deficit proposed by Reagan in his fiscal 1983 budget. But it took months to come up with an alternative budget strategy.

In the end, Congress did no better than Reagan in holding down the deficit. Nonetheless, it succeeded in setting priorities in its own way. Reagan agreed to accept some modest cuts in the defense buildup he wanted. More significantly, the president abandoned his insistence that taxes were only for cutting, and allowed himself to be convinced that raising $98.3 billion in new taxes over the next three years was an essential ingredient for economic recovery.

Budget Resolution

The compromise budget plan was incorporated in the first fiscal 1983 budget resolution. Congress approved the resolution June 23, nearly six weeks after the statutory May 15 deadline. It had taken five frustrating months — and House rejection of a series of alternative budgets — to win approval of the measure, which forecast a $103.9 billion fiscal 1983 deficit.

To hold the deficit to that level, the resolution included reconciliation instructions that required authorizing committees to come up with $20.9 billion in increased revenues and $6.57 billion in fiscal 1983 spending cuts.

The measure, which did not require the president's signature, also included language that would automatically convert the budget targets it set into binding fiscal 1983 spending ceilings if a second budget resolution was not approved by Oct. 1, the beginning of the new fiscal year.

The economic upturn projected for the second quarter of 1982 never materialized. And by Oct. 1, with unemployment at a post-World War II high and recovery not yet in sight, the budget outlook had grown significantly worse.

Under the combined pressures of the sagging economy and the impending midterm elections, Congress not surprisingly decided to avoid another round of difficult budget votes. Thus the first budget resolution became binding, even though its budget projections were generally regarded as unreasonably optimistic.

By the time the 97th Congress closed up shop in December, officials were talking about a fiscal 1983 deficit approaching $200 billion, nearly double the level projected in the budget resolution approved six months earlier.

Reconciliation

That sharp increase occurred even though Congress carried out the deficit reduction measures required by S Con Res 92 in two reconciliation bills cleared in mid-August. The bills were expected to raise $98.3 billion in additional revenues and reduce anticipated spending by $30.8 billion over fiscal 1983-85.

When combined, the measures were expected to reduce the federal deficit by about $130 billion by fiscal 1985. The budget resolution had called for $125.5 billion in deficit reductions over the three-year period.

Appropriations Tangle

Because the budget struggle consumed so much time, the appropriations process lagged far behind schedule. When fiscal 1983 began Oct. 1, only two of the 13 regular annual appropriations bills had been signed into law.

Two omnibus continuing appropriations measures were needed to keep the government running.

The first stopgap funding measure provided money only through Dec. 17.

The second provided $389 billion in full-year funding for agencies covered by the six regular appropriations bills that did not clear before adjournment — including the giant Defense and Labor-Health and Human Services-Education measures. Congress completed action on the measure Dec. 20, after Senate-House conferees bowed to Reagan's veto threats by dropping money for emergency jobs programs that both chambers had included in the bill. Reagan signed the measure Dec. 21, four days after much of the government had technically run out of funds.

Since the second continuing resolution was to run through the end of the fiscal year, lawmakers started the 98th Congress in 1983 with a clean appropriations slate for the first time since 1980.

Supplemental Vetoes

In addition to the protracted fight over the budget, the fiscal 1983 appropriations cycle was held up by two long battles over supplemental funding bills for fiscal 1982.

Congress handed Reagan his first big budget defeat Sept. 10 when it overrode his veto of a $14.2 billion supplemental bill. The president wanted more for defense and less for social programs than the bill provided, but his attempts to portray the bill as a "budget-buster" backfired as Congress insisted on its right to help set spending priorities.

Earlier in the year, Congress spent 16 weeks fashioning an "urgent" supplemental that the president would sign. Reagan vetoed two earlier versions because of money added for an emergency housing bailout. The House failed to override the vetoes.

—By Dale Tate

Budget Totals Compared, Fiscal 1977-83

(in billions of dollars)

	Budget Authority	Outlays*	Revenues*	Deficit*
Fiscal Year 1977				
Ford Budget	$433.4	$394.2	$351.3	$ — 43.0
First Resolution	454.2	413.3	362.5	— 50.8
Second Resolution	451.55	413.1	362.5	— 50.6
Third Resolution	472.9	417.45	347.7	— 69.75
Third Resolution amended	470.2	409.2	356.6	— 52.6
Actual	464.4	402.7	357.8	— 44.9
Fiscal Year 1978				
Ford Budget	480.4	440.0	393.0	— 47.0
Carter Revisions	507.3	459.4	401.6	— 57.7
First Resolution	503.45	460.95	396.3	— 64.65
Second Resolution	500.1	458.25	397.0	— 61.25
Actual	500.4	450.8	402.0	— 48.8
Fiscal Year 1979				
Carter Budget	568.2	500.2	439.6	— 60.6
First Resolution	568.85	498.8	447.9	— 50.9
Second Resolution	555.65	487.5	448.7	— 38.8
Revised Second Resolution	559.2	494.45	461.0	— 33.45
Actual	556.7	493.6	465.9	— 27.7
Fiscal Year 1980				
Carter Budget	615.5	531.6	502.6	— 29.0
First Resolution	604.4	532.0	509.0	— 23.0
Second Resolution	638.0	547.6	517.8	— 29.8
Revised Second Resolution	658.9	572.65	525.7	— 46.95
Actual	658.8	579.6	520.0	— 59.6
Fiscal Year 1981				
Carter Budget	696.1	615.8	600.0	— 15.8
Carter Revisions	691.3	611.5	628.0	+ 16.5
First Resolution	697.2	613.6	613.8	+ 0.2
Second Resolution	694.6	632.4	605.0	— 27.4
Revised Second Resolution	717.5	661.35	603.3	— 58.05
Actual	718.4	657.2	599.3	— 57.9
Fiscal Year 1982				
Carter Budget	809.8	739.3	711.8	— 27.5
Reagan Revision	772.4	695.3	650.3	— 45.0
First Resolution[1]	770.9	695.45	657.8	— 37.65
Revised Second Resolution	777.67	734.10	628.4	— 105.7
Actual	779.9	728.4	617.8	— 110.6
Fiscal Year 1983				
Reagan Budget	801.9	757.6	666.1	— 91.5
First Resolution[2]	822.39	769.82	665.9	— 103.92
Reagan Revision[3]	847.4	805.2	597.5	207.7

[1] *Second resolution merely reaffirmed figures in first resolution.*
[2] *First resolution became binding Oct. 1, 1982.*
[3] *Included in administration's fiscal 1984 budget.*

 Reagan Budget

Reagan Budgets 1983 Deficit of $91.5 Billion

Asking Congress to "persevere, to stay the course, to shun defeat," President Reagan proposed a fiscal 1983 budget showing unprecedented deficits — $91.5 billion for that year and $98.6 billion for 1982 — even with major new cuts in domestic programs.

"The first year of the 97th Congress will be remembered for its decisive action to hold down spending and cut tax rates," Reagan said in a message formally delivered Feb. 8. "Clearly there is a great deal more to be done." *(Text, p. 6-E)*

Despite the advice of a number of his own aides for prescriptions that might have reduced the deficit substantially, Reagan did not propose any major new tax increases. Nor did he take the scalpel to the $221 billion proposed fiscal 1983 defense budget.

Supporting this position in his budget message to Congress, the president said, ". . . our incentive-minded tax policy and our security-based defense programs are right and necessary for long-run peace and prosperity, and must not be tampered with in a vain attempt to cure deficits in the short run."

Instead, to curb the size of the deficit the administration proposed a $55.9 billion "Deficit Reduction Plan" that would cut domestic spending — both entitlements and discretionary programs — impose user fees, revise some tax benefits and undertake so-called "management initiatives."

Even if this plan were adopted in toto the deficit would still hit $91.5 billion — a relatively slight dip from the record-setting $98.6 billion deficit the Office of Management and Budget (OMB) predicted for fiscal 1982. According to White House estimates, total outlays for fiscal 1983 would reach $757.6 billion; budget authority, $801.9 billion; and receipts, $666.1 billion.

The administration's forecast for future deficits was not much more heartening. The prospect of a balanced budget — a campaign theme of both the president and many of his Republican colleagues — drifted into the mists of fiscal 1988 and beyond. The White House estimate for the fis-

cal 1984 deficit was $82.9 billion, and for fiscal 1985, $71.9 billion.

Unlike the warm reception given Reagan's plan to trim the budget in 1981 — a plan that had projected a budget surplus in fiscal 1984 — the reaction to the "Deficit Reduction Plan" on Capitol Hill was skeptical. But OMB Director David A. Stockman predicted that when Congress looked at the "hard, stark choices . . . they will understand very quickly that unless measures of magnitude that we've proposed by way of savings are adopted, that there could well be a severe threat to the economic recovery."

Economic Outlook

The administration continued to defend the economic policy course it originally charted and predicted that economic growth would "snap back" after the middle of the year.

Murray L. Weidenbaum, chairman of the Council of Economic Advisers, said Feb. 6 that the administration was "projecting that the current recession will be over by midyear and will be followed by sustained economic growth and reduced inflation." Weidenbaum contended that this upbeat outlook was supported by recent data.

The administration's forecast for the annual average unemployment rate peaked at 8.9 percent for calendar year 1982, dropping to 7.9 percent for 1983. The forecast also reflected a continued downturn in the rate of in-

flation during both 1982 and 1983, when the Consumer Price Index (CPI) would increase 7.3 percent and 6 percent respectively.

But as Reagan's budget pointed out, a change in any of the major economic variables could substantially change the budget outlook.

While most economists generally agreed with the unemployment figures, there was less support for the administration's contention that inflation would dip so low during 1983.

But the greatest skepticism centered on the administration's projections that inflation-adjusted economic growth as measured by the gross national product (GNP) would reach 5.2 percent in 1983, and that from the second half of 1982 through 1987 the average rate of growth would be 4.7 percent. That would make this period the strongest period of growth — with the exception of the early 1960s — since World War II.

The Congressional Budget Office (CBO) in its "Baseline Budget Projections for Fiscal Years 1983-87" estimated that inflation-adjusted GNP would grow by only 4.4 percent in 1983. Those projections were not strictly comparable to the administration's, but still reflected fundamental disagreements.

The principal reason economists doubted the administration's economic growth projections involved the current monetary policy set by the Federal Reserve Board and generally supported by the administration.

The Fed's monetary policy in-

The Budget Totals

(Fiscal years, in billions of dollars)

	1981 actual	1982 estimate	1983 estimate	1984 estimate
Receipts	599.3	626.8	666.1	723.0
Outlays	657.2	725.3	757.6	805.9
Deficit	−57.9	−98.6	−91.5	−82.9
Budget authority	718.4	765.5	801.9	858.0

Budget Terminology

The federal budget is the president's financial plan for the federal government. It accounts for how government funds have been raised and spent, and it proposes financial policies. It covers the **fiscal year.** Fiscal year 1983 began Oct. 1, 1982, and ended Sept. 30, 1983.

The budget discusses **receipts**, amounts the government expects to raise in taxes; **budget authority**, amounts agencies are allowed to obligate or lend; and **outlays**, amounts actually paid out by the government in cash or checks during the year. Examples of outlays are funds spent to buy equipment or property, to meet the government's liability under a contract or to pay the salaries of employees. Outlays also include net lending — the difference between disbursements and repayments under government lending programs.

The purpose of the budget is to establish priorities, and to chart the government's **fiscal policy**, which is the coordinated use of taxes and expenditures to affect the economy.

Congress adopts its own budget in the form of **budget resolutions.** The **first budget resolution**, due May 15, sets overall goals for tax and spending, broken down among major budget categories, called **functions.** The **second budget resolution,** due Sept. 15, sets binding budget figures.

An **authorization** is an act of Congress that establishes government programs. It defines the scope of programs and sets a ceiling for how much can be spent on them. Authorizations do not actually provide the money. In the case of authority to enter contractual obligations, though, Congress authorizes the administration to make firm commitments for which funds must later be provided. Congress also occasionally includes mandatory spending requirements in an authorization in order to ensure spending at a certain level.

An **appropriation** provides money for programs, within the limits established in authorizations. An appropriation may be for a single year, a specified period of years, or an indefinite number of years, according to the restrictions Congress wishes to place on spending for particular purposes.

Appropriations generally take the form of **budget authority**. Budget authority often differs from actual outlays. That is because, in practice, funds actually spent or obligated during a year may be drawn partly from the budget authority conferred in the year in question and partly from budget authority conferred in previous years.

---

volved keeping a tight rein on the growth of money, yet the economic growth predicted by the administration for 1983 and beyond could not occur if a restrictive monetary policy were continued, most economists believed. Tight monetary policy could accommodate such healthy rates of economic growth only if velocity — the rate at which money changes hands throughout the economy — hit historically high levels.

The administration denied that the Fed's monetary policy would inhibit growth. At a press briefing Feb. 9 on the Council of Economic Advisers' Economic Report, Weidenbaum said, " Concerns that the Federal Reserve's targets for money growth are not compatible with the vigorous upturn in economic activity envisioned later in 1982 are unjustified."

But CBO cited "the risk of an unprecedented clash between monetary and fiscal policy that could produce either a flat, no-growth economy with a spike in interest rates driving the economy into recession once again."

The administration contended, however, that rates on 91-day Treasury bills would average 11.7 percent in 1982 and only 10.5 percent in 1983. CBO estimated that these rates would average 12 percent in 1982 and 13.2 percent in 1983.

Interest rates, the administration maintained, would not be driven up by the high deficits — real and projected. The administration argued that the savings incentives provided in the 1981 tax bill would create enough private savings to prevent "crowding out" in the credit markets.

At a Feb. 6 briefing, Treasury Secretary Donald T. Regan said that deficits have "no effect" on interest rates. He maintained that a big boost in savings would make it easy to finance the deficits and provide a "very rapid increase" in capital investment.

Certainly one of the most critical factors for the outcome of Reagan's economic policy was what the Federal Reserve Board would do.

In testimony before both the House and Senate Banking committees during the week of Feb. 8, Fed Chairman Paul A. Volcker said the central bank would continue to pursue its restrictive monetary growth targets, aiming for a 2.5 percent to 5.5 percent growth of the basic money supply during 1982. But he said it might be "acceptable" if growth rates were near the top of that range.

Volcker had consistently maintained that monetary policy alone cannot hold down inflation — that fiscal policy must share the burden.

"I think we all know that without action [to hold down the deficit] we would be on a collision course," Volcker told the House Banking Committee Feb. 10.

Fiscal Policy

The administration characterized its fiscal 1983 budget as providing two fundamental changes: "A new environment to foster economic prosperity, and a rational and lean realignment of domestic programs combined with an adequate defense."

The spending growth projected in the fiscal 1983 budget continued on the downward trend started in fiscal 1982. The budget document noted that spending grew at a rate of 17 percent in 1980. According to OMB, spending growth would decline to 10 percent in 1982 and 4 percent in 1983.

Total outlays in fiscal 1983 would increase by only $32 billion over fiscal 1982, OMB said. "In real terms, spending growth will average less than 1 percent in the 1982-87 period, as compared to 4 percent in the 1976-1981 period," the budget stated.

The fiscal policy that the budget reflected, according to the document, would result in "radically asymmetrical patterns of budget growth in the years ahead." That meant that future growth in the budget would be limited to just three areas: defense, Social Security, and medical care. These three areas accounted for 62 percent of the 1983 budget.

On the other hand the "budget margin for discretionary programs and lower priority activities will shrink after the tax reduction program is fully effective," the budget said.

According to OMB, all outlays together except for defense, interest and social insurance would decrease from 8.1 percent of GNP in 1981 to 5.6 percent in 1983.

Principally as a result of the 1981 tax cut, federal receipts as a share of national output would decline to 19 percent in 1983 and to 18.3 percent by 1987. If the tax cut had not been enacted the share would have been 21.7 percent in 1983. Total receipts would increase by $39.3 billion from fiscal 1982 through fiscal 1983.

Deficit Problem

Critics of Reagan's policies had contended that the enacted tax cuts were one of the primary reasons for the large, continuing deficits in the forecast. The budget projected that the deficit for fiscal 1985 would be $71.9 billion; for fiscal 1986, $66 billion; and for fiscal 1987, $53.2 billion.

But the president provided other rationales for the deficit problem.

First, Reagan stated in his budget message, "the most important setback to our budgetary timetable is the recession now under way."

Another major cause for the deficits, Reagan said, was the rising cost of interest payments on a trillion-dollar debt.

The lowering of the rate of inflation, Reagan said, was itself another cause for the deficit because lower inflation means lower tax receipts.

Finally, Reagan blamed Congress for failing in 1981 to make all the spending cuts he requested. The most important failure, he maintained, was that Congress "discarded" his plan to ensure solvency of Social Security. In fact, the administration eventually backed away from his plan, and Reagan proposed a task force to study Social Security and report by January 1983. *(Social Security, p. 53)*

Deficit Reduction Plan

In order to avoid deficits in the "triple digit range" for fiscal 1983 and the future, the administration advanced its Deficit Reduction Plan.

For fiscal 1983 the plan encompassed $43 billion in proposed savings and $12.8 billion in increased revenues, according to OMB.

However, the budget also proposed spending increases totaling

$21.4 billion — the largest portion of it for defense. Since the $55.9 billion reduction plan was offset by these increases, the overall budget would reduce the deficit by only $34.5 billion in fiscal 1983. *(Chart, p. 196)*

The administration estimated that its plan would cut deficits by $84 billion in fiscal 1984 and $99 billion in fiscal 1985. Without the plan, the deficit in fiscal 1983 would be $147 billion; in fiscal 1984, $167 billion; and in fiscal 1985 it would be $171 billion.

The Deficit Reduction Plan was composed of five elements, involving both outlay reductions and revenue increases. Cuts in discretionary programs would save $14.2 billion in fiscal 1983. Changes in entitlement programs, accounting for $11.7 billion in fiscal 1983 deficit reductions, would include revisions in programs affecting food stamps, federal retirees' cost-of-

living increases and medical care for the poor and elderly.

Increases in user fees — for nuclear waste, airports and Coast Guard services, among others — would total $2.5 billion in fiscal 1983.

Management initiatives in fiscal 1983, such as selling underused federal property, reducing the federal work force and restraining federal pay, accelerating the leasing of Outer Continental Shelf (OCS) land for oil and gas drilling, and improving tax collection, would net $20.3 billion, the administration said.

Finally, revisions in the tax code, including changes that would restrict the use of tax-exempt industrial development bonds, repeal energy tax credits for business and increase the minimum tax on corporations would raise $7.2 billion in fiscal 1983. *(Tax legislation, p. 29)*

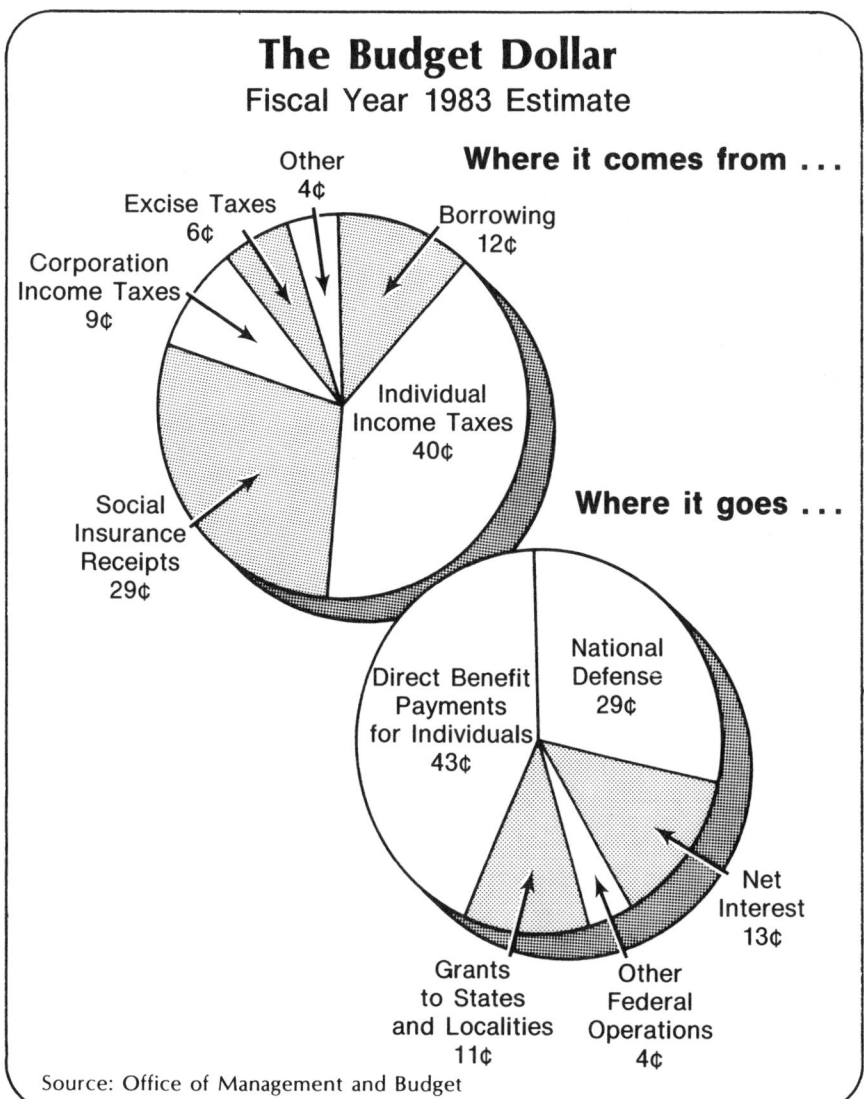

The Budget Dollar
Fiscal Year 1983 Estimate

Where it comes from . . .

Other 4¢
Excise Taxes 6¢
Corporation Income Taxes 9¢
Borrowing 12¢
Individual Income Taxes 40¢
Social Insurance Receipts 29¢

Where it goes . . .

Direct Benefit Payments for Individuals 43¢
National Defense 29¢
Net Interest 13¢
Grants to States and Localities 11¢
Other Federal Operations 4¢

Source: Office of Management and Budget

Reagan Administration Economic Assumptions

(Calendar years; dollar amounts in billions)

Item	Actual 1980	FORECAST			ASSUMPTIONS			
		1981[1]	1982	1983	1984	1985	1986	1987
Major economic indicators:								
Gross national product, percent change, fourth quarter over fourth quarter:								
Current dollars	9.4	9.3	10.4	11.0	10.0	9.4	9.1	8.9
Constant (1972) dollars	−0.3	0.7	3.0	5.2	4.9	4.6	4.3	4.3
GNP deflator (percent change, fourth quarter over fourth quarter)	9.8	8.6	7.2	5.5	4.9	4.6	4.6	4.4
Consumer Price Index (percent change, fourth quarter over fourth quarter)[2]	12.6	9.4	6.6	5.1	4.7	4.6	4.6	4.4
Unemployment rate (percent, fourth quarter)	7.5	8.4	8.4	7.6	6.8	6.2	5.6	5.2
Annual economic assumptions:								
Gross national product:								
Current dollars:								
Amount	2,626	2,922	3,160	3,524	3,883	4,258	4,651	5,068
Percent change, year over year	8.8	11.3	8.1	11.5	10.2	9.7	9.2	9.0
Constant (1972) dollars:								
Amount	1,481	1,510	1,513	1,591	1,670	1,750	1,827	1,905
Percent change, year over year	−0.2	2.0	0.2	5.2	5.0	4.7	4.4	4.3
Incomes:								
Personal income	2,160	2,404	2,641	2,887	3,121	3,411	3,723	4,057
Wages and salaries	1,344	1,483	1,605	1,747	1,887	2,065	2,256	2,458
Corporate profits	246	230	215	260	314	330	317	334
Price level:								
GNP deflator:								
Level (1972 = 100), annual average	177.4	193.6	208.9	221.5	232.5	243.4	254.6	266.0
Percent change, year over year	9.0	9.1	7.9	6.0	5.0	4.7	4.6	4.5
Consumer Price Index:[2]								
Level (1967 = 100), annual average	247.0	272.3	292.1	309.5	323.8	339.2	354.8	370.8
Percent change, year over year	13.5	10.3	7.3	6.0	4.6	4.8	4.6	4.5
Unemployment rates:								
Total, annual average	7.1	7.6	8.9	7.9	7.1	6.4	5.8	5.3
Insured, annual average[3]	3.8	3.5	4.9	4.3	3.7	3.2	2.8	2.4
Federal pay raise, October (percent):[4]								
Civilian	9.1	4.8	5.0	5.0	5.0	5.0	5.0	5.0
Military	11.7	14.3	8.0	7.6	5.5	5.0	5.0	5.0
Interest rate, 91-day Treasury bills (percent)[5]	11.5	14.1	11.7	10.5	9.5	8.5	7.0	5.5

1. *Preliminary actual data.*

2. *CPI for urban wage earners and clerical workers. Two versions of the CPI are now published. The index shown here is that currently used, as required by law, in calculating automatic cost-of-living increases for indexed federal programs.*

3. *This indicator measures unemployment under state regular unemployment insurance as a percentage of covered employment under that program. It does not include recipients of extended benefits under that program.*

4. *General schedule pay raises become effective in October — the first month of the fiscal year. Thus, the October 1982 pay raise will set new pay scales that will be in effect during fiscal year 1983.*

5. *Average rate on new issues within period. These projections assume, by convention, that interest rates decline with the rate of inflation. They do not represent a forecast of interest rates.*

SOURCE: Fiscal 1983 Budget

1982 Revisions

Although administrations often have to revise their deficit numbers for the prior fiscal year upward in a new budget, the jump in the fiscal 1982 deficit projection more than doubled from the administration's last formal estimate. The midyear revision in July 1981 estimated a $42.5 billion fiscal 1982 deficit. The number soared to $98.6 billion in the new budget.

The budget outlined a total of $9.06 billion in budget authority for proposed 1982 supplemental appropriations, excluding requests for increased pay costs. The supplemental requests included more than $2.6 billion for defense, $2.4 billion for the Environmental Protection Agency and $1.9 billion for the Labor Department.

In addition to the supplemental requests, the administration proposed 1982 rescissions totaling $10.655 billion. These rescissions included more than $9.4 billion from the Department of Housing and Urban Development and more than $1 billion from the Department of Education.

According to OMB figures, the "grand total" of rescissions minus supplementals would cut 1982 budget authority by $1.527 billion.

The proposed Deficit Reduction Plan also would affect the fiscal 1982 deficit. The administration estimated that the plan would save $2.6 billion in fiscal 1982 and increase revenues by $300 million.

Current Services

The 1974 Budget Act (PL 93-344) required the president to supply Congress with estimates of outlays and budget authority that would be needed to maintain current government services at the same level as the fiscal year in progress, with no changes in policy. These figures, known as the "Current Services Estimates," can be used as a baseline to measure the budget's proposed changes and year-to-year growth.

In 1982, instead of using these estimates as a baseline in the main budget document, OMB used what it called "current services with adequate defense." This reflected the current services spending level for all non-defense programs, plus a level of defense spending that included proposed increases. The effect of using this baseline was that the magnitude of the defense increases was obscured in the context of the total budget.

The more complete current services estimate, presented by OMB in a

separate document, showed that without policy changes, receipts for fiscal 1983 would total $653.3 billion; outlays would be $779.3 billion; budget authority $833.9 billion and the deficit $126 billion.

Current service outlays rose $52.9 billion from 1982 to 1983.

Income security, national defense, interest and health functions accounted for the largest dollar increase in current services outlays. According to OMB, the higher figures were the result of the increase in the number of beneficiaries, cost-of-living adjustment, higher prices and increased borrowing requirements.

Current services outlays for Medicare and Medicaid alone increased $8.8 billion, OMB noted.

Defense outlays jumped $15.8 billion from the 1982 number. The October 1982 pay raise accounted for $4.9 billion of the increase.

Credit Budget

In 1981 Reagan attempted, unsuccessfully, to cut the size of the government's loan and loan-guarantee programs. In 1982 he proposed merely to limit their growth.

The budget recommended an overall increase of 2.7 percent in loan activity for a total of $147.3 billion in fiscal 1983. For fiscal year 1982, credit activities would increase 7.3 percent to $143.4 billion.

New federal direct loan obligations for fiscal 1983 would total $49 billion; loan guarantee commitments would be $98.4 billion.

Major proposals to reduce the growth in credit included plans to: reduce loan commitments for mortgage-backed securities by Government National Mortgage Association (GNMA); reduce direct loans for the Export-Im-

port bank; and eliminate direct loans offered by the Small Business Administration.

Increases, however, were proposed for military aid abroad and mortgage programs that come under the Federal Housing Administration and the Veterans Administration.

Program Highlights

National Defense. The Reagan administration proposed to continue its policy of beefing up national defense by increasing fiscal 1983 outlays to $221.1 billion — up from $187.5 billion in fiscal 1982.

Budget authority for the entire defense function would be $263 billion in fiscal 1983.

The Defense Department's budget authority would increase from $214.1 billion to $257.5 billion. Of that $43.4 billion increase, the department estimated that $29.8 billion would be above inflation — a real increase of about 13.2 percent.

Much of the large increase reflected a decision to try to fully estimate the likely cost of weapons and buy them in a way most likely to reduce total cost in the long run. Typically, this means higher initial costs.

The most dramatic of these "spend now; save later" plans would fund two nuclear-powered aircraft carriers at a total cost $6.8 billion in fiscal 1983 budget authority.

According to the department, doing it this way under a single contract would save $750 million and get the second ship into service in the fleet 21 months earlier than if they were funded separately, a few years apart as usual.

International Affairs. The Reagan budget proposed a dramatic,

Budget Receipts by Source

(In billions of dollars)

| | 1981 actual | Estimate | | | | |
		1982	1983	1984	1985	1986
Individual income taxes	285.9	298.6	304.5	322.9	362.0	401.5
Corporation income taxes	61.1	46.8	65.3	83.7	88.2	83.9
Social insurance taxes and contributions	182.7	206.5	222.5	242.5	273.1	304.0
Excise taxes	40.8	43.0	41.7	41.5	40.8	39.2
Other	28.7	31.9	32.1	32.5	32.5	32.4
Total	599.3	626.8	666.1	723.0	796.6	861.0

Fiscal 1983 Budget by Function: $757.6 Billion in . . .

(in millions of dollars†)

	BUDGET AUTHORITY‡			OUTLAYS		
	1981	1982 est.	1983 est.	1981	1982 est.	1983 est.
NATIONAL DEFENSE						
Military Defense	$178,386	$214,060	$257,469	$156,096	$182,800	$215,900
Atomic Energy Defense Activities	3,651	4,673	5,506	3,398	4,498	5,155
Defense-Related Activities	373	137	58	276	204	13
Deductions #	−4	−4	—	−4	−4	—
TOTAL	$182,405	$218,865	$263,033	$159,765	$187,497	$221,068
INTERNATIONAL AFFAIRS						
Foreign Economic and Financial Assistance	$ 4,499	$ 4,529	$ 4,764	$ 4,215	$ 4,277	$ 4,327
International Security Assistance	2,543	3,486	4,663	3,131	3,485	3,835
Conduct of Foreign Affairs	1,471	1,624	1,809	1,347	1,543	1,794
Foreign Information and Exchange Activities	551	588	746	525	599	655
International Financial Programs	15,844	8,352	6,241	2,007	1,265	1,455
Deductions #	−95	−97	−97	−95	−97	−97
TOTAL	$ 24,812	$ 18,482	$ 18,126	$ 11,130	$ 11,074	$ 11,968
GENERAL SCIENCE, SPACE AND TECHNOLOGY						
General Science and Basic Research	$ 1,541	$ 1,533	$ 1,679	$ 1,483	$ 1,660	$ 1,572
Space Flight	3,187	3,578	3,983	3,053	3,462	3,992
Space, Science, Applications and Technology	1,359	1,381	1,526	1,384	1,344	1,462
Supporting Space Activities	450	508	618	444	481	613
Deductions #	−5	−5	−5	−5	−5	−5
TOTAL	$ 6,533	$ 6,995	$ 7,800	$ 6,359	$ 6,942	$ 7,633
ENERGY						
Energy Supply	$ 2,224	$ 3,689	$ 3,418	$ 5,362	$ 4,554	$ 2,965
Energy Conservation	728	163	27	757	736	326
Emergency Energy Preparedness	2,791	191	242	3,280	227	302
Energy Information, Policy and Regulation	1,089	871	712	940	964	690
Deductions #	−62	−69	−69	−62	−69	−69
TOTAL	$ 6,769	$ 4,846	$ 4,330	$ 10,277	$ 6,413	$ 4,215
NATURAL RESOURCES AND ENVIRONMENT						
Water Resources	$ 4,163	$ 3,916	$3,376	$ 4,215	$ 4,106	$ 3,407
Conservation and Land Management	2,749	2,031	1,393	2,576	2,249	1,521
Recreational Resources	1,287	1,228	1,156	1,632	1,648	1,383
Pollution Control and Abatement	2,981	3,639	3,566	5,169	5,384	4,613
Other Natural Resources	1,500	1,548	1,470	1,485	1,569	1,507
Deductions #	−1,553	−2,330	−2,520	−1,553	−2,330	−2,520
TOTAL	$ 11,128	$ 10,030	$ 8,440	$ 13,525	$ 12,626	$ 9,911
AGRICULTURE						
Farm Income Stabilization	$ 5,049	$ 8,037	$ 5,289	$ 3,993	$ 7,041	$ 2,926
Agricultural Research and Services	1,559	1,576	1,580	1,540	1,596	1,572
Deductions #	38	−4	−4	38	−4	−4
TOTAL	$ 6,646	$ 9,609	$ 6,865	$ 5,572	$ 8,633	$ 4,494
COMMERCE AND HOUSING CREDIT						
Mortgage Credit and Thrift Insurance	$ 3,178	$ 4,061	$ 1,646	$ 651	$ 925	$ −184
Postal Service	1,343	619	500	1,343	619	500
Other Advancement of Commerce	2,022	1,603	1,282	1,959	1,728	1,284
Deductions #	−7	−8	−8	−7	−8	−8
TOTAL	$ 6,537	$ 6,275	$ 3,419	$ 3,946	$ 3,265	$ 1,591
TRANSPORTATION						
Ground Transportation	$ 18,236	$14,357	$ 12,317	$ 17,100	$ 14,728	$ 13,045
Air Transportation	4,082	3,648	4,463	3,850	3,730	3,968
Water Transportation	2,592	3,002	2,279	2,420	2,778	2,575
Other Transportation	109	86	113	110	89	111
Deductions #	−99	−97	−70	−99	−97	−70
TOTAL	$ 24,920	$ 20,996	$ 19,102	$ 23,381	$ 21,228	$ 19,628
COMMUNITY AND REGIONAL DEVELOPMENT						
Community Development	$ 4,811	$ 4,286	$ 4,460	$ 5,111	$ 5,066	$ 4,349
Area and Regional Development	2,626	1,928	1,801	2,708	2,848	2,732
Disaster Relief and Insurance	737	459	452	1,604	503	237
Deductions #	−30	−51	−55	−30	−51	−55
TOTAL	$ 8,143	$ 6,621	$ 6,658	$ 9,394	$ 8,366	$ 7,263

... Expenditures, $801.9 Billion in Spending Authority

(in millions of dollars†)

	BUDGET AUTHORITY‡			OUTLAYS		
	1981	1982 est.	1983 est.	1981	1982 est.	1983 est.
EDUCATION, TRAINING, EMPLOYMENT, SOCIAL SERVICES						
Elementary, Secondary and Vocational Education	$ 6,713	$ 5,280	$ 4,417	$ 7,043	$ 7,092	$ 5,467
Higher Education	6,913	6,552	4,789	6,790	6,982	6,346
Research and General Education Aids	1,286	1,186	1,060	1,223	1,304	1,273
Training and Employment	9,109	3,945	2,955	9,241	5,439	2,764
Other Labor Services	606	585	637	587	584	633
Social Services	5,935	5,989	4,968	6,531	6,400	5,101
Deductions #	—13	—31	—32	—13	—31	—32
TOTAL	$ 30,550	$23,507	$ 18,794	$ 31,402	$ 27,770	$ 21,552
HEALTH						
Health Care Services	$ 63,462	$ 73,955	$ 72,468	$ 60,351	$ 67,961	$ 72,675
Health Research	3,757	3,824	3,969	3,836	3,839	3,941
Education and Training of Health Care Work Force	665	460	337	779	637	451
Consumer and Occupational Health and Safety	1,077	1,012	1,052	1,042	1,017	1,055
Deductions #	—25	—16	—17	—25	—16	—17
TOTAL	$ 68,936	$ 79,234	$ 77,808	$ 65,982	$ 73,437	$ 78,105
INCOME SECURITY						
General Retirement and Disability Insurance	$139,431	$157,531	$170,741	$145,024	$162,268	$175,650
Federal Employee Retirement and Disability	28,777	33,567	34,992	17,547	19,361	21,062
Unemployment Compensation	19,048	21,006	22,249	19,664	25,213	22,598
Housing Assistance	26,105	6,649	—3,854	6,942	8,247	8,884
Food and Nutrition Assistance	16,573	15,785	13,784	16,202	15,569	13,772
Other Income Security	19,985	17,784	19,664	19,721	20,213	19,770
TOTAL	$249,918	$252,322	$257,576	$225,099	$250,870	$261,736
VETERANS' BENEFITS AND SERVICES						
Income Security	$ 13,210	$ 14,524	$ 15,024	$12,909	$ 14,070	$ 14,843
Education, Training and Rehabilitation	2,351	1,945	1,666	2,254	1,883	1,557
Hospital and Medical Care	6,919	7,640	8,324	6,965	7,594	8,108
Housing	—	—	—95	201	—68	—863
Other Benefits and Services	690	683	743	662	680	741
Deductions #	—3	—3	—3	—3	—3	—3
TOTAL	$ 23,167	$ 24,789	$ 25,660	$ 22,988	$ 24,155	$ 24,383
ADMINISTRATION OF JUSTICE						
Federal Law Enforcement Activities	$ 2,350	$ 2,479	$ 2,671	$ 2,384	$ 2,468	$ 2,643
Federal Litigative and Judicial Activities	1,485	1,388	1,427	1,493	1,393	1,423
Federal Correctional Activities	352	367	383	361	376	386
Criminal Justice Assistance	169	140	67	473	318	162
Deductions #	—13	—35	—23	—13	—35	—23
TOTAL	$ 4,343	$ 4,339	$ 4,525	$ 4,698	$ 4,521	$ 4,592
GENERAL GOVERNMENT						
Legislative Functions	$ 1,031	$ 1,194	$ 1,217	$ 1,036	$ 1,200	$ 1,204
Executive Direction and Management	108	92	104	99	94	101
Central Fiscal Operations	2,679	2,855	3,154	2,600	2,802	3,092
General Property and Records Management	577	369	362	169	428	192
Central Personnel Management	162	136	139	159	136	140
Other General Government	763	707	660	745	687	656
Deductions #	—195	—200	—377	—195	—200	—377
TOTAL	$ 5,125	$ 5,152	$ 5,259	$ 4,614	$ 5,146	$ 5,008
GENERAL PURPOSE FISCAL ASSISTANCE						
General Revenue Sharing	$ 4,573	$ 4,573	$ 4,573	$ 5,140	$ 4,576	$ 4,573
Other General Purpose Fiscal Assistance	1,678	1,846	2,123	1,716	1,841	2,113
TOTAL	$ 6,251	$ 6,419	$ 6,696	$ 6,856	$ 6,417	$ 6,686
INTEREST						
Interest on the Public Debt	$ 95,503	$115,700	$132,900	$ 95,503	$115,700	$132,900
Other Interest	—12,966	—16,606	—20,364	—12,967	—16,605	—20,364
TOTAL	$ 82,537	$ 99,094	$112,536	$ 82,537	$ 99,095	$112,536
CIVILIAN AGENCY PAY RAISES	$ —	$ 392	$ 757	$ —	$ 376	$ 743
CONTINGENCIES	—	—	—	—	—	—
FRAUD, WASTE AND ABUSE	—	—1,000	—1,000	—	1,000	1,000
UNDISTRIBUTED DEBT COLLECTION	—	—	—1,000	—	—	—1,000
OFFSETTING RECEIPTS	$—30,319	$—31,501	$—43,475	$—30,319	$—31,501	$—43,475
GRAND TOTAL	$718,400	$765,464	$801,910	$657,204	$725,331	$757,638

† Figures may not add to totals due to rounding.   *‡ Primarily appropriations.*   **Less than $500 thousand.*   *# For offsetting receipts.*

SOURCE: Fiscal 1983 Budget

Budget Outlays
Constant 1983 Dollars

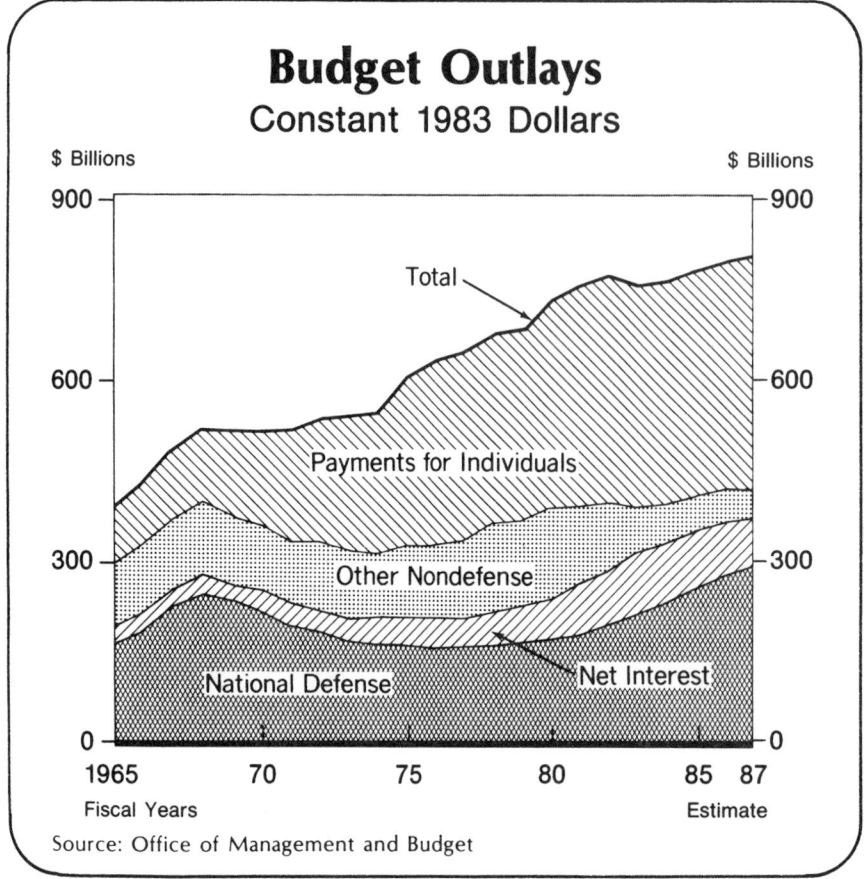

$ Billions

$ Billions

900 — — 900

600 — — 600

Total

Payments for Individuals

300 — — 300

Other Nondefense

National Defense   Net Interest

0 — — 0

1965   70   75   80   85   87

Fiscal Years   Estimate

Source: Office of Management and Budget

44 percent increase over fiscal 1982 spending for military-related loans and grants to other countries. The military and military-related aid budget would rise from $4.0 billion in fiscal 1982 to $5.8 billion in 1983.

At the same time, however, the administration planned to hold down increases in aid to poor countries for economic development.

Politically it would be difficult for Reagan to approve any of his $9.4 billion fiscal 1983 foreign aid budget — a $1.4 billion increase from 1982 — since Congress was traditionally reluctant to vote for foreign aid in an election year. In addition, congressional aides said House Democrats on the Foreign Affairs Committee would resist making broad changes in the two-year authorization bill approved in 1981.

Energy. Assuming the dismantlement of the Department of Energy (DOE), Reagan's fiscal 1983 funding for energy programs that normally made up DOE's budget was cut 10 percent from the fiscal 1982 level to $11.8 billion. The budget envisioned a transfer of most functions to the Commerce Department under a new

agency to be called the Energy Research and Technology Administration.

Weapons programs, however, would increase 17 percent — up $815 million to $5.5 billion.

Reagan's energy budget refocused funding from President Carter's emphasis on coal, conservation and solar to nuclear energy. Fission and fusion made up about $1.5 billion of the $2.2 billion for energy research.

The budget reflected a $1.5 billion savings for the strategic petroleum reserve by using leftover fiscal 1982 money to buy oil in 1983.

Natural Resources and Environment. A major part of the president's Deficit Reduction Plan involved the sale of offshore oil and gas leases and "unneeded" federal land at full market prices. The sale of the offshore leases, the administration estimated, would net more than $8 billion in fiscal 1983. And the sale of federal lands would bring in $17 billion from fiscal 1983-87.

The Environmental Protection Agency's (EPA) fiscal 1983 operating funds totaled $961.3 million — a 12 percent cut from the amount expected

to be spent in fiscal 1982 and 29 percent less than was spent in fiscal 1981.

Almost half of Reagan's $8.4 billion environment budget was designated for construction of federal dams, irrigation projects, waterways and ports. Only 42 percent of the budget would be used to fight pollution and build sewage treatment plants.

The EPA budget prompted objections from both Democrats and Republicans, as well as environmental groups who called it a "strangulation budget" that would cut EPA spending by almost 40 percent from pre-Reagan days, after adjusting for inflation.

Federal Workers. Reagan proposed to cut the federal work force by 75,000 people by the end of 1984, and another 75,000 by 1987. The first 75,000 reduction was expected to yield $2.1 billion in budget authority savings beginning in fiscal 1985.

The administration also asked Congress to limit the annual cost-of-living adjustment to federal retirees to the increase in the Consumer Price Index (CPI) or the annual pay raise for federal workers, whichever was less.

Pay raises for civilian white- and blue-collar workers also would be limited — to 5 percent in October 1982.

Transportation. Reagan proposed to further reduce federal involvement in transportation programs and transfer program costs to states, localities and transportation users.

A limit of $7.8 billion was set on obligations from the Highway Trust Fund, down from estimated obligations of $8.2 billion in fiscal 1982. Some mass transit capital programs were increased, but operating subsidies were slashed to $640 million — down from more than $1 billion.

Amtrak, the subsidized passenger railroad, would receive $600 million in budget authority — not enough to maintain a national system, supporters contended.

Education. The budget called for a continued reduction of the federal role in education, symbolized by the dismantlement of the Department of Education. The department would be replaced by the Foundation for Education Assistance.

Cuts totaling 21 percent would affect education programs, with deep cuts in Title I, compensatory educa-

Budget Changes from Existing Policy‡

(In billions of dollars)

	Fiscal Year	
	1982	1983

Decreases in Outlays

	1982	1983
National defense:		
Entitlements (retired pay)	0	−0.1
Management initiative (civilian employee pay raise)	0	−0.6
Stockpile sales	0	−0.4
Subtotal, national defense	0	−1.1
Non-defense:		
Entitlements:		
Guaranteed student loans	−0.2	−0.8
Medicare	−0.3	−2.5
Medicaid	−0.3	−2.0
Railroad retirement	0	−2.0
Civil Service retirement and disability	−*	−0.5
Food stamps	−0.3	−2.4
Aid to families with dependent children	−0.2	−1.2
Supplemental security income	−0.1	−0.3
Other entitlements	−0.1	−1.2
Subtotal, entitlements	−1.4	−12.8
Management initiatives:		
Civilian agency pay raise	—	−0.8
Other allowances	−1.0	−2.0
Outer Continental Shelf receipts†	0	−8.4
Federal property disposition†	0	−1.0
Other	−0.1	−2.0
Subtotal, management initiatives	−1.1	−14.2
Net interest	0	−2.7
Higher user fees†	0	−1.2
Other non-defense		
Energy programs	−*	−0.9
Natural resources and environment	0.1	−0.7
Transportation	*	−1.6
Education	−0.1	−1.2
Employment and training (net)	*	−2.2
Social services	−0.1	−1.0
Housing assistance	−*	−0.6
Other income security and health	−*	−1.8
All other (net)	0.1	−1.1
Subtotal, other non-defense	−0.1	−11.1
Subtotal, non-defense	−2.6	−41.9
Total, decreases	**−2.6**	**−43.0**

Increases in Outlays

	1982	1983
National defense:		
Department of Defense—military	1.3	19.3
Other national defense	*	0.3
Subtotal, national defense	1.3	19.7
Non-defense:		
Foreign military sales credit	0	0.1
Economic support fund	0	0.3
Federal Aviation Administration	0.1	0.5
Sewage treatment construction grants	0	0.4
Internal Revenue Service	0.1	0.4
Subtotal, non-defense	0.2	1.8
Total, increases	**1.5**	**21.4**

Changes in Receipts

	1982	1983
Tax revisions:		
Completed contract accounting	0	3.3
Business energy tax credits	0	0.1
Tax-exempt revenue bonds	0	−0.2
Modified coinsurance	0	1.1
Construction period interest and taxes	0	0.5
Corporate minimum tax	0	2.3
Subtotal, tax revisions	0	7.2
Improved tax collection and enforcement:		
Withholding on interest and dividends	0	2.0
Acceleration of corporate tax payments	0	1.4
Internal Revenue Service staff increase	0.2	2.1
Subtotal, improved tax collection and enforcement	0.2	5.5
Airport and Airway Trust Fund	0.1	1.2
Railroad retirement	0	−1.7
Federal employee hospital insurance taxes	0	0.6
Other	*	0.1
Total	**0.3**	**12.8**

*Less than $50 million.
† Receipts treated as reductions in outlays.
‡ Changes from Current Services Estimates.

SOURCE: Office of Management and Budget

Overall Fiscal Change

	1982	1983
Net change in Outlays	−1.1	−21.7
Net change in Deficit	−1.4	−34.5

Deficits in Perspective

FISCAL YEAR	DEFICIT (−) or SURPLUS (+)		NET INTEREST	
	Amount in Billions	Percent of GNP	Amount in Billions	Percent of Outlays
1964	−5.9	1.0	8.2	6.9
1965	−1.6	.2	8.6	7.3
1966	−3.8	.5	9.4	7.0
1967	−8.7	1.1	10.3	6.5
1968	−25.2	3.0	11.1	6.2
1969	+3.2	.4	12.7	6.9
1970	−2.8	.3	14.4	7.4
1971	−23.0	2.2	14.8	7.0
1972	−23.4	2.1	15.5	6.7
1973	−14.8	1.2	17.3	7.1
1974	−4.7	.3	21.4	8.0
1975	−45.2	3.1	23.2	7.2
1976	−66.4	4.0	26.7	7.3
1977	−44.9	2.4	29.9	7.5
1978	−48.8	2.3	35.4	7.9
1979	−27.7	1.2	42.6	8.7
1980	−59.6	2.3	52.5	9.1
1981	−57.9	2.0	68.7	10.5
1982†	−98.6	3.2	83.0	11.4
1983†	−91.5	2.7	96.4	12.7

† Estimated   SOURCE: Office of Management and Budget

The budget deficits projected by President Reagan for fiscal years 1982 and 1983 were not out of line with past experience — especially for a recession period — when they were considered in relation to the size of the gross national product (GNP).

That relationship does not give the whole picture of federal deficits, however. Deficits are financed by borrowing, and the interest paid to carry the debt is itself a significant and growing item in the federal budget.

The Reagan budget, reflecting not only cumulative deficits but also high market interest rates, allocated a record-high share of federal spending to cover interest costs.

---

tion for the disadvantaged, Pell grants and work-study.

The administration also called for major changes in the Guaranteed Student Loan program by making graduate and professional students ineligible and requiring a needs test for all students.

Legal Services. Reagan again asked Congress to abolish the Legal Services Corporation, which provided free legal aid to the poor in civil cases, and to eliminate the remnants of Justice Department programs that provided grants to state and local governments to assist in fighting crime. Congress refused to eliminate these

programs in 1981.

Income Security. Reagan asked Congress to eliminate the trade adjustment assistance (TAA) cash benefit as of July 1, 1982. TAA, which was designed to help workers who lose their jobs as a result of competition from imports, was cut substantially by Congress in 1981. The proposed changes would mean an outlay savings of $26 million in fiscal 1982 and $108 million in fiscal 1983.

The administration also proposed eliminating the Railroad Retirement Board beginning in 1983. The railroad retirement system would be broken into two parts.

While no major changes were called for in unemployment compensation, the administration estimated that outlays would be reduced from $25.2 billion in fiscal 1982 to $22.6 billion, anticipating a drop in the unemployment rate and reflecting eligibility changes made in 1981.

Health. While specifics of major health reform legislation were not included in the budget, the Reagan administration proposed cuts totaling nearly $4 billion in outlays from Medicare and Medicaid. These cuts, combined with administrative changes, the Department of Health and Human Services said, would cut nearly $5 billion from health costs in fiscal 1983.

Total Medicare outlays for fiscal 1983 would be $55.4 billion; for Medicaid $17.1 billion and for the states' portion of Medicaid $15.5 billion. Budget authority for all health programs would be $77.8 billion, compared with $79.2 billion in fiscal 1982.

One proposal would reduce various federal matching rates for Medicaid expenditures. Another would charge Medicaid beneficiaries a dollar or two per visit to the doctor or hospital to discourage use. Yet another budget strategy contemplated across-the-board cuts in what the federal government would pay hospitals for Medicare patients.

Welfare. The budget sought major changes in welfare programs.

The president proposed cutting the core income support programs for the poor — Aid to Families with Dependent Children (AFDC), food stamps and Supplemental Security Income (SSI) — by a total of $3.7 billion in fiscal 1983.

Legislative changes needed to accomplish those savings included reductions in food stamp and AFDC benefits to recipients of federal low-income energy assistance, elimination of work "incentives" for food stamp recipients, and toughened eligibility standards for disabled applicants for SSI.

States would be required to set up AFDC "workfare" programs, under which adult recipients would have to perform community service work in exchange for their benefits.

Federal funding for state administration of welfare programs would be reduced. Strict penalties for states that made errors in handing out benefits would be imposed.

The budget did not reflect a wel-

Budget Authority and Outlays by Agency

(in millions of dollars)

DEPARTMENT OR OTHER UNIT	BUDGET AUTHORITY			OUTLAYS		
	1981 actual	1982 estimate	1983 estimate	1981 actual	1982 estimate	1983 estimate
Legislative branch	1,247	1,423	1,465	1,209	1,502	1,450
The Judiciary	653	741	842	637	730	824
Executive Office of the President	103	90	102	96	92	99
Funds appropriated to the President	14,662	11,036	11,483	7,010	6,370	6,936
Agriculture	28,169	30,251	24,748	26,034	29,442	23,533
Commerce [1]	11,160	10,044	9,730	11,484	11,646	9,862
Defense — Military [2,3]	178,386	214,060	257,469	156,096	182,800	215,900
Defense — Civil	3,097	2,918	2,292	3,148	2,991	2,286
Health and Human Services [2]	225,844	251,358	268,411	228,115	252,938	274,165
Housing and Urban Development	33,350	13,020	685	14,033	14,614	13,130
Interior [1,2]	6,359	2,929	3,270	6,775	3,139	3,270
Justice [1,2]	2,457	2,454	2,644	2,752	2,643	2,727
Labor	29,452	26,623	26,418	30,084	32,075	26,451
State	2,332	2,541	2,673	1,897	2,183	2,447
Transportation [4]	23,710	20,300	18,438	22,509	20,567	18,980
Treasury [2]	92,681	110,308	124,957	93,372	110,022	124,545
Environmental Protection Agency	3,025	3,674	3,590	5,241	5,434	4,644
National Aeronautics and Space Administration	5,518	5,936	6,608	5,421	5,827	6,577
Veterans Administration	23,133	24,754	25,621	22,904	24,134	24,356
Other independent agencies [1,2]	63,383	63,114	55,181	48,706	48,306	40,187
Allowances [5]	—	−608	−1,243	—	−624	−1,257
Undistributed offsetting receipts:						
Employer share, employee retirement	−6,371	−7,560	−8,353	−6,371	−7,560	−8,353
Interest received by trust funds	−13,810	−16,080	−16,122	−13,810	−16,080	−16,122
Rents and royalties on the Outer Continental Shelf lands	−10,138	−7,861	−18,000	−10,138	−7,861	−18,000
Federal surplus property disposition	—	—	−1,000	—	—	−1,000
Total budget authority and outlays	718,000	765,464	801,910	657,204	725,331	757,638

[1] *The budget proposes dismantlement of the Department of Energy (DOE), effective October 1, 1982. Budget data for activities previously performed by DOE are included in the agencies that are proposed to assume these activities.*

[2] *The budget proposes dismantlement of the Department of Education (DEd), effective October 1, 1982. Budget data for activities previously per-*formed by DEd are included in the agencies that are proposed to assume these responsibilities.

[3] *Includes allowances for civilian and military pay raises for Department of Defense.*

[4] *Includes allowance for military pay raises for the Coast Guard.*

[5] *Includes allowances for civilian agency pay raises and contingencies.*

SOURCE: Fiscal 1983 Budget

fare program swap with the states Reagan had announced he would propose for fiscal 1984.

Jobs Programs. Reagan proposed cutting jobs programs to $2.4 billion in budget authority in fiscal 1983, two-thirds below the fiscal 1981 level of $7.1 billion. The Comprehensive Employment and Training Act (CETA) would be replaced by a new block grant to states. The available funds could only be used for training — not for public service jobs. And unlike past CETA training programs, participants would not be paid.

Agriculture. Total fiscal 1983 outlays for the Agriculture Depart- ment — for both farm and feeding programs — were estimated at $23.5 billion, compared with $29.4 billion for fiscal 1982, or about a 20 percent decrease.

The policy directions of the fiscal 1983 budget were the same as in the 1982 budget: eliminate federal lending for rural development; reduce the lending by the Rural Electrification Administration and cut severely into funds for soil and water conservation.

Slated for increases — though not generous ones — were agricultural research, some export market development activities, federal crop insurance, and forest production.

Housing. The budget proposed a major shift in housing policy that would scrap most subsidized programs in favor of cash vouchers for the poor and limit new construction to units for the elderly and handicapped.

Some 107,000 existing units would be placed under the new voucher program in 1983. Vouchers would average about $2,000 per year and be issued to qualified tenants who would shop for housing and negotiate rent directly with their landlords.

The administration, however, proposed continuation of the popular Community Development and Urban Development Action Grants. ∎

First Budget Resolution Becomes Binding

Beset by election-year pressures stemming from a lingering recession and soaring federal deficits, Congress in 1982 made no effort to adopt a second, binding budget resolution for fiscal 1983.

Instead, lawmakers included in the first resolution (S Con Res 92) a provision stipulating that the budget targets set in that measure automatically would become binding if Congress did not approve a second resolution by the Oct. 1 beginning of the fiscal year. They thus bypassed provisions of the Congressional Budget Act of 1974 (PL 93-344) that mandated approval of a second resolution by Sept. 15 annually.

Congress completed action on S Con Res 92 June 23, nearly six weeks after the statutory May 15 deadline. It had taken five frustrating months to win approval of the measure, which projected deficits above the politically critical $100 billion mark — $103.92 billion in fiscal 1983 and $105.7 billion in 1982.

Senate-House conferees were able to get the figures that low only by accepting controversial accounting practices used by House Republicans to pass their version of the resolution (H Con Res 352) on the House floor June 10.

The final version of S Con Res 92 called for budget authority of $822.39 billion, outlays of $769.82 billion and revenues of $665.9 billion for fiscal 1983. It also revised fiscal 1982 budget levels and set preliminary budget targets for fiscal 1984-85. Other provisions established appropriate levels for the public debt and set limits on federal credit activity. *(Budget totals, box, below)*

The resolution continued the previous year's pattern of cutting back the size of domestic programs while providing massive increases in military spending. It called for deficit reduction measures amounting to $76.8 billion in fiscal 1983 and $378.5 billion over fiscal 1983-85.

As its primary means of enforcing the budget targets, the resolution relied on the reconciliation procedure that was used during 1981 to enact President Reagan's fiscal 1982 budget cuts. Under this process, the resolution included specific instructions ordering congressional committees to draft legislation making the actual spending cuts and revenue increases.

The reconciliation instructions ordered $6.57 billion in spending cuts and $20.9 billion in revenue increases in fiscal 1983; the rest of the assumed fiscal 1983 savings were to be achieved through management savings, lower interest payments and other sources over which Congress had little control. *(Reconciliation bill, p. 199)*

The resolution estimated the deficit would drop from $103.9 billion in fiscal 1983 to $60 billion by fiscal 1985. The non-partisan Congressional Budget Office (CBO) calculated, however, that the measure would produce a $116.4 billion deficit in fiscal 1983, declining to $92.7 billion in fiscal 1985. Spending for fiscal 1983, according to CBO, would be $775.5 billion, instead of the $769.8 billion contained in the resolution.

The reliability of the budget's numbers was questioned in both houses. "It is a budget package wrapped in deceit, based on phony figures, erroneous assumptions and questionable projections — particularly with regard to deficit levels," charged Rep. Ted Weiss, D-N.Y.

Those who voted for the resolution did so grudgingly. "...Even though this budget resolution is no one's cup of tea, it is the only one we have," said Rep. Bill Frenzel, R-Minn.

Background

President Reagan's budget, submitted to Congress Feb. 8, projected a $91.5 billion deficit for the year ending Sept. 30, 1983, even with major new cuts in domestic programs. *(Reagan budget, p. 175)*

CBO, which re-estimated the president's budget using its own economic assumptions and technical analysis, predicted that even if Reagan's entire deficit reduction plan were put into law, the deficit would hit $120.6 billion in fiscal 1983 and nearly $140 billion in fiscal 1985 — almost twice the level projected by the administration. (In its April budget revisions, the White House boosted its estimate of the fiscal 1983 deficit to $100.5 billion.)

From the moment it was released, the president's fiscal blueprint was criticized almost universally among members of Congress. Reagan had asked Congress to make what most members considered Draconian cuts in domestic spending while boosting the military budget to unprecedented levels. He made his request in the midst of a severe recession and only months before the 1982 elections.

Democrats, still smarting from the humiliating budget defeats inflicted by Reagan in 1981, protested that they would not work on a budget compromise unless the president became involved. *(1981 Almanac pp. 247, 256)*

To avert a stalemate, White House Chief of Staff

Budget Totals, Fiscal 1982-85

(In billions of dollars)

	Senate	House	Conference
Fiscal 1982			
Budget authority	$777.6	$779.30	$777.67
Outlays	740.8	729.20	734.10
Revenues	623.0	628.40	628.40
Deficit	−117.8	−100.80	−105.70
Fiscal 1983			
Budget authority	835.7	800.38	822.39
Outlays	784.3	765.17	769.82
Revenues	668.4	665.90	665.90
Deficit	−115.9	−99.27	−103.92
Fiscal 1984			
Budget authority	897.5	862.60	878.47
Outlays	833.3	815.98	821.93
Revenues	741.4	738.00	738.00
Deficit	−91.9	−77.98	−83.93
Fiscal 1985			
Budget authority	973.3	948.50	960.61
Outlays	890.7	874.96	881.36
Revenues	825.5	821.40	821.40
Deficit	−65.2	−53.56	−59.96

James A. Baker III began a series of private — and ultimately unsuccessful — negotiations with congressional leaders March 25. The compromise efforts ran into two major stumbling blocks: the president's unwillingness to repeal part of the personal tax cut enacted in 1981 and the reluctance of House Speaker Thomas P. O'Neill Jr., D-Mass., to trim Social Security benefits. Reagan and O'Neill tried rhetorically to set the stage so that each might blame the other if the discussions failed.

The talks of the White House-congressional negotiating team — dubbed the "Gang of 17" — collapsed in a final meeting between Reagan and O'Neill in the Capitol April 28. The Senate Budget Committee began drafting a budget resolution the following day.

Senate Committee Action

Budget gridlock was broken on May 6 when the Budget Committee, by a 12-8 party-line vote, adopted a newly drafted fiscal plan embraced by Reagan.

The resolution, reported May 10 (S Con Res 92 — S Rept 97-385), called for $95 billion in tax increases and $40 billion in savings in Social Security programs over fiscal 1983-85.

The Budget Committee's plan targeted outlays at $779.1 billion and revenues at $667.0 billion in fiscal 1983. That reduced the projected deficit for the fiscal year to $106.1 billion, compared to $182 billion if current policy remained unchanged.

The committee's budget figures were calculated from a revised baseline budget that had been accepted earlier by administration and congressional negotiators. The baseline budget was an estimate of spending and revenue under current law, plus defense spending increases proposed by Reagan. *(Committee targets, box, p. 188)*

The catalyst for committee approval of the plan was provided May 5 by the panel's chairman, Pete V. Domenici, R-N.M.

On that day the committee rejected Reagan's February budget 20-0. Then the panel's Republicans agreed to work with Domenici to craft a package based on a proposal unveiled by the chairman a day earlier.

That plan envisaged $125 billion in higher revenues over three years, and possibly some alteration of the third year of Reagan's individual tax cut enacted in 1981 (PL 97-34). Domenici told the committee, "I do not rule out a freeze on the third year of the scheduled tax cut if that is the final element that a compromise of this magnitude hinges upon." *(Tax bill, 1981 Almanac p. 91)*

The White House then was forced to recognize that unless it became directly involved and made some concessions, the Senate committee would move on its own.

After the president met with his key advisers to provide new budget guidelines, Domenici and Senate Majority Leader Howard H. Baker Jr., R-Tenn., met with White House Chief of Staff Baker and Office of Management and Budget (OMB) Director David A. Stockman on Capitol Hill. The administration and GOP congressional leaders merged their numbers, and each made concessions to come up with a fiscal plan acceptable both to the president and the members.

Domenici agreed to scale back the size of the revenue increases, thus removing the threat of retreat on the tax cut. The president agreed to go out front on the Social Security issue.

Domenici then caucused with GOP members of the panel, who agreed to support the proposal, and the outcome was assured. That night Domenici told the committee, "I submit it tonight after negotiations with the White House as a budget the president will support and take to the people." The committee agreed, in principle, to the outline of the plan by a party-line vote of 11-10.

The next day, May 6, Reagan pledged his support for the plan. He said the package would "continue to bring down the growth in federal spending." He added, "It should . . . reassure financial markets by sharply reducing projected deficits next year and in the years beyond."

The committee continued its work that day, with Republicans successfully fending off every Democratic effort to increase spending in such areas as education, job training, law enforcement and food stamps. The GOP package was approved intact.

Social Security Uproar

While Majority Leader Baker was predicting the resolution "would fly" in the Senate, Democrats and moderate Republicans blasted key elements of the plan.

Democrats centered their attack on what in 1981 proved to be the most vulnerable issue for the president — Social Security. Senate Minority Leader Robert C. Byrd, D-W.Va., claimed the GOP proposal's call for a three-year, $40 billion reduction in Social Security benefits amounted to "mortgaging the economic future of the elderly to finance the economic folly" of Reagan's three-year tax plan.

Baker staved off adoption of an amendment offered by Daniel Patrick Moynihan, D-N.Y., to the defense authorization bill (S 2248) that would have repudiated the Budget panel's action on Social Security. *(Defense bill, p. 77)*

Baker's ploy was to offer an alternative — an amendment that put the Senate on record as supporting no more "corrective" actions on Social Security than were "absolutely necessary" to keep the system solvent.

With this counter-amendment in the wings, the Senate tabled the Moynihan proposal May 11 by a vote of 51-44. It went on the next day to approve amendments protecting Social Security, 91-7. *(Votes 97, 101, pp. 20-S, 21-S)*

Background of Plan

The broad outlines of the fiscal plan reported by the Budget Committee had been around since the fall of 1981, when Domenici tried to convince the president to call for additional spending reductions and revenue increases in the second fiscal 1982 budget resolution. *(1981 Almanac p. 267)*

The significance of the new package was that domestic programs — both discretionary spending and benefit programs — suffered the largest share of the cuts, as they did in spending reductions enacted in 1981. *(1981 cuts, 1981 Almanac p. 256)*

Reagan's proposed increases in defense spending escaped relatively unscathed. And the increases in revenues were relatively modest, compared to the $122 billion that the president had apparently acquiesced in a week earlier in the bipartisan budget discussions.

The package's deficit reduction plans amounted to a savings of $75.9 billion in fiscal 1983, $147 billion in 1984 and $193 billion in 1985.

The economic assumptions underlying the resolution estimated that during calendar 1983 the rate of inflation, as measured by the Consumer Price Index, would be 6.9 percent, the unemployment rate would be 8 percent, the rate of interest on three-month Treasury bills would be

Senate Budget Committee's Targets[1]

Changes from Revised Baseline[2]
(billions of dollars)

	Fiscal Years			
	1982	**1983**	**1984**	**1985**
Revenues				
Revised Baseline	623.0	645.0	702.0	780.0
Revenue increases	—	+20.0	+35.0	+40.0
New user fees	—	+2.0	+2.0	+2.0
Committee target	623.3	667.0	739.0	822.0
Outlays				
Revised baseline	742.3	827.0	918.0	1,012.5
Defense (excluding pay, entitlements)	−0.5	−5.0	−7.0	−10.0
Civilian pay raises	—	−3.9	−6.3	−8.5
Military pay raises	—	−1.6	−3.0	−4.0
Non-defense discretionary programs	−0.8	−5.7	−12.5	−20.1
Cost-of-living adjustments	−0.1	−2.7	−5.1	−7.2
Other entitlement programs	—	−7.2	−11.4	−15.0
Management savings	—	−8.9	−12.1	−12.1
Net Interest:				
Lower rates	−0.1	−8.0	−19.1	−27.8
Lower deficits	−0.1	−4.9	−16.5	−29.3
Total outlay savings	−1.6	−47.9	−93.0	−134.0
Committee target	740.7	779.1	825.0	878.5
Social Security				
Committee target	—	−6.0	−17.0	−17.0
Deficit (-) or surplus (+)				
Revised baseline	−119.3	−182.0	−216.0	−232.5
Proposed changes	+1.6	+75.9	+147.0	+193.0
Committee target	−117.7	−106.1	−69.0	−39.5

[1] *First Budget Resolution, as approved by committee.*
[2] *Revised baseline is estimate of current policy levels, together with Reagan's proposed defense increases.*

Source: Senate Budget Committee

This chart shows the spending cuts and revenue increases proposed by the Senate Budget Committee in the fiscal 1983 budget resolution it approved May 6.

The committee cast its proposal in terms of changes from a "revised baseline" budget that was an estimate of spending and revenue under current law, together with defense spending increases proposed by President Reagan. The "revised baseline" was established during talks between the administration and congressional leaders that broke down April 28.

13.2 percent and the growth in real gross national product (GNP) would be 4.4 percent.

Major Proposals

Following is a summary of the major proposals contained in the resolution agreed to by the Senate committee. All of the savings are in outlay numbers.

Revenues. The plan called for tax increases of $20 billion in fiscal 1983, $35 billion in 1984 and $40 billion in 1985, plus $2 billion in new user fees each year. The Budget Committee had no authority to tell the Finance Committee, which has jurisdiction over revenues, how to raise taxes.

Social Security. According to Domenici, the minimum needed to assure the solvency of the trust fund that provided basic Social Security benefits beyond July 1983 was $6 billion in fiscal 1983, $17 billion in 1984 and $17 billion in 1985. The Finance Committee would have to meet these targets in reducing the cost of the Social Security program. Finance would have the option of changing Social Security programs — by reducing benefits or tightening eligibility — increasing Social Security taxes, or both.

The Finance panel was given mandatory instructions requiring it to report Social Security reform legislation by Dec. 1. Congress would have to return after the Nov. 2 elections for a "lame-duck" session to tackle Social Security legislation.

COLAs. Cost-of-living adjustments (COLAs) for all entitlement programs — except Social Security, Supplemental Security Income and food stamps — would be frozen for one year in fiscal 1983, at 1982 levels. In fiscal years 1984 and 1985 the affected programs would receive a 4 percent inflation increase.

Targeted Entitlement Savings. Other savings from mandatory entitlement programs, such as Medicaid, welfare and food stamps, would total $33.6 billion over three years.

Non-Defense Discretionary Spending. All spending depending on appropriations, except for defense, would be held at the fiscal 1982 baseline budget authority levels during the next three fiscal years. The savings from this freeze would amount to $5.7 billion in fiscal 1983, $12.5 billion in 1984 and $20.1 billion in 1985.

Defense. The increase in defense spending would be shaved by $5 billion in fiscal 1983, $7 billion in 1984 and $10 billion in 1985.

Civilian and Military Pay Raises. The resolution assumed a one-year pay freeze for both military and civilian employees, although readiness-related pay increases for the military would be allowed. Civilian employees would receive a 4 percent pay raise in fiscal 1984 and 1985. The savings from these freezes would amount to $27.3 billion over three years.

Management Savings. Savings totaling $33.1 billion over three years would come from a variety of areas including disposal of surplus federal property, improved debt collection and reduction in waste, fraud and abuse.

Net Interest Savings. The interest savings, which would total $105.6 billion over three years, reflected the assumption that enactment of this plan would reduce interest rates six-tenths of a percentage point beginning in July 1982, with further reductions later reaching 2.5 percentage points.

Procedural Flaps

Before finally voting on the resolution, the committee had a heated debate over several procedural issues included in the measure.

The draft of the resolution included language that would have made the spending levels in it binding if, by Sept. 15, Congress had not adopted a second budget resolution.

Domenici argued that because of the difficulty in getting budget resolutions through Congress the provision would provide "some validity in the area of appropriations."

But two Democrats, Gary Hart, Colo., and Joseph R. Biden Jr., Del., strenuously objected. If the change were made in the first resolution, Hart argued, it would mean "waiving fundamental elements" of the Budget Act.

Domenici backed off, and the language making the first resolution binding was removed.

Also dropped in the face of Democratic objections was proposed language that would have made an increase in the federal debt ceiling part of the reconciliation instructions given the Finance Committee.

Debt ceiling increases ordinarily were passed as part of the budget resolution in the House, but voted on separately in the Senate. If the ceiling increase were included as part of reconciliation, as proposed in Domenici's draft resolution, the debt ceiling increase could not be amended or used as a political football, as was often the case.

The resolution did contain reconciliation instructions requiring the Finance Committee to report legislation dealing with revenues and targeted entitlements and the committees on Agriculture, Labor and Human Resources, Governmental Affairs, Armed Services, Commerce, and Veterans' Affairs to report targeted entitlement and non-Social Security COLA reductions to the Budget Committee by June 18.

The resolution included language calling on the Federal Reserve to re-evaluate its monetary targets "if Congress acts to restore fiscal responsibility and reduces projected budget deficits in a substantial and permanent way." The same language also was included in the measure reported by the House Budget Committee.

House Committee Action

The House Budget Committee May 13 approved its version of the first resolution, which envisioned a $103.85 billion deficit in fiscal 1983, dropping to $34.65 billion in fiscal 1985. The resolution was reported May 17 (H Con Res 345 — H Rept 97-521).

The committee's 17-12 vote followed party lines, with conservative Democrat Phil Gramm, Texas, abstaining. And while liberal Democrat David R. Obey, Wis., voted to report the committee proposal, he said he would fight on the floor for an alternative resolution.

"I simply don't think you lead with your bottom line," Obey said. "It's like selling your soul to the devil before you're tempted."

Even Budget Chairman James R. Jones, D-Okla., acknowledged that the committee's plan was merely a "first step." Majority Leader Jim Wright, D-Texas, called it "a very good start."

The resistance to tampering in any way with Social

Budget Totals Approved by Senate, House Committees

(Fiscal years, in billions of dollars)

	1983		1984		1985	
	House Committee	Senate Committee	House Committee	Senate Committee	House Committee	Senate Committee
Budget authority	$ 828.00	$ 831.70	$ 888.40	$ 892.30	$ 952.85	$ 966.00
Outlays	780.55	779.10	826.40	825.00	881.20	878.50
Revenues	676.70	667.00	753.65	739.00	846.55	822.00
Deficit	−103.85	−106.10	−72.75	−69.00	−34.65	−39.50

Security in an election year was just as strong and negative in the House as in the Senate.

During the House committee's markup, Jack F. Kemp, R-N.Y., offered an amendment to remove Social Security from the unified budget. "I just don't think there is any other way we can take Social Security out of the political arena but to move it off-budget," Kemp asserted.

Jones said he thought a proposal of this magnitude should not be attached to a budget resolution and that Congress should wait for the recommendations of the National Commission on Social Security Reform before acting on such a measure.

The committee then adopted, 16-13, a substitute to the Kemp amendment urging the Ways and Means Committee to review the proposal to take Social Security off-budget.

House Budget Plan

The resolution approved by the House committee had a bottom line very close to the Senate committee's plan — the total deficits over three years were only $3 billion apart — but the makeup of the proposal was starkly different.

The major differences between the two were that the House plan included larger tax increases, deeper defense cuts, smaller domestic spending cuts and no action on Social Security.

The deficits would be slightly lower in the House committee's resolution, dropping from $103.85 billion in fiscal 1983 to $72.75 billion in fiscal 1984 and $34.65 billion in fiscal 1985.

The House panel's deficit reduction proposals totaled $77.5 billion in fiscal 1983, $142.55 billion in fiscal 1984 and $197.5 billion in fiscal 1985. *(Reductions compared, box, this page)*

Economic assumptions adopted by the House committee were identical to those used by the Senate panel.

The only challenge to those assumptions came from Kemp, who with Ed Bethune, R-Ark., offered an amendment to change the entire baseline from which the budget was calculated. Kemp asserted that the fiscal 1982 deficit currently reported by the Treasury Department was running substantially below projections. He said a lower deficit in the current year would affect deficits in future years.

Kemp maintained that the committee's baseline, which was agreed to during the high-level negotiations by the administration and the majority staffs of the House and Senate Budget committees, overestimated the cost of defense and other outlays, underestimated revenues and overestimated Social Security cost-of-living adjustments.

The committee rejected by an 8-21 vote his amendment to lower baseline deficit projections to $105 billion in fiscal 1982, $155.1 billion in fiscal 1983, $172 billion in fiscal 1984 and $186.6 billion in fiscal 1985.

In other action during the markups, the committee adopted amendments by:

• Norman Y. Mineta, D-Calif., to transfer approximately $1 billion in outlays over the next three fiscal years from defense to space programs, to maintain the current schedule for space shuttle operations.

• Adam Benjamin Jr., D-Ind., to add $400 million in outlays annually in fiscal 1983, 1984 and 1985 for the Coast Guard, Amtrak and Interstate highways.

• Richard A. Gephardt, D-Mo., to increase revenues by $1.9 billion and outlays by $942 million over three years, to provide up to 13 weeks' additional unemployment benefits. The revenue would be raised by lowering the threshold at

which an individual must start paying taxes on his unemployment benefits. This amendment also increased outlays by $290 million over three years to change welfare program disregards.

• Obey and Les Aspin, D-Wis., to restore the full COLAs for veterans and railroad retirees, thus increasing outlays by $2.75 billion over the next three fiscal years.

Major House Proposals

Following is a summary of the major proposals agreed to by the House Budget Committee. All of the savings are in outlay numbers.

Revenues. The plan called for revenue increases of $30.7 billion in fiscal 1983, $50.65 billion in fiscal 1984 and $65.5 billion in fiscal 1985 — a total of $147 billion. Although the committee could not make specific recommendations on how to achieve these added revenues, such large increases would be difficult to accomplish without touching the 1981 tax cuts.

The Senate committee's plan would raise $52 billion less in revenues than the House panel's — $95 billion over

---

Deficit Reduction Plans

(Fiscal 1983-85, in billions of dollars)

	Senate Committee	House Committee
Baseline Deficits	$630	$630
Adjustments for COLAs and 1982 supplementals	—	−1
Adjusted deficits	630	629
Deficit Reduction Plan		
Management initiatives	−33	−43
User fees (outlays and revenues)	−6	−6
Federal pay, retirement	−43	−29
Discretionary freeze	−39	−33
Add-backs to discretionaries	—	+8
Targeted entitlement reform	−33	−14
Other minor changes	—	−2
Defense (except pay, retirement)	−22	−47
Revenue increases	−95	−147
Social Security benefit cuts or tax increases	−40	—
Interest rates	−55	−55
Debt service	−51	−50
Total, deficit reduction	−416	−418
Remaining Deficits	$214	$211

Note: Figures may not add due to rounding.

Source: House Budget Committee

---

the next three fiscal years. Both committees approved a $6 billion increase in user fees in fiscal 1983-85.

COLAs, Federal Pay. COLA increases for federal employees and retired military personnel would be capped for the next three years at 4 percent. Pay increases during these three years also would be limited to 4 percent. The freezes would save $4.7 billion in fiscal 1983, $9.7 billion in fiscal 1984, and $14.2 billion in fiscal 1985. Total House committee savings would be $29 billion, compared to $43 billion in the Senate resolution.

The Senate measure would freeze most COLAs for one year — although Social Security was not touched — and would provide 4 percent increases in fiscal 1984 and 1985. It also would freeze federal pay for one year, except for military readiness-related personnel, and provide a 4 percent increase in fiscal 1984 and 1985.

Entitlement Savings. Unspecified savings from entitlement programs such as Medicaid, welfare and food stamps would be $3 billion in fiscal 1983, $4.65 billion in fiscal 1984 and $6.65 billion in fiscal 1985 — a total of $14 billion over three years. The Senate resolution called for considerably higher savings — $33.8 billion over three years.

Non-Defense Discretionary Spending. Although most non-defense discretionary spending programs would be frozen at the fiscal 1982 baseline budget authority level, the House budget resolution added back money in certain areas and made policy assumptions to accommodate job training and other programs. This made the total savings in these programs lower than the Senate resolution's. Savings in discretionary spending in the House resolution would be $4.9 billion in fiscal 1983, $10.6 billion in fiscal 1984 and $17.2 billion in fiscal 1985. Total non-defense discretionary program savings in the Senate resolution would be $38.3 billion.

Defense. The House resolution would cut defense spending increases by a total of $47 billion. In fiscal 1983 the reduction would be $8.9 billion, in fiscal 1984 $15.6 billion and in fiscal 1985 $22.75 billion. This compared to a three-year reduction of $22 billion in the Senate resolution. The House committee's recommendation assumed 5 percent real growth in defense spending; the Senate's assumed about a 7 percent rate.

Procedural Difficulties

Jones tried in the House committee, as Domenici had in the Senate panel, to include several procedural changes in the resolution. Like Domenici, Jones was rebuffed.

In the House the focal point of the controversy was reconciliation, the mechanism for achieving the budget savings included in the resolution.

The 1981 budget reconciliation battles — in which the work of most of the authorizing committees was cast aside in favor of an administration-GOP congressional package — had left a bitter taste with most House committee chairmen. *(1981 reconciliation bill, 1981 Almanac p. 256)*

Ways and Means Chairman Dan Rostenkowski, D-Ill., was especially sensitive to problems with reconciliation, since his committee would have to make the lion's share of the cuts.

At his insistence, the House Budget Committee's resolution included no date for reporting back legislation increasing revenues and making entitlement benefit changes. Under the Senate resolution, committees would have to report reconciliation legislation to the Budget committees by June 18.

Jones also wanted to include a provision that would have automatically made the first resolution binding if a second resolution were not adopted by Sept. 25.

Jones' proposal presented problems with the Appropriations Committee because of enforcement procedures relating to spending ceilings, and the provision was dropped, as it had been by Domenici.

Senate Floor Action

The Senate made substantial modifications in the resolution reported by its Budget Committee before approving S Con Res 92 May 21 by a 49-43 vote. *(Vote 153, p. 28-S)*

Acceding to pressure from moderate Republican senators and to partisan sniping from Democrats, Senate GOP leaders decided to remove from the Budget Committee's resolution provisions that would have reduced the cost of Social Security benefits by $40 billion over the next three years.

Once the modifications were made, in a closed-door Republican caucus, Senate Republicans successfully fended off most Democratic amendments — including two that were directed at eliminating the third year of the individual income tax cuts enacted in 1981.

The deletion of Social Security savings and additional funds for domestic programs increased the fiscal 1983 deficit under the modified Senate resolution from $106.1 billion to $115.4 billion. By fiscal 1985 the deficit would drop to $64.4 billion.

GOP Modifications

Before beginning to vote on amendments, the Senate had to modify the resolution reported by the Senate Budget Committee to incorporate the changes approved by the Republican caucus.

The Republicans were able to make these changes without a floor vote because of a Senate rule that allowed the majority of a committee to modify a measure on the floor as long as it had not yet been amended.

In major changes from the Budget Committee's package, the modified resolution:

● Removed Social Security solvency savings. However, it included reconciliation instructions requiring the Finance and Ways and Means committees to approve legislation by Dec. 1 that would make the Social Security trust funds solvent.

● Increased revenues $6.2 billion in fiscal 1983-1985.

● Reduced the savings from Medicaid by $6.2 billion over three years.

● Eliminated $2 billion in savings from the guaranteed student loan program.

● Added back money for 12 programs in which fiscal 1981 deferrals lowered the budget authority level in fiscal 1982. This added $3.4 billion over three years.

● Provided additional funds for space and science; housing; veterans' pensions, compensation and health programs; and postal service. These changes added $2.5 billion in fiscal 1983 spending.

● Added $4.4 billion over three years for interest costs due to higher deficits.

In all, the revisions increased outlays a total of $9.3 billion in fiscal 1983, $22.3 billion in fiscal 1984 and $24.9 billion in fiscal 1985.

The Senate modifications increased taxes by $107.2 billion, reduced the increase in defense spending by $22

billion, and reduced all domestic spending programs — including entitlements — $70.8 billion.

Successful Amendments

Democrats — and a few Republicans — made repeated attempts throughout the week of debate to increase funds for some domestic programs and reduce funds for others.

The Democrats were successful on very few occasions. The most costly Democratic amendment adopted, by a 57-40 vote May 21, was one offered by Jim Sasser, D-Tenn., to restore the full COLA for railroad retirees, as well as fund "windfall" provisions of a 1974 Railroad Retirement Act, and money for railroad retirement field offices. *(Vote 139, p. 26-S)*

The total cost of the amendment would be $1.7 billion in fiscal 1982-85. Republicans twice tried to fend off Sasser by proposing less costly modifications of his amendment, but their amendments were tabled. *(Votes 135, 138, pp. 25-S, 26-S)*

The Senate also agreed, by voice vote, to amendments by:

● Dale Bumpers, D-Ark., adding $18.6 million in fiscal 1983-85 for childhood immunization programs.

● John H. Chafee, R-R.I., adding $76.5 million in fiscal 1983-85 for maternal and child health care.

Tax Cuts

The most telling rebuff to the Democrats came May 20 when the Senate rejected 32-68 an amendment offered by Ernest F. Hollings, D-S.C., to repeal the third installment of the 1981 individual income tax cut and add that amount to the $107.2 billion in increased revenues required under the resolution over the next three years.

Hollings lost 19 Democrats but picked up five Republicans on the roll call, which was the first up-or-down Senate vote on Reagan's tax cut in 1982. *(Vote 132, p. 25-S)*

Following the Hollings vote, Minority Leader Byrd offered a "sense of the Senate" amendment advising the Finance Committee, as part of its revenue-raising package, that the Senate favored deferral of the third year of the tax cut or eliminating it entirely and replacing it with a "fiscally prudent" tax cut as opposed to "new regressive taxes on Americans."

The Senate rejected the Byrd amendment almost as soundly, by a 35-63 vote. *(Vote 133, p. 25-S)*

Few Close Votes

There were very few close votes during Senate floor action.

One amendment, offered by Nancy Landon Kassebaum, R-Kan., to reduce outlays for defense spending by $13.9 billion over the next three years, concerned Senate GOP leaders, however. Kassebaum argued that the amendment would "slow the pace at which such a [defense] buildup would take place to a rate consistent with sound economic policy."

The amendment was tabled on a 53-44 vote, even though 14 Republicans voted with her. *(Vote 125, p. 24-S)*

The closest vote came on a proposal by Gary Hart, D-Colo., to restore $931 million in fiscal 1983-85 for Title I education programs for disadvantaged children, and for handicapped children. The amendment was defeated 48-51. Hart lost again when his motion to reconsider the amendment was tabled 51-49. *(Votes 129, 130, p. 25-S)*

Other amendments rejected included proposals by:

● John Melcher, D-Mont., and Dennis DeConcini, D-

Ariz., to reduce outlays for foreign aid by $7 billion in fiscal 1982-85. Rejected 27-73. *(Vote 128, p. 24-S)*

● Lawton Chiles, D-Fla., to restore full COLAs for veterans' pensions and compensation benefits, fund veterans' hospitals and clinics at the administration's request level, and assume only $150 million of legislative savings recommended by the Veterans' Affairs Committee. Rejected 46-53. *(Vote 134, p. 25-S)*

● Byrd, D-W.Va., to extend unemployment benefits an additional 13 weeks in states suffering high unemployment, at a cost of $1.1 billion in fiscal 1982-84. Tabled 52-42. *(Vote 140, p. 26-S)*

House Rule for Debate

The House May 21 adopted by voice vote a complicated rule to govern House floor debate on its resolution.

This so-called "king of the mountain" rule provided for votes on seven alternatives to the measure reported by the Budget Committee, plus a number of perfecting amendments.

The major alternatives were:

● A bipartisan package produced by Minority Leader Robert H. Michel, R-Ill., ranking Budget Committee Republican Delbert L. Latta, R-Ohio, OMB Director Stockman and members of the conservative Democratic "Boll Weevils" and moderate Republican "Gypsy Moths" who had ensured Reagan's success in 1981.

● The so-called "moderate bipartisan" plan, sponsored by a group of Gypsy Moths as well as a group of Budget Committee Democrats.

● The Jones-Budget Committee resolution as reported.

The chief differences among the Michel-Latta package, the moderate bipartisan plan and the Budget Committee resolution involved defense spending, tax increases and non-defense discretionary spending.

The Michel plan took the smallest bite out of the increase in defense spending — lopping $22 billion over the next three years off the president's request compared to the moderate bipartisan plan's $45.7 billion reduction and the Budget Committee's $47.4 billion cut.

On the other hand, the Michel plan called for the lowest amount of new taxes over the next three years — $95 billion, compared to the $138.4 billion in tax increases in the bipartisan moderate plan and $146.9 billion in the Budget Committee's version of the resolution.

The biggest chunk of cuts in the Michel plan came in the non-defense discretionary area. These programs would be reduced by $45.8 billion in the Michel plan, compared to $32.4 billion in the moderate bipartisan plan and $32.7 billion in the committee resolution.

In one other major difference, both the Michel plan and the Budget Committee resolution called for a 4 percent freeze in COLAs for federal employee and military pension plans, while the moderate bipartisan group did not touch COLAs.

Complex Procedure

Before voting on the three major alternatives, the rule decreed that the House was to vote on four "Category A" options:

● A plan offered by Rep. George Miller, D-Calif., — known as the "pay as you go" budget — that would balance the budget by fiscal 1985.

● A liberal plan — known as the Obey budget for its chief sponsor.

- An alternative drafted by the Black Caucus.
- A balanced budget plan sponsored by California Republicans John H. Rousselot and William E. Dannemeyer.

Following votes on these four plans, the House was to move to the three major, or "Category B," alternatives. All three were to be considered simultaneously, and all perfecting amendments could be offered to all of the plans.

Once consideration of the perfecting amendments was completed, the House was to vote on 1) Michel-Latta, 2) moderate bipartisan and 3) Jones-Budget Committee. The last alternative to win a majority of the votes would prevail.

Rules Committee Chairman Richard Bolling, D-Mo., acknowledged that the rule was "necessarily very complicated," adding that as "far as I know it's unique."

Minority Whip Trent Lott, R-Miss., a Rules Committee member, said when the panel approved the rule by voice vote May 20, "I think it [the rule] gives everybody a fair and even shot."

Initial House Floor Action

House leaders of both parties had warned for weeks that no budget package could win approval in the chamber. On May 27 the House proved them dead right.

In the course of defeating eight budget alternatives, during a session that extended into the early hours of May 28, the House illustrated just how divided it was over the framework of a fiscal 1983 budget.

It also showed members' disdain for the budget process itself. In addition to casting aside all budget options for fiscal 1983, the House agreed to amendments that eliminated the only enforcement teeth in the budget resolution: the ability to hold back appropriations bills if they exceeded spending allocation levels.

No one came out of the budget battle unscathed. The House action handed President Reagan his first House budget defeat and provided clear signs that the solid wall of GOP votes that pushed through the administration's 1981 economic plan was crumbling.

Meanwhile, the House Democrats' budget track record remained unblemished — they had not won a single budget fight since Reagan was elected.

Budget Chairman Jones and ranking minority member Latta agreed that the complex procedure under which the initial budget was debated was a "tragic mistake." Jones pledged to try to "narrow the differences" and offer members a clear choice between two alternative plans.

Following the House defeat, Minority Leader Michel told members it was clear to him that for a budget to pass it would have to move "several degrees to the right."

Michel singled out one amendment — offered by Ohio Democrat Mary Rose Oakar — to restore Medicare funding in fiscal 1983 to current services levels while taking an equivalent amount out of defense — as the key to the defeat of the Reagan-backed Michel-Latta substitute. "That was the margin of difference," Michel argued.

The Michel-Latta budget, which of the major alternatives garnered the highest number of votes, was defeated 192-235. *(Vote 121, p. 34-H)*

The moderate-bipartisan, or Aspin, substitute (named after sponsor Les Aspin, D-Wis.) was defeated 137-289. *(Vote 122, p. 36-H)*

The Budget Committee plan, as amended, was defeated 171-253. *(Vote 123, p. 36-H)*

Speaker O'Neill closed debate on the final option — the Budget Committee resolution as originally reported.

"We come to the moment of decision," he said. "The hour is late. Most Americans have retired for the evening. Tomorrow morning, when they wake up, I want them to know that Congress did its job and passed a budget."

But the House defeated the Budget Committee's plan, 159-265. *(Vote 124, p. 36-H)*

Oakar: The 'Key'

When the House began its fifth day of debate on the budget May 27, both Democratic and Republican leaders thought the volatile Medicare issue — which had replaced Social Security in the Democrats' strategy as providing the clearest distinction between the GOP plan and the two others — had been put to rest.

The night before, Henry A. Waxman, D-Calif., told the House that he did not want an amendment he had planned to offer to become "the engine that drives the [Republican] budget." His proposal would have added $16.3 billion in Medicare funds over the next three years to the GOP substitute.

All of the three major budget alternatives included cuts in Medicare funding. But the Michel-Latta plan cut the deepest — $23.3 billion over three years. The Jones and the moderate-bipartisan plans each cut $9.3 billion from fiscal 1983-85. Waxman's amendment would have offset the increase in money for Medicare by increasing taxes in the GOP plan by $19.5 billion over three years.

According to Wright, Waxman met that night with the House leadership, along with other members involved in the Medicare issue, and was assured there was no way the Ways and Means Committee — with jurisdiction over Medicare — could come up with Medicare cuts of the size included in the GOP substitute.

That meant that during reconciliation — when the House would convert the targeted savings in the budget resolution into actual legislation — the Republicans would have to offer a floor amendment to meet the Medicare savings targets, and they would have to fight for it. That would take the Medicare issue out of the Democrats' hands. Waxman, convinced that Medicare could not in practice be cut as deeply as the Republican plan called for, decided not to offer his amendment.

At that same meeting, however, several members reported to the leadership that the move to add the Oakar amendment to the Republican plan would lose. Their calculation was that since the amendment also would reduce defense spending, Republicans would not vote for it — and Democrats, who now believed they had the Republicans on the run on Medicare, would not need to vote for Oakar.

But a combination of unforeseen forces surprised both sides. And the end result preordained the ultimate defeat of the GOP plan.

The debate on the amendment was clear-cut. "You have a choice of choosing between our older and disabled people in the country and the price of a cost overrun of a helicopter," Oakar said.

Opponents, including ranking Ways and Means Republican Barber B. Conable Jr., N.Y., argued that the Republicans were not cutting Medicare, just reducing the size of the growth in the program. Conable said that over the next three years Medicare would grow 31.3 percent.

When the vote began, members watched as many of their colleagues — 64 at one point — voted "present."

Most of those voting present were conservative Republicans who wanted to send a signal to their leaders that they were unhappy with the GOP package. They objected

both to the size of the deficit — over $100 billion in fiscal 1983 — and the $95 billion in increased taxes over three years.

Democrats, seeing another chance to cast their Republican colleagues as the ones that would "choose a 40-year-old battleship over their 80-year-old mother," as one Democrat put it, voted for Oakar. With all members up for re-election, Republicans and conservative Democrats began voting "aye" too.

By then the "present" votes were turning to "nays," but the momentum was behind the proposal. The Oakar amendment to the GOP plan was agreed to 228-196. The House then added it to the moderate-bipartisan substitute, 328-94, and to the Budget Committee plan by voice vote. *(Votes 110, 111, p. 32-H)*

After the vote, a Michel aide despondently noted that it would be "a small miracle if we are able to pull it off with that kind of baggage on it." The baggage was a $4.85 billion increase in Medicare funding in fiscal 1983 and a decrease in defense outlays of the same amount.

One of the conservatives who voted present was Bill Archer, R-Texas. Archer told reporters following the vote that there was a "growing nucleus" of conservatives who believed the deficit must fall below $100 billion in fiscal 1983. This core conservative group decided to vote against all of the major alternatives.

Before the Fall

When the House began debating the resolution May 21, it had before it, under a complex procedure, seven distinct alternatives and 68 perfecting amendments. The measure as reported provided an eighth option.

The four "Category A" alternatives were debated and defeated by the next day:

● California liberal Miller's "pay as you go" plan, would have frozen all spending at current levels. Any increase in spending would have had to be offset by either increases in taxes or cuts in other spending areas.

"What is clear to me is that the financial markets of this country, and the people we represent, do not expect miracles from the Congress, but they do expect truth," Miller said.

His plan was defeated 181-225. *(Vote 90, p. 26-H)*

● The House next defeated, 152-268, a plan authored by Obey that would have provided additional funds for job training, mass transit, veterans' medical care and other domestic programs and paid for these add-ons by dramatically increasing taxes — $233 billion over the next three years. Obey argued that his plan would "preserve the guts" of domestic spending. *(Vote 91, p. 26-H)*

● A package put together by the Congressional Black Caucus was rejected, 86-322. This plan also would have increased aid to education, job training and health care. Just as in the Obey plan, these domestic programs would be paid for by large increases in new taxes from fiscal 1983-85. *(Vote 92, p. 28-H)*

● The Category A plan that came closest to winning was the balanced budget package offered by two California conservative Republicans, Rousselot and Dannemeyer. In order to reach a balanced budget in fiscal 1983, the Rousselot-Dannemeyer plan would have cut domestic spending $113.9 billion in fiscal 1983 and by 1985 would have reduced spending in these programs $452.2 billion. "We've talked about it, we've discussed it, now we can vote for it," Rousselot told his colleagues. The balanced budget plan was defeated 182-242. *(Vote 94, p. 28-H)*

Major Options

By the final day of debate, with action on amendments completed, the House had before it three options that fully pleased none of the sponsors but had fairly comparable bottom lines.

The differences among the three major contenders — the Michel-Latta plan, the moderate-bipartisan plan and the Jones-House Budget Committee plan — were in the ways the money was divided.

The Michel budget wound up, according to House Budget Committee calculations reflecting the authors' figures, with a fiscal 1983 deficit of $103.50 billion. It would have cut the least from defense spending and raised taxes the least. Large cuts, however, were made in both entitlement and discretionary spending.

The breakdown of the Michel budget showed that for the next three fiscal years entitlement cuts would have totaled $29.05 billion, discretionary cuts $42.6 billion, defense cuts $26.8 billion and additional revenues $95 billion.

The Jones-Budget Committee plan, as amended, called for the highest increase in revenues and the smallest cuts in entitlement and discretionary programs.

The Jones budget, which according to its authors would have resulted in a $105 billion fiscal 1983 deficit, called over the next three fiscal years for $12.5 billion in entitlement cuts, $22.8 billion in non-defense discretionary cuts, $50.15 billion in defense cuts and $146.9 billion in new revenues.

Finally, the moderate-bipartisan or Aspin plan had the highest defense cuts and fell in between the other two alternatives in all other areas. The plan would have resulted, over the next three fiscal years, in $13.25 billion in entitlement cuts, $29.8 billion in discretionary cuts, $54.55 billion in defense cuts and $134.8 billion in new revenues.

This moderate-bipartisan plan, according to its authors, also would have produced the smallest fiscal 1983 deficit — $97.2 billion.

Amendments Accepted

During the course of floor consideration, the House adopted several amendments to one or all of the substitutes. These amendments included proposals by:

● Silvio O. Conte, R-Mass., to the Michel substitute, increasing budget authority by $963 million and outlays by $737 million in fiscal 1983, for a variety of education programs including handicapped education, Head Start and vocational education. Adopted 343-72. *(Vote 108, p. 32-H)*

● W. G. "Bill" Hefner, D-N.C., to add $300 million in budget authority and $250 million in outlays to all three substitutes in fiscal 1983 for veterans' hospitals.

● Steny Hoyer, D-Md., to all three substitutes, to provide for a 5 percent pay increase for federal employees instead of the 4 percent increase assumed by all the substitutes. The amendment added $398 million to the fiscal 1983 deficit. Adopted 259-159. *(Vote 113, p. 32-H)*

● Thomas J. Downey, D-N.Y., to Jones and Michel, to provide a full cost-of-living adjustment for all federal civilian and military personnel. The amendment added $500 million to the deficit in fiscal 1983, $1.65 billion in fiscal 1984 and $2.9 billion in fiscal 1985. Adopted 327-94. *(Vote 114, p. 34-H)*

Turf Fight

In the midst of the turmoil over substantive issues came a successful move by Appropriations Committee Chairman Jamie L. Whitten, D-Miss., to remove what little

enforcement language the budget resolution contained.

Whitten's amendment removed a provision of H Con Res 345 that called for the deferred enrollment, until adoption of the second budget resolution, of any appropriations bill that exceeded the allocations provided to the Appropriations Committee under the first resolution. Any bill going over this amount would be held at the desk and could not be sent to the president for his signature.

Whitten argued that the Appropriations Committee had "a splendid record on holding down spending." If the Budget Committee could meet its deadlines, the Appropriations Committee could move ahead with its work, he maintained.

But since the Budget Committee and the House did not act quickly enough, Whitten said, Appropriations was forced to write money bills under unrealistic constraints of time and changing conditions.

Ralph Regula, R-Ohio, a member of the Budget Committee, responded, "If we adopt this amendment we would really de-fang the Budget Act." Regula said Congress had, at the outset, to decide what its priorities were. "Once we establish those priorities we have to follow them — or we lose the impact of the Budget Act."

Opposing Whitten, Budget Chairman Jones said, "I regret that we're having this jurisdictional squabble when we ought to be talking about economic policy."

In the vote on the amendment, many members who were disturbed over the power and pervasive influence of the Budget Committee and the budget process showed their discontent by voting with the Appropriations chairman.

The Whitten amendment was added to all three substitutes: by a 73-72 teller vote to the moderate-bipartisan plan, by a 212-205 vote to the GOP plan, and finally by voice vote to the committee plan. *(Vote 119, p. 34-H)*

House Approval

By squeezing the deficit down below $100 billion and maintaining party discipline, the House Republican leadership was able June 10 to eke out a narrow victory and win approval of a first budget resolution for fiscal 1983 (H Con Res 352).

The victory came on a vote in favor of a GOP-sponsored amendment to a revised measure reported by the Budget Committee June 7 (H Rept 97-597). *(Vote 134, p. 40-H)*

Following the defeat of H Con Res 345 on the House floor May 28, the Budget Committee had met June 3 and agreed to report the president's February budget, to be used as a vehicle for House votes on two alternative plans drafted by the Republicans and the Democrats. If both alternatives failed, the House would have had to vote on the Reagan budget. That was a prospect the Republicans clearly did not relish, since there was virtually no support for the president's original blueprint.

Budget Chairman Jones once again was the shepherd for a losing Democratic budget, defeated 202-225. *(Vote 133, p. 40-H)*

The amended resolution was adopted by a 219-206 margin. *(Vote 135, p. 40-H)*

The House-passed resolution envisioned a $99.27 billion deficit, while the version approved by the Senate (S Con Res 92) showed a deficit just under $116 billion.

The House resolution required the Ways and Means Committee to come up with $20.9 billion in new revenues

for fiscal 1983. And it required seven committees to draft savings totaling $4.2 billion in budget authority in fiscal 1983 and $8.1 billion in outlays.

The decisive 220-207 House vote came on what was called the Latta plan after its primary sponsor, the ranking Budget Committee Republican. GOP leaders referred to it as the "bipartisan" plan.

Forty-six Democrats voted with 174 Republicans on the vote for Latta, while only 15 Republicans, mostly moderate "Gypsy Moths," voted against their party's plan.

Thirty-three members — 25 Democrats and eight Republicans — who had voted against an earlier GOP budget voted for the new one.

The mood on the House floor was sober and weary. After the debacle of May 27-28, when the House turned down eight budget options — including major plans advanced by each party — many members wanted to pass a budget just to get it over with.

"I am going to hold my nose a little," said North Carolina Democrat Hefner, "and vote for Jones." He added, "I'll hold my nose a lot if it fails and vote for Latta, simply because we have to have a budget...."

The specter of what would happen without a budget was raised often. Minority Whip Lott said there would be "nothing but chaos and confrontation the rest of the year" if the House did not adopt a resolution.

Democratic leaders, while decrying the Republican budget as inhumane, also called on members to vote for at least one of the budgets. Majority Leader Wright asked "every member of this House to exercise that choice."

House Budget Plan

The budget resolution adopted by the House followed the same pattern as the Senate's — making further and even deeper cuts in entitlement and discretionary domestic spending while allowing sizable increases for defense and maintaining the third year of individual tax cuts.

In the area of entitlements, the House budget called for a total of $7.4 billion in targeted savings in fiscal 1983 — and a total of $32.6 billion during fiscal 1983-85.

Republicans added $1.7 billion in fiscal 1983 back into Medicare from their previously defeated budget. But the new plan also called for additional savings totaling $834 million in Medicaid, $414 million for public assistance, $837 million in food stamps and nutrition programs, and a total of $108 million in changes in trade adjustment assistance and guaranteed student loans.

In discretionary programs, the House budget would freeze employment and training programs at the fiscal 1982 level and reduce spending for non-medical veterans' programs, the Federal Trade Commission, Urban Development Action Grants, fossil fuel research and development, and postal subsidies.

Other parts of the House deficit-reduction package included an additional 1 percent reduction in the federal work force and $800 million more in cuts for foreign aid. Outlays for international affairs would be $11.2 billion compared to $12.05 billion in the original GOP plan.

In defense spending, the House plan called for larger cutbacks in President Reagan's proposed increase than the Senate version did. The House resolution included $253.57 billion in budget authority and $213.97 billion in outlays in fiscal 1983. The Senate-passed version called for $251.7 billion in budget authority and $215.3 billion in outlays.

The House plan cut $7.85 billion in fiscal 1983 outlays from Reagan's defense request, while the Senate measure

cut $5 billion. Over three years the House budget would cut $28.45 billion from his defense increase. The Senate's would shave $22 billion.

Democratic Alternative

The Democratic leadership said its budget would be true to the party's traditional principles, and additions to its previously rejected budget reflected that philosophy.

The Democrats started out with the resolution approved by the House Budget Committee and rejected on the floor in May. But then they added approximately $3 billion for domestic programs — much of that reflecting amendments that were agreed to during the May 27 floor debate on the defeated resolution, H Con Res 345.

The inclusion of these programs, without offsetting increases in revenues, brought the deficit in the Democratic program up to $107.45 billion in fiscal 1983. The Democratic plan's deficit would have dropped to $78.4 billion in fiscal 1984 and $41.9 billion in fiscal 1985.

Total outlays in fiscal 1983 under the Democratic alternative would have been $784.1 billion; total fiscal 1983 revenues would have been $676.7 billion.

Final Deficit Reductions

(Fiscal years, in billions of dollars)

	1983	1984	1985
Baseline Deficit	$ 182.0	$ 216.0	$ 232.5
Adjustments to baseline	−1.3	−1.4	−1.5
Adjusted baseline deficit	180.7	214.6	231.0
Deficit Reduction Measures			
Revenue increases	20.0	35.0	40.0
User fees (revenues)	0.9	1.0	1.4
Defense (except pay and entitlements)	7.6	8.2	10.5
Federal pay raises	5.2	9.0	11.8
Non-defense discretionary programs	6.3	10.2	18.8
COLAs	0.5	1.8	3.1
Other entitlement savings	5.9	9.0	10.4
Management savings	13.6	17.0	15.8
User fees (spending offsets)	1.1	1.4	1.7
Other program reductions	1.2	1.3	1.1
Net interest:			
Lower rates	8.0	19.1	27.8
Lower deficits	6.5	17.7	28.6
Total deficit reduction	76.8	130.7	171.0
Remaining Deficits	$ 103.9	$ 83.9	$ 60.0

Note: Figures may not add due to rounding.

Source: Senate Budget Committee

Conference Action

Congressional conferees, dominated by Republicans from both houses, June 17 approved a conference agreement on the resolution (H Rept 97-614) that envisioned budget deficits of $103.9 billion in fiscal 1983 and $105.7 billion in 1982.

The agreement, primarily based on a compromise drafted behind closed doors by Senate and House Republicans and modified slightly by the full conference, called for fiscal 1983 revenues of $665.9 billion, including $20.9 billion in tax increases and other money-raising measures, and outlays of $769.8 billion.

Democrats at the conference, led by House Budget Chairman Jones, left it up to GOP members from both houses to settle a "family squabble" on the basic outline of a compromise.

Even though the final agreement was closer to the House's version than to the Senate's, House Minority Leader Michel acknowledged that he would have problems convincing conservatives to vote for the budget.

"We'll have some real heartburn" over the deficits, Michel said. But he predicted, "With all the blood, sweat and tears that went into this thing I think I can sell some people. And by swallowing hard, they'll vote for it in sufficient numbers."

Controversial Figures

Democrats criticized the figures in the final resolution because Republicans had departed from budget assumptions previously agreed upon by House, Senate and White House representatives and calculated by the Congressional Budget Office.

"I feel very strongly we are underestimating where the deficit is going to be," Jones said. Hollings, the Senate Budget Committee's ranking Democrat, declared, "We know it's out of whole cloth. We know it."

Senate Budget Chairman Domenici defended the final agreement's deficit projections, although he previously had insisted that the Senate stick with the CBO numbers in its version of S Con Res 92. "It has about as much realism as any budget we've produced," Domenici said.

The final agreement revised the "baseline" deficit — the amount assumed if the budget made no policy changes from current law except to approve President Reagan's defense increases — from the $182 billion figure that had been used by budget leaders since the "Gang of 17" talks with Reagan that collapsed in April.

The revised baseline deficit was stated in the agreement at $180.7 billion. Similar adjustments were made in several program areas.

For example, the agreement rejected CBO's estimate for the cost of Reagan's defense program, thus reducing projected defense outlays and the deficit for 1983 by $1.84 billion.

The agreement also accepted Reagan administration estimates — rejected by CBO as too optimistic — for receipts from offshore oil leasing, thus reducing the projected 1983 deficit by $3.8 billion.

The conferees used the House Republicans' revenue estimate for fiscal 1982 to lower the projected deficit for the year by $5.4 billion.

These and similar deficit reductions — which Democrats claimed existed only on paper — also reduced projected costs for net interest, one of the fastest growing elements of the federal budget, for fiscal 1982-85.

Shift Toward House

Besides accepting the accounting methods from the House-approved budget, the conference agreement moved toward the House's position in several program areas.

It accepted the House provisions on the defense budget. And it cut foreign aid deeply below the Senate level, which dissenters said would cripple U.S. military aid efforts.

The final resolution embodied the House's deeper level of cuts in education, employment and social services programs, as well as agriculture. It took the higher House level of spending for health.

In some program areas, however, the agreement either accepted the Senate position or fell somewhere between the two houses' versions.

On the question of COLAs and pay raises for federal employees and retirees, the final resolution generally followed the House's more generous recommendations. The Senate would have frozen employee pay and granted no COLAs for federal beneficiaries. But the agreement accepted the House proposal for a 4 percent annual increase.

The final resolution took the Senate's higher spending levels for transportation and for the category of science, space and technology.

The agreement included lower spending approved by the Senate for community and regional development and ended up between the two houses' versions on commerce and housing credit. But Domenici said it still allowed for a $3 billion housing aid program included in a pending conference agreement on the urgent fiscal 1982 supplemental appropriations bill (HR 5922). The bill subsequently was vetoed. *(Story, p. 219)*

On domestic programs, the agreement was a compromise between the House emphasis on cutting benefit programs for the poor, such as food stamps, Medicaid and Aid to Families With Dependent Children (AFDC), and the deeper Senate cuts in the largely middle-class Medicare program.

Program Levels

It was in these domestic programs that Democrats had the most success in softening the impact of the GOP compromise proposal, although they emphasized that the final product still was unacceptable to most in their party.

The Republican proposal, which generally split the difference between the two houses' versions, called for fiscal 1983 outlay reductions of $1.1 billion in child nutrition and food stamps, $3.6 billion in Medicare, $900 million in Medicaid, $400 million in AFDC, $200 million in Supplemental Security Income (SSI), $100 million in child support enforcement and $250 million for subsidized housing.

The GOP-controlled Senate delegation agreed to modify this plan, however, by accepting an amendment advanced by Jones to restore $200 million for food stamps and nutrition, $200 million for Medicaid and $10 million for AFDC and SSI combined.

Jones' amendment, which also included a $200 million restoration of space funds, was the Democrats' major success in altering the GOP budget.

Democratic proposals that failed included efforts by

Fiscal 1983 Targets Become Binding

Although the validity of the figures in the first fiscal 1983 budget resolution was widely questioned, the House and Senate Budget committees put off until the 98th Congress any effort to revise or update them.

Noting that action on fiscal 1983 appropriations bills was "far from complete," Senate Budget Committee Chairman Pete V. Domenici, R-N.M., told colleagues Oct. 1 that changes in the budget resolution should be put off "to give the appropriations process the time necessary to run its course without the intrusion of policy changes in the middle of that action." Budget revisions could be considered in connection with the first fiscal 1984 budget resolution, Domenici said.

Because Congress did not adopt a second resolution before the fiscal year began Oct. 1, the preliminary targets set in S Con Res 92 became binding limits on fiscal 1983 spending decisions.

Pending adoption of a revised resolution, congressional spending decisions for fiscal 1983 would be governed by provisions of S Con Res 92 that called for budget authority of $822.39 billion, outlays of $769.818 billion, revenues of $665.9 billion and a deficit of $103.918 billion.

Spending legislation also was required to remain within the following limits for various program areas, as set in S Con Res 92 *(in billions of dollars)*:

Function	Budget Authority	Outlays
National defense	$ 253.566	$ 213.966
International affairs	15.900	11.500
General science, space and technology	7.800	7.600
Energy	4.800	4.500
Natural resources and environment	9.500	10.950
Agriculture	6.692	9.042
Commerce and housing credit	7.100	2.837
Transportation	21.450	19.900
Community and regional development	6.900	7.700
Education, training, employment and social services	26.832	26.205
Health	79.569	77.816
Income security	274.797	270.895
Veterans benefits and services	24.560	23.823
Administration of justice	4.540	4.650
General government	4.800	4.650
General purpose fiscal assistance	6.500	6.500
Interest	113.200	113.200
Allowances	−3,016.000	−2,816.000
Undistributed offsetting receipts	−43.100	−43.100
Total	**$ 822.390**	**$ 769.818**

Rep. Thomas J. Downey, N.Y., to restore more of the social spending, Sen. Lawton Chiles, Fla., to retain more funds for law enforcement, Rep. Adam Benjamin Jr., Ind., to add funds for transportation, and Stephen J. Solarz, N.Y., to undo the foreign aid cuts.

Foreign Aid Fight

Foreign aid proved to be the most hard-fought issue as the conference dragged on late into the night of June 17.

With vocal support from Senate Republican Rudy Boschwitz, Minn., Solarz argued to restore the $600 million in fiscal 1983 foreign affairs outlays that the GOP compromise proposal had cut from the Senate-passed version of the resolution.

The aid cuts, they argued, would have to come out of military programs critical to U.S. foreign policy. The Senate-passed level encompassed Reagan's foreign aid request, and the aid proponents early in the conference brandished a letter from Reagan supporting it.

Boschwitz said the budget would force deep cuts in Foreign Military Sales (FMS) credits for Egypt and Israel, and deny 16 nations — including El Salvador — any FMS aid at all.

But Domenici and Latta turned back the Solarz effort. If the foreign aid funds were put back into the budget, they said, the conference agreement could not pass the House.

"If this amendment succeeds there isn't going to be any compromise," Latta said.

Domenici said he had talked to Reagan. "He indicated to me that he wants a budget," the Senate chairman said. "He would prefer the Senate level of funding . . . but if this was the best we could do to get a budget we should proceed."

The Senate delegation defeated Solarz' efforts on a 5-5 vote, with Republican Boschwitz joining the losing Democratic faction.

Deficit Reductions

To help reach a total of $76.8 billion in deficit reductions from the revised baseline deficit of $180.7 billion in fiscal 1983, the resolution called for $20.9 billion in revenue increases.

That target, which included $900 million in proposed new user fees, was the same level proposed by the House and $2.5 billion below the Senate's figure. The resolution also called for another $1.1 billion in user fees to offset spending.

In defense, the resolution envisioned reductions of $7.6 billion below the baseline level of Reagan's defense proposal for fiscal 1983. The figure for that reduction was distorted by the accounting changes, however. Domenici said the defense savings — stated in terms comparable to the Senate figures — actually would be much closer to the $5 billion cut by the Senate.

The compromise contemplated fiscal 1983 savings of $5.2 billion from the federal pay-raise cap and $500 million from the cap on COLAs.

Non-defense discretionary programs — domestic programs funded by appropriations — would be cut $6.3 billion below the baseline level, and other entitlement savings would come to $5.9 billion.

Management savings, including the controversial estimate for oil leasing, would net $13.6 billion.

The resolution envisioned fiscal 1983 savings of $1.2 billion in miscellaneous other programs, and $14.5 billion from interest savings.

Enforcement

As its primary means of enforcing the budget targets, the resolution included reconciliation instructions ordering congressional committees to draft legislation making the actual spending cuts, which the Budget committees would combine into omnibus legislation for each house to vote on.

The resolution required House committees to report their reconciliation legislation by Aug. 1. Senate committees had until July 20, except for Finance, which had to act by July 12.

Domenici noted that the specific reconciliation instructions included in the agreement did not cover all the spending cuts targeted by the resolution. "I think ultimately something a little stronger will be required" for enforcement, he said.

The compromise resolution did include another enforcement provision, which Domenici had tried and failed to have included in the original Senate version: If Congress did not approve a second budget resolution by Oct. 1, S Con Res 92 automatically would become the binding version.

But in a step back from the kind of budget discipline Domenici had pressed for, the agreement deleted a Senate-passed requirement that congressional committees report by Dec. 1 legislation making revisions in Social Security.

The resolution retained Senate language, also included in the House committee version and the House Republican substitute, telling the Federal Reserve to reconsider its tight-money policy as deficits were reduced.

The provision stated the "sense of Congress" that if projected budget deficits were reduced substantially and permanently, the Fed "shall re-evaluate its monetary targets in order to assure that they are fully complementary to a new and more restrained fiscal policy."

Credit Budget

The final version of S Con Res 92 included House provisions that imposed formal restraints on the total size of federal lending and loan-guarantee programs. Such programs, largely beyond the reach of the conventional budget process, had expanded rapidly in the past decade and had enlarged the federal presence in private credit markets.

The fiscal 1982 budget resolutions had included non-binding targets for credit programs, but the enforcement provisions directed at credit ceilings in S Con Res 92 marked Congress' first attempt to give its credit budget teeth.

Adoption of the temporary credit enforcement mechanism represented a modest but significant victory for members of Congress who had crusaded to make such procedures a permanent part of the congressional budget process.

The credit provisions included in the budget resolution imposed binding restraints on credit programs, similar to curbs on spending programs enforced under the Budget Act.

The resolution set overall ceilings for each of the three major types of federal credit programs: direct loan obligations, primary loan guarantee commitments and secondary loan guarantee commitments. Following the format of the president's credit budget, the measure also divided these totals among broad budget functions such as national defense, agriculture and income security.

In addition, the budget resolution allocated to congressional spending committees — principally the Appropriations panels, but also including a handful of authorizing

committees — subtotals limiting the amount of credit that could be authorized for each type of program within each committee's jurisdiction.

The spending committees, in turn, were required to subdivide their allocations among their own subcommittees.

The key enforcement provision in the resolution blocked floor consideration of any bills that would cause the resolution's totals for direct loan obligations or loan guarantee commitments to be exceeded.

Another provision of the resolution required any authorizations for new direct loan or loan guarantee programs to be subject to limits in appropriations bills.

The budget resolution set the following limits on federal credit programs in fiscal 1983:

● $59.7 billion on new direct loan obligations — authority for agencies to make federal loans available to non-federal recipients.
● $101.9 billion on new primary loan guarantee commitments — authority for agencies to offer federal guarantees that loans provided by non-federal sources to non-federal recipients will be repaid.
● $68.3 billion for new secondary loan commitments — authority for agencies to offer guarantees of loans already guaranteed by other federal programs. ∎

Reconciliation Savings: $130 Billion by 1985

Congress completed action in August on two massive "reconciliation" bills, designed to carry out the deficit reduction instructions incorporated in the first fiscal 1983 budget resolution.

● The Omnibus Reconciliation Act of 1982 (HR 6955 — PL 97-253), cleared Aug. 18, cut anticipated federal spending by $13.3 billion over fiscal 1983-85. The measure tightened spending on government pensions, farm programs, food stamps, federal home loans and veterans' benefits.

● The Tax Equity and Fiscal Responsibility Act of 1982 (HR 4961 — PL 97-248), cleared Aug. 19, was expected to provide $98.3 billion in increased revenues and cut $17.5 billion from projected spending for Medicare, Medicaid, welfare and savings bond programs over fiscal 1983-85.

When combined, the measures were expected to reduce the federal deficit by about $130 billion by fiscal 1985. The budget resolution Congress cleared June 23 (S Con Res 92) had included reconciliation instructions requiring Senate and House committees to come up with about $125.5 billion in deficit reductions over the three-year period.

The budget resolution assumed total deficit reductions of $378.5 billion over fiscal 1983-85, only part of which was to be achieved through reconciliation. Only $27.47 billion of the $76.8 billion assumed for fiscal 1983 was required by the reconciliation instructions, for example. The rest of the assumed fiscal 1983 savings were to come from a variety of sources, including nearly $28.2 billion over which Congress had almost no control: $13.7 billion in management savings and $14.5 billion in lower interest payments.

The budget cuts were measured against spending estimates for the coming year — not against the prior year's spending. The savings were calculated from a baseline established by the Congressional Budget Office (CBO), which projected spending for programs as they existed under current law and then adjusted the figures to take into account anticipated inflation.

The 1982 reconciliation cuts were far less sweeping than those approved in the previous year's reconciliation measure. In the 1981 package (PL 97-35), dozens of federal programs were reshaped as Congress slashed spending by $130.6 billion for fiscal 1982-84. *(1981 Almanac p. 256)*

Reconciliation Requirements

The reconciliation process was created by the 1974 Congressional Budget Act (PL 93-344) as a mechanism for carrying out budget savings sought by Congress. Under the process, authorizing committees could be required to recommend changes in existing law to achieve savings specified in the budget resolution. The committees' legislative savings measures would be incorporated in omnibus legislation and taken to the floor by the Senate and House Budget committees for single up-or-down votes in each chamber.

The reconciliation language included in the fiscal 1983 budget resolution required House committees to report spending-cut and revenue-raising measures by Aug. 1. Senate committees were to report their reconciliation measures by July 20, except for the Finance Committee, which was given a July 12 deadline.

Finance and the House Ways and Means Committee carried the heaviest burden in making the spending cuts, since they had jurisdiction over the bulk of entitlement programs — programs that guaranteed a certain level of benefits to persons who met the requirements set by law.

These two committees also were instructed to raise $20.9 billion in new revenues in fiscal 1983 and a total of $98.3 billion in taxes in fiscal 1983-85.

Their reconciliation instructions assumed the revenue-raising measures would include $900 million in user fees in fiscal 1983 and a total of $3.3 billion in user fees in fiscal 1983-85.

Senate Committees

Taken together, eight Senate committees were required to make fiscal 1983 spending reductions totaling $6.57 billion in outlays. For fiscal 1983-85 the committees were required to report legislation cutting spending by $27.15 billion.

Following is a breakdown of the proposed cuts each committee was directed to make for fiscal 1983-85. The committees were not bound to make the specific program reductions assumed in the reconciliation instructions, but they were required to meet the reduction targets.

Agriculture. Cuts in food stamps: $779 million in 1983; $1.08 billion in 1984; $1.4 billion in 1985.

Armed Services. Four percent cap on cost-of-living adjustments (COLAs) for both military and Public Health Service retirees: $213 million in 1983; $693 million in 1984; $1.23 billion in 1985.

Banking. Federal Housing Administration (FHA) mortgage premiums: $695 million in 1983; $697 million in 1984; and $687 million in 1985.

Senate, House Reconciliation Instructions

(By fiscal year, in millions of dollars)

	1983 Budget Authority	1983 Outlays	1984 Budget Authority	1984 Outlays	1985 Budget Authority	1985 Outlays
SENATE COMMITTEES						
Spending reductions						
Agriculture	$ −779	$ −779	$ −1,083	$ −1,083	$ −1,428	$ −1,428
Armed Services	−213	−213	−693	−693	−1,231	−1,231
Banking	—	−695	—	−697	—	−687
Commerce	−4	−4	−15	−15	−27	−27
Finance	−1,106	−4,429	−1,444	−5,564	−1,740	−5,976
Foreign Relations	—	−2	−2	−8	−4	−15
Governmental Affairs	—	−374	−240	−1,053	−534	−1,793
Veterans	−77	−77	−155	−155	−155	−155
Total spending reductions	−2,179	−6,573	−3,632	−9,268	−5,119	−11,312
Revenue increases						
Finance	—	+20,900	—	+36,000	—	+41,400
(User-fee portion)	—	(+900)	—	(+1,000)	—	(+1,400)
Total reconciliation instructions	—	$ −27,473	—	$ −45,268	—	$ −52,712
HOUSE COMMITTEES						
Spending reductions						
Agriculture	$ −779	$ −779	$ −1,083	$ −1,083	$ −1,428	$ −1,428
Armed Services	−213	−213	−693	−693	−1,231	−1,231
Banking	—	−695	—	−697	—	−687
Energy and Commerce	−514	−675	−741	−739	−815	−811
Foreign Affairs	—	−2	−2	−8	−4	−15
Merchant Marine	−4	−4	−15	−15	−27	−27
Post Office	—	−376	−242	−1,061	−538	−1,808
Veterans	−77	−77	−155	−155	−155	−155
Ways and Means	−593	−3,755	−705	−4,827	−928	−5,168
Total	−2,180	−6,576	−3,636	−9,278	−5,126	−11,330
(Less double counting*)	1	3	4	10	7	18
Total spending reductions	−2,179	−6,573	−3,632	−9,268	−5,119	−11,312
Revenue increases						
Ways and Means	—	+20,900	—	+36,000	—	+41,400
(User-fee portion)	—	(+900)	—	(+1,000)	—	(+1,400)
Total reconciliation instructions	—	$ −27,473	—	$ −45,268	—	$ −52,712

Resulting from dual committee jurisdiction.

Commerce. Four percent cap on Coast Guard retirees' COLAs: $4 million in 1983; $15 million in 1984; and $27 million in 1985.

Finance. Medicare: $3.16 billion in 1983; $4.12 billion in 1984; $4.2 billion in 1985.

Medicaid: $674 million in 1983; $737 million in 1984; and $808 million in 1985.

Aid to Families with Dependent Children (AFDC): $390 million in 1983; $400 million in 1984; and $401 million in 1985.

Supplemental Security Income (SSI): $158 million in 1983; $254 million in 1984; $368 million in 1985.

Child support enforcement: $45 million in 1983; $51 million in 1984; and $159 million in 1985.

Foreign Relations. Four percent cap on foreign service retirees' COLAs: $2 million in 1983; $8 million in 1984; $15 million in 1985.

Governmental Affairs. Four percent cap on civil service retirement and COLAs: $374 million in 1983; $1.05 billion, 1984; $1.79 billion, 1985.

Veterans' Affairs. Four percent cap on COLAs, compensation changes, unspecified entitlement changes: $77 million in 1983; $155 million in 1984; $155 million in 1985.

House Committees

Nine House committees were directed to report reconciliation cuts.

Agriculture. Cuts in food stamps: $779 million in 1983; $1.08 billion in 1984; $1.42 billion in 1985.

Armed Services. Four percent cap on military and Public Health Service retirees' COLAs: $213 million in 1983; $693 million in 1984; $1.23 billion in 1985.

Banking. FHA premiums: $695 million in 1983; $697 million in 1984; and $687 million in 1985.

Energy and Commerce. Medicaid: $674 million in 1983; $737 million in 1984; $811 million in 1985. Four percent cap on Public Health Service retirees' COLAs: $1 million in 1983; $2 million in 1984; $3 million in 1985.

Foreign Affairs. Four percent cap on foreign service retirees' COLAs: $2 million in 1983; $8 million in 1984; $15 million in 1985.

Merchant Marine and Fisheries. Four percent cap on Coast Guard retirees' COLAs: $4 million in 1983; $15 million in 1984; $27 million in 1985.

Post Office and Civil Service. Civil service retirement and COLA cap plus foreign service COLA cap: $376 million in 1983; $1.06 billion in 1984; $1.8 billion in 1985.

Veterans' Affairs. Four percent cap on COLAs, compensation changes, unspecified entitlement cuts; $77 million in 1983; $155 million in 1984; $155 million in 1985.

Ways and Means. Medicare: $3.16 billion in 1983; $4.12 billion in 1984; and $4.24 billion in 1985. AFDC: $390 million in 1983; $400 million in 1984; $401 million in 1985. SSI: $158 million in 1983; $254 million in 1984; $368 million in 1985. Child Support enforcement: $45 million in 1983; $51 million in 1984; $159 million in 1985.

Tax Reconciliation Bill

With the belated backing of the Reagan administration, Congress Aug. 19 approved HR 4961. The Tax Equity and Fiscal Responsibility Act of 1982 was expected to raise $98.3 billion in revenues over fiscal 1983-85, mostly by closing loopholes and clamping down on tax evasion. *(Details of action, tax provisions, p. 29)*

The measure's $17.5 billion total spending reduction included cuts in major income support programs for the poor, as well as savings of $13.3 billion in Medicare, the health care program for the elderly, and $1.9 billion resulting from payment of variable interest rates on U.S. savings bonds. *(Outlay savings, box, this page; Medicare-Medicaid story, p. 471, welfare, p. 476)*

The bill had an irregular legislative history. Although the Constitution stipulates that revenue legislation must originate in the House, the Democratic-controlled Ways and Means Committee chose to sit back and let the Republican-controlled Senate sweat out a politically unpopular tax increase package on its own. As a result, the tax/spending reconciliation measure was put together in the Senate Finance Committee and then attached to HR 4961, a miscellaneous tax bill passed by the House in 1981.

The Finance Committee reported the bill on schedule July 12 (S Rept 97-494), and the Senate passed it July 23 by a largely party-line vote of 50-47. *(Vote 257, p. 44-S)*

The Senate action was the first major test of congressional willingness to comply with the reconciliation instructions in the budget resolution. Despite strong pressure from lobbyists and general unwillingness among members to raise taxes during an election year, the Finance Committee

HR 4961 Outlay Savings

(Fiscal years, in millions of dollars)

	1983	1984	1985
Medicare	$2,879	$4,430	$5,998
Medicaid	275	364	502
Aid to families with dependent children (AFDC)	85	95	163
Child support enforcement (CSE)	92	141	151
Supplemental security income (SSI)	116	126	144
Unemployment compensation (UC)	−81	49	49
Debt management	329	691	858
Total savings	$3,695	$5,896	$7,865

Note: This table does not reflect the additional food stamp outlays of $184 million, and additional Medicaid outlays of $111 million resulting from two Medicare provisions over the three-year period. Thus the total net outlays savings are $17,161 million. The table reflects the savings to each of the programs identified. The minus sign (−) for 1983 in unemployment compensation represents additional outlays.

Source: Conference report on HR 4961

tee package was kept largely intact. As passed, it met the spending and revenue requirements of the budget resolution.

The House, still anxious to keep its distance from legislation that would raise $99 billion in taxes and cut $17 billion from spending over three years, decided July 28 to go directly to conference on the Senate-passed bill, bypassing action by the Ways and Means Committee and House floor debate. The bypass strategy was adopted after Ways and Means Democrats overwhelmingly rejected a revenue-raising package proposed by Chairman Dan Rostenkowski, D-Ill., July 21.

Democrats and some Republicans, including ranking Ways and Means Republican Barber B. Conable Jr., R-N.Y., insisted that the House bypass was the only practical way to get tax increases enacted quickly in an election year. Nonetheless, the motion to go to conference won approval by only a narrow margin, 208-197. *(Vote 213, p. 62-H)*

The conference agreement, reported Aug. 17 (H Rept 97-760), was crafted over eight grueling days of meetings. The final bill, which won the endorsement of both President Reagan and House Speaker Thomas P. O'Neill Jr., D-Mass., mirrored closely the measure approved by the Finance Committee and passed by the Senate.

O'Neill and his Democratic lieutenants were critical to the 226-207 House vote to approve the conference report Aug. 19. Without the support of 123 Democrats the conference report would have gone down to defeat. Only 103 Republicans voted for the measure; 89 voted against it. *(Vote 289, p. 84-H)*

In the Republican-controlled Senate the vote was more clear-cut. Although 11 Republicans jumped ship, nine Democrats voted for the measure on the final 52-47 tally that cleared the bill for the president's signature. *(Vote 337, p. 55-S)*

Reagan signed the bill Sept. 3 (PL 97-248).

Omnibus Reconciliation Bill

Congress earlier had handed President Reagan another budget victory when both houses Aug. 18 gave final approval to a three-year, $13.3 billion package of spending cuts contained in HR 6955. The House adopted the conference report on the bill (H Rept 97-759) by a 243-176 vote, and the Senate cleared the measure 67-32. *(House vote 277, p. 82-H; Senate vote 335, p. 55-S)*

The CBO estimated that HR 6955 would save $3.3 billion in fiscal 1983, $4.8 billion in fiscal 1984 and $5.2 billion in fiscal 1985.

The bill's most significant provision, providing three-year savings of $4.1 billion, limited inflation adjustments for certain federal retirees. Budget leaders claimed the move was a first step toward controlling automatic increases in federal benefits.

"This is a historic change," said Pete V. Domenici, R-N.M., chairman of the Senate Budget Committee. "In the past, automatic cost-of-living adjustments have led to spending growth of as much as $26 billion in a single year." *(COLA story, p. 514)*

Other major elements of the bill included cuts of $4.2 billion in dairy price supports and $1.9 billion from food stamps during the next three years. *(Farm, food stamp cuts, p. 255)*

The measure saved $2 billion in an FHA home loan program and $552 million in veterans' benefits. It also decreased the number of members on the Federal Communications Commission (FCC) and the Interstate Commerce Commission (ICC), for three-year savings of $1 million.

House Budget Committee Chairman James R. Jones, D-Okla., said many members were "holding their noses" as they voted for the cuts.

The most troublesome points, he said, were the bill's dairy and crop reduction programs and the cap on COLAs for federal retirees under age 62.

Some Republicans grumbled that the 1982 reconciliation bill did not lower spending enough. But many agreed with Rep. Delbert L. Latta, R-Ohio, ranking minority member on the Budget Committee, who conceded that the savings were "not chicken feed."

Although the administration disputed the CBO estimate of $13.3 billion in savings, claiming instead that HR 6955 reduced spending by $10.4 billion, officials backed the bill as a key to lower deficits, eased interest rates and economic recovery.

The discrepancy in the figures was because of "an honest difference of opinion" between administration and congressional offices about the projected savings from farm program changes, according to Edwin L. Dale Jr., spokesman for the Office of Management and Budget (OMB).

Senate Action

The Senate passed its version of the omnibus reconciliation bill (S 2774 — S Rept 97-504) by a 72-24 vote Aug. 5. The measure, reported by the Budget Committee July 26, aimed to reduce projected spending by a total of $12.6 billion over the next three fiscal years. *(Vote 299, p. 50-S)*

The package included reductions in agriculture, veterans' and banking programs, as well as a 4 percent cap on COLAs for federal and military retirees. Savings in the measure amounted to $2.5 billion in fiscal 1983.

During floor debate the Senate rejected a number of amendments to retain various spending programs.

Unemployment Benefits. Before overwhelmingly approving the reconciliation package, Republicans were forced to accept a "sense of the Senate" amendment, offered by Ohio Democrat Howard M. Metzenbaum, directing conferees on HR 4961, the tax/spending reconciliation bill, to approve up to 13 weeks of additional unemployment benefits. *(Unemployment benefits, p. 43)*

Republicans went along with the non-binding Metzenbaum amendment when it became clear he had the votes to attach the costly unemployment benefits to the reconciliation measure. The amendment sailed through 84-13. *(Vote 291, p. 49-S)*

COLA Fight. The only attempt to take a big chunk out of the savings measure came Aug. 4, when Donald W. Riegle Jr., D-Mich., offered an amendment to eliminate the cap on COLAs for federal and military retirees — with the exception of members of Congress.

Adoption of the Riegle amendment would have eliminated nearly half of the bill's three-year savings, $5 billion. The amendment was defeated 48-51. *(Vote 289, p. 49-S)*

Riegle argued that federal and military retirees should not be treated differently from others receiving federal retirement benefits: Social Security recipients and railroad retirees. "I think what Congress and what the Senate are being asked to decide now is whether we want our retirees all on an equal footing," he said.

But Ted Stevens, R-Alaska, noted that the federal retirement fund was already so far in deficit that $12 billion would have to be transferred from the general Treasury to maintain its solvency. "It is time Congress understands that the federal retirement system cannot withstand the peregrinations of politicians," he said.

Agriculture Amendments. The only other area of controversy involved farm programs. Several attempts were made to increase the agriculture savings, but only one succeeded.

The largest cuts would have resulted from an amendment offered by Paula Hawkins, R-Fla., to lower dairy price supports from the current level of $13.10 per hundredweight to $12.60 on the date of enactment and to $12.00 on Jan. 1, 1983.

Hawkins said the amendment would save $1.2 billion over three years and benefit consumers by $2 billion over the same period.

But Thad Cochran, R-Miss., noted that the bill would freeze dairy price supports for savings of $1.5 billion over the next three years. Further reforms, if necessary, would be considered by the Agriculture Committee before the end of the session, he said.

Hawkins' amendment was tabled 65-33. Another amendment to limit dairy price supports, offered by S. I. "Sam" Hayakawa, R-Calif., also failed, 48-49. *(Votes 293, p. 49-S; 298, p. 50-S)*

The Senate did, however, adopt an amendment by David L. Boren, D-Okla., setting up a program to pay farmers for not growing wheat, corn and feed grains. While costing the government money in the first year, the program would save $400 million over three years.

Boren said farmers would receive $120 per acre for the 10 percent additional wheat acreage they set aside and $150 per acre for corn and feed grains set aside. The House Agriculture Committee adopted a similar program in its reconciliation bill.

Senate Provisions

As passed by the Senate, S 2774 provided for the following savings, broken down by committee jurisdiction:

Agriculture: $4.6 billion in budget authority and outlays in fiscal 1983-85. The legislation would:

● Reauthorize the food stamp program for three years and make certain reforms. Food stamp spending would be capped at $11.9 billion in fiscal 1983, $12.3 billion in fiscal 1984 and $13.2 billion in fiscal 1985.

● Continue the Puerto Rico nutrition block grant at $825 million annually and give states the option to convert food stamps to a similar block grant.

● Eliminate scheduled increases in milk price support levels by maintaining the current $13.10 per hundredweight minimum support level through fiscal 1985.

● Require that part of the expected wheat, feed grain, cotton and rice support deficiency payments be paid to farmers in advance at the time of enrollment in the program.

● Authorize use of Commodity Credit Corp. funds to increase agricultural exports by subsidizing interest rates on export loans and direct export subsidies. The net effect of the higher exports would be to reduce price support expenditures by $188 million over three years.

● Require the secretary of agriculture to offer a combination paid diversion/acreage reduction program for wheat, corn and other feed grains. The program would save $400 million over three years.

Armed Services: $2.1 billion in budget authority and outlays in fiscal 1983-85. The reductions were achieved by limiting COLAs to 4 percent annually in fiscal 1983-85 for recipients of military and public health service pensions.

Banking, Housing and Urban Affairs: $2.1 billion in budget authority and outlays over the three-year period. The savings were achieved by allowing the FHA to collect a lump-sum premium from a lender when the FHA insured a mortgage. Under existing law, the FHA premium was amortized over the life of the mortgage.

Commerce, Science and Transportation: $48 million in budget authority and outlays in fiscal 1983-85. The savings were achieved by limiting the COLA to 4 percent for each fiscal year for recipients of Coast Guard retirement pensions. In addition, the maximum size of the FCC was reduced to five members, and the ICC to seven members.

Foreign Relations: $6 million in budget authority and $25 million in outlays in fiscal 1983-85. The savings were achieved by limiting the COLA to 4 percent for each fiscal year for recipients of foreign service retirement pensions.

Governmental Affairs: $777 million in budget authority, $3.1 billion in outlays and $149 million in increased revenues, for a total deficit reduction of $3.2 billion over the three-year period. The legislation would:

● Limit the COLA to 4 percent in each fiscal year for the civil service retirement program.

● Reduce civil service retirement outlays and increase revenues by closing loopholes in current law and allow disability recipients to adjust their earnings levels to stay on the rolls.

● Limit early retirement for civil service employees, reduce benefits to early retirees and require payment for credited service transferred from other retirement systems.

Veterans' Affairs: $562 million in budget authority and $560 million in outlays in fiscal 1983-85. The bill would:

● Eliminate by fiscal 1985 college benefits for dependents of veterans with non-service connected disabilities.

● Impose a user fee on VA home loans beginning Oct. 1, 1983.

● Make other changes in compensation and pension provisions, such as rounding down benefit checks to the next lowest dollar and delaying payments until the first full month of entitlement.

House Action

While the Senate was acting on its omnibus bill, the House was addressing its reconciliation requirements in a number of separate measures.

The piecemeal approach was part of a Democratic strategy to force Republicans into a series of potentially embarrassing election-year votes on budget cuts. Republicans, who had hoped to accomplish the cuts in an omnibus bill, charged the Democrats with subverting the budget process.

After passing measures making cuts in veterans' programs (HR 6782), housing programs (HR 6812), federal pension programs (HR 6862) and agriculture programs (HR 6892), the House Aug. 10 folded the four bills into an omnibus measure (HR 6955), which it passed by voice vote.

The House took these actions on the individual bills.

● **HR 6782.** The bill, which also included non-reconciliation provisions, was reported by the Veterans' Affairs Committee July 23 (H Rept 97-660) and passed by the House July 27 on a 400-0 vote. Savings totaled $550 million over fiscal 1983-85. After its reconciliation provisions were transferred to HR 6955, HR 6782 — PL 97-306 went on to enactment Oct. 14. *(Vote 205, p. 60-H; story, p. 488)*

● **HR 6812.** In reporting the bill July 29 (H Rept 97-683), the Banking Committee rejected its reconciliation instructions by approving only $5 million in fiscal 1983 savings. Committee Democrats — who later reversed their position — claimed they would save more than the mandated $2.1 billion for fiscal 1983-85 if Congress enacted two other House-passed banking bills: the Net Worth Guarantee Act (HR 6267) and the so-called regulators bill (HR 4603). *(Banking legislation, p. 45)*

Before passing HR 6812 by voice vote Aug. 5, the House adopted, 337-69, an amendment to provide $2.1 billion in additional savings over three years by requiring home buyers to pay a lump sum premium for FHA mortgage insurance. *(Vote 235, p. 70-H)*

● **HR 6862.** As passed by the House Aug. 3, 268-128, HR 6862 was a token reconciliation bill that reduced federal pensions by only $113 million during fiscal 1983-85. *(Vote 225, p. 66-H; details of pension action, p. 514)*

The House refused to clamp a 4 percent lid on COLAs for federal retirees, snubbing its instructions to slash $3.2 billion from pension payments over the three-year period. The Post Office and Civil Service Committee, which drafted the bill, also had rejected the 4 percent COLA cap. Although the House action directly affected only civil service retirees, the decision would have a domino effect on military, foreign service and other federal retirees.

● **HR 6892.** The agriculture reconciliation bill was reported by the Agriculture Committee Aug. 2 (H Rept 97-687) and passed by the House Aug. 10 by a 268-121 vote. Three-year savings in farm and food stamp programs totaled $4.6 billion. *(Vote 246, p. 74-H; details of agriculture action, p. 255)*

Conference Action

Conferees wrapped up their work the night of Aug. 16, and House Budget Chairman Jones brought the conference

report (H Rept 97-759) to the House floor the next day.

Jones said conferees had produced a package that saved at least $2 billion more than the $11 billion ordered by the budget resolution.

"To those of you who were concerned that this body did not have the will to carry out the spending cuts mandated of it, I think you can support this conference report and go back home and explain that not only did you meet the targets, but you actually cut spending even more than you were required to do," Jones said.

But to his surprise, a little-noticed point in the bill caused a scare on the House floor that led members to recommit the conference report in a 266-145 vote. *(Vote 274, p. 80-H)*

The provision, inserted in the conference report by Alaska Sen. Stevens, would have required a government commission to recommend new pay rates for members of Congress, federal judges and top-level bureaucrats by Nov. 15, 1982, instead of in 1984 as required by current law.

The president could send the commission's recommendations to Congress, and unless both chambers vetoed the proposal within 30 days, the new rates would take effect automatically.

The provision also was in the fiscal 1982 supplemental appropriations bill (HR 6863) but later removed. *(Supplemental, p. 219)*

In a "Dear Colleague" letter circulated Aug. 17 before the reconciliation vote, Reps. Patricia Schroeder, D-Colo., Doug Walgren, D-Pa., and Bob Shamansky, D-Ohio, warned that "a vote for reconciliation is a vote to increase your own pay."

They said the so-called "Quadrennial Commission" could raise congressional salaries to $85,000 from the current $60,662 a year. The pay raise would go into effect in December, when Congress was not likely to be in session to veto it, they said.

At the end of the normal 15-minute roll call, the vote was 209-191 to recommit the bill to conference. Then, in what Majority Whip Thomas S. Foley, D-Wash., described as "a whiff of panic," more than 50 members switched their votes to avoid any appearance of giving themselves a raise.

Budget leaders quickly reconvened the conference and sliced out the Stevens provision. They returned to the floor Aug. 18, when Jones said, "There are no more excuses to vote against this bill."

Four hours after the House acted, the Senate conducted a cursory debate on the conference report. Most objections came from senators representing dairy and grain states and areas heavily populated by federal retirees.

One vocal opponent was William Proxmire, D-Wis., a frequent proponent of spending restraint who was up for re-election in a state with a huge dairy industry.

"I will vote against the conference report because the dairy provisions amount to an absolute, total, unmitigated disaster for dairy farmers in Wisconsin and throughout the nation," he said.

Republican Domenici could not resist the opportunity to take a poke at Proxmire after his remarks.

"I really cannot believe what I heard," the Budget Committee chairman said. "He is always willing to cut someone else's program, when he comes to this floor talking about fiscal responsibility, [and now] he would have the tunnel vision to vote against a $13.3 billion deficit reduction on the basis that the milk pricing subsidy in this bill is devastatingly low."

Another critic of HR 6955 was Ernest F. Hollings, D-

S.C., ranking minority member of the Budget Committee.

Hollings said he would not support the conference report because he believed the COLA reduction for retirees under age 62 shifted the burden to military retirees.

Final Provisions

As signed into law Sept. 8, HR 6955 (PL 97-253) included the following major provisions:

● **Agriculture.** The bill made two major changes in farm policies. One required new payments to farmers for not growing major crops; the other froze dairy price supports at current levels. HR 6955 also curbed inflation adjustments in food stamp benefits and tightened eligibility for the food stamp program. The changes were expected to cut $6.6 billion from projected spending in fiscal 1983-85. *(Details, p. 255)*

● **Federal Pensions.** The bill reduced inflation adjustments in pensions for federal retirees under age 62 in fiscal 1983-85. It delayed by one month the effective date of COLAs for all federal retirees in each of the three years. Three-year savings from these changes were estimated at $4.1 billion. *(Details, p. 514)*

● **FHA Insurance Premiums.** The bill required home buyers to pay a lump-sum premium for FHA mortgage insurance, instead of spreading payments over the life of a mortgage.

Conferees included House provisions requiring refunds of the premium if a home was sold in the early years of the mortgage, and proof by the secretary of housing and urban development (HUD) that the advance premium program was sound.

The savings from early collection of the fees was estimated at about $2 billion during the next three years.

HR 6955 also authorized $50.2 million in fiscal 1983 for the Bureau of the Mint.

The conference agreement dropped a House provision limiting expenses for the offices of the Treasury and HUD secretaries and the New York City and Chrysler Corp. loan guarantee programs.

● **Veterans' Affairs.** Instead of making $387 million in cuts as ordered by the budget resolution, conferees slashed spending by about $552 million for the three fiscal years.

To save costs, the bill imposed a new user fee on VA-backed home loans equal to .5 percent of the amount guaranteed.

It also delayed payment of certain compensation and pension benefits, rounded benefit checks down to the next lowest dollar and changed the effective date for benefit reductions caused by a change in dependency status.

A House Veterans' Affairs Committee aide said the excess savings allowed conferees to drop two early cuts that would have ended a correspondence training program and stopped benefit payments to students between the ages of 18 and 23.

● **Regulatory Agencies.** The FCC was reduced to five members from its authorized level of seven by July 1, 1983. Conferees estimated that the savings would be $100,000 in fiscal 1983 and $500,000 annually thereafter.

The ICC was reduced to five members from its authorized level of 11 on a phased basis to be completed by Dec. 31, 1985. A member's term would be reduced to five years, from seven. The saving was estimated at $475,000 a year.

Although the ICC had been authorized for 11 members, in recent years there had been only seven or fewer appointed.

Urgent Supplemental Signed After 2 Vetoes

Sixteen weeks and two vetoes after it was first reported by the House Appropriations Committee, the fiscal 1982 "urgent" supplemental appropriations bill finally cleared Congress July 15 in a form that satisfied President Reagan. He signed the measure into law July 18 (HR 6685 — PL 97-216).

HR 6685 was the fourth bill passed in the long battle between Congress and the president over spending levels. Approved by conferees July 14, it contained $5.4 billion in new spending and $5.8 billion in rescissions. The conferees took pains to mollify the president, who vetoed two earlier versions of the measure, HR 5922 and HR 6682. *(Guide to bills, box, this page)*

Both chambers approved the conference report July 15 by overwhelming margins. Enactment of the bill came just in time to avert large-scale layoffs among federal employees. Some furloughs already had taken place because of the lack of funds provided by the measure.

During its lengthy legislative history, the bill that started out as a non-controversial "housekeeping" measure became the vehicle for an emergency housing bailout proposal and a bruising House-Senate fight over congressional tax breaks, in addition to the confrontation with the president over spending.

Reagan won two important victories in his campaign against over-budget spending when the House twice voted to sustain his vetoes of the earlier versions of the bill:

● A June 24 attempt to override his veto of HR 5922 was defeated 253-151. *(Vote 165, p. 48-H)*

● On July 13 the House failed by a 242-169 vote — 32 votes short of the two-thirds needed — to override the veto of HR 6682. *(Vote 170, p. 50-H)*

Along with funds to pay employees of the departments of Labor, Health and Human Services and other agencies, HR 6685 contained $2.4 billion for sewer construction grants, $1.3 billion for guaranteed student loans and $1 billion for food stamps. It did not contain a multibillion-dollar program of mortgage interest rate subsidies for buyers of new homes that had been included in HR 5922.

HR 6685 also re-established the $3,000 annual limit on business-related tax deductions claimed by members of Congress for Washington living expenses. Members had been under heavy criticism since Congress gave itself a tax break in 1981 by replacing the longstanding $3,000 limit with a minimum, automatic $75-a-day deduction. *(1981 action, 1981 Almanac p. 400)*

Provisions

As signed into law, HR 6685 (PL 97-216) included the following supplemental appropriations for fiscal 1982 and rescissions of previous appropriations:

Labor Department

Employment and Training Administration	
Program administration	
(by transfer)	$ (8,742,000)
Summer youth employment	45,000,000
Employment Standards Administration	
Salaries and expenses (by transfer)	(4,259,000)
Bureau of Labor Statistics	
Salaries and expenses (by transfer)	(5,623,000)

Department of Health and Human Services

Health Services (community health centers, maternal and child health block grant, university-affiliated facilities)	$60,080,000
Health resources — nursing research grants	1,000,000
Work Incentives (WIN) program	35,000,000
Inspector General (by transfer)	(13,941,000)
Refugee and entrant assistance	20,000,000

Education Department

Guaranteed Student Loan program	1,300,000,000
Departmental management	5,650,000

ACTION	2,000,000
President's Commission for the Study of Ethical Problems in Medicine	309,000
Corporation for Public Broadcasting	
Public Broadcasting Fund (for fiscal 1984)	24,400,000

Housing and Urban Development

Low-income housing projects (operating subsidies)	198,000,000
Rescission of budget authority:	
Annual contributions for assisted housing	−4,098,640,000
Rent supplements	−1,750,480,000

Environmental Protection Agency

Sewage treatment construction grants	2,400,000,000

Transportation Department

Coast Guard	17,500,000
Federal-aid highway program	91,000,000

Civil Aeronautics Board

Payments to air carriers	20,158,000

Interstate Commerce Commission

Payments for directed rail service	8,000,000

Guide to Bills

During the maneuvering over the "urgent" supplemental appropriations for fiscal 1982, Congress considered four different measures:

HR 5922, originally a routine, non-controversial $4.9-billion bill, to which a $3 billion emergency housing aid program and a $3,000-a-year limit on members' tax deductions were added. Reagan vetoed it June 24 and the House upheld him.

HR 6645, an abortive attempt by the House to pass a stopgap funding measure without the $3,000 tax deduction limit. It passed the House June 23 but did not pass the Senate.

HR 6682, a $5.9 billion bill identical to HR 5922 except that it dropped the housing plan. Reagan vetoed it June 25 and the House July 13 sustained the veto.

HR 6685, a $4.5 billion bill containing only the most urgently needed funds, plus the $3,000 tax deduction limit. It cleared Congress July 15 and was signed into law July 18 (PL 97-216).

Treasury Department

Bureau of Government Financial Operations	$ 81,604,000
Bureau of Alcohol, Tobacco and Firearms	23,825,000
Customs Service	14,865,000
Postal Service	42,000,000
General Services Administration	
Inspector General	500,000
Merit Systems Protection Board	4,006,000
Office of the Special Counsel	238,000
U.S. Tax Court	1,530,000
Commerce Department	
General administration	3,171,000
Economic Development Administration (by transfer)	(3,500,000)
National Oceanic and Atmospheric Administration	2,000,000
Agriculture Department	
Food stamps	1,006,616,000
Defense Department	
Army Corps of Engineers — flood control	40,000,000
Total new budget authority	$ 5,448,452,000
Rescissions	$—5,849,120,000

Legislative Provisions

Members' Tax Deductions. Limited to $3,000 a year business-related income tax deductions that could be claimed by individual members of Congress for Washington, D.C., living expenses.

Polish Loans. Prohibited the use of government funds to make loan guarantee payments to banks for loans made to the government of Poland, unless Poland was declared to be in default or the president certified to Congress, on a monthly basis, that such payments were in the national interest.

Mine Safety. Transferred jurisdiction over the surface mining of stone, clay, colloidal phosphate, sand and gravel to the Mine Safety and Health Administration (MSHA), from the Occupational Safety and Health Administration (OSHA).

● Prohibited MSHA from classifying potash mines as "gassy" on the basis of air samples containing methane gas, unless the classification was based on formal rule-making after Nov. 5, 1981.

Sewer Construction. Provided that funding for a sewage treatment project for the New York City Convention Center be provided from the following sources: one-third from the total sewage treatment funding in the bill for all states, one-third from the allocation to New Jersey and one-third from the allocation to New York state.

Amtrak. Allowed Amtrak officers to hold railroad stock, despite an existing conflict-of-interest prohibition, provided they did not participate in decisions relating to the railroad in which they held stock, and made full disclosure of their holdings. The provision specifically was intended for W. Graham Claytor Jr., who was nominated to be president of Amtrak but had substantial holdings in the Southern Railway Co.

BATF. Prohibited reorganization of the Bureau of Alcohol, Tobacco and Firearms before Sept. 30, 1982; required approval of the House and Senate Appropriations committees for any reorganization plan after that.

Postal Service. Provided that the additional funds in the bill for the Postal Service be used to rescind postage cost increases for non-profit mailers.

United Nations. Prohibited the United States' share of funding for the United Nations and other international organizations from being available for the Palestine Liberation Organization, the South West Africa Peoples Organization or Cuba.

Education. Required the Education Department to allocate fiscal 1982 funds for Supplemental Educational Opportunity Grants to states in the same ratio as funds were allocated in fiscal 1981.

NASA. Established minimum funding levels for certain National Aeronautics and Space Administration (NASA) programs.

Watershed Projects. Required the Agriculture Department to begin work on at least 15 watershed protection and flood control projects in fiscal 1982.

Public Health Service. Prohibited the use of funds to implement any plan phasing down the Public Health Service Commissioned Corps.

Action on HR 5922

The first "urgent" supplemental for fiscal 1982, HR 5922, was reported by the House Appropriations Committee March 23 (H Rept 97-469). It contained a total of $4,868,934,000 in net new budget authority.

The biggest item in the bill was $2.4 billion for the Environmental Protection Agency's sewer construction grant program.

A more controversial item was the $1.3 billion for the guaranteed student loan program. The funds were needed to cover the cost of interest subsidies on federally guaranteed loans made by banks to college students. The existing fiscal 1982 appropriation for the program was $1.8 billion.

The administration had requested a student loan supplemental of $978 million. To bring the additional cost of the program down to that level, it proposed to tack on a series of money-saving legislative changes in the program. The proposals, which were rejected by the committee, included provisions limiting loan amounts to individual students and doubling the fee banks could charge when making a loan to a student.

The third largest item in the bill was a $1 billion increase in funding authority for the Government National Mortgage Association (Ginnie Mae), which provides support for various kinds of mortgages.

The committee rejected the administration's request for a $9.4 billion rescission of funds for subsidized housing. Instead, it recommended rescinding $100 million and deferring $3.8 billion to fiscal 1983.

Most of the other funds in the bill were housekeeping items needed to allow agencies to continue normal operations and prevent staff furloughs.

Amendments Rejected. The Appropriations Committee rejected two significant amendments March 23.

Sidney R. Yates, D-Ill., offered an amendment to rescind $1.9 billion in funds already appropriated for procurement, research and development for the B-1 bomber. The amendment was rejected 22-27.

William H. Gray III, D-Pa., proposed an unsuccessful amendment that would have cut out $5 million of the funds in the bill for the Coast Guard. Gray said the funds were to be used by the Coast Guard to carry out its policy of stopping and turning back boats containing Haitian refugees bound for the United States, outside of U.S. territorial waters.

Budget Problems

HR 5922 needed special protection from the Rules Committee to come to the floor because it provided for new spending at a time when total government outlays for fiscal 1982 were well over the $695 billion limit set by the binding second budget resolution (S Con Res 50) approved by Congress in December 1981. *(1981 Almanac p. 267)*

The Budget Committee certified in February that fiscal 1982 spending already approved by Congress would be $738 billion. Under the 1974 Congressional Budget Act (PL 93-344), any new spending bill that came to the floor was subject to a point of order for violating the ceiling. HR 5922 thus required a waiver of the budget ceiling provision in order to be brought to the floor.

The Appropriations Committee said all the items in the bill were urgent, and thus the whole measure deserved a waiver. The Budget Committee felt only a few items were so time-sensitive that they could not wait until Congress passed a third budget resolution. It recommended only a limited waiver of the budget ceiling rule, which would leave most items open to points of order.

The Rules Committee took a middle ground. The rule adopted March 30 (H Res 415) allowed a budget waiver for most of the items in HR 5922, but allowed points of order against a number of them.

The committee also refused to allow a housing aid amendment to be offered to the measure, saying it would be legislation on an appropriations bill, which is barred by House rules.

Housing Assistance

Even with all the squabbling over the budget waiver, the bill's biggest problem came from a group of Republicans who wanted to use HR 5922 as a vehicle to aid the housing industry, which was in a deep slump because of the recession and high interest rates.

Led by Tom Corcoran, R-Ill., and Thomas B. Evans Jr., R-Del., they introduced an amendment to take $1 billion from the $15 billion in funding authority available to the U.S. Synthetic Fuels Corp., and give it to the Department of Housing and Urban Development to be used for state mortgage revenue bonds financing low-interest housing loans.

Corcoran and Evans were outspoken opponents of the synfuels corporation and had introduced legislation to abolish it. The corporation was established by Congress in 1980. *(1980 Almanac p. 477)*

The amendment was adamantly opposed by House Majority Leader Jim Wright, D-Texas, an ardent synfuels supporter. Taking $1 billion away from that program was unacceptable to him.

The Rules Committee action barring their amendment meant that Evans and Corcoran had to change or defeat the rule — a possibility the Democratic leadership took so seriously that it avoided bringing the issue to a vote.

Despite repeated warnings about the dire consequences of failing to quickly approve the funding bill, floor action on HR 5922, originally scheduled for early April, was delayed for more than a month. Republicans repeatedly criticized the Democrats for failing to act on the "urgent" measure, saying the bill was being postponed because the Democrats did not want to let Republicans take credit for helping housing.

Finally, under increasing pressure to do something to aid the housing industry, the leadership agreed to back a different, Democratic-sponsored amendment to subsidize mortgage interest costs for home buyers.

The Democratic alternative was crafted by Jerry M. Patterson, D-Calif., and Les AuCoin, D-Ore. While co-opting the widespread political support for emergency housing aid, their plan did not take money from the synfuels program. It also provided a more direct form of interest rate subsidy to home buyers than the GOP plan.

Seeking to broaden support for some kind of housing aid, Evans and Corcoran tried to get the two Democrats to consolidate the two proposals. House leaders then, at a May 4 meeting, agreed to accept the Patterson-AuCoin plan. "They realized that the Evans-Corcoran amendment would gain a lot of support from Democrats who felt we needed to do something now," Patterson said.

In order for the Patterson-AuCoin amendment to be added to HR 5922, the bill was pulled from the House schedule and Rules Chairman Richard Bolling, D-Mo., announced that his committee would meet May 11 to report a new rule that would allow consideration of the amendment.

Minority Whip Trent Lott, R-Miss., incensed that the Democrats would manipulate the rule to allow their own amendment but block the Republican proposal, sought to force a vote on the original rule. He invoked a seldom-used House rule that allowed him to bring up H Res 415 on a point of personal privilege. His May 6 motion to cut off debate and order an immediate vote on the rule was agreed to, 240-158. The rule was then adopted, 338-54. *(Votes 58, 59, p. 18-H)*

Lott's maneuvering had little effect, however, since the Rules Committee went ahead and reported a new rule May 11 (H Res 461) and H Res 415 was never used. Besides allowing consideration of the Democratic housing amendment, H Res 461 also allowed Budget Act waivers for all items in the bill. The original rule had angered Appropriations Chairman Jamie L. Whitten, D-Miss. — he felt a rule granting only a partial waiver for the bill was an infringement on the jurisdiction of his committee — and Bolling agreed to change it.

House Floor Action

Despite the strong possibility of a veto, the House May 12 passed HR 5922 with a $1 billion amendment for new home mortgage assistance.

The emergency housing aid, which would provide interest-rate subsidies for an estimated 74,000 low- and middle-income home buyers, was added to the bill by a 343-67 vote. *(Vote 68, p. 22-H)*

The bill then passed by voice vote.

With the addition of the new program and an extra $23 million for refugee assistance, total new fiscal 1982 spending in HR 5922 came to $5.9 billion.

Well before the bill passed, the prospect that the House would add the $1 billion to it had prompted threats of a veto. Office of Management and Budget Director David A. Stockman opposed any amendments to HR 5922, and President Reagan denounced any "budget-busting bailout" for the housing industry.

Housing Aid

The Patterson-AuCoin housing amendment was part of a $2 billion jobs-creation package announced by the Democratic leadership May 7. Sponsors said the emergency aid was needed to keep the housing industry from complete

collapse under the weight of high interest rates. *(Jobs package, p. 59)*

Under the amendment, a home buyer with income at or below 130 percent of the median income for his area could qualify for a government subsidy that would reduce his mortgage interest rate by 4 to 6 percentage points. The subsidy would be available for five to seven years, on mortgages up to $67,500; in certain high-cost areas, mortgages up to $90,000 would be eligible. The aid would be available only for homes on which construction began no earlier than one year prior to the program's enactment — a provision designed to help builders unload their inventory of new homes.

The housing aid plan was seen as a possible precursor to a round of emergency funding programs for recession-wracked industries. The lopsided vote for the amendment indicated that, even as it was struggling to reduce the federal deficit, Congress found it hard to resist providing help for troubled industries.

Floor action on HR 5922 took place with a smoothness and lack of controversy that concealed the bitter partisan wrangling that preceded it. Convinced that the Democratic leadership had the votes to pass the Patterson-AuCoin amendment, Evans and Corcoran did not challenge the rule that allowed it to be offered, and the rule was adopted by voice vote. The Patterson-AuCoin amendment then passed easily, with support from Evans, Corcoran and a majority of Republicans.

Balanced Budget Amendment

In other action on HR 5922, the House voted to abolish a long-forgotten provision of a 1978 law that required the federal budget to be balanced by fiscal year 1981.

The impetus for that action was an amendment by Robert S. Walker, R-Pa., to block the expenditure of funds in the housing section of HR 5922 until the federal budget was balanced. Walker said Congress should begin to comply with the 1978 provision, which had been tacked onto an International Monetary Fund bill (PL 95-435) by Sen. Harry F. Byrd Jr., Ind.-Va. *(1978 Almanac p. 424)*

But adoption of the amendment would have killed not only the new housing program but the $2.4 billion for sewer grants and the other items in the bill. The amendment was rejected, 132-276. *(Vote 69, p. 22-H)*

Silvio O. Conte, R-Mass., however, warned that the 1978 provision could still be in effect. "I imagine that after today there are going to be people bringing suits against the federal government for violating the law," he said.

So, with the support of Democratic members of the Appropriations Committee, Conte proposed an amendment to eliminate the 1978 provision. His amendment was adopted by voice vote without debate — in fact, without any explanation at all of its contents.

Other Amendments

The House also adopted, by voice vote, a Mike Lowry, D-Wash., amendment to provide an additional $23.3 million for refugee assistance. The funds were to reimburse 21 states that had been temporarily unable to implement federal regulations reducing to 18 months from 36 months the period during which refugees and Cuban and Haitian entrants were eligible for special welfare and health benefits.

It also rejected, 186-220, a John H. Rousselot, R-Calif., amendment that would have had the effect of leaving jurisdiction over surface mining operations with OSHA, rather than MSHA. *(Vote 70, p. 22-H)*

Senate Committee Action

HR 5922 emerged from the Senate Appropriations Committee May 18 loaded with controversial provisions on sensitive political issues.

One of these, repealing the automatic $75-a-day tax deduction for members of Congress, proved to be a major stumbling block for the bill. House leaders had tacitly supported the deduction when it slipped through Congress in 1981.

As reported by the Senate committee (S Rept 97-402), HR 5922 contained $6.3 billion in new 1982 spending, compared to $5.9 billion in the House-passed bill. It also included $7.6 billion in housing program rescissions, compared to only $100 million in the House bill.

The committee added funds for several programs not included in the House bill, including $1 billion for food stamps, $210.6 million for community service employment for older Americans and $64.6 million for community health centers, maternal and child health block grants, developmental disabilities research and nursing research grants.

The administration request for additional food stamp funds had come too late for inclusion in the House bill. The other funds were not requested by the administration.

The Senate committee also added to the House-passed funding levels for several programs, and added a $24.4 million fiscal 1984 advance appropriation for the Corporation for Public Broadcasting.

Members' Tax Deductions

Reacting to heavy public criticism of the 1981 tax break for Congress, the committee voted 13-9 for an amendment that would require members to substantiate their business-related tax deductions.

The amendment, sponsored by Mack Mattingly, R-Ga., would end the Internal Revenue Service regulation that allowed members to automatically deduct $75 in Washington living expenses, without substantiation, for every day of the year except for congressional recesses of more than four days. However, the amendment did not include a provision sponsored by William Proxmire, D-Wis., to reimpose the $3,000 annual limit on deductions that had existed until 1981.

Debate focused on the serious political damage that apparently had been inflicted on incumbent members by the tax deduction. Many taxpayers felt the deduction gave members an unfair advantage, and the issue had become a key one in a number of congressional campaigns.

Jake Garn, R-Utah, attributed the public criticism of the deduction to unfair reporting by the press. "Never have I seen the press so dishonestly report an issue," he said, while acknowledging that the deduction had saved him $3,822 on his 1981 taxes.

Polish Loans

Despite administration opposition, the committee voted by a wide margin to prohibit the U.S. government from making payments to banks for overdue Polish loans unless it declared Poland in default or the president certified that payment would be in the national interest.

Robert W. Kasten Jr., R-Wis., chairman of the Appropriations Subcommittee on Foreign Operations, added the provision to the bill. An effort by Thad Cochran, R-Miss., to delete it was rejected, 4-15.

A similar amendment had been defeated by the Senate

in February. *(Story, p. 230)*

Kasten argued that the administration's policy toward Poland was not pushing the military government there to relax martial law. "It is time to stand up for Poland by declaring the military government in default," he said.

Cochran said President Reagan and Secretary of State Alexander M. Haig Jr. both opposed the default provision. "The default would serve no other purpose that has not already been achieved by the sanctions imposed by the president," he argued.

Another foreign policy provision added to the bill by the committee would allow the Pentagon to spend up to $50,000 to train Brazilian military officers. Military aid to Brazil was barred under U.S. laws aimed at halting the spread of nuclear weapons.

Housing Aid

The committee included in HR 5922 a $1 billion appropriation and a $5.1 billion, five-year authorization for a new program providing mortgage interest rate subsidies for moderate-income buyers of new homes.

The House-passed bill contained the $1 billion appropriation, but the authorization for that spending was put in legislation (HR 6294) approved separately by the House. The authorization approved by the Senate committee was identical to a bill (S 2226) sponsored by Richard G. Lugar, R-Ind., and reported by the Senate Banking Committee April 27. *(Housing bills, p. 40)*

But while it approved the $1 billion mortgage aid program, the Appropriations Committee cut other housing funds much more deeply than the House had. In an effort to increase the chance of Reagan signing the bill, the committee deleted the $1 billion appropriation for Ginnie Mae, intended for purchase of mortgages on subsidized housing projects, and approved rescissions of $7.6 billion in subsidized housing funds.

Senate Floor Action

By the time the Senate passed HR 5922 May 27, the $1 billion housing aid amendment had grown into a $5.1 billion program of mortgage interest rate subsidies for buyers of new homes.

The Senate voted 69-23 for an amendment by Lugar to not only authorize but appropriate the full $5.1 billion for the program. It then passed the bill 73-19. *(Votes 167, 168, p. 29-S)*

The Lugar amendment brought total fiscal 1982 supplemental spending in HR 5922 to $10.5 billion, along with the $7.6 billion in rescissions.

Lugar Amendment

Under the Lugar amendment, originally crafted by the home building and lumber industries, families with incomes of up to $30,000 a year could get subsidies to lower their interest rate by up to 4 percent, on mortgages up to $67,500. In certain high-cost areas, families making up to $37,000 a year would be eligible for subsidies, on mortgages up to $77,625. Subsidies would be available for five years.

Unlike the House-passed plan, Lugar's amendment provided aid only for houses built or substantially rehabilitated after enactment of the bill and before Jan. 1, 1983 — a provision designed to stimulate new housing construction.

Lugar, whose state had a 12.5 percent unemployment rate, consistently referred to his plan as a jobs bill rather than a housing industry bailout. He argued that "the federal government is going to have to take action this year to counter unemployment," and predicted that his plan would create 700,000 new jobs.

Approval of the amendment was a defeat for President Reagan, who opposed the plan on budgetary grounds. Administration officials and Senate critics of the proposal, especially William L. Armstrong, R-Colo., warned that it could lead to a flood of "bailouts" for other troubled industries such as automobiles, agriculture and airlines.

Maneuvering Over Amendment

The Senate took four days to pass HR 5922, with most of the time spent in behind-the-scenes negotiations over the fate of the housing program.

While a number of complex procedural questions were involved, the basic situation was fairly simple: Lugar had the votes to pass the housing amendment, but Armstrong had the ability to delay it indefinitely. In between the two was Majority Leader Howard H. Baker Jr., R-Tenn., who wanted to pass the bill in time to depart on a scheduled trip to China May 28.

Baker worked out a plan to break the deadlock. One part of the strategy was to invoke cloture, thus limiting debate on the bill, which the Senate did by a 95-2 vote May 27. *(Vote 160, p. 28-S)*

In return for Armstrong's support of the cloture motion, Lugar agreed not to challenge a ruling of the chair that his housing aid amendment was out of order as not germane. Germaneness rules under cloture are very strict.

Although Lugar could have moved to overturn the ruling of the chair, and would have needed only a majority vote to win, Senate leaders felt that would set a bad precedent by weakening the cloture rule against extraneous amendments.

Instead, Lugar moved to suspend the germaneness rule, a procedure requiring a two-thirds majority. His motion — the key procedural vote — was agreed to, 63-27, and the housing aid amendment then passed, 69-23. *(Votes 165, 167, p. 29-S)*

In agreeing to Lugar's motion, the Senate made parliamentary history. It was the first time since the cloture rule was adopted in 1917 that the Senate had voted to suspend the rule prohibiting non-germane amendments after cloture had been invoked.

Members' Taxes, Polish Loans

In other action on the bill, the Senate voted 70-23 for a Proxmire amendment to restore the $3,000 annual limit on business-related tax deductions claimed by members of Congress. *(Vote 163, p. 29-S)*

The amendment went beyond the Appropriations Committee provision, which ended the automatic $75-a-day deduction approved by Congress in 1981 but would have allowed members to deduct any amount of substantiated living costs as a business expense.

The Senate also voted 83-10 to oppose the Reagan administration's policy of not requiring a declaration of default before providing payments for overdue loans to Poland. *(Vote 162, p. 29-S)*

The strong Senate support for the provision reflected growing frustration with Poland's continuing martial law rule, and a continuing split within the Reagan administration. Defense Secretary Caspar W. Weinberger favored a default declaration, but Secretary of State Haig opposed the tactic.

Other Amendments

The Senate also:

● Adopted, 76-19, an Alan J. Dixon, D-Ill., amendment to provide $38.4 million for the Work Incentive program for welfare recipients, after rejecting, 46-48, an amendment to provide $76.8 million as in the House bill. *(Votes 154, 157, p. 28-S)*

● Adopted, 52-38, a Dale Bumpers, D-Ark., amendment to preserve OSHA's jurisdiction over the surface mining of clay, sand and gravel, instead of transferring it to MSHA, as the committee bill provided. *(Vote 164, p. 29-S)*

● Adopted by voice vote an Edward M. Kennedy, D-Mass., amendment to provide an extra $63 million for summer youth jobs.

● Adopted an amendment worked out by Ted Stevens, R-Alaska, and Quentin N. Burdick, D-N.D., adding an extra $62 million for the Postal Service, to be used to reduce postage rates for non-profit mailers.

Conference Action

Conferees reached agreement June 10 on the spending provisions of HR 5922, but remained deadlocked over the issue of tax deductions for members of Congress.

Under heavy public pressure, the House voted June 9 to accept the Senate provision repealing the tax break members of Congress voted themselves in 1981. But House conferees retaliated by demanding that the Senate accept an $18,200 annual ceiling on outside income earned by senators, setting off a bitter House-Senate struggle that again delayed final action on the bill.

As reported by conferees (H Rept 97-605), HR 5922 contained new spending totaling $8.9 billion, and $5.7 billion in rescissions. The conference agreement included $3 billion for the housing assistance program — a compromise between the $5.1 billion approved by the Senate and the $1 billion backed by the House.

Of the total, $2.5 billion was to provide mortgage subsidies on newly built homes, for families with incomes up to $30,000 a year. Another $400 million was designated for mortgages on homes that had been built but not sold; the rest was for subsidies on homes in high-cost areas.

Conferees compromised on the Polish loan repayment provision, allowing payments if the president declared them to be in the "national interest."

The Senate amendment providing $50,000 for training of Brazilian military officers was dropped.

Tax Deductions

The conference action on congressional tax deductions unleashed a torrent of resentment and recriminations on all sides. House members angrily attacked Senate members, senators argued bitterly among themselves and just about everybody jumped on the press.

Although many House members were reluctant to give up the tax break they had won in 1981, they were unwilling to defend it publicly or to vote for it on the record. So when Patricia Schroeder, D-Colo., obtained a roll-call vote June 9 on a motion to instruct House conferees to accept the Senate provision restoring the $3,000 limit, the outcome was assured. The motion was agreed to, 356-43. *(Vote 129, p. 38-H)*

By a closer vote of 176-218, the House rejected a motion by John T. Myers, R-Ind., to instruct the conferees to agree to eliminate the automatic $75-a-day deduction

without restoring the $3,000 limit. That would have allowed members of Congress to claim whatever business-related deductions for Washington living expenses they could substantiate. *(Vote 128, p. 38-H)*

While they were forced by Schroeder's motion to accept the Senate provision, House conferees were furious with the Senate. They accused senators of hypocrisy for taking away the tax break while continuing to receive large honoraria from interest groups.

Garn responded that House members were "just as gutless" as senators on the issue. He attributed public attacks on the tax breaks to dishonest reporting by the press, which he called "a bunch of damned barracudas." Garn also lashed out at Proxmire, sponsor of the Senate provision. "You used this vehicle for political purposes because you're running this year," he shouted.

Rep. Vic Fazio, D-Calif., proposed that the House accept the Senate provision, with an amendment to impose on senators a limit on outside earned income, including honoraria, of 30 percent of congressional pay, or about $18,200 a year. The House already had that same limit. Fazio's motion was agreed to 10-8.

While they did not seriously consider the House proposal, Senate conferees narrowly rejected a compromise plan offered by Stevens. The amendment, defeated 10-11, would have adjusted the $3,000 limit on deductions according to the increase in consumer prices since 1952, when the limit was imposed. Under the amendment, the limit would have been about $10,800 in 1982.

Final Action on HR 5922

The House adopted the conference report on HR 5922 by voice vote June 16, but voted 381-29 for a motion by Fazio to insist that the Senate accept the $18,200-a-year limit on honoraria. *(Vote 143, p. 42-H)*

House members already had an $18,200 limit, and in any case they generally received far less in honoraria than senators. They averaged $5,237 in 1981, while the average senator received $19,575.

Supporters of the limit argued that the large fees for speaking engagements received by some members of Congress, especially senators, threatened the integrity of the legislative process. "I am fed up with [senators] posing for holy pictures on congressional pay and then running around collecting $60,000 in outside income," said David R. Obey, D-Wis.

The only opposition to the limit came from the most vocal backers of restoring the $3,000 tax deduction limit, such as Schroeder. She argued that the honoraria limit, even if justifiable in the abstract, was actually just a ploy by House members who wanted to defeat the Senate's tax deduction amendment.

Earlier, in what was viewed as a test of sentiment on the emergency housing program, the House adopted the rule (H Res 502) for consideration of the conference report by a 257-155 vote — less than the two-thirds that would be needed to override a veto of the bill. *(Vote 140, p. 42-H)*

Stockman had renewed the veto threat June 15, saying the administration opposed the $3 billion emergency housing aid program.

Like the original version of the bill, the conference report needed a waiver from the Budget Act. Lott led the fight against it. Noting that the Budget Committee had voted 11-6 against granting a waiver, he warned that a

waiver would weaken the Budget Act's controls on spending.

Budget Committee Chairman James R. Jones, D-Okla., said there would be room for the spending in the bill under the final fiscal 1982 budget limits contained in the fiscal 1983 budget resolution.

Although House Republicans had overwhelmingly supported a housing "bailout" originally, under the pressure of a probable veto they switched to opposition. While they voted 128-52 for the $1 billion aid program in the original bill, they voted 41-142 against the rule on the conference report.

By votes of 312-96 and 299-104, the House agreed to accept the Senate-passed rescissions in funding for assisted housing and rent supplements. *(Votes 141, 142, p. 42-H)*

Senate Action

The Senate approved the conference report on HR 5922 by voice vote June 21. The bill did not clear, however, because the Senate refused to accept the House-added Fazio amendment limiting senators' outside income. The Senate rejected the provision by a 54-41 vote June 22. *(Vote 191, p. 33-S)*

Stripped-Down Bill (HR 6645)

Faced with the Senate opposition to the outside income limit and anxious not to delay the start of the House's Independence Day recess, the House leadership adopted a new strategy. Dropping both the tax deduction and outside income limits, the Appropriations Committee quickly brought to the floor a completely new bill (HR 6645).

The $4.5 billion bill included temporary funding, through July 20, for those 17 agencies and programs that were in danger of shutting down because of lack of funds while the House was in recess. It did not contain the housing funds or more than 40 other items in HR 5922 that were considered less time-sensitive.

The House passed HR 6645 by voice vote June 23, and the Senate leadership agreed to rush it through the Senate.

But the Senate refused to go along with the stripped-down "urgent interim stopgap supplemental," as Appropriations Committee Chairman Mark O. Hatfield, R-Ore., called it.

Ignoring Hatfield's plea to pass the new bill without amendment so that it could be cleared quickly and sent to the president before the House began its recess, the Senate first moved to add Proxmire's amendment repealing the 1981 tax break for Congress and restoring the $3,000-a-year limit on members' deductions — the same amendment on HR 5922 that had angered the House and prompted it to add the honoraria limit for senators.

Hatfield warned that accepting the amendment would "open the floodgates" to a variety of other amendments, and said he would ask the leadership to pull the bill from the Senate calendar if the amendment passed. But the Senate rejected his motion to table the amendment by a vote of 21-76. *(Vote 195, p. 34-S)*

Lugar then moved to add the $3-billion conference version of his housing stimulus program to the Proxmire amendment. Armstrong raised a point of order against it on the grounds that it was legislation on an appropriations bill.

The chair agreed with Armstrong, but Lugar appealed the ruling, and the Senate backed Lugar, rejecting the ruling of the chair 33-66. It then passed the Lugar amendment, 70-27. *(Votes 196, 197, p. 34-S)*

HR 5922 Cleared

At that point — before any more amendments could be offered — Hatfield announced that the House leadership had agreed to accept the Senate version of the conference report on HR 5922, dropping the amendment limiting honoraria.

The Senate then suspended action on HR 6645, and the House — by voice vote, with only about 45 members on the floor — agreed to drop the Fazio amendment. That cleared HR 5922, and the bill was immediately sent to the White House for the expected veto.

First Veto

President Reagan vetoed HR 5922 June 24, saying it would increase the 1983 deficit by $1.3 billion and add at least $5 billion to federal spending over the next few years.

Reagan also said the housing subsidy program established by the bill would set a bad precedent. *(Veto text, p. 24-E)*

The veto was the fifth of Reagan's presidency. Housing lobbyists said it meant prospects of any major help for housing were dead for the year. Even aside from the president's opposition, time would run out on the building season before another measure could get through Congress, industry spokesmen said.

The House sustained the veto by a 17-vote margin the same day. The vote was 253-151. A two-thirds majority (270 in this case) of both houses is needed to override a veto. *(Vote 165, p. 48-H)*

Republican members, who had voted 128-52 for the original version of the emergency housing program, voted 53-131 against the bill on the override attempt. House Democratic leaders said they would make the veto a key issue in the fall election campaign.

"The consequences should be very severe for anyone who voted for [the housing bill] in the first place and then cowers and cringes and genuflects and kisses the president's, uh, ring," said Wright.

HR 6682, HR 6685

After the defeat of the override attempt, House Democratic leaders June 24 decided to pass two different bills.

The first was a $5.9 billion measure (HR 6682) that quickly became known as the "fat" bill. It was identical to HR 6645 except that the amendment restoring the tax deduction limit was included.

The House passed the measure by a vote of 267-106. *(Vote 166, p. 48-H)*

Lest a veto of that bill left government agencies without funds during Congress' Independence Day recess, the House also passed a fallback position — a $4.5 billion "skinny" bill (HR 6685) good only through July 20, one week after Congress was to return from the recess. It passed 342-25. *(Vote 167, p. 48-H)*

HR 6685 included $2.4 billion for sewer construction grants, $1.3 billion for the guaranteed student loan program and $335 million for food stamps.

It also contained the provision restoring the $3,000 limit on members' business-related tax deductions, but not the $18,200 limit on honoraria and other outside earned income.

The Senate passed HR 6682 June 24 by a 59-26 vote, clearing it for the president. *(Vote 199, p. 35-S)*

Second Veto

Reagan vetoed HR 6682 June 25, showing that he was prepared to use his veto weapon against spending bills that exceeded his budget by relatively small amounts even if they did not contain controversial "bailouts" such as the new housing program. He said the bill contained "excessive and unrequested budget authority totaling nearly $1 billion." *(Veto text, p. 25-E)*

In something of a surprise to Congress, Reagan also threatened to veto HR 6685, on grounds that it also exceeded his budget. It had been widely expected that he would sign that bill, since it cost considerably less than the two vetoed bills.

Senate Action on HR 6685

So the Senate passed a revised version of HR 6685 June 29 and left for its Independence Day recess, leaving the "urgent" funding needs unmet and agency heads scrambling to find ways to pay employees and keep programs in operation.

House leaders urged Reagan "to do whatever is possible" to avoid federal employee layoffs, but declined to call members back early from their recess to act on the bill.

The Senate version of HR 6685 was put together by Hatfield to meet the approval of Stockman. It contained $5.3 billion in new fiscal 1982 appropriations and $5.7 billion in rescissions. It passed by voice vote.

While he insisted the Senate was not "playing dead" or being "rolled over" by the executive branch, Hatfield presented the Stockman-approved bill to the Senate as a package that could not be altered without risking a veto.

Stockman had cited three main objections to the House-passed bill. He said it did not provide needed funds for administration of the Commerce and Education departments, it added $350 million to the president's request for other programs, and its July 20 expiration date for most of the funding in the bill was unworkable.

The revised version made deeper cuts in housing programs than the House bill provided. At the same time, Hatfield assuaged Senate pride by including a number of amendments that had been added by the Senate during the first round of action on HR 5922 but were dropped from the House version of HR 6685.

The Senate bill also included a long list of legislative provisions that were in HR 5922 but dropped from HR 6685. Funding in the bill, including the administrative funds for the Commerce and Education departments, would continue through Sept. 30, 1982.

Before passing the bill, the Senate defeated two Democratic-sponsored amendments. One, by Kennedy, adding $63 million for summer youth jobs, was tabled 55-37, and an effort by Donald W. Riegle Jr., D-Mich., to restore the $3 billion housing program was tabled 48-44. *(Votes 200, 201, p. 36-S)*

The biggest items in the bill were the $2.4 billion for sewer construction grants, $1.3 billion for student loans and $1 billion for food stamps. The bill rescinded $4.1 billion from assisted housing and $1.6 billion from rental housing subsidies, and dropped the $150 million for Ginnie Mae in the House-passed measure.

Senate-approved amendments added back to the bill included $60 million for health services, $24.4 million for the Corporation for Public Broadcasting and $40 million for emergency dredging by the Army Corps of Engineers.

Also included were the $3,000 annual limit on members' tax deductions and the ban on government payments for loans made to Poland unless the Polish government was found to be in default or the president certified to Congress that the payments were in the national interest.

Second Override Attempt

Back from its recess, the House voted July 13 on whether to override Reagan's second veto of a supplemental funding bill. But without the popular emergency housing aid program included in HR 5922, HR 6682 had little prospect of winning a two-thirds House majority, and the attempt failed by an even wider margin than the first one — 242-169. *(Vote 170, p. 50-H)*

While 53 Republicans and 200 Democrats voted to override the first veto, on HR 6682 only 39 Republicans voted to override, along with 203 Democrats.

Wright said the vote was a test of whether the House was "subservient" to the wishes of Reagan and Stockman. He noted that the alternative to the vetoed bill was the Senate-passed version of HR 6685, which he said was written in "direct obeyance and obedience to the command" of Stockman.

Minority Leader Robert H. Michel, R-Ill., said the veto should be sustained because the bill contained $1 billion in spending not requested by the administration.

Conference Action on HR 6685

After voting to sustain the veto of HR 6682, the House went to conference with the Senate on HR 6685.

Hatfield said he was willing to accept some of the House's spending provisions as long as the total amount in the conference agreement did not exceed the amount in the Senate-passed bill. Stockman had made clear that he would recommend signing the bill if it went not more than $390 million over the administration's budget, and the Senate bill measured up.

Conferees worked out an agreement July 14 (H Rept 97-632) that added back funds for summer youth jobs, nursing research, refugees, highway aid and the Postal Service. To compensate for the additional spending, they agreed to rescind an additional $171 million from the rental housing supplement program.

The final bill provided $5.4 billion in appropriations and $5.8 billion in rescissions, compared to Reagan's original request of $4.5 billion in spending and $7.7 billion in rescissions.

The House adopted the conference report July 15 by a 389-13 vote. The Senate approved it later the same day, 91-6, clearing it for the president. *(House vote 176, p. 52-H; Senate vote 214, p. 39-S)* ∎

Military Construction

Congressional efforts to pressure U.S. allies to pay more of the cost of the common defense were turned up another notch by the conference report on the $7 billion military construction appropriations bill for fiscal 1983.

The bill (HR 6968 — PL 97-323) gave the Pentagon about half the $178.6 million it requested to construct facilities in Egypt that would be used as a base for oper-

Military Construction Appropriations, Fiscal 1983

HR 6968 made the following appropriations for military construction projects in fiscal 1983:

Service	Reagan Request	House Passed	Senate Passed	Final Appropriation
Army	$1,100,200,000	$ 941,570,000	$ 982,810,000	$ 929,720,000
Navy	1,208,300,000	1,120,813,000	1,047,040,000	1,080,750,000
Air Force	2,081,800,000	1,420,825,000	1,657,457,000	1,551,414,000
Defense Agencies	408,900,000	289,145,000	305,143,000	339,770,000
NATO Infrastructure	375,000,000	325,000,000	325,000,000	325,000,000
Guard and Reserve	261,500,000	285,458,000	261,500,000	285,458,000
Family Housing	2,896,203,000	2,739,514,000	2,642,834,000	2,653,004,000
(debt reduction)[1]	−124,076,000	−124,076,000	−124,076,000	−124,076,000
Homeowners Assistance Fund	4,000,000	2,000,000	2,000,000	2,000,000
Total	$8,211,827,000	$7,000,249,000	$7,099,708,000	$7,043,040,000

[1] *Not counted as new budget authority*

ations in the Persian Gulf. But the conferees barred any use of the funds until the secretary of defense certified that negotiations were under way seeking support from Japan and the NATO allies for the U.S. defense buildup in the gulf region.

They also refused to fund some airfield improvements in Europe, which the Air Force insisted were vital, but which the conferees said should be paid for by NATO.

The bill approved funds requested for a project that was part of a multi-year program to re-station U.S. troops in West Germany. But it barred use of those funds until the Bonn government agreed to pay for most of the multi-year plan.

The conference report (H Rept 97-913) was adopted by voice vote in each house on Oct. 1. The bill was signed into law on Oct. 15.

House Committee Action

The House Appropriations Committee reported HR 6968 Aug. 11 (H Rept 97-726). As reported, the bill appropriated $7,000,249,000 for Pentagon construction programs in fiscal 1983.

This included $4.38 billion for construction of military projects and $2.74 billion to build and operate military family housing units. The housing appropriation included $124 million applied to debt reduction that was not counted as new budget authority.

Gross reductions in the administration request, which totaled $1.445 billion, were partly offset by $250 million appropriated for unbudgeted programs added to the companion authorization bill (HR 6214), and approved by the Appropriations Committee. Most of the additions were for projects located in districts represented by House Armed Services Committee members. *(Authorization, p. 101)*

The largest of those add-ons was a $41 billion headquarters building for the Army's Forces Command at Ft. McPherson, Ga. That project made Georgia the second largest beneficiary of the bill among states. Its $267.7 million in construction funds was exceeded only by the $410.9 million earmarked for projects in California.

Georgia also hosted the largest single project in the administration's construction request: $148.3 million to continue construction of a base at King's Bay for Trident missile-firing submarines. The base was scheduled to begin operation in 1989.

The military construction subcommittees of both the Appropriations panel and the Armed Services Committee were chaired by Georgia Democrats, Bo Ginn and Jack Brinkley, respectively.

The committees' cuts included nearly $200 million earmarked for construction in Europe, and nearly $300 million associated with the construction of bases for U.S. operations in the Indian Ocean and Persian Gulf region.

The lack of formal agreements granting U.S. access rights to bases in Egypt and the Azores was cited as one factor in the cuts for those projects. But the "burden-sharing" issue clearly was the dominant factor in the committee's cuts in European projects and its opposition to current plans for a Rapid Deployment Force base at Ras Banas, Egypt.

In its report, House Appropriations underscored its concern with the scope of unilateral actions to increase U.S. military capability abroad.

"Although some of these actions are justified to defend U.S. vital interests," the panel said, "the benefits derived affect the whole region, and therefore the costs should be more equitably shared."

The committee had issued similar complaints for several years; each year its willingness to act on the complaints seemed to grow. *(1981 Almanac p. 306; 1980 Almanac p. 166)*

NATO Construction

The Appropriations Committee said it was unhappy not only with unilateral U.S. funding of overseas construction programs, but more fundamentally with increased U.S. military commitments abroad at a time when U.S. allies in Europe and elsewhere were decreasing their defense efforts.

The panel cited a raft of programs to deploy new weapons in Europe or improve the combat readiness of units already on the continent, that would require an estimated $541 million in U.S. construction costs. The projects

would increase by an estimated 22,035 the number of U.S. military personnel and dependents living in Europe.

NATO Infrastructure. The committee approved $325 million of the $375 million requested for the annual U.S. contribution to the Infrastructure — NATO's kitty for construction projects of common benefit.

The panel commended the program, but complained that it was too small to meet all the construction requirements that the committee thought should be paid for by the alliance.

The Pentagon should make up most of the committee's reduction, according to the report, by stepping up its efforts to recoup from the alliance the U.S. funds that had been spent on projects that were eligible for Infrastructure funding. The Pentagon frequently had asked Congress for such "pre-financing" of projects with U.S. funds because they would have to wait several years for Infrastructure funding.

The committee protested that of $280 million due from NATO for such pre-financed projects, the Pentagon expected to collect only $35 million to $40 million in fiscal 1983.

Of the total, projects costing $150 million had not yet even been scheduled for repayment in future years, the panel said. If that $150 million was not at least scheduled for future repayment by the time the fiscal 1984 appropriations bill came to the panel, it warned, it would consider reducing the U.S. Infrastructure payment by that amount to force the issue.

The panel reiterated its proposal that the allies increase their collective share of the annual Infrastructure budget to offset the cost to the United States of building military facilities in the Indian Ocean and Persian Gulf region. The lack of direct allied contributions to those facilities had been a particularly sore point to some members, who pointed out that the bases were intended to defend Persian Gulf oil supplies that were far more critical to the European allies and Japan than to the United States.

The committee also complained that U.S. contractors were obtaining few Infrastructure contracts — particularly for the use of U.S. structural steel. There was some question as to whether they were being allowed to compete fairly for the contracts, the panel said, and it said the matter would be thoroughly investigated in 1983.

European Air Bases. The panel denied $40.3 million requested for various Air Force projects in Europe that, it said, should be funded through the NATO Infrastructure.

Of this amount, $28.6 million was to construct fuel and ammunition supply dumps and aircraft parking ramps at so-called "co-located operating bases." These were European-owned air bases that would host U.S. combat planes flown to the continent as reinforcements in case of war.

Cruise Missile Bases. Of the $85.4 million requested to construct bases in Europe for ground-launched cruise missiles, the committee approved $36 million. And it denied $30.5 million earmarked for dependents' schools and $18.5 million for family housing at the missile bases.

Both actions echoed the position taken in the companion authorization bill, as did the panel's order that the Air Force build only austerely equipped bases, with no facilities for personnel to be accompanied by their families. This was because the declared administration goal in arms control talks with the Soviet Union had been to bar all such long-range missiles from Europe. If a treaty embodying

that goal were to be ratified, much of the U.S. investment in cruise missile bases would be lost.

Master Re-stationing Plan. The committee evidently concurred in the authorizing bill's denial of $37.2 million for construction at two bases in West Germany where the Army hoped to re-station three battalions currently stationed more than a hundred miles to the west.

This so-called Master Re-stationing Plan (MRP) was intended both to replace old and inadequate facilities and to move the units closer to their planned defensive positions. The committee said the plan was estimated to cost $1.2 billion.

The committee applauded the Pentagon's efforts to elicit financial support for the plan from West Germany. But it expressed "disappointment" that the German government had not yet made any firm funding commitments to the plan. The panel reiterated its position that the Bonn government should pay for the whole program, partly because its territory would then be better defended and partly because it would obtain the valuable real estate in several urban areas that would be vacated by the U.S. units.

The committee hinted that it might wind up approving the $37.2 million request, for bases at Vilsek and Wildflecken, if West Germany were to act favorably on the plan prior to the Senate-House conference on HR 6968.

Persian Gulf, Indian Ocean

Denial of $178.6 million for facilities at Ras Banas, at the southern end of Egypt's Red Sea coast, accounted for more than half of the committee's reduction in funds associated with the deployment of U.S. forces to the Indian Ocean and Persian Gulf area. *(Box, p. 216)*

Other Facilities. The Appropriations Committee agreed with the Armed Services panel that proposed air-cargo facilities at Lajes air base in the Portuguese-owned Azores Islands should not be built until a formal agreement guaranteeing U.S. access was in hand.

Both committees deleted the $55.7 million request from their respective bills.

The other large reduction related to U.S. plans for the Persian Gulf was a cut of $51.1 million in the $60.35 million request for construction in Oman. The remaining $9.25 million was the amount authorized, because of uncertainty in construction plans. But the Appropriations Committee said it would support the entire request once the plans were clarified and authorized by Congress.

The committee approved $71.9 million of the $80.6 million requested for Navy facilities on Diego Garcia, a British-owned atoll in the Indian Ocean. However, the committee approved the entire $36.5 million Air Force request for Diego Garcia.

The committee also approved the requests to complete the modernization and expansion of facilities in two other countries: $30 million for air and naval facilities in Somalia and $8.3 million for naval facilities in Kenya.

Honduras Air Bases

The request for $21 million to improve two airfields in Honduras was deleted because it had not been authorized in the House version of the construction authorization bill. That was because the U.S.-Honduras agreement guaranteeing U.S. access to the bases after they were improved was not signed until after the House Armed Services Committee reported the authorization bill.

The committee said that the proposed access to Hon-

duras could prove valuable, but it ordered the Pentagon to provide an analysis of the long-term construction and operation costs that would be entailed.

In considering the companion construction authorization bill, the House rejected, 109-280, an amendment that would have barred the airfield construction in Honduras.

MX Missile Construction

The committee denied the entire request ($207 million) associated with the MX intercontinental missile, because the administration had not yet decided how the missile should be based. But it approved $30 million requested for planning and design work on the program and recommended transfer to the same use of $20 million appropriated for MX construction in fiscal 1982.

The committee insisted that these design funds not be spent until the administration had chosen a specific basing plan for MX. And the bill included a provision that barred the use of any funds to design construction projects for a specific MX deployment site until the administration had complied with the National Environmental Policy Act. This would include preparation of an environmental impact statement.

Barracks and Family Housing

The panel added to the bill $100 million for barracks and $30 million for increased maintenance of family housing in Europe. This would increase from 24,000 to 29,300 the number of personnel who could be housed in barracks funded by the bill.

The report complained that the services were not budgeting enough money to replace dilapidated barracks and ordered them to plan on building enough new barracks in each of the next several years to house 30,000 to 35,000 people.

The committee also complained that the services' estimates for new housing units were too high. "The department has clearly failed to consider prevailing market conditions and industry trends in formulating its request," its report said. The panel made a 10 percent cut in the $249 million family housing request, but it ordered the services to build the number of units requested in the budget — "to stimulate good bids."

Other Reductions

The following reductions also were recommended in the administration request:

● $85 million across-the-board cut to reflect the currently depressed condition of the construction market which, the committee surmised, should yield lower than projected bids for many fiscal 1983 projects.

● $42.5 million requested to cover cost overruns in constructing a huge Air Force wind tunnel at Tullahoma, Tenn., for testing jet engines. The committee said the Air Force should continue paying for cost overruns in the project by re-programming funds appropriated for other projects, with congressional approval.

To allow for that, the committees assigned the Air Force only $5 million of the $85 million across-the-board reduction, compared to $40 million each for the Army and Navy.

● $35 million requested to lease a large block of land in the Mariana Islands. The panel said this request was deferred without prejudice pending a study of the proposal by the General Accounting Office.

● $18.3 million to construct a manufacturing facility at

Pine Bluff, Ark., for a new type of lethal nerve gas weapon, called binary munitions. In debating the 1983 defense authorization bill (S 2248), the House voted 3-2 against beginning production of the weapons; funds for the weapons subsequently were deleted from that bill. *(Story, p. 77)*

House Floor Action

The House passed HR 6968 by a vote of 325-31 late in the evening of Aug. 19. *(Vote 291, p. 86-H)*

The House first rejected by a vote of 34-322 an amendment by David R. Obey, D-Wis., that would have reduced each appropriation in the bill by 30.8 percent. Obey, a staunch opponent of the pending constitutional amendment requiring a balanced federal budget, described his proposal as a "put-up-or-shut-up" test of whether members really were willing to live with a balanced budget requirement. To balance the budget in fiscal 1983, he estimated, all appropriations bills would have to be cut by 30.8 percent. *(Vote 290, p. 86-H)*

Also rejected, by voice vote, was an amendment by Robert S. Walker, R-Pa., that would have barred the expenditure of any funds that would violate existing laws requiring a balanced federal budget. Walker had offered this amendment to several money bills in recent weeks.

Senate Action

The Senate Appropriations Committee reported its version of HR 6968 Sept. 22. The Senate passed the bill intact Sept. 27 by voice vote.

Committee Report

As reported by the Appropriations Committee Sept. 22, HR 6968 provided $16.3 million less than the military construction appropriation for fiscal 1982 (HR 4241 — PL 97-106).

The committee report (S Rept 97-572) complained that the Pentagon was sacrificing construction to protect weapons programs, which were covered by a separate appropriations bill (HR 6957), in the face of congressional insistence on budget cuts.

The administration had offered to give up $1.4 billion of its $8.2 billion military construction request during negotiations with Congress over the first budget resolution for fiscal 1983 (S Con Res 92), the committee noted.

But it warned, "Without the docks for the ships, without the runways and hangars for the planes, without the maintenance facilities for wheeled and tracked vehicles, and without the launching sites for missiles, all of the funds spent on these systems would be of no use."

Savings. In order to meet the spending cuts mandated by the budget resolution, the committee dropped from the bill $300 million worth of projects that had not been requested but had been added by the House.

These included $100 million for a barracks and $41 million for a headquarters building at Fort McPherson, Ga.

However, the panel said it hoped the Pentagon would be able to fund several of those projects during fiscal 1983 anyway, using money left over from budgeted projects. Lower-than-anticipated bids could be expected because of the depressed construction industry, it said. Accordingly, the Senate panel restored the $85 million the House bill had cut across-the-board in anticipation of these lower bids.

House, Senate Committees Disagree . . .

Congress in 1982 sharply pared back the administration's plans for facilities at Ras Banas, at the southern end of Egypt's Red Sea coast.

Conferees on the fiscal 1983 military construction appropriations bill (HR 6968 — PL 97-323) approved $91 million of the $125.6 million requested for Air Force facilities at Ras Banas and none of the $53 million requested for Army facilities.

The Pentagon plan was for the site to serve as a staging area and supply base for ground and air forces flown from the United States to intervene in the Persian Gulf region. The fiscal 1983 request had been approved in full by the Senate and rejected in full by the House.

House Committee Complaints

The House Appropriations Committee cited several grounds for denying the $178.6 million requested in fiscal 1983 for a military "facility" at Ras Banas in Egypt. To avoid offending local authorities, the Pentagon refused to use the word "base" to describe its new Middle East installations.

The committee's foremost complaint was that NATO allies and Japan were not doing enough to protect their oil supplies in the Persian Gulf region.

Among the other complaints about Ras Banas:

● The committee said the facility had grown too elaborate and expensive with an estimated 500 buildings and a total cost of $948 million, including equipment that would be stored at the base. Originally, the project had been presented to Congress as a "bare base" with concrete slabs where Army units could temporarily pitch tents and supply dumps could be established.

Later additions to the plan included facilities to operate B-52 bombers and concrete block barracks for Army ground combat troops, instead of concrete slabs on which the troops could pitch tents.

Army officials had told the committee that the block buildings would be cheaper than tents and could be adapted for use as a hospital in case of war.

During House debate on HR 6968 on Aug. 19, Bill Nelson, D-Fla., said the currently planned construction cost would be $522 million. The rest of the committee's estimate came from equipment that the Pentagon would need anyway, even if it were stored elsewhere, he said.

● The Appropriations panel also complained that, alone among the countries near the Persian Gulf in which U.S. facilities were being built, Egypt had signed no formal agreement guaranteeing U.S. access to the site.

During a March 31 hearing on the request, Military Construction Subcommittee Chairman Bo Ginn, D-Ga.,

pointed out that in his letter offering U.S. use of the facility, former Egyptian President Anwar Sadat spoke of temporary U.S. facilities for the purpose of assisting any Arab or Moslem country requesting help to repel attack.

"What limitations would this base have in terms of an attack on Israel, Kenya, Somalia or other non-Muslim countries in the Persian Gulf [region]?" Ginn asked.

"I think in all the contingencies we would be involved in [against] radical states which the Soviets support, we could count on the use of Ras Banas," responded Defense Department official David M. Ransom.

In a similar vein, the Senate Appropriations Committee dismissed the significance of a formal country-to-country agreement in its report on the fiscal 1982 supplemental appropriations bill (HR 6863).

"The committee is satisfied that our present relationship with Egypt fully supports the development of the rear staging base at Ras Banas," the Senate panel said.

● The heat, wind and flood potential of the site and its distance from the Persian Gulf might severely limit its operational value, according to House Appropriations.

Nelson countered that the weather at the site was one of its strongest pluses. Because of its coastal location, he said, temperatures typically were lower than at inland sites in Egypt or Saudi Arabia, he maintained. And he said that a 1977 flood of the site was the first such incident in 100 years.

● The committee said that in planning what to build at Ras Banas, the Pentagon had made no allowance for the access U.S. forces would have to facilities in friendly Persian Gulf states.

"Clearly the United States cannot be expected to assist in maintaining the security of these nations without this access," the panel said.

But according to Nelson, the Pentagon regarded the site's distance from the potential front lines as an asset. Troops and supplies assembled at Ras Banas could be flown to the gulf region in the Air Force's workhorse transport plane, the C-130 Hercules. But the base itself would be beyond the range of easy air attack from most of the radical states in the region.

Senate Committee

In its report on the bill, the Senate Appropriations Committee declared its wholehearted support for the Ras Banas plan: "The time has arrived to demonstrate substantively our resolve to maintain our vital interests in the area," the report said.

The report essentially endorsed the Defense Department's rejoinder to the House committee's arguments:

The committee also cut $87 million by deferring projects it did not regard as critical, including gymnasiums, chapels, family service centers and schools for dependents.

Persian Gulf, Indian Ocean

Unlike the House committee, the Senate panel provided full funding for facilities at Ras Banas, in Egypt, and approved the full amount requested for facilities in Oman

— $60.35 million, of which the House had approved only $9.25 million.

But because of limitations set by a conference agreement on the companion authorization bill (S 2586), the Appropriations Committee approved only a portion of the requests for two other large facilities associated with U.S. plans for the Persian Gulf:

● For projects at the U.S.-owned base nearest the Per-

. . . About Plans for Ras Banas 'Facility'

● The report estimated the project's current cost at $439 million, 16 percent less than the $522 million estimated by the Pentagon in August. The House committee more than doubled the current cost estimate by including equipment the Senate panel said would have to be bought whether or not the Ras Banas facility was built.

● According to the Senate report, U.S. access rights to the facility were assured, for all practical purposes, by former Egyptian President Anwar Sadat's offer of the facility, Mubarak's reaffirmation of that offer, and the wide support for the project within the Egyptian government.

● The Senate committee said the site's hot climate was acceptable and its distance from potential Persian Gulf trouble spots was an asset: It would be near enough to support a U.S. expedition, but too far away to be attacked by radical states.

The committee insisted that Ras Banas' usefulness for defending oil routes outweighed two other arguments made by the House committee: that the base was superfluous because of other available facilities and that U.S. allies should do more to offset costs of defending the region.

Conference Action

The conference committee on HR 6968 approved $91 million of the $125.6 million requested for Air Force facilities at Ras Banas and none of the $53 million requested for Army facilities.

Conferees nearly split the difference and imposed three conditions on the use of the $91 million:

● The total cost of the facility should not exceed $350 million. The Pentagon's most recent cost estimate for its current plan was $439 million. Conferees said they intended the facility to be a "bare base," with only the minimum essential construction.

● The Pentagon was to obtain from the government of Egypt "further written assurances" on the availability of Ras Banas for U.S. use. The secretary of defense also was required to give the Appropriations committees a letter detailing his understanding of "how, when and for what purposes the government of Egypt will allow the United States to use the Ras Banas facility."

● Before any of the Ras Banas funds were obligated, the conferees said, "the secretary of defense should certify through specific documentation that negotiations have proceeded with our NATO and Japanese allies which would insure either direct funding or indirect offset funding support for the [U.S.] Persian Gulf program."

By "indirect offset funding," the conferees meant that allies could pay a larger share of the cost of U.S.

military construction projects in their own territory.

Third Time Down

The deletion of the Army funds for Ras Banas marked the third congressional setback for the Ras Banas plan in two years.

In the fiscal 1982 military construction appropriations bill (PL 97-106), Congress rejected all but $14.3 million of the $120.7 million requested for facilities at Ras Banas. *(1981 Almanac p. 306)*

The Ras Banas money also was eliminated from the fiscal 1982 supplemental appropriations bill (HR 6863 — PL 97-257), cleared by Congress Aug. 20. The House committee deleted the $104 million request for Ras Banas from that bill. *(Supplemental, p. 219)*

Indian Ocean Projects

Aside from the Army's Ras Banas project, Congress in 1982 continued to support most of the president's requests for projects to bolster the U.S. capacity to respond rapidly to crises in the Indian Ocean and Persian Gulf regions.

For most of the projects, construction began in fiscal 1981, when Congress appropriated $252.9 million for installations in the region. Congress appropriated an additional $440.7 million in fiscal 1982. *(1980 Almanac p. 168; 1981 Almanac p. 310)*

	Fiscal 1983	
	Request	Appropriation
Diego Garcia		
Navy facilities expansion	$ 80,630,000	$ 53,395,000
Air Force facilities expansion	36,550,000	4,550,000
Ras Banas, Egypt		
Army RDF base	53,000,000	0
Air Force RDF base	125,600,000	91,000,000
Somalia		
Navy facilities expansion	30,000,000	30,000,000
Kenya		
Navy facilities expansion	8,300,000	8,300,000
Oman		
Air Force facilities expansion	60,350,000	60,350,000
Portugal		
Lajes (Azores) air base	56,490,000	0
TOTAL	$450,920,000	$247,595,000

sian Gulf, on the British island of Diego Garcia, the committee approved $53.4 million for the Navy and $4.55 million for the Air Force. The administration had requested $80.6 million for the Navy and $36.5 million for the Air Force.

● The committee approved none of the $55.7 million request to expand air transport facilities at Lajes airfield in the Portuguese Azores.

MX Missile

Of the $207 million requested for construction associated with the MX missile, the committee approved $40 million for projects it said would be required regardless of where and how the missile was based.

The Senate panel also restored $45 million the House had cut from the request for MX design work.

The committee dropped a House provision that barred

the use of any MX funds for specific deployment sites until all provisions of the National Environmental Policy Act had been complied with. But it directed the Air Force to spend none of the funds for MX planning and design until the president had notified Congress of his MX basing decision and Congress had approved it.

NATO Construction

The Senate panel echoed — but in more subdued tones — House complaints that U.S. allies were shirking their fair share of defense costs.

The Senate committee concurred in the House reduction of $50 million from the $375 million request for the U.S. contribution to the NATO Infrastructure — the alliance's fund for construction of common-use facilities. The two committees agreed that $40 million of the cut should be made up by repayments to the United States from the Infrastructure for facilities that were eligible for Infrastructure funding but which were funded unilaterally by the United States.

European Air Bases. The Senate committee approved $28 million to build fuel and ammunition dumps at European-owned air bases that would host U.S. combat planes flown in as reinforcements in wartime. The House had refused to fund these so-called "co-located operating bases."

Cruise Missile Bases. Restoring $49 million cut by the House, the Senate panel approved the entire $85.4 million request for bases in Europe for ground-launched cruise missiles (GLCMs).

But the committee denied an additional $49 million requested for family housing and dependents' schools at the GLCM bases since they had been denied authorization in S 2586.

Master Restationing Plan. Contrary to the House bill, the Senate committee approved $37.2 million requested for construction at two bases in Germany, near the eastern border.

The panel emphasized that new billets would improve conditions for U.S. troops.

Honduras Airfields

The Senate committee approved a $21 million request to improve two airfields in Honduras.

An agreement with Honduras completed May 7 allowed U.S. access to these two bases (and to a third) and permitted U.S. improvements.

Other Provisions

The Senate committee approved a $35 million request to lease a large block of land in the Mariana Islands, which the House had rejected.

Also included in the Senate version was $7.92 million of $18.3 million requested to begin constructing a manufacturing facility for new lethal chemical weapons, called binary munitions. The House had rejected the request, noting that Congress had refused to authorize the new weapons.

The Senate panel said the portion of the request it approved was earmarked to clean up earlier chemical weapons activities, whether or not binary production ever was approved.

Concurring in the House position, the committee refused the $42.5 million requested to cover cost overruns in constructing a wind tunnel at Tullahoma, Tenn., to test jet engines.

Conference Report

As reported Sept. 30, the conference report on HR 6968 (H Rept 97-913) appropriated $7.043 billion for military construction projects, including the construction and operation of military family housing units.

This was $1.17 billion less than President Reagan's request. It was $42.8 million more than had been approved by the House and $57.7 million less than the Senate bill.

Persian Gulf, Indian Ocean

Conferees professed their support for U.S. efforts to develop military options in the Persian Gulf region, funding all projects to the authorized levels.

However, they complained: "Neither our NATO allies nor Japan, who import 70 percent of their oil from the Persian Gulf, have taken sufficient steps to support facility construction in the region or to develop other types of offsets to the large U.S. investment."

Military construction bills had served for several years as the vehicles for congressional complaints about allied defense efforts. *(1981 Almanac pp. 234, 306)*

The conferees approved $91 million of the $125.6 million requested for Air Force facilities at Ras Banas, at the southern end of Egypt's Red Sea coast, and none of the $53 million requested for Army facilities. *(Box, p. 216)*

Because of reductions made by the companion authorization bill (S 2586), the conferees sharply cut funds for facilities on Diego Garcia. Both houses also had denied the entire $56.49 million request for transport facilities at Lajes air base in the Azores.

European Construction

Conferees approved $37.2 million for bases at Vilseck and Wildflecken in West Germany. Three U.S. Army battalions stationed 100 miles to the west would be moved to those sites, closer to East Germany and Czechoslovakia. The House had denied the funds for this Master Restationing Plan.

But the conferees insisted that before the $26.5 million budgeted for Vilseck could be spent, the Pentagon would have to notify the Appropriations panels that West Germany had agreed to "substantially assume the cost of the restationing plan." The limitation did not apply to the Wildflecken projects ($10.7 million), which were not officially part of the MRP package.

For bases in England and Sicily to house ground-launched cruise missiles, the conferees agreed on $75 million. Both houses had agreed to dispense with family-oriented facilities at the two bases, which they said should be kept to a very austere standard.

The conferees also approved $13 million requested for an underground wartime command post at a secret location for U.S. forces in Europe.

Air Base Improvements. For the fourth time in as many years, the Pentagon was unable to win approval for construction of fuel and ammunition storage dumps at European-owned airfields that would host U.S. fighter units flown to the continent in case of war. The conferees rejected the request for $28 million and said that NATO should pay for it, since the improvement in Western Europe's defenses was of mutual benefit.

MX Missile Facilities

Conferees approved only $16.7 million of the $207 million requested for construction associated with the MX

intercontinental missile. The authorization bill and the two versions of the appropriations bill refused the funds associated with a particular method of deploying the missile.

The funds approved were for logistic facilities at Newark, Ohio and Hill Air Force Base in Utah. Both would be needed to service the missile no matter how it was based.

Also retained in the conference report was a House provision barring the expenditure of any MX-related design funds for specific deployment sites, until "all terms, conditions and requirements of the National Environmental Policy Act are complied with."

Pentagon officials said this provision was consistent with their plan to incorporate a "legislative environmental impact statement" in the president's Dec. 1 MX recommendation to Congress. This would greatly shorten the time needed to prepare a formal statement on the specific sites. The Air Force already had gone through several stages of the environmental statement process for MX.

Honduras Airfield

To extend the runway and build storage facilities at the airfield in Comayagua, Honduras, the conferees approved $13 million. Similar improvements at another Honduras airfield ($8 million) were deferred without prejudice.

Under an agreement with Honduras concluded in May, U.S. forces would be entitled to use the bases in return for the U.S. improvements.

Other Issues

Since Congress had rejected the administration's plan to begin production of a new kind of lethal chemical weapon (called a binary munition), both houses had dropped the $10.38 million requested for a plant to manufacture the weapon in Pine Bluff, Ark.

But the conferees went along with the Senate to provide $7.92 million requested for a waste-treatment unit and landfill to handle contaminated soil at facilities at Pine Bluff as a result of previous chemical weapons activities.

The conferees recommended $33 million of the $35 million requested for a long-term lease on a large area on Tinian and Farallon de Medinilla Islands, near Guam, for possible future military use. But they directed the Pentagon to report on whether an outright purchase would be more cost-effective than the proposed lease.

The rejected $2 million was to develop a park.

Following the lead of the conferees on the construction authorization bill, the appropriations conferees listed projects at 25 sites which they said should be paid for by savings that likely would be realized in carrying out the fiscal 1983 military construction budget.

None of these projects had been requested by the administration, but they all were added to the military construction authorization bill by the House Armed Services Committee. Most of the projects were located in districts represented by members of that committee. ∎

Congress Overrides Veto of Supplemental

Smacking President Reagan with his first significant budget defeat, Congress Sept. 10 overrode his veto of a $14.2 billion supplemental appropriations bill (HR 6863).

The House voted 301-117 Sept. 9 to override, with the Democrats almost totally united and 81 Republicans joining the majority to vote against the president. *(Vote 299, p. 90-H)*

The Republican-controlled Senate nailed down the override the next day by voting 60-30 — the exact two-thirds majority required — to pass the bill. Twenty-one Republicans deserted the president and voted to override. *(Vote 341, p. 57-S)*

"I'm not angry," Reagan said after the vote. "I'm just terribly hurt."

Earlier in the year, Congress had failed to override Reagan's vetoes of two other "urgent" supplemental spending bills (HR 5922, HR 6682). *(Story, p. 205)*

Reagan vetoed HR 6863 Aug. 28, saying it would "bust the budget" by nearly $1 billion. He said it cut his request for defense spending by $2 billion while providing $918 million more than he wanted for social programs. *(Veto message text, p. 25-E)*

Most members rejected Reagan's characterization of HR 6863 as a budget-buster, however, noting that the bill actually provided $1.9 billion less than his total requests for fiscal 1982 supplemental appropriations.

Democrats accused Reagan of playing politics and sacrificing money for the handicapped and the elderly to fund the military and foreign aid. Republicans suggested he had been misinformed and ill-advised before vetoing the bill. Several blamed David A. Stockman, Reagan's budget director, for the bad advice. Stockman had recommended a veto.

Members of both parties who supported the override said the key issue was asserting Congress' right to set spending priorities along with the president.

The bill, which became law as a result of the override (PL 97-257), was needed to allow the government to pay its employees, including members of the military, through the end of September. The biggest chunk of money in the measure — $6.1 billion — was to cover pay raises that went into effect in October 1981. If the veto had been sustained, thousands of federal workers could have been furloughed.

Besides the money for pay, HR 6863 included funding for Reagan's new Caribbean Basin Initiative (CBI) and for some 100 programs that were running short of money in the last weeks of fiscal 1982, which ended Sept. 30.

It also — against the president's wishes — contained funds for community service jobs for the elderly, college assistance for low-income students and education aid for disadvantaged children. Heavy lobbying by senior citizens' and education groups vitally interested in those funds was credited with shoring up support for the override votes.

Provisions

As enacted over President Reagan's veto, HR 6863 (PL 97-257) provided $14,578,111,924 in new fiscal 1982 budget authority and rescinded previous appropriations of $400,846,000, for a net new spending total of $14,177,265,924. *(Appropriations, box, p. 220)*

Major spending items included:

● $6.1 billion for salary increases for federal government employees, including $5.2 billion for employees of the Defense Department.

● $5 billion in increased borrowing authority for the Commodity Credit Corporation, which finances farm price

support and loan programs.

● $42 million for construction of new federal prison facilities, including $22 million for a prison in Phoenix and $17 million for a new detention center for illegal aliens. The bill stipulated that unless the administration obtained congressional approval for another site, the detention facility must be built in Oklahoma or Louisiana.

● $61 million for the State Department, including $49 million for security improvements at embassy posts abroad.

● $179 million for military personnel programs, $48 million for pay for military retirees, $62 million for operation and maintenance funds for the armed services, and $32.3 million for military family housing maintenance.

● $146 million for military weapons procurement, including $120 million to allow the Air Force to buy two new KC-10 cargo-tanker aircraft.

● $64 million for Energy Department weapons production programs, including $14 million for weapons research and production, $36 million for production of nuclear materials and $10 million for military nuclear waste programs.

Foreign Aid, CBI. The bill appropriated $407 million for economic and military aid to foreign countries, including $350 million for the Caribbean Basin Initiative (CBI) and $56 million in military assistance. It:

● Provided that the CBI funds would be available upon enactment of authorizing legislation or on Sept. 15, 1982, whichever came first, and would remain available until March 31, 1983.

● Earmarked the CBI funds as follows: Not more than $75 million for El Salvador and $10 million for Guatemala; not less than $20 million for eastern Caribbean nations, $41 million for the Dominican Republic, $10 million for Haiti, $50 million for Jamaica, $10 million for Belize, $70 million for Costa Rica, $35 million for Honduras, $2 million for the Inter-American Foundation and $2 million for the American Institute for Free Labor Development; $25 million unallocated.

● Barred funds for any of those countries that did not cooperate in preventing the entry of narcotic drugs into the United States from those countries.

● Provided that the CBI funds could not be spent "in any manner inconsistent" with a 1962 law (PL 87-733), restated in HR 6863, declaring that the United States would use any means, including military force, to stop Cuban subversion in the Western Hemisphere or the use of Cuba by the Soviet Union as a base for nuclear weapons. Also provided that nothing in the restatement of PL 87-733 was to be interpreted as authorization for the president to use U.S. troops outside the limitations of the War Powers Act (PL 93-148).

Other foreign and military aid items included:

● $50 million for aid to victims of the Israeli invasion of Lebanon.

● $2 million for new Military Assistance Program (MAP) grants. The bill also authorized the administration to shift $25 million in MAP grants from Sudan's account so as to make available $10 million in grants for Honduras, $5 million for Somalia, $2 million for Costa Rica and $10 million for Portugal.

● $50 million in Foreign Military Sales loans for Sudan, with repayment to be forgiven, and $125 million for initial funding of a Special Defense Acquisition Fund, to be used to keep in stock items frequently requested by foreign nations that bought weapons or military services from the U.S. government.

Domestic Programs. The bill also appropriated:

Appropriations

HR 6863 (PL 97-257) appropriated the following amounts for fiscal 1982:

Increased Pay Costs	$ 6,145,002,640
General Supplemental Appropriations	
Agriculture	5,000,000,000
State, Justice, Commerce	149,951,000
Defense	435,354,000
Energy and Water	64,300,000
Foreign Operations	406,543,000
Housing and Urban Development, Related Agencies	150,000
Interior, Related Agencies	223,939,000
Labor, Health and Human Services, Education, Related Agencies	790,984,000
Legislative Branch	8,757,325
Military Construction	45,000,000
Transportation	340,020,000
Treasury, Postal Service, General Government	567,264,959
Subtotal	$ 8,032,263,284
Total	**$14,177,265,924**

● $30 million for the National Park Service to acquire park lands, $4 million for a national fish research center in Florida and $2 million to help rebuild the burned-down Filene Center at Wolf Trap Farm Park for the Performing Arts in Virginia.

● $13 million for reclamation at abandoned mines, $65 million for firefighting in the national forest system and $30 million for Indian programs, including $11 million for health facilities.

● $211 million for the community service employment program for older Americans.

● $20 million for grants to states for administering additional federal unemployment benefits, plus "such sums as are necessary" for the extended benefits, which were authorized by the tax increase/spending cut bill (HR 4961 — PL 97-248). *(Story, p. 29)*

● $11.5 million for the Centers for Disease Control, including $6 million for childhood immunization programs and $4 million for venereal disease programs.

● $10 million for research on mental health and alcohol and drug abuse, and $7 million for health planning.

● $112 million for grants to states to help pay for the Medicaid health care program for the poor.

● $148 million for grants to local school systems to help educate disadvantaged children, $27 million for education of the handicapped and $2.5 million for vocational and adult education programs.

● $217 million for student financial assistance to help low-income students attend college.

● $8.5 million for House and Senate offices, including $1.2 million for salaries and contingent expenses of the Senate and $6 million for contingent expenses in the House.

● $33.5 million for the Coast Guard and $119 million for the Federal Aviation Administration. The bill also pro-

vided $30 million for the Federal Railroad Administration, $37 million in grant money for the Urban Mass Transportation Administration and $113 million in federal grants to states for interstate highways; none of these funds were requested by the administration.

● $607 million for contributions to federal employee health insurance programs and to the civil service retirement and disability fund.

Legislative Provisions

● Specified minimum numbers of employees the Energy Department was required to maintain in programs funded by Congress over the administration's objections.

● Expressed the sense of Congress that new administration regulations affecting education of the handicapped should not go into effect until Congress had an opportunity to veto them, either in a special session after the election or at the beginning of the 98th Congress.

● Barred the use of federal funds to service the debt owed to the United States by Poland unless the president provided Congress with a report saying it was in the national interest to do so or if the debt was declared in default.

● Required the administration to immediately release $3.25 billion in recaptured assisted housing funds; also provided that in fiscal 1983, $89 million be made available for public housing modernization.

● Required the Defense Department to burn U.S. (Pennsylvania) coal at installations overseas, instead of coal available locally.

● Authorized the continued detention of 1,100 Cubans who had been ordered deported but whom Cuba would not take back.

House Committee Action

The House Appropriations Committee reported HR 6863 July 27 (H Rept 97-673). As reported, the bill contained a total of $14.6 billion in new fiscal 1982 budget authority and $265 million in rescissions. The total was about $1.3 billion below the administration's supplemental spending requests of $15.7 billion, the committee said.

The bulk of the money in the bill — about 85 percent — was for mandatory spending items that Congress was required by law to provide. These included federal employee pay ($6.2 billion), new borrowing authority for the CCC ($5 billion), federal employee retirement and health programs ($607 million) and Medicaid ($142 million).

The bill was well over the administration requests for social programs and transportation, but about $1.9 billion below the proposed amount for defense spending.

The committee added $211 million to the bill for community service employment for the elderly, $148 million for education for the disadvantaged, $169 million for college student aid and $197 million for interstate highways. It also added funds for subsidized housing programs of the Government National Mortgage Association (Ginnie Mae), increasing to $600 million the $500 million approved by the housing subcommittee.

Spending for social programs would have been even higher if the committee had included the full $553 million request for Medicaid. The committee said the additional $411 million was not needed. However, ranking Republican Silvio O. Conte, Mass., said the reduction was a "phony cut" that would have to be made up later.

By an 18-13 party-line vote, the committee approved a 14 percent cut in pay supplementals requested for employees of the executive office of the president. Offered by Edward R. Roybal, D-Calif., the amendment affected offices such as the National Security Council and the Office of Management and Budget, but not the White House Office itself.

Defense Cuts. The committee refused the administration's request for $101 million for initial construction work on a $1 billion air base at Ras Banas, Egypt, which would be used for a rapid deployment force for the Persian Gulf. While not opposed to a base in the area, the committee said it considered the plans too costly and said they were not based on a formal agreement with Egypt.

For other Defense Department programs, the bill included $368 million, compared with the request of $2.4 billion. The committee also refused to modify a number of administrative provisions that the administration said hampered military relations with NATO.

The panel deferred action on the CBI pending resolution of a dispute over other foreign aid programs. But it provided $50 million for emergency humanitarian aid for the people of Lebanon.

In addition to supplemental spending, HR 6863 contained $265 million in rescissions, bringing net new spending in the bill to $13.8 billion. Most of the rescinded funding was from the Postal Service subsidy, which the committee said could be cut without affecting service or mail rates.

Controversial Issues

In hopes of avoiding the lengthy delays that held up HR 6685, the committee agreed not to include provisions on two controversial subjects: emergency housing aid and limits on senators' reimbursement for travel expenses. But members insisted on adding limits on senators' outside income, also an emotional subject.

Carroll A. Campbell Jr., R-S.C., attempted to resurrect a Republican housing assistance amendment originally offered by Thomas B. Evans Jr., R-Del., and Tom Corcoran, R-Ill., to HR 5922, the first version of the urgent supplemental. Campbell said his amendment, which would take $1 billion from the synfuels program to fund state mortgage-subsidy programs, was less likely to be vetoed than the original, $3 billion proposal.

However, he was persuaded to withdraw it to avoid a veto confrontation over HR 6863, too.

Outside Income. Committee members were still smarting over the Senate's successful amendment to the earlier supplemental, restoring a $3,000 annual limit on business-related tax deductions claimed by members of Congress for their Washington, D.C., living expenses. So they again retaliated by proposing a statutory limit on outside income earned by members of Congress, equal to 30 percent of their congressional salaries.

The amendment, by Vic Fazio, D-Calif., would limit honoraria and other earned income of senators to about $18,000 a year. The limit already applied to House members under House rules.

Congress had lifted a $25,000-a-year statutory limit on outside income in 1981, as part of a deal under which House members won abolition of the $3,000 tax deduction limit and Senate members got the right to earn unlimited honoraria. If the Senate was going to renege on that deal by restoring the tax deduction limit, said Fazio, the House should strike back by imposing a limit on senators' outside income. *(1981 action, 1981 Almanac p. 290)*

Conte also sought to limit senators' reimbursements for travel expenses in their home states. His amendment was aimed specifically at Sen. William Proxmire, D-Wis., who had led the fight to restore the limit on members' tax deductions. Conte said Proxmire frequently used Senate funds for meals and hotels while in his home state.

When it was pointed out that the amendment could have problems because congressional rules barred the House and Senate from interfering in each other's internal affairs, Conte agreed to withdraw it. But he said he would offer it to the fiscal 1983 legislative appropriations bill.

Fazio's amendment then was approved by voice vote.

House Floor Action

The House passed HR 6863 July 29 by a vote of 282-111, after an amendment to add money for the Caribbean Basin Initiative was ruled out of order. *(Vote 218, p. 64-H)*

The $350 million CBI aid fell prey to parliamentary objections from members opposed to assistance to El Salvador. It was the most hotly debated issue during House consideration of the bill.

George Miller, D-Calif., raised a point of order and blocked a vote on the amendment. His objection, sustained by the chair, was that legislation authorizing the aid had not been passed.

The Foreign Affairs Committee had reported authorizing legislation July 15, but it remained in limbo because of opposition to trade and investment incentives Reagan wanted to offer Caribbean and Central American nations. *(CBI, p. 151)*

Miller and other administration critics had said they would attack the CBI aid to protest Reagan's July 27 certification of El Salvador for continued U.S. arms aid. They said the government of El Salvador should not get military assistance unless it halted human rights abuses and made peace with leftist rebels there. *(Story, p. 137)*

Besides dealing a severe blow to the CBI, Miller's move also torpedoed a compromise worked out by members of the Appropriations Subcommittee on Foreign Operations to approve $52 million in supplemental fiscal 1982 military aid along with the CBI aid.

Reagan had asked for extra military aid of $301.5 million, including $35 million for El Salvador, but subcommittee Democrats rejected that request. Instead, they worked out an agreement with Jack F. Kemp, R-N.Y., who was sponsoring amendments to add $350 million for the CBI and $77 million in military aid to the bill. The Democrats agreed to support the CBI aid if arms aid was limited to $52 million — $25 million for Sudan, $17 million for Honduras and $10 million for Somalia.

Miller's point of order effectively doomed that compromise, and subcommittee members protested vehemently that their agreement had been scuttled. They said committee Chairman Jamie L. Whitten, D-Miss., should have asked the Rules Committee to waive the rule allowing points of order against appropriations for programs not yet authorized by Congress.

As offered on the floor by Foreign Operations Subcommittee Chairman Clarence D. Long, D-Md., the CBI amendment contained $75 million for El Salvador, close to the amount in the Foreign Affairs Committee's CBI authorization bill. It was adopted by voice vote.

Reagan originally had asked for $128 million in CBI funds for El Salvador, leading critics to charge that the CBI was a "front" for funneling additional aid to El Salvador.

Other Changes

Other than the acrimonious debate on aid to the Caribbean, floor action on HR 6863 proceeded smoothly, without major amendments.

The only significant changes in the committee bill were due to points of order raised against certain sections. The most important of these was deletion of the $600 million appropriation for subsidized housing programs of Ginnie Mae because it lacked an authorization.

Also because of the leadership's tactic of bringing the bill to the floor without a rule waiving points of order, both Republicans and Democrats were prevented from offering emergency housing aid amendments. Legislation authorizing an emergency housing program had not been passed.

Three provisions disapproving administration requests for deferral of funds also were killed on points of order.

By voice vote, the House also rejected three amendments on social issues offered by Robert S. Walker, R-Pa. The amendments would have barred the use of funds in the bill to enforce racial or sexual quotas in hiring, admissions or contracting or to prevent voluntary prayer in the public schools, and prohibited spending funds in the bill if federal outlays exceeded federal revenues in the fiscal year.

Senate Committee Action

The Senate Appropriations Committee reported its version of HR 6863 Aug. 3 (S Rept 97-516).

Heeding the warning of Appropriations Chairman Mark O. Hatfield, R-Ore., that "the risk of a veto increases in direct proportion to the number of add-ons," the panel approved few amendments to increase spending over the recommendations of its subcommittees.

The bill was considerably closer to the recommendations of the administration than the version passed by the House. The Senate bill contained $14 billion in net new spending; most importantly, it included $355 million for the CBI package of economic assistance. The House bill was similar in total spending ($13.8 billion) but contained more for domestic programs and less for defense-related programs than the Senate measure.

The most extensive debate in the Senate committee was on the related issues of CBI aid and military aid to El Salvador.

Patrick J. Leahy, D-Vt., urged the panel to cut the entire $35 million recommended by the Foreign Operations Subcommittee for military aid to El Salvador. He said James L. Buckley, under secretary of state for security assistance, had agreed during House action on HR 6863 to leave it out.

But subcommittee Chairman Robert W. Kasten Jr., R-Wis., said that offer was made as part of the compromise needed to get the CBI through the House. Since the compromise fell through, Kasten said, the administration had returned to support of the aid.

Leahy's amendment was rejected 4-19. However, the committee did agree to an amendment by Daniel K. Inouye, D-Hawaii, to cut El Salvador aid to $20 million.

Leahy also sought to drop the CBI aid from the bill on the grounds that the program had not yet been authorized, but his amendment was rejected, 3-20.

Besides the CBI aid, the Senate bill included $17 million in new appropriations and $25 million in reprogrammed funds for foreign military aid, not included in the House bill. The money would go to El Salvador, Honduras and Somalia. The panel also included the requested $3.5

million for military training of foreign officials and $50 million in foreign military sales credits for the Sudan.

The $492.8 million provided for the Defense Department was $125.2 million more than the House bill contained, but still $1.9 billion below the administration's request. The committee rejected funding requests of $801 million for operations and maintenance and $797 million for procurement. It said they were not of sufficient urgency to be included in the supplemental but would be considered as part of fiscal 1983 defense appropriations.

Like the House committee, the Senate panel denied for the time being the $101 million requested for construction of a military base at Ras Banas, Egypt.

The committee reaffirmed its support for continued work on the new Philip A. Hart Senate Office Building, which had been under criticism since the mid-1970s. The building was nearly completed and was estimated to cost at least $137 million.

HR 6863 contained no new funds for the building, but Proxmire, one of its chief critics, moved to delete $4.2 million in already appropriated funds for it. The money was to be used for a third Senate gym, a multimedia hearing room and staff offices — projects that Proxmire said were of low priority.

J. Bennett Johnston, D-La., said the new hearing room was needed to relieve a shortage of committee meeting rooms and to provide permanent facilities for television coverage.

Proxmire's amendment was rejected 3-19.

Senate Floor Action

The Senate passed its version of HR 6863 by voice vote Aug. 11 after adding funds for unemployed workers and a bailout of the ailing copper industry. It also took a partisan series of votes on foreign aid that were aimed mostly at the fall elections.

In two long days of debate, the Senate made few substantive changes in the bill. As passed, the measure appropriated $14 billion, although the actual total could be higher because of the adoption of an amendment providing "such sums as may be necessary" for additional unemployment compensation benefits to workers whose basic 26-week entitlement had run out.

Foreign Aid Amendments

By a party-line vote of 42-54, the Senate rejected a Leahy amendment to delete the $355 million for the CBI as well as other funds for economic and military aid to foreign countries. *(Vote 303, p. 51-S)*

Democrats argued that the spending could not be justified when the government was cutting most other areas of the budget. They also noted that Congress had not passed an authorization for the program.

Similar partisan splits occurred on two other foreign aid votes. The Senate decided, 53-46, to essentially overrule a procedural point made by Leahy that the foreign aid funding should be eliminated because it had not been authorized. It also tabled (killed), 55-40, an amendment by Christopher J. Dodd, D-Conn., to halve the bill's funding for the Caribbean. *(Votes 302, 304, p. 51-S)*

In an action some senators claimed was aimed mostly at the fall elections, the Senate voted 68-28 for an amendment by Steven D. Symms, R-Idaho, stating that it was U.S. policy to block Cuban expansionism by any means necessary, including military force. *(Vote 306, p. 51-S)*

An effort by Foreign Relations Committee Chairman Charles H. Percy, R-Ill., to table the proposal failed, 30-65. A subsequent effort by Percy to replace the wording of Symms' amendment with language that was less harsh also failed, 47-52. *(Votes 305, 308, p. 51-S)*

Coming down on multiple sides of the issue, five senators, including three up for re-election, voted first to kill the Symms amendment, then to pass it, and then voted for the Percy amendment to soften the Symms language.

Of the 30 senators running for re-election in 1982, 21 voted for the Symms amendment.

Congressional, Executive 'Perks'

Proxmire offered an amendment to prohibit the spending of $736,400 to furnish a gymnasium for senators in the new Hart office building. Proxmire said senators already had two gyms which most of them did not use.

The main defense of the new gym came from Johnston, who said it could also serve as a hearing room.

The Senate tabled Proxmire's amendment, 50-48. *(Vote 300, p. 50-S)*

The day after saving its exercise facility, the Senate by voice vote adopted an amendment prohibiting the commissioner and the chief lawyer of the Internal Revenue Service from using federal funds for renovating their offices at an estimated cost of $135,000. Dennis DeConcini, D-Ariz., who offered the amendment, said such costly improvements could not be justified at a time of federal penny-pinching.

Money Added

High unemployment rates spurred the Senate to approve supplemental unemployment benefits. It voted 96-3 for an amendment by Harrison "Jack" Schmitt, R-N.M., to appropriate an undetermined amount for extended unemployment benefits. Schmitt said the amendment was necessary to allow the benefits to begin as soon as Congress passed the bill authorizing them. *(Vote 309, p. 51-S)*

Schmitt, facing a tough re-election fight, also won Senate approval of an amendment to help the ailing copper industry, a major employer in his state. The amendment, which the Office of Management and Budget (OMB) estimated would cost between $197 million and $464 million, required that the proceeds from all sales of materials from the government's strategic materials stockpile be used to buy U.S. copper for the stockpile. To prevent the government from buying surplus copper, which was in ample supply, it required that the copper purchased must have been mined and smelted after July 31, 1982.

Dale Bumpers, D-Ark., argued that the stockpile was for military preparedness and was not something to use to create jobs. But the Senate adopted the amendment, 55-44. *(Vote 310, p. 52-S)*

Another chunk of money added to HR 6863 by the Senate was a $48 million amendment by Dodd for supplemental educational opportunity grants for needy students.

The Senate also adopted an amendment by Ted Stevens, R-Alaska, adding $160,000 to fund and convene a government commission to come up with new pay rates for members of Congress, federal judges and senior bureaucrats. The commission was not scheduled to meet until 1984, but under the amendment, its recommendations would be made by Nov. 15, 1982. The president would send the recommendations to Congress and they would go into effect automatically unless both chambers objected within 30 days — a reversal of existing law that required both houses to vote to approve a raise.

Other Amendments

The Senate also adopted amendments including:

● By Lowell P. Weicker Jr., R-Conn., stating that it was the sense of Congress that proposed Education Department regulations affecting the rights of handicapped children should not become effective until Congress had a chance to vote on them. The amendment was adopted 93-4. *(Vote 301, p. 50-S)*

● By John C. Danforth, R-Mo., to make available previously appropriated funds for the bankrupt Rock Island and Milwaukee railroads.

● By Johnston, to increase the likelihood that the government would build a $17 million facility to detain illegal aliens in Allen Parish, La., a high-unemployment area.

Conference, Final Action

After compromising on funding levels and other differences between the House and Senate bills, conferees agreed to a $14.2 billion version of the measure Aug. 12. They filed their report Aug. 13 (H Rept 97-747).

Conferees agreed to include $350 million for the CBI in the bill, but only after reducing funding for El Salvador and stripping $186 million in Senate-approved foreign military sales credits from the bill. Conte told the conference the CBI funding was "the linchpin" necessary for getting Reagan's signature on the bill. Conte also proposed a compromise of $75 million in foreign military sales, but that was rejected by House conferees on an 8-11 vote.

Conferees retained the Senate amendment stating that it was U.S. policy to block Cuban expansionism by any means necessary, although House members dismissed it as "meaningless rhetoric."

Conferees retained Schmitt's amendment providing funds for extended unemployment benefits, but they could not agree on his amendment to aid the copper industry, so it was sent back to the House for a separate vote.

The Stevens amendment providing for new pay raise recommendations for members of Congress also was returned to the House for a vote. Conferees reported it in technical disagreement.

The conferees dropped the House provision limiting senators' outside earnings. The House gave up on the issue after the Senate eliminated funds for House members' expenses and for House staff pay increases. When conferees removed the limit on senators' earnings, they also restored the money for the House.

House Action

The House adopted the conference report on HR 6863 Aug. 18 by a 348-67 vote. *(Vote 280, p. 82-H)*

By a 62-339 vote, it rejected the Senate provision requiring that proceeds of sales of material from the national defense stockpile be used to buy copper for the stockpile. *(Vote 283, p. 84-H)*

Western members argued that the provision was necessary. "The facts are that since the first of the year, the copper industry has flat gone to hell," said John J. Rhodes, R-Ariz. But Roybal, who had opposed the provision in conference, said the law required the stockpile to be used for defense purposes, not for economic or budget policy.

The House accepted the Senate amendment providing $350 million for the CBI by a vote of 281-129. Part of the reason members agreed to it was to get Reagan to sign the bill, although several argued that it was the wrong time to spend money for a new foreign aid program, while

domestic programs were being cut and taxes raised. *(Vote 281, p. 82-H)*

Despite a number of complaints that congressional pay ($60,662 a year) was too low, the House by voice vote stripped from the conference agreement the provision that could have given members a raise after the fall elections. Rep. Patricia Schroeder, D-Colo., blasted the amendment as a "back door" method of giving members a raise without having to vote on it.

Senate Action

The Senate approved the House-modified conference report by voice vote just before leaving for its Labor Day recess Aug. 20.

Before the vote, Carl Levin, D-Mich., insisted on getting a vote on his proposal to restore college student benefits provided to children of deceased and disabled Social Security recipients. The benefits had been cut by the 1981 budget reconciliation bill (PL 97-35). *(1981 Almanac p. 119)*

Levin offered his proposal as an amendment to HR 6863 but was defeated, 42-47. *(Vote 339, p. 56-S)*

Veto Threats

Although conferees expressed hope that Reagan would sign HR 6863 because it included funding for his CBI program, OMB officials began warning of a veto as soon as the legislation cleared.

Stockman complained that the bill underfunded defense programs by about $2 billion while providing $918 million more than President Reagan wanted for social programs. The $918 million included $367 million that had been contained in the urgent supplemental bill (HR 6682) vetoed by Reagan in June, Stockman said, and $872 million would be a restoration of funds Congress had included in a stopgap funding resolution Reagan vetoed in 1981. *(1981 Almanac p. 294)*

The administration particularly objected to the $211 million in the bill for community service jobs for the elderly, $148 million for education aid for poor children and $217 million in aid for low-income college students. Stockman also complained about language in the bill requiring the Energy Department to maintain specific numbers of employees in energy programs not favored by the administration.

Senate Majority Whip Stevens said Aug. 19 that Stockman was giving Reagan bad advice. "I don't think anything is to be gained by vetoing this one," Stevens said. "A veto would be overridden in the Senate. I'm confident of that. The president is being advised on the basis of confrontational politics with the Congress."

Other members, many normally supporters of the president, also said they would vote to override a veto.

Despite those warnings, Reagan vetoed the bill Aug. 28. He accused Congress of reverting to "old spendthrift habits" that would undermine efforts to reduce federal deficits and interest rates.

Along with Stockman, Treasury Secretary Donald T. Regan had urged Reagan to veto the bill, while Secretary of State George P. Shultz and Defense Secretary Caspar W. Weinberger urged him to sign it. Shultz wanted the CBI funding in the bill, and Weinberger warned that a veto would leave the Defense Department without funds to pay the armed forces.

However, under pressure from OMB, a scheme was devised by which the Pentagon was allowed to delay its

payroll contributions to Social Security and federal income tax withholding, saving about $700 million and enabling it to meet its Aug. 31 payroll.

Defense officials said they would be unable to meet the Sept. 15 payroll without a supplemental appropriation, however.

Override Votes

House. One day after returning from its Labor Day recess, the House voted 301-117 Sept. 9 to override the veto of HR 6863. *(Vote 299, p. 90-H)*

The total was 22 votes more than the two-thirds majority required for an override. It surprised Democratic leaders, who had worked to override but had not anticipated as much help from Republican members as they got. Democrats voted 220-13 for the override, Republicans 81-104.

Just before the vote, Majority Leader Jim Wright, D-Texas, appealed to GOP members, 130 of whom had voted for the bill initially. He said the vote would show how many would stand by their earlier positions and "how many are going to let the White House lead them around with a ring in their nose like a prize bull at the county fair."

Urging Republicans to stick with Reagan, Minority Leader Robert H. Michel, R-Ill., tried to defuse two of the reasons members were giving to override. He said the president had agreed to accept in a later supplemental the $211 million in HR 6863 for community service jobs for the elderly, and not to seek additional fiscal 1982 funding for defense.

But the promises came too late, according to some. Sid Morrison, Wash., GOP freshman whip, said a number of Republicans already had told the press or lobbyists for senior citizen groups that they would vote to override and could not switch. Joel Pritchard, R-Wash., who voted to override, said he might have voted to sustain had he known earlier about Reagan's willingness to compromise on money for the elderly and defense. "But I only learned of it an hour before the vote," he said. Other members said they had little faith the funds would be included in a later bill.

Conte, the senior Republican on the Appropriations Committee, who had advised Reagan to sign the bill, was a leader in the effort to override the veto. "You just don't have 435 robots up here in Congress that are going to vote in lockstep," Conte said after the vote. The veto was "an affront to Congress," he added.

Many members who had been willing to switch their positions and vote to sustain Reagan's earlier vetoes of spending bills were unwilling to do so this time. For example, when Reagan vetoed HR 6682 in June, 57 members who originally voted for the bill voted to sustain the veto.

But only 22 of those 57 members voted to sustain the veto of HR 6863.

Although the defectors gave a variety of reasons, they generally denied the bill was a "budget-buster" and defended Congress' right to set spending priorities. Many said they would not vote to cut funds for certain programs such as education and jobs for the elderly.

Senate Vote

After the unexpected loss in the House, the White House put intensive lobbying pressure on the Senate. Reagan personally called senators and his aides urged senators to back the president. Several members who had been out of town were flown back to Washington. Vice President George Bush presided over the vote.

Hatfield, surprised by the House vote, had to catch a red-eye flight from Oregon to lead the Senate fight for the override. He called the override debate the most difficult of his 16 years in the Senate. He said it was the first time since the GOP gained control of the Senate in 1981 that he had taken the floor to oppose Reagan, "but there comes a time when conscience and principle transcend loyalty to party and president." Hatfield said Reagan acted on "very poor advice." He said he was told the president vetoed the bill not even knowing there was $211 million in it for elderly employment programs.

Several senators, including Mark Andrews, R-N.D., and Alfonse D'Amato, R-N.Y., said they had been called by Reagan and asked to vote with him but said they could not.

Defense of the veto was limited to Finance Committee Chairman Robert Dole, R-Kan.; Majority Leader Howard H. Baker Jr., R-Tenn., and Harry F. Byrd Jr., Ind.-Va.

Dole and Baker spoke only briefly. Dole said, "I don't suggest we're busting the budget but I don't want to bust the president either." Baker said the bipartisan partnership created by passage of the tax bill would be at an end if the veto was not sustained, and the country would perceive that Congress was losing the fiscal discipline it had only recently gained. Byrd said the bill would "add tremendously to the spending of government."

After all 90 senators present had voted, the vote was 62-28 to override. Stevens and fellow Alaskan Frank H. Murkowski, R, then switched their votes from aye to nay, making the final vote 60-30. When the results of the vote were announced, Baker and Dole were still unsuccessfully trying to persuade Charles E. Grassley, R-Iowa, to vote to sustain. *(Vote 341, p. 57-S)*

Of the 11 Republicans running for re-election, seven voted against Reagan, two with him and two were absent. All 19 Democrats up for re-election either voted to override or were absent. Only three Democrats voted to sustain the president: Johnston and Russell B. Long of Louisiana and Howell Heflin of Alabama.   ∎

First Continuing Resolution: Oct. 1-Dec. 17

Before beginning its election recess, Congress Oct. 1 cleared a measure (H J Res 599 — PL 97-276) to provide temporary funding for most government agencies for the first 11 weeks of fiscal 1983.

Although lawmakers did not complete action on the continuing appropriations resolution before the fiscal year began Oct. 1, there appeared to be no disruptions in government activity as a result of the one-day delay.

H J Res 599, which expired Dec. 17, was intended to provide stopgap funding until the regular fiscal 1983 appropriations measures were enacted. Spending levels under the resolution were generally those of the House- or Senate-passed bill or the current operating level, whichever was lowest. The resolution provided full-year funding for

the legislative branch, eliminating the need for further action on that bill.

Congress had cleared only one regular fiscal 1983 appropriations bill before the fiscal year began. That measure (HR 6956) provided funds for the Department of Housing and Urban Development (HUD) and a number of independent agencies. A second bill (HR 6968), funding military construction programs, cleared Oct. 1.

Before its final adjournment Dec. 23, Congress was forced to approve a further continuing resolution (HJ Res 631) to maintain funding for agencies covered by the six regular appropriations bills that did not clear before the session ended. *(Story, p. 238)*

Provisions

As signed into law Oct. 2, H J Res 599 (PL 97-276) provided funding through Dec. 17 at the following levels:

● Agencies included in five appropriations measures were to be funded at the level approved by either the House or the Senate, or reported by their Appropriations committees, whichever was lower.

The five appropriations measures were: Agriculture (HR 7072); State-Justice-Commerce-Judiciary (HR 6957); District of Columbia (HR 7144, S 2917); Transportation (HR 7019); and Treasury-Postal Service (HR 7158, S 2916).

● Agencies included in the Labor-Education-Health and Human Services (HR 7205), Energy-Water (HR 7145) and Interior bills were to be funded at current operating levels.

● Foreign Operations programs were to be funded at the rate provided in the fiscal 1982 bill or the budget estimate, whichever was lower.

● Defense (S 2951) was to be funded at a compromise fiscal 1983 level of $228.7 billion in budget authority with certain restrictions upon new procurement.

● Military Construction programs were to be funded at the level in the regular annual appropriations bill (HR 6968), cleared by Congress Oct. 1.

● Legislative Branch programs (HR 7073, S 2939) were to be funded for the full year, generally at the rate in the Senate-reported bill. The bill's pay cap on upper-level federal employees, however, expired with the stopgap resolution. *(Legislative funds, p. 236)*

The continuing resolution also:

● Included off-budget appropriations for Strategic Petroleum Reserve oil acquisition and transportation.

● Expanded the prohibition against using funds for activities related to leasing in wilderness areas to conform more closely to the provisions of the House-passed Wilderness Protection Act.

● Apportioned funds for urban and non-urban mass transportation grants so that 75 percent was based on the 1980 census and 25 percent was based on the 1970 census.

● Allowed the secretary of transportation to spend unobligated fiscal 1982 contract authority for grants-in-aid to airports in the first month of fiscal 1983 on a discretionary basis.

● Prohibited the disposal of any large public land tracts and real estate holdings until certain evaluations of the land were accomplished. Also, Congress had to be notified of the property to be disposed of and the plans for carrying out that disposal.

● Provided up to $85 million for the purchase of copper for the national security stockpile. This provision expired with the continuing resolution.

● Authorized the secretary of the Treasury to regulate

the entry of steel mill products in order to monitor and enforce foreign export restraints.

● Provided duty-free treatment for imported steam.

● Extended the International Coffee Agreement, which authorized the president to regulate the importation of coffee, until the expiration of the continuing resolution.

● Provided an annual pay increase of 6.6 percent to working air traffic controllers.

● Continued existing provisions of law prohibiting 1) federally funded abortions and 2) bars on the implementation of voluntary prayer programs in public schools.

House Committee Action

As reported by the House Appropriations Committee Sept. 16 (H Rept 97-834), H J Res 599 extended funding through Feb. 28, 1983.

The committee rejected 17-24 an attempt by ranking Republican Silvio O. Conte, Mass., to limit H J Res 599 to

---

Stopgap Funding on Rise

H J Res 599 reflected Congress' increasing reliance on continuing appropriations resolutions to fund government programs.

A 1981 study by the General Accounting Office found that 74 continuing resolutions were enacted between fiscal 1962 and fiscal 1981 — at least one per year and an average of four.

During the 1960s and early 1970s, the scope of the continuing resolutions was fairly narrow. Typically, they funded a few agencies whose programs were controversial or whose appropriations bills had become burdened with controversial amendments.

Starting in the late 1970s, continuing resolutions became more sweeping in scope and duration. That expansion was widely attributed to the 1974 Congressional Budget Act (PL 93-344), which established a time frame for appropriations action.

Under the Budget Act, Congress could not consider appropriations bills before adoption of the first budget resolution, technically due May 15, each year. It was supposed to complete appropriations action by the seventh day after Labor Day, well in advance of the Oct. 1 start of the fiscal year. But when the first resolution was delayed, a frequent occurrence, the appropriations deadline became very difficult to meet.

Congress found it necesssary to approve four continuing resolutions for fiscal 1982. None of the 13 fiscal 1982 appropriations bills had been completed before the year began Oct. 1, 1981. Three never emerged from Congress, and the final continuing resolution (PL 97-161) provided full-year funding for seven departments and various agencies covered by those measures: Labor-Health and Human Services-Education; Commerce-Justice-State-Judiciary; and Treasury-Postal Service-General Government. *(Fiscal 1982 continuing resolution, p. 236)*

For the first eight months of fiscal 1981, stopgap funding (PL 96-536) was needed for programs covered by five regular bills. And in fiscal 1980, six measures — including Defense and Labor-Health, Education and Welfare — never cleared.

Congress' final 1982 adjournment date.

Chairman Jamie L. Whitten, D-Miss., argued that the committee "should not take it upon ourselves to make a leadership decision."

The only other controversy involved defense spending, for which substantial increases were projected in fiscal 1983. As approved by the committee, H J Res 599 generally limited spending to current operating levels. But it set spending for defense programs at the current rate of operations only until the regular appropriations bill was reported in the House. The rate would then be adjusted to reflect the House-reported bill and subsequent House action. Two attempts to put all government agencies on equal footing with defense failed.

House Floor Action

The House approved the resolution on a 242-161 vote Sept. 22. *(Vote 336, p. 100-H)*

The House made only one change in the bill, advancing the expiration date from Feb. 28, 1983, to Dec. 15, 1982. The new date was proposed by Whitten to accommodate administration requests that Congress return after the election to complete work on funding bills.

The House rejected 188-215 a motion by Conte to recommit the bill with instructions to make the resolution expire at the *sine die* adjournment of the 97th Congress. *(Vote 335, p. 100-H)*

Conte argued that the adjournment date expiration would give the Congress more flexibility to "complete the public's business" and pass a number of regular fiscal 1983 appropriations bills before it quit work for the year.

But Whitten countered that a set expiration date would give House leaders more control over what could become a lengthy lame-duck session.

Adoption of the continuing resolution followed objections by some members over a rule preventing any changes other than a switch in the expiration date. Several had amendments waiting in the wings, including ones to reduce direct military aid to Israel and to delete funding for the Clinch River breeder reactor. The rule was adopted, however, 280-120. *(Vote 334, p. 100-H)*

Several members criticized the resolution for the special treatment accorded defense appropriations.

Senate Committee Action

The Senate Appropriations Committee reported the resolution Sept. 23 (S Rept 97-581).

The committee pegged defense spending to the Senate-reported appropriations bill (S 2951) — or at an annual rate of $233.4 billion, $28.1 billion higher than the current operating level provided by the House version of H J Res 599.

James A. McClure, R-Idaho, successfully offered an amendment that added language eliminating the authority of the Federal Trade Commission (FTC) to regulate professionals and to ban "unfair" advertisements. That language was part of a Senate Commerce Committee authorization bill (S 2499).

The committee voted to ban spending to process applications for oil and gas leasing in designated or candidate wilderness areas, a provision also included in the House resolution. It circumvented the Senate Energy and Natural Resources Committee, where a House-passed permanent wilderness leasing ban was still bottled up.

Senate Floor Action

It took the Senate more than 13 hours to work its way through a flood of amendments to a final 72-26 vote on the continuing resolution Sept. 29. *(Vote 373, p. 63-S)*

Majority Leader Howard H. Baker Jr., R-Tenn., clearly frustrated by the rush of amendments, admonished his colleagues that if they did not begin to restrain themselves or move more quickly, he might ask for an emergency one-week continuing resolution. That would have forced Congress to stay in session an additional week, eating up precious campaign time.

"We simply cannot do the country's work this way," Baker said.

Although senators persisted in bringing up their amendments, the time for debate was reduced and many were accepted by voice votes.

Successful amendments included one offered by Daniel Patrick Moynihan, D-N.Y, stating the sense of the Senate that Congress should reject any proposal to impose a "means" test on eligibility or benefits under the Medicare program. The Senate adopted that amendment on a 70-29 vote after adding language proposed by Dale Bumpers, D-Ark., urging the president to proclaim Oct. 10 as National Peace Day. *(Vote 369, p. 62-S)*

All major Democratic efforts, either to add funds for jobs or to reduce spending for defense, were defeated.

The closest defeat — 48-49 — came on an amendment offered by Bumpers and Gordon J. Humphrey, R-N.H., that would have prohibited the use of funds for the Clinch River nuclear breeder reactor. *(Vote 365, p. 62-S)*

Bumpers argued that the reactor, which the General Accounting Office estimated would cost $8.8 billion if completed, was a "technological turkey." He said the Clinch River reactor could not be completed until 1990 "and by that time the technology will be 16 years out of date."

Baker, who said the reactor was not "conceived as a Tennessee project," countered that "the United States must explore the avenues for the production of power in the next century."

Howard M. Metzenbaum, D-Ohio, unsuccessfully offered an amendment to liberalize unemployment benefits by changing provisions in current law that would lop between 28 and 30 states off the 13-week extended benefits program. Metzenbaum's amendment also would have continued supplemental unemployment benefits, just approved in the tax/spending cut bill (HR 4961), until the national unemployment rate dipped to 8.7 percent — the rate included in the fiscal 1983 budget resolution. *(Supplemental benefits, p. 43)*

Finance Chairman Robert Dole, R-Kan., argued that the Metzenbaum amendment would be a "giant step backwards" from the unemployment benefit reforms Congress had adopted. The amendment was defeated 47-51. *(Vote 366, p. 62-S)*

An attempt by Edward M. Kennedy, D-Mass., to attach the $1 billion public works jobs package approved by the House earlier in September also failed. Kennedy said the package was needed to help the chronically unemployed. But Dan Quayle, R-Ind., characterized it as another "repudiated Comprehensive Education Training Act program." *(Vote 372, p. 63-S; jobs bill, p. 39)*

The ranking Democrat on the Budget Committee, Ernest F. Hollings, S.C., offered an amendment, which was killed 50-46, to preclude any obligation or expenditure of funds for procurement of the MX missile until the basing

mode had been approved. *(Vote 370, p. 63-S)*

Backing the Hollings amendment, Carl Levin, D-Mich., said, "We're not even buying a pig in a poke — we don't even have a poke to put it in."

"If we adopt this amendment, they'll be dancing in the streets in Moscow," warned Armed Services Chairman John Tower, R-Texas.

Jesse Helms, R-N.C., failed in an effort to block use of compulsory labor union dues for political purposes. Helms said "a lot of Americans just don't think it's fair" for unions to use their members' dues to make political contributions. The Senate tabled his proposal 62-37. *(Vote 368, p. 62-S)*

Conference Action

Conferees reached agreement on the bill Sept. 30 (H Rept 97-914).

When the House-Senate conference began, Senate Appropriations Committee Chairman Mark O. Hatfield, R-Ore., joked that he had dropped about 50 of the Senate-approved amendments in the Capitol Rotunda on his way over from the Senate. "I admit we have put a lot of garbage in it," Hatfield said.

House Appropriations Chairman Whitten lamented that the Senate version "attacked the whole idea of being a continuing resolution — it's a catchall legislative bill."

Conferees nonetheless accepted most of the Senate amendments, including those that did not directly affect appropriations.

Defense Compromise

The single thorniest issue for conferees was the level of defense spending. Since the House Appropriations Committee had not reported a defense appropriations bill, the House set the level of defense funding at the current operating level — or an annual rate of $205.3 billion in fiscal 1983 budget authority. The Senate version contained its Appropriations Committee's defense level of $233.4 billion.

The compromise reached by the conferees funded defense at an annual level of $228.7 billion in budget authority. It banned new starts for major new programs, including procurement of MX missiles and construction of the second of two nuclear carriers sought by the president. Advance procurement for the other aircraft carrier and other defense projects included in the 1982 spending base could go forward.

"It is reluctantly that we accepted this agreement," said Senate Defense Appropriations Subcommittee Chairman Ted Stevens, R-Alaska. During the conference, Stevens received a telephone call from Defense Secretary Caspar W. Weinberger asking that conferees allow funding to proceed for two nuclear carriers. Stevens claimed the delay in starting work on the second carrier could cost the government $150 million.

But House Defense Appropriations Chairman Joseph P. Addabbo, D-N.Y., argued that the "House has a right to act" on decisions on major new weapons procurement. Addabbo said his panel would return a week earlier than the rest of Congress to report a defense funding measure.

Included in the defense continuing appropriations was an extension of the expiration date for enlistment and re-enlistment bonuses for the military service until Dec. 17, 1982.

Foreign Aid, Social Programs

Senate conferees quickly accepted the House's lower funding levels for foreign aid despite warnings from Senate Foreign Operations Subcommittee Chairman Robert W. Kasten Jr., R-Wis., that it was a level "no one believes we can live with."

The spending level for foreign aid, which reflected the current operating rate under the fiscal 1982 foreign aid appropriations bill, was set at an annual rate of $9.7 billion. The Senate continuing appropriations measure provided $11.1 billion, which included funds contained in supplemental legislation (HR 6863) approved Sept. 10.

In accepting House foreign aid levels, the Senate agreed to a provision that continued aid to Israel at fiscal 1982 levels, which amounted to $50 million more in grant arms aid than President Reagan's fiscal 1983 request.

Many of the Senate amendments related to the Labor-Health and Human Services (HHS)-Education section of the continuing resolution. Under the stopgap funding bill, these departments would be funded at the current operating level, including all supplemental bills.

While House conferees rejected $296.5 million in forward funding for the Older Americans Act and $50 million in advance funding for vocational education basic state grants, they accepted most other Senate amendments.

Conferees accepted Senate amendments that would provide:

- $39 million for childhood immunization programs.
- $34 million for grants and contracts to hospitals and medical schools for residencies in family medicine.
- $800 million for processing Medicare claims.
- $18 million for the Runaway and Homeless Youth Act.
- $5 million for nursing research.

Other Senate amendments accepted by the conferees:

- Stipulated that certain states would be required to pass through at least 90 percent of funds allotted to them to local community action agencies.
- Required preliminary education impact aid payments equal to 75 percent of the amount of aid received in the previous year.
- Stated the sense of Congress in opposition to "any proposal to impose a 'means test' on eligibility for the Medicare program or benefits provided by the Medicare program."
- Imposed restrictions on the activities of the Legal Services Corporation and its grantees.

Final Action

The Senate cleared the funding measure by voice vote late Oct. 1, following final House approval by a 290-123 vote. *(Vote 364, p. 110-H)*

House debate was punctuated with complaints about the omnibus procedure. "In the name of expediency, we have rolled all of our appropriations into a single foul-smelling lump," said Rep. Bill Frenzel, R-Minn.

Air Controllers. With little debate the House yielded to the Senate on an amendment in disagreement that provided a 6.6 percent annual pay increase for air traffic controllers.

But it rejected 128-267 an amendment by Rep. William D. Ford, D-Mich., that would have permitted the administration to rehire former controllers. *(Vote 365, p. 110-H)*

Rep. Gene Snyder, R-Ky., said the House should de-

feat the Ford amendment and provide a pay increase for "those air traffic controllers who did not, like so many of their colleagues, go on strike last August."

Peace Day. The House dropped a provision, adopted by the Senate and agreed to by conferees, setting Oct. 10 as National Peace Day. There was no debate over the deletion in the House, but the Peace Day proposal caused an uproar in the Senate.

"This amendment is not innocent but will give aid and comfort to the enemies of this country," Jeremiah Denton, R-Ala., told his Senate colleagues.

The idea for National Peace Day was suggested by Peace Links, an organization headed by Betty Bumpers, the wife of Sen. Bumpers, Denton said. He described Peace Links as a group guided by a 14-organization advisory board and said four of these organizations were "either Soviet controlled or openly sympathetic with and advocates for communist foreign policy objectives."

Moments after Denton's speech, Bumpers jumped to his feet to defend his wife and decry the prospect of another era of "McCarthyism."

"When a resolution like that becomes subversive, you can kiss everything that has made this country what it is goodbye," Bumpers said.

In the end, National Peace Day was excluded from the measure.

Trade Issues. The Senate included, and the House conferees accepted, several amendments affecting trade and tariffs. One amendment permitted duty-free imports of steam; another authorized the secretary of the Treasury to regulate the entry of imported steel mill products.

Frenzel and Sam Gibbons, D-Fla. — both members of the House Ways and Means Committee, which had jurisdiction over trade matters — protested the House conferees' acceptance of the Senate amendments. Frenzel said the Senate had not acted on 59 House-passed duty suspension bills over the past two years. ∎

Continued Funding, FY 1982

After first going on record in favor of lower salaries, tougher tax deduction rules and public disclosure of tax returns for members of Congress, the Senate March 31 decided instead to forget the whole thing and pass an emergency funding measure without amendment.

By an 81-18 vote the Senate passed the continuing resolution (H J Res 409 — PL 97-161), providing funding for the seven departments and various independent agencies whose regular fiscal 1982 appropriations bills had not been enacted. *(Vote 79, p. 16-S)*

The House had passed the resolution (H Rept 97-465) March 24 by a 299-103 vote. *(Vote 40, p. 12-H)*

Senate acceptance of the House-passed version of the measure, and President Reagan's subsequent signature, prevented a shutdown of the seven departments similar to the one that had halted most government activities in November 1981. The deadline for final approval of the resolution was midnight March 31, when the preceding continuing resolution (H J Res 370 — PL 97-92) expired. *(PL 97-92, 1981 Almanac p. 329)*

H J Res 409 simply extended the funding levels contained in PL 97-92 through Sept. 30, the end of fiscal year 1982. Included in the measure were funds for the departments of Labor, Education, Commerce, Justice, State,

Treasury, and Health and Human Services.

Congressional Pay, Taxes

But it was congressional pay, not funding levels, that generated the most controversy and threatened to prevent final action on the resolution before the deadline.

Under heavy pressure from the Republican leadership, the Senate reversed itself and agreed to kill amendments restricting pay and tax deductions. Passage of the resolution with the amendments would have forced a conference with the House, which probably could not have been completed in time to prevent a lapse in funding authority.

The key amendment, offered by William L. Armstrong, R-Colo., would have restored a $3,000 limit on business-related tax deductions claimed by members of Congress. An earlier fiscal 1982 continuing resolution (PL 97-51) had removed the longstanding limit. *(Background, 1981 Almanac pp. 290, 400; later action, p. 542)*

On four separate roll-call votes, the Senate affirmed its support for Armstrong's amendment. The removal of the tax deduction limit — with its estimated $7,000 a year increase in disposable income for the average member of Congress — had attracted widespread public criticism.

Under regulations issued by the Treasury Department, members were currently allowed to deduct up to $75 for each "congressional" day. They did not have to substantiate their expenses, or even be in Washington, to claim the deduction. The new rules would allow members to claim about $16,000 a year in additional business deductions.

Armstrong said that the new rules gave an unfair advantage to members of Congress. He argued that Congress should return the law to the way it was before passage of PL 97-51, and then start thinking about rewriting the rules that applied to members' taxes.

Assistant Majority Leader Ted Stevens, R-Alaska, defended the increased deductions as compensation for the pain suffered by senators in having to live in the nation's capital. "I know of no town that has a worse crime standard, a worse set of schools, a worse circumstance to live and work in than the city of Washington," he said.

In response to Armstrong's amendment, Stevens offered an amendment to reduce salaries of members of Congress by 10 percent, beginning April 1. The amendment, which would have cut pay to $54,596.25 a year from $60,662.50, was adopted 63-36. *(Vote 75, p. 15-S)*

In addition, a Paul E. Tsongas, D-Mass., amendment to require printing of members' tax returns in the *Congressional Record* was approved 55-43. *(Vote 70, p. 14-S)*

However, the Senate rejected an amendment by Arlen Specter, R-Pa., to require members to provide substantiation for their business-related tax deductions. Specter said his amendment would treat members of Congress like other taxpayers, who must be able to prove their deductions. The amendment was rejected 37-60. *(Vote 67, p. 14-S)*

All three amendments initially approved by the Senate, however, were eventually eliminated by a technical point of order. Unwilling to reject the Armstrong amendment outright, the Senate instead found that the Armstrong amendment, and the Stevens and Tsongas amendments attached to it, constituted legislation on an appropriations bill, and was therefore out of order. The ruling of the chair against the Armstrong amendment was upheld by a 51-48 vote. *(Vote 77, p. 16-S)*

Ironically, the Senate had voted on exactly the same parliamentary question, in the opposite way, in September 1981. At that time, the Senate overturned a ruling of the

chair that Stevens' amendment to eliminate the $3,000 tax deduction limit was out of order.

Busing Amendment

Once the Armstrong amendment was out of the way, there was only one potential obstacle to final passage of the resolution — the effort by Jesse Helms, R-N.C., to force the House to act on his anti-busing amendment.

Along with J. Bennett Johnston, D-La., Helms had sponsored a successful amendment to the Justice Department authorization bill (S 951) that would virtually eliminate court-ordered busing. The Senate passed the bill March 2. *(Authorization, p. 385)*

House Democratic leaders opposed the amendment, however, and Helms warned that they would seek to kill it by not acting on the bill. To pressure them into acting, he proposed an amendment to H J Res 409 that would have cut off Justice Department funding on May 31.

Helms agreed to withdraw his amendment so that action on the resolution could be completed. ∎

Emergency Supplementals

Congress Feb. 10 completed action on two fiscal 1982 supplemental appropriations bills, providing emergency funding for farm price supports, home heating aid for the poor and unemployment compensation.

Price Supports, Polish Debt

One of the bills (H J Res 389 — PL 97-147), appropriating $5 billion for the Commodity Credit Corporation (CCC) was cleared over the objections of members who said it would indirectly ease financial pressure on Poland's martial law government.

The appropriation was intended to pay debts the CCC owed the Treasury for funds borrowed in past years to finance payments to farmers under federal crop loan and price support programs. The Poland issue arose because the Reagan administration had decided to let the CCC pay U.S. banks $71.3 million that Poland failed to pay in January on loans guaranteed by the CCC.

The decision was controversial because the administration allowed the CCC to acquire Poland's debt without forcing the banks to declare Poland in default, a step that normally was mandatory.

The United States had imposed economic sanctions against both Poland and the Soviet Union as a result of the Dec. 13, 1981, imposition of martial law in Poland.

Final action on H J Res 389 came when the House accepted, by a 264-62 vote, a Senate amendment adding $123 million for low-income energy assistance administered by the Department of Health and Human Services. *(Vote 7, p. 2-H)*

The Senate had added the fuel subsidy to H J Res 389 earlier Feb. 10 by a vote of 85-10, on an amendment by Edward M. Kennedy, D-Mass. *(Vote 7, p. 3-S)*

The House had passed the energy aid by 342-62 on Feb. 9 as a separate bill (H J Res 392). *(Vote 4, p. 2-H)*

The House also had passed the CCC appropriation on Feb. 9 by a vote of 320-86. *(Vote 3, p. 2-H)*

Votes on Poland Issue

In its only direct action on the Poland issue, the House

rejected, 152-256, a motion by Jerry Lewis, R-Calif., to send the bill back to committee with instructions to add a prohibition against payment of guaranteed loans to Poland. *(Vote 2, p. 2-H)*

Lewis and other conservatives argued that before getting CCC funds, U.S. banks should be forced to declare Poland in default and seize Polish assets. They said that would force the Soviet Union to come up with funds to restore Poland's international credit rating, or else face a halt of Western commerce with Poland, leading to further deprivation of its populace and more popular pressure on the government.

Supporters of the CCC funding argued that blocking it to get at Poland's authorities would only penalize American farmers owed money by the CCC. Some said that forcing a Polish default risked provoking a world economic crisis.

Jamie L. Whitten, D-Miss., chairman of the House Appropriations Committee, said the $5 billion appropriation could not be used for Poland anyway, since its sole purpose was to pay off CCC debts to the Treasury. He said the bill was urgent if the CCC was to make payments to some 233,000 farmers who needed the funds to finance 1982 plantings.

But Lewis and others said paying off CCC debts to the Treasury was the same as restoring the CCC's ability to borrow; that meant giving the CCC borrowing authority to finance its assumption of Poland's debt to the banks.

Similar opposition arose in the Senate. Daniel Patrick Moynihan, D-N.Y., offered an amendment to prohibit the CCC from assuming any of Poland's debt absent a declaration of default by the banks, unless the president reported monthly to Congress on how U.S. national security was served by assuming Poland's debt without a declaration of default. The Senate rejected Moynihan's amendment by a vote of 39-55. *(Vote 6, p. 3-S)*

Unemployment Compensation

The other emergency supplemental (H J Res 391 — PL 97-148) provided $2.3 billion for the unemployment insurance program and the U.S. Employment Service.

The House passed the appropriation (H J 391) by a 398-3 vote Feb. 9. *(Vote 5, p. 2-H)*

The Senate passed the measure, without amendment, by a 95-0 vote Feb. 10. *(Vote 8, p. 3-S)*

The Reagan administration had requested the additional funding, which was made necessary by higher than predicted unemployment rates.

The funding provided by the resolution was for four different accounts. The biggest part, $1.45 billion, was for federal loans to states that had exhausted their unemployment trust funds. Another $500 million was for the federal share of the extended benefits program, which provided an additional 13 weeks of benefits to the unemployed.

The remaining $343 million was for administration of the unemployment benefits program, and for the U.S. Employment Service. Of that amount, $133 million was to be used to hire additional staff to process the increased volume of unemployment insurance claims.

Much of the debate on the resolution concerned the $210 million supplemental for the U.S. Employment Service, which funded state jobs search programs. Sponsors of the resolution said the additional funds were needed to support a total staff level of 24,800. Because of a shortage of funds, some states had laid off or were preparing to lay off some of their employment service workers.

Although Reagan had requested additional funds for the employment service, Moynihan said the administration really wanted to do away with the program. He said that there had been an "aborted attempt by this administration to dismantle the U.S. Employment Service."

While Congress completed action on the appropriations for the CCC, unemployment and low-income energy, it did not act on another supplemental that had been reported by the House Appropriations Committee Feb. 4. H J Res 390 (H Rept 97-427), providing $2.4 billion for Environmental Protection Agency sewer grants, was not brought to the House floor. The sewer grant appropriation subsequently was folded into another supplemental funding bill. *(Urgent supplemental, p. 205)* ∎

$46.9 Billion for HUD, Independent Agencies

Congress Sept. 29 sent to the president the fiscal 1983 appropriations bill for the Department of Housing and Urban Development (HUD) and various independent agencies.

The measure (HR 6956 — PL 97-272), the first regular appropriations bill to be cleared by Congress in 1982, contained no funds for the federal government's major subsidized housing programs. The House-Senate conference committee that established the final funding levels in the bill deferred action on government-assisted housing because Congress had not passed the required authorizing legislation for those programs. *(Story, p. 68)*

As cleared, PL 97-272 provided $46.9 billion for other HUD programs and for 17 independent agencies.

The bill was about $100 million less than the House had provided Sept. 15 in a bill that did not include subsidized housing. The Senate, however, had included subsidized housing in the $47.5 billion bill it approved Sept. 24; the final bill was $360 million more than the Senate had provided for the programs retained in the final bill.

President Reagan had proposed $46.6 billion for the programs kept in the final bill. In 1982, $46.8 billion was appropriated for those programs.

In addition to HUD, the largest funding in PL 97-272 went to the Veterans Administration (VA) ($24.1 billion); the National Aeronautics and Space Administration (NASA) ($6.8 billion); the general revenue sharing program, administered by the Treasury Department ($4.6 billion); and the Environmental Protection Agency (EPA) ($3.7 billion).

Both the House and Senate by voice votes Sept. 29 approved the conference agreement on HR 6956, completing congressional action on the measure.

Final Appropriations

As signed into law Sept. 30, HR 6956 (PL 97-272) appropriated the following amounts for fiscal 1983 *(in thousands of dollars)*:

	Budget Request	Final Amount
Department of Housing and Urban Development		
Community Development	$ 3,908,000	$ 3,908,000
Subsidized Housing Programs	*	*
Other Housing Programs	1,432,748	1,735,248
Policy Development and Research	20,000	18,000
Fair Housing Assistance	5,700	5,700
Management and Administration	321,001	307,500
Total, HUD	$ 5,687,449	$ 5,974,448

	Budget Request	Final Amount
Independent Agencies		
American Battle Monuments Commission	10,669	10,669
Cemeterial expenses, Army	6,689	6,682
Consumer Information Center	1,299	1,351
Consumer Product Safety Commission	33,508	33,508
Council on Environmental Quality	926	926
Treasury Department:		
General Revenue Sharing	4,573,622	4,573,622
Environmental Protection Agency	3,635,392	3,719,688
Federal Emergency Management Agency	850,287	549,898
Federal Home Loan Bank Board	(66,160)	(66,160)
National Aeronautics and Space Administration	6,612,900	6,809,200
National Credit Union Administration	(600,000)	(600,000)
National Science Foundation	1,069,400	1,092,200
Neighborhood Reinvestment Corporation	15,512	15,512
Office of Consumer Affairs	1,987	1,947
Office of Science and Technology Policy	1,839	1,839
Selective Service System	23,386	22,700
Veterans Administration	24,118,343	24,081,218
GRAND TOTAL	**$46,643,208**	**46,895,408**

* *The legislation deferred action on subsidized housing programs; the president had requested a rescission of $5,353,113,000.*

House Committee Action

The House Appropriations Committee reported HR 6956 (H Rept 97-720) Aug. 10 with an appropriation totaling $47 billion in fiscal 1983 for HUD and the independent agencies, excluding subsidized housing. The overall funding level was about $349 million higher than the administration requested for corresponding programs and $571 million more than the fiscal 1982 appropriation.

The committee version, which was ordered reported by voice vote, contained no funds for several government subsidized housing programs. Legislation dealing with housing aid was still being considered by the House and Senate Banking committees at the time HR 6956 was being drafted.

Edward P. Boland, D-Mass., chairman of the Appropriations Committee's HUD-Independent Agencies Subcommittee, explained that assisted housing was deferred to allow the other panels to make their recommendations.

HUD Programs

The committee recommended $5.9 billion for HUD. The housing programs not funded were assisted housing, rent supplements, low-rent public housing loans and the Government National Mortgage Association special assistance fund (Ginnie Mae tandem program).

Reagan had requested $5.7 billion for the HUD programs included in the bill. For the subsidized housing programs that were not funded, the administration submitted rescission requests of $2.4 billion for assisted housing and $2.8 billion for rent supplement contract authority.

Although the bill contained funds for existing contracts for housing assistance programs, no new budget authority was provided that would allow the government to enter into new contracts for assisted housing.

Major housing items funded by the bill included:

Housing Payments. The bill matched Reagan's request of $9.5 billion for housing payments mandated by existing contracts. Those included Section 8 housing assistance and rent supplements, Section 235 homeownership assistance, Section 236 rental housing assistance, low-income public housing and college housing programs. (The $9.5 billion was not part of the appropriations — new budget authority — in the bill.)

Elderly or Handicapped Housing. The panel approved a loan limit of $453 million for Section 202 housing for the elderly and handicapped, the same loan limit requested by the administration. That would provide an estimated 10,000 housing units.

Operating Subsidies. The committee added $275 million to the administration's request to subsidize the operations of low-income housing. The funding would be maintained at the existing level of $1.35 billion.

Community Development. The House committee bill contained $3.4 billion for Community Development Block Grants, $11 million less than Reagan wanted. For Urban Development Action Grants, the bill provided $340 million, a $100 million decrease from the president's request. The committee report said the panel anticipated a carry-over of $100 million from unused 1982 funds earmarked for grants to small cities.

Solar Energy Bank. Reagan wanted to halt funding for the Solar Energy and Energy Conservation Bank, but the committee approved $25 million.

Environmental Protection Agency

The committee recommended $3.7 billion for EPA, $72 million more than the administration's request and $5 million more than the fiscal 1982 appropriation.

The biggest increase was for abatement, control and compliance programs, for which the committee added $53 million to the administration's proposal, for an appropriation of $364.6 million. The additional money was intended to be used for air and water quality programs and waste treatment assistance.

For research and development, the committee approved $121.2 million, $12.5 million more than Reagan proposed. EPA salaries and expenses were set at $545 million, an increase of $6.9 million from the administration's recommendation.

The Hazardous Substance Response Trust Fund, known as "Superfund," received $230 million, the amount the administration requested.

The committee approved $2.4 billion for waste water construction grants. That amount equaled the fiscal 1982 funding level and the Reagan 1983 request.

Veterans Administration

A total of $24.1 billion was recommended for VA programs, $15 million less than Reagan wanted. The fiscal 1982 appropriation was $24 billion.

For compensation and pensions for disabled veterans, the committee approved Reagan's request of $13.4 billion. The committee recommended $7.5 billion for veterans' medical care, $16.8 million more than requested. The extra money was to go for nursing staff and community nursing home care.

Major construction would be funded by the bill at $427 million, and $686 million would be allocated for general operating expenses.

National Aeronautics and Space Administration

The committee recommended $6.8 billion for NASA, a $193.8 million increase in the administration's request. The fiscal 1982 appropriation was $5.9 billion.

Of the NASA appropriation, $5.5 billion was for research and development. This was $208.8 million more than Reagan proposed. The committee cut the administration's budget for construction by $5 million, to $95 million, and the requested appropriation for research and program management by $10 million, to $1.2 billion.

The additional money was earmarked for development of the Centaur space transportation system, an advanced communications test satellite, for planetary mission operations and analysis and for aeronautics.

In setting the appropriation for NASA, the committee agreed to a $1.78 billion cap on funding for the space shuttle, and a $1.8 billion ceiling was placed on space flight operations.

National Science Foundation

For the NSF, the committee recommended $1.1 billion, a $40 million increase in the Reagan request. For fiscal 1982, $993.7 million had been appropriated.

The bill included $40 million for science education, $25 million more than the administration recommended.

Arguing that "this nation is faced with the specter of pervasive science illiteracy," the committee report said the additional money should be used for pre-college teacher training and for promotion of science education and enhanced opportunities in the sciences for minorities.

Federal Emergency Management Agency

The committee cut Reagan's FEMA request by $120.5 million. The total funding recommended was $729.8 million, compared to an administration request of $850.3 million. Funding for fiscal 1982 was $585.3 million.

Boland said the reduction came from the administration's proposal for civil defense spending. Reagan had recommended a $119 million increase in the 1982 funding level for a "crisis relocation" program. "They came up with a program that's terribly flawed," Boland added.

Other Programs

Council on Environmental Quality. The committee met the administration's request for $926,000 for the Council on Environmental Quality, a $7,000 increase from fiscal 1982.

Office of Science and Technology Policy. The White House science office received $1.6 million, $261,000 less than Reagan proposed. The fiscal 1983 funding in the bill equaled the fiscal 1982 level.

Treasury Department Revenue Sharing. The

general revenue sharing programs for local governments, administered by the Treasury Department, was allocated $4.6 billion for fiscal 1983, equal to the administration request and the 1982 level.

Consumer Product Safety Commission. For salaries and expenses, the committee matched Reagan's request of $33.5 million. The 1982 funding was $31.7 million.

Selective Service System. The committee approved $22.4 million for salaries and expenses for the Selective Service System, a $1 million reduction in the administration request.

American Battle Monuments Commission. The committee recommended $10.7 million for salaries and expenses of the commission, which is responsible for the design, construction and maintenance of all cemeteries and war memorials outside the United States that commemorate Americans who have served abroad in the armed services since 1917.

The 1982 funding level was $10.5 million.

Amendments

George M. O'Brien, R-Ill., tried to revive a proposal to help the depressed housing industry by providing federally subsidized home mortgages for buyers of new homes. His amendment was rejected in committee by voice vote. A similar proposal introduced earlier in 1982 had led to Reagan's June 24 veto of a supplemental appropriations bill (HR 5922). *(Supplemental appropriations bill, story p. 205)*

Sidney R. Yates, D-Ill., offered an amendment to ban the use of EPA funds to register pesticides containing toxaphene, a carcinogen. The committee approved his amendment by voice vote.

House Floor Action

The House approved HR 6956 Sept. 15 by a vote of 343-38. *(Vote 314, p. 94-H)*

As passed, the bill was about $357 million larger than President Reagan requested for comparable programs.

On the floor, an additional $4.5 million was added to the bill. The extra money was earmarked for pollution abatement programs of the EPA.

The House also adopted an amendment barring the EPA from using funds in the bill to impose sanctions on states that had not complied with vehicle emission inspection rules.

The House made no attempt to add funds for the federally assisted housing that had been deferred in committee.

Boland said he eventually would recommend no more than $9.6 billion in new budget authority for subsidized housing in order to stay within the $56.6 billion ceiling set by the first budget resolution for programs in HR 6956. *(First budget resolution, story, p. 186)*

The budget resolution had allowed $10.4 billion for assisted housing, but because HR 6956 exceeded budget ceilings in other categories, funding for housing could not exceed $9.6 billion unless appropriations were reduced in some other category.

Based on Boland's pledge to stay within the overall budget ceiling, White House officials said Reagan would support the bill.

In fiscal 1982 approximately $13.3 billion was appropriated for low-income housing. The year before, Congress had provided nearly $32 billion. *(1980 Almanac p. 172)*

Floor Amendments

Changes to Clean Air Act. The most controversial amendment offered during the House debate was by Doug Walgren, D-Pa., to prohibit the use of EPA funds to implement mandatory state inspection and maintenance programs dealing with automobile emissions. The amendment imposed a one-year moratorium on the emission standards program.

Existing law required that states having air quality designated as substandard establish mandatory annual inspections of motor vehicles if they could not improve their air by December 1982. Walgren said EPA had notified 11 states that it would impose sanctions for their failure to require inspections.

"This is a very unpopular program," Walgren said. "In Pennsylvania, for example, the state Legislature refused to appropriate funds for an inspection and maintenance program and then even overrode a veto by the governor in order to protect their constituents from the expense and inconvenience of an automobile inspection and maintenance program."

Walgren argued that the moratorium was reasonable because of public resistance to the program and because Congress was considering changes in the Clean Air Act that could alter the automobile emissions standards.

Opponents called the amendment, adopted 200-184, "a major weakening of our Clean Air Act." *(Vote 313, p. 94-H)*

Said Republican Bill Green of New York, "What we have done in Clean Air Act amendments in the past to improve the quality of the air by restrictions on motor vehicles will, to all intents and purposes, be significantly dissipated if this amendment is allowed to pass."

"If we adopt this amendment, we are sentencing communities to unhealthy air for an unlimited period of time," added Toby Moffett, D-Conn.

The House in 1981 rejected a similar amendment by seven votes. *(1981 Almanac p. 336)*

Although environmentalists lost a round with Walgren's amendment, they scored a victory with the approval of an amendment by Ron Wyden, D-Ore.

Wyden's proposal, agreed to by voice vote, barred the use of EPA funds to relax health standards regulating carbon monoxide. EPA had proposed regulations that environmentalists said would harm air quality by allowing carbon monoxide levels to exceed EPA standards for up to five days, instead of one day, during a year.

EPA Funding. Several attempts were made to add money for EPA. But only the $4.5 million was approved. Green warned that additional funds for EPA would have to be taken from the $9.6 billion reserved by Boland for housing aid.

The House rejected, 131-263, an amendment by James H. Scheuer, D-N.Y., to increase funding for EPA research and development activities by $25 million. *(Vote 311, p. 94-H)*

Rejected by voice vote was an amendment by Albert Gore Jr., D-Tenn., to increase funding for EPA salaries and expenses by $10.1 million. Later, Gore offered a compromise to increase funding for EPA abatement, control and compliance by $4.5 million. That amendment, approved by voice vote, included $900,000 for an environmental study of the Chesapeake Bay.

NASA Centaur Program. Another controversy erupted over a proposal to delete $140 million for a NASA plan to integrate the Centaur space transportation system into the space shuttle program. The amendment, intro-

duced by Ronnie G. Flippo, D-Ala., was rejected by a 77-316 vote. *(Vote 312, p. 94-H)*

Senate Committee Action

The Senate Appropriations Committee reported HR 6956 (S Rept 97-549) on Sept. 16.

HUD Programs

Unlike the House, which had withheld all funding for housing assistance programs, the Senate panel appropriated $3.8 billion for assisted housing, $9.5 billion less than the amount approved in fiscal 1982.

As reported, the Senate committee version totaled $47.5 billion. The Senate bill was ordered reported Aug. 18.

Overall, the Senate committee recommended approximately $7 billion for HUD programs. In addition to the $3.8 billion for assisted housing, the committee provided $1.3 billion for low-income housing project operating subsidies and a $725 million loan limit on Section 202 housing for the elderly and the handicapped.

The loan limit approved by the panel for Section 202 housing would provide for about 16,000 housing units for the elderly and handicapped, 6,000 more than the administration and the House recommended. The House and the administration approved a $453 million loan limit. In 1982 the ceiling was $799 million.

Other housing appropriations included in the Senate committee's version were:

Federal Housing Administration (FHA), Government National Mortgage Association (GNMA). A $39.8 billion ceiling — $200 million below that of fiscal 1982 — was approved for FHA guaranteed loans. The administration requested $35 billion and the House version contained $40 billion.

GNMA was given a $68.3 billion limit on mortgage-backed securities, the same as the House ceiling and the 1982 level. President Reagan requested $38.4 billion.

Solar Energy Bank. The committee provided $15 million for the Solar Energy and Energy Conservation Bank. The administration wanted to abolish the bank, but the House approved a $25 million appropriation. With leftover 1982 funds and the new budget authority provided by the Senate bill, 36,000 solar and conservation aids could be supported.

Block Grants/Urban Development Grants. The committee matched the House-approved $3.4 billion for Community Development Block Grants. It also restored $100 million cut by the House Appropriations Committee for Urban Development Action Grants, increasing the amount to the $440 million requested by the administration.

Other Agencies

Environmental Protection Agency. The committee recommended $3.7 billion for EPA, about $70 million more than the administration requested. The proposal was basically the same as the 1982 appropriation and the House-approved amount.

For research and development, the Senate panel suggested $115 million, $6 million more than Reagan wanted. The increase includes funds for Great Lakes research, a phosphate processing study and other priority studies.

The panel added $53.4 million for abatement, control and compliance, for a 1983 appropriation of $365 million. The extra money would be used mainly to restore state grants for air, water quality and waste management.

Agreeing with the House and the administration, the Senate committee approved $2.4 billion for basic construction grants.

The Senate panel deleted the House committee amendment banning pesticides containing toxaphene.

Federal Emergency Management Agency. The committee proposed $586.7 million — $263.4 million less than Reagan requested — for FEMA disaster relief, local aid, emergency planning and administrative expenses. The House had appropriated $729.8 million, and the fiscal 1982 amount was $585.3 million.

The Senate panel said it cut the administration's disaster relief request by $195 million because $531 million was available from previous years. About $70 million of the FEMA cut was made in civil defense programs; the panel said the proposed civil defense plan should be thoroughly reviewed before the full budget request was considered.

The bill also included $39.2 million for national flood insurance, the same amount recommended by the House, but $2.4 million less than Reagan proposed. The flood insurance program received $328 million in 1982.

National Aeronautics and Space Administration. Total NASA funding provided by the panel came to $6.4 billion, compared to $6.6 billion requested and $6.8 billion approved by the House. The 1982 level was $6 billion.

National Science Foundation. The panel set NSF funding at $1.1 billion, the same as the administration request but $37 million less than the House provided. The Senate committee omitted an additional $25 million provided by the House for science education.

Veterans Administration. A total of $24 billion was proposed for the VA, about the same as the administration's request. The committee provided the full request of $13.4 billion for compensation and pensions and $7.5 billion for veterans' medical care.

General Revenue Sharing. For the general revenue sharing program administered by the Treasury Department, the committee provided $4.6 billion, the same as the request, the House version and the 1982 level.

Consumer Product Safety Commission. The committee approved the administration request of $33.5 million for the CPSC. The House had approved the same amount.

Senate Floor Action

The Senate passed HR 6956 Sept. 24 by a 73-11 vote. *(Vote 357, p. 61-S)*

An amendment by Daniel Patrick Moynihan, D-N.Y., to add $39.3 million for EPA research and $30 million for the hazardous waste cleanup program (Superfund) was turned down. Moynihan said the additional money would bring EPA's research budget up to the fiscal 1982 level of $154.3 million.

But Jake Garn, R-Utah, chairman of the Appropriations' HUD-Independent Agencies Subcommittee, argued that extra money for EPA would dip into funds needed for housing assistance. "In the past two years," Garn said, "most of the cuts have come from housing. Every time we add something to the bill, usually for EPA, it has to come from housing."

A Garn motion to table the Moynihan amendment was agreed to by a 44-40 vote, thereby killing it. *(Vote 356, p. 61-S)*

Six other Senate amendments were approved:

● By Moynihan, to prohibit for 90 days the use of HUD funds to enforce regulations increasing tenant rent contributions for subsidized housing. Voice vote. (The amendment subsequently was dropped in conference when action was deferred on funding for subsidized housing.)

● By William L. Armstrong, R-Colo., to require the State Department to investigate reports that slave labor was being used to build the trans-Siberian pipeline. Roll call, 80-1. (The amendment subsequently was dropped in conference.) *(Vote 355, p. 61-S)*

● By William Proxmire, D-Wis., to reduce the committee-approved civil defense funding by $28.8 million, thus bringing the program's appropriation to the authorization level of $152.3 million. Voice vote.

● By Patrick J. Leahy, D-Vt., to bar a reduction-in-force at the EPA staff in fiscal 1983. Voice vote.

● By Larry Pressler, R-S.D., to provide $1.25 million for a housing demonstration project for the elderly and handicapped. Voice vote.

● By Howard H. Baker Jr., R-Tenn., and Robert C. Byrd, D-W.Va., to order the Capitol Architect not to spend funds to construct a gymnasium in the Hart Senate Office Building or to spend funds to operate the Dirksen Senate Office Building gym. *(Story, p. 539)*

Appropriations Compared

	House-passed Appropriations	Senate-passed Appropriations
Department of Housing and Urban Development		
Community Development	$ 3,797,000,000	$ 3,908,000,000
Housing Programs	* 1,739,748,000	2,804,531,000
Policy Development	20,000,000	18,000,000
Fair Housing Assistance	5,700,000	5,700,000
Management and Administration	308,501,000	307,500,000
Total, HUD	$ 5,870,949,000	$ 7,043,731,000
Independent Agencies		
American Battle Monuments Commission	10,669,000	10,669,000
Cemeterial expenses, Army	6,689,000	6,682,000
Consumer Information Center	1,299,000	1,351,000
Consumer Product Safety Commission	33,508,000	33,508,000
Council on Environmental Quality	926,000	926,000
Treasury Department: General Revenue Sharing	4,573,622,000	4,573,622,000
Environmental Protection Agency	3,712,242,000	3,699,620,200
Federal Emergency Management Agency	729,795,000	557,457,000
Federal Home Loan Bank Board	(66,160,000)	(66,160,000)
National Aeronautics and Space Administration	6,806,700,000	6,394,800,000
National Credit Union Administration	(600,000,000)	(600,000,000)
National Science Foundation	1,109,400,000	1,072,768,000

	House-passed Appropriations	Senate-passed Appropriations
Neighborhood Reinvestment Corporation	15,512,000	15,512,000
Office of Consumer Affairs	1,947,000	1,947,000
Office of Science and Technology Policy	1,578,000	1,839,000
Selective Service System	22,386,000	22,986,000
Veterans Administration	24,103,017,000	24,066,459,000
GRAND TOTAL	$47,000,239,000	$47,503,877,200

*The House did not approve any funding for subsidized housing.

Conference Report

A conference report on HR 6956 (H Rept 97-891) was filed Sept. 29

The conference agreement contained no new budget authority for the government's annual contributions for Section 8 low-income rental housing, rent supplements, low-rent public housing loans or the Government National Mortgage Association's tandem program for the purchase of mortgages at below-market interest rates.

By not providing funds for these programs, Congress partly satisfied the Reagan administration's goal of phasing out federal aid for low-income housing construction. Reagan in February 1982 had proposed a rescission of more than $5 billion for these programs. Congressional acquiescence was not seen as necessarily permanent because a supplemental housing appropriations bill could be considered in the remaining months of fiscal 1983. However, Congress did not complete action in 1982 on legislation to reorganize subsidized housing programs.

"We never intended that our action would eliminate a housing program. The intent was to get the authorizing committees and the administration to agree on what kind of program they want," said Debbi Bowman, an aide to the House HUD-Independent Agencies Subcommittee.

According to Bowman, any supplemental funds eventually approved would be spent on those housing programs retained in the bill if Congress failed to approve an authorization bill for fiscal 1983. Although Reagan proposed to scrap major low-income housing programs, his endorsement of Congress' fiscal 1983 budget resolution — which did include funds for subsidized housing — indicated he probably would allow additional appropriations for them in 1983, according to Edwin L. Dale, the administration's spokesman for the Office of Management and Budget (OMB).

The budget resolution provided $10.4 billion for assisted housing in fiscal 1983. Dale said the administration would accept that much money as long as the total appropriations in the bill fell within the budget limits.

The House version of the bill contained no funds for subsidized housing, while the Senate-passed bill provided $3.8 billion. "We thought we should take what we can get at this point, rather than defer it to the future," said Sen. Garn, in explaining why the Senate had included some subsidized funds. Garn subsequently agreed to drop the Senate funds from HR 6956 because he objected to the $9.6 billion proposed by House conferees.

Other Conference Action

Environmental Protection Agency. Conferees on HR 6956 dropped the two House-passed provisions that

would have altered the EPA clean air programs. One would have imposed a one-year moratorium on EPA vehicle emission inspections. Garn argued that the amendment was too controversial in the Senate, where some senators had threatened to filibuster the provision. The other House amendment would have deleted language barring the use of EPA funds to relax carbon monoxide health standards.

Conferees said a House provision prohibiting the use of EPA funds to register pesticides containing toxaphene, a suspected carcinogen, would take effect unless EPA issued final regulations dealing with toxaphene within 60 days of the bill's enactment.

NASA. Conferees left unresolved the question of how much the Defense Department should reimburse NASA for the use of the space shuttle. The Senate, but not the House, wanted to transfer $409 million from defense funds to the NASA budget to cover the Pentagon's share of shuttle launch costs.

It was decided to let conferees handling the fiscal 1983 NASA authorization bill (HR 5890 — PL 97-324) resolve how the reimbursement would be carried out. If the plan were approved, the NASA appropriation in HR 6956 would be reduced by the amount of the transfer from the Defense Department. *(NASA authorization, p. 519)* ∎

Congress' Funding in Continuing Resolution

For the fourth year in a row, Congress sidestepped the sticky problem of voting on its own operating funds.

Money for running the House and Senate — but not members' salaries — was included in the first continuing appropriations resolution (H J Res 599 — PL 97-276), passed Oct. 1. But unlike the measure's other provisions, which expired Dec. 17, legislative appropriations were approved through Sept. 30, 1983, the end of fiscal 1983. *(First continuing resolution, p. 225)*

As a result, providing operating funds for the legislative branch was not debated on the floor of the House or the Senate before the Nov. 2 elections — a great relief to many members who feared the political consequences of voting themselves money. However, the legislators could not avoid the topic for long.

Expiring Dec. 17 along with most of the other provisions in the continuing resolution was a cap on the pay of members of Congress, federal judges and senior government officials. And in the lame-duck session, House members voted themselves a 15 percent raise, while senators opted instead to permit themselves unlimited outside earnings, including honoraria from speeches and appearances. *(Details, p. 544)*

Background

Congress had not passed a separate legislative appropriations bill since 1978, receiving its money instead through a series of continuing resolutions.

In 1979 the legislative appropriations bill was defeated in the House and never reintroduced, and in 1980 the House passed a bill but the Senate failed to act. *(1979 Almanac p. 271; 1980 Almanac p. 176)*

In 1981, neither the Senate nor the House ever brought a legislative appropriations bill to the floor, and full-year funding was again provided in a temporary spending measure. *(1981 Almanac p. 286)*

Members decided to follow the same safe route in 1982. Particularly in the House, the legislative funding measure had become the target for an array of amendments cutting legislators' pay and perquisites.

Those amendments offered members an unpalatable choice: They could vote for cuts and take a financial loss, or vote against them and almost certainly suffer some political consequences. By sheltering the bill inside a continuing resolution, members spared themselves that dilemma.

"There is a feeling we are better off not forcing members to vote on their own appropriations," complained Sen.

Mack Mattingly, R-Ga., chairman of the Senate Appropriation's Legislative Branch Subcommittee. "But I feel we cheat the American people when we take the easy way out and do not face up squarely to this issue."

Mattingly said he would insist on following normal procedures for the fiscal 1984 legislative funding bill, even if it required reversing appropriations protocol and initiating the bill in the Senate.

Members' Pay Excluded

As cleared by Congress, H J Res 599 provided $1.336 billion for Congress and its related agencies in fiscal 1983 — a cut of almost $30 million from fiscal 1982.

For the first time, however, the measure did not include members' pay, which totaled more than $36 million in fiscal 1983. Members' pay was made a permanent appropriation, not requiring annual approval, by a provision in a 1981 continuing appropriations resolution. By removing their own pay from the annual appropriations process, members had hoped to reduce the controversy that had surrounded legislative appropriations bills. *(1981 Almanac p. 290)*

If members' pay was included, the total approved was a shade higher than the 1982 figure.

Provisions

As cleared, H J Res 599 contained the following funding for the legislative branch in fiscal 1983. Fiscal 1982 funding is shown in column one. *(Figures are in thousands of dollars.)*

	Fiscal 1982	Fiscal 1983
Congressional Operations		
Senate	$ 228,034	$ 229,534
House	380,386	348,836
Joint Items	84,472	64,168
Office of Technology Assessment	12,169	12,575
Congressional Budget Office	13,226	14,825
Architect of the Capitol	74,388	87,705
Congressional Research Service	31,605	33,851
Government Printing Office (congressional printing)	84,843	81,747
Subtotal	909,123	873,241

Related Agencies	Fiscal 1982	Fiscal 1983
Botanic Gardens	2,351	1,827
Library of Congress	163,518	169,828
Architect of the Capitol	8,785	5,371
Copyright Royalty Tribunal	487	449
Government Printing Office (other than congressional printing)	45,008	40,082
General Accounting Office	236,000	244,900
Subtotal	456,149	462,457
GRAND TOTAL	$1,365,272	$1,335,698

House Action

Praising itself for fiscal austerity, the House Appropriations Committee Sept. 9 approved a $1.1 billion fiscal 1983 legislative branch appropriations bill.

The measure (HR 7073) included an amendment blocking members from getting a 4 percent pay raise Oct. 1. They would automatically have gotten the raise if the amendment did not become law.

The committee said the measure was $37 million less than the amount appropriated in fiscal 1982. However, the panel did not mention that HR 7073 did not include more than $29 million that was in the 1982 bill for salaries for members.

Aside from the $29 million "saving," the committee cut official mail costs by $20 million.

Untouched by OMB

The bill contained funding to pay the salaries of congressional staff, to run the Capitol and congressional buildings and to run several associated agencies, such as the General Accounting Office (GAO), the Government Printing Office (GPO) and the Library of Congress.

Like other parts of the federal budget, the totals in the bill were sent to Congress as a formal request from the president. But unlike funding for other government agencies, appropriations requests from the legislative branch were untouched by the Office of Management and Budget (OMB), the administration's budgetary watchdog.

In the case of House programs, the clerk of the House assembled funding requests and forwarded them to the president, who in turn sent them back to Capitol Hill in the form of a formal budget request. However, OMB auditors did not give those programs the same scrutiny, or subject them to the same reductions, that often were imposed on other agencies. The Senate request similarly was forwarded through the president.

The bill reported by the House committee did not include funds for the operation of the Senate, which traditionally were inserted by that chamber. Approximately $263 million was requested.

Details of the Bill

As reported (H Rept 97-801) by the Appropriations Committee, the bill would have provided $622 million for congressional operations and $463 million for the legislative agencies.

House Operations. The bill would have provided $349 million specifically for the House. The largest portion was for staff salaries: $144 million for the personal staffs of members, approximately $78 million for committee staffs and $42 million for salaries of House supporting officers, such as the doorkeeper, the clerk, police officers and the chaplain. Other items in this account included:

● $82 million for "allowances and expenses," including $50 million for members' expenses, $8.3 million for supplies and $45,000 for automobiles.

● $2.7 million for House leadership offices, including $676,000 for the Speaker, $617,000 for the minority leader and $555,000 for the majority leader. These were increases of between 5.3 percent and 7.7 percent over fiscal 1982.

Joint Expenses. The bill would have provided $64 million for offices funded jointly by the House and Senate. This total included:

● $55 million for official mail costs of members.

● $2.4 million for the Joint Economic Committee.

● $633,000 for the attending physician's office, the Capitol medical facility.

● $945,000 for Capitol police expenses. Another $15 million was in the bill for the House share of police salaries. The total, including the Senate portion to be added later, would have provided salaries for 1,190 Capitol police officers. This did not include 157 special police officers employed by the Library of Congress.

Additional Accounts. The bill also contained funding for other congressional support offices and for running the Capitol complex, including:

● $12.6 million for the Office of Technology Assessment.

● $14.2 million for the Congressional Budget Office.

● $34 million for the Congressional Research Service of the Library of Congress.

● $82 million for the GPO printing of congressional documents.

● $66.4 million for the architect of the Capitol, including $20 million to run the three House office buildings, $23 million to operate the Capitol power plant, $9 million to run the Capitol building, $5 million for the Capitol grounds and $4.5 million to buy property near the Capitol.

Other Agencies. The bill contained $463 million for several congressional agencies including:

● $1.8 million for the Botanic Garden, which provided plants for members' offices.

● $170 million for the Library of Congress in addition to the $34 million provided for the research service.

● $40 million for the GPO for non-congressional printing.

● $245 million for the GAO. The committee said work by the GAO in 1981 resulted in $8.4 billion in savings.

● $300,000 for restoration of the Congressional Cemetery.

General Provisions. The bill also blocked members of Congress and senior civil servants from getting a 4 percent pay raise Oct. 1 along with other federal white-collar workers.

Senate Action

After adding about $250 million for Senate operations, the Senate Appropriations Committee approved its fiscal 1983 legislative branch appropriations bill (S 2939 — S Rept 97-573) Sept. 22. The bill included $1.335 billion for congressional operations. Like HR 7073, the measure would have prevented a 4 percent pay raise for members of Congress and senior bureaucrats from taking effect Oct. 1.

Both bills then were included in each chamber's version of the continuing resolution (H J Res 599). ∎

2nd 1983 Continuing Resolution: $379 Billion

It was four days late and caused many frayed nerves, but the second continuing appropriations resolution for fiscal 1983 was finally signed into law Dec. 21 (H J Res 631 — PL 97-377).

Both the House and Senate approved the conference agreement on the measure Dec. 20 — the House by an unrecorded 232-54 vote, the Senate on a 55-41 roll call. *(Senate vote 455, p. 75-S)*

No one was totally satisfied with the $379 billion measure, which was required because only three of the regular fiscal 1983 appropriations bills had been signed into law by the time the existing continuing resolution (PL 97-276) expired at midnight Friday, Dec. 17. (Four additional bills cleared before Congress adjourned.) Technically, much of the government was without funds during the four-day lapse. *(Box, p. 241; PL 97-276, p. 225)*

Among other complaints, Democrats were unhappy about conference committee action to drop money for emergency jobs programs. The Reagan administration and congressional advocates of the MX missile were angry that the final agreement contained no funds to build the controversial weapon.

In both cases, however, the final conference decisions were based on pragmatism.

Just before he proposed dropping the jobs money in conference, House Appropriations Committee Chairman Jamie L. Whitten, D-Miss., talked about the futility of including the funds in the bill, given President Reagan's vow to veto the measure if it included a jobs program.

"I think the time is so short, there is nothing to be gained by insisting on our position. . . . It's just a case of recognizing reality," Whitten said.

And before he described the compromise on the MX missile, Senate Defense Appropriations Subcommittee Chairman Ted Stevens, R-Alaska, reluctantly admitted, "It's not what the administration wants, but it's good or better than what they might have expected getting from the House position." (The House rejected the administration's request for $988 million to begin MX production).

The final bill provided $2.5 billion in fiscal 1983 research and development funds for the MX. Of that amount, $560 million was "fenced." In other words, it could not be used for full-scale engineering development of the basing system for the MX until Congress approved the basing plan. Another $215 million could be spent for the basing system. And research money totaling $1.7 billion could be used to acquire missiles for testing. Once a basing plan was approved, the missiles could be deployed.

The resolution also provided a 15 percent pay raise for House members — to $69,800 a year — plus salary increases of up to 15 percent for about 32,000 other senior government officials.

Although the congressional pay raise was expected to be very controversial, conferees were able to finesse the issue. They denied senators a pay raise while allowing House members to receive the $9,138 salary hike they had voted themselves. Conferees then removed any limit on the amount of outside income senators could earn, including honoraria for speeches, a source of substantial income for many of them.

Among the other difficult issues in conference:
• Money, though less than the administration had re-

quested, was provided for the Clinch River nuclear breeder reactor.

• A provision prohibiting federal employees' health benefit plans from paying for abortions was eliminated.

• Funding for the Federal Trade Commission was continued, and a limitation on the agency's role in regulating professionals was dropped.

Despite the general unhappiness with the conference agreement, some members took a small measure of cheer from the expiration date of the resolution — Sept. 30, 1983. That meant that for the first time since 1980, Congress would start the new year with a clean appropriations slate.

Major Provisions

As cleared, H J Res 631 contained the following fiscal 1983 funding levels and general provisions for agencies whose regular appropriations bills had not become law:

Commerce-Justice-State-Judiciary: Provided funding for programs in the bill at the lower of the House-passed or Senate-reported rate. *(Details, p. 246)*

• Provided that eligible recipients for Economic Development Administration (EDA) funds in fiscal 1982 would remain eligible in fiscal 1983.

• Provided $241 million for the Legal Services Corporation (LSC); limited compensation of members of the board of directors for services to the corporation and prohibited reimbursement for private club membership and severance payments exceeding those paid to comparable government employees. *(LSC, p. 412)*

• Established a director general of U.S. and Foreign Commercial Services in the Commerce Department's International Trade Administration.

• Provided $1.5 million for a White House Conference on Productivity.

• Provided $63.6 million for the Federal Trade Commission, with no restrictions on agency efforts to regulate professionals. *(FTC, p. 347)*

Defense: Provided $232 billion in budget authority for fiscal 1983. *(Details, p. 77)*

In addition to the provisions on the MX missile, H J Res 631:

• Deleted all production funds for the Pershing II missile, although $30 million in operations and maintenance funds was provided for the training of missile crews.

• Amended the expiration date of the enlistment and re-enlistment bonus programs from Dec. 17, 1982, to March 30, 1983.

• Limited the number of active U.S. military personnel stationed onshore in Europe to the fiscal 1982 level; allowed the president to waive this limit if he found that overriding national security needs required such action.

Energy and Water Projects: Funded programs in the bill at the fiscal 1982 level. *(Details, p. 292)*

• Provided $181 million for the Clinch River breeder reactor. However, no construction of permanent structures could be initiated in fiscal 1983, and $1 million was made available to study ways of reducing federal expenditures for the project. *(Story, p. 292)*

• Included funds for the O'Neill irrigation project in Nebraska and the Garrison Diversion project in North Dakota.

• Barred the use of funds to extend the Tennessee-Tombigbee waterway south from Demopolis, Ala.

• Limited new budget authority for atomic energy defense activities to $5.7 billion.

Foreign Operations: Provided $11.2 billion in fiscal 1983. *(Details, p. 242)*

• Provided $2.48 billion for Israel — $785 billion in economic assistance under the Economic Support fund and $1.7 billion in foreign military credit sales ($750 million of the credits would be forgiven).

• Provided $2.075 billion for Egypt, including $750 million in economic assistance and $1.32 billion in foreign military credit sales, $425 million of which was forgiven.

• Provided direct lending authority of $4.4 billion for the Export-Import Bank, and guaranteed lending authority of $9 billion.

Housing and Urban Development: Although the president had signed the fiscal 1983 appropriations bill for the Department of Housing and Urban Development into law late in September (PL 97-272), H J Res 631 contained $8.65 billion for assisted housing and $2.5 billion for public housing modernization. *(PL 97-272, p. 231)*

Interior: The regular Interior appropriations bill (HR 7356) cleared Congress Dec. 19, but H J Res 631 provided $200 million for state low-income energy assistance and weatherization programs from amounts held in escrow as a result of petroleum pricing and allocation violations. *(HR 7356, p. 262)*

Labor, Health and Human Services, Education: Provided $89.1 billion for the three departments and related agencies in fiscal 1983, plus $6.9 billion in advance funding for fiscal 1984 and $130 million for 1985. *(Details, p. 250)*

Legislative Branch: Legislative branch appropriations for fiscal 1983 became law in October (PL 97-276), but H J Res 631 provided pay increases for certain government employees. A maximum cost-of-living increase of 15 percent was to be provided to senior executive, legislative and judicial employees and officials, except senators. House members were to have their pay raised to $69,800. The limit on the amount of outside income senators could earn was removed. *(Details, p. 236)*

Treasury-Postal Service: Provided funding for programs in the bill at the lower of the House-passed or Senate-reported rate. *(Details, p. 273)*

• Provided $789 million for the "revenue forgone" subsidy of the U.S. Postal Service, which subsidized free and reduced-rate mail for certain non-profit organizations.

• Provided $770 million for rental of space for federal agencies by the General Services Administration.

• Prohibited the relocation, consolidation or reduction of U.S. Customs offices in Duluth, Minn.; Superior or Milwaukee, Wis.; Bridgeport or Hartford, Conn.; Portland, Ore.; Miami, Fla.; St. Albans, Vt., or Anchorage, Alaska.

• Provided for the hiring of 200 additional special agents for the U.S. Secret Service.

Miscellany

As usual, a number of special interest provisions — known on Capitol Hill as "cats and dogs" — survived and were included in the 300-page continuing resolution.

For instance, Sen. Robert Dole, R-Kan., succeeded in including a provision eliminating the requirement that records be kept on the sale of .22 caliber rimfire ammunition.

Another section of the bill provided $1.7 million for

payments to the state of Hawaii for people afflicted with Hansen's disease, or leprosy.

Conferees also accepted an amendment by Sen. Bill Bradley, D-N.J., designating a part of the New Jersey Turnpike as part of the Interstate Highway System, and one by Sen. Bob Packwood, R-Ore., exempting the transportation of broken, crushed or powdered glass from the jurisdiction of the Interstate Commerce Commission.

One of the most keenly lobbied special-interest amendments was one referred to as the "Ted Turner" amendment, named for the owner of the Cable News Network. House conferees fought the inclusion of a provision to provide temporary relief for cable television operators, including Turner, who recently had their copyright royalty fees increased. But they finally agreed to a compromise that would not raise the fees until March 15; meanwhile, the cable owners would try to resolve the issue in court.

House Committee Action

The House Appropriations Committee reported the resolution Dec. 10 (H Rept 97-959) after attaching a $5.4 billion Democratic jobs program to the massive stopgap funding bill.

Jobs Package. The job-creation package contained increased funding for some three dozen existing federal programs ranging from rural waste disposal to government auto purchases. In addition, there was money for two new efforts — a $1 billion emergency jobs program run by the Labor Department and $50 million for emergency food and shelter programs, to be distributed by the United Way of America and other private groups.

In drafting the plan, Democratic leaders made sure there were funds for a wide range of interest groups and every region of the country.

The $1 billion emergency jobs program was to be concentrated in areas with unemployment rates over 9 percent. The estimated 160,000 jobs created by the new program on local repair and rehabilitation projects were to be reserved for the long-term unemployed.

The package included:

• Federal buildings repair; $200 million.

• Highway and railroad repair; $440 million.

• Health programs, including repair of Veterans Administration hospitals; $115 million.

• Public housing modernization; $200 million.

• Community development projects; $1.2 billion.

• Small business programs; $282 million.

• Parks, forests and wildlife projects; $220 million.

• Rural water and development projects; $322 million.

• Prison construction; $95 million.

• Water control and flood prevention projects; $177 million.

• Emergency jobs; $1 billion.

• Job training; $232 million.

• Day care; $50 million.

• Emergency food and shelter; $50 million.

• Military housing construction; $489 million.

• Weatherization of low-income family homes; $250 million.

• Government purchase of domestic autos; $100 million.

Funding Levels. The continuing resolution provided funding through March 15, 1983, at the following rates for those appropriations measures not already signed into law:

• District of Columbia, Interior, State-Justice-Commerce and Treasury-Postal Service at the level of the

House- or Senate-passed bill, whichever was lower. No funds were included for the Federal Trade Commission.

● Defense and Labor-Health and Human Services-Education at the House-passed rate.

● Energy-Water, at the current rate.

● Transportation and Agriculture at the conference report level if not approved by Dec. 17.

● Foreign aid, at the lower of the fiscal 1982 appropriations level or the budget estimate, with several exceptions. The committee agreed to an amendment by Clarence D. Long, D-Md., transferring $600 million in funds to the Export-Import Bank; increasing forgiven loans to Israel by $200 million above the fiscal 1982 level; and increasing low-interest loans to Egypt by $25 million.

In addition to these funds, the resolution included $9.7 billion for subsidized housing programs.

House Floor Action

The House passed H J Res 631 Dec. 14 by a 204-200 vote. *(Vote 426, p. 126-H)*

Silvio O. Conte, R-Mass., the ranking Republican on the Appropriations Committee, relayed to his colleagues a warning given by President Reagan at a meeting earlier that day: "I don't give a damn whether it is Friday night [Dec. 17] and the whole government is brought to a standstill. I will not sign the continuing resolution with a jobs bill in it."

But Majority Leader Jim Wright, D-Texas, asked, "Who does he [the president] think he is. . . . The Constitution did not convey upon him the role of 'Big Daddy.'"

A motion by Conte to send the bill back to committee with instructions to delete the jobs program failed 215-191. *(Vote 425, p. 126-H)*

The House resolution carried other controversial baggage. By a vote of 303-109 the House voted itself a 15 percent pay raise. An amendment to retain the current cap on congressional pay was defeated on a tie 208-208 vote. *(Votes 420, 421, p. 124-H)*

Funding, except for close-down costs, for the much debated Clinch River reactor was deleted on a 217-196 vote. And amendments denying money for two water projects — the O'Neill unit in Nebraska (245-144) and the Garrison Diversion water project in North Dakota (252-152), were also approved. *(Votes 422, 423, p. 124-H; vote 424, p. 126-H)*

The House adopted an administration-opposed amendment requiring that at least 50 percent of the bilateral assistance funds provided by the Agency for International Development be used to finance projects that benefit the "truly poor." The vote was 227-184. *(Vote 419, p. 124-H)*

One non-controversial amendment was approved. It allowed recipients of Supplemental Security Income (SSI) to receive assistance from private non-profit organizations or public utilities without having their SSI benefits reduced or eliminated as a result of receiving such payments.

Senate Committee Action

Before reporting H J Res 631 Dec. 15, the Senate Appropriations Committee made several major revisions in the House-passed resolution.

Instead of the $5.4 billion jobs program in the House bill, the Senate committee included $1.2 billion for a variety of public works projects. Committee Chairman Mark O.

Hatfield, R-Ore., said this money was not for "leaf-raking activities ... but a reasonable, responsible approach in constructive activities."

Among the jobs projects funded under the Senate measure were: rural water and waste treatment plants; support for small business; Indian housing and school construction; weatherization of schools and hospitals; job training; and mass transit.

The Senate committee deleted the 15 percent pay raise agreed to by the House, as well as language limiting outside earnings to 30 percent of a member's salary.

Stevens, the Senate majority whip, told committee members he had conducted a nose count and there were not enough votes in the Senate to approve a pay raise. He argued that the pay issue ought to be resolved in conference. And while it was clear the Senate would not agree to a pay increase for itself, Stevens said, that did not bar approval of a salary hike for House members and other federal workers.

In other action, the Senate committee voted to keep the level of American troops in Europe at the number on land at the end of fiscal 1982. The defense appropriations bill cleared by the committee Sept. 23 held the number of troops to the fiscal 1980 level.

Funding Levels. As reported by the Senate committee, the resolution provided funding at the following rates for those appropriations measures not already signed into law:

● Agriculture, District of Columbia, and Transportation at the conference levels.

● Defense, State-Justice-Commerce, and Labor-Health and Human Services-Education at the Senate-reported level.

● Treasury-Postal Service-General Government at the Senate or House-passed level, whichever was lower.

● Foreign Assistance at the fiscal 1982 level, with adjustments to reflect the levels in the Senate-reported bill.

● Energy-Water at the current rate.

Senate Floor Action

The Senate began consideration of the measure late Dec. 16. Debate continued through that night and into the next, when the existing continuing resolution expired. The Senate resumed work on H J Res 631 Dec. 18, and was about ready to vote on final passage when John P. East, R-N.C., one of the group of conservatives filibustering the highway/gas tax bill (HR 6211), took to the floor to prevent the final vote. East hoped that by holding the funding bill hostage he could prevent a final vote on the gas tax. *(Highway bill, p. 317)*

After some parliamentary maneuvering, the leadership finally regained control of the floor. But East's actions meant that the final vote was put off until Dec. 19. Conferees were actually meeting and working out the final agreement when the Senate voted 63-31 to approve the continuing resolution. *(Vote 451, p. 75-S)*

Three GOP leaders — Majority Leader Howard H. Baker Jr., Tenn., Budget Committee Chairman Pete V. Domenici, N.M., and Finance Committee Chairman Dole — lost 46-50 when they tried to strike the jobs program from the bill. *(Vote 434, p. 73-S)*

"It seems we've gotten into a bidding war with the House," Domenici said. He characterized the House jobs program as "pork barrel personified."

But Hatfield argued that it was "the only opportunity

the Senate will have" to show it cared about jobs creation.

Several committee amendments had close calls. One that retained funds for the Clinch River breeder reactor was approved 49-48. *(Vote 422, p. 71-S)*

Dale Bumpers, D-Ark., tried to cut the Clinch River breeder from the bill. "This is supposed to be a demonstration project, yet it's not demonstrating anything," he said.

But Baker — in whose home state of Tennessee the reactor project was located — said, "I believe we have to do something for the future."

Another amendment, which deleted House abortion language, also squeaked by on a 49-48 vote. *(Vote 425, p. 72-S)*

Idaho Republican James A. McClure's amendment to prohibit the FTC from spending money to regulate professionals was tabled 59-37. *(Vote 424, p. 71-S)*

The Senate did reject 43-52 a committee amendment that deleted a House-passed provision committing $50 million for emergency food and shelter for the unemployed. *(Vote 428, p. 72-S)*

Defense, Other Amendments

Before the final vote, the Senate took action on dozens of other amendments, including a series relating to defense spending. *(Roll-call votes 418-450, pp. 71-S — 75-S)*

On most of those votes, the Senate generally came down on the side of the administration, overturning several Appropriations Committee provisions that would have irritated U.S. allies. Some of these victories proved fleeting, however, as they were later dropped by conferees.

The Senate refused, on a 52-45 vote, to cut $5.6 billion from the $232 billion defense appropriation, and upheld the administration position on other defense issues by larger margins. A move to drop one of two $3.4 billion nuclear-powered aircraft carriers funded by the bill, for instance, was killed 67-31. *(Votes 435, 436, p. 73-S)*

Happily for the administration, the Senate accepted an amendment on the MX missile that reflected some compromise by the White House as well as by staunch defenders of the military budget. The vote to withhold funding until the basing plan for the missile was decided was 56-42. *(Vote 420, p. 71-S)*

But it also accepted by voice vote an amendment by Gary Hart, D-Colo., that would block the first flight test of the missile until Congress had approved a specific basing method. An effort to delete funds for the purchase of five missiles was blocked on a 70-28 vote. *(Vote 419, p. 71-S)*

Non-defense amendments agreed to by the Senate included those:

• By John W. Warner, R-Va., to provide $200 million to states for low-income energy assistance and weatherization. Adopted 76-19. *(Vote 432, p. 72-S)*

• By Dan Quayle, R-Ind., to provide payments equal to certain Social Security benefits to widows and children of members of the armed forces who died in service or as a result of service-related disabilities. The benefits had been eliminated by the 1981 budget reconciliation act (PL 97-35).

• By Dennis DeConcini, D-Ariz., to establish limits on payments to the directors and officers of the Legal Services Corporation.

• By William Proxmire, D-Wis., prohibiting planning for or construction of any additional Senate office building.

• By Wendell H. Ford, D-Ky., to expedite grants to states for abandoned land reclamation projects.

Final Action

Approval of the conference agreement (H Rept 97-980) Dec. 20 followed the same pattern as floor action; the House spent one hour debating the measure, the Senate four.

House Majority Leader Jim Wright, D-Texas, summed up the sentiment of the House leadership when he told colleagues that while he was "bitterly disappointed" that the jobs section had been dropped, "... for now we have the responsibility to keep the government functioning."

Senate Democrats, however, were not quite so sanguine over the decision to delete all money for jobs programs.

"I think it is a tragedy that the jobs part of this bill was tossed over the side," said Donald W. Riegle Jr., D-Mich. "The fact that a pay raise survives and the jobs program does not is something that cannot be defended."

Senate Appropriations Chairman Hatfield agreed that it was "distressing" to see the jobs programs dropped. But he said he had already begun work on another jobs program

---

Shutdown Averted

For the third time in 14 months, a snarl over stopgap spending brought several federal agencies to the brink of a shutdown Dec. 21.

Between midnight Friday, Dec. 17 and about 2 p.m. on Tuesday, Dec. 21, when President Reagan signed the second fiscal 1983 continuing resolution (H J Res 631 — PL 97-377), a large part of the government was technically broke.

While Congress haggled over the measure during the weekend and then waited for Reagan to sign the bill, hundreds of thousands of federal workers faced possible furloughs. The Justice Department had ruled in 1980 that agencies could not continue operating in the absence of approved funding. *(1980 Almanac p. 233)*

The Office of Personnel Management (OPM) estimated that between 400,000 and 800,000 "non-essential" employees would have been affected at the departments of Commerce, Defense, Education, Energy, Health and Human Services, Justice, Labor, State and Treasury and several agencies.

Unlike Nov. 23, 1981, when thousands of federal workers were sent home for the day when Reagan vetoed a stopgap spending bill, preparations for a closing moved more slowly this time. *(1981 Almanac p. 298)*

"Technically, we're in a shutdown mode," OPM spokesman Mark Tapscott said Dec. 20. "But we're just telling agencies to stretch out the time it takes for the shutdown. It was done with more dispatch last year." Although workers were uncertain about their status Dec. 20, they were told to report to work Dec. 21 when it appeared Reagan would sign the bill.

In addition to the November 1981 partial shutdown — which cost the government more than $80 million in wasted time, according to one study — layoffs almost occurred again March 31, when Congress and Reagan nearly missed a deadline for passage of an earlier emergency funding measure.

that he hoped he could persuade the president to include in the fiscal 1984 budget. "I'm not throwing in the towel on this," Hatfield said.

The two top congressional Republicans — House Minority Leader Robert H. Michel, Ill., and Senate Majority Leader Baker — also indicated they would fight for jobs legislation when the new Congress convened in January.

Senate Budget Chairman Domenici said preliminary figures showed that the conference agreement was about $2.3 billion in outlays over the amount allowed by the fiscal 1983 budget resolution (S Con Res 92) — "about one-half of 1 percent on a total allocation of about $460 billion."

The final bill was about $12 billion under the budget target for budget authority, Domenici said.   ∎

Foreign Aid Appropriations

Over the opposition of the Reagan administration, Congress increased military aid to Israel for fiscal 1983. But the increase was substantially less than what Israel and its staunchest allies in Congress had wanted.

The aid increases were included in the foreign aid portion of the fiscal 1983 continuing resolution (H J Res 631 — PL 97-377), cleared on Dec. 20.

H J Res 631 included $11.2 billion for "foreign operations" in fiscal 1983, of which $8.1 billion was for foreign economic, military and development aid programs. For budget purposes those amounts did not count several billion dollars for guaranteed loans. *(Chart, p. 245)*

The remainder of the foreign operations category of H J Res 631 was accounted for by the Export-Import Bank. The bank was authorized $13.4 billion in fiscal 1983, but for technical reasons only $3.1 billion of that amount counted as part of the $11.2 billion total in the bill.

The bill provided about half of the $2.3 billion increase in military aid that Reagan had sought for fiscal 1983.

House-Senate conferees on the measure warned the administration not to return with new requests for the money that had been denied.

Any request for additional money "must be in response to serious emergency needs," the conferees said in the report on H J Res 631. "A simple re-requesting of those items which the conferees have provided under the regular fiscal 1983 budget estimates will not be considered genuine needs resulting from real foreign policy problems."

Neither chamber took up a regular foreign aid appropriations bill for fiscal 1983. The House Appropriations Committee never wrote such a measure. The Senate committee approved a separate aid bill (S 3075) on Dec. 2; the full Senate, on a 57-41 vote on Dec. 16, incorporated the bulk of that measure into its version of H J Res 631. *(Vote 418, p. 71-S)*

Aid to Israel

The continuing resolution gave Israel an increase over its past aid levels and over the request of President Reagan. But the measure sharply cut the amount of aid for Israel that had been approved earlier in December by the Senate Appropriations Committee over the objections of the Reagan administration. The full Senate had adopted $475 million in grant aid increases for Israel when it passed the continuing resolution.

The issue of aid to Israel crept up on Congress in 1982. During the spring, the House Foreign Affairs and Senate Foreign Relations committees quietly voted increases in grants for Israel as part of the fiscal 1983 foreign aid authorization bills (HR 6370, S 2608). Neither of those bills ever reached the floor. *(Authorization, p. 156)*

Israel's June 1982 invasion and subsequent occupation of Lebanon led many members of Congress to argue that it was time to hold the line on aid to Israel.

But supporters of Israel continued to work for an aid increase. Their chance came early in December, when the Senate Appropriations Committee finally began work on a foreign aid bill. With the backing of Chairman Robert W. Kasten Jr., R-Wis., and ranking Democrat Daniel K. Inouye, D-Hawaii, the subcommittee approved the Israel figures that had been proposed in May by the Foreign Relations Committee.

The full Appropriations Committee approved the same amount two days later, in its $11.6 billion fiscal 1983 foreign aid appropriations bill (S 3075). The committee issued its report (S Rept 97-672) the next day.

The committee bill boosted economic aid for Israel in fiscal 1983 to $910 million, from the $785 million requested by Reagan and provided in 1982. The bill also put that aid on more concessional terms than Reagan had wanted; the president asked that two-thirds of the money be given as a grant and the rest as a loan, but the committee voted to make the entire $910 million a grant.

The committee bill also gave Israel $850 million in military loans that would not have to be repaid — $350 million more than Reagan had requested. Israel would receive another $850 million in military loans to be repaid at market interest rates.

Administration vs. Israel

The Appropriations Committee action capped a week of furious lobbying that pitted the administration against the pro-Israeli lobby in an unusual debate over Israel's policies and U.S. support for them.

On Nov. 30, as the Senate subcommittee prepared to draft its aid bill with the increases for Israel, President Reagan met with the counterpart House Foreign Operations Appropriations Subcommittee and adamantly opposed the add-ons for Israel. Reagan was attempting, unsuccessfully, to get the House panel to begin work on an aid bill. The House Democratic Caucus decided later that day not to proceed with an aid measure.

The administration, which apparently had been caught napping by Kasten's behind-the-scenes maneuvering, in early December launched a public campaign opposing any increases in aid to Israel.

In letters sent to Capitol Hill Dec. 1 and 9, the State Department said increasing aid to Israel would require cuts in aid for other countries and would undercut the Middle East peace process. The first letter was signed by Kenneth W. Dam, the deputy secretary of state who was filling in for Secretary of State George P. Shultz who was out of the country at the time. Shultz signed the Dec. 9 letter.

The letters first said countries such as Spain, Portugal, Turkey and Pakistan would suffer if aid to Israel were increased.

On the second issue, the letters referred by implication to Israeli Prime Minister Menachem Begin and his policies toward Lebanon and the occupied West Bank of the Jordan River. "By appearing to endorse and reward Israel's policies," they said, increasing aid "could strengthen the

hand of those who are content with the status quo, while calling into question among others the U.S. commitment to an equitable outcome."

The latter phrase was an apparent reference to Egypt. Administration officials had argued privately that Egypt would be offended because the increase for Israel would upset a balance of U.S. aid to the two countries.

The letters were countered by the American Israel Public Affairs Committee, the pro-Israel lobby. It claimed Reagan had sought an aid cut that would "send a dangerous signal of abandonment [of Israel] to Israel's enemies."

Israeli officials bitterly complained about the administration's opposition to increased aid. Foreign Minister Yitzhak Shamir on Dec. 4 called it "an unfriendly act" that "endangers the peace process."

One House conferee on H J Res 631 later said some members felt that the Israeli government had exerted "pressure" on Congress to approve the high Senate figures.

House, Conference Action

The House version of the continuing resolution, passed Dec. 14, struck a middle line on aid to Israel. It put direct military grants for Israel at $750 million, compared to the $500 million administration request and the $850 million approved by the Senate. And the House bill kept economic

aid for Israel at the $785 million request level, but decreed that all of it would be a grant; Reagan had requested that only about two-thirds of the economic aid be a grant.

To avoid ruffling Egypt's feathers, the House bill added $25 million for military grants to Egypt, bringing that nation's total to $425 million.

The final bill increased economic and military aid to Israel for fiscal 1983 by $300 million over fiscal 1982, including an additional $200 million in military grants. But the bill also gave Israel $225 million less in military and economic grants than the Senate had approved.

Conferees adopted all the House figures for Israel and Egypt. *(Chart, below)*

From the Reagan administration's point of view, the final bill was an important victory because it basically maintained a rough balance between Israel and Egypt in the amount of U.S. aid they were to receive.

Nevertheless a State Department official said the administration was reluctant to accept any increases over Reagan's request for Israel.

By all accounts, House Foreign Operations Appropriations Subcommittee Chairman Clarence D. Long, D-Md., was the key figure in the House-Senate conference committee on the foreign aid portions of H J Res 631. Long and four other conferees drafted the foreign aid provisions dur-

---

Military and Economic Aid to Egypt and Israel

Following are the fiscal 1982 and 1983 amounts for military and economic aid to Egypt and Israel. The fiscal 1982 amounts were appropriated in PL 97-121; the fiscal 1983 amounts were included in the continuing resolution (H J Res 631). In addition to the amounts listed below, each of the fiscal 1983 totals for Egypt includes $2 million for military training.

	Fiscal 1982 Amount	Fiscal 1983 Reagan Request	Fiscal 1983 House Bill	Fiscal 1983 Senate Bill	Fiscal 1983 Continuing Resolution
ISRAEL:					
Forgiven loans	$550 million	$500 million	$750 million	$850 million	$750 million
Loans to be repaid at market interest rates	850 million	1.2 billion	950 million	850 million	950 million
Military Aid (subtotal)	$ 1.4 billion	$ 1.7 billion	$ 1.7 billion	$ 1.7 billion	$1.7 billion
Economic Support Fund	785 million (all grants)	785 million (525 million grants, 260 million loans)	785 million (all grants)	910 million (all grants)	785 million (all grants)
Total Assistance	$2.185 billion	$2.485 billion	$2.485 billion	$2.61 billion	$2.485 billion
EGYPT:					
Forgiven loans	200 million	400 million	425 million	400 million	425 million
Loans to be repaid at market interest rates	700 million	900 million	900 million	900 million	900 million
Military Aid (subtotal)	$ 900 million	$ 1.3 billion	$1.325 billion	$ 1.3 billion	$1.325 billion
Economic Support Fund	750 million (all grants)	750 million (500 million grants, $250 million loans)	750 million (all grants)	750 million (all grants)	750 million (all grants)
Total Assistance	$1.625 billion	$2.052 billion	$2.077 billion	$2.052 billion	$2.077 billion

ing a five-hour, closed-door session on Dec. 19. Their work was upheld by the full conference committee.

Although an unrelenting supporter of Israel in the past, Long held out against fellow foreign aid conferees who wanted to keep the Senate's increases for Israel.

"I'm a friend of Israel, but I'm a practical politician and an American first," Long said in an interview. "These increases that Israel wanted were excessive."

Long said the other conferees "beat on me" to get the higher figures, but he said he resisted and held out for lower amounts that had been approved by the House.

"I warned them that if I was sandbagged [in conference], I would come back and oppose the foreign aid bill in the House," Long said.

Kasten said he was forced to recede because Long "was simply intransigent and unwilling to negotiate or even discuss negotiation."

Though disappointed that he was unable to win the full increases for Israel, Kasten said the amount approved by conferees was "adequate for Israel's security needs."

Arms vs. Development

Although it kept a basic balance between aid to Israel and Egypt, the continuing resolution did little toward maintaining the politically important balance between military and development aid. The bill provided $1.2 billion of the $2.3 billion in additional military aid that Reagan had requested for fiscal 1983, while holding the line on economic and development aid programs at near-1982 levels.

For several years there had been a heated dispute between liberals, who wanted more money for development programs aimed at helping other nations overcome poverty, and conservatives, who emphasized the need for military aid for America's allies.

In 1981, the two sides battled to a draw when writing the fiscal 1982 foreign aid appropriations bill (PL 97-121). *(1981 Almanac p. 339)*

The dispute grew bitter in 1982 when the Reagan administration asked Congress to approve large increases in military aid, both as a supplemental to fiscal 1982 spending and for regular 1983 spending. Several key House Democrats accused the administration of reneging on a 1981 compromise agreement. Kasten and other Republicans in both houses fought for Reagan's requests.

Military Aid

As it became obvious that Congress would not pass regular foreign aid authorization and appropriations bills for 1983, the administration launched a campaign emphasizing the need for military and economic aid to several countries that host U.S. military bases. In each case, the United States had recently negotiated a base-access agreement, or was in the process of doing so.

As worked out by conferees, H J Res 631 came close to providing the military aid for those countries sought by the administration, but at the expense of most other aid recipients.

The bill provided $5.273 billion for military aid programs in fiscal 1983 — $1.0896 billion less than Reagan had requested. The final figure was about halfway between the Senate and House amounts.

Of the total, $3.638 billion was for arms loans that carried market interest rates and were guaranteed by the U.S. government, and $1.5 billion was for several grant programs.

Conferees earmarked the following amounts for countries with U.S. bases: Turkey, $290 million in guaranteed loans and $110 million in grants; Portugal, $52.5 million in guaranteed loans and $37.5 million in grants; Spain, $400 million in guaranteed loans. Conferees also earmarked $75 million in guaranteed loans and $25 million in grants for Morocco, with which the United States was negotiating for use of several military facilities.

Turkey was the only one of those countries whose aid was cut by conferees. Reagan had requested $465 million in total military aid for Turkey; H J Res 631 provided $400 million.

Conferees did not earmark funds for Greece and the Philippines, the two other countries that received aid in return for hosting U.S. bases. However, the existing fiscal 1983 foreign aid authorization law (PL 97-113) earmarked $280 million for Greece. *(1981 Almanac p. 162)*

When combined with the amounts for Israel and Egypt, the earmarks in H J Res 631 consumed most of the military aid in the bill. After the earmarks, the bill provided only $970.5 million for guaranteed loans and $117.5 million for grants to enable other countries to buy American weapons. That was about $700 million less than Reagan had requested for other countries.

The bill kept a lid on the Economic Support Fund (ESF), a program of grants and loans that bolstered the economies of key U.S. allies and friends. The ESF program was part of the administration's "security assistance" package and was generally considered an adjunct of military aid.

The bill included $2.661 billion for that program — $85 million above fiscal 1982 and $225 million less than Reagan had requested. Most of the aid, $1.5 billion, was earmarked for Israel and Egypt.

Development Aid

On the other side of the ledger, H J Res 631 kept a tight rein on programs aimed at developing the economies of poor countries. Liberal Democrats in the House, such as David R. Obey of Wisconsin and Matthew F. McHugh of New York, who had championed those programs in recent years, were not among the conferees who wrote the foreign aid parts of H J Res 631.

The bill provided $3.9 billion for U.S. contributions to international development banks, such as the World Bank, and organizations such as the United Nations; $1.5 billion of that amount was counted as new budget authority and the rest was for loan guarantees. The total was about $84 million above fiscal 1982 and $235 million less than Reagan's request.

Included in the $3.9 billion was $700 million, the same as fiscal 1982, for the fiscal 1983 U.S. contribution to the International Development Association (IDA). Reagan had requested $945 million but the administration made little effort to win approval for that amount.

At the urging of Daniel K. Inouye, D-Hawaii, the Senate Appropriations Committee had approved $800 million for IDA. But the full Senate knocked the figure back to $700 million on an amendment by Jesse Helms, R-N.C. The Helms amendment survived a tabling motion Dec. 18 by a 44-46 vote. *(Vote 449, p. 75-S)*

IDA was the World Bank agency that made low-interest loans to the world's poorest countries. President Carter in 1979 promised to contribute $3.24 billion to IDA over fiscal years 1981-83; Reagan in 1981 stood by the overall

Foreign Aid Appropriations, Fiscal 1983

The following chart shows amounts in new budget authority of the revised Reagan administration request, the House- and Senate-approved amounts, and the final amounts for foreign aid appropriations in fiscal 1983. Foreign aid programs were included in a continuing resolution, PL 97-377.

(Figures in parentheses show program limitations; except for a portion of the Export-Import Bank limits, the limitations do not count as new budget authority. Figures for development banks include paid-in capital, which counts as new budget authority. Callable capital for the banks is not included.)

Program	Revised Request	House-Passed Amount	Senate-Passed Amount	Final Amount
Inter-American Development Bank	$ 284,100,437	$ 263,423,620	$ 237,423,437	$ 284,100,437
International Bank for Reconstruction and Development	126,041,553	126,041,553	126,041,553	126,041,553
International Development Association	945,000,000	700,000,000	700,000,000	700,000,000
Asian Development Bank	131,882,575	122,247,297	131,882,575	131,882,575
African Development Fund	50,000,000	50,000,000	40,000,000	50,000,000
International Organizations and Programs	238,650,000	215,438,000	227,450,000	249,002,000
Subtotal, multilateral aid	$ 1,775,674,565	$ 1,477,150,470	$ 1,462,797,565	$ 1,541,026,565
Agriculture aid	700,000,000	700,000,000	697,000,000	700,000,000
Population aid	211,000,000	211,000,000	206,100,000	211,000,000
Health aid	133,405,000	133,405,000	123,512,000	133,405,000
Education aid	103,550,000	103,550,000	103,550,000	103,550,000
Energy, technical, selected development aid	140,288,000	137,200,000	137,200,000	140,288,000
Science and technology	10,000,000	10,000,000	10,000,000	10,000,000
American schools and hospitals abroad	7,500,000	20,000,000	20,000,000	20,000,000
International disaster assistance	25,000,000	27,000,000	25,000,000	25,000,000
Sahel development	93,757,000	93,757,500	77,000,000	93,757,000[1]
Foreign Service retirement and disability	35,403,000	32,552,000	35,403,000	35,403,000
Economic Support Fund	2,886,000,000	2,576,000,000	2,886,000,000	2,661,000,000[2]
Peace-keeping	43,474,000	43,474,000	31,100,000	31,100,000
AID operating expenses	376,000,000	331,000,000	331,000,000	335,000,000
Trade and development program	10,500,000	10,500,000	10,500,000	10,500,000
International Narcotics Control	40,000,000	36,700,000	36,700,000	36,700,000
Inter-American Foundation	10,634,000	12,000,000	12,000,000	12,000,000
Peace Corps	97,500,000	105,000,000	109,000,000	109,000,000
Migration, refugee assistance	419,000,000	419,000,000	395,000,000	395,000,000
Anti-terrorism program	5,000,000	0	5,000,000	0
Subtotal, bilateral aid	$ 5,348,011,000	$ 5,002,138,500	$ 5,251,065,000	$ 5,062,703,000
Military assistance program grants	557,000,000	176,512,000	367,000,000	290,000,000[3]
International military education and training	53,700,000	38,488,000	53,700,000	45,000,000
Foreign military sales: forgiven loans	950,000,000	1,175,000,000	1,300,000,000	1,175,000,000[4]
Foreign military sales: guaranteed loans	(4,323,300,000)	(3,383,500,000)	(3,973,300,000)	(3,638,000,000)[5]
Defense acquisition fund limitation	(475,000,000)	0	(200,000,000)	(125,000,000)
Subtotal, military aid	$ 1,560,700,000	$ 1,390,000,000	$ 1,720,700,000	$ 1,510,000,000
Total, new budget authority	$ 8,684,385,565	$ 7,869,288,970	$ 8,434,562,565	$ 8,113,729,565
Housing guaranty program	(150,000,000)	(150,000,000)	(150,000,000)	(150,000,000)
Overseas Private Investment Corporation				
Direct loans	(10,000,000)	(10,000,000)	(10,000,000)	(10,000,000)
Loan guarantees	(100,000,000)	(100,000,000)	(100,000,000)	(100,000,000)
Export-Import Bank total limitation	(11,846,253,000)	(13,635,115,000)	(13,415,115,000)	(13,415,115,000)[6]
Direct loans	(3,830,000,000)	(4,400,000,000)	(4,400,000,000)	(4,400,000,000)
Loan guarantees	(8,000,000,000)	(9,220,000,000)	(9,000,000,000)	(9,000,000,000)
Administration	(16,253,000)	(15,115,000)	(15,115,000)	(15,115,000)
Grand total, including new budget authority impact of Ex-Im Bank limitations	$11,240,385,565	$10,987,288,970	$11,552,562,565	$11,231,729,565

[1] *Includes $2 million for the African Development Foundation.*
[2] *Includes $785 million for Israel and $750 million for Egypt.*
[3] *Includes $110 million for Turkey, $37.5 million for Portugal and $25 million for Morocco.*
[4] *Includes $750 million for Israel and $425 million for Egypt.*

[5] *Includes $400 million for Spain, $290 million for Turkey, $75 million for Morocco and $52.5 million for Portugal.*
[6] *A portion of the Ex-Im Bank limitations counts as new budget authority, resulting in the difference between the Total and Grand Total.*

amount but decided to make the contribution in four, rather than three, years. As of the end of fiscal 1982, the United States had contributed $1.2 billion. Thus, with the 1983 appropriation, the U.S. contribution over the three years was be $1.9 billion.

H J Res 631 also held the line on bilateral U.S. development aid programs, including those administered by the Agency for International Development (AID). AID programs were funded at $1.298 billion, the administration request, which was only $3 million above fiscal 1982.

As a signal of their dissatisfaction with the administration's handling of foreign aid, liberals managed to attach to the bill an amendment directing the president to attempt to use at least 40 percent of development funds to help those living in "absolute poverty." The AID administrator was directed to report to Congress within six months on the implementation of that provision.

The House added the provision to H J Res 631 on Dec. 14 by a 227-184 vote. *(Vote 419, p. 124-H)*

The provision was strongly opposed by the administration, which had sought to shift the emphasis in foreign aid away from traditional anti-poverty programs and toward efforts to help development of the private sector in Third World countries.

Conferees included the essence of the House provision, but they deleted a stipulation that would have raised the percentage of development funds going to poverty projects to 50 percent, starting in fiscal 1984.

To satisfy House liberals, conferees also earmarked $85 million in ESF for development programs, and provided $24 million for the International Fund for Agricultural Development.

Other Aid Issues

Export-Import Bank. In marked contrast to previous years, H J Res 631 held the line on spending authority for the Export-Import Bank, the government agency that issued loans and loan guarantees to support exports by American companies.

The bill included $4.4 billion for direct, below-market-rate loans, the same amount as fiscal 1982. It also approved $9 billion for guaranteed loans at market rates; that was a decrease of $220 million from fiscal 1982.

Covert Action vs. Nicaragua. The Senate on Dec. 18 rejected an attempt by liberals to put Congress on record in opposition to the administration's reported aid to groups that were seeking to overthrow the Sandinista government of Nicaragua.

By a 56-38 vote, the Senate tabled an amendment to H J Res 631 by Christopher J. Dodd, D-Conn., declaring that

funds should not be used, directly or indirectly after Jan. 20, 1983, "in support of irregular military forces or paramilitary groups operating in Central America." *(Vote 441, p. 74-S)*

Dodd said the administration's support for anti-Sandinista forces, based in Honduras, threatened "a far more expanded conflict in Central America than already exists."

The House had passed a watered-down version of a similar amendment Dec. 8 during action on the fiscal 1983 defense appropriations bill (HR 7355). That provision was adopted by House-Senate conferees on the defense section of the continuing resolution. *(Defense story, p. 277)*

IAEA. Conferees included $10 million for the annual U.S. contribution to the International Atomic Energy Agency (IAEA) in fiscal 1983. But the administration was prohibited from making that contribution unless the United Nations-related body retreated on its decision to dump Israel from its membership. Reagan had requested $14.5 million for the agency.

Pakistan. Conferees accepted a Senate-passed provision aimed at cutting off military sales and aid to Pakistan if it transferred sensitive U.S. military equipment to a communist country. Sponsored by John Glenn, D-Ohio, the amendment had been approved by the Senate Dec. 18 on an 85-10 vote. In describing his amendment to the Senate, Glenn said it was directed at Pakistan, but did not say what had prompted it. *(Vote 444, p. 74-S)*

The amendment required the president, before providing sensitive equipment to any country, to certify to Congress that he had "reliable assurances" that the country would not transfer the equipment to a communist country without U.S. approval.

During consideration of H J Res 631, Glenn also raised in the Senate his objections to an administration decision to install the most advanced form of radar warning equipment on 40 F-16 jets that Pakistan was buying from the United States.

Glenn offered an amendment that would require the president to return to Congress to seek approval of that decision. But he withdrew the amendment when Charles H. Percy, R-Ill., chairman of the Senate Foreign Relations Committee, inserted in the *Congressional Record* the text of a committee letter asking Reagan to get congressional approval for the sale.

Anti-terrorism. Conferees denied a request for $5 million to begin a program helping friendly nations combat terrorism. Conferees complained that the administration had not supplied sufficient details about what countries would receive aid or what type of aid they were to receive. ∎

State, Justice, Commerce Funds in Stopgap Bill

The second continuing appropriations resolution (H J Res 631 — PL 97-377) cleared Dec. 20 provided $9.26 billion for the departments of State, Justice and Commerce, the federal judiciary and 20 related agencies in fiscal 1983.

The final appropriation was $398.1 million more than the Reagan administration request of $8.87 billion.

It was $259.54 million more than the bill passed by the House Dec. 9 (HR 6957 — H Rept 97-721) and $8 million more than a Senate bill that was reported by the Senate

Appropriations Committee (S 2956 — S Rept 97-584) Sept. 24 and then amended in the Senate version of the stopgap funding bill.

It was the third year in a row that Congress failed to act on the regular appropriations bill for these agencies. *(1981 Almanac p. 364)*

Drug Task Forces

Among the appropriations was $127.5 million for a new anti-drug program proposed by President Reagan in Octo-

ber. The money would be used to create 12 teams around the country to combat major drug trafficking. The agencies involved would be the Federal Bureau of Investigation (FBI), the Drug Enforcement Administration (DEA) and the Customs Service.

"The top priority of these task forces will be to disrupt the intricate distribution and sales network set up by organized criminal enterprises engaged in drug trafficking throughout the nation," a Justice Department memo explained.

The conference report on the funding bill (H Rept 97-980) stipulated that law enforcement officials report to Congress each year on the progress of the task forces. The conferees said the task force report should include specifically whether the supply of drugs such as heroin and cocaine had been reduced in the task force areas and whether there was an increase in the seizure and forfeiture of assets from illegal drug enterprises.

The funding bill also included money for several programs President Reagan wanted to abolish or severely restrict, including the Legal Services Corporation (LSC); a program to help states combat juvenile delinquency; the Economic Development Administration; and public telecommunications facilities grants, which help finance new public TV and radio operations.

Legal Services Corporation

The continuing resolution included new provisions concerning the operation of the LSC. Some of the new restrictions came in direct response to disclosures that members of the LSC board of directors appointed by Reagan had collected unprecedented consulting fees. *(LSC, p. 412)*

The funding bill stated that board members could collect only actual out-of-pocket expenses and consulting fees for attendance at board meetings.

Another provision barred any officer or employee of the LSC from collecting severance pay different from that accorded other federal employees, and from being reimbursed for membership in a private club. This was in response to a contract that the LSC board chairman, William F. Harvey, negotiated with the new president, Donald P. Bogard, an Indianapolis lawyer who once was Harvey's law student.

The funding bill included other restrictions on corporation activities, most of which had been incorporated in stopgap funding legislation that kept the LSC alive throughout fiscal 1982. *(1981 Almanac p. 412)*

Provisions

As cleared, H J Res 631 (PL 97-377) made the following State, Justice, Commerce appropriations for fiscal 1983 *(in thousands of dollars)*:

	Administration Request	Final Amount
Department of Commerce	$1,366,010	$1,747,700
Department of Justice	2,793,587	2,864,062
Department of State	1,893,882	1,863,145
The Judiciary	851,133	791,007
Related Agencies		
Arms Control and Disarmament Agency	15,142	15,142
Board for International Broadcasting	117,184	90,300

Related Agencies	Administration Request	Final Amount
Commission on Civil Rights	11,626	11,626
Commission on Security and Cooperation in Europe	550	550
Commission on Wartime Relocation and Internment of Civilians	——	300
Chrysler Corp. Loan Guarantee Program:		
Administrative Expenses	1,211	1,211
Equal Employment Opportunity Commission	144,937	142,771
Federal Communications Commission	74,446	79,817
Federal Maritime Commission	10,428	11,500
Federal Trade Commission	60,838	63,638
International Communication Agency	665,700	545,449
International Trade Commission	19,737	19,150
Japan-United States Friendship Commission	1,700	1,700
Legal Services Corp.	265,000*	241,000
Marine Mammal Commission	594	822
Maritime Administration	86,313	118,413
Office of the United States Trade Representative	10,100	10,100
Radio Broadcasting to Cuba	12,952	——
Securities and Exchange Commission	84,300	88,040
Small Business Administration	378,700	556,729
TOTAL	**$8,866,070**	**$9,264,172**

Submitted directly by the Legal Services Corporation.

House Committee

The House Appropriations Committee reported HR 6957 Aug. 10 (H Rept 97-721), approving $9.07 billion in fiscal 1983 appropriations for the Commerce, Justice and State departments that included funding for several programs the Reagan administration wanted to phase out.

Among the endangered programs protected by the panel were the LSC, which financed legal services for the poor; the Economic Development Administration (EDA); the Sea Grant Program, designed to protect marine resources and foster ocean commerce; and public telecommunications facilities grants, which helped finance new public TV and radio facilities.

HR 6957 provided $398.77 million more than the administration requested for these departments and $546.69 million more than fiscal 1982 budget authority.

Commerce Department

The committee recommended $1.73 billion for the Commerce Department, $370.71 million above the budget request but $25.92 million below fiscal 1982 funding. The bulk of the increase over the request was to fund the EDA, Sea Grant and public telecommunications programs.

EDA. The committee provided $193.45 million for EDA, an agency designed to foster economic growth primarily in depressed communities. It earmarked $168.5 million for economic development assistance grants, which covered such things as public works and community planning assistance. The administration requested no program

spending for EDA and only 54 percent of 1982 administrative funds to monitor and close out agency operations.

U.S. Travel and Tourism Administration. The committee provided the full request of $5.03 million for the agency, which promoted foreign travel to the United States. The amount was $2.57 million below the 1982 appropriation. The House July 20 failed to pass a $10 million authorization bill for the agency.

National Oceanic and Atmospheric Administration (NOAA). HR 6957 provided $867.19 million for NOAA, $117.56 million above the president's request and $27.12 million above the 1982 appropriation. The appropriation included $25 million for the Sea Grant program.

National Telecommunications and Information Administration. The committee recommended $27.42 million for this agency, which developed national telecommunications and information policy, provided grants for planning construction of public TV and radio facilities and managed federal use of the airwaves.

Of the total, $15 million was for planning and construction grants for public radio and TV facilities. The administration requested no funds for the grant program, saying it was no longer necessary.

Related Agencies

Maritime Administration. The committee provided $118.41 million, $35 million more than requested. It recommended $25 million, not requested by the administration, for construction subsidies to help U.S. builders compete with foreign shipyards. The bill also included $454 million, the full request, for payment of operating subsidies to those who ran U.S.-flag vessels to help them compete with foreign-operated vessels.

Chrysler Loan Guarantee. HR 6957 provided the full budget request of $1.21 million for administrative expenses to carry out the Chrysler Loan Guarantee Program. The office was designed to make sure the Chrysler Corporation followed provisions of the loan guarantee act of 1979 (PL 96-185.) *(1979 Almanac p. 285)*

Federal Communications Commission (FCC). The committee recommended $79.5 million for the FCC, $5.05 million above the budget request and $2.6 million above 1982 funding. The report said the increase meant the FCC would not have to terminate 300 employees and furlough all others for three days. FCC commissioners had testified that proposed reductions would seriously hamper the FCC's ability to manage its projected workload.

Federal Trade Commission (FTC). The panel voted $63.64 million for the FTC, $2.8 million more than requested but $5.14 million less than 1982 funding. The funding level was designed to retain some of the 145 positions the president proposed to cut.

Justice Department

HR 6957 provided $2.7 billion for the Justice Department, $59.67 million more than the budget request and $234.06 million above fiscal 1982 spending. The increase over the budget request resulted primarily from the addition of $70 million for the Juvenile Justice and Delinquency Prevention Program. The administration asked no funds for the program, which provided grants to help states combat juvenile delinquency.

Immigration and Naturalization Service (INS). The committee voted $488.92 million for the INS, $35.68 million less than requested. The report said the funding proposal was $60.36 million above fiscal 1982 ap-

propriations and reflected an increase of $28.33 million and 15 positions to handle newly arrived immigrants.

FBI. The panel provided $799.48 million for the FBI, $147,000 above the budget request and $59.87 million more than 1982 funding. It included $570,000 for training of state and local law enforcement officials to supplement a previous appropriation. The committee report said the training program was "crucial" to helping stop crime.

Federal Prison System. The committee voted $424.04 million for the federal prison system, $29.78 million above the budget request and $46.12 million more than fiscal 1982 funding. The bulk of the increase over Reagan's request, $22 million, was for construction of a new federal prison in central Arizona to help cope with a growing federal inmate population.

Legal Services Corporation. The committee provided $241 million for the LSC in fiscal 1983, $24 million less than the corporation requested in its direct presentation to Congress. This was the same amount as the fiscal 1982 appropriation. The committee included by reference a number of new restrictions on LSC lawyers approved by the House in 1981.

Civil Rights Commission. The committee recommended $11.63 million for the commission, the full budget request, but $692,000 less than fiscal 1982 funding.

The Federal Judiciary

HR 6957 provided $799.34 million for operations of the federal judiciary, including the Supreme Court, federal appeals and district courts and several specialized courts. The recommendation was $51.79 million less than the judiciary requested but $89.48 million above 1982 spending.

The major cut in the funding sought by the judiciary was for operations of the federal appeals and district courts. Within that category, the committee recommended $16.74 million less than requested for space and facilities. It provided no funds for proposed renovations of existing libraries and creation of satellite libraries, saying these could be financed from existing court funds.

State Department

HR 6957 included $1.87 billion for the State Department — $28.88 million less than requested but $196.54 million more than fiscal 1982 appropriations. The bulk of the reduction from the request — $21.7 million — came from salaries and expenses. The bill provided $999.83 million for this. The committee said the amount nonetheless was $109.07 million more than the 1982 appropriation and included funds to continue strengthening political and economic analysis at key posts abroad.

The committee said $15 million of the reduction came from gains in the value of the U.S. dollar against foreign currencies.

Related Agencies

International Communication Agency (ICA). The panel voted $538.17 million, $105.83 million less than the budget request, for the ICA, which ran the Voice of America and other international communication programs.

The bulk of the reduction came in the recommendation for acquisition and construction of radio facilities. The committee provided $25 million for this purpose, $90 million less than requested but $6 million more than the 1982 funding. The report said the money, coupled with leftover funds from previous appropriations, should provide adequate resources for construction of new high-power trans-

mitting facilities in Sri Lanka and Botswana.

The committee said it did not provide all the funds sought for new facilities because construction had not proceeded as quickly as anticipated and not all of the money could be spent in fiscal 1983.

Radio Broadcasting to Cuba. The committee did not approve a $7.7 million appropriation for broadcasting to Cuba. The report noted that authorizing legislation for the new station, Radio Marti, had not been enacted. *(Story, p. 147)*

House Floor Action

The House Dec. 9 approved a $9 billion version of HR 6957 after decisively rejecting an amendment that would have sliced 40 percent from the allocation for the Legal Services Corporation (LSC).

The vote on the bill was 234-125. *(Vote 406, p. 120-H)*

Amendments on school prayer and school busing, which in the past had provoked heated debate, were adopted with barely a ripple.

An amendment by Robert S. Walker, R-Pa., to prevent the Justice Department from blocking any "voluntary" school prayer program was adopted by voice vote with no debate.

A similar amendment was adopted on the fiscal 1982 appropriations bill, which was never enacted. Adopted 243-153 was an amendment by James M. Collins, R-Texas, to bar Justice Department involvement in lawsuits that could lead to busing for racial balance. *(Vote 402, p. 120-H)*

This amendment had been added to previous appropriations bills, although not the fiscal 1982 bill. However, it never had been enacted.

FTC Fight Averted

A bitter fight over restrictions on the Federal Trade Commission (FTC) was averted after James J. Florio, D-N.J., a supporter of the FTC, successfully raised a point of order against the agency's $63.64 million appropriation because no FTC authorization bill had been cleared. The funds were then struck from the bill.

On Dec. 1 the House passed an FTC authorization bill that barred the agency from regulating doctors and other professionals (HR 6995). The Senate Commerce Committee approved a bill with similar restrictions (S 2499 — S Rept 97-451), but Commerce Chairman Bob Packwood, R-Ore., who opposed the bill, blocked consideration by the full Senate. *(Background, p. 347)*

Under House rules, appropriations were not permitted for programs that were not authorized. This was often waived by the Rules Committee, but at the request of FTC supporters, no such waiver was given on HR 6957.

Florio's point of order meant that no FTC amendments were allowed.

On Dec. 10, the House Appropriations Committee by 20-25 refused to add FTC funding to the continuing appropriations resolution that Congress had to pass before adjournment. Neal Smith, D-Iowa, chairman of the State, Justice, Commerce Subcommittee, said such a move would simply provoke another House floor fight. He said the Senate would add the FTC funds when the stopgap money bill reached it.

As passed by the House, HR 6957 was $481.65 million above fiscal 1982 appropriations and $334.13 million above the administration's fiscal 1983 request of $8.67 billion. The House bill was $93.66 million under a bill (S 2956 — S

Rept 97-584) reported Sept. 24 by the Senate Appropriations Committee.

Both the House and Senate bills included funding for programs the Reagan administration had sought to abolish: $241 million for the LSC; $70 million for juvenile justice programs; $193.45 million for the Economic Development Administration; and $15 million for public telecommunications facilities grants, which helped finance new public TV and radio facilities.

Legal Services Corporation

The 90-minute debate on the LSC amendment was the most spirited.

The current appropriation, and the funding level recommended in HR 6957, was $241 million — a 25 percent reduction from the agency's $321 million allocation in fiscal 1981.

F. James Sensenbrenner Jr., R-Wis., proposed cutting LSC funding to $100 million, but his amendment was rejected 121-269. *(Vote 403, p. 120-H)*

Sensenbrenner contended the agency was "overfunded" and should be forced to operate on a more restrictive budget.

Sam B. Hall Jr., D-Texas, was Sensenbrenner's most ardent supporter. He contended that in its eight-year existence, the agency had gone "completely beyond the scope of what was intended in its charter." Hall said he would like to see the agency's entire appropriation deleted.

However, Sensenbrenner's proposal ran into bipartisan opposition, as a dozen Republicans and Democrats rose to defend the corporation.

Several members said they had received complaints from their districts about the number of offices that already had been closed down because of previous budget cuts.

They also pointed out that the corporation's leadership had been in limbo for the past year because of controversy surrounding President Reagan's nominations to the board of directors. Bob Shamansky, D-Ohio, said it would be "grossly unfair and improper to kill the whole program" because of administrative problems in Washington.

Senate Committee Action

The Senate Appropriations Committee Sept. 24 reported a $9.1 billion version of the fiscal 1983 appropriations bill (S 2956 — S Rept 97-584) for the Commerce, Justice and State Departments that, like its House counterpart, included funding for several programs the Reagan administration wanted to phase out.

Among the programs protected by the panel were the Legal Services Corporation, at the House level of $241 million; juvenile justice programs, at the House level of $70 million; the Economic Development Administration, at $168.5 million, $25 million below the House level; and public telecommunications facilities grants, which helped finance new public TV and radio facilities, at the House level of $15 million.

The committee acted even though the House had not acted on its measure (HR 6957 — H Rept 97-721).

The Senate bill was $427.49 million above Reagan's request and $28.7 million above the House committee bill.

It continued existing restrictions on Federal Trade Commission authority, including the ability of Congress to block agency rules.

Provisions Compared

The following is a comparison of the budget authority requested by President Reagan and appropriated under HR 6957 *(in thousands of dollars)*:

Agency	Budget Request	House-passed Appropriation	Senate Committee Appropriation
Department of Commerce	$1,366,010	$1,733,424	$1,744,148
Department of Justice	2,793,587	2,704,352	2,705,272
Department of State	1,893,882	1,867,378	1,864,289
Judiciary	851,133	799,340	792,407
Related Agencies	1,961,358	1,900,134	1,992,167
Fiscal 1983 Total	**$8,866,070**	**$9,004,628**	**$9,098,283**

Provisions

The measure included the following major provisions:

Commerce Department. A total of $1.74 billion was provided for the department, $9.4 million more than the House bill and $380 million above Reagan's request.

A major part of the appropriation was $887.9 million for the National Oceanic and Atmospheric Administration. That was $20.8 million more than the House bill and $138 million more than the administration request.

The appropriation for the Small Business Administration was $547.9 million, $18 million more than the House proposal and $169 million above the administration request. The major difference between the House and Senate bills was a Senate provision that allocated $25 million for small business loans to disabled veterans and Vietnam War veterans.

Justice Department. The committee recommended $2.7 billion for the Justice Department, nearly $60 million above the administration bill. The committee provided the FBI $806 million, $7 million more than the House bill and the administration request. For the Immigration and Naturalization Service, $488 million — the same as the House bill — was provided. The administration had recommended $524 million.

The panel gave the Drug Enforcement Administration $247 million, nearly $2 million more than the House bill and $242,000 more than Reagan asked. Included was $2.5 million to restore nearly 100 positions.

State Department. The committee recommended $1.86 billion for the State Department — $3 million less than the House bill and $32 million under the administration request. The panel recommended a reduction of $24.8 million for salaries and expenses and denied a $5.9 million request for information and communication systems.

The recommendation included $1.8 million to reopen and operate seven consulates, authorized in the State Department authorization bill (PL 97-241) cleared Aug. 11. *(Story, p. 135)*

Like the House panel, the Senate committee did not provide money for radio broadcasting to Cuba because Congress had not approved an authorization for this program, known as Radio Marti.

The Judiciary. A total of $792 million was recommended for the federal judiciary, including the Supreme Court, the federal appeals and district courts, and several specialty courts. The amount was $6.9 million less than the House bill and $58.7 million under the request.

The committee report said the reduction from the House bill resulted largely from a freeze on rental payments to the General Services Administration. ∎

$96.2 Billion Labor-HHS-ED Funding Cleared

Congress Dec. 20 cleared fiscal 1983 appropriations for the departments of Labor, Health and Human Services (HHS) and Education (ED) and related agencies.

The funding was included in the continuing appropriations resolution, which President Reagan signed into law Dec. 21 (H J Res 631 — PL 97-377). As cleared, H J Res 631 contained the full text of the regular fiscal 1983 Labor-HHS-ED appropriations bill (HR 7205). *(Continuing resolution, p. 238)*

The continuing resolution provided $89.1 billion in fiscal 1983 funds for the three departments and related agencies, plus $7 billion in fiscal 1984 funds and $130 million for fiscal 1985, for a grand total of $96.2 billion.

The spending total in the bill did not reflect the huge amounts for Social Security and other permanent programs that did not require annual appropriations. Taken together, fiscal 1983 spending for the three departments and related agencies was expected to be at least $318.1 billion.

Legislative History

The House Appropriations Committee reported HR 7205 Sept. 29, and the House passed it Dec. 1. The Senate Appropriations Committee reported its version Dec. 8, but the bill never went to the floor.

Conferees on H J Res 631 in effect held a separate conference to reconcile the differences between the House-passed bill and the Senate committee version of HR 7205. They included their agreement on HR 7205 as part of H J

Res 631.

Action on the measure was in marked contrast to the legislative histories of past Labor-HHS-ED appropriations bills. There was little in 1982 of the bitter controversy over subjects such as abortion and school busing that held up the funding bills in previous years. The last time Congress cleared a Labor-HHS-ED appropriations bill was in 1978. The departments and agencies had been funded by continuing resolutions ever since. (*1981 action, 1981 Almanac p. 331*)

H J Res 631 extended a number of limitations on the use of funds that were already in existing law. For example, it barred the use of funds in the bill to pay for abortions unless the life of the mother was in danger, and restricted inspections by the Occupational Safety and Health Administration (OSHA).

Funding Levels Increased

Funding levels in the Labor-HHS-ED section of H J Res 631 were well above those initially requested by the Reagan administration. In some cases, the increases reflected higher estimates for "mandatory" entitlement programs, but discretionary spending also was increased, particularly for education programs. (Mandatory programs are those in which payments are mandated by law or are fixed by federal matching formula.)

The administration's budget requests for a number of entitlement programs, such as Medicare and Medicaid, assumed the enactment of cost-saving legislative changes. But since Congress approved changes in only a few of the entitlement programs during 1982, the funding levels in the budget request were too low to meet the full needs of the programs.

For Aid to Families with Dependent Children and other welfare programs, for example, the administration asked for an appropriation level of $5.3 billion, which assumed legislative savings of $1.2 billion. Most of those changes were not approved by Congress. So conferees on H J Res 631 had to include a much higher figure — $6.7 billion.

The House bill had retained the administration figures for most of the entitlement programs. But the Senate Appropriations Committee sought to fund the programs fully, and conferees generally adopted the Senate levels.

On discretionary programs, the sharpest differences with the administration came over education spending. The administration had sought deep cuts in ED funding, bringing the department down $4.7 billion from its fiscal 1982 level. H J Res 631 provided education funding that was slightly above the 1982 level and significantly higher than the administration requests. For example, the administration requested $1.9 billion for compensatory education for the disadvantaged — a $1.1 billion cut from the year before. Conferees on H J Res 631 approved $3.2 billion for the program.

Provisions

As signed into law, H J Res 631 (PL 97-377) provided the following amounts for the Departments of Labor, HHS and Education and related agencies:

Labor Department	Budget Request	Final Amount
Employment and Training Administration		
Program administration	$ 81,068,000	$ 91,465,000

Labor Department	Budget Request	Final Amount
Employment and training assistance	2,387,000,000	3,764,000,000
Dislocated workers	——	25,000,000
Community service employment for older Americans	——	281,950,000
Federal unemployment benefits	35,000,000	230,000,000
Grants to states for unemployment insurance and employment services	22,200,000	22,200,000
Advances to unemployment trust fund	4,572,000,000	5,411,000,000
Labor-Management Services Administration	60,153,000	58,077,000
Employment Standards Administration	1,183,196,000	1,183,196,000
Occupational Safety and Health Administration	206,256,000	205,256,000
Mine Safety and Health Administration	153,828,000	153,828,000
Bureau of Labor Statistics	120,143,000	120,143,000
Departmental Management	91,905,000	91,931,000
Inspector General	38,133,000	38,133,000
Total, Labor Department	**$8,950,882,000**	**$11,676,179,000**

Health and Human Services	Budget Request	Final Amount
Health Services	937,732,000	1,018,563,000
Preventive Health Services	299,792,000	290,701,000
National Institutes of Health		
Cancer	955,449,000	983,576,000
Heart, Lung and Blood	577,143,000	622,745,000
Dental Research	74,462,000	78,860,000
Arthritis, Diabetes, and Digestive and Kidney Diseases	379,422,000	412,182,000
Neurological and Communicative Disorders and Stroke	274,505,000	295,719,000
Allergy and Infectious Diseases	246,043,000	273,581,000
General Medical Sciences	345,621,000	369,561,000
Child Health and Human Development	233,575,000	253,655,000
Eye	131,550,000	141,561,000
Environmental Health Sciences	157,448,000	164,367,000
Aging	84,556,000	93,996,000
Research resources	191,024,000	213,804,000
John E. Fogarty International Center	10,147,000	10,147,000
National Library of Medicine	46,043,000	46,043,000
Director	24,283,000	24,683,000
Buildings	17,500,000	17,500,000
Alcohol, Drug Abuse and Mental Health Administration	805,682,000	854,061,000

Health and Human Services	Budget Request	Final Amount
Health Resources Administration	168,411,000	284,963,000
Health services management	109,563,000	96,694,000
Health maintenance organization loans	2,500,000	——
Retirement pay	85,433,000	78,861,000
Health Care Financing Administration	29,479,567,000	30,056,165,000
(Fiscal 1984 advance)	(4,470,000,000)	(5,105,600,000)
Social Security Administration		
Payments to Social Security trust funds	855,213,000	855,213,000
Black lung payments	1,102,000,000	1,093,000,000
Supplemental Security Income	8,891,362,000	8,515,483,000
Assistance payments	4,555,976,000	5,975,548,000
(Fiscal 1984 advance)	(1,327,203,000)	(1,718,000,000)
Child support enforcement	284,877,000	347,500,000
(Fiscal 1984 advance)	(112,500,000)	(118,000,000)
Low-income energy aid	1,300,000,000	1,975,000,000
Refugee resettlement	532,152,000	585,000,000
Social services	1,974,126,000	2,450,000,000
Programs for special populations	1,611,704,000	1,757,014,000
Child welfare	410,920,000	572,669,000
Work incentives	——	270,760,000
Community services	103,500,000	360,500,000
Departmental management	158,143,000	158,143,000
Inspector General	71,267,000	71,267,000
(Fiscal 1984 advance)	(10,000,000)	(10,000,000)
Office for Civil Rights	19,163,000	19,163,000
Policy research	14,718,000	14,718,000
Subtotal, HHS	**$57,522,572,000**	**$61,702,966,000**
(Fiscal 1984 advance)	**(5,919,703,000)**	**(6,951,600,000)**
Education Department		
Compensatory education	1,942,000,000	3,167,894,000
Special programs	433,000,000	534,500,000
Bilingual education	94,534,000	138,057,000
Impact aid	286,880,000	480,000,000
Handicapped education	845,668,000	1,110,252,000
Rehabilitation services	650,000,000	1,036,727,000
Vocational education	500,000,000	816,500,000
College student assistance	1,800,000,000	3,567,800,000
Guaranteed student loans	2,484,631,000	3,100,500,000
Higher education	271,352,000	385,525,000
Higher education facilities loans	20,143,000	20,143,000
Education research, statistics	62,392,000	64,203,000
Overseas activities	516,000	516,000
Libraries	——	80,320,000
Special institutions	228,421,000	228,500,000
Civil rights	44,868,000	44,868,000
Departmental management	222,000,000	222,000,000
Inspector General	12,840,000	12,840,000
Subtotal, Education Department	**$ 9,899,245,000**	**$15,011,145,000**
Related Agencies		
Action	117,721,000	129,321,000

Related Agencies	Budget Request	Final Amount
Corporation for Public Broadcasting (Fiscal 1985 advance)	(85,000,000)	(130,000,000)
Federal Mediation and Conciliation Service	20,190,000	21,321,000
Federal Mine Safety and Health Review Commission	3,686,000	3,686,000
National Commission on Libraries and Information Science	——	674,000
National Commission on Student Financial Assistance	840,000	840,000
National Labor Relations Board	133,000,000	124,045,000
National Mediation Board	3,618,000	5,468,000
Occupational Safety and Health Review Commission	6,316,000	6,316,000
Railroad Retirement Board	350,250,000	430,250,000
Soldiers' and Airmen's Home	26,718,000	26,718,000
Subtotal, related agencies	**$ 662,339,000**	**$ 748,639,000**
(Fiscal 1985 advance)	**(85,000,000)**	**(130,000,000)**
Grand Total, Fiscal 1983	**$77,035,038,000**	**$89,138,929,000**
(Fiscal 1984 advance)	**(5,919,703,000)**	**(6,951,600,000)**
(Fiscal 1985 advance)	**(85,000,000)**	**(130,000,000)**

House Committee Action

The House Appropriations Committee reported HR 7205 on Sept. 29 (H Rept 97-894).

As approved by the committee, the bill contained a total of $85.4 billion. That was $5.3 billion over President Reagan's budget request, mostly because the committee refused to accept proposed deep cuts in education programs.

But the committee seriously under-funded a number of mandatory entitlement programs, so appropriations in the bill would not be sufficient to cover actual spending for the three departments and related agencies.

Entitlement spending in the bill was based on administration budget requests, which assumed some $4 billion in legislative savings that the committee said were unlikely to be enacted. In addition, the bill did not contain funds for four programs, including job training, that had not been authorized by the time the committee acted. The administration had requested $3.1 billion for the four programs.

Labor Department

The committee approved $6 billion for Labor Department programs, $502.7 million less than the administration's request and $872 million below fiscal 1982 funding.

However, the reduction was achieved by appropriating only $3.8 billion for advances to the unemployment trust fund — $774 million less than the budget estimate. If that amount proved insufficient, additional spending for the mandatory program would be required in the future.

In addition, the bill did not include funding for job training programs, since legislation (S 2036) authorizing a new training program had not cleared Congress at the time the bill was reported. The administration requested $2.4 billion for job training, and other estimates had assumed

that the programs would receive about $3.8 billion. (Congress subsequently cleared S 2036 on Oct. 1.) *(Story, p. 39)*

Employment for the Elderly. Reflecting the strong political support for programs for the elderly, the committee included $277.1 million for the community service employment program for older Americans. The administration had not sought any funds for the program. The committee estimated the funding in the bill would maintain the existing employment level of 54,200 jobs.

OSHA. For the Occupational Safety and Health Administration, $202.3 million was provided. That was $4 million less than the budget request, a savings achieved by reducing funds for outside contracts.

The committee rejected an administration proposal to delete language, added to appropriations bills in past years, to limit OSHA activities. Among the restrictions in the bill were those exempting small employers in relatively safe industries from routine inspections and prohibiting OSHA inspections of businesses that had been inspected by state safety agencies in the preceding six months.

Health and Human Services

HR 7205 provided $64.2 billion for HHS — $58.3 billion for fiscal 1983, plus $5.9 billion in advance appropriations for 1984. The total was $1.3 billion above the budget request and $2.3 billion above the 1982 total.

The bulk of the increases over the budget were in appropriations for the National Institutes of Health (NIH), low-income energy assistance and human development programs.

The bill did not include funds for health planning, professional standards review organizations (PSROs) or refugee programs because authorizing legislation had not been completed. And it substantially under-funded certain entitlement programs; the difference would have to be made up in a subsequent supplemental bill.

Health Services. For the Health Services Administration, HR 7205 provided $1 billion — $65.3 million over the budget but $193.9 million less than 1982 funding.

Virtually all of the increase over the budget was for community health service programs. The bill contained $841.2 million for primary care, maternal and child care programs, for which the administration sought $775.7 million. Since Congress had not accepted the administration's proposal to merge the existing community health centers block grant and programs for black lung services, migrant health and family planning, the committee provided separate funding for the programs. The maternal and child health care block grant, established in 1981, received $373 million, $23 million more than the administration asked.

While providing more than the budget request for community health services, the bill cut funding for health professions education below the budget proposal and well below the 1982 level. Funding for the National Health Service Corps, health professions student assistance and nursing student aid totaled $129.3 million, compared with $169.9 million in 1982 and a $131.2 million budget request.

Centers for Disease Control. The preventive health programs of the Centers for Disease Control received $318.4 million — $18.6 million over the budget.

Childhood immunization programs were funded above budget levels. HR 7205 provided $34.9 million for the programs, which combat measles, rubella, poliomyelitis, mumps, diphtheria, pertussis and tetanus. The $6 million increase over the budget was enough to maintain immuni-

zations at the 1982 level, the committee said.

The panel also restored a proposed $1.8 million cut in research and surveillance of herpes.

National Institutes of Health. The bill provided $4 billion for the research institutes. The administration had requested $3.7 billion, a modest increase over the 1982 level of $3.6 billion.

The committee rejected an administration proposal to require research institutions to absorb 10 percent of the indirect costs of research projects (a project's share of the institution's utilities, administration and maintenance costs). But it did order a study to see whether federal projects were bearing a disproportionate share of some institutions' costs.

Each of the 11 NIH institutes received some increase over the budget request. As in 1982, the institute with the highest funding level was the National Cancer Institute, with $981.4 million. The Institute for Arthritis, Diabetes, Digestive and Kidney Diseases received $408.5 million.

Drug Abuse. The committee increased funding for the Alcohol, Drug Abuse and Mental Health Administration by $29.9 million over the budget, for a total of $768.1 million.

The panel allotted $432 million for alcohol, drug abuse and mental health block grants to states. It provided additional funds for federal research and training programs in these areas.

Health Resources. HR 7205 contained a major increase over the budget request for the Health Resources Administration, allowing $213.6 million, $79.2 million over the budget. The increase was due in part to the inclusion of $29 million to repay a federally guaranteed loan made to Meharry Medical College, a black institution in Nashville, Tenn. HR 7205 also provided $42.7 million for nurse training and other nursing student aid programs, which the administration wanted to cut sharply or eliminate.

Health Care Financing. The bill contained $17.9 billion, the administration estimate, for the federal share of state Medicaid costs. However, the committee said the estimate assumed greater savings than would be achieved by program changes ordered by the tax increase/spending cut bill (HR 4961 — PL 97-248), so supplemental funding would be needed. *(HR 4961, p. 29)*

The bill provided $15.6 billion for payments to the Medicare trust fund, for costs not covered by workers' payroll contributions.

Welfare Programs. As with the Medicaid funding, the committee approved amounts for welfare programs that were below the expected required funding. For Aid to Families with Dependent Children and related programs, for example, it allowed the budget estimate of $5.3 billion. But the estimate assumed certain legislative savings unlikely to be enacted, the panel said, so future supplemental funding would be required.

The committee provided the amount requested ($284.9 million) for the Child Support Enforcement program, although it said the program consistently had cost more to administer than it had reduced welfare costs.

It provided $1.9 billion for low-income energy assistance, a $550 million increase over the budget.

Human Development. For human development programs, the bill provided $4.8 billion — $663.3 million more than the budget but $488.2 million less than 1982. The increases went largely to three areas: programs for the aging, work incentives for welfare recipients, and community services block grants.

The bill provided $646.7 million for programs for the aging, a $78.6 million increase over the budget. It continued the work incentive (WIN) program, which provided training and support services to welfare recipients, at the 1982 level of $280.8 million; the administration wanted to eliminate the program. And it provided $360.5 million for community services block grants, which the administration sought to reduce to $103.5 million, less than one-third its 1982 level.

Education Department

HR 7205 appropriated $14.3 billion for the Education Department, $324.1 million less than the 1982 level but $4.4 billion more than the administration requested.

Elementary, Secondary Education. The core program of federal aid to elementary and secondary education, compensatory education assistance to the disadvantaged, was funded at $3 billion. That was the same as the comparable 1982 funding level and represented a rejection of the administration's call for a $1.1 billion cut.

Two other programs remained at the 1982 level, thus escaping administration cuts. Bilingual education was funded at $138.1 million, $43.5 million over the budget. The new education block grant received $483.8 million, $50.8 million over the budget.

Other education funding exceeded both the 1982 level and the budget request. Impact aid for schools educating children whose parents worked or lived on federal property was given $475 million — $18.8 million over the 1982 figure and $188.1 million over the budget. Spending for handicapped education was set at $1.1 billion, $258 million over the budget and $35.1 million over 1982. Rehabilitation services for the handicapped received $1 billion, $385.2 million over the budget and $83.1 million over 1982.

Adult and vocational education programs were similarly successful, receiving $829.5 million — $329.5 million over the budget and $94.5 million over 1982.

Higher Education. The committee accepted for the time being the administration's funding level for the costliest student aid program, guaranteed student loans (GSL), but it gave other key programs significant increases.

For Pell grants, HR 7205 provided the 1982 level of $2.4 billion; the administration had sought only $1.4 billion. The college work-study program also was funded at the 1982 level, $528 million — $130.5 million above the budget request.

The committee included funds for three higher education programs the administration wanted to eliminate: supplemental educational opportunity grants, $355.4 million; capital contributions to institutional loan programs, $178.6 million, and state student incentive grants, $73.7 million.

While the GSL program received the budget request of $2.5 billion, the committee said that funding would be insufficient.

Related Agencies

HR 7205 provided $129.1 million for the volunteer agency ACTION — $11.4 million over the budget. The Corporation for Public Broadcasting was given an advance fiscal 1985 appropriation of $130 million — $45 million more than requested. The bill also contained $430 million — $80 million more than the budget request — to provide dual benefits to retirees who were eligible for both railroad retirement and Social Security benefits.

House Floor Action

The House passed HR 7205 Dec. 1 by a vote of 330-70. *(Vote 377, p. 114-H)*

In sharp contrast to House action on similar funding bills in the past, the bill sailed through the House with surprising ease. The House spent less than two hours on the measure and considered no major amendments.

The House approved a handful of amendments that added $31.6 million to the bill. It did not reduce any funding levels set by the Appropriations Committee.

Sponsors of the bill conceded that it fell well short of the funding levels needed to cover entitlements and other mandatory spending programs. The Appropriations Committee estimated that supplemental money would be needed for health and welfare entitlements and for four programs whose funding was deferred pending completion of authorizing legislation.

Bill Frenzel, R-Minn., complained that passage of a bill without full funding for mandatory and entitlement programs "gives the committee a smokescreen behind which discretionary programs can be overspent." Frenzel also said the bill was some $6 billion over the outlay target set by the fiscal 1983 congressional budget resolution (S Con Res 92). *(Budget resolution, p. 186)*

The Appropriations Committee said the bill was below the resolution's target amount for budget authority, although members acknowledged that supplemental appropriations required to fully fund all the programs in the bill would bring it very close to that limit.

The social programs funded by HR 7205 came in for high praise from House members, who made no effort to reduce any spending in the bill.

The bill "is both fiscally responsible and humanly responsive," said Silvio O. Conte, Mass., ranking Republican on the Appropriations Committee.

The House by voice vote adopted three amendments that added:

● $4 million for OSHA. Sponsored by Larry E. Craig, R-Idaho, the amendment increased OSHA's fiscal 1983 funding to $206.3 million and removed a provision barring the agency from contracting out development of health and safety standards. OSHA director Thorne G. Auchter had opposed the committee-backed restriction that required use of in-house staff for all such projects.

● $2.6 million for the Centers for Disease Control. The amendment, which brought CDC funding to $321 million, would fund additional work against acquired immune deficiency, a syndrome that made people highly susceptible to infections and cancers. Sponsor Edward R. Roybal, D-Calif., said the extra funds were needed to combat the rapid growth of the disease, which was particularly prevalent among homosexuals.

● $25 million for human development services in HHS. Sponsor Thomas M. Foglietta, D-Pa., said the funds would bring spending for nutrition programs for the elderly up to their authorized level.

Senate Committee Action

The Senate Appropriations Committee agreed Dec. 7 to add $7 billion to the Labor-HHS-Education appropriations bill passed by the House Dec. 1. The panel filed its report on the measure Dec. 8 (S Rept 97-680).

The committee bill totaled $92.3 billion — $84.7 of it for fiscal 1983. Most of the increase over the House amount

was for mandatory entitlement spending.

Harrison "Jack" Schmitt, R-N.M., chairman of the Appropriations Subcommittee on Labor, HHS and Education, said the bill, together with $4.5 billion in expected supplemental funding for programs whose authorizations had not been enacted, would be just below the spending allocation given it by the budget resolution. Approval of any amendments adding substantial amounts of money to the measure would put it over the ceiling and jeopardize the chances for presidential approval, he said.

Schmitt said the Reagan administration had agreed to support the $60.2 billion in entitlement spending in the Senate bill, which was significantly higher than the $54.4 billion included in the House bill.

"We've tried to make the entitlements realistic. We have assurances that we will not be held accountable for increases in the entitlements," Schmitt said.

Entitlement funding in the Senate bill included $19.7 billion for Medicaid, $7.3 billion for Aid to Families with Dependent Children (AFDC) and $3.1 billion for guaranteed student loans. The comparable House figures were $17.9 billion for Medicaid, $6.1 billion for AFDC and $2.5 billion for student loans. The Senate bill also included slightly higher funding levels for discretionary programs than the House bill.

Committee Amendments

During markup, the Appropriations Committee added a total of $30 million to the bill as approved by Schmitt's subcommittee Dec. 2.

The panel also fought another battle in the long-running dispute over moving the headquarters of the National Institute for Occupational Safety and Health (NIOSH) to Atlanta from Rockville, Md.

Thomas F. Eagleton, D-Mo., proposed a ban on funds to carry out the proposed move, which had aroused intense opposition from the affected employees. The House-passed bill contained the prohibition, but the Senate subcommittee dropped it. Eagleton said the administration had already begun to make the transfer, despite the existing ban under the fiscal 1982 NIOSH appropriation. His amendment was rejected 6-16.

The biggest funding increase over the subcommittee bill was a $25 million add-on for nutrition programs for the elderly. Schmitt sponsored the amendment, which would bring funding for the popular programs to $381 million.

Other amendments added $2 million for OSHA and $1.7 million for traditionally black medical, dental and veterinary schools.

The committee rejected an amendment by Arlen Specter, R-Pa., to add $7 million for the runaway youth program and another by Dennis DeConcini, D-Ariz., to add $4.8 million to the veterans' cost of instruction program aiding colleges and universities that enrolled veterans.

James Abdnor, R-S.D., offered a successful amendment to protect impact aid funding for school districts with large numbers of students who were military dependents. The amendment would ensure that school districts in which 20 percent or more of the students had a parent who both lived and worked on federal property would receive 100 percent of their fiscal 1981 payments for each such child. Payments for such students in less heavily impacted school districts would be 90 percent of the 1981 level. ∎

$34 Billion Voted for Farm, Food Programs

Congress Dec. 15 gave final approval to a $34 billion fiscal 1983 appropriations bill for federal farm and food programs.

The funding measure (HR 7072 — PL 97-370) provided $31,733,548,000 in new budget authority, compared with an amended administration request of $31,833,247,000. A transfer of $2,287,346,000 from a special customs receipt fund known as the Section 32 fund brought total spending available in PL 97-370 to $34,020,894,000.

The House had passed a $23 billion bill Sept. 21, and the Senate had approved a $25 billion version Sept. 28. The fiscal 1982 appropriation for agriculture programs was $31,841,329,000.

The final version worked out by House-Senate conferees dropped or softened controversial dairy, conservation, farm-loan and credit program provisions that had elicited a veto threat from Office of Management and Budget (OMB) Director David A. Stockman.

Supplemental budget requests — totaling $8.8 billion — were forwarded to Congress by OMB after the House and Senate had passed the bill. The administration requested an additional $6.7 billion for the Commodity Credit Corporation (CCC), whose price support programs were being heavily used by financially squeezed farmers. The other supplemental requests were for higher food program spending levels that both the House and Senate insisted upon.

Total funding for the CCC in HR 7072 came to $10.5 billion. It was the first time that observers could remember price support programs costing nearly as much as food stamps, which were funded at $10.8 billion. Among rural development programs, the Farmers Home Administration (FmHA) received the largest appropriation — $2.75 billion.

Final action came Dec. 15 when the Senate adopted the conference agreement on the bill by voice vote. The House had approved the measure earlier the same day by a 324-73 vote. *(Vote 431, p. 126-H)*

Final Appropriations

As enacted into law, HR 7072 made the following appropriations for fiscal 1983:

Agriculture Programs	Budget Request	Final Amount
Office of the Secretary	$ 5,406,000	$ 3,884,000
Standard Level User Charges*	——	56,377,000
Advisory Committees*	——	1,398,000
Departmental Administration	13,647,000	13,166,000
Governmental and Public Affairs	7,288,000	6,677,000
Congressional Affairs	464,000	439,000
Inspector General	33,769,000	27,943,000

Agriculture Programs	Budget Request	Final Amount
General Counsel	13,689,000	12,386,000
Federal Grain Inspection Service	5,195,000	5,369,000
Agricultural Research Service	468,548,000	452,378,000
Cooperative State Research Service	232,103,000	244,966,000
Extension Service	311,911,000	328,672,000
National Agricultural Library	9,016,000	8,849,000
Animal and Plant Health Inspection Service	229,919,000	270,301,000
Food Safety and Inspection Service	319,876,000	315,557,000
Economic Research Service	40,584,000	37,751,000
Statistical Reporting Service	53,694,000	51,035,000
Agricultural Cooperative Service	3,683,000	4,639,000
World Agricultural Outlook Board	1,535,000	1,403,000
Agricultural Marketing Service	33,768,000	35,279,000
Packers and Stockyards Administration	8,564,000	8,668,000
Agricultural Stabilization & Conservation Service	62,046,000	62,962,000
Federal Crop Insurance Corporation	716,936,000	528,433,000
Commodity Credit Corporation	10,466,057,000	10,466,057,000
Subtotal	**$13,040,675,000**	**$12,951,493,000**
Rural Development Programs		
Office of Rural Development Policy	2,501,000	2,000,000
Farmers Home Administration	2,754,219,000	2,572,551,000
Rural Electrification Administration	30,431,000	29,036,000
Soil Conservation Service	515,816,000	592,925,000
Agricultural Stabilization & Conservation Service	56,000,000	211,300,000
Subtotal	**$ 3,358,000,000**	**$ 3,407,812,000**
Domestic Food Programs		
Child Nutrition Programs	963,310,000	896,324,000
Special Milk Program	——	20,100,000
Women, Infants & Children (WIC) Program	1,060,000,000	1,060,000,000
Commodity Supplemental Food Program	32,600,000	32,600,000
Food Stamps	10,815,657,000	10,815,657,000
Nutrition Assistance for Puerto Rico	825,000,000	825,000,000
Food Donations Programs	153,200,000	156,266,000
Food Program Administration	85,477,000	82,146,000
Nutrition Information	8,289,000	8,089,000
Subtotal	**$13,943,533,000**	**$13,896,189,000**
International Programs		
Foreign Agricultural Service	79,207,000	74,454,000
Food for Peace (PL 480)	1,028,000,000	1,028,000,000

International Programs	Budget Request	Final Amount
Office of International Cooperation and Development	3,703,000	3,578,000
Subtotal	**$ 1,110,910,000**	**$ 1,106,032,000**
Other Agencies		
Food and Drug Administration	356,163,000	349,130,000
Commodity Futures Trading Commission	22,999,000	22,892,000
Subtotal	**$ 379,162,000**	**$ 372,022,000**
TOTAL	**$31,833,247,000**	**$31,733,548,000**
Section 32 Transfers	$ 2,219,419,000	$ 2,287,346,000

New accounts created by the House Appropriations Committee to consolidate spending for these functions.

House Committee Action

The House Appropriations Committee Sept. 9 reported the fiscal 1983 agriculture appropriations bill (HR 7072 — H Rept 97-800).

As reported, the bill provided $23,066,954,000 in new budget authority for farm and food programs, a decrease of about $3.7 billion from the $26.8 billion appropriated in fiscal 1982.

Although the bill, according to committee estimates, was $16.7 million below the president's budget request and $3.2 billion below the amount allocated for food and farm programs in the fiscal 1983 budget resolution, the panel did not appropriate funds for major federal feeding programs, such as food stamps, for the entire year. Those programs would need more than $2 billion in supplemental appropriations to continue them to the end of fiscal 1983.

Stockman's Objections

In a Sept. 9 letter to Committee Chairman Jamie L. Whitten, D-Miss., and ranking minority member Silvio O. Conte, R-Mass., OMB Director Stockman warned that the president would not sign the bill because of the "undesirable spending increases."

Stockman's complaints were based only in part on the committee's departures from the president's budget requests. In other instances, Stockman apparently objected to the panel's failure to accept all the assumptions underlying the fiscal 1983 budget resolution (S Con Res 92). *(Story, p. 186)*

His specific objections were that the bill:

● Exceeded the budget resolution's allocation for non-entitlement agriculture programs by $206 million.

● Funded major federal food programs for eight to 10 and one-half months, instead of the entire fiscal year.

● Mandated a $500 million farm export fund that, he said, "would increase . . . the federal deficit."

● Continued, with certain qualifications, a prohibition on all federal lending to Poland. Stockman said such action "would continue to undermine administration efforts to maintain maximum economic pressure on Poland and could seriously damage the credibility of all government guarantee programs."

The committee recommended the following appropriations:

Agriculture Programs

For price support, research, crop insurance and other

basic farm programs, the committee recommended $6.3 billion, about $35 million below the budget request and about $3 billion less than the fiscal 1982 appropriation.

The major difference between the two fiscal years was a reduction in HR 7072 of $3.3 billion in the fund that reimbursed the CCC for losses in price support, loan, disaster and other farm programs. The committee's reduction in reimbursements, to $3.8 billion from a fiscal 1982 level of $7 billion, followed the budget request and reflected the fact that Congress earlier in the year had approved $5 billion for reimbursements through an urgent supplemental agriculture appropriations bill (H J Res 389 — PL 97-147). *(Story, p. 230)*

The Stockman letter, however, contended that the CCC still would need an additional $578 million. HR 7072 instructed the CCC to earmark at least $500 million for direct loans to finance commodity exports to aid the ailing farm economy. The provision was intended, according to committee aides, to supersede a provision in the regular fiscal 1982 supplemental appropriations bill (HR 6863 — PL 97-257) that was enacted over the president's veto. Language in that measure stated that "no more than" $500 million could be spent on CCC loans. *(Story, p. 219)*

The bill also prohibited the use of any government funds to make loan guarantee payments to banks on loans to the government of Poland, unless Poland were declared in default on earlier unpaid loans or the president certified to Congress each month that such payments were in the national interest. This provision continued a similar prohibition enacted earlier.

The panel provided $451.5 million for the Agricultural Research Service, $17 million less than requested and $19 million more than provided in fiscal 1982. It added $15 million to the request for the popular agriculture extension service, for a total of $327 million, including $3 million for the urban gardening program.

The committee added $39 million to the Animal and Plant Health Inspection Service, for a total of $269 million. The report characterized severe budget reductions in an assortment of pest-specific control programs as "tantamount to a dismantling of programs which have proven . . . very effective."

The panel provided $316 million for the Food Safety and Inspection Service, about $4 million less than requested. It assumed a $2 million savings, proposed in the president's budget, that would result if Congress gave the secretary authority he requested to relax inspection regulations by permitting occasional federal surveillance of meat and poultry processing plants. Existing law required continuous federal inspection.

The Agriculture Subcommittee had provided $176,000 to continue the dairy indemnity program, which the administration proposed to end. The full committee raised that figure to $7 million at the request of Rep. Daniel K. Akaka, D-Hawaii. The additional funds were intended for Hawaiian milk producers, whose herds had been condemned because of exposure to the pesticide heptachlor.

As it had done in 1981, the panel allotted significantly less money than requested for operating expenses of the expanded crop insurance program and for the fund from which the Federal Crop Insurance Corporation (FCIC) made payments for its losses. The insurance program was intended eventually to replace farm disaster payments.

But while the president requested $716.9 million, the committee provided only $605 million. It cited FCIC testimony that "optimistic assumptions of the rate of growth of the . . . program have not been realized." About a third less insurance was in force than originally estimated for the year, and the government insurance agency, unlike private insurers, did not need "large idle reserves," the committee said in its report.

Rural Development

The committee provided a total of $3.4 billion, some $34 million more than the administration requested and $912 million more than was allocated in fiscal 1982.

Farmers Home Administration (FmHA). The committee nearly doubled the rural housing insurance fund request, providing $4.4 billion. The biggest increase was for insured rural housing loans, for which the committee provided $3.2 billion compared with a request of $1.1 billion.

The committee also changed the financing mechanism for the rural rental assistance payments program and, according to Stockman, claimed $398 million in savings it was not entitled to make in the first fiscal 1983 budget resolution.

The Agricultural Credit Insurance Fund, which made farming, recreation and emergency loans to individuals and associations, was allotted $74 million more than the budget request, including $30 million for soil conservation loans, which the administration proposed to end.

For the Rural Development Insurance Fund, the committee recommended $75 million more than was requested for water and sewer facility loans, for a total of $375 million. The committee disregarded a budget request to eliminate industrial development guaranteed loans and provided $300 million, the same amount as granted in fiscal 1982. The panel told the department to choose projects "that will produce jobs as rapidly as possible."

Rural Electrification Administration (REA). The panel generally ignored proposed REA budget reductions, providing $400 million more than requested, for a fiscal 1983 total of $1.1 billion in insured loans for rural electrical and telephone systems, and $985 million more than requested for guaranteed electric loans. It also restored $30 million for the Rural Telephone Bank.

The Reagan budget request had reduced REA sharply, arguing that funding for it was an unwarranted subsidy to non-urban consumers of such services.

As in earlier years, the committee largely ignored budget requests to slash spending for anti-erosion work on individual farms and for larger-scale conservation projects. Its recommendation of $190 million for watershed and flood prevention operations exceeded the budget by $72 million. For the Agricultural Conservation Program, which paid for individual farm conservation projects if farmers shared the cost, the panel provided $190 million — $134 million more than the budget request.

Food Programs

By terminating funds for three major feeding programs well before the end of fiscal 1983, the committee recommended billions of dollars less than it estimated the programs actually would require.

In each case, the committee suggested that the lower budget estimates drawn up by the administration were based on legislative changes that had not occurred. The committee said its funding was intended to continue the programs at current levels and recommended that the administration request supplemental appropriations to carry out the programs after the cutoff dates.

For child nutrition programs, including school lunches,

the panel provided an appropriation of $544 million, plus a transfer of Section 32 funds (funded by customs receipts), for a total of $2.8 billion. The committee said this amount was intended to finance the program through Aug. 15, 1983. The committee predicted that an additional $322.7 million would be needed to finish out the year at the current levels.

For the Women, Infants and Children (WIC) program, $652 million was provided, the same figure used in the 1983 budget request. The committee, however, specified that these funds were to carry the program only through May 15, 1983.

The committee rejected an administration plan to transfer the WIC program to the Department of Health and Human Services, where it would be included as part of a new block grant. It praised WIC's effectiveness, suggesting that its beneficial "impact on infant mortality, chronic ill health, birth defects and subnormal development averts major medical expenditures and reduces outlays in programs such as Medicaid," federal disability and special education.

For food stamps, $9.5 billion was provided through July 15, 1983. The committee report indicated that an additional $2.2 billion would be required to finish the year at current spending levels.

The committee criticized what it called "the continuing pattern of unrealistic budget estimates for the food stamp program. This action leads to periodic crises which tend to call into question the ability of the government to run the program effectively, and which force Congress into eleventh-hour action." It directed the Agriculture Department to work out "a more feasible and less wasteful" procedure and to report any funding shortfalls immediately to Congress.

The committee also continued two other food programs that the administration's budget slated for extinction: the $28 million special milk program and a $33 million commodity food program that supplemented WIC benefits. The amount for the commodity program included $900,000 for pilot projects to supply extra food to the elderly.

International Programs, Agencies

The committee met the budget request of $1.028 billion for Food for Peace (PL 480) food donations abroad and low-interest loans for food purchases by foreign nations.

For the Food and Drug Administration (FDA), the bill cut nearly $26 billion from the requested amount for salaries and expenses, providing a total of $330 million. It also told the agency to maintain a special program to promote approval of "orphan drugs" — those that were overlooked by drug companies because they did not seem likely to yield enough profits to justify the expensive drug-approval process.

House Floor Action

The House Sept. 21 passed HR 7072 without amendment by a margin of more than two-to-one, despite Stockman's threat to recommend a presidential veto. The final vote was 264-105. *(Vote 325, p. 96-H)*

Before passing the bill, the House rejected, 125-246, an amendment offered by Robert S. Walker, R-Pa., to stretch the bill's $9.5 billion appropriation for food stamps to cover the full fiscal year. *(Vote 324, p. 96-H)*

Walker complained that the bill "institutionalized" supplemental appropriations, making it difficult to curb

federal spending. He said that the House should write money-saving changes into food stamp law, to keep spending within the $9.5 billion.

E. Thomas Coleman, R-Mo., responded, "We might kid ourselves that if we go with this amendment, that we are saving a couple of billion dollars more, but we all know that come next year when the money runs out and the people start writing us and clamoring that they are running out of food stamps, we know we are going to provide some sort of relief."

Senate Committee Action

Without waiting for the House to act, the Senate Appropriations Committee Sept. 16 reported a bill (S 2911 — S Rept 97-545) providing $25,155,989,000 in new budget authority for agriculture and related programs in fiscal 1983.

That amount was $2.1 billion more than the president requested but $149,000 less than the committee's allocation in the fiscal 1983 budget resolution for outlays for agriculture and food programs and related agencies. Additional money to keep food programs going for the entire fiscal year accounted for most of the $2.1 billion difference between the Senate committee bill and the House-passed figure.

The bill elicited some praise from Stockman for the way it treated food stamps and other feeding programs. Although the Senate panel provided for full-year funding at levels that were well over the budget request, Stockman commended the committee for funding the food programs within the fiscal 1983 budget resolution allocation. Stockman nevertheless found it necessary to warn that it would be "difficult for the administration to accept the bill in its present form" because of its "false savings."

The Senate panel also retained a House-passed, half-billion-dollar export promotion fund opposed by the administration.

After reporting its own bill, the Senate committee on Sept. 22 inserted the language of S 2911 under the House numbered bill and filed a renumbered report (S Rept 97-566) to go with HR 7072. The House bill, as amended, then was sent to the full Senate.

Agriculture Programs

For price support, research, crop insurance and other basic farm programs, the bill provided $6.3 billion, nearly $84 million less than the budget request and almost $49 million less than the House figure.

The panel approved $455 million for the Agricultural Research Service, $13 million less than the budget request and nearly $4 million more than the House amount.

The committee occasionally substituted its own priorities for those of the House. For example, it erased a $9 million House fund for operation of a human nutrition center at Tufts University in Boston, Mass., and instead earmarked $6 million for the Agriculture Department's nutrition center in North Dakota.

For the extension service, the panel provided $326.6 million, compared with a House figure of $327 million and a budget request of $312 million.

The Senate committee exceeded the House amount by $3.8 million and the budget request by $42.8 million in its $273 million allotment for the Animal and Plant Health Inspection Service. It reiterated a House warning against undercutting "proven" programs and added that adminis-

tration testimony had failed to provide "compelling justifications for [budget] reductions of such magnitude."

For the Food Safety and Inspection Service, the Senate committee provided $316 million, the same as the House amount. Like the House, it assumed savings from enactment of an administration proposal to permit periodic federal surveillance of meat and poultry processing plants instead of the continuous inspection required under existing law.

The committee also agreed with the House version in providing $7 million for the dairy indemnity program that the administration wanted to end. Almost all of the funds were intended to compensate Hawaiian milk producers for contamination of their herds by the pesticide heptachlor.

The Senate panel went significantly further than the House in trimming the budget request for the Federal Crop Insurance Corp. The committee's $528 million figure was $189 million lower than the budget request and $77 million less than the House aproved. "Lower-than-projected participation" in the program justified these cuts, the committee said in its report.

For reimbursement of CCC losses, the panel provided $3.8 billion, the same as the budget request and the House amount. Like the House, the Senate committee approved a requirement that the CCC spend not less than $500 million in fiscal 1983 in direct loans to finance exports of American farm commodities.

Rural Development

The committee approved a total of $3.4 billion for programs providing loans and grants to individual farms and for public services such as telephone, electric, water and waste disposal, conservation and industrial development. The committee's figure exceeded the budget request by $64 million and the House bill by $30 million.

Farmers Home Administration (FmHA). The committee provided a total of $4.5 billion for rural housing insurance, compared with a budget request of $2.3 billion and a House figure of $4.4 billion. The largest increase, as in the House bill, went for insured rural housing loans: $3.4 billion, compared with a $1.1 billion budget request. The committee ignored an administration request not to fund rent supplements; instead, it provided $174 million, $100 million more than the House.

In several rural rental housing programs, the committee recommended increases that, taken together, exceeded the budget request by $740 million. It said that since fewer Americans could afford to own homes, "the demand for affordable rental housing continues to increase."

For the Agricultural Credit Insurance Fund, which provides farming, recreation and emergency loans to individuals and associations, the Senate panel followed the budget requests and the House recommendations on most loan levels. It dropped a $22 million House increase for insured real estate loans but retained a $30 million appropriation added by the House for soil conservation loans that the administration had not requested.

The committee's $1.1 billion for the Rural Development Insurance Fund was $25 million less than the House figure but $350 million more than the budget request. Included was $300 million for water and sewer facility loans, $75 million less than the House and the same amount as requested. Also included was $350 million, $50 million more than the House, for guaranteed industrial development loans. The president did not want any funding of that program.

Rural Electrification Administration (REA) and Conservation Programs. Like the House, the Senate committee retained 1982 funding levels, totaling $1.1 billion, for REA insured electric and telephone loans. The administration had requested that those REA accounts be cut by $400 million. The committee also agreed with the House in adding $985 million to the $3.8 billion budget request for guaranteed electric loans and $30 million for the rural telephone bank. (Insured electric loans were made by the federal government, while guaranteed loans were made by banks or other private lenders, with a guarantee that the federal government would repay most of the loan if the borrower defaulted.)

Expressing concern over what it called "unacceptable" soil erosion problems, the panel increased the funding for conservation programs. The largest increase was for watershed and flood prevention operations of the Soil Conservation Service. The panel provided $195 million — $77 million more than the request and $5 million more than the House bill. Like the House, it provided $190 million for anti-erosion work on individual farms, for which farmers shared the costs. The budget had requested $56 million.

Food Programs

While the House accepted the budget requests for major food programs but cut the programs off months before the end of the fiscal year, the Senate committee provided full-year funding and significantly more money.

For child nutrition programs, including school lunches, the Senate bill provided $896 million, plus a transfer of Section 32 customs receipts, for a total of $3.2 billion. That was $352 million more than the House amount and the budget request.

For the Women, Infants and Children (WIC) program, the committee provided $1.06 billion, exceeding the House bill and the budget request by $408 million. Even that level of funding could force 100,000 persons out of the program, which served about 2.4 million people, according to the committee.

In its report, the Senate panel reiterated a House statement that, by improving the nutrition of needy pregnant and nursing women and young children, the WIC program prevented larger federal expenditures for such programs as Medicaid and special education. It criticized an administration plan to allow WIC food packages to include such items as chocolate milk and heavily sugared cereals. The committee barred implementation of "any regulation that would not maintain or enhance the nutritional integrity of foods available under WIC." It also rejected an administration proposal to transfer the program to the Department of Health and Human Services.

For food stamps, the committee provided $10.9 billion, $1.4 billion more than the House bill and the budget request. The higher Senate committee figure still was $404 million below fiscal 1982 spending and was consistent with program changes made in the budget reconciliation bill. (Details, p. 479)

However, the committee report noted that the total also assumed that inflation and unemployment rates would be "consistent with the administration's current projections," warning that food stamps would cost more should the projections prove "too optimistic." It barred benefit reductions without Congress "being given ample opportunity to consider required supplemental funding."

The committee expressed concern at the "apparent inadequacy" of the administration's model for predicting

food stamp costs, suggesting that "the relationship between food stamp costs and unemployment rates may not be accurate."

The committee also continued the special milk program and a food program that supplemented WIC, neither of which the administration wished to continue.

International Programs, Agencies

The Senate committee matched the House in meeting the budget request of $1.028 billion for Food for Peace (PL 480) contributions. Like the House, it reduced a $356 million request for Food and Drug Administration salaries and expenses by $26 million.

Senate Floor Action

The Senate Sept. 28 passed HR 7072 with amendments by a vote of 84-14. *(Vote 364, p. 62-S)*

The $25,155,989 Senate-passed version of the bill exceeded Reagan's budget requests by more than $2 billion. It also was larger than the House bill by the same amount, largely because the Senate provided full-year funding for food stamps and other food programs.

There were no attempts during the Senate debate to lower the committee's spending recommendations for food programs, nor were there concerted efforts to drop other features of the bill opposed by the administration.

During the floor debate, Thad Cochran, R-Miss., chairman of the Senate Appropriations Committee's Agriculture Subcommittee, acknowledged that the $10.9 billion in the Senate bill for food stamps was much more than the president had requested, but he pointed out that Congress had not approved all the program changes on which Reagan's request was based.

Amendments

Besides flouting a number of the administration's budget priorities, the Senate bill was a vehicle for two successful amendments dealing with conservation and dairy surpluses.

Cultivation on Erodible Land. The first amendment, which sponsors called the "sod buster" amendment, barred the payment of price supports, farm loans, crop insurance and other farm programs funded by the bill to farmers who cultivated highly erodible land, as determined by the soil classification system of the Soil Conservation Service (SCS). The amendment was adopted 69-29. *(Vote 360, p. 61-S)*

William L. Armstrong, R-Colo., sponsor of the amendment, argued that it was "counterproductive" for the federal government to bankroll farming practices that promoted erosion. He said Colorado farmers had plowed up thousands of acres of fragile sod in recent years "in a futile attempt to grow crops."

Given the scarcity of federal funds, the size of farm surpluses and the seriousness of erosion throughout the nation, federal dollars should not finance farming on fragile land, he said.

Armstrong said farm and conservation groups uniformly supported his amendment. But Cochran warned that the plan would be impossible to administer.

SCS official Keith Schmude said the amendment could take tens of millions of acres out of production.

Milk Content Standards. An amendment by S. I. "Sam" Hayakawa, R-Calif., to raise federal minimum standards for the amount of solids (protein, lactose and butterfat) in fresh milk, was adopted by voice vote after the Senate rejected, 28-70, a motion by Cochran to table, and thus kill, the proposal. *(Vote 363, p. 62-S)*

Hayakawa said his amendment would use up surplus dry milk because most dairymen would have to mix dry milk with their fresh milk to bring it up to the higher standard. The enriched milk tasted better and was more nutritious so consumers would buy more of it, Hayakawa maintained.

The senator acknowledged that milk would cost more, but he said "consumers are going to pay for the milk in one fashion or the other" — either at the grocery store or through the tax-supported federal dairy price support program.

Hayakawa said the higher solids standards in his amendment were the same as those that had been in force in California since the early 1970s. Those standards generally required producers to add some non-fat dry milk to fluid milk. Hayakawa said the nutritional value of milk would go up 20 to 33 percent under the new standard. Californians bought 23 percent more milk than the national average, he added.

Rudy Boschwitz, R-Minn., said the change was widely supported by dairy farmers in his state.

Cochran protested that the appropriations bill was an inappropriate vehicle for the amendment and argued that, at least in his state, consumers could not pay higher milk prices.

"Just because it is happening in California does not mean it is going to happen in Alabama or Mississippi or some of the other states that are not blessed with all the resources people may have in California," he said.

E. Linwood Tipton, executive vice president of the International Association of Ice Cream Manufacturers and of the Milk Industry Foundation, said the amendment would increase retail milk prices far more than Hayakawa indicated.

He predicted price hikes for raw milk of 5 cents a gallon for whole milk to 17 cents a gallon for low-fat milk. That would translate into even higher retail price hikes, Tipton warned. The foundation represented fluid milk processors and distributors.

Patrick B. Healy, secretary of the National Milk Producers Federation, endorsed the amendment and disputed Tipton's price predictions. He said farmers would not profit, but "I don't know what the hell the handlers will charge consumers."

Emergency Loans. The Senate adopted by voice vote an amendment by Walter D. Huddleston, D-Ky., and David L. Boren, D-Okla., to extend the economic emergency loan program for a year, provide $600 million in insured loans and mandate a one-year deferral of FmHA loan repayments for farmers meeting certain criteria. The amendment was accepted after the Senate rejected, 37-60, a Cochran tabling motion. *(Vote 362, p. 61-S)*

The provisions of the amendment had been approved by the Senate Agriculture Committee Sept. 27 as a separate bill (S 2960 — S Rept 97-591). The deferral language and loan program extension, plus lower limits on the maximum size of individual economic emergency loans, had been passed by the House Sept. 9 as part of another bill (HR 5831) setting new lending ceilings for FmHA loans. *(Story, p. 364)*

Huddleston said farm income had fallen for the third consecutive year and that there was "every indication that [in 1983] ... we are going to see U.S. net farm income fall

to about one-half of what it was just a few years ago." He said his amendment would give farmers a little breathing room, at negligible costs to the federal government.

Paula Hawkins, R-Fla., chairman of the Agriculture subcommittee with jurisdiction over farm credit programs, called the amendment "a dramatic political move late in an election year" and "window dressing for November."

Agriculture Committee Chairman Jesse Helms, R-N.C., also objected that the amendment would unduly restrict FmHA operations. He said the agency already was rescheduling and deferring loans on a case-by-case basis.

FmHA foreclosures totaled only one-fourth of 1 percent of its loans, and delinquencies had dropped from 58 percent in January 1981 to 25 percent in August 1982, according to Helms. As for the emergency loans, Helms said, "We simply do not have $600 million to put into this program."

Farm Exports. Also adopted by voice vote was an amendment by David Durenberger, R-Minn., to require implementation by Nov. 20, 1982, of a standby export program authorized by the 1981 farm bill (PL 97-98). That program provided for commodity export subsidies if the president judged them to be necessary to offset the effects of subsidies used by other nations. *(PL 97-98, 1981 Almanac p. 535)*

Durenberger said nothing had been done to put the new program in place and that it would be "a useful tool" for the U.S. delegation at trade talks scheduled for November.

Economic Forecasts. The Senate adopted by voice vote an amendment by Alan J. Dixon, D-Ill., to require that at least $66,000 be spent to prepare and publish quarterly forecasts of farm-sector receipts, production costs and net income for the 1983 crop year.

Earlier in the year the Agriculture Department had stopped publishing net income forecasts, which it had produced routinely since the 1940s, according to Dixon. He said Congress, lobbyists, farmers and agribusinesses needed to share "the same statistical information as a starting point for debate" on farm issues, and that failure to publish the forecasts heightened fears about farmers' economic problems.

WIC Funding. Budget Committee Chairman Pete V. Domenici, R-N.M., won approval by voice vote of an amendment to drop language in the bill requiring the administration to spend appropriated funds for the WIC special nutritional program, but only on condition that the administration promise not to propose any spending rescissions for the popular program in fiscal 1983.

The committee had written the directive into the bill because OMB delayed allocating WIC funds in 1981, causing the WIC program in one state to cease temporarily, according to Thomas F. Eagleton, D-Mo., the ranking Democrat on the Appropriations' Agriculture Subcommittee.

Domenici argued that the language violated the budget act and said OMB had authorized him "to state that the administration will not seek any deferrals or rescissions in the WIC program in 1983."

Grain Storage. The Senate rejected, 48-50, an amendment by Edward Zorinsky, D-Neb., to require storage payments to farmers in the grain reserve program to equal those made by the Agriculture Department to commercial storage facilities. *(Vote 361, p. 61-S)*

Zorinsky said paying more to commercial facilities was unfair. But Helms said they had higher costs for bonds and

insurance and had to guarantee higher quality grain.

Appropriations Compared

As passed by the House and Senate, HR 7072 made the following appropriations for fiscal 1983 *(in thousands of dollars)*:

	House-Passed Appropriation	Senate-Passed Appropriation
Agriculture Programs	$ 6,322,717	$ 6,274,229
Rural Development Programs	3,393,036	3,422,730
Domestic Food Programs	11,876,954	13,977,362
International Programs	1,102,525	1,109,539
Related Agencies	371,722	372,129
Total	$23,066,954	$25,155,989
Section 32 Transfers	2,287,346	2,287,346

Conference Report

A conference report (H Rept 97-957) on the bill was filed Sept. 10.

To assure enactment of HR 7072, House and Senate conferees at committee sessions Dec. 2 and 7 agreed to administration requests to drop controversial dairy and conservation amendments and revise a half-billion-dollar export loan fund.

In their final meeting Dec. 10, conferees settled the funding levels for the WIC special nutrition program and made implementation of a $500 million export credit fund optional.

However, conferees approved funding of major food programs at levels well above the original budget requests after forcing OMB Director Stockman to submit new requests totaling $1.8 billion for these programs. The new supplemental requests eliminated a major basis for earlier veto threats by Stockman, and the changes in dairy, conservation and farm credit provisions met other OMB objections.

"Everybody came out happy," House Appropriations Committee Chairman Whitten said.

Partial Funding Issue

The major difference between the House and Senate versions was that the House funded food stamps, child nutrition and WIC programs for only part of the fiscal year, assuming that supplemental appropriations enacted in 1983 would continue them. The Senate had provided full-year funding. Both bills assumed spending rates for these programs that were higher than the original budget requests.

Whitten refused to drop the less than full-year funding tactic without additional budget requests from the administration that recognized the need for higher spending levels. Eagleton objected, saying that the administration would allow WIC to die before requesting more money. He argued that the Senate plan should be approved.

Two new budget requests from Stockman arrived in time for conference action Dec. 7. They raised the administration requests to $10.8 billion for food stamps and $896 million for the nutrition programs. (Additional funds from customs receipts raised the total for the nutrition programs

to $3.2 billion.) On Dec. 9 OMB requested an extra $1.06 billion for WIC and $32.6 million for another supplemental nutrition program. These were approved by conferees Dec. 10.

Commodity Credit Corporation

In a decision that reflected mounting financial problems in the agriculture sector, conferees agreed to an additional $6.7 billion, for a total of $10.5 billion, for the CCC. The additional funds were requested by the administration because continuing low market prices had greatly increased farmers' use of CCC-run loan and grain reserve programs.

Dairy Programs

Another major conference decision was to drop the Senate-passed Hayakawa amendment to raise the federal minimum standard for the total solids content of fresh milk.

Whitten nearly succeeded Dec. 7 in inserting a second dairy plan into the bill. He proposed to cancel an unpopular 50-cent deduction in the price support payment of $13.10 per hundred pounds that farmers received, unless the administration put the federally owned dairy surplus up for sale to the highest bidder. Whitten argued that dairymen should not have to pay for storing products that the federal government was withholding from the market.

Reagan farm officials had been threatening for months to dump the dairy surplus on world markets at cut-rate prices, but the administration was not united on that strategy. Whitten's amendment would have forced such dumping, overriding objections from the State Department.

Sen. Cochran objected to the Whitten proposal, arguing that using the appropriations bill to change regulations already in existence was improper.

Senate conferees refused to accept Whitten's plan on a 4-4 tie vote.

Other Changes

In other action, the conferees:

● Eliminated the Senate-passed Armstrong amendment that would have withheld price supports and other farm program benefits from farmers who plowed up easily erodible land.

● Retained a one-year extension of the economic emergency loan program of the Farmers Home Administration that the Reagan administration wanted to end.

To avoid having to incorporate the program's $600 million appropriation in the congressional budget totals, conferees changed the program from insured to guaranteed loans.

● Dropped Senate-passed language mandating a one-year deferral of FmHA loan repayments to farmers meeting certain criteria. Instead, conferees added language to the conference report advising federal lenders to treat financially troubled farmers leniently.

● Reversed the effect of Senate language that barred the use of highly sugared cereals and chocolate milk in the WIC program, to permit these items to enter the program.

● Dropped a Senate-passed amendment requiring the administration to put into place an export subsidy program authorized by the 1981 farm bill. In addition to making use of the fund optional, conferees changed the language to specify that $500 million was to be the maximum amount that could be spent on the program. Both the House and Senate had specified that it would be the minimum amount that would be made available.   ∎

Congress Clears Interior Appropriations Bill

Congress Dec. 19 cleared for President Reagan a $7.5 billion fiscal 1983 appropriations bill (HR 7356 — PL 97-394) for the Interior Department and related agencies.

Final action came when the Senate Dec. 19 by voice vote approved a conference report (H Rept 97-978) on the bill that the House had adopted Dec. 18 by a 282-63 vote. *(Vote 453, p. 132-H)*

The conference report settled significant House-Senate differences in a number of areas — more often by addition than by subtraction. The final $7,500,025,000 bill was well above the $7,386,522,000 version originally passed by the House and the $7,391,607,000 bill passed by the Senate.

As cleared, the bill gave Reagan $923,065,000 more than the $6,576,960,000 in new budget authority he had requested. Much of the increase came in resource protection programs, energy conservation, and research on synfuels and alternative energy technologies.

The total funding was $136.21 million above the final fiscal 1982 appropriation.

HR 7356 raised an estimated $20.67 billion in revenue — nearly three times the appropriations it provided — through oil, gas and mineral leasing, timber sales and other activities.

As cleared, HR 7356 reined in Interior Secretary James G. Watt on two major issues where environmentalists had charged his interest in energy development was threatening natural resources. It banned until Sept. 30, 1983, oil and gas drilling in areas designated or under consideration as federally protected wilderness. *(Wilderness leasing, p. 461)*

It also exempted the California coastline north from Morro Bay to the Oregon line, and key areas off the New Jersey coast as well, from Watt's ambitious plan to offer most U.S. offshore areas for oil and gas leasing over the next five years.

The Senate had voted such protection only for the New Jersey coastal area and four northern California basins that had been exempted from leasing under the fiscal 1982 Interior appropriations bill. *(1981 Almanac p. 369)*

The House version included the entire California coastline north of Santa Maria. Conferees compromised on an area smaller than the House sought, but larger than the Senate wanted to protect.

The conference agreement cleared by Congress also included legislative language aimed at extending the deadline for lawsuits aimed at resolving certain Indian claims that arose prior to 1966. *(Story, p. 530)*

Final Provisions

The following is a comparison of the budget authority requested by President Reagan and appropriated under HR 7356 by Congress (*in millions of dollars*);

Agency	Budget Request	Final Amount
Interior Department	$3,551	$3,905
Energy Department	443	808
U.S. Forest Service	1,494	1,533
Other Agencies	1,089	1,254
Total	$6,577	$7,500

House Committee Action

The House Appropriations Interior Subcommittee approved HR 7356 Nov. 18, and the full committee reported it Dec. 2 (H Rept 97-942), voting $7.387 billion in funds for fiscal 1983. The total was $809.56 million above the $6.577 billion sought by President Reagan.

The bill reported by the committee extended until Sept. 30, 1983, the ban on oil and gas leasing in wilderness areas that had been included in the first continuing appropriations resolution for fiscal 1983 (H J Res 599 — PL 97-276). (*1st continuing resolution, p. 225*)

It also renewed and expanded a ban on offshore leasing along the California coast that was part of the fiscal 1982 Interior appropriations bill.

The committee voted major increases over Reagan's budget requests for park land acquisition, energy conservation, fossil energy research and development — especially "synfuels" projects. It also substantially increased, over the administration request, funding for the National Endowment for the Arts and the National Endowment for the Humanities.

House Floor Action

The House passed HR 7356 Dec. 3 by a 275-73 vote. (*Vote 388, p. 116-H*)

As passed, the bill was essentially unchanged from the $7.387 billion version reported by the Appropriations Committee.

During the floor debate, however, the House added new language to the ban on oil and gas leasing off the California coast. It adopted an amendment by Rep. Jim Courter, R-N.J., that banned leasing in certain environmentally sensitive fish and shellfish breeding grounds off the coast of New Jersey. Courter said the ban affected 1.5 percent of tracts to be offered for sale in April 1983.

Parks

The House approved expenditures of $260.2 million for the Land and Water Conservation Fund, which finances acquisition of federal and state park land. Of that, $75 million was earmarked for the states. The Reagan administration had requested $69.4 million for the federal part of the fund but sought to eliminate the state grants entirely. Congress had appropriated $149.2 million for the fund in fiscal 1982.

In the category of park management, the administra-

tion requested $482.5 million, up from $473.7 million appropriated in fiscal 1982. The House increased that total to $511.2 million.

Energy

Some of the sharpest differences with Reagan were evident in the energy area, as the House voted far more funds than the president sought for conservation and for fossil energy research and development.

In fiscal 1982, Congress appropriated some $145.4 million in new budget authority for energy conservation. Reagan sought to slash that to $21.8 million in fiscal 1983, but the House refused to go along — providing $317.8 million directly and another $64 million through transfers from other programs.

Funding for fossil energy research and development was set at $413 million in fiscal 1982, but Reagan asked only $105 million for fiscal 1983. This category involved synfuel projects such as coal gasification and other exotic fuel processing and combustion technologies. Again, the House refused to go along with Reagan's cuts, voting to provide $297 million for this program.

Senate Committee Action

The Senate Appropriations Committee Dec. 8 approved a $7.392 billion version of HR 7356 after stripping from the House-passed version some riders aimed at thwarting Reagan administration energy and land policies.

However, the Senate panel joined the Democratic-controlled House in continuing until Sept. 30, 1983, an existing ban on oil and gas leasing in federal wilderness areas and areas under study for wilderness designation.

The House bill took sharp issue with nearly every major policy thrust by Interior Secretary Watt: offshore drilling, wilderness oil and gas leasing, park land acquisition, park maintenance, energy conservation, synfuels research, coal leasing, payments in lieu of taxes, Indian health and education, and the arts and humanities endowments.

But the Senate bill, influenced by James A. McClure, R-Idaho, chairman of the Senate Appropriations Interior Subcommittee, was more in line with Watt's proposals.

Both versions exceeded the administration's $6.6 billion budget request.

Wilderness Leasing

The critical test of strength on the long-simmering wilderness leasing issue came Dec. 8 in a series of four votes that in effect sent to the Senate floor the legislative language favored by environmentalists.

The House Aug. 12 passed a bill (HR 6542) banning wilderness leasing, but that measure and a companion Senate bill (S 2801) introduced by Henry M. Jackson, D-Wash., remained bottled up in the Senate Energy and Natural Resources Committee, which McClure also chaired.

In the full Appropriations Committee, Dennis DeConcini, D-Ariz., proposed an amendment to HR 7356 that was equivalent to S 2801.

McClure offered as a substitute an amendment that would ban leasing in areas designated or recommended as wilderness areas but would permit it in areas under study for wilderness; would legislatively declare the "sufficiency" of environmental impact statements for the U.S. Forest Service's last nationwide wilderness study (RARE II),

blocking further legal challenges by environmentalists; and would allow seismic testing in wilderness oil exploration.

Both sides agreed to divide the McClure amendment into its three parts, with separate votes on each.

The first vote was on language to allow explosive seismic testing. The panel rejected such testing 11-13 on a roll-call vote. The second part of McClure's amendment, language to exclude wilderness study areas from the leasing ban, was rejected 3-5 on a show of hands. The third part, declaring the legal sufficiency of RARE II environmental impact statements, was rejected 3-6 on a show of hands.

The committee then approved DeConcini's original amendment on a voice vote.

Offshore Drilling

Like the House, the Senate Appropriations Committee banned spending to process leases for energy exploration on certain parts of the outer continental shelf (OCS).

This ban partly thwarted a controversial five-year OCS leasing plan that Watt approved July 21. Watt hoped to speed energy development by offering oil companies leases of up to one billion acres, nearly the entire OCS, over the next five years. *(Story, p. 448)*

The House bill renewed and expanded a ban on leasing in four basins off the northern California coast that was part of the fiscal 1982 Interior appropriations bill. It included all of the California coastline north of Santa Maria, but excluded the Santa Barbara Channel where large oil discoveries were announced in November.

Added on the House floor was a separate ban covering certain environmentally sensitive fish and shellfish breeding grounds off the coast of New Jersey.

The bill approved by Senate Appropriations, however, was less restrictive of drilling. It included only the four northern California basins that were in the 1982 bill.

The Senate committee added $3.7 million to the $115.1 million the House voted to manage offshore leasing. The administration had estimated that revenues as high as $15 billion could come from the leases in fiscal 1983 — but that estimate was not expected to be met.

Parks

The House approved expenditures of $260.2 million for the Land and Water Conservation Fund, which was used for acquisition of federal and state park land, while the Senate Appropriations Committee approved $203.9 million.

Senate Appropriations also approved an amendment adopted in subcommittee that increased the fee visitors pay for using transportation facilities in national parks when those facilities required federal subsidies. The measure had originally applied only to the shuttle bus at Yosemite National Park, but was expanded to cover other parks as well.

Generally, national parks fared better in the House than in Senate Appropriations or in the administration's budget request. In the critical category of park management, the administration requested $482.5 million, up from $473.7 million appropriated in fiscal 1982. The House increased that to $511.2 million, but the Senate committee reduced the funding to $478.7 million.

Abandoned Mine Reclamation

One of the items that significantly raised the total in the bill sent by the Interior Subcommittee to Senate Appropriations was an amendment offered by Walter D.

Huddleston, D-Ky., to add $200 million to the Abandoned Mine Reclamation Fund as a jobs-creating measure for economically depressed Appalachian coal states.

McClure agreed to create room under the budget ceiling for part of Huddleston's request by a series of small cuts totaling $51.6 million in what he called the "big-ticket items" — park land acquisition, energy research, energy conservation, Indian programs and national parks.

In return, Huddleston reduced his mine reclamation request to $55 million for fiscal 1983. He said it was unlikely the states could spend the money much faster than that because of administrative hurdles to be cleared in the mine reclamation program. McClure pledged that as states demonstrated a capacity to spend more, he would join in asking for a supplemental appropriation to provide the funds.

Coal Leasing

Administration coal-leasing policies also came under attack in a rider offered by Sen. Dale Bumpers, D-Ark., who moved to cut $2.13 million from the Bureau of Land Management's (BLM) budget for processing coal leases. That amount had been added by the Senate Appropriations Interior Subcommittee to the $13.66 million approved by the House. Bumpers said that extra money would allow BLM to lease an additional 3.7 billion tons of coal in two sales this year.

Bumpers and other critics of administration coal policy said the Treasury was not receiving fair market value for coal lands Watt leased, because BLM had set minimum bids too low and was quickly selling large amounts of coal at a time when coal company reserves were high. McClure, however, said that some of those reserves had to be dedicated through long-term contracts to minehead power plants to make construction of the plants economically feasible.

Bumpers, admitting he lacked the votes to approve his amendment in committee, withdrew it, saying he would offer it on the floor.

Payments in Lieu of Taxes

In areas where the federal government holds large areas of land within a municipality, Congress appropriates funds to compensate local governments for the tax revenues they could not collect on federal lands.

Despite its "new federalism" policy initiative, the Reagan administration proposed only $45 million for such payments in fiscal 1983 as compared to levels close to $100 million actually appropriated in fiscal 1980, 1981 and 1982.

The House voted payments of $95.5 million and the Senate committee raised them to $96.3 million.

Forest Service

U.S. Forest Service programs accounted for a sizable part of the increase made by Senate Appropriations over the House bill. The administration requested $1.494 billion for all Forest Service programs, and the House approved a spending level of $1.485 billion. But the Senate subcommittee raised that to $1.522 billion.

That increase came in spending for timber sales and road construction. While such funding was favored by the badly depressed U.S. timber industry, environmentalists opposed too much road construction and said the timber industry could not sell the timber it had already bought from the government.

Energy Research, Conservation

For fossil energy research and development — mainly "synfuels" such as gasified or liquefied coal and other exotic fuel processing and combustion technologies — the House voted $297 million, but the Senate Appropriations Committee slashed that to about $242.5 million.

A similar tug of war took place on energy conservation. At their peak in fiscal 1980, federal energy conservation programs received $750 million in appropriations. Funding declined to $145.4 million in new budget authority in fiscal 1982, and Reagan requested $21.8 million for fiscal 1983.

The House refused to go along with the administration, voting to appropriate $317.8 million in new budget authority and transfer another $64 million to that purpose from other accounts — for a total of $381.8 million.

The Senate Appropriations Committee voted a total of $293.5 million for energy conservation.

Indian Programs

The House approved total spending of $1.775 billion for Indian programs in nine categories in its version of HR 7356. That was $45.9 million above the administration request for those categories, and down $11.9 million from the amount appropriated in the same bill for fiscal 1982.

The House and the Senate committee approved spending close to the administration's $1.022 billion request for the Bureau of Indian Affairs.

But in Department of Health and Human Services Indian programs, the administration proposed a cut from 1982 levels to $613.3 million, the House moved that up to $682.5 million, and the Senate committee voted $654.5 million.

Arts, Humanities Endowments

Both the House and the Senate committee voted more funds than the administration sought for federal cultural programs, particularly those administered by the National Endowment for the Arts and the National Endowment for the Humanities.

The administration proposed $196.9 million in total for both programs, while the House approved $274.4 million and the Senate committee reported $273.9 million.

Senate Floor Action

The Senate passed HR 7356 Dec. 14 by 84-9. *(Vote 404, p. 69-S)*

The action came after two days of debate during which the Senate adopted several minor amendments and a slightly modified version of the wilderness leasing ban approved by the Appropriations Committee.

Among the amendments adopted by voice vote was one by Sen. William Armstrong, R-Colo., to permit the secretary of interior to lease off-tract sites to the holder of a federal oil shale lease to facilitate extraction of the oil. Armstrong said the authority was needed because at least one oil shale project in Colorado had been shut down since operators lacked authority to dispose of spent oil shale at an offsite location.

The only major floor fight occurred over a proposed amendment by Bumpers to delete from the bill $2.3 million for the Bureau of Land Management's coal leasing program. The House had cut that much from the administration's $15.79 million budget request for coal leasing.

Bumpers argued that the administration was not getting fair value for its coal leases, and that deletion of the

funds would block the leasing of another 2.7 billion tons of coal in late 1983. "I have serious reservations about why we should be leasing land when we have got coal leases galore," Bumpers said.

McClure said that deleting the $2 million would mean the loss in 1983 of $12 million in bonuses that would be bid if the coal leases were put up for sale. "So to save $2 million we lost $12 million. That is not a particularly good deal," he said.

The Bumpers amendment was narrowly defeated, 47-48. *(Vote 400, p. 68-S)*

Interior Department

The total administration request for the Interior Department was $3.52 billion. The House raised the amount to $3.71 billion, and the Senate boosted it still further to $3.82 billion.

In some areas where the House bill differed sharply from Reagan's request, the Senate was more sympathetic. For national park operations, for example, the administration asked $539.70 million, up slightly from the $521.53 million Congress appropriated in fiscal 1982. The House boosted this to $567.73 million, but the Senate cut it back to about $537 million.

On the other hand, both chambers voted far more than the $69.37 million Reagan had sought for park land acquisition under the Land and Water Conservation Fund. The Senate approved $203.88 million, and the House voted $260.23 million.

Mindful of high unemployment in Appalachian coal fields, both chambers added to Reagan's $97.65 million request for the Abandoned Mine Reclamation Fund. The House pushed the total up to $126.61 million, and the Senate approved $152.65 million.

Forest Service

The administration sought $1.49 billion for the U.S. Forest Service. The House voted $1.48 billion, but the Senate approved $1.55 billion, with big increases for timber sales and road construction.

The Senate cut out the entire $20 million the House had voted for the Youth Conservation Corps, hewing to the administration's request for no funds.

Energy Department

Both House and Senate gave the administration far more for the Energy Department than the $443.06 million it requested. The House approved $926.76 million in new budget authority, while the Senate voted $826.15 million.

Much of that increase came in fossil energy research and development — mostly "synfuels" projects. While the administration requested $106.90 million for fossil research, the House approved $297.06 million and the Senate $247.51 million.

Much of the remaining Energy Department add-on came in energy conservation programs. The administration had asked $21.8 million — which would have ended most energy conservation programs now run by the department. But the House refused to go along, giving conservation programs $317.79 million in new budget authority. The Senate voted $264.53 million in new budget authority for the programs. Both bills allotted additional funds for conservation programs through transfers.

Approved in the Interior appropriations bill — but not included in its totals — was a hefty $2.07 billion expenditure for buying oil to put in the Strategic Petroleum Re-

serve, the funding requested by the administration. That amount compared with $3.68 billion for fiscal 1982 and $2.69 billion for fiscal 1981.

Formerly counted in budget totals, the Strategic Petroleum Reserve went "off-budget" in fiscal 1982, when pressure to cut the budget and fill the reserve mounted simultaneously. *(1981 Almanac p. 449)*

Conference

House-Senate conferees reached agreement late Dec. 16 on a $7.5 billion compromise version of HR 7356 (H Rept 97-978).

One conference compromise involved funds for coal leasing on federal lands in the West.

Conferees adopted the Senate funding levels but voted delays of at least three months for two coal lease sales planned in fiscal 1983, putting one of them off until fiscal 1984.

Another compromise involved the Youth Conservation Corps, which Reagan and the Senate had sought to eliminate but the House had funded at $20 million. Conferees kept the program alive at a funding level of $10 million.

The conference committee increased funding for strip mining enforcement and abandoned mine reclamation above levels in either the House or Senate bills, and also boosted funding for the U.S. Forest Service, primarily for timber sales. ∎

D.C. Appropriations Bill

Congress Dec. 18 cleared for the president a bill (HR 7144 — PL 97-378) making fiscal 1983 appropriations for the District of Columbia.

Final action came when the Senate by voice vote adopted a conference report (H Rept 97-972) on the measure that the House had approved Dec. 17 by a 288-79 vote. *(Vote 448, p. 132-H)*

Final Provisions

The measure appropriated $524,180,100 in federal funds and $1,998,841,900 in funds from the District's own treasury. The federal funding was $55.69 million less than requested by President Reagan and nearly $33 million less than the fiscal 1982 appropriation. It was the same level approved by the Senate Dec. 7, and $21.29 million below the House version.

The allocation from the District's own treasury was $7.1 million below the president's request but $33.08 million above fiscal 1982 appropriations. It was $27.19 million more than the House figure but $71.07 million less than the Senate had approved.

The bill included a federal payment to the city for revenue losses and operating costs associated with its role as the national capital; payment for water and sewer services; retirement fund contributions; loans to the District for capital projects; and funds for libraries, day care and other city services. The public schools received $306 million, the full budget request.

It also included $3.1 million for a special effort to reduce crime in the city. The money was to go to the city's police department to purchase equipment and to the U.S. attorney's office to hire more prosecutors.

The conference agreement also contained $20 million

for retirement of an accumulated deficit, and funds for two local jobs programs cut by the House.

House Action

HR 7144 was reported by the House Appropriations Committee Sept. 21 (H Rept 97-849).

It was passed by voice vote Sept. 30.

As passed, the bill appropriated $545.5 million in federal funds, including a federal payment to the city of $336.6 million. It provided for expenditures of $1.97 billion from the District's own treasury.

The bill included language to withhold the federal payment until there were at least 3,880 officers on the city's police force. Rep. Julian C. Dixon, D-Calif., chairman of the Appropriations D.C. Subcommittee, said that number of officers had been mandated and funded since 1981, but the total complement never had been hired.

During House floor debate, points of order were sustained against language in the bill that sought to prohibit the city from booking certain events at its new Washington Convention Center. The Appropriations Committee had recommended banning such events as concerts or theatrical productions that could place the center in competition with existing facilities in the region.

Del. Walter E. Fauntroy, D-D.C., raised the point of order, arguing that the provision violated House rules by legislating on an appropriations bill. His objection was sustained.

Senate Action

The Senate passed HR 7144 Dec. 7 after adopting an amendment that removed proposed restrictions on the use of the city's new $100 million convention center.

The spending measure was approved 71-22. *(Vote 393, p. 67-S)*

The Senate bill included $27.5 million more than the version passed by the House Sept. 30 and $16 million more than the fiscal 1982 appropriation. However, it rescinded $48.8 million in previously appropriated capital loan authority that was never used, according to Alfonse D'Amato, R-N.Y., chairman of the District of Columbia Appropriations Subcommittee.

In addition to the federal funds, the Senate bill allowed spending of $2 billion from the District's own treasury for operating expenses and capital outlay projects. The House bill approved $1.97 billion in spending from the city's treasury.

Convention Center. Floor debate focused on language in the bill that would have prohibited the District from using its convention center for concerts, athletic events and other entertainment activities that could place the center in competition with existing facilities in the region.

The Senate agreed by voice vote to delete the restrictive language, which also was removed from the House bill in September.

Thomas F. Eagleton, D-Mo., sponsor of an amendment to strike the language, said the provision amounted to "dictatorial" congressional intrusion into the District's affairs. He warned that the city would lose money if the center could be used only for conventions or trade shows.

Eagleton also charged that efforts to limit the center's use were based on "the greed of Mr. Abe Pollin," owner of the Capital Centre in Landover, Md., a nearby arena that could face competition from the new facility.

But Patrick J. Leahy, D-Vt., who wanted to restrict

convention center activities, said Eagleton's amendment would allow the city "to enter into a commercial enterprise with none of the risks which most business people have to take."

A Leahy-D'Amato compromise to allow concerts and athletic games if they were for educational or charitable purposes was defeated 40-54. Eagleton's amendment was then adopted by voice vote. *(Vote 392, p. 66-S)* ∎

$10.6 Billion Approved for DOT, Agencies

President Reagan Dec. 18 signed into law (HR 7019 — PL 97-369) a $10.6 billion appropriations bill for the Department of Transportation (DOT) and related agencies in fiscal 1983.

Both the House and Senate by voice votes Dec. 16 adopted a conference committee compromise (H Rept 97-960) on the measure, clearing the bill for the president.

The conference agreement, filed Dec. 13, appropriated about $250 million more than Reagan's original request and $74 million less than his amended request. The conference total was $103 million less than appropriated in regular and supplemental appropriations for transportation in fiscal 1982.

The House version, passed Sept. 21, would have provided almost $11.2 billion in fiscal 1983; the Senate bill, passed Dec. 2, would have appropriated $10.96 billion.

The final bill did not include any funds for federal highway and mass transit programs that states and communities with federal approval substitute for planned Interstate Highway additions; this was because some $883 million in new budget authority had been appropriated for that purpose by the so-called first continuing appropriations resolution for fiscal 1983 (PL 97-276) enacted in late October. That emergency measure was needed to continue the operations of federal departments and agencies, including DOT, whose regular appropriation had not been approved by Congress by the start of the fiscal year. *(Story, p. 225)*

The compromise did contain a provision denying highway funds to states that did not permit trucks 102-inches wide on primary and Interstate highways, up from the current federal minimum of 96 inches. Efforts to delete the proposal had failed in the Senate.

The agreement also appropriated $500,000, inserted in the Senate version, to help states compensate billboard owners for signs taken down in accordance with highway beautification law.

Highlights of the bill included:

● A ceiling of $8.1 billion on spending from the Highway Trust Fund for fiscal 1983 highway construction and related programs, an increase of $400 million over Reagan's request of $7.7 billion. The fiscal 1982 ceiling was $8 billion. A highway and mass transit authorization that hiked highway taxes by five cents was later enacted (HR 6211 — PL 97-424) and set the trust fund ceiling at $12.1 billion. *(Story, p. 317)*

● A ceiling of $600 million on obligations from the Airport and Airway Trust Fund for airport development, $150 million more than Reagan originally requested but which matched an amended request in September.

● $2.4 billion for the Coast Guard, including $1.5 billion for operating expenses.

● $700 million for Amtrak, the federally subsidized passenger railroad, $100 million more than requested. *(Amtrak authorization, 1981 Almanac p. 565)*

● $3.2 billion for urban mass transit programs, including $1.6 billion for discretionary grants for urban capital projects, such as bus and rail purchases, and $1.2 billion for formula grants for both operating and capital subsidies. Reagan had requested a total of $3.15 billion for transit.

Final Appropriations

As cleared by Congress, HR 7019 (PL 97-369) appropriated the following amounts for fiscal 1983:

	Budget Request	Final Appropriation
Department of Transportation		
Office of the Secretary	$ 49,500,000	$ 44,900,000
Coast Guard	2,280,817,350	2,402,848,350
Federal Aviation Administration	3,129,841,000	3,298,197,000
Federal Highway Administration	161,305,000	13,177,000
National Highway Traffic Safety Administration	81,600,000	74,000,000
Federal Railroad Administration	831,575,000	919,675,000
Urban Mass Transportation Administration	3,150,075,000	3,200,831,000
Research and Special Programs Administration	21,300,000	20,022,000
Office of the Inspector General	24,946,000	24,946,000
Subtotal	9,730,959,350	9,998,596,350
Related Agencies		
Architectural and Transportation Barriers Compliance Board	—	2,020,000
National Transportation Safety Board	17,700,000	19,970,000
Civil Aeronautics Board	72,900,000	71,525,000
Interstate Commerce Commission	69,000,000	65,600,000
Panama Canal Commission	452,589,000	434,024,000
U.S. Railway Association	2,000,000	2,950,000
Washington Metropolitan Area Transit Authority	51,663,569	51,663,569
Subtotal	665,852,569	647,752,569
GRAND TOTAL	$10,396,811,919	$10,646,348,919

House Committee Action

The House Appropriations Committee reported HR 7019 on Aug. 19 (H Rept 97-783).

The committee criticized cutbacks in the administration's transportation budget, recommending $802.5 million more than Reagan requested. The committee bill provided almost $11.2 billion in new budget authority for the Transportation Department (DOT) and related agencies in fiscal 1983 — $943 million more than Congress approved in regular and supplemental transportation appropriations bills for fiscal 1982.

The committee said it did not agree with the executive branch "that the budget requested by the administration is sufficient to meet our transportation challenges. As past experience has shown, decreases in capital investments result in the deferral of necessary construction and maintenance work and a more rapid deterioration of our transportation facilities."

There was "an essential federal role in developing, maintaining and improving our transportation system," the committee said, pointing out that "despite this traditional federal support" the administration's requests "were nearly 20 percent less than the fiscal year 1981 appropriations."

MAJOR FUNDING

As reported, major transportation programs funded by the bill were:

Office of the Secretary

The bill provided $37.5 million for the transportation secretary's office, $4 million less than requested for fiscal 1983 but $3 million more than the 1982 appropriation. The committee expressed dissatisfaction with the size of the secretary's policy staff, and it directed that any staff reductions in 1983 be taken primarily from this office.

Coast Guard

The committee bill recommended $2.295 billion for the Coast Guard, $357.8 million more than the administration's original request, but only $14.6 million more than its amended request. The committee version was $122.2 million less than the 1982 level because of a one-time transfer of $300 million from the Defense Department for fiscal 1983.

The bill included about $1.6 billion for operating expenses, $213.8 million more than provided in fiscal 1982. The total was intended to provide a total staffing level of 37,425 military positions and 4,757 civilian positions, the number requested by the administration. Also approved was $287 million for capital acquisition, construction and improvement programs.

The committee directed the Coast Guard to restore aircraft patrols in Alaska. It said law enforcement activities in the Southeast should not "be maintained at the expense of other vital national and international interests of this country." The panel asked the Coast Guard for an analysis of the Haitian refugee interdiction operation to determine the cost effectiveness of continuing the current level of operations.

Federal Aviation Administration (FAA)

The panel recommended $2.456 billion for FAA operations and maintenance of the national air traffic control system, $93 million less than requested but $361.8 million more than the 1982 level. The panel's recommendation included $1 billion from the Airport and Airway Trust Fund, although the administration requested $2 billion from the trust fund, which was financed by taxes on airline tickets and general aviation fuel.

The committee denied $61 million requested by the administration for increased pay for air traffic controllers pending enactment of the authorizing legislation. The panel approved 1,899 new staff positions at air traffic control centers and towers.

The committee approved $375.5 million in new budget authority, plus $7.45 million in transferred funds from other accounts, for modernizing facilities and equipment for the airway system. The $375.5 million was $49.47 million less than requested.

The committee deferred action on another $300 million the administration planned to request after aviation tax legislation was enacted. The request was made in September. The tax bill (HR 4961 — PL 97-248) was signed into law Sept. 3. The funds were to be used for the administration's multibillion-dollar modernization of the air traffic control system.

Federal Highway Administration (FHWA)

The committee recommended $8.5 billion in fiscal 1983 for highway programs, including the $8 billion ceiling on contract authority obligations from the trust fund. The new budget authority recommended by the panel was $652.67 million more than requested by the administration and $112.2 million more than the 1982 level.

Much of the increase was due to a proposed $500 million appropriation for highway projects that states and communities substituted for previously planned Interstate Highway segments. Reagan had requested $150 million.

National Highway Traffic Safety Administration (NHTSA)

The committee recommended $170 million for NHTSA programs, $11.4 million more than the budget request and $2.6 million more than the 1982 level. The total included a $100 million ceiling on obligations for state and community highway safety grants. The administration had requested $77 million.

The committee provided $70 million for NHTSA operations and research, $11.6 million less than requested and $4.9 million less than appropriated for 1982.

Federal Railroad Administration (FRA)

As reported, the bill included $12.3 million for the FRA administrator's office, $3.3 million less than requested for fiscal 1983. The FRA budget, under the committee bill, would be funded at $1.03 billion, $202.8 million more than the budget request but $267.96 million less than the 1982 amount.

The panel recommended $23.2 million in new budget authority for certain railroad safety programs plus $2 million in transfer funds. The administration requested $29.3 million. The committee concurred with an administration decision not to provide any funds for a federal program that had financed 50 percent of the salaries and expenses of state rail safety inspectors.

An additional $20 million was provided for labor protection benefits for employees of Conrail, the federally subsidized freight railroad. The panel also recommended

$115 million, the same as the budget request, for improvements to the Northeast rail corridor, which ran from Washington, D.C., to Boston. *(1981 Almanac p. 561)*

The $788 million approved by the committee for Amtrak was the same as the authorized amount for fiscal 1983. Amtrak officials said the budget request of $600 million would have required suspending service on 37 percent of its route.

Urban Mass Transportation Administration (UMTA)

The panel recommended a total of $3.64 billion in fiscal 1983 for UMTA activities, $493 million more than Reagan proposed but $82 million less than the 1982 appropriation.

While the administration had requested $1 billion for urban formula grants, the committee provided $1.3 billion. That amount still was $65 million less than the 1982 appropriation. The portion of the formula grants program that could be used for operating subsidies was funded at $735 million, almost $300 million more than Reagan requested. The administration sought to end operating subsidies by fiscal 1985.

The $1.63 billion for discretionary capital grants was $50.5 million less than the 1982 level; but that year's appropriation had included $220 million in previously deferred appropriations and $11 million in transfer funds.

In its report, the committee said $880 million should be transferred from the discretionary grant program to the formula program if the authorizing legislation were enacted.

The committee included $365 million for transit projects that replaced certain Interstate segments dropped by the states and communities. The budget had included $400 million for transit projects; $538 million had been provided in fiscal 1982.

Civil Aeronautics Board (CAB)

The bill included $24.35 million for the CAB, a decrease of $150,000 from the budget request and $1.15 million less than the 1982 level. The panel noted that the board's authority over fares and rates ended Dec. 31, 1982, as a result of the 1978 airline deregulation law (PL 95-504). *(1978 Almanac p. 496)*

The committee provided $48.4 million, the full budget request, for subsidies to air carriers to continue service to small communities. One of these programs, funded by the committee at $14 million for fiscal 1983, ended Sept. 30, 1983, as a result of the deregulation law.

Interstate Commerce Commission (ICC)

The committee provided $66.3 million for the ICC, $2.7 million less than requested and $3.85 million less than the 1982 appropriation. The amount was less than the administration's proposal because the committee said the General Services Administration (GSA) was charging too much for office space.

United States Railway Association (USRA)

The USRA received $2 million under the committee bill, the full budget request but $7 million less than appropriated for 1982. USRA, which monitored Conrail, was scheduled to go out of business by the end of 1983. *(1981 Almanac p. 561)*

The committee noted that it had not received a budget request for Conrail subsidies, and thus did not include any funds for the freight system in the bill. Conrail in 1981

made its first profit after five years of losses. The committee prohibited the sale or transfer of any Conrail securities held by the federal government without prior approval of the House and Senate Appropriations committees.

House Floor Action

Disregarding warnings that Reagan might veto the measure because of its cost, the House Sept. 21 passed HR 7019 by a 268-119 vote. *(Vote 323, p. 96-H)*

It provided $802.5 million more than Reagan requested.

The overall appropriations in the House-approved bill was the same as that recommended by the Appropriations Committee.

Veto Threat

Reagan advisers let it be known they could not recommend that the president sign the bill. "A distinct veto signal was sent" to House members, a spokesman for the Office of Management and Budget (OMB) said.

The bill was below the fiscal 1983 budget resolution allocations for new discretionary budget authority for transportation programs by only $81 million. Administration officials argued that when expected additional requests were incorporated, transportation appropriations actually would be $525 million above the allocations. Opponents also contended that the bill was $750 million above targets for outlays.

The bill's sponsors said the $11.2 billion total was essential to help maintain the nation's transportation network, even though they recognized the need for budgetary restraint.

Amendments

By a 154-221 vote, the House rejected an amendment offered by Lawrence Coughlin, R-Pa., ranking minority member of the Appropriations Transportation Subcommittee, that would have cut $320 million from various DOT programs. For example, $100 million would have been struck from mass transit formula grants and $88 million from Amtrak subsidies. *(Vote 321, p. 96-H)*

"It seems to me that it is worth taking this very modest step to try and assure that we have a bill that will be enacted into law and will be signed by the president," Coughlin said.

But William Lehman, D-Fla., acting subcommittee chairman, opposed the amendment, saying, "I do not agree that we can reduce highway, rail and transit programs by $320 million and still have a bill which is responsible and responsive to the transportation needs of our nation."

The House also rejected, by a 38-349 vote, an amendment by David R. Obey, D-Wis., that would have cut all accounts and programs in the bill by 33.8 percent. *(Vote 322, p. 96-H)*

Coast Guard

The House adopted an amendment offered by Gerry E. Studds, D-Mass., to increase Coast Guard operating funds by transferring $14 million from its retired pay account. It was approved by voice vote, bringing the total operating funds for the Coast Guard to over $1.6 billion. It did not affect the total new budget authority contained in the bill.

Senate Committee Action

The Senate Appropriations Committee Sept. 16 reported its version of the fiscal 1983 DOT appropriations bill (S 2914 —S Rept 97-546), providing $11.56 billion in new budget authority.

Rather than wait for the House to complete its deliberations, the panel considered its own bill in an effort to speed up action on the measure. On Sept. 22 the committee incorporated its version in the House-numbered bill and refiled its report with a new number (S Rept 97-567).

As reported, HR 7019, according to the committee, was $836 million larger than the president's budget after including supplemental budget requests of $323.5 million sought by the administration but not formally sent to Congress by the time the committee considered the bill. Not counting the supplemental amount, the committee version still was $512.5 million more than the budget request.

The committee said there could be no substantial economic growth and improvement in the balance of trade "without a strong, steadfast and certain commitment to the continued improvement in our transportation investments."

"Good roads are not a luxury," the committee argued. "They are an essential component to running an efficient transportation system. Our nation's economic strength depends to an increasing degree on our ability to compete with production from abroad. The cost of transportation is a significant component of that cost."

For that reason, the panel explained, it had recommended a higher ceiling ($8.1 billion) on obligations from the Highway Trust Fund than did the administration ($7.7 billion).

While the committee did not make specific recommendations, it did say the federal government should exercise its power to raise additional revenue for building and repairing the nation's highways and mass transit systems. The existing 4-cents-a-gallon gasoline tax did not raise enough funds, the panel said.

Transportation Secretary Drew Lewis throughout the year had lobbied for a 5-cents-a-gallon increase in the tax, and Congress eventually approved the hike as its last major legislative action of the 1982 lame-duck session. *(Details, p. 317)*

Office of the Secretary

The bill provided $41.7 million in new budget authority for the transportation secretary's office in fiscal 1983, $4.2 million more than provided by the House and the same as the administration request. The panel disagreed with the House Appropriations Committee's directive that any additional staff reductions in fiscal 1983 should be made primarily in the secretary's policy staff.

Coast Guard

The committee recommended a total of $2.45 billion for the Coast Guard, $155 million more than the House-passed bill and $169 million more than requested.

Of the amount appropriated, $425 million, including $9 million by transfer from other accounts, was allocated for the acquisition, construction and improvement of Coast Guard vessels, aircraft and aids to navigation. The House bill provided $287 million, including $9 million by transfer.

The committee agreed with the House that the Coast Guard should provide an analysis of the Haitian refugee interdiction operation to determine the cost effectiveness of continuing the current level of activity.

Federal Aviation Administration (FAA)

The bill provided $2.468 billion for FAA operations and maintenance of the air traffic control system and $55.6 million for a new FAA headquarters administration account. The total was $26 million less than Reagan requested but $67 million more than the House had recommended. Of the total, less than $1.5 billion was sought from the Airport and Airway Trust Fund. Reagan requested $2 billion from the trust fund, and the House provided $1 billion.

The committee met the administration request for $61 million for a pay raise for air traffic controllers. The House committee had refused to consider it until authorizing legislation had been enacted. Both the Senate panel and the House concurred with the request for 1,899 new staff positions at air traffic control centers and towers.

The Senate committee provided $725 million for modernizing facilities and equipment for the airway system, the same as that proposed by the administration. The House deferred action on $300 million of the request because the administration had not officially asked for the funds.

Federal Highway Administration (FHWA)

A total FHWA program level of $8.499 billion for fiscal 1983 was approved by the Senate panel; this amount was $628 million more than the request and $24 million less than the House version.

The Senate panel provided $375 million for highway projects substituted for previously planned additional Interstate Highway segments. The House had included $500 million. Reagan requested $150 million.

The bill also barred funds from being apportioned to any state having a truck width limitation other than 102 inches on Interstate or other qualifying federal-aid highways. Existing federal law limited truck widths to 96 inches in most states. The timber industry, in particular, had pushed for wider trucks because of loading problems. *(Truck size issue, 1981 Almanac p. 582)*

The panel recommended $500,000 to help states compensate owners for the removal of advertising billboards along highways. The House bill did not include any money.

National Highway Traffic Safety Administration (NHTSA)

The committee recommended $170.6 million for NHTSA in fiscal 1983, $633,000 more than the House approved and $12 million more than the budget request. The Senate bill included a ceiling of $92.5 million on obligations for state and community highway safety grants, $5.5 million more than requested and $7.5 million less than the House provided.

The committee provided $78.1 million for NHTSA operations, $8.1 million more than the House and about $3.5 million less than requested.

Federal Railroad Administration (FRA)

The committee provided a total of almost $1.1 billion for the FRA, $193 million more than the budget request and $18 million more than the House-passed bill. The Senate version included $15.2 million for the office of the FRA administrator, almost $3 million more than the House bill.

The panel included $28 million for railroad safety, about $4.8 million more than the House bill but $1.3 million less than the administration request. Another $1.9 million in carryover funds was provided. The panel recommended $2.4 million for railroad safety grants to the states. The House and the administration wanted to end the program.

Also in the Senate-reported bill was $20 million for labor protection benefits for employees of Conrail. The House bill provided the funds by transfer from another Conrail account. And the panel concurred with the House and provided the full budget request of $115 million for the Northeast rail corridor improvement project.

Although the committee did not increase the existing Amtrak subsidy of $735 million, it ordered the passenger railroad to maintain all routes that were in operation in fiscal 1982. The panel said the need for fiscal restraint and statutory requirements mandating Amtrak cost-cutting made it difficult to increase the appropriation.

Urban Mass Transportation Administration (UMTA)

The bill provided a total of $3.45 billion for UMTA in fiscal 1983, $301.5 million more than requested and $192 million less than provided by the House.

The panel recommended $1.2 billion for urban formula grants; the House provided $1.3 billion and Reagan proposed $1 billion. The portions of the formula grants program that could be used for mass transit operating subsidies were funded at $875 million, $75 million less than the House bill and $235 million more than the budget request.

The $1.62 billion for discretionary capital grants provided by the committee was $8.3 million less than that in the House bill, but $103 million more than the administration requested.

Also included in the Senate bill was $225 million for mass transit programs that replaced the proposed additions to the Interstate Highway System. This amount was $140 million less than the House provided and $25 million less than the administration requested.

Civil Aeronautics Board (CAB)

The panel recommended $21.9 million for the CAB, a reduction in the administration's request of $2.6 million, which would result in the loss of 57 positions, according to the committee. The board's authority over fares and rates ended Dec. 31, 1982.

The committee included $48.4 million, the full budget request, for subsidies to air carriers to continue service to small communities. The committee proposed to terminate on Oct. 1, 1982, a year earlier than the House bill, another program that had provided aid to continue services to small communities. However, the Senate committee bill provided $13.5 million in phase-out subsidies.

Interstate Commerce Commission (ICC)

The committee recommended $65.6 million for the ICC, $3.4 million less than requested and $700,000 less than the House approved. The reduction in the administration request was due partly to a freeze on payments to the GSA for office space.

United States Railway Association (USRA)

The USRA received $2.95 million under the committee bill, $950,000 more than the House provided and the administration requested. The committee said the additional funds were included because litigation and other costs were

higher than previously thought. *(1981 Almanac p. 561)*

The bill also barred the sale or transfer of any Conrail securities held by the federal government without the approval of both the House and Senate Appropriations committees.

St. Lawrence Seaway

The committee agreed to cancel the St. Lawrence Seaway's obligation to repay the government $110 million for the waterway's construction costs. The seaway had paid $25 million in principal and $38 million in interest. *(1970 Almanac p. 374; 1954 Almanac p. 490)*

Senate Floor Action

The Senate Dec. 2 passed an amended version of HR 7019 by voice vote. The Senate bill contained $10.96 billion in new budget authority — $243 million less than the House-passed bill; $560 million more than the administration's original budget request; and about $236 million more than its amended request.

The Senate bill set an $8.1 billion ceiling on obligations from the Highway Trust Fund for highway construction and related programs and a $600 million ceiling on obligations from the Airport and Airway Trust Fund for airport development.

About $2.5 billion was included for FAA operations and maintenance of the air traffic control system.

Amendments

Interstate Highway Additions. The Senate-passed bill did not include $600 million that had been approved by the Senate Appropriations Committee for highway and transit projects in place of additions to the Interstate Highway network. The Senate by voice vote accepted two amendments sponsored by Sen. Mark Andrews, R-N.D., chairman of the Appropriations Transportation Subcommittee, to delete those funds. The money had been appropriated for a full year by the stopgap continuing appropriations resolution (H J Res 599 — PL 97-276) passed just before the November election recess. This was the only change made by the Senate in the appropriations levels recommended by the committee.

Truck Widths. Most of the Senate debate focused on the provision requiring states to allow 102-inch-wide trucks on primary and Interstate highways.

Thomas F. Eagleton, D-Mo., and Harrison "Jack" Schmitt, R-N.M., opposed the change, contending that pending highway authorization legislation already provided for the wider trucks in exchange for increases in heavy-truck highway taxes. Contending that the larger trucks would do more damage to the nation's roads, they offered an amendment to delete the provision from the bill.

Andrews argued that the 102-inch standard would allow for better loading, thereby reducing a truck's bounce on the highways. In addition, he said wider trucks would result in savings of $3.5 billion a year in food costs to consumers because more food could be carried in a single truck.

Before voting on the Eagleton amendment, the Senate ruled, by a vote of 67-27, that the width provision was germane to the appropriations bill. *(Vote 388, p. 65-S)*

The Senate then rejected the amendment by a 31-62 vote. *(Vote 389, p. 65-S)*

Provisions Compared

As passed by the House and Senate, HR 7019 made the following appropriations for fiscal 1983:

	Senate-Passed Appropriations	House-Passed Appropriations
Department of Transportation		
Office of the Secretary	$ 49,500,000	$ 39,532,000
Coast Guard	2,441,148,350	2,286,447,350
Federal Aviation Administration	3,425,139,0000	2,984,548,000
Federal Highway Administration	13,282,000	512,677,000
National Highway Traffic Safety Administration	78,133,000	70,000,000
Federal Railroad Administration	1,024,491,000	986,394,000
Urban Mass Transportation Administration	3,226,531,000	3,643,500,000
Research and Special Programs Administration	21,300,000	20,022,000
Office of the Inspector General	24,946,000	24,946,000
Subtotal	10,304,470,350	10,568,066,350
Related Agencies		
Architectural and Transportation Barriers Compliance Board	20,020,000	1,900,000
National Transportation Safety Board	19,970,000	19,970,000
Civil Aeronautics Board	70,300,000	72,750,000
Interstate Commerce Commission	65,600,000	66,300,000
Panama Canal Commission	439,426,000	416,750,000
U.S. Railway Association	2,950,000	2,000,000
Washington Metropolitan Area Transit Authority	51,663,569	51,663,569
Subtotal	651,929,569	631,333,569
GRAND TOTAL	$10,956,399,919	$11,199,399,919

Conference Report

A conference report on HR 7019 (H Rept 97-960) was filed Dec. 13. The final compromise appropriated about $250 million more than Reagan's original budget request and $74 million less than his amended request.

The compromise was $103 million less than Congress had approved in the regular and supplemental appropriations bills for transportation in fiscal 1982. *(1981 Almanac p. 358)*

The House version of the measure, passed Sept. 21, provided almost $11.2 billion for fiscal 1983. The bill passed by the Senate Dec. 2 appropriated $10.96 billion.

Highways, Mass Transit

House-Senate conferees did not include any funds for highways and mass transit projects that were proposed in place of additional Interstate Highway segments. In October, $883 million for these projects had been appropriated

for the fiscal year by the first fiscal 1983 continuing appropriations resolution (PL 97-276).

As agreed to by the conferees, the bill set an $8.1 billion ceiling for fiscal 1983 on obligations from the Highway Trust Fund for highway construction and related programs. The House bill had set an $8 billion ceiling, and the Senate version contained an $8.1 billion cap. Reagan had requested a ceiling of $7.7 billion.

Under the DOT appropriations conference agreement, states would have to allow 102-inch-wide trucks on their highways; the maximum allowable had been 96 inches. This change also was included in HR 6211.

The conference agreement also included a $500,000 appropriation, added by the Senate, to help states compensate billboard owners for signs taken down in accordance with the federal highway beautification law. The House had not included any funds.

The compromise bill also appropriated a total of $3.201 billion for mass transit. The Senate provided $3.227 billion, and the House approved $3.644 billion. Reagan had requested $3.15 billion.

Of the total, $1.2 billion was intended for mass transit formula grants, which may be used for operating or capital expenses. The final appropriation was the same as the Senate-approved figure, $100 million more than the House provided and almost $200 million more than Reagan requested. Another $1.606 billion of the total appropriation was allocated for transit discretionary grants, which funded capital projects such as bus facilities. The Senate had included $1.621 billion, while the House had provided $1.630 billion. Reagan requested $1.518 billion.

The mass transit program subsequently was altered by enactment of the authorization (HR 6211), which created a block grant formula program that could be used for operating and capital costs.

Other Conference Decisions

The final version of the DOT appropriations bill also:

● Set a ceiling of $600 million on obligations from the Airport and Airway Trust Fund for airport development projects. This ceiling was the same as that provided by both the House and Senate and contained in the amended administration request.

● Appropriated $625 million for Federal Aviation Administration (FAA) facilities and equipment, allowing the administration to begin its multibillion-dollar program to modernize the national air traffic control system.

The administration had sought $725 million, but the conferees questioned whether the full budget request could be obligated for spending during fiscal 1983.

The conference agreement also provided $2.516 billion for FAA operations of the airway system and headquarters administration, a compromise between the House level of $2.456 billion and the Senate amount of $2.523 billion.

Of the agreed upon amount, $1.264 billion was slated to come from the Airport and Airway Trust Fund. The final amount from the trust fund was $200 million less than the Senate bill provided; the House measure provided $1 billion.

Reagan had requested that $2 billion of FAA operating costs be paid for through the trust fund. Congress historically had resisted efforts to use the trust fund for FAA operations because the aviation taxes were established originally to finance airport development. Reagan had argued that airport users should pay FAA operating costs.

● Appropriated $700 million for Amtrak. That amount

was less than both the House level of $788 million — the amount previously authorized — and the Senate level of $735 million.

Amtrak officials said they could manage with a $700 million appropriation because about $80 million in unspent capital funds were available from fiscal 1982.

• Appropriated the Senate-approved level of $1.518 billion for Coast Guard operations, rather than the House level of $1.587 billion.

The bill also provided $409 million for acquisition, construction and improvement of Coast Guard vessels, aircraft and navigation aids.

The House bill appropriated $287 million, while the

Senate bill provided $425 million.

• Appropriated $5 million from the National Recreational Boating Safety and Facilities Improvement Fund; the Senate approved $10 million while the House did not approve any funds.

The boating fund, which was intended to aid state boating safety programs, was made up of revenue from a 4-cents-a-gallon tax on motorboat fuel, up to a total of $20 million. No monies had been appropriated from the fund since it was established in 1980 (PL 96-451).

• Canceled the St. Lawrence Seaway's debt to the federal government of $110 million for original construction costs. ∎

Treasury, Postal Funds in Continuing Measure

Funding for the Treasury Department, Postal Service, executive offices and several independent agencies was included in the second continuing resolution (H J Res 631 — PL 97-377) after Congress failed to complete action on the regular fiscal 1983 appropriations bill for those agencies.

The stopgap funding measure cleared Dec. 20 provided a total of $10,876,737,000 in new budget authority for the Treasury Department, Postal Service, executive offices and other agencies for fiscal 1983. That was $358.92 million more than President Reagan had requested and $681.08 million more than the fiscal 1982 appropriations.

The House passed its version of the regular fiscal 1983 Treasury, Postal Service appropriations bill (HR 7158 — H Rept 97-854) Nov. 30.

The Senate Appropriations Committee had approved a separate measure (S 2916 — S Rept 97-547) Sept. 16, but the full Senate took no action on either bill.

It was the third year in a row that the agencies were funded in a continuing appropriations resolution. *(1981 Almanac p. 355; 1980 Almanac p. 227)*

Postal Subsidies, BATF, Taxpayer Aid

The biggest increase over the president's budget came in the funding for postal subsidies. The president had recommended $500 million in subsidies, but Congress voted $789 million.

Congress also voted $145 million for the Bureau of Alcohol, Tobacco and Firearms (BATF), which Reagan had sought to abolish. The administration's plan to eliminate the agency and redistribute its responsibilities to the U.S. Secret Service and U.S. Customs Service ran into fierce opposition from gun owners and the liquor industry.

The liquor industry wanted to preserve a regulatory apparatus it was familiar with, while the gun lobby — led by the National Rifle Association, a frequent harsh critic of the BATF — did not want to see firearms law enforcment in the hands of the Secret Service, a highly respected and efficient police agency.

Both House and Senate added $50 million to the president's request to maintain at existing levels various Internal Revenue Service (IRS) taxpayer services that Reagan wanted to drop, including toll-free telephone assistance. Although this provision was not in dispute, the conferees went out of their way to emphasize the importance Congress placed on keeping those services in place.

Private School Tax Exemptions

Upset by an early 1982 Reagan administration attempt

to reverse a longstanding IRS policy barring tax exemptions for private schools that discriminate, both the House and Senate rejected floor amendments that would have prevented the IRS from implementing some revisions of its anti-discrimination rule that were proposed in 1978 and modified in 1979.

During House debate on HR 7158, Rep. Robert K. Dornan, R-Calif., offered the same amendment he had successfully pressed in prior years to prohibit expenditure of any funds in the bill to implement the revised IRS rules. But this time, his amendment was defeated by a voice vote.

In the Senate, a similar amendment by Jesse Helms, R-N.C., was tabled (killed) Dec. 18 during debate on the continuing appropriations resolution by a vote of 61-29. *(Vote 450, p. 75-S)*

Although many in Congress in years past criticized the proposed IRS rule revisions as too sweeping, there was never any attempt to reverse the anti-discrimination policy itself.

In 1982, members in both chambers argued that Congress should not be legislating on the tax-exemption issue at a time when the Supreme Court was weighing a challenge to the existing IRS rules. *(Private school tax exemptions, p. 397)*

Provisions

As cleared by Congress, H J Res 631 contained the following appropriations in new budget authority for the Treasury Department, Postal Service, executive offices and certain independent agencies *(in thousands of dollars)*:

Agency	Budget Request	Final Amount
Treasury Department		
Office of the Secretary	$59,752	$37,000
International affairs	—	20,000
Federal Law Enforcement Training Center	12,913	12,500
Bureau of Government Financial Operations	183,267	248,000
Bureau of Alcohol, Tobacco and Firearms	—	145,000
U.S. Customs Service	560,524	553,700
Bureau of the Mint	55,365	53,200
Bureau of the Public Debt	210,045	201,000
Internal Revenue Service	2,917,159	2,948,190

Agency	Budget Request	Final Amount
Treasury Department		
Payment where energy credit exceeds liability for tax	300	300
U.S. Secret Service	301,882	235,000
Subtotal	4,301,207	4,453,890
U.S. Postal Service		
Payment to the Postal Service Fund	500,000	789,000
Subtotal	500,000	789,000
Executive Office of the President		
President's Compensation	250	250
Office of Administration	13,640	12,904
The White House Office	22,164	21,300
Executive Residence	3,878	3,800
Official Residence of the Vice President	281	275
Special Assistance to the President	1,483	1,475
Council of Economic Advisers	2,115	2,100
Office of Policy Development	2,653	2,600
National Security Council	3,976	3,900
Office of Management and Budget	36,109	33,000
Office of Federal Procurement Policy	2,486	2,400
Property Review Board	445	445
Unanticipated Needs	1,000	1,000
Subtotal	90,480	85,449
Independent Agencies		
Administrative Conference of the United States	1,339	1,100
Advisory Commission on Intergovernmental Relations	1,920	1,900
Advisory Committee on Federal Pay	204	200
Committee for Purchase of Products from the Blind and Other Handicapped	653	653
Federal Election Commission	9,880	9,700
General Services Administration	513,288	441,137
Office of Personnel Management	5,044,066	5,041,448
Merit Systems Protection Board	23,949	22,760
Federal Labor Relations Authority	15,745	15,500
U.S. Tax Court	15,083	14,000
Subtotal	5,626,127	5,548,398
Grand Total	$10,517,814	$10,876,737

House/Senate Committee Action

The House Appropriations Subcommittee on Treasury-Postal Service-General Government Aug. 11 approved a fiscal 1983 spending bill totaling roughly $10.8 billion.

The subcommittee agreed to a provision barring the use of federal employee health insurance benefit funds for abortion, an item that had prevented final Senate action on the 1982 Treasury, Postal Service appropriations bill.

The full House Appropriations Committee Sept. 22 approved HR 7158 (H Rept 97-854) providing $10.772 billion in fiscal 1983, $284 million more than the administration's original proposal of $10.488 billion.

The Senate bill (S 2916 — S Rept 97-547), reported Sept. 16 and revised Sept. 22 by the Senate Appropriations Committee, provided $10.527 billion.

The biggest increase over the administration's budget was for the Postal Service. Both committees recommended a $708 million subsidy, compared to the president's request for $500 million. Both bills also provided funds for the BATF.

The Senate bill included restrictions on the renovation of government offices and a ban on the use of chauffeurs to drive government officials between their homes and offices. The chauffeur limits did not apply to Cabinet officers, ambassadors and other high-level diplomats.

S 2916 also included language reducing funding for executive branch consultants by 20 percent in fiscal 1983.

The House committee achieved savings by holding to 1982 levels the rent that the General Services Administration (GSA) charged other agencies for office space. The administration and the Senate committee proposed increasing rental fees for government agencies.

Treasury Department

The Senate committee recommended $4.32 billion for the Treasury Department, compared to $4.27 billion sought by the administration. The House panel allowed $4.4 billion. The fiscal 1982 appropriation was $4.1 billion.

Bureau of Alcohol, Tobacco and Firearms. The administration recommended abolishing the agency and merging its functions with the Secret Service and Customs Service. Both panels rejected the idea, with S 2916 providing $148 million and HR 7158 allocating $145 million for BATF. The fiscal 1982 level was $142 million.

U.S. Customs Service. The Senate committee recommended $537 million, $6.5 million more than the administration wanted. The House panel recommended $528.7 million. Fiscal 1982 funding was $527 million.

Bureau of the Mint. The Mint would receive $53.2 million under S 2916, about $2 million less than Reagan and the House panel wanted, and $1.7 million more the 1982 level.

Internal Revenue Service (IRS). The Senate committee recommended $2.9 billion for the IRS, $19 million less than Reagan proposed and $50 million less than the House panel suggested. In 1982, the IRS received $2.7 billion.

Both panels voted $50 million to continue toll-free telephone assistance to taxpayers, a program Reagan wanted to eliminate.

To achieve savings beyond those sought by Reagan, the Senate committee reduced the administration's request for data processing, office rental fees and salaries and expenses.

Secret Service. The Senate panel suggested $235

million, $66.9 million less than the administration wanted. The House committee called for $220 million, while the 1982 funding was $194 million.

U.S. Postal Service

The $708 million payment for the Postal Service fund was to cover the revenue loss from free and reduced-rate mail, including second-class publications such as rural newspapers and third-class letters from non-profit groups.

The administration proposed $500 million for revenue foregone. In 1982 the appropriation was $915.5 million.

The Senate panel included language prohibiting the Postal Service from closing or consolidating small post offices or curtailing six-day mail delivery in fiscal 1983. It also included a provision precluding the mandatory implementation of the nine-digit ZIP codes in fiscal 1983.

White House, Other Agencies

For the executive office of the president, the Senate committee recommended $85.5 million, $5 million less than Reagan requested. The House panel called for about $85 million, while the 1982 appropriation was $82 million.

Federal Election Commission (FEC). Both panels would give the FEC $9.7 million. The funding would be $180,000 less than Reagan proposed, but $525,600 more than in 1982.

General Services Administration (GSA). Total funding was $775.1 million in S 2916 and about $443.8 million in the House bill. The administration proposed $513.3 million. The 1982 funding was $476.6 million.

The House committee report said holding GSA rental fees to 1982 levels would result in government-wide savings of about $350 million.

Federal Personnel Activities. The committees recommended $5.1 billion for federal employee costs, including the government payment for retiree and employee health benefits and payments to the civil service retirement and disability fund. The level was about equal to the administration's request. In 1982, funding was $4.8 billion.

For the Office of Personnel Management, the Senate panel called for $100 million, $4.5 million less than the 1982 appropriation and $2.6 million less than Reagan's request. HR 7158 recommended $100.8 million.

House Floor Action

In its first post-election spending vote, a cost-conscious House Nov. 30 cut 2 percent from all discretionary funds in HR 7158.

By 193-172, the House slashed $117 million from the proposed $10.8 billion spending bill (HR 7158 — H Rept 97-854). Members then approved the pared down $10.7 billion measure by a 269-98 vote. *(Votes 375, 376, p. 112-H)*

Even with the cut, HR 7158 exceeded President Reagan's budget request by almost $200 million. And, according to the Office of Management and Budget (OMB), the bill contained nearly $900 million more in budget authority for discretionary programs than the fiscal 1983 budget resolution (S Con Res 92) allowed.

During debate on HR 7158, the House broke with a three-year precedent by rejecting a rider that would have prohibited implementation of revised IRS regulations regarding the tax-exempt status of private schools.

The amendment, which was attached to every House-passed Treasury-Postal Service spending bill since fiscal

1980, would have prevented the IRS from enforcing regulations denying tax-exempt status to racially discriminatory schools unless the regulations were in effect prior to Aug. 22, 1978. It was defeated by voice vote.

Abortion Benefits

There was no discussion Nov. 30 of a provision in HR 7158 that barred the use of federal employee health benefits to pay for abortions — an item that stirred up controversy in earlier years. No effort was made to strike the language, which allowed abortion payments providing the life of the mother would be endangered if the fetus were carried to term.

The biggest increase over the administration's budget was for the Postal Service. The House approved a subsidy of about $700 million for free and reduced-rate mail for certain non-profit organizations, compared to the president's request for $500 million.

The House also voted about $50 million more for the U.S. Customs Service than the $499 million requested by Reagan. Edward R. Roybal, D-Calif., chairman of the Appropriations Subcommittee on Treasury-Postal Service, said the added funds would prevent personnel cutbacks of 2,300 employees that would have been necessary if Reagan's funding request had been approved.

HR 7158 also provided funds for the BATF, an agency the administration wanted to abolish.

Other offices funded by HR 7158 included the Bureau of the Mint, IRS, Secret Service, Federal Election Commission, General Services Administration, Office of Personnel Management and the executive office of the president, which included OMB.

The 2 Percent Cut

As reported Sept. 22 by the House Appropriations Committee, HR 7158 exceeded Reagan's request by $284 million. White House officials claimed the bill exceeded the congressional budget resolution by $993 million in budget authority for discretionary programs, and was $775 million above the Treasury subcommittee's allowance.

Clarence E. Miller, R-Ohio, GOP floor manager for HR 7158 and sponsor of the amendment cutting 2 percent from non-mandatory spending, said he received "conflicting signals" from the White House concerning how much the administration wanted to cut from the bill. Miller said he recommended the 2 percent reduction because "I thought that was the most the House would stand for."

Under Miller's amendment, no line item could be reduced by more than 4 percent. The cut would not affect about $4.9 billion in mandatory spending, such as federal employee health benefits and payments to the civil service retirement and disability fund.

Roybal opposed the cut, saying it "would have a very detrimental effect on the overall basic operations of this government." Roybal said the reduction would affect revenue collected by the IRS because the agency could lose tax agents. "It would also mean that Customs, for one example, would have to reduce its activities with regard to the trafficking of illegal drugs being smuggled into this country," he said.

However, it was not clear following the House vote precisely where the mandated cuts would be made. Although the 2 percent reduction could be applied across-the-board to discretionary programs, the executive branch would have the flexibility to cut up to 4 percent from any one program, while leaving others intact.

The IRS and Private Schools

The most sensitive issue during debate on HR 7158 involved IRS regulations affecting private and religious schools.

The IRS had a 12-year-old policy of denying tax exemptions to schools that racially discriminate. In 1978, the IRS proposed stringent regulations that would have revoked the tax-exempt status of private schools that failed to meet certain criteria aimed at demonstrating they did not discriminate on the basis of race.

The rules came under fire in Congress, and although they were modified in 1979, they never took effect. During debate on HR 7158, Rep. Dornan offered the same amendment he had pressed successfully in the past prohibiting the use of Treasury Department funds to implement the revised IRS rules. This time, however, his amendment was rejected by voice vote.

In January, the Reagan administration announced it was ending the IRS policy of denying exemptions to segregated schools, unless Congress expressly authorized the IRS to do so.

That decision provoked an uproar in Congress and elsewhere, and the administration backed off. The matter remained in limbo at year's end, pending a decision by the U.S. Supreme Court. The court was reviewing the tax-exemption issue in the cases of *Goldsboro Christian Schools v. United States* and *Bob Jones University v. United States*, involving two schools that discriminated against blacks as a matter of religious belief and practice.

Dornan argued that without his amendment, "the private and religious schools of this nation once again [would] find themselves threatened by the IRS and by federal courts engaged in social engineering."

But his amendment drew fire from several Democrats, who called it a threat to civil rights advancement and said that Congress should not get into the tax-exemption issue until the Supreme Court ruled on it. "This amendment comes under the guise of a prohibition on spending by the IRS. But it is really a civil rights issue because it hampers the ability of the IRS in its efforts to eliminate racial discrimination in private schools," Roybal said.

After the House rejected his amendment by a voice vote, Dornan offered another rider that would have barred the use of funds to implement any IRS ruling denying a charitable deduction for contributions to tax-exempt religious schools. This amendment, which was included in Treasury-Postal Service spending bills for the past three years, was also defeated by voice vote.

The House also rejected by voice vote an amendment by Philip M. Crane, R-Ill., prohibiting the use of any funds to issue new regulations depriving private schools of tax-exempt status.

Other Amendments

In other action, a point of order was sustained against language in HR 7158 that sought to limit OMB's power to "interfere with the rule-making authority of any regulatory agency." The committee inserted that language because members were concerned about the aggressive role OMB had played in reviewing the cost and paperwork implications of rules proposed by regulatory agencies.

The administration, however, opposed the provision. "This language could seriously compromise three of the president's most important policy priorities: strict budgetary control, regulatory reform, and paperwork reduction," a White House policy statement said.

The language was deleted after Frank Horton, R-N.Y., argued that it consisted of legislation on an appropriations bill, which violated House rules.

The House by voice adopted the following amendments to HR 7158:

● By Silvio O. Conte, R-Mass., an administration-backed proposal to add $25 million to the Customs Service. The money was to be used to expand Project Exodus, a program to prevent the illegal export of high-technology equipment to the Soviet Union and its allies.

● By Ron Wyden, D-Ore., to prohibit the Customs Service from closing its facility in Portland, Ore.

● By Michael D. Barnes, D-Md., to prohibit the use of IRS funds to reduce taxpayer assistance services below 1982 funding levels. The administration had wanted to eliminate toll-free telephone assistance and walk-in help for taxpayers, but the Appropriations Committee had preserved the program. Barnes' amendment reinforced the panel's action.

● By Robert W. Edgar, D-Pa., to prohibit the General Services Administration from contracting out positions for which veterans had preference in hiring. The positions included guards, elevator operators, messengers and custodians in government buildings.

Conference

In addition to resolving relatively minor differences over funding levels, House-Senate conferees also settled some substantive questions.

Abortion. The conference committee deleted a House-passed provision that barred the use of federal employee health benefits to pay for abortions except when the life of the mother was endangered.

Secret Service Agents. The conferees agreed to insert language proposed by the Senate directing the Secret Service to hire an additonal 200 special agents. In its report (S Rept 97-547) the Senate committee had noted that due to limited hiring and low attrition rates, some 60 percent of Secret Service agents were age 35 or older. "This trend must not be allowed to continue in view of the physical and psychological demands" placed on agents, the committee said, referring in particular to the Secret Service's responsibility to protect the president and other top officials.

Chauffeured Officials. Dropped from the bill was another Senate provision that had all but prohibited the chauffeuring of government officials between their homes and offices. Conferees directed the General Accounting Office to study the use of government vehicles and chauffeurs for such purposes and to report to Congress by June 1, 1983.

Customs Offices. The conferees prohibited the reduction of Customs Service regions below nine, and barred any Customs office closings or consolidations, and any reductions in personnel or programs. However, the conferees said the House and Senate Appropriations committees would examine the restrictions in hearings on fiscal 1984 appropriations for the Customs Service, and would work with the agency to find cost savings.

Contracting Out. Conferees also adopted House language that prohibited the contracting out of federal jobs for which veterans had preference. ∎

Defense Bill Cuts 7 Percent; Deletes MX

For the second year in a row, President Reagan won congressional approval for the bulk of his defense buildup.

In spite of apparently growing concern about the level of defense spending in an era of economic trauma, Congress cut only 7 percent of the president's budget request for defense in fiscal 1983. The $232 billion allocation for defense was by far the biggest item in the fiscal 1983 continuing resolution (H J Res 631 — PL 97-377), cleared by Congress Dec. 20 and signed by Reagan Dec. 21. *(Continuing resolution, p. 238)*

The 7 percent cut — $17.585 billion — represented the biggest congressional cut in a defense request since the early 1970s. But the bulk of the cut came from routine congressional efforts to tighten bureaucratic belts. The most dramatic instance was a $2.3 million reduction in the size of the annual pay hike for Pentagon employees, an austerity measure imposed on all federal agencies.

According to the two Defense Appropriations subcommittees, a subsantial amount of the reduction came from changes in the facts of life since the budget initially was drafted. One example was the $833 million cut in fuel purchase funds, reflecting the continuing decline in petroleum prices.

Just over half the total reduction — $8.9 billion — came from procurement accounts. But procurement funds were flatly denied for only a few major programs, with the rest of the cuts coming from production slowdowns.

The bill took three major swipes at Reagan's defense program: It deleted funds for production of the MX missile and directed Reagan to come up with a better plan for basing the MX than the "dense pack" system he had proposed Nov. 22; it cut funds for production of the Pershing II missile that was to be based in Europe; and it included provisions that were bound to irritate U.S. allies in Europe.

But the MX and Pershing provisions did not ring the death knell for those strategic weapons. The action on MX amounted to yet another postponement of a final decision on what to do with the much-debated missile; congressional leaders made it clear that they supported the Pershing program, but wanted solid proof that the missile would work as advertised.

Otherwise, the bill included funds for nearly all other major weapons programs requested by the president, including the B-1 bomber, one Trident submarine, two nuclear-powered aircraft carriers, two *Los Angeles*-class attack submarines, and reactivation of the battleship *Iowa*. One major exception was Reagan's $54 million request for production of a new family of chemical weapons, called binary munitions. That request had been denied during action on the defense authorization bill (S 2248 — PL 97-252). *(Authorization bill, p. 77)*

H J Res 631 appropriated $232.026 billion for defense programs in fiscal 1983, including $231.603 billion in new budget authority and $423 million in transfers of unused authority from previous years.

The final amount was $17.585 billion below Reagan's amended request, and $1.3 billion above the House-passed level and $1.7 billion below the Senate-passed amount. The comparable fiscal 1982 amount was $205.7 billion.

By putting the defense spending measure into the continuing resolution, Congress failed for the first time in

at least 30 years to pass a separate defense appropriations bill. However, leaders of the two Appropriations committees noted that the defense provisions of H J Res 631 represented complete legislation and, unlike most continuing resolutions, were not based on a mere continuation of spending levels from the previous year.

The House passed a regular defense appropriations bill (HR 7355) on Dec. 8. The Senate incorporated its bill (S 2951) into the continuing resolution.

Although Reagan signed the bill despite his objections to the MX and Pershing provisions, some of the president's congressional allies on defense and foreign policy matters expressed strong reservations about the bill.

John Tower, R-Texas, chairman of the Senate Armed Services Committee, took to the floor during debate on the conference report to condemn the final bill.

Noting that the conference report deleted many Senate-passed provisions, Tower said it "will have serious adverse consequences for U.S. national security policy and will needlessly jeopardize the mutual security relationships which we have enjoyed with our allies."

Tower complained especially about the final MX provisions, which he said "effectively precluded fair and reasoned consideration" of the issue by Congress in 1983 because the bill gave the Appropriations committees, rather than the Armed Services committees, jurisdiction over key legislation on the MX basing system. H J Res 631 was written by the Appropriations committees.

MX Missile

Reagan's request for $3.5 billion in MX programs was the most heatedly contested defense issue in the House-Senate conference committee on H J Res 631.

The rejection of Reagan's MX budget — the first time Congress ever had denied production of a major nuclear weapon requested by a president — was a powerful political blow to the program.

In their key action, the conferees accepted a House amendment deleting all of the $988 million that Reagan requested for production of the first five MXs.

This money had been deleted by the House Dec. 7 in a stunning upset for the president. House conferees, led by Defense Appropriations Subcommittee Chairman Joseph P. Addabbo, D-N.Y., reportedly were adamant in refusing to budge on the issue. Addabbo long had opposed the missile, and he used the leverage of the House's 245-176 vote to bolster his position in the House-Senate conference. *(Vote 398, p. 118-H)*

Conferees coupled the deletion of MX production funds with other provisions aimed at giving Congress the right to block a basing system for the missile. Reagan had proposed deploying 100 of the missiles in a "dense pack" in Wyoming. But that proposal encountered strong, if not overwhelming opposition in Congress, largely because of skepticism about the elaborate theories used to justify the system. *(Dense pack, p. 120)*

In the other MX provisions, H J Res 631:

● Approved $2.509 billion for research and development on the MX missile and its basing system. Of this amount, $1.734 billion was for research and development on the missile itself — that amount was approved without restrictions — and conferees agreed that missiles produced in the

Department of Defense Appropriations, Fiscal 1983

Following are the Department of Defense appropriations for fiscal 1983 under H J Res 631 (PL 97-377). The chart shows the fiscal 1982 appropriation (which includes a supplemental appropriation), President Reagan's revised request, the amounts approved by the House and Senate, and the final amount approved in a compromise House-Senate conference committee.

(in thousands of dollars)

Program	FY1982 Appropriation	Administration Request	House-Passed Amount	Senate-Passed Amount	Final Amount
Personnel	$ 42,737,017	$ 47,902,500	$ 45,136,265	$ 43,810,320	$ 45,066,808
Retired personnel	14,986,000	16,510,800	16,154,800	16,228,800	16,154,800
Operations and maintenance	62,646,310	71,087,451	66,894,464	67,363,622	67,279,010
Procurement	64,987,785	89,616,914	79,820,133	83,012,879	80,287,703
Research and development	19,859,148	24,398,894	22,114,054	22,876,984	22,704,284
Special foreign currency	3,083	3,800	3,800	3,800	3,800
Related agencies	98,295	92,050	106,976	106,700	107,156
Total, new budget authority	**$205,317,638**	**$249,612,409**	**$230,230,492**	**$233,403,105**	**$231,603,561**
(Transfer from previous appropriations)	426,626	0	520,072	345,900	423,163
Total funding available	**$205,744,264**	**$249,612,409**	**$230,750,564**	**$233,749,005**	**$232,026,724**

development stage could later be deployed once Congress approved a basing system for MX.

The remaining $775 million in research and development money was earmarked for the basing system itself. Of that amount, conferees approved $215 million without restrictions on how or when it could be spent. The remaining $560 million was for full-scale engineering development of the basing system, and conferees agreed that it would not be spent until both houses of Congress had approved a permanent basing system by concurrent resolution.

Conferees retained a Senate-passed provision requiring the president to report to Congress on his choice of a basing system on or after March 1, 1983. The amendment provided for expedited consideration in both houses of a resolution to approve the basing system; the most important provision limited debate in either house to 50 hours, thus eliminating the possibility of a Senate filibuster of a resolution to approve the MX basing system.

● Adopted a Senate provision prohibiting any flight testing of MX missiles until both houses of Congress had approved expenditures for the MX basing mode.

Ted Stevens, R-Alaska, chairman of the Senate Defense Appropriations Subcommittee, said the House conferees made a "significant concession" in agreeing to allow eventual deployment of missiles that had been produced during research and development. That agreement would enable the Pentagon to begin deploying the missile by 1986 — its current target date, Stevens said.

Pershing II Missile

Conferees accepted a House provision deleting $493.3 million for production of Pershing II nuclear-tipped missiles that were designed to strike Soviet territory from bases in Western Europe. The House Appropriations Committee had denied the administration budget request, saying the Army needed to conduct additional tests on the missile. The United States was scheduled to begin deploying Pershing II missiles in Europe by December 1983.

Conferees said they would consider a renewed request for Pershing II funds once the Army had successfully completed flight testing of the missile. Conferees approved $30 million to allow the Army to continue training and other services leading up to deployment of the missile.

Several 1982 tests of the missile failed or were postponed. Conference committee members emphasized that they supported the 1979 NATO decision to deploy long-range nuclear missiles, including the Pershing II, to offset similar Soviet missiles aimed at Western Europe. Pershing IIs funded in fiscal 1982 could be used to meet the agreed deployment deadline of December 1983, they said.

But the NATO plan's future depended less on having missiles on hand in December than on fending off antinuclear arms political pressure within several NATO countries. And as Congress wrestled with the defense funding question in late 1982, administration officials warned in vain that any apparent interruption of the Pershing program, even for technical purposes, would lend political momentum to the European opponents of the deployment plan.

Troops in Europe

Conferees adopted a modified version of a Senate Appropriations Committee provision limiting the number of active-duty U.S. military personnel stationed onshore in Europe to 315,600, the level authorized at the end of fiscal 1982. But the president could waive that limitation if he declared to Congress that "overriding national security requirements" made such action necessary.

The conference action essentially overrode an earlier proposal by the Senate Defense Appropriations Subcommittee to reduce the number of troops in Europe by 18,900. The troop cut had been sponsored by Stevens, as part of the subcommittee's regular defense spending bill (S 2951).

On a related issue, the conferees accepted a modified version of a Senate Appropriations Committee budget-cutting initiative to disband the 4,000-man Third Brigade

of the First Cavalry Division, stationed in West Germany. The committee action had been weakened by the full Senate on Dec. 17. Conferees adopted the Senate provision, which deleted $35 million in operating funds for the brigade in Europe, but allowed the Pentagon to decide by March 30, 1983, whether to save the money by disbanding the brigade or by making cuts elsewhere if it determined the brigade to be "essential."

NATO Provisions

The conference report took several actions bound to irritate U.S. allies in Europe. For the most part, the provisions were aimed at signaling congressional dissatisfaction with the level of European defense spending. Each of the provisions reduced U.S. funding for NATO-related programs, thus implying that European nations would have to make up the difference.

Conferees retained an existing ban on storing equipment in Europe for more than four U.S. Army divisions. The Pentagon wanted to store, in so-called POMCUS sites, the tanks and other heavy equipment for six divisions that could be flown to Europe in case of crisis.

The conference bill also rejected a Senate provision that would have enabled the Pentagon to spend $44.3 million to buy equipment to be used in wartime by West German reservists assigned to provide transportation and supply support to U.S. combat units.

On the final issue relating to the European allies, the conferees rejected a Senate compromise on the issue of "specialty metals," which were high-temperature alloys used in jet engines and other weapons. Several European countries made those metals.

The Senate had adopted a provision allowing the Pentagon to buy defense items, and parts of defense items, containing specialty metals that were made outside the United States. Conferees accepted more restrictive House language that allowed the purchase, under previous agreements, only of foreign-made weapons containing specialty metals.

Strategic Warfare

In addition to denying MX procurement funds, the conferees also dropped from the bill $15 million added by the Senate to replace 50 single-warhead Minuteman II missiles with triple warhead Minuteman IIIs then in storage. The switch, which some conservatives had touted for years, had been included in the initial fiscal 1983 Pentagon request, but was sacrificed on budgetary grounds in the spring.

Bombers. Both houses had approved without change the $4.6 billion request for procurement of the first seven production-line versions of the B-1 bomber and for continued development of the plane.

Conferees approved $532.2 million of $554.6 million requested to modernize existing B-52 bombers. The new changes included electronic gear to jam enemy radar and equipment to let the planes carry long-range nuclear-armed cruise missiles.

For procurement of the cruise missiles, the conferees approved $548.2 million of the $664.5 million request. Both houses had agreed that procurement of the current cruise missile type should be slowed in preparation for the imminent switch to production of an improved version.

The administration's decision to retire three squadrons of the oldest version of the B-52 — the "D" model

planes —was approved.

Submarine Missiles. For the 10th Trident missile launching submarine, the conferees approved the $1.462 billion provided by the Senate. The House had trimmed from that figure $34 million earmarked as a contingency fund for the program. The conferees restored that management reserve, but warned the Navy they would provide no additional funds for this ship in the future. The Navy said the current appropriation should be sufficient.

Funds were approved for 66 Trident I submarine missiles as approved by the Senate ($633.7 million) rather than 72 as requested and approved by the House ($685.3 million). The Senate position was that production of that missile should be slowed since all new missile subs beginning with the ninth Trident ship (funded in fiscal 1981) would carry the larger and more powerful Trident II.

Both houses had approved the $366.7 million requested for Trident II development.

Conferees also adjusted the funding for the several versions of the Tomahawk long-range cruise missile, including the nuclear-armed version that could be fired against ground targets from submarines designed to hunt other ships. Because of testing problems with the missile, the final bill contained $229.8 million to procure 100 missiles — some of which would be the nuclear-armed type — instead of the $271 million requested for 120. But after Congress adjourned, the Navy reportedly decided on a far-reaching reorganization of the Tomahawk program because of problems with the missile's cost, performance and development schedule. Accordingly, it was not clear how many missiles the appropriated funds would buy.

Ground Combat

Procurement of 855 new M-1 tanks was approved, as funded by the House ($1.36 billion) rather than 720 tanks as allowed by the Senate ($1.21 billion). But the conferees ordered the Army to hold production to the lower rate until tests had demonstrated that the tank's engine and transmission would take the wear and tear of use.

Both houses had agreed on appropriations to procure 600 M-2 armored troop carriers ($783.3 million) and to modernize some 450 existing M-60 tanks ($162.9 million).

Tank Hunting. Both houses had approved the request for 48 Apache (AH-64) anti-tank helicopters. A $15 million disagreement over funding was resolved in favor of the lower, House-passed figure ($695.3 million).

Also in both versions of the bill was $357.3 million for 20 A-10 anti-tank planes. The planes were requested in the budget but had been dropped from the authorization bill (S 2248) at the insistence of the Senate Armed Services Committee. The conferees included a Senate-passed provision that barred expenditure of the funds until approved by the two Armed Services committees. They also ordered the Pentagon to request such approval by the Armed Services panels, which appeared unlikely nonetheless.

Tower, chairman of the Senate committee, called the conferees' decision to approve the funding a "horrible example" of "congressional pork in the defense bill." The A-10 was a favorite project of Rep. Addabbo, who represented a Long Island district near where the Grumman Corp. built the plane.

Both houses had approved the request for 12,000 TOW anti-tank guided missiles, and a minor funding disagreement was resolved in favor of the higher, House-passed amount ($134.7 million).

But the Senate conferees prevailed in denying all funds for procurement of the Viper, a short-range anti-tank missile ($113.7 million had been requested). The Senate position was that the missile was too puny to deal with modern Soviet tanks. The conferees added $10 million to conduct a test comparing the Viper and several similar foreign-made weapons.

Anti-Aircraft Weapons. Conferees approved the higher, House-passed appropriations for procurement of two types of anti-aircraft missiles:

● $779.1 million for 376 Patriot long-range missiles. The Senate had cut the buy to 287 missiles ($687.3 million) citing production delays.

● $214.6 million for 2,256 Stinger portable short-range missiles. The Senate had trimmed $42.5 million because of test problems.

Both houses had approved $148.9 million for British-made Rapiers, short-range missiles that would be operated by allied troops to defend U.S. air bases in Europe.

The request for 96 Sergeant York anti-aircraft tanks (formerly called DIVAD) also had been approved in both bills and conferees agreed on the higher, Senate-passed appropriation level ($471.1 million).

Rocket Contract. There had been no disagreement about appropriating $368.9 million to continue procurement of so-called MLRS artillery rockets that could lob hundreds of explosive grenades or dozens of anti-tank mines up to 20 miles.

But the conferees accepted the House position to approve an additional $53.2 million to begin a multi-year contract with LTV Corp. for future purchase of the missiles. The Senate had ordered the Army instead to equip a second contractor to produce the rockets and to hold a competition between the two contractors for each of the next several years' purchases of rockets.

Airlift and Sealift

The two houses had been in substantial agreement over several programs intended to improve the Pentagon's ability to transport combat units to distant spots. So on those issues, the conference report simply incorporated the points of agreement and smoothed out minor differences.

For air transport, both houses had taken the same basic approach, approving the administration plan to buy 50 more C-5 transport planes while making gestures toward powerful members of Congress who supported alternative purchases.

The conference report approved $800 million to begin purchasing the C-5s and $94 million in new appropriations to buy used, wide-body transports from U.S. airlines. The C-5 proposal had encountered a buzz-saw of lobbying by critics who favored instead the purchase of used Boeing 747s.

Conferees also transferred to the account for the wide-body purchase $50 million appropriated in prior years but not spent, and told the Air Force to assign the planes to the Air National Guard.

The conferees also added to the bill $60 million to continue development of the C-17 wide-body transport, designed to carry heavy equipment into primitive airstrips. This was the alternative favored by the Senate bill (which appropriated $200 million), and particularly by Senate Defense Appropriations Subcommittee Chairman Stevens. Since only $1 million had been authorized for C-17 devel-

opment, the conferees directed the Pentagon to request approval of the added funding from the two Armed Services committees.

Both houses had agreed to the request for $915 million for procurement of KC-10 aircraft, a version of the DC-10 jetliner modified to haul cargo and to refuel other planes in midair. But both the Senate and House had reduced the appropriation by $120 million and made up that amount from funds appropriated in earlier years but not spent.

Each version of the bill also had approved only $44 million of the $322.6 million requested to modify four high-speed commercial cargo ships so they could carry tanks and other heavy, military cargo.

Amphibious Attack. The conference report also incorporated the two bodies' concurrence in the request for new amphibious ships, from which Marine Corps units would fight their way ashore against opposing forces. (The air transports and conventional ships typically would be useful only to reinforce areas under the control of friendly military forces.)

The bill appropriated $379.2 million to procure an additional LSD-41 class ship, designed to carry combat vehicles and the landing barges to haul them ashore. An additional $37.8 million was approved for components of a sister ship to be requested in fiscal 1984. Also included was $55 million for components of a large helicopter carrier designed to carry 1,800 Marines. The $1.3 billion ship was due to be requested in fiscal 1984.

Naval Warfare

The conferees followed the House's action in denying contingency funds that were included in the amounts requested for several major warships.

The conference report approved two nuclear-powered aircraft carriers ($6.6 billion), modernization of the battleship *Iowa* ($300.8 million), and three cruisers intended to protect the carriers against Soviet cruise missiles ($2.9 billion). These amounts reflected an overall reduction of $419.3 million from the Senate-passed amounts, nearly all of it reflecting the denial of the contingency funds.

The Senate prevailed in dropping from the bill $94 million requested for components that would be used in modernization of another battleship, the *Missouri*, to be requested in fiscal 1984.

Both houses had approved the request for $138.6 million to design a new class of destroyers (the DDG-51s, formerly called DDGX) that would be equipped as anti-cruise missile escort ships but would be cheaper than the current class of escort cruisers. The conferees dropped $14.5 million the Senate had added to the Navy research budget to speed up development of an improved engine and an improved sub-detecting sonar for the new ship.

Sub Hunting. Both houses had supported the request for two *Los Angeles*-class nuclear-powered submarines designed to hunt other subs. The conference agreed on the House-passed appropriation of $1.004 billion, dropping $23 million requested for a contingency fund. The request for $416 million to buy components that would be used in future sub construction had been approved without change in both houses.

For two escort frigates designed to protect convoys against submarine attack, the conferees agreed on $646.3 million, directing the Navy to use an additional $35 million appropriated for this program but not needed in fiscal 1982.

Conferees adopted the lower, House-passed amounts for procurement of two small, sub-hunting helicopters that were carried by most U.S. surface warships. For 27 Seahawks (formerly called LAMPS III), $576.1 million was approved, $40.6 million less than the Senate-passed amount. For 18 smaller Sea Sprites, the conference report allowed $150 million, $15.4 million less than the Senate figure.

Auxiliary Ships. The Senate had denied funds for a mid-ocean refueling tanker, on grounds that the first ship of the class was not yet far enough along in construction to be sure that the design was ready for mass production.

The House had approved $179.6 million of the $210.2 million requested for the ship, saying that favorable negotiations with the shipbuilder should result in the lower cost. But the House turned down an additional $109.8 million to begin a multi-year contract for construction of additional tankers, saying the Navy had not made its case for mass producing the ship. The conferees approved $173 million for the tanker.

The House had denied the request for four minesweepers ($371.6 million) on the same grounds the Senate had cited in the tanker case: Construction of the first ship of that new design had not gone far enough to prove the design ready for production.

The conferees approved $100 million for one minesweeper, but ordered the Navy to buy it from a second shipyard, so there would be more than one source of these ships. The Navy planned to buy 24 of these oceangoing minesweepers.

Tactical Air Combat

The two houses had agreed on the appropriations for Air Force fighter planes: 39 F-15s ($1.24 billion) and 120 smaller F-16s ($1.71 billion), each amount only slightly smaller than the administration request.

Similarly, for most types of Navy combat planes, the conferees had to reconcile only minor disagreements in the funding level for the number of planes requested by the administration. The conference report provided:

- $235.2 million for 8 A-6E bombers;
- $875 million for 24 F-14 fighters;
- $2.136 billion for 84 F-18 fighters.

The conferees also approved $702 million for 21 Harriers —small, vertical-takeoff bombers used by the Marine Corps. The administration had requested 18 of the planes ($677.1 million).

The two houses also had agreed to provide $100 million to continue developing LANTIRN, a combined radar and infrared viewing system to allow fighters to fly low and find ground targets at night.

Conferees approved a total of $62.6 million — $19.9 million for the Navy and $42.7 million for the Air Force — to develop a smaller version of the Tomahawk cruise missile that could be fired from fighters to attack enemy airfields. The Senate had cut $15 million of the Navy portion of the program.

Personnel Costs

The largest single reduction from the president's February 1982 budget request was a $2.33 billion cut in the allowance for the annual federal pay raise. Reagan's $4 billion request assumed an 8 percent military pay hike and a 5 percent raise for all other federal workers. But during

budget negotiations with Congress in the spring, Reagan agreed to a 4 percent raise across-the-board.

The House position, adopted by the conferees, was that all departments would be given funds to cover only three-quarters of that raise and would make up the rest of the pay hike from other funds appropriated in fiscal 1983.

Authority for enlistment and re-enlistment bonuses was extended through March 31, 1983, by the conference report, thereby setting a deadline for early legislation to extend those programs.

The bonus authority had expired Dec. 17 with the first continuing resolution, H J Res 599 — PL 97-276, (which provided stopgap funding in the absence of a defense appropriations bill).

Administration proposals to liberalize reimbursement of service members' moving costs were turned down for the most part. Of seven proposals — costing $273.8 million — the conferees approved only two — costing $4.1 million. The conferees complained that the Pentagon's transfer policies required too many moves at government expense and asked the General Accounting Office to recommend policy changes.

Medical Benefits. A Senate-passed increase of $120 million in the budget for the military dependents' hospital and medical insurance program (called CHAMPUS) was approved by the conferees. This brought the CHAMPUS appropriation up to $1.199 billion.

And the conferees restored $93 million the House had taken from the medical programs of the four armed services to use for part of the CHAMPUS funding.

Guard, Reserve Forces

The conference report added to the budget several hundred million dollars for equipment earmarked for National Guard and Reserve units, including:

- $53.9 million for 11 Cobra anti-tank helicopters;
- $209 million for 10 Hercules transport planes in various versions;
- $125 million for trucks and other equipment.

Miscellaneous Items

The conferees agreed with the House in making two large cuts it insisted would have no impact on Pentagon operations.

They dropped $1 billion from the request for operating expenses and told the Defense Department to make up the reduction with funds drawn from a cash reserve that was maintained to compensate for any decline in the purchasing power of dollars spent overseas on training exercises and other operational purposes. According to the House Appropriations panel, that account had gotten far larger than was necessary because of the dollar's recent strength against most foreign currencies.

The conference committee also cut $833 million — slightly less than the House reduction — from the request for fuel because of the declining cost of petroleum.

But the conference report retained $300 million the House had cut to force the Pentagon to draw that amount out of the so-called stock funds the department uses to buy commodities that are subject to price fluctuations. As with the foreign currency stabilization fund, the House panel had argued that the stock funds had accumulated too much cash.

Waste Alleged. The conferees also agreed on the following cuts in areas that had routinely come under attack for years as sanctuaries of waste and abuse:

● $91 million cut from the requests for consultants, the amount reduced by the House. The Senate had trimmed $116.1 million from consultant accounts. The conference report approved $735.7 million for consultants and studies.

● $89.9 million from travel funds. The House had cut only $2.5 million from these accounts, and the Senate cut $109.6 million. For travel, the conference report appropriated $1.323 billion.

● $85 million that it ordered the Pentagon to make up by recovering from foreign governments the full administrative cost of foreign arms sales. The House had cut $100 million for this purpose.

Corporate Research. The conferees also approved a House-passed cut of $386 million from funds intended to reimburse contractors for their independently conducted, militarily relevant research and for the cost of preparing bids on defense contracts. The intent of the action was to hold these funds to $2.1 billion.

The conferees ordered the Pentagon to begin identifying these costs as a separate budget item beginning in fiscal 1985. The Army's $1.4 billion budget for delivering new weapons to units in the field and putting them into service was cut by $156.25 million. This split the difference between the Senate cut of $187.5 million and the House reduction of $125 million. The committees agreed that this simply reflected delays in scheduled deliveries of weapons from the contractors.

The Navy's $3.1 billion budget for ship and aircraft overhaul was trimmed by $153.1 million, the amount cut by the Senate. The House had reduced this account by $103.5 million.

Rapid Deployment Force. Conferees permitted the Defense Department to proceed with its plans to transform the Rapid Deployment Force into a unified command responsible only for the Persian Gulf and Middle East regions.

Covert Action. Conferees retained a House-passed provision prohibiting the Pentagon or the Central Intelligence Agency from furnishing military equipment or support to any non-government group for the purpose of overthrowing the government of Nicaragua or provoking a military exchange between Nicaragua and Honduras.

House Committee Report

The House Appropriations Committee reported HR 7355 on Dec. 2 (H Rept 97-943).

The committee recommended an appropriation of $231,103,492,000 in new budget authority and transferred to the fiscal 1983 program an additional $520 million appropriated but not spent for defense programs in earlier years. Reagan's request, revised in November, was for $249,612,409,000, including $4 billion for the annual pay raise for military members and civilian Pentagon employees.

The committee's $17.99 billion cut (counting the additional funds transferred) was by far the largest reduction of a defense appropriations request in recent years, amounting to 7.2 percent. Even so, the bill was $25.88 billion higher than the corresponding fiscal 1982 appropriations.

"With record deficits facing this country," the committee said, the Pentagon should "share with other non-defense programs in helping to reduce federal spending."

MX Missile

The MX intercontinental missile survived in the House Appropriations Committee on a 26-26 vote on Dec. 2. Defense Subcommittee Chairman Addabbo needed a majority of the committee for his motion to delete from the bill $988 million to buy five MXs.

While approving $3.5 billion for MX procurement and research and development, Appropriations did agree to two amendments that would "fence in," or withhold, the money until March 15, 1983.

The fight to save the MX engendered a high-powered lobbying effort that included intercontinental phone calls from Reagan and Secretary of State George P. Shultz in Brazil, and Defense Secretary Caspar W. Weinberger in Belgium, where he was attending a NATO meeting.

Addabbo acknowledged the impact of the administration lobbying. He said there was "tremendous lobbying by the president, the secretary of defense, the secretary of state, everyone from the administration has been calling every member."

In addition to the administration's lobbying, Senate Armed Services Committee Chairman Tower sent letters to congressional colleagues urging them not to delete funds for the MX missile during the lame-duck session, but to wait until 1983, after the "dense pack" basing proposal was fully aired.

In offering the amendment to delete procurement money for the MX missile Addabbo argued that "nobody knows what 'dense pack' is."

Addabbo asked his colleagues: "How could you go back to your districts and say we are going to give a gift of $988 million to the Air Force without us knowing where we're going?" Addabbo also said he had received a petition signed by 1,300 people in Wyoming who "don't want it."

But Jack Edwards, R-Ala., and others argued that keeping funds for the MX missile in the bill was needed to keep the Soviets at the bargaining table in strategic arms talks. Edwards said: "It is essential that we are perceived worldwide as willing to build that deterrent," while at the same time "saying to the Soviets, 'We're serious, why don't you get serious.' "

The last member to cast his vote, the deciding 26th "no" vote, was Bill Alexander, D-Ark. Alexander, who did not make up his mind until the last moment, said: "I wanted to get it [the MX] to the floor." But he added he was still "undecided on the ultimate issue of deploying the MX in 'dense pack.' "

The committee defeated other amendments offered by Addabbo to make major reductions in spending.

By voice vote, the committee defeated an amendment to reduce MX missile research and development funds from $1.7 billion to $500 million and cut basing development money from $715 million to $500 million.

Few Major Changes

Despite the size of its reduction, the committee ordered very few changes in the shape of Reagan's planned defense program. The trouble-plagued Pershing II missile was the only major weapons program requested for which the panel flatly refused to approve production funds.

Pay Cap. The largest single reduction, $2.33 billion, was made in the annual pay raise, which in previous years had been included in supplemental appropriations bills.

Bookkeeping Changes. Another large slice of the reduction came from what amounted to bookkeeping

changes the committee insisted would have no impact on Pentagon operations. These cuts included:

• $1 billion to be replaced with funds drawn from an account the Pentagon maintained to compensate for any decline in the purchasing power of the dollars spent overseas for training exercises and other operational purposes. According to the committee, the account had ballooned to far larger than was necessary because of the dollar's strength against foreign currencies.

• $300 million to be replaced with funds drawn out of the so-called "stock funds" that the Pentagon used to buy commodities that were subject to price fluctuations. As with the foreign currency fund, the committee decided the stock funds had accumulated too much cash.

• $850 million for fuel oil, because of the decline in petroleum prices, and $109 million for enriched uranium ore to fuel nuclear-powered warships, because the money was in the Energy Department spending bill (HR 7145).

Reserves. An additional $724.8 million that was trimmed from Navy procurement accounts had been earmarked for "management reserves" to cover unanticipated problems or design changes in weapons programs. The panel complained that the Navy's formula for calculating reserve requests was not justified and that the money was put to other use without congressional scrutiny.

Research. Another large bite — $386 million — came from funds intended to reimburse contractors for their independent militarily relevant research and for the cost of preparing bids on defense contracts. The committee emphasized that it approved of Pentagon payment for both kinds of contractor activity. But the panel wanted those costs identified as a separate budget item, rather than being assigned to procurement contracts awarded to the contractors, which was the current practice.

Defense Department estimates of both kinds of costs for fiscal 1983 averaged $2.486 billion. The committee ordered the payments limited to no more than $2.1 billion, and it reduced the procurement appropriations by an amount equal to the balance.

Waste. In its annual pattern, the committee also made reductions in several accounts that it had attacked for years as sanctuaries of waste and mismanagement.

The largest of these was a $267.7 million reduction in ammunition procurement, based on a General Accounting Office report that cited cost changes, production inefficiencies and schedule slippages in various ammunition production lines. The panel also trimmed a total of $150.6 million from various accounts to force a reduction in the Pentagon's use of outside consultants.

Strategic Warfare

In addition to approving procurement of five MX missiles and seven B-1 bombers ($4.033 billion), the committee approved a secret amount to develop the "stealth" bomber, designed to evade enemy detection.

The panel approved the B-1 funding by defeating, 15-29, an amendment to delete it.

The panel recommended a $33 million reduction in the $554.6 million requested to modernize existing B-52 bombers to carry long-range, air-launched cruise missiles (ALCM). Citing budget restraints, the committee also agreed reluctantly with the Pentagon's decision to retire three of the oldest squadrons of B-52s, the D-model planes.

Citing Air Force plans to phase out production of the current ALCMs in favor of an improved model, the committee cut procurement of the current model from 440 to

330, a reduction of $112 million. It also trimmed $4.3 million from the request for components for future purchases of the current model, and $20 million from the request for continued development of that missile. The committee approved without change the requests for the improved ALCM: $160 million for development and $30.7 million for components.

Tridents. Consistent with the companion defense authorization bill, the committee recommended one Trident missile-firing submarine ($1.4 billion) rather than the two requested ($2.2 billion). It also approved with minor reductions the request for 72 Trident I missiles ($685 million).

Approved without change was the administration request for $366.7 million to develop a larger version of the Trident missile, called the D-5, that would be accurate enough to destroy enemy land-based missiles in their armored, underground silos.

But the panel was more wary of the Pentagon's plan to speed up the equipping of attack submarines with long-range, nuclear-armed Tomahawk cruise missiles intended for land targets. "The program to date has had a record of marginally acceptable testing," the committee said.

It approved procurement of 109 missiles rather than 120, and approved a plan to have 52 of them produced by a second contractor who would compete for future Tomahawk contracts with General Dynamics Inc. Meanwhile, the committee ordered General Dynamics to produce the missiles only at the current rate, rather than the higher rate included in the budget.

European Nuclear Missiles

The committee also cited testing problems to justify its denial of $498.3 million requested to procure an additional 91 Pershing II missiles.

"The committee sees little merit in continuing to fund production of Pershing II until the Army can document a series of successful tests," the panel said.

The committee declared that its intent was "to send the unmistakable signal that the system when fielded will operate exactly as required, without doubt." The 21 Pershing IIs funded in fiscal 1982 could be used to meet NATO's December 1983 deadline for matching the Soviet missiles, the committee said.

The ground-launched cruise missile (GLCM) which also was planned for deployment in Europe to offset the Soviet missiles, was a version of the Navy's Tomahawk. So the panel imposed reductions on the Air Force GLCM program similar to those imposed on the Navy version: $73.5 million for 45 of the proposed 120 missiles and $11.1 million for GLCM components.

Ground Combat

The committee's principal changes in the requests for major ground combat weapons reflected action taken by the Armed Services committees in the authorization bill.

Amounts approved included $1.4 billion to buy 855 M-1 tanks and $162.9 million to modernize existing M-60 tanks. According to the Appropriations panel, the Army should be able to modernize 453 of the older tanks for that amount instead of the planned 360 because two contractors were competing for the job, thus driving down the price.

The request for 96 UH-60A Blackhawk troop-carrying helicopters was approved at the reduced funding level set by the authorization bill ($568.9 million). The committee cut $65 million from the request for 48 AH-64 Apache

tank-hunting helicopters, approving $695.3 million.

Missile Battles. The committee squared off against its Senate counterpart on two Army missile programs.

It approved $36 million of the $113.7 million requested for the Viper, short-range anti-tank missile, which Congress ordered the Pentagon in 1981 to test against foreign competitors. The Senate Appropriations Committee had barred any further procurement of Viper, citing its inability to penetrate the front armor of new Soviet tanks.

The House committee also approved with minor restrictions an Army plan to award a multi-year contract for production of 20-mile-range artillery rockets. The Senate committee had voted to order the Army instead to set up a second contractor who could compete with the current contractor for each year's purchase of the rockets.

Mobility Forces

The committee basically approved the administration's request to begin buying additional C-5 long-range cargo planes, though incorporating minor funding changes from the authorization bill. The C-5 amount was $847.5 million, including funds for components and spare parts.

The panel also included $60 million, which had been added to the authorization bill, to buy three wide-body commercial jets. The panel said these should be assigned to Air National Guard units. The $60 million was intended to mollify members who had attempted to kill the revival of the Lockheed Corp. C-5 production line in favor of buying Boeing 747s.

Tanker Planes. The committee approved the request for a $915 million installment on a multi-year contract for KC-10 tanker planes. But the committee recommended only $795 million in new appropriations, making up the difference by transferring $120 million from unused appropriations from earlier years.

The committee approved $375 million of the $490 million requested to equip existing KC-135 tanker planes with new engines. It added to the bill a total of $115 million to equip some of the tankers with used airliner engines that were more powerful than current ones. These tankers would be assigned to the Air National Guard.

Rapid Deployment. The panel denied $278.6 million of the $322.6 million requested to modify four high-speed commercial cargo ships to carry Army tanks and other combat gear. Four of the ships were then being modified. The $44 million approved by the committee was to buy parts for future modifications.

Naval Warfare

All of Reagan's requests for major warships were approved by the committee with relatively small reductions that denied the requests for management reserves.

Approved essentially as requested were funds for two aircraft carriers ($6.56 billion), two attack submarines ($1 billion), modernization of the battleship *Iowa* ($300 million) and components to be used in fiscal 1984 to modernize the battleship *Missouri* ($94 million).

The committee rejected an amendment to delete the funding for one carrier on an 18-34 vote.

The panel basically approved the request for two other classes of warships, but ordered design changes. It recommended $2.9 billion for three cruisers equipped with the Aegis anti-missile defense system, but told the Navy not to equip the ship with the LAMPS III anti-submarine helicopter. And the committee approved $666.4 million for two, smaller missile-armed frigates and ordered the Navy to develop an improved radar for them.

Air Combat

The committee appropriated the amounts authorized for Air Force fighter planes: $1.24 billion for 39 F-15s and $1.71 billion for 120 smaller F-16s.

Like the Senate Appropriations Committee, the House panel recommended $357.3 million for 20 A-10 tank-hunting planes. But the funds would be available only if separately authorized, and the authorization bill had ended the A-10 program.

Carrier Planes. Most Navy aircraft programs were approved essentially intact. But the committee denied all funds requested for management reserves, and it made several additional cuts on the grounds that recent contract negotiations had yielded price reductions.

The committee recommended $2.14 billion of the $2.44 billion requested for F/A-18 fighters, though insisting that was enough to buy the planned 84 planes. The panel approved $248.2 million of the $283.7 million requested for components that would be used in future F/A-18 procurement. And it barred the Navy from assigning any of the planes to light bomber squadrons until it met all of the performance criteria originally set for bomber missions.

Manpower

At the end of fiscal 1983, there was to be a total of 2,127,444 active duty military personnel under the committee's bill. This was 18,844 more than the limit at the end of fiscal 1982 but 20,156 fewer than the administration originally had requested for fiscal 1983.

To meet the defense limitations imposed by the first budget resolution (S Con Res 92), the Pentagon informally had reduced its manpower request by 18,100 members. Compared to that revised figure, the committee made deeper cuts in the Navy and Air Force but smaller reductions in the Army. Compared to the original February budget request, the committee's manpower reductions trimmed spending in the bill by $234.2 million.

Among the changes to which the Pentagon had agreed was early retirement of 22 Navy ships, which allowed the committee to cut $248.9 million from the bill.

Bonuses. The panel approved $616.15 million of the $763.75 million requested for enlistment and re-enlistment bonuses. Noting that the services were having no trouble getting enough enlistments and re-enlistments and that bonuses went to one of every 9.5 new recruits and to half of re-enlistees, the committee told the Pentagon to be more selective in awarding bonuses.

The committee also curtailed several proposed new fringe benefits, approving $72.98 million of $376.75 million requested for them. For instance, the committee dropped 75 percent of the $86.3 million requested to increase allowances for moving expenses.

Reserves. Reflecting Congress' traditional solicitude for the Reserve and National Guard forces, the committee added to the bill $517.4 million for their programs. Among the additions were funds for 11 Cobra anti-tank helicopters ($56.9 million), 10 copies of various versions of the C-130 transport plane ($209 million), and $6.8 million to equip a National Guard battalion with the new M-1 tank.

NATO Issues

The committee refused to drop two provisions included in the fiscal 1982 defense bill that the administra-

tion warned would damage relations with other NATO members by blocking planned procurement for U.S. forces of foreign-made equipment.

But the committee accepted modifications to those provisions that had been included in earlier defense bills. The general prohibition on the purchase abroad of "specialty metals" would be waived for the purchase of foreign-made weapons under existing agreements. And the ban on the foreign purchase of automobiles and pickup trucks would be waived for purchases under existing contracts with the United Kingdom, Italy and West Germany.

The committee took several other NATO-related actions:

● It retained the ban on storing equipment at POMCUS sites in Europe for more than four Army divisions.

● It denied $44 million for equipment to be used in wartime by West German reservists assigned to provide supply and transportation support to U.S combat units.

● It cut $25 million from the $55.7 million earmarked to reimburse West German landowners for damage caused by U.S. units during military exercises. As in each of the last few years, the panel said claims payments should be reduced to induce the West German government to pay more of the costs of keeping U.S. forces in that country.

House Floor Action

In a major symbolic defeat for President Reagan, the House voted 245-176 on Dec. 7 to drop from the bill $988 million to buy the first five production-line versions of the MX missile.

The vote marked the first time in recent history that either house of Congress had rejected a president's request to fund a strategic weapons program. *(Vote 398, p. 118-H)*

The House went on to pass the $231 billion defense bill Dec. 8 on a 346-68 vote. *(Vote 400, p. 118-H)*

The House later incorporated most provisions of HR 7355 into the continuing resolution for fiscal 1983, H J Res 631.

As passed by the House, HR 7355 cut some $19 billion from Reagan's $249 billion request, but made few major changes in the president's arms buildup. Most of the reduction came from hundreds of relatively small cuts made because of technical problems or management judgments.

MX Battle

While cutting the MX production funds, the House approved $2.5 billion to continue research and development on the missile.

"Congress is still for the MX, is undecided but skeptical on dense pack, and is against procurement of the missile before you've decided on the basing mode," said Les Aspin, D-Wis., a frequent Pentagon critic who voted to cut the MX funds.

Despite strong lobbying by the administration, the House majority, including 50 Republicans, broke with the longstanding tradition of congressional deference to the president and the Pentagon on complex weapons issues.

The House rejected repeated administration warnings that a vote against MX would undermine the U.S. bargaining position in arms reduction talks with Moscow. That argument typically had carried great weight on Capitol Hill.

"We must move forward with the MX to have any hope of achieving meaningful progress at the arms negotia-

tions in Geneva," Reagan said in a letter to all members the day before the MX vote.

The administration contended that unless deployment of MX was likely, Moscow would have no incentive to agree to reductions in its ICBM force.

During the two-hour House debate, some MX opponents denounced this logic. "The history of the arms race shows that weapons which are intended to force the other side to the negotiating table simply add more momentum to the arms race," said Mike Lowry, D-Wash.

And Addabbo argued that MX production was not yet necessary. To whatever extent the bargaining argument for MX was correct, he said, continued development of the missile would provide U.S. negotiators with adequate leverage. He sponsored the amendment cutting the MX funds.

Dense Pack. Opponents of the MX procurement funding also stressed the novel and untested character of the "dense pack" deployment system.

By the time the House voted on the issue, only a handful of members had been briefed on dense pack, which was disputed even within the Joint Chiefs of Staff and marked a radical change from previous notions of how to defend the missile from Soviet attack.

Dense pack was attacked by some members for violating the common-sense rule against putting all one's eggs in a single basket. Les AuCoin, D-Ore., likened it to the decision by military chiefs in Hawaii before the Japanese attack on Pearl Harbor, that "the one way to make sure the planes would be safe is to cluster them on the runway.... They got blown to smithereens."

But Defense Subcommittee member Joseph M. McDade, R-Pa., and others said they simply needed more time to analyze the approach. In voting for the Addabbo amendment, they seemed to be rejecting Reagan's argument that support for the missile procurement money did not constitute an irrevocable commitment to dense pack.

In a Dec. 10 press conference, called to urge the Senate to restore the MX funds, Reagan held fast to his position. He hinted at a willingness to jettison dense pack if Congress proposed a more acceptable basing method, but he insisted on the need for the missile.

"Next year as we have more time, I would welcome a vigorous debate on the best way to base the missile," he said. "I agree that more time is needed before we achieve a consensus in Congress on the basing mode."

The insistence by MX foes on casting the Addabbo amendment in terms of a vote on dense pack, Reagan said, was "lacking a little in honesty."

Budget Symbol. According to several members and aides on both sides of the MX battle, the state of the economy and the political lessons of the November elections also were important factors in the House vote.

The huge defense bill offered members their first opportunity since the election to cast a symbolic vote for restraining the Pentagon budget. Democratic gains in November were widely read as reflecting public sentiment to trim Reagan's defense plan.

"The MX has become a symbol . . . of the over-costliness of the Reagan military budget," declared Sidney R. Yates, D-Ill. "Every other national program is being held hostage to the military budget."

Carroll Hubbard Jr., a Kentucky Democrat who typically supported Pentagon requests, put the argument more colorfully. "Right or wrong, the words 'Here come the Russians,' nowadays do not scare Kentuckians half as much as 'Here come the creditors.'"

Among the expensive and controversial weapons in the bill, including the B-1 bomber and two nuclear-powered aircraft carriers, the MX apparently emerged as the sacrificial goat largely because of skepticism over dense pack.

MX Vote. The administration's defeat by a margin of 69 votes was a dramatic turnaround from a July 21 House vote on the same issue. Acting on the defense authorization bill (S 2248 — PL 97-252), the House turned aside, 212-209, an amendment by Nicholas Mavroules, D-Mass., that would have deleted the MX production money. *(Vote 188, p. 56-H)*

Forty-three House members who had voted against the Mavroules amendment in July switched to support the Addabbo amendment; among them were 22 Southern Democrats, 13 Republicans and eight Northern Democrats. Nine Republicans changed in the opposite direction.

Between Dec. 2, when the Appropriations Committee rejected Addabbo's amendment on a tie vote, and Dec. 7, Mavroules and Norman D. Dicks, D-Wash., who co-sponsored the Addabbo amendment, ardently canvassed their colleagues for support. Their efforts were meshed with a lobbying campaign by a coalition of groups that came close to beating Reagan on the nuclear weapons "freeze" vote in August. Prominent among them were the Council for a Livable World, Common Cause, Friends of the Earth, and church groups, but none of the major labor unions that had joined in the freeze campaign.

Other Amendments

On the broader issue of overall defense funding levels, Addabbo called the MX vote "a forerunner of things to come." He also predicted that cost increases would make the B-1 bomber vulnerable to congressional attack in 1983.

But House members' zeal for challenging the Reagan defense plan apparently was spent in the Dec. 7 MX battle. The next day the House rejected by voice votes Addabbo amendments to cut procurement funds for the B-1 and one of the two nuclear-powered aircraft carriers. The B-1 amendment would have deleted $4 billion to buy the first seven B-1 planes and components for future planes. The other amendment would have deleted $3.56 billion of the $6.6 billion earmarked for two carriers.

Addabbo abandoned a fight to cut another $1.5 billion from the $2.5 billion budgeted to continue development of MX. He accepted a substitute amendment by Jack Edwards that extended from March 15 to April 30 a committee-imposed ban on expenditure of $560 million of the amount earmarked for developing an MX basing system.

F/A-18 Fighter. An amendment by Bruce F. Vento, D-Minn., that would have ended procurement of the Navy's F/A-18 jet after the bill's purchase of 84 planes was rejected by voice vote. The proposal would have dropped the $248.2 million earmarked for components that would be used in F/A-18s procured in the fiscal 1984 budget.

A longtime F-18 critic, Vento said his amendment would leave enough planes to fill Marine Corps fighter squadrons, while blocking the purchase of any for use by the Marines and the Navy as small bombers. The plane had been designed to perform both missions. But in recent tests it had fallen short of some of the performance specifications for the bombing role, including maximum range.

Covert Actions. By a vote of 411-0, the House adopted an amendment by Edward P. Boland, D-Mass., barring the Pentagon or the CIA from using funds in the bill to provide military aid to any non-governmental group "for the purpose of overthrowing the government of Nica-

ragua or provoking a military exchange between Nicaragua and Honduras." *(Vote 399, p. 118-H)*

This was a substitute for a more restrictive amendment by Tom Harkin, D-Iowa, that would have barred assistance to non-governmental groups "for the purpose of . . . carrying out military activities in or against Nicaragua."

Harkin cited press reports that the CIA was aiding groups seeking to overthrow the government of Nicaragua.

Rejected by voice vote were two amendments that would have reduced procurement funds in the bill:

● By Marge Roukema, R-N.J., to cut $2.7 billion across-the-board from the bill's procurement accounts.

● By Jim Courter, R-N.J., to cut $117.57 million from the $377.7 million recommended for development of an anti-ballistic missile defense for U.S. ICBMs. The committee figure was $350 million below Reagan's request.

The House adopted by voice vote two amendments restoring to the bill a total of $115 million that had been dropped by the Appropriations Committee:

● By Edwards, restoring $55 million for components to be used in a large helicopter carrier that could haul 1,800 Marines. The administration planned to request $1.3 billion for the ship in its fiscal 1984 budget.

● By Addabbo, adding back $60 million for Reserve and National Guard personnel.

Senate Committee Action

The $233.4 billion defense bill (S 2951) reported Sept. 23 by the Senate Appropriations Committee was about 5 percent below Reagan's request, but it funded all major weapon programs, most of them at or near the budgeted levels.

During committee action on the bill, the B-1 bomber never was challenged, and an effort to fund only one nuclear-powered aircraft carrier rather than two was overwhelmingly rejected.

The Defense Subcommittee had tentatively deferred initial procurement of MX missiles, but quickly reversed itself when the administration warned that the action would undermine the U.S. bargaining position in arms control talks with Moscow.

As reported (S Rept 97-580), the bill cut $12.1 billion from Reagan's $245.5 billion request for new appropriations. But that reduction was partly offset by the committee's transfer to fiscal 1983 accounts of $346 million appropriated in prior years (but not spent) for various defense programs.

More than half the total reduction — $6.48 billion — came from the procurement accounts, reduced by 6.9 percent.

An additional $1.14 billion came from two sets of price reductions: $700 million could be trimmed from operating costs paid overseas because of the dollar's growing strength against several foreign currencies, according to the panel; the $9 billion fuel budget could be cut by $440 million because oil prices had softened since the budget was submitted in February.

The appropriation bill provided $5.48 billion less than had been included in the companion defense authorization bill. The latter bill covered every program in S 2951 except military personnel costs. Again, the procurement accounts showed the biggest differences, $3.1 billion lower than the ceilings set by the earlier bill.

Budget Ceilings. The most critical threshold facing S 2951 in the Appropriations Committee was the ceiling

allocated to the Defense Subcommittee under the first concurrent budget resolution (S Con Res 92).

Appropriations Chairman Mark O. Hatfield, R-Ore., told defense panel Chairman Stevens that he simply would not accept a bill from the subcommittee that exceeded the allowed ceilings of $238.5 billion in budget authority and $201.3 billion in projected outlays.

Stevens' panel met the budget authority limit with relative ease, but had to strain mightily to meet the outlay ceilings. When allowance was made for other outlay reductions for which the Defense Subcommittee could take credit, projected outlays for fiscal 1983 had to be reduced by $8.7 billion below the amount projected from Reagan's request for the bill.

After several days of hardball politicking between the subcommittee and Defense Secretary Weinberger, the panel met the $8.7 billion target. As reported by the Appropriations Committee, the projected defense outlays under S 2951 were estimated at $200.3 billion.

Who's on First? As it had done in 1981, the Senate committee reported its version of the defense bill without waiting for House action, which was deferred until after the election recess. The committee said early action on the Senate version of the bill was needed to establish a realistic base for Pentagon spending under the continuing resolution. *(1981 Almanac p. 311)*

"It is not the committee's intent to overturn the traditions of Congress that have established the House as the normal originating body for appropriations measures," the Senate panel declared.

Manpower Issues

Calling for an end to "the steady growth in military manpower," the committee approved less than half of the president's proposal to increase by 37,600 the number of active duty military personnel.

The bill funded a manpower level at the end of fiscal 1983 of 2,125,200 — compared to the level of 2,110,000 which prevailed at the end of fiscal 1982 — for a reduction of $220.4 million from Reagan's request.

Troops in Europe. The committee said it was "greatly disturbed that the U.S. commitment to European security in terms of force levels and defense expenditures continues to escalate while our NATO allies' share of defense steadily declines."

Accordingly, it ordered the number of military personnel stationed in Europe to be held at the fiscal 1980 level of 331,700, thereby cutting the bill by $49.9 million. The committee also directed the disbanding of a cavalry brigade stationed in West Germany, saying it said would reduce the bill by an additional $42 million.

Bonuses and Benefits. Partly because of recent hikes in military compensation, the panel cut several proposed new fringe benefits, reducing the bill by $322 million.

For the same reason, and because the services had had an easier time recruiting and retaining members during the recession, the committee trimmed $22.9 million from the request for enlistment bonuses and $138 million from the request for re-enlistment bonuses.

The panel also cut $230 million from the request for personnel transfers. It said that fewer moves would be made than had been budgeted, partly because the proportion of senior personnel, who were transferred less frequently, was increasing.

Guard and Reserve Emphasis. In contrast to its opposition to increases in the active duty force, the com-

mittee approved with enthusiasm the budgeted increase of 62,300 in the size of the National Guard and Reserve component forces. During the spring budget negotiations, the administration had proposed scaling back that increase, to save $140 million.

"The committee is convinced that by augmenting the strength and capabilities of the Guard and Reserve forces, the military readiness of the armed forces can be maintained at a lower cost with no degradation to combat effectiveness," according to the report.

The panel directed the defense secretary to convene a panel of non-government experts to report to Congress by July 1 on missions that could be performed as well — and more cheaply — by Guard and Reserve forces rather than active duty forces.

In keeping with Congress' traditional responsiveness to the politically potent Guard and Reserve organizations, the panel funded several programs that had been added to the president's budget by the two Armed Services committees to improve the equipment of Guard and Reserve units.

These included:

● $31.2 million to buy equipment and protective clothing to operate under chemical attack and in cold weather conditions;

● $200 million for trucks, artillery and other equipment to be selected by the various Guard and Reserve components;

● $145 million for eight C-130 transport planes for the Air National Guard;

● $136.5 million to replace the engines on 28 midair refueling tankers flown by the Air National Guard with more fuel-efficient engines stripped off second-hand commercial jetliners.

Operations and Maintenance

Two perennial targets of congressional budgeteers came in for the usual trimming: $109.5 million was taken from the request for travel costs and $191.1 million from the request for various contract consultants.

Another large block of reductions came from cuts that the committee insisted were mandated by facts of life: $187.5 million from the Army because, the panel said, new equipment was being introduced into the field more slowly than had been planned; $60 million from the Navy, because planned ship modernizations were lagging behind their timetables; $47.5 million from the Navy because the Trident missile-launching submarines were entering service behind schedule.

An additional cut of $200.8 million reflected the committee's judgment that the Navy was unduly optimistic about the rate at which its ships and planes could be overhauled and maintained. Of that reduction, $175.8 million came from canceling the overhauls for four ships the committee decided to retire and for three ships that would be overhauled a year later than planned.

"The planned number of complex vessel overhauls would exceed previous demonstrated performance," the panel said.

The remaining $25 million cut was to hold the total amount of time Navy planes would be flown to 1.8 million hours, the same total as was budgeted in fiscal 1982. A planned increase of 81,000 hours would put too heavy a workload on the Navy's aircraft maintenance schedule, the committee said.

Mirroring the authorization bill, the committee also dropped $190 million from an Air Force maintenance ac-

count for technical bookkeeping reasons.

Force Cuts. In addition to these reductions that the committee implied would be essentially painless, it also approved cuts in the forces in the field.

Deferring the planned activation of a new Air Force wing saved $40 million. The deferral had also been directed by the defense authorization bill.

By retiring 22 ships a few years ahead of schedule — the Navy's 17 oldest destroyers and its five oldest amphibious landing ships — the panel saved $123.2 million. The authorization bill had retired only 13 destroyers and none of the amphibious ships.

The committee also dropped $100 million requested as a contingency fund to allow senior commanders to meet unforeseen crises. It told the Pentagon to accommodate unforeseen requirements within its budget.

Strategic War Forces

The committee slowed some strategic weapons programs to a modest extent, but neither of the symbols of the administration's nuclear buildup — the B-1 bomber and the MX missile — was significantly affected.

The Defense Subcommittee had tentatively proposed sharp restraints on funding for the MX and Pershing II missiles. But the panel quickly acceded to the administration's insistence that any sign that Congress might kill either program would undermine U.S. negotiating leverage in arms control talks with Moscow.

ICBMs. To procure the first five production-line MX missiles and associated equipment, the committee recommended $988 million, the amount authorized. The administration had requested $1.45 billion for nine missiles.

Also recommended was $1.67 billion to continue development of MX and $775 million to develop a basing technique for the missile. Echoing a provision of the authorization bill, the committee directed that $715 million of the basing development money not be available for spending until the president had made a specific basing method recommendation to Congress.

The committee complained that the Air Force had given too low a priority to a research program studying more exotic improvements in ICBMs. It approved only the $50 million requested rather than the $60 million authorized for that program, but it told the service to develop a plan to pursue promising developments in the area.

Bombers, Cruise Missiles. The B-1 bomber program was funded as requested: $3.39 billion for the first nine production-line planes; $475 million for components to be used in planes funded in fiscal 1984; and $753.5 million to continue development of the plane.

Procurement of air-launched cruise missiles (ALCMs), to be launched from B-52 bombers flying outside Soviet airspace, was cut from the 440 missiles requested to 350, for a reduction of $125 million. But the panel maintained the slowdown was intended to bring production of the missiles into line with the rate at which B-52s were being modified to carry them. And it said the Air Force was considering development of an improved cruise missile to replace the ALCM.

Submarine-Launched Missiles. For the 10th in a class of submarines designed to launch Trident ballistic missiles, the committee recommended $1.46 billion, along with $81.3 million to procure components that would be used on the next two ships in the class.

The administration had requested funds for two Trident subs, but a reduction to one ship had been agreed to

during negotiations on the first budget resolution.

The number of Trident I missiles was cut to 66, from the 72 requested, for a savings of $65.8 million. The committee based this cut on the fact that all Trident subs beginning with the ship funded in fiscal 1981 were to be built to carry a much larger, more accurate missile, called the Trident II.

The committee provided $173 million to procure 71 long-range Tomahawk missiles, some of which were to be nuclear-armed, to be deployed on attack submarines and other warships. This was a reduction of 49 missiles ($98 million) from the request.

European Missiles. The request for 91 Pershing II missiles was approved ($498.3 million). But the request for a ground-launched version of the Tomahawk cruise missile (the so-called GLCM) was cut from 120 missiles to 100, a reduction of $47.3 million.

Tank, Anti-Tank Warfare

For procurement of M-1 tanks, the committee recommended $1.35 billion, of which $140.9 million had been appropriated but not spent for other purposes in earlier years. This would allow purchase of "at least" 720 tanks, the panel said, and an additional $363.9 million would buy components for 840 tanks in fiscal 1984.

The authorization bill had approved $1.56 billion for 855 M-1s.

Also included in the bill was the authorized amount for 600 M-2 infantry carriers, which also were equipped with anti-tank missiles ($783.3 million).

The authorized amount ($114.7 million) was provided to begin procurement of "off the shelf" lightweight armored vehicles that would be easier for the Army and Marine Corps to transport into remote areas.

Anti-Tank Weapons. Based on anticipated price reductions, the committee trimmed the request for TOW anti-tank guided missiles by $13.2 million, to $132 million. TOWs had a range of about two miles and were fired from simple launch tubes mounted on tripods and on various Army vehicles and helicopters.

But the panel flatly refused to allow any further funding for a smaller, short-range anti-tank rocket, called Viper, thus cutting the bill by $113 million. Viper was intended as a small, "throw-away" weapon that could be carried by an infantryman and used as a last-ditch defense against tanks. But the Senate committee complained that it had grown too expensive and would be unable to penetrate the front armor of new Soviet tanks.

The committee told the Pentagon to continue a comparative test of other weapons, which Congress mandated in 1981, and to pick one with "frontal kill capability against modern tanks." Because of the design of tank armor and because a missile usually hit it at a shallow angle, penetrating the front of a Russian T-72 tank reportedly was equivalent to penetrating a steel slab about 20 inches thick.

Rockets and Jobs. Continued procurement of large artillery rockets was funded as requested ($368.9 million). These so-called MLRS missiles could carry hundreds of explosive grenades or dozens of anti-tank mines up to 20 miles.

But the committee rejected a request for $53.2 million to begin work on a multi-year contract for the rockets, ordering the Army instead to make preparations with a second contractor, who then could compete for each year's buy of rockets beginning in 1986. Accordingly, the committee added $20 million to equip the competing plant.

During the markup of S 2951, the MLRS issue had been hotly contested by Sens. Dale Bumpers, D-Ark., and J. Bennett Johnston, D-La. Vought Corp., the current MLRS contractor who would receive the proposed multi-year contract, manufactured the rockets in Arkansas. Thiokol Corp., the potential competitor, would manufacture its share of the procurement in Louisiana.

Anti-Tank Helicopters. To continue production of the Apache (AH-64) anti-tank helicopter, the committee approved the authorized amount ($710 million) for 48 planes. Also included in the bill was $115 million for components to be used in the fiscal 1984 purchase of Apaches and $249.2 million for the laser-guided Hellfire anti-tank missiles with which the Apache was armed.

The committee expressed its support of the Army's plan to equip 578 existing scout helicopters with lasers to control the missiles shot from Apaches. But it complained about cost increases in the program and approved only $110.9 million of the $120.9 million request.

The panel also said that the Army and the Defense Department were not moving fast enough to develop small, cheap, remote-controlled airplanes that could be used for several missions, including carrying lasers to guide missiles and bombs. It ordered the Army to provide an eight-year plan for these so-called "remotely piloted vehicles" by June 30, 1983.

Behind the Lines. The committee approved $32.5 million to develop a so-called "conventional stand-off weapon" — a missile designed to release several anti-tank homing warheads over enemy tank formations dozens of miles behind the front line. It would be fired from ground launchers by the Army and from airplanes by the Air Force and was planned for production by 1986.

The Pentagon believed that such weapons could badly disrupt a Soviet ground attack, since Russian plans relied heavily on prompt arrival of waves of fresh reinforcements to exploit any battlefield success.

But the committee protested that the budget and timetable for developing an airborne radar used to locate MLRS targets were too uncertain. It provided $15 million of the $19.76 million requested for the so-called battlefield data system and called for more precise planning information.

Anti-Aircraft Defense

Citing production delays, the committee trimmed $117.8 million from the $805.1 million request for Patriot, long-range anti-aircraft missiles, a reduction from 376 missiles to 287.

The panel also cut $42.5 million from the $214.6 million request for Stinger anti-aircraft missiles, fired by infantrymen from little bazooka-like launchers. This was because an improvement in the missile's infrared homing device was not yet ready for production, the committee said. It added $4 million to the Army research budget to complete tests of the modification.

Like the authorizing committees, the Appropriations panel added $50 million to the request for British-built Rapier anti-aircraft missiles. The Pentagon had requested $98 million for the short-range missiles to be used by British troops to protect U.S. air bases in Britain. The added funds were to buy more weapons to be used to protect U.S. air bases on the European mainland.

For 96 Sergeant York anti-aircraft tanks (formerly called DIVADs), to protect tank columns against Soviet missile-firing helicopters, the committee approved $471.1

million. It cut $50 million requested for the program's management reserve, but approved the requested $74.4 million for components to be used in future Yorks.

Chemical Warfare

Following the authorization bill, the committee dropped the $54 million requested to procure binary chemical weapons. During action on the authorization bill, the request had won approval by a very narrow margin in the Senate, but was decisively rejected in the House.

The Appropriations panel also dropped $2.7 million from the $13.7 million request for Army research on chemical weapons. The reduction was aimed at a program to develop additional types of binary weapons.

The committee also provided $36.2 million to buy Army gas masks instead of the $49.6 million requested to begin buying a new, more expensive model. After an eight-year development effort, the Army had decided to abandon the new mask because it made it no easier for the wearer to perform certain tasks, such as looking through optical equipment. The committee also dropped $2.5 million budgeted to continue development of the new mask.

Naval Warfare

The committee approved, unchanged, the requests for $6.8 billion to build two nuclear-powered aircraft carriers and for $323.4 million to finish modernizing the battleship *Iowa* as a cruise-missile launcher.

But it rejected the $94 million request to begin modernization of a third battleship, the *Missouri*. Refurbishing of the *New Jersey* had been completed.

The panel also dropped the request for $210.2 million to build an oiler to refuel combat ships in mid-ocean and $109.8 million for components to be used on another oiler next year. It explained that, though construction of the first ship of this class was to have begun in fiscal 1982, the contract would not be let until fiscal 1983. A delay in funding the succeeding ships would ensure that the design and cost estimates were firm, according to the committee.

Submarine Hunting. Approved without change were the requests for $1 billion to build two nuclear-powered submarines of the *Los Angeles* class, designed to hunt Soviet subs, and for $416 million for components to be used in additional subs in the future.

The committee approved $631.4 million for two escort frigates, $35 million less than the request. But it said the reduction could be offset by a $35 million saving in the price of the frigates ordered in fiscal 1982.

The request for $3.06 billion to build three cruisers was reduced by $49.6 million to remove from the ships sonars and equipment associated with LAMPs III anti-submarine helicopters.

The cruisers were built around the Aegis, computer-controlled anti-aircraft system, and were designed to protect naval task forces against waves of Soviet cruise missiles. Accordingly, some critics had insisted that they did not need to carry their own anti-submarine systems, but the Navy wanted to equip the ships to operate independently as well as in fleets.

The surveys and investigations staff of the House Appropriations Committee had issued a report questioning the stability of the cruiser, but the Navy staunchly defended the ship.

The committee approved the $616.7 million authorized to buy 27 LAMPS III helicopters, which was to be the principal anti-submarine weapon of most of the Navy's

surface ships. This $241.7 million reduction in the request was part of the negotiated budget package. The panel also added to the bill $9 million to test whether a new engine would improve the range and weapons payload of the smaller, cheaper LAMPS I anti-submarine helicopter.

The $138.6 million request to design a new class of guided missile-armed destroyers (called DDG-51s) was approved. But the committee added $14.5 million to ensure that an improved propulsion system and sonar would be ready in time to go into the first ship of the class. And it added $60 million to continue development of laser-guided artillery for the ship, something greatly desired by the Marine Corps to support amphibious landings.

The authorization bill barred expenditure of any funds for DDG-51 until the Navy produced a plan to equip the first ship with the laser-guided artillery.

Aerial Combat

The authorized amounts were recommended for: 39 F-15 fighters ($1.24 billion); components for future F-15s ($162 million); and 120 smaller F-16 fighters ($1.7 billion). For future F-16 components, the panel recommended $223.3 million as requested instead of the $323.3 million authorized.

Future Fighters. For a comparative test of improved versions of the F-15 and F-16 — the so-called F-15E and F-16E — the authorized $47 million was recommended by Senate Appropriations. The Air Force originally had planned to choose one model and buy 400 copies in the mid-1980s to attack ground targets deep behind enemy lines. But reportedly, the service recently had been considering procurement of both planes.

The committee insisted that only one of the modified fighters could be afforded.

The panel also added $50 million to the $10.2 million requested to test improved versions of existing jet engines that would be used by the new "E model" planes, among others. This program had been the subject of intense political maneuvering by the Pratt & Whitney division of United Technologies, which made the F-100 engine that powered the F-15 and F-16, and General Electric Co., which had a fighter version of the F-101 engine.

The Air Force insisted that the modified engine was to be chosen on the basis of reliability rather than power, maintaining that both competitors were powerful enough for its needs. But Pratt & Whitney supporters worried that the greater thrust of the F-101 would work to their disadvantage. The added funds were to let Pratt & Whitney boost the thrust of the F-100.

The committee also added to the bill a provision requiring that any new jet engine be accompanied by a performance warranty.

To continue development of the LANTIRN infrared viewing and radar system to allow fighters to fly low and find ground targets at night, the committee approved $100 million of the $103.76 million requested. Setting the stage for a battle with the authorizing committees, it also included a provision barring the use of any funds to have a competition between LANTIRN, which the committee said was on schedule and within budget, and any other night-fighting system. The authorization bill had ordered a test between one part of LANTIRN and the night-viewing system built for the Navy's F-18 fighter.

To develop an entirely new Air Force fighter for the 1990s, the committee approved $23 million, the authorized

amount, of the $27.3 million request. Of the approved amount, $18.7 million was to develop a new engine.

Rapid Deployment Forces

For rapid transport of supplies in emergencies, the committee provided $750 million to buy C-5B transport planes, including $100 million for advance procurement of parts, and added the $200 million to accelerate development of the smaller C-17. It also recommended a total of $915 million for procurement of KC-10 tanker planes by a multi-year contract. Of that amount, $120 million had been appropriated in the fiscal 1982 supplemental but had not been spent.

The seaborne component of the Pentagon's plans for landing troops in the Persian Gulf fared less well than the air transport package. The committee denied the $278.6 million of the $322.6 million requested to modify four high-speed cargo ships to carry tanks and other heavy vehicles. Four of these so-called SL-7 ships already were being modified, and the committee said it did not want all eight ships to be undergoing conversion simultaneously.

The remaining $44 million was to buy components for the eventual conversions.

Another reduction of $40 million, copied from the authorization bill, reflected delays in the Navy's plan to charter converted cargo ships as mobile storage depots for the tanks and other heavy equipment for troops that could be flown to the Persian Gulf or other trouble spots.

The committee added a provision barring the formal evolution of the Rapid Deployment Force command into an independent command for Southwest Asia, similar to the other overseas commands, such as the European Command. This change, announced in 1981, was scheduled for Jan. 1, 1983. The panel said it had been given no explanation for narrowing the organization's responsibility to one region.

More fundamentally, the committee appeared to view the issue as another facet of the argument over allied burden-sharing. "Our European and Japanese allies, who have a far greater dependence and thus a far greater stake in the stability of Southwest Asia, should be expected to assume an appropriate responsibility for the military defense of the region," it said.

Pentagon Lobbying

The committee included a provision barring the use of federal funds either directly or indirectly to lobby Congress. Defense Subcommittee Chairman Stevens had professed great irritation at the intensity of lobbying by the Pentagon and by the competing contractors in May when the Senate debated whether to buy C-5 transport planes or used commercial Boeing 747s.

Senate Floor Action

The Senate committee on Dec. 15 incorporated most provisions of S 2951 into the fiscal 1983 continuing resolution, H J Res 631.

During the Senate's initial action on H J Res 631 on Dec. 16-17, administration supporters achieved a draw on a proposed cut in U.S. troop strength in Europe.

The administration won on several other issues that had been the focus of congressional anger over the relatively low defense budgets of major U.S. allies, but some of these victories proved fleeting because the Senate provi-

sions were dropped or changed in the final version of the resolution.

The Senate also rejected a $5.6 billion cut in the continuing resolution's $232 billion defense appropriation. And it upheld the administration position on other defense issues by larger margins, for example turning back a proposal to drop funding for one of two $3.4 billion aircraft carriers.

In a late addendum to its vote to support a White House-backed position on procurement of the MX missile, the Senate accepted by voice vote an amendment by Gary Hart, D-Colo., that blocked the first flight test of the MX until Congress approved a specific method for basing the missile.

The Senate on Dec. 16 had adopted, 56-42, an administration-backed provision that postponed a decision on MX basing until mid-1983. *(Vote 420, p. 71-S)*

NATO Issues

As reported by the Senate Appropriations Committee, the resolution allowed the Pentagon to retain 315,600 personnel in Europe, the number authorized at the end of fiscal 1982. But the resolution made that a ceiling. The administration had planned to increase European troop strength in fiscal 1983. The president could override the troop ceiling for reasons of national security.

In addition, the Senate Dec. 17 adopted an amendment by Sam Nunn, D-Ga., that dropped a requirement that the Army disband the 4,000-man brigade stationed at Wiesbaden in West Germany. The funds to operate the brigade would have to be diverted from other programs, subject to the approval of the congressional defense committees.

The Nunn amendment also allowed the Pentagon to fund the U.S. share of two NATO programs that the Appropriations Committee had barred in the regular defense bill (S 2951) and the continuing resolution:

● The so-called "host nation support" plan under which 93,000 West German reservists would be equipped to perform security, supply and transport jobs for U.S. units in wartime;

● Storage of the tanks and other heavy equipment for two Army divisions in POMCUS sites in Europe.

As with the restored Army brigade, the Nunn amendment added no funds to the resolution for the host nation support plan or the two POMCUS sites. It provided that up to $49.3 million for the two programs could be diverted from other projects, subject to approval by the Armed Services and Appropriations committees.

Burden-Sharing Debate. Nunn had the backing of an array of Armed Services and Foreign Relations Committee members during Senate debate on the issue. He insisted that his disagreement with the Appropriations panel was over tactics rather than over the basic premise that U.S. allies should bear a larger share of the cost of the common defense.

The POMCUS expansion and joint U.S.-German funding of the host-nation support agreement both were part of a package deal under which the United States would expand its plans to reinforce the continent, and the European NATO members would provide more support for U.S. troops.

"We cannot expect to improve allied burden-sharing if we fail to fund our share of key programs designed for that purpose," he told the Senate.

Supporters of the amendment emphasized that the

host-nation support agreement set a new precedent within NATO, which in the past had assumed that each country was responsible for the supply and transport only of its own troops. Under the new agreement, West Germany would provide the manpower and some of the budget for such services to U.S. troops.

But the Senate and House Appropriations committees each had objected to the planned U.S. absorption of some of the costs of the West German support troops.

"If after the hard and lengthy negotiations that produced this cost-sharing formula, we now ask the Germans to pay the entire cost," Nunn warned, "the program is dead."

Stevens accepted the amendment, arguing that his subcommittee had been more interested in the projected savings than in the specific policy changes. And he said that when he visited Europe in November, NATO commanders had placed a high priority on the POMCUS and host-nation support programs.

But he underscored the committee's fundamental unhappiness with NATO burden-sharing, a feeling that appeared to be widely shared in both houses of Congress.

"We have repeatedly stated our concern for the level of support coming from our allies. We view it to be disproportionately low," Stevens said.

Buy American. The Senate on Dec. 17 also adopted by voice vote an amendment by Tower slightly relaxing legal restrictions on Pentagon procurement of foreign-made equipment containing specialty metals.

Provisions put in effect by the fiscal 1982 appropriations bill (PL 97-114) allowed the Pentagon to buy finished weapons that included foreign-processed specialty metals. The administration and senior members of the Senate Armed Services and Foreign Relations committees had warned that a flat ban on procurement of foreign metals would nullify agreements with NATO allies and Israel.

The Tower amendment expanded the exemption to allow purchase of weapons parts and subassemblies that included non-U.S. processed specialty metals. Tower said such items accounted for most U.S. defense purchases abroad.

$5.6 Billion Cut

Also on Dec. 17, Slade Gorton, R-Wash., proposed a $5.6 billion reduction in the defense total for the continuing resolution. The operations and maintenance accounts would have been exempted from the 3.3 percent cut, which was aimed at the procurement accounts.

Gorton justified the reduction partly by the fact that inflation was lower than had been forecast when the fiscal 1983 budget was drafted, so the Pentagon should need less money to buy the same amount of equipment.

But the cut also was a recognition of "the weakening national consensus for massive increases in the national defense budget," Gorton said.

He predicted that Congress would reject the continued large defense spending increases that would be needed to follow through on the large procurement increases in fiscal 1983. The weapons purchases authorized in 1983 would have to be paid for in years to come.

If steps were not taken in 1982 to restrain future spending commitments, Gorton warned, "we shall find that the steps we will be taking in two or three years will require much greater cuts in readiness and in weapons systems themselves."

Stevens objected that his subcommittee already had met the requirements of the first budget resolution (S Con Res 92), which mandated several billion dollars in cuts from Reagan's 1983 defense budget.

Stevens said his plan had trimmed $16 billion in budget authority from the president's defense request. And he said it would be practically impossible to allocate another $5.6 billion reduction to specific projects before the conference committee met on the continuing resolution.

Charles H. Percy, R-Ill., warned against across-the-board cuts as a general rule, saying that they "inevitably penalize the most efficient operations and lead to budget padding when agencies submit their requests."

In general, the 52-45 vote to table the Gorton amendment had liberals supporting Gorton and conservatives opposed. But several conservatives, including Armed Services Committee members Harry F. Byrd Jr., Ind.-Va., and Roger W. Jepsen, R-Iowa, opposed the tabling motion. *(Vote 435, p. 73-S)*

Smaller Reduction. The Senate approved by voice vote a Tower amendment to reduce the defense portion of the resolution by a total of $356 million. The amendment cut funds for several programs that were not authorized or that were authorized at levels lower than the continuing resolution.

The cuts included:
- $64.2 million for the C-2 Navy cargo plane;
- $328.3 million for the Air Force A-10 tank-hunting bomber;
- $100 million for the C-17, a long-range Air Force cargo plane, formerly called the CX.

The amendment also added to the resolution $82 million for F-16 fighters and $53.9 million for the HARM missile, launched from fighters to home in on anti-aircraft radars.

Tower's amendment also allowed the Navy to use up to $29 million of its appropriation to continue operating five amphibious ships that the Appropriations Committee had recommended retiring to save money. The amendment did not alter a committee provision to retire 17 old Navy destroyers.

Carrier Battle

The battle over nuclear carriers followed the pattern of previous years, with liberals accounting for nearly all support for an amendment by Hart and Carl Levin, D-Mich., that would have dropped one of the two $3.4 billion ships from the resolution. The motion to table (kill) the amendment was agreed to 67-31. *(Vote 436, p. 73-S)*

As a member of Senate Armed Services, Hart had tried for years to force the Navy to deploy a larger fleet of smaller carriers. He argued that continuing to build only huge, 1,000-foot-long carriers would doom the Navy to a small number of powerful ships that the Russians could deluge with cruise missiles launched from bombers and submarines.

To dramatize the point that the administration was spending money on large weapons at the expense of maintenance and combat readiness, the Hart-Levin amendment would have added $76 million to the account for Navy aircraft overhauls. This was the amount by which cancellation of one carrier would reduce defense outlays in fiscal 1983.

Levin complained: "This bill sacrifices essential combat readiness on the altar of glamorous weapons procurement."

But he failed to swing debate from the issue of small vs. large carriers.

Other Amendments

The Senate adopted, 73-25, an amendment by William S. Cohen, R-Maine, allowing the Pentagon to transform the Rapid Deployment Force (RDF) into a major command, equal in status to the Pacific and European commands. The RDF would be responsible only for U.S. military action in the Indian Ocean and the Persian Gulf region. *(Vote 437, p. 73-S)*

As a practical matter, planning by the RDF had focused on the Persian Gulf region since October 1981. But Stevens and several other members of the Defense Appropriations panel objected to the creation of a regionally limited command. In part, they feared it would commit the United States to unilateral defense of a region whose oil supplies were less critical to this country than to its allies.

The Senate also voted 70-27 to table an amendment by David Pryor, D-Ark., to drop from the resolution $245 million earmarked for procurement of the Maverick infrared homing missile, designed to let airplanes attack tanks. *(Vote 438, p. 73-S)* ∎

Energy/Water Funds

Congress did not complete action in 1982 on the fiscal 1983 appropriations bill for energy and water projects (HR 7145).

Although both the House and Senate Appropriations committees reported the measure, neither chamber took action on it. So funds for the Department of Energy (DOE) and related agencies, the Army Corps of Engineers, the Bureau of Reclamation and several independent agencies were included in the fiscal 1983 continuing appropriations resolution (H J Res 631 — PL 97-377). *(Story, p. 238)*

H J Res 631 continued funding for most of the programs in the bill at the fiscal 1982 level through the remainder of fiscal 1983. The fiscal 1982 funding bill provided a total of $12.5 billion. *(1981 Almanac p. 301)*

An increase was allowed, however, for DOE's nuclear defense activities. The bill contained $5.7 billion for atomic energy defense operations in fiscal 1983, up from $4.8 billion in 1982.

Funds for a number of other energy programs were included in the fiscal 1983 Interior appropriations bill (HR 7356 — PL 97-394). *(Story, p. 262)*

Clinch River, Tenn-Tom

Action on HR 7145, and on the energy and water sections of H J Res 631, was dominated by debate over funding for two controversial programs: the Clinch River nuclear breeder reactor and the Tennessee-Tombigbee ("Tenn-Tom") waterway in Alabama and Mississippi.

Money for both projects was included in H J Res 631, but opposition to their funding grew stronger in 1982. For the first time in the 12-year history of the Clinch River project, the House voted to kill it, and the Senate twice backed the funding by one-vote margins. Conferees on the continuing resolution kept the project alive.

Funding was set at $181 million, substantially less than the $252 million requested by the administration but enough to keep work moving. H J Res 631 allowed continuation of site preparation and engineering activities but

prohibited the construction of major new facilities or the signing of new construction contracts.

Major credit for the continued funding of the multibillion-dollar project went to Senate Majority Leader Howard H. Baker Jr., R-Tenn., whose state was the home of the reactor site.

The Clinch River power plant, located near Oak Ridge, Tenn., was designed to demonstrate the feasibility of breeder reactors, which ran on plutonium and produced, as a byproduct, more plutonium than they consumed. Ever since it was first authorized in 1970, the project had been fought by environmentalists. In the preceding two years, they were joined in their opposition by a growing number of fiscal conservatives who believed the reactor was not economically feasible and was draining too much money from the federal budget.

H J Res 631 also contained funds for the 232-mile-long Tenn-Tom waterway, which was designed to carry barges from Appalachian coal fields to the Gulf Coast. Proponents of the project argued that it was nearly completed and that putting it in mothballs would cost more than finishing it.

But H J Res 631 prohibited use of federal funds to make any improvements in the waterway south of Demopolis, Ala., a point about mid-way between the Tennessee River and the Gulf of Mexico. Work on that portion of the project had never been authorized by Congress.

House Committee Action

The House Appropriations Committee Sept. 21 reported a $13.6 billion version of HR 7145 (H Rept 97-850).

Before reporting the bill, the committee added almost a quarter of a billion dollars to the Reagan administration's request for water projects. Many of the extra dollars would go for projects in the home districts and states of committee members.

The bill as reported contained $227 million for the Clinch River breeder reactor and $186 million for the Tennessee-Tombigbee waterway.

When the committee approved HR 7145 by voice vote, John T. Myers, Ind., senior Republican on the energy subcommittee, called it an "all-American bill" with something in it for almost all committee members. He said the bill was under budget and that he had been assured by David A. Stockman, director of the Office of Management and Budget, that it would not be vetoed.

Clinch River

During markup, Lawrence Coughlin, R-Pa., a longtime opponent of Clinch River, offered an amendment to kill that project. But he withdrew it, saying he would make his fight on the House floor. In 1981, Coughlin lost a 14-24 vote in committee on Clinch River.

A coalition of taxpayer groups, environmental organizations, members of Congress and others formed to fight the breeder reactor project. After losing by only 20 votes in 1981 on a floor amendment to kill the Clinch River project, opponents believed they had the votes to succeed in 1982.

The Energy Department had estimated that the project, a favorite of the administration and of Baker, would cost $3.6 billion. Opponents said it would cost between $5 billion and $10 billion. About $1.3 billion already had been spent but construction had not begun. Bulldozers began clearing the site on Sept. 22, 1982.

Advocates of breeder reactors argued that they were the next logical step in the evolution of nuclear power and

that Clinch River should be completed to make sure the technology was available in the future. Opponents said breeder reactors would not be economical until well into the next century, if then, and that Clinch River represented an obsolete technology.

In 1981, the House rejected an amendment to kill the project by a vote of 186-206. The Senate voted 48-46 to table (kill) a similar amendment.

Tenn-Tom Canal

House opponents of the Tennessee-Tombigbee Waterway came even closer to killing that project in 1981 than they did Clinch River, losing by only 10 votes — 198-208.

In 1982, the Appropriations Committee included $186 million in HR 7145 for Tenn-Tom. It said about $1.3 billion already had been spent on it, of a projected total of $1.8 billion. Killing the project would mean that money had been wasted, and 2,800 people would be added to the unemployment rolls, the committee said. It said the canal was needed to deal with expected increases in coal exports.

The canal had been authorized since the 1940s. It would stretch 232 miles, connecting the Tennessee and Tombigbee rivers and providing a direct route to the Gulf Coast for barge traffic.

Opponents had been fighting it for years. They claimed the canal would cost as much as $3 billion and that it was not economically practical.

Energy Funding

As reported by the House committee, HR 7145 contained $8.5 billion for DOE, $282 million less than the administration requested.

Although the committee total came in under the request, the panel added money to almost every energy area except military weapons programs. The budget savings were achieved by a combination of a cut in the weapons area and some "creative accounting;" two large nuclear programs were put into a revolving fund.

Most of the money cut from the energy area was pumped back into the bill's water projects.

Research and Development. The committee provided $1.9 billion for energy research and development, $259 million more than the president's request. It included $180 million for solar programs ($108 million more than requested); $50 million for geothermal energy ($40 million over the request); $43 million for electric energy systems (no money requested); $648 million for nuclear fission programs ($66 million more than requested); $469 million for nuclear fusion ($25 million over the request); $182 million for environmental programs ($13 million more than requested), and $283 million for basic energy research.

Nuclear Fuel Cycle. The committee created a new appropriation account to include funding for Clinch River, nuclear waste and the government's processing of uranium for the utility industry. Because it anticipated a certain amount of revenue from uranium enrichment and nuclear waste activities, it appropriated only $54 million for the account even though almost $2.4 billion would be spent.

The committee estimated the government would take in from utilities about $2 billion in revenues for uranium enrichment and $300 million from a nuclear waste fund that had not yet been authorized. (The nuclear waste fund was subsequently authorized.) *(Story, p. 304)*

The bill provided about $1.9 billion for uranium enrichment, including $600 million for a new, controversial enrichment facility being built at Portsmouth, Ohio.

The committee included $227 million for the Clinch River breeder program in addition to other breeder research money funded in the research portion of the bill.

It provided $185 million for civilian nuclear waste activities; $50 million to be spent exploring a DOE site near Richland, Wash., for a nuclear waste dump and $57 million to be spent for a similar purpose at DOE's Nevada test site.

Military Programs. Traditionally, DOE and its predecessor agencies designed and built nuclear weapons for the Defense Department. HR 7145 included $5.8 billion for this function, $108 million less than requested.

In this account the committee provided $3.4 billion for "weapons activities," including $756 million for research and development, $449 million for testing, and $1.959 billion for weapons production and surveillance.

It provided $1.3 billion for the production of nuclear materials for weapons, including $394 million for operating production reactors, $237 million for processing these materials and $70 million for research on a laser isotope process that, among other things, could enable the government to use burned civilian reactor fuel for weapons materials.

The committee provided $516 million for managing the nuclear waste from the defense program, which constituted about 90 percent by volume of the nation's total radioactive waste. The funding included $274 million for continuing to store the liquid wastes in temporary facilities, $94 million for work on long-term waste technology and $111 million for continued construction of a waste repository near Carlsbad, N.M.

Water Projects

According to Tom Bevill, D-Ala., chairman of the Energy and Water Development Subcommittee, HR 7145 contained funding for 327 separate water projects. Most of them (244) were funded through the Army Corps of Engineers, which would get $2.972 billion, $236 million more than the administration requested. The rest were funded through the Interior Department's Bureau of Reclamation, which would get $947 million, $13 million more than the budget request.

The committee said in its report that the administration "has not addressed the total national water policy issue." It said water projects "make an enormous contribution to America," often deriving far more in benefits than they cost.

Although Bevill said there was no money in the bill for new water projects, the committee included legislative language modifying more than a dozen water projects, including the controversial Central Arizona Project.

Among funding added by the committee for water projects was $7 million for navigation on Alabama's Coosa River, in Bevill's district; $500,000 for a deep water ship channel in Sacramento, Calif., home area of subcommittee Democrat Vic Fazio, and $1 million for flood control at Skiatook Lake, Okla. A $35 million authorization for this project also was included in the bill. The project would affect the districts of House Budget Committee Chairman James R. Jones, D, and Mike Synar, D, according to Edward R. Osann, director of the National Wildlife Federation's water resources program.

For subcommittee member Wes Watkins, D-Okla., the panel added a new authorization for a water supply system at Sardis Lake and $500,000 to design it, as well as an extra $1 million in construction funds for flood control.

The committee authorized and provided $5 million for a flood control project on the Lower San Joaquin River in

California which Osann said would affect the districts of Tony Coelho, D, and Norman D. Shumway, R. It also provided $8 million for flood control work on Yatesville Lake, Ky., which would affect the district of Carl D. Perkins, D, chairman of the House Education and Labor Committee, according to Osann.

The bill included $10 million for the Central Arizona Project. It also provided an open-ended authorization for the project, removing the $100 million ceiling in current law. Osann said the project's total cost could be $550 million.

Related Agencies

The committee provided $475 million for the Nuclear Regulatory Commission — along with a good deal of criticism of the agency, which regulated the nuclear industry. The bill appropriated $415 million of the total, requiring $60 million to come from licensing fees.

It also provided $89 million for the Federal Energy Regulatory Commission — $29 million in appropriated funds and $60 million to be raised by the agency in fees.

The bill also contained $486 million for the five federal power marketing administrations, including $276 million for the Bonneville Power Administration and $174 million for the Western Area Power Administration.

HR 7145 included $2.7 million, not requested by the administration, for the Appalachian Regional Commission; $145 million for Appalachian regional development programs, mostly for highway construction; $127 million for the Tennessee Valley Authority, $7 million more than requested, and $500,000 for the Water Resources Council, for which the president did not request anything.

Senate Committee Action

The Senate Appropriations Committee Dec. 2 approved a $13.5 billion version of the energy-water appropriations bill (S 3079 — S Rept 97-673).

The committee included $195 million for the Clinch River breeder reactor and $186 million for the Tennessee-Tombigbee waterway. It also, by an 11-8 vote, adopted an amendment by Walter D. Huddleston, D-Ky., to increase funding for Appalachian development programs by 75 percent, bringing them in line with the House-approved appropriation of $145 million.

Senate Floor Action

While HR 7145 did not come to the floor in either House or Senate, there were major floor battles in both chambers over continuation of the Clinch River project.

The first floor fight over Clinch River came during Senate action on H J Res 599, the first continuing appropriations resolution for fiscal 1983. *(Story, p. 225)*

By a 48-49 vote, the Senate Sept. 29 rejected an amendment to delete funding for the project. *(Vote 365, p. 62-S)*

The amendment, sponsored by Dale Bumpers, D-Ark., and Gordon J. Humphrey, R-N.H., was supported by a coalition of liberals and fiscal conservatives, backed by environmental, taxpayer, labor and church groups. It took high-pressure lobbying by the White House and Baker to defeat it.

Bumpers called the reactor a "technological turkey." He said it could not be completed until 1990 "and by that time the technology will be 16 years out of date."

Study of Federal Power Pricing Halted

Led by members from the big public-power states of Washington, Oregon, Idaho and Tennessee, Congress short-circuited an administration study that members feared might result in higher prices for federal power.

Since the 1930s, power consumers in the Southeast and Northwest had enjoyed the benefits of low-cost federal hydroelectricity — and their representatives in Congress wanted to keep it that way.

An amendment barring the use of federal funds to conduct a study of federal power pricing was attached to the first fiscal 1983 continuing appropriations resolution (H J Res 599 — PL 97-276) Sept. 29. It was sponsored by Senate Energy Committee Chairman James A. McClure, R-Idaho, and other senators from public-power states.

The amendment was retained in the final conference version of that bill, and later was also included in the second continuing resolution (H J Res 631 — PL 97-377), which funded the Department of Energy (DOE) through fiscal 1983. *(Stories, pp. 225, 238)*

The study would have considered ways to raise rates on power sold by the Tennessee Valley Authority (TVA), the Bonneville Power Administration and other federal power marketing agencies, to a level more in line with other electric rates.

Sen. Henry M. Jackson, D-Wash., said such a change might triple rates for some consumers in the Northwest, and Sen. Jim Sasser, D-Tenn., claimed it would raise rates by 25 percent for households in the Tennessee Valley.

The head of the administration study group, William A. Niskanen, contended that artificially low federal power rates distorted the distribution of the nation's resources and could lead to excessive energy consumption in some regions.

The Office of Management and Budget (OMB) saw in the study a chance to raise revenues and cut the federal budget deficit. An analysis by the American Public Power Association suggested that a power price increase could bring in more than $1 billion a year in additional federal revenue.

Sasser denounced the study as "an effort by David Stockman [director of OMB] to find ways of reducing the bulging budget deficit at the expense of the families and businesses consuming public power."

Rep. Albert Gore Jr., D-Tenn., also objected to the idea in the House Sept. 20. "Public power is not a device to raise money for the federal Treasury," he said. "It is designed as a device to lift the standard of living for the people in the areas served."

Sasser and McClure both scored the administration for beginning the study in secrecy, without consulting Congress.

Cheap Public Power

Since the New Deal days of the 1930s, it had been government policy to provide cheap public power in certain areas of the country. *(Background on public power policy, Congress and the Nation Vol. I, p. 771)*

The TVA was established in 1933 to provide electricity for residents of the Appalachian region. The Bonneville Power Administration followed soon afterwards, to market power produced by federal dams along the Columbia River. Four other federal power marketing authorities subsequently were established. Together, the agencies sold electricity in more than 30 states.

Prices charged by federal power agencies were based on historical costs — the costs of a facility at the time of its completion. As a result, hydropower from dams completed decades ago was much less costly than electricity generated by coal and nuclear plants, built when construction costs were higher.

Cheap federal hydropower was a major reason for the wide variation in electricity rates across the United States. A 1980 study by the Midwest Research Institute found that average rates ranged from 1.48 cents per kilowatt hour in Seattle to 11.8 cents in Connecticut — a variance of 800 percent.

Baker insisted that "the United States must explore the avenues for the production of power in the next century."

By a similar one-vote margin, the Senate early Dec. 17 agreed to include funds for the project in H J Res 631, the second continuing appropriations resolution for fiscal 1983. It rejected a Bumpers amendment to delete the funding by a 49-48 vote. *(Vote 422, p. 71-S)*

House Floor Action

House action on H J Res 631 saw a dramatic turnaround on Clinch River: for the first time, the House voted against funding for the project.

By a 217-196 vote, the House Dec. 14 adopted a Coughlin amendment to delete Clinch River funds from H J Res 631. *(Vote 422, p. 124-H)*

Environmentalists who had tried to kill the project since its inception were jubilant. But the major factor in the House switch was a group of fiscal conservatives, many of whom philosophically favored advancing nuclear power but voted against the project because of its rapidly rising costs.

"I have supported Clinch River since I first came to Congress," said Phil Gramm, D-Texas. "But as we look at the budget deficit, we have got to set a new, higher standard for spending." Gramm was one of 35 members who backed the project in 1981 but turned against it Dec. 14. *(Vote switches, box, p. 296)*

Backers of Clinch River knew their support in the House was eroding and had hoped to avoid a vote. They were taken by surprise Dec. 13 when the Rules Committee agreed to allow Coughlin to offer an amendment to H J Res 631 to delete the funding.

During floor debate, proponents attempted to portray Clinch River as an employment opportunity. "Over 3,500 jobs are at stake on this vote," Bevill said.

In addition to taking out Clinch River funds, the

Vote Switches

Thirty-five House members who voted for Clinch River funding in 1981 opposed it Dec. 14. They were:

Republicans (19): Bailey, Mo.; Coats, Ind.; Courter, N.J.; Coyne, Pa.; Gingrich, Ga.; Hillis, Ind.; Jeffries, Kan.; Kramer, Colo.; LeBoutillier, N.Y.; Lent, N.Y.; Lott, Miss.; McCollum, Fla.; Rogers, Ky.; Shumway, Calif.; Thomas, Calif.; Vander Jagt, Mich.; Walker, Pa.; Whittaker, Kan.; Wolf, Va.

Democrats (16): Addabbo, N.Y.; Byron, Md.; de la Garza, Texas; Derrick, S.C.; Dicks, Wash.; Ford, Mich.; Gramm, Texas; Hawkins, Calif.; Huckaby, La.; Kogovsek, Colo.; Long, Md.; Mavroules, Mass.; Roemer, La.; Russo, Ill.; Stokes, Ohio; Volkmer, Mo.

Sixteen members switched from opposition in 1981 to support on the Dec. 14 vote:

Republicans (11): Benedict, W.Va.; R. W. Daniel, Va.; Dornan, Calif.; Hunter, Calif.; Hyde, Ill.; Marlenee, Mont.; Siljander, Mich.; Smith, Ore.; Stanton, Ohio; Staton, W.Va.; Williams, Ohio.

Democrats (5): Brinkley, Ga.; Dorgan, N.D.; Luken, Ohio; Mineta, Calif.; Yatron, Pa.

House also approved amendments to delete funding for two controversial water projects — the O'Neill irrigation unit in Nebraska and the Garrison Diversion water project in North Dakota.

The Nebraska project was entangled in a court challenge, and both the House and Senate Appropriations committees had eliminated funds for it pending a court decision. But because H J Res 631 provided for water project funding at the 1982 level, David E. Bonior, D-Mich., said money could still be spent for the project.

Bonior's amendment to prohibit funding for the O'Neill unit was adopted 245-144. *(Vote 423, p. 124-H)*

Silvio O. Conte, R-Mass., offered the amendment to delete funds for the Garrison Diversion project. Conte said the project, which would drain wetlands, would violate U.S.

boundary water treaties with Canada and destroy duck habitat. His amendment was adopted 252-152. *(Vote 424, p. 126-H)*

Conference Action

Although the Clinch River project was defeated in the House and survived only by one vote in the Senate, conferees on H J Res 631 decided to retain funding for it.

However, conferees also provided for a study of future funding sources for the project that would not add to the federal deficit. The conference agreement (H Rept 97-980) included $1 million for DOE to explore the possibility of greater participation by the private sector in the breeder project and to look at other sources of financing; the department was directed to report to Congress on its findings by March 15, 1983.

(Under an existing cost-sharing agreement, private utility companies were expected to contribute $19 million to the Clinch River project in fiscal 1983.)

Conferees also included funds in H J Res 631 for the Tenn-Tom waterway project. But they accepted a Senate provision, sponsored by John H. Chafee, R-R.I., to prohibit the use of funds to either study or construct any improvements in the waterway south of Demopolis, Ala.

Tenn-Tom opponents claimed that additional, costly work would be needed on the waterway from Demopolis south to the seaport of Mobile to accommodate barge traffic to the Gulf of Mexico.

Conferees dropped House amendments to eliminate funding for the O'Neill and Garrison water projects, thus continuing the projects for another year.

After dropping Conte's amendment on the Garrison project, however, conferees added language stipulating that money could not be used to construct features affecting the water that flowed into Canada. The project was expected to need $4 million in fiscal 1983.

While the conference agreement generally set fiscal 1983 funding levels at the fiscal 1982 levels, it provided an increase for DOE's nuclear defense activities. Conferees provided $5.7 billion for atomic energy defense operations, up from $4.8 billion in fiscal 1982. ∎

Energy

A week before Christmas in 1982, oil ministers from the 13 member nations of the Organization of Petroleum Exporting Countries (OPEC) gathered in Vienna, hoping to tighten their grasp on the world's oil supplies.

Two days later they adjourned in disarray. They had agreed to hold 1983 oil production to 18.5 million barrels a day, but they could not agree on how to allocate that production among the members. And without individual country quotas, their cartel was powerless.

The Vienna meeting was probably not the end of OPEC, but it was a fitting end to a year in which the oil cartel lost most of its influence over world energy supplies. The continued slump in oil demand, prolonged by world recession, left a large glut on the market that depressed prices and rendered OPEC virtually impotent.

In the United States, increased domestic supplies enabled the country to cut its oil imports 16 percent from 1981, down 53 percent from their peak in 1977. And though OPEC stuck to its $34-a-barrel price, Mexico and other non-OPEC producers were selling their petroleum well below that level, and discounts even were being offered by many of the OPEC producers.

The cost of oil purchased by U.S. refiners dropped steadily throughout the year. Once expected to top $50 in 1982, the price per barrel went instead from $33.95 in January to $31.39 in September.

That in turn caused the prices of petroleum products to decline for the first time in a decade. The average U.S. retail gasoline price fell from $1.34 a gallon in January to $1.28 in October; heating oil dropped from $1.22 to $1.19.

With the failure of the OPEC meeting, most energy analysts predicted that prices would continue a steady decline throughout 1983. The Department of Energy projected its optimism even further, estimating that increases in domestic energy supplies would outstrip increases in demand through the year 2000, resulting in a 43 percent drop in imports.

The oil glut caused severe problems in oil-producing developing nations that had banked on rising revenue from oil exports. Mexico was perhaps the most severely hit, and OPEC members such as Algeria, Ecuador, Gabon, Indonesia, Iran, Iraq, Nigeria and Venezuela also suffered.

But in the United States, which met 47 percent of its energy needs with oil, the fall in prices was a welcome blessing. It contributed to the substantial decrease in inflation. It also enabled government policy-makers, for the second year in a row, to largely ignore energy issues, which skyrocketing oil prices had forced them to deal with throughout the 1970s.

With an eye toward future oil supply disruptions, however, Congress did pass a bill establishing procedures for filling the nation's Strategic Petroleum Reserve and for putting that oil on the market in the event of a new oil crisis. *(Story, p. 301)*

Natural Gas

While oil prices fell, natural gas prices rose, defying all the rules of textbook economics.

Like oil, gas was in surplus. Supplies were plentiful, and there were even scattered reports of excess gas being burned off at wells. Depressed demand was 3 percent below the level of 1981.

But unlike oil, gas continued to rise in price in spite of the glut. Estimates by the Energy Information Administration put the average price of home heating gas almost 18 percent above year-earlier levels.

Natural gas warmed about 55 million households and supplied 27 percent of the nation's energy needs. As a result, the rapid rise in gas prices caused howls of protest by users throughout the nation. And members of Congress, responsive to the complaints, introduced dozens of legislative proposals for dealing with the problem.

None of those proposals made much progress in the 97th Congress, but they laid the seeds for a debate which seemed certain to reach full bloom in 1983.

Some members suggested the solution to rising prices was the reimposition of price controls, which were being removed gradually according to the schedule established by the Natural Gas Policy Act of 1978.

The Reagan administration, on the other hand, attributed the problems to the controls themselves. Oil prices, administration officials noted, had been decontrolled and were behaving admirably in the face of a glut. Immediate, full decontrol of natural gas producer prices would enable that market to operate properly too, and cause prices to fall, these officials predicted.

Both arguments were somewhat simplistic. Strict controls on the wellhead price of gas probably would have resulted in supply shortages at some point in the future, just as they had in 1976 and 1977. But immediate and full decontrol of wellhead prices, on the other hand, could have led to even faster price hikes, since many gas pipelines were tied to long-term contracts that forced them to buy more expensive gas even when cheaper gas was available. Furthermore, federal regulation of the pipelines — which Reagan did not propose to eliminate — enabled them to pass on the cost of gas to the consumers, thus reducing incentives to bring prices down.

Several members of Congress attempted during the lame-duck session to tack amendments onto the highway/gas tax bill that would address these problems, but the amendments were rejected, leaving the issue to the 98th Congress to solve. *(Story, p. 317)*

The Senate did pass a resolution urging that all available funds be used to help low-income natural gas consumers pay their skyrocketing gas bills, and funds for low-income energy assistance and home weatherization were increased in the final fiscal 1983 continuing appropriations resolution. *(Story, p. 238)*

Nuclear Energy

Faced with excess supplies of other fuels, enthusiasm for nuclear energy waned. Nuclear power accounted for only 4 percent of U.S. energy consumption during the year.

As had been the case for several years, no new nuclear plants were ordered in 1982, and none were expected to be ordered in the near future. Some new units, such as Pennsylvania Power & Light Co.'s Susquehanna-1 reactor, were brought into service. But others, such as Iowa Power and Light Co.'s 2,270-megawatt Vandalia reactor, were canceled or delayed.

The Reagan administration continued its pro-nuclear stance, requesting increased funds for the Clinch River (Tenn.) breeder reactor while decreasing funds for all other types of energy research.

But congressional interest in nuclear technology had clearly fallen. After 10 years of support for Clinch River, the House in December voted 217-196 to kill funding for the project. The breeder escaped death in the Senate by only one vote on two different occasions. *(Story, p. 292)*

"I think the Clinch River breeder reactor is an extremely valuable project," said Rep. Robert S. Walker, R-Pa., one of those who voted against the breeder for the first time in 1982, "but I am also on the Energy Development Subcommittee and I see how Clinch River is eating into the totality of research funds."

When new Energy Secretary Donald P. Hodel went before the Senate Energy Committee for confirmation hearings in December, he heard a similar story. Sen. John Heinz, R-Pa., complained that the president's budget was cutting back funds for energy conservation, solar and coal technology research but pumping ever more money into nuclear technology. "I think you will find you have all your eggs in one basket, not just marked nuclear, but marked breeder reactor," Heinz said.

The disillusionment with nuclear power was heightened by stories emanating from the Pacific Northwest, where a public power project started in the 1970s was turning into a financial disaster.

The Washington Public Power Supply System, nicknamed "Whoops," originally had planned to build five huge nuclear plants to meet projected electricity demand in the region. But that demand never materialized, and cost overruns were enormous. Two of the five plants — which were 17 and 23 percent complete, respectively — were canceled. And utility firms in the region were told they must pay $7 billion in principal and interest on those plants even though they would never be put into operation.

As a result of its ambitious construction program, the system was strapped with the greatest long-term, tax-exempt bond debt in U.S. history. Payment of that debt, by one estimate, would cause electricity bills in the region to quadruple. As 1982 drew to a close, "Whoops" seemed to be barreling toward a massive default.

With the proliferation of new nuclear power plants brought to a halt, attention turned toward maintaining those already in operation.

Firms that specialized in engineering, handling of nuclear waste or the brokerage of nuclear fuel reported an increase in business during 1982. And estimates suggested that utilities and the U.S. government would spend more than $24 billion a year for the completion and upkeep of their nuclear facilities through the 1980s.

Congress also did its part to aid the maturing nuclear power industry. After four years of bickering, it completed work Dec. 20 on a plan for establishing both temporary and permanent federal repositories for the highly radioactive waste that was piling up at civilian nuclear power reactors throughout the country. *(Story, p. 304)*

Coal, Synthetic Fuels

The consumption and production of coal in the United States in 1982 stayed very close to the levels of the year before, after having grown steadily for a decade. Total production during the year was estimated to reach 797 million short tons, up from 602 million tons a decade earlier. Coal accounted for 22 percent of U.S. energy needs in 1982. The Department of Energy predicted that its use would increase through the decade.

The development of synthetic fuels stayed on the back burner during 1982. With traditional fuels in surplus, energy companies lost interest in high-cost synthetic projects.

The U.S. Synthetic Fuels Corp., the government agency established in 1980 to promote synthetic fuel programs, had great difficulty finding projects worthy of its aid. And one of the three synfuels projects that had received government subsidies — the Colony Project in western Colorado — collapsed in May because of soaring costs and the declining prospects for synthetic fuels.

With interest in synfuels development declining, some members of Congress introduced bills to abolish the corporation; others attempted to divert the $15 billion authorized for its activities to other uses.

Energy Policy

With the aftershocks of the oil crises of the 1970s past, the need for a national energy policy seemed greatly diminished during 1982. Few people argued that energy should be treated as just another commodity, but few gave it the emphasis it had received during the previous decade.

The Reagan administration continued to push for abolition of the five-year-old Energy Department and the merging of its key functions into the Department of Commerce. That plan, however, met resistance from a number of influential Republican senators and made virtually no progress in Congress. *(Story, p. 303)*

When the new energy secretary, Hodel, went before the Senate for confirmation in December, he acknowledged the lack of support for abolishing the department. And unlike his predecessor, James B. Edwards, Hodel said the abolition plan was by no means his top priority.

Speaking to the Senate Energy Committee, Hodel reiterated the administration's belief that most energy problems should be left to the marketplace for solution. The market, he argued, could stimulate production, moderate prices, encourage conservation and provide appropriate distribution of energy better than government legislation.

Hodel did say, however, that the federal government still had four other critical missions in energy policy:

● Completion of the Strategic Petroleum Reserve, which was to be used as the primary means for ensuring against future energy supply disruptions.

● Development of long-range, high-risk, high-payoff energy technologies that industry was either unable or unwilling to undertake.

● Development of fundamental scientific and engineering knowledge that could be used for new energy developments or for assessing the health, safety and environmental effects of energy developments.

● Continuation of defense programs for the development, testing and production of nuclear weapons.

—By Alan Murray

Energy Preparedness Legislation Enacted

After months of extended negotiations and veto threats, President Reagan Aug. 3 signed into law an energy preparedness bill cleared by Congress July 30 (S 2332 — PL 97-229).

The president had vetoed an earlier version of the legislation (S 1503) in March, and Congress failed to override the veto. That bill would have given Reagan authority to allocate oil supplies and control prices during a severe petroleum shortage — powers Reagan said he did not want. *(Story, p. 301)*

S 2332 represented a compromise between the president, who wanted to let the energy marketplace determine allocation and prices, and Congress, which wanted government controls available for use in an emergency.

The compromise bill required Reagan to fill the nation's Strategic Petroleum Reserve (SPR) faster than he wanted. But it basically left intact his desire to rely on the marketplace in times of shortage.

To obtain the legislation, Congress tied it to a provision of the vetoed bill that Reagan did want — a provision extending a limited antitrust defense for U.S. oil companies that shared petroleum supply information with the International Energy Agency (IEA). The oil companies had said they would not participate in IEA activities without it. *(Story, p. 299)*

Provisions

As signed into law, S 2332 (PL 97-229):

IEA Antitrust Defense. Extended through Dec. 31, 1983, the antitrust defense for companies sharing information with the International Energy Agency.

Strategic Petroleum Reserve. Required the president to fill the SPR at a rate of at least 300,000 barrels of oil a day, unless he certified that to do so would not be in the national interest.

● Set an absolute minimum fill rate of 220,000 barrels a day, or higher if funds were available.

● Required that the minimum fill rate be maintained until the SPR contained at least 500 million barrels of oil, and that the president "seek to" continue that rate until the reserve reached its authorized level of 750 million barrels. The SPR contained about 260 million barrels of oil at the time of enactment.

● Authorized the storage of SPR oil in existing "interim storage facilities," such as above-ground steel tanks or tanker ships; permitted the use of up to 10 percent of funds provided for the SPR for the leasing of such interim storage space.

● Required the president to seek congressional approval under the 1974 Impoundment Control Act of any plans to spend less money for SPR oil than Congress appropriated.

Emergency Plans, Reports. Required the president to send to Congress by Dec. 1, 1982, a plan for distributing oil from the SPR in times of shortage. This "drawdown" plan would take effect when submitted; it would not require congressional approval. Any subsequent changes to the plan, however, would require congressional approval. The plan must be accompanied by a report describing under what conditions the president would consider using SPR oil.

● Required the president to send to Congress by Nov. 15, 1982, a memorandum of law describing his existing author-ity to deal with a severe energy shortage. The memorandum would be prepared by the attorney general.

● Required the president to send Congress by Dec. 31, 1982, a comprehensive plan for responding to a severe energy supply interruption or other energy emergency.

● Required the secretary of energy to analyze the impact on the U.S. economy and on consumers of relying on the free market to allocate petroleum supplies and determine prices during a severe energy shortage. The report must be submitted to Congress within one year of enactment, along with recommendations on policies to deal with problems related to the shortage.

● Required the administration to continue to collect information on the pricing, supply and distribution of petroleum products. The Reagan administration had sought to discontinue this data collection.

● Required the president to send to Congress by Dec. 31, 1982, a report on the feasibility and cost of creating regional petroleum reserves, along with a list of potential sites for such reserves; also required a second report on the feasibility of creating a strategic alcohol fuel reserve.

Senate Action

The Senate Energy Committee reported S 2332 May 13 (S Rept 97-393), and the Senate passed it May 26 by a vote of 88-7, after rejecting White House pleas to reduce the minimum fill rate required by the bill for the Strategic Petroleum Reserve. *(Vote 156, p. 28-S)*

The bill extended until August 1983 the antitrust defense for the oil companies that shared information with the IEA.

But, continuing its fight with the administration over U.S. preparedness for a disruption of oil imports, the Energy Committee tacked onto the extension provisions requiring that the president fill the SPR at the rate of 300,000 barrels of oil a day and write contingency plans for an oil shortage.

Reagan protested that the rate set by the committee would cost the government an extra $3.6 billion over two years. But Energy Committee Chairman James A. McClure, R-Idaho, who had led the fight for the earlier vetoed Standby Petroleum Allocation Act, said the nation did not have the capability to respond to an oil emergency and should fill the SPR as fast as possible.

The Senate rejected, 44-51, a White House-backed amendment, offered by Budget Committee Chairman Pete V. Domenici, R-N.M., to set the minimum fill rate at 208,000 barrels a day — the amount for which the president had budgeted. *(Vote 155, p. 28-S)*

The administration planned to spend $5.8 billion on SPR in the next two years, Domenici said, but the higher rate would require $9.4 billion. Waving a May 24 letter from Reagan that said the extra spending was not justified, Domenici said the higher rate would add to the federal deficit. He also said Reagan had more than doubled the size of the reserve he inherited from President Carter.

"This president has done a fantastic job of filling SPR," Domenici said. He asked the Senate to give the president flexibility to fill the reserve faster if economic conditions permitted, but not to tie Reagan's hands.

Domenici framed the issue as one of budget discipline, arguing that the Senate needed to stand firm against bud-

get increases. But McClure and others argued that it probably would be cheaper in the long run to buy more oil while it was in plentiful supply and prices were relatively low. McClure noted that even with the fill rate required by the bill, the administration would be limited to whatever

IEA Antitrust Exemption

Legislation extending a limited antitrust defense for U.S. oil companies participating in activities of the International Energy Agency (IEA) was extended four times in 1982.

The IEA, located in Paris, coordinates a 21-nation energy program aimed at reducing international oil demand, increasing stockpiles and sharing available oil supplies in an energy emergency. Twenty-one U.S. oil companies participated in IEA programs in 1982; they insisted they would not do so without immunity from antitrust prosecution. U.S. antitrust laws prohibited information-sharing and market allocation activities.

The exemption for the oil companies, originally provided by Sec. 252 of the 1975 Energy Policy and Conservation Act (PL 94-163), was extended twice in 1981. The last extension was until April 1, 1982. *(1981 Almanac p. 446)*

An extension until July 1, 1983, was included in the Standby Petroleum Allocation Act (S 1503) cleared by Congress March 3. However, that bill was vetoed and Congress upheld the veto. *(Story, p. 301)*

Congress then passed a two-month extension of the antitrust defense (S 1937 — PL 97-163), good until June 1. Several senators wanted to amend the bill to require the president to do more contingency planning for a possible oil crisis — the issue over which Reagan vetoed S 1503. But their efforts were blocked by the threat of a filibuster March 31 as the Senate prepared to leave for its Easter vacation, and the Senate approved the simple two-month extension by voice vote.

The House Energy and Commerce Committee had approved a 15-month extension (HR 5789 — H Rept 97-474) March 30, but the House April 1 agreed to the Senate's shorter extension by a 211-163 vote, then passed the bill 374-3. *(Votes 50, 51, p. 16-H)*

When it became clear that legislation providing a longer extension of the antitrust defense (S 2332, HR 6337) would not be finished by the June 1 expiration of the existing law, Congress passed another 30-day extension (S 2575 — PL 97-190) just before leaving on its Memorial Day recess. The Senate passed the bill May 27, the House May 28; Reagan signed it June 1.

House Energy and Commerce Committee Chairman John D. Dingell, D-Mich., sought House approval June 24 of another 30-day extension. But he was blocked by the panel's ranking Republican, James T. Broyhill, N.C. An aide said Broyhill was "fed up" with Congress' practice of granting short extensions rather than a single long-term extension of the immunity.

Congress passed one more stopgap extension (S 2651 — PL 97-217) July 15, two weeks after the existing exemption had expired. It ran until Aug. 1.

On July 30, Congress finally cleared the energy preparedness bill (S 2332 — PL 97-229) that extended the exemption through Dec. 31, 1983.

amount Congress decided to appropriate for oil purchases.

McClure said that although Reagan called for a fill rate of 208,000 barrels a day in his fiscal 1983 budget, he actually planned to put only about 180,000 barrels a day into the reserve. The constraint was the slowly expanding capacity of the Gulf Coast salt domes to hold more oil.

S 2332 would allow temporary storage of SPR oil in leased facilities, such as above-ground tanks or in tanker ships, until more salt dome space was ready.

Henry M. Jackson, Wash., ranking Democrat on the Energy Committee, said it was absolutely vital for national security reasons to fill the reserve as quickly as possible. Jackson accused the administration of "fiddling while Rome burns when it comes to energy."

House Action

The House Energy and Commerce Committee reported its energy emergency preparedness bill May 24 (HR 6337 — H Rept 97-585, Part I). The bill also was referred to the Merchant Marine and Fisheries Committee, which reported it June 22 (Part II).

The House passed the bill June 23 by a vote of 396-3. *(Vote 163, p. 48-H)*

The House bill — which the administration preferred to the Senate version — ordered the president to fill the SPR at a minimum rate of 200,000 barrels of oil a day, while urging him to fill it at the rate of 300,000 barrels a day if he found it "fiscally prudent to do so."

At a 200,000-barrel-a-day fill rate, the SPR would contain 500 million barrels by the end of 1985, according to Philip R. Sharp, D-Ind., chairman of the House Energy and Commerce Subcommittee on Fossil and Synthetic Fuels. That would last more than 250 days in the event of a Middle East oil cutoff, Sharp said. The reserve held about 145 days' worth of oil at the time of the House vote, he said.

HR 6337 also extended the antitrust exemption for oil companies sharing petroleum supply data with the IEA for three years, until June 30, 1985.

The House rejected, 110-282, an amendment by Marc L. Marks, R-Pa., that would have required the administration to store 140 million barrels of SPR oil in above-ground steel tanks. *(Vote 162, p. 48-H)*

Marks, whose district's steel mills had been hard-hit by the ailing economy, said the amendment would create 8,000 to 9,000 new jobs in the steel industry and would save money in the long run over the cost of other storage methods.

Sharp opposed the amendment. He said Marks' claims of cost savings were disputed by the administration and had not yet been examined by the Energy Committee.

By voice vote, the House approved an amendment by Dan Glickman, D-Kan., requiring the administration to report to Congress by the end of the year on the feasibility of using alcohol fuels to supplement the SPR. Glickman said converting the nation's surplus wheat and corn into fuel might cost the government less than commodity price supports and storage costs.

A Merchant Marine Committee amendment to the bill also was adopted by voice vote. As reported by the Energy Committee, the bill waived the preparation of environmental impact statements if existing oil storage facilities were used to accommodate temporarily a portion of the SPR. The Merchant Marine amendment clarified that the waiver applied only to storage facilities in existence as of July 1, 1982, and not substantially enlarged or modified thereafter.

Other provisions of the House bill required the administration to continue to collect data from the states on petroleum product pricing and consumption and to prepare a series of reports on the effect of an oil shortage and the steps the government could take to alleviate it.

Conference, Final Action

A House-Senate conference committee July 21 agreed on a compromise version of S 2332 that required an SPR fill rate of 300,000 barrels of oil a day unless the president certified that to do so would not be in the national interest. The absolute minimum would be 220,000 barrels a day.

The conferees also compromised on Dec. 31, 1983, as the expiration date for the IEA antitrust exemption.

The conference report (S Rept 97-663) was filed July 23. The House approved it July 29 by voice vote, and the Senate followed suit July 30. ∎

Veto of Standby Oil Allocation Bill Upheld

The Senate handed President Reagan an unexpected victory March 24, upholding his veto of a standby petroleum allocation bill (S 1503).

Under intense White House pressure, 27 senators — 24 Republicans and three Democrats — reversed their earlier position on the bill and voted with the president. The vote was 58-36 to override — five votes shy of the two-thirds needed. *(Vote 63, p. 13-S; vote switches, box, p. 302)*

With 94 senators voting, 32 negative votes were needed to sustain the veto. The House also would have had to go along by a two-thirds vote for the override to occur.

Congress cleared S 1503 March 3; Reagan vetoed it March 20. The bill was intended to replace the Emergency Petroleum Allocation Act of 1973 — known as EPAA — which expired Sept. 30, 1981. That law, enacted during an Arab embargo on oil shipments to the United States, required the president to control oil allocation and prices during a petroleum emergency. *(1973 Almanac p. 623)*

The vetoed bill would have left it up to the president's discretion whether to invoke controls during a severe oil shortage. Nevertheless, administration officials opposed the legislation throughout congressional consideration, arguing that the marketplace — not the government — should allocate oil.

It was the first time Congress had tried to override a Reagan veto. The veto was Reagan's third; in 1981 he vetoed a continuing appropriations resolution (H J Res 357) and a bankruptcy measure (HR 4353). *(1981 Almanac pp. 294, 436)*

Senate Turnaround

Reagan's victory in the Senate surprised even some of his own lobbyists. Three weeks earlier, the Senate had approved the conference report on S 1503 by a vote of 86-7.

The main force behind the bill had been Senate Energy Committee Chairman James A. McClure, R-Idaho. He contended that it would be better to enact standby presidential authority to deal with an oil shortage before the power was needed, rather than be forced by public pressure to act during a crisis, as was the case in 1973.

McClure and other supporters of the bill were as surprised as opponents were by the Senate vote to sustain the veto. They had been looking ahead to an override fight in the House, where the president had more support — but the Senate vote put an end to any House effort to override.

The House had approved the conference report on S 1503 by a 246-144 vote, and sponsors had been preparing for an override vote on March 31.

In vetoing S 1503, Reagan said he already had sufficient power under other laws to protect national security and assure essential public services in an oil crisis. He also said the bill could be counterproductive to preparedness efforts if businesses and individuals believed the government would come to their rescue in a shortage. *(Text of veto message, p. 17-E)*

Reagan did want one provision of S 1503, however — an extension of the antitrust defense for U.S. oil companies that shared petroleum supply information with the International Energy Agency (IEA). The provision was expiring and the oil companies said they would not participate in IEA activities without it. After the veto of S 1503, Congress used this extension as a vehicle to obtain a compromise energy preparedness bill (S 2332) that Reagan signed into law Aug. 3. *(Story, p. 299; IEA extensions, p. 300)*

Action on S 1503

S 1503 — the Standby Petroleum Allocation Act (SPAA) — passed the Senate Oct. 29, 1981, by a vote of 85-7. The House passed a similar bill (HR 4700) Dec. 14, 1981, by a 244-136 vote. Conferees were unable to fashion a compromise version before Congress adjourned Dec. 15. *(1981 Almanac p. 451)*

Meeting early in the second session, the conference committee generally melded the two bills, filing its report Feb. 11 (S Rept 97-313). The conferees dropped a House provision that would have required the president to write a detailed plan for distributing oil from the Strategic Petroleum Reserve in an emergency.

The conference version of the bill gave the president power to allocate petroleum supplies when he declared there was a "severe petroleum supply shortage." It did not specifically define such a shortage but said it would be one with a major impact on the country, and one which the free market could not deal with. The president could set prices only where necessary to carry out his oil allocation plan; he could not order gasoline rationing under the bill.

The Senate approved the conference report March 2, 86-7. The House approved it March 3, 246-144, clearing the measure. *(Senate vote 42, p. 8-S; House vote 13, p. 4-H)*

In the Senate, there was little opposition to the legislation. McClure said the measure would give Reagan broad, flexible powers that he would need in a severe oil shortage. J. Bennett Johnston, D-La., also argued that the free market could not handle large-scale disruptions of oil imports. He noted that S 1503 was written so that it would expire just before the end of Reagan's first term. "We can trust Ronald Reagan not to misuse and abuse this grant of discretionary authority," Johnston said.

Don Nickles, R-Okla., and Bill Bradley, D-N.J., argued against the bill but attracted only seven votes against it — the same seven they got when the bill originally passed the

Senate. Nickles claimed the bill would create an extensive bureaucracy and that consumers would "end up on the short end of the stick."

Bradley, the only Senate Democrat who voted against the bill, said the marketplace should allocate oil but the government should provide a buffer against the high prices that would occur by "recycling" to individuals the revenues from federal oil taxes. The Senate rejected his recycling plan during action on the bill in 1981.

In the House, bill manager Philip R. Sharp, D-Ind., argued that the United States was not prepared to handle a reduction in oil imports. He described the bill as "national security" legislation.

House Republicans generally denounced the bill, saying it would mean a return to massive government controls on oil that they said failed in past shortages. James T. Broyhill, R-N.C., said "it would send the wrong signals to the marketplace," causing petroleum users to believe "Uncle Sugar" would bail them out in a shortage. Clarence J. Brown, R-Ohio, urged House members not to "make the same mistake you made before" with EPAA. Opponents disparagingly referred to the bill as the "son of EPAA."

Not all House Republicans opposed the bill; 56 voted for it. Tom Tauke, R-Iowa, sought GOP support, describing the measure as a bill tailored for Reagan. He said it would "provide very limited and very temporary authorities, only to be implemented by a president who is known for his adherence to free-market principles."

Administration Opposition

Administration lobbyists did not oppose the conference report in the Senate but did lobby against final passage in the House. However, they got only eight more opposing votes than in December, when 136 members voted against the bill.

Fourteen House members — 12 Republicans and two Democrats — switched from their original support of the bill to opposition; six — four Republicans and two Democrats — switched from opposition to support.

Opponents circulated a paper saying the administration "strongly opposed" the conference report, and that "the secretary of energy and the president's senior advisers will recommend that the president veto the measure."

According to a memorandum prepared by a senior Energy Department official, "This bill is bad for America, bad for energy policy and bad for the administration."

Noting that Reagan had promised in his 1980 election campaign to eliminate federal energy allocation rules, the memorandum said the president's signature on the bill would compromise his free-market policy.

Provisions of S 1503

As cleared by Congress, S 1503:

● Required the president to send Congress a standby petroleum allocation regulation within 180 days. The regulation must include a program for allocating crude oil among refiners, although the president would not be forced to implement this program. It could include a system of price controls on petroleum products. Congress would have 30 days to review the regulation but would not have veto power over it.

● Required the president to declare that there was a "severe petroleum supply shortage" before putting the standby regulation into effect. Such a shortage was not precisely defined, but generally it would have to have a "major adverse impact" on the nation's security, on the economy or on a particular region.

● Allowed either chamber of Congress to veto the plan by passing a resolution of disapproval within 15 days of the president's declaration of a severe shortage.

● Allowed any regulation that was implemented to remain in effect for no more than 90 days unless the president determined that a severe shortage continued to exist. In that case, the regulation could be extended for 60 days. After that, the president would have to again send a regulation to Congress, which it could disapprove.

● Prohibited the president from including in the plan any rationing program, tax, tariff or user fee.

● Exempted from any allocation plan petroleum stocks held before the shortage was declared, if the oil was intended for consumption by the company that owned it. This protection would not apply to oil held by refiners that was intended to be refined and sold to consumers.

● Included the same list of priority users of petroleum that had been in EPAA, including agricultural users, refiners and public services, such as fire and police agencies.

● Pre-empted state laws dealing with oil allocation and pricing. However, the bill would not void state laws providing odd-even gasoline sales or minimum purchase restrictions.

● Allowed state governors to ask the president for permission to implement a state set-aside program under which the governor could allocate up to 5 percent of the petroleum supply within a state. The president would have 10 days to approve or reject the program.

● Required the president to continue to collect information on the pricing, supply and distribution of oil products at the same level at which such information was being collected in September 1981.

● Required several studies: analyzing the economic impact of U.S. reliance on free-market allocation and pricing of oil during a severe shortage; whether tax incentives were needed to ensure the building of private oil stocks and to ensure that those stocks were drawn down during an emergency; and how oil stocks held by the United States and its allies would be coordinated internationally during an emergency.

---

27 Senators Switch Votes

Twenty-seven senators — 24 Republicans and three Democrats — March 24 reversed their previous position and voted to sustain President Reagan's veto of S 1503. The Senate passed the bill 85-7 on Oct. 29, 1981, and approved the conference report 86-7 on March 2, 1982. *(Vote 340, 1981 Almanac p. 57-S; Vote 42, p. 8-S)*

The following senators switched from support of the bill to support of the president:

Republicans: Howard H. Baker Jr., Tenn.; Rudy Boschwitz, Minn.; Alfonse D'Amato, N.Y.; Jeremiah Denton, Ala.; Robert Dole, Kan.; John P. East, N.C.; Barry Goldwater, Ariz.; Orrin G. Hatch, Utah; S. I. "Sam" Hayakawa, Calif.; John Heinz, Pa.; Jesse Helms, N.C.; Nancy Landon Kassebaum, Kan.; Paul Laxalt, Nev.; Richard G. Lugar, Ind.; Charles McC. Mathias Jr., Md.; Frank H. Murkowski, Alaska; Bob Packwood, Ore.; Alan K. Simpson, Wyo.; Arlen Specter, Pa.; Robert T. Stafford, Vt.; Ted Stevens, Alaska; John Tower, Texas; Malcolm Wallop, Wyo., and John W. Warner, Va.

Democrats: Lloyd Bentsen, Texas; David L. Boren, Okla., and Howell Heflin, Ala.

● Extended until July 1, 1983, antitrust exemptions for oil companies that shared information with the International Energy Agency.

● Terminated the bill's authority on Dec. 31, 1984.

Veto, Override Fight

In the days before Reagan announced his decision to veto the bill, lobbyists both for and against it bombarded the White House with calls and visits.

Supporters of the bill included the National Governors' Association (18 governors called the White House); the nation's utilities, eight major oil companies, petroleum refiners and marketers, agricultural organizations, consumer groups and large labor organizations including the AFL-CIO and the Teamsters.

McClure and four other influential Republican senators (Majority Leader Howard H. Baker Jr., Tenn.; Finance Committee Chairman Robert Dole, Kansas; Budget Committee Chairman Pete V. Domenici, N.M.; and David Durenberger, Minn.) went to the White House March 18 and pleaded with Reagan to let S 1503 become law.

Immediately after they left, three House Republicans — Broyhill, Tom Corcoran, Ill., and Trent Lott, Miss. — were ushered into his office to urge a veto. Also lobbying the White House against the bill were a few smaller oil companies, several airlines, the Holiday Inns motel chain and a host of large industrial petroleum users including General Motors, Bethlehem Steel and Goodyear.

Senate Vote

When the Senate voted March 24 to uphold Reagan's veto, 27 senators reversed their earlier position on the bill and voted with the president. *(Box, p. 302)*

Among those who switched were Baker and Dole, who just six days earlier had urged Reagan to veto the bill. Also switching their votes, to McClure's displeasure, were the chairmen of three of his Energy subcommittees: John W. Warner, R-Va.; Frank H. Murkowski, R-Alaska, and Malcolm Wallop, R-Wyo.

On the morning of the vote, McClure and other backers of the bill believed they had votes to spare in overriding the veto. Even Energy Department lobbyists believed the Senate would vote to override. But by mid-afternoon, as the White House phone calls began coming in, the vote prediction got much closer. The tide had swung completely when the vote was taken about 5 p.m.

"We had the vote at 3 p.m.," said one lobbyist supporting the bill. "But the longer they talked, the more the phones rang and the more votes we lost. It was just a case of straight-up muscle by the White House."

When the White House lobbying barrage began, most of the lobbyists supporting the bill were meeting to devise strategy for the override fight in the House. A frantic phone call from McClure's staff brought them scurrying back to the Senate in hopes of rescuing what had been presumed to be an easy victory.

Johnston tried to get an early vote, but McClure held off to allow several senators a chance to speak.

Reagan personally called 10 senators urging them to switch positions, a White House spokesman said. Vice President Bush called several senators, and others in the administration also worked the phones just before the vote.

McClure said after the vote that some administration officials had pressured some organizations lobbying for the bill to back off. McClure said he guessed that the decision

by several major oil companies not to continue pushing for the bill after the veto resulted in Texas' two senators reversing their votes to support Reagan.

During debate on the override, Henry M. Jackson, Wash., ranking Democrat on the Energy Committee, said the veto would have the American people believe the country was prepared for an oil interruption. But, he said, the administration had no contingency plans for dealing with an oil shortage, while political turmoil in the Middle East made such a shortage increasingly likely.

Howard M. Metzenbaum, D-Ohio, said the veto meant that "if there is another supply cutoff from the Middle East, the oil companies will decide who will get the scarce supplies of crude oil, gasoline and heating oil. And the oil companies, not the federal government, will decide what the price will be for the fuels that make this country run."

After the vote, McClure credited Reagan's persuasive powers for the outcome. But he said the issue was one that should not have provoked the political confrontation that it did. McClure warned Reagan that "he had better pray, as he has never prayed before, that there be no interruption of petroleum supplies during his term of office."

Reagan called the Senate vote "an expression of confidence that our marketplace and the good sense of the American people provide our best lines of defense against any future interruptions of energy supplies." ■

DOE Dismantlement

Congress took no action on President Reagan's proposal to abolish the Department of Energy (DOE) and shift most of its responsibilities to other agencies, principally the Commerce Department.

Reagan had promised during his 1980 presidential campaign to scrap the department, which was created in 1977. *(1977 Almanac p. 609)*

Reagan argued that the marketplace, not a government agency, should solve energy problems.

Legislation to dismantle DOE was introduced in the Senate May 24 (S 2562), but influential members of both parties gave it a chilly reception. No sponsors could even be found to introduce a bill in the House until August, when Frank Horton, R-N.Y., and James T. Broyhill, R-N.C., finally agreed to do so. They introduced HR 6972 Aug. 11.

By year's end, Reagan's new energy secretary, Donald P. Hodel, told the Senate Energy Committee he realized there was little support in Congress for the proposal and that it was no longer a top priority of his department.

Reagan first outlined his plan to abolish DOE and send most of its programs to the Commerce Department when he submitted his fiscal 1983 budget Feb. 6. However, the legislation introduced in May differed substantially from the original proposal.

The original plan had been delayed for months because of infighting within the administration over how DOE would be divided up. Much of the struggle reportedly was between Interior Secretary James G. Watt and Commerce Secretary Malcolm Baldrige, both of whom wanted some of DOE's programs.

There also was controversy over where to put DOE's defense activities — the research and production of nuclear weapons, which accounted for nearly half the department's budget; 13 senators wrote Reagan, asking him not to put those activities under either Commerce or Interior.

Baldrige emerged the big winner when the original plan was announced Feb. 6. Reagan said he would ask Congress to transfer about 70 percent of DOE's programs to a new Energy Research and Technology Administration in the Commerce Department. The remaining energy programs would go to Interior.

However, key senators still had objections to the plan, many of them having to do with loss of committee jurisdiction over programs that would be transferred to other departments. After months of negotiations, the administration scrapped its original proposal and called instead for two new deputy secretaries of commerce — one for nuclear weapons programs and one for all other energy programs. A few other energy functions would be transferred to the Justice, Interior and Agriculture departments.

S 2562 was referred to the Senate Governmental Affairs Committee, HR 6972 to the House Government Operations and Energy and Commerce committees. No further action was taken.

Both the House and Senate had backed creation of the Energy Department by large margins, and Baldrige acknowledged that there was no real constituency for abolishing it. On the other hand, numerous groups felt their interests would best be served by retaining the existing energy structure.

In addition, key members of Congress, such as Senate Energy Committee Chairman James A. McClure, R-Idaho, were concerned about the signal that dropping energy as a Cabinet-level department would send to the nation and the world. And while the administration claimed the reorganization would save money, the Congressional Budget Office said it would not result in significant savings. ∎

Comprehensive Nuclear Waste Plan Enacted

Congress Dec. 20 cleared legislation (HR 3809) establishing a national plan for the disposal of highly radioactive nuclear waste, after resolving in a few hectic hours disputes that had stalled waste legislation for four years.

President Reagan signed the measure into law on Jan. 7, 1983 (PL 97-425).

A comprehensive nuclear waste bill had died in the closing hours of the 96th Congress in 1980, and the legislation's progress through the 97th Congress was laborious. Its fate was in doubt up to its final passage.

The Senate passed a bill in April, but with seven House committees claiming a share of jurisdiction, the House did not pass a waste bill until Dec. 2. It differed significantly from the Senate bill in several key areas. A compromise agreement was forged by the bill's managers in both chambers, but various portions of it remained in dispute as the lame-duck session drew to a close.

Finally, the Senate took up the compromise Dec. 20 during a break in its end-of-session action, and worked through more than 20 amendments in as many minutes. The measure was then adopted by voice vote.

Senate action was made possible when bill sponsors agreed to accept an amendment by William Proxmire, D-Wis., giving the states a stronger say over a federal decision to put a nuclear waste dump within their borders. Both the House and Senate had rejected such amendments, but Proxmire said that unless his provision was accepted he would filibuster against the bill, which would have killed it so late in the session.

A few hours later, the House accepted the Senate amendments at the urging of Interior Committee Chairman Morris K. Udall, D-Ariz., who said any attempts to change the bill at that late hour would certainly kill it.

The final House vote, clearing the bill for the president, was 256-32. *(Vote 457, p. 134-H)*

Permanent, Temporary Storage

HR 3809 set a timetable for establishing a permanent, underground repository for high-level nuclear waste by the mid-1990s and provided for some temporary federal storage of waste, including spent (burned) fuel from civilian nuclear reactors, in the meantime.

A state could veto a federal government decision to place a waste repository within its borders and, under Proxmire's amendment, the veto would stand unless both houses of Congress voted to override it.

The bill also called for developing plans by 1985 to build "monitored, retrievable storage" (MRS) facilities, where wastes could be kept for 50 to 100 years or more and then be removed for permanent disposal or for reprocessing.

The waste program, which was expected to cost billions of dollars, would be funded through what would amount to a tax on nuclear-generated electricity.

The nuclear power industry, faced with a growing accumulation of highly radioactive spent fuel in storage pools at nuclear power plants across the nation, had pushed for a waste bill for years. But the legislation was obstructed by the attempts of various members of Congress to prevent the location of waste dumps in their states or districts.

Environmental groups also opposed the final bill. They said its environmental protections were inadequate and that it would result in unnecessary and potentially dangerous shipments of spent fuel around the country.

Provisions

As signed into law, HR 3809 (PL 97-425):

Permanent Repositories. Required the secretary of energy, within 180 days of enactment, to issue guidelines for the recommendation of sites for nuclear waste repositories.

● Required the secretary to study five potential sites for the location of a permanent, underground repository and to recommend three of those sites to the president by Jan. 1, 1985, for further site characterization studies.

● Required that five more potential sites, including at least three not included in the first five, be studied and three of them recommended to the president by July 1, 1989, as possible sites for a second repository.

● Required an environmental assessment of each potential repository site, including a description of the decision process by which the site was recommended and an assessment of the regional and local impacts of locating a repository at the site.

● Set other guidelines for the Department of Energy (DOE) to follow in locating a site, and required it to hold public hearings in the vicinity of each site considered.

● Barred placement of a repository where its surface facility would be in a highly populated area or adjacent to a one-square-mile area with a population of 1,000 or more.

● Required the president to review site recommendations and to approve or disapprove them within 60 days, or within six months if he found that the energy secretary had submitted insufficient information on which to base a decision.

● Provided for site characterization activities by the Energy Department at candidate sites. Such activities could include excavation, drilling of deep shafts and possibly the burial of a small quantity of radioactive material at the site for testing.

● Required the president to submit to Congress by March 31, 1987, his recommendation of one site for the first repository, and by March 31, 1990, his recommendation for a second repository site; allowed the president to extend the deadlines by one year if he determined that such an extension was necessary; also allowed him to recommend additional repository sites if he wished.

● Required the energy secretary to apply to the Nuclear Regulatory Commission (NRC) within 90 days of the site selection for authority to construct a repository; required the NRC to act on the application for the first repository by Jan. 1, 1989, and for the second by Jan. 1, 1992.

● Provided that the repository could be used for the storage of either spent fuel or the high-level radioactive waste that results from reprocessing. (There was no commercial fuel reprocessing in the United States in 1982.) Spent fuel would have to be retrievable.

● Limited the amount of high-level waste or spent fuel that could be placed in the first repository to the equivalent of 70,000 metric tons of heavy metal, until a second repository was built.

● Provided that the federal government would take title to the waste or spent fuel deposited in a repository.

● Required a full environmental impact statement once a site was selected by DOE to be recommended to the president for a repository.

● Provided for judicial review of any final decision or action of the energy secretary, the president or the NRC in the process of selecting a site for and constructing a waste repository.

Spent Fuel Storage. Authorized DOE to provide up to 1,900 metric tons of storage capacity for temporary storage of spent fuel from civilian nuclear reactors. The spent fuel could be transported to an existing, federally owned nuclear facility, stored in casks or other mobile storage equipment there or at a reactor site, or stored in new storage facilities built by the government at the reactor site. (The requirement that the spent fuel be stored at a federally owned facility would preclude the use of the privately owned facilities at Morris, Ill., Barnwell, S.C., and West Valley, N.Y., for spent fuel storage, bill sponsors said.)

● Stipulated that this away-from-reactor (AFR) storage would be available only for waste from utilities that had filled the storage space at a reactor site and could not reasonably provide adequate additional storage at the site.

● Required that spent fuel be moved from the temporary storage facilities within three years after a permanent waste repository went into operation.

● Barred AFR storage at a site that was a candidate site for a permanent waste repository.

● Required an environmental impact statement for storage of more than 300 metric tons of spent fuel, and an environmental assessment for storage of less than that amount.

● Provided that the costs of interim storage would be paid with fees collected from utilities making use of the storage.

● Provided that the federal government would take title to the spent fuel at the reactor site and would be responsible for transporting it to the storage facility.

● Required the NRC to establish procedures for licensing new technologies that would increase the capacity of storage pools at reactors and thus reduce the need for temporary federal storage facilities.

● Authorized a demonstration program for the dry storage of spent fuel at reactor sites.

Monitored, Retrievable Storage. Required the secretary of energy to report to Congress by June 1, 1985, on the need for and the feasibility of a monitored, retrievable storage facility; specified that the report was to include five different combinations of proposed sites and facility designs, involving at least three different sites.

● Required environmental assessments of the sites.

● Provided that, if Congress decided to proceed with an MRS facility, it would have to be licensed by the NRC.

● Barred construction of an MRS facility in a state under consideration for a permanent waste repository.

State Participation, Veto. Required that the Energy Department consult closely throughout the site selection process with states or Indian tribes that might be affected by the location of a waste facility.

● Allowed a state (governor or legislature) or Indian tribe to veto a federal decision to place a waste repository or an AFR facility holding 300 tons or more of spent fuel within its borders; provided that the veto would stand unless it was overruled by a vote of both houses of Congress within 90 days.

Fees. Established a Nuclear Waste Fund, composed of fees levied against utilities, to pay for the costs of constructing and operating a permanent repository; set the fee at one mill per kilowatt-hour of nuclear electricity generated. Utilities also would be charged a one-time fee for storage of spent fuel generated before enactment of the bill.

● Directed the energy secretary to study alternative means of financing the construction and operation of nuclear waste facilities, including the feasibility of establishing a private corporation for such purposes.

Test and Evaluation Facility. Required DOE, within one year of enactment, to identify three potential sites, in at least two different geologic media, for a facility to test and evaluate the characteristics and feasibility of underground waste storage. The tests conducted at the facility would supplement the repository locating process.

Other Provisions. Provided that nothing in the bill would affect existing federal, state or local laws governing the transportation of spent fuel or high-level radioactive waste.

● Exempted waste resulting from atomic energy defense activities from most provisions of the bill; required that, if military waste were put into a civilian repository, the government must pay its pro rata share of the cost of development, construction and operation of the repository.

● Authorized impact assistance payments to states or Indian tribes to offset any costs resulting from the location of a waste facility within their borders.

● Required the NRC to issue regulations within one year governing the training and qualifications of civilian nuclear power plant employees.

● Directed the NRC to establish procedures and financial arrangements for the closure of low-level radioactive waste sites.

● Provided for increased U.S. cooperation with and technical assistance to non-nuclear-weapons nations in the field of spent fuel storage.

● Established an Office of Civilian Radioactive Waste Management in DOE to carry out the act's provisions.

Background

Although there had long been broad general agreement on the need for legislation to establish a comprehensive national policy for the disposal of highly radioactive nuclear waste, no such legislation had been enacted during the nearly 40 years that nuclear waste had been generated in the United States.

The administration, the nuclear industry and utility companies were especially anxious to have a bill.

Nuclear waste, which remains dangerously radioactive for thousands of years, was being kept in various types of temporary storage. The bulk of the waste came from the production of nuclear weapons; about 77 million gallons of military waste, in liquid form, was stored in steel tanks, mostly in South Carolina, Washington state and Idaho.

In the private sector, the nation's 82 nuclear plants burned uranium fuel to produce electricity. Highly radioactive burned (spent) fuel rods were stored in pools of water at the reactor sites, but many utilities said they were running out of storage space.

The Energy Department had been examining potential waste storage sites for several years, causing public anxiety in the states being considered. The NRC had ruled that, before selecting a permanent repository site, the government must consider at least three different sites in at least two different kinds of geologic formations.

The sites considered the leading contenders for a permanent repository were basalt formations at the government's Hanford, Wash., Nuclear Reservation; volcanic tuff formations at its Nevada nuclear test site, and several salt formations in Utah, Texas, Louisiana and Mississippi. Salt and granite formations in other states also had been surveyed, but not explored in great detail. *(Map, this page)*

The most likely sites for away-from-reactor storage of spent fuel were considered to be defunct or never-used privately owned reprocessing facilities at Morris, Ill., Barnwell, S.C., and West Valley, N.Y.

None of the states under consideration wanted a waste facility, and their representatives generally fought vigorously to prevent one being placed within their borders. The lone exception was Rep. Sid Morrison, R-Wash., whose district included the Hanford site; he said his constituents were comfortable with nuclear facilities and would welcome the jobs a repository would create.

Earlier Legislative Action

Both the House and Senate passed waste disposal bills in 1980 but they could not agree on a common version in the final days of the lame-duck session, and the legislation died. *(1980 Almanac p. 494)*

Congress set to work on the problem again in 1981. The Senate Energy and Environment committees approved different versions of a waste bill (S 1662) in the fall and filed a joint report Nov. 30 (S Rept 97-282). In the House, the Science and Technology Committee also reported a bill late in the year (HR 5016 — H Rept 97-411,

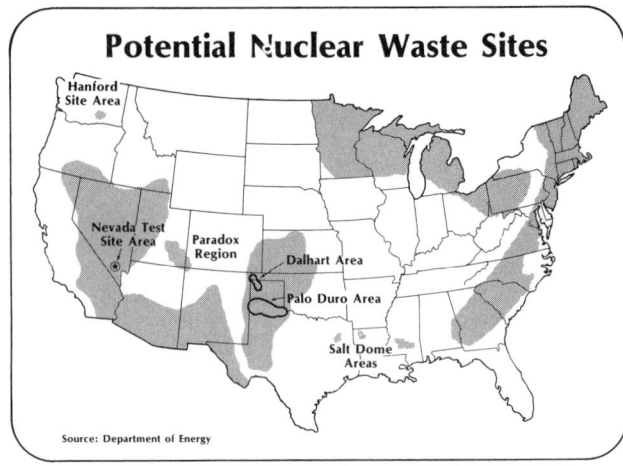

Potential Nuclear Waste Sites

Source: Department of Energy

The shaded areas are the areas determined by the Department of Energy (DOE) to be potential sites for permanent repositories for highly radioactive nuclear waste. The prime areas under consideration in 1982 were basalt formations at Hanford, Wash.; formations of volcanic tuff at the government's nuclear test facility in Nevada, and several different salt formations, including salt domes in Texas, Louisiana and Mississippi and bedded salt formations in Texas (Dalhart and Palo Duro) and southeastern Utah (the Paradox region). DOE also had surveyed salt formations in Ohio, Michigan, New York and Pennsylvania, had begun examining granite formations in Minnesota and was negotiating to do so in Michigan and Wisconsin.

Part I, filed Dec. 15, 1981). *(1981 Almanac p. 455)*

Senate sponsors had hoped for floor action before adjournment, but the measure was put over until 1982.

1982 Senate Committee Action. In March 1982, the Senate Energy and Environment committees agreed on a compromise bill to take to the floor after the Easter recess. The compromise consisted mostly of the Environment Committee version of S 1662, with the understanding that provisions on which the committees disagreed would be thrashed out on the floor.

The Senate Armed Services Committee set the stage for one floor fight when it voted 9-2 March 25 to strip provisions relating to military waste from the bill. The inclusion of military waste — which constituted about 90 percent of the nation's total volume of nuclear waste — was the issue that killed the 1980 waste legislation.

Armed Services filed its report on the bill on March 25 (S Rept 97-327).

Senate Floor Action

The Senate passed S 1662 April 29, 69-9, after turning aside complaints of senators who feared their states would be selected for waste dumps. *(Vote 93, p. 20-S)*

The action delighted the nuclear industry and the Reagan administration, both of which lobbied hard to make sure the measure passed essentially as written.

Environmental groups, however, were dismayed over the bill's rapid timetable for finding a permanent home for the nation's radioactive waste. They also were unhappy with provisions allowing the government to provide interim storage for utilities' spent fuel, which they regarded as a "bailout" for the nuclear industry. The closest votes in two days of floor debate came over this issue; amendments to delete the AFR storage provisions from the bill were killed by 47-43 and 46-43 votes.

As passed by the Senate, S 1662 set a fast timetable for a nuclear waste repository. It called for the selection of three potential sites for a permanent, underground repository by 1984, and the selection of one of them by the president by 1986. The facility would go into operation in the mid-1990s. Potential sites for a second repository would be recommended by 1987 and the site selected by 1989.

Military waste would be put into the repositories along with civilian waste unless the president ruled that it be kept separate for reasons of national security, public health and safety, cost or efficiency.

The bill also required the government to examine the concept of monitored, retrievable storage — man-made facilities near the earth's surface, built to hold waste for hundreds of years — as an alternative to permanent repositories. Within one year of enactment, DOE would have to send Congress detailed plans for building one or more such facilities.

Some members of Congress from potential geologic repository states, principally Sen. J. Bennett Johnston, D-La., had pushed this idea. The concept was opposed by environmentalists, who said they did not want to saddle future generations with the waste. But supporters said it would be safer to build a facility than to depend on the stability of geologic formations for thousands of years. Several European nations had chosen this type of storage, Johnston said.

To finance the waste program, S 1662 established a fee of one mill per kilowatt-hour of nuclear electricity generated, or one cent per 10 kilowatt-hours. During floor debate, supporters of the bill said the fee would bring in about $300 million a year at first, rising to $1 billion a year when all reactors then under construction had gone into operation. While this fee would cover only waste generated after enactment of the bill, utilities would be charged a similar fee for the spent fuel they already had created and sent to an AFR storage facility.

The Senate bill allowed storage of spent fuel in a federal AFR for up to 12 years before it would have to be shipped to a reprocessing center, a permanent repository or a long-term MRS facility.

The bill required the government to work closely with affected states and Indian tribes in siting waste facilities. If a state or tribe objected to a federal decision to put a repository within its borders, one chamber of Congress would have to agree for the objection to stand. The bill also authorized impact assistance payments to states or localities where an AFR or a repository was located, to "mitigate social or economic impacts" associated with the facility.

Floor Debate

AFR Storage. During floor consideration of S 1662, senators from the three states where away-from-reactor storage for spent fuel was considered most likely to be located — South Carolina, Illinois and New York — tried unsuccessfully to delete the AFR section of the bill.

Led by Strom Thurmond, R-S.C., they argued that an AFR was not needed; they said spent fuel could be kept at reactor sites until a permanent waste disposal facility was built. Storage pools at reactors could be redesigned, the spent fuel compacted or a new dry storage method used, they said.

But Energy Committee Chairman James A. McClure, R-Idaho, the bill's floor manager, said the AFR provision in the bill was limited. Utilities would have to do everything

possible to find room to store the spent fuel at reactor sites before the government would take it, he said. Utilities also would have to pay for government storage.

Environmental lobbyists blasted a federal AFR program as a bailout of the utility industry. But getting an AFR in the bill was the industry's top priority, and its lobbyists were out in force during the debate.

The Senate tabled Thurmond's amendment 47-43, then by a 46-43 vote tabled a motion to reconsider that action. *(Votes 88, 89, p. 19-S)*

State Role. The Senate also refused to give states a stronger role in the siting of nuclear waste repositories.

S 1662 required the federal government to work closely with states in which it was considering building a waste repository. If this process of "consultation and concurrence" failed, the bill allowed the state to object to the repository. That objection would stand if either the House or Senate passed a resolution backing the state.

Senators from potential repository states felt that was not enough protection. Proxmire proposed giving states an absolute veto. But McClure said no state wanted a repository and that the amendment would result in 50 state rejections.

Proxmire's amendment was tabled, 70-19. *(Vote 86, p. 19-S)*

Howard W. Cannon, D-Nev., then offered a more moderate amendment that would allow a state's objection to stand unless both houses of Congress passed a resolution overriding the state. That would put the burden on the federal government to convince Congress of the need for the repository within that state, Cannon said.

Cannon's amendment also was tabled, 52-40. *(Vote 87, p. 19-S)*

Timetable. John C. Stennis, D-Miss., sought to slow the timetable for selecting a repository site. He complained that the bill required three sites to be picked in 1984 — before a survey of the entire country was due to be completed in 1986. (Salt domes in Mississippi already had been studied for a possible repository, so a fast timetable increased that state's chances of being selected.)

Stennis proposed delaying the schedule by three years to allow the survey to be completed before any sites were picked. "What is a delay of three years compared to a program of 10,000 years?" he asked, noting that nuclear waste remained hazardous for thousands of years.

But Alan K. Simpson, R-Wyo., called the amendment "delay for delay's sake," and the Senate voted 63-27 to table it. *(Vote 90, p. 19-S)*

Thad Cochran, R-Miss., also tried to delay the timetable by offering an amendment to require that of the first three sites initially considered for a repository, one must be in a granite formation. His amendment also was tabled, 83-5. *(Vote 91, p. 19-S)*

Military Waste. The Senate by voice vote adopted an amendment by Simpson and Gary Hart, D-Colo., to have the government plan on burying military waste in the same facility as civilian waste unless the president determined that a separate military repository was needed.

The Armed Services Committee had objected to such a provision but agreed not to fight the amendment after it was clear that Simpson and Hart had the votes to win.

House Committee Action

Seven committees had some jurisdictional stake in nuclear waste legislation in the House. Three — Science

and Technology, Interior, and Energy and Commerce — shared primary jurisdiction. Four others — Armed Services, Rules, Judiciary, and Merchant Marine and Fisheries — had jurisdiction over certain sections, although the latter two took no action on the bill.

The Science Committee reported a waste bill Dec. 15, 1981 (HR 5016 — H Rept 97-411, Part I). Under that bill, the government would quickly pick potential sites for a repository and build a test facility to gain public confidence in its ability to safely dispose of nuclear waste.

The Interior Committee approved a more comprehensive bill (HR 3809) March 17. It filed its report April 27 (H Rept 97-491, Part I).

Interior's bill had a somewhat slower schedule for picking repository sites; it also included limited relief for the utilities' spent fuel problem. It would allow government storage of spent fuel only as a last resort; the government would not buy or build an AFR but would store the spent fuel only at existing federal facilities.

The committee rejected an amendment drafted by the Armed Services Committee staff that would have exempted military waste from the provisions of the bill.

Armed Services then exercised its claim on the bill. It approved its version of HR 3809 July 15, stipulating that the bill's provisions would not apply to waste from the production of nuclear weapons. However, rejecting the urging of its leaders, the panel voted 26-6 to give states a substantial voice in the location of a military waste facility.

The committee filed its report on the bill July 16 (H Rept 97-491, Part II).

Energy and Commerce Fight

The Energy and Commerce Committee, which shared primary jurisdiction over the bill, was slow to act because two key members were unable to reach agreement on several controversial provisions. The committee did not report a bill until Aug. 20 (HR 6598 — H Rept 97-785, Part I).

Richard L. Ottinger, D-N.Y., chairman of the Energy Conservation and Power Subcommittee, and James T. Broyhill, N.C., the committee's senior Republican, were at odds for months, principally over the issue of whether to provide federal storage for spent fuel. Ottinger opposed the idea, while Broyhill, whose district included several nuclear reactors said to be running out of storage space, wanted a large federal AFR.

The two also differed on what to do about military waste. Broyhill wanted to exempt it from the bill; Ottinger felt it was just as hazardous to the public as civilian waste and should be covered by the same environmental and state participation requirements.

Compromise efforts failed, and finally, on June 16, both men introduced their own proposals. Broyhill's bill generally reflected the wishes of the nuclear industry and the Reagan administration. Broyhill referred to it as a "bipartisan compromise" because it was cosponsored by Phil Gramm, D-Tex. Ottinger's plan was geared more toward the concerns of environmentalists and the states.

Subcommittee Action. Ottinger's subcommittee June 23 rejected his plan and adopted Broyhill's, with only a few minor modifications, by a lopsided 16-5 vote.

However, the margin obscured the sharp divisions within the panel on several controversial issues. Because of the close votes on those issues and the relatively weaker number of industry advocates on the full committee, Ottinger promised to press for reconsideration of a number of provisions there.

It was clear early in the markup that Ottinger's proposal lacked the votes for approval, so its supporters — most of the panel's Democrats — concentrated on offering amendments to Broyhill's plan, to add health, safety, procedural and environmental safeguards to the waste site selection process. However, of the seven such amendments on which there were recorded votes, all but one were defeated by a coalition of all of the subcommittee's Republicans and two or three conservative Southern Democrats.

Full Committee Action. The Energy and Commerce Committee approved HR 6598 by voice vote Aug. 4 after more than a dozen close votes on amendments were settled.

During five days of markup, the whip hand was held by Broyhill, who kept Republicans in line and got help from a handful of Southern Democrats led by Gramm. The coalition, backed strongly by a bevy of administration and nuclear industry lobbyists, lost very few votes. Amendments sought by environmental lobbyists were beaten back repeatedly.

The Broyhill coalition defeated attempts to delete the bill's AFR storage provisions, although an amendment by Edward R. Madigan, R-Ill., made clear that AFR storage could not be provided at three privately owned facilities, including one in Illinois. A Mike Synar, D-Okla., amendment providing that AFR storage was to be used only as a last resort, if storage at the reactor sites could not be expanded, also was defeated, 17-25.

Under the bill, a state's objection to a federal decision to give it a waste repository would stand if either the House or Senate passed a resolution upholding that objection. James D. Santini, D-Nev., whose state was a prime candidate for a repository, wanted stronger language that would allow an objection to stand unless both chambers passed a resolution opposing it. His amendment lost 18-23.

An Edward J. Markey, D-Mass., amendment to have the bill cover military waste was replaced with a Broyhill substitute exempting military waste. The substitute was adopted 24-18.

Several committee members wanted an independent commission created to make sure that the federal government was impartial in selecting a repository location. But an amendment by Ron Wyden, D-Ore., to do so failed on a 21-21 tie. An amendment by Al Swift, D-Wash., to create a somewhat less powerful commission was first approved, 23-19, but was then replaced by a Broyhill substitute amendment calling for a much weaker commission.

The only substantial amendment won by committee Democrats was a Swift provision to allow court challenges by states or citizens' groups at the time the government was examining a potential repository site. After first losing 20-22, Swift modified his proposal slightly and won 22-20.

As written, the Broyhill bill contained a population density exemption that would keep a repository from being built at Richton, Miss., where a salt formation was being examined as a possible site. The amendment was sought by Trent Lott, R-Miss., a member of the Rules Committee. However, as it was affected by other amendments, the formula was mistakenly rewritten to essentially exclude almost all areas of the country, including the prime sites being considered.

When Republicans tried to correct the problem, the markup degenerated into a parochial brawl. W. J. "Billy" Tauzin, D-La., tried to add language that effectively would rule out sites in Mississippi, Louisiana and Texas. He called the amendment a "safety valve." Santini called it an "escape hatch." The proposal lost 20- 22.

The committee then rejected, 21-21, a Corcoran amendment to correct the earlier population language. The bill thus contained a population restriction that would exclude all potential sites. Staff members said it would have to be "fixed."

Compromise Bill

In a last-minute push to get a waste bill passed before Congress recessed for the fall election campaigns, House committee leaders crafted a compromise measure (HR 7187), introduced Sept. 24.

The bulk of the 142-page bill was written by leaders of the Interior and Energy committees. Interior Chairman Udall was generally credited with keeping negotiations moving when they stalled, as they often did.

The final compromise was elusive. Twice, the committee leaders went to the Rules Committee expecting to present a bill to take to the floor, but they were unable to produce a written deal for Rules to consider. The second time, on Sept. 23, Rules Chairman Richard Bolling, D-Mo., told Udall, Science Committee Chairman Don Fuqua, D-Fla., and Energy and Commerce Chairman John D. Dingell, D-Mich., to have the bill printed that evening. They managed to do it the next day.

The bill required the government to choose a site for a permanent waste repository by 1987 and to build it by about 2000. It also authorized federal storage of up to 2,000 tons of spent fuel for which utilities could not provide storage; required the government to design an MRS facility within one year, and provided for construction of a smaller, test version of a permanent repository, to be built and put into operation by 1990.

The test facility, included at the insistence of the Science Committee, would not be licensed by the NRC as the larger one would, and states would not be given any power to object to it.

However, at the insistence of the Rules Committee, the bill did give the states a powerful voice in the location of a permanent repository. If a state objected to a decision to put a waste dump within its borders, the objection would stand unless both the House and Senate voted to override it. The administration and the nuclear industry felt such a provision would give the states too much power, making it potentially impossible for the government to build a repository anywhere. States also could veto an AFR facility, and the veto would stand unless it was overridden by a vote of both houses of Congress.

The bill allowed the military to bury its waste in a separate facility not subject to the environmental and judicial procedures required for the civilian dump. States could veto a military repository, with a two-house vote required to overrule it.

Rules Committee Action

The committee leaders who drafted the compromise waste bill sought to speed House consideration by obtaining a rule for floor consideration that would severely limit amendments to the controversial legislation. But the Rules Committee Sept. 28 decided to allow more than 30 amendments to be offered.

The committee was persuaded by the arguments of Markey and other members that parts of the bill were so important and contentious that they should be subject to a full debate by the the House. Markey had about a dozen amendments he wanted to offer.

Several Rules members had a strong personal interest in floor amendments themselves. For example, Butler Derrick, D-S.C., whose state was a likely site for an AFR, had vowed to try to block any bill that provided AFR storage, and Lott wanted to be sure the bill contained a population formula that would prevent a repository from being located in his district.

House Floor Action

The House began debating the nuclear waste bill Sept. 30 but could not finish before leaving for the election recess. It took up the bill again Nov. 29, and worked on it for three days before finally passing it Dec. 2, by voice vote.

For floor debate, the House considered the text of HR 7187, the compromise bill, under the bill number of HR 3809.

As passed by the House, HR 3809 provided for the development of a permanent repository, with the site to be selected by 1987; provision of a limited amount of interim, away-from-reactor storage for spent fuel; the design of an MRS facility, and construction of a small test and evaluation repository by 1990. Military waste for the most part was excluded from the bill.

State Veto Power

The major debate during House consideration was over how much power states should have to reject a federal decision to give them a waste repository.

The House adopted a Broyhill amendment that would make it more difficult for a state to veto a federal decision to place a permanent waste repository within its boundaries.

As written, the bill allowed a state veto to stand unless both houses of Congress voted to override it within 90 days and the president signed the joint resolution. Under the amendment, the state would have to convince one house of Congress to vote to uphold its veto.

The amendment was adopted 190-184 Nov. 29 and reaffirmed Dec. 2 by a vote of 213-179. *(Votes 372, 384, pp. 112-H, 114-H)*

Broyhill argued that without his amendment, "we could spend several years ... and several hundred million dollars in making the selection and then have a governor veto the project, overriding the decision of this Congress, overriding the decision that had been made by the president. ... I think that is going too far."

The amendment brought the House bill one step closer to the Senate bill, which also required a one-house vote of Congress to sustain a veto of a permanent repository.

The House rejected an amendment by Manuel Lujan Jr., R-N.M., that would have made an identical change in the state veto provision for interim storage facilities. Lujan's amendment was defeated 181-194 on Nov. 29. As a result, the bill allowed a veto of an interim facility to stand unless Congress passed a joint resolution overriding it. *(Vote 370, p. 112-H)*

An attempt by Thomas E. Petri, R-Wis., to give states an absolute veto over a permanent repository was defeated by voice vote Dec. 2.

MRS Controversy

The House by voice vote Nov. 29 adopted a Udall amendment to give DOE five years instead of two for completion of a study on monitored, retrievable storage of nuclear waste.

That moved the House bill further from the Senate-

passed measure, which required completion of the MRS study within one year of enactment. As a result, the chief Senate advocate of MRS storage, Johnston, predicted the bill would never be enacted. Johnston wanted to expedite development of an MRS system in hopes it would displace plans for long-term storage of waste in underground geologic formations such as the salt domes under his state.

Udall wanted to move ahead quickly on permanent waste storage. "This MRS technology is not the best answer to our national nuclear waste problem," he told the House.

Parochial Concerns

The House defeated several amendments designed by members to keep waste facilities out of their districts.

Lott lost, 81-296, Nov. 29 on his proposal to bar a repository at any site adjacent to an area where more than 1,000 people lived within one square mile — a prohibition that would have disqualified the site under consideration in his district. *(Vote 371, p. 112-H)*

"We are going to be tested on this amendment and a half dozen more like it," said Udall, opposing the amendment. "They usually don't come right out and say it, but they say in effect, 'You can't put this in my district or in my state.' "

The House also rejected an amendment by Stanley N. Lundine, D-N.Y., that would have eliminated the bill's provisions for interim storage of nuclear waste. Lundine argued that utilities did not really need the extra storage space; if the government provided interim storage, he said, the utilities would not make the changes needed to accommodate their own additional waste. AFR storage also would mean that more nuclear wastes would be transported around the nation, possibly with dangerous consequences, he said.

Lundine's amendment also stemmed in part from his concern that the West Valley facility in his district was a prime candidate for interim storage. His amendment was defeated 84-308. *(Vote 373, p. 112-H)*

Markey, an opponent of nuclear power, offered the most amendments to the bill, but with little success. His proposal to increase reimbursement to states for the costs of having a test storage facility located within their boundaries was defeated 72-321. And his amendment to extend all the provisions of the bill to military waste lost 105-281. *(Votes 382, 383, p. 114-H)*

Determined to see waste legislation enacted, Udall opposed the military waste amendment, as he did several others, for fear its adoption would kill the bill's chances of passage. "There are some pretty good arguments made by [Markey]," Udall said, "but we have got to this late stage of the session and we have got to put first things first. . . . This bill has a lot of baggage already that makes it pretty hard to carry."

Another Markey amendment to tighten environmental restrictions in the location of a permanent repository was rejected by voice vote. Markey did succeed in attaching one amendment to the bill by voice vote that allowed either a state legislature or a governor to initiate veto proceedings.

Compromise, Final Action

Udall, after shepherding the bill through the House, hoped the Senate would accept the House version. Instead, Senate Energy Committee staff, in consultation with key members, drafted a compromise bill, which McClure introduced Dec. 13.

The Senate took up the measure Dec. 20. McClure said it had been kept free of provisions that would prevent the location of a waste dump in any particular state or district. The bill did contain Lott's amendment barring construction of a repository whose surface facility would be next to a square-mile area with a population of 1,000 or more. Lott hoped the provision would eliminate from consideration a potential repository site in his district, but staff aides said it was not clear whether it would have the desired effect.

In another area of controversy, the compromise bill set a two-and-a-half-year timetable for the development of plans for one or more MRS facilities. Johnston had insisted that DOE complete its MRS study in one year; Udall wanted to allow five years for completion of the study. The compromise was agreed to by Johnston and Udall.

The Senate abandoned its requirement that repository site recommendations to the president be accompanied by a full environmental impact statement, adopting instead House language allowing a less stringent "environmental assessment."

Among the amendments to the compromise adopted on the Senate floor Dec. 20 was Proxmire's, increasing the power of the states to override a federal government decision to locate a waste repository within their boundaries.

Both the Senate- and House-passed bills contained so-called "one-house sustain" provisions; a state that objected to a repository would have to convince one house of Congress to uphold its objection for the veto to stand. Proxmire's amendment changed that to a "two-house override" — allowing a state to effectively veto a repository unless both chambers acted to override the veto.

In other Senate action on the compromise bill, Thurmond succeeded in adding three amendments tightening restrictions on the location of temporary federal storage. One ensured fuller participation by states in the location of temporary storage facilities. Another provided impact aid to states receiving those facilities. The third required that spent fuel must be moved from a temporary federal storage facility within three years after a permanent repository went into operation.

An amendment by John Glenn, D-Ohio, provided for cooperative international research in the storage of spent nuclear fuel. Another, by Lowell P. Weicker Jr., R-Conn., authorized the NRC to establish a training program for the operators of civilian nuclear plants.

The Senate accepted the compromise bill, as amended, by voice vote.

The House, despite some complaints about the Senate's reversal on the state veto provision and about the rule for consideration of the compromise, approved it a few hours later, 256-32. The rule (H Res 636 — H Rept 97-983) allowed no amendments and provided that the vote on adoption of the rule was also the vote on the bill. ∎

NRC Authorization Bill Finally Cleared

Some last-minute parliamentary maneuvering and a compromise on uranium import restrictions enabled Congress Dec. 16 to clear legislation authorizing fiscal 1982 and 1983 funding for the Nuclear Regulatory Commission (NRC).

The measure (HR 2330 — PL 97-415), reported by

House and Senate committees in the spring of 1981, was intended to take effect in 1982. But it was dogged by controversy throughout the 97th Congress, and barely slipped by in the last days of the lame-duck session. Its passage took so long that fiscal 1982 and the first quarter of fiscal 1983 were over by the time it was signed into law.

President Reagan signed the bill Jan. 3, 1983.

The legislation authorized appropriations totaling $485.2 million in fiscal 1982 and $513.1 million in fiscal 1983 for the NRC.

It contained controversial "interim licensing" provisions allowing the NRC to issue temporary licenses to new nuclear plants so that they could begin operating before the completion of public hearings on them. The commission also could issue amendments to existing licenses before hearings were held on the changes. The nuclear industry had sought the expedited licensing provisions; environmental groups opposed them.

Other controversial provisions in the bill were one prohibiting the government from using the plutonium in spent (burned) fuel from civilian nuclear reactors to make atomic weapons, and another delaying NRC regulations governing the cleanup of radioactive uranium mill tailings. The Defense Department had opposed the spent fuel provision, while the uranium tailings issue held up action on the bill for months.

Another controversial provision that had threatened to kill the legislation was dropped from the final bill. It would have triggered a moratorium on uranium imports if they exceeded 37.5 percent of U.S. uranium consumption.

The Senate had attached the protectionist provision at the insistence of Sen. Pete V. Domenici, R-N.M., whose state was the center of the financially ailing U.S. uranium industry. After veto threats and objections from the House Ways and Means Committee, the House refused to accept the conference version of the amendment. Domenici finally agreed to a compromise under which Congress passed a separate resolution (S Con Res 135) requiring a comprehensive study of the domestic uranium mining and milling industry.

Although uranium imports accounted for only about 12 percent of the domestic market in 1982, low-cost imports from Canada and Australia had been rising rapidly as a result of recently discovered supplies. The Domenici amendment upset those countries and the Reagan administration, which generally fought such trade restrictions.

Provisions

As signed into law, HR 2330 (PL 97-415):

Funding. Authorized appropriations of $485 million in fiscal 1982 and $513 million in fiscal 1983 for the NRC. The 1983 authorization included $77 million for regulation of nuclear reactors, $70 million for inspection and enforcement of NRC regulations, $47 million for safeguarding nuclear materials and $257 million for nuclear regulatory research.

The bill specified that $6 million be made available for licensing work on the controversial Clinch River breeder reactor, being built by the Department of Energy (DOE) in Tennessee. It also authorized $18 million for NRC regulatory research on the project. *(Clinch River, p. 292)*

The bill authorized spending of $5.5 million on gascooled nuclear reactors, which could be used in areas of the West where there was not sufficient water to support standard water-cooled reactors.

Safety Goal. Required the NRC to issue a safety goal for nuclear reactors by Dec. 31, 1982.

Three Mile Island. Prohibited the use of any NRC funds for cleaning up or repairing the nuclear reactor at Three Mile Island, Pa., damaged in 1979 in the nation's worst nuclear accident; also prohibited any discharge of radioactive water relating to the accident. The plant, known as TMI, had been idle since the accident. *(Related story, p. 313)*

Nuclear Plant Licensing. Allowed the NRC, through Dec. 31, 1983, to issue temporary operating licenses for new nuclear reactors before the completion of public hearings, if it determined that there would be no danger to the public health or the environment. Initially, an interim license would allow a reactor to run at only 5 percent of its total power, but NRC eventually could allow reactors to run at full power on a temporary license.

● Allowed the NRC to issue amendments to existing licenses of nuclear plants before holding public hearings on the changes, if it found that a change would present "no significant hazard" to the public.

This change, known as the "Sholly amendment," would make moot a case pending before the U.S. Supreme Court at the time the bill was cleared. A lower court had ruled that the NRC must hold public hearings before issuing any licensing amendments, including ones as minor as a change in the name of a reactor.

Quality Assurance. Beefed up the NRC's quality assurance program by requiring the commission to have at least one resident inspector at every nuclear plant under construction, where construction was at least 15 percent complete.

Spent Fuel. Prohibited the government from using the plutonium in burned fuel from civilian nuclear reactors to make atomic weapons.

Nuclear Sabotage. Set criminal penalties of up to 10 years in prison and a fine of not more than $10,000 for anyone convicted of willfully damaging a nuclear plant or waste storage facility.

Uranium Mill Tailings. Suspended NRC regulations governing the cleanup of uranium mill tailings until the Environmental Protection Agency (EPA) issued environmental standards; required EPA to issue the standards by October 1983 and to take the cost of cleaning up the tailings into consideration in writing the standards.

● Allowed state governments to adopt alternative proposals for the cleanup of mill tailings if they wished.

● Required DOE to clean up mill tailings near an inactive uranium mill at Edgemont, S.D., that had been operated by the Tennessee Valley Authority (TVA).

Uranium Study. S Con Res 135, which the House parliamentarian said had the same effect as an amendment to HR 2330, required the president to conduct a comprehensive study of the domestic uranium mining and milling industry. It also provided that if, in the next 10 years, uranium imports exceeded 37.5 percent of total U.S. demand or threatened to impair national security, the secretary of energy should investigate whether imports should be restricted for national security reasons.

Background

For several years, authorization bills for the NRC had become tied up in controversy because of nuclear-related provisions. Congress did not pass an authorization for fiscal 1980 until the year was more than half over, and it never

passed one at all for fiscal 1981. *(1980 Almanac p. 502)*

The main hang-up on those bills was nuclear power plant safety and the different ways members sought to address the problem in the wake of the TMI accident.

In 1981 most of the controversy centered on proposals to allow temporary licensing of nuclear reactors before completion of the NRC's lengthy hearing process. The nuclear industry insisted such provisions were needed to avoid operating delays for about a dozen plants, although by 1982 it appeared that only one utility would be affected, and that delay was only expected to be about two months.

Environmental groups opposed accelerated licensing procedures on grounds public safety could be endangered.

Both House and Senate committees reported NRC authorization bills in the spring of 1981, but the House did not pass HR 2330 until November of that year. In the Senate, floor consideration was delayed repeatedly as amendments on cleaning up radioactive waste at uranium mills and on the use of commercial fuel for military weapons were negotiated. Faced with the threat of a filibuster in the last days of the session, the Senate put off action on its bill (S 1207) until 1982. *(1981 Almanac p. 444)*

Senate Action

After voting 88-9 to ban the use of spent fuel to make nuclear weapons for the military, the Senate passed HR 2330 March 30 by a 97-0 vote. *(Votes 64, 65, p. 14-S)*

Spent fuel was fuel that had been burned in civilian nuclear power plants; it contained elements that could be used for the production of weapons. The amendment to bar such use was the main focus of the Senate debate, and its adoption was a rebuff to the Reagan administration and to the chairman of the Senate Armed Services Committee.

Interim licensing of new nuclear reactors, a controversial issue during House consideration of the bill, was not an issue on the Senate floor.

Spent Fuel for Weapons

The amendment barring the use of spent fuel for weapons production was sponsored by the bill's floor managers, Alan K. Simpson, R-Wyo., and Gary Hart, D-Colo., chairman and ranking minority member of the Energy and Public Works Subcommittee on Nuclear Regulation. Hart was the main force behind it.

The Senate had adopted a similar Hart amendment in 1981, as part of the fiscal 1982 energy and water appropriations bill, but the amendment was later dropped in conference. *(1981 Almanac pp. 301, 458)*

The amendment was aimed at heading off some high-level interest in the Reagan administration, as well as in the congressional Armed Services committees, in using the plutonium in burned commercial fuel to make weapons.

Traditionally, the civilian nuclear program and military weapons production had been kept separate. But planned increases in nuclear warheads were expected to require more plutonium than existing government reactors could produce. Rather than build expensive new reactors, some officials suggested refining the plutonium in spent commercial fuel, which the administration testified would be cheaper.

Hart said that "would, in effect, turn commercial nuclear power plants into bomb-making factories. It would seriously undermine U.S. efforts to halt the spread of nuclear weapons to countries that do not now have them."

Hart and Simpson said using spent fuel for weapons

also would be a public relations disaster for the nuclear industry, which already was having significant image problems. "This could be the death knell for commercial nuclear power in the United States," said Simpson, who described himself as pro-nuclear. Simpson said he believed the military could meet its plutonium needs without resorting to commercial spent fuel.

John W. Warner, R-Va., and Henry M. Jackson, D-Wash., tried to defuse the amendment by offering a substitute that would permit the use of spent fuel for weapons only if the president certified that it was necessary for national security. But the substitute could not be offered under the parliamentary agreement the Senate had adopted to debate the bill.

John Tower, R-Texas, chairman of the Senate Armed Services Committee, fought the amendment. He said there was no justification for eliminating "an important national security option."

"I suspect the Kremlin would be delighted with this amendment. Here we go again — giving up an important national security option unilaterally and unnecessarily," Tower said. He noted that the Armed Services Committee had rejected such an amendment to the nuclear waste bill (S 1662), and said it did not make sense to build new government reactors to produce plutonium for weapons, at a cost of several billion dollars, while spent fuel loaded with plutonium was piling up at civilian reactor sites around the country. *(Nuclear waste bill, p. 304)*

The administration, in letters from Deputy Defense Secretary Frank C. Carlucci and Energy Secretary James B. Edwards, opposed the amendment but did not actively lobby to defeat it.

Some observers believed the lopsided vote in favor of the amendment was strengthened by growing grass-roots support for limiting nuclear weapons production.

Uranium Tailings, Imports

By voice vote March 30, the Senate adopted a Domenici amendment that would bolster the sagging domestic uranium industry in two ways:

● It would delay the implementation of NRC regulations requiring the cleanup of radioactive uranium mill tailings. The industry said the regulations were too harsh and expensive.

● It also required that at least 80 percent of uranium used by U.S. utilities must be produced in the United States.

The dispute over cleaning up tailings — the voluminous, sandlike radioactive waste produced in the mining and processing of uranium ore — was the main reason the NRC bill did not make it to the Senate floor in 1981. After the bill was reported, Domenici indicated he wanted a delay in implementing the regulations on cleaning up tailings at active uranium mines, several of which were located in his state.

At many mines, tons of tailings had been piled up, allowing dangerous radioactivity to be spread by wind and water. In some cases, tailings had been used in the construction of schools and homes.

Congress had passed a law (PL 95-604) in 1978 requiring the cleanup of abandoned mines and the establishment of regulations for controlling tailings at active mines. EPA was supposed to set health standards for tailings but it failed to act, so the NRC in 1980 issued its own regulations. Implementation of the regulations had been delayed once by an amendment to the fiscal 1982 energy-water appropri-

ations bill, but Domenici wanted to delay them again through an amendment to the NRC authorization measure.

Other Amendments

Without controversy or recorded votes, the Senate March 22 approved several other amendments, including:

● By Simpson, to reduce NRC's fiscal 1982 authorization by $10 million, reflecting what Simpson called current restraints on the federal budget.

● By James Abdnor, R-S.D., to give the Energy Department authority to begin cleaning up uranium tailings near a uranium mill at Edgemont, S.D. The TVA, which owned the mill, was cleaning up the mill site itself, but the NRC found that about 130 pieces of private property nearby had to be cleaned up, at a cost of about $300,000.

● By Wendell H. Ford, D-Ky., to get the NRC to pay more attention to quality assurance in the construction of new reactors. Ford offered the amendment because two plants being built adjacent to his state, one in Ohio and one in Indiana, had had serious construction problems. "At this moment, it is very possible that nuclear plants are being built in such a way that they present a danger to the public health and safety," Ford said.

Conference Action

After six months of sporadic negotiations, House-Senate conferees Sept. 16 agreed on a compromise version of HR 2330. The conference report (H Rept 97-884) was filed Sept. 28.

In place of Domenici's amendment requiring U.S. utilities to use at least 80 percent domestic uranium, the conference agreement called for a two-year moratorium on new contracts for uranium imports if imports rose above 37.5 percent of U.S. consumption. The conferees said imports above this level could endanger national security.

However, U.S. Trade Representative William E. Brock III indicated that the provision could lead to a veto of the bill. In a Sept. 15 letter, Brock said the administration could not accept such an automatic trigger for a moratorium on uranium imports.

On the mill tailings issue, conferees required EPA to issue standards for the cleanup of tailings by October 1983. The NRC then would have to issue new regulations, which would have to take economic costs into consideration.

The conference agreement allowed the NRC to issue interim licenses through the end of 1983 if environmental and safety reviews of the new reactor had been completed. It also allowed the commission to make minor changes in license requirements for nuclear reactors without holding public hearings.

Without discussion, conferees retained the Senate amendment prohibiting the use of burned fuel from civilian nuclear reactors for the production of nuclear weapons. They also retained Senate language that would expand the NRC's program of checking the quality of construction at new plants.

Final Action

The Senate approved the conference report on HR 2330 Oct. 1 by voice vote.

However, the likelihood of floor fights over several controversial provisions prevented final House action before the campaign recess, and a vote on clearing the measure was put off until the lame-duck session.

The conference report drew objections from two House committees. The Ways and Means Committee objected to the restrictions on uranium imports. Armed Services members objected to several provisions, including the one prohibiting the government from using the plutonium in spent fuel to make atomic weapons.

The objectionable provisions had been added by the Senate and were accepted or modified by conferees. The House committee leaders planned to raise points of order against them as non-germane and, if necessary, to seek separate votes and full debate on each one, staffers said.

Besides complaining that the Senate-added provisions had not been considered by their panels, the committee leaders cited numerous substantive objections. Ways and Means leaders, for example, said in a "Dear Colleague" letter that the uranium import restrictions could have a detrimental effect on both foreign relations and U.S. energy prices.

House Action

The House, by a 241-148 vote Dec. 2, agreed to drop the uranium imports restriction from the conference report on HR 2330. *(Vote 385, p. 116-H)*

Bill Frenzel, R-Minn., who offered the motion, said the provision would be an "unfair trade barrier" and might result in retaliation by Australia and Canada, the major uranium exporters.

The House voted to keep the Senate-added provision barring the government from using spent fuel from civilian reactors to make plutonium for nuclear weapons. By a 107-281 vote, it rejected a motion by Samuel S. Stratton, D-N.Y., to drop the provision. *(Vote 386, p. 116-H)*

The House then approved the remainder of the conference report by voice vote and sent it back to the Senate for final consideration.

Uranium Imports Compromise

Under a compromise worked out between Domenici and Rep. Morris K. Udall, D-Ariz., Domenici allowed the House-amended conference report on HR 2330 — without the uranium import restriction — to clear the Senate Dec. 17 by voice vote.

But at the same time the Senate passed a concurrent resolution (S Con Res 135), also by voice vote, "correcting" HR 2330 by adding a section on uranium imports.

That section did not contain an automatic trigger for import restrictions, but it did require the president to conduct a comprehensive study of the domestic uranium mining and milling industry. It also provided that if, in the next 10 years, uranium imports exceeded 37.5 percent of total U.S. demand or threatened to impair national security, the secretary of energy should investigate whether imports should be restricted for national security reasons.

The House passed the concurrent resolution Dec. 20 by voice vote. Parliamentarians said it had the same effect as an amendment to the bill. ∎

Three Mile Island Cleanup

The Senate Energy Committee March 31 approved legislation (S 1606) to force the nation's nuclear utilities to pay part of the cost of cleaning up the reactor at Three Mile Island, Pa., damaged in 1979 in the nation's worst nuclear accident.

However, the sharply divided Environment and Public Works Committee July 27 voted 10-6 to report the bill without recommendation, and the measure was never brought to the Senate floor for a vote. The two committees filed a joint report Aug. 13 (S Rept 97-524).

The House Interior Committee held hearings on several cleanup proposals, but no bill was reported in that chamber.

The effort to devise a plan to help finance the cleanup, estimated to cost at least $1 billion, was spearheaded by politicians from the area served by the Three Mile Island (TMI) plant. They said the cleanup was a national problem and its completion would benefit all utilities.

The legislation foundered because of opposition to requiring ratepayers and shareholders of all nuclear utilities to share in the cost, and because of fears that it would set a precedent for future federal "bailouts" for financially troubled utilities.

Background

The accident at Three Mile Island occurred March 28, 1979. A valve stuck open on TMI-2, one of two reactors at the island in the Susquehanna River near Harrisburg, Pa., causing a loss of cooling water. The nuclear fuel core overheated and, at least partially, melted. Area residents were evacuated when it was feared a hydrogen explosion might rip the reactor building apart. *(1979 Almanac pp. 694, 696)*

Most of the radioactive water was removed from the reactor building and the building adjoining it. But the toughest part of the cleanup remained: decontaminating the reactor building and then dealing with the reactor core. General Public Utilities Corp. (GPU), owner of the plant, estimated the work would cost more than $1 billion. Insurance payments provided $300 million, but with that money running out, GPU had slowed the cleanup.

Although the plant was not leaking radioactivity, Pennsylvania politicians feared it could as time went by. They wanted it cleaned up as soon as possible.

Gov. Richard L. Thornburgh, R-Pa., proposed a cost-sharing plan under which the federal government, the nation's utilities and nuclear manufacturers would pay about half the cost of the cleanup, with the other half coming from payments by GPU, its customers and the states of Pennsylvania and New Jersey.

Thornburgh said he had President Reagan's support for the idea, but the White House commitment was less than the $190 million the governor had in mind. The administration only agreed to provide $123 million in research funds, and the General Accounting Office said only about half of that amount actually would go toward GPU's cleanup costs.

Rep. Allen E. Ertel, D-Pa., in whose district the TMI plant was located, pushed a different plan. He introduced legislation (HR 2512) in 1981 to establish a quasi-public insurance corporation to provide additional property insurance to nuclear utilities, and provide a retroactive payment to cover three-fourths of the cost of the TMI cleanup; GPU eventually would have to repay half of the funds it received. Sen. John Heinz, R-Pa., introduced a similar plan in the Senate (S 1606).

Ertel's bill failed to gain the support of the Pennsylvania House delegation, the administration or the nuclear industry. Hearings were held by the House Interior and

Energy and Commerce committees, but no action was taken. Ertel subsequently introduced a simplified version of the bill (HR 5962) that would collect $37.5 million a year for the cleanup from nuclear utilities.

In September 1982, the Edison Electric Institute (EEI), an association of investor-owned utilities, proposed that the utilities' share of TMI cleanup costs be raised through an annual fee on all utilities, plus a surcharge on nuclear utilities. EEI officials said this would raise $192 million over six years. The plan required legislation to order utilities to contribute.

It was that legislation — the only part of Thornburgh's proposal that required congressional action — that was considered by the Senate Energy Committee. It was drafted as an amendment to S 1606.

The American Public Power Association (APPA) opposed efforts to spread TMI cleanup costs to the nation's electrical users, saying it would set a bad precedent. APPA officials said GPU could raise its rates enough to finance the entire cleanup and still not have the highest electric rates in the region.

The Union of Concerned Scientists also opposed legislation that would allow utilities to pass their share of cleanup costs through to electric consumers, in effect creating a "national tax" on electricity to help clean up Three Mile Island. Electric rates already had risen more than 80 percent over the past year in some areas of the country, a spokesman for the group noted.

Energy Committee Action

The Senate Energy Committee approved a revised version of S 1606 March 31 by a vote of 12-8, after heavy lobbying by supporters of a TMI cleanup aid plan.

The amended version of the bill was written by Heinz and Bill Bradley, D-N.J., whose states received power from TMI, and lobbyists for EEI and GPU.

As approved by the committee, the bill would require U.S. nuclear utilities to pay a fee of 28 cents per kilowatt of nuclear generating capacity, up to a maximum of $1.6 million a year per utility, for six years. The fee would generate about $177 million toward the cost of cleaning up the damaged TMI reactor.

As originally drafted, the bill would have required all of the nation's utilities, even those not using nuclear power, to help finance the cleanup. But to secure votes for the measure, Heinz rewrote it to apply only to utilities that owned nuclear power plants.

The legislation was further amended by J. Bennett Johnston, D-La., to exempt utilities that had nuclear plants under construction but did not have any operating nuclear reactors. Johnston particularly wanted to protect Gulf States Utilities Co., which was building its first nuclear plant. To win votes for the bill, Heinz agreed to the amendment, which reduced the amount the bill would bring in by $20 million, to $170 million.

Heinz also agreed to an amendment by Gordon J. Humphrey, R-N.H., to give state utility commissions discretion on whether utilities would be allowed to pass their costs under the bill on to electric consumers. Humphrey subsequently voted against the bill anyway; he said the free market should deal with the cleanup problem — not a government-imposed bail-out funded by the nation's electric users. ■

Transportation/Commerce/Consumers

The enactment in 1982 of legislation increasing special taxes to help finance highway, mass transit and airport improvements required both Congress and the Reagan administration to make significant compromises.

The most important transportation initiative — to finish the Interstate Highway System and make needed highway, bridge and transit repairs — became stalled during the regular session. Members did not want to take the political chance of passing a gasoline tax hike needed to finance the improvements without President Reagan's approval. There also were jurisdictional disputes over the highway program in the House and disagreements over ansit changes in the Senate. *(Story, p. 317)*

But supporters found new impetus in the November elections. Many members read the election results to mean that voters were deeply concerned about the rising unemployment rate. At the same time, the nation's crumbling transportation infrastructure — the cratered highways, inadequate bridges, broken down buses and poor subway tracks — caught the attention of members and the media.

Supporters described the highway and transit measure as a "jobs bill" and launched a major drive to pass it during the lame-duck session. They said it would create an estimated 300,000 jobs.

A major obstacle was Reagan's continued rejection of the gas tax increase. But after it became clear that the bipartisan leadership of Congress would push for the transportation aid and gas tax increase, Reagan jumped on the bandwagon.

With Transportation Secretary Drew Lewis deeply committed to the legislation, Congress and the administration worked fairly smoothly on the bill. A major trade-off concerned mass transit operating subsidies. Earlier threats of a presidential veto of subsidies for mass transit operations beyond fiscal 1984 dissolved. However, members in turn agreed to make deeper cuts in operating subsidies than many had wanted.

The administration also dropped its "New Federalism" proposal to turn back urban and rural road programs to the states, largely in an effort to reduce opposition to the overall bill. Some key members representing both rural and urban interests opposed the turnback.

Lewis had been working all year developing a coalition to support the gas tax legislation. He had gotten mass transit interests behind the bill by promising the first major diversion of gas tax monies — 1 cent a gallon — for public transportation. And he brought along highway builders, who previously opposed gas tax revenues for non-highway uses, by pushing for increased road funding.

Trucking interests fiercely fought increased highway-use taxes, but the tenuous remaining coalition of supporters succeeded in the closing hours of the session in passing the Transportation Assistance Act of 1982. The legislation authorized a record $71 billion-plus over four years for highways and mass transit and increased the gasoline tax a nickel, to a total of 9 cents a gallon, the first hike in the levy since 1959.

Airports, Air Traffic Control

The dormant federal airport development program was another transportation area that required significant compromises of Congress and the administration to achieve revival. *(Story, p. 333)*

The airport development program had expired in 1980, partly because of disputes over the program's direction. The aviation taxes that financed airport development also expired or were reduced. *(1980 Almanac p. 267)*

The major areas that required trade-offs between Congress and the administration or between the Senate and the House included the following:

● **Defederalization.** The Senate had won administration support for the concept of dropping the major airports from the development program and allowing them to negotiate with the airlines for development funds. But the House continued to oppose it. The Senate abandoned its demand to defederalize the airports in an effort to rejuvenate the program, and the basic structure of the program was left intact.

● **Taxes.** The aviation taxes, which comprised the Airport and Airway Trust Fund and helped finance aviation programs, terminated or were reduced when the original legislation expired.

The general aviation gasoline tax dropped to 4 cents a gallon, down from 7 cents, and the jet fuel tax expired. Reagan sought steep increases. He proposed general aviation gas levels of 12 cents a gallon in fiscal 1982, rising to 20 cents in fiscal 1987; and jet fuel taxes of 14 cents a gallon, rising to 22 cents in the same period.

Congress came under conflicting pressures. The active general aviation lobby resisted the proposed taxes. At the same time, Reagan said funds for airport development and the modernization of the air traffic control system, which Congress wanted, were contingent on the tax increases.

Congress and the administration compromised on a final bill that set a tax of 12 cents a gallon for aviation gasoline and 14 cents for jet fuel. The funds were authorized for development and airway system improvements.

● **Air Traffic Control System.** Congress partly met Reagan's demand for increased use of the trust fund for operating the air traffic control system. Reagan contended that aviation users, not the general taxpayer, should bear the major portion of the costs of federal aviation programs. However, Congress historically resisted using the trust fund for operations, contending that the taxes were passed with the intention of being used for airport development, not operations.

Other Major Legislation

Congress continued its efforts to relax federal and state regulation of transportation, and buses became the fourth transportation industry to undergo significant deregulation in as many years. As with previous legislation

involving airlines, railroads and trucking, the bus legislation was intended to promote competition within the industry by allowing companies to respond quickly to changing marketplace conditions with less interference from government. *(Story, p. 336)*

The greatest concern expressed was whether lifting regulations would result in a reduction in service to small towns in rural areas. Supporters contended that there were provisions to protect small towns.

Besides making it easier for companies to expand operations and to change their rates, the bill also provided for the eventual elimination of antitrust immunity for joint rate-setting.

Maritime bills did not do as well in 1982. Measures that would broaden antitrust immunity for ocean liner charters and allow U.S.-flag ship operators to buy foreign vessels and still be eligible for federal operating subsidies were blocked in the Senate by Howard M. Metzenbaum, D-Ohio. *(Stories, pp. 342, 343)*

Supporters of the antitrust bill said it would help make the U.S.-flag ocean liner fleet more competitive with foreign vessels in international trade. Opponents, led by Metzenbaum, argued that the legislation was a bailout for an inefficient industry and would lead to higher consumer prices for imported goods.

Metzenbaum also blocked the subsidy measure because he opposed providing federal operating funds to companies that bought foreign-built ships.

Legislation making it easier for companies to secure rights of way across railroad properties for construction of coal slurry pipelines was approved by House and Senate committees, but then went nowhere. The railroad industry, the major hauler of coal, continued to lobby intensely against the legislation. Coal slurry is pulverized coal mixed with water and then carried by pipe.

The president's proposals for "user fees" to recover federal costs for certain Coast Guard services and port operations and improvements and to increase inland waterway fees again failed to win congressional support.

Railroad Strike

With unemployment on the rise and the economy worsening, Congress quickly acted to end a four-day national railroad strike that had threatened to throw one million people out of work and cost the economy $1 billion a day. *(Story, p. 335)*

Many members had to convince themselves that the situation was serious enough to overcome their opposition to intervening in the collective bargaining process. The measure passed by Congress ordered the 26,000 striking members of the Brotherhood of Locomotive Engineers back to work and imposed the settlement recommended by a presidential Emergency Board. The settlement barred the union from striking through June 30, 1984.

Communications

Efforts spanning several years to update telecommunications policy came to an abrupt halt in 1982. *(Story, p. 331)*

A 1981 Senate bill to restructure the American Telephone & Telegraph Co. (AT&T) and deregulate much of the telecommunications industry was superseded Jan. 8,

1982, when the Justice Department and AT&T announced a settlement to an antitrust case. The agreement resulted in the telephone monopoly's making its local telephone operating companies independent businesses.

Key members in the House and some senators still believed that legislation was needed to supplement the settlement and to prevent undue increases in telephone rates. The Energy and Commerce Committee and its Telecommunications Subcommittee worked to modify the settlement, but the bill was opposed by AT&T, which called on its stockholders and employees to write to their representatives.

Telecommunications Subcommittee Chairman Timothy E. Wirth, D-Colo., withdrew his bill in July because of what he charged was AT&T's campaign of "fear and distortion" against the measure and dilatory tactics that made it impossible to finish a bill.

Consumers

Consumer advocates won both victories and suffered defeats during the session.

Congress exercised its power for the first time to veto a Federal Trade Commission (FTC) regulation. Consumer advocates had supported the rule, which would have required used-car dealers to disclose information about known major defects in the automobiles they sold.

Used-car dealers lobbied extensively for the veto, contending that the rule would require expensive inspections. Consumer advocates argued that the rule specifically did not require inspections. *(Story, p. 346)*

But following that defeat, consumer groups won against the American Medical Association (AMA), which was pushing to exempt doctors and other professionals from FTC antitrust jurisdiction. The doctors argued that the FTC was interfering in the quality of care. *(Story, p. 347)*

FTC officials, the administration and consumer groups said no group should be above the law. The agency, FTC officials said, was interested only in anti-competitive behavior by professionals, such as boycotts and price-fixing.

Parliamentary maneuvering and lobbying by FTC supporters blocked the exemption for professionals and other new curbs on FTC authority. The agency's authorization expired Sept. 30, and no new authorization was approved, but the FTC still received its fiscal 1983 appropriation. *(Story, p. 238)*

Also, consumer groups, along with trial lawyers, opposed legislation approved by a Senate committee that would have limited business liability for damages caused by defective products. The measure did not reach the Senate floor. *(Story, p. 330)*

Lewis Resignation

After Congress cleared the highway and mass transit bill, Lewis announced his resignation, effective Feb. 1, 1983. Considered one of Reagan's most capable Cabinet members, Lewis became chief executive officer of Warner Amex Cable Communications Inc.

Reagan tapped Elizabeth Hanford Dole, his assistant for public liaison and wife of Senate Finance Committee Chairman Robert Dole, R-Kan., to succeed Lewis.

—By Judy Sarasohn

Taxes Hiked to Finance Roads, Mass Transit

A bill authorizing a record $71 billion for highway construction, road repairs and mass transit, and increasing the gasoline tax for the first time since 1959 was cleared in the closing hours of the 97th Congress.

The legislation (HR 6211 — PL 97-424) was sent to President Reagan after a battle-weary Senate Dec. 23 concluded marathon sessions by adopting the conference report (H Rept 97-987) by a vote of 54-33. Reagan signed the bill Jan. 6, 1983. *(Vote 465, p. 77-S)*

Conferees reached agreement Dec. 21, and the House adopted the conference report the same day by a vote of 180-87 and adjourned. Senate action, however, continued to be delayed by filibusters by conservative Republicans who opposed the tax increase. The Senate invoked cloture for a final time Dec. 23 by a vote of 81-5 before adopting the conference report. *(House Vote 459, p. 134-H; Senate Vote 464, p. 77-S)*

The $71 billion authorized through fiscal 1986 was a record amount for the federal highway and mass transit program, according to the Transportation Department. The previous high was the 1978 authorization of $54 billion (PL 95-599). *(1978 Almanac p. 576)*

The Transportation Assistance Act of 1982 raised the gasoline tax five cents, to a total of 9 cents a gallon, beginning April 1, 1983. Truck taxes were increased substantially, but as a trade-off, states were required to allow bigger and heavier trucks on the highways.

The fuel tax change was expected to raise an additional $5.5 billion a year to repair deteriorating roads and transit systems, finish the Interstate Highway System and provide jobs for some of the 12 million unemployed Americans.

In addition to constituting the first increase in the gas tax since 1959, the legislation made a number of other policy changes. One cent of the increased gas tax was earmarked for mass transit, the first substantial diversion of the Highway Trust Fund for public transportation purposes.

Congress established a new block grant program for mass transit and, over the objections of the Reagan administration, continued operating subsidies beyond fiscal 1984.

Also, Congress agreed to allocate more mass transit funds by formulas based on service factors rather than population. Northern cities heavily dependent on mass transit despite declining populations sought formulas that would favor cities with existing service.

States were guaranteed that their highway aid apportionments would equal at least 85 percent of the highway taxes paid by their motorists. The law also allowed states to defer a portion of their local share of federally-funded projects in fiscal 1983 and 1984.

In addition to attempting to provide jobs in road construction and repairs, the bill extended unemployment benefits.

Jobs-Bill Label

Congressional committees had scrapped their multi-year authorization bills earlier in the year because of the uncertainty over revenues that followed the initial refusal of President Reagan to endorse the gas tax hike on which the proposals were predicated. A stop-gap bill extending the basic highway authorizations for one-year was enacted (S 2574 — PL 97-327). *(Details below)*

The proposals were revived, however, after the November elections, when unemployment reached more than 10 percent. The legislation was wrapped in the aura of a "jobs bill" that would provide some 300,000 jobs and begin the repair of the crumbling physical infrastructure of the nation. *(Infrastructure box, p. 320)*

The effort quickly drew bipartisan support in Congress.

Reagan, at the urging of Transportation Secretary Drew Lewis, eventually endorsed the tax increases, labeling them as "user-fees." He supported HR 6211 not as a jobs bill but as a start in repairing the transportation system.

Senate Democrats unsuccessfully tried to attach their jobs plan to HR 6211. Their amendment would have eliminated the fuel tax increase, provided a "light" public works program funding small-scale projects such as bridge-painting, and financed the highway program by trimming the scheduled July 1983 tax cut for upper-income taxpayers.

The trucking industry lobbied intensely against the bill because of the higher truck taxes. Officials of the American Trucking Associations contended that the tax burden would force some companies out of business.

Senate Passage Delayed

The House Dec. 7 in a session that began the day before, voted 262-143 to pass the bill. *(House Vote 396, p. 118-H)*

Senate action, however, was blocked by Republican Senators who objected to the tax increases. Their delaying tactics forced weekend and early morning sessions, leaving tempers badly frayed.

The frustration and anger was expressed by S. I. "Sam" Hayakawa, R-Calif., to John P. East, R-N.C, as East filibustered during the Dec. 18 session.

"Does the senator from North Carolina believe that his own wisdom is so great that no opinions on this matter on this floor matter but his own.... Why does he demean himself by associating himself with clods and peasants and idiots like us?" Hayakawa said.

Opponents contended they had a responsibility to fight what they called bad legislation. "I know that tempers of senators under the circumstances have been frayed, but I hope upon reflection during the holiday season they realize that on some future occasions they may be in the same position," said Jesse Helms, R-N.C., who spearheaded the opposition.

The Senate passed its version by a 56-34 vote in a session that began Dec. 20. *(Votes 463, p. 76-S)*

Other Highlights

The House-passed bill authorized $71.3 billion over four years for highways and transit systems. The Senate version authorized $70.4 billion over five years for highways and $12.3 billion over three years for transit.

The bill, as cleared, authorized $53.6 billion for fiscal 1983-1986 to complete the Interstate Highway System and make major highway and bridge repairs.

The legislation set a $12.1 billion ceiling on obligations from the Highway Trust Fund for highway construction and related programs for fiscal 1983, increasing to $14.45 billion in fiscal 1986. The trust fund was comprised of highway taxes.

Although primarily described as a highway and transit

repair measure, the bill authorized $4 billion annually for new Interstate Highway construction in fiscal 1984-1987.

Mass Transit. In addition, the measure authorized $17.76 billion for mass transit systems in fiscal 1983-1986 and created a new block grant program for capital and operating expenses.

While the funds available for transit subsidies were cut by 20 percent from the fiscal 1982 level for the largest cities, Congress did not allow the even deeper cuts sought by the administration.

It also hiked the highway user taxes of heavy trucks. The maximum tax for an 80,000-pound truck would increase from $240 a year to $1,600, July 1, 1984. The tax would hit $1,900 on July 1, 1988.

In addition to the highway provisions, the bill appropriated $475 million from the Airport and Airway Trust Fund balance, along with earlier appropriations, for airport development projects in fiscal 1983-1985. (*Airport Tax, p. 333*)

And it mandated the spending of another $400 million from various trust funds for forest development, state boating safety programs and fisheries development. Senate Commerce Committee Chairman Bob Packwood, R-Ore., said those provisions would create another 82,000 jobs.

Final Provisions

As cleared by Congress, the Transportation Assistance Act of 1982:

● Authorized $4 billion for Interstate construction each year for fiscal 1984-1990. A one-year authorization (PL 97-327) cleared before the November recess provided for $3.225 billion in 1984. Although listed, the fiscal 1988-1990 authorizations traditionally were not included in the totals.

New Federalism

Not included in any of the highway bills was the president's "New Federalism" plan to return responsibility for rural and urban road programs to the states, along with $2.2 billion in highway tax monies to pay for them. (*1981 Almanac p. 583*)

Administration officials said they did not push the proposal in order to minimize controversy. City officials had opposed the federalism plan, fearing the states would not fund urban needs. Key members of Congress also had objected to it.

Reagan first proposed the change in early 1981. And in a Nov. 30, 1982, letter to Congress, Reagan said he "remains committed to Federalism and will strive to return to state and local governments programs that are primarily of local interest and responsibility."

A "redirected" federal role in highway programs also was among the alternatives examined in a December report by the Congressional Budget Office (CBO).

If states took greater responsibility for highways, the current 4-cents-a-gallon fuel tax would be adequate for the federal highway programs at least until 1986, CBO said. A temporary 2.4-cents-a-gallon federal fuel tax hike might be needed to help the states, the report said.

CBO, however, did not make any recommendations to Congress.

Earlier law (PL 94-280) authorized $3.625 billion a year for 1985-1990. (*1976 Almanac p. 641*)

Under this program, states could obligate their apportionment of Interstate federal aid one year before the authorization.

● Provided that no state receive less than one-half of 1 percent of the total Interstate apportionment.

● Set a ceiling on obligations from the Highway Trust Fund of $12.1 billion for fiscal 1983; $12.75 billion, 1984; $13.55 billion, 1985; and $14.45 billion, 1986.

● Authorized the following amounts; the 1983 figures included funds previously authorized by PL 97-327:

Primary Highways. $1.85 billion in fiscal 1983; $2.1 billion, 1984; $2.3 billion, 1985; and $2.45 billion, 1986.

Rural Highways. $650 million each year for fiscal 1983-1986.

Urban Highways. $800 million each year for fiscal 1983-1986.

● Required states beginning in fiscal 1984 to spend at least 40 percent of the funds for Primary, rural and urban highways on major repair work, except under certain circumstances.

● Authorized $1.95 billion in fiscal 1984 for Interstate reconstruction, repairs, resurfacing and rehabilitation — known as the "4-R" program — up from $800 million previously authorized; $2.4 billion, 1985; $2.8 billion, 1986; and $3.15 billion, 1987.

● Authorized out of the Highway Trust Fund $257 million in fiscal 1983 for highway projects that communities and states substituted for planned Interstate Highway segments, $700 million annually for 1984 and 1985, and $725 million for 1986. The 1983 funds would be added to $518 million previously appropriated from general revenues.

● Changed the formula for apportioning funds for Primary Highways, which were major urban and rural roads. The existing formula included factors on population, land area and miles of Primary routes. Under the change, a state would receive the higher amount from either the existing formula or a new one based only on urban and rural population. The amount would be reduced to keep the apportionments within the authorized level.

● Authorized $300 million in fiscal 1983 specifically for discretionary funds for special high-cost Interstate segments. Under existing law, about $200 million a year in Interstate monies unused by states reverted to this fund.

● Apportioned bridge repair and replacement funds by a formula based on the latest inventory of bridge needs and state costs of completing the work.

● Provided for a number of demonstration projects, including one in cooperation with the State of Vermont to illustrate the feasibility of reducing the time and cost required to complete highway projects not on the Interstate System. The measure authorized $50 million from the Highway Trust Fund for the Vermont project.

● **Truck Size, Weight.** Set standards for truck size and weight. States were required to allow trucks up to 80,000 pounds on Interstate Highways, up from 73,280 pounds, or lose federal highway funds.

Vehicle lengths were set at 48 feet for a single truck trailer or 28 feet for each semitrailer in a double combination. States could not regulate overall length or bar twin-trailer trucks. The limits applied to Interstate and qualified Primary routes.

● Directed the transportation secretary to report to Congress within one year on the potential benefits and costs to shippers, receivers, truck operators and the general public

State-by-State Highway Aid

Following are the amounts the states received in actual highway aid in fiscal year 1982, the amounts they will be eligible for in fiscal 1983 as a result of the increased taxes contained in new highway-gas tax legislation, and an estimate of fiscal 1984 aid (*in thousands of dollars*).

State	1982	1983	1984 (estimate)	State	1982	1983	1984 (estimate)
Alabama	$ 156,800	$ 217,298	$ 230,013	Nevada	$ 47,667	$ 66,089	$ 71,243
Alaska	107,639	141,043	150,741	New Hampshire	41,067	53,775	57,292
Arizona	105,466	145,082	161,796	New Jersey	180,107	267,003	287,668
Arkansas	75,770	113,009	123,540	New Mexico	63,489	91,022	100,295
California	671,676	907,299	1,009,593	New York	396,545	590,797	645,029
Colorado	118,393	164,909	204,417	North Carolina	148,492	249,304	278,699
Connecticut	137,053	185,382	256,408	North Dakota	53,070	73,439	78,927
Delaware	35,273	48,723	52,114	Ohio	214,526	411,881	459,483
Florida	312,060	405,032	451,607	Oklahoma	89,932	163,314	182,547
Georgia	251,562	329,630	351,745	Oregon	97,630	132,475	158,870
Hawaii	81,206	98,860	102,251	Pennsylvania	341,122	470,283	513,286
Idaho	55,300	72,038	77,165	Rhode Island	80,167	96,970	150,031
Illinois	256,532	389,834	488,444	South Carolina	106,693	141,564	152,374
Indiana	109,539	237,871	265,769	South Dakota	52,816	75,629	81,887
Iowa	94,734	142,687	209,552	Tennessee	141,186	213,273	268,026
Kansas	98,755	147,676	157,373	Texas	438,686	755,403	843,737
Kentucky	171,896	214,524	228,629	Utah	81,143	108,975	116,849
Louisiana	249,646	290,598	302,525	Vermont	41,518	52,118	55,667
Maine	43,213	57,958	61,614	Virginia	208,728	268,229	285,170
Maryland	268,817	335,146	363,617	Washington	221,215	280,354	294,140
Massachusetts	170,525	221,341	235,119	West Virginia	113,236	158,774	165,759
Michigan	188,959	339,330	378,377	Wisconsin	110,211	176,703	196,653
Minnesota	158,686	197,623	223,541	Wyoming	51,855	75,452	82,632
Mississippi	71,171	128,245	137,580	Dist. of Columbia	51,991	63,229	68,021
Missouri	131,699	236,947	255,716	Puerto Rico	29,479	42,782	47,176
Montana	66,738	99,948	109,084				
Nebraska	68,255	100,781	113,266	**TOTAL**	**$7,659,934**	**$11,047,607**	**$12,343,057**

Source: Federal Highway Administration

from a national intercity network for longer, combination trucks.

● Increased federal assistance by 5 percent for highway and bridge surfacing or restoration projects done with recycled materials. The federal share could be 80 to 85 percent of the cost, depending on the type of project.

● Provided, beginning in fiscal 1985, that a state require proof of payment of the federal truck highway use tax before registering the vehicle or face the loss of up to 25 percent of its federal highway funds.

● Directed the secretary to arrange for a study by the National Academy of Sciences of the effects of twin-trailer trucks on the Interstate Highway System.

● Allowed a state to defer payment of its share of projects funded by increased highway monies for fiscal 1983 and 1984. If it did not "repay" that share, then half of the balance would be deducted from its apportionment for 1985 and half for 1986.

● Clarified that Davis-Bacon Act requirements applied to major repair projects on federally aided highways, as well as to new construction. The Davis-Bacon Act required wages for federally funded projects be paid at the prevailing rates of the area.

● Required that each state's highway apportionment be equal to at least 85 percent of the highway taxes its motorists paid into the Highway Trust Fund. The 1-cent-per-gallon fuel tax revenue slated for mass transit would not be included. The bill authorized such sums as necessary out of the trust fund to provide the 85 percent floor.

● Authorized $50 million annually in fiscal 1983-1986 for demonstration railroad relocation projects.

● Authorized $100 million a year from the Highway Trust Fund for emergency highway projects.

● Authorized $3 million for the House Public Works Committee to contract for the preparation of a national public works inventory and assessment and a preliminary analysis of existing data.

● **Buy America.** Required that cement, steel and manufactured products used in federally funded highway and certain transit projects, such as rail tracks and bus garages, be American-made if they cost no more than 25 percent more than foreign products. The differential was set at 10 percent for mass transit buses and rail cars. The requirement could be waived if the transportation secretary determined that it was inconsistent with the public interest or that the product was not reasonably available.

● Authorized $1.6 billion in fiscal 1983 for bridge repairs and replacement, including an earlier authorization (PL 97-327); $1.65 billion, 1984; $1.75 billion, 1985; and $2.05 billion, 1986.

● Authorized $200 million annually for fiscal 1983-1986 to eliminate highway hazards.

● **NHTSA.** Authorized $100 million annually for fiscal 1985 and 1986 for National Highway Traffic Safety Administration (NHTSA) highway safety programs.

● Authorized $20 million out of the total NHTSA authorization annually for fiscal 1985 and 1986 for enforcing the national 55-miles-per-hour speed limit. The bill directed the transportation secretary to arrange with the National Academy of Sciences for a study on the benefits of the speed limit and whether state laws provided a substantial deterrent to violations of the limit.

● Set a ceiling of $100 million annually for fiscal 1985 and 1986 on Highway Trust Fund obligations for NHTSA highway safety programs and a limit of $10 million a year for 1985 and 1986 for Federal Highway Administration safety programs.

● Authorized $190 million annually for fiscal 1983-1986 for railroad-highway crossing projects.

● Encouraged each state to prohibit the sale of alcoholic beverages to people under 21 years of age.

Mass Transit

● Authorized a total of $4.098 billion in fiscal 1983 for mass transit; $4.471 billion, 1984; $4.54 billion, 1985; and $4.65 billion, 1986.

● Provided that of the total authorized for transit, $1.6 billion be for discretionary capital grants in fiscal 1983; $1.25 billion, 1984; $1.1 billion, 1985 and $1.1 billion, 1986. Those monies would be available for major capital projects, such as new bus facilities.

● Authorized $68 million for rural formula grants in fiscal 1983. The program would be folded into the urban formula block grant program in fiscal 1984.

● Authorized $365 million in fiscal 1983 for transit projects substituted for planned Interstate Highway segments; $380 million, 1984; $390 million, 1985; and $400 million, 1986.

● **Block Grants.** Created a block grant program for transit funds allocated by formula. The monies would be available on an annual grant basis for capital and operating expenses, rather than on a project-by-project basis.

Of the total, the bill authorized $779 million for block grants in fiscal 1983; $2.75 billion, 1984; $2.95 billion, 1985; and $3.05 billion, 1986. The existing formula program was authorized at $1.2 billion in fiscal 1983, and then folded into the block grant program.

● Restricted the use of block grant funds for mass transit operating expenses. Cities over one million population could use funds amounting to 80 percent of their 1982 operating subsidy level for transit operating costs. Cities from 200,000 to one million, could use up to 90 percent of the 1982 level; and cities under 200,000 could use up to 95 percent.

In fiscal 1983 and 1984, communities could use up to 100 percent of their 1982 operating subsidy level for operating costs, but they would lose some of their capital funds as a penalty.

● Apportioned most rail funds by a formula based 60 percent on miles of revenue-producing service and 40 percent on the total miles of routes.

Also an "incentive tier" was included, starting in fiscal

1984, to provide additional monies based on the number of miles of passenger service and the cost of moving passengers.

● Apportioned bus monies to cities over 200,000 by a formula based 50 percent on population and 50 percent on bus vehicle miles in service.

Also an "incentive tier" was included to provide additional monies based on passenger service and the cost of moving the passengers.

Bus funds would be apportioned to cities under 200,000 by formula based on population.

Taxes

● Increased the federal 4-cents-a-gallon fuel tax to 9-cents-a-gallon for gas, diesel fuel and motorboat fuel. The tax would be effective April 1, 1983, through Sept. 30, 1988.

● Exempted methanol and ethanol from the fuel tax if they were not producing petroleum or natural gas.

● Exempted gasohol, a mixture of alcohol and gasoline, from 5 cents a gallon of the tax.

● Exempted state and local governments; intercity, school and local buses; farm vehicles and off-highway business vehicles from the fuel tax.

● Continued the 4-cents-a-gallon tax exemption for taxicabs.

● Repealed taxes on lubricating oil, truck parts and tread rubber.

● Set a 12 percent tax on the retail sale price of trucks over 33,000 pounds and truck trailers over 26,000 pounds, effective April 1, 1983. The tax was 10 percent of manufacturer's sale price for trucks and trailers over 10,000 pounds.

● Set new graduated highway use taxes for trucks, generally effective July 1, 1984, through June 30, 1988. The maximum tax for 80,000-pound trucks was increased from $240 to $1,600, July 1, 1984; $1,700, July 1, 1986; $1,800, July 1, 1987; and $1,900, July 1, 1988.

● Set new graduated taxes for tires over 40 pounds, exempting most passenger car tires. The bill charged 15 cents for each pound between 40 and 70; 30 cents for each pound between 70 and 90; 50 cents for each pound over 90. The tax would be effective Jan. 1, 1984. The tax had been 9.75 cents per pound for all tires.

● Codified the Highway Trust Fund as part of the Internal Revenue Code.

● Extended the authority for the Highway Trust Fund through Sept. 30, 1988.

● Increased the cap from $20 million to $45 million on motorboat fuel tax revenues transferred annually from the Highway Trust Fund to the National Recreational Boating Safety and Facilities Improvement Fund. The boating fund's balance could not exceed $45 million. The boating fund monies were intended for state boating safety programs and boating facilities.

● Provided that if unfunded authorizations exceeded two years of Highway Trust Fund receipts, state apportionments would be reduced proportionately.

● Created an account in the trust fund for monies from 1 cent of the fuel tax hike for transit capital projects.

Miscellaneous

● Authorized $10 million in fiscal 1984 for state development of programs to enforce federal commercial vehicle safety regulations; $20 million, 1985; $30 million, 1986; $40 million, 1987; and $50 million, 1988.

The federal share for the costs of such programs was set at 80 percent.

Infrastructure Repairs: Trillion-Dollar Job

The crumbling infrastructure — the foundation of roads, bridges, transit and other facilities upon which the nation depended to deliver essential services — took the congressional spotlight immediately after the November elections.

Some members of Congress had toiled unsuccessfully for months to move legislation to create jobs and increase transportation and public works funding. But the high unemployment rate, along with the Democratic election victories in the House and the near wins in the Senate, pushed jobs and the problems of structural decay further up on the congressional agenda.

Members returning for the lame-duck session focused on programs that would create public works jobs repairing deteriorating waterlines, sewage treatment plants, public buildings and transportation facilities to help some of the 12 million unemployed Americans. A number of efforts were made to attach public-works programs to various bills. *(Story, p. 317)*

The legislation (HR 6211 — PL 97-424) that was passed involved a substantial portion of the infrastructure: highways and mass transit. The bill authorized $71 billion to finish the Interstate Highway System and for road, bridge and mass transit improvements. The measure raised an additional $5.5 billion a year to help pay for the programs by increasing the gas tax a nickel a gallon, to a total of 9 cents.

Trillion-Dollar Job

Estimates of the costs of making all needed repairs to public facilities ranged from several hundred billion dollars to $3 trillion.

Despite the costs, administration officials and members of Congress agreed a start should be made.

Ray A. Barnhart, administrator of the Federal Highway Administration (FHWA), said of the highway network:

"It constitutes a large part of living costs. If we have poor highways, those costs will increase. Ninety percent of everything we eat, wear or use travels by the highways."

The types of "infrastructure" needs were varied. Transportation Secretary Drew Lewis, the Associated General Contractors of America and others cited examples such as these:

● One out of five bridges in the nation needed immediate major repairs. The life of a bridge was about 50 years, and 40 percent already were more than 40 years old.

● More than 4,000 miles, or 10 percent, of the Interstate Highway System needed replacement or major repairs. More than 26,000 miles would require major repairs through 1995.

● If highway conditions continued to decline at their current rate, the average motorist's costs could increase by up to 25 percent in 1995 because of the wear and tear on automobiles and increased gasoline use.

● Twenty percent of all subway cars were more than 25 years old, while the design life generally was about 20 years. Sixty-seven percent of all track needed upgrading.

● Capital needs for transit replacement and repairs would total $50 billion over the next 10 years.

● A study for the House Wednesday Group made up of Republican members said more than one-half of the nation's communities had wastewater treatment systems at full capacity and could not support further economic development.

Maintenance Deferred

Federal officials and others blamed age and deferred maintenance for the deterioration of the roads, bridges and other facilities.

For example, Interstate Highways built when the program began in the late 1950s and many bridges built earlier had outlived their design. Also, unanticipated increases in traffic added to wear and tear. Some bridges were structurally sound but could not sustain modern traffic loads, requiring big trucks to detour.

The economic straits of all levels of government confronted with competing needs had led to the postponing of much of the necessary maintenance. A 1982 Urban Institute study noted that the most distressed older cities had the slowest growing tax bases and were under financial pressure to defer capital spending on their facilities.

Developing cities faced problems that were more associated with their growth. Their roads and water systems were not built to sustain the growth they had experienced, and they were under pressure to emphasize new construction rather than maintenance.

High Costs

An official of the Office of Management and Budget (OMB) said the OMB did not have an overall estimate of total needs. But various groups provided figures involving some segments of the nation's infrastructure.

A 1981 report by the Transportation Department and FHWA said from $275 billion to $363 billion in federal and state funds was needed to maintain federally aided roads in their 1978 condition. Transportation officials said $60 billion was needed to rebuild and repair bridges on and off federally aided systems.

A 1980 survey by the Environmental Protection Agency said the states needed $119.9 billion through the year 2000 to upgrade and repair sewage treatment plants, interceptor sewers and other lines. Of that total, $91.2 billion was for backlog projects.

Pat Choate, who prepared the House Wednesday Group's May 18 report, estimated total needs at $2.5 trillion to $3 trillion just to maintain existing levels of service. He said national public works investments shrank from 3.6 percent of gross national product in 1965 to less than 1.7 percent in 1980.

All levels of government spent about $80 billion in 1980 on public works, he said, with the federal government spending 10 percent of the funds directly and providing 40 percent to state and local governments.

The contractors group, representing an industry in which unemployment exceeded 20 percent, said $909.9 billion was required for established infrastructure improvements, not including the needs of private health facilities, police stations, firehouses, libraries and prisons.

● Protected trucking employees from dismissal or discipline for filing a complaint regarding the violation of a commercial motor vehicle safety rule.

● **Unemployment Benefits.** Provided up to six weeks of extra unemployment benefits to thousands of workers for whom regular and extended payments had run out. *(Story, p. 43)*

● **Conventions.** Allowed certain tax deductions for business conventions held on U.S. cruise ships, as long as they stopped at U.S. ports or those of U.S. possessions. The deduction was limited to $2,000 for most individuals and $1,000 for a married individual filing a separate return. *(Story, p. 51)*

● **Utility Companies.** Forgave three California utility companies of over $2 billion in tax liability, which they were required to pass on to consumers. *(Story, p. 52)*

● **Ocean Dumping.** Imposed a two-year ban on ocean dumping of low-level radioactive wastes. The only exception allowed was for research-related dumping under certain conditions. *(Story, p. 459)*

● **Airport Funds.** Appropriated $475 million over fiscal 1983-1985 from the Airport and Airway Trust Fund balance, above earlier authorized funds, for airport development projects.

● Appropriated $401 million over fiscal 1983-1985 from the Reforestation Trust Fund, the boating trust fund and the Saltonstall-Kennedy Fund. The funds would be used for forest redevelopment, state boating safety programs and boating facilities, and fisheries development.

Background

Key members of Congress increasingly had become concerned about completing the Interstate System while faced with escalating costs and the need to maintain what roads were in place. The 42,500 mile system, begun in 1956, was 96 percent complete.

Although the Interstate Highway construction authorizations were established for the decade, most of the other highway and mass transit authorizations were due to expire Sept. 30.

The gasoline and other highway taxes making up the Highway Trust Fund that financed highway constructions and repair programs also needed to be extended beyond Sept. 30, 1984.

In May, congressional committees reported legislation (HR 6211, S 2574, S 2606) authorizing funds for highways and transit. But the lack of support from the president for increasing the gas tax, divisions among members over structuring a new mass transit program, jurisdictional disputes and the press of other business prevented floor action on major legislation during the regular session.

House Public Works Committee Chairman James J. Howard, D-N.J., one of the key promoters of the highway bill (HR 6211), said Congress would not pass a gas tax increase without Reagan's endorsement.

Transportation Secretary Lewis had argued all year for a highway tax hike plan that would raise $5.5 billion a year, the equivalent of a 5-cent-a-gallon increase in the gas levy.

Appealing to the president's policy of requiring beneficiaries of a service to pay for that service, Lewis described the taxes as "user fees" because they went into the Highway Trust Fund that financed highway programs. *(User fees, 1981 Almanac, p. 580)*

Lewis' original plan called for a 4-cents-a-gallon hike in the fuel tax to raise $4.4 billion, with the rest of the

revenue coming from increases in other highway levies, such as the truckers' highway use tax.

But Reagan May 18 shelved the Lewis proposal. The president said he would consider it again during deliberations on the fiscal 1984 budget.

Supporters of the legislation were disheartened when Reagan Sept. 28 responded to a reporter's question about a gas tax increase by saying, "Unless there's a palace coup and I'm overtaken or overthrown, no, I don't see the necessity for that."

Lame-Duck Session

But after the elections and faced with the prospect of a lame-duck session, interest in the highway and mass transit legislation was renewed. Key backers promoted HR 6211 as a "jobs bill."

Lewis pushed again for the gas tax increase, and although Reagan reviewed the plan Nov. 10 with Lewis and other Cabinet officials, he made no decision.

House Speaker Thomas P. O'Neill Jr., D-Mass., and Senate Majority Leader Howard H. Baker Jr., R-Tenn., announced Nov. 22 that they would work together in the lame-duck session for enactment of gas tax legislation to help counter unemployment.

Reagan jumped on the bandwagon Nov. 23, endorsing a gas tax increase bill as a vitally needed effort to repair the transportation infrastructure.

"There's no question but obviously there will be some employment with it, but it is not a jobs bill as such. It is a necessity. It's a problem that we have to meet, and we'd be doing this if there were no recession at all," Reagan said.

In fact, Martin S. Feldstein, chairman of the president's Council of Economic Advisers, warned that a gas tax hike "may actually increase unemployment during the first year or two," because motorists would have less money to spend on consumer goods.

The administration's tax plan called for the entire $5.5 billion to come from a hike in the gas and diesel fuel tax, although there would be changes in other highway taxes. The plan also funneled 1 cent per gallon of the tax to mass transit for capital projects, providing an estimated $1.1 billion a year.

Reagan said the tax plan did not conflict with his Sept. 28 statement that he did not see the necessity for the increase. He said he meant he would not support a gas tax hike to provide general revenues.

The administration bill presented to the lame-duck Congress (S 3044) proposed authorizing about $100 billion over six years to complete the Interstate System, repair highways and bridges, shore up mass transit systems and related projects. Of that total, almost $20 billion would go to transit.

House Committee Action

HR 6211 originally was reported (H Rept 97-555) May 17 by the House Public Works Committee. The bill would have authorized more than $70 billion over four years for highways and mass transit, and created a transit block grant program.

The bill, however, was contingent on increases in the gas tax and other highway levies. After Reagan decided to shelve the tax proposal, the panel Aug. 10 slashed its ambitious bill to a one-year $16.7 billion measure.

The new version, for example, cut Interstate Highway construction to $3.525 billion in fiscal 1984, down from the

original bill's level of $4 billion.

Despite the cuts and bipartisan backing for the legislation, administration officials still had serious concerns about the funding level for highways and continuing mass transit operating subsidies.

The new version of the bill would have established a ceiling of $8.8 billion on obligations from the Highway Trust Fund for road construction and related programs in fiscal 1983, a reduction from the original proposal of $12.2 billion. But the administration had asked for a limit of $7.7 billion.

Also the bill continued operating subsidies for mass transit systems. Reagan wanted to cut the subsidies to $640 million in fiscal 1983 and eliminate them after fiscal 1984. He contended that they were not a suitable use of federal funds and they encouraged operating inefficiencies.

Transit operators and cities, however, argued that they needed federal aid to keep buses and subways running, especially at a time when financially strapped cities and states were being asked to take over the costs of other federal programs. *(Story, p. 536)*

Turf Fight

A jurisdictional dispute between the House Public Works and Ways and Means Committees prevented the scaled-down version of HR 6211 from being taken up by the House before the authorizations expired Sept. 30 and the Congress recessed for the November elections.

The Public Works panel had jurisdiction over highways, and the Ways and Means Committee had jurisdiction over the Highway Trust Fund and the highway taxes that fed it.

Howard contended that a highway tax bill (HR 7092 — H Rept 97-838) reported Sept. 17 by Ways and Means, and designed to be added as a title to HR 6211, would have given Ways and Means authority over highway construction and maintenance programs. The bill would have extended the Highway Trust Fund and the existing highway taxes.

"He's trying to take my jurisdiction," Howard said, referring to Ways and Means Committee Chairman Dan Rostenkowski, D-Ill.

Rostenkowski denied that was his intent. He said the bill was necessary to allow his committee to fulfill its responsibility to ensure the solvency of the trust fund. He said his panel needed to "review" overall highway authorizations to be sure the trust fund taxes were sufficient to finance them.

The two chairmen could not reach a compromise, and the Rules Committee would not report a rule to provide for House consideration of HR 6211.

Substitute Bill Passed

With the Sept. 30 deadline to reauthorize the highway programs past, the Senate Oct. 1 took up S 2574 (S Rept 97-421), reported May 26 by the Environment and Public Works Committee. Committee Chairman Robert T. Stafford, R-Vt., offered an amendment, which was adopted, cutting the bill from a four-year authorization to a one-year, $8.6 billion authorization.

Before passage of the bill, Mark Andrews, R-N.D., offered an amendment that would have required states by Oct. 1, 1983, to allow 102-inch wide trucks on federal highways, up from the present 96 inches. But a substitute sponsored by Thomas F. Eagleton, D-Mo., and Harrison "Jack" Schmitt, R-N.M., to give states the discretion to

permit the wider trucks, passed by a vote of 47-45. The bill was then passed by voice vote. *(Vote 380 p. 64-S)*

On the same day, Howard sought unanimous consent to bring a new bill to the House floor, bypassing committee. The bill (HR 3197) would have authorized $8.87 billion for highways for fiscal 1983 and extended the trust fund and highway taxes for a year, until Oct. 1, 1985. The extension was required by law (PL 84-627) to provide enough revenue to cover existing highway obligations and those proposed by Howard's new bill. *(1965 Almanac p. 398)*

Rostenkowski objected because the bill did not include the Ways and Means Committee provisions and blocked consideration of the measure.

Howard then offered an amendment to substitute for S 2574, which Rostenkowski did not try to block. The substitute, accepted by voice vote, authorized about $5 billion for Interstate construction and other highway programs. The funds would carry states for three to six months, supporters said.

The authorizations were low enough to stay within anticipated trust fund revenues and avoid triggering the need to extend the trust fund and taxes, thereby skirting the jurisdictional dispute.

The Senate accepted the change, also on Oct. 1, clearing the measure (PL 97-327) for the president.

As cleared by Congress, S 2574:

● Authorized $3.225 billion in fiscal 1984 for Interstate construction, down from the existing authorization of $3.625 billion for fiscal 1984.

● Directed the transportation secretary to apportion the 1984 Interstate funds to the states.

● Provided that other highway authorizations be reduced according to a formula based on the length of time covered by a resolution (H J Res 599 — PL 97-276) that provided temporary funding for government operations, or a reduction of less than one-fourth. *(Story, p. 225)*

● Authorized the following amounts, to be reduced by the formula: $1.5 billion for Primary Highways; $400 million, rural road; $800 million, urban roads; $900 million, bridge repairs and replacement; $200 million for elimination of highway hazards; and $190 million for rail-highway crossings.

House Floor Action

House Public Works members drafted a substitute for HR 6211 when they returned from the elections recess Nov. 29. The substitute authorized about $71 billion over four years for highway and transit and created a public transportation block grant program, similar to the original bill.

The Ways and Means Committee Dec. 3 approved gas and truck tax changes that would be offered as a tax title to HR 6211 on the floor.

The gas tax would be increased to 9 cents a gallon from April 1, 1983, through Sept. 30, 1988. Trucks over 80,000 pounds would pay $2,000, up from $240, beginning Jan. 1, 1984. The tax on trucks under 33,000 pounds would be repealed. Also in the package was a provision to funnel 1 cent per gallon of the fuel tax to mass transit projects.

The House began consideration of the bill Dec. 6 and finally passed it by a vote of 262-143 in the early hours of Dec. 7. As amended, the bill authorized $71.3 billion over four years. *(Vote 396, p. 118-H)*

Although the final vote was overwhelming, supporters originally feared for its passage when the House by a narrow 197-194 vote adopted the rule (H Res 620) Dec. 6

providing for floor consideration of the measure. *(Vote 389, p. 116-H)*

Also, Howard and Secretary Lewis were worried that they might lose votes because of ill feelings from a series of angry debates on Davis-Bacon Act wage requirements and other issues.

It was not until the 236-169 vote at 12:30 a.m., Dec. 7, to accept the Ways and Means Committee highway tax package that supporters breathed easier. *(Vote 395, p. 118-H)*

Fight Over the Rule

The rule allowed amendments to the highway and transit portions of the bill but not to the Ways and Means tax title.

Members opposing the fuel or truck taxes fought the rule. "Now is not the time to impose unreasonable financial burdens on the trucking community," Arlan Stangeland, R-Minn., said.

Richard L. Ottinger, D-N.Y., and Henry S. Reuss, D-Wis., chairman of the Joint Economic Committee, urged replacing the gas tax hike with a cap on the third year of the income tax cut. They said the cap would raise $7 billion in revenues that could be used for highway and transit programs.

But the bill's supporters argued that significant changes in the taxes would jeopardize passage.

Major Amendments

The House by voice votes adopted two amendments designed to head off opposition from states concerned about losing funds. The amendments were offered by Public Works Committee Chairman Howard.

One required that each state receive at least 85 cents in highway apportionments for each $1 that its motorists paid into the Highway Trust Fund.

The second allowed states to defer their matching share of road projects funded by the revenues from the gas tax increase in fiscal 1983. The states would have to repay the money or have their future aid cut.

Other major amendments considered by the House included:

● **Davis-Bacon Act Requirements.** Three votes were taken on proposals to waive or weaken Davis-Bacon Act prevailing wage requirements.

Sponsors said the requirements resulted in inflated wages. Without Davis-Bacon, up to 30,000 more jobs could be created by the bill, Charles W. Stenholm, D-Texas, argued.

Existing law applied the requirements to "initial construction." Administration officials said that the law applied to new construction or reconstruction. But they contended that it did not apply to other major repair projects.

Howard argued that Davis-Bacon had always applied to all major highway repairs. The bill struck the word "initial" to ensure that traditional practice be continued, he said.

Stenholm's amendment to waive Davis-Bacon wage requirements for all road projects funded by Highway Trust Fund monies was rejected 174-223. *(Vote 391, p. 116-H)*

The second amendment, by Buddy Roemer, D-La., to restore the word "initial," was rejected 191-194. The third, by Robert S. Walker, R-Pa., barring Davis-Bacon from "limiting legitimate job opportunities" was rejected 149-217. *(Vote 392, p. 116-H; Vote 394, p. 118-H)*

● **Buy America.** An amendment expanding "Buy America" requirements was adopted by a division vote of 54-46.

The proposal, by Douglas Applegate, D-Ohio, required that all cement, steel and manufactured products bought with U.S. highway and transit funds be U.S.-made unless they were not reasonably available. Buses and rail car parts could be 50 percent foreign-made, but the vehicles must be assembled in the United States.

"Buy America" law required that U.S. products be bought for federally funded transit and highway projects if they cost no more than 10 percent more than foreign products, and the law could be waived for public interest reasons. Administration officials said the amendment was too protectionist, and planned to seek changes in the Senate.

Applegate said a stronger law was needed because of high unemployment and inequities in trade laws.

● **Highway Beautification.** An amendment by E. Clay Shaw Jr., R-Fla., to delete language eliminating federal compensation for billboard owners whose signs were taken down by states was rejected by voice vote.

The bill would continue state responsibility for controlling outdoor advertising. A state could lose up to 10 percent of its highway funds if the secretary determined that its program to control billboards was inadequate.

Howard said that although the current law (PL 89-285) required a 75 percent federal share of compensation costs, Congress had not provided enough monies to fund the program properly. At the current pace of federal funding, it would take 1,600 years and an estimated $1 billion to remove the remaining illegal billboards, he said. At least, he said, the bill would continue billboard control standards.

The provision later was dropped in conference.

● **High Cost Projects.** An amendment by Ted Weiss, D-N.Y., to delete provisions directing the secretary to give top priority for $300 million in Interstate Highway discretionary funds to completing high-cost Interstate segments was rejected 21-329. *(Vote 393, p. 118-H)*

Weiss and environmental groups said high-cost projects were not necessarily worthy ones and the bill encouraged adding frills to projects. Supporters of the bill said it would prevent projects from becoming even more costly because of delays.

House Provisions

As passed by the House, HR 6211:

● Authorized $4 billion for Interstate Highway construction annually for fiscal 1984-1990.

● Provided that no state would lose funds as a result of the legislation.

● Set a general ceiling on obligations from the Highway Trust Fund of $12.2 billion for fiscal 1983; $12.7 billion, 1984; $13.5 billion, 1985; and $14.4 billion, 1986.

● Authorized the following amounts; the 1983 figures included funds previously authorized by PL 97-327.

Primary Roads. $2 billion in fiscal 1983; $2.1 billion, 1984; $2.2 billion, 1985; and $2.5 billion, 1986.

Rural Roads. $600 million annually in fiscal 1983-1986.

Urban Highways. $800 million annually in fiscal 1983-1986.

● Authorized $2.1 billion in fiscal 1984 for the "4-R" program; $2.4 billion, 1985; $2.8 billion, 1986; and $3.1 billion, 1987.

● Authorized out of the Highway Trust Fund $275 million in fiscal 1983 for highway projects substituted for planned Interstate Highway segments and $775 million annually for 1984-86.

● Changed the formula for apportioning funds for Primary Highways to one based on urban and rural population. The existing formula included factors based on population, land area and miles of Primary routes. The change would shift funds from sparsely populated but large states, to more urbanized states.

● Changed the formula for 4-R Interstate funds to one based on vehicle miles traveled on Interstate highways, and gasoline and diesel fuel usage. The existing formula was based on traffic and lane miles. The new formula was designed to take into better account truck wear on highways.

● Authorized $300 million in fiscal 1983 specifically for Interstate discretionary funds to be used for special high-cost Interstate segments.

● Eliminated the requirement that the federal government pay 75 percent of the cost of compensating a billboard owner for taking down a highway billboard as required by law. States would have to pay the entire compensation, rather than 25 percent share under existing law.

Also, states would be required to control the erection, maintenance and, in certain circumstances, removal of outdoor advertising signs along highways. If the secretary determined that a state did not properly control outdoor advertising, the state could lose up to 10 percent of its federal highway funds.

● Allowed bigger trucks on the highways. The new standards required states to allow trucks weighing up to 80,000 pounds on all Interstate Highways.

Vehicle length limitations were set at 48 feet for a single truck trailer or 28 feet for each trailer in a double combination. The length limitations did not include the truck tractor, and states could not regulate the overall length. No state could bar twin-trailer trucks.

States would have to allow 102-inch-wide trucks, up from the current limit of 96 inches.

● Provided that a state must require proof of payment of the federal heavy-truck tax from a truck operator before registering the truck. Failure to comply could result in the loss of federal highway funds. The provision would be effective Jan. 1, 1985.

● Clarified that the Davis-Bacon Act wage requirements applied to major repairs of federally aided highways, as well as to new construction.

● Allowed a state to defer payment of its share of projects funded by the tax hike for fiscal 1983 until 1984. If it did not pay that share, 50 percent of the balance would be deducted from its federal highway funds for 1985 and 50 percent for 1986.

● Provided that every state's federal highway apportionment was equal to at least 85 percent of the tax revenue its highway users paid into the Highway Trust Fund. The 1-cent-per-gallon fuel tax revenue for mass transit would not be included in this provision. The bill also authorized $420 million in fiscal 1983 and such sums as may be necessary for 1984-1986 to provide the 85 percent floor.

Safety

● Authorized $1.5 billion in fiscal 1983 for bridge repairs and replacement; $1.6 billion, 1984; $1.7 billion, 1985; and $2.1 billion, 1986.

● Authorized $200 million annually for fiscal 1983-1986 for projects eliminating highway hazards.

● Authorized $100 million annually for fiscal 1985-86 for National Highway Traffic Safety Administration (NHTSA) highway safety programs.

Of the funds authorized, $20 million for each of fiscal 1985 and 1986 would be obligated for enforcing the 55 miles-per-hour speed limit. Also, the bill provided that the transportation secretary not approve highway projects for any state whose laws did not constitute a substantial deterrent to violations of the speed limit.

● Set a ceiling of $100 million a year for fiscal 1983-1986 for obligations for NHTSA highway safety programs, and a ceiling of $10 million a year for 1983-86 for Federal Highway Administration highway safety programs.

Mass Transit

● Authorized a total of $3.8 billion in fiscal 1983 for mass transit; $4 billion, 1984; $4.2 billion, 1985; and $4.5 billion, 1986.

● Provided that of the total authorized for transit, $928 million was for discretionary capital grants in fiscal 1983; $978 million, 1984; $1 billion, 1985 and $1.1 billion, 1986.

● Authorized $82 million for non-urban formula grants in fiscal 1983; $86 million, 1984; $91 million, 1985; and $96 million, 1986.

● Created a block grant program for transit funds allocated by formula on an annual grant basis.

Of the total authorized for transit, $2.7 billion was authorized for block grants in fiscal 1983; $2.8 billion, 1984; $3 billion, 1985; and $3.2 billion, 1986.

Most bus funds would be apportioned by a formula based 50 percent on population factors and 50 percent on revenue-generating bus service. Most rail funds would be apportioned by a formula based 70 percent on miles of revenue-producing service and 30 percent on the total miles of routes.

Cities under 200,000 population would receive funds apportioned on population factors, based on the latest federal census.

● Allowed block grant funds to be used for either capital or operating expenses, under certain conditions. Funds could be used up to the fiscal 1982 level for transit operating subsidies.

Other provisions were included to encourage communities to use block grant funds otherwise available for operating subsidies to pay for capital costs and maintenance projects.

● Required that all cement, steel and manufactured products used in federally funded highway and transit projects be American-made, unless not reasonably available. Buses and rail cars could be 50 percent foreign-made but must be assembled in the United States.

Taxes

● Increased the federal 4-cents-a-gallon fuel tax to 9 cents a gallon for gasoline, diesel fuel, special motor fuels and motorboat fuel. The tax would be in effect from April 1, 1983, until Oct. 1, 1988.

● Exempted methanol or ethanol fuels not made from petroleum from the entire fuel tax.

●Exempted gasohol from the first 4-cents-a-gallon charge, but not from the new 5-cents portion.

● Exempted state and local government vehicles; intercity, school and local buses; farm vehicles and non-highway business uses from the fuel tax.

● Continued the 4-cents-a-gallon tax exemption for taxi-cabs.

● Repealed taxes on lubricating oil, truck parts and accessories.

● Set a 12 percent tax on the retail sale price of trucks over 33,000 pounds and truck trailers over 26,000 pounds, effective April 1, 1983, until Oct. 1, 1988.

● Established new graduated highway use taxes for heavy trucks, effective Jan. 1, 1984, until Oct. 1, 1988. The $3-per-1,000-pounds annual tax for trucks more than 26,000 pounds was repealed.

The levy for trucks 80,000 pounds and more was set at a flat $2,000 fee.

● Charged 25 cents per pound for tires over 100 pounds. The existing tax was 9.75 cents per pound for all tires.

● Charged 25 cents per pound for tread rubber for tires over 100 pounds, a change from the current tax of 5 cents a pound for all tires.

● Extended the authority for the Highway Trust Fund through Sept. 30, 1988, and codified the fund as part of the Internal Revenue Code.

● Provided that if unfunded authorizations exceeded two years of trust fund receipts, state apportionments would be reduced proportionally.

● Increased the $20 million cap to $45 million on transfers of motorboat fuel tax revenues from the Highway Trust Fund to the National Recreational Boating Safety and Facilities Improvement Fund.

The boating fund monies were intended for state boating safety programs and boating facilities.

● Established a mass transit account within the Highway Trust Fund for revenues received from 1-cent-per-gallon of the fuel tax after March 31, 1983.

The funds would be available only for capital programs, including new transit rail systems.

Senate Committee Action

The major highway measure S 2574 (S Rept 97-421) on the Senate side was reported May 26 by the Environment and Public Works Committee. The bill would have authorized more than $38 billion through fiscal 1986 for highways. That was the measure that eventually was cleared by Congress before the elections recess as a $5 billion one-year authorization.

The Senate Banking Committee had approved a stop-gap mass transit bill (S 2606) May 28 (no written report) that would have authorized a total of $3.1 billion in fiscal 1983, without major changes in the program. Members of the committee were sharply divided over a new structure for the program and did not reach a compromise until the lame-duck session.

The chief stumbling blocks were the level of transit operating subsidies and the formula for allocating rail funds. The committee GOP leadership wanted deep cuts in operating subsidies, opposed by Republican and Democratic senators representing cities dependent on mass transit. Senators from rail cities disagreed on how much the formula for allocating rail funds should account for service and track miles.

When the senators returned for the lame-duck session, the committees and key senators developed new legislation. The Environment and Public Works Committee Dec. 9 reported a new highway bill (S 3043 — S Rept 97-676), which authorized $70.4 billion over 5 years for highway programs.

The Finance Committee Dec. 9 approved its own tax package and substituted it for all of the House language in HR 6211. The panel's version of HR 6211 included a 9-cent-a-gallon gas tax through fiscal 1989. The highway use taxes on trucks would be phased in over three years, beginning Jan. 1, 1984, and the maximum tax on 80,000-pound trucks would be $1,600.

Richard G. Lugar, R-Ind., and Alfonse D'Amato, R-N.Y., developed a compromise mass transit bill (S 3072), which authorized $12.3 billion over three years and created a block grant program. Transit operating subsidies would be continued, although with cuts of up to 20 percent, except under special circumstances. Lugar was chairman of the Banking panel's Housing and Urban Affairs Subcommittee, which had jurisdiction over transit, and D'Amato was a subcommittee member. The bill was discharged from committee Dec. 3.

The Commerce Committee Dec. 6 approved a highway safety title to the administration bill (S 3044), similar to a bill (S 1402) the panel reported in 1981 and to a bill (S 1390) passed by the Senate in 1980. The title set federal standards for truck length and width, gave the transportation secretary broader authority to issue safety rules for commercial motor vehicles, established a grant program to help states enforce motor carrier safety regulations and protected employees who reported safety violations. *(1981 Almanac p. 582; 1980 Almanac p. 260)*

The length standards included 48 feet for a semi-trailer unit, or 28 feet for semi-trailers operating in a double combination. States must allow trucks meeting these standards on Interstate Highways or other qualified highways. No state could bar the operation of a twin-trailer truck. Also, the title barred states from prohibiting 102-inch wide trucks on Interstates or other qualified roads.

In addition, the Commerce panel's proposal authorized an additional $475 million over three years for airport development projects.

Senate Floor Action

The Senate leadership plan was to call up the Finance Committee's version of HR 6211 as the main bill and then to incorporate all of the committees' measures into an amendment as a substitute, to be offered by Baker.

But when the Senate took up the bill Dec. 10, action was immediately stalled by a filibuster by Gordon J. Humphrey, R-N.H., Don Nickles, R-Okla., and Helms. They objected to a Baker motion to proceed to consider the bill. Their filibuster efforts were joined later by East.

That filibuster was broken Dec. 13 when the Senate invoked cloture to cut off debate on the motion. The vote was 75-13, 15 more than the 60 votes required by Senate rules. *(Vote 397, p. 68-S)*

The Senate then took up the Baker substitute. Opponents were ready to filibuster again and in fact, did resort to some delaying tactics. But action also was slowed by numerous amendments to the substitute, including some proposed by Republican and Democratic supporters of the bill.

Although cloture motions were filed on both the substitute and the bill, Baker did not seek a quick vote on them because cloture would rule out some prospective amendments.

Once cloture was invoked on a measure, debate was limited to no more than 100 hours, and no new amendments could be offered except by unanimous consent. Non-

germane amendments and dilatory motions were barred.

The Senate accepted a number of unrelated tax amendments, including one that allowed deductions for business conventions held on cruise ships.

Jobless Benefits

A GOP attempt to table, or kill, an amendment by Carl Levin, D-Mich., to extend umemployment benefits an extra two to five weeks eventually led to the defeat of the cloture motions to limit debate on the legislation.

The Levin plan had been part of a Democratic job-creation package, and the Democrats wanted a vote on it. The leadership tried to table it and lost 47-50, with some Republican desertions. *(Vote 411, p. 70-S)*

Some Republicans thought they could avoid a vote on the Levin amendment by invoking cloture. However, Democratic supporters of the Levin amendment voted against cloture, thereby denying the leadership the required 60 votes. Cloture failed 48-50 on the substitute and 5-93 on the original bill. *(Votes 412, 413, p. 70-S)*

Finance Committee Chairman Robert Dole, R-Kan., and Levin then reached a compromise to extend benefits up to six weeks but at a lower cost. Dole said the compromise, targeted at the states hardest hit by unemployment, would cost $530 million rather than the $900 million price tag of Levin's original amendment. The compromise was adopted 93-4. *(Vote 416, p. 70-S)*

Trucks

Another major amendment adopted by the Senate Dec. 16 reduced the substitute's tax on heavy trucks. The amendment, offered by Rudy Boschwitz, R-Minn., was approved 96-1. *(Vote 417, p. 71-S)*

The amendment provided that the maximum tax on trucks 80,000 pounds or more would be $1,200 — down from the Finance Committee's proposal of $1,600.

In earlier action the Senate tabled, 48-37, an amendment by David Pryor, D-Ark., that would have eliminated the increases in heavy-truck taxes as well the truck size provisions. *(Vote 410, p. 70-S)*

Democratic Jobs Plan

In a 44-53 party-line vote, the Senate Dec. 14 rejected the Democrats' fiscal 1983 , $5.3 billion job-creation/supplemental jobless benefit amendment. *(Vote 402, p. 68-S)*

The amendment — the Senate Democrats' alternative jobs creation plan — would have eliminated the 5-cents-a-gallon increase in fuel taxes and financed the highway repair program by trimming the scheduled July 1983 tax cut for upper-income taxpayers.

The proposal would have raised $24.9 billion over three years and cost $18.9 billion.

As offered on the floor, the amendment would not have changed the highway, bridge and mass transit repairs portion of the bill. The core of the Democrats' proposal was a $2 billion "light" public works program funding small-scale projects such as bridge-painting and public housing repair.

Minority Leader Robert C. Byrd, D-W.Va., said the amendment would provide a total of 411,000 jobs. The Democrats pounded away at the high unemployment under the Reagan administration.

"The fact is that since Ronald Reagan got his job, four million Americans have lost theirs," Edward M. Kennedy, D-Mass., said.

Natural Gas Amendment

The Senate defeated an amendment, proposed by Nancy Landon Kassebaum, R-Kan., aimed at limiting increases in natural gas heating bills.

The amendment would have allowed the Federal Energy Regulatory Commission (FERC) to annul or modify "take-or-pay" provisions in contracts requiring a pipeline company to pay for natural gas it had contracted for whether it took that gas or not. The amendment also would have frozen wellhead prices at the Oct. 1 level until Jan. 1, 1985.

The take-or-pay contracts resulted in companies buying more expensive gas than necessary, Kassebaum said. Natural gas producers demanded the contracts during the mid-1970s, when supplies were short, and the pipelines agreed to them for fear of being caught short, she said. Although there was a surplus of supplies, companies were unable to take advantage of cheaper gas.

Opposing the amendment, J. Bennett Johnston, D-La., a member of the Energy and Natural Resources Committee, said the situation was too complicated to be dealt with in such a short time.

By a 56-38 vote, the Senate tabled the first portion of the amendment, dealing with take-or-pay contracts. It tabled the second portion, dealing with the price freeze, 62-33. *(Votes 405, 406, p. 69-S)*

Subsequently, the Senate adopted a resolution (S Res 515) directing the FERC to consider ways to correct the contract problems. The resolution, proposed by Energy Committee Chairman James A. McClure, R-Idaho, was adopted 90-3. *(Vote 407, p. 69-S)*

The measure also said that pipeline companies and producers should enter into negotiations to eliminate the contract problems, and that available federal aid should be provided to low-income natural gas consumers.

Delays

After the vote on unemployment benefits, the Democrats were willing to vote on passage. However, the earlier rejections of cloture left the leadership vulnerable to a filibuster by Helms and his allies.

In an effort to pressure the opponents into allowing a vote on the bill, Baker held up action on a continuing resolution (H J Res 631) needed to prevent the shutdown of federal offices at midnight Dec. 17. *(Story, p. 238)*

But at 10 p.m. Dec. 16, it was the GOP leaders who felt the pressure of the Dec. 17 deadline. Still faced with a deadlock, Baker asked the Senate to temporarily lay aside the highway bill and take up the funding resolution.

The Democrats had agreed to drop all of their remaining amendments and vote on the bill if the Republicans would do the same. But after two GOP caucuses, Baker said, the Republicans could not reach an agreement to vote on the bill.

Before laying aside the bill, Baker telephoned Reagan. He said the president was "pretty angry" about the situation.

Continued Fight

Sen. East took on the battle against the highway bill Dec. 18 in an unusual Saturday session. He argued that while the bill might create new jobs in the construction industry, the tax increases would cost jobs in other fields. He called it a "jobs transfer bill."

He delayed passage of the continuing resolution to prevent the Senate from finishing that bill and going on to

the highway measure.

East contended that he was not obstructing the orderly consideration of business. He said the Senate had failed to invoke cloture on the bill Dec. 16, and thus should not return to the measure during the lame-duck session.

By a vote of 89-5, the Senate Dec. 19 invoked cloture on Baker's substitute amendment to HR 6211. *(Vote 452, p. 75-S)*

In a Dec. 20 session that extended beyond midnight, the Senate by a vote of 71-24 adopted the Baker substitute as amended. *(Vote 457, p. 76-S)*

Senate leaders said 400 amendments had been filed on the Baker substitute. But time ran out on most of them because of the limits set by cloture rules and agreements.

One of the major amendments lost in the crunch was one by Banking Committee Chairman Jake Garn, R-Utah, that would have made further cuts in mass transit operating subsidies. Transportation Department officials had said that the deeper cuts were necessary to avoid a presidential veto, but, in the end, they said they were satisfied with the bill.

Garn withdrew his amendment Dec. 20, in exchange for an agreement by Bill Bradley, D-N.J., to drop an amendment that would have modified penalties for transit systems using certain federal funds for operating costs.

Other Amendments

Some of the amendments considered by the Senate included proposals by:

● Lloyd Bentsen, D-Texas, to move up the 1983 income tax cut to April 1, from July 1, and to defer 5 percent of the cut until the federal budget deficit was eliminated. Rejected 40-54, Dec. 14. *(Vote 403, p. 68-S)*

● Howard M. Metzenbaum, D-Ohio, to require that only steel and cement manufactured in the United States be used in federal highway and bridge programs. Tabled, and thereby killed, 51-47, Dec. 15. *(Vote 408, p. 69-S)*

● Paul E. Tsongas, D-Mass., to reallocate $16 billion in new highway construction funds authorized in the bill to repair projects. Rejected 17-74, Dec. 15. *(Vote 409, p. 70-S)*

● Dale Bumpers, D-Ark., to the Baker substitute, to require that each state receive at least 85 percent of the transit revenues derived from 1-cent-a-gallon of the gas tax increase that its motorists would pay. Tabled, and thereby killed, 52-44, Dec. 20. *(Vote 456, p. 75-S)*

● Nickles, to remove a provision of the Baker substitute relating to Davis-Bacon Act requirements that an area's prevailing wage rate be paid on federally funded highway projects. The provision clarified that the Davis-Bacon Act applied to major highway repairs as well as new construction. Tabled, and thereby killed, 48-46, Dec. 19. *(Vote 453, p. 75-S)*

● Donald W. Riegle Jr., D-Mich., to exempt families with incomes of $10,000 or less from the gas tax increase. Tabled, and thereby killed, 50-42, Dec. 19. *(Vote 454, p. 75-S)*

Senate Provisions

As passed by the Senate, HR 6211:

● Authorized $3.625 billion in fiscal 1984 for Interstate Highway construction; $3.8 billion, 1985; $3.8 billion, 1986; and $4 billion annually for 1987-1990.

● Authorized $1.7 billion in fiscal 1983 for Primary Highways; $2.1 billion, 1984; $2.4 billion, 1985; $2.4 billion, 1986; $2.6 billion, 1987.

● Authorized $614.5 million in fiscal 1983 for rural roads

and $700 million annually for 1984-1987.

● Authorized $629 million in fiscal 1983 for urban roads and $800 million annually for 1984-1987.

● Authorized $1.7 billion in fiscal 1983 for bridge repair and replacement; $1.7 billion, 1984; $1.8 billion, 1985; $2 billion, 1986; and $2 billion, 1987.

● Authorized $316.7 million in fiscal 1983 for highway safety improvement; $400 million annually for 1984-1987.

● Required that every state receive at least one-half of 1 percent of the total Interstate apportionment.

● Required each state beginning in fiscal 1984 to spend at least 60 percent of the funds for Primary, rural and urban highways on major repairs, except under certain circumstances.

● Authorized $1.8 billion in fiscal 1984 for the Interstate 4-R program; $2.4 billion, 1985; $2.8 billion, 1986; $3.2 billion, 1987; and $3.4 billion, 1988.

● Authorized $500 million in fiscal 1983 from the Highway Trust Fund for highway projects substituted for planned Interstate Highway segments; $600 million, 1984; and $650 million annually for 1985-1987.

● Apportioned bridge monies by formula based on factors including the average national cost of bridge work.

● Authorized $100 million annually for emergency highway projects.

● Clarified that Davis-Bacon Act wage requirements apply to major repair projects on federally aided highways, as well as to new construction.

● Set a ceiling of $12 billion in fiscal 1983 on obligations from the Highway Trust Fund for highway construction and related programs; $12.8 billion, 1984; $13.6 billion, 1985; $14.5 billion, 1986; $14.9 billion, 1987.

● Allowed a state under certain circumstances to defer payment of its share of the cost of a highway project funded by the gas tax increase in fiscal 1983. If the state did not "repay" its deferred match by Sept. 30, 1984, 50 percent of the amount would be taken from its federal highway apportionments in fiscal 1985 and 50 percent in 1986.

● Required each state's federal highway apportionment to equal at least 85 percent of the highway taxes that its motorists paid. The gas tax revenues for mass transit would not be included.

● Authorized $526 million annually for fiscal 1983-1987 for transit projects substituted for planned Interstate Highway segments.

● Required all states to allow 80,000-pound trucks on Interstate Highways.

● Increased the federal share by 5 percent for highway and bridge surfacing or restoration done with recycled materials.

Mass Transit

● Authorized a total of $3.69 billion for mass transit in fiscal 1983; $4.3 billion, 1984; and $4.3 billion, 1985.

● Created a formula block grant program that could finance both transit capital and operating costs.

Bus funds for cities of populations over 200,000 would be apportioned 50 percent by miles of revenue service and 50 percent by population.

Rail funds would be apportioned by formula based 60 percent on miles of revenue service and 40 percent on route miles.

● Set restrictions on the use of block grant funds for mass transit operating expenses. Operating subsidies for cities of one million population or more could not exceed 80

percent of the fiscal 1982 level of operating assistance. The subsidies for cities of 200,000 to one million population could not exceed 90 percent; and subsidies for cities under 200,000 could not exceed 95 percent.

A city could use block grant funds up to the fiscal 1982 level of operating subsidies to pay for transit operations in fiscal 1983 and 1984, but it would lose some capital funds as a penalty.

● Authorized $550 million in fiscal 1983 from the transit account of the Highway Trust Fund for transit capital projects, and $1.1 billion in each of 1984 and 1985.

Safety

● Gave the transportation secretary broader authority to establish rules to ensure safety in loading and operating commercial motor vehicles.

● Protected truck employees from dismissal or discipline for filing a complaint about violations of commercial motor vehicle safety rules.

● Authorized $10 million in fiscal 1984 for grants to states to enforce commercial motor vehicle safety regulations; $20 million, 1985; $30 million, 1986; and $40 million, 1987; and $50 million, 1988.

● Authorized $13 million annually for fiscal 1985-1988 for Federal Highway Administration safety programs.

● Authorized $100 million annually for fiscal 1985-1988 for NHTSA highway safety programs.

● Authorized $31 million annually for fiscal 1985-1988 for NHTSA highway safety research.

● Set length standards for trucks, including not less than 48 feet for a semi-trailer unit, or 28 feet for semi-trailers operating in a double combination. States had to allow trucks meeting these standards on Interstate Highways or any other qualifying federally aided highway. No state could regulate the overall length of a truck, and no state could bar the operation of a twin-trailer truck.

● Barred states from prohibiting 102-inch wide trucks on Interstates or other qualifying federally aided highways.

Taxes

● Increased the gas and diesel fuel tax by a nickel a gallon, to a total of 9 cents a gallon, from April 1, 1983 through Sept. 30, 1989.

● Exempted gasohol from the full 9-cents-a-gallon tax.

● Exempted methanol or ethanol fuels produced from a substance other than petroleum or natural gas.

● Exempted state and local governments; intercity, local and school buses; farm and non-highway business uses from the fuel tax.

● Exempted taxicabs from 4 cents a gallon of the fuel tax.

● Established new graduated taxes for tires. The taxes were set at 10 cents a pound for the first 50 pounds; 15 cents a pound for the next 50 pounds; and 25 cents a pound for weight over 100 pounds.

● Increased the 5-cents-a-gallon tax on tread rubber to 6 cents a gallon.

● Retained the 6-cents-a-gallon tax on lubricating oil.

● Set a 12 percent retail tax on new trucks over 33,000 pounds and trailers over 26,000 pounds, through Sept. 30, 1988.

● Increased the tax on truck parts and accessories to 10 percent, up from 8 percent, for trucks or trailers over 10,000 pounds.

● Established new graduated taxes for heavy trucks, with a maximum levy of $1,200 for 80,000-pound trucks.

The tax for trucks from 33,000-55,000 pounds would be $80 plus $10 per 1,000 pounds over 33,000; from 55,000-70,000 pounds, $300 plus $20 per 1,000 pounds over 55,000 pounds; and from 70,000-80,000, $600 plus $60 per 1,000 pounds over 70,000.

● Extended the authority for the Highway Trust Fund through Sept. 30, 1989.

● Set the cap on fuel tax revenue transferred to the boating trust fund at $45 million a year.

● Established an account within the Highway Trust Fund for revenues from 1-cent a gallon on the fuel tax for mass transit capital programs.

Miscellaneous

● Appropriated $475 million over fiscal 1983-1985 from the Airport and Airway Trust Fund balance, in addition to previously authorized funds, for airport development projects.

● Appropriated $401 million over fiscal 1983-1985 from the Reforestation Trust Fund, the boating trust fund and the Saltonstall-Kennedy Fund. The funds would be used for forest redevelopment, state boating safety programs and boating facilities, and fisheries development.

● Provided up to six weeks of extra unemployment benefits to thousands of workers for whom regular and extended payments had run out.

● Included a number of miscellaneous unrelated tax law changes including:

● **Tax Deductions.** Allowed certain deductions for business conventions held on U.S. cruise ships, as long as they stopped at U.S. ports or those of U.S. possessions. The deduction was limited to $2,000 for most individuals and $1,000 for a married individual filing a separate return.

● **Utility Companies.** Forgave three California utility companies of over $2 billion in tax liability, which they were required to pass on to consumers.

● **Safe-Harbor Leasing.** Provided that there would be no government recapture of safe-harbor leasing tax benefits upon the sale of qualified aircraft in a bankruptcy situation to a person who used the property predominantly outside the United States.

Conference Action

Despite members' growing impatience to go home for the Christmas holiday, negotiations on the Senate and House versions of the legislation took all day, Dec. 21, before a compromise was reported (H Rept 97-987).

The compromise followed the four-year structure of the House bill, generally authorizing funds through fiscal 1986 for highways and mass transit.

The 9-cent-a-gallon gas tax would be effective from April 1, 1983, to Sept. 30, 1988, which actually was an extension of four years because the 4-cent-a-gallon levy was due to expire Oct. 1, 1984.

A new tax on heavy trucks was established to be phased in July 1, 1984. The maximum tax for 80,000-pound trucks was set at $1,600 July 1, 1984, increasing to $1,900 July 1, 1988.

While the total authorization was about the same as the House bill, it did not include unspecified authorizations to ensure that every state received federal highway apportionments amounting to at least 85 percent of the highway taxes that its motorists paid.

Under the compromise, states were allowed to defer their matching share of highway projects funded by the tax

increase for two years.

Highway Formula

Conferees bogged down over the insistence by House members that the formula for allocating funds for Primary Highways — major urban and rural roads — be based on population. The House formula would have favored the urbanized Eastern states and California, at the expense of the large but sparsely populated Western states.

The conferees agreed to allow a state to receive the higher amount from either the existing formula, which included land area and highway mileage factors, or a new one based only on urban and rural population. The amount would be reduced to keep the apportionments within the authorized level.

The conferees also did not accept the House changes in the formula for allocating major repair monies for the Interstates. The House had wanted to focus on car and truck fuel use, which would have benefited the urbanized states. The existing formula was based on traffic and lane miles.

Also eliminated from the final bill was a House provision that would have eliminated federal compensation for highway billboards that were taken down.

Mass transit subsidies were cut along the lines of the Senate bill, up to 20 percent of the fiscal 1982 amount for the largest cities. But, there was a provision included to allow communities to spend up to their fiscal 1982 level in exchange for some of their capital funds.

The protectionist "Buy America" provision of the House bill also was moderated in the compromise.

Conferees also accepted the unemployment benefits extension and some unrelated tax provisions included in the Senate bill.

The 102-inch width provision for trucks was left out of the compromise because it had been included in a previously passed appropriations bill (HR 7019 — PL 97-369). *(Story, p. 267)* ∎

Product Liability

Business and consumer groups were sharply divided over proposed legislation that would limit business liability for damages caused by defective products.

The legislation (S 2631) was approved by the Senate Commerce Committee. But it did not reach the floor, and there was no action in the House.

Business representatives argued that they had been seriously hurt by high liability insurance premiums, demands for large cash awards, legal costs, differing state laws and the uncertainty of whether a product currently thought safe later might be deemed otherwise.

Also, some companies said they had been sued even when their particular element of a product was not dangerous or when the user altered the product after it was purchased.

But trial lawyers and consumer advocates contended that the bill unfairly limited the rights of people to sue for damages when they were injured by defective products.

The bill's sponsor, Consumer Subcommittee Chairman Robert W. Kasten Jr., R-Wis., said it would "pinpoint responsibility" for harm caused by products.

"I believe it brings uniformity and predictability into the process. We're not limiting anybody," he said.

Senate Commerce Committee

The bill, reported Dec. 1 (S Rept. 97-670), would have preempted state law on all matters of product liability governed by the measure. Jurisdiction would remain with state courts, except where there currently was a basis for federal jurisdiction.

It would have set standards for manufacturers' and sellers' responsibilities and for determining if a product was unreasonably dangerous. Under the bill, for example, the manufacturer would be liable if the claimant established that the product was unreasonably dangerous in construction, in design, or because of a failure to provide adequate warnings or instructions.

The claimant would have to show that the unreasonably dangerous aspect of the product was the significant cause of the injury for which the manufacturer should be held responsible.

According to the committee bill, a product would be unreasonably dangerous in construction if it deviated from the manufacturer's design or performance specifications, or from otherwise identical units of the same product line. A product would be unreasonably dangerous in design if a reasonably prudent manufacturer would not have used the design.

Damages awarded to a claimant, however, would be reduced in proportion to his own responsibility for the injury. The allocation of responsibility would account for whether the claimant knew about the product's defective condition and voluntarily used the product or assumed the risk of harm.

And the bill, under certain circumstances, would have set a 25-year time limit on liability for claims against capital goods. A capital good was a product used in trade or business or held for production of income.

Legal Uncertainty

In 1981, consumer advocates had joined business groups to support a bill that made it easier for businesses to obtain product liability insurance. That act (PL 97-45) generally pre-empted state laws that restricted the formation of business groups for self-insurance. *(1981 Almanac p. 573)*

That measure, however, did not address the touchy issues of defining what was a suitable cause for suit and who might be liable for any damages, as the Kasten bill did.

Arguing in support of the 1982 bill, businesses and insurers said the current system of torts — legal wrongs or injuries for which a person was entitled to compensation — needed revision. Tort law had been developed mostly by states on a case-by-case basis.

They said the tort system and diverse state laws created an environment of legal uncertainty, making the practice of insuring for product liability increasingly risky.

Backing the bill was the Product Liability Alliance, which represented more than 200 businesses and trade groups, including the National Association of Wholesaler-Distributers, National Association of Manufacturers and U.S. Chamber of Commerce.

Jay Angoff of Congress Watch, a consumer advocacy group, argued against enacting a federal statute, saying that "common law or court law can change as time and technology change."

Other opponents included the Association of Trial Lawyers of America and the Consumer Federation of America. ∎

AT&T Bill Dropped, Killing Rewrite Efforts

In a surprise announcement, Rep. Timothy E. Wirth, D-Colo., July 20 withdrew his bill (HR 5158) to modify a proposed antitrust settlement between the American Telephone & Telegraph Co. (AT&T) and the Justice Department, effectively killing any congressional overhaul of the telecommunications industry in 1982.

The Senate in 1981 had passed a bill (S 898) that was more limited than either the Wirth measure or the proposed settlement. Wirth had revised his 1981 version of HR 5158 in order to address what he considered gaps left by the proposed court agreement. *(1981 Almanac p. 555)*

In announcing the withdrawal of his bill, Wirth charged that AT&T had waged a campaign of "fear and distortion" against HR 5158 and had used dilatory tactics that made it impossible to finish the bill.

"In the 97th Congress, we are left with only 27 legislative days to complete work on the most significant telecommunications bill since the 1930s," Wirth said in a statement to the Energy and Commerce Committee July 20.

"The only way to pass legislation now would be to accept an agreement dictated by AT&T," he said.

The Senate bill had in effect been superseded Jan. 8, when AT&T and the Justice Department announced an antitrust agreement under which AT&T would shed its 22 local operating companies in exchange for the right to enter unregulated and computer-oriented markets.

Wirth's measure would have gone beyond the antitrust settlement in restricting AT&T's activities. While AT&T originally pushed for legislation, it vehemently opposed Wirth's bill, contending that it unfairly limited its operations while making it easier for other telecommunications firms to compete.

AT&T said Congress should delay legislation until the agreement was approved and urged its one million employees, three million stockholders and 190,000 retirees to object to Wirth's bill. Thousands of letters protesting the legislation poured into House offices.

HR 5158 had been unanimously approved by Wirth's telecommunications subcommittee March 25. After seven days of markup by the full committee, Wirth July 20 still claimed he had the votes to report the bill out of committee.

But Wirth said the procedural delays used by committee members sympathetic to AT&T — such as forcing a formal reading of the 130-page bill and conducting extensive debate on each amendment — were likely to continue on the House floor and if the bill passed, in conference with the Senate. He also said AT&T tried to have the bill referred to House committees ranging from Agriculture to Ways and Means.

A Wirth aide said the congressman decided to abandon his effort July 19, after a five-hour negotiating session between AT&T and committee staffers failed to produce a compromise.

Supporters had said that HR 5158 was needed to prevent undue increases in local telephone rates, to protect the viability of local telephone companies after they were separated from AT&T and to guard against potential anticompetitive actions by a restructured AT&T.

The bill would have barred AT&T from using revenue from regulated long-distance service to subsidize unregulated, competitive businesses. It also would have prevented AT&T from transmitting its own electronic publishing services and would have allowed the divested companies to sell new telephone equipment.

Antitrust Agreement

Wirth's decision to stop work on HR 5158 was initially interpreted as a victory for AT&T, which wanted Congress to postpone legislation and allow the proposed court settlement to become effective. However, U.S. District Judge Harold H. Greene of Washington, D.C., Aug. 11 called for changes in the settlement, some of which addressed concerns raised by Wirth and others.

AT&T and the Justice Department had announced the proposed antitrust settlement Jan. 8 while a trial was in progress before Greene in Washington, D.C. The plan required AT&T to divest itself of 22 local telephone operating companies, representing $87 billion of the firm's assets. In exchange, AT&T would be allowed to enter the lucrative data-processing and other unregulated fields denied to it by a consent decree settling an earlier antitrust case.

Greene said the settlement was in the public interest, but he said modifications to ensure the financial strength of the local operating companies and to limit telephone rate increases would be necessary.

One of the proposed modifications would give Greene the authority to approve AT&T's reorganization plan under the settlement.

Greene said he would resume the antitrust trial if AT&T and the Justice Department did not agree to the modifications. The two parties accepted the changes Aug. 19, and the new agreement was approved by Greene Aug. 24.

Court Modifications

The modifications approved by the court:

● Allowed the local operating companies to produce the *Yellow Pages* advertising directories. The original settlement would have transferred *Yellow Pages* to AT&T. HR 5158 and S 898 would allow the local companies to retain the *Yellow Pages* revenue, estimated at more than $2 billion a year.

Greene said production of *Yellow Pages* by the local operating companies would generate a substantial subsidy for local telephone rates.

● Allowed the local operating companies to market customer premises equipment, such as ordinary telephones. The original settlement would have transferred the equipment to AT&T.

Permitting the local companies to market the equipment would "provide needed competition for AT&T," Greene said.

● Barred AT&T from engaging in electronic publishing over its own transmission facilities, although it would be allowed to offer limited electronic directory and weather services. The court could lift the restriction after seven years unless it found that competitive conditions required an extension.

Greene said the electronic publishing industry was still in infancy, and if AT&T were allowed into the industry now "there would be a substantial risk not only that it would stifle the efforts of other electronic publishers but

that it would acquire a substantial monopoly over the generation of news. . . . Such a development would strike at a principle which lies at the heart of the First Amendment: that the American people are entitled to a diversity of sources of information."

Newspaper publishers succeeded in including restrictions in HR 5158 and S 898 generally barring AT&T's entry into electronic publishing over its own lines.

House Committee Action

The House Telecommunications Subcommittee March 25 approved a substitute to a bill introduced in 1981 by Wirth.

AT&T immediately attacked the new version of HR 5158, contending that it unfairly and severely restricted the firm while making it easier for other telecommunications companies to compete. In a press conference, company officials said they would ask their one million employees and three million stockholders to object to the bill.

The subcommittee approved the bill by a 15-0 vote.

James E. Olson, vice chairman of the AT&T board, contended that HR 5158 could disrupt the nation's telephone system by placing substantial burdens on AT&T's long-distance operations.

He said the bill's requirement that AT&T form a separate subsidiary for long-distance operations would restrict business dealings between the subsidiary and the parent company, including AT&T's research and manufacturing arms, Bell Laboratories and Western Electric.

Proposed Limits

As passed by subcommittee, HR 5158:

• Required AT&T to place its regulated long-distance service in a subsidiary with accounting and employees separate from the unregulated operations. Neither the Jan. 8 antitrust settlement nor the modified version would require a subsidiary.

• Barred the unregulated AT&T parent company from owning transmission facilities outside the long-distance subsidiary. This was to ensure that AT&T did not concentrate on a new, unregulated long-distance service and neglect the existing network. The original settlement would allow AT&T to own long-distance transmission lines.

• Required that the valuation of assets be completed after the operating companies were divested. The settlement would provide for the valuation of assets before divestiture.

The valuation of assets, such as a local company's long-distance facilities, would determine the extent to which the operating companies would be compensated for those assets after they were spun off from AT&T.

• Allowed divested companies to offer *Yellow Pages,* which produced about $2 billion a year in revenues nationally. The original settlement would have transferred *Yellow Pages* to AT&T, but the modified agreement allowed the local companies to produce the directories.

• Allowed operating companies to keep customer terminal equipment currently in use, such as telephones, and to receive the lease revenues from the equipment for nine years. After five years, the companies could sell, but not manufacture, new telephones and other terminal equipment through separate subsidiaries.

The settlement would transfer customer equipment to AT&T. The bill also would allow AT&T to provide the equipment. ∎

Airline Pact

Language requiring the payment of benefits under certain circumstances to airline employees affected by mergers, acquisitions and other transactions was dropped from a bill (HR 5930 — PL 97-309) before being cleared by Congress Sept. 30.

The bill, originally a routine aviation insurance measure, became the focus of a battle between the airline industry and pilots when the labor protection requirement was tacked on during the first conference on the measure. Airlines opposed the provision because of its potential cost.

The first conference report (H Rept 97-722), filed Aug. 10, was recommitted Aug. 12 by the Senate by a vote of 59-38 on the grounds that the provision exceeded the scope of the conference. *(Vote 318, p. 53-S)*

The final conference report (H Rept 97-864), filed Sept. 23, kept the Senate provision allowing the Civil Aeronautics Board (CAB) to continue its discretionary authority to impose such benefits through Jan. 1, 1985. The report was adopted by the Senate Sept. 30 by voice vote and cleared by the House by voice vote the same day.

The new agreement gave Congress time to determine how it wanted to deal with the labor protection issue by extending the CAB authority over domestic mergers and other transactions through Jan. 1, 1985.

The 1978 airline deregulation act (PL 97-504) had required the transfer of CAB authority over domestic mergers and other transactions to the Justice Department Jan. 1, 1983. The final conference agreement did not change the 1978 provision for the CAB to retain authority over international cases until Jan. 1, 1985. *(1978 Almanac p. 496)*

Prior to deregulation, the CAB required airlines in merger cases to pay up to 60 percent of a furloughed employee's average salary for up to five years, compensate employees moved to lesser paying jobs and provide other benefits. Since 1978, the board had included those benefits in merger cases only when requested by management and labor.

Provisions

As signed by the president Oct. 14, HR 5930:

• Reauthorized the aviation war risk insurance program through Sept. 30, 1987. The program (PL 95-163) provided federal insurance for certain aviation risks that commercial insurers would not cover. *(1977 Almanac p. 559)*

• Required the National Transportation Safety Board (NTSB) to withhold from public disclosure cockpit voice recordings associated with accidents. The NTSB was required to make public relevant portions of the communications at the time of its public hearing on the accident or no later than 60 days after the accident.

• Provided that no less than three NTSB members must have technical or other special qualifications in the fields of accident reconstruction, safety engineering, human factors, transportation safety or regulation.

Legislative History. The bill was reported from the House Public Works and Transportation Committee May 17 (H Rept 97-519) and passed by the House June 2 under suspension of the rules. It was passed by the Senate amended June 21, after the Commerce, Science and Technology Committee had been discharged. The amendments concerned the cockpit voice recordings, NTSB appointments and the CAB language. ∎

Tax Bill Revives Dormant Airport Program

The multibillion-dollar tax hike legislation (HR 4961 — PL 97-248) cleared by Congress Aug. 19 also revived a dormant airport development program, and raised airline ticket and general aviation fuel taxes.

Airport development aid legislation expired in 1980 and the taxes were reduced or dropped entirely. The expiration meant that no new monies were going into the Airport and Airways Trust Fund, which financed the development program. The remaining taxes were deposited into other accounts. *(1981 Almanac p. 570; 1980 Almanac pp. 267, 159)*

The Senate Commerce and House Public Works committees had reported authorizing bills (S 508, HR 2643) in 1981 but were unable to bring them to the floor. The stalemate was caused partly by disagreement over the direction of the program.

The final 1982 measure involved trade-offs between the two chambers, and Congress and the administration over the development program's structure, tax levels and how much of the aviation tax revenues should be spent on operating the air traffic control system.

The bottleneck was broken when the Senate Finance Committee, in its search for revenues to reduce the federal deficit, decided to include increased and new aviation taxes in the 1982 omnibus tax bill. *(Tax bill story, p. 29)*

Sen. Bob Packwood, R-Ore., a member of the finance panel and chairman of the Commerce Committee, obtained the support of the Commerce Committee majority to add authorizations for the airport program to the tax bill. In addition to airport development, the authorizations involved such programs as noise abatement, facilities and equipment, and engineering.

One of his goals was to ensure that the aviation taxes were not spent on non-airport projects. Packwood and others feared that a fragile industry coalition supporting the airport package would be split if the authorizations were not tied to the taxes in the same bill, specifying how they would be spent.

Packwood said that if the authorizations were removed, he would work to strike the aviation taxes from the bill, which would derail the tax package.

But the tactic drew harsh criticism on the floor from senators such as Howard W. Cannon, D-Nev., who charged that it was a backdoor effort to enact proposals that had not been approved by the entire Commerce Committee.

"This maneuver is simply an effort to avoid open debate and fair consideration of this legislation," Cannon, ranking minority member of the Commerce panel, said in floor debate July 20.

"If an aviation bill of this scope can be passed without having been the subject of a single Commerce Committee meeting, then we might as well declare jurisdiction rules void and have a free-for-all," he declared.

Packwood retorted that he was not circumventing Senate rules and that the committee had discussed the issues previously. He prevailed, and the Senate-passed tax bill included authorizations for the airport aid program and for the Federal Aviation Administration (FAA) operation of the air traffic control system.

The House, which sent the tax bill to conference without debate, later accepted the program as revised by the conferees.

Summary of Agreement

Conferees on HR 4961 from the House Public Works and Senate Commerce committees agreed Aug. 5 to increase the use of aviation tax monies to help pay the FAA's costs of running the nation's air traffic system.

Congress historically had resisted using the airport trust fund for FAA operations, contending that the aviation taxes feeding the fund were intended only for airport development. President Reagan had sought to shift the cost of operations from general taxpayers to aviation users by raising the aviation ticket and fuel taxes and using them to pay operating costs.

The conference agreement (H Rept 97-760) established formulas for authorizing operations funding, amounting to $1.462 billion in fiscal 1983, up from the 1982 level of $800 million. Reagan had sought a $2 billion share from the trust fund for a proposed $2.55 billion program to operate the air traffic control system.

The conferees put strings on the authorizations to help ensure that monies for airport development projects would be spent. For example, if all of the development money was not allocated, the funds for FAA operations would be reduced. Some members were concerned that the administration might hold up development funds to reduce budget deficits.

The conferees dropped a Senate provision allowing for voluntary airport "defederalization," which would have permitted airports to withdraw from the federal development aid program and negotiate with airlines for monies.

Senate Finance and House Ways and Means Committee conferees set the airline passenger ticket tax and general aviation fuel levies at the Senate-passed levels: 8 percent for the ticket tax, up from 5 percent; 12-cents-a-gallon general aviation fuel levy, up from 4 cents, and imposed a 14-cents-a-gallon jet fuel tax. The jet fuel tax had expired.

The Ways and Means Committee May 12 reported a bill (HR 4800 — H Rept 97-510) that would have set a 5 percent ticket tax and 12-cents-a-gallon levies for general aviation and jet fuel. HR 4800 was going to be folded into the Public Works Committee airport development bill (HR 2643) if the authorization measure had reached the floor.

Final Provisions

As cleared by Congress, HR 4961:

● **Taxes:** Raised $2.8 billion in various taxes for the Airport and Airway Trust Fund by making changes that included: increasing the passenger ticket tax from 5 percent to 8 percent; raising the general aviation gasoline tax from 4 cents a gallon to 12 cents a gallon; imposing a 14-cent-a-gallon tax on jet fuel; and reinstating the 5 percent air freight waybill and $3 international departure ticket taxes.

The taxes would expire after four years unless extended by Congress. The new taxes would go into effect Sept. 1, 1982.

●**Airport Program:** Continued the requirement that the transportation secretary periodically review and revise the plan for the national airport system.

● Authorized $450 million in fiscal 1982 for airport development and noise abatement projects; $600 million,

1983; $793.5 million, 1984; $912 million, 1985; $1.017 billion, 1986; and $1.017 billion, 1987. Unused authorizations could be carried over.

Those were the Senate levels. The House committee bill authorized $450 million in fiscal 1982 and $600 million in 1983.

• Authorized $261 million in fiscal 1982 for facilities and equipment; $725 million, in 1983; $1.393 billion, 1984; $1.407 billion, 1985; $1.377 billion, 1986; and $1.164 billion, 1987. Unused authorizations could be carried over. The funds would help finance the administration's multibillion-dollar program to modernize the air traffic control system.

• Authorized $72 million for research, engineering and development in fiscal 1982; $134 million, 1983; $286 million, 1984; $269 million, 1985; $215 million, 1986; and $193 million, 1987.

• Authorized $800 million in fiscal 1982 from the Airport and Airway Trust Fund for FAA operations and maintenance of the air traffic control system.

• Established formulas for authorizing funds from the Airport and Airway Trust Fund for FAA operations and maintenance of the air traffic control system. The formulas based the operation funds on the level of funding made available each year for airport development.

A House conferee staffer said the formulas amounted to $1.462 billion in fiscal 1983 for operations if the full airport development authorization was spent; $1.245 billion, 1984; $1.271 billion, 1985; $1.306 billion, 1986; and $1.362 billion, 1987.

And, the bill provided for the reduction in trust fund monies for operations if facilities and equipment monies were not spent.

The Senate tax bill authorized $1.559 billion in fiscal 1983; $1.355 billion, 1984; $1.363 billion, 1985; $1.388 billion, 1986; and $1.444 billion, 1987.

HR 2643 would have authorized trust fund expenditures of up to 50 percent of the total amount appropriated for operations in fiscal 1983, or about $964 million.

• Required the transportation secretary within one year of enactment to submit a report to Congress on whether, and to what extent, airports that have the ability to finance their capital and operating needs without federal aid should be made ineligible to receive airport development and planning funds.

• Provided for apportionment of development funds to primary airports based on a passenger enplanement formula that is the same as in existing law. The amount apportioned to each primary airport would be increased by 10 percent in fiscal 1984, 20 percent in 1985, 25 percent in 1986 and 30 percent in 1987.

• Provided that a primary airport receive not less than $200,000 or more than $12.5 million in development apportionments in any fiscal year. The total amount of all apportionments based on enplanements may not exceed 50 percent of the amount authorized in a fiscal year.

• Allocated an apportionment to states of 12 percent of airport development funds to pay for projects at general aviation and reliever airports, which are general aviation airports designed to relieve congestion at major airports.

• Allowed a primary airport to use the larger of $200,000 or 60 percent of its apportionment for terminal facilities. The funds may be used for terminals only afer all necessary safety, security and passenger enplaning-deplaning facilities have been provided.

• Allocated out of total airport development authorizations 10 percent for the development and improvement of reliever airports; 8 percent for noise abatement projects; and 5.5 percent for commuter airports.

Legislative Action

In floor debate on the tax bill, Cannon complained that no committee Democrats had agreed to Packwood's revisions of the authorizations in S 508 that were added to the tax measure.

Cannon said the aviation tax levels were too high for the amount planned to be spent on airport programs and too much would be diverted from development to FAA operations. He said the Senate should debate separate aviation legislation.

He tried to have the language stricken on the floor but was blocked by Packwood's parliamentary maneuvering.

The Finance Committee reported the legislation in the form of two committee amendments to the tax bill. The first provided for the tax changes, and the second was the airport program. Before the Senate could consider the second amendment, Packwood offered his own amendment that provided for the authorizations with some changes.

Cannon raised a point of order that the Packwood amendment was non-germane to the bill, but the chair ruled that it was germane because the two Finance amendments brought the airport issues into the legislation. However, the chair said the original committee amendment on the airport program would have been out of order if it had been the one pending because Finance did not have jurisdiction over airports.

The Senate voted 53-44 affirming the ruling of the chair that the Packwood amendment was germane. *(Vote 230; p. 41-S)*

Minority Leader Robert C. Byrd, D-W.Va., then moved that the bill be recommitted with instructions to delete the authorizations. "Let us not do indirectly what we cannot do directly," he said.

Packwood replied that levying the aviation taxes without targeting them for aviation purposes "does worse violence" than attaching the authorizations to the tax bill.

The Byrd motion was defeated by a vote of 43-54, and the Packwood amendment was adopted 93-5. *(Votes 231, 232, p. 41-S)*

Background

An FAA proposal made public Jan. 28 proposed a $9 billion modernization program involving high-capability computers and greatly increased automation to handle the heavier air traffic expected in the future. It would improve communications, save fuel, reduce accident risks and eventually result in a $25 billion savings in operating and maintenance costs, the FAA said.

A key element of the plan was criticized by the Rand Corp., a consultant hired by the FAA to analyze the plan. Rand said the proposal shifted too much decision-making from human controllers to computers, raising potential safety problems. However, FAA officials and other consultants maintained that the program was safe.

Reagan requested $725 million for equipment in fiscal 1983 to begin the modernization plan and $450 million for airport development. But the development funds and $300 million of the equipment monies were contingent on enactment of Reagan's proposed increase in the taxes.

The president proposed raising the aviation tax to 12 cents a gallon in fiscal 1982, increasing to 20 cents by 1987;

the jet fuel tax would be 14 cents, increasing to 22 cents by 1987. The ticket tax would go to 8 percent.

Legislation raising the taxes, but not as high as Reagan wanted, was eventually enacted. ∎

Rail Strike Ended

Congress Sept. 22 quickly enacted legislation to end a four-day national railroad strike that had threatened to throw one million people out of work and cost the economy $1 billion a day.

Hours after the House voted 383-17 to adopt a Senate-approved resolution (S J Res 250) to send railroad workers back to their jobs, President Reagan signed the measure (PL 97-262). He said it would "protect the jobs of our people and keep both factories and farms at work." *(Vote 333, p. 98-H)*

The legislation, initiated by the administration, ordered the 26,000 striking members of the Brotherhood of Locomotive Engineers (BLE) back to work and imposed the settlement recommended earlier by a presidential Emergency Board. The settlement prohibited the union from striking through June 30, 1984.

Mining, Auto Industry

Members of Congress and administration officials were reluctant to intervene in the collective bargaining process. But with the recession continuing and the unemployment rate standing at 9.8 percent, most felt they had no choice.

The strike, which began at 12:01 a.m. Sept. 19, affected 117 railroads outside the Northeast and was quickly felt by coal mines and the auto industry. General Motors closed its truck assembly plant in St. Louis Sept. 20. Eight coal mines in West Virginia were closed.

The administration estimated that 300,000 to 500,000 workers had been idled. Also, 150,000 commuters, primarily in Chicago, were sent scurrying for other transportation.

Conrail, the federally subsidized freight railroad in the Northeast, had reached its own labor agreement in 1981 and was not affected by the strike. Amtrak passenger lines in the Northeast also were not affected.

While members were concerned about alienating organized labor, they had received signals from other unions that there would be no retaliation on the issue at the polls.

Rex Hardesty, spokesman for the AFL-CIO, said the organization was "bothered on principle" by the proposal. But, he added, "In this deep a recession, the shutdown of America's railroads was more harm than the public could take."

Background

The rail industry had concluded agreements with 12 of the 13 rail unions. Negotiations began in 1981, but the BLE in June notified the National Mediation Board that it intended to strike July 11 over unresolved contract issues.

Reagan exercised his authority July 8 under the Railway Labor Act of 1926 to establish a cooling-off period and to create an Emergency Board to recommend a settlement. The union would be free to strike Sept. 19 if no agreement was reached. *(Congress and the Nation Vol. I, pp. 626, 570)*

The settlement recommended by the board Aug. 19 provided for a 28.8 percent pay and cost-of-living increase over a 39-month period, retroactive to April 1981.

It also allowed the engineers to continue negotiations to maintain their wage advantage over other crew members. Other crew members, represented by the 135,000-member United Transportation Union (UTU), could receive productivity payments during the settlement period — through June 30, 1984 — that might result in some being paid more than engineers.

However, under the settlement, engineers would not be allowed to strike over the wage differential issue through June 30, 1984. The engineers objected, and the dispute led to the Sept. 19 walkout.

The average salary for engineers was $37,000 a year, while conductors were paid $32,000, and brakemen, $27,000.

During congressional hearings Sept. 21, Transportation Secretary Drew Lewis warned that a resolution providing another cooling-off period for the BLE might unravel the tentative UTU agreement, which had not been ratified.

UTU President Fred Hardin told the House Energy and Commerce Committee that if Congress ordered a cooling-off period and new negotiations for the BLE, the UTU would want to be able to renegotiate its settlement.

James J. Florio, D-N.J., chairman of the House panel's Transportation Subcommittee, opposed the resolution, contending that a congressionally mandated settlement including a no-strike clause was a "radical" action.

Lewis said Congress had intervened several times in rail labor disputes since 1963. The last time was in 1971 when Congress cleared a bill (PL 92-17) to end a two-day strike. That law gave the Brotherhood of Railway Signalmen a wage hike, barred further strikes through Oct. 1, 1971, and directed negotiations to continue. *(1971 Almanac p. 171)*

Congressional Action

The Senate Labor Committee Sept. 21 reported S J Res 250 (no written report), and the Senate passed it by voice vote that evening.

The House panel reported an identical measure (H J Res 600 — H Rept 97-853) Sept. 22. The full House approved the Senate resolution after rejecting 37-361 a Florio amendment that would have suspended the strike for 140 days while negotiations resumed. *(Vote 332, p. 98-H)* ∎

Tourism Funding

The U.S. Travel and Tourism Administration received funding at a $7.6 million annual rate for fiscal 1983 even though a bill authorizing funds for the agency had been rejected by the House.

The appropriation was included in the stopgap government funding bill (H J Res 599 — PL 97-276) approved by Congress Oct. 1. The amount was the same as approved by the Senate in its version of the continuing appropriations resolution but was about $2.6 million more than the House bill (HR 6258) proposed. *(Story, p. 225)*

The House failed July 20 to suspend the rules and pass the bill, which would have authorized $10 million in fiscal 1983 for the agency. The vote was 241-167; a two-thirds majority (272) was required for passage. *(Vote 181, p. 54-H)*

Opponents argued that increased funding could not be justified. The agency, created in 1981 to replace the U.S. Travel Service to promote foreign travel to this country,

was authorized to receive $8.6 million in fiscal 1982. *(1981 Almanac p. 574)*

HR 6258 had been reported from the Energy and Commerce Committee May 18 (H Rept 97-568). ∎

NHTSA Authorization

Congress Oct. 1 cleared legislation (HR 6273 — PL 97-332) that prohibited the National Highway Traffic Safety Administration (NHTSA) from requiring independent tire dealers and distributors to complete tire registration forms.

Instead, the dealers must furnish purchasers with a registration form containing the tire identification numbers, which they could then return directly to tire manufacturers.

The bill was cleared when the Senate by voice vote passed a measure approved by the House June 14. The bill had been reported May 19 by the House Energy and Commerce Committee (H Rept 97-576) and by the Senate Commerce Committee July 27 (S Rept 97-505).

The legislation also authorized $51.4 million in fiscal 1983 for NHTSA activities; $55 million, fiscal 1984; and $58.7 million, fiscal 1985. This was consistent with the administration's budget request for fiscal 1983.

Tire registration was used to notify owners of defective tires that could cause accidents. ∎

Bill Easing Intercity Bus Regulation Cleared

Legislation to relax federal and state regulation of the intercity bus industry was approved by Congress in 1982, making buses the fourth transportation industry to undergo significant deregulation in as many years.

The House Aug. 19 by voice vote adopted the conference report (HR 3663 — H Rept 97-780) on the bill. By an 84-8 vote, the Senate Aug. 20 adopted the report, clearing the measure for the president. *(Vote 338, p. 56-S)*

Regulatory reform laws affecting railroads (PL 96-448) and trucks (PL 96-296) were passed in 1980 and for airlines (PL 95-504), in 1978. *(1980 Almanac pp. 248, 242; 1978 Almanac p. 496)*

Rep. Glenn M. Anderson, D-Calif., chairman of the Public Works Surface Transportation Subcommittee, said the conference agreement went further toward deregulation than a measure originally adopted by the House in November 1981. *(1981 Almanac p. 581)*

The final legislation (PL 97-261) was designed to promote competition within the bus industry, and between buses and private cars and airlines. Its supporters said the bill allowed bus carriers to respond quickly to changing marketplace conditions with less interference from government, particularly by the states. It pre-empted some state rules such as ones barring buses from picking up or dropping off passengers on intermediate points along routes.

The measure eased the way for new companies to start up service and for existing carriers to expand operations. Unprofitable routes could be dropped more easily, and companies could change their rates with less government interference.

At the same time, the bill set the stage for the elimination of immunity from antitrust laws now allowed for collective rate-making.

Rural Service

In contrast to the sometimes sharp controversy over some of the other transportation deregulation laws, the bus bill was relatively non-controversial and had the backing of the industry. The greatest concern expressed by members of Congress was whether relaxing government regulation would result in a reduction in service to small towns.

"I continue to be concerned that this legislation, if passed, would mean that bus transportation service to rural communities would be reduced or eliminated, and the quality of life for those people would be diminished," Senate Minority Leader Robert C. Byrd, D-W.Va., said in explaining why he would vote against it.

Senate Commerce Committee Chairman Bob Packwood, R-Ore., said service to small towns had been maintained in Florida, which had deregulated the industry there and that the bill contained protection for rural travelers and shippers.

The compromise was worked out informally by key House and Senate members, bus industry representatives and administration officials.

One sticking point was restrictions on Canadian and Mexican truck and bus carriers operating in the United States. U.S. truckers had complained that Mexican laws prevented them from doing business in Mexico and that regulations and laws in Canada had unfairly limited them.

Administration officials feared that the House measure would have been too harsh and warned that the president might veto it.

The House had given the Interstate Commerce Commission (ICC) discretion to deny applications of Mexican or Canadian companies if it determined that their governments did not treat Americans as favorably as they treated their own companies; and prohibited the ICC from issuing permits if Americans in those countries were not given operating authority from those governments.

The compromise, accepted by the administration, prohibited operating permits for Canadian and Mexican carriers for two years and allowed the president to lift or modify the moratorium.

Provisions

As cleared by Congress, the Bus Regulatory Reform Act of 1981:

● **National Policy.** Directed the ICC to reduce regulation and promote competition.

● Called for national policy guidelines requiring the ICC to cooperate with states on transportation matters and requiring the commission to ensure that federal reform initiatives were not nullified by state actions. The measure also provided guidelines for the regulation of motor carriers — trucks and buses — to include maintaining service to small towns and shippers, and maintaining a sound and competitive privately owned motor carrier system.

● **Entry.** Directed the ICC to permit a bus company to operate if it is "fit, willing and able" to provide the service, unless the ICC found, on the basis of evidence presented by an objector, that the service would not be consistent with the public interest.

● Directed the ICC to authorize a company to provide regular-route service entirely in one state over an existing interstate route unless the intrastate service would have a significant adverse effect on a competing commuter bus operation. The ICC also must allow intrastate service to points along a new interstate route unless it found that the service was not consistent with the public interest. The burden of proof would be on the objector.

● Provided that the ICC, in making findings relating to the public interest, consider national transportation policy, the value of competition, the impact on service to small communities and whether issuance of the permit would impair the ability of any other carrier to provide a substantial portion of its regular-route service.

The public interest finding would not apply to interstate service for any community not regularly served by a bus company; service that would substitute for discontinued rail or commercial air passenger service for a community when the discontinuance meant that there would not be any rail and commercial air service; and interstate service to any community that was about to lose other bus service.

● Required that determinations on fitness and public interest be made on a case-by-case basis rather than by an industrywide rule-making proceeding.

● Barred any bus carrier from protesting an application to provide service or for the removal of an operating restriction except under certain conditions, such as the objector already having had the authority to handle the traffic being sought and being willing and able to provide the service.

● Barred the ICC for two years following enactment from granting operating authority to Canadian or Mexican truck and bus carriers. The president could extend the moratorium for either country if that country was substantially prohibiting U.S. carriers from receiving authority to provide service within its boundaries. The president could lift or modify the moratorium if he found it was in the national interest and if he first notified the Congress.

● **Restrictions Removed.** Provided that an ICC certificate to provide interstate transportation was deemed to authorize round-trip operations where only one-way authority currently existed, and special and charter transportation from all points in a state in any instance in which the transportation authority was limited.

● Required the ICC within 90 days upon a carrier's request to remove any restriction on transportation to intermediate points on the carrier's interstate route, unless the ICC found, on the basis of evidence presented by an objector, that the service would adversely affect a competing commuter bus operation.

● Allowed a carrier to transport special or charter passengers in the same vehicle with regular-route passengers.

● **Rates.** Established a rule of rate-making that must be considered by the ICC in determining whether rates were reasonable. The rule would authorize revenue levels adequate to allow a well-managed carrier to cover costs and earn a fair return.

● **Antitrust.** Prohibited carriers belonging to a rate bureau from discussing or voting on any single-line rate as of Jan. 1, 1983, and barred carriers as of Jan. 1, 1984, from discussing or voting on any joint rate. Single-line rates were charges for service handled by one carrier, while joint rates were charges for service handled by more than one.

The ban would not apply to general industry rate changes. Antitrust immunity would remain for broad changes in tariff structure, changes in promotional and innovative fares, and support services for members.

● Required a study commission to report to Congress by Jan. 1, 1984, on the collective rate-making process for general rate and innovative fare changes, and whether there was a need for continued antitrust immunity for collective rate-making. The commission also by Jan. 1, 1984, would report on the impact of bus legislation on the elderly.

● **Zone of Rate Freedom.** Allowed carriers to raise or decrease rates within a "zone of rate freedom" without ICC approval.

The ICC would not be allowed to suspend, revise or revoke the rate because it was unreasonably high or low if the change was not more than 10 percent above or 20 percent below the rate in effect one year prior to the proposed charge. One year later, the zone would change to 15 percent above to 25 percent below the effective rate. Two years later the zone would be 20 percent above to 30 percent below the effective rate. By the third year, regulation of independent rates generally would be eliminated except when a rate is predatory or discriminatory.

A carrier must notify the ICC that it wants its rate considered pursuant to this provision. Antitrust laws would apply to proposals for using the zone. Use of general rate increases would count against the upward zone.

● **Special, Charter Rates.** Prohibited the ICC from suspending, revising or revoking a rate for special or charter service except on the basis that the rates were predatory. Collective consideration of special operations or charter service would be eliminated.

● Provided that entry for contract bus carriers would be based on a "fit, willing and able" entry test, defined as a carrier meeting safety and insurance requirements.

● Exempted brokers for bus service from ICC regulation except for requirements for bonds or insurance. A broker was someone other than a bus carrier who arranged bus transportation for compensation.

● **Service Reductions.** Lessened restrictions on a bus company's ability to reduce or abandon service.

A carrier would have to meet certain conditions before the ICC could approve its proposal to reduce service, such as the carrier must be requesting to reduce or abandon both intrastate and interstate service along a route, the carrier must show that a state had denied or not acted finally on its request, and the carrier must have notified the governor, appropriate state agency and affected communities that it intended to petition the ICC for action.

The ICC would have to approve the request unless an objector showed that discontinuing the service was inconsistent with the public interest or that continuing the service was not an unreasonable burden on commerce. In making that determination, the ICC would have to consider national policy; whether the carrier was receiving or had received an offer of financial assistance; whether there was reasonable alternative service; whether interstate and intrastate revenues for the service to be stopped were less than the variable costs of providing the transportation; and whether granting the request would adversely affect commuter buses. The carrier would bear the burden of proving that continuing the service was a financial hardship.

The ICC could order the carrier to continue service for up to 165 days. The legislation also pre-empted state laws relating to discontinuance or reduction in certain intrastate service unless the laws required notice of up to 30 days.

● **State Regulation.** Required the ICC to establish

rates, rules or practices applicable to intrastate service if the carrier had a request denied or not acted upon finally by a state agency, and if the ICC determined that the rate, rule or practice in effect caused unreasonable discrimination against or imposed an unreasonable burden on interstate commerce. The carrier must notify the state and interested parties.

State rate-making authority over intrastate rates of solely intrastate carriers would not be affected.

● Barred a state from enacting or enforcing any law or rule relating to scheduling of bus service except to the extent of requiring up to 30 days' notice of changes.

● Directed the ICC to cooperate with states to establish standards and procedures that promote uniformity.

● **Miscellaneous.** Provided for the ICC to suspend a carrier's operating permit in an expedited manner if the carrier was operating in a way that was an imminent hazard to public health or property.

● Allowed the ICC to provide administrative aid to local governments and small carriers that wanted to participate in proceedings dealing with pre-emption of state authority.

● Required a bus carrier to give priority for jobs to employees laid off for other than cause within 10 years of enactment of the legislation. The ICC was directed to keep a list of available bus jobs.

● Provided that the legislation became effective on the 60th day after enactment.

Senate Action

Before adopting its version of the bill June 30, the Senate by voice vote accepted a committee amendment that helped win the general support of the administration. The amendment softened the provision restricting Canadian trucking operations in the United States.

The Senate bill originally would have placed a moratorium on ICC approval of operating applications from foreign truck firms until the president negotiated an agreement ensuring fair treatment for U.S. truckers in that country.

The amendment barred the ICC from issuing a permit to a Canadian or Mexican trucking firm for two years but allowed the U.S. trade representative to remove or modify the restriction for reasons of national interest.

The bill was approved in an 85-10 vote. *(Vote 206, p. 37-S)*

The Senate Commerce Committee May 11 ordered the bill reported by a vote of 15-1, with Larry Pressler, R-S.D., casting the only negative vote. Pressler said he was concerned that the measure might result in less service in rural areas. The report (S Rept 97-411) was filed May 20. ∎

FCC Lottery Rules

The Federal Communications Commission (FCC) was ordered to establish rules for granting broadcast licenses by random selection under legislation cleared for the president Aug. 19.

Although the bill (HR 3239 — PL 97-259) did not require that a lottery be used instead of the current method of comparative hearings on applications, Congress insisted that regulations for a lottery be established. The 1981 budget reconciliation law (PL 97-35) directed the FCC to establish a lottery, but the commission did not do so,

contending that the requirements were unworkable. *(1981 Almanac p. 569)*

HR 3239 was cleared for the president when the House accepted the conference report (H Rept 97-765) on the measure by voice vote. Earlier Aug. 19 the Senate accepted the report.

The measure was a collection of various communications bills (S 929, S 2181, HR 5008, HR 6162) substituted by the Senate Aug. 18 for the language of a bill (HR 3239) passed by the House in 1981. The original version of HR 3239 had been incorporated in the 1981 reconciliation act. *(1981 Almanac p. 569)*

NTIA. The new legislation also authorized $12.9 million in fiscal 1983 for the National Telecommunications and Information Administration (NTIA), which developed telecommunications policy. It authorized $11.8 million in 1984. President Reagan had requested $12.4 million in fiscal 1983.

The conferees said they "do not expect" NTIA to eliminate its program for aiding the construction of public broadcasting facilities, as Reagan proposed. The 1981 reconciliation act authorized $15 million in fiscal 1983 for facilities construction.

The conferees said a lottery for granting some types of broadcast licenses may be helpful in reducing the regulatory process, and may promote diversity in information sources and media ownership.

They "encouraged" the FCC to use a lottery for the granting of licenses for low power television stations because of "huge backlogs which would otherwise significantly delay service to the public if the traditional comparative hearing process were relied upon."

The bill directed the FCC to adopt rules within 180 days of enactment for a random selection system and required that "significant preference" be given to minority groups to help increase diversification of ownership of mass media outlets. The conference report provided guidelines for establishing a lottery.

Provisions

As cleared by Congress, the Communications Amendments Act of 1981 also:

● Authorized the FCC to eliminate the individual licensing of citizens band (CB) radio operators.

● Allowed the FCC to use amateur radio operators on a voluntary basis to administer and update amateur radio license examinations. Also the bill permitted the FCC to accept the volunteer services of amateur radio and CB operators to monitor radio frequencies for violation of FCC rules.

● Repealed a provision of a 1978 law (PL 95-234) that would have terminated the existing formula used by the FCC for determining the reasonableness of rates charged for cable television attachments to utility poles. *(1978 Almanac p. 475)*

● Made clear that the FCC had jurisdiction over intrastate radio communications. This provision was necessary to ensure that the FCC could charge CB radio operators with violation of commission rules.

● Required the FCC to establish minimum standards for televisions and other home electronic equipment to reduce their susceptibility to radio interference.

● Allowed the FCC to grant radio operator licenses to aliens eligible for employment in the United States.

● Relaxed the existing bar against FCC employees having an interest in a firm involved in wire or radio communi-

cations. The new standard would prohibit ownership only when there was a significant interest in communications, manufacturing or sales activities subject to FCC regulation.

● Established rules for FCC regulation of private land mobile services and eased the process for granting private land mobile licenses. Private land mobile services include emergency and business vehicle radios.

● Directed the NTIA to conduct a study of U.S. long-range international telecommunications goals. ∎

Coast Guard Authorization

Members of Congress, critical of President Reagan's wanting to trim Coast Guard funding while increasing other defense spending, cleared a bill Sept. 29 authorizing more than the president requested.

The measure (S 2252 — PL 97-322) authorized $2.38 billion for Coast Guard activities in fiscal 1983 and $2.68 billion in fiscal 1984. The president had requested $1.99 billion in new budget authority in fiscal 1983 compared to about $2 billion in fiscal 1982. The bill was $800 million over the first budget resolution.

The administration argued that its position was a responsible one in poor economic times and that it provided for adequate incremental improvements. Many members of Congress, however, complained that the Coast Guard had been assigned additional duties without corresponding increases in funds.

"The Coast Guard of today is in very deep trouble. The service simply cannot continue to function competently without additional funds," said Gerry E. Studds, D-Mass., chairman of the House Merchant Marine and Fisheries subcommittee on the Coast Guard.

Rep. Walter B. Jones, D-N.C., chairman of the Merchant Marine Committee, said the funding hike was needed to cover military pay and benefits increases, higher fuel costs, a program to interrupt boats carrying Haitians trying to illegally enter the United States, and to prevent closings or reduced operations at Coast Guard facilities.

The bill was cleared when the House accepted Senate amendments raising some funding in a bill the Senate had passed earlier.

Besides the specific authorizations listed, the final measure assumed the authorization of "such sums as may be necessary" for retired pay in fiscal 1983 and 1984. That would amount to $332 million in 1983, a Senate Commerce Committee aide said.

Senate Action

The Senate had approved S 2252 May 5 by voice vote after key senators said the Coast Guard did not have adequate funding to perform its duties. The Coast Guard is responsible for rescue service; military backup; enforcement of fisheries, immigration and drug laws; and environmental protection.

The bill, reported by the Senate Commerce Committee April 26 (S Rept 97-361), authorized about $2.62 billion for the Coast Guard in fiscal 1983.

It provided $550 million in fiscal 1983 for acquisitions and improvements to navigation aids and vessels, while Reagan requested $19.2 million in new authority and proposed using previously appropriated funds.

S 2252 authorized $1.7 billion for operations and maintenance in fiscal 1983 and $2 billion in 1984; $550 million

for acquisition, construction and improvements of navigation aids, facilities and vessels in fiscal 1983 and $650 in 1984; $29 million for research in fiscal 1983 and $32 million in 1984; and $336 million for retirement pay and medical benefits in fiscal 1983 and $396 million in 1984.

It also authorized an end-of-year strength for active duty personnel of 41,500 and allowed the Coast Guard to operate navigation aids by contract with any person or public authority.

House Action

The House July 15 by a vote of 348-25 essentially accepted the recommendations of its Merchant Marine and Fisheries Committee and authorized funding exceeding both the Senate and presidential levels. *(Vote 178, p. 52-H)*

The bill reported May 17 (HR 5617 — H Rept 97-563, Pt. I-II) was $1 billion more than Reagan proposed for the Coast Guard's major accounts in fiscal 1983 and $273 million more than the Senate bill.

HR 5617 would permit a total of $2.55 billion in fiscal 1983 for Coast Guard operations; acquisition, construction and improvement of navigation aids and vessels (ACI); research; and bridge alterations. The Senate committee and administration proposals included authorizations for other activities not under the House panel's jurisdiction.

The bill authorized $2.759 billion in fiscal 1984.

For fiscal 1983, the bill authorized $1.842 billion for operating expenses; $670 million for acquisition, construction and improvements of navigation aids and vessels; $30 million for research and development; and $12.7 million for alteration or removal of bridges.

For fiscal 1984, the House authorized $2.026 billion for operating expenses; $700 million for acquisitions, construction and improvements; and $33 million for research and development.

Unlike the Senate bill, which included specific amounts for Coast Guard retirement pay, the House bill authorized "such sums as may be necessary" for pensions.

Compromise

The House then attached its language to S 2252 and passed the Senate bill.

In an effort to reach a compromise and avoid a conference, the Senate Sept. 27 by voice vote agreed to increase its previously approved fiscal 1983 authorization for operations by $100 million.

The Senate did not change its fiscal 1984 authorizations. Also remaining the same was the fiscal 1983 authorization of $550 million for acquisition and construction of aids to navigation, vessels and aircraft, the other major Coast Guard authorization. ∎

Drunk Driving

States that crack down on drunk driving were made eligible for extra highway safety funds under compromise legislation approved by Congress.

The bill (HR 6170 — PL 97-364) authorized $125 million in extra highway safety funds in fiscal 1983-1985 for states that enacted stricter drunk driving laws.

The House passed the bill by voice vote Sept. 29, and the Senate by voice vote Oct. 1 cleared the measure.

The legislation also authorized $9.1 million for fiscal 1983-1987 to computerize and maintain the National

Driver Register, which is intended to help states identify drivers with a history of serious traffic offenses. The Reagan administration had proposed eliminating funding for the register in fiscal 1982 but later supported it.

Legislative History

Senate. The Senate passed a bill (S 2158 — S Rept 97-360) May 11 that would allow states to receive grants if they passed laws requiring 90-day suspension of a driver's license for the first failure of a chemical sobriety test, a one-year suspension for subsequent violations, a minimum 48-hour jail term for repeat offenders and impoundment for at least 90 days of a motor vehicle operated by anyone whose license was suspended or revoked under drunk-driving laws.

The bill, reported April 26 by the Senate Commerce Committee, authorized $25 million in fiscal 1983 for the grants and $50 million in fiscal 1984. It also authorized $6.8 million for fiscal 1983-1985 to maintain and computerize the National Driver Register.

House. The House Public Works Committee included language in its highway and mass transit bill (HR 6211) to provide incentive grants to states adopting certain minimum standards. Its bill, however, would authorize $25 million in fiscal 1983 and $50 million each in fiscal 1984 and 1985.

A separate bill reported Sept. 23 (HR 6170 — H Rept 97-867) by the Committee on Public Works and Transportation was designed as a compromise. It followed the funding authorized by the earlier House bill but was less restrictive in its requirements than the Senate legislation.

Chief House sponsors James J. Howard, D-N.J., chairman of the Public Works Committee, and Michael D. Barnes, D-Md., said drunk driving was responsible for the highway deaths of 25,000 people and the injury of 650,000 people last year.

"In the last two years, the total amounted to more than died during the entire Vietnam War," Howard said.

Additional Provisions

As approved by the House and Senate, HR 6170 would provide incentive grants in fiscal 1983-1985 to states that enacted stricter drunk driving laws. The money would be in addition to existing safety programs. To be eligible, a state must require:

● That any motorist with a .1 percent blood-alcohol level be deemed to be driving while intoxicated.

● Prompt suspension or revocation of a driver's license for at least 90 days for a person convicted of drunk driving, and at least one year for a repeat offender.

● A mandatory jail sentence of 48 consecutive hours or at least 10 days community service for anyone convicted of drunk driving more than once in five years.

● Increased enforcement of state drunk driving laws supported by increased publicity.

States would be eligible for additional money if they included other measures, such as establishing a system to track repeat offenders, setting a minimum drinking age of 21 years old and impounding a vehicle operated by a motorist whose license was suspended or revoked for drunk driving. The eligibility criteria would be determined by the transportation secretary.

The legislation authorized $25 million in fiscal 1983 and $50 million annually in fiscal 1984 and 1985. It also provided $9.1 million for fiscal 1983-1987 to computerize and maintain the National Driver Register. ∎

Public Broadcast Funds

Supporters of public broadcasting succeeded in 1982 in obtaining the full $130 million in federal subsidies they said they needed for fiscal 1984 and 1985.

Congressional action came after the Corporation for Public Broadcasting (CPB) launched a lobbying campaign to try to reverse budget cuts of previous years.

Although Congress had authorized $130 million annually for fiscal 1984 and 1985, the corporation was to receive only $105.6 million for fiscal 1984 under stopgap funding measures passed in 1981 and 1982 (PL 97-92, PL 97-161). *(1981 Almanac p. 329; story, p. 229)*

The CPB said that the $130 million was the minimum required for survival. Spokesmen predicted that less would result in a loss of quality programming and could put some stations out of business.

"Many stations are on the razor's edge. Maybe what is necessary [to convince Congress] is for 20 stations to go under," S. L. Harrison, CPB director of corporate communications, said as the lobbying drive began in early January.

Arguments

Pressed by President Reagan to reduce overall spending, Congress in 1981 slashed previously appropriated fiscal 1983 broadcasting funds to $137 million from $172 million.

But Congress overrode the administration's authorization request of $110 million and $100 million for fiscal 1984 and 1985 and provided for $130 million for each of those two years. *(1981 Almanac p. 567)*

The administration had argued that the general taxpayer should not finance the entertainment of a few and that the reductions in government aid could be made up in private donations.

In response, CPB supporters said the subsidies were justified because public broadcasting provided the nation with special cultural and educational diversity.

They pointed out that public television was available to 90 percent of U.S. households with TV sets and public radio was accessible to 65 percent of the American public.

They also contended that the federal funds helped to draw private donations by financing quality programs. Public broadcasting also received funds from state and local governments and businesess that underwrote programs.

The CPB was established by Congress in 1967 to promote public broadcasting and to distribute money to public stations. The advance funding mechanism was created in 1975 to insulate broadcasters from political pressures and to promote long-range planning.

Funding Scenario

CPB sought $24.4 million to bring the $105.6 million funding for fiscal 1984 up to the authorized level.

The funds were contained in two supplemental appropriations bills vetoed by President Reagan (HR 5922, HR 6682).

They remained in the third supplemental appropriation measure (HR 6685 — PL 97-216), which the president signed July 18.

CPB succeeded in obtaining the full $130 million for fiscal 1985 in the continuing resolution cleared by the lame-duck Congress and signed into law Dec. 21 (H J Res 631 — PL 97-377). ∎

Broadcast Deregulation

A Senate-passed bill significantly reducing federal regulation of radio and television broadcasting died when the House failed to act before the 97th Congress adjourned.

The bill (S 1629 — S Rept 97-292), passed by voice vote March 31, was similiar to legislation the Senate had attached to the 1981 budget reconciliation bill (PL 97-35). Key House members blocked that effort, contending there was not enough competition in broadcasting to warrant lifting federal regulation. *(1981 Almanac p. 569)*

S 1629 would have codified steps taken by the Federal Communications Commission (FCC) to deregulate radio broadcasting, such as barring the agency from imposing public affairs programming requirements.

Also, the bill would have eliminated the radio and TV license renewal procedure of comparing the existing licensee with competing applicants. Licenses generally would be renewed unless there had been serious legal violations. Separate legislation (HR 3239) instructing the FCC to prepare for license lotteries was enacted in 1982. *(Story, p. 338)*

In addition, an amendment accepted by the Senate by voice vote would have required fees for such FCC services as facility construction permits and station assignment and transfer.

Supporters of the legislation contended the regulations and comparative license renewal process were not necessary to ensure diverse programming. Critics argued that the rules protected public access to scarce airwaves and the comparative renewal procedure promoted attention to public needs.

A staff member of the House Energy and Commerce Telecommunications Subcommittee said key members had not changed their opinions against substantial deregulation.

S 1629 had been reported (S Rept 97-292) by the Commerce, Science and Transportation Committee Dec. 10. ∎

Cable TV Control

Cities and other interest groups succeeded in 1982 in short-circuiting the efforts of cable television operators to free themselves from local government control.

The controversy involved legislation reported Aug. 10 by the Senate Commerce Committee (S 2172 — S Rept 97-518) that would sharply restrict local regulation of cable television.

Mayors, state and county officials, consumer advocates and labor representatives lobbied against the measure. They succeeded in 1981 in knocking similar restrictions out of a telecommunications bill (S 898) approved by the Senate. *(1981 Almanac p. 558)*

They contended that the bill would be an unwarranted federal intrusion into local government affairs, would unfairly restrict local regulation of rates that a cable customer must pay and would require cities to renew an operator's franchise automatically.

Cable operators said the bill would resolve their difficulties with overlapping and uncertain regulation that had impeded development. It also would help them compete with unregulated telecommunications companies, they added.

Controversies

One major controversy involved rates and franchise fees. Currently, local governments and cable firms established long-term agreements that provided the terms and conditions of the franchise, including the use of public rights-of-way. Generally a company was granted a monopoly and agreed to pay the government a portion of its revenues.

The bill would give the federal government jurisdiction over cable unless otherwise provided by law, thereby pre-empting conflicting state or local laws.

Cities and other government entities would be allowed to regulate rates for basic service — re-transmission of over-the-air television signals and providing public and educational programming — but no level of government would be allowed to regulate the rates for other cable service. Nor would any government entity be allowed to regulate other cable-provided telecommunication services, such as electronic banking or publishing.

The cities and others objected to those changes.

The bill also would require a city to renew a franchise if the cable company met certain criteria, such as the company having substantially complied with the terms of the franchise.

The cities objected that the provision would require a city to treat an agreement as a perpetual franchise. But cable supporters argued that operators, who did not begin to earn a profit until late in the franchise term, should have a reasonable expectation that the franchise would be renewed as long as they met the criteria of the franchise and the bill.

The bill also barred any government agency from prohibiting the ownership of a cable system by anyone because of his control of another media interest, such as a television station or newspaper. The committee said this provision would eliminate current FCC restrictions on cable cross-ownership. ∎

Coal Slurry Pipelines

Rail interests and other opponents of coal slurry pipelines succeeded in 1982 in fending off legislation to ease pipeline construction.

Although committees in both chambers reported legislation, neither bill reached the floor, largely because of the strong opposition. Coal slurry is crushed coal mixed with water and shipped by underground pipe; the water is later reclaimed and the coal burned to generate electricity.

Railroads and rail unions traditionally have argued that giving pipeline companies the right of federal eminent domain to condemn land, including railroad rights of way, would be unfair and would cost them business and jobs. Railroads were the major haulers of coal. *(1981 Almanac p. 578)*

"We have a right to protest the government fostering a competitor," Daniel L. Lang, a spokesman for the Association of American Railroads, said.

Also, some Western states fought the legislation, contending it would pre-empt their rights to allocate scarce water.

In addition, President Reagan became the first president to come out against federal eminent domain for slurry lines since it was proposed by President Kennedy in 1962. Reagan said it would encroach on states' rights.

Slurry supporters — electric utilities, pipeline companies, non-rail unions, coal interests and some consumer advocates — had contended that railroads had blocked pipelines from crossing their properties in an attempt to prevent competiton. They said competition would help reduce the cost of coal, and thus lower electricity costs.

A new coalition called the Alliance for Coal and Competitive Transportation lobbied members from the Northeast and Midwest who had traditionally opposed coal slurry bills.

Committee Action

HR 4230 (H Rept 97-423, Pt. I) was reported Jan. 29 by the House Interior and Insular Affairs Committee. The Public Works and Transportation Commitee voted 24-21 to approve the bill July 28. Its report (Pt. II) was filed Aug. 10.

The Senate Energy and Natural Resources Committee reported a similar bill (S 1844 — S Rept 97-528) Aug. 17 after several days of contentious markup. Opponents delayed action by offering a flurry of amendments before the committee voted 14-6 Aug. 5 to approve the bill.

The Public Works bill was reported with only one amendment, a "buy American" provision requiring pipeline companies to use construction materials produced in the United States.

Critics, spearheaded by Robert W. Edgar, D-Pa., and Bud Shuster, R-Pa., had offered more than a dozen other amendments, many of which would have effectively gutted the bill. They held off a final vote for nearly two days with roll-call votes, quorum calls and full use of the time allowed for debate.

Committee Chairman James J. Howard, D-N.J., responded to those tactics by continuing the markup session into the evening of July 28.

Similar Patterns

The pattern of support and opposition was similar in both the House and Senate panels: Members from the South and West tended to support the proposal, and members from Midwestern and Eastern coal-producing states tended to oppose it.

Strong proponents of the bill in the House Public Works Committee were John B. Breaux and Buddy Roemer, both Louisiana Democrats. The chief sponsor on the Senate Energy Committee was J. Bennett Johnston, also a Louisiana Democrat.

The House committee version of the bill gave the Interstate Commerce Commission the authority to regulate the pipelines.

The Senate panel granted the regulatory authority to the Department of Energy.

Water Issues

Both measures left to the states another issue critical to the pipelines' future: water rights.

Slurry pipelines would use substantial amounts of water, and unlike many other users of water, they would not return it to the area from which it came. The longest proposed pipelines would move coal from Western states that were as water-poor as they were coal-rich. Potential water costs had been one of the biggest objections to slurry pipelines among Westerners.

Neither bill allowed pipelines to use water or transfer it between states without the permission of the state from which the water came.   ∎

Ship-Buying Aid Founders

Legislation that would have allowed U.S.-flag ship operators to buy foreign vessels without losing their federal operating subsidies died because Congress was unable to clear it before the lame-duck session ended Dec. 23.

Sen. Howard M. Metzenbaum, D-Ohio, blocked consideration of a compromise (S 2336 — H Rept 97-961) filed by Senate and House conferees Dec. 13 because he opposed providing operating subsidies to companies that bought foreign-built ships.

The provision had been included in the bill passed by the Senate June 24; the House bill did not have similar language.

Temporary Program Stops

The lack of a new law left U.S.-flag operators without federal construction subsidies to acquire U.S.-built ships. If they bought foreign ships, they would lose their federal operating subsidies.

The domestic construction subsidies were eliminated in 1981 in the budget reconciliation act (PL 97-35). The act also established a temporary program allowing U.S. companies to buy foreign vessels or ships rebuilt in foreign yards and to continue to receive federal operating subsidies. *(1981 Almanac p. 570)*

Prior to the 1981 change in law, ships had to be built in domestic yards to qualify for operating subsidies.

Congressional staffers said the old law effectively meant that an American company accepting operating subsidies had to own only American-built ships.

The subsidies were intended to help U.S.-flag companies and yards to compete with foreign operators and shipbuilders.

The Senate bill extended the buy-foreign provision for fiscal 1983, while the House bill did not change the law.

Operating subsidies for domestically built ships continued, however. The $454.01 million in operating subsidies authorized by the bill was included in the continuing appropriations resolution (H J Res 631). *(Story, p. 238)*

Conference Agreement

The conference agreement authorized $572.423 million in fiscal 1983 for maritime programs, the same as provided by the House bill and $30.6 million more than requested by President Reagan. The Senate bill authorized $541.8 million.

As approved by the conferees, the compromise would have:

• Authorized $454.01 million for operating subsidies.

• Authorized $15.3 million for research and development.

• Authorized $78.1 million for operations and training, including $17.3 million for the U.S. Merchant Marine Academy at Kings Point, N.Y., and $17.8 million for state maritime academies.

• Authorized $25 million for the acquisition of three ships for the National Defense Reserve Fleet. Under that program, the administration acquired obsolete commercial vessels from companies for the fleet in exchange for a credit against the construction or purchase of a new U.S. vessel.

• Allowed U.S.-flag ship operators to build, reconstruct or acquire ships outside the United States until Oct. 1, 1983, and be able to receive operating subsidies. The compromise did not include a Senate provision that would have

allowed the operators to benefit from a tax deferral program now allowed only for American-built ships.

● Limited the administration's authority to deny or defer requests for construction loan guarantees that met the legislated criteria of existing law.

● Required annual authorizations for the Federal Maritime Commission beginning in fiscal 1984.

Legislative History

The House bowed to administration pressure and passed a maritime authorization (HR 5723) Sept. 28 that eliminated construction subsidies. The House Merchant Marine and Fisheries Committee May 17 reported the bill (H Rept 97-539), including $100 million for construction subsidies. The subsidies were dropped before the measure was brought up on the floor.

After approving its bill by voice vote, the House substituted its language for that of a Senate bill (S 2336).

The Senate June 24 passed S 2336 by voice vote and without debate. The bill as reported May 20 by the Commerce Committee (S Rept 97-408) did not include construction subsidies. ▮

Maritime Antitrust Bill

Legislation sought by maritime interests and the Reagan adminstration to grant broad antitrust immunity to international ocean liner cartels was among the casualties of the 1982 lame-duck session of Congress.

Although the House Sept. 15 overwhelmingly approved an antitrust bill (HR 4374), supporters were unable to obtain a Senate vote before adjournment. Sen. Howard M. Metzenbaum, D-Ohio, objected to bringing up what he called "atrocious" legislation. At one point late in the lame-duck session, compromise language worked out by key members was attached to another bill (HR 3420), but Metzenbaum blocked that too.

Supporters contended that the measure would clarify congressional intent in the 1916 Shipping Act that the liner cartels, or conferences, should be exempt from antitrust laws that prohibit price-fixing and other joint activities. They said judicial interpretations and regulatory actions impeded the financially troubled American merchant marine from competing in a worldwide industry that accepted joint activities as routine.

Among those pushing for the bill were the National Maritime Council, which represented carriers, labor and shipyards; the National Industrial Traffic League, representing 1,800 shippers and business groups; Council of American-Flag Ship Operators; Labor-Management Maritime Committee; American Farm Bureau Federation; port groups; Union Carbide Corp.; ARCO Chemical Co.; Du Pont; Ford Motor Co.; and the Council of European & Japanese National Shipowners Association.

Opposition came from members who resisted grants of antitrust immunity to business in general and from a coalition including the Consumer Federation of America, Consumers Union, Congress Watch, National Farmers Union and the Public Interest Economics Foundation's National Institute of Economics and Law.

They contended that by greatly expanding immunity, the bills would allow companies acting in concert to raise shipping rates for exports and imports, resulting in higher costs to consumers.

House Action

The House Sept. 15 voted 350-33 to suspend the rules and pass the bill (HR 4374), a procedure that prevented opponents from offering amendments. The required two-thirds majority was achieved easily. *(Vote 304, p. 92-H)*

During debate, Merchant Marine and Fisheries Committee Chairman Walter B. Jones, D-N.C., and Judiciary Committee Chairman Peter W. Rodino Jr., D-N.J., the floor managers of the bill, said the measure included protections for shippers to offset the liners' power and to ensure competition. For example, shippers would be allowed to seek a limited antitrust immunity from the Justice Department to form their own councils to negotiate with cartels for more favorable rates.

"It represents a careful balancing of the interests of the ocean carriers, the shippers who pay for their services and the ultimate consumers," Rodino said during debate Sept. 13.

But opponents argued that the bill would result in higher consumer prices for imported goods. They also warned that it would set a bad precedent for other industries.

"The bill provides a bailout for an inefficient American industry, a bailout through a kind of off-budget financing by imposing the burden of monopolistic prices on American consumers and exporters," said Don Edwards, D-Calif., a Judiciary Committee member and leading opponent of the bill. He said shipping rates would rise 20 percent.

Edwards contended that the vote was so lopsided because of heavy lobbying by maritime unions and liner companies controlled by big businesses, such as R. J. Reynolds Industries Inc., LTV Inc. and Holiday Inns Inc.

"We got rolled over," Edwards moaned. "I tip my hat to the job they did, regrettably. It was a magnificent, hard-hitting lobbying effort."

Jones credited "a tremendous selling job done by all the supporters of the bill, including those in the private sector."

The bill was reported by the Merchant Marine Committee June 16 (H Rept 97-611, Parts I and II). The Judiciary Committee July 30 reported a compromise worked out with the Merchant Marine panel. The Judiciary bill was more restrictive than the original bill in its grant of antitrust immunity for cartel activities.

Key members agreed to further modifications, and it was that new version that was presented to the House.

House Provisions

As approved by the House, HR 4374:

● Allowed ocean common carriers to meet in conferences to discuss and fix rates and conditions of service; pool cargo and revenues; restrict sailings between ports; regulate the volume or character of traffic; and engage in preferential or cooperative working arrangements among themselves or with marine terminal operators; and enter into agreements to regulate or prevent competition among themselves.

● Required carriers in conferences to file agreements on authorized activities with the Federal Maritime Commission (FMC), which could reject any agreement that failed to comply with the law. An agreement automatically would become effective 45 days after filing, unless rejected by the FMC because it violated the act.

The burden of proving the violation would be on the complainant. The FMC would be allowed to suspend the effective date of an agreement up to 180 days.

• Required cartel agreements to allow membership for any carrier willing to service a particular trade, or route, and to permit any member to withdraw from the conference without penalty upon reasonable notice.

• Allowed members of a conference that used a loyalty contract with shippers to take independent action on rates or services under certain conditions. A loyalty contract granted a discount to a shipper that committed all or some of its cargo to the conference. Loyalty contracts tended to bolster conference strength. Independent action would allow a shipper to convince a member of the conference to offer better rates than provided in the loyalty contract.

• Established guidelines for loyalty contracts. The contract must be available to all shippers on equal terms and cover only those goods available to the shipper at the time. The shipper, carrier and conference must be allowed to terminate the contract on 90 days' notice. The contract also must provide for a discount of no more than 15 percent.

Once the rate became effective, it could be increased only after 90 days' notice, except by agreement of the shipper.

• Exempted from antitrust laws any agreement filed under the legislation and any activity or agreement within the scope of the legislation, even if it was in violation of the measure, as long as it was entered into in the "reasonable belief" that it was allowed. Also exempted was any agreement relating to transportation services within or between foreign countries, whether or not via the United States; loyalty contracts; and any agreement or activity to provide terminal facilities outside the United States.

• Barred the private recovery of damages or injunctive relief under the Clayton Act for violation of the legislation.

• Allowed shippers to form a council that could receive certification from the U.S. attorney general that the council's bargaining with a cartel would not be likely to result in a violation of the antitrust laws.

• Required carriers and conferences to file public tariffs of rates, charges and practices with the FMC.

• Allowed a shipper and a carrier or conference to enter into a "service contract" that specified the rate and promised service for specific commitment of cargo.

• Prohibited any new rates resulting in increased costs to shippers from becoming effective less than 30 days after filing with the FMC. The FMC could waive the requirement. Any decrease in rates could become effective upon filing.

• Barred a carrier controlled by a foreign nation from maintaining unjustly low rates or unreasonable rules. The FMC may reject or suspend any charge or rule that the carrier could not demonstrate to be just and reasonable. The president could require the FMC to stay a rejection or suspension for defense or foreign policy reasons.

• Prohibited any carrier from forming a joint venture with others operating in the same trading route if the action "substantially reduces competition." This would not apply if such activity resulted in efficiency improvements that outweighed reductions in competition, and if the activity furthered foreign policy interests of the United States.

A joint venture was a consortium or agreement that would result in a new service operated for the benefit of the agreeing carriers and that eliminated all competition among the parties in the trading route.

• Provided that conduct undertaken by a line in the "reasonable belief" that it was consistent with a cartel agreement would be presumed not to violate the law. The burden of proving the action was in violation would be on the complainant. If the FMC determined that the conduct violated the law, the carrier would not be liable for certain reparations.

• Barred any carrier alone or in conjunction with others from charging rates not specified by tariff; rebating any portion of its rates except in accordance with its tariffs; providing any privilege, concession, or facility other than specified by tariff; or retaliating against a shipper because the shipper patronized another carrier or filed a complaint.

Carriers would be barred from engaging in any unfair or discriminatory practice regarding rates, space accommodations and the handling of freight, and from predatory practices to eliminate competition. Also prohibited would be the pooling of net losses or net profits.

• Barred any conference or group of carriers from boycotting or taking other concerted actions "resulting in a refusal to deal"; restricting the ability of a shipper to select a carrier in a competing trade, an ocean tramp or a bulk carrier; and restricting members' use of technological innovations.

Also barred would be a predatory practice designed to eliminate the participation of any non-member carrier or to deny the entry of a new competitor in a trading route.

• Allowed the FMC on its own or upon complaint to investigate alleged violations of the act, and to order a carrier to pay reparations to an injured party.

• Authorized the FMC on its own initiative or at the request of the U.S. attorney general or Federal Trade Commission to investigate conduct pursuant to an agreement for pooling traffic or revenues if the FMC believed that such conduct "substantially reduces competition." The FMC could reject, modify or terminate an agreement except under certain conditions.

• Provided for civil penalties of up to $5,000 for each violation of the act. In the case of willful violations, the penalty would be up to $25,000.

• Allowed the FMC to exempt any activity from the act if the exemption would not substantially impair effective regulation and would not likely result in any significant lessening of competition in any U.S. trading route. Before the FMC could exempt any activity, it would have to allow federal offices and agencies to comment.

• Extended a provision of a 1981 law that allowed a freight forwarder to arrange a shipment in which he had a direct or indirect interest as long as no compensation was received. *(1981 Almanac p. 570)*

• Created a commission to make recommendations about the deregulation of ocean shipping, including the impact of antitrust laws upon U.S.-foreign relations.

Senate Action

The bill reported by the Senate Commerce Committee May 25 (S Rept 97-414) was similar to a measure (S 2585) passed by the Senate in 1980. However, the new bill eliminated a requirement that the FMC approve a conference agreement before it became effective. *(1980 Almanac p. 259)*.

Provisions

As reported, S 1593 would:
• Set objectives to encourage rates and practices to be

internationally competitive and to allow common carriers "complete" immunity from antitrust laws for international liner activities.

● Allowed carriers to meet in conferences to discuss and fix rates and conditions of services; pool earnings, losses and traffic; restrict the number of sailings; prevent competition; and consult with shippers or shipper groups on general rate levels, practices and services.

● Allowed marine terminal operators to jointly fix rates and service conditions, and pool earnings or traffic.

● Permitted shippers to establish councils to discuss general rate levels, practices or services; agree on positions; and consult with any carrier or conference regarding general rate levels, practices or services. The councils could not actually negotiate common rates.

● Required carriers to file agreements on authorized activities with the FMC, which could reject any agreement that failed to comply with the law. An agreement would become effective 45 days after filing.

● Required conferences to provide reasonable terms for admission and readmission to conference membership. Any member may withdraw from membership without penalty upon reasonable notice.

Conferences would have to include procedures for considering shippers' requests and complaints.

● Allowed members of a conference that used a loyalty contract with shippers to take independent action on rates or services under certain conditions.

● Required every shippers' council agreement to provide for voluntary membership and allowed members the right of independent action with any carrier or conference.

● Allowed any carrier or conference to use a loyalty contract under certain conditions.

● Extended antitrust immunity to conference activities permitted by the legislation; any agreement or activity that related solely to ocean services within or between foreign countries; and any activity that related to shippers and councils organized under foreign laws and operating outside the United States, even when affecting U.S. cargo.

● Required carriers, conferences and terminal operators to file tariffs of rates, rules and practices with the FMC.

● Allowed a shipper and a carrier or conference to enter into a "service contract" that specified the rate and the promised services for specific commitment of cargo.

● Barred any increase in existing rates earlier than 30 days after filing with the FMC, except under special circumstances. A decrease could become effective upon filing. The FMC would not review the rate level for reasonableness.

● Prohibited a carrier owned or controlled by a foreign country from maintaining unjustly low rates or unreasonable rules. If the FMC rejected the rates or rules, the president could require the commission to stay its order for national defense or foreign policy reasons.

● Continued prohibitions against rebating, the offering of discounts or kickbacks lower than filed tariff rates in order to secure cargo. *(1979 Almanac p. 349)*

● Prohibited any carrier alone or in conjunction with others from charging more than the rates listed in its tariffs or retaliating against a shipper because the shipper patronized another carrier.

A carrier could not make any unjustly discriminatory contract with a shipper or port in regards to rates, services and access to cargo. Also, carriers could not collectively engage in predatory practices to eliminate competition. ▪

Alaska Railroad

Congress Dec. 21 completed action on legislation (HR 3420 — PL 97-468) providing for the transfer of the Alaska Railroad to the state of Alaska, thereby ending a bitter dispute between two senators.

The compromise, worked out by Senate Majority Whip Ted Stevens, R-Alaska, and Sen. Howard M. Metzenbaum, D-Ohio, provided for the U.S. Railway Association (USRA) to determine the fair market value of the railroad. That appraisal would then be used in negotiations for the sale of the federally owned railroad. The state would not have to buy the railroad if it did not like the price.

Metzenbaum had blocked passage until the waning hours of the lame-duck session of legislation to turn the railroad over to the state, contending that it was a federal giveaway.

Stevens accused Metzenbaum of being an obstructionist. Metzenbaum at one time called Stevens "the Alaskan oil and gas senator."

The compromise was tacked onto HR 3420, an unrelated measure making technical changes in pipeline safety law. The Senate and House cleared the bill by voice votes Dec. 21.

Also tacked onto the bill were a number of railroad provisions from other measures (HR 6308, S 1879, S 1500, S 2301, S 2430). The bill included funding authorizations for labor protection benefits to Rock Island Railroad employees and transition costs for transferring Conrail commuter lines to other agencies.

Parliamentary Maneuvers

The House and Senate passed differing versions of HR 3420, to authorize pipeline safety programs, in 1981. *(1981 Almanac p. 582)*

In an effort to break the 1982 deadlock on the Alaska Railroad measure, the House Dec. 20 called up the Senate-passed version of HR 3420 and eliminated the pipeline safety authorizations and other provisions. It then attached Alaska rail transfer language, other railroad provisions and a shipping antitrust measure, and requested a conference with the Senate. *(Maritime antitrust, p. 343)*

The maneuver was designed to head off a Metzenbaum filibuster and allow the Alaska bill to be brought up on the Senate floor.

Metzenbaum also was blocking consideration of a Commerce Committee shipping antitrust bill (S 1593), which would broaden antitrust immunity for ocean liner cartels.

Sidestepping a conference on HR 3420, the Senate Dec. 21 substituted the Stevens-Metzenbaum Alaska Railroad compromise and stripped the shipping provisions from the bill. The House then accepted the new Senate version, clearing the bill.

Alaska Dispute

The House had included in an omnibus railroad bill (HR 6308 — H Rept 97-571, Pts. I and II), passed Aug. 12, a provision that would have transferred the Alaska Railroad to the state. The state would have been required to pay an amount equal to 75 percent of the net liquidation value of the rail properties. The Congressional Budget Office said one estimate of the cost was $183 million but added that the final figure might be substantially different.

Metzenbaum had blocked Senate floor action on a bill, reported by the Commerce Committee June 22 (S 1500 — S Rept 97-479), that would have transferred the railroad to the state for no payment. The state would have been responsible for the railroad's liabilities and obligations.

But while the state was willing to take over the railroad, it did not want to pay for it. Alaska officials contended the state would be responsible for more than $100 million in necessary improvements, and the transfer would be subject to costly employee protection conditions and probably to existing claims to some railroad lands.

Stevens said the railroad had been for sale on the private market since 1970, but there had been no offers. He noted that the railroad moved heavy equipment to four military bases in Alaska.

Metzenbaum contended that the railroad and its properties might be worth more than $500 million. "I think the Alaska Railroad bill is just nothing more than a boondoggle for one state," he said in the early morning hours of Dec. 21 during debate with Stevens over the railroad.

However, he and Stevens subsequently worked out a compromise that established a process for determining the value of the railroad and transferring it to the state.

As passed by the House, HR 6308 also authorized $52 million in fiscal 1983 for the Federal Railroad Administration (FRA) safety programs and $52.7 million in 1984; authorized $75 million to pay transition costs of the transfer of Conrail commuter lines to an Amtrak subsidiary and other agencies; and required the appropriation of all the $2.5 billion authorized for the Northest Corridor project.

Other Provisions

As cleared, HR 3420 also:

● Authorized a $35 million grant for labor protection benefits for former Rock Island Railroad employees. Earlier legislation (PL 96-254) had required that $75 million be paid in benefits to former employees of the bankrupt railroad. But the Supreme Court March 2 struck down the provision, saying it was unconstitutional for Congress to pass a bankruptcy law applying to only one bankrupt organization.

● Authorized $75 million for the transition costs of the transfer of Conrail commuter lines to an Amtrak subsidiary and other commuter agencies. The funds would be in addition to $50 million previously authorized to help in the transfer of commuter lines inherited by Conrail, the federally subsidized freight railroad. *(1981 Almanac p. 561)*

● Required the eventual appropriation of the entire $2.5 billion authorized for the Northeast Corridor improvement project and identified specific improvements to be accomplished. The corridor runs from Washington, D.C., to Boston. The administration in 1981 announced it would reduce the scope of the project and spend only $2.19 billion. *(1981 Almanac p. 566; 1980 Almanac p. 238)*

● Authorized $52 million in fiscal 1983 and $55.3 million in fiscal 1984 for Federal Railroad Administration (FRA) safety programs.

● Required the transportation secretary within one year after enactment to issue rules to require that the construction, maintenance and operation of rail equipment be done in a manner to increase the safety of passengers.

● Authorized $55 million for fiscal 1983-1985 for a loan program that helped railroads repair and rebuild facilities and equipment.

● Authorized $15.6 million in fiscal 1983 for the Office of the Administrator of the FRA.

FTC Rule Vetoed

The Federal Trade Commission's rule requiring car dealers to disclose information about auto defects in 1982 became the first victim of the FTC legislative veto Congress had enacted in 1980.

The rule was blocked May 26 — the last day allowed by law for congressional action — when the House voted 286-133 to endorse a resolution of disapproval (S Con Res 60). The Senate had agreed to the same resolution by a vote of 69-27 May 18. *(House vote 101, p. 30-H; Senate vote 121, p. 24-S)*

While legislative vetoes had been included in about 200 laws, the 1980 FTC authorization act (PL 96-252) was the first to permit Congress to veto any rule of the independent agency. Both chambers had to adopt a resolution of disapproval. The president's signature was not required. Floor action to disapprove the rule in 1981 had been blocked by a parliamentary maneuver. *(1981 Almanac p. 582; 1980 Almanac p. 233)*

The Consumers Union of the United States challenged the constitutionality of the veto in the U.S. Court of Appeals for the District of Columbia *(Consumers Union of the United States Inc. v. FTC)*. It argued that the veto process was invalid because the president's signature was not required and noted that the Constitution required approval by both houses and review by the president to enact a law.

The appeals court Oct. 22 overturned the veto, and the Senate appealed the decision to the U.S. Supreme Court.

Legislative vetoes involving other agencies were also under fire, but some cases involved narrow grounds not applicable to the veto of the FTC rule.

The veto of the rule was criticized by FTC Commissioner Patricia P. Bailey, who led the agency's fight to prevent the veto.

"A review of the congressional calendar reveals that the used-car rule was the major consumer protection initiative that has been considered by the Congress during this session," Bailey said.

The vetoed rule, issued in 1981 after almost 10 years of investigations, hearings and deliberations, would have required used-car dealers to disclose major known defects in automobiles and the extent of warranty coverage.

Dealers contended that expensive inspections would be required to protect them from possible litigation, thereby adding to the cars' cost. Industry officials said they would support warranty disclosure.

Consumer advocates and other supporters of the rule said it was a modest consumer protection measure and did not require inspections.

After the House action, James J. Florio, D-N.J., chairman of the House Energy and Commerce Committee's consumer subcommittee, predicted that special interests, "smelling blood," would seek further limits on the FTC during consideration of the agency's reauthorization.

However, additional limits were not approved because the authorizing legislation died in a dispute over a provision exempting doctors and other professionals from FTC regulation. *(FTC authorization, p. 347)*

Senate Action

The Senate used-car debate May 18 on the veto pitted Commerce Committee Chairman Bob Packwood, R-Ore., a supporter of the rule, against Robert W. Kasten Jr., R-Wis., chairman of the panel's Consumer Subcommittee.

Packwood said a veto of the FTC rule would send a message that "We endorse shabby practices. We endorse cheating. We will take no action against those who would deliberately deceive."

Joining Packwood, were Slade Gorton, R-Wash., and John C. Danforth, R-Mo., both of whom had been attorneys general of their states. The National Association of Attorneys General supported the rule.

Gorton said the rule would benefit both consumers and "the best and most principled dealers" by offering customers more information, preventing potential complaints and helping dealers compete against less principled businessmen.

Packwood added that the Magnuson-Moss Act (PL 93-637) required the FTC to decide whether to issue a rule on used-car warranties and practices. *(1974 Almanac p. 327)*

Support for Veto

Kasten argued for the veto, saying the issue was one of states' rights. He said that while there may be a need for consumer protection, the rule was an unnecessary federal intrusion in an area best left to state regulation and enforcement.

"I believe that we should not be afraid to use the legislative veto and other tools that are available to regain control of the government," he said.

Packwood noted that no group representing state interests testified for the veto.

Larry Pressler, R-S.D., chief sponsor of S Con Res 60, charged that the rule would give more protection to dealers than to consumers. Dealers, he said, could say they were unaware of any major defects even if that were not true.

Pressler also argued that the rule would add $150 for inspections to the cost of a car and create enormous paperwork burdens for dealers.

Senate Committee. The Senate Commerce Committee March 29 ordered the resolution of disapproval (S Con Res 60) reported by a 12-5 vote. The resolution was reported May 12.

House Action

An overwhelming rejection of the used-car rule seemed certain after the House May 26 voted 317-92 to limit debate on the resolution. Energy and Commerce Committee Chairman John D. Dingell, D-Mich., offered the motion, but Toby Moffett, D-Conn., a supporter of the rule, had sought the entire 10 hours of debate allowed by the 1980 FTC law. *(Vote 100, p. 30-H)*

Car dealers lobbied heavily for the veto. Reports filed with the Federal Election Commission showed that the political action committee of the National Automobile Dealers Association (NADA) gave more than $1 million to the campaign coffers of members of Congress from 1979 through 1980.

NADA officials said the contributions were not tied to specific legislation. And members who received the contributions said they were not influenced by the money.

However, Moffett charged that Congress was being manipulated by a special interest group that "pumped

hundreds of thousands of dollars into members' campaigns."

"[W]hat we have at work here is money influencing political decisions. It embarrasses me," Thomas J. Downey, D-N.Y., added.

Supporters of the rule argued that it provided consumer protection without hurting honest dealers.

"There is no burden on the dealer that makes this rule particularly burdensome, except the burden of telling the truth to the used-car purchaser," Florio said.

Others warned that a veto of the used-car rule would have a chilling effect on other FTC proposals.

But critics said the rule would result in higher car prices.

Gary A. Lee, R-N.Y., said the rule was "intellectually dishonest" in saying that inspections would not be required but then delineating procedures for carrying out inspections.

He also said the rule would be "anti-consumer" because it would not affect private sales, which accounted for 50 percent of the market. "The casual market provides no consumer protection for the buyer as the purchaser accepts the vehicle as is," he said.

House Committee. The House Energy and Commerce Comittee May 5 approved the resolution of disapproval by a 26-14 vote. It was reported (H Rept 97-586) May 25. It had been approved April 21 6-4 by Florio's Commerce, Transportation and Tourism Subcommittee. ∎

FTC Restrictions

The Federal Trade Commission (FTC) escaped having new restrictions imposed on its powers in 1982, despite a drive by business and professional organizations.

The chief target involved FTC efforts to regulate doctors and other professional groups. The American Medical Association (AMA), which lobbied for an exemption for the professionals from agency authority, argued that the FTC had no mandate from Congress to regulate professions already licensed by states and that the agency was interfering in quality of care issues.

Agency spokesmen and their supporters countered that the FTC authority was needed to prevent professionals and their associations from conducting boycotts, price-fixing and other activities that limited competition, led to higher consumer costs and reduced the choice of services.

The battle over new restrictions was fought on several fronts: the agency reauthorization, its appropriations and a continuing resolution providing funding for the government.

The House Dec. 1 passed a bill (HR 6995 — H Rept 97-809, Parts 1 and 2) reauthorizing the agency after adopting an amendment exempting professionals from FTC jurisdiction. It also limited FTC regulation of unfair or deceptive business practices or false advertising.

But Senate opponents of the exemption blocked an authorization (S 2499 — S Rept 97-451) that contained it, thereby preventing the two chambers from agreeing to a compromise bill with the exemption. The 1980 authorization (PL 96-252) for the agency expired Sept. 30. *(1980 Almanac p. 233)*

On Dec. 9, House supporters of the FTC used a parliamentary maneuver to knock funding for the agency out of the 1983 State-Justice-Commerce Appropriations bill (HR

6957). That headed off attempts to attach the exemption and other new restrictions to the funding measure.

Then, Dec. 17 while considering the second continuing resolution (H J Res 631 — PL 97-377) that included funding for the FTC, Senators staved off efforts to add an exemption for professionals to the bill. The measure that cleared Dec. 20 eventually dropped the mild language included by the Senate. *(Stories, pp. 246, 238)*

The continuing resolution provided an appropriation of $63.6 million for fiscal 1983 for the agency. It also continued the restrictions provided by the FTC's expired authorization, such as congressional authority to veto agency rules.

The victory against new restrictions came after Congress earlier in the year used that legislative veto authority for the first time against an FTC rule, when it blocked the FTC's used-car rule. *(Story, p. 346)*

Authorizations

House Committee. The House Energy and Commerce Committee Sept.15 reported its authorization (HR 6995 — H Rept 97-809, Part 1). It had ordered the bill reported by voice vote Aug. 18.

The panel rejected an amendment offered by William E. Dannemeyer, R-Calif., that would have reduced the authorized funding to the level requested by President Reagan. The amendment proposed $60.8 million in fiscal 1983; $55.1 million, 1984; and $54.6 million, 1985. The 1982 authorization was $80 million. The bill would authorize $66.08 million in fiscal 1983 for FTC activities; $70.7 million, 1984; and $75.65 million, 1985.

As reported, HR 6995:

● Defined an unfair act or practice that could be regulated as one that caused or was likely to cause substantial injury to consumers, which was not reasonably avoidable and which was not outweighed by benefits to consumers or to competition.

Those standards were part of FTC policy but were not written into law. Some consumer advocates argued that a statutory definition would limit FTC flexibility.

● Allowed the FTC to consider a rule against unfair or deceptive acts or practices or false advertisements only if it had issued two or more cease and desist orders regarding the act, practice or ad; or if it had "reason to believe" that a pattern of such conduct existed.

● Barred the FTC from conducting investigations or prosecutions of an agricultural cooperative for practices covered by the 1922 Capper-Volstead Act, which gave farmer co-ops a measure of antitrust immunity. But, the FTC would be allowed to scrutinize co-ops that went beyond the 1922 act.

● Allowed Congress to veto an FTC rule if both chambers passed a resolution of disapproval. The president's signature would not be required.

The Rules Committee, which also had jurisdiction over the legislative veto issue, reported an amendment (H Rept 97-809, Part 2) Sept. 20 that would strike the veto provision from the bill.

House Floor Action. The House adopted an exemption amendment backed by the AMA and others before passing the bill Dec. 1. The amendment, offered by Thomas A. Luken, D-Ohio, was accepted 245-155. *(Vote 379, p. 114-H)*

Before adopting the Luken amendment, the House rejected by 195-208 a substitute offered by James T. Broyhill, R-N.C., ranking minority member of the Energy

and Commerce Committee. *(Vote 378, p. 114-H)*

The substitute would have clarified FTC jurisdiction so that any business conducted under the "state action doctrine" could not be challenged. The doctrine provided that anti-competitive activity required and supervised by states would not fall under federal jurisdiction.

Broyhill's proposal had bipartisan support and was endorsed by the FTC and by the Reagan administration.

Luken argued that Congress had never given the FTC the power to regulate professionals. His amendment placed a moratorium on FTC actions against professional groups until Congress specifically granted it the authority.

Besides the exemption for professions, the House slashed FTC funding authorizations by more than $40 million over three years. The cuts, proposed by Dannemeyer, were accepted by a 241-158 vote. *(Vote 380, p. 114-H)*

The House rejected by voice vote the Rules Committee amendment that would have struck the legislative veto.

Senate Committee. The Senate Commerce Committee May 28 reported an authorization bill (S 2499 — S Rept 97-451). The bill had been approved May 11 by a 12-3 vote, over the objections of Chairman Bob Packwood, R-Ore., and Howard W. Cannon, D-Nev., ranking minority member. The other negative vote was cast by Slade Gorton, R-Wash.

An amendment to bar the FTC from regulating professions licensed by states proposed by Ted Stevens, R-Alaska, was accepted by a 10-5 vote. Stevens said that FTC regulation was an unnecessary extension of federal bureaucracy into state matters.

As approved by committee, S 2499:

● Authorized $60.8 million for the FTC in fiscal 1983, $55.1 million in 1984 and $54.6 million in 1985.

● Exempted state-licensed professionals, including doctors and lawyers, from FTC regulation.

● Barred the FTC from regulating ads on the basis that they were unfair.

● Limited FTC authority to regulate other unfair business practices. The bill defined unfair practices as those that had "caused or are likely to cause substantial injury to consumers, which is not reasonably avoidable" and were not outweighed by benefits to consumers or competition.

● Prevented the FTC from taking action against alleged anti-competitive activities by agricultural cooperatives until after the agriculture secretary determined that a challenged activity was outside the scope of the 1922 Capper-Volstead Act. The 1922 act gave farm cooperatives a measure of immunity from antitrust laws.

● Extended the two-house legislative veto of an FTC rule.

Other Action

Rep. James J. Florio, D-N.J., and Sen. Warren B. Rudman, R-N.H., prevented the House and Senate from attaching restrictions on the FTC to either its fiscal 1983 appropriations bill (HR 6957) or the continuing appropriations resolution into which the FTC appropriations were ultimately folded.

Florio, a supporter of the FTC, was chairman of the Energy and Commerce panel's Commerce, Transportation and Tourism Subcommittee, which oversaw the agency. When the House considered the appropriations bill Dec. 9, Florio successfully raised a point of order against the agency's appropriation because no authorization bill had been cleared. The funds were then stricken from the bill.

When the FTC was deleted from the bill, restrictions

on the agency could not be added to it.

The FTC funds were included in the continuing resolution reported by the Senate Appropriations Committee. Also included by the panel was a Rudman amendment that effectively allowed the antitrust regulation of professionals by the FTC as long as it did not interfere with state laws governing training and experience requirements.

The AMA opposed the Rudman language. And when the Senate considered the resolution Dec. 17, James A. McClure, R-Idaho, offered an amendment that would have barred the use of funds by the FTC to regulate professionals already regulated by states. McClure argued that otherwise the FTC still would be able to regulate legitimate activities by professionals. By a 59-37 vote, the Senate agreed to Rudman's motion to table, or kill, the McClure amendment. *(Vote 424, p. 71-S)*

When House and Senate conferees worked out a compromise on the continuing resolution, they also deleted the Rudman language, thus eliminating any restriction on FTC regulation of professionals. ∎

Agriculture

The deteriorating farm economy forced the Reagan administration to make a striking change in its farm policy in 1982.

By the end of the year, the administration was poised to offer farmers both cash and "payments in kind" of surplus crops to not plant wheat, cotton and other major crops in 1983. The goal of the program was to retire as much as half the nation's cropland. *(Story, p. 361)*

Administration officials insisted that the program was a temporary expedient to eliminate the enormous surpluses of major commodities that had accumulated in the nation's storage bins and warehouses. No previous administration, Democratic or Republican, had attempted a production cutback of such magnitude.

Top Agriculture Department (USDA) officials, such as Deputy Secretary Richard E. Lyng, acknowledged that when they took office in 1981, they hardly expected to launch sweeping — if temporary — production curbs. Secretary John R. Block came to Washington advocating all-out production by farmers, with minimum government intervention.

Estimates of farm income for 1982 were so grim that early in the year, USDA stopped publishing them. When pressed to defend that move, Block and his economists usually said that income predictions were meaningless because it was so difficult to anticipate weather, world markets and other variables.

But Block also told a Senate subcommittee, "The truth is, the department doesn't want to give validity to the horror stories. The forecasts give credence to what farmers around the country are saying and feeling."

What farmers were saying was that 1982 was the worst year for agriculture since the Depression of the 1930s. Farm-income and parity figures, dipping to 50-year lows, seemed to bear that out. Parity, the economic index of farmers' purchasing power, stood at 57 percent in December; the previous low of 58 occurred in 1932. The final 1981 figure was 61 percent.

Export Safety-Valve

The underlying problem was that world markets had gone sour while farm production peaked. Global recession and aggressive competition for markets by other agricultural exporters lessened demand for American commodities. The continuing strength of the U.S. dollar, compared with other currencies, was also damaging. It meant that although U.S. commodities were selling for bargain-basement prices, their cost in foreign currencies kept rising to uncompetitive levels.

For more than 10 years, U.S. farm policy and individual farmers' decisions to gear up production had been based on an assumption that the world would buy as much as America could grow.

But in 1982, for the first time in a decade, U.S. farm exports instead declined in value, to $40.5 billion, from a record 1981 level of $43.5 billion.

The slump coincided with the second year in a row of record high yields. USDA officials reported that America was ending the year with surpluses unequaled in magnitude for 20 years.

"Ending stocks" — commodities for which there was no commercial demand at the end of the year — were estimated at about 150 million metric tons. That was nearly enough to meet the nation's domestic needs for a full year.

There were other disheartening statistics too. Farm loan delinquencies rose. Private banks expected that as many as one-fourth of their farm customers would fail to qualify for financing another year.

The growth in farm land values, which had supported much farm borrowing for expansion during the 1970s, turned around. Agricultural land values registered a 1 percent decline in March.

Farm Income Declines

Not until September did USDA come forth with a 1982 net farm income estimate of $19 billion. That was a sharp drop from a 1979 high of $32.7 billion and about the same as 1981.

During the year, however, unofficial department estimates and projections by private economic forecasters had placed net farm income as low as $15 billion to $16 billion. The department did not publish its total until September, when it could include some $4 billion in early payments to farmers. The advance payments were for one type of price supports known as deficiency payments, and for farmers promising to retire farm land in the coming crop year.

The pre-election injecton of cash had been proposed by the administration and approved by Congress, which increased the amount that could be paid out before customary dates.

In all, the government spent an unprecedented $12 billion in fiscal 1982 to prop up farm income; that included the $4 billion in advances for deficiency and land diversion payments, price support and reserve loans to farmers, and about $2 billion in payments under the surplus-swollen dairy program.

The total was about four times the annual average for the preceding decade.

USDA historians said that while total farm income figures, adjusted for inflation, were the same as those of the Depression, the comparison was not totally valid.

Fifty years ago, there were more farmers to divide up the income and no federal programs such as farm loans and price supports, they said. And, by 1982, off-farm jobs had become a major source of income for farm families.

Nevertheless, as one department publication observed in November, "Pretty generally, it was a bad year."

Other Developments

The president extended the U.S.S.R.—U.S. grain sales trade agreement for one year, but Soviet buyers showed little interest in American grain and instead concluded major new sales agreements with Canada and other competing suppliers.

Reagan sought to stimulate sales when he announced Oct. 15 that if Soviet buyers completed contract and delivery agreements by specified deadlines, he would guarantee delivery for 23 million metric tons of grain. The grain sales agreement's basic guarantee had covered a minimum of 6 million tons. The offer had little visible effect on depressed grain markets.

Europeans, incensed at Reagan's efforts to cut off sales of technology and equipment for a Soviet natural gas pipeline, criticized the grain offer.

Sugar Quotas. The administration departed conspicuously from its advocacy of free trade in May when the president announced an immediate restriction on the amount of sugar imported into the United States. A world glut had pushed sugar prices so low that the federal government was faced with program payments to sugar producers of as much as $800 million. The quota survived an unsuccessful lawsuit by outraged sugar refiners.

GATT Talks. High-level trade talks in Geneva, Switzerland in November failed to produce any change in European farm export subsidies. American farmers believed the subsidies were a contributing factor to their financial problems.

American delegates to the meeting of the General Agreement on Tariffs and Trade (GATT) sought unsuccessfully to win a freeze and then a gradual elimination of subsidies by all producing nations. But European officials refused even to discuss their commodity subsidies. When USDA officials returned to Washington, they renewed threats of retaliation, but later softened their statements after resuming discussions with European trade officials.

Blended Credit. Using funds appropriated to promote exports, the administration launched what it called a "blended credit" program, in which interest-free federal loans could be used in combinations with federally guaranteed commercial loans to provide lower-interest financing for farm exports.

Committee Changes

It was difficult to distinguish the effect of farm problems from other factors in the November congressional elections. Still, the election cost the House Agriculture Committee its ranking minority member William C. Wampler, Va., and committee veterans Paul Findley, Ill., and Tom Hagedorn, Minn. All three Republicans had stoutly defended administration farm priorities in committee. Other committee Republicans who were defeated were John L. Napier, S.C., and Clint Roberts, S.D.

The Senate Agriculture committee lost one Republican, S. I. "Sam" Hayakawa, Calif., to retirement.

—By Elizabeth Wehr

Western Reclamation Water Law Rewritten

Congress intervened in a long-running dispute between environmentalists and Western farmers over the use of subsidized water from federal reclamation projects by substantially rewriting a 1902 water law.

The bill (S 1409 — PL 97-293) cleared by Congress Sept. 29 increased the number of acres of land irrigated by low-cost federal water that an individual could own. The old limit set by the 1902 water law was 160 acres per individual or 320 acres for a farmer and spouse; the new one was 960 acres for an individual or small corporation.

The bill also permitted water service to leased acreage beyond the new ownership limit and raised the price of that water, bringing the government closer to recovering the costs of constructing and operating the massive Western water projects. Another provision repealed the 1902 requirement that farmers live on or near their irrigated farms.

Environmentalists decried what they viewed as a giveaway to large corporate farms. They had wanted strict enforcement of the 160-acre limit to force the breakup of large agricultural operations and to redistribute the irrigated land to small farmers.

Supporters of the bill said that the final measure reflected modern farm practices and that the new prices — raised significantly for the first time since 1902 — would correct inequities while promoting water conservation.

Sharp differences required a House-Senate conference. The House had set the basic ownership limit at 960 acres, while the Senate established it at 1,280 acres. The chambers also differed on conditions under which water contracts could be reopened and the price of water increased to reflect real costs.

Morris K. Udall, D-Ariz., chairman of the House Interior and Insular Affairs Committee, refused to go to conference until an unrelated Indian water dispute was settled. Eventually, the reclamation provisions (HR 5539) were incorporated along with the Indian water rights matter into S 1409, a bill to enlarge a Wyoming dam. *(Story, p. 449)*

The conference, however, was stormy. The first three sessions Sept. 14, 15 and 16 were dominated by Sen. Howard M. Metzenbaum, D-Ohio, who had almost single-handedly delayed Senate voting on its original bill to win concessions.

Metzenbaum repeatedly told conferees that farmers should pay more for water than either the House or Senate bill required. His persistent complaints about "subsidies to people who don't need subsidies" prompted a dry lecture from Udall on the broad public benefits of federal investments. Udall noted that Midwesterners were not asked to repay the government for publicly financed watershed projects and other improvements.

Metzenbaum's pressures had some effect, however. To assuage him, conferees adopted a combination of the House- and Senate-passed formulas determining the rate of interest to be charged farmers in repaying the cost of reclamation projects and added a minimum rate of 7.5 percent. The Senate had no minimum, and the House minimum was 5 percent. They also modified House language permitting farmers to evade the new limits by following the old law.

The conference agreement (H Rept 97-855, S Rept 97-568) filed Sept. 22 was approved by the Senate Sept. 24 by voice vote and by the House, also by voice vote, Sept. 29, clearing the measure for the president.

Final Provisions

As signed by the president, PL 97-293:

BUFFALO BILL DAM

● Authorized $106.7 million for building and operating enlargements of the Buffalo Bill Dam and Reservoir in Wyoming.

RECLAMATION WATER

Acreage Limits and Water Prices

● Stipulated that new acreage limits and payment provisions applied to contracts made with the secretary of the interior after the effective date of the act and to existing contracts that were revised to provide additional benefits or to conform to the new law.

● Permitted water districts to choose whether to comply with the new law or to stay under the old law with its 160-acre ownership limit.

● Required farms in districts governed by existing law to pay "full cost" for water for acreage in excess of 160 acres, with the cost calculated under a new formula beginning four and one half years after enactment. "Full cost" referred to the amount required to recover federal expenses for construction and operation of the water projects.

● Permitted individual farms in districts choosing the old law to elect instead to comply with the new law.

● Changed the acreage an individual or corporation of 25 persons or fewer could own to be eligible to receive subsidized water from 160 acres to 960 acres. A larger corporation or other legal entity of more than 25 persons could own up to 640 acres. Permitted farms to lease unlimited additional acreage but required payment of the new full-cost rate for reclamation water used on the extra land.

● Required owners of land exceeding the new ownership limits to put such land under "recordable contract" with the secretary of the interior, to be sold. The sale must take place within 10 years, as under existing law, for excess land owned at the time of enactment. For contracts completed after enactment, the sale must take place within 5 years.

● Permitted owners with land under recordable contract at enactment to revise those contracts to conform with the more generous new ownership limits.

● Affirmed that owners with land under recordable contract at enactment would have a full 10 years to sell the land, not including delays caused by the secretary. The secretary had imposed a moratorium on recordable contract sales in 1976 after a court found fault with the way some sales were conducted. The moratorium was still in force in the very large Westlands district in California when Congress acted.

● Permitted delivery of subsidized water to land exceeding the new ownership limits only if it was under recordable contract and only for the period of the contract. But, permitted an additional 18 months of subsidized water service for land under contract at the time of enactment, if those contracts had expired so that full-cost payments would start as soon as the moratorium was lifted.

● Established new full-cost payment rates for water service to leased acreage exceeding new owned acreage limits.

For individuals and small corporations in existing reclamation projects, the new rate would apply to leased acreage in excess of 960 acres; the existing subsidized rate would apply on owned or leased land up to 960 acres. For larger corporations receiving water before Oct. 1, 1981, the new rate would apply to land in excess of 320 acres.

The new rate would reflect unpaid project construction costs, plus interest, as determined by an average of all Treasury obligations at the time expenditures for a project were made. The interest rate formula followed the House proposal, except conferees specified that the interest rate could not drop below 7.5 percent.

Individuals in new projects and larger legal entities receiving water after Oct. 1, 1981, also would pay a new rate reflecting unpaid construction costs but with a different interest rate formula as passed by the Senate, and also with a 7.5 percent minimum.

Individuals and small corporations in new projects would pay the new rate for acreage in excess of 960 acres; larger corporations would pay it on all their land.

● Required annual updating, for all irrigated acreage, of the rates for payments by water users for the operation and maintenance of the projects. Under existing law, some contracts required updating every five years, while others set a single rate for the life of the user's 40-year contract.

● Required farmers in districts covered by the new law to certify to the secretary that they complied with it, specifying how many acres they leased, and also certifying that their rent reflected a "reasonable" value for the irrigation water. (This provision was intended to discourage evasion of acreage and pricing limits by token leases.)

Other Reclamation Provisions

● Directed the secretary to promote water conservation and required water districts to develop conservation plans, with goals and timetables for achieving them.

● Repealed the requirement that a farmer must live on or near the farm to be eligible for project water.

● Permitted subsidized water service to acreage in excess of the new limits if the land was less productive because of such factors as a short growing season or high altitude.

● Exempted land irrigated by Corps of Engineers projects from acreage limits, except for projects designated by federal statute as part of a federal reclamation project or corps projects in which reclamation construction had created ways to control or convey water to farm land.

● Ended acreage and pricing restrictions in districts that had repaid project construction costs, but barred lump sum or accelerated repayment unless such repayment was permitted by existing contract. Required the secretary to provide certificates affirming that full payment had been made and that the land was no longer subject to acreage and payment restrictions. Affirmed the validity of certificates already issued before enactment.

● Exempted from the new ownership limits land held in trust for one or several individuals whose interest did not exceed the limits; land receiving water for not more than a year because of unusually large water supplies; land acquired by involuntary foreclosure or similar process; land so isolated as to be unworkable unless included in a larger farm; and land under contract that required contract-holders to reduce groundwater pumping by the amount of reclamation water they received.

Only the Central Arizona Project qualified for the last exemption; for that project, still to be completed, landowners would be allowed 10-year recordable contracts from the time water delivery began.

● Permitted religious or charitable organizations (those that qualified for federal tax exemption) to be treated as landowners, if the farming was done by the organization and if the proceeds went to charity.

● Permitted temporary use of project water that exceeded demand, for municipal, industrial or other purposes but only under contract requiring payment.

● Authorized suits against the United States regarding reclamation water contracts.

● Required the agriculture secretary to report to Congress, one year after enactment, on production on reclamation-irrigated land of crops considered to be in surplus supply; also, for projects existing at enactment, specified that any limit on water for irrigating surplus crops expired 10 years after the first authorization of the project.

● Provided a blanket validation of district contracts from before Oct. 1, 1981, dealing with "co-mingled" water from reclamation and non-reclamation sources.

● Required a public comment process on new or amended district contracts for reclamation water.

PAPAGO INDIANS

● Authorized reclamation water service for the Papago Indian tribe; authorized a total of $39.8 million in federal appropriations for a tribal trust fund, construction of irrigation facilities and other purposes; specified new limits on tribal use of groundwater; and established procedures for tribal waivers of certain water rights and legal action.

Background

The rancorous dispute over the 1902 reclamation statute had been simmering for years.

The old limit of 160 acres for an owner or 320 acres for an owner and spouse had largely been evaded. Some of the nation's largest federally irrigated farms, particularly in California, covered thousands of acres, although much of the acreage was operated under lease. The question of whether lease arrangements violated the spirit of the 1902 law was at the heart of the dispute.

The old acreage limit had been poorly enforced for generations because of federal laxity, confusion created by later statutes and contradictory interpretations by courts and federal officials.

In 1976, a California group, Land is for People, won a federal court ruling that the group interpreted as an affirmation of the 160-acre limit.

President Carter's interior secretary, Cecil D. Andrus, set about enforcing the limit with a vigor that alarmed much of the farm community and the large corporations with interests in massive farms, particularly in California.

Congress had grappled periodically with the issue since then. The Senate passed a reclamation rewrite in 1979, and the House committee reported a bill in 1980. *(1979 Almanac, p. 688; 1980 Almanac, p. 598)*

In 1981, budget matters pushed the issue off the agenda until December, when the House Interior Subcommittee on Water and Power Resources held hearings.

Interior Secretary James G. Watt said then that if Congress did not promptly amend the 1902 act, he would have no choice but to enforce it.

House Committee Action

The House Interior Committee Feb. 24 completed a rewrite of the 1902 statue. The committee bill (HR 5539 — H Rept 97-458) reported March 15 expanded the acreage limit to 960 acres. It made no change in the basic charge to landowners for the subsidized water.

It permitted water districts, the quasi-public agencies that provided water to individual farms, to choose to remain under the old statute or to observe the new one, and allowed individual farmers in districts choosing the old law to bring themselves under the new one. For most farmers with large holdings, the new law would mean escape from a requirement to sell off excess irrigated acreage.

The committee bill also permitted a farmer to lease an unlimited number of acres that could be watered by federal projects, in addition to the 960 acres owned outright. The farmer would pay for the additional water at a higher rate intended to recoup the costs of the reclamation project.

The committee rewrite meant that about 97 percent of reclamation-irrigated farms would not have to change their present arrangements, Udall said. The remaining 3 percent occupied about 30 percent of federally watered land.

In a hefty catalog published in February of ways to reduce the federal deficit, the Congressional Budget Office (CBO) had observed that farms paid what they could afford for federal water, not what it cost to produce it. Increasing water fees to cover costs, estimated at $50 per acre foot, could save $22 million in 1983 and $375 million in five years, CBO said. If rates were increased to a market level of roughly $100 per acre foot, net receipts in five years would total $800 million, according to CBO.

(An acre foot is the volume needed to cover an acre of land with one foot of water.)

Reaction to Bill

Gordon Nelson of the Farm-Water Alliance was pleased with the bill and predicted smooth sailing for the measure. Nelson, a leading lobbyist for groups seeking liberalization of the old law, also said that the higher rates for water on leased land would not be a major problem for operators of large farms.

Environmentalists and others expressed outrage.

"Yech," was the response of George Ballis of Land is for People. "It's as if we spent 25 years uncovering a crime wave, and Congress handled it by declaring the criminal actions legal," he complained.

Brent Blackwelder of the Environmental Policy Center agreed that the higher water rates would have little impact on large leased farms. "You average the subsidy and the higher cost, and you're still not paying anything like the full price. It's a helluva deal," he said.

House Floor Action

Floor action was temporarily delayed by Richard Bolling, D-Mo., chairman of the House Rules Committee. Bolling said only that he had "some trouble with the bill personally;" he had opposed a 1980 bill that died in the House. A rule was granted May 4, and the House on May 6 approved the bill. *(1980 Almanac p. 598)*

The 228-117 vote passing the measure was a major victory for supporters because the House had strongly resisted earlier attempts to liberalize the law. Still, the nearly 2-to-1 vote occurred amid signs that the legislation was not out of the political woods. *(Vote 61, p. 20-H)*

Sen. Richard G. Lugar, R-Ind., had put a hold on a Senate committee bill (S 1867) setting larger acreage limits to explore alternatives, a Lugar aide said.

Rep. George Miller, D-Calif., told the House that he would fight any move to "ramrod the Senate committee's proposal down the throats of the House in a conference committee." Miller also warned: "I would gladly lead the effort to kill any legislation which weakens the bill before us today."

Bitter Debate

Debate on HR 5539 occasionally turned bitter. Opponents charged that the legislation continued billion-dollar subsidies to wealthy Western agribusinesses. They succeeded in tightening certain provisions through amendments, though they did not change the basic thrust of the legislation. They lost by voice vote on an amendment offered by David F. Emery, R-Maine, to shrink the size of farms receiving subsidized water to 640 acres.

Environmentalists had hoped to block the bill entirely, claiming that it legitimized flagrant and unfair violations of the 1902 law.

Proponents argued that it simply recognized modern farming practices and that western agriculture needed a resolution to the long-running controversy. The higher water prices, they said, would eventually bring about the changes sought by environmentalists.

Among amendments approved by the House:

● By Dale E. Kildee, D-Mich., to permit water service to continue for corporations consisting of more than 18 shareholders if the corporations were receiving project water on or before Oct. 1, 1981, and if they did not own or lease land in excess of 160 acres; and permitted new contracts with corporations not receiving project water on or before Oct. 1, 1981, calling for the corporation to pay the full cost for all water. Adopted, 220-160. *(Vote 60, p. 20-H)*

The committee bill had permitted the larger corporations, like individuals, to receive subsidized water on up to 960 acres of owned land, with a higher rate for additional leased acreage.

● By Kildee, canceling the secretary of the interior's authority to waive civil penalties for violation of certain water provisions. Adopted by voice vote.

● By John N. Erlenborn, R-Ill., to require the Interior Department to review recent internal audits showing poor management in the Bureau of Reclamation, and to act on auditors' recommendations. Adopted by voice vote.

● By Robert W. Edgar, D-Pa., to require water contractholders to develop and carry out conservation measures and to authorize the secretary of the interior to penalize water waste with a surcharge or other measures. Adopted by voice vote.

Senate Committee Action

In a surprise move April 21, the Senate Energy and Natural Resources Committee by a vote of 18-1 approved a bill (S 1867) that greatly enlarged the acreage limit. Metzenbaum voted "no" by proxy, and Lowell P. Weicker Jr., R-Conn., did not vote.

The Senate panel had been expected to wait until after the House acted, but when that bill was delayed in the House Rules Committee, the Senate panel acted to meet the May 15 deadline for reporting legislation with an impact on the fiscal 1983 budget.

Its report (S Rept 97-373) was filed April 29.

Bills Compared

Unlike the House bill, which permitted water districts and individuals to choose whether to observe the new law or the 80-year-old statute it would replace, the Senate committee bill would apply uniformly.

The old law limited to 160 acres the amount of federally irrigated land a farmer could own, or 320 acres for a farmer and spouse.

S 1867 set an absolute ownership limit of 1,280 acres, with additional leasing permitted up to a total farm size of 2,080 acres, to be eligible for subsidized rates. For farms exceeding that limit, a new "full cost" rate designed to recoup government expenses would apply to all leased acreage. A corporate entity of more than 25 persons could own up to 640 acres and lease the remainder.

Full-cost water under S 1867 would be more expensive than under the House bill because the Senate formula used interest rates reflecting current costs to the government of financing a project. According to Interior Department officials, that figure was about 9.4 percent at the time the Senate panel acted, compared with a figure as low as 2 or 3 percent for some projects under the House formula.

Senate Floor Action

The Senate late July 16 approved the bill after an agreement by key members ended a day of delaying actions by Metzenbaum. The bill passed 49-13 after the pact was approved 60-5. *(Vote 228, 227, p. 41-S)*

Some of the major changes made by the agreement were similar to amendments sought by environmentalists and farm critics of the legislation that were voted down during earlier debate July 14 and July 15.

The compromise was agreed to by Senate Energy Committee Chairman James A. McClure, R-Idaho, Malcolm Wallop, R-Wyo., and Metzenbaum. According to Wallop, an amendment circulated but never formally offered by Mark O. Hatfield, R-Ore., was a key part of the pact that broke the impasse.

The compromise reduced the acreage allowance from 2,080 acres to 1,280 acres. It allowed farms of that size to continue to receive reclamation water under existing subsidized rates. As in the original bill, farmers could also receive water on additional acreage, but at a higher cost.

Also changed was a complex formula for the price larger farms would have to pay for the additional water.

Also, the compromise added language to promote the conservation of reclamation water; clarified conditions under which a farmer receiving reclamation water under a flawed contract could sue the federal government; established rules, with a congressional veto, for validation of existing water contracts; and shortened to five years, from 10 years, the period in which certain farm lands that exceeded the new acreage limit must be sold by their owners.

Metzenbaum did not detail his objections to the bill, telling the Senate simply, "This is bad legislation." He delayed action with repeated quorum calls and by offering unlimited amendments. He could use these tactics because the bill had been brought to the floor under an unusual time agreement that permitted unlimited amendments and effectively precluded formal procedures such as cloture that could have stopped him.

His tactics so angered his opponents that at one point Senate Majority Whip Ted Stevens, R-Alaska, told him that he was "violating one of the basic rules of the Senate, which is to be a gentleman."

Metzenbaum replied, "I'm not worried about my reputation as a gentleman in opposing legislation of this kind."

The extent of Metzenbaum's isolation became clear when the Senate rejected his first amendment on July 16 by a 7-75 vote. *(Vote 226, p. 40-S)*

The proposal would have cut out a provision repealing the requirement that farmers using reclamation water live on or near their farm. Afterwards, Wallop snapped, "I think [that] vote gives some indication as to the mood of the Senate, and I would hope that that might not be lost on the senator from Ohio."

But Metzenbaum continued to stall until a late afternoon negotiating session attended by Wallop, McClure, Metzenbaum and others produced the compromise.

Earlier Debate

Most of the debate July 15 was dominated by unsuccessful attempts by Lugar, William Proxmire, D-Wis., and J. James Exon, D-Neb., to impose much higher costs on farmers using the reclamation water.

Lugar suggested that the subsidy was unfairly concentrated in the hands of the West's largest farmers. He said that out of 47,000 farming operations served by reclamation water, the 435 largest farms contained nearly one-fifth of all the federal irrigated acreage.

McClure called Lugar's statistics "totally false." McClure also argued that the effect of Lugar's and Proxmire's amendment would be to force Western farmers to "recapitalize" their farms — in effect, re-buy their basic assets at the current higher interest rates. Irrigation water service, like land, was a capital cost, McClure said.

The first Lugar-Proxmire amendment of July 15, rejected by a 39-58 vote, would have based the formula on the current cost of money to the federal government — about 14 percent at the time of debate, compared to a committee figure of a little more than 9 percent. *(Vote 215, p. 39-S)*

The second version offered by Proxmire on July 15 and killed by a 56-39 vote on a motion to table by Wallop, would have permitted subsidized water to be used by farms up to 960 acres and charged the higher rate for irrigation of additional acreage. *(Vote 218, p. 39-S)*

The Senate by voice vote agreed to an amendment by Alan Cranston, D-Calif., that would permit free use of water from reclamation projects that was flushed through a system to combat salinity or otherwise improve water quality, or that was in excess supply because of flood conditions.

The Senate rejected by a 39-58 vote an amendment by Dale Bumpers, D-Ark., that would have required competitive bidding for all leasing of oil and gas exploration rights on federally owned lands. *(Vote 217, p. 39-S)*

Other Amendments

In other action, the Senate:

● Rejected by a 22-65 vote an amendment by Exon to limit owned acreage to 960 acres and to eliminate a provision for additional water service, at a higher price, to farms exceeding the acreage limit. *(Vote 220, p. 40-S)*

● Rejected by a 29-55 vote an amendment by Daniel Patrick Moynihan, D-N.Y., to compel higher payments for the "full-cost" water and to mandate studies of the feasibility of bringing Corps of Engineers' water projects under reclamation rules for reimbursement by farm water users. *(Vote 223, p. 40-S)*

The Senate substituted its language for the text of HR 5539 before passing the bill July 16. ∎

Industry-Backed Tobacco Bill Cleared

Congress July 15 approved legislation (HR 6590) aimed at eliminating costs to taxpayers of the federal tobacco program.

The legislation represented a critical victory for tobacco interests, who hoped that it would defuse criticism of the controversial program.

Final action came when the House by voice vote accepted minor amendments added by the Senate to the House-passed bill. President Reagan signed the bill July 20 (PL 97-218).

The legislation, sponsored by Rep. Charlie Rose, D-N.C., was in response to a mandate contained in the 1981 omnibus farm bill (PL 97-98) that the tobacco program be run at no net cost to taxpayers, other than administrative expenses. *(1981 Almanac p. 535)*

HR 6590 obligated growers who used the program to reimburse the federal government for losses resulting from the price-support loans that the program provided farmers. They were required to make new "contributions" for this purpose to special funds run by their cooperative marketing associations.

The measure also directed institutional owners of acreage allotments and marketing quotas for flue-cured tobacco to sell these federal "licenses to grow" to farmers who would use them. The bill did not disturb allotment and quota leasing arrangements between individuals.

The industry-backed package of changes in the tobacco program was found inadequate by an anti-smoking coalition of health groups. They criticized its continuation of federal involvement with a product that endangered human health.

Final Provisions

As cleared by Congress, HR 6590:

● Required tobacco producers, as a condition for holding allotments and quotas, to make payments into special funds operated by cooperative tobacco marketing associations. Also required payments, but beginning with the 1983 crop, by owners who leased their quotas. Required the funds to repay the federal government for losses of principal and interest from tobacco price-support loans, which are administered through the associations.

● Authorized the secretary of agriculture to reduce the support rate for any grade of tobacco determined to be in surplus. Such reductions could not bring the weighted average support rate for all types of tobacco below 65 percent of what the rate would have been without the reduction. In a year when there would have been no increase, the overall average could not be less than that of the previous year. (The support rates were based on 1959 tobacco prices, updated by a formula.)

● Permitted an individual producer of flue-cured tobacco in a surplus year to sell up to 10 percent of his crop in a special auction. Such tobacco would not be eligible for price support loans.

● Permitted an owner of a flue-cured tobacco quota to sell the quota to any "active" tobacco farmer within his county and defined an "active grower" as one who "shared the risk" of producing a crop in at least one out of three years preceding the sale. "Sharing the risk" could include investing in at least 20 percent of crop costs or leasing the allotment or quota.

A buyer who failed to "share the risk" of a tobacco crop within 18 months of purchase would be required to sell the allotment or quota. A buyer could not so reduce his acreage, after purchase of the quota, that the quota covered more than 50 percent of his land; to comply with this requirement, he must either buy more land or forfeit a portion of the quota. (This provision was intended to encourage farmers to diversify their crops and not have the bulk of their land in tobacco.)

● Required that allotments and quotas sold to comply with other provisions of the bill should be available to farmers who certified that they intended to become tobacco producers.

● Prohibited leasing of quotas and allotments in the fall, except during natural disaster conditions.

● Required that any corporate or institutional owner of an allotment or quota that was not "significantly involved" in managing or using the land for farming, must sell the allotment or quota by Dec. 1, 1983, or forfeit it. Forfeited quotas would be redistributed by county Agricultural Conservation and Stabilization committees.

House Action

HR 6590 moved quickly through the House, pushed by Rose's desire to have it become law before July 15, the beginning of the 1982 tobacco marketing year.

Rose's House Agriculture Subcommittee on Tobacco and Peanuts marked up the bill June 15, and the full committee reported it June 18 (H Rept 97-613).

The bill was criticized by Paul Findley, R-Ill., who said that it did not go far enough in charging tobacco farmers for the cost of their program. The bill did not require farmers to pay for the administrative costs of the program, estimated at $15.9 million in fiscal 1983.

The bill then passed the House by voice vote June 21. Rose fended off delaying objections in the House but only by promising hearings to foes of the program, led by Rep. Bob Shamansky, D-Ohio.

Anti-smoking forces muted their objections in the House in return for pledges from Rose that he would give them a chance to air their views and offer legislation in the full House Agriculture Committee in 1983.

Rose also promised hearings on two cost issues. One was a proposal that growers also should pay the administrative costs of their program; the second was an unusual tobacco credit procedure used by the Commodity Credit Corporation that lost the federal government nearly $2 million in interest in 1979-80, according to the General Accounting Office.

Senate Action

The Senate passed HR 6590 by a 77-17 vote July 14. *(Vote 213, p. 38-S)*

Backers had sought to bring the bill to the floor before the July 4th congressional recess so that it could become law before the July 15 beginning of the crop year. The Senate Agriculture Committee reported the measure, with amendments, June 24 (no written report). The amendments required farmers of flue-cured and burly tobacco to contribute to the costs of their program.

However, efforts to move the legislation quickly through the Senate were blocked by the leading critic of the tobacco program, Thomas F. Eagleton, D-Mo. After Eagleton prevented quick action on the bill, Agriculture Secretary John R. Block postponed the beginning of the marketing year until July 22.

Prior to passing HR 6590, the Senate refused by a 49-47 vote to subject the controversial program to the periodic congressional review that other major farm programs must endure. *(Vote 212, p. 38-S)*

The 49-47 Senate vote came on a motion by Majority Leader Howard H. Baker Jr., R-Tenn., to kill an amendment by Eagleton. Eagleton proposed to end tobacco price-support loans in 1985, when other farm authorizations expired. The permanently authorized tobacco program was not subject to reauthorization.

He charged that opponents feared routine reauthorizations because "they know the program is so odious, or so odiferous [sic] that a second or third look will reveal more of the shortcomings of this peculiarly popular program."

Jesse Helms, R-N.C., called Eagleton's amendment "unnecessary" and "destructive" and said it "borders on being frivolous." Other opponents of the amendment warned that reauthorization would destabilize tobacco farming.

Walter D. Huddleston, D-Ky., a major advocate of the measure, said that the "big hope" of supporters of the legislation was that it would "lead to the possibility of a totally independent program down the road." Reducing federal involvement in tobacco, he said, lessened opportu-nities for attacks on the program.

Huddleston and his colleagues said that the true target of critics of the program was America's smoking habits. When Eagleton complained of what he called his own "addiction" to cigarettes, Huddleston shot back, "Don't blame the little tobacco farmer for any weakness you may have."

In the only other recorded vote during floor action July 14, the Senate agreed 56-40 to a Baker motion to kill an Eagleton amendment that would have given the secretary of agriculture more discretion to set tobacco price support levels than the bill provided. *(Vote 210, p. 38-S)*

Senate Amendments

By voice votes, the Senate accepted amendments by:
- Eagleton, to require that allotments and quotas sold to comply with other provisions of the bill should be available to farmers who certify that they intend to become tobacco producers.

As written, the bill would have shut out farmers not already involved in tobacco production, Eagleton said.
- J. James Exon, D-Neb., to express the sense of Congress that the president should immediately resume negotiations on renewing the expiring Soviet grain sales agreement.
- Eagleton, as amended by a Huddleston substitute, to reduce the amount of tobacco "floor sweepings" that warehousemen may sell and to double civil cash penalties for exceeding the limit.
- Eagleton, to drop a new authorization for special auction tobacco sales in surplus years.

Farm Programs Cut in Reconciliation

Two farm policy changes aimed at reducing grain and dairy surpluses were included in the omnibus budget reconciliation measure (HR 6955) approved by Congress Aug. 18.

One provided new advance payments to farmers who agreed not to grow major crops. The theory was that the reduced production would lead to higher market prices and subsequently decrease the amounts the government would have to pay in the future for price supports to bolster farm income.

The second change had the effect of cutting up to $1 from the existing dairy price support of $13.10 per hundred pounds, unless dairymen reduced milk production sharply.

However, the final bill dropped controversial House dairy provisions that would have established an industry-dominated board that in some cases could have set the level of price supports and could have levied assessments on farmers to pay for promotional programs.

The measure reduced projected increases in major farm and food stamp programs by $6.6 billion over three years (fiscal 1983-85), according to Congressional Budget Office (CBO) estimates. The reduction was nearly twice the amount mandated by the congressional budget resolution (S Con Res 92). *(Budget reconciliation bill, p. 199; fiscal 1983 budget resolution, p. 186; food stamps, p. 479)*

Final action on the legislation came Aug. 18 when both houses adopted a conference report on the bill (H Rept 97-759). President Reagan signed HR 6955 on Sept. 8 (PL 97-253).

Conference Compromise

The biggest money-saver in the compromise was the dairy plan conferees accepted during their third and final meeting Aug. 16. The dairy program, whose costs were estimated at nearly $2 billion in fiscal 1982, was the most difficult point to resolve; in earlier meetings, the conferees agreed to wheat and grain provisions.

The conferees dropped a House proposal that would have established a two-tier price support system and empowered a new, industry-dominated board to establish the rate of support for a portion of surplus dairy production.

The proposal, written by the National Milk Producers Federation, would have made dairy farmers pay part of the cost of buying and storing millions of pounds of surplus butter, cheese and dry milk.

The administration and some members, however, objected to the cash outlays required and maintained that the plan was antithetical to the policy of minimal government interference in agriculture.

The conferees rejected the plan and instead froze price supports at $13.10 per hundred pounds for the next two years, canceling scheduled annual increases.

Under the final legislation, the government was still required to buy all surplus products at the price of $13.10 per hundred pounds. But the secretary could withhold up to $1 of each $13.10 from payments to dairymen, unless surplus production fell below specified amounts. The withholding was expected to "return" more than $1 billion each

year to the Treasury that would otherwise have been paid out in price supports.

In all, the dairy changes were expected to lower projected spending for the program by $4.2 billion in fiscal years 1983-85, according to CBO. Three-year savings in wheat, feed grain and rice program changes were estimated at $274 million.

Provisions

As enacted into law, the agriculture section of HR 6955:

Dairy Program

● Froze price supports at the current level of $13.10 per hundred pounds for fiscal years 1983 and 1984. For fiscal 1985, the price support would be whatever level of parity $13.10 translated into as of Oct. 1, 1983 — estimated in 1982 at about 61.2 percent, which would convert to about $14.05 per hundred pounds for fiscal 1985.

● Authorized the agriculture secretary to deduct 50 cents per hundred pounds from milk price support payments from Oct. 1, 1982, through fiscal 1985, unless federal purchases of surplus dairy products dropped below 5 billion pounds of milk equivalent annually.

● Authorized the secretary to deduct a second 50 cents per hundred pounds from milk price support payments from April 1, 1983, through fiscal 1985, unless purchases of surplus dairy products dropped below 7.5 billion pounds annually. The secretary could not make the second deduction until he had implemented a program rebating the deduction to farmers who reduced their production.

● Expanded authority of the Commodity Credit Corporation to dispose of federally owned surplus dairy products by donations abroad and to needy households in the United States, with donations overseas coordinated with other aid programs.

Farm Programs

● Required early payments to farmers of one type of price supports known as deficiency payments for fiscal 1982 and 1983. Deficiency payments were paid by the government to farmers when the market price of a commodity failed to reach a higher target price set by law.

● Increased commodity loan rates to $3.65 a bushel for wheat and $2.65 a bushel for corn, 10 cents a bushel more than existing law provided. The rate determined how much a farmer could borrow against his crops.

● Required the secretary of agriculture to offer a 20 percent diversion for wheat, 15 percent for corn and 20 percent for rice.

In each case, a producer must retire the specified acreage to qualify for price supports and other farm programs, and for special diversion payments on 5 percent of his land. The special payment rates were set at $3 a bushel for wheat, $3 per hundredweight for rice and $1.50 a bushel for corn, with the secretary having the authority to lower the rates by 10 percent.

● Mandated that each fiscal year through 1985, from $175 million to $190 million in Commodity Credit Corporation funds be devoted to export promotion.

Food Stamps

The food stamp provisions of the budget reconciliation bill are detailed elsewhere in this volume. *(Story, p. 479)*

House Action

Committee

Separate reconciliation bills (HR 6313, dairy; HR 6793, grain) were considered by various House legislative committees. They subsequently were combined in a clean bill (HR 6892), which became the reconciliation budget-cutting vehicle for final House committee and floor action on farm programs.

The House Agriculture Committee reported HR 6892 on Aug. 2 (H Rept 97-687).

Cuts in the farm programs resulted in the committee exceeding its reconciliation obligations, established in the budget resolution, by a projected $1.3 billion. The changes in the dairy, grains, cotton and rice programs, when added to revisions in food stamps, reduced anticipated federal spending by $4.6 billion in fiscal 1983-85, according to CBO estimates. The panel's three-year reconciliation savings target was $3.3 billion.

The CBO estimates were challenged by administration officials, who contended that, instead of saving money, the bill would add at least $1 billion in new costs. Committee member Paul Findley, R-Ill., also complained that the committee's savings were "ephemeral" and damaging to agriculture in the long run.

But committee members were under strong pressure not only to meet budget reconciliation goals but also to put some cash into the hands of farmers to help them through a third year of high interest rates and depressed market prices. For major crops, the committee authorized payments to farmers who took land out of production.

Former House Agriculture Committee Chairman Thomas S. Foley, D-Wash., sponsor of the committee's wheat and feed-grain plan, said the bill would make the production controls more attractive to farmers and thereby "save some taxpayer dollars." The theory behind Foley's provisions was that if enough farm land was taken out of production, the total supply of grain would shrink, and market prices would rise. And higher market prices would save money for the federal government because farmers' use of price support programs would lessen.

The Reagan administration objected to the cash outlays required by the plan and also disapproved of federal intervention in farmers' production decisions. The deteriorating farm economy, however, had prompted the administration in July to adopt modest production controls for both the 1982 wheat and feed grains crops and for the 1983 wheat crop. Agriculture Secretary John R. Block asked wheat farmers to retire 20 percent of their land in 1983. Those doing so would qualify for advance payment of half their estimated deficiency payments — one type of price support.

Findley objected that a strategy to boost U.S. grain prices while shrinking supplies would invite foreign competitors like Brazil and Canada to increase their own production. The United States would lose more of the world market to competitors, and price-depressing surpluses at home would continue, he predicted.

Amendments Considered. In three days of debate July 27-29, the committee:

● Rejected amendments by Findley to drop the loan rate increases for wheat and feed grains, and to cut the volume of surplus dairy products the federal government was required to buy.

● Adopted amendments by Jerry Huckaby, D-La., to mandate paid land diversion programs for cotton and rice

similar to those for wheat and feed grains.

● Adopted an amendment by Tom Harkin, D-Iowa, to authorize the Agriculture Department to perform the functions of a newly authorized board representing the dairy industry until the board could be appointed. The purpose of the amendment was to speed implementation of the committee's changes in the dairy program so that the panel could claim greater savings in fiscal 1983.

Provisions

As reported by the House Agriculture Committee, HR 6892 contained the following major provisions:

Dairy Programs. For the dairy program, the committee froze current support levels for three years and authorized lower payment rates for a portion of surplus production, with rebates for farmers who cut back production. A newly created industry board would set the lower rates.

The panel hoped to discourage the enormous gains in productivity that increased federal price-support outlays in 1982 to an estimated $2 billion. The government was required to buy, at a fixed price, all butter, dried milk and cheese that was not sold to the public. The Agriculture Department currently bought about 10 percent of all domestic dairy products.

Wheat. The committee raised the loan rate for wheat to $3.80 a bushel in 1983, instead of to $3.55, the 1983 level announced by the Agriculture Department. It also required the secretary to offer a 1983 set-aside program in which producers would take 25 percent of their acreage out of production and receive federal payments for 10 percent of their acreage, at a rate of $3.00 per bushel of expected yield as determined by a formula. (For example, a farmer with 100 acres would retire 25, and receive payments for 10 of those acres.)

Corn. The committee raised the loan rate for corn to $2.71 per bushel, with comparable adjustments for other feed grains. (The 1982 corn rate was $2.55.) The secretary was required to offer a 1983 set-aside program if he estimated that the 1982 crop would exceed 7.3 billion bushels. Producers were to retire 20 percent of their acreage, with payment on 10 percent, at $1.50 a bushel.

Rice. The committee required the secretary to offer a 1983 set-aside program for rice if he estimated that the 1982 crop would exceed 145 million hundredweight. Producers were to retire 20 percent of their acreage, with payment on 10 percent at a rate of $3.00 per hundredweight.

Cotton. The committee required the secretary, if he offered an acreage reduction program in upland cotton, to make payments at a rate of 25 cents per pound on a fourth of the retired acres.

Wheat, Corn and Cotton. The committee required producers to retire the full amount of their acreage to qualify for payments on part of the idled land and or to qualify for price support loans, the farmer-held reserve, farm storage facility loans or the deficiency payments. Farmers were required to observe conservation practices on the land they took out of production. The secretary was required to pay a farmer half the diversion payments as soon as possible after he enrolled in the program.

Food Stamps. The committee was closely divided on the food stamp program but nevertheless approved cuts totaling $1.3 billion over fiscal 1983-85. The reductions were substantially less than the $2.6 billion in cuts approved earlier by the Senate Agriculture Committee. The

CBO estimated the committee's action would save $334 million in 1983, $431 million in 1984 and $561 million in 1985. The reconciliation package extended the authorization for the federal food stamp program through fiscal 1985.

Floor Action

The House passed HR 6892 without amendments Aug. 10 by a 268-121 vote. *(Vote 246, p. 74-H)*

The special rule under which HR 6892 was brought to the floor permitted only two amendments in addition to an Agriculture Committee amendment. They were a Republican substitute, which proposed some additional cuts in food stamps, and a Foreign Affairs Committee amendment to subject dairy product donations authorized by the bill to the administrative procedures used in the Food for Peace (PL 480) program.

The GOP plan was rejected by a 181-210 vote, and the Foreign Affairs amendment was adopted by voice vote. *(Vote 244, p. 74-H)*

Efforts by opponents of the bill to defeat the rule, and then to recommit the bill to the Agriculture Committee, failed by votes of 230-156 and 145-245, respectively. *(Vote 242, p. 72-H; vote 245, p. 74-H)*

A major objection to the bill voiced by Republicans, according to Delbert L. Latta, R-Ohio, ranking minority member of the House Budget Committee, was that neither the farm nor the food-stamp provisions saved the required amounts, despite CBO estimates.

The House bill's proposed dairy industry board, empowered to set some dairy price supports, assess dairymen for promotional activities and dispose of some dairy surpluses, was criticized as unconstitutional and monopolistic.

Latta also warned that the dairy plan would not discourage overproduction as promised, asserting that it would hike price supports to $16 per hundredweight by 1985, compared with the current $13.10 level.

Defenders of the bill insisted that the dairy plan would save money by reducing production and that the bill's payments to farmers for retiring cropland were essential. "I know members have heard time after time about the problems of our farmers. Let me tell them, this time our farmers really have problems," Berkley Bedell, D-Iowa, said.

Senate Action

Committee

The Senate Agriculture Committee, July 26, reported S 2774 (S Rept 97-504) focusing on food stamps and the dairy program to reach its reconciliation savings goals.

Meeting in June and July, the committee approved legislative changes providing an estimated $4.1 billion in savings from the two programs over three fiscal years (1983-85). The budget resolution had instructed the panel to find three-year savings of $3.3 billion.

Since together, the food stamp and dairy program savings were more than enough to meet the reconciliation goal, the committee decided to try to help the ailing farm economy by authorizing additional funds for two agricultural programs. The panel called for advance payment to eligible farmers under the deficiency payment program of price supports for major crops. The committee also approved spending of up to $190 million for subsidies to promote agricultural exports.

Dairy Program Cuts. The dairy changes approved

by the committee froze the existing price support levels for milk. The committee agreed to retain the existing milk price support level ($13.10 per hundredweight) through fiscal 1985. The 1981 farm bill (S 884 — PL 97-98) had called for annual increases in the price level, reaching $14.60 by 1985. *(1981 Almanac p. 535)*

Floor Action

The omnibus reconciliation bill approved by the Senate Aug. 5 (S 2774) included reductions in agriculture, veterans' and banking programs, as well as a 4 percent cap on cost-of-living adjustments (COLAs) for federal and military retirees. Savings in the measure amounted to $2.5 billion in fiscal 1983.

With the approval of S 2774, the Senate had exceeded its savings goal for the next three years.

Besides the cost-of-living adjustment for federal workers, the only other area of controversy involved farm programs. Several attempts were made to increase the agriculture savings, but only one succeeded.

The largest cuts would have resulted from an amendment offered by Paula Hawkins, R-Fla., to lower dairy price supports from the current level of $13.10 per hundredweight to $12.60 on the date of enactment and to $12.00 on Jan. 1, 1983.

Hawkins said the amendment would save $1.2 billion over three years and benefit consumers by $2 billion over the same period, by reducing retail prices of dairy goods.

Supporting the amendment, John H. Chafee, R-R.I., said, "I am for dairy farmers, I am for dairy cows. I like Guernseys and Jerseys and Holsteins. They are all favorites. But we should not be pouring so much money into them, or on them or under them."

But Thad Cochran, R-Miss., argued that the bill would freeze dairy price supports for savings of $1.5 billion over the next three years. Further reforms, if necessary, would be considered by the Agriculture Committee before the end of the session, he said.

Hawkins' amendment was tabled 65-33. Another amendment to limit dairy price supports, offered by S. I. "Sam" Hayakawa, R-Calif., also failed, 48-49.

The Senate did, however, adopt an amendment by David L. Boren, D-Okla., setting up a program to pay farmers for not growing wheat, corn and feed grains. While costing the government money in the first year, the program would save $400 million over three years.

Boren said farmers would receive $120 per acre for the 10 percent additional wheat acreage they set aside and $150 per acre for corn and feed-grains set aside.

The House Agriculture Committee adopted a similar program in its reconciliation bill.

Major Provisions

As passed by the Senate, S 2774 provided for agriculture savings of $4.6 billion in budget authority and outlays in fiscal 1983-85. The legislation would:

● Eliminate scheduled increases in milk price support levels by maintaining the current $13.10 per hundredweight minimum support level through fiscal 1985.

● Require that part of the expected wheat, feed grain, cotton and rice support deficiency payments be paid to farmers in advance at the time of enrollment in the program.

● Authorize use of Commodity Credit Corporation funds to increase agricultural exports by subsidizing interest rates on export loans and direct export subsidies. The net effect of the higher exports would be to reduce price support expenditures by $188 million over three years.

● Require the secretary of agriculture to offer a combination paid diversion/acreage reduction program for wheat, corn and other feed grains. The program would save $400 million over three years. ∎

Giveaway Bills Fail

The Reagan administration failed to win congressional endorsement in 1982 of a major change in farm policy involving payments of federally owned commodities to farmers who reduced acreage.

However, it announced in early January 1983 it would proceed without legislation. *(Box p. 362)*

The Democratic House approved a bill (HR 7439) Dec. 18 involving the so-called payment-in-kind (PIK) program. The bill bypassed committee. However, a more elaborate Senate version (S 3074) became bogged down by deadline pressures. The Agriculture Committee had approved it Dec. 13 (no written report).

Senators testily objected to considering the bill, citing the gas-tax filibuster of Agriculture Committee Chairman Jesse Helms, R-N.C. Shortly after midnight Dec. 20, when Helms told the Senate that PIK legislation was "vital," Paul E. Tsongas, D-Mass., said he would object to consideration of the bill even though he supported it. "I will not participate in anything that rewards" obstructionists, Tsongas declared. *(Gas tax, p. 317)*

Both bills were intended to address what Agriculture Secretary John R. Block called relatively minor changes in the law needed to protect the program from potential lawsuits. Block said the changes would clarify authority he already had.

One would exempt commodity payments in kind from a $50,000 limit on federal farm program payments to an individual farmer. The second would exempt them from a requirement that commodities owned by the Commodity Credit Corporation (CCC) could not be sold for less than 110 percent of the price at which grain could be sold out of the farmer-held reserve.

(The CCC was the Agriculture Department agency that operated price support programs. It became the owner of wheat, corn and other farm commodities when farmers defaulted on federal loans. The reserve program permitted farmers to borrow from the federal government if they agreed to keep their crops in storage and not sell them until market prices reached a fixed "release" level.)

New Program

Under the new program, Block hoped to idle up to half the nation's farm land in 1983. Farmers who agreed to take their land out of production would be paid in corn, wheat and other surplus commodities, in addition to cash payments already announced by Block.

No previous administration had sought a production control program of such magnitude, according to Block's deputy secretary, Richard E. Lyng.

The driving force behind the plan was the massive surpluses in corn, wheat and other major commodities that had been building up for more than a year. Block wanted to rid the nation of the surpluses, while heading off yet another glut in 1983 and giving farmers some income. The

payments in kind could be converted to cash or used as collateral for bank loans, according to Agriculture Department officials.

Surpluses deeply depressed farm prices and drove up the costs of federal price support programs. In fiscal 1982, these programs cost the federal government $12 billion.

Congressional Consideration

On Dec. 9, in addition to requesting the two changes in farm law, Block also asked Congress to freeze one type of price supports, known as target prices, at 1983 levels. The supports were scheduled to rise automatically in 1984 and 1985; the administration believed the increases would inappropriately encourage farmers to grow even more.

On Dec. 13, despite some members' doubts about the PIK plan, the Senate Agriculture Committee unanimously approved legislation (S 3074) making the two law changes Block wanted but not changing target prices. The bill was a rewrite of legislation introduced by Thad Cochran, R-Miss., and Walter D. Huddleston, D-Ky. Cochran's agricultural production subcommittee had endorsed it earlier that day.

S 3074 went beyond the administration's request in several areas. It authorized bonus gifts of grain, cotton, rice or other surplus commodities to foreign purchasers of American farm goods and to domestic processors who planned ultimately to export the processed commodity.

Another section guaranteed minimum prices for farmers when they sold their PIK stocks, even if the federal government had to give them cash payments to make up the difference between a low market price and the level set by the bill.

Other sections expanded CCC authority to donate surplus stocks to needy people at home and abroad, and provided special treatment in the PIK program for farmers who owned more than one farm or who "double-cropped" (planted more than one major crop per year on the same acreage).

The House Agriculture Committee quickly called a hearing Dec. 16 and grilled Block on the plan. When House members asked Block if he would operate the program without legislation, he cited legal problems but said, "We may have the authority and the inclination to go ahead."

The bill ultimately approved by the House involved only the two legal changes sought by the administration.

Dramatic Policy Change

Participation in the PIK program would be voluntary, and Agriculture Department officials said they intended the program to be short-lived — one or two years at the most.

Nevertheless, the decision to seek massive reductions in the volume of grain, cotton and rice grown by U.S. farmers was an extraordinary turnaround for the Reagan administration. Basic GOP farm philosophy held that farmers should profit from growing and selling all they could, with minimal federal intervention. Block had routinely scoffed at the notion of shrinking farm production.

In June, for example, he declared that "we aren't going to be providing any encouragement to idle land or divert it from food crops. I hope we never again find ourselves in the position we were in during the early 1970s, when 62 million acres of farm land were out of production."

Concerns also surfaced during committee hearings. Members worried that the plan:

● Offered no immediate relief to small farmers who

lacked financial backing. Block maintained that the most hard-pressed farmers would benefit the most because they could avoid the costs of planting and still have stocks to sell at harvest time.

● Threatened the survival of rural businesses by cutting deeply into sales of fertilizer, farm equipment and other farm-related products. USDA said representatives of those industries disliked the plan but thought it might be better than continuing low prices for commodities.

● Might fail to head off new surpluses, because farmers tended to retire infertile land for compliance purposes. Block contended that the sheer size of the program and the fact that PIK payments would be based on a farmer's yield would pull fertile acreage out of production.

Block and his chief economist William G. Lesher repeatedly stressed that PIK would not dramatically improve the farm economy in the next 12 months. Lesher said farm prices might go up in 1983, but not by more than 5 percent. He estimated the PIK program would save the government about $3 billion in fiscal 1983-85 ($5 billion if Congress canceled target price increases).

Block said the plan's major benefit would be to assure the economic recovery of agriculture two or three years from now, by eliminating the surpluses that "hang over the market like the dark clouds of a summer thunderstorm." ∎

PIK Program Announced

President Reagan announced Jan. 11, 1983, that the federal government would pay farmers in surplus wheat, corn, cotton and rice to not plant those crops in 1983.

Although Congress in 1982 failed to enact bills to initiate the payment-in-kind (PIK) program, Agriculture Department (USDA) lawyers had resolved legal questions and the government would institute the program administratively, Agriculture Secretary John R. Block explained.

The administration had wanted Congress to exempt it from two statutory limits. One specified that total federal price support payments to individual farmers not exceed $50,000 a year; the second set a minimum price at which federally owned surplus commodities could be sold.

USDA attorneys believed they neutralized the limits by ensuring that farmers received only commodities, not cash, for PIK transactions.

Under the program, wheat, corn, grain sorghum, cotton and rice farmers who joined previously announced acreage reduction programs could receive PIK payments for retiring an additional 10 to 30 percent of their land.

Payment rates were 95 percent of yield per acre for wheat and 80 percent for other crops. Payments would be with crops that farmers had used as collateral for federal price support and farmer-held reserve loans, or from stocks that had become federal property because of default by farmers on the loans.

Payments would be made at harvest times, and to avert dumping the crops on the market and depressing prices, the government would pay storage costs for 5 months or, for reserve crops, 12 months.

Conflicts Doom Passage of Pesticide Bill

Congress was unable in 1982 to reconcile conflicts surrounding a rewrite of federal pesticide law, despite nearly a year of negotiations among interested groups.

Although the House passed a two-year reauthorization (HR 5203 — H Rept 97-566) of the Federal Insecticide, Fungicide and Rodenticide Act (FIFRA), sharp conflicts among environmentalists, pesticide makers and farm groups kept the bill from reaching the Senate floor before adjournment. The Environmental Protection Agency (EPA), which administered federal pesticide programs, could continue its activities with appropriated funds.

The programs involved the registration with the federal government of chemicals used to kill insects, rodents, funguses and plants. To obtain registration — in effect a license to sell a product — manufacturers had to submit data to EPA. The last major rewrite of the law was in 1978. *(1978 Almanac p. 697)*

Key controversies in 1982 were whether stricter state registration laws could pre-empt federal statutes, whether individuals would be able to sue to stop violations of pesticide laws and the confidentiality of industry information filed with state and federal governments.

The House had endorsed major industry proposals when it passed its bill. But it also voted strongly against new limits on state regulation that the industry said it needed to avoid having to comply with many varied state laws. It also eliminated a section the industry wanted restricting access to information.

The House also reinstated the right of individuals to sue that its Agriculture Committee had omitted. The AFL-CIO, migrant farm groups and environmentalists backed the right to sue while the American Farm Bureau Federation objected that it could be used to harass farmers.

Senate Committee. The bill was reported by the Senate Agriculture Committee Sept 20 (S Rept 97-551). The report pleased the industry but drew strong objections from state agriculture officials and environmental and labor groups. There was no right to sue provision.

The bill added five years to manufacturers' patentlike right to market a product without competition and gave the industry new legal ammunition against damaging disclosures of manufacturing secrets. It also imposed new restraints on state authority to regulate pesticides.

The conflicting demands surfaced in the form of amendments by Sen. Robert T. Stafford, R-Vt., and several senatorial "holds" on the measure that blocked floor consideration. Sen. Howard M. Metzenbaum, D-Ohio, also objected to sections extending the time period in which a firm would have exclusive sales, which industry officials said was needed to protect their research investment.

House Action

Before reporting its bill May 17, the Agriculture Committee by a vote of 22-19 canceled a provision to permit farm workers, pesticide factory workers or others who might have been injured by violations of the law to sue for relief in federal courts.

The bill restricted public access to information about the health and safety of pesticides in response to industry arguments that the information constituted trade secrets. Another provision included new protections for workers who protested violations of the law.

The House considered the bill July 26 and before passing it Aug. 11, by a vote of 352-56, reinstated the right to sue and killed the industry-backed provisions involving state pesticide regulation and confidentiality. *(Vote 253, p. 76-H)*

Although the Reagan administration objected that the funding levels were too high, there was no effort to amend the bill to lower them. The bill authorized up to $56.4 million for federal pesticide programs in fiscal 1983, compared with the $44.2 million ceiling sought by the administration.

It also provided for an increase of up to 6 percent of fiscal 1983 funding for the following fiscal year, and up to $4 million annually in matching grants to states or Indian tribes for pesticide licensing and applicator training programs.

The final bill still honored some major industry objectives, and Luther W. Shaw, vice president for public affairs of the National Agricultural Chemicals Association, said he was generally pleased. The bill extended by five years the period of time in which a company could sell a new pesticide or a pesticide approved for a new use, without competition from other manufacturers.

And the new right for individuals to sue was much narrower than a provision permitting companies to collect triple damages. An individual lawsuit could yield neither damage payments nor attorneys' fees — only an injunction against the violation of the federal law.

Industry Defeats

State Regulation. The most emphatic industry defeat came when the House scrapped new limits on state authority to regulate pesticides more strictly than the federal government. The vote on the amendment offered by Tom Harkin, D-Iowa, to drop the limits was 250-154. *(Vote 252, p. 76-H)*

Harkin attributed his success to the amendment's appeal to both environmentalists and advocates of states' rights — "a combination that's hard to beat," he said. Lobbying by the National Association of State Departments of Agriculture and other state officials also was a critical factor, he added.

Manufacturers' allies such as William M. Thomas, R-Calif., said the limits were needed to protect them from the expense of meeting many different state regulations. The disputed section would have set deadlines for state regulatory decisions and would have permitted the EPA administrator to overrule some state requests to manufacturers for health and safety data.

Harkin's primary argument was that the disputed section violated states' rights and would create a "Rube Goldberg system, a spaghetti-works type of nightmare."

Until the end of July, the Reagan administration had objected to the new restraints but then dropped its opposition.

Confidentiality. The second industry-backed section that the House dropped would have kept certain types of information about pesticides from public view for five years after submission by the company to EPA. Industry spokesmen said they needed to protect their costly research from competitors.

Opponents said the section would keep independent scientists from scrutinizing the industry research on which regulatory decisions were made. Some 41 distinguished scientists wrote a letter expressing "grave concern," about the restraints, and the American Association for the Advancement of Science also notified members of their objections.

Elliott H. Levitas, D-Ga., proposed wiping out the entire series of committee restrictions on the release of companies' data, at home and abroad. He and the scientists especially objected to stringent protections for a new category of registration data on innovative methods and technology.

When George E. Brown Jr., D-Calif., chairman of the subcommittee with jurisdiction over the legislation, suggested that only that section be dropped, Levitas agreed to the compromise, and the House approved it by voice vote.

Suits. The third industry loss came when the House adopted, by voice vote, an amendment by Leon E. Panetta, D-Calif., permitting the individual lawsuits.

The House also agreed by voice vote to an amendment by Albert Lee Smith Jr., R-Ala., that directed the EPA administrator to protect unborn children. Smith said that pesticide misuse had been associated with miscarriages and birth defects.

Senate Action

The bill reported by the Senate Agriculture Committee gave pesticide manufacturers important legal tools to use against competitors, individuals who compromised trade secrets and state regulators.

Key senators called the bill a compromise, but it sparked swift and bitter complaints from state government officials, national environmental and labor groups, and an organization of grass-roots groups known as the National Coalition Against the Misuse of Pesticides.

The opponents objected to new restrictions on state regulation, and the omission of a right for farm workers and others to sue to stop violations of pesticide law.

The Senate panel used a reauthorization bill (S 2620) drafted by Chairman Jesse Helms, R-N.C., as a markup vehicle, and then substituted its completed version for the language of the House bill before reporting it.

Helms' bill followed the House version in extending the time period for manufacturers' rights to the exclusive marketing of their products.

Like the House bill, it beefed up penalties for violations of the confidentiality of trade-secret data submitted to EPA as part of the process of obtaining federal approval to market a pesticide.

Helms also had included an industry-backed provision to protect data characterized by manufacturers as "new or innovative technology."

The language permitted scientists to examine the data but barred publication or discussion for five years.

Environmental groups, the March of Dimes and a number of distinguished scientists objected sharply that the section would keep them from evaluating decisions of regulators relating to the health and safety of pesticides. The House dropped the section, and the Senate panel also eliminated it, as part of a compromise package offered by Sen. Patrick J. Leahy, D-Vt.

Elimination of the technology section pleased environmentalist and health groups but did not buy their support.

State Regulation

The restrictions on state regulatory programs were added in committee as an amendment by S. I. "Sam" Hayakawa, R-Calif., and David L. Boren, D-Okla. Their amendment resembled the scuttled House version in setting special conditions on requests from state regulators for more health and safety data from manufacturers than the federal program required.

Like the House measure, the Senate committee bill also set deadlines for state action and required registration — permission to market a product — if states failed to act in time on applications. The only major change from the House version was that federal courts, not EPA, would arbitrate disputes over state data requests.

J. B. Grant, executive secretary of the National Association of State Departments of Agriculture, said any restriction on state authority was unacceptable.

His organization played a major role in persuading House members to drop the state restrictions, but he said the group was not consulted on the Hayakawa amendment. ∎

Firearms for Border Patrols

Congress completed action Sept. 30 on a bill (HR 2035 — PL 97-312) permitting Agriculture Department "tick inspectors" to carry firearms when they patroled the U.S.-Mexico border to prevent livestock smuggling. The inspectors often encountered drug smugglers or illegal aliens.

The bill was reported (H Rept 97-515) by the House Agriculture Committee May 13 and passed the House by voice vote May 18.

The Senate Agriculture Committee reported the bill (S Rept 97-569) Sept. 22. The Senate passed it by voice vote Sept. 29 after adopting an amendment requiring imported grapes to meet quality standards of domestic federal marketing orders.

The House accepted the amended bill, clearing it for the president Sept. 30. It was signed into law Oct. 14. ∎

FmHA Authorization

Bills reauthorizing funding for the Farmers Home Administration (FmHA) died when the Senate failed to act before adjournment.

A measure approved Sept. 9 by the House, in addition to setting overall lending limits for fiscal 1983-85, also would have allowed financially-pressed farmers to put off repaying certain federal loans. The bill, HR 5831, was passed by a 372-39 vote. *(Vote 298, p. 90-H)*

The Senate, however, did not act on its companion measure. The bill reported May 26 by the Senate Agriculture Committee (S 2314 — S Rept 97-422) did not contain a loan deferral provision.

The administration objected strongly to authorizing postponement of FmHA loan repayments. The House bill required deferral to be granted if a farmer could show that his financial problems were not caused by bad management but by circumstances beyond his control, such as national economic conditions.

Advocates said that the depressed farm economy justified deferrals. But Tom Hagedorn, R-Minn., objected that

deferral was an unwarranted "gift" of foregone interest to certain farmers. Hagedorn suggested that all FmHA farm borrowers, whether they had financial problems or not, would try to avoid loan payments next year.

The House bill also exceeded lending ceilings requested in the president's budget and did not include the administration request to limit spending for emergency loans for physical disasters. Furthermore, the House accepted by voice vote an amendment by Jack Hightower, D-Texas, to continue the expiring economic emergency program for another year, also against administration wishes.

Provisions

House. HR 5831 was reported May 17 by the House Agriculture Committee, with a supplemental report filed June 2 (H Rept 97-553, Pt. 1 & II). As passed by the House, the bill reauthorized the following annual ceilings for fiscal 1983-85: real estate loans, $1 billion; farm operating loans, $1.5 billion; emergency disaster loans, in amounts as needed; insured water and sewer facility loans, $500 million; industrial development loans, $1 billion; insured community facility loans, $300 million.

The administration had requested $775 million for real estate loans; $300 million for water and waste facilities; $130 million for community facility loans; and $1.5 billion

for emergency disaster loans instead of an open-ended authorization.

The House bill made other changes designed to increase the availability of loans to hard-pressed farmers.

Senate Committee. The Senate committee also ignored the administration request to cap emergency loans for physical disasters such as drought and to end FmHA financing of rural businesses.

Its bill reauthorized the following loan levels for fiscal years 1983-85: real estate: $818 million; farm operating, $1.6 billion, with 15 percent earmarked for limited-resource borrowers; emergency disaster, in amounts as needed; insured water and sewer facility, $300 million; industrial development, $400 million; and community facility loans, $130 million.

Instead of ending the industrial development loans as requested by the administration, the committee added $100 million to the current fiscal year's authorization for a total of $400 million and raised to 20 percent, from 10 percent, the equity required of borrowers. It also lowered to 80 percent, from 90 percent, the federal loan guarantee and decided to give highest priority for the loans to areas with high unemployment and other economic problems.

The secretary was authorized to make FmHA borrowers buy federal crop insurance where it was available. ∎

Commodity Futures Trading Bill Cleared

President Reagan Jan. 10, 1983, signed into law a bill (HR 5447 — PL 97-444) requiring that the president guarantee the delivery of American farm exports for up to nine months even if he should decide to impose a trade embargo.

Despite an earlier threat of a veto, conferees on the bill reauthorizing the Commodity Futures Trading Commission (CFTC) through Sept. 30, 1986, had agreed Dec. 9, 1982, to retain the so-called "contract sanctity" rider added by the Senate.

The Senate approved the conference agreement (H Rept 97-964) by voice vote Dec. 15; the House followed suit Dec. 16, clearing the measure for the president.

The contract sanctity amendment barred the president from restricting the export of any agricultural commodity under contract at the time an embargo was imposed, if delivery was scheduled within 270 days.

Sponsored by Sen. David R. Durenberger, R-Minn., the provision had been adopted by voice vote before the Senate passed its version of the bill Oct. 1. The bill passed Sept. 23 by the House had no similar language.

Supporters said the guarantee was needed because America's reputation as a reliable supplier of food had been damaged severely by the 1980 embargo on grain sales to the Soviet Union and by earlier trade restraints. *(1980 Almanac p. 93)*

User Fees Added

Other provisions of HR 5447 were intended to strengthen the hand of state law enforcement officials and individuals against fraudulent commodity operators. The bill also ratified an important jurisdictional agreement between the CFTC and the Securities and Exchange Commission (SEC).

In addition, under a compromise worked out between

the commodities industry and the Office of Management and Budget, the final legislation affirmed CFTC authority to charge the industry fees for such services as approval of contracts. Both the House and Senate had rejected attempts to include administration-backed fees on individual commodities transactions, but conferees added the "service fee" language to avert another veto threat to the bill.

The fees would return about $3 million a year to the Treasury, according to Richard G. Lugar, R-Ind., chairman of the Senate Agriculture subcommittee with jurisdiction over the CFTC.

The administration originally had wanted Congress to authorize transaction fees to raise enough revenue to cover most of the CFTC's annual $23 million budget. But the industry objected that the fees would drain financial support from its new, self-regulatory group, the National Futures Association (NFA), and neither the House nor the Senate included the transaction fees in their CFTC bills.

The bill set a deadline by which the NFA must actively share regulatory responsibilities with the CFTC.

Contract Sanctity Issue

The bill's guarantee on delivery of agricultural exports, with an exception only for national emergency or war, drew objections from the State Department because it restricted the president's freedom to act in the future. But because the trade guarantee had wide support within the financially troubled farm community, administration officials had avoided making public objections to it.

Sen. Robert Dole, R-Kan., told conferees Dec. 9 that he and other supporters of the provision had offered to soften the language in conference if the State Department would agree to negotiate a long-term grain sale agreement with the Soviet Union. But "to try to reason with the State Department is, as in any administration, impossible," Dole said.

Futures Industry Definitions

Following are definitions of terms used in the futures trading industry:

Commodity Futures Trading Commission (CFTC): A five-member federal board authorized by Congress in 1974 and charged with ensuring proper execution of customer orders and preventing unlawful manipulation, price distortion, fraud, cheating, fictitious trades and misuse of customer funds. Among its duties are licensing exchanges, registering brokers and certain other professionals, auditing records and bank accounts, monitoring trading, and prosecuting violators.

Futures Contract: A firm commitment to deliver or to receive a specified quantity and grade of a commodity during a designated month, with the price being determined by public auction among exchange members.

Leverage Contract: A standardized agreement calling for delivery of a commodity with payments against the total cost spread out over a period of time.

Option: A unilateral contract which gives the buyer the right to buy or sell a specified quantity of a commodity at a specific price within a specified period of time, regardless of the market price of that commodity.

Sources: Senate Agriculture Committee and *Using the Futures Market in Financial Planning* by Raymond M. Leuthold and P. Jon van Blokland, University of Illinois at Urbana-Champaign, College of Agriculture, Cooperative Extension Service.

Although department officials did not respond to his offer, Dole added, "now, at the last minute, they're calling frantically and saying, 'you've got to change this.'"

Administration officials sought, without success, to convince farm lobbyists and their congressional allies that they did not need the statutory guarantee because Reagan repeatedly had pledged to avoid trade embargoes, except in extreme circumstances.

But supporters insisted a statutory guarantee was needed to assure foreign purchasers that U.S. export commitments would be honored despite an embargo or other foreign policy action.

During House debate on the conference report, Foreign Affairs Committee Chairman Clement J. Zablocki, D-Wis., noted that the amendment normally would have been within the jurisdiction of his committee, and that he did not consider it a precedent for future Agriculture Committee action on export matters.

Provisions

As cleared by Congress, HR 5447:

• Authorized funding as needed for activities of the CFTC through Sept. 30, 1986.

• **CFTC-SEC Accord.** Affirmed exclusive CFTC jurisdiction over commodity futures contracts and options on futures, including futures and options on so-called exempted securities, such as instruments of the Government National Mortgage Association and Treasury bills, but not on municipal securities.

• Barred CFTC jurisdiction over options on securities, including groups or indexes of securities, in effect affirming the jurisdiction of the Securities and Exchange Commission (SEC).

• Prohibited futures or options on futures on individual corporate bonds and securities or on municipal securities.

• Stated that nothing in the Commodity Exchange Act, the basic CFTC legislation, applied to options on foreign currency traded on a national securities exchange. The effect of the provision was to permit trading on such options on both commodity and stock exchanges.

• Affirmed CFTC jurisdiction over futures and options on futures on a group or index of securities, and spelled out standards for approval of contracts on such indexes. Barred CFTC approval of an application for this type of trading if the SEC found within 45 days, or 90 days in some circumstances, that the contract did not meet specified criteria.

• Affirmed CFTC jurisdiction over commodity pools except where pool transactions were subject to securities law, as in securities issued by pools.

• Broadened existing disclosure authority to permit the CFTC to give information on potentially disruptive transactions or market operations to a registered futures association or self-regulatory securities association.

Other Provisions

• Expanded categories of individuals subject to various commodity law provisions; made officials of commodity firms responsible for acts of their employees and agents under specified conditions.

• Affirmed that U.S. residents who sold foreign futures were subject to federal registration requirements and other regulations. (Federal regulations required individuals involved in futures and related transactions to register with the CFTC.)

• Explicitly barred the CFTC from regulating foreign markets.

• Expanded CFTC authority to set speculative limits, and affirmed the authority of contract markets and other licensed exchanges to set such limits for futures or option transactions; made violation of a market limit a violation of federal law, if the CFTC had approved the market limit.

• Authorized the CFTC to implement a three-year pilot program on trading in agricultural options, and then to generally permit such trading, but only 30 days after reporting to the Agriculture committees of Congress on its ability adequately to regulate such trading.

• Required large traders to keep certain financial records even if exempted from routine reporting rules.

• Eliminated a $15,000 ceiling for claims eligible for arbitration by markets or a registered futures association; made merchants who were not members of a market eligible for its arbitration process. Repealed a ban on mandatory settlement payments not agreed to by both parties.

• Revised rules for the CFTC's reparations program, and limited eligibility for the program to registrants.

• Affirmed CFTC authority to set temporary emergency margin levels and to fix position limits retroactively. (A margin was the amount of money or collateral that must be deposited by a client or broker to insure against loss on futures contracts; a position limit was the maximum interest an individual could hold on a commodity future or on all futures in one commodity.)

• Authorized the CFTC to restrict or cancel registration for specified causes; upgraded to felonies certain illegal actions, such as manipulating the price of a commodity or a

futures market or transmitting false market information.

● Authorized states to enforce relevant state or federal laws against illegal commodity transactions occurring outside regulated exchanges and outside the regulatory structure of the CFTC.

● Authorized states to enforce anti-fraud sections of the Commodity Exchange Act in state courts, against persons registered as required by the federal law. Exempted floor brokers and registered futures associations from such state enforcement and authorized the CFTC to intervene in these proceedings.

● Required the commodity industry's self-regulatory group, the National Futures Association (NFA), to put into operation a specific regulatory program, as directed by the CFTC, by Sept. 30, 1985. Authorized the CFTC to require the NFA or similar self-regulatory groups to take over certain CFTC responsibilities, such as registration of commodity brokers and others involved in futures transactions.

● Authorized the CFTC to regulate leverage transactions as soon as practicable. (A leverage contract was an agreement calling for delivery of a commodity with payments made in installments.)

● Authorized private lawsuits, with certain limitations, against commodity dealers, trading advisers or contract markets by individuals who had been harmed by violation of the Commodity Exchange Act occurring on or off regulated markets.

● Required the Federal Reserve Board, with the assistance of the CFTC, the SEC and the Treasury, to conduct a study and report to Congress by Sept. 30, 1984, on the effect of futures and options trading on the economy, including the effect on capital investment in industry and business; also required that the study examine the impact of stock index futures on the securities on which they were based and on capital formation, with recommendations for legislation if needed.

● Directed the CFTC to conduct a two-year study on commodities trading by individuals, such as company officials, who had information not generally available to the public, and to report on whether the commission had enough authority to prevent abuses in such "insider trading."

● Restated existing authority for the CFTC to charge fees for such services as rule enforcement reviews of commodity exchanges; barred imposition of "user" fees or fees on individual commodities or options transactions.

● Authorized the CFTC to deny the use of futures markets or impose other sanctions against persons violating the statutory requirement that large commodity export sales be reported to the Agriculture Department.

Trade Guarantee

● Barred the president from prohibiting or restricting the export of any agricultural commodity that was under contract at the time the president imposed an embargo or other restriction on trade, if the contract provided for delivery of the commodity within 270 days of the imposition of such a restriction. However, the bill permitted restrictions on contracted agricultural sales abroad in time of war or national emergency.

Background

Congressional committees struggled throughout 1982 to revise the regulation of an industry whose rapid growth in new directions made some members uneasy.

At issue was how to treat the fast-growing trade in new hybrid financial instruments. The new instruments based so-called "forward" or future contracts on conventional stocks or bonds that were used by corporations and units of government to raise capital.

Future contracts typically set a price for a given commodity on a specified date in the future. An option permitted an owner to buy or sell at a certain price in the future but imposed no obligation to do so. *(Box, p. 366)*

Those types of contracts had been used for decades by buyers and sellers of agricultural commodities as a form of insurance against price changes, and by speculators.

Inflation made them attractive to dealers in nonfarm goods during the past decade, and the market responded with ingenious new variations. Futures or options were available, for example, on foreign currency, Treasury bonds, housing bonds and stock indexes.

Congress fueled the trend in 1974 when it wrote an unusually inclusive definition of "commodity" into the statute (PL 93-463) creating the CFTC. But fierce competition over new products between securities and futures industries continued to inspire occasional congressional plans for dismembering the CFTC. *(1974 Almanac p. 215)*

In December 1981, the CFTC and SEC voluntarily divided up much of the disputed turf, deciding which types of transactions would be regulated by each agency. However, on March 23, the U.S. Appeals Court in Chicago ruled against one section of the accord, finding that the SEC did not have authority to regulate non-stock options on such instruments as mortgages bought and resold through the Government National Mortgage Association (GNMA).

The decision, in effect, took from securities brokers a new business that had been granted them by the agreement. Congressional ratification of the agreement would overrule the court and give that business back to them.

The accord also:

● Affirmed exclusive CFTC jurisdiction over commodity futures contracts and options on futures, including futures and options on so-called exempted securities such as GNMAs and Treasury bills.

● Barred CFTC jurisdiction over options on securities, including groups or indexes of securities, in effect affirming SEC jurisdiction.

● Prohibited futures or options on individual corporate bonds and securities or on municipal securities.

● Stated that nothing in the commodities statute applied to options on foreign currency traded on a national securities exchange. The effect was to permit trading on such options on both commodity and stock exchanges.

● Affirmed CFTC jurisdiction over futures on a group or index of securities, and spelled out standards for approval of contracts on such indexes. Provided for public comment and SEC review of index contracts and in the event of an SEC objection, a CFTC hearing and judicial appeal by the SEC.

● Affirmed CFTC jurisdiction over commodity pools, except where pool transactions were subject to securities law, as in securities issued by pools.

House Committee Action

Although the CFTC was under the Agriculture Committee jurisdiction, the House Energy and Commerce Committee, which had jurisdiction over the SEC, requested referral of the legislation.

Chairman John D. Dingell, D-Mich., disapproved

strongly of the accord. He complained in an April 23 hearing held by the Commerce Subcommittee on Telecommunications, Consumer Protection and Finance that the CFTC was positioned to claim jurisdiction over securities and "eliminate competition from securities exchanges, much like PAC-men moving across a video screen."

"This trend must be stopped," he added.

The subcommittee hearing signaled deep skepticism in and out of Congress about the wisdom of the CFTC-SEC agreement.

Although witnesses generally advised prompt congressional approval of the accord to eliminate uncertainties affecting markets, many also said it was time for Congress to rework regulation of financial markets. Some suggested merging the commodities and securities agencies.

Subcommittee Chairman Timothy E. Wirth, D-Colo., said, "I believe our task should be more than just to allocate various financial instruments to a particular agency."

Some witnesses from the securities industry urged either a much larger regulatory role for the SEC than the accord provided or strict securities-type regulation in futures markets, including protections for consumers. They suggested that the CFTC was neither competent nor interested in protecting customers.

CFTC Chairman Philip Johnson stressed that differing styles of regulation by the CFTC and SEC reflected deep functional differences between futures and securities trading. He suggested that the two agencies continue working informally to solve regulatory problems.

In response to complaints that futures markets offered customers too little protection, Johnson indicated that his industry's reputation for fast, high-risk, high-stakes trading protected consumers by discouraging all but the most sophisticated and affluent from participating.

Like Johnson, SEC Chairman John S. R. Shad urged approval of the accord. But Shad also remarked that "as a theoretical matter, it is the commission's view that the agency which has authority over the underlying instrument or 'commodity' should have authority over all derivative interests in such instrument."

Another concern raised was whether trading in the financial hybrids diverted capital from more productive, long-term investments. Those who defended such new instruments as options on stock indexes said that by acting as insurance against inflation, the instruments could actually encourage capital formation.

The Agriculture Committee made relatively minor changes in its subcommittee bill. As reported May 17 (H Rept 97-565) the bill ratified the CFTC-SEC agreement.

Commerce Committee

Before approving the funding reauthorization June 16, the Energy and Commerce Committee agreed to changes expressing Chairman Dingell's misgivings.

The first change gave the SEC power to veto CFTC approval of contracts on futures on an index or group of securities. This change disturbed one portion of the CFTC-SEC agreement ratified by the bill as reported by the House Agriculture Committee. The agreement only permitted the SEC to review applications for such contracts, object, and appeal through the courts if the CFTC disregarded its objections.

The second change broadened the scope of a study of the futures industry mandated by the Agriculture panel and shifted lead responsibility for the study from the CFTC to the Federal Reserve Board.

House Floor Action

On Sept. 23 the House approved a four-year reauthorization by a 319-59 vote, after rejecting an amendment that would have levied fees on individual futures transactions. *(Vote 343, p. 102-H)*

The bill strengthened the federal and state regulators in several respects and authorized the CFTC to delegate to the NFA key regulatory functions, such as registration of persons active in the futures markets.

The House Sept. 23 also passed by voice vote a related bill (HR 6156) making changes in federal securities statutes to make them conform to the CFTC-SEC agreement. HR 6156 had been reported June 24 by the House Energy and Commerce Committee and July 30 by the Agriculture Committee (H Rept 97-626 Pts. I & II).

During consideration of HR 5447, Barber B. Conable Jr., R-N.Y., proposed imposing fees of 6 cents per transaction for each contract traded by a member of an exchange or a self-regulatory organization such as the NFA; 12 cents for non-members; and $3 for options and leverage transactions.

But the House disregarded Conable's arguments that the fees would be a negligible cost and that other regulated financial industries had long borne similar fees. The amendment was rejected 170-216. *(Vote 342, p. 102-H)*

Conable maintained that taxpayers should not pay for futures regulation since the benefits went mainly to a relatively small group of futures traders.

But Thomas A. Daschle, D-S.D., and Dan Rostenkowski, D-Ill., insisted that the nation as a whole benefited from the price-setting and risk-sharing functions of the futures market.

Ways and Means Committee Chairman Rostenkowski also objected that the fees amounted to a tax that had not been approved by his tax-writing committee and that it was "unprecedented to provide revenue powers" to a regulatory agency. Conable's amendment allowed the CFTC to suspend or reduce fees. In other action, the House:

● Adopted by a 7-5 standing vote an Energy and Commerce Committee amendment that enhanced SEC jurisdiction over futures and options on futures on a group or index of securities.

The agreement and the Agriculture Committee bill affirmed CFTC authority over those transactions, provided for SEC review of applications to the CFTC for index contracts and permitted SEC lawsuits if the securities agency disapproved a CFTC decision.

The committee amendment approved by the House barred CFTC approval of an index contract if the SEC determined, within a few months, that the contract did not meet certain criteria.

● Adopted by voice vote a second Energy and Commerce amendment broadening a study on futures and related instruments, and making the Federal Reserve the lead agency for the study.

● Adopted by voice votes clarifying amendments relating to private lawsuits and to the assumption of regulatory functions by the NFA.

● Adopted by voice vote an amendment by Neal Smith, D-Iowa, that required large export sales of commodities such as wheat to be reported to the CFTC within 48 hours, and to be made public by the next working day. An existing Agriculture Department reporting system was too slow, Smith said.

● Adopted by an 18-0 standing vote a Smith amendment

that prohibited trading on a commodity by individuals with "insider" information on that commodity that was not generally available to the public.

Senate Action

The Senate Agriculture Committee reported its bill May 6 (S 2109 — S Rept 97-384). A companion measure conforming security laws to the CFTC-SEC agreement was reported May 12 by the Banking Housing and Urban Affairs Committee (S 2260 — S Rept 97-390).

In floor debate, the Senate rejected a transaction fee amendment by a 27-66 vote before passing its CFTC bill Oct. 1 and attaching the language to the House bill. *(Vote 381, p. 64-S)*

In arguing for his proposal to guarantee export contracts, Durenberger said that a series of embargoes beginning in 1973 had damaged America's reputation abroad as a "reliable supplier" of food.

Richard G. Lugar, R-Ind., speaking in support of the amendment, said that before President Carter's 1980 embargo on grain sales to the Soviet Union, America's share of growth in the world commodities market was 76 percent. (That is, for every 100-bushel increase in world wheat sales, 76 bushels were American wheat.) After the embargo, that share dropped to 54 percent, Lugar said.

The Senate also considered the following amendments:
● By William V. Roth Jr., R-Del., to give states the authority to prosecute persons registered under the Commodity Exchange Act under state commodities or securities anti-fraud statutes. Adopted by voice vote.
● By Charles H. Percy, R-Ill., to set time limits on CFTC reivew of futures association rules. Adopted by voice vote.
● By Percy to facilitate the assumption of certain CFTC registration functions by the National Futures Association. Adopted by voice vote.

In separate action, the Senate by a 91-0 vote passed the House companion bill on security laws (HR 6156), clearing the bill for the president. The bill was signed into law (PL 97-303) Oct. 13. *(Vote 382, p. 64-S)*

Major Differences

Major differences in the two CFTC authorizations bills included:
● The House had no provision to match the Senate's sweeping ban on agricultural trade embargoes.
● The Senate bill continued CFTC funding for two years, anticipating reconsideration of transaction fees then. The House approved a four-year reauthorization.

● A House-passed change in one section of the CFTC-SEC accord that gave the SEC more authority to block CFTC decisions on trading in stock index futures and options.
● A Senate-passed authorization for state officials to bring anti-fraud actions against both on-exchange and off-exchange transactions. That provided an exception to what had been exclusive CFTC jurisdiction over transactions in commodities exchanges.
● House-passed authority for private lawsuits for violations of commodity law filed by individuals, contract markets, clearing organizations or registered futures associations.
● Senate-passed authority for the CFTC to require a registered futures association, such as the NFA, to perform registration functions, including denial or revocation of registration.

The House bill required a registered futures association to implement a number of regulatory programs within two years, such as audits and enforcement among members.
● A House-passed prohibition on "insider" trading — transactions by individuals with information that was not generally available to the public on a commodity.
● A House-passed requirement that export commodity sales be made public by the CFTC shortly after they were contracted. ∎

Government Gasohol

Mountains of federally owned surplus grain could be converted to alcohol fuel for use by government agencies or for sale in commercial markets under a bill cleared by Congress Oct. 1.

The measure (HR 6142 — PL 97-358) authorized the Commodity Credit Corporation (CCC), the financial arm of the Agriculture Department that operated price support programs, to convert to fuel the grain it had accumulated as a result of price support loan defaults.

Rep. E. "Kika" de la Garza, D-Texas, chairman of the Agriculture Committee, said the bill could help alleviate pressure caused by the record grain production predicted by the Agriculture Department.

The bill had been reported by his panel Sept. 26 (H Rept 97-874) and was passed by the House by voice vote under suspension of the rules Sept. 28. After discharging the Senate Agriculture Committee Oct. 1, the Senate approved the bill by voice vote. ∎

Law Enforcement/Judiciary

Congress in 1982 renewed and strengthened the landmark Voting Rights Act of 1965, but other major legislation handled by the House and Senate Judiciary committees failed to clear.

Despite the Republican takeover of the Senate in 1981 and a generally conservative mood in Congress, none of the New Right's social proposals on abortion, busing and school prayer was enacted.

They were derailed by a combination of tactical blunders by their proponents, tough politicking by their foes and a liberal House Judiciary Committee that preserved its standing as the graveyard of many conservative initiatives.

Although the Senate passed a constitutional amendment requiring a balanced federal budget, a similar proposal was handily rejected in the House one month before the November elections.

The Senate also passed a wide-ranging immigration reform bill. While a similar House bill made it to the House floor late in the lame-duck session, it proved too controversial to handle in the brief time available.

The Supreme Court June 28 struck down the bankruptcy court system created by Congress in 1978. Although the justices gave Congress until Dec. 24 to come up with new legislation, none was enacted. The U.S. Judicial Conference, the policy-making arm of the federal judiciary, quickly put in effect interim rules for handling bankruptcy cases.

Congress made at least modest progress on anti-crime bills, although for the third time since 1977 a massive criminal code revision failed to pass. A bill designed to make the federal government more sensitive to victims and witnesses of crime was cleared, along with a bill that made it a federal crime to kill or assault high federal officials.

An anti-crime package whose main provisions focused on combating drug trafficking was cleared by Congress but vetoed at the last minute by President Reagan. The president heeded objections from administration officials to a provision that would have created a new Cabinet-level office to coordinate drug enforcement.

Voting Rights

The voting rights bill, cleared June 23, was the most important legislation to move from the Judiciary committees to the president's desk in the 97th Congress.

The main section of the bill extended for 25 years the enforcement section of the 1965 law. This required nine states and portions of 13 others to get Justice Department approval for any election law changes.

Another part of the bill made it easier to challenge election systems by specifying that violations could be proved by showing that certain election procedures resulted in discrimination.

As civil rights groups had expected, the bill's journey through the Republican Senate was considerably more dif-

ficult than House consideration in 1981.

The Reagan administration declined to testify during House voting rights hearings. After the House passed its bill, the administration announced support for extending the enforcement section but opposition to the so-called "results" test for proving discrimination. The administration wanted a test requiring proof that a challenged election procedure was adopted with intent to discriminate.

The issue dominated two months of hearings before the Constitution Subcommittee, whose chairman, Orrin G. Hatch, R-Utah, sided with the administration. The full committee was deadlocked, but one day before it was to meet, Robert Dole, R-Kan., announced that he had put together a compromise version of a "results" test. It subsequently was approved by the committee.

The bill ran into a week-long filibuster on the Senate floor, but it passed intact June 18 on an 85-8 vote. The House then accepted the Senate version of the bill.

Social Issues

Senate conservatives anxious to pass anti-abortion and anti-busing legislation got off to a fast start in 1981, but they ended up in 1982 with nothing to show for their efforts.

Language that would have virtually eliminated court-ordered busing passed the Senate March 2 as a rider to a bill authorizing Justice Department programs. The bill first came to the floor June 16, 1981, but it was stymied by a filibuster led by Sen. Lowell P. Weicker Jr., R-Conn. Nearly nine months later, Weicker finally dropped his delaying tactics.

When the bill reached the House, it was promptly and permanently buried in a House Judiciary subcommittee.

Although the Senate Judiciary Committee approved a proposed constitutional amendment sponsored by Hatch that was designed to restrict abortion, the measure never was considered by the full Senate.

It was competing for support among anti-abortion groups with legislative proposals sponsored by Sen. Jesse Helms, R-N.C., that would have given states the authority to enact anti-abortion laws.

When a proposed time agreement that would have allowed votes on both proposals fell apart, Helms tried to attach his language to a bill raising the public debt limit. The abortion amendment actually was added to another debt-ceiling amendment that sought to allow "voluntary" prayer in the public schools. The amendments immediately sparked filibusters that Helms and his supporters were unable to cut off, and both died on procedural votes.

Immigration

An eleventh-hour House effort to pass an immigration reform bill died when the House leadership Dec. 18 took the controversial bill off the floor.

It was a painful defeat for chief sponsor Romano L. Mazzoli, D-Ky., who had worked for a year with his Senate counterpart, Alan K. Simpson, R-Wyo, to draft a bill they believed could garner bipartisan support. The legislation was designed to curb the flow of illegal aliens while granting amnesty to the millions of undocumented workers already in the United States. The main enforcement tool was to be sanctions against employers who knowingly hired illegal aliens.

Despite vehement opposition from Hispanic groups, the bill passed the Senate easily Aug. 17 by an 80-19 vote. In the House, the Mazzoli measure faced many more roadblocks. It drew Judiciary Committee opposition from liberals concerned about discrimination that might result from the sanction provisions, and from conservatives who argued that the amnesty provisions were too lenient and the sanctions scheme too cumbersome for employers.

The committee finally approved an amended bill Sept. 22, but it was too late for House action before the November election recess. By the time Congress returned for the lame-duck session, lobbying against the bill had intensified, and the Democratic leadership became increasingly leery about pushing the legislation. Some 300 amendments were filed, indicating the depth of the opposition.

After five hours of general debate and consideration of a single amendment, House leaders pulled the bill from the floor Dec. 18.

Bankruptcy Courts

Despite a June 28 Supreme Court ruling invalidating the existing bankruptcy court system, Congress failed to act on legislation to restructure those courts.

In its decision, the court said Congress in 1978 had given bankruptcy judges, who were appointed for fixed terms, too much authority and too little independence.

The court first set an Oct. 4 deadline for congressional action, then extended it to Dec. 24 when Congress failed to act. But when the 97th Congress adjourned without resolving the problem, the justices refused to grant another extension. That left the bankruptcy system in legal limbo at year's end, operating under a stopgap rule put forward by the U.S. Judicial Conference.

A proposal championed by House Judiciary Chairman Peter W. Rodino Jr., D-N.J., would have given bankruptcy judges lifetime appointments and put them on equal footing with federal district court judges. That plan, which called for 227 new judgeships, was approved by the Judiciary Committee but never considered by the full House.

Key senators balked at the Rodino approach until the Justice Department announced its support for the lifetime judgeships. Although various Senate proposals were put together, none was ever considered. The issue became tangled in a dispute over revising the law on consumer bankruptcies.

Crime

Reagan's veto of the anti-crime package meant that little major law enforcement legislation was enacted.

The most significant bill authorized judges to order restitution to a victim who sustained personal injury or property loss, made it a felony to harass crime victims and witnesses, and called for revocation of bail for any defendant who tried to intimidate a witness.

Two other cleared bills were aimed at protecting high government officials. One made it a federal crime to kill, kidnap or assault specified federal officials. It was prompted by the March 30, 1981, shooting of President Reagan and three other men.

The other bill made it a federal crime to threaten to kidnap the president, a former president, presidential candidates or anyone else entitled to Secret Service protection.

Despite objections from the Justice Department, Congress cleared a bill that revised and extended the special prosecutor law enacted following the Watergate scandal.

The bill tightened the standard that triggered appointment of a special prosecutor to investigate alleged wrongdoing by high government and campaign officials and shortened the list of officials covered by the law.

Legal Services Corporation

As in 1981, Reagan tried to abolish the Legal Services Corporation (LSC) but Congress refused to go along. Instead, it appropriated $241 million for the LSC for fiscal 1983, the same level as fiscal 1982 spending.

Only nine of the 11 individuals Reagan named to the LSC board of directors were nominated officially, and none was confirmed. He appointed the nine during the December 1981 congressional recess, which meant they were allowed to serve until the end of 1982 without Senate confirmation.

Two of the most conservative board members, William F. Harvey, the chairman, and William Olson, drew opposition from a majority of senators. Prior to a Senate vote on their nominations, Reagan withdrew the entire slate.

During the 1982 election recess, the president appointed two other LSC board members. They continued to serve in the first session of the 98th Congress.

During House subcommittee oversight hearings Dec. 14, it was disclosed that LSC board members appointed by Reagan had collected unprecedented consulting fees. As a result of the disclosures, new provisions were put into the second continuing appropriations resolution limiting board members' compensation to out-of-pocket expenses and consulting fees for attendance at board meetings.

Another new provision barred LSC employees from receiving severance pay different from that accorded any federal employee, and barred reimbursement for membership in a private club. Both restrictions were adopted in reaction to a contract Harvey negotiated with the new corporation president. It provided for a year's severance pay and private club membership at government expense.

Judgeships

In 1982 President Reagan made 48 appointments to the federal district and appeals courts. It was not a good year for women, blacks and Hispanics, who had made substantial gains in representation on the federal bench during the Carter administration. All but four of Reagan's appointments went to white males. Two women and two Hispanics were named to district court seats.

Overall in his first two years, Reagan made 89 judicial appointments, including naming Sandra Day O'Connor as the first woman to serve on the Supreme Court.

In addition to the O'Connor appointment, Reagan in 1981 named a woman to the federal district bench who had been a U.S. Tax Court judge. He also elevated a black district court judge to an appeals court position.

Administration officials said they were proud of their court appointments, adding that they had made a concerted effort to find qualified judges who shared the president's conservative philosophy.

—By Nadine Cohodas

Voting Rights Act Extended, Strengthened

The House June 23 cleared for the president a bill (HR 3112) extending the enforcement section of the 1965 Voting Rights Act for 25 years and making it easier to prove certain voting rights violations.

President Reagan signed the bill into law June 29 (PL 97-205), even though he had harbored reservations about earlier versions of the measure.

At the White House for the signing ceremony were Senate Republicans who helped put the final compromise bill together and prominent civil rights leaders, many of whom had criticized the administration's performance on civil rights in general and the voting rights extension in particular.

Reagan, in signing the extension measure, called the right to vote "the crown jewel of American liberties" and said the legislation "proves our unbending commitment to voting rights."

Final congressional action came when the House, without debate and by unanimous consent, accepted the Senate version of the legislation.

The Senate June 18 had amended HR 3112 to conform with its own version (S 1992 — S Rept 97-417) and then passed it by a vote of 85-8, one day after a handful of conservative senators led by Jesse Helms, R-N.C., ended a filibuster against it. *(Vote 190, p. 33-S)*

The House originally passed HR 3112 (H Rept 97-227) Oct. 5, 1981, by a 389-24 vote. That version of the bill called for a permanent extension of Section Five, the enforcement provision of the law, rather than the 25-year extension ultimately enacted. *(1981 Almanac p. 415)*

The Heart of the Bill

The bill sent to President Reagan had four major elements. First, it extended Section Five for 25 years. Without congressional action, Section Five would have become ineffective Aug. 6, 1982. It required 9 states and portions of 13 others to get Justice Department approval before making any changes in election laws or procedures.

Second, starting in 1984, the bill permitted covered jurisdictions to bail out from Section Five if they could prove to a three-judge panel in the District of Columbia that they had a clean voting rights record for the previous 10 years.

Third, the bill allowed certain voting rights violations under Section Two of the law to be proved by showing that an election law or procedure had resulted in discrimination. Section Two, which is a permanent part of the law and applies nationwide, bars states and political subdivisions from adopting election laws or procedures that deny or hamper the right to vote. The new language in HR 3112 overturned a 1980 Supreme Court ruling in the case of *Mobile v. Bolden* that an intent to discriminate must be shown to prove a violation. *(1980 Almanac p. 9-A)*

Fourth, the bill extended until 1992 provisions requiring certain areas of the country to provide bilingual election materials. These provisions would have expired in 1985 without further congressional action.

Strong Southern Support

In both chambers, the bill received widespread bipartisan support and strong backing from Southern legislators — even though it was primarily the South that was affected by the Section Five enforcement provision requiring nine states and portions of 13 others to get Justice Department approval for any changes in their election laws and procedures.

In the House, 71 Southern Democrats voted in 1981 to approve HR 3112, while 14 Southern Democratic senators voted for the bill June 18. When the law was first passed in 1965, 33 Southern Democrats in the House and five in the Senate voted for the measure. When Section Five was extended in 1970, 34 Southern Democrats in the House and four in the Senate voted for it. And when it was extended again in 1975, 56 Southern Democrats in the House and 11 in the Senate voted for the extension.

The steady upward trend in Southern support for the Voting Rights Act reflected not only changing social and political mores but — more directly — a dramatic increase since 1965 in the number of blacks registered to vote in the South and their growing clout at the polls.

The law was widely considered the most effective civil rights measure ever enacted.

Victory for Civil Rights Groups

The final passage of HR 3112 represented a major victory for a coalition of civil rights groups that included black, Hispanic, labor, religious and civic organizations.

When the 97th Congress began, leaders of these groups started working in Washington and with their own organizations across the country to put together an educational and lobbying campaign to persuade members that the 1965 act needed to be extended a third time.

The 18-month campaign included numerous briefings for congressional staffers and the press in Washington and the creation of coalitions in virtually all 50 states. They were organized under an umbrella group, the Leadership Conference on Civil Rights, whose executive director, Ralph Neas, coordinated virtually all of the lobbying efforts.

Washington lobbyists flew around the country at various times to appear on television interview shows and to talk with newspaper editorial boards in an effort to put pressure on representatives and senators who were considered swing votes.

Laura Murphy, a lobbyist with the American Civil Liberties Union, cited two major factors in the civil rights groups' success.

"We were able to substantiate all of our claims when it came to discrimination against minority voters," she said. "The facts were there, and from all of the covered jurisdictions."

The second major element, she said, was the lack of any funded opposition to extending the enforcement provisions.

Provisions

As cleared by Congress, HR 3112 included these major provisions:

● Allowed private parties, under Section Two of the act, to prove a voting rights violation by showing that an election law or procedure had been imposed or applied in a manner that "results" in voting discrimination. The provision specified that a court would have to look at the "totality of circumstances" in determining whether a voting

rights violation had been proved.

• Specified that in a Section Two lawsuit there was no right to proportional representation for a minority group and that lack of proportional representation was only one circumstance a court could consider.

• Extended Section Five, the pre-clearance mechanism, for 25 years. This required nine states and portions of 13 others to obtain Justice Department approval before making any changes in their election laws or procedures.

• Provided a new bailout section to take effect in 1984 allowing a jurisdiction to bail out from Section Five coverage if it could show a three-judge panel in the District of Columbia that it had a clean voting rights record for the preceding 10 years. The current bailout provision remained in effect until Aug. 5, 1984.

• Required as proof of a clean record the following: local authorities had not used any voting test or device in a discriminatory way; there had been no final judgment of a federal court finding a violation of the voting rights law; there had been no consent decree, settlement or agreement entered into concerning voting rights violations; the attorney general had not been required to send in federal examiners to help register voters; local officials had complied with the pre-clearance requirement by making all required submissions to the Justice Department, and had repealed all election law changes the department objected to; and the jurisdictions had made "constructive efforts" to bring minority groups into the election process and to end any intimidation or harassment of prospective voters.

• Extended until 1992 provisions requiring certain areas of the country to provide bilingual election materials.

• Authorized any voter who was blind, disabled or unable to read to receive assistance in voting from a person of his or her choice, except that such assistance could not be provided by the voter's employer or union officer.

The Administration Position

Despite repeated requests, Reagan administration officials declined to testify on voting rights in 1981, and HR 3112 went through the House Judiciary Committee and the House without guidance from the administration.

On Jan. 19, one day before Senate Judiciary subcommittee hearings on voting rights were to begin, the Justice Department abruptly asked for a week's delay.

The move came as the administration was embroiled in a separate civil rights controversy over its changing positions on granting tax exemptions to private schools that discriminated against blacks. *(Story, p. 397)*

But Thomas DeCair, a Justice Department spokesman, denied suggestions that the administration was reluctant to go public with its Voting Rights position in such a political climate. "There's nothing to that," he said.

Orrin G. Hatch, R-Utah, chairman of the Senate Judiciary Constitution Subcommittee, agreed to the postponement and rescheduled the first hearing for Jan. 27.

Hatch's decision to abide by the department's request touched off an angry response from civil rights groups, although they were more upset with the department than with the senator.

The civil rights groups were no more pleased when the hearings did get under way Jan. 27 with testimony by Attorney General William French Smith.

Smith told the Constitution Subcommittee that the Reagan administration supported extending Section Five, the pre-clearance provisions of the Voting Rights Act, but

for 10 years rather than permanently, as provided in the House bill.

He said the administration also favored provisions allowing covered jurisdictions to bail out, but he declined to elaborate.

In his testimony, Smith said the administration also supported an extension of provisions requiring bilingual election materials in certain areas of the country. These provisions were added in 1975. Although they were not due to expire until 1985, Hispanic groups, in particular, pushed for their extension along with Section Five.

However, the attorney general said the administration strongly opposed any move to allow violations under Section Two of the act to be proved by looking at electoral results, preferring to maintain the "intent" standard set forth by the Supreme Court in *Mobile v. Bolden*.

Smith said President Reagan and the Justice Department believed that anyone challenging an existing voting practice or procedure should be required to show that it was adopted with an intent to discriminate.

With a standard focusing on results, such as the one written into the House-passed HR 3112, "quotas would be the end result," Smith said. At-large election systems for local councils and boards could come under challenge, and "the only ultimate logical result would be proportional representation," he said.

Administration Attacked

Smith's testimony drew sharp criticism from Democratic Sens. Edward M. Kennedy, Mass., and Howard M. Metzenbaum, Ohio, and from Benjamin L. Hooks, executive director of the NAACP.

"We are not seeking proportional representation," Hooks declared. "We are strongly seeking the unfettered right to vote. All the administration is trying to do is make it much harder for those who are outside who are trying to get in."

Sparks flew when Kennedy launched into a speech about the administration's alleged insensitivity to minorities. He said there was "a crisis of confidence" in the administration's commitment to protect the rights of women, blacks and Hispanics. The Massachusetts Democrat specifically pointed to the decision — later modified — to grant tax exemptions to private schools that discriminated against blacks.

When Kennedy finished, Smith countered that "it is the injection of this kind of political rhetoric that makes it difficult to diagnose and analyze legislation.

"What we're talking about is good vs. bad legislation, and bad legislation is not made good through general, broad political, rhetorical attacks," Smith said.

The Intent Issue

The whole standard-of-proof issue emanated from a 1980 Supreme Court decision involving at-large elections in Mobile, Ala. In that decision, a plurality of the court ruled that those challenging the election procedure had to prove it was adopted with an intent to discriminate. They said discrimination was not proved simply by showing that no black had been elected to the City Commission even though blacks made up one-third of the city's population.

Civil rights groups and members of Congress who agreed with their position said the Supreme Court misinterpreted Section Two. That section prohibited the use of any voting procedure or practice to deny or abridge the right of any citizen to vote because of race or color. The

provision was not up for renewal in 1982, but it became embroiled in the debate when the House inserted the "results" test in HR 3112.

The House bill made clear that voting rights violations could be proved by showing that an election procedure "results in the denial or abridgment" of the right to vote.

Although Section Five was considered the law's major enforcement tool, civil rights groups argued that Section Two played an equally important role because it covered the entire nation and allowed citizens to challenge election procedures that were in place before the 1965 act.

The intent-vs.-results issue dominated two months of Senate hearings. Hatch, chairman of the Constitution Subcommittee, agreed with the administration on Section Two and argued vigorously for the intent standard articulated by the Supreme Court.

Echoing the administration's concerns, Hatch contended that a results test would threaten thousands of local at-large election systems and lead to proportional representation of minorities on local governing bodies.

Senate Action

The Subcommittee Vote

Hatch's subcommittee completed hearings on the voting rights issue March 1. On March 24, the panel approved a 10-year extension of Section Five but refused to incorporate the "results" test of the House bill into Section Two, thereby leaving the Supreme Court's "intent" standard intact.

The party-line vote belied the broad bipartisan support enjoyed by the House version. S 1992, as introduced Dec. 16, 1981, by Kennedy and Sen. Charles McC. Mathias Jr., R-Md., was a carbon copy of the House bill. By the time the subcommittee acted, it had 65 Senate sponsors.

Hatch's panel voted 3-2 to amend S 1992 into the simple 10-year extension measure, then ordered it reported to the full Judiciary Committee by a unanimous vote.

Ironically the subcommittee action saw Judiciary Chairman Strom Thurmond, R-S.C., a member of the Constitution Subcommittee, voting to extend Section Five without modification. Thurmond had said after assuming the Judiciary chairmanship in 1981 that he would try to alter that section, which made it virtually impossible for the six Southern states originally covered by the 1965 act — including Thurmond's — to "bail out" from the preclearance requirement. The House bill extended Section Five permanently but slightly relaxed the criteria for "bailout" after 1984.

New Legal Twist: Mobile Revisited

Adding a new twist to an already heated legal and political debate was an April 15 determination by an Alabama federal judge that Mobile's at-large city election system was discriminatory and was adopted a century ago with the intent to discriminate against blacks.

The ruling came on the very voting rights case that led civil rights advocates to seek a change in Section Two on the standard of proof needed to establish a voting rights violation.

In the case of *Mobile v. Bolden*, the Supreme Court ruled it was not enough to show that blacks never had been elected to the City Commission even though they made up about one-third of Mobile's population. The court said those challenging the system had to prove it was adopted

with the intent to keep blacks from winning office.

The justices sent the case back to Alabama to be reconsidered in light of this opinion. On April 15, U.S. District Court Judge Virgil Pittman issued a 61-page opinion finding that Mobile's at-large system had indeed been enacted with the intent to discriminate against blacks.

Both sides in the "intent" debate promptly sought to use Pittman's decision as support for their positions.

In an April 20 letter to senators, the Leadership Conference on Civil Rights contended that Pittman's opinion amply demonstrated "the wastefulness and unfairness" of the intent test.

The letter noted that Pittman had to explore more than 100 years of Alabama history to reach his determination. Retrial of the case after the 1980 Supreme Court decision took more than 6,000 hours of lawyers' time, 4,000 hours of the time of expert witnesses and paralegals, and more than a year of the judge's time.

Besides such inconvenience and expense, the civil rights group said, an intent test was irrelevant because in most instances it did not focus on present circumstances.

On the other side, the Justice Department — which had argued vigorously against the "results" test — said the decision showed that "intent" was provable. On April 16, Robert A. McConnell, assistant attorney general for legislative affairs, wrote to Judiciary members contending that "it is now clear beyond doubt" that there was no factual basis for saying intent was too difficult to prove.

On April 20, William Bradford Reynolds, head of the Justice Department's civil rights division and a vigorous advocate of the "intent" test, likewise asserted that the Pittman decision "put to rest" claims that intent could not be proved.

The Dole Compromise

In the weeks following markup of S 1992 by Hatch's subcommittee, it rapidly became apparent that the full Judiciary Committee was sharply polarized on the bill, with Sens. Robert Dole, R-Kan., and Howell Heflin, D-Ala., holding the balance of power.

Nine Judiciary members were publicly supporting the House-passed version of the voting rights extension, while seven opposed it. Dole and Heflin kept their own counsel, although Dole began working with other senators and with administration officials in pursuit of a compromise.

Dole's efforts focused directly on the nettlesome Section Two "intent" issue, and on May 3 he announced that a compromise had been reached. Helping to draft it were Kennedy and Mathias, original cosponsors of the voting rights extension.

Blacks inside the administration and mainline congressional Republicans urged Reagan to support the compromise, arguing a strong bill was likely to pass in any event, and the president gave his endorsement.

The compromise had two main provisions — one altering the standard of proof for privately initiated voting rights suits and the other revising the Section Five enforcement section. A third less controversial section extended until 1992 voting rights protection for non-English-speaking voters.

The most sensitive part of the compromise dealt with Section Two, the provision allowing private voting rights suits. The Dole compromise kept the House "results" test but added a section spelling out how the test could be met. Its language was taken directly from a 1973 Supreme Court case, *White v. Register*, that involved the dilution of mi-

nority votes in two Texas counties. The new language stated that a violation could be proved "if, based on the totality of circumstances, it is shown that the political processes leading to nomination or election in the state or political subdivision are not equally open to participation" by minority groups.

Concerning proportional representation, the compromise stated that "nothing in this section establishes a right to have members of a protected class [minority groups] elected in numbers equal to their proportion in the population."

Although the compromise was tailored to meet his concerns, Hatch professed dissatisfaction with the Dole proposal. In lengthy remarks, he contended that despite the added language on the "results test," thousands of at-large systems in the country would be in jeopardy if the bill was enacted.

"This language amounts to little more than cosmetics. . . . The consequences of the bill will be to inject racial considerations into more and more political decisions that formerly had nothing to do with race," Hatch said.

He contended that courts would be able to undo electoral systems simply by looking at how many minority members were on a city council or commission, for example, and then finding one other factor indicating bias, such as segregated housing or racial bloc voting.

The other major part of the Dole compromise extended Section Five for 25 years, rather than 10 years, as approved by the Constitution Subcommittee, or permanently, as called for by the House version. The compromise also kept the new House bailout provisions.

The Dole proposal required congressional review of Section Five and the bailout after 15 years, although Dole said that Congress could review these provisions at any time prior to 1997.

The Judiciary Committee Vote

On May 4, the Dole compromise was adopted by the Judiciary Committee by a 14-4 vote, with Thurmond, Hatch, John P. East, R-N.C., and Jeremiah Denton, R-Ala., voting against it.

The committee then voted 17-1 to send the legislation to the Senate, with East casting the lone dissenting vote. He claimed the bill was "punitive and vexatious" and called it "a slap in the face to the South."

East offered 10 amendments that opponents said would weaken the bill, but only one was accepted. By a 10-8 vote the committee agreed to language that would bar an officer or agent of a voter's labor union from assisting the voter in the voting booth. This amended a provision in the bill that allowed assistance to blind or disabled voters and voters unable to read or write.

The provision originally had barred assistance only from a voter's employer or an agent of the employer. East argued that if an employer was barred from helping a voter, a union official also should be barred.

East offered one amendment barring a judge from considering the use of an at-large system as part of the evidence of discrimination in a Section Two case. He said that without such language, at-large systems would be suspect, despite contentions by others to the contrary. But his amendment was rejected 5-13.

Another amendment that would have allowed lawsuits under Section Five to be heard in local federal courts rather than in the District of Columbia was rejected 6-12. The full House had rejected a similar proposal when it considered HR 3112. *(Key Votes, 1981 Almanac p. 8-C)*

An East amendment that would have required all Section Two cases to be heard in the District of Columbia instead of in local federal courts was rejected 4-14.

Kennedy pointed out that Section Two cases were privately initiated, while Section Five cases that were tried in Washington involved the federal government and state or local governments. He said it would be inefficient and difficult to have the Justice Department "running all over the country" trying cases.

Senate Passage

The Senate June 18 amended HR 3112 to conform with its own version, S 1992, and then passed the measure by an 85-8 vote. *(Vote 190, p. 33-S)*

Voting "nay" were Republicans Helms and East, both of N.C.; S. I. "Sam" Hayakawa, Calif.; Denton, Ala.; Gordon J. Humphrey, N.H.; Steven D. Symms and James A. McClure, both of Idaho, and Independent Harry F. Byrd Jr., Va.

Before approving the bill, the Senate — by substantial majorities — rejected 15 amendments that chief sponsors Mathias, Dole and Kennedy contended would weaken the measure. The sponsors wanted to prevent all but technical amendments in order to avoid a conference with the House, where sponsors of HR 3112 had said they would accept the Senate bill if it passed without substantive change from the version approved by the Judiciary Committee.

Debate on S 1992 began in earnest June 17 after Helms gave up a desultory filibuster he had waged since June 9. Helms, East, Denton and Byrd had tied up the Senate with speeches attacking S 1992 and with repeated requests for quorum calls. Their filibuster came on a motion to take up S 1992, which the Senate finally agreed to June 17 by a vote of 97-0. *(Vote 174, p. 31-S)*

Several factors apparently persuaded Helms to give up his stalling tactics, including a June 17 announcement by Majority Leader Howard H. Baker Jr., R-Tenn., that the Senate would not take up any other business until the voting rights bill was completed, thus postponing several other measures Helms was interested in.

A second factor that helped cut off Helms' filibuster was the growing irritation of his Republican colleagues, most of whom supported S 1992 and were anxious to move on to other legislation. One Senate GOP leader noted that Helms "isn't making any friends" with his strategy.

Once work on the bill began, the vote on the first proposed floor amendment clearly indicated that the bill's sponsors and civil rights lobbyists had succeeded in building unshakeable support for the measure.

The amendment, offered by East, would have deleted the new "results" standard for proving certain voting rights violations. The amendment was rejected 16-81. *(Vote 175, p. 31-S)*

A second East amendment that would have barred federal judges from requiring proportional representation or quotas for minorities as a remedy for a violation was rejected 14-81. *(Vote 176, p. 31-S)*

A Helms amendment authorizing judges to order proportional representation or require quotas as a remedy was rejected 1-94. *(Vote 177, p. 31-S)*

Among the other amendments rejected were those by:

● East, to allow lawsuits under Section Five to be heard in local federal courts, rather than in Washington, D.C., by a vote of 31-65. *(Vote 178, p. 32-S)*

● East, to ease the new bailout requirements, by a vote

of 19-78. *(Vote 179, p. 32-S)*

● Ted Stevens, R-Alaska, to allow states to bail out even if all of their counties were not eligible to escape coverage, by a vote of 32-58. *(Vote 181, p. 32-S)*

● Stevens, to incorporate the results test of Section Two of the act in the bailout provisions, which were in another section, by a vote of 38-59. *(Vote 180, p. 32-S)*

● Hayakawa, to delete from the bill all requirements for bilingual election materials, by a vote of 32-54. *(Vote 182, p. 32-S)*

● Thad Cochran, R-Miss., to extend nationwide the Section Five requirement for Justice Department approval of election law changes, by 16-74. *(Vote 183, p. 32-S)*

House Accepts Senate Amendments

After the months of controversy in the Senate, final House action on HR 3112 was anticlimactic. The House June 23 accepted the Senate amendments without debate and by unanimous consent.

There was only one moment of minor fireworks. Rep. Henry J. Hyde, R-Ill., angry he was not consulted about the procedure used to clear the bill, resigned from the subcommittee that had handled it.

Hyde, ranking Republican on the House Judiciary Civil and Constitutional Rights Subcommittee, initially opposed a Section Five extension. But after hearing a month of testimony, he publicly stated his support for the extension and began to work with Democrats on a compromise proposal.

Hyde's proposal ultimately was not accepted, and instead Democrats put together a compromise with Republicans F. James Sensenbrenner Jr., Wis., and Hamilton Fish Jr., N.Y.

However, Hyde did vote to report the bill to the House and to pass it.

When subcommittee Chairman Don Edwards, D-Calif., chief sponsor of HR 3112, rose to compliment Hyde for his work on the measure, the Illinois Republican stormed off the House floor. Moments later, he resigned from Edwards' panel. ∎

ERA Dies Three States Short of Ratification

The proposed Equal Rights Amendment (ERA) to the Constitution officially died June 30, three states short of the 38 needed to ratify it.

No state had approved the ERA since 1978, when Congress extended the original March 22, 1979, ratification deadline. *(1978 Almanac p. 773)*

Fifteen states, most of them in the South, never ratified the ERA: Alabama, Arizona, Arkansas, Florida, Georgia, Illinois, Louisiana, Mississippi, Missouri, Nevada, North Carolina, Oklahoma, South Carolina, Utah and Virginia.

Idaho, Tennessee and Nebraska rescinded their pro-ERA votes. The Kentucky Legislature rescinded its vote in favor of the ERA in March 1978 but the resolution was vetoed by the lieutenant governor, who was acting as governor. The South Dakota Legislature passed a resolution in 1979 declaring that its earlier ratification of the ERA would become void if the amendment were not finally approved by the original March 22, 1979, deadline.

The operative language of the proposed amendment was short and to the point:

"Equality of rights under the law shall not be denied or abridged by the United States or by any state on account of sex."

However, the proposal stirred a national political and social debate out of all proportion to its seeming simplicity.

ERA Background

Congressional approval of the ERA was no easier than the ratification fight. The amendment finally was approved by Congress March 22, 1972, 49 years after it was first introduced.

Although the House Judiciary Committee handily approved the bill by a 32-3 vote June 22, 1971, supporters had to work to defeat two restrictive amendments on the House floor. The measure was passed Oct. 12 on a 354-24 vote, a margin substantially greater than the two-thirds necessary. *(1971 Almanac p. 656)*

The Senate did not take up the ERA until 1972. The Judiciary Committee aproved the bill by a 15-1 vote March 14, 1972. The only senator voting against it was Sam J. Ervin Jr., D-N.C. (1954-74), who led a vigorous floor battle to block the proposal. *(1972 Almanac p. 199)*

But after four days of debate in which nine Ervin amendments were defeated, the Senate approved the resolution March 22 by an 84-8 vote.

Less than two hours after the Senate acted, Hawaii became the first state to ratify the amendment.

By early 1978, 35 states had ratified the ERA, but with the March 22, 1979, deadline approaching, amendment supporters knew they were in trouble. They launched a campaign to extend the ratification period.

After months of furious lobbying and often heated debate, Congress on Oct. 6 gave final approval to a resolution extending the ratification deadline by 39 months, until June 30, 1982.

The Court Challenge

The legality of that extension was soon challenged. After Idaho in 1978 voted to rescind its 1973 ratification of the ERA, a group of anti-ERA state legislators and other officials sued the General Services Administration (GSA), which maintained the official list of ratifying states, seeking to force removal of Idaho from the list.

Pro-ERA forces and the Justice Department sought unsuccessfully to remove Judge Marion Callister, of the federal district court in Idaho, from hearing the case because he was a Mormon, and his church opposed the ERA.

However, on Dec. 23, 1981, Callister ruled that Congress exceeded its power when it extended the ERA ratification period in 1978, and that states could rescind their approval of the amendment if they acted within the period available for ratification.

After Callister's adverse ruling, both the National Organization for Women (NOW) and the Justice Department appealed directly to the Supreme Court. NOW asked for expedited consideration of the appeal, but the Justice Department — which was under fire from conservative political groups opposed to the ERA — said such speed would be "inadvisable."

On Jan. 25, 1982, the Supreme Court agreed to hear

the cases of *NOW v. Idaho* and *Carmen v. Idaho* but denied NOW's request for expedited action.

The court did not hear arguments in the case during its 1981-82 term, and on Oct. 4, 1982, the first day of its 1982-83 term, the court dismissed the ERA cases as moot.

Not only did the justices dismiss the cases as moot, they also vacated the lower court decision, wiping it off the law books and rendering it useless as a precedent, a partial victory for those challenging it.

Doom in June

Despite a massive fund-raising and lobbying effort in 1982, ERA supporters were dealt three crushing blows in June, when state legislatures in North Carolina, Florida and Illinois rejected the amendment.

Women's rights activists conceded defeat almost a week before the June 30 deadline, marking the end of a 10-year battle.

At a June 24 news conference, Eleanor Smeal, president of the National Organization for Women (NOW), which led the ERA drive, said that women's groups would concentrate on electing women and their male backers to state legislatures. They would also use lawsuits and such political tools as boycotts and demonstrations to improve women's rights in the business sector, she said.

Smeal was sharply critical of the Republican Party, which she contended led the attack on the amendment. In somewhat softer terms, she also complained that while the Democratic Party included the ERA in its platform for the 1980 election, the amendment and women's rights generally were not high enough on the party's agenda.

President Reagan opposed the ERA, although he did not take an active role in trying to defeat it. By contrast, President Carter and his wife, Rosalynn, strongly supported the amendment, and though it was to no avail, they lobbied legislators extensively in key states while Carter was in office.

Supporters, Foes Looking Ahead

On June 30, the day the ERA officially died, its leading supporters and most vociferous foes all held press conferences to mark its passing and look toward the future.

Phyllis Schlafly, the head of Stop ERA and a leading opponent of the amendment, proclaimed ERA "not only dead now but forever in this century."

She said the amendment had been given three years "of artificial life" by the news media since the ratification deadline was extended in 1979.

Schlafly said ERA failed because her supporters could show it would lead to erosion of family life and the draft of women for military service.

"The gift that we give to Americans today," she said, "is to assure the young women today and for all future years that they will forever be exempted from the military draft."

Pro-ERA leaders vowed to continue their fight. Smeal released a list of 137 Republican state legislators she said opposed the ERA. While she did not say that these 137 would be targeted specifically in upcoming elections, Smeal said NOW would advise women "to vote selectively on the basis of a candidate's stands on women's rights issues."

Kathy Wilson, head of the National Women's Political Caucus, at a separate press conference released her group's "dirty dozen" list of 12 state legislators who she said played strategic roles in defeating the ERA in seven states. Only two were Republicans.

Wilson blamed the ERA's defeat on the seniority system in state legislatures, which she contended gave anti-ERA legislators key political positions. "The seniority system gave power to the unrepresentative few, small-minded men who became our true adversaries in this decade of struggle for equality," she said.

"We will continue to change the political complexion of the legislatures at large. With more feminists in the ring, these men will never again be the ring leaders."

New Effort Begun

Even before ERA was put to rest, an identical constitutional amendment was introduced in the House.

On June 24, six days before the ERA died, Rep. Mario Biaggi, D-N.Y., dropped an identical constitutional amendment (H J Res 529) into the House hopper.

And July 14, two weeks after the ratification deadline passed, another — identically worded — amendment (S J Res 213, H J Res 533) was introduced.

The new Senate amendment had 51 cosponsors, led by Paul E. Tsongas, D-Mass., and Bob Packwood, R-Ore. A two-thirds majority — 67 if all members vote — is required to pass a constitutional amendment.

In the House, where the effort was headed by Democratic Reps. Don Edwards, Calif., Peter W. Rodino Jr., N.J., and Patricia Schroeder, Colo., and Republican Rep. Margaret M. Heckler, Mass., sponsors claimed 205 supporters. This was well short of the two-thirds majority (290) that would be needed if all members voted.

However, no action was taken on the new ERA before the 97th Congress adjourned. Senate Majority Leader Howard H. Baker, R-Tenn., said shortly after the original version died June 30 that he favored a "cooling off" period before starting the congressional debate all over again. ∎

LEAA Goes Out of Business

Fourteen years after its creation, the Law Enforcement Assistance Administration (LEAA) went quietly out of business April 15, a demise ordered by Attorney General William French Smith but preordained in the final years of the Carter administration.

In its somewhat troubled life, the grant agency dispensed nearly $8 billion to local law enforcement agencies for programs such as improved police equipment, shelters for homeless youth and special local task forces to prosecute "career criminals." In recent years, however, LEAA was criticized for requiring too much red tape in its grant program and for wasting money on Dick Tracy-type gadgetry.

The LEAA's official end came by order of Attorney General Smith, who announced Dec. 30, 1981, that the agency would be out of business by April 15. The agency came to a practical end March 20, when all LEAA personnel either were transferred to related law enforcement divisions or laid off.

Four LEAA programs continued after April 15 but were operated through the Office of Justice Assistance, Research and Statistics (OJARS), the government's umbrella law enforcement assistance agency. They were: a benefit program that paid $50,000 to the survivors of police officers killed in action, a regional organized crime intelligence center, a drug treatment program and a program that helped local police run "sting" operations.

The death knell of the LEAA was sounded in 1979

when Congress, after lengthy skirmishing, passed a bill restructuring the agency and giving supervisory authority to OJARS. Research and statistical work previously done by the LEAA was transferred to the newly created National Institute of Justice and the Bureau of Justice Statistics. *(Background, 1978 Almanac p. 370)*

The LEAA had not had a separate appropriation since fiscal 1980, and President Carter did not ask for money for the LEAA in his revised fiscal 1981 budget. ▪

Employee Claims Settlement

The Senate July 16 cleared for the president a bill (HR 4688 — PL 97-226) increasing from $15,000 to $25,000 the amount the United States can pay in claims settlements to military personnel and civilian government employees.

The measure, which amended the 1964 Military and Civilian Employees Claims Act (PL 88-558), was reported from the House Judiciary Commitee March 8 (H Rept 97-452) and passed by the House March 18 under suspension of the rules.

In the Senate, a companion bill (S 1739) was reported from the Judiciary Committee June 24 (S Rept 97-482) and passed July 14, a proceeding that was subsequently vacated in favor of passage of HR 4688. ▪

Missing Children Legislation

A bill (HR 6976 — PL 97-292) aimed at allowing the federal government to help locate missing children was cleared for the president Oct. 1.

Final action came when the Senate adopted a conference report on the measure (H Rept 97-911) one day after the House had done so.

As cleared, the bill authorized entry into the FBI's central crime computer of descriptive data about missing children. If state and local officials failed to enter the information, parents or guardians could have the FBI do so.

The legislation also required inclusion in the FBI computer of a clearinghouse file listing descriptions of unidentified bodies that have been found anywhere in the country. Many of these are children.

Background

Every year, according to federal government estimates, some 1.5 to 1.8 million children are missing from their homes. A majority are runaways who eventually are found unharmed.

But at the end of each year, almost 10 percent of the missing children cases remain unsolved.

The FBI's National Crime Information Center (NCIC) was established in 1967 to centralize criminal history records and to maintain a list of stolen property and persons wanted for crimes.

In 1975, the NCIC started a missing persons file, allowing state and local police to enter information about missing persons into the system. But only a small fraction of the children missing from their homes each year were ever reported to the FBI computer.

Sen. Paula Hawkins, R-Fla., chief sponsor of the Senate version of the missing children bill (S 1701), said that a survey of 25 of the nation's 35 largest police departments

showed only 10 to 14 percent of the missing children had been reported to the NCIC missing persons file.

According to Hawkins, the file was not better used for three major reasons: "a feeling that missing children were a 'domestic dispute,' best handled on the local level; lack of awareness about the availability of the system; [and] reluctance to use limited manpower to update the NCIC files periodically."

Rep. Paul Simon, D-Ill., sponsor of the House bill, said, "When your car is stolen, your local police are able to flash a description that is instantly available to 50,000 departments nationwide. But if your child is stolen, you may be on your own."

HR 6976 was designed to encourage the NCIC to accept more specific information on missing persons, such as blood type, dental records and scars that would be helpful in identifying children. Currently, the file information generally was limited to the person's name, address, height, weight, date of birth, Social Security number, driver's license number or other statistical information, which was of little use in locating children.

In addition, the bill established a national clearinghouse registry for detailed descriptions of unidentified bodies that could then be checked against the descriptions of missing persons. Approximately 2,000 to 5,000 unidentified dead are found each year.

Legislative History

Hawkins, chairman of the Labor Subcommittee on Investigations and Oversight, which conducted a yearlong probe of the missing children problem, pushed hard for enactment of HR 6976.

On Nov. 12, 1981, she successfully attached similar language to HR 4169, a State, Justice, Commerce appropriations bill. However, the bill never cleared. *(1981 Almanac p. 364)*

On Nov. 19, 1981, she attached language to H J Res 357, a continuing appropriations resolution for fiscal 1982. But the provisions were subsequently dropped in conference, and the entire measure was subsequently vetoed by Reagan in any event. *(1981 Almanac p. 294)*

On July 30 and Aug. 19, 1982, the Senate and House Judiciary committees, respectively, approved separate versions (S 1701, HR 6976) of the missing children legislation that was finally enacted into law.

The major difference between the two bills involved the mechanism for getting data on missing children entered into the NCIC computer.

As approved by the Senate committee, S 1701 (S Rept 97-853) would have allowed parents, next of kin, or the legal guardian of missing children to get entries put into the NCIC file. The parent, next of kin or guardian would have to notify the state or local law enforcement agency with investigatory jurisdiction over the matter before having the information put into the missing persons file.

Hawkins argued strongly that parental access to the system was necessary to ensure that information on missing children would in fact be entered in the NCIC file, given past usage patterns.

The FBI opposed parental access, and the House Judiciary Committee heeded the agency's concerns (H Rept 97-820). One House committee aide said members were concerned about local FBI offices being swamped with parents who wanted agents to go out and look for their children. The staffer said that the NCIC missing persons file was designed to help local police do their job, not to have the

federal government supplant local law enforcement.

The House Sept. 20 suspended the rules and passed HR 6976 by voice vote. The Senate Sept. 23 passed S 1701, also by voice vote.

The compromise worked out in conference Sept. 30 allowed parents to determine from FBI field offices whether local or state law officers had entered information about missing children into the master computer.

FBI Director William H. Webster wrote Rep. Don Edwards, D-Calif., a sponsor of the House bill, stating that the FBI would enter information about a child in the computer if state and local officers refused to cooperate. The language of Webster's letter was not part of the final bill, but it was included in the conference report. ∎

Manufacturing Clause Kept

Congress July 13 voted overwhelmingly to override President Reagan's veto and enact a copyright bill (HR 6198 — PL 97-215) intended to protect the American printing industry.

The action came on the seventh veto of Reagan's presidency, his first to be overridden.

The vote in the House was 324-86, 50 more than the two-thirds majority (274) needed. The vote in the Senate was 84-9, 22 more than the two-thirds (62) required. *(Vote 169, p. 50-H; vote 209, p. 38-S)*

The bill enacted over the president's objections was a one-paragraph measure that extended until 1986 the "manufacturing clause" in U.S. copyright law. This clause required most books and periodicals written in English by U.S. authors to be printed and bound in the United States or Canada to receive full copyright protection.

Reagan said in his July 8 veto message that the clause, first enacted in 1891, was no longer necessary because the U.S. printing industry "is now one of the most modern and efficient in the world." He also said that countries trading with the U.S. had complained about the clause. *(Text of veto message, p. 25-E)*

Book publishers and authors also opposed extension of the clause. They argued that it amounted to discrimination against a class of copyright owners and had hamstrung the American publishing industry.

But the U.S. printing industry and organized labor argued that expiration of the clause would result in a massive loss of business to foreign printing companies, particularly those in Southeast Asia.

The Jobs Issue

A June 15, 1981, report by the Labor Department said eliminating the manufacturing clause could cost up to 367,000 domestic jobs in printing and related industries.

Republican and Democratic supporters of HR 6198 made much of the Labor Department report in debate July 13 on the override motions.

They were helped by a quickly mobilized lobbying effort from organized labor. On July 12, the AFL-CIO hand-delivered letters to all House members urging them to override the veto. And lobbyists from several unions stood outside the House chamber July 13 exhorting members to vote their way.

As soon as the House voted, the lobbyists hurried to the Senate, where they buttonholed members and passed around their letter.

Rep. Harold S. Sawyer, R-Mich., perhaps the most vocal House supporter of HR 6198, said that extending the clause did not amount to a new trade protection. "This is something that has been on the books for 91 years," he said.

"... If there were a time to repeal the manufacturing clause or to allow it to expire, this certainly is not the time," he declared, citing high unemployment figures.

Sawyer concluded his remarks by waving a 1981 newspaper article from *The Straits Times* of Singapore talking about "brighter days ahead for Singapore printers" if the manufacturing clause expires.

"I say if we want to help Singapore and Hong Kong and Taiwan, then let us go ahead and sustain this veto," Sawyer said.

A handful of House members, including Republicans Dan Lungren, Calif., Barber B. Conable Jr., N.Y., and Bill Frenzel, Minn., supported the veto. They called the bill protectionist and said it undermined U.S. efforts to improve trade with other countries.

In the Senate, Judiciary Chairman Strom Thurmond, R-S.C., said he was convinced the president had gotten bad advice on the bill. Thurmond voiced irritation that Reagan vetoed the bill without telling GOP leaders ahead of time. He said the administration had never expressed concern about the bill while it was pending.

Legislative History

HR 6198 was reported by the House Judiciary Committee May 19 (H Rept 97-575) and then referred to the Ways and Means Committee. That panel approved the bill June 10.

The House passed HR 6198 by voice vote June 15 under suspension of the rules.

The Senate Judiciary Committee approved an identical bill (S 1880) on June 23, but published no report on the measure. The full Senate adopted the House version June 30, sending the bill to the president. ∎

Record Piracy Bill Cleared

Congress May 10 cleared a bill (S 691 — PL 97-180) increasing the penalties for record, tape and film piracy and counterfeiting.

Final action came when the House approved the Senate bill, which was identical to a House bill (HR 3530) it had passed by voice vote minutes earlier under suspension of the rules. The Senate had passed S 691 (S Rept 97-274) in 1981. *(1981 Almanac p. 437)*

The House Judiciary Committee reported HR 3530 on April 29 (H Rept 97-495).

The bill was designed to curb the illegal reproduction and sale of copyrighted records, films and tapes, which sponsor Rep. Robert W. Kastenmeier, D-Wis., called "a highly sophisticated business that has grown into a billion-dollar-a-year industry."

As cleared by Congress, S 691 provided:

● A maximum penalty of five years' imprisonment or a fine of up to $250,000 or both for illegally reproducing and distributing as many as 1,000 records or 65 films during a 180-day period.

● A one-year prison term, a $25,000 fine or both for copyright infringements of a lesser volume.

Current penalties were $10,000 or one year in prison or both for a first offense, $25,000 or two years, or both, for any subsequent offense. ∎

Filibuster Dooms Controversial Antitrust Bill

Proponents of a controversial antitrust bill (S 995), one of the most heavily lobbied measures of the 97th Congress, gave up their fight Dec. 2 after two efforts to cut off a Senate filibuster failed in lopsided votes.

Senate Judiciary Committee Chairman Strom Thurmond, R-S.C., chief sponsor of the legislation, said he could not in good conscience insist that the Senate continue working on the measure when it seemed clear that opponents had the votes to keep the filibuster going.

The first vote to invoke cloture and limit debate was 38-58, 22 votes short of the three-fifths majority (60) needed. It would have ended debate on the Judiciary Committee version of the bill. *(Vote 386, p. 65-S)*

The second cloture vote was on the bill as originally introduced, and it failed 44-51. *(Vote 387, p. 65-S)*

The outcome was a victory for Max Baucus, D-Mont., Howard M. Metzenbaum, D-Ohio, and Warren B. Rudman, R-N.H., who led the opposition to S 995.

S 995 was a bill to change the 1914 Clayton Act to allow defendants in price-fixing suits to apportion damages among themselves according to their share of the price-fixing scheme, a practice known as "contribution."

Price-fixers currently were each liable for all damages involved in a price-fixing conspiracy, regardless of each defendant's level of participation.

The Supreme Court ruled May 26, 1981, that there was no right of contribution in existing antitrust laws. The court said it was up to Congress to write contribution into the statutes. *(Texas Industries v. Radcliff Materials Inc., 1981 Almanac p. 10-A)*

S 995 also made it more difficult for some defendants to work out advantageous settlements at the expense of other defendants. As reported April 26 by the Senate Judiciary Committee (S Rept 97-359), this provision could have saved millions of dollars for companies that were defendants in pending antitrust cases.

A bill similar to S 995 was approved by the Senate Judiciary Committee in 1979, but it never was considered by the full Senate. *(1979 Almanac p. 388)*

Claim Reduction

The provisions of S 995 to permit "contribution," or the apportionment of damages among defendants in a price-fixing case, were relatively non-controversial.

Lobbying pressures centered around a second feature of S 995 that required a judge to subtract from the total damages awarded a plaintiff an amount proportionate to any settling defendant's share of liability, even if the actual settlement were less. Such "claim reduction" was intended to prevent some defendants from settling for far less money than their actual share of the conspiracy.

Currently, if a plaintiff settled with one defendant in a $100 million conspiracy for $10 million, the plaintiff would only have to subtract $10 million from the total he sought from the remaining defendants — even if the defendant who settled was responsible for $50 million of the overcharges in the price-fixing scheme.

Under S 995, the plaintiff would have to reduce his claims against the remaining defendants by $50 million.

The bill as originally introduced made the changes in damage awards applicable only to cases initiated after the date of enactment. But the Judiciary Committee version of

the bill allowed a judge to apply the claim reduction principle to pending cases if he believed it would be "inequitable under all the circumstances" not to do so.

The Lobbying Campaign

S 995 spawned an intense and expensive lobbying campaign directed at whether the damage award changes should be applied to pending cases.

Pressing for such a provision were Georgia Pacific Co., Weyerhaeuser Co. and Willamette Industries, defendants in a lawsuit over irregularities in plywood product sales; and Milliken & Co., of South Carolina, the defendant in an antitrust suit brought by Burlington Industries over price fixing on textile machinery.

One of the companies lobbying for the bill, Mead Corp., had contended it could be liable for up to $750 million in damages if the law was not changed. But Mead announced Sept. 7 that it had reached a $45 million settlement with plaintiffs in its price-fixing case. Nonetheless, Mead officials and their lawyers continued to press for passage of S 995.

Among the well-known lobbyists arguing for pending-case application were former Attorneys General Griffin B. Bell and Benjamin R. Civiletti; a former Watergate prosecutor, Philip A. Lacovara; and two former Senate Judiciary Committee members, Birch Bayh, D-Ind. (1963-81), and Sam J. Ervin Jr., D-N.C. (1954-74).

S 995 provoked strenuous opposition from plaintiffs in price-fixing suits, who claimed it was a bailout for the defendant companies. They said current law needed to remain stringent to act as a deterrent to price fixers. To apply the claim reduction principle to pending cases, they asserted, was to change the rules in the middle of the game and deprive plaintiffs of the chance to collect adequate damages from remaining defendants.

Stuart E. Eizenstat, a top aide to former President Jimmy Carter, was among those lobbying in opposition to the pending-case provision.

It was only the perseverance of Thurmond that pushed S 995 to the floor at all during the brief lame-duck session that began Nov. 29.

Ever since he maneuvered the bill out of the Judiciary Committee March 31, Thurmond had been pressing Majority Leader Howard H. Baker Jr., R-Tenn., for floor action.

Mark Goodin, Thurmond's press secretary, characterized as "absolute nonsense" allegations by opponents of the bill that Thurmond was pushing the legislation simply to help Milliken, a South Carolina company. He said Thurmond supported the bill because it corrected inequities in the current law.

Committee Action

The Senate Judiciary Committee approved S 995 by a 12-6 vote March 31 and formally reported it April 26 (S Rept 97-359).

Two proposals on the pending-case issue were rejected before the committee approved a version offered by Thurmond and Republicans Paul Laxalt, Nev., and Orrin G. Hatch, Utah.

The first, offered by Thurmond on behalf of Jeremiah Denton, R-Ala., was an amendment to make the claim-reduction provisions applicable only to cases filed after

March 31, 1982. It would not affect the rights that parties had acquired in cases pending before that date. Baucus, a cosponsor of the amendment, sought to withdraw the proposal prior to a vote, but Thurmond wouldn't allow it. The amendment was rejected 6-11, with Howell Heflin, D-Ala., voting "present."

Baucus then offered another amendment to make the bill applicable only to cases filed after the date of enactment. This proposal failed 6-10, with Heflin and Arlen J. Specter, R-Pa., voting present.

The committee then approved the Thurmond-Laxalt-Hatch amendment by a 10-7 vote. It would apply the claim-reduction principle to pending cases if a court determined that "it would be inequitable in light of all the circumstances" not to do so.

The amendment also specified that no agreement to settle, compromise or release a claim against any party in a case could be rescinded unless all parties involved agreed in writing. ∎

Threats to Public Officials

On Sept. 28, Congress cleared a bill (HR 6168 — PL 97-297) making it a federal crime to threaten to kidnap the president, a former president, presidential candidates or any other person entitled to Secret Service Protection. Currently, there was no one federal statute covering kidnap threats, and the Secret Service was hampered, according to the bill's sponsors, by having to rely on various state laws.

The House passed HR 6168 by unanimous consent Aug. 16. The bill had been approved July 20 and was reported Aug. 11 by the House Judiciary Committee (H Rept 96-725).

In the Senate, the measure was referred to the Judiciary Committee, but the committee was discharged and the bill was placed on the calendar Sept. 16.

The Senate passed it Sept. 28, clearing it for President Reagan. ∎

Crimes Against Officials

Congress Sept. 22 cleared for President Reagan a bill (S 907 — PL 97-285) making it a federal crime to kill, kidnap or assault specified U.S. government officials.

Final action came when the Senate accepted House amendments to the bill.

The House passed S 907 under suspension of the rules Sept. 14, just hours after it had been amended and reported (H Rept 97-803) by the House Judiciary Committee.

The Senate passed its version of the bill (S Rept 97-320) May 5.

The measure covered Supreme Court justices, senior presidential and vice presidential aides, Cabinet officers and nominees, second-ranking officials in each department and the director of the Central Intelligence Agency.

Penalties ranged from one year in prison, a $5,000 fine or both for assaults, to life imprisonment for murder, manslaughter, kidnapping and an attempt or conspiracy to harm the covered officials.

Currently, crimes against these officials were prosecuted under laws of the states in which the offenses occurred.

The House committee amended the Senate bill to include nominees for Cabinet posts and the director of the Central Intelligence Agency, and to make clear that the government would not have to prove that a defendant knew a harmed official was protected under federal law.

The bill grew out of the March 30, 1981, shooting of President Reagan and three other men. *(Reagan shooting, 1981 Almanac p. 6; legislative response, 1981 Almanac p. 420)* ∎

Victims, Witnesses of Crime

In a session that began Oct. 1, Congress cleared a bill (S 2420) designed to make the federal courts more sensitive to crime victims and witnesses. President Reagan signed the measure into law (PL 97-291) Oct. 12.

Although the bill did not create an outright victim compensation program, it did require judges to order restitution to victims in most cases involving violations of federal criminal statutes.

"With the passage of this bill, we have taken an important step to assure those who are victimized that they will receive at least the same considerations and protections which are currently extended to the accused," said Sen. John Heinz, R-Pa.

The version of the legislation sent to President Reagan early Oct. 2 was a compromise worked out by House and Senate Judiciary staffers and approved by both chambers in the last hours of a marathon session before Congress recessed for the Nov. 2 elections.

Provisions

As cleared, S 2420 contained the following major provisions:

● Strengthened and clarified existing law concerning harassment of crime victims and witnesses.

● Made it a felony, punishable by a fine of up to $250,000 and a prison term of up to 10 years or both, to seek to intimidate victims or witnesses of crime through physical force or threats of such force.

● Allowed a prosecutor to seek a court order to protect a victim or witness from intimidation by a particular person. The so-called "protective order" could cover the family of the victim or witness as well.

● Provided for revocation of bail for a defendant who tried to intimidate a victim or witness.

● Required the sentencing report on a defendant to include a "victim's impact statement" providing information on the financial, social, psychological and physical impact of the crime on the victim.

● Authorized a judge to order restitution to the victim in cases involving loss of property or personal injury to cover uninsured medical expenses, property losses and funeral and burial expenses, if appropriate. The judge would have to cite reasons if restitution was not ordered.

The bill that eventually cleared did not contain two provisions that were in S 2420 as passed by the Senate Sept. 14. One would have made the federal government civilly liable for bodily injury caused by a person who either escaped or was prematurely released from federal custody because of the federal government's "gross negligence."

The other section would have expanded the attorney general's authority to relocate or protect any witness or potential witness.

Legislative History

S 2420 was approved by the Senate Judiciary Committee Aug. 16 and formally reported Aug. 19 (S Rept 97-532).

It was passed by the Senate Sept. 14 by voice vote.

In the House, the bill was referred to the Judiciary Committee. But that panel was discharged without acting, and the measure passed the House by voice vote Sept. 30. ∎

Pretrial Services Program

Congress Sept. 15 cleared for the president legislation (S 923 — PL 97-267) to expand nationwide 10 demonstration pretrial services programs designed to help judges decide who should be released on bail.

Final action came when the House by a vote of 367-20 adopted the conference report (H Rept 97-792) on the bill. *(Vote 309, p. 92-H)*

The Senate had approved the report Aug. 20. The Senate originally passed S 923 June 18, 1981. *(1981 Almanac p. 433)*

The House passed a similar though not identical bill (HR 3481 — H Rept 97-56) May 11 by a vote of 369-30. *(Vote 64, p. 20-H)*

That measure had been reported May 19, 1981, by the House Judiciary Committee.

The demonstration programs were created in 1974 as part of the Speedy Trial Act (PL 93-619), which set deadlines for trying those charged with crimes. *(1974 Almanac p. 295; 1979 Almanac p. 376)*

Through the programs, pretrial services officers collected information about a defendant and gave it to a judge prior to a bail decision. If bail was granted, the officers supervised released defendants, notified the judge about any violation of bail conditions and recommended changes in release conditions.

As cleared by Congress, S 923 required the creation of pretrial services programs in all 95 federal judicial districts. The House bill had provided for a more limited program expansion.

The bill provided that information collected in a pretrial report must remain confidential unless it was needed for a bail hearing. The information was not admissible on the issue of guilt in a criminal proceeding unless the proceeding concerned a crime committed while the defendant was on pretrial release or related to his failure to appear for a proceeding involving pretrial release. ∎

Anti-Arson Legislation

Congress Sept. 28 cleared a bill (HR 6454) designed to simplify the prosecution of federal arson cases and to upgrade the offense of arson to major-crime status.

President Reagan signed the measure into law (PL 97-298) on Oct. 12.

Final congressional action came when the House by voice vote accepted amendments to the bill adopted by the Senate, which had passed the measure Sept. 22.

HR 6454 was reported July 28 by the House Judiciary Committee (H Rept 97-678). It was passed by the House Aug. 2.

The measure was designed to clarify that arson involving property used in or affecting interstate or foreign commerce constituted a federal offense. To prosecute an arson case as a federal crime under current law, authorities had to show that damage to burned property was the result of an explosion. HR 6454 eliminated that requirement.

Rep. William J. Hughes, D-N.J., chief House sponsor, said the old requirement often necessitated extensive investigation even in cases where it was established that the fire in question was intentionally set.

Major-Crime Status

The Senate adopted an amendment by John Glenn, D-Ohio, elevating arson to major-crime status for purposes of the FBI's Uniform Crime Reports. This reporting system, designed to permit evaluation of fluctuations in the volume of major crimes, already tracked murder, rape, robbery, aggravated assault, burglary, larceny and motor vehicle theft.

Glenn said arson was a "deadly, billion-dollar crime" that each year killed 1,000 people, injured more than 3,000 and caused direct property losses of at least $1.7 billion.

It was also, he said, "the nation's fastest growing crime, quadrupling during the last decade and increasing tenfold in dollar losses.... Arson represents 25 percent of all fires and also 25 percent of our fire insurance premiums."

Glenn said that arson was the costliest crime, with an average 1981 loss per incident of $9,399, compared to $3,173 per auto theft, the next most costly.

In the past, he said, the U.S. Fire Administration found it "impossible to accurately measure the arson problem and its various components."

Adding the offense to the FBI's statistical reports on serious crimes "will help focus public attention on this burgeoning problem," Glenn said.

"Increased public awareness will in turn put pressure on legislators, officials, the insurance industry and others to develop effective solutions to the arson epidemic that plagues our nation," he concluded. ∎

Secret Service Zones

The Senate Oct. 1 cleared for President Reagan a bill (HR 4468 — PL 97-308) authorizing the Secret Service to establish cordoned-off zones of protection around anyone entitled to Secret Service protection.

Currently, although the Secret Service generally set up protective zones around all individuals it was responsible for guarding, it was a crime to violate only the zone around the president. The Secret Service also provided protection to the vice president, candidates for president and vice president, the president-elect and vice president-elect, and the families of these officials; visiting heads of state and distinguished foreign visitors for whom the president authorized protection.

The change embodied in HR 4468 was recommended by the House Select Committee on Assassinations (H Rept 95-1828) in 1978 and by the Treasury Department. *(1978 Almanac p. 211)*

The maximum fine for violating a protection zone was increased to $1,000 from $300; persons convicted of the offense could also face up to a year in prison.

HR 4468 was reported March 8 by the House Judiciary Committee (H Rept 97-451) and passed March 18 under suspension of the rules. ∎

Theft of Nuclear Materials

Congress Oct. 1 sent President Reagan a bill (HR 5228 — PL 97-351) making it a federal crime to unlawfully obtain nuclear materials and use them to threaten or physically harm individuals.

Penalties ranged from 20 years and/or a $250,000 fine up to life imprisonment for cases involving serious injury or death.

The measure, designed to deter nuclear terrorism, was necessary to implement a 1979 convention on protecting nuclear materials that the United States signed with 33 other countries. The Senate ratified that convention July 30, 1981. *(Vote 241, 1981 Almanac p. 41-S)*

The convention was first proposed by Secretary of State Henry A. Kissinger in 1974 and was called for by Congress in the 1978 Nuclear Non-Proliferation Act. *(1978 Almanac p. 350)*

The purpose of the convention, according to Rep. William J. Hughes, D-N.J., chief House sponsor of HR 5228, was "to establish general levels of physical security" during the international shipment and domestic use, storage and transportation of nuclear material. Hughes said another purpose was to require signatories to establish "appropriate responses" to serious offenses involving nuclear material. HR 5228, he said, was such a response.

The New Jersey Democrat noted that the convention's provisions guaranteed that violators would find no safe haven in any of the party countries. They must either be prosecuted, he said, or extradited to a nation that would prosecute.

The bill set penalties in cases involving death or serious bodily injury of up to $250,000 in fines or imprisonment for up to life, or both.

Other offenses carried penalties of up to $250,000 in fines, up to 20 years in prison, or both.

Serious bodily injury was defined in the bill to cover injuries that involved a substantial risk of death, extreme physical pain, protracted and obvious disfigurement, protracted loss or impairment of a body function or mental faculty.

In addition to prohibiting the misuse of nuclear materials, HR 5228 authorized the attorney general to seek enforcement help from the military in certain emergencies.

House Action

HR 5228 was reported June 24 by the House Judiciary Committee (H Rept 97-624).

The House passed the bill July 20 by 396-9 under suspension of the rules, a procedure that bars amendments and requires a two-thirds vote. *(Vote 180, p. 54-H)*

Reps. Thomas N. Kindness, R-Ohio, and F. James Sensenbrenner Jr., R-Wis., who were among the nine opponents, argued during debate July 19 that the death penalty should be provided in circumstances involving the death of another person.

Sensenbrenner had offered a death penalty amendment when the House Judiciary Committee approved the bill June 15, but his proposal was rejected 8-20.

Chief sponsor William J. Hughes, D-N.J., told the House that no hearings had been held on the death penalty. He noted that capital punishment raised problems "politically and morally for many members of this body," and said its inclusion in the nuclear terrorism bill would jeopardize the legislation.

Senate Action

In the Senate, the measure was referred to the Judiciary Commitee, but that panel was later discharged and HR 5228 was placed on the Senate calendar Aug. 5 along with a companion bill (S 1446).

On Sept. 14, the Senate first amended and then passed HR 5228, indefinitely postponing any action on the companion measure. The changes involved the definition of "attempts" and "conspiracy" to commit offenses prohibited under the bill.

The House agreed to certain of the amendments Sept. 28, disagreed to others and returned the bill to the Senate. On Oct. 1, the Senate concurred in the House action, clearing the bill. ∎

Patent Fee Restructuring

Congress Aug. 12 cleared for the president a bill (HR 6260 — PL 97-247) authorizing operations of the U.S. Patent and Trademark Office for fiscal 1983-1985 and restructuring patent fees.

Final action came when the Senate approved the bill by voice vote. The House had passed it June 8.

The bill authorized appropriations of $76 million for fiscal 1983 and "such sums as may be necessary" for the other two years. Revenues from various fees for patents and registered trademarks were expected to give the patent office a total fiscal 1983 budget of $154.9 million.

HR 6260 also authorized a $2.5 million increase in the fiscal 1982 authorization of the patent office, for a total of $121.5 million.

New Fee Structure

The legislation established a two-tier system for payment of patent user fees, requiring large firms to pay at a level that recoups 100 percent of patent application and maintenance costs while individual inventors, small firms and non-profit organizations pay at a rate designed to recoup 50 percent of costs.

The Reagan administration originally sought legislation (S 2211) that would have required all recipients of U.S. patents to pay fees set by the patent commissioner at a level recovering 100 per cent of costs. But Congress refused to go along with that approach.

HR 6260 was reported from the House Judiciary Committee on May 17 (H Rept 97-542) and passed June 8 under suspension of the rules.

In the Senate, it was reported from the Judiciary Committee July 6, but no written report was issued. ∎

Trademark Amendments

The Senate Sept. 29 cleared for the president a bill (HR 5154 — PL 97-296) making clear that state and local governments could not require alteration of federally registered trademarks on signs, brochures, posters, stationery and the like.

The House Sept. 20 suspended the rules and passed HR 5154, which had been reported Aug. 19 from the Judiciary Committee (H Rept 97-778).

The Senate accepted the House version without

amendment Sept. 20.

The bill amended the 1946 Lanham Trademark Act, which provided federal regulation of trademarks. HR 5154 grew out of a 1978 Nevada case involving Century 21 Real Estate Inc., in which a three-judge federal court decided that the Lanham act did not block the Nevada Real Estate Commission from regulating the use of a federally registered trademark. Nevada had sought to require local real estate brokers to modify the trademarked logos of their companies to meet state requirements.

Nevada was not alone. A number of other jurisdictions also sought to regulate display of such trademarks, especially in the real estate business.

The committee report made clear that HR 5154 was intended only to restrict a state's authority concerning the name of a franchise holder within a trademark. The bill did not cover a state's ability to control the use of trademarks in advertising. ∎

Senate Passes Anti-Busing Rider to Justice Bill

The Senate March 2 approved a fiscal 1982 authorization bill for the Justice Department that carried the toughest anti-busing rider ever approved by either chamber of Congress. But the measure (S 951) died in the House.

The House Judiciary Committee approved its own fiscal 1983 authorization bill (HR 6297) on May 11, but that legislation never reached the House floor.

It was the third year in a row that the department's regular authorization became mired down. In contrast to other years, however, Congress made no attempt to pass a temporary authorization measure. *(1981 Almanac p. 428)*

The Justice Department's last stopgap authorization (HR 4608 — PL 97-76) expired Feb. 1, 1982. But the department, with the blessing of the House and Senate Judiciary committees, continued operating under various continuing appropriations resolutions.

Senate Action

The Anti-Busing Rider

After an on-again-off-again eight-month fight, the Senate voted 58-38 Feb. 4 to add sweeping anti-busing language to a fiscal 1982 Justice Department authorization bill (S 951). *(Vote 2, p. 2-S)*

The action was not unexpected. In September 1981, the Senate had approved identical language by voice vote after cutting off a three-month filibuster led by Lowell P. Weicker Jr., R-Conn.

Because of the way the amendment was put together, however, a second vote was needed to make it part of the bill. Weicker led another filibuster after the September vote, but cloture on the amendment was invoked Dec. 10. This led to the Feb. 4 vote.

The amendment, sponsored by Jesse Helms, R-N.C., and J. Bennett Johnston, D-La., was the most stringent anti-busing measure ever approved by either house. It barred the Justice Department from bringing any legal action that could lead, directly or indirectly, to court-ordered busing; prohibited federal courts from ordering busing except in narrowly defined circumstances; and allowed the attorney general to file suit on behalf of students who believed they had been bused in violation of the standards. This last provision opened the way for overturning existing busing orders.

The only new development in the battle over the anti-busing amendment was a decision by Barry Goldwater, R-Ariz., hero of the "old right," to speak out against efforts by the "new right" to curb the power of the federal courts to address inflammatory social issues such as busing, abortion and school prayer.

In a floor statement Feb. 4, Goldwater denounced such efforts as a threat to the constitutional separation of powers and the independence of the judiciary.

Cloture Invoked

The Senate Feb. 9 voted to invoke cloture and choke off debate on S 951. The 63-33 vote, three more than the 60 needed, came nearly eight months after the Senate took up S 951. It did not, however, put an end to Weicker's delaying tactics. *(Vote 4, p. 3-S)*

An agreement for a final vote was not reached until Feb. 25, when Weicker gave up on the filibuster he had been conducting against the legislation since June 16, 1981.

Weicker's filibuster was reminiscent of the wrangling that occurred during Senate fights in the 1960s over civil rights legislation. But in that era, it was Southern conservatives who used the Senate rules to stall the passage of civil rights legislation championed by Northerners.

Since June 16, 1981, the reverse had been true — Southerners were trying to push through legislation to undo what the civil rights laws and the Supreme Court had wrought, while Weicker and his allies used the very tactics they once deplored to obstruct passage of the legislation.

The turning points in the eight-month fight were three cloture votes to end the filibuster: Sept. 16, 1981, on a Johnston amendment; Dec. 10, 1981, on a Helms amendment; and Feb. 9, on the bill itself.

The last cloture vote limited debate on S 951 to 100 hours and capped the number of amendments that could be considered.

Weicker agreed to permit a final vote on the bill March 2 when it became clear that he had little chance of stalling proceedings much beyond Feb. 25.

Although the Connecticut Republican had filed some 604 amendments before cloture was invoked Feb. 9, the vast majority were ruled out of order.

Part of Weicker's problem was Johnston's parliamentary skill. Shortly before the Feb. 9 cloture vote, Johnston introduced a new text of his anti-busing amendment. Some 250 of Weicker's amendments had been drafted as changes to the earlier language, and thus they would have been ruled out of order as soon as Weicker brought them up.

All-Night Session

Weicker could see his battle drawing to a close when Baker kept the Senate in session from 10 a.m. Feb. 24 until 1:21 a.m. Feb. 25. During those hours, 46 of Weicker's amendments were ruled out of order in rapid succession.

Early in the evening of Feb. 24, the Senate rejected an anti-busing proposal offered by Slade Gorton, R-Wash., that was even more sweeping than Johnston's language.

The amendment was rejected by a 42-49 vote after the Senate by a 40-51 margin rejected a motion to table (kill) the amendment. *(Votes 23, 21, p. 6-S)*

The Gorton amendment would have barred any federal or state court, agency or department from implementing a plan that assigned students to public schools based on race. Thus, the amendment even would have barred a school board from voluntarily developing a desegregation plan that called for busing.

Heflin Amendment

Before passing S 951, the Senate March 2 by 72-22 adopted an amendment of Howell Heflin, D-Ala., to allow the Justice Department to participate in any proceeding to "remove or reduce" the requirement of busing under existing court orders. *(Vote 38, p. 8-S)*

This amounted to a restriction on the Helms-Johnston proposal that Heflin said was necessary to assure the proper resolution of any case that was reopened. Otherwise, Heflin said, a judge would find himself reviewing a case that Justice had participated in but unable to hear from the department during that review.

Final Passage

The Senate March 2 passed S 951 as amended by the anti-busing language. The vote was 57-37. *(Vote 39, p. 8-S)*

Weicker said that he had not abandoned his fight against the legislation. "This bill will not become law," he vowed, thumping his desk for emphasis.

House Committee Action

In an effort to keep S 951 out of the hostile clutches of the House Judiciary Committee, Rep. Robert A. Young, D-Mo., March 10 introduced a resolution asking that the measure be sent directly to the House floor. His resolution was sent to the Rules Committee, along with a similar one introduced March 11 by Reps. Henson Moore, R-La.; Ronald M. Mottl, D-Ohio; L. A. "Skip" Bafalis, R-Fla., and Carroll Hubbard Jr., D-Ky.

Despite such efforts, S 951 was sent to the House Judiciary Committee March 22.

On May 25, Rep. James M. Collins, R-Texas, filed a discharge petition aimed at prying S 951 from the Judiciary Committee, but he never was able to gather the 218 signatures, a majority of the House membership, needed to do so. The bill remained lodged in committee at year's end.

The House Bill: HR 6297

Although it ignored S 951, the House Judiciary Committee May 11 approved a $2.66 billion fiscal 1983 authorization for Department of Justice (DOJ) programs.

The bill (HR 6297) authorized $69 million more than the $2.59 billion sought by the Reagan administration in a request submitted to the committee May 10.

Following were some of the major expenditures authorized in the fiscal 1983 House bill:

● **FBI,** $799.33 million. This was the same as the administration proposal.

● **Drug Enforcement Administration,** $256.44 million. The administration proposed $246.95 million.

● **Immigration and Naturalization Service,** $571.65 million. The administration proposed $524.6 million.

● **Federal prison system,** $394.25 million. This was the same as the administration proposal.

● **General legal activities,** $136.56 million. This was the same as the administration proposal. The bill earmarked $2.75 million for investigating and prosecuting alleged Nazi war criminals. M. Caldwell Butler, R-Va., offered an amendment to delete the earmarking, but his proposal was rejected by voice vote. ∎

Revision of Special Prosecutor Law Cleared

In the session that began Dec. 16, Congress cleared legislation (S 2059) that revised and extended for five years the special prosecutor law that was enacted following the Watergate scandal. President Reagan signed the bill Jan. 3 (PL 97-409).

Final action came when the Senate by voice vote accepted relatively minor amendments to the bill adopted by the House Dec. 13.

Generally, the bill tightened the standards that trigger appointment of a special prosecutor to investigate alleged wrongdoing by high government and campaign officials. It also shortened the list of officials covered by the law, reduced the number of years individuals were covered and changed the name of the special prosecutor to independent counsel.

Without congressional action, the special prosecutor law, Title VI of the Ethics in Government Act (PL 95-521), would have expired Oct. 1, 1983. *(1978 Almanac p. 835)*

The Justice Department had opposed a reauthorization, contending that the attorney general was fully capable of handling any federal investigation, regardless of its political sensitivity. However, a Justice Department spokesman said of the legislation, "We recognize it as a political reality."

Provisions

As cleared by Congress, S 2059 included the following provisions:

● Changed the name of the special prosecutor to an independent counsel.

● Changed the standard that would trigger a preliminary investigation of covered officials to allow the attorney general to consider the credibility of the accuser and the specificity of the information received.

● Required the appointment of an independent counsel only when the attorney general "finds reasonable grounds to believe that further investigation or prosecution is warranted." This replaced the current standard, which required a special prosecutor unless the information received "is so unsubstantiated that no further investigation is warranted."

● Allowed the attorney general to seek an independent counsel if he determined that an investigation by him or any other Justice Department officer might result in a personal financial or political conflict of interest.

● Modified the list of persons covered to include only officials who occupied top-level executive positions close to either the president or the attorney general.

Watergate Revisited: A Legislative Legacy

The Watergate scandal began on June 17, 1972, with the infamous break-in at Democratic National Committee headquarters and culminated Aug. 9, 1974, with the resignation of President Nixon.

The effects of the scandal did not end then, however. Throughout most of the ensuing decade, Congress considered and passed reform proposals that were born during the Watergate period.

Some sweeping new laws bearing on executive branch powers, such as the 1973 War Powers Act (PL 93-148) and the Congressional Budget and Impoundment Control Act of 1974 (PL 93-344), had nothing to do with Watergate but much to do with a related weakening of the Nixon presidency.

On the other hand, several specific recommendations of the Senate Watergate Committee — especially those urging revisions in federal criminal law that covered more precisely acts like those of the Watergate burglars and conspirators — never were enacted. *(Committee report, Watergate: Chronology of a Crisis, p. 730)*

But the roots of several public laws were traced directly to Watergate. This legislation included two landmark acts governing political campaigns and government ethics, as well as other laws more limited in scope.

Watergate was not the only factor involved in the reform legislation. It was shaped over a period of years and was affected by many crosscurrents in Congress. But the Watergate legacy was clearly evident.

Following is a description of the most significant laws rooted in Watergate:

FEDERAL ELECTIONS CAMPAIGN AMENDMENTS OF 1974 (PL 93-443). Technically a package of amendments to the Federal Election Campaign Act of 1971 (PL 92-225), the 1974 legislation actually was a comprehensive rewrite of U.S. election law. *(1974 Almanac p. 611)*

The new law tightened financial disclosure requirements, set low contribution limits and expenditure ceilings for all federal election campaigns, established public financing for presidential primary and general election campaigns and created the Federal Election Commission (FEC) to enforce the law.

The campaign act was amended again in 1976 to partially restore and revise major parts of the 1974 law struck down by the Supreme Court. The 1976 campaign act amendments (PL 94-283) reconstituted the FEC and revised financial limits in the law. *(1976 Almanac p. 459)*

ETHICS IN GOVERNMENT ACT OF 1978 (PL 95-521). This broad law was the second piece of major reform legislation to grow out of the Watergate period. The act:

● Established a mechanism for appointing a special prosecutor to investigate allegations against high government officials;

● Set detailed financial disclosure requirements for the president, vice president, high executive branch officials, Supreme Court justices, federal judges, top judicial employees, members of Congress, key congressional aides and candidates for federal office;

● Placed new restrictions on business activities of federal workers who leave government;

● Established an Office of Government Ethics in the executive branch to regulate ethical conduct and monitor compliance with ethics laws.

Although the 1978 law could be traced directly to Watergate, by the time it finally was enacted it had been shaped by three major factors: the Watergate scandal itself; the reform movement inside Congress, which in 1977 produced Senate and House ethics codes that later were embodied in the law; and ethics proposals advanced by President Carter. *(1978 Almanac p. 835)*

PRESIDENTIAL RECORDS. A 1978 law (PL 95-591), which grew out of Watergate-era controversy over Nixon's claim to ownership of his presidential papers and tape recordings made in the White House, declared that most records of future presidents, beginning in 1981, would be public property. *(1978 Almanac p. 799)*

Congress first had applied that principle in 1974 by passing legislation (PL 93-526) specifically directed at Nixon's tapes and papers. The 1974 law, which nullified an agreement between Nixon and the General Services Administration (GSA), directed GSA to keep the Nixon materials and not destroy any of them without congressional permission. *(1974 Almanac p. 654)*

SECRET SERVICE SPENDING. Angered over spending of more than $17 million by the Secret Service at Nixon's private homes, Congress in 1976 passed legislation (PL 94-524) to restrict such expenditures in the future. *(Congress and the Nation Vol. IV, p. 826)*

FBI DIRECTOR'S TERM. Congress in 1976 attached a provision setting a 10-year term for the director of the Federal Bureau of Investigation to legislation extending the Law Enforcement Assistance Administration (PL 94-503).

The decision to limit the director's term reflected a reaction to the FBI's compromised independence during the Watergate cover-up, as well as concern over the agency's excessive independence before that period under the late FBI director, J. Edgar Hoover. *(Congress and the Nation Vol. IV, p. 604)*

DISCLOSURE OF TAX RETURNS. The Watergate investigation revealed that the Nixon White House had sought from the Internal Revenue Service (IRS) the tax returns of people considered to be political enemies.

As part of the Tax Reform Act of 1976 (PL 94-455), Congress put strict new limits on disclosure of tax return information to anyone outside the IRS. *(1976 Almanac p. 49)*

The section retained current coverage of Cabinet members and the director and deputy director of the Central Intelligence Agency and the commissioner of the Internal Revenue Service. Lower-echelon presidential appointees and campaign officials previously covered were omitted.

● Provided that persons covered under the legislation remained covered for two years after they left office.

● Provided attorneys' fees for the subject of an investigation if no indictment was brought and if the subject's costs would not have been incurred by a private citizen in similar circumstances.

● Permitted the attorney general to remove the independent counsel for "good cause." The current law provided for removal on the grounds of "extraordinary impropriety" or mental and physical disability.

Background

The Watergate Connection

The special prosecutor law traced its origins to the legal aftermath of the bungled break-in June 17, 1972, at the Democratic National Committee headquarters at the Watergate office building in Washington, D.C. *(1972 Almanac p. 90)*

Within a year, Senate hearings were under way and "Watergate" came to encompass a wide variety of suspect matters, including a White House cover-up of criminal activities, political sabotage and kickbacks, spending on presidential properties and President Richard M. Nixon's income taxes. *(1973 Almanac p. 1007)*

The idea of a special prosecutor emerged April 30, 1973, when the Senate Judiciary Committee refused to confirm Elliot Richardson as attorney general until he had appointed a special prosecutor for the Watergate investigation.

But it was not until five years later, in 1978, that the special prosecutor law was enacted as Title VI of the Ethics in Government Act (PL 95-521). *(1978 Almanac p. 835)*

The legislation was an amalgam of several proposals with a common theme: that an independent investigator was needed to handle politically sensitive cases. The objective was to eliminate a potential conflict of interest in having the attorney general, a political appointee, investigate the president who appointed him or other top executive branch officials.

The special prosecutor law was just one of several to emerge from Watergate. The magnitude of the scandal spurred Congress to enact the entire Ethics in Government Act, which covered financial disclosure for top government officials and post-government work restrictions for those officials. In addition, Congress passed a wide-ranging campaign reform law in 1974 and several less sweeping measures in the years that followed. *(Box, p. 387)*

Experience to Date

By the end of 1982, the special prosecutor law had been called into play 11 times and in only three instances had a special prosecutor been appointed. None of the investigations produced enough evidence to warrant a prosecution.

The first two of these cases involved drug use allegations against Hamilton Jordan, then chief of Jimmy Carter's White House staff, and Timothy Kraft, then campaign manager for the Carter-Mondale Presidential Committee.

Neither investigation produced enough evidence to warrant a prosecution, yet they consumed considerable time and money. The Jordan case, for example, cost $215,621, according to the Justice Department.

The third case, involving corruption allegations surrounding Labor Secretary Raymond J. Donovan, also did not result in any prosecution. It was closed Sept. 13, 1982, with an announcement by special prosecutor Leon Silverman that there was "insufficient credible evidence" to support allegations of Donovans's ties to organized crime and labor corruption. *(Donovan probe, p. 67)*

In addition to these cases, there were eight instances in which the attorney general conducted a preliminary investigation after receiving allegations involving individuals covered by the act.

Information was available about only three of the cases, each of which generated considerable publicity. In the first, Attorney General Griffin B. Bell concluded Feb. 1, 1979, that there was no "factual substantiation" of allegations that President Carter and Vice President Walter F. Mondale illegally solicited or received political contributions at a White House luncheon to help pay off Democratic Party debts.

Attorney General William French Smith came to a similar conclusion concerning allegations of misconduct involving former national security adviser Richard V. Allen, who resigned Jan. 4, 1982. *(1981 Almanac p. 186)*

In the third case, Smith also declined to pursue an investigation of CIA Director William J. Casey for allegedly violating the foreign agents registration law in 1976, when he represented Indonesia as a private lawyer before the Treasury Department and the Internal Revenue Service.

Information on the other preliminary investigations was not available because of strict anti-disclosure provisions in the special prosecutor act.

S 2059: The Overhaul

Legislation (S 2059) to revamp the law was introduced Feb. 3 by Sen. William S. Cohen, R-Maine, chairman of the Oversight of Government Management Subcommittee of the Governmental Affairs Committee, and Carl Levin, D-Mich., the ranking subcommittee Democrat. Their action followed hearings in May 1981 and an extensive subcommittee report in October 1981 that concluded the attorney general needed more flexibility in administering the law.

Cohen had more than a passing familiarity with the events that led Congress to enact the special prosecutor law in the first place. In 1974, as a freshman House member, he was one of seven Republicans on the House Judiciary Committee to vote in favor of impeaching President Richard M. Nixon, following an inquiry touched off by the Oct. 20, 1973, firing of Archibald Cox, the first Watergate special prosecutor. *(1974 Almanac p. 867)*

Senate Action

Subcommittee Hearings

Despite the infrequent application of the act, Cohen had little trouble finding witnesses anxious to testify about its operation. The law was never popular with attorneys general, who believed that its very existence implied that they were incapable of conducting impartial investigations of high government officials.

"The special prosecutor statute is predicated on the assumption that the attorney general will lack impartiality, or at least will be perceived to do so, in any investigation

and prosecution of senior administration members. I do not believe this conclusion to be warranted in the ordinary case," Richardson wrote in a Feb. 10 letter to Cohen. However, Richardson, like most of the witnesses who testified in 1981, agreed that some type of special prosecutor provision remained necessary to assure the public that high officials suspected of wrongdoing would not get special treatment from the Justice Department.

The Reagan administration took a different view. In his testimony, Rudolph Giuliani, associate attorney general, called for repeal of the act. He contended the law was unconstitutional because it involved the judiciary — through the appointment of a special prosecutor — in the enforcement of laws, an executive branch function.

Attorney General Smith voiced similar concerns in an April 17, 1981, letter to Senate Legal Counsel Michael Davidson.

Cohen, disturbed by the Justice Department's statements, wrote in his panel's report that "the subcommittee is gravely concerned that Attorney General Smith's announcement doubting the constitutionality of the present law will undermine the operation of the provisions in the next case that arises under the act."

Trouble Spots

Several of the 1981 witnesses, including former Attorney General Benjamin R. Civiletti, who served under Carter, Washington lawyer Lloyd Cutler, a former Carter White House aide, and Arthur Christie, the special prosecutor in the Jordan case, said the standards for triggering the appointment of a special prosecutor should be tightened.

The current law required the attorney general to seek a special prosecutor unless he could conclude that the matter was so unsubstantiated that no further investigation or prosecution was warranted.

Referring to the Jordan case, Civiletti said that although he concluded the charges against Jordan were unsubstantiated, he could not close the case. He said that despite an extensive FBI investigation, several pertinent witnesses had not been questioned and could not be without subpoenas to appear before a grand jury.

Civiletti, Richardson and Cutler also said the law did not allow the attorney general sufficient discretion in weighing the initial evidence to determine whether to ask for a special prosecutor.

The subcommittee report highlighted a number of other problem areas. Chief among them were provisions spelling out which officials were covered under the law.

The panel concluded that the current law covered both too few individuals and too many — too few because it did not cover a president's family; too many because it applied to many executive branch officials whose prosecution would not raise conflict-of-interest problems.

The subcommittee pointed to allegations involving President Carter's brother Billy and his involvement with the Libyan government to illustrate problems with the act. No special prosecutor was appointed to look into alleged illegalities because Billy Carter was not a government official and was not covered by the act. Instead, a special panel of the Senate Judiciary Committee was created to look into how the Justice Department and the White House handled the legal ramifications of Billy Carter's foreign dealings. *(1980 Almanac p. 392)*

Cohen's subcommittee also determined that the act covered people for too long a time. The report pointed out that some persons could be covered for 16 years — eight years during the terms of the president who appointed them and another eight years if a new president of the same party were elected and served two terms.

Committee, Senate Approval

Cohen's subcommittee approved S 2059 by letter poll June 2. Before sending the bill to the full committee, the panel adopted an amendment to allow the attorney general to seek independent counsel in cases that raised a conflict of interest, even if the person involved was not otherwise covered by the act.

The full Governmental Affairs Committee approved the bill June 17, the tenth anniversary of the Watergate break-in, and formally reported it July 14 (S Rept 97-496).

The bill was passed by the full Senate by voice vote Aug. 12.

House Action

The House passed S 2059 Dec. 13 when it suspended the rules and voted 347-37 to approve the measure. *(Vote 414, p. 122-H)*

The House returned the measure to the Senate after adopting three amendments to restrict the bill's coverage that had been recommended by the Judiciary Committee's Subcommittee on Administrative Law and Governmental Relations. Neither the subcommittee nor the full House Judiciary Committee ever formally acted on the bill, which had been referred to them after Senate passage Aug. 12.

One of the House amendments deleted a provision in the Senate bill that specifically covered members of a president's family. However, under another provision, the attorney general was given discretion to appoint a special prosecutor in a case involving a presidential family member.

The Senate bill allowed appointment of a special prosecutor if there was so much as an appearance of financial or political conflict; the House struck this provision.

The Senate bill required coverage for up to five years after leaving office. The House reduced the period to two years. ∎

Bankruptcy Court Impasse

The Supreme Court Dec. 23 refused to give Congress any more time to restructure the bankruptcy courts it had found unconstitutional in a June 28 decision.

As a result of the court's action, an interim rule for handling bankruptcy cases went into effect Dec. 27. It was written by the U.S. Judicial Conference, the policy-making arm of the federal judiciary.

When the court struck down the bankruptcy court provisions of a 1978 bankruptcy reform law June 28, the justices gave Congress until Oct. 4 to come up with a revised system. But Congress failed to meet that deadline, and the court extended it to Dec. 24.

After it became clear Dec. 22 that Congress again would not act, the solicitor general asked the court for a second extension, until March 25, 1983. House and Senate leaders told Justice Department officials that bankruptcy reform would be a priority issue in the 98th Congress.

In a simple order Dec. 23 that had no written explanation, the court refused to grant another stay.

The Temporary Rules

Opinions differed on the effect of the Supreme Court's refusal to grant another extension. Bankruptcy practitioners contended that chaos would result because parties would not be sure whether the bankruptcy courts could hear the matters under dispute. The lawyers and many bankruptcy judges argued that it was often difficult to differentiate a "straight" bankruptcy issue from an ancillary issue that must be transferred to a federal district judge.

The Judicial Conference, on the other hand, maintained that such lines could be drawn without excessive difficulty, and its temporary rule reflected that view. Basically, the stopgap rule maintained the existing bankruptcy court structure and provided that all bankruptcy cases be initially filed in these courts.

Bankruptcy judges would retain their authority to handle clear bankruptcy issues. However, a federal district judge could intervene on his own or at the request of a party in the case to handle issues not considered to be bankruptcy matters.

Background

On June 28, the court ruled 6-3 that the existing bankruptcy system, adopted in 1978, was unconstitutional. *(Northern Pipeline Construction Co. v. Marathon Pipeline Co., p. 12-A)*

The 1978 reform law (PL 95-598) was designed to make the handling of bankruptcy cases more efficient by allowing bankruptcy judges to hear not only bankruptcy matters but also a myriad of civil issues that might be related to a bankrupt party. *(1978 Almanac p. 179)*

Prior to enactment of that law, bankruptcy "referees" were appointed by federal district judges and acted as adjuncts to the court. They could handle only bankruptcy matters, with no authority over ancillary matters.

The court majority said the bankruptcy judges, who were appointed by the president for specified terms, were given too much power and too little independence. The majority noted that bankruptcy judges had basically the same authority as federal district judges. However, those judges were appointed for life under Article III of the Constitution and were immune from salary cuts. Bankruptcy judges were appointed by the president for 14-year terms, with no protection against salary cuts.

The structure created by the 1978 law was a compromise hammered out in conference after the Senate refused to go along with a House plan to make bankruptcy judges "Article III" appointees, just like federal district judges.

Chief Justice Warren E. Burger dissented from the June 28 decision. In 1978, Burger had opposed Article III status for bankruptcy judges and had lobbied against such proposals. *(1978 Almanac p. 180)*

Legislative History

House Action

Anticipating the court's adverse ruling, House Judiciary Chairman Peter W. Rodino Jr., D-N.J., introduced legislation April 20 to give bankruptcy judges Article III status, thus setting up a replay of the 1978 House-Senate struggle.

The House Judiciary Committee Aug. 19 approved a bill (HR 6978) to elevate the judges to the status of federal district court judges. The measure was formally reported Sept. 15 (H Rept 97-807).

However, the bill was referred to the House Appropriations Committee for consideration of its fiscal ramifications, and that panel Sept. 29 reported it unfavorably. (Pt. II)

Democratic House leaders opposed the bankruptcy court legislation because it would have given President Reagan some 227 new judges to appoint.

Senate Action

As was the case in 1978, the Senate Judiciary Committee was cool to the Article III approach.

In the final hours before Congress began its election recess Oct. 2, Sen. Robert Dole, R-Kan., chairman of the Senate Judiciary Courts Subcommittee, tried unsuccessfully to push through an omnibus bill that covered not only the court problem but other bankruptcy issues as well.

The measure would have provided for bankruptcy cases to be heard in the district court, eliminating separate bankruptcy courts. Instead, the bankruptcy judges would comprise a division within the district court.

Dole's proposal also included a section to make it harder for individuals to declare bankruptcy and wipe out their debts, provisions expediting procedures for handling bankruptcies involving grain elevators, and a section designed to make it easier to resolve legal issues when a shopping center tenant goes bankrupt.

Sen. Howard M. Metzenbaum, D-Ohio, objected to the consumer bankruptcy provisions and threatened to filibuster the bill when Dole tried to bring it up. *(Consumer bankruptcy, p. 391)*

Late Oct. 1, the Senate passed as separate measures a grain elevator bill (S 3037) and the shopping center bill (S 2297). Both subsequently died in the House. *(Grain elevators, p. 395; shopping center leases, below)*

The Supreme Court Oct. 4 gave Congress almost 12 weeks of breathing space to come up with legislation revising the nation's bankruptcy courts.

At the request of Solicitor General Rex Lee, the court extended its original Oct. 4 deadline until Dec. 24.

Senate and House staffers negotiated through the election recess and into the lame-duck session, seeking a compromise solution to the impasse. But their efforts failed to produce agreement. ∎

Shopping Center Leases

The Senate Oct. 1 passed a bill (S 2297) designed to protect the financial interests of shopping center owners and tenants in the event that a tenant went bankrupt. But the legislation died in the House.

The Senate Judiciary Committee approved S 2297 Aug. 4 by voice vote and formally reported it Aug. 17 (S Rept 97-527). In the House, the measure was referred to the Judiciary Committee, which took no action on it.

Among other things, the bill would have required the administrator of a bankrupt estate to decide within 60 days whether to keep the lease of a bankrupt tenant or let it revert to the shopping center owner, who could then find a new tenant. The bill specified that any assignment of the unexpired lease could not disrupt the tenant mix of the shopping center.

Chief sponsor Orrin G. Hatch, R-Utah, said new proce-

dures for shopping center bankruptcies were required because a 1978 bankruptcy reform law (PL 95-598) did not afford enough protection for shopping center owners who wanted to fill vacancies created by bankruptcies. *(1978 Almanac p. 179)* ∎

Consumer Bankruptcy Bill

The Senate Judiciary Committee April 21 approved legislation to make it much more difficult for individuals to declare bankruptcy and start their financial lives anew. However, the measure went no further in the 97th Congress.

The bill, S 2000, formally reported May 27 (S Rept 97-446), would have allowed creditors to exact payment for debts from a person's future income after he filed for bankruptcy — an idea Congress had rejected in previous rewrites of the bankruptcy laws over the last four decades.

The credit industry put on a strong lobbying effort to persuade members of Congress that the bankruptcy code — revised in 1978 — needed another retooling.

The industry argued that the 1978 changes (PL 95-598) made it too easy for individuals to declare bankruptcy and escape their debts. To support their claim, creditors cited a 1981 survey by Purdue University's Credit Research Center concluding that a sizable percentage of persons filing for bankruptcy could pay off their debts with time. The credit industry commissioned the study. *(1978 revisions, 1978 Almanac p. 179)*

The credit industry also said that since 1979, the number of individual bankruptcies filed had more than doubled, from 196,976 in fiscal 1979 to 452,145 between July 1, 1980, and June 30, 1981. The statistics were from the Administrative Office of the U.S. Courts.

House Judiciary hearings March 23 and March 25 indicated a bankruptcy revision bill had little chance of House passage in 1982, even though some 260 members cosponsored HR 4786, a companion to S 2000.

Opponents said that a poor economy, and not the new bankruptcy code, had brought consumers into the bankruptcy courts in increasing numbers. They noted that business bankruptcies, which were covered in the 1978 law but would not be affected by S 2000, had risen at the same rate as individual bankruptcies. This indicated, they said, that general economic conditions — and not the 1978 law — were responsible for increasing bankruptcies of all sorts.

Future Income Provision

The most controversial provision in S 2000 concerned eligibility for "Chapter 7" bankruptcy — a process allowing an individual debtor to discharge his debts, liquidate his assets and start over.

The bill would have required the bankruptcy court to consider a debtor's future income in deciding whether the person qualified for a straight bankruptcy. If the debtor could pay off "a reasonable" portion of non-mortgage debts through another procedure in the bankruptcy code, then he would be ineligible for a straight bankruptcy.

The court would determine future income on the basis of information supplied by the debtor. Income considered by the court would have to come from a source available to the debtor at the time of the proceeding, such as the person's current job, or from a source certain to supply income within 12 months, such as trust funds.

The court could exempt a debtor from the future income provision if its application would result in hardship.

Opponents of these provisions said there were practical problems inherent in the scheme — including the creation of new litigation over eligibility for straight bankruptcy; the difficulty of devising standards for determining who could pay debts from future income; problems of uniform application of such standards; and involving a court too heavily in a debtor's daily life in determining what future income would be parceled out to creditors.

Metzenbaum Blocks Action

In the final hours before Congress began its election recess Oct. 2, Sen. Robert Dole, R-Kan., chairman of the Senate Judiciary Courts Subcommittee, tried unsuccessfully to push through an omnibus bill that contained the consumer bankruptcy provisions along with proposals to overhaul the bankruptcy courts. *(Court proposals, p. 389)*

But Sen. Howard M. Metzenbaum, D-Ohio, objected to the consumer bankruptcy provisions and threatened to filibuster the bill when Dole tried to bring it up.

Metzenbaum also blocked Dole from bringing up S 2000 during the lame-duck session following the Nov. 2 elections. ∎

Balanced Budget Amendment Fails in House

The Senate in 1982 approved a constitutional amendment to require a balanced federal budget, but the measure was rejected in the House.

Despite pre-election jitters and pressure from President Reagan, the House Oct. 1 rejected a proposed constitutional amendment (H J Res 350) that would have required Congress to adopt a balanced federal budget each year unless a three-fifths majority voted to allow a deficit.

The Senate Aug. 4 adopted a similar but not identical constitutional amendment (S J Res 58) by a vote of 69-31, two more than the necessary two-thirds majority. *(Vote 288, p. 49-S)*

That measure had been reported from the Senate Judiciary Committee July 10, 1981. *(1981 Almanac p. 427)*

H J Res 350 reached the House floor only after its supporters succeeded in gathering the 218 petition signatures needed to discharge the House Judiciary Committee from considering it. The committee, dominated by members opposed to the amendment, had kept the measure bottled up for months.

The House vote was 236-187, 46 short of the two-thirds majority of those present and voting (282 in this case) required to pass a constitutional amendment. *(Vote 363, p. 108-H)*

Twenty Republicans joined 167 Democrats in rejecting the proposal, which would have required a balanced budget except in time of war or when three-fifths of the entire Congress voted for deficit spending.

Before the decisive vote, the House also rejected a Democratic alternative that would have made the president responsible for submitting a balanced budget to Congress. That proposed constitutional amendment went down

to defeat 77-346. *(Vote 362, p. 108-H)*

Congressional defeat of the amendment was expected to spur renewed efforts in the states to force the calling of a constitutional convention on the balanced-budget issue. As of Oct. 1, 31 states had called for such a convention, three short of the 34 needed.

Background

The Convention Drive

Since 1975, the National Taxpayers Union had been leading a campaign in state legislatures to force Congress to call a constitutional convention to consider a balanced budget amendment.

Previous amendments to the Constitution had been approved by two-thirds of each house of Congress and then ratified by three-fourths of the states; the convention approach had not been used since the Founding Fathers first wrote the nation's basic governing document nearly 200 years ago.

After a lull of two years, the drive to add a balanced-budget amendment to the Constitution acquired new momentum in 1982, in large part because of concern about ballooning federal budget deficits. *(Box, next page)*

On Jan. 31, 1982, Alaska became the 31st state to adopt a resolution calling for a convention. Two-thirds of the states, or 34, had to act before Congress would be required to call a convention.

In addition to the 31 state legislatures that had adopted convention resolutions by the end of 1982, a single chamber in nine other states also had approved such proposals.

Many members of Congress conceded that the convention drive gave impetus to the congressionally initiated balanced-budget proposals.

Indeed, four amendments that were currently part of the Constitution were approved by Congress only after a number of states had first sought a constitutional convention to debate them. These were the amendments requiring direct elections of U.S. senators, repealing Prohibition, limiting presidents to two terms and providing for presidential succession in case of the chief executive's disability.

Convention Obstacles

Significant obstacles remained to the convention route. It was one thing for states to demand a convention as a spur to congressional action; it would be quite another matter actually to hold one.

While Article V of the Constitution provided that a convention must be called if two-thirds of the states (34) requested one, no procedures existed for either calling or running such a convention.

For example, even if 34 states passed resolutions calling for a convention, it was not clear that all 34 resolutions would be valid. There were no rules on whether the resolutions had to have identical wording, or even whether they had to be limited to a particular subject. Likewise, no one knew how delegates would be selected, who would pay for the convention and what authority Congress would have in setting convention guidelines.

The Senate Judiciary Committee's Constitution Subcommittee on Nov. 3, 1981, approved a bill (S 817) to establish procedures for a constitutional convention. But the full Judiciary Committee was sharply divided over the issue of how much power Congress should have over the convention process, and the bill never emerged from committee. *(1981 Almanac p. 435)*

Senate Action

Measure Moves to the Floor

The Senate Judiciary Committee approved S J Res 58 on May 19, 1981, and formally reported it July 10, 1981 (S Rept 97-151). However, the measure went no further that year. The House Judiciary Subcommittee on Monopolies and Commercial Law held hearings on a companion measure (H J Res 2), but took no action.

S J Res 58 remained dormant for the first six months of 1982, but Majority Leader Howard H. Baker Jr., R-Tenn., finally called it up July 12 for consideration by the full Senate.

Judiciary Chairman Strom Thurmond, R-S.C., argued that only a constitutional amendment would force Congress to balance the federal budget. He noted that previous attempts to require such action by law had had no effect.

"Congress has violated its own laws in recent years in enacting federal budgets that are not balanced.... A constitutional amendment is the only way. Congress must obey the Constitution," Thurmond said.

Opponents, led by Sen. Charles McC. Mathias Jr., R-Md., and Max Baucus, D-Mont., counterattacked July 13. Noting Congress had approved a fiscal 1983 budget with a deficit of more than $100 billion, Mathias said the public would wonder how members "can sit here, with our hands folded piously before us, and vote for a constitutional amendment for a balanced budget.... I do not think we should use the Constitution as a fig leaf to cover our embarrassment over the deficit," he said.

Amendments Adopted

Before the vote on final passage, the Senate adopted two amendments to the balanced-budget proposal. Proponents had tried to fend off all amendments, hoping to avoid a conference with the House, but they were unsuccessful.

The first amendment, which was cleared in advance with Thurmond and Orrin G. Hatch, R-Utah, the other chief sponsor of S J Res 58, was proposed by Pete V. Domenici, R-N.M., chairman of the Senate Budget Committee.

The amendment made clear that neither the president nor Congress would gain new fiscal powers if S J Res 58 were to become part of the Constitution, a provision primarily designed to prevent the president from impounding appropriated funds to balance the budget. It allowed Congress to enact legislation to implement the amendment. And it broadened the fiscal base for determining national income.

The Domenici amendment was adopted July 27 by a 97-0 vote. *(Vote 261, p. 45-S)*

On Aug. 3, the Senate adopted by 51-45 an amendment requiring a three-fifths congressional vote to increase the debt ceiling — something Congress had to do almost annually to keep government running. *(Vote 277, p. 47-S)*

The debt ceiling proposal was offered by William L. Armstrong, R-Colo., and David L. Boren, D-Okla. It was designed to do two things — freeze the debt ceiling at the time the constitutional amendment was ratified and then require a three-fifths vote to raise it beyond that level.

Armstrong — long a champion of budget austerity — said he considered his proposal a "friendly" amendment

Red-Ink Budgets: How the Pattern Developed

(in millions of dollars)

Fiscal year	Budget receipts	Budget outlays	Surplus or deficit (−)	Fiscal year	Budget receipts	Budget outlays	Surplus or deficit (−)
1921	5,571	5,062	+509	1954	69,719	70,890	−1,170
1922	4,026	3,289	+736	1955	65,469	68,509	−3,041
1923	3,853	3,140	+713	1956	74,547	70,460	+4,087
1924	3,871	2,908	+963	1957	79,990	76,741	+3,249
1925	3,641	2,924	+717	1958	79,636	82,575	−2,939
1926	3,795	2,930	+865	1959	79,249	92,104	−12,855
1927	4,013	2,857	+1,155	1960	92,492	92,223	+269
1928	3,900	2,961	+939	1961	94,389	97,795	−3,406
1929	3,862	3,127	+734	1962	99,676	106,813	−7,137
1930	4,058	3,320	+738	1963	106,560	111,311	−4,751
1931	3,116	3,577	−462	1964	112,662	118,584	−5,922
1932	1,924	4,659	−2,735	1965	116,833	118,430	−1,596
1933	1,997	4,598	−2,602	1966	130,856	134,652	−3,796
1934	3,015	6,645	−3,630	1967	148,906	157,608	−8,702
1935	3,706	6,497	−2,791	1968	152,973	178,134	−25,161
1936	3,997	8,442	−4,425	1969	186,882	183,645	+3,236
1937	4,956	7,733	−2,777	1970	192,807	195,652	−2,845
1938	5,588	6,765	−1,177	1971	187,139	210,172	−23,033
1939	4,979	8,841	−3,862	1972	207,309	230,681	−23,373
1940	6,361	9,456	−3,095	1973	230,799	245,647	−14,849
1941	8,621	13,634	−5,013	1974	263,224	267,912	−4,688
1942	14,350	35,114	−20,764	1975	279,090	324,245	−45,154
1943	23,649	78,533	−54,884	1976	298,060	364,473	−66,413
1944	44,276	91,280	−47,004	1977	355,559	400,506	−44,948
1945	45,216	92,690	−47,474	1978	399,561	448,368	−48,807
1946	39,327	55,183	−15,856	1979	463,302	490,997	−27,694
1947	38,394	34,532	+3,862	1980	517,112	576,675	−59,563
1948	41,774	29,773	+12,001	1981	599,272	657,204	−57,932
1949	39,437	38,834	+603	1982	617,766	728,375	−110,609
1950	39,485	42,597	−3,112	1983 est	597,494	805,202	−207,708
1951	51,646	45,546	+6,100	1984 est	659,702	848,483	−188,781
1952	66,204	67,721	−1,517	1985 est	724,318	918,515	−194,197
1953	69,574	76,107	−6,533				

Data prior to 1940 are for the administrative budget.

SOURCE: Fiscal 1984 Budget

and disagreed with senators such as Hatch, who feared it would damage the legislation's prospects for enactment.

Armstrong prevailed after liberals, who saw the amendment as a way to weaken S J Res 58, formed an impromptu coalition with conservatives and voted for the proposal.

Majority Leader Howard H. Baker Jr., R-Tenn., immediately moved to reconsider the vote. But his motion to reconsider was rejected 40-56. *(Vote 278, p. 47-S)*

Amendments Rejected

Except for the Armstrong and Domenici amendments, sponsors were successful in turning back a total of 27 proposals during the debate.

Among those rejected were the following:

● By Wendell Ford, D-Ky., to require the president to submit a balanced budget to Congress. Rejected 45-53. *(Vote 259, p. 45-S)*

● By Slade Gorton, R-Wash., and Warren B. Rudman,

R-N.H., to clarify and restrict the authority of the federal judiciary to interpret the amendment. Rejected 45-51. *(Vote 271, p. 46-S)*

● By Howell Heflin, D-Ala., an amendment to allow deficit spending, by majority vote, in the case of an "unforeseen and imminent threat to the national security." Rejected 47-51. *(Vote 284, p. 48-S)*

● By Carl Levin, D-Mich., an amendment that would allow deficit spending, by majority vote, if Congress by a three-fifths vote declared a national emergency. Rejected 37-60. *(Vote 283, p. 48-S)*

● By Charles McC. Mathias Jr., R- Md., and Max Baucus, D-Mont., an amendment making the provisions of S J Res 58 statutory only. Rejected 28-67. *(Vote 273, p. 47-S)*

● By J. James Exon, D-Neb., an amendment requiring the president to submit to Congress a statement of receipts and outlays for each fiscal year. Rejected 45-52. *(Vote 280, p. 48-S)*

Provisions

As passed by the Senate, S J Res 58 included the following provisions:

● Required Congress to adopt a balanced federal budget before the beginning of each fiscal year.

● Allowed deficit spending only by a three-fifths majority of the entire Congress.

● Made the debt ceiling permanent at the time the amendment took effect and required any increase to be approved by a three-fifths majority of Congress.

● Barred an increase in total receipts in any fiscal year that was greater than the rate of increase in "national income" in the previous year unless a majority of the whole Congress passed a bill to raise taxes.

● Allowed the amendment to be waived when a declaration of war was in effect.

● Defined total receipts as "all receipts of the United States except those derived from borrowing" and defined total outlays to mean "all outlays of the United States except those for repayment of the debt principal."

● Gave Congress the authority to enforce and implement the amendment by "appropriate legislation."

● Made the amendment effective for the second fiscal year beginning after its ratification.

Senate Passage

The Senate approved S J Res 58 on Aug. 4 by a vote of 69-31, two more than the two-thirds majority (67) that was required to pass it. *(Vote 288, p. 49-S)*

Final passage came after 11 days of debate. President Reagan, who had publicly urged adoption of the measure, called four or five senators just before the vote to seek support for S J Res 58.

Minority Leader Robert C. Byrd, D-W.Va., and Appropriations Committee Chairman Mark O. Hatfield, R-Ore., the last senators to be recorded, provided the final two votes for the majority.

House Committee Action

For most of the 97th Congress, H J Res 350 remained bottled up in the House Judiciary Committee, where the Monopolies and Commercial Law Subcommittee held intermittent hearings..

On Aug. 18, the subcommittee adopted two amendments that substantially weakened the proposed constitutional amendment.

The first, offered by William J. Hughes, D-N.J., struck a section limiting any tax increase to the percent of national income growth in the previous year, unless Congress approved a larger tax increase by a majority vote.

Henry J. Hyde, R-Ill., complained that the amendment killed "the heart of the bill," because the deleted section was the only provision discouraging Congress from raising taxes to avoid deficits.

Another amendment required the president to submit a balanced budget to Congress before each fiscal year and barred deficit spending in fiscal "periods" rather than fiscal years.

The Discharge Drive

On July 12, Rep. Barber B. Conable Jr., R-N.Y., chief sponsor of H J Res 350, filed a petition to discharge the Rules Committee from handling a rule he had drafted (H Res 450) that provided for immediate House consideration of the balanced-budget amendment.

By July 15, Conable had collected 104 of the 218 signatures needed to discharge a committee from considering a measure before it. By Aug. 5, the total had climbed to 185. And by late September, Conable was within 16 votes of his goal.

Finally, on Sept. 29 a group of Republicans led by Conable and Vice President George Bush, with help from conservative Texas Democrat Phil Gramm, rounded up the last 16 signatures needed on the discharge petition.

Once 218 people — a majority of the House membership — had signed such a petititon, the relevant panel had to either act on the measure before it or let the House vote directly.

The Democratic Alternative

When Conable had 218 signatures, Speaker Thomas P. O'Neill Jr., D-Mass., met with other Democratic leaders and decided to force the issue. Rather than let Reagan brand them as obstructionists, and wary of letting Conable control the time under normal discharge procedures, the Democrats decided to call for a vote Oct. 1. But they decided to do so under a rule (H Res 604) drafted by the Democratic-controlled Rules Committee.

The quick vote apparently caught the amendment's sponsors off guard. Minority Leader Robert H. Michel, R-Ill., conceded, "We didn't have enough time to gear up our machinery."

The rule called first for consideration of a Democratic substitute sponsored by Bill Alexander, D-Ark., and then for action on a Conable proposal identical to H J Res 350.

Whichever proposal was the last adopted by majority vote would then be voted on as the proposed amendment and would need a two-thirds majority to pass.

The Alexander amendment, unlike the Conable proposal, would have required the president to submit a balanced budget to Congress. Congress would have to adopt such a budget unless members voted by simple majority to declare a "national emergency." In that case, deficit spending would be allowed.

After Alexander's proposal was rejected 77-346, Conable decided not to offer his amendment as the rule provided because it was identical to the underlying proposal, H J Res 350. *(Vote 362, p. 108-H)*

But H J Res 350 itself then went down to defeat, 46 votes short of the two-thirds majority needed. *(Vote 363, p. 198-H)* ∎

State Justice Institute

The Senate Aug. 10 passed by voice vote a bill (S 537) creating a State Justice Institute to provide technical and financial aid to state courts. However, the bill was never approved by the House.

The bill, reported July 31 by the Senate Judiciary Committee (S Rept 97-175), authorized expenditures of $20 million in fiscal 1983 and $25 million in fiscal 1984-85.

Sponsor Howell Heflin, D-Ala., said state courts deserved federal help because they handled 95 percent of the country's lawsuits and most of its criminal cases. A similar bill was passed by the Senate in 1980 but died in the House. *(1980 Almanac p. 408)* ∎

Supreme Court Police

Congress Dec. 13 cleared for the president a bill (HR 6204 — PL 97-390) to clarify and expand the authority of the Supreme Court's 70 police officers.

Final action came when the House accepted the Senate version of the measure. The House had passed HR 6204 Aug. 16. The Senate took up the bill Oct. 1, adopted two amendments and sent it back to the House.

As cleared, HR 6204 authorized court police to protect the justices and their official guests anywhere in the country.

The bill also made clear that Supreme Court police could carry their firearms off the Supreme Court premises while performing their duties, such as taking a person arrested on Supreme Court grounds to a police station. Currently, only those police who also were deputized U.S. marshals could carry their weapons off the court's grounds.

Under the Senate amendments accepted by the House, the off-premises authority would end after three years. The Supreme Court marshal must report to Congress each year on the cost of the off-premises protection.

The legislation, requested by Chief Justice Warren E. Burger, took on added significance in the wake of a July 15 attack on Justice Byron R. White at a speaking engagement in Salt Lake City, Utah. White was seated, awaiting his turn to speak, when he was pummeled by a man who said he was upset by court decisions on school busing and pornography.

House Committee Debate

HR 6204 was approved July 20 by the House Judiciary Committee by a vote of 22-5 and reported Aug. 10 (H Rept 97-704).

During debate on the bill, some committee members expressed concern about giving the Supreme Court guards new authority. "There is nothing more inappropriate for the court than to have a police force," said Thomas N. Kindness, R-Ohio.

Rep. Carlos J. Moorhead, R-Calif., said the Supreme Court police should be only a "guard service" and should not be "running around the country with weapons."

Sam B. Hall, D-Texas, whose Administrative Law and Governmental Relations Subcommittee recommended the bill, responded that the measure was narrowly drawn and was only intended to provide protection for the justices and court personnel. ∎

Court Jurisdiction Review

By voice vote Oct. 1, the Senate passed a bill (S 675) establishing a 14-member commission to study the jurisdiction of the federal and state courts and recommend changes to improve the handling of legal problems nationwide.

However, the House did not act on the measure.

Under S 675, the commission was given two years after members were appointed to send a preliminary report on its findings to the president and Congress. A final report would be required in 10 years.

The members would be appointed by the president, the Senate, the House, the chief justice and the Conference of Chief Justices of state courts. ∎

Grain Elevator Bankruptcies

The Senate Oct. 1 passed a bill (S 3037) to expedite procedures for handling bankruptcies involving grain elevators, but the measure died in the House.

It was the fourth time in the 97th Congress that the Senate had sought to provide special treatment for producers affected by the failure of grain elevators or other farm storage facilities.

In each instance, the legislation was blocked by House Judiciary Chairman Peter W. Rodino Jr., D-N.J.

The Senate attached grain elevator bankruptcy provisions to an omnibus farm bill (S 884) passed Sept. 18, 1981. However, the provisions were subsequently dropped in conference with the House after Rodino objected that they had not gone through his Judiciary Committee, which had jurisdiction over bankruptcy matters. *(1981 Almanac p. 547)*

On Sept. 22, 1981, the Senate passed a separate bill (S 1365 — S Rept 97-168) setting out specific time limits for resolving claims against the bankrupt party. But the House took no action on the legislation.

Finally, the Senate Dec. 8, 1981, attached the grain elevator language as a rider to a bill (HR 4482) creating a new federal appeals court to handle patent cases. *(1981 Almanac p. 431)*

But the amendment was stripped off by the House March 9 before HR 4482 was returned to the Senate for final clearance. *(Appeals court bill, next page)* ∎

Mandatory Jurisdiction

The House Sept. 20 suspended the rules and passed a bill (HR 6872) to give the Supreme Court greater discretion in deciding which cases it would hear. However, the Senate failed to act on the measure.

The bill, reported Sept. 16 by the House Judiciary Committee (H Rept 97-824), eliminated the court's "mandatory" jurisdiction — certain types of cases it currently had to review, even if the justices dismissed them without full-blown consideration.

HR 6872 would have allowed the Supreme Court to choose which of these cases it wanted to hear, just as it did with most other cases. Chief sponsor Robert W. Kastenmeier, D-Wis., said the bill was "an attempt to bring rationality to the method by which the Supreme Court selects which cases to hear."

All nine justices had urged Congress to enact the bill as one means of easing the Supreme Court's ever-growing workload.

A similar bill in the 96th Congress was bottled up in the House after the Senate added a provision barring federal courts, including the Supreme Court, from hearing any school prayer cases. *(1979 Almanac p. 404)*

HR 6872 had two other major provisions. One would apply federal workers' compensation to federal jurors injured while on jury duty. This was incorporated into a separate bill (S 2863) that was cleared by Congress Dec. 21. *(Story, next page)*

The second deleted 85 provisions in various federal laws that granted expedited court treatment for certain types of cases.

The bill gave priority status to only three types of cases — those involving personal liberty, such as a claim

that one was imprisoned in violation of the Constitution; cases involving requests for temporary restraining orders or preliminary injunctions; and cases where "good cause" had been shown.   ∎

Service of Process in Suits

Congress Dec. 21 cleared legislation (HR 7154 — PL 97-462) to allow complaints in federal lawsuits to be served on parties by regular mail and to shift the cost of doing so to plaintiffs.

Final action came when the Senate accepted the version of the bill passed by the House Dec. 15.

Currently, federal marshals personally served complaints on the parties named in a lawsuit. The bill allowed marshals to continue serving complaints in three instances — when ordered by a federal judge; when the United States initiated a suit; and if the case involved an indigent.

Under the new law, the plaintiff was responsible for mailing the complaint to the named defendants with a postage-paid reply form included. If no reply was received within a certain time, the plaintiff must find other means to serve the complaint.

Foreign Agent Registration

In an unrelated section, the bill also increased the penalty for failing to register as a foreign agent with the State Department. The current penalty was $5,000; it was raised to $75,000 under the bill.

This provision amounted to a compromise with the Senate, which had raised the penalty to $50,000 but had included a host of other changes in the foreign agents registration act opposed by House members.   ∎

New Federal Appeals Court

The Senate March 22 cleared for the president a bill (HR 4482) to create a new U.S. Court of Appeals for the Federal Circuit, primarily to handle patent cases.

President Reagan signed the measure into law (PL 97-164) on April 2, and the new court held its inaugural session in Washington on Oct. 1.

Final congressional action came as the Senate by voice vote concurred in an amendment adopted by the House March 9 stripping from the bill an unrelated provision dealing with grain elevator bankruptcies. The bankruptcy provision had been attached by the Senate Dec. 8, 1981. *(Grain elevator bankruptcies, p. 395)*

HR 4482 (H Rept 97-312) was passed by the House Nov. 18, 1981. A companion measure (S 1700 — S Rept 97-275) was passed by the Senate Dec. 8. After passage, Sen. Robert Dole, R-Kan., floor manager of the bill, called up the House version and amended it to conform with the provisions of S 1700. *(1981 Almanac p. 431)*

The House and Senate passed similar bills in the 96th Congress but could not agree on a final version before the Congress ended. *(1980 Almanac p. 404)*

The New Appeals Court

As cleared by Congress, HR 4482 created a new appellate court by consolidating the existing U.S. Court of Cus-

toms and Patent Appeals with the appellate division of the current U.S. Court of Claims.

Although the new appellate court was on the same footing as the existing 12 appeals courts, it differed in its jurisdiction. Where the other circuit courts hear cases by region, the new court takes cases by subject matter from all over the nation.

It was given exclusive jurisdiction over appeals from all U.S. district courts in patent cases and certain other specified cases, as well as appeals from the Merit Systems Protection Board.

Other Provisions

HR 4482 also created a new trial-level court, the U.S. Claims Court, to handle cases currently heard by the trial division of the U.S. Court of Claims. These generally are cases in which the government is a defendant, such as legal disputes over contracts with government agencies.

In addition, HR 4482 authorized federal district courts to experiment with a variety of methods for recording court proceedings, from traditional shorthand and court-reporting devices to "electronic sound recordings."

And it changed the method of computing interest owed by the government in certain civil cases in which it was ultimately found liable. Currently, the goverment paid 4 percent interest or, in cases involving state laws, the rate set by those laws.

Under HR 4482, the interest would be computed at a rate equivalent to that paid on one-year Treasury bills. ∎

New Judgeships Blocked

The Senate Judiciary Committee Sept. 21 approved a bill creating 45 additional federal judgeships to alleviate pressures from growing caseloads at the trial and appellate levels.

The bill, never formally reported, went no further.

Eleven of the new judgeships recommended by the committee would have been permanent seats on federal appeals courts, divided among seven judicial circuits. Three were temporary seats on the 9th U.S. Circuit Court of Appeals, which encompassed nine Western states, Guam and the Northern Mariana Islands.

The remaining 31 slots were for federal district courts, spread out over several states. Seven of the district court seats were to be temporary.

As approved by the Judiciary Committee, the bill followed the recommendations of the U.S. Judicial Conference, the federal judiciary's policy-making arm.

The committee rejected an amendment by Sen. John P. East, R-N.C., that would have created a commission to monitor the performance of judges to "ensure compliance with standards of good behavior."   ∎

Federal Juror Law Revisions

Legislation (S 2863 — PL 97-463) revising some of the laws concerning federal jurors was cleared by Congress Dec. 21.

Final action came when the House accepted the bill as passed by the Senate Dec. 20.

As cleared, the bill provided for attorneys' fees for

jurors who had court-appointed lawyers to help them in cases involving an employer who discriminated against an employee because of jury service. Under current law, fees were available only to lawyers privately retained.

The bill also provided for using regular mail to send jury summonses rather than registered or certified mail, as under current law.

The third part of the bill made federal jurors eligible for workers' compensation for jury-related injuries.

Under current law, only federal employees who happened also to be serving on a jury were eligible for such compensation. ∎

Tax-Exempt Private Schools

The Reagan administration touched off a furor Jan. 8 when it announced it was reversing a 12-year-old government policy of denying tax-exempt status to private schools that discriminated against blacks.

The administration also said that it planned to grant such status to Bob Jones University and the Goldsboro Christian Schools, which were before the Supreme Court appealing an Internal Revenue Service (IRS) denial of such status.

The announcement brought a torrent of criticism from the civil rights community, but it was hailed by fundamentalist religious schools, many of which had been denied tax exemptions because of their racial policies.

Apparently surprised by the vehement response, President Reagan reversed himself Jan. 12 and said he was preparing a bill that would explicitly authorize the IRS to deny exemptions to segregated schools. The legislation was sent to Congress Jan. 18, but it never advanced beyond the hearing stage in either the House or Senate.

Reagan also backed off his plan to grant tax-exempt status to Bob Jones University and the Goldsboro schools, and said the Supreme Court should go ahead and decide those cases. Oral arguments were conducted Oct. 12, but the justices had issued no decision by year's end.

The Court Test

The court agreed in October 1981 to hear the cases of *Bob Jones University v. United States, Goldsboro Christian Schools v. United States*. Both schools discriminated against blacks as a matter of religious belief and practice. For this reason, the IRS revoked the tax-exempt status that Bob Jones University had enjoyed prior to 1971 and denied such status to the Goldsboro Schools.

Both institutions went to court to challenge the IRS action, contending primarily that it violated their First Amendment freedom to act in accord with their religious beliefs. The 4th U.S. Circuit Court of Appeals rejected that argument, and the schools appealed to the Supreme Court.

In September 1981 court filings, the Justice Department said federal tax laws required the government to deny tax exemptions to racially discriminatory organizations.

But the Reagan administration reversed positions Jan. 8, saying that without express authorization from Congress, the IRS lacked the authority to deny tax-exempt status to schools simply because they pursued racially discriminatory policies.

At that time, the IRS reported that some 111 private

schools were ineligible for tax-exempt status because of racial discrimination.

The IRS Regulation

The origin of the tax exemption controversy was in a July 1970 IRS regulation to bar segregated schools from tax-exempt status.

Such status conferred two major benefits on institutions. First, the qualifying institutions received exemptions from federal income, Social Security and unemployment taxes. Second, contributors to such institutions could claim deductions for their contributions, enhancing the institutions' ability to raise money.

The IRS regulation came as a case involving Mississippi schools, *Green v. Connally*, was working its way through the federal courts.

In 1971, a three-judge panel in the District of Columbia ruled that a proper interpretation of the Internal Revenue Code barred racially discriminatory schools from getting federal tax exemptions. The court said that even though the case involved only Mississippi schools, it would be illegal to grant exemptions to similar schools elsewhere. The decision later was upheld by the Supreme Court in a memorandum of affirmance.

The decision was one of several barring assistance, such as textbooks and athletic facilities, to schools that discriminated. *(CQ Guide to the U.S. Supreme Court, p. 602)*

In 1975 the IRS provided a set of guidelines for schools that wished to retain their exempt status. Late in 1978, the IRS proposed new, more stringent regulations, but these drew strong criticism from Congress and never went into effect.

In the fiscal 1980 Treasury, Postal Service appropriations bill (PL 96-74), Congress added a provision barring the IRS from issuing new rules on the tax-exempt status of private schools practicing racial discrimination. *(1979 Almanac p. 197)*

A similar provision was included in the fiscal 1981 Treasury, Postal Service bill. Because that measure did not clear before Congress adjourned, the provision was put into the second continuing resolution (PL 96-536). *(1980 Almanac p. 218)*

With an eye to the pending Supreme Court cases, the House Nov. 30 by voice vote rejected a similar amendment to the fiscal 1983 Treasury, Postal Service appropriations bill (HR 7158) proposed by Rep. Robert K. Dornan, R-Calif. Although that bill did not clear prior to adjournment, no private-school language was included in the continuing appropriations resolution (H J Res 631 — PL 97-377) that funded the Treasury Department — including the IRS — for fiscal 1983.

The Mississippi Case

A federal judge in Washington told the Justice Department Feb. 4 it would be in contempt of court if it tried to grant tax exemptions to private, segregated schools in Mississippi.

Since the 1971 *Green* ruling, the department had been under a court order to deny exemptions to such schools in Mississippi. William Bradford Reynolds, assistant attorney general for civil rights, told U.S. District Judge George L. Hart the department had no plans to violate the court order.

Civil rights lawyers went to court Feb. 4 seeking to have the injunction applied nationwide, but Hart said he

had no authority to make such a ruling.

Coleman Named

Saying that it could not defend the IRS position in the *Bob Jones* and *Goldsboro* cases, the administration suggested the court appoint someone else to do so.

In April, the court appointed William T. Coleman, a noted black attorney and former transportation secretary in the Ford administration, to argue in behalf of the IRS that the lower court's ruling should be upheld.

Coleman, a Republican, in 1948 was the first black Supreme Court clerk, serving Justice Felix Frankfurter. He participated as a "friend of the court" in the private school cases.

Coleman's brief, filed Aug. 25, contended that "recognition of tax exemption [for these schools] would be utterly inconsistent with federal law and fundamental national policy condemning racial discrimination in public and private education...."

He argued that "Congress has been fully aware of the IRS decision on this issue since the day it was made, and has repeatedly refused to alter the IRS ruling," thereby indicating its approval of it. If the First Amendment had any effect on this matter, he added, "it is to prohibit special tax preferences for religiously motivated racial discrimination."

The Justice Department brief, filed in February, argued that the IRS lacked authority to deny these schools tax exemptions because of their racial policies. However, it stated that the government agreed the denial of tax-exempt status did not violate any First Amendment rights.

Attorneys for the schools attacked the IRS policy as both unauthorized and unconstitutional.

When the two cases were argued before the high court Oct. 12, 1982, one of the largest crowds of the past decade showed up for the occasion.

Congressional Inaction

Hostile Hill Reception

Despite a reluctant — even hostile — Congress, the Reagan administration initially pressed for legislation specifically allowing the IRS to deny tax exemptions to private schools that discriminated on the basis of race.

However, hearings on Capitol Hill Feb. 1 and Feb. 4 made clear that its proposals (HR 5313, S 2024) faced a very tough time.

Most members of Congress saw no need for the bill, believing such exemptions already were prohibited by law.

At a House Ways and Means Committee hearing Feb. 4, some Democrats were openly skeptical of the administration's rationale for proposing a bill.

Rep. William M. Brodhead, D-Mich., told Deputy Attorney General Edward C. Schmults and Deputy Treasury Secretary R. T. McNamar that he was "appalled" by their testimony in support of the legislation.

"It's the shabbiest, most unbelievable bunch of crap" I've heard since I've been here," Brodhead said.

There rarely were more than two Republicans on hand during the daylong hearing, and none of them jumped to the defense of administration witnesses.

Chairman Dan Rostenkowski, D-Ill., said he was "struck by the carelessness — or naiveté — with which the administration reversed longstanding civil rights law." He

said he found "no justification" for the administration's contention that legislation was needed to give the IRS legal authority to do what it had been doing for almost 12 years.

Earlier Feb. 4, a panel of law professors sharply criticized the administration's legal reasoning in calling for new legislation. And two former IRS commissioners — one from the Nixon administration and one from the Carter administration — told House Ways and Means members they believed the law was clear in giving the IRS authority to deny tax breaks to segregated private schools.

Administration Adamant

Attorney General William French Smith, Treasury Secretary Donald T. Regan and their top subordinates stood firm in the face of such criticism. Schmults and McNamar insisted Feb. 1 in the Senate Finance Committee and again Feb. 4 in the House that specific legislation was needed. They contended that since 1970, when the IRS began denying tax-exemptions to segregated schools, the IRS had been acting in effect without legal authority.

"There is no shifting of position," McNamar said in an interview.

The White House confirmed Feb. 5 that the president had not changed his mind. "The president still firmly believes legislation is needed," said Robin Gray, a staff assistant in the White House press office.

Schmults said that "painstaking analysis" by Justice could find no support for IRS authority to deny exemptions to segregated schools. He said the *Green* case was insufficient because the Supreme Court simply affirmed it by memorandum instead of handing down a full-scale opinion. He cited a note in a subsequent Supreme Court case he said supported his view.

Schmults also said that there was no legal justification for interpreting existing IRS regulations to require that an educational institution also be considered "charitable" to be eligible for a tax exemption.

One of the main legal theories underlying IRS policy since 1970 was that an institution had to be considered "charitable" to be entitled to exempt status. Under decades-old case law, "charitable" had been defined to mean following public policy, and the IRS had determined that there was a strong public policy against racial discrimination.

Under sharp questioning, Schmults and Reynolds said they believed that all that was necessary for an exemption under the IRS code would be a determination that an institution was a bona fide educational one, even if it was set up to teach students how to murder or kidnap.

Deep Internal Divisions

Internal IRS and Justice Department memos turned over to the congressional committees showed deep disagreement between lower ranking officials, who supported IRS procedures, and the politically appointed heads of the Treasury and Justice departments.

On Feb. 3 more than half of the 176 attorneys in the Justice Department's civil rights division wrote a letter to Reynolds expressing "serious concern" about the administration's position.

The law professors testifying Feb. 4 were unanimous in their condemnation of the administration's position.

Michael I. Sanders, a former Justice and Treasury tax attorney and an adjunct law professor at Georgetown University, said he would give the administration a failing grade on its legal analysis. "It's flat wrong," he said. "I

don't understand it. As a former Justice Department attorney, I'm embarrassed by that analysis."

No Further Action

The February hearings constituted the only congressional response to Reagan's plea for new legislation on the tax-exemption issue. Neither House nor Senate committees went to markup on the bills, as Congress left the issue to the Supreme Court to decide. ∎

Foreign Nations, Antitrust

Congress Dec. 15 cleared for the president a bill (S 816 — PL 97-393) eliminating the right of foreign governments to recover triple damages in U.S. antitrust suits.

Final action came when the Senate concurred in House amendments. Before passing the bill Dec. 13, the House modified it to conform to the version (HR 5106) passed by the House April 27.

S 816 put other nations on the same footing as the U.S. government, limiting them to collecting actual damages in U.S. antitrust cases. But it allowed "a truly commercial" enterprise owned by a foreign government to collect triple damages in an antitrust suit if certain standards were met.

S 816, which was passed by the Senate in July 1981, modified the Supreme Court's 1978 *Pfizer Inc. v. Government of India* decision, which held that foreign governments could sue for triple damages in U.S. courts to recover financial losses resulting from violations of U.S. antitrust laws. *(1981 Almanac p. 434)*

The House version of S 816 — which was the version ultimately cleared — differed in three respects from the Senate's.

First, the Senate version denied recovery to a foreign government unless its laws provided the United States with remedies for antitrust violations. The House bill did not include this provision, which was opposed by the State and Justice departments. Officials said the provision could be interpreted by U.S. allies as an attempt to impose U.S. antitrust law on them and would be difficult to enforce.

Second, the Senate bill applied to pending cases; the House version was silent on the matter. Third, the Senate version made no exception for commercial enterprises owned by foreign governments.

House Action

The House Judiciary Committee reported HR 5106 March 31 (H Rept 97-476).

The House approved the bill April 27 by voice vote under suspension of the rules, which required a two-thirds majority of those present and voting for passage.

One House provision not in the Senate version allowed a "truly commercial" enterprise owned by a foreign government to collect triple damages in an antitrust suit under certain specified conditions.

Robert McClory, R-Ill., ranking Judiciary Committee Republican, explained: "Our committee decided that there was no convincing reason why our antitrust laws should have, for example, one rule for Renault, which is owned by the French government, and another rule for Peugeot, which is privately owned. . . .

"Consequently, HR 5106 contains an express four-part test for determining whether a commercial entity of a foreign state is eligible for treble damages, as are its privately owned competitors." ∎

Tris Reimbursement Bill

For the second time in four years, Congress cleared legislation (S 823 — PL 97-395) allowing companies to seek federal reimbursement for losses resulting from the sale of Tris-treated children's sleepwear.

Final action came Dec. 14 when the Senate by voice vote accepted the version of the bill that the House had passed by voice vote Dec. 13 under suspension of the rules.

The Senate originally passed its version of S 823 (S Rept 97-130) June 18, 1981. *(1981 Almanac p. 432)*

Since then, Senate Judiciary Chairman Strom Thurmond, R-S.C., had pushed the House to consider the legislation. On two occasions, Thurmond attached S 823 to unrelated bills in the hope of obtaining House approval, but he failed in both attempts.

The House finally acted after the Judiciary Subcommittee on Administrative Law and Governmental Relations considered S 823, amended it and sent the bill directly to the floor without full Judiciary Committee action.

S 823 was designed to permit compensation of companies who used the chemical Tris in the early 1970s in an effort to meet federal regulations requiring that children's sleepwear be made flame-resistant, only to run afoul of a 1977 decision by the Consumer Product Safety Commission (CPSC) banning Tris as a "hazardous substance." Manufacturers were required to repurchase all unsold or unwashed garments made from Tris-treated fabric.

Congress cleared a Tris reimbursement bill in 1978, but President Carter vetoed it. *(1978 Almanac p. 520)*

Provisions

As cleared, S 823 included the following provisions:

● Allowed companies to file claims in the U.S. Claims Court to recover the cost of producing Tris-treated goods and transportation costs associated with the return of the sleepwear. It also provided for recovery of costs associated with lawful disposal of Tris-treated products. (This is broader than the Senate provision, which allowed compensation only for a company's transportation costs in returning the sleepwear to manufacturers.)

No recovery would be allowed for lost profits.

● Established a set of standards by which judges would determine whether compensation was due.

● Prohibited a judge from ordering compensation, or the attorney general from agreeing to a settlement, unless a company produced proof of lawful disposal of Tris-treated products. (This provision was not in the Senate bill.)

● Barred recovery by a claimant who knowingly allowed the export of Tris-treated products after the CPSC published its ban on the export of such products on June 14, 1978. (This provision was not in the Senate bill.)

● Required successful claimants to repay the Small Business Administration for any loans granted or guaranteed because of losses resulting from the Tris ban. (This provision was not in the Senate bill.)

S 823: Legislative History

The Senate passed S 823 (S Rept 97-130) on June 18, 1981, but the House did not act on it. On Dec. 16, the last day of the 1981 session, Thurmond added the Tris bill to legislation providing a charter for an organization for former members of Congress. But the House refused to accept the measure.

In 1982, as Congress rushed toward its election recess, Senate Judiciary Chairman Strom Thurmond, R-S.C., for the second year in a row tried to push the Tris bill through as a rider to a separate piece of legislation.

On Sept. 30, Thurmond attached a Tris amendment to a House-passed antitrust bill (HR 5106) involving foreign governments, and the Senate passed the measure. *(Pfizer bill, p. 399)*

The House, however, did not act on the amended HR 5106 before leaving Washington early Oct. 2.

Instead, the House waited until the lame-duck session and then passed S 823 as amended by its Judiciary subcommittee. ∎

Patent Term Extension Dies

Legislation extending the patent term for up to seven years for drug manufacturers, chemical companies and others whose products are subject to pre-marketing federal regulatory review died when Congress adjourned.

The House Sept. 15 refused to suspend the rules and pass a patent term extension bill (HR 6444). The vote was 250-132, five votes short of the two-thirds margin required to pass the bill under suspension of the House rules. Chief sponsor Robert W. Kastenmeier, D-Wis., had wanted to get the bill approved under suspension to ward off amendments he feared would weaken the measure. *(Vote 305, p. 92-H)*

The Senate had passed a similar but not identical measure (S 255 — S Rept 97-138) on July 9, 1981. *(1981 Almanac p. 431)*

HR 6444 had been reported by the House Judiciary Committee Aug. 4 (H Rept 97-696).

A patent, which gave the developer certain exclusive rights, currently lasted 17 years, a time limit not changed since it was put into effect in 1861.

HR 6444 applied to drugs, medical devices, food additives, pesticides and chemicals subject to regulation under the Toxic Substances Control Act.

Companies that needed federal approval before marketing patented items pushed hard for HR 6444. Makers of brand-name drugs, for example, complained that the federal review process often consumed so many years that less than half the time under a patent remained when an agency finally granted marketing approval.

House Floor Debate

During House floor debate Sept. 13, Kastenmeier said the purpose of the legislation was to spur development by granting longer patents for those items that required extensive investment and research.

Kastenmeier said testimony before his subcommittee as well as a congressional study "confirms the link between an effective commercial patent term and innovation."

Judiciary Chairman Peter W. Rodino Jr., D-N.J., another supporter, asserted the bill would not enhance the profits of companies. "Rather, the purpose of the bill is to channel existing profits into further research by ensuring adequate patent term to amortize investments in research," he said.

Rodino quoted statistics showing that the effective patent life for items affected by the bill had declined since 1966 from 14.6 years to 6.8 years.

Opponents led by Barney Frank, D-Mass., and E. Clay Shaw Jr., R-Fla., disputed the sponsors' arguments. Shaw said the bill protected name-brand drugs from competition for too long and would bring "a continuation of the high price of drugs which has now lasted for 17 years."

"The people who are bitten are the consumers," he said, adding that the elderly would be hurt the most seriously because they used 25 percent of the drugs that were consumed and often had a limited income.

Frank said patent extensions should not be granted to compensate for time needed for experimentation with a drug, but only for the time it took a federal agency to review a patented item after research and experimentation had been completed.

Henry A. Waxman, D-Calif., chairman of the House Energy Subcommittee on Health and the Environment, noted that in the 1981 tax bill (PL 97-34), Congress gave businesses, including the drug companies, a 25 percent tax credit for research and development spending. That, he argued, should be assistance enough for the drug industry. *(Tax bill, 1981 Almanac p. 91)* ∎

Surplus Property Donations

The Senate by voice vote May 26 passed a bill (S 1422) authorizing the federal government to donate surplus property to any state for building or modernizing criminal justice facilities.

The measure was referred to the Government Operations Committee in the House, but it went no further in the 97th Congress.

S 1422 was reported March 16 by the Senate Governmental Affairs Commitee (H Rept 97-322). It was designed to make additional space available to states to ease prison overcrowding.

The bill provided that if any donated property ceased to be used or maintained for criminal justice purposes, the United States could reclaim it. ∎

Air Disaster Treaty

A proposed treaty that would have set new limits on passenger recoveries in international air crashes failed to win Senate approval in the 97th Congress.

The treaty, known as Montreal Protocol 3, was negotiated by the Ford administration in 1975, with the United States taking the lead role. By the end of 1982, it had been ratified by only a handful of countries; most were waiting for the United States to ratify the treaty before they did.

A major concern of the Ford, Carter and Reagan administrations, all of which supported the treaty, was preserving this country's standing in international diplomacy.

"At stake is our credibility in the international aviation community and the ability to negotiate effectively in the future," said Secretary of State Alexander M. Haig Jr., in a March 1982 letter to Majority Leader Howard H. Baker Jr., R-Tenn.

Although the Foreign Relations Committee approved the treaty Nov. 17, 1981 (S Rept 97-45) by a 16-1 vote, the agreement was not considered by the full Senate.

A handful of senators led by Ernest F. Hollings, D-S.C., objected to the pact and threatened to force a time-consuming floor fight.

A two-thirds vote of the Senate was needed to approve ratification.

The treaty's most vigorous opponent was the American Trial Lawyers Association (ATLA), whose members parlayed hometown contacts with senators and $214,000 in campaign contributions since 1980 into effective lobbying.

Another lawyers' group, the American Bar Association (ABA), joined forces with the Air Transport Association (ATA) — the airlines' representative — to push the treaty. They contended it would provide adequate and fair recoveries to air crash victims and avoid the lengthy litigation often required under existing law.

Limiting Liability

The debate over Montreal Protocol 3 centered on the treaty's limited liability provision, which would have applied to U.S. citizens on virtually all international flights, not just those to and from the United States.

If a plane on an international flight went down for any reason, all passengers could recover up to about $120,000 in "provable economic damages" — a term used to define the loss of future income suffered by the victim or the victim's family as a result of the crash.

Passengers would not have to prove that the accident resulted from someone's negligence. They or their survivors would have to establish only the amount of economic damage suffered.

In addition, U.S. citizens flying on any airline could recover up to another $200,000 from a fund created by a $2 surcharge on their tickets. This fund also would cover any hospital or medical expenses related to the accident for the rest of the passenger's life.

The fund would be monitored by the Civil Aeronautics Board and administered by the Prudential Insurance Company of America. It would be reviewed at least biennially to determine whether the limit should be raised or the surcharge lowered.

Under an existing treaty in force since 1934, a passenger traveling on a ticket written in the United States — such as for New York to Paris to Rome to New York — could recover up to $75,000 from the airline for economic damages resulting from a crash on any leg of the trip.

Currently, recoveries were limited to $10,000 or $20,000 for crashes involving trips on tickets not written in the United States. The amount varied depending on which of two existing international agreements applied. This covered, for example, a U.S. citizen who was in New Delhi, India, and bought a ticket there for a trip to Karachi, Pakistan, and then was involved in a crash.

An exception to all of these limits existed if the passenger could have his case tried in the United States and could prove the airline engaged in "willful misconduct." The exception would have been eliminated by Protocol 3, and it was this provision that touched off the opposition of trial lawyers.

Defending the Limit

The treaty's backers contended the Montreal package had enough benefits to outweigh the loss of "willful misconduct" suits. The ATA and the ABA argued that the $120,000 recovery limit from an airline coupled with the $200,000 available from the supplemental fund provided both an adequate and certain damage award. The ATA cited a State Department study showing that the average recovery since 1977 in an international case was $65,200; in a domestic case, the average was $180,600.

While spokesmen for these groups conceded that some passengers won large recoveries, they argued that such awards were rare. The recovery limit in the protocol — $320,000 when the $200,000 supplemental was included — was more than the actual awards in 88.3 percent of the cases since 1977 involving both international and domestic air crashes, according to the study.

The treaty's proponents also said a liability limit was a fact of life for any international agreement. One ATA memo called it "fundamental in obtaining an international liability accord. Many nations of the world have vigorously opposed the high liability standards promoted by the United States and flatly rejected the concept of unlimited liability," the memo said.

The Trial Lawyers' Case

The trial lawyers contended the Montreal proposal was unfair because it stripped victims of their right to sue wrongdoers for unlimited damages.

Howard A. Specter, a Pittsburgh lawyer and president of the ATLA, said the protocol "serves no purpose other than to take away rights of victims to benefit international air carriers and the foreign governments that own most of the foreign airlines."

Lee S. Kreindler, a New York City lawyer who specialized in aviation cases and helped the ATLA develop its strategy, called the treaty proposal "nonsense." In a December 1981 letter to colleagues he predicted grave consequences if the measure passed. "I see a clear and present danger of a major invasion, on a national level, of our tort [personal injury] system," he wrote.

The trial attorneys focused most of their attention on what they considered the inadequacy of the $320,000 liability limit. One long question-answer memo prepared by the aviation specialists asserted that "settlements in the $600,000 and above range are not uncommon."

Cases have in fact gone to trial, the memo said, and "on the question of 'willful misconduct' juries have been prone to find willful misconduct to avoid the limitation on a passenger's damages."

Specter scoffed at the notion that willfulness rarely was proven. "Do you honestly believe that [airline] companies and insurance carriers settle cases on the basis of willfulness when there is none?" he asked. "There is a real possibility of demonstrating willfulness or the carriers wouldn't have to be concerned." ∎

Cable TV Copyright Bill

A bill (HR 5949) clarifying the broadcast rights of cable television operators died in the Senate when the 97th Congress adjourned.

The measure spelled out the rights of cable television operators to retransmit copyrighted material broadcast by non-cable stations. It also restored certain protections for broadcast stations that had been eliminated in 1981 by the Federal Communications Commission (FCC).

HR 5949 was passed by the House Sept. 28, and sponsors were hoping to win Senate approval quickly even though no committee had scrutinized the bill. But key senators requested that the measure be referred jointly to the Judiciary and Commerce committees.

Although the Senate Judiciary Committee held 1981 hearings on the subject of cable-TV copyright liability, there was no Senate bill on the subject.

The administration opposed HR 5949.

House Action

The House Sept. 28 passed HR 5949 by a 347-53 vote. *(Vote 351, p. 104-H)*

Chief sponsor Robert W. Kastenmeier, D-Wis., said the bill represented a compromise among the National Association of Broadcasters, the Cable Television Association, the Motion Picture Association of America, the National Association of Public Television Stations and the National Association of Religious Broadcasters.

Professional sports organizations opposed the measure, claiming it did not provide enough protection against rebroadcasting games without adequate compensation.

HR 5949 was reported May 17 by the House Judiciary Committee and Sept. 24 by the Energy and Commerce Committee (H Rept 97-559, Parts I and II).

One significant Commerce Committee amendment, accepted by the House, made clear that any cable system having 36 or fewer channels must carry at least one non-entertainment commercial station, such as a station oriented to religious broadcasts, if there was such a station within the cable system's area. Staffers said the amendment, sponsored by Rep. James M. Collins, R-Texas, resulted from heavy lobbying by religious broadcasters, who wanted to be sure of access to viewers via cable systems.

As passed by the House, HR 5949 included the following major provisions:

● Retained current law requiring cable systems to pay a compulsory license fee to the Copyright Royalty Tribunal for use of copyrighted materials. This spared cable systems from having to negotiate directly with every copyright holder when they retransmitted a signal involving copyrighted material.

The license fee, which took effect in 1978 pursuant to 1976 copyright law revisions, covered retransmission of an unlimited number of distant broadcast signals. The tribunal was set up under the 1976 law (PL 94-553) to set royalty fees and distribute them to copyright holders. *(1976 Almanac p. 494)*

● Provided protection from cable competition to broadcast stations that held exclusive rights to specific programs and motion pictures within their area. Exclusivity would run for the duration of a contract on a series. For movies, an independent station could get protection for up to 300 movies each quarter of a calendar year, and a network affiliate could get protection for 100 movies each quarter.

The exclusivity provision was to be phased in over two years, starting with cable and broadcast systems in the nation's top 50 markets.

● Required any cable television system to carry up to three non-commercial, educational stations regardless of the size of the station's audience.

● Codified an FCC regulation allowing a local professional team the option of blacking out cable transmission of its games within a 35-mile radius. However, a cable system capable of transmitting a distant signal could beam another game into the area. ∎

Home Video Recording

In hopes that the Supreme Court would resolve the issue, Congress took no action in 1982 on legislation to clarify the applicability of copyright laws to home videotape recordings.

The high court heard arguments Jan. 18, 1983, in the case of *Sony Corporation of America v. Universal City Studios.*

In that case, the 9th U.S. Circuit Court of Appeals ruled Oct. 19, 1981, that the use of Sony Betamax home video recorders to tape television programs — even for purely private use — amounted to copyright infringement.

Sony appealed, and the Supreme Court June 14 agreed to review the decision.

The appeals court said it could find no explicit exemption from copyright law for home video recording in the Copyright Act of 1976 (PL 94-553). This was a major overhaul of copyright law that raised royalties paid to songwriters by record-makers and extended new protections to periodical and book writers. It also imposed copyright liability on three industries that were heavy users of copyrighted material but previously had not paid royalties for it: public broadcasters, cable television systems and jukebox operators. *(1976 Almanac p. 494)*

Legislative Response

Within days of the appeals court ruling, bills were introduced by several members of Congress in an effort to overturn the decision. First to be heard from were Sen. Dennis DeConcini, D-Ariz., (S 1758) and Rep. Stan Parris, R-Va., (HR 4808).

Their measures would protect the estimated three million Americans with home video recorders from being charged with copyright violations if they simply recorded television programs for their own use.

The bills specified that no copyright infringement would be involved in recording copyrighted works on a video recorder if the recording was made for private use only and was not sold commercially.

Supporters of the legislation contended that the artists already had been compensated for their work by the network or cable system that purchased programs or movies. Home video machines, they argued, were not used to create movie libraries but to allow owners to view programs at a time other than that scheduled by a network.

The entertainment industry, which was unhappy with the DeConcini-Parris legislation, quickly found members of Congress willing to offer bills more to its liking.

In December 1981, Sen. Charles McC. Mathias Jr., R-Md., along with Majority Leader Howard H. Baker Jr., R-Tenn., and Minority Leader Robert C. Byrd, D-W.Va., introduced an amendment to S 1758 that included DeConcini's language protecting home tapers but went a step further.

It would have required the manufacturers of video machines and blank cassettes to pay a royalty on each machine and blank tape.

The amount of the royalty would be set by the Copyright Royalty Tribunal, which was established under the 1976 law. The tribunal likewise would be responsible for distributing the royalty fees to those who owned copyrights on their creative material.

Rep. Don Edwards, D-Calif., introduced similar legislation Feb. 9. This bill (HR 5705) was amended March 3 to include audio machines — ordinary tape recorders — and audio tapes. The Mathias legislation was similarly amended March 1.

Despite vigorous lobbying by the entertainment industry on one side and the makers and distributors of video recorders on the other, the legislation went nowhere in either chamber. ∎

Senate Kills Abortion, School Prayer Riders

Using three procedural votes, the Senate Sept. 23 ended a six-week debate on the divisive issues of prayer in public schools and abortion.

Since Aug. 16, a handful of senators led by Lowell P. Weicker Jr., R-Conn., Max Baucus, D-Mont., and Bob Packwood, R-Ore., had filibustered anti-abortion and prayer amendments that Jesse Helms, R-N.C., sought to attach to an unrelated bill (H J Res 520) raising the public debt ceiling. *(Debt ceiling, p. 44)*

One amendment designed to ban abortion was laid aside Sept. 15 by a 47-46 vote, moments after the Senate failed, 50-44, to shut off the filibuster. *(Votes 344, 343, p. 58-S)*

The other amendment would have barred the federal courts, including the Supreme Court, from hearing any "voluntary" school prayer case. It was intended to open the way for restoration of public school prayer — banned by the Supreme Court in a series of decisions — because the court would no longer have the authority to strike down such prayer programs.

The prayer amendment was stripped off the debt bill Sept. 23 when Majority Leader Howard H. Baker Jr., R-Tenn., moved to return the bill to the Finance Committee with instructions to send an unencumbered measure back to the Senate.

Baker's motion was approved handily 79-16. *(Vote 352, p. 60-S)*

"We have reached that place after a month where the opportunity to debate these issues has ended," Baker said. "The Senate has exhausted the possibility of enacting reasonable legislation, and it is time to move on."

No House Action

In the House, the abortion and prayer issues never really surfaced in 1982. The Judiciary Committee, chaired by Peter W. Rodino Jr., D-N.J., and dominated by liberals, showed no interest in dealing with legislation on those issues.

Of the panel's 28 members, nine were considered liberal Democrats, three were moderate Democrats and three were moderate Republicans inclined to oppose social-issue legislation.

Abortion

A preoccupation with economic issues kept the abortion issue off center stage for most of the 97th Congress, even in the Senate where Helms and his allies were pressing for action on the subject.

In 1981, two Senate Judiciary subcommittees approved separate anti-abortion measures. The Separation of Powers Subcommittee chaired by John P. East, R-N.C., on July 9, 1981, approved S 158, which declared that human life begins at conception and allowed states to approve anti-abortion laws. On Dec. 16, 1981, the Constitution Subcommittee headed by Orrin G. Hatch, R-Utah, approved a proposed constitutional amendment (S J Res 110) giving Congress and the states joint authority to enact legislation restricting or banning abortion. *(1981 Almanac p. 425)*

S J Res 110: Hatch Amendment

S J Res 110, which was sponsored by Hatch, was approved March 10, 1982, by the full Judiciary Committee and reported June 8 (S Rept 97-465). It was the first time since the Supreme Court's 1973 *Roe v. Wade* decision legalizing abortion that any committee of Congress had approved anti-abortion legislation.

S J Res 110 was approved 10-7. Voting for it were Republicans Strom Thurmond, S.C.; Paul Laxalt, Nev.; Robert Dole, Kan.; Alan K. Simpson, Wyo.; Charles E. Grassley, Iowa; Jeremiah Denton, Ala.; East and Hatch, along with Democrats Dennis DeConcini, Ariz., and Joseph R. Biden Jr., Del.

Opposing the amendment were Republicans Charles McC. Mathias Jr., Md., and Arlen Specter, Pa., and Democrats Edward M. Kennedy, Mass.; Robert C. Byrd, W. Va.; Howard M. Metzenbaum, Ohio; Patrick J. Leahy, Vt., and Max Baucus, Mont.

Howell Heflin, D-Ala., was absent and did not vote.

Split in Anti-Abortion Ranks

Although anti-abortion groups were happy with the March 10 vote, they were badly split over which legislation to support. The Hatch amendment was supported by at least two major organizations, the National Right to Life Committee and the National Conference of Catholic Bishops.

But a number of other anti-abortion groups, including the Washington-based March for Life, backed S 158, the so-called "human life bill."

The divisions within the anti-abortion ranks contributed to delays in further action on either measure.

Compromise Measures

In an effort to unify the splintered anti-abortion forces, both Helms and Sen. Mark O. Hatfield, R-Ore., introduced new legislation in the spring of 1982.

Helms proposed S 2148, which resembled S 158, the "human life bill," but did not entirely bar the federal courts from striking down new state anti-abortion laws that might result from its enactment. Instead, S 2148 authorized appeals directly to the Supreme Court.

Hatfield introduced S 2372, which made permanent a ban on using federal funds for abortion unless the life of the mother were endangered and stated that "unborn children who are subjected to abortion are living members of the human species."

Neither measure was acted on in 1982, however.

The Supreme Court: New Cases

The Supreme Court injected a new element in the abortion debate when it agreed May 24 to review five separate cases from Ohio, Missouri and Virginia involving various restrictions on abortion imposed by state and local governments. *(Akron Center for Reproductive Health v. City of Akron, City of Akron v. Akron Center for Reproductive Health; Planned Parenthood of Kansas City v. Ashcroft, Ashcroft v. Planned Parenthood of Kansas City; Simopoulos v. Virginia)*

None of the cases directly challenged the 1973 *Roe v. Wade* decision regarding a woman's first-trimester right to an abortion. But the cases took on national significance when the Reagan administration in September filed a brief suggesting that the court defer to the political process on

the abortion issue, leaving "further refinements" of the law to legislative bodies.

Arguments in the new cases were heard Nov. 30, but the court reached no decision on them by year's end.

The Debt Ceiling Rider

The Senate's long-promised debate on abortion began Aug. 16 and promptly turned into a filibuster that ranged over the subjects of school prayer and the scope of the federal courts' authority.

The vehicle for getting the social issues to the Senate floor was a bill (H J Res 520) to increase the public debt limit to $1.29 trillion. Congress had to pass the measure by Sept. 30, when an earlier debt limit was due to expire.

When Helms and his allies said in June that they intended to tack anti-abortion and "voluntary" school prayer legislation onto the debt limit bill, the majority leader said he would not oppose such a move.

For a month prior to consideration of the debt ceiling bill, Baker worked with Helms, Packwood and other senators seeking a time agreement for votes on two major anti-abortion measures.

One was S 2148, Helms' bill declaring that a fetus is a "person" under the Constitution and entitled to protection, permanently banning federal funding for abortion or research and medical procedures related to abortion, and granting a direct appeal to the Supreme Court for challenges to any new anti-abortion laws.

The other measure was S J Res 110, Hatch's proposed constitutional amendment to give Congress and the states joint authority to restrict abortions.

The time agreement fell through the week of Aug. 9 when Helms, apparently fearing he lacked the votes to pass S 2148, wanted the right to amend it. Packwood refused to agree.

Parliamentary Wrangling, Prayer Proposal

When the debt ceiling bill was called up Aug. 16, Helms immediately moved to amend it. He offered a proposal that simply said "Title II." A moment later Packwood was recognized by the presiding officer, and for the next few hours, until the Senate recessed, he read from a book on the history of abortion since 1800. The filibuster resumed Aug. 17 after the Senate finished other business.

On Aug. 18, after some parliamentary maneuvering, Helms, rather than Packwood, got control of the Senate floor and promptly introduced an amendment to prevent the Supreme Court and the lower federal courts from handling cases concerning "voluntary" school prayer.

He then offered an abortion amendment to the prayer measure that resembled S 2148. But to garner support, Helms removed the congressional determination that a fetus is "a person" under the Constitution.

Instead, the amendment included congressional "findings" that the Supreme Court erred in its 1973 decision legalizing abortion by "not recognizing the humanity of the unborn" and by not entitling them to protection under the Constitution.

As soon as Helms offered his amendments, Weicker proposed an amendment making clear that the Justice Department and the federal courts had authority to fully enforce the Constitution. Max Baucus, D-Mont., then offered an amendment to Weicker's proposal stating the sense of the Congress that the federal courts should still hear constitutional claims.

A Helms motion to table the Weicker amendment was rejected 38-59. *(Vote 334, p. 55-S)*

Under Senate rules, the vote, in combination with the Baucus amendment to Weicker's proposal, closed off further moves by Helms to amend H J Res 520, and the filibuster resumed.

Cloture Tests

On Sept. 9, the Senate failed to invoke cloture on the abortion proposal by 41-47, 19 votes short of the 60 needed to carry the motion. *(Vote 340, p. 57-S)*

President Reagan directly joined the abortion debate Sept. 8 when he sent one letter to Baker and another to nine senators, whom the White House would not identify, urging support for cloture and Helms' abortion proposal.

In his letter to Baker, the president said that abortion was "a subject about which I feel very deeply," and he said the Senate should have the opportunity to "stand up and be counted on what I think is one of the most important issues of our time."

White House spokesman Larry Speakes said Reagan also telephoned six senators from Air Force One while he was enroute to Kansas.

Speakes said Reagan would take "no position" on Helms' prayer amendment even though Attorney General William French Smith had said the proposal was unwise because it would have deprived the Supreme Court of jurisdiction over prayer cases.

Reagan's moves were seen as a direct response to criticism from conservative supporters who were upset that he had not taken a more active role in pushing abortion and prayer legislation.

But Reagan's last-minute efforts on the Helms proposals had little visible effect; 18 Republicans voted against the Baker cloture petition.

On Sept. 13, a second cloture motion — this one offered by Helms — went down to defeat 45-35, 15 votes short of the 60 needed. *(Vote 342, p. 58-S)*

Helms tried again on Sept. 15, but his cloture motion again failed, 50-44, 10 votes short of the three-fifths required. *(Vote 343, p. 58-S)*

Moments later, on a motion by S. I. "Sam" Hayakawa, R-Calif., the Senate voted 47-46 to table the Helms anti-abortion amendment. *(Vote 344, p. 58-S)*

Opponents of the Helms proposal were helped by groups seeking to keep abortion legal that by 1982 began to rival the anti-abortion movement in grass-roots organization.

"A lot of Americans became quite aroused in the last 12 months," said William Hamilton, director of the Washington office of Planned Parenthood. "In the broadest sense, a lot of senators have been persuaded by pressure from home that the politic place to be is on our side...."

The Helms votes were preceded Sept. 15 by a surprise announcement by Hatch that he was withdrawing S J Res 110, his proposed constitutional amendment to give Congress and the states joint authority to restrict abortions.

Hatch said there was insufficient time left in the 97th Congress to consider his amendment.

Hatch said that divisions among anti-abortion interest groups over what legislative approach to take made it difficult to mobilize support behind any proposal.

School Prayer

The school prayer issue drew less attention — and less action — during the 97th Congress.

The Reagan Proposal

President Reagan May 17 sent Congress his proposal for a constitutional amendment to allow organized voluntary prayer in public schools, and Thurmond, chairman of the Senate Judiciary Committee, introduced the measure (S J Res 199) May 18.

The Reagan proposal said: "Nothing in this Constitution shall be construed to prohibit individual or group prayer in public schools or other public institutions. No person shall be required by the United States or any state to participate in prayer."

No action was taken on the amendment by Thurmond's committee.

The Debt Ceiling Debate

Not until the Senate began debate on the debt ceiling bill did the prayer issue finally move to the fore.

On Aug. 18, Helms introduced an amendment to the debt bill that would have prevented the Supreme Court and lower federal courts from handling cases concerning "voluntary" school prayer.

He then offered his anti-abortion amendment as an amendment to the prayer rider. From that point on, the two emotionally charged issues were intertwined.

But opponents of the two proposals seized and held the initiative during the Senate's debate on them. Weicker,

Packwood and Baucus repeatedly charged that Helms' amendments were "court-stripping" proposals that would undermine the constitutional separation of powers and cripple the federal judiciary.

Speaking of the prayer proposal, Baucus said Sept. 16 that the real issue before the Senate was "whether we here today set in motion the vicious and pernicious precedent of removing the Supreme Court's power and right to enforce the Constitution."

Four times Helms tried to muster the votes needed to invoke cloture and shut off the liberal filibuster against his prayer amendment. And four times he failed — by margins of 50-39 Sept. 20, 53-47 Sept. 21, 54-46 Sept. 22 and 53-45 Sept. 23. *(Votes 345, 346, 347 and 349, pp. 59-S, 60-S)*

The Final Blow

Moments after the final cloture vote, Helms moved to send the debt bill back to the Finance Committee with instructions that it be returned to the Senate floor with his prayer amendment incorporated but without any other amendments.

At Baker's request, Barry Goldwater, R-Ariz., moved to table, and thereby kill, Helms' motion. Goldwater's motion was adopted 51-48. *(Vote 350, p. 60-S)*

Goldwater had tried to derail the Helms prayer amendment Sept. 22, but his motion to table the proposal was rejected 47-53. *(Vote 348, p. 59-S)* ∎

Immigration Reform Measure Dies in House

A last-ditch effort to pass a wide-ranging immigration reform bill failed Dec. 18 when the House was unable to complete action on the measure before adjournment.

The legislation (HR 7357 — H Rept 97-890, Parts I & II) died from a combination of ailments — opposition from Hispanics, organized labor, the business community and civil rights groups; an unenthusiastic House leadership; and lack of time.

The bill was an ambitious package that included sanctions against employers who knowingly hire illegal aliens; an amnesty program to give legal status to the millions of undocumented workers already in the country; a temporary worker program primarily for the agriculture industry; and new, restrictive procedures for handling asylum, deportation and exclusion cases.

The Senate Aug. 17 had passed a bill (S 2222 — S Rept 97-485) sponsored by Sen. Alan K. Simpson, R-Wyo., that was similar to HR 7357, and House sponsors had hoped this would be an incentive to members to move on the legislation.

But the measure ran into trouble from a growing number of interest groups as it awaited floor action. House Speaker Thomas P. O'Neill Jr., D-Mass., was frank in stating that the only reason he scheduled the bill at all was because President Reagan and Attorney General William French Smith had asked him to.

Chief sponsor Romano L. Mazzoli, D-Ky., who was given a standing ovation Dec. 18 for his efforts, admitted disappointment in failing to get the bill passed. But he said he planned to introduce the measure in the next Congress.

Background

The immigration reform legislation was introduced

March 17 by Simpson and Mazzoli, chairmen of the Senate and House Judiciary subcommittees on immigration and refugees.

The legislation represented the first comprehensive proposed overhaul of the nation's immigration laws in 30 years, since enactment of the 1952 McCarran-Walter Act (PL 82-414). *(Congress and the Nation Vol. I, p. 222)*

HR 7357 began life as HR 5872; it became HR 6514 when reported from the House Judiciary Committee (H Rept 97-890, Part I) and underwent a second change of bill number before reaching the House floor in December.

Both the House and Senate bills grew out of extensive hearings and study by the two immigration subcommittees in 1981.

The measures incorporated some but not all of a sweeping immigration proposal made by the Reagan administration in July 1981. *(1981 Almanac p. 422)*

The administration proposal (S 1765, HR 4823) did not call for a national identity card, a central element of the Simpson-Mazzoli proposal. It laid out a different scheme for employer sanctions and for granting legal status to aliens who entered the country illegally; and it included broad presidential emergency powers, such as closing highways, harbors and airports to stem the tide of illegal aliens.

The proposed emergency powers elicited immediate and strong adverse reaction when they were disclosed in October 1981. They were not included in the Simpson-Mazzoli bill, and that eliminated one source of potential controversy.

Several others remained, however, including the employer sanctions provision, amnesty for illegal aliens already in the United States, expansion of the existing temporary worker program and a cap on legal immigration. All became the focus of intense interest group lobbying.

Senate Committee Action

Subcommittee Approval

The House and Senate subcommittees held joint hearings on the immigration reform legislation in April, and on May 6, Simpson's subcommittee approved S 2222 by voice vote after making a number of changes in the bill.

The subcommittee softened the employer sanctions provisions to impose criminal penalties only on employers who engaged in a "pattern or practice" of hiring illegal aliens.

The panel voted to shift prime responsibility for management of the H-2 temporary worker program from the Labor Department to the attorney general. This program, named after the section of the 1952 law that allowed such employment, allowed foreign workers into the country temporarily if the secretary of labor certified that an employer needed the workers and could not find them in the domestic job market.

Full Committee Amendments

The full Senate Judiciary Committee approved S 2222 May 27 after amending it to increase the number of undocumented aliens who would be eligible after enactment to become permanent U.S. residents. The bill was formally reported June 9 (S Rept 97-485).

The May 27 vote to report the measure was 16-1, with Edward M. Kennedy, D-Mass., casting the lone dissenting vote. Kennedy said he was concerned about potential discrimination against Hispanics, in particular, that could result from a provision imposing sanctions on employers who hired illegal aliens.

Kennedy's major success during the committee markup came when the panel by an 8-6 vote adopted his amendment making undocumented aliens who were in this country by Jan. 1, 1982, eligible for permanent resident status.

As introduced, the Simpson bill would have granted permanent residence to persons who entered the United States before Jan. 1, 1978. Temporary resident status would have been given to aliens who arrived between Jan. 1, 1978, and Jan. 1, 1980, and after two years they would have been eligible for permanent resident status.

Paul Laxalt, R-Nev., who voted for the Kennedy proposal, said he was concerned that aliens who came to this country between 1980 and 1982 would be in legal limbo, constantly facing the threat of deportation. After the vote, Laxalt, the son of Basque immigrants, turned to an aide and said, "That could have been a Laxalt wandering around 60 years ago."

The legalization provisions were of great concern to local government officials, who feared that a host of undocumented aliens — previously afraid of using public services — would suddenly emerge and put new financial strains on already pressed communities.

After persistent lobbying by organized labor, principally the AFL-CIO, the committee adopted an amendment concerning the hiring of foreign temporary workers during a labor dispute. Organized labor contended that the bill as originally drafted would have eased restrictions on hiring foreigners during certain labor disputes.

The provision agreed to by voice vote May 27 barred hiring of foreign workers during a strike or other labor dispute as defined by existing Labor Department and Immigration and Naturalization Service regulations.

On a 4-10 vote, the committee rejected a Kennedy amendment that would have kept prime responsibility for writing temporary-worker regulations with the Labor Department.

As he had in subcommittee, Kennedy sought to require that at the end of three years, the president certify that employer sanctions had not been used in a discriminatory manner. His amendment was rejected 3-12.

As approved by the committee, S 2222 provided a new procedure for handling asylum claims, a remedy afforded persons who had fled their own countries and already were on U.S. property.

Anyone claiming asylum would be entitled to a hearing before an administrative law judge, whose decisions could be appealed to a new U.S. Immigration Board. The board could reverse any decision not supported by substantial evidence. There would be no judicial review, unless certain constitutional issues were involved or unless the attorney general disagreed with a board decision. Then the attorney general could take the case to court.

A Kennedy amendment, rejected by a 7-8 vote, would have allowed judicial review if a pattern or practice of discrimination in asylum cases were alleged.

Administration Concerns

The administration joined the debate on the legalization issue July 11 when Attorney General William French Smith sent Senate Judiciary Chairman Strom Thurmond, R-S.C., a letter expressing "serious concerns" about the amnesty provisions. Smith said he believed the bill, if enacted, would cost state governments $3.9 billion in 1983-86 for welfare and other social services and cost the federal government $6.3 billion in that period.

Smith also said he feared the amnesty section could encourage, rather than deter, more illegal immigration.

President Reagan in 1981 urged Congress to adopt an amnesty program for illegal aliens, but he wanted to grant them permanent resident status only after 10 years of continuous residence in the United States.

In his July 11 letter, Smith proposed granting permanent residence to aliens here before Jan. 1, 1976, with temporary residence status for those here between 1976 and Jan. 1, 1981.

Simpson disputed Smith's amnesty cost estimates, contending they were based on an assumption that illegal aliens would use welfare and other social services at the same high rate as refugees.

Both Simpson and Mazzoli said that unlike refugees, who fled their countries for political reasons, illegal aliens usually came to the United States specifically to work. There was no reason to assume they would quit their jobs and go on welfare once they became legal residents, the two men argued.

Senate Floor Action

The Senate passed S 2222 Aug. 17 by a vote of 80-19. *(Vote 329, p. 54-S)*

The final vote came after the Senate had rejected all but one amendment opposed by chief sponsor Simpson and the Reagan administration.

That amendment, offered by S. I. "Sam" Hayakawa, R-Calif., and adopted 78-21, said it was the sense of the Congress that "English be declared the official language of the United States." *(Vote 325, p. 53-S)*

The only other major amendment adopted was a com-

promise proposal by Charles E. Grassley, R-Iowa, that tightened the provisions granting amnesty to illegal aliens already in the United States and created a block grant program to reimburse states for costs associated with legalized aliens. The administration supported the Grassley amendment, which was adopted 84-16 on Aug. 12. *(Vote 316, p. 52-S)*

Hispanic leaders were angered by the bill, primarily because of the employer sanction provisions, which they believed would exacerbate discrimination against Hispanics, and because of the scaled-down amnesty provisions.

The Amnesty Amendment

The most significant change in the bill was the Grassley amnesty amendment, which sharply restricted legalization for aliens. The amendment:

● Moved from Jan. 1, 1978, to Jan. 1, 1977, the date by which illegal aliens had to enter the United States to become eligible for permanent resident status under the amnesty provisions.

● Denied these permanent residents federal benefits, such as food stamps, for three years.

● Moved from Jan. 1, 1982, to Jan. 1, 1980, the date by which illegal aliens had to enter the United States to be given temporary-resident status. (The amendment kept the committee provision that denied federal benefits to temporary residents.)

● Required temporary residents to wait three years before applying to become permanent residents.

● Established a block grant program to reimburse states primarily for medical assistance and disability payments made to aliens whose status was legalized under the bill.

Kennedy opposed the amendment, contending it would maintain "a subclass of people" — those who came after Jan. 1, 1980, and who would continue to face exploitation by employers, landlords and others.

But Grassley said any cutoff date would be arbitrary. He said it was fair to require an alien to live in the United States for some time before being granted legal status.

An amendment by Jesse Helms, R-N.C., to eliminate the entire amnesty program was rejected 17-82. *(Vote 315, p. 52-S)*

Rejected Amendments

Among amendments rejected Aug. 12, 13 and 17 were those:

● By Dale Bumpers, D-Ark., to give Congress, except in emergency situations, 30 days in which to veto any presidential proposal to admit more than 75,000 refugees to the United States each year. Rejected 41-45. *(Vote 322, p. 53-S)*

● By Kennedy, to terminate the employer sanctions after three years unless the president certified they had not resulted in discrimination. Rejected 22-69. *(Vote 321, p. 53-S)*

● By John Tower, R-Texas, to ease the employer sanction provisions. Rejected 14-85. *(Vote 327, p. 54-S)*

Provisions

As passed by the Senate, S 2222 included, in addition to the amnesty section, the following major provisions:

● Made it unlawful to knowingly hire, refer for employment or recruit for employment an illegal alien.

● Allowed employers to rely upon a person's existing documents, such as a passport or driver's license, to establish eligibility to work. The employer must determine

whether the documents "reasonably appeared to be genuine" and must complete a form attesting to such document review.

● Required the administration to develop within three years a "secure" system, such as a special identity card, for determining work eligibility.

● Set a six-month grace period after enactment to permit employers to become familiar with the law and provided a warning for the first violation in the next six months.

● Set a civil penalty of $1,000 per illegal alien hired for the first violation after the warning period and $2,000 per alien for the second violation.

● Provided a criminal penalty only if an employer was found to have engaged in a "pattern or practice" of hiring illegal aliens.

● Exempted employers of three or fewer workers from the requirement to examine aliens' documents for work eligibility.

● Authorized summary exclusion for aliens who were determined at the port of entry to have no "reasonable basis" for legal entry and who had not applied for asylum.

● Provided for a general, informal hearing during an exclusion proceeding if an alien requested asylum.

● Created a new nine-member U.S. Immigration Board to be appointed by the attorney general and provided new, specially trained immigration judges, appointed by the attorney general, to handle asylum claims, deportation and exclusion cases.

● Provided for "informal, non-adversarial" hearings on asylum claims by persons already in the United States. The applicant would be entitled to counsel at government expense, to present evidence and to examine and cross-examine witnesses.

● Eliminated judicial review in deportation and asylum cases except if particular constitutional claims were involved.

● Authorized $20 million for fiscal 1983 to establish the U.S. Immigration Board, train new immigration judges and promulgate new rules.

● Created a ceiling of 425,000 per year for legal immigrants.

● Provided that 350,000 visas among the 425,000 be allotted for family reunification and that 75,000 be reserved for "special" immigrants as defined in the bill.

● Provided that visas for immediate relatives of U.S. citizens, which were not restricted, be subtracted each year from the total number of visas allowed for family reunification.

● Eliminated the existing visa preference for brothers and sisters of adult U.S. citizens.

● Allowed specified foreign students "with exceptional ability" to become legal immigrants without first having to leave the United States for two years, and set a 5,000 visa limit for such students.

● Expanded the existing "H-2 program" that permitted temporary entry of aliens, primarily as seasonal agricultural workers.

● Gave the attorney general final approval of regulations implementing the H-2 program, after consulting with the Labor and Agriculture departments. Agriculture currently had no role in administering the program.

● Allowed the labor secretary to approve a request for H-2 workers if the secretary certified that the employer could not find sufficient workers who would be "available at the time and place needed" and that such hiring would not

adversely affect the wages and working conditions of similarly employed workers in the United States.

● Deleted the existing requirement that an employer must make a nationwide search for workers before seeking permission to hire foreign workers.

● Prohibited the labor secretary from certifying foreign workers for an employer during a strike or lockout in the course of a labor dispute.

House Committee Action

Mazzoli's Immigration, Refugees and International Law Subcommittee unanimously approved the immigration legislation May 19 after adopting amendments that weakened the measure's enforcement sections and made a temporary-worker program more palatable to the agriculture industry.

Subcommittee Amendments

By a vote of 4-3, the subcommittee adopted an amendment by Dan Lungren, R-Calif., to exempt from sanctions employers with no more than three employees.

The Senate bill gave employers of three or fewer workers an exemption from certain paper-work requirements but kept civil and criminal sanctions for all employers.

The panel also adopted another Lungren amendment that allowed a criminal penalty only if a judge determined an employer had engaged in a "pattern or practice" of knowingly hiring illegal aliens. This was the same as the Senate version.

The bill gave the president three years to develop a "secure sytem" for determining a person's eligibility to work. Until then, an employer could rely on a person's existing documents such as a driver's license or passport to determine work eligibility.

The panel adopted an amendment allowing the president to determine that no new system was needed and that existing documents could be made secure enough for an eligibility system.

The panel adopted an amendment by Hamilton Fish Jr., R-N.Y., that would protect — under certain circumstances — owners and chief officers of multi-state, multi-employer businesses from criminal sanctions for actions by their employees throughout the country. Top corporate officials would not face criminal penalties if their companies had taken steps to assure that employees complied with the law and if top officials had no knowledge that, in spite of such instructions, the law was being violated.

The panel made a number of changes in the temporary-worker program, which under current law allowed foreign workers into the country for up to 11 months if the labor secretary certified that the employer seeking foreign labor needed workers, could not find them in the United States, and that such employment would not have an adverse effect on wages of domestic employees doing similar work.

Over the last decade, an average of about 18,300 workers were certified each year, according to the Labor Department.

The subcommittee adopted an amendment shifting prime responsibility for making regulations for the program from the Labor Department to the attorney general. It also gave the Agriculture Department a say in developing the regulations — a move long sought by growers whose antipathy toward the Labor Department was legend.

The panel accepted a Lungren amendment retaining the current 11-month limit for H-2 workers. The bill had limited their stay to eight months.

The panel adopted another Lungren amendment that narrowed one aspect of the certification process. The original version barred employment of aliens unless there would be no adverse effect on wages and working conditions of similar employees in the United States as a whole. The Lungren amendment required looking at the effect on wages only in "the area of intended employment."

The subcommittee adopted a Mazzoli amendment raising the overall immigration ceiling from 425,000 per year to 450,000. Another Mazzoli amendment raised from 325,000 to 375,000 the number of visas within the total that could be granted to reunite families in this country.

The panel adopted a Mazzoli amendment that eased regulations for granting visas to Amerasian children — those fathered by U.S. servicemen in Southeast Asia. The amendment included a 50,000-person, 10-year limit, but the panel accepted a Frank amendment that deleted the numerical limit while keeping the 10-year provision.

Full Committee Amendments

The full House Judiciary Committee approved the immigration reform bill Sept. 22 after restricting the program to provide amnesty for illegal aliens already in the United States.

The bill, renumbered HR 6514, was approved by voice vote after four days of consideration punctuated by contentious debate.

Moments before final approval, a motion to send the bill back to the Immigration Subcommittee — effectively killing it — was barely defeated. The vote on the motion by Sam B. Hall Jr., D-Texas, was 13-15.

Earlier in the day, the committee had voted 16-12 to provide 100 percent reimbursement to the states for three years after enactment to cover amnesty costs — those associated with legalizing the status of aliens already in this country.

The Reagan administration, Judiciary Chairman Peter W. Rodino Jr., D-N.J., and chief sponsor Mazzoli all opposed the amendment, which was sponsored by Don Edwards, D-Calif.

Rodino reportedly told Justice Department officials that unless they could persuade some of the six Republicans who sided with Edwards to change their votes, the bill was doomed.

Deputy Attorney General Edward C. Schmults was dispatched to the Judiciary Committee meeting room, where he and Robert A. McConnell, the department's legislative liaison, worked on the Republican members.

On a second vote two hours later, the Edwards amendment was rejected 13-15. Three Republicans — Harold S. Sawyer, Mich., and Bill McCollum and E. Clay Shaw Jr., both Fla., switched their votes. The Floridians said they still supported the amendment but feared it could kill the bill by forcing a referral to the Appropriations Committee.

At Rodino's urging, the committee voted 15-12 to eliminate provisions in the bill setting a rigid ceiling of 450,000 immigrants per year and sharply restricting visas available for immediate relatives of U.S. citizens and permanent residents.

Two motions by McCollum to delete the entire amnesty section were rejected 12-16 and 11-17.

As approved by the subcommittee, HR 6514 granted permanent resident status to persons who entered the United States before Jan. 1, 1978. Such persons would be

entitled to most forms of public assistance. Temporary resident status would be available for those aliens who had been in the United States since Jan. 1, 1980. They could seek permanent resident status after two years. Only federal emergency medical care and aid for the blind, aged and disabled would be available.

The committee adopted an amendment by Lungren that was virtually identical to the Senate bill and more restrictive than the House subcommittee version. It would grant permanent residency to those aliens who were in the United States by Jan. 1, 1977, rather than 1978.

These aliens would be denied most forms of public assistance for three years.

The 1980 date for temporary resident status was retained, but temporary residents would have to wait three years before adjusting to permanent resident status — as in the Senate bill. They would be denied all forms of federal assistance, including emergency aid, for a total of six years.

An amendment by Fish was adopted to provide emergency medical aid for permanent and temporary residents, and assistance for those who are blind, aged and disabled.

Following the defeat of his reimbursement proposal, Edwards offered a revised amendment that authorized 100 percent reimbursement to the states for amnesty costs if funds were available. This proposal was adopted 16-12.

The Edwards amendment replaced a section in the Lungren amendment that would have created a block grant program, like that in the Senate bill, to compensate states for legalization costs.

On Sept. 21, the committee, by voice vote, adopted a package of amendments to the temporary worker program that had been vigorously sought by organized labor.

The principal modification essentially restored current law concerning the administration of the program, keeping control with the Labor Department.

Labor Committee Referral

After the Judiciary Committee completed work on the immigration bill, it was referred to the Education and Labor Committee for consideration of provisions involving the temporary worker program.

That committee Dec. 1 voted to send the measure (HR 6514) to the Rules Committee.

With only brief debate, the panel approved changes that strengthened the Labor Department's role in operating the temporary worker program.

The bill also was referred to the Agriculture, Ways and Means, and Energy and Commerce committees, but those panels did not act on it.

The Education Committee adopted an amendment by George Miller, D-Calif., that not only retained Labor Department authority over the program but in some areas actually strengthened Labor's role beyond existing law.

Among the key elements of the amendment were provisions that made regulations governing the treatment of workers part of the actual law and barred the attorney general from allowing temporary workers into the country unless the Labor Department certified the workers were necessary. Under existing law, the attorney general, in special circumstances, could admit workers despite the lack of Labor certification that such workers were needed.

House Floor Action

On Dec. 8, the Rules Committee granted a rule (H Res 623) for handling the immigration measure that provided for virtually unlimited amendments.

The Rules panel heard testimony on HR 7357 from 21 members, and their remarks highlighted the intense opposition the bill faced.

By the time the House began work on the bill Dec. 16, some 300 amendments had been filed.

The measure did not have priority status with the House leadership. Speaker O'Neill said Dec. 17 that he had scheduled the bill for floor action only because the White House had asked him to do so.

Hispanic Opposition

While the bill had a core of strong supporters, including the Reagan administration, it had generated controversy among a variety of interest groups. The most vociferous opponents were Hispanics, who contended that the employer sanction provisions would exacerbate existing job discrimination. Dozens of the proposed amendments to the bill were aimed at altering the sanctions to meet their concerns.

Edward R. Roybal, D-Calif., chairman of the Congressional Hispanic Caucus, said HR 7357 was "an affront to those the bill will affect."

"There is no reform in this bill whatsoever," he said. He contended that employer sanctions would not keep illegal aliens out of the United States, citing a General Accounting Office report that a survey of 20 countries with sanctions found they were ineffective.

Hispanic organizations worked with the Congressional Hispanic Caucus to prepare more than 100 amendments on the sanction provisions alone.

Tony Coehlo, D-Calif., in one of several emotional speeches on the bill, told colleagues Dec. 17, "It is much easier to discriminate against someone who has dark hair, dark eyes and dark skin. It is easy to identify those people, and it is easy to assume immediately that those people are illegal and everybody else is legal."

More than once, Roybal told colleagues he would call for recorded votes on each of his amendments, a process that could have taken many hours.

Antonia Hernandez, head of the Washington office of the Mexican American Legal Defense and Education Fund, pointed to one crucial factor that made the difference between the House and the Senate, which passed S 2222 by a lopsided vote.

"In the Senate," she said, "there is not one single person of color, and it takes a person of color, an Hispanic, a black, to say the things we were saying."

Other Opposition

The Hispanics had ample help from other quarters in opposing parts of the bill.

Many segments of the business community opposed employer sanctions, although for reasons different from those cited by Hispanics. Business representatives, led by the U.S. Chamber of Commerce, said they were concerned about turning employers into private immigration officials who would have to check documents and keep too many records about whom they interviewed, hired or rejected.

Black leaders liked some parts of the measure but were concerned about strict asylum and exclusion provisions they feared would discriminate against Haitians seeking refuge in the United States. They had strong support on this point from the American Civil Liberties Union and several lawyers' groups around the country.

Finally, there was organized labor. The AFL-CIO, the

most active labor organization working on immigration reform, generally supported the House and Senate bills. The unions were enthusiastic about the sanction provisions, seeing them as protection for American workers.

But labor representatives made clear they also had a vital interest in keeping tight control over any temporary worker program. This put them at odds with the agricultural industry, which was worried about an adequate supply of labor to harvest crops.

Labor representatives told the House leadership they would not support HR 7357 unless the Labor Committee version prevailed. That seemed to be the straw that broke the camel's back. ∎

Aliens in Virgin Islands

A bill (HR 3517) making 7,000 to 10,000 aliens living in the U.S. Virgin Islands eligible to become permanent U.S. residents was cleared by Congress Sept. 8. President Reagan signed the measure into law (PL 97-271) Sept. 30.

Final action came when the House, by voice vote, accepted Senate amendments to the bill.

HR 3517 was originally passed by the House Nov. 4, 1981. *(1981 Almanac p. 435)*

It was reported by the Senate Judiciary Committee Aug. 18 (S Rept 97-529) and passed by the full Senate Aug. 20 by voice vote.

As cleared, HR 3517 granted permanent resident status to any alien who was admitted to the Virgin Islands as a temporary worker and had resided there continuously since June 30, 1975.

The Temporary Worker Program

In the 1950s and 1960s, a large number of alien workers — most from nearby islands — went to the U.S. Virgin Islands to relieve the acute labor shortage that developed during the territory's economic boom period. The workers entered under the H-2 temporary worker program, but the Virgin Islands became a permanent home for the workers and their families.

HR 3517 abolished the temporary worker program for the islands on grounds that no labor shortage requiring importation of alien workers was anticipated in the foreseeable future.

However, the Senate added a provision not in the House bill that allowed entertainers and athletes to continue working on the islands on a temporary basis.

Under HR 3517, an alien seeking to become a permanent resident had to make an application to the attorney general within one year of the bill's enactment.

Restrictions on Visas

Unlike other sections of immigration law, HR 3517 gave the secretary of state discretionary authority to restrict the right of new permanent residents to use the existing visa preference system to have relatives join them on the islands.

While acknowledging that such limitations were unprecedented, the Senate Judiciary Committee said in its report, "The committee is convinced that these restrictions are necessary to prevent a further influx of new immigrants to the already over-populated and resource-strained U.S. Virgin Islands." ∎

'Amerasian' Immigration

Congress Oct. 1 cleared for the president a bill (S 1698 — PL 97-359) to enable "Amerasian" children, young Southeast Asians fathered by Americans, to immigrate to the United States.

Final action came when first the House and then the Senate approved minor changes worked out by chief House and Senate supporters or their aides. The Senate had passed the measure Sept. 28 by a voice vote.

S 1698 was virtually identical to HR 808, introduced by Rep. Stewart B. McKinney, R-Conn. Provisions on Amerasians were also part of a major immigration reform bill (HR 7357) that was approved by the House Judiciary Committee but died in the waning days of the 97th Congress. *(Immigration reform, p. 405)*

Sen. Jeremiah Denton, R-Ala., chief sponsor of S 1698, said he and Carl Levin, D-Mich., were pushing the bill "because we believe that our country has too long ignored its responsibility to the abandoned offspring of our citizens in Asia."

Provisions

As cleared, S 1698:

● Allowed unmarried Amerasians to apply for admission to the United States under the "first preference" for visa allocations, a category reserved for unmarried sons and daughters of U.S. citizens.

● Authorized the attorney general to approve petitions for Amerasians if he had reason to believe the applicant was born after 1950 in Korea, Thailand, Vietnam, Laos, or Kampuchea (Cambodia) and was fathered by a U.S. citizen. The attorney general would consult private organizations in the country of the applicant's birth to make such a determination, considering such factors as the physical appearance of the petitioner, a birth certificate and proof of past financial support from a U.S. citizen thought to be the father.

● Required the attorney general to obtain a guarantee of financial support from a sponsor who was a U.S. citizen or permanent resident and was at least 21 years old. The guarantee of support would have to be signed in the presence of a U.S. immigration official.

● Required the sponsor to agree to be financially responsible for the applicant at 125 percent above the poverty threshold for five years or until the applicant reached the age of 21, whichever was longer. ∎

Refugee Admissions Pared

For the second year in a row, the Reagan administration, in consultation with Congress, reduced the number of refugees authorized to enter the United States.

The final authorization, published in the *Federal Register* Oct. 19, set an admission limit of 90,000 refugees for fiscal 1983. Some 64,000 of them, about two-thirds of all those authorized to enter the United States in fiscal 1983, were from Southeast Asia.

The overall ceiling for refugee admissions was down 50,000 from the fiscal 1982 authorized level of 140,000 and 127,000 from the fiscal 1981 authorized level of 217,000.

According to congressional testimony by Justice and State Department officials, the fiscal 1983 reduction re-

sulted largely from a more stable atmosphere in Southeast Asia and the imposition of martial law in Poland, which had restricted the number of persons allowed to leave that country.

Three-Year Downward Trend

The lowered 1983 refugee admission level reflected a downward trend over the last three years in the actual admission of refugees. *(Chart, below)*

In fiscal 1980, 215,000 refugees were admitted, according to the State Department. That number dropped to 159,252 in fiscal 1981 and to 97,297 in fiscal 1982.

The admission figures since fiscal 1980 grew out of a new process for admitting refugees set up in the 1980 refugee reform act (PL 96-212). The legislation broadened the definition of a refugee and established a new admissions mechanism based on yearly consultations with Congress. *(1980 Almanac p. 378)*

It also established a federally funded resettlement program for refugees, which Congress reauthorized for one year in a bill (HR 5879 — PL 97-363) cleared Oct. 1. *(Story, p. 413)*

Prior to 1980, most refugees entered the country under special provisions of the immigration laws designed to help those fleeing Southeast Asia and the Soviet Union.

Setting the Ceiling

The administration proposed a refugee admission level of 98,000 for fiscal 1983, but after consultations with the immigration subcommittees of the House and Senate Judiciary committees, the figure was lowered to 90,000. This was the level recommended by the Senate subcommittee.

In a letter to President Reagan, the subcommittee said its lower figure was based on conditions in Southeast Asia and Eastern Europe.

In the House, Rep. Romano L. Mazzoli, D-Ky., chairman of Judiciary's immigration subcommittee, recommended admitting 86,000 refugees. Other panel members supported the administration's request.

In a letter to Reagan, Mazzoli said the administration's original 68,000 allotment for Southeast Asia was too high because the number of refugees from that area was down.

Mazzoli also mildly chastised the administration for being too willing to admit as refugees those people who fled communist countries while turning down those who fled non-communist countries.

U.S. Refugee Admissions

	Actual admissions fiscal 1981	Actual admissions fiscal 1982	Authorized admissions fiscal 1983
Asia	131,139	73,522	64,000
Soviet Union/ Eastern Europe	20,148	13,536	15,000
Near East	3,829	6,304	6,000
Africa	2,119	3,356	3,000
Latin America/ Caribbean	2,017	579	2,000
TOTAL	159,252	97,297	90,000

Source: State Department

This was a particularly troublesome issue in handling the applications of Haitians who fled their homeland and sought asylum in the United States. (An asylum applicant, like a refugee, must have a well-founded fear of persecution in his homeland.) For the most part, neither the Carter nor the Reagan administration was willing to treat Haitians as refugees or grant them asylum. "Not everyone emerging from Southeast Asia is a refugee," Mazzoli wrote. "And by the same token, not everyone emerging from Central America or the Caribbean is an economic migrant. The Refugee Act requires each such application to be considered objectively on its own merits. . . ." ∎

Extradition Revision Dies

After moving quietly through the Senate and two House committees, a bill to revise U.S. extradition procedures stalled short of the House floor.

HR 6046 was reported June 24 by the House Judiciary Committee and Aug. 3 by the Foreign Affairs Committee (H Rept 97-627, Parts I & II).

The Senate passed its version of the bill (S 1940 — S Repts 97-331, 97-475) Aug. 19 by voice vote after it had been considered by the Senate Judiciary and Foreign Relations committees.

Many extradition laws had been in force without change since 1882. House and Senate panels that looked at the statutes agreed that reforms were needed, in large part to deal with instances of international terrorism.

But a coalition of religious and civil rights groups led by the American Civil Liberties Union spent months lining up House members to challenge the bill if it surfaced on the House floor.

The major focus of controversy was the protection of persons in the United States from prosecution in their own countries for "political offenses." There was disagreement over how to define a political offense and how to determine the motives of a country seeking to extradite someone from the United States. Also in dispute was who should decide whether a political offense was involved.

Political Offense: A Definition

During extradition hearings, a person had the right to claim that he was being sought for a political offense and should not be extradited. Federal judges, with help from the State Department, traditionally had decided on a case-by-case basis whether to accept such claims.

However, the courts generally had refused to look into the motives of the requesting country and had developed a doctrine of "non-inquiry" in such matters. The State Department, not the courts, had determined whether a country was seeking extradition to punish a person because of his or her political beliefs.

Both House and Senate bills redefined a "political offense" in similar fashion, and it was this section of the legislation that stirred the most controversy.

Current law defined a political offense as an act "committed in the course of or incidental to a violent political disturbance such as war, revolution or rebellion."

HR 6046 stated that "except in extraordinary circumstances" a political offense did not include airplane hijacking; attacks against internationally protected persons, such as diplomats; homicide, serious assault, rape and kidnap-

ping; the taking of hostages; an offense involving the use of a firearm that endangered another person; manufacturing, importing, distributing or selling narcotics or dangerous drugs; or an attempt or conspiracy to commit those crimes.

The House committee report said members wanted to "emphasize the need for the court to conduct a balancing test in assessing whether particular conduct constitutes a political offense." Major factors to be considered included international legal obligations, political neutrality (of the United States) and "the need to punish reprehensible conduct."

Opponents argued that the new definition was riddled with so many exceptions that it could end up denying protection in the United States to persons traditionally accorded a safe haven, most commonly refugees fleeing repressive regimes.

Christopher H. Pyle, a constitutional law professor at Mount Holyoke College, said in House testimony that HR 6046 "would virtually destroy the political-crimes defense."

"By its terms," he said, "a modern-day Alfred Dreyfus, who in the course of fighting his way out of an unjust imprisonment on Devil's Island seriously injured one of his torturers and commandeered a prison boat, holding its

crew hostage until he was free, would be extraditable for each of those actions."

Who Decides?

The Reagan administration wanted to give the secretary of state, rather than the judiciary, discretion to determine whether a political offense had been committed in the country seeking extradition.

Neither the House bill nor the measure passed by the Senate included that change. However, the bill originally approved by the Senate Judiciary Committee did give the secretary such authority, subject to limited judicial review. It was amended by the Senate Foreign Relations Committee to ensure that federal courts would continue to make "political offense" determinations.

The Senate bill required a person fighting extradition to prove "by clear and convincing evidence" that the crime for which he was sought was a political offense. The House bill required proof by the lesser "preponderance of the evidence."

Both bills codified the judicial doctrine of "non-inquiry" by making clear that only the secretary of state can look into the requesting country's motives for extradition. ∎

LSC Kept Alive; Reagan Board Unconfirmed

Although President Reagan for the second year in a row tried to abolish the Legal Services Corporation (LSC), Congress kept the agency alive through funding in the second fiscal 1983 continuing appropriations resolution (H J Res 631 — PL 97-377).

That measure allotted $241 million for the LSC in fiscal 1983, the same funding Congress provided through a series of continuing resolutions in fiscal 1982. *(1981 Almanac p. 412)*

The action was necessitated by the failure of Congress to complete action on the regular fiscal 1983 appropriations bill for the State, Justice, Commerce departments and certain other agencies, including the LSC. *(Story, p. 246)*

The corporation was created in 1974 to provide legal aid to the poor in civil cases, and reauthorized in 1977 after protracted congressional debates over the proper role of legal aid programs. *(Background, 1977 Almanac p. 587; 1974 Almanac p. 489)*

The LSC Board: All Unconfirmed

LSC lawyers, the agency's clients and its supporters in the legal community contended that by appointing members to the LSC governing board who were hostile to the corporation, Reagan tried to do by the backdoor what he could not accomplish through the front.

In 1982, only nine of the LSC's 11 board members were nominated officially and none was confirmed. By year's end, Reagan had withdrawn all nine of his nominees.

Seven LSC board members were appointed during the December 1981 congressional recess and later were nominated for their positions, along with two other people.

While Congress was away for its election recess, Reagan Oct. 23 made two surprise recess appointments to the board. This gave acting Chairman William Harvey, a conservative University of Indiana law professor, the full complement of 11 members prior to an Oct. 29 board meeting to select a new president of the corporation.

The new appointees were Dan Rathbun, 23, a student at Christendom College, Front Royal, Va., and Frank Donatelli, 33, a Washington lawyer with solid conservative connections. Donatelli had served as a board member of the National Conservative Political Action Committee and as executive director of Young Americans for Freedom. He also worked in Reagan's 1980 campaign.

A bipartisan group of 32 senators sent Reagan a letter Oct. 28 objecting to his making the recess appointments so close to the board meeting and in a manner that precluded Senate consideration of those appointments.

Picking an LSC Board President

Legal aid lawyers and outside supporters of the agency feared that the LSC presidency might be offered either to Robert D'Agostino, a former Justice Department official who wrote a controversial memo in 1981 suggesting that blacks were more likely than whites to be emotionally disturbed, or to Alfred S. Regnery, a deputy assistant attorney general in the department's lands division who had suggested in the past that the corporation be eliminated. Regnery was once an aide to Sen. Paul Laxalt, R-Nev.

In the 48 hours before the board meeting, the corporation's main office in Washington, D.C., was peppered with telegrams from lawyers around the country opposed to those possible choices.

But when the meeting took place Oct. 29, the LSC board voted to offer the presidency to Donald P. Bogard, an Indiana lawyer who had no poverty law experience and was director of litigation for Stokely Van Camp Inc., a large food processing company in Indianapolis.

Bogard had helped represent Stokely in lawsuits filed against the company by migrant workers represented by legal services lawyers. The lawsuits involved alleged labor law violations by the company.

Bogard said he saw no conflict of interest in serving as LSC president but declined to elaborate on why his in-

volvement in litigation directly against a legal services program would not constitute such a conflict.

Bogard accepted the LSC job Nov 10. His contract was effective Dec. 13.

The Senate could confirm or reject LSC board nominees, but it had no power over their choice of a president, who actually ran the corporation.

Reagan Nominees Withdrawn

In a surprise move Dec. 8, Reagan withdrew his nine pending LSC board nominees after 52 senators signed a letter saying they would not support his three most conservative nominees — Harvey; William J. Olson, a former officer of the Young Americans for Freedom and National Conservative Political Action Committee; and George E. Paras, whose nomination had stalled in the Labor and Human Resources Committee.

Under their recess appointments, Donatelli and Rathbun could serve until the end of 1983.

The previous LSC board, appointed by President Carter, had filed suit in federal court against the Reagan board, contending that LSC board members could not be appointed constitutionally during a recess of Congress. That suit was dismissed Sept. 30, but the plaintiffs filed an appeal Oct. 29.

Reining in Reagan Appointees

Following disclosures that Reagan's appointees to the LSC board had collected unprecedented consulting fees, members of Congress acted on three fronts to control the board.

Corporation records made public Dec. 14 at a House Judiciary subcommittee meeting showed the 11-member board collected $156,000 in fees in 1982, more than twice the level of any previous board. Harvey, the chairman, and Olson collected $25,028 and $19,721, respectively.

In addition, the two-year contract negotiated by Harvey for Bogard, his former law student and the new LSC president, provided Bogard with one year's severance pay if he was fired before his contract expired; membership in a private club of his own choosing; and two free trips each month through June 15, 1983, to Indianapolis, his home.

According to the Office of Personnel Management, federal workers in their first 10 years were entitled to a week's severance pay for each year worked. Under this plan, Bogard, who did not start work until Dec. 13, would not have been entitled to a full week's pay until Dec. 13, 1983.

Congress added provisions to the stopgap funding bill (H J Res 631) sharply restricting fees that could be paid LSC board members and barring any officer or employee of the LSC from collecting severance pay different from that accorded other federal employees.

In another move, all seven members of a House Judiciary subcommittee and 10 Democratic senators in two separate letters asked the General Accounting Office to look into "possible improprieties" concerning the board's consulting fees and Bogard's contract.

Finally, two other letters were sent directly to President Reagan expressing concern about the LSC. Rep. Harold S. Sawyer, R-Mich., a member of the House Judiciary subcommittee with LSC oversight, told Reagan that the conduct of his appointees "is an embarrassment to us and is becoming a political liability to you." And members of the Wednesday Group, a coalition of moderate Republicans, in a letter signed by 31 representatives and four

senators, urged Reagan to ensure that future board nominees were "outstanding attorneys committed to the fair and effective legal representation of the poor...."

Restrictions on LSC Activities

H J Res 631 included restrictions on the use of the LSC appropriations that had been part of previous funding bills. Some of the restrictions were altered, and certain new ones were added to clamp down on the fees collected by Reagan's appointees to the LSC board.

Included in the continuing resolution were provisions that:

● Prevented legal services lawyers from representing illegal aliens, allowing representation only for aliens admitted lawfully as immigrants, married to a U.S. citizen or admitted as refugees. This provision was in HR 3480, an authorization bill that passed the House in 1981 but never passed the Senate.

● Maintained restrictions enacted in earlier funding bills on composition of local boards that govern legal aid programs. One of the requirements was participation by state, county or local bar groups in appointing attorney members of the local boards.

● Eased a restriction against LSC lawyers lobbying by allowing legal aid lawyers to respond to requests from legislators on subjects within the lawyers' expertise, such as the effect of legislation on the elderly. A regulation adopted by the national LSC board of directors had allowed lawyers to respond only to questions relating to appropriations, authorizations or LSC oversight.

● Maintained restrictions on filing class actions lawsuits against local, state or federal agencies, but eased restrictions from the previous funding law. The earlier funding measure had allowed class actions so long as they were in compliance with regulations issued by the national LSC board. Congress changed this in PL 97-377 after members became concerned over the highly restrictive regulations proposed by Reagan's LSC board members.

The new language allowed class action suits if they were approved by the local office project director and were in conformance with local guidelines; if the class was made up of eligible clients; and if the project director determined that the government agency challenged would not change the policy in dispute.

● Maintained funding for programs that currently received LSC money until action to the contrary was taken by corporation directors confirmed by the Senate, as the LSC authorizing law required.

● Limited compensation to LSC board members to an attendance fee not to exceed the highest daily rate for a GS-15 federal employee, plus travel expenses in accord with government regulations.

● Prohibited reimbursement of LSC board members or employees for membership dues in private clubs.

● Specified that any severance paid LSC board members or employees could not exceed that available to all federal employees. ∎

Refugee Program Renewed

The Senate Oct. 1 cleared for the president a bill (HR 5879 — PL 97-363) reauthorizing for one year refugee resettlement programs established in 1980.

The bill was passed by the House June 22.

HR 5879 set no overall funding limit for fiscal 1983 but

rather provided "such sums as necessary." There were two exceptions — $100 million was authorized for social services such as language and job training, and $14 million for health monitoring and treatment of refugees.

The programs reauthorized under the legislation were established in a 1980 refugee reform law (PL 96-212). That measure established a new definition of refugees, created a more orderly process for their entry into the United States, provided for executive branch consultation with Congress, raised the number of refugees allowed into the country each year under normal conditions, and set up a resettlement program coordinated by the Office of Refugee Resettlement within the Department of Health and Human Services. *(1980 Almanac p. 378)*

The 1980 law also stated that the resettlement office could reimburse states for "up to 100 percent" of the cash and medical assistance provided refugees during their first 36 months in the United States. HR 5879 struck the words "up to" in order to clarify congressional intent that refugee resettlement costs should be treated as a federal responsibility.

Some 750,000 refugees, most of them from Indochina and Cuba, entered the country since 1975, straining government programs everywhere.

State officials had expressed mounting dissatisfaction with the 1980 law, contending in particular that federal officials did not provide enough notice before refugees' arrival.

Another major concern was the high number of refugees receiving some sort of welfare benefits; best estimates put the figure at 70 percent. Several provisions in HR 5879 were designed to meet state officials' concerns and to get better control over resettlement programs.

Major Provisions

In addition to the funding sections, the bill included major provisions that:

● Made clear that the Office of Refugee Resettlement was to develop a refugee placement plan to keep new refugees out of areas such as Florida that already had a large number of refugees. Exceptions would be made for immediate relatives of refugees already settled.

● Required consultation with state and local government officials about refugee placement.

● Required a refugee to participate in an available job or language training program in order to receive cash assistance. Assistance would be terminated if a refugee refused a suitable job offer, and it would not be available for full-time college students.

● Required voluntary agencies working with refugees to notify local welfare agencies when a refugee got a job offer. The refugee would have to be told of the notification and warned that cash aid would be available only if there was no suitable job offer.

● Required welfare agencies to notify voluntary agencies when a refugee had applied for welfare.

Legislative History

The House Judiciary Committee approved the bill May 12 (H Rept 97-541).

The House passed HR 5879 June 22 by a 357-58 vote. *(Vote 154, p. 46-H)*

By voice vote, the House adopted an amendment by John Edward Porter, R-Ill., requiring the Office of Refugee Resettlement to study and report to Congress by Sept. 30, 1983, on the feasibility of establishing refugee orientation centers.

The Reagan administration had wanted an authorization of at least two years. But supporters of a one-year bill said annual reviews permitted better congressional oversight.

HR 5879 was approved Sept. 28 by the Senate Judiciary Committee (S Rept 97-638), and cleared Oct. 1. ∎

Electronic Surveillance

The Senate March 25 passed a bill (S 1640) clarifying procedures for obtaining a court order authorizing electronic surveillance. But the measure died in the House Judiciary Committee.

The bill would have required a federal agency — in most instances the FBI — to indicate whether a break-in was necessary to install an electronic listening device.

Court orders would not be required, however, in emergency situations involving imminent danger of death or serious injury to any person. Current law already allowed emergency surveillance for situations involving "conspiratorial activities" threatening national security or "characteristic of organized crime."

The bill retained current requirements that a court order be obtained within 48 hours of an emergency surveillance.

The measure was approved by the Senate Judiciary Committee by voice vote March 2 and reported March 8 (S Rept 97-319).

S 1640 was similar to legislation approved by the Senate on June 9, 1980 (S 1717). Both measures were introduced in response to a 1979 Supreme Court decision that the Fourth Amendment did not require law enforcement agents, in seeking a court order permitting electronic surveillance, to say specifically that a break-in was necessary to install the listening devices. *(1980 Almanac p. 377; 1979 Almanac p. 30-A)* ∎

Curbing False Identification

Congress Dec. 19 cleared for the president a bill (HR 6946 — PL 97-398) designed to curb the spread of false identification documents such as drivers' licenses and birth certificates.

Final action came when the Senate by voice vote adopted a conference report (H Rept 97-975) on the bill. The House had adopted the report Dec. 17. Except for two modifications, the measure that cleared was the same as that passed by the House Sept. 14.

Provisions

As cleared by Congress, the bill included the following major provisions:

● Made it a federal offense to produce false identification documents or transfer them, knowing they were stolen or counterfeit; to possess such documents with the intent to use them or to transfer five or more of them; and to make, transfer or possess equipment intended for use in making counterfeit identification papers.

● Made it a federal offense to possess stolen or false identification documents that had been or appeared to

have been issued by the United States if the possessor knew that such documents were stolen or counterfeit. (This was not in the original House bill.)

● Provided a fine of up to $25,000 or a prison term up to five years or both if the production or transfer involved federally issued documents or a birth certificate, driver's license or personal identification card; the production of more than five false identification documents; or the production or transfer of equipment used to make false documents.

● Provided a fine of up to $15,000 and a prison term of up to three years for offenses involving any other type of production or transfer of false identification documents.

● Made it a misdemeanor for anyone making private identification documents with birth dates and then sending them through the mail or in interstate commerce to fail to clearly imprint a disclaimer that the document was not a government document. This provision was not in the original House bill. Proponents said it was intended to help sellers of alcoholic beverages "avoid being fooled by unfamiliar, unofficial identification."

Legislative History

The House Judiciary Committee Aug. 10 approved and Sept. 10 reported the false identification bill (H Rept 97-802).

Chief sponsor William J. Hughes, D-N.J., said the bill was aimed primarily at drug traffickers, terrorists and traffickers in stolen and illegal firearms who used false identifications to launder proceeds of crimes and "perpetrate frauds against businesses and the government."

Hughes said testimony before his Crime Subcommittee made clear that federal legislation was needed to help curb interstate shipment of false documents, such as state drivers' licenses.

"Since a state cannot investigate or prosecute misuse of its instruments in another state, recourse to federal criminal sanctions is the only effective deterrent available," Hughes said.

He added that forged identification could be responsible for as much as $10 billion in losses annually to government agencies and consumers.

Hughes said there were mail-order houses that provided false identifications and "blatantly advertised" their ability to make documents "in whatever name you want to start over again...."

The House approved the bill Sept. 14 by voice vote.

The Senate passed HR 6946 on Oct. 1 after amending the measure. The Senate added a provision aimed at those who made false identification documents and shipped them interstate to persons under the age of 21. It also adopted another amendment, sought by the Justice Department, expanding the offense concerning possession of false ID documents.

The Senate asked for a conference, and the House agreed. The conference report (H Rept 97-975) was filed in the House Dec. 17. ∎

Bill Easing Gun Law Dies

Spurred by heavy lobbying from the National Rifle Association (NRA), the Senate Judiciary Committee April 21 approved a bill (S 1030) making it easier to buy and sell firearms. But the measure went no further in 1982.

The bill, formally reported June 18 (S Rept 97-476), was approved 13-3. Opposing it were Edward M. Kennedy, D-Mass., who had tried with only partial success to strengthen the measure; Howard M. Metzenbaum, D-Ohio; and Charles McC. Mathias Jr., R-Md.

S 1030 substantially revised the 1968 Gun Control Act (PL 90-618). *(1968 Almanac p. 549)*

Among other things, it lifted most prohibitions on gun sales across state lines, permitted sales through the mail between individuals who had previously met face-to-face, loosened licensing requirements and required proof of intent in order to establish any violation of the act.

At Kennedy's urging, the committee by an 8-5 vote adopted an amendment requiring a 14-day waiting period for the purchase of a handgun. During that time, the seller would be required to notify local police for a check to determine whether the prospective buyer was barred under the law from owning a gun. Such a waiting period had been recommended in 1981 by the attorney general's Task Force on Violent Crime, but it was opposed by the NRA. *(1981 Almanac p. 420)*

The committee also adopted another Kennedy amendment requiring a sentence of two-to-five years for any federal crime committed with a gun.

However, the panel rejected by a 3-12 vote a major Kennedy amendment that would have kept all existing controls on the sale of handguns.

Background

The chief sponsor of S 1030 was James A. McClure, R-Idaho, who had tried since he came to the Senate in 1973 to modify the 1968 law.

Providing impetus for the bill was a strong and growing dissatisfaction among gun owners and dealers with the 1968 law, enacted in the aftermath of the assassinations of Dr. Martin Luther King Jr. and Robert F. Kennedy.

The 1968 law did a number of things, including barring the mail order or interstate shipment of firearms and ammunition. It also refined licensing procedures for those manufacturing, importing, selling or collecting guns. The law banned importation of most firearms, but it did not ban imports of gun parts.

The Judiciary Committee sought for months to mark up the gun bill, but prior to April 21, it either was unable to get a quorum or bogged down in arguments over the bill.

Although a companion House bill (HR 3300) sponsored by Harold L. Volkmer, D-Mo., had 171 cosponsors, House Judiciary Chairman Peter W. Rodino Jr., D-N.J., and other senior committee Democrats opposed it and the bill never went anywhere. ∎

Criminal Code Revision Dies

Efforts to revise the federal criminal code in the 97th Congress were effectively doomed April 27 when the Senate failed by 15 votes to cut off debate on a motion to consider a code reform bill (S 1630).

The vote was 45-46, well short of a majority, let alone the 60 "aye" votes needed to invoke cloture on the motion to consider the bill (S 1630). Both liberals and conservatives joined in blocking cloture. *(Vote 84, p. 19-S)*

Senate Judiciary Chairman Strom Thurmond, R-S.C., chief sponsor of S 1630, later mobilized a bipartisan group of senators behind a trimmed-down anti-crime package (S

2572) that contained many features from the code revision bill but dropped its most controversial provisions. The measure was introduced May 26 and placed directly on the Senate calendar, bypassing the Judiciary Committee.

Rep. Robert McClory, R-Ill., ranking Republican on the House Judiciary Committee, introduced an identical bill (HR 6497) May 26, but no action was taken on it. The House Judiciary Criminal Justice Subcommittee held numerous hearings on revising criminal laws, but no omnibus bill was approved by the panel in the 97th Congress.

S 2572 was passed by the Senate Sept. 30, 95-1, but it went no further. *(Vote 379, p. 64-S)*

However, some of the components of S 2572 ultimately were included in an omnibus anti-crime bill (HR 3963) vetoed by President Reagan in the waning days of the 97th Congress.

Background: Code Reform History

S 1630 was the third complete criminal code overhaul in five years to be approved by the Senate Judiciary Committee. *(Background, 1981 Almanac p. 432)*

The effort to revise federal criminal laws dated back to 1966, when a National Commission on Reform of Federal Criminal Laws was created. The commission's report resulted in the introduction Jan. 4, 1973, of the first omnibus code bill, S 1 — a proposal that was immediately controversial, especially among civil libertarians who considered it harmful to individual rights. *(1973 Almanac p. 374)*

The Senate Judiciary Committee did not act on S 1, but in 1977 the panel approved a "descendant" of that measure, S 1437, which was passed by the Senate Jan. 30, 1978, after eight days of debate. The bill went nowhere in the House Judiciary Committee, however. *(1978 Almanac p. 165)*

In the 96th Congress, the Senate committee approved yet another code revision, S 1722, on Dec. 4, 1979. On July 2, 1980, the House Judiciary Committee approved its own version, HR 6915. But the measure went no further. *(1980 Almanac p. 393)*

In past code fights, the most vocal lobbyists were the American Civil Liberties Union, the National Committee Against Repressive Legislation and various business groups.

In the 97th Congress, however, a new player was added — the Moral Majority. Although this conservative group was interested in the code during the 96th Congress, it did not play a particularly active lobbying role.

This time around, Dr. Ronald S. Godwin, Moral Majority's vice president, testified in both the House and Senate. The group sent out numerous press releases and newsletters and had lobbied selected members.

In testimony before the House Judiciary Committee, Godwin offered a sweeping denunciation of HR 1647 and HR 4711. He said they "would permit a wide range of obscene materials to be transmitted through the public mails, would inhibit local communities in the prosecution of the dissemination of pornography . . . and would in several other areas alter existing law to lessen the public perception of the seriousness of crimes involving moral turpitude."

S 1630: Senate Filibuster

S 1630 was approved by the Senate Judiciary Committee Nov. 18, 1981, and formally reported Jan. 25, 1982 (S Rept 97-307). *(1981 Almanac p. 432)*

By the time it reached the Senate floor in April, a trio of conservative Republicans — Jesse Helms, N.C., James A. McClure, Idaho, and Jeremiah Denton, Ala. — had filed more than 60 proposed amendments to S 1630. Many were controversial, covering such subjects as the death penalty, obscenity crimes and sexual offenses. An aide to Helms said the senator also was likely to offer an amendment barring the federal courts — including the Supreme Court — from handling school prayer cases, and possibly an amendment outlawing abortions.

Efforts to reach a unanimous consent agreement on the amendments were unsuccessful. Without such consent, the amendments would have been ruled out of order because they expanded the scope of the bill.

Thurmond attributed the cloture defeat to the reluctance of many senators to deal with controversial issues in an election year. "Too many members of Congress don't want to face these hot issues this year. That's the bottom line," he said.

The Second Try: S 2572

S 2572, considerably more limited than the criminal code bill, was carefully drafted to include only provisions with widespread support.

Major provisions included a preventive detention section allowing judges to jail before trial defendants considered "dangerous" to the community; a new sentencing scheme that virtually abolished parole and established a sentencing commission to write sentencing guidelines; increased penalties for drug trafficking; and new protections for top government officials and federal witnesses.

Thurmond, Sen. Joseph R. Biden Jr., D-Del., ranking Judiciary Committee Democrat, and Majority Leader Howard H. Baker Jr., R-Tenn., July 1 worked out an unusual time agreement specifying eight controversial matters that could not be included in the bill or offered as amendments.

Among them was a provision revising the insanity defense that was deleted from the bill. It would have redefined insanity so that the plea could be used successfully only by individuals so deranged they lacked the requisite mental state to commit the crime they were charged with.

Under current federal law, the defense applied to a person who by reason of a mental disease or defect did not have substantial capacity to conform his conduct to the law and to appreciate that his conduct was wrong.

Interest in the insanity issue skyrocketed after a federal court jury June 21 found John W. Hinckley Jr. not guilty by reason of insanity in the March 30, 1981, shooting of President Reagan and three other men. *(Insanity bill, p. 418)*

The administration supported the insanity provision of S 2572 and tried to see that it was kept in the bill.

But Howell Heflin, D-Ala., a former state Supreme Court chief justice, insisted that the insanity provision be withdrawn. Otherwise, he said, he would object to the bill coming up. Heflin said the insanity issue needed more study. Thurmond finally agreed to delete the provision.

In addition to the insanity issue, the time agreement specified that several other controversial matters could not be part of the bill, including provisions to re-establish a federal death penalty; allow federal prosecutions for extortion during labor disputes; restrict the authority of federal courts over such matters as busing, abortion and school prayer; restrict the use of "habeas corpus," a post-trial procedure allowing defendants to challenge their convictions; and amend the 1968 gun control act.

The time agreement and narrow focus of S 2572 helped win it easy Senate passage Sept. 30. Sen. Charles McC. Mathias Jr., R-Md., cast the lone dissenting vote. Mathias said he opposed the bill's proposed sentencing scheme, which called for creation of a seven-member sentencing commission to write sentencing guidelines for federal judges. Mathias offered an amendment to strike the provision, but it was rejected by voice vote.

In an effort to speed House consideration, the Senate sponsors attached the crime package to a House-passed bill (HR 3963) concerning a drug offenders program, sent the measure back to the House and asked for a conference. HR 3963 was cleared for the president Dec. 20 but Reagan vetoed it Jan. 14, 1983. *(Story, p. 419)* ▮

Reagan's Judicial Selections

At the mid-point of President Reagan's four-year term, assessments of his judicial appointment record varied sharply according to the perspective of the viewer.

Administration officials were proud of the president's selections and believed Reagan was balancing off scores of "activist" judges appointed by President Carter.

Conservative groups, such as the Washington Legal Foundation and the Free Congress Foundation, also found much to applaud in Reagan's selections. Their spokesmen said that for the most part, Reagan had appointed high-caliber people who generally shared the president's conservative political philosophy.

Few Women, Minorities Named

But groups representing women, blacks and Hispanics were disappointed and angry. All but seven of the president's 89 appointees to lifetime federal judgeships were white males, and these groups felt shut out of the judicial selection process — in sharp contrast to the influence and record gains they achieved during the Carter administration.

Reagan did appoint Sandra Day O'Connor as an associate justice of the Supreme Court, making her the first woman to serve on the nation's highest court. Women's groups praised the O'Connor appointment, but they saw nothing else to cheer in the president's record. Black and Hispanic representatives held the same view.

Of 19 appointments to federal appeals courts, none went to a woman or Hispanic. One black was appointed, and he already was serving as a federal district judge.

In his first two years, Reagan made 69 federal district court appointments. None went to blacks, three went to women and two to Hispanics. The Hispanic appointments were on the federal bench of Puerto Rico, traditional positions for Hispanics. No Hispanics were appointed to posts in the 50 states. *(Previous Reagan appointments, 1981 Almanac p. 410)*

In 1982, Reagan made 48 appointments. All but four went to white males. Two women and the two Hispanics were named to district court seats.

In his first two years in office, President Carter made 12 appointments to the appeals courts. Three of them went to blacks. Of Carter's 52 district court appointments, six were blacks, six were women and two were Hispanics, according to the Justice Department.

With passage of the 1978 Omnibus Judgeship Act (PL 95-486) that gave him 152 new federal judgeships, Carter ended his presidency having appointed 40 women, 38 blacks and 16 Hispanics to the federal bench — more than any other president. *(Judgeship act, 1978 Almanac p. 173; comparative chart, see next page)*

To help him select appeals court nominees, Carter established commissions to suggest candidates. The Reagan administration abolished the commissions; Justice Department officials, who helped the president with judicial selections, said the panels were unnecessary.

A Shift in Philosophy

"I think the Reagan administration has taken full advantage of the prerogatives of the presidency. They put on the bench those kind of people who are compatible with their ideology and political commitment. That was true of the Carter administration as well," said Sheldon Goldman, a political science professor at the University of Massachusetts and an authority on federal judicial selection.

Jonathan C. Rose, a Justice Department official who was heavily involved in judicial appointments, basically agreed with Goldman. "Philosophy certainly has been a factor with regard to our appointments. I think it is entirely appropriate," said Rose, head of the Office of Legal Policy.

"I think that the president came to office realizing that his predecessor had appointed people of a judicial philosophy which was quite different [from Reagan's]. By and large, Carter tended to appoint people who have a very activist role in mind for the judiciary, who believe that judicial intervention can solve all manner of problems that might better be left to political intervention.

"The number of appointments was so massive that we would have been derelict in our responsiblity if we did not pay some attention to our obligation to try to produce some semblance of balance," Rose said.

Dan Popeo, head of the Washington Legal Foundation, a business-oriented law and research organization, said he was "very pleased" with the quality of Reagan's appointments, particularly to the appeals courts. Among the appointees were several well-known, conservative law professors.

"I don't think he's given anyone in the judicial community a reason to cry foul," Popeo said. "If anyone is crying foul, they, themselves, are playing politics and are not worrying about good judicial competence."

Women, Minorities Displeased

Spokesmen for groups representing women, blacks and Hispanics assessed the Reagan appointments entirely differently.

"The nature of the judicial selection process is so closed at this point and the likelihood of getting first-quality women or blacks through the process is so remote, that people have sort of given up," said Susan Ness, a consultant on judicial selection who had monitored the process for five years.

Gladys Kessler, a District of Columbia Superior Court judge who was president of the National Association of Women Judges, said the number of women appointed "is shockingly low considering that there is a large pool of extremely qualified women."

Like other women lawyers, Ness and Kessler contended the Reagan administration was applying a double standard in selecting judges. "They are asking questions and applying a political litmus test different for women than for men," Kessler said, pointing in particular to ques-

tions about "reproductive freedom."

She cited the case of Judith Whittaker, a respected Missouri lawyer who was in line for an appeals court seat. Her nomination was derailed in 1981 by conservative groups who contended that she was a staunch supporter of legalized abortion.

Rose conceded he was unhappy with the Whittaker result, but he said that the "political leadership of the state found it impossible to support her."

Spokesmen for Hispanic groups were more resigned than angry in discussing Reagan's appointments.

"We are not surprised at the number of Hispanics appointed. This president is not doing anything for Hispanics," said Arnold Torres, head of the League of United Latin American Citizens. Antonia Hernandez, director of the Washington office of the Mexican American Legal Defense and Educational Fund, agreed: "I think what has happened is that they have made a political decision that Hispanics are not important enough to contend with."

Althea T. L. Simmons, director of the NAACP's Washington office, was equally disheartened. "We certainly knew that we would lose on judgeships with the new administration," she said. "We did, however, believe that there would be some attempt to have tokenism with reference to judges. I could not even call this tokenism."

Rose defended the administration's selection and appointment process. "We approach this from a different philosophy than the Carter administration. We did not adopt a view that we should strive for a quota or a goal of a particular number of women or minorities to be put on the federal bench," he said.

"We wanted to first see that the people we nominated were of the highest possible quality."

Rose said, however, that the administration was "actively working to try to improve the record."

Quality of Judges

Rose claimed that the Reagan appointees were of a higher caliber than many of the Carter appointees. "I know

there are people on the federal bench who are giving our U.S. attorneys significant problems," Rose said.

Popeo, of the Washington Legal Foundation, was even stronger in his criticism. "Carter did a great disservice by putting judicial candidates on the bench because they needed minorities," he said. "I don't think the majority were made on the basis of their qualifications. If the Carter administration wants to take that as an insult, that's just what I intended it to be."

It was difficult to measure how accurate such criticism was. Carter's judges had been on the bench such a short time that no sufficient record existed to judge their performances.

The only constant was the ratings of the American Bar Association (ABA), which for 34 years had reviewed the qualifications of presidential appointees. Comparing the two administrations, the ABA results showed little difference. Of all Carter appointments, 6.1 percent were given the highest rating, exceptionally well qualified, while 6.7 percent of Reagan's appointees received this rating.

The designation "well qualified" was given to 49.6 percent of the Carter appointees and 46 percent of Reagan's appointees. A "qualified" rating was given to 43.1 percent of Carter's appointees and 47 percent of Reagan's appointees.

An "unqualified" rating was given to 1.1 percent of Carter's appointees but to none of Reagan's appointees. (The percentages do not add up precisely to 100 because of rounding.)

Despite these figures, Rose said he still believed Reagan's appointees were more qualified. He suggested that the ABA lowered its standards for Carter's women and minority nominees. "I have the general impression they may have applied less rigorous standards for people from these groups," Rose said.

Asked about Rose's comments, Brooksley Born, chairman of the ABA committee that rated judicial nominees, said, "I think we apply consistent standards. During the Carter administration, with minority groups and women, we did adopt a policy that in evaluating experience we would recognize that women and minorities had entered the profession in large numbers in recent years and that their opportunity for advancement might have been limited.

"There were a number of women we felt were qualified, for example, even though they had not been in practice for 12 years." The ABA generally had considered 12 years' experience to be the minimum necessary to qualify for a federal judgeship. ∎

Judicial Nominees

U.S. Court of Appeals

	Women	Blacks	Hispanics
Johnson	2.5%	5.0%	Not available
Nixon	0	0	Not available
Ford	0	0	Not available
Carter	19.6	16.1	3.6
Reagan	0	5.3	0

U.S. District Court

	Women	Blacks	Hispanics
Johnson	1.6%	3.3 %	2.5%
Nixon	0.6	2.8	1.1
Ford	1.9	5.8	1.9
Carter	14.1	14.1	6.8
Reagan	4.3	0	2.9

Source: The Johnson, Nixon and Ford statistics are from a study by Sheldon Goldman of the University of Massachusetts at Amherst. The Carter and Reagan percentages were compiled by Congressional Quarterly based on figures from the Justice Department.

Insanity Defense Unchanged

When John W. Hinckley Jr. June 21 was found not guilty by reason of insanity in the 1981 shooting of President Reagan and three other men, it prompted a flood of congressional proposals to change the insanity defense in federal criminal trials. But none was cleared by the 97th Congress.

The day after the federal court verdict, members in both chambers introduced bills to sharply restrict the insanity defense and revived proposals already pending.

Attorney General William French Smith, in an unusual post-trial news conference June 22, urged Congress to act. "There must be an end to the doctrine that allows so

many persons to commit crimes of violence, to use confusing procedures to their own advantage, and then to have the door open to them to return to the society which they victimized," he said.

Hinckley Verdict Prompts Outrage

The response on Capitol Hill reflected widespread public outrage at the verdict in the Hinckley case, which grew out of the March 30, 1981, assassination attempt at the Washington Hilton Hotel. *(1981 Almanac p. 6)*

Following the verdict, the 27-year-old defendant was committed to St. Elizabeths Hospital in the District of Columbia for a minimum of 50 days to undergo additional psychiatric evaluations. Both his family and his attorneys said they would not seek his release until convinced he was no longer a danger to himself or others.

The verdict came after the presiding judge told a jury of seven women and five men that it could only convict Hinckley if the prosecution had proved "beyond a reasonable doubt" that Hinckley was not suffering from a mental disease or defect, or that he nonetheless had substantial capacity both to conform his conduct to the requirements of the law and to appreciate the wrongfulness of his conduct.

The jury, confronted with days of sharply conflicting testimony from defense and prosecution psychiatrists, found itself unable to dismiss all doubts about Hinckley's sanity.

On June 24, just three days after the verdict, a Senate Judiciary subcommittee summoned five members of the Hinckley jury to testify about the verdict and the insanity law. All five jurors testified that they believed Hinckley had some type of mental disability they could not ignore. "We had that mental problem to deal with," said Maryland T. Copelin. "We just couldn't shut that out."

The Focus for Change

The legislative proposals focused on three main issues — redefining legal insanity, creating a new verdict for someone found to be guilty but mentally ill, and shifting the burden of proof on the question of insanity.

According to the American Bar Association (ABA), a majority of states and the federal courts required the prosecution to prove beyond a reasonable doubt that the defendant was sane at the time of the crime. A "respectable minority," the ABA said, put the burden of proof on the defendant to show by "a preponderance of the evidence" that he was insane.

Idaho and Montana abolished the insanity defense. Five states had a "guilty but mentally ill" verdict: Michigan, Illinois, Indiana, Georgia and New Mexico.

The ABA specialist said that a major concern with some of these state laws was that a person adjudged guilty but mentally ill had no right to treatment. Instead, many of those convicted were sent directly to prison with no medical help.

The "guilty but mentally ill" verdict was a feature in some bills introduced in Congress. The judge would sentence the defendant and determine whether treatment was needed. If so, the defendant would be placed in an institution until found to be well. At that time, he would serve out the rest of his sentence in prison.

Another proposal, which was part of an omnibus crime bill (S 2572), would have replaced the current insanity definition with a new verdict of "not guilty only by reason of insanity." A defendant would have to prove that, because of a mental disease or defect, he did not have the requisite state of mind — such as intent — to commit the crime with which he was charged. *(S 2572, p. 415)*

Sen. Orrin G. Hatch, R-Utah, a sponsor of the bill, said this would apply to someone who thought, for example, that when he shot a person, he was shooting a cabbage.

If a jury returned this verdict, the defendant would be confined in an appropriate mental institution until a judge determined by a preponderance of the evidence that he had recovered.

Sen. Arlen Specter, R-Pa., sponsored another proposal (S 2658) that would have required the defendant to prove by clear and convincing evidence that he was insane.

No Action Taken

The provision revising the insanity defense was deleted from S 2572, the omnibus anti-crime package, July 1 under an unusual time agreement worked out by Senate leaders.

The Reagan administration had supported the insanity provision of S 2572 and tried to see that it was kept in the bill. On July 1, the day the time agreement was worked out, Attorney General Smith wrote a letter to Baker backing the provision.

"In short, we believe that reform of the insanity defense is urgently needed to restore public confidence in the criminal justice system," Smith wrote, adding that the S 2572 proposal was a "well thought out and considered approach — not an emotional response to the public furor" over the Hinckley decision.

Senate Judiciary Chairman Strom Thurmond, R-S.C., read Smith's letter to colleagues, but Howell Heflin, D-Ala., a former state Supreme Court chief justice, insisted that the insanity provision be withdrawn. Otherwise, he said, he would object to the bill coming up. Heflin said the insanity issue needed more study.

Thurmond finally agreed to delete the provision. No further action was taken on the insanity defense during the 97th Congress. ∎

Reagan Vetoes Package of Anti-Crime Bills

President Reagan Jan. 14, 1983, vetoed a package of anti-crime legislation (HR 3963) that had been cleared by Congress Dec. 20. *(Veto message, p. 28-E)*

The anti-crime measure, which incorporated a number of bills approved earlier by one chamber or the other, was put together in House-Senate staff negotiations in the closing days of the 97th Congress.

Final action came Dec. 20 when the Senate, by voice vote, accepted the House package. The House had adopted the measure under suspension of the rules earlier in the day by a 271-27 vote. *(Vote 456, p. 134-H)*

HR 3963 began in 1981 as a simple three-year reauthorization of a program to provide drug abuse monitoring and treatment to convicted federal offenders released on parole or probation. *(1981 Almanac p. 437)*

Appended to it in December 1982 was an amendment

containing a new grant program to help states combat crime; increased fines for drug traffickers and provisions allowing forfeiture of property related to illegal drug enterprises; new penalties for tampering with drugs, food or other consumer products; a "career criminal" provision that would allow certain repeat offenders to be tried in federal court; and a new federal drug enforcement office to direct national and international drug enforcement operations.

The Reagan Veto

Reagan vetoed HR 3963 primarily because of objections from administration officials to the new centralized anti-drug office the bill would have created. Informally termed a "drug czar," the new position was to be a Cabinet-level office with authority over existing agencies involved in anti-drug law enforcement.

A senior Justice Department official told reporters Jan. 14, 1983, that the Justice, State and Treasury departments all opposed the proposed new drug office because they feared it "had a tremendous potential for disruption" of existing law enforcement projects. The official called the drug czar proposal "a band-aid, a gimmick" that would "create more paperwork, not arrests."

He said a drug czar would mean "sweeping changes in the executive branch." Such an office would "undermine the authority of Cabinet officers and alter the chain of command" within existing agencies, such as the FBI and Drug Enforcement Administration, the Justice official said.

The official said Justice also opposed the provision in HR 3963 that would have allowed federal prosecution of repeat state offenders under specified circumstances. He said the department opposed language giving local prosecutors power to veto a decision by federal prosecutors to take jurisdiction over a case. He said the bill had "grave constitutional" problems and raised "practical concerns."

The administration supported the bill's other provisions, the official said, but concerns about the drug czar and the "career criminal" provisions prevailed.

Half a Loaf

During House floor debate Dec. 20, William J. Hughes, D-N.J., chief sponsor of the House bill and chairman of the House Judiciary Crime Subcommittee, praised HR 3963 as a useful anti-crime package. But Thomas N. Kindness, R-Ohio, complained that the legislation amounted to "a pitiful dribble of legislation."

Missing from the bill were two controversial proposals — bail reform, to allow expanded pretrial detention, and a completely new federal sentencing scheme that set standardized fines and prison terms and virtually abolished parole. These had been included in an omnibus crime package (S 2572) containing remnants of a criminal code revision that was approved by the Senate Sept. 30 but never passed by the House. *(Criminal code, p. 415)*

As approved by Congress, HR 3963 included the following major elements:

Drug-Dependent Offenders

The program reauthorized by the original version of HR 3963 provided for the examination of all convicted federal offenders released on parole or given probation to determine if they were drug users.

Drug abuse treatment and monitoring, largely through urinalysis, was to be provided to help defendants end their drug dependence.

The House Judiciary Committee reported the original version Oct. 21, 1981 (H Rept 97-283) and the full House passed it Oct. 26, 1981.

The bill as approved in 1982 authorized $4.5 million for fiscal 1983, $5.5 million for fiscal 1984 and $6.5 million for fiscal 1985.

Drug Offense Penalties

Title I of the amendment to HR 3963 was essentially the drug penalty measure (HR 7140 — H Rept 97-883) reported Sept. 28 by the House Judiciary Committee and passed by the House the same day. The measure passed the Senate with amendments Oct. 1, and then was rolled into HR 3963.

This title included the following provisions:

● Increased substantially the penalties for manufacturing and trafficking in drugs, and for sales of drugs. For example, the maximum fine for manufacturing and trafficking in amphetamines was increased from $15,000 to $250,000 for individuals, and $1 million if an association was involved. The maximum fines for manufacturing and trafficking in heroin or cocaine were increased from $25,000 to $250,000, with a maximum $1 million fine if more than one individual or an organization was involved.

● Created a new, alternative fine allowing a judge, instead of assessing fixed penalties, to fine offenders up to twice their gross profits or proceeds.

● Provided for forfeiture to the government of property in all felony drug cases. The bill authorized courts to restrain the transfer of property that might be subject to forfeiture and to order the seizure of property to ensure its availability for a forfeiture proceeding. The Senate had passed a broader forfeiture bill (S 2320 — S Rept 97-520), covering cases other than those involving drugs. But it accepted the House version.

● Established a $10 million fund from forfeiture proceeds in fiscal 1984 and 1985 to be used for enforcement of federal drug laws.

● Expanded the authority of U.S. Customs officials, in civil proceedings, to dispose of property related to drug operations.

Justice Assistance Act

Title II of the amendment to HR 3963 created a new anti-crime assistance program for states and local communities, a successor to the now-defunct Law Enforcement Assistance Administration. The House and Senate had passed differing versions of a bill (HR 4481) to provide grants for fiscal 1983 and 1984.

HR 4481 was reported Oct. 26, 1981, by the House Judiciary Committee (H Rept 97-293) and passed Feb. 10, 1982. *(1981 Almanac p. 433)*

The Senate passed HR 4481 on Dec. 9 after amending it to incorporate provisions of S 2411, reported Sept. 24 by the Senate Judiciary Committee (S Rept 97-587)

This title of HR 3963 contained the following provisions:

● Created an Office of Justice Assistance to administer a program of about $130 million in block grants to states. Funds would be available for proven programs such as drug treatment projects, undercover operations to recover stolen property and programs within prosecutors' offices to pro-

vide speedy trials of repeat offenders.

● Created a discretionary grant program authorized at about $35 million for programs that train judges, prosecutors, and other law enforcement officials and provide technical assistance for criminal court systems.

● Required states and local communities to match any federal grant.

● Based the amount of block grants on population.

● Provided that the minimum block grant for any state would be $250,000, which the state would then parcel out for projects specified under the law.

● Provided grants for law enforcement emergencies.

● Authorized funding for fiscal 1983 and fiscal 1984 for two anti-crime research agencies, the Bureau of Justice Statistics and the National Institute of Justice, at an annual $25 million each, their current funding level.

● Authorized creation of an assistant attorney general for justice assistance who would oversee the Office of Justice Assistance, the Bureau of Justice Statistics and the National Institute of Justice.

Other Anti-Crime Measures

Title III of the amendment to HR 3963 included four different measures.

Anti-Tampering Provisions

The first part of Title III was a revision of a Senate bill (S 3048) to make tampering with food and drug products a federal felony. The measure was largely a response to the seven deaths that occurred in October when unsuspecting consumers ingested Extra-Strength Tylenol capsules that had been laced with cyanide.

S 3048 was reported Dec. 8 by the Senate Judiciary Committee, but no written report was filed. It was passed Dec. 17.

This section included the following provisions:

● Made it a felony for anyone, with an intent to cause bodily harm, to tamper with drugs, food, cosmetics or other devices and thereby cause bodily injury or death.

● Provided for a fine of up to $20,000, a prison term of up to five years, or both, for attempted tampering.

● Provided a fine of up to $100,000, life in prison, or both, of death or serious bodily harm resulted.

● Provided a fine of up to $100,000, up to 20 years in prison, or both, in any other case of actual tampering.

The Senate bill had included penalties for cases involving an intent to damage the reputation of another's business. This was stricken from the final version.

Protecting Intelligence Officers

Part two of Title III included elements of a Senate bill (S 2552) that made it a federal crime to assault or murder certain designated intelligence officials. The bill was reported Sept. 23 (S Rept 97-575) by the Judiciary Committee and passed by the Senate Oct. 1.

The version adopted in the conference report covered fewer intelligence personnel than the original Senate bill. Currently, an attack on an intelligence official was covered by the law of the state in which the offense occurred.

Career Criminals

Part three of Title III was a bill (S 1688 — S Rept 97-585) passed by the Senate Sept. 30 giving federal courts jurisdiction to try "career criminals" — repeat offenders — who used a firearm in burglaries or robberies, provided they had at least two prior convictions for such crimes.

This section was one of two that prompted Reagan's veto. Its major provisions included the following:

● Gave the federal courts authority to handle criminal cases involving state offenses if the defendant used a firearm to commit a crime and had been convicted at least twice before in state court of robbery, burglary, or an attempt or conspiracy to commit such an offense.

● Set a mandatory minimum 15-year prison term, a fine of $10,000, or both, for those convicted under the new law. No parole or probation would be allowed.

● Required a federal prosecutor to obtain consent from the local prosecuting authority or from the U.S. attorney general or his top assistants. These officials had to determine there was a sufficient federal interest to take the case and that a federal prosecution would "likely result in a significantly faster trial or lengthier sentence."

● Gave local prosecutors veto authority over a federal request to take a case authorized under the legislation.

New Federal Drug Office

The last section of Title III established a new Cabinet-level office to direct and coordinate national and international operations for combating drug trafficking. This provision, which drew heated objections from departments already involved in drug enforcement, was part of S 2572, passed Sept. 30 by the Senate.

Under HR 3963, the director of the proposed Office of National and International Drug Operations and Policy would have been appointed by the president and confirmed by the Senate. This "drug czar" would have had authority to order other Cabinet officials, including the attorney general, to follow his priorities. ∎

Environment

The year 1982 was one of confrontation and stalemate between the Reagan administration and congressional Democrats over environmental issues.

The spirit of the year was accurately if unwittingly summed up at its end by Environmental Protection Agency (EPA) Administrator Anne M. Gorsuch. "The time for compromise has passed," she said Dec. 20, responding to a House vote four days earlier citing her for contempt of Congress for failing to turn over documents sought by a House committee investigating EPA's enforcement of the "superfund" hazardous waste law.

That uncompromising spirit — equally evident among many of the administration's critics — led to deadlock on much major environmental legislation in 1982.

As a result of the Gorsuch contempt vote, the year ended with Congress and EPA headed into court for a constitutional showdown that was likely to test the fundamental powers of each branch.

An earlier contempt recommendation against Interior Secretary James G. Watt was averted by a compromise March 18. That dispute concerned subpoenaed documents on Cabinet consideration of how Canadian energy policy affected U.S. companies.

Stalemate

During 1982, environmentalists and their congressional allies proved they had the strength to stop just about any legislative initiative aimed at dismantling the environmental laws of the preceding decade.

At the same time, the administration showed it could block new environmental legislation it strongly opposed. Three of President Reagan's 15 vetoes during the 97th Congress came in the area of the environment and natural resources. Reagan vetoed bills designating Florida wilderness lands, settling a dispute over water rights of Arizona's Papago Indians, and setting specific EPA research and development priorities. Congress did not attempt to override any of the vetoes, although the Papago bill was scaled down, repackaged with a reclamation water reform bill the administration wanted, and eventually signed into law.

Five major environmental laws of the 1970s came due for reauthorization during the 97th Congress, but Congress did not finish action on any of them. They were the Clean Air Act (PL 95-95); the Clean Water Act (PL 95-217, except for Title II); the Federal Insecticide, Fungicide, and Rodenticide Act (PL 92-517); the Safe Drinking Water Act (PL 96-63); and the Ocean Dumping Act (PL 92-532).

All remained on the books and were funded through appropriations. But they carried over as "unfinished business" onto the agenda of the 98th Congress.

There were two major reasons for the inaction: the main focus of the 97th Congress was on budget and economic matters, and members were locked in stalemate over whether and how to change the status quo.

On a number of occasions, the Democratic-controlled House passed measures supported by environmental groups, only to see them languish in the Republican-controlled Senate. These ranged from a bill to strengthen a major hazardous waste law to legislation protecting national parks from overuse and encroaching development.

Budget Cuts

While the administration proposed major cuts in environmental and natural resource programs, Congress generally held overall fiscal 1983 appropriations close to fiscal 1982 levels. But that preserved deep cuts the administration proposed and Congress enacted in many programs in fiscal 1982.

EPA's operating budget was slashed from $1.3 billion in fiscal 1981 to $1.09 billion in 1982. While the administration requested $961 million for 1983, Congress appropriated $1.04 billion.

One of the biggest cuts at EPA was in research and development. Congress appropriated $227.2 million for fiscal 1983 — more than the $219 the administration requested, but well below the 1982 level of $270.5 million and the 1981 level of $358 million.

Congress appropriated some $7.5 billion for the Interior Department and related agencies in fiscal 1983, $923 million more than the $6.6 billion Reagan requested.

That did not include $2.07 billion in "off-budget" appropriations to buy oil for the Strategic Petroleum Reserve (SPR). While the final amount was up slightly from the $7.36 billion enacted for 1982 (not counting the SPR), it was still down from fiscal 1981 spending of $12.06 billion, which included the SPR.

The fiscal 1983 Interior appropriations bill restored funds Reagan had sought to cut from energy conservation, fossil fuels research, park land acquisition, historic preservation, and the arts and humanities endowments.

Clean Air Act

The biggest legislative struggle of the year was over reauthorization of the Clean Air Act, one of the most technical and complex of all federal laws. Industry groups had hoped — and environmental groups had feared — that the Reagan administration would push a major relaxation of the law through the 97th Congress.

Industry complained that the law saddled it — and ultimately consumers — with billions of dollars in cleanup costs. Environmentalists countered that air pollution, left unchecked, cost as much or more in damage to human health, crops and property.

The act affected a wide range of industries, especially steel, coal, autos, chemicals, petroleum and electric utilities. Clean air legislation excited intense regional rivalries, because one region's economic mainstay was often another's major polluter.

The political pressures of an election year proved too intense to allow a workable reauthorization compromise.

The Senate Environment and Public Works Committee, chaired by Robert T. Stafford, R-Vt., reported out a carefully constructed "fine-tuning" of the existing law. But even though that bill represented a virtual consensus of the committee, it faced a bruising battle on the floor, and Senate leaders never called it up.

In the House Energy and Commerce Committee, Chairman John D. Dingell, D-Mich., took a different approach, attempting to settle some issues by tests of raw voting power. Dingell led a faction supporting major relaxations of the existing law, while Health and Environment Subcommittee Chairman Henry A. Waxman, D-Calif., fought to strengthen current law. Neither side was able to gain a lasting advantage, and the panel finally abandoned all attempts at a markup.

Despite its inconclusive nature, the 1982 clean air maneuvering did much to pinpoint the issues that needed to be settled before a bill could pass. These included acid rain, toxic air pollutants, auto and truck emission controls, and programs to prevent deterioration of air that was cleaner than required by the national standards.

Wilderness Leasing

One of the major clashes between the administration and Congress came over the issue of oil and gas leasing in areas either designated as federally protected wilderness or under consideration for such designation.

Early in his tenure, Watt had vowed to open wilderness areas to leasing in the interests of energy development. Existing law permitted leasing until the end of 1983, when a permanent ban on such activity was to take effect. But until Watt took office, very few wilderness leases had actually been granted.

Environmentalists and their allies in Congress reacted angrily to Watt's plans, and the secretary agreed to a moratorium lasting until the end of the 97th Congress.

But that still left a one-year "window" before the permanent ban was to take effect. Congress in effect slammed that window shut with a rider to the fiscal 1983 Interior appropriations bill that banned oil and gas leasing in wilderness and wilderness study areas.

Endangered Species

One of the year's more significant accomplishments was a three-year reauthorization of the Endangered Species Act. It streamlined, but did not significantly relax, provisions prohibiting trade in such species and protecting their habitats.

Logging, mining and electric utility groups had complained the law often blocked or delayed government and private projects. Environmentalists argued that genetic diversity was important to the health of the global ecosystem and that some species facing extinction promised important benefits to mankind.

The Reagan administration had sought to include potential economic costs among the factors to be weighed in deciding whether to list a species as endangered, but Congress specified that such determinations had to be made solely on biological grounds.

All sides said they could live with the compromise bill Congress cleared.

Oil Royalties, Barrier Islands

Two measures cleared by Congress were "good government" bills with broad bipartisan support.

One was expected to save hundreds of millions of dollars by tightening the system for collecting oil and gas royalties on federal lands. That bill grew out of recommendations by a special commission set up by Watt.

A second bill banned federal subsidies for development on undeveloped coastal barrier islands. Proponents, including the administration, argued it made little sense for the federal government to pay for development twice — once to promote it, and again to compensate for inevitable damages by flooding and erosion in these areas.

Administrative Actions

Many important environmental decisions were made not in Congress but in the Interior Department and EPA. The administration moved forward in 1982 with a long agenda of major and minor rule changes aimed at relieving the burden of regulation on industries and promoting energy development.

Despite Watt's apparent defeat on wilderness leasing, the Interior Department's annual report suggested that he had gained more ground in the regulatory arena than he had lost in the legislative one.

Federal oil and gas leasing for onshore public lands climbed dramatically. The tonnage of coal leased grew even more rapidly, with the total including the largest federal coal lease sale in history, for the Powder River region in Montana and Wyoming.

Watt in 1982 also adopted a five-year offshore leasing program that could open up offshore tracts dozens of times faster than the historical rate. However, the rate of actual leasing went down in 1982 compared with 1981.

During 1982, Congress cleared five bills designating wilderness on national forest lands totaling 123,571 acres in Florida, West Virginia, Missouri, Indiana, and Alabama. Congress also designated as wilderness 8,440 acres of the Cumberland Island National Seashore in Georgia. But Watt made far more progress in the opposite direction — administratively removing some 805,000 Bureau of Land Management acres from wilderness study. And President Reagan on Jan. 14, 1983, vetoed the Florida wilderness bill, subtracting 49,150 acres from Congress' total.

When it disagreed with agency actions, Congress could rarely do much more than raise a fuss. But in some cases, that was enough. After noisy congressional protests, for example, EPA backed off from a decision to suspend an existing ban on dumping toxic liquid wastes into unlined landfills, and from plans to consider relaxing or repealing restrictions on lead in gasoline.

During the 97th Congress, Interior Department officials appeared at 383 congressional hearings. EPA officials appeared at 97 hearings between Oct. 1, 1981, and the end of 1982.

All those hearings were symptomatic of a growing sense of distrust, especially on the part of House Democrats, of the administration's willingness to carry out the nation's existing environmental laws.

But Congress itself remained sharply divided over the need for revising some of those laws. The November elections appeared to strengthen the hand of members who favored retaining or toughening existing environmental laws. But it remained to be seen whether the 98th Congress would be more successful than its predecessor in passing clean air and clean water bills, hazardous waste measures and other major environmental legislation.

—By Joseph A. Davis

Congress Fails to Act on Clean Air Rewrite

Despite the threat of sanctions against hundreds of counties that could not meet a Dec. 31 deadline for compliance with national air quality standards, the 97th Congress failed to approve a rewrite of the Clean Air Act.

The Environmental Protection Agency (EPA) warned Nov. 15 that it would impose construction bans and grant cutoffs on up to 472 counties nationwide unless Congress extended the law's deadlines, although EPA later revised that estimate downward to about 150 counties. *(Sanctions, p. 426)*

And President Reagan, in an Oct. 13 statement, listed passage of a Clean Air Act reauthorization as one of his five top economic priorities, saying such action, "while protecting the environment, will make it possible for industry to rebuild its productive base and create more jobs."

But neither threats nor exhortations had any effect on the House Energy and Commerce Committee, which deadlocked Aug. 19 over a massive air act rewrite (HR 5252) favored by industry and the Reagan administration and never resumed its markups.

Senate leaders made no effort to schedule floor action on a very different reauthorization measure (S 3041) that was approved by the Senate Environment and Public Works Committee Aug. 19 and formally reported Nov. 15 (S Rept 97-666).

Although the Senate bill was approved by a 15-1 committee vote, it was certain to face a major battle on the floor, with dozens of proposed amendments expected. With little time remaining in the 97th Congress and a crush of other business to deal with, Senate leaders had no desire to put such a massive and controversial measure on the floor.

Both committees had devoted months of work to the clean air issue, beginning in 1981, but they were never able to reconcile the demands of competing interest groups anxious to see the landmark anti-pollution law rewritten along lines to their own suiting. *(1981 Almanac p. 505)*

Although the law's authorization expired in 1981, clean air regulations remained on the books. Funding to enforce the law was provided through appropriations bills, the most recent of which was the fiscal 1983 appropriations bill (HR 6956 — PL 97-272) for the Department of Housing and Urban Development and certain independent agencies, including EPA. *(HUD appropriations bill, p. 231)*

Background

The Clean Air Act (PL 91-604) was enacted in 1970 and extended and amended in 1977 (PL 95-95).

The original 1970 act required EPA to establish safe concentrations for seven major air pollutants and set a 1975 deadline for states to meet those national standards. *(1970 Act, Congress and the Nation Vol. III, p. 757)*

When it appeared most states would not meet the deadline, Congress in 1977 extended it to 1982, or, for areas with severe auto-related pollution, to 1987. *(1977 Almanac p. 627)*

The law, the most complex and far-reaching environmental measure ever enacted, directed EPA to set two types of national air quality standards, primary and secondary, without regard for the cost of compliance.

Primary standards were to protect human health with a margin of safety for vulnerable populations such as the elderly. Secondary standards were to prevent damage to such things as crops, buildings, water, visibility and materials. *(Clean Air Act Summary, 1981 Almanac p. 510)*

HR 5252: The House Vehicle

Early in 1981, two major clean air bills were introduced in the House. HR 4400, sponsored by Reps. Bob Traxler, D-Mich., and Elwood Hillis, R-Ind., dealt only with automobile emission standards. HR 3471, sponsored by James T. Broyhill, R-N.C., and Edward R. Madigan, R-Ill., focused exclusively on air pollution from factories and other stationary sources.

On Dec. 16, 1981, the day Congress adjourned for the year, these measures were effectively supplanted by HR 5252, introduced by Rep. Thomas A. Luken, D-Ohio, a member of both the full House Energy and Commerce Committee and its Subcommittee on Health and the Environment, which was reviewing the reauthorization of the Clean Air Act.

HR 5252 included many provisions of the earlier bills and was cosponsored by Traxler, Hillis, Broyhill, Madigan and Energy Committee Chairman John D. Dingell, D-Mich.

The bill extended air quality deadlines, eliminated or relaxed existing sanctions, overhauled requirements for controlling pollution in areas with pristine air, and doubled allowable emissions of the two major auto pollutants, carbon monoxide and nitrogen oxides.

EPA Administrator Anne M. Gorsuch said the bill generally reflected the 11 principles President Reagan wanted Congress to follow in rewriting the law. *(Principles, 1981 Almanac p. 507)*

She told the House subcommittee Feb. 17 that the administration supported most provisions of HR 5252.

Industry and a number of labor unions also quickly announced support for the bill, but environmentalists denounced it.

S 3041: The Senate Vehicle

The Senate Environment and Public Works Committee, which began work on a Clean Air Act reauthorization Nov. 17, 1981, did not start with a fresh bill. Instead, the panel plowed through the existing law section by section, a procedure that forced members who favored changes to muster a majority of the panel each time they wanted to propose a modification.

As the pace of markups quickened in 1982, Environment Chairman Robert T. Stafford, R-Vt., continued to insist that nothing more than a "fine-tuning" of the existing law was needed.

Stafford did propose his own package of limited changes in February 1982, including extensions in deadlines for states to meet national air quality standards and new proposals for combating acid rain.

But throughout the Senate markups, Stafford and other supporters of the existing clean air law remained in clear control of the committee.

Senate Committee

In February, the Senate committee resumed where it had left off in 1981 — plodding through the Clean Air Act

The Sharp Teeth of the Clean Air Act . . .

No law as sweeping as the Clean Air Act could be effective without teeth, and by the end of 1982, it appeared that numerous communities around the nation might begin to feel the bite of that landmark anti-pollution legislation sometime in 1983.

Under the Clean Air Act, the nation was divided into local "air quality control regions" — not always along county boundaries but often similar to counties in scale. *(1970 Act, Congress and the Nation Vol. III, p. 757; 1977 amendments, 1977 Almanac p. 627)*

The act required the Environmental Protection Agency (EPA) to set "national ambient air quality standards" — goals for the quality of air in general circulation rather than for the gas coming out of smokestacks.

As of 1982, EPA had set seven "primary," or health-related, standards. An area that had not met any one of those primary standards was called a "non-attainment area" for the pollutant in question. The law required every air quality region to meet the primary standards by Dec. 31, 1982, except in certain narrowly defined cases where extensions were possible.

No specific deadlines were set for "secondary" standards, or those pertaining to visibility, protection of crops and other factors not related to human health.

Areas not meeting the deadline for primary standards, and not given extensions, faced certain penalties, or "sanctions." One was a ban on EPA issuance of permits for the construction or modification of major stationary sources of the pollutant in question. Sources of other pollutants would not be affected by the construction ban.

The construction ban would not necessarily apply to a whole state, county, or air quality region, since the law defined a non-attainment area as the area not meeting the standard.

Beginning in the early 1970s, states were required to classify their air quality regions according to whether they had attained the primary standards.

They also were required to draw up plans ("State Implementation Plans," or SIPs) for meeting the standards in non-attainment areas.

An air quality area could be subject to another sanction — the cutoff of federal grants for highways and clean air programs — if the state failed to submit a satisfactory plan for that area to EPA or failed to implement its plan. This provision applied to non-attainment areas with transportation-related problems, such as smog. The deadline for application of this sanction in some areas was as early as July 1, 1979.

Sanctions: The Numbers Game

As the clock ran out on the midnight, Dec. 31, 1982, deadline for meeting national air quality standards, the major question became whether the sanctions would be imposed. EPA administrator Anne M. Gorsuch warned state environmental officials Nov. 3: "December 31st is coming and the law has not been changed. We're going to enforce the law. When you all start screaming, don't scream at me," she said. "Scream at Congress, because they're the only ones that can do anything about it.

"We're going to have about 600 counties that aren't going to be in attainment," Gorsuch told the state officials. Speaking of the "serious dislocation" that could result, she urged them, "Please speak to your congressman."

A. Alan Hill, chairman of the Council on Environmental Quality, put the number of affected counties at "about 700" in a speech to the Environmental Industry Council Nov. 23. That group consisted of leaders from industries affected by pollution control requirements.

But in a list dated Nov. 15, EPA reduced to 472 its estimate of the number of counties facing possible sanctions. Those 472 were counties that had been formally designated as non-attainment areas, most of them in 1978. EPA expected some to attain the standards by Dec. 31, and the agency said in early January 1983 that the total failing to meet the standards was probably only 150 counties.

An EPA analysis of the Nov. 15 list showed 199 counties flunking the standards for particulates, 65 for sulfur dioxide, 52 for carbon monoxide, 302 for ozone and 11 for nitrogen dioxide. Those figures added to more than 472 because some counties failed to attain standards for more than one pollutant.

Six states and the District of Columbia did not have to worry about the Dec. 31 deadline, because they had either attained all standards or had received extensions, according to the analysis: North Dakota, Alaska, Connecticut, Delaware, New Jersey, and North Carolina.

But seven other states had half the non-attainment counties nationwide, each with 19 or more counties in non-attainment: California, Illinois, Louisiana, Michigan, New York, Ohio and Pennsylvania.

While business groups such as the U.S. Chamber of Commerce had joined EPA in warning of dire consequences if Congress failed to act, some environmentalists suggested that the emphasis on looming sanctions was meant to pressure Congress into passing a broad reauthorization of the Clean Air Act in 1982. They speculated that industry groups might have less chance of getting the relaxed clean air provisions they wanted out of the House in 1983 because of membership changes resulting from the Nov. 2 elections.

EPA Plans

A Nov. 18 draft policy memo sent by EPA Assistant Administrator Kathleen M. Bennett to the agency's regional administrators outlined how the agency planned to deal with non-attainment areas once the deadline expired.

According to the memo, EPA "will presume that areas listed as non-attainment by the end of the year may not be attaining the standards. If a state believes that areas listed as non-attainment are in fact attainment areas, and can make a reasonable demonstration to that effect, we encourage it to apply for redesignation."

Before EPA could impose sanctions, it had to find the state plan for that area "inadequate" in a formal rule-making process. The memo said EPA intended to start

. . . EPA Sanctions for Non-Compliance

this process promptly by proposing such findings for all non-attainment areas in the *Federal Register* by Jan. 31, 1983.

The memo also stated EPA's intention to divide non-attainment areas into two groups: those it believed could "demonstrate timely attainment" and those it believed could not. The agency planned to delay any final action on the first group "until the supporting data can be gathered and evaluated, and until the area can be formally redesignated."

EPA did not announce in 1982 how many areas would be in each category, although states were awaiting the information anxiously.

To know for sure which areas attained the standards by Dec. 31, EPA and the states needed the most recent air quality data. Getting that information was expected to take time. The states were responsible for compiling it, and EPA normally received the information about three months after the states did.

Under its draft plan, however, EPA did not intend to wait for that data before putting the sanction machinery into motion.

Sanction Delays Likely

Once EPA published its preliminary notice that it found certain areas' plans inadequate, several months normally had to pass before that finding could be made final. That requirement was imposed by rule-making procedures under the Administrative Procedure Act and the Clean Air Act itself. Other procedural requirements were expected to engender further delay.

Furthermore, not all non-attainment areas automatically faced sanctions. Under the law, it depended on what pollutants were putting them in violation. The law allowed extensions until Dec. 31, 1987, under certain strict conditions, for areas violating standards for ozone and carbon monoxide. Thirty-one states had requested extension of the deadline for these pollutants.

While the list of 472 non-attainment counties excluded those which had been granted extensions to 1987, it was not clear how many of those remaining on the list had pending requests for extensions.

On the other hand, those areas already granted extensions had to submit a revised SIP to EPA by July 1, 1982, and adverse EPA action on those plan revisions could add some counties to the list of 472.

In a Nov. 4 memo to EPA regional administrators, Bennett announced her determination to speed up drastically the normal 14-month timetable for processing such plan revisions.

Particulates: Standard Revision

Some 199 counties were in violation of the standard for particulates — small particles of dust, soot, or other substances fine enough to float through the air. That standard was currently undergoing review and revision — something required by the Clean Air Act before Dec. 31, 1980, but not yet completed.

Scientists generally agreed that the particles most dangerous to human health were the smallest ones, because they were inhaled deepest into the lung. EPA's review of the particulate standard focused on pegging the health-related "primary" standard to particles of a specific size. The present standard included all particle sizes.

One EPA official said the new standard could be formally proposed by the agency by early 1983. The agency's last published schedule, or "regulatory agenda," put action as far away as May 1983. Thus, EPA appeared to be trying to speed up issuance of the new standard.

Many areas that did not meet the current particulate standard were expected to meet the new one. That would further shrink the list of non-attainment areas — although no one knew by how much.

EPA officials cautioned, however, that while shifting the focus to small particles could bring some areas into attainment, much depended on the *amount* of such particles allowed by the standard and the time over which measurements were averaged.

Even if EPA proposed a particulate standard that some non-attainment areas could meet, that might not get those areas off the hook. A proposed standard had no legal force — so the areas still had failed to attain the existing legal standard as of Dec. 31, 1982.

A proposed new particulate standard would have to wait at least 90 days before becoming final, and probably more. EPA staff familiar with the process said it had never taken less than a year for a major ("primary") air quality standard, adding that this was one of the most controversial in the last decade.

But while EPA staff said a new particulate standard would not provide relief from sanctions for non-attainment areas "except in a psychological sense," others said they would make the sanctions moot for particulates.

State Concerns

Although the states were anxious for an end to the uncertainty over the provisions of any Clean Air Act rewrite, they did not appear terribly worried about the threat of EPA sanctions under the existing law.

"I don't think the deadlines will work fast. It could take six months to two years," said S. William Becker, executive secretary of the State and Territorial Air Pollution Program Administrators. "We believe a responsible EPA will take the time necessary, get the data, and go through the process."

Becker said he did not think the potential construction ban would have immediate severe impacts, noting: "There are not many new plants being built these days."

It was difficult to predict how long Congress could take to resolve disputes and pass a bill. In 1977, the last time the Clean Air Act was reauthorized, the 95th Congress started with a bill that was much further along in the legislative process than the 1982 legislation — it had been approved by a House-Senate conference committee late in the 94th Congress.

Even so, it was Aug. 4 before the final bill cleared Congress that year.

section by section, discussing proposed changes for days on end before voting on them, as Stafford sought to produce a "consensus" bill.

The committee chairman paused only long enough to denounce HR 5252, the industry-backed bill introduced in the House on the last day of the 1981 session.

"Practically every important provision in the Clean Air Act would be repealed if HR 5252 were to become law," Stafford said on the Senate floor Feb. 11.

Stafford Proposals

Not until the end of that month did Stafford finally introduce a package of proposed changes to the existing law to serve as a focal point for committee debate. His package did not deal with the system for protecting areas with pristine air nor with a number of vehicle-emission issues, problems that were being addressed by other committee members. Instead, the chairman proposed amendments that would have:

● Established a 31-state acid rain region in the Northeast in which sulfur dioxide and oxides of nitrogen emissions could not exceed levels that were present Jan. 1, 1981, and where 10 million tons of sulfur dioxide had to be removed from emissions within 10 years.

● Made emissions of any air pollutant that adversely affected the public health or welfare in another state a violation of the act, and required the polluting plants to install "reasonably available control technology."

● Provided a 10-year period during which the EPA could not require a plant that had installed "best available control technology" to comply with more stringent requirements, except for newly regulated toxic pollutants.

● Simplified the review process for state clean-air plans.

● Given the EPA three years to determine whether more than 100 chemical air pollutants were hazardous to human health and should be regulated.

● Retained EPA's authority to impose a construction ban in certain circumstances in dirty-air areas.

● Extended until 1984 the current 1982 deadline for states to meet national air quality standards.

● Allowed states an extension of the 1984 deadline until 1985 if they could show that they would meet federal standards for sulfur dioxide, nitrogen oxides and particulates, and until 1987 for ozone and carbon monoxide.

● Allowed states with exceptionally difficult pollution problems to have until 1992 to meet the national standards, if they took all reasonably available actions to control pollution, including imposing an inspection and maintenance program for automobile emission control devices.

PSD, Sanctions

As markups continued intermittently into March, committee members talked repeatedly of the need to develop a bill with broad support.

A big step toward that objective was taken March 23, when the committee voted 15-1 to adopt changes in the section of the law designed to prevent significant deterioration (PSD) of air quality in areas with air cleaner than required by the national standards.

The amendment, drafted by Gary Hart, D-Colo., and amended by Slade Gorton, R-Wash., and Pete V. Domenici, R-N.M., allowed states to "opt out" under certain circumstances of the increment system of controlling pollution in areas other than national parks and wilderness, where maximum controls would be retained.

Business groups opposed the amendment because it

was based on what industry claimed was largely inaccurate computer modeling used for determining the background levels of air pollution before setting limits on how much new pollution would be allowed in a given area.

Auto Emissions, Sanctions

The committee May 5 approved three minor changes in existing auto pollution control provisions, but showed no inclination to loosen those standards significantly.

The panel approved 14-0 an amendment that slightly relaxed standards, and the deadlines for meeting them, for cars and light-duty trucks in high-altitude states.

The committee approved a second amendment, offered by ranking Democrat Jennings Randolph, W.Va., that adjusted restrictions on the import of foreign cars not certified to be in compliance with the clean air law.

And it adopted by voice vote an amendment offered by Frank H. Murkowski, R-Alaska, requiring EPA to conduct a two-year study of problems with driveability and pollution control with cars in cold climates.

On May 6, the committee unanimously approved compromise language slightly relaxing sanctions to be imposed on communities failing to meet clean air standards and giving the federal government greater flexibility in applying those sanctions.

The committee then broke off markups for nearly two months.

Acid Rain

George J. Mitchell, D-Maine, who introduced an acid rain control bill (S 1706) Oct. 6, 1981, proposed a modified version June 29 that was endorsed by Stafford, Daniel Patrick Moynihan, D-N.Y., and Environmental Pollution Subcommittee Chairman John H. Chafee, R-R.I.

Mitchell's proposal, among other things:

● Established a 31-state acid rain control region consisting of all states bordering or east of the Mississippi River.

● Required reduction of annual sulfur dioxide emissions in this region by 10 million tons below the 1980 level of roughly 22 million tons.

● Set a 12-year deadline for achieving that reduction through innovative technologies, and a 10-year deadline for doing so with conventional approaches.

● Set a six-year deadline for any source choosing to achieve its reduction by switching to low-sulfur fuel.

● Provided for economic growth by allowing sulfur dioxide emissions from new sources to be offset by reductions in existing emissions until 1994.

● Allowed governors of the 31 states one year in which to decide how to allocate the reduction among themselves. After that, a formula would be imposed.

● Speeded up research on acid rain by an inter-agency task force, requiring a comprehensive report after three years — before major investments were made in controls.

The committee July 22 approved 15-0 a modified version of Mitchell's amendment that mandated a reduction of 8 million tons per year in sulfur dioxide emissions below 1980 levels in a 31-state region.

As adopted, the provision would not have become fully effective for 12 years.

Senate Bill Reported

After nine months of markups, the Senate committee Aug. 19 completed its work on the clean air reauthorization bill. By 15-1, the panel ordered the measure reported. Steven D. Symms, R-Idaho, was the lone dissenter.

The bill, formally reported Nov. 15 (S 3041 — S Rept 97-666), authorized expenditures of $177 million for fiscal 1983 and $200 million for each of the succeeding four years.

During its final markup session, the committee adopted an amendment on hazardous pollutants offered by Randolph that required EPA to decide within six years whether 40 pollutants should be listed as hazardous and made subject to special regulation. This was somewhat milder than a proposal adopted by the House Energy Committee that would have automatically listed 37 pollutants as hazardous if EPA failed to decide within four years whether they should be so listed.

The panel also adopted language that prevented any increase over current levels of lead in gasoline. This bolstered a recent EPA decision to strengthen existing rules requiring a phasedown of lead in gasoline, and it was a rebuff to the Office of Management and Budget, which sought relaxation of those rules.

The committee rejected 5-10 an amendment by Alan K. Simpson, R-Wyo., that would have eliminated the "percentage reduction" provision of current law. That provision required utilities and factories to remove a certain percentage of sulfur oxides from their stack gases. The effect was to require installation of costly scrubbers, largely eliminating incentives to switch to low-sulfur Western coal.

The committee adopted an amendment by Hart requiring EPA to conduct research on indoor air pollution.

It also agreed to relax deadlines and technology requirements for non-ferrous smelters, a provision designed to help the copper industry.

Major Provisions: S 3041

As reported, S 3041 made a number of modifications in the Clean Air Act but did not significantly relax any of its provisions. Some of the most important provisions:

● Reduced the extent of the review EPA was required to conduct of state and local clean-air decisions, particularly routine and non-controversial ones.

● Retained existing PSD provisions to protect pristine air in parks and wilderness areas but allowed states to "opt out" of the current increment system for attainment of national clean-air standards elsewhere.

● Retained existing control standards limiting auto emissions to 3.4 grams per mile for carbon monoxide and 1.0 gram per mile for oxides of nitrogen.

● Barred EPA from rolling back existing 1984 standards for emissions of hydrocarbon and carbon monoxide from heavy-duty trucks, thereby effectively requiring installation of catalytic converters.

● Slightly relaxed certain emission standards, and the deadlines for meeting them, for light-duty trucks and vans.

● Required cars and light-duty trucks sold for use in high-altitude areas to meet the same emission standards as those sold for low-altitude areas, although this could be accomplished by certain EPA-approved dealer adjustments or modifications after the vehicle left the factory.

● Retained the "percentage reduction" provision of current law that required utilities and factories to remove a certain percentage of sulfur oxides from their stack gases.

● Extended from Dec. 31, 1982, to Dec. 31, 1984, the deadline for states to meet national primary air quality standards, provided a state certified it had implemented all measures in an approved or promulgated implementation plan. If acceptable plans were submitted, deadlines could be extended to 1985 or 1987, depending on the pollutant.

● Extended from Dec. 31, 1987, to Dec. 31, 1992, the

deadline for certain areas with severe auto-related pollution to meet national standards, provided they implemented all reasonably available control technologies, imposed an offset program and set up a vehicle inspection and maintenance program.

● Gave EPA slightly more flexibility in imposing sanctions, such as a cutoff of highway funds, on areas that failed to submit or implement an acceptable plan for meeting air quality standards.

● Required EPA to identify within 60 days at least 20 substances or materials suspected of being hazardous air pollutants, and to decide within two years whether to list those substances as toxic pollutants.

● Required EPA to identify within one year another 20 substances or materials thought to be toxic pollutants and to decide within five years whether to list them as such.

● Required EPA to establish emission standards for hazardous pollutants based on the best available control technology that was adequate to protect public health with an adequate margin for safety.

● Required an 8-million-ton reduction in emissions of sulfur dioxide from 31 Eastern and Midwestern states over the next 12 years in an effort to curb acid rain.

● Prohibited emission of air pollutants that adversely affected the public health or welfare in another state, and required installation of reasonably available control technology on any existing major source of such pollution within two years after a finding that it had committed a violation.

House Subcommittee Action

The Dingell-Waxman Split

In the House Energy Health and Environment Subcommittee, a bitter split developed between a faction led by Chairman Henry A. Waxman, D-Calif., who did not favor a major overhaul of the act, and members allied with Dingell and Luken, who were pushing for approval of HR 5252, the industry-backed reauthorization bill.

Detroiter Dingell, chairman of the full House Energy Committee, was anxious to get HR 5252 out of Waxman's subcommittee in order to help the beleaguered auto industry, which was based in part in his home district.

Waxman's panel began work Feb. 25, with the chairman offering his own proposed rewrite (HR 5555) as a markup vehicle. He claimed it was more "moderate and constructive" than HR 5252.

Luken then offered a revised version of HR 5252, designed to defuse charges that the original gutted the Clean Air Act, and Waxman agreed to let Luken's bill be offered, section by section, as an amendment to HR 5555.

Dingell Group in Control

The first clean air vote of 1982 came March 4, when Waxman and his allies lost an 8-12 vote on an amendment to tighten up provisions in HR 5252 that allowed states to "fast-track" so-called "non-controversial" changes in state plans for controlling air pollution.

That initial 8-12 vote set the pattern for the remainder of the subcommittee's markups, which continued until March 24. Again and again, the panel's Republicans voted in a bloc, joined by Democrats Luken, Dingell, Phil Gramm, D-Texas, and Richard C. Shelby, D-Ala.

Among the amendments rejected 8-12 by the subcommittee in the opening days of its markup sessions was a

proposal by Toby Moffett, D-Conn., to delete a provision allowing EPA to let states approve or disapprove both controversial and non-controversial state plans and plan revisions.

Also defeated 8-12 was an amendment by Waxman to delete a provision giving states two more years — on top of the seven they already had — to meet national clean-air standards when a new pollutant was regulated by EPA.

Acid Rain

The House subcommittee twice refused to insert provisions in HR 5252 to control acid rain.

Moffett the week of March 8 tried to insert most provisions of HR 4829, an acid rain bill he had introduced in 1981. If adopted, it would have mandated that sulfur dioxide emissions in the Eastern United States be reduced by 10 million tons per year in order to control acid rain.

The amendment established an allotment formula for reducing sulfur dioxide emissions in 31 states located either east of or adjacent to the Mississippi River.

Sulfur dioxide (SO_2) particles in the atmosphere combined with water vapor to cause vinegar-like acid rain that was killing fish in many lakes in the Eastern United States and in Canada.

Many scientists believed that SO_2 emissions from coal-burning Midwestern power plants, carried east by prevailing winds, were a major contributor.

"Instead of addressing the problem of acid rain, HR 5252 makes the problem worse," charged Waxman, noting that the Luken bill would eliminate some stringent emission controls for plants in dirty-air areas.

Opponents argued, however, that it could cost from $3 billion to $7 billion a year to remove 10 percent of the East's SO_2, and that not enough was known about how acid rain occurred to spend that kind of money yet.

"We haven't the vaguest idea where the SO_2 comes from," said Dingell. "We could spend massive amounts of money and still wind up with an acid rain problem just as bad as we have now."

He also argued that Moffett's allotment formula was inequitable because the Midwest would have to clean up more of its emissions than the Northeast.

Moffett replied that the Northeast was already doing more than its share to clean up SO_2 emissions by using coal that contained much less sulfur than that used in the Midwest.

Dingell also argued that utility bills in the Midwest would increase by 50 to 100 percent under Moffett's proposal.

Doug Walgren, D-Pa., who — like Moffett — normally sided with Waxman in seeking to strengthen HR 5252, said he reluctantly opposed the amendment because of its cost and regional inequities.

"I am very satisfied that enough is known to take some action, but what is being proposed is truly burdensome," Walgren said.

The amendment was then rejected, 7-13.

Walgren then offered his own acid rain proposal, saying that "any bill that does not address the acid rain problem is seriously flawed." Walgren's proposal would have required EPA to review available research on acid rain every two years. If the research indicated that federal action was necessary to prevent or limit acid rain, the EPA administrator would be required to issue regulations implementing such federal controls.

Walgren's amendment was defeated by voice vote.

Prevention of Significant Deterioration

In the week of March 8, the subcommittee tackled the much-criticized "prevention of significant deterioration" (PSD) provisions of the act, which outlined a complex program to prevent degradation of air quality in areas that had air cleaner than the national standards. The law set up three classes of PSD areas ranging from Class I, having the cleanest air, to Class III, where the air was allowed to become the dirtiest, up to the national standards.

The PSD program specified that pollution could increase in Class II and III areas only by incremental levels, forcing states to limit the amount of pollution new factories could produce.

Under the 1977 amendments to the law, 158 national parks and wilderness areas were designated as Class I areas, where no increases in pollution would be allowed. The rest of the country was designated as Class II, where slight increases in pollution would be allowed. Any national park, park addition, monument, primitive area or wildlife reserve established after 1977 was designated as Class II.

Rep. Ron Wyden, D-Ore., offered three amendments designed to retain anti-pollution protections in such federally owned recreation areas.

One, defeated by voice vote, would have restored the Class II increment system entirely.

The second, defeated 8-12, would have continued the increments only for national lands of special significance, such as recreation areas.

The third would have redesignated specific national parks, monuments and wilderness areas — including California's Redwood and Sequoia national parks — from Class II to the more restrictive Class I. The amendment was defeated 8-12.

Vehicle Inspection

The panel three times rejected attempts to restore to HR 5252 provisions in existing law regarding on-the-road inspections of vehicle pollution-control devices, or to add new language addressing the problem.

Under current law, if a state could not clean up its vehicular pollution (carbon monoxide and ozone) by the 1982 deadline, it could receive an extension until 1987, but only if it established a vehicle-inspection program.

HR 5252 required "cost-effective" inspection programs only in urban areas with a population of more than 500,000 where the ozone or carbon monoxide levels in 1981 exceeded the national standards by more than 50 percent.

An amendment offered by Moffett that would have retained current provisions of the law was defeated 6-14. On this amendment, both Walgren and Barbara A. Mikulski, D-Md., joined the prevailing coalition, saying existing inspection programs in many cases were ineffective and highly unpopular with drivers.

"Maryland's program is a real turkey," said Mikulski. "It exempts some of the largest polluters like buses, heavy-duty trucks, and polluting vehicles if the cost of improvement is high."

The votes on vehicle inspection and acid rain were the only ones during the week of March 8 that were decided by margins other than 8-12.

Toxic Pollutants

The subcommittee on March 17 rejected a proposal to beef up controls on toxic air pollutants.

By an 8-12 vote, the panel defeated an amendment by James J. Florio, D-N.J., to force the EPA to finish its study

of 37 toxic pollutants within one year or declare each of them to be hazardous. The pollutants had been under study at the agency for four years.

Since the 1970 version of the clean-air law (PL 91-604) mandated that the EPA control toxic air pollutants, the agency had listed only seven and issued emission standards for just four — asbestos, beryllium, mercury and vinyl chloride.

"We cannot afford to let the EPA procrastinate anymore," Florio argued.

Luken, who opposed the amendment, quoted a March 10 letter from EPA stating that it could not conduct the reviews required by law within the one-year time frame.

Subcommittee Approval

HR 5252 was approved March 24 by the Health and Environment Subcommittee. The vote was 13-7.

As approved, the measure relaxed existing emission standards for both automobiles and factories. It also extended by up to 11 years the current 1982 deadline for states to meet national clean-air standards.

To allow more industrial growth in Western states, the bill relaxed protections on visibility in and around the national parks, allowing up to twice as much air pollution in some of those areas.

It also eliminated the law's mandatory ban on construction in dirty-air areas that could not meet national clean-air deadlines. The ban, which often led opponents to call the act an "anti-growth" law, could be imposed on a selective basis by the EPA but would not be mandatory.

Waxman, who had introduced HR 5555 as the markup vehicle when the panel started work Feb. 25, asked unanimous consent to report a "clean" bill, or one with a new number. But, in an unusual move, Rep. Thomas J. Bliley Jr., R-Va., insisted that the final bill bear the number of Waxman's measure, presumably because of the negative publicity HR 5252 had received in heavy grass-roots lobbying by environmentalists.

Bliley denied that his action was prompted by negative publicity for HR 5252. "We had originally asked the chairman to use HR 5252 as the markup vehicle," said Bliley. "But he insisted that we use HR 5555. I felt that since we had used it in markup we should follow the regular order and report it out, as amended."

House Committee Action

First Cracks in Dingell Coalition

Cracks began appearing in the bipartisan coalition supporting an industry-backed rewrite of the Clean Air Act almost as soon as the full House Energy and Commerce Committee began consideration of the bill March 30.

Aided by eight Republicans and three other Democrats, Dingell had guided the measure through the Health and Environment Subcommittee largely untouched, repeatedly beating back attempts by Subcommittee Chairman Waxman to add amendments favored by environmental groups.

In its first action, the full committee agreed to change the number on the bill from HR 5555 to HR 5252, as Waxman had requested once his own bill was replaced by the industry-backed version.

By the comity soon disappeared.

The first signal that Dingell would find the full committee hard to control occurred when Waxman won voice-

vote approval of an amendment to tighten up deadlines for complying with certain clean-air regulations. Dingell did not ask for a vote, indicating that he did not have the votes to beat Waxman.

Waxman's amendment reduced from nine to seven years the amount of time states would have to revise their state air-cleanup plans and comply with new regulations issued by the EPA to control pollutants not now regulated.

After the vote, Waxman said, "I think this committee is in a real state of flux. I'm sensing a lot of uneasiness among members about voting for a bill that will have us retreat from clean air."

By pairing relaxations of auto emission standards with provisions easing pollution-control requirements for factories, Dingell hoped to hold together his tenuous coalition. But Waxman said after the vote on deadline delays that he and his allies were "beginning to feel we have a real chance to beat back the auto sections" of HR 5252.

Coal Scrubbers: East-West Split

A third leg of Dingell's strategy which appeared shaky was a decision to retain a controversial "percentage reduction" requirement of existing law in an effort to win support for his auto provisions from members from Midwestern and Eastern coal-producing states.

The panel April 1 delayed a vote on an amendment by Gramm to scrap that provision, which in effect mandated that all coal-burning utilities install equipment to "scrub" sulfur dioxide from their emissions regardless of how much sulfur the coal contained.

The provision, added to the law in 1977 and retained by HR 5252, was designed to protect coal producers and mining jobs in Eastern and Midwestern states, which produced most of the country's high-sulfur coal.

Gramm argued that the scrubbing requirement was not cost-effective and did not produce significant environmental benefits.

If his amendment to delete the scrubbing requirement passed, it could have alienated some key Midwestern members of Dingell's coalition, such as Madigan of Illinois, ranking subcommittee Republican. But Gramm was also a member of the coalition, and like Madigan, was lobbying heavily for his position.

When the vote on the scrubbing amendment was deferred, Madigan asked Dingell for assurances that he would not be asked to vote on Dingell's auto-emission relaxations until the scrubber issue had been resolved.

"I think we ought to establish procedures here, or something is going to fall apart," warned Madigan.

Dingell promised Madigan that the scrubber issue would be settled before the committee voted on the automobile sections of the bill.

Acid Rain

Tempers flared April 22, when Moffett and Madigan each claimed to have been insulted by the other's conduct in committee consideration of the acid rain issue.

Acidic rainfall was of particular concern to members from the Northeast, where many lakes and streams could no longer support aquatic life because of increased acidity. These members blamed the problem on the sulfur dioxide pumped into the air by coal-burning Midwestern utilities.

Moffett drafted an amendment to limit the amount of sulfur dioxide coal-fired utilities could discharge. However, members from the Midwest and from coal-producing states said that not enough was known about acid rain to justify

the expensive equipment that would be required. Madigan said that Moffett's approach of limiting utility emissions would cost $300 billion in increased utility bills and would not solve the acid rain problem because other sources produce sulfur dioxide.

Instead, Madigan proposed an amendment calling for acceleration of the government's current study of acid rainfall and authorizing federal grants to help areas hurt by acid rain. It was adopted 27-5, although Moffett claimed members had not been given enough notice that it would be offered.

Waxman called the Madigan amendment "a fraud and a sham" designed to allow members to say they had done something about acid rain. He said providing grant money for the Northeast was like paying the medical bills of people who got emphysema from breathing dirty air instead of cleaning the air.

Deadlines and Backsliding

Also during the week of April 19, the committee approved an amendment by Timothy E. Wirth, D-Colo., to limit the bill's extension of deadlines for communities to meet clean air standards. Current law put the deadlines at the end of 1982.

As drafted in subcommittee, HR 5252 would have allowed communities to seek an extension until 1987 and another delay until 1993. The Wirth amendment required clean air standards to be met by December 1987 for all pollutants except carbon monoxide and ozone. Standards for the latter two would have to be met by 1993.

Dingell, Luken and William E. Dannemeyer, R-Calif., opposed the amendment as too inflexible. The committee, however, approved it by a 22-19 vote; 19 Democrats and three Republicans supported it, 14 Republicans and five Democrats opposed it. Five of six subcommittee chairmen voted against Dingell, who chaired the sixth subcommittee.

Waxman attributed this "significant victory" to lobbying over the Easter recess. On other votes, the committee:

● Adopted by voice vote an amendment by Broyhill that Broyhill said would give states flexibility to adjust factory emissions during the deadline extension. Broyhill insisted it would not allow pollution to increase — "backsliding" — during the extension; Waxman claimed it would result in two or three times more pollution in some areas. A later proposal by Waxman to reverse the Broyhill amendment was defeated 15-26.

● Rejected 16-24 a Waxman amendment to require modern pollution control equipment to be installed when parts of factories were rebuilt.

● Rejected by voice vote an amendment by Walgren to limit to $75 annually the amount an individual car owner could be forced to pay to meet vehicle emission standards.

PSD: The First Breaking Point

The House committee's drive to rewrite the Clean Air Act screeched to a halt April 29, with industry lobbyists scrambling to patch up their shaky coalition.

Environmental lobbyists won a major victory April 28 when the committee adopted an amendment that would keep tight controls on air pollution in areas that were now cleaner than the national standards. When lobbyists for industry found they could not round up enough support to reverse that vote, committee Chairman Dingell called for the hiatus in markup activity.

The showdown came over the complex program to prevent degradation of air quality in areas that had air cleaner than the national standards. This "prevention of significant deterioration" (PSD) program set up three classes of PSD areas ranging from Class I, having the cleanest air, to Class III, where the air was allowed to become the dirtiest, up to the national standards.

Class I areas included national parks and wilderness areas. Almost no pollution increases were allowed in these areas. Class II areas were all other regions with air cleaner than the national standards. States could redesignate some of these as Class III, but no state had done so.

The PSD program specified that pollution could increase in Class II and III areas only by incremental levels, forcing states to limit the amount of pollution new factories could produce.

As written by the Health and Environment Subcommittee, HR 5252 would have eliminated Class II and III designations, allowing pollution up to national standards in those areas. The incremental system would have been eliminated except for those states that chose to design their own such system. Supporters believed this could facilitate industrial growth in areas with clean air.

When the committee met April 27, Rep. Ron Wyden, D-Ore., offered an amendment to eliminate only the Class III designation. Under his amendment, states could opt to take areas out of the Class II designation, except protected federal lands for which the category was required. For those areas remaining Class II, the incremental system would continue.

Wyden called it a reasonable compromise, noting a similar amendment had been adopted 15-1 by the Senate Environment Committee.

But Dingell and Broyhill, the committee's senior Republican, opposed the amendment. They said it would be as unworkable as the current law. Broyhill offered a substitute that would have gutted the Wyden proposal.

Wyden had the votes, however. On April 28, the committee rejected the Broyhill substitute by a 17-19 vote and approved the Wyden amendment 25-13.

Afterwards, industry lobbyists went to work trying to persuade members on the prevailing side to switch their positions. When those switches could not be found, Dingell on April 29 called off further markup sessions until at least the week of May 10 and possibly the week of May 17.

"They're worried about their coalition holding together," Waxman said. "He [Dingell] wants more lobbying time. There's been a steady erosion of their votes to the point that many of them are saying they want a more moderate bill."

An administration official said the business community had become complacent and had not been working hard enough for the bill. At the moment, he said, "it's a game of chicken."

The Key Votes: Toxic Pollutants

Environmentalists Aug. 11 won a pair of key votes in the House committee in a test of strength that proved to be the death knell of HR 5252.

As the panel resumed work on clean air following a three-month layoff, its members defeated by 20-21 a hazardous pollutants amendment backed by Dingell. The committee then approved, 22-20, an alternative backed by Waxman.

The amendment adopted by the committee was proposed by Florio and amended by W. J. "Billy" Tauzin, D-La. It gave EPA four years to determine whether 37 substances the agency had identified as potential carcinogens

were hazardous or not, and it automatically listed them as hazardous if EPA made no determination within that time.

The version backed by Dingell was proposed by Republican Broyhill of North Carolina and amended by Democrat Luken of Ohio. It set a similar deadline for EPA consideration, but it allowed the agency to delay a decision on whether to list a pollutant as hazardous if it found there was insufficient information to decide either way.

Once EPA listed a substance as a hazardous air pollutant under current law, it had to set emission standards that protected public health with an "ample margin of safety" for the most sensitive groups of people, such as children, asthmatics, or the elderly.

This requirement was the "main obstacle" to carrying out the current law, according to Luken and other critics, because it could require zero emissions of some hazardous pollutants. Such stringent controls were so costly that EPA was holding back from findings that would impose them — always waiting for just slightly stronger evidence on the need for them.

Both alternatives considered by the Energy Committee — the Broyhill-Luken amendment and the Florio-Tauzin amendment — struck out the margin-of-safety requirement for national standards. The Florio-Tauzin amendment adopted by the panel still required standards stringent enough to protect public health, but left that determination to EPA.

The pending business before the committee when it resumed air act markups Aug. 10 was the Broyhill hazardous pollutants amendment, which he had offered as a substitute for the Florio amendment to HR 5252.

During 8½ hours of debate and maneuvering, the committee took three major votes.

The first was on Luken's amendment to the Broyhill substitute. Luken's amendment, which he called "a real compromise between the Broyhill and Florio amendments," added the option for EPA to make a finding of insufficient information. It also adopted the tighter timetable used in the Florio amendment for EPA decisions on whether to list the 37 substances named. Instead of automatic listing, the Luken amendment would have allowed citizen suits to force action if EPA failed to meet the timetable.

Tauzin and Florio criticized the Luken amendment, contending the judicial review provision was too weak and charging the proposal removed health considerations from the setting of emission standards, basing them instead on existing technology alone. Don Ritter, R-Pa., a supporter of the Luken amendment, said that was not true.

The Luken amendment was approved by a 25-17 vote, and Waxman, who opposed it, acknowledged later that "We seemed to have lost that vote." But it was not regarded as a final test of strength at the time.

Doug Walgren, D-Pa., one member who voted for Luken but later switched to join Waxman, explained he felt that to vote against Luken would have risked ending up with a worse bill if Broyhill won the uncertain vote that still lay ahead.

At that point, under a previous agreement with Chairman Dingell, Tauzin offered his amendment to the Florio amendment. The committee approved Tauzin's amendment by voice vote.

It softened the Florio automatic listing provision by requiring EPA to publish a notice before listing a pollutant and allowing any person (or corporation) to petition EPA to conduct hearings and make a definite determination on the pollutant in question.

With the stage set for the decisive vote between the Florio-Tauzin compromise and the Broyhill-Luken alternative, and with the outcome still unclear, Waxman stalled, offering the first of what promised to be an endless series of amendments to HR 5252. The first was defeated by voice vote, and the skirmishing dragged on until the committee had to adjourn for other business.

After losing another vote, 9-28, on one of his amendments the next morning, Waxman stunned the audience in the meeting room by announcing that he would offer no more amendments and calling for a final vote on hazardous pollutants.

He and Florio had the votes — enough to defeat the Broyhill-Luken package by one vote and approve the Florio-Tauzin proposal by two votes. They drew enough support from "moderate" swing voters, Republicans and Democrats alike, to prevail.

Auto Emissions

In a key vote Aug. 17, the House committee adopted a provision relaxing current automobile emission standards, but not as much as U.S. automakers and their congressional allies originally wanted.

The panel voted to weaken existing automobile emission standards that were already being met by many 1981 and 1982 cars, thereby obviating the need for some anti-pollution equipment.

In a move sought by Dingell, members approved 26-16 a compromise auto emissions amendment offered by Philip R. Sharp, D-Ind., that was looser than present law but stricter than the original language of HR 5252.

Sharp's amendment was resisted by Waxman, who offered 10 amendments aimed at restoring the standards to levels in current law. All were defeated.

Throughout the markup of HR 5252, the Dingell-Broyhill group consistently prevailed on auto-emission issues, pulling 23 to 26 members of the 42-member committee while Waxman's side mustered only 16 to 19 votes.

As originally written, HR 5252 would have doubled the allowable emissions of carbon monoxide (CO) and nitrogen oxides (NOx) for gasoline-powered passenger cars, raising the CO standard to 7.0 grams per mile from 3.4 grams per mile, and raising the NOx standard to 2.0 grams per mile from 1.0.

The Sharp amendment returned the NOx standard to the 1.0 grams per mile of current law, but kept the 7.0-grams-per-mile CO standard.

Waxman charged that Sharp's amendment went beyond temporary relief for the beleaguered auto industry. In arguing against the 7.0-gram CO standard, Waxman said the committee had heard no testimony that automakers were having any technological trouble meeting the tighter 3.4-gram standard. He said the cost savings would be only about $30 per car.

Dingell and the industry set the figure higher. Automakers said that if both standards were relaxed, they could remove about $360 worth of pollution-control equipment, saving $60 for equipment to control CO and $300 for equipment to control NOx.

Dingell, arguing in support of Sharp's amendment, said that 69 percent of the autos manufactured in 1982 had been given EPA waivers allowing them to emit up to 7.0 grams per mile of CO. But Waxman quoted General Motors as saying that 70 percent of the cars with waivers met the tighter 3.4-gram standard anyway.

Sharp defended the 7.0-gram standard, saying the existing standard had caused driveability problems with small cars. His Muncie-centered district was dotted with auto-related industries, many of them hit by layoffs.

While environmentalists charged HR 5252 increased allowable auto emissions, auto industry supporters liked to put that increase in the context of the overall reduction achieved since the Clean Air Act was first enacted in 1970.

Dingell noted that the 2.0-gram standard for NOx initially proposed in HR 5252 required removal of 92 percent of the NOx in the uncontrolled emission — as compared to the 96 percent removal achieved by the 1.0-gram standard.

Ritter noted that without controls, CO emissions would total 88 grams per mile. A 3.4-gram standard would reduce the fleetwide average to 26.3 grams per mile, while a 7.0-gram CO standard produced a fleetwide average of 26.6 grams per mile, he said.

Emissions from old cars raised the fleetwide average emissions well above levels achieved by cars in the current model year. Dingell repeatedly pointed out that total emissions would continue to decrease as these old cars were replaced by new ones.

Environmentalists, however, said that some of the problem was caused by newer cars whose pollution control devices were not working right. They criticized several provisions in HR 5252 that they said weakened programs to make sure pollution control devices continued to work.

Sharp's amendment also loosened NOx standards for light diesel cars and trucks by setting them at 1.5 grams instead of the 1.0 grams in current law, and by allowing NOx emissions as high as 2.0 grams if particulates (another pollutant) were reduced. HR 5252 originally contained no such allowance for diesels.

Sharp said this amendment, which was backed by diesel car manufacturers, would take advantage of a trade-off inherent in existing pollution control technology in which NOx reductions could only be achieved at the expense of particulates, and vice versa. But Waxman said newer devices could reduce both simultaneously.

Sharp's amendment also required a study by the National Academy of Sciences on the health effects of different levels of auto emissions. The study would be submitted to EPA by March 1985 and then sent to Congress, along with EPA's recommendations, within 120 days.

Deadlines

The Clean Air Act Amendments of 1977 (PL 95-95) set 1981 as the deadline for achievement of national standards for mobile source emissions. It allowed EPA to waive the 3.4-gram CO standard (not to exceed 7.0 grams) for 1981 and 1982 if public health did not require it and if the technology to achieve it did not exist. It also allowed a four-year waiver of the 1.0-gram NOx standard, not to exceed 1.5 grams, for diesel engines and for innovative technology having potential air quality or fuel economy benefits.

Another waiver was authorized for small manufacturers such as American Motors Corp. that depended on pollution control devices produced by other companies. They were allowed a two-year waiver, until 1983, to meet the 1.0-gram NOx standard.

There were other deadline extensions under separate requirements for high-altitude areas, where cars emitted more pollution because of the way lower atmospheric pressure affected carburetion and combustion. Present law allowed pollution limits higher than those at sea level, but

only through model year 1983, when high-altitude cars would have to meet sea-level standards.

HR 5252 did not change the basic deadlines in current law, but it enlarged the opportunities for administrative waivers of those deadlines by EPA, which had used such authority often. Nearly all the 1981 cars met the NOx standard. During the Carter administration, only 30 percent of the 1981 fleet got waivers from the 3.4-gram standard for CO. During the Reagan administration, 70 percent of the 1982 cars were granted waivers from that standard.

HR 5252, for one thing, extended authorization for the high-altitude waiver past model year 1983.

It also extended the "innovative technology" waiver — which was limited to 50,000 vehicles per year per manufacturer under the present law. HR 5252 allowed this waiver for up to 200,000 vehicles per manufacturer per year.

High-Altitude Emissions

The House committee rejected, 17-25, a compromise proposal on high-altitude emissions that was adopted 14-0 in the Senate Environment and Public Works Committee on Aug. 5.

Current law required all cars to meet the national standards by 1984, regardless of where they were driven. To do that in high-altitude areas, the 95 percent of U.S. cars currently driven at low altitudes would have needed extra controls that EPA in July 1981 estimated would cost more than $4 billion over five years. (Until 1984, high-altitude standards could be looser.)

The high-altitude amendment rejected by the House committee would have eased national requirements slightly for cars sold at high altitudes — just enough to allow the standards to be met by retuning existing low-altitude equipment rather than installing additional equipment.

The Breakdown

The House committee, still bitterly divided, Aug. 19 broke off markups on HR 5252 as Congress departed for its Labor Day recess.

"I'm not sure it's dead yet," said Tauzin, "but lately when we've cut into it, it hasn't bled."

Despite intermittent negotiations among members of the Energy Committee, no additional markups occurred before the Nov. 2 elections.

And if there was some question about the bill's vitality before the elections, it was obvious by the time the lame-duck session began that HR 5252 was dead for the 97th Congress. Leaders in both houses were insisting upon a stripped-down agenda, and the complex and controversial clean-air reauthorization was not on their priority list. House Energy never resumed its work on the bill.

A few members talked of putting together a simple bill that merely extended national air quality deadlines for a few years so that EPA would not put in motion the sanctions machinery of the existing law. But that idea generated no discernible enthusiasm.

Environmentalists believed they could get a better bill from the next Congress. Industry groups and their allies feared a simple extension might relieve all pressures on Congress to take a careful look at the existing law.

Nearly everyone realized it would be well into 1983 before EPA could even begin to punish local jurisdictions failing to meet the standards, and most assumed that the 98th Congress could deal with the problem before that happened. ∎

Endangered Species Act Reauthorized

Congress Sept. 30 cleared for the president a three-year reauthorization (HR 6133 — PL 97-304) of the 1973 Endangered Species Act. The measure retained most existing protections for species threatened with extinction, but it streamlined enforcement of the law.

Final action came when the House by voice vote adopted a conference report (H Rept 97-835) on the measure that the Senate had approved Sept. 20, also by voice vote.

The act, itself considered endangered by environmentalists early in the year, was actually changed very little by Congress.

As cleared, HR 6133 authorized appropriations of almost $39 million annually for three years. The Reagan administration had asked for a one-year reauthorization.

The bill shortened from two years to one year the deadline by which the Interior Department had to act on a petition to list a species as endangered. It also rejected administration policy of weighing economic factors in listing decisions, requiring them to be made solely on biological grounds.

Final Provisions

As cleared by Congress, HR 6133 contained the following major provisions:

● Set a one-year deadline for the Interior Department to decide whether to list or delist a species after it received a petition containing substantial evidence on such questions. The current deadline was two years, and environmentalists had criticized the Reagan administration for dragging its feet on listing decisions.

● Set a similar one-year deadline for decisions on petitions to revise a designation of critical habitat.

● Required listing decisions to be made solely on the biological question of whether the species was endangered or threatened. Current administration policy had been to weigh potential economic costs in listing decisions as well.

● Continued to permit consideration of economic factors in decisions on designating critical habitats.

● Provided that a decision by the interior secretary to reject petitions should be subject to judicial review.

● Allowed federal agencies (or, through them, applicants for federal permits) to enter into early, informal consultations with the Interior Department on whether a project would jeopardize any endangered species. Current rules did not allow consultation before a formal permit application, which left less leeway for the applicant to change his plans.

● Eliminated the threat of criminal penalties or project shutdown for industries that took threatened species incidentally in the course of other activities. This change applied only if the industry filed a plan with Interior in advance and had taken measures to minimize such "incidental takings," and if the taking would not jeopardize the existence of the species.

● Streamlined the current exemption mechanism in a way meant to reduce processing time from 360 days to 190 days. Without changing the standards for granting exemptions from the act's provisions, the bill substituted a secretarial report on whether they should be granted for a report by a review board.

● Encouraged introduction of captive-bred populations of an endangered species into the wild through special provisions for "experimental" populations that would not trigger the law's full protective mechanisms.

● Continued the exemption from trade restrictions for certain finished scrimshaw (carved whale bone) products, to allow sale of pre-1973 stockpiles under tight safeguards.

● Required the interior secretary to submit a justification to Congress within 90 days if the United States failed to take certain actions under the Convention on International Trade in Endangered Species of Wild Fauna and Flora.

● Abolished the International Convention Advisory Commission, which advised the secretary on matters related to the trade convention.

● Declared it to be the policy of Congress that the federal government would cooperate with states and local agencies to resolve water resource issues involving endangered species.

● Authorized appropriations for each of the fiscal years 1983, 1984, and 1985 of up to $27 million for the Interior Department, $3.5 million for the Commerce Department, $1.85 million for the Agriculture Department, $6 million for grants to states, and $600,000 for the interior secretary and the Endangered Species Committee to be used in administering the exemptions process. For carrying out obligations under the Convention on International Trade, it authorized $150,000 for each of the fiscal years 1983 and 1984 and $300,000 for fiscal 1985.

● Increased the maximum share of costs for which states could receive grants under the act from 66.6 percent to 75 percent for single-state projects and from 75 percent to 90 percent for multi-state projects.

Background

The 1973 law (PL 93-205) made it a federal offense to buy, sell, possess, export, or import any species listed as endangered or threatened, or any product made from such a species. It also required federal agencies to ensure that their projects do not jeopardize a listed species or adversely affect its habitat. Agencies must obtain a permit by consulting with the Interior Department for land-based species or the Commerce Department for marine species. *(1973 Almanac p. 670)*

In instances where no feasible alternative could be found, a proposed federal project could be exempted from provisions of the act. However, industry critics claimed this process had been cumbersome and time-consuming.

The law had engendered controversy since 1978, when it led to a temporary halt in construction of the Tennessee Valley Authority's Tellico Dam near Knoxville, Tenn., because the structure threatened the habitat of the endangered snail darter, a three-inch fish.

In another instance, the law was used to block construction of the proposed Dickey-Lincoln dam in northern Maine in order to protect a variety of snapdragon known as the furbish lousewort. The project was eventually modified to change the area that would be flooded.

Mostly in response to the Tellico controversy, Congress in 1978 set up a Cabinet-level board, usually referred to as the "God committee," that could permit construction of federal projects even if they might kill off species pro-

tected by the endangered species law. And in 1979, Congress exempted the Tellico Dam from protection of the law in a provision attached to the fiscal 1980 energy and water appropriations bill. *(1978 Almanac p. 707; 1979 Almanac pp. 223, 661)*

Before enactment of HR 6133, the Reagan administration had added only two new species to the endangered list, although more than one hundred candidates for listing were under consideration. The two additions, both made in 1982, were a tiny crustacean that lives in only one known place, the waters of Washington's National Zoo, and an orchid found at two sites in Brazos County, Texas.

Environmental groups complained about the slow pace of the listing process. They also protested the administration's policy of weighing potential economic costs in deciding whether to add a species to the endangered list.

On the other hand, industries that needed federal permits for their projects complained that the existing law did permit them to learn soon enough whether a project would jeopardize an endangered species or its critical habitat.

Legislative History

House Committee Action

HR 6133 was approved May 5 by the House Merchant Marine and Fisheries Committee (H Rept 97-567).

Sponsor John B. Breaux, D-La., chairman of the House Merchant Marine subcommittee that drafted the bill, noted HR 6133 was endorsed by "all the major environmental groups" and was at least accepted, if not supported, by many industry groups.

At its markup session, the House committee adopted a half-dozen amendments to HR 6133, including ones that would:

● Require a designation of critical habitat within one year after a listing.

● Specify that if the United States voted against adding a species to the Convention on International Trade in Endangered Species (CITES) list and failed to enter a reservation to that treaty, the secretary of state must provide a written justification to the House Merchant Marine and Senate Environment committees.

● Tighten an exemption that permited carvers who had

whale parts in stock prior to the law's enactment in 1973 to continue selling scrimshaw.

● Ensure that agencies or industries that consulted with the interior secretary under Section 7 of the act to minimize danger to species would not be barred from proceeding with a project by Section 9 prohibitions against the "taking" of endangered species.

Senate Committee Action

The Senate Environment and Public Works Committee May 11 approved a similar bill (S 2309) sponsored by Sen. John H. Chafee, R-R.I. The bill was reported May 26 (S Rept 97-418).

Committee action came after staff members in both chambers negotiated for months with industry representatives, state wildlife managers and environmentalists on changes that would streamline the existing law without weakening its substantive protections for plants, fish, birds and animals threatened with extinction.

Interior Secretary James G. Watt had sought only a one-year reauthorization, but Chafee said the decision to report a longer extension should not be viewed as a "rebuff" of Watt.

"He would have preferred a one-year reauthorization, that's true. But it was not a major bone of contention," Chafee said May 11.

The Senate committee adopted only minor technical amendments May 11. But its Environmental Pollution Subcommittee May 5 adopted several substantive changes in S 2309, including amendments that would:

● Reduce from two years to one the deadline for a final decision on whether to add or remove a species from the endangered list. This amendment brought S 2309 into accord with the House bill on the listing timetable.

● Prohibit removal of endangered or threatened plants from federal lands.

● Direct federal agencies to consider state water rights when working to protect endangered species.

Floor Action/Conference

The House passed HR 6133 on June 8, and the Senate approved it June 9 after substituting the language from its own bill, S 2309. House-Senate conferees filed their report on the measure Sept. 17 after resolving minor differences between the two versions.   ∎

Congress Clears Barrier Islands Legislation

Congress Oct. 1 sent to the president a bill (S 1018 — PL 97-348) to ban federal subsidies for development on undeveloped coastal barrier islands.

The measure, which had the support of both the Reagan administration and environmental groups, represented one of the few environmental initiatives to clear the 97th Congress.

Slightly differing versions of the legislation were passed Sept. 23 by the Senate and Sept. 28 by the House (HR 3252).

The Senate Oct. 1 disagreed to the House amendments, and a House-Senate conference hastily reconciled the differences. The conference report (H Rept 97-928) was then adopted by voice vote, first by the Senate and then by the House, clearing the bill for the president.

Provisions

HR 3252, as cleared by Congress:

● Established a Coastal Barrier Resources System consisting of those barrier landforms listed in a series of maps accompanying the bill.

● Allowed 180 days for the interior secretary, in consultation with state and local officials, to make "minor and technical" changes to the boundaries of the system.

● Allowed certain nearby coastal landowners to have their property added to the Coastal Barrier Resource System upon request, even if it did not technically qualify.

● Required the interior secretary to review the maps every five years and revise them to reflect changes caused by natural forces.

● Prohibited, with certain exceptions, new expenditures or financial aid for construction or purchase of roads, airports, boat landings, bridges, causeways and other structures on lands within the system.

● Prohibited federal spending to stabilize or prevent erosion of inlets, shorelines or inshore areas of the system, except where an emergency threatens life, land, or property adjacent to a unit of the system.

● Defined new expenditures as those for which specific appropriations or legally binding commitments for financial aid had not been made before the date of enactment.

● Allowed projects for the study, management, protection and enhancement of fish and wildlife, including land acquisition, habitat stabilization and recreation projects.

● Allowed spending needed for exploration, extraction or transportation of energy resources in coastal areas.

● Allowed maintenance of existing channel improvements and related structures such as jetties, including disposal of dredge spoil.

● Allowed maintenance or replacement, but not expansion, of publicly owned or operated roads or structures that were essential links in a larger system.

● Allowed essential military activities and construction and operation of Coast Guard facilities.

● Allowed, if consistent with the purposes of the act, navigational aids, scientific research, emergency actions to protect property and public safety, maintenance and replacement of public roads, non-structural or natural shoreline stabilization projects, and projects under the Land and Water Conservation Fund Act of 1965 or Coastal Zone Management Act of 1975.

● Allowed federal spending on programs unrelated to development — such as old age benefits or student loans.

● Required the director of the Office of Management and Budget to certify annually to Congress that each federal agency concerned had complied with the act.

● Required the interior secretary, after consulting with the governors of coastal states and allowing for public comment, to submit to Congress within three years a report containing recommendations for the conservation of coastal barrier resources and for changes to the boundaries or elements of the system.

● Prohibited, beginning Oct. 1, 1983, issuance of federal flood insurance under the National Flood Insurance Act of 1968 for any new construction or structural improvements within the system.

● Authorized a total of $1 million to be expended over three fiscal years (1983-85) to carry out the act.

Background

Barrier islands stretch along the Atlantic and Gulf coasts from Maine to Mexico. They act as buffers protecting the coastline, delicate wetlands and estuaries from the full force of hurricanes and ocean storms.

These islands and other coastal landforms were unstable as a result of erosion, flooding and other natural forces. Consequently, they could be very poor places to build houses, roads, and other structures. Not only were the houses likely to wash away, but human activity could damage fragile dunes and wetlands.

The government often paid twice for barrier island development: once to subsidize the original construction and again to bail out property owners hit by disaster.

In testimony at Senate hearings, Interior Secretary James G. Watt estimated that the federal government had spent more than $800 million in the past six years to assist development on barrier islands, not counting federal flood insurance. Without new legislation, he said, the total could reach $5.5 billion to $11 billion over the next 20 years.

The 1981 budget reconciliation act (PL 97-35) prohibited the sale of federal flood insurance on coastal barriers after Oct. 1, 1983, and the more extensive 1982 bill retained that ban. *(1981 Almanac p. 521)*

Legislative History

Senate Committee Action

S 1018 was approved April 28 by the Environmental Pollution Subcommittee of the Senate Environment and Public Works Committee.

A list specifying the barrier islands that would be affected by the legislation also was approved by the subcommittee without opposition.

The full Environment and Public Works Committee approved the legislation May 13 by a 13-0 vote, and it was formally reported May 26 (S Rept 97-419).

Senate Floor Action

The Senate passed S 1018 by voice vote Sept. 23 after adopting an amendment establishing a new set of map boundaries for coastal lands covered under the bill. Also adopted was an amendment prohibiting the sale of federal flood insurance for new or substantially improved structures on covered islands.

Another amendment adopted by the Senate gave coastal barrier landowners one year to voluntarily have their land included in the Coastal Barrier Resources System. Sen. Strom Thurmond, R-S.C., said that while the amendment grew out of the wishes of certain property owners on Daufuskie Island, S.C., it would apply nationwide. In effect, it allowed coastal barrier property owners with undeveloped land near an area covered by the bill to opt for inclusion under the protective provisions of S 1018, thereby shielding their land from development pressures.

House Committee Action

In the House, HR 3252 was introduced in April by Rep. Thomas B. Evans, R-Del.

The House Merchant Marine and Fisheries Committee Sept. 16 approved the bill by voice vote. It was formally reported Sept. 21 (H Rept 97-841).

The measure was then referred to the Banking, Finance and Urban Affairs Committee and to the Public Works and Transportation Committee, but those panels were discharged Sept. 22 without acting on the bill.

HR 3252 sparked controversy only when it came to mapping out precisely what lands would be covered.

Developers and landowners in several coastal states lobbied to keep their property outside the barrier system boundaries, and the map lines approved by the House committee differed somewhat from those in the Senate bill.

House Floor Action

The House Sept. 28 suspended the rules and passed HR 3252 by a 399-4 vote. *(Vote 350, p. 104-H)*

It then vacated the action and passed S 1018 after substituting language of HR 3252, sending the bill to conference.

Noting the broad support for the bill, chief sponsor Evans inquired, "When have you ever seen a bill endorsed

by the National Wildlife Federation, the National Taxpayers' Union and the American Red Cross?"

Conference

When House-Senate conferees met Oct. 1, the main issue before them was reconciling varying versions of the map boundaries for the coastal barrier system. The agreement reached added land in Rhode Island, Delaware, North Carolina, Florida and Mississippi, and deleted land in Maine, New York, South Carolina and Alabama.

The conference report clarified the definition of prohibited federal "financial assistance" to exclude programs unrelated to development, such as old-age benefits or student loans. It also included a Senate provision allowing certain landowners to be added to the Coastal Barrier Resource System at their own request, even if they did not technically qualify.

Conferees also kept a Senate provision allowing state coastal zone management agencies to propose minor changes in the boundaries of the system. ∎

Mount St. Helens Measure

Congress Aug. 17 cleared for the president a bill (HR 6530 — PL 97-243) creating a Mount St. Helens National Volcanic Monument in the Washington state area devastated by the volcano's May 18, 1980, eruption.

Final action came when the House by a 393-8 vote adopted a conference report (H Rept 97-748) on the bill. The Senate had adopted the report Aug. 13, one day after conferees agreed on a compromise version of the legislation. *(Vote 275, p. 82-H)*

As cleared by Congress, the measure set aside as a national monument an area of about 110,000 acres. The House had originally approved a 115,000-acre monument and the Senate a 105,400-acre version. The Reagan administration had requested only 84,700 acres for the area in an October 1981 Forest Service land management plan.

The House passed HR 6530 by voice vote July 19; the Senate followed suit July 21.

The measure gave the secretary of agriculture authority to make minor adjustments in the monument boundaries after giving public notice. The monument was to be administered as part of the Agriculture Department's National Forest system.

The area was set aside primarily for the purposes of resource preservation and scientific research, with other uses such as logging, recreation, hunting, and fishing allowed only insofar as they were compatible with those purposes.

The monument included roughly 30,000 acres of nonfederal lands owned mainly by the Weyerhaeuser Co., Burlington Northern Inc. and Washington state. It also included parts of the Gifford Pinchot National Forest. The private lands were to be exchanged voluntarily for other nearby federal lands.

Provisions

As cleared by Congress, HR 6530:

• Designated a Mount St. Helens National Volcanic Monument to be administered by the U.S. Forest Service.

• Established boundaries that included approximately 110,000 acres, giving the agriculture secretary authority to make minor adjustments after notice to the public and Congress.

• Extended the boundary of the Gifford Pinchot National Forest to include certain lands affected by the 1980 eruption.

• Set the timber valuation date at July 1, 1982, for non-federal lands (because of possible damage by insects or disease if acquisition was delayed).

• Limited federal authority to acquire state-owned lands to exchange only. (The Senate version permitted either exchange or donation.)

• Specified a tract-by-tract exchange package for acquisition of Weyerhaeuser and Burlington Northern lands. (The Senate version had established a "pool" of national forest lands to be used in working out exchange agreements.)

• Directed the agriculture secretary to draw up a full-scale management plan for the area within three years.

• Authorized the agriculture secretary to take actions to protect life and property in and near the monument.

• Limited the construction of new roads in the area.

• Withdrew lands in the monument from mineral leasing, except for valid existing rights.

• Required acquisition of mineral and geothermal interests within the monument area to be through exchange only, not purchase.

• Allowed "full use" of the area for scientific research and permitted motor vehicle access for administrative and emergency purposes.

• Limited commercial timber harvesting in the area to the minimum amount needed to control fire, insects, and disease and to protect monument resources and public safety.

• Limited timber hauling on national forest roads within the area to what was necessary and harmless.

• Authorized hunting and fishing within the area, subject to state and federal law, except where designated no-hunting areas were set up.

• Established a nine-member Mount St. Helens Scientific Advisory Board to advise the agriculture secretary on the management and protection of the natural and scientific resources of the monument.

Committee Action

The Senate Energy and Natural Resources Committee June 16 approved and June 23 reported its version (S 2133 — S Rept 97-481) of the bill, which called for a 105,400-acre national volcanic area.

HR 6530 won approval in the House Interior Subcommittee on Public Lands and National Parks on June 14.

The House Agriculture Subcommittee on Forests, Family Farms, and Energy approved a bill (HR 5773) identical to HR 6530 on June 10. Both bills set aside 115,000 acres.

HR 6530 was formally reported July 15 by both the House Interior and House Agriculture committees (H Rept 97-636, Parts I and II). ∎

CEQ Funds/Oil Leasing Ban

President Reagan Oct. 18 signed into law a bill (S 1210 — PL 97-350) reauthorizing spending for the Council on Environmental Quality (CEQ) for three years and barring oil, gas and mineral leasing on certain federal lands in the state of Washington.

The bill was cleared by Congress Oct. 1 when the Senate accepted minor House amendments to the bill on its second round of consideration by both chambers.

The bill, which amended the Environmental Quality Improvement Act of 1970 (PL 91-224), authorized only $44,000 per year for the CEQ in fiscal 1982-84. However, the three-member advisory council had a continuing $1 million annual authorization under the 1969 National Environmental Policy Act (NEPA — PL 91-190).

The $1,044,000 total authorization was the same as the Reagan administration request for fiscal 1982, but nearly 13 percent higher than the administration's $926,000 proposal for fiscal 1983. It represented a 72 percent slash from fiscal 1981 CEQ spending.

A companion House bill (HR 1953 — H Rept 97-50) was reported May 18, 1981, from the Merchant Marine and Fisheries Committee at the $44,000 funding level. It was passed Sept. 22, 1981, and the House then vacated the action and passed S 1210 after substituting the provisions of HR 1953. *(1981 Almanac p. 531)*

The Senate originally passed S 1210 on June 2, 1981. That version of the bill in combination with the continuing NEPA authorization provided the CEQ a total authorization of $2,544,000 for fiscal 1982.

Oil and Gas Leasing

Before approving S 1210 (S Rept 97-116) a second time, the Senate by voice vote June 14, 1982, adopted an amendment by Sens. Slade Gorton, R-Wash., and Henry M. Jackson, D-Wash., to bar energy and mineral leasing on lands managed by the U.S. Forest Service that fall within the drinking-water watershed of Seattle and Tacoma, Wash.

In early April, the Interior Department's Bureau of Land Management (BLM) announced it had granted five oil and gas exploration leases on the lands in the Mount Baker-Snoqualmie National Forest. The controversial action was taken despite objections from the Forest Service and the existence of a cooperative agreement between the service and the cities calling for management practices designed to protect the watershed.

The leases drew vehement protests from the cities and from the state's entire congressional delegation, and BLM eventually canceled them.

But Gorton and Jackson decided to make sure they could not be reinstated.

In floor remarks June 14, Gorton charged that the administration's environmental policy "is that oil and gas exploration, even where there is no known oil and gas reserves, outweighs the protection of the natural forested areas in which the population of two large American cities draws its drinking water. I do not believe that this is a good policy."

Jackson criticized the Interior Department's "helter-skelter approach" to oil and gas leasing on public lands. The Washington Democrat said the department's "act first and think later" policy "is bound to stimulate widespread opposition to development, even in circumstances where development would be appropriate."

After the leasing ban amendment was adopted, the Senate concurred in the House funding-cut amendments to S 1210 by a 76-0 vote. *(Vote 171, p. 31-S)*

The House subsequently accepted the oil leasing amendment and returned the measure to the Senate with a few minor changes. It was cleared for President Reagan Oct. 1. ∎

Florida Keys Exchange

The House June 21 cleared for the president a bill (S 1519 — PL 97-211) to implement a land exchange in the Florida Keys between the Interior Department and a private company, Charles River Breeding Laboratories.

The firm bred rhesus monkeys for medical research on all but 25 acres of Raccoon Key, an island. Those 25 acres belonged to the federal wilderness system. S 1519 authorized an exchange of the 25 acres for a nearby island, 73-acre North Cudjoe Key, which the company bought to transfer to the government.

The Senate Energy and Natural Resources Committee reported the bill May 3 (S Rept 97-377) and the full Senate passed it May 10.

The House Interior and Insular Affairs Committee reported it June 7 (H Rept 97-599) without amendment. ∎

Wolf Trap Reconstruction

President Reagan Oct. 14 signed into law a bill (HR 7293 — PL 97-310) authorizing up to $17 million in federal grants and loans to help rebuild the Filene Center at Wolf Trap Park Farm, Va. The theater for the performing arts, part of the national park system, was destroyed by fire April 4.

Differences between House and Senate versions of the legislation were settled by the introduction Oct. 1 of a compromise measure (HR 7293) that was quickly cleared by voice vote, first in the House and then in the Senate.

The park, including the Filene Center, was established as a unit of the national park system in 1966, largely on land donated by Mrs. Jouett Shouse. The Wolf Trap Foundation handles the arts programming for the center under a cooperative agreement with the National Park Service.

As a federally owned facility, the Filene Center had no insurance. The Wolf Trap Foundation agreed to raise enough funds from private contributions to pay half the estimated $18 million cost of reconstruction.

HR 6875, the original House version of the legislation, was reported Sept. 16 from the House Interior and Insular Affairs Committee (H Rept 97-825) and passed Sept. 20 by the House.

It authorized a $9 million federal grant to the Wolf Trap Foundation and loans equal to twice the amount raised by the foundation from private sources, up to a maximum of $8 million.

The bill also instructed the interior secretary to obtain assurances from the Federal Aviation Agency (FAA) that there were legally enforceable controls on air and noise pollution from nearby Dulles Airport, which the FAA owns, and from existing and planned roads in the Dulles access corridor.

A companion measure (S 1999) was reported Sept. 10 by the Senate Energy and Natural Resources Committee (S Rept 97-542). But it was supplanted by the final compromise version, HR 7293.

The compromise left unchanged the $17 million authorization limit for grants and loans to help rebuild the Filene Center at the park.

But it relaxed slightly the original House provisions regarding allowable noise levels from Dulles Airport and its

access roads. As cleared, HR 7293 set the maximum at 52-54 decibels, the level currently allowed and specified by the Senate bill (S 1999). Virginia had objected that it could not meet tighter limits and that they would complicate noise-

control work already set in motion. The cleared bill authorized use of funds for roadside barriers and other noise control measures, as well as reconstruction of the Filene Center.

Reagan Vetoes EPA Research Authorization

President Reagan Oct. 22 vetoed a bill (S 2577) authorizing $282 million in fiscal 1983 and $298 million in fiscal 1984 for Environmental Protection Agency (EPA) research and development.

Reagan charged that provisions in the bill requiring a balance of interest group representation on EPA's Science Advisory Board threatened the scientific objectivity of the board. He also complained that the bill set a higher spending limit than he wanted and reduced the EPA administrator's flexibility in several areas. *(Veto message, p. 30-E)*

The Senate Nov. 30 laid the bill aside indefinitely, after Robert T. Stafford, R-Vt., chairman of the Senate Environment and Public Works Committee, and Slade Gorton, R-Wash., chairman of the Subcommittee on Toxic Substances and Environmental Oversight, recommended to Majority Leader Howard H. Baker Jr., R-Tenn., that no override be attempted.

A vetoed bill is returned to the chamber where it originated. While mustering the two-thirds majority needed for an override of S 2577 was considered possible in the House, it was deemed impossible in the Republican-controlled Senate, which had to act first.

The Senate passed S 2577 by voice vote June 10, while the House passed an amended version 314-92 on Aug. 17. *(Vote 272, p. 80-H)*

Congress finally cleared the bill Oct. 1.

The veto did not mean an end to EPA research programs, since Congress on Sept. 29 funded them in the fiscal 1983 appropriations bill (HR 6956 — PL 97-272) for the Department of Housing and Urban Development and various independent agencies, including EPA. *(HUD appropriations, p. 231)*

However, S 2577 attached a number of strings to authorized spending that were not part of the appropriations measure. These included mandates for research on energy-related pollution and indoor air pollution, and provisions which earmarked 20 percent of total funding for long-term research.

Provisions

As cleared, S 2577 included the following major provisions:

● Authorized $282 million for EPA research and development in fiscal 1983 and $298 million in fiscal 1984, including $15 million per year earmarked from the "superfund" for cleanup of hazardous waste dumps. The fiscal 1983 allocation was well above the $215.88 million requested for fiscal 1983 by the administration.

In HR 6956, the HUD-Independent Agencies fiscal 1983 appropriations bill, Congress appropriated $119 million specifically for EPA research, although the addition of research-related salaries and expenses brought the total to $227.2 million.

● Earmarked 20 percent of the authorized funding for long-term research.

● Prohibited EPA from transferring more than 10

percent of the funds for any program to another program without congressional approval.

● Prohibited major manpower reductions without notification of Congress.

● Established a new process for nominating members of EPA's Science Advisory Board and directed the administrator to include representatives from industry, consumers, academic institutions, the states, and the general public.

● Mandated an indoor air pollution study, a national environmental monitoring program, and a special program on health and ecological effects of energy production.

The Reagan Veto

In his Oct. 22 veto message, Reagan placed major emphasis on provisions requiring a balance of interest group representation on EPA's Science Advisory Board. The board was set up by the Environmental Research, Development and Demonstration Act of 1978 (PL 95-477), which gave the EPA administrator authority to select all but one member of the board. The only selection criterion in the law was that each board member "be qualified by education, training or experience to evaluate scientific and technical information on matters referred to the board...." *(1978 Almanac p. 681)*

S 2577 added a new requirement, stating, "The administrator shall select persons nominated for the board to ensure that board membership is fairly balanced in terms of points of view represented and the functions to be performed by the board. In order to provide this balance, the board membership must represent the states, industry, labor, academia, consumers and the general public."

In his veto message, Reagan said, "This requirement runs counter to the basic premise of modern scientific thought as an objective undertaking in which the views of special interests have no role."

Reagan said S 2577 contained "a number of other objectionable features," including a higher spending limit than he wanted, a requirement that 20 percent of the authorized funding be earmarked for basic research, and language mandating what he called "a duplicative and wasteful effort to create another national environmental monitoring network."

Congressional Reaction

Rep. James H. Scheuer, D-N.Y., the bill's primary House sponsor and the chairman of the House Science Subcommittee on Natural Resources, Agriculture Research and Environment, called the veto "political."

A Scheuer spokesman pointed out that part of the disputed provision in the vetoed bill merely echoed language in the Federal Advisory Committee Act of 1972 (PL 92-463). The language requiring balance was, in fact, taken from section 5(b)(2) of that act.

But requirements for representation of specific interest groups were not in the 1972 act, although such require-

ments applied to science panels for other agencies, such as the Food and Drug Administration. The Scheuer spokesman said the legislative history of the 1972 act demonstrated its purpose was "to avoid dominance of the committee by a single interest."

As of Oct. 22, EPA Administrator Anne M. Gorsuch had appointed 31 members to the science board. Biographical information supplied by EPA indicated that virtually all were affiliated with universities or scientific organizations. Three members were employed directly by industry, although these also had academic credentials. None of the other interests mentioned in the vetoed bill was represented.

Neither environmentalists nor bill sponsors claimed that the current committee was not balanced. They did, however, say the bill was intended to prevent imbalance from developing.

Legislative History

Background

Throughout 1981 and 1982, there was growing concern in Congress about the deep cuts made in EPA's research budget since President Reagan took office.

EPA was responsible for administering most of the nation's environmental laws, including those aimed at combating air and water pollution, purifying drinking water, cleaning up hazardous wastes and controlling the disposal of toxic chemicals.

Research was critical to the agency's ability to determine safe levels of pollutants and contaminants and to assess the best technology for controlling them.

However, a combination of spending reductions and inflation chopped EPA's "real dollar" research budget nearly in half over the first two years of Reagan's term.

Senate Action

As approved May 10 and reported May 26 (S Rept 97-428) by the Senate Environment and Public Works Committee, S 2577 was a one-year bill authorizing $264 million for EPA research in fiscal 1983 and earmarking for research another $15 million from the so-called "Superfund" for the cleanup of hazardous waste dumps.

The bill, however, made no substantive changes in existing law.

The Senate passed S 2577 by voice vote June 10.

House Committee Action

The House Science and Technology Committee May 18 reported its own bill (HR 6323 — H Rept 97-574) authorizing expenditures of $296.77 million in fiscal 1983 and $310.88 million in fiscal 1984 for EPA research and development programs.

The measure, approved by voice vote, also included new strings on how EPA could spend the funds.

Like S 2577, it called for funding levels well above the administration's fiscal 1983 request of $215.88 million. But again like the Senate bill, it left EPA's research authorization at a level far below the agency's fiscal 1981 research appropriation of $342.56 million.

Before approving HR 6323, the House Science Committee by voice vote rejected a one-year authorization proposal by Rep. William Carney, R-N.Y., that would have funded EPA research at a level just $7 million above the Reagan request.

House Floor Approval

The House passed HR 6323 on Aug. 17 after reducing the funding authorization to $277.9 million for fiscal 1983 and $291 million for fiscal 1984. The fiscal 1983 authorization was the same level as fiscal 1982 appropriations but some $62 million more than the $215.9 million the administration wanted.

The major increases over Reagan's budget came in funding levels for air, water, hazardous waste and energy pollution research. Such research is the underpinning for EPA pollution control standards.

In urging approval of the bill, Scheuer noted the funding proposed by Reagan was $126.7 million below the actual appropriation for fiscal 1981. He said that when inflation was taken into account, the administration's request, "measured in real dollars, represented a 50-percent reduction in environmental research since President Reagan took office."

A cut of such magnitude, he said, "goes far beyond what can be offset by management improvements and cuts into the very heart of EPA's research function."

Rep. William Carney, R-N.Y., tried unsuccessfully to trim the bill to a funding level closer to Reagan's budget. "We would all like to live in a world where we could have the amounts of money necessary to carry out the programs in Cadillac fashion. But unfortunately, realities of today do not dictate that we can go along at that pace," Carney said.

Floor Amendments

Carney proposed a substitute that called for a one-year authorization of $225.5 million, or $9.6 million more than the administration requested.

But Science Committee Chairman Don Fuqua, D-Fla., promptly offered an amendment to Carney's substitute that called for an authorization of $277.9 million in fiscal 1983 and $291 million in fiscal 1984. The amendment brought the bill's fiscal 1983 funding level into line with the one-year version (S 2577) passed June 10 by the Senate.

The Fuqua amendment was adopted, 244-153. *(Vote 270, p. 80-H)*

The House then adopted the Carney substitute, as amended by Fuqua, 394-7. *(Vote 271, p. 80-H)*

Final Action

Congress cleared the measure Oct. 1 when both chambers concurred in amendments embodying a compromise worked out between the Senate Environment and Public Works Committee and the House Science and Technology Committee. ∎

Water Rights Bill Vetoed

President Reagan June 1 vetoed a bill (HR 5118) aimed at settling a seven-year legal battle over water supplies between the Papago Indian Tribe and major water users in the Tucson, Ariz., metropolitan area. But a compromise version was subsequently approved as part of a major reclamation reform bill (S 1409 — PL 97-293) that was cleared Sept. 29.

Rep. Morris K. Udall, D-Ariz., sponsor of the bill, took the lead in seeking a compromise satisfactory to the administration. Udall, who originally threatened to seek an override of the veto, pulled back from that position June 4, admitting his chances of gaining an override in the House

were not promising.

Enactment of S 1409 settled the water rights dispute out of court and cleared the way for further construction of the Central Arizona Project, a $1.7 billion water diversion project consisting of 400 miles of aqueducts and dams.

That project was first proposed in 1963 by Interior Secretary Stewart L. Udall, the brother of Morris. The plan was authorized in 1968 (PL 90-537) and was scheduled to deliver its first flow of water in 1985. *(Congress and the Nation Vol. II, p. 513)*

Under the settlement provided in S 1409, the Papago Indians relinquished all further claims to water in the basins underlying the Tucson area and agreed to cooperate with regional water management plans. In exchange, they were assured an adequate annual water supply.

Background

The Legal Dispute

HR 5118, the bill Reagan vetoed, reflected an agreement among the Indian tribe, miners, farmers, and the city of Tucson aimed at ensuring an adequate yearly water supply to two Papago Indian reservations.

In 1975 the United States filed suit on behalf of the Papago Indian Tribe against the major water users in the Tucson metropolitan area. The Indians charged these users with diminishing their water supply through pumping near the reservation. In the suit, the tribe sought payment for damages and an injunction barring further pumping of groundwater by non-Indian members of the community.

According to the House Interior and Insular Affairs Committee report (H Rept 97-422) on HR 5118, the Tucson metropolitan area was one of the largest communities in the world solely dependent on groundwater for its municipal and industrial needs.

The Veto Message

Reagan's veto was the fourth of his presidency. In his message the president said, "HR 5118 is a multi-million dollar bailout of local, public and commercial interests at the expense of federal taxpayers throughout the nation." *(Veto text, p. 24-E)*

He also complained that the United States was not a party to negotiations that led to a proposed agreement that "asks the federal government to pay the settlement share of the mining companies and other local water users whose share should more properly be borne by the defendants themselves."

Reagan said the legislation could cost the government an initial $112 million and another $5 million annually, although a report by the Senate Select Committee on Indian Affairs (S Rept 97-375) estimated the total cost of the settlement at $65 million.

Udall's Rebuttal

In a letter to Reagan released June 4, Udall called the president's veto "ill-advised and unfair."

He objected to Reagan's labeling the bill a "bailout," saying the government could not expect the "present-day citizens" of the areas involved in the long-running dispute to bear the entire financial burden of the settlement.

He said the federal government should help the Western states resolve water rights claims just as it helped in settling Indian land claims in the Eastern states.

Udall also took issue with the president's claim that

the United States was not a party to the negotiations. He said representatives from the Bureau of Reclamation and the Army Corps of Engineers were at the bargaining table and "had every opportunity to actively participate and to represent the interest of the federal government."

They did not do so, he said, because the administration had no policy on the settlement of Indian claims nor a program for participation in such negotiations.

Legislative History

The Original Version: HR 5118

HR 5118 was reported Jan. 29 by the House Interior and Insular Affairs Committee (H Rept 97-422) and was passed by the House March 4 by a vote of 311-50. *(Vote 17, p. 6-H)*

In the Senate, it was reported April 29 by the Select Indian Affairs Committee (S Rept 97-375) and passed, amended, by voice vote May 11.

The House May 12 agreed to Senate amendments, with further modifications that the Senate accepted by voice vote May 13, clearing the bill for the president.

The Rewrite: S 1409

After the veto, a new bargaining team, this time including representatives of both the legislative and executive branches, renegotiated the settlement. The new agreement was incorporated into a three-part omnibus bill (S 1409) that was passed by both the House and Senate the week of Aug. 16.

The vehicle, S 1409, started its legislative life as a simple Wyoming dam authorization bill. By the time it cleared Congress, it included:

● Title I, the original S 1409, authorizing construction of the Buffalo Bill Dam and Reservoir in Wyoming.

● Title II, legislation revising acreage limits on land eligible for federally subsidized reclamation water in Western states. This was a compromise version of reclamation reform bills (HR 5539, S 1867) passed by the House May 6 and by the Senate July 16. *(Story, p. 353)*

● Title III, the rewritten version of the vetoed bill (HR 5118) involving Papago Indian water rights.

Final action on the reclamation reform legislation was anxiously awaited by the Reagan administration and its Western backers. Although the Senate passed its version of the bill July 16, Rep. Morris K. Udall, D-Ariz., chairman of the House Interior and Insular Affairs Committee, refused to go to conference on it until he got a resolution of the unrelated Papago Indian water dispute.

The Senate originally passed S 1409, which then simply authorized the Buffalo Bill Dam in Wyoming, on June 22.

The House added the provisions on Papago water rights and reclamation reform and passed the whole package on Aug. 17.

That would have set up a conference where only the House version of the Papago and reclamation bills was on the negotiating table. To put its own version on the table as well, the Senate amended S 1409 to include the added provisions and on Aug. 20 passed the package.

House-Senate conferees filed their report on S 1409 on Sept. 22 (H Rept 97-855, S Rept 97-568), and the Senate agreed to it Sept. 24.

Final action came when the House accepted the report by voice vote Sept. 29.

Buffalo Bill Dam

The Buffalo Bill Dam provisions constituted the first major new authorization of a reclamation water project in six years. The bill authorized $106.7 million in federal appropriations for building and operating enlargements to an existing dam and reservoir.

Wyoming, mindful of administration demands for cost-sharing on federal water projects, had already appropriated $47 million for the Buffalo Bill project, a far larger state share of the costs than usual.

Papago Indians

The new Indian water rights agreement, embodied in S 1409, authorized a total of $39.8 million in federal appropriations, although much of that amount would be held in a special Treasury trust fund. Net outlays under the budget for the first year after enactment of the law would be $9.75 million.

The bill also authorized reclamation water service for the Papago Indian tribe and construction of irrigation facilities; specified new limits on tribal use of groundwater; and established procedures for tribal waivers of certain water rights and legal action. ∎

Georgia Wilderness Bill

The Senate Aug. 19 cleared for the president a bill (S 1119 — PL 97-250) to adjust the boundary of Crater Lake National Park in Oregon and to designate as wilderness certain lands in the Cumberland Island National Seashore in Georgia.

Final action on the measure, which designated 8,440 acres of the seashore as wilderness and 11,718 as potential wilderness, came when the Senate by voice vote concurred in an amendment made to the bill by the House.

The section on the Cumberland Island wilderness area was essentially the same as S 2569, reported by the Senate Committee on Energy and Natural Resources on Aug. 18 (S Rept 97-531).

The original Crater Lake version of S 1119 was reported Oct. 7, 1981, by the Senate Energy and Natural Resources Committee (S Rept 97-205) and was passed by the Senate Oct 21, 1981.

The bill was reported from the House Interior and Insular Affairs Committee Dec. 10, 1981, (H Rept 97-383) and was passed by the House, with amendments, on Dec. 15, 1981. ∎

WEB Pipeline Project

The House Sept. 23 agreed to Senate amendments and cleared for the president a bill (HR 4347) authorizing construction of the WEB Pipeline, which would bring water to some 30,000 people in rural South Dakota.

President Reagan signed the measure into law Sept. 30 (PL 97-273).

The project was meant to partially compensate South Dakota for some 540,000 acres flooded since 1944 by the federally funded Pick-Sloan flood control and power project on the Missouri River.

The bill authorized several studies of other potential water developments that could also compensate the state.

These included a reformulation of the Pollock-Herreid irrigation unit; the possible use of return flows from the Garrison project in North Dakota for irrigation and domestic use in South Dakota; and alternative uses for the Oahe irrigation project, which was stopped by local opposition in 1977 after $41 million had been spent on construction.

Under an agreement with the Carter administration, authorization of the WEB project depended on deauthorization of the Oahe project, estimated to cost as much as $900 million, by Sept. 30, 1981. Congress did not deauthorize Oahe, but the Reagan administration no longer insisted on this linkage.

HR 4347 was expected to have the effect of blocking further construction on Oahe, but it did not formally deauthorize the project.

The bill was reported May 17 from both the House Interior and Insular Affairs Committee and the House Agriculture Committee (H Rept 97-524, Parts I and II).

It was passed by the House June 8 under suspension of the rules.

The measure was reported Aug. 2 from the Senate Energy and Natural Resources Committee (S Rept 97-514) and was passed by the Senate Aug. 19. ∎

Urgent Reclamation Repairs

The House Sept. 20 cleared for the president a bill (S 1628 — PL 97-275) that allowed use of Bureau of Reclamation emergency repair funds for work on projects that involved municipal or industrial water supply as well as irrigation and power generation.

The measure amended the Emergency Fund Act of 1948. That law set up a fund to finance emergency repairs of irrigation or power facilities of Bureau of Reclamation projects. S 1628 simply made the fund available for emergency repairs to any Bureau of Reclamation project.

In addition, it authorized use of the fund for facilities constructed under the Small Reclamation Projects Act of 1956 and the Distribution System Loans Act of 1956.

Similar legislation was introduced in the 96th Congress, but it never moved beyond hearings in the Senate Energy and Natural Resources Committee.

S 1628 was reported by the Senate Energy Committee on April 27 (S Rept 97-363) and passed by voice vote May 10 by the full Senate.

The House Interior and Insular Affairs Committee reported the bill Aug. 19 (H Rept 97-769), and it was passed by voice vote Sept. 20. ∎

Interstate Waste Compact

The Senate Sept. 20 cleared for the president a bill (HR 5288 — PL 97-278) granting congressional approval to a compact between New Hampshire and Vermont for construction and operation of a facility that would burn solid wastes to produce electricity for communities in both states.

The House passed the bill by voice vote Aug. 16. Under the Constitution, congressional approval is required for interstate compacts. The legislatures of the two states had already approved the solid waste compact.

HR 5288 was reported Aug. 11 by the House Judiciary

Committee (H Rept 97-724). In the Senate, the Judiciary Committee took no action on a companion bill (S 1915) introduced by the four Vermont and New Hampshire senators. Instead, the House bill was held at the desk and called up by unanimous consent.

The agreement between the two New England states was the first such interstate compact to be developed under the 1976 Resource Conservation and Recovery Act (RCRA), which governed the disposal of solid and hazardous wastes. *(RCRA reauthorization, p. 456)*

Rep. Robert McClory, R-Ill., told the House the agreement marked a significant change of attitude toward the disposal of solid wastes.

"Once the source of perpetual controversy among communities, solid waste disposal has turned into a hidden bonanza for all participants," McClory said.

Technology now made it possible to convert waste into electric power, while separation of solid wastes facilitated recovery of metals for reuse, he noted. ∎

Central Arizona Project

Congress Dec. 9 cleared for the president a bill (S 2177 — PL 97-373) authorizing more than $200 million in additional spending on portions of the huge Central Arizona Project to bring Colorado River water to the arid Tucson and Phoenix regions.

Final action came when the House by voice vote accepted technical amendments to the House-passed version of the bill that the Senate had adopted Dec. 8.

As cleared, S 2177 authorized cost indexing estimated to add from $350 million to $500 million to the $100 million originally authorized for non-Indian distribution systems to deliver the project's water from the main aqueducts to the eventual users.

The 1968 law that first authorized the Central Arizona Project authorized $100 million for non-Indian distribution and drainage facilities. Construction of these facilities had not yet begun, because water from the project was not available for irrigation until fiscal 1985. Meanwhile, construction costs had gone up. Although other parts of the original law included inflation indexing, the part authorizing distribution and drainage systems did not.

As cleared, S 2177 included a House amendment that required project beneficiaries to share at least 20 percent of the cost of the distribution facilities.

Legislative History

The Senate Energy and Natural Resources Committee reported S 2177 on May 12 (S Rept 97-389).

The measure was passed by the Senate May 19.

The House Interior and Insular Affairs Committee approved the measure by voice vote Aug. 11 and reported Pt. 1 Aug. 19 and Pt. 2 Sept. 14 (H Rept 97-776).

The House Sept. 30 passed the bill by voice vote after adopting an amendment requiring local and state governments to bear 20 percent of distribution and drainage project costs.

The amendment, offered by Bruce F. Vento, D-Minn., was supported by Republican fiscal conservatives and Democratic environmentalists. It required non-federal interests to pay their share "up front," as construction proceeded, rather than permitting them to reimburse the U.S. Treasury later at low interest, as in the past. ∎

Sikes Act Amendments

Legislation (HR 1952 — PL 97-396) to reauthorize conservation programs on military and other federally owned lands was cleared for the president Dec. 17.

Final action came when the House concurred in amendments to the bill that had been adopted by the Senate Dec. 16.

As cleared, HR 1952 amended the 1960 Sikes Act, which provided for cooperative federal-state management of fish and wildlife on military reservations.

The Sikes Act was modified in 1968 and 1974 to authorize development of comprehensive plans for conservation and rehabilitation of fish and wildlife on lands owned by several government agencies, not just the military. The agencies affected by the Sikes Act control over 600 million acres of fish, wildlife and plant habitat.

HR 1952 clarified federal-state responsibilities on such issues as habitat improvement, rehabilitation and protection of threatened and endangered species of fish, wildlife and plants on government lands.

The measure authorized expenditures of $28.5 million annually in fiscal 1983 and 1984, and $26.5 million in fiscal 1985.

Included in the total was an authorization of $2 million annually in fiscal 1983 and 1984 to complete a study of the decline of the striped bass population in Atlantic coastal waters. The study, ordered by Congress in 1979, was to determine why striped bass populations had been declining since 1970. The fish was popular among both commercial and recreational fishermen, and was of considerable economic significance to Atlantic coastal states.

HR 1952 exempted the secretaries of Interior and Agriculture from advertising and competitive bidding regulations under the Federal Property and Administrative Services Act of 1949. This was intended to free the agencies from the time-consuming process of justifying why state agencies rather than other organizations or individuals should receive contracts under the Sikes Act.

Legislative History

HR 1952 was reported May 18, 1981, by the House Merchant Marine and Fisheries Committee (H Rept 97-49). It was passed by the full House Sept. 21, 1981, under suspension of the rules.

The measure was approved with minor amendments May 6, 1982, by the Senate Environment and Public Works Committee and was formally reported May 25. (S Rept 97-413).

The Senate passed the amended bill June 9.

The House returned it to the Senate Sept. 30 with an additional amendment designed to clarify the authority of the Interior Department's Fish and Wildlife Service to carry out certain "sting-type" operations to stop trafficking in protected wildlife.

This amendment was accepted by the Senate Dec. 16 with some technical changes granting comparable authority to the National Marine Fisheries Service. The Senate also added an amendment deleting two small coastal areas in Texas from the boundaries of the Coastal Barrier Resources System established under a separate bill (S 1018 — PL 97-348) cleared by Congress Oct. 2. *(Coastal barriers legislation, p. 436)*

The House accepted these amendments Dec. 17, clearing HR 1952 for the president. ∎

National Trails Legislation

The House May 11 passed a bill (HR 861) designating three new national scenic trails and authorizing the study of six other routes for possible inclusion in the national trail system. However, the measure died in the Senate.

The bill, reported from the House Interior and Insular Affairs Committee Oct. 7, 1981 (H Rept 97-267), was passed by a vote of 389-6. *(Vote 65, p. 20-H)*

HR 861, sponsored by Rep. Phillip Burton, D-Calif., was a scaled-down version of legislation that was approved by both the House and Senate in 1980 but stalled short of enactment. *(1980 Almanac p. 617)*

As passed, it designated three new scenic trails: the Potomac Heritage, Natchez Trace and Florida trails. Studies were authorized for six additional routes: the General Crook, Beale Wagon Road, Juan Bautista da Anza, Trail of Tears, Illinois and Jedediah Smith trails.

The bill authorized total expenditures of $3.6 million in fiscal 1983-1986, with $2.5 million earmarked for land acquisition and development of the Natchez Trace Trail.

The measure forbade entrance fees for any national recreational area, national wild and scenic river area or any portion of the national trail system. In addition, it prohibited entrance fees at national parks where the cost of collecting them would exceed the revenue from such fees.

This provision was opposed by the administration. President Reagan, in his fiscal 1983 budget, proposed increasing revenues by $63 million per year by increasing existing entrance fees at national parks and by imposing new fees at recreation and wilderness areas where currently none were collected.

Background

The National Trails System Act (PL 90-543) was enacted in 1968 to promote the development of a national network of scenic trails, beginning with the Appalachian Trail from Maine to Georgia and the Pacific Crest Trail through Washington, Oregon and California. The law was later amended to include historic trails. *(Background, 1968 Almanac p. 477)*

National trails, which could be established only by an act of Congress, were usually located in remote areas and were reserved primarily for hiking and camping.

HR 861, as introduced, contained the text approved by the Senate in 1980. However, after additional hearings in 1981, the House Committee on Interior and Insular Affairs Oct. 7 reported a revised version (H Rept 97-267) that eliminated most of the items requiring future federal expenditures.

The bill deleted four of the trails initially proposed for inclusion to permit additional review by the Interior Department.

In addition, it placed a greater reliance on citizen participation than ever required before under the law.

The 1980 version of the trails bill would have authorized $19.5 million for land acquisition and development of the Natchez Trace National Scenic Trail. But because the Senate refused to spend that much money, HR 861 authorized only $2.5 million for acquisition and development of the Natchez.

No federal purchases were authorized for the other two trails, the Potomac Heritage and the Florida Trails, which would be carved out of existing national forest and park lands.

Senate Committee Action

The Senate Energy and Natural Resources Committee approved the bill Sept. 15 and reported it Sept. 23 (S Rept 97-577).

The Senate panel deleted a House provision barring entrance fees at national recreation areas, scenic rivers or trails.

With a crowded agenda and limited time available in the lame-duck session, the full Senate never considered the national trails bill. ∎

National Park Protection Bill

The House Sept. 29 suspended the rules and passed a bill (HR 5162) aimed at protecting national parks not only from nearby resource development but also from too many visitors and the actions of governmental agencies.

In the Senate, the measure was referred to the Energy and Natural Resources Committee, which took no action on it.

The House vote was 319-84. The wide margin of victory came in spite of opposition to the bill by the Reagan administration. *(Vote 353, p. 104-H)*

As passed, HR 5162 required the National Park Service (NPS), an arm of the Interior Department, to identify and address threats to individual parks and to the system as a whole.

The park service was required to submit a "State of the Parks Report" to Congress every two years, detailing park problems and ways to solve them. The bill also required creation of a resource management plan for each park.

It set up a consultation and review process to ensure that the parks were not harmed either by Interior Department actions or by actions taken by other federal agencies.

Administration Opposed

Interior Secretary James G. Watt stated his objections to the bill in a Sept. 27 letter read by Dick Cheney, R-Wyo., during debate on the bill.

"We believe ... that HR 5162 is unnecessary, duplicates existing laws and administrative programs, creates more red tape, and imposes inflexible requirements on resource management efforts that should remain flexible enough to apply available staff and funds to changing needs," he said.

Watt also said the bill was opposed by the Office of Management and Budget and would have "adverse" budgetary impacts. It authorized $750,000 annually for three years to be used for planning grants to local governments.

State of the Parks

"Nearly all of the national parks are being degraded or threatened with degradation in significant ways from activities both within and outside of their boundaries, and the trend is worsening," countered John F. Seiberling, D-Ohio, chairman of the Interior Subcommittee on Public Lands and National Parks.

Seiberling cited a May 1980 National Park Service report to Congress that detailed 4,345 specific threats to parks. That report concluded that the leading internal threat to the parks was overuse and excess visitation. Wil-

derness Society chairman and former Wisconsin Sen. Gaylord Nelson (1963-81) told a Feb. 3 subcommittee hearing that park visits had jumped from 3 million in 1930 to 33 million in 1950, 300 million in 1980 and 327 million in 1981.

The subcommittee also heard of external threats to the parks, often on adjacent land, such as the following:

● Energy developers applied for geothermal steam leases within one mile of some Yellowstone National Park thermal features, threatening not only grizzly bears but Old Faithful itself, Nelson said.

● The Department of Energy proposed siting a high-level nuclear waste disposal facility, complete with its own power plant, on Bureau of Land Management land within one-half mile of the Canyonlands National Park.

● Fishing interests in southern Florida were trying to reverse an NPS decision to phase out commercial fishing in Everglades National Park by 1985. Farmers wanted to reopen the park to commercial tomato-growing, which required pesticides, according to Nathaniel Reed, former assistant interior secretary for fish, wildlife, and parks.

House Committee Action

HR 5162 was approved Sept. 22 and reported Sept. 28 (H Rept 97-881) by the House Interior and Insular Affairs Committee.

The measure had been approved by the subcommittee Sept. 16 in the form of a substitute that incorporated some aspects of similar bills: HR 5552, introduced by Seiberling; HR 5976, introduced by Douglas K. Bereuter, R-Neb.; and HR 5973, introduced by Pat Williams, D-Mont.

The subcommittee defeated an amendment offered by Larry E. Craig, R-Idaho, requiring the interior secretary to provide reasonable alternatives to any local action he decided to oppose under the bill. The subcommittee approved an amendment removing a citizen's right to sue for compliance with the act, along with 10 other amendments, most technical.

The full committee approved an amendment preserving an exemption under the 1980 Alaska National Interest Lands Conservation Act, which allowed special and traditional uses to continue within Alaskan national parks. The committee also approved an amendment restricting lawsuits under the act to the federal court in the district where the park was located and limiting relief to temporary, rather than permanent, injunction.

Also adopted by the committee was an amendment applying the act to lands "nearby" and "within" the park boundaries, as well adjacent lands. Defeated was an amendment that would have let state legislatures and governors define adjacent lands. ∎

Risk Analysis Legislation

The House Aug. 2 suspended the rules and passed a bill (HR 6159) to improve "risk analysis" by federal agencies charged with protecting life, health and the environment.

The Senate Commerce Committee Dec. 6 approved a similar measure (S 3006) Dec. 6, but the full Senate failed to act on the measure.

Risk analysis was defined as the process of "quantifying a risk and determining an acceptable level of that risk for an individual, group, society or the environment."

HR 6159 authorized no new spending. Instead, it would have set up a research and demonstration program to determine whether and how to use risk analysis in developing federal health, environmental and safety-related regulations.

The program, designed to cover nine agencies, was to be under the joint aegis of the Office of Management and Budget and the White House Office of Science and Technology Policy.

Covered agencies included the Food and Drug Administration, the Environmental Protection Agency, the Occupational Safety and Health Administration, the Food Safety and Inspection Service, the Nuclear Regulatory Commission, the Department of Energy, the Consumer Product Safety Commission, the Federal Aviation Administration, and the Department of Transportation.

The bill was reported June 24 from the House Science and Technology Committee (H Rept 97-625).

Senate Action

S 3006 was introduced Oct. 1 by Sen. Harrison "Jack" Schmitt, R-N.M., and approved Dec. 6 by the Commerce Committee. No hearings were held, and no written report published.

As approved, the measure covered only five agencies rather than the nine of the House bill. Eliminated were the Nuclear Regulatory Commission, the Departments of Transportation and Energy and the Federal Aviation Administration. ∎

Oil, Gas Royalty Collection

The House Dec. 21 sent to the president a bill (HR 5121 — PL 97-451) to reform the system for collecting royalties for oil and gas produced on federal lands, tightening the government's grip on hundreds of millions of dollars in revenue previously lost or stolen.

As cleared, HR 5121 gave the interior secretary broad authority to overhaul and oversee a tightened system of inspections, record-keeping, reporting, auditing and security at oil and gas production sites. It also set new penalties for violations.

Rep. Edward J. Markey, D-Mass., who along with James D. Santini, D-Nev., introduced HR 5121, called passage of the bill "a big victory for consumers who have not been getting a fair return for the use of their land by oil and gas companies."

Before Congress completed action on the legislation, the House and Senate battled over a proposal to allow the interior secretary to raise the royalties collected by the federal government on certain non-competitive oil and gas leases.

That provision, included in the version of the bill passed by the House Sept. 29, gave the interior secretary discretion to raise the royalty rate to $16\frac{2}{3}$ percent of the dollar value of oil at the wellhead. The rate was currently set by statute at $12\frac{1}{2}$ percent.

The Senate Dec. 6 passed its own version of the bill without the royalty raise.

But the originator of the royalty raise proposal, Rep. George Miller, D-Calif., and the bill's House managers insisted on keeping it, and that set off a struggle between the House and Senate. The measure went back and forth between the chambers three times before the House finally

gave in and dropped the provision.

Background

The Reagan administration supported the measure, which grew out of recommendations from a special commission set up by Interior Secretary James G. Watt in July 1981 to investigate charges of mismanagement, underpayment and theft.

The Commission on Fiscal Accountability of the Nation's Energy Resources issued a scathing report Jan. 21 charging that the federal government was losing $200 million to $500 million annually due to oil thefts and royalty underpayments by oil companies.

That commission found that accounting and collection procedures were outmoded, enforcement was weak, penalties were insufficient, and security on well sites was lax.

The report said oil company royalties, which should reach $14 billion a year by 1990, were collected almost totally on the honor system.

"The government has no way of verifying independently how much oil and gas are taken from leases on federal and Indian lands," said Commission Chairman David F. Linowes. "Site security is deficient. Theft of oil is common."

Allegations of irregularities, dating back to 1959, had earlier been made by the General Accounting Office, Congress, various states, Indian communities and the U.S. Geological Survey (USGS).

The problems became even more acute in recent years as oil prices increased, and Watt announced that he wanted to expand oil and gas exploration on federal lands.

Major Overhaul Announced

The commission's report prompted Watt to announce a major overhaul of the Interior Department's royalty collection system designed to plug loopholes and crack down on the thefts and underpayments.

The program was shifted from the scientifically oriented USGS to a new Minerals Management Service. Watt also said he would institute tighter internal controls and hire and train new field inspectors.

In addition, Watt called for new legislation to tighten collection procedures and management.

Provisions

As cleared by Congress, HR 5121 including the following major provisions:

● Required thorough record-keeping and reporting by operators, leaseholders and holders of interests in leases.

● Required lease operators to set up and carry out site security plans to prevent theft.

● Required lease operators to notify the interior secretary not later than the fifth business day after any new well began production or any old well commenced new production.

● Required transporters of oil from leases to document where it came from and where it was going.

● Required royalty payments on lost or wasted oil and gas.

● Directed the interior secretary to conduct annual inspections of every lease site producing significant quantities of oil or gas.

● Required the federal government to pay proceeds from royalties promptly on a monthly schedule and to provide a complete statement accounting for the payment, to states and Indian tribes owed such royalty payments.

● Required bonding of persons who handled royalties to insure their liability for losses.

● Authorized the interior secretary or those he appointed to carry out appropriate law enforcement actions, including power to stop and inspect vehicles.

● Authorized the interior secretary to conduct needed hearings, investigations, audits and inspections, with power to issue and enforce subpoenas.

● Required the inspector general of the Interior Department to conduct an annual audit of the system.

● Provided that late payments of royalties be charged interest at the Internal Revenue Service rate, with the interest to be paid in appropriate shares to Indian tribes and the states.

● Set civil penalties of up to $500 per day for minor violations of the act if they were not corrected within 20 days of notice and up to $5,000 per day if not corrected within 40 days.

● Set penalties of up to $10,000 per day for anyone who "knowingly and willfully" failed to make required royalty payments, refused to permit inspection or audit or failed to comply with reporting requirements of the act.

● Provided civil penalties of up to $25,000 for anyone who knowingly or willfully submitted false reports, stole oil or gas from a lease site or trafficked in stolen oil or gas.

● Set a criminal penalty of $50,000 fine or two years imprisonment or both for the most serious knowing and willful violations of the act.

● Authorized the secretary to delegate to states and Indian tribes power to conduct inspections, audits and investigations.

● Authorized the interior secretary to reinstate certain terminated leases.

● Required the interior secretary to submit to Congress an annual report on the royalty management system.

Legislative History

House Action

The House Interior and Insular Affairs Subcommittee on Mines and Mining held a hearing on HR 5121 on Jan. 27. The panel approved the measure March 25.

The full Interior Committee approved the bill by a 31-4 vote Sept. 15 and formally reported it Sept. 23 (H Rept 97-859).

The House Sept. 29 suspended the rules and passed HR 5121 by voice vote.

Senate Action

The Senate Energy and Natural Resources Committee approved its version of the bill (S 2305) on July 27 and formally reported it July 30 (S Rept 97-512). The 20-0 committee vote ended a marathon nine-session markup stalled by the objections of John Melcher, D-Mont.

Although wording in the Senate committee bill and the House bill differed considerably, the substance was quite similar.

Rep. Morris K. Udall, D-Ariz., chairman of the House Committee on Interior and Insular Affairs, and Sen. James A. McClure, R-Idaho, chairman of Senate Energy, directed their staffs to negotiate a single text combining the best elements of both.

When S 2305 came up Dec. 6 on the Senate floor,

McClure offered a substitute amendment embodying the negotiated text (minus a provision on increasing royalty rates, which the House staff still insisted on).

The Senate adopted that text by voice vote, substituted it for the text of the House-passed HR 5121, and passed the bill by voice vote.

One key difference between the Senate committee and House bills was the ceiling on criminal penalties they allowed for knowing or willful violations of their requirements. The compromise bill set a limit of a $50,000 fine or two years imprisonment, or both. The Senate committee version set civil fines of $25,000 per violation for each day the violation continued and allowed on top of that any criminal penalties available under existing federal law — typically a fine of $10,000 and five or 10 years' imprisonment. The House version allowed fines up to $100,000 and jail terms up to five years.

Another key difference was that the Senate committee bill allowed the interior secretary to delegate to individual states the authority to collect royalties due the federal government. The House bill did not allow states to collect federal royalties, and the compromise version did not either.

Melcher had vigorously opposed the state collection proposal. "Nothing could do more to compound the confusion which is inevitable under the new system than the imposition on top of it of all the multiple, possible contradictory systems of regulation, reporting, and accounting involving state authorities."

States and Indian tribes collected their own royalties or severance taxes on oil or gas produced, and when well production was not properly reported, they lost revenue just as the federal government did. Both the compromise bill and earlier versions allowed the interior secretary to make arrangements for states or tribes to carry out inspections, audits, and investigations on federal leases — possibly helping the U.S. Treasury as well as their own.

The compromise bill also included a provision allowing reinstatement of certain terminated leases, which was passed by the House but omitted from the Senate committee version. When oil and gas leaseholders failed to pay certain rental fees due the federal government, the government had to automatically terminate those leases under current law.

Members of Congress often got appeals for help from persons who had bought a lease only to find it was terminated for non-payment of rentals by a previous leaseholder. One result, staff said, was that Congress passed more than a dozen private relief bills for reinstatement of leases in 1982 alone, using up legislative time and effort.

The reinstatement provision in the compromise bill gave the interior secretary authority to settle these cases administratively, subject to tight requirements meant to ensure the federal Treasury got payments due it. ∎

Offshore Leasing Revenues

The House Sept. 29 passed a bill (HR 5543) to allocate part of federal revenues from offshore oil and gas leasing to state coastal resource management programs designed to soften the impact of offshore drilling. But the measure died in the Senate.

The House vote was 260-134. *(Vote 356, p. 106-H)*

HR 5543 would have set aside up to $300 million of the estimated $10 billion to $15 billion in yearly revenue anticipated from the Reagan administration's controversial five-year offshore leasing plan.

Of the funds set aside, 10 to 20 percent would go to the National Sea Grant College Program, a program of marine research and technical assistance. The remainder would be divided, as block grants, among the coastal and Great Lakes states according to a five-part formula that would take into account:

● Actual Outer Continental Shelf (OCS) leasing and production from waters adjacent to a state.
● Planned OCS lease sales under the five-year plan.
● The quantity of coastal energy activities and facilities affecting a state's coastal zone.
● A state's shoreline mileage.
● Population in a state's coastal counties.

States with federally approved coastal zone management programs would qualify for a minimum grant of at least one-half of 1 percent of the amount available for block grants nationwide.

States would have to use 30 percent of these block grants for activities authorized under the 1972 Coastal Zone Management Board.

Another 20 percent would be earmarked for management of fisheries and marine life, including programs under the Commercial Fisheries Research and Development Act and the Anadromous (upstream-spawning) Fish Conservation Act.

A further 10 percent would go to activities under the Coastal Energy Impact Program.

The remaining 40 percent could be spent, with virtually no strings attached, for "the enhancement and management of natural resources."

The bill also contained provisions meant to encourage states to pass through some of their block grants to local governments.

A Piece of the Action

"Coastal states will finally have a small share of revenues attributable to extraction of oil and gas from federal offshore lands," said Walter B. Jones, D-N.C., chairman of the Committee on Merchant Marine and Fisheries.

"Other [inland] states for years have shared, under the Mineral Leasing Act and other laws, huge sums for the extraction of resources from federal lands," Jones noted.

The Reagan administration proposed termination of the Coastal Zone Management, Sea Grant and Coastal Energy Impact programs — and major budget reductions for the two fisheries programs.

The administration opposed HR 5543 on grounds that it would take revenue away from the federal Treasury. One of the administration's main purposes in stepping up offshore leasing was to reduce the federal budget deficit.

But Norman E. D'Amours, D-N.H., chairman of the Merchant Marine Subcommittee on Oceanography, said, "If the states cannot act as partners in this process, they are going to act to obstruct the process through litigious means." If that happens, he said, "billions of dollars ... could be lost to the federal Treasury by unnecessary delays."

D'Amours noted that in fiscal 1981, inland states received $781 million as a result of mineral development on federal lands. Under HR 5543, coastal states would get just $300 million per year.

Some 34 states, territories and possessions could have been eligible to receive funds under the bill.

Background

The Five-Year OCS Plan

The Reagan administration in April 1981 unveiled plans to offer oil companies leases on up to one billion acres, nearly the entire Outer Continental Shelf (OCS), over the next five years.

The plan faced stiff opposition from environmental groups and from many coastal states concerned about the impact of offshore drilling not only on their beaches but also on commercial fishing industries.

The OCS plan, which grew out of Reagan campaign pledges to speed up offshore leasing, was meant not only to increase U.S. domestic energy production, but also to raise revenue for the deficit-ridden federal government.

The administration by September 1982 was estimating fiscal 1983 revenues from such leasing at $15.33 billion, a figure revised downward from the estimate in Reagan's original 1983 budget. But the Congressional Budget Office and General Accounting Office said actual revenues were likely to be even lower.

The Outer Continental Shelf Lands Act Amendments of 1978 (PL 95-372) required the interior secretary to submit a proposed leasing plan to Congress at least 60 days before final issuance. This would give Congress a chance to comment on the plan and allow the secretary to accommodate congressional concerns before making the plan final. *(1978 Almanac p. 668)*

Watt's OCS plan was first proposed in April 1981. He submitted the proposal to Congress May 11, 1982, and he approved it July 21, 11 days after the 60-day period expired.

Too Much, Too Fast?

Critics of the leasing plan charged that the oil industry had neither the interest nor the ability to explore one billion acres over five years.

In the middle of a worldwide oil glut, exploratory drilling in 1982 was way down. A count by Hughes Tool Co. showed 2,600 onshore drilling rigs at work in the United States at midyear, compared to a record 4,530 in December 1981. That suggested oil companies either had all the oil they could handle, or were not making enough profit to search for more.

For offshore rigs, the picture was slightly different. The worldwide fleet of offshore rigs was stretched to its limits, with close to 100 percent in use, and was growing fast during 1980 and 1981. In 1982, the rate of use fell to 91 percent worldwide and 80 percent in the Gulf of Mexico.

Fair Market Value?

Watt said his plan "will enhance the national security, provide jobs, and protect the environment while making America less dependent on foreign oil sources."

"The market will select the lease tracts instead of the government," Watt said. "Fair market value will be set by competition, not solely on government economic models."

It was precisely the opposite — a lack of significant competition — that troubled some critics. In 13 recent sales, 58 percent of all OCS tracts leased received two or fewer bids, and 38 percent received only one bid, according to Interior.

Yet in 1982, with oil more plentiful than it had been for years, Watt sought to offer almost 40 times as much offshore acreage during the next five years as had been offered in the previous 28 years. Critics feared that the U.S. Treasury would not be getting its due.

In the 1978 OCS law, Congress required the Interior and Energy departments to seek "fair market value" for oil and gas leases.

Heretofore, Interior estimated a fair price for each tract offered. Under the new plan, it evaluated only tracts receiving bids and only about 35 percent of those.

Interior said this approach pared the unnecessary costs of pricing tracts that did not receive bids — historically, about half of those offered.

"I think it's going to hurt," says Michael Kavanaugh, director of research for Public Interest Economics, a non-profit research and public advocacy group. "The combination of accelerated leasing and very loose tract evaluation is going to cost the public billions of dollars in fiscal 1983."

Congressional Opposition

Watt's five-year plan prompted a July 9 letter of protest from three senators and 26 House members, including Speaker Thomas P. O'Neill Jr., D-Mass.

"The OCS plan you have endorsed ... consistently underestimates the potential for significant damage to the environment," the letter stated. "It precludes the appropriate and mandated participation of the states which will be directly affected by OCS leasing. It invites and unnecessarily encourages costly and time-consuming opposition by seeking to circumvent or ignore established procedures to bring about consensus on controversial points."

The letter was sparked by Edward J. Markey, D-Mass., chairman of the House Interior Subcommittee on Oversight and Investigations. Watt earlier declined to attend a June 14 hearing on his OCS plan held jointly by Markey's panel and the Interior Subcommittee on Mines and Mining, chaired by James D. Santini, D-Nev. Interior spokesmen said Watt was unable to attend the June 14 hearing because of scheduling conflicts. Subcommittee staff, however, said Watt was offered virtually any day during the 60-day comment period and "refused" to testify. ∎

Dam Safety Repair Bill Dies

Legislation to increase the authorization for safety repairs to 56 federally built dams died in the Senate when Congress adjourned.

The House passed a dam repair bill (HR 3208) April 29 after amending it on the floor, 212-140, to include administration-backed language that would have required local beneficiaries of federal dams to share in the cost of the repairs. *(Vote 53, p. 18-H)*

The Senate Energy and Natural Resources Committee reported its own version of the bill (S 956 — S Rept 97-533) on Aug. 19 — without the cost-sharing provision approved by the House. But the measure went no further.

Background

Both bills would have amended the 1978 Reclamation Safety of Dams Act (PL 95-578), which was enacted in the aftermath of the collapse of the Teton Dam in Idaho. *(1978 Almanac p. 723)*

HR 3208 and S 956 would have increased the existing $100 million authorization to $650 million — the minimum the Reagan administration said was needed to do the work.

In testimony Jan. 26 before the House Interior Committee's Water and Power Resources Subcommittee, Reclamation Commissioner Robert Broadbent said most of the dams in need of repair were built in the early 1900s in the 17 Western states served by the Interior Department's Bureau of Reclamation.

The repairs were needed because the dams were built before current earthquake and flood prediction techniques were developed.

"This committee cannot sit here and refuse to authorize money to fix dams the federal government built," said Rep. Don H. Clausen, R-Calif., ranking GOP member of the subcommittee. The repairs, he said, meant "life and death to thousands of Westerners who live downstream from federal dams."

Cost-Sharing

Administration officials urged both committees in both the House and Senate to amend HR 3208 and S 956 to require cost-sharing by those who benefited from the federally built dams covered by the legislation.

In an April 22, 1982, letter to Senate Energy Chairman James A. McClure, R-Idaho, David C. Russell, acting assistant interior secretary, said the administration "is committed to reducing the federal budget and believes that beneficiaries of federal projects should, in most cases, contribute to those projects."

Russell said the "long-range effects of correcting safety problems without cost sharing or reimbursement is to make all replacement of existing investment free to its users and beneficiaries, and place the total cost on the general taxpayer."

The administration urged adoption of an amendment allocating safety repair costs according to the various functions served by the dam — irrigation, hydroelectric power, municipal supply, recreation and other purposes. Costs allocated to irrigation would be reimbursable to the government by the user within 50 years of completion of work. No interest payment would be required, however, and payment would be waived if irrigators were unable to pay.

Municipal, industrial and commercial power users, as well as recreation and fish and wildlife projects, would be required to pay back their share of costs over 50 years with interest.

This proposal would put repayment of dam safety costs on the same footing as original construction costs for reclamation projects under existing law.

Previous administrations likewise asked Congress to require more cost-sharing by irrigators, but Congress rejected the idea five times.

Current law required that those who benefited from the dams pay only for repairs that resulted from normal wear and tear or improper operation and maintenance — not for structural deficiencies.

House Action

The House Interior and Insular Affairs Committee approved HR 3208 March 24 and reported it April 1 (H Rept 97-478).

As introduced, the bill would have increased the spending ceiling from $100 million to $450 million. The bill was amended in the Water and Power Resources Subcommittee to authorize up to $650 million.

The House passed the measure April 29 by a vote of 335-9. *(Vote 54, p. 18-H)*

Before passing the bill, the House adopted an amendment sponsored by Rep. Gerald B. H. Solomon, R-N.Y., and backed by the Reagan administration requiring those who benefited from federal irrigation dams to share in the cost of the repairs.

In the past, Congress repeatedly turned down such cost-sharing proposals in connection with dam repairs. But in the current climate of concern over budget deficits, Solomon's amendment was adopted by a 212-140 margin. *(Vote 53, p. 18-H)*

Senate Committee Action

Before approving S 956 Aug. 18, the Senate Energy Committee amended it to authorize replacement instead of repair of an existing dam if that was the most cost-effective method of alleviating safety hazards.

A second committee amendment authorized safety modifications of nine dams that had been included in reclamation projects by various laws passed by Congress but were not owned by the federal government.

As approved by the Senate committee, the bill did not include cost-recovery provisions sought by the administration and adopted by the House. Instead, it left unchanged current requirements that irrigators and others who benefited from the dams pay only for repairs necessitated by normal wear and tear or improper operation and maintenance — not for structural deficiencies. ∎

Oil Spill Liability Limits

The House Dec. 13 suspended the rules and passed by voice vote a bill (HR 5906) clarifying limits on liability for oil spills from offshore drilling. However, the Senate failed to act on the measure.

HR 5906 amended Title III of the Outer Continental Shelf Lands Act Amendments of 1978 (PL 95-372), which set up an Offshore Oil Pollution Compensation Fund financed by a tax on offshore oil. Persons economically damaged by offshore spills could make claims against the fund, which in turn could sue those responsible for the spill. *(Background, 1978 Almanac p. 670)*

The 1978 law set a $35 million limit on damages that could be obtained from operators of offshore oil rigs, but left them with unlimited liability for the costs of cleaning up the spills.

The House bill changed that to a total liability limit of $75 million for both damages and cleanup costs.

"The inclusion of both cleanup and damage costs within the liability limit will provide industry with a greater degree of certainty about the upper limit of costs which it will be called on to bear in the event of a major pollution incident," said Gerry E. Studds, D-Mass., chairman of the House Merchant Marine and Fisheries Subcommittee on Coast Guard and Navigation.

The bill also sought to spell out clearly who was financially responsible for damage and cleanup costs in oil spills from offshore rigs: leaseholders, holders of exploratory drilling permits, drillers, owners and operators of pipelines and vessels, or other parties. The present law had been interpreted by the U.S. Coast Guard, which enforced it, as holding drilling contractors responsible and leaseholders free from liability.

The amended bill imposed a general liability on the

leaseholder for any spill coming from his lease. But it also spelled out conditions under which others involved in the operation would be liable and the limits on their liability.

For example, drilling contractors would be liable for spills originating on or above the water surface — up to $250,000 or $300 per gross ton of drilling equipment, whichever was greater. That amount would range from $4.5 million to $10.5 million for most drillers. Similar provisions applied to other parties. Beyond that limit, the leaseholder would be liable for remaining costs up to the $75 million cap.

The bill also allowed those involved in a drilling operation to obtain "hold harmless" and indemnity agreements from other parties.

"This provision does not allow responsible parties to escape liability," said John B. Breaux, D-La. "It does allow, however, parties operating on the outer continental shelf to decide among themsleves the issue of who will ultimately pay cleanup or damage costs in the event a polluting event occurs."

The House Merchant Marine Committee had approved the bill by voice vote Aug. 3 and reported it (H Rept 97-861) on Sept. 23.

There was no comparable bill in the Senate, which took no action on HR 5906 in the waning days of the 1982 session. ∎

Gorsuch Cited for Contempt of Congress

The House Dec. 16 voted to hold Anne M. Gorsuch, administrator of the Environmental Protection Agency (EPA), in contempt of Congress for refusing, on President Reagan's orders, to turn over documents sought by two House panels.

The action came on a 259-105 vote. Gorsuch was the first Cabinet-level federal official ever cited for contempt of Congress. *(Vote 444, p. 130-H)*

Earlier in the year, Reagan March 28 averted a threatened House contempt citation of Interior Secretary James G. Watt when he sent to Capitol Hill certain papers Watt had refused to give the House Energy and Commerce Committee. But negotiations that continued up to the House contempt vote failed to resolve the Gorsuch case. *(Watt confrontation, p. 454)*

The Gorsuch contempt citation grew out of efforts of the House Public Works Committee and the House Energy and Commerce oversight subcommittee to obtain documents on EPA's enforcement of the 1980 "superfund" hazardous waste cleanup law. *(Superfund, 1980 Almanac p. 584)*

Justice Refuses to Prosecute

The Justice Department, which normally would be responsible for prosecuting the charge, immediately filed a civil suit in U.S. District Court in Washington, D.C., seeking to block any further action on the contempt citation. Department officials said Dec. 17 that they expected the civil suit to forestall any prosecution.

In its suit, the department argued that production of the documents sought by the House would "unconstitutionally contravene" the privilege of the executive branch to "ensure the confidentiality of its law enforcement files and its deliberative process."

Lawyers for the House Dec. 30 asked the court to dismiss the Justice Department suit. While acknowledging that the contempt charge raised some major constitutional issues, they said the Justice Department suit was so flawed the court should throw it out without addressing those issues. House lawyers said Gorsuch could raise any constitutional claims of executive privilege in the context of criminal proceedings on the contempt charge.

Impeachment Threat

The Justice Department's refusal to prosecute the contempt citation prompted Rep. Elliott H. Levitas, D-Ga., chairman of the House Public Works subcommittee that originated the contempt move, to call Dec. 20 for a Judiciary Committee inquiry into whether there were grounds for impeachment of Attorney General William French Smith. No such inquiry was scheduled by year's end.

Levitas said Smith had "failed to faithfully execute the law and is engaging, in my judgment, in an obstruction of justice."

Levitas and other House members said that under the law, once the Speaker of the House certified a contempt citation, it was the "duty" of the appropriate U.S. attorney "to bring the matter before the grand jury for its action."

Justice officials saw it differently. They said asking the courts to decide an important constitutional question was a reasonable way to settle it, not an impeachable offense.

In a Dec. 29 letter to Judiciary Chairman Peter W. Rodino Jr., D-N.J., Levitas said, "the question also arises whether a special prosecutor should be appointed" to prosecute the contempt charge against Gorsuch.

Congress Dec. 16 cleared and President Reagan Jan. 3, 1983, signed into law a reauthorization (S 2059 — PL 97-409) of the post-Watergate special prosecutor law that, among other provisions, allowed the attorney general to seek appointment of a special prosecutor if investigation by Justice Department officials might involve a political conflict of interest. *(Special prosecutor bill, p. 386)*

Levitas enclosed a Dec. 27 letter to House Speaker Thomas P. O'Neill Jr., D-Mass., from Stanley S. Harris, U.S. attorney for the District of Columbia, in which Harris noted that he was responsible for prosecuting all civil suits in his jurisdiction and all federal criminal offenses — meaning both the Justice Department suit seeking to block the contempt citation and the contempt charge itself.

"The U.S. attorney's letter clearly spells out his conflict of interest," Levitas said in his letter to Rodino.

Background

The House vote to cite Gorsuch for contempt of Congress arose out of basic questions about how well the Reagan administration was enforcing hazardous waste laws.

The contempt citation was based upon Gorsuch's refusal to comply with a subpoena covering virtually every document EPA had on 160 hazardous waste sites given early priority for cleanup under the 1980 "superfund" law. *(Superfund law, 1980 Almanac p. 584)*

Gorsuch said that amounted to about 787,000 pages, of which she had withheld only 74 documents. Levitas said it was the withheld documents his subcommittee was interested in.

Executive Privilege, Contempt of Congress

The clash between Congress and Anne M. Gorsuch, head of the Environmental Protection Agency (EPA), over EPA enforcement documents posed the first major test of "executive privilege" since President Nixon tried to withhold White House tapes from Watergate prosecutors.

Nixon was unsuccessful, as a unanimous Supreme Court in July 1974 ruled that his claim of executive privilege must yield to the ongoing criminal prosecution of Watergate defendants. *(1974 Almanac p. 879)*

The Gorsuch case involved the same sort of legal issue that existed in the Nixon case — defining the limits of executive privilege when that doctrine collided with the interests of another branch of government.

There were some important differences between the cases, however. In the Nixon matter, the dispute was between a president protecting his own private communications and the judicial system.

In the Gorsuch case, the clash did not involve personal, presidential communications but rather an agency within the executive branch trying to keep certain documents from the legislative branch. Congressional staffers working on the case resisted the notion that executive privilege was involved at all.

The House Dec. 16 voted Gorsuch in contempt of Congress for refusing to give a House Public Works and Transportation subcommittee documents relating to the enforcement of the $1.6 billion "superfund" law designed to pay for the cleanup of abandoned hazardous waste dumps.

Gorsuch said she acted on written orders from President Reagan, dated Nov. 30, in which he instructed her to withhold certain documents because their dissemination outside the executive branch "would impair my solemn responsibility to enforce the law."

The White House contended some of the documents subpoenaed by the House Public Works oversight subcommittee concerned potential litigation and could jeopardize enforcement of the superfund law.

Executive Privilege

In addition to helping refine the limits of executive privilege, the Gorsuch case offered a new opportunity for defining the scope of congressional contempt authority. The case marked the first time a person was held in contempt of Congress for refusing to produce information because of executive privilege.

Most prior contempt cases involved private persons who refused to testify or produce documents based on other reasons, such as the Constitution's Fifth Amendment privilege against self-incrimination.

Although the House transmitted its contempt citation to the Justice Department for prosecution, the department immediately said it would not prosecute. Instead, it filed a lawsuit Dec. 16 challenging the constitutionality of the subpoena.

A major element of the department's case rested on the Nixon tapes decision. While the Supreme Court ordered Nixon to turn over the White House tapes, the justices did find a constitutional underpinning for the

concept of "presidential" privilege. But the privilege, they indicated, is not absolute.

Writing for the court, Chief Justice Warren E. Burger said, "Nowhere in the Constitution . . . is there any explicit reference to a privilege of confidentiality, yet to the extent this interest relates to the effective discharge of a President's powers, it is constitutionally based."

Nixon lost his case because the court determined that the interests of the ongoing Watergate trial outweighed the president's "generalized interest in confidentiality" of his communications.

In the Gorsuch case, the Justice Department based Reagan's arguments on a claim that the Constitution implied a privilege of the executive to ensure the confidentiality of law enforcement files and of the process of policy deliberation.

The claim of executive privilege dated back to 1792, when President George Washington said he had the authority to decide what documents should be given to Congress concerning an army defeat in the Northwest Territory.

As it turned out, none of the papers concerning the army's devastating loss was deemed confidential, but most researchers nonetheless considered the clash to mark the first claim of executive privilege.

According to a Justice Department memo released after the Gorsuch contempt proceedings, presidents had relied on executive privilege 64 times.

Between the Nixon tapes case and the Gorsuch contempt citation, there had been only two instances of presidents seeking to withhold documents from Congress. During the Carter administration, a House subcommittee sought documents concerning executive branch deliberations on President Carter's decision to impose a conservation fee on imports of crude oil and gasoline. Ultimately, some — but not all — of the documents were given to the subcommittee, and the panel did not pursue documents that directly involved deliberations with the president.

In 1981, Reagan ordered Interior Secretary James G. Watt to withhold documents sought by a subcommittee concerning Canadian reciprocity under a mineral leasing law. After months of negotiations — which included a recommended contempt citation against Watt — the matter was resolved March 18, 1982, when members were allowed access to certain documents for one day. *(Watt confrontation, p. 454)*

Congressional Contempt Power

The congressional contempt power had almost as long a history as the doctrine of executive privilege. *(CQ Guide to Congress 3rd Edition, p. 163)*

In 1821 the Supreme Court held that the power of contempt was inherent under the Constitution. Without it, the court said, Congress was "exposed to every indignity and interruption that rudeness, caprice or even conspiracy may meditate against it." In decisions since then, however, the court imposed certain limits on the contempt power, basically to protect witnesses from unwarranted punishment at the hands of Congress.

The Justice Department claimed that the withheld documents included "sensitive memoranda or notes by EPA attorneys and investigators reflecting enforcement strategy, legal analysis, lists of potential witnesses, settlement considerations and similar materials the disclosure of which might adversely affect a pending enforcement action, overall enforcement policy or the rights of individuals."

RCRA and Superfund

The confrontation with Gorsuch had been building since spring, when some members of Congress began questioning EPA's enforcement of the nation's hazardous waste laws. There were two major hazardous waste laws. The first, the 1976 Resource Conservation and Recovery Act (RCRA — PL 94-580), dealt with the disposal of both solid and hazardous wastes. *(1976 Almanac p. 199)*

The House Sept. 8 passed a bill (HR 6307) to reauthorize and strengthen RCRA. But the Senate Environment and Public Works Committee was unable to reach agreement on that bill or a companion measure, S 2432, and the legislation died when Congress adjourned Dec. 23. *(RCRA, p. 456)*

The other major hazardous waste law, the Comprehensive Environmental Response, Liability and Compensation Act of 1980 (PL 96-510), created a $1.6 billion "superfund" to pay for cleanup of abandoned hazardous waste dumps. Congress had struggled to draft such legislation since shortly after the 1977 Love Canal discovery near Niagara Falls, N.Y.

Some 86 percent of the fund came from a tax on the chemical and oil industries, while the rest came from congressional appropriations. Congress had to appropriate the money to EPA after it came into the fund.

The fund was meant to pay for immediate cleanup of dump sites, avoiding time-consuming lawsuits over who was responsible for them. The law also contained liability provisions under which the government could recover the cleanup costs and collect damages from dumpers.

Enforcement Questioned

Because the superfund law was not passed until Dec. 3, 1980, the Reagan administration was the first to implement the measure.

Under the law, EPA was supposed to draw up a list of priority cleanup sites by July 1981 and to update that list at least annually.

The agency first put together an interim list of 115 sites in October 1981. It added 45 more in July 1982, and on Dec. 20, four days after the contempt citation, EPA released a proposed list of the 418 dump sites it considered most dangerous to public health. They received top priority in the superfund program and were to be eligible for federal cleanup funds as soon as final rule-making was completed after a two-month comment period. Gorsuch called the list a sign of the agency's progress in enforcing the law.

But congressional critics such as Rep. James J. Florio, D-N.J., said that compiling a list was no substitute for cleanup action. And they charged that under the law, the final list was actually due more than a year earlier.

"Serious questions have been raised by my committee and others regarding the integrity of several superfund site settlements and negotiations with private parties," Florio said during the contempt proceedings against Gorsuch.

Florio also said that through fiscal 1982, the superfund "had accumulated an unexpended balance of $364 million, while only $88 million had been expended on site cleanup and related work." Florio charged that EPA had completed cleanups on only three sites of the 160 first listed as priority sites.

EPA officials, however, put the number of finished cleanups at five. They said state-EPA agreements had been worked out on 112 sites, funding begun for feasibility and engineering studies at 70 sites, and actual physical cleanup commenced at 21 sites (not counting those completed). Actual cleanup, they said, could take up to three years.

EPA also took issue with Florio's spending figures, saying Congress had appropriated a total of $265 million to EPA from the fund, and that EPA had spent $221 million of that, or 83 percent.

Florio asserted that the Reagan administration had dramatically slowed legal enforcement of hazardous waste laws. He said that from fiscal 1980 to 1981, referrals of civil hazardous waste cases from EPA to the Justice Department for prosecution dropped from 46 cases to eight. That included cases under both the superfund law and RCRA.

EPA said it reached settlements in the cases of 39 sites with private parties numbering in the hundreds — whose contributions saved the fund $121 million in cleanup costs. EPA said 43 superfund cases had been referred to the Justice Department for enforcement action.

Florio's charges echoed those in a report (H Rept 97-968) filed by the House Public Works and Transportation Committee, which recommended the Gorsuch contempt citation.

"Our preliminary finding suggests that many hazardous waste sites are not being fully cleaned up, that chemical companies responsible for cleanup costs are not being held liable for their full share of the cleanup costs in every instance," said Levitas, chairman of that panel's Subcommittee on Investigations and Oversight.

"We have got to find out whether sweetheart deals are being made in the settlement of cases," Levitas said.

One example of the kind of information sought by the committee was an undated draft memo from James D. Bunting, acting deputy associate EPA enforcement counsel, about the settlement of a case against the Inmont Corp., a paint manufacturer EPA wanted to pay for cleanup of a dump site in Santa Fe Springs, Calif.

EPA delivered the memo to the House Energy and Commerce Subcommittee on Oversight and Investigations for an April 2 hearing, but later refused to turn over the document to the Public Works panel because it was "enforcement sensitive."

Thornton Field, a former Gorsuch special assistant currently with EPA's Office of Legal and Enforcement Counsel, acknowledged in the hearing that he had told Inmont that EPA was willing to settle for $700,000, which was $150,000 less than EPA's negotiating position at the time. The agency finally settled for $700,000, according to testimony.

House Action

Committee Vote

The House Public Works Subcommittee on Investigations and Oversight voted 9-2 Dec. 2 to cite Gorsuch for contempt for failing to comply with a subpoena served upon her Nov. 22. The full House Public Works and Transportation Committee followed suit Dec. 10, voting 28-11 to recommend that the House adopt the contempt citation.

The committee vote was along party lines, with 27 Democrats voting for the contempt citation and 11 Repub-

Watt Contempt Vote Averted

President Reagan sent a batch of closely held presidential papers to the Capitol March 18, thus avoiding a House vote on whether to hold his interior secretary, James G. Watt, in contempt of Congress.

Members of the House Energy and Commerce Subcommittee on Oversight and Investigations were given four hours to peruse seven documents concerning the Cabinet's consideration of the effect of Canadian energy policy on U.S. companies.

The documents had been subpoenaed by the subcommittee in 1981. After Reagan invoked executive privilege and refused to let Watt comply with the subpoena, the Energy and Commerce Committee voted Feb. 25 to hold Watt in contempt.

If the full House had approved the contempt resolution, Watt could have faced trial and, if convicted, imprisonment for up to a year.

The House had never voted a Cabinet officer in contempt.

But on Dec. 16, it found Anne M. Gorsuch, administrator of the Environmental Protection Agency, in contempt for refusing — on Reagan's orders — to turn over documents regarding her agency's enforcement of a 1980 law on cleanup of hazardous waste dumps.

To avoid the confrontation with Watt, Chairman John D. Dingell, D-Mich., proposed that committee members and staff be allowed to review the papers in question for eight hours. The White House offered a compromise, which was accepted: four hours' review, for members only.

Six of the Oversight subcommittee's 17 members — four Democrats and two Republicans — showed up to read the papers March 18. Some, including Dingell, took detailed notes; they were not allowed to make photocopies. A White House aide and a Capitol policeman made sure no one else read the papers.

Dingell aides said the arrangement sustained the right of Congress to see presidential documents.

Background

The dispute with Watt arose in July 1981 when the Energy and Commerce Subcommittee on Oversight and Investigations began looking into charges that some Canadian companies were using unfair advantages under Canadian law to try to acquire American energy firms, including St. Joe Minerals Corp., Conoco Inc. and Cities Service Co.

In August, the panel asked Watt for Interior Department documents dealing with whether Canada was still entitled to reciprocal status under laws governing the leasing of mineral rights on federal lands.

Watt refused to provide some of the documents, and the subcommittee voted in September to subpoena them.

Claiming executive privilege for the first time, Reagan said in October that the documents, which included material prepared for the Cabinet and State Department cables from Canada, would not be provided.

Early in February, Watt decided Canada was entitled to reciprocal status, which allowed Canadian firms to produce minerals on U.S. government-owned lands. Such status was supposed to be denied to countries that did not provide similar rights to U.S. companies.

Committee Action

The subcommittee voted 11-6 Feb. 9 to hold Watt in contempt. Marc L. Marks, R-Pa., the senior Republican on the panel, joined the 10 Democrats in voting for the contempt citation.

The full Energy and Commerce Committee followed suit Feb. 25.

The committee split 23-19 along party lines, with Democrats generally seeking to punish Watt and Republicans supporting him. Marks again was the only Republican to vote with the Democrats against the White House. Two Texas Democrats — Phil Gramm and Ralph M. Hall — voted with the Republicans against the resolution.

Committee Chairman John D. Dingell, D-Mich., who also chaired the subcommittee, said the committee had "bent over backwards" trying to reach an agreement with the White House on the papers. "We extended offers at every opportunity to meet the legitimate needs of each separate and co-equal branch of the government," he said, but "our good-faith efforts have been met with a combination of benign neglect and bureaucratic puffery."

Dingell said White House counsel Fred F. Fielding had offered to discuss the papers with him and the committee's ranking Republican, James T. Broyhill, N.C.

But Dingell refused because, he said, all members of the committee should be entitled to the material. Dingell offered to accept the documents in closed session and not release them to the public without a vote, but the White House refused.

Broyhill said the administration had provided "95 percent" of the papers requested and defended Reagan's right to withhold the rest. He offered a motion to allow the committee to sue the president for the documents in federal court, but Dingell ruled the motion was not germane.

Marks tried to convince his fellow Republicans that the contempt proceeding was not a partisan issue. He suggested the White House might be preventing Watt from turning over the material as a way to "dump" him. But James M. Collins, R-Texas, insisted it was a partisan issue. "Let's be clear about that," he said. "This committee is trying to embarrass the president of the United States."

Collins claimed the Democrats had not cited Carter administration officials for similar refusals to provide material. But Albert Gore Jr., D-Tenn., reminded Collins that the same subcommittee had voted to hold Carter's secretary of health, education and welfare, Joseph A. Califano Jr., in contempt in 1978, when Collins was the senior Republican on the subcommittee.

licans voting against it. The only Republican defector was Guy V. Molinari, R-N.Y., who voted "aye." Five Republicans voted "present."

In its report (H Rept 97-968), the Public Works Committee noted the subpoena was issued as part of the subcommittee's oversight investigation of EPA's enforcement of the superfund law. "Refusal to provide the subpoenaed documents has prevented the subcommittee from obtaining information necessary to the discharge of its responsibilities and duties," the committee report said.

House Floor Debate

The House vote Dec. 16 was preceded by a relatively brief but sometimes heated debate.

James J. Howard, D-N.J., chairman of the Public Works Committee, said his panel had tried but failed to avoid the confrontation through a negotiated settlement. Indeed, efforts continued up until moments before the vote.

Gerald B.H. Solomon, R-N.Y., said the contempt move "fails to recognize that EPA has agreed to turn over to the subcommittee a substantial amount of information" and that Gorsuch was withholding the remaining documents on direct orders of the president.

"The legal issues involved in this matter are extremely complex and should have been analyzed more carefully," Solomon said.

Mike Synar, D-Okla., said that if the House voted down the contempt citation, "we will effectively be letting this administration — and all future administrations — know that we will allow them to pick and choose what information will be provided to Congress. More important, we will be allowing any executive branch agency to throw the enforcement-sensitive cloak over virtually any information."

The Legal Battle

In asking the court to dismiss the Justice Department's suit, the House asserted that under the Constitution, members of Congress could not be sued for legislative actions.

"It is beyond doubt that voting, reporting and debating or anything done in the chamber or committee cannot serve as a basis for suit," the House motion said.

It further argued that the executive branch had no standing to sue, partly because it had not yet been injured. And the House lawyers said that the department's suit in the name of the "United States of America" as sovereign against the "House of Representatives of the United States" created a legal absurdity — because it amounted to the plaintiff suing itself. No single branch of government had a right to lay claim to the name "United States of America," the House contended.

On Dec. 29, the day before the House motion to dismiss was filed, the Justice Department filed an amended complaint, a rewrite of its original suit that appeared to anticipate some of the legal arguments raised by the House.

Justice added Gorsuch as a plaintiff, along with language claiming Congress "injured" the plaintiffs by "impairing their ability to meet their obligation to execute the laws of the United States faithfully," by impeding their exercise of constitutional powers and "by damaging their reputation for obedience to the rule of law."

Justice dropped its request for an injunction to keep Congress from further efforts to enforce its outstanding subpoena, asking only for a declaration by the courts that Gorsuch either had complied with the subpoena — or that, if she had not, her non-compliance was lawful.

The department based its case on a claim that the Constitution implied a privilege of the executive to ensure the confidentiality of law enforcement files and of the policy deliberation process.

Reagan, in a Nov. 30 communication to Gorsuch, wrote:

"Because dissemination of such documents outside the executive branch would impair my solemn responsibility to enforce the law, I instruct you and your agency not to furnish copies of this category of documents to the subcommittees in response to the subpoenas."

The Dec. 30 House motion called the Justice Department civil suit an "impermissible usurpation of the legislative function." The House said the suit was an "attempt to erect law by executive fiat, substituting *ad hoc* civil review for the duly enacted statutory and judicially approved provisions" of the criminal contempt statute.

Confidentiality: Who Decides?

Another separation-of-powers issue that arose in the dispute concerned the question of who had ultimate authority to declare specific documents sensitive and off-limits to public disclosure.

What really sparked the whole dispute, according to the House committee report, was an EPA decision in September that committee investigators could not have access to EPA enforcement files unless those files had been "pre-screened" by EPA officials. Taking the position that disclosure to Congress could be tantamount to public disclosure, the agency asserted that its duty was to make a decision on each document before disclosing it to Congress.

The Justice Department argued it had a duty to protect the confidentiality of open law enforcement files. Such files could contain unsubstantiated allegations of wrongdoing against individuals, and their disclosure could harm the reputations of those individuals and jeopardize government sources of information, the department said.

Moreover, the department said, disclosure before allegations were substantiated could jeopardize the success of any eventual prosecution — by warning a wrongdoer of any investigation under way or by subjecting investigators to congressional pressure.

In an Oct. 25 letter to John D. Dingell, D-Mich., chairman of the House Energy and Commerce Committee, EPA went even further, noting that some of the companies accused of hazardous waste dumping were located in the districts of members of the Energy subcommittee that was also looking into enforcement of the superfund law.

"Potential defendants could gain access to sensitive prosecutorial documents through their elected representatives," the EPA letter to Dingell said.

Albert Gore Jr., D-Tenn., called that statement "an insult to the Congress." Norman Y. Mineta, D-Calif., said Congress had for years kept secret Central Intelligence Agency documents that it needed to see.

House lawyers, while admitting some need for confidentiality, said it was up to Congress to provide such protection.

"It is our responsibility to discipline our members if they act improperly," said Bill Green, R-N.Y., referring to the possiblity of leaks. "I do not think the executive branch can deny us documents on the assumption that our members will act improperly." ∎

RCRA Reauthorization Dies

The House Sept. 8 passed a bill (HR 6307) to reauthorize and tighten the nation's principal law governing the management and disposal of hazardous wastes, but the measure died in the Senate.

The Senate Environment and Public Works Committee on May 27 formally reported a more modest reauthorization bill (S 2432 — S Rept 97-445), but the full Senate never acted.

The 317-32 House vote came after members turned aside all efforts to weaken the bill. *(Vote 295, p. 88-H)*

Background

Much of the impetus for the House bill came from members' concern that the Reagan administration was not vigorously enforcing hazardous waste disposal laws. It was this concern, in fact, that led to the Dec. 16 contempt of Congress citation voted by the House against Environmental Protection Agency (EPA) Administrator Anne M. Gorsuch. *(Story, p. 451)*

The Resource Conservation and Recovery Act (RCRA, PL 94-580) was enacted as an amendment to the 1965 Solid Waste Disposal Act. It was the basis for management of the nation's hazardous waste and for encouraging conservation and recovery of valuable materials and energy from solid wastes. *(1976 Almanac p. 199)*

Although the law sailed through Congress with little opposition in 1976, there had been growing controversy since then over EPA's efforts to enforce sections of the legislation designed to provide "cradle-to-grave" regulation of the generation, transportation, treatment, storage and disposal of hazardous wastes.

The agency did not issue its first major package of hazardous waste regulations until May 1980, and it had barely begun to implement them before the Reagan administration took office. Since then, EPA was hit with severe budget reductions and progress on several programs slowed accordingly.

According to the House Energy Committee report on HR 6307 (H Rept 97-570), final permits had been issued for only two of the nation's 9,980 waste treatment, storage or disposal facilities that were in existence prior to Nov. 19, 1980.

In addition, EPA under Reagan suspended several key regulations. Although vehement protests from the public and members of Congress persuaded EPA to reinstate in March a ban that it lifted in February on the disposal of containerized liquid wastes in unlined landfills, the agency still sought to allow 25 percent of future landfill capacity to be reserved for such containerized wastes.

In the past, barrels of dangerous chemicals were buried at conventional landfills. But after several years the drums could disintegrate, and unless the landfills were lined with an impermeable material, the chemicals could leak into nearby water supplies, as occurred in 1977 at the Love Canal neighborhood in Niagara Falls, N.Y.

The disposal ban, which went into effect in November 1981, was part of the "interim" standards for toxic waste disposal set under RCRA while EPA developed permanent standards.

EPA announced Feb. 25 that it was suspending the ban for 90 days, while comments were received on a new proposal — developed with the help of the Chemical Manufacturers Association — to allow up to 25 percent of a landfill's capacity to be used for hazardous liquids.

The Hazardous Waste Treatment Council and the Environmental Defense Fund promptly asked the U.S. District Court in Washington, D.C., to order EPA to restore the ban.

Several members of the House also denounced the proposal. Rep. Elliott H. Levitas, D-Ga., chairman of the House Public Works Committee's Oversight and Investigations Subcommittee, convened an oversight hearing March 10 to grill EPA on why the ban was lifted.

"It would appear that the very type of control that would preclude the occurrence of future 'Love Canals' has been abandoned by the agency that is supposed to protect our waters," Levitas said.

At a public hearing March 11, Rep. Guy V. Molinari, R-N.Y., called the action "the equivalent of opening all jails for a period of 90 days, to determine if the criminals within could possibly pose a threat to the public on the outside."

In the face of such negative reaction, EPA retreated, announcing March 17 that it was reinstating the ban on disposal of containers with "free-standing" liquid visible inside.

Environmentalists and state hazardous waste control officials still planned to fight the proposal to allow 25 percent of a landfill to be used for hazardous waste disposal.

EPA also stirred controversy when it suspended a requirement that the nation's 50,000 to 60,000 hazardous waste producers file annual statements with the government explaining how they had disposed of their wastes. The reporting requirement was part of the "cradle-to-grave" monitoring of hazardous wastes mandated by Congress in 1976 when it passed RCRA.

EPA said instead of requiring the voluminous paperwork, it would send questionnaires to 10 percent of the companies to ask if they were complying with the law.

An EPA spokesman said that the random samples would be a more cost-effective and efficient way of collecting the information, but he admitted that there would be no way to verify the accuracy of the information because no on-site inspections would be made.

Environmental groups complained that abolishing the individual company reports would eliminate important tools for private citizens wanting to know what local manufacturers were doing with their toxic wastes.

House Committee Action

HR 6307 was approved May 11 by the House Committee on Energy and Commerce and reported May 18 (H Rept 97-570).

Although the bill was approved by voice vote, 11 of the committee's 18 Republicans, led by ranking GOP member James T. Broyhill, N.C., published dissenting or minority views on various sections of the measure.

Major Provisions

As approved by the Energy Committee, the bill authorized appropriations of $108.5 million in fiscal year 1983 and $111.5 million in fiscal 1984. The total was more than $30 million above the Reagan administration's request for RCRA.

The bill gave EPA four years either to issue permits for hazardous-waste land disposal facilities or shut them

down, and six years to issue or deny permits for other types of facilities.

It extended the law's coverage to many generators of small quantities of hazardous waste exempt from RCRA under existing law.

And it banned within 12 to 18 months the injection of liquid hazardous wastes into or above an underground source of drinking water. It gave EPA one year to issue regulations to minimize placement of hazardous liquid wastes into sanitary landfills.

Second Committee Referral

The Energy Committee had primary responsibility for the bill, which was introduced by Reps. James J. Florio, D-N.J., and Norman F. Lent, R-N.Y., but it was subsequently referred to the House Public Works and Transportation Committee for consideration of the water-related sections.

That committee approved the measure June 9 after amending it to enlarge the membership of a proposed National Groundwater Commission to study groundwater contamination.

House Floor Action

Closing Loopholes

During House floor debate, Florio said HR 6307 closed "several major loopholes in RCRA coverage which allow as much hazardous waste to escape regulation as is covered by RCRA controls."

The most controversial of those "loopholes" was the current exemption for businesses that generate, store or transport only small quantities of hazardous wastes — defined as less than 1,000 kilograms (kg) per month. The bill as passed by the House exempted only those handling no more than 100 kg per month.

Phil Gramm, D-Texas, contended the lower cutoff would load small businesses with "mountains of paperwork" for little demonstrable environmental benefit. He cited an Aug. 1 letter from EPA Administrator Gorsuch supporting his position.

While Gramm pointed to a recent EPA study concluding that RCRA-exempt small sources generated less than 1 percent of all hazardous waste, Florio cited two other studies saying the figure was closer to 8 percent.

The small-quantities provision would affect gas stations, dry cleaners and even schools. Florio noted that 20 states had already made their own laws tighter than RCRA in this regard, and he said that his compromise included provisions meant to ease the paperwork burden for small-quantity waste generators.

Also controversial was a provision in the committee substitute spelling out the right of an injured party to sue in court under state and federal common law for relief of problems caused by hazardous waste.

Dannemeyer unsuccessfully sought to strike this provision, saying plaintiffs should be limited to suing under RCRA so that businesses and municipalities knew exactly what set of rules to follow. It was unfair to subject them to the uncertainty of common law, he argued.

Florio and his allies, however, said federal common law remedies were needed in cases where EPA had not yet issued rules and where interstate lawsuits arose that were not covered under state law. He noted that the National Association of Attorneys General supported the language in the committee substitute.

Amendments Rejected

By a 148-183 vote, members rejected an amendment offered by Gramm that would have deleted provisions in the bill that for the first time extended the law's regulations to small-quantity generators of hazardous wastes. *(Vote 293, p. 88-H)*

Also rejected, 85-255, was an amendment by Dannemeyer that would have restricted to the provisions of RCRA itself the right of citizens to file lawsuits involving hazardous wastes. *(Vote 294, p. 88-H)*

Senate Committee Action

The Senate Environment and Public Works Committee May 27 reported its own RCRA reauthorization bill (S 2432 — S Rept 97-445).

The measure, which made little change from existing law, authorized funding at a level of $88.6 million annually for fiscal 1983 and 1984.

It also called for a National Academy of Sciences study on the threats of hazardous waste to humans, the environment and to groundwater.

Under HR 6307, EPA was given four years either to issue permits for hazardous-waste land disposal facilities or close them down, and six years to issue or deny permits for other types of disposal facility.

Although the Senate committee report said EPA's "permitting process is proceeding at much too slow a pace," S 2432 did not attempt to write deadlines into the law.

Although the issue of small-quantity waste generators was discussed by the Senate committee, it was not addressed in S 2432.

Even though the Senate bill made no change in existing law apart from authorizing a National Academy of Sciences study, Environment Committee members made clear in their report that they were not satisfied with EPA's implementation of RCRA.

"Uncertainties and delays in the agency's regulatory development efforts have resulted in far less progress than the Congress anticipated in developing a nationwide program to regulate hazardous waste management practices ... from the time waste is generated until final disposal.

"The agency is urged to take the steps necessary to expedite the development and promulgation of all the necessary standards and regulations for the safe handling and disposal of hazardous wastes to ensure that the public health and welfare are adequately protected," the report said.   ∎

National Park Visitor Facilities

The Senate Dec. 21 cleared for President Reagan a bill (HR 7316 — PL 97-433) to set up a fund blending public and private sector money to finance repair of National Park Service visitor facilities.

Final action came when the Senate by voice vote accepted the bill as passed by the House Dec. 10.

Before passing the bill by voice vote, the House had adopted a substitute amendment approved Dec. 8 by the House Interior and Insular Affairs Committee (H Rept 97-953). The amendment made the House bill identical to legislation (S 2715) approved Dec. 7 by the Senate Energy and Commerce Committee.

As cleared, HR 7316 established a special fund for the

repair, renovation or replacement of visitor facilities in the national parks.

The bill set aside fees paid by national park concession-holders for use in the upkeep of food and lodging facilities owned by the federal government.

HR 7316 applied to more than 1,000 buildings owned by the federal government in national parks, including cabins, small motels, lodges, restaurants, utility buildings and employee dormitories used to support those facilities.

Many of the buildings were old and run down. But Director Russell E. Dickenson told the House committee the National Park Service had to focus available rehabilitation funds on "life safety problems" in larger park hotels and motels.

The National Park System Visitor Facilities Fund set up under HR 7316 would go toward "reconstruction, rehabilitation, replacement, improvement, relocation, or removal" of the smaller facilities that tended to fall to the bottom of Park Service priority lists.

Fees, Matching Grants

The fund was to consist primarily of franchise fees and building user fees paid to the Park Service by concession holders. According to Dickenson, those fees currently produced total revenue of about $5.2 million per year.

The bill also authorized annual appropriations to the fund of up to $1 million, which could be spent only to the extent that the money was matched dollar-for-dollar by cash or in-kind contributions from the private sector.

Work under the visitor facilities fund was to be carried out by the National Park Foundation, a federally chartered, quasi-private, tax-exempt organization authorized by Congress in 1967 to accept gifts for the benefit of the National Park System.

While parks affected by the program were spread out over 34 states, more than half the buildings involved were in six national parks: Grand Canyon, Olympic, Bryce Canyon, Glacier Bay, Grand Teton, and Mammoth Cave. ■

Timber Relief Bill Fails

The Senate Energy and Natural Resources Committee Sept. 28 approved by 13-2 a timber industry relief bill (S 2805) sought by members from the economically depressed Pacific Northwest.

However, a threatened filibuster by Howard M. Metzenbaum, D-Ohio, kept the bill from the Senate floor, and it went no further.

The question of whether the bill should apply only to small companies was raised by Metzenbaum, who wanted an amendment limiting relief to operators qualifying under Small Business Administration rules.

Metzenbaum voiced a number of concerns about the bill, including the effect it would have on housing prices. He left the meeting shortly before the roll was called, protesting that he had not had a chance to raise all of his questions or offer intended amendments. He subsequently cast a "nay" vote, joining Gordon J. Humphrey, R-N.H., in opposition.

The Reagan administration, which had philosophic objections to most "bailout" bills, opposed S 2805. Assistant Agriculture Secretary John B. Crowell Jr. testified against it during hearings Aug. 17.

Provisions

As approved by the Energy Committee, the bill would have let logging companies out of contracts to buy timber from the national forests. Many of these contracts were signed two or three years earlier, before the bottom fell out of the housing market.

Under the contracts, timber companies promised to pay the United States prices current at the time, which were far above those prevailing in 1982's depressed market. As a result, those who were able to sell timber at all sometimes ended up doing so at prices below what it cost them.

Mark O. Hatfield, R-Ore., who introduced S 2805 along with five other Northwestern senators, said logging companies on the verge of bankruptcy could go under if forced to purchase the timber under the contracts.

The relief bill was eyed with suspicion by timber interests from Southeastern states, who feared a competitive disadvantage. The timber industry in the Northwest depended more heavily on public lands than that in the Southeast. And the Northwest produced more construction lumber — whose marketability was closely keyed to housing — while the Southeast tended to grow trees more suited to pulp products, such as paper, not so sensitive to economic recession.

Some of the healthier companies feared that as the timber from forgiven contracts came back onto the market at lower prices, it would drive down prices in all regions.

But changes made by Hatfield after hearings on the bill defused some concerns of the Southeastern timber interests. The measure required timber from terminated contracts to be resold "in an orderly fashion," within the annual limits otherwise set on the normal timber sales program. Hatfield and J. Bennett Johnston, D-La., also added an amendment setting a cap of 4.1 billion board feet per year on all federal timber sales in the Pacific Northwest for fiscal years 1983 and 1984. This was below the 5.3 billion board feet previously planned for fiscal 1983.

The bill applied to lands under both Agriculture Department and Interior Department jurisdiction.

It authorized the government to terminate, at the request of the purchaser, all obligation to purchase up to 40 percent of the timber specified in any contract bid before Jan. 1, 1982. Or, if the purchaser preferred, the government could terminate contract obligations to buy up to 15 million board feet, or one entire contract bid before Jan. 1, 1981.

In addition to those cancellations, the government could forgive one further contract, for no more than 10 million board feet, bid before Jan. 1, 1981, but after all the purchaser's other terminated contracts.

Purchasers must pay a fee, not to exceed $20,000 per contract, to defray contract termination costs.

The bill also allowed the government to stretch out timber sale contracts for as much as five years without imposing penalty fees normally assessed for late performance.

Another key provision allowed companies that spent money to build logging roads in national forests to transfer credit for that spending to other timber contracts or other purchasers. Current law allowed companies to credit the cost of a road toward the purchase price of the timber hauled on it. But some companies said they spent more on roads than the timber was worth to them.

Although conservation groups like the Wilderness Society supported the general concept of timber industry

relief, they worried that the road-credit provision would encourage construction of new forest roads in areas scarcely worth logging.

The road-credit provision, they noted, stayed in effect permanently, while most other provisions of the relief bill expired in one year.

Sponsors of S 2805 warned that unless help was provided, many small timber companies could go out of business during the current slump.

"At stake here is the survivability of the small and medium-sized operator," said Henry M. Jackson, D-Wash., a cosponsor of the bill. "I think this is a very serious emergency." ∎

No Clean Water Act Rewrite

After months of delay, the Reagan administration May 25 unveiled its proposals for rewriting the Clean Water Act, but Congress took no action on them.

The amendments sought by the administration did not make as many changes in the act as a set of Environmental Protection Agency (EPA) proposals leaked earlier in the year. But they still promised to be controversial, and committees preoccupied with other business found no time to tackle them.

The Senate Environment and Public Works Committee May 27 reported a one-year reauthorization (S 2590 — S Rept 97-443) of the Clean Water Act at a funding level of $299.3 million, but the Senate never acted on it.

The administration proposed authorizations of $146.3 million in fiscal 1983 funding, the same as the president's budget request. It provided $13 million for pollution-control demonstration and information, $40.9 million for grants to state pollution-control programs, and $92.4 million for general administration. The Clean Water Act (PL 92-500) was enacted in 1972 and amended in 1977 (PL 95-217). In the absence of a reauthorization bill, programs established under the law continued to be funded through appropriations measures and clean water regulations remained on the books. *(1972 Act, Congress and the Nation Vol. III, p. 792; 1977 Amendments, 1977 Almanac p. 697)*

Major Provisions

The administration's proposal would have:

● Extended from July 1, 1984, to July 1, 1988, the deadline for industries that dump wastes directly into rivers and streams to install the "Best Available Technology" (BAT) for treating toxic wastes and the "Best Conventional Technology" (BCT) for treating non-toxic pollutants. Although the deadline was set in 1977 amendments to the act (PL 92-217), EPA delayed issuing rules for most BAT categories and said industries would not have enough time to comply with the rules because of that delay.

● Extended to July 1, 1984, the deadline for EPA to issue effluent guidelines for BAT and BCT. EPA said more work was needed to finish these highly technical rules, including those covered in a court-ordered deadline for toxic discharges. In 1981, EPA cut the budget for the Effluent Guidelines Division, saying work on these rules was virtually complete.

● Extended from 1983 to 1988 the deadline for municipal sewage treatment plants to comply with minimum ("secondary") treatment levels required by EPA under the act. Since most cities and towns still relied on federal grants to fund 75 percent of construction costs for new or improved sewage facilities, their rate of progress depended on the rate of congressional funding.

● Made optional the current requirement for EPA to issue "categorical pre-treatment standards," which set industry-by-industry standards for treating toxic waste before it is discharged into municipal sewage systems. The proposal kept general pre-treatment provisions, which required cities to prohibit toxic discharges that pass through or interfere with their sewage treatment plants. The effect of the administration bill was to give local sewer agencies leeway to design their own pre-treatment programs.

● Authorized EPA to charge fees to process applications for exemptions from some of the act's more stringent industrial treatment requirements. This proposal was in line with the administration's user-fee philosophy, expressed in many of its legislative proposals this year.

● Specified that "new source performance standards" (NSPS) would apply to a plant only if construction began after the final NSPS rule was issued. Currently, the rules applied if construction began after the rule was proposed.

● Authorized the EPA administrator to assess civil penalties of up to $10,000 a day for clear violations of the act. Currently, only courts could impose such penalties.

● Authorized new criminal penalties of up to $50,000 per day and two years' imprisonment for knowing violations of certain parts of the act.

● Redefined dams as "non-point sources" not subject to the discharge permit rules. This had been EPA's traditional reading of the law, but a recent court ruling reversed it. The new language overturned the court decision.

● Expanded the scope of the president's authority to exempt federal facilities from pollution-control rules when he found it in the "paramount interest" of the United States for military operations.

● Extended from five years to 10 years the term for industrial and municipal discharge permits. The administration contended the longer term would reduce EPA's permit-writing workload and provide greater certainty for industrial investments in pollution control. Environmentalists said it would reduce EPA's leverage over dischargers, legitimize obsolete control equipment and leave the permits unresponsive to changing water conditions. ∎

Ocean Dumping Legislation

The House Sept. 20 suspended the rules and passed by voice vote a bill (HR 6113) to reauthorize and strengthen the law regulating the ocean dumping of dredged materials, industrial wastes and other materials. However, the measure was never approved by the Senate.

Congress did clear, as part of an unrelated highway gas tax bill (HR 6211), a two-year ban on ocean dumping of low-level radioactive wastes. *(Gas tax bill, p. 317)*

The House ocean dumping bill reflected a compromise between the Merchant Marine and Fisheries Committee and the Public Works and Transportation Committee designed to balance environmental concerns against the need for ocean disposal sites for dredge spoil from coastal harbors and waterways.

Merchant Marine reported the measure May 17; Public Works followed suit July 29 (H Rept 97-562, Parts I and II).

Background

HR 6113 amended title I of the Marine Protection, Research and Sanctuaries Act of 1972. *(PL 92-532 — Congress and the Nation Vol. III, p. 798)*

The 1972 law authorized EPA to issue permits for the ocean dumping of waste materials. But under the law, EPA could issue such permits only if it determined that dumping would not harm the marine environment or endanger public health. The permit must specify the type and quantity of material to be dumped, how long it could be dumped, and where it was to be dumped. The law allowed, but did not require, EPA to designate sites for such dumping.

In January 1977, EPA designated 140 historically used dump sites for interim use while it conducted the required studies. The studies dragged on, and in 1980, the National Wildlife Federation sued EPA to challenge the continued authorization of dumping at unstudied or interim sites. The suit was settled in September 1980 with an agreement that required EPA to finish its studies and act on 48 of the most heavily used sites by March 1983. To meet the court-approved schedule, EPA asked that its fiscal 1982 authorization be raised from $2 million to $4.2 million.

The House committees, however, criticized EPA's rate of progress. A schedule EPA gave to the committee in March "indicates that ... EPA has fallen ... up to 23 months behind the court-approved schedule," the committees' report said. Of the 141 dump sites currently designated, 12 had final designation and the rest had interim status.

House Floor Action

The only House member to speak against HR 6113 was Robert S. Walker, R-Pa., who said the Reagan administration opposed the measure, in part because its $4.2 million authorization level for fiscal 1983 exceeded the president's budget request of $3.5 million.

Environmentalists, despite some qualms of their own, supported the final bill.

"I have serious reservations about using the ocean to dump society's wastes because of the easy convenience of ocean dumping," said Norman E. D'Amours, D-N.H., one of the bill's sponsors.

"As a common-access resource, the ocean is not protected by the same economic and political forces that protect private property.... It is up to the members of Congress to provide a voice for the ocean and to ensure that the ocean has sufficient protection," he said.

The 1972 law authorized the Environmental Protection Agency (EPA) to issue permits for the ocean dumping of waste materials, but only if it determined that dumping would not harm the marine environment or endanger public health. The permit must specify the type and quantity of material to be dumped, how long it could be dumped, and where it was to be dumped. The law allowed, but did not require, EPA to designate sites for such dumping.

As passed by the House, HR 6113 made the site designation mandatory, not discretionary. It gave the agency six months to draw up a schedule for site designations and gave citizens the right to sue to force EPA to stick to its schedule.

Radioactive Wastes: Gas Tax Bill

Another major section of the bill imposed a two-year moratorium on any dumping of low-level radioactive wastes, a move designed to head off EPA plans to permit such dumping for the first time since 1970.

It was essentially this provision that was inserted into the highway gas tax legislation (HR 6211) in the waning days of the 97th Congress.

The only exception to the moratorium allowed was for research-related dumping, and even that would have to meet elaborate safeguards against environmental risks and receive approval of both House and Senate in a joint resolution.

The two-year moratorium on ocean dumping of low-level radioactive waste was to give Congress time to look at Navy proposals to dump contaminated soils from the Manhattan Project and to scuttle decommissioned nuclear submarines.

Opposed by environmentalists, the sub-scuttling proposal heated up in 1982 as Glen Sjoblom, who advocated the program for the Navy, was appointed head of EPA's radiation office.   ∎

Deep Seabed Mining Bill

The Senate Dec. 19 passed without amendment and cleared for President Reagan a bill (HR 6120 — PL 97-416) to reauthorize for fiscal 1983 and 1984 the Deep Seabed Hard Mineral Resources Act.

HR 6120 was cleared when the Senate by unanimous consent discharged the Energy and Natural Resources Committee from further consideration of the bill. That panel had received the bill after the House passed it Dec. 13 by voice vote.

House opponents of the measure earlier called it a signal to the nations signing the Law of the Sea Treaty that the United States would take no part in sharing of technology for mining deep sea minerals.

But the bill's proponents claimed the treaty, which the United States had not signed by the end of 1982, required a giveaway of the technological edge of U.S. companies to the third world without providing anything in return.

Law of the Sea Treaty

The bill reauthorized the 1980 law, which provided a temporary legal framework for deep seabed mining until the United States approved an international treaty on the subject. *(1980 Almanac p. 595)*

But U.S. mining companies feared that the Law of the Sea Treaty approved by the United Nations April 30 would deprive them of the returns from the lead they held in seabed mining technology.

That treaty, signed by 117 nations in Jamaica Dec. 10, declared seabed resources to be the "common heritage of mankind." It established a global authority to regulate seabed mining, and a global enterprise to which private mining companies would be required to sell their technology.

The Reagan administration opposed the treaty, and the United States, along with some 46 other nations, did not sign it.

Provisions

HR 6120 was reported May 17 by House committees on Merchant Marine and Fisheries, Interior and Insular Affairs and Foreign Affairs (H Rept 97-522, Parts 1, 2 and 3).

As passed by the House, the bill authorized $1,469,000

for fiscal 1983 and $2,150,000 for fiscal 1984 to carry out the seabed mining program, which was under the National Oceanic and Atmospheric Administration (NOAA).

Under present law and the reauthorization, NOAA was to develop regulations and issue licenses for seabed mineral exploration and commercial recovery. The agency was also responsible for protecting the environment, conserving seabed resources, and assuring the safety of life and property in relation to seabed mining.

NOAA also was to participate in negotiations with other countries that had seabed minerals programs, seeking to win recognition of U.S. licenses in return for U.S. recognition of their licenses.

Certain parts of the ocean floor contained rich deposits of minerals such as cobalt, manganese, nickel and copper. Although the technology for recovering them was expensive and complicated, it was feasible enough to have aroused commercial interest. Four mining companies to date had applied to NOAA for exploratory licenses covering 10 sites.

These minerals, especially cobalt, manganese and nickel, were considered as strategic or critical minerals because they were essential to alloys needed for advanced aircraft and weapons, as well as other industrial technologies.

However, according to John B. Breaux, D-La., the United States imported 91 percent of the cobalt it consumed, 98 percent of its manganese and 72 percent of its nickel. ∎

Congress Bans Wilderness Oil, Gas Leasing

Environmentalists scored a victory in 1982 on a wilderness oil and gas leasing issue that had smoldered for most of the 97th Congress.

Congress Dec. 19 cleared for President Reagan a $7.5 billion fiscal 1983 appropriations bill for the Interior Department (HR 7356 — PL 97-394) that included language banning such leasing until Sept. 30, 1983. *(HR 7356, p. 262)*

The legislation prohibited any spending during fiscal 1983 to issue oil and gas leases in areas either designated by Congress for protection as wilderness areas, or being considered for such protection.

That still left a three-month "window" between Sept. 30, 1983, the end of the fiscal year, and Jan. 1, 1984, when a permanent ban on wilderness leasing was to take effect under the 1964 Wilderness Act. *(Congress and the Nation Vol. I, p. 1063)*

However, Interior Secretary James G. Watt promised Dec. 30 that he would not try to "slip things through" that 90-day "window of opportunity."

BLM Lands Dropped From Study Category

But Watt infuriated environmentalists Dec. 27, when he announced removal of more than 805,000 acres of Bureau of Land Management (BLM) lands from study for possible wilderness designation. The decision grew out of rulings by the Interior Board of Land Appeals, which held that BLM could not name as wilderness study areas three different categories of lands:

• Parcels smaller than 5,000 acres, whose inclusion as study areas was optional under a 1976 law. Interior estimated that 340,526 acres in 10 Western states were affected.

• "Split estates," lands where the surface was owned by the federal government but the underground mineral rights were owned privately. Interior estimated 464,975 acres in eight Western states were in this category.

• Areas contiguous to federal wilderness or wilderness candidate areas. The board said these could not be named study areas simply because they adjoined other lands, but had to qualify on their own merits. Acreage figures for this category were not available.

Interior spokesmen stressed dropping the lands from the wilderness study category did not mean they would immediately revert to the "multiple use" category, which could include logging or drilling.

Environmentalists said Watt's action on the study lands showed hostility to wilderness preservation, and they expressed mistrust of Watt's stated intentions on the leasing ban.

On Jan. 13, 1983, six environmental groups filed suit in a federal district court in Sacramento, Calif., charging that Watt had acted illegally in removing the 800,000 acres from wilderness study status. Their suit asked the court to return the land to its prior status and to block Watt from authorizing any development on it.

The Interior Department issued a statement in response to the suit saying, "Our decision was based on a reading of the applicable laws by an impartial body of administrative law judges. We are confident the courts will support our determination."

Anti-Leasing Bills Supplanted

The appropriations rider obviated the need for action on separate legislation to ban oil and gas leasing in wilderness and wilderness study areas.

The House had passed its version of such a measure (HR 6542) on Aug. 12 by a 340-58 vote. *(Vote 259, p. 78-H)*

A Senate bill (S 2801) containing similar provisions had 54 cosponsors. But it was blocked from reaching the floor by delays in the Senate Energy and Natural Resources Committee.

Background

The leasing ban grew out of congressional displeasure with early efforts by Watt to open up the nation's federally designated wilderness areas to oil and gas leasing.

In May 1981, the House Interior and Insular Affairs Committee invoked a little-used provision of the 1976 Federal Land Policy and Management Act to force Watt to close three popular Montana wilderness areas to such leasing. The secretary later agreed to a moratorium on oil and gas leasing in all wilderness or wilderness candidate areas until the end of the 97th Congress. *(1981 Almanac p. 525)*

However, that left a one-year "window" until Jan. 1, 1984, when the permanent ban on all wilderness leasing was to take effect under provisions of the 1964 Wilderness Act.

Limited Leasing to Date

Under the Wilderness Act of 1964 (PL 88-577), all the nation's non-park wilderness was left open for oil and gas exploration until Dec. 31, 1983. After that date, no new

exploratory leases could be issued, but claims already filed could continue to be developed indefinitely.

However, since the law was enacted, only 50 oil and gas leases had been granted in existing wilderness or wilderness candidate areas administered by the U.S. Forest Service, although 891 applications for oil and gas leases were pending on those lands in early 1982. Almost no mining or drilling had been allowed on the 12,000 acres of BLM wilderness.

Most of the oil drilling so far had occurred on federal land being studied by the agencies or reviewed by Congress for future wilderness designation. The BLM had granted about 5,000 oil and gas leases covering 26 percent of the 24 million acres it was studying for possible wilderness recommendation. The Forest Service had issued at least 337 leases on its 19.5 million acres being reviewed by Congress or studied by the agency for possible future wilderness designation.

Oil companies had filed 745 applications for additional leases on Forest Service study areas. The BLM did not have any consolidated figures on how many applications were pending on its study areas.

Watt's Plan

Congress was caught by surprise Feb. 21 when Watt, reversing the position he had taken early in 1981, said he wanted to close the nation's wilderness to oil and mineral development for the next 18 years.

Watt proposed closing wilderness areas while the government surveyed them and reported to Congress every five years on what minerals it was finding. After the year 2000, Congress could vote to open some areas to development if it determined such a step was needed.

Because the measure was silent on what would become of all wilderness acreage after the year 2000, it caused consternation among some in Congress and the environmental community who feared it would lift wilderness protections after that date. Another provision raising some hackles set deadlines for Congress to act on pending wilderness proposals or they would be "released" for non-wilderness uses such as logging.

"The Watt proposal would be the most sweeping and devastating *anti*-wilderness bill I have ever seen," said Rep. John F. Seiberling, D-Ohio, chairman of the House Interior and Insular Affairs Committee's Public Lands Subcommittee.

"I have learned to look for 'fishhooks' in Mr. Watt's glittering proposals," he continued. "This particular one appears to be an attempt by the secretary to portray himself as pro-wilderness when actually developing legislation to gut the nation's wilderness system."

Environmental groups, who initially hailed Watt's proposal when he announced it on network television Feb. 21, changed their tune when draft copies of the legislation leaked out of the Interior Department later.

"This bill is a duplicitous hoax," said William Turnage, executive director of the Wilderness Society, who had earlier called Watt's plan "a real victory for wilderness protection."

Under Watt's plan, no drilling or mining would be allowed in the wilderness areas unless ordered by the president because of an urgent national need — such as an energy or strategic mineral shortage. Congress would have 60 days in which to pass legislation blocking such presidential action, but that bill would have to be signed by the president.

The proposal included controversial "release" language giving Congress until Jan. 1, 1985, to act on 1979 recommendations for wilderness designation by the Carter administration as part of its wilderness review of roadless forest service areas (RARE II). If Congress failed to act, the areas would be released for other uses, such as logging and mining. *(RARE II bills, p. 464)*

Such "release" language — favored by timber and mining interests — had been proposed for national forest wilderness areas by Sens. S. I. Hayakawa, R-Calif., and Jesse Helms, R-N.C. (S 842), but their measure never emerged from the Senate Energy Committee.

House Committee Action

HR 6542: The Leasing Ban Bill

Key members of the House Interior Committee introduced HR 6542, the separate leasing ban legislation, on June 8. Sponsors included Chairman Morris K. Udall, D-Ariz., ranking Republican Manuel Lujan Jr., N.M., and Seiberling, chairman of the Subcommittee on Public Lands and National Parks.

The bill covered not only lands already designated as wilderness but also lands recommended or being studied for wilderness status. It allowed energy or mineral prospecting and inventories "compatible with the preservation of the wilderness environment," but not seismic surveys using explosives. And it allowed the president to seek congressional approval for mineral development on any specific tract of withdrawn land in cases of "urgent national need."

HR 6542 was approved June 18 by the Interior Subcommittee on Public Lands and National Parks, with only technical amendments.

The House Interior and Insular Affairs Committee approved the bill by a 34-7 vote June 24 and formally reported it July 19 (H Rept 97-638).

The bill approved by the House committee covered about 33 million acres of land that was either already designated as wilderness or was recommended or being studied for wilderness status. No land in Alaska was included, because that state had been dealt with separately in 1980 Alaska lands legislation. *(1980 Almanac p. 575)*

'Release' Language

The House bill contained no release language, but some senators favored such a provision, according to Rep. Lujan. The New Mexico Republican made the statement after a June 23 meeting with GOP members from both chambers, including Sen. James A. McClure, R-Idaho, chairman of the Senate Energy and Natural Resources Committee.

Also at the meeting were Interior Secretary Watt and John B. Crowell Jr., assistant secretary of agriculture for natural resources and environment.

An amendment adding release language to HR 6542 was offered in the House Interior Committee by Bill Hendon, R-N.C., but was fended off on a point of order raised by Seiberling. The Ohio Democrat, a cosponsor of the bill, said such an amendment should be considered as part of a comprehensive wilderness bill, instead of the "narrowly drawn" HR 6542, which was designed to address only the energy and mineral leasing issue. Interior Chairman Udall sustained Seiberling's point of order.

Democrats used this same strategy to defeat four of

the 11 amendments offered in committee. They were hoping to build a record that would help them repel amendments on the House floor.

But when Udall ruled that one amendment offered by Don Young, R-Alaska, was clearly out of order, Young retorted: "The only thing clear-cut is that you've got the votes."

The only major amendment adopted by the committee permitted "hard-rock" mineral leasing to continue on certain forest lands — primarily in the East — otherwise withdrawn from leasing.

An earlier version of this amendment, which was opposed by some Eastern members, on June 23 left the committee split 22-20 in favor. But a compromise version was worked out overnight, and it was adopted by voice vote June 24.

House Floor Action

The House passed the leasing ban legislation Aug. 12 by a 340-58 vote. *(Vote 259, p. 78-H)*

Before passing HR 6542, the House by voice vote rejected an amendment by Rep. Don Young, R-Alaska, to allow leasing in wilderness study areas, which made up about 14 million acres of the 33 million acres covered by the bill. Also rejected, 115-281, was a Young amendment to allow surface use of explosives during seismic exploration of wilderness areas. *(Vote 258, p. 76-H)*

In urging support for HR 6542, the bill's proponents said Watt had been completing paper work on pending lease applications so that he could move quickly when the moratorium expired. About 1,000 applications covering some 3 million acres of wilderness were before him at the time of the House vote.

Young, the most vocal opponent of HR 6542, called it a reaction "to emotional claptrap perpetrated by the no-growth elite in this country who wish to deny the American people access to the resources that they need to cheaply heat their homes and schools and run their automobiles."

But Seiberling cited an Oak Ridge National Laboratory estimate that only 2 to 3 percent of the nation's undiscovered oil and gas lay under wilderness or wilderness candidate areas.

First Continuing Resolution

Appropriations Rider

Although HR 6542 won overwhelming approval in the House, it quickly became bottled up in the Senate Energy Committee, along with S 2801, a companion measure sponsored by Sen. Henry M. Jackson, D-Wash.

Fearful that the legislation would not emerge in time for final action by the 97th Congress, backers of the wilderness leasing ban adopted a new tactic in September.

In the House Appropriations Committee, an amendment offered by Sidney R. Yates, D-Ill., prohibiting the use of federal funds to process wilderness lease applications was added to H J Res 599, the first continuing appropriations resolution for fiscal 1983. *(H J Res 599, p. 225)*

The Senate Appropriations Committee approved the wilderness leasing ban as well, adopting an amendment offered by McClure himself.

Even though the bill was open to amendment on the floor of the Republican-controlled Senate, the leasing ban

survived. In fact, it was amended by voice vote on the Senate floor to bring it into line with S 2801.

Some environmentalists were bewildered to see McClure and Jackson, on opposite sides of S 2801, cosponsoring the amendment.

McClure's support for the processing freeze was best understood as a reaffirmation and clarification of the terms of the existing leasing moratorium — rather than a change of heart on the basic wilderness leasing issue.

McClure's opposition to the leasing ban was not as absolute as sometimes pictured. His main concern, according to a spokesman, was for adding "release" provisions to the bill.

Such provisions would set a deadline for Congress to act on recommended wilderness areas; any that were not included in the wilderness system by the deadline would become available for other uses.

Watt himself sent a letter Sept. 23 to Mark O. Hatfield, R-Ore., chairman of the Senate Appropriations Committee, urging the panel to adopt the processing freeze.

"It has come to my attention that there are those in Congress who still question my sincerity regarding the moratorium I imposed on leasing in the wilderness areas," Watt wrote.

"This additional period will hopefully allow the Congress to act on our suggestions for a permanent solution to this vexing issue."

H J Res 599, with the leasing ban attached, was cleared in the session that began Oct. 1 (PL 97-276). It expired Dec. 17.

Interior Appropriations Bill

House Committee, Floor Action

The wilderness leasing ban was next written into the regular fiscal 1983 Interior appropriations bill (HR 7356) reported Dec. 2 from the House Appropriations Committee (H Rept 97-942).

The language approved by the committee banned oil and gas leasing, and mineral surveys, in all designated wilderness areas, in all congressionally designated wilderness study areas, and in all Forest Service RARE II areas recommended for wilderness designation or for further planning. The ban extended until Congress had made a final determination of the status of lands not already formally designated as wilderness.

The committee noted its prohibition did not extend to BLM lands under study for possible wilderness designation, but it said the Interior Department "should take whatever action is necessary to ensure the Congress' prerogative to designate BLM wilderness study areas as wilderness is not foreclosed by leasing or mineral survey activities."

The bill was passed by the full House Dec. 3 by a 275-73 vote. There was no discussion of the leasing ban during floor debate on the measure. *(Vote 388, p. 116-H)*

Senate Committee, Floor Action

A critical test of strength on the wilderness leasing issue came in a series of four votes Dec. 8 in the Senate Appropriations Committee that sent to the floor the legislative language most favored by environmentalists. Dennis DeConcini, D-Ariz., proposed an amendment to HR 7356 that was equivalent to S 2801, the Senate counterpart

to House-passed wilderness leasing legislation, which remained bottled up in the Energy and Natural Resources Committee.

McClure, who chaired the Appropriations Interior Subcommittee as well as the Senate Energy Committee, offered as a substitute an amendment that would ban leasing in areas designated or recommended as wilderness areas but permit it in areas under study for wilderness; legislatively declare the "sufficiency" of environmental impact statements for the U.S. Forest Service's last nationwide wilderness study (RARE II), blocking further legal challenges by environmentalists; and allow seismic testing in wilderness oil exploration.

Both sides agreed to divide the McClure amendment into its three parts, with separate votes on each.

The first vote was on language to allow explosive seismic testing. The panel rejected such testing 11-13 on a rollcall vote. The second part of McClure's amendment, language to exclude wilderness study areas from the leasing ban, was rejected 3-5 on a show of hands. The third part, declaring the legal sufficiency of RARE II environmental impact statements, was rejected 3-6 on a show of hands.

The committee then approved DeConcini's original amendment on a voice vote.

Senate Floor Action

The Senate approved the leasing ban Dec. 14 when it adopted a substitute amendment offered by John Melcher,

D-Mont., to an amendment to HR 7356 offered by McClure.

Both McClure's amendment and Melcher's substitute contained the key points that proponents of the leasing ban had sought. Both applied to areas designated as wilderness, areas recommended for wilderness, or areas under planning or study for wilderness. Both included a ban on seismic surveys using explosives in designated wilderness areas.

The Melcher substitute settled a dispute over whether McClure's language would allow the Interior Department to issue prospecting permits for U.S. Forest Service lands. Melcher said his substitute would ensure that each agency issued permits only for its own lands.

The Senate adopted the Melcher amendment by voice vote, and later passed the Interior appropriations bill by a vote of 84-9. *(Vote 404, p. 69-S)*

Conference/Final Action

The Senate wilderness leasing language was adopted by House-Senate conferees, who reached agreement on the final version of HR 7356 late Dec. 16. The conference report on the bill (H Rept 97-978) was filed the following day.

The House agreed to the conference report Dec. 18 by a 282-63 vote, and the Senate followed suit by voice vote Dec. 19, clearing the legislation for the president. *(Vote 453, p. 132-H)*

President Reagan signed the bill into law Dec. 30. ∎

Congress Clears RARE II Wilderness Bills

The 97th Congress cleared legislation designating federal wilderness areas in five states — but other state wilderness bills died as the clock ran out.

The measures sent to President Reagan were part of a patchwork of state-by-state legislation that grew out of the second Roadless Area Review and Evaluation (RARE II) inventory of some 62 million acres in the 187-million-acre National Forest System.

That inventory, which was commenced in June 1977, came to an end in April 1979, when the Carter administration recommended that 15.4 million acres of forest land in 36 states be designated as wilderness, with an additional 12 million acres recommended for further planning and study.

The RARE II recommendations did not take effect automatically. Only Congress could designate federal wilderness areas, a laborious state-by-state process.

The 96th Congress passed RARE II legislation covering seven states — Idaho, Colorado, Louisiana, Missouri, New Mexico, South Carolina and South Dakota. *(Background, 1979 Almanac p. 688; 1980 Almanac p. 617)*

Alaska was covered in special legislation (PL 96-487) cleared Nov. 12, 1980, that granted wilderness protection to some 56.7 million acres in that state. *(1980 Almanac p. 575)*

The 97th Congress cleared RARE II bills covering five states — Florida, West Virginia, Missouri, Indiana and Alabama.

But Reagan on Jan. 14, 1983, vetoed the Florida measure (HR 9) because he opposed provisions calling for compensation of companies with pending applications to strip-mine phosphate from some of the lands covered by

the bill.

Other RARE II bills that died in the 97th Congress included measures for California (HR 4083), Montana (S 2110), Wyoming (S 2118) and Oregon (HR 7340).

Florida

The House Dec. 20 cleared a Florida wilderness bill (HR 9) settling issues that had been in dispute for four successive Congresses. But Reagan vetoed the measure Jan. 14, 1983.

Final congressional action came when the House concurred in a Senate amendment that provided a way of settling certain phosphate claims in national forest lands covered by the bill.

The Senate had passed the bill, with its amendment, on Dec. 19. The measure was approved Dec. 7 by the Senate Energy and Natural Resources Committee, but no written report was filed.

HR 9 was originally reported by the House Interior and Insular Affairs Committee Dec. 11, 1981, (H Rept 97-402) and passed by the House Dec. 15, 1981. *(1981 Almanac p. 531)*

As cleared, the measure designated as wilderness seven areas totaling approximately 49,150 acres in the Apalachicola, Ocala, and Osceola national forests in Florida.

Phosphate Mining Banned

It also prohibited the interior secretary from issuing phosphate strip-mining leases in the Osceola National Forest unless the president declared that "there is a clear and

present national need for the phosphate resulting from a domestic shortage...," and both House and Senate adopted a joint resolution approving the move.

The leasing ban provision was complicated by the fact that four companies had filed applications before 1972 for leases to mine phosphate in 52,253 acres covering roughly one-third of the Osceola National Forest. The four companies were Kerr-McGee Corp., Global Exploration Co., Monsanto Chemical Products Co., and Pittsburgh and Midway Coal Mining Co. The applications gave the companies certain rights to any valuable and recoverable deposits of phosphate rock they found in those areas.

The bill set up a mechanism to compensate those companies for rights they would lose as a result of the leasing ban. Upon giving up those rights, the companies would get monetary credits based on the fair market value of the replacement cost of the unmined recoverable phosphate in the ground.

The value of the phosphate would be discounted for the costs of mining it and of complying with applicable federal, state and local laws, such as those requiring the companies to reclaim the land after mining. The bill also required the companies to deduct taxes and inflation costs resulting from an annual limit of 10 percent on the payout of credits from the government to the companies.

Sen. Paula Hawkins, R-Fla., estimated the final cost of the settlement at no more than $74 million. But the administration said the compensation could cost as much as $200 million.

Reagan Veto

On Jan. 13 Interior Secretary James G. Watt denied the pending applications for preference-right leases to mine phosphate in Florida's Osceola National Forest. Those applications had been the basis for the claims the wilderness bill would have compensated.

The next day, Reagan vetoed HR 9, citing its compensation provisions as the reason. *(Veto messge, p. 35-E)*

"As our actions demonstrate, we ... support Congress' aim of denying phosphate mining there, but this bill, with its purchase of what we have found to be legally invalid 'rights' to mine phosphate, is simply not the vehicle that meets the objectives," Watt said.

Watt said he was denying the lease applications because Interior Department environmental studies had concluded that the Osceola forest lands could not be adequately reclaimed if strip-mining were allowed.

Environmental groups criticized Reagan's veto of HR 9, saying Watt's denial of the lease applications could be appealed to the courts, leaving the forest open to risk of phosphate mining. The president said, however, that the legislation would have recognized mineral rights that "might not otherwise have existed."

West Virginia

The Senate Dec. 20 concurred in a House amendment and cleared for presidential signature a bill (HR 5161 — PL 97-466) designating as wilderness three areas of West Virginia's Monongahela National Forest — Cranberry, Laurel Fork North and Laurel Fork South. The areas totaled about 47,800 acres.

The House on Dec. 20 had sent the bill to the Senate with an amendment authorizing $2.2 million to be paid to Pocahontas and Webster counties, W.Va., to compensate for tax revenues they would lose as a result of the bill.

The Senate had amended the bill on Dec. 18 to change language that would compensate the CSX Corp. for mineral rights it held in the 35,600-acre Cranberry area.

The original version, reported May 17 by the House Interior Committee (H Rept 97-561) and passed June 14 by the House, had directed the Interior Department to acquire all privately owned mineral rights in the Cranberry Wilderness area through a swap of equally valuable federally owned mineral rights under other lands. The Dec. 18 Senate amendment substituted a monetary credit that could be applied toward other federal oil, gas or mineral leases the company might seek.

While this compensation mechanism was similar to that included in the Florida wilderness bill (HR 9) that Reagan vetoed Jan. 14, 1983, the mineral rights involved in the West Virginia bill were different.

HR 5161 released for other uses all RARE II areas in West Virginia not officially designated as wilderness under this legislation. Their status would not be subject to new Forest Service review until the mid 1990s.

Missouri

Paddy Creek Wilderness

The Senate Dec. 19 concurred by voice vote in a House amendment and sent to the president a bill (S 1965 — PL 97-407) to establish the 6,888-acre Paddy Creek Wilderness Area in Mark Twain National Forest, Missouri.

The bill had been approved Sept. 15 and reported Sept. 20 (S Rept 97-554) by the Senate Energy and Natural Resources Committee. It was passed by the Senate in the session that began Oct. 1.

In the House, the Paddy Creek Wilderness measure was approved Dec. 8 and reported Dec. 9 (H Rept 97-949) by the Interior and Insular Affairs Committee.

The full House Dec. 15 failed by a vote of 250-143 to suspend the rules and pass S 1965. A two-thirds majority of those present and voting (262 in this case) was needed. *(Vote 430, p. 126-H)*

However, the Rules Committee sent the bill back to the House floor a day later, and it was passed 367-23 after the House adopted a substitute proposed by Rep. Wendell Bailey, R-Mo., and agreed to by Rep. John F. Seiberling, D-Ohio, chairman of the House Interior subcommittee on public lands. *(Vote 442, p. 130-H)*

The substitute amendment released from further wilderness consideration certain other lands in Missouri. The release, however, did not apply to RARE II "further planning areas," thus leaving alive the possibility of wilderness designation in the future for the proposed 17,562-acre Irish Wilderness, the only remaining "further planning" area in the state.

Irish Wilderness Bill Dies

A bill (S 1964) to create the Irish Wilderness died Dec. 16 when the House by a 186-191 vote failed to adopt a rule (H Res 628) providing for consideration of the measure. *(Vote 438, p. 128-H)*

Opponents complained there had been no field hearing to give local residents in the affected region a chance to express their views on the wilderness proposal.

In addition, the Reagan administration opposed creation of the Irish Wilderness because the area could contain lead deposits.

S 1964 was approved Sept. 15 and reported Sept. 20 by

the Senate Energy and Natural Resources Committee (S Rept 97-553). It was passed by the full Senate in a session that began Oct. 1.

In the House, S 1964 was approved Dec. 8 and reported Dec. 13 (H Rept 97-962) by the Interior Committee.

Alabama

The House Dec. 20 passed and cleared for the president a bill (S 2953 — PL 97-411) establishing the 6,780-acre Cheaha Wilderness in the Talladega National Forest in Alabama.

The measure had been passed by the Senate Dec. 19 after winning approval from the Senate Energy Committee Dec. 7.

An earlier statewide RARE II measure (HR 6011) passed Aug. 4 by the House had designated the Cheaha Wilderness and added approximately 28,500 acres to the Sipsey Wilderness in the Bankhead National Forest. But that measure never cleared.

Indiana

The House Dec. 13 by voice vote suspended the rules and cleared for the president a bill (S 2710 — PL 97-384) setting aside as wilderness some 12,953 acres in Indiana's Hoosier National Forest.

The measure, which was passed by the Senate in the session that began Oct. 1, had been reported Dec. 9 (H Rept 97-948) by the House Interior Committee.

Final congressional action marked the end of nearly a decade of negotiations over how much acreage to include in the wilderness area. Although there were more than 20 million acres of land in Indiana, this Charles C. Deam Wilderness was the first federally designated wilderness area in the state. The area was named after Indiana's first state forester.

S 2710 was approved Sept. 15 and formally reported (S Rept 97-557) Sept 20 by the Senate Energy and Natural Resources Committee. It was passed by the full Senate in the session that began Oct. 1.

Bills That Failed

Wyoming

The Senate Dec. 15 passed and sent to the House a bill (S 2118) designating as wilderness 678,449 acres of national forest land in eight areas of Wyoming. But the measure went no further in the 97th Congress.

The Carter administration had recommended wilderness protection for 713,900 acres, and the Reagan administration originally recommended it for 996,000 acres, although the areas were not strictly comparable.

As passed by the Senate, S 2118 included "release" language that would have freed up for non-wilderness uses such as logging or oil drilling lands considered for wilderness but not designated as such.

The Wyoming wilderness measure was approved Sept. 15 by the Senate Energy and Natural Resources Committee and reported Sept. 23 (S Rept 97-574).

It was steered through committee by Sen. Malcolm Wallop, R-Wyo., but it was opposed by environmentalists and by Ed Herschler, Wyoming's Democratic governor. They were unhappy with the amount of land designated for wilderness protection and with the release language in the

bill. Critics said the land would be released for too long before it could again be considered for wilderness designation.

Oregon

The House Interior and Insular Affairs Committee Dec. 8 approved and Dec. 9 reported a bill (HR 7340 — H Rept 97-951) to designate as wilderness some 1,006,375 acres of national forest land in Oregon, with another 112,500 acres set aside for further wilderness study.

However, the full House Dec. 15 failed by 247-141 to muster the two-thirds majority needed (259 in this case) to suspend the rules and pass the bill, and the measure went no further in the 97th Congress. *(Vote 429, p. 126-H)*

The Reagan administration opposed the bill, arguing that it protected too much land from logging and other development activities. The total wilderness acreage designated under the bill was roughly three times the amount recommended for such protection under the state's RARE II evaluation, the administration said.

Montana

The Senate Energy and Natural Resources Committee Dec. 7 approved a bill (S 2110) to establish a wilderness area in Montana named after former Sen. Lee Metcalf, D-Mont. (House 1953-1961, Senate 1961-1978).

However, the measure was never passed by the Senate and it died when Congress adjourned.

California

For the second Congress in a row, legislation to designate as wilderness millions of acres of land in California was passed by the House but died in the Senate.

The bill (HR 4083) was passed by the House July 17, 1981. It would have given wilderness protection to 2.1 million acres of national forest lands and 1.4 million acres of national park land in the state. *(1981 Almanac p. 524; 1980 Almanac p. 617)*

HR 4083 was referred to the Senate Energy Committee July 21, 1981, but that panel never acted on it. ∎

Water Resources Bill Dies

The Senate June 21 passed by voice vote a bill (S 2494) authorizing $21.1 million annually in federal grants to state water resources research programs. The House, however, failed to act on the measure.

The bill was designed to save a program formerly operated under the Interior Department's Office of Water Research and Technology (OWRT), which the Reagan Administration succeeded in eliminating at the end of fiscal 1982. No funding for the OWRT was provided in the fiscal 1983 Interior appropriations bill (HR 7356) cleared Dec. 19. *(Interior appropriations, p. 262)*

There were currently water research institutes at land grant universities in 54 states and territories. Under the bill, each would have been eligible for a federal matching grant of up to $150,000 per year through fiscal 1987.

States would have had to put up one dollar for every federal dollar for the first two years, three state dollars for two federal dollars the second two years, and two state dollars for every federal dollar in the last year. It also would have required more of the state contribution to be in cash (rather than in kind) than the previous program under

the Water Research and Development Act of 1978. *(1978 Almanac p. 721)*

Separate from the state grants, $13 million annually would have been authorized for specific water research project grants on various subjects.

The Senate Environment and Public Works Committee reported the bill May 27 (S Rept 97-441).

The measure was identical to Title III of a more comprehensive water bill (S 1095 — S Rept 97-120) that was reported by the committee May 15, 1981. It stalled because Interior Secretary James G. Watt and some of his Senate allies opposed provisions calling for creation of an independent board to coordinate national water policy. *(1981 Almanac p. 526)*

Health/Education/Welfare

A deepening recession and the results of 1981 budget cuts kept Congress from approving many major changes in social programs during 1982.

With a soaring unemployment rate, which neared 11 percent by year's end, Congress became less interested in cutting the programs. Cuts approved in 1982 were small compared to the billions of dollars in savings ordered by the 1981 budget reconciliation act. *(1981 Almanac p. 256)*

While they generally escaped deep spending cuts at the hands of Congress, however, health, education and welfare programs, and the people who relied on them, came under increasing stress in 1982.

Programs such as Aid to Families with Dependent Children (AFDC), Medicaid and guaranteed loans for college students experienced for the first time the full effects of the 1981 spending cuts.

Important changes resulting from the budget cuts, combined with the economic recession, included:

● A shift of welfare funds from the working poor to the non-working poor.

● An increased health cost burden on private health insurers and patients, combined with a cut in services.

● Reductions in enrollment at many private colleges and universities and layoffs of public school teachers.

Welfare and Poverty

The number of poor people in the United States increased significantly in 1982. But budget cuts held down the number receiving welfare and other forms of assistance to the poor, ending two decades of rapid growth in the programs.

The ranks of the poor were swelling even before the onset of 1982's severe economic problems. The Census Bureau estimated that the percentage of people living in poverty grew from 11.7 percent in 1979 to 13.2 percent in 1980 and to 14 percent in 1981. Some 2.2 million people entered the poverty population in 1981, bringing the total number living in poverty to 32 million.

The increase in 1982 was even greater, poverty experts believed. As high unemployment in many areas dragged on, more and more jobless workers exhausted their unemployment benefits. They became the "new poor," dependent on government programs for the first time in their lives.

By year's end, there were believed to be several million people with no money and no place to stay. Many laid-off workers abandoned the hard-hit Midwest to look for jobs in the "Sun Belt," only to end up living in their cars when they found there was no work there either.

While the poverty population obviously was growing, experts were divided over who should be classified as poor. There was a lot of argument over whether to count "in-kind" income — federal benefits that came in the form of goods, such as food stamps and housing subsidies, rather

than cash. Census Bureau estimates of poverty did not count in-kind benefits in determining a person's income.

Conservative economists argued that the poverty rate actually was lower than the census estimates, since inclusion of the value of in-kind benefits would raise many people's incomes over the poverty line. The Census Bureau estimated that the poverty rate would fall by almost half if in-kind benefits were counted as income.

While the economy worsened, budget cuts enacted in 1981 began to tighten eligibility for welfare programs, and limit benefits. Combined with the 1981 tax reductions, the budget cuts produced a substantial shift of income from the poor to the rich.

The Congressional Budget Office estimated that the average family with an income below $10,000 a year lost $240 worth of benefits from the budget cuts, while families with annual incomes over $80,000 saved an average of $15,130 from the tax cuts.

The welfare cuts fell most heavily on the working poor, who got federal benefits to supplement their small earned incomes. By sharply reducing food stamps and other benefits to those with earned income, the cuts were a disincentive to work, anti-poverty groups argued. They predicted many poor workers would quit their jobs and go completely on welfare.

Meanwhile, the 1981 reconciliation law was increasing the emphasis on work requirements for welfare recipients. Some two dozen states established "workfare" programs, under which recipients performed public service work for their communities in exchange for benefits.

There were 10.4 million people on the AFDC rolls in 1982, down from 11.1 million in 1981. The drop was not as great in food stamp participation; 22.2 million received food stamps in 1982, compared to 22.4 million in 1981.

Education

Some of the most dramatic changes in social programs in 1982 came in the area of higher education. Budget cuts and the recession combined to produce these trends:

● Enrollment in colleges and universities leveled off, and was expected to decline in the near future. The National Center for Education Statistics estimated that 12.5 million students were enrolled in postsecondary education in the fall of 1982, a very small rise from the 12.4 million in 1981.

● Students were shifting from more expensive private colleges to public institutions. Full-time freshman enrollment went down by 4 percent at private schools in 1982, according to the National Institute of Independent Colleges and Universities, while public colleges and universities held their own. The loss of freshmen was a serious problem for the independent colleges, since it meant the loss of about a quarter of a billion dollars in tuition revenues over the following four years.

● Private education increasingly was limited to students from middle- and upper-income families. Private colleges reported they had experienced a dramatic loss of students from families with incomes below $24,000.

● Students made less use of federally subsidized guaranteed student loans. The volume of loans in 1982 fell about 25 percent from the 1981 level.

● The number of college students receiving the basic form of federal aid, Pell grants, remained at about 2.5 million. Aid was slightly more targeted on low-income students than it had been the year before.

● Traditionally black institutions experienced particularly severe problems, with freshman enrollment at some black schools falling by 12 percent.

Health

Developments with major implications for health care in America occurred largely outside the confines of congressional health committees in 1982. Certain states took the lead in developing strategies to curb the growth of health care expenditures, especially in Medicaid, the federal-state health care program for the poor. And the secretary of health and human services (HHS), Richard S. Schweiker, moved administratively to relax a number of regulations affecting hospitals and drug manufacturers.

Schweiker, for example, dropped a requirement that hospitals post notices advising patients of the availability of charity care, and abandoned a Carter administration proposal to require pharmacists to give patients information leaflets when they bought any of the 10 most commonly prescribed drugs.

Unhappy consumer groups complained that the Food and Drug Administration (FDA) had cut its enforcement actions by two-thirds in the first 18 months of the Reagan administration. FDA officials maintained that they achieved the same results by using more negotiation, and less coercion, with regulated industries.

In Congress, there were signs of friction between the American Medical Association (AMA) and the hospital industry on the one hand, and their traditional allies on Capitol Hill. The AMA alienated many of its best moderate and conservative Republican friends in Congress during its bitter — and unsuccessful — campaign against Federal Trade Commission regulation of doctors. *(Story, p. 347)*

Meanwhile, statistics pointed up the failure of a multi-year campaign by hospitals to voluntarily keep their expenses within certain limits. In sharp contrast to declining inflation rates in the economy, prices for medical care continued to rise substantially, led by hospital cost increases. In the first quarter of fiscal 1982, while the overall Consumer Price Index increased at an annual rate of 1 percent, medical care went up 10.2 percent; prices for hospital care rose 15 percent, doctors' fees 9.7 percent.

Industry claims that hospital officials could best curb their own expenditures had been a telling argument against President Jimmy Carter's abortive drive for federal regulation of hospital cost increases in 1979. The emerging flaws in the voluntary cost control program prompted Sen. Robert Dole, R-Kan., to suggest in March that Congress might have erred in rejecting Carter's plan. Dole, chairman of the Senate Finance Committee, had been an influential opponent of the plan. Dole's committee later endorsed two sweeping limits on Medicare payments to hospitals, which were enacted as part of the 1982 tax bill (PL 97-248). *(Tax bill, p. 29; 1979 action, 1979 Almanac p. 512)*

Spending limits agreed to in the congressional budget resolution forced committees responsible for Medicare and Medicaid to devise new ways to curb the rapid growth of spending in those programs. Congress acted on these changes without much systematic evidence of the impact on hospitals, doctors and patients of budget-cutting changes enacted in 1981. (Health statistics generally lagged by as much as two or three years.)

Using the 1981 changes in Medicaid law, states began changing eligibility standards for the program and restricting patient access to certain doctors or hospitals. California, for example, negotiated payment rates with hospitals, then required Medicaid patients to seek treatment only at hospitals winning contracts from the state to care for them. Michigan designated willing doctors as "primary providers," responsible for full case management of Medicaid patients; without a referral from the primary physician, pharmacies, emergency rooms and other medical facilities could not be paid by Medicaid for services to the patient.

Some states began asking Medicaid beneficiaries to pay nominal amounts for medical services; the payments were intended less as a source of new income than as a barrier to overuse of medical services.

Health officials hoped these changes could both save money and improve the quality of care of the poor, by discouraging episodic use of hospital emergency services and assuring some continuity of treatment. But changes of this type also quietly eroded the basic premise of Medicaid: that America's poor, with the government footing the bill, would enjoy the same unfettered access to medical facilities and private doctors as everyone else. The realities of Medicaid, whose patients clogged overburdened public hospitals and clinics, had always fallen short of that goal.

One outcome of state Medicaid changes was that the growth of program outlays slowed dramatically. Compared with 1981, Medicaid expenditures rose 8.6 percent in fiscal 1982; in the previous year, the rate of increase was 18.1 percent. It was the first time since the program began in 1966 that the annual growth rate in spending had dropped below double-digit figures.

If Medicaid's growth rate slowed, that of Medicare did not. Medicare financed medical care for the elderly and disabled. At the end of July, HHS reported that the costs of Medicare payments had risen 21.5 percent since 1980, with hospital costs the driving factor.

A state program to control hospital expenditures became the model for a major administration proposal to curb Medicare hospital spending, submitted to Congress just before the end of the year. The plan was based on the New Jersey system of setting standard payment rates or prices for each of 467 different medical conditions.

Little was heard during the year of the administration's "new federalism" plan to relieve states of their share of Medicaid expenditures if states would take full responsibility for welfare and food stamps. President Reagan announced the scheme in his State of the Union address, but many state officials were unwilling to take over the two expensive non-medical programs. While some were attracted by the possibility of escaping soaring medical care inflation in Medicaid, defenders of more generous state Medicaid programs feared the administration would choose a "lowest common demoninator" approach in an all-federal Medicaid program. That could mean less care for the poor and working poor.

—By Harrison Donnelly and Elizabeth Wehr

Congress Votes Cuts in Medicare, Medicaid

Congress made numerous changes in Medicare and Medicaid in 1982 in an effort to reduce federal outlays for the health programs in fiscal 1983-85. The changes would cut spending for the programs by an estimated $14.4 billion over the three years, nearly two and one-half times the amount pruned from the programs in 1981.

The changes were included in HR 4961 (PL 97-248), the massive tax increase/spending cuts bill cleared Aug. 19. The measure contained a total of $98.3 billion in tax increases and $17.5 billion in spending cuts. *(Story, p. 29)*

The bulk of the spending reductions made by the bill — $13.3 billion — came in Medicare, the massive federal health care program for the elderly and disabled. Savings were estimated at $2.9 billion in fiscal 1983, $4.4 billion in 1984 and $6 billion in 1985.

Another $1.14 billion was cut from projected spending for Medicaid, the state-federal health care program for the poor. Projected savings in that program were estimated at $275 million in fiscal 1983, $364 million in 1984 and $502 million in 1985.

The principal cost-cutting changes made by the bill were new ceilings on Medicare payments to hospitals and doctors. The legislation also required employers to offer Medicare-eligible workers comparable coverage under their company health plans, and required federal employees to pay the 1.3 percent payroll tax for Medicare coverage, a move designed to raise $2.5 billion over three years.

The bill also included several benefit expansions, which advocates said would save money over the long run by encouraging the use of less expensive forms of care. These included Medicare coverage for hospice care of terminally ill patients, a new payment system to promote Medicare enrollments in the prepaid health plans known as health maintenance organizations (HMOs), and Medicaid coverage for certain disabled children kept at home rather than in a hospital.

Congress rejected several proposals to require elderly Medicare patients to pay more out of their own pockets for their care, but it did permit states to require Medicaid beneficiaries to pay nominal fees for health care services.

HR 4961 also repealed the Professional Standards Review Organization (PSRO) program, which the administration had sought to eliminate. Instead, the bill provided for peer review of Medicare and Medicaid claims by physician review boards under contract with the Department of Health and Human Services (HHS).

Critics of the cost-cutting changes, such as Democratic Reps. Henry A. Waxman, Calif., and Charles B. Rangel, N.Y., chairmen of the House subcommittees with jurisdiction over Medicare and Medicaid, warned that reducing federal spending on the programs would simply shift costs onto others —hospitals, state and local governments, private insurers, and the poor and elderly beneficiaries of the programs themselves. But the budget resolution adopted by Congress required spending reductions in the programs of $13.7 billion in 1983-85, so members generally felt they had little choice but to agree to the cuts.

Congress already had made a number of cost-cutting changes in Medicare and Medicaid as part of the 1981 budget reconciliation bill (PL 97-35). Those cuts were expected to reduce federal spending on the programs by $5.8 billion. *(1981 Almanac p. 477)*

Provisions

Following are the legislative changes made in Medicare and Medicaid by HR 4961 (PL 97-248):

Medicare

Hospital Reimbursement. Established two new limits on reimbursement rates for hospitals:

● The first change expanded an existing limit that restricted payments to a hospital for routine operating costs (bed, board and routine nursing) to no more than 108 percent of the average of such costs of similar hospitals. The new limit would apply to both routine and ancillary services, such as laboratory work or drugs, and to average costs-per-case. It would limit payment to an individual hospital to no more than 120 percent of the average for similar hospitals in fiscal 1983, 115 percent in 1984 and 110 percent in 1985 and following years.

Rural hospitals with fewer than 50 beds were exempted from the limit, and adjustments were allowed for psychiatric hospitals, those with large numbers of Medicaid, uninsured low-income and/or Medicare patients, and certain other hospitals.

● The second limit, effective for up to three years beginning in fiscal 1983, restricted the overall annual rate of increase in a hospital's payments for operating costs, calculated on a per-case basis. Payments would be the previous year's amount, increased by the same percentage that an index of hospital wages and prices went up, plus 1 percent.

A hospital whose costs rose less in a year than the amount calculated by this formula could keep part of the difference; one whose costs rose more than the formula permitted could get one-fourth of its "excess" costs reimbursed in the first two years of the program, but none thereafter. The secretary of HHS was authorized to adjust an individual hospital's target rate up or down, for case mix or other factors.

● Permitted the secretary to calculate Medicare payments under state standards instead of the new federal limits, in states with cost control programs that met certain criteria.

● Required HHS to submit to Congress, within five months of enactment, a procedure for "prospective" payments to hospitals and nursing homes. Payments under this procedure would be a set amount each year, based on an institution's anticipated costs of caring for Medicare patients. Under existing law, charges were calculated after services were rendered.

The new plan could not take effect unless authorized by Congress.

● Required the HHS secretary to implement existing law to end a private-room subsidy for hospitals, create a single payment limit for nursing facilities and home health services, and end duplicate payments for outpatient services.

● Required the secretary to implement existing law on payments to hospital-based doctors, such as pathologists. The law restricted payments under Part B (the portion of Medicare that covers physician services) to services provided directly by doctors, and required Part A (hospitalization) rates for related services, such as laboratory work, not performed directly by the doctors.

● Barred payments for services calculated on a percent-

age basis, as when a laboratory received a percentage of total payments to a hospital, but exempted services where percentage arrangements were customary or provided incentives for efficiency.

● Suspended payments to hospitals for the last six weeks of fiscal years 1983 and 1984, so that the payments would be made after the beginning of the following fiscal year.

● Canceled the 5 percent "differential" added to routine nursing costs to cover what hospitals and nursing facilities claimed were higher costs of caring for the elderly.

● Barred reimbursement of hospitals and skilled nursing facilities for charity care given to fulfill requirements of the Hill-Burton Act, which provided hospital construction funds.

● Prohibited Medicare reimbursement to hospitals for costs of actions taken directly to influence employees' views of unionization.

Other Reimbursement Provisions. Canceled a special reimbursement rate that paid hospital-based radiologists and pathologists 100 percent of their charges. The effect would be to treat them the same as other doctors, who received 80 percent of "reasonable" charges from Medicare (adjusted to reflect the beneficiary's annual deductible).

● Prohibited reimbursements for surgical assistants in teaching hospitals, except in unusual medical circumstances.

● Required health-care providers to pay interest on Medicare overpayments when they delayed returning these funds to the government; also required the government to pay interest on money it delayed sending to hospitals to make up for underpayments.

Federal Employee Coverage. Made federal employees eligible for Medicare coverage, and required them to pay the 1.3 percent Federal Insurance Contributions Act (FICA) tax for their coverage.

Under existing law, federal employees did not pay the tax but about 80 percent of retired federal employees over age 65 received Medicare coverage anyway because of previous non-government employment or through their spouses.

Employer Health Plans. Required employers to offer the same health insurance coverage to 65-to-69-year-old workers and their dependents that they provided for younger workers, and made Medicare the secondary payer for those covered by a company plan. In effect, Medicare would become a supplementary insurance plan for those individuals choosing private coverage, the reverse of what existing law provided. Employees who chose not to join their employer's health plan would continue to receive their primary coverage from Medicare.

Employers with fewer than 20 employees were exempted from the provision.

HMO Enrollment. Authorized prospective payments to HMOs that enrolled Medicare beneficiaries, at rates that could be adjusted for such factors as age, sex and health status of beneficiaries; set certain conditions for plans that enrolled these beneficiaries.

Hospice Care. Authorized payments for hospice services for terminally ill patients, through Sept. 30, 1986, with some limitations, such as a 5 percent co-payment for covered drugs.

Extended Care. Authorized the HHS secretary to end a requirement that a patient must be hospitalized for at least three days to qualify for coverage of treatment in a skilled nursing facility, if the secretary determined that

such a change would not increase program costs.

Ineffective Drugs. Reaffirmed a provision of the 1981 reconciliation bill that barred Medicare and Medicaid payments for drugs that had not met Food and Drug Administration standards for effectiveness.

Premiums. Stipulated that premium rates for Medicare Part B coverage (for physician services) should be set to ensure that premiums would cover 25 percent of program costs. Existing law provided for gradual premium rate increases, but since 1974 the proportion of program costs paid by beneficiaries, through premiums, had declined from 47 percent to about 24 percent.

As of July 1, 1982, the monthly premium was $12.20; with the change made by HR 4961, premiums would be $13.70 (instead of $13.10) beginning July 1, 1983, and $15.30 (instead of $14), beginning July 1, 1984.

The existing method of calculating Part B premium rates would resume July 1, 1985.

Merchant Seamen. Authorized eligible merchant seamen to enroll in Medicare Part B without a late-enrollment penalty, through Dec. 31, 1982. Seamen lost access to Public Health Service care in 1981, and normally would be subject to a late enrollment penalty.

Worker Standards. Extended through Sept. 30, 1983, the HHS secretary's authority to determine the proficiency of health care workers, including those in clinical laboratories, who did not meet certain educational standards.

Audit, Medical Review. Increased by $45 million a year funding for audit and medical review activities by the fiscal intermediaries that administered the Medicare program.

Medicaid

● Permitted states to require Medicaid beneficiaries to pay nominal fees for medical services; exempted children, services for medical emergencies, pregnancy and family planning, patients in nursing homes, and welfare recipients enrolled in HMOs.

● Permitted states to put liens on the property of permanently institutionalized beneficiaries, to recover costs of medical services to the beneficiary, but only if the home was not needed by the patient, his dependents or certain others. Also permitted states, in certain circumstances, to deny Medicaid for a period of time to individuals who sold their homes below market prices.

● Repealed existing error rate reduction targets and instead required states to lower program error rates to 3 percent, beginning in fiscal 1983. Also delayed for six months, until mid-1983, penalties for failure to comply with error rate reduction targets.

● Stipulated that the value of an individual's burial policy would not be included in his financial assets when determining Medicaid or Supplemental Security Income (SSI) eligibility; also permitted states to exclude such assets from individual eligibility calculations for Medicaid.

The change was made in response to news stories about a disabled Virginia woman, Mattie Dudley, who lost Medicaid coverage because the value of her burial policy pushed her assets just above eligibility standards. When she gave the policy away, she still was ineligible because the state contended that under federal law, she had improperly divested herself of an asset to qualify for the program.

● Permitted states to provide Medicaid coverage on an outpatient basis for disabled children who under existing law qualified for SSI and Medicaid only while they were in

a hospital or other institution.

This change broadened a special exception made for one such child — Katie Beckett of Cedar Rapids, Iowa — after President Reagan cited her hospitalization as an example of problems with federal health policy.

- Delayed for six months after enactment HHS regulations loosening survey and certification requirements for nursing homes.
- Authorized Medicaid funding for American Samoa.

Peer Review Organizations

- Repealed the existing Professional Standards Review Organization (PSRO) program and instead required the secretary of HHS to provide for peer review of Medicare and Medicaid claims by contracting for such reviews with organizations composed largely of practicing physicians, to be known as Provider Reimbursement Review Boards.
- Barred review contracts with organizations owned by or affiliated with providers. The intent was to prevent hospitals or other providers from reviewing their own claims.
- Exempted the peer-review organizations from the Freedom of Information Act (requiring disclosure to the public upon request). Required disclosure to an appropriate state agency, with enough information to identify a particular practitioner or institutional provider, in cases where there appeared to be a risk to the public health. Also required disclosure of specific information, on request, to federal or state agencies concerned with program fraud and abuse, and to state licensure or certification agencies.
- Barred the secretary of HHS from terminating an existing PSRO until he had contracted with a review organization to take over its functions.
- Directed the secretary to create statewide review areas by consolidating existing PSRO areas, but permitted a locality or region with a high volume of services to be treated as a separate review area.
- Empowered peer-review organizations, through fiscal intermediaries, to deny payment for services they found to be part of a pattern of "inappropriate" use, but only if the provider had been given a chance to correct the problem and had failed to do so.
- Permitted states or other entities, such as private insurers, to use the peer review organizations; authorized federal matching payments of 75 percent for reviewing Medicaid claims.

Background

In his Feb. 8 budget message, President Reagan asked Congress to cut nearly $3.6 billion from projected spending for Medicare and Medicaid in fiscal 1983. Another $1 billion would be cut through administrative changes not requiring legislative action, he said.

Even with the proposed reductions, federal outlays for the two health programs would be $72.7 billion in 1983 and $79.6 billion in fiscal 1984, compared to $68 billion in fiscal 1982, according to the Office of Management and Budget (OMB). Fiscal 1983 outlays for Medicare were estimated at $55.4 billion, and for Medicaid, $17.1 billion; in addition, the states were expected to spend another $15.5 billion to provide Medicaid services.

About 47 million persons — nearly one out of every five Americans — would be covered by one of the two programs in 1983, according to the budget.

The administration asked Congress to bring federal

employees under Medicare; require employers to include workers aged 65-69 in their company health plans; index the deductible for Part B Medicare coverage to the Consumer Price Index; require beneficiaries to pay 5 percent of the cost of home health visits, to reduce "unnecessary utilization;" end special payment provisions for radiologists and pathologists, and reduce federal payments to hospitals by 2 percent.

In Medicaid, the administration sought to require co-payments of $1 to $2 per visit or per day of hospitalization of beneficiaries, to make them more "cost-conscious"; cut federal payments for optional services such as clinics or drugs; end federal matching payments for state purchases of Medicare coverage for the elderly poor; require states to eliminate all errors by 1986, with a reduction in funds for those that failed to achieve a zero error rate; permit states to require children of institutionalized Medicaid beneficiaries to pay part of the cost of their parents' care and to place liens on the property of those beneficiaries to facilitate recovery of Medicaid costs after their death.

The administration also repeated its 1981 request to kill the PSRO program.

Among the changes the president said would be made administratively were ending certain allowances to hospitals that the administration considered unrelated to Medicare beneficiary services, and setting a single rate for services, such as dialysis, that were offered by both hospitals and free-standing facilities.

Spending Limits

Congress balked at the president's budget, and efforts to fashion a compromise acceptable to both sides ended in failure. It was not until June 23 that Congress cleared the fiscal 1983 budget resolution (S Con Res 92) — the measure that established congressional spending limits for the year. *(Budget resolution, p. 186)*

Among the spending cuts congressional committees were required to make in fiscal 1983-85 to meet the limits set by the resolution were reductions totaling $13.7 billion in the Medicare and Medicaid programs ($11.5 billion in Medicare, $2.2 billion in Medicaid).

Senate Action

The Senate Finance Committee started the ball rolling on congressional compliance with the budget resolution by voting June 24 to cut $15.2 billion from Medicare and Medicaid spending over the next three years — $1.5 billion more than it was required to cut.

The committee completed action on its spending cuts and tax increases July 12, and reported them as part of its budget reconciliation package (HR 4961 — S Rept 97-494).

Chairman Robert Dole, R-Kan., had called for quick action on spending cuts to counter "widespread skepticism" in financial markets that Congress could cut the budget deficit.

The committee called for a major restructuring of the way the government reimbursed hospitals for Medicare patients, which would increase out-of-pocket costs for both Medicare and Medicaid recipients. By a 13-6 vote, it approved a package of 20 program changes that would shift costs from the government to hospitals, doctors, businesses that employed older workers, and individuals enrolled in the two programs.

The biggest new money-savers were two limits on what Medicare paid hospitals, and the requirement that employ-

ers include workers over the age of 65 in company health plans, thus making Medicare the secondary payer for individuals working past the age of 65. Three-year savings from this change would total $1.4 billion.

Savings from the hospital reimbursement changes were estimated at $670 million in fiscal 1983 and $5.6 billion over three years.

One change was to impose new, annual percentage caps on how much Medicare would pay for "ancillary services" such as X-rays and laboratory services. Under existing law, only payments for "routine" services such as bed and board were so restricted. For both, payments could not exceed 110 percent of the previous year's level.

The second provision set overall limits, for various types of hospitals, on how much their Medicare payments could rise each year. For three years, beginning Oct. 1, 1982, reimbursement increases would be held to 110 percent of the preceding year's level.

Meanwhile, HHS was directed to write legislation to put Medicare payments to hospitals and nursing homes on a "prospective" basis, instead of being paid after services were rendered, as under the existing system. The new system, intended to make health institutions more cost-conscious, would pay a fixed sum at the beginning of each year for anticipated costs of caring for Medicare patients.

Another major Medicare change, with three-year savings of $1.4 billion, would place a 5 percent cap on annual increases in physician fee payments. The committee also restricted payments for hospital-based specialists in radiol-

ogy and pathology. Opponents said the changes would result in higher out-of-pocket payments by beneficiaries, either for additional physician charges or for more private supplementary insurance.

The committee also voted to increase both premiums and deductibles under "Part B," the optional portion of Medicare that paid physician fees, and required beneficiaries to pay 5 percent of the cost of home health care visits.

Another change, which neither lowered nor raised program costs, would facilitate enrollment of Medicare beneficiaries in prepaid health plans (HMOs).

The biggest Medicaid savings provision would eliminate federal matching funds for states that bought Medicare Part B coverage for their elderly Medicaid beneficiaries, for three-year savings of $649 million. The committee also agreed to let states require Medicaid patients to pay "nominal" fees of 50 cents to $3 per visit for hospital care.

Among the revenue-raising provisions of HR 4961, the committee voted to require federal employees to pay the 1.3 percent FICA tax for Medicare coverage.

Senate Floor Action

The Senate passed HR 4961 early July 23 by a largely party-line vote of 50-47. *(Vote 257, p. 44-S)*

Surprisingly little opposition was raised to the spending cuts of $4.2 billion for fiscal 1983, $6 billion in 1984 and $7.3 billion in 1985 in health and welfare programs that were included in the package.

An amendment by David Durenberger, R-Minn., to reduce the Medicare cuts was the only major change to the spending side of the package. His proposal, adopted 99-0, restored approximately $400 million in Medicare spending over the three-year period. *(Vote 236, p. 42-S)*

Under Durenberger's amendment, the bill would leave the deductible for part B at the 1982 level of $75 for 1983, and increase it to approximately $78 in 1984 and $80 in 1985. The committee bill would have raised the deductible each year, up to approximately $89 in 1985, to reflect increases in the cost of living.

The amendment also would end, or "sunset," after 1985 the provision requiring Medicare premiums to equal approximately 25 percent of program costs. It also revised a committee provision requiring a 5 percent co-payment (estimated to be about $2 a visit in 1983) for home health care visits by making the first 20 visits free.

The Durenberger plan was adopted after an attempt by Max Baucus, D-Mont., to eliminate all three Medicare provisions from the bill. That would have increased program spending by $1.5 billion over three years.

Baucus' proposal was rejected 46-53, but eight Republicans voted for it. Durenberger's promise to offer a compromise package was credited with preventing more GOP defections. *(Vote 235, p. 42-S)*

An amendment by John Heinz, R-Pa., to allow Medicare reimbursement for hospice care for the terminally ill also was adopted.

The Republican concessions on Medicare were among several changes Dole agreed to in an attempt to ensure passage of the carefully crafted package.

House Committee Action

The House Ways and Means Committee, which had jurisdiction over Medicare, July 15 endorsed a package of reductions in the projected growth of the program in fiscal 1983-85.

Means Test for Medicare?

Congress expressed its opposition in September to "any proposal to impose a 'means test' on eligibility for the Medicare program or benefits provided by the Medicare program."

The action followed news reports that the Reagan administration was considering such a proposal as a way of saving money in the fiscal 1984 budget.

Congressional Democrats reacted angrily to the reports, and sense-of-Congress resolutions opposing a means test were introduced in both chambers. Sponsors said limiting Medicare coverage only to persons who demonstrated financial need would profoundly alter the character of the Medicare program and would be a breach of faith with the American people.

Among those introducing resolutions of disapproval were Rep. Peter A. Peyser, D-N.Y., and Sens. Gary Hart, D-Colo.; Daniel Patrick Moynihan, D-N.Y., and Edward M. Kennedy, D-Mass.

Moynihan offered his resolution Sept. 29 as an amendment to the fiscal 1983 continuing appropriations resolution (H J Res 599). The Senate adopted it 70-29. *(Vote 369, p. 62-S)*

Conferees accepted the amendment, so it became part of the stopgap funding measure (PL 97-276). *(Story, p. 225)*

Medicare was established in 1965 as part of the Social Security system, to provide health insurance to people over 65 and to the disabled, regardless of income. About 26 million elderly and three million disabled persons were enrolled in 1982. *(Background, Congress and the Nation Vol. II, p. 751)*

The committee bill (HR 6878), approved in an unusual closed-door meeting, would reduce Medicare spending by about $12 billion in fiscal 1983-1985. The budget resolution called for cuts of $11.5 billion.

The committee's action surprised some observers since Chairman Dan Rostenkowski, D-Ill., had warned during debate on the budget resolution that it would be difficult, if not impossible, for the committee to come anywhere near the Medicare savings required by the resolution. The panel's Health Subcommittee, chaired by Rangel, made only $5.9 billion in cuts, leaving it up to the full committee to make the rest.

According to committee member John H. Rousselot, R-Calif., the Democrats waited for the Republicans to push for the cuts and planned to blame the GOP for the reductions in the politically sensitive programs.

The major source of savings in the committee bill was new restraints on payments to hospitals, similar to those in the Senate bill. The panel also called on the secretary of HHS to develop a prospective reimbursement plan for hospitals by Dec. 31, 1982, and put it into effect by July 1, 1983, unless Congress disapproved it. Savings from that change were estimated at $5.65 billion in fiscal 1983-85.

The committee rejected one major money-saver in the Senate measure: the requirement that employers include Medicare-eligible workers in their private health insurance plans. But it agreed to make federal employees subject to the hospital insurance portion of Social Security taxes.

It also authorized a voucher system for Medicare beneficiaries who chose to leave the federal program and buy private health insurance instead. Sponsors estimated the provision would add $50 billion to Medicare expenditures in three years, but eventually would save money.

Also adopted by the committee were provisions that:

● Increased funding for audit and medical review of Medicare contractors. (Estimated savings: $730 million in 1983-85)

● Reaffirmed, for purposes of claiming reconciliation savings, five sections of existing law that the administration was planning to enforce anyway. They would give Medicare contractors goals and greater authority for reducing wasteful spending; restrict reimbursements to hospital-based physicians; end payments to physicians for "overhead" expenses associated with outpatient services they provided in hospitals; end special private-room payments, and establish a single system of limits on payments for nursing facilities and home health services. (Estimated savings: $2.35 billion)

● Suspended payments to hospitals for the last six weeks of fiscal 1982-1983; payments would be made after the start of the following fiscal years. (Net cost: $20 million in 1985)

● Authorized payments for hospice services to terminally ill Medicare patients from Aug. 1, 1983, until Sept. 30, 1986. (Estimated savings: $13 million)

● Prohibited payments for surgical assistants in teaching hospitals except in certain circumstances. (Estimated savings: $335 million)

● Required health-care providers to pay interest on Medicare overpayments when they delayed returning the funds to the government; also required the government to pay interest on money it delayed sending to hospitals to make up for underpayments. (Estimated savings: $70 million)

● Barred hospitals from being reimbursed for charity care given to fulfill requirements of the Hill-Burton Act. (Estimated savings: $52 million)

● Barred reimbursement of hospitals for costs associated with actions taken to discourage unionization.

● Authorized the HHS secretary to end a requirement that a patient must be hospitalized at least three days to qualify for coverage of treatment in a skilled nursing facility, if the change would not add to program costs.

● Authorized advance payments to prepaid health plans that enrolled Medicare beneficiaries.

● Barred most payments for services calculated on a percentage basis.

Commerce Committee Action

The Energy and Commerce Committee, which had jurisdiction over Medicaid and Part B of Medicare, approved a short list of changes in those programs July 28, and filed its report Aug. 17 (HR 6877 — H Rept 97-757).

Although a stormy session had been expected, deliberations went smoothly and the final package, approved by voice vote, came within several hundred million dollars of reaching the committee's reconciliation savings goal.

The Health Subcommittee did not meet on reconciliation proposals. Instead, its chairman, Waxman, brought to the committee a compromise package constructed by him, ranking Republican Edward R. Madigan, Ill., full committee Chairman John D. Dingell, D-Mich., and ranking Republican James T. Broyhill, N.C.

Waxman said he was unhappy about cutting the programs, but that the compromise package was a "damage-control" tactic to forestall more harmful changes. Waxman had said during debate on the budget resolution in May that regardless of the reconciliation instructions that were ultimately adopted, the House Democratic leadership would not go along with health budget reductions of the size sought by the administration.

The budget resolution directed the Energy and Commerce Committee to reduce projected spending for Medicaid by $2.219 billion in fiscal 1983-85. The panel nearly achieved the savings goal, recommending changes to reduce spending by $2.059 billion. However, only $683 million of the savings came from changes in Medicaid. The remainder came from revisions in Medicare. Exercising its jurisdiction over Medicare "Part B," the optional plan that covered physician services, the committee adopted two new restraints on payments to doctors.

The committee also included in its budget package a plan it had approved in 1981 (HR 3399 — H Rept 97-119) to promote enrollment of Medicare beneficiaries in HMOs. HMOs offered comprehensive medical services for a fixed annual fee and their internal budgeting was thought to hold down medical expenditures, but participation by Medicare patients had been discouraged by Medicare's method of paying for services after they were delivered.

Like the Senate bill, the Energy and Commerce bill provided for Medicare enrollments in the prepaid plans by authorizing advance payment of the plans' fees. The House committee stipulated that the change not take place until the secretary of HHS devised an actuarially sound, money-saving way of calculating the fees.

The plan was not as broad as the Ways and Means Committee's voucher system, which would allow Medicare beneficiaries to leave the federal program and buy comparable private services instead, either from a prepaid plan or under conventional health insurance.

Energy and Commerce also included provisions slightly loosening Medicaid eligibility in two respects. It allowed states to include the "working poor" in the pro-

gram; many of these individuals had lost Medicaid coverage along with welfare benefits because of a 1981 tightening of eligibility standards. It also allowed states to provide coverage for medical care of disabled children living at home, if the children would be eligible if hospitalized.

The committee agreed to cancel existing restrictions on states that chose to require Medicaid recipients to pay nominal fees for services, but exempted from such co-payments children, pregnant women, emergency services, family planning and care of institutionalized individuals who already paid for part of their care. It limited co-payments to $1 per hospital day or outpatient visit for recipients whose participation in Aid to Families with Dependent Children (AFDC) qualified them for Medicaid, but allowed co-payments of up to $4 for non-emergency visits to emergency rooms.

The committee permitted states to put liens on property of permanently institutionalized beneficiaries and to recover costs of medical services to a beneficiary by disposing of the property, but only if it was unneeded by the beneficiary or his dependents. Existing law authorized such liens only after the death of a beneficiary.

The bill also permitted states, in certain circumstances, to deny Medicaid to individuals who sold their homes below market prices.

The committee modified a scheduled reduction in federal matching rates by allowing states to regain 1 percent of their federal matching funds if they created a hospital rate review program meeting certain standards or took other steps that effectively reduced their rates of increase in hospital costs by 2 percent, compared with average national hospital costs. Existing law allowed states to regain matching funds only if a qualified cost control program was in place by July 1, 1981.

Medicare provisions approved by the committee:

● Limited the July 1, 1982, increase in payment for physician fees to 4 percent more than the previous year's rate, based on an economic index; however, permitted physicians agreeing to accept "assignment" for all Medicare patients to receive the full 8.8 percent scheduled increase. (Estimated savings: $830 million)

● Canceled a special reimbursement rate that paid hospital-based radiologists and pathologists 100 percent of their charges instead of 80 percent of "reasonable" charges, like other physicians. (Estimated savings: $570 million)

● Authorized merchant seamen to enroll in Medicare Part B (physician services coverage) from 20 days after enactment until Dec. 31, 1982, without financial penalty. Under existing law, the seamen, who lost access to Public Health Service care in 1981, would have to pay a financial penalty for late enrollment. (Cost: $22.2 billion)

Final Legislative Action

In an unusual procedure, the House decided by a 208-197 vote July 28 to skip floor votes on HR 4961 and instead go directly to conference with the Senate on the bill. *(Vote 213, p. 62-H)*

Because the House had not passed the bill, House conferees were not formally bound by the committees' reconciliation decisions, but those actions constituted strong recommendations.

The conferees agreed on the least controversial Medicare-Medicaid provisions during sessions Aug. 3, 4 and 5. They accepted proposals to extend Medicare coverage to hospice care for terminally ill patients and to authorize a

new payment method for Medicare beneficiaries who wanted to enroll in prepaid health plans. They also agreed to let states impose nominal co-payments on Medicaid beneficiaries, with certain exemptions, and liens against the homes of certain institutionalized Medicaid recipients.

However, three days of deadlock over other health and welfare cuts were not broken until Aug. 12. The hang-up occurred because some House Democrats wanted to restore some of the cuts made in Medicaid and welfare programs by the 1981 reconciliation bill. By some estimates, these restorations would have added $1 billion to the costs of the programs in fiscal 1983-85.

The House add-ons were adamantly opposed by Sen. Russell B. Long, D-La., ranking Senate Democrat on the conference committee. House conferees finally yielded after senators agreed to go along with several welfare and unemployment provisions the House supported.

Among proposals rejected by conferees were provisions that would cap physician-fee increases, require co-payments for home health care services and increase the deductible for Medicare Part B.

The conferees inserted in the bill a provision, not included in either the Senate or House committee bills, barring HHS from implementing certain proposed changes in nursing home certification requirements for a period of six months after enactment of the bill. The conferees said the moratorium was intended to allow time for further review of the controversial regulations.

The conference report (H Rept 97-760), filed Aug. 17, was approved by the House Aug. 19 by a vote of 226-207. *(Vote 289, p. 84-H)*

The Senate approved it the same day by a 52-47 vote, clearing it for the president. *(Vote 337, p. 55-S)* ∎

Welfare Spending Cuts

Congress in 1982 approved changes in federal welfare programs designed to cut an estimated $1.1 billion from anticipated spending for those programs in fiscal 1983-85. However, it refused to slash welfare spending as deeply as the Reagan administration wanted.

The changes were incorporated in the massive tax increase/spending cuts bill cleared by Congress Aug. 19 (HR 4961 — PL 97-248). *(Story, p. 29)*

Changes were made in the core federal welfare program, Aid to Families with Dependent Children (AFDC), in child support enforcement and in the Supplemental Security Income (SSI) program for the aged, blind and disabled. Savings over the three-year period were estimated at $343 million in AFDC, $384 million in child support enforcement and $386 million in SSI.

Among other things, the bill allowed states to require AFDC applicants and recipients to participate in job search programs, increased penalties for states with high error rates in the administration of benefits and reduced welfare payments through a variety of administrative provisions. It did not include a mandatory "workfare" program for welfare recipients or new block grant proposals for child welfare and emergency assistance, as President Reagan had urged.

The administration proposed spending cuts totaling $7.7 billion in federal welfare programs. But the Senate, following the lead of the Finance Committee, agreed to cut only about one-fourth of that.

The House Ways and Means Committee, in an effort to meet budget reconciliation requirements, included a modified package of cuts in its tax increase/spending cuts bill (HR 6878), but the full House declined to vote on the controversial measure. House Democrats attempted in conference on HR 4961 to restore a number of cuts made in health and welfare programs in 1981, but Senate conferees held firm against any spending additions and the effort failed.

Congress had made numerous changes in the welfare programs in 1981, as part of the fiscal 1982 budget reconciliation bill (PL 97-35). The Congressional Budget Office estimated those changes would result in savings of $1.2 billion in fiscal 1982 and $1.4 billion in each of fiscal years 1983 and 1984. *(1981 Almanac p. 473)*

Provisions

HR 4961 (PL 97-248) made the following changes in federal welfare programs:

AFDC

• Required states to round their need standards and monthly benefit amounts in the AFDC program to the next lower dollar.

• Provided for prorating of AFDC benefits during a recipient's first month on the program according to the date on which the application was filed.

• Excluded from the program families in which the father was absent because of military service.

• Permitted states to require AFDC applicants and recipients to participate in a program of employment search beginning at the time of application.

• Required that a portion of the income of unrelated adults who shared living quarters with an AFDC family be included in calculating the family's AFDC benefits.

• Increased penalties paid by states whose error rates in awarding AFDC benefits exceeded 4 percent in fiscal 1983 and 3 percent in 1984 and 1985.

• Allowed states the option, for two additional years, of operating a Work Incentive (WIN) demonstration program authorized by the 1981 reconciliation law.

Child Support Enforcement

• Repealed a provision of the 1981 reconciliation law that required states to charge a 10 percent fee for child support payments collected on behalf of non-AFDC families; permitted the states to charge a reasonable fee.

• Allowed collection of child support payments from the pay of a member of the armed forces if the absent parent was two months behind in his payments.

• Allowed states to retain a portion of child support payments collected for an AFDC family if the state had already paid benefits to the family for the month during which the child support funds were collected.

• Reduced the federal matching rate for state costs of operating the child support enforcement program.

Supplemental Security Income

• Established a prorating procedure under which SSI benefit levels for recipients during their first month on the program would be determined according to the day of the month on which they applied or met eligibility requirements. Under existing law, recipients received a full month's benefits regardless of what day of the month they applied.

• Provided for rounding of a recipient's benefit amounts to the next lower dollar.

• Required that SSI benefits be reduced in the first month in which a recipient received a cost-of-living increase in Social Security payments.

• Excluded from countable resources, for eligibility purposes, burial spaces for an individual or members of his immediate family. Burial funds of up to $1,500 each for the individual and his or her spouse also would be excluded if specifically set aside for this purpose.

• Allowed states to shift from the aggregate spending option to the state supplementation payment level option.

• Clarified the authority to credit states for unnegotiated SSI benefit checks which were "state supplementation only" checks.

Reagan Welfare Proposals

In his fiscal 1983 budget, released Feb. 6, President Reagan proposed major cost-cutting changes in all of the big income security programs for the poor and elderly except Social Security. *(Reagan budget, p. 175)*

Several of the programs were among the so-called "social safety net" programs Reagan had promised in 1981 to protect from budget cuts. *(1981 Almanac p. 461)*

Critics said the proposed cuts would have a harsh impact on the poor, who already had lost substantial federal aid under the 1981 reconciliation bill.

Several themes ran through the administration proposals: mandatory work requirements for welfare recipients; "targeting" of benefits on the most needy by reducing benefits to persons with relatively higher incomes; reductions of "overlapping" benefits by counting federal assistance from one program in calculating eligibility and benefits for another, and a crackdown on inefficient administration of programs by penalizing states for errors in the payment of benefits.

Reagan had made many of the same proposals in 1981, but Congress rejected them.

AFDC. Legislative changes sought for AFDC would save $1.2 billion in fiscal 1983, bringing total costs of the program down to $5.5 billion. The changes would save a total of $5.9 billion by fiscal 1987, the administration said.

Reagan proposed to reduce the size of welfare payments by counting benefits from other government programs, such as low-income energy assistance, as income in calculating AFDC eligibility and benefits. Under existing law, such payments were not counted.

He also proposed to count other sources of income, such as part of the income of unrelated adults who lived with an AFDC family. The savings in living costs achieved by sharing a household with other people not on AFDC also would be taken into account in computing a family's needs. Families that shared a house with others would have lower living expenses and thus would receive lower welfare benefits.

Families that got benefits because the father was absent while in the military would be dropped from the program. Parents whose youngest child was 16 or older also would lose AFDC benefits, although the child would still be eligible for some benefits until age 18.

The administration proposed to eliminate the $61 million AFDC emergency assistance program and to include it in a block grant with low-income energy assistance instead. Congress rejected a similar proposal in 1981. *(1981 Almanac p. 488)*

Noting that less than half the states had decided to set up work experience programs authorized by the 1981 reconciliation law, the administration proposed to force states to do so. Welfare recipients would have to find private jobs or perform public service work in exchange for their benefits, and applicants would have to exhaust all possible opportunities for finding work before they could get welfare benefits.

Reagan also proposed to eliminate the work incentive (WIN) program, which helped welfare recipients find jobs and provided job training and social services for them, and to restructure the child support enforcement program, rewarding states that did a good job of collecting child support money from absent parents.

In an effort to improve state administration of welfare benefits, Reagan proposed to limit federal matching for state costs of administering welfare programs and to impose much stricter penalties for states that paid excess welfare benefits.

Under existing law, the federal government paid half the cost of state administration of the AFDC, food stamp and Medicaid programs. Under the new plan — known as the combined welfare administration block grant — states would get a fixed amount to operate the programs, with no specific matching requirement. Funding for the administrative grants would be set 5 percent below the federal share of administrative costs in fiscal 1982.

States would have four years to eliminate errors in payment of welfare benefits. Under existing law, the federal government penalized states that had welfare error rates (payments to ineligible persons or in excessive amounts) above 4 percent. Reagan proposed to reduce the allowable error rate by one percentage point a year, until by 1986 no error would be allowed. The federal government then would not reimburse states for any welfare payments made in error.

SSI. Somewhat less drastic changes were requested in the SSI program, although by fiscal 1987 the estimated annual savings of the proposals would be $1.1 billion, according to the budget.

In addition to some technical changes that were also applied to AFDC and food stamps (such as "prorating" the first month's benefits according to the day on which benefits were applied for and rounding benefit amounts down to the lower dollar), the budget called for elimination of the $20-a-month unearned income disregard used in setting SSI benefits for new recipients. Under existing law, working SSI recipients, like food stamp recipients, could deduct part of their job income before calculating benefits. Reagan's proposal would result in benefit reductions for new applicants.

Standards for determining whether an applicant was truly disabled also would be tightened. To receive SSI disability payments, applicants would have to show that they were expected to be disabled for at least two years, compared to one year under existing law. They also would have to show that they were medically disabled — unable to undertake substantial gainful employment. Under existing practice, benefits could be awarded to workers who were partially disabled and could show that there was little chance they would be able to find new work.

Other Programs. Reagan's budget called for deep cuts in social service programs and a consolidation of existing programs into new block grants, including a child welfare block grant. The new grant would be formed of the existing child welfare, foster care, adoption assistance and child welfare training programs. Funding for the combined program would be $380 million, a 27 percent reduction from the 1981 level.

Congress in 1981 refused to include child welfare programs in a social services block grant. *(1981 Almanac p. 488)*

Reagan also proposed to turn funding for state rehabilitation services for the handicapped into a block grant and reduce its funding by 30 percent from the 1981 level, to $663 million.

Other budget proposals in the welfare area included:

● Deep funding cuts in two block grants established by the 1981 budget reconciliation law. The social services block grant's funding was set at $1.97 billion, a $426 million reduction from fiscal 1982. The community services block grant would get $100 million, a 79 percent reduction in community services funding since 1981.

● Elimination of Volunteers in Service to America (VISTA), and a cut in outlays for the ACTION volunteer agency to $119 million from $133 million.

● A reduction in funding for programs for refugees and Cuban and Haitian entrants. Predicting a decline in the number of new refugees and savings from more restrictive aid policies, the budget called for reductions in funding authority to $532 million, from $670 million in 1982.

Legislative Action

Senate Committee. The Senate Finance Committee — the first panel to act on spending reductions mandated by the congressional budget resolution for fiscal 1983 (S Con Res 92) — made changes designed to pare $2.1 billion from federal spending for welfare programs in fiscal 1983-85 — only about one-fourth of the cut sought by the administration.

The changes were folded into the committee's budget reconciliation package and reported July 12 (HR 4961 — S Rept 97-494).

The committee agreed to $1.6 billion in cuts in AFDC, child support enforcement and SSI. It agreed to end AFDC parent benefits when the youngest child turned 16; include all children, even those earning income, in determining a family's AFDC benefit, and count the income of an unrelated adult in the AFDC household as part of the family income. It also agreed to round SSI and AFDC benefit payments down to the next lowest dollar and to prorate benefits according to the day of the month the application was made or eligibility requirements were met.

The committee rejected the administration proposal to require welfare recipients to participate in "workfare" programs, although it did include a provision requiring applicants for AFDC to undertake efforts to find employment.

The committee also rejected proposed cuts in the social services block grant program and consolidation of child welfare services into block grants.

A major savings proposal was the imposition of penalties on states that had high error rates in administering AFDC. The committee also agreed to repeal the AFDC emergency assistance program.

Provisions adopted by the committee included: a reduction in SSI benefits beginning in the first month in which a recipient received a cost-of-living increase in Social Security payments; authority for the Social Security Administration to recover amounts paid to individuals in excess of their correct SSI benefits by reducing their payments under the Social Security or Black Lung programs,

and a requirement that a teen-age mother be eligible for AFDC only if she lived with her own parent, and that the income of that parent be taken into account in determining whether the girl and her baby were eligible for benefits.

Senate Floor Action. The Senate passed HR 4961 by a 50-47 vote in the session which began July. It made no changes in the welfare spending provisions. *(Vote 257, p. 44-S)*

House Committee Action. The House Ways and Means Committee, in an unusual closed-door meeting July 15, agreed to fiscal 1983-85 spending cuts of $20.9 billion to meet its budget reconciliation target.

Although the bulk of the reductions were in Medicare, the panel agreed to make limited savings in AFDC, SSI and unemployment compensation. Among the welfare provisions agreed to was one that would allow states to insist that individuals look for jobs before they began receiving AFDC payments.

The committee filed no written report on its spending cuts/revenue raising bill (HR 6878).

The panel had been expected to vote down many of the proposed cuts in committee, thus forcing Republicans to offer amendments on the House floor making reductions in the politically sensitive health and welfare programs. Instead, the committee held its meeting in private, took no recorded votes and came out with savings close to what it was instructed to achieve.

House Floor. In an unusual move, the House voted to skip floor votes on the spending cut/tax increase package of the Ways and Means Committee and the spending cuts endorsed by the Energy and Commerce Committee. Instead, it went directly to conference on HR 4961.

Conference Action. In conference, House Democrats attempted unsuccessfully to restore some of the cuts made in Medicaid and AFDC in 1981. By some estimates, the changes would have added $1 billion to the cost of the programs in fiscal 1983-85.

Sen. Russell B. Long, D-La., ranking Senate Democrat on the conference committee, adamantly opposed the move, arguing that conferees should be "trying to get the genie back in the bottle as far as spending is concerned."

The conferees eventually agreed to a spending package that cut income security programs such as AFDC and SSI by $1.1 billion over the three-year period. The conference agreement on the spending cuts and tax increases was filed Aug. 17 (H Rept 97-760).

Final Action. The House adopted the conference report Aug. 19, 226-207, despite attacks by liberal Democrats on the cuts in Medicare, AFDC and other social programs. The Senate approved the measure Aug. 19, 52-47, clearing it for the president. *(House vote 289, p. 84-H; Senate vote 337, p. 55-S)*   ∎

More Changes Made in Food Stamp Program

Congress again made changes in the food stamp law in 1982, in an effort to hold down the soaring costs of the program. The revisions were expected to save $1.9 billion in fiscal 1983-85; they would not reduce federal spending for the program, but simply slow its rate of growth.

The changes, along with changes in farm programs, were included in an omnibus fiscal 1983 budget reconciliation bill cleared Aug. 18 (HR 6955 — PL 97-253). *(p. 199)*

Together, the changes would cut anticipated spending for farm and food programs in the three fiscal years by $6.6 billion, the Congressional Budget Office estimated — nearly twice the amount of savings mandated by the fiscal 1983 budget resolution (S Con Res 92). *(p. 186)*

HR 6955 cut an estimated $548 million from projected fiscal 1983 spending for food stamps, which recipients could exchange for food at grocery stores. The bill placed a "cap" of $12.87 billion on food stamp spending in fiscal 1983, $13.14 billion in 1984 and $13.93 billion in 1985.

The federal government spent $11.3 billion on the program in fiscal 1982. About 22 million persons — nearly one of every 10 Americans — received food stamps in 1982.

For recipients, the revisions made in the program by HR 6955 would mean less generous adjustments in benefits to account for rising food prices, and tighter eligibility standards. The bill also strengthened work requirements and authorized pilot projects in which recipients would lose their food stamps if they did not work at least 20 hours a week. States were required to reduce their error rates in awarding food stamp benefits or lose some of the federal funds they received for administering the program.

Congress rejected proposals by the Reagan administration and by several conservative Republican senators to make deeper cuts in the program and to put a greater share of the burden of the cuts on recipients.

Conferees on the bill rejected a Senate-passed plan to let states substitute cash payments for food stamps. They also canceled a program, enacted in 1981, that had allowed the substitution of cash for food stamps in Puerto Rico.

Congress had made numerous changes in the food stamp law in 1981, but could not agree on future spending levels or inflation adjustments for the program. So the program was reauthorized for only one year, necessitating further action in 1982. *(1981 action, 1981 Almanac p. 466)*

Provisions

The food stamp provisions of HR 6955 (PL 97-253):

Spending Levels. Reauthorized the food stamp program for three years. Set authorization levels, or spending caps, of $12.874 billion for fiscal 1983, $13.145 billion for 1984, and $13.933 billion for 1985, including $825 million a year for Puerto Rico.

The authorizations included a 5 percent "cushion" on top of a basic estimate of projected costs, to allow appropriations to rise if poor economic conditions brought more people into the program than anticipated.

Benefits. Delayed scheduled adjustments in the "thrifty food plan," the government's list of low-cost foods whose price determined the value of stamps given to beneficiaries.

The bill called for the plan to be updated on Oct. 1, 1982, to reflect food price changes for the 21 months ending June 30, 1982, minus 1 percent. The Oct. 1, 1983, and Oct. 1, 1984, adjustments would reflect food price changes for the 12 months ending the preceding June, also minus 1 percent. The Oct. 1, 1985, adjustment would reflect food price changes for the 12 months ending in the preceding June, but without the 1 percent reduction.

● Delayed the next inflation adjustment of the standard deduction, used in determining benefits, until Oct. 1, 1983. The deduction, which was $85 a month in 1982, would be adjusted July 1, 1983.

● Required that food stamp benefits be rounded down to the nearest dollar. Previously, benefits had been rounded up or down to the nearest dollar.

● Barred payments of prorated benefits of less than $10 a month and revised certain dates for prorating.

● Barred benefit increases to a household whose income dropped because of a penalty for non-compliance with welfare laws.

Eligibility. Provided that a permanently disabled individual aged 60 or older, who was unable to prepare his or her own food and who lived with others, could, along with his or her spouse, qualify for food stamps as a separate household if the gross income of the people with whom the disabled person lived was no more than 65 percent above the official poverty line.

● Made disabled veterans and their survivors eligible for food stamps under certain circumstances.

● Disqualified from the program households with net monthly incomes (after various expense disregards and deductions) above 100 percent of the federal poverty level, unless the household contained an elderly or disabled member. In addition, to be eligible for food stamps, a household's gross monthly income must not exceed 130 percent of the poverty level. In 1982, the poverty level as used in the food stamp program was $9,300 a year in net income for a non-farm family of four.

● Allowed states to use a standard utility allowance in calculating a household's expenses to determine eligibility.

● Required that accessible pension funds and savings or retirement accounts be counted in determining eligibility for food stamps, except in certain circumstances.

● Permitted households to qualify for food stamps if all members received Aid to Families with Dependent Children (AFDC) and if the household's gross income did not exceed 130 percent of the federal poverty level.

● Permitted states to allow certain types of households to report their incomes less frequently than every month; also permitted states to revise periodic reporting rules to conform with AFDC reporting requirements.

● Specified that college or other postsecondary students could qualify for food stamps only if they had a child under age 6 (or under age 12 if no satisfactory child care was available) and received AFDC benefits.

● Allowed the secretary of agriculture to determine the beginning of the disqualification period for food stamp participants who voluntarily quit their jobs without good cause. Lengthened the period of ineligibility to 90 days, from 60 days. Specified that federal, state or local government employees who lost their jobs because they participated in a strike would be considered as having voluntarily quit.

Work Requirements. Permitted states to require that unemployed food stamp applicants — as well as recipients — actively look for work.

● Applied work registration requirements to parents or caretakers of young children when there was another able-bodied parent or caretaker in the household. Under existing law, persons responsible for the care of children under 6 were exempt from work registration requirements. The effect of the change was to require the second parent or caretaker to look for work when the youngest child in a household became 6 years old.

● Authorized four pilot projects to determine the effect of disqualifying individuals who did not work at least 20 hours a week or participate in a workfare program.

● Ended an automatic exemption from the workfare requirement for food stamp recipients who spent at least 20 hours a week in a work incentive program, but permitted states to continue the exemption if they wished. Also revised the maximum number of workfare hours required of a recipient, and provided for some reimbursements to states for workfare administrative expenses.

Administration. Authorized the agriculture secretary to limit the use of food stamps for purchases from house-to-house tradesmen to cases where access to grocery stores was limited.

● Permitted the secretary to limit the number of households for which one individual could serve as an authorized representative and to establish verification standards for such households and representatives.

● Required that food stamps be supplied within five days of application to destitute migrant or seasonal farm workers with liquid assets of less than $100, or to households with gross incomes lower than $150 a month.

● Required states to establish a system for determining periodically that no individual was receiving food stamps in more than one jurisdiction in the state.

● Permitted states to require food stamp applications to be included in applications for AFDC or general assistance; also permitted states to make food stamp eligibility determinations on the basis of AFDC or general assistance files. Affirmed that food stamp eligibility could continue after disqualification from AFDC, and that food stamp disqualification decisions must be made separately.

● Required states to determine, at least every year, that people who had been "cashed out" of the program were not still receiving food stamps in addition to cash payments.

● Permitted the agriculture secretary to require states to issue food stamp cards, for use in an automatic data processing system, instead of stamps, if he determined that such a system was necessary to control fraud and abuse.

● Doubled, to $10,000, the maximum civil penalty for each violation of food stamp law by stores. Established disqualification periods for violators, with permanent disqualification for a third violation for trafficking in food stamps or related documents. Also authorized the secretary to require bonds from disqualified stores that wished to re-enter the program.

● Permitted states to keep part of the funds they recovered from fraudulent issues of food stamps, unless the state made a mistake in issuing them.

● Required states to reduce payment error rates to 9 percent for fiscal year 1983, 7 percent for fiscal 1984, and 5 percent for fiscal 1985 and thereafter. Those failing to meet the goals would lose some of their administrative funds.

Puerto Rico. Barred Puerto Rico from distributing its share of federal food stamp funds in the form of cash after Oct. 1, 1983, thus ending the nutritional assistance block grant program for the commonwealth that was established by the 1981 budget reconciliation act (PL 97-35).

Administration Proposal

The Reagan administration, in its Feb. 6 budget, proposed to cut food stamp spending by nearly 20 percent in fiscal 1983. It requested savings of $2.3 billion, to bring the cost of the program to $9.6 billion, from the 1982 level of $11.3 billion.

Some of the proposed changes would have sharply reduced benefits to recipients with earned income.

The working poor would have been most severely affected by a proposal to eliminate the "earned income disregard." That provision allowed recipients with jobs to exclude 18 percent of their work income from the calculations that determined benefits. The 1981 reconciliation law already had reduced it to 18 percent from 20 percent.

A further cut in benefits to recipients with relatively higher incomes would have been achieved by increasing the "benefit reduction rate." Under existing law, benefits were reduced by 30 cents for each dollar of income (after various deductions were taken into account). President Reagan sought to raise that to 35 cents. Thus, for each $100 of income, a food stamp recipient would lose $35 in food stamp benefits.

The administration also proposed to count energy assistance as income in determining benefits; require food stamp applicants to look for a job; eliminate benefits to persons eligible for less than $10 a month in food stamps; round benefits down to the next dollar, and require states to lower their error rates in determining eligibility and benefits or lose administrative funds. It also proposed that the nutritional block grant for Puerto Rico, established by the 1981 reconciliation law, be expanded to include the U.S. island territories.

Congress rejected Reagan's budget, but it did agree in its own budget resolution to make cuts in the food stamp program totaling $3.2 billion — $779 million in fiscal 1983, $1.08 billion in 1984 and $1.4 billion in 1985.

Senate Committee Action

The Senate Agriculture Committee worked on a reauthorization of the food stamp program in May and June. In sessions July 15 and 16, it wrapped its legislative changes into its budget reconciliation package.

The committee approved changes designed to provide savings of $815 million in fiscal 1983, $846 million in 1984 and $908 million in 1985.

Despite the cuts, the legislation approved by the committee was something of a victory for food stamp advocates, especially Nutrition Subcommittee Chairman Robert Dole, R-Kan. The savings were achieved by provisions — such as slowing the inflation updating of benefits or penalizing states with poorly administered programs — that were expected to have less impact on recipients than those sought by committee Chairman Jesse Helms, R-N.C.

Dole also was successful in adding to the committee's part of the reconciliation bill a three-year reauthorization for the food stamp program, which he said would give it a respite from the repeated changes made in it by Congress in recent years.

In addition, the bill contained spending ceilings on the program — $11.9 billion in fiscal 1983, $12.3 billion in fiscal 1984 and $13.2 billion in fiscal 1985 — that were expected to allow ample room to meet program costs.

Most of the reconciliation savings effected by the committee already had been obtained during several months of intermittent markup of food stamp reauthorizing legislation. The main bills before the panel were S 2352, introduced by Helms, and S 2493, by Dole. An administration bill (S 2392) and another (S 2480) by S. I. "Sam" Hayakawa, R-Calif., also were considered. Helms' bill would have cut $2.3 billion from food stamp costs in fiscal 1983, the same as the administration request. Dole's bill provided for cuts of $780 million.

It was clear throughout the markups that the committee was unwilling to go as far as Helms would have liked in scaling back the program. His efforts were blocked repeatedly by Dole, whose argument that the program should not have to bear further sharp cuts after being cut severely in 1981 had the support of committee Republicans such as Rudy Boschwitz, Minn., and Thad Cochran, Miss., as well as most committee Democrats.

The food stamp savings made by the committee exceeded its $779 million reconciliation target for fiscal 1983 but fell short in 1984 and 1985. The committee approved cuts in federal dairy programs to make up the difference.

Major Savings Provisions

The largest single savings provision adopted by the committee was to delay the inflation indexing of the thrifty food plan. The delays would cause benefit levels to fall behind increases in the cost of food, for a three-year savings of more than $800 million.

The committee also assumed that $600 million in savings could be obtained by penalizing states that had high error rates in the distribution of benefits. By 1985, states that handed out more than 5 percent of their food stamps incorrectly — to ineligible people or in amounts in excess of what recipients were supposed to get — would face reductions in federal funding of their administrative costs of operating the program.

The committee achieved additional savings by adopting a Dole proposal to delay the indexing of various income deductions used in calculating benefit amounts.

As part of the reauthorizing legislation included in the reconciliation proposal, the committee included a Helms provision allowing states to establish their own nutritional block grants in place of the food stamp program. The amendment would allow states to use their share of food stamp funds to operate nutritional programs, without federal guidelines other than the goal of improving the nutritional status of low-income people. (Puerto Rico already had been given such authority under the 1981 reconciliation bill. It began its new program July 1, 1982, distributing cash instead of food stamps to needy residents.)

Patrick J. Leahy, D-Vt., said the provision seemed to go against the trend of recent years, under which Congress had sought to place restrictions on the food stamp program to ensure that it be used for food. "After all the years of tightening up the program, aren't we just opening up the door and saying, 'here's a check, God love you, go out and buy food and don't stop to buy a little Ripple' [wine]?" Leahy wondered.

The committee adopted but later dropped an amendment, sponsored by Helms and Hayakawa, to terminate food stamp assistance to the unemployed. In its place, the panel approved a provision offered by Dole and Walter D. Huddleston, D-Ky., to add teeth to existing rules that required able-bodied recipients to seek work.

The Helms-Hayakawa amendment originally was adopted June 14 by an 11-5 vote. It would have required states to cut off food stamp benefits to jobless adults whose unemployment insurance had run out. It was modified by the committee to provide that, as an alternative, states could establish "workfare" programs to let recipients work off the value of their benefits in community service jobs. Able-bodied food stamp recipients then would have to accept available jobs with private employers or local governments if they wanted to continue receiving benefits.

People who were honestly looking for jobs but could not find them could continue to get stamps.

The committee also tightened the definition of a "household" unit eligible to apply for stamps. Existing law allowed people who lived in the same house but did not eat together to apply for stamps separately. The amendment required that all related persons living together be treated as a single household, unless one was elderly or disabled.

Senate Floor Action

The Senate Aug. 5 adopted an omnibus reconciliation bill (S 2774) containing the Agriculture Committee-approved changes in the food stamp program. The vote was 72-24. *(Vote 299, p. 50-S)*

There were no floor amendments changing the committee's food stamp provisions.

The bill reauthorized the program through fiscal 1985 and set spending ceilings of $11.9 billion in fiscal 1983, $12.3 billion in 1984 and $13.2 billion in 1985. It continued the Puerto Rico nutrition block grant at $825 million a year, and gave the states the option of converting their food stamp programs to a similar block grant.

House Committee Action

The House Agriculture Committee July 28 approved cuts totaling $1.3 billion in the food stamp program in fiscal 1983-85, as part of its budget reconciliation bill (HR 6892). The report was filed Aug. 2 (H Rept 97-687).

The committee was closely divided over food stamp issues. The outcome of several key amendments was decided by one- and two-vote margins.

The reductions approved by the committee were substantially less than those made by the Senate bill. The CBO estimated the changes would save $334 million in 1983, $431 million in 1984 and $561 million in 1985.

Most of the savings were achieved by imposing penalties on states with poorly run food stamp programs and by a variety of relatively small changes in accounting procedures used to determine benefit levels.

The committee approved an amendment by E. Thomas Coleman, R-Mo., to set spending ceilings on the program of $12.6 billion in fiscal 1983, $12.9 billion in 1984 and $13.7 billion in 1985.

However, Coleman amendments to impose more stringent penalties on states that made frequent errors in distributing food stamps and to slow the inflation updating of food stamp benefit levels in future years were defeated.

In another significant action, the committee reaffirmed the decision of its Nutrition Subcommittee to bar Puerto Rico from distributing its share of federal food stamp funds in the form of cash after Oct. 1, 1983.

The reconciliation package included a reauthorization for the food stamp program through fiscal 1985.

Spending Cap

The long-running fight over statutory limits on food stamp spending was won in the Agriculture Committee this time by proponents of a tight-fitting "cap."

Congress repeatedly had imposed spending ceilings on food stamps in recent years, only to have to raise them when the program needed more money to continue full operation.

Supporters of a cap argued that it gave Congress some control over the program's rapid growth. Opponents, such

as Dan Glickman, D-Kan., said the needs of the program were so dependent on unforeseen economic conditions that there was no way to set a realistic cap for the future.

Leon E. Panetta, D-Calif., a member of the Budget Committee, called predictions about future costs of the program "guesstimates" based on debatable assumptions about unemployment and inflation rates.

Coleman based his spending levels on CBO projections of future food stamp costs, including savings already made by the committee. Glickman proposed a substitute allowing a "cushion" for unexpected cost increases in the program; the cushion would be 5 percent in 1983, 7.5 percent in 1984 and 10 percent in 1985, above CBO projections. Under Glickman's amendment, the spending limits for the program would be $13.2 billion in 1983, $13.8 billion in 1984 and $14.9 billion in 1985.

Glickman's amendment was rejected 21-22, and Coleman's was then adopted 10-4.

Error Rates

The House committee refused to go further than the Senate committee in punishing states with high error rates in their food stamp programs.

Like the Senate panel, the Nutrition subcommittee had set a goal of a 5 percent error rate — the percentage of stamps that were given out to the wrong people or in excess of the amounts to which people were entitled — by 1985. The subcommittee called for reducing the federal share of state administrative costs in operating the food stamp program in states that failed to meet that goal.

Coleman's amendment, while maintaining the 5 percent goal, would have made greater reductions in administrative funding for states that failed to meet it. After 1985, states would lose $1 of administrative funding for each dollar they distributed in error, above the 5 percent error rate. "If they lose dollar for dollar, we're going to get their attention," Coleman said. The tougher sanctions would save an additional $120 million in 1984 and 1985.

The amendment was rejected 21-22.

Puerto Rico, Inflation Updates

Despite a plea from Resident Commissioner Baltasar Corrada, New Prog.-Puerto Rico, the committee insisted that Puerto Rico stop giving cash to its poor residents in place of food stamps, as provided by the 1981 reconciliation bill.

Worried that the cash-out would undermine the program's goal of improving the nutrition of the poor, the Nutrition subcommittee had voted to prohibit Puerto Rico from distributing cash food grants after Oct. 1, 1983. But subcommittee Chairman Fred Richmond, D-N.Y., proposed to drop that provision, thus allowing Puerto Rico to continue the cash program.

While not a committee member, Corrada was given an opportunity to argue that Puerto Rico deserved a chance to see if the cash program would work. If not, he said, then the six-month study in the bill would give Congress enough evidence to block the cash distribution in 1983.

Richmond's amendment to drop the subcommittee provision was defeated 10-11.

The committee fell short of the savings achieved by the Senate panel in part because it refused to slow the inflation adjustment of food stamp benefit levels.

Coleman proposed saving an additional $430 million over three years by delaying the indexing of the thrifty food plan. He said the amendment would lead to small

losses of benefits — $3 a month for a very poor family of four. But Richmond said recipients already had fallen well behind food price inflation and could not afford to lose more.

Coleman's amendment was rejected 20-22.

House Floor Action

The House passed HR 6892 without amendments Aug. 10 by a 268-121 vote. *(Vote 246, p. 74-H)*

The rule under which the bill was brought to the floor permitted only two amendments in addition to an Agriculture Committee amendment. One of these was a Republican substitute, which made some additional cuts in food stamps. It failed 181-210. *(Vote 244, p. 74-H)*

Opponents' efforts to defeat the rule and later to recommit the bill to the Agriculture Committee also were defeated.

The chief objection to the bill, voiced by Delbert L. Latta, R-Ohio, ranking minority member of the House Budget Committee, was that neither the food stamp nor the farm provisions would save the amounts required by the budget resolution, although the CBO said they would.

The provisions of HR 6892 later were folded into the omnibus reconciliation bill, HR 6955.

Conference Action

Conferees on the reconciliation bill Aug. 13 agreed on food stamp savings provisions that generally split the difference between the $2.1 billion worth of cuts approved by the Senate and the $1.3 billion approved by the House.

Because of House objections, they rejected a Senate-passed plan to let states substitute cash payments for food stamps. They also followed the House in canceling the short-lived cash program in Puerto Rico.

The conferees accepted a modified version of the Senate plan to slow inflation adjustments in the thrifty food plan, and approved four pilot projects requiring food stamp recipients to work 20 hours a week or participate in a workfare program.

The conference report on the bill was filed Aug. 16 (H Rept 97-759). The House and Senate both approved it Aug. 18, and President Reagan signed the bill into law Sept. 8. ∎

Congress Rejects Proposed Student Aid Cuts

Frustrated by Education Department delays in issuing regulations and determined to head off Reagan administration efforts to cut back student aid, Congress Sept. 29 cleared legislation setting the rules for college student assistance programs for the 1983-84 school year.

The bill (S 2852 — PL 97-301) also restored eligibility for student aid to some 50,000 veterans who had lost it as a result of legislation passed in 1981. Another provision made it possible for the Student Loan Marketing Association (Sallie Mae), the federally chartered corporation that provided capital for student loan programs, to continue borrowing funds on the private money markets.

The legislation, which mandated extension of student aid regulations already in place for the 1982-83 school year into the following year, primarily affected Pell grants and guaranteed student loans. The regulations set the amounts a student's family was expected to contribute to his education, depending on their income. That in turn determined how much assistance the student could receive, when compared with his educational costs.

The Education Department (ED) had issued proposed regulations Aug. 2 — four months after they were due — that could have resulted in a $1.2 billion reduction in student aid funding.

In effect, S 2852 barred ED from increasing the share of college costs that a student's family was expected to provide. It would ensure that about the same number of students would be eligible for aid in 1983-84 as were eligible in 1982-83.

The bill also set the maximum Pell grant at $1,800, or 50 percent of the cost of attendance, for the 1983-84 school year. The administration had wanted to cut the maximum grant to $1,600, from the existing level of $1,670.

Although S 2852 went against administration policy, President Reagan signed it into law Oct. 13. But he said he would not be bound by a "legislative veto" provision allowing either chamber of Congress to veto ED regulations for the 1984-85 school year.

In 1981 Congress blocked ED regulations that would have barred most college students in families with incomes over $15,000 a year from getting grants. It also set guidelines for the department to follow in writing future rules. Members complained that delays in issuing regulations made it difficult for colleges, students and parents to know how much aid would be available and to plan accordingly. *(1981 Almanac p. 495)*

Provisions

As cleared by Congress, S 2852 (PL 97-301):

● Required the Education Department (ED) to use the same rules for calculating the expected family contribution to a student's educational costs in the 1983-84 school year that it used in 1982-83, with certain adjustments.

● Also required ED to use the adjusted 1982-83 rules in 1984-85, if it failed to publish new rules by May 15, 1983.

● Provided that 1984-85 regulations issued by ED could be overturned by a vote of one house of Congress.

● Continued through the 1983-84 school year the existing maximum on individual Pell grants of $1,800 or 50 percent of a student's cost of attending school.

● Reserved $30 million of the fiscal 1982 supplemental appropriation (PL 97-257) for Pell grants for the purpose of restoring Pell grant aid to those veterans who lost it when a 1981 law (PL 97-92) required that all GI Bill payments to veterans be considered as student aid in computing Pell grant eligibility; required instead that one-third of GI Bill benefits be considered as aid.

● Established a formula for reduction of Pell grants in case appropriations were insufficient to fund all awards, so that low-income students whose families were expected to contribute $200 or less would receive their full awards.

● Provided that if funding for supplemental educational opportunity grants, the college work-study program or national direct student loans in fiscal 1983-85 was less than the fiscal 1981 funding level, the available funds would be

Changes in Higher Education Assistance

Program, number of participants in 1981-82 school year	Description of program	Spending Levels		Changes in program made in 1981-82
		Fiscal 1980	**Fiscal 1983***	
Pell Grants 2.5 million	Basic grant support for students from low- and middle-income families; pays up to half of a student's college costs.	$2.415 billion	$2.419 billion	Maximum grant to low-income students increased to $1,800, from $1,670 in 1981-82, but aid to middle-income students reduced. Size of grants held constant in the face of tuition increases averaging 39% in public colleges, 23% in private colleges. Other changes affected some of the 80,000 veterans receiving GI Bill benefits who also were eligible for Pell grants. GI Bill benefits were counted as student aid in determining Pell grant awards, in effect excluding veterans at low-cost schools from Pell grants; reduction partially restored by Congress in September 1982.
Guaranteed Student Loans 3.8 million	Federally backed bank loans to students; interest paid while student is in school and subsidized at below-market rates thereafter.	$4.8 billion**	$5.9 billion**	"Needs test" imposed on student borrowers with family incomes in excess of $30,000 a year; 5% "origination fee" subtracted from loan amount; interest on related parental loan program increased to 14% from 9%.
National Direct Student Loans 800,000	Federal contribution to revolving loan accounts established by colleges.	$286 million	$178.6 million	Authorization and appropriation reduced; interest rate on loans increased to 5%, from 4%.
Social Security 760,000	Payments to student dependents of retired, disabled or deceased workers.	$1.6 billion	$800 million	New students excluded from program; benefits to those already on the program phased out by 1985.
Supplemental Educational Opportunity Grants 440,000	Funds provided to colleges to distribute as grants to needy students.	$370 million	$355.4 million	Appropriations reduced.
Campus Work-Study 950,000	Funds provided to institutions to hire students for part-time jobs.	$550 million	$528 million	Appropriations reduced.
State Student Incentive Grants 295,000	Matching funds for state student aid programs.	$76.75 million	$73.7 million	Appropriations reduced.

* As set by fiscal 1983 continuing resolution (PL 97-276).
** Loan volume. Federal costs were $1.6 billion in 1980, $3.1 billion in 1983.

Based on figures supplied by U.S. Department of Education and the American Council on Education.

allocated to the states in the same ratio as the 1981 funds.

● Extended for two years, through Sept. 30, 1984, the waiver of the presumption that the federal government had the first claim on assets if the Student Loan Marketing Association (Sallie Mae) were to declare bankruptcy.

● Terminated on Aug. 1, 1983, Sallie Mae's authority to consolidate loans held by students.

● Imposed certain disclosure requirements on banks making loans to students.

Background

S 2852 was part of the long-running fight between the Reagan administration and Congress over federal spending for college student assistance.

Bowing to budget pressures, Congress had made substantial cost-saving changes in student aid programs in 1981. *(Chart, p. 484; 1981 cuts, 1981 Almanac p. 493)*

But throughout 1982 it resisted administration attempts to make further cuts in the costly but politically popular programs.

In his Feb. 6 budget, President Reagan proposed deep cuts in aid to higher education, particularly in the Guaranteed Student Loan (GSL) program.

Since 1978, when GSL eligibility was extended to all students, regardless of income, the program had become the fastest growing entitlement program in the federal budget.

Nearly four million students had GSLs in 1982, and the government was spending more than $3 billion a year to subsidize the interest on those loans. Students could borrow up to $2,500 a year. The interest rate on GSLs was 9 percent; the government paid all of the interest while a student was in school and any interest over 9 percent after he left school.

Reagan proposed to save $762 million in fiscal 1983 by making graduate and professional students ineligible for GSLs; doubling the 5 percent fee charged when a loan was taken out; applying a "need" test to all students seeking loans and raising the expected family contribution to a student's educational costs, among other things.

He also proposed to slash spending on Pell grants, the principal government aid program for low-income students, from $2.2 billion in 1982 to $1.4 billion in 1983 and $1 billion in 1984 and 1985. The administration estimated that would cut about 700,000 students from the program and reduce the maximum grant to $1,600 a year.

The budget called for the elimination of several other aid programs, including Supplemental Educational Opportunity Grants.

Congress Rejects Proposals

Confronted with massive lobbying by colleges, students and their parents, Congress refused to go along with the administration's higher education proposals.

The House Appropriations and Education and Labor committees rejected them outright. The Senate Budget Committee agreed to changes in the GSL program that would have saved about $144 million, mainly by eliminating the interest subsidy on loans paid by the government while students were in school. But, under pressure from Republicans up for re-election, Senate Republican leaders later dropped the proposal. *(Budget resolution, p. 186)*

A showdown over student aid developed during consideration of the fiscal 1982 supplemental appropriations bill (HR 6863). The measure contained less for defense and

---

Other Student Aid Actions

Congress in 1982 voted to bar federal aid to male college students who failed to register with the Selective Service System.

It did so with an amendment attached to the fiscal 1983 defense authorization bill (S 2248 — PL 97-252).

The amendment originally was offered in the House by Gerald B. H. Solomon, R-N.Y. It was adopted 303-95 on July 28, and was accepted by conferees on the bill. *(Vote 211, p. 62-H)*

Solomon told the House that the 93 percent of eligible men who had complied with the law and registered "sorely resent the other 7 percent of Americans who have either intentionally or unintentionally chosen not to register."

An amendment requiring the Department of Education to transmit to the Selective Service System the information needed to enforce the provision was adopted by voice vote.

A substitute amendment by Paul Simon, D-Ill., that would have exempted from the aid ban anyone informing Selective Service in writing that he had religious or moral objections to registration was first gutted and then killed. *(Story, p. 77)*

Social Security Benefits. In other action affecting student aid, an attempt to restore benefits to college-age children of deceased and disabled Social Security recipients was rejected in the Senate.

Carl Levin, D-Mich., offered the proposal as an amendment to a fiscal 1982 supplemental appropriations bill (HR 6863). The Senate rejected it, 42-47. *(Vote 339, p. 56-S; story, p. 219)*

The benefits had been cut by the 1981 budget reconciliation bill (PL 97-35). *(1981 Almanac p. 119)*

---

more for social programs — including $217 million for Pell grants — than Reagan wanted.

Reagan vetoed the appropriations bill on grounds it was a "budget-buster" but Congress overrode the veto. *(Story, p. 219)*

Another source of controversy between the administration and Congress was ED's repeated delays in issuing regulations governing who would get student aid and how much they would get. Several sets of regulations were withdrawn because of congressional opposition, and had to be rewritten.

Veterans' Complaints

There was a flood of complaints in 1982 from veterans who found themselves deprived of student aid as a result of congressional action in 1981.

Previously, veterans who got GI Bill assistance often were able to get Pell grants as well. Only half of their veterans' benefits were counted as income in determining Pell grant eligibility.

In 1981, however, Congress provided in a continuing appropriations resolution (PL 97-92) that all GI benefits be considered as direct student aid. That eliminated up to 50,000 veterans from Pell grant eligibility. *(1981 Almanac p. 329)*

Legislative Action

S 2852 sped through Congress with little opposition. The only real problem came when the administration threatened a veto if the final version contained a Senate provision allowing states to consolidate student loans.

Senate Action. The Senate Labor and Human Resources Committee reported the bill Sept. 9 (S Rept 97-538), and the Senate passed it by voice vote Sept. 16.

The main focus of the Senate bill was on Sallie Mae borrowing, and the measure originally was known as the Sallie Mae Technical Amendments. The goal of the Sallie Mae provision was to reassure private lenders that they would have a chance at getting their money back in the unlikely event that the corporation went bankrupt. However, the provision would remain in effect for only two years, giving Congress further opportunity to review the whole issue of Sallie Mae's purpose and operations.

Another provision of the Senate bill authorized state agencies to consolidate student loans. States could buy up multiple loans owed by individual students to banks, and convert them into a single loan with an easier repayment schedule. The administration said the provision would cost up to $200 million a year.

The bill also restored eligibility for Pell grants for the veterans who had lost it in 1981.

House Action. The House Education and Labor Committee reported a companion bill Sept. 16 (HR 7048 — H Rept 97-814). The measure passed the House 381-19 Sept. 22 under suspension of the rules. *(Vote 331, p. 98-H)*

Both the committee report and House floor debate concentrated on the Education Department's apparent inability to meet congressional deadlines for student aid program regulations. Sponsors of the bill stressed that delays in regulations spread confusion and doubt among the people who administered the aid programs and the students who depended on them.

Besides restoring the eligibility of veterans who had lost their Pell grants in 1981, the House bill also set aside $30 million from the fiscal 1982 Pell grant supplemental appropriation to be used for veterans.

Conference Action. Conferees approved a compromise version of the bill Sept. 23. They agreed to drop the Senate provision allowing consolidation of student loans, thus clearing the way for administration approval of the bill. They accepted the House provision setting aside $30 million for Pell grants for veterans, with an amendment requiring that one-third of GI Bill benefits be counted as direct student aid.

The Senate approved the conference report (S Rept 97-589) Sept. 27, the House Sept. 29, both by voice vote. President Reagan signed the measure into law Oct. 13. ∎

Education Regulations

Congress killed one set of education regulations issued by the Reagan administration in 1982, and forced the withdrawal of another.

Regulations dealing with compensatory education for disadvantaged children and other elementary and secondary education programs were rejected by a congressional veto. Others, dealing with the education of handicapped children, were withdrawn by the Education Department (ED) in the face of congressional opposition.

The proposed regulations would have loosened federal controls over the programs. The administration contended they would give more flexibility to program administrators, while retaining basic protections for those affected by the regulations.

Opposition came from interest groups and members of Congress who feared that the flexibility given to administrators would lead to inadequate services.

There also was the traditional institutional conflict over Congress' right to control executive departments. The regulations drew bipartisan opposition as attempts to undermine Congress' authority.

Handicapped Education

ED's proposed rules for handicapped education sought to remove many of the requirements imposed on local schools under the 1975 Education for All Handicapped Children Act (PL 94-142). *(1975 Almanac p. 651)*

The changes were viewed by critics as an effort by ED to scuttle the landmark law in the face of Congress' refusal to do so.

Issued Aug. 4, the regulations would have allowed states and local schools to set their own guidelines, standards and timetables in meeting the mandate of providing an "appropriate" education to the handicapped. For example, the list of health-related services schools had to provide to handicapped students was reduced. Another proposed change would weaken the role of parents in determining the types of services given to their children.

ED also proposed to loosen a key provision of the law — the "mainstreaming" requirement. The law required that, if possible, schools teach handicapped children in the same classrooms with non-handicapped students. The new regulations would allow schools to keep handicapped students out of regular classrooms if their presence caused serious disruptions.

Education Secretary T. H. Bell insisted the proposal would maintain the basic protections of the 1975 law while removing unneeded regulatory requirements added since it was enacted. But the plan ran into heavy criticism from the well-organized handicapped education lobby and its congressional allies, such as Lowell P. Weicker Jr., R-Conn., chairman of the Senate Subcommittee on the Handicapped.

Lobby groups like the National Education Association and the Children's Defense Fund said taking handicapped children out of regular classrooms would mark a return to the "asylum attitude" of the past.

Opposition was strong enough that a resolution to overturn the regulations could have passed. But the regulations had only been proposed in draft form, so Congress could not take formal action to block them. They were scheduled to be issued in final form in early November, when Congress would not be in session.

So Weicker offered an amendment to the fiscal 1982 supplemental appropriations bill (HR 6863) on Aug. 10, expressing the sense of Congress that ED should not put handicapped education regulations into effect before Congress had a chance to vote on them. The Senate adopted the amendment 93-4, and the provision was retained in the final version of the bill. *(Vote 301, p. 50-S)*

Although the provision was a non-binding expression of congressional sentiment, it showed the depth of opposition to the regulations. On Sept. 29, Bell announced that he was withdrawing six of the controversial changes, including those allowing schools to keep handicapped children out of

regular classrooms if they were considered disruptive, weakening the requirement that schools obtain parental consent in planning the education of their handicapped children and freeing schools from having to provide certain medical services.

However, Bell refused to withdraw the entire set of regulations. In response, the House Education and Labor Committee reported a resolution Sept. 30 (H Res 558 — H Rept 97-906) stating the sense of the House in opposition to the regulations as a whole. The resolution was never brought to the floor, but supporters said the administration was unlikely to push for the regulations in the face of Congress' disapproval.

Other Education Programs

Another controversy centered around regulations issued by the Education Department July 29 to implement provisions of the 1981 budget reconciliation bill (PL 97-35). The regulations covered changes ordered by Congress in the compensatory education program for disadvantaged children, the cornerstone of federal aid to elementary and secondary schools, as well as a new block grant formed from smaller education programs. *(1981 Almanac p. 499)*

While most of the regulations were not controversial, one was designed to conform to a goal of the Education Department under the Reagan administration: reduction or elimination of the jurisdiction of the General Education Provisions Act (GEPA) over education programs.

GEPA, enacted in 1968, established a host of procedural and funding guidelines for federal elementary and secondary education programs. It also allowed Congress to block education regulations by a two-house veto. The Reagan administration, like the Carter administration before it, opposed legislative veto provisions.

Arguing that GEPA requirements limited the flexibility of states in operating education programs, the administration proposed regulations for the compensatory education and block grant programs stating that most GEPA provisions did not apply to them.

From the congressional point of view, the key effect of eliminating GEPA jurisdiction was that it would deprive Congress of the power to block future regulations for the programs. Local educators also feared that the programs would not be "forward-funded" if they were not governed by GEPA. GEPA required that federal funds for most education programs be provided a year in advance so educators could plan for the next school year.

The regulations brought an especially heated reaction from Congress because the authors of the block grant legislation in 1981 had explicitly stated that they intended GEPA to apply to it. ED insisted the legislative history of the block grants was ambiguous and thus did not mandate the applicability of GEPA.

Faced with the possible loss of its ability to veto regulations and angered by the apparent flouting of its intentions, Congress moved quickly to block the administration's proposed changes. The House Education and Labor Committee Aug. 5 reported a resolution to overturn the rules (H Con Res 388 — H Rept 97-701). The House approved it unanimously on Aug. 10 (363-0), and the Senate approved it by voice vote the same day. *(House vote 241, p. 72-H)*

In the wake of the congressional veto, ED officials said they would rewrite the regulations and make GEPA applicable. ∎

Veterans' Health Programs

Congress Aug. 20 cleared legislation (HR 6350 — PL 97-251) designed to deal with a shortage of nurses at the nation's veterans' hospitals.

There were nearly 1,000 nursing vacancies in Veterans Administration (VA) hospitals as of June 30, VA officials said. As a result, some wards had had to be closed, nursing staffs were overworked and many nurses were leaving. They blamed the nationwide shortage of nurses and stiff competition for the existing supply.

HR 6350 gave the VA new flexibility to offer pay and educational incentives to help attract and retain nurses, and contained several other provisions affecting veterans' programs.

The bill was reported May 17 by the House Veterans' Affairs Committee (H Rept 97-543), and passed the House June 15 by a 390-0 vote under suspension of the rules. *(Vote 137, p. 42-H)*

The Senate Veterans' Affairs Committee reported its version of the bill June 8 (S 2385 — S Rept 97-467). The Senate substituted it for the text of HR 6350 and passed it by voice vote June 21.

Veterans' committee leaders worked out the differences without a formal conference. Their compromise version was approved by voice vote of the House Aug. 19 and the Senate Aug. 20.

Provisions

As signed into law, HR 6350 (PL 97-251):

● Provided that nurses who worked two 12-hour regularly scheduled tours of duty over a weekend in a VA health care facility would be considered to have worked a full basic workweek, if the VA administrator decided that was necessary to obtain or retain adequate nursing services.

● Allowed payment at the "weekend" rate for VA nurses working on Saturdays, at the administrator's discretion. Under existing law, only Sunday work qualified for the higher rate.

● Allowed full-time VA employees to participate in the VA health professional scholarship program on a part-time basis, rather than full-time, if they wished.

● Extended for one year, through Sept. 30, 1983, the VA's authority to contract for hospital and medical care for eligible veterans in Puerto Rico and the Virgin Islands; directed the VA to present a plan by Dec. 1, 1982, for providing care for those veterans on a permanent basis.

● Allowed survivors and dependents of severely disabled veterans to become eligible again for the civilian health and medical program (CHAMPVA) if they had lost eligibility by becoming eligible for Medicare but then had exhausted their Medicare benefits.

● Extended for one year a VA alcohol and drug treatment and rehabilitation pilot program and the deadline for a report on the program. The program was extended through Sept. 30, 1983, the report date to March 31, 1984.

● Extended for four years, through fiscal 1986, a program for matching-fund grants to states for the construction of state veterans' homes and nursing homes.

● Required the VA administrator to report to Congress by July 1, 1985, on the VA's experience with flexible and compressed work schedules under a federal employees' "flexitime" law (PL 97-221) enacted in July. ∎

Disabled Veterans Get Cost-of-Living Hike

Congress Sept. 29 cleared legislation (HR 6782 — PL 97-306) granting a 7.4 percent cost-of-living raise to disabled veterans and making changes in various veterans' education and employment programs.

The final bill, a compromise negotiated by staff rather than by a conference committee, was approved by voice vote in the House Sept. 28 and in the Senate Sept. 29.

About 2.3 million disabled veterans and 319,000 widows and children received disability benefits.

Several of the bill's provisions were aimed at the 685,000 unemployed Vietnam-era veterans — "clearly one of the hardest hit portions of our labor force," according to Senate Minority Leader Robert C. Byrd, D-W.Va.

Besides providing the cost-of-living boost to veterans with service-connected disabilities and their survivors, HR 6782 consolidated Labor Department veterans' employment programs, established a new employment and training program aimed at Vietnam-era veterans and extended for one year the deadline for veterans to use education benefits for vocational and secondary education programs.

Major Provisions

As signed into law, HR 6782 (PL 97-306):

● Authorized a 7.4 percent cost-of-living increase, effective Oct. 1, 1982, in compensation for veterans with service-connected disabilities and for survivors of service members or veterans who died from service-connected injuries.

● Increased compensation for dependents of disabled veterans and for certain blinded veterans.

● Made members of the Senior Reserve Officers' Training Corps (SROTC) eligible for disability compensation.

Education Programs. Made voluntary, instead of mandatory, the veterans' representatives ("vet reps") program, which provided educational benefits counseling to veterans returning to college.

● Eliminated a requirement that schools providing Veterans Administration (VA)-approved vocational courses must show that at least half their graduates had found jobs in the career field for which training was provided.

● Eased restrictions on the payment of vocational rehabilitation subsistence allowances to veterans jailed as the result of a felony to allow payment to those living in a halfway house or participating in a work release program.

● Barred VA educational payments to jailed veterans convicted of a felony if tuition and fees for the course were paid by another federal, state or local program or if no fees were charged for the course.

● Limited the VA's authority to deny eligibility for education benefits to Vietnam-era veterans enrolled in vocational education, on-the-job training, apprenticeship or secondary education programs. Veterans could be denied eligibility only after a case-by-case review. Extended the eligibility period for one year, to Dec. 31, 1984.

Employment. Clarified the responsibilities of and made administrative improvements in the operation of the Labor Department's veterans' employment office.

● Expanded the responsibilities of the directors of state veterans' employment programs to include such duties as ensuring that discrimination complaints were resolved in a timely manner.

● Established a national employment and training program for veterans; authorized grants to local, state and non-profit organizations to operate the programs.

● Required federal contractors to report annually to the secretary of labor on veteran hiring activity.

Other Provisions. Reinstated the $300 burial benefit for indigent veterans. The 1981 Budget Reconciliation Act (PL 97-35) had ended the benefit for veterans with non-service-connected injuries whose deaths occurred after Oct. 1, 1981. *(1981 Almanac p. 399)*

● Provided that contracting out for services would be permitted within the VA health care system, but only where patient care would not suffer and where savings of at least 15 percent would result.

● Authorized the VA to guarantee loans made to veterans to refinance a manufactured (mobile) home or to purchase a lot for the unit.

● Provided that a minimum of two years of military service was required for eligibility for all federal veterans' rights and benefits.

Legislative History

The provisions in the final bill originally were contained in two separate House bills, HR 6782 and HR 6794.

The House Veterans' Affairs Committee reported HR 6782, containing the 7.4 percent boost in disability compensation, July 23 (H Rept 97-660). The House passed it July 27, 400-0, under suspension of the rules, a procedure that barred amendments and required a two-thirds vote for passage. *(Vote 205, p. 60-H)*

In September, the House passed a separate bill dealing with veterans' education and employment programs. That bill (HR 6794 — H Rept 97-799) was reported by the Veterans' Affairs Committee Sept. 9 and passed the House Sept. 20 by voice vote under suspension of the rules.

The Senate Veterans' Affairs Committee Sept. 17 reported a measure combining compensation, employment and education provisions (S 2913 — S Rept 97-550). The Senate approved that bill by voice vote Sept. 24.

Staff members then worked out an informal agreement ironing out the differences between the bills.

The Senate side agreed to accept the House provision setting up the new employment and training program for Vietnam-era veterans. The program would provide grants to state and local government and private non-profit agencies to set up the training programs.

The House accepted a Senate provision extending the period during which Vietnam-era veterans could use their GI bill benefits for on-the-job training, vocational or secondary school courses.

The provision was a reaction to stringent VA rules that had limited use of the benefits.

The House refused to accept a Senate provision authorizing chiropractic care under the VA health care program.

And the Senate refused to accept a House provision that would have terminated the Veterans' Educational Assistance Program (VEAP) on March 30, 1983, unless the president recommended to Congress by Jan. 15, 1983, that it continue and neither chamber passed a resolution of disapproval by March 30.

According to House Veterans' Affairs Chairman G. V. "Sonny" Montgomery, D-Miss., few veterans used the program, and of those who did enroll, almost 40 percent had dropped out.

Tuition Tax Credit

After cutting back benefits to parents of private school students and adding new anti-discrimination protections, the Senate Finance Committee Sept. 23 reported a version of President Reagan's tuition tax credit proposal (HR 1635 — S Rept 97-576).

However, there was no further action on the issue, and the legislation died when Congress adjourned.

Had it reached the Senate floor, the bill faced a possible filibuster from Ernest F. Hollings, D-S.C., as well as vigorous lobbying opposition from public education groups.

Most of the aid under the plan would have gone to parents of students in Catholic parochial schools, which enrolled the bulk of the nation's five million private school students.

Reagan said tuition tax credits were needed because parents were hard-pressed to pay both private school tuition and taxes to support the public schools. "Our proposal is intended to relieve that dual financial burden threatening to usurp the traditional right of parents to direct the education of their children," he said.

As reported, the bill would have provided tax credits equal to half of private school tuition costs, up to a maximum of $300 per child by 1985. The credits would have been available only for tuition at private elementary and secondary schools, not for college tuition. The committee reduced the benefit levels proposed by the administration to limit the budgetary drain of the program.

Although Reagan had supported tuition tax credits during his 1980 campaign, the administration did not submit its legislative proposal to Congress until mid-1982. The legislation followed the outlines given by Reagan in an April 15 speech to a Catholic education organization.

"It would have had a much better chance if the president had put it in his budget this year," said Russell Shaw of the U.S. Catholic Conference.

Catholic groups had put considerable pressure on the administration to offer the plan. New York parochial school supporters delivered 750,000 letters in support of the credits to Washington shortly before Reagan's proposal was announced.

Public education groups mobilized against the proposal. "There can be no justification for spending billions of dollars for private and church-related schools at a time when the Reagan administration says it can't afford to support the public schools," said Willard McGuire, president of the National Education Association (NEA).

The NEA was a member of the National Coalition for Public Education, which was formed by the major Washington-based interest groups to fight tuition tax credits.

Civil libertarians also opposed the plan. They argued that the credits would be unconstitutional — a form of state assistance to religion. In addition, civil rights groups feared that tuition credits would help segregationist schools.

Background

Congress came close to approving tuition tax credits the last time it seriously considered the issue, in 1978. After a bruising lobbying battle between public and private school interests, the tuition tax credits for elementary and secondary education were dropped in a House-Senate conference. *(1978 Almanac p. 248)*

But the 1978 fight was different in a number of crucial ways from the struggle over Reagan's proposal. Most importantly, the 1982 plan had presidential support, while the earlier legislation faced a certain veto from President Carter if it had cleared Congress.

In addition, the fate of tax credits in 1978 was tied up with the subject of college student aid. Expansion of aid to college students had strong support at the time, and the legislation that passed both the House and Senate was aimed originally at providing tax credits for college tuition.

Then, the House was much more supportive than the Senate of tax credits for elementary and secondary education. The House adopted an elementary and secondary tuition amendment on the floor but the Senate rejected it.

There were a number of tuition tax credit proposals in Congress prior to 1978, mainly aimed at helping to offset rising college costs. The Senate passed college tuition tax credit amendments in 1976 and 1977, but they were dropped in conference with the House, which was more interested in credits for elementary and secondary school students. *(1977 Almanac p. 161; 1976 Almanac p. 61)*

The Supreme Court in 1973 ruled that a New York state law providing tax credits for private elementary and secondary schools was unconstitutional. *(CQ Guide to the U.S. Supreme Court, p. 468)*

Details of Reagan Plan

In announcing his tuition tax credit proposal before the National Catholic Educational Association in Chicago April 15, Reagan stressed that its benefits would be focused on low- and middle-income families who wanted to send their children to private schools.

"We do not seek to aid the rich, but those lower- and middle-income federal taxpayers who are most strapped by inflation, oppressive taxation and the recession that grips us all," the president said. He said the majority of parents with children in private elementary and secondary schools had incomes of $25,000 a year or less.

"I would like to think we are offering help to the inner-city child who faces a world of drugs and crime, the child with special needs, and the families who still believe the Lord's Prayer will do less harm than good in the classroom," Reagan added.

Reagan proposed a relatively small credit — no more than $100 per student to begin with. That would make it a more significant factor for parents of students in parochial schools, where tuitions were low, than for those attending exclusive prep schools with very high tuitions.

Under the proposal, parents would receive an income tax credit equal to 50 percent of tuition in a non-profit, private elementary or secondary school. The limit on the credit for each child would be $100 in 1983, $300 in 1984 and $500 in 1985.

The rich would not be eligible for credits. Parents with incomes over $50,000 a year would receive only partial credits. Those with incomes over $75,000 would get no credits.

Cost estimates released by the Treasury Department showed revenue losses because of the credits of $100 million in fiscal 1983, $600 million in 1984, $1 billion in 1985 and $1.4 billion in 1986.

The outline of the president's proposal promised to include protections against use of the credits for segregated schools, but the specifics of those limits were not spelled out until the administration legislation (S 2673) was introduced June 23.

Finance Committee Action

Under prodding from Reagan and a coalition of Catholic and conservative lobby groups, the Finance Committee Sept. 16 approved the tuition tax credit legislation by an 11-7 vote. Since tax bills must originate in the House, the committee substituted its bill, S 2673, for the text of HR 1635, a minor House-passed tax measure.

Committee Chairman Robert Dole, R-Kan., acknowledged that chances appeared slim for final congressional approval of the legislation in the remainder of the session. "I'm just following the urging of the president," Dole said. "He hasn't been around here long enough to believe that Congress can't do things."

Civil rights forces won a significant victory when the committee added a key provision blocking the tax credit from taking effect until either Congress or the Supreme Court acted to prohibit tax-exempt status for segregated schools.

Dole and the administration were forced to accept several compromises to get the legislation out of committee. Benefit levels were reduced, bringing the bill's cost down to $2.1 billion in fiscal 1984-87. There would be no revenue loss in fiscal 1983.

As reported, the bill provided a tax credit equal to half of private elementary or secondary school tuition, up to a maximum of $100 per child in 1983, $200 in 1984 and $300 in succeeding years. Under Reagan's original proposal, the credit would have reached $500 a year per child. The bill was to take effect July 31, 1983.

Parents with incomes of up to $50,000 a year could get the credit under the committee bill. The administration had proposed credits for families with incomes up to $75,000.

Besides tying the effective date of the bill to resolution of the tax-exemption issue, the committee also accepted a series of White House-backed amendments strengthening protections against tax credits for parents of students in schools that discriminated on the basis of race.

Civil Rights Issue

The civil rights protections in the bill were by far the most controversial issue of the markup.

The committee was nearly evenly split between two opposing forces. Bill Bradley, D-N.J., with support from civil rights groups, argued that the administration bill indirectly could benefit segregated schools. Allies of the "Christian school" movement feared that stronger civil rights provisions would lead to government interference in their schools.

The fight in committee was closely related to the broader issue of tax exemptions for segregated schools. A case on that subject was pending before the Supreme Court. *(Story, p. 397)*

Markup of the bill, which began in August, had been delayed after Bradley and others raised concerns about the adequacy of civil rights protections. Recognizing the political importance of the issue, the administration came up with a compromise package, which was adopted unanimously by the committee.

The original bill established legal procedures under which schools could be found to have discriminated on racial grounds, thus making their students ineligible for credits. The administration amendments allowed anyone to bring a complaint against an allegedly discriminatory school, instead of just the victims of discrimination, as under the original bill. The changes also would make it easier for the attorney general to prove that a school was discriminatory.

In addition, the amendments excluded discriminatory schools from tax credit eligibility until they showed that they no longer discriminated. The original bill would have made schools automatically re-eligible after three years.

However, Bradley wanted more than the administration proposal. He offered an amendment to establish procedures for the Internal Revenue Service (IRS) to oversee the racial policies of private schools.

That was anathema to conservative supporters of the tax credits. According to Robert Baldwin of the Citizens for Educational Freedom, adoption of the amendment would have killed the bill.

After the committee initially adopted Bradley's amendment, Dole proposed a compromise to put off the question of IRS enforcement until the tax-exempt status issue was resolved. Dole's amendment was adopted with Bradley's support.   ∎

Incentives for 'Orphan Drug' Makers Voted

Backers of a bill to promote the development of more drugs for rare, disabling diseases guided the legislation to completion in the final days of the 97th Congress.

The House passed the final compromise bill (HR 5238) Dec. 14 and the Senate cleared it Dec. 17, both by voice vote. Despite objections to the measure within his administration, President Reagan signed it into law Jan. 4, 1983 (PL 97-414).

The bill was intended to encourage drug companies to invest in developing drugs for diseases such as Huntington's disease, myoclonus and others that afflicted so few people that development costs exceeded likely profits.

Sales of such "orphan drugs" could be expected to bring in $3 million to $5 million a year, compared with costs of as much as $70 million for testing a drug and bringing it through the Food and Drug Administration (FDA) approval process, according to drug industry spokesmen.

The bill authorized tax credits and grants to promote the development of these rare-disease drugs. It also authorized seven years of exclusive marketing rights for rare-disease drugs that were not patentable. Other sections of the measure were designed to ease regulatory barriers for orphan drug approval by directing the FDA to tell a manufacturer precisely what tests it would require before granting approval to market a drug.

Treasury officials had objected to sections of the bill that would allow drug makers to claim tax credits for what they spent to test new drugs on human patients, required before a drug could be approved by the FDA. It was estimated that the provisions would cost the government $75 billion in lost revenues over the five-year life of the bill.

Attorney General William French Smith reportedly also objected to a provision, added to the bill by the Senate, requiring the development of statistical tables on exposure to open-air nuclear bomb testing in the 1950s and cancer in

humans exposed to fallout from the tests. The department had been defending the government in a major lawsuit brought on behalf of persons exposed to radiation during those tests.

The House originally passed the bill Sept. 28. The Senate dropped the House-approved tax credits and substituted loans for drug development costs before approving the measure Oct. 1. The Senate also added a number of unrelated amendments, including an authorization for start-up funds for home health services and the provision requiring the Department of Health and Human Services (HHS) to develop the statistics on exposure to nuclear tests and cancer in humans exposed to fallout from the tests.

The final version of the bill retained these and other Senate-passed amendments, and authorized both grants for orphan drug development and a modified version of the tax credit. The compromise was worked out informally, without a conference.

Provisions

As signed into law, HR 5238 (PL 97-414):

Drug Development. Authorized the secretary of health and human services, at the request of a manufacturer or sponsor, to designate drugs for treatment of a rare disease or condition — that is, one that occurred so infrequently in the United States that costs of developing the drug appeared to exceed potential profits.

● Required the secretary, at the request of the sponsor of a drug for a rare illness, to specify required clinical and non-clinical tests the drug must undergo for approval, if the secretary found the drug qualified as a rare-disease drug.

● Provided that a company winning approval to market a designated drug that was not patentable could have exclusive marketing rights for seven years after approval. However, provided that other companies could be allowed to sell such a drug within the first seven years if the original marketer was unable to produce enough of the drug for all individuals with the disease or if the original marketer consented to sales by another company.

● Directed the secretary to encourage developers of orphan drugs to design clinical trials that would permit persons afflicted with a disease who needed the drug to join the experimental group, if there was no other drug to treat their condition.

● Established a federal Orphan Products Board, with representatives of the FDA, the National Institutes of Health (NIH) and other agencies, to promote development of drugs, biologicals and devices for rare illnesses, by evaluating approval procedures, coordinating research, and other activities.

● Authorized tax credits for half of a drug developer's costs in clinical (human) trials of drugs meeting the bill's criteria for designation. (It was expected that the secretary of the Treasury would generally recognize the designation decisions of the secretary of HHS, but the bill provided for an independent decision by the Treasury secretary that a drug did not meet rare disease specifications for purposes of the credit.)

● Authorized the tax credit for testing expenses paid or obligated after Dec. 31, 1982, and before Jan. 1, 1988; allowed the credit for testing done outside the United States in certain circumstances; barred the credit for investigators eligible for grants authorized by the bill.

● Permitted, in addition to the tax credit, a partial tax deduction on the expenses for which the credit could be claimed.

● Authorized $4 million a year in fiscal years 1983-85 for grants to drug researchers to defray the costs of certain clinical tests of designated drugs.

● Required annual reports to Congress on orphan drug research at NIH and at the federal alcohol, drug abuse and mental health institutes; also required reports on the use of the drug tax credits and grants and on the activities of the Orphan Products Board.

Home Health Care. Authorized $5 million a year in fiscal 1983-84 for grants and loans to public and non-profit private groups, and loans to for-profit groups, to pay start-up costs of establishing and operating home health programs.

● Stipulated that grants and loans should go to entities in areas without adequate home health care services, particularly areas where transportation to existing health care services was inadequate or areas with a large percentage of old, poor or disabled residents.

● Specified that, to qualify for loans, for-profit entities must be fiscally sound, must be unable to obtain a loan from non-federal lenders and must pay interest comparable to what it cost the federal government to raise the money. Public and private non-profit groups must meet standards set by HHS to qualify for grants.

● Authorized $2 million a year in fiscal 1983-84 for grants and contracts to establish training programs for homemaker health aides; specified standards for such programs; provided that programs to train persons aged 50 or older would have high priority.

● Required the secretary of HHS to report results of the program to the health committees of Congress by Jan. 1, 1984, with recommendations about legislation to improve the provision of these services by the end of the following year; also required reports on payment methods for home health care funded by federal programs and on methods to combat fraud and abuse in Medicare and Medicaid.

● Authorized demonstration projects to identify patients suitable for home health services.

Radiation and Cancer. Required the secretary of HHS to conduct research and develop analyses that would lead to "credible" estimates of: the risk of thyroid cancer associated with exposure to Iodine 131; individuals' exposure to Iodine 131 by fallout from nuclear bombs, and Americans' exposure to Iodine 131 by fallout from above-ground nuclear bomb tests in Nevada during the 1950s. Required a report to Congress on these activities within a year of enactment.

● Required the secretary to develop and publish, within a year of enactment, statistical tables showing the risk of cancer associated with exposure to radiation, with such variables as size of radiation dose, age at time of exposure, time elapsed between exposure and development of cancer, and other factors. Required simultaneous publication of assessments of the accuracy of the tables and formulas used to devise them.

Other Provisions. Required HHS to fund at least 10 comprehensive sickle cell disease research centers at medical schools.

● Authorized $400,000 in fiscal 1983 and $800,000 in fiscal 1984 for nurse-anesthetist training programs.

● Revised the allocation formula for alcohol, drug abuse and mental health block grants.

● Provided an extended period of patent protection for a product cleared for interstate sales by the FDA and then subjected to a stay of the regulation permitting sales, if such a stay was in effect on Jan. 1, 1981. The provision was designed specifically for a low-calorie sweetener, Aspartame.

House Action

The House Energy and Commerce Committee unanimously approved HR 5238 on Sept. 15 and filed its report Sept. 17 (H Rept 97-840). The House passed the measure Sept. 28 by voice vote under suspension of the rules, a procedure that barred amendments and required a two-thirds majority for passage.

The House bill contained only provisions relating to orphan drugs. Advocates of the legislation said special incentives were necessary to persuade drug-makers to make the drugs commercially available to rare-disease victims.

Under the bill, drug companies could claim a tax credit equal to 90 percent of the cost of conducting human clinical investigations of orphan drugs, for each year in which the costs were incurred. Sponsors said the credit would cover about 45 percent of total drug development costs. It would expire Dec. 31, 1989.

The long duration of the tax credit provision (seven years) was meant to recognize that clinical trials of new drugs, a major expenditure for drug makers, could take as long as five years. Manufacturers claiming the credit could not also claim a separate research and development credit in the tax code.

The bill also allowed partial tax deductions for drug testing costs. The credits and deductions together would cost the Treasury about $15 million a year for five years in lost revenue, according to Henry A. Waxman, D-Calif., chairman of the Energy and Commerce Subcommittee on Health and chief sponsor of the bill.

Waxman had cleared the tax provisions with the chairman of the tax-writing House Ways and Means Committee, Dan Rostenkowski, D-Ill.

Senate Action

The Senate passed HR 5238 Oct. 1 by voice vote, after knocking out the House-passed tax credit provisions and adding a number of other amendments.

The Labor and Human Resources Committee had not acted on the bill nor on a similar bill (S 2130) by Nancy Landon Kassebaum, R-Kan., that had been referred to it in February.

Because of objections from Robert Dole, R-Kan., and Russell B. Long, D-La., chairman and ranking minority member of the Senate Finance Committee, the Senate bill did not include the seven-year tax credit for drug development that was in the House version. Instead, the Senate bill authorized a total of $50 million over three years for grants to companies for drug development costs.

Dole and Long appeared dead set against tax credits. "We hope that nobody will try to slip any tax credit in later on," Dole told the Senate. Long elicited an assurance from bill manager, Orrin G. Hatch, R-Utah, chairman of the Labor and Human Resources Committee, that he would "confer with the Finance Committee ... and obtain their approval" before accepting a tax credit in conference.

Home Health Care

One of the numerous "pet projects" added to the bill by the Senate was a section authorizing $14 million over two years for grants and loans to create home health care services and train aides to work in the services.

Home health care as defined by the bill included homemaking services, such as housekeeping and preparing meals, to enable ailing elderly or disabled people to receive medical treatments at home instead of in a hospital or nursing home.

A more ambitious home health care bill (S 234) sponsored by Hatch and Bob Packwood, R-Ore., had been reported by the Labor and Human Resources Committee March 23 (S Rept 97-325). Besides funding training and service programs, S 234 would expand Medicare coverage to include home health care and provide tax credits for individuals providing such care for dependents living at home instead of in an institution.

Hatch told the Senate that "in spite of the obvious need for these services, many of my colleagues remain skeptical" about the bill. He disputed the $2 billion cost estimate for the measure made by the Congressional Budget Office (CBO), saying CBO analysts had not taken into consideration savings that would result from keeping people out of costly hospitals and nursing homes.

Hatch said his scaled-down home health amendment to HR 5238 would "demonstrate that Congress has heard the voice of the people and is prepared to maintain the foundation upon which we can build a comprehensive home health care program in the near future."

Other Senate Amendments

The Senate bill also mandated studies that Hatch hoped would ease the way for compensating victims of cancer allegedly caused by radioactive fallout from above-ground nuclear bomb testing in the Nevada desert in the 1950s.

A radiation compensation bill (S 1483) approved by the Labor and Human Resources Committee April 20 had become bogged down in criticisms of the statistical methods it authorized for deciding damages in victim lawsuits. The studies mandated by Hatch's amendment were meant to answer those criticisms. *(S 1483, p. 493)*

The Senate also added provisions reauthorizing federal funding for training nurse-anesthetists, making a number of technical corrections in health statutes and providing a longer patent for the low-calorie sweetener Aspartame.

Aspartame was first approved for use as a food additive by the FDA in 1974. The agency stayed its approval, however, after receiving allegations that the substance could cause brain damage in children and that there were problems with animal studies on the substance. After further investigation satisfied the FDA that the substance was not harmful and the studies were valid, the agency approved marketing of Aspartame in July 1981.

The amendment, tailored to the regulatory history of the sweetener without mentioning it by name, was offered by Robert C. Byrd, D-W.Va., on behalf of Howell Heflin, D-Ala.

The Senate bill also directed the Reagan administration to honor congressionally mandated specifications for primary health care block grants authorized in 1981. *(1981 Almanac p. 483)*

Edward M. Kennedy, D-Mass., ranking minority member of the Labor and Human Resources Committee, said

regulation writers at HHS had ignored congressional directives for the program, which funded community health centers.

Kennedy said another provision of the Senate bill, requiring a minimum of 10 federally funded research centers on sickle cell disease, would block administration efforts to cut back on these centers. The proposed cutbacks, Kennedy said, sent "an ominous message to America's black community, a message which says that a disease which affects primarily blacks is of little interest to the Congress."

Final Action

Backers of the legislation fought an expected veto by generating substantial publicity after the final compromise version cleared Congress Dec. 17.

Their campaign included a public letter to Reagan from victims of rare diseases and their representatives, and a pre-Christmas press conference on Capitol Hill urging him to give disease sufferers a holiday gift of "hope" by signing the bill.

Waxman's staff alerted more than 40 newspapers to the issue and later advised the White House that at least 17 major newspapers had printed editorials in favor of the bill. Major television networks also covered the issue repeatedly and sympathetically.

At the Dec. 21 press conference, Waxman defended giving tax credits to drug companies to make orphan drugs. Saying the bill would allow drug manufacturers to take a tax write-off of 73 cents for every dollar spent on human drug testing, Waxman suggested that cost was minimal compared with tax breaks backed by the administration and Congress "for the oil industry and for some of the wealthiest people in our society."

Waxman deflected suggestions that profitable drug companies should make orphan drugs available as a humanitarian act, without the multimillion-dollar tax break, and said hints that they would profit inappropriately from the legislation were unfair. Even with the bill's financial incentives, he said, drug makers probably still would lose money making orphan drugs because comparatively few people would buy them. "The legislation only means that they will lose less money," Waxman said. ∎

Radiation Compensation

Legislation to provide an unusual new legal remedy to persons exposed to radioactive fallout during open-air atomic bomb tests in the 1950s was approved by the Senate Labor and Human Relations Committee in April. However, it bogged down in the Judiciary Committee and never made it to the Senate floor.

The bill (S 1483) was sponsored by Labor and Human Resources Chairman Orrin G. Hatch, R-Utah. Residents of Utah and neighboring states who lived downwind from the Nevada test site would have been the prime beneficiaries. Scientists had reported a higher-than-expected incidence of certain types of cancer among this population.

Hatch said the government owed these people a special debt because it exposed them to hazardous levels of radiation and misled them about the risks they faced; he argued that if there was at least a 10 percent chance that fallout from the tests caused cancer in an individual, that individual should be able to collect money damages from

the government. His bill would have made it easier for such persons to do so.

Medical statisticians had told Congress they had devised a method that could become the legal basis for damage payments to radiation victims. Their novel statistical procedure could deal with uncertainties of cancer causation without, as one witness said, "opening wide the doors to the U.S. Treasury." S 1483 would have written the procedure into law.

However, well-placed senators and the insurance industry did not share the scientists' confidence in the new methodology. Skeptics, including representatives of the Reagan administration, warned that the bill could be enormously expensive and could set costly precedents for claims from veterans, nuclear industry workers or individuals exposed to environmental pollutants.

Unable to dislodge the bill from the Judiciary Committee, Hatch had to settle for attaching an amendment to an "orphan drug" bill cleared by Congress Dec. 17 (HR 5238 — PL 97-414) that required the secretary of health and human services (HHS) to develop the statistical tables on radiation and cancer. *(Story, p. 490)*

No action was taken in the House on a bill (HR 6052), similar to Hatch's, introduced by Dan Marriott, R-Utah.

Background

Existing law did not bar lawsuits against the federal government by cancer victims who blamed their illness on exposure to radiation from atom bomb tests. About 2,000 such suits were pending in 1982, according to Hatch.

But to win, Hatch said, a plaintiff had to prove three things: that the radiation was the most immediate likely cause of his cancer, that there was a better than 50 percent chance that the radiation did cause it, and that the government was negligent in exposing him to the radiation.

Hatch believed few, if any, test victims could meet that standard because science could not distinguish biologically between cancers caused by radiation and those caused by other agents. What science could do, he said, was render relatively sophisticated judgments on how likely it was that an individual's cancer was caused by the radiation. Hatch proposed to amend federal tort law to make this new methodology grounds for suits against the government by those exposed to the bomb tests.

Under his bill, a court could award damages to an individual who proved that he met probability criteria laid out in the new statistical tables. A plaintiff would not have to prove either federal negligence or a direct cause-and-effect relationship between his cancer and the bomb tests.

That meant that some awards inevitably would go to people whose cancers were not caused by the tests, Hatch admitted. But he said his bill was narrowly drafted to make successful claims difficult. He estimated successful suits would number in the hundreds, although the total could be higher.

The proposal drew skepticism from some fellow senators and outright opposition by the Reagan administration. Witnesses from the Defense and Energy departments and the Veterans Administration said it could set an undesirable precedent for claims relating to other instances of exposure to radiation or to toxic substances such as dioxins. It also could disrupt the nuclear energy industry and military nuclear operations, Defense officials said, by casting doubt on existing radiation exposure safety standards.

The insurance industry also warned that if the concept of basing compensation on statistical tables were extended, the financial risks on which insurance premiums were based would become totally unpredictable and insuring nuclear and chemical industries would be extremely difficult and "prohibitively expensive."

Committee Action

The Labor and Human Resources Committee agreed by a 14-1 vote April 20 to report S 1483.

Don Nickles, R-Okla., voted "no." He warned that the bill would invite thousands of lawsuits, some for cancers unrelated to the atomic testing.

Provisions. As approved by the committee, S 1483:

● Required the secretary of HHS, within 60 days of enactment, to publish a list of types of cancer that had been demonstrated to be related to exposure of a human population to ionizing radiation.

● Required the secretary, within a year of enactment, to publish tables expressing, in percentage terms, statistical probabilities that various doses of ionizing radiation caused radiation-related cancers. Variables used in the tables would include types of cancer, radiation doses, sex, age at time of exposure, and time between exposure and onset of cancer. The tables would be updated every four years.

● Authorized suits for damages against the federal government by individuals (or estates of deceased individuals) with radiation-related cancers diagnosed after Jan. 1, 1952, that appeared to be related to the bomb tests. The suits must be started within two years of enactment of the bill or two years after the cancer was diagnosed, whichever was later.

● Authorized release of federal data or records related to such a suit, but with deletions of materials that were classified or required by executive order to remain secret for national defense or foreign policy reasons. Permitted private examination by a court of deleted materials, to ascertain radiation dose levels, among other things.

● Authorized payment for damages to any individual who, using the tables, could demonstrate a "probability of causation" of at least 10 percent that his cancer was caused by fallout, or "rainout," from open-air atomic bomb tests conducted at the government's Nevada test site between Jan. 1, 1951, and July 31, 1962. (There had been speculation that radiation from the tests was released in rain as far away as Ohio and New York.)

● Authorized damage awards of $50,000 to $500,000, with the amount prorated to reflect an individual's probability figure. The individual would bear the burden of proving a "best estimate" of his individual exposure.

Judiciary Committee Action

The Senate Judiciary Subcommittee on Agency Administration approved S 1483 May 6 and sent it on to the full Judiciary Committee, after adding several amendments. But Hatch, who also sat on Judiciary, was unable to move the measure to the top of that committee's agenda, and subcommittee Chairman Charles E. Grassley, R-Iowa, said that if it did come up, he would ask that it be referred to the U.S. Court of Appeals for a review of its merits.

Grassley introduced a resolution of referral (S Res 416), which required approval by one house of Congress — in this case, the Senate. The court would, in effect, conduct a "trial" of both the new method and the validity of claims made under it, a procedure that could take as long as a year. The court's final opinion would be treated as advice to Congress.

Grassley's plan to seek court review of S 1483 appealed to Judiciary members such as Alan K. Simpson, R-Wyo., who sympathized with the bill's aims but were concerned with its implications.

Grassley said the Congressional Budget Office had estimated that claims relating to just one type of cancer associated with the bomb tests could cost as much as $14 billion.

The Judiciary subcommittee amended S 1483 to exclude veterans and to limit awards to actual damages only. Another amendment, aimed at reducing the bill's precedent-setting potential, specified that it would not be part of the broad statute on claims against the federal government.

The panel approved the bill by unanimous vote, after lengthy discussion of its potential cost and on whether to weight its novel legal test more in favor of victims, as Howard M. Metzenbaum, D-Ohio, urged.   ∎

National Institutes of Health

Congress failed to complete action on bills to reauthorize funding for the National Institutes of Health (NIH) devoted to research on cancer, heart, lung and blood diseases and to create a new national research institute on arthritis and related diseases.

The House passed a three-year reauthorization bill (HR 6457) for the cancer and heart-lung-blood institutes Sept. 30, along with authority for a new research institute on arthritis.

However, the Senate never took up that bill or a less costly Senate bill (S 2311), reported in May, reauthorizing the cancer and heart-lung-blood institutes. Key senators were reluctant to debate a controversial House-passed amendment, sponsored by Rep. William E. Dannemeyer, R-Calif., that would have banned medical research on living human fetuses in most instances.

In a last-minute effort to salvage the arthritis institute, a separate authorization (S 1939) was discharged from the Labor and Human Resources Committee and passed by the Senate Dec. 20. However, Dannemeyer objected to bringing the bill to the House floor, and the measure died.

There had been a strenuous lobbying campaign for a separate arthritis institute. *(Box, p. 495)*

Although the authorization bills did not clear, fiscal 1983 funding for the affected health programs was included in the continuing appropriations resolution (H J Res 631 — PL 97-377). *(Story, p. 238)*

Separate reauthorization bills for the federal research institutes on alcoholism and drug abuse also failed to clear. *(Story, p. 496)*

Senate Committee Action

The Senate Labor and Human Resources Committee April 27 approved a three-year reauthorization (S 2311) for the National Cancer Institute and the National Heart, Lung and Blood Institute. The committee report was filed May 28 (S Rept 97-461).

By an 8-8 tie vote, the panel rejected an attempt by Lowell P. Weicker Jr., R-Conn., to add to the bill an extension of the federal health planning system, which the Reagan administration wanted to kill. The program's existing authorization was scheduled to expire Sept. 30. *(Health*

planning, p. 497)

Weicker argued that health care was too important and too expensive to develop without planning. The planning system was aimed at discouraging duplicate or unneeded medical services by requiring hospitals to get prior approval of major expansions or equipment purchases.

Weicker said he would offer the amendment again when the bill came up on the Senate floor.

The seven committee Democrats voted for Weicker's amendment; committee Republicans did not.

Committee Chairman Orrin G. Hatch, R-Utah, preferred to let the planning law expire. At his request, the committee amended the NIH bill to cancel penalties for non-compliance with it.

Provisions

As reported, S 2311:

● Reauthorized the National Cancer Institute, the National Heart, Lung and Blood Institute and the National Library of Medicine for three years, with funding increases above the previous fiscal year's level of 6 percent in fiscal 1983, 5.5 percent in 1984 and 5 percent in 1985. The administration had requested a 3 percent increase in overall NIH funding for fiscal 1983, although that was unevenly distributed among the different institutes.

● Continued for three years the advisory boards for arthritis, diabetes, kidney and urologic diseases.

● Lengthened contracts for cancer research and treatment centers to five years, from three years. (The contracts were renewable.)

● Raised to $50,000, from $35,000, the ceiling on direct costs for cancer and heart-lung-blood grants that could be funded without approval by advisory boards.

● Reauthorized health information and health promotion activities, including the Office of Disease Prevention and Health Promotion. Repealed authority for sports medicine and physical fitness programs.

● Reauthorized for two years the President's Commission for the Study of Ethical Problems in Medicine and Biomedical and Behavioral Research; authorized $1.1 million in fiscal 1983 and $1.4 million in 1984.

● Required two new annual reports from NIH, on efforts to improve grant and contract accountability and peer review, and on disease prevention and health promotion.

● Repealed health planning act sanctions against states that failed to meet certain requirements.

● Extended for six months the deadline for states to begin providing most community services block grant money to local governments, rather than funneling it through community action agencies. The 1981 budget reconciliation law (PL 97-35) required the changeover, for states opting to take the block grants, by Sept. 30, 1982. As many as 10 states need additional time to make the changeover, according to Thomas F. Eagleton, D-Mo. *(Block grants, 1981 Almanac p. 483)*

House Committee Action

The House Energy and Commerce Committee Aug. 23 reported a three-year, $6.6 billion authorization for national research institutes on cancer, heart-lung-blood diseases, arthritis and certain other diseases (HR 6457 — H Rept 97-791).

The funding levels were set by the committee to provide for a real 5 percent growth each year, in addition to inflation.

Arthritis Institute Urged

Arthritis sufferers and organizations representing them came close to winning creation of a separate, new national research institute for that disease in 1982.

The election-year mobilization of the well-organized arthritis lobby, backed by the organized elderly and several arthritics in high places, easily overcame protests from the Reagan administration and the medical community that the proposed new Institute of Arthritis and Musculoskeletal Diseases would be a questionable use of scarce federal health dollars.

A provision creating the new institute was attached to a House-passed bill (HR 6457) reauthorizing the National Institutes of Health (NIH), but the Senate never took up its NIH bill (S 2311). On Dec. 20 the Senate passed a separate bill authorizing an arthritis institute (S 1939), but Rep. William E. Dannemeyer, R-Calif., objected to bringing that bill up on the House floor, so the legislation died. *(NIH bill, p. 494)*

Under the existing NIH structure, arthritis research was financed through the National Institute of Arthritis, Diabetes and Digestive and Kidney Diseases. Giving arthritis separate billing, proponents said, would bring higher visibility, stronger leadership, more money and a better chance of relief for the nation's 37 million arthritis sufferers.

"Although one in three families is affected, only 1 percent of the NIH budget has been allocated to arthritis research," said Rep. Ron Wyden, D-Ore. "Arthritis . . . has been lost in the shuffle."

NIH officials disagreed. They said arthritis research, funded at more than $60 million in 1981, had grown faster than research in other areas, more than doubling since 1976. A new institute, they said, would create $4 million in new administrative costs, money that in a time of tight budgets would be siphoned away from other priorities.

Joining the administration in opposing the new institute were several medical organizations, including the American Medical Association. "We just think creating yet another administrative unit doesn't necessarily mean better research or more research," said Dr. John S. Zapp, director of AMA's Washington office.

Critics warned that if the new arthritis institute was approved, others would follow close behind.

Philanthropist Mary Lasker, a force in the enlargement of NIH for three decades, and the Arthritis Institute spearheaded the campaign for the new institute. The proposal initially met resistance from key Republicans in the House and Senate, but as the lobbying effort grew, some skeptics either backed off or joined as cosponsors. Like the administration, several decided it would be fruitless to fight the idea.

Barry Goldwater, R-Ariz., who underwent a hip replacement in 1981 due to arthritis, was the most avid Senate advocate of a new institute. Steven D. Symms, R-Idaho, whose wife suffered from an arthritis-related disease, also pressed colleagues into support. Labor and Human Resources Committee Chairman Orrin G. Hatch, R-Utah, was cool initially, but after considerable pressure from arthritic constituents and colleagues, he enlisted as a cosponsor Aug. 15.

The bill provided explicit statutory authorizations for the 11 existing National Institutes of Health, some of which had been created administratively. It also authorized creation of a new research institute on arthritis, and mandated increased emphasis on disease prevention.

Efforts to require the health institutes to go through the normal authorization process required of almost all other federal agencies had been a matter of controversy for several years. In 1980, after a long lobbying campaign by the nation's health research establishment, Congress backed off and agreed not to require statutory authorizations for those institutes. The Cancer and Heart-Lung-Blood Institutes were the only ones that had been authorized by statute. *(1980 Almanac p. 463)*

NIH supported biomedical research at universities and medical schools as well as conducting its own research. It accounted for about 68 percent of federal health research spending. The research community argued that subjecting the institutes to the congressional authorization process would "politicize" research decisions.

Ron Wyden, D-Ore., offered the amendment to authorize creation of a new Institute of Arthritis and Musculoskeletal Diseases. Under the existing NIH structure, arthritis research funding was lumped together with that for diabetes and digestive and kidney diseases. Advocates of a separate institute said arthritis research was "lost in the shuffle."

House Floor Action

The House took up HR 6457 Sept. 22, but broke off debate after Edward R. Madigan, Ill., ranking Republican on the Energy and Commerce Subcommittee on Health, objected to the bill's funding levels and its recodification of statutory authority for the National Institutes of Health.

Madigan suggested the bill's author, Henry A. Waxman, D-Calif., chairman of the Health subcommittee, was laying groundwork for direct congressional intervention in NIH administrative decisions. Waxman denied any intention to meddle in NIH affairs and said a recent article in a medical publication suggesting otherwise was "an absolute misstatement of my position."

The House finally passed HR 6457 by voice vote Sept. 30, despite strong objections by Republicans to its funding increases for the health institutes.

Fetal Research

Passage of the bill came after a heated debate on an amendment by Dannemeyer to prohibit NIH funding for any research or experimentation on human fetuses while they were alive.

Waxman objected that the amendment would bar key research techniques such as sampling amniotic fluid or fetal tissues, and cited treatments already developed from such research for critical fetal health problems. Waxman said federal regulations already barred most research involving fetuses.

Barbara A. Mikulski, D-Md., also opposed the amendment, saying, "Women . . . want this research because we want to live and we want our babies to live and we want our babies to be healthy."

Dannemeyer said the amendment was a necessary defense of human life. Robert K. Dornan, R-Calif., claiming that a small minority of researchers were "sick . . . mentally disturbed," threatened that unless Waxman helped work out an amendment on the issue, "I am going to call a spade

a spade and start putting out ghastly color photographs . . . of what you and others are trying to protect."

The House approved Dannemeyer's amendment, 260-140. *(Vote 358, p. 106-H)*

Funding Levels

James T. Broyhill, R-N.C., offered a substitute reducing the funding levels in the bill. He said his amendment would allow 7 percent NIH growth in 1983 over 1982, while the committee bill would increase funding by 11 percent in 1983 and more than double that amount by 1985. He also said the bill's recodification of NIH authority was "unnecessary and potentially disruptive."

Members opposing Broyhill praised the research supported by NIH, and Waxman argued that medical research could ultimately reduce health care costs. The Broyhill substitute was rejected, 130-275. *(Vote 359, p. 106-H)* ∎

Drug, Alcohol Research

Congress in 1982 failed to complete action on legislation reauthorizing funding for programs of the federal research institutes on alcoholism and drug abuse.

The House passed a three-year reauthorization (HR 6458) Sept. 20 and the Senate passed a two-year bill (S 2365) Oct. 1. Sponsors met informally and agreed on a compromise version; they also agreed to tack on a one-year extension of the controversial federal health planning system, followed by its repeal in 1985. *(Health planning, p. 497)*

The compromise also contained a provision extending for 90 days a presidential commission on biomedical ethics.

The House passed the compromise version of HR 6458 Dec. 16, but the Senate did not take up the bill before adjournment, and the measure died.

Although the bill did not clear, funding for the institutes and for the health planning system was included in the fiscal 1983 continuing appropriations resolution cleared Dec. 20 (H J Res 631 — PL 97-377). *(Story, p. 238)*

House Action

The House Energy and Commerce Committee reported HR 6458 Aug. 19 (H Rept 97-768) and the House passed the bill Sept. 20 by voice vote under suspension of the rules, a procedure that barred floor amendments and required a two-thirds vote for passage.

The bill provided a three-year authorization of funding for research, training and public information programs of the National Institute on Alcohol Abuse and Alcoholism and the National Institute on Drug Abuse.

For the alcohol institute, the bill authorized appropriations of up to $33 million in fiscal 1983, $50 million in 1984 and $75 million in 1985. For the drug abuse institute, it authorized $47 million, $53 million and $59 million for the three years.

Robert S. Walker, R-Pa., said during floor debate that the Reagan administration "has some problems with this bill" because the funding levels exceeded the president's budget request by 30 to 66 percent.

Edward R. Madigan, R-Ill., acknowledged that the funding levels exceeded the budget request, but he said they were within the limits of the congressional budget resolution. Madigan was ranking minority member of the

Energy and Commerce Subcommittee on Health.

Subcommittee Chairman Henry A. Waxman, D-Calif., argued that a strong commitment to research was essential to combat serious national problems with alcohol and drug abuse. He placed the social and economic costs of drug and alcohol abuse at $60 billion a year, and said as many as 13 million Americans were problem drinkers.

HR 6458 mandated a new emphasis on disease prevention for the two institutes and the National Institute of Mental Health. It also established formal procedures for peer review, for research contracts awarded by the three institutes, and for handling accusations of scientific misconduct by researchers working on institute grants.

Senate Action

Despite complaints from the chairman of the subcommittee with jurisdiction that the bill was too expensive, the Senate Oct. 1 passed S 2365, reauthorizing for two years the institutes on alcohol and drug abuse.

Gordon J. Humphrey, R-N.H., told the Senate he "wholeheartedly supported" research and dissemination of information on alcohol and drug problems, but he said the bill's funding levels were too high in light of existing economic conditions and the size of the federal deficit.

At the request of the Reagan administration, the Labor and Human Resources Committee had increased the funding levels approved by Humphrey's Subcommittee on Alcoholism and Drug Abuse. The committee reported the bill June 8 (S Rept 97-468).

Committee Chairman Orrin G. Hatch, R-Utah, speaking for the bill on the floor, described alcoholism and drug abuse as "our society's two most serious health problems" — and both "completely preventable."

After passing S 2365 by voice vote, the Senate substituted the text of its bill for the more expensive, three-year House authorization (HR 6458).

For the National Institute on Alcohol Abuse and Alcoholism, the Senate bill authorized $32.9 million a year in fiscal 1983 and 1984. For the National Institute on Drug Abuse, it authorized $46.4 million for each year.

The bill also revised reporting requirements for the institutes and for the White House Office of Drug Abuse Policy, and required uniform data reporting in the alcohol, drug abuse and mental health block grant program. ∎

Health Planning System

The embattled federal health planning system escaped death or severe modification in 1982, despite the Reagan administration's desire to kill it.

The controversial program was kept alive by the fiscal 1983 continuing appropriations resolution (H J Res 631 — PL 97-377) after the failure of efforts to reauthorize it as optional block grants to the states.

Supporters of planning, recognizing that they did not have the votes to keep the system alive in its existing form, had agreed to support the block grant idea, which was put forward by Republicans, principally Rep. Edward R. Madigan, Ill. The Republicans had no particular fondness for the program but felt some sort of planning program was needed to help hold down medical cost increases, at least until the administration came up with its long-promised "pro-competition" legislation to deregulate the health care delivery system.

The House passed a health planning bill (HR 6173) Sept. 24 and included a modified version of the program in another bill (HR 6458), passed Dec. 16, reauthorizing the federal research institutes on alcoholism and drug abuse. *(Story, p. 496)*

However, the Senate did not act on either bill. Lowell P. Weicker Jr., R-Conn., tried to add an extension of the planning system to legislation (S 2311) reauthorizing the National Cancer Institute and the National Heart, Lung and Blood Institute, but failed on an 8-8 tie vote. Weicker planned to offer a similar amendment on the Senate floor, but the bill never was brought up. *(Story, p. 494)*

The continuing resolution funded the program at the fiscal 1982 level of $64.4 million. The president had requested only $2 million.

Background

Created in 1974 (PL 93-641) and extended in 1979 (PL 96-79), the planning system was intended to equalize the distribution of health care facilities and services in the United States. Its main focus came to be attempting to hold down health care costs by curbing unneeded hospital expansions and duplication in the provision of health services and purchase of major medical equipment. Under the law, a hospital must obtain a "certificate of need" from the state before proceeding with major changes.

The program funded local planning groups, known as health systems agencies (HSAs), which were controlled by locally selected boards made up of consumers and providers of health care. The HSAs were to review any proposed expansion of health services or facilities in their areas. Supporters of the program contended that it helped hold down health care costs, but opponents called it unnecessary federal regulation.

The Reagan administration wanted to phase out the program. In 1981, Congress declined to kill it, but, as part of the budget reconciliation legislation (PL 97-35), substantially reduced its funding while extending its authorization for one year. Federal spending for the program previously had been running about $130 million a year. *(Background, 1981 action, 1981 Almanac p. 476)*

Senate Committee Action

The Senate Labor and Human Resources Committee April 27 refused to resuscitate the planning system it once helped to create. The program was scheduled to expire Sept. 30.

By an 8-8 tie vote, the panel rejected Weicker's amendment to add a reprieve for the program to the NIH reauthorization bill (S 2311). Weicker said health care was too important and too expensive to develop without planning.

Weicker's amendment would continue the program for three years but would make state participation optional. It included funds for states that wanted to substitute pro-competition health policies for planning. It also provided for new data collection so that comparisons of medical costs could be made between states with and without planning systems.

The seven committee Democrats voted for Weicker's amendment; committee Republicans did not, although Dan Quayle, Ind., and Paula Hawkins, Fla., said they were concerned with rising health care costs, and Hawkins warmly praised Florida's health planning program. Haw-

kins and Quayle told staff aides to continue working on the issue, with the idea of moving a less ambitious version of Madigan's block grant plan on the Senate floor.

Committee Chairman Orrin G. Hatch, R-Utah, wanted to let the program expire. States might choose to continue planning, he said, but the federal program had become "a bureaucratic morass" that added costs and "stifled creative development of medical care." Hatch said the prior-approval process known as "certificate of need" had become "the shrillest problem we've got in health care today." A hospital could spend $50,000 to $1 million on the process of acquiring a certificate, Hatch claimed.

Permitting the planning act to expire would not automatically end certificate-of-need procedures, since they were based on state law. But it would take away financial support for state certification programs.

In addition to defeating Weicker's amendment, the committee amended the NIH bill, at Hatch's request, to cancel penalties for non-compliance with the federal health planning law.

House Committee Action

The House Energy and Commerce Committee May 13 voted 23-19 for Madigan's plan to convert the health planning system into an optional block grant program with much-reduced funding and powers.

The panel then, by voice vote May 20, decided to remove the provision from its NIH reauthorization bill (HR 6338) and instead to report it as a separate bill (HR 6173). The committee report was not filed until Aug. 20 (H Rept 97-784).

In an unusual reversal of roles, opponents of planning backed the block grant plan, while Henry A. Waxman, D-Calif., chairman of the panel's Health Subcommittee and a strong advocate of the existing system, opposed it. Waxman claimed the plan would effectively kill the planning system, but he was unable to block it in committee.

Madigan's bill represented a much-disputed middle ground in a struggle that continued for weeks, mostly in private meetings, before the committee agreed to report it. Madigan had forged a majority of conservatives and moderates on the committee to support his plan.

The conservatives, led by Richard C. Shelby, D-Ala., sided with Madigan after finding that they lacked enough votes for their preferred choice — immediate repeal of planning. The Health Subcommittee May 11 had rejected Shelby's motion to repeal the system by an 8-12 vote.

Waxman's plan to reauthorize the existing system, with some changes to enhance state power, also had failed on a 10-10 tie.

Madigan and Shelby wanted to put the committee on record as supporting their version of the health planning extension, hoping this would head off moves to incorporate a stronger planning provision in any omnibus budget reconciliation legislation.

Following committee approval of the Madigan plan, Waxman worked out an agreement with him, Shelby, Committee Chairman John D. Dingell, D-Mich., and ranking minority member James T. Broyhill, R-N.C., that the bill would move forward but that they would all support a package of modifications when the measure reached the House floor.

Provisions. As approved by the committee, HR 6173 authorized $40 million for planning block grants in fiscal 1983 and $42 million in 1984. It made the program optional instead of mandatory, with block grants for states choosing to take them. It appeared to eliminate support for non-profit local planning agencies; states could fund planning by units if they were part of local government, but the statutory requirement for local input into certificate-of-need (CON) decisions at the state level would end.

The bill also greatly increased the dollar thresholds for projects that had to go through CON review, and specified that only "new" services were subject to review. It would require CON review only for a project with a capital expenditure of $5 million or more, or annual operating costs of more than $1 million. In certain circumstances, states could adopt lower thresholds of $1 million in capital expenditures or $500,000 in annual operating expenses. CON review was required for hospitals, nursing facilities and similar institutions, but not for health maintenance organizations, equipment in independent clinical laboratories or doctors' offices.

Existing thresholds, set by the 1981 reconciliation bill, required CON review for projects with capital expenditures of over $600,000, all equipment purchases of over $400,000, and new services generating annual operating costs of $250,000 or more.

The new thresholds were expected to cut the number of projects undergoing review by 50 percent.

Lobbying

Madigan's bill was supported by the Federation of American Hospitals, the American Hospital Association and the National Council of Community Hospitals, whose counsel, John Hoff, helped draft it.

Lobbying hard for changes in what members considered "unworkable" portions of the bill was a coalition including the American Health Planning Association, the National Governors' Association, the Washington Business Group on Health, Blue Cross and Blue Shield Associations, commercial health insurers, the National Association of Counties and the Catholic Health Association, representing 632 hospitals and 261 nursing homes across the country.

The groups lobbying for changes in Madigan's bill said its dollar thresholds were too high to curb many unnecessary health service expenditures. They also objected to the fact that states would be ineligible for block grant money if they chose to set lower thresholds.

Pro-planning testimony by insurers and corporate purchasers of employee health insurance also made a strong impression on members who usually voted against any form of health regulation. The business witnesses argued that planning was an important cost-control tool.

House Floor Action

The House passed HR 6173 Sept. 24 by a vote of 302-14, after lowering funding levels and making certain other changes in the version reported by the Energy and Commerce Committee. *(Vote 348, p. 104-H)*

Madigan and Waxman had drafted a second bill (HR 7040), printed at the end of the committee report, and asked the House to substitute that for the committee bill. The House agreed by voice vote.

The bill would virtually end strict requirements that states operate CON programs and maintain dual networks of local and state planning agencies. Its funding authorizations were about 60 percent below fiscal 1980 levels for health planning — $32 million in fiscal 1983 and $33.6 million in 1984, compared with committee levels of $40

million and $42 million. The authorization was for grants to states, to support certificate-of-need programs and development of health plans.

The substitute set certain conditions of eligibility for the grants, established procedures for continuing the existing program until the new program was operative and repealed existing law, including penalties for non-compliance, when the new program was in place.

Later Action

In the final days of the 97th Congress, a two-year reauthorization for the national institutes on drug and alcohol abuse (HR 6458) became a last-minute vehicle for continuing the health planning system. The House passed the bill Dec. 16.

Sponsors had agreed to tack a one-year extension of the existing health planning law, followed by its repeal in 1985, onto the bill.

However, the Senate did not take up the bill before adjournment. ∎

Cigarette Labeling

Tobacco industry objections and a Reagan administration turnaround torpedoed bills (S 1929, HR 5653) to require new, more alarming health warning labels on cigarettes.

A new anti-smoking coalition that included the American Lung Association, American Cancer Society and American Heart Association had enlisted the support of conservatives, moderates and liberals of both parties in Congress for stronger labeling requirements. The coalition also had won a qualified endorsement of the labeling plan from the administration.

The secretary of health and human services (HHS), Richard S. Schweiker, and other administration health officials had spoken out strongly against smoking, calling it the chief preventable cause of death in the United States.

But on March 16, five days after strongly endorsing new labels at a House hearing, Dr. Edward N. Brandt Jr., assistant secretary for health in HHS, told the Senate Labor and Human Resources Committee the administration was reconsidering the issue.

Neither bill ever moved out of committee. Orrin G. Hatch, R-Utah, chairman of the Senate panel, attempted to mark up the bill July 29, but a talkathon by John P. East, a Republican from the tobacco-growing state of North Carolina, blocked consideration of the measure.

Since 1970, cigarette packaging, print advertisements and billboards had been required to carry the words, "Warning: The Surgeon General Has Determined That Cigarette Smoking Is Dangerous To Your Health." But that warning was so shopworn and vague that many Americans ignored it, according to Hatch and Rep. Henry A. Waxman, D-Calif., chairman of the House Energy and Commerce Subcommittee on Health.

Hatch, Sen. Bob Packwood, R-Ore., and Waxman were the principal sponsors of the bills to mandate tougher, rotating warning labels for cigarettes. The bills also would have required cigarette makers to state the levels of "tar," nicotine and carbon monoxide produced by a cigarette when smoked, and to disclose, for the first time, what chemicals they added to cigarettes for flavoring and other purposes.

Opponents of the bills said the labeling plan was unnecessary, unconstitutional, expensive and unfair. They said most Americans already knew of the allegations against smoking, and that warning labels had little impact. Americans spent about $21 billion on cigarettes in 1980.

Although the percentage of the U.S. population that smoked had declined from 42 percent in 1965 to 32 percent in 1982, the surgeon general's 1982 annual report estimated that 111,000 Americans a year were dying of lung cancer, three times as many as 20 years earlier. The report said smoking also could cause cancers of the larynx, mouth, esophagus, bladder, kidneys and pancreas; chronic lung disease such as emphysema; coronary heart disease; miscarriages and birth defects. ∎

Science Education

Caught in a conflict between two House committees, legislation to expand the federal role in science education lost its chance for congressional action in 1982.

The bill (HR 7130) was reported by the House Science and Technology Committee Oct. 5 (H Rept 97-933, Part I). The Education and Labor Committee approved major amendments to the bill on Nov. 30, and filed its report (Part II) Dec. 2.

HR 7130 and dozens of related bills introduced during the 97th Congress sought to restore science to the prominent role in federal education policy that it had in the years following the launching of the Soviet Sputnik satellite in 1957. The National Science Foundation (NSF) and the American Association for the Advancement of Science (AAAS) had warned that the deteriorating quality of science instruction could leave the United States without the trained people needed to compete in the world economy.

There were shortages of mathematics, science and engineering teachers at both the high school and college levels, mainly because trained people could earn much more in industry than they could teaching. There also were serious deficiencies in the equipment used to train students. The average equipment in engineering school laboratories was 14 years old, and the NSF estimated the cost of upgrading science teaching equipment could run to $4 billion.

There also was concern that students who did not become professional scientists were leaving school without the basic understanding of science needed to function in the modern world. Scores on science and math achievement tests taken by high school students had fallen steadily for a decade. Fewer students were taking science and math courses beyond the most basic level, and the courses they did take often were taught by teachers who lacked adequate science and math qualifications. Only about one-third of U.S. high school students finished three years of math, while in Japan, for example, virtually all college-bound students took four years of math. Students in the Soviet Union also received much more math and science instruction, beginning earlier in their education, than Americans did.

House Committee Differences

The main difference between the House panels was over who would shape a new science education program.

Science and Technology. The Science Committee had sought exclusive jurisdiction over the bill. Its bill emphasized applied science and grants to universities, with funds distributed through the NSF according to evalua-

tions of projects by panels of scientists.

The committee wanted to establish a structure for a national science education policy, as well as specific programs to attack current problems. Its bill gave general authority to federal agencies to engage in activities aimed at encouraging training of specialists in their areas, with congressional approval required for specific training proposals.

A Coordinating Council on Engineering and Scientific Manpower established by the bill would be responsible for overseeing the status of science manpower training and proposing strategies to improve it.

The biggest share of funding under the bill would go to an Engineering and Science Manpower Fund administered by the NSF. The bill provided $20 million in fiscal 1983 and $40 million in each of fiscal years 1984-87 for the fund, which would provide matching grants to encourage development of new ways to strengthen science training.

The bill also authorized $30 million in fiscal 1983, rising to $85 million in 1987, for four smaller programs: modernization of college science teaching equipment; community college training of high-technology technicians; research grants for young college faculty members to encourage them to continue teaching, and improvement of science and math teaching and instructional materials in elementary and secondary schools.

Education and Labor. The Education and Labor Committee had to fight to gain a share of jurisdiction over the bill, and amended it to distribute funds through the Education Department, largely by formula to states and local schools.

While they agreed that something needed to be done about science education, committee members were sharply critical of the bill reported by the Science panel. They said they and most education interest groups had been left out of the development of the bill. Chairman Carl D. Perkins, D-Ky., was particularly angered by the Science Committee provision giving the NSF control over grant distribution.

In place of the Science Committee's small elementary and secondary education program, providing teacher training and research through NSF, Perkins' committee proposed to establish a program of direct grants to states and local school districts, run by the Education Department. Each local school district with a science program would be eligible for payments according to a formula based on the number of its students and the average per-pupil spending in the state. Districts could use the funds to improve instruction in science, math, foreign languages or technology.

The committee also amended the Science bill to allow state vocational education agencies, as well as community colleges, to receive technical training funds. It deleted the Science Committee provision authorizing government agencies to encourage training. ∎

Health Promotion

A two-year reauthorization of health information and health promotion programs (HR 6384) passed the House Sept. 13, but the Senate did not act on the measure.

The House passed the bill by voice vote under suspension of the rules, a procedure that barred floor amendments and required a two-thirds vote for passage. The Energy and Commerce Committee had reported it Aug. 19 (H Rept 97-767).

The existing authorization for the programs, included in a 1979 nurse training bill (PL 96-76), expired Sept. 30. *(1979 Almanac p. 506)*

HR 6384 authorized $8 million in fiscal 1983 and $9 million in 1984 for grants and contracts to foster research and programs dealing with health information and health promotion, preventive health services and "education in the appropriate use of health care." The funds would be in addition to money appropriated under the preventive health and health services block grant to the states, approved by Congress as part of the 1981 budget reconciliation bill (PL 97-35). *(1981 Almanac p. 483)*

While the states had the primary responsibility for funding health promotion programs under the block grant system, the Energy and Commerce Committee said the research and information functions conducted by the federal Centers for Disease Control and the Department of Health and Human Services still were essential.

The reauthorization of the health promotion programs originally was included in a broader measure (HR 6338) approved by the Energy and Commerce Subcommittee on Health May 11. But that bill, which also dealt with the National Institutes of Health, assistance to medical libraries, the health planning system and other programs, was divided into several separate bills before being reported by the full committee. Subcommittee Chairman Henry A. Waxman, D-Calif., split off the health information and promotion provisions and introduced them as HR 6384, which was approved by the committee June 2.

In the Senate, an omnibus health programs extension bill (S 2311) was reported by the Labor and Human Resources Committee May 28 but was never brought to the floor. *(Story, p. 494)*

Despite the failure of the authorization bills to clear, the various health programs were continued in the fiscal 1983 continuing appropriations resolution cleared by Congress Dec. 20 (H J Res 631 — PL 97-377). ∎

NIOSH Transfer

Disagreement over a proposed transfer of the National Institute of Occupational Safety and Health (NIOSH) from the Centers for Disease Control (CDC) to the National Institutes of Health (NIH) killed a House health bill (HR 6355) Sept. 15.

In addition to transferring NIOSH, the bill would have authorized funding for the training of nurse anesthetists, allowed the use of community health center grants to build as well as operate health centers, and made various technical corrections in health provisions of the hastily written 1981 budget reconciliation act (PL 97-35). *(1981 Almanac p. 483)*

The House voted 227-165 for the bill, but that was short of the two-thirds vote needed to pass it under suspension of the rules, the procedure under which it was brought to the floor. *(Vote 308, p. 92-H)*

The suspension procedure was intended to be used with noncontroversial bills. The NIOSH transfer was highly controversial, opponents pointed out. They said the transfer was simply an effort by disgruntled NIOSH employees and their supporters in Congress to reverse an administration order to move the agency from the Washington, D.C., area to Atlanta, headquarters of the CDC. NIH was located in the Washington area. ∎

Education Bills Vetoed

President Reagan in January 1983 pocket-vetoed two education bills cleared by Congress in the last week of the lame-duck session.

One bill (S 2623) authorized federal assistance to the nation's 18 tribally controlled community colleges. The other (HR 7336) made numerous amendments to the 1981 Education Consolidation and Improvement Act (ECIA).

If the president failed to sign a bill within 10 days of receiving it (excluding Sundays), and Congress had adjourned, the bill died without a formal veto. Congress adjourned Dec. 23.

Indian Colleges. Reagan announced Jan. 4 that he was withholding his signature from the Tribally Controlled Community Colleges Act (S 2623), which cleared Congress Dec. 20. The bill authorized funds for construction of new facilities at the Indian schools, plus $5 million a year to fund endowments.

The House Education and Labor Committee had reported a companion bill Aug. 12 (HR 6485 — H Rept 97-736). The Senate Indian Affairs Committee reported S 2623 Dec. 13 (S Rept 97-681); the Senate passed it Dec. 16. The House substituted its provisions and passed S 2623 Dec. 17. The Senate adopted the conference report on the bill (H Rept 97-979) Dec. 19, the House Dec. 20, both by voice vote.

Reagan rejected the bill's contention that support of the colleges was part of the federal government's trust responsibility toward Indian tribes. He also opposed spending money on a new building program. *(Veto text, p. 33-E)*

ECIA Amendments. On Jan. 12 Reagan pocket-vetoed HR 7336, which amended the 1981 Education Consolidation and Improvement Act (ECIA). ECIA, passed as part of the fiscal 1982 budget reconciliation act (PL 97-35), made changes in the Title I program of aid to disadvantaged children and combined 28 education programs into a block grant to the states. *(1981 Almanac p. 499)*

HR 7336 cleared Congress Dec. 20, three days after it was reported by the House Education and Labor Committee. Both the House and Senate passed it by voice vote, without objections.

The bill was designed to "dispel ambiguities, eliminate unintended results and correct drafting errors" that arose because of the haste with which the reconciliation bill was enacted, according to the Education and Labor Committee. Among other things, it would have increased school districts' flexibility in targeting aid to disadvantaged children; made clear that Title I aid could be provided to private school pupils, preschool children of migrant workers and Indian children, and made clear that Education Department regulations on ECIA programs were subject to congressional review.

Introduced Nov. 30 by Bill Goodling, Pa., ranking Republican on the Elementary, Secondary and Vocational Education Subcommittee, the bill was reported Dec. 17 by the Education and Labor Committee (H Rept 97-977) and passed the House the same day. The Senate passed it Dec. 20.

In his memorandum of disapproval, Reagan took issue with the bill's assertion that providing aid to Indian children was part of the government's "trust responsibility" to Indians — the same argument he made in vetoing the Indian colleges bill. He also said the bill would hamper administration efforts to help children of migrant workers, and called the congressional veto provision an "unwarranted intrusion" on executive branch authority. *(Veto text, p. 34-E)*

Congress earlier in the year had overturned a set of education regulations in a battle over the same issue. *(Story, p. 486)* ∎

Quality of Teaching

The House Dec. 13 rejected legislation (H J Res 429) urging states to establish commissions on teacher excellence to evaluate the quality of teaching in their schools.

The vote was 225-153, 27 votes short of the two-thirds majority needed to pass under suspension of the rules, the procedure under which the measure was brought to the floor. *(Vote 411, p. 122-H)*

Reported by the Education and Labor Committee Aug. 12 (H Rept 97-735), H J Res 429 would not have required states to do anything. Instead, it recommended that each state set up a commission to evaluate its teachers and study ways to improve their performance.

Sponsor Paul Simon, D-Ill., chairman of the Postsecondary Education Subcommittee, said the resolution was in response to growing concerns about the future supply of first-rate teachers. He noted that many teachers, particularly of science and mathematics, were leaving the profession. *(Related story, p. 499)*

Simon argued that, while the federal government could do little to improve teacher quality directly, it could encourage states to look at the situation themselves.

The ranking Republican on the committee, John N. Erlenborn, Ill., opposed the bill as an unwarranted federal intrusion into state concerns. ∎

ED Dismantlement

Congressional reaction to President Reagan's plan to dismantle the Education Department (ED) was so cool that the administration decided not to push legislation to demote the department from a Cabinet agency to an independent foundation.

The department, created by a 1979 law (PL 96-88), had been in operation since 1980. *(1979 Almanac p. 465)*

Reagan pledged during the 1980 presidential campaign to abolish it. To many conservatives, ED was a symbol of federal government intrusion into areas they considered of purely local concern. Reagan said in his State of the Union message in January that dismantling ED also would result in "major savings." Details of his plan to turn it into a foundation were outlined in the administration's fiscal 1983 budget. *(State of the Union message, p. 3-E)*

Senate Majority Leader Howard H. Baker Jr., R-Tenn., and William V. Roth Jr., R-Del., chairman of the Senate Governmental Affairs Committee, did not like the foundation plan, and showed no inclination to act on it if it were introduced. Roth's committee had jurisdiction over government reorganization plans.

In the House, the idea also faced strong opposition from Government Operations Committee Chairman Jack Brooks, D-Texas.

Although ED was not universally popular in the educa-

tion community when it was created, virtually all education interest groups mobilized in support of it when it was threatened with dismantlement. Educators feared its abolition was part of a broader administration effort to cut federal aid to education.

Even critics of the department were ambivalent about the foundation proposal. They saw any federal education agency, even a smaller one, as a symbol of federal intrusion into the traditional local control of education.

Reagan Proposal

Reagan's foundation proposal was an uneasy compromise between his promise to get rid of ED and Education Secretary T.H. Bell's reluctance to allow education to be submerged in some other, larger department, as it was before it was made into a separate department.

The plan was to convert much of ED into an independent Foundation for Educational Assistance, which would retain control over major grant programs for the education of disadvantaged and handicapped children; distribute financial aid to college students, and be responsible for educational research and statistics.

Some 28 programs would be transferred to other departments; 23 would be terminated, along with 11 federal boards and commissions. With the transfers and terminations, the foundation would have 4,800 employees, 1,400 fewer than ED had in fiscal 1981 and 1,200 fewer than in 1982.

The administration's recommendation that the foundation have reduced authority over civil rights laws was expected to be a source of controversy in any congressional consideration of the plan. The foundation would retain responsibility for investigations of complaints about violations of civil rights laws in education and for negotiations to obtain voluntary compliance with the laws. But litigation of civil rights cases would be transferred to the Justice Department.

The Lawyers' Committee for Civil Rights Under Law said that would cripple federal efforts to ensure equal access to educational opportunities. ∎

Child Nutrition Programs

The House Sept. 29 went on record in opposition to one part of President Reagan's proposed "New Federalism" plan — transferring school lunch and other federal child nutrition programs to the states.

By voice vote under suspension of the rules, the House approved a resolution (H Con Res 384) expressing congressional opposition to the proposed transfer. The suspension procedure, intended for non-controversial measures, required a two-thirds vote for passage.

The "sense-of-Congress" resolution was reported by the House Education and Labor Committee Sept. 24 (H Rept 97-870). Although not binding, its passage was an indication of the political difficulties facing Reagan's proposal to shift many social programs to the states.

The federalism plan, proposed in Reagan's State of the Union message in January, was never sent to Congress, although the administration in July released a tentative list of programs to be "turned back" to the states. *(State of the Union message, p. 3-E; list of programs, p. 536)*

Some 120 House members had signed on as sponsors of H Con Res 384, which said the federal government should retain primary responsibility for child nutrition programs and that the programs should not be converted into a block grant. In the Senate, Robert Dole, R-Kan., chairman of the Agriculture Subcommittee on Nutrition, had 32 cosponsors for a companion resolution (S Con Res 121), but it was never brought to the floor for a vote.

Although the bipartisan support for the measures seemed to promise a tough future for Reagan's federalism proposal, resolution sponsor Bill Goodling, R-Pa., said he thought the child nutrition programs were a special case, unlike the other turnback programs. "I don't think there is anything more unique than child nutrition," Goodling said. "A lot of other things won't meet this kind of opposition" in Congress, he suggested.

Lobby groups such as the American School Food Service Association (ASFSA) hoped the resolution would serve as a pre-emptive strike against inclusion of the child nutrition programs in the new federalism shift. "We want the resolution to lock people into position on the issue," said ASFSA counsel Marshall Matz.

Hearings

The administration's proposal to turn child nutrition programs over to the states was denounced at a Sept. 21 hearing on the issue by the Education and Labor Subcommittee on Elementary and Secondary Education. Witnesses said it would lead to the end of the national commitment to good nutrition for children.

No administration witnesses testified, but President Reagan and other officials had argued that operation of the programs by the states would make them more efficient and responsive to the people.

Supporters of the existing programs said experience since enactment of the 1981 budget reconciliation bill (PL 97-35), which cut federal child nutrition spending by $1.5 billion, showed that states would be unwilling or unable to pay for child nutrition programs on their own. *(1981 action, 1981 Almanac p. 497)*

"Not one state moved to pick up the slack," said Gene White, a California state official representing the ASFSA. "Three million children have been forced from the school lunch program, yet we are not aware of any state that has increased its financial commitment one penny," he said.

In addition, argued Dr. Julius B. Richmond of the Harvard Medical School, states probably would not be able to run child nutrition programs as well as the federal government. "Nutrition is a national, not a state issue," the former U.S. surgeon general insisted. He said the states varied widely in their technical capacities, financial resources and political will to operate nutrition programs. ∎

New GI Bill Proposals

The House Armed Services Committee joined the Veterans' Affairs Committee in calling for a new GI Bill program of education benefits to entice young people to join the military, but legislation to establish the program never made it to the House floor.

Armed Services reported the bill May 17 (HR 1400 — H Rept 97-80, Part II) — a full year after the Veterans' Affairs Committee acted on it. *(Background, 1981 action, 1981 Almanac p. 472)*

Pentagon officials had said they needed the program to attract more qualified young people into the armed

forces. In 1979, for the first time since the all-volunteer military began in 1973, all four branches of the service failed to reach their recruiting goals; recruiting also fell short in 1980. In addition, some military commanders complained that the quality of the personnel they were getting was poor; they hoped the prospect of new educational benefits would attract more middle-class youths of college aptitude to join the service.

Eligibility for the previous GI Bill expired in 1976.

Although prospects for enactment of a new GI Bill were considered good when the 97th Congress opened in 1981, interest waned for several reasons. As the recession continued and jobs became scarcer, more young people were joining the armed forces anyway; in 1981 and 1982 the services met their recruiting quotas, with "quality" also going up. In addition, the growing federal deficit put a damper on the creation of any costly new programs. Internal Pentagon bickering also created problems for the bill.

Although President Reagan had pledged during the 1980 campaign to back a new GI bill, the administration withdrew its endorsement as budget pressures mounted. The chairman of the Senate Veterans' Affairs Committee, Alan K. Simpson, R-Wyo., also said he could not support new educational benefits during lean economic times while recruiting was good.

Veterans' organizations such as the American Legion and the Veterans of Foreign Wars, were on record as favoring a new GI Bill, but they gave it a low priority and did not lobby for it. The organizations were concentrating on fighting proposed budget cuts in the VA health care system.

Veterans' Affairs Committee Bill

As reported by the Veterans' Affairs Committee in 1981, HR 1400 would have provided persons who enlisted in the military for at least three years with an education stipend of $300 a month for up to 36 months, or more if needed to attract recruits for certain hard-to-fill jobs. It also provided education benefits for persons signing up for the reserves or National Guard.

The bill allowed the military to grant leaves of absence to career personnel seeking to use their benefits. It also entitled service members, after 10 years of service, to transfer their education benefits to a spouse or child if they wished, rather than using them themselves.

The Congressional Budget Office (CBO) estimated the bill would cost $381 million a year in 1985, $1.2 billion in 1990 and $1.4 billion a year in 1994. The benefits would be paid by the Veterans Administration (VA).

The VA sent the committee a letter opposing the bill but did not actively lobby against the measure.

Administration Proposal

In February 1982, the Department of Defense (DOD) introduced its own GI Bill proposal. The plan was similar to HR 1400. It would cost the government about $1 billion a year. However, the armed services, not the VA, would have to pay for the program, and it would have to be funded on an accrual basis — meaning the services would have to begin putting money aside for benefits to be paid in the future.

Service officials, who already had to deal with budget cuts, said they did not want a GI Bill if they had to pay for it. They wanted the VA to fund the program.

In March, DOD told Congress that the administration wanted no new GI Bill benefits.

Armed Services Committee Bill

The Pentagon's decision not to seek a bill upset congressional backers of new GI benefits. The Armed Services Committee decided to move ahead with a modified version of HR 1400 anyway. It approved the amended bill by a vote of 40-1 May 11, and filed its report May 17 (H Rept 97-80, Part II).

The Armed Services version authorized a basic education entitlement for military people of $200 a month for 36 months, to be paid by the VA. For people with critical skills, DOD could add an extra stipend of up to $400 a month. Service members who served five years beyond the initial enlistment period would be entitled to an additional $100 a month in education benefits. DOD could add another $300 to this supplemental benefit. The maximum benefit available under the bill for a full-time student would be $1,000 a month for 36 months.

DOD could allow service members with more than 10 years' service to transfer their education benefits to their dependents, but this would not be an automatic entitlement, as it would under the Veterans' Affairs bill.

The Armed Services bill also included a "cash-out" provision, allowing re-enlisting service members to give up their education benefits in exchange for 25 percent of the value in cash.

The bill required that DOD fund its portion of the program on an accrual basis, while the VA would pay for benefits as they became due.

CBO estimated the Armed Services bill would cost about $187 million in 1987, $392 million in 1990 and $757 million in 1995. ∎

Asbestos Compensation

The Aug. 26 declaration of bankruptcy by the Manville Corporation, the nation's largest maker of asbestos products, spurred congressional interest in establishing a system for compensating victims of asbestos-related diseases. Hearings were held but no legislation was enacted in 1982.

Manville's surprise action was widely viewed as a tactic to force Congress to contribute federal funds to compensate ailing asbestos workers. A smaller asbestos firm, UNR Industries Inc., of Chicago, also had filed for bankruptcy earlier in the summer.

Officials of both companies said they were overwhelmed by the anticipated costs of settling pending and future lawsuits by victims of asbestos-related diseases. Manville officials put the costs of settlement at $2 billion for their company alone; 16,500 lawsuits already had been filed and thousands more were expected. Manville said its insurance companies had refused to pay the claims.

One insurance company official told Congress that liability generated by asbestos-related product liability suits was likely to reach $38.2 billion, and could go as high as $90 billion.

An estimated 13 million workers were exposed to asbestos in their jobs between 1940 and 1980. The mineral was widely used as a fireproofing agent and as a sound and moisture barrier in buildings and ships, until it was discovered that asbestos fibers lodged in the lungs could cause cancer and other lung diseases.

The industry insisted the government shared responsibility for workers' exposure to asbestos and so should share the costs of compensating disabled workers and the fam-

ilies of deceased workers.

Manville's move created a new sense of urgency but little visible sympathy for the company in Congress. The bankruptcy filing effectively stopped all Manville payments due either to conventional creditors or to plaintiffs in asbestos damage suits; it also halted any new lawsuits. Manville officials did not envision the dissolution of the company; they said filing for reorganization under the 1978 bankruptcy law (PL 95-598) was intended to ensure that the corporation remained financially sound. *(Bankruptcy law, 1978 Almanac p. 179; 1982 revisions, p. 389)*

Legislation

George Miller, D-Calif., chairman of the House Education and Labor Subcommittee on Labor Standards, and several other members of Congress had been trying for several years to establish a compensation system for asbestos disease victims. Miller mounted four subcommittee hearings in 1982 to set the stage for action on occupational health in the 98th Congress. The House Energy and Commerce Subcommittee on Investigations and Oversight also held a hearing in August.

Miller introduced legislation (HR 5735) to create industry-financed compensation funds for victims of diseases associated with both asbestos and uranium. The bill also authorized industry-financed occupational health research and monitoring of workers exposed to other hazardous substances. Miller's larger goal was to force manufacturers generally to clean up hazardous or unhealthful working environments, by saddling them with the full cost of occupational diseases — also a long-term legislative goal of organized labor.

Asbestos bills also were introduced by Sen. Gary Hart, D-Colo., whose state was the home base of the giant Manville Corporation, and Rep. Millicent Fenwick, R-N.J., whose district housed Manville's predecessor, Johns-Manville. Her constituents included many asbestos disease victims.

Hart's bill (S 1643) set minimum federal standards for asbestos compensation, with appeals to the federal government if state workers' compensation awards failed to meet those standards. Funding would come from the industry and from the government, if federal fault could be shown. The asbestos industry had formed a coalition to lobby for Hart's bill.

Fenwick's first asbestos bill in 1977 combined federal and industry financing for asbestos victims, but her 1982 bill (HR 5244) dropped federal payments and added an assessment on the tobacco industry. (Asbestos workers who smoked had a higher incidence of cancer than those who did not.)

Until Manville filed for bankruptcy, Miller, Fenwick and Hart had been stymied by congressional lack of interest in the compensation issue and by deep disagreements among the various groups interested in the legislation. Asbestos companies, their insurers, business groups, the Reagan administration, ailing former asbestos workers and their attorneys held widely differing views on whether the government should contribute to asbestos compensation — and whether Congress should address the issue at all.

Many in Congress were reluctant to set an expensive new precedent for compensating victims of environmental exposure to toxic substances. The high costs and administrative problems of existing federal compensation programs — for coal miners' "black lung" disease and for longshoremen's injuries — made even their supporters wince.

The asbestos industry said the government should contribute to a worker compensation fund because federal agencies had failed to adequately state the dangers faced by asbestos workers. World War II shipbuilding activities and federal sales of unlabeled asbestos also were cited to justify claims on the Treasury for asbestos compensation. About half of the claims against the industry stemmed from wartime exposures in shipyards.

A substantial legal industry had grown up to handle asbestos claims. These lawyers claimed that asbestos victims opposed any legislation relieving the industry of financial responsibility, preferring to sue for compensation.

Reagan administration officials said the government already had shouldered its share of responsibility for asbestos because disabled workers relied heavily on benefits of Medicare, Social Security disability and other federal programs. Millions of dollars also had been paid out under the Federal Employees Compensation Act to disabled asbestos victims who were directly employed by the government. ∎

Animal Welfare

Animal welfare groups conducted a vigorous campaign for legislation to reform the way laboratory animals were treated, but no bill was enacted in 1982.

The House Science and Technology Committee reported a bill Aug. 19 (HR 6928 — H Rept 97-777, Part I). But the Energy and Commerce Committee, which shared jurisdiction, did not act on the measure, and the Senate Labor and Human Resources Committee took no action on a companion bill (S 2948) introduced by Robert Dole, R-Kan.

The bills would have required labs receiving federal funds to set up animal care committees to monitor the experimental use of animals; set standards for the animals' care and treatment, and provided awards to researchers who developed alternatives to animal experimentation. The House bill also would have required accreditation of laboratories.

Many researchers feared the real goal of the legislation was halting the use of animals in scientific research, although sponsors said it was simply intended to encourage researchers to improve the care and treatment of animals and, where possible, to use alternative research methods.

Researchers generally opposed the legislation, which was known as the Humane Care and Development of Substitutes for Animals in Research Act. They said it would be too costly, would replace a voluntary system with a mandatory one and would have a chilling effect on experiments.

Background

Some 60 million to 100 million animals were used in scientific research programs each year, according to the Humane Society of the United States. The animals, including monkeys, pigs, dogs, cats, rats and mice, were used in everything from high school biology classes to medical school and university labs and pharmaceutical, cosmetics and pesticide company testing facilities.

The federal government supported a large portion of this research, primarily through grants to medical school, university and other laboratories. The National Institutes of Health (NIH) provided the largest chunk of money: $3.4 billion a year in fiscal 1982 for health research and development out of a total of $5 billion for all federal research

support, according to NIH figures. Private companies, including chemical and cosmetics firms, matched NIH spending, devoting about $3.4 billion a year to research and testing, including animal experimentation.

Researchers said they had reduced their use of animals over the years and developed alternatives such as the use of tissue or bacterial cultures, mathematical or computer models. Laboratory animal use in the United States decreased by about 40 percent between 1968 and 1978, according to Franklin M. Loew, dean of the Tufts University School of Veterinary Medicine.

Congress first regulated the care and treatment of laboratory animals when it passed the Animal Welfare Act in 1966 (PL 89-544). The act required private and federally funded laboratories using animals to register with the Agriculture Department (USDA) and to submit to periodic unannounced inspections. It also established standards that included minimum requirements for housing, feeding, watering, sanitation, shelter and veterinary care. Laboratories that violated the act were subject to criminal penalties. *(1966 Almanac p. 365)*

Other federal agencies also tried to ensure high-quality care for laboratory animals. For example, NIH required non-government laboratories it funded to be accredited by the American Association for Accreditation of Laboratory Animals or assure NIH in writing that high-quality care would be provided. The labs also had to set up animal care committees to oversee the animals' welfare.

But animal welfare groups complained that the federal monitoring system was inadequate. Their concerns fueled the drive for reform legislation, with September 1981 revelations of mistreatment of animals at an NIH-funded lab in Silver Spring, Md., giving the movement impetus.

Legislation

As reported by the House Science Committee, HR 6928 required federally funded labs using research animals to be accredited; labs would have 10 years to upgrade their facilities. The bill also required labs to set up animal care committees, including one veterinarian and one individual from outside the institution, to monitor the use of research animals and inspect facilities at least twice a year. No lab could receive a federal grant unless it justified pain to the animals in terms of its research goals and withheld anesthetics from the animals only for scientifically necessary reasons.

Under HR 6928, the animal care committees would have more clout than the existing panels. The twice-yearly inspections and the scrutiny of research projects were designed to give them backbone, although the Science Committee said it did not intend that their activities "supplant or interfere with the normal peer review process" of evaluating research proposals.

Researchers generally opposed the idea, for fear the panels would try to control their work.

However, the part of the bill to which the research community objected the most vigorously was the requirement that laboratories be accredited. The Congressional Budget Office estimated that modernizing animal care facilities to meet accreditation standards would cost institutions $500 million. The Senate bill called for a one-year study of the costs.

The plan would be "an economic hardship . . . that will require the reduction or elimination of existing medical and scientific research projects," Reps. F. James Sensenbrenner Jr., R-Wis., Edwin B. Forsythe, R-N.J., and

Harold L. Volkmer, D-Mo., wrote in dissenting views to the Science Committee report.

Jobs for Older Americans

Congress in 1982 expressed strong support for the community service employment program for older Americans, which the Reagan administration wanted to close down.

The Senate July 1 voted 89-6 for a resolution (S Res 340) opposing the termination of the program. *(Vote 208, p. 37-S)*

The Labor and Human Resources Committee had approved the resolution unanimously.

The vote on the resolution came just two days after the Senate, at the administration's insistence, agreed to drop a $210.6 million appropriation for the program from the "urgent" supplemental appropriations bill (HR 6685). The Senate Appropriations Committee had added the funding to the bill. *(Story, p. 205)*

However, Congress insisted on adding the funds to a later supplemental funding bill (HR 6863). The president vetoed the bill because of his opposition to funding for the jobs program and several education aid programs, but Congress overrode his veto. Heavy lobbying by senior citizen organizations for the jobs program was instrumental in the override vote. *(Story, p. 219)*

Congress in 1981 had reauthorized the jobs program for the elderly for three years. The program provided jobs in hospitals, libraries, day care centers and senior citizen programs for about 54,000 low-income elderly Americans. *(1981 Almanac p. 496)*

Conservation Corps

The House voted twice in 1982 to establish a new program to put unemployed young people to work on conservation and rehabilitation projects on federal and state lands, but the program — known as the American Conservation Corps (ACC) — was not enacted.

The ACC would have replaced two similar programs — the Youth Conservation Corps and the Young Adult Conservation Corps — which the Reagan administration planned to terminate.

Ignoring administration opposition, the House June 9 voted 291-102 to establish the new program. The bill (HR 4861) was passed under suspension of the rules, a procedure that barred amendments and required a two-thirds vote for passage. *(Vote 127, p. 38-H)*

The legislation had been reported by the Interior Committee May 4 and by Education and Labor May 17 (H Rept 97-500, Parts I & II).

Under the program, youths aged 16-25 would be hired for year-round or summer jobs in national parks, forests or other public lands. Disadvantaged youths and those from high-unemployment areas would be given special consideration. Corps members would be paid the minimum wage and could not displace regular federal employees.

The bill authorized $50 million in fiscal 1983 and $250 million a year in fiscal 1984-89, with funding to come from federal revenues generated by such activities as oil and gas leasing and timber sales. States would have to put up 15

percent matching funds.

Proponents said the program would help alleviate high youth unemployment while also helping to conserve public resources. Opponents said the nation could not afford it in a time of tight budget constraints.

John N. Erlenborn, R-Ill., called the program a "warmed-over" version of the two expiring programs, which he said were not cost-effective or targeted on the neediest youths. He urged the House to address youth unemployment problems when it considered the Job Training Partnership Act (HR 5320) instead. *(Story, p. 39)*

On Dec. 14, the House attached the provisions of HR 4861 to an unrelated Senate-passed bill (S 1501) known as the Educational Mining Act, which provided for the transfer of certain lands in Alaska to the University of Alaska. However, the Senate Dec. 19 deleted the House amendment, and the House concurred in the Senate action the following day. Rep. John F. Seiberling, D-Ohio, sponsor of the ACC bill, said the Senate had agreed to give the program serious consideration in the 98th Congress.

No action was taken in 1982 on a Senate bill to create a conservation corps (S 2061). ∎

Congress and Government

Congress in 1982 did not find time to pass all of the annual appropriations bills, but members were able to give a pay raise to representatives and to scrap outside income restrictions for senators.

Breaking nearly 200 years of tradition, the 97th Congress ended with representatives making more than senators for the first time. With the exception of one year — 1795-96 — when senators got $7 a day and representatives $6, members of Congress have been paid the same salary.

In 1981, members were roundly criticized for giving themselves a tax break that could have amounted to about $16,500 each. Stung by the criticism Congress in July 1982 repealed that tax break, although members were allowed to benefit from it for the 1981 tax year.

When the subject of a pay raise reared its head before Congress' election recess, the House quickly squelched it. As part of the first continuing appropriations resolution, the House included a cap to prevent members and senior government officials from getting the 4 percent raise that went to other government workers Oct. 1.

But members' reluctance to take a pay raise faded after the November elections. With critical help from lame-duck representatives who no longer had to worry about re-election, the House in December approved a 15 percent raise, increasing congressional pay from $60,662.50 a year to $69,800.

At the same time, the Senate voted to repeal its rule that would have limited the outside earnings of senators to about $9,100 a year. The rule had been passed in 1977 as a condition for members to get a $12,900 pay raise, but the effective date had been delayed until Jan. 1, 1983.

The Senate scrapped it entirely in December 1982, with the help of 14 senators who had voted for the rule in 1977.

With the change, senators could earn as much as they chose in business income, legal fees or in honoraria for speeches or appearances.

The House and Senate then struck a deal. Representatives got the pay increase and kept limits on their own outside income. Senators did not get the pay raise but were allowed unlimited outside earnings. Some members of the House actually felt the Senate got the better deal, noting that in 1981 some senators earned as much as $48,000 in honoraria.

The raise also affected the top ranks of the federal government, from Cabinet officers to senior bureaucrats, about 32,000 people in all.

Getting raises of up to 15 percent, senior bureaucrats went from a maximum of $59,500 a year to up to $68,400. Members of the Cabinet went from $69,630 annually to $80,100.

The raises also caused another break with tradition. In some cases, Senate aides made more than their bosses, who remained at $60,662.50.

Senate Turmoil

Senators spent days late in the winter of 1982 debating the expulsion of a colleague, who spared himself some disgrace by resigning before a vote could be taken to throw him out.

Sen. Harrison A. Williams Jr., D-N.J. (1959-82), was the only senator among the seven members of Congress caught in the FBI's Abscam sting operation. In Abscam, undercover agents, posing as wealthy Arabs, offered bribes to public officials.

A federal jury convicted Williams in May 1981 on nine counts including bribery, conspiracy and receipt of an unlawful gratuity. The following August, the Senate Ethics Committee called Williams' conduct "ethically repugnant" and recommended unanimously that he be expelled. But Senate floor action did not begin until March 1982.

In five grueling days of debate, Williams maintained, as he had throughout his trial, that he had committed no crime, arguing that the wrongdoing had been on the part of the government.

But with an unusually large number of senators listening on the floor, leaders of the Ethics Committee laid out the case against Williams.

Finally, just hours before the Senate was to vote on expulsion, a vote that Williams seemed certain to lose, he resigned.

Senators seemed collectively relieved. The Senate had not expelled one of its members since the Civil War and no senator had ever been expelled on grounds other than treason or disloyalty.

At the same time, the Senate set up a special committee to examine the Abscam undercover operation, particularly the nagging question of whether politicians had been targeted on the basis of their politics.

Although not giving Abscam a totally clean bill of health, the committee concluded in December that there was no political targeting of public officials. The panel recommended legislation and guidelines for future undercover operations by government agents.

Filibuster Season

But the debate over Williams was not nearly so rending for the Senate as the filibusters that punctuated 1982 from spring through the end of the year.

When adjournment finally came in December, senators left town tired and bitter, with many of them muttering about the need for changes in Senate rules.

One of the last votes taken in 1982 was on a cloture motion to shut off a filibuster on a bill to increase the gasoline tax to pay for highway repairs. With that filibuster a handful of conservative Republicans had blocked action for days and delayed adjournment.

Majority Leader Howard H. Baker Jr., R-Tenn., who had essentially lost control of the Senate during the gasoline tax debate, said at the end of the year that he would

consider rules changes to prevent a few senators from obstructing the will of the majority.

Conservative senators were not the only ones who used filibusters, a delaying tactic one senator called a "verbal sit-in." A group of liberals and moderates filibustered in September to block approval of amendments dealing with abortion and prayer in public schools.

By year's end, as filibusters became a regular parliamentary procedure, senatorial courtesy vanished. Senators shouted at one another, later regretting their remarks and making changes in the *Congressional Record*.

House Scandals

In late June, while Congress was out of town on vacation, members were rocked by published charges of homosexual relations between members and pages, the young boys and girls who ran errands at the Capitol.

At the same time, reports surfaced that police were investigating a cocaine ring operating in the Capitol, possibly involving members of Congress.

The House ethics committee appointed a special counsel to investigate the charges, Joseph A. Califano Jr., secretary of Health, Education and Welfare in the Carter administration.

His report, issued after five months of investigation, found no truth in the charges of illicit sexual activity. And the two pages who had made most of the claims admitted to either lying or exaggerating. However, in December, Califano said he was still looking into separate charges of drug use and distribution.

The House's image also was damaged in August when Rep. Fred Richmond, D-N.Y. (1975-82), resigned his seat as part of a plea-bargain with federal prosecutors and agreed not to seek re-election. (The portion of the plea bargain involving his re-election was later voided by a federal judge.)

Richmond pleaded guilty to income tax evasion, possession of marijuana and making an illegal payment to a federal employee. He was sentenced in November to spend one year and one day in federal prison.

—By Andy Plattner

Sen. Williams Resigns, Averts Expulsion

Sen. Harrison A. Williams Jr., D-N.J., resigned his seat March 11, averting expulsion by his peers and enabling Congress to close out its investigation of members' wrongdoing turned up by the FBI during its Abscam political corruption probe. *(Background, 1981 Almanac p. 383)*

Williams, 62, resigned just hours before the Senate was expected to vote on expelling him — a vote that seemed certain to go against the 23-year Senate veteran. He was the last remaining member of Congress, and the only senator, to have been convicted on charges growing out of Abscam and investigated by congressional ethics panels.

By leaving the Senate voluntarily, Williams avoided becoming the first senator to be expelled since the Civil War and the first in history to be ejected on grounds other than treason or disloyalty. *(Previous House and Senate expulsion and censure proceedings, CQ Guide to Congress 3rd Edition, p. 828)*

Williams' resignation brought to seven the total number of members expelled or forced from Congress after being implicated in the FBI Abscam operation.

Only one of the seven — Rep. Michael "Ozzie" Myers, D-Pa. (1976-80) — actually was expelled, though three others — Sen. Williams and Reps. John W. Jenrette Jr., D-S.C. (1975-80), and Raymond F. Lederer, D-Pa. (1977-81) — resigned from Congress to stop expulsion proceedings against them.

Another three members convicted in federal district court — Reps. Richard Kelly, R-Fla. (1975-81), John M. Murphy, D-N.Y. (1963-81), and Frank Thompson Jr., D-N.J. (1955-81) — were defeated for re-election before the House could act against them.

All seven were handed fines and prison sentences as a result of their Abscam convictions, though all remained free pending appeals.

The convictions of Lederer, Murphy, Thompson and Myers were upheld Sept. 3 by a federal appeals court in New York. The court also upheld the convictions of several other Abscam defendants: Angelo J. Errichetti, former mayor of Camden, N.J.; Louis C. Johanson, a former member of the Philadelphia City Council; and Howard C. Criden, a Philadelphia lawyer.

However, Kelly was ordered acquitted May 13 by U.S. District Judge William B. Bryant of the District of Columbia. Bryant's action came in response to a defense motion for an acquittal judgment based on government violation of Kelly's due process rights. The government appealed that decision.

Most Troubling Case

Of charges against the seven legislators, the case against Williams was perhaps the most troubling to members of Congress.

While the other Abscam defendants appeared in government-produced video and audio tapes to be eager participants in the government's bribery scheme, Williams actually turned down a cash bribe when undercover agents offered him one.

Williams was convicted — not of accepting an offer of cash in exchange for promises of legislative favors — but for his participation in an extremely complicated business scheme involving a hidden interest in a mining venture owned by several of Williams' friends.

During Williams' criminal trial in Brooklyn, N.Y., prosecutors alleged that he had accepted a hidden 18 percent interest in a titanium mining company in return for a promise to use his influence to obtain government contracts to buy the mine output.

A key part of the deal was that government undercover agents, masquerading as wealthy Arabs and their associates, had promised to loan the mining company $100 million. The prosecutors said Williams knew when he accepted the stock that the loan would benefit him directly. The prosecutors also argued — and produced recordings to prove — that Williams later had promised to use his influence to help one of the supposed Arabs gain permanent U.S. residency.

Throughout his trial, the Ethics Committee's hearings and Senate floor debate on expulsion, Williams argued that he had committed no crime at all. Instead, he maintained that the government agents had "manufactured" the crimes of which he was accused after their other attempts to incriminate him had failed.

It was this possibility that most disturbed Williams' colleagues and in the wake of Williams' resignation, the Senate created an eight-member select committee to investigate the possibility of Justice Department and FBI misconduct in Abscam. Charles McC. Mathias Jr., R-Md., was named to chair the panel, which was created March 25. *(Box, next page)*

But ultimately most senators said in floor debate that they were convinced both that Williams' conduct was a separate issue from the government's and that he actually had committed offenses serious enough to merit expulsion.

Williams' resignation took effect at the close of Senate business on March 11. Although he resigned before finishing out his term, he was entitled to full pension rights and retained the right of all former senators to enter the Senate chamber.

Steps to Resignation

The March 3 opening of the Senate debate on Williams' expulsion was one of the final steps in a long series of events and delays that had begun about 25 months before, when the existence of the Abscam investigation became public in February 1980.

On May 1, 1981, Williams was convicted by a federal court jury on nine counts, including bribery, conspiracy, receipt of an unlawful gratuity, accepting outside compensation for the performance of official duties and interstate travel in aid of a racketeering enterprise.

On Aug. 24 the Senate Select Ethics Committee, relying heavily on the court conviction and the same evidence that had been presented during the trial, concluded that Williams' conduct had been "ethically repugnant" and recommended unanimously that he be expelled.

Senate debate on the committee's expulsion resolution (S Res 204) eventually was set for Feb. 2. But on Jan. 25 Williams fell on the ice outside his New Jersey home, which aggravated a hernia condition and required emergency surgery. Debate was put off until Feb. 23.

On Feb. 16, Williams was sentenced by U.S. District Judge George C. Pratt in Brooklyn to three years in prison and a $50,000 fine for his May 1 convictions. (The sentencing initially had been set for Jan. 26, but was delayed

Panel Probed Government's Abscam Role

During the expulsion proceeding against Sen. Harrison A. Williams Jr., D-N.J., some of his supporters asked the Senate to judge not Williams but the Department of Justice and the FBI.

Most senators participating in the debate said the conduct of Williams and that of the department were separate issues. But there appeared to be wide agreement in the chamber that the government had misbehaved in pursuing congressional targets of the undercover Abscam operation.

A select committee to investigate those charges was set up March 25 and issued its final report Dec. 16.

During its nine-month investigation, the panel found that the Abscam operation had uncovered wrongdoing but that law enforcement agencies did not exert enough management control over the undercover probe.

Early in the deliberations, chief counsel James F. Neal, a Nashville, Tenn., attorney and former associate Watergate special prosecutor, suggested that the committee's investigation should attempt to establish:

● What the Justice Department and FBI policies were concerning the conduct of undercover operations.

● How those policies squared with law and democratic principles.

● Whether those policies actually were followed.

● What should be done about any problems turned up by the panel's investigation.

Responding to many of these points, the panel recommended enactment of legislation that would guide agents about appropriate undercover activity and that would indemnify those harmed during an undercover operation. It also appealed to undercover investigators to balance civil liberty and law enforcement concerns.

Creation, Organization

The study of alleged government misconduct in Abscam was urged by Sens. Daniel K. Inouye, D-Hawaii, and Alan Cranston, D-Calif., during the expulsion proceeding that culminated in Williams' resignation March 11. The New Jersey Democrat, convicted of bribery as a result of Abscam, resigned before the Senate could expel him.

Following the Williams proceeding, the Senate voted March 25 by voice vote to approve a resolution that set up an eight-member panel to investigate the Abscam operation.

The panel was given until Dec. 15 to complete its work and to issue a final report. The committee's authorization expired one month later.

The panel elected Sen. Charles McC. Mathias Jr., R-Md., its chairman and Walter D. Huddleston, D-Ky., its vice chairman.

At a brief organizational session March 31, lawmakers also decided to have a bipartisan staff rather than the more common arrangement of separate staffs for Republicans and Democrats.

The four GOP members named to the select committee by the Senate Republican leadership on March 29 were: Mathias, James A. McClure, Idaho; Warren B. Rudman, N.H.; and Alan K. Simpson, Wyo. In addition to Huddleston, Democrats named March 25 were Dennis DeConcini, Ariz.; Inouye; and Patrick J. Leahy, Vt.

Preliminary Report

In a preliminary report released Aug. 18, the committee said it found no information that would have "materially affected" the bribery trials of former members of Congress and other politicians who were snared in the probe.

But the report had plenty of criticism for the government's undercover investigation in the late 1970s. It said law enforcement officers could have conducted the investigation with greater attention to effective supervision, management and control of the operation.

Of particular concern to senators during the Williams expulsion debate was the question of whether federal investigators had targeted individual members of a particular party or faction. The report said it "found no indication of targeting of specific individuals in the Abscam operation before their names were mentioned by middlemen."

However, the report said that middlemen's claims that certain politicians could be bribed were not sufficiently corroborated by the FBI before many of the politicians were offered bribes by agents posing as Arab sheiks.

Middlemen named 58 public officials as persons who could be bribed. Twenty bribe meetings with FBI agents actually occurred and 12 officials were subsequently convicted, the report said.

Final Report

In its final report, the committee called for legislation and federal guidelines to better control undercover law enforcement operations. The panel gave Abscam a "mixed review," with the good outweighing the bad.

But the panel also warned of the improper use of undercover techniques that "create risks to citizens' property, privacy, and civil liberties, and may compromise law enforcement itself."

Moreover, the report continued, "the undercover technique may on occasion create crime where none would otherwise have existed."

The select committee found that the "central task" of those involved with undercover techniques was to create a system that gave the public a balanced program of effective law enforcement and the preservation of civil liberties.

Specifically, members recommended a new federal law concerning entrapment. They also called for a new standard of "reasonable suspicion" before undercover agents offered someone the opportunity to commit a crime. And they recommended that the government indemnify individuals harmed during an undercover probe.

In addition, it called on Congress to pass legislation requiring the attorney general to create guidelines governing all undercover operations and to require the FBI, the Drug Enforcement Administration and the Immigration and Naturalization Service to conduct their undercover activities according to the attorney general's guidelines.

because of Williams' fall. However, the senator's co-defendant, Alexander Feinberg, was sentenced at that time, to three years in prison and a $40,000 fine.)

On Feb. 18, Majority Leader Howard H. Baker Jr., R-Tenn., further delayed Senate debate on expulsion until March 3. The postponement came at the request of Williams, who said he had not fully recovered from his surgery.

Five Days of Debate

Debate on the expulsion resolution eventually lasted five days, and ended with Williams' resignation.

On March 4, Williams pleaded with his colleagues to reject the Ethics Committee's "preposterous" expulsion recommendation.

"I have not committed a crime, nor have I acted improperly," Williams said. "I stand before you today, strong in my resolve, innocent of any wrongdoing and confident that you shall find me so."

He argued that it was government undercover investigators — not himself — who had behaved wrongly. His ensnarement in "the Abscam net," he said, resulted from an attempt by the government "to manufacture crime out of nothing."

"This appearance [of wrongdoing] has been created by the government," Williams said. Abscam was simply "an attempt to get me to appear to be doing something criminal," he maintained.

Joining Williams in his defense were Sen. Daniel K. Inouye, D-Hawaii, and Minority Whip Alan Cranston, D-Calif.

Inouye had volunteered in late November 1981 to act as Williams' counsel during the expulsion proceeding. He did so, he said at the time, in order to assure Williams "his day in court."

Ethics Panel Argument

The case against Williams for the Ethics Committee was presented March 3 by Vice Chairman Howell Heflin, D-Ala. He argued that the evidence upheld the case against Williams, regardless of the government's conduct.

"At any point in this drawn out, sordid affair," Heflin said, "Sen. Williams could have said, 'Wait a minute. What you're proposing is wrong. This is not what I had in mind. I can't be involved in this.'

"But he didn't. He stayed; he discussed; he agreed; he promised; he pledged — to abuse his office, his public trust, for which now he must be expelled."

Heflin argued for Williams' expulsion during a detailed dissection of the evidence lasting nearly three hours.

"If a member of this body really knows right from wrong," Heflin said, "if he or she truly believes that a public office is a public trust, if he or she genuinely cares about the integrity of this institution, then that member would not hesitate for a moment to get up and walk out — walk away from sleazy characters swearing like sailors; walk away from talk about sheiks and deals and hiding interests and protection and concealment; walk away from talk about government contracts and influence and 'who you know' and 'you're the deal.' Walk away, in other words, from obvious impropriety."

Williams' Defense

Williams' March 4 presentation of his defense took about three hours. Most of the time he appeared at ease, although as the day wore on he sometimes seemed to ramble.

He spoke while standing at his Senate desk, reading from a lengthy text resting on a lectern. He was flanked on either side by his lawyers. Williams earlier had asked that his lawyers be able to speak on the Senate floor, but this request was turned down by Senate leaders.

During the months leading up to the debate, Williams also had asked Senate leaders for an opportunity to subpoena witnesses — including FBI and Justice Department officials as well as a linguist, a psychologist and a trial juror in his federal court case who reportedly changed his mind about Williams' guilt — and cross-examine them on the Senate floor.

But Williams dropped the idea after colleagues expressed little support for such an undertaking. Instead, during the debate he asked that several government memorandums as well as a lengthy linguistic analysis of the surreptitiously recorded Abscam video and audio tapes be read into the record by the Senate clerk.

Williams had filed suit Nov. 23, 1981, in an effort to block Senate consideration of the expulsion resolution unless members agreed to let him examine witnesses and be represented by his attorney. The suit was dismissed Feb. 3 after U.S. District Judge Louis F. Oberdorfer of the District of Columbia ruled that Williams should have waited to file the suit until after the Senate had turned down his requests.

Before beginning his presentation, Williams asked the Senate to permit him to speak under oath — in order, he said, to waive "any constitutional protection I might have as a senator" against perjury charges. The Constitution protects members of Congress from prosecution for anything they say on the House or Senate floor.

However, the New Jersey Democrat dropped the idea when senators suggested that an oath on this occasion might suggest that senators would be less truthful in the future if they did not first take an oath.

In addition, Majority Leader Baker told Williams that no oath could override the Constitution.

Williams acknowledged to his colleagues that he was putting them in an uncomfortable position by requiring them to judge a fellow senator. But he said he would not apologize.

"I could have made it easier for all of you, my colleagues, by resigning, as some counseled," he said. "But in conscience, I had no choice."

Williams said the Ethics Committee's case against him consisted solely of "tainted" government evidence from the FBI investigation. In attempting to incriminate him, he said, the government itself had been guilty of perjury, conspiracy, obstruction of justice, forgery, fraud and impersonation of a foreign dignitary.

'Good Spirit and Good Heart'

However, by March 11, as the proceeding neared its end and as expulsion began to look more likely, Williams sounded bitter about his colleagues' apparent refusal to let him remain in the Senate. But he said he was leaving "in good spirit and good heart and strong resolve to continue the things that I believe in and that I've enjoyed."

All 99 other senators as well as Vice President George Bush were in the chamber when Williams announced his intention to resign.

During an often rambling, 25-minute farewell speech laced with biblical references and quotations, he continued to argue that the Senate had erred in moving "prematurely" toward expelling him before all the evidence was in

Rep. Richmond Resigns

Rep. Fred Richmond, D-N.Y., resigned from the House Aug. 25 and, as part of an unusual plea-bargain with federal prosecutors, agreed not to run again.

In U.S. district court in Brooklyn, Richmond, 58, pleaded guilty to three federal charges: income tax evasion, possession of marijuana and making an illegal payment to a federal employee.

In return for his guilty plea and resignation, the government agreed not to prosecute him for other actions it had been investigating, including cocaine possession and his arranging for a prison escapee, using an alias, to be put on the House payroll.

However, the part of the plea bargain involving Richmond's resignation and re-election was voided by U.S. District Judge Jack B. Weinstein Nov. 10 on grounds that it was an "unconstitutional interference by the executive with the legislative branch of government" and that it "conflicted with the fundamental right of the people to elect their representatives."

Also on Nov. 10, Richmond was sentenced to a year and one day in federal prison and fined $20,000. He reported to the federal prison camp at Allenwood, Pa., on Dec. 6.

In a written statement Aug. 25, Richmond said, "These acts to which I have pled guilty were irresponsible, unnecessary, foolish and wrong."

The House ethics committee, which had been investigating the allegations against Richmond, dropped its probe when he resigned.

Richmond's seat remained vacant until the beginning of the 98th Congress in January 1983.

The only felony charge to which he pleaded guilty, tax evasion, involved Richmond's 1980 income, which he admitted in court was understated on his return. He did not report funds paid by his company, Walco National Corp., for his New York apartment. Failure to report the payment reduced Richmond's tax liability by approximately $50,000.

He acknowledged possessing marijuana, which he said was obtained from his congressional staff.

The final charge was illegally supplementing the salary of a Navy civilian employee, who was not named by prosecutors. Richmond admitted arranging to have $7,420 in college tuition paid for the daughter of the Navy employee, who had helped obtain government contracts for a ship repair facility in Brooklyn.

A liberal, urban Democrat, Richmond chaired the Agriculture Subcommittee on Domestic Marketing, Consumer Relations and Nutrition and was perhaps the most outspoken House advocate of food stamps.

Richmond, one of the wealthiest representatives, came to Congress in 1975. A patron of the arts, he had worked to increase federal subsidies to museums and creative artists and in 1981 founded a Congressional Arts Caucus aimed at preserving funding for the National Endowment for the Arts.

Richmond had had an earlier brush with the law in 1978 when he was arrested on a morals charge. The charges were dropped after he completed a psychiatric treatment program. *(1978 Almanac p. 14)*

on possible government misconduct in Abscam.

He acknowledged that he previously had insisted he would never resign. But he said his colleagues had convinced him that if he did not resign, he would surely be expelled.

Williams added that he found resignation to be a more palatable alternative after Minority Whip Cranston and Inouye assured him that the Senate would continue to pursue the question of government misconduct in Abscam.

By moving to expel him, he said, each senator "stands accused" of failing to protect the chamber's integrity from the Justice Department's "invasion of our collective rights and privileges."

"I did not wish to see the Senate bring dishonor to itself by expelling me," Williams said.

"To bring the battle here — it was a vow I made to fight the wretchedness of it all at every opportunity," Williams said. "It was an ordeal for me, but I took it on without embarrassment."

"I have fought a good fight," he concluded, quoting St. Paul. "I have finished my course. I have kept the faith. . . .

"I have been been strengthened. I thank you, all of you."

Salutes, Congratulations

After Williams concluded his remarks, several senators rose to salute his decision and to congratulate the Senate on the dignity of the expulsion proceeding.

"The Senate has passed through yet another of the many gates of history, and it has done so with honor and with courage," said Ethics Chairman Malcolm Wallop, R-Wyo.

"Sen. Williams believes he has been wronged, been victimized by the government, and has fought long and hard for what he believes in," added Vice Chairman Heflin. "For that fight based on conviction, I believe he deserves our respect, irrespective of what we may think about his conduct on tape in this sordid matter called Abscam."

"During the past several days, the Senate has been on trial in a tragedy that has no heroes," said Minority Leader Robert C. Byrd, D-W.Va. "Sorrowful though it is, [Williams] has chosen to take a course that only he could choose, but a course that I respect and believe to be right."

Inouye then delivered Williams' letter of resignation to Bush, who turned it over to the Senate clerk to be read. The letter instructed the Senate to inform New Jersey Gov. Thomas H. Kean, R, that a vacancy existed.

(On April 12, Kean named Republican businessman Nicholas F. Brady, 52, to fill the remaining 10 months of Williams' term. The move increased the GOP Senate majority by one, to 54-46. Brady was named as a caretaker and did not seek re-election.)

The Senate then recessed briefly to enable Williams' colleagues to wish him well. Williams remained in the Senate chamber for nearly 15 minutes, shaking the hands of aides and pages as well as senators.

Outside the chamber, Williams met his wife, Jeanette, who had watched the entire proceeding from the gallery, and the two left the Capitol together.

Later, Williams was cheered as he entered a nearby Senate office building for a news conference.

Censure Effort Fizzles

Until March 11, Williams had stiffly resisted suggestions from several of his colleagues that he resign and save them the anguish of going through an expulsion vote.

The week before, Williams had been buoyed by an effort by Cranston to soften the expulsion resolution into a censure measure and allow Williams to remain.

Cranston had argued that the numerous allegations of government misconduct in Abscam indicated the lesser punishment was merited. In any case, Cranston had said, censure would not preclude senators from later expelling Williams if the misconduct allegations were found to be groundless.

But a series of painstaking analyses of the evidence in the case by Ethics leaders Wallop and Heflin appeared to hold sway in the Senate and puncture Williams' hopes.

Beginning on March 9, senator after senator — among them some of Williams' closest associates — rose to announce that they had decided to vote for expulsion rather than censure.

That same day, Majority Leader Baker indicated that a poll of Senate Republicans had found near unanimous support for Williams' expulsion.

That night, after the Senate recessed for the evening, Williams told reporters that Republican senators had voted as a party during a GOP caucus to support his expulsion.

However, the next morning, Baker took the Senate floor to deny Williams' account. "At every meeting of the [Republican] Conference," Baker said, "there has been an admonition to 'keep your minds open and to hear the arguments on this matter and not to make statements in public.'"

'Tawdry, Greedy Enterprise'

Perhaps the most dramatic speech of the entire proceeding occurred late March 9, when Sen. Thomas F. Eagleton, D-Mo., the self-described "showcase liberal" on the Ethics panel and a longtime associate of Williams, took the floor to say he opposed Cranston's censure proposal and would vote for expulsion.

"I ask 98 of my colleagues," Eagleton said. "Would any of you have engaged in this tawdry, greedy enterprise? If your silent answer of inner conscience is in the affirmative, then do your soul a favor by serving out your term and passively fading into deserved oblivion.

"Sen. Williams has not had the good grace and good judgment to withdraw from this body. We should not perpetrate our own disgrace by asking him to stay."

Another dramatic moment occurred the next day, when Sen. Patrick J. Leahy, D-Vt., a former district attorney, indicated that he would support the expulsion recommendation.

As Leahy began to sit down, Williams leaped to his feet and asked him to answer a few questions.

Williams then asked Leahy whether, with his background as a prosecutor, he would have behaved as Abscam prosecutor Thomas H. Puccio did in his pursuit of Williams. When the senator had been offered a bribe and had refused it, Williams said, Puccio had cut off Williams' explanation of why he had turned it down by making a telephone call into the FBI undercover meeting room where the session with Williams was taking place.

Puccio "was hiding in another room, watching me," Williams said. "It was the prosecutor of my case who stopped my opportunity to explain exactly why . . . I was going to live under the law."

Leahy responded that he had found Puccio's conduct in Abscam to have been "reprehensible, outrageous, disturbing." But, he added, "that is not the issue before us today."

Williams was further wounded when Bill Bradley, a fellow Democrat and the junior senator from New Jersey, said he would vote for expulsion because Williams' misconduct had gone to "the core of democratic government — the faith people extend to political institutions."

Following Williams' resignation, Bradley told a reporter the decision had "drained" him. "This is the toughest decision I've had to make," he said.

'Filled with Doubt'

Speaking in Williams' defense in the days prior to his resignation were Sens. S. I. "Sam" Hayakawa, R-Calif., and John Melcher, D-Mont., in addition to Cranston and Inouye.

Cranston spoke almost daily to press his case for censure as well as for a Senate probe of the FBI's alleged wrongdoing.

Inouye delivered two lengthy speeches on Williams' behalf, the first of which occurred March 3.

The government's conduct in Abscam, Inouye said, "adds up to an encroachment on the legislative branch that we cannot tolerate if we are to be a separate but equal branch of government."

"None of us is safe. . . . This could have happened to any one of us," Inouye said. "It is only by a very tortured reading [of the evidence] that there is any wrongdoing at all," Inouye said, maintaining that Williams' worst crime might have been that he had behaved like "a fool."

"I do not feel that a senator should be expelled because he's a fool or did foolish things," Inouye said. "Maybe his most serious crime is that he embarrassed us."

In the second speech, delivered March 10, he reiterated his belief that Williams should not be expelled because the case against him was "filled with doubt and multiple plausible interpretation of the evidence."

Inouye added: "Well, my dear colleagues, let us not punish Pete because he caused us pain and embarrassment, because editorials urge us to do so, or because it is the politically expedient thing to do. Or because he has not had the good grace to resign."   ∎

Prompt Pay Act

Legislation to encourage the federal government to pay its bills on time was signed into law by President Reagan May 21.

The Delinquent Payments Act of 1981 (S 1131 — PL 97-177) had been pushed by the Slow Pay Coalition, a group of 41 trade associations.

The bill gave agencies 30 days to make payments, with a 15-day grace period before interest penalties began to accrue. Once the grace period expired, interest would accumulate from the 31st day at a rate to be set by the Treasury secretary.

The bill had been reported by the Senate Governmental Affairs Committee Dec. 14, 1981, (S Rept 97-302) and was passed by voice vote by the Senate the next day. The House Governmental Operations Committee reported its version March 18 (HR 4709 — H Rept 97-461). On March 23 the House voted 396-0 to suspend the rules and pass the bill. The House then amended its language to the Senate bill. *(Vote 35, p. 10-H)*

The Senate agreed to the House amendment May 11, clearing the measure for the president.   ∎

Reconciliation Cut Federal Retirees' COLAs

Cost-of-living hikes for federal retirees under age 62 were reduced for three fiscal years and all federal pension increases were delayed one month under the budget reconciliation conference agreement adopted by Congress Aug. 18.

The compromise (HR 6955 — H Rept 97-759) rejected a proposed across-the-board 4 percent cap on retirees' annual cost-of-living adjustments (COLA) and instead cut COLAs for younger retirees in half. The measure also ended the practice of awarding COLAs each March; they would be granted in April 1983, May 1984 and June 1985. *(Reconciliation, p. 199)*

Civil service, military, intelligence and foreign service retirees also were affected by the changes, which were expected to reduce spending by about $3.3 billion through fiscal 1985.

The compromise also eliminated "double-dipping" by military retirees who collected both military and civil service benefits, and made technical changes in computing pay for federal workers and retirees, for a total three-year savings of about $4.1 billion.

The issue of limiting federal pension COLAs was one of the most difficult for the House-Senate reconciliation conferees to resolve in the three days of meetings Aug. 13-16.

The first budget resolution (S Con Res 92) called for reducing anticipated pension expenses by more than $5 billion by placing a 4 percent ceiling on federal pension COLA increases. The House rejected the COLA limit Aug. 3 and approved cuts of only $113 million. The Senate accepted the cap Aug. 5.

Conference Agreement

About 1.9 million civil service retirees and 2.2 million military retirees were affected by the pension changes.

By reducing benefits for pensioners below age 62, the compromise attempted to focus cuts on individuals who left military or civil service work at an early age but who still might hold other jobs.

All survivors, disabled retirees and retirees above age 62 would get a full COLA in Spring 1983, equal to the increase in the Consumer Price Index (CPI). The accord projected a 6.6 percent COLA in fiscal 1983, 7.2 percent in 1984 and 6.6 percent in 1985.

Retirees under 62 would receive only 50 percent of the COLA. According to estimates, that would amount to a 3.3 percent inflation adjustment in 1983.

If the CPI were higher than assumed, pensioners under 62 would receive the 50 percent COLA, plus the difference between the projected and the actual CPI.

Several senators protested that the compromise shifted the burden to military annuitants because early military retirees greatly outnumbered civil service pensioners under 62. Senate aides said there were about 980,000 military retirees under 62, compared to 150,000 civil service retirees below that age.

Rep. William D. Ford, D-Mich., chairman of the Post Office and Civil Service Committee, noted, however, that military retirees would have lost $2.1 billion under the proposed 4 percent COLA cap. Under the half-COLA compromise, their benefits would be slashed by $2.2 billion, he said.

Other Provisions

To achieve a total of $4.089 billion in savings, the federal pension provisions of HR 6955 also:

● Delayed by one month the date COLAs took effect. Instead of awarding COLAs March 1 annually, they would be issued in April 1983, May 1984 and June 1985. The 13-month payment, combined with the half-COLA for retirees under 62, would save approximately $3.3 billion.

● Eliminated "double-dipping" by military retirees who obtained federal jobs, by reducing an individual's civilian pay by the amount of his military retiree COLA. This would save about $143 million during the three-year period.

● Changed the method of computing general schedule pay for current federal workers, by calculating pay on the basis of 2,087 hours annually rather than 2,080 hours. Conferees said this would cost most federal employees about $6 a year. It would save the budget about $266 million.

● Altered the method for reclassifying employees as non-disabled after they have received disability benefits. This would save approximately $11 million a year.

● Required that the interest rate on certain retirement fund deposits equal the average yield on obligations in which the retirement fund was invested, starting in 1985. Also determined that an employee must have left his job for at least 31 days before a refund of retirement contributions may be made, instead of the current three days. The changes would increase fiscal 1985 revenues by $33 million.

● Mandated that pension benefits be rounded down to the next lowest dollar, instead of to the nearest whole dollar. This would save $33 million in the three years.

● Delayed the date pensioners would receive their first payment from the day after they ended work to the first day of the month following retirement. This would not apply to individuals retiring involuntarily or on disability. It would save $80 million.

● Adjusted the way military service was counted toward civil service retirement benefits, to resolve a problem of dual coverage by the military and civil service systems.

One change stated that employees hired after the bill's enactment would not receive military service credit toward a civil service pension unless the employees deposited to the Civil Service Retirement Fund an amount equal to the calculated contributions for their military service. The provisions would save $37 million during the three years and would increase revenues by $94 million in fiscal 1984 and $22 million in fiscal 1985.

● Required that a significant reduction in force or a reduction in pay must occur before a worker may retire early, before age 55. The bill provided that a reasonable offer of a position would preclude an individual from eligibility for early retirement.

Under existing law, a major reorganization of an agency could authorize early retirement for any individual in that agency whether or not jobs were abolished or pay was reduced. This provision would save $65 million during the three-year period.

The conferees also accepted a House provision guaranteeing at least a 4 percent pay raise to current federal employees in October 1983 in the event President Reagan submitted an alternative pay plan that proposed limiting

pay raises to less than 4 percent.

● Prohibited anyone from receiving more in an annuity than the current salary of the position from which they retired.

Committee Action

House. The Post Office and Civil Service Committee July 21 ignored its budget instructions and refused to place the 4 percent cap on COLAs.

The Democratic-dominated panel was the first committee to defiantly reject the cuts ordered in the first budget resolution. Instead of making $376 million in fiscal 1983 reconciliation cuts as ordered, the House panel agreed to reduce civil service pension benefits by only $32 million. The committee also had been directed to make cuts of $1.061 billion in fiscal 1984 and $1.808 billion in 1985, for a cumulative savings of $3.2 billion. Because the COLA limit by law also would apply to military and other federal retirees, the total savings would be more than $5 billion. Without a limit on COLAs, federal pension payments would be tied to increases in the Consumer Price Index.

However, the panel voted 18-8 to cut $32 million in retirement benefits in fiscal 1983, and $81 million in 1984 and 1985, for a total of $113 million for the three years.

Most of the savings ordered by the budget resolution were to have come from the 4 percent freeze on retiree COLAs, but Democrats charged that the limit would be unfair.

"During the last three years, as a result of the budget process [federal retirees] have been repeatedly, and in my view, callously squeezed," Ford said.

William E. Dannemeyer, R-Calif., offered an amendment to impose the cap, but it was rejected by voice vote.

Senate. The Governmental Affairs Committee, facing similar instructions July 20, cut $302 million from retirement benefits in 1983. The panel by a vote of 10-5 approved the 4 percent ceiling on COLAs and made other changes to meet its total savings of $3.2 billion.

The committee defeated 5-9 an amendment by Carl Levin, D-Mich., to limit annual COLAs to the Consumer Price Index minus 2 percentage points for the next three years. A committee aide said the amendment would have taken $800 million from the COLA savings the panel needed to make.

An amendment by Mack Mattingly, R-Ga., accepted by voice vote and included in the conference agreement, froze COLAs for former top-level workers whose pension benefits were higher than the salaries current employees now earn in the same jobs. This could limit pension increases for former members of Congress.

The panel also adopted other administrative changes in the civil service retirement system to save $32 million in fiscal 1983, $156 million in 1984 and $147 million in 1985.

Floor Action

House. The House set the stage for a partisan clash over budget reconciliation when it voted July 28 to allow the COLA issue to be considered individually, rather than as part of an omnibus money-saving bill.

Instead of following the 1981 format in which all reconciliation items were considered in a single package, the House voted 240-170 to consider federal pension spending cuts separately from other fiscal 1983 budget reductions. *(1981 Almanac p. 256)*

The decision furthered the Democratic strategy of forcing Republicans into a series of potentially embarrassing election-year votes on budget cuts. Republicans, who had hoped to accomplish the cuts in an omnibus bill, charged the Democrats with subverting the budget process.

The vote occurred on a rule (H Res 536) for floor consideration of HR 6862, which dealt with the recommendations of the Post Office and Civil Service Committee for federal retirees. *(Vote 207, p. 62-H)*

The rule permitted an amendment to be offered imposing a 4 percent cap on COLA increases. Republicans were expected to offer the amendment.

The decision to hold a separate vote on the COLAs angered Republican leaders. "We are not considering reconciliation in the context of fiscal responsibility," charged Minority Leader Robert H. Michel, R-Ill. "We are being forced to consider individual bills tailored to embarrass and frustrate those in this House who supported the budget resolution in June."

But Leon E. Panetta, D-Calif., chairman of the Budget Committee Reconciliation Task Force, said, "Members cannot come here and support a budget resolution that calls for certain cuts and then hide from the ability to vote up or down on those cuts."

Panetta pointed out that just the day before, the House handled veterans' reconciliation as a separate item (HR 6782) without dissent. The veterans' cuts, however, matched the reconciliation instructions. *(Story, p. 488)*

Majority Leader Jim Wright, D-Texas, said that the rule's approval would merely allow individual cuts to be discussed "in the sunlight and open air where the public can see exactly what we are for and what we are against."

Democratic Attack

Democrats used the debate to attack the 1981 Republican-dominated budget process, contending that the huge Gramm-Latta package allowed Congress to surreptitiously repeal or change 436 laws.

The vote on the rule was generally along party lines, with Republicans who had large federal retiree clusters in their districts joining Democrats in support of the rule.

House sentiment against cutting federal pensions was evident May 27, when the House rejected the 4 percent cap by a 327-94 margin in an early budget vote. *(Vote 114, p. 34-H)*

But the House accepted the principle when the 4 percent COLA limit was wrapped into the budget resolution adopted June 23.

On Aug. 3, the House refused to clamp the 4 percent lid on COLAs, rejecting one of the biggest spending cuts in the $27 billion budget package. Instead, by a 268-128 vote the House passed a token reconciliation bill (HR 6862) that reduced pensions by only $113 million during the three-year period. *(Vote 225, p. 66-H)*

The Republicans avoided a direct vote on capping pensions, even though they originally planned to offer the amendment to impose the 4 percent ceiling.

They instead offered a motion to recommit HR 6862 to the Post Office and Civil Service Committee with instructions to make reductions as ordered by the budget resolution. The motion was rejected 160-236. *(Vote 224, p. 66-H)*

The Senate Aug. 5 accepted the 4 percent ceiling as part of its omnibus reconciliation bill (S 2774). Donald W. Riegle Jr., D-Mich., had tried Aug. 4 to lift the 4 percent COLA cap in S 2774. His amendment was defeated. ∎

Flexitime Extended

Legislation permitting flexible work hours for federal employees for three more years was signed (S 2240 — PL 97-221) by President Reagan July 23, ending a dispute between the administration and employee unions that had threatened to end the experiment.

The Office of Personnel Management (OPM) had demanded stronger management control over flexible hours for the 325,000 workers in the program. The unions wanted to keep decisions on flexitime within contract negotiations.

The disagreement led to the defeat March 2 of a House bill (HR 5366) to permanently authorize flexitime. The program was to expire March 29, and the measure failed by 10 votes to obtain the two-thirds majority needed for passage under suspension of the rules. The vote was 255-142. *(Vote 11, p. 4-H)*

Senate efforts to reach a compromise collapsed March 18, partly over the management control issue and partly because of an attempt to amend the bill (S 2240) to change private sector labor practices.

A few days later, Congress enacted a simple four-month extension (S 2254) to keep the program going while the administration and unions worked on a compromise. The extension was approved March 22 by the Senate by voice vote and cleared March 23 by the House by a vote of 361-33. It was signed into law (PL 97-160) March 26. *(Vote 38, p. 12-H)*

S 2240, the later three-year compromise authorization supported by both the administration and unions, was adopted by the Senate June 30 by a 93-2 vote and cleared by voice vote by the House July 12. *(Vote 203, p. 36-S)*

The Experiment

A three-year, nationwide experiment in flexible schedules for federal employees was authorized by Congress in 1978 (PL 95-390). *(1978 Almanac, p. 790)*

Agencies could choose to use flexitime, which staggered arrival and departure times within an eight-hour day; or condensed schedules, which permitted employees to meet their 80-hour biweekly work requirement in less than 10 days; or a combination. A compressed workweek could involve four 10-hour days each week, for example.

Under the 1978 legislation, federal managers had to negotiate flexible schedules with employees represented by unions, or a majority of non-unionized workers had to vote in favor of flexible hours before they were implemented in a certain office.

OPM estimated that more than 325,000 federal workers in 1,500 offices voluntarily participated in the project.

"If no legislation is passed by March 29, it would create a lot of havoc," said Robert Honig, director of the Federal Government Services Task Force. "People would more than likely be asked to change their schedules. It could create traffic jams and mass confusion."

Supporters of alternative work schedules said the plan improved government efficiency, extended hours of service to the public and reduced gasoline consumption by saving a day's commuting for many employees.

House Action

The House Post Office and Civil Service Committee reported HR 5366 Feb. 22 (H Rept 97-433). The bill permanently authorized federal agencies to set flexible and compressed work schedules for their employees. It provided broad management discretion in limiting the use of flexible time to prevent disruption of agency operations. But the measure also required agencies to negotiate with employee unions before setting up flexible work schedules.

While an administration study found the program generally had been successful, officials argued that productivity, public service and cost-effectiveness should be given more weight in deciding whether to use flexitime or compressed schedules.

As evidence of problems with the program, OPM Director Donald Devine cited the absence of employees on Mondays and Fridays in one agency and employee fatigue in another because of 10-hour days.

David Messing, legislative liaison in OPM, said the administration disliked HR 5366 because it left too much decision-making to labor-management negotiations.

Instead, the administration wanted the sole right to abandon flexible hours if they reduced productivity, lowered the level of public service or increased costs, he said.

When the measure reached the floor March 2, it failed by 10 votes to obtain the two-thirds majority needed for passage under suspension of the rules.

Senate Action

An effort led by Sen. Ted Stevens, R-Alaska, to renew the program fell apart when negotiations with the administration broke down.

Stevens, chairman of the Governmental Affairs Civil Service and Post Office Subcommittee, tried to get unanimous consent March 18 to bring a bill (S 2240) directly to the floor without committee action. But he was blocked when other senators objected.

Stevens' compromise would have given management more power to end an alternative work schedule, while retaining union rights to negotiate hours as part of contract talks. Stevens also recommended that disputes about the abolishment of flexitime be subjected to the Federal Services Impasses Panel.

In addition to continued administration opposition, a major obstacle was the intent of William L. Armstrong, R-Colo., to use the bill as a vehicle to amend the Walsh-Healey Act of 1936 by dropping the requirement that federal contractors pay overtime for work done in excess of eight hours each day.

Armstrong did offer the amendment when a new compromise was brought to the floor June 30 after the flexitime program had been granted the emergency extension.

The amendment was supported by the administration and business lobbies. But the AFL-CIO and federal unions opposed it, largely because it threatened the traditional eight-hour day.

Armstrong argued that government contractors' employees should have the same right to flexitime as federal workers.

Stevens said Armstrong in 1981 had introduced the language as a separate bill (S 398), but it had not emerged from the Labor and Human Resources panel. Stevens suggested the labor committee should handle the issue.

The amendment, Stevens said, "deserves review by the Senate and by the Congress. But I say to the Senate that it should not be on this bill."

The proposal was tabled by a vote of 49-46, and the bill passed by 93-2. *(Votes 202, 203 p. 36-S)*

The compromise gave agency heads 90 days during which they could unilaterally cancel existing flexitime if the programs increased costs, reduced productivity or diminished public service. On the floor, however, Stevens added an amendment allowing unions to bargain for substitute plans to replace those discarded by management.

S 2240 allowed agencies and unions to negotiate decisions to begin or end new flexitime programs. Impasses would be resolved by the Federal Service Impasses Panel.

The bill had been reported by the Governmental Affairs panel April 28 (S Rept 97-365). ∎

Roosevelt Memorial

Thirty-seven years after the death of Franklin Delano Roosevelt, Congress approved construction of a major memorial to the nation's longest-serving president.

Final action came July 14, when the House cleared for the president legislation (S J Res 95 — PL 97-224) authorizing construction of an FDR memorial on a 27-acre site in West Potomac Park in Washington, D.C. The site is near the Tidal Basin and the Lincoln and Jefferson memorials.

The new memorial will consist of a 14-foot-high garden wall winding past the cherry trees that edge the Tidal Basin and around waterfalls, pools, gardens and sculptures. It was designed by architect Lawrence Halperin and approved in 1979 by the Commission on Fine Arts and by the Franklin Delano Roosevelt Commission, which will supervise the project.

Before sending the authorizing legislation to President Reagan, the House approved an identical version (H J Res 400) by a vote of 254 to 151. It then adopted the Senate number, and cleared the resolution. *(Vote 174, p. 50-H)*

The Committee on House Administration had reported H J Res 400 on May 17 (H Rept 97-556).

The Senate passed S J Res 95 by voice vote March 8. It was reported by the Rules and Administration Committee on Feb. 8 (S Rept 97-311).

As cleared, the legislation authorized the appropriation of whatever funds were necessary for the construction, operation and maintenance of the monument by the National Park Service. The Congressional Budget Office estimated the cost of construction at $31 million and the annual maintenance cost at $1 million.

The House rejected, by a vote of 158-247, an amendment by Robert S. Walker, R-Pa., to prohibit expenditure of any funds under the bill until such time as the federal budget is balanced. *(Vote 173, p. 50-H)*

Background

A memorial to Roosevelt, whose four election victories made him president for longer than any other chief executive had been the subject of controversy for decades.

Before his death, Roosevelt reportedly told Supreme Court Justice Felix Frankfurter that he wanted no memorial bigger than a desk. The only existing memorial — a solid block of marble installed in 1965 opposite the National Archives building in Washington — is about desk size. It bears the simple inscription "In memory of Franklin Delano Roosevelt January 30, 1882 — April 12, 1945," and it was paid for through private donations.

Congress in 1955 passed legislation (PL 84-372) establishing the Franklin Delano Roosevelt Memorial Commission to plan a permanent Washington memorial to the nation's 32nd president.

Four years later, in 1959, the site in West Potomac Park was set aside for that purpose (PL 86-214).

It had been estimated that in the past 20 years, more than 500 attempts were made to design an appropriate FDR memorial. Two formal design proposals were considered and rejected, and the one finally accepted was scaled back to reduce its cost.

Living Memorial

In a related action, the House March 23 by a vote of 288-107 passed HR 4750 authorizing a study on the possibility of making the Warm Springs, Ga., area a living memorial to Roosevelt. FDR died in Warm Springs. *(Vote 32, p. 10-H)*

The study was to address ways of preserving and using the property known as the Little White House, built by Roosevelt in 1931; associated pools and springs; the rehabilitation center and the 10,000-acre Franklin Delano Roosevelt State Park.

The measure was reported by the Interior and Insular Affairs Committee (H Rept 97-460) on March 18. The Senate took no action on the bill. ∎

Small Business Research Bill Survives Critics

A bill (S 881 — PL 97-219) guaranteeing small businesses a share of the federal research budget survived a treacherous journey through a half-dozen critical committees and was signed into law by the president July 22.

The legislation had been diluted substantially from its original version because of strong opposition.

The measure was endorsed by the Reagan administration and nearly 200 cosponsors, who argued that small firms had been slighted in competition for federal contracts and grants, with most money going to big corporations and universities.

But the proposal faced strenuous criticism from major universities and the American Electronics Association. They argued that the program would siphon federal research dollars away from universities and that mandatory set-asides were wasteful because they required agencies to spend their annual quotas of grants regardless of the need for such spending.

In addition, six House committees took exception to the plan. Those panels — Energy and Commerce, Veterans' Affairs, Science and Technology, Foreign Affairs, Armed Services and Select Committee on Intelligence — wanted to remove agencies from the bill.

Little opposition had been raised when the Senate unanimously passed a similar bill in December 1981 or when the House Small Business Committee by a 40-0 vote approved its version in October. By Spring, however, a late lobbying drive by critics was taking effect.

The House Small Business Committee held new hearings and revised the bill before bringing it to the floor. The new version excluded from the set-aside provision all funds for in-house government research and development (R&D); the CIA, National Security Council and Defense Intelligence Agency; and the Agency for International Develop-

ment's international research centers and grants to foreign governments.

It also lowered the set-aside from the original 3 percent to 1.25 percent, bringing it more in line with the 1 percent stipulated in a bill passed by the Senate in 1981. The set-aside applied to agencies with R&D budgets of more than $100 million. *(1981 Almanac p. 401)*

The Senate cleared the measure for the president June 29 by accepting by voice vote the House-passed bill.

No new funds were required for the program, which used monies already in the government's aggregate research and development budget, estimated at about $40 billion a year. The 1.25 percent set-aside would amount to about $375 million annually.

Provisions

As signed into law, S 881:

● Stated that while small companies were the main source of significant innovations, the vast majority of federally funded R&D was conducted by large businesses, universities and government laboratories. It also stated that small businesses were "particularly capable of developing research and development results into new products."

● Established that the purposes of the bill were to stimulate technological innovation; use small businesses to meet federal R&D needs; and increase private, commercial innovations derived from federal R&D projects.

● Created Small Business Innovation Research (SBIR) programs, under which a portion of a federal agency's R&D budget was to be reserved for awards to small business concerns.

● Established a three-phase process to award funds to small companies. In the first phase, small business ideas would be evaluated according to their "scientific and technical merit and feasibility."

Projects demonstrating technical and economic viability could qualify for phase-two awards. Commercialization of the results would be left to the private sector in phase three. In the last phase, federal agencies could issue non-SBIR contracts to the firms for products or processes to be used by the government.

● Required federal agencies with R&D budgets of more than $100 million — not including in-house research — to spend specific percentages of that budget for small businesses. The percentage would increase from 0.2 percent in the first fiscal year of the program's operation to 0.6 percent in the second year, 1.0 percent in the third year, and 1.25 percent for the fourth year and each subsequent year.

● Allowed a five-year phase-in for agencies with extramural R&D budgets of more than $10 billion, a provision that currently applied only to the Defense Department. Such agencies must spend 0.1 percent in the first year; 0.3 percent in the second; 0.5 percent in the third; 1.0 percent in the fourth; and 1.25 percent in the fifth and subsequent years.

● Placed a limit on the percentage of basic research funds that may be spent on SBIR projects. The cap would equal the set-aside percentages established above.

● Exempted from the SBIR programs the Agency for International Development's support of international research centers or grants to foreign countries. It also excluded all intelligence agencies from the requirements of the bill.

● Required that agencies with R&D budgets greater than $20 million establish goals for small business participation. The percentage of R&D funding earmarked for small companies by these goals must not be less than the amount spent on small businesses by the agency during the preceding fiscal year.

● Ordered the Small Business Administration (SBA), within 120 days of the bill's enactment, to issue guidelines for SBIR programs. The guidelines were to include a uniform method for soliciting SBIR proposals, outside peer review for phase-two proposals, and protection of sensitive information provided by small companies as part of their proposals.

● Allowed exemptions to the SBA guidelines when national security or intelligence functions would be jeopardized.

House Action

The Small Business Innovation Development Act (HR 4326) was approved by the House June 23 by a vote of 353-57 and its language amended to S 881. Consideration began June 17. *(Vote 159, p. 46-H)*

Although the Small Business Committee on May 18 revised the bill it had reported Nov. 20 (H Rept 97-349 Pt. 1), some critical committee members still were not satisfied.

During floor debate, they attempted to exempt several agencies from the set-aside program, but they succeeded only in removing the intelligence community from the scope of the bill.

Paul N. McCloskey Jr., R-Calif., the most outspoken critic, said he believed it passed because "everybody in this House wants to help small business in an election year."

"It's a $377 million theft from the public Treasury," he said, referring to the amount earmarked for small firms.

"It gives preference to the one segment of the small business community that doesn't need it. We're not talking about mom-and-pop shops. We're talking about people with Ph.Ds. They get more than their share," he said.

The House easily accepted by voice vote an amendment by Edward P. Boland, D-Mass., chairman of the Permanent Select Committee on Intelligence, to expand the exemption for intelligence agencies to exclude all intelligence research done by the government. He argued that intelligence research would not be compatible with the open, competitive nature of the small business innovation program.

Larry P. McDonald, D-Ga., offered an amendment to remove the entire Department of Defense and the Department of Energy's atomic energy defense programs from the scope of the bill. He claimed that the Pentagon already awarded a good portion of its contracts to small businesses, and that the new program would harm the competitive bidding process.

John H. LaFalce, D-N.Y., a chief sponsor of the bill, responded that McDonald's proposal "would tremendously harm the bill by taking out a huge percentage of the total federal R&D dollar." The amendment was defeated 80-295. *(Vote 150, p. 44-H)*

Later, however, the House agreed by voice vote to an amendment exempting the atomic energy defense programs.

An amendment to exclude health-related research under the Department of Health and Human Services was offered by Henry A. Waxman, D-Calif., chairman of the

Energy and Commerce subcommittee on health. It was rejected 164-193. *(Vote 151, p. 44-H)*

Waxman argued that the set-aside would take money away from basic medical research because small firms would not be interested in conducting such inquiries.

A proposal by William C. Wampler, R-Va., to exempt funds for federal-state cooperative agricultural research ventures was defeated by a division vote of 13-34.

Voluntary Compliance Rejected

Perhaps the most crucial amendment offered came from the Science and Technology Committee and challenged the basic philosophy of a mandatory set-aside.

The committee's proposal, defeated 118-290, would have eliminated the compulsory nature of the program. Instead, it would have required certain agencies with R&D budgets above $100 million to reserve a portion of that budget for small firms. Congress, however, would then establish the actual amount the agencies would provide for small businesses, using the normal authorization and appropriations process. *(Vote 155, p. 46-H)*

Don Fuqua, D-Fla., chairman of the Science and Technology Committee, said the amendment was intended to "put the Congress back in the driver's seat" to control agency R&D spending.

"A mandatory set-aside will allow the executive branch to reallocate funds otherwise authorized and appropriated by the Congress," Fuqua said.

But opponents argued that it would gut the bill by failing to ensure that agencies spend a certain amount on small firms.

Other Amendments

The House also accepted by voice vote the following amendments:

● By Henry B. Gonzalez, D-Texas, to encourage technological innovation programs that maximize the use of firms owned and operated by minorities. Agreed to by voice vote.

● By Elliott H. Levitas, D-Ga., to provide a six-year "sunset" provision for the legislation, requiring the program to expire in October 1988. Agreed to by voice vote.

● By McCloskey, to require the General Accounting Office to study the effect of the bill on federal R&D activities and report to Congress in five years. Agreed to by voice vote. ∎

NASA Authorization

Congress authorized $6.773 billion for the National Aeronautics and Space Administration (NASA) in fiscal 1983, $160 million more than the Reagan administration requested.

A conference agreement on HR 5890 (H Rept 97-897) provided $124.9 million more than the House recommended and $160 million more than the Senate wanted. The Senate had matched the president's request of $6.61 billion.

The House agreed to the report Oct. 1 by a vote of 284-83, clearing the measure for the president. The Senate approved the measure by voice vote Sept. 30. It was signed into law (PL 97-324) Oct. 15. *(Vote 366, p. 110-H)*

The bill authorized NASA to begin production of a fifth orbiter for the space shuttle fleet. It also restored $281 million the Senate had cut for operating costs related to

space shuttle launching of military cargo.

The most controversial issue in the conference involved Senate language that would have required the Defense Department to reimburse NASA for the full cost of placing its cargo on the shuttle. The conferees settled on a provision directing the NASA administrator to set prices needed to recover the "fair value" of carrying Pentagon payloads into orbit on the shuttle.

HR 5890 exceeded the administration's request because of additions in the Centaur upper stage program for the shuttle and in aeronautical research and technology activities, according to Rep. Ronnie G. Flippo, D-Ala., chairman of the House Science and Technology subcommittee on space.

The largest share of the NASA budget was devoted to the space shuttle. It was authorized at $1.8 billion, about $80 million more than the administration proposed.

The bill also authorized the National Oceanic and Atmospheric Administration Landsat activities, which provided satellite scanning of the Earth's surface. The measure provided for user fees and a plan to transfer future civil applications of such remote-sensing satellite systems to the private sector when Congress determined that a transfer would be in the national interest.

HR 5890 authorized $36 million less than Congress appropriated for NASA for fiscal 1983 in a bill (HR 6956 — H Rept 97-891 — PL 97-272) that cleared Sept. 29 and was signed by President Reagan the next day. *(Story, p. 231)*

Legislative History

House. The House authorized $6.65 billion, $35.1 million more than the Reagan administration requested. Approved in a 277-84 vote May 13, HR 5890 stayed within the president's request for space activities, while adding $35.1 million for aeronautical programs. The largest portion of the space budget, $1.7 billion, would go to the reusable Space Shuttle. *(Vote 74, p. 22-H)*

The bill was reported from the Science and Technology Committee May 5 (H Rept 97-502).

Senate. The Senate Commerce Committee May 28 reported a measure (S 2604 — S Rept 97-449) that matched the administration's request.

The Senate June 9 passed HR 5890 after substituting its text for the House-passed version. ∎

Smithsonian Museum

The Senate cleared for the President June 9 a bill (HR 5659 — PL 97-203) authorizing a new museum for African art and a center for Eastern art in the Smithsonian Institution. It was signed into law June 24.

The bill, as passed by the House (H Rept 97-534) June 3, authorized $36.5 million in federal funds and required a matching amount of private money for construction of the art showcases near the original Smithsonian building in Washington, D.C. The measure had been reported May 17 from the Public Works and Transportation Committee.

The Senate June 9 also passed a bill (S 2390 — S Rept 97-432) authorizing extra fiscal 1983 appropriations for the Smithsonian of $782,000 and $1 million in each of fiscal 1984 and 1985.

The bill had been reported by the Rules and Administration Committee May 26. ∎

NSF Authorization

Legislation authorizing $1.089 billion in fiscal 1983 for the National Science Foundation (NSF) won House approval May 19 in a 282-111 vote. *(Vote 80, p. 24-H)*

The bill (HR 5842 — H Rept 97-485) was passed after a floor fight in which Larry Winn Jr., R-Kan., failed in an effort to cut the authorization by $30 million to bring it in line with the administration's $1.069 billion request.

Winn wanted to take the $30 million from science and engineering education activities. But Don Fuqua, D-Fla., chairman of the Science and Technology Committee, argued that the money was necessary to meet the nation's need for science teachers and engineers.

Although Winn's amendment was accepted 194-191, the House then approved 203-188 an amendment by Peter A. Peyser, D-N.Y., restoring $20 million to the bill. The final bill contained $10 million less than the Science and Technology Committee had proposed in reporting the legislation April 26. *(Votes 76-79, p. 24-H)*

HR 5842 also authorized $1.085 billion for NSF in fiscal 1982. Fuqua said the 1982 authorization was identical to that contained in HR 1520, which passed the House in September 1981. The Senate, however, did not act on that bill. *(1981 Almanac p. 403)*

Two Senate committees approved fiscal 1983 NSF authorization bills that also exceeded the president's request.

The Commerce, Science and Technology Committee May 20 reported a $1.09 billion authorization (S 2551 — S Rept 97-407), which, like the House measure, was $20 million more than the administration proposal.

The Labor and Human Resources Committee May 28 reported a $1.084 billion authorization (S 2349 — S Rept 97-457), or $15 million higher than the administration's request.

Debt Collection Act

President Reagan Oct. 25 signed a bill (HR 4613 — PL 97-365) designed to help the federal government collect billions of dollars in unpaid federal debts.

The House Sept. 30 accepted, with minor changes, amendments the Senate had added to the bill Sept. 28 by a vote of 96-2. The House had originally passed the bill May 5. The Senate, in the session that started Oct. 1, cleared the bill by voice vote Oct. 2. *(Vote 359, p. 61-S)*

HR 4613 authorized the government to enlist the aid of credit bureaus and collection agencies in tracking down delinquent borrowers. *(Background, 1981 Almanac p. 401)*

It required individuals to provide Social Security numbers when applying for a federal loan, permitted federal agencies to give collection firms the addresses of delinquent borrowers obtained from Internal Revenue Service (IRS) files, allowed wage deductions from federal employees who were delinquent in repaying government loans and imposed interest and penalty charges on overdue government debts.

Chief Senate sponsor Charles H. Percy, R-Ill., said studies by the General Accounting Office and the Office of Management and Budget indicated that as of Sept. 30, 1979, delinquent federal debts amounted to more than $25 billion. The total had grown since then, he added. "The consequences of these substantial losses are both serious and wide-ranging," Percy said.

"If we do not crack down on those defaulting on a government loan," he said, "how can we justify asking our honest constituents to make sacrifices to cut federal spending?"

HR 4613 exempted credit bureaus from the requirements of the 1974 Privacy Act (PL 93-579) for purposes of listing any debts an individual might owe the federal government. Previously, if credit bureaus used federal debt information in compiling an individual's financial history, they became subject to the Privacy Act, which allowed individuals to inspect, challenge or amend their credit records. *(1974 Almanac p. 292)*

Credit bureaus, already subject to the 1970 Fair Credit Reporting Act disclosure and truth-in-reporting requirements, declined to list federal debts because they did not want to be subject to two sets of rules. Thus, individuals who did not repay federal loans did not have to worry about blemishing their credit records.

Legislative History

The Senate Governmental Affairs Committee reported its version of the debt collection bill (S 1249 — S Rept 97-378) July 17, 1981. It contained the Privacy Act exemption for credit bureaus and permitted addresses from IRS files to be given to collection agencies and credit bureaus.

The Senate Finance Committee Dec. 3 reported S 1249 (S Rept 97-287) with several tax-related provisions, including one providing IRS addresses to debt collectors only.

As reported April 29, 1982, by the House Ways and Means Committee, HR 4613 (H Rept 97-496) dealt only with IRS-related issues. For example, it would have allowed IRS addresses to go not only to debt collectors, but also to credit bureaus.

The House passed HR 4613 by a 402-3 vote May 5. It passed a separate debt collection bill (HR 2811 — H Rept 97-42) by voice vote May 18 that contained the Privacy Act exemption for credit bureaus. *(Vote 55, p. 18-H)*

House and Senate staff reached an agreement on a compromise version that dropped the provision giving IRS addresses to credit bureaus and cut to 15 percent, from 25 percent, the amount that could be deducted from federal employees' wages to pay back a federal debt. It was this compromise that the Senate approved Sept. 28.

Provisions

As signed, PL 97-365:

● Permitted federal agencies, except the IRS, to contract with private collection agencies for collection services.

● Exempted credit bureaus from Privacy Act restrictions.

● Allowed mailing addresses obtained from the IRS to be provided to private debt collectors.

● Required individuals to supply their Social Security numbers when applying for federal loans.

● Permitted deductions of up to 15 percent of a federal employee's salary, after taxes and retirement contributions, to pay off overdue debts owed the government.

● Authorized the IRS to tell other federal agencies whether an applicant for a government loan had an outstanding tax liability.

● Required agencies to charge interest and penalties on overdue debts.

● Made it a federal offense to assault federal employees collecting debts owed the federal government.

Franking Law Changes

The Senate Rules Committee voted unanimously Feb. 26 to delay at least until the end of the 97th Congress the ability of senators to make statewide mailings of franked letters addressed to "postal patron." The effect of the change was that senators had to continue to put a specific name and address on each piece of mail on which their signature franks served as postage stamps.

A law revising the congressional franking statute (PL 97-69), and allowing postal-patron mailings, was passed by Congress in 1981. But the Senate Rules Committee decided to delay implementation of the law after the Senate sergeant-at-arms reported that if every senator made four such mailings a year, the Senate would have to hire an additional 166 employees and would exceed its budget by $57 million. *(1981 Almanac p. 394)*

House members had been able to make districtwide postal-patron mailings since 1973.

In a related development, a special three-judge panel of the U.S. District Court for the District of Columbia Sept. 7 dismissed a lawsuit filed in 1973 by Common Cause, the self-styled citizens' lobby, challenging the congressional franking privilege. Members have enjoyed free mailing privileges since the 1st Congress in 1789.

Common Cause argued that the free mailing privilege gave incumbents an unfair political advantage, thus denying challengers equal protection of the law. The court said the franking privilege "confers a substantial advantage to incumbent congressional candidates over their challengers," but it found no constitutional violation. Common Cause appealed the decision to the U.S. Supreme Court. ∎

Tax-Exempt Aid

A bill allowing White House press secretary James S. Brady to accept contributions from tax-exempt charitable organizations to defray his medical expenses was cleared by Congress in 1982.

Brady was seriously wounded in the March 30, 1981, assassination attempt on President Reagan. *(1981 Almanac p. 6)*

The legislation (S 2333) bypassed committees and was approved by voice vote April 1 by both the House and Senate. It exempted federal employees injured during an assassination or kidnapping attempt from a law forbidding federal workers from accepting any remuneration from sources outside the government.

It was signed into law April 13 (PL 97-171). ∎

Olympic Coins

A bill allowing the federal government to market coins commemorating the 1984 Los Angeles Olympic Games was signed into law (S 1230 — PL 97-220) by the president July 22.

The legislation represented a triumph for Rep. Frank Annunzio, D-Ill., who led a prolonged battle to prevent private firms from selling the coins.

His proposal, approved by the House May 20 by a vote of 302-84, gave the Treasury responsibility for marketing the coins. Annunzio's plan was a substitute for a version of

S 1230 passed by the Senate in December 1981 and approved by the House Banking, Finance and Urban Affairs Committee allowing private marketing of the coins. Annunzio argued that more money would go to athletes under his plan. *(Vote 84, 26-H)*

The Senate by voice vote accepted the House amendments July 1, clearing the measure for the president. S 1230 had been reported by the House Banking, Finance and Urban Affairs Committee March 2 (H Rept 97-554) and by the Senate Banking, Housing and Urban Affairs Committee Oct. 30, 1981 (S Rept 97-264).

As cleared, the bill required the government to mint 52 million coins in three designs. Annunzio said $600 million would go to the Olympic committees if all the coins were sold. ∎

Freedom of Information Act

Congress did not complete action on legislative proposals backed by the Reagan administration to place new restrictions on the Freedom of Information Act (FOIA).

Despite months of negotiations, differences between those in favor of shielding more government data from the public and those who preferred broad access to government records presented too great an obstacle in the 97th Congress.

The proposed changes in FOIA became a touchy issue, particularly in an election year, because of intense news media opposition.

Although a Senate committee in May approved changes in FOIA, the legislation was never considered by the full Senate in 1982.

There was no action on the issue by the House, either. Rep. Glenn English, D-Okla., chairman of the Government Operations Committee's Information Subcommittee, had refused to hold hearings on the bill until the Senate completed action.

"On the House side, we didn't see the pressing need to make major changes that Senator Hatch and the [Reagan] administration saw," English said.

Background

The FOIA was enacted in 1966 to make previously classified government files available to the public. Changes in the law enacted in 1974 over the veto of President Gerald R. Ford broadened access to certain information and were intended to remove bureaucratic obstacles erected to thwart implementation of the act. *(Congress and the Nation Vol. IV, p. 805)*

President Reagan and various members of Congress, including the chairman of the Senate Judiciary Committee's Constitution Subcommittee, Orrin G. Hatch, R-Utah, maintained that the FOIA had been misused.

They sought certain changes in the law to ensure greater protection against disclosure of vital government records, particularly those having some relation to national security or law enforcement. They also were sympathetic to appeals by businessmen for changes that would shield more information that corporations were required to submit to the federal government, including federal regulatory agencies.

In 1981, Hatch proposed changes allowing the attorney general to protect information about federal investigations of organized crime and terrorism, giving agencies more

time to release government files and making it more difficult for the public to see information supplied by businesses. Supporting Hatch were the Justice Department and
the Central Intelligence Agency, which argued that the
public's right to know had to be balanced against national
security interests.

Opposing any new restrictions were the news media,
public interest and academic groups. They contended that
some of Hatch's proposals would give the government new
powers to withhold information.

1981 Action

Many of the FOIA changes sought by Hatch and the
administration were included in a bill (S 1730) approved by
a 3-2 vote of Hatch's Constitution Subcommittee in December 1981. *(1981 Almanac p. 404)*

The subcommittee measure gave government agencies
the authority to establish uniform fees to search for and
copy requested documents that reflected the actual cost of
such services. The government was allowed to charge extra
for technological information having a commercial value.

The subcommittee bill also gave agencies more time to
answer FOIA requests. Critics said the change would allow
the government to drag out its response time. The exact
length of the time limits was left unresolved by the panel.

After businesses complained that FOIA was responsible for trade secrets being released to competitors, the
subcommittee included provisions giving companies the
opportunity to protest disclosure of any information they
might be asked to submit to the government. Opponents
argued that public health and safety could be jeopardized if
certain data supplied to the government — for example, on
food and drugs, consumer goods, pollution hazards and
employment practices — were not available to the public.

The subcommittee measure also gave broad new powers to the attorney general to exempt all information relating to terrorism, organized crime and foreign counterintelligence investigations. And it made it easier for the CIA to
go to court to stop disclosure of information the agency
considered to be sensitive.

1982 Compromise Bill

After the measure had been approved by the subcommittee at the end of the first session, critics in and out of
Congress became aroused, charging that the subcommittee
measure went too far.

An alliance of public interest groups, including the
American Civil Liberties Union, Ralph Nader's Public Citizen Litigation Group and Common Cause, fought to preserve the greatest possible public access to government
records.

But Hatch faced his stiffest opposition from press
groups worried that his bill would hamper their ability to
write stories based on government files.

The center of press lobbying was the Joint Washington
Media Committee, including representatives of the American Newspaper Publishers Association, the American Society of Newspaper Editors, the National Newspaper Association, the National Association of Broadcasters, the
Radio-Television News Directors Association, the Society
of Professional Journalists and the Reporters Committee
for Freedom of the Press.

From the outset, all of the media groups were unified
in their feelings about FOIA. They said the existing act
worked well and did not need substantial revisions. The

opposition eventually forced Hatch to make compromises.

The media group met with Hatch's subcommittee
counsel Randy Rader for more than six months, discussing
each provision of the legislation.

Hatch gradually gave ground on provisions until April,
when Rader presented the press group with a substitute
bill. The senator backed away from proposals to protect
business data submitted to the government, to let the
government seal files on terrorism investigations and to
charge service fees for processing information requests.

"A minimum count of what Hatch has given up from
his subcommittee bill is 62 amendments in a 25-page bill,"
said Robert E. Feidler, a Judiciary staffer for Sen. Dennis
DeConcini, D-Ariz., who was involved in the negotiations.

"We have rolled back a tremendous amount," said
Rader. "I hope the other side will recognize this is a genuine compromise."

The compromise resulted from negotiations among
Sens. Hatch, who had sponsored the more restrictive mea-
sure, Patrick J. Leahy, D-Vt., DeConcini, and Charles E.
Grassley, R-Iowa.

Judiciary Committee Action

The Senate Judiciary Committee on May 20, 1982,
approved the compromise package of amendments to S
1730. The bill then was ordered reported by a unanimous
vote. However, a report on the committee bill was never
issued during the session.

As ordered reported, S 1730 created new limits on
public access to files dealing with organized crime, government informants and the Secret Service. The bill also allowed the withholding of information that "could reasonably be expected to cause a clearly unwarranted invasion"
of personal privacy.

The bill set new fees for processing FOIA requests but
waived them for reporters, scholars and non-profit public
interest groups. It also authorized the government to
charge commercial users royalties for valuable technical
information.

Reaction. The compromise won praise from lobbyists
and lawmakers on both sides of the issue, who agreed that
the bill managed to limit public access to certain federal
records without creating excessive government secrecy.

"It's such a vast improvement over what Senator
Hatch first introduced," said Richard M. Schmidt, general
counsel for the American Society of Newspaper Editors. "It
really preserves the essence of the Freedom of Information
Act, for which we're thankful. It helps preserve the people's
right to know."

Geoffrey Stewart, special counsel to the Justice Department's Office of Legal Policy, said department officials
were pleased with the new protections for records dealing
with confidential informants, organized crime and the use
of FOIA by imprisoned felons.

"The bill that came out gave the law enforcement area
very much what it needed," Stewart said, adding that the
Justice Department still wanted more restraints on the
release of records for terrorism probes.

Lobbyists for some business groups, including the
Chamber of Commerce, said they were disappointed S 1730
did not include a wider exclusion of business data. But they
praised the new procedures requiring agencies to notify
businesses before releasing information and language giving them the right to a court review of an agency disclosure.

"What we have done this year is just going to be the
starting point for discussion in the next Congress," pre-

dicted Gary D. Lipkin, assistant general counsel of the National Association of Manufacturers (NAM).

Until lobbying began last year on FOIA, "many senators thought everything was hunky-dory. They were amazed to find there was a problem with FOIA," Lipkin said. "Next year, business lobbyists won't be met with amazement when they say FOIA needs to be changed."

S 1730 Provisions. As modified, the bill included the following major changes in the law:

● Allowed the attorney general to seal files on organized crime investigations for up to eight years.

● Expanded protection for government informers by limiting access to records that "could reasonably be expected" to disclose the identity of a confidential source.

● Excluded Secret Service records related to that agency's protective role from FOIA's disclosure rules.

● Created a new exemption from FOIA for technical data that was not allowed to be exported from the United States without a license.

● Required a federal agency to notify a company when anyone requested information that the firm labeled as sensitive when it submitted the data to the government. The bill also gave businesses new rights to challenge an agency's decision to release the records, at both the agency level and in court.

● Changed the FOIA time limits in which an agency was required to release requested documents. Instead of the existing law's 10-day extension for "unusual circumstances" warranting a delay, an agency was given an extra 30 days to answer a FOIA inquiry. S 1730 also expedited access to files for anyone who could show a compelling need for the information.

● Allowed agencies to charge individuals for the cost of processing requested documents, in addition to the fees they already were charging for searching for and duplicating files.

● Permitted the government to charge royalty fees for commercially valuable technological information obtained by the government at a substantial cost to taxpayers.

● Barred the release of records that "could reasonably be expected to constitute a clearly unwarranted invasion of personal privacy."

● Allowed the attorney general to issue regulations restricting the use of FOIA by imprisoned felons. The bill also allowed agencies to turn down FOIA requests by non-U.S. citizens.

● Prevented the use of FOIA to circumvent judicial discovery rules by giving an agency the right not to respond to a FOIA request from a litigant in a pending government case. ∎

Regulatory Reform Bill Stalled in House

Regulatory reform legislation (HR 746, S 1080) was effectively killed Dec. 9 when the House Rules Committee held a second hearing on the House measure but recessed without clearing the bill for floor action.

A lethal dose of talking by committee and subcommittee chairmen opposed to the measure, coupled with a lack of enthusiasm by House Democratic leaders, doomed the bill for the 97th Congress.

The regulatory reform legislation, which was supported by business lobbyists and the Reagan administration, would have revamped federal rule-making procedures to give Congress, the White House and the courts more control over the way regulations were promulgated and adopted.

As the first overhaul of the Administrative Procedure Act since it was written in 1946, the measure would have subjected major proposed rules to cost-benefit analysis and changed the way regulations were challenged in court. Supporters said it would streamline and reduce the cost of rule-making.

The Senate unanimously passed its version of the regulatory reform bill March 24. But the House bill, reported by the Judiciary Committee Feb. 25, ran into opposition from committee chairmen. A coalition of public interest groups also fought the legislation, arguing that it would hamper regulations needed to protect public health and safety. *(Background, 1981 Almanac p. 404; 1980 Almanac p. 526)*

One of the more controversial issues involved in the regulatory reform debate concerned the legislative veto. While both the Senate and House bills permitted Congress to override federal regulations, they differed in particulars. The tougher Senate provision allowed a two-house legislative veto, without presidential review, of most regulations issued by executive and independent agencies.

Although Congress had attached some form of legislative veto to other laws, the veto had never before been used so broadly. A decision was pending by the U.S. Supreme Court on the constitutionality of the legislative veto.

In other 1982 action on the issue, Congress exercised legislative veto authority first enacted in 1980 (PL 96-252) to block a Federal Trade Commission rule requiring used-car dealers to disclose auto defects. That veto was overturned by an appellate court Oct. 22. *(Story, p. 346)*

Senate Floor Action

The Senate passed S 1080 March 24 by a 94-0 vote. The bill had been reported by the Judiciary (S Rept 97-284) and Governmental Affairs (S Rept 97-305) committees in 1981. *(Vote 62, p. 13-S)*

Paul Laxalt, R-Nev., chief sponsor of S 1080, said the measure improved rule-making procedures "so regulations will be more effective and less costly."

"After all the years of people talking about making government work better, we've actually sat down and done something that will," said Patrick J. Leahy, D-Vt., who with Laxalt led the bipartisan drive for a regulatory relief bill.

The keystone of the Regulatory Reform Act was the introduction of cost-benefit analysis into the federal rule-making process.

Each agency would have to decide whether the benefits of a proposed rule outweighed its costs. The "regulatory analysis" would be conducted on major rules — those that generated $100 million a year in compliance and enforcement costs.

The president, through the Office of Management and Budget (OMB) or another designee, was given the power to make sure both independent and executive agencies com-

plied with the cost-benefit requirement. However, time limits to the review were added, and an amendment approved just before passage required OMB to make public information about its role in a rule-making procedure.

The legislation also made legal challenges to agency decisions easier by removing the benefit of doubt often given to agencies under existing law.

Several provisions of S 1080, including the requirement for cost-benefit studies, already were in practice in executive departments under an order issued by Reagan Feb. 17, 1981. The Senate bill codified some of those provisions and extended them to independent agencies, such as the Nuclear Regulatory Commission, the Securities and Exchange Commission and the Federal Communications Commission.

Legislative Veto

While most differences on S 1080 were ironed out before the complex bill reached the floor, the legislative veto proposal was a sticking point because of administration opposition to a veto that did not require a presidential signature.

However, the veto amendment sponsored by Harrison "Jack" Schmitt, R-N.M., Carl Levin, D-Mich., and 48 others was adopted by a 69-25 vote after an effort to table the proposal failed. *(Vote 58, p. 13-S)*

The implementation of most rules would be delayed 45 days while congressional committees reviewed them. If a committee recommended disapproval of a regulation, each chamber would have an additional 30 days to act. A majority of both houses would have to reject the rule for it to be blocked.

About 200 laws with legislative veto provisions were already on the books. The Senate measure would have applied the veto across-the-board to all agencies, except the Department of Defense, the Internal Revenue Service and rules dealing with rates, wages, prices or mergers, Schmitt said.

Proponents of the veto argued that Congress needed to reclaim the power it had delegated to regulatory agencies because bureaucrats often misinterpreted the intent of congressional policies.

"We created a class of people who were insulated from the political process and then we turned over to them ... the implementation of our laws," Levin said. "It was wrong to give such vast powers to an essentially unaccountable fourth branch of government."

Critics argued that the timing was wrong for the proposal because of the pending Supreme Court decision.

"Let us wait for the Supreme Court to speak," said John C. Danforth, R-Mo., whose motion to table the Schmitt amendment was defeated 23-70. *(Vote 57, p. 13-S)*

Leahy argued against the proposal. "The legislative veto is one of the bad elements of the bill," Leahy said. "It will spawn all kinds of special interest groups on the right and left, who will be up here asking us to second-guess agency actions."

As a safeguard, the Senate adopted an amendment to sever the veto provision if the Supreme Court found the legislative veto unconstitutional.

Regulatory Analysis

The requirement that agencies weigh the costs of their proposed rules against the benefits would apply to major new regulations, defined as those that had an annual effect on the economy of $100 million or more in "reasonably quantifiable direct and indirect costs."

The president also could designate up to 75 rules a year as major on the grounds that they would substantially increase costs or prices for wage earners, consumers, industries or other groups. Such a designation would then mandate a regulatory analysis by the proposing agency.

In the analysis, an agency must explain how the benefits of a proposed rule justified its costs and show that a rule would be cost-effective, compared to other alternatives that would achieve the same goal.

OMB, the office the president was expected to designate to monitor agency compliance with the cost-benefit requirement, could establish guidelines for those tests. OMB could review procedures followed by an agency but could not comment on the substance of a rule.

The limits on OMB's power were made explicit in an amendment submitted by John Glenn, D-Ohio, who wanted to insulate independent agencies from White House interference.

Under Glenn's amendment, the president or his designee must comment on cost-benefit studies of proposed and final rules within 30 days of each analysis. The time limit was designed to prevent the president from holding up enactment of rules by stalling on a procedural review of the cost-benefit study.

The amendment also excluded certain independent agencies from executive branch supervision. Glenn originally proposed that all independent agencies be excluded but the compromise, adopted by voice vote, exempted only the Federal Election Commission, the Nuclear Regulatory Commission and certain Federal Communications Commission regulations.

Another safeguard against OMB meddling was an amendment by Levin requiring agencies to place written comments from OMB on proposed rules in a public file and to explain why significant changes were recommended. Levin had wanted OMB to log all oral comments it made to agencies, but after the administration warned that such activity could bring rule-making to a "screeching halt," Levin dropped that requirement. His amendment was adopted 92-0. *(Vote 61, p. 13-S)*

Court Role Strengthened

An amendment by Dale Bumpers, D-Ark., adopted by voice vote, instructed judges not to presume an agency's interpretation of law was necessarily correct, placing a greater burden on the agency to support its position.

It was designed to eliminate a tradition of judicial deference to agency expertise, and as a Bumpers aide said, "It takes the bureaucratic thumb off the scales of justice."

The version adopted was a compromise reached by Bumpers and the administration, in which Bumpers conceded that courts should "give the agency interpretation such weight as it warrants."

In other action, the Senate:

● Defeated, 27-65, an amendment by Thomas F. Eagleton, D-Mo., intended to prevent judicial review of major rule determination under the $100 million test. *(Vote 59, p. 13-S)*

● Adopted by voice vote an amendment by Jim Sasser, D-Tenn., requiring regulators to estimate a rule's cost to state and local governments and identify federal funds available to pay such costs.

● Adopted by voice vote a Leahy amendment clarifying that S 1080's cost-benefit standards did not apply to regulations implementing laws that preclude consideration of

costs such as health and civil rights legislation.

Senate Provisions

As passed by the Senate, S 1080:

General Rule-Making
● Required agencies to publish a notice of proposed rule-making in the *Federal Register.*

● Ordered that the notice contain the time, place and nature of the rule-making proceeding, a brief explanation of the need for and objectives of the proposed rule, an explanation of the statutory authority under which the rule was proposed, the suggested provisions of the rule and a statement specifying where the file of the rule-making proceeding might be inspected.

● Directed agencies to include in the notice a statement seeking ideas from the public for alternative methods to achieve the rule's objectives that were more effective or less burdensome than the approach used in the proposed rule.

● Required that agencies give interested parties at least 60 days to participate in the rule-making by submitting written data, views or arguments.

● Allowed agencies to use other procedures to enhance public comment, such as sending direct notice of a proposed rule to persons who would be substantially affected, or conducting informal public hearings. An agency's decision whether to use such procedures would not be subject to judicial review.

● Provided that for a major rule, participation should include the opportunity for oral presentations, including cross-examination of agency witnesses.

● Allowed judicial review of major rule-making procedures when outside parties made a timely objection, or when the failure to use the procedure precluded a "fair consideration" of a central issue.

● Required an agency to publish the final rule in the *Federal Register* at least 30 days before the rule was to take effect. The notice must explain the need for, objectives of and statutory authority for the rule; discuss significant issues raised during rule-making, including alternatives considered and why they were rejected; and explain how the factual basis for the rule was supported in the rule-making file.

● Ordered an agency to maintain a public file for each rule-making proceeding. The file must include the notice of proposed rule-making, all written comments, a transcript of any public hearing and copies of factual and methodological material used in connection with the rule-making.

● Required that the file also contain copies of all written material, including drafts of the proposed and final rule, submitted by the agency to the president or his designee for a review of their regulatory impact. The agency also must include a written explanation of the reasons for any significant changes it made in the drafts of a rule in response to comments from the president or his designee as part of the regulatory review.

● Prohibited judicial review of an agency's file-keeping unless an agency violation precluded fair public consideration of a key issue.

● Banned the use of appropriated funds to pay the expenses of persons participating in agency proceedings, unless otherwise authorized by statute.

Regulatory Analysis
● Exempted from regulatory analysis rules dealing with

rates, wages, prices, services, corporate or financial structures, reorganizations, mergers or acquisitions, or accounting practice. Also exempted rules dealing with military and foreign affairs.

● Excluded from regulatory analysis rules relating to monetary policy of the Federal Reserve Board; rules issued by the Internal Revenue Service, Federal Election Commission and Tennessee Valley Authority; and certain rules issued by the Federal Communications Commission and the Food and Drug Administration.

● Exempted until June 30, 1985, rules dealing with the viability of federally insured depository institutions.

● Defined a major rule as one that the agency, president or the president's designee determined was likely to have an annual effect on the economy of $100 million or more in "reasonably quantifiable direct and indirect costs"; or a rule that would cause a substantial increase in costs or prices; or would have an adverse effect on competition, employment, investment, productivity, the environment, public health or safety.

● Defined "costs" and "benefits" as reasonably identifiable, significant social and economic costs and benefits, including beneficial and adverse effects, that were likely to be direct or indirect results of a rule.

● Provided that an agency or the president might determine that a rule was major under the $100 million test. Agencies and the president could designate major rules under the second definition, but the president was limited to 75 rules a year in this category and had to make the designation within 30 days of the publication of the notice of proposed rule-making. All major rules would be subject to cost-benefit studies.

● Required a preliminary regulatory analysis to be published with the notice of proposed rule-making. The preliminary analysis must describe costs and benefits of a proposed rule, including those that could not be quantified. The analysis also must include a brief description of alternatives that would achieve the goal of the rule.

● Mandated that the preliminary analysis identify federal funds available to pay state and local governments the costs incurred from a proposed rule.

● Ordered that the analysis describe how the benefits of a proposed rule justified its costs and how the recommended rule would be cost-effective, compared to other alternatives that would achieve the same goal. This would not apply when cost-benefit tests were inconsistent with the agency's enabling statute.

● Required agencies to publish a final regulatory analysis with the final rule.

● Stipulated that the final regulatory analysis contain a description of the costs, benefits and alternatives to a rule.

Unless otherwise prohibited, the final analysis must show that the benefits justified the costs and that the rule was more cost-effective than the alternatives.

● Clarified that the regulatory analysis requirements did not alter rule-making standards used under other statutes.

Court Comment on 'Major' Status
● Barred judicial review of a determination by the president or his designee that a rule was a major one, or of the failure to make such a designation.

● Allowed courts to set aside an agency's determination of whether a rule was major under the $100 million test only if the court found the determination was clearly erroneous in light of information available to the agency when it made the decision. Designation by an agency under the

subjective criteria would not be reviewable.

Executive Oversight

● Gave the president authority to establish procedures for agency compliance with regulatory analysis and authorized the president to "monitor, review and ensure agency implementation" of the procedures.

● Provided an opportunity for public comment on the procedures, and mandated that the procedures lead to speedy completion of the rule-making.

● Limited the president's review of a preliminary and final regulatory analysis to 30 days following receipt of each study. The president could extend the deadlines 30 days for good cause.

● Permitted the president to delegate the oversight authority to the vice president or to another Executive Office official who had been confirmed by the Senate.

● Exempted Nuclear Regulatory Commission rules from executive oversight provisions.

Periodic Review of Rules

● Required agencies to review their existing major rules within 10 years of the act's effective date.

● Ordered each agency to publish a proposed schedule for review of existing major rules not later than nine months after the effective date of this section. One year after the section became effective, each agency must publish a final schedule for review of existing major rules.

● Mandated that new major rules and amended rules be reviewed within 10 years of their effective date or the date they were amended.

● Allowed the president or his designee to grant agencies up to a five-year extension for reviewing specific rules.

● Required agencies to allow at least 60 days for public comment on rules that would be renewed without change.

● Stated that if an agency failed to review a rule within the prescribed period, it must immediately publish in the *Federal Register* a notice proposing to repeal or renew the rule, and it must complete a review within 180 days.

● Ordered each agency to publish an agenda in April and October of rules the agency would be acting on during the next 12 months.

● Required the president in May and November to publish a calendar of major rules on which agencies would be acting in the next 12 months.

● Ordered the president to report annually to Congress on the government's regulatory activities.

Scope of Judicial Review

● Stated that a court could find an agency action or finding unlawful if it was arbitrary or capricious, unconstitutional, in excess of the agency's statutory authority, in violation of procedures required by law, unsupported by substantial evidence in the record or unsubstantiated by facts.

● Prohibited a court from making a presumption either in favor of or against an agency action. It stipulated, however, that "in reaching its independent judgment concerning an agency's interpretation of a statutory provision, the court shall give the agency interpretation such weight as it warrants."

● Allowed a court to determine whether the factual basis of a rule had substantial support in the rule-making file.

● Mandated that when suits challenging an agency action were brought in two or more courts, the case would be heard in the court in which the first proceeding was insti-

tuted. However, if less than five days elapsed between the filing of each suit, the hearing court would be randomly selected.

General Provisions

● Exempted federal, state and local government officials from terms of the Federal Advisory Committee Act.

● Granted federal courts authority to resolve jurisdictional disputes between two or more regulatory agencies involving public utilities.

● Authorized the head of a federal agency to adopt as a federal rule a state or local regulation or procedure that duplicated a federal regulation or procedure.

● Provided that if any part of the act were held invalid, the remainder of the act would not be affected.

Legislative Veto

● Exempted from congressional review any rule dealing with rate-making, military and foreign affairs, and certain Internal Revenue Service activities.

● Exempted from congressional review any rule issued in response to an emergency.

● Established that no proposed final rule could become effective until 45 days of continuous session of Congress elapsed after the rule had been sent to Congress and appropriate committees.

● Allowed congressional committees to use the 45-day period to report a resolution of disapproval of a rule. If a committee reported such a resolution, a rule could not become effective for another 30 days of congressional session, while one chamber considered the resolution of disapproval. If the first chamber agreed to the resolution, another 30 days would be set aside for consideration by the other house. If both houses agreed to the resolution, the rule would be nullified.

● Allowed a resolution of disapproval to be brought directly to the floor if a committee did not report a resolution within 30 days of the date the final rule was sent to Congress, and if one-fifth of the members signed a discharge petition. In the second chamber, a committee would have 20 days to report a resolution of disapproval before a discharge petition would be allowed.

● Established that a rule could become effective at any time after the day on which either chamber defeated a resolution of disapproval.

● Precluded a rule from becoming effective if Congress adjourned *sine die* before the expiration of the 45-day period cited above.

● Allowed a rule to take effect if an agency transmitted a proposed final rule to Congress at least 45 days before the day on which Congress adjourned *sine die* and if neither house adopted a resolution of disapproval prior to the adjournment date.

● Established procedures for House and Senate consideration of a resolution of disapproval of a recommended rule.

Effective Date

● Provided that the bill take effect Jan. 1, 1983, for new rule-making after that date. The bill would not affect proceedings that began before the effective date.

● Provided that the periodic review, calendar and agenda provisions take effect six months after the date of enactment.

● Provided that the venue provisions take effect three months after the enactment date.

House Committee Action

The House bill, HR 746, was reported by the Judiciary Committee Feb. 25 (H Rept 97-435). But further action on the legislation was delayed by the resignation in March of its chief sponsor, George E. Danielson, D-Calif., who accepted a California judgeship. Sam B. Hall Jr., D-Texas, was named chairman of Danielson's Administrative Law Subcommittee April 1.

As reported, HR 746 differed from the Senate bill in three key areas: the autonomy given to independent federal agencies, the ability of Congress to overturn agency-issued regulations and the scope of judicial review of regulations.

Legislative Veto. While both bills gave Congress new power to override federal regulations, the veto mechanism differed in the two versions.

As passed by the Senate, a majority of both houses of Congress must veto a regulation in order to block it, but no presidential sign-off was needed.

The legislative veto in the House bill would allow both chambers to overturn proposed rules in a joint resolution, but it also would require the president's signature.

HR 746 limited the legislative veto to "major" rules, defined as those with an annual cost of $100 million or more. In contrast, the Senate version applied to nearly all rules proposed by independent and executive agencies.

A stricter legislative veto was expected to be offered as a floor amendment by Rep. Elliott H. Levitas, D-Ga. His proposal (HR 1776), which had 251 cosponsors, would allow one house to overturn a rule, but it would give the other chamber the opportunity to override the first veto. No presidential signature would be required.

Presidential Supervision. Another major difference between the two bills was the amount of freedom that independent agencies were given from presidential supervision.

Both measures ordered agencies to conduct studies weighing the costs against the benefits of proposed major rules. They also gave the president, who was expected to designate OMB to act in his behalf, authority to oversee the rule-making process.

But the House bill created a mostly advisory role for OMB, while the Senate version gave OMB more authority to ensure compliance with its procedures for cost-benefit tests.

Moreover, the House measure exempted 19 independent agencies such as the Federal Trade Commission from OMB oversight of the cost-benefit analysis. The Senate bill excluded only the Federal Election Commission, the Nuclear Regulatory Commission and certain Federal Communications Commission rules from executive branch supervision.

Judicial Review. Like the Senate bill, the House proposal gave more direction to the courts on their role in reviewing agency decisions. But the House version did not include Senate-adopted provisions that made it easier to legally challenge agency actions.

Rules Consideration

Seven months after HR 746 was reported by the Judiciary Committee and one day before Congress recessed for its eight-week election break, the Rules Committee began consideration of the measure.

After expressing early reservations about the bill, House Democratic leaders had met during the summer with business and administration officials to develop a compromise.

The Rules Committee was reviewing that compromise, which was to be offered as a substitute to the committee bill amendment by Sam B. Hall Jr., D-Texas, and Thomas N. Kindness, R-Ohio, the chairman and a minority member respectively of the Judiciary Administrative Law Subcommittee.

In one key change, the compromise gave the president or his designee authority to ensure that independent agencies complied with the bill's procedures for cost-benefit tests.

The original version exempted 19 independent agencies from presidential supervision in this area.

The new version was vehemently opposed by several committee leaders and by a coalition of environmental, labor, consumer and civil rights groups.

The committee heads, led by Energy and Commerce Committee Chairman John D. Dingell, D-Mich., argued that the bill would erode statutes within their committees' jurisdiction and would increase the power of the Office of Management and Budget at the expense of Congress.

Opponents described the legislation as a "regulatory paralysis" bill that would produce more red tape and would undermine health, safety, environmental and other consumer protection laws.

After a Sept. 30 hearing dominated by Dingell's criticisms of the measure, Rules Chairman Richard Bolling, D-Mo., pledged to return to the bill during the lame-duck session.

Bolling kept his promise Dec. 9, when he held a two-hour hearing. But like the first meeting, the session was dominated by the bill's opponents.

Some objections were to the rule requested by Hall, who asked that only two amendments be allowed: the Hall-Kindness substitute amendment, and a legislative veto amendment by Levitas.

"I'm very concerned that a bill of this enormous magnitude, which affects the entire operation of government, could come before the floor without an open rule," said Dan Glickman, D-Kan. Glickman was one of several Judiciary Committee members who complained that the panel never had a chance to review the Hall-Kindness substitute.

"At this late hour, will we as members have an adequate opportunity to assess this legislation? I think not," said Jack Brooks, D-Texas, chairman of the Government Operations Committee.

Several members attacked the legislation on substantive grounds, arguing that the proposed cost-benefit analysis of regulations could be cumbersome and expensive itself.

Others said it would dismantle consumer protection laws, while providing regulatory relief for special interests.

Other than Hall, Levitas was the only member to testify in favor of HR 746. Levitas described the bill's opponents as a "verbal Moral Majority."

"They are very noisy, but their noise is much greater than their numbers," he said.

Levitas said the committee's failure to report the bill with a rule "would be an abandonment of responsibility by this committee and a breach of faith."

But with the session rapidly drawing to a close, the Rules Committee showed no appetite for wrestling with the complex and controversial legislation.

The panel broke off hearings after nine House members had spoken against HR 746. Another 25 witnesses were awaiting an opportunity to testify. ∎

Groundless Page Sex Charges Prompt Reforms

Congress focused on its page system in 1982 after reports were published alleging sexual activity and cocaine use involving pages and members.

A five-month investigation by the House ethics committee found no truth in the highly publicized allegations of illicit sexual relations, but a special House commission and a Senate management panel recommended that changes be made in the page program, which brought young boys and girls to Washington to run errands for members.

The ethics committee investigation was headed by Joseph A. Califano Jr., secretary of health, education and welfare during the Carter administration.

Califano's 114-page report, issued Dec. 14, strongly implied that the media failed to substantiate rumors of sexual activity before publishing them. But he noted that while the allegations were false, the complete lack of after-work supervision for pages was a serious problem.

A separate Justice Department investigation into the allegations of homosexual activities between members of Congress and pages was closed Aug. 31 after officials were unable to corroborate charges made by Leroy Williams, a former page.

Continuing into 1983 was a Califano investigation into separate allegations of drug use and distribution. The Justice Department also was investigating Capitol drug use at year's end.

Through 1982, the ethics committee probe had cost about $400,000, Califano estimated, including the salaries of nine lawyers, seven investigators and three researchers.

Chronology of Events

Califano's report gave the following account of the events leading to the public allegations:

On June 30 and July 1, CBS television aired news reports, including interviews with two unidentified pages, that said pages had been the victims of sexual misconduct on the part of House members.

Those reports were followed by stories in newspapers, magazines and on other television networks about the sexual misconduct allegations. The stories also included reports of an alleged drug distribution ring at the Capitol, possibly involving the pages.

The page-sex charges were traced to the two pages who appeared on CBS.

One of them, Williams, an 18-year-old former page from Arkansas, told CBS, other reporters and the ethics committee that he had engaged in homosexual relations with three members of Congress and had arranged a liaison between a senator and a male prostitute. He later admitted he lied about these relationships.

The other page, Jeffrey Opp, 16, of Colorado, told CBS and federal investigators of several incidents of homosexual approaches by members of Congress. Opp later said he had exaggerated and called the television interview "a 16-year-old kid satisfying his ego."

In late spring, after rumors of a page scandal had circulated on Capitol Hill, CBS reporter John Ferrugia began asking pages about improper activities on the part of members of Congress. On June 9, he contacted Opp, who told the ethics committee that Ferrugia said he had been investigating homosexual activities of congressmen. Opp

said that Ferrugia named individual members and their sexual preference. Opp testified that he was flattered by the attention and began repeating some of Ferrugia's stories.

Opp also told two staff members of his sponsor, Patricia Schroeder, D-Colo., of the allegations of illicit sex.

The two staffers testified that they contacted Ferrugia, who told them he had learned of a widespread homosexual ring among senior government officials. The staffers set up a meeting between Opp and Justice Department officials, who decided to investigate Opp's stories. It was the opening of this investigation that CBS used as the "news peg" for airing its interviews with Williams and Opp.

The Califano report indicated that the allegations snowballed after the first CBS report, with other reporters picking up the story and talking to pages, none of whom had direct knowledge of sexual activity between pages and members but some of whom had heard Opp's or Williams' stories.

Califano had asked Ferrugia to talk to investigators about the sex allegations, but Ferrugia, with the backing of CBS, declined. In a letter to Califano, CBS said Ferrugia "acted entirely properly in his investigation and reporting of this story."

Ethics Committee

The ethics committee investigation began after the House voted 407-1 July 13 to authorize an investigation into allegations of:

● Improper or illegal sexual activity by members or congressional employees.

● Illicit use or distribution of drugs by members or employees.

● Preferential treatment by members or employees to those people, including pages, who may have provided either drugs or sexual favors.

The investigation resolution (H Res 518) gave the panel, formally known as the Committee on Standards of Official Conduct, broad subpoena power to force the testimony of witnesses. It also allowed the committee to receive information from law enforcement agencies and to prohibit other members of Congress from having access to that information. *(Vote 171, p. 50-H)*

Majority Leader Jim Wright, D-Texas, who authored the resolution, said the powers were identical to those the committee had been given during its investigations of Abscam and of allegations of Korean influence peddling. *(Abscam, 1980 Almanac p. 513; "Koreagate," 1978 Almanac p. 803)*

On July 27, Rep. Louis Stokes, D-Ohio, chairman of the ethics committee, named Califano as special counsel to head the investigation. Califano said he had been asked to proceed "as expeditiously as possible," but that no deadline had been set.

Page Program Revisions

Almost as soon as the page charges surfaced in late June, members and congressional staff complained that the pages were not adequately supervised or housed.

And a special House commission and a Senate management panel were commissioned to look into the program.

The House panel, the Speaker's Commission on Pages, released its recommendations Aug. 16. It had been created in July by Speaker Thomas P. O'Neill Jr., D-Mass. Its recommendations, which dealt primarily with the ages, supervision and education of pages, recommended that the system be retained but improved. The Senate group, the Senate Management Board made similar recommendations July 14.

For most of its history, Congress had employed young boys to run errands and do housekeeping chores. In the last decade, female pages also had been employed. Pages originally had been used to fill inkwells, light oil lamps and candles and keep fireplaces going, but their duties had changed to include carrying documents between the Capitol building and members' offices, making sure necessary papers were in the House and Senate chambers, running errands and taking messages for members.

During the academic year, there were 101 pages — 30 in the Senate and 71 in the House. Both employed more in the summer. The Senate pages ranged in age from 14-18; House pages were between 16 and 18. They were appointed by individual members for periods of a few months to two years and were paid about $750 a month. They had to find their own housing, and usually stayed in boarding houses or shared apartments. Pages attended school early in the morning at classrooms in the Library of Congress. The school was operated by the District of Columbia public school system.

In 1976, House Doorkeeper James T. Molloy, overseer of the House pages, had tried to warn Congress of the "potential time bomb" of unsupervised young pages. In hearings on the page school, Molloy told the House Education and Labor Committee that Congress had authorized construction of a page dormitory in 1970 but never appropriated the money to build it.

Molloy said the lack of supervision "is an area very truly that needs to be investigated by the House. It could be a potential black eye to the House of Representatives."

At the same hearings, a former page said there had been a serious drug problem among a few pages but that when he had tried to bring the problem to light, he was told by his supervisors in the Republican cloakroom to ignore it.

The Speaker's commission found that the page system was "essential to the efficient functioning of Congress." The panel consisted of Rep. Bill Alexander, D-Ark., chairman; Rep. John T. Myers, R-Ind.; Doorkeeper Molloy; Joel Jankowsky, a lobbyist who was an assistant to former Speaker Carl Albert, D-Okla. (1947-77), and former Rep. Charles E. Wiggins, R-Calif. (1967-79).

The commission rejected proposals to use college students or senior citizens as pages. It said pages should be 11th graders who were at least 16 years old and who would serve for only one semester. To monitor the program, it recommended creation of a Page Board, consisting of the House Speaker, majority leader and minority leader.

The board was created Nov. 30 with the passage of H Res 611.

The panel also recommended that pages be housed in an old hotel that had been converted to House offices, that resident counselors be appointed and that the page school be improved. The House began converting two floors of the building to a dormitory, where pages would be required to live, and authorized the hiring of a resident supervisor.

The recommendations were similar to those of the Senate Management Board, which concluded that only 11th graders should be pages, that they should be housed in a single dormitory and get more supervision, and that their school should be improved. The board consisted of the secretary of the Senate, the Senate sergeant-at-arms, the architect of the Capitol and the staff director of the Senate Rules Committee.

The Senate also established an advisory board and was expected to require its pages to live at the dormitory beginning in the fall of 1983.

In addition, the House Administration Subcommittee on Personnel and Police met briefly July 15 to discuss the page system, which fell under the subcommittee's jurisdiction. Chairman Joseph G. Minish, D-N.J., said the pages needed more supervision, a dormitory and a better school. Minish introduced a bill (HR 6762) to establish a board to oversee the page program.

Bill Goodling, R-Pa., introduced a bill (HR 6745) to require pages to be at least 18 years old, which would eliminate the need for the school.

Neither of the bills was enacted.

Cocaine Investigation

Much of the public information about the investigation into the alleged Capitol cocaine ring came from Rep. Robert K. Dornan, R-Calif., who revealed he had let an undercover District of Columbia narcotics detective pose as a member of his staff.

When he agreed to help with the investigation in March 1981, he said, there was no hint of members' involvement, just staff.

In April 1982 police arrested three men said to be distributing cocaine in the Capitol. And a federal grand jury began focusing on pushers, not users, who allegedly included members of Congress, according to published reports.

That investigation and the drug probe by the House ethics committee both were continuing at year's end. ∎

House Chaplain Vote

The House reaffirmed by a 388-0 vote March 30 its right to appoint a chaplain and to open each day's session with prayer. *(Vote 42, p. 14-H)*

The symbolic action on a House resolution (H Res 413) was intended to signal members' concern over a March 9 decision by the U.S. Court of Appeals for the District of Columbia that could ultimately require both House and Senate to get rid of their chaplains or to stop paying them.

A three-judge panel of the appeals court ruled 2-1 that Congress' appointment of official chaplains was open to challenge on constitutional grounds by ordinary taxpayers.

The resolution said the court ruling "implied a lack of respect" for Congress and declared that the House considered its practice of employing a chaplain to be "an appropriate and constitutional exercise."

The decision came in a suit filed in June 1980 by Madalyn Murray O'Hair, Jon Garth Murray and the Society of Separationists, an atheist organization. The suit charged that using government money to support the chaplains' activities violated the First Amendment requirement that "Congress shall make no law respecting an establishment of religion." *(1980 Almanac p. 559)*

The decision overturned a January 1981 ruling by U.S. District Judge Louis F. Oberdorfer that the suit should be dismissed without consideration of its merits. He ruled that

the suit centered on a "political question" inappropriate for the court to judge and that O'Hair and Murray lacked standing to sue.

The appeals court ruled that Congress could choose its officers and make its rules only so long as the Constitution was not violated. The effect of its ruling was to send the suit back to the district court for a decision on the case on its merits. The government took the case to the full appeals court, which heard arguments Oct. 27 but had issued no decision at year's end. ∎

House Bicentennial Office

The House voted 230-97 Dec. 17 for a resolution (H Res 621) establishing a House Office for the Bicentennial to be staffed by a professional historian appointed by the Speaker. Its purpose was to prepare for the celebration of the 200th anniversary of Congress in 1989. *(Vote 450, p. 132-H)*

Sponsors said the historian would be temporary, because authority for the office would expire in 1989. A resolution (H Res 581) calling for a permanent House historian had been defeated in September on a 132-180 vote. *(Vote 347, p. 104-H)*

The Senate had had a Historical Office since 1975 at a 1982 cost of more than $155,000. Opponents of both House resolutions said the measures would cost too much. The expenses and salary of the historian under H Res 621 would come from the contingent fund of the House. ∎

Indian Claims Legislation

Legislation extending the time limit for American Indian tribes to bring lawsuits in certain damage cases was defeated by the House Dec. 13. But three days later, its provisions were included in the conference agreement on the fiscal 1983 Interior appropriations bill (HR 7356).

That appropriations measure, with the Indian claims language incorporated, was cleared by Congress Dec. 19 and signed Dec. 30 by President Reagan (PL 97-394). *(Story, p. 262)*

Background

The legislation was designed to extend the deadline for legal action on about 17,000 Indian claims that arose before 1966. The claims came from Indians who said they were illegally stripped of land, money or fishing rights by a variety of private and governmental parties. As trustee for Indian affairs, the federal government was responsible for filing lawsuits to press these claims.

Congress had already renewed the statute of limitations three times; the latest extension was due to expire Dec. 31. Congress was also pressed to act before adjournment because a federal judge ruled Nov. 17 that the government had failed to properly represent the Indians.

U.S. District Judge Howard Corcoran in Washington, D.C., said the government had to file lawsuits for the Indians by Dec. 31 or submit legislation by Dec. 15 to resolve claims it would not pursue through the courts. The government appealed that ruling, which was temporarily stayed by an appellate court.

If the statute of limitations had run out Dec. 31 without government action on the cases, the United States would have been barred from starting lawsuits to recover money damages for Indian claims arising before July 18, 1966.

The Reagan administration initially opposed another extension of the time limit, maintaining that government attorneys could wrap up the cases administratively by Dec. 31. But after Corcoran's ruling, the administration dropped its opposition to another extension.

Provisions

As cleared by Congress, the Interior appropriations bill (HR 7356) included the following Indian claims provisions:

● Required the secretary of interior, within 90 days of enactment of this law, to publish in the *Federal Register* a list of all pending pre-1966 Indian claims, broken down tribe-by-tribe, reservation-by-reservation or state-by-state.

● Gave Indian tribes six months after publication of the list to submit to the Interior Department any additional pre-1966 claims they believed should be considered for litigation or legislative resolution.

● Gave the interior secretary 30 more days to publish a revised list of pending claims, incorporating any new ones submitted during the six-month comment period.

● Kept alive all Indian claims on the initial and revised lists pending action by the secretary of interior either rejecting a particular Indian claim or proposing legislation to settle it. Set no deadline for such action, but required notice of any claim rejection to be published in the *Federal Register*.

● Set a one-year statute of limitations on the filing of lawsuits pursuing any claims the secretary of interior explicitly rejected in a notice published in the *Federal Register*.

● Set a three-year deadline for the filing of suits on any claim for which the interior secretary submitted a proposed legislative solution, or a report to Congress, with the time to begin running from the date of the legislative submission or report.

Legislative History

Virtually identical Indian claims bills (S 2978, H J Res 553) were introduced in 1982 by Sen. William S. Cohen, R-Maine, chairman of the Senate Indian Affairs Committee, and by Rep. Morris K. Udall, D-Ariz., chairman of the House Interior Committee.

S 2978 was reported Sept. 29 by the Indian Affairs Committee. There was no written report. Cohen, however, explained the purpose of the bill on the Senate floor at the time it was reported.

"To simply allow these claims to lapse — to administratively shove them under the rug — is damaging to the law; it is damaging to the Congress; and ultimately, it is damaging to this country," Cohen said. He warned that the government, as trustee for the Indians, could be held liable for the value of the claims if it failed to take some action to resolve them.

S 2978 never came to a vote of the full Senate.

In the House, H J Res 553 was reported Dec. 10 by the Interior Committee (H Rept 97-954) and called up on the floor Dec. 13.

During floor debate on the Indian claims legislation, Udall — like Cohen — warned that if the statute of limitations ran out before any disposition had been made of the old claims, the government could be held liable for not fulfilling its responsibility as trustee for the Indians.

However, several House members argued Dec. 13 that Congress had renewed the statute of limitations enough.

"We must end this litigation process, which has our taxpayers over a barrel. We are paying for the litigation, and we are paying for the claims," said Ron Marlenee, R-Mont.

"In shutting this legal door, I think the rights of individuals who have a clear and just claim can be handled by private relief legislation," he said.

The House voted 228-153 in favor of suspending the rules and passing H J Res 553, but the measure fell short of the two-thirds majority of those present and voting (254, in this case) necessary for passage under that procedure. *(Vote 417, p. 124-H)*

At that point, backers of the legislation switched tactics. Instead of trying a second time to pass a separate bill, on Dec. 16 they attached the Indian claims language to the conference agreement on the Interior Appropriations bill (HR 7356). Three days later, that measure was cleared for the president. ∎

Mail Fraud Bill Fails to Clear

Legislation making it easier for the U.S. Postal Service to crack down on fraudulent mail-order schemes was passed by both the House and Senate in 1982, but the measure (S 1407) did not clear Congress.

The Senate passed S 1407 in May, but the House did not take up its version (HR 7044) until the lame-duck session in December.

The House approved HR 7044 Dec. 13 by a 320-61 vote, then adopted the Senate bill number (S 1407) to ready the legislation for a House-Senate conference. *(Vote 413, 122-H)*

However, with time running out in the session and significant differences separating the two chambers, no further action was taken on the bill.

Background

The mail fraud legislation grew out of hearings by the House Select Committee on Aging on fraud against the elderly. Committee Chairman Claude Pepper, D-Fla., said the elderly, who often used the mails to purchase goods and to invest money, were the most frequent victims of fraud. They were especially vulnerable to medical quackery, land promotions, false insurance sales and work-at-home deals, he said.

More than 300 members of the House joined Pepper in cosponsoring HR 3973, the predecessor bill to HR 7044. In the Senate, David Pryor, D-Ark., ranking minority member of the Governmental Affairs Post Office subcommittee, sponsored S 1407 with 25 other senators.

"Mail fraud has grown in epidemic proportions in recent years," Pryor said. "According to the Postal Service, postal inspectors last year received more than 200,000 complaints of mail fraud or misrepresentation, completed more than 4,400 investigations and saw nearly 1,400 would-be swindlers convicted of mail fraud."

"For about 100 years the Post Office Department has been charged with the responsibility of combating mail fraud. Yet we have not given them sufficient tools to follow through with the task," Pryor testified at a House subcommittee hearing in May.

To address the problem, both measures gave the chief

postal inspector the same subpoena power already held by inspectors general in other federal agencies.

The postal inspector was given authority to seek access to any books, records, documents or other material related to an investigation. An inspector could, for example, demand in writing to see inventory records to ascertain that advertised products existed in quantities sufficient to meet orders. If the operator resisted, the inspector could ask a court to implement the order.

Secondly, the Postal Service was granted authority to quickly obtain samples of an advertised product to begin an immediate inquiry into suspected misrepresentation. Postal authorities currently had to send for items by mail, and some operators delayed delivery until a late date, giving them time to close shop and escape scrutiny before the product was delivered.

Also, the bills authorized a civil penalty of up to $10,000 per day against anyone who violated an order to stop engaging in fraudulent schemes.

Currently, the postal inspector could protect the public under a criminal mail fraud statute and a civil false representation statute enacted more than a century ago, according to Charles P. Nelson, acting chief postal inspector.

Under these statutes, the principal sanction was an administrative "mailstop order" that prevented a consumer's money from reaching the scheme operator and required that the money be returned to the sender.

"The underlying expectation is that if the operator of the scheme is cut off from his profits, he must either reform his promotion to avoid misrepresentation or cease marketing his product by mail," Nelson told the Postal Personnel subcommittee July 22.

Nelson said the present statutes contained defects that prevented adequate law enforcement. One problem was that a mail-stop order often arrived too late to catch up with operators who had moved on to new addresses. Another weakness was the lack of sanctions against promoters who evaded false representation orders by changing their names, for example.

Senate Action

The Senate Governmental Affairs Subcommittee on Civil Service, Post Office and General Services held hearings on S 1407 in 1981.

The full Governmental Affairs Committee reported the bill April 29, 1982 (S Rept 97-392).

Before approving the bill, the full committee added a provision requiring the Postal Service to issue guidelines for the use of subpoenas, or "written demands," as the bill called them. The panel also provided that the U.S. district courts, rather than the Postal Service, would enforce subpoenas.

The legislation slid through the Senate without opposition May 19.

House Hearings

When House hearings began May 20 on HR 3973, postal committee leaders sounded alarms about the legislation's potential infringement on constitutional rights.

Rep. William D. Ford, D-Mich., chairman of the Post Office and Civil Service Committee, argued that the Postal Service already had extensive police powers.

"It is none of our business what people put in [the mail]. It is between the person who mails it and the person who receives it," Ford said.

David Minton, Washington counsel of the Magazine Publishers Association, testified that giving postal inspectors the power to search books and records could impinge upon the rights of religious, educational, philanthropic and other groups that send second- and third-class mail.

"The little Bible churches and evangelical groups who today enjoy absolute protection against the prying eyes of the government would be subject to having their books opened, their membership examined and further difficulties imposed upon them by the government," Minton said.

John Shattuck, Washington director of the American Civil Liberties Union (ACLU), told congressmen July 20 that the expanded inspection authority could invade the privacy of businesses and their customers.

The bill also could tread on First Amendment rights by making it easier for the Postal Service to censor or suppress literature or advertising, he said.

Minton said it would be more appropriate to use other government agencies — such as the FBI, the Secret Service or the Federal Trade Commission with its quasi-judicial powers — to apprehend and prosecute mail fraud.

Some of the strongest opposition to the legislation came from the National Health Federation, a 20,000-member organization that was concerned about post office interference with health books.

Clinton Ray Miller, the federation's executive director, argued that the Postal Service had no business stopping the distribution of information that was unproven or contrary to prevailing medical or scientific opinion. Miller complained that the Postal Service already "can be depended upon to abuse and misuse policy authority," and he said new powers would worsen that situation.

Compromise

The full House Post Office and Civil Service Committee Sept. 28 approved and Oct. 4 reported a compromise version of the mail fraud bill (HR 7044 — H Rept 97-932) that contained safeguards designed to protect privacy rights, freedom of expression and due process rights.

The one dissenter was William E. Dannemeyer, R-Calif., who described the bill as "an abomination."

"If this bill passes in its present form, I think it's unconstitutional," Dannemeyer said. "It [violates] the right against unreasonable search and seizure by the government."

By wide margins, the committee defeated a series of amendments by Dannemeyer to restrict the new Postal Service powers. Dannemeyer's proposals were backed by the ACLU, which opposed the legislation.

Among the changes made in response to criticism of the original bill, HR 7044:

● No longer allowed the Postal Service to investigate and impose penalties for fraudulent schemes that did not rely on the mails, such as telephone sales.

● Allowed a court to conduct independent fact-finding on the grounds for penalties authorized by the bill. The bill allowed penalties of up to $10,000 per day against anyone who violated an order to stop engaging in fraudulent schemes.

● Created objective standards for issuance of subpoenas, which the bill referred to as "civil investigative demands."

● Required postal inspectors to inform individuals of their rights and privileges before issuing an investigative demand.

● Adopted the Federal Trade Commission's "mirror image" doctrine to protect advertisements for books and

other publications as long as the advertisement accurately reflected the item's contents and was designed merely to promote the sale of the book or publication.

● Required the postmaster general to develop a consumer education program on false representation schemes.

The compromise was endorsed by the Reagan administration. The Justice Department had voiced concerns about the first bill, but supported HR 7044. The independent Postal Service supported both versions of the bill.

During markup sessions Sept. 22 and Sept. 28, the committee rejected amendments by Dannemeyer that would have stopped the Postal Service from initiating its own complaints against suspected mail fraud operators, and would have required that search warrants be issued by a federal magistrate before a mailer's records could be examined.

The panel also rejected Dannemeyer amendments to exclude tax-exempt, non-profit organizations from the bill's provisions; to allow a person being investigated to inspect government files related to his case; and to reduce the $10,000-a-day penalty for repeat offenders to $1,000 a day.

While Dannemeyer argued that a $10,000 fine "is excessive," Ford countered that "to any mailer, $1,000 a day is really cheap overhead to continue doing business."

"I'm a little tired of always thinking of the rights of the potential criminal and not the victim of the crime," said committee member Mary Rose Oakar, D-Ohio, who backed the bill.

House Floor Action

The House passed HR 7044 Dec. 13 by a vote of 320-61. *(Vote 413, p. 122-H)*

As passed, HR 7044 did not contain a controversial proposal to give the Postal Service authority to issue civil investigative demands, similar to subpoenas, to examine books, records or other material related to a mail fraud investigation.

Although that provision had been included in the bill when it was reported by the Post Office Committee, it was stricken at Ford's recommendation.

The Senate-passed version (S 1407 — S Rept 97-392) gave the Postal Service more enforcement powers, including subpoena authority. But Ford and civil liberties groups warned that it could dangerously expand the Postal Service's police powers.

"HR 7044 is intended to plug holes in the existing postal law without infringing on anyone's constitutional rights," Ford said after proposing the revisions. "It has built-in procedural and substantive protections to insure that the new investigative and enforcement authority which we are granting is used properly and prudently," he added.

New powers given to the Postal Service under HR 7044 included the authority to quickly buy an advertised product or service that could be part of a mail scam. Presently, the Postal Service often faced a long wait to obtain a questionable product, and an operator could fill all his orders and shut down before the Postal Service could halt his mail deliveries.

HR 7044 also authorized the Postal Service to issue cease and desist orders to perpetrators of mail-order schemes, and to seek civil penalties against violators. Penalties under the legislation would be up to $10,000 per day for anyone who violated an order to stop engaging in fraudulent conduct. ∎

Financial Integrity Act

A bill (HR 1526 — PL 97-255) to target fraud, waste and mismanagement in the federal government by requiring each federal agency to submit an annual report to the president on its internal accounting and administrative controls was cleared by Congress Aug. 19.

Final action came when the House accepted the version of the bill approved by the Senate by voice vote Aug. 4.

HR 1526 was reported May 14, 1981, by the House Government Operations Committee (H Rept 97-38) and passed by the full House May 18, 1981, under suspension of the rules.

In the Senate, the measure was referred to the Governmental Affairs Committee, which reported a companion bill (S 864) on Feb. 11, 1982 (S Rept 97-312).

When the full Senate took up the legislation Aug. 19, it inserted the text of S 864 into HR 1526, and approved the House measure.

"Passage of S 864 means that the head of each federal agency will be held accountable for his agency's internal control system," said William V. Roth Jr., R-Del., chairman of the Governmental Affairs Committee. "In other words, we can fix the blame, if necessary. Or, on the other hand, give a well-deserved pat on the back." ∎

Reports to Congress Cut

The Senate Dec. 8 passed and sent to President Reagan a bill (HR 6005 — PL 97-375) eliminating or modifying some 77 reports that executive branch agencies previously were required to submit to Congress on a regular basis.

The House had passed the bill by voice vote Sept. 20. Although the measure was referred to the Governmental Affairs Committee in the Senate, that panel was discharged without acting, and the bill was passed by the full Senate without amendment.

The legislation was introduced at the request of the Office of Management and Budget (OMB), which had recommended the elimination or modification of 200 reports.

HR 6005 was approved Aug. 10 and reported Sept. 14 by the House Government Operations Committee (H Rept 97-804). At the recommendation of other House committees, the panel pared to 77 the list of 200 reports OMB had targeted.

The other reporting requirements were left intact, according to the Government Operations report, "because committees indicated the reports are either still useful and pertinent in overseeing government programs and the activities they contain, or they contain substantive material which should be the subject of in-depth hearings by the relevant committees prior to any change in the law."

The Congressional Budget Office estimated that HR 6005, as cleared by Congress, would save the government approximately $4 million annually. ∎

King Memorial Approved

The Senate Dec. 20 cleared a resolution (H Con Res 153) calling for a bust or statue of the Rev. Dr. Martin Luther King Jr. to be placed in the U.S. Capitol.

The civil rights leader, who was slain April 4, 1968, at the age of 39, thus became the first black person to be represented among the building's statues.

H Con Res 153, which did not require the president's signature, had been passed by the House Sept. 15, 1981.

The resolution allowed expenditures of up to $25,000 on the memorial, which was to be chosen in a design competition sponsored by the Joint Committee on the Library.

"It is fitting to honor Dr. King in the halls of the Capitol, because it was the U.S. Congress that translated many of his most important goals into reality. His influence on our nation's laws was profound," said Sen. Charles McC. Mathias Jr., R-Md., a sponsor of the resolution and vice chairman of the library committee.

Twice before, in 1976 and 1979, the House had passed resolutions authorizing the erection of a memorial to King, only to see the proposals become snagged in the Senate.

In addition, bills had been introduced repeatedly since King's assassination to make his Jan. 15 birthday a national holiday. None had cleared, although committees in both the House and Senate approved such legislation in 1979. *(1979 Almanac p. 584)*

Congress in 1980 did enact legislation (PL 96-428) establishing a Martin Luther King Jr. National Historic Site in Atlanta, Ga. *(1980 Almanac p. 615)* ∎

Surplus Property Donation

The House Dec. 13 cleared for President Reagan a bill (S 1444 — PL 97-380) allowing the federal government to donate to state and local governments surplus military equipment loaned to them for civil defense purposes.

Final action came when the House accepted without amendment the bill passed by the Senate Oct. 1. It was identical to a companion measure (HR 1856) that had been reported by the House Government Operations Committee Sept. 30 and the House Armed Services Committee Oct. 5 (H Rept 97-910, Parts I and II).

Since 1971, the federal government had loaned trucks, trailers, bulldozers, pumps and other equipment to state and local governments for civil defense uses.

"Literally thousands of small communities across our nation rely heavily on military surplus equipment to help them meet their civil defense needs," said Senate sponsor Strom Thurmond, R-S.C. Giving them the equipment, he said, would allow them to modify it to conform more closely to their needs.

As cleared, S 1444 authorized the General Services Administration to transfer ownership of military surplus property to state or local governments holding it on the date of enactment. The Federal Emergency Management Agency had to certify that the equipment was still being used for civil defense purposes. ∎

OMB Funds Study Mandated

The Senate Oct. 1 cleared for President Reagan a bill (S 2386 — PL 97-326) designed to ensure that the Office of Management and Budget (OMB) compiled and published data on the geographic distribution of federal funds.

Final action came when the Senate, by voice vote,

accepted an amended version of the bill that had been passed by the House Sept. 28 by voice vote.

As cleared, the bill required OMB to prepare a report detailing federal spending in each state, county, congressional district and municipality for fiscal 1983 through fiscal 1985.

Existing data sources would be used for the OMB report, so no new funding was required.

Background

Since 1968, the government had reported on the geographic distribution of federal funds for about 1,800 programs to states, counties, congressional districts, and cities with over 25,000 population. These reports were produced by the Community Services Administration (CSA), acting as agent for OMB. But when the CSA was abolished in October 1981 by the omnibus budget reconciliation (PL 97-35), OMB discontinued production of the reports.

Starting in fiscal 1983, OMB proposed to replace the old reports with one that would provide data only on state-by-state distribution of federal funds.

But Congress balked, insisting on the more detailed breakdowns. "Such information would be especially useful today, given the major changes being proposed in federal budget policies and in intergovernmental relations," said the House Government Operations Committee in reporting its version of the funding report bill (HR 7096 — H Rept 97-878).

S 2386 was reported May 28 by the Senate Governmental Affairs Committee (S Rept 97-473) and passed July 29 by the full Senate.

In the House, the Government Operations Committee Sept. 28 reported HR 7096 (H Rept 97-878), which the full House passed later that day before adopting the Senate bill number and returning the amended legislation to the Senate for final approval. ∎

Earthquake Hazards Bill

The Earthquake Hazards Reduction Act (S 2273) was cleared by the Senate Dec. 16 by voice vote, sending it to the president who signed the bill into law (PL 97-464) Jan. 12, 1983.

The measure, which won House approval Sept. 14, authorized $63.4 million in fiscal 1983 for a multi-agency effort to reduce the risks to life and property from future earthquakes. The bill authorized "such sums as may be necessary" for fiscal 1984.

Funds provided under the program were devoted to the first phase of an earthquake prediction network that would conduct research on the nature of earthquakes and analyze earthquake possibilities by developing seismic risk maps for the entire nation.

S 2273 was reported April 20 by the Senate Commerce Committee (S Rept 97-336) and passed April 29 by the Senate.

In the House, a companion measure (HR 6272) was reported May 17 by the Interior and Insular Affairs Committee and by the Science and Technology Committee (H Rept 97-535, Pts. I and II).

HR 6272 was passed by voice vote Sept. 14 under suspension of the rules. The action was then vacated and the House passed S 2273 after amending it to conform to HR 6272.

The two chambers swapped amendments Oct. 1 as Congress struggled to recess for the Nov. 2 elections, but did not complete action on the bill until the lame-duck session. ∎

Contract Disputes Veto

President Reagan Oct. 15 vetoed a little-noticed bill (HR 1371) affecting interest payments by the federal government to contractors. Congress made no effort to override the veto, and the measure died.

The legislation, which Congress cleared in the session that began Oct. 1, would have amended the Contract Disputes Act of 1978. *(Background, 1978 Almanac p. 205)*

The bill made clear that interest the government was required to pay to contractors on claims in excess of $50,000 would begin running the date such claims were submitted. Claims were submitted when contractors incurred unexpected expenses and a dispute arose over who should bear the cost. Interest was paid only to claimants who prevailed in such disputes.

The vetoed bill also would have changed the 1978 act by requiring the Treasury secretary to set interest rates to be paid contractors. The secretary had such authority under PL 92-41, but that law pertained to the Renegotiation Board, which was terminated in 1979. The comptroller general of the United States had urged Congress to pass legislation clarifying the Treasury secretary's authority.

The Interest Dispute

The House passed HR 1371 by voice vote June 1, 1981.

The Senate Governmental Affairs Committee reported the bill Sept. 24, 1982, with an amendment clarifying that the period for which interest was payable for an approved claim would begin from the date the contracting officer received the claim. There was no written report.

The House Judiciary Committee, in reporting HR 1371 May 18, 1981 (H Rept 97-47), said the 1978 law already provided that submission of a claim was the starting point for interest to begin to run.

The committee acknowledged some agencies disagreed with this interpretation, but it said those agencies were misreading the 1978 law.

In his Oct. 15 veto message, however, Reagan insisted that current law required interest to begin only from the date a claim was certified, or deemed to be accurate. *(Veto message text, p. 30-E)*

Reagan said he had no quarrel with the language in the bill giving the Treasury secretary authority to set interest rates on contractors' claims.

But the president objected to the Senate-added language requiring interest to begin from the time a claim was submitted, without regard to the certification date.

Reagan said the provision was inconsistent with the 1978 law's goal of discouraging "the submission of inflated claims against the government by requiring contractors to certify that their claims are made in good faith and are accurate and complete to the best of their knowledge.

"By permitting interest to run from the date a claim is submitted, instead of from the date of certification, as current law provides, HR 1371 could result in a large increase in governmental obligations without any corresponding benefits to the claims resolution process," he said. ∎

D.C. Federal Payment

Congress Oct. 1 cleared for President Reagan legislation (S 2457 — PL 97-334) authorizing a $361 million federal payment to the District of Columbia for fiscal 1983.

The payment authorization, up from $336.6 million in fiscal 1982, was intended to compensate the city for revenue losses and operating costs associated with its role as the nation's capital, such as the property taxes foregone on federal buildings and grounds.

The federal payment authorized in S 2457 was the level requested by President Reagan.

The bill was reported May 28 by the Senate Governmental Affairs Committee (S Rept 97-471) and passed by the Senate by voice vote June 21.

The House District of Columbia Committee May 13 reported a companion measure (HR 5595 — H Rept 97-512), and the full House passed that bill Aug. 12 by a 279-122 vote. *(Vote 261, p. 78-H)*

The House subsequently adopted the Senate bill number, and House-Senate conferees worked out minor differences between the two bills. The conference report (H Rept 97-931) was agreed to by both chambers in the session that began Oct. 1, clearing the bill for the president. ∎

Capitol Historical Society

The Senate Dec. 21 passed and sent to President Reagan a bill (HR 4491 — PL 97-447) exempting from District of Columbia sales taxes the U.S. Capitol Historical Society's sales on the Capitol grounds.

The House Dec. 13 had approved the bill clarifying that the non-profit society was not subject to the sales tax, and that the Capitol, the site of the sales, was not within the District's jurisdiction.

"In providing this exemption for the society, it is in no way the committee's intent to establish a precedent regarding the tax status of the other federally chartered organizations or institutions operating in the District of Columbia," said Sen. Charles McC. Mathias Jr., R-Md., chairman of the Governmental Affairs Subcommittee on the District of Columbia.

The bill grew out of a dispute between the District and the society, which since 1964 had run a souvenir stand in the Capitol. The District in 1981 sued the organization for nearly $750,000 in back sales taxes. The United States countersued, arguing that as a federal instrumentality, the society was not subject to state or local taxes.

The U.S. District Court for the District of Columbia ruled in favor of the federal government Sept. 3, 1982. The city appealed Nov. 4.

The District opposed the legislation on the grounds that the city could lose millions of dollars in tax revenue if such tax exemptions became widespread.

But members of Congress were incensed at the city's attempts to tax an entity operating on the very grounds of the Capitol. "The District of Columbia government has been ill advised to try to impose its sales tax as though the society were a normal commercial institution operating on private property," said Barber B. Conable Jr., R-N.Y., when the House passed the bill on Dec. 13.

HR 4491 was reported March 5 by the House Judiciary Committee (H Rept 97-445). ∎

Uniform Relocation Act

The Senate Aug. 5 approved legislation to reform a law governing the relocation of individuals and businesses displaced by federal projects, but the House failed to act on the bill.

The Uniform Relocation Assistance bill (S 2363 — S Rept 97-487) was reported July 1 by the Senate Governmental Affairs Committee and passed by the Senate by voice vote Aug. 5.

A companion House measure (HR 6171) died in the House Public Works and Transportation Committee.

S 2363 was "designed to establish a policy of fair and equitable treatment for persons displaced by federally funded programs," said David Durenberger, R-Minn., chairman of the Governmental Affairs Subcommittee on Intergovernmental Relations.

Durenberger said the bill made more than 40 changes in the present law, the Uniform Relocation Act of 1970. They included expanding the act's scope to cover persons displaced by rehabilitation and demolition projects by the Department of Housing and Urban Development (HUD); consolidating the regulations governing the act; authorizing a payment of up to $10,000 for displaced small businesses and non-profit organizations; and making several management revisions.

The bill raised the ceiling on moving payments to compensate for inflation, leaving the amount up to local officials. It also changed the formula for subsidizing the rents of displaced persons to reflect a person's ability to pay, although it lowered the total payment ceiling from $4,000 to $3,000.

S 2363 would have saved approximately $8 million annually, according to the Congressional Budget Office. ∎

NOAA Authorization Fails

Congress failed to clear a two-year reauthorization bill (HR 6324) for the atmospheric, climatic and ocean pollution activities of the National Oceanic and Atmospheric Administration (NOAA).

The House approved the legislation Aug. 17 by a 340-65 vote. *(Vote 273, p. 80-H)*

The Senate passed an amended version in the session that began Dec. 16, but the changes it adopted were never considered by the House, which adjourned Dec. 21.

The bill would have authorized $544 million in fiscal 1983 and $576.5 million in fiscal 1984 for all NOAA research activities and selected operations.

More than half of the increase over Reagan's request was earmarked to continue two polar-orbiting weather satellites; the administration had wanted to fund only one.

The bill also authorized more funding than Reagan requested for research on atmospheric and ocean pollution, the Great Lakes, weather modification and solar flares.

Although the authorization never cleared, Congress provided funding for the NOAA activities under the second continuing appropriations resolution (H J Res 631 — PL 97-377) for fiscal 1983. *(Story, p. 238)*

The House Merchant Marine and Fisheries Committee reported HR 6324 on May 17 and the House Science and Technology Committee followed suit May 18 (H Rept 97-557, Pts. I and II). ∎

Congress Cool to Reagan's 'New Federalism'

President Reagan used his first State of the Union address Jan. 26 to unveil a sweeping proposal to transform the federal system, but his "new federalism" got a cold shoulder from Congress and the states.

In fact, administration attempts to translate the president's proposal into specific legislation bogged down completely during talks with state and local officials and interest groups. No legislation was submitted by Reagan, and Congress made no effort to initiate its own.

Reagan unveiled a broad outline of the new federalism package Jan. 26, making it the centerpiece of his first State of the Union address. *(State of the Union, p. 3-E)*

The federalism proposal, involving a phased swap of some $47 billion in programs and revenues between Washington and the states beginning in fiscal 1984, in effect was a request that Congress dismantle much of the domestic empire it had built up over decades.

Reagan's proposal called for a dramatic shift of some 40 social, transportation and community development programs — and revenues to help pay for them in the early phase — to states.

Reagan also proposed a "swap" of the three principal welfare programs for the poor. The federal government would assume the full costs of the Medicaid health program, while states took over food stamps and Aid to Families with Dependent Children (AFDC).

"In a single stroke, we will be accomplishing a realignment that will end cumbersome administration and spiraling costs at the federal level while we ensure these programs will be more responsive to both the people they are meant to help and the people who pay for them," Reagan said.

Administration officials said details of the plan had not been been set, pending consultations with congressional, state and local leaders.

Governors Cautious

The initial reaction from governors and county officials was cautiously supportive, but mayors — particularly from big cities — were more wary.

"You have to judge whether the glass is half full or half empty. But the president has come a long way," said Gov. Richard A. Snelling, R-Vt., chairman of the National Governors' Association (NGA).

The welfare swap was viewed as a mixed blessing by the governors. Many had advocated one part of the swap, the transfer of Medicaid costs to the federal government. States currently paid part of the costs of the program of health care for the poor.

But, along with the Medicaid shift, governors had sought another shift in a direction opposite that of the Reagan plan — giving welfare costs as well to the federal government, in exchange for state assumption of costs in areas such as education.

"Most governors would prefer that the national government took AFDC, food stamps and Medicaid and give us an even amount in programs of a more everyday concern like sewers," said Gov. Lamar Alexander, R-Tenn.

As for the the other part of Reagan's federalism proposal — the transfer of a broad array of federal programs to the states, to be funded at the outset by a new federal trust fund and eventually by the states' own revenues — governors expressed concern about the fate of the less

wealthy states. Under the proposal, states beginning in 1991 would be on their own to raise funds for the programs or pare the government services and benefits.

Both Snelling and Alexander stressed that the transfer would have to be accompanied by a mechanism to ensure federal support for states with limited capacities to raise more money through excise or other taxes.

"The president's proposal has no chance of getting to first base unless it takes into account the differences between rich and poor states," Alexander said.

Snelling, along with Sen. David Durenburger, R-Minn., suggested that the federalism plan should include some form of long-range revenue adjustment to help equalize fiscal disparities among states. But budget director David A. Stockman indicated that the administration was reluctant to go along with such an effort.

Local Interests

A key question for city and county officials was whether their interests would be protected under the new plan. Under the proposal, funds that had been provided to localities by federal categorical programs would first be converted into a single huge grant to states. By 1991, federal support would be ended, and states could provide money as they chose.

Administration officials argued that the proposal contained guarantees against a cutoff of funds to cities and counties. During the transition period, there would be "pass-through" provisions requiring states to give some of the money to lower levels of government.

After 1991, the officials predicted, the political power of urban voters in the state legislatures would make sure that the big cities were not unfairly deprived of funds. "There is no reason to believe that by 1991 the states won't be just as sensitive to their cities' needs as the federal government is now," said presidential counselor Edwin Meese III.

New York City Mayor Edward I. Koch described the provisions requiring states to turn over funds to cities as "inadequate." But James Seeley, a lobbyist for Los Angeles, was hopeful that his city would be treated well in the distribution of funds by the state Legislature. "It could end up as a plus for us, because we're obviously closer to Sacramento than we are to Washington," Seeley said.

The welfare swap held out benefits for counties, observed Bernard F. Hillenbrand, executive director of the National Association of Counties, because it would give many counties control as well as financial responsibility over welfare programs.

In many large urban states, Hillenbrand explained, counties administered welfare payments and paid a share of the costs. Yet they had to follow federal rules in running the programs. "We've had no policy input into those programs for two decades. Until now, all we did was pay. Under the new basis, we might have something to say about it," he said.

The Original Plan

Welfare Swap

Reagan proposed terminating AFDC and food stamps

as federal programs, and providing for a complete federal takeover of Medicaid.

Beginning in fiscal 1984, AFDC and food stamps would cease to exist as federal programs, thus essentially ending federal income assistance programs for people who were not either elderly or disabled. At the same time, the federal government would begin paying all Medicaid costs.

According to documents released by the administration, the swap would be financially advantageous to states. In fiscal 1984, the documents said, AFDC and food stamps would cost the states $16.5 billion. In return, they would save $19.1 billion in Medicaid costs.

Those state savings would grow, the administration maintained, until by fiscal 1987 the states would be spending only $17.6 billion on welfare while saving $25.4 billion on Medicaid.

However, those figures were based on very specific assumptions that cast the savings for states in the best light. According to Office of Management and Budget (OMB) spokesman Edwin L. Dale, the fiscal 1984 estimates for the cost of AFDC and food stamps assumed enactment of some $4 billion in cuts before transfer of the programs.

AFDC and food stamps cost about $19.5 billion in fiscal 1982, $3 billion more than what the administration projected they would cost two years later.

By contrast, the estimates for Medicaid costs assumed continuation of existing policy without cuts.

Snelling said NGA estimates showed the swap would be unfavorable to the states by some $3 billion.

Another major unanswered question about the swap was whether states would remain under some sort of federal standards for their own welfare programs. Critics of the proposal worried that some states would use their savings from Medicaid for non-welfare purposes, leaving the former recipients with little or no aid.

Administration documents said the proposal would include maintenance-of-effort provisions requiring that current welfare recipients not have their basic benefits reduced while the states took over.

But Snelling said the states would reject "grandfathering" provisions requiring them to carry all current recipients. "If the notion is that there will be no removal from the rolls, that cannot happen. We won't say that we will pay for welfare and food stamps and you will tell us who to give them to," he said.

Program Turnback

The other part of the federalism proposal was far more complex, involving transition provisions, "super revenue sharing," a new federal trust fund and a graduated reduction in federal excise taxes.

The transition was to begin in fiscal 1984 with the establishment of a trust fund financed by revenues from existing federal excise taxes — part of the oil windfall profits tax ($16.7 billion), taxes on tobacco ($2.7 billion), alcohol ($6.1 billion), telephones ($.3 billion) and a portion of the tax on gasoline ($2.2 billion). In all, the trust fund would have revenues estimated at $28 billion in fiscal 1984.

Trust fund money would be fully available to states during the 1984-87 period. States would be allocated trust fund money in the same proportion as they got federal money from the various categorical grant programs being replaced during the period 1979-81.

On top of that formula, however, there would be one further adjustment: Part of the trust fund money would be used to compensate states that had lost funds because of the Medicaid-AFDC-food stamp swap.

States could elect to use their funds in two ways during 1984-1987:

● Those that wanted to continue to participate in the existing categorical programs could do so. Their trust fund money would be used to reimburse the federal agencies that gave them the categorical grants.

● Alternately, states could begin to receive their trust fund money in the form of a single federal grant. They could use the money much as they pleased, although some of it would have to be turned over to local governments. They would have to turn over all the money for programs that had gone directly to local governments in the past, such as mass transit; 15 percent of funds for most of the other programs would have to be given to the localities.

The super revenue sharing funds would replace 40 or more existing categorical programs. The administration estimated that the combined value of those programs would be $30.2 billion in fiscal 1984.

The administration specifically excluded certain programs from turnback. It said that compensatory education for the disadvantaged, handicapped and higher education, the Head Start preschool program, interstate highways and certain regulatory programs definitely would not be part of the proposal.

Combining the two proposals, the administration estimated that state and local governments would incur new costs of $46.7 billion in fiscal 1984. In return, they would receive savings from Medicaid and money from the trust fund totaling $47.1 billion.

The turnback proposal would enter a new phase in fiscal 1988. At that point, the remaining programs would be terminated, and states would begin to receive money only through the trust fund.

The trust fund money then would start to dry up. Each year, federal excise taxes and the trust fund would be reduced by 25 percent. Under existing law, the oil windfall profits tax already was scheduled to begin phasing out in 1988. *(1980 Almanac p. 473)*

States would be free to raise their own taxes to make up the difference. The federal excise taxes would be eliminated after 1991, as would the trust fund money for states. From then on, states would be on their own.

Winners and Losers

The biggest outstanding question about the new federalism proposal was whether it could be designed to avoid great regional disparities that would hurt some states severely and give bonuses to others. Even accepting the administration's prediction that the welfare swap would not hurt states in the aggregate, it was obvious that the proposal had substantial potential for redirecting federal aid among different states.

Administration officials emphasized that they wanted to design the new system to prevent regional differences. "The program is completely neutral on that front," Stockman told reporters.

Without the compensating money from the trust fund that the Reagan proposals envisioned, the Medicaid-AFDC-food stamp swap was likely to yield a major redirection of federal aid. In general, the swap would help big industrial states with generous Medicaid programs, and hurt poorer Southern states that had relied heavily on food stamps.

A chart distributed by the White House showed the regional impact of the swap in fiscal 1984. By far the

biggest winner from the Medicaid savings was New York, which would give up $4 billion in Medicaid costs while assuming only $1.7 billion in AFDC and food stamps — a net savings of $2.3 billion.

Other states that would get major gains from the swap were California ($494 million), Massachusetts ($251 million), Minnesota ($299 million) and Wisconsin ($337 million).

By contrast, Mississippi could lose $184 million. Even worse off would be Florida, which faced $281 million in losses. The 13 Southern states would lose a total of $1.3 billion from the swap.

According to the chart, fund distribution from the trust fund would be altered to balance each state's gains or losses from the welfare swap. So New York would get only $789 million from the trust fund, while taking on $3.1 billion worth of programs; Mississippi would get $563 million in exchange for $379 million in programs.

Medicaid Standards

Another troublesome question involved the standards for Medicaid assistance under total federal control.

States currently set their own standards, which varied widely. All states had to provide aid to recipients of other welfare programs. Thirty also gave Medicaid to other "medically needy" low-income persons. States also differed greatly on the scope of services provided to recipients.

That disparity posed a major problem for the design of a national Medicaid system. If a single national standard were set, presumably it would be somewhere in the middle, between the generous standard of New York and the more restrictive rules of Mississippi.

That would be a bonus for poor people in Mississippi, since many would become newly eligible for medical assistance. But it could harm people in New York, since many who had benefited from the state's liberal standards would lose their Medicaid.

Of course, New York could continue to provide medical assistance to all those who had gotten Medicaid in the past. But instead of sharing the costs for all previous recipients with the federal government, the state would have to pay the medical care costs for all those above the national standard on its own. So all the state's savings from the swap could be lost.

Reagan vowed in his speech that "this administration has not and will not turn its back on America's elderly or America's poor." But critics of the proposal warned that it could seriously hurt poor people who depended on AFDC and food stamps.

Administration officials said the proposal would include provisions to ensure that the poor were not cut off by the states. Meese also said that changes in social mores over the preceding 20 years would prevent states from abandoning the poor.

But some major changes in the programs under state control seemed likely. With many state budgets under tight fiscal constraints, there could be a strong tendency to use some of the Medicaid savings for non-welfare programs.

"The pressure to shift substantial sums to other state functions with more powerful constituencies will be overwhelming," argued Robert Greenstein of the Center on Budget and Policy Priorities.

Greenstein, former administrator of the Agriculture Department's Food and Nutrition Service, said no state would be able to cope with the administrative difficulties of establishing its own food stamp program. Most would probably add the value of food stamps to welfare checks, he

said. That would end the unique nature of the food stamp program, which alone among welfare programs was available to all those who were poor, even if they were not members of families with dependent children, elderly or disabled.

Greenstein and others warned that welfare reductions in Southern states would spur renewed migration of poor people to states like New York and California that kept more generous benefits.

Revisions Promised

After months of negotiations with state and local officials, Reagan announced July 13 that he would send Congress his long-delayed new federalism legislation by the end of the month.

But the announcement proved premature. Although the administration disclosed some alterations in the new federalism proposal, no legislation ever went to Capitol Hill in 1982.

The thrust of Reagan's revised plan remained the same: Responsibility for AFDC and at least 30 other federal programs would be shifted to state and local governments.

The transfer of almost $40 billion in costs would be offset in part by lifting most state responsibility for Medicaid. In addition, state and local governments would get money from a new, temporary trust fund to replace the aid they currently got from grant programs that would be eliminated.

The program transfers would begin in fiscal 1984. The package would be phased in over eight years.

Reagan said in making his announcement before a meeting of the National Association of Counties in Baltimore, Md., that "significant changes" had been made since the State of the Union outline.

Neither the president nor the White House disclosed many details, but they did point to some specific changes.

Meeting State, Local Complaints

The biggest difference was that Reagan's original proposal to transfer the food stamp program to the states along with AFDC was dropped. Concerns about the costs of such welfare programs had overshadowed negotiations over the package.

In response to complaints by local officials, the administration included in the revised plan a requirement that local governments be guaranteed the same share of aid passed through from states that localities traditionally had received from direct federal grants.

The administration also moved to allay fears of state and local officials that grant programs would be subjected to budget cuts before the transfer began.

Under the revised package, the White House pledged to base the total of the new trust fund's budget on the total amount Congress approved for fiscal 1983 to fund the programs that eventually would be eliminated by the "turnback" proposal.

The scope of the "turnback" — involving the non-welfare grant programs that would be eliminated — was reduced from that envisioned at the time of Reagan's state of the union address. The administration dropped its call to eliminate several programs, including Urban Development Action Grants; aid for migrant health and black lung clinics; Women, Infants and Children grants; Interstate highway transfers; and some other highway programs.

The White House in July released the following list — which it said still was not final — of programs included in the proposed turnback:

Education and Training

Vocational rehabilitation
Vocational adult education
State block grants for education and rehabilitation
Comprehensive Employment and Training Act
Work Incentive

Energy Assistance

Low-income home energy assistance

Social, Health and Nutrition Services

Child Nutrition
Child welfare, foster care and adoption assistance
Runaway youth, child abuse
Social services block grant
Legal Services
Community services block grant
Prevention block grant
Alcohol, drug abuse and mental health block grant
Primary care health care centers
Maternal and child health block grant
Primary care research and development
Family planning

Transportation

Highways:
- Urban
- Secondary
- Appalachian highways

Urban Mass Transit Administration:
- Construction
- Operating

Community Development and Facilities

Water and Sewer:
- Grants
- Loans

Community Facilities Loans
Community Development Block Grants
Waste water treatment grants ∎

Hart Building Opens

The new Hart Senate Office Building finally opened its doors Nov. 22, 10 years after the project was conceived. *(1981 Almanac p. 393, 1972 Almanac p. 691)*

Plagued by cost overruns and considerable criticism, the building was named after the late Sen. Philip A. Hart, D-Mich. (1959-76). It was the third office building for senators, and had 50 office suites.

Critics charged that although Congress had spent most of the past two years slicing federal programs, fiscal austerity was not applied to the new structure. With a price tag of nearly $137.7 million, it was the nation's most expensive federal building.

A bill (HR 6666) increasing the authorization for the Madison Building of the Library of Congress to $138.8 million, which would have made it the most expensive building, did not clear Congress in 1982. *(Story, p. 540)*

The Hart building would have been even more expensive if Congress had not capped spending in 1979 when the estimate ballooned to $175 million.

First authorized in 1972, the building had often been a source of political embarrassment for senators as costs skyrocketed and representatives, who had built expensive suites for themselves in the $135 million Rayburn building, labeled Hart a palace.

The controversy continued as the opening day approached.

On Aug. 17, the Senate voted to stop construction of a $736,000 gymnasium in the new building. The 98-0 vote came on an amendment by Majority Leader Howard H. Baker Jr., R-Tenn., to the resolution (H J Res 520) to increase the national debt ceiling. "We're going to kill this snake once and for all," Baker told reporters. Baker's amendment did not save money earmarked for the new gym; it simply assured that the funds would be used for other items in the new building. *(Vote 330, p. 54-S; debt limit, p. 44)*

Earlier, on Aug. 10, the Senate had killed an amendment by William Proxmire, D-Wis., to prohibit the spending of $736,400 to furnish the gymnasium. Proxmire complained the Senate already had two gymnasiums and did not need a third in the Hart building.

The main defense of the gym came from J. Bennett Johnston, D-La., who said it also could serve as a hearing room.

Proxmire's amendment, offered to the fiscal 1982 supplemental appropriations bill (HR 6863), was ruled out of order and his appeal from the ruling was tabled (killed) on a 50-48 vote. *(Vote 300, p. 50-S; supplemental appropriations, p. 219)*

A Look Inside

Despite the criticism, Capitol Architect George M. White said the one-million-square-foot building was built for "as little as possible."

White, who acknowledged that structures built to house politicians were routinely criticized, said that if the building had cost $100 million, "we'd still get criticized. We might as well spend a little more and get it right."

The Hart building's predecessors, the Russell and Dirksen buildings, were finished, respectively, in 1909 at a cost of $8.4 million and in 1958 for $24.2 million. Under the new arrangement, 14 senators had space in Dirksen and 36 in Russell.

The nine-story Hart building, located northeast of the Capitol on Constitution Avenue, was constructed of white, Vermont marble with long, vertical windows indented in its sides. A spacious atrium, with a Tennessee pink marble floor, was designed to provide natural light to every suite of offices.

White called the structure "a contemporary design based on classical proportions...I like it. It will be an exciting building to work in. It should be the first choice of senators."

Each of the 50 office suites contained about 5,700 square feet of office space, White said, compared to about 2,400 square feet in existing offices. In addition to quarters for senators, the new building provided about 70,000 square feet of offices for committee staffs and a "multimedia" hearing room with broadcast coverage facilities built in.

Each office suite had space on two floors with a con-

Madison Building Funding

The House voted 188-186 Sept. 9 to increase to $138.8 million the authorization for the new Madison Building of the Library of Congress, which would have made it the most expensive government building ever. The vote was 186-186 when the roll call ended, but House leaders rounded up two more votes to pass the bill (HR 6666). However, it never made it through the Senate before the end of the session. *(Vote 302, p. 90-H)*

Although the Madison Building had already been completed, the bill increased the construction authorization by $8.1 million. The additional money was necessary to pay claims made by the contractor. The Senate's new Hart Office Building, which opened after the Nov. 2 elections, had been limited by Congress to a cost ceiling of $137.7 million.

necting staircase. This arrangement was made, White explained, to allow senators' personal offices to have 16-foot ceilings. The higher ceilings, in about 15 percent of the building, were designed "to capture a feeling of dignity." Offices in the Russell building had 16-foot ceilings. Unlike the older office buildings, there were no separate entrances for senators to their offices.

Originally, the Hart offices were to have had wood paneling, but that plan was scrapped in 1979 when the Senate became cost conscious. Also canceled was a rooftop restaurant for senators on the ninth floor and special switches for senators to dim their office lights.

Space remained unfinished for both the restaurant and the gymnasium. But in early 1983, the Senate found $8 million to buy modular furniture, which had been canceled to save money. The $8 million came from the unspent portion of a three-year old legislative branch appropriation.

The Senate also found a way to get the $400,000 needed to fill the building's huge atrium with a stabile designed by Alexander Calder just before his 1976 death. Former Sen. Nicholas F. Brady, R-N.J. (1982), agreed to raise the money, which also had been cut from the building's budget.

Background

The Hart building was first authorized as an extension to the Dirksen building in 1972 at an estimated cost of $48 million. White said that he spun that number out of his head only two weeks after being asked what such a building might cost.

He said the first meaningful estimate was $85 million, a figure that came after the design was completed in 1974. By 1978, the estimated cost was up to $135 million. But later that year, when the Senate tried to add money to cover the increase to an appropriations bill, the House refused. Normally, the House and Senate deferred to each other on the affairs of only one chamber. *(1978 Almanac p. 71)*

In July 1979, a consulting firm estimated the final cost at $175 million, although White disputed the estimate. After eliminating such items as the wood paneling, the Senate voted a total of $142.6 million for the building. *(1979 Almanac p. 227)*

But the House still balked, insisting that the total be no more than $137.7 million, a ceiling that became law (PL 96-69).

Senate TV Bill Died

Although Majority Leader Howard H. Baker Jr., R-Tenn., made television and radio coverage of the Senate his first legislative priority when he assumed the post in January 1981, he was unable to persuade his colleagues to go along.

A resolution (S Res 436) providing a plan for TV and radio coverage of Senate proceedings never came to a floor vote because of strong opposition, and it died with the end of the 97th Congress. The plan had been approved by the Senate Rules Committee July 21 on a 7-5 party line vote.

Earlier, the Senate had considered, but not approved, another broadcast resolution (S Res 20) reported by the Rules Committee in 1981. That bill fell prey to a filibuster led by Russell B. Long, D-La. *(1981 Almanac, p. 391)*

The House had had complete television and radio coverage of its proceedings since 1979, but the Senate had never allowed it. Both chambers continued to prohibit the taking of still pictures by news photographers.

Senate Floor Action

Baker had brought S Res 20 to the Senate floor in February. The resolution allowed continuous coverage of the Senate chamber by both television cameras and radio microphones. It left the details — such as when coverage would begin and who would control the cameras — up to the Rules Committee.

Long led the Democratic opposition to the plan. Democrats favored an alternative plan permitting only radio coverage, or perhaps part-time television coverage, of Senate deliberations.

The Senate began preliminary debate on S Res 20 Feb. 2. The first important action came Feb. 4, when the Senate voted 92-3 to consider the resolution. *(Vote 3, 2-S)*

Long argued that televising the Senate would be a "very great mistake and a net minus to the Senate." He said senators would give more frequent and longer speeches and that television would attract senators to the floor when they should be attending committee sessions.

Other Democrats argued that the television plan would be too costly.

Baker and Rules Committee Chairman Charles McC. Mathias Jr., R-Md., disputed Long's argument.

"I do not think we are 100 moths fascinated by the candle of television," Mathias said.

"Whether we like it or not, we are what we are," Baker said. "We are elected by our constituents to serve them according to our talents, our disposition, our convictions ... We are a composite cross-section of this nation commissioned to debate the public's business in a public way."

Baker was unsuccessful in his efforts to cut off Long's filibuster. His first cloture motion against the filibuster failed by a 47-51 vote April 20. The count for the cloture motion was 13 shy of the 60 votes needed to cut off debate, and four short of the 51 votes needed to approve the resolution. *(Vote 81, p 18-S)*

Before the Senate could vote on a second cloture motion, Baker reached a compromise with the Democrats that sent the proposal back to the Rules Committee for rewriting. By a 95-1 vote, the Senate April 21 adopted an amendment to S Res 20 offered jointly by Baker and Minority Leader Robert C. Byrd, D-W.Va. *(Vote 83, p. 18-S)*

The amendment gave the Rules Committee 60 days to draft a complete plan for broadcast coverage of debates. It

required Rules to seek the Senate's final approval of all aspects of the plan before it could be carried out. In addition, it struck from the resolution a requirement that the Senate broadcasts provide complete gavel-to-gavel coverage of the chamber's actions.

In an earlier action April 20, the Senate rejected 46-51 an attempt by Jennings Randolph, D-W.Va., to tack onto the measure a requirement that senators vote from their desks. *(Vote 82, p. 18-S)*

Committee Report

The Rules Committee reported a new broadcast resolution (S Res 436) July 21. The Senate had acted June 15 to extend the 60-day deadline for action set by S Res 20.

In reporting S Res 436 (S Rept 97-506), the Rules Committee said coverage would not require any changes in existing Senate rules, including those controlling voting and length of speeches.

The committee said television and radio coverage would be gavel-to-gavel to provide a complete documentary, free from editorial analysis. Only the senator actually speaking would be televised. The cameras would not pan the chamber or show the reactions of senators to what was said.

The report said Senate employees would operate the cameras by remote control. Pictures and sound would be provided free to news organizations. Tapes could not be used for political or commercial purposes.

Six cameras would be installed in the Senate chamber. No new lights would be needed, but the wattage of existing lights would be increased. To pay for coverage, the resolution would authorize spending of $3.5 million.

When the panel marked up the resolution July 21, Wendell H. Ford, D-Ky., holding the proxies of the four other committee Democrats, tried to delay action until after a commission studying Senate rules issued its report in 1983. Ford was defeated 5-7 on a party-line vote.

The vote was identical on a Ford amendment to allow only radio, not television, coverage.

In minority views appended to the report, the Democrats said their main reason for opposing television coverage was cost, which they said probably would be closer to $5 million.

The effect of television coverage on the operation of the Senate should be studied, they continued, while radio coverage, which would be relatively inexpensive ($54,000), should be implemented immediately.

They argued that the presence of television could lead to more, longer and less relevant speeches, as well as more posturing by senators. ∎

Federal Employee Pay

A 4 percent pay raise for federal employees went into effect Oct. 1, when Congress accepted President Reagan's recommendation to hold the annual increase to that figure.

No legislative action was necessary for the pay hike to take effect for about 1.4 million white-collar federal workers. But either house of Congress had authority to veto Reagan's proposal by Sept. 30.

Congressional salaries had been linked to federal employee pay since 1975. But Congress, in the first continuing appropriations resolution for fiscal 1983, blocked the raise for its own members. *(Continuing resolution, p. 225)*

Instead, Congress in December voted to raise the pay of House members 15 percent, to $69,000 from $60,662.50. Although senators' salaries remained at the lower figure, the Senate voted to eliminate from its rules a provision that would have limited the outside earnings of senators beginning in 1983. *(Congressional pay, p. 544)*

Reagan Recommendation

Reagan followed Congress' lead Aug. 26 when he recommended the 4 percent pay raise for federal employees.

In his Feb. 8 budget, Reagan proposed a 5 percent increase for federal civilian workers. But Congress reduced it to 4 percent in the fiscal 1983 budget resolution (S Con Res 92). *(Budget resolution, p. 186)*

Congress repeated its intent to allow a 4 percent in-

Office, Travel Funds

While the House was noisily voting to raise its pay, members' office accounts and travel allowances were being increased in more quiet fashion. *(Pay raise, p. 544)*

On Dec. 9, the House Administration Committee increased members' office accounts by 10 percent and travel allowances by 15 percent effective Jan. 3, 1983. The changes did not require full House approval.

Before the increase, each representative got $47,300 a year as his base allowance for official expenses. The money was used primarily for stationery and office equipment. In 1983, this office account increased to $52,000.

For travel within the United States, each member got an allowance based on how far his district was from the capital. Before the increase, members who lived less than 500 miles away got 30 cents per mile. Those who lived more than 3,000 miles away got 18 cents per mile, with several categories in between. In January 1983, the range became 21 to 35 cents a mile.

The adjustments were based on higher prices for office equipment and for air fare, a committee spokesman said. The last increase came in May 1981. *(1981 Almanac p. 390)*

Also on Dec. 9, the panel made clear that members could not be reimbursed for hotel stays in the same city or town as their legal residence. The action affected those who did not maintain a home in their districts.

Members still would be able to be reimbursed for staying in hotels in their districts that were distant from their hometowns. Whether the distance was great enough to warrant reimbursement was up to the individual member.

Senate Accounts. Senators paid for travel expenses out of their office accounts, which in 1982 ranged from $33,000 to $143,000, based on a combination of state population and distance from Washington.

Effective Jan. 1, 1983, those accounts were increased by 10 percent, according to the Senate Rules Committee staff. The change, the first adjustment since 1979, was included in the first fiscal 1983 continuing appropriations resolution (PL 97-276), which was enacted in October. *(Story, p. 225)*

crease in the budget reconciliation conference report (HR 6955 — H Rept 97-759) adopted Aug. 18. The report said if Reagan submitted a pay adjustment of less than 4 percent and either House vetoed the proposal, the pay raise would be 4 percent. *(Reconciliation, p. 199)*

Reagan's proposal was far less than the 18.47 percent raise that a survey found would be needed to keep pace with pay rates in the private sector. The salary study was made by the president's pay advisers, a panel consisting of Labor Secretary Raymond J. Donovan, Office of Management and Budget Director David A. Stockman and Office of Personnel Management (OPM) Director Donald Devine.

Under the Federal Pay Comparability Act of 1970, federal white-collar wages must be annually adjusted to achieve comparability with similar private sector jobs. *(Congress and the Nation Vol. III, p. 454)*

But Reagan noted that the act allowed him to propose an alternative "if such action is appropriate because of economic conditions."

Recent presidents had not called for the full increase suggested in the comparability report. In 1981, workers received a 4.8 percent raise, although the pay board said a 15.1 percent hike was necessary for comparability. *(1981 Almanac p. 396)*

The salary hike did not affect wages for U.S. postal workers or the estimated 500,000 federal blue-collar workers, whose pay was adjusted separately, OPM officials said. ■

Congressional Tax Breaks

A controversial 1981 provision providing generous tax breaks for members of Congress was repealed July 15 when the lawmakers cleared an "urgent" supplemental spending bill for fiscal 1982 (HR 6685 — PL 97-216). *(Story, p. 205)*

Later in the year a pay raise for House members and removal of limits on senators' outside earnings were passed as part of the second fiscal 1983 continuing resolution (H J Res 631 — PL 97-377). *(Story, pp. 544, 238)*

The urgent supplemental limited to $3,000 a year business-related tax deductions that could be claimed by individual members of Congress for Washington, D.C., living expenses. A more generous tax deduction had been approved on the last day of the session in 1981. The 1981 actions were intended to enable members to deduct from their income taxes more of the expenses they incurred while in Washington. *(1981 Almanac pp. 400, 290)*

According to Treasury Department regulations approved Jan. 13, 1982, those more generous provisions allowed members to deduct $75 a day for each "congressional day" in a given year, without having to substantiate their expenses with receipts or be in Washington on those days. They could deduct more if expenses, such as rent or depreciation on a Washington home, were documented.

The new regulations translated into a 1981 deduction of at least $19,200 for senators and $19,650 for House members. The numbers were different for the two chambers because the House met more days in 1981. Previous law allowed members an automatic deduction of $3,000 a year for their Washington expenses. So the new legislation provided an additional deduction of at least $16,200 for senators and $16,650 for House members in 1981.

Repeal Efforts

The more generous tax rules provoked a raft of unfavorable publicity for members of Congress as taxpayers flooded Capitol Hill and the Internal Revenue Service (IRS) with angry letters and phone calls protesting the members' tax treatment.

The outcry prompted the Senate to debate repeal as part of the fiscal 1982 continuing resolution (H J Res 409 — PL 97-161). *(Story, p. 229)*

During debate, senators went on record in favor of lower salaries, tougher tax deduction rules and public disclosure of tax returns for members of Congress, but then on March 31, under heavy pressure from the Republican leadership, the Senate reversed itself and agreed to kill amendments restricting pay and tax deductions.

Passage of the resolution with the amendments would have forced a conference with the House that probably could not have been completed in time to prevent a lapse in funding authority. The deadline for final approval of the resolution was midnight March 31, when the preceding continuing resolution (H J Res 370 — PL 97-92) expired. The new bill simply extended the funding levels in PL 97-92 through Sept. 30, the end of the fiscal year. *(PL 97-92, 1981 Almanac p. 329)*

Senate acceptance of the House-passed version, and President Reagan's subsequent signature, prevented a shutdown of seven government departments.

However, the controversy over congressional pay had threatened to prevent final action on the resolution before the deadline.

The key Senate amendment, offered by William L. Armstrong, R-Colo., would have restored the $3,000 limit on business-related tax deductions claimed by members.

On four separate roll-call votes, the Senate affirmed its support for Armstrong's amendment. Armstrong said the new rules gave an unfair advantage to members of Congress. He argued that Congress should return the law to the way it was before repeal of the rule and then start thinking about rewriting the regulations that applied to members' taxes.

Assistant Majority Leader Ted Stevens, R-Alaska, defended the increased deductions as compensation for the pain suffered by senators in having to live in the nation's capital. "I know of no town that has a worse crime standard, a worse set of schools, a worse circumstance to live and work in than the city of Washington," he said.

In response to Armstrong's amendment, Stevens offered an amendment to reduce salaries of members of Congress by 10 percent, beginning April 1. The amendment, which would have cut pay to $54,596.25 a year from $60,662.50, was adopted 63-36. *(Vote 75, p. 15-S)*

In addition, a Paul E. Tsongas, D-Mass., amendment to require printing of members' tax returns in the *Congressional Record* was approved 55-43. *(Vote 70, p. 14-S)*

However, the Senate rejected an amendment by Arlen Specter, R-Pa., to require members to provide substantiation for their business-related tax deductions. Specter said his amendment would treat members of Congress like other taxpayers, who must be able to prove their deductions. The amendment was rejected 37-60. *(Vote 67, p. 14-S)*

All three amendments initially approved by the Senate, however, were eventually eliminated by a technical point of order. Unwilling to reject the Armstrong amendment outright, the Senate instead found that the Armstrong amendment, and the Stevens and Tsongas amendments attached to it, constituted legislation on an appropriations bill, and was therefore out of order. The ruling of the chair against the Armstrong amendment was

upheld by a 51-48 vote. *(Vote 77, p. 16-S)*

Ironically, the Senate had voted on exactly the same parliamentary question, in the opposite way, in September 1981. At that time, the Senate overturned a ruling of the chair that Stevens' amendment to eliminate the $3,000 tax deduction limit was out of order.

The Next Round

Next, the fate of the expanded tax deductions became entangled in the urgent fiscal 1982 supplemental appropriations bill (HR 5922).

On May 27, the Senate voted 70-23 in favor of an amendment by William Proxmire, D-Wis., to restore the $3,000 annual limit on business-related tax deductions claimed by members of Congress beginning in 1982. The Appropriations Committee had voted to end the automatic $75-a-day deduction, but not to restore the $3,000 limit. *(Vote 163, p. 29-S)*

Many House members were privately reluctant to give up the increased tax deductions, which saved them several thousand dollars each in 1981 taxes. But they were unwilling to defend the tax breaks publicly, or to vote for them on the record.

So on June 9 when Patricia Schroeder, D-Colo., obtained a roll-call vote on an amendment to a motion to instruct House conferees to accept the Senate provision restoring the $3,000 limit, the outcome was assured. The amendment was adopted, 356-43. *(Vote 129, p. 38-H)*

By a closer vote of 176-218, the House rejected a motion by John T. Myers, R-Ind., to instruct the conferees to agree to eliminate the automatic $75-a-day deduction without restoring the $3,000 limit. That would have allowed members of Congress to claim whatever business-related deductions for Washington living expenses they could substantiate. *(Vote 128, p. 38-H)*

(The House Ways and Means Committee June 10 added a provision similar to the Myers proposal to a debt-limit bill (HR 6550), but another bill, minus the tax provision (HR 6595), was reported June 16 after some Democrats objected to inclusion of the tax provision. *(Debt limit, p. 44)*)

In a House-Senate conference committee June 10, the House, under heavy public pressure, accepted the provision repealing the tax breaks. But House conferees then retaliated by demanding that the Senate accept an $18,200 annual ceiling on outside income earned by senators.

The conference action unleashed a torrent of resentment and recriminations on all sides. House members angrily attacked Senate members, senators argued bitterly among themselves and just about everybody jumped on the press.

While they were forced by Schroeder's amendment to accept the Senate provision, House conferees clearly were furious with the Senate. They accused senators of hypocrisy for taking away the tax break while continuing to receive large honoraria from interest groups.

"You got a bunch of fat cats up there raking in the big bucks. They can be big statesmen because they can collect those big honoraria," said Silvio O. Conte, R-Mass.

Jake Garn, R-Utah, the most outspoken Senate opponent of restoring the $3,000 limit, responded that House members were "just as gutless" as senators on the issue. He attributed public attacks on the tax breaks to dishonest reporting by the press, which he called "a bunch of damned barracudas." Garn also lashed out at Proxmire, sponsor of the Senate provision. "You used this vehicle for political

purposes because you're running this year," he shouted.

The motion to accept the Senate tax break provision but also to limit senators' outside earnings to 30 percent of congressional pay, or about $18,200 a year, was offered by Rep. Vic Fazio, D-Calif. It was approved 10-8. The House already had that limit.

While they did not seriously consider the House proposal, Senate conferees narrowly rejected a compromise plan offered by Stevens. The amendment, defeated 10-11, would have adjusted the $3,000 limit on deductions according to the increase in consumer prices since 1952, when the limit was imposed. Under the amendment, the limit would be about $10,800 in 1982.

House-Senate Battle

When the conference report reached the House floor June 16 members approved it by voice vote, but then voted 381-29 to insist that the Senate accept the $18,200-a-year limit on honoraria and other outside earnings in return for restoration of the $3,000 limit on business-related tax deductions for Washington living expenses. *(Vote 143, p. 42-H)*

The average senator received $19,575 in honoraria in 1981. House members already had an $18,200 annual limit and generally received far less in honoraria than senators; they averaged $5,237 in 1981.

Supporters of the limit argued that the large fees for speaking engagements received by some members of Congress, especially senators, threatened the integrity of the legislative process. "I am fed up with [senators] posing for holy pictures on congressional pay and then running around collecting $60,000 in outside income," complained David R. Obey, D-Wis.

The only opposition to the limit came from the most vocal backers of restoring the $3,000 tax deduction limit, such as Schroeder. She argued that the honoraria limit, even if justifiable in the abstract, was actually just a ploy by House members who wanted to defeat the Senate's tax deduction amendment.

"I don't think anybody really believes the Senate will stand still for the honoraria limit," Schroeder said. She said the real goal of House sponsors of the limit was to pressure the Senate into a compromise on the tax deduction.

The Senate approved the conference report on HR 5922 (H Rept 97-605) June 21 by voice vote. But the bill did not clear because senators refused to accept Fazio's amendment establishing the $18,200 limit on outside income. The Senate voted 54-41 against that provision on June 22. *(Vote 191, p. 33-S)*

Faced with the Senate opposition to the outside income limit, and anxious not to delay the start of their recess, the House leadership adopted a new strategy.

HR 5922 had been threatened with a veto because it contained an expensive program to aid the ailing housing industry. That problem coupled with the fight over congressional benefits prompted the Appropriations Committee to bring to the floor a completely new bill (HR 6645).

That $4.5 billion measure included temporary funding, through July 20, for 17 agencies and programs that were in danger of shutting down because of lack of funds while the House was in recess. It did not contain the housing funds, more than 40 other parts of HR 5922 that were viewed as being less time-sensitive or the tax deduction and outside income limits.

The House passed HR 6645 by voice vote June 23, and the Senate leadership agreed to rush it through the Senate.

But the Senate refused to go along with the stripped-down "urgent interim stopgap supplemental," as Appropriations Committee Chairman Mark O. Hatfield, R-Ore., called it.

Ignoring Hatfield's plea to pass the new bill without amendment so that it could be cleared quickly and sent to the president before the House began its recess, the Senate first moved to add the Proxmire amendment restoring the $3,000-a-year limit on deductions for Washington living expenses.

Hatfield warned that accepting the Proxmire amendment would "open the floodgates" to a variety of other amendments, and said he would ask the leadership to pull the bill from the Senate calendar if the amendment passed. But the Senate rejected his motion to table the amendment by a vote of 21-76. *(Vote 195, p. 34-S)*

Richard G. Lugar, R-Ind., then moved to add the $3 billion conference version of his housing stimulus program, which the president opposed, to the Proxmire amendment. Armstrong, who had fought the housing industry "bailout" from the beginning, raised a point of order against the amendment on the grounds that it was legislation on an appropriations bill. The chair agreed with Armstrong, but Lugar appealed the ruling, and the Senate backed Lugar, rejecting the ruling of the chair by a vote of 33-66. It then adopted the Lugar amendment, 70-27. *(Votes 196, 197, p. 34-S)*

At that point — before any more amendments could be offered — Hatfield announced that the House leadership had agreed to accept the Senate version of the conference report on HR 5922, dropping the amendment limiting honoraria.

The Senate then suspended action on HR 6645, and the House — by voice vote, with only about 45 members on the floor — agreed to drop the Fazio amendment. That cleared HR 5922, and the bill was immediately sent to the White House, where it was vetoed by President Reagan June 24 because it contained a housing stimulus package. *(Veto message, p. 24-E)*

Post-Veto Action

Unable to muster the votes necessary for an override, Congress cleared a second supplemental (HR 6682), which the president vetoed June 25 complaining that it, too, was too expensive. A third bill (HR 6685), containing only the most urgently needed funding — and the $3,000 a year tax deduction limit — was passed June 24 by the House, which then left town for the Independence Day recess.

However, the White House made it clear that the House version of HR 6685 still was not acceptable to the president, and a new version was passed by the Senate June 29.

After the July 4 recess, the House went to conference with the Senate on HR 6685. A compromise (H Rept 97-632) adopted July 14 contained $5.4 billion in new spending and $5.8 billion in rescissions — plus the reinstatement of the $3,000 limit.

The Senate adopted the conference report July 15 by a 91-6 vote. The House earlier the same day had approved the report by a 389-13 vote. *(House vote 176, p. 52-H; Senate vote 214, p. 39-S)*

In January of 1983, Sen. Russell B. Long, D-La., introduced a bill (S 70) that would remove the $3,000 limit and allow members of Congress to deduct business expenses the same as any other citizen. "It simply provides equal treatment," Long said of his bill.   ∎

Congressional Pay Raise

In a break with nearly two centuries of tradition, Congress decided in 1982 to pay larger salaries to House members only while allowing senators to earn unlimited amounts in outside income, including honoraria. *(Pay history, box, p. 546)*

The unusual arrangement was included in the second fiscal 1983 continuing appropriations resolution (H J Res 631 — PL 97-377), which was cleared by Congress Dec. 20. *(Story, p. 238)*

The resolution provided a $9,138 pay raise for House members, bringing their annual salaries to $69,800 effective Dec. 18. Senators remained at an annual salary of $60,662.50 but were allowed to earn as much as they chose in outside income, including legal fees, business income and honoraria for speeches and articles. Outside earnings for representatives continued to be limited by the House rules to 30 percent of members' salaries, or $20,940. A limit on outside earned income for senators equal to 15 percent of their congressional salaries, or about $9,100, would have gone into effect Jan. 1, 1983 if the Senate had not acted to change its own rules. *(Details below)*

The continuing resolution also provided salary increases of up to 15 percent for about 32,000 senior government employees. The pay of Cabinet officers went from $69,630 a year to $80,100; senior bureaucrats went from $59,500 to up to $68,400.

The raises also affected House and Senate staffers, although their precise pay levels were set by the members for whom they worked. Senate staffers were eligible for increases, although their bosses were not. The result was the possibility that some aides could end up making more than the senators for whom they worked.

Without congressional action, members would have received an automatic 27 percent raise Dec. 18, when an earlier pay cap expired. That cap had been included in the first fiscal 1983 continuing resolution (H J Res 599 — PL 97-276), which expired Dec. 17. *(Story, p. 225)*

Earlier in the year, members had voted to limit a controversial tax break they had voted themselves in 1981. *(Story, p. 542)*

Chronology of Events

The House, suffering from election year jitters, was the first chamber to confront the possibility of increasing its own pay, but it shunned the plan quickly.

The prospect of a congressional pay raise surfaced the week of Aug. 16 while Congress was putting final touches on two key bills.

One, the omnibus reconciliation bill (HR 6955) making budget cuts, was delayed for a day and sent back to a conference committee to delete the offending provision. *(Story, p. 199)*

The other, the fiscal 1982 supplemental appropriations bill (HR 6863), simply had the pay provision stripped from it on the House floor while a number of members complained that their pay was too low. *(Story, p. 219)*

The issue arose courtesy of Senate Majority Whip Ted Stevens, R-Alaska, who had long been an advocate of increasing pay for members. Stevens had inserted a provision in the two bills that would have convened a special session of a government commission to examine pay rates for members of Congress, federal judges, Cabinet officers and senior bureaucrats.

The Quadrennial Review Commission was not scheduled to meet until 1984. Under Stevens' amendment, the panel would have made pay recommendations to President Reagan by Nov. 15 — just after the 1982 congressional elections — for transmission to Congress. Raises suggested by the commission would have been effective in 30 days unless both the House and Senate voted them down.

Rep. Patricia Schroeder, D-Colo., blasted the amendment as a "backdoor" pay raise that Congress would never get a chance to vote on if it did not meet after the Nov. 2 elections. In 1980, she said, the commission had recommended members be paid $85,000 annually, and in 1982, if convened, she estimated it would suggest $96,400 a year.

She also complained that the Stevens amendment reversed a 1977 law (PL 95-19) that required both House and Senate to vote for a pay raise for members. *(1977 Almanac p. 753)*

When the conference agreement on the reconciliation bill reached the House floor Aug. 17, Schroeder, Doug Walgren, D-Pa., and Bob Shamansky, D-Ohio, issued a letter warning members that a vote for the agreement would be interpreted as a vote to raise their own pay.

The House hastily voted 266-145 to send the bill back to conference. Initially, the vote was much closer, but when it was apparent Schroeder would succeed, 61 members who had opposed recommitting the bill switched their votes. *(Vote 274, p. 80-H)*

Rep. Leon E. Panetta, D-Calif., told reporters the House was so sensitive over pay "that people started jumping out the windows when it came up. I turned around and all I saw was feet."

The conference committee quickly deleted the Stevens language and sent the reconciliation bill back to the House floor Aug. 18 for passage. Later that evening, by voice vote, the House also removed the provision from the supplemental appropriations bill.

Rep. Vic Fazio, D-Calif., supported removing the pay issue from the bill but defended the need for raises. "Obviously, we are in an election period and it is not a good time to talk about these things," he said.

Rep. David R. Obey, D-Wis., said members treated public discussions of their pay like "an unmentionable social disease."

Rep. Ken Holland, D-S.C., who was leaving Congress because of compensation, said, "Somebody like me with four children, the first beginning college next week, just cannot remain in Washington under the pay that is provided."

The Senate agreed to the House deletion of the pay question from the reconciliation bill on Aug. 18 and from the supplemental appropriation on Aug. 20.

First Continuing Resolution

The next rounds of the pay raise fight were during congressional action on the two continuing appropriations resolutions (H J Res 599, H J Res 631) for fiscal 1983.

With the threat of congressional elections still facing them, members were chary of a pay raise battle when they considered H J Res 599 in September. Without any apparent opposition, the final version of the resolution contained a provision barring members of Congress and senior bureaucrats from receiving the 4 percent pay raise recommended by President Reagan for federal white-collar workers, which took effect Oct. 1. *(Story, p. 225)*

The Dec. 17 expiration of that resolution meant that

Congress had to reconsider the issue after the elections. Before it did so, however, a new element came into play — the General Accounting Office (GAO) reported that members were eligible for a pay raise of 27.2 percent, bringing their annual pay to $77,300. That was the amount that members would have gotten if they had not rejected cost-of-living increases for themselves four times in the preceding five years.

Second Continuing Resolution

House Action

When it considered H J Res 631 Dec. 14, the House took the politically painful step of voting for a 15 percent, $9,100 annual raise. The vote was 303-109. But the key vote came when the House rejected an amendment to limit pay to current levels. That amendment failed on a tie vote, 208-208. *(Votes 420, 421, p. 124-H)*

In an attempt to gain some bargaining leverage with the Senate, the House also added a section limiting all members of Congress, including senators, to outside earnings of 30 percent.

As passed by the House Dec. 14, the continuing resolution also contained a raise for Cabinet officers and senior bureaucrats, whose pay had been under the ceilings Congress had imposed on its own salaries in recent years. Cabinet officers would go from $69,630 to $80,100 annually; senior bureaucrats from $59,500 to $68,400.

Doubting that Congress would approve members' salaries of $77,300 a year, as the GAO had ruled, Legislative Appropriations Subcommittee Chairman Fazio wrote an amendment to limit the raise to 15 percent, or $69,800.

Under the rule providing for floor consideration of the bill, the House was to vote first on the Fazio amendment and then on an amendment by Bob Traxler, D-Mich., to continue the pay cap, which would give members no raise at all.

Armed with large charts and graphs, Fazio said members' pay had lost much of its purchasing power in the last several years as Congress rejected cost-of-living raises.

Clair W. Burgener, R-Calif., who was retiring from Congress, also supported the raise. "If we continue to neglect adequate pay for this body, we are going to end up with two kinds of people in this House: a combination of millionaires and ne'er-do-wells."

Rules Committee Chairman Richard Bolling, D-Mo., who also was retiring, called the vote for more pay a test of courage. "If we have not the courage to deal with our own pay, what makes anybody think we have the courage to deal with the great issues of the world?"

But Sam B. Hall Jr., D-Texas, said, "I cannot go back and tell 3,500 men and women who were let off from Lone Star Steel last August, who are living on a meager existence of approximately $250 every two weeks and maybe not that much, that it is time for me to raise my salary as a member of this House."

When the House voted first on the Fazio amendment, many members who were opposed to an increase voted for Fazio because his amendment provided a smaller raise — 15 percent — rather than the 27 percent they would have received if the House adopted no limit on pay. Fazio's amendment was approved 303-109.

Traxler, whose amendment would have prohibited any raise, then argued that although members might have needed a pay raise, "the timing is very poor," and he

Members' Pay History: From $6 a Day

Even before the 1st Congress met in 1789, compensation for national legislators was a difficult issue in the fledgling United States.

In 1787, the Constitutional Convention debated whether senators — who it was thought would represent the wealthy — would even be paid. In 1789, Congress set pay for members of both chambers at $6 a day.

Except for one year when senators got $7, that rate was maintained through 1815. In 1816, Congress scrapped the daily rate and enacted an annual salary of $1,500. The increase was condemned by the public. Nine members resigned over the issue and a number who voted for the raise were defeated that year, including Rep. Daniel Webster of New Hampshire. The outcry was so great that in 1817 Congress returned to a daily rate, $8 a day. The pay stayed the same for 38 years.

In 1856, Congress went back to an annual salary — $3,000, retroactive to 1855. In 1866, pay was raised to $5,000, retroactive to 1865. But at the close of the 42nd Congress in 1873, a third retroactive raise boomeranged. Salaries were hiked to $7,500 a year, retroactive to 1871 — a two-year, 50 percent raise. The move was attacked as a "salary grab" and a "back-pay steal." In 1874, pay was set back to $5,000, where it remained for 34 years.

In 1907, pay was raised to $7,500, and in 1925, to $10,000. But during the Depression, Congress took a pay cut; salaries were cut to $9,000 in 1932 and to $8,500 in 1933. In 1935, pay was restored to $10,000 a year, where it remained until 1947. Then members began getting $12,500 a year plus a $2,500 tax-free expense allowance. In 1951, Congress made the expense allowance taxable.

In 1953, Congress created a commission to study judicial and congressional salaries. The commission recommended a $10,000 raise, but Congress did not act until 1955, when a $22,500 annual salary for members was enacted. The expense allowance was scrapped.

In 1964, the House killed a bill providing another $10,000 raise. But after the 1964 primary elections were over, the House and Senate agreed to a $7,500 hike, bringing salaries to $30,000 a year. *(History of congressional pay, CQ Guide to Congress, 3rd edition, p. 569)*

Quadrennial Commission

In 1967, Congress tried to defuse the dilemma of dealing with its own pay. It established a Commission on Executive, Legislative and Judicial Salaries, which would meet every four years to recommend pay changes for top officials in all three branches of government. It would make its recommendations to the president, who then would send his recommendation to Congress.

In 1969, this quadrennial review commission endorsed a $12,500 raise for members, and salaries were increased to $42,500. In 1973, President Nixon delayed appointing commissioners and recommendations did not go to Congress until 1974, an election year. No increase was passed.

In 1975, congressional leaders, consulting secretly with the Ford administration, wrote legislation tying members' salaries to the annual pay increase for civil servants. Congress would automatically get the raise unless either chamber rejected it. The plan, approved by

Congress only five days after most members learned of it, resulted in a 5 percent raise, bringing pay to $44,600. Again reaction was loud and negative. In 1976, an election year, Congress decided against taking a raise.

In 1977, the third quadrennial commission recommended a $57,500 salary, but only if a strong ethics code were adopted. Congress enacted the $57,500 salary and restrictions on outside income for members — restrictions that were relaxed later. It also required both chambers to approve, by recorded votes, all increases in pay for federal workers, including members of Congress.

In 1978, Congress decided to defer rather than reject its annual raise, which was 5.5 percent that year. In 1979, the raise was scheduled to be 7 percent, which, when compounded with the deferred raise from 1978, would have provided an increase of 12.9 percent, or more than $7,400. After weeks of feuding over the size of the raise, Congress settled on a 5.5 percent hike. That brought salaries up to $60,662.50, the current level.

In the 1980 lame-duck session, Sen. Ted Stevens, R-Alaska, introduced an amendment to increase pay to $70,900 a year, the amount President Carter had recommended after hearing from the fourth quadrennial commission. The Senate defeated the proposal.

1981 Action

Congress did not vote itself a direct pay raise in 1981, but it did a lot of other things with congressional pay. While rejecting the 4.8 percent raise they would have received along with other federal workers, members adopted a new procedure enabling them to get future annual raises automatically, without a vote. And, rather than having to approve an annual appropriations bill to pay members, Congress made its pay a permanent appropriation. *(1981 Almanac p. 286)*

In the same law (PL 97-51), Congress eliminated the $25,000-a-year limit on the amount members could collect in honoraria for speeches or articles. The change affected only senators, because House rules continued to prevent members from getting more than 15 percent of their salary in honoraria. That limit was changed later in 1981 to 30 percent, or $18,200.

Congress also gave itself a tax break, which ran into heavy public criticism. Members had been allowed an income tax deduction of up to $3,000 a year for Washington, D.C., living expenses. In 1981, this limit was lifted. It was estimated then that the change would provide the typical member with the equivalent of a $10,500 pay raise. However, under regulations approved by the Treasury Department in January 1982 the change gave members an additional deduction of $16,500 on 1981 taxes.

Congress backed down and repealed the tax break in July 1982, although members were allowed to benefit from it for the 1981 tax year. *(Tax break, p. 542)*

In the 1982 lame-duck session, in a break with nearly two centuries of tradition, Congress voted a $9,138 pay raise for House members only while allowing senators to earn unlimited amounts in outside income, including honoraria. The change brought House members' salaries to $69,800 effective Dec. 18. Senators remained at $60,662.50. *(Story, p. 544)*

suggested that the issue be deferred until the economy improved.

As the 15 minutes allotted for the vote on Traxler ran out, the amendment seemingly was defeated on a 198-201 tally. But after several other members were permitted to vote, the amendment was ahead 209-204.

However, amid considerable confusion on the House floor, more members were allowed to vote and others changed their votes. Even Speaker Thomas P. O'Neill Jr., D-Mass., who customarily did not vote, cast a vote against the amendment. Finally, with the amendment ahead 208-207, lame duck Robert K. Dornan, R-Calif., voted no, and the amendment failed on a 208-208 tie.

It was the vote of Dornan and the other 70 lame ducks who voted on the Traxler amendment that sealed its fate. Lame ducks opposed the amendment by 2-to-1, 24-47. While Republicans overall supported Traxler 121-65, the 48 Republican lame ducks who were voting opposed his amendment 21-27.

Senate Action

The Senate Appropriations Committee quickly deleted both the pay raise and the outside earnings limit when it marked up the continuing resolution Dec. 15.

The version of H J Res 631 passed by the Senate Dec. 19 incorporated the Appropriations Committee action.

J. James Exon, D-Neb., offered a floor amendment Dec. 17 to continue the pay cap and also repeal a provision passed in 1981 that gave Congress automatic cost-of-living raises without a vote. *(1981 Almanac p. 286)*

Stevens tried to table the amendment but failed on a 24-71 vote. *(Vote 439, p. 73-S)*

However, the amendment was then ruled out of order as legislation on an appropriations bill.

Conference Action

During Dec. 19 conference action on H J Res 631, senators agreed to allow House members, but not themselves, to get a raise, along with other senior government officials. In exchange, House members agreed to drop the 30 percent limit on senators' outside income.

Although representatives got more in their paychecks, House Appropriations Chairman Jamie L. Whitten, D-Miss., insisted that senators were getting a better deal because they could collect far more in outside income than the size of the raise.

"I just want to point out that the Senate is going to get much more of an increase than we are," Whitten said.

The average senator received $19,575 in honoraria in 1981, compared to $5,237 for House members.

Senators and representatives always had received the same salary except in 1795-96, when senators received $7 a day compared to $6 a day for representatives.

The House and Senate both adopted the conference report Dec. 20.

Senate Outside Income

While members were debating the pay raise question, action on compensation for senators also had been proceeding on a separate track.

On Dec. 14, by a vote of 54-38, senators adopted a resolution (S Res 512) overturning a limit on outside earned income scheduled to go into effect Jan. 1, 1983. *(Vote 401, p. 68-S)*

The change meant that senators could earn an unlimited amount in addition to their salaries. If the Senate had not acted, senators would have been limited to outside earnings of about $9,100 — 15 percent of their salaries — in 1983.

The Senate action on outside earned income limits was the culmination of a lengthy and complex legislative history, stretching over several years, that always was closely tied to the question of pay raises.

As a condition for taking a $12,900 raise in 1977, both House and Senate agreed to strict ethics codes for members. One provision in both codes limited the outside earnings of senators and representatives to 15 percent of their salary.

This limit was to apply only to earned income, such as honoraria for speeches or legal work, but not to unearned income, such as dividend payments. A separate 1976 law (PL 94-283) had limited the net amount members could receive from honoraria for speeches, appearances or articles to $25,000 annually.

In 1979, the Senate voted to put off the 15 percent limit in its own rules until Jan. 1, 1983. *(1979 Almanac p. 578)*

In 1981, Congress repealed the $25,000 honoraria limit contained in the 1976 law. Although the change came late in 1981, 25 senators still earned more than $25,000 in honoraria in 1981. *(1981 Almanac p. 286)*

But without a change in the Senate rules, senators would have been limited to about $9,100 in outside income in 1983, including honoraria. House rules limited representatives to outside earned income of 30 percent — about $18,200 — of their congressional salaries.

The Senate adopted S Res 512 with little debate and no spoken opposition. Sen. Jake Garn, R-Utah, who led senators in 1981 by making $48,000 in honoraria, said, "It seems to me that it is a matter of conscience between each individual senator and his constituency."

Garn noted that the outside income would continue to be subject to public disclosure requirements. ∎

SPECIAL REPORTS

CQ

CQ Supreme Court Term (1981-82)

O'Connor Influence Felt at Supreme Court

Change comes slowly to the U.S. Supreme Court, but change was clearly evident in the term that ended July 2. For the first time, a woman participated in the court's decisions, but Justice Sandra Day O'Connor's importance ran far beyond her gender — and beyond her generally conservative views.

In a term that began Oct. 5, 1981, barely two weeks after O'Connor was sworn in, the court seemed to be emerging from a dozen years of fragmented votes and confused opinions.

Some deep divisions remained, especially on issues involving individual and criminal rights. But a new clarity of expression and coherence of reasoning were reflected in many of the court's decisions as the justices resolved some issues left in legal limbo by ambiguous rulings of the last few years and sharpened their focus on a number of remaining questions.

Although it was far too early to draw a detailed portrait of O'Connor as a justice, it was clear that her experience as an assistant state attorney general, state legislator and state judge made her more aware than any other justice of the difficulties faced by police, lawyers, judges and other state officials when they try to comply with confusing and unclear directives from the nation's highest court. *(O'Connor appointment, 1981 Almanac p. 409)*

The court O'Connor joined on Sept. 25, 1981, was a panel of aging veterans. At 51, she was at least 20 years the junior of most of her colleagues. All of them except Justice John Paul Stevens had served together at least 10 years and three — Justices William J. Brennan Jr., Byron R. White and Thurgood Marshall — were members of the court under Chief Justice Earl Warren (1953-1969).

But this long period of shared service had not resulted in any consensus among the justices on major issues. Indeed, on a number of important questions, the justices were in chronic disagreement. Even if they concurred on *what* to do in a particular case, they frequently disagreed on *why* they were doing it.

Early in 1981, the *Harvard Law Review* noted that since Chief Justice Warren E. Burger succeeded Warren in June 1969, there had been more plurality decisions — those on which fewer than five justices agreed — than there had been in the entire previous history of the court.

The editors of the *Harvard Law Review* pointed out the problems such rulings cause: "The Supreme Court has a role beyond that of resolving individual disputes," they wrote. "It serves as a guide for private parties, legislatures, lower courts, and its own future decisions. . . . More than a mere agreement on the result is needed; without a majority rationale for the result, the Supreme Court abdicates its responsibility to the institutions and parties depending on it for direction."

In the 1980-1981 term, the court decided six cases in which a majority of the participating justices could not agree on the reasoning for the eventual result. In the 1981-1982 term, only half as many cases were decided by such a fragmented court.

Conservative Trends

Two distinct conservative trends were evident in the court's rulings this term. First, the justices were inclined to place more power and responsibility in the hands of state and local officials — and less in the federal government. And second, the court was disposed — even more than in the 1970s — to back the arguments of police, prosecutors and state judges and to reject those of defendants.

O'Connor's vote contributed to the strength of these trends. She quickly became a fully participating member of the court, and she provided an articulate voice for the court's conservative core — Chief Justice Burger and William H. Rehnquist, her fellow Arizonan and Stanford University Law School classmate.

But two factors militated against a quick characterization of O'Connor as a staunch conservative.

One was the fact that neither she nor the court came down on the conservative side of every issue. The court issued a number of notable rulings expanding the Constitution's protection for individual rights and enlarging the bounds of First Amendment protection. O'Connor joined the majority in some of these rulings.

A second cause for caution was the fact that justices often changed as they gained seasoning on the nation's highest court. When Justice Harry A. Blackmun first joined the court in 1970, he and Chief Justice Burger were quickly dubbed the "Minnesota Twins." The men shared a friendship, a home state, and a seemingly "look-alike" conservative voting record. But as the years passed, Blackmun and Burger diverged more and more. And in the 1981-82 term, Blackmun voted against the chief justice 53 times out of the 93 instances when the court divided on a case.

Presidential Immunity

One major issue that split Burger and Blackmun this term was the question of whether presidents were immune from damage suits. In a case involving former President Richard M. Nixon, the court ruled 5-4 that chief executives had absolute immunity from such suits for all official actions during their tenure. Burger voted with the majority; Blackmun dissented.

Federal-State Balance

Time and again in its history, the court had been called on to find the proper balance between state power and federal authority in a particular area or situation. In the 1981-1982 term, dozens of cases required the court to consider the allocation of power within the federal system.

Since the New Deal presidency of Franklin Delano Roosevelt, the Supreme Court generally had favored the expansion of federal power at the expense of state prerogatives. Symbolic of this shift was the moribund state of the 10th Amendment — the last provision of the original Bill of Rights. That amendment declared that all powers which the Constitution did not explicitly delegate to the federal government or deny to the states "are reserved to the States, respectively, or to the people."

The "court-packing fight" of the Roosevelt era was in large measure brought on by the court's vigorous use of this amendment to strike down substantial portions of Roosevelt's New Deal program. After the court's turnabout in 1937 to favor expansion of federal power — the famed "switch in time that saved nine" — the 10th amendment fell into disuse.

But in two cases this term, states argued that Congress had again violated this amendment. In both cases, the states lost. The court held that workers on the state-owned Long Island Railroad in New York had a federally protected right to strike, and that Mississippi had to comply with directives of the 1978 Public Utility Regulatory Policy Act. But in the Mississippi case, a four-person minority, for whom Justice O'Connor spoke, gave the 10th Amendment new life, arguing it prohibited the very sort of federal interference that Mississippi was protesting.

In other cases involving state powers, the court upheld New York's child pornography law, backed an anti-busing amendment to California's constitution, upheld that state's law forbidding aliens to hold jobs as peace officers and backed a city ordinance in Illinois banning "head shops" that sold drug paraphernalia.

The justices struck down as unconstitutional Alaska's scheme for giving long-term residents a larger share of its oil revenues than newcomers, Washington state's anti-busing law, Illinois' law governing business takeover attempts, and Idaho and New Mexico's method of calculating the income tax owed them by multinational corporations.

Moving into a new and sensitive area of the law, the court told New York it must stiffen its standard for proving parents unfit to continue caring for their children, but it refused to expand the power of federal courts to intervene in state decisions concerning custody and parental fitness.

Cities joined an expanding group of those liable to antitrust suits as the court ruled they did not share the immunity of states to those charges. Among other groups whose liability in such cases was enlarged this term were engineers, doctors, insurance companies and medical associations.

With decisions focusing on two sensitive areas in federal-state relations, taxes and crime, the court curtailed the power of federal judges to interfere in state affairs.

The court held that taxpayers who felt a state tax system was being administered so unfairly that it violated their constitutional rights could not use a federal damage suit to protest that system. And it ruled that Congress had forbidden federal judges either to halt the collection of a state tax or to declare that tax unconstitutional.

State prisoners often claimed their convictions were obtained in violation of their constitutional rights, seeking a writ of *habeas corpus* from a federal court. If granted, that writ usually meant the prisoner went free. In one of her first opinions, Justice O'Connor wrote for the court that all claims raised in such a petition first had to be presented to the state courts. If they had not been, she said, the federal judge had to dismiss the request for relief.

In a pair of subsequent cases involving *habeas corpus* requests based on claims the prisoner failed to raise at the the time of his trial, O'Connor wrote opinions setting out a strict standard for judging such claims. Federal judges should grant the writ of *habeas corpus* and overturn the state conviction, she wrote, only if the prisoner could show

good reason for his failure to make the claim at his trial and actual prejudice to his case as a result of the alleged constitutional flaw. "Federal intrusions into state criminal trials," wrote O'Connor, "frustrate both the states' sovereign power to punish offenders and their good faith attempts to honor constitutional rights."

Individual Rights

Despite this court's strong conservative streak, it continued to demonstrate a willingness to take up for those "underclasses" in society for whom no one else would speak. In a landmark ruling expanding the meaning of the Constitution's promise of equal protection, the court held that states had to provide illegal alien children with a free public education.

In another important ruling, the court held for the first time that the Constitution guaranteed mentally retarded persons who lived in state institutions the right to a certain measure of safety, freedom and training sufficient to ensure that safety and freedom of movement.

The court held that Washington state's anti-busing initiative denied minority residents their constitutional rights, but said an anti-busing amendment to California's constitution did not violate the U.S. Constitution.

In the area of job bias, the court on the one hand interpreted broadly the exemption that Title VII of the 1964 Civil Rights Act provided for seniority systems that might seem discriminatory. On the other hand, the court held that Congress gave the federal government the authority to oversee the employment practices of schools and school districts that received federal education funds.

In ruling that a state-supported all women's school violated the constitutional guarantee of equal protection when it denied a male applicant admission to its nursing program, the court seemed to adopt a stiffer standard for weighing such sex-discrimination cases.

O'Connor wrote for the majority that laws which treated men and women differently would be found valid only if they were supported by an "exceedingly persuasive justification" for the different treatment of the sexes.

First Amendment

The court resolved a broad spectrum of First Amendment cases during the term. In a long-running lawsuit arising out of a 1966 civil rights boycott of merchants in Port Gibson, Miss., the court unanimously held that the First Amendment protected those who took part in such a boycott from being held liable for any damages that resulted. The justices found, however, that the First Amendment did not protect political boycotts by labor unions from a prohibition in federal labor law against secondary boycotts. The case involved a work stoppage by longshoremen who protested the 1980 Soviet invasion of Afghanistan.

In another major ruling, the court said the decision of a school board to remove certain books from the shelves of secondary school libraries had to be examined in light of the freedoms guaranteed by the First Amendment.

Child pornography — material that depicted a child engaged in sexual conduct — was outside the protection of the First Amendment, the court declared, upholding New York's law against distribution of such material. ∎

—By Elder Witt

MAJOR DECISIONS, 1981-1982 TERM
CRIMINAL LAW

Search and Seizure

Washington v. Chrisman, decided by a 6-3 vote, Jan. 13, 1982. Burger wrote the opinion; White, Brennan and Marshall dissented.

A policeman who arrested a student and accompanied him to the student's room could properly search that room without a warrant and seize evidence for use in court against the student and his roommate. The "plain view" exception to the warrant requirement of the Fourth Amendment permits a law enforcement officer to seize clearly incriminating evidence when it is discovered in a place where the officer has the right to be. Once an officer places someone under arrest he has the right to remain at that person's elbow at all times.

United States v. Ross, decided by a 6-3 vote, June 1, 1982. Stevens wrote the opinion; White, Brennan and Marshall dissented.

Police officers who have stopped a vehicle and who have probable cause to suspect that drugs or other contraband are somewhere in it may search the entire vehicle as thoroughly as if they had a warrant, including all containers and packages found in the vehicle which might contain the object of the search. The contrary holding in *Robbins v. California* (1981) — requiring police to obtain a warrant to search such containers — is rejected. *(1981 Almanac p. 5-A)*

United States v. Johnson, decided by a 5-4 vote, June 21, 1982. Blackmun wrote the opinion; White, Burger, Rehnquist and O'Connor dissented.

The court's 1980 ruling in *Payton v. New York* that police may not, without a warrant or consent, enter a home to arrest its occupant applies to invalidate the 1977 arrest of a man whose case was still on appeal when the 1980 ruling was announced. *(1980 Almanac p. 5-A)*

Taylor v. Alabama, decided by a 5-4 vote, June 23, 1982. Marshall wrote the opinion; O'Connor, Burger, Powell and Rehnquist dissented.

A confession obtained, without physical coercion, from a suspect who was taken into custody without probable cause or a warrant and who was warned of his constitutional rights before confessing is inadmissible in court because it is the product of an illegal arrest.

Double Jeopardy

Oregon v. Kennedy, decided by a 9-0 vote, May 24, 1982. Rehnquist wrote the opinion.

A defendant is not deprived of his constitutional protection against double jeopardy when he is tried again on theft charges after a mistrial was declared in his first trial, at his request, because the prosecutor called him a "crook" during the trial.

Tibbs v. Florida, decided by a 5-4 vote, June 7, 1982. O'Connor wrote the opinion; White, Brennan, Marshall and Blackmun dissented.

When a defendant's conviction has been reversed by a state appeals court which finds the guilty verdict contrary to the weight of the evidence presented at the trial, a retrial is not barred by the Fifth Amendment protection against double jeopardy. The reversal simply affords the defendant a second opportunity to seek an acquittal.

Due Process

United States v. Goodwin, decided by a 7-2 vote, June 18, 1982. Stevens wrote the opinion; Brennan and Marshall dissented.

The court will not presume prosecutorial vindictiveness, in violation of the due process clause, in every case in which a lesser charge is changed to a greater one prior to trial. The court refused to reverse the felony conviction of a man who was charged with a felony only after he asserted his right to a jury trial on misdemeanor charges arising out of the same incident. Without proof of prosecutorial vindictiveness, the court refused to presume such misconduct on the part of the government.

United States v. Valenzuela-Bernal, decided by a 7-2 vote, July 2, 1982. Rehnquist wrote the opinion; Brennan and Marshall dissented.

An individual charged for transporting an illegal alien failed to demonstrate that he was denied his Fifth Amendment right to due process and his Sixth Amendment right to compel the presence of witnesses by the government's deportation of two of his illegal alien passengers after the government concluded that they possessed no evidence material to his prosecution.

Speedy Trial

United States v. MacDonald, decided by a 6-3 vote, March 31, 1982. Burger wrote the opinion; Marshall, Brennan and Blackmun dissented.

The Sixth Amendment guarantee of the right to a speedy trial applies to the period between arrest and indictment, not to the period after military charges have been dismissed against a suspect and before a civilian indictment has been obtained. Thus an Army doctor, initially charged by the military with the murder of his wife and daughters, was not denied his speedy trial right by the delay of several years between dismissal of the military charges and institution of the civilian charges.

The Sixth Amendment right to a speedy trial is not primarily intended to prevent prejudice to the defense caused by passage of time. That interest is protected by the due process clause and statutes of limitations. The speedy trial guarantee is intended to limit the impairment of liberty of an accused before trial and to shorten the disruption of life caused by unresolved criminal charges.

Fair Trial

Smith v. Phillips, decided by a 6-3 vote, Jan. 25, 1982. Rehnquist wrote the opinion; Marshall, Brennan and Stevens dissented.

A defendant's due process right to a fair trial was not violated simply because a juror in the case was applying for a job with the prosecutor's office as the murder trial was in process. The trial judge, in a hearing on the situation, found "beyond a reasonable doubt" that this situation did not result in any prejudice to the defendant.

"Due process does not require a new trial every time a juror has been placed in a potentially compromising situation. Were that the rule, few trials would be constitutionally acceptable.... Due process means a jury capable and willing to decide the case solely on the evidence before it,

and a trial judge ever watchful to prevent prejudicial occurrences and to determine the effect of such occurrences when they happen," declared the majority.

Cruel and Unusual Punishment

Eddings v. Oklahoma, decided by a 5-4 vote, Jan. 19, 1982. Powell wrote the opinion; Burger, White, Blackmun and Rehnquist dissented.

The death sentence imposed upon a defendant who was 16 when he killed a state patrolman must be set aside — and the sentence reconsidered by lower courts — because the sentencing judge refused to consider such potentially mitigating factors as the defendant's unhappy childhood and alleged emotional disturbance at the time of the crime. The Eighth Amendment requires that the sentencing authority in capital cases consider all relevant aspects of the individual offender's character and record and the circumstances of the particular crime.

Zant v. Stephens, decided by a 6-3 vote, May 3, 1982. *Per curiam* opinion; Brennan, Marshall and Powell dissented.

The court returned this case to the Georgia Supreme Court, asking it to explain what basis there was in state law for holding a death sentence still valid after the state court had set aside one of the aggravating circumstances justifying the death penalty.

Hopper v. Evans, decided by votes of 9-0 and 7-2, May 24, 1982. Burger wrote the opinion; Brennan and Marshall dissented in part.

The court reinstated the death sentence imposed on a convicted killer under an Alabama death penalty law subsequently held constitutionally defective. The court explained that the constitutional flaw in the statute was irrelevant to this individual's case.

Enmund v. Florida, decided by a 5-4 vote, July 2, 1982. White wrote the opinion; O'Connor, Burger, Powell and Rehnquist dissented.

It is cruel and unusual punishment, disproportionate to the actions of the defendant, for the driver of a getaway car to be sentenced to death after he is convicted of first-degree murder and robbery when he did not himself witness the killings or kill the victims.

"Robbery is a serious crime deserving serious punishment. It is not, however ... 'so grievous an affront to humanity that the only adequate response may be the penalty of death,'" wrote the majority.

Excessive Bail

Murphy v. Hunt, decided by an 8-1 vote, March 2, 1982. *Per curiam* opinion. White dissented.

The court dismissed a case challenging as unconstitutional a Nebraska law that precludes bail before trial for defendants charged with forcible sexual offenses when the proof or the presumption is great that they committed the crime charged. The court held this case moot because the pretrial period had passed; the defendant had been tried and could not benefit from a ruling on pre-trial bail.

General

Ralston v. Robinson, decided by a 6-3 vote, Dec. 2, 1981. Marshall wrote the opinion; Stevens, Brennan and O'Connor dissented.

A person sentenced initially under the rehabilitation-oriented Youth Corrections Act of 1950 who subsequently receives an adult sentence for crimes committed in prison may be treated thereafter as an adult if the judge imposing the adult term determines that the youth will not benefit from further treatment under the Youth Corrections Act.

McElroy v. United States, decided by an 8-1 vote, March 23, 1982. O'Connor wrote the opinion; Stevens dissented.

Federal law barring the transportation of forged securities in interstate commerce does not require proof that the security was forged *before* traveling across state lines, but only that the security was forged at some point *and* was transported in interstate commerce.

Williams v. United States, decided by a 5-4 vote, June 29, 1982. Blackmun wrote the opinion; White, Brennan, Marshall and Burger dissented.

Federal law making it a crime to make a false statement or to willfully overvalue an asset in order to influence the action of certain financial institutions does not apply to the deposit of "bad checks" in federally insured banks.

CIVIL RIGHTS

Schools

Washington v. Seattle School District No. 1, decided by a 5-4 vote, June 30, 1982. Blackmun wrote the opinion; Powell, Burger, Rehnquist and O'Connor dissented.

A 1978 voter-initiated state law prohibiting school boards from voluntarily using busing and pupil reassignment to desegregate public schools violates the equal protection clause. The law, Initiative 350, is clearly racially discriminatory in intent and operation and restructures the process deciding education policy in the state, removing decisions about the voluntary use of busing from local school boards to the state level.

Crawford v. Board of Education of City of Los Angeles, decided by an 8-1 vote, June 30, 1982. Powell wrote the opinion; Marshall dissented.

Proposition 1, a 1979 voter-initiated amendment to the state constitution denying state courts the power to order busing unless it is needed to remedy a specific violation of the U.S. Constitution, is permissible under the equal protection clause. This change in the state constitution simply adopts for state courts the standard federal courts use in deciding when to order busing for school desegregation.

Jobs

Logan v. Zimmerman Brush Co., decided by a 9-0 vote, Feb. 24, 1982. Blackmun wrote the opinion.

A handicapped man was denied his right to due process when his complaint of job discrimination was dismissed by a state fair employment practices commission because the commission had failed to act on the matter within the time set by law.

Zipes v. TWA Inc., Independent Federation of Flight Attendants v. TWA Inc., decided by an 8-0 vote, Feb. 24, 1982. White wrote the opinion; Stevens did not participate in the decision.

A federal court acted within its authority when it

awarded retroactive seniority to stewardesses grounded by an airline because they became mothers, when no similar restriction was imposed on male flight attendants who became fathers. The award of retroactive seniority was appropriate even for stewardesses who filed their claims later than the legal deadline. It was not necessary that the stewardesses file charges with the Equal Employment Opportunity Commission before filing the lawsuit against their former employer.

American Tobacco Co. v. Patterson, decided by a 5-4 vote, April 5, 1982. White wrote the opinion; Brennan, Marshall, Blackmun and Stevens dissented.

Workers challenging a seniority system as discriminatory under the 1964 Civil Rights Act must prove *both* that it had an adverse effect on women or minorities *and* that it was adopted with the intent to discriminate against those workers.

When Congress exempted *bona fide* seniority systems from challenge under the 1964 Act, unless they were adopted with the intent to discriminate, it included that exemption in both systems then in effect *and* those adopted after the act's passage, the court held.

Pullman-Standard v. Swint, United Steelworkers v. Swint, decided by a 7-2 vote, April 27, 1982. White wrote the opinion; Marshall and Blackmun dissented.

A court of appeals erred when it overturned a trial court finding that a seniority system used by the Pullman-Standard Co., a manufacturer of railroad cars, was not intended to discriminate against black workers. Unless it found that the trial court's conclusion was clearly erroneous, the appeals court should have sent the matter back to the trial court for consideration of additional evidence relevant to the question of discriminatory intent.

Kremer v. Chemical Construction Co., decided by a 5-4 vote, May 17, 1982. White wrote the opinion; Blackmun, Brennan, Marshall and Stevens dissented.

Once a state court has upheld a state agency's finding that there is no basis for a charge of job discrimination, a federal court may not re-litigate that issue in a case brought under title VII of the 1964 Civil Rights Act.

In 1790 Congress passed a law directing that all U.S. courts afford the same full-faith-and-credit to state court judgments that would apply in the state's own courts. That law, still in effect, was not superseded by title VII.

General Telephone Company of the Southwest v. Falcon, decided by votes of 9-0 and 8-1, June 14, 1982. Stevens wrote the opinion; Burger dissented in part.

An individual who alleges that he was denied a *promotion* because he is Mexican-American may not bring a class action on behalf of employees who were denied *employment* for that reason.

Sumitomo Shoji America v. Avagliano, decided by a 9-0 vote, June 15, 1982. Burger wrote the opinion.

A company constituted under the laws of the United States or a single state is a company of the United States, subject to the laws of the United States, and not eligible for the exemption contained in certain treaties made by the United States that allows foreign corporations operating in the United States to hire as they wish, free of the fair employment requirements of U.S. law.

Connecticut v. Teal, decided by a 5-4 vote, June 21, 1982. Brennan wrote the opinion; Powell, Burger, Rehnquist and O'Connor dissented.

An employer sued for violating the Civil Rights Act of 1964 by using a non-job-related test to select candidates for promotion when that test excludes more blacks than whites from consideration for promotion may not use as a complete defense the "bottom line" argument that in fact, more eligible blacks than whites are promoted.

Ford Motor Co. v. Equal Employment Opportunity Commission, decided by a 6-3 vote, June 28, 1982. O'Connor wrote the opinion; Blackmun, Brennan and Marshall dissented.

An employer charged with discrimination in hiring can terminate the period for which he may be held liable to the claimant for back pay by unconditionally offering the claimant the job he had previously refused to offer — even if this offer does not include seniority retroactive to the date of the alleged discriminatory refusal.

Housing

Havens Realty Corp. v. Coleman, decided by a 9-0 vote, Feb. 24, 1982. Brennan wrote the opinion.

Under the Fair Housing Act of 1968, "testers" — persons who inquire about available housing primarily to collect evidence of alleged discrimination — have legal standing to sue landlords or Realtors when they uncover discriminatory practices. The law grants all persons a legal right to truthful information about available housing, and this right is violated when rental agents give false information to a black "tester."

Sex Discrimination

North Haven Board of Education v. Bell, decided by a 6-3 vote, May 17, 1982. Blackmun wrote the opinion; Powell, Burger and Rehnquist dissented.

Title IX of the Education Amendments of 1972 — which provides that "no person ... shall, on the basis of sex, be excluded from participation in, be denied the benefits of, or be subjected to discrimination under any education program or activity receiving federal financial assistance" — authorizes federal monitoring of the employment practices, as well as the treatment of students, of recipient school districts, colleges and universities.

The sanction for violating this prohibition — termination of federal funds — is program-specific; that is, funds are to be terminated only to programs in which discrimination has been found to exist.

Mississippi University for Women v. Hogan, decided by a 5-4 vote, July 1, 1982. O'Connor wrote the opinion; Burger, Blackmun, Powell and Rehnquist dissented.

The policy of a state-supported university that has historically admitted only women to its school of nursing violates the constitutional guarantee of equal protection when applied to deny admission to a man merely because of his sex. To justify a law that classifies individuals on the basis of sex an "exceedingly persuasive justification" must be presented. The state did not meet that test in this case.

Damage Suits

O'Dell v. Espinoza, dismissed May 3, 1982. *Per curiam* opinion.

The court dismissed for want of jurisdiction a case from Colorado in which that state's supreme court had allowed the children of a man killed by Denver police to bring a civil rights damage suit against the police. Because the state supreme court had sent this case back for trial, the U.S. Supreme Court found that its decision was not a final judgment in the case subject to review by the nation's highest court.

Patsy v. Board of Regents of the State of Florida, decided by a 7-2 vote, June 21, 1982. Marshall wrote the opinion; Powell and Burger dissented.

An individual need not exhaust all available state administrative remedies for a grievance before filing a civil rights damage suit in federal court against the individuals responsible for denying him his constitutional or other federal rights under color of state law.

Rendell-Baker v. Kohn, decided by a 7-2 vote, June 25, 1982. Burger wrote the opinion; Brennan and Marshall dissented.

The receipt of substantial state funds by a private school does not make the actions of the school, in discharging teachers or other employees, state action. Such discharges are not action "under color of state law" and cannot form the basis for civil rights damage suits against the school. "Acts of such private contractors do not become acts of the government by reason of their significant or even total engagement in performing public contracts," stated the court.

Blum v. Yaretsky, decided by a 7-2 vote, June 25, 1982. Rehnquist wrote the opinion; Brennan and Marshall dissented.

The fact that a business is regulated by the state does not convert the actions of the business into state action. A state will normally be held responsible for a private decision only when it has exercised coercive power or provided so much encouragement that the choice made must be considered the choice of the state.

The action of privately owned and operated nursing homes in tranferring patients from nursing homes to less intensive care facilities is not "state action" even though the transferred patients are Medicaid recipients, for whose care the state reimburses the nursing home, and the transfers are in accord with federal Medicaid regulations. The decision to transfer a particular patient is made not by any state official, but by physicians and nursing home administrators.

Lugar v. Edmondson Oil Co., decided by a 5-4 vote, June 25, 1982. White wrote the opinion; Burger, Powell, Rehnquist and O'Connor dissented.

The action of a creditor in obtaining a writ of attachment against the property of his debtor, a writ obtained from and enforced with the aid of state officials, a county clerk and sheriff, is state action and action under color of state law. The creditor may thus be sued for damages if the debtor feels that the attachment denied him his constitutional right to due process.

General Building Contractors Association v. Pennsylvania, decided by a 7-2 vote, June 29, 1982. Rehnquist wrote the opinion; Brennan and Marshall dissented.

An employer may not be held liable to a civil rights damage suit by persons alleging that the union hiring hall, which the employer is obligated to use as part of a collective bargaining agreement, engages in racial discrimination unless there is proof that the employers intended to discriminate.

INDIVIDUAL RIGHTS

Aliens

Cabell v. Chavez-Salido, decided by a 5-4 vote, Jan. 12, 1982. White wrote the opinion; Blackmun, Brennan, Marshall and Stevens dissented.

California may require that all peace officers be U.S. citizens, even when the category is a broad one, encompassing deputy probation officers. Such officers both exercise and symbolize the power of the political community and it is reasonable that they be required to be citizens.

Plyler v. Doe, Texas v. Certain Named and Unnamed Undocumented Alien Children, decided by a 5-4 vote, June 15, 1982. Brennan wrote the opinion; Burger, Rehnquist, White and O'Connor dissented.

The 14th Amendment guarantees the equal protection of the laws to illegal aliens present in the United States. They are clearly persons within the jurisdiction of the state in which they reside, even if they have entered the country and that state illegally. Texas, therefore, may not deny illegal alien children a free public education; there is no national policy nor sufficient state interest presented to justify this action.

Toll v. Moreno, decided by a 7-2 vote, June 28, 1982. Brennan wrote the opinion; Rehnquist and Burger dissented.

A state university policy of denying in-state status for purposes of tuition to non-immigrant aliens who live in the state because members of their families work nearby for international organizations is invalid under the supremacy clause because it conflicts with the national policy that encourages these aliens to establish a domicile in this country and provides them significant tax exemptions.

Children

City of Mesquite v. Aladdin's Castle Inc., decided by votes of 9-0 and 7-2, Feb. 23, 1982. Stevens wrote the opinion; Powell and White dissented in part.

Sidestepping a ruling on whether or not children have a constitutional right to play coin-operated video games in shopping malls, the court sent this case back to a lower court for clarification of the appeals court ruling that an ordinance strictly limiting the use of such arcades by children was unconstitutional.

Mills v. Habluetzel, decided by a 9-0 vote, April 5, 1982. Rehnquist wrote the opinion.

Once a state grants children the right to support from their natural fathers, the equal protection guarantee of the 14th Amendment prohibits the state from making it more difficult for illegitimate children than for legitimate children to exercise that right, unless the additional restrictions placed on the assertion of this right by illegitimate children are substantially related to a legitimate state interest. Texas unduly burdens this right by requiring that any suit brought to establish a child's paternity be brought within the first year of the child's life.

Citizens

Zobel v. Williams, decided by an 8-1 vote, June 14, 1982. Burger wrote the opinion; Rehnquist dissented.

Alaska violated the guarantee of equal protection when it provided for distribution of an oil and gas income dividend to each resident based on the number of years he or she had lived in Alaska since 1959, the year Alaska became a state. Alaska showed no valid state interest that was rationally served by distinguishing between individuals who were living in Alaska in 1959 and those who had come there to live since.

Handicapped Persons

Board of Education of Hendrick Hudson Central School District v. Rowley, decided by a 6-3 vote, June 28, 1982. Rehnquist wrote the opinion; White, Brennan and Marshall dissented.

The Education for all Handicapped Children Act of 1975 obliged school districts receiving funds under the act to provide each handicapped student a free appropriate public education. But it did not obligate the state to provide all the aid necessary to ensure that a student realizes his or her maximum potential. Instead, the law requires only the provision of personalized instruction accompanied by sufficient support services to permit the child to benefit educationally from that instruction.

DUE PROCESS

Mentally Retarded Persons

Youngberg v. Romeo, decided by a 9-0 vote, June 18, 1982. Powell wrote the opinion.

Mentally retarded persons in state institutions have a constitutional right to safe conditions, freedom of movement and sufficient training to enable them to move safely and freely within that institution. The guarantee against deprivation of personal liberty without due process of law means that such persons will only be restrained or allowed to remain in less than completely safe conditions as a result of the decision of a qualified professional.

Mentally Ill Persons

Mills v. Rogers, decided by a 9-0 vote, June 18, 1982. Powell wrote the opinion.

The court sent back to the appeals court, for reconsideration in light of an intervening decision by the Massachusetts Supreme Judicial Court, a case involving the successful claim by mental patients at a Massachusetts hospital that they had a constitutional right, under the due process guarantee, to refuse treatment with anti-psychotic drugs.

Parents

Santosky v. Kramer, decided by a 5-4 vote, March 24, 1982. Blackmun wrote the opinion; Rehnquist, Burger, White and O'Connor dissented.

Natural parents have a right to due process at state proceedings to terminate their parental rights over their children. Parents have a fundamental liberty interest in the care, custody and management of their children which they do not lose simply because they are not model parents. The interests involved in such a proceeding require that the state's charge that parents are unfit be proved by more than just a fair preponderance of the evidence. The state's

charge must be proved by at least clear and convincing evidence before a state may completely and irrevocably terminate the rights of parents in their child.

Tenants

Greene v. Lindsey, decided by a 6-3 vote, May 17, 1982. Brennan wrote the opinion; O'Connor, Burger and Rehnquist dissented.

A Kentucky law that permits service of process by posting summons on the door of tenant's apartment in public housing, where notices are "not infrequently" removed by children before being seen by occupants, does not comply with an essential requirement of due process — that tenants be adequately notified of pending eviction proceedings.

FIRST AMENDMENT

Freedom of Expression

Princeton University v. Schmid, decided by an 8-0 vote, Jan. 13, 1982. *Per curiam* opinion; Brennan did not take part in consideration of this case.

The court dismissed this case after hearing it argued, finding that Princeton University lacked the standing to challenge a ruling by the New Jersey Supreme Court that a non-student's First Amendment rights were violated when he was prosecuted for trespassing after he distributed political materials on the university campus without obtaining permission from university officials.

In re R. M. J., decided by a 9-0 vote, Jan. 25, 1982. Powell wrote the opinion.

State rules governing advertising by attorneys may regulate such speech only to the extent necessary to prevent deceptive or misleading ads. Missouri infringed too far upon the First Amendment guarantee of freedom of expression when it restricted the categories of information that could be provided in lawyers' ads and specified the phrases to be used to describe areas of legal practice.

Brown v. Hartlage, decided by a 9-0 vote, April 5, 1982. Brennan wrote the opinion.

Kentucky applied its campaign law too strictly when it voided a candidate's election as county commissioner because he had promised, if elected, to serve at a reduced salary. The state court held that this promise violated an anti-bribery election law forbidding candidates to promise anything of value to anyone in order to obtain that person's vote. The Supreme Court disagreed, declaring that in applying the law to this case, the state was impermissibly curtailing a candidate's First Amendment freedom of expression.

Board of Education, Island Trees Union Free School District #26 v. Pico, decided by a 5-4 vote, June 25, 1982. Brennan announced the court's decision in an opinion joined by three other justices; White concurred in the decision; Burger, Powell, Rehnquist and O'Connor dissented.

The decision of a local school board to remove certain books from high school and junior high school libraries is subject to certain restrictions imposed by the First Amendment guarantee of freedom of ideas and expression. The court sent to trial a case in which several students chal-

lenged such school board action. The justices directed the lower court to ascertain whether the board had acted to remove unpopular ideas from the library, which would be impermissible under the First Amendment, or to remove vulgar and irrelevant material from the library, which would be permissible.

Freedom of Religion

Widmar v. Vincent, decided by an 8-1 vote, Dec. 8, 1981. Powell wrote the opinion; White dissented.

A state university violates the First Amendment guarantee of freedom of expression when it denies use of its buildings and grounds to a recognized student group — while allowing other such groups use of those facilities — just because the excluded group wishes to hold religious meetings there. Once a university creates a forum generally open for use by student groups, it may not deny access to that forum to certain groups because of the subject of their meetings.

Valley Forge Christian College v. Americans United for Separation of Church and State, decided by a 5-4 vote, Jan. 12, 1982. Rehnquist wrote the opinion; Brennan, Marshall, Blackmun and Stevens dissented.

A citizens' group that could not demonstrate a clear "injury" as a result of the transfer of surplus federal property to a church-related school lacks standing to bring a federal suit challenging that transfer as a violation of the First Amendment ban on state action "establishing" religion.

Larson v. Valente, decided by a vote of 5-4, April 21, 1982. Brennan wrote the opinion; White, Rehnquist, Burger and O'Connor dissented.

Minnesota violated the Constitution's "establishment" clause and engaged in an official preference for certain denominations when it exempted from the registration and reporting requirements of state law those religious organizations that receive more than half their financial support from their members. The Supreme Court held the state law invalid in a case brought by the Unification Church of the Rev. Sun Myung Moon.

Right of Access

Globe Newspaper Co. v. Superior Court, decided by a 6-3 vote, June 23, 1982. Brennan wrote the opinion; Burger, Rehnquist and Stevens dissented.

First Amendment rights of access to criminal trials are violated by a Massachusetts law mandating the closing of sex-crime trials to press and public during the testimony of a victim who is a minor.

Child Pornography

New York v. Ferber, decided by a 9-0 vote, July 2, 1982. White wrote the opinion.

Pornographic depictions of children are outside the protection of the First Amendment. State laws prohibiting the promotion of sexual performances by children under 16 do not violate the First Amendment.

Boycotts

National Association for the Advancement of Colored People v. Claiborne Hardware Co., decided by an 8-0 vote, July 2, 1982. Stevens wrote the opinion; Marshall did not participate in the decision.

A non-violent 1966 boycott by civil rights demonstrators of the shops of white merchants in Port Gibson, Miss., was speech and conduct protected by the First Amendment. Violence, however, is not protected by the First Amendment, and a state court may assess damages against those responsible for such violence. But such liability must be based on a record that reflects the individuals' participation in violent activity; it may not be lodged against individuals or a group simply on the basis of association.

ELECTION LAWS

Voting Rights

Hathorn v. Lovorn, decided by an 8-1 vote, June 15, 1982. O'Connor wrote the opinion; Rehnquist dissented.

State courts have both the power and the obligation to decide whether changes in election laws and procedures require pre-clearance with federal authorities under the Voting Rights Act of 1965. State courts must refrain from issuing any orders that conflict with the Voting Rights Act.

Rogers v. Lodge, decided by a 6-3 vote, July 1, 1982. White wrote the opinion; Powell, Rehnquist and Stevens dissented.

In order to find an at-large system of electing county officials unconstitutional in violation of the 14th and 15th Amendments, courts must determine that the system is discriminatory in intent as well as effect.

A court may consider indirect as well as direct evidence of intent, however, wrote White, who explained that " 'an invidious discriminatory purpose may often be inferred from the totality of the relevant facts, including the fact, if it is true, that the law bears more heavily on one race than another.' "

Evidence permissible in such cases may include evidence of the exclusion of blacks from the political process, of official insensitivity to the needs of blacks, and the socio-economic status of an area's blacks.

Campaign Finance

Federal Election Commission v. Democratic Senatorial Campaign Committee, National Republican Senatorial Committee v. Democratic Senatorial Campaign Committee, decided by a vote of 9-0, Nov. 10, 1981. White wrote the opinion.

The Federal Election Campaign Act of 1971 does not preclude national party committees from enlarging the amount they may legally spend in an election by assuming the spending authority granted by law to state party committees and making those expenditures as agents of the state committees.

Citizens Against Rent Control/Coalition for Fair Housing v. City of Berkeley, decided by an 8-1 vote, Dec. 14, 1981. Burger wrote the opinion; White dissented.

Citizens have a First Amendment right to contribute as much as they wish to groups opposing or supporting ballot issues, and that right is violated when a city limits such contributions to $250. Such a limit infringes upon the First Amendment guarantees of freedom of expression and the right of association. "Contributions by individuals to support concerted action by a committee advocating a position on a ballot measure is beyond question a very significant form of political expression," stated the court.

Common Cause v. Schmitt, Federal Election Commission v. Americans for Change, decided by a 4-4 vote, Jan. 19, 1982. O'Connor did not participate.

The evenly divided court upheld, without opinion, a lower court's ruling that Congress violated the First Amendment's guarantee of free speech when it limited to $1,000 the amount an independent and unauthorized political action committee could spend in a presidential campaign.

Bread Political Action Committee v. Federal Election Commission, decided by a 9-0 vote, March 8, 1982. O'Connor wrote the opinion.

Avoiding a decision on a challenge to federal election law provisions that limit solicitation by trade associations of political contributions from their members' stockholders and officers, the court held that under federal election law such trade associations and political action committees may not win expedited review of their challenges to such provisions. Expedited review of such challenges is available only to national committees of political parties, eligible voters and the Federal Election Commission.

General

Rivera-Rodriguez v. Popular Democratic Party, decided by a 9-0 vote, June 7, 1982. Burger wrote the opinion.

Puerto Rico may, by law, vest in a political party the power to fill an interim vacancy in the Legislature resulting from the death of an incumbent member of that party. This does not violate the Constitution's guarantees of equal protection or freedom of political association.

BUSINESS LAW

Antitrust

Community Communications Co. Inc. v. City of Boulder, Colo., decided by a 5-3 vote, Jan. 13, 1982. Brennan wrote the opinion; Rehnquist, Burger and O'Connor dissented; White did not participate in the decision.

Boulder's ordinance imposing a three-month moratorium on expansion of cable television systems within the city limits — a period within which the city invited competing systems to enter the market — is not immune from challenge under federal antitrust laws.

Such city action is not "state action" exempt from such challenge under *Parker v. Brown*, 317 U.S. 341, because it is not taken to further a clearly expressed state policy.

Kaiser Steel Corp. v. Mullins, decided by a 6-3 vote, Jan. 13, 1982. White wrote the opinion; Brennan, Marshall and Blackmun dissented.

A coal producer, party to a collective bargaining contract with the United Mine Workers that included provisions, not enforced for years, which the producer considered in violation of federal antitrust and labor laws, may raise the defense of their illegality when charged with failing to comply with the questionable provisions.

As a general rule, federal courts must defer to the National Labor Relations Board on such questions, but a federal court has a duty to determine whether or not a contract is in line with federal law before acting to enforce that contract.

American Society of Mechanical Engineers v. Hydrolevel Corp., decided by a 6-3 vote, May 17, 1982. Blackmun wrote the opinion; Powell, White and Rehnquist dissented.

Professional engineering societies and other nonprofit membership organizations that issue standards and codes used in various areas of industry may be held liable under the antitrust laws for violations of those laws by their members. This liability, held the court, extends at least to actions of society members and "agents" taken with the apparent authority of the organization.

Arizona v. Maricopa County Medical Society, decided by a 4-3 vote, June 18, 1982. Stevens wrote the opinion; Powell, Burger and Rehnquist dissented; Blackmun and O'Connor did not participate.

An agreement among competing physicians setting the maximum fees they would charge certain insurance companies for services to their policyholders amounts to price-fixing in violation of federal antitrust laws.

Blue Shield of Virginia v. McCready, decided by a 5-4 vote, June 21, 1982. Brennan wrote the opinion; Rehnquist, Burger, O'Connor and Stevens dissented.

An individual whose insurance company refused to reimburse her for services provided by a psychologist, although it would have paid for those same services had they been provided by a psychiatrist, has standing to sue the insurance company and the state psychiatric association for triple damages under the Clayton Act. She has suffered injury as a result of their allegedly anti-competitive activity, even though she was not its primary target.

Union Labor Life Insurance v. Pireno, decided by a 6-3 vote, June 28, 1982. Brennan wrote the opinion; Rehnquist, Burger and O'Connor dissented.

An insurance company's practice of obtaining advice from a peer review committee of the state chiropractic association on what fees charged by chiropractors to patients are reasonable and should be reimbursed by the company is not immune from scrutiny under the antitrust laws as part of the "business of insurance."

Banking

Fidelity Federal Savings & Loan Association v. de la Cuesta, decided by a 6-2 vote, June 28, 1982. Blackmun wrote the opinion; Powell did not participate; Rehnquist and Stevens dissented.

State efforts to prohibit enforcement of "due-on-sale" clauses in home loan instruments — which allow the mortgage lender to demand immediate payment in full whenever the mortgaged property is sold or transferred — are pre-empted by federal regulations issued by the Federal Home Loan Bank Board. The regulations grant federal savings and loan associations the right to include such clauses in their loan agreements. The Federal Home Loan Bank Board acted in accord with the authority granted it by Congress in the Home Owners' Loan Act of 1933 to regulate federal savings and loan associations.

Bankruptcy

Railway Labor Executives' Association v. Gibbons, decided by a vote of 9-0, March 2, 1982. Rehnquist wrote the opinion.

Congress may not pass bankruptcy laws that apply to

the affairs of only one bankrupt organization. The Constitution gives Congress the power to "establish . . . uniform Laws on the subject of bankruptcies throughout the United States."

The Rock Island Transition and Employee Assistance Act of 1980 (PL 96-254) applied only to the Rock Island Railroad, providing special protection to its employees not available to the employees of other bankrupt railroads. Thus that law violated the uniformity standard of the Constitution's bankruptcy clause. It was the first time that the court had held a federal bankruptcy act unconstitutional for this reason.

Northern Pipeline Construction Co. v. Marathon Pipe Line Co., United States v. Marathon Pipe Line Co., decided by a 6-3 vote, June 28, 1982. Brennan announced the decision in an opinion joined by three justices; Rehnquist and O'Connor concurred in the judgment; White, Burger and Powell dissented.

Congress acted in violation of Article III, which provides that federal judicial power should be exercised only by federal judges whose independence is assured by life tenure and fixed compensation, when it enacted provisions of the 1978 Bankruptcy Reform Act creating a new corps of bankruptcy judges who lack these guarantees of independence but have jurisdiction over all civil cases related to a bankrupt person or organization.

Regulation

American Medical Association v. Federal Trade Commission, decided by a 4-4 vote, March 23, 1982. Blackmun did not take part in consideration of the case.

The evenly divided court affirmed an appeals court ruling that the Federal Trade Commission has jurisdiction to order a non-profit medical association to lift its restrictions on the dissemination of price information by doctors and its ban on advertising of physicians' services and alternative forms of medical care.

Southern Pacific Transportation Co. v. Commercial Metals Co., decided by a 9-0 vote, April 27, 1982. Blackmun wrote the opinion.

A railroad's violation of credit regulations issued by the Interstate Commerce Commission does not bar the railroad from collecting a lawful freight charge from a shipper who is in fact liable for that charge.

Securities

Marine Bank v. Weaver, decided by a 9-0 vote, March 8, 1982. Burger wrote the opinion.

Neither a certificate of deposit pledged to guarantee a loan nor a related agreement sharing a company's future profits with the guarantor of the loan is a "security" within the meaning of the Securities Exchange Act of 1934, and so these actions are not covered under the anti-fraud provisions of that law.

Merrill Lynch, Pierce, Fenner & Smith v. Curran, New York Mercantile Exchange v. Leist, Clayton Brokerage Co. v. Leist, Heinhold Commodities v. Leist, decided by a 5-4 vote, May 3, 1982. Stevens wrote the opinion; Powell, Burger, Rehnquist and O'Connor dissented.

Private investors in commodity futures, as well as federal regulators, have the right to seek enforcement in court of federal laws governing trading in commodity futures.

Investors may sue their brokers and the exchanges for damages in cases involving fraud or market manipulation. This private right to sue in such cases existed before enactment of the 1974 law creating the Commodity Futures Trading Commission and was left untouched by Congress in the passage of that law.

Shipping

Griffin v. Oceanic Contractors Inc., decided by a 7-2 vote, June 30, 1982. Rehnquist wrote the opinion; Stevens and Blackmun dissented.

A federal district court has no discretion to limit the period for which a wage penalty is assessed under the Jones Act against a vessel owner for wages wrongly withheld from a seaman. This penalty must be assessed for each day that payment of the wages is withheld.

Taxation

United States v. Vogel Fertilizer Co., decided by a 7-2 vote, Jan. 13, 1982. Brennan wrote the opinion; Blackmun and White dissented.

The court struck down as invalid a Treasury regulation concerning the definition of a controlled group of corporations described as a "brother-sister controlled group." The Treasury defined such a group as two or more corporations in which the same five or fewer persons own large percentages of stock "singly or in combination." The court said that under the Internal Revenue Code, such a group must be defined as two or more corporations in which the same five or fewer persons own large portions of stock in *each* of the "controlled" companies.

Merrion v. Jicarilla Apache Tribe, Amoco Production Co. v. Jicarilla Apache Tribe, decided by a 6-3 vote, Jan. 25, 1982. Marshall wrote the opinion; Stevens, Rehnquist and Burger dissented.

Indian tribes may constitutionally impose severance taxes upon companies or individuals who develop mineral resources on Indian lands and remove them from those lands. Congress has the power to deny tribes that authority, but it has not done so, leaving with the tribes their inherent power to impose such taxes.

Jewett v. Commissioner of Internal Revenue, decided by a 6-3 vote, Feb. 23, 1982. Stevens wrote the opinion; Blackmun, Rehnquist and O'Connor dissented.

A person who waits 33 years to disclaim a contingent interest in a testamentary trust waited too long for that disclaimer to exempt that interest from federal gift taxes.

Diedrich v. Commissioner of Internal Revenue, decided by an 8-1 vote, June 15, 1982. Burger wrote the opinion; Rehnquist dissented.

Individuals who give property on the condition that the recipient pay the resulting gift tax receive taxable income to the extent that the gift tax exceeds the donor's investment in the gift.

Trademarks

Inwood Laboratories Inc. v. Ives Laboratories Inc., decided by a 9-0 vote, June 1, 1982. O'Connor wrote the opinion.

Manufacturers of a generic drug equivalent to a trademarked product are not guilty of trademark infringement because they marketed their drug in capsules which

looked just like those of the trademarked product unless it is shown that they intentionally induced pharmacists to substitute the generic for the trademarked drug contrary to prescription specifications, or that they continued to supply the generic drug to pharmacists whom they knew were engaging in such mislabeling of drugs.

LABOR LAW

National Labor Relations Board v. Hendricks County Rural Electric Membership Corp., Hendricks County Rural Electric Membership Corp. v. National Labor Relations Board, decided by votes of 6-3 and 5-4, Dec. 2, 1981. Brennan wrote the opinion; Burger, Rehnquist, O'Connor and Powell dissented.

The only "confidential employees" exempt from the protection of federal labor law are those who enjoy the confidence of company officials involved in setting and carrying out labor relations policy. This exemption does not extend to secretaries and all employees who have access to some confidential information.

Charles D. Bonanno Linen Service Inc. v. National Labor Relations Board, decided by a 5-4 vote, Jan. 12, 1982. White wrote the opinion; Burger, Rehnquist, O'Connor and Powell dissented.

An impasse in bargaining between a multi-employer group and a union does not justify the unilateral withdrawal of an employer from the bargaining unit.

United Mine Workers of America Health and Retirement Funds v. Robinson, decided by a 9-0 vote, March 8, 1982. Stevens wrote the opinion.

The Labor Management Relations Act does not authorize federal courts to review the provisions of a collective-bargaining agreement for reasonableness — including such provisions setting eligibility standards for health and welfare funds.

U.S. Industries/Federal Sheet Metal Inc. v. Director, Office of Workers' Compensation Programs, U.S. Department of Labor, decided by a 6-2 vote, March 23, 1982. Stevens wrote the opinion; Brennan and Marshall dissented; O'Connor did not participate in the decision.

An appeals court erred when it presumed that an injury first noticed at home by a workman was in fact the result of an accident at work and thus made him eligible for disability benefits under the Longshoremen's and Harbor Workers' Compensation Act.

International Longshoremen's Association, AFL-CIO v. Allied International Inc., decided by a 9-0 vote. Powell wrote the opinion.

The refusal by an American longshoremen's union to unload cargo shipped from the Soviet Union — a step taken in protest of the Russian invasion of Afghanistan — is a secondary boycott, illegal under the National Labor Relations Act. The application of this ban on secondary boycotts to this boycott does not infringe on the First Amendment rights of the union and its members.

Finnegan v. Leu, decided by a 9-0 vote, May 17, 1982. Burger wrote the opinion.

A union president who, after his election, removed from their union posts 15 individuals who under union

constitution served at his pleasure and who had actively supported his opponent in the union election did not violate their First Amendment rights as guaranteed in federal labor law. That guarantees the free speech rights of members, not the tenure of union officers.

Woelke & Romero Framing Inc. v. National Labor Relations Board, Pacific Northwest Chapter of the Associated Builders & Contractors Inc. v. National Labor Relations Board, Oregon-Columbia Chapter, Associated General Contractors of America v. National Labor Relations Board, decided by a 9-0 vote, May 24, 1982. Marshall wrote the opinion.

Federal labor law permits construction unions operating under collective bargaining agreements to demand that contractors use subcontractors that recognize the union.

Summit Valley Industries Inc. v. Local 112, United Brotherhood of Carpenters and Joiners of America, decided by a 9-0 vote, June 1, 1982. Marshall wrote the opinion.

A company or individual who successfully brings unfair labor practice charges against a union may, under the Labor Management Relations Act, seek damages to compensate him for injuries sustained as a result of the unfair labor practice — but attorneys' fees incurred by the complainant during the proceedings concerning the unfair labor practice charge before the National Labor Relations Board are not a proper element of those damages.

Jackson Transit Authority v. Local Div. 1285, Amalgamated Transit Union, decided by a 9-0 vote, June 7, 1982. Blackmun wrote the opinion.

Labor disputes between the employees of a publicly owned transit system — which changed from private to public hands with aid provided through the Urban Mass Transportation Act of 1964 — and the management of the transit system should be resolved in state courts, not federal courts. By providing for the preservation of transit systems employees' bargaining rights, the 1964 Act did not create a federal cause of action allowing those rights to be enforced in federal court.

United Steelworkers of America v. Sadlowski, decided by a 5-4 vote, June 14, 1982. Marshall wrote the opinion; White, Burger, Brennan and Blackmun dissented.

A United Steelworkers rule barring contributions by non-members to candidates for union office does not violate the provisions of the Labor Management Reporting and Disclosure Act of 1959, which guarantees union members freedom to sue and freedom of speech and assembly. The rule does affect those rights, but it is justified by the union's interest in ensuring that non-members do not unduly influence union affairs.

Jacksonville Bulk Terminals Inc. v. International Longshoremen's Association, decided by a 6-3 vote, June 24, 1982. Marshall wrote the opinion; Burger, Powell and Stevens dissented.

The Norris-LaGuardia Act, which bars federal courts from enjoining any strike involving or growing out of a labor dispute, denies a federal court the power to enjoin a politically motivated longshoremen's boycott of cargo coming from or going to the Soviet Union, even though that boycott was in violation of a no-strike clause and an arbitration clause in the union's collective bargaining contract.

ENERGY AND ENVIRONMENT

Weinberger v. Catholic Action of Hawaii/Peace Education Project, decided by a 9-0 vote, Dec. 1, 1981. Rehnquist wrote the opinion.

The Department of Defense does not have to formulate and release a "hypothetical environmental impact statement" on the potential consequences of storing nuclear weapons at a naval base in Hawaii. Congress provided in the National Environmental Policy Act (PL 91-190) that public disclosure of required environmental impact statements was subject to provisions of the Freedom of Information Act. Since information about the site of nuclear weapons is classified, any impact statement that would reveal such information is exempt from disclosure under the Freedom of Information Act.

Watt v. Energy Action Educational Foundation, decided by a 9-0 vote, Dec. 1, 1981. O'Connor wrote the opinion.

The interior secretary has discretion to decide whether to experiment with non-cash-bonus bidding systems for offshore leasing. The 1978 Outer Continental Shelf Lands Act Amendments (PL 95-372) required a five-year period of experimentation with new bidding systems but did not demand experimentation with specific alternative systems.

Weinberger v. Romero-Barcelo, decided by an 8-1 vote, April 27, 1982. White wrote the opinion; Stevens dissented.

Federal courts have some discretion in determining proper remedies for violations of the Federal Water Pollution Control Act. The justices held that a federal district court acted within permissible limits when it allowed the U.S. Navy to continue target practice on an island off Puerto Rico while it sought a permit for discharging ordnance into the coastal waters, as required under the law. An appeals court had ruled that the district court should have ordered a halt to the target practice until the permit was obtained.

Federal Energy Regulatory Commission v. Mississippi, decided by votes of 9-0 and 5-4, June 1, 1982. Blackmun wrote the opinion; Powell, O'Connor, Burger and Rehnquist dissented in part.

Congress was within its power to regulate interstate commerce when it passed the Public Utility Regulatory Policies Act of 1978 (PL 95-617) directing state utility regulatory commissions to consider adopting certain rate-design and regulatory standards and to follow certain procedures when acting on those standards. (The majority held that PL 95-617 did not infringe upon powers reserved to the states under the 10th Amendment, but the four dissenters disagreed and said the law should be held unconstitutional.)

STATE POWERS

G. D. Searle & Co. v. Cohn, decided by votes of 8-1 and 7-2, Feb. 24, 1982. Blackmun wrote the opinion; Powell and Burger dissented in part; Stevens dissented.

A state law that bars the effect of the statute of limitations for suits against corporations based in other states that have no one in that state upon whom legal process may be served does not vacate the Constitution's promises of equal protection and due process. The effect of such a law in this case was to allow individuals to sue a corporation for the ill effects of a medication 11 years after the ill effects were evident, even though there is normally a two-year statute of limitation on such suits.

New England Power Co. v. New Hampshire, Massachusetts v. New Hampshire, Roberts v. New Hampshire, decided by a 9-0 vote, Feb. 24, 1982. Burger wrote the opinion.

A ban imposed by New Hampshire on out-of-state sales of hydroelectric power produced at plants located on its rivers is unconstitutional, a clear violation of the intent behind the grant to Congress of the power to regulate interstate commerce. This ban was "precisely the sort of protectionist regulation that the commerce clause declares off-limits to the states."

Village of Hoffman Estates v. Flipside, decided by an 8-0 vote, March 3, 1982. Marshall wrote the opinion; Stevens did not participate in the decision.

Cities are not barred by the Constitution from approving and enforcing ordinances regulating "head shops" that sell items designed or marketed for use with illegal drugs. If activities encouraging illegal drug use can be considered "speech" within the meaning of the First Amendment, then it is speech proposing an illegal transaction, which may — consistent with that amendment's guarantee — be regulated or banned entirely by the government.

United Transportation Union v. Long Island Rail Road Co., decided by a 9-0 vote, March 24, 1982. Burger wrote the opinion.

Applying the Railway Labor Act, which guarantees railroad workers the right to strike, to a state-owned railroad does not interfere so far into state affairs that it violates the 10th Amendment, even if the act displaces a state law forbidding strikes by state employees.

Congressional authority to regulate labor matters in the railroad industry has long been recognized. It is essential that this authority be extended in uniform fashion nationwide and not be displaced by state action. The 10th Amendment protects a state from federal interference that impairs its ability to carry out its essential functions, but operating a railroad is not one of those essential functions.

Cory v. White, decided by a 6-3 vote, June 14, 1982. White wrote the opinion; Powell, Marshall and Stevens dissented.

The 11th Amendment forbids the federal courts to entertain suits brought by citizens against a state without the state's consent. This bars a suit in federal court, under the Federal Interpleader Act, initiated by the administrator of the estate of billionaire Howard Hughes in order to resolve conflicting claims by the states of California and Texas that Hughes was domiciled in their state at the time of his death.

Clements v. Fashing, decided by a 5-4 vote, June 25, 1982. Rehnquist wrote the opinion; Brennan, Marshall, Blackmun and White dissented.

Texas does not violate the guarantee of equal protection by barring certain public officers from running for the state Legislature during the term for which they have been elected to another public office. Nor does the law, which

creates a vacancy in an office whenever its holder announces his candidacy for some other state or federal office, violate the equal protection guarantee.

Alfred L. Snapp & Son Inc. v. Puerto Rico, decided by an 8-0 vote, July 1, 1982. White wrote the opinion; Powell did not participate in the ruling.

Puerto Rico has standing to bring a *parens patriae* suit against Virginia apple growers, charging them with violating federal law concerning temporary migrant farm workers. Puerto Rico has a quasi-sovereign interest in the general well-being of its citizens, which this suit is brought to protect.

Florida Department of State v. Treasure Salvors Inc., decided by a 5-4 vote, July 1, 1982. Stevens announced the court's decision in an opinion joined by three justices; Brennan concurred; White, Powell, Rehnquist and O'Connor dissented.

The 11th Amendment does not bar a federal court from issuing a warrant of arrest directing federal seizure of artifacts taken from a sunken offshore vessel that are in the possession of state officials.

Property Rights

Texaco Inc. v. Short, Pond v. Walden, decided by a 5-4 vote, Jan. 12, 1982. Stevens wrote the opinion; Brennan, White, Marshall and Powell dissented.

A state has the power to enact and enforce a law providing for the extinguishment of mineral rights that have been unused for 20 years; application of this law to extinguish such rights without any notice or hearing does not violate the constitutional guarantee of due process, the constitutional ban on impairment of contracts or the prohibition on the taking of property without just compensation.

Loretto v. Teleprompter Manhattan CATV Corp., decided by a 6-3 vote, June 30, 1982. Marshall wrote the opinion; Blackmun, Brennan and White dissented.

A New York law requiring a landlord to permit installation of cable television facilities upon his property in return for a nominal fee results in a "taking" of private property for public use without just compensation, a violation of the Fifth Amendment. This installation is a "permanent physical occupation of property," which the court has traditionally viewed as a taking of property.

Regulation

Edgar v. MITE Corp., decided by a 6-3 vote, June 23, 1982. White wrote the opinion; Marshall, Brennan and Rehnquist dissented.

The Illinois Business Takeover Act, which imposes stricter requirements on companies bidding to take over other companies than does the federal Williams Act, is unconstitutional because it imposes burdens on interstate commerce that outweigh the local interests argued in justification of the state law.

Rice v. Norman Williams Co., decided by a 9-0 vote, July 1, 1982. Rehnquist wrote the opinion.

A California law that allows a liquor wholesaler to import only those brands of liquor for which he has been designated an "authorized agent" by the distiller is not invalid on its face as being in conflict with federal antitrust law, nor is it pre-empted by federal law governing the distribution of alcohol, nor is it in violation of the constitutional guarantees of equal protection or due process.

Sporhase v. Nebraska, decided by a 7-2 vote, July 2, 1982. Stevens wrote the opinion; Rehnquist and O'Connor dissented.

Groundwater is an article of commerce subject to congressional regulation. Nebraska violated the commerce clause when it conditioned the export of its groundwater on the grant, by the recipient state, of reciprocal rights to take water from that state.

State Courts

Ridgway v. Ridgway, decided by a 5-3 vote, Nov. 10, 1981. Blackmun wrote the opinion; Powell, Rehnquist and Stevens dissented; O'Connor did not participate.

A serviceman's designation of his beneficiary under the Servicemen's Group Life Insurance Act (PL 89-214) cannot be overridden by a state court, even if that designation is in direct conflict with the provisions of a divorce decree and settlement.

Underwriters National Assurance Co. v. North Carolina Life & Accident & Health Insurance Guaranty Association, decided by a 9-0 vote, March 24, 1982. Marshall wrote the opinion.

The Constitution requires that, "Full faith and credit shall be given in each state to the public acts, records, and judicial proceedings of every other state." Under this provision, the judgment of an Indiana court on a matter was conclusive upon the merits of that matter in North Carolina courts and should be honored in those courts.

Taxation

United States v. New Mexico, decided by a 9-0 vote, March 24, 1982. Blackmun wrote the opinion.

Corporations holding contracts with the federal government to manage government-owned facilities are not "instrumentalities of the United States" and are not exempt from state gross-receipts and compensating-use taxes imposed upon all persons doing business within the states. Immunity from state taxes is appropriate only when the tax falls on the U.S. government itself, or on an agency or instrumentality so closely connected to it that the two cannot realistically be viewed as separate.

ASARCO Inc. v. Idaho State Tax Commission, decided by a 6-3 vote, June 29, 1982. Powell wrote the opinion; O'Connor, Blackmun and Rehnquist dissented.

The due process clause bars a state from levying a tax upon income outside the proper reach of the state's tax power. Idaho may not properly include within ASARCO's taxable income (for purposes of calculating ASARCO's state tax liability) part of the dividends and other payments that ASARCO received from its subsidiary corporations outside the state, because there is no showing that the parent and the subsidiaries form a "unitary business."

F. W. Woolworth Co. v. Taxation and Revenue Department of New Mexico, decided by a 6-3 vote, June 29, 1982. Powell wrote the opinion; O'Connor, Blackmun and Rehnquist dissented.

New Mexico may not tax part of the dividends that a multinational corporation receives from its foreign subsidiaries unless it is shown that those foreign subsidiaries

constitute a unitary business with the parent corporation.

Ramah Navajo School Board v. Bureau of Revenue of New Mexico, decided by a 6-3 vote, July 2, 1982. Marshall wrote the opinion; Rehnquist, White and Stevens dissented.

Federal law denies New Mexico the power to tax the gross receipts of a non-Indian construction company paid by a tribal school board for the construction of a school on the reservation.

INTERSTATE BOUNDARIES

Tennessee v. Arkansas, decree issued Dec. 14, 1981.

The court approved a decree defining a disputed part of the boundary between Tennessee and Arkansas.

OFFSHORE LANDS

California ex rel. State Lands Commission v. United States, decided by a 9-0 vote, June 18, 1982. White wrote the opinion.

The court ruled that the United States, not California, owned approximately 184 acres of land along the California coast that had been created through accretion to land already owned by the United States.

FEDERAL COURTS

Fair Assessment in Real Estate Association Inc. v. McNary, decided by a 9-0 vote, Dec. 1, 1981. Rehnquist wrote the opinion.

The principle of comity restrains federal courts from hearing taxpayer damage suits brought to seek remedy for the operation of an allegedly unconstitutional state tax system. Taxpayers with such complaints should seek a remedy in state courts; the decisions of those courts in their cases may ultimately be reviewed in federal courts.

Piper Aircraft Co. v. Reyno, Hartzell Propeller v. Reyno, decided by a 4-3 vote, Dec. 8, 1981. Marshall wrote the opinion; White, Stevens and Brennan dissented; Powell and O'Connor did not participate in the decision.

A federal court may properly dismiss a lawsuit, finding that another court or another country provides a more convenient forum for resolution of the dispute, even if the law of the alternative forum is less favorable to the persons bringing the suit.

White v. New Hampshire Department of Employment Security, decided by a 9-0 vote March 2, 1982. Powell wrote the opinion.

Individuals who successfully sue state and local governments for violating their constitutional rights are not bound by the 10-day limit set out in federal procedural rules in requesting that they be awarded their attorneys' fees under the Civil Rights Attorney's Fees Awards Act of 1976. They may make such a request more than 10 days after their victory.

Rose v. Lundy, decided by an 8-1 vote, March 3, 1982. O'Connor wrote the opinion; Stevens dissented.

Federal courts presented with a petition from a state prisoner for a writ of *habeas corpus* that contains several constitutional claims, some of which have been pursued in state courts and some of which have not, should dismiss that petition. State inmates must give state courts the first opportunity to address such constitutional complaints. An inmate whose petition is dismissed for this reason may either delete from his petition the claims not presented to state courts and file it again in federal court, or he may return to the state courts to pursue his complaints there.

Lane v. Williams, decided by a 6-3 vote, March 23, 1982. Stevens wrote the opinion; Marshall, Brennan and Blackmun dissented.

Two men who pleaded guilty to burglary in state court and later claimed they were denied due process because they were not informed that their negotiated sentences included mandatory three-year paroles may not obtain a writ of *habeas corpus* from federal courts eliminating the mandatory parole term because they have now served those terms and their cases are moot. Their cases would not be moot had they sought nullification of their plea bargains and the opportunity to plead anew.

Engle v. Isaac, decided by votes of 6-3 and 7-2, April 5, 1982. O'Connor wrote the opinion; Stevens, Brennan and Marshall dissented.

State prisoners seeking collateral review of their convictions through a writ of *habeas corpus* from a federal court must show both cause for their failure to raise a constitutional objection at the time of their trial and actual prejudice as a result of the alleged constitutional violation before the writ can be granted.

United States v. Frady, decided by a 6-1 vote, April 5, 1982. O'Connor wrote the opinion; Brennan dissented; Burger and Marshall did not participate.

A federal prisoner seeking collateral review of his conviction in an effort to vacate his sentence on the grounds of error occurring at his trial may not win relief unless he can prove cause for his failure to object to the error during his trial and actual prejudice as a result of the alleged error.

Insurance Corporation of Ireland Ltd. v. Compagnie des Bauxites de Guinea, decided by a 9-0 vote, June 1, 1982. White wrote the opinion.

A federal district court did not deny due process to a corporation sued before it that was not a resident of the United States and that failed to comply with discovery orders seeking evidence relating to the existence of contacts with the United States when the district court simply assumed that such contacts existed and that jurisdiction was established.

Army and Air Force Exchange Service v. Sheehan, decided by a 9-0 vote, June 1, 1982. Blackmun wrote the opinion.

The Tucker Act does not give federal courts jurisdiction over a suit against the U.S. government for money damages brought by a former government employee who alleges that he was discharged in violation of his right to due process.

California v. Grace Brethren Church, United States v. Grace Brethren Church, Grace Brethren Church v. United States, decided by a 7-2 vote, June 18, 1982. O'Connor

wrote the opinion; Stevens and Blackmun dissented.

The Tax Injunction Act deprives federal courts of jurisdiction to issue an injunction halting state collection of unemployment compensation tax when there is a speedy and efficient remedy, as in this case. That law also denies a federal court the power to declare the state law unconstitutional as an infringement on the First Amendment rights of certain religious schools not affiliated with churches.

Middlesex County Ethics Committee v. Garden State Bar Association, decided by a 9-0 vote, June 21, 1982. Burger wrote the opinion.

A federal court should abstain from considering a challenge to the constitutionality of disciplinary rules and proceedings against an attorney charged with unethical conduct so long as that proceeding is under way within the jurisdiction of a state court and provides the attorney an opportunity to raise his constitutional claims before that body.

Foremost Insurance Co. v. Richardson, decided by a 5-4 vote, June 23, 1982. Marshall wrote the opinion; Powell, Burger, Rehnquist and O'Connor dissented.

Federal admiralty jurisdiction extends to accidents occurring on navigable waters between two boats involved solely in recreational use.

Lehman v. Lycoming County Children's Services Agency, decided by a 6-3 vote, June 30, 1982. Powell wrote the opinion; Blackmun, Brennan and Marshall dissented.

Federal courts do not have jurisdiction to consider petitions for *habeas corpus* relief brought by parents challenging state court action terminating their parental rights to their children.

OFFICIAL IMMUNITY

Polk County v. Dodson, decided by an 8-1 vote, Dec. 14, 1981. Powell wrote the opinion; Blackmun dissented.

Public defenders, although paid by the state, owe their primary loyalty to the clients they represent and do not act "under color of state law" in that capacity. Therefore, they cannot be sued under the federal civil rights damage statute, Section 1983, for negligent representation. When performing certain other functions, public defenders may be acting under color of state law and thus be liable to such suits, but not when performing the traditional function of counsel to a criminal defendant.

Finley v. Murray, dismissed May 17, 1982, without dissent.

In a *per curiam* (unsigned) statement, the court said that it should not have agreed to hear arguments in this case, which presented the question of the immunity of a circuit court clerk from a damage suit charging him with violating the civil rights of a woman arrested on the basis of an invalid warrant he issued.

Nixon v. Fitzgerald, decided by a 5-4 vote, June 24, 1982. Powell wrote the opinion; White, Brennan, Marshall and Blackmun dissented.

Presidents are absolutely immune from civil damage suits for all official actions taken while in office. The court ruled in a case involving the claim of former Air Force cost analyst A. Ernest Fitzgerald that he lost his job, as punishment for his disclosure in congressional testimony of massive cost overruns on a defense transport plane, as a result of a White House conspiracy involving former President Richard Nixon. The majority said the electoral process and the impeachment mechanism provide sufficient remedy for presidential wrongdoing. The four dissenters said the ruling "places the president above the law" and was "a reversion to the old notion that the king can do no wrong."

Harlow v. Fitzgerald, decided by an 8-1 vote, June 24, 1982. Powell wrote the opinion; Burger dissented.

Presidential aides do not have absolute immunity from civil rights damage suits by individuals who claim they have been denied their rights by those aides acting in their official capacity. A presidential aide can establish such immunity if he shows that the "responsibilities of his office embrace[d] a function so sensitive as to require a total shield from liability."

Presidential aides, like other executive officials, enjoy qualified immunity from such damage suits. The court set out a new standard for courts to use in weighing a qualified immunity defense. The court held that "government officials performing discretionary functions generally are shielded from liability for civil damages insofar as their conduct does not violate clearly established statutory or constitutional rights of which a reasonable person would have known." The court abandoned an earlier test that required inquiry into the motivation of the official in committing the challenged act.

Velde v. National Black Police Association, decided by a 7-0 vote, June 30, 1982. Powell and Stevens did not participate. *Per curiam* opinion.

The court sent this case back to a lower court. It involved federal officials who were sued for failing to cut off federal aid to force recipient police departments to halt discrimination against women and blacks. The court said the lower court should consider this case in light of the ruling in *Harlow v. Fitzgerald (above)*.

SOCIAL SECURITY

United States v. Lee, decided by a 9-0 vote, Feb. 23, 1982. Burger wrote the decision.

Congress exempted from Social Security taxes only self-employed individuals whose religious beliefs forbid them to participate in the Social Security system. This does not allow an Amish farmer and carpenter who employs other members of his sect to refuse to pay Social Security taxes on their wages.

Although paying his workers' Social Security taxes may interfere with the right of the farmer to the free exercise of his religious beliefs, some such burdens may be justified if necessary to realize an overriding governmental interest. The government's interest in the fiscal vitality of the Social Security system is such an overriding interest.

Blum v. Bacon, decided by a 9-0 vote, June 14, 1982. Marshall wrote the opinion.

A New York law that denies emergency cash assistance, a program set up with federal funding under the Social Security Act, to recipients of Aid to Families with Dependent Children, and denies this aid in any form to

reimburse welfare recipients for lost or stolen welfare checks, is invalid because it conflicts with federal regulations forbidding inequitable treatment of individuals under the emergency assistance program.

Medicare

United States v. Erika, decided by a 9-0 vote, April 20, 1982. Powell wrote the opinion.

The Court of Claims lacks jurisdiction to review challenges to decisions by private insurance companies concerning the amount of benefits payable under part of the Medicare program.

Schweiker v. McClure, decided by a 9-0 vote, April 20, 1982. Powell wrote the opinion.

The federal statutory scheme under which hearings on claims under the Medicare program are conducted by private insurance company employees does not deny Medicare claimants their due process rights, even though it is the insurance company which has already once denied the benefit claim.

Medicaid

Herweg v. Ray, decided by an 8-1 vote, Feb. 23, 1982. Rehnquist wrote the opinion; Burger dissented.

A federal Medicaid regulation limiting the period during which a state may assume that the income of a non-institutionalized spouse is available to pay the expenses of an institutionalized spouse is a permissible exercise of federal authority under the Social Security Act.

Schweiker v. Hogan, decided by a 9-0 vote, June 21, 1982. Stevens wrote the opinion.

Income requirements imposed by the Social Security Act for federal reimbursement of Medicaid benefits are not unconstitutional even when they result, under a state Medicaid program, in lower benefits for some low-income, retired and disabled workers than for welfare recipients.

FREEDOM OF INFORMATION

McNichols v. Baldrige, Baldrige v. Shapiro, decided by votes of 9-0, Feb. 24, 1982. Burger wrote the opinion.

Congress explicitly provided that all raw census data reported by or on behalf of individuals should remain confidential, and neither the Freedom of Information Act nor the discovery provisions of federal court rules may be used to force disclosure of such information. The court thus blocked efforts of officials from Denver, Colo., and Essex County, N.J., to obtain certain address lists used by 1980 census-takers in their areas. Both areas claimed their populations had been under-counted by census-takers who incorrectly described certain dwellings as vacant.

U.S. Department of State v. The Washington Post Co., decided by a 9-0 vote, May 17, 1982. Rehnquist wrote the opinion.

The exemption from disclosure under the Freedom of Information Act for "personnel and medical files and similar files the disclosure of which would constitute a clearly unwarranted invasion of personal privacy" encompasses information that may exist elsewhere in the public domain. The State Department could, under this exemption, refuse to disclose documents indicating whether two Iranian nationals held valid U.S. passports.

Federal Bureau of Investigation v. Abramson, decided by a 5-4 vote, May 24, 1982. White wrote the opinion; Blackmun, Brennan, O'Connor and Marshall dissented.

The FBI may refuse, under an exemption provided by the Freedom of Information Act for law enforcement files, to disclose information contained in "name check" summaries prepared for the Nixon White House on certain public figures. This information had originally been collected for such files but was transmitted to the White House in summary form. The court held that it was still exempt.

FOREIGN AFFAIRS

Weinberger v. Rossi, decided by a 9-0 vote, March 31, 1982. Rehnquist wrote the opinion.

When Congress in 1971 banned job discrimination against U.S. citizens on military bases overseas unless such discrimination was permitted by a treaty, it used the word 'treaty' to include executive agreements with other nations as well as formal treaties ratified by the Senate. The court upheld executive agreements with other nations that give preferential treatment to citizens of nations where U.S. military bases are located.

GOVERNMENT EMPLOYEES

United States v. Clark, decided by a 9-0 vote, Jan. 12, 1982. O'Connor wrote the opinion.

A federal employee who is promoted from the wage system pay scheme to the general schedule pay system is not entitled by law to an automatic two-step increase in pay; this automatic increase applies only to promotions and transfers within the general schedule pay system. ∎

Nominations and Confirmations

Conservatives Block Some Reagan Nominees

President Reagan's nominees for two Cabinet vacancies in 1982 — George P. Shultz as secretary of state and Donald P. Hodel as secretary of energy — were confirmed by the Senate with almost no controversy.

Martin S. Feldstein, the president's choice for another prestigious post, that of chairman of the Council of Economic Advisers (CEA), ran into some Democratic opposition but also was confirmed.

Nominees to several other high-level positions encountered greater obstacles. In contrast to his first year in office, in 1982 the president's chief difficulties in winning approval of his nominations for high-level executive branch positions came from conservatives in his own party rather than from liberal Democrats.

The conservative opposition was led by Sen. Jesse Helms, R-N.C. Helms' tactics resulted in infighting between Senate factions — leaving some of the president's choices caught in the middle — over issues that had little to do with the nominees' qualifications. Several nominees opposed by the conservatives were not confirmed.

Bipartisan opposition sidetracked other appointees. Reagan late in the year withdrew the nominations of nine members of the Legal Services Corporation (LSC) board of directors when it became clear that the three most conservative nominees faced difficulty winning confirmation.

The Senate confirmed 3,555 civilian nominations in 1982. Seven nominations failed, 21 were withdrawn, and 47 remained unconfirmed at year's end.

Cabinet Nominees

Shultz. To succeed Alexander M. Haig Jr., who abruptly resigned as secretary of state on June 25, Reagan nominated George P. Shultz, an economist and business executive and a veteran Cabinet official.

The volatile Haig had come under increasing criticism from some high administration officials, including Defense Secretary Caspar W. Weinberger, over various foreign policy issues. Weinberger had won a long intramural dispute with Haig over economic sanctions against the Soviet Union.

In contrast to Haig, flamboyant and known for his jealous jousting over policy turf, Shultz' calm demeanor during two days of hearings before the Senate Foreign Relations Committee, and his circumspect responses to senator's questioning, quickly reassured members of the committee. His nomination was approved 17-0 on July 14.

The following day, acting rapidly because of crises in the Middle East and problems in U.S.-European relations, the Senate confirmed Shultz, 97-0. *(Vote 216, p. 39-S)*

Shultz proposed no dramatic departures from the policies Haig had pursued. During the hearings, Shultz dispelled concerns raised by his years as a Bechtel executive by pledging that his experience with the firm would not color his views on the Mideast. Shultz joined Bechtel Group Inc. in 1974 and had been president of the worldwide construction and engineering firm since December 1980.

Bechtel had grossed $11.6 billion in 1981, about half from business dealings outside the United States, including about 12 percent from the Middle East. Some senators had feared Bechtel's ties with the Arabs would influence Shultz' Mideast policies, to the detriment of Israel.

While Shultz said he would cultivate stronger ties with the Arabs, and that solving the Palestinian issue was "fundamental" to peace in the Middle East, he also assured the panel of his firm commitment to the security of Israel.

Hodel. Donald P. Hodel was appointed Nov. 5 to replace James B. Edwards as secretary of energy. Edwards had resigned the same day.

Since Congress was not in session at the time, Hodel's was a recess appointment, which took effect immediately. He nevertheless would have to win Senate confirmation by the end of the regular 1983 session.

The Senate Energy Committee favorably reported the nomination Dec. 7 by a 19-1 vote, with Paul E. Tsongas, D-Mass., casting the lone "no" vote. It was not so much a vote against Hodel, Tsongas said, as a vote against Interior Secretary James G. Watt. Hodel had been Watt's under secretary.

Edward M. Kennedy, D-Mass., called the nomination "a distressing continuation of this administration's record of dismal appointments in the area of environment and energy."

The Senate Dec. 8 confirmed Hodel by a vote of 86-8. *(Vote 395, p. 67-S)*

Economic Policy

Feldstein. Martin S. Feldstein was confirmed Dec. 8 as a member of the Council of Economic Advisers. The vote was 77-18. *(Vote 394, p. 67-S)*

Feldstein had been serving as acting chairman of the CEA since Sept. 8. He replaced Murray L. Weidenbaum, who resigned July 22.

Confirmation came after Feldstein agreed to testify before the Joint Economic Committee Dec. 9. He had been criticized for refusing to testify before his nomination was confirmed.

The Senate Banking Committee had approved the nomination on a party-line vote. Panel Democrats expressed reservations about Feldstein, a Harvard University economics professor and head of the National Bureau of Economic Research, because "his statements suggest he is insufficiently sensitive to the economic distress facing the country today."

Martin. Preston Martin was routinely confirmed by the Senate March 30 for a 14-year term as a member of the Federal Reserve Board. Martin, whose term began Feb. 1, 1982, was to serve as vice chairman of the board for four years.

A California businessman, Martin had served as chairman of the Federal Home Loan Bank Board during the Nixon administration.

He had been an aide to President Reagan when Reagan was governor of California.

Membership of Federal Regulatory Agencies, 1982

Civil Aeronautics Board

(Five members appointed for six-year terms; not more than three members from one political party; agency due to expire Jan. 1, 1985.)

Member	Party	Term Expires	Nominated	Confirmed by Senate
Clinton D. McKinnon (C)	R	12/31/85	10/6/81	10/26/81
George A. Dalley	D	12/31/82	8/3/79	3/6/80
Elizabeth E. Bailey	R	12/31/83	7/8/77	7/28/77
Gloria Schaffer	D	12/31/84	7/13/78	9/13/78
James R. Smith	I	12/31/86	7/25/80	8/27/80

Commodity Futures Trading Commission

(Five members appointed for five-year terms; not more than three members from one political party.)

Member	Party	Term Expires	Nominated	Confirmed by Senate
Philip F. Johnson (C)	R	4/15/84	5/12/81	6/4/81
James M. Stone	D	4/15/83	1/15/79	4/10/79
Susan M. Phillips	R	4/15/85	9/10/81	10/27/81
Kalo A. Hineman	R	6/19/86	12/10/81	12/15/81
Fowler C. West	D	4/15/87	9/17/82	10/1/82

Consumer Product Safety Commission

(Five members appointed for seven-year terms; not more than three members from one political party.)

Member	Party	Term Expires	Nominated	Confirmed by Senate
Nancy H. Steorts (C)	R	10/26/84	7/13/81	7/27/81
Edith B. Sloan	D	10/26/83	1/20/78	2/28/78
Samuel D. Zagoria	R	10/26/85	9/29/78	10/10/78
Stuart M. Statler	R	10/26/86	6/14/79	7/26/79
Vacancy				

Federal Communications Commission

(Seven members appointed for seven-year terms; not more than four members from one political party.)

Member	Party	Term Expires	Nominated	Confirmed by Senate
Mark S. Fowler (C)	R	6/30/86	4/27/81	5/14/81
Joseph R. Fogarty	D	6/30/83	6/21/76	9/8/76
James H. Quello	D	6/30/84	7/8/81	7/31/81
Anne P. Jones	R	6/30/85	1/15/79	3/21/79
Henry M. Rivera	D	6/30/87	7/8/81	7/31/81
Mary Ann Weyforth-Dawson	R	6/30/88	5/12/81	6/4/81
Stephen A. Sharp	R	6/30/83	5/24/82	10/1/82

Federal Election Commission

(Six members appointed for six-year terms; not more than three members from one political party.)

Member	Party	Term Expires	Nominated	Confirmed by Senate
Frank P. Reiche (C)	R	4/30/85	5/1/79	7/25/79
John W. McGarry	D	4/30/83	1/15/79	2/21/79
Joan D. Aikens	R	4/30/83	1/26/82	7/1/82
Thomas E. Harris	D	4/30/85	5/1/79	6/19/79
Lee Ann Elliott	R	4/30/87	1/26/82	7/1/82
Danny Lee McDonald	D	4/30/87	1/26/82	7/1/82

Federal Energy Regulatory Commission

(Five members appointed to staggered four-year terms; not more than three members from one political party.)

Member	Party	Term Expires	Nominated	Confirmed by Senate
Charles M. Butler III (C)	R	10/20/83	5/12/81	6/4/81
John D. Hughes	D	10/20/83	5/1/80	8/27/80
Georgianna Sheldon	R	10/20/84	5/14/81	6/4/81
Anthony G. Sousa	R	10/20/84	6/30/81	7/27/81
Oliver G. Richard III	D	10/20/85	7/16/82	8/19/82

Federal Reserve System Governors

(Seven members appointed for 14-year terms; no statutory limitation on political party membership.)

Member	Party	Term Expires	Nominated	Confirmed by Senate
Paul A. Volcker (C)	D	1/31/92	8/17/79	8/2/79
Nancy H. Teeters	D	1/31/84	8/28/78	9/15/78
J. Charles Partee	I	1/31/86	12/8/75	12/19/75
Henry C. Wallich	R	1/31/88	4/12/79	6/12/79
Emmett J. Rice	D	1/31/90	4/12/79	6/12/79
Lyle E. Gramley	D	1/31/94	3/21/80	5/15/80
Preston Martin	R	1/31/96	1/11/82	3/31/82

Federal Trade Commission

(Five members appointed for seven-year terms; not more than three members from one political party.)

Member	Party	Term Expires	Nominated	Confirmed by Senate
James C. Miller III (C)	R	9/25/88	7/16/81	9/21/81
David A. Clanton	R	9/25/83	7/20/76	7/26/76
Michael J. Pertschuk	D	9/25/84	3/25/77	4/6/77
Patricia P. Bailey	R	9/25/87	6/10/80	6/26/80
George W. Douglas	D	9/25/89	9/20/82	12/16/82

Interstate Commerce Commission

(Eleven members appointed for seven-year terms; not more than six members from one political party. President Carter decided to cut the commission's size by not filling vacancies.)

Member	Party	Term Expires	Nominated	Confirmed by Senate
Reese H. Taylor Jr. (C)	R	12/31/84	5/5/81	6/16/81
Reginald E. Gilliam Jr.	I	12/31/82	12/12/79	4/2/80
J. J. Simmons III	D	12/31/85	12/18/81	4/1/82
Frederic N. Andre	R	12/31/87	9/24/81	3/16/82
Malcolm M. B. Sterrett	R	12/31/87	9/24/81	2/9/82
Heather J. Gradison	R	12/31/88	3/22/82	6/16/82
Vacancy				

Nuclear Regulatory Commission

(Five members appointed for five-year terms; not more than three members from one political party.)

Member	Party	Term Expires	Nominated	Confirmed by Senate
Nunzio J. Palladino (C)	R	6/30/86	6/11/81	6/19/81
John F. Ahearne	D	6/30/83	5/18/78	7/21/78
Victor Gilinsky	D	6/30/84	5/15/79	6/27/79
Thomas M. Roberts	R	6/30/85	7/9/81	7/31/81
James K. Asselstine	I	6/30/87	4/26/82	5/13/82

Securities and Exchange Commission

(Five members appointed for five-year terms; not more than three members from one political party.)

Member	Party	Term Expires	Nominated	Confirmed by Senate
John S. R. Shad (C)	R	6/5/86	4/1/81	4/8/81
John R. Evans	R	6/5/83	6/11/79	9/18/79
Bevis Longstreth	D	6/5/84	6/23/82	8/20/82
Barbara S. Thomas	D	6/5/85	7/29/80	9/8/80
James C. Treadway Jr.	R	6/5/87	7/22/82	8/19/82

Foreign Policy

Opposition by Helms and other conservatives killed two Reagan nominations to the Arms Control and Disarmament Agency (ACDA): Robert T. Grey Jr. as deputy director and Norman Terrell as director of the ACDA's bureau of nuclear weapons control.

The opposition was based partly on the nominees' role in nuclear arms control in previous administrations. On a broader level, Helms and his colleagues used the nominations as a basis for challenging what they saw as the administration's abandonment of a sufficiently tough stance in arms talks with the Soviet Union.

Terrell's nomination was withdrawn Nov. 30. Grey's nomination was sent to the Senate Dec. 8, but Helms prevented it from coming to a vote. The White House withdrew the nomination Jan. 4, 1983.

The threat of a conservative filibuster also shelved the nominations of Richard R. Burt to be assistant secretary of state for European affairs and Richard T. McCormack to be assistant secretary of state for economic affairs. Both nominations were debated briefly by the Senate Dec. 8, but neither was brought to a vote. The nominations were expected to be resubmitted in 1983.

Sen. Helms objected to articles Burt had written while he was a reporter for *The New York Times*, and Sen. Orrin G. Hatch, R-Utah, implied that Burt disagreed with administration policies.

In apparent retaliation, Sen. Joseph R. Biden Jr., D-Del., threatened to block the nomination of McCormack, who had worked for Helms from 1979 to 1981.

In other action:

Nickel. The Senate March 29 confirmed Herman W. Nickel as ambassador to South Africa in spite of complaints from some groups that he had a relaxed attitude toward that nation's racial policies. The Senate approved Nickel by voice vote.

At his confirmation hearings before the Senate Foreign Relations Committee March 19, Nickel cited his "implacable opposition" to South Africa's policy of apartheid. But representatives of church groups maintained that Nickel, a journalist, actually favored closer relations with the white South African government.

Maino. The Senate Sept. 29 by voice vote confirmed Theodore C. Maino as ambassador to Botswana. The Senate confirmed him despite an unusually strong complaint from the American Foreign Service Association, a private group composed of active and retired Foreign Service officers, that the California contractor and Republican campaign contributor was unqualified for the post.

Civil Rights Commission

President Reagan bowed to strong protests by civil rights groups Feb. 26 and withdrew his latest choice for a post on the six-member U.S. Civil Rights Commission.

A White House spokesman later explained that the Rev. B. Sam Hart, a black Philadelphia radio evangelist whom Reagan had picked for the post, asked that his name be withdrawn, and Reagan complied.

Hart provoked controversy as soon as he was nominated. He said he opposed busing for school desegregation, the Equal Rights Amendment and the concept of homosexual rights.

Pennsylvania's two Republican senators, John Heinz and Arlen Specter, were unhappy with Reagan's choice. Both said they had not been consulted on the selection, and

Heinz said he had strong reservations about Hart's qualifications.

Legal Services Corporation

President Reagan Dec. 8 withdrew the nominations of nine members of the Legal Services board of directors after 52 senators signed a letter saying they would not support three of Reagan's choices.

The White House said some of the other six nominees to the 11-member board were not "philosophically in tune" with Reagan's policies.

Eight of the nine nominations were before the Senate. The ninth had been held up in the Labor and Human Resources Committee.

Since taking office, Reagan had tried to abolish the LSC, which provided legal aid to the poor. Congress refused to kill it. Reagan then named to the board members he hoped would substantially restrict LSC activities. (*Legal Services Corporation, p. 412*)

The two most controversial nominees were William F. Harvey, an Indiana University law professor, and William J. Olson, a former officer of the Young Americans for Freedom and the National Conservative Political Action Committee.

The other nominee the 52 senators said they would not support was George E. Paras, whose nomination was still in committee.

Harvey, appointed during a congressional recess in 1981, was chairman of the board. He and the eight others whose nominations were withdrawn were all recess appointees and could serve only until the end of the 97th Congress. Two other members, Dan Rathbun and Frank Donatelli, were named during the 1982 election recess and could serve through 1983.

1982 Confirmations

Listed below are 148 persons appointed by President Reagan to major federal posts and confirmed by the Senate in 1982. Information is given in the following order: name of office, salary (as of confirmation date), appointee, legal residence, last occupation before appointment, selected political or public policy posts held, date of birth, party affiliation (where available) and confirmation date.

EXECUTIVE OFFICE OF THE PRESIDENT

Council of Economic Advisers

Member and chairman, $60,662.50 — **Martin S. Feldstein;** Belmont, Mass.; professor, Harvard University (1969-82); chairman, Subcommittee on Capital Investments, President's Private Sector Survey on Cost Control (1981-82); Nov. 25, 1939; Independent; Dec. 8.

Member, $58,500 — **William Poole VII;** Providence, R.I.; professor, Brown University (1974-82); visiting economist, Reserve Bank of Australia (1980-81); consultant, Federal Reserve Bank of Boston (1974-82); June 19, 1937; Republican; Dec. 10.

Council on Environmental Quality

Member, $58,500 — **Nancy A. Maloley;** Washington, D.C.; senior staff member, policy development, White House (1981-82); legislative assistant to U.S. Sen Richard G. Lugar (1977-81); April 13, 1946; Republican; July 26.

Office of Management and Budget

Deputy director, $59,500 — **Joseph R. Wright Jr.;** Washington, D.C.; deputy secretary, Commerce Department (1981-82); assistant secretary for administration, Agriculture Department (1973-76); Sept. 24, 1939; Republican; April 20.

CABINET DEPARTMENTS

Department of Agriculture

Assistant secretary for governmental and public affairs, $58,500 — **Wilmer D. Mizell Sr.;** Winston-Salem, N.C.; public relations representative, Southern Tool Manufacturing Co. Inc. (1978-82); assistant secretary, Commerce Department (1975-77); U.S. representative, North Carolina (1969-75); Aug. 13, 1930; Republican; Aug. 18.

Assistant secretary for science and education, $58,500 — **Orville G. Bentley;** Urbana, Ill.; dean, College of Agriculture, University of Illinois (1965-82); consultant, Board for International Food and Agricultural Development, Agency for International Development (1976-79); March 6, 1918; Republican; Dec. 8.

Department of Commerce

Deputy secretary, $60,662.50 — **Guy W. Fiske;** McLean, Va.; under secretary, Energy Department (1981-82); Sept. 28, 1924; Republican; June 24.

Under secretary for economic affairs, $59,500 — **Robert G. Dederick;** Washington, D.C.; assistant secretary, Commerce Department (1981-82); member, economic advisory board, Commerce Department (1968-70, 1975-76); Nov. 18, 1929; Republican; Aug. 4.

National Oceanic and Atmospheric Administration

Associate administrator, $58,500 — **James W. Winchester;** Pass Christian, Miss.; owner, Business and Engineering Consultants Inc. (1977-82); director, National Oceanic and Atmospheric Administration Data Buoy Office (1972-77); Nov. 7, 1916; Republican; March 15.

Department of Defense

Deputy secretary, $60,662.50 — **W. Paul Thayer;** Dallas; chairman and chief executive officer, The LTV Corp. (1970-82); Nov. 23, 1919; Dec. 16.

Assistant secretary of the Air Force for research, development and logistics, $67,200 — **Thomas E. Cooper;** Alexandria, Va.; professional staff member, U.S. House of Representatives Armed Services Committee (1977-82); May 31, 1943; Dec. 21.

Department of Education

Under secretary, $59,500 — **Gary L. Jones;** Fairfax, Va.; deputy under secretary for planning, budget and evaluation, Education Department (1981-82); director, research and policy coordination, Reagan for President (1979-80); assistant to U.S. Sen. Robert P. Griffin (1970-73); May 6, 1944; Republican; Oct. 1.

Assistant secretary for civil rights, $58,500 — **Harry M. Singleton;** Washington, D.C.; deputy assistant secretary for congressional affairs, Commerce Department (1981-82); minority chief counsel, U.S. House of Representatives District of Columbia Committee (1979-81); April 10, 1949; Republican; Oct. 1.

Assistant secretary for elementary and secondary education, $58,500 — **Lawrence F. Davenport;** Reston, Va.; associate director for domestic and anti-poverty operations, ACTION (1981-82); provost, San Diego Community College District (1979-81); Oct. 13, 1944; Republican; Oct. 1.

Assistant secretary for postsecondary education, $58,500 — **Edward M. Elmendorf;** Springfield, Va.; deputy assistant secretary, student financial assistance, Education Department (1981-82); president, Johnson State College (1974-80); Aug. 1, 1939; Republican; Dec 16.

Department of Energy

Secretary, $69,630 — **Donald P. Hodel;** Lake Oswego, Ore.; under secretary, Interior Department (1981-82); energy consultant (1978-81); deputy administrator and then administrator, Bonneville Power Administration (1969-77); May 23, 1935; Republican; Dec. 8.

Assistant secretary for management and administration, $58,500 — **Martha O. Hesse;** Chicago; executive director, President's Task Force on Management Reform (1982); associate deputy secretary, Commerce Department (1981-82); Aug. 14, 1942; Republican; Dec. 8.

Federal Energy Regulatory Commission

Member for term expiring Oct. 20, 1985, $58,500 — **Oliver G. Richard III;** Lafayette, La.; partner, Hayes, Durio & Richard (1981-82); legislative assistant to U.S. Sen. J. Bennett Johnston (1977-81); Oct. 11, 1952; Democrat; Aug. 19.

Department of Health and Human Services

National Institutes of Health

Director, $58,500 — **James B. Wyngaarden;** Bethesda, Md.; chairman, department of medicine, School of Medicine, Duke University (1967-82); Oct. 19, 1924; Democrat; April 27.

Department of Housing and Urban Development

Assistant secretary for housing and federal housing commissioner, $58,500 — **Philip Abrams;** West Newton, Mass.; deputy assistant secretary, Housing and Urban Development Department (1981-82); treasurer, Abreen Corp. (1966-81); Nov. 13, 1939; Republican; Sept. 29.

Department of Justice

Immigration and Naturalization Service

Commissioner, $58,500 — **Alan C. Nelson;** Lafayette, Calif.; deputy commissioner, Immigration and Naturalization Service (1981-82); Oct. 18, 1933; Republican; Feb. 8.

Department of State

Deputy secretary, $60,662.50 — **Walter J. Stoessel Jr.;** Washington, D.C.; under secretary for political affairs, State Department (1981-82); U.S. ambassador to the Federal Republic of Germany (1976-81); U.S. ambassador to the Soviet Union (1974-76); Jan. 24, 1920; Republican; Feb. 8.

Under secretary for political affairs, $59,500 — **Lawrence S. Eagleburger;** Daytona Beach, Fla.; assistant secretary for European affairs, State Department (1981-82); U.S. ambassador to Yugoslavia (1977-81); deputy under secretary, State Department (1975-77); executive assistant to secretary, State Department (1973-75); Aug. 1, 1930; Republican; Feb. 10.

Assistant secretary for congressional relations, $58,500 — **Powell A. Moore;** Alexandria, Va.; assistant to the president for legislative affairs, White House (1981-82); Jan. 5, 1938; Republican; Feb. 4.

Assistant secretary for international organization affairs, $58,500 — **Gregory J. Newell;** McLean, Va.; special assistant and director of appointments and scheduling to President Ronald Reagan (1981-82); consultant to U.S. Sen. Robert Dole (1978-79); staff assistant to President Gerald R. Ford (1975-77); Aug. 30, 1949; Republican; May 27.

Secretary, $69,630 — **George P. Shultz;** Stanford, Calif.; various positions leading to president and director, Bechtel Group (1974-82); secretary of the Treasury (1972-74); director, Office of Management and Budget (1970-72); secretary of labor (1969-70); Dec. 13, 1920; Republican; July 15.

Under secretary for security assistance, science and technology, $59,500 — **William Schneider Jr.**; Rockville Centre, N.Y.; associate director for national security and international affairs, Office of Management and Budget (1981-82); staff associate, Defense Subcommittee, U.S. House of Representatives Appropriations Committee (1977-81); Nov. 20, 1941; Republican; Aug. 19.

Counselor, $59,500 — **James L. Buckley**; Norwich, Conn.; under secretary for coordination of security assistance programs, State Department (1981-82); U.S. senator, New York (1971-77); March 9, 1923; Republican; Aug. 20.

Assistant secretary for public affairs, $58,500 — **Robert Hughes**; Orleans, Mass.; associate director for programs, International Communication Agency (1981-82); April 28, 1930; Independent; Aug. 18.

Deputy secretary, $60,662.50 — **Kenneth W. Dam**; Chicago; professor, University of Chicago Law School (1964-71, 1974-82); consultant, Federal Trade Commission (1975-76); Aug. 10, 1932; Republican; Sept. 22.

Under secretary for economic affairs, $59,500 — **W. Allen Wallis**; Rochester, N.Y.; chancellor, trustee and professor, University of Rochester (1970-82); member of transition team for International Communication Agency (1981); Nov. 5, 1912; Sept. 22.

Under secretary for management, $59,500 — **Jerome W. Van Gorkom**; Lake Forest, Ill.; chairman, Chicago School Finance Authority (1981-82); executive official and then chief executive officer, Trans Union Corp. (1956-81); Aug. 6, 1917; Dec. 10.

Assistant secretary for East Asian and Pacific affairs, $58,500 — **Paul D. Wolfowitz**; Washington, D.C.; director of policy planning, State Department (1981-82); professor, School of Advanced International Studies, Johns Hopkins University (1980-81); deputy assistant secretary for regional planning, Defense Department (1977-80); Dec. 22, 1943; Dec. 16.

Ambassadors

At-large for refugee affairs, $60,662.50 — **Howard Eugene Douglas**; Vienna, Va.; member, policy planning staff, State Department (1981-82); Oct. 5, 1940; March 4.

Chile, $58,500 — **James Daniel Theberge**; Washington, D.C.; special adviser on inter-American affairs, Defense Department (1981-82); ambassador to Nicaragua (1975-77); Dec. 28, 1930; March 2.

Philippines, $60,662.50 — **Michael Hayden Armacost**; Bethesda, Md.; deputy assistant secretary, State Department (1980-82); deputy assistant secretary, Defense Department (1978-80); April 15, 1937; Feb. 10.

South Africa, $59,500 — **Herman W. Nickel**; Washington, D.C.; member, board of editors, *Fortune* (1977-81); Oct. 23, 1928; March 29.

Jamaica, $59,500 — **William A. Hewitt**; Rock Island, Ill.; chairman and chief executive officer, Deere & Co. (1964-82); member, President's Commission for a National Agenda for the Eighties (1980-81); member, Trilateral Commission (1973-81); Aug. 9, 1914; Republican; Sept. 29.

Republic of Botswana, $58,500 — **Theodore C. Maino**; San Luis Obispo, Calif.; president, Maino Construction Co. Inc. (1954-82); Oct. 29, 1913; Sept. 29.

At-large ambassador for non-proliferation policy, $68,400 — **Richard T. Kennedy**; Washington, D.C.; U.S. representative, International Atomic Energy Agency (1981-present); under secretary for management, State Department (1981); member, Nuclear Regulatory Commission (1975-80); deputy assistant to the president for national security and senior staff member, National Security Council (1969-75); Dec. 24, 1919; Republican; Dec. 10.

Commonwealth of the Bahamas, $67,200 — **Lev E. Dobriansky**; Alexandria, Va.; professor, Georgetown University (1960-82); Nov. 9, 1918; Dec. 10.

Rank of ambassador while serving as special assistant to the secretary and special negotiator for the Middle East peace process, $67,200 — **Richard Fairbanks**; Washington, D.C.; assistant secretary for congressional relations, State Department (1981-82); partner, Beveridge, Fairbanks & Diamond (1974-81); associate

director, White House Domestic Council (1971-74); Feb. 10, 1941; Republican; Dec. 16.

Department of the Treasury

Assistant secretary for economic policy, $58,500 — **Manuel H. Johnson Jr.**; Fairfax, Va.; acting assistant secretary for economic policy, Treasury Department (1982); deputy assistant secretary for economic policy, Treasury Department (1981-82); associate professor, George Mason University (1980-81); Feb. 10, 1949; Republican; Dec. 10.

INDEPENDENT AGENCIES

ACTION

Deputy director of the Peace Corps, $58,500 — **Edward A. Curran**; Rock Hall, Md.; director, National Institute of Education, Education Department (1981-82); member of transition team for Education Department (1981); Aug. 22, 1933; Republican; Oct. 1.

Deputy director, $67,200 — **Betty H. Brake**; Oklahoma City; deputy assistant director, Older Americans Volunteer Programs, ACTION (1981-82); co-chairperson and executive director, Reagan for President Committee and Reagan-Bush Committee, Oklahoma division (1979-80); May 14, 1920; Republican; Dec. 21.

Central Intelligence Agency

Deputy director, $59,500 — **John N. McMahon**; Bethesda, Md.; various positions leading to executive director, Central Intelligence Agency (1951-82); July 3, 1929; June 9.

Civil Aeronautics Board

Member for term expiring Dec. 31, 1988, $58,500 — **Diane Kay Morales**; Houston; deputy assistant secretary, Office of Territorial and International Affairs, Interior Department (1981-82); special assistant to the secretary, Interior Department (1981-82); July 11, 1946; Republican; Dec. 16.

Commodity Futures Trading Commission

Commissioner for term expiring April 13, 1987, $58,500 — **Fowler C. West**; Waco, Texas; staff director, U.S. House of Representatives Agriculture Committee (1972-82); administrative assistant to Rep. W. R. Poage (1971-72); July 6, 1940; Democrat; Oct. 1.

Environmental Protection Agency

Assistant administrator for water, $58,500 — **Frederic A. Eidsness Jr.**; Washington, D.C.; consultant, Environmental Protection Agency (1981-82); vice president, BMML Inc. (1978-81); Dec. 1, 1944; Republican; March 23.

Assistant administrator for solid waste and emergency response, $58,500 — **Rita M. Lavelle**; Arlington, Va.; director of communications, Aerojet Liquid Rocket Co. (1979-82); publications assistant to Gov. Ronald Reagan (1969-71); Sept. 8, 1947; Republican; March 31.

Equal Employment Opportunity Commission

Member for term expiring July 1, 1985, $58,500 — **Cathie A. Shattuck**; Boulder, Colo.; private law practice (1970-82); July 18, 1945; Republican; March 2.

Member for term expiring July 1, 1984, $58,500 — **Tony E. Gallegos**; Pico Rivera, Calif.; various positions leading to manager, equal employment program, Douglas Aircraft Co. (1952-82); Feb. 13, 1924; Democrat; April 14.

Member for term expiring July 1, 1986, $58,500 — **Clarence Thomas**; Bethesda, Md.; assistant secretary for civil rights, Edu-

cation Department (1981-82); June 23, 1948; Republican; May 6.

Member for term expiring July 1, 1987, $58,500 — **William A. Webb;** Pittsburgh; deputy attorney general, Pennsylvania (1980-82); senior staff counsel, U.S. House of Representatives Select Committee on Assassinations (1977-79); Oct. 22, 1943; Republican; Oct 1.

Export-Import Bank of the United States

First vice president and vice chairman, $58,500 — **Charles E. Lord;** Washington, D.C.; acting comptroller of the currency, Treasury Department (1981-82); senior adviser to comptroller of the currency, Treasury Department (1979-81); April 26, 1928; Republican; March 15.

Member of board of directors, $58,500 — **Richard W. Heldridge;** Alexandria, Va.; consultant, Export-Import Bank of the United States (1982); president and chief executive officer, California Commerce Bank of San Jose (1975-80); Sept. 18, 1918; Republican; Aug. 4.

Member of board of directors, $58,500 — **Rita M. Rodriguez;** Chicago; professor, University of Illinois (1978-82); Sept. 6, 1942; Independent; Oct. 1

Member of board of directors, $58,500 — **James E. Yonge;** Fort Lauderdale, Fla.; chairman of the board, North Ridge Bank (1979-82); Jan. 12, 1932; Democrat; Oct 1.

Federal Communications Commission

Member for term expiring June 30, 1989, $58,500 — **Stephen A. Sharp;** Alexandria, Va.; general counsel, Federal Communications Commission (1981-82); legal assistant to FCC Commissioner Margita E. White (1976-78); June 10, 1947; Republican; Oct. 1.

Federal Election Commission

Member for term expiring April 30, 1983, $58,500 — **Joan D. Aikens;** Swarthmore, Pa.; member, Federal Election Commission (1975-82); vice president and account executive, Lew Hodge Communications (1974-75); May 1, 1928; Republican; July 1.

Member for term expiring April 30, 1987, $58,500 — **Lee Ann Elliott;** Skokie, Ill.; vice president, Bishop, Bryant & Associates (1970-82); June 26, 1927; Republican; July 1.

Member for term expiring April 30, 1987, $58,500 — **Danny Lee McDonald;** Oklahoma City; general administrator, Oklahoma Corporation Commission (1979-82); Aug. 26, 1946; Democrat; July 1.

Federal Home Loan Bank Board

Member for term expiring June 30, 1982, $58,500 — **James Jay Jackson**; Reston, Va.; executive vice president, Fidelity Savings & Loan Association (1974-82); July 31, 1948; Democrat; March 4.

Member for term expiring June 30, 1986, $58,500 — **James Jay Jackson**; Reston, Va.; member, Federal Home Loan Bank Board (1982); executive vice president, Fidelity Savings and Loan Association (1974-82); July 31, 1948; Democrat; June 24.

Federal Mediation and Conciliation Service

Director, $59,500 — **Kay McMurray;** Bethesda, Md.; consultant and arbitrator (1977-82); chairman and member, National Mediation Board (1972-77); March 18, 1918; Republican; July 20.

Federal Mine Safety and Health Review Commission

Member for term expiring Aug. 30, 1988, $67,200 — **Richard V. Backley;** Fairfax, Va.; member, Federal Mine Safety and Health Review Commission (1978-82); administrative law judge, Civil Aeronautics Board (1975-78); July 21, 1927; Dec. 21.

Member for term expiring Aug. 30, 1988, $67,200 — **L. Clair Nelson;** McLean, Va.; vice president and general counsel, then

senior vice president, Champion International Corp. (1967-82); June 2, 1918; Republican; Dec. 21.

Federal Trade Commission

Commissioner for term expiring Sept. 25, 1989, $58,500 — **George W. Douglas;** Austin, Texas; president, Southwest Econometrics Inc. (1976-82); associate professor, University of North Carolina (1973-76); economist, Office of the Secretary, Transportation Department (1968-69); Aug. 10, 1938; Democrat; Dec. 16.

Interstate Commerce Commission

Member for term expiring Dec. 31, 1987, $58,500 — **Malcolm M. B. Sterrett**; Bethesda, Md.; vice president and general counsel, U.S. Rail Association (1980-82); minority staff director, U.S. Senate Commerce, Science and Transportation Committee (1976-80); Sept. 21, 1942; Republican; Feb. 9.

Member for term expiring Dec. 31, 1987, $58,500 — **Frederic N. Andre**; Paoli, Ind.; business and financial consultant (1977-82); June 25, 1933; Republican; March 16.

Member for term expiring Dec. 31, 1985, $58,500 — **J. J. Simmons III**; Muskogee, Okla.; vice president, Amerada Hess Corp. (1970-82); March 26, 1925; Democrat; April 1.

Member for term expiring Dec. 31, 1988, $58,500 — **Heather J. Gradison**; Washington, D.C.; various positions leading to rate officer, Southern Railway System (1974-82); Sept. 6, 1952; Republican; June 16.

National Credit Union Administration

Member for term expiring April 10, 1985, $58,500 — **Elizabeth F. Burkhart;** Washington, D.C.; associate deputy administrator, Veterans Administration (1981-82); deputy treasurer, Reagan-Bush Compliance Committee (1980); controller, George Bush for President Committee (1979-80); July 19, 1935; Republican; July 20.

National Foundation on the Arts and Humanities
National Endowment for the Humanities

Chairman, $59,500 — **William J. Bennett;** Chapel Hill, N.C.; president and director, National Humanities Center (1979-82); July 31, 1943; Feb. 8.

National Mediation Board

Member for term expiring July 1, 1984, $58,500 — **Walter C. Wallace;** New York, N.Y.; corporate counsel and director of industrial relations, Multiplant (1980-82); assistant secretary for manpower, Labor Department (1960-61); March 25, 1924; Republican; Oct. 1.

National Transportation Safety Board

Member for term expiring Dec. 31, 1986, $58,500 — **Donald D. Engen;** Alexandria, Va.; senior associate, Ketron Inc. (1980-82); May 28, 1924; Republican; June 16.

Nuclear Regulatory Commission

Member for terms expiring June 30, 1982, and June 30, 1987, $59,500 — **James K. Asselstine;** Alexandria, Va.; associate counsel, U.S. Senate Committee on Environment and Public Works (1981-82); staff attorney, Nuclear Regulatory Commission (1977-78); assistant counsel, Congressional Joint Committee on Atomic Energy (1975-77); June 7, 1948; Independent; May 13.

Postal Rate Commission

Member for term expiring Oct. 16, 1986, $58,500 — **John W.**

Crutcher; Alexandria, Va.; investment manager (1980-82); office manager, Dole for President Committee (1979-80); administrative assistant to U.S. Sen. Robert Dole (1974-75); lieutenant governor, Kansas (1965-69); Dec. 19, 1916; Republican; March 8.

Member for term expiring Oct. 14, 1982, $58,500 — **Henry R. Folsom;** Arlington, Va.; consultant, Water Resources Agency (1981); July 19, 1913; Republican; March 8.

Commissioner for term expiring Oct. 14, 1988, $58,500 — **Henry R. Folsom;** Hockessin, Del.; commissioner, Postal Rate Commission (1982); consultant, Water Resources Agency (1981-82); engineer, E. I. du Pont de Nemours Co. (1937-73); July 19, 1913; Republican; Dec. 8.

Securities and Exchange Commission

Member for term expiring June 5, 1987, $58,500 — **Bevis Longstreth;** New York City; member, Securities and Exchange Commission (1981-82); Jan. 29, 1934; Democrat; Aug. 20.

Member for term expiring June 5, 1987, $58,500 — **James C. Treadway Jr.;** Washington, D.C.; partner, Dickstein, Shapiro & Morin (1970-82); May 21, 1943; Republican; Aug. 19.

Small Business Administration

Administrator, $59,500 — **James C. Sanders;** Washington, D.C.; associate administrator for management, Small Business Administration (1981-82); Nov. 7, 1926; Republican; March 29.

U.S. Information Agency

Associate director for educational and cultural affairs, $58,500 — **Ronald L. Trowbridge;** Falls Church, Va.; acting associate director for educational and cultural affairs, International Communication Agency (1981-82); director, office of private sector programs and office of policy, planning and review, International Communication Agency (1981); Dec. 4, 1937; Republican; May 10.

Associate director for broadcasting (Voice of America), $58,500 — **Robert J. Hughes;** McLean, Va.; associate director for programs, International Communication Agency (1982); April 28, 1930; Independent; July 1.

Associate director, $58,500 — **W. Scott Thompson;** Chestnut Hill, Mass.; associate professor, Fletcher School of Law and Diplomacy (1969-82); White House Fellow (1975-76); Jan. 1, 1942; Republican; Sept. 22.

Associate director for broadcasting (Voice of America), $58,500 — **Kenneth Y. Tomlinson;** Chappaqua, N.Y.; staff writer, associate editor and then senior editor, *Reader's Digest* (1968-82); Aug. 3, 1944; Republican; Dec. 10.

U.S. International Development Cooperation Agency
Agency for International Development

Assistant administrator, $58,500 — **John R. Bolton;** Vienna, Va.; general counsel, Agency for International Development (1981-82); Oct. 20, 1948; Republican; Feb. 8.

Assistant administrator, $58,500 — **Otto J. Reich;** McLean, Va.; special assistant to the administrator, Agency for International Development (1981-82); Oct. 16, 1945; March 4.

Assistant administrator for Asia, $58,500 — **Charles W. Greenleaf Jr.;** Alexandria, Va.; senior adviser to administrator, Agency for International Development (1981-82); member, Presidential Personnel Office, White House (1981); director, Office of George Bush, Reagan-Bush Campaign Committee (1980); March 13, 1941; Republican; Aug. 18.

Deputy administrator, $59,500 — **Jay F. Morris;** Adelphi, Md.; assistant administrator for external relations, Agency for International Development (1981-82); executive recruiter, Presidential Personnel Office, White House (1981); legislative assistant to U.S. Sen. James B. Pearson (1967-71); Feb. 21, 1941; Republican; Oct. 1.

U.S. International Trade Commission

Member for term expiring June 16, 1984, $58,500 — **Veronica A. Haggart;** Washington, D.C.; partner, Heron, Haggart, Ford, Burchette & Ruckert (1981-82); Sept. 6, 1949; Republican; March 8.

U.S. Merit Systems Protection Board

Chairman for term expiring March 1, 1986, $59,500 — **Herbert E. Ellingwood;** McLean, Va.; deputy counsel to President Ronald Reagan (1981-82); legal affairs secretary to Gov. Ronald Reagan (1969-74); March 5, 1931; Republican; May 5.

Member for term expiring March 1, 1988, $58,500 — **Dennis M. Devaney;** Columbia, Md.; associate, Tighe, Curhan, Reukauf & Case (1979-82); Feb. 25, 1946; Democrat; Aug. 20.

Special counsel, $58,500 — **K. William O'Connor;** Falls Church, Va.; inspector general, Community Services Administration (1981); special counsel for interagency coordination and staff director, President's Executive Group, White House (1980-81); Aug. 1, 1931; Republican; Sept. 29.

U.S. Synthetic Fuels Corp.

Inspector general for term expiring May 3, 1989, salary to be set by Synthetic Fuels Corp. board — **Samuel K. Lessey Jr.;** Hancock, N.H.; investment adviser, Shearson, Hammell & Co. (1974-82); Oct. 9, 1923; Republican; May 3.

Deputy inspector general for term expiring May 3, 1989, salary to be set by Synthetic Fuels Corp. board — **Robert W. Gambino;** Vienna, Va.; director of security, Central Intelligence Agency (1975-80); Nov. 16, 1926; Republican; May 3.

Veterans Administration

Deputy administrator for veterans' affairs, $59,500 — **Everett Alvarez Jr.;** Rockville, Md.; deputy administrator, Peace Corps (1981-82); Dec. 23, 1937; Aug. 20.

Administrator, $60,662.50 — **Harry N. Walters;** McLean, Va.; assistant secretary of the Army for manpower and reserve affairs, Defense Department (1981-82); president and chief executive officer, Potsdam Paper Corp. (1977-81); July 4, 1936; Republican; Dec. 16.

JUDICIARY

U.S. Circuit Courts

Judge, District of Columbia Circuit, $74,300 — **Robert H. Bork;** Washington, D.C.; partner, Kirkland & Ellis (1981-82); solicitor general, Justice Department (1973-77); March 1, 1927; Feb. 8.

Judge, 6th Circuit, $74,300 — **Leroy J. Contie Jr.;** Akron, Ohio; judge, U.S. District Court, Northern District of Ohio (1971-82); April 2, 1920; Republican; March 4.

Judge, 6th Circuit, $74,300 — **Robert B. Krupansky;** Cleveland; judge, U.S. District Court, Northern District of Ohio (1970-82); Aug. 15, 1921; Republican; March 4.

Judge, 8th Circuit, $74,300 — **John R. Gibson;** Kansas City, Mo.; judge, U.S. District Court, Western District of Missouri (1981-82); Dec. 20, 1925; Republican; March 4.

Judge, 7th Circuit, $74,300 — **John L. Coffey;** Milwaukee; judge, state Supreme Court, Wisconsin (1978-82); April 15, 1922; March 18.

Judge, 2nd Circuit, $74,300 — **George C. Pratt;** Syosset, N.Y.; judge, U.S. District Court, Eastern District of New York (1976-82); May 22, 1928; June 18.

Judge, 5th Circuit, $74,300 — **E. Grady Jolly;** Jackson, Miss.; partner, Jolly, Miller & Milam (1977-82); Oct. 3, 1937; July 27.

Judge, 5th Circuit, $74,300 — **Patrick E. Higginbotham;** Dallas; judge, U.S. District Court, Northern District of Texas

(1976-82); Dec. 16, 1938; Republican; July 27.

Judge, District of Columbia, $74,300 — **Antonin Scalia;** McLean, Va.; professor of law, University of Chicago (1977-82); March 11, 1936; Republican; Aug. 5.

Judge, 6th circuit, $74,300 — **Harry W. Wellford;** Memphis, Tenn.; judge, U.S. District Court, Western District of Tennessee (1971-82); Aug. 6, 1924; Republican; Aug. 20.

Judge, 8th Circuit, $74,300 — **George G. Fagg;** Marshalltown, Iowa; judge, second judicial district, Iowa (1972-82); April 30, 1934; Oct. 1.

U.S. District Courts

Judge, Northern District of California, $70,300 — **Eugene F. Lynch;** San Francisco; judge, Superior Court, San Francisco County (1975-82); Dec. 2, 1931; Republican; March 4.

Judge, Middle District of Florida, $70,300 — **Elizabeth A. Kovachevich;** St. Petersburg, Fla.; judge, State Circuit Court, Florida (1973-82); Dec. 14, 1936; Republican; March 4.

Judge, Northern District of Indiana, $70,300 — **Michael S. Kanne;** Rensselaer, Ind.; judge, Circuit Court, Jasper County (1972-82); Dec. 21, 1938; Feb. 8.

Judge, Northern District of Indiana, $70,300 — **James T. Moody;** Hobart, Ind.; U.S. magistrate, Northern District of Indiana (1979-82); judge, Superior Court, Lake County (1972-79); June 16, 1938; Republican; Feb. 8.

Judge, Eastern District of California, $70,300 — **Robert E. Coyle;** Fresno, Calif.; partner, McCormick, Barstow, Sheppard, Coyle & Wayte (1961-82); May 6, 1930; Republican; March 31.

Judge, Northern District of Illinois, $70,300 — **William T. Hart;** Aurora, Ill.; partner, Schiff Hardin & Waite (1961-82); Feb. 4, 1929; Republican; April 20.

Judge, Northern District of Illinois, $70,300 — **John A. Nordberg;** Chicago; judge, Circuit Court, Cook County (1976-82); June 18, 1926; Republican; April 20.

Judge, District of Maryland, $70,300 — **Walter E. Black Jr.;** Baltimore; partner, Clapp, Somerville, Black & Honemann (1968-82); July 7, 1926; Republican; April 20.

Judge, Western District of New York, $70,300 — **Michael A. Telesca;** Rochester, N.Y.; judge, Surrogate's Court, Monroe County (1973-82); Nov. 25, 1929; Republican; April 20.

Judge, Middle District of Pennsylvania, $70,300 — **William W. Caldwell;** Harrisburg, Pa.; judge, Pennsylvania Court of Common Pleas, 12th District (1970-82); Nov. 10, 1925; Republican; March 18.

Judge, Western District of Pennsylvania, $70,300 — **Carol Los Mansmann;** Pittsburgh; professor, Duquesne Law School (1974-82); Aug. 7, 1942; Republican; March 18.

Judge, Western District of Pennsylvania, $70,300 — **Glenn E. Mencer;** Smethport, Pa.; judge, Commonwealth Court, Pennsylvania (1970-82); May 18, 1925; Republican; March 18.

Judge, District of Colorado, $70,300 — **John P. Moore;** Denver; U.S. bankruptcy judge, Colorado (1975-82); Oct. 14, 1934; Republican; June 24.

Judge, District of Columbia, $70,300 — **Thomas P. Jackson;** Washington, D.C.; partner, Jackson, Campbell & Parkinson (1964-82); Jan. 10, 1937; Republican; June 24.

Judge, Northern District of Florida, $70,300 — **Maurice M. Paul;** Orlando, Fla.; judge, State Circuit Court, Florida (1973-82); May 16, 1932; Republican; June 18.

Judge, District of Hawaii, $70,300 — **Harold M. Fong;** Honolulu; partner, Fong & Miho (1978-82); April 28, 1938; Republican; June 18.

Judge, Eastern District of Louisiana, $70,300 — **A. J. McNamara;** Metairie, La.; partner, Hailey, McNamara, McNamara & Hall (1971-82); member, Louisiana House of Representatives (1976-80); June 9, 1936; Republican; June 18.

Judge, Eastern District of Louisiana, $70,300 — **Henry A. Mentz Jr.;** Hammond, La.; partner, Mentz & Gorrell (1981-82);

Nov. 10, 1920; Republican; June 24.

Judge, Northern District of Ohio, $70,300 — **John W. Potter;** Toledo, Ohio; judge, 6th District Court of Appeals, Ohio (1969-82); mayor, Toledo, Ohio (1961-67); Oct. 25, 1918; Republican; June 18.

Judge, Central District of California, $70,300 — **Richard A. Gadbois Jr.;** San Marino, Calif.; judge, Superior Court, Los Angeles County (1972-82); June 18, 1932; July 27.

Judge, Southern District of California, $70,300 — **J. Lawrence Irving;** San Diego; partner, Irving & Butz (1976-82); Feb. 16, 1935; Republican; July 28.

Judge, district of Puerto Rico, $70,300 — **Jaime Pieras Jr.;** Santurce, Puerto Rico; attorney, Jaime Pieras Jr. (1979-82); May 19, 1924; July 13.

Judge, Northern District of Alabama, $70,300 — **William M. Acker Jr.;** Birmingham, Ala.; partner, Dominick, Fletcher, Yeilding, Acker, Wood & Lloyd (1971-82); Oct. 27, 1927; Republican, Aug. 18.

Judge, District of Columbia, $70,300 — **Thomas F. Hogan;** Chevy Chase, Md.; partner, Furey, Doolan, Abell & Hogan (1981-82); May 31, 1938; Republican; Aug. 20.

Judge, Central District of Illinois, $70,300 — **Michael M. Mihm;** Peoria, Ill.; attorney, Michael M. Mihm (1980-82); May 18, 1943; Aug. 5.

Judge, Western District of Missouri, $70,300 — **Ross T. Roberts;** Joplin, Mo.; partner, Roberts and Fleischaker (1976-82); Nov. 28, 1938; Republican; Aug. 20.

Judge, District of Rhode Island, $70,300 — **Bruce M. Selya;** Providence, R.I.; partner, Selya and Iannuccillo Inc. (1974-82); May 27, 1934; Republican; Aug. 18.

Judge, Central District of California, $70,300 — **Edward Rafeedie;** Malibu, Calif.; judge, Superior Court of California, Los Angeles County (1971-82); Jan. 6, 1929; Republican; Sept. 22.

Judge, Eastern District of North Carolina, $70,300 — **James C. Fox;** Wilmington, N.C.; partner, Murchison, Fox & Newton (1960-82); Nov. 6, 1928; Sept. 29.

Judge, Northern District of Ohio, $70,300 — **David D. Dowd Jr.;** Massillon, Ohio; partner, Black, McCuskey, Souers and Arbaugh (1981-82); judge, Supreme Court of Ohio (1980-81); judge, Ohio Court of Appeals, 5th District (1975-80); Jan. 31, 1929; Republican; Sept. 22

Judge, District of Puerto Rico, $70,300 — **Raymond L. Acosta;** Hato Rey, Puerto Rico; U.S. district attorney, Puerto Rico (1980-82); May 31, 1925; Sept. 29.

Judge, Northern District of Illinois, $70,300 — **Paul E. Plunkett;** Glenview, Ill.; partner, Mayer, Brown & Platt (1978-82); July 9, 1935; Republican; Dec. 10.

Judge, District of New Jersey, $70,300 — **John W. Bissell;** Montclair, N.J.; judge, New Jersey Superior Court (1981-82); June 7, 1940; Republican; Dec. 10.

Judge, Eastern District of New York, $70,300 — **Frank X. Altimari;** Old Westbury, Conn.; justice, New York Supreme Court, 10th Judicial District (1974-82); Sept. 4, 1928; Republican; Dec. 10.

Judge, Middle District of North Carolina, $70,300 — **Frank W. Bullock Jr.;** Greensboro, N.C.; associate and then partner, Douglas, Ravenel, Hardy, Crihfield & Bullock (1973-82); Nov. 3, 1938; Dec. 10.

Judge, Northern District of Ohio, $73,100 — **Sam H. Bell;** Silver Lake Village, Ohio; judge, Ohio Court of Appeals, 9th District (1977-82); Dec. 31, 1925; Republican; Dec. 21.

U.S. Tax Court

Judge, $70,300 — **Mary Ann Cohen;** Santa Monica, Calif.; partner, Abbott & Cohen (1969-82); July 16, 1943; Republican; Aug. 16.

Judge, $70,300 — **Lapsley W. Hamblen Jr.;** Alexandria, Va.; deputy assistant attorney general, Justice Department (1982); Dec. 25, 1926; Republican; Aug. 16.   ∎

POLITICAL REPORT

CQ

 Election '82

Lasting Election Effects Likely in House

As published in the Nov. 6, 1982, Weekly Report.

Whatever the short-term effect on President Reagan's fortunes may be, the 1982 election is likely to change the politics of the House of Representatives for years to come.

A combination of redistricting and recession produced a huge crop of 81 House freshmen — 57 of them Democrats. In the past 30 years, only three other elections have brought in that many new Democrats. When the party's caucus meets in January, more than one-fifth of its members will be there for the first time.

A big congressional class is a little like a baby boom in the population. It speaks with disproportionate weight over its life span in the institution. And its members tend to move the chamber's politics toward the themes and issues that brought them there in the first place.

The Democratic "Watergate Babies" of 1974 campaigned on clean government and institutional reform. When they arrived on Capitol Hill, they immediately forced an end to traditional House practices of seniority and secrecy. The 52 new Republicans in 1980 came to town preaching supply-side economics, and their sheer numbers were important in generating the peer pressure that forced a virtually unanimous GOP vote for the 1981 Reagan tax cut. This year's new Democrats are unlikely to do anything that dramatic in the next few months. But over a longer period of time, they may set the scene for a Democratic cohesiveness that has not existed in any recent Congress.

The new Democrats of 1982 will go down as the group that resurrected traditional liberal issues from the graveyard to which all but a tiny element of the party had consigned them over the course of the 1970s.

Hardly any of these newcomers campaigned as avowed liberals. Most went out of their way to refer to themselves as fiscal conservatives. But the labels are not important. The vast majority of these people built their campaigns around a defense of the social programs the administration has been seeking to cut back. And those are the political commitments, however labeled, that they will carry with them into the 98th Congress.

In a curious way, President Reagan himself made all this possible. By abandoning the traditional GOP high ground of balanced-budget politics in favor of supply-side economics, he allowed resourceful Democratic candidates to come up with a new mixture of issues that proved to have remarkable power. He allowed the Democratic Party to proclaim itself the party of social programs *and* low deficits.

In diverse districts throughout the country, Democrats offered a simple, if potentially contradictory, political program: protect the existing service programs (without creating any new ones), hold increases in defense spending to a minimum, cancel the third year of the Reagan tax cut and hope that the result is a deficit low enough to claim economic progress.

That is not exactly the set of new ideas Democrats would like to provide as the party out of power. But the fact is, it worked. It is one important reason why there will be 26 fewer Republicans in the 98th Congress.

Southern Surprise

As common as these themes were throughout the country, they were most important in the South and Southwest, where the 1982 elections produced a result both unexpected and full of implications for the future.

If one thing seemed certain about 1982, it was that the reapportionment of 17 seats from the Frost Belt to the Sun Belt would move the House almost that many votes in a conservative direction, no matter which party managed to win the seats.

SENATE

97th Congress: Democrats 46*
Republicans 54

98th Congress: Democrats 46
Republicans 54

HOUSE

97th Congress: Democrats 241†
Republicans 192

98th Congress: Democrats 269‡
Republicans 166

* Includes Harry F. Byrd Jr., Va., elected as an independent. †Two vacancies.

‡ Includes Georgia's 4th and 5th districts, where elections were held Nov. 30.

That simply did not happen. The new House will have 23 freshman Democrats from Southern and Southwestern states (excluding California), and a look at their records yields only three (Richard Ray of Georgia, I. T. "Tim" Valentine Jr. of North Carolina and Tom Vandergriff of Texas) apparent candidates for Boll Weevil status. The rest seem likely to settle somewhere within the national Democratic Party mainstream, ranging from the moderate right to, in a couple of cases, the outspoken left.

Jim McNulty of Arizona is a personal friend and close ally of his state's liberal elder statesman, Rep. Morris K. Udall. Ronald Coleman of Texas was the legal adviser to Mexican-American clothing workers during a protracted strike in El Paso. Lindsay Thomas of Georgia campaigned on the need for the United States to "provide the leadership toward meaningful nuclear disarmament." Robert M. Tallon Jr. of South Carolina owes his election to his district's large and politically active black community, which will remain his most important constituency.

These and other Sun Belt freshmen stand in marked contrast to the Southern newcomers of 1978, a contingent that included such conservative Democratic stalwarts as Phil Gramm and Charles W. Stenholm of Texas. That group contributed in large numbers to the conservative coalition that brought about passage of the initial Reagan program.

As individuals, the Boll Weevil incumbents fared exceptionally well at the polls in 1982. Not one of them lost in the general election, and many were unopposed. But as a group, they face some serious problems. In the short run, conservative Southern Democrats have probably lost their role as the balance of power between the chamber's national Democrats and the Reagan administration. Speaker Thomas P. O'Neill Jr. should now have the votes to win most direct tests of strength, and the more tentative of the Boll Weevils — the ones who have always been more enamored of balanced budgets than of supply-side tax cuts — seem certain to drift away from President Reagan in the coming months.

More important in the long run, the arrival of a large moderate contingent from the Sun Belt creates new opportunities for the Democratic leaders, especially Majority Leader Jim Wright of Texas. Over several Congresses, a skillful centrist course by

the leadership could knit together a national Democratic Party in the House that would make the conservative coalition obsolete, at least in its traditional form. In the end, that may not happen. But the 1982 election appears to have provided Wright and O'Neill with the resources.

A Splintered GOP

Election '82 will change House GOP politics in a much different way. For the past two Congresses, House Republicans have acted with remarkable unanimity, ignoring political differences in their constituencies to preach tax-cut politics in 1978 and 1980 and to implement it in 1981.

Part of this was the work of the Republican National Committee and the GOP congressional campaign committee, which set up training programs for these Republicans as challengers, designed advertising for them and provided the financing that allowed them to win.

This national strategy worked beautifully as long as GOP candidates could focus criticism on the Carter administration and the spending habits of House Democrats. But 1982 was a different story.

Even though many GOP candidates worked hard to create an image of independence, the White House and national party units ultimately made this very difficult. President Reagan's continued emphasis on the economy and his "Stay the Course" advertising theme nationalized the campaign beyond any ability of House Republican candidates to localize it.

This problem ended the careers of several otherwise strong Republican incumbents who had established records of independence but who found themselves trapped in economically troubled districts by their 1981 votes for the Reagan program.

GOP freshmen Jim Dunn in Michigan, James L. Nelligan in Pennsylvania and Lawrence J. DeNardis in Connecticut lost narrowly in districts where their 1981 votes became a major issue. Ironically, DeNardis lost while a neighboring Democratic district was falling to a Republican whose views were similar to his but who had not been in office to vote for the Reagan program in 1981.

What all this signals is a denationalizing of House Republican politics, away from musketeer loyalty and toward whatever works for members

in their own districts. Democrats have always operated this way, and moderate GOP members who survived in 1982 are likely to see it as the way to survive in 1984 and beyond.

This poses an obvious problem for the Reagan administration; on many issues in the next Congress, Democratic leaders are likely to attract the 15 or 20 moderate Republican votes they used to be able to count on before party loyalty became such a preoccupation of the GOP. And Republican moderates should be able to cast such votes without the peer pressure that made those decisions difficult in the last Congress.

One Republican likely to ponder this problem is the House minority leader, Robert H. Michel of Illinois. Elected easily for two decades as a symbol of upright small-town conservatism, Michel now represents a declining industrial constituency that may respond better to a liberal Republican emphasis on jobs and social services. Michel went down the line for Reagan in the 97th Congress, and almost paid the price for it; another 5,000 Democratic votes would have ended his career. He thus has a strong personal incentive to opt for a looser approach to Republican loyalty.

Senate Largely Unchanged

The Senate is a shorter story. For all practical purposes, it will be the same next year as it was this year. The party ratio remains 54-46 Republican, only two incumbents were defeated, and of the five senators who will give way to newcomers, only veteran Democrat Howard W. Cannon of Nevada was a major player in Senate politics.

But in the current Senate, stability represents a real change. Massive turnover throughout the 1970s created a chamber lacking in institutional memory; each set of newcomers barely made the acquaintance of colleagues before another huge group was brought in. When the 97th Congress convened in 1981, a majority of the majority party (27 of 53 Republicans) had been in office two years or less.

The 1982 election gives the Senate a useful period of personal continuity. That could eventually lead to fewer of the one-man filibusters and displays of open hostility that marked the last two years. If so, many senators may come to feel that the winner of the election was the institution. ∎

Impact of Reaganomics:

House Vote: Major Midterm Setback for the Republicans

Democrats scored a 26-seat gain in the U.S. House on Nov. 2, as voters expressed antipathy toward President Reagan's economic program but stopped short of repudiating it altogether.

The outcome revealed an unusual degree of voter frustration with a party only two years into national power. The electorate is usually kinder to a party facing its first midterm election after capturing the White House.

Jimmy Carter's Democratic Party lost only 11 House seats in the 1978 midterm election. Republicans under Richard M. Nixon dropped 12 in 1970.

The Republican loss this year was the worst suffered by any party at the two-year point in 60 years — since the GOP under Warren G. Harding lost 75 seats in 1922.

According to the unofficial returns from 435 districts, Democrats won 269 seats to 166 seats for the GOP, giving the Democrats a 103-seat advantage. This total included Colorado's 6th District, whose newly elected GOP representative, Jack Swigert, died Dec. 27, and two districts in Georgia where redistricting problems forced postponement of the election until Nov. 30. Both Georgia seats were retained by incumbent Democrats. *(State-by-state returns, p. 23-B)*

Going into the election, Democrats held 241 seats and Republicans 192, with vacancies in two districts formerly occupied by Democrats.

Twenty-six Republican incumbents and three sitting Democrats were beaten, nearly a mirror image of the 1980 election, in which the GOP lost three incumbents and unseated 28 Democratic members.

Democrats scored a net gain of two in the 36 districts left open by the retirement, primary defeat or death of an incumbent. In the 22 open districts created by redistricting, Democrats won 12, the GOP 10. *(Redistricting analysis, p. 12-B)*

East: Pennsylvania Debacle

In a year when voters obviously were concerned that Reagan was charting a course that veered too sharply to the right, an unusual number of the defeated incumbents were moderate Eastern Republicans, some of whom had sharply questioned the president's policies.

The worst news for Republicans came from Pennsylvania, where four of the party's incumbents lost. In the 3rd District, two-term Rep. Charles F. Dougherty was defeated by Democratic state Rep. Robert A. Borski, even though Dougherty's opposition to urban aid cuts and other Reagan policies had helped him earn endorsements from some labor unions.

Republican Rep. Jim Coyne in the 8th District opposed more military aid to El Salvador and called for the resignation of Interior Secretary James G. Watt, but such stands were not enough to overcome former U.S. Rep. Peter H. Kostmayer, the liberal Democrat who lost to Coyne in 1980.

In a Pennsylvania contest where

U.S. House

97th Congress		98th Congress	
Democrats	241*	Democrats	269†
Republicans	192	Republicans	166‡
Democrats			
Net gain			26
Freshmen			57
Incumbents re-elected			212
Incumbents defeated			3
Republicans			
Net Loss			26
Freshmen			24
Incumbents re-elected			142
Incumbents defeated			26

* *Two vacancies.*

†*Includes the 4th and 5th districts in Georgia, where elections were held Nov. 30.*

‡*Includes Jack Swigert who died Dec. 27.*

both parties had more than the usual amount of pride at stake, GOP Rep. Eugene V. Atkinson lost decisively to state Rep. Joseph P. Kolter in the 4th District. Atkinson left the Democratic Party in 1981 to signal his belief that Reagan policies would bring economic recovery to the steel-producing 4th. Prominent national politicians from both parties campaigned in the district, and Kolter forced Atkinson on the defensive by accusing him of betraying the average working person when he joined the GOP.

The fourth incumbent GOP loser in Pennsylvania was freshman James L. Nelligan, defeated by Frank Harrison in the 11th District.

The moderate Republican incumbent in Connecticut's 3rd District fell victim to one of the election's biggest upsets. Freshman Rep. Lawrence J. DeNardis, a leader of the GOP's "Gypsy Moth" faction, was a solid favorite to defeat Democrat Bruce A. Morrison. But Morrison built an extensive grass-roots organization that brought him victory by a very slim margin.

During 15 years in office, Republican Rep. Margaret M. Heckler established a reputation as a pro-consumer representative with a strong independent streak. But the independents and Democrats who backed Heckler in past years deserted her this time, and she lost to Democratic Rep. Barney Frank, a liberal who managed to focus voters' attention on Heckler's 1981 votes for Reagan's economic proposals. Redistricting paired the two in Massachusetts' 4th District.

Another casualty in the ranks of the left-of-center Eastern GOP was New Jersey Rep. Harold C. Hollenbeck, challenged by Democrat Robert G. Torricelli in New Jersey's 9th District. Like several other challengers to moderate Republicans, Torricelli found that voters wanting to send an anti-Reagan message were receptive to the argument that it would more likely be received if delivered in a Democratic package.

Oddly enough, some of the most impressive Republican showings came in pockets of the industrial Northeast where economic conditions were bad, but where resourceful GOP candidates managed to prevent the opposition from saddling them with the failures

of Reaganomics.

Republican Nancy L. Johnson took the Connecticut seat being vacated by Democrat Toby Moffett, a Senate candidate, and John R. McKernan Jr. eked out a narrow win in Maine's 1st, where the departing incumbent was a Republican but where a return to Democratic control had been expected. And in Pennsylvania's 21st, where GOP Rep. Marc L. Marks decided to retire after a close escape in 1980, Republican Thomas J. Ridge was a surprise winner by fewer than 1,000 votes.

The 21st, dominated by its blue-collar ethnic population in Erie, was one case where the incumbent's departure helped. Marks voted for the Reagan budget and tax cuts in 1981 (although later he was critical of the administration), and would have had to defend them in a campaign. Ridge, had he been in office in 1981, would almost certainly have voted the same way. But since he was not there, he was not restricted in his efforts to declare independence.

Midwest: Illinois Revolt

Evidence of Middle America's skepticism over Reaganomics was clearly seen in Illinois, where Democrats picked up two GOP seats and frightened several other Republican incumbents. Sagging domestic demand for agricultural machinery and other heavy equipment had forced layoffs at important Illinois employers, and workers were grumbling that Reagan-imposed trade sanctions on equipment sales to the Soviet Union robbed Americans of foreign contracts that could have helped preserve jobs.

Voters in the Peoria-based 18th District gave the White House one of its worst scares: 13-term Republican Robert H. Michel, the House minority leader, nearly lost to 31-year-old labor lawyer G. Douglas Stephens. Reagan campaigned personally for Michel; in a speech after the ballots were counted, Michel interpreted his narrow margin as a signal that some adjustments in the president's programs were necessary.

Falling into Democratic hands was the 17th District, where state Sen. Kenneth G. McMillan, a conservative Republican, lost to Democrat Lane Evans, a lawyer from Rock Island. Strong support from right-leaning rural voters enabled McMillan to defeat moderate GOP Rep. Tom Railsback in the primary. But in the general election, McMillan could not cut into Ev-

U.S. House Members Defeated				
		Terms		Terms
Albert Lee Smith Jr., R-Ala.		1	Peter A. Peyser, D-N.Y.	5
Don H. Clausen, R-Calif.		10	Eugene Johnston, R-N.C.	1
John H. Rousselot, R-Calif.		8	Bill Hendon, R-N.C.	1
Lawrence J. DeNardis, R-Conn.		1	Ed Weber, R-Ohio	1
Thomas B. Evans Jr., R-Del.		3	Bob Shamansky, D-Ohio	1
Paul Findley, R-Ill.		8	Charles F. Dougherty, R-Pa.	2
Joel Deckard, R-Ind.		2	Jim Coyne, R-Pa.	1
Margaret M. Heckler, R-Mass.		8	James L. Nelligan, R-Pa.	1
Jim Dunn, R-Mich.		1	Eugene V. Atkinson, R-Pa.	2
Tom Hagedorn, R-Minn.		4	John L. Napier, R-S.C.	1
Arlen Erdahl, R-Minn.		2	Clint Roberts, R-S.D.	1
Wendell Bailey, R-Mo.		1	Robert W. Daniel Jr., R-Va.	5
Harold C. Hollenbeck, R-N.J.		3	William C. Wampler, R-Va.	9
John LeBoutillier, R-N.Y.		1	David Michael Staton, R-W.Va.	1
Leo C. Zeferetti, D-N.Y.		4		

ans' backing in the industrialized Rock Island-Moline portion of the district.

Republican Rep. Paul Findley was the victim of economic troubles and a redistricting plan that made his 20th District skirt tortuously around conservative Illinois farm land and suburban territory to include every available blue-collar Democrat. Findley was defeated by Richard J. Durbin, a lawyer whose campaign was financed in part by pro-Israel organizations unhappy with Findley's ties to the Palestine Liberation Organization.

As in the Eastern states, Midwestern voters disenchanted with the Reagan administration vented their anger on some Republicans who have tried to pull their party to the center. Ohio's 9th District turned out freshman GOP Rep. Ed Weber, who sought to avoid being labeled a Reagan lackey by lobbying for more money for Urban Development Action Grants and by opposing cutbacks in Social Security payments. Strong support from organized labor in the 9th helped elect Democrat Marcy Kaptur, a former urban affairs specialist in the Carter White House.

Minnesota Republican Rep. Arlen Erdahl billed himself as an independent-minded "fiscal conservative with a social conscience," but he lost the 6th District to state Sen. Gerry Sikorski, who had fought against social program cuts in the Legislature and was popular with education and labor groups.

The swing to the Democratic Party was more pronounced in Minnesota than in neighboring farm states.

Also losing was 1st District GOP Rep. Tom Hagedorn, a conservative unseated by state Sen. Timothy J. Penny. Gaining the 1st and 6th districts gave Minnesota Democrats a 5-3 edge in the state's House delegation, an advantage they had not held since the 1978 election.

Elsewhere in the Midwest, Democratic state Rep. Alan Wheat scored a landmark victory for blacks in Missouri's 5th District, which includes Kansas City and some of its suburbs. Wheat defeated Republican state Rep. John A. Sharp to become the first black in modern times to win a district that was neither predominantly black nor overwhelmingly liberal. The Democratic incumbent, Rep. Richard Bolling, retired at the end of the 97th Congress.

In some economically troubled regions of the Midwest, though, Republican incumbents held on better than expected. This was largely due to the strength of young GOP members who took over in 1980 and applied the usual formula of tireless constituent service and aggressive self-promotion.

Two of the seats that seemed most likely to fall were the Wisconsin 3rd and the Minnesota 2nd, both Democratic until 1980 and both devastated by collapsing farm prices. But the incumbents in these districts, 31-year-old Steve Gunderson in Wisconsin and 30-year-old Vin Weber in Minnesota, both won comfortably. Even more surprising, in Iowa's hard-hit 3rd District, was the comfortable re-election of 58-year-old freshman Republican Rep. Cooper Evans, who lacked the aggressiveness or flair for

personal campaigning that helped Weber and Gunderson.

South: Border Resurgence

Resurgence of traditional Democratic voting habits in five Southern and border states — Virginia, West Virginia, North Carolina, South Carolina and Tennessee — produced a gain of nine Democratic seats, more than one-third of the party's nationwide net gain of 26 districts.

Two Republican incumbents lost in Virginia, and Democrats added a third seat occupied by a Republican who had retired there. In the 4th District, state Rep. Norman Sisisky unseated GOP Rep. Robert W. Daniel Jr., a staunch Reagan supporter. Sisisky's victory came with considerable help from blacks, who comprised 40 percent of the district's population.

Democrat James R. Olin was the first Democrat in 30 years to win Virginia's 6th District, represented for the past decade by retiring Rep. M. Caldwell Butler. Olin, a retired corporate executive, drew support from a variety of quarters — labor and teachers' groups, black leaders and much of the Roanoke financial community.

The new Democrat from Virginia's 9th District, state Sen. Frederick C. Boucher, was a narrow winner over GOP Rep. William C. Wampler. Boucher was an advance man in George McGovern's 1972 presidential campaign, and his House bid was actively backed by the United Mine Workers, a potent force in the district's coal fields.

Wampler's defeat removed the only Republican seeking re-election who had ever served in a House GOP majority. He was a member of the 83rd Congress (1953-55).

West Virginia went into the election with a House delegation split 2-2 and emerged with four Democratic winners. The most dramatic philosophical shift came in the 3rd District, where pro-labor populist state Sen. Bob Wise defeated first-term GOP Rep. David Michael Staton, who was one of the Religious Right's leading voices in Congress.

Staton tried to shift attention away from the economy by talking about his opposition to abortion and his support for school prayer, but that strategy won him only 42 percent of the vote.

In South Carolina's 6th District, black voters were pivotal to the success of Democratic state Rep. Robert M. Tallon Jr., who defeated first-term Republican Rep. John L. Napier. Blacks made up 41 percent of the district's population, and in 1980 their strong support for Abscam-tainted incumbent John W. Jenrette nearly re-elected him in spite of his personal problems. Tallon inherited Jenrette's organization and made good on Democratic claims that Napier's win two years ago was an aberration.

North Carolina's two new Democratic House members were likely to vote a moderate-to-liberal line in the House, in sharp contrast to the Republicans they replaced. In the 6th District, lawyer Charles Robin Britt defeated GOP Rep. Eugene Johnston, a conservative businessman who was a surprise 1980 winner over Democratic Rep. Richardson Preyer. Britt, who managed Preyer's 1978 campaign, kept voters' attention focused on Johnston's controversial personality and criticized his down-the-line support for Reagan.

In 1980, the North Carolina 11th went Republican for the first time in 50 years, but the occupancy of GOP Rep. Bill Hendon turned out to be brief. Hendon lost to Democrat James McClure Clarke, a wealthy 65-year-old state senator whose stands on most social, economic and environmental issues were in line with national Democratic policy.

Clarke and Britt were the leading edge of a strong reaction by North Carolina voters against the National Congressional Club, the political action committee founded by Sen. Jesse Helms to advance his conservative causes. The club assisted several Republican candidates in the state, putting primary emphasis on replacing 4th District Democratic Rep. Ike Andrews with former University of North Carolina athletic director William Cobey Jr.

From the outset, Andrews was rated no better than an even chance to win. When he was arrested Oct. 2 for drunken driving, some thought his fate was sealed. But as the election approached, voters became increasingly irritated with the club's extensive activities on Cobey's behalf, and Andrews pulled out a stunning victory. All the other club-supported House candidates lost, most by lopsided margins, in an outcome that could be a bad omen for Helms' own re-election chances in 1984.

In the new 4th District in Tennessee, lawyer Jim Cooper handily defeated Cissy Baker, daughter of the Senate majority leader, Howard H. Baker Jr. Cooper was the youngest member of the 98th Congress.

The GOP scored some scattered gains in the South. In Mississippi's open 2nd District, Republican Webb Franklin defeated state Rep. Robert G. Clark, who was the first black since Reconstruction to win a Democratic congressional primary in Mississippi. Republican businessman Don Sundquist of Memphis upset Democrat Bob Clement in Tennessee's open 7th District.

Thanks to redistricting, the GOP also took two newly created seats in Florida.

West: The Remap Story

Redistricting was responsible for virtually all of the changes in the

---

Primary, Special Election Victories

The voting for the House ended Nov. 30, when elections were held in two Georgia districts. The balloting in the two Atlanta-area constituencies was postponed because of redistricting problems.

In the 4th District, incumbent Democrat Elliott H. Levitas turned back GOP nominee Dick Winder, winning 38,758 votes (65.5 percent) to Winder's 20,418 (34.5 percent), according to unofficial returns. The other Democratic incumbent, Wyche Fowler Jr., who is white, defeated two blacks in the black-majority 5th. Fowler received 53,264 votes (80.8 percent) against independent state Rep. J. E. "Billy" McKinney, who won 9,049 votes (13.7 percent), and GOP nominee Paul Jones, who won 3,633 votes (5.5 percent).

In Indiana, voters Nov. 2 also cast ballots in the vacant 1st District in a special election to fill the seat for the rest of the 97th Congress. Democrat Katie Hall won both the special election and the balloting for the 98th Congress. In the special election, she beat her GOP foe, Thomas W. Krieger, 70,716 votes (63.3 percent) to 40,999 (36.7 percent). The seat was vacated by the death of Democratic Rep. Adam Benjamin Jr. in September.

Western state delegations. Republicans picked up five newly created districts: the Colorado 6th, Nevada 2nd, Oregon 2nd, Utah 3rd and Washington 8th. Also, the GOP gained a seat in Arizona as party-switching Rep. Bob Stump won his first election as a Republican.

Those Republican additions helped cushion the impact of a devastating partisan Democratic remap in California. Before the election, Republicans held 21 of that state's 43 seats. Thanks mostly to the artful map-drawing of Democratic Rep. Phillip Burton, the election gave Democrats a 28-17 advantage in the delegation. Republican incumbents Don H. Clausen and John H. Rousselot lost, four of five newly created open districts went Democratic and two formerly Republican open districts were won by Democrats. *(California details, p. 12-B)*

Republicans were thwarted in their attempt to gain the new Arizona 5th, as Democratic former state Sen. Jim McNulty defeated GOP state Sen. Jim Kolbe, whose allies in the Arizona Senate tried to craft the 5th to suit his needs. As expected, Democrat Bill Richardson won the new 3rd District in New Mexico.

Surge and Struggle

In one sense, the 1982 results contradicted a well-established rule of modern House elections, the famous "sophomore surge," in which incumbents gained strongly in their first bid for re-election. Half the 26 Republicans who were unseated Nov. 2 were freshmen, a much higher percentage than in recent years. But on average, members of the GOP class of 1980 ran 2 percentage points ahead of their showing as challengers two years ago. Democrats seeking their first re-election surged an impressive 12.3 points.

Several of the 13 defeated GOP freshmen lost because they ran in new territory where they had little time to practice the constituent courtship that normally guaranteed re-election.

Michigan's Jim Dunn provided a good example. Less than six months before the election, map makers gave him massive amounts of new territory in heavily Democratic Pontiac. He lost that part of the district overwhelmingly, which caused him to fall just short districtwide against Democrat Bob Carr, whom he had defeated in the old district in 1980.

A similar casualty on the Democratic side was Bob Shamansky, whose Columbus-based district was given more than 50,000 new constituents in Republican Licking County, and who lost his district by about 5,000 votes.

Party Switchers: One Win, One Loss

One lesson of the 1982 election: If you want to switch parties, do it in a congenial locale.

Rep. Eugene V. Atkinson jumped from the Democrats to the Republicans in 1981, and was defeated in 1982 in his Pennsylvania district, whose steel-producing economy had been ravaged by the recession. Another life-long Democrat, Rep. Bob Stump of Arizona's 3rd District, also ran as a Republican but with far happier results — he won handily.

The GOP-controlled Legislature rearranged Atkinson's 4th District to reduce its Democratic registration edge. The result, however, was still a Democratic constituency with high unemployment. Labor unions branded Atkinson a traitor and made him a priority target. State Rep. Joseph P. Kolter, a staunch labor Democrat, defeated him by 3-to-2.

Stump, by contrast, had a consistent conservative record that his constituents long had appreciated. Democrat Pat Bosch, a former bank official, gave him little trouble. Stump beat his opponent by about as much as Kolter defeated Atkinson.

House: Newcomers, Losers, Lame Ducks

State	District	Winner	Loser	Incumbent
Alabama	6	Ben Erdreich (D)	Albert Lee Smith Jr. (R)	Smith
Arizona	1	John McCain (R)	William E. Hegarty (D)	John J. Rhodes (R)[1]
	5	Jim McNulty (D)	Jim Kolbe (R)	New District
California	1	Douglas H. Bosco (D)	Don H. Clausen (R)	Clausen
	6	Barbara Boxer (D)	Dennis McQuaid (R)	John L. Burton (D)[1]
	12	Ed Zschau (R)	Emmett Lynch (D)	Paul N. McCloskey Jr. (R)[2]
	18	Richard Lehman (D)	Adrian C. Fondse (R)	New District
	26	Howard L. Berman (D)	Hal Phillips (R)	New District
	27	Mel Levine (D)	Bart W. Christensen (R)	Robert K. Dornan (R)[2]
	34	Esteban Torres (D)	Paul R. Jackson (R)	New District
	37	Al McCandless (R)	Curtis P. "Sam" Cross (D)	New District
	43	Ron Packard (R write-in)	Roy "Pat" Archer (D) Johnnie R. Crean (R)	Clair W. Burgener (R)[1]
	44	Jim Bates (D)	Shirley M. Gissendanner (R)	New District
Colorado	6	Jack Swigert (R)*	Steve Hogan (D)	New District
Connecticut	3	Bruce A. Morrison (D)	Lawrence J. DeNardis (R)	DeNardis
	6	Nancy L. Johnson (R)	William E. Curry Jr. (D)	Toby Moffett (D)[2]
Delaware	AL	Thomas R. Carper (D)	Thomas B. Evans Jr. (R)	Evans
Florida	6	Kenneth H. "Buddy" MacKay (D)	Ed Havill (R)	New District
	9	Michael Bilirakis (R)	George H. Sheldon (D)	New District
	12	Tom Lewis (R)	Brad Culverhouse (D)	New District
	13	Connie Mack III (R)	Dana N. Stevens (D)	L. A. "Skip" Bafalis (R)[3]
	16	Larry Smith (D)	Maurice Berkowitz (R)	New District

* Died Dec. 27.

State	District	Winner	Loser	Incumbent
Georgia	1	Lindsay Thomas (D)	Herb Jones (R)	Bo Ginn (D)[3]
	3	Richard Ray (D)	Tyron Elliott (R)	Jack Brinkley (D)[1]
	8	J. Roy Rowland (D)	No Republican candidate	Billy Lee Evans (D)[4]
Illinois	5	William O. Lipinski (D)	Daniel J. Partyka (R)	John G. Fary (D)[5]
	17	Lane Evans (D)	Kenneth G. McMillan (R)	Tom Railsback (R)[5]
	20	Richard J. Durbin (D)	Paul Findley (R)	Findley
Indiana	1	Katie Hall (D)	Thomas H. Krieger (R)	No incumbent[6]
	6	Dan Burton (R)	George E. Grabianowski (D)	New District
	8	Francis X. McCloskey (D)	Joel Deckard (R)	Deckard
Kansas	2	Jim Slattery (D)	Morris Kay (R)	Jim Jeffries (R)[1]
Maine	1	John R. McKernan Jr. (R)	John M. Kerrey (D)	David F. Emery (R)[2]
Michigan	6	Bob Carr (D)	Jim Dunn (R)	Dunn
	17	Sander Levin (D)	Gerald E. Rosen (R)	William M. Brodhead (D)[1] James J. Blanchard (D)[3]
Minnesota	1	Timothy J. Penny (D)	Tom Hagedorn (R)	Hagedorn
	6	Gerry Sikorski (D)	Arlen Erdahl (R)	Erdahl
Mississippi	2	Webb Franklin (R)	Robert G. Clark (D)	David R. Bowen (D)[1]
Missouri	5	Alan Wheat (D)	John A. Sharp (R)	Richard Bolling (D)[1]
Nevada	1	Harry Reid (D)	Peggy Cavnar (R)	James D. Santini (D)[2]
	2	Barbara Vucanovich (R)	Mary Gojack (D)	New District
New Jersey	9	Robert G. Torricelli (D)	Harold C. Hollenbeck (R)	Hollenbeck
New Mexico	3	Bill Richardson (D)	Marjorie Bell Chambers (R)	New District
New York	3	Robert J. Mrazek (D)	John LeBoutillier (R)	LeBoutillier
	11	Edolphus Towns (D)	James W. Smith (R)	No incumbent[7]
	12	Major R. Owens (D)	David Katan Sr. (R)	Shirley Chisholm (D)[1]
	25	Sherwood L. Boehlert (R)	Anita Maxwell (D)	Donald J. Mitchell (R)[1]
North Carolina	2	I. T. "Tim" Valentine Jr. (D)	John W. Marin (R)	L. H. Fountain (D)[1]
	6	Charles Robin Britt (D)	Eugene Johnston (R)	Johnston
	11	James McClure Clarke (D)	Bill Hendon (R)	Hendon
Ohio	7	Michael Dewine (R)	Roger D. Tackett (D)	Clarence J. Brown (R)[3]
	9	Marcy Kaptur (D)	Ed Weber (R)	Weber
	12	John R. Kasich (R)	Bob Shamansky (D)	Shamansky
	19	Edward F. Feighan (D)	Richard G. Anter II (R)	Ronald M. Mottl (D)[5]
Oregon	2	Bob Smith (R)	Larryann Willis (D)	New District
Pennsylvania	3	Robert A. Borski (D)	Charles F. Dougherty (R)	Dougherty
	4	Joseph P. Kolter (D)	Eugene V. Atkinson (R)	Atkinson
	8	Peter H. Kostmayer (D)	Jim Coyne (R)	Coyne
	11	Frank Harrison (D)	James L. Nelligan (R)	Nelligan
	17	George W. Gekas (R)	Larry J. Hochendoner (D)	Allen E. Ertel (D)[3]
	21	Thomas J. Ridge (R)	Anthony "Buzz" Andrezeski (D)	Marc L. Marks (R)[1]
South Carolina	5	John Spratt (D)	John S. Wilkerson (R)	Ken Holland (D)[1]
	6	Robert M. Tallon Jr. (D)	John L. Napier (R)	Napier
Tennessee	4	Jim Cooper (D)	Cissy Baker (R)	New District
	7	Don Sundquist (R)	Bob Clement (D)	New District
Texas	3	Steve Bartlett (R)	James L. McNees Jr. (D)	James M. Collins (R)[2]
	5	John Bryant (D)	Joe Devaney (R)	Jim Mattox (D)[8]
	16	Ronald Coleman (D)	Pat B. Haggerty (R)	Richard C. White (D)[1]
	25	Mike Andrews (D)	Mike Faubion (R)	New District
	26	Tom Vandergriff (D)	Jim Bradshaw (R)	New District
	27	Solomon P. Ortiz (D)	Jason Luby (R)	New District
Utah	3	Howard C. Nielson (R)	Henry Huish (I)[9]	New District
Virginia	1	Herbert H. Bateman (R)	John J. McGlennon (D)	Paul S. Trible Jr. (R)[2]
	4	Norman Sisisky (D)	Robert W. Daniel Jr. (R)	Daniel
	6	James R. Olin (D)	Kevin G. Miller (R)	M. Caldwell Butler (R)[1]
	9	Frederick C. Boucher (D)	William C. Wampler (R)	Wampler
Washington	8	Rodney Chandler (R)	Beth Bland (D)	New District
West Virginia	1	Alan B. Mollohan (D)	John F. McCuskey (R)	Robert H. Mollohan (D)[1]
	2	Harley O. Staggers Jr. (D)	J. D. Hinkle Jr. (R)	Cleve Benedict (R)[2]
	3	Bob Wise (D)	David Michael Staton (R)	Staton
Wisconsin	5	Jim Moody (D)	Rod K. Johnston (R)	Henry S. Reuss (D)[1]

1 Retired.   2 Ran for Senate.   3 Ran for Governor.   4 Defeated in primary runoff.   5 Defeated in primary.
6 Incumbent Democratic Rep. Adam Benjamin Jr. died before the election.   7 Incumbent Democratic Rep. Fred Richmond resigned before the election.   8 Ran for state attorney general.   9 Huish, a Democrat, missed the filing deadline and ran as an independent.

House Membership in the 98th Congress

ALABAMA
1. Jack Edwards (R)
2. William L. Dickinson (R)
3. Bill Nichols (D)
4. Tom Bevill (D)
5. Ronnie G. Flippo (D)
6. Ben Erdreich (D)#
7. Richard C. Shelby (D)

ALASKA
AL Don Young (R)

ARIZONA
1. John McCain (R)#
2. Morris K. Udall (D)
3. Bob Stump (R)
4. Eldon Rudd (R)
5. Jim McNulty (D)#

ARKANSAS
1. Bill Alexander (D)
2. Ed Bethune (R)
3. John Paul Hammerschmidt (R)
4. Beryl Anthony Jr. (D)

CALIFORNIA
1. Douglas H. Bosco (D)#
2. Gene Chappie (R)
3. Robert T. Matsui (D)
4. Vic Fazio (D)
5. Phillip Burton (D)
6. Barbara Boxer (D)#
7. George Miller (D)
8. Ronald V. Dellums (D)
9. Fortney H. "Pete" Stark (D)
10. Don Edwards (D)
11. Tom Lantos (D)
12. Ed Zschau (R)#
13. Norman Y. Mineta (D)
14. Norman D. Shumway (R)
15. Tony Coelho (D)
16. Leon E. Panetta (D)
17. Charles Pashayan Jr. (R)
18. Richard Lehman (D)#
19. Robert J. Lagomarsino (R)
20. William M. Thomas (R)
21. Bobbi Fiedler (R)
22. Carlos J. Moorhead (R)
23. Anthony C. Beilenson (D)
24. Henry A. Waxman (D)
25. Edward R. Roybal (D)
26. Howard L. Berman (D)#
27. Mel Levine (D)#
28. Julian C. Dixon (D)
29. Augustus F. Hawkins (D)
30. Matthew G. Martinez (D)
31. Mervyn M. Dymally (D)
32. Glenn M. Anderson (D)
33. David Dreier (R)
34. Esteban Torres (D)#
35. Jerry Lewis (R)
36. George E. Brown Jr. (D)
37. Al McCandless (R)#
38. Jerry M. Patterson (D)
39. William E. Dannemeyer (R)
40. Robert E. Badham (R)
41. Bill Lowery (R)
42. Dan Lungren (R)
43. Ron Packard (R)#

House Lineup††

Democrats 269   Republicans 166

Freshman Democrats - 57
#Freshman Representative
Freshman Republicans - 24
†Former Representative
††Includes Georgia's 4th and 5th districts,
where elections were held Nov. 30.

---

44. Jim Bates (D)#
45. Duncan L. Hunter (R)

COLORADO
1. Patricia Schroeder (D)
2. Timothy E. Wirth (D)
3. Ray Kogovsek (D)
4. Hank Brown (R)
5. Ken Kramer (R)
6. Jack Swigert (R)#*

CONNECTICUT
1. Barbara B. Kennelly (D)
2. Sam Gejdenson (D)
3. Bruce A. Morrison (D)#
4. Stewart B. McKinney (R)
5. William R. Ratchford (D)
6. Nancy L. Johnson (R)#

DELAWARE
AL Thomas R. Carper (D)#

FLORIDA
1. Earl Hutto (D)
2. Don Fuqua (D)
3. Charles E. Bennett (D)
4. Bill Chappell Jr. (D)
5. Bill McCollum (R)
6. Kenneth H. MacKay (D)#
7. Sam Gibbons (D)
8. C.W. Bill Young (R)
9. Michael Bilirakis (R)#
10. Andy Ireland (D)
11. Bill Nelson (D)
12. Tom Lewis (R)#
13. Connie Mack III (R)#
14. Daniel A. Mica (D)
15. E. Clay Shaw Jr. (R)
16. Larry Smith (D)#
17. William Lehman (D)
18. Claude Pepper (D)
19. Dante B. Fascell (D)

GEORGIA
1. Lindsay Thomas (D)#
2. Charles Hatcher (D)
3. Richard Ray (D)#
4. Elliott H. Levitas (D)
5. Wyche Fowler Jr. (D)
6. Newt Gingrich (R)
7. Larry P. McDonald (D)
8. J. Roy Rowland (D)#
9. Ed Jenkins (D)
10. Doug Barnard Jr. (D)

HAWAII
1. Cecil Heftel (D)
2. Daniel K. Akaka (D)

IDAHO
1. Larry E. Craig (R)
2. George Hansen (R)

ILLINOIS
1. Harold Washington (D)
2. Gus Savage (D)
3. Marty Russo (D)
4. George M. O'Brien (R)
5. William O. Lipinski (D)#
6. Henry J. Hyde (R)
7. Cardiss Collins (D)
8. Dan Rostenkowski (D)
9. Sidney R. Yates (D)
10. John Edward Porter (R)
11. Frank Annunzio (D)
12. Philip M. Crane (R)
13. John N. Erlenborn (R)
14. Tom Corcoran (R)
15. Edward R. Madigan (R)
16. Lynn Martin (R)
17. Lane Evans (D)#
18. Robert H. Michel (R)
19. Daniel B. Crane (R)
20. Richard J. Durbin (D)#
21. Melvin Price (D)
22. Paul Simon (D)

INDIANA
1. Katie Hall (D)#
2. Philip R. Sharp (D)
3. John Hiler (R)
4. Dan Coats (R)
5. Elwood Hillis (R)
6. Dan Burton (R)#
7. John T. Myers (R)
8. Francis X. McCloskey (D)#
9. Lee H. Hamilton (D)
10. Andrew Jacobs Jr. (D)

IOWA
1. Jim Leach (R)
2. Tom Tauke (R)
3. Cooper Evans (R)
4. Neal Smith (D)
5. Tom Harkin (D)
6. Berkley Bedell (D)

KANSAS
1. Pat Roberts (R)
2. Jim Slattery (D)#
3. Larry Winn Jr. (R)
4. Dan Glickman (D)
5. Bob Whittaker (R)

KENTUCKY
1. Carroll Hubbard Jr. (D)
2. William H. Natcher (D)
3. Romano L. Mazzoli (D)

4. Gene Snyder (R)
5. Harold Rogers (R)
6. Larry J. Hopkins (R)
7. Carl D. Perkins (D)

LOUISIANA
1. Bob Livingston (R)
2. Lindy (Mrs. Hale) Boggs (D)
3. W. J. "Billy" Tauzin (D)
4. Buddy Roemer (D)
5. Jerry Huckaby (D)
6. Henson Moore (R)
7. John B. Breaux (D)
8. Gillis W. Long (D)

MAINE
1. John R. McKernan Jr. (R)#
2. Olympia J. Snowe (R)

MARYLAND
1. Roy Dyson (D)
2. Clarence D. Long (D)
3. Barbara A. Mikulski (D)
4. Marjorie S. Holt (R)
5. Steny H. Hoyer (D)
6. Beverly B. Byron (D)
7. Parren J. Mitchell (D)
8. Michael D. Barnes (D)

MASSACHUSETTS
1. Silvio O. Conte (R)
2. Edward P. Boland (D)
3. Joseph D. Early (D)
4. Barney Frank (D)
5. James M. Shannon (D)
6. Nicholas Mavroules (D)
7. Edward J. Markey (D)
8. Thomas P. O'Neill Jr. (D)
9. Joe Moakley (D)
10. Gerry E. Studds (D)
11. Brian J. Donnelly (D)

MICHIGAN
1. John Conyers Jr. (D)
2. Carl D. Pursell (R)
3. Howard Wolpe (D)
4. Mark Siljander (R)
5. Harold S. Sawyer (R)
6. Bob Carr (D)†#
7. Dale E. Kildee (D)
8. Bob Traxler (D)
9. Guy Vander Jagt (R)
10. Don Albosta (D)
11. Robert W. Davis (R)
12. David E. Bonior (D)
13. George W. Crockett Jr. (D)
14. Dennis M. Hertel (D)
15. William D. Ford (D)
16. John D. Dingell (D)
17. Sander Levin (D)#
18. William S. Broomfield (R)

MINNESOTA
1. Timothy J. Penny (D)#
2. Vin Weber (R)
3. Bill Frenzel (R)
4. Bruce F. Vento (D)
5. Martin Olav Sabo (D)
6. Gerry Sikorski (D)#

* Died Dec. 27.

House Membership in the 98th Congress

7. Arlan Stangeland (R)
8. James L. Oberstar (D)

MISSISSIPPI
1. Jamie L. Whitten (D)
2. Webb Franklin (R)#
3. G. V. "Sonny" Montgomery (D)
4. Wayne Dowdy (D)
5. Trent Lott (R)

MISSOURI
1. William Clay (D)
2. Robert A. Young (D)
3. Richard A. Gephardt (D)
4. Ike Skelton (D)
5. Alan Wheat (D)#
6. E. Thomas Coleman (R)
7. Gene Taylor (R)
8. Bill Emerson (R)
9. Harold L. Volkmer (D)

MONTANA
1. Pat Williams (D)
2. Ron Marlenee (R)

NEBRASKA
1. Douglas K. Bereuter (R)
2. Hal Daub (R)
3. Virginia Smith (R)

NEVADA
1. Harry Reid (D)#
2. Barbara Vucanovich (R)#

NEW HAMPSHIRE
1. Norman E. D'Amours (D)
2. Judd Gregg (R)

NEW JERSEY
1. James J. Florio (D)
2. William J. Hughes (D)
3. James J. Howard (D)
4. Christopher H. Smith (R)
5. Marge Roukema (R)
6. Bernard J. Dwyer (D)
7. Matthew J. Rinaldo (R)
8. Robert A. Roe (D)
9. Robert G. Torricelli (D)#
10. Peter W. Rodino Jr. (D)
11. Joseph G. Minish (D)
12. Jim Courter (R)
13. Edwin B. Forsythe (R)
14. Frank J. Guarini (D)

NEW MEXICO
1. Manuel Lujan Jr. (R)
2. Joe Skeen (R)
3. Bill Richardson (D)#

NEW YORK
1. William Carney (R)
2. Thomas J. Downey (D)
3. Robert J. Mrazek (D)#
4. Norman F. Lent (R)
5. Raymond J. McGrath (R)
6. Joseph P. Addabbo (D)
7. Benjamin S. Rosenthal (D)
8. James H. Scheuer (D)
9. Geraldine A. Ferraro (D)
10. Charles E. Schumer (D)

11. Edolphus Towns (D)#
12. Major R. Owens (D)#
13. Stephen J. Solarz (D)
14. Guy V. Molinari (R)
15. Bill Green (R)
16. Charles B. Rangel (D)
17. Ted Weiss (D)
18. Robert Garcia (D)
19. Mario Biaggi (D)
20. Richard L. Ottinger (D)
21. Hamilton Fish Jr. (R)
22. Benjamin A. Gilman (R)
23. Samuel S. Stratton (D)
24. Gerald B. H. Solomon (R)
25. Sherwood L. Boehlert (R)#
26. David O'B. Martin (R)
27. George C. Wortley (R)
28. Matthew F. McHugh (D)
29. Frank Horton (R)
30. Barber B. Conable Jr. (R)
31. Jack F. Kemp (R)
32. John J. LaFalce (D)
33. Henry J. Nowak (D)
34. Stanley N. Lundine (D)

NORTH CAROLINA
1. Walter B. Jones (D)
2. I. T. "Tim" Valentine Jr. (D)#
3. Charles Whitley (D)
4. Ike Andrews (D)
5. Stephen L. Neal (D)
6. Charles Robin Britt (D)#
7. Charlie Rose (D)
8. W. G. "Bill" Hefner (D)
9. James G. Martin (R)
10. James T. Broyhill (R)
11. James McClure Clarke (D)#

NORTH DAKOTA
AL Byron L. Dorgan (D)

OHIO
1. Thomas A. Luken (D)
2. Bill Gradison (R)
3. Tony P. Hall (D)
4. Michael G. Oxley (R)
5. Delbert L. Latta (R)
6. Bob McEwen (R)
7. Michael Dewine (R)#
8. Thomas N. Kindness (R)
9. Marcy Kaptur (D)#
10. Clarence E. Miller (R)
11. Dennis E. Eckart (D)
12. John R. Kasich (R)#
13. Don J. Pease (D)
14. John F. Seiberling (D)
15. Chalmers P. Wylie (R)
16. Ralph Regula (R)
17. Lyle Williams (R)
18. Douglas Applegate (D)
19. Edward F. Feighan (D)#
20. Mary Rose Oakar (D)
21. Louis Stokes (D)

OKLAHOMA
1. James R. Jones (D)
2. Mike Synar (D)
3. Wes Watkins (D)

4. Dave McCurdy (D)
5. Mickey Edwards (R)
6. Glenn English (D)

OREGON
1. Les AuCoin (D)
2. Bob Smith (R)#
3. Ron Wyden (D)
4. James Weaver (D)
5. Denny Smith (R)

PENNSYLVANIA
1. Thomas M. Foglietta (D)
2. William H. Gray III (D)
3. Robert A. Borski (D)#
4. Joseph P. Kolter (D)#
5. Richard T. Schulze (R)
6. Gus Yatron (D)
7. Robert W. Edgar (D)
8. Peter H. Kostmayer (D)†#
9. Bud Shuster (R)
10. Joseph M. McDade (R)
11. Frank Harrison (D)#
12. John P. Murtha (D)
13. Lawrence Coughlin (R)
14. William J. Coyne (D)
15. Don Ritter (R)
16. Robert S. Walker (R)
17. George W. Gekas (R)#
18. Doug Walgren (D)
19. Bill Goodling (R)
20. Joseph M. Gaydos (D)
21. Thomas J. Ridge (R)#
22. Austin J. Murphy (D)
23. William F. Clinger Jr. (R)

RHODE ISLAND
1. Fernand J. St Germain (D)
2. Claudine Schneider (R)

SOUTH CAROLINA
1. Thomas F. Hartnett (R)
2. Floyd Spence (R)
3. Butler Derrick (D)
4. Carroll A. Campbell Jr. (R)
5. John Spratt (D)#
6. Robert M. Tallon Jr. (D)#

SOUTH DAKOTA
AL Thomas A. Daschle (D)

TENNESSEE
1. James H. Quillen (R)
2. John J. Duncan (R)
3. Marilyn Lloyd Bouquard (D)
4. Jim Cooper (D)#
5. Bill Boner (D)
6. Albert Gore Jr. (D)
7. Don Sundquist (R)#
8. Ed Jones (D)
9. Harold E. Ford (D)

TEXAS
1. Sam B. Hall Jr. (D)
2. Charles Wilson (D)
3. Steve Bartlett (R)#
4. Ralph M. Hall (D)
5. John Bryant (D)#
6. Phil Gramm (D)
7. Bill Archer (R)

8. Jack Fields (R)
9. Jack Brooks (D)
10. J. J. Pickle (D)
11. Marvin Leath (D)
12. Jim Wright (D)
13. Jack Hightower (D)
14. Bill Patman (D)
15. E. "Kika" de la Garza (D)
16. Ronald Coleman (D)#
17. Charles W. Stenholm (D)
18. Mickey Leland (D)
19. Kent Hance (D)
20. Henry B. Gonzalez (D)
21. Tom Loeffler (R)
22. Ron Paul (R)
23. Abraham Kazen Jr. (D)
24. Martin Frost (D)
25. Mike Andrews (D)#
26. Tom Vandergriff (D)#
27. Solomon P. Ortiz (D)#

UTAH
1. James V. Hansen (R)
2. Dan Marriott (R)
3. Howard C. Nielson (R)#

VERMONT
AL James M. Jeffords (R)

VIRGINIA
1. Herbert H. Bateman (R)#
2. G. William Whitehurst (R)
3. Thomas J. Bliley Jr. (R)
4. Norman Sisisky (D)#
5. Dan Daniel (D)
6. James R. Olin (D)#
7. J. Kenneth Robinson (R)
8. Stan Parris (R)
9. Frederick C. Boucher (D)#
10. Frank R. Wolf (R)

WASHINGTON
1. Joel Pritchard (R)
2. Al Swift (D)
3. Don Bonker (D)
4. Sid Morrison (R)
5. Thomas S. Foley (D)
6. Norman D. Dicks (D)
7. Mike Lowry (D)
8. Rodney Chandler (R)#

WEST VIRGINIA
1. Alan B. Mollohan (D)#
2. Harley O. Staggers Jr. (D)#
3. Bob Wise (D)#
4. Nick J. Rahall II (D)

WISCONSIN
1. Les Aspin (D)
2. Robert W. Kastenmeier (D)
3. Steve Gunderson (R)
4. Clement J. Zablocki (D)
5. Jim Moody (D)#
6. Thomas E. Petri (R)
7. David R. Obey (D)
8. Toby Roth (R)
9. F. James Sensenbrenner Jr. (R)

WYOMING
AL Dick Cheney (R)

No Rightward Shift:

Redistricting Bitter Disappointment to GOP

In 1982, reapportionment, the rise of the Sun Belt and the decline of the Frost Belt were supposed to catch up with the Democrats, setting in motion a decade of conservative and Republican advance of power in the House. But it did not work out that way.

The Sun Belt proved the Republicans' greatest disappointment. The nationwide shift in population away from the industrial North gave Southern and Western states 17 new districts, and the GOP at one time hoped to take at least a dozen. But Democratic legislative cartography and unfriendly federal court action got in the way, and in the end Democrats won 10 of the 17. *(Chart, next page)*

Democrats also managed to sidestep the brunt of district losses in the Northeast and Midwest. Legislative map makers eliminated Republican seats in Illinois and New Jersey, even though the population decline had been in urban, Democratic areas. On Nov. 2, anti-Republican economic resentments took over, bringing victory to several Democrats in new districts that were nominally Democratic but had been voting conservatively in recent years. In all, in the 10 Northern states that lost districts, Republicans came out 18 seats short of where they stood before the election.

In most of the 11 states that gained seats, the GOP seemed the natural heir to demographic changes. All 11 were carried by Ronald Reagan in the 1980 presidential race, and eight went for Republican Gerald R. Ford in 1976.

Nonetheless, legislatures or courts in six of the states drew new districts favoring or leaning to Democrats. And contrary to prediction, not one of these new constituencies nominated a conservative Democrat. As a result, liberals (including four Hispanics) made up a large portion of the Sun Belt's new House contingent.

California Scheming

The Democrats' greatest boost came in California, where Democratic Rep. Phillip Burton masterminded a remap that dissolved three GOP-held seats and diluted a fourth enough to fatally weaken the incumbent. And although population gains entitled California to only two additional districts,

Burton managed to give his party five new seats while strengthening its grip on most of the districts it already held.

Three of the new California Democratic seats were in the Los Angeles area, where liberals Howard Berman, Mel Levine and Esteban Torres all won convincing victories. A new district in San Diego and one around Fresno also sent liberal Democrats to the House.

Burton particularly galled California Republicans by doing in the seats of GOP incumbents Barry M. Goldwater Jr. and Robert K. Dornan, both of whom ran unsuccessfully for the GOP nomination for the U.S. Senate. He also dismembered the district of his arch-nemesis in the California delegation, conservative GOP Rep. John H. Rousselot.

Rousselot eventually decided to run in a reshaped 30th District won in a special election earlier in 1982 by Democrat Matthew G. Martinez. Although Rousselot had the edge in campaign sophistication and experience, he was unable to overcome the new district's strongly Democratic character.

In New Mexico, the Democratic-controlled Senate and the state's U.S. House members prevailed over a conservative coalition in the state House to create a northern 3rd District that was two-thirds Hispanic and Indian, and heavily Democratic. Democrat Bill Richardson, who is half Hispanic, won that seat on Nov. 2. In Tennessee,

which also gained one seat, Democratic lawyer Jim Cooper won an impressive victory over Republican Cissy Baker, daughter of the Senate majority leader, in a new, Democratic-leaning 4th District.

In Arizona, which gained one seat, a compromise plan was drawn after Hispanics charged that their voting strength had been diluted in a map drawn by the GOP-dominated Legislature. The new 5th District was crafted by the Republican who eventually ran there, state Sen. Jim Kolbe. Nonetheless, Kolbe, a moderate Republican who appealed largely to upper middle-class professionals, narrowly lost to liberal former state Sen. Jim McNulty. McNulty's small-town appeal pulled in support from rural Democrats who in the past routinely supported the GOP.

Republicans expected to win at least one of the three new Texas districts, but instead they were shut out. In the Republican-leaning 26th District between Dallas and Fort Worth, the winner by the slimmest of margins was conservative Democrat Tom Vandergriff, former mayor of Arlington. He defeated Republican Jim Bradshaw, former Fort Worth mayor pro tempore. In the southeastern 27th, which is 61.5 percent Hispanic, Democrat Solomon Ortiz easily became Texas' third Hispanic House member. Liberal Democratic lawyer Mike Andrews handily took south Houston's 25th District.

Incumbent *vs.* Incumbent Contests

District		Vote Total	Percent
Calif. 30	Matthew G. Martinez (D)	60,033	54%
	John H. Rousselot (R)	51,058	46
Mass. 4	Barney Frank (D)	121,632	59
	Margaret M. Heckler (R)	82,862	41
Mo. 4	Ike Skelton (D)	96,114	55
	Wendell Bailey (R)	79,255	45
N.Y. 14	Leo C. Zeferetti (D)	50,601	42
	Guy V. Molinari (R)	66,781	57
N.Y. 22	Peter A. Peyser (D)	68,424	41
	Benjamin A. Gilman (R)	89,687	54
S.D. AL	Thomas A. Daschle (D)	144,013	52
	Clint Roberts (R)	133,986	48

1983 House Makeup, Party Gains and Losses

	97th Congress			98th Congress			Gain/		97th Congress			98th Congress			Gain/
	Seats	Dem.	Rep.	Seats	Dem.	Rep.	Loss		Seats	Dem.	Rep.	Seats	Dem.	Rep.	/Loss
Ala.	7	4	3	7	5	2	+1D/-1R	Neb.	3	0	3	3	0	3	
Alaska	1	0	1	1	0	1		Nev.	1	1	0	2	1	1	+1R
Ariz.	4	2	2	5	2	3	+1R	N.H.	2	1	1	2	1	1	
Ark.	4	2	2	4	2	2		N.J.	15	8	7	14	9	5	+1D/-2R
Calif.	43	22	21	45	28	17	+6D/-4R	N.M.	2	0	2	3	1	2	+1D
Colo.	5	3	2	6	3	3	+1R	N.Y.	39	22	17	34	20	14	-2D/-3R
Conn.	6	4	2	6	4	2		N.C.	11	7	4	11	9	2	+2D/-2R
Del.	1	0	1	1	1	0	+1D/-1R	N.D.	1	1	0	1	1	0	
Fla.	15	11	4	19	13	6	+2D/+2R	Ohio	23	10	13	21	10	11	-2R
Ga.	10	9	1	10	9*	1*		Okla.	6	5	1	6	5	1	
Hawaii	2	2	0	2	2	0		Ore.	4	3	1	5	3	2	+1R
Idaho	2	0	2	2	0	2		Pa.	25	12	13	23	13	10	+1D/-3R
Ill.	24	10	14	22	12	10	+2D/-4R	R.I.	2	1	1	2	1	1	
Ind.	11	6	5	10	5	5	-1D	S.C.	6	2	4	6	3	3	+1D/-1R
Iowa	6	3	3	6	3	3		S.D.	2	1	1	1	1	0	-1R
Kan.	5	1	4	5	2	3	+1D/-1R	Tenn.	8	5	3	9	6	3	+1D
Ky.	7	4	3	7	4	3		Texas	24	19	5	27	22	5	+3D
La.	8	6	2	8	6	2		Utah	2	0	2	3	0	3	+1R
Maine	2	0	2	2	0	2		Vt.	1	0	1	1	0	1	
Md.	8	7	1	8	7	1		Va.	10	1	9	10	4	6	+3D/-3R
Mass.	12	10	2	11	10	1	-1R	Wash.	7	5	2	8	5	3	+1R
Mich.	19	12	7	18	12	6	-1R	W.Va.	4	2	2	4	4	0	+2D/-2R
Minn.	8	3	5	8	5	3	+2D/-2R	Wis.	9	5	4	9	5	4	
Miss.	5	4	1	5	3	2	+1R/-1D	Wyo.	1	0	1	1	0	1	
Mo.	10	6	4	9	6	3	-1R								
Mont.	2	1	1	2	1	1		**TOTALS**	**435**	**243**	**192**	**435**	***269**	***166**	**+26D/-26R**

Georgia 4th and 5th districts included in calculations. Elections were held in those districts on Nov. 30.

Republicans' biggest gains came in Florida, where two of the state's four new seats were placed firmly in GOP hands. The new 9th, in the Tampa-St. Petersburg area, and the 12th, which sprawls across the southern portion of the state, both chose Republicans after closely fought campaigns. The new 6th, in the central part of the state, and the 16th, just north of Miami, were earmarked for Democrats all along.

The GOP also picked up one seat each in Colorado, Nevada, Oregon, Utah and Washington. None of those gains came at the expense of Democratic seats, however, as some Republican legislators had initially planned; Democrats still held a majority of the delegations of Washington and Oregon, and the partisan balance was even in Nevada and Colorado.

In the Northeast and Midwest, Democrats used redistricting and the national Democratic tide to deny Republicans their apparent advantages of population shift.

In Illinois and New Jersey, where population losses forced the removal of two seats and one seat, respectively, Democratic legislatures dissolved existing GOP districts to bring delegation sizes down. They also left several

Republican incumbents weaker: In New Jersey, GOP Rep. Harold C. Hollenbeck lost his seat in a 9th District that had gained several Democratic towns; in Illinois, GOP Rep. Paul Findley was evicted from a 20th District that had picked up three traditionally Democratic counties and lost Republican territory.

In Michigan, the Democratic Legislature dissolved the district held by Democrat James J. Blanchard, who had given it up for his successful gubernatorial bid. At the same time, however, legislators cut Republican territory out of the 6th District of freshman GOP Rep. Jim Dunn and gave Dunn staunchly Democratic Pontiac and its western Oakland County suburbs. Dunn lost the 6th to Democrat Bob Carr, whom he had unseated two years before. Although Carr trailed in the portion of the district that he held until 1980, he pulled in a 10,000-vote margin in the depression-plagued Pontiac area.

Even in Northern states where Republicans controlled the redistricting process, Democrats managed to post gains or cut their losses. In Indiana, which lost one seat, the GOP-dominated Legislature drew a map designed to cost Democrats two or three

seats; however, the new map not only galvanized Democrats in other states to work to offset those losses, it ended up costing Democrats only one seat even in Indiana.

Only in Ohio did a change in a district prove fatal to a Democratic incumbent facing a challenger.

In the 12th District, freshman Rep. Bob Shamansky saw his constituency lose Democratic portions of Columbus and gain rural and conservative territory. Shamansky was unseated by New Right Republican John R. Kasich.

No clear trend emerged from the six contests in which incumbents were paired in newly drawn districts.

Those with the edge in familiar territory won three. New York GOP Reps. Benjamin A. Gilman and Guy V. Molinari, and Missouri Democrat Ike Skelton all were given districts in which a majority of the voters were from their old districts. (Chart, previous page)

In Massachusetts, however, Democrat Barney Frank defeated Republican Margaret M. Heckler in a district with a Democratic registration advantage, but in which 70 percent of the residents had been represented by Heckler.   ▪

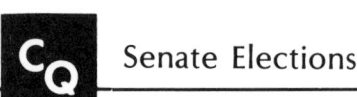 Senate Elections

Partisan Balance Unchanged:

Senate Election: A Dull Affair Compared to 1980's Upheaval

If the 1980 Senate elections marked a tidal wave that dramatically reshaped the political landscape, the balloting in 1982 created no more than a gentle swell. It barely disturbed the status quo.

The only thing remarkable about the 1982 Senate results was the sheer absence of change. Not only did the party ratio remain the same — 54 Republicans and 46 Democrats — but 95 of the 100 senators returned to Washington. The class of five newcomers was the smallest such group in the 68-year history of popular Senate elections.

That sort of stability was itself a dramatic reversal of recent election trends. During the past decade, a Senate seat had been one of the most difficult offices in U.S. politics to hold. While re-election rates for House incumbents regularly had run above 85 percent, senators were struggling against well-financed challengers and effective special interest groups.

In both 1976 and 1978 less than 65 percent of Senate incumbents won re-election. Two years ago, the rate tumbled to 55 percent as a conservative, anti-incumbent tide swept Democratic senators from office across the country.

But there was no national tide visible in Senate contests in 1982, and the cry of "throw the bums out" was barely audible. Of 30 incumbents who sought re-election, all but two — Republican Harrison "Jack" Schmitt of New Mexico and Democrat Howard W. Cannon of Nevada — won re-election. And Cannon came within 6,000 votes of victory. *(State-by-state results, p. 18-B)*

In both 1976 and 1978, 18 new senators were elected. In 1980, there were 20. But when the Senate assembled in January 1983, it seemed like a homecoming reunion. *(Freshmen senators, box, p. 17-B)*

The New Class

Three members of the tiny freshman class were Republicans: former Nevada state Sen. Chic Hecht, 53, who ousted Cannon; San Diego Mayor Pete Wilson, 49, who defeated California Gov. Edmund G. Brown Jr. for the seat of retiring GOP Sen. S. I. "Sam" Hayakawa; and U.S. Rep. Paul S. Trible Jr., 35, who edged out Virginia Lt. Gov. Richard J. Davis for the seat that was vacated by Harry F. Byrd Jr., who ran as an independent but caucused with Senate Democrats.

The two new Democratic senators were New Mexico state Attorney General Jeff Bingaman, 39, who retired Schmitt, and New Jersey computer executive Frank R. Lautenberg, 58, who defeated Rep. Millicent Fenwick. The New Jersey contest was for the seat formerly held by Democratic Sen. Harrison A. Williams Jr. but occupied by Republican Nicholas F. Brady, who was appointed as a caretaker after Williams' resignation in April. *(Senate newcomers, box, p. 16-B)*

The Senate outcome was neither the "ratifying" election that Republicans had hoped for after their sweep of 1980, nor the "correcting" election

U.S. Senate	
97th Congress	**98th Congress**
Democrats 46*	Democrats 46
Republicans 54	Republicans 54

Democrats	
Freshmen	2
Incumbents re-elected	18
Incumbents defeated	1
Howard W. Cannon, Nev.	

Republicans	
Freshmen	3
Incumbents re-elected	10
Incumbents defeated	1
Harrison "Jack" Schmitt, N.M.	

*Includes the seat of Independent Sen. Harry F. Byrd Jr., Va., who retired.

that Democrats had wanted. But there were favorable results for both parties. Republicans kept their beachhead on Capitol Hill, ensuring that Ronald Reagan would be the first Republican president since Herbert Hoover to have a GOP Senate majority throughout his four-year term.

Democrats broke even in an election that could have relegated them to minority status in the Senate for a long time. Of the 33 seats that were contested this year, the Democrats were defending 19 (not including Byrd's seat). They ended up winning 60.6 percent of the races — a figure almost identical to the one in the House, where Democrats took just over 61 percent.

And with 19 of the 33 seats up in 1984 belonging to the Republicans, Democrats could think realistically of regaining control of the Senate in January 1985. That was not the case after their battering in 1980. As Democrats looked ahead to 1982, many foresaw another debacle at the polls. But as the economy worsened, Democratic leaders became cautiously optimistic that their party could pick up the five seats that would give them a Senate majority.

They came closer to making it than the final partisan tally indicated. While the Democrats held nearly all their 19 seats with solid majorities, Republicans retained theirs by much smaller margins. The GOP lost only two of the 13 seats that it was defending, but in six others Republican candidates struggled to victory with no more than 53 percent of the vote.

The Endangered Five

In 1982, embattled incumbents were mostly moderate Republicans with Frost Belt constituencies. They proved to be a more resilient group than the band of liberal Democrats that was ousted in 1980.

These GOP senators were up against the stagnant economy and traditional Democratic voting strength in their states. Five were especially threatened: John H. Chafee in Rhode Island, John C. Danforth in Missouri, David Durenberger in Minnesota, Robert T. Stafford in Vermont and Lowell P. Weicker Jr. in Connecticut. All capitalized on their independence

Senate Membership in 98th Congress

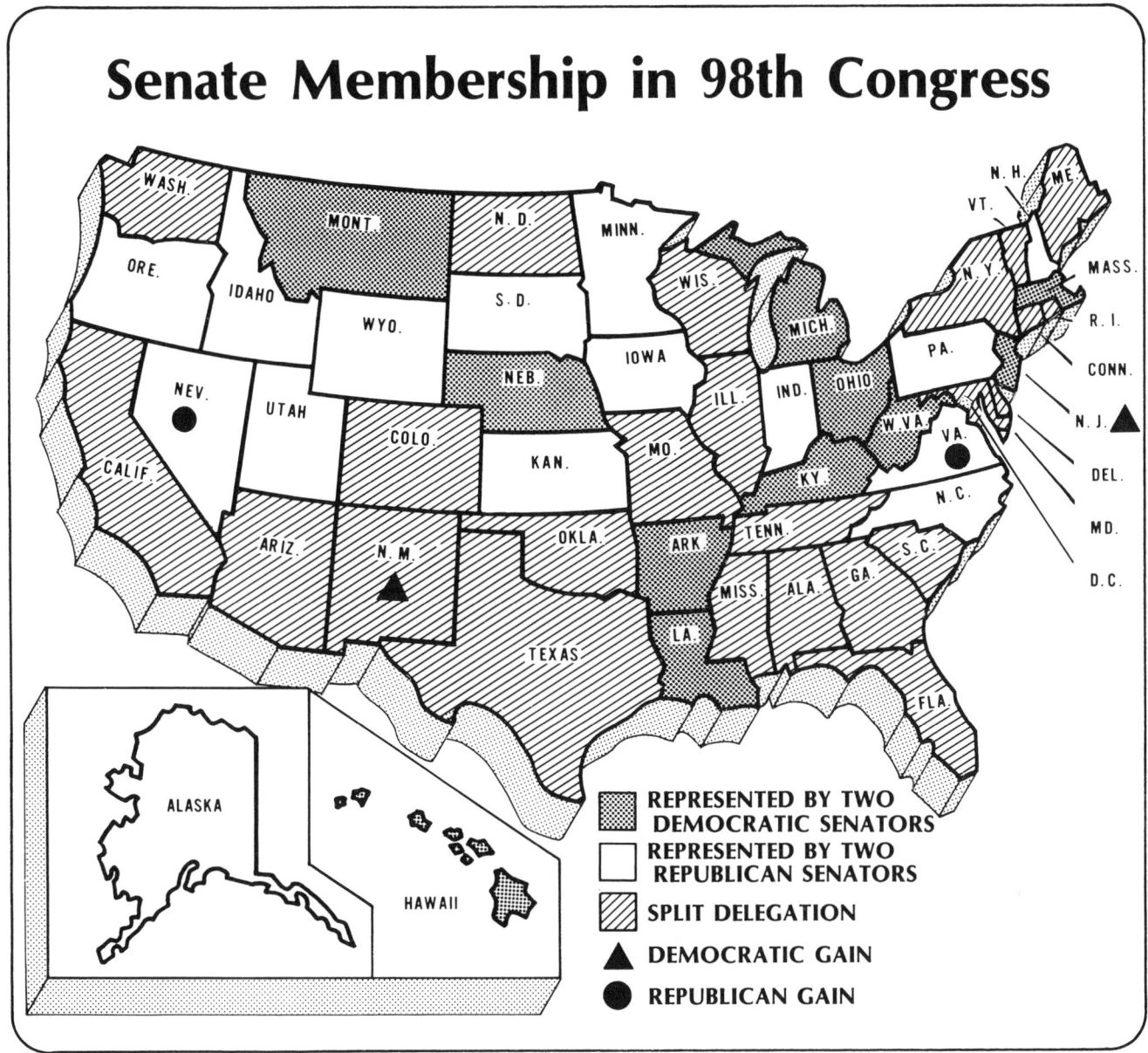

REPRESENTED BY TWO DEMOCRATIC SENATORS

REPRESENTED BY TWO REPUBLICAN SENATORS

SPLIT DELEGATION

▲ DEMOCRATIC GAIN

● REPUBLICAN GAIN

and their personal popularity to fend off Democratic efforts to tie them to what the Democrats said were failures of Reaganomics.

The endangered GOP five established themselves — as liberal Democrats Gary Hart of Colorado and Patrick J. Leahy of Vermont did in 1980 — as survivors in what was a bad year for their party. It was hard to imagine a stronger group of incumbents for the Republican Party to throw at the opposition in a difficult year. By and large, the GOP newcomers chosen in 1978 and 1980 would not have fared as well had they been up in 1982.

Despite the quality of the Republican candidates, however, there were some anxious moments. In state after

state, seemingly large leads early in the fall of 1982 dwindled sharply by Election Day.

Chafee, Danforth, Stafford and Weicker won re-election with 51 percent of the vote. Durenberger drew 53 percent. For all but Stafford it was a significant drop from their previous elections.

Chafee defeated former Rhode Island Attorney General Julius C. Michaelson in a state where Reagan drew his lowest share of the vote (37 percent) in 1980. Weicker had to withstand two rivals, Democratic Rep. Toby Moffett and conservative third-party entry Lucien DiFazio (who was backed by the New Right). He also had to buck a solid Democratic guber-

natorial victory. Stafford had to overcome a lackluster primary showing in which two conservative challengers combined drew a majority of the vote.

Durenberger won a bit more easily, but had to fend off a strong Democratic tide in Minnesota and a lavishly financed campaign by his challenger, department store heir Mark Dayton. The wealthy Dayton threatened the all-time Senate spending record — the $7.5 million spent by Sen. Jesse Helms, R-N.C., in 1978 — in an unsuccessful effort to ride the Democratic tide that removed the governorship and two House seats from GOP control.

All of the endangered five, with the exception of Durenberger, were

able to outspend significantly their rivals (even Durenberger had a solid $3 million campaign chest). And the economy, though a definite liability, was not as devastating in their states as it was in the industrial heart of the Frost Belt. In Connecticut, Minnesota, Missouri, Rhode Island and Vermont, the latest statewide unemployment rate was below 10 percent.

The worst unemployment tended to be in states with liberal Democratic incumbents, most of whom would have lost if forced to run against the Reagan tide in 1980. In this category were Donald W. Riegle Jr. of Michigan, where unemployment was around 15 percent, and Howard M. Metzenbaum of Ohio, where the rate was 12.5 percent. Both won new terms Nov. 2 with 58 percent of the vote.

Personalities, Local Issues

Although the 1982 election was advertised as a national referendum on the Reagan administration, the few Senate turnovers seemed to hinge on personalities and local issues.

In Nevada, Cannon was crippled by the residue from a bitter, closely fought primary contest with Rep. James D. Santini. He was hurt further in the closing days of the campaign by adverse publicity from a trial of Teamsters officials in Chicago. They were accused of conspiring to bribe Cannon to secure his help in defeating a trucking deregulation bill. Although he accepted no bribe and had been completely cleared of any wrongdoing, the late publicity helped ensure his narrow loss to Hecht.

Reagan could take some credit for Hecht's victory. The president, who carried Nevada in 1980 with 62 percent of the vote, made a late campaign appearance on Hecht's behalf.

Cannon was one of the last remnants of the fabled Democratic class of 1958, which included Edmund S. Muskie, Eugene J. McCarthy and

New Jersey Democratic Senator-elect Frank R. Lautenberg

Philip Hart, and which set the tone of Senate politics for nearly two full decades. The only two members of that class who were still in office at the start of the 98th Congress were Robert C. Byrd and Jennings Randolph, both of West Virginia.

New Mexico was a state where last-minute campaigning by Reagan had little impact. Voters seemed to accept Democratic charges that Schmitt was a loner with little impact on the Senate. Although Schmitt outspent the politically unscarred Bingaman, he lost by 8 percentage points.

In the contest to succeed Harry F.

Byrd Jr. in Virginia, neither candidate wanted to be positioned too close or too far from Reagan. The president visited Richmond in late September to boost Trible, but the candidate's strategists were careful not to invite Reagan back before the election lest he motivate angry Democratic voters.

Democrat Davis launched a series of negative advertisements depicting Trible as callous and ambitious, but made little effort to tie him to Reagan. Davis' managers viewed the president as personally popular among Virginia's large body of conservative white voters. Their strategy nearly worked, but Trible's early start and superior

Senate: Newcomers, Switched Seats, Losers

State	97th	98th	Winner	Loser	Lame Duck
California	R	R	Pete Wilson	Edmund G. Brown Jr.	S. I. "Sam" Hayakawa*
Nevada	D	R	Chic Hecht	Howard W. Cannon	Cannon
New Jersey	R	D	Frank R. Lautenberg	Millicent Fenwick	Nicholas F. Brady*
New Mexico	R	D	Jeff Bingaman	Harrison "Jack" Schmitt	Schmitt
Virginia	I†	R	Paul S. Trible Jr.	Richard J. Davis	Harry F. Byrd Jr.*

*Retired.
† Sen. Harry F. Byrd Jr., elected as an independent, caucused with the Democrats.

financing helped produce a 2 percentage point victory.

In the other open seat contests, in California and New Jersey, Reagan and national themes took a back seat to the colorful personalities of Brown and Fenwick. Both lost to less flamboyant rivals who promised they would be more effective legislators.

Few Surprises

In recent elections, pollsters had noted late shifts in voter preferences that produced some totally unexpected results. In 1978, former airline pilot Gordon J. Humphrey came out of nowhere to unseat veteran Democratic Sen. Thomas J. McIntyre of New Hampshire. In 1980, former Georgia GOP Chairman Mack Mattingly was a similar long shot who came from way back to oust 24-year incumbent Herman E. Talmadge.

But in 1982 there were landslides rather than surprises, especially among the Democrats. Of the 19 Democratic incumbents who sought reelection, all but Cannon won with at least 54 percent of the vote.

That included veteran Mississippi Democrat John C. Stennis, who drew his first serious challenge since he initially won his seat in a 1947 special election. Republicans were hopeful that Stennis' age — he would be 87 by the end of his sixth full term — would lead to a voter revolt. But he projected the image of a vigorous elder statesman and won by nearly 2-to-1.

Stennis' margin was matched by 74-year-old North Dakota veteran Quentin N. Burdick, who drew his highest percentage since he was first elected to the Senate in 1960.

The National Conservative Political Action Committee (NCPAC) ran a strident campaign which sought to portray Burdick as too liberal for North Dakota. But, as was the case virtually everywhere NCPAC was involved in the 1982 elections, its effort backfired or had little effect.

Rather than softening up Democratic incumbents as they did in 1980, NCPAC's negative ads seemed to galvanize Democratic support and spur fund raising. Maryland's Paul S. Sarbanes, a NCPAC target for more than a year, drew 63 percent of the vote, up 7 percentage points from his last race. Senate Minority Leader Robert C. Byrd, who also had concerted NCPAC opposition, was an even bigger winner in West Virginia.

The 18 victorious Democratic incumbents won with percentages rang-

Senate Freshmen, 1914-1982

Year	Freshmen Senators	Democrats	Republicans	Others
1914	10	7	3	
1916	19	8	11	
1918	17	6	11	
1920	17	4	13	
1922	19	12	6	1
1924	13	3	10	
1926	15	8	7	
1928	11	1	10	
1930	19	14	5	
1932	16	16	0	
1934	13	13	0	
1936	16	13	2	1
1938	13	5	8	
1940	12	5	7	
1942	13	3	10	
1944	14	8	6	
1946	23	6	17	
1948	18	14	4	
1950	14	6	8	
1952	16	6	10	
1954	14	7	7	
1956	10	6	4	
1958	18	15	3	
1960	9	7	2	
1962	12	9	3	
1964	8	6	2	
1966	7	2	5	
1968	15	5	10	
1970	11	5	5	1
1972	13	8	5	
1974	11	9	2	
1976	18	10	8	
1978	20	9	11	
1980	18	2	16	
1982	5	2	3	

ing from 54 percent for Montana's John Melcher to 82 percent for Hawaii's virtually unopposed Spark M. Matsunaga. His GOP opponent raised less than $5,000, and it showed.

Edward M. Kennedy of Massachusetts, who normally is near the top of the Democratic vote charts, drew a solid 61 percent against GOP electronics executive Raymond Shamie. But it was Kennedy's lowest Senate percentage in 20 years and only a modest sendoff for a prospective presidential bid in 1984.

Kennedy's Senate vote was matched by Maine's George J. Mitchell, who was appointed in 1980 when Muskie resigned to become secretary of state. Mitchell looked like a sure loser earlier in 1982, but capitalized on the gaffes of GOP Rep. David F. Emery to win handily.

Altogether, there were 13 Democrats who won with at least 60 percent of the vote. In each region there were several of these big winners, with a low of two in the West and a high of five in the East.

But among Republicans, only Pennsylvania's John Heinz reached 60 percent. The state's 11 percent unemployment rate made Pennsylvania fertile ground for a Democratic challenge. But the wealthy Heinz far out-raised his opponent and so skillfully distanced himself from Reagan that he won the endorsement of the state AFL-CIO.

The only other GOP winners who were able to come close to 60 percent were in the staunchly Republican Rocky Mountain region — Utah's Orrin G. Hatch and Wyoming's Malcolm Wallop. ∎

Senate Membership in the 98th Congress

Democrats 46   Republicans 54

Freshman Senators - 5

Seats Switched Parties D to R - 2*   Seats Switched Parties R to D - 2

> **Senators elected in 1982 are *italicized***
>
> **# Freshman Senators**
>
> **✔ Seat switched parties**

ALABAMA
Howell Heflin (D)
Jeremiah Denton (R)

ALASKA
Frank H. Murkowski (R)
Ted Stevens (R)

ARIZONA
Dennis DeConcini (D)
Barry Goldwater (R)

ARKANSAS
Dale Bumpers (D)
David Pryor (D)

CALIFORNIA
Alan Cranston (D)
Pete Wilson (R)#

COLORADO
Gary Hart (D)
William L. Armstrong (R)

CONNECTICUT
Christopher J. Dodd (D)
Lowell P. Weicker Jr. (R)

DELAWARE
Joseph R. Biden Jr. (D)
William V. Roth Jr. (R)

FLORIDA
Lawton Chiles (D)
Paula Hawkins (R)

GEORGIA
Sam Nunn (D)
Mack Mattingly (R)

HAWAII
Daniel K. Inouye (D)
Spark M. Matsunaga (D)

IDAHO
James A. McClure (R)
Steven D. Symms (R)

ILLINOIS
Alan J. Dixon (D)
Charles H. Percy (R)

INDIANA
Richard G. Lugar (R)
Dan Quayle (R)

IOWA
Charles E. Grassley (R)
Roger W. Jepsen (R)

KANSAS
Robert Dole (R)
Nancy Landon Kassebaum (R)

KENTUCKY
Wendell H. Ford (D)
Walter D. Huddleston (D)

LOUISIANA
J. Bennett Johnston (D)
Russell B. Long (D)

MAINE
George J. Mitchell (D)
William S. Cohen (R)

MARYLAND
Paul S. Sarbanes (D)
Charles McC. Mathias Jr. (R)

MASSACHUSETTS
Edward M. Kennedy (D)
Paul E. Tsongas (D)

MICHIGAN
Carl Levin (D)
Donald W. Riegle Jr. (D)

MINNESOTA
Rudy Boschwitz (R)
David Durenberger (R)

MISSISSIPPI
John C. Stennis (D)
Thad Cochran (R)

MISSOURI
Thomas F. Eagleton (D)
John C. Danforth (R)

MONTANA
Max Baucus (D)
John Melcher (D)

NEBRASKA
J. James Exon (D)
Edward Zorinsky (D)

NEVADA
✔ *Chic Hecht (R)#*
Paul Laxalt (R)

NEW HAMPSHIRE
Gordon J. Humphrey (R)
Warren B. Rudman (R)

NEW JERSEY
Bill Bradley (D)
✔ *Frank R. Lautenberg (D)#*

NEW MEXICO
✔ *Jeff Bingaman (D)#*
Pete V. Domenici (R)

NEW YORK
Daniel Patrick Moynihan (D)
Alfonse M. D'Amato (R)

NORTH CAROLINA
John P. East (R)
Jesse Helms (R)

NORTH DAKOTA
Quentin N. Burdick (D)
Mark Andrews (R)

OHIO
John Glenn (D)
Howard M. Metzenbaum (D)

OKLAHOMA
David L. Boren (D)
Don Nickles (R)

OREGON
Mark O. Hatfield (R)
Bob Packwood (R)

PENNSYLVANIA
John Heinz (R)
Arlen Specter (R)

RHODE ISLAND
Claiborne Pell (D)
John H. Chafee (R)

SOUTH CAROLINA
Ernest F. Hollings (D)
Strom Thurmond (R)

SOUTH DAKOTA
James Abdnor (R)
Larry Pressler (R)

TENNESSEE
Jim Sasser (D)
Howard H. Baker Jr. (R)

TEXAS
Lloyd Bentsen (D)
John Tower (R)

UTAH
Jake Garn (R)
Orrin G. Hatch (R)

VERMONT
Patrick J. Leahy (D)
Robert T. Stafford (R)

VIRGINIA
✔ *Paul S. Trible Jr. (R)#*
John W. Warner (R)

WASHINGTON
Henry M. Jackson (D)
Slade Gorton (R)

WEST VIRGINIA
Robert C. Byrd (D)
Jennings Randolph (D)

WISCONSIN
William Proxmire (D)
Robert W. Kasten Jr. (R)

WYOMING
Alan K. Simpson (R)
Malcolm Wallop (R)

*Includes the seat of retiring Virginia Sen. Harry F. Byrd Jr., an independent. Byrd caucused with the Democrats and voted with them on Senate organizational matters.

Years of Expiration of Senate Terms

— 1984 —

(33 Senators: 19 Republicans, 14 Democrats)

Armstrong, William L. (R Colo.)
Baker, Howard H. Jr. (R Tenn.)
Baucus, Max (D Mont.)
Biden, Joseph R. Jr. (D Del.)
Boren, David L. (D Okla.)
Boschwitz, Rudy (R Minn.)
Bradley, Bill (D N.J.)
Cochran, Thad (R Miss.)
Cohen, William S. (R Maine)
Domenici, Pete V. (R N.M.)
Exon, J. James (D Neb.)

Hatfield, Mark O. (R Ore.)
Heflin, Howell (D Ala.)
Helms, Jesse (R N.C.)
Huddleston, Walter D. (D Ky.)
Humphrey, Gordon J. (R N.H.)
Jepsen, Roger W. (R Iowa)
Johnston, J. Bennett (D La.)
Kassebaum, Nancy Landon (R Kan.)
Levin, Carl (D Mich.)
McClure, James A. (R Idaho)
Nunn, Sam (D Ga.)

Pell, Claiborne (D R.I.)
Percy, Charles H. (R Ill.)
Pressler, Larry (R S.D.)
Pryor, David (D Ark.)
Randolph, Jennings (D W.Va.)
Simpson, Alan K. (R Wyo.)
Stevens, Ted (R Alaska)
Thurmond, Strom (R S.C.)
Tower, John (R Texas)
Tsongas, Paul E. (D Mass.)
Warner, John W. (R Va.)

— 1986 —

(34 Senators: 22 Republicans, 12 Democrats)

Abdnor, James (R S.D.)
Andrews, Mark (R N.D.)
Bumpers, Dale (D Ark.)
Cranston, Alan (D Calif.)
D'Amato, Alfonse (R N.Y.)
Denton, Jeremiah (R Ala.)
Dixon, Alan J. (D Ill.)
Dodd, Christopher J. (D Conn.)
Dole, Robert (R Kan.)
Eagleton, Thomas F. (D Mo.)
East, John P. (R N.C.)
Ford, Wendell H. (D Ky.)

Garn, Jake (R Utah)
Glenn, John (D Ohio)
Goldwater, Barry (R Ariz.)
Gorton, Slade (R Wash.)
Grassley, Charles E. (R Iowa)
Hart, Gary (D Colo.)
Hawkins, Paula (R Fla.)
Hollings, Ernest F. (D S.C.)
Inouye, Daniel K. (D Hawaii)
Kasten, Robert W. Jr. (R Wis.)
Laxalt, Paul (R Nev.)

Leahy, Patrick J. (D Vt.)
Long, Russell B. (D La.)
Mathias, Charles McC. Jr. (R Md.)
Mattingly, Mack (R Ga.)
Murkowski, Frank H. (R Alaska)
Nickles, Don (R Okla.)
Packwood, Bob (R Ore.)
Quayle, Dan (R Ind.)
Rudman, Warren B. (R N.H.)
Specter, Arlen (R Pa.)
Symms, Steven D. (R Idaho)

— 1988 —

(33 Senators: 13 Republicans, 20 Democrats)

Bentsen, Lloyd (D Texas)
Bingaman, Jeff (D N.M.)
Burdick, Quentin N. (D N.D.)
Byrd, Robert C. (D W.Va.)
Chafee, John H. (R R.I.)
Chiles, Lawton (D Fla.)
Danforth, John C. (R Mo.)
DeConcini, Dennis (D Ariz.)
Durenberger, David (R Minn.)
Hatch, Orrin G. (R Utah)
Hecht, Chic (R Nev.)

Heinz, John (R Pa.)
Jackson, Henry M. (D Wash.)
Kennedy, Edward M. (D Mass.)
Lautenberg, Frank R. (D N.J.)
Lugar, Richard G. (R Ind.)
Matsunaga, Spark M. (D Hawaii)
Melcher, John (D Mont.)
Metzenbaum, Howard M. (D Ohio)
Mitchell, George J. (D Maine)
Moynihan, Daniel Patrick (D N.Y.)
Proxmire, William (D Wis.)

Riegle, Donald W. Jr. (D Mich.)
Roth, William V. Jr. (R Del.)
Sarbanes, Paul S. (D Md.)
Sasser, Jim (D Tenn.)
Stafford, Robert T. (R Vt.)
Stennis, John C. (D Miss.)
Trible, Paul S. Jr. (R Va.)
Wallop, Malcolm (R Wyo.)
Weicker, Lowell P. Jr. (R Conn.)
Wilson, Pete (R Calif.)
Zorinsky, Edward (D Neb.)

CQ Gubernatorial Elections

Republicans Surrender Seven Statehouses

Hurt by losses in the economically distressed Midwest, Republicans saw their hold on the nation's governorships dwindle to 16 in the Nov. 2 election. The Democrats controlled statehouses in 34 states.

The GOP's net loss of seven statehouses — they dropped nine and picked up two — ended a comeback in the party's gubernatorial fortunes. Republicans had been posting gains since 1977, when they hit a low point of 12 governors' chairs. *(Results, p. 23-B)*

Their 1982 performance in governors' races stood in vivid contrast to the results for the U.S. Senate, where the GOP maintained its majority at the same level as before the election.

Of the Republican governors' seats that switched to the Democrats, five were in the Midwest, where the recession had been most acute, hitting both manufacturing and farming. Michigan, Minnesota, Nebraska, Ohio and Wisconsin opted for Democrats. Republican incumbents were retiring in all these states except Nebraska, where Gov. Charles Thone was turned out by about 10,000 votes.

The Illinois governor, Republican James R. Thompson, won by the smallest of margins in a tight contest against former Democratic Sen. Adlai E. Stevenson III. The outcome of the Illinois race was certified Nov. 22, but the results were the subject of continued legal wrangling through December. South Dakota's William J. Janklow, the other Midwestern GOP governor who sought re-election, enjoyed a comfortable victory.

Republicans also encountered a setback in their progress in the South. They held four of the region's 13 governorships in 1982; in 1983, they had just two. Frank D. White of Arkansas and William Clements of Texas were ousted. Only Tennessee's Lamar Alexander won re-election.

In addition, Democrats took over GOP statehouses in Alaska and Nevada. Republicans assumed power in California, where George Deukmejian edged Democrat Tom Bradley and in New Hampshire, where GOP challenger John Sununu unseated Democratic incumbent Hugh Gallen.

Each party had six open seats at stake. Democrats held all theirs except for California. Republicans managed to retain only Iowa.

Comebacks

The election marked a personal comeback for four Democratic former governors. George C. Wallace, who had served three previous terms as governor of Alabama, assembled a populist coalition of blue-collar whites and blacks to overcome a conservative law-and-order Republican, Montgomery Mayor Emory Folmar.

In Arkansas, Bill Clinton won his rematch against White, the Republican who ousted him in 1980.

In Massachusetts, Michael S. Dukakis cruised past an aristocratic Republican opponent, John Winthrop Sears. Dukakis' real test was in the Sept. 14 Democratic primary, when he unseated the man who had defeated him in 1978, Edward J. King.

And in Minnesota, Rudy Perpich was returned to the post he had lost in 1978 when Republicans not only ousted him but won both of the state's U.S. Senate seats. The Republican who beat Perpich in 1978, Albert H. Quie, did not run in 1982; the state government's rocky finances eroded

his personal standing, and he decided to retire. Perpich outpolled a moderate Republican businessman, Wheelock Whitney.

U.S. House members did not fare spectacularly in their efforts to move up to governor in 1982. Republican L. A. "Skip" Bafalis was trounced in Florida. Democrat Allen E. Ertel compiled a more impressive vote while losing to incumbent Republican Richard L. Thornburgh in Pennsylvania. The third U.S. House member running, Democrat James J. Blanchard, won Michigan's gubernatorial contest, although by only 52 percent in a state badly damaged by the recession.

The nation remained without a female governor, a result of the defeat of former U.S. Attorney Roxanne Conlin in Iowa and Lt. Gov. Madeleine M. Kunin in Vermont. Both were Democrats. In 1980, there were two women governors; one resigned because of ill health (Connecticut's Ella T. Grasso, who died early in 1981) and the other was defeated in a primary (Dixy Lee Ray in Washington).

In California, voters passed up the opportunity to choose the country's first elected black governor. Deukmejian, the state attorney general and a white Republican, narrowly beat Los Angeles Mayor Bradley, a black Democrat.

All but two of the 17 new governors had government experience. In addition to the four ex-governors, two were lieutenant governors and one was a former lieutenant governor, two were state attorneys general and three were former attorneys general. One was a U.S. House member, one was a state representative and one was a former state representative.

The remaining two, both Democrats, had business backgrounds. Bill Sheffield in Alaska was a hotel owner and Bob Kerrey in Nebraska was a restaurateur.

Iowa Republican Terry Branstad was the youngest of the new governors at 35, and Wallace of Alabama the oldest at 63.

In other balloting, Democrats increased their hold in state legislatures. Before the election, Democrats con-

---

Governorships

Current lineup		1983	
Democrats	27	Democrats	34
Republicans	23	Republicans	16

Democrats

Net Gain	+7
Incumbents re-elected	13
Incumbents defeated	1
Hugh Gallen, N.H.	

Republicans

Net Loss	−7
Incumbents re-elected	6
Incumbents defeated	4
Frank D. White, Ark.	
Charles Thone, Neb.	
Robert F. List, Nev.	
William Clements, Texas	

Governors for 1983

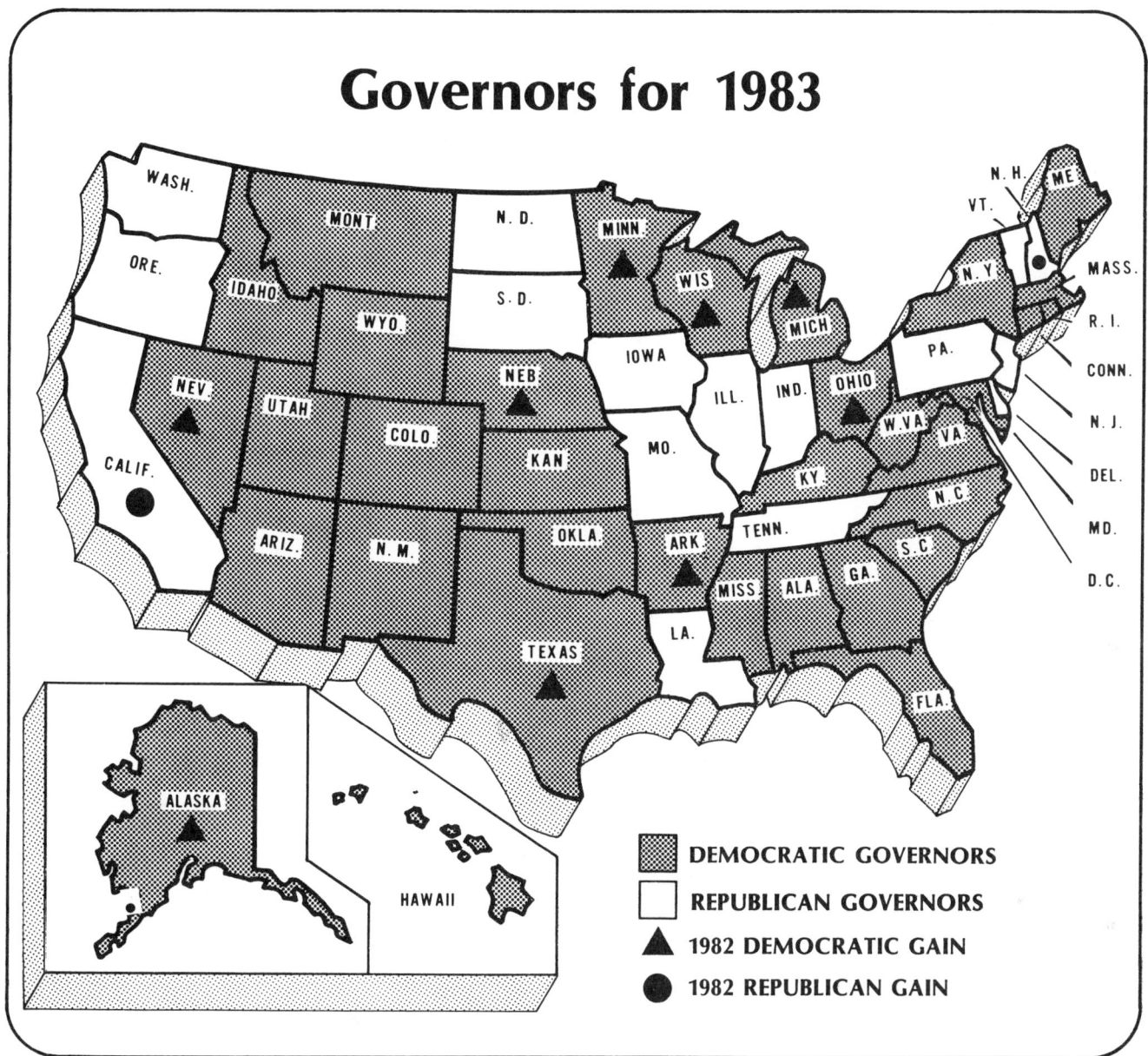

DEMOCRATIC GOVERNORS

REPUBLICAN GOVERNORS

▲ 1982 DEMOCRATIC GAIN

● 1982 REPUBLICAN GAIN

trolled both houses in 28 states, Republicans had both in 15 states and the legislatures were split between the parties in six. According to a tally by the National Conference of State Legislatures, the new lineup was Democrats with both chambers in 34 states, Republicans with both in 11 and four split. Nebraska had a non-partisan Legislature.

The Economy

The election for governor in Ohio, where unemployment had reached double-digit levels, illustrated the Republicans' weakness in the Midwest. GOP Gov. James A. Rhodes was ineligible for a third consecutive term.

The Republican nominee, U.S.

Rep. Clarence J. Brown, could not withstand former Lt. Gov. Richard F. Celeste's charge that his House record was too conservative for the beleaguered state. Rhodes had prevailed over Celeste in their 1978 match.

Even strong Republican incumbents were weakened by the sour economy. In Pennsylvania, Democrat Ertel surprised Gov. Thornburgh by coming within 100,000 votes of victory. The confident Thornburgh, who refused to back off from his support for Reaganomics, had ignored Ertel for most of the campaign. Ertel capitalized on the governor's Reagan ties to win big margins out of Philadelphia and in the recession-ridden steel region around Pittsburgh.

Personal Factors

As usual, personal factors had a lot to do with the election outcomes.

Democrat Conlin was favored to win the Iowa Statehouse until it was disclosed in July that she and her husband had paid no state income taxes in 1981.

New York's Lew Lehrman did not find GOP economics quite the burden that fellow Republicans did elsewhere. Millionaire Lehrman blended calls for big supply-side tax cuts, a strong law-and-order appeal and heavy spending to hold Lt. Gov. Mario M. Cuomo to 51 percent of the vote. Cuomo, an unabashed liberal, was thought to be farther ahead of Lehrman. Nevertheless, Cuomo won a clear victory and be-

1983 Occupants of the Nation's Statehouses

Here is a list of the governors and governors-elect of the 50 states, and the years in which each office is next up for election. The names of governors elected in 1982 are *italicized*. Asterisks (*) denote incumbents re-elected.

Alabama — *George C. Wallace (D) 1986*
Alaska — *Bill Sheffield (D) 1986*
Arizona — *Bruce Babbitt (D) 1986**
Arkansas — *Bill Clinton (D) 1984*
California — *George Deukmejian (R) 1986*
Colorado — *Richard D. Lamm (D) 1986**
Connecticut — *William A. O'Neill (D) 1986**
Delaware — Pierre S. "Pete" du Pont IV (R) 1984
Florida — *Robert Graham (D) 1986**
Georgia — *Joe Frank Harris (D) 1986*
Hawaii — *George Ariyoshi (D) 1986**
Idaho — *John V. Evans (D) 1986**
Illinois — *James R. Thompson (R) 1986*
Indiana — Robert D. Orr (R) 1984
Iowa — *Terry Branstad (R) 1986*
Kansas — *John Carlin (D) 1986**
Kentucky — John Y. Brown (D) 1983
Louisiana — David C. Treen (R) 1983
Maine — *Joseph E. Brennan (D) 1986**
Maryland — *Harry R. Hughes (D) 1986**
Massachusetts — *Michael S. Dukakis (D) 1986*
Michigan — *James J. Blanchard (D) 1986*
Minnesota — *Rudy Perpich (D) 1986*
Mississippi — William Winter (D) 1983
Missouri — Christopher S. "Kit" Bond (R) 1984

Montana — Ted Schwinden (D) 1984
Nebraska — *Bob Kerrey (D) 1986*
Nevada — *Richard H. Bryan (D) 1986*
New Hampshire — *John H. Sununu (R) 1984*
New Jersey — Thomas H. Kean (R) 1985
New Mexico — *Toney Anaya (D) 1986*
New York — *Mario M. Cuomo (D) 1986*
North Carolina — James B. Hunt Jr. (D) 1984
North Dakota — Allen I. Olson (R) 1984
Ohio — *Richard F. Celeste (D) 1986*
Oklahoma — *George Nigh (D) 1986**
Oregon — *Victor G. Atiyeh (R) 1986**
Pennsylvania — *Richard L. Thornburgh (R) 1986**
Rhode Island — *J. Joseph Garrahy (D) 1984**
South Carolina — *Richard Riley (D) 1986**
South Dakota — *William J. Janklow (R) 1986**
Tennessee — *Lamar Alexander (R) 1986**
Texas — *Mark White (D) 1986*
Utah — Scott M. Matheson (D) 1984
Vermont — *Richard A. Snelling (R) 1984**
Virginia — Charles S. Robb (D) 1985
Washington — John Spellman (R) 1984
West Virginia — John D. "Jay" Rockefeller IV (D) 1984
Wisconsin — *Anthony S. Earl (D) 1986*
Wyoming — *Ed Herschler (D) 1986**

came New York's first governor of Italian heritage.

Clements' brash and abrasive personality had much to do with his loss. The first Republican governor in Texas since Reconstruction, he once declared that "legislators are a dime a dozen."

Republican Robert F. List, defeated in Nevada, had a different problem with his personality. Critics found him indecisive. Also, his "Tax Shift" program — which lowered property taxes and raised sales levies — was a failure.

In Nebraska, Kerrey scored points against Thone by saying the governor had done little to help the state's ailing farm economy. Thone had another liability — he campaigned in 1978 as a tax cutter but ended up raising the sales and income taxes.

In Arkansas, Clinton accused White of failing to attract new industry to ease the state's high level of joblessness. He also painted White as too close to utility executives at a time when utility rates had been raised.

Democrat Hugh Gallen owed much of his defeat in New Hampshire to his refusal to take "the pledge" not to impose a sales or income tax. The state's budget problems had led the governor to hint that such taxes might be needed. This gave Republican John Sununu an opening to blast "Gallenomics."

In Alaska, former state House Speaker Tom Fink, a Republican, had his strength sapped by a Libertarian candidate. State Rep. Dick Randolph captured 12 percent of the vote, most of which would have gone to Fink. In Arizona, however, the well-known Libertarian candidate, former U.S. Rep. Sam Steiger, played no role in the failure of state Senate President Leo Corbet to dislodge incumbent Democrat Bruce Babbitt. Babbitt drubbed Republican Corbet by 2-to-1.

Race Questions

The subterranean issue of race was an important factor in assessing Bradley's defeat in California. Deukmejian removed his campaign manager, Bill Roberts, in early Octo-

ber for saying publicly that a hidden anti-black vote would benefit the Republican candidate. As Roberts saw it, these white voters would not admit to a pollster that they opposed Bradley because of his race, but would respond differently at the polls.

Deukmejian whittled away Bradley's early lead by linking the mayor to the controversial, outgoing governor, Democrat Edmund G. Brown Jr. Brown's presence on the ballot with Bradley — he ran unsuccessfully for the Senate — likely held down Bradley's vote. Duekmejian also knocked Bradley for reducing the size of his city's police force.

Meanwhile, Wallace managed to overcome his segregationist past and captured the Alabama governorship with the help of blacks.

A key to Wallace's bid for the black vote was black reaction to the Republican candidate, Montgomery Mayor Folmar, whose strong stands on law-and-order issues made Wallace appear liberal. Folmar often carried a pistol and accompanied police on raids.

 Election Results

Returns for Governor, Senate and House

Following are final 1982 vote returns for the Senate, House and governorships, compiled by Congressional Quarterly from results furnished by the secretaries of state or election boards in the 50 states.

All candidates are included who were listed on the ballot. Due to the exclusion of scattered write-in votes from this chart and the results of rounding numbers in computing percentages, the totals do not always equal 100 percent. The box below shows party designation symbols.

* indicates incumbents.

X denotes unopposed candidates.

- denotes minor parties for which the vote was not available.

ALABAMA

	Vote Total	Per-cent
Governor		
George C. Wallace (D)	650,538	57.6
Emory Folmar (R)	440,815	39.1
John Dyer (P)	4,364	0.4
Leo Suiter (C)	17,936	1.6
Henri Klingler (LIBERT)	7,671	0.7
John L. Jackson (NDPA)	4,693	0.4
Martin Boyers (S)	2,578	0.2
House		
1 Steve Gudac (D)	54,315	37.2
Jack Edwards (R)*	89,901	61.6
Bill Springer (LIBERT)	1,812	1.2
2 Billy Joe Camp (D)	81,904	49.6
William L. Dickinson (R)*	83,290	50.4
3 Bill Nichols (D)*	100,864	96.3
Richard Landers Jr. (LIBERT)	3,920	3.7
4 Tom Bevill (D)*	X	100.0
5 Ronnie G. Flippo (D)*	108,807	80.7
Leopold Yambrek (R)	24,593	18.2
Kenneth Ament (LIBERT)	1,474	1.1
6 Ben Erdreich (D)	88,029	53.2
Albert Lee Smith Jr. (R)*	76,726	46.4
Charles Ewing (LIBERT)	632	0.4
7 Richard C. Shelby (D)*	124,070	96.8
James Jones (LIBERT)	4,058	3.2

ALASKA

	Vote Total	Per-cent
Governor		
Bill Sheffield (D)	89,918	46.1
Tom Fink (R)	72,291	37.1
Joseph Vogler (AKI)	3,235	1.7
Richard L. Randolph (LIBERT)	29,067	14.9
House		
AL Dave Carlson (D)	52,011	28.7
Don Young (R)*	128,274	70.8

ARIZONA

	Vote Total	Per-cent
Governor		
Bruce Babbitt (D)*	453,795	62.5
Leo Corbet (R)	235,877	32.5
Sam Steiger (LIBERT)	36,649	5.0
Senator		
Dennis DeConcini (D)*	411,970	56.9
Pete Dunn (R)	291,749	40.3
Randall Clamons (LIBERT)	20,100	2.8
House		
1 William E. Hegarty (D)	41,261	30.5
John McCain (R)	89,116	65.9
Richard K. Dodge (LIBERT)	4,850	3.6
2 Morris K. Udall (D)*	73,468	70.9

	Vote Total	Per-cent
Roy B. Laos (R)	28,407	27.4
Jessica Sampson (YSA)	1,799	1.7
3 Pat Bosch (D)	58,644	36.7
Bob Stump (R)*	101,198	63.3
4 Wayne O. Earley (D)	44,182	30.4
Eldon Rudd (R)*	95,620	65.7
Richard A. Stauffer (LIBERT)	5,664	3.9
5 Jim McNulty (D)	82,938	49.7
Jim Kolbe (R)	80,531	48.3
Richard D. Auster (LIBERT)	3,332	2.0

ARKANSAS

	Vote Total	Per-cent
Governor		
Bill Clinton (D)	431,855	54.7
Frank D. White (R)*	357,496	45.3
House		
1 Bill Alexander (D)*	124,208	64.8
Chuck Banks (R)	67,427	35.2
2 Charles L. George (D)	82,913	46.1
Ed Bethune (R)*	96,775	53.9
3 Jim McDougal (D)	69,089	34.0
John Paul Hammerschmidt (R)*	133,909	66.0
4 Beryl Anthony Jr. (D)*	121,256	65.6
Bob Leslie (R)	63,661	34.4

Abbreviations for Party Designations

AD	—Anti-Drug	LIBERT	—Libertarian
AKI	—Alaskan Independence	LU	—Liberty Union
AM	—American	NA	—New Alliance
AMI	—American Independent	NDPA	—National Democratic Party of Alabama
BGG	—Bipartisan Good Government	NF	—Nuclear Freeze
C	—Conservative	NP	—Nonpartisan
CIT	—Citizens	NU	—New Union
COM	—Communist	P	—Prohibition
CONSU	—Consumers	PFP	—Peace and Freedom Party
CST	—Constitution	R	—Republican
D	—Democratic	RTL	—Right to Life
DFL	—Democratic Farmer-Labor	SOC	—Socialist
F LIBERT	—Free Libertarian	SOC LAB	—Socialist Labor
FP	—Free People's	SOC WORK	—Socialist Workers
I	—Independent	TAX	—Taxpayers
I-D	—Independent-Democrat	UN	—Unity
I-R	—Independent-Republican	WF	—World Federalist
JI	—Jeffersonian Independent	WL	—Workers League
L	—Liberal	YSA	—Young Socialist Alliance

	Vote Total	Percent

CALIFORNIA

Governor

Tom Bradley (D)	3,787,669	48.1
George Deukmejian (R)	3,881,014	49.3
James C. Griffin (AMI)	56,249	0.7
Dan P. Dougherty (LIBERT)	81,076	1.0
Elizabeth Martinez (PFP)	70,327	0.9

Senator

Edmund G. Brown Jr. (D)	3,494,968	44.8
Pete Wilson (R)	4,022,565	51.5
Theresa "Tena" Dietrich (AMI)	83,809	1.1
Joseph Fuhrig (LIBERT)	107,720	1.4
David Wald (PFP)	96,388	1.2

House

1	Douglas H. Bosco (D)	107,749	49.8
	Don H. Clausen (R)*	102,043	47.2
	David Redick (LIBERT)	6,374	3.0
2	John A. Newmeyer (D)	81,314	40.5
	Gene Chappie (R)*	116,172	57.9
	Howard Fegarsky (PFP)	3,126	1.6
3	Robert T. Matsui (D)*	194,680	89.6
	Bruce A. Daniel (LIBERT)	16,222	7.5
	John C. Reiger (PFP)	6,294	2.9
4	Vic Fazio (D)*	118,476	63.9
	Roger B. Canfield (R)	67,047	36.1
5	Phillip Burton (D)*	103,268	57.9
	Milton Marks (R)	72,139	40.5
	Justin Raimondo (LIBERT)	2,904	1.6
6	Barbara Boxer (D)	96,379	52.4
	Dennis McQuaid (R)	82,128	44.6
	Howard C. Creighton (LIBERT)	3,191	1.7
	Timothy-Allen Albertson (PFP)	2,366	1.3
7	George Miller (D)*	126,952	67.2
	Paul E. Vallely (R)	56,960	30.2
	Terry L. Wells (AMI)	2,205	1.2
	Rich Newell (LIBERT)	2,752	1.4
8	Ronald V. Dellums (D)*	121,537	55.9
	Claude B. Hutchison Jr. (R)	95,694	44.1
9	Fortney H. "Pete" Stark (D)*	104,393	60.7
	Bill J. Kennedy (R)	67,702	39.3
10	Don Edwards (D)*	77,263	62.7
	Bob Herriott (R)	41,506	33.7
	Edmon V. Kaiser (AMI)	2,109	1.7
	Dale Burrow (LIBERT)	2,403	1.9
11	Tom Lantos (D)*	109,812	57.1
	Bill Royer (R)	76,462	39.7
	Nicholas W. Kudrovzeff (AMI)	1,250	0.7
	Chuck Olson (LIBERT)	2,920	1.5
	Wilson Branch (PFP)	1,928	1.0
12	Emmett Lynch (D)	61,372	33.5
	Ed Zschau (R)	115,365	63.0
	Bill White (LIBERT)	6,471	3.5
13	Norman Y. Mineta (D)*	110,805	65.9
	Tom Kelly (R)	52,806	31.4
	Al Hinkle (LIBERT)	4,553	2.7
14	Baron Reed (D)	77,400	36.6
	Norman D. Shumway (R)*	134,225	63.4
15	Tony Coelho (D)*	86,022	63.7
	Ed Bates (R)	45,948	34.0
	Stephen L. Gerringer (LIBERT)	3,073	2.3
16	Leon E. Panetta (D)*	142,630	85.4
	G. Richard Arnold (R)	24,448	14.6
	Anne Nixon Ball (R write-in)	—	—
17	Gene Tackett (D)	68,364	46.0

		Vote Total	Percent
	Charles Pashayan Jr. (R)*	80,271	54.0
18	Richard Lehman (D)	92,762	59.5
	Adrian C. Fondse (R)	59,664	38.3
	Marshall William Fritz (LIBERT)	3,501	2.2
19	Frank Frost (D)	66,042	35.8
	Robert J. Lagomarsino (R)*	112,486	61.1
	R. C. Gordon-McCutchan (LIBERT)	4,198	2.3
	Charles J. Zekan (PFP)	1,520	0.8
20	Robert J. Bethea (D)	57,769	31.9
	William M. Thomas (R)*	123,312	68.1
21	George Henry Margolis (D)	46,412	24.1
	Bobbi Fiedler (R)*	138,474	71.8
	Daniel Wiener (LIBERT)	7,881	4.1
22	Harvey L. Goldhammer (D)	46,521	23.5
	Carlos J. Moorhead (R)*	145,831	73.6
	Robert T. Gerringer (LIBERT)	5,870	2.9
23	Anthony C. Beilenson (D)*	120,788	59.6
	David Armor (R)	82,031	40.4
24	Henry A. Waxman (D)*	88,516	65.0
	Jerry Zerg (R)	42,133	31.0
	Jeff Mandel (LIBERT)	5,420	4.0
25	Edward R. Roybal (D)*	71,106	85.5
	Daniel John Gorham (LIBERT)	12,060	14.5
26	Howard L. Berman (D)	97,383	59.6
	Hal Phillips (R)	66,070	40.4
27	Mel Levine (D)	108,347	59.5
	Bart W. Christensen (R)	67,479	37.0
	Zack Richardson (LIBERT)	6,391	3.5
28	Julian C. Dixon (D)*	103,469	78.9
	David Goerz (R)	24,473	18.7
	David W. Meleney (LIBERT)	3,210	2.4
29	Augustus F. Hawkins (D)*	97,028	79.8
	Milton R. MacKaig (R)	24,568	20.2
30	Matthew G. "Marty" Martinez (D)*	60,905	53.9
	John H. Rousselot (R)*	52,177	46.1
31	Mervyn M. Dymally (D)*	86,718	72.4
	Henry C. Minturn (R)	33,043	27.6
32	Glenn M. Anderson (D)*	84,663	58.0
	Brian Lungren (R)	57,863	39.6
	Eugene E. Ruyle (PFP)	3,473	2.4
33	Paul Servelle (D)	55,514	32.2
	David Dreier (R)*	112,362	65.2
	Phillips P. Franklin (LIBERT)	2,251	1.3
	James Michael Noonan (PFP)	2,223	1.3
34	Esteban Torres (D)	68,316	57.2
	Paul R. Jackson (R)	51,026	42.8
35	Robert E. Erwin (D)	52,349	31.7
	Jerry Lewis (R)*	112,786	68.3
36	George E. Brown Jr. (D)*	76,546	54.3
	John Paul Stark (R)	64,361	45.7
37	Curtis P. "Sam" Cross (D)	68,510	38.5
	Al McCandless (R)	105,065	59.1
	Marc R. Wruple (LIBERT)	4,297	2.4
38	Jerry M. Patterson (D)*	73,914	52.4
	William F. Dohr (R)	61,279	43.4
	Anita K. Barr (LIBERT)	5,989	4.2
39	Frank G. Verges (D)	46,681	26.0
	William E. Dannemeyer (R)*	129,539	72.2
	Frank Boeheim (PFP)	3,152	1.8
40	Paul Haseman (D)	52,546	26.1
	Robert E. Badham (R)*	144,228	71.5
	Maxine Bell Quirk (PFP)	4,826	2.4
41	Tony Brandenburg (D)	58,677	28.8
	Bill Lowery (R)*	140,130	68.9
	Everett Hale (LIBERT)	4,654	2.3
42	James P. Spellman (D)	58,690	28.3

		Vote Total	Percent
	Dan Lungren (R)*	142,845	69.0
	John S. Donohue (PFP)	5,514	2.7
43	Roy "Pat" Archer (D)	57,995	32.1
	Johnnie R. Crean (R)	56,297	31.1
	Ron Packard (R write-in)	66,444	36.8
44	Jim Bates (D)	78,474	65.0
	Shirley M. Gissendanner (R)	38,447	31.8
	Jim Conole (LIBERT)	3,904	3.2
45	Richard Hill (D)	50,148	29.2
	Duncan L. Hunter (R)*	117,771	68.6
	Jack R. Sanders (LIBERT)	3,839	2.2

COLORADO

Governor

Richard D. Lamm (D)*	627,960	65.7
John D. Fuhr (R)	302,740	31.7
Paul Grant (LIBERT)	19,349	2.0
Earl F. Dodge (P)	3,496	0.4
Alan Gummerson (SOC WORK)	2,476	0.2

House

1	Patricia Schroeder (D)*	94,969	60.3
	Arch Decker (R)	59,009	37.4
	Robin White (LIBERT)	3,619	2.3
2	Timothy E. Wirth (D)*	101,194	61.8
	John C. Buechner (R)	59,580	36.4
	Charles Jackson (LIBERT)	2,862	1.8
3	Ray Kogovsek (D)*	92,384	53.4
	Tom Wiens (R)	77,409	44.8
	Stormy Mon (LIBERT)	2,439	1.4
	Henry John Olshaw (I)	656	0.4
4	Charles L. "Bud" Bishopp (D)	45,750	30.2
	Hank Brown (R)*	105,550	69.8
5	Tom Cronin (D)	57,392	40.5
	Ken Kramer (R)*	84,479	59.5
6	Steve Hogan (D)	56,598	35.6
	Jack Swigert (R)†	98,909	62.1
	J. Craig Green (LIBERT)	3,605	2.3

CONNECTICUT

Governor

William A. O'Neill (D)*	578,264	53.4
Lewis B. Rome (R)	497,773	45.9
Walter J. Gengarelly (LIBERT)	7,839	0.7

Senator

Toby Moffett (D)	499,146	46.1
Lowell P. Weicker Jr. (R)*	545,987	50.4
Lucien DiFazio (C)	30,212	2.8
James A. Lewis (LIBERT)	8,163	0.7

House

1	Barbara B. Kennelly (D)*	126,798	68.1
	Herschel A. Klein (R)	58,075	31.2
	Daniel Landerfen (LIBERT)	1,237	0.7
2	Sam Gejdenson (D)*	95,254	55.8
	Tony Guglielmo (R)	74,294	43.5
	Donald W. Wood (LIBERT)	1,255	0.7
3	Bruce A. Morrison (D)	90,638	50.0
	Lawrence J. DeNardis (R)*	88,951	49.0
	Joelle R. Fishman (COM)	696	0.4
	Michael R. Cohen (LIBERT)	1,164	0.6
4	John A. Phillips (D)	71,110	42.9
	Stewart B. McKinney (R)*	93,660	56.4
	Lothar Frank (LIBERT)	1,127	0.7
5	William R. Ratchford (D)*	101,362	58.5
	Neal B. Hanlon (R)	70,808	40.8
	Jerry Brennan (LIBERT)	1,203	0.7

†Died Dec. 27.

	Vote Total	Per-cent
6 William E. Curry Jr. (D)	92,178	47.7
Nancy L. Johnson (R)	99,703	51.7
Monte Dunn (LIBERT)	1,091	0.6

DELAWARE

Senator

David N. Levinson (D)	84,413	44.2
William V. Roth Jr. (R)*	105,357	55.2
Charles A. Baker (AM)	537	0.3
Lawrence D. Sullivan (LIBERT)	653	0.3

House

AL Thomas R. Carper (D)	98,533	52.4
Thomas B. Evans Jr. (R)*	87,153	46.3
Mary D. Gise (AM)	1,109	0.6
David Nuttall (CIT)	558	0.3
Richard A. Cohen (LIBERT)	711	0.4

FLORIDA

Governor

Robert Graham (D)*	1,739,553	64.7
L. A. "Skip" Bafalis (R)	949,023	35.3

Senator

Lawton Chiles (D)*	1,636,857	61.7
Van Poole (R)	1,014,551	38.3

House

1 Earl Hutto (D)*	82,482	74.5
J. Terry Bechtol (R)	28,285	25.5
2 Don Fuqua (D)*	79,096	61.7
Ron McNeil (R)	49,084	38.3
3 Charles E. Bennett (D)*	73,713	84.1
George Grimsley (R)	13,921	15.9
4 Bill Chappell Jr. (D)*	83,830	66.9
Larry Gaudet (R)	41,399	33.1
5 Dick Batchelor (D)	49,042	41.2
Bill McCollum (R)*	69,939	58.8
6 Kenneth H. "Buddy" MacKay (D)	85,799	61.3
Ed Havill (R)	54,058	38.7
7 Sam Gibbons (D)*	85,317	74.2
Ken Ayers (R)	29,624	25.8
8 C. W. Bill Young (R)*	X	100.0
9 George H. Sheldon (D)	90,673	48.8
Michael Bilirakis (R)	94,993	51.2
10 Andy Ireland (D)*	X	100.0
11 Bill Nelson (D)*	101,625	70.6
Joel Robinson (R)	42,323	29.4
12 Brad Culverhouse (D)	73,886	47.4
Tom Lewis (R)	81,864	52.6
13 Dana N. Stevens (D)	71,206	34.9
Connie Mack III (R)	132,906	65.1
14 Daniel A. Mica (D)*	128,627	73.0
Steve Mitchell (R)	47,542	27.0
15 Edward J. Stack (D)	67,058	42.9
E. Clay Shaw Jr. (R)*	89,128	57.1
16 Larry Smith (D)	91,869	67.9
Maurice Berkowitz (R)	43,343	32.1
17 William Lehman (D)*	X	100.0
18 Claude Pepper (D)*	72,137	71.2
Ricardo Nunez (R)	29,156	28.8
19 Dante B. Fascell (D)*	74,274	58.9
Glenn Rinker (R)	51,925	41.1

	Vote Total	Per-cent

GEORGIA

Governor

Joe Frank Harris (D)	734,090	62.8
Bob Bell (R)	434,496	37.2

House

1 Lindsay Thomas (D)	65,625	64.1
Herb Jones (R)	36,799	35.9
2 Charles Hatcher (D)*	X	100.0
3 Richard Ray (D)	74,626	71.0
Tyron Elliott (R)	30,537	29.0
4 Elliott H. Levitas (D)*	38,758	65.5
Dick Winder (R)	20,418	34.5
5 Wyche Fowler Jr. (D)*	53,264	80.8
Paul Jones (R)	3,633	5.5
J. E. "Billy" McKinney (I)	9,049	13.7
6 Jim Wood (D)	50,459	44.7
Newt Gingrich (R)*	62,352	55.3
7 Larry P. McDonald (D)*	71,647	61.1
Dave Sellers (R)	45,569	38.9
8 J. Roy Rowland (D)	X	100.0
9 Ed Jenkins (D)*	86,514	77.0
Charles Sherwood (R)	25,907	23.0
10 Doug Barnard Jr. (D)*	X	100.0

HAWAII

Governor

George Ariyoshi (D)*	141,043	45.2
D. G. Anderson (R)	81,507	26.2
Frank F. Fasi (I-D)	89,303	28.6

Senator

Spark M. Matsunaga (D)*	245,386	80.1
Clarence J. Brown (R)	52,071	17.0
E. F. Bernier-Nachtwey (I-D)	8,953	2.9

House

1 Cecil Heftel (D)*	134,779	89.9
Rockne H. Johnson (LIBERT)	15,128	10.1
2 Daniel K. Akaka (D)*	132,072	89.2
Amelia Oy Fritts (LIBERT)	6,856	4.6
Gregory B. Mills (NP)	9,080	6.2

IDAHO

Governor

John V. Evans (D)*	165,365	50.6
Philip E. Batt (R)	161,157	49.4

House

1 Larry LaRocco (D)	74,388	46.3
Larry E. Craig (R)*	86,277	53.7
2 Richard Stallings (D)	76,608	47.7
George Hansen (R)*	83,873	52.3

ILLINOIS

Governor

Adlai E. Stevenson III (D)	1,811,027	49.3
James R. Thompson (R)*	1,816,101	49.4
Bea Armstrong (LIBERT)	24,417	0.7
John E. Roche (TAX)	22,001	0.6

House

1 Harold Washington (D)*	172,641	97.3
Charles Allen Taliaferro (R)	4,820	2.7
2 Gus Savage (D)*	140,827	87.0
Kevin Walker Sparks (R)	20,670	12.8
Joseph Zvonkovach (write-in)	288	0.2
3 Marty Russo (D)*	137,391	74.0
Richard D. Murphy (R)	48,268	26.0
4 Michael A. Murer (D)	66,323	45.4
George M. O'Brien (R)*	79,842	54.6

	Vote Total	Per-cent
5 William O. Lipinski (D)	110,351	75.4
Daniel J. Partyka (R)	35,970	24.6
6 Leroy E. Kennel (D)	45,237	31.6
Henry J. Hyde (R)*	97,918	68.4
7 Cardiss Collins (D)*	133,978	86.5
Dansby Cheeks (R)	20,994	13.5
8 Dan Rostenkowski (D)*	124,318	83.4
Bonnie Hickey (R)	24,666	16.6
9 Sidney R. Yates (D)*	114,083	66.5
Catherine Bertini (R)	54,851	32.0
Sheila Jones (AD)	2,595	1.5
10 Eugenia S. Chapman (D)	63,115	41.0
John Edward Porter (R)*	90,750	59.0
11 Frank Annunzio (D)*	134,755	72.6
James F. Moynihan (R)	50,967	27.4
12 Daniel G. DeFosse (D)	40,108	30.7
Philip M. Crane (R)*	86,487	66.2
Joan T. Jarosz (LIBERT)	4,101	3.1
13 Robert Bily (D)	49,105	30.2
John N. Erlenborn (R)*	113,423	69.8
14 Dan McGrath (D)	53,914	35.4
Tom Corcoran (R)*	98,262	64.6
15 Tim L. Hall (D)	53,303	33.7
Edward R. Madigan (R)*	105,038	66.3
16 Carl R. Schwerdtfeger (D)	66,877	42.8
Lynn Martin (R)*	89,405	57.2
17 Lane Evans (D)	94,483	52.8
Kenneth G. McMillan (R)	84,347	47.2
18 G. Douglas Stephens (D)	91,281	48.4
Robert H. Michel (R)*	97,406	51.6
19 John Gwinn (D)	87,231	47.9
Daniel B. Crane (R)*	94,833	52.1
20 Richard J. Durbin (D)	100,758	50.4
Paul Findley (R)*	99,348	49.6
21 Melvin Price (D)*	89,500	63.6
Robert H. Gaffner (R)	46,764	33.3
Sandra L. Climaco (BGG)	4,344	3.1
22 Paul Simon (D)*	123,693	66.2
Peter G. Prineas (R)	63,279	33.8

INDIANA

Senator

Floyd Fithian (D)	828,400	45.6
Richard G. Lugar (R)*	978,301	53.8
Raymond James (AM)	10,586	0.6

House

1 Katie Hall (D)	89,369	56.9
Thomas H. Krieger (R)	66,921	42.6
Jesse Smith (SOC WORK)	806	0.5
2 Philip R. Sharp (D)*	107,298	56.2
Ralph W. Van Natta (R)	83,593	43.8
3 Richard C. Bodine (D)	83,046	48.8
John Hiler (R)*	86,958	51.2
4 Roger M. Miller (D)	60,054	35.1
Dan Coats (R)*	110,155	64.3
John B. Cameron (AM)	1,029	0.6
5 Allen B. Maxwell (D)	67,238	38.9
Elwood Hillis (R)*	105,469	61.1
6 George E. Grabianowski (D)	70,764	35.1
Dan Burton (R)	131,100	64.9
7 Stephen S. Bonney (D)	70,249	37.7
John T. Myers (R)*	115,884	62.3
8 Francis X. McCloskey (D)	100,592	51.4
Joel Deckard (R)*	94,127	48.1
Robert F. Arnove (CIT)	1,006	0.5
9 Lee H. Hamilton (D)*	121,094	67.1
Floyd E. Coates (R)	58,532	32.4
Stephen Arnold (CIT)	913	0.5
10 Andrew Jacobs Jr. (D)*	114,674	66.7

	Vote Total	Per-cent
Michael A. Carroll (R)	56,992	33.2
David W. Ellis (SOC WORK)	197	0.1

IOWA

Governor

Roxanne Conlin (D)	483,291	46.5
Terry Branstad (R)	548,313	52.8
Marcia J. Farrington (LIBERT)	3,307	0.3
Jim Bittner (SOC)	2,767	0.3

House

1	William E. Gluba (D)	61,734	40.8
	Jim Leach (R)*	89,585	59.2
2	Brent Appel (D)	69,539	41.1
	Tom Tauke (R)*	99,478	58.9
3	Lynn G. Cutler (D)	83,581	44.5
	Cooper Evans (R)*	104,072	55.5
4	Neal Smith (D)*	118,849	66.1
	Dave Readinger (R)	60,534	33.6
	Bill Douglas (SOC)	584	0.3
5	Tom Harkin (D)*	93,333	58.9
	Arlyn E. Danker (R)	65,200	41.1
6	Berkley Bedell (D)*	101,690	64.3
	Al Bremer (R)	56,487	35.7

KANSAS

Governor

John Carlin (D)*	405,772	53.2
Sam Hardage (R)	339,356	44.4
Frank W. Shelton Jr. (AM)	6,136	0.8
James H. Ward (LIBERT)	7,595	1.0
Warren C. Martin (P)	4,404	0.6

House

1	Kent Roth (D)	51,079	30.2
	Pat Roberts (R)*	115,749	68.4
	Kent Earnest (LIBERT)	2,305	1.4
2	Jim Slattery (D)	86,286	57.4
	Morris Kay (R)	63,942	42.6
3	William L. Kostar (D)	53,140	38.3
	Larry Winn Jr. (R)*	82,117	59.2
	Gene R. Blair (LIBERT)	3,439	2.5
4	Dan Glickman (D)*	107,326	73.9
	Gerald Caywood (R)	35,478	24.5
	Karl Peterjohn (LIBERT)	2,363	1.6
5	Lee Rowe (D)	47,676	31.1
	Bob Whittaker (R)*	103,551	67.6
	John L. Conger (LIBERT)	1,894	1.3

KENTUCKY

House

1	Carroll Hubbard Jr. (D)*	X	100.0
2	William H. Natcher (D)*	49,571	73.8
	Mark T. Watson (R)	17,561	26.2
3	Romano L. Mazzoli (D)*	92,849	65.1
	Carl Brown (R)	45,900	32.2
	Dan Murray (LIBERT)	608	0.4
	Craig Honts (SOC)	400	0.3
	Norbert D. Leveronne (I)	2,840	2.0
4	Terry L. Mann (D)	61,937	45.3
	Gene Snyder (R)*	74,109	54.2
	Paul Thiel (LIBERT)	704	0.5
5	Doye Davenport (D)	28,285	34.8
	Harold Rogers (R)*	52,928	65.2
6	Don Mills (D)	49,839	41.4
	Larry J. Hopkins (R)*	68,418	56.8
	Ken Ashby (LIBERT)	1,185	1.0
	Don B. Pratt (I)	917	0.8

	Vote Total	Per-cent
7 Carl D. Perkins (D)*	82,463	79.4
Tom Hamby (R)	21,436	20.6

LOUISIANA

House

1	Bob Livingston (R)*	X	100.0
2	Lindy (Mrs. Hale) Boggs (D)*	X	100.0
3	W. J. "Billy" Tauzin (D)*	X	100.0
4	Buddy Roemer (D)*	X	100.0
5	Jerry Huckaby (D)*	X	100.0
6	Henson Moore (R)*	X	100.0
7	John B. Breaux (D)*	X	100.0
8	Gillis W. Long (D)*	X	100.0

MAINE

Governor

Joseph E. Brennan (D)*	281,066	61.1
Charles L. Cragin (R)	172,949	37.6
J. Martin Bachon (I)	2,573	0.5
Vern Warren (I)	3,650	0.8

Senator

George J. Mitchell (D)*	279,819	60.9
David F. Emery (R)	179,882	39.1

House

1	John M. Kerry (D)	118,884	47.9
	John R. McKernan Jr. (R)	124,850	50.4
	Gregory J. Fleming (I)	4,221	1.7
2	James Patrick Dunleavy (D)	68,086	33.4
	Olympia J. Snowe (R)*	136,075	66.6

MARYLAND

Governor

Harry R. Hughes (D)*	705,910	62.0
Robert A. Pascal (R)	432,826	38.0

Senator

Paul S. Sarbanes (D)*	707,356	63.5
Lawrence J. Hogan (R)	407,334	36.5

House

1	Roy Dyson (D)*	89,503	69.3
	C. A. Porter Hopkins (R)	39,656	30.7
2	Clarence D. Long (D)*	83,318	52.6
	Helen Delich Bentley (R)	75,062	47.4
3	Barbara A. Mikulski (D)*	110,042	74.2
	H. Robert Scherr (R)	38,259	25.8
4	Patricia O'Brien Aiken (D)	47,947	38.8
	Marjorie S. Holt (R)*	75,617	61.2
5	Steny H. Hoyer (D)*	83,937	79.6
	William P. Guthrie (R)	21,533	20.4
6	Beverly B. Byron (D)*	102,596	74.4
	Roscoe Bartlett (R)	35,321	25.6
7	Parren J. Mitchell (D)*	103,496	87.9
	M. Leonora Jones (R)	14,203	12.1
8	Michael D. Barnes (D)*	121,761	71.3
	Elizabeth W. Spencer (R)	48,910	28.7

MASSACHUSETTS

Governor

Michael S. Dukakis (D)	1,219,109	59.4
John W. Sears (R)	749,679	36.6
Rebecca Shipman (LIBERT)	17,918	0.9
Frank Rich (I)	63,068	3.1

Senator

Edward M. Kennedy (D)*	1,247,084	60.8
Raymond Shamie (R)	784,602	38.3

	Vote Total	Per-cent
Howard Katz (LIBERT)	18,878	0.9

House

1	Silvio O. Conte (R, D)*	X	100.0
2	Edward P. Boland (D)*	118,215	72.6
	Thomas P. Swank (R)	44,544	27.4
3	Joseph D. Early (D)*	X	100.0
4	Barney Frank (D)*	121,802	59.5
	Margaret M. Heckler (R)*	82,804	40.5
5	James M. Shannon (D)*	140,177	84.7
	Angelo Laudani (LIBERT)	25,224	15.2
6	Nicholas Mavroules (D)*	117,723	57.8
	Thomas H. Trimarco (R)	85,849	42.2
7	Edward J. Markey (D)*	151,305	77.8
	David Basile (R)	43,063	22.2
8	Thomas P. O'Neill Jr. (D)*	123,296	74.9
	Frank Luke McNamara Jr. (R)	41,370	25.1
9	Joe Moakley (D)*	102,665	64.1
	Deborah R. Cochran (R)	55,030	34.3
	Valerie Eckart (SOC WORK)	2,527	1.6
10	Gerry E. Studds (D)*	138,418	68.7
	John E. Conway (R)	63,014	31.3
11	Brian J. Donnelly (D)*	X	100.0

MICHIGAN

Governor

James J. Blanchard (D)	1,561,291	51.4
Richard H. Headlee (R)	1,369,582	45.1
James Phillips (AMI)	7,356	0.2
Richard Jacobs (LIBERT)	15,603	0.5
Tim Crane (SOC WORK)	3,682	0.1
Martin McLaughlin (WL)	1,980	0.1
Robert Tisch (I)	80,288	2.6

Senator

Donald W. Riegle Jr. (D)*	1,728,793	57.7
Philip E. Ruppe (R)	1,223,288	40.9
Daniel Eller (AMI)	12,660	0.4
Bette Erwin (LIBERT)	19,131	0.6
Steve Beumer (SOC WORK)	4,335	0.2
Helen Halyard (WL)	6,085	0.2

House

1	John Conyers Jr. (D)*	125,517	96.7
	Bill Krebaum (LIBERT)	3,186	2.4
	Eddie Benjamin (WL)	1,140	0.9
2	George Wahr Sallade (D)	53,040	32.5
	Carl D. Pursell (R)*	106,960	65.4
	Barbara J. McKenna (LIBERT)	3,412	2.1
3	Howard Wolpe (D)*	96,842	56.3
	Richard L. Milliman (R)	73,315	42.6
	Lizzie M. Hudson (AMI)	693	0.4
	Robert S. Holderbaum (LIBERT)	1,111	0.7
4	David A. Masiokas (D)	56,877	38.8
	Mark Siljander (R)*	87,489	59.7
	Robert C. Drenkhahn (AMI)	690	0.5
	Richard Wagner (LIBERT)	1,544	1.0
5	Stephen V. Monsma (D)	87,229	46.9
	Harold S. Sawyer (R)*	98,650	53.1
6	Bob Carr (D)	84,778	51.4
	Jim Dunn (R)*	78,388	47.5
	James E. Hurrell (LIBERT)	1,818	1.1
7	Dale E. Kildee (D)*	118,538	75.4
	George R. Darrah (R)	36,303	23.1
	Dennis L. Berry (LIBERT)	1,842	1.2
	David Freund (WL)	568	0.3
8	Bob Traxler (D)*	113,515	91.0
	Sheila M. Hart (LIBERT)	11,219	9.0
9	Gerald D. Warner (D)	60,932	35.1

	Vote Total	Per- cent
Guy Vander Jagt (R)*	112,504	64.9
10 Don Albosta (D)*	102,048	60.1
Lawrence W. Reed (R)	66,080	39.0
William Spiers (LIBERT)	1,558	0.9
11 Kent Bourland (D)	69,181	39.5
Robert W. Davis (R)*	106,039	60.5
12 David E. Bonior (D)*	103,851	65.9
Ray Contesti (R)	52,312	33.2
Keith P. Edwards (LIBERT)	1,501	0.9
13 George W. Crockett Jr. (D)*	108,351	88.0
Letty Gupta (R)	13,732	11.1
Fred Mazelis (WL)	1,107	0.9
14 Dennis M. Hertel (D)*	116,421	95.0
Harold H. Dunn (LIBERT)	6,175	5.0
15 William D. Ford (D)*	94,950	72.8
Mitchell Moran (R)	33,904	26.0
Guy R. Collins (AMI)	1,555	1.2
16 John D. Dingell (D)*	114,006	73.7
David K. Haskins (R)	39,227	25.3
Susan Apstein (SOC WORK)	1,071	0.7
Paul Scherrer (WL)	450	0.3
17 Sander Levin (D)	116,901	66.6
Gerald E. Rosen (R)	55,620	31.7
Virginia L. Cropsey (LIBERT)	2,955	1.7
18 Allen J. Sipher (D)	46,545	25.7
William S. Broomfield (R)*	132,902	73.3
Joseph Cote (LIBERT)	1,813	1.0

MINNESOTA

Governor

	Vote Total	Per- cent
Rudy Perpich (DFL)	1,049,104	58.8
Wheelock Whitney (I-R)	711,796	39.9
Franklin H. Haws (LIBERT)	6,323	0.3
Kathy Wheeler (SOC WORK)	10,332	0.6
Tom McDonald (I)	7,984	0.4

Senator

Mark Dayton (DFL)	840,401	46.6
David Durenberger (I-R)*	949,207	52.6
Fred G. Hewitt (LIBERT)	5,870	0.3
Jeffrey M. Miller (NU)	3,300	0.2
Bill Onasch (SOC WORK)	5,897	0.3

House

1 Timothy J. Penny (DFL)	109,257	51.2
Tom Hagedorn (I-R)*	102,298	47.9
Clare H. Jarvis (LIBERT)	1,965	0.9
2 James W. Nichols (DFL)	103,243	45.5
Vin Weber (I-R)*	123,508	54.5
3 Joel Saliterman (DFL)	60,993	26.4
Bill Frenzel (I-R)*	166,891	72.1
Richard Laybourn (CIT)	3,427	1.5
4 Bruce F. Vento (DFL)*	153,494	73.2
Bill James (I-R)	56,248	26.8
5 Martin Olav Sabo (DFL)*	136,634	65.5
Keith W. Johnson (I-R)	61,184	29.4
Kathryn Anderson (CIT)	8,143	3.9
Thomas Wicklund (LIBERT)	2,491	1.2
6 Gerry Sikorski (DFL)	109,246	50.8
Arlen Erdahl (I-R)*	105,734	49.2
7 Gene Wenstrom (DFL)	107,062	49.7
Arlan Stangeland (I-R)*	108,254	50.3
8 James L. Oberstar (DFL)*	176,392	76.7
Marjory L. Luce (I-R)	53,467	23.3

MISSISSIPPI

Senator

John C. Stennis (D)*	414,099	64.2
Haley Barbour (R)	230,927	35.8

House

	Vote Total	Per- cent
1 Jamie L. Whitten (D)*	79,726	70.9
Fran Fawcett (R)	32,750	29.1
2 Robert G. Clark (D)	71,536	48.4
Webb Franklin (R)	74,450	50.3
William V. Harris (I)	1,887	1.3
3 G. V. "Sonny" Montgomery (D)*	114,530	93.1
James Bradshaw (I)	8,519	6.9
4 Wayne Dowdy (D)*	79,977	52.6
Liles Williams (R)	69,469	45.6
Eddie L. McBride (I)	2,770	1.8
5 Arlon "Blackie" Coate (D)	22,634	21.5
Trent Lott (R)*	82,884	78.5

MISSOURI

Senator

Harriett Woods (D)	758,629	49.1
John C. Danforth (R)*	784,876	50.9

House

1 William Clay (D)*	102,656	66.1
William E. White (R)	52,599	33.9
2 Robert A. Young (D)*	100,770	56.5
Harold L. Dielmann (R)	77,433	43.5
3 Richard A. Gephardt (D)*	131,566	77.9
Richard Foristel (R)	37,388	22.1
4 Ike Skelton (D)*	96,388	54.8
Wendell Bailey (R)*	79,565	45.2
5 Alan Wheat (D)	96,059	57.9
John A. Sharp (R)	66,664	40.1
Kathie A. Fitzgerald (SOC WORK)	1,141	0.7
Alan H. Deright (I)	2,125	1.3
6 Jim Russell (D)	79,053	44.7
E. Thomas Coleman (R)*	97,993	55.3
7 David A. Geisler (D)	89,549	49.5
Gene Taylor (R)*	91,391	50.5
8 Jerry Ford (D)	76,413	46.9
Bill Emerson (R)*	86,493	53.1
9 Harold L. Volkmer (D)*	99,228	60.8
Larry E. Mead (R)	63,942	39.2

MONTANA

Senator

John Melcher (D)*	174,861	54.4
Larry Williams (R)	133,789	41.7
Larry Dodge (LIBERT)	12,412	3.9

House

1 Pat Williams (D)*	100,087	59.7
Bob Davies (R)	62,402	37.2
Don Doig (LIBERT)	5,113	3.1
2 Howard Lyman (D)	65,815	44.2
Ron Marlenee (R)*	79,968	53.7
Westley F. Deitchler (LIBERT)	3,154	2.1

NEBRASKA

Governor

Bob Kerrey (D)	277,436	50.7
Charles Thone (R)*	270,203	49.3

Senator

Edward Zorinsky (D)*	363,350	66.6
Jim Keck (R)	155,760	28.5
Virginia Walsh (I)	26,443	4.9

House

1 Curt Donaldson (D)	45,676	24.9
Douglas K. Bereuter (R)*	137,675	75.1
2 Richard M. Fellman (D)	70,431	43.1
Hal Daub (R)*	92,639	56.7

	Vote Total	Per- cent
3 Virginia Smith (R)*	X	100.0

NEVADA

Governor

Richard H. Bryan (D)	128,132	53.4
Robert F. List (R)*	100,104	41.8
Dan Becan (LIBERT)	4,621	1.9
None of the Above	6,894	2.9

Senator

Howard W. Cannon (D)*	114,720	47.7
Chic Hecht (R)	120,377	50.1
None of the Above	5,297	2.2

House

1 Harry Reid (D)	61,901	57.5
Peggy Cavnar (R)	45,675	42.5
2 Mary Gojack (D)	52,265	41.3
Barbara Vucanovich (R)	70,188	55.5
Teresa Vuceta (LIBERT)	4,043	3.2

NEW HAMPSHIRE

Governor

Hugh Gallen (D)*	132,287	46.4
John H. Sununu (R)	147,774	51.9
Meldrim Thomson Jr. (I)	4,785	1.7

House

1 Norman E. D'Amours (D)*	76,281	54.9
Robert C. Smith (R)	61,876	44.6
William C. Mackenzie (I)	752	0.5
2 Robert L. Dupay (D)	37,854	29.1
Judd Gregg (R)*	92,098	70.9

NEW JERSEY

Senator

Frank R. Lautenberg (D)	1,117,549	50.9
Millicent Fenwick (R)	1,047,626	47.7
Henry Koch (LIBERT)	9,934	0.5
Julius Levin (SOC LAB)	5,580	0.3
Claire Moriarty (SOC WORK)	3,726	0.2
Robert T. Bastien (I)	2,955	0.1
Rose Zeidwerg Monyek (I)	1,830	0.1
Martin E. Wendelken (I)	4,745	0.2

House

1 James J. Florio (D)*	110,570	73.3
John A. Dramesi (R)	39,501	26.2
Jerry Zeldin (LIBERT)	493	0.3
Patrick J. McCann (SOC LAB)	327	0.2
2 William J. Hughes (D)*	102,826	68.0
John J. Mahoney (R)	47,069	31.2
Bruce Powers (LIBERT)	1,233	0.8
3 James J. Howard (D)*	104,055	62.3
Marie Sheehan Muhler (R)	60,515	36.2
John Kinnevy III (CIT)	785	0.5
Lee A. Gesner Jr. (LIBERT)	701	0.4
Lawrence D. Erickson (SOC)	436	0.3
Joseph B. Hawley (I)	504	0.3
4 Joseph P. Merlino (D)	75,658	46.5
Christopher H. Smith (R)*	85,660	52.7
Bill Harris (LIBERT)	662	0.4
Eugene A. Creech (WF)	241	0.2
Paul B. Rizzo (I)	374	0.2
5 Fritz Cammerzell (D)	53,659	33.5
Marge Roukema (R)*	104,695	65.3
William J. Zelko Jr. (LIBERT)	2,004	1.2
6 Bernard J. Dwyer (D)*	100,418	68.1
Bertram L. Buckler (R)	46,093	31.3
Charles M. Hart (LIBERT)	920	0.6

	Vote Total	Percent
7 Adam K. Levin (D)	70,978	43.2
Matthew J. Rinaldo (R)*	91,837	56.0
Donald B. Siano (LIBERT)	1,294	0.8
8 Robert A. Roe (D)*	89,980	70.7
Norm Robertson (R)	36,317	28.5
Sidney J. Pope (LIBERT)	1,000	0.8
9 Robert G. Torricelli (D)	99,090	53.0
Harold C. Hollenbeck (R)*	86,022	46.0
Robert Shapiro (LIBERT)	1,767	1.0
10 Peter W. Rodino Jr. (D)*	76,684	82.6
Timothy Lee Jr. (R)	14,551	15.7
Katherine Florentine (LIBERT)	958	1.0
Christine Keno (I)	659	0.7
11 Joseph G. Minish (D)*	105,607	64.3
Rey Redington (R)	57,099	34.8
Richard Roth (LIBERT)	1,531	0.9
12 Jeff Connor (D)	57,049	32.3
Jim Courter (R)*	117,793	66.8
Harold F. Leiendecker (LIBERT)	1,610	0.9
13 George Callas (D)	65,820	39.1
Edwin B. Forsythe (R)*	100,061	59.5
Paula Volpe (CIT)	955	0.6
Don Smith (CST)	651	0.4
Leonard T. Flynn (LIBERT)	769	0.4
14 Frank J. Guarini (D)*	94,021	74.3
Charles J. Catrillo (R)	28,257	22.3
Louis J. Sicilia (LIBERT)	471	0.4
Kenneth Famularo (I)	921	0.7
Jack Murphy (I)	1,704	1.3
Herbert H. Shaw (I)	1,232	1.0

NEW MEXICO

Governor

	Vote Total	Percent
Toney Anaya (D)	215,840	53.0
John B. Irick (R)	191,626	47.0

Senator

	Vote Total	Percent
Jeff Bingaman (D)	217,682	53.8
Harrison "Jack" Schmitt (R)*	187,128	46.2

House

	Vote Total	Percent
1 Jan Alan Hartke (D)	67,534	47.6
Manuel Lujan Jr. (R)*	74,459	52.4
2 Caleb Chandler (D)	50,599	41.6
Joe Skeen (R)*	71,021	58.4
3 Bill Richardson (D)	84,669	64.5
Marjorie Bell Chambers (R)	46,466	35.4
David Arturo Fernandez (write-in)	158	0.1

NEW YORK

Governor

	Vote Total	Percent
Mario M. Cuomo (D, L)	2,675,213	50.9
Lew Lehrman (R, C, I)	2,494,827	47.5
John J. Northrup (F LIBERT)	16,913	0.3
Nancy Ross (NA)	5,277	0.1
Diane Wang (SOC WORK)	3,766	0.1
Robert J. Bohner (RTL)	52,356	1.0
Jane Benedict (UN)	6,353	0.1

Senator

	Vote Total	Percent
Daniel Patrick Moynihan (D,L)*	3,232,146	65.1
Florence Sullivan (R, C, RTL)	1,696,766	34.1
James J. McKeown (F LIBERT)	23,379	0.5
Steven Wattenmaker (SOC WORK)	15,206	0.3

House

	Vote Total	Percent
1 Ethan C. Eldon (D)	49,787	36.1

	Vote Total	Percent
William Carney (R, C, RTL)*	88,234	63.9
2 Thomas J. Downey (D)*	80,951	63.9
Paul G. Costello (R, C)	42,790	33.8
Lewis VanDenEssen (RTL)	2,971	2.3
3 Robert J. Mrazek (D)	93,846	51.8
John LeBoutillier (R, C)*	83,238	46.0
Richard G. Bohner (RTL)	4,049	2.2
4 Robert P. Zimmerman (D, L)	63,390	36.3
Norman F. Lent (R, C)*	105,241	60.4
John J. Dunkle (RTL)	5,717	3.3
5 Arnold J. Miller (D, L)	67,002	38.8
Raymond J. McGrath (R, C)*	100,485	58.1
Thomas J. Boyle (RTL)	4,911	2.8
Richard Horan (F LIBERT)	490	0.3
6 Joseph P. Addabbo (D, R, L)*	95,483	95.9
Mark E. Scott (C)	4,074	4.1
7 Benjamin S. Rosenthal (D, L)*	84,013	77.2
Albert Lemishow (R, C, RTL)	24,832	22.8
8 James H. Scheuer (D, L)*	91,830	89.5
John T. Blume (C)	10,741	10.5
9 Geraldine A. Ferraro (D)*	75,286	73.2
John J. Weigandt (R)	20,352	19.8
Ralph G. Groves (C, RTL)	6,011	5.9
Patricia A. Salargo (L)	1,171	1.1
10 Charles E. Schumer (D, L)*	89,852	79.2
Stephen Marks (R, C)	21,726	19.1
Alice J. Bertolotti (RTL)	1,873	1.7
11 Edolphus Towns (D)	39,357	83.7
James W. Smith (R)	4,449	9.5
Joseph N. O. Caesar (C, RTL)	1,357	2.9
Patrick W. Giagnacova (L)	1,488	3.2
Susan C. Zarate (SOC WORK)	359	0.7
12 Major R. Owens (D, L)	44,586	90.5
David Katan Sr. (R)	3,215	6.5
David E. Rosenstroch (C)	1,005	2.1
Jahn-Clymer Francis (RTL)	453	0.9
13 Stephen J. Solarz (D, L)*	68,549	80.5
Leon F. Nadrowski (R, C, RTL)	14,257	16.8
James M. Gay (C)	2,324	2.7
14 Leo C. Zeferetti (D)*	51,728	42.9
Guy V. Molinari (R, C, RTL)*	67,626	56.1
Carl F. Grillo (L)	1,276	1.0
15 Betty G. Lall (D, L)	55,483	44.8
Bill Green (R)*	66,262	53.6
Henry Van Rossem (C)	1,953	1.6
16 Charles B. Rangel (D, R, L)*	76,626	97.5
Michael T. Berns (C)	1,261	1.6
Veronica Cruz (SOC WORK)	718	0.9
17 Ted Weiss (D, L)*	113,172	85.0
Louis S. Antonelli (R, C, RTL)	19,928	15.0
18 Robert Garcia (D, R, L)*	57,009	98.9
Rafael Perez (POPULAR)	655	1.1
19 Mario Biaggi (D, R, L, RTL)*	118,803	93.7
Michael J. McSherry (C)	7,438	5.9
Eva Chertov (SOC WORK)	584	0.4
20 Richard L. Ottinger (D)*	98,425	56.5
Jon S. Fossel (R, C)	72,005	41.3
Florence T. O'Grady (RTL)	3,798	2.2
21 J. Morgan Strong (D)	38,664	24.8
Hamilton Fish Jr. (R, C)*	117,460	75.2
22 Peter A. Peyser (D)*	73,124	42.0
Benjamin A. Gilman (R)*	92,266	52.9
Charles C. Beck (C)	4,877	2.8
Richard Bruno (RTL)	4,019	2.3
23 Samuel S. Stratton (D)*	164,427	76.1
Frank Wicks (R, NF)	41,386	19.2
Mark A. Dunlea (CIT)	1,119	0.5
John G. Dow (L)	8,492	3.9
Patricia A. Mayberry		

	Vote Total	Percent
(SOC WORK)	659	0.3
24 Roy Esiason (D)	49,441	26.1
Gerald B. H. Solomon (R, C, RTL)*	140,296	73.9
25 Anita Maxwell (D)	70,793	42.4
Sherwood L. Boehlert (R)	93,071	55.8
Donald J. Thomas (RTL)	2,963	1.8
26 David P. Landy (D)	43,208	28.4
David O'B. Martin (R, C)*	108,962	71.6
27 Elaine Lytel (D, L)	79,209	44.2
George C. Wortley (R)*	95,290	53.2
Thomas M. Hunter (C)	2,783	1.5
George Hyrcza (RTL)	1,904	1.1
28 Matthew F. McHugh (D, L)*	100,665	56.4
David F. Crowley (R, C)	75,991	42.5
Mark Masterson (RTL)	2,003	1.1
29 William C. Larsen (D)	47,463	30.2
Frank Horton (R)*	104,412	66.4
Edwin Lundberg (C)	5,370	3.4
30 Bill Benet (D)	48,764	27.9
Barber B. Conable Jr. (R)*	119,105	68.2
Richard G. Baxter (C)	3,853	2.2
David J. Valone (RTL)	2,898	1.7
31 James A. Martin (D, L)	43,843	24.7
Jack F. Kemp (R, C)*	133,462	75.3
32 John J. LaFalce (D, L)*	116,386	91.4
Raymond R. Walker (R, C)	8,638	6.8
Timothy J. Hubbard (RTL)	2,359	1.8
33 Henry J. Nowak (D, L)*	126,091	84.1
Walter J. Pillich (R, C)	19,791	13.2
James Gallagher (RTL)	4,095	2.7
34 Stanley N. Lundine (D)*	99,502	60.2
James J. Snyder (R, C)	63,972	38.7
Genevieve F. Ronan (RTL)	1,806	1.1

NORTH CAROLINA

House

	Vote Total	Percent
1 Walter B. Jones (D)*	79,954	81.3
James F. McIntyre III (R)	17,478	17.8
Bobby Yates Emory (LIBERT)	910	0.9
2 I. T. "Tim" Valentine Jr. (D)	59,617	53.5
John W. Marin (R)	34,293	30.8
Sue Lamm (LIBERT)	1,426	1.3
H. M. Michaux Jr. (write-in)	15,990	14.4
3 Charles Whitley (D)*	68,936	63.5
Eugene "Red" McDaniel (R)	39,046	36.0
Marshall Sprague (LIBERT)	491	0.5
4 Ike Andrews (D)*	70,369	51.3
William Cobey Jr. (R)	64,955	47.4
Fritz Prochnaw (LIBERT)	1,720	1.3
5 Stephen L. Neal (D)*	87,819	60.3
Anne Bagnal (R)	57,083	39.2
Naudeen Beek (LIBERT)	631	0.4
Merly Lynn Farber (SOC WORK)	174	0.1
6 Charles Robin Britt (D)	68,696	53.8
Eugene Johnston (R)*	58,244	45.7
J. Erik Christensen (LIBERT)	679	0.5
7 Charlie Rose (D)*	68,529	71.0
Edward Johnson (R)	27,015	28.0
Richard Hollenbeak (LIBERT)	990	1.0
8 W. G. "Bill" Hefner (D)*	71,691	57.4
Harris D. Blake (R)	52,417	41.9
Don Scoggins (LIBERT)	830	0.7
9 Preston Cornelius (D)	47,258	41.9
James G. Martin (R)*	64,297	57.0
David Braatz (LIBERT)	1,231	1.1
10 James T. Broyhill (R)*	80,904	92.7
Jhon Rankin (LIBERT)	6,360	7.3

	Vote Total	Per-cent
11 James McClure Clarke (D)	85,410	49.9
Bill Hendon (R)*	84,085	49.2
Linda Janka (LIBERT)	1,552	0.9

NORTH DAKOTA

Senator

	Vote Total	Per-cent
Quentin N. Burdick (D)*	164,873	62.8
Gene Knorr (R)	89,304	34.0
Anna Bourgois (I)	8,288	3.2

House

	Vote Total	Per-cent
AL Byron L. Dorgan (D)*	186,534	71.6
Kent H. Jones (R)	72,241	27.7
Don J. Klingensmith (P)	1,724	0.7

OHIO

Governor

	Vote Total	Per-cent
Richard F. Celeste (D)	1,981,882	59.0
Clarence J. Brown (R)	1,303,962	38.9
Phyllis Goetz (LIBERT)	39,114	1.2
Kurt O. Landefeld (I)	14,279	0.4
Erwin J. Reupert (I)	17,484	0.5

Senator

	Vote Total	Per-cent
Howard M. Metzenbaum (D)*	1,923,767	56.7
Paul E. Pfeifer (R)	1,396,790	41.1
Philip Herzing (LIBERT)	36,103	1.1
Alicia Merel (I)	38,803	1.1

House

	Vote Total	Per-cent
1 Thomas A. Luken (D)*	99,143	63.5
John "Jake" Held (R)	52,658	33.7
James A. Berns (LIBERT)	4,386	2.8
2 William J. Luttmer (D)	53,169	34.2
Bill Gradison (R)*	97,434	62.7
Charles K. Shrout Jr. (LIBERT)	2,948	1.9
Joseph I. Lombardo (I)	1,827	1.2
3 Tony P. Hall (D)*	119,926	87.7
Kathryn E. Brown (LIBERT)	16,828	12.3
4 Robert W. Moon (D)	57,564	35.4
Michael G. Oxley (R)*	105,087	64.6
5 James R. Sherck (D)	70,120	44.8
Delbert L. Latta (R)*	86,450	55.2
6 Lynn Alan Grimshaw (D)	63,435	40.8
Bob McEwen (R)*	92,135	59.2
7 Roger D. Tackett (D)	65,543	42.0
Michael Dewine (R)	87,842	56.2
John B. Winer (LIBERT)	2,761	1.8
8 John W. Griffin (D)	49,877	33.6
Thomas N. Kindness (R)*	98,527	66.4
9 Marcy Kaptur (D)	95,162	57.9
Ed Weber (R)*	64,459	39.3
David Muir (LIBERT)	1,217	0.7
Susan A. Skinner (I)	1,785	1.1
James J. Somers (I)	1,594	1.0
10 John M. Buchanan (D)	57,983	36.7
Clarence E. Miller (R)*	100,044	63.3
11 Dennis E. Eckart (D)*	93,302	60.9
Glen W. Warner (R)	56,616	36.9
Jim Russell (LIBERT)	3,324	2.2
12 Bob Shamansky (D)*	82,753	47.3
John R. Kasich (R)	88,335	50.5
Russell A. Lewis (LIBERT)	3,939	2.2
13 Don J. Pease (D)*	92,296	61.2
Timothy Paul Martin (R)	53,376	35.4
James S. Patton (LIBERT)	5,053	3.4
14 John F. Seiberling (D)*	115,629	70.5

	Vote Total	Per-cent
Louis A. Mangels (R)	48,421	29.5
15 Greg Kostelac (D)	47,070	29.8
Chalmers P. Wylie (R)*	104,678	66.3
Steve Kender (LIBERT)	6,139	3.9
16 Jeffrey R. Orenstein (D)	57,386	34.2
Ralph Regula (R)*	110,485	65.8
17 George D. Tablack (D)	80,375	44.9
Lyle Williams (R)*	98,476	55.1
18 Douglas Applegate (D)*	X	100.0
19 Edward F. Feighan (D)	111,760	58.8
Richard G. Anter II (R)	72,682	38.3
Thomas Pekarek (LIBERT)	3,129	1.6
Kevin G. Killeen (I)	2,371	1.3
20 Mary Rose Oakar (D)*	133,603	85.6
Paris T. LeJeune (R)	17,675	11.3
Milton R. Norris (LIBERT)	2,844	1.8
Louise Haberbush (I)	1,930	1.3
21 Louis Stokes (D)*	132,544	86.1
Alan G. Shatteen (R)	21,332	13.9

OKLAHOMA

Governor

	Vote Total	Per-cent
George Nigh (D)*	548,159	62.1
Tom Daxon (R)	332,207	37.6
Allah-U Akbar Allah-U Wahid (I)	2,764	0.3

House

	Vote Total	Per-cent
1 James R. Jones (D)*	76,379	54.1
Richard C. Freeman (R)	64,704	45.9
2 Mike Synar (D)*	111,895	72.6
Lou Striegel (R)	42,298	27.4
3 Wes Watkins (D)*	121,670	82.2
Patrick K. Miller (R)	26,335	17.8
4 Dave McCurdy (D)*	84,205	65.0
Howard Rutledge (R)	44,351	34.3
Charles T. Emerson (I)	507	0.4
Marshall A. Luse (I)	441	0.3
5 Dan Lane (D)	42,453	28.9
Mickey Edwards (R)*	98,979	67.2
Paul E. Trent (I)	5,777	3.9
6 Glenn English (D)*	102,811	75.4
Ed Moore (R)	33,519	24.6

OREGON

Governor

	Vote Total	Per-cent
Ted Kulongoski (D)	374,316	35.9
Victor G. Atiyeh (R)*	639,841	61.4
Paul J. Cleveland (LIBERT)	27,394	2.7

House

	Vote Total	Per-cent
1 Les AuCoin (D)*	118,638	53.8
Bill Moshofsky (R)	101,720	46.2
2 Larryann Willis (D)	85,495	44.4
Bob Smith (R)	106,912	55.6
3 Ron Wyden (D)*	159,416	78.3
Thomas H. Phelan (R)	44,162	21.7
4 James Weaver (D)*	115,448	59.1
Ross Anthony (R)	80,054	40.9
5 J. Ruth McFarland (D)	98,952	48.8
Denny Smith (R)*	103,906	51.2

PENNSYLVANIA

Governor

	Vote Total	Per-cent
Allen E. Ertel (D)	1,772,353	48.1
Richard L. Thornburgh (R)*	1,872,784	50.8
Lee Frissell (CONSU)	13,101	0.4

	Vote Total	Per-cent
Richard D. Fuerle (LIBERT)	10,252	0.3
Mark Zola (SOC WORK)	15,495	0.4

Senator

	Vote Total	Per-cent
Cyril H. Wecht (D)	1,412,965	39.2
John Heinz (R)*	2,136,418	59.3
Liane Norman (CONSU)	16,530	0.5
Barbara I. Karkutt (LIBERT)	19,244	0.5
Kipp M. Dawson (SOC WORK)	18,951	0.5

House

	Vote Total	Per-cent
1 Thomas M. Foglietta (D)*	103,626	72.3
Michael Marino (R)	38,155	26.6
Lisa Brannan (CONSU)	1,063	0.7
Ralph Mullinger (LIBERT)	572	0.4
2 William H. Gray III (D)*	120,744	76.1
William C. Saunders (LIBERT)	2,726	1.7
Milton Street (I)	35,205	22.2
3 Robert A. Borski (D)	97,161	50.1
Charles F. Dougherty (R)*	94,497	48.7
Carolyn Berger (CONSU)	980	0.5
Bruce Bishkin (LIBERT)	435	0.2
Mike Finley (SOC WORK)	881	0.5
4 Joseph P. Kolter (D)	100,481	60.1
Eugene V. Atkinson (R)*	64,539	38.6
Sam Blancato (CONSU)	2,082	1.3
5 Bob Burger (D)	44,170	32.8
Richard T. Schulze (R)*	90,648	67.2
6 Gus Yatron (D)*	108,230	72.0
Harry B. Martin (R)	42,155	28.0
7 Robert W. Edgar (D)*	105,775	55.4
Steve Joachim (R)	85,023	44.6
8 Peter H. Kostmayer (D)	83,242	50.3
Jim Coyne (R)*	80,928	48.9
Hans G. Schroeder (LIBERT)	483	0.3
Albert H. Reef (I)	882	0.5
9 Eugene J. Duncan (D)	49,583	34.9
Bud Shuster (R)*	92,322	65.1
10 Robert J. Rafalko (D)	49,868	32.5
Joseph M. McDade (R)*	103,617	67.5
11 Frank Harrison (D)	90,371	53.5
James L. Nelligan (R)*	78,485	46.5
12 John P. Murtha (D)*	96,369	61.1
William N. Tuscano (R)	54,212	34.4
Joseph E. Krill (I)	7,059	4.5
13 Martin J. Cunningham Jr. (D)	59,709	35.2
Lawrence Coughlin (R)*	109,198	64.3
Nicholas Kyodnieus (LIBERT)	917	0.5
14 William J. Coyne (D)*	120,980	74.9
John R. Clark (R)	32,780	20.3
Richard E. Calligiuri (LIBERT)	5,437	3.3
William R. Kalman (SOC WORK)	2,380	1.5
15 Richard J. Orloski (D)	58,002	42.2
Don Ritter (R)*	79,455	57.8
16 Jean D. Mowery (D)	37,364	28.7
Robert S. Walker (R)*	93,034	71.3
17 Larry J. Hochendoner (D)	61,974	42.4
George W. Gekas (R)	84,291	57.6
18 Doug Walgren (D)*	101,807	54.2
Ted Jacob (R)	84,428	45.0
William A. Lewis Jr. (LIBERT)	1,448	0.8
19 Larry Becker (D)	41,787	29.2
Bill Goodling (R)*	101,163	70.8
20 Joseph M. Gaydos (D)*	127,281	76.0
Terry T. Ray (R)	38,212	22.8
David L. Travis (LIBERT)	1,935	1.2
21 Anthony "Buzz" Andrezeski (D)	79,451	49.8
Thomas J. Ridge (R)	80,180	50.2
22 Austin J. Murphy (D)*	123,716	78.7

	Vote Total	Per-cent
Frank J. Paterra (R)	32,176	20.5
Deann Rathbun (SOC WORK)	1,323	0.8
23 Joseph J. Calla Jr. (D)	49,297	34.8
William F. Clinger Jr. (R)*	92,424	65.2

RHODE ISLAND

Governor

	Vote Total	Per-cent
J. Joseph Garrahy (D)*	247,208	73.3
Vincent Marzullo (R)	79,602	23.6
Hilary Salk (CIT)	7,033	2.1
Peter Van Daam (JI)	3,405	1.0

Senator

Julius C. Michaelson (D)	167,283	48.8
John H. Chafee (R)*	175,495	51.2

House

1 Fernand J. St Germain (D)*	97,254	60.7
Burton Stallwood (R)	61,253	38.3
Gertrude M. Jayne Fowler (I)	1,624	1.0
2 James V. Aukerman (D)	76,769	44.4
Claudine Schneider (R)*	96,282	55.6

SOUTH CAROLINA

Governor

Richard Riley (D)*	468,819	69.8
William D. Workman Jr. (R)	202,806	30.2

House

1 W. Mullins McLeod (D)	52,916	44.9
Thomas F. Hartnett (R)*	63,945	54.3
Walter Smith (LIBERT)	971	0.8
2 Ken Mosely (D)	50,749	41.5
Floyd Spence (R)*	71,569	58.5
3 Butler Derrick (D)*	77,125	90.4
Gordon T. Davis (LIBERT)	8,214	9.6
4 Marion E. Tyus (D)	40,394	36.7
Carroll A. Campbell Jr. (R)*	69,802	63.3
5 John Spratt (D)	69,345	67.6
John S. Wilkerson (R)	33,191	32.4
6 Robert M. Tallon Jr. (D)	62,582	52.5
John L. Napier (R)*	56,653	47.5

SOUTH DAKOTA

Governor

Mike O'Connor (D)	81,136	29.1
William J. Janklow (R)*	197,426	70.9

House

AL Thomas A. Daschle (D)*	142,122	51.6
Clint Roberts (R)*	133,530	48.4

TENNESSEE

Governor

Randy Tyree (D)	500,937	40.4
Lamar Alexander (R)*	737,963	59.6

Senator

Jim Sasser (D)*	780,113	61.9
Robin L. Beard (R)	479,642	38.1

House

1 Jessie J. Cable (D)	27,580	22.8
James H. Quillen (R)*	89,497	74.1
James B. "Peppy" Fields (I)	3,778	3.1
2 John J. Duncan (R)*	X	100.0
3 Marilyn Lloyd Bouquard (D)*	84,967	61.8
Glen Byers (R)	49,885	36.3
Henry Ford Brock (I)	2,640	1.9

	Vote Total	Per-cent
4 Jim Cooper (D)	93,453	66.1
Cissy Baker (R)	47,865	33.9
5 Bill Boner (D)*	109,282	80.2
Laural Steinhice (R)	27,061	19.8
6 Albert Gore Jr. (D)*	X	100.0
7 Bob Clement (D)	72,359	49.5
Don Sundquist (R)	73,835	50.5
8 Ed Jones (D)*	93,945	74.9
Bruce Benson (R)	31,527	25.1
9 Harold E. Ford (D)*	112,143	72.4
Joe Crawford (R)	40,812	26.4
Isaac Richmond (I)	1,874	1.2

TEXAS

Governor

Mark White (D)	1,697,870	53.2
William Clements (R)*	1,465,937	45.9
Bob Poteet (CIT)	8,065	0.3
David Hutzelman (LIBERT)	19,143	0.6

Senator

Lloyd Bentsen (D)*	1,818,223	58.6
James M. Collins (R)	1,256,759	40.5
Lineaus Hooper Lorette (CIT)	4,564	0.1
John E. Ford (LIBERT)	23,494	0.8

House

1 Sam B. Hall Jr. (D)*	100,685	97.5
John Traylor (LIBERT)	2,598	2.5
2 Charles Wilson (D)*	91,762	94.3
Ed Richbourg (LIBERT)	5,584	5.7
3 James L. McNees Jr. (D)	28,223	21.8
Steve Bartlett (R)	99,852	77.1
Jerry R. Williamson (LIBERT)	1,453	1.1
4 Ralph M. Hall (D)*	94,134	73.8
Peter J. Collumb (R)	32,221	25.3
Bruce Iiams (LIBERT)	1,141	0.9
5 John Bryant (D)	52,214	64.8
Joe Devaney (R)	27,121	33.7
John Richard Bridges (CIT)	459	0.6
Richard Squire (LIBERT)	732	0.9
6 Phil Gramm (D)*	91,546	94.5
Ron Hard (LIBERT)	5,288	5.5
7 Dennis Scoggins (D)	17,866	14.0
Bill Archer (R)*	108,718	85.0
Bill Ware (LIBERT)	1,338	1.0
8 Henry E. Allee (D)	38,041	42.6
Jack Fields (R)*	50,630	56.8
Mike Angwin (LIBERT)	547	0.6
9 Jack Brooks (D)*	78,965	67.6
John W. Lewis (R)	35,422	30.3
Dean Allen (LIBERT)	2,510	2.1
10 J. J. Pickle (D)*	121,030	90.1
Bradley Louis Rockwell (CIT)	4,511	3.4
William G. Kelsey (LIBERT)	8,735	6.5
11 Marvin Leath (D)*	83,236	96.4
Tom Kilbride (LIBERT)	3,136	3.6
12 Jim Wright (D)*	78,913	68.9
Jim Ryan (R)	34,879	30.5
Ed Olson (LIBERT)	743	0.6
13 Jack Hightower (D)*	86,376	63.6
Ron Slover (R)	47,877	35.2
Rod Collier (LIBERT)	1,567	1.2
14 Bill Patman (D)*	76,851	60.7
Joe Wyatt Jr. (R)	48,942	38.6
Glenn Rasmussen (LIBERT)	919	0.7
15 E. "Kika" de la Garza (D)*	76,544	95.7
Frank L. Jones III (LIBERT)	3,458	4.3
16 Ronald Coleman (D)	44,024	53.9
Pat B. Haggerty (R)	36,064	44.2

	Vote Total	Per-cent
Catherin A. McDivitt (LIBERT)	1,583	1.9
17 Charles W. Stenholm (D)*	109,359	97.1
James Cooley II (LIBERT)	3,271	2.9
18 Mickey Leland (D)*	68,014	82.6
C. Leon Pickett (R)	12,104	14.7
Thomas P. Bernhardt (LIBERT)	2,215	2.7
19 Kent Hance (D)*	89,702	81.6
E. L. Hicks (R)	19,062	17.3
Mike Read (LIBERT)	1,206	1.1
20 Henry B. Gonzalez (D)*	68,544	91.5
Roger V. Gary (LIBERT)	4,163	5.6
Benedict D. La Rosa (I)	2,213	2.9
21 Charles S. Stough (D)	35,112	24.6
Tom Loeffler (R)*	106,515	74.5
Jeffrey J. Brown (LIBERT)	1,243	0.9
22 Ron Paul (R)*	X	100.0
23 Abraham Kazen Jr. (D)*	51,690	55.3
Jeff Wentworth (R)	41,363	44.2
Parker Abell (LIBERT)	475	0.5
24 Martin Frost (D)*	63,857	72.8
Lucy P. Patterson (R)	22,798	26.1
David Guier (LIBERT)	998	1.1
25 Mike Andrews (D)	63,974	60.4
Mike Faubion (R)	40,112	37.9
Barbara Coldiron (CIT)	963	0.9
Jeff Calvert (LIBERT)	864	0.8
26 Tom Vandergriff (D)	69,782	50.1
Jim Bradshaw (R)	69,438	49.9
27 Solomon P. Ortiz (D)	66,604	64.0
Jason Luby (R)	35,209	33.8
Steven R. Roberts (LIBERT)	2,231	2.2

UTAH

Senator

Ted Wilson (D)	219,482	41.3
Orrin G. Hatch (R)*	309,332	58.3
Lawrence R. Kauffman (AM)	953	0.2
George Mercier (LIBERT)	1,035	0.2

House

1 A. Stephen Dirks (D)	66,006	37.2
James V. Hansen (R)*	111,416	62.8
2 Frances Farley (D)	78,981	46.2
Dan Marriott (R)*	92,109	53.8
3 Howard C. Nielson (R)	108,478	76.9
Henry A. Huish (I-D)	32,661	23.1

VERMONT

Governor

Madeleine M. Kunin (D)	74,394	44.0
Richard A. Snelling (R)*	93,111	55.0
John L. Buttolph (LIBERT)	801	0.5
Richard F. Gottlieb (LU)	850	0.5

Senator

James A. Guest (D)	79,340	47.2
Robert T. Stafford (R)*	84,449	50.3
Ion Laskaris (CIT)	897	0.5
Bo Adlerbert (LIBERT)	892	0.5
Jerry Levy (LU)	774	0.5
Michael Hackett (I)	1,463	0.9

House

AL Mark A. Kaplan (D)	38,296	23.2
James M. Jeffords (R)*	114,191	69.2
Robin Lloyd (CIT)	6,409	3.9
George Trask (LIBERT)	1,407	0.9
Peter Diamondstone (LU)	2,794	1.7
Morris Earle (I)	1,733	1.1

	Vote Total	Per-cent

VIRGINIA

Senator

Richard J. Davis (D)	690,839	48.8
Paul S. Trible Jr. (R)	724,571	51.2

House

1	John J. McGlennon (D)	62,379	43.7
	Herbert H. Bateman (R)	76,926	53.9
2	G. William Whitehurst (R)*	X	100.0
3	John A. Waldrop Jr. (D)	63,946	40.8
	Thomas J. Bliley Jr. (R)*	92,928	59.2
4	Norman Sisisky (D)	80,695	54.4
	Robert W. Daniel Jr. (R)*	67,708	45.6
5	Dan Daniel (D)*	X	100.0
6	James R. Olin (D)	68,192	49.7
	Kevin G. Miller (R)	66,537	48.5
	Robert L. Fariss (I)	2,395	1.8
7	Lindsay G. Dorrier Jr. (D)	46,514	36.3
	J. Kenneth Robinson (R)*	76,752	59.8
	David J. Toscano (I)	4,950	3.9
8	Herbert E. Harris II (D)	68,071	48.6
	Stan Parris (R)*	69,620	49.7
	Austin W. Morrill Jr. (I)	2,373	1.7
9	Frederick C. Boucher (D)	76,205	50.4
	William C. Wampler (R)*	75,082	49.6
10	Ira M. Lechner (D)	75,361	46.0
	Frank R. Wolf (R)*	86,506	52.7
	Scott R. Bowden (I)	2,162	1.3

WASHINGTON

Senator

Henry M. Jackson (D)*	943,655	68.9
Doug Jewett (R)	332,273	24.3
Jesse Chiang (I)	20,251	1.5
King Lysen (I)	72,297	5.3

House

1	Brian Long (D)	59,444	32.4
	Joel Pritchard (R)*	123,956	67.6
2	Al Swift (D)*	101,383	59.6
	Joan Houchen (R)	68,622	40.4
3	Don Bonker (D)*	97,323	60.1
	J. T. Quigg (R)	59,686	36.8
	O'Dean Williamson (I)	5,049	3.1
4	Charles D. Kilbury (D)	45,990	28.6
	Sid Morrison (R)*	112,148	69.8
	Michael Leroy Burns (FP)	2,530	1.6
5	Thomas S. Foley (D)*	109,549	64.3
	John Sonneland (R)	60,816	35.7
6	Norman D. Dicks (D)*	89,985	62.5
	Ted Haley (R)	47,720	33.2
	Jayne H. Anderson (I)	6,193	4.3
7	Mike Lowry (D)*	126,313	70.9
	Bob Dorse (R)	51,759	29.1
8	Beth Bland (D)	59,824	43.0
	Rodney Chandler (R)	79,209	57.0

WEST VIRGINIA

Senator

Robert C. Byrd (D)*	387,170	68.5
Cleve Benedict (R)	173,910	30.8
William B. Hovland (SOC WORK)	4,234	0.7

House

1	Alan B. Mollohan (D)	79,529	53.2
	John F. McCuskey (R)	70,069	46.8
2	Harley O. Staggers Jr. (D)	87,904	64.0
	J. D. Hinkle Jr. (R)	49,413	36.0

Rep. Claude Pepper, D-Fla., celebrates his re-election victory.

	Vote Total	Per-cent

3	Bob Wise (D)	84,619	57.9
	David Michael Staton (R)*	60,844	41.6
	Adrienne Benjamin (SOC WORK)	787	0.5
4	Nick J. Rahall II (D)*	91,184	80.5
	Homer L. Harris (R)	22,054	19.5

WISCONSIN

Governor

Anthony S. Earl (D)	896,812	56.8
Terry J. Kohler (R)	662,838	41.9
James P. Wickstrom (CST)	7,721	0.5
Larry Smiley (LIBERT)	9,734	0.6
Peter Seidman (I)	3,025	0.2

Senator

William Proxmire (D)*	983,311	63.7
Scott McCallum (R)	527,355	34.1
Sanford G. Knapp (CST)	4,463	0.3
George Liljenfeldt (LIBERT)	7,947	0.5
William Osborne Hart (I)	21,807	1.4

House

1	Les Aspin (D)*	95,055	61.0
	Peter N. Jannson (R)	59,309	38.1
	Arthur F. Jackson (LIBERT)	1,438	0.9
2	Robert W. Kastenmeier (D)*	112,677	60.6
	Jim Johnson (R)	71,989	38.7
	David Beito (LIBERT)	1,368	0.7
3	Paul Offner (D)	75,132	42.8
	Steve Gunderson (R)*	99,304	56.6
	Kenneth P. Van Doren (LIBERT)	1,027	0.6

	Vote Total	Per-cent

4	Clement J. Zablocki (D)*	129,557	94.5
	John Gudenschwager (CST)	946	0.7
	Nicholas P. Youngers (LIBERT)	4,064	3.0
	John F. Baumgartner (I)	2,421	1.8
5	Jim Moody (D)	99,713	63.6
	Rod K. Johnston (R)	54,826	34.9
	William G. McCuen Jr. (LIBERT)	1,498	1.0
	Walter G. Beach (I)	526	0.3
	Cheryll Y. Hidalgo (I)	353	0.2
6	Gordon E. Loehr (D)	59,922	35.0
	Thomas E. Petri (R)*	111,348	65.0
7	David R. Obey (D)*	122,124	68.0
	Bernard A. Zimmerman (R)	57,535	32.0
8	Ruth C. Clusen (D)	74,436	42.0
	Toby Roth (R)*	101,379	57.2
	Anthony Theisen (LIBERT)	1,336	0.8
9	F. James Sensenbrenner Jr. (R)*	X	100.0

WYOMING

Governor

Ed Herschler (D)*	106,427	63.1
Warren A. Morton (R)	62,128	36.9

Senator

Rodger McDaniel (D)	72,466	43.3
Malcolm Wallop (R)*	94,725	56.7

House

AL	Ted Hommel (D)	46,041	28.9
	Dick Cheney (R)*	113,236	71.1

Election Results, Congress and Presidency, 1854-1982

Election Year	Congress Elected	HOUSE Members Elected Dem.	Rep.	Misc.	HOUSE Gains/Losses Dem.	Rep.	SENATE Members Elected Dem.	Rep.	Misc.	SENATE Gains/Losses Dem.	Rep.	PRESIDENCY Elected	Popular Vote Plurality
1854	34th	83	108	43			42	15	5			Pierce (D)	
1856	35th	131	92	14	+ 48	− 16	39	20	5	− 3	+ 5	Buchanan (D)	498,209
1858	36th	101	113	23	− 30	+ 21	38	26	2	− 1	+ 6		
1860	37th	42	106	28	− 59	− 7	11	31	7	−27	+ 5	Lincoln (R)	487,764
1862	38th	80	103		+ 38	− 3	12	39		+ 1	+ 8		
1864	39th	46	145		− 34	+ 42	10	42		− 2	+ 3	Lincoln (R)	414,299
1866	40th	49	143		+ 3	− 2	11	42		+ 1	0	Johnson (R)	
1868	41st	73	170		+ 24	+ 27	11	61		0	+19	Grant (R)	309,380
1870	42nd	104	139		+ 31	− 31	17	57		+ 6	− 4		
1872	43rd	88	203		− 16	+ 64	19	54		+ 2	− 3	Grant (R)	763,664
1874	44th	181	107	3	+ 93	−96	29	46		+10	− 8		
1876	45th	156	137		− 25	+ 30	36	39	1	+ 7	− 7	Hayes (R)	−251,746
1878	46th	150	128	14	− 6	− 9	43	33		+ 7	− 6		
1880	47th	130	152	11	− 20	+ 24	37	37	2	− 6	+ 4	Garfield (R)	9,457
1882	48th	200	119	6	+ 70	− 33	36	40		− 1	+ 3	Arthur (R)	
1884	49th	182	140	2	− 18	+ 21	34	41		− 2	+ 2	Cleveland (D)	23,737
1886	50th	170	151	4	− 12	+ 11	37	39		+ 3	− 2		
1888	51st	156	173	1	− 14	+ 22	37	47		0	+ 8	Harrison (R)	−95,096
1890	52nd	231	88	14	+ 75	− 85	39	47	2	+ 2	0		
1892	53rd	220	126	8	− 11	+ 38	44	38	3	+ 5	− 9	Cleveland (D)	365,516
1894	54th	104	246	7	−116	+120	30	44	5	− 5	+ 6		
1896	55th	134	206	16	+ 30	− 40	34	46	10	− 5	+ 2	McKinley (R)	597,012
1898	56th	163	185	9	+ 29	− 21	26	53	11	− 8	+ 7		
1900	57th	153	198	5	− 10	+ 13	29	56	3	+ 3	+ 3	McKinley (R)	861,668
1902	58th	178	207		+ 25	+ 9	32	58		+ 3	+ 2	Roosevelt (R)	
1904	59th	136	250		− 42	+ 43	32	58		0	0	Roosevelt (R)	2,544,298
1906	60th	164	222		+ 28	− 28	29	61		− 3	− 3		
1908	61st	172	219		+ 8	− 3	32	59		+ 3	− 2	Taft (R)	1,268,449
1910	62nd	228	162	1	+ 56	− 57	42	49		+10	−10		
1912	63rd	290	127	18	+ 62	− 35	51	44	1	+ 9	− 5	Wilson (D)	2,173,466
1914	64th	231	193	8	− 59	+ 66	56	39	1	+ 5	− 5		
1916	65th	210	216	9	− 21	+ 23	53	42	1	− 3	+ 3	Wilson (D)	582,576
1918	66th	191	237	7	− 19	+ 21	47	48	1	− 6	+ 6		
1920	67th	132	300	1	− 59	+ 63	37	59		−10	+11	Harding (R)	7,020,023
1922	68th	207	225	3	+ 75	− 75	43	51	2	+ 6	− 8	Coolidge (R)	
1924	69th	183	247	5	− 24	+ 22	40	54	1	− 3	+ 3	Coolidge (R)	333,217
1926	70th	195	237	3	+ 12	− 10	47	48	1	+ 7	− 6		
1928	71st	163	267	1	− 32	+ 30	39	56	1	− 8	+ 8	Hoover (R)	6,429,579
1930	72nd	216	218	1	+ 53	− 49	47	48	1	+ 8	− 8		
1932	73rd	313	117	5	+ 97	−101	59	36	1	+12	−12	Roosevelt (D)	7,068,817
1934	74th	322	103	10	+ 9	− 14	69	25	2	+10	−11		
1936	75th	333	89	13	+ 11	− 14	75	17	4	+ 6	− 8	Roosevelt (D)	11,073,102
1938	76th	262	169	4	− 71	+ 80	69	23	4	− 6	+ 6		
1940	77th	267	162	6	+ 5	− 7	66	28	2	− 3	+ 5	Roosevelt (D)	4,964,561
1942	78th	222	209	4	− 45	+ 47	57	38	1	− 9	+ 10		
1944	79th	243	190	2	+ 21	− 19	57	38	1	0	0	Roosevelt (D)	3,594,993
1946	80th	188	246	1	− 55	+ 56	45	51		−12	+13	Truman	
1948	81st	263	171	1	+ 75	− 75	54	42		+ 9	− 9	Truman (D)	2,188,054
1950	82nd	234	199	2	− 29	+ 28	48	47	1	− 6	+ 5		
1952	83rd	213	221	1	− 21	+ 22	47	48	1	− 1	+ 1	Eisenhower (R)	6,621,242
1954	84th	232	203		+ 19	− 18	48	47	1	+ 1	− 1		
1956	85th	234	201		+ 2	− 2	49	47		+ 1	0	Eisenhower (R)	9,567,720
1958	86th	283	154		+ 49	− 47	64	34		+17	−13		
1960	87th	263	174		− 20	+ 20	64	36		− 2	+ 2	Kennedy (D)	118,574*
1962	88th	258	176	1**	− 4	+ 2	67	33		+ 4	− 4		
1964	89th	295	140		+ 38	− 38	68	32		+ 2	− 2	Johnson (D)	15,951,296
1966	90th	248	187		− 47	+ 47	64	36		− 3	+ 3		
1968	91st	243	192		− 4	+ 4	58	42		− 5	+ 5	Nixon (R)	510,314
1970	92nd	255	180		+ 12	− 12	55	45		− 4	+ 2		
1972	93rd	243	192		− 12	+ 12	57	43		+ 2	− 2	Nixon (R)	17,999,528
1974	94th	291	144		+ 43	− 43	61†	38		+ 3†	− 3		
1976	95th	292	143		+ 1	− 1	62	38		0	0	Carter (D)	1,682,970
1978	96th	277	158		− 11	+ 11	59	41		− 3	+ 3		
1980	97th	243	192		− 33	+ 33	47	53		−12	+12	Reagan (R)	8,420,270
1982	98th	269	166		+ 26	− 26	46	54		0	0		

* Includes divided Alabama elector slate votes.

** Vacancy — Rep. Clem Miller (D-Calif. 1959-62) died Oct. 6, 1962, but his name remained on the ballot and he received a plurality.

 State Legislatures

Democrats Recoup State Legislature Losses

Democrats turned the tables on the GOP in state legislative elections Nov. 2, recouping most of the chambers taken by the Republicans in the past two elections and ending a six-year decline in the number of legislatures under Democratic control.

Aided by a strong showing in congressional and gubernatorial elections across the country — and, in some instances, redrawn legislative districts — the Democrats raised from 28 to 34 the number of states in which they controlled both houses. When most legislatures reconvened in January 1983, the GOP controlled both houses in 11 states — a net loss of four from the end of the 1982 legislative session. In four states, neither party controlled both chambers, down from six before the elections. Nebraska maintained its unique non-partisan, unicameral system.

Democrats reclaimed four of the five chambers captured by the GOP in 1980, winning back the lower houses in Illinois, Montana and Washington and picking up two seats to establish a tenuous one-seat edge in the Ohio Senate. Although the GOP held on to the Pennsylvania Senate, a shift of two seats returned the Democrats to power in Pennsylvania's lower house after four years of Republican control. *(Chart, next page)*

Republicans did manage to add one new legislature to their column. Gaining one seat in Alaska's upper house, Republicans broke the tie that resulted from the 1980 election and resumed control of the chamber. An additional five-seat gain enabled them to capture the House. However, GOP strength was undercut somewhat by the election of Democrat Bill Sheffield as Alaska's governor. Republican gains brought them within one seat of the Democrats in Wisconsin's upper chamber; they trailed by a mere two seats in the upper houses in Michigan and New Mexico.

Democratic Coups

The Democrats' most significant gains came in Iowa and Washington — they seized both chambers from the GOP in each state. In Iowa, where control of the Legislature had seesawed back and forth over the past decade, Democrats picked up seven seats in the upper

house and 15 in the lower house. The victories avenged Democratic losses in 1978, when the Republicans assumed control of both chambers.

A gain of 12 seats propelled the Democrats to victory in Washington's lower house, snatched from their hands by the GOP in 1980. Explaining the Republicans' sizable losses, Rob Hodges of the Washington state GOP Communications Office claimed that in many cases "it came down to personality. A lot of the [state] House members who lost were first-term members." A shift of one seat returned the Democrats to power in the Senate.

Democrats further eroded Republicans' strength elsewhere around the country. In Delaware, they picked up nine seats to claim the lower chamber and so garnered complete control of the Legislature. Seizing Maine's upper house, the Democrats exerted complete control in that state's Legislature. Control of Montana's Legislature was split between the two parties as a result of a 12-seat gain the Democrats made in the lower house. Democrats scored their biggest advance in North Dakota, grabbing 28 seats to capture the lower chamber and split control of the Legislature.

State Redistricting

In Illinois, Democrats won roughly a 19-seat majority in the state House, erasing the five-seat GOP edge that had existed before the election. Democratic gains were largely

Party Control of State Legislatures After 1982 Elections

DEMOCRATS CONTROL BOTH HOUSES
REPUBLICANS CONTROL BOTH HOUSES
NEITHER PARTY CONTROLS BOTH HOUSES
NON-PARTISAN UNICAMERAL LEGISLATURE

1983 New Party Lineup of State

State	Governor	1983 Legislature[2]	Oct. 1982 Upper House			Oct. 1982 Lower House			Jan. 1983 Upper House		
Alabama	D	D	35 D,	0 R		101 D,	4 R		32 D,	3 R	
Alaska	● D	● R	10 D,	10 R		22 D,	16 R,	2 L	● 9 D,	11 R	
Arizona	D	R	14 D,	16 R		17 D,	43 R		12 D,	18 R	
Arkansas	● D	D	34 D,	1 R		93 D,	7 R		32 D,	3 R	
California	● R	D	23 D,	17 R		48 D,	32 R		25 D,	15 R	
Colorado	D	R	13 D,	22 R		25 D,	40 R		14 D,	21 R	
Connecticut	D	D	23 D,	13 R		82 D,	69 R		23 D,	13 R	
Delaware	R	● D	12 D,	9 R		16 D,	25 R		13 D,	8 R	
Florida	D	D	27 D,	13 R		81 D,	39 R		32 D,	8 R	
Georgia	D	D	51 D,	5 R		157 D,	23 R		49 D,	7 R	
Hawaii	D	D	17 D,	8 R		39 D,	12 R		20 D,	5 R	
Idaho	D	R	12 D,	23 R		14 D,	56 R		14 D,	21 R	
Illinois	R	● D	30 D,	29 R		86 D,	91 R		33 D,	26 R	
Indiana	R	R	15 D,	35 R		37 D,	63 R		18 D,	32 R	
Iowa	R	● D	21 D,	29 R		45 D,	55 R		● 28 D,	22 R	
Kansas	D	R	16 D,	24 R		53 D,	72 R		16 D,	24 R	
Kentucky	D	D	29 D,	9 R		76 D,	24 R		29 D,	9 R	
Louisiana	R	D	39 D,	0 R		94 D,	10 R,	1 Ind.	39 D,	0 R	
Maine	D	● D	16 D,	17 R		82 D,	69 R		● 23 D,	10 R	
Maryland	D	D	40 D,	7 R		127 D,	14 R,	1 Ind.	41 D,	6 R	
Massachusetts	D	D	32 D,	8 R		127 D,	32 R,	1 Ind.	32 D,	8 R	
Michigan	● D	D	24 D,	14 R		64 D,	46 R		20 D,	18 R	
Minnesota	● D	D	44 D,	23 R		70 D,	64 R		42 D,	25 R	
Mississippi	D	D	48 D,	4 R		116 D,	4 R,	2 Ind.	48 D,	4 R	
Missouri	R	D	23 D,	11 R		110 D,	53 R		22 D,	12 R	
Montana	D	● X	22 D,	28 R		43 D,	57 R		24 D,	26 R	
Nebraska	● D			Non-partisan Unicameral							
Nevada	● D	D	15 D,	5 R		26 D,	14 R		17 D,	4 R	
New Hampshire	● R	R	10 D,	14 R		160 D,	240 R		10 D,	14 R	
New Jersey	R	D	21 D,	19 R		43 D,	37 R		21 D,	19 R	
New Mexico	D	D	23 D,	19 R		41 D,	29 R		22 D,	20 R	
New York	D	X	25 D,	35 R		88 D,	62 R		25 D,	36 R	
North Carolina	D	D	40 D,	10 R		96 D,	24 R		45 D,	5 R	
North Dakota	R	● X	11 D,	39 R		27 D,	73 R		18 D,	35 R	
Ohio	● D	● D	15 D,	18 R		56 D,	43 R		● 17 D,	16 R	
Oklahoma	D	D	37 D,	11 R		73 D,	28 R		34 D,	14 R	
Oregon	R	D	22 D,	8 R		33 D,	27 R		21 D,	9 R	
Pennsylvania	R	● X	24 D,	26 R		100 D,	103 R		23 D,	27 R	
Rhode Island	D	D	43 D,	7 R		82 D,	18 R		43 D,	7 R	
South Carolina	D	D	41 D,	5 R		106 D,	18 R		41 D,	5 R	
South Dakota	R	R	10 D,	25 R		21 D,	49 R		9 D,	26 R	
Tennessee	R	D	21 D,	11 R, 1 Ind.		58 D,	39 R,	2 Ind.	22 D,	11 R	
Texas	● D	D	23 D,	8 R		112 D,	38 R		25 D,	5 R,	1 V
Utah	D	R	7 D,	22 R		17 D,	58 R		5 D,	24 R	
Vermont	R	R	12 D,	17 R		64 D,	84 R,	2 Ind.	13 D,	17 R	
Virginia	D	D	31 D,	9 R		65 D,	33 R,	1 Ind.	31 D,	9 R	
Washington	R	● D	24 D,	25 R		42 D,	56 R		● 25 D,	24 R	
West Virginia	D	D	27 D,	7 R		78 D,	22 R		31 D,	3 R	
Wisconsin	● D	D	19 D,	14 R		60 D,	39 R		16 D,	16 R,	1 V
Wyoming	D	R	11 D,	19 R		23 D,	39 R		11 D,	19 R	

Oct. 1982 Upper House[4]	Oct. 1982 Lower House[4]	Jan. 1983 Upper House[4]	Jan. 1983 Lower House[4]
1,182 Democrats	3,296 Democrats	1,215 Democrats	3,425 Democrats
748 Republican	2,193 Republicans	720 Republicans	2,015 Republicans
1 Independent	2 Libertarians	2 Vacancies	7 Independents
	10 Independents		4 Undecided
			2 Vacancies

Sources: National Conference of State Legislatures, and secretaries of state.

Legislatures[1]

Jan. 1983 Lower House	Upper House Gains	Lower House Gains
97 D, 8 R	+3 R	+4 R
● 19 D, 21 R	+1 R	+5 R
21 D, 39 R	+2 R	+4 D
93 D, 7 R	+2 R	No Change
47 D, 33 R	+2 D	+1 R
25 D, 40 R	+1 D	No Change
87 D, 64 R	No Change	+5 D
● 25 D, 16 R	+1 D	+9 D
84 D, 36 R	+5 D	+3 D
156 D, 24 R	+2 R	+1 R
43 D, 8 R	+3 D	+4 D
19 D, 51 R	+2 D	+5 D
● 68 D, 49 R, 1 Und.	+3 D	Und.[5]
43 D, 57 R	+3 D	+6 D
● 60 D, 40 R	+7 D	+15 D
53 D, 72 R	No Change[3]	No Change
76 D, 24 R	No Change[3]	No Change[3]
94 D, 10 R, 1 Ind.	No Change[3]	No Change[3]
93 D, 57 R, 1 Und.	+7 D	Und.
123 D, 19 R	+1 D	+5 R
130 D, 30 R	No Change	+3 D
63 D, 47 R	+4 R	+1 R
77 D, 57 R	+2 R	+7 D
116 D, 4 R, 2 Ind.	No Change[3]	No Change[3]
110 D, 53 R	+1 R	No Change
● 55 D, 45 R	+2 D	+12 D
23 D, 19 R {2 Ind., 1 Und.}	+2 D*	+5 R*
156 D, 241 R	No Change	Und.
43 D, 37 R	No Change[3]	No Change[3]
45 D, 25 R	+1 R	+4 D
99 D, 51 R	+1 R*	+11 D
99 D, 21 R	+5 D	+3 D
● 55 D, 51 R	+7 D*	+28 D*
64 D, 35 R	+2 D	+8 D
76 D, 25 R	+3 R	+3 D
36 D, 24 R	+1 R	+3 D
●102 D, 101 R	+1 R	+2 D
85 D, 15 R	No Change[3]	+3 D
103 D, 20 R, 1 V	No Change[3]	Und.
15 D, 55 R	+1 R	+6 R
60 D, 38 R, 1 Ind.	+1 D	+2 D
114 D, 36 R	Und.	+2 D
17 D, 58 R	+2 R	No Change
65 D, 84 R, 1 V	+1 D*	Und.
66 D, 33 R, 1 Und.	No Change	Und.
● 54 D, 44 R	+1 D	+12 D
88 D, 12 R	+4 D	+10 D
58 D, 41 R	Und.	+2 R
25 D, 38 R, 1 Ind.	No Change	+2 D*

KEY TO SYMBOLS: *D — Democrat; R — Republican; L — Libertarian; Ind. — Independent; Und. — Undecided; V — Vacancy; ● — changed party control; * — Due to the addition of seats through redistricting, one party's gains may not equal the other's losses.*

[1]*The number of seats controlled is based on Nov. 2 elections using unofficial election results as of Nov. 11. Official canvasses and recounts could change lineups; vacancies may occur before legislatures meet, which also might change lineups.*

[2]*Column Key: D — Democrats control both houses; R — Republicans control both houses; X — neither party has complete control.*

[3]*No election held.*

[4]*Totals do not include Nebraska, which has a 49-seat unicameral non-partisan Legislature.*

[5]*Illinois voters approved a 1980 state constitutional amendment to reduce the size of the state's lower house from 177 seats to 118 seats.*

the result of newly apportioned state House districts drawn according to a 1980 amendment to the state constitution that reduced the size of the House by one third and provided for representatives to be elected within single-member districts. Under the old system, three House members were elected at large from within each state Senate district.

After the Legislature proved unable to agree on a legislative remap, Democrats won control of the independent board set up to draw the new lines. The result was a set of House district lines designed to eliminate the minimal GOP presence in Chicago, weaken Republican strength in several suburban and downstate districts and shore up marginally Democratic seats in southern Illinois.

In Iowa, where Democrats gained control of both the House and the Senate, the role of reapportionment was less clear. "In Iowa we have honest-to-God, non-partisan reapportionment," commented University of Iowa political scientist Samuel Patterson. Democratic gains there, he said, were simply part of a strong Democratic showing throughout the Midwest.

But Gordon McKenzie, Iowa GOP press secretary, noted that reapportionment did have an effect on incumbents. "It was the first time some people had run in new districts," he maintained. "Also, in many cases, an incumbent was pitted against an incumbent." Several Republican incumbents, he said, found themselves facing Republican colleagues in the primary.

National Party Strategies

In contrast to recent years, national Republican involvement in state legislative contests in 1982 was relatively muted. In 1980, the Republican National Committee (RNC) mounted a $2.9 million effort aimed at winning control of state legislatures. In 1982, the RNC spent some $600,000 in direct contributions to candidates; another half million dollars was distributed by GOPAC, an independent political action committee set up by Republicans prior to the 1980 elections to give help to GOP legislative candidates.

The Republican effort in 1980 was spurred by the GOP hopes of taking control of enough state legislatures to help the party — or at least minimize harm done to it — through redistricting based on the 1980 census.

In 1982, however, with redistricting finished for the decade in most states, the RNC's local elections division switched gears. Rather than trying to win control of legislatures by funding GOP candidates, most of its resources went into sending operatives into the field to help candidates and local party workers develop campaign knowledge and sophistication. The goal was not only to help build the party at the local level, but, taking note of the large number of former state legislators in Congress, to develop a pool of potential congressional candidates. More than half of the 81 new U.S. House members elected in 1982 were or had been state legislators.

The Democratic National Committee (DNC) was somewhat more active in local elections in 1982 than two years before, when it all but ignored local races. The DNC's political affairs division worked with state party officials in 16 states to develop a local campaign apparatus capable of being used at all political levels. The phone and mail lists, data bases and local political consulting services that the DNC and state party organizations developed were used to help state legislative candidates as well as candidates for higher office. ∎

VOTING STUDIES

CQ

C
Q Key Votes

Reagan Support Fades in Key Votes of 1982

Key House and Senate votes in 1982 showed clearly that congressional support of the Reagan administration's legislative agenda was beginning to deteriorate.

While the White House was able to hold a majority of the Republican-controlled Senate on a few economic issues, House Democrats — often with significant help from Republican colleagues — went against the administration on almost all key votes.

Not only did the votes reflect growing doubts about the Reagan economic program, but they were also evidence of members' concerns about their own future at the polls.

Both houses, for instance, voted to override Reagan's veto of a $14.2 billion supplemental appropriations bill. Few members up for re-election were willing to vote against funding for education programs and jobs for the elderly.

But this was only one in a series of White House defeats. Both houses rejected the administration's fiscal 1983 budget as unrealistic and adopted their own.

Against Reagan's wishes, the House voted for a $1 billion mortgage subsidy program and later for a $5.4 billion jobs program. The Senate passed $5.1 billion in housing aid. But both houses backed off after a presidential veto in one case and the threat of one in another.

One of Reagan's pet projects, a constitutional amendment to balance the budget, failed in the House, although the Senate went along with the president.

The House handed Reagan the first presidential defeat on a major nuclear arms program by voting against procurement of the controversial MX missile. The House also rejected an administration plan to produce chemical weapons.

The Senate voted for production of the MX, but it barred spending on the missile until some compromise could be reached on a basing mode.

In a move to protect the oversight authority of its committees, the House passed a resolution citing Environmental Protection Agency Administrator Anne M. Gorsuch for contempt of Congress for refusing, on Reagan's orders, to turn over documents subpoenaed by a subcommittee. The vote culminated a confrontation that had mounted all year between the House and the Reagan administration over enforcement of environmental laws.

Even some administration "victories" were hardly that. Passage by both houses of legislation raising $98.3 billion in taxes over three years was more a tribute to efforts by congressional Republicans to reduce the budget deficit. Administration support for the tax hikes was reluctant and belated.

The House agreed to weaken a measure that would have forced Reagan to lift economic sanctions against the Soviet Union, but the three-vote margin showed strong congressional unhappiness with administration policy.

And the administration secured House rejection of a nuclear freeze resolution — but by only two votes.

So-called social issues made little headway in either chamber. Faced with a filibuster, the Senate voted to lay aside an anti-abortion measure.

Congress did pass a Reagan-backed bill to raise taxes for repairing the nation's highways and mass transit systems, but it did so in large part due to bipartisan recognition of the need for an economic stimulus and jobs initiative before year's end.

The House and Senate also voted themselves a little economic stimulus.

The House agreed to raise members' salaries and the Senate voted to eliminate limits on senators' outside earnings.

Senate Key Votes

1. Fiscal 1983 Budget

Congress gave short shrift to President Reagan's fiscal 1983 budget, in marked contrast to its ratification of Reagan's initial budget in 1981. But it took the lawmakers months to fashion their own substitute for the president's blueprint, which had called for further sweeping cuts in domestic spending combined with unprecedented increases in military programs.

Senate Republicans ultimately succeeded May 21 in pushing through their fiscal 1983 budget proposal (S Con Res 92) on a near party-line vote of 49-43: R 46-2; D 3-41 (ND 1-28, SD 2-13).

Senate action followed the collapse of prolonged efforts by White House and bipartisan congressional negotiators to draft a compromise plan. The White House agreed to some concessions only after the Republican-controlled Senate Budget Committee unanimously repudiated the president's budget and prepared to report a budget resolution the administration did not support.

Senate Republicans successfully fended off Democratic attempts to restore funding for many domestic programs and to repeal the third installment of the 1981

individual income tax cut. But in order to secure passage, GOP leaders acceded to pressure from moderate Republicans and partisan sniping from Democrats to eliminate from the resolution reported by the Budget Committee a proposal to reduce the cost of Social Security benefits by $40 billion over three years.

The Senate-passed resolution called for $784.3 billion in spending, $668.4 billion in revenues and a $115.9 billion deficit in fiscal 1983. The measure included reconciliation instructions that required Senate and House committees to recommend legislative savings to meet the resolution's deficit reduction targets.

The House June 10 adopted a Republican substitute for President Reagan's fiscal 1983 budget by a narrow 220-207 margin. *(House key vote 3)*

2. Emergency Housing Aid

Senate Republicans signaled their willingness to break with President Reagan over providing aid to the troubled economy when they voted May 27 for a $5.1 billion housing aid program. Despite Reagan's strong opposition to the housing industry "bailout," the Senate approved the amendment offered by Richard G. Lugar, R-Ind., by a vote of 69-23: R 29-20; D 40-3 (ND 27-1, SD 13-2).

The amendment to the fiscal 1982 "urgent" supplemental appropriations bill (HR 5922) would have provided mortgage interest rate assistance to buyers of new homes. It would have allowed families with incomes of up to $37,000 a year to get subsidies to lower their interest rate by up to 4 percentage points on mortgages of up to $77,600.

Under heavy political pressure to do something about high unemployment in an election year, Lugar and other Republican backers of the amendment argued that high interest rates were preventing all but the wealthiest families from being able to buy a new home. They said interest rate subsidies would spur new construction, create up to 700,000 new jobs and help lead the economy out of its deep recession.

Although the aid was reduced to $3 billion in conference with the House, which had passed a $1 billion housing measure, Reagan followed through on his threat to veto the bill, and the housing program never went into effect. *(House key vote 1)*

3. Tobacco Price Supports

The perils-of-Pauline existence of the tobacco price-support program was illustrated by a July 14 Senate vote of 49-47: R 29-23; D 20-24 (ND 7-23, SD 13-1) to preserve the program's permanent status in law.

The vote came the week before the Senate soundly overrode tobacco state efforts to kill a plan to double the excise taxes on cigarettes and then adopted a conciliatory compromise to repeal the increase on Sept. 30, 1985.

At issue July 14 was an industry-backed bill (HR 6590) designed to silence tobacco's critics by making new assessments on tobacco growers to help pay the costs of the price-support program. The vote killed an amendment by Sen. Thomas F. Eagleton, D-Mo., that would have ended tobacco's permanent authorization by continuing it just through 1985, when other major commodity programs were scheduled to expire.

Permanent status in the past helped tobacco allies evade debate and votes on the program. Nevertheless, foes had become more and more vocal, criticizing what they called a politically protected "feudal" system of federal allotments and quotas, which amounted to licenses to grow the lucrative crop.

In 1981, critics forced a series of votes on the program. At one point the Senate came within 11 votes of canceling the program altogether, and the 1981 farm bill (PL 97-98) required that the program be operated at no net cost to the Treasury.

4. Western Water Law

Moving to end a longstanding fight between environmentalists and Western farmers, Congress rewrote an 80-year-old law governing the use of federal irrigation water on private farm land. The bill cleared by Congress raised the price farmers pay for some of the water and greatly increased the number of federally irrigated acres an individual could farm.

Advocates said the changes recognized modern farming practices in Western states that were served by federal water reclamation projects. They also claimed that the new law would encourage water conservation and the development of smaller farms, as environmentalists wanted. But angry environmental groups were not satisfied and called the measure a sellout to large corporate farms, some of which controlled thousands of cheaply irrigated acres.

Acting on those objections, Sen. Howard M. Metzenbaum, D-Ohio, delayed floor action on the measure for several days, using quorum calls and other dilatory tactics. He broke off his mini-filibuster only when bill sponsors agreed to offer a compromise amendment raising prices for some of the water above those of the committee bill and reducing new farm acreage limits somewhat. On July 16, the Senate adopted the compromise by a 60-5 vote.

With the logjam broken, the Senate then passed the bill (HR 5539) by a 49-13 vote, clearing the way for a House-Senate conference and enactment of the law: R 30-3; D 19-10 (ND 12-10, SD 7-0).

5. Tax/Spending Reconciliation

One of the most difficult pieces of legislation to be enacted in the 97th Congress was a bill (HR 4961) to raise taxes $98.3 billion and to cut spending $17.5 billion over three years.

Not only did it come shortly before the midterm elections, but support of the measure meant an about-face for many members from the tax-cutting themes they had espoused the year before. In addition, provisions calling for higher tobacco taxes and the withholding of tax from interest and dividend income proved particularly troublesome to many members.

But in the end, Senate Finance Committee Chairman Robert Dole, R-Kan., was able to push a carefully crafted package through the reluctant Senate. He did so in part by threatening to take the bill back to committee and substitute even more unpopular tax hikes for any provisions defeated on the floor.

Members were caught in a bind since they already had voted to raise the $98.3 billion as a deficit-reducing measure in the fiscal 1983 budget resolution (S Con Res 92) adopted May 21. *(Senate key vote 1)*

The final vote on passage of the bill early July 23 was close — 50-47: R 49-3; D 1-44 (ND 0-30, SD 1-14). Democrats, with the exception of Independent Harry F. Byrd Jr., Va., who caucused with the minority party, did nothing to help Republicans out of their fiscal predicament.

That left the House with two choices: to come up with its own tax-increase package or go directly to conference with the Senate. By a 208-197 vote, the House July 28

opted to proceed to conference. *(House key vote 5)*

6. Balanced Budget Constitutional Amendment

Balanced-budget lobbying groups and Senate fiscal conservatives scored a victory Aug. 4 as the Senate approved a proposed constitutional amendment (S J Res 58) requiring a balanced federal budget except in times of declared war or when three-fifths of the Congress agreed to deficit spending. The vote was also a victory for President Reagan, who endorsed the amendment even as he presided over record deficits.

The vote was 69-31, two more than the two-thirds of those present and voting (67 in this case) required to pass a constitutional amendment: R 47-7; D 22-24 (ND 9-22, SD 13-2).

Despite election-year jitters and pressure from Reagan, the House subsequently defeated the balanced budget amendment 236-187, 46 votes short of the two-thirds required. *(House key vote 9)*

S J Res 58 won the backing of Robert Dole, R-Kan., chairman of the Finance Committee, and Pete V. Domenici, R-N.M., chairman of the Budget Committee, although Domenici did not support the measure until he secured a package of amendments he said added more flexibility to the amendment. Appropriations Chairman Mark O. Hatfield, R-Ore., also voted for the measure.

Proponents contended that a constitutional amendment was needed to force fiscal discipline upon Congress. But opponents said the amendment was unworkable and complained that while Congress would have to adopt a balanced budget, the president could submit a document with deficit spending.

Opponents conceded at the outset, however, that their fight was a tough one. They said many senators were unwilling to oppose the amendment publicly because it would look like a vote against the concept of balanced budgets.

7. Cap on Federal COLAs

Efforts to limit automatic cost-of-living adjustments (COLAs) in federal retirement programs illustrated the difficulties confronting Congress as it set out to curb spending under government entitlement programs, which guarantee a certain level of benefits to all persons who meet the requirements set by law.

Although the fiscal 1983 budget resolution (S Con Res 92) had recommended a 4 percent cap on COLAs for federal and military retirees to meet its deficit reduction requirements, a more modest limit on COLA spending barely squeaked through Congress as part of the Omnibus Reconciliation Act of 1982.

The Senate Aug. 4 narrowly defeated by a 48-51 vote — R 10-44; D 38-7 (ND 30-1, SD 8-6) — an amendment to eliminate a 4 percent COLA cap for federal and military retirees from its version of the reconciliation bill (S 2774).

The Senate action came one day after the House snubbed its reconciliation instructions by refusing to impose the COLA cap. Senate-House conferees ultimately settled on a plan to delay federal COLA increases by one month in each of the next three years and to cut in half COLAs for federal retirees under age 62, for three-year budget savings of $4.1 billion.

Budget leaders applauded the move as a first step toward controlling automatic increases in Social Security and other federal benefit programs. "This is a historic change," said Senate Budget Committee Chairman Pete V. Domenici, R-N.M.

8. Veto Override

Smacking President Reagan with his first significant budget defeat, Congress Sept. 10 overrode his Aug. 28 veto of a $14.2 billion supplemental appropriations bill (HR 6863) that he called a "budget buster."

Reagan objected that the bill cut his request for defense spending while providing $918 million too much for social spending — money he had not requested and some of which he had previously vetoed.

Members of Congress denied the bill was a budget buster. They pointed out that it was nearly $2 billion under Reagan's total request for additional fiscal 1982 funding. Congress, they said, had simply put its own stamp on the spending priorities, allowing less for the military and more for education and jobs for senior citizens.

Returning from its Labor Day recess, the House voted to override the veto Sept. 9 by a vote of 301-117. *(House key vote 7)*

Worried by the unexpectedly strong override vote in the House, the White House lobbied furiously to get senators to stick with the president. It even arranged to have several flown back to Washington for the vote. But despite Reagan's personal pleas to many senators and the presence of Vice President George Bush in the chamber, the Republican-controlled Senate Sept. 10 also voted to override. The margin was as close as it could get — 60-30, the exact two-thirds majority required: R 21-26; D 39-4 (ND 31-0, SD 8-4).

Appropriations Committee Chairman Mark O. Hatfield, R-Ore., who had caught a late-night flight from Oregon to lead the Senate fight for the override, said Reagan had acted on "very poor advice."

Of the 11 Republican senators up for re-election in 1982, seven voted against Reagan, two voted with him and two were absent.

9. Abortion

Efforts to pass anti-abortion legislation came to a halt in the Senate Sept. 15 after members grew weary of a filibuster and voted to lay aside a proposal designed to virtually ban abortion.

The vote marked the end of an 18-month drive by a handful of senators and interest groups who had hoped that the Republican takeover of the Senate in the 97th Congress would result in legislation sharply restricting a woman's right to an abortion.

The showdown came on an anti-abortion amendment by Sen. Jesse Helms, R-N.C., to unrelated debt limit legislation (H J Res 520). A week-long effort by President Reagan in support of the Helms proposal was to no avail, as one-third of the Senate's Republicans voted with a majority of its Democrats to kill the amendment.

The vote on the motion to table, and thus kill, the Helms anti-abortion amendment, which technically was an amendment to a separate Helms school prayer amendment to the debt bill, was 47-46: R 18-33; D 29-13 (ND 22-7, SD 7-6).

The underlying school prayer amendment was derailed Sept. 23 when the Senate by a 79-16 vote adopted a motion by Majority Leader Howard H. Baker Jr., R-Tenn., to recommit the debt ceiling measure to the Finance Committee with instructions to strip off all amendments.

Throughout the six-week Senate debate on abortion and school prayer, opponents labeled both Helms amendments "court-stripping" proposals, charging they would

unwisely and unconstitutionally infringe upon the power of the federal courts to review laws enacted by the states and Congress.

10. Senators' Income Limits

In 1977, as a condition for taking a $12,900 pay raise, both House and Senate agreed to strict ethics codes for members. One provision in both codes limited the outside earnings of senators and representatives to 15 percent of their salaries.

This limit was to apply only to earned income, such as honoraria for speeches or legal work, not to unearned income, such as dividend payments. A separate 1976 law (PL 94-283) had limited the net amount members could receive in honoraria for speeches, appearances or articles to $25,000 annually.

However, in 1979, when the 15 percent limit on outside income in the Senate was to take effect, members voted to delay the effective date until Jan. 1, 1983.

And in 1981, Congress repealed the $25,000 honoraria limit. Some senators earned as much as $48,000 that year.

As the 1983 effective date for the 15 percent limit approached, the Senate Dec. 14, with little debate, approved a resolution (S Res 512) abolishing that restriction as well. The vote was 54-38: R 39-12; D 15-26 (ND 9-19, SD 6-7).

Fourteen senators who had voted for the 15 percent limit in 1977 switched in 1982 and voted to abolish it.

No House action was required. The change meant that senators could earn as much as they chose beyond their Senate salary by giving speeches, practicing law or any other legal means.

The Senate's decision also laid the groundwork for a salary deal with the House. As part of the second continuing resolution (H J Res 631), representatives, who retained a 30 percent limit on outside income, got a 15 percent pay raise. Senators got no raise but had no ceilings on outside income. *(House key vote 12)*

11. MX Missile

President Reagan won the Senate round of his battle to begin production of the MX missile, but only after he had substantially compromised with congressional critics of the so-called "dense pack" basing method.

On Nov. 22, Reagan proposed deployment of 100 MXs in heavily armored underground silos close together. He argued that attacking Soviet missile warheads would destroy each other while leaving most of the MXs unscathed.

He argued that the new, more powerful land-based MX missile was needed to offset Moscow's arsenal of ICBM warheads, which were more numerous and more powerful than current U.S. weapons. He also maintained that the Russians would agree to reduce their nuclear arsenals only if confronted by clear indications that the United States would match Soviet forces if no arms control agreement was reached.

The House voted Dec. 7 against appropriating money for procurement of the missile. *(House key vote 11)*

On Dec. 15, the Senate Appropriations Committee adopted 16-12 an amendment that left the MX procurement money in the second fiscal 1983 continuing resolution (H J Res 631) that contained appropriations for the Defense Department, but barred its expenditure until Congress approved an MX basing method by concurrent resolution.

The White House and senior senators of both parties

who supported MX then drafted an amendment to the committee provision that would guarantee congressional action within 45 days of the time the president submitted a report to Congress on dense pack and various alternative basing methods. This would preclude a filibuster against a resolution to approve a basing method.

On Dec. 17, the Senate adopted the administration-sanctioned amendment 56-42: R 41-12; D 15-30 (ND 6-24, SD 9-6).

12. Clinch River Breeder Reactor

Twice in 1982, the Senate by a one-vote margin chose to continue funding for the controversial Clinch River nuclear breeder reactor.

The votes were a test of strength for Senate Majority Leader Howard H. Baker Jr., R-Tenn., whose state was the home of the Clinch River site. Support for the project in both houses of Congress had been declining in recent years, and traditionally pro-nuclear conservative groups such as the Heritage Foundation had gone on record against it.

"If it were not for the majority leader, if it were not being built in his state, it would long ago have been terminated," Dale Bumpers, D-Ark., said Dec. 17, after the Senate upheld the project for the second time. Baker reportedly herded some of his Republican colleagues who were reluctant to take a stand on the issue onto the Senate floor during the final minutes of the vote.

That vote came just three days after the House had voted 217-196 to kill Clinch River. *(House key vote 13)*

A compromise agreement later was worked out in conference that continued funding at the 1982 level for engineering and site preparation but prohibited construction of any major facilities.

The Clinch River project, authorized in 1970, was designed to demonstrate the feasibility of breeder reactors — nuclear power reactors that run on plutonium and create, as a byproduct, more plutonium than they consume. The reactor originally was scheduled to be completed in 1983 but because of controversy and delays, ground was not broken until September 1982. Official cost estimates of the project soared from $700 million to $3.6 billion, while the need for the reactor became more difficult to demonstrate.

The Senate first took up the issue Sept. 29, when it defeated a Bumpers amendment to delete Clinch River funds from the first fiscal 1983 continuing appropriations resolution (H J Res 599). After losing by a single vote then, opponents hoped they could win the vote on the second continuing resolution (H J Res 631) in December. But the Appropriations Committee amendment reinstating the Clinch River funds, which had been deleted by the House, passed 49-48: R 38-14; D 11-34 (ND 4-26, SD 7-8).

13. Doctors, Federal Trade Commission

Congressional allies of the Federal Trade Commission (FTC) blocked an attempt to exempt doctors and other professionals from agency jurisdiction.

Their success came seven months after both the House and Senate overwhelmingly vetoed an FTC rule requiring used-car dealers to disclose information about auto defects.

The American Medical Association (AMA) had lobbied successfully to include the exemption for doctors and other state-regulated professionals in a House-passed authorization bill and a Senate committee bill. The AMA said that Congress had not given the FTC authority to regulate doctors and that the agency had interfered with quality of care issues.

Administration officials, the FTC and others argued that the FTC had authority to regulate anti-competitive business practices of professionals, such as price-setting and boycotts, and should be allowed to retain that power.

Opponents of the exemption blocked it on three fronts: an FTC authorization, a regular appropriations bill and the second fiscal 1983 continuing appropriations resolution.

They prevented Senate consideration of an FTC authorization bill that contained the exemption, thereby avoiding a House-Senate conference on the authorization.

Then because there was no authorization, the supporters succeeded in getting the House to delete FTC funds from the regular fiscal 1983 State, Justice, Commerce appropriations (HR 6957). That prevented new FTC restrictions, including the exemption for professionals, from being attached to the appropriations bill.

However, the second fiscal 1983 continuing appropriations resolution then before the Senate (H J Res 631) included FTC monies and continued some existing curbs, such as the congressional veto over agency rules. The measure also contained a provision by Warren B. Rudman, R-N.H., allowing the FTC to regulate doctors as long as it did not interfere with state laws governing professional training and experience requirements. Rudman, an opponent of the exemption for professionals, argued that no group should be above the law.

In a session that began Dec. 16, James A. McClure, R-Idaho, offered an amendment to bar the use of FTC funds to regulate professionals. The Senate by a vote of 59-37 adopted a Rudman motion to table, or kill, the McClure amendment: R 31-21; D 28-16 (ND 23-7, SD 5-9).

That allowed the Senate to go to conference with the House with only the less restrictive Rudman language under consideration. When the provision was dropped by the conferees, FTC supporters claimed victory, as did the AMA, which opposed the Rudman provision because even with its qualifications, it gave explicit congressional approval to FTC regulation of professionals.

14. Job Creation

Reacting to a mounting unemployment rate and Democratic election gains, the Senate Appropriations Committee added $1.2 billion for jobs under a variety of public works programs to its version of the second fiscal 1983 continuing appropriations resolution (H J Res 631).

Appropriations Committee Chairman Mark O. Hatfield, R-Ore., argued that "this was the only opportunity the Senate will have" in the lame-duck session to show its concern about jobs.

But Budget Committee Chairman Pete V. Domenici, R-N.M., called the jobs money "pork-barrel personified." He said the Senate should not engage in a bidding war with the House, which had included $5.4 billion for job creation in its version of the funding bill.

Domenici, along with Majority Leader Howard H. Baker Jr., R-Tenn., and Finance Committee Chairman Robert Dole, R-Kan., sought to delete the $1.2 billion for jobs during floor action early Dec. 17. Their amendment was defeated 46-50: R 39-12; D 7-38 (ND 3-27, SD 4-11).

In the House, a Republican motion to recommit the continuing resolution to the Appropriations Committee with instructions to delete the $5.4 billion for jobs programs was rejected 191-215. *(House key vote 14)*

Although both the Senate and House versions of the continuing resolution thus included money for jobs pro-

grams, conferees bowed to President Reagan's veto threats and dropped the jobs funding from the final measure.

15. Highway-Gas Tax Bill

A series of filibusters and a host of amendments threatened Senate passage of a bill to raise gasoline taxes for the first time since 1959. The legislation (HR 6211) increasing highway taxes to finance highway, bridge and mass transit improvements had been wrapped in the aura of a jobs bill, winning both bipartisan congressional support and the backing of the president.

In contrast to the House, which had comfortably approved the package one day after a 197-194 vote Dec. 6 on adoption of a rule for its consideration, the Senate staggered through days and nights of marathon sessions punctuated by bitter debate before passing its version of the bill in a session that began Dec. 20. *(House key vote 10)*

The filibusters started as soon as the Senate began considering the bill Dec. 10. It was unclear whether there would be enough time in the lame-duck session for the Senate to pass the bill and go to conference with the House.

Supporters contended that the bill was necessary to complete the Interstate Highway System, repair the nation's deteriorating transportation infrastructure and help create more than 300,000 new jobs. Under the measure, the gas tax was increased a nickel, to a total of 9 cents a gallon, to raise an additional $5.5 billion a year to help pay for the improvements. Heavy trucks also had to pay higher taxes.

Four Republicans — Jesse Helms, N.C., John P. East, N.C., Gordon J. Humphrey, N.H., and Don Nickles, Okla. — objected to the tax increases, contending that a recession was a bad time to hike taxes.

Their tactics forced a series of time-consuming parliamentary manuevers that left tempers frayed and prompted intensified lobbying by the administration and highway interests. Finally, the Senate passed the bill 56-34: R 35-15; D 21-19 (ND 14-12, SD 7-7).

The Senate version authorized about $70 billion for highways through fiscal 1987 and about $12 billion for mass transit through fiscal 1985, and increased gas and other highway taxes.

A conference report authorizing more than $71 billion for highways and mass transit over four years was adopted by the House Dec. 21. Filibusters continued to delay Senate action until Dec. 23, when it adopted the report.

House Key Votes

1. Emergency Housing Aid

Facing growing pressure to do something for the recession-hit housing industry, House Democratic leaders agreed to back a $1 billion mortgage interest rate subsidy program. The measure, added as an amendment to the fiscal 1982 "urgent" supplemental appropriations bill (HR 5922), was adopted May 12 by a vote of 343-67: R 128-52; D 215-15 (ND 149-6, SD 66-9).

The amendment was the first in a series of job-creation proposals pushed by House Democrats in 1982 in an effort to counter rapidly rising unemployment.

Actually, the Democratic leadership initially did not want to include the program in the supplemental funding bill, which contained a number of time-sensitive appropriations needed to keep government agencies in operation. President Reagan opposed the housing "bailout," and it

seemed destined to lead to a veto of the whole bill.

But the amendment was needed to forestall House approval of a Republican-backed amendment that threatened one of the pet projects of Majority Leader Jim Wright, D-Texas: the synthetic fuels program. Thomas B. Evans Jr., R-Del., and Tom Corcoran, R-Ill., were proposing an amendment to take $1 billion from funds already appropriated for the synfuels program, to be used to create low-interest housing loans.

When it appeared that the House would approve the Evans-Corcoran amendment, the Democrats came up with their own housing aid program that did not take money from synfuels. With strong lobbying support from the housing industry, the amendment carried easily.

The Senate subsequently passed a $5.1 billion housing aid program. *(Senate key vote 2)*

Conferees compromised on a $3 billion program, but Reagan carried out his veto threat and the program never became law.

2. Medicare Funding

In a clear-cut guns vs. butter vote that led to defeat of the first fiscal 1983 budget resolution (H Con Res 345), the House May 27 agreed to increase Medicare outlays by $4.85 billion while cutting defense spending by the same amount.

The 228-196 vote — R 64-125; D 164-71 (ND 136-20, SD 28-51) — came on an amendment offered by Mary Rose Oakar, D-Ohio, to the administration-backed substitute for the resolution.

Democrats saw in the Oakar amendment a chance to cast their Republican colleagues as people who would "choose a 40-year-old battleship over their 80-year-old mother," as one Democrat put it. Republicans who opposed defense cuts were nonetheless reluctant to be portrayed as voting against the elderly in an election year.

House Minority Leader Robert H. Michel, R-Ill., said adoption of the Oakar amendment was the "margin of difference" that meant defeat for the GOP budget plan. The Oakar amendment also was added to the other major budget alternatives the House was considering, all of which went down to defeat May 27-28.

3. Fiscal 1983 Budget

On its second attempt to pass a budget resolution, the House June 10 adopted a Republican substitute for President Reagan's fiscal 1983 budget, which had been sent to the floor by the House Budget Committee (H Con Res 352). This was the final repudiation of the Reagan budget.

The Senate May 21 had adopted its own version of a fiscal 1983 budget resolution by a vote of 49-43. *(Senate key vote 1)*

By squeezing the deficit below $100 billion and maintaining party discipline, House Republican leaders eked out a narrow 220-207 — R 174-15; D 46-192 (ND 9-151, SD 37-41) — victory for the substitute, named after the ranking Republican member of the Budget Committee, Delbert L. Latta, Ohio. The specter of continued stalemate and fiscal chaos helped assure approval of the resolution, which subsequently passed by a 219-206 margin.

The measure called for $765.17 billion in spending, $665.90 billion in revenues and a $99.27 billion deficit in fiscal 1983. The House resolution followed the same pattern as the Senate version — making further cuts in entitlement and discretionary domestic spending while allowing sizable increases for defense and maintaining the third installment of the 1981 individual income tax cut.

4. Chemical Weapons

The House July 22 rejected an administration move to begin production of a new type of lethal, chemical weapons called "binary munitions."

The administration maintained that the new weapons were needed to prod the Soviet Union to negotiate a chemical weapons ban and to deter use of the large Soviet chemical weapons arsenal. Current U.S. chemical weapons were inadequate for either purpose, the administration argued, because they were becoming unsafe to handle due to internal chemical reactions.

But opponents of production of binary weapons warned that production of the new arms would surrender the valuable propaganda leverage the United States had gained by abstaining from chemical weapons production for the past 13 years. Most of the opponents also maintained that the new weapons were militarily unnecessary. Existing chemical weapons stocks were sufficient to force enemy troops to don clumsy and tiring protective suits and masks, they said.

The showdown came during debate on the fiscal 1983 defense authorization bill (HR 6030) when the House in effect rejected the administration position 192-225: R 112-72; D 80-153 (ND 27-132, SD 53-21).

5. Tax Increases

With an election looming in November, House Democrats gladly let the Republican-controlled Senate take the lead in putting together a tax-increase bill to help reduce the federal budget deficit. *(Senate key vote 5)*

Even though the Constitution requires all tax legislation to originate in the House, Ways and Means Committee Chairman Dan Rostenkowski, D-Ill., made it clear early on that he saw the deficit as a Republican problem and raising taxes as a Republican responsibility.

When the Senate did produce its own package July 22, it was attached to a minor House-passed measure (HR 4961) to address the technical niceties of the Constitution.

That left the House with two choices: to come up with its own tax-increase package or to go directly to conference with the Senate. After a short-lived attempt to produce a tax-hike plan within Ways and Means, Rostenkowski decided it was hopeless. Even if one could pass the committee, floor passage looked doubtful.

The committee agreed to bypass the House and go directly to conference on the Senate bill. The House agreed July 28 by a vote of 208-197: R 44-137; D 164-60 (ND 116-35, SD 48-25).

Despite considerable rhetoric that the House was shirking its constitutional duties, many members were relieved that they would not have their fingerprints on the politically troublesome legislation.

6. Nuclear Freeze

The administration averted by the narrowest of margins a major symbolic rebuff to its nuclear arms policy when the House Aug. 5 rejected a call for a nuclear weapons "freeze."

The freeze proposal had its roots in a far-flung grassroots movement that had swelled through the spring, fueled largely by doubts that the administration was seriously committed to seeking arms control agreements with Moscow.

As reported by the House Foreign Affairs Committee in late June, the freeze resolution (H J Res 521) called on the United States and Soviet Union to decide "when and

how to achieve a mutual verifiable freeze" on the testing, production and deployment of nuclear arms.

This was a direct challenge to the administration's position that the U.S.-Soviet nuclear balance currently was tilted to Moscow's advantage.

The administration and congressional backers drafted an alternative that also called for a "freeze," but with the qualification that it be at "equal and substantially reduced levels," thus endorsing Reagan's position that the current U.S. nuclear weapons deficit would have to be erased in any arms control agreement.

Despite ferocious White House lobbying, Reagan's position prevailed in the House by a margin of only two votes. A switch by one member would have created a tie that would have defeated the administration's alternative.

The administration-backed substitute was approved 204-202: R 151-27; D 53-175 (ND 11-149, SD 42-26).

7. Veto Override

When President Reagan vetoed a $14.2 billion fiscal 1982 supplemental appropriations bill (HR 6863) Aug. 28, he called it a budget buster. While cutting his request for defense spending, he said, the measure contained $918 million for social spending that he had not requested and some of which had been in previously vetoed bills.

But members of Congress insisted the president was simply wrong in his accounting. They noted that the bill was nearly $2 billion under his total request for additional fiscal 1982 funding, and said they supported increased funding for education and for jobs for senior citizens.

When the House returned from its Labor Day recess, a sizable bloc of angry Republicans joined unified Democrats in supplying the two-thirds majority for the House to override the veto. They did it with 22 votes to spare. The Sept. 9 vote to override the president was 301-117: R 81-104; D 220-13 (ND 157-1, SD 63-12).

The Senate made the override stick the next day by a vote of 60-30. It was Reagan's first significant budget defeat. *(Senate key vote 8)*

The president tried to block the override in the House, promising members he would sign a subsequent bill containing employment money for the elderly and that he would not seek additional funds for defense. But the promises came too late for many members who had already committed themselves while in their districts to vote to override. Senior citizen groups and education organizations had lobbied hard for the override.

Helping to lead the House effort against Reagan was Rep. Silvio O. Conte, Mass., the senior Republican on the Appropriations Committee. Calling the veto an affront to Congress, Conte said, "You just don't have 435 robots up here in Congress that are going to vote in lockstep."

8. Pipeline Sanctions

A close vote in the House of Representatives helped prod President Reagan to drop his most visible effort to punish the Soviet Union for its interference in Poland. The vote may also have sparked a reassessment by Congress and the administration of the effectiveness of conducting economic war for political purposes.

The key vote was on Sept. 29, when the House voted 206-203 to weaken a bill (HR 6838) that would have forced Reagan to lift the most controversial of a series of economic sanctions he had imposed on the Soviet Union. A broad range of members in both parties complained that the sanctions hurt American workers and businesses more than

the Soviets. The breakdown on the vote was R 124-57; D 82-146 (ND 41-111, SD 41-35).

The closeness of the vote demonstrated the depth of congressional unhappiness with an important element of Reagan's foreign policy. Administration officials lobbied vigorously against the bill, arguing that passage of it would undercut negotiations then under way between the United States and its European allies on trade with the Soviets.

The sanctions prohibited American companies, their foreign subsidiaries and foreign companies using U.S. licenses from selling to the Soviet Union equipment or technology for the transmission or refining of oil and gas. One goal of the sanctions was to prevent the Soviets from using U.S. technology to build a 2,600-mile natural gas pipeline from Siberia to Western Europe.

Reagan himself lifted the pipeline-related sanctions on Nov. 13, saying they had accomplished the purpose of demonstrating U.S. concern with Soviet pressure on Poland. Reagan also said the United States and its Western allies had agreed to conduct a study of ways to limit future trade that bolstered the Soviet economy.

Administration critics, however, said Reagan was merely heeding the signal he had been given by the House vote: that there was little political support for the sanctions, which had failed to change Soviet behavior and had ruptured relations between the United States and its closest allies. American business leaders said the failure of the sanctions on those counts should make the administration more hesitant in the future to use trade as a political weapon.

9. Balanced Budget Constitutional Amendment

Despite pressure from President Reagan and pre-election jitters, the House Oct. 1 rejected a proposed constitutional amendment to require a balanced federal budget (H J Res 350).

The vote on the measure was 236-187, 46 short of the two-thirds majority of those present and voting (282 in this case) required to pass a constitutional amendment: R 167-20; D 69-167 (ND 12-147, SD 57-20).

The vote ended a three-day struggle that featured some arm-twisting by Vice President George Bush and an appearance by President Reagan Sept. 30 to drum up support for the amendment.

The maneuvering had begun in earnest Sept. 29 when a group of Republicans led by Bush and Barber B. Conable Jr., R-N.Y., rounded up the last 16 signatures on a discharge petition that pried H J Res 350 from a hostile House Judiciary Committee that had kept the legislation buried for a year.

The Senate Aug. 4 had approved its own version of a balanced budget amendment by a 69-31 vote, two more than the two-thirds required. *(Senate key vote 6)*

Giving impetus to the drive for a balanced budget amendment was a seven-year-old effort by outside groups led by the National Taxpayers Union to force the calling of a constitutional convention to consider such a proposal.

Under Article V of the Constitution, a convention must be called if two-thirds of the states (34) request one. At the end of 1982, 31 states had made such a request, although there was no agreement on whether all 31 convention calls were valid.

10. Highway-Gas Tax Bill

The opposition of the trucking industry to substantial increases in highway-use taxes for heavy trucks posed a

strong threat to House passage of legislation to raise funds for highway, bridge and mass transit improvements.

The bill raised fuel taxes a nickel, for a total of 9 cents a gallon, and increased the maximum highway use tax for an 80,000-pound truck to $2,000, up from $240.

Truckers, contending that the tax increases were too severe, lobbied intensely against the bill. Although there was general backing for the legislation (HR 6211), a fragile coalition of cities, road builders, public transit operators, Republicans, Democrats, administration officials and others was not sure that the House would be able to pass the measure.

Members opposing the truck or fuel taxes attacked the rule (H Res 620) because it allowed amendments to the highway and transit portions of the bill but not to the tax title. They almost succeeded in blocking floor consideration. The rule was adopted Dec. 6 by 197-194: R 59-114; D 138-80 (ND 112-34, SD 26-46).

The bill's supporters, who argued that significant changes in the taxes would jeopardize passage, breathed easier when the House accepted the tax title by a vote of 236-169 at 12:30 a.m., Dec. 7. The House later passed the bill by a 262-143 vote.

In the Senate, a filibuster by a handful of opponents led by Jesse Helms, R-N.C., delayed action on the gas tax bill until just before Christmas. But the measure finally passed Dec. 21 by a 56-34 vote. *(Senate key vote 15)*

11. MX Missile

The House vote Dec. 7 against initial procurement of MX missiles marked the first time that either house of Congress had voted against a major nuclear arms program requested by a president.

Despite strong White House objections, the House deleted from the fiscal 1983 defense appropriations bill (HR 7355) $988 million earmarked for procurement of the first five production line versions of the MX.

The large House majority included liberals who long had opposed MX in any form, for fear that it would elicit from Moscow a further escalation in the arms race. But they were joined by moderates and conservatives who were alarmed at the cost of Reagan's defense buildup and suspicious of the technical feasibility of the so-called "dense pack" basing method for the missile.

In this technique, announced by Reagan on Nov. 22, 100 MXs would be placed close together in heavily armored underground silos. The administration argued that explosions from attacking Soviet missile warheads would destroy other Soviet missiles while leaving most of the MXs unscathed.

Reagan argued that the new, more powerful land-based missile was needed to offset Moscow's arsenal of ICBM warheads, which are more numerous and more powerful than current U.S. weapons. And he said that the new missile was needed to give the Russians an incentive to agree to nuclear arms reductions.

The vote against MX procurement was 245-176: R 50-138; D 195-38 (ND 151-7, SD 44-31).

The Senate Dec. 17 returned MX procurement money to the second fiscal 1983 continuing appropriations resolution but barred its expenditure unless Congress approved a basing mode. *(Senate key vote 11)*

12. House Pay Raise

After more than three years without a pay raise, Congress in December 1982 gave House members a 15 percent

increase, bringing salaries to $69,800 a year. Senators stayed at the old rate of $60,662.50.

In October, as part of the first fiscal 1983 continuing appropriations resolution (H J Res 599) Congress had voted to cap its pay, blocking what members then believed would be a 4 percent raise. The resolution, however, was to expire Dec. 17.

While Congress was in its post-election recess, confusion arose over the exact size of the raise members would get if the cap were lifted. The General Accounting Office ruled Dec. 10 that the increase actually would be 27.2 percent. The higher figure included several cost-of-living raises from previous years that Congress had voted not to take.

The issue came to a House vote Dec. 14 as part of the second fiscal 1983 continuing resolution (H J Res 631). Supporters of a raise offered an amendment limiting it to 15 percent — about $9,100. Faced with a raise of either 27.2 percent or 15 percent, the House supported the lower figure on a 303-109 vote.

But then Bob Traxler, D-Mich., offered an amendment to continue the freeze on congressional pay, keeping salaries at $60,662.50.

Only because of substantial help from lame-duck members, who no longer had to answer to the voters, the Traxler amendment failed on a tie, 208-208: R 121-65; D 87-143 (ND 46-109, SD 41-34).

The 71 lame ducks who voted on the Traxler amendment opposed it by 2-to-1, 24-47. While Republicans voted 121-65 for the amendment, 48 Republican lame ducks voted 21-27 against it.

The pay raise for House members but not senators was contained in the final version of the bill. The Senate agreed not to take a raise for itself, but senators retained their prerogative to earn unlimited amounts in outside income. *(Senate key vote 10)*

The result was the first time that representatives had made more than senators. Since the 1st Congress in 1789, members of both chambers had been paid the same, except for one year, 1795-96, when senators were paid $7 a day and representatives $6.

13. Clinch River Breeder Reactor

More than a decade of House support for the controversial Clinch River nuclear breeder reactor ended Dec. 14 when members voted 217-196 to deny funds for the project.

Environmentalists were jubilant. They had opposed the project since its inception, questioning its safety and arguing that it would increase supplies of plutonium that could be used to manufacture nuclear weapons.

But it was budget concerns that finally led the House to reverse its stance on the breeder. Expressing the sentiment of many members who had backed the project previously but voted against it in 1982, Phil Gramm, D-Texas, said, "I have supported Clinch River since I first came to Congress. But as we look at the budget deficit, we have got to set a new higher standard for spending."

The House action was reversed by the Senate three days later, by a one-vote margin, but it nevertheless marked a watershed in the history of the breeder reactor. *(Senate key vote 12)*

The Clinch River project, located near Oak Ridge, Tenn., was authorized in 1970. It was designed to demonstrate the feasibility of breeder reactors — nuclear power reactors that run on plutonium and create as a byproduct more plutonium than they consume. The reactor originally

was scheduled for completion in 1983, but it was surrounded by controversy and plagued with delays. Ground was not broken until September 1982. In the meantime, official cost estimates soared from $700 million to $3.6 billion; more than $1.3 billion already had been spent.

The need for the project also had become more difficult to demonstrate. The growth in electricity demand, once expected to rise at a long-term average of 7 percent a year, was projected in 1982 to rise at an average pace of 3 percent a year. And new uranium deposits had been found, reducing fears of a fuel shortage for traditional — and less costly — light water reactors.

Faced with these circumstances, 19 Republicans and 16 Democrats who had supported funding for Clinch River in 1981 voted against it in 1982. The amendment by Lawrence Coughlin, R-Pa., to bar the use of funds for the project was attached to the second fiscal 1983 continuing appropriations resolution (H J Res 631) by a vote of 217-196: R 80-102; D 137-94 (ND 121-33, SD 16-61).

14. Job Creation

The House Appropriations Committee included $5.4 billion for jobs programs in its version of the second fiscal 1983 continuing appropriations resolution (H J Res 631).

In addition to adding funds for existing programs, the measure provided $1 billion for a new jobs program to be run by the Labor Department and $50 million for emergency food and shelter to be distributed by private voluntary agencies.

Many House Republicans opposed the jobs program on grounds that it was a scattershot approach, with a little money for projects in almost every congressional district. They also argued that President Reagan would veto the bill if the funds were included.

A Republican motion to recommit the bill to the Appropriations Committee with instructions to delete the $5.4 billion in jobs money failed Dec. 14 on a 191-215 vote: R 171-7; D 20-208 (ND 2-150, SD 18-58).

Although the Senate version of the resolution also included money for jobs programs, conferees dropped the jobs funding from the final measure to avert a presidential veto. *(Senate key vote 14)*

15. Auto Domestic Content Requirements

As unemployment rose during 1982, so did protectionist sentiment in Congress.

Most of the legislative proposals were directed toward Japan, whose exports to the United States during the year exceeded its imports from the United States by more than $20 billion. "While Japanese cars invade our highways, American workers pay for the defense of Japan," complained Rep. Don J. Pease, D-Ohio.

The most drastic piece of protectionist legislation considered during the year was the domestic content bill (HR 5133). Drafted by the United Auto Workers union (UAW), the measure would have required all companies selling more than 100,000 cars a year in the United States to use a certain proportion of U.S. labor and parts. Toyota and Nissan (Datsun), the major Japanese manufacturers, would have been forced to use 70 to 75 percent domestic content in the cars they sell here. Toyo Kogyo (Mazda) and Honda would have had to achieve ratios of between 20 and 40 percent.

The bill came under heavy attack from the Reagan administration and from free-traders in Congress. U.S. Trade Representative William E. Brock III called it "the worst piece of economic legislation since the 1930s."

But the UAW lobbied fervently for the bill, and the opposition was much less intense. On Dec. 15, the measure passed the House by a vote of 215-188: R 44-130; D 171-58 (ND 132-20, SD 39-38).

The vote was largely a symbolic one. Even the bill's supporters admitted that it had little chance of passing the Senate in the closing days of the lame-duck session. But they argued that House passage would send a clear signal to Japan, encouraging that nation to change its trading practices.

The signal, however, was made considerably less clear by an amendment successfully sponsored by lame-duck Rep. Millicent Fenwick, R-N.J. Fenwick's amendment said the measure should not "supersede" any "treaty, international convention or agreement on tariffs and trade." The bill's opponents said the domestic content requirements clearly violated the General Agreement on Tariffs and Trade, and therefore Fenwick's amendment "gutted" the bill.

16. Gorsuch Contempt of Congress

Congress and the Reagan administration were at loggerheads on environmental issues for most of the 97th Congress. But a Dec. 16 House vote to cite Environmental Protection Agency (EPA) Administrator Anne M. Gorsuch for contempt of Congress escalated that underlying political conflict into a constitutional showdown. Gorsuch was the highest ranking executive branch official to be cited for contempt of Congress.

Especially in the Democratic-controlled House, members accused the Reagan administration of failing to enforce adequately major provisions of environmental laws that Congress had passed during the 1970s.

The contempt vote grew out of efforts by two House subcommittees to oversee EPA enforcement of the 1980 "superfund" law for cleanup of abandoned hazardous waste dumps. On written orders from President Reagan, Gorsuch withheld enforcement documents subpoenaed by the House Public Works and Transportation Subcommittee on Investigations and Oversight.

The disputed documents included enforcement strategies, legal analysis, witness lists and "settlement considerations." The administration claimed its pursuit of pending cases could be jeopardized if the documents were to become public or fall into the hands of defendants. Subcommittee Chairman Elliott H. Levitas, D-Ga., said that early evidence showed companies responsible for hazardous waste dumping were not being held liable for their full share of cleanup costs and that the documents were needed "to find out whether sweetheart deals are being made."

More than one-third of all House Republicans voting on the contempt resolution (H Res 632) joined most Democrats in the final vote of 259-105: R 55-101; D 204-4 (ND 145-2, SD 59-2). Some of those Republicans said protection of congressional prerogatives outweighed their loyalty to the party leadership or the administration.

Instead of referring the charge against Gorsuch to the U.S. attorney for the District of Columbia for presentation to a grand jury, the procedure called for under the criminal contempt statute, the Justice Department filed a civil suit seeking to block further action on the House citation. The House Dec. 30 filed a motion seeking dismissal of that suit, claiming all constitutional issues involved in the separation-of-powers clash could be resolved in the course of proceedings on the criminal contempt charge. ∎

	1	2	3	4	5	6	7	8
ALABAMA								
Denton	Y	?	Y	Y	Y	Y	N	N
Heflin	Y	Y	Y	?	N	Y	Y	N
ALASKA								
Murkowski	Y	N	?	?	Y	Y	N	N
Stevens	?	Y	Y	Y	Y	Y	Y	N
ARIZONA								
Goldwater	Y	N	Y	Y	-	Y	N	N
DeConcini	-	Y	N	Y	N	Y	Y	Y
ARKANSAS								
Bumpers	N	Y	N	?	N	N	Y	Y
Pryor	N	Y	?	Y	N	Y	Y	Y
CALIFORNIA								
Hayakawa	Y	N	Y	+	Y	Y	N	N
Cranston	N	Y	Y	Y	N	N	Y	Y
COLORADO								
Armstrong	Y	N	Y	Y	Y	Y	N	N
Hart	N	N	N	Y	N	N	Y	Y
CONNECTICUT								
Weicker	N	Y	?	?	-	N	Y	Y
Dodd	N	Y	N	?	N	N	Y	Y
DELAWARE								
Roth	Y	N	N	N	Y	Y	N	Y
Biden	N	Y	N	N	N	N	Y	Y
FLORIDA								
Hawkins	Y	Y	Y	+	N	Y	Y	Y
Chiles	N	Y	Y	?	N	Y	Y	Y
GEORGIA								
Mattingly	Y	N	Y	Y	N	Y	N	N
Nunn	N	Y	Y	Y	N	Y	N	Y
HAWAII								
Inouye	N	?	Y	Y	-	N	Y	Y
Matsunaga	N	Y	Y	Y	N	N	Y	Y
IDAHO								
McClure	Y	N	Y	Y	Y	Y	N	?
Symms	Y	N	Y	Y	Y	Y	N	N
ILLINOIS								
Percy	Y	?	N	+	Y	Y	N	N
Dixon	N	Y	N	N	N	Y	Y	Y
INDIANA								
Lugar	Y	Y	N	Y	Y	Y	N	?
Quayle	Y	Y	N	Y	Y	Y	N	?

	1	2	3	4	5	6	7	8
IOWA								
Grassley	Y	Y	Y	Y	Y	Y	N	Y
Jepsen	Y	Y	N	?	Y	Y	N	Y
KANSAS								
Dole	Y	N	Y	Y	Y	Y	N	N
Kassebaum	Y	N	Y	?	Y	N	N	N
KENTUCKY								
Ford	N	Y	Y	Y	N	N	Y	Y
Huddleston	N	Y	Y	Y	N	Y	Y	Y
LOUISIANA								
Johnston	N	N	Y	N	Y	N	N	N
Long	N	Y	Y	Y	N	Y	N	N
MAINE								
Cohen	Y	N	N	X	Y	N	N	Y
Mitchell	N	Y	N	?	N	N	Y	Y
MARYLAND								
Mathias	Y	Y	N	X	Y	N	N	Y
Sarbanes	N	Y	Y	N	N	N	Y	Y
MASSACHUSETTS								
Kennedy	N	Y	N	+	N	N	Y	Y
Tsongas	N	Y	N	N	N	N	Y	Y
MICHIGAN								
Levin	N	Y	N	N	N	N	Y	Y
Riegle	N	Y	N	X	N	N	Y	Y
MINNESOTA								
Boschwitz	Y	Y	Y	?	Y	Y	N	N
Durenberger	?	+	N	+	Y	Y	Y	Y
MISSISSIPPI								
Cochran	Y	Y	Y	?	Y	Y	N	?
Stennis	Y	Y	Y	?	N	Y	?	#
MISSOURI								
Danforth	Y	Y	N	Y	Y	Y	N	Y
Eagleton	N	Y	N	Y	N	N	Y	Y
MONTANA								
Baucus	N	Y	N	Y	N	N	Y	Y
Melcher	-	Y	Y	#	N	Y	Y	Y
NEBRASKA								
Exon	N	Y	N	?	N	Y	Y	Y
Zorinsky	Y	Y	N	N	N	Y	Y	Y
NEVADA								
Laxalt	Y	Y	Y	Y	Y	Y	N	N
Cannon	N	+	N	#	N	Y	Y	Y

	1	2	3	4	5	6	7	8
NEW HAMPSHIRE								
Humphrey	Y	N	N	Y	Y	Y	N	N
Rudman	Y	Y	Y	Y	Y	Y	N	Y
NEW JERSEY								
Brady	Y	N	Y	#	Y	Y	N	N
Bradley	N	Y	N	N	N	N	Y	Y
NEW MEXICO								
Domenici	Y	N	Y	Y	Y	Y	N	Y
Schmitt	+	?	Y	#	Y	Y	N	#
NEW YORK								
D'Amato	Y	Y	N	+	Y	Y	N	Y
Moynihan	N	Y	N	N	N	N	Y	Y
NORTH CAROLINA								
East	Y	N	Y	Y	Y	Y	N	N
Helms	N	Y	Y	Y	Y	Y	N	N
NORTH DAKOTA								
Andrews	Y	Y	Y	?	Y	Y	Y	Y
Burdick	N	Y	Y	?	N	Y	Y	Y
OHIO								
Glenn	N	Y	?	Y	N	N	Y	Y
Metzenbaum	N	Y	N	N	N	N	Y	Y
OKLAHOMA								
Nickles	Y	N	N	+	Y	Y	N	N
Boren	N	Y	Y	?	N	Y	N	Y
OREGON								
Hatfield	+	Y	N	Y	Y	N	N	Y
Packwood	Y	Y	N	Y	Y	Y	N	Y
PENNSYLVANIA								
Heinz	Y	Y	N	?	Y	N	Y	Y
Specter	Y	Y	N	N	Y	Y	Y	?
RHODE ISLAND								
Chafee	Y	Y	N	Y	Y	N	N	Y
Pell	N	+	N	Y	N	N	N	Y
SOUTH CAROLINA								
Thurmond	Y	Y	Y	Y	Y	Y	N	N
Hollings	N	Y	Y	?	N	Y	N	+
SOUTH DAKOTA								
Abdnor	Y	Y	Y	?	Y	Y	N	Y
Pressler	?	+	Y	+	Y	Y	Y	Y
TENNESSEE								
Baker	Y	N	Y	Y	Y	Y	N	N
Sasser	N	Y	Y	+	N	Y	Y	Y

	1	2	3	4	5	6	7	8
TEXAS								
Tower	Y	Y	Y	Y	Y	Y	N	X
Bentsen	N	Y	Y	Y	N	Y	Y	?
UTAH								
Garn	Y	Y	N	Y	Y	Y	N	N
Hatch	Y	Y	N	Y	Y	Y	N	N
VERMONT								
Stafford	+	Y	Y	?	Y	Y	Y	Y
Leahy	N	Y	N	X	N	N	Y	Y
VIRGINIA								
Warner	Y	N	Y	Y	Y	Y	Y	N
Byrd¹	N	N	Y	?	Y	Y	N	N
WASHINGTON								
Gorton	Y	Y	N	Y	Y	N	N	Y
Jackson	N	Y	N	Y	N	N	N	Y
WEST VIRGINIA								
Byrd	N	Y	N	Y	N	Y	Y	Y
Randolph	N	Y	N	Y	N	N	Y	Y
WISCONSIN								
Kasten	Y	Y	N	Y	Y	Y	N	N
Proxmire	N	Y	N	N	N	Y	N	Y
WYOMING								
Simpson	Y	N	N	Y	Y	Y	N	N
Wallop	Y	N	N	Y	Y	Y	N	N

ND - Northern Democrats   SD - Southern Democrats (Southern states - Ala., Ark., Fla., Ga., Ky., La., Miss., N.C., Okla., S.C., Tenn., Texas, Va.)   ¹Byrd elected as an independent.

1. S Con Res 92. First Budget Resolution, Fiscal 1983. Adoption of the concurrent resolution to set budget targets for the fiscal year ending Sept. 30, 1983, as follows: budget authority, $835.7 billion; outlays, $784.3 billion; revenues, $668.4 billion; and deficit, $115.9 billion. The resolution also set preliminary goals for fiscal 1984-85, revised binding budget levels for fiscal 1982 and included reconciliation instructions requiring Senate and House committees to recommend legislative savings to meet the budget targets. Adopted 49-43: R 46-2; D 3-41 (ND 1-28, SD 2-13), May 21, 1982.

2. HR 5922. Urgent Supplemental Appropriations, Fiscal 1982. Lugar, R-Ind., amendment to establish a new subsidy program to provide mortgages at below-market interest rates for buyers of new homes. The amendment contained a fiscal 1982 appropriation of $5.1 billion. Adopted 69-23: R 29-20; D 40-3 (ND 27-1, SD 13-2), May 27, 1982. A "nay" was a vote supporting the president's position.

3. HR 6590. Tobacco Program Revisions. Baker, R-Tenn., motion to table (kill) the Eagleton, D-Mo., amendment to authorize tobacco price support loans through 1985 (thus ending permanent authorization for these loans). Motion agreed to 49-47: R 29-23; D 20-24 (ND 7-23, SD 13-1), July 14, 1982.

4. HR 5539. Reclamation Law Amendments. Passage of the bill to increase acreage limitations for farms irrigated by water from reclamation projects, to raise the price for some of that water, and to make other changes in federal reclamation laws. Passed 49-13: R 30-3; D 19-10 (ND 12-10, SD 7-0), July 16, 1982.

5. HR 4961. Budget Reconciliation Tax Increases/Spending Cuts. Passage of the bill to increase taxes $99 billion for fiscal years 1983-85 and to cut welfare, Medicare and Medicaid spending $17 billion for the same three years, in compliance with reconciliation instructions in the fiscal 1983 budget resolution (S Con Res 92). Passed 50-47: R 49-3; D 1-44 (ND 0-30, SD 1-14), in the session which began July 22, 1982.

6. S J Res 58. Balanced Budget/Tax Limitation Amendment. Passage of the joint resolution to propose an amendment to the Constitution to require a balanced budget at the beginning of each fiscal year unless a three-fifths majority of Congress agreed to deficit spending. The amendment could be waived during the time of a declared war. Passed 69-31: R 47-7; D 22-24 (ND 9-22, SD 13-2), Aug. 4, 1982. A two-thirds majority of those present and voting (67 in this case) of both houses is required for passage of a joint resolution proposing an amendment to the Constitution. A "yea" was a vote supporting the president's position.

7. S 2774. Omnibus Reconciliation Act. Riegle, D-Mich., amendment to delete provisions that would impose a 4 percent cap on cost-of-living adjustments for federal and military retirees but retain the cap for members of Congress who retire after the date of the bill's enactment. Rejected 48-51: R 10-44; D 38-7 (ND 30-1, SD 8-6), Aug. 4, 1982.

8. HR 6863. Supplemental Appropriations, Fiscal 1982. Passage, over President Reagan's Aug. 28 veto, of the bill to appropriate $14,578,111,924 in new fiscal 1982 budget authority for federal military and civilian pay raises, commodity credit programs, defense and other programs, and to rescind $400,846,000 in previously appropriated funds. Passed (thus enacted into law) 60-30: R 21-26; D 39-4 (ND 31-0, SD 8-4), Sept. 10, 1982. A two-thirds majority of those present and voting (60 in this case) of both houses is required to override a veto. A "nay" was a vote supporting the president's position. (The House voted to override the veto the previous day (see vote 7, p. 14-C).)

	9	10	11	12	13	14	15
ALABAMA							
Denton	N	N	Y	Y	N	Y	N
Heflin	N	N	Y	Y	N	N	N
ALASKA							
Murkowski	N	Y	Y	Y	Y	Y	Y
Stevens	Y	Y	Y	Y	N	Y	Y
ARIZONA							
Goldwater	N	#	?	#	?	?	?
DeConcini	N	-	Y	N	N	N	Y
ARKANSAS							
Bumpers	Y	Y	N	N	Y	N	N
Pryor	Y	Y	N	N	Y	N	N
CALIFORNIA							
Hayakawa	Y	Y	Y	Y	Y	Y	Y
Cranston	Y	Y	N	N	Y	N	?
COLORADO							
Armstrong	N	Y	Y	N	N	Y	N
Hart	Y	Y	N	N	Y	N	Y
CONNECTICUT							
Weicker	Y	Y	N	Y	Y	N	Y
Dodd	Y	Y	N	N	Y	N	Y
DELAWARE							
Roth	Y	Y	Y	N	N	Y	Y
Biden	N	N	N	N	Y	N	N
FLORIDA							
Hawkins	N	N	Y	Y	Y	Y	N
Chiles	N	N	Y	N	Y	Y	Y
GEORGIA							
Mattingly	N	N	Y	Y	Y	Y	N
Nunn	Y	N	Y	N	Y	Y	Y
HAWAII							
Inouye	Y	Y	N	N	N	N	N
Matsunaga	Y	X	N	N	N	N	Y
IDAHO							
McClure	N	Y	Y	Y	N	Y	Y
Symms	N	Y	Y	Y	N	Y	Y
ILLINOIS							
Percy	Y	Y	Y	N	Y	Y	Y
Dixon	Y	Y	N	N	Y	N	Y
INDIANA							
Lugar	N	Y	Y	N	Y	Y	Y
Quayle	N	Y	Y	N	Y	Y	Y

	9	10	11	12	13	14	15
IOWA							
Grassley	N	N	Y	Y	N	Y	Y
Jepsen	N	Y	Y	Y	N	Y	Y
KANSAS							
Dole	N	Y	Y	Y	Y	Y	Y
Kassebaum	Y	Y	N	N	Y	Y	Y
KENTUCKY							
Ford	N	N	N	N	N	N	N
Huddleston	N	N	N	Y	N	N	Y
LOUISIANA							
Johnston	-	#	Y	Y	N	N	
Long	N	N	Y	Y	?	N	Y
MAINE							
Cohen	Y	N	Y	N	Y	N	Y
Mitchell	Y	N	N	N	Y	N	N
MARYLAND							
Mathias	Y	#	N	Y	Y	?	Y
Sarbanes	Y	N	N	N	Y	N	Y
MASSACHUSETTS							
Kennedy	Y	N	N	N	Y	N	-
Tsongas	Y	Y	N	N	Y	N	Y
MICHIGAN							
Levin	Y	N	N	N	Y	N	Y
Riegle	Y	N	N	N	Y	N	N
MINNESOTA							
Boschwitz	N	Y	Y	N	Y	Y	Y
Durenberger	N	Y	N	N	Y	Y	Y
MISSISSIPPI							
Cochran	N	Y	Y	Y	N	N	N
Stennis	N	Y	Y	Y	N	N	Y
MISSOURI							
Danforth	N	Y	Y	Y	Y	Y	Y
Eagleton	N	N	N	N	Y	N	N
MONTANA							
Baucus	Y	N	N	N	Y	N	Y
Melcher	Y	N	N	N	N	N	Y
NEBRASKA							
Exon	N	N	Y	N	N	Y	N
Zorinsky	N	N	Y	Y	N	Y	N
NEVADA							
Laxalt	N	Y	Y	Y	N	Y	Y
Cannon	?	N	Y	Y	Y	N	?

	9	10	11	12	13	14	15
NEW HAMPSHIRE							
Humphrey	N	Y	Y	N	Y	Y	N
Rudman	Y	Y	Y	Y	Y	N	Y
NEW JERSEY							
Brady	Y	Y	Y	Y	Y	Y	Y
Bradley	Y	N	N	N	Y	N	N
NEW MEXICO							
Domenici	N	Y	Y	Y	N	Y	Y
Schmitt	Y	X	Y	Y	N	N	Y
NEW YORK							
D'Amato	N	Y	Y	Y	Y	N	Y
Moynihan	Y	?	N	N	Y	N	?
NORTH CAROLINA							
East	N	N	Y	Y	N	Y	N
Helms	N	N	Y	Y	N	Y	N
NORTH DAKOTA							
Andrews	N	N	N	Y	N	Y	Y
Burdick	Y	N	N	Y	Y	N	Y
OHIO							
Glenn	+	Y	?	-	?	?	Y
Metzenbaum	Y	N	N	N	Y	N	N
OKLAHOMA							
Nickles	N	N	Y	N	N	Y	N
Boren	?	N	Y	Y	Y	N	Y
OREGON							
Hatfield	N	Y	N	X	Y	N	?
Packwood	Y	Y	N	N	Y	N	Y
PENNSYLVANIA							
Heinz	+	Y	N	N	Y	N	?
Specter	Y	Y	N	Y	Y	N	Y
RHODE ISLAND							
Chafee	Y	Y	N	N	Y	N	Y
Pell	Y	N	N	N	Y	N	Y
SOUTH CAROLINA							
Thurmond	N	Y	Y	Y	Y	Y	Y
Hollings	Y	Y	N	N	N	N	?
SOUTH DAKOTA							
Abdnor	N	N	Y	Y	Y	Y	Y
Pressler	N	N	N	Y	N	Y	Y
TENNESSEE							
Baker	X	Y	Y	Y	Y	Y	Y
Sasser	Y	X	N	Y	N	N	N

	9	10	11	12	13	14	15
TEXAS							
Tower	Y	Y	Y	Y	N	Y	N
Bentsen	Y	Y	Y	N	N	N	Y
UTAH							
Garn	N	Y	Y	Y	N	Y	N
Hatch	N	Y	Y	Y	-	Y	-
VERMONT							
Stafford	#	Y	N	N	Y	N	Y
Leahy	Y	Y	N	N	Y	N	Y
VIRGINIA							
Warner	N	Y	Y	Y	Y	Y	Y
Byrd¹	Y	Y	Y	N	Y	Y	Y
WASHINGTON							
Gorton	Y	Y	Y	Y	Y	Y	Y
Jackson	Y	N	Y	Y	Y	N	+
WEST VIRGINIA							
Byrd	Y	N	Y	N	Y	N	Y
Randolph	N	Y	N	N	N	N	Y
WISCONSIN							
Kasten	N	N	Y	N	Y	Y	N
Proxmire	N	N	N	N	Y	N	N
WYOMING							
Simpson	Y	Y	Y	Y	N	Y	N
Wallop	Y	Y	Y	Y	N	?	N

KEY

Y Voted for (yea).
\# Paired for.
\+ Announced for.
N Voted against (nay).
X Paired against.
- Announced against.
P Voted "present".
C Voted "present" to avoid possible conflict of interest.
? Did not vote or otherwise make a position known.

Democrats   *Republicans*

ND - Northern Democrats   SD - Southern Democrats (Southern states - Ala., Ark., Fla., Ga., Ky., La., Miss., N.C., Okla., S.C., Tenn., Texas, Va.)   ¹Byrd elected as an independent.

9. H J Res 520. Temporary Debt Limit Increase. Hayakawa, R-Calif., motion to table (kill) the Helms, R-N.C., amendment designed to ban abortion, which was an amendment to the Helms amendment (stripping the Supreme Court of jurisdiction to review any case involving voluntary prayers in public schools) to the committee version of the bill. Motion agreed to 47-46: R 18-33; D 29-13 (ND 22-7, SD 7-6), Sept. 15, 1982.

10. S Res 512. Outside Income of Senators. Adoption of the resolution to abolish the limit in the Senate rules on the total income senators may receive from outside sources, including money for speeches and articles. Adopted 54-38: R 39-12; D 15-26 (ND 9-19, SD 6-7), Dec. 14, 1982.

11. H J Res 631. Continuing Appropriations, Fiscal 1983/MX Missile. Jackson, D-Wash., amendment to bar the use of funds in the bill for procurement of the MX missile until Congress by concurrent resolution had approved a basing mode for it; set out procedures for congressional consideration of the concurrent resolution, and required the president to submit a detailed report on basing mode options to Congress by March 1, 1983. Adopted 56-42: R 41-12; D 15-30 (ND 6-24, SD 9-6), in the session which began Dec. 16, 1982. A "yea" was a vote supporting the president's position.

12. H J Res 631. Continuing Appropriations, Fiscal 1983/Clinch River. Appropriations Committee amendment to drop the House-approved provision in the bill eliminating construction funds for the Clinch River (Tenn.) nuclear breeder reactor. Adopted 49-48: R 38-14; D 11-34 (ND 4-26, SD 7-8), in the session which began Dec. 16, 1982. A "yea" was a vote supporting the president's position.

13. H J Res 631. Continuing Appropriations, Fiscal 1983/Federal Trade Commission. Rudman, R-N.H., motion to table (kill) the McClure, R-Idaho, amendment to bar the use of funds by the Federal Trade Commission to investigate or make rules relating to the medical or other professions that were licensed and regulated by the states. Motion agreed to 59-37: R 31-21; D 28-16 (ND 23-7, SD 5-9), in the session which began Dec. 16, 1982. A "yea" was a vote supporting the president's position.

14. H J Res 631. Continuing Appropriations, Fiscal 1983. Domenici, R-N.M., amendment to delete the section of the joint resolution providing $1.2 billion for public works jobs. Rejected 46-50: R 39-12; D 7-38 (ND 3-27, SD 4-11), in the session which began Dec. 16, 1982. A "yea" was a vote supporting the president's position.

15. HR 6211. Transportation Assistance Act of 1982. Passage of the bill to authorize approximately $70 billion for highways through fiscal 1987 and approximately $12 billion for transit through fiscal 1985, and increase gasoline and other highway taxes. Passed 56-34: R 35-15; D 21-19 (ND 14-12, SD 7-7), in the session which began Dec. 20, 1982. A "yea" was a vote supporting the president's position.

1. HR 5922. Urgent Supplemental Appropriations, Fiscal 1982. Boland, D-Mass., amendment to provide $1 billion to the Department of Housing and Urban Development for mortgage interest subsidy payments to home buyers with family income not exceeding 130 percent of the median income for their area. Adopted 343-67: R 128-52; D 215-15 (ND 149-6, SD 66-9), May 12, 1982.

2. H Con Res 345. First Budget Resolution, Fiscal 1983. Oakar, D-Ohio, amendment, to the Latta, R-Ohio, substitute, to increase budget authority by $400 million and outlays by $4.85 billion for health programs in fiscal 1983 to accommodate Medicare funding at current services levels, and to make corresponding reductions in defense programs. Adopted 228-196: R 64-125; D 164-71 (ND 136-20, SD 28-51), May 27, 1982.

3. H Con Res 352. First Budget Resolution, Fiscal 1983. Latta, R-Ohio, substitute for the president's fiscal 1983 budget submission, to set budget targets for the fiscal year ending Sept. 30, 1983, as follows: budget authority, $800.38 billion; outlays, $765.17 billion; revenues, $665.9 billion; and deficit, $99.27 billion. Adopted 220-207: R 174-15; D 46-192 (ND 9-151, SD 37-41), June 10, 1982.

4. HR 6030. Defense Department Authorizations, Fiscal 1983. Courter, R-N.J., substitute for the Zablocki, D-Wis., amendment, to ban the production of binary munitions unless one existing chemical weapon were destroyed for each new binary weapon built. Rejected 192-225: R 112-72; D 80-153 (ND 27-132, SD 53-21), July 22, 1982. A "yea" was a vote supporting the president's position. (The Zablocki amendment to delete $54 million earmarked for procurement of binary chemical munitions and barring the use of any authorized funds for that program subsequently was adopted.)

5. HR 4961. Budget Reconciliation Tax Increases/Spending Cuts. Rostenkowski, D-Ill., motion to disagree to the Senate amendments to the bill and to agree to a conference requested by the Senate. Motion agreed to 208-197: R 44-137; D 164-60 (ND 116-35, SD 48-25), July 28, 1982.

6. H J Res 521. Nuclear Arms Freeze. Broomfield, R-Mich., substitute to call for a nuclear weapons freeze by the United States and the Soviet Union at equal and substantially reduced levels. Adopted 204-202: R 151-27; D 53-175 (ND 11-149, SD 42-26), Aug. 5, 1982. A "yea" was a vote supporting the president's position. (As reported, the resolution had called for the United States and the Soviet Union to decide when and how to implement an immediate freeze on nuclear arms.)

7. HR 6863. Supplemental Appropriations, Fiscal 1982. Passage, over President Reagan's Aug. 28 veto, of the bill to appropriate $14,578,111,924 in new fiscal 1982 budget authority for federal military and civilian pay raises, commodity credit programs, defense and other programs, and to rescind $400,846,000 in previously appropriated funds. Passed 301-117: R 81-104; D 220-13 (ND 157-1, SD 63-12), Sept. 9, 1982. A two-thirds majority of those present and voting (279 in this case) of both houses is required to override a veto. A "nay" was a vote supporting the president's position. (The Senate also voted to override the veto *(see vote 8, p. 12-C)*, so the bill was enacted.)

8. HR 6838. Soviet Economic Sanctions. Broomfield, R-Mich., motion to recommit the bill to the Foreign Affairs Committee with instructions to insert an amendment repealing economic sanctions against the Soviet Union 90 days after enactment of the bill, provided that during that period the president certified to Congress that the Soviet Union was not using forced labor on certain construction projects. The original bill would have immediately repealed economic sanctions against the Soviet Union. Motion agreed to 206-203: R 124-57; D 82-146 (ND 41-111, SD 41-35), Sept. 29, 1982. A "yea" was a vote supporting the president's position.

KEY

Y	Voted for (yea).
#	Paired for.
+	Announced for.
N	Voted against (nay).
X	Paired against.
-	Announced against.
P	Voted "present".
C	Voted "present" to avoid possible conflict of interest.
?	Did not vote or otherwise make a position known.

Democrats   **Republicans**

	1	2	3	4	5	6	7	8
ALABAMA								
1 *Edwards*	Y	N	Y	Y	Y	Y	Y	Y
2 *Dickinson*	Y	N	Y	Y	N	Y	N	N
3 Nichols	N	N	Y	Y	Y	Y	?	Y
4 Bevill	Y	Y	N	Y	N	Y	Y	Y
5 Flippo	Y	Y	Y	N	Y	N	Y	Y
6 *Smith*	Y	N	Y	Y	N	Y	N	Y
7 Shelby	Y	N	Y	Y	N	Y	Y	Y
ALASKA								
AL *Young*	N	N	Y	Y	Y	Y	#	Y
ARIZONA								
1 *Rhodes*	N	?	Y	?	Y	Y	Y	Y
2 Udall	Y	Y	N	N	Y	N	Y	N
3 *Stump*	N	N	Y	N	Y	?	?	Y
4 *Rudd*	N	N	Y	N	Y	N	?	Y
ARKANSAS								
1 Alexander	Y	N	N	Y	N	N	N	N
2 *Bethune*	N	N	Y	N	N	Y	N	Y
3 *Hammerschmidt*	Y	N	Y	Y	N	Y	Y	Y
4 Anthony	Y	Y	N	Y	N	Y	N	Y
CALIFORNIA								
1 *Chappie*	N	N	Y	?	N	Y	Y	Y
2 *Clausen*	Y	N	N	Y	N	Y	Y	Y
3 Matsui	Y	Y	N	N	Y	N	Y	N
4 Fazio	Y	Y	N	Y	N	Y	N	N
5 Burton, J.	?	?	X	?	?	N	Y	?
6 Burton, P.	Y	Y	N	N	Y	N	Y	N
7 Miller	Y	Y	N	N	Y	N	Y	N
8 Dellums	Y	Y	N	N	Y	N	Y	N
9 Stark	Y	Y	N	N	Y	N	Y	N
10 Edwards	Y	Y	N	N	Y	N	Y	N
11 Lantos	Y	Y	N	N	Y	N	Y	N
12 *McCloskey*	?	N	Y	N	Y	N	N	N
13 Mineta	Y	N	N	N	Y	N	Y	N
14 *Shumway*	N	N	Y	N	Y	N	Y	N
15 Coelho	Y	Y	N	N	Y	N	Y	N
16 Panetta	Y	N	N	N	Y	N	Y	N
17 *Pashayan*	Y	Y	Y	N	Y	N	Y	Y
18 *Thomas*	Y	N	Y	N	Y	N	Y	N
19 *Lagomarsino*	Y	N	Y	N	Y	N	Y	N
20 *Goldwater*	?	N	#	Y	N	?	N	Y
21 *Fiedler*	Y	N	Y	N	Y	N	Y	N
22 *Moorhead*	N	N	Y	N	Y	N	Y	N
23 Beilenson	N	N	N	N	Y	N	Y	N
24 Waxman	Y	Y	N	N	Y	N	Y	Y
25 Roybal	Y	Y	N	N	Y	N	Y	N
26 *Rousselot*	N	N	Y	N	Y	N	Y	N
27 *Dornan*	N	N	?	Y	?	?	N	Y
28 Dixon	Y	Y	N	N	Y	N	Y	N
29 Hawkins	?	Y	N	N	Y	N	Y	N
30 Martinez[1]				N	Y	N	Y	N
31 Dymally	?	Y	N	N	?	N	Y	N
32 Anderson	Y	Y	N	N	Y	N	Y	N
33 Grisham	?	N	Y	N	Y	N	Y	N
34 *Lungren*	N	N	Y	N	Y	N	Y	N
35 *Dreier*	?	N	Y	N	Y	N	Y	N
36 Brown	Y	Y	N	N	Y	N	Y	N
37 *Lewis*	Y	N	Y	N	Y	N	Y	N
38 Patterson	Y	Y	N	N	Y	N	Y	N
39 *Dannemeyer*	N	N	N	Y	N	Y	N	Y
40 *Badham*	N	N	Y	N	Y	N	Y	N
41 *Lowery*	Y	N	Y	N	Y	N	Y	N
42 *Hunter*	N	N	Y	N	Y	N	Y	N
43 *Burgener*	Y	N	Y	?	Y	Y	N	Y
COLORADO								
1 Schroeder	Y	Y	N	N	Y	N	?	Y
2 Wirth	Y	N	N	N	Y	N	Y	N
3 Kogovsek	Y	Y	N	N	Y	N	Y	Y
4 *Brown*	N	Y	Y	N	Y	N	Y	N

	1	2	3	4	5	6	7	8
5 *Kramer*	N	N	Y	Y	N	Y	N	Y
CONNECTICUT								
1 Kennelly	Y	Y	N	N	Y	N	Y	Y
2 Gejdenson	Y	Y	N	N	Y	N	Y	N
3 *DeNardis*	Y	Y	N	N	N	Y	N	N
4 *McKinney*	Y	Y	N	N	N	N	Y	N
5 Ratchford	Y	Y	N	N	Y	N	Y	N
6 Moffett	Y	Y	N	N	?	N	Y	?
DELAWARE								
AL *Evans*	Y	Y	Y	N	N	N	Y	Y
FLORIDA								
1 Hutto	Y	N	Y	N	Y	Y	Y	Y
2 Fuqua	Y	N	Y	N	?	Y	Y	Y
3 Bennett	Y	N	N	Y	N	Y	Y	N
4 Chappell	Y	N	Y	N	Y	N	Y	?
5 *McCollum*	Y	N	Y	N	Y	N	Y	Y
6 *Young*	Y	N	Y	N	Y	N	Y	?
7 Gibbons	N	N	Y	Y	N	Y	N	Y
8 Ireland	Y	N	Y	Y	N	Y	N	Y
9 Nelson	Y	N	Y	Y	Y	Y	Y	Y
10 *Bafalis*	Y	N	Y	?	?	?	?	?
11 Mica	Y	Y	N	N	Y	N	Y	Y
12 *Shaw*	N	N	Y	N	N	Y	N	Y
13 Lehman	Y	Y	N	N	Y	N	Y	N
14 Pepper	Y	Y	N	-	?	N	Y	N
15 Fascell	N	Y	N	N	Y	N	Y	N
GEORGIA								
1 Ginn	?	N	Y	?	?	Y	Y	Y
2 Hatcher	Y	N	Y	Y	Y	Y	Y	Y
3 Brinkley	Y	Y	Y	Y	Y	Y	Y	Y
4 Levitas	Y	N	Y	N	Y	Y	Y	Y
5 Fowler	Y	Y	N	N	Y	N	Y	N
6 *Gingrich*	Y	N	Y	N	Y	N	Y	N
7 McDonald	N	N	Y	Y	Y	N	Y	N
8 Evans	Y	N	Y	N	Y	Y	?	Y
9 Jenkins	Y	N	Y	N	Y	N	Y	Y
10 Barnard	Y	N	Y	Y	Y	Y	Y	Y
HAWAII								
1 Heftel	?	Y	Y	Y	Y	N	Y	N
2 Akaka	Y	Y	N	Y	N	Y	N	N
IDAHO								
1 *Craig*	Y	N	Y	N	N	Y	N	Y
2 *Hansen*	N	N	Y	Y	N	Y	N	Y
ILLINOIS								
1 Washington	Y	Y	N	N	N	N	Y	N
2 Savage	Y	Y	N	N	N	Y	N	N
3 Russo	Y	Y	N	N	Y	N	Y	N
4 *Derwinski*	Y	N	Y	N	Y	N	Y	Y
5 Fary	Y	Y	N	N	Y	N	Y	N
6 *Hyde*	Y	N	Y	N	Y	N	Y	N
7 Collins	Y	N	N	N	N	N	Y	N
8 Rostenkowski	Y	Y	N	N	Y	N	Y	N
9 Yates	Y	Y	N	N	?	N	Y	N
10 *Porter*	Y	Y	N	N	Y	N	Y	N
11 Annunzio	Y	Y	N	N	Y	N	Y	N
12 *Crane, P.*	N	N	Y	N	Y	N	Y	N
13 *McClory*	Y	N	Y	N	Y	?	N	Y
14 *Erlenborn*	N	N	Y	N	Y	N	?	N
15 *Corcoran*	N	N	Y	N	Y	N	Y	N
16 *Martin*	N	N	Y	N	N	N	N	N
17 *O'Brien*	Y	N	Y	Y	#	Y	Y	X
18 *Michel*	N	N	Y	N	Y	N	Y	N
19 *Railsback*	Y	Y	Y	N	Y	X	N	X
20 *Findley*	Y	Y	N	N	Y	N	Y	N
21 *Madigan*	Y	N	Y	Y	Y	N	Y	N
22 *Crane, D.*	N	N	Y	N	Y	N	Y	N
23 Price	Y	N	Y	Y	Y	Y	Y	Y
24 Simon	Y	Y	N	N	Y	N	Y	N
INDIANA								
1 Hall[2]								
2 Fithian	Y	Y	N	N	N	N	Y	N
3 *Hiler*	Y	N	Y	N	Y	N	Y	N
4 *Coats*	Y	N	Y	Y	Y	Y	Y	N
5 *Hillis*	Y	N	Y	Y	Y	N	Y	N
6 Evans	Y	N	Y	N	?	Y	Y	N
7 *Myers*	Y	N	Y	N	Y	N	Y	N
8 *Deckard*	Y	N	Y	Y	Y	N	Y	N
9 Hamilton	Y	Y	Y	Y	N	N	Y	N
10 Sharp	Y	N	Y	N	N	N	Y	N
11 Jacobs	Y	N	N	Y	N	N	Y	N
IOWA								
1 *Leach*	Y	Y	Y	N	N	N	Y	N
2 *Tauke*	Y	N	Y	N	Y	N	Y	N
3 *Evans*	Y	Y	Y	N	Y	N	Y	N
4 Smith	Y	Y	N	N	Y	N	Y	N
5 Harkin	Y	Y	N	N	N	N	Y	N
6 Bedell	Y	Y	N	N	Y	N	Y	N

ND - Northern Democrats   SD - Southern Democrats

	1	2	3	4	5	6	7	8
KANSAS								
1 ***Roberts***	N	N	Y	N	N	Y	N	N
2 ***Jeffries***	N	N	Y	Y	N	Y	N	Y
3 ***Winn***	Y	N	Y	Y	N	Y	N	Y
4 Glickman	Y	N	N	N	Y	N	Y	N
5 ***Whittaker***	N	N	Y	N	N	Y	N	Y
KENTUCKY								
1 Hubbard	Y	N	N	Y	N	Y	N	Y
2 Natcher	Y	Y	N	N	N	N	Y	N
3 Mazzoli	Y	N	N	N	Y	N	Y	N
4 ***Snyder***	N	Y	Y	Y	N	Y	N	Y
5 ***Rogers***	Y	N	Y	Y	N	Y	Y	Y
6 ***Hopkins***	Y	Y	Y	N	N	Y	Y	Y
7 Perkins	Y	Y	N	N	N	N	Y	N
LOUISIANA								
1 ***Livingston***	?	N	Y	Y	N	Y	N	Y
2 Boggs	Y	Y	N	Y	Y	N	Y	N
3 Tauzin	Y	N	Y	Y	N	Y	N	N
4 Roemer	N	N	Y	Y	Y	Y	N	N
5 Huckaby	Y	N	Y	Y	Y	Y	Y	N
6 ***Moore***	Y	N	Y	Y	N	Y	N	N
7 Breaux	Y	N	Y	?	Y	Y	Y	N
8 Long	Y	Y	N	Y	Y	?	Y	Y
MAINE								
1 ***Emery***	Y	Y	Y	N	Y	Y	Y	Y
2 ***Snowe***	Y	Y	Y	N	Y	N	Y	N
MARYLAND								
1 Dyson	Y	Y	Y	Y	Y	Y	Y	Y
2 Long	N	N	N	N	Y	N	Y	Y
3 Mikulski	?	Y	N	N	Y	N	Y	Y
4 ***Holt***	N	Y	Y	Y	N	Y	Y	Y
5 Hoyer	Y	Y	N	N	Y	N	Y	N
6 Byron	Y	Y	Y	Y	Y	Y	Y	Y
7 Mitchell	Y	Y	N	N	?	N	Y	N
8 Barnes	Y	Y	N	-	N	N	Y	N
MASSACHUSETTS								
1 ***Conte***	Y	Y	Y	N	Y	N	Y	N
2 Boland	Y	Y	N	N	Y	N	Y	N
3 Early	N	Y	N	N	?	N	Y	Y
4 Frank	Y	Y	N	N	N	N	Y	Y
5 Shannon	Y	Y	N	N	N	N	Y	N
6 Mavroules	Y	Y	N	N	Y	N	Y	Y
7 Markey	Y	Y	N	N	Y	N	Y	N
8 O'Neill[3]						N	Y	
9 Moakley	Y	Y	N	N	Y	N	Y	N
10 ***Heckler***	Y	Y	N	N	N	N	Y	Y
11 Donnelly	N	N	N	N	Y	N	Y	Y
12 Studds	Y	Y	N	N	N	N	Y	N
MICHIGAN								
1 Conyers	Y	Y	N	N	Y	N	Y	Y
2 ***Pursell***	Y	Y	Y	N	Y	N	Y	N
3 Wolpe	Y	Y	N	N	Y	N	Y	N
4 ***Siljander***	Y	N	Y	Y	?	Y	N	Y
5 ***Sawyer***	Y	N	Y	N	N	Y	N	Y
6 ***Dunn***	Y	N	Y	N	N	Y	Y	N
7 Kildee	Y	Y	N	N	N	N	Y	N
8 Traxler	Y	Y	N	N	Y	N	Y	N
9 ***Vander Jagt***	Y	N	Y	N	Y	Y	Y	Y
10 Albosta	Y	Y	N	N	Y	N	Y	N
11 ***Davis***	Y	Y	Y	Y	N	Y	Y	Y
12 Bonior	Y	Y	N	N	?	N	Y	Y
13 Crockett	Y	?	N	N	Y	N	Y	N
14 Hertel	Y	Y	N	N	Y	N	Y	N
15 Ford	Y	Y	N	N	Y	N	Y	N
16 Dingell	Y	Y	N	Y	Y	N	Y	N
17 Brodhead	Y	Y	N	N	Y	N	Y	N
18 Blanchard	Y	Y	N	N	?	N	Y	?
19 ***Broomfield***	Y	N	Y	Y	N	Y	N	Y
MINNESOTA								
1 ***Erdahl***	Y	N	Y	N	N	N	Y	N
2 ***Hagedorn***	N	N	Y	Y	N	Y	N	Y
3 ***Frenzel***	N	N	Y	N	Y	Y	N	N
4 Vento	Y	Y	N	N	Y	N	Y	N
5 Sabo	Y	Y	N	N	Y	N	Y	N
6 ***Weber***	N	N	Y	N	N	Y	N	N
7 ***Stangeland***	Y	Y	Y	Y	N	Y	Y	N
8 Oberstar	Y	Y	N	N	Y	N	Y	N
MISSISSIPPI								
1 Whitten	Y	Y	N	N	N	?	Y	N
2 Bowen	Y	N	N	?	Y	N	?	N
3 Montgomery	Y	N	Y	Y	Y	Y	N	Y
4 Dowdy	Y	Y	N	Y	?	N	Y	N
5 ***Lott***	Y	N	Y	Y	Y	Y	N	Y
MISSOURI								
1 Clay	Y	Y	N	?	?	N	Y	?
2 Young	Y	N	Y	Y	Y	N	Y	N
3 Gephardt	N	N	Y	Y	Y	N	Y	N
4 Skelton	Y	N	Y	Y	N	?	Y	?
5 Bolling	Y	Y	?	Y	Y	?	Y	N
6 ***Coleman***	Y	Y	Y	?	N	Y	Y	Y
7 ***Taylor***	N	N	Y	Y	N	Y	N	N
8 ***Bailey***	Y	N	Y	N	N	Y	N	N
9 Volkmer	Y	Y	Y	Y	N	N	Y	N
10 ***Emerson***	Y	N	Y	?	N	Y	Y	N
MONTANA								
1 Williams	Y	Y	N	N	N	N	Y	N
2 ***Marlenee***	Y	Y	Y	Y	N	Y	N	N
NEBRASKA								
1 ***Bereuter***	Y	Y	Y	N	N	Y	Y	Y
2 ***Daub***	Y	Y	Y	N	N	Y	N	Y
3 ***Smith***	Y	Y	Y	N	N	Y	Y	N
NEVADA								
AL Santini	Y	Y	N	?	N	Y	Y	?
NEW HAMPSHIRE								
1 D'Amours	Y	Y	N	N	N	N	Y	Y
2 ***Gregg***	N	N	Y	N	N	N	N	Y
NEW JERSEY								
1 Florio	Y	Y	N	N	N	N	Y	N
2 Hughes	Y	Y	N	N	N	N	Y	Y
3 Howard	Y	Y	N	N	Y	N	Y	N
4 ***Smith***	Y	Y	N	N	N	N	Y	Y
5 ***Fenwick***	?	Y	Y	N	N	N	Y	N
6 ***Forsythe***	Y	Y	Y	N	Y	Y	N	#
7 ***Roukema***	N	Y	Y	N	N	N	Y	N
8 Roe	Y	Y	N	N	N	N	Y	N
9 ***Hollenbeck***	Y	Y	N	N	N	N	Y	N
10 Rodino	Y	Y	N	N	Y	N	Y	N
11 Minish	Y	Y	N	N	Y	N	Y	Y
12 ***Rinaldo***	Y	Y	N	N	N	N	Y	Y
13 ***Courter***	Y	Y	Y	Y	N	Y	N	Y
14 Guarini	Y	Y	N	N	Y	N	Y	N
15 Dwyer	Y	Y	N	N	Y	N	Y	N
NEW MEXICO								
1 ***Lujan***	Y	Y	Y	Y	N	#	N	Y
2 ***Skeen***	N	N	Y	Y	N	Y	N	Y
NEW YORK								
1 ***Carney***	Y	N	Y	Y	N	Y	N	Y
2 Downey	Y	Y	N	N	Y	N	Y	N
3 ***Carman***	Y	N	Y	N	N	Y	N	Y
4 ***Lent***	Y	Y	Y	Y	N	Y	Y	Y
5 ***McGrath***	Y	Y	Y	N	N	-	Y	Y
6 ***LeBoutillier***	Y	Y	Y	Y	N	Y	Y	?
7 Addabbo	Y	Y	N	N	Y	N	Y	Y
8 Rosenthal	Y	?	N	N	Y	X	Y	N
9 Ferraro	Y	Y	N	N	Y	N	Y	N
10 Biaggi	Y	Y	N	N	Y	N	Y	Y
11 Scheuer	Y	Y	N	N	Y	N	Y	?
12 Chisholm	Y	?	N	N	Y	N	Y	N
13 Solarz	Y	Y	N	N	Y	N	Y	N
14 Richmond[4]	Y	Y	N	N	Y	N		
15 Zeferetti	Y	Y	N	N	Y	N	Y	Y
16 Schumer	Y	Y	N	N	Y	N	?	N
17 ***Molinari***	Y	Y	Y	N	N	Y	Y	Y
18 ***Green***	N	Y	N	N	N	N	Y	Y
19 Rangel	Y	Y	N	N	Y	N	Y	N
20 Weiss	Y	Y	N	N	Y	N	?	?
21 Garcia	Y	?	N	N	Y	N	Y	N
22 Bingham	Y	?	N	N	Y	N	Y	N
23 Peyser	Y	Y	N	N	Y	N	Y	Y
24 Ottinger	Y	Y	N	N	N	N	Y	Y
25 ***Fish***	Y	Y	Y	N	Y	Y	Y	N
26 ***Gilman***	Y	Y	N	Y	N	Y	Y	Y
27 McHugh	Y	Y	N	N	N	N	Y	N
28 Stratton	Y	N	N	Y	Y	Y	Y	N
29 ***Solomon***	Y	N	Y	?	N	Y	N	Y
30 ***Martin***	Y	N	Y	Y	N	Y	Y	Y
31 ***Mitchell***	Y	N	Y	Y	N	Y	Y	Y
32 ***Wortley***	Y	N	Y	Y	N	Y	Y	Y
33 ***Lee***	Y	Y	Y	N	-	Y	Y	Y
34 ***Horton***	Y	Y	Y	N	N	N	Y	N
35 ***Conable***	N	N	Y	Y	Y	Y	Y	N
36 LaFalce	Y	Y	N	N	N	N	Y	N
37 Nowak	Y	Y	N	N	N	N	Y	Y
38 ***Kemp***	N	N	N	Y	N	Y	N	Y
39 Lundine	Y	Y	N	N	Y	N	Y	N
NORTH CAROLINA								
1 Jones	Y	Y	N	Y	Y	Y	Y	N
2 Fountain	Y	N	Y	Y	N	Y	Y	Y
3 Whitley	Y	N	Y	Y	Y	Y	Y	Y
4 Andrews	Y	N	N	Y	N	?	Y	Y
5 Neal	?	N	N	Y	N	N	Y	Y
6 ***Johnston***	N	N	Y	Y	N	Y	N	Y
7 Rose	Y	N	N	N	Y	N	Y	N
8 Hefner	Y	N	N	Y	Y	Y	Y	Y
9 ***Martin***	Y	N	Y	N	N	Y	N	Y
10 ***Broyhill***	N	N	Y	Y	Y	Y	N	Y
11 ***Hendon***	Y	N	Y	Y	N	Y	Y	Y
NORTH DAKOTA								
AL Dorgan	Y	Y	N	N	Y	N	Y	N
OHIO								
1 ***Gradison***	N	N	Y	Y	N	Y	N	N
2 Luken	Y	Y	N	N	Y	N	Y	N
3 Hall	Y	Y	N	N	N	N	N	N
4 ***Oxley***	Y	N	Y	N	N	Y	N	N
5 ***Latta***	N	N	Y	Y	Y	Y	N	Y
6 ***McEwen***	Y	N	Y	N	N	Y	N	Y
7 ***Brown***	?	Y	Y	?	?	?	?	?
8 ***Kindness***	Y	N	Y	Y	N	Y	N	Y
9 ***Weber***	Y	Y	Y	N	N	Y	Y	N
10 ***Miller***	N	N	Y	Y	Y	Y	N	Y
11 ***Stanton***	?	?	Y	Y	Y	Y	N	N
12 Shamansky	Y	Y	N	N	Y	N	Y	N
13 Pease	Y	Y	N	N	Y	N	Y	N
14 Seiberling	Y	Y	N	N	Y	N	Y	N
15 ***Wylie***	Y	Y	Y	Y	N	?	N	?
16 ***Regula***	Y	N	Y	N	Y	Y	Y	Y
17 ***Ashbrook***[5]				Y	N	Y	N	Y
18 Applegate	Y	Y	N	Y	Y	N	Y	Y
19 ***Williams***	Y	Y	Y	N	N	Y	Y	N
20 Oakar	Y	Y	N	N	?	N	Y	Y
21 Stokes	Y	Y	N	N	Y	N	Y	N
22 Eckart	Y	Y	N	N	N	N	Y	N
23 Mottl	Y	Y	N	Y	N	N	Y	Y
OKLAHOMA								
1 Jones	Y	N	N	N	Y	N	Y	N
2 Synar	Y	N	N	N	N	-	Y	N
3 Watkins	Y	N	N	Y	Y	N	Y	Y
4 McCurdy	Y	N	Y	N	N	Y	Y	N
5 ***Edwards***	Y	N	Y	N	Y	Y	N	Y
6 English	Y	N	N	Y	N	Y	Y	Y
OREGON								
1 AuCoin	Y	Y	N	N	Y	N	Y	N
2 ***Smith***	Y	N	Y	Y	N	Y	N	Y
3 Wyden	Y	Y	N	N	Y	N	Y	N
4 Weaver	Y	Y	N	N	Y	N	Y	N
PENNSYLVANIA								
1 Foglietta	?	Y	N	N	Y	N	Y	Y
2 Gray	Y	Y	N	N	Y	N	Y	N
3 Smith	?	Y	N	N	?	Y	Y	Y
4 ***Dougherty***	Y	Y	N	Y	Y	Y	Y	Y
5 ***Schulze***	Y	N	Y	Y	N	#	Y	?
6 Yatron	Y	Y	N	N	N	N	Y	Y
7 Edgar	Y	Y	N	N	N	N	Y	N
8 ***Coyne, J.***	Y	N	Y	Y	N	Y	Y	Y
9 ***Shuster***	Y	Y	Y	N	N	Y	Y	Y
10 ***McDade***	Y	Y	Y	N	Y	#	Y	N
11 ***Nelligan***	Y	Y	Y	Y	N	Y	Y	Y
12 Murtha	Y	N	N	Y	Y	Y	Y	Y
13 ***Coughlin***	Y	N	Y	N	Y	Y	Y	Y
14 Coyne, W.	Y	Y	N	N	Y	N	Y	N
15 ***Ritter***	Y	Y	Y	Y	N	Y	N	Y
16 ***Walker***	N	N	Y	N	N	Y	N	Y
17 Ertel	Y	Y	N	N	N	N	Y	?
18 Walgren	Y	Y	N	N	Y	N	Y	N
19 ***Goodling***	N	N	Y	N	N	P	Y	N
20 Gaydos	Y	Y	N	N	Y	Y	Y	Y
21 Bailey	Y	N	N	Y	Y	Y	Y	Y
22 Murphy	Y	Y	N	Y	Y	N	Y	Y
23 ***Clinger***	N	N	Y	Y	N	Y	Y	N
24 ***Marks***	Y	Y	N	?	?	Y	Y	?
25 ***Atkinson***	Y	Y	Y	Y	Y	Y	N	Y
RHODE ISLAND								
1 St Germain	Y	Y	N	N	N	N	Y	N
2 ***Schneider***	+	Y	N	N	Y	N	Y	N
SOUTH CAROLINA								
1 ***Hartnett***	N	N	Y	Y	Y	Y	N	Y
2 ***Spence***	Y	N	Y	Y	N	Y	N	Y
3 Derrick	Y	Y	N	N	Y	N	Y	N
4 ***Campbell***	?	N	Y	Y	N	Y	N	Y
5 Holland	Y	Y	?	Y	Y	?	Y	Y
6 ***Napier***	Y	N	Y	Y	N	Y	N	Y
SOUTH DAKOTA								
1 Daschle	Y	Y	N	N	N	N	Y	N
2 ***Roberts***	Y	N	Y	N	N	Y	Y	N
TENNESSEE								
1 ***Quillen***	Y	Y	Y	Y	Y	Y	N	Y
2 ***Duncan***	Y	Y	Y	Y	Y	Y	Y	Y
3 Bouquard	Y	N	N	Y	N	?	Y	N
4 Gore	Y	Y	N	Y	Y	N	Y	N
5 Boner	Y	Y	N	Y	N	N	Y	Y
6 ***Beard***	Y	N	Y	Y	X	?	Y	?
7 Jones	Y	Y	Y	?	?	?	Y	N
8 Ford	?	Y	N	N	?	X	Y	N
TEXAS								
1 Hall, S.	Y	N	Y	N	N	Y	N	Y
2 Wilson	Y	N	Y	Y	Y	Y	Y	Y
3 ***Collins***	N	N	Y	Y	?	?	X	?
4 Hall, R.	Y	N	Y	Y	N	Y	N	N
5 Mattox	?	Y	N	N	Y	?	#	?
6 Gramm	N	N	Y	Y	Y	Y	N	Y
7 ***Archer***	Y	N	Y	Y	Y	Y	N	N
8 ***Fields***	Y	N	Y	Y	N	Y	N	Y
9 Brooks	Y	N	N	Y	Y	N	Y	N
10 Pickle	Y	Y	Y	N	Y	Y	Y	N
11 Leath	N	N	Y	Y	?	Y	Y	Y
12 Wright	Y	N	N	Y	Y	N	Y	N
13 Hightower	Y	N	Y	N	Y	Y	Y	N
14 Patman	Y	N	Y	Y	Y	Y	N	Y
15 de la Garza	Y	Y	N	Y	Y	Y	Y	Y
16 White	Y	N	Y	Y	Y	Y	Y	Y
17 Stenholm	N	N	Y	Y	Y	Y	N	Y
18 Leland	Y	Y	N	N	Y	N	Y	N
19 Hance	N	N	Y	Y	Y	Y	Y	Y
20 Gonzalez	Y	Y	N	N	N	N	Y	Y
21 ***Loeffler***	Y	N	Y	Y	Y	Y	N	Y
22 ***Paul***	N	N	Y	N	N	Y	N	N
23 Kazen	Y	N	N	Y	N	Y	Y	Y
24 Frost	Y	Y	N	Y	Y	N	Y	N
UTAH								
1 ***Hansen***	?	N	Y	Y	?	Y	N	Y
2 ***Marriott***	Y	N	Y	Y	N	Y	?	Y
VERMONT								
AL ***Jeffords***	Y	Y	N	N	Y	N	Y	N
VIRGINIA								
1 ***Trible***	Y	N	Y	Y	N	Y	N	Y
2 ***Whitehurst***	Y	N	Y	Y	N	Y	N	Y
3 ***Bliley***	Y	N	Y	Y	N	Y	N	Y
4 ***Daniel, R.***	Y	N	Y	Y	N	Y	N	Y
5 Daniel, D.	Y	N	Y	Y	Y	Y	Y	?
6 ***Butler***	N	N	Y	Y	Y	Y	N	Y
7 ***Robinson***	Y	N	Y	Y	N	Y	Y	Y
8 ***Parris***	Y	Y	Y	N	N	Y	Y	Y
9 ***Wampler***	Y	Y	Y	Y	N	Y	Y	Y
10 ***Wolf***	Y	Y	Y	Y	N	Y	Y	Y
WASHINGTON								
1 ***Pritchard***	Y	N	Y	N	Y	N	Y	N
2 Swift	Y	N	N	N	Y	N	Y	N
3 Bonker	Y	N	N	N	Y	N	Y	N
4 ***Morrison***	Y	N	Y	Y	Y	Y	Y	Y
5 Foley	Y	N	N	N	Y	N	Y	N
6 Dicks	Y	N	N	Y	Y	N	Y	N
7 Lowry	Y	Y	N	N	Y	N	Y	N
WEST VIRGINIA								
1 Mollohan	Y	Y	N	Y	Y	Y	Y	Y
2 ***Benedict***	Y	N	Y	N	Y	Y	N	N
3 ***Staton***	Y	N	Y	Y	N	Y	N	Y
4 Rahall	Y	Y	N	N	?	N	Y	Y
WISCONSIN								
1 Aspin	Y	N	N	N	Y	N	Y	N
2 Kastenmeier	Y	Y	N	N	N	N	Y	N
3 ***Gunderson***	Y	Y	Y	N	N	N	Y	N
4 Zablocki	Y	Y	N	N	Y	N	Y	N
5 Reuss	Y	Y	N	N	Y	N	Y	N
6 ***Petri***	N	Y	Y	Y	N	Y	Y	Y
7 Obey	Y	Y	N	N	Y	N	Y	N
8 ***Roth***	Y	N	Y	N	N	Y	N	Y
9 ***Sensenbrenner***	Y	N	N	N	N	Y	N	Y
WYOMING								
AL ***Cheney***	N	N	Y	Y	Y	Y	N	Y

1. Rep. Matthew G. Martinez, D-Calif., sworn in July 15, 1982, to succeed George E. Danielson, D, who resigned March 9, 1982.

2. Rep. Katie Hall, D-Ind., sworn in Nov. 29, 1982, to succeed Adam Benjamin Jr., D, who died Sept. 7, 1982.

3. Rep. Thomas P. O'Neill Jr., D-Mass., as Speaker, votes at his own discretion.

4. Rep. Fred Richmond, D-N.Y., resigned, Aug. 25, 1982.

5. Rep. Jean S. Ashbrook, R-Ohio, sworn in July 12, 1982, to succeed her husband, John M. Ashbrook, R, who died April 24, 1982.

Southern states - Ala., Ark., Fla., Ga., Ky., La., Miss., N.C., Okla., S.C., Tenn., Texas, Va.

9. H J Res 350. Balanced Budget Constitutional Amendment. Passage of the joint resolution to propose an amendment to the Constitution to require Congress to adopt a balanced federal budget every year, except in time of war, unless a three-fifths majority of Congress agreed to deficit spending. Rejected 236-187: R 167-20; D 69-167 (ND 12-147, SD 57-20), Oct. 1, 1982. A two-thirds majority of those present and voting (282 in this case) of both houses is required for passage of a joint resolution proposing an amendment to the Constitution. A "yea" was a vote supporting the president's position.

10. HR 6211. Transportation Assistance Act of 1982. Adoption of the rule (H Res 620) providing for House floor consideration of the bill to authorize funds for highway and mass transit programs for fiscal 1983-1986 and to increase gasoline and other highway taxes. Adopted 197-194: R 59-114; D 138-80 (ND 112-34, SD 26-46), Dec. 6, 1982.

11. HR 7355. Department of Defense Appropriations, Fiscal 1983. Addabbo, D-N.Y., amendment to delete $988 million for procurement of five MX missiles. Adopted 245-176: R 50-138; D 195-38 (ND 151-7, SD 44-31), Dec. 7, 1982. A "nay" was a vote supporting the president's position.

12. H J Res 631. Continuing Appropriations, Fiscal 1983/Pay Raise. Traxler, D-Mich., amendment to retain the existing cap on salaries of members of Congress at $60,662.50 a year. Rejected 208-208: R 121-65; D 87-143 (ND 46-109, SD 41-34), Dec. 14, 1982.

13. H J Res 631. Continuing Appropriations, Fiscal 1983/Clinch River. Coughlin, R-Pa., amendment to bar use of funds provided by the joint resolution for research and development, design or construction of the Clinch River breeder reactor. Adopted 217-196: R 80-102; D 137-94 (ND 121-33, SD 16-61), Dec. 14, 1982. A "nay" was a vote supporting the president's position.

14. H J Res 631. Continuing Appropriations, Fiscal 1983/Jobs. Conte, R-Mass., motion to recommit the joint resolution to the Appropriations Committee with instructions to delete jobs program funding (Title II) and add $44 million in funding for Radio Liberty. Motion rejected 191-215: R 171-7; D 20-208 (ND 2-150, SD 18-58), Dec. 14, 1982. A "yea" was a vote supporting the president's position.

15. HR 5133. Automobile Domestic Content Requirements. Passage of the bill to require automakers to use set percentages of U.S. labor and parts in automobiles they sell in the United States. Passed 215-188: R 44-130; D 171-58 (ND 132-20, SD 39-38), Dec. 15, 1982. A "nay" was a vote supporting the president's position.

16. H Res 632. Contempt of Congress Proceedings Against Anne M. Gorsuch. Adoption of the resolution to cite Environmental Protection Agency Administrator Anne M. Gorsuch for contempt of Congress for refusing to furnish certain documents under subpoena to the House Public Works and Transportation Subcommittee on Investigations and Oversight. Adopted 259-105: R 55-101; D 204-4 (ND 145-2, SD 59-2), Dec. 16, 1982.

KEY

- Y Voted for (yea).
- # Paired for.
- + Announced for.
- N Voted against (nay).
- X Paired against.
- - Announced against.
- P Voted "present".
- C Voted "present" to avoid possible conflict of interest.
- ? Did not vote or otherwise make a position known.

Democrats   *Republicans*

	9	10	11	12	13	14	15	16
ALABAMA								
1 Edwards	Y	Y	N	Y	N	Y	N	?
2 Dickinson	Y	N	N	Y	N	Y	N	N
3 Nichols	Y	N	N	Y	N	Y	Y	?
4 Bevill	Y	?	N	Y	N	Y	N	Y
5 Flippo	Y	Y	N	Y	N	N	Y	#
6 Smith	Y	N	N	Y	N	Y	Y	N
7 Shelby	Y	N	N	Y	N	N	N	Y
ALASKA								
AL Young	Y	N	N	N	N	Y	?	?
ARIZONA								
1 Rhodes	N	Y	N	N	?	?	?	?
2 Udall	N	Y	Y	N	Y	N	Y	Y
3 Stump	Y	N	N	Y	N	Y	N	N
4 Rudd	Y	N	N	Y	N	Y	N	N
ARKANSAS								
1 Alexander	N	?	?	N	N	N	#	?
2 Bethune	N	N	N	Y	Y	Y	N	Y
3 Hammerschmidt	Y	N	N	Y	N	Y	N	N
4 Anthony	Y	Y	Y	N	N	N	N	Y
CALIFORNIA								
1 Chappie	Y	N	N	?	?	#	N	N
2 Clausen	Y	Y	N	Y	N	Y	X	N
3 Matsui	N	Y	Y	N	Y	N	Y	Y
4 Fazio	N	Y	Y	N	Y	N	Y	Y
5 Burton, J.	N	Y	Y	?	?	X	#	Y
6 Burton, P.	N	Y	Y	N	Y	N	Y	Y
7 Miller	N	Y	Y	N	Y	N	Y	Y
8 Dellums	N	Y	Y	N	Y	N	Y	Y
9 Stark	N	Y	Y	N	Y	N	Y	Y
10 Edwards	N	Y	Y	N	Y	N	Y	Y
11 Lantos	N	?	Y	Y	Y	N	Y	?
12 McCloskey	?	?	Y	N	Y	N	Y	
13 Mineta	N	Y	Y	N	N	N	Y	Y
14 Shumway	Y	N	Y	N	Y	Y	N	N
15 Coelho	N	Y	Y	N	Y	N	Y	Y
16 Panetta	N	Y	Y	Y	N	Y	Y	Y
17 Pashayan	Y	Y	N	Y	N	Y	N	N
18 Thomas	Y	Y	N	N	Y	#	N	?
19 Lagomarsino	Y	Y	N	Y	N	Y	N	N
20 Goldwater	?	N	N	?	N	?	?	?
21 Fiedler	Y	Y	N	N	Y	N	N	N
22 Moorhead	Y	N	N	Y	N	Y	N	N
23 Beilenson	N	Y	Y	?	?	N	Y	Y
24 Waxman	N	Y	Y	N	Y	N	N	Y
25 Roybal	N	Y	Y	N	N	Y	Y	Y
26 Rousselot	Y	Y	N	N	Y	N	Y	N
27 Dornan	Y	Y	N	Y	N	Y	N	N
28 Dixon	N	Y	Y	N	Y	N	Y	Y
29 Hawkins	N	Y	Y	N	Y	N	Y	Y
30 Martinez	N	Y	Y	?	?	N	Y	Y
31 Dymally	N	Y	Y	N	Y	N	Y	?
32 Anderson	Y	Y	Y	N	Y	N	Y	Y
33 Grisham	Y	N	N	Y	N	Y	N	N
34 Lungren	Y	N	N	Y	N	Y	N	N
35 Dreier	Y	N	N	Y	N	Y	N	N
36 Brown	N	Y	Y	N	Y	N	?	?
37 Lewis	Y	N	N	Y	N	Y	N	?
38 Patterson	N	?	Y	N	Y	N	Y	Y
39 Dannemeyer	Y	N	N	Y	N	Y	N	N
40 Badham	#	N	N	N	N	X	X	
41 Lowery	Y	Y	N	N	Y	N	N	N
42 Hunter	Y	N	Y	N	Y	N	Y	Y
43 Burgener	Y	Y	N	N	N	Y	N	X
COLORADO								
1 Schroeder	N	N	Y	Y	Y	?	?	Y
2 Wirth	N	Y	Y	Y	Y	N	Y	Y
3 Kogovsek	N	Y	Y	Y	Y	N	N	Y
4 Brown	Y	N	N	Y	Y	Y	N	N

	9	10	11	12	13	14	15	16
5 Kramer	Y	N	N	Y	Y	Y	N	N
CONNECTICUT								
1 Kennelly	N	Y	Y	N	Y	N	Y	Y
2 Gejdenson	N	N	Y	N	Y	N	Y	Y
3 DeNardis	N	?	Y	N	Y	?	N	Y
4 McKinney	N	N	Y	Y	Y	Y	Y	Y
5 Ratchford	N	Y	Y	N	Y	N	Y	Y
6 Moffett	N	Y	Y	N	Y	?	Y	?
DELAWARE								
AL Evans	Y	Y	N	N	Y	?	N	?
FLORIDA								
1 Hutto	Y	N	N	N	N	N	N	Y
2 Fuqua	Y	N	Y	N	N	N	N	#
3 Bennett	Y	Y	Y	N	N	N	N	Y
4 Chappell	#	N	N	N	N	N	N	Y
5 McCollum	Y	N	N	Y	Y	N	N	Y
6 Young	Y	N	N	Y	N	Y	N	Y
7 Gibbons	Y	Y	N	Y	N	N	N	Y
8 Ireland	Y	N	N	Y	N	Y	N	?
9 Nelson	Y	Y	N	N	N	N	N	Y
10 Bafalis	Y	?	?	N	N	Y	N	N
11 Mica	Y	Y	Y	N	N	N	Y	Y
12 Shaw	Y	Y	N	Y	Y	N	N	N
13 Lehman	N	?	Y	?	?	?	?	?
14 Pepper	N	Y	Y	N	N	N	Y	Y
15 Fascell	N	?	Y	Y	Y	N	Y	?
GEORGIA								
1 Ginn	Y	N	N	N	N	N	Y	Y
2 Hatcher	Y	N	N	N	N	N	N	Y
3 Brinkley	Y	N	N	N	N	N	N	Y
4 Levitas	Y	N	?	Y	Y	Y	Y	Y
5 Fowler	N	Y	Y	N	Y	Y	Y	Y
6 Gingrich	Y	N	N	Y	Y	Y	Y	N
7 McDonald	Y	N	N	Y	N	Y	N	N
8 Evans	Y	N	N	?	?	N	?	?
9 Jenkins	Y	Y	Y	Y	N	Y	Y	Y
10 Barnard	Y	N	Y	N	N	N	N	Y
HAWAII								
1 Heftel	N	?	Y	N	Y	N	Y	Y
2 Akaka	N	Y	Y	N	N	N	Y	Y
IDAHO								
1 Craig	Y	N	N	Y	N	Y	N	X
2 Hansen	Y	N	N	Y	N	Y	N	N
ILLINOIS								
1 Washington	N	?	Y	?	Y	N	Y	Y
2 Savage	N	?	Y	N	Y	N	Y	Y
3 Russo	N	Y	Y	N	Y	N	Y	Y
4 Derwinski	Y	Y	N	N	N	Y	N	N
5 Fary	N	Y	Y	?	?	X	Y	Y
6 Hyde	Y	N	N	N	N	N	N	Y
7 Collins	N	Y	Y	N	N	N	Y	Y
8 Rostenkowski	N	Y	Y	N	N	N	N	Y
9 Yates	N	Y	Y	N	Y	N	?	Y
10 Porter	Y	N	Y	N	N	Y	N	N
11 Annunzio	N	Y	Y	N	Y	N	Y	Y
12 Crane, P.	Y	N	N	Y	Y	Y	N	N
13 McClory	Y	Y	N	N	N	N	N	Y
14 Erlenborn	Y	Y	N	N	N	Y	N	N
15 Corcoran	Y	Y	N	Y	N	Y	N	N
16 Martin	Y	Y	Y	Y	Y	Y	Y	Y
17 O'Brien	Y	Y	Y	N	Y	N	Y	?
18 Michel	Y	Y	N	Y	N	N	Y	N
19 Railsback	Y	Y	Y	?	?	?	Y	?
20 Findley	Y	N	Y	N	Y	Y	?	Y
21 Madigan	Y	N	N	Y	N	Y	N	N
22 Crane, D.	Y	N	N	Y	N	Y	N	?
23 Price	N	N	N	N	N	N	N	Y
24 Simon	N	Y	Y	N	Y	N	Y	Y
INDIANA								
1 Hall¹		Y	Y	N	Y	N	Y	Y
2 Fithian	N	N	N	Y	N	?	N	Y
3 Hiler	Y	N	N	Y	Y	N	N	N
4 Coats	Y	N	Y	N	Y	Y	N	?
5 Hillis	Y	?	N	Y	Y	N	Y	N
6 Evans	N	?	Y	N	N	N	N	Y
7 Myers	Y	N	N	N	Y	N	N	N
8 Deckard	Y	?	Y	Y	Y	N	Y	Y
9 Hamilton	N	N	Y	N	Y	N	Y	Y
10 Sharp	N	N	Y	Y	N	Y	N	Y
11 Jacobs	Y	N	Y	Y	N	Y	N	Y
IOWA								
1 Leach	Y	N	Y	Y	Y	Y	Y	Y
2 Tauke	Y	N	Y	N	Y	N	Y	X	Y
3 Evans	Y	N	Y	N	Y	N	Y	Y
4 Smith	N	Y	Y	N	N	N	N	Y
5 Harkin	N	Y	Y	Y	N	Y	N	Y
6 Bedell	N	N	Y	Y	Y	N	N	Y

ND - Northern Democrats   SD - Southern Democrats

	9	10	11	12	13	14	15	16
KANSAS								
1 ***Roberts***	Y	N	Y	Y	N	Y	N	N
2 ***Jeffries***	Y	N	N	Y	Y	Y	N	X
3 ***Winn***	Y	?	N	N	N	Y	N	N
4 Glickman	N	N	Y	Y	Y	N	N	Y
5 ***Whittaker***	Y	N	Y	Y	Y	Y	N	Y
KENTUCKY								
1 Hubbard	Y	N	Y	Y	N	Y	Y	?
2 Natcher	Y	Y	Y	Y	N	N	Y	Y
3 Mazzoli	N	Y	Y	N	N	N	Y	Y
4 ***Snyder***	Y	Y	Y	Y	Y	Y	Y	?
5 ***Rogers***	Y	N	N	Y	Y	Y	Y	N
6 ***Hopkins***	Y	N	Y	Y	Y	Y	Y	Y
7 Perkins	N	N	Y	Y	N	N	Y	Y
LOUISIANA								
1 ***Livingston***	Y	N	N	N	N	Y	N	Y
2 Boggs	N	Y	Y	N	N	N	Y	Y
3 Tauzin	Y	N	N	Y	N	Y	Y	Y
4 Roemer	Y	N	Y	Y	Y	Y	Y	Y
5 Huckaby	Y	N	Y	Y	Y	Y	N	?
6 ***Moore***	Y	N	N	Y	Y	Y	N	Y
7 Breaux	Y	Y	N	N	N	N	N	Y
8 Long	N	Y	Y	N	N	N	Y	Y
MAINE								
1 ***Emery***	Y	?	N	Y	Y	Y	?	N
2 ***Snowe***	Y	N	Y	Y	Y	Y	N	Y
MARYLAND								
1 Dyson	Y	Y	Y	Y	N	N	Y	Y
2 Long	N	Y	Y	Y	Y	N	Y	?
3 Mikulski	N	Y	Y	Y	Y	N	Y	Y
4 ***Holt***	Y	N	N	N	N	Y	N	?
5 Hoyer	N	Y	Y	N	Y	N	Y	Y
6 Byron	Y	?	Y	Y	Y	N	N	Y
7 Mitchell	N	Y	Y	Y	Y	N	Y	Y
8 Barnes	N	?	Y	N	Y	N	Y	Y
MASSACHUSETTS								
1 ***Conte***	N	?	Y	N	Y	Y	Y	Y
2 Boland	N	Y	Y	Y	Y	N	Y	Y
3 Early	N	Y	Y	N	Y	N	Y	Y
4 Frank	N	Y	Y	Y	Y	N	Y	?
5 Shannon	N	Y	Y	N	Y	N	Y	Y
6 Mavroules	N	Y	Y	N	Y	N	Y	Y
7 Markey	N	Y	Y	N	Y	N	Y	Y
8 O'Neill[2]				N				
9 Moakley	N	Y	Y	N	Y	N	Y	Y
10 ***Heckler***	N	Y	?	N	Y	?	?	?
11 Donnelly	N	Y	Y	N	Y	N	N	Y
12 Studds	N	N	Y	N	Y	N	Y	Y
MICHIGAN								
1 Conyers	N	N	Y	N	Y	N	Y	Y
2 ***Pursell***	Y	N	Y	Y	Y	Y	?	?
3 Wolpe	N	Y	Y	Y	Y	N	Y	Y
4 ***Siljander***	Y	N	N	Y	N	Y	Y	N
5 ***Sawyer***	Y	N	N	Y	Y	Y	N	N
6 ***Dunn***	Y	?	N	Y	Y	Y	Y	N
7 Kildee	N	Y	Y	Y	Y	N	Y	Y
8 Traxler	N	Y	Y	Y	Y	N	Y	Y
9 ***Vander Jagt***	Y	N	N	Y	Y	Y	N	?
10 Albosta	N	N	Y	Y	Y	N	Y	Y
11 ***Davis***	Y	N	N	Y	N	N	Y	Y
12 Bonior	N	Y	Y	Y	Y	N	Y	Y
13 Crockett	N	Y	Y	N	Y	N	Y	Y
14 Hertel	N	Y	Y	Y	Y	N	Y	Y
15 Ford	N	Y	Y	N	Y	N	Y	Y
16 Dingell	N	Y	Y	N	Y	N	Y	Y
17 Brodhead	N	Y	Y	N	Y	N	Y	Y
18 Blanchard	?	?	?	?	?	?	#	?
19 ***Broomfield***	Y	N	N	N	Y	Y	Y	?
MINNESOTA								
1 ***Erdahl***	Y	N	Y	Y	?	Y	N	Y
2 ***Hagedorn***	Y	N	N	?	?	?	?	?
3 ***Frenzel***	Y	N	Y	N	Y	Y	N	Y
4 Vento	N	Y	Y	N	Y	N	Y	Y
5 Sabo	N	Y	Y	N	Y	N	Y	Y
6 ***Weber***	Y	N	Y	Y	Y	Y	N	Y
7 ***Stangeland***	Y	N	N	Y	N	Y	N	N
8 Oberstar	N	N	Y	N	Y	N	Y	Y
MISSISSIPPI								
1 Whitten	Y	Y	Y	N	N	N	Y	Y
2 Bowen	Y	Y	N	N	N	N	N	Y
3 Montgomery	Y	Y	N	?	N	Y	N	Y
4 Dowdy	Y	Y	Y	N	N	N	Y	Y
5 ***Lott***	Y	Y	N	N	Y	Y	N	N
MISSOURI								
1 Clay	N	Y	Y	N	Y	N	Y	Y
2 Young	N	Y	Y	N	N	N	Y	Y
3 Gephardt	N	Y	Y	Y	Y	N	Y	Y
4 Skelton	Y	?	?	N	N	N	Y	Y
5 Bolling	N	Y	?	N	?	?	?	?
6 ***Coleman***	Y	N	N	N	N	Y	Y	Y
7 ***Taylor***	Y	?	N	Y	N	Y	N	N
8 ***Bailey***	Y	N	N	Y	Y	Y	N	N
9 Volkmer	Y	N	Y	Y	Y	N	Y	Y
10 ***Emerson***	Y	N	N	Y	N	Y	N	N
MONTANA								
1 Williams	N	N	Y	N	Y	N	Y	Y
2 ***Marlenee***	Y	?	N	N	N	Y	N	N
NEBRASKA								
1 ***Bereuter***	Y	N	N	Y	N	Y	N	Y
2 ***Daub***	Y	N	N	Y	N	Y	N	N
3 ***Smith***	Y	N	Y	Y	N	Y	N	N
NEVADA								
AL Santini	Y	?	?	Y	N	?	N	?
NEW HAMPSHIRE								
1 D'Amours	N	Y	Y	Y	Y	N	?	Y
2 ***Gregg***	Y	Y	Y	Y	Y	Y	N	N
NEW JERSEY								
1 Florio	N	?	Y	N	Y	N	Y	Y
2 Hughes	N	N	Y	Y	Y	N	Y	Y
3 Howard	N	Y	Y	N	Y	N	Y	Y
4 ***Smith***	Y	Y	Y	Y	Y	Y	N	Y
5 ***Fenwick***	Y	Y	Y	N	Y	Y	N	Y
6 ***Forsythe***	?	Y	Y	N	N	Y	?	N
7 ***Roukema***	N	N	Y	Y	N	Y	N	Y
8 Roe	N	N	Y	N	N	N	Y	Y
9 ***Hollenbeck***	N	Y	Y	N	N	?	Y	N
10 Rodino	N	Y	Y	N	Y	N	Y	Y
11 Minish	N	Y	Y	N	Y	N	Y	Y
12 ***Rinaldo***	N	Y	Y	Y	Y	N	N	Y
13 ***Courter***	Y	N	N	Y	Y	Y	N	Y
14 Guarini	X	Y	Y	N	Y	N	Y	Y
15 Dwyer	N	Y	Y	N	N	N	Y	Y
NEW MEXICO								
1 ***Lujan***	Y	N	N	Y	N	Y	N	N
2 ***Skeen***	Y	N	N	Y	N	Y	N	N
NEW YORK								
1 ***Carney***	Y	?	N	N	N	Y	N	N
2 Downey	N	Y	Y	N	Y	N	Y	Y
3 ***Carman***	Y	Y	N	N	Y	Y	N	N
4 ***Lent***	Y	Y	Y	N	Y	Y	N	N
5 ***McGrath***	Y	Y	Y	N	Y	Y	N	N
6 ***LeBoutillier***	Y	?	N	Y	Y	Y	?	?
7 Addabbo	N	Y	Y	N	Y	N	Y	Y
8 Rosenthal	N	Y	Y	?	Y	N	Y	?
9 Ferraro	N	Y	Y	N	Y	N	Y	Y
10 Biaggi	N	Y	Y	N	N	N	Y	Y
11 Scheuer	N	Y	Y	N	Y	N	Y	Y
12 Chisholm	N	?	Y	N	Y	N	Y	Y
13 Solarz	N	Y	Y	N	Y	N	Y	Y
14 Richmond[3]								
15 Zeferetti	N	?	Y	N	N	N	?	Y
16 Schumer	N	Y	Y	N	Y	N	Y	Y
17 ***Molinari***	Y	?	N	N	Y	Y	N	Y
18 ***Green***	Y	N	Y	N	Y	Y	N	N
19 Rangel	N	Y	Y	N	Y	N	Y	Y
20 Weiss	N	N	Y	N	Y	N	Y	Y
21 Garcia	N	Y	Y	N	Y	N	Y	?
22 Bingham	N	Y	Y	N	Y	?	N	Y
23 Peyser	N	Y	Y	N	Y	N	Y	Y
24 Ottinger	N	N	Y	N	Y	N	Y	Y
25 ***Fish***	Y	Y	N	N	Y	Y	Y	Y
26 ***Gilman***	N	N	N	Y	Y	Y	Y	Y
27 McHugh	N	Y	Y	N	Y	N	N	Y
28 Stratton	N	Y	N	N	N	N	Y	Y
29 ***Solomon***	Y	N	N	Y	Y	Y	Y	N
30 ***Martin***	Y	N	N	Y	Y	Y	N	Y
31 ***Mitchell***	Y	N	N	Y	Y	Y	N	Y
32 ***Wortley***	Y	Y	N	Y	Y	Y	Y	N
33 ***Lee***	Y	N	N	Y	N	Y	Y	?
34 ***Horton***	N	N	Y	Y	N	Y	Y	?
35 ***Conable***	Y	Y	N	Y	N	Y	N	Y
36 LaFalce	N	N	Y	N	Y	N	Y	Y
37 Nowak	N	N	Y	N	Y	N	Y	Y
38 ***Kemp***	N	N	N	N	Y	Y	N	?
39 Lundine	N	N	Y	N	Y	N	Y	?
NORTH CAROLINA								
1 Jones	Y	Y	Y	N	N	N	Y	?
2 Fountain	Y	N	N	N	N	Y	N	Y
3 Whitley	Y	N	N	Y	N	N	N	Y
4 Andrews	Y	N	Y	N	N	N	N	Y
5 Neal	Y	N	Y	Y	Y	N	N	Y
6 ***Johnston***	Y	Y	N	N	?	Y	N	N
7 Rose	Y	Y	Y	Y	N	N	N	?
8 Hefner	Y	N	?	Y	N	N	N	Y
9 ***Martin***	Y	N	N	N	N	Y	N	N
10 ***Broyhill***	Y	N	N	Y	N	Y	N	N
11 ***Hendon***	Y	?	N	Y	N	Y	N	N
NORTH DAKOTA								
AL Dorgan	N	Y	Y	Y	N	N	Y	Y
OHIO								
1 ***Gradison***	Y	Y	Y	Y	Y	Y	N	Y
2 Luken	N	Y	Y	N	N	N	Y	Y
3 Hall	N	Y	Y	N	Y	N	Y	Y
4 ***Oxley***	Y	N	N	Y	N	Y	N	N
5 ***Latta***	Y	Y	N	N	Y	Y	Y	N
6 ***McEwen***	Y	N	N	Y	N	Y	Y	N
7 ***Brown***	Y	Y	N	Y	N	Y	?	N
8 ***Kindness***	Y	N	N	Y	N	?	Y	N
9 ***Weber***	Y	N	N	Y	Y	Y	N	N
10 ***Miller***	Y	N	N	Y	N	Y	Y	Y
11 ***Stanton***	Y	?	N	N	N	Y	N	?
12 Shamansky	N	Y	Y	Y	Y	N	Y	Y
13 Pease	N	Y	Y	Y	Y	N	Y	Y
14 Seiberling	N	N	Y	N	Y	N	Y	Y
15 ***Wylie***	Y	Y	N	Y	Y	Y	Y	N
16 ***Regula***	Y	N	N	Y	N	Y	Y	Y
17 ***Ashbrook***	Y	N	N	N	N	Y	N	?
18 Applegate	Y	Y	Y	Y	Y	N	Y	Y
19 ***Williams***	Y	N	Y	Y	N	N	Y	#
20 Oakar	N	Y	Y	Y	Y	N	Y	Y
21 Stokes	N	Y	Y	N	Y	N	#	Y
22 Eckart	Y	Y	Y	Y	Y	N	Y	Y
23 Mottl	Y	?	N	Y	N	N	Y	Y
OKLAHOMA								
1 Jones	N	N	Y	Y	N	N	N	Y
2 Synar	N	N	Y	Y	Y	Y	N	Y
3 Watkins	Y	Y	Y	Y	N	N	Y	Y
4 McCurdy	Y	N	Y	Y	Y	Y	Y	Y
5 ***Edwards***	?	N	N	Y	Y	Y	N	Y
6 English	Y	N	Y	Y	N	Y	Y	Y
OREGON								
1 AuCoin	N	Y	Y	Y	?	N	N	Y
2 ***Smith***	Y	N	Y	Y	N	Y	N	Y
3 Wyden	N	Y	Y	Y	Y	N	N	Y
4 Weaver	N	N	Y	?	Y	N	Y	Y
PENNSYLVANIA								
1 Foglietta	N	Y	Y	N	Y	N	Y	Y
2 Gray	N	Y	Y	N	Y	N	Y	Y
3 Smith	N	Y	Y	N	N	?	Y	?
4 ***Dougherty***	N	Y	?	N	?	N	Y	?
5 ***Schulze***	Y	Y	N	?	?	?	?	?
6 Yatron	N	N	Y	Y	N	N	Y	Y
7 Edgar	N	Y	Y	N	Y	N	Y	Y
8 ***Coyne, J.***	Y	?	N	Y	Y	Y	?	N
9 ***Shuster***	Y	Y	?	?	?	?	?	?
10 ***McDade***	N	Y	Y	N	Y	N	Y	N
11 ***Nelligan***	N	Y	N	N	Y	N	Y	Y
12 Murtha	N	Y	N	N	N	N	Y	Y
13 ***Coughlin***	Y	Y	Y	N	Y	Y	Y	N
14 Coyne, W.	N	Y	Y	N	N	N	Y	Y
15 ***Ritter***	Y	N	N	Y	Y	Y	Y	N
16 ***Walker***	Y	N	N	Y	Y	Y	N	N
17 Ertel	N	N	Y	N	Y	N	Y	Y
18 Walgren	N	Y	Y	Y	Y	N	Y	Y
19 ***Goodling***	Y	N	Y	N	Y	Y	Y	Y
20 Gaydos	N	Y	Y	Y	N	N	Y	Y
21 Bailey	N	Y	N	N	N	N	Y	Y
22 Murphy	N	N	Y	N	N	N	Y	Y
23 ***Clinger***	Y	Y	Y	Y	Y	Y	N	N
24 ***Marks***	N	?	Y	N	N	N	Y	Y
25 ***Atkinson***	Y	?	N	Y	N	Y	N	N
RHODE ISLAND								
1 St Germain	N	Y	Y	N	Y	N	Y	Y
2 ***Schneider***	N	N	Y	Y	Y	Y	Y	Y
SOUTH CAROLINA								
1 ***Hartnett***	Y	N	N	N	N	Y	N	N
2 ***Spence***	Y	N	N	Y	N	Y	N	N
3 Derrick	Y	Y	Y	N	Y	Y	N	#
4 ***Campbell***	Y	N	N	N	N	Y	N	?
5 Holland	N	N	Y	N	N	N	N	?
6 ***Napier***	Y	N	N	N	N	Y	N	N
SOUTH DAKOTA								
1 Daschle	Y	N	Y	Y	Y	Y	?	Y
2 ***Roberts***	Y	N	N	Y	N	Y	N	N
TENNESSEE								
1 ***Quillen***	Y	N	N	Y	N	Y	N	N
2 ***Duncan***	Y	N	N	Y	N	Y	N	N
3 Bouquard	Y	N	Y	Y	N	N	N	Y
4 Gore	N	N	Y	Y	N	N	N	Y
5 Boner	Y	N	Y	Y	N	N	Y	Y
6 ***Beard***	Y	N	N	Y	?	?	X	?
7 Jones	Y	N	Y	Y	N	N	Y	Y
8 Ford	N	N	Y	N	N	N	Y	Y
TEXAS								
1 Hall, S.	Y	N	N	Y	N	N	Y	Y
2 Wilson	Y	N	N	?	N	?	Y	Y
3 ***Collins***	Y	N	N	Y	Y	Y	N	N
4 Hall, R.	Y	N	N	Y	N	N	Y	Y
5 Mattox	N	?	?	N	Y	N	Y	Y
6 Gramm	Y	N	N	Y	Y	Y	N	N
7 ***Archer***	Y	Y	N	Y	N	Y	N	?
8 ***Fields***	Y	Y	N	Y	N	Y	N	N
9 Brooks	N	Y	Y	N	N	N	Y	Y
10 Pickle	Y	Y	Y	Y	N	N	N	Y
11 Leath	Y	N	N	N	N	N	N	?
12 Wright	N	Y	Y	N	N	N	Y	Y
13 Hightower	Y	N	N	Y	N	N	N	Y
14 Patman	Y	N	N	Y	N	N	N	Y
15 de la Garza	Y	N	N	Y	Y	N	N	Y
16 White	Y	N	N	N	N	N	N	Y
17 Stenholm	Y	N	N	Y	N	Y	N	Y
18 Leland	N	?	Y	N	Y	N	Y	Y
19 Hance	Y	?	N	Y	N	N	N	Y
20 Gonzalez	N	N	Y	N	N	N	Y	Y
21 ***Loeffler***	Y	N	N	Y	N	Y	N	N
22 ***Paul***	Y	N	Y	Y	Y	Y	N	Y
23 Kazen	Y	N	N	Y	N	N	N	Y
24 Frost	N	Y	Y	N	Y	N	Y	Y
UTAH								
1 ***Hansen***	Y	N	N	Y	N	Y	N	N
2 ***Marriott***	Y	N	N	Y	N	Y	N	N
VERMONT								
AL ***Jeffords***	N	N	Y	N	Y	Y	N	Y
VIRGINIA								
1 ***Trible***	Y	N	N	N	Y	Y	N	N
2 ***Whitehurst***	Y	Y	N	Y	N	Y	N	N
3 ***Bliley***	Y	N	N	N	N	Y	N	N
4 ***Daniel, R.***	Y	Y	N	N	N	Y	N	N
5 Daniel, D.	?	N	N	N	N	Y	N	Y
6 ***Butler***	Y	N	N	N	N	Y	N	N
7 ***Robinson***	Y	N	N	N	N	Y	N	N
8 ***Parris***	Y	Y	N	Y	N	Y	N	Y
9 ***Wampler***	Y	N	N	N	N	Y	N	N
10 ***Wolf***	Y	N	N	N	Y	Y	N	N
WASHINGTON								
1 ***Pritchard***	N	Y	Y	N	Y	Y	N	Y
2 Swift	N	N	Y	N	Y	N	Y	Y
3 Bonker	N	-	Y	N	Y	N	N	Y
4 ***Morrison***	Y	N	N	Y	N	Y	N	N
5 Foley	N	Y	Y	N	N	N	N	Y
6 Dicks	N	Y	Y	N	Y	N	Y	Y
7 Lowry	N	Y	Y	N	Y	N	N	Y
WEST VIRGINIA								
1 Mollohan	N	Y	N	N	N	N	Y	Y
2 ***Benedict***	Y	N	N	Y	N	Y	N	N
3 ***Staton***	Y	Y	N	N	N	Y	N	N
4 Rahall	N	N	Y	N	Y	N	Y	Y
WISCONSIN								
1 Aspin	N	N	Y	Y	Y	N	Y	Y
2 Kastenmeier	N	N	Y	N	Y	N	Y	Y
3 ***Gunderson***	Y	N	Y	Y	Y	Y	N	Y
4 Zablocki	N	Y	Y	N	N	N	Y	Y
5 Reuss	N	Y	Y	N	Y	N	N	Y
6 ***Petri***	Y	N	Y	Y	Y	Y	N	Y
7 Obey	N	N	Y	N	Y	N	Y	Y
8 ***Roth***	Y	N	N	Y	N	Y	Y	N
9 ***Sensenbrenner***	Y	N	Y	Y	Y	Y	N	Y
WYOMING								
AL ***Cheney***	Y	N	N	Y	N	Y	N	N

1. Rep. Katie Hall, D-Ind., sworn in Nov. 29, 1982, to succeed Adam Benjamin Jr., D, who died Sept. 7, 1982.

2. Rep. Thomas P. O'Neill Jr., D-Mass., as Speaker, votes at his own discretion.

3. Rep. Fred Richmond, D-N.Y., resigned, Aug. 25, 1982.

Southern states - Ala., Ark., Fla., Ga., Ky., La., Miss., N.C., Okla., S.C., Tenn., Texas, Va.

 Presidential Support

Honeymoon Is Over:

Presidential Support Study Shows Reagan Rating Fell 10 Percentage Points in 1982

If 1981 was President Reagan's honeymoon with Congress, Congressional Quarterly's annual study of presidential support showed that by 1982, the bloom was off the rose.

For some Democrats, in fact, the link to Reagan looked more like a love affair with an unhappy ending. And even some Republicans found less than total bliss with their president.

A number of members who voted regularly with Reagan found themselves out of a job as a result of the November elections. And some Democrats who were unusually loyal to the Republican president learned after the election that their party was unhappy with their choice of a GOP political mate.

One Democrat — Rep. Phil Gramm of Texas — was thrown off the House Budget Committee for his fealty to Reagan. Two other Democrats who appealed for forgiveness were given stern warnings. And a handful of others were denied the committee assignments they sought.

Success Rate

Following are the annual percentages of presidential victories since 1953 on congressional votes where the presidents took a clear-cut position:

Eisenhower		Nixon	
1953	89.0%	1969	74.0%
1954	82.8	1970	77.0
1955	75.0	1971	75.0
1956	70.0	1972	66.0
1957	68.0	1973	50.6
1958	76.0	1974	59.6
1959	52.0		
1960	65.0	**Ford**	
		1974	58.2%
		1975	61.0
Kennedy		1976	53.8
1961	81.0%		
1962	85.4	**Carter**	
1963	87.1	1977	75.4%
		1978	78.3
Johnson		1979	76.8
1964	88.0%	1980	75.1
1965	93.0		
1966	79.0	**Reagan**	
1967	79.0	1981	82.4%
1968	75.0	1982	72.4

CQ's study of 196 votes on which Reagan declared a position showed that his support was down from 1981. The president's overall score was 72.4 percent, a reduction of 10 percentage points from 1981. *(Box, this page)*

The majority of the 196 votes used in the study — 119 — were in the Republican-controlled Senate; the other 77 were in the Democratic-controlled House. *(Votes, p. 21-C)*

On Senate votes on which he took a position, Reagan won 83.2 percent of the time, a drop of 5.1 percentage points from the 1981 level, according to the study. On House votes on which he took a position, he won 55.8 percent of the time, a drop of 16.6 percentage points from the 1981 level. *(1981 study, 1981 Almanac p. 18-C)*

Limitations of Study

Although the study reflected that Reagan had more political troubles on Capitol Hill than in 1981, it does not measure how much of his program actually was approved. And as a precise measure of a member's loyalty to the White House, it should be used with caution.

First, the study counted only issues that reached a roll-call vote on the House or Senate floor. Aspects of the president's agenda that are scuttled or rejected before they reach the floor, compromised behind closed doors or whisked through by voice vote were not counted.

Second, the study counted only votes where the president indicated clear personal support or opposition. Third, all votes were given equal weight; no distinction was made between major and minor votes, narrow victories and lopsided margins, administration proposals and congressional initiatives. *(Ground rules, p. 20-C)*

Therefore, for example, Reagan's slim victory on a $98.3 billion package of tax increases, a heavily lobbied piece of legislation, counted the same as the Senate's unanimous confirmation of George P. Shultz as secretary of state.

Finally, issues that took many roll calls to resolve may have influenced the study more than issues settled by a single vote. The classic recent example was in 1978, when President Carter's Senate support score was dramatically enhanced by winning 55 roll calls — mostly procedural — related to ratification of the Panama Canal treaties.

In 1982, some issues were controversial enough to require a number of roll calls to resolve the issues. For example, 30 Senate roll calls were related to a proposed constitutional amendment requiring a balanced federal budget and 16 were related to Senate consideration of a wide-ranging immigration reform bill, giving those subjects extra importance in calculating President Reagan's support score.

A reporter or researcher interested in how an individual member of Congress voted on the administration's program is advised to look at the specifics of the member's legislative actions, including his or her record on CQ's selection of key votes. *(Key votes, p. 3-C)*

Still, the presidential support score is a rough measure of the relationship between Congress and the president. Over time, it reflects numerically the rises and dips in relations between the two branches of government, and individual scores show how members fit the trends. *(Sena-*

tors' 1982 scores, p. 24-C; House members' scores, p. 22-C)

The study was started in 1953 and was long considered an indicator of the president's success on Capitol Hill. A closer reading of the study's ground rules showed its limitations as a measure of executive clout, but not all readers have been discriminating in using the figures.

During the 1980 presidential campaign, for example, President Carter's supporters, citing his 77 percent support score in 1979, claimed that Congress had passed four-fifths of the Carter agenda. A Carter aide later conceded that CQ's statistics had been "mistranslated or misused." However, the aide claimed that the study itself was "reasonably misleading." *(Carter 1980 score, 1980 Almanac p. 17-C)*

The Reagan Record

With his lowered support scores in 1982, Reagan broke something of a tradition with all of his predecessors since Eisenhower. The support scores of most recent presidents increased in their second year in office. *(Success rate, box, p. 18-C)*

Not surprisingly, Republicans agreed with Reagan more often than Democrats, although GOP support was down from the previous year.

Senate Republicans. Senate Republicans on the average voted with Reagan on 74 percent of the roll calls counted, down from a record-breaking 80 percent in 1981.

Strom Thurmond, R-S.C., chairman of the Senate Judiciary Committee, tied with Majority Leader Howard H. Baker Jr., R-Tenn., for top support honors, voting with Reagan 89 percent of the time.

Two senators who had considerable influence over Reagan's economic proposals were next in line. Robert Dole, R-Kan., chairman of the Finance Committee and responsible for all tax legislation, voted with Reagan on 86 percent of the applicable votes. Pete V. Domenici, R-N.M., chairman of the Budget Committee, voted with him 85 percent of the time.

Some of Reagan's most conservative GOP colleagues wavered in the ranks, particularly over his last initiative of the year, a highway bill that included a gasoline tax hike. Jesse Helms and John P. East of North Carolina led the fight against the measure.

Helms' support score was 75 percent, down nine points from 1981. East's score was 77 percent, down seven points.

For one Republican, Harrison "Jack" Schmitt, N.M., loyalty to Reagan apparently was not a political asset. Schmitt voted with the president on 71 percent of the roll calls in the study, a shade below the party average of 74 percent but good enough to get Reagan out to New Mexico for a campaign appearance. It didn't help. Schmitt was defeated for re-election.

The president's most consistent Republican opponent was John H. Chafee, R-R.I., who voted against him 45 percent of the time. Chafee was re-elected in November.

Senate Democrats. The Democrats' average support score dipped to 43 percent, from 49 percent in 1981. Democrats showing the highest support were all Southerners: Harry F. Byrd Jr., an independent who caucused with the Democrats, at 75 percent; John C. Stennis, Miss., 71 percent, and Sam Nunn, Ga., 70 percent. Daniel Patrick Moynihan, D-N.Y., opposed Reagan the most (71 percent).

Although Howard W. Cannon, D-Nev., had only a 34 percent support score, his distance from Reagan did not bring re-election. Hampered by the residue of a tough primary fight and beset by damaging publicity coming from a trial of Teamsters officials in Chicago, he lost to Republican Chic Hecht.

House. In the House, Republican support for Reagan dropped from 68 percent in 1981 to 64 percent in 1982. Democratic support slipped from 42 percent to 39 percent. The most supportive Republican was Dan Lungren, R-Calif., at 90 percent. The most supportive Democrat was Gramm, at 84 percent.

The Republican who opposed the president most often was Margaret M. Heckler, Mass., at 56 percent. She was

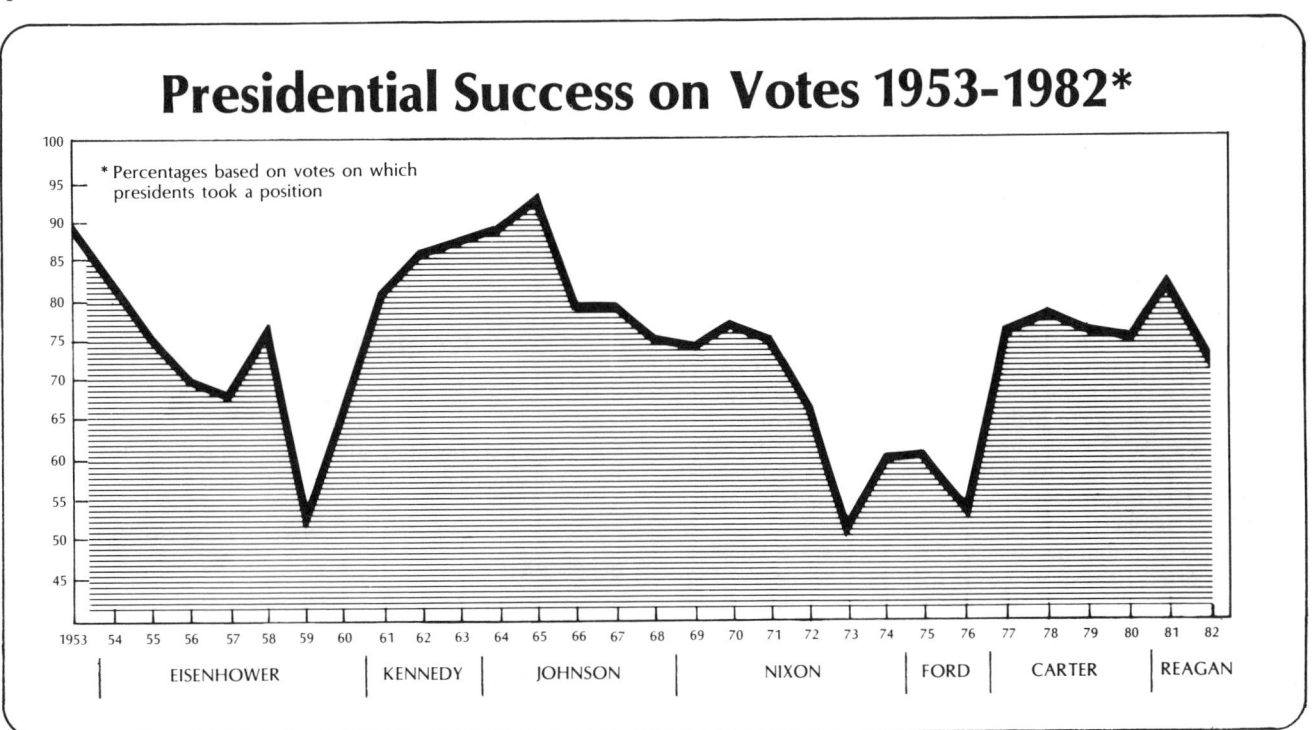

Presidential Success on Votes 1953-1982*

* Percentages based on votes on which presidents took a position

Ground Rules for CQ Presidential Support-Opposition

Presidential Issues — CQ tries to determine what the president personally, as distinct from other administration officials, does and does not want in the way of legislative action by analyzing his messages to Congress, press conference remarks and other public statements and documents. Members must be aware of the position when the vote is taken.

Borderline Cases — By the time an issue reaches a vote, it may differ from the original form in which the president expressed himself. In such cases, CQ analyzes the measure to determine whether, on balance, the features favored by the president outweigh those he opposed or vice versa. Only then is the vote classified.

Some Votes Excluded — Occasionally, important measures are so extensively amended on the floor that it is impossible to characterize final passage as a victory or defeat for the president.

Procedural Votes — Votes on motions to recommit, to reconsider or to table often are key tests that govern the legislative outcome. Such votes are necessarily included in the presidential support tabulations.

Appropriations — Generally, votes on passage of appropriations bills are not included in the tabulations, since it is rarely possible to determine the president's position on the revisions Congress almost invariably makes in the sums allowed. However, votes on amendments to cut or increase specific funds requested in the president's budget are included.

Failure to Vote — In tabulating the support or opposition scores of members on the selected presidential-issue votes, CQ counts only "yea" and "nay" votes on the ground that only these affect the outcome. Most failures to vote reflect absences because of illness or official business. Failures to vote lower both support and opposition scores equally.

Weighting — All presidential-issue votes have equal statistical weight in the analysis.

Changed Positions — Presidential support is determined by the position of the president at the time of a vote, even though that position may be different from an earlier position, or may have been reversed after the vote was taken.

---

defeated for re-election, and despite her opposition score, Reagan appointed her to his Cabinet Jan. 12, 1983.

The Democrat with the highest opposition score was Ronald V. Dellums, Calif., at 81 percent.

The House results provided an interesting study of the consequences of presidential support. The best example was Gramm. When the Democrats organized for the 98th Congress in January 1983, Gramm was thrown off the Budget Committee. Gramm resigned from his seat and said he would run for re-election as a Republican.

Two other Democrats who showed strong fealty to the president were not punished as severely as Gramm, but their colleagues left no doubt that future wandering from the party would not be countenanced. G. V. "Sonny" Montgomery, Miss., with a support score of 74 percent, was allowed to keep his post as chairman of the Veterans' Affairs Committee, but only by a 16-11 vote of the Democratic Steering and Policy Committee, which makes committee assignments.

Buddy Roemer, D-La., whose support score was 75 percent, was given a seat on the Banking, Finance and Urban Affairs Committee over the protests of other party members. To calm some angered committee members, the panel was expanded to include two other Democrats.

Three other Democrats with scores well above the party average — Roy Dyson, Md., Doug Barnard Jr., Ga., and John B. Breaux, La. — were not given the committee posts they sought.

Among Republicans defeated Nov. 2 were a number who supported Reagan well over half the time on the CQ votes, including Eugene Johnston, N.C., 84 percent; Albert Lee Smith Jr., Ala., 81 percent; David Michael Staton, W.Va., 78 percent; Robert W. Daniel Jr., Va., 75 percent; Bill Hendon, N.C., 71 percent; James L. Nelligan, Pa., 62 percent; John LeBoutillier, N.Y., 60 percent; William C. Wampler, Va., 58 percent; and Jim Coyne, Pa., 56 percent.

Average Scores

Following are composites of Democratic and Republican scores for 1982 and 1981:

| | 1982 | | 1981 | |
	Dem.	Rep.	Dem.	Rep.
SUPPORT				
Senate	43%	74%	49%	80%
House	39	64	42	68
OPPOSITION				
Senate	51	21	45	15
House	51	27	50	26

Regional Averages

SUPPORT

Regional presidential support scores for 1982; scores for 1981 are in parentheses:

	East	West	South	Midwest
DEMOCRATS				
Senate	34% (40)	38% (46)	55% (60)	42% (46)
House	34 (35)	34 (38)	50 (56)	34 (36)
REPUBLICANS				
Senate	64 (74)	75 (82)	80 (85)	77 (81)
House	56 (64)	70 (70)	70 (73)	62 (67)

OPPOSITION

Regional presidential opposition scores for 1982; scores for 1981 are in parentheses:

	East	West	South	Midwest
DEMOCRATS				
Senate	62% (52)	54% (44)	41% (35)	53% (49)
House	56 (57)	56 (54)	41 (37)	56 (57)
REPUBLICANS				
Senate	31 (21)	18 (11)	17 (11)	19 (16)
House	35 (31)	18 (21)	23 (22)	30 (29)

*(CQ defines regions of the United States as follows: **East:** Conn., Del., Maine, Md., Mass., N.H., N.J., N.Y., Pa., R.I., Vt., W.Va. **West:** Alaska, Ariz., Calif., Colo., Hawaii, Idaho, Mont., Nev., N.M., Ore., Utah, Wash., Wyo. **South:** Ala., Ark., Fla., Ga., Ky., La., Miss., N.C., Okla., S.C., Tenn., Texas, Va. **Midwest:** Ill., Ind., Iowa, Kan., Mich., Minn., Mo., Neb., N.D., Ohio, S.D., Wis.)*

Highest Scorers — Support

Highest individual scorers in presidential support — those who voted most often for Reagan's position in 1982:

SENATE

Democrats		Republicans	
Byrd, Va. [1]	75%	Baker, Tenn.	89%
Stennis, Miss.	71	Thurmond, S.C.	89
Nunn, Ga.	70	Dole, Kan.	86
Zorinsky, Neb.	64	Domenici, N.M.	85
Chiles, Fla.	63	Quayle, Ind.	84
Bentsen, Texas	61	Grassley, Iowa	84
Heflin, Ala.	61	Lugar, Ind.	83
Johnston, La.	61	Garn, Utah	83
DeConcini, Ariz.	61	Warner, Va.	83
Boren, Okla.	60	Mattingly, Ga.	82
Long, La.	59	Laxalt, Nev.	82
Exon, Neb.	55	Brady, N.J.[2]	82
		Simpson, Wyo.	82

HOUSE

Democrats		Republicans	
Gramm, Texas	84%	Lungren, Calif.	90%
McDonald, Ga.	83	Cheney, Wyo.	87
Stump, Ariz.[3]	82	Corcoran, Ill.	87
Roemer, La.	75	Bliley, Va.	86
Stenholm, Texas	74	Hiler, Ind.	86
Montgomery, Miss.	74	Fields, Texas	84
Daniel, Va.	70	Johnston, N.C.	84
Leath, Texas	66	Loeffler, Texas	84
English, Okla.	65	Hansen, Idaho	84
Gibbons, Fla.	65	Latta, Ohio	83
Bennett, Fla.	65	Lagomarsino, Calif.	83
		Michel, Ill.	83
		Hunter, Calif.	83

[1] *Elected as an independent, but caucuses with Democrats.*
[2] *Not eligible for all presidential-issue votes in 1982.*
[3] *Stump was elected to the 97th Congress as a Democrat and to the 98th Congress as a Republican.*

High Scorers — Opposition

Highest individual scorers in presidential opposition — those who voted most often against Reagan's position in 1982:

SENATE

Democrats		Republicans	
Moynihan, N.Y.	71%	Chafee, R.I.	45%
Eagleton, Mo.	68	Weicker, Conn.	44
Matsunaga, Hawaii	66	Specter, Pa.	44
Inouye, Hawaii	66	Heinz, Pa.	39
Cranston, Calif.	66	Mathias, Md.	38
Riegle, Mich.	66	Cohen, Maine	31
Sarbanes, Md.	65	Hatfield, Ore.	29
Kennedy, Mass.	64	Durenberger, Minn.	28
Metzenbaum, Ohio	64	Stafford, Vt.	27
		Rudman, N.H.	27

HOUSE

Democrats		Republicans	
Dellums, Calif.	81%	Heckler, Mass.	56%
Seiberling, Ohio	75	Hollenbeck, N.J.	56
Kastenmeier, Wis.	74	Schneider, R.I.	56
Mitchell, Md.	74	McKinney, Conn.	52
Ottinger, N.Y.	73	DeNardis, Conn.	52
Washington, Ill.	73	Leach, Iowa	52
Rodino, N.J.	71	Snowe, Maine	52
Roybal, Calif.	71	Smith, N.J.	51
Miller, Calif.	71	Findley, Ill.	49
		Rinaldo, N.J.	49

Presidential Support and Opposition: House

1. Reagan Support Score, 1982. Percentage of 77 Reagan-issue recorded votes in 1982 on which representative voted "yea" or "nay" *in agreement* with the president's position. Failures to vote lower both Support and Opposition scores.

2. Reagan Opposition Score, 1982. Percentage of 77 Reagan-issue recorded votes in 1982 on which representative voted "yea" or "nay" *in disagreement* with the president's position. Failures to vote lower both Support and Opposition scores.

KEY		
† Not eligible for all recorded votes in 1982 (sworn in after Jan. 25, died or resigned during session, or voted "present" to avoid possible conflict of interest).		
Democrats *Republicans*		

	1	2
ALABAMA		
1 *Edwards*	71	22
2 *Dickinson*	75	14
3 Nichols	52	38
4 Bevill	55	44
5 Flippo	49	40
6 *Smith*	81	16
7 Shelby	60	40
ALASKA		
AL *Young*	45	26
ARIZONA		
1 *Rhodes*	43	18
2 Udall	38	56
3 *Stump*	82	13
4 *Rudd*	78	13
ARKANSAS		
1 Alexander	40	49
2 *Bethune*	58	31
3 *Hammerschmidt*	65	32
4 Anthony	48	43
CALIFORNIA		
1 *Chappie*	66	19
2 *Clausen*	61	35
3 Matsui	40	60
4 Fazio	36	58
5 Burton, J.	4	18
6 Burton, P.	22	60
7 Miller	26	71
8 Dellums	17	81
9 Stark	23	64
10 Edwards	27	68
11 Lantos	31	57
12 *McCloskey*	45	21
13 Mineta	40	60
14 *Shumway*	78	16
15 Coelho	44	52
16 Panetta	42	55
17 *Pashayan*	71	22
18 *Thomas*	79	10
19 *Lagomarsino*	83	16
20 *Goldwater*	42	9
21 *Fiedler*	71	27
22 *Moorhead*	78	21
23 Beilenson	38	53
24 Waxman	36	58
25 Roybal	23	71
26 *Rousselot*	69	9
27 *Dornan*	61	5
28 Dixon	32	55
29 Hawkins	34	60
30 Martinez [1]	32†	55†
31 Dymally	22	56
32 Anderson	51	49
33 *Grisham*	70	6
34 Lungren	90	8
35 *Dreier*	78	17
36 Brown	32	51
37 *Lewis*	81	16
38 Patterson	38	55
39 *Dannemeyer*	81	17
40 *Badham*	78	6
41 *Lowery*	78	17
42 *Hunter*	83	14
43 *Burgener*	65	4
COLORADO		
1 Schroeder	29	65
2 Wirth	34	62
3 Kogovsek	36	62
4 *Brown*	68	32

	1	2
5 *Kramer*	79	19
CONNECTICUT		
1 Kennelly	34	66
2 Gejdenson	36	60
3 *DeNardis*	36	52
4 *McKinney*	40	52
5 Ratchford	35	62
6 Moffett	12	26
DELAWARE		
AL *Evans*	56	38
FLORIDA		
1 Hutto	62	34
2 Fuqua	47	40
3 Bennett	65	35
4 Chappell	45	17
5 *McCollum*	78	17
6 *Young*	74	16
7 Gibbons	65	29
8 Ireland	60	17
9 Nelson	60	36
10 *Bafalis*	43	5
11 Mica	52	43
12 *Shaw*	77	23
13 Lehman	26	56
14 Pepper	36	47
15 Fascell	39	51
GEORGIA		
1 Ginn	22	31
2 Hatcher	43	42
3 Brinkley	57	42
4 Levitas	55	42
5 Fowler	45	48
6 *Gingrich*	70	26
7 McDonald	83	17
8 Evans	45	23
9 Jenkins	40	49
10 Barnard	60	31
HAWAII		
1 Heftel	39	47
2 Akaka	40	53
IDAHO		
1 *Craig*	75	23
2 *Hansen*	84	12
ILLINOIS		
1 Washington	13	73
2 Savage	17	62
3 Russo	30	62
4 *Derwinski*	70	9
5 Fary	53	38
6 *Hyde*	75	17
7 Collins	25	65
8 Rostenkowski	44	44
9 Yates	19	53
10 *Porter*	60	32
11 Annunzio	51	43
12 *Crane, P.*	79	18
13 *McClory*	66	18
14 *Erlenborn*	78	12
15 *Corcoran*	87	13
16 *Martin*	49	48
17 O'Brien	53	29
18 *Michel*	83	12
19 *Railsback*	44	35
20 *Findley*	48	49
21 *Madigan*	68	27
22 *Crane, D.*	74	17
23 Price	57	38
24 Simon	31	56
INDIANA		
1 Hall [2]	50†	50†
2 Fithian	23	52
3 *Hiler*	86	14
4 *Coats*	71	29
5 *Hillis*	65	30
6 Evans	31	52
7 *Myers*	70	27
8 *Deckard*	43	45
9 Hamilton	47	52
10 Sharp	42	57
11 Jacobs	39	60
IOWA		
1 Leach	45	52
2 Tauke	49	47
3 *Evans*	55	44
4 Smith	40	56
5 Harkin	26	69
6 Bedell	40	57

1. Rep. Matthew G. Martinez, D-Calif., sworn in July 15, 1982, to succeed George E. Danielson, D, who resigned March 9, 1982. Danielson's 1982 presidential support score was zero; opposition was 100 percent.

2. Rep. Katie Hall, D-Ind., sworn in Nov. 29, 1982, to succeed Adam Benjamin Jr., D, who died Sept. 7, 1982. Benjamin's 1982 presidential support score was 50 percent; opposition was 50 percent.

3. Rep. Thomas P. O'Neill Jr., D-Mass., as Speaker, votes at his own discretion.

4. Rep. Fred Richmond, D-N.Y., resigned Aug. 25, 1982.

5. Rep. Jean S. Ashbrook, R-Ohio, sworn in July 12, 1982, to succeed her husband, John M. Ashbrook, R, who died April 24, 1982. John Ashbrook's 1982 presidential support score was 11 percent; opposition was 11 percent.

ND - Northern Democrats   SD - Southern Democrats

	1	2
KANSAS		
1 Roberts	62	36
2 Jeffries	78	14
3 Winn	70	23
4 Glickman	47	53
5 Whittaker	65	35
KENTUCKY		
1 Hubbard	55	42
2 Natcher	48	52
3 Mazzoli	44	53
4 Snyder	68	32
5 Rogers	70	29
6 Hopkins	58	39
7 Perkins	43	56
LOUISIANA		
1 Livingston	79	14
2 Boggs	42	52
3 Tauzin	57	36
4 Roemer	75	25
5 Huckaby	51	38
6 Moore	75	25
7 Breaux	58	27
8 Long	44	51
MAINE		
1 Emery	47	42
2 Snowe	47	52
MARYLAND		
1 Dyson	55	43
2 Long	49	51
3 Mikulski	31	68
4 Holt	66	17
5 Hoyer	38	57
6 Byron	56	40
7 Mitchell	22	74
8 Barnes	35	56
MASSACHUSETTS		
1 Conte	52	45
2 Boland	39	56
3 Early	36	52
4 Frank	34	62
5 Shannon	34	62
6 Mavroules	40	56
7 Markey	32	62
8 O'Neill [3]		
9 Moakley	39	52
10 Heckler	35	56
11 Donnelly	38	60
12 Studds	32	66
MICHIGAN		
1 Conyers	22	60
2 Pursell	42	42
3 Wolpe	34	66
4 Siljander	56	18
5 Sawyer	65	34
6 Dunn	47	48
7 Kildee	36	64
8 Traxler	27	61
9 Vander Jagt	53	36
10 Albosta	27	68
11 Davis	45	47
12 Bonior	26	58
13 Crockett	18	65
14 Hertel	32	64
15 Ford	30	62
16 Dingell	44	55
17 Brodhead	31	64
18 Blanchard	8	26
19 Broomfield	65	26
MINNESOTA		
1 Erdahl	51	42
2 Hagedorn	66	25
3 Frenzel	74	25
4 Vento	34	65
5 Sabo	35	64
6 Weber	61	38
7 Stangeland	57	31
8 Oberstar	34	65
MISSISSIPPI		
1 Whitten	40	53
2 Bowen	43	30
3 Montgomery	74	23
4 Dowdy	30	45
5 Lott	75	17
MISSOURI		
1 Clay	19	43
2 Young	45	44
3 Gephardt	44	53

	1	2
4 Skelton	48	34
5 Bolling	18	23
6 Coleman	56	32
7 Taylor	65	29
8 Bailey	62	31
9 Volkmer	35	60
10 Emerson	58	34
MONTANA		
1 Williams	35	61
2 Marlenee	55	31
NEBRASKA		
1 Bereuter	75	25
2 Daub	74	26
3 Smith	70	29
NEVADA		
AL Santini	30	31
NEW HAMPSHIRE		
1 D'Amours	34	53
2 Gregg	68	30
NEW JERSEY		
1 Florio	32	66
2 Hughes	43	57
3 Howard	35	64
4 Smith	49	51
5 Fenwick	51	44
6 Forsythe	35	36
7 Roukema	62	34
8 Roe	35	60
9 Hollenbeck	40	56
10 Rodino	26	71
11 Minish	36	61
12 Rinaldo	45	49
13 Courter	64	25
14 Guarini	34	60
15 Dwyer	39	57
NEW MEXICO		
1 Lujan	74	23
2 Skeen	82	16
NEW YORK		
1 Carney	75	21
2 Downey	38	58
3 Carman	81	14
4 Lent	66	27
5 McGrath	61	34
6 LeBoutillier	60	25
7 Addabbo	26	57
8 Rosenthal	22	48
9 Ferraro	34	58
10 Biaggi	34	52
11 Scheuer	35	60
12 Chisholm	18	48
13 Solarz	38	58
14 Richmond [4]	22†	48†
15 Zeferetti	36	45
16 Schumer	29	64
17 Molinari	52	36
18 Green	51	42
19 Rangel	31	69
20 Weiss	18	56
21 Garcia	26	58
22 Bingham	35	56
23 Peyser	36	53
24 Ottinger	23	73
25 Fish	45	44
26 Gilman	53	42
27 McHugh	39	53
28 Stratton	51	38
29 Solomon	60	26
30 Martin	62	27
31 Mitchell	51	38
32 Wortley	68†	24†
33 Lee	60	23
34 Horton	39	47
35 Conable	82	14
36 LaFalce	38	57
37 Nowak	34	65
38 Kemp	71	22
39 Lundine	30	61
NORTH CAROLINA		
1 Jones	39	44
2 Fountain	56	35
3 Whitley	51	44
4 Andrews	45	47
5 Neal	42	44
6 Johnston	84†	11†
7 Rose	32	49
8 Hefner	47	48

	1	2
9 Martin	75	25
10 Broyhill	78	21
11 Hendon	71	23
NORTH DAKOTA		
AL Dorgan	36	62
OHIO		
1 Gradison	75	22
2 Luken	34	58
3 Hall	36	57
4 Oxley	77	17
5 Latta	83	14
6 McEwen	58	34
7 Brown	19	1
8 Kindness	66	26
9 Weber	81	19
10 Miller	70	30
11 Stanton	40	14
12 Shamansky	39	55
13 Pease	38	61
14 Seiberling	23	75
15 Wylie	56	35
16 Regula	64	35
17 Ashbrook [5]	79†	19†
18 Applegate	39	57
19 Williams	48	47
20 Oakar	31	61
21 Stokes	27	65
22 Eckart	31	64
23 Mottl	39	49
OKLAHOMA		
1 Jones	51	47
2 Synar	43	55
3 Watkins	49	45
4 McCurdy	58	36
5 Edwards	68	23
6 English	65	35
OREGON		
1 AuCoin	30	61
2 Smith	74	16
3 Wyden	30	69
4 Weaver	21	69
PENNSYLVANIA		
1 Foglietta	32	56
2 Gray	21	65
3 Smith	34	39
4 Dougherty	44	39
5 Schulze	57	31
6 Yatron	40	56
7 Edgar	30	62
8 Coyne, J.	56	39
9 Shuster	56	23
10 McDade	40	45
11 Nelligan	62	34
12 Murtha	53	39
13 Coughlin	65	34
14 Coyne, W.	42	57
15 Ritter	73	26
16 Walker	68	32
17 Ertel	9	30
18 Walgren	34	61
19 Goodling	61	36
20 Gaydos	38	61
21 Bailey	55	44
22 Murphy	35	57
23 Clinger	65	35
24 Marks	16	31
25 Atkinson	69	31
RHODE ISLAND		
1 St Germain	39	57
2 Schneider	38	56
SOUTH CAROLINA		
1 Hartnett	74	19
2 Spence	74	26
3 Derrick	36	52
4 Campbell	71	21
5 Holland	47	38
6 Napier	58	30
SOUTH DAKOTA		
1 Daschle	31	62
2 Roberts	58	30
TENNESSEE		
1 Quillen	69	29
2 Duncan	68	30
3 Bouquard	47	47
4 Gore	45	52
5 Boner	40	42
6 Beard	49	14

	1	2
7 Jones	29	43
8 Ford	27	56
TEXAS		
1 Hall, S.	55	44
2 Wilson	47	30
3 Collins	48	12
4 Hall, R.	58	42
5 Mattox	18	42
6 Gramm	84	14
7 Archer	82	18
8 Fields	84	14
9 Brooks	44	44
10 Pickle	53	43
11 Leath	66	30
12 Wright	48	48
13 Hightower	56	40
14 Patman	62	36
15 de la Garza	49	32
16 White	58	39
17 Stenholm	74	26
18 Leland	26	68
19 Hance	62	31
20 Gonzalez	45	53
21 Loeffler	84	16
22 Paul	53	44
23 Kazen	58	42
24 Frost	34	58
UTAH		
1 Hansen	77	12
2 Marriott	65	25
VERMONT		
AL Jeffords	44	47
VIRGINIA		
1 Trible	55	23
2 Whitehurst	69	22
3 Bliley	86	13
4 Daniel, R.	75	21
5 Daniel, D.	70	19
6 Butler	77	13
7 Robinson	77	19
8 Parris	58	38
9 Wampler	58	36
10 Wolf	56	39
WASHINGTON		
1 Pritchard	44	45
2 Swift	42	56
3 Bonker	39	55
4 Morrison	70	29
5 Foley	39	51
6 Dicks	40	53
7 Lowry	34	62
WEST VIRGINIA		
1 Mollohan	42	36
2 Benedict	65	26
3 Staton	78	17
4 Rahall	29	58
WISCONSIN		
1 Aspin	42	48
2 Kastenmeier	26	74
3 Gunderson	56	44
4 Zablocki	45	49
5 Reuss	31	61
6 Petri	53	40
7 Obey	38	57
8 Roth	57	38
9 Sensenbrenner	60	36
WYOMING		
AL Cheney	87	10

Southern states - Ala., Ark., Fla., Ga., Ky., La., Miss., N.C., Okla., S.C., Tenn., Texas, Va.

State / Senator	1	2	State / Senator	1	2	State / Senator	1	2
ALABAMA			**IOWA**			**NEW HAMPSHIRE**		
Denton	71	14	*Grassley*	84	16	*Humphrey*	81	18
Heflin	61	39	*Jepsen*	78	20	*Rudman*	73	27
ALASKA			**KANSAS**			**NEW JERSEY**		
Murkowski	79	11	*Dole*	86	13	*Brady* ¹	82†	8†
Stevens	74	18	*Kassebaum*	78	19	Bradley	37	63
ARIZONA			**KENTUCKY**			**NEW MEXICO**		
Goldwater	65	14	Ford	32	60	*Domenici*	85	15
DeConcini	61	34	Huddleston	48	50	*Schmitt*	71	17
ARKANSAS			**LOUISIANA**			**NEW YORK**		
Bumpers	30	63	Johnston	61	37	*D'Amato*	71	26
Pryor	45	49	Long	59	30	Moynihan	28	71
CALIFORNIA			**MAINE**			**NORTH CAROLINA**		
Hayakawa	75	18	*Cohen*	67	31	*East*	77	22
Cranston	26	66	Mitchell	35	63	*Helms*	75	25
COLORADO			**MARYLAND**			**NORTH DAKOTA**		
Armstrong	76	22	*Mathias*	51	38	*Andrews*	74	24
Hart	37	56	Sarbanes	25	65	Burdick	50	50
CONNECTICUT			**MASSACHUSETTS**			**OHIO**		
Weicker	40	44	Kennedy	29	64	Glenn	35	45
Dodd	35	61	Tsongas	33	51	Metzenbaum	32	64
DELAWARE			**MICHIGAN**			**OKLAHOMA**		
Roth	77	20	Levin	34	63	*Nickles*	81	19
Biden	34	61	Riegle	24	66	Boren	60	38
FLORIDA			**MINNESOTA**			**OREGON**		
Hawkins	72	23	*Boschwitz*	77	22	*Hatfield*	61	29
Chiles	63	32	*Durenberger*	60	28	*Packwood*	75	24
GEORGIA			**MISSISSIPPI**			**PENNSYLVANIA**		
Mattingly	82	13	*Cochran*	77	20	*Heinz*	55	39
Nunn	70	29	Stennis	71	27	*Specter*	55	44
HAWAII			**MISSOURI**			**RHODE ISLAND**		
Inouye	28	66	*Danforth*	71	19	*Chafee*	54	45
Matsunaga	28	66	Eagleton	29	68	Pell	36	59
IDAHO			**MONTANA**			**SOUTH CAROLINA**		
McClure	68	24	Baucus	44	53	*Thurmond*	89	9
Symms	79	20	Melcher	49	43	Hollings	44	45
ILLINOIS			**NEBRASKA**			**SOUTH DAKOTA**		
Percy	76	17	Exon	55	40	*Abdnor*	78	17
Dixon	45	50	Zorinsky	64	34	*Pressler*	70	24
INDIANA			**NEVADA**			**TENNESSEE**		
Lugar	83	15	*Laxalt*	82	14	*Baker*	89	8
Quayle	84	15	Cannon	34	37	Sasser	42	55

KEY

† Not eligible for all recorded votes in 1982 (sworn in after Jan. 25, died or resigned during session, or voted "present" to avoid possible conflict of interest).

Democrats   *Republicans*

State / Senator	1	2
TEXAS		
Tower	80	15
Bentsen	61	33
UTAH		
Garn	83	16
Hatch	79	13
VERMONT		
Stafford	64	27
Leahy	37	62
VIRGINIA		
Warner	83	17
Byrd ²	75	24
WASHINGTON		
Gorton	76	24
Jackson	36	60
WEST VIRGINIA		
Byrd	40	60
Randolph	37	63
WISCONSIN		
Kasten	77	22
Proxmire	50	50
WYOMING		
Simpson	82	14
Wallop	71	18

ND - Northern Democrats   SD - Southern Democrats (Southern states - Ala., Ark., Fla., Ga., Ky., La., Miss., N.C., Okla., S.C., Tenn., Texas, Va.)

Presidential Support and Opposition: Senate

1. Reagan Support Score, 1982. Percentage of 119 Reagan-issue recorded votes in 1982 on which senator voted "yea" or "nay" *in agreement* with the president's position. Failures to vote lower both Support and Opposition scores.

2. Reagan Opposition Score, 1982. Percentage of 119 Reagan-issue recorded votes in 1982 on which senator voted "yea" or "nay" *in disagreement* with the president's position. Failures to vote lower both Support and Opposition scores.

1. Sen. Nicholas F. Brady, R-N.J., sworn in April 20, 1982, to succeed Harrison A. Williams Jr., D, who resigned March 11, 1982. Williams' 1982 presidential support score was 50 percent; opposition was 50 percent.
2. Sen. Harry F. Byrd Jr., Va., elected as an independent.

 Voting Participation

Voting Participation High Despite Campaign Duties

Despite the lure of election-year campaigning, voting participation by members of Congress in 1982 dropped only slightly from the high mark established the year before.

The high voting rate may have stemmed partly from the fairly low number of votes taken in the second session of the 97th Congress, which was preoccupied with budget matters most of the year.

It may also have been a tribute to deft scheduling of votes by leaders in either chamber to avoid Mondays and Fridays, when members were most likely to be back in their home districts.

Statistically, the member least likely to miss a vote would have been a Republican senator from the South or Midwest. But while transportation problems encountered by Westerners may have caused them to average a few points lower, geography was not always the most important factor.

Congressional Quarterly's study of 1982 voting participation showed that members of Congress on average voted on 90 percent of the votes taken, 2 percent less often than in 1981 when members scored higher than they had at any time in the previous 30 years.

Scores are traditionally lower in election years, when members must campaign for re-election. In 1980, the average for all members was 87 percent.

The voting participation study is the closest approach to an attendance record for Congress, but it is only an approximation. *(Definition, box, p. 26-C)*

As is traditional, Republicans voted more often than Democrats in 1982. Senate Democrats have outscored their Republican counterparts in only four of the last 31 years; House Democrats only twice. Three senators and four representatives had perfect scores for voting participation, and 14 representatives voted less than 60 percent of the time. The lowest Senate score was 71 percent.

Chamber, Party Scores

There were 924 recorded votes taken in the House and Senate in 1982, 426 fewer than the record 1,350 votes in 1978 and 88 more than in 1981. There were 465 Senate votes in 1982, 18 fewer than in 1981 and 223 fewer than the record 688 in 1976.

The House took 459 votes in 1982, 375 fewer than the record 834 in 1978 and 106 more than in 1981.

Voting participation was higher in the Senate than in the House. The average score for senators in 1982 was 94 percent; for representatives, 89 percent. House members scored 91 percent in 1981, senators 93 percent.

House Republicans on average voted 90 percent of the time in 1982, compared to 92 percent in 1981. Democratic House members scored 88 percent in 1982, 90 percent in 1981.

In the Senate, Republicans scored 95 percent, Demo-

crats 94 percent. In 1981, Senate Republicans scored 94 percent, Democrats 92 percent.

For the two chambers together, the 1982 scores were 91 percent for Republicans and 89 percent for Democrats. In 1981, Republicans led Democrats 93 percent to 91 percent.

Republican senators from the Midwest and South led members from all regions in both chambers, voting 96 percent of the time. The lowest regional score came from Republican House members from the West: 87 percent.

Individual Highs and Lows

Two Democratic senators, William Proxmire of Wisconsin and Robert C. Byrd of West Virginia, and one Republican, Slade Gorton of Washington, answered every roll call in 1982.

Proxmire last missed a vote in 1966 and extended his record of consecutive votes to 7,972. Sixteen other senators — five Democrats and 11 Republicans — scored 99 percent.

Four representatives, all Democrats, had perfect scores in 1982: William H. Natcher of Kentucky, Charles En Bennett of Florida, Dale E. Kildee of Michigan and Abraham Kazen Jr. of Texas. Natcher has not missed a vote since his election to Congress in 1954 and extended his record to 9,013 consecutive votes.

The lowest scoring senator was Republican Barry Goldwater of Arizona, 71 percent. The lowest scoring Democratic senator was Howard W. Cannon of Nevada, 81 percent. Cannon in 1982 fought closely contested primary and general election battles, losing his seat in the latter.

The lowest scoring representative was Democrat John L. Burton of California, who did not seek re-election. He

---

Absences

Among members of Congress absent for a day or more in 1982 because they were sick or because of illness or death in their families were:

Senate Democrats: Bentsen, Texas; Biden, Del.; Pryor, Ark.

Senate Republicans: Cochran, Miss.; Goldwater, Ariz.; Mattingly, Ga.

House Democrats: Alexander, Ark.; AuCoin, Ore.; Bolling, Mo.; Bouquard, Tenn.; Phillip Burton, Calif.; D'Amours, N.H.; Dyson, Md.; Fary, Ill.; Florio, N.J.; Foley, Wash.; Ford, Tenn.; Hall, Ohio; Hutto, Fla.; Lantos, Calif.; Lowry, Wash.; Mavroules, Mass.; Mikulski, Md.; Neal, N.C.; Rosenthal, N.Y.; Russo, Ill.; Smith, Pa.; Weiss, N.Y.; Yates, Ill.; Young, Mo.; Zeferetti, N.Y.

House Republicans: Bethune, Ark.; Broyhill, N.C.; Dannemeyer, Calif.; Deckard, Ind.; DeNardis, Conn.; Fiedler, Calif.; Forsythe, N.J.; Lujan, N.M.; McDade, Pa.; Miller, Ohio; Rudd, Ariz.; Schneider, R.I.; Shuster, Pa.; Smith, Ore.; Stanton, Ohio; Wolf, Va.

Failure to vote often is due to conflicting duties. Members frequently have to be away from Washington on official business. Leaves of absence, not listed here, are granted members for these purposes.

voted on 25 percent of the votes in 1982. Clarence J. Brown of Ohio was the lowest scoring House Republican, 33 percent. Brown ran for, and lost, the Ohio governorship.

State Delegations

The Senate delegations with the highest voting participation scores in 1982 were Indiana, New Hampshire, North Carolina, West Virginia and Wisconsin, all 99 percent; and Georgia, Iowa, Maine and Virginia, all 98 percent.

In the House, the highest scoring delegations with two or more members were Nebraska, 99 percent; New Mexico, 97 percent; and Colorado and Kentucky, both 96 percent.

Party Scores

Composites of Democratic and Republican voting participation scores for 1982 and 1981:

	⌐1982⌐		⌐1981⌐	
	Dem.	**Rep.**	**Dem.**	**Rep.**
Senate	94%	95%	92%	94%
House	88	90	90	92

Regional Scores

Regional voting participation breakdowns for 1982 with 1981 scores in parentheses:

	East	**West**	**South**	**Midwest**
DEMOCRATS				
Senate	94% (90)	90% (89)	95% (94)	95% (95)
House	88 (90)	88 (89)	89 (91)	88 (90)
REPUBLICANS				
Senate	94% (93)	93% (92)	96% (96)	96% (97)
House	89 (93)	87 (89)	91 (93)	91 (93)

(CQ defines regions of the United States as follows: **East:** *Conn., Del., Maine, Md., Mass., N.H., N.J., N.Y., Pa., R.I., Vt., W.Va.* **West:** *Alaska, Ariz., Calif., Colo., Hawaii, Idaho, Mont., Nev., N.M., Ore., Utah, Wash., Wyo.* **South:** *Ala., Ark., Fla., Ga., Ky., La., Miss., N.C., Okla., S.C., Tenn., Texas, Va.* **Midwest:** *Ill., Ind., Iowa, Kan., Mich., Minn., Mo., Neb., N.D., Ohio, S.D., Wis.)*

Highest Scorers

SENATE

Democrats		**Republicans**	
Proxmire, Wis.	100%	Gorton, Wash.	100%
Byrd, W.Va.	100	Garn, Utah	99
Zorinsky, Neb.	99	Quayle, Ind.	99
Randolph, W.Va.	99	Specter, Pa.	99
Baucus, Mont.	99	Helms, N.C.	99
Leahy, Vt.	99	Humphrey, N.H.[1]	99
Bradley, N.J.	99	Nickles, Okla.	99
Nunn, Ga.	98	Rudman, N.H.	99
Levin, Mich.	98	Warner, Va.	99
Mitchell, Maine	98	East, N.C.	99
Byrd, Va.[1]	98	Grassley, Iowa	99
		Kasten, Wis.	99

HOUSE

Democrats[2]		**Republicans**	
Natcher, Ky.	100%	Brown, Colo.	99%
Bennett, Fla.	100	Smith, Neb.	99
Kildee, Mich.	100	Lagomarsino, Calif.	99
Kazen, Texas	100	Daub, Neb.	99
Matsui, Calif.	99	Sensenbrenner, Wis.	99
Roemer, La.	99	Shaw, Fla.	99
Howard, N.J.	99	Snowe, Maine	99
Perkins, Ky.	99	Bereuter, Neb.	99
Wolpe, Mich.	99	Clinger, Pa.	99
Brinkley, Ga.	99	Robinson, Va.	99
Mineta, Calif.	99	Walker, Pa.	99
Studds, Mass.	99	Moore, La.	99
Patman, Texas	99	Loeffler, Texas	99
Gore, Tenn.	99	Regula, Ohio	99
Anderson, Calif.	99	Gunderson, Wis.	99
Hughes, N.J.	99		

Lowest Scorers

SENATE

Democrats[3]		**Republicans**	
Cannon, Nev.	81%	Goldwater, Ariz.	71%
Glenn, Ohio	82	Schmitt, N.M.	86
Inouye, Hawaii	83	Heinz, Pa.	86
		Weicker, Conn.	86

HOUSE

Democrats		**Republicans[4]**	
John Burton, Calif.	25%	Brown, Ohio[1]	33%
Bolling, Mo.	40	Goldwater, Calif.	39
Blanchard, Mich.	41	Marks, Pa.	39
Moffett, Conn.	41	Stanton, Ohio	48
Ertel, Pa.	47	Bafalis, Fla.	49
Chisholm, N.Y.	49	McCloskey, Calif.	57
Ginn, Ga.	51	Rhodes, Ariz.	62
Mattox, Texas	59	Beard, Tenn.	66

[1] *Not eligible for all votes in 1982.*
[2] *Another Democrat, Adam Benjamin Jr., Ind., who died Sept. 7, 1982, also scored 99 percent.*
[3] *Another Democrat, Harrison A. Williams Jr., N.J., who resigned March 11, 1982, scored 27 percent.*
[4] *Another Republican, John M. Ashbrook, Ohio, who died April 24, 1982, scored 27 percent.*

ALABAMA		**IOWA**		**NEW HAMPSHIRE**		**KEY**
Denton	91†	*Grassley*	99	*Humphrey*	99†	
Heflin	97	*Jepsen*	97	*Rudman*	99	† Not eligible for all recorded votes in 1982 (sworn in after Jan. 25, died or resigned during session, or voted "present" to avoid possible conflict of interest).
ALASKA		**KANSAS**		**NEW JERSEY**		
Murkowski	93	*Dole*	98	*Brady* [1]	93†	
Stevens	95	*Kassebaum*	96	Bradley	99	
ARIZONA		**KENTUCKY**		**NEW MEXICO**		
Goldwater	71#	Ford	97	*Domenici*	98	# Member absent a day or more in 1982 due to illness or illness or death in family.
DeConcini	92	Huddleston	94	*Schmitt*	92	
ARKANSAS		**LOUISIANA**		**NEW YORK**		
Bumpers	94	Johnston	95	*D'Amato*	97	Democrats *Republicans*
Pryor	95#	Long	95	Moynihan	96	
CALIFORNIA		**MAINE**		**NORTH CAROLINA**		
Hayakawa	92	*Cohen*	98	*East*	99	
Cranston	89	Mitchell	98	*Helms*	99	
COLORADO		**MARYLAND**		**NORTH DAKOTA**		
Armstrong	97	*Mathias*	88	*Andrews*	98	
Hart	94	Sarbanes	91	Burdick	95	
CONNECTICUT		**MASSACHUSETTS**		**OHIO**		**TEXAS**	
Weicker	86	Kennedy	91	Glenn	82	*Tower*	95
Dodd	88	Tsongas	93	Metzenbaum	94	Bentsen	95#
DELAWARE		**MICHIGAN**		**OKLAHOMA**		**UTAH**	
Roth	97	Levin	98	*Nickles*	99	*Garn*	99
Biden	94#	Riegle	92	Boren	94	*Hatch*	92
FLORIDA		**MINNESOTA**		**OREGON**		**VERMONT**	
Hawkins	92	*Boschwitz*	98	*Hatfield*	87	*Stafford*	90
Chiles	97	*Durenberger*	88	*Packwood*	98	Leahy	99
GEORGIA		**MISSISSIPPI**		**PENNSYLVANIA**		**VIRGINIA**	
Mattingly	97#	*Cochran*	93#	*Heinz*	86	*Warner*	99
Nunn	98	Stennis	92	*Specter*	99	Byrd [2]	98†
HAWAII		**MISSOURI**		**RHODE ISLAND**		**WASHINGTON**	
Inouye	83	*Danforth*	92	*Chafee*	97	*Gorton*	100
Matsunaga	90	Eagleton	97	Pell	94	Jackson	94
IDAHO		**MONTANA**		**SOUTH CAROLINA**		**WEST VIRGINIA**	
McClure	95	Baucus	99	*Thurmond*	92	Byrd	100
Symms	97	Melcher	88	Hollings	92	Randolph	99
ILLINOIS		**NEBRASKA**		**SOUTH DAKOTA**		**WISCONSIN**	
Percy	92	Exon	94	*Abdnor*	97	*Kasten*	99
Dixon	97	Zorinsky	99	*Pressler*	90	Proxmire	100
INDIANA		**NEVADA**		**TENNESSEE**		**WYOMING**	
Lugar	98	*Laxalt*	95	*Baker*	95	*Simpson*	95
Quayle	99	Cannon	81	Sasser	95	*Wallop*	91

ND - Northern Democrats   SD - Southern Democrats (Southern states - Ala., Ark., Fla., Ga., Ky., La., Miss., N.C., Okla., S.C., Tenn., Texas, Va.)

Voting Participation Scores: Senate

Voting Participation, 1982. Percentage of 465 roll calls in 1982 on which senator voted "yea" or "nay."

1. Sen. Nicholas F. Brady, R-N.J., sworn in April 20, 1982, to succeed Harrison A. Williams Jr., D, who resigned March 11, 1982. Williams' 1982 voting participation score was 27 percent.
2. Sen. Harry F. Byrd Jr., Va., elected as an independent.

Voting Participation Scores: House

Voting Participation, 1982. Percentage of 459 recorded votes in 1982 on which representative voted "yea" or "nay."

<table>
<tr><td colspan="2">KEY</td></tr>
<tr><td>†</td><td>Not eligible for all recorded votes in 1982 (sworn in after Jan. 25, died or resigned during session, or voted "present" to avoid possible conflict of interest).</td></tr>
<tr><td>#</td><td>Member absent a day or more in 1982 due to illness or illness or death in family.</td></tr>
<tr><td colspan="2">Democrats   *Republicans*</td></tr>
</table>

ALABAMA
1	*Edwards*	91
2	*Dickinson*	87
3	Nichols	87
4	Bevill	96
5	Flippo	89
6	*Smith*	92
7	Shelby	96

ALASKA
AL	*Young*	67

ARIZONA
1	*Rhodes*	62
2	Udall	90
3	Stump	93
4	*Rudd*	90#

ARKANSAS
1	Alexander	90#
2	*Bethune*	91#
3	*Hammerschmidt*	98
4	Anthony	91

CALIFORNIA
1	*Chappie*	87
2	*Clausen*	96
3	Matsui	99
4	Fazio	96
5	Burton, J.	25
6	Burton, P.	82#
7	Miller	92
8	Dellums	89
9	Stark	87
10	Edwards	95
11	Lantos	87#
12	*McCloskey*	57
13	Mineta	99
14	*Shumway*	95
15	Coelho	91
16	Panetta	98
17	*Pashayan*	93
18	*Thomas*	84
19	*Lagomarsino*	99
20	Goldwater	39
21	*Fiedler*	97#
22	*Moorhead*	97
23	Beilenson	89
24	Waxman	90
25	Roybal	96
26	*Rousselot*	76
27	*Dornan*	67
28	Dixon	81
29	Hawkins	84
30	Martinez [1]	86†
31	Dymally	79
32	Anderson	99
33	*Grisham*	71
34	*Lungren*	95
35	*Dreier*	90
36	Brown	85
37	*Lewis*	93
38	Patterson	92
39	*Dannemeyer*	98#
40	*Badham*	80
41	*Lowery*	92
42	*Hunter*	95
43	*Burgener*	74

COLORADO
1	Schroeder	94
2	Wirth	95
3	Kogovsek	95
4	*Brown*	99

5	*Kramer*	97

CONNECTICUT
1	Kennelly	98
2	Gejdenson	95
3	*DeNardis*	78#
4	*McKinney*	83
5	Ratchford	96
6	Moffett	41

DELAWARE
AL	*Evans*	86

FLORIDA
1	Hutto	95#
2	Fuqua	87
3	Bennett	100
4	Chappell	67
5	*McCollum*	95
6	*Young*	90†
7	Gibbons	92
8	Ireland	68
9	Nelson	94
10	*Bafalis*	49†
11	Mica	95
12	*Shaw*	99
13	Lehman	75†
14	Pepper	86
15	Fascell	84

GEORGIA
1	Ginn	51
2	Hatcher	84
3	Brinkley	99
4	Levitas	96
5	Fowler	86
6	*Gingrich*	91
7	McDonald	98
8	Evans	66
9	Jenkins	89
10	Barnard	91

HAWAII
1	Heftel	80
2	Akaka	88

IDAHO
1	*Craig*	91
2	*Hansen*	94

ILLINOIS
1	Washington	81
2	Savage	62
3	Russo	93#
4	*Derwinski*	82
5	Fary	91#
6	*Hyde*	95†
7	Collins	90
8	Rostenkowski	90
9	Yates	78#
10	*Porter*	94
11	Annunzio	96
12	*Crane, P.*	88
13	*McClory*	86
14	*Erlenborn*	85
15	*Corcoran*	97
16	*Martin*	96
17	O'Brien	80
18	*Michel*	93
19	*Railsback*	77
20	*Findley*	92
21	*Madigan*	90
22	*Crane, D.*	91
23	Price	95
24	Simon	85

INDIANA
1	Hall [2]	98†
2	Fithian	79
3	*Hiler*	97
4	*Coats*	98
5	*Hillis*	91
6	Evans	76
7	*Myers*	98
8	*Deckard*	83#
9	Hamilton	98
10	Sharp	98
11	Jacobs	91

IOWA
1	*Leach*	95
2	*Tauke*	94
3	*Evans*	98
4	*Smith*	97
5	Harkin	93
6	Bedell	96

1. Rep. Matthew G. Martinez, D-Calif., sworn in July 15, 1982, to succeed George E. Danielson, D, who resigned March 9, 1982. Danielson's 1982 voting participation score was 89 percent.
2. Rep. Katie Hall, D-Ind., sworn in Nov. 29, 1982, to succeed Adam Benjamin Jr., D, who died Sept. 7, 1982. Benjamin's 1982 voting participation score was 99 percent.
3. Rep. Thomas P. O'Neill Jr., D-Mass., as Speaker, votes at his own discretion.
4. Rep. Fred Richmond, D-N.Y., resigned Aug. 25, 1982.
5. Rep. Jean S. Ashbrook, R-Ohio, sworn in July 12, 1982, to succeed her husband, John M. Ashbrook, R, who died April 24, 1982. John Ashbrook's 1982 voting participation score was 27 percent.

ND - Northern Democrats   SD - Southern Democrats

KANSAS
1 Roberts 96
2 Jeffries 89
3 Winn 94
4 Glickman 98
5 Whittaker 97

KENTUCKY
1 Hubbard 91
2 Natcher 100
3 Mazzoli 95
4 Snyder 98
5 Rogers 95
6 Hopkins 97
7 Perkins 99

LOUISIANA
1 Livingston 93
2 Boggs 86
3 Tauzin 97
4 Roemer 99
5 Huckaby 90
6 Moore 99
7 Breaux 83
8 Long 93

MAINE
1 Emery 81
2 Snowe 99

MARYLAND
1 Dyson 94#
2 Long 92
3 Mikulski 94#
4 Holt 86
5 Hoyer 96
6 Byron 93
7 Mitchell 88
8 Barnes 95

MASSACHUSETTS
1 Conte 97
2 Boland 88
3 Early 88
4 Frank 93
5 Shannon 94
6 Mavroules 90#
7 Markey 94
8 O'Neill [3]
9 Moakley 92
10 Heckler 82
11 Donnelly 93
12 Studds 99

MICHIGAN
1 Conyers 73
2 Pursell 73
3 Wolpe 99
4 Siljander 78
5 Sawyer 98
6 Dunn 94
7 Kildee 100
8 Traxler 87
9 Vander Jagt 88
10 Albosta 92
11 Davis 89
12 Bonior 86
13 Crockett 63
14 Hertel 88
15 Ford 81
16 Dingell 95
17 Brodhead 91
18 Blanchard 41
19 Broomfield 88

MINNESOTA
1 Erdahl 91
2 Hagedorn 85
3 Frenzel 96
4 Vento 97
5 Sabo 96
6 Weber 96
7 Stangeland 92
8 Oberstar 95

MISSISSIPPI
1 Whitten 92
2 Bowen 83
3 Montgomery 95
4 Dowdy 82
5 Lott 93

MISSOURI
1 Clay 69
2 Young 86#
3 Gephardt 94
4 Skelton 83
5 Bolling 40#
6 Coleman 93
7 Taylor 95
8 Bailey 93
9 Volkmer 97
10 Emerson 96

MONTANA
1 Williams 84
2 Marlenee 89

NEBRASKA
1 Bereuter 99†
2 Daub 99
3 Smith 99

NEVADA
AL Santini 62

NEW HAMPSHIRE
1 D'Amours 89#
2 Gregg 95

NEW JERSEY
1 Florio 93#
2 Hughes 99
3 Howard 99
4 Smith 98
5 Fenwick 87
6 Forsythe 74#
7 Roukema 94
8 Roe 94
9 Hollenbeck 88
10 Rodino 94
11 Minish 97
12 Rinaldo 95
13 Courter 88
14 Guarini 95
15 Dwyer 96

NEW MEXICO
1 Lujan 96#
2 Skeen 98

NEW YORK
1 Carney 90
2 Downey 94
3 Carman 96
4 Lent 91
5 McGrath 97
6 LeBoutillier 83
7 Addabbo 80
8 Rosenthal 66#
9 Ferraro 91
10 Biaggi 75
11 Scheuer 93
12 Chisholm 49
13 Solarz 97
14 Richmond [4] 67†
15 Zeferetti 75#
16 Schumer 93
17 Molinari 94
18 Green 92
19 Rangel 92
20 Weiss 78#
21 Garcia 77
22 Bingham 83
23 Peyser 91
24 Ottinger 84
25 Fish 87
26 Gilman 96
27 McHugh 93
28 Stratton 89
29 Solomon 92
30 Martin 91
31 Mitchell 86
32 Wortley 94†
33 Lee 77
34 Horton 88
35 Conable 94
36 LaFalce 90
37 Nowak 95
38 Kemp 86
39 Lundine 88

NORTH CAROLINA
1 Jones 81
2 Fountain 84
3 Whitley 96
4 Andrews 88
5 Neal 81#
6 Johnston 90†
7 Rose 76
8 Hefner 92†
9 Martin 92
10 Broyhill 97#
11 Hendon 92

NORTH DAKOTA
AL Dorgan 97

OHIO
1 Gradison 96
2 Luken 90
3 Hall 84#
4 Oxley 92
5 Latta 94
6 McEwen 94
7 Brown 33†
8 Kindness 94
9 Weber 98
10 Miller 98#
11 Stanton 48#
12 Shamansky 95
13 Pease 97
14 Seiberling 95
15 Wylie 93
16 Regula 99
17 Ashbrook [5] 96†
18 Applegate 84
19 Williams 90
20 Oakar 93
21 Stokes 93
22 Eckart 97
23 Mottl 88

OKLAHOMA
1 Jones 96
2 Synar 96
3 Watkins 90
4 McCurdy 90
5 Edwards 87
6 English 98

OREGON
1 AuCoin 81#
2 Smith 92#
3 Wyden 98
4 Weaver 89

PENNSYLVANIA
1 Foglietta 83
2 Gray 84
3 Smith 63#
4 Dougherty 78
5 Schulze 84
6 Yatron 93
7 Edgar 92
8 Coyne, J. 88
9 Shuster 78#
10 McDade 85#
11 Nelligan 95
12 Murtha 86
13 Coughlin 96
14 Coyne, W. 97
15 Ritter 98
16 Walker 99
17 Ertel 47
18 Walgren 94
19 Goodling 94
20 Gaydos 93
21 Bailey 97
22 Murphy 91
23 Clinger 99
24 Marks 39
25 Atkinson 88

RHODE ISLAND
1 St Germain 93
2 Schneider 92#

SOUTH CAROLINA
1 Hartnett 92
2 Spence 98
3 Derrick 86
4 Campbell 90
5 Holland 71
6 Napier 89

SOUTH DAKOTA
1 Daschle 92
2 Roberts 86

TENNESSEE
1 Quillen 94
2 Duncan 97
3 Bouquard 94#
4 Gore 99
5 Boner 88
6 Beard 66
7 Jones 78
8 Ford 82#

TEXAS
1 Hall, S. 96
2 Wilson 76
3 Collins 73
4 Hall, R. 98
5 Mattox 59
6 Gramm 97
7 Archer 97
8 Fields 97
9 Brooks 86
10 Pickle 95
11 Leath 94
12 Wright 94
13 Hightower 97
14 Patman 99
15 de la Garza 86
16 White 94
17 Stenholm 95
18 Leland 86
19 Hance 93
20 Gonzalez 95
21 Loeffler 99
22 Paul 96
23 Kazen 100
24 Frost 92

UTAH
1 Hansen 85
2 Marriott 92

VERMONT
AL Jeffords 89

VIRGINIA
1 Trible 80
2 Whitehurst 92
3 Bliley 97
4 Daniel, R. 97
5 Daniel, D. 92
6 Butler 87
7 Robinson 99
8 Parris 96†
9 Wampler 94
10 Wolf 96#

WASHINGTON
1 Pritchard 87
2 Swift 96
3 Bonker 88
4 Morrison 97
5 Foley 94#
6 Dicks 97
7 Lowry 95#

WEST VIRGINIA
1 Mollohan 82
2 Benedict 90
3 Staton 96
4 Rahall 83

WISCONSIN
1 Aspin 92
2 Kastenmeier 98
3 Gunderson 99
4 Zablocki 93
5 Reuss 89
6 Petri 97
7 Obey 94
8 Roth 94
9 Sensenbrenner 99

WYOMING
AL Cheney 92

Southern states · Ala., Ark., Fla., Ga., Ky., La., Miss., N.C., Okla., S.C., Tenn., Texas, Va.

 Party Unity

Republican Unity Drops:

Democrats Overtake GOP In Party-Line Vote Loyalty

Party unity during the second session of the 97th Congress generally declined among Republicans in both houses, but was on the rebound among Democrats.

GOP party unity dropped from 76 percent on the votes studied in 1981 to 71 percent in 1982, while Democrats voted the party line 72 percent of the time, compared to 69 percent in 1981.

Congressional Quarterly's annual study of party unity shows that a majority of Democrats voted against a majority of Republicans on 40 percent of the recorded votes. In 1981, the parties split on 43 percent of the votes.

The study looked only at those votes in figuring party unity voting scores.

In the Senate, the percentage of partisan votes went down from 48 percent in 1981 to 43 percent in 1982, the lowest level since 1977. In the House, the percentage of votes on which a majority of Democrats voted against a majority of Republicans declined from 37 percent in 1981 to 36 percent in 1982.

A decline in party-line voting took place among Senate Republicans and moderate House GOP lawmakers. In 1981, Republican senators voted with their party on party-line votes 81 percent of the time; in 1982, they voted the party line only 76 percent of the time. Party unity among Senate Democrats went from 71 to 72 percent.

In the House, where the fiercest battles over President Reagan's programs raged, party loyalty, as measured by CQ, went down for Republicans, but up for Democrats.

House Democrats saw an increase in their party unity score, from 69 percent in 1981 to 72 percent in 1982. GOP House members displayed party loyalty 69 percent of the time, down from 74 percent in 1981.

Among Northern Republicans in the House, party

Definitions

Party Unity Votes. Recorded votes in the Senate and House that split the parties, a majority of voting Democrats opposing a majority of voting Republicans.

Party Unity Scores. Percentage of Party Unity votes on which a member votes "yea" or "nay" *in agreement* with a majority of his party. Failure to vote, even if a member announced his stand, lowers his score.

Opposition-to-Party Scores. Percentage of Party Unity votes on which a member votes "yea" or "nay" *in disagreement* with a majority of his party. A member's Party Unity and Opposition-to-Party scores add up to 100 percent only if he voted on all Party Unity votes.

unity dropped from 72 percent in 1981 to 67 percent in 1982.

Scores for opposition-to-party voting decreased slightly for Democrats and increased for Republicans. Democrats voted against the party line 20 percent of the time in 1982, as opposed to 23 percent in 1981. For Republicans, party opposition crept up to 21 percent in 1982, as opposed to 18 percent in 1981.

Some individual House members showed particularly sharp changes in their scores. Doug Barnard Jr., D-Ga., a member of the conservative "Boll Weevil" faction, increased his party unity score from 26 in 1981 to 46 in 1982. Claudine Schneider, R-R.I., a leader of the liberal/moderate "Gypsy Moths" group in the House, dropped from 44 in 1981 to 20 in 1982.

Party Unity Scoreboard

The following table shows the proportion of Party Unity recorded votes in recent years:

	Total Recorded Votes	Party Unity Recorded Votes	Percentage of Total
1982			
Both Chambers	924	369	40
Senate	465	202	43
House	459	167	36
1981			
Both Chambers	836	363	43
Senate	483	231	48
House	353	132	37
1980			
Both Chambers	1,135	470	41
Senate	531	243	46
House	604	227	38
1979			
Both Chambers	1,169	550	47
Senate	497	232	47
House	672	318	47
1978			
Both Chambers	1,350	510	38
Senate	516	233	45
House	834	277	33
1977			
Both Chambers	1,341	567	42
Senate	635	269	42
House	706	298	42
1976			
Both Chambers	1,349	493	37
Senate	688	256	37
House	661	237	36
1975			
Both Chambers	1,214	584	48
Senate	602	288	48
House	612	296	48

Victories, Defeats

	Senate	House	Total
Democrats won, Republicans lost	55	106	161
Republicans won, Democrats lost	147	61	208
Democrats voted unanimously	5	0	5
Republicans voted unanimously	10	2	12

Party Scores

Party Unity and Opposition-to-Party scores below are composites of individual scores and show the percentage of time the average Democrat and Republican voted with his party majority in disagreement with the other party's majority. Failures to vote lower both Party Unity and Opposition-to-Party scores. Averages are closer to House figures because the House has more members.

	1982		1981	
	Dem.	Rep.	Dem.	Rep.
Party Unity	72%	71%	69%	76%
Senate	72	76	71	81
House	72	69	69	74
Opposition	20%	21%	23%	18%
Senate	23	19	21	14
House	19	22	23	19

Sectional Support, Opposition

SENATE	Support	Opposition
Northern Democrats	78%	17%
Southern Democrats	59	36
Northern Republicans	74	21
Southern Republicans	86	12

HOUSE	Support	Opposition
Northern Democrats	79%	11%
Southern Democrats	56	35
Northern Republicans	67	23
Southern Republicans	78	15

Party Unity History

Composite Party Unity scores showing the percentage of time the average Democrat and Republican voted with his party majority in partisan votes in recent years:

Year	Democrats	Republicans
1982	72%	71%
1981	69	76
1980	68	70
1979	69	72
1978	64	67
1977	67	70
1976	65	66
1975	69	70

Individual Scores

Highest Party Unity Scores. Those who in 1982 most consistently voted with their party majority against the majority of the other party:

SENATE

Democrats		Republicans	
Levin, Mich.	92%	Garn, Utah	93%
Sarbanes, Md.	91	Symms, Idaho	93
Leahy, Vt.	91	Laxalt, Nev.	93
Eagleton, Mo.	91	Thurmond, S.C.	92
Riegle, Mich.	89	Dole, Kan.	91
Mitchell, Maine	89	Murkowski, Alaska	91
Metzenbaum, Ohio	88	Armstrong, Colo.	91
Bradley, N.J.	87	Domenici, N.M.	90
		Mattingly, Ga.	90

HOUSE

Democrats		Republicans	
Howard, N.J.	98 %	Smith, Ore.	94%
Roybal, Calif.	95	Dannemeyer, Calif.	93
Oberstar, Minn.	95	Corcoran, Ill.	93
Dwyer, N.J.	94	Shumway, Calif.	93
Solarz, N.Y.	94	Hansen, Idaho	93
Vento, Minn.	94	Moorhead, Calif.	92
Matsui, Calif.	93	Bliley, Va.	92
Hall, Ind.	93[1]	Hiler, Ind.	92
Edwards, Calif.	93	Walker, Pa.	92
		Loeffler, Texas	92

Highest Opposition-to-Party Scores. Those who in 1982 most consistently voted against their party majority:

SENATE

Democrats		Republicans	
Byrd, Va. [1, 2]	68%	Weicker, Conn.	58%
Zorinsky, Neb.	51	Mathias, Md.	50
Stennis, Miss.	51	Chafee, R.I.	50
Johnston, La.	48	Specter, Pa.	49
Long, La.	47	Heinz, Pa.	43
Proxmire, Wis.	43	Durenberger, Minn.	41

HOUSE

Democrats		Republicans	
Stump, Ariz. [3]	93%	Schneider, R.I.	74%
McDonald, Ga.	90	Hollenbeck, N.J.	71
Gramm, Texas	87	Rinaldo, N.J.	71
Stenholm, Texas	78	Conte, Mass.	62
Daniel, Va.	76	Green, N.Y.	60
Roemer, La.	68	Heckler, Mass.	59
Montgomery, Miss.	66	Jeffords, Vt.	58
Leath, Texas	64	Smith, N.J.	57
Tauzin, La.	63	DeNardis, Conn.	57
Shelby, Ala.	63	Davis, Mich.	56
Ralph Hall, Texas	60	Gilman, N.Y.	56

[1] *Not eligible for all party unity votes in 1982.*
[2] *Byrd elected as an independent, but caucused with Democrats.*
[3] *Stump served as a Democrat in the 97th Congress, but was elected to the 98th Congress as a Republican.*

Party Unity and Party Opposition: House

1. Party Unity, 1982. Percentage of 167 House Party Unity recorded votes in 1982 on which representative voted "yea" or "nay" *in agreement* with a majority of his party. (Party unity roll calls are those on which a majority of voting Democrats opposed a majority of voting Republicans. Failures to vote lower both Party Unity and Party Opposition scores.)

2. Party Opposition, 1982. Percentages of 167 House Party Unity recorded votes in 1982 on which representative voted "yea" or "nay" *in disagreement* with a majority of his party.

KEY

† Not eligible for all recorded votes in 1982 (sworn in after Jan. 25, died or resigned during session, or voted "present" to avoid possible conflict of interest).

Democrats   *Republicans*

	1	2
ALABAMA		
1 *Edwards*	68	29
2 *Dickinson*	76	11
3 Nichols	46	43
4 Bevill	70	26
5 Flippo	66	29
6 *Smith*	85	7
7 Shelby	35	63
ALASKA		
AL *Young*	50	25
ARIZONA		
1 *Rhodes*	44	20
2 Udall	86	7
3 Stump	3	93
4 *Rudd*	87	6
ARKANSAS		
1 Alexander	72	17
2 *Bethune*	80	15
3 *Hammerschmidt*	79	20
4 Anthony	63	31
CALIFORNIA		
1 *Chappie*	81	5
2 *Clausen*	67	29
3 Matsui	93	5
4 Fazio	92	7
5 Burton, J.	25	1
6 Burton, P.	87	2
7 Miller	92	4
8 Dellums	90	5
9 Stark	85	4
10 Edwards	93	4
11 Lantos	87	4
12 *McCloskey*	38	25
13 Mineta	91	8
14 *Shumway*	93	2
15 Coelho	81	11
16 Panetta	86	14
17 *Pashayan*	82	14
18 *Thomas*	71	8
19 *Lagomarsino*	90	10
20 *Goldwater*	40	3
21 *Fiedler*	81	18
22 *Moorhead*	92	5
23 Beilenson	81	5
24 Waxman	87	7
25 Roybal	95	2
26 *Rousselot*	75	5
27 *Dornan*	68	5
28 Dixon	79	7
29 Hawkins	81	5
30 Martinez ¹	82†	6†
31 Dymally	78	4
32 Anderson	66	32
33 Grisham	63	8
34 *Lungren*	90	5
35 *Dreier*	87	2
36 Brown	85	5
37 *Lewis*	84	13
38 Patterson	84	12
39 *Dannemeyer*	93	5
40 *Badham*	73	6
41 *Lowery*	88	10
42 *Hunter*	84	10
43 *Burgener*	64	10
COLORADO		
1 Schroeder	75	19
2 Wirth	84	9
3 Kogovsek	84	11
4 Brown	89	11

	1	2
5 *Kramer*	81	16
CONNECTICUT		
1 Kennelly	92	8
2 Gejdenson	92	4
3 *DeNardis*	25	57
4 *McKinney*	38	51
5 Ratchford	87	6
6 Moffett	46	1
DELAWARE		
AL *Evans*	51	34
FLORIDA		
1 Hutto	54	43
2 Fuqua	54	36
3 Bennett	55	45
4 Chappell	40	28
5 *McCollum*	91	8
6 *Young*	74†	17†
7 Gibbons	62	35
8 Ireland	22	50
9 Nelson	62	33
10 *Bafalis*	36†	10†
11 Mica	74	23
12 *Shaw*	84	16
13 Lehman	66†	3†
14 Pepper	85	4
15 Fascell	71	10
GEORGIA		
1 Ginn	40	22
2 Hatcher	53	35
3 Brinkley	69	31
4 Levitas	51	45
5 Fowler	70	17
6 *Gingrich*	78	18
7 McDonald	10	90
8 Evans	35	29
9 Jenkins	47	44
10 Barnard	46	47
HAWAII		
1 Heftel	71	14
2 Akaka	81	8
IDAHO		
1 *Craig*	85	7
2 *Hansen*	93	4
ILLINOIS		
1 Washington	74	7
2 Savage	63	7
3 Russo	81	15
4 *Derwinski*	67	16
5 Fary	81	11
6 *Hyde*	79†	19†
7 Collins	86	6
8 Rostenkowski	80	14
9 Yates	75	4
10 *Porter*	66	28
11 Annunzio	85	11
12 *Crane, P.*	81	5
13 *McClory*	63	23
14 *Erlenborn*	75	16
15 *Corcoran*	93	5
16 *Martin*	65	31
17 O'Brien	56	26
18 *Michel*	81	16
19 *Railsback*	38	37
20 *Findley*	52	38
21 *Madigan*	65	26
22 *Crane, D.*	87	6
23 Price	80	15
24 Simon	81	4
INDIANA		
1 Hall ²	93†	5†
2 Fithian	66	17
3 *Hiler*	92	5
4 *Coats*	84	13
5 *Hillis*	71	22
6 Evans	72	13
7 *Myers*	84	16
8 *Deckard*	44	35
9 Hamilton	66	33
10 Sharp	69	28
11 Jacobs	62	29
IOWA		
1 *Leach*	43	54
2 *Tauke*	51	41
3 *Evans*	59	40
4 Smith	83	17
5 Harkin	83	12
6 Bedell	80	17

1. Rep. Matthew G. Martinez, D-Calif., sworn in July 15, 1982, to succeed George E. Danielson, D, who resigned March 9, 1982. Danielson's 1982 party unity score was 100 percent.

2. Rep Katie Hall, D-Ind., sworn in Nov. 29, 1982, to succeed Adam Benjamin Jr., D, who died Sept. 7, 1982. Benjamin's 1982 party unity score was 85 percent; opposition was 15 percent.

3. Rep. Thomas P. O'Neill Jr., D-Mass., as Speaker, votes at his own discretion.

4. Rep. Fred Richmond, D-N.Y., resigned Aug. 25, 1982.

5. Rep. Jean S. Ashbrook, R-Ohio, sworn in July 12, 1982, to succeed her husband, John M. Ashbrook, R, who died April 24, 1982. John Ashbrook's 1982 party unity score was 20 percent; opposition was zero.

ND - Northern Democrats   SD - Southern Democrats

	1	2
KANSAS		
1 *Roberts*	86	11
2 *Jeffries*	91	4
3 *Winn*	82	12
4 Glickman	74	26
5 *Whittaker*	84	12
KENTUCKY		
1 Hubbard	43	47
2 Natcher	74	26
3 Mazzoli	75	22
4 *Snyder*	74	24
5 *Rogers*	73	20
6 *Hopkins*	77	22
7 Perkins	81	19
LOUISIANA		
1 *Livingston*	76	20
2 Boggs	78	13
3 Tauzin	35	63
4 Roemer	32	68
5 Huckaby	46	46
6 *Moore*	80	17
7 Breaux	44	42
8 Long	84	12
MAINE		
1 *Emery*	50	30
2 *Snowe*	53	46
MARYLAND		
1 Dyson	68	29
2 Long	78	17
3 Mikulski	90	7
4 *Holt*	69	19
5 Hoyer	92	5
6 Byron	44	49
7 Mitchell	85	6
8 Barnes	89	6
MASSACHUSETTS		
1 *Conte*	35	62
2 Boland	86	7
3 Early	86	5
4 Frank	81	10
5 Shannon	90	4
6 Mavroules	85	7
7 Markey	90	3
8 O'Neill [3]		
9 Moakley	89	5
10 *Heckler*	25	59
11 Donnelly	84	13
12 Studds	92	8
MICHIGAN		
1 Conyers	68	8
2 *Pursell*	38	40
3 Wolpe	88	11
4 *Siljander*	74	7
5 Sawyer	67	32
6 Dunn	66	30
7 Kildee	92	8
8 Traxler	84	7
9 *Vander Jagt*	62	28
10 Albosta	83	12
11 *Davis*	37	56
12 Bonior	85	5
13 Crockett	68	4
14 Hertel	80	9
15 Ford	90	1
16 Dingell	90	7
17 Brodhead	85	7
18 Blanchard	42	1
19 *Broomfield*	72	20
MINNESOTA		
1 *Erdahl*	58	33
2 *Hagedorn*	72	10
3 *Frenzel*	78	18
4 Vento	94	5
5 Sabo	92	5
6 *Weber*	80	18
7 *Stangeland*	80	17
8 Oberstar	95	4
MISSISSIPPI		
1 Whitten	66	27
2 Bowen	62	19
3 Montgomery	29	66
4 Dowdy	68	18
5 *Lott*	78	19
MISSOURI		
1 Clay	74	5
2 Young	67	20
3 Gephardt	71	24

	1	2
4 Skelton	40	41
5 Bolling	42	6
6 *Coleman*	67	28
7 Taylor	87	9
8 Bailey	87	8
9 Volkmer	66	34
10 *Emerson*	88	9
MONTANA		
1 Williams	81	11
2 *Marlenee*	73	17
NEBRASKA		
1 *Bereuter*	77	23
2 *Daub*	86	14
3 *Smith*	82	18
NEVADA		
AL Santini	32	32
NEW HAMPSHIRE		
1 *D'Amours*	68	23
2 *Gregg*	84	15
NEW JERSEY		
1 Florio	87	7
2 Hughes	80	19
3 Howard	98	2
4 *Smith*	41	57
5 *Fenwick*	50	40
6 *Forsythe*	54	21
7 *Roukema*	57	39
8 Roe	83	12
9 *Hollenbeck*	19	71
10 Rodino	92	5
11 Minish	90	7
12 *Rinaldo*	26	71
13 *Courter*	65	24
14 Guarini	89	7
15 Dwyer	94	5
NEW MEXICO		
1 *Lujan*	83	14
2 *Skeen*	90	10
NEW YORK		
1 *Carney*	69	20
2 Downey	92	4
3 *Carman*	86	13
4 *Lent*	60	32
5 *McGrath*	66	31
6 *LeBoutillier*	71	16
7 Addabbo	83	5
8 Rosenthal	65	4
9 Ferraro	90	3
10 Biaggi	72	8
11 Scheuer	91	6
12 Chisholm	57	2
13 Solarz	94	4
14 Richmond [4]	81†	1†
15 Zeferetti	64	8
16 Schumer	91	4
17 *Molinari*	62	33
18 *Green*	32	60
19 Rangel	87	5
20 Weiss	74	4
21 Garcia	77	4
22 Bingham	78	7
23 Peyser	89	4
24 Ottinger	89	9
25 *Fish*	41	51
26 *Gilman*	41	56
27 McHugh	89	8
28 Stratton	56	35
29 *Solomon*	85	9
30 *Martin*	77	19
31 *Mitchell*	49	41
32 *Wortley*	71	22
33 *Lee*	60	15
34 *Horton*	39	50
35 *Conable*	72	23
36 LaFalce	80	10
37 Nowak	90	8
38 *Kemp*	68	23
39 Lundine	74	11
NORTH CAROLINA		
1 Jones	65	22
2 Fountain	33	57
3 Whitley	50	47
4 Andrews	59	30
5 Neal	48	32
6 *Johnston*	81	4
7 Rose	63	19
8 Hefner	57†	39†

	1	2
9 *Martin*	84	7
10 *Broyhill*	86	13
11 *Hendon*	84	9
NORTH DAKOTA		
AL Dorgan	81	17
OHIO		
1 *Gradison*	76	20
2 Luken	77	14
3 Hall	73	14
4 *Oxley*	81	13
5 *Latta*	85	12
6 *McEwen*	77	18
7 Brown	36	7
8 *Kindness*	87	8
9 Weber	78	20
10 Miller	80	18
11 Stanton	33	14
12 Shamansky	87	8
13 Pease	87	11
14 Seiberling	91	5
15 Wylie	63	29
16 Regula	65	34
17 Ashbrook [5]	88†	6†
18 Applegate	64	31
19 Williams	41	48
20 Oakar	83	11
21 Stokes	91	4
22 Eckart	87	10
23 Mottl	63	28
OKLAHOMA		
1 Jones	63	32
2 Synar	79	17
3 Watkins	60	33
4 McCurdy	48	43
5 *Edwards*	78	13
6 English	43	57
OREGON		
1 AuCoin	76	7
2 *Smith*	94	3
3 Wyden	92	7
4 Weaver	77	11
PENNSYLVANIA		
1 Foglietta	81	5
2 Gray	80	5
3 Smith	51	8
4 *Dougherty*	26	53
5 *Schulze*	63	15
6 Yatron	71	23
7 Edgar	84	10
8 *Coyne, J.*	63	27
9 *Shuster*	60	13
10 McDade	36	55
11 *Nelligan*	61	36
12 Murtha	68	21
13 *Coughlin*	65	34
14 Coyne, W.	91	7
15 *Ritter*	83	16
16 *Walker*	92	8
17 Ertel	49	6
18 Walgren	80	16
19 *Goodling*	74	24
20 Gaydos	77	17
21 Bailey	82	16
22 Murphy	71	19
23 *Clinger*	61	38
24 *Marks*	12	32
25 *Atkinson*	57	32
RHODE ISLAND		
1 St Germain	90	8
2 *Schneider*	20	74
SOUTH CAROLINA		
1 *Hartnett*	88	8
2 *Spence*	84	15
3 Derrick	70	22
4 *Campbell*	80	11
5 Holland	49	24
6 *Napier*	63	25
SOUTH DAKOTA		
1 Daschle	80	14
2 *Roberts*	75	11
TENNESSEE		
1 *Quillen*	68	26
2 *Duncan*	68	28
3 Bouquard	56	38
4 Gore	89	11
5 Boner	72	21
6 *Beard*	59	8

	1	2
7 Jones	59	25
8 Ford	81	6
TEXAS		
1 Hall, S.	39	59
2 Wilson	51	30
3 *Collins*	72	5
4 Hall, R.	40	60
5 Mattox	51	6
6 *Gramm*	10	87
7 *Archer*	90	8
8 *Fields*	89	9
9 Brooks	70	16
10 Pickle	57	36
11 Leath	31	64
12 Wright	79	16
13 Hightower	54	44
14 Patman	47	52
15 de la Garza	67	25
16 White	49	46
17 Stenholm	17	78
18 Leland	84	5
19 Hance	46	49
20 Gonzalez	84	14
21 *Loeffler*	92	8
22 *Paul*	83	15
23 Kazen	51	49
24 Frost	82	12
UTAH		
1 *Hansen*	77	8
2 *Marriott*	75	20
VERMONT		
AL *Jeffords*	35	58
VIRGINIA		
1 *Trible*	63	18
2 *Whitehurst*	78	16
3 *Bliley*	92	5
4 *Daniel, R.*	87	11
5 Daniel, D.	19	76
6 *Butler*	77	13
7 *Robinson*	91	9
8 *Parris*	66	31
9 *Wampler*	74	24
10 *Wolf*	69	28
WASHINGTON		
1 *Pritchard*	47	41
2 Swift	90	7
3 Bonker	79	10
4 *Morrison*	78	22
5 Foley	83	12
6 Dicks	89	8
7 Lowry	92	5
WEST VIRGINIA		
1 Mollohan	73	17
2 *Benedict*	74	17
3 Staton	83	14
4 Rahall	77	10
WISCONSIN		
1 Aspin	77	15
2 Kastenmeier	89	10
3 *Gunderson*	74	26
4 Zablocki	87	8
5 Reuss	84	6
6 *Petri*	71	28
7 Obey	86	11
8 *Roth*	73	22
9 *Sensenbrenner*	84	16
WYOMING		
AL *Cheney*	83	7

Southern states - Ala., Ark., Fla., Ga., Ky., La., Miss., N.C., Okla., S.C., Tenn., Texas, Va.

	1	2		1	2		1	2
ALABAMA			**IOWA**			**NEW HAMPSHIRE**		
Denton	82†	10†	*Grassley*	82	17	*Humphrey*	84†	16†
Heflin	57	42	*Jepsen*	83	16	*Rudman*	79	20
ALASKA			**KANSAS**			**NEW JERSEY**		
Murkowski	91	5	*Dole*	91	8	*Brady* ¹	81†	13†
Stevens	85	8	*Kassebaum*	74	24	Bradley	87	13
ARIZONA			**KENTUCKY**			**NEW MEXICO**		
Goldwater	63	11	Ford	75	24	*Domenici*	90	9
DeConcini	52	36	Huddleston	64	28	*Schmitt*	72	14
ARKANSAS			**LOUISIANA**			**NEW YORK**		
Bumpers	86	11	Johnston	47	48	*D'Amato*	76	22
Pryor	73	23	Long	50	47	Moynihan	86	11
CALIFORNIA			**MAINE**			**NORTH CAROLINA**		
Hayakawa	82	14	*Cohen*	62	36	*East*	89	11
Cranston	81	10	Mitchell	89	11	*Helms*	87	13
COLORADO			**MARYLAND**			**NORTH DAKOTA**		
Armstrong	91	9	*Mathias*	39	50	*Andrews*	71	29
Hart	85	12	Sarbanes	91	3	Burdick	81	17
CONNECTICUT			**MASSACHUSETTS**			**OHIO**		
Weicker	32	58	Kennedy	83	5	Glenn	67	17
Dodd	82	12	Tsongas	78	11	Metzenbaum	88	5
DELAWARE			**MICHIGAN**			**OKLAHOMA**		
Roth	76	22	Levin	92	6	*Nickles*	85	15
Biden	79	17	Riegle	89	3	Boren	52	42
FLORIDA			**MINNESOTA**			**OREGON**		
Hawkins	73	23	*Boschwitz*	71	28	*Hatfield*	57	27
Chiles	59	37	*Durenberger*	45	41	*Packwood*	67	32
GEORGIA			**MISSISSIPPI**			**PENNSYLVANIA**		
Mattingly	90	7	*Cochran*	88	9	*Heinz*	47	43
Nunn	57	41	Stennis	42	51	*Specter*	50	49
HAWAII			**MISSOURI**			**RHODE ISLAND**		
Inouye	74	14	*Danforth*	72	21	*Chafee*	47	50
Matsunaga	80	12	Eagleton	91	7	Pell	75	19
IDAHO			**MONTANA**			**SOUTH CAROLINA**		
McClure	85	9	Baucus	80	18	*Thurmond*	92	5
Symms	93	6	Melcher	63	23	Hollings	73	20
ILLINOIS			**NEBRASKA**			**SOUTH DAKOTA**		
Percy	65	29	Exon	64	33	*Abdnor*	88	10
Dixon	76	20	Zorinsky	49	51	*Pressler*	67	20
INDIANA			**NEVADA**			**TENNESSEE**		
Lugar	85	14	*Laxalt*	93	5	*Baker*	88	8
Quayle	87	12	Cannon	63	18	Sasser	72	25

KEY

† Not eligible for all recorded votes in 1982 (sworn in after Jan. 25, died or resigned during session, or voted "present" to avoid possible conflict of interest).

Democrats　　*Republicans*

	1	2
TEXAS		
Tower	86	11
Bentsen	54	41
UTAH		
Garn	93	7
Hatch	80	12
VERMONT		
Stafford	53	36
Leahy	91	9
VIRGINIA		
Warner	87	13
Byrd ²	30†	68†
WASHINGTON		
Gorton	78	22
Jackson	78	18
WEST VIRGINIA		
Byrd	81	19
Randolph	74	24
WISCONSIN		
Kasten	83	16
Proxmire	57	43
WYOMING		
Simpson	83	13
Wallop	82	10

ND - Northern Democrats　　　SD - Southern Democrats (Southern states - Ala., Ark., Fla., Ga., Ky., La., Miss., N.C., Okla., S.C., Tenn., Texas, Va.)

Party Unity and Party Opposition: Senate

1. Party Unity, 1982. Percentage of 202 Senate Party Unity votes in 1982 on which senator voted "yea" or "nay" *in agreement* with a majority of his party. (Party Unity roll calls are those on which a majority of voting Democrats opposed a majority of voting Republicans. Failures to vote lower both Party Unity and Party Opposition score.)

2. Party Opposition, 1982. Percentage of 202 Senate Party Unity votes in 1982 on which senator voted "yea" or "nay" *in disagreement* with a majority of his party.

1. Sen. Nicholas F. Brady, R-N.J., sworn in April 20, 1982, to succeed Harrison A. Williams Jr., D, who resigned March 11, 1982. Williams' 1982 party unity score was 14 percent; opposition was zero.
2. Sen. Harry F. Byrd Jr., Va., elected as an independent.

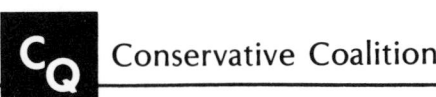 Conservative Coalition

Conservative Success Wanes As Democratic Loyalty Grows

President Reagan's prime source of congressional clout, the conservative coalition of Republicans and Southern Democrats, waned in strength during 1982 after peaking in the previous year, according to a CQ analysis of voting in both houses.

In the second session of the 97th Congress, the conservative coalition came together less frequently and, when it did show up, won fewer votes than it did in 1981.

A 7 percentage point decline in the coalition's winning percentage in 1982 coincided with erosion of congressional support for President Reagan's positions. The decline also occurred during a year when party loyalty was up among Democrats, and down — dramatically, in some individual cases — among Republicans. *(Presidential Support, p. 18-C; Party Unity, p. 30-C)*

Success Rate Drops

On those recorded votes where majorities of Republicans and Southern Democrats voted together against a majority of Northern Democrats, they won 85 percent of the time in 1982. In 1981, the rate of wins for the conservative coalition was a record high 92 percent. *(1981 Almanac, p. 35-C)*

The 1982 figure reversed a three-year strengthening trend, but even with the coalition's lessened success rate, its strength was still impressive.

In 1957, the first year CQ began studying the coalition's voting patterns, its success rate was 89 percent.

After 1957, the trend of the coalition's success was downward until 1965, when the victory rate hit bottom at 33 percent. The rate peaked again in 1971, after which it declined to 52 percent in 1978.

Since 1978, there had been a gradual upswing in the coalition's annual success rate.

As defined by CQ in analyzing House and Senate votes, the coalition's score refers to recorded votes on which majorities of Southern Democrats and Republicans vote the same way and in opposition to a majority of Northern Democrats. It does not reflect any sort of organized conservative entity, nor any philosophic definitions of conservatism. *(Definitions, box, this page)*

The coalition appeared in 18 percent of recorded votes during 1982. Last year, the coalition showed up in 21 percent of recorded votes.

The coalition scores reflected waning presidential popularity, and the twin pressures of elections and party discipline.

In 1982 in the House, where all seats were up for election, the average Southern Democrat voted with the coalition 66 percent of the time — a drop of 4 points.

Comparatively few Democratic Southerners in the Senate faced re-election in 1982, and their coalition support score rose to 73 percent, from 71 percent in 1981.

Republicans in both houses, however, supported the coalition a little less consistently in 1982.

Senate Republican support for the coalition dropped from 80 percent to 76 percent, and House support declined from 77 percent in 1981 to 75 percent in 1982.

Individual Members' Scores

Among Senate Republicans, John P. East, N.C., and Jesse Helms, N.C., voted most often with the coalition in 1982, both scoring 99 percent. Strom Thurmond, R-S.C., who registered a perfect 100 percent in 1981, voted with the coalition 86 percent of the time in 1982. The Southern Democratic senators voting most consistently with the coalition in 1982 were J. Bennett Johnston, La., and Harry F. Byrd Jr., Ind.-Va., whose scores of 93 percent and 89 percent respectively were unchanged from 1981. Although elected as an independent, Byrd caucused with the Democrats.

Among House Southern Democrats, Rep. Charles W. Stenholm, Texas, voted most often with the coalition in 1982 (93 percent) while his colleague, Rep. Phil Gramm of Texas dropped 10 percentage points below his 99 percent score of the previous year.

Reps. Tom Loeffler of Texas and Joe Skeen of New Mexico were the House Republicans with the highest coalition support scores — 100 percent.

Coalition Strained

As in 1981, conservative coalition support ensured Reagan of repeated wins on money matters. But narrow wins — and losses — on certain high-visibility issues suggested the weakened state of the coalition, particularly in the House.

In July, the administration won a House test on funding for the MX, but the vote was on a face-saving compromise, which was approved by just three votes. *(Vote 188, p. 56-H)*

MX funding was later deleted.

In August, the coalition gave Reagan a two-vote victory on the nuclear weapons freeze vote in the House. *(Vote 237, p. 72-H)*

A third important coalition vote in September kept the House, by three votes, from scrapping economic sanctions that Reagan had imposed on the Soviet Union. *(Vote 354, p. 104-H)*

House votes where the coalition appeared but lost included a restoration of Medicare funding and votes against binary chemical munitions. *(Vote 110, p. 32-H; votes 193, 194, 195, p. 58-H)*

In the Senate, the coalition lost six times when it joined repeated attempts by Jesse Helms to end a filibuster on an anti-abortion rider to a school prayer amendment Helms was sponsoring.

The coalition suffered a seventh loss on the prayer amendment itself when Barry Goldwater, R-Ariz., a conservative himself, moved to kill it. The prayer amendment would have barred federal courts, including the Supreme Court, from hearing "voluntary" school prayer cases. It was intended to pave the way for the restoration of public school prayer. *(Votes 342, 343, 345, 346, 347, 349, 350, pp. 58-S—60-S)*

Coalition Appearances, 1963-82

Following is the percentage of the recorded votes for both houses of Congress on which the coalition appeared:

1963	17%	1973	23%
1964	15	1974	24
1965	24	1975	28
1966	25	1976	24
1967	20	1977	26
1968	24	1978	21
1969	27	1979	20
1970	22	1980	18
1971	30	1981	21
1972	27	1982	18

Coalition Victories, 1963-82

Year	Total	Senate	House
1963	50%	44%	67%
1964	51	47	67
1965	33	39	25
1966	45	51	32
1967	63	54	73
1968	73	80	63
1969	68	67	71
1970	66	64	70
1971	83	86	79
1972	69	63	79
1973	61	54	67
1974	59	54	67
1975	50	48	52
1976	58	58	59
1977	68	74	60
1978	52	46	57
1979	70	65	73
1980	72	75	67
1981	92	95	88
1982	85	90	78

Average Scores

Following are the composite conservative coalition support and opposition scores for 1982 (scores for 1981 are in parentheses):

	Southern Democrats	Republicans	Northern Democrats
Coalition Support			
Senate	73% (71)	76% (80)	28% (27)
House	66 (70)	75 (77)	24 (28)
Coalition Opposition			
Senate	23% (23)	18% (15)	65% (66)
House	25 (23)	18 (17)	68 (65)

Regional Scores

Following are the parties' coalition support and opposition scores by region for 1982 (scores for 1981 are in parentheses):

SUPPORT

	East	West	South	Midwest
DEMOCRATS				
Senate	19% (15)	34% (33)	73% (71)	35% (37)
House	23 (25)	23 (26)	66 (70)	26 (31)
REPUBLICANS				
Senate	53% (59)	83% (84)	91% (93)	77% (82)
House	62 (67)	82 (82)	85 (86)	74 (77)

OPPOSITION

	East	West	South	Midwest
DEMOCRATS				
Senate	74% (76)	57% (57)	23% (23)	59% (60)
House	68 (67)	69 (67)	25 (23)	66 (61)
REPUBLICANS				
Senate	41% (35)	11% (10)	4% (4)	19% (15)
House	31 (29)	9 (9)	9 (9)	19 (19)

*(CQ defines regions of the United States as follows: **East:** Conn., Del., Maine, Md., Mass., N.H., N.J., N.Y., Pa., R.I., Vt., W.Va. **West:** Alaska, Ariz., Calif., Colo., Hawaii, Idaho, Mont., Nev., N.M., Ore., Utah, Wash., Wyo. **South:** Ala., Ark., Fla., Ga., Ky., La., Miss., N.C., Okla., S.C., Tenn., Texas, Va. **Midwest:** Ill., Ind., Iowa, Kan., Mich., Minn., Mo., Neb., N.D., Ohio, S.D., Wis.)*

Individual Scores

SUPPORT

Highest Coalition Support Scores. Those who voted with the conservative coalition most consistently in 1982:

SENATE

Southern Democrats		Republicans	
Johnston, La.	93%	East, N.C.	99%
Byrd, Va. [1]	89	Helms, N.C.	99
Bentsen, Texas	88	Domenici, N.M.	97
Boren, Okla.	87	Mattingly, Ga.	97
Long, La.	85	Symms, Idaho	97

Northern Democrats	
Zorinsky, Neb.	86%
DeConcini, Ariz.	74
Exon, Neb.	70
Melcher, Mont.	59
Byrd, W.Va.	56

HOUSE

Southern Democrats		Republicans	
Stenholm, Texas	93%	Loeffler, Texas	100%
White, Texas	90	Skeen, N.M.	100
McDonald, Ga.	90	Hammerschmidt, Ark.	99
Kazen, Texas	90	Bliley, Va.	97
Whitley, N.C.	90	Robinson, Va.	97
Montgomery, Miss.	90	Corcoran, Ill.	97
Hutto, Fla.	89	Moorhead, Calif.	96
Gramm, Texas	89	Campbell, S.C.	96
		Hansen, Idaho	95
		Dreier, Calif.	95

Northern Democrats	
Stump, Ariz. [2]	96%
Byron, Md.	79
Skelton, Mo.	73
Stratton, N.Y.	70
Murtha, Pa.	64
Dyson, Md.	62
Anderson, Calif.	59
Young, Mo.	58
Hamilton, Ind.	58
Mollohan, W.Va.	58

[1] *Byrd, Va., was elected as an independent, but caucused with Democrats.*

[2] *Stump was elected to the 97th Congress as a Democrat and to the 98th Congress as a Republican.*

OPPOSITION

Highest Coalition Opposition Scores. Those who voted against the conservative coalition most consistently in 1982:

SENATE

Southern Democrats		Republicans	
Bumpers, Ark.	74%	Chafee, R.I.	69%
Hollings, S.C.	36	Weicker, Conn.	60
Sasser, Tenn.	36	Specter, Pa.	59

1982 Coalition Votes

Following is a list of all 1982 Senate and House votes on which the conservative coalition appeared. The votes are listed by CQ vote number and may be found beginning on pages 1-S and 1-H.

SENATE VOTES (94)

Coalition Victories (85) — 2, 4, 5, 9, 10, 11, 12, 18, 25, 26, 29, 32, 33, 34, 35, 39, 53, 54, 59, 87, 88, 89, 94, 111, 112, 113, 114, 118, 125, 132, 152, 164, 166, 204, 210, 211, 212, 215, 218, 220, 223, 225, 241, 243, 244, 260, 263, 264, 266, 267, 268, 269, 270, 272, 273, 276, 281, 282, 287, 288, 299, 305, 306, 310, 312, 313, 314, 318, 319, 335, 348, 365, 372, 384, 394, 405, 406, 419, 420, 423, 427, 436, 441, 449, 455.

Coalition Defeats (9) — 70, 115, 342, 343, 345, 346, 347, 349, 350.

HOUSE VOTES (73)

Coalition Victories (57) — 61, 91, 96, 101, 103, 105, 106, 112, 115, 116, 117, 122, 135, 141, 142, 151, 153, 188, 190, 196, 200, 210, 211, 215, 216, 227, 237, 238, 239, 248, 249, 250, 254, 255, 265, 269, 274, 277, 282, 284, 308, 311, 313, 354, 358, 365, 372, 374, 378, 379, 380, 383, 384, 402, 434, 447, 454.

Coalition Defeats (16) — 60, 70, 94, 110, 193, 194, 195, 293, 305, 349, 355, 363, 389, 392, 421, 422.

Pryor, Ark.	35	Mathias, Md.	57
Ford, Ky.	33	Cohen, Maine	52

Northern Democrats	
Levin, Mich.	94%
Leahy, Vt.	88
Kennedy, Mass.	88
Eagleton, Mo.	87
Riegle, Mich.	86

HOUSE

Southern Democrats		Republicans	
Leland, Texas	86%	Schneider, R.I.	74%
Ford, Tenn.	64	Hollenbeck, N.J.	73
Gonzalez, Texas	60	Green, N.Y.	67
Pepper, Fla.	59	Heckler, Mass.	66
Frost, Texas	59	Leach, Iowa	62
Lehman, Fla.	55	DeNardis, Conn.	62
Gore, Tenn.	53	Conte, Mass.	58
Synar, Okla.	52	Rinaldo, N.J.	58
Mazzoli, Ky.	49	Jeffords, Vt.	55
Fascell, Fla.	49	Gilman, N.Y.	52

Northern Democrats	
Dellums, Calif.	96%
Edwards, Calif.	93
Schumer, N.Y.	92
Phillip Burton, Calif.	92
Roybal, Calif.	92
Vento, Minn.	92
Ottinger, N.Y.	92
Markey, Mass.	92

Conservative Coalition Support and Opposition: House

1. Conservative Coalition Support, 1982. Percentage of 73 conservative coalition recorded votes in 1982 on which representative voted "yea" or "nay" *in agreement* with the position of the conservative coalition. Failures to vote lower both support and opposition scores.

2. Conservative Coalition Opposition, 1982. Percentage of 73 conservative coalition recorded votes in 1982 on which representative voted "yea" or "nay" *in disagreement* with the position of the conservative coalition. Failures to vote lower both support and opposition scores.

KEY

† Not eligible for all recorded votes in 1982 (sworn in after Jan. 25, died or resigned during session, or voted "present" to avoid possible conflict of interest).

Democrats   *Republicans*

	1	2
ALABAMA		
1 *Edwards*	93	7
2 *Dickinson*	89	4
3 Nichols	88	7
4 Bevill	75	19
5 Flippo	75	19
6 *Smith*	88	4
7 Shelby	86	10
ALASKA		
AL *Young*	66	15
ARIZONA		
1 *Rhodes*	51	11
2 Udall	29	62
3 Stump	96	0
4 *Rudd*	90	1
ARKANSAS		
1 Alexander	60	34
2 *Bethune*	85	11
3 *Hammerschmidt*	99	1
4 Anthony	71	21
CALIFORNIA		
1 *Chappie*	82	4
2 *Clausen*	88	12
3 Matsui	19	81
4 Fazio	29	67
5 Burton, J.	1	29
6 Burton, P.	3	92
7 Miller	7	90
8 Dellums	4	96
9 Stark	5	88
10 Edwards	7	93
11 Lantos	29	66
12 *McCloskey*	44	29
13 Mineta	32	67
14 *Shumway*	89	4
15 Coelho	37	59
16 Panetta	36	63
17 *Pashayan*	81	14
18 *Thomas*	84	7
19 *Lagomarsino*	93	7
20 *Goldwater*	47	3
21 *Fiedler*	93	5
22 *Moorhead*	96	3
23 Beilenson	11	82
24 Waxman	12	86
25 Roybal	8	92
26 *Rousselot*	74	7
27 *Dornan*	73	4
28 Dixon	15	73
29 Hawkins	16	73
30 Martinez [1]	10†	73†
31 Dymally	11	74
32 Anderson	59	41
33 *Grisham*	77	7
34 *Lungren*	93	7
35 *Dreier*	95	1
36 Brown	12	79
37 *Lewis*	89	10
38 Patterson	26	67
39 *Dannemeyer*	90	10
40 *Badham*	88	4
41 *Lowery*	93	7
42 *Hunter*	90	5
43 *Burgener*	71	5
COLORADO		
1 Schroeder	16	82
2 Wirth	19	79
3 Kogovsek	29	67
4 *Brown*	75	25

	1	2
5 *Kramer*	89	8
CONNECTICUT		
1 Kennelly	26	74
2 Gejdenson	15	82
3 *DeNardis*	27	62
4 *McKinney*	44	49
5 Ratchford	15	82
6 Moffett	1	47
DELAWARE		
AL *Evans*	62	32
FLORIDA		
1 Hutto	89	10
2 Fuqua	75	16
3 Bennett	81	19
4 Chappell	66	10
5 *McCollum*	93	7
6 *Young*	84	5
7 Gibbons	64	32
8 Ireland	75	5
9 Nelson	78	19
10 *Bafalis*	38†	6†
11 Mica	63	34
12 *Shaw*	90	10
13 Lehman	21†	55†
14 Pepper	23	59
15 Fascell	44	49
GEORGIA		
1 Ginn	45	8
2 Hatcher	79	8
3 Brinkley	74	25
4 Levitas	73	23
5 Fowler	48	44
6 *Gingrich*	75	12
7 McDonald	90	8
8 Evans	56	14
9 Jenkins	77	15
10 Barnard	88	5
HAWAII		
1 Heftel	41	42
2 Akaka	32	58
IDAHO		
1 *Craig*	86	8
2 *Hansen*	95	0
ILLINOIS		
1 Washington	10	74
2 Savage	8	77
3 Russo	32	68
4 *Derwinski*	75	14
5 Fary	51	47
6 *Hyde*	86	8
7 Collins	7	85
8 Rostenkowski	42	56
9 Yates	4	70
10 *Porter*	62	32
11 Annunzio	47	52
12 *Crane, P.*	89	7
13 *McClory*	64	19
14 *Erlenborn*	84	11
15 *Corcoran*	97	3
16 *Martin*	58	41
17 *O'Brien*	68	14
18 *Michel*	89	10
19 *Railsback*	45	37
20 *Findley*	48	45
21 *Madigan*	70	21
22 *Crane, D.*	86	7
23 Price	48	47
24 Simon	16	73
INDIANA		
1 Hall [2]	7†	87†
2 Fithian	25	63
3 *Hiler*	93	5
4 *Coats*	82	18
5 *Hillis*	81	11
6 Evans	26	53
7 *Myers*	89	11
8 *Deckard*	52	38
9 Hamilton	58	42
10 Sharp	36	64
11 Jacobs	26	74
IOWA		
1 *Leach*	36	62
2 *Tauke*	53	44
3 *Evans*	55	42
4 Smith	30	67
5 Harkin	12	86
6 Bedell	25	74

ND - Northern Democrats   SD - Southern Democrats

1. *Rep. Matthew G. Mortinez, D-Calif., sworn in July 15, 1982, to succeed George E. Danielson, D, who resigned March 9, 1982. Danielson was not eligible for any conservative coalition votes in 1982.*

2. *Rep. Katie Hall, D-Ind., sworn in Nov. 29, 1982, to succeed Adam Benjamin Jr., D, who died Sept. 7, 1982. Benjamin's 1982 conservative coalition support score was 43 percent; opposition was 57 percent.*

3. *Rep. Thomas P. O'Neill Jr., D-Mass., as Speaker, votes at his own discretion.*

4. *Rep. Fred Richmond, D-N.Y., resigned Aug. 25, 1982.*

5. *Rep. Jean S. Ashbrook, R-Ohio, sworn in July 12, 1982, to succeed her husband, John M. Ashbrook, R, who died April 24, 1982. John Ashbrook was not eligible for any conservative coalition votes in 1982.*

Member	1	2
KANSAS		
1 Roberts	84	14
2 Jeffries	86	7
3 Winn	88	7
4 Glickman	45	53
5 Whittaker	82	16
KENTUCKY		
1 Hubbard	86	11
2 Natcher	63	37
3 Mazzoli	49	49
4 Snyder	85	15
5 Rogers	86	12
6 Hopkins	78	21
7 Perkins	52	47
LOUISIANA		
1 Livingston	84	11
2 Boggs	52	38
3 Tauzin	82	15
4 Roemer	77	23
5 Huckaby	75	14
6 Moore	86	12
7 Breaux	64	14
8 Long	48	44
MAINE		
1 Emery	63	23
2 Snowe	58	40
MARYLAND		
1 Dyson	62	37
2 Long	42	56
3 Mikulski	18	79
4 Holt	81	11
5 Hoyer	25	71
6 Byron	79	15
7 Mitchell	8	81
8 Barnes	18	73
MASSACHUSETTS		
1 Conte	40	58
2 Boland	37	60
3 Early	19	70
4 Frank	15	78
5 Shannon	7	89
6 Mavroules	25	70
7 Markey	8	92
8 O'Neill [3]		
9 Moakley	25	70
10 Heckler	23	66
11 Donnelly	33	60
12 Studds	10	90
MICHIGAN		
1 Conyers	8	75
2 Pursell	45	37
3 Wolpe	11	88
4 Siljander	79	1
5 Sawyer	84	14
6 Dunn	68	29
7 Kildee	10	90
8 Traxler	25	68
9 Vander Jagt	77	14
10 Albosta	36	63
11 Davis	62	29
12 Bonior	12	71
13 Crockett	3	75
14 Hertel	21	68
15 Ford	8	77
16 Dingell	25	74
17 Brodhead	3	90
18 Blanchard	8	38
19 Broomfield	82	12
MINNESOTA		
1 Erdahl	62	36
2 Hagedorn	84	10
3 Frenzel	77	21
4 Vento	5	92
5 Sabo	10	89
6 Weber	74	25
7 Stangeland	85	10
8 Oberstar	10	89
MISSISSIPPI		
1 Whitten	49	34
2 Bowen	58	27
3 Montgomery	90	5
4 Dowdy	44	34
5 Lott	88	11
MISSOURI		
1 Clay	3	67
2 Young	58	33
3 Gephardt	56	40
4 Skelton	73	14
5 Bolling	15	29
6 Coleman	75	14
7 Taylor	89	5
8 Bailey	79	15
9 Volkmer	55	41
10 Emerson	85	10
MONTANA		
1 Williams	16	79
2 Marlenee	82	12
NEBRASKA		
1 Bereuter	79	21
2 Daub	84	16
3 Smith	81	19
NEVADA		
AL Santini	47	22
NEW HAMPSHIRE		
1 D'Amours	42	44
2 Gregg	77	19
NEW JERSEY		
1 Florio	18	75
2 Hughes	40	59
3 Howard	10	90
4 Smith	52	47
5 Fenwick	42	48
6 Forsythe	52	30
7 Roukema	60	37
8 Roe	33	66
9 Hollenbeck	21	73
10 Rodino	11	88
11 Minish	23	73
12 Rinaldo	41	58
13 Courter	78	14
14 Guarini	23	71
15 Dwyer	22	78
NEW MEXICO		
1 Lujan	79	15
2 Skeen	100	0
NEW YORK		
1 Carney	81	11
2 Downey	11	88
3 Carman	90	7
4 Lent	71	27
5 McGrath	66	29
6 LeBoutillier	82	12
7 Addabbo	14	75
8 Rosenthal	5	64
9 Ferraro	15	79
10 Biaggi	29	59
11 Scheuer	14	82
12 Chisholm	4	52
13 Solarz	11	86
14 Richmond [4]	2†	70†
15 Zeferetti	23	52
16 Schumer	7	92
17 Molinari	67	30
18 Green	30	67
19 Rangel	10	88
20 Weiss	7	79
21 Garcia	10	82
22 Bingham	11	74
23 Peyser	10	85
24 Ottinger	7	92
25 Fish	49	44
26 Gilman	45	52
27 McHugh	19	81
28 Stratton	70	23
29 Solomon	78	10
30 Martin	88	7
31 Mitchell	75	16
32 Wortley	81	16
33 Lee	64	18
34 Horton	55	36
35 Conable	71	21
36 LaFalce	21	73
37 Nowak	14	86
38 Kemp	81	14
39 Lundine	22	74
NORTH CAROLINA		
1 Jones	56	32
2 Fountain	85	10
3 Whitley	90	5
4 Andrews	67	22
5 Neal	59	25
6 Johnston	84	8
7 Rose	60	32
8 Hefner	87†	10†
9 Martin	89	10
10 Broyhill	85	10
11 Hendon	90	5
NORTH DAKOTA		
AL Dorgan	33	64
OHIO		
1 Gradison	81	18
2 Luken	36	56
3 Hall	30	60
4 Oxley	90	10
5 Latta	93	5
6 McEwen	77	18
7 Brown	37	5
8 Kindness	88	8
9 Weber	82	18
10 Miller	78	22
11 Stanton	32	8
12 Shamansky	30	63
13 Pease	16	81
14 Seiberling	12	84
15 Wylie	60	26
16 Regula	75	23
17 Ashbrook [5]	92†	4†
18 Applegate	56	41
19 Williams	59	37
20 Oakar	22	70
21 Stokes	10	86
22 Eckart	21	78
23 Mottl	40	53
OKLAHOMA		
1 Jones	63	32
2 Synar	44	52
3 Watkins	74	19
4 McCurdy	79	19
5 Edwards	81	12
6 English	82	16
OREGON		
1 AuCoin	15	71
2 Smith	88	4
3 Wyden	8	90
4 Weaver	11	79
PENNSYLVANIA		
1 Foglietta	18	77
2 Gray	8	84
3 Smith	34	36
4 Dougherty	58	30
5 Schulze	73	11
6 Yatron	52	44
7 Edgar	5	88
8 Coyne, J.	64	25
9 Shuster	60	18
10 McDade	53	41
11 Nelligan	78	21
12 Murtha	64	30
13 Coughlin	56	42
14 Coyne, W.	26	74
15 Ritter	78	21
16 Walker	84	16
17 Ertel	16	34
18 Walgren	23	73
19 Goodling	66	30
20 Gaydos	42	55
21 Bailey	56	44
22 Murphy	41	49
23 Clinger	77	23
24 Marks	22	27
25 Atkinson	73	21
RHODE ISLAND		
1 St Germain	23	71
2 Schneider	22	74
SOUTH CAROLINA		
1 Hartnett	88	8
2 Spence	93	5
3 Derrick	56	41
4 Campbell	96	1
5 Holland	62	11
6 Napier	82	11
SOUTH DAKOTA		
1 Daschle	34	56
2 Roberts	79	11
TENNESSEE		
1 Quillen	88	11
2 Duncan	93	5
3 Bouquard	73	22
4 Gore	47	53
5 Boner	60	32
6 Beard	67	3
7 Jones	52	23
8 Ford	19	64
TEXAS		
1 Hall, S.	79	18
2 Wilson	63	15
3 Collins	62	11
4 Hall, R.	81	19
5 Mattox	22	41
6 Gramm	89	10
7 Archer	89	10
8 Fields	92	8
9 Brooks	55	38
10 Pickle	74	19
11 Leath	88	4
12 Wright	56	36
13 Hightower	79	21
14 Patman	88	12
15 de la Garza	67	19
16 White	90	5
17 Stenholm	93	4
18 Leland	8	86
19 Hance	75	18
20 Gonzalez	34	60
21 Loeffler	100	0
22 Paul	62	34
23 Kazen	90	10
24 Frost	40	59
UTAH		
1 Hansen	85	5
2 Marriott	93	4
VERMONT		
AL Jeffords	38	55
VIRGINIA		
1 Trible	79	7
2 Whitehurst	90	4
3 Bliley	97	3
4 Daniel, R.	93	5
5 Daniel, D.	88	4
6 Butler	78	12
7 Robinson	97	1
8 Parris	74†	24†
9 Wampler	93	5
10 Wolf	78	15
WASHINGTON		
1 Pritchard	49	41
2 Swift	26	73
3 Bonker	33	58
4 Morrison	89	11
5 Foley	40	55
6 Dicks	36	63
7 Lowry	11	89
WEST VIRGINIA		
1 Mollohan	58	29
2 Benedict	82	12
3 Staton	93	7
4 Rahall	23	55
WISCONSIN		
1 Aspin	41	53
2 Kastenmeier	12	88
3 Gunderson	68	32
4 Zablocki	38	55
5 Reuss	16	77
6 Petri	70	30
7 Obey	18	79
8 Roth	78	18
9 Sensenbrenner	70	30
WYOMING		
AL Cheney	93	3

Southern states - Ala., Ark., Fla., Ga., Ky., La., Miss., N.C., Okla., S.C., Tenn., Texas, Va.

	1	2		1	2		1	2
ALABAMA			**IOWA**			**NEW HAMPSHIRE**		
Denton	86	3	*Grassley*	86	12	*Humphrey*	80†	20†
Heflin	79	17	*Jepsen*	86	12	*Rudman*	69	31
ALASKA			**KANSAS**			**NEW JERSEY**		
Murkowski	89	1	*Dole*	85	10	*Brady* [1]	74†	15†
Stevens	90	4	*Kassebaum*	77	21	Bradley	14	85
ARIZONA			**KENTUCKY**			**NEW MEXICO**		
Goldwater	62	14	Ford	66	33	*Domenici*	97	3
DeConcini	74	20	Huddleston	72	24	*Schmitt*	88	3
ARKANSAS			**LOUISIANA**			**NEW YORK**		
Bumpers	20	74	Johnston	93	6	*D'Amato*	78	17
Pryor	56	35	Long	85	11	Moynihan	14	84
CALIFORNIA			**MAINE**			**NORTH CAROLINA**		
Hayakawa	77	18	*Cohen*	47	52	*East*	99	1
Cranston	7	84	Mitchell	16	84	*Helms*	99	1
COLORADO			**MARYLAND**			**NORTH DAKOTA**		
Armstrong	96	4	*Mathias*	33	57	*Andrews*	82	17
Hart	14	79	Sarbanes	2	78	Burdick	48	51
CONNECTICUT			**MASSACHUSETTS**			**OHIO**		
Weicker	26	60	Kennedy	2	88	Glenn	26	51
Dodd	5	85	Tsongas	7	77	Metzenbaum	4	85
DELAWARE			**MICHIGAN**			**OKLAHOMA**		
Roth	83	16	Levin	5	94	*Nickles*	95	5
Biden	28	67	Riegle	4	86	Boren	87	10
FLORIDA			**MINNESOTA**			**OREGON**		
Hawkins	77	13	*Boschwitz*	54	43	*Hatfield*	45	45
Chiles	83	15	*Durenberger*	39	48	*Packwood*	59	40
GEORGIA			**MISSISSIPPI**			**PENNSYLVANIA**		
Mattingly	97	2	*Cochran*	85	3	*Heinz*	41	46
Nunn	82	16	Stennis	83	9	*Specter*	40	59
HAWAII			**MISSOURI**			**RHODE ISLAND**		
Inouye	17	65	*Danforth*	76	18	*Chafee*	30	69
Matsunaga	14	82	Eagleton	12	87	Pell	17	78
IDAHO			**MONTANA**			**SOUTH CAROLINA**		
McClure	88	3	Baucus	31	67	*Thurmond*	86	4
Symms	97	2	Melcher	59	35	Hollings	55	36
ILLINOIS			**NEBRASKA**			**SOUTH DAKOTA**		
Percy	56	35	Exon	70	26	*Abdnor*	96	2
Dixon	39	54	Zorinsky	86	14	*Pressler*	77	13
INDIANA			**NEVADA**			**TENNESSEE**		
Lugar	84	16	*Laxalt*	86	3	*Baker*	88	6
Quayle	86	14	Cannon	49	26	Sasser	62	36

	1	2
TEXAS		
Tower	91	6
Bentsen	88	10
UTAH		
Garn	93	6
Hatch	90	6
VERMONT		
Stafford	46	43
Leahy	12	88
VIRGINIA		
Warner	96	2
Byrd [2]	89	10
WASHINGTON		
Gorton	76	24
Jackson	37	60
WEST VIRGINIA		
Byrd	56	44
Randolph	53	47
WISCONSIN		
Kasten	88	12
Proxmire	54	46
WYOMING		
Simpson	91	6
Wallop	86	5

KEY

† Not eligible for all recorded votes in 1982 (sworn in after Jan. 25, died or resigned during session, or voted "present" to avoid possible conflict of interest).

Democrats   *Republicans*

ND - Northern Democrats   SD - Southern Democrats (Southern states - Ala., Ark., Fla., Ga., Ky., La., Miss., N.C., Okla., S.C., Tenn., Texas, Va.)

Conservative Coalition
Support and Opposition: Senate

1. Conservative Coalition Support, 1982. Percentage of 94 conservative coalition votes in 1982 on which senator voted "yea" or "nay" *in agreement* with the position of the conservative coalition. Failures to vote lower both support and opposition scores.

2. Conservative Coalition Opposition, 1982. Percentage of 94 conservative coalition votes in 1982 on which senator voted "yea" or "nay" *in disagreement* with the position of the conservative coalition. Failures to vote lower both support and opposition scores.

1. Sen. Nicholas F. Brady, R-N.J., sworn in April 24, 1982, to succeed Harrison A. Williams Jr., D, who resigned March 11, 1982. Williams' 1982 conservative coalition support score was zero; opposition was 6 percent.
2. Sen. Harry F. Byrd Jr., Va., elected as an independent.

LOBBY
REGISTRATIONS

CQ

November 1981 Registrations

Citizens' Groups

ALLIANCE TO SAVE ENERGY, 1925 K St. N.W., Washington, D.C. 20006. Filed for self 11/19/81. Legislative interest — "Promotion of energy efficiency. Authorizations, appropriations, tax credits, depreciation provisions...." Lobbyist — Linda P. Gallagher.

CONSUMER FEDERATION OF AMERICA, Washington, D.C. Lobbyist — Robert C. Eckhardt, 1750 Pennsylvania Ave. N.W., Washington, D.C. 20006. Filed 11/3/81. (Former U.S. rep., D-Texas, 1967-81.) Legislative interest — "...Natural Gas Policy Act."

GEORGE WASHINGTON UNIVERSITY STUDENT ASSOCIATION, 800 21st St. N.W., Washington, D.C. 20052. Filed 11/4/81. Legislative interest — "All legislation impacting on post-secondary schools, post-secondary education, and the Washington, D.C. metropolitan area." Lobbyist — Joseph Subic Jr.

NATIONAL AUDUBON SOCIETY, 950 Third Ave., New York, N.Y. 10022. Filed for self 11/5/81. Legislative interest — "All legislation relating to environment/natural resources/population issues." Lobbyist — M. Rupert Cutler.

NATIONAL INSURANCE CONSUMER ORGANIZATION, 344 Commerce St., Alexandria, Va. 22314. Filed for self 11/13/81. Legislative interest — "...HR 4497, Insurance Sales Deregulation Act." Lobbyists — J. Robert Hunter, James H. Hunt, V. Michele Lavin, Theresa Rose Hanczor.

NATIONAL RIGHT TO WORK COMMITTEE, 8001 Braddock Road, Springfield, Va. 22160. Filed for self 11/5/81. Legislative interest — "...proposals related to compulsory unionism in private industry, farm labor, public sector employees." Lobbyist — Rex B. Wackerle.

THE NATIONAL TAX LIMITATION COMMITTEE, Washington, D.C. Lobbyist — Charls E. Walker Associates Inc., 1730 Pennsylvania Ave. N.W., Washington, D.C. 20006. Filed 11/13/81. Legislative interest — "...proposals for altering federal budget procedures."

THE PATRIOTS FOUNDATION INC., 986 Atherton Drive, Salt Lake City, Utah 84107. Filed for self 11/19/81. Legislative interest — Not specified. Lobbyists — William L. Allen, Richard T. Cardall.

RENEWABLE ENERGY INSTITUTE, Washington, D.C. Lobbyist — Nossaman, Krueger & Marsh, 445 S. Figueroa St., Los Angeles, Calif. 90071 and 1140 19th St. N.W., Washington, D.C. 20036. Filed 11/16/81. Legislative interest — "...authorizations and appropriations for Dept. of Energy, tax incentives (S 750, S 1288), and other matters pertinent to the research, development and commercialization of renewable energy."

TAXPAYERS FOR FEDERAL PENSION REFORM, P.O. Box 7755, Philadelphia, Pa. 19101. Filed for self 11/23/81. Legislative interest — "Reform pensions offered by federal government as employer, for its employees...." Lobbyist — Harold P. Mueller III.

Corporations and Businesses

AMERICAN EXPRESS CO., Washington, D.C. Lobbyist — Terrence H. Klasky, 1201 Pennsylvania Ave. N.W., Washington, D.C. 20004. Filed 11/19/81. Legislative interest — "General financial institutions legislation."

BANNEKER ASSOCIATES, Washington, D.C. Lobbyist — Gray and Co., 3255 Grace St. N.W., Washington, D.C. 20007. Filed 11/4/81. Legislative interest — "...urban renewal and real estate development."

BARETTA CORP., Washington, D.C. Lobbyist — Gray and Co., 3255 Grace St. N.W., Washington, D.C. 20007. Filed 11/4/81. Legislative interest — "...the contract with Department of Defense to replace the Colt-.45 as the standard military issue handgun."

CHASE MANHATTAN BANK, New York, N.Y. Lobbyist — Milbank, Tweed, Hadley & McCloy, 1 Chase Manhattan Plaza, New York, N.Y. 10005 and 1747 Pennsylvania Ave. N.W., Washington, D.C. 20006. Filed 11/23/81. Legislative interest — "HR 4353 and S 863 (proposed amendments to the Bankruptcy Act)...."

CSL ENERGY CONTROLS INC., Los Angeles, Calif. Lobbyist — Manatt, Phelps, Rothenberg & Tunney, 1200 New Hampshire Ave. N.W., Washington, D.C. 20036. Filed 11/20/81. (Former U.S. Rep. James C. Corman, D-Calif., 1961-81, was listed as agent for this client.) Legislative interest — "...commercial and industrial energy tax credits." Lobbyist — Koteen & Burt, 1150 Connecticut Ave. N.W., Washington, D.C. 20036. Filed 11/4/81. Legislative interest — "...S 750, 'The Industrial Energy Security Tax Incentive Act of 1981'; S 1288, 'The Commercial Business Energy Tax Credit Act of 1981'...."

COMINCO AMERICAN INC., Spokane, Wash. Lobbyist — Garvey, Schubert, Adams & Barer, 1000 Potomac St. N.W., Washington, D.C. 20007. Filed 11/13/81. Legislative interest — "HR 4186, providing for moratorium upon acquisitions of U.S. firms by Canadian interests...."

CONSOLIDATED NATURAL GAS CO., Pittsburgh, Pa. 15222. Lobbyist — Robert C. Eckhardt, 1750 Pennsylvania Ave. N.W., Washington, D.C. 20006. Filed 11/20/81. (Former U.S. rep., D-Texas, 1967-81.) Legislative interest — "Legislation relaxing or removing application of Holding Company Act to gas utilities...S 189, S 190, S 191."

CORNING GLASS WORKS, Corning, N.Y. 14831. Filed for self 11/30/81. Legislative interest — "...energy production and conservation, Clean Air Act amendments, taxation, export administration, international trade laws, anti-dumping code amendments, telecommunications and matters affecting road, rail and air transportation." Lobbyist — Carl T. Johnson, 1800 K St. N.W., Washington, D.C. 20006.

COURTNEY & ASSOCIATES, 632 F St. N.E., Washington, D.C 20002. Filed for self 11/20/81. Legislative interest — "...small business concerns."

CRAY RESEARCH INC., 1440 Northland Drive, Mandota Heights, Minn. 55120. Filed for self 11/3/81. Legislative interest — "...federal use of supercomputers, export and other trade policy related to supercomputers...." Lobbyist — Frank Brett Berlin, 1919 Pennsylvania Ave. N.W., Washington, D.C. 20006.

CRYSTAL OIL CO., Shreveport, La. Lobbyist — Fulbright & Jaworski, 1150 Connecticut Ave. N.W., Washington, D.C. 20036. Filed 11/18/81. Legislative interest — "Legislation affecting Title 26 of the U.S. Code."

DAIRYMEN INC., 10140 Linn Station Road, Louisville, Ky. 40223. Filed for self 11/24/81. Legislative interest — "...dairy farmers and dairy cooperatives." Lobbyist — Joseph J. Westwater.

DOW CHEMICAL CO., Midland, Mich. Lobbyist — Shank, Irwin, Conant, Williamson & Grevelle, 1300 19th St. N.W., Washington, D.C. 20036. Filed 11/6/81. Legislative interest — "...opposition to the addition of other chemicals to Section 122 of the Clean Air Act without further scientific and economic evaluation and justification."

EXXON CORP., 1251 Avenue of the Americas, New York, N.Y. 10020. Filed for self 11/4/81. Legislative interest — Not specified. Lobbyist — Amy R. Hammer, 1899 L St. N.W., Washington, D.C. 20036.

FEDERAL NATIONAL MORTGAGE ASSOCIATION, 3900 Wisconsin Ave. N.W., Washington, D.C. 20016. Filed for self 11/6/81. Legislative interest — "...HR 4515, HR 4603, S 1702, S 1703 and S 1720." Lobbyist — Nicholas J. Spiezio.

FOOTHILLS PIPE LINES (YUKON) LTD., Calgary, Alberta, Canada. Lobbyist — McHenry & Staffier, 1300 19th St. N.W., Washington, D.C. 20036. Filed 11/12/81. Legislative interest — "H [J] Res 341 and S [J] Res 115."

FORD MOTOR CO., Dearborn, Mich. Lobbyist — Wilmer, Cutler & Pickering, 1666 K St. N.W., Washington, D.C. 20006. Filed 11/3/81. Legislative interest — "Clean Air Act, HR 4400...."

GENERAL MOTORS CORP., Detroit, Mich. Lobbyist — Dickinson, Wright, Moon, Van Dusen & Freeman, 1901 L St. N.W., Washington, D.C. 20036. Filed 11/12/81. Legislative interest — "Defense procurement, automotive research."

THE GHK COMPANIES, Oklahoma City, Okla. Lobbyist — Hale and Dorr, 1201 Pennsylvania Ave. N.W., Washington, D.C. 20004. Filed 11/25/81. Legislative interest — "...legislation affecting oil and gas exploration and production, including tax and regulatory matters ... taxation of intangible drilling costs."

GLOBAL EXPLORATION & DEVELOPMENT CORP., Lakeland, Fla. Lobbyist — Sylvester Ligsukis, 1320 19th St. N.W., Washington, D.C. 20036. Filed 11/2/81. Legislative interest — "...phosphate mining the Osceola National Forest, Florida...."

HILLSDALE COUNTY RAILWAY CO., Hillsdale, Mich. Lobbyist — Wald, Harkrader & Ross, 1300 19th St. N.W., Washington, D.C. 20036. Filed 11/19/81. Legislative interest — "...transportation appropriations bill, HR 4209."

HUDSON SECURITIES INC., New York, N.Y. Lobbyist — Davis, Polk & Wardwell, 1575 I St. N.W., Washington, D.C. 20005. Filed 11/24/81. Legislative interest — "Matters affecting foreign banks ownership of affiliates in the United States (12 U.S.C. 3106)."

INDEX, Minneapolis, Minn. Lobbyist — Terrence H. Klasky, 1201 Pennsylvania Ave. N.W., Washington, D.C. 20004. Filed 11/19/81. Legislative interest — Not specified.

KANSAS CITY SOUTHERN RAILWAY, Kansas City, Mo. Lobbyist — Brown & Roady, 1333 New Hampshire Ave. N.W., Washington, D.C. 20036. Filed 11/20/81. Legislative interest — "coal slurry pipeline legislation, HR 4230...."

LISBON ASSOCIATES INC., 515 Madison Ave., New York, N.Y. 10022. Filed for self 11/30/81. Legislative interest — "...HR 3659 — for, HR 4035 — for." Lobbyist — Jeffrey L. Farrow.

THE LOUIS DREYFUS CORP., Stamford, Conn. Lobbyist — Martin, Ryan, Haley & Associates Inc., 1015 15th St. N.W., Washington, D.C. 20005. Filed 11/30/81. Legislative interest — Not specified.

MARATHON OIL CO., Findlay, Ohio. Lobbyist — Jones, Day, Reavis & Pogue, 1735 I St. N.W., Washington, D.C. 20006. Filed 11/12/81. Legislative interest — "Antitrust and energy legislation ... HR 4930, an amendment to the Energy Policy and Conservation Act...."

MARION LABORATORIES INC., Kansas City, Mo. Lobbyist — Martin, Ryan, Haley & Associates Inc., 1015 15th St. N.W., Washington, D.C. 20005. Filed 11/30/81. Legislative interest — Not specified.

MISSION RESOURCES, Oakland, Calif. Lobbyist — Nossaman, Krueger & Marsh, 445 S. Figueroa St., Los Angeles, Calif. 90071 and 1140 19th St. N.W., Washington, D.C. 20036. Filed 11/16/81. Legislative interest — "In favor of enactment of legislation authorizing non-lease development of Indian lands to overcome the restrictions of the Indian Non-Intercourse Act (25 U.S.C. 177) and the Omnibus Indian Mineral Leasing Act (25 U.S.C., section 396a et seq.)...."

MORGAN GUARANTY TRUST COMPANY OF NEW YORK, New York, N.Y. Lobbyist — Davis, Polk & Wardwell, 1575 I St. N.W., Washington, D.C. 20005. Filed 11/4/81. Legislative interest — "Bankruptcy legislation."

PANHANDLE PRODUCING CO., San Antonio, Texas. Lobbyist — O'Neill and Haase, 1333 New Hampshire Ave. N.W., Washington, D.C. 20036. Filed 11/12/81. Legislative interest — "...to repeal or modify section 110 of the Natural Gas Policy Act of 1978."

PELICAN TERMINAL CO., Houston, Texas. Lobbyist — Vinson & Elkins, First City National Bank Building, Houston, Texas 77002. Legislative interest — "...legislation authorizing local cost-sharing of costs and construction, operation and maintenance of deep-draft channel for Port of Galveston."

REPUBLIC AIRLINES, Washington, D.C. Lobbyist — Gray and Co., 3255 Grace St. N.W., Washington, D.C. 20007. Filed 11/4/81. Legislative interest — "...airline industry interests within the federal government."

ROCKWELL INTERNATIONAL CORP., Arlington, Va. Lobbyist — Hansell, Post, Brandon & Dorsey, 1747 Pennsylvania Ave. N.W., Washington, D.C. 20006. Filed 11/17/81. Legislative interest — "...strategic bomber programs." Lobbyist — Patton, Boggs & Blow, 2550 M St. N.W., Washington, D.C. 20037. Filed 11/12/81. Legislative interest — "Defense appropriations bills: favor funding of the president's defense program, including the B-1."

ROHM AND HAAS CO., Philadelphia, Pa. Lobbyist — Nancy Weinberg, 1899 L St. N.W., Washington, D.C. 20036. Filed 11/12/81. Legislative interest — "...bills relating to the manufacture, sale and use of chemicals and allied products."

ROYAL HAWAIIAN CRUISES INC., San Francisco, Calif. Lobbyist — Dickinson, Wright, Moon, Van Dusen & Freeman, 1901 L St. N.W., Washington, D.C. 20036. Filed 11/30/81. Legislative interest — "Against HR 3782, waiving Merchant Marine Act restrictions."

ST. VINCENT'S MEDICAL CENTER OF RICHMOND, Staten Island, N.Y. Lobbyist — Powell, Goldstein, Frazer & Murphy, 1110 Vermont Ave. N.W., Washington, D.C. 20005. Filed 11/9/81. Legislative interest — "...HR 4560."

THE SCOTT CO., 8 Jacana Road, Hilton Head, S.C. 29928. Filed for self 11/13/81. Legislative interest — "Legislation affecting coastal development...." Lobbyist — James M. Scott.

SILVERCREST INDUSTRIES INC., Long Beach, Calif. Lobbyist — Witkowski, Weiner, McCaffrey & Brodsky, 1575 I St. N.W., Washington, D.C. 20005. Filed 11/9/81. Legislative interest — "...Military Construction Authorization Act (HR 3455 and S 1408) and the Military Construction Appropriations Act (HR 4242)."

SMITH, BARNEY, HARRIS, UPHAM & CO., New York, N.Y. Lobbyist — Cladouhos & Brashares, 1750 New York Ave. N.W., Washington, D.C. 20006. Filed 11/6/81. Legislative interest — "Legislation affecting industrial development bonds."

SPERRY CORP., 2000 L St. N.W., Washington, D.C. 20036. Filed for self 11/12/81. Legislative interest — "...taxes, telecommunications, agriculture, international affairs and regulations." Lobbyist — Joseph H. McCaulay.

STURM, RUGER & CO. INC., Southport, Conn. Lobbyist — Donald E. Santarelli, 2033 M St. N.W., Washington, D.C. 20036. Filed 11/4/81. Legislative interest — "...legislation dealing with product liability."

TELESCIENCES INC., Moorestown, N.J. Lobbyist — Metzger, Shadyac & Schwarz, One Farragut Square South, Washington, D.C. 20006. Filed 11/6/81. Legislative interest — "...telecommunications industry."

VENTURE ENTREPRENEURS INC., 1201 San Marco Blvd., Jacksonville, Fla. 32207. Filed for self 11/2/81. Legislative interest — "...Import/Export bank functions...." Lobbyist — Jack Dillon.

WILMORE CITY DEVELOPMENT INC., Long Beach, Calif. Lobbyist — Witkowski, Weiner, McCaffrey & Brodsky, 1575 I St. N.W., Washington, D.C. 20005. Filed 11/9/81. Legislative interest — "...Military Construction Authorization Act (HR 3455 and S 1408) and the Military Construction Appropriations Act (HR 4242)."

YAMAHA MOTOR CO. LTD., Iwata-Shi, Japan. Lobbyist — Peabody, Lambert & Meyers, 1150 Connecticut Ave. N.W., Washington, D.C 20036. Filed 11/23/81. Legislative interest — "Opposing HR 4868...."

International Relations

CANADIAN EMBASSY, Washington, D.C. Lobbyist — Wellford, Wegman, Krulwich, Gold & Hoff, 1015 18th St. N.W., Washington, D.C. 20036. Filed 11/2/81. Legislative interest —

"Legislation concerning acid rain, including HR 3471...."

GOVERNMENT OF NICARAGUA, Managua, Nicaragua. Lobbyist — Powell, Goldstein, Frazer & Murphy, 1110 Vermont Ave. N.W., Washington, D.C. 20005. Filed 11/10/81. Legislative interest — "Foreign assistance legislation affecting Nicaragua, S 1196, S 1802."

Labor Groups

AMALGAMATED TRANSIT UNION, AFL-CIO, 5025 Wisconsin Ave. N.W., Washington, D.C. 20016. Filed 11/18/81. Legislative interest — Not specified. Lobbyist — Marc P. Gabor.

CONTINENTAL AIRLINE EMPLOYEES ASSOCIATION, Los Angeles, Calif. Lobbyist — Francis Associates Ltd., 316 Pennsylvania Ave. S.E., Washington, D.C. 20003. Filed 11/9/81. Legislative interest — "...S 8626."

NATIONAL EDUCATION ASSOCIATION, Washington, D.C. Lobbyist — Francis Associates Ltd., 316 Pennsylvania Ave. S.E., Washington, D.C. 20003. Filed 11/5/81. Legislative interest — Not specified.

State and Local Governments

ALASKA STATE SENATE, TRANSPORTATION COMMITTEE, Juneau, Alaska. Lobbyist — Billig, Sher & Jones, 2033 K St. N.W., Washington, D.C. 20006. Filed 11/16/81. Legislative interest — "...Alaska Railroad, specifically including S 1500 and HR 4278."

BAY AREA RAPID TRANSIT DISTRICT, Oakland, Calif. Lobbyist — Anderson, Hibey, Nauheim & Blair, 1605 New Hampshire Ave. N.W., Washington, D.C. 20009. Filed 11/18/81. Legislative interest — "...urban mass transit."

CANAVERAL PORT AUTHORITY, Cape Canaveral, Fla. Lobbyist — Cramer, Hoffman & Haber, 1320 19th St. N.W., Washington, D.C. 20036. Filed 11/2/81. Legislative interest — "...federal assistance to ports or railways for enhanced coal transportation or processing facilities ... Ports & Navigation Improvement Act of 1980...."

CITY OF MIAMI, Miami, Fla. Lobbyist — Cramer, Hoffman & Haber, 1320 19th St. N.W., Washington, D.C. 20036. Filed 11/2/81. Legislative interest — "Any legislation, including budget authorization, or appropriation which may affect federal funding or federal programs for the city of Miami, Florida."

COUNCIL OF STATE HOUSING AGENCIES, Washington, D.C. Lobbyist — Gray and Co., 3255 Grace St. N.W., Washington, D.C. 20007. Filed 11/4/81. Legislative interest — "...tax exempt revenue bonds."

DADE COUNTY, Miami, Fla. Lobbyist — Cramer, Hoffman & Haber, 1320 19th St. N.W., Washington, D.C. 20036. Filed 11/2/81. Legislative interest — "Any legislation, including budget authorization, or appropriation which may affect federal funding or federal programs for Dade County, Florida."

GUAM AIRPORT AUTHORITY, Tamuning, Guam. Lobbyist — Cook, Purcell, Hansen & Henderson, 1015 18th St. N.W., Washington, D.C. 20036. Filed 11/25/81. Legislative interest — "Sunset of Civil Aeronautics Board ... HR 4514 — Visa Waiver legislation — Guam."

METROPOLITAN ATLANTA RAPID TRANSIT AUTHORITY, Atlanta, Ga. Lobbyist — Anderson, Hibey, Nauheim & Blair, 1605 New Hampshire Ave. N.W., Washington, D.C. 20009. Filed 11/18/81. Legislative interest — "...urban mass transportation."

OAKLAND COUNTY DEPARTMENT OF PUBLIC WORKS, Pontiac, Mich. Lobbyist — Dickinson, Wright, Moon, Van Dusen & Freeman, 1901 L St. N.W., Washington, D.C. 20036. Filed 11/12/81. Legislative interest — "Clean water amendments."

STATE OF NORTH DAKOTA, Bismarck, N.D. Lobbyist — Duncan, Weinberg & Miller, 1775 Pennsylvania Ave. N.W., Washington, D.C. 20006. Filed 11/6/81. Legislative interest — "Energy and Water Development Appropriations bill for 1982...."

Trade Associations

AIR TRANSPORT ASSOCIATION OF AMERICA, Washington, D.C. Lobbyist — Curtis, Mallet-Prevost, Colt & Mosle, 1735 I St. N.W., Washington, D.C. 20006. Filed 11/19/81. Legislative interest — "Ratification by U.S. Senate of Montreal Protocols to Warsaw Convention...." Lobbyist — O'Melveny & Myers, 1800 M St. N.W., Washington, D.C. 20036. Filed 11/19/81. Legislative interest — "Senate ratification of Montreal Protocols 3 and 4."

AMERICAN COUNCIL OF LIFE INSURANCE INC., 1850 K St. N.W., Washington, D.C. 20006. Filed for self 11/23/81. Legislative interest — Not specified. Lobbyist — R. Scott Rinn.

AMERICAN HEALTH PLANNING ASSOCIATION, 1601 Connecticut Ave. N.W., Washington, D.C. 20009. Filed for self 11/4/81. Legislative interest — "Health Planning and Resources Development Act of 1974." Lobbyist — Harry P. Cain.

AMERICAN HOSPITAL ASSOCIATION, 840 North Lake Shore Drive., Chicago, Ill. 60611. Filed for self 11/23/81. Legislative interest — "...legislation which may affect the health of the American people." Lobbyists — Lynn S. Hart, Sharon L. Hildebrandt, 444 North Capitol St. N.W., Washington, D.C. 20001.

AMERICAN MARITIME ASSOCIATION, Washington, D.C. Lobbyist — Gray and Co., 3255 Grace St. N.W., Washington, D.C. 20007. Filed 11/4/81. Legislative interest — Not specified.

AMERICAN NUCLEAR ENERGY COUNCIL, 410 First St. S.E., Washington, D.C. Filed for self 11/25/81. Legislative interest — "Matters pertaining to nuclear energy, non-proliferation, reactor safety." Lobbyist — James F. Brown.

AMERICAN PETROLEUM INSTITUTE, 2101 L St. N.W., Washington, D.C. 20037. Filed for self 11/17/81. Legislative interest — Not specified. Lobbyist — James R. McCarthy.

AMERICAN SOCIETY OF ASSOCIATION EXECUTIVES, 1575 I St. N.W., Washington, D.C. 20005. Filed for self 11/2/81. Legislative interest — Not specified. Lobbyist — R. William Taylor.

AMERICAN SUBCONTRACTORS ASSOCIATION, 8401 Corporate Drive, Landover, Md. 20785. Filed for self 11/30/81. Legislative interest — "S 1782, zero retention bill; Slow Payment Act (HR 4709)...." Lobbyist — Michael Roybal.

AMERICAN TUNABOAT ASSOCIATION, San Diego, Calif. Lobbyist — James P. Walsh, 4403 Klingle St. N.W., Washington, D.C. 20016. Filed 11/6/81. Legislative interest — "HR 4169, fiscal year 1982 State, Justice, Commerce appropriations bill; the Magnuson Fishery Management and Conservation Act (16 U.S.C. 1901), S 1564 and HR 4457, amendments to the Magnuson Act; the Fishermen's Protective Act (22 U.S.C. 1971); the Atlantic Tuna Convention Act (16 U.S.C. 971); the Tuna Convention Act (16 U.S.C. 951)...."

ASSOCIATION FOR EQUAL ACCESS TO NATURAL GAS MARKETS AND SUPPLIES, Denver, Colo. Lobbyist — Shank, Irwin, Conant, Williamson & Grevelle, 1300 19th St. N.W., Washington, D.C. 20036. Filed 11/5/81. Legislative interest — "...amending the Natural Gas Act, PL 95-617 ... to provide for greater market access for producers and consumers to natural gas supplies."

COOPERATIVE LEAGUE OF THE U.S.A., 1828 L St. N.W., Washington, D.C. 20036. Filed for self 11/23/81. Legislative interest — Not specified. Lobbyist — Thomas G. Krajewski.

CUTTING TOOL MANUFACTURERS ASSOCIATION AND METAL CUTTING TOOL INSTITUTE, Cleveland, Ohio. Lobbyist — Michael R. Graul, 1725 DeSales St. N.W., Washington, D.C. 20036. Filed 11/13/81. Legislative interest — "...legislation which relates to defense, labor, tax issues...."

DISTILLED SPIRITS COUNCIL OF THE U.S. INC., 425 13th St. N.W., Washington, D.C. 20004. Filed for self 11/6/81. Legislative interest — "...taxes, labeling, ingredient and health warning, container deposit, franchise, method of business laws, liquor control laws...." Lobbyist — Llewellyn H. Gerson.

EDISON ELECTRIC INSTITUTE, Washington, D.C. Lobbyist — John A. C. Gibson, 1815 Corcoran St. N.W., Washington, D.C. 20009. Filed 11/5/81. Legislative interest — "Black Lung Benefits Act, Black Lung Benefits Revenue Act and all amend-

ments thereto."

FAR EAST CONFERENCE, New York, N.Y. Lobbyist — Lillick, McHose & Charles, 1333 New Hampshire Ave. N.W., Washington, D.C. 20036. Filed 11/2/81. Legislative interest — "Shipping Act of 1981; Shipping Act Amendments of 1981; S 1593 and HR 4374."

FLORIDA BANKERS ASSOCIATION, Orlando, Fla. Lobbyist — Terrence H. Klasky, 1201 Pennsylvania Ave. N.W., Washington, D.C. 20004. Filed 11/19/81. Legislative interest — "HR 4401."

GLASS PACKAGING INSTITUTE, Washington, D.C. Lobbyist — O'Neill and Haase, 1333 New Hampshire Ave. N.W., Washington, D.C. 20036. Filed 11/12/81. Legislative interest — "...beverage container legislation such as S 709."

MANUFACTURED HOUSING INSTITUTE, Arlington, Va. Lobbyist — Patrick Di Chiro, 3586 Powder Mill Road, Beltsville, Md. 20705. Filed 11/12/81. Legislative interest — "...housing legislation, specifically mobile and modular...."

MID-CONTINENT OIL & GAS ASSOCIATION, 1111 Thompson Building, Tulsa, Okla. Filed for self 11/9/81. Legislative interest — Not specified. Lobbyist — Nicholas J. Bush, 1919 Pennsylvania Ave. N.W., Washington, D.C. 20006.

MOTION PICTURE ASSOCIATION OF AMERICA INC., Lobbyist — Akin, Gump, Strauss, Hauer & Feld, 1333 New Hampshire Ave. N.W., Washington, D.C. 20036. Filed 11/5/81. Legislative interest — "...copyright law ... HR 4783, HR 4794, HR 4808 and S 1758."

NATIONAL ASSOCIATION OF AIRCRAFT & COMMUNICATIONS SUPPLIERS INC., 7360 Laurel Canyon Blvd., North Hollywood, Calif. 91605. Filed for self 11/16/81. Legislative interest — "Opposition to portions of the proposed Freedom of Information Act legislation (S 1730, S 1751 and HR 4805)...." Lobbyist — Joseph J. Petrillo.

NATIONAL ASSOCIATION FOR ASSOCIATION POLITICAL ACTION COMMITTEES, McLean, Va. Lobbyist — Taft, Stettinius & Hollister, First National Bank Center, Cincinnati, Ohio 45202 and 1800 Massachusetts Ave. N.W., Washington D.C. 20036. Filed 11/19/81. Legislative interest — "...federal election campaign law revision."

NATIONAL ASSOCIATION OF COIN LAUNDRY EQUIPMENT OPERATORS, Tucson, Ariz. Lobbyist — Sonosky, Chambers, Sachse & Guido, 1050 31st St. N.W., Washington, D.C. 20007. Filed 11/16/81. Legislative interest — "...S J Res 93 and HR 3840."

NATIONAL ASSOCIATION OF REALTORS, 777 14th St. N.W., Washington, D.C. 20005. Filed for self 11/30/81. Legislative interest — "...tax relief; independent contractor; S 31, Repeal of Family Rental Tax; fair housing; alternative mortgage instruments; public lands management; Clean Air Act; and Depository Institutions Act." Lobbyist — Frank West.

NATIONAL BARREL & DRUM ASSOCIATION, Washington, D.C. Lobbyist — Taft, Stettinius & Hollister, First National Bank Center, Cincinnati, Ohio 45202 and 1800 Massachusetts Ave. N.W., Washington, D.C. 20036. Filed 11/19/81. Legislative interest — "...energy tax credit matters ... S 750."

NATIONAL FERTILIZER SOLUTIONS ASSOCIATION, 8823 North Industrial Road, Peoria, Ill. 61615. Filed for self 11/16/81. Legislative interest — "Matters affecting the production, marketing and application of fluid fertilizer." Lobbyist — Dennis E. Brown.

NATIONAL HEALTH CARE FINANCING ASSOCIATION, Suite 230, The Exchange, Atlanta, Ga. 30339. Filed for self 11/23/81. Legislative interest — "Health care financing." Lobbyist — H. Radford Bishop.

NATIONAL RESTAURANT ASSOCIATION, Washington, D.C. Lobbyist — Manatt, Phelps, Rothenberg & Tunney, 1200 New Hampshire Ave. N.W., Washington, D.C. 20036. Filed 11/12/81. (Former U.S. Rep. James C. Corman, D-Calif., 1961-81, was listed as agent for this client.) Legislative interest — "To amend Internal Revenue Code, section 119."

NATIONAL RETAIL MERCHANTS ASSOCIATION, Washington, D.C. Lobbyist — Weil, Gotshal & Manges, 1101 Connecticut Ave. N.W., Washington, D.C. 20036. Filed 11/2/81.

Legislative interest — "...amendments to the Communications Act of 1954 ... S 898."

NATURAL GAS SUPPLY ASSOCIATION, 1025 Connecticut Ave. N.W., Washington, D.C. 20036. Filed for self 11/23/81. Legislative interest — "...oversight of the Natural Gas Policy Act of 1978, and amending same with a view toward assuring a more adequate supply of natural gas for the consumer and national defense." Lobbyist — Robert Slaughter.

PACIFIC WESTBOUND CONFERENCE, San Francisco, Calif. Lobbyist — Lillick, McHose & Charles, 1333 New Hampshire Ave. N.W., Washington, D.C. 20036. Filed 11/2/81. Legislative interest — "Shipping Act of 1981; Shipping Act Amendments of 1981; S 1593, HR 4374."

SOUTHWEST KANSAS IRRIGATION ASSOCIATION, Ulysses, Kansas. Lobbyist — Allen Harris, 1330 Classen Building, Oklahoma City, Okla. 73106. Filed 11/20/81. Legislative interest — "...natural gas decontrol, the Natural Gas Policy Act...."

SUGAR USERS GROUP, Washington, D.C. Lobbyist — O'Neill and Haase, 1333 New Hampshire Ave. N.W., Washington, D.C. 20036. Filed 11/17/81. Legislative interest — "Food and Agriculture Act of 1981...."

TASK FORCE ON CREATIVE FINANCE FOR MANUFACTURED HOUSING, Washington, D.C. Lobbyist — Witkowski, Weiner, McCaffrey & Brodsky, 1575 I St. N.W., Washington, D.C. 20005. Filed 11/9/81. Legislative interest — "...Financial Institutions Restructuring Act of 1981 (S 1720), the Thrift Institutions Restructuring Act (S 1703) and the Deposit Insurance Flexibility Act of 1981 (HR 4603)."

TEXAS COUNTY IRRIGATION AND WATER RESOURCES ASSOCIATION, Ulysses, Kansas. Lobbyist — Allen Harris, 1330 Classen Building, Oklahoma City, Okla. 73106. Filed 11/20/81. Legislative interest — "...natural gas decontrol, the Natural Gas Policy Act...."

U.S. CANE SUGAR REFINERS' ASSOCIATION, Washington, D.C. Lobbyist — Jackie Lloyd, 3240 Whitebirch Drive, West Covina, Calif. 91793. Filed 11/18/81. Legislative interest — "Legislation involving sugar supports in agriculture bill."

Miscellaneous

AMERICAN COLLEGE OF NEUROPSYCHOPHARMACOLOGY, Nashville, Tenn. Lobbyist — Perito, Duerk, Carlson & Pinco, 1140 Connecticut Ave. N.W., Washington, D.C. 20036. Filed 11/13/81. Legislative interest — "Health and Human Services appropriations bill, HR 4560."

AMERICAN COLLEGE OF NURSE-MIDWIVES, 1522 K St. N.W., Washington, D.C. 20005. Filed for self 11/16/81. Legislative interest — "Maternal and child health legislation, general health and welfare legislation...." Lobbyist — Sally Austen Tom.

WILLIAM T. CURTIS, 1200 Maine Ave. S.W., Washington, D.C. 20024. Filed for self 11/5/81. Legislative interest — "...leasing government land under [District of Columbia] control...."

WILLIAM M. MacKENZIE, 5908 Columbia Pike, Falls Church, Va. 22041. Filed for self 11/13/81. Legislative interest — "Thermal insulation and small business."

JOHN C. MARTIN, 4640 South Orange Blossom Trail, Orlando, Fla. Filed for self 11/13/81. Legislative interest — "Emergency medical services...."

KENNETH MICHAEL ROBINSON, 306 6th St. N.W., Washington, D.C. 20001. Filed for self 11/12/81. Legislative interest — "Title 18, Title 28 ... bail bond reform and gun control proposals."

RULE OF LAW COMMITTEE, Washington, D.C. Lobbyist — Steptoe & Johnson, 1250 Connecticut Ave. N.W., Washington, D.C. 20036. Filed 11/17/81. Legislative interest — "Export administration authorization, fiscal year 1982-83, S 1112, HR 3567."

PHILIP P. SOUTH, 400 Maine Ave. S.W., Washington, D.C. 20024. Filed for self 11/9/81. Legislative interest — "...leasing government land under [District of Columbia] control...."

LLOYD V. TEMME, 915 15th St. N.W., Washington, D.C. 20005. Filed for self 11/23/81. Legislative interest — "...Social Security, tax limitations and reductions, welfare reform, constitutional issues including separation of church and state, maintenance of individual liberties...."

WAR AGAINST WOMEN, 1710 Giles, Roseburg, Ore. 97470. Filed for self 11/17/81. Legislative interest — "Removal of women from importance and responsibility."

SUNNY L. WHITE, 400 Maine Ave. S.W., Washington, D.C. 20024. Filed for self 11/9/81. Legislative interest — "...leasing government land under [District of Columbia] control...."

December 1981 Registrations

Citizens' Groups

AMERICAN RIVERS CONSERVATION COUNCIL, 323 Pennsylvania Ave. S.E., Washington, D.C. 20003. Filed for self 12/8/81. "...additions to the National Wild and Scenic River System and other proposals which protect rivers...." Lobbyists — Patricia Munoz, Ron Vlaskamp.

COMMITTEE FOR PROPOSITION THIRTY, P.O. Box 915, Hartselle, Ala. 35640. Filed for self 12/11/81. Legislative interest — Not specified. Lobbyist — Alvin L. Abercrombie.

COMMITTEE ON NORTH-SOUTH ISSUES, Anderson Hall, The American University, Washington, D.C. 20016. Filed for self 12/8/81. Legislative interest — Not specified. Lobbyist — Gino Jon DeMarco.

NATIONAL AUDUBON SOCIETY, 645 Pennsylvania Ave. N.W., Washington, D.C. 20003. Filed for self 12/15/81. Legislative interest — "...Interior appropriations, Forest Service appropriations, Endangered Species Act (for), Clean Water Act, HR 3252/S 1018 Barrier Islands (for)." Lobbyist — C. Eugene Knoder.

NATIONAL BUSINESS AND ECONOMIC FREEDOM COUNCIL, 418 C St. N.E., Washington, D.C. 20002. Filed for self 12/16/81. Legislative interest — "...Tax and IRS matters, specifically support for HR 4093, The Taxpayers Protection Act." Lobbyist — Gary L. Jarmin.

NATIONAL CONSERVATIVE POLITICAL ACTION COMMITTEE, Arlington, Va. Lobbyist — Pearson & Co., 103 W. Cedar St., Alexandria, Va. 22301. Filed 12/1/81. Legislative interest — "Federal Election Commission."

NATIONAL RIFLE ASSOCIATION OF AMERICA, 1600 Rhode Island Ave. N.W., Washington, D.C. 20036. Filed for self 12/16/81. Legislative interest — "...all aspects of the acquisition, possession and use of firearms and ammunition as well as legislation relating to hunting and wildlife conservation." Lobbyist — Mary Karen Jolly.

PUBLIC CITIZEN INC., 2000 P St. N.W., Washington, D.C. 20036. Filed for self 12/14/81. Legislative interest — "S 1730 and S 1751, to amend the Freedom of Information Act, 5 U.S.C. section 552." Lobbyists — Diane B. Cohn, Katherine A. Meyer.

SIERRA CLUB, San Francisco, Calif. Filed for self 12/9/81. Legislative interest — Not specified. Lobbyist — Lawrence F. Williams, 300 Pennsylvania Ave. N.W., Washington, D.C. 20003.

THE WILDERNESS SOCIETY, 1901 Pennsylvania Ave. N.W., Washington, D.C. 20006. Filed for self 12/11/81. Legislative interest — "Alaska national interests lands bill, other pieces of legislation affecting the state of Alaska." Lobbyist — Tom Robinson. Filed for self 12/16/81. Legislative interest — "Forest Service issues." Lobbyist — V. Alaric Sample Jr.

Corporations and Businesses

ASARCO, Washington, D.C. Lobbyist — Gray and Co., 3255 Grace St. N.W., Washington, D.C. 20007. Filed 12/1/81. Legislative

interest — "...environmental legislation."

BERETTA CORP., Washington, D.C. Lobbyist — Gray and Co., 3255 Grace St. N.W., Washington, D.C. 20007. Filed 12/1/81. Legislative interest — "...contract with DOD to replace the Colt-.45 as the standard military issue handgun."

COASTAL CORP., Houston, Texas. Lobbyist — Abadie & Hudson, P.O. Box 2787, Baton Rouge, La. 70821. Filed 12/7/81. Legislative interest — "...S 506."

CONTINENTAL RESOURCES CO., Washington, D.C. Lobbyist — Miles & Stockbridge, 1701 Pennsylvania Ave. N.W., Washington, D.C. 20006. Filed 12/2/81. Legislative interest — "...Coal Distribution and Utilization Act of 1981."

FIREMAN'S FUND INSURANCE COMPANIES, San Francisco, Calif. Lobbyist — The Hannaford Co. Inc., 1225 19th St. N.W., Washington, D.C. 20036. Filed 12/10/81. Legislative interest — Not specified.

CARL M. FREEMAN ASSOCIATES, Potomac, Md. Lobbyist — Wyman, Bautzer, Rothman, Kuchel & Silbert, 600 New Hampshire Ave. N.W., Washington, D.C. 20037. Filed 12/9/81. Legislative interest — "Legislation concerning the protection of the Barrier Islands including S 2686 and HR 5981."

GERBER PRODUCTS CO., Fremont, Mich. Lobbyist — Eugene J. Hardy, 1100 17th St. N.W., Suite 1000, Washington, D.C. 20036. Filed 12/30/81. Legislative interest — "HR 463, 746, 914, 1201, 1425, 1894, 1937, 1964, 2400, 2889, 3636, 3670, 4014, 4031, 4126, 4503, 4700, 4975, 5159, 5160, 5252; S 255, 524, 683, 702, 708, 734, 823, 857, 884, 905, 922, 1080, 1247, 1442, 1503, 1700, 1716, 1748."

HILLSDALE COUNTY RAILWAY CO., Hillsdale, Mich. Lobbyist — Wald, Harkrader & Ross, 1300 19th St. N.W., Washington, D.C. 20036. Filed 12/6/81. Legislative interest — "...obtain federal rail assistance in fiscal 1982, including assistance under the redeemable preference shares program for which monies are included in the transportation appropriations bill, HR 4209...."

HTB CORP., Washington, D.C. Lobbyist — Gray and Co., 3255 Grace St. N.W., Washington, D.C. 20007. Filed 12/1/81. Legislative interest — "...defense legislation."

LORAL CORP., New York, N.Y. Lobbyist — Wilkie, Farr & Gallagher, 818 Connecticut Ave. N.W., Washington, D.C. 20006. Filed 12/4/81. Legislative interest — "Defense appropriations bill, HR 4995."

THE MAY CO., St. Louis, Mo. Lobbyist — Sisk, Foley, Hultin & Driver, 2501 M St. N.W., Washington, D.C. 20037. Filed 12/11/81. Legislative interest — "In support of legislation permitting the use of industrial revenue bonds."

MERRILL LYNCH LIFE AGENCY INC., New York, N.Y. Lobbyist — Morgan, Lewis & Bockius, 1800 M St. N.W., Washington, D.C. 20036. Filed 12/11/81. Legislative interest — "S 1888 and HR 5004."

MILLIKEN & CO., Spartanburg, S.C. Lobbyist — Johnson, Smith and Hibbard, 220 N. Church St., Spartanburg, S.C. 29304. Filed 12/30/81. Legislative interest — "...enactment of S 995 or similar legislation."

MORGAN GUARANTY TRUST COMPANY OF NEW YORK, New York, N.Y. Lobbyist — Anderson, Hibey, Nauheim & Blair, 1605 New Hampshire Ave. N.W., Washington, D.C. 20009. Filed 12/2/81. Legislative interest — "Bankruptcy legislation."

NATIONWIDE MUTUAL INSURANCE CO., Columbus, Ohio. Lobbyist — Thomas L. Ashley, 1730 Pennsylvania Ave. N.W., Washington, D.C. 20006. Filed 12/14/81. (Former U.S. rep., D-Ohio, 1955-81.) Legislative interest — "...HR 5004."

NORTHWEST ALASKAN PIPELINE CO., Washington, D.C. Lobbyist — McCamish, Ingram, Martin & Brown Inc., 1800 M St. N.W., Washington, D.C. 20036. Filed 12/14/81. Legislative interest — "All issues relating to natural gas."

PETRO-LEWIS CORP., Denver, Colo. Lobbyist — Tucker and Brown, Western Federal Savings Building, Denver, Colo. 80202. Filed 12/8/81. Legislative interest — "S 1660, HR 4626, to validate certain placer mining claims in Hot Springs County, Wyoming...."

ST. JOE MINERALS CORP., Washington, D.C. Lobbyist — Richard W. Bliss, 1899 L St. N.W., Washington, D.C. 20036.

Filed 12/9/81. Legislative interest — "All legislation dealing with the Alaska Natural Gas Transportation System, including H J Res 341."

SHEARSON/AMERICAN EXPRESS INC., New York, N.Y. Lobbyist — Elizabeth Jane Robbins, 43 D St. S.E., Washington, D.C. 20003. Filed 12/1/81. Legislative interest — "Tax exempt mortgage revenue bonds."

SOUTHERN PACIFIC COMMUNICATIONS CO., 1828 L St. N.W., Washington, D.C. 20036. Filed for self 12/4/81. Legislative interest — "S 898 - Telecommunications Competition and Deregulation Act of 1981...." Lobbyist — E. J. Kushan.

STENCEL AERO ENGINEERING CORP., Arden, N.C. Lobbyist — Vorys, Sater, Seymour & Pease, 1828 L St. N.W., Washington, D.C. 20036. Filed 12/14/81. Legislative interest — "...military procurements."

TDI/WINSTON NETWORK INC., New York, N.Y. Lobbyist — Epstein, Becker, Borsody and Green, 1140 19th St. N.W., Washington, D.C. 20036. Filed 12/2/81. Legislative interest — "...transit advertising in the District of Columbia ... FTC and FCC authorizations and appropriations."

UNION PACIFIC CORP., 345 Park Ave., New York, N.Y. 10022. Filed for self 12/10/81. Legislative interest — "...railroad industry, petroleum industry, natural gas industry, nuclear industry, mining industry with particular reference to coal, natural soda ash and uranium." Lobbyist — Eugene P. Kopp, 1120 20th St. N.W., Washington, D.C. 20036.

WARNER COMMUNICATIONS/FRANKLIN MINT, Philadelphia, Pa. Lobbyist — Gray and Co., 3255 Grace St. N.W., Washington, D.C. 20007. Filed 12/1/81. Legislative interest — "...legislation concerning Franklin Mint commemorative coins."

WILSHIRE TERRACE COOPERATIVE HOUSING CORP., Los Angeles, Calif. Lobbyist — Latham, Watkins & Hills, 1333 New Hampshire Ave. N.W., Washington, D.C. 20036. Filed 12/4/81. Legislative interest — "Amendment of section 216 of the Internal Revenue Code."

WNET/13, New York, N.Y. Lobbyist — Mintz, Levin, Cohn, Ferris, Glovsky & Popeo, 1015 15th St. N.W., Washington, D.C. 20005. Filed 12/10/81. Legislative interest — "Appropriations for public broadcasting."

International Relations

EMBASSY OF INDIA, Washington, D.C. Lobbyist — Baron/Canning and Co. Inc., 540 Madison Ave., New York, N.Y. 10022. Filed 12/3/81. (Former U.S. Rep. Seymour Halpern, R-N.Y., 1959-73, was listed as agent for this client.) Legislative interest — "General matters pertaining to U.S.-Republic of India relations."

Labor Groups

AMALGAMATED TRANSIT UNION, AFL-CIO, 5025 Wisconsin Ave. N.W., Washington, D.C. 20016. Filed for self 12/8/81. Legislative interest — Not specified. Lobbyist — Robert A. Molofsky.

AMERICAN ASSOCIATION OF RETIRED PERSONS, 1909 K St. N.W., Washington, D.C. 20049. Filed for self 12/1/81. Legislative interest — "Improved Social Security and Medicare/Medicaid laws, Older Americans Act amendments, improved tax treatment of older Americans, improved nursing home standards, consumer protection legislation, employment of older workers, transportation for the elderly, no-fault insurance, housing for the elderly." Lobbyist — Jack E. Christy.

INDUSTRIAL UNION OF MARINE & SHIPBUILDING WORKERS OF AMERICA, AFL-CIO, LOCAL 9, 340 N. Broad Ave., Wilmington, Calif. 90744. Lobbyist — Manatt, Phelps, Rothenberg & Tunney, 1200 New Hampshire Ave. N.W., Washington, D.C. 20036. Filed 12/4/81. (Former U.S. Rep. James C. Corman, D-Calif., 1961-81, was listed as agent for this client.) Legislative interest — "In opposition to S 1182...."

NATIONAL RETIRED TEACHERS ASSOCIATION, 1909 K St. N.W., Washington, D.C. 20049. Filed for self 12/1/81.

Legislative interest — "Improved Social Security and Medicare/Medicaid laws, Older Americans Act amendments, improved tax treatment of older Americans, improved nursing home standards, consumer protection legislation, employment of older workers, transportation for the elderly, no-fault insurance, housing for the elderly." Lobbyist — Jack E. Christy.

State and Local Governments

STATE OF ALASKA, Juneau, Alaska. Lobbyist — Wickwire, Lewis, Goldmark & Schorr, 500 Maynard Building, Seattle, Wash. 98104. Filed 12/14/81. Legislative interest — "Legislation providing for the transfer of the Alaska Railroad to the State of Alaska, S 1500, HR 4278."

AMERICAN SAMOA, Pago Pago, American Samoa. Lobbyist — Richard W. Bliss, 1899 L St. N.W., Washington, D.C. 20036. Filed 12/3/81. Legislative interest — "All legislation dealing with clean air, including the fiscal year 1981 and 1982 budgets."

DELAWARE RIVER PORT AUTHORITY, Camden, N.J. Lobbyist — Ballard, Spahr, Andrews & Ingersoll, 1850 K St. N.W., Washington, D.C. 20006. Filed 12/3/81. Legislative interest — "...Port development legislation and user fees."

PHILADELPHIA PORT CORP., Philadelphia, Pa. Lobbyist — Ballard, Spahr, Andrews & Ingersoll, 1850 K St. N.W., Washington, D.C. 20006. Filed 12/3/81. Legislative interest — "...Port development legislation and user fees."

TOLEDO-LUCAS COUNTY PORT AUTHORITY, Toledo, Ohio. Lobbyist — Thomas L. Ashley, 1730 Pennsylvania Ave. N.W., Washington, D.C. 20006. Filed 12/14/81. (Former U.S. rep., D-Ohio, 1955-81.) Legislative interest — "Port development legislation - S 1586, S 1692, HR 4627, HR 4862."

Trade Associations

AMERICAN HOSPITAL ASSOCIATION, 840 N. Lakeshore Drive, Chicago, Ill. 60611. Filed for self 12/18/81. Legislative interest — Not specified. Lobbyist — Marcia L. Desmond, 444 N. Capitol St. N.W., Washington, D.C. 20001.

AMERICAN MARITIME ASSOCIATION, Washington, D.C. Lobbyist — Gray and Co., 3255 Grace St. N.W., Washington, D.C. 20007. Filed 12/1/81. Legislative interest — Not specified.

AMERICAN TRUCKING ASSOCIATIONS, Washington, D.C. Lobbyist — Gray and Co., 3255 Grace St. N.W., Washington, D.C. 20007. Filed 12/1/81. Legislative interest — "...trucking, highway and tax legislation."

AMERICAN WOOD PRESERVERS INSTITUTE, 1651 Old Meadow Road, McLean, Va. 22102. Filed for self 12/14/81. Legislative interest — "...Federal Insecticide, Fungicide and Rodenticide Act, the Toxic Substances Control Act ... the Resource Conservation and Control Act ... the Clean Water Act, the Comprehensive Environmental Response, Compensation and Liability Act and the Occupational Safety and Health Act...." Lobbyist — Walter G. Talarek.

THE ASSOCIATED GENERAL CONTRACTORS OF AMERICA, 1957 E St. N.W., Washington, D.C. 20006. Filed for self 12/8/81. Legislative interest — "Highway and transportation legislation." Lobbyists — Jack O. Andresen, Michael E. Kennedy.

ASSOCIATION OF TRIAL LAWYERS OF AMERICA, 1050 31st St. N.W., Washington, D.C. 20007. Filed for self 12/4/81. Legislative interest — "...admiralty, automobile reparation, aviation, consumer protection, criminal law, the environment, health, the administration of justice, legal services and workers' compensation." Lobbyist — Anita S. Warren.

AUTOMOTIVE DISMANTLERS AND RECYCLERS ASSOCIATION, Washington, D.C. Lobbyist — Wyman, Bautzer, Rothman, Kuchel & Silbert, 600 New Hampshire Ave. N.W., Washington, D.C. 20037. Filed 12/9/81. Legislative interest — "All legislation concerning motor vehicle theft prevention including HR 4325 and S 1676."

CALIFORNIA SAVINGS & LOAN LEAGUE, 9800 S. Sepulveda Blvd., Los Angeles, Calif. 90045. Filed for self 12/31/81. Legislative interest — "...HR 5135; HR 5136; HR 4603; S 1703; S

1720; S 1721." Lobbyist — Richard J. Perry Jr., 1575 I St. N.W., Washington, D.C. 20005.

COUNCIL OF LARGE PUBLIC HOUSING AUTHORI-TIES, Boston, Mass. Lobbyist — Roisman, Reno & Cavanaugh, 1016 16th St. N.W., Washington, D.C. 20036. Filed 12/15/81. Legislative interest — "...increased appropriations for operating subsidies for low-income housing...."

HEALTH INSURANCE ASSOCIATION OF AMER-ICA, Washington, D.C. Lobbyist — Gray and Co., 3255 Grace St. N.W., Washington, D.C. 20007. Filed 12/1/81. Legislative interest — Not specified.

MANUFACTURERS OF EMISSION CONTROLS AS-SOCIATION, 1800 K St. N.W., Washington, D.C. 20006. Filed for self 12/7/81. Legislative interest — "...reauthorization of a strong Clean Air Act, opposing enactment of HR 4400 (the Traxler-Hillis bill)...." Lobbyist — Sara Sibley.

MINNESOTA PETROLEUM COUNCIL, 300 Northern Federal Building, St. Paul, Minn. 55102. Filed for self 12/31/81. Legislative interest — Not specified. Lobbyist — Darrel D. Bunge.

NATIONAL ASSOCIATION OF FEDERAL CREDIT UNIONS, 1111 N. 19th St., Arlington, Va. 22209. Filed for self 12/31/81. Legislative interest — "S 1607 interest/dividend exclusion, S 1703 Thrift Institution Restructuring Act, S 1720 Financial Institutions Restructuring and Service Act, S 1721 Deposit Insurance Consolidation Act, S 1406/HR 2501 federal pre-emption of state usury laws, S 2000/HR 4786 Bankruptcy Improvements Act, HR 4603 Regulators' bill, Money Market Share Accounts, Tax-Deferred Savings Vehicles."

NATIONAL ASSOCIATION OF HOME BUILDERS, Washington, D.C. Lobbyist — Gray and Co., 3255 Grace St. N.W., Washington, D.C. 20007. Filed 12/1/81. Legislative interest — "...housing legislation and legislation affecting the Job Corps program."

NATIONAL ASSOCIATION OF PUBLIC HOSPI-TALS, Washington, D.C. Lobbyist — Califano, Ross & Heineman, 1575 I St. N.W., Washington, D.C. 20005. Filed 12/15/81. Legislative interest — Not specified.

NATIONAL ASSOCIATION OF REALTORS, 777 14th St. N.W., Washington, D.C. 20005. Filed for self 12/15/81. Legislative interest — "...tax relief; independent contractor; S 31, Repeal of Family Rental Tax; fair housing; alternative mortgage instruments; public lands management; Clean Air Act; and Depository Institutions Act." Lobbyist — Debbie Shannon.

NATIONAL ASSOCIATION OF TRUCK STOP OPER-ATORS, 700 N. Fairfax St., Alexandria, Va. 22314. Filed for self 12/30/81. Legislative interest — "...fuel and energy issues, labor issues, trucking regulation, agricultural issues (as they relate to food service), regulatory reform...." Lobbyist — Betty Carolyn Horn.

NATIONAL MUSIC PUBLISHERS ASSOCIATION INC., New York, N.Y. Lobbyist — Elizabeth Jane Robbins, 43 D St. S.E., Washington, D.C. 20003. Filed 12/1/81. Legislative interest — "Copyright legislation... S 1758 and HR 4794, HR 4808 and HR 4783 exempting home recording of copyright works from copyright infringement."

ORGANIZATION OF HEATER MANUFACTURERS, Franklin, Tenn. Lobbyist — Lord, Day & Lord, 1120 20th St. N.W., Washington, D.C. 20036. Filed 12/23/81. Legislative interest — "Implementation of the United States Generalized System of Preference for less developed countries under the provisions of the Trade Act of 1974 as amended."

SALT INSTITUTE, 206 N. Washington St., Alexandria, Va. 22314. Filed for self 12/6/81. Legislative interest — "...labeling of sodium in food products...." Lobbyist — William E. Dickinson.

THE SMALL BUSINESS COALITION FOR POLLU-TION CONTROL, Dayton, Ohio. Lobbyist — Vorys, Sater, Seymour & Pease, 1828 L St. N.W., Washington, D.C. 20036. Filed 12/9/81. Legislative interest — "...SBA pollution facilities loan guarantee program."

THE UTILITY GROUP, Washington, D.C. Lobbyist — O'Brien & Fierce, 1828 L St. N.W., Washington, D.C. 20036. Filed 12/16/81. Legislative interest — "Diversification amendments to

the Public Utility Holding Company Act, S 1870...."

WESTERN COTTON GROWERS ASSOCIATION, 1101 17th St. N.W., Washington, D.C. 20036. Filed for self 12/3/81. Legislative interest — "S 884." Lobbyist — James H. Lake.

Miscellaneous

JEFF SAMUEL ALLDER, 911 Walker St., Houston, Texas 77052. Filed for self 12/10/81. Legislative interest — Not specified.

PUBLIC HEALTH HOSPITAL PRESERVATION AND DEVELOPMENT AUTHORITY, Seattle, Wash. Lobbyist — Wickwire, Lewis, Goldmark & Schorr, 500 Maynard Building, Seattle, Wash. 98104. Filed 12/17/81. Legislative interest — "...to secure transfer of the Seattle Public Health Service Hospital to the PHHPDA...."

JAMES P. PURVIS, Spokane, Wash. Lobbyist — Hudson, Creyke, Koehler & Tacke, 1744 R St. N.W., Washington, D.C. 20009. Filed 12/16/81. Legislative interest — "Private bill for the relief of James P. Purvis."

JOE ROSS, 842 Donaghey Building, Little Rock, Ark. 72201. Filed for self 12/10/81. Legislative interest — Not specified.

JAMES L. SOUTH, 8607 Dixie Place, McLean, Va. 22102. Filed for self 12/9/81. Legislative interest — Not specified.

January 1982 Registrations

Citizens' Groups

AMERICAN CANCER SOCIETY, New York, N.Y. Lobbyist — Bayh, Tabbert & Capehart, 1575 I St. N.W., Washington, D.C. 20005. Filed 1/13/82. Legislative interest — "...cancer research and cancer control."

THE AMERICAN LEGION, 700 N. Pennsylvania St., Indianapolis, Ind. Filed for self 1/10/82. Legislative interest — "...children and youth ... economics ... internal affairs ... national security ... veterans' affairs and rehabilitation ... Americanism ... foreign relations...." Lobbyist — Alan M. Olszewski, 1608 K St. N.W., Washington, D.C. 20036.

AMERICAN RIVERS CONSERVATION COUNCIL, 323 Pennsylvania Ave. S.E., Washington, D.C. 20003. Filed for self 1/11/82. Legislative interest — "...National Wild and Scenic Rivers System...." Lobbyists — Patricia Munoz, Ron Vlaskamp.

COALITION FOR ENVIRONMENTAL-ENERGY BALANCE, Columbus, Ohio. Lobbyist — Porter, Wright, Morris & Arthur, 37 W. Broad St., Columbus, Ohio 43215. Filed 1/11/82. Legislative interest — "...proposed amendments to the Clean Air Act, 42 U.S.C. section 7401 *et. seq.*, specifically."

FEDERATION FOR AMERICAN IMMIGRATION REFORM, 2028 P St. N.W., Washington, D.C. 20036. Filed for self 1/18/82. Legislative interest — Not specified. Lobbyist — Mary Lou Tanton.

HANDGUN CONTROL INC., Washington, D.C. Lobbyist — Wilmer, Cutler & Pickering, 1666 K St. N.W., Washington, D.C. 20006. Filed 1/20/82. Legislative interest — "...in support of Handgun Crime Control Act of 1981, S 974, HR 3200; in opposition to Federal Firearms Reform Act, S 1030, HR 3300."

NATIONAL ASSOCIATION OF ARAB AMERICANS, 1825 Connecticut Ave. N.W., Washington D.C. 20009. Filed for self — 1/11/82. Legislative interest — "Middle East related legislation, fiscal year 1982 Foreign Assistance Act, amendments to the Internal Revenue Code sections 911 and 913; S 408, HR 911." Lobbyist — Georgia Abraham.

NATIONAL RIFLE ASSOCIATION OF AMERICA, 1600 Rhode Island Ave. N.W., Washington D.C. 20036. Filed for self 1/13/82. Legislative interest — "...all aspects of the acquisition, possession, and use of firearms and ammunition ... hunting and wildlife conservation." Lobbyist — David S. Marshall.

PLANNED PARENTHOOD OF NEW YORK CITY INC., 380 Second Ave., New York, N.Y. 10010. Filed for self 1/10/82. Legislative interest — "Reproductive health care ... Title

X of the Public Health Service Act, Hyde amendment which restricts access to Medicaid funded abortions." Lobbyist — May Del Rio Dorfman.

SIERRA CLUB, 530 Bush St., San Francisco, Calif. 94108. Filed for self 1/20/82. Legislative interest — Not specified. Lobbyist — Debbie Sease, 330 Pennsylvania Ave. S.E., Washington, D.C. 20003.

TENTH PROLIFE CONGRESSIONAL DISTRICT ACTION COMMITTEE, 3443 Hancock Bridge Parkway, North Fort Myers, Fla. 33903. Filed for self 1/18/82. Legislative interest — "...the Hatch human life amendment...." Lobbyist — Alfred E. Johnson.

Corporations and Businesses

ADVANCE PUBLICATIONS INC., Staten Island, N.Y. Lobbyist — Dow, Lohnes & Albertson, 1225 Connecticut Ave. N.W., Washington, D.C. 20036. Filed 1/11/82. Legislative interest — "...S 1695, S 1733, S 1734."

ADVANCED FUEL SYSTEMS INC., 118 N. Indiana Ave., Wichita, Kan. 67214. Filed for self 1/12/82. Legislative interest — "Legislation concerning alternative fuels and natural gas pricing and availability." Lobbyist — Stephen M. Goldberg, 1945 Gallows Road, Vienna, Va. 22180.

ANHEUSER-BUSCH COMPANIES INC., One Busch Place, St. Louis, Mo. 63118. Filed for self 1/5/82. Legislative interest — "...supports HR 1880 ... HR 2360 ... S 1328 ... S 169 ... S 995 ... HR 3269 and S 1215 ... opposes S 709 and HR 2498...." Lobbyists — Louis A. Gatti, Richard F. Keating, 1211 Connecticut Ave. N.W., Washington, D.C. 20036.

THE BOEING CO., Rosslyn, Va. Lobbyist — C & B Associates, 1750 New York Ave. N.W., Washington, D.C. 20006. Filed 1/12/82. Legislative interest — "Opposed to H Con Res 194."

CELP, Beltsville, Md. Lobbyist — Beatty & McNamee, 4316 Hamilton St., Hyattsville, Md. 20781. Filed 1/14/82. Legislative interest — "Passive income limitations on Subchapter S corporations ... Internal Revenue Code section 1372(e)(5)."

CHAMPION INTERNATIONAL CORP., Washington D.C. Lobbyist — Shea & Gould, 330 Madison Ave., New York, N.Y. 10017. Filed 1/11/82. Legislative interest — "Section 904(f), Internal Revenue Code."

THE COASTAL CORP., Nine Greenway Plaza, Houston, Texas 77046. Filed for self 1/8/82. Legislative interest — "Energy issues." Lobbyist — Steven Edward Some, 1333 New Hampshire Ave. N.W., Washington, D.C. 20036.

COBB, GREEN & ASSOCIATES, P.O. Box 974, Las Vegas, Nev. 89125. Filed for self 1/15/82. Legislative interest — "...HR 3789, HR 4965, S 1704, S 1849."

CONSOLIDATED FREIGHTWAY CORP., Menlo Park, Calif. Lobbyist — Bregman, Abell & Kay, 1900 L St. N.W., Washington, D.C. 20036. Filed 1/8/82. Legislative interest — "...tax classification of over-the-road trailers."

DEMINEX U.S. OIL CO., Dallas, Texas. Lobbyist — Kilgore & Kilgore Inc., 1800 First National Bank Building, Dallas, Texas 75202. Filed 1/8/82. Legislative interest — "...will support legislation, not yet introduced into Congress, to amend section 613A(d)(4) of the Internal Revenue Code to exclude foreign refining from the definition of the refining of crude oil."

DIRECT BROADCAST SATELLITE CORP., Bethesda, Md. Lobbyist — Pepper, Hamilton & Scheetz, 1777 F St. N.W., Washington, D.C. 20006. Filed 1/11/82. Legislative interest — Not specified.

DOW CHEMICAL U.S.A., 1800 M St. N.W., Washington, D.C. 20036. Filed for self 1/19/82. Legislative interest — "All bills involving patents and trademarks; Food, Drug and Cosmetic Act; bills involving Agent Orange; bills involving food additives." Lobbyist — John J. Osick.

ELECTRONIC DATA SYSTEMS CORP., 229 Pennsylvania Ave. S.E., Washington, D.C. 20003. Lobbyist — O'Connor & Hannan, 1919 Pennsylvania Ave. N.W., Washington, D.C. 20006. Filed 1/18/82. Legislative interest — "...health-related legislation." Filed for self 1/10/82. Legislative interest — "...health care, National Health Insurance, banking, insurance, retailing and utili-

ties." Lobbyist — John D. Lacopo.

GENERAL DYNAMICS CORP., St. Louis, Mo. Lobbyist — Pepper, Hamilton & Scheetz, 1777 F St. N.W., Washington, D.C. 20006. Filed 1/11/82. Legislative interest — "Legislation affecting the communications industry; S 898, HR 5108."

GENERAL PUBLIC UTILITIES CORP., Harrisburg, Pa. Lobbyist — Shaw, Pittman, Potts & Trowbridge, 1800 M St. N.W., Washington, D.C. 20036. Filed 1/12/82. Legislative interest — "Legislation dealing with the clean-up of nuclear waste."

GENERAL TELEPHONE AND ELECTRONICS CORP., Washington, D.C. Lobbyist — Mintz, Levin, Cohn, Ferris, Glovsky & Popeo, 1015 15th St. N.W., Washington, D.C. 20005. Filed 1/11/82. Legislative interest — "...Communications Act."

GRAEPER-VAN NOY-WAGNER INC., Colorado Springs, Colo. Lobbyist — Hamel, Park, McCabe & Saunders, 888 16th St. N.W., Washington, D.C. 20006. Filed 1/11/82. Legislative interest — "...amendments to the Telecommunications Act of 1981, HR 5158."

HAMPSHIRE ENERGY, Milwaukee, Wis. Lobbyist — Charls E. Walker Associates Inc., 1730 Pennsylvania Ave. N.W., Washington, D.C. 20006. Filed 1/10/82. Legislative interest — "...legislation affecting synthetic fuel development and business energy property investment tax credit."

HIGHLY ENTERPRISE CORP., Bothell, Wash. Lobbyist — Birch, Horton, Bittner and Monroe, 1140 Connecticut Ave. N.W., Washington, D.C. 20036. Filed 1/7/82. Legislative interest — "...issues related to fishing."

HIRAM WALKER & SONS INC., P.O. Box 33006, Detroit, Mich. 48232. Filed for self 1/19/82. Legislative interest — "...HR 322, HR 460, HR 967, HR 1800, HR 2251, HR 2488, HR 2644, HR 3637, HR 4121, HR 4545, HR 4761, H J Res 370, S 671, S 1543." Lobbyist — Nancy H. Jessick, 425 13th St. N.W., Washington, D.C. 20004.

INEXCO OIL CO., Houston, Texas. Lobbyist — Butler, Binion, Rice, Cook & Knapp, 1747 Pennsylvania Ave. N.W., Washington, D.C. 20006. Filed 1/12/82. Legislative interest — "Legislation affecting stock options."

INTERNATIONAL BUSINESS MACHINES CORP., Old Orchard Road, Armonk, N.Y. 10504. Filed for self 1/11/82. Legislative interest — "...legislative matters dealing with telecommunications, patents and copyrights." Lobbyist — Randolph C. Lumb, 1801 K St. N.W., Washington, D.C. 20006.

JACQUES BOREL ENTERPRISES INC., New York, N.Y. Lobbyist — Powell, Goldstein, Frazer & Murphy, 1110 Vermont Ave. N.W., Washington, D.C. 20005. Filed 1/8/82. Legislative interest — "...section 119 of the Internal Revenue Code...."

JOINT TRAWLERS (NORTH AMERICA) LTD., Gloucester, Mass. Lobbyist — Nossaman, Krueger & Marsh, 1140 19th St. N.W., Washington, D.C. 20036. Filed 1/13/82. Legislative interest — "...fisheries legislation."

LEAR SIEGLER INC., 2040 E. Dyer Road, Santa Ana, Calif. 92705. Filed for self 1/6/82. Legislative interest — "...S 694 ... HR 4995 ... HR 3515...." Lobbyist — Gordon L. Murray, 1911 Jefferson Davis Highway, Arlington, Va. 22202.

LIFELINE SYSTEMS INC., Waltham, Mass. Lobbyist — Wald, Harkrader & Ross, 1300 19th St. N.W., Washington, D.C. 20036. Filed 1/10/82. Legislative interest — "Home health legislation, including support of HR 3921."

MCI COMMUNICATIONS CORP., 1133 19th St. N.W., Washington, D.C. 20036. Filed for self 1/13/82. Legislative interest — "...HR 5158 and any similar bills...." Lobbyist — Charles W. Franz.

MIDCON CORP., Chicago, Ill. Lobbyist — Gardner, Carton & Douglas, 1875 I St. N.W., Washington, D.C. 20006. Filed 1/11/82. Legislative interest — "Energy legislation."

MILLIKEN & CO., Spartanburg, S.C. Lobbyist — Johnson, Smith and Hibbard, 220 N. Church St., Spartanburg, S.C. 29304. Filed 1/10/82. Legislative interest — "...enactment of S 995 or similar legislation."

MOBIL CORP., New York, N.Y. Lobbyist — James B. Pearson, 1333 New Hampshire Ave. N.W., Washington, D.C. 20036. Filed 1/8/82. (Former U.S. sen., R-Kan., 1962-78.) Legisla-

tive interest — "...legislation related to energy matters ... including legislation relating to corporate mergers."

NATIONAL FOOTBALL LEAGUE, New York, N.Y. Lobbyist — Covington & Burling, 1201 Pennsylvania Ave. N.W., Washington, D.C. 20044. Filed 1/11/82. Legislative interest — "...including but not limited to the application of the antitrust laws to professional sports...."

NIPPON ELECTRIC CO. LTD., New York, N.Y. Lobbyist — Paul, Weiss, Rifkind, Wharton & Garrison, 345 Park Ave., New York, N.Y. 10154. Filed 1/19/82. Legislative interest — "...bills relating to the telecommunications industry including S 898 and HR 5158."

PAGE AIRWAYS, Rochester, N.Y. Lobbyist — F. Nordy Hoffmann and Associates Inc., 400 North Capitol St. N.W., Washington, D.C. 20001. Filed 1/11/82. Legislative interest — Not specified.

PALMER COMMUNICATIONS INC., Des Moines, Iowa. Lobbyist — Dow, Lohnes & Albertson, 1225 Connecticut Ave. N.W., Washington, D.C. 20036. Filed 1/11/82. Legislative interest — "...S 1695, S 1733, S 1734...."

ROADWAY EXPRESS INC., Akron, Ohio. Lobbyist — Bregman, Abell & Kay, 1900 L St. N.W., Washington, D.C. 20036. Filed 1/8/82. Legislative interest — "...tax classification of over-the-road trailers."

ROGERS & COWAN INC., Beverly Hills, Calif. Lobbyist — Mark A. Siegel & Associates Inc., 400 North Capitol St. N.W., Washington, D.C. 20001. Filed 1/7/82. Legislative interest — "Legislation concerning the Philippines."

ST. GEORGE TANAQ CORP., Anchorage, Alaska. Lobbyist — Birch, Horton, Bittner and Monroe, 1140 Connecticut Ave. N.W., Washington, D.C. 20036. Filed 1/7/82. Legislative interest — "Fishing-related legislation and fiscal year 1982 Department of Interior appropriations bills."

SANTA FE INDUSTRIES INC., 224 S. Michigan Ave., Chicago, Ill. 60604. Filed for self 1/10/82. Legislative interest — "...taxes, Mineral Leasing Act revisions, oil spill liability, federal allocation and price controls on natural gas, crude oil and petroleum products...." Lobbyist — R. Ray Paabo, 1100 Connecticut Ave. N.W., Washington, D.C. 20036.

SECURITY LIFE OF DENVER, Denver, Colo. Lobbyist — Paul, Hastings, Janofsky & Walker, 1050 Thomas Jefferson St. N.W., Washington, D.C. 20007. Filed 1/12/82. Legislative interest — "Taxation of life insurance companies."

STEPHENS OVERSEAS SERVICES INC., 1101 Connecticut Ave. N.W., Washington, D.C. 20036. Filed for self 1/8/82. Legislative interest — "Banking, small business, international and corporate regulatory issues." Lobbyist — T. Glenn Johnston.

U.S. TELEPHONE COMMUNICATIONS INC., 108 S. Akard St., Dallas, Texas 75202. Filed for self 1/13/82. Legislative interest — "S 898, Telecommunications Deregulation and Competition Act." Lobbyist — Susan Buck.

UNIVERSAL LEAF TOBACCO CO. INC., Richmond, Va. Lobbyist — Busby, Rehm & Leonard, 1629 K St. N.W., Washington, D.C. 20006. Filed 1/13/82. Legislative interest — Not specified.

WESTINGHOUSE ELECTRIC CORP., Washington, D.C. Lobbyist — White, Fine & Verville, 1156 15th St. N.W., Washington, D.C. 20005. Filed 1/10/82. Legislative interest — "...legislative matters concerning nuclear power, nuclear equipment export, the Export-Import Bank of the United States, the Clinch River Breeder Reactor...." Lobbyist — F. Nordy Hoffmann and Associates Inc., 400 North Capitol St. N.W., Washington, D.C. 20001. Filed 1/11/82. Legislative interest — Not specified.

International Relations

ARAB REPUBLIC OF EGYPT, Cairo, Egypt. Lobbyist — Neill and Co. Inc., 1025 Connecticut Ave. N.W., Washington, D.C. 20036. Filed 1/6/82. Legislative interest — "...Administration's military and economic assistance programs insofar as they may relate to the Arab Republic of Egypt...."

CANADIAN COALITION ON ACID RAIN, Toronto.

Lobbyist — Ernest Michael Perley, 105 Davenport Road, Toronto M5R 1H6. Filed 1/8/82. Legislative interest — "...revising and extending authorizations under the Clean Air Act of 1970, as amended."

WASHINGTON OFFICE ON AFRICA, Washington, D.C. Lobbyist — Kenneth Zinn, 1720 Q St. N.W., Washington, D.C. 20009. Filed 1/14/82. Legislative interest — Not specified.

Labor Groups

AMERICAN ASSOCIATION OF RETIRED PERSONS, 1909 K St. N.W., Washington, D.C. 20049. Filed for self 1/18/82. Legislative interest — "Support of improved Social Security and Medicare/Medicaid laws, Older Americans Act Amendments, improved tax treatment of older Americans, improved nursing home standards, consumer protection legislation, employment of older workers, transportation of the elderly, no-fault insurance, housing for the elderly." Lobbyist — Jo Reed.

AMERICAN ASSOCIATION OF SCHOOL ADMINISTRATORS, 1801 N. Moore St., Arlington, Va. 22209. Filed for self 1/13/82. Legislative interest — "...Department of Education Organization Act ... full funding of federally authorized programs ... youth employment...." Lobbyist — Claudia Mansfield Austin.

CONTINENTAL EMPLOYEES ASSOCIATION, Rosslyn, Va. Lobbyist — C & B Associates, 1750 New York Ave. N.W., Washington, D.C. 20006. Filed 1/12/82. Legislative interest — "Amendment to tax bill S 626, allowing Continental employees to establish an ESOP [employees stock option plan]...."

EPIC, Washington, D.C. Lobbyist — F. Nordy Hoffmann and Associates Inc., 400 North Capitol St. N.W., Washington, D.C. 20001. Filed 1/11/82. Legislative interest — Not specified.

MARINE ENGINEERS BENEFICIAL ASSOCIATION, Washington, D.C. Lobbyist — F. Nordy Hoffmann and Associates Inc., 400 North Capitol St. N.W., Washington, D.C. 20001. Filed 1/11/82. Legislative interest — Not specified.

NATIONAL FEDERATION OF FEDERAL EMPLOYEES, 1016 16th St. N.W., Washington, D.C. 20036. Filed for self 1/12/82. Legislative interest — Not specified.

NATIONAL RETIRED TEACHERS ASSOCIATION, 1909 K St. N.W., Washington, D.C. 20049. Filed for self 1/18/82. Legislative interest — "Support of improved Social Security and Medicare/Medicaid laws, Older Americans Act Amendments, improved tax treatment of older Americans, improved nursing home standards, consumer protection legislation, employment of older workers, transportation of the elderly, no-fault insurance, housing for the elderly." Lobbyist — Jo Reed.

State and Local Governments

COUNCIL OF STATE HOUSING AGENCIES, Washington, D.C. Lobbyist — Kirkpatrick, Lockhart, Hill, Christopher & Phillips, 1900 M St. N.W., Washington, D.C. 20036. Filed 1/19/82. (Former U.S. Rep. Garry E. Brown, R-Mich., 1967-79, was listed as agent for this client.) Legislative interest — "Legislation affecting issuance of tax-exempt mortgage revenue bonds."

SANTA ANA RIVER FLOOD PROTECTION AGENCY, Santa Ana, Calif. Lobbyist — Jensen, Sanders & McConnell, 244 Maryland Ave. N.E., Washington, D.C. 20002. Filed 1/8/82. Legislative interest — "Legislation authorizing the Army Corps of Engineers to continue with the Santa Ana River Flood Control Project."

STATE OF MONTANA, Helena, Mont. Lobbyist — C & B Associates, 1750 New York Ave. N.W., Washington, D.C. 20006. Filed 1/12/82. Legislative interest — "Opposed to bill S 178 limiting state's coal severance tax."

STATE OF WASHINGTON, Olympia, Wash. Lobbyist — Donald W. Whitehead, 1120 Connecticut Ave. N.W., Washington, D.C. 20036. Filed 1/14/82. Legislative interest — "Public Works and Development Act of 1965, as amended and other legislation dealing with regional commissions."

Trade Associations

AMERICAN FUR INDUSTRY INC., New York, N.Y. Lobbyist — Kiefer & Morrison, 15th St. N.W., Washington, D.C. 20005. Filed 1/10/82. Legislative interest — "Wildlife legislation: 16 U.S.C. section 1531 *et. seq.*; 16 U.S.C. section 701 *et. seq.*; 16 U.S.C. 1361 *et. seq.*; and Bankruptcy Act."

AMERICAN GROUP PRACTICE ASSOCIATION INC., 20 S. Quaker Lane, Alexandria, Va. 22314. Filed for self 1/15/82. Legislative interest — Not specified. Lobbyist — Donald W. Fisher, 3814 Ivanhoe Lane, Alexandria, Va. 22310.

AMERICAN HOSPITAL ASSOCIATION, 840 N. Lakeshore Drive, Chicago, Ill. 60611. Filed for self 1/20/82. Legislative interest — Not specified. Lobbyists — Marcia L. Desmond, Frank J. Kinney, Martin A. Wall, 444 North Capitol St. N.W., Washington, D.C. 20001.

AMERICAN PETROLEUM INSTITUTE, 2101 L St. N.W., Washington, D.C. 20037. Filed for self 1/7/82. Legislative interest — Not specified. Lobbyists — Darrel D. Bunge, 300 Northern Federal Building, St. Paul, Minn. 55102; Charles E. Harman Jr., 230 Peachtree St. N.W., Atlanta, Ga. 30303.

THE AMERICAN WATERWAYS OPERATORS INC., 1600 Wilson Blvd., Arlington, Va. 22209. Filed for self 1/13/82. Legislative interest — Not specified. Lobbyists — Brian J. Chiasson, Patricia D. Yoder.

ASSOCIATION OF AMERICAN RAILROADS, 1920 L St. N.W., Washington, D.C. 20036. Filed for self 1/12/82. Legislative interest — Not specified. Lobbyist — William H. Darden, 412 First St. S.E., Washington, D.C. 20003.

ASSOCIATION OF EXECUTIVE RECRUITING CONSULTANTS INC., New York, N.Y. Lobbyist — Powell, Goldstein, Frazer & Murphy, 1110 Vermont Ave. N.W., Washington, D.C. 20005. Filed 1/8/82. Legislative interest — Not specified.

THE ASSOCIATED GENERAL CONTRACTORS OF AMERICA, 1957 E St. N.W., Washington, D.C. 20006. Filed for self 1/11/82. Legislative interest — Not specified. Lobbyists — Jack O. Andresen, Michael E. Kennedy.

CHAMBER OF COMMERCE OF THE UNITED STATES, 1615 H St. N.W., Washington, D.C. 20062. Filed for self 1/11/82. Legislative interest — Not specified. Lobbyist — Jean C. Statler.

CHEMICAL SPECIALTIES MANUFACTURERS ASSOCIATION, 1001 Connecticut Ave. N.W., Washington, D.C. 20036. Filed for self 1/10/82. Legislative interest — Not specified. Lobbyist — Warren E. Stickle.

COMMITTEE FOR TITLE XI VESSEL FINANCING, Washington, D.C. Lobbyist — Kominers, Fort, Schlefer & Boyer, 1776 F St. N.W., Washington, D.C. 20006. Filed 1/12/82. Legislative interest — "Preservation and enlargement of authorization under Title XI, Merchant Marine Act, 1936 and clarification of executive authority to limit same."

COOPERATIVE LEAGUE OF THE USA, 1828 L St. N.W., Washington, D.C. 20036. Filed for self 1/10/82. Legislative interest — "...National Consumer Cooperative Bank, HUD financing, eligibility of cooperatives for mortgage revenue bond funding and access to credit markets...." Lobbyist — Matthew B. Slepin.

DISTILLED SPIRITS COUNCIL OF THE UNITED STATES, 425 13th St. N.W., Washington, D.C. 20004. Filed for self 1/5/82. Legislative interest — Not specified. Lobbyist — Geoffrey G. Peterson.

THE FARMERS' EDUCATIONAL AND CO-OPERATIVE UNION OF AMERICA, 1012 14th St. N.W., Washington, D.C. 20005. Filed for self 1/15/82. Legislative interest — "...labor, health, medical care and welfare, taxation, revenue, tariffs, farm price support, crop insurance, farm credit, REA, public power, natural resources, marketing and distribution of farm commodities, exportation and importation of agricultural products, foreign aid, defense, reclamation, education, marketing and consumer cooperatives, social security, reciprocal trade agreements, transportation, and antitrust legislation." Lobbyist — Carl W. Ek.

FUR CONSERVATION INSTITUTE OF AMERICA, New York, N.Y. Lobbyist — Kiefer & Morrison, 805 15th St. N.W., Washington, D.C. 20005. Filed 1/8/82. Legislative interest — "Wildlife legislation: 16 U.S.C. section 1531 *et. seq.*; 16 U.S.C. section 701 *et. seq.*; 16 U.S.C. section 1361 *et. seq.*; Bankruptcy Act."

INVESTMENT COMPANY INSTITUTE, 1775 K St. N.W., Washington, D.C. 20006. Filed for self 1/8/82. Legislative interest — "...S 1424 ... S 1427 ... S 1720 ... S 1888 ... HR 1916 ... HR 2591 ... HR 2916 ... HR 3058 ... HR 3097 ... HR 3230 ... HR 3456 ... HR 2980 ... HR 4049 ... HR 5004 ... HR 5053...." Lobbyist — Julie Domenick.

MOTION PICTURE ASSOCIATION OF AMERICA, Washington, D.C. Lobbyist — Wexler and Associates Inc., 1616 H St. N.W., Washington, D.C. 20006. Filed 1/11/82. Legislative interest — "...to obtain passage, with amendments, of S 1758, to amend Title 17 of the U.S.C." Lobbyist — Hill and Knowlton Inc., 1425 K St. N.W., Washington, D.C. 20005. Filed 1/18/82. Legislative interest — "...changes in copyright law affecting videotaping, particularly S 1758...." Filed for self 1/18/82. Legislative interest — "...changes in the Copyright Act of 1976, as amended, HR 3528, HR 3560, HR 3844; antitrust legislation related to export trade, S 144, S 734, S 795, S 816, HR 1648, HR 1799, HR 2326, HR 2459, HR 2812; legislation that deals with a rewrite of the Communications Act of 1934, as amended; federal procurement of audiovisual materials; censorship of motion pictures and television programs; and miscellaneous tax bills. Betamax legislation (S 1758, HR 4783, HR 4794, HR 4808, HR 5250)...." Lobbyists — Fritz Attaway, Edward Cooper, John Giles, Nancy Thompson, Jack Valenti.

NATIONAL ASSOCIATION OF CROP INSURANCE AGENTS, Anoka, Minn. Lobbyist — Linda Vickers, 1706 23rd St. South, Arlington, Va. 22202. Filed 1/5/82. Legislative interest — Not specified.

NATIONAL ASSOCIATION OF FEDERAL CREDIT UNIONS, 1111 N. 19th St., Arlington, Va. 22209. Filed for self 1/10/82. Legislative interest — "...S 1607 ... S 1703 ... S 1720 ... S 1721 ... S 1406/HR 2501 ... S 2000/HR 4786 ... HR 4603...." Lobbyists — Mal Nestlerode, Michael G. Troop.

NATIONAL ASSOCIATION OF MANUFACTURERS, 1776 F St. N.W., Washington, D.C. 20006. Filed for self 1/8/82. Legislative interest — "General energy legislation, including but not limited to natural gas decontrol, synthetic fuels, energy taxes, coal conversion, energy conservation and commercialization of energy technologies." Lobbyist — Bonnie G. Bird.

NATIONAL CABLE TELEVISION ASSOCIATION INC., 1724 Massachusetts Ave. N.W., Washington, D.C. 20036. Filed for self 1/10/82. Legislative interest — "Amendments to the Communications Act of 1934...." Lobbyist — James B. Hedlund.

NATIONAL COAL CONSUMERS ALLIANCE, Minneapolis, Minn. Lobbyist — Rogers & Wells, 1666 K St. N.W., Washington, D.C. 20006. Filed 1/11/82. Legislative interest — "... to limit exorbitant state taxation of coal, specific legislative interest in the following bills: S 178, HR 1313."

NATIONAL FROZEN FOOD ASSOCIATION, Hershey, Pa. Lobbyist — Victoria R. Calvert, 600 Maryland Ave. S.W., Washington, D.C. 20005. Filed 1/20/82. Legislative interest — "Energy legislation."

NATIONAL HOME FURNISHINGS ASSOCIATION, 405 Merchandise Mart, Chicago, Ill. 60654. Filed for self 1/11/82. Legislative interest — "...tax bills, retail and consumer credit, interest rate deregulation, and Consumer Bankruptcy Reform legislation." Lobbyist — Vickie L. Erickson, 900 17th St. N.W., Washington, D.C. 20006.

NATIONAL OCEAN INDUSTRIES ASSOCIATION, 1050 17th St. N.W., Washington, D.C. 20036. Filed for self 1/6/82. Legislative interest — "...oceanography, conservation, development of natural resources, and environmental quality." Lobbyist — Phillip A. Clark.

NATIONAL UTILITY CONTRACTORS ASSOCIATION, 1235 Jefferson Davis Highway, Arlington, Va. 22202. Filed for self 1/12/82. Legislative interest — "All matters pertaining to the interests of small business and to water and sewer contracting, particularly the Clean Water Act." Lobbyists — William G. Harley, David F. McDermitt.

ORGANIZATION OF HEATER MANUFACTURERS, Franklin, Tenn. Lobbyist — Lord, Day & Lord, 1120 20th St. N.W., Washington, D.C. 20036. Filed 1/14/82. Legislative interest — "Implementation of the United States Generalized System of Preference for less developed countries under the provisions of the Trade Act of 1974."

RUBBER MANUFACTURERS ASSOCIATION, 1901 Pennsylvania Ave. N.W., Washington, D.C. 20006. Filed for self 1/6/82. Legislative interest — "...energy, environment, economics, product liability, and industrial relations." Lobbyist — Frank T. Ryan.

THE SECURITIES GROUPS, Washington, D.C. Lobbyist — C & B Associates, 1750 New York Ave. N.W., Washington, D.C. 20006. Filed 1/12/82. Legislative interest — "...commodity tax straddles amendment to tax bill S 626."

THE UNITED STATES CANTALOUPE GROWERS & IMPORTERS ASSOCIATION, Hidalgo, Texas. Lobbyist — Barnes, Richardson & Colburn, 1819 H St. N.W., Washington, D.C. 20006. Filed 1/14/82. Legislative interest — "...the elimination of the duty on cantaloupes which are imported during the period of the year when there is no domestic production of cantaloupes...."

Miscellaneous

MR. FAYE STEWART, Eugene, Ore. Lobbyist — Schwabe, Williamson, Wyatt, Moore & Roberts, 1000 Potomac St. N.W., Washington, D.C. 20007. Filed 1/11/82. (Former U.S. Rep. Robert B. Duncan, D-Ore., 1963-67, 1975-81, was listed as agent for this client.) Legislative interest — "Domestic preference in government contracts."

February Registrations

Citizens' Groups

ALLIANCE FOR JUSTICE, 600 New Jersey Ave. N.W., Washington, D.C. 20001. Filed for self 2/8/82. Legislative interest — "Regulatory reform legislation (S 1080) ... Legal Services Corporation reauthorization (HR 3480) ... limitations on awards of attorney's fees (S 585)...." Lobbyist — Nan Aron.

AMERICAN FRIENDS OF KIRYAT SANZ LANIADO HOSPITAL, New York, N.Y. Lobbyist — Whitman and Ransom, 522 Fifth Ave., New York, N.Y. 10036 and 1333 New Hampshire Ave. N.W., Washington, D.C. 20036. Filed 2/16/82. Legislative interest — "Legislation relating to the International Security and Development Cooperation Act."

CITIZEN/LABOR ENERGY COALITION, 1300 Connecticut Ave. N.W., Washington, D.C. 20036. Filed for self 2/4/82. Legislative interest — "...price controls on oil and gas, the formation of a public energy corporation, horizontal and vertical divestiture of the largest oil companies, the solar band and other conservation measures, adequate fuel assistance for low income persons, a federal oil import authority, establishment of an office of Special Prosecutor to investigate pricing and supply violations, and elimination of oil industry tax subsidies." Lobbyist — Michael Podhorzer.

COMMON CAUSE, 2030 M St. N.W., Washington, D.C. 20036. Filed for self 2/19/82. Legislative interest — "...S 509, HR 1986 ... HR 3603, S 884 ... S Res 20 ... HR 18 and S 10 ... S Res 58 and H J Res 10 ... S 708 ... S 895, HR 3112 ... HR 3471 ... HR 4144 ... S 939, HR 3480 ... S 1078 ... S 1760 ... S 1760, S 415, S 158, HR 900 ... S 193, HR 4882...." Lobbyists — Ellen Block, Alice Daniel, Don Simon.

EASTERN BAND OF CHEROKEE INDIANS, Cherokee, N.C. Lobbyist — Terrance J. Brown Associates, 1331 H St. N.W., Washington, D.C. 20005. Filed 2/16/82. Legislative interest — "Snyder Act, PL 93-638...."

EIGHTH PROLIFE CONGRESSIONAL DISTRICT ACTION COMMITTEE, 6308 Midnight Pass Road, Sarasota,

Fla. 33581. Filed for self 2/17/82. Legislative interest — "For passage of S J Res 110 (the Hatch Amendment) or other proposed Human Life Amendments." Lobbyist — S. C. Michaelis.

FOOD RESEARCH AND ACTION CENTER, 1319 F St. N.W., Washington, D.C. 20004. Filed for self 2/17/82. Legislative interest — "...all bills relating to the Food Stamp Act of 1964 ... National School Lunch Act ... Child Nutrition Act of 1966 ... surplus commodities and commodity donations legislation ... Title VII of the Older Americans Act of 1965 ... and portions of the Social Security Act." Lobbyists — Carolyn Brickey, Jack Mark Stolier.

FRIENDS OF THE COLUMBIA GORGE, 113 W. 1st, Vancouver, Wash. 98660. Filed for self 2/8/82. Legislative interest — Not specified. Lobbyist — Dave Cannard.

HELEN KELLER NATIONAL CENTER, Sands Point, N.Y. Lobbyist — Hoffheimer & Johnson, 1120 20th St. N.W., Washington, D.C. 20036. Filed 2/12/82. Legislative interest — "... Rehabilitation Act of 1973; HR 5191...."

HELP INC., 1400 S. Joyce St., Arlington, Va. 22202. Filed for self 2/26/82. Legislative interest — Not specified. Lobbyist — Robert S. Pelton.

MINIMUM TAX COALITION, Washington, D.C. Lobbyist — Gray and Co., 3255 Grace St. N.W., Washington, D.C. 20007. Filed 2/22/82. Legislative interest — "Including but not limited to corporate minimum tax on tax preferences."

NATIONAL ALLIANCE FOR HYDROELECTRIC ENERGY, Washington, D.C. Lobbyist — Thaxter, Lipez, Stevens, Broder & Micoleau, 1825 K St. N.W., Washington, D.C. 20006. Filed 2/5/82. Legislative interest — "...hydroelectric power generation and regulation."

NATIONAL PUBLIC RADIO, 2025 M St. N.W., Washington, D.C. 20036. Filed for self 2/16/82. Legislative interest — "...rescission for CPB [Corporation for Public Broadcasting]; S 720, Radio Deregulation Act of 1981; CPB appropriation for fiscal year 1985." Lobbyist — Bruce C. Wolpe.

NATIONAL SKEET SHOOTING ASSOCIATION, San Antonio, Texas. Lobbyist — Christopher L. Davis, 1920 N St. N.W., Washington, D.C. 20036. Filed 2/25/82. Legislative interest — "Matters of general interest to clay target shooting sports persons."

THE NATURE CONSERVANCY, Arlington, Va. Lobbyist — W. J. Chandler Associates, 1717 Massachusetts Ave. N.W., Washington, D.C. 20036. Filed 2/23/82. Legislative interest — "...wildlife and plant conservation, biological research, land conservation and management, federal activities affecting Conservancy programs or property, the tax status of non-profit organizations, tax incentives for land conservation, and natural resource inventory programs."

RED LAKE BAND OF CHIPPEWA INDIANS, Red Lake, Minn. Lobbyist — Terrance J. Brown Associates, 1331 H St. N.W., Washington, D.C. 20005. Filed 2/16/82. Legislative interest — "Snyder Act, PL 93-638...."

SIERRA CLUB, 530 Bush St., San Francisco, Calif. 94108. Filed for self 2/16/82. Legislative interest — "...regulatory reform ... clean air, clean water, hazardous materials, population growth...." Lobbyist — Judith Kunofsky.

UNITED SOUTH AND EASTERN TRIBES, Nashville, Tenn. Lobbyist — Terrance J. Brown Associates, 1331 H St. N.W., Washington, D.C. 20005. Filed 2/16/82. Legislative interest — "Snyder Act, PL 93-638...."

VOCATIONAL INDUSTRIAL CLUBS OF AMERICA INC., P.O. Box 3000, Leesburg, Va. 22075. Filed for self 2/25/82. Legislative interest — "Any legislation affecting vocational education." Lobbyist — Larry W. Johnson.

THE WILDERNESS SOCIETY, 1901 Pennsylvania Ave. N.W., Washington, D.C. 20006. Filed for self 2/10/82. Legislative interest — "Issues concerning Northwestern United States wilderness areas." Lobbyist — Jean Durning, 1424 Fourth Ave., Seattle, Wash. 98101.

WILDLIFE LEGISLATIVE FUND OF AMERICA, 50 W. Broad St., Columbus, Ohio 43215. Filed for self 2/19/82. Legislative interest — "Any legislation affecting hunting, fishing, trapping and wildlife management." Lobbyist — Carol Alice

Porter, 1050 17th St. N.W., Washington, D.C. 20036.

WOMEN'S LEGAL DEFENSE FUND, 2000 P St. N.W., Washington, D.C. 20036. Filed for self 2/17/82. Legislative interest — "...employment discrimination; equal education; domestic relations; and federal appointments." Lobbyists — Arkie Byrd, Meshall Thomas.

Corporations and Businesses

ALABAMA POWER CO., 600 N. 18th St., Birmingham, Ala. 35291. Filed for self 2/5/82. Legislative interest — "...amendments to Clean Air Act; waste management bills; and S 1080 regulatory reform." Lobbyist — Julian H. Smith Jr.

AMERICAN CYANAMID CO., Wayne, N.J. Lobbyists — Dawson Mathis and Associates, 6712 Old McLean Village Drive, McLean, Va. 22101. Filed 2/25/82. (Former U.S. Rep. Dawson Mathis, D-Ga., 1971-81, was listed as agent for this client.) Legislative interest — "All legislation affecting agricultural pesticides and other agriculture-related products of the company." Filed for self 2/25/82. Legislative interest — "Legislation affecting the welfare of the chemical, pharmaceutical and consumer products industries ... tax, economic, labor policies, government regulation of business, international commercial and economic policy." Lobbyist — St. Clair J. Tweedie, 1575 I St. N.W., Washington, D.C. 20005.

AMERICAN PRESIDENT LINES, Oakland, Calif. Lobbyist — Preston, Thorgrimson, Ellis & Holman, 1776 G St. N.W., Washington, D.C. 20006. Filed 2/23/82. Legislative interest — "Matters with respect to funding levels and programs authorized under the Merchant Marine Act, 1936, as amended. Fiscal year 1983 authorization and appropriation bills. Foreign taxation of U.S.-flag ocean carriers."

AM GENERAL INC., Washington, D.C. Lobbyist — Paul, Hastings, Janofksy & Walker, 1050 Thomas Jefferson St. N.W., Washington, D.C. 20007. Filed 2/12/82. Legislative interest — "Revision of Clean Air Act."

APPLE COMPUTER CORP., Cupertino, Calif. Lobbyist — Eric R. Fox, 1700 Pennsylvania Ave. N.W., Washington, D.C. 20006. Filed 2/22/82. Legislative interest — "Amendments to the Internal Revenue Code pertaining to charitable contributions of inventory."

BECHTEL POWER CORP., Gaithersburg, Md. Lobbyist — Charles W. Sandford, 11202 Farmland Drive, Rockville, Md. 20852. Filed 2/25/82. Legislative interest — Not specified.

BELRIDGE CAPITAL CORP., New York, N.Y. Lobbyist — Thomas L. Burgum & Associates, 499 South Capitol St. S.W., Washington, D.C. 20003. Filed 2/5/82. Legislative interest — "To monitor tax legislation."

BENEFICIAL MANAGEMENT CORPORATION OF AMERICA, Wilmington, Del. Lobbyist — C. B. Neely Jr., P.O. Box 829, Raleigh, N.C. 27602. Filed 2/26/82. Legislative interest — "S 2000, HR 4786."

CARMA-SANDLING GROUP, Irvine, Calif. Lobbyist — Jensen, Sanders & McConnell, 1200 N. Main St., Santa Ana, Calif. 9270l and 244 Maryland Ave. N.E., Washington, D.C. 20002. Filed 2/18/82. Legislative interest — "Housing and land development issues."

CENTRAL AND SOUTH WEST CORP., 2700 One Main Place, Dallas, Texas 75202-3963. Filed for self 2/3/82. Legislative interest — "The Clean Air Act...." Lobbyist — John L. Wood.

CENTRAL AND SOUTH WEST SERVICES INC., 2700 One Main Place, Dallas, Texas 75250. Filed for self 2/18/82. Legislative interest — "...Clean Air Act amendments ... Settlement Discounts Tax Act of 1981 ... amendments to Public Utility Holding Company Act of 1935 ... Coal Pipeline Act of 1981 ... nuclear waste legislation...." Lobbyist — Thomas M. Hagan, 1510 American Bank Tower, Austin, Texas 78701.

DAILY EXPRESS INC., Carlisle, Pa. Lobbyist — Baker & McKenzie, 815 Connecticut Ave. N.W., Washington, D.C. 20006. Filed 2/22/82. Legislative interest — "Technical amendment to Section 266 of the Economic Recovery Tax Act of 1981."

DEL SMITH & CO., 5218 Kings Park Drive, Springfield, Va. 22151. Filed for self 2/11/82. Legislative interest — "ADAP bill (aviation) ... highway bill." Lobbyist — Del Smith.

DIGITAL EQUIPMENT CORP., 111 Powdermill Road, Maynard, Mass. 01754. Filed for self 2/16/82. Legislative interest — "...legislation affecting the manufacture, sale and service of computers and associated peripheral equipment and related software and supplies." Lobbyist — Michael A. Aisenberg, 8300 Professional Place, Landover, Md. 20785.

DUTY FREE SHOPPERS LTD., Honolulu, Hawaii. Lobbyist — Patton, Boggs & Blow, 2550 M St. N.W., Washington, D.C. 20037. Filed 2/26/82. Legislative interest — "Customs Service Authorization Act. Support certain changes to reauthorization legislation relating to duty free bonded warehouses."

E. M. GRAVES & CO. INC., Southport, Conn. Lobbyist — Thomas L. Burgum & Associates, 499 South Capitol St. S.W., Washington, D.C. 20003. Filed 2/5/82. Legislative interest — "Monitor tax legislation ... the FmHA B & I and other guaranteed loan programs."

FIRST NATIONAL MONETARY CORP., Southfield, Mich. Lobbyist — Simon, Deitch, Siefman & Tucker, 4000 Town Center, Southfield, Mich. 48075. Filed 2/25/82. Legislative interest — "...trading of commodity futures and the Commodity Futures Trading Commission, HR 5447 and S 2109."

FRUITDALE TELEPHONE CO., Peakesville, Miss. Lobbyist — Thomas L. Burgum & Associates, 499 South Capitol St. S.W., Washington, D.C. 20003. Filed 2/5/82. Legislative interest — "...the Rural Electrification Administration."

GATX TERMINALS CORP., Chicago, Ill. Lobbyist — Vinson & Elkins, 1101 Connecticut Ave. N.W., Washington, D.C. 20036. Filed 2/11/82. Legislative interest — "Clean Air Act amendments, HR 5252."

GEOSOURCE INC., Houston, Texas. Lobbyist — Baker & McKenzie, 815 Connecticut Ave. N.W., Washington, D.C. 20006. Filed 2/23/82. Legislative interest — "Technical amendment to Section 422A of the Economic Recovery Tax Act of 1981."

GETTY OIL CO., 3810 Wilshire Blvd., Los Angeles, Calif. 90010. Filed for self 2/12/82. Legislative interest — "...tax legislation, windfall profit tax, Strategic Petroleum Reserve, synfuels legislation, petroleum divestiture (HR 1362, S 326), superfund (HR 85 and S 681), clean air (HR 1817, HR 2219 and S 63)." Lobbyist — Robert N. Borens, 1701 Pennsylvania Ave. N.W., Washington, D.C. 20006.

THE GOODYEAR TIRE AND RUBBER CO., 1144 E. Market St., Akron, Ohio 44316. Filed for self 2/18/82. Legislative interest — "...the Regulatory Reform Act of 1981, product liability legislation, changes to the Clean Air and Clean Water Acts." Lobbyist — Isabel E. Hyde, 1800 K St. N.W., Washington, D.C. 20006.

GOVERNMENT RESEARCH & DEVELOPMENT CORP., Washington, D.C., and Blanco, Texas. Lobbyist — Birch, Horton, Bittner and Monroe, 1140 Connecticut Ave. N.W., Washington, D.C. 20036. Filed 2/24/82. Legislative interest — "Enactment of gross income tax system and a study of problems relating to implementation of a gross income tax system."

ILLINOIS BELL TELEPHONE CO., Chicago, Ill. Lobbyist — C. G. Pete Milligan, 4360 N.E. Joe's Point, Stuart, Fla. 33494. Filed 2/24/82. Legislative interest — "...legislation affecting the communications industry, including corporate, financial, and tax issues (e.g., HR 1524)."

INLAND STEEL CORP., Chicago, Ill. Lobbyist — Charls E. Walker Associates Inc., 1730 Pennsylvania Ave. N.W., Washington, D.C. 20006. Filed 2/4/82. Legislative interest — "...refundability of the investment tax credit, or items relating to taxation of leasing transactions."

JOHN ADAMS ASSOCIATES, 1825 K St. N.W., Washington, D.C. 20006. Filed for self 2/8/82. Legislative interest — "Preservation and strengthening of the Clean Air Act, pro-consumer legislation ... and establishment of a non-commercial home use exemption for consumer use of video cassette recorders." Lobbyist — Peter H. Kostmayer (Former U.S. rep., D-Pa., 1977-81.).

LOYAL TRUST, Dallas, Texas. Lobbyist — Sutherland, Asbill & Brennan, 1666 K St. N.W., Washington, D.C. 20006. Filed 2/24/82. Legislative interest — "Legislation to make technical

corrections to Section 6166 of the Internal Revenue Code."

MERRILL LYNCH & CO., New York, N.Y. Lobbyist — Rogers & Wells, 200 Park Ave., New York, N.Y. 10166. Filed 2/9/82. Legislative interest — "Erisa legislation generally and S 1541, Retirement Income Incentives and Administrative Simplification Act of 1981, specifically."

NATIONAL BASKETBALL ASSOCIATION, New York, N.Y. Lobbyist — Baraff, Koerner, Olender & Hochberg, 2033 M St. N.W., Washington, D.C. 20036. Filed 2/8/82. Legislative interest — ". . .legislation dealing with sports."

NATIONAL FOOTBALL LEAGUE, New York, N.Y. Lobbyists — Akin, Gump, Strauss, Hauer & Field, 1333 New Hampshire Ave. N.W., Washington, D.C. 20036. Filed 2/9/82. Wexler and Associates Inc., 1616 H St. N.W., Washington, D.C. 20006. Filed 2/23/82. Legislative interest — ". . .including but not limited to the application of the antitrust laws to professional sports."

NATIONAL GYPSUM CO., Dallas, Texas. Lobbyist — Foley & Lardner, 777 E. Wisconsin Ave., Milwaukee, Wis. 53202. Filed 2/1/82. Legislative interest — ". . .non-navigability determination."

NATIONAL STEEL CORP., Pittsburgh, Pa. Lobbyist — Charls E. Walker Associates Inc., 1730 Pennsylvania Ave. N.W., Washington, D.C. 20006. Filed 2/4/82. Legislative interest — ". . .refundability of the investment tax credit, or items relating to taxation of leasing transactions."

NORTH AMERICAN SOCCER LEAGUE, New York, N.Y. Lobbyist — Baraff, Koerner, Olender & Hochberg, 2033 M St. N.W., Washington, D.C. 20036. Filed 2/8/82. Legislative interest — ". . .legislation dealing with sports."

NORTHWEST PIPELINE CORP., 315 E. 200 South, Salt Lake City, Utah 84110. Filed for self 2/3/82. Legislative interest — ". . .natural gas policy." Lobbyist — Judy M. Sullivan, 1120 20th St. N.W., Washington, D.C. 20036.

THE PROCTER & GAMBLE CO., Cincinnati, Ohio. Lobbyist — George D. Carpenter, 7162 Reading Road, Cincinnati, Ohio 45222. Filed 2/11/82. Legislative interest — "To amend the Clean Air Act. . . ."

PUBLICKER INDUSTRIES INC., Greenwich, Conn. Lobbyist — Thomas L. Burgum & Associates, 499 South Capitol St. S.W., Washington, D.C. 20003. Filed 2/5/82. Legislative interest — "To seek repeal of the surcharge on imported alcohol and to promote the passage of HR 1989 and S 1843."

REFRIGERATED TRANSPORT INC., Forest Park, Ga. Lobbyist — Dawson Mathis and Associates, 6712 Old McLean Village Drive, McLean, Va. 22101. Filed 2/16/82. (Former U. S. Rep. Dawson Mathis, D-Ga., 1971-81, was listed as agent for this client.) Legislative interest — "Trucking and related business."

REPUBLIC STEEL CORP., Cleveland, Ohio. Lobbyist — Charls E. Walker Associates Inc., 1730 Pennsylvania Ave. N.W., Washington, D.C. 20006. Filed 2/4/82. Legislative interest — ". . .refundability of the investment tax credit, or items relating to taxation of leasing transactions."

ROADWAY EXPRESS INC., 1501 Wilson Blvd., Arlington, Va. 22209. Filed for self 2/17/82. Legislative interest — "Trucking, taxes, general business; S 1402 (for), S 1748 (for), HR 5223 (for)." Lobbyist — Timothy P. Lynch.

SAFT AMERICA INC., Valdosta, Ga. Lobbyist — Dawson Mathis and Associates, 6712 Old McLean Village Drive, McLean, Va. 22101. Filed 2/16/82. (Former U.S. Rep. Dawson Mathis, D-Ga., 1971-81, was listed as agent for this client.) Legislative interest — "Procurement of military equipment and supplies and related matters."

SANDOZ INC., Route 10, East Hanover, N.J. Filed for self 2/11/82. Legislative interest — "Health care related issues; national health insurance; patent term restoration, HR 1937." Lobbyist — Herbert Allen Ailsworth, 1050 17th St. N.W., Washington, D.C. 20036.

SENECA AND ASSOCIATES INC., Washington, D.C. Lobbyist — Beard and Associates, P.O. Box 2394, Columbia, Md. 21045. Filed 2/26/82. Legislative interest — ". . .revisions in reclamation laws dealing with the prohibition against growing certain crops (HR 5539); revisions in federal oil shale leasing programs (S

1484); appropriations for Indian water resource development through the Department of Interior and related agencies appropriations bill for fiscal year 1983."

SCHOENEMAN INC., New York, N.Y. Lobbyist — Paul Tendler Associates Inc., 1899 L St. N.W., Washington, D.C. 20036. Filed 2/26/82. Legislative interest — ". . .domestic economic matters and international trade."

SONY CORPORATION OF AMERICA, 9 West 57th St., New York, N.Y. 10019. Lobbyist — McNair, Glenn, Konduros, Corley, Singletary, Porter & Dibble, 1155 15th St. N.W., Washington, D.C. 20005. Filed 2/4/82. Legislative interest — "S 1758." Filed for self 2/4/82. Legislative interest — ". . .amend Title 10 of the U.S. Code - S 1758 . . . S 1242 . . . HR 4783 . . . HR 4808 . . . HR 5250 . . . amend Internal Revenue Code of 1954 - HR 1983 . . . S 655." Lobbyist — Sadami Wada.

SOUTHERN SHIPBUILDING CORP., Slidell, La. Lobbyist — Kirkpatrick, Lockhart, Hill, Christopher & Phillips, 1900 M St. N.W., Washington, D.C. 20036. Filed 2/9/82. Legislative interest — "Amendments to Longshoremen's & Harbor Workers' Compensation Act Section 1182. . . ."

SPACE SERVICES INC., P.O. Box 4, Houston, Texas 77001. Filed for self 2/16/82. Legislative interest — "Regulation of private outer space ventures. . . ." Lobbyist — Charles M. Chafer, 2550 M St. N.W., Washington, D.C. 20037.

SQUIBB CORP., 40 West 57th St., New York, N.Y. 10019. Filed for self 2/18/82. Legislative interest — ". . .health and tax matters." Lobbyist — John G. Ryan, 1700 K St. N.W., Washington, D.C. 20006.

TOYOTA MOTOR CO. LTD., Aichi-Ken, Japan. Lobbyist — Rivkin, Sherman and Levy, 900 17th St. N.W., Washington, D.C. 20006. Filed 2/19/82. Legislative interest — "Amendments to the Clean Air Act . . . passive restraint and auto safety legislation (including S 1887, S 1676, HR 3183, HR 3184, HR 3237, HR 3151)."

UNITED CALIFORNIA BANK, Los Angeles, Calif. Lobbyist — Stuart A. Lewis, 1919 Pennsylvania Ave. N.W., Washington, D.C. 20006. Filed 2/17/82. Legislative interest — "HR 4986."

VISA U.S.A. INC., P.O. Box 8999, San Francisco, Calif. 94128. Filed for self 2/18/82. Legislative interest — "Legislation and regulation of retail banking services and the telecommunication systems needed to provide these services." Lobbyist — Louise L. Roseman, 1620 I St. N.W., Washington, D.C. 20006.

WARNER COMMUNICATIONS INC., New York, N.Y. Lobbyist — Gray and Co., 3255 Grace St. N.W., Washington, D.C. 20007. Filed 2/22/82. Legislative interest — "Including but not limited to home taping legislation."

WEST TEXAS UTILITIES CO., P.O. Box 841, Abilene, Texas. Filed for self 2/2/82. Legislative interest — Not specified. Lobbyist — Don Welch.

WESTERN AIRLINES, Los Angeles, Calif. Lobbyist — Jack Ferguson Associates Inc., 203 Maryland Ave. N.E., Washington, D.C. 20002. Filed 2/11/82. Legislative interest — "Air transportation policy. . . ."

Labor Groups

COMMITTEE FOR FARMWORKER PROGRAMS, Washington, D.C. Lobbyist — Boasberg, Klores, Feldesman & Tucker, 2101 L St. N.W., Washington, D.C. 20037. Filed 2/5/82. Legislative interest — "All legislation affecting farm workers, and particularly reauthorization of Section 303 of CETA."

FEDERAL EMPLOYEES POLITICAL ACTION COMMITTEE, 210 7th St. S.E., Washington, D.C. 20003. Filed for self 2/4/82. Legislative interest — Not specified. Lobbyist — Dennis M. Reardon.

NATIONAL TREASURY EMPLOYEES UNION, 1730 K St. N.W., Washington, D.C. 20006. Filed for self 2/8/82. Legislative interest — ". . .legislation dealing with employment conditions, compensation, retirement and other matters affecting Federal employees and annuitants." Lobbyist — Patrick F. Smith Jr.

TEAMSTERS LOCAL 959, Anchorage, Alaska. Lobbyist — Birch, Horton, Bittner and Monroe, 1140 Connecticut Ave.

N.W., Washington, D.C. 20036. Filed 2/24/82. Legislative interest — "Transportation excise tax bill, S 2075; Alaska Railroad bill, S 1500."

State and Local Governments

ADAMS COUNTY, Brighton, Colo. Lobbyist — Webster & Sheffield, 1200 New Hampshire Ave. N.W., Washington, D.C. 20036. Filed 2/16/82. Legislative interest — "Airport and Airways Development Act and Department of Transportation appropriation bills; S 508 and HR 2643."

COUNCIL OF STATE HOUSING AGENCIES, Washington, D.C. Lobbyist — Gray and Co., 3255 Grace St. N.W., Washington, D.C. 20007. Filed 2/2/82. Legislative interest — "Including but not limited to tax exempt revenue bonds."

SENECA COUNTY, Waterloo, N.Y. Lobbyist — Hale and Dorr, 1201 Pennsylvania Ave. N.W., Washington, D.C. 20004. Filed 2/9/82. Legislative interest — "Legislation affecting Indian land claims made in the eastern United States which may involve Seneca County's interests."

TOWN OF MASHPEE, Mashpee, Mass. Lobbyist — Hale and Dorr, 1201 Pennsylvania Ave. N.W., Washington, D.C. 20004. Filed 2/19/82. Legislative interest — "Legislation affecting Indian land claims made in the eastern United States which may involve the town of Mashpee's interests."

Trade Associations

AMERICAN ASSOCIATION OF HOMES FOR THE AGING, Washington, D.C. Lobbyist — Lawrence S. Hoffheimer, 1120 20th St. N.W., Washington, D.C. 20036. Filed 2/12/82. Legislative interest — "Medicare/Medicaid long-term care amendments, housing for elderly legislation, Older Americans Act and social service programs...."

AMERICAN BAR ASSOCIATION, 1155 E. 60th St., Chicago, Ill. 60637. Filed for self 2/8/82. Legislative interest — Not specified. Lobbyist — Irene R. Emsellem, 1800 M St. N.W., Washington, D.C. 20036.

AMERICAN BUSINESS CONFERENCE, 1025 Connecticut Ave. N.W., Washington, D.C. 20036. Filed for self 2/11/82. Legislative interest — "... tax and regulatory reform legislation for high-growth, mid-range business organizations ... the Reagan tax program." Lobbyists — Patricia A. Jeffers, Nancy A. Nagy.

AMERICAN CONGRESS ON SURVEYING & MAPPING, 210 Little Falls St., Falls Church, Va. 22046. Filed for self 2/10/82. Legislative interest — "(HR 4399/S 706) Federal Land Survey Act, (HR 4000/S 1153) Surface Mining Control and Reclamation Act of 1977...." Lobbyist — John M. Palatiello.

AMERICAN FEED MANUFACTURERS ASSOCIATION, 1701 N. Fort Myer Drive, Arlington, Va. 22209. Filed for self 2/10/82. Legislative interest — "...S 1080 regulatory reform, S 1442 food safety, HR 5252 Clean Air Act amendments, and H J Res 305 animal husbandry studies." Lobbyist — Steven L. Kopperud.

AMERICAN PETROLEUM INSTITUTE, Washington, D.C. Lobbyist — McNair, Glenn, Konduros, Corley, Singletary, Porter & Dibble, 1155 15th St. N.W., Washington, D.C. 20005. Filed 2/8/82. Legislative interest — "S 326."

AMERICAN SOCIETY OF ASSOCIATION EXECUTIVES, 1575 I St. N.W., Washington, D.C. 20005. Filed for self 2/4/82. Legislative interest — "...HR 990 tax reform act for associations; revisions of Federal Election Commission regulations." Lobbyist — Robert H. Steel.

AMERICAN SOCIETY OF PHOTOGRAMMETRY, 210 Little Falls St., Falls Church, Va. 22046. Filed for self 2/10/82. Legislative interest — "(HR 4399/S 706) Federal Land Survey Act, (HR 4000/S 1153) Surface Mining Control and Reclamation Act of 1977...." Lobbyist — John M. Palatiello.

ASSOCIATED BUILDERS AND CONTRACTORS, 444 North Capitol St. N.W., Washington, D.C. 20001. Filed for self 2/16/82. Legislative interest — Not specified. Lobbyist — Ellen B. Brown.

THE BUSINESS ROUNDTABLE, Washington, D.C. Lobbyist — McNair, Glenn, Konduros, Corley, Singletary, Porter & Dibble, 1155 15th St. N.W., Washington, D.C. 20005. Filed 2/4/82. Legislative interest — "S 995."

COMMITTEE FOR TITLE XI VESSEL FINANCING, Washington, D.C. Lobbyist — O'Brien & Fierce, 1828 L St. N.W., Washington, D.C. 20036. Filed 2/19/82. Legislative interest — "Increase Title XI loan guarantee authority of Maritime Administration from $12 billion to $15 billion."

COMMUNICATION INDUSTRIES ASSOCIATION OF JAPAN, Tokyo, Japan. Lobbyist — Anderson, Hibey, Nauheim & Blair, 1605 New Hampshire Ave. N.W., Washington, D.C. 20009. Filed 2/19/82. Legislative interest — "Opposition to sectoral trade reciprocity legislation affecting the communications industry, including HR 5158."

COMPETITIVE TELECOMMUNICATIONS COALITION, Washington, D.C. Lobbyists — O'Connor & Hannan, 1919 Pennsylvania Ave. N.W., Washington, D.C. 20006. Filed 2/16/82; Pierson, Ball & Dowd, 1200 18th St. N.W., Washington, D.C. 20036. Filed 2/16/82; Williams & Jensen, 1101 Connecticut Ave. N.W., Washington, D.C. 20036. Filed 2/12/82. Legislative interest — "...telecommunications industry."

FOOD MARKETING INSTITUTE, 1750 K St. N.W., Washington, D.C. 20006. Filed for self 2/12/82. Legislative interest — Not specified. Lobbyists — Lars E. Peterson, William F. Sutherland.

GEORGIA AGRICULTURAL COMMODITY COMMISSION FOR PEANUTS, Tifton, Ga. Lobbyist — Dawson Mathis and Associates, 6712 Old McLean Village Drive, McLean, Va. 22101. Filed 2/16/82. (Former U.S. Rep. Dawson Mathis, D-Ga., 1971-81, was listed as agent for this client.) Legislative interest — "Peanut and peanut product legislation."

GROCERY MANUFACTURERS OF AMERICA, Washington, D.C. Lobbyist — Kirkpatrick, Lockhart, Hill, Christopher & Phillips, 1900 M St. N.W., Washington, D.C. 20036. Filed 2/8/82. Legislative interest — "Sodium labeling; in support of HR 5160 and opposition to HR 4031."

HAWAIIAN SUGAR PLANTERS' ASSOCIATION, Aiea, Hawaii. Filed for self 2/10/82. Legislative interest — Not specified. Lobbyist — Elin Peltz, 1511 K St. N.W., Washington, D.C. 20005.

HOME RECORDING RIGHTS COALITION, Washington, D.C. Lobbyist — Mintz, Levin, Cohn, Ferris, Glovsky & Popeo, 1015 15th St. N.W., Washington, D.C. 20005. Filed 2/8/82. Legislative interest — "Exemption from copyright infringement for home recording of over-the-air video programs for non-commercial use."

INTERNATIONAL DISTRICT HEATING ASSOCIATION, Washington, D.C. Lobbyist — Buchanan, Ingersoll, Rodewald, Kyle & Buerger, 1735 I St. N.W., Washington, D.C. 20006. Filed 2/22/82. Legislative interest — "District Heating and Cooling Tax Incentives Act...."

JAPAN FISHERIES ASSOCIATION, Tokyo, Japan. Lobbyist — Garvey, Schubert, Adams & Barer, Bank of California Center, Seattle, Wash. 98164. Filed 2/16/82. Legislative interest — "S 1669, HR 5002...."

NATIONAL ASSOCIATION OF REALTORS, Washington, D.C. Lobbyist — McNair, Glenn, Konduros, Corley, Singletary, Porter & Dibble, 1155 15th St. N.W., Washington, D.C. 20005. Filed 2/9/82. Legislative interest — Not specified.

PHARMACEUTICAL MANUFACTURERS ASSOCIATION, Washington, D.C. Lobbyists — Barbara S. Blaine and John David Reaves, 910 16th St. N.W., Washington, D.C. 20006. Filed 2/12/82. Legislative interest — "The Patent Term Restoration Act of 1981, HR 1937...." Lobbyist — McNair, Glenn, Konduros, Corley, Singletary, Porter & Dibble, 1155 15th St. N.W., Washington, D.C. 20005. Filed 2/14/82. Legislative interest — "...Patent Term Restoration Act, S 225, HR 1937...."

RECORDING INDUSTRY OF AMERICA INC., New York, N.Y. Lobbyist — Williams & Jensen, 1101 Connecticut Ave. N.W., Washington, D.C. 20036. Filed 2/24/82. Legislative interest — "Copyright law particularly concerning *Universal City Studio Inc. v. Sony Corp. of America.*"

SERVICE STATION DEALERS OF AMERICA, Washington, D.C. Lobbyist — Price & Glover, 1001 Connecticut Ave. N.W., Washington, D.C. 20036. Filed 2/17/82. Legislative interest — "S 326 and HR 1362...."

Miscellaneous

THE BELZ INSTITUTE OF ISRAEL, Brooklyn, N.Y. Lobbyist — Whitman & Ransom, 522 Fifth Ave., New York, N.Y. 10036 and 1333 New Hampshire Ave. N.W., Washington, D.C. 20036. Filed 2/16/82. Legislative interest — "...the International Security and Development Cooperation Act."

March Registrations

Citizens' Groups

ALLIANCE OF THIRD CLASS NON-PROFIT MAILERS, Washington, D.C. Lobbyist — James M. Hanley and Associates, 1301 Pennsylvania Ave. N.W., Washington, D.C. 20004. Filed 3/5/82. (Former U.S. Rep. James M. Hanley, D-N.Y., 1965-81, was listed as agent for this client.) Legislative interest — Not specified.

CHRISTIAN VOICE MORAL GOVERNMENT FUND, 418 C St. N.E., Washington, D.C. 20002. Filed for self 3/15/82. Legislative interest — "...moral issues that would have an impact on the religious communities; i.e.: support for school prayer and anti-abortion legislation." Lobbyist — A. Donald Evans.

NATIONAL TAX LIMITATION COMMITTEE, 1523 L St. N.W., Washington, D.C. 20005. Filed for self 3/18/82. Legislative interest — "Constitutional Amendment limiting federal spending (S J Res 58, H J Res 350)." Lobbyist — Lewis K. Uhler, P.O. Box 513, Loomis, Calif. 95650.

THE REDUCE OUR DEBT FOUNDATION, P.O. Box 29021, 2645 E. Washington, Phoenix, Ariz. 85038. Filed for self 3/18/82. Legislative interest — "Selling of federally held lands to reduce the national debt." Lobbyists — Fred Hervey, Robert E. Hutchinson, Jill A. Moline.

SIERRA CLUB, 228 East 45th St., New York, N.Y. 10017. Filed for self 3/3/82. Legislative interest — "Ocean dumping and ports aspects of waterway and water resources issues." Lobbyist — Michael N. Garabedian.

UNITED STATES STUDENT ASSOCIATION, 2000 P St. N.W., Washington, D.C. 20036. Filed for self 3/8/82. Legislative interest — "...student financial aid; educational opportunities for disadvantaged students, women, minorities, and disabled students; Selective Service registration; and access to government documents and information (Freedom of Information Act)." Lobbyist — Edward R. Hanley.

Corporations and Businesses

AGRIGENETICS CORP., Denver, Colo. Lobbyist — Fried, Frank, Harris, Shriver & Kampelman, 600 New Hampshire Ave. N.W., Washington, D.C. 20037. Filed 3/15/82. Legislative interest — "...to amend the Internal Revenue Code of 1954, subsection 1235, as amended."

AIRCO INC., Montvale, N.J. Lobbyist — McNair, Glenn, Konduros, Corley, Singletary, Porter & Dibble, Bankers Trust Towers, Columbia, S.C. Filed 3/8/82. Legislative interest — "S 255...."

ALARM DEVICE MANUFACTURING CO., Syosset, N.Y. Lobbyist — Harris Communications Inc., 80 Trowbridge St., Cambridge, Mass. 02138. Filed 3/9/82. Legislative interest — "S 898; HR 5158...."

AM GENERAL CORP., 14250 Plymouth Road, Detroit, Mich. 48232. Filed for self 3/4/82. Legislative interest — "General automotive and military related legislation including such interests as federal budgets, Clean Air Act and foreign assistance

legislation." Lobbyists — Frank S. Besson III, Fred C. Fielding, 1129 20th St. N.W., Washington, D.C. 20036.

AMERICAN EXPRESS CO., Washington, D.C. Lobbyist — Patton, Boggs & Blow, 2550 M St. N.W., Washington, D.C. 20037. Filed 3/8/82. Legislative interest — "S 2198, the tax compliance bill. Against section pertaining to reporting of charge card tips."

AMERICAN HOECHST CORP., Route 202-206 North, Somerville, N.J. 08876. Filed for self 3/4/82. Legislative interest — "...Clean Air Act Amendments; Clean Water Act Amendments; natural gas deregulation; product liability legislation; patent legislation; trade legislation; food safety legislation." Lobbyist — Jay T. Scheck Jr., 1101 Connecticut Ave. N.W., Washington, D.C. 20036.

BECKEL, FINCHEM, TORRICELLI & ASSOCIATES, 1731 21st St. N.W., Washington, D.C. 20009. Filed for self 3/9/82. Legislative interest — "HR 5158, The Telecommunications Act of 1981." Lobbyist — Robert G. Beckel.

BELCHER TOWING CO., Miami, Fla. Lobbyist — Ginsburg, Feldman, Wail and Bress, 1700 Pennsylvania Ave. N.W., Washington, D.C. 20006. Filed 3/8/82. Legislative interest — "To oppose the imposition of increased fees on users of inland waterways and deep-draft ports and harbors; ...S 809; S 810; S 169; HR 2959; HR 2962."

BURLINGTON NORTHERN INC., Seattle, Wash. Lobbyist — Perkins, Coie, Stone, Olsen & Williams, 1110 Vermont Ave. N.W., Washington, D.C. 20005. Filed 3/19/82. Legislative interest — "...the natural resources and energy areas."

THE CIRCLE K CORP., P.O. Box 20230, 4500 S. 40th St., Phoenix, Ariz. 85036. Filed for self 3/18/82. Legislative interest — "All pieces of legislation which could affect the convenience store industry." Lobbyists — Fred Hervey, Robert E. Hutchinson, Jill A. Moline.

COMMUNICATIONS SATELLITE CORP., 950 L'Enfant Plaza S.W., Washington, D.C. 20024. Filed for self 3/11/82. Legislative interest — "...HR 1957, the International Communications Reorganization Act of 1981 and S 271, the International Record Carrier Competition Act of 1981." Lobbyist — Robert E. Bernier.

CONTROL DATA CORP., P.O. Box O, 8100 34th Ave. S., Minneapolis, Minn. 55440. Filed for self 3/2/82. Legislative interest — "...trade, regulatory agencies and taxation." Lobbyists — James F. Hogg, Lois D. Rice, 1201 Pennsylvania Ave. N.W., Washington, D.C. 20004.

CSX CORP., Richmond, Va. Lobbyist — Collier, Shannon, Rill & Scott, 1055 Thomas Jefferson St. N.W., Washington, D.C. 20007. Filed 3/3/82. Legislative interest — "Antitrust legislation including ... HR 1242 and ... S 995...."

DEMINEX U.S. OIL CO., Lock Box 340, Plaza of the Americas, North Tower, Dallas, Texas 75201. Lobbyist — Kilgore & Kilgore Inc., 1800 First National Bank Building, Dallas, Texas 75202. Filed 3/12/82. Legislative interest — "...legislation ... to amend subsection 613A(d)(4) of the Internal Revenue Code to exclude foreign refining from the definition of the refining of crude oil." Filed for self 3/12/82. Legislative interest — "...legislation ... to amend subsection 613A(d)(4) of the Internal Revenue Code to exclude foreign refining from the definition of the refining of crude oil." Lobbyist — Wolfgang Reinecke.

DESERT PALACE INC., Las Vegas, Nev. Lobbyist — Rogers & Wells, 200 Park Ave., New York, N.Y. 10166. Filed 3/17/82. Legislative interest — "...HR 4592...."

DOW CHEMICAL CO., Washington, D.C. Lobbyist — Beveridge & Diamond, 1333 New Hampshire Ave. N.W., Washington, D.C. 20036. Filed 3/10/82. Legislative interest — "Congressional action affecting the Clean Air Act."

DOW CORNING CO., Midland, Mich. Lobbyist — Ropes & Gray, 1200 New Hampshire Ave. N.W., Washington, D.C. 20036. Filed 3/1/82. Legislative interest — "Increase protection of confidential business information from disclosure under Freedom of Information Act; S 1730...."

DGA INTERNATIONAL INC., Washington, D.C. Lobbyist — Gale W. McGee Associates, 1201 Pennsylvania Ave. N.W., Washington, D.C. 20004. Filed 3/24/82. (Former U.S. Sen. Gale W.

McGee, D-Wyo., 1959-77, was listed as agent for this client.) Legislative interest — "...Caribbean Basin program."

ENERGY RESEARCH CORP., Danbury, Conn. Lobbyist — Patton, Boggs & Blow, 2550 M St. N.W., Washington, D.C. 20037. Filed 3/26/82. Legislative interest — "Fiscal year 1983 DOE [Department of Energy] appropriations. In favor of increased appropriations for fuel cells program."

FARMLAND INDUSTRIES INC., Kansas City, Mo. Lobbyist — Stinson, Mag & Fizzell, 2100 CharterBank Center, Kansas City, Mo. 64105. Filed 3/10/82. Legislative interest — "ERISA matters, PL 93-406...."

FEDERAL NATIONAL MORTGAGE ASSOCIATION, Washington, D.C. Lobbyist — Powell, Goldstein, Frazer & Murphy, 1110 Vermont Ave. N.W., Washington, D.C. 20005. Filed 3/22/82. Legislative interest — "...banking and housing legislation."

FLORIDA EAST COAST RAILWAY CO., St. Augustine, Fla. Lobbyist — Smathers, Symington & Herlong, 1700 K St. N.W., Washington, D.C. 20006. Filed 3/29/82. Legislative interest — "Legislation affecting small railroads...."

GATX CORP., Chicago, Ill. Lobbyist — Mayer, Brown & Platt, 888 17th St. N.W., Washington, D.C. 20006. Filed 3/9/82. Legislative interest — "...amendments to the Internal Revenue Code."

GENERAL PUBLIC UTILITIES CORP., 100 Interpace Parkway, Parsippany, N.J. 07054. Lobbyist — Perkins, Coie, Stone, Olsen & Williams, 1110 Vermont Ave. N.W., Washington, D.C. 20005. Filed 3/19/82. Legislative interest — "Legislation affecting nuclear plant operation." Filed for self 3/15/82. Legislative interest — "Proposed legislation to facilitate the funding of decontamination and cleanup expenses resulting from the accident at Three Mile Island nuclear generating station, Unit No. 2." Lobbyist — B. H. Cherry.

HALLMARK CARDS INC., 25th & McGee, Kansas City, Mo. 64108. Filed for self 3/29/82. Legislative interest — "...postal and communications matters...." Lobbyist — Christopher E. Clouser.

HAYES INC., Port Arthur, Texas. Lobbyist — Kutak, Rock & Huie, 1101 Connecticut Ave. N.W., Washington, D.C. 20036. Filed 3/31/82. Legislative interest — "Tax matters affecting industrial development bonds."

HOUSTON NATURAL GAS CORP., 1700 N. Moore St., Arlington, Va. 22209. Filed for self 3/15/82. Legislative interest — "S 2074, Natural Gas Production & Market Adjustment Act of 1982; HR 5252, amendment to the Clean Air Act; S 810, The Waterways User Tax; S 2027, study of causes and effect of acid rain; and HR 4230, coal slurry pipelines." Lobbyist — Terence H. Thorn.

IFG LEASING CO., 511 Central Ave., Great Falls, Mont. 59403. Filed for self 3/2/82. Legislative interest — "Amendments to the Internal Revenue Code, including proposals affecting safe harbor leasing and the minimum tax." Lobbyist — Mark A. Clark.

INTERNATIONAL FUTURES EXCHANGE (BERMUDA) LTD., Hamilton, Bermuda. Lobbyist — Pierson, Ball & Dowd, 1200 18th St. N.W., Washington, D.C. 20036. Filed 3/3/82. Legislative interest — "...the Futures Trading Act of 1982; S 2109 and HR 5467."

INTEX HOLDINGS (BERMUDA) LTD., Hamilton, Bermuda. Lobbyist — Pierson, Ball & Dowd, 1200 18th St. N.W., Washington, D.C. 20036. Filed 3/3/82. Legislative interest — "...the Futures Trading Act of 1982; S 2109 and HR 5467."

THE JOURNAL CO., Milwaukee, Wis. Lobbyists — H. Stewart Dunn Jr., Steven S. Snider, 1700 Pennsylvania Ave. N.W., Washington, D.C. 20006. Filed 3/31/82. Legislative interest — "...the interest deduction limitation under Section 163(d) of the Internal Revenue Code."

KIAWAH ISLAND CO., P.O. Box 12910, Charleston, S.C. 29142. Filed for self 3/16/82. Legislative interest — "...federal flood insurance and coastal barriers ... S 1018 and HR 3252, 42 United States Code, Chapter 50...." Lobbyists — W. Allen Ball, Mark Permar.

THE LEAFFER CO. INC., Sherborn, Mass. Lobbyist — Jim Casey, 3470 Mildred Drive, Falls Church, Va. 22042. Filed

3/18/82. Legislative interest — "...development of hydroelectric power."

THE LONDON GOLD FUTURES MARKET, London, England. Lobbyist — Arnold & Porter, 1200 New Hampshire Ave. N.W., Washington, D.C. 20036. Filed 3/18/82. Legislative interest — "HR 5447 ... S 2109 ... and other legislation relating to United States regulation of commodities sales."

THE LONDON INTERNATIONAL FINANCIAL FUTURES EXCHANGE LTD., London, England. Lobbyist — Arnold & Porter, 1200 New Hampshire Ave. N.W., Washington, D.C. 20036. Filed 3/18/82. Legislative interest — "HR 5447 ... S 2109 ... and other legislation relating to United States regulation of commodities sales."

MARLEX PETROLEUM INC., Long Beach, Calif. Lobbyist — Akin, Gump, Strauss, Hauer & Feld, 1333 New Hampshire Ave. N.W., Washington, D.C. 20036. Filed 3/2/82. Legislative interest — "...tax-exempt revenue bonds."

MERRILL LYNCH COMMODITIES INC., New York, N.Y. Lobbyist — Rogers & Wells, 1666 K St. N.W., Washington, D.C. 20006. Filed 3/18/82. Legislative interest — "...HR 5447 and S 2109, to reauthorize the Commodities Futures Trading Commission."

METAL MARKET & EXCHANGE COMPANY LTD., London, England. Lobbyist — John V. Rainbolt, 1800 K St. N.W., Washington, D.C. 20006. Filed 3/4/82. Legislative interest — "...Commodity Exchange Act, as amended ... S 2109, HR 5447." Lobbyist — Arnold & Porter, 1200 New Hampshire Ave. N.W., Washington, D.C. 20036. Filed 3/18/82. Legislative interest — "HR 5447 ... S 2109 ... and other legislation relating to United States regulation of commodities sales."

NATIONAL CONSUMER COOPERATIVE BANK, 2001 S St. N.W., Washington, D.C. 20009. Filed for self 3/24/82. Legislative interest — "...banking, cooperatives and taxation, especially those related to the Bank's federal charter; (PL 95-351 as amended)." Lobbyists — Robert J. Conlan, John X. Ward.

OGLETHORPE POWER CORP., Atlanta, Ga. Lobbyist — Sutherland, Asbill & Brennan, 3100 First National Bank Tower, Atlanta, Ga. 30303. Filed 3/25/82. Legislative interest — "Revisions to the safe harbor leasing provisions of the Economic Recovery Tax Act."

PETRO-LEWIS CORP., Denver, Colo. Lobbyist — Wellford, Wegman, Krulwich, Gold & Hoff, 1015 18th St. N.W., Washington, D.C. 20036. Filed 3/25/82. Legislative interest — "S 1660; HR 4626; to validate certain placer mining claims in Hot Springs County, Wyoming...."

POTLATCH CORP., Washington, D.C. Lobbyist — Charls E. Walker Associates Inc., 1730 Pennsylvania Ave. N.W., Washington, D.C. 20006. Filed 3/11/82. Legislative interest — "...refundability of the investment tax credit or items relating to taxation of leasing transactions."

THE RENDON CO., 1321 Pennsylvania Ave. S.E., Washington, D.C. 20009. Filed for self 3/23/82. Legislative interest — Not specified. Lobbyists — Gordon Jack Dover, John W. Rendon Jr.

ROWAN COMPANIES INC., Houston, Texas. Lobbyist — David P. Stang, 1629 K St. N.W., Washington, D.C. 20006. Filed 3/25/82. Legislative interest — "Employee stock option plans."

SECURITY LIFE OF DENVER, Security Life Building, Denver, Colo. 80202. Filed for self 3/24/82. Legislative interest — "Taxation of life insurance companies." Lobbyist — Judith Richards Hope, 1050 Thomas Jefferson St. N.W., Washington, D.C. 20007.

C. A. SHEA & CO. INC., One World Trade Center, New York, N.Y. 10048. Filed for self 3/3/82. Legislative interest — "Customs laws and surety bonding, Title 19 United States Code." Lobbyists — Harvey Barrison, 291 Broadway, New York, N.Y. 10007; James M. Gorman, 258 W. Clinton Ave., Tenafly, N.J. 07670; John J. Sheppard, 267 Westervelt Place, Englewood Cliffs, N.J. 07632.

SOLITRON DEVICES INC., Riviera Beach, Fla. Lobbyist — Windels, Marx, Davies & Ives, 1800 M St. N.W., Washington, D.C. 20036 and 51 W. 51st St., New York, N.Y. 10019. Filed 3/9/82. Legislative interest — "Support of private legislation relieving employer of tax liability for abandoned asset."

SONY CORPORATION OF AMERICA, New York, N.Y. Lobbyist — Leva, Hawes, Symington, Martin & Oppenheimer, 815 Connecticut Ave. N.W., Washington, D.C. 20006. Filed 3/24/82. Legislative interest — "...HR 4808, HR 5250, HR 4783, HR 5488, HR 5705, S 1758...."

SOUTHERN CALIFORNIA GAS CO., Los Angeles, Calif. Lobbyist — Shannon, Heffernan, Moseman & Goren, 1875 I St. N.W., Washington, D.C. 20006. Filed 3/22/82. Legislative interest — "HR 1524 ... S 232...."

SPACE SERVICES INC., Houston, Texas. Lobbyist — Andrews & Kurth, 1747 Pennsylvania Ave. N.W., Washington, D.C. 20006. Filed 3/24/82. Legislative interest — "...regulation of private commercial outer space ventures."

THE STANDARD OIL CO. (OHIO), Cleveland, Ohio 44115. Filed for self 3/26/82. Legislative interest — Not specified. Lobbyist — Douglas M. Webb, 1111 19th St. N.W., Washington, D.C. 20036.

TANDY CORP., Fort Worth, Texas. Lobbyist — Hamel, Park, McCabe & Saunders, 888 16th St. N.W., Washington, D.C. 20006. Filed 3/30/82. Legislative interest — "...Telecommunications Act of 1982...."

TEXASGULF INC., Stamford, Conn. Lobbyist — Kilgore & Kilgore Inc., 1800 First National Bank Building, Dallas, Texas 75202. Filed 3/8/82. Legislative interest — "...to amend subsection 613A(d)(4) of the Internal Revenue Code to exclude foreign refining from the definition of crude oil."

TWENTIETH CENTURY-FOX FILM CORP., Los Angeles, Calif. Lobbyist — Williams & Connolly, 1000 Hill Building, Washington, D.C. 20006. Filed 3/16/82. Legislative interest — "...the tax credit employee stock ownership plans, (principally section 409A of the Internal Revenue Code)."

UNIFI INC., 7201 W. Friendly Road, Greensboro, N.C. 27413. Filed for self 3/16/82. Legislative interest — Not specified. Lobbyist — Betty Jane Leonard, P.O. Box 21368, Greensboro, N.C. 27420.

UNITED DISTRIBUTION CO., Falmouth, Mass. Lobbyist — Robert N. Smith, 21 East Long Lake Road, Bloomfield Hills, Mich. 48013. Filed 3/11/82. Legislative interest — "Low-income energy assistance legislation...."

UNITED STATES FILTER CORP., 522 Fifth Ave., New York, N.Y. 10036. Filed for self 3/10/82. Legislative interest — "Legislation concerning energy and power production, transportation and use including but not limited to (a) equipment and products, and (b) engineering and other services ... domestic and foreign construction." Lobbyist — Clifton T. Hilderley Jr., 1025 Connecticut Ave. N.W., Washington, D.C. 20036.

WARNER COMMUNICATIONS INC., Washington, D.C. Lobbyist — Stroock & Stroock & Lavan, 1150 17th St. N.W., Washington, D.C. 20036. Filed 3/4/82. Legislative interest — "Eliminating tariffs on various categories of toys...."

WASTE MANAGEMENT INC., 600 Maryland Ave. S.W., Washington, D.C. 20024. Filed for self 3/11/82. Legislative interest — Not specified. Lobbyists — Scott Charles Clarkson, Jack J. Schramm.

WESTINGHOUSE ELECTRIC CORP., 2119 Gateway Center, Pittsburgh, Pa. 15222 and 1801 K St. N.W., Washington, D.C. 20006. Lobbyist — Beckel, Finchem, Torricelli and Associates Inc., 1731 21st St. N.W., Washington, D.C. 20009. Filed 3/8/82. Legislative interest — "Buy America legislation...." Lobbyist — Dilworth, Paxson, Kalish & Kauffman, 1819 H St. N.W., Washington, D.C. 20006. Filed 3/25/82. Legislative interest — "...amendments to the Clean Air Act." Lobbyist — McNair, Glenn, Konduros, Corley, Singletary, Porter & Dibble, 1155 15th St. N.W., Washington, D.C. 20005. Filed 3/22/82. Legislative interest — "Legislation affecting the nuclear industry."

WHEELABRATOR-FRYE INC., Hampton, N.H. Lobbyist — Miller & Chevalier, 1700 Pennsylvania Ave. N.W., Washington, D.C. 20006. Filed 3/26/82. Legislative interest — "In support of an exception to the Administration's February 26, 1982, industrial development bond proposal for resource recovery facilities."

WHITTAKER CORP., Los Angeles, Calif. Lobbyist — Daniel J. Edelman Inc., 1730 Pennsylvania Ave. N.W., Washington, D.C. 20006. Filed 3/17/82. Legislative interest — "...health care legislation."

YELLOW FREIGHT SYSTEM INC., 10990 Roe Ave., Shawnee Mission, Kan. 66207. Filed for self 3/11/82. Legislative interest — "All legislation affecting the trucking industry."

Y & M STEEL CONTRACTORS INC., Millersville, Md. Lobbyist — Tietz & O'Connell, 107 W. Jefferson St., Rockville, Md. 20850. Filed 3/5/82. Legislative interest — Not specified.

International Relations

THE REPUBLIC OF INDONESIA, Washington, D.C. Lobbyist — White & Case, 1747 Pennsylvania Ave. N.W., Washington, D.C. 20006. Filed 3/9/82. Legislative interest — "...ensuring fair treatment for the Republic of Indonesia under Foreign Assistance Act appropriations legislation."

Labor Groups

AMERICAN FEDERATION OF MUSICIANS, 1500 Broadway, New York, N.Y. 10036. Filed for self 3/10/82. Legislative interest — "HR 4376 ... HR 4377 ... H J Res 151 ... HR 1805...." Lobbyist — Ned H. Guthrie, 209 Hayes Ave., Charleston, W.Va. 25314.

AMERICAN FEDERATION OF STATE, COUNTY AND MUNICIPAL EMPLOYEES (AFL-CIO), 1625 L St. N.W., Washington, D.C. 20036. Filed for self 3/4/82. Legislative interest — Not specified. Lobbyist — Charles M. Loveless.

AMERICAN GUILD OF AUTHORS AND COMPOSERS, New York, N.Y. Lobbyist — Charls E. Walker Associates Inc., 1730 Pennsylvania Ave. N.W., Washington, D.C. 20006. Filed 3/11/82. Legislative interest — "...issues relating to the home copying of copyrighted audio materials."

BUILDING AND CONSTRUCTION TRADES DEPARTMENT (AFL-CIO), Washington, D.C. Lobbyist — Arnold & Porter, 1200 New Hampshire Ave. N.W., Washington, D.C. 20036. Filed 3/29/82. Legislative interest — "Legislation with respect to the travel expenses of construction workers ... S 1342...."

State and Local Governments

METROPOLITAN TRANSIT AUTHORITY, New York, N.Y. Lobbyist — Brown & Roady, 1333 New Hampshire Ave. N.W., Washington, D.C. 20036. Filed 3/29/82. Legislative interest — Not specified.

PUERTO RICO FEDERAL AFFAIRS ADMINISTRATION, Washington, D.C. Lobbyist — Stroock & Stroock & Lavan, 1150 17th St. N.W., Washington, D.C. 20036. Filed 3/23/82. Legislative interest — "In favor of removing restrictions on travel to and from Puerto Rico by boat."

Trade Associations

AEROSPACE INDUSTRIES ASSOCIATION OF AMERICA, Washington, D.C. Lobbyist — Miller & Chevalier, 1700 Pennsylvania Ave. N.W., Washington, D.C. 20006. Filed 3/29/82. Legislative interest — "In opposition to the Administration's proposal of February 26, 1982, pertaining to the tax accounting treatment of long-term contracts." Lobbyist — Charls E. Walker Associates Inc., 1730 Pennsylvania Ave. N.W., Washington, D.C. 20006. Filed 3/11/82. Legislative interest — "...the completed contract method of accounting for income and deductions attributable to long-term contracts entered into by aerospace industries."

AMERICAN ASSOCIATION OF EQUIPMENT LESSORS, Arlington, Va. Lobbyist — Jones & Winburn, 1101 15th St. N.W., Washington, D.C. 20005. Filed 3/8/82. Legislative interest — "...the leasing provisions of the Economic Recovery Tax Act of 1981, or other matters of taxation relating to the business of leasing."

AMERICAN ASSOCIATION OF RETIRED PERSONS, 1909 K St. N.W., Washington, D.C. 20049. Filed for self 3/8/82. Legislative interest — Not specified. Lobbyist — Marty Corry.

AMERICAN COUNCIL OF LIFE INSURANCE INC., 1850 K St. N.W., Washington, D.C. 20006. Lobbyist — Bernard M. Shapiro, 1801 K St. N.W., Washington, D.C. 20006. Filed 3/24/82. Legislative interest — Not specified. Filed for self 3/24/82. Legislative interest — Not specified. Lobbyist — Lawrence P. Higgins.

AMERICAN ELECTRONICS ASSOCIATION, Washington, D.C. Lobbyist — O'Brien, Fierce & Eberle, 1828 L St. N.W., Washington, D.C. 20036. Filed 3/17/82. Legislative interest — Not specified.

AMERICAN TRUCK DEALERS, McLean, Va. Lobbyist — David P. Stang, 1629 K St. N.W., Washington, D.C. 20006. Filed 3/15/82. Legislative interest — "HR 2936."

CALIFORNIA AIR TANKER OPERATORS ASSOCIATION, Sacramento, Calif. Lobbyist — A-K Associates Inc., 1225 8th St., Sacramento, Calif. 95814. Filed 3/17/82. Legislative interest — "Federal legislation regarding rules and regulations relating to air tanker services relative to firefighting, agricultural spraying and services rendered for air services government contracts."

COALITION FOR EMPLOYMENT THROUGH EXPORTS, Washington, D.C. Lobbyist — Powell, Goldstein, Frazer & Murphy, 1110 Vermont Ave. N.W., Washington, D.C. 20005. Legislative interest — "...U.S. export policy issues."

CONTINENTAL ASSOCIATION OF RESOLUTE EMPLOYERS, 511 C St. N.E., Washington, D.C. 20002. Filed for self 3/8/82. Legislative interest — "...HR 4326 ... HR 4709 ... HR 5022 ... HR 5419...." Lobbyists — Robert G. Allen, Robin Risso, Kevin Rowland.

FARMERS FOR FAIRNESS, Camilla, Ga. Lobbyist — Shaw, Pittman, Potts & Trowbridge, 1800 M St. N.W., Washington, D.C. 20036. Filed 3/16/82. Legislative interest — "...section 702 ('National Poundage Quota and Farm Poundage Quota') of the Agriculture and Food Act of 1981...."

FEDERATION SUISSE DES ASSOCIATIONS DE FABRICANTS D'HORLOGERIE, Bienne, Switzerland. Lobbyist — Arnold & Porter, 1200 New Hampshire Ave. N.W., Washington, D.C. 20036. Filed 3/24/82. Legislative interest — "...HR 5758 and any related bills that may be introduced concerning the provision of incentives for the manufacture of watches in the Virgin Islands."

GOVERNMENT GUARANTEED LOAN COMMITTEE, PUBLIC SECURITIES ASSOCIATION, New York, N.Y. Lobbyist — Neece, Cator & Associates Inc., 1050 17th St. N.W., Washington, D.C. 20036. Filed 3/29/82. Legislative interest — "Government guaranteed loans; Small Business Administration guaranteed loan program."

GROCERY MANUFACTURERS OF AMERICA INC., 1010 Wisconsin Ave. N.W., Washington, D.C. 20007. Filed for self 3/24/82. Legislative interest — "...legislation affecting the production or processing of grocery and related products, including HR 4031 and HR 5160." Lobbyist — William Lincoln Spoor.

HOME RECORDING RIGHTS COALITION, 1015 15th St. N.W., Washington, D.C. 20006. Filed for self 3/1/82. Legislative interest — "Participate in legislative process involving passage of Home Videotape." Lobbyist — Stanton P. Sender.

INDEPENDENT GAS PRODUCERS COMMITTEE, Oklahoma City, Okla. Lobbyist — Casey, Lane & Mittendorf, 815 Connecticut Ave. N.W., Washington, D.C. 20006. Filed 3/29/82. Legislative interest — "...field prices for old flowing gas pursuant to the National Gas Policy Act of 1978, PL 95-621." Lobbyist — Wexler and Associates Inc., 1616 H St. N.W., Washington, D.C. 20006. Filed 3/18/82. Legislative interest — "...to oppose the decontrol of field prices for old flowing gas pursuant to the Natural Gas Policy Act of 1978, PL 95-621."

INTERNATIONAL ASSOCIATION OF DRILLING CONTRACTORS, Washington, D.C. Lobbyist — David P. Stang, 1629 K St. N.W., Washington, D.C. 20006. Filed 3/15/82. Legislative interest — "Legislation involving oil spill liability provisions of the OCSLAA of 1978."

MOTOR CARRIER LAWYERS ASSOCIATION, Austin, Texas. Lobbyist — Kent and O'Connor Inc., 1919 Pennsylvania Ave. N.W., Washington, D.C. 20006. Filed 3/9/82. Legislative interest — "HR 3663...."

MOTOR VEHICLE MANUFACTURERS ASSOCIATION OF THE UNITED STATES INC., 300 New Center Building, Detroit, Mich. 48202. Filed for self 3/22/82. Legislative interest — Not specified. Lobbyist — Charles H. Lockwood II.

NATIONAL APARTMENT ASSOCIATION, 1825 K St. N.W., Washington, D.C. 20006. Filed for self 3/10/82. Legislative interest — "All legislation affecting multifamily housing, including housing authorization legislation and tax treatment of multifamily investment." Lobbyist — Scott L. Slesinger, 7105 Oakridge Ave., Chevy Chase, Md. 20815.

NATIONAL ASSOCIATION OF DEVELOPMENT COMPANIES, Washington, D.C. Lobbyist — Neece, Cator & Associates Inc., 1050 17th St. N.W., Washington, D.C. 20036. Filed 3/29/82. Legislative interest — "Section 503 Certified Development Corporations; Small Business Investment Act."

NATIONAL ASSOCIATION OF REAL ESTATE DEVELOPERS, Chicago, Ill. Lobbyist — Powell, Goldstein, Frazer & Murphy, 1110 Vermont Ave. N.W., Washington, D.C. 20005. Filed 3/22/82. Legislative interest — "...housing legislation."

NATIONAL BULK VENDORS ASSOCIATION, Chicago, Ill. Lobbyist — Leighton, Conklin, Lemov, Jacobs & Buckley, 2033 M St. N.W., Washington, D.C. 20036. Filed 3/22/82. Legislative interest — "...HR 5838, HR 5801...."

NATIONAL COALITION OF TELECOMMUNICATIONS USERS AND PROVIDERS, 115 D St. S.E., Washington, D.C. 20003. Filed for self 3/9/82. Legislative interest — "HR 5158, The Telecommunications Act of 1981...." Lobbyists — Barbara Ann Cebuhar, Calvin Reginald Greene Jr., Joe M. Norton Jr., Kathleen A. O'Neill, Martin H. Rogol.

NATIONAL COUNCIL FOR INDUSTRIAL INNOVATION, Cambridge, Mass. Lobbyist — Powell, Goldstein, Frazer & Murphy, 1110 Vermont Ave. N.W., Washington, D.C. 20005. Filed 3/2/82. Legislative interest — "...HR 4326, S 881."

NATIONAL FOREST PRODUCTS ASSOCIATION, 1619 Massachusetts Ave. N.W., Washington, D.C. 20036. Filed for self 3/15/82. Legislative interest — "...Forest Service appropriations, federal land management policies, wilderness proposals, housing and mortgage finance, public financing, lobby law reform, RARE II Review Act of 1981, regulatory reform and taxation." Lobbyist — Tricia L. Swift.

NATIONAL MILK PRODUCERS FEDERATION, Washington, D.C. Lobbyist — Barnett & Alagia, 1627 K St. N.W., Washington, D.C. 20006. Filed 3/3/82. Legislative interest — Not specified.

NATIONAL MULTI HOUSING COUNCIL, 1800 M St. N.W., Washington, D.C. 20036. Filed for self 3/11/82. Legislative interest — "Legislation affecting the development and availability of multifamily housing in particular opposition to rent control; overly restrictive condo conversion regulations and tax incentives." Lobbyist — Stephen D. Driesler.

NATIONAL MUSIC PUBLISHERS ASSOCIATION, New York, N.Y. Lobbyist — Pierson, Ball & Dowd, 1200 18th St. N.W., Washington, D.C. 20036. Filed 3/12/82. Legislative interest — "...Home Video Recording Act of 1982; HR 4783; HR 4808; HR 4794; HR 5488; HR 5705; S 1758...."

NATIONAL PASSENGER TRAFFIC ASSOCIATION, New York, N.Y. Lobbyist — Stein, Davidoff, Malito, Katz & Hutcher, 1775 Broadway, New York, N.Y. 10019. Filed 3/29/82. Legislative interest — "...HR 4147, HR 5102, S 1450."

NATIONAL RETIRED TEACHERS ASSOCIATION, 1909 K St. N.W., Washington, D.C. 20049. Filed for self 3/8/82. Legislative interest — Not specified. Lobbyist — Marty Corry.

NATIONAL VENTURE CAPITAL ASSOCIATION, Washington, D.C. Lobbyist — Neece, Cator & Associates Inc., 1050 17th St. N.W., Washington, D.C. 20036. Filed 3/29/82. Legislative interest — "Treasury Rule 385."

NEW YORK SHIPPING ASSOCIATION INC., 80 Broad St., New York, N.Y. 10004. Filed for self 3/18/82. Legislative interest — "HR 4374, S 1593, regulatory reform bills to amend the Shipping Act ... 46 United States Code subsection 801, *et seq.*...." Lobbyist — Pauline B. Reeping, 1750 New York Ave.

N.W., Washington, D.C. 20006.

PHARMACEUTICAL MANUFACTURERS ASSOCIATION, Washington, D.C. Lobbyist — Pierson, Ball & Dowd, 1200 18th St. N.W., Washington, D.C. 20036. Filed 3/24/82. Legislative interest — "Patent Term Restoration Act of 1981; HR 1937...."

SLURRY TRANSPORT ASSOCIATION, Washington, D.C. Lobbyist — F/P Research Associates, 1700 K St. N.W., Washington, D.C. 20006. Filed 3/31/82. Legislative interest — "General federal energy transportation issues, specifically the coal slurry pipeline legislation (HR 4230 and S 1844)."

SMALL BUSINESS DEVELOPMENT CENTER DIRECTORS ASSOCIATION, Washington, D.C. Lobbyist — Neece, Cator & Associates Inc., 1050 17th St. N.W., Washington, D.C. 20036. Filed 3/29/82. Legislative interest — "Small Business Act and Small Business Investment Act of 1958."

SMALL BUSINESS UNITED, Waltham, Mass. Lobbyist — Neece, Cator & Associates Inc., 1050 17th St. N.W., Washington, D.C. 20036. Filed 3/29/82. Legislative interest — "...S 881; HR 4326."

SOCIETY FOR NUTRITION EDUCATION, 1736 Franklin St., Oakland, Calif. 94612. Filed for self 3/18/82. Legislative interest — "Food/nutrition information and education issues; school lunch, NET, WIC, farm bill; authorizing and appropriating legislation; food safety regulations." Lobbyist — Elizabeth Shipley-Moses, 1107 Jackson Court, Falls Church, Va. 22046. Filed 3/18/82. Legislative interest — "Food/nutrition information and education issues; school lunch, NET, WIC, farm bill; authorizing and appropriating legislation; food safety regulations."

SOUTHEASTERN LUMBER MANUFACTURERS ASSOCIATION, Forest Park, Ga. Lobbyist — Neece, Cator & Associates Inc., 1050 17th St. N.W., Washington, D.C. 20036. Filed 3/29/82. Legislative interest — "Housing/timber industry issues, S 1080...."

STOCK INFORMATION GROUP, Washington, D.C. Lobbyist — Sutherland, Asbill & Brennan, 1666 K St. N.W., Washington, D.C. 20006. Filed 3/24/82. Legislative interest — "...tax proposals affecting the life insurance industry."

WASHINGTON STATE CHARTER BOAT ASSOCIATION, Westport, Wash. Lobbyist — Carmody, Syrdal, Danelo & Klein, Fourth and Blanchard Building, Seattle, Wash. 98121. Filed 3/12/82. Legislative interest — "...16 United States Code 1801 *et seq....*"

Miscellaneous

WILLIAM M. BEUTE, 25 Broadway, Clark, N.J. 07066. Filed for self 3/23/82. Legislative interest — "Education and small business."

CENTRAL STATES SOUTHEAST AND SOUTHWEST AREAS HEALTH AND WELFARE AND PENSION FUNDS, Chicago, Ill. Lobbyists — Arent, Fox, Kintner, Plotkin & Kahn, 1815 H St. N.W., Washington, D.C. 20006. Filed 3/11/82. (John C. Culver, D-Iowa, U.S. Senate 1975-81, U.S. House 1965-75, was listed as agent for this client.) Legislative interest — "...legislative treatment (tax and regulatory) relating to pension plan formulations, benefit programs and payments and permitted investments." Lobbyists — Thompson & Crawford, 1575 I St. N.W., Washington, D.C. 20005. Filed 3/26/82. Legislative interest — "...legislative treatment (tax and regulatory) relating to pension plan formulations, benefit programs and payments and permitted investments."

COUNCIL OF STATE HOSPITAL FINANCE AUTHORITIES, 35 E. Wacker Drive, Chicago, Ill. 60601. Lobbyist — Williams & Connolly, 839 17th St. N.W., Washington, D.C. 20006. Filed 3/23/82. Legislative interest — "Legislation proposed by the Administration amending section 103(a)(2) of the Internal Revenue Code as it will affect hospital revenue bonds issued on behalf of private nonprofit hospitals...." Filed for self 3/25/82. Legislative interest — "Legislation proposed by the Administration amending section 103(a)(2) of the Internal Revenue Code as it will affect hospital revenue bonds issued on behalf of private nonprofit hospitals...." Lobbyist — George C. Phillips Jr.

HELEN WODELL HALBACH ESTATE, Gladstone, N.J. Lobbyist — Alcorn, Bakewell & Smith, One American Row, Hartford, Conn. 06103. Filed 3/26/82. Legislative interest — "...HR 2583; S 1983...."

JOINT TASK FORCE ON FEDERAL FINANCIAL ASSISTANCE FOR LAW STUDENTS, 11 Dupont Circle N.W., Washington, D.C. 20036. Lobbyist — Milbank, Tweed, Hadley & McCloy, 1747 Pennsylvania Ave. N.W., Washington, D.C. 20006. Filed 3/11/82. Legislative interest — "...guaranteed student loan programs for law and other graduate school students." Filed for self 3/24/82. Legislative interest — "...guaranteed student loan programs for law and other graduate school students." Lobbyist — Bruce I. Zimmer.

ELAINE J. K. LEGAS SWOPE, 3907 Minden Road, Wheaton, Md. 20906. Filed for self 3/18/82. Legislative interest — "HR 268; S 1361 ... HR 1641; HR 3039; HR 835; HR 4710...."

GERALD M. SYRKETT, 617 Hamlin St. N.E., Washington, D.C. 20017. Filed for self 3/1/82. Legislative interest — Not specified.

April Registrations

Citizens' Groups

ALLIANCE TO SAVE ENERGY, 1925 K St. N.W., Washington, D.C. 20006. Filed for self 4/12/82. Legislative interest — "...HR 4035 ... HR 2876 ... S 239 ... HR 3982 ... HR 4390...." Lobbyists — Robin Miller, Michael W. Reid.

AMERICAN PUBLIC HEALTH ASSOCIATION, Washington, D.C. Lobbyist — Gerald R. Connor, 6500 Wisconsin Ave., Chevy Chase, Md. 20815. Filed for self 4/30/82. Legislative interest — "Amendments to the Public Health Service Act; amendments to Titles XVIII and XIX of the Social Security Act."

ASBESTOS COMPENSATION COALITION, Washington, D.C. Lobbyist — Barnett & Alagia, 1627 K St. N.W., Washington, D.C. 20006. Filed 4/22/82. Legislative interest — "...HR 5737 and related bills, and proposed Occupational Disease Compensation Improvement Act...."

CENTER ON BUDGET AND POLICY PRIORITIES, 236 Massachusetts Ave. N.E., Washington, D.C. 20002. Filed for self 4/15/82. Legislative interest — "...HR 3603, HR 4119, S 2352...." Lobbyist — Robert Greenstein.

CITIES IN SCHOOLS INC., Atlanta, Ga. Lobbyist — Roger Tilles, 1111 19th St. N.W., Washington, D.C. 20036. Filed 4/16/82. Legislative interest — Not specified.

COALITION FOR UNIFORM PRODUCT LIABILITY LAW, 1901 L St. N.W., Washington, D.C. 20036. Lobbyist — Steptoe & Johnson, 1250 Connecticut Ave. N.W., Washington, D.C. 20036. Filed 4/12/82. Legislative interest — "...HR 5214...." Filed for self 4/12/82. Legislative interest — "...HR 5214...." Lobbyist — Barbara L. Vandegrift.

COMMON CAUSE, 2030 M St. N.W., Washington, D.C. 20036. Filed for self 4/9/82. Legislative interest — "...HR 4070 ... HR 3603, S 884 ... S Res 20 ... HR 18, S 10 ... S Res 58, H J Res 10 ... S 708 ... S 1730 ... S 1992 ... the Clean Air Act ... S 393, HR 3480 ... S 1760, S 951, S 1647, S 158 ... S 193, HR 4882...." Lobbyists — Laurie Duker, Richard Mark, Kathleen Sheekey.

CONGRESS OF ADVOCATES FOR THE RETARDED INC., New York, N.Y. Lobbyist — Gerald R. Connor, 6500 Wisconsin Ave., Chevy Chase, Md. 20815. Filed 4/30/82. Legislative interest — "Amendments to the Developmental Disabilities Act; amendments to Titles XVIII and XIX of the Social Security Act; other legislation affecting the mentally retarded."

CONSERVATIVES FOR IMMIGRATION REFORM INC., 227 Massachusetts Ave. N.E., Washington, D.C. 20002. Filed for self 4/27/82. Legislative interest — "Support effective enforcement of immigration laws and reforms such as employer sanctions. Oppose amnesty for illegal aliens." Lobbyist — Phil Kent.

NATIONAL COALITION TO BAN HANDGUNS, 100 Maryland Ave. N.E., Washington, D.C. 20002. Filed for self 4/9/82. Legislative interest — "...'Firearm Owners Protection Act' (S

1030/HR 3300) . . . 'Handgun Crime Control Act of 1981' (S 974/HR 3200) . . . legislation that would amend the Gun Control Act of 1968 (Chapter 44 of title 18, United States Code; Public Law 90-618) . . . proposed reorganization of the Bureau of Alcohol, Tobacco and Firearms. . . ." Lobbyist — Clarke Rupert.

NATIONAL OUTDOOR COALITION, Fontana, Calif. Lobbyist — John Russell Deane III, 1607 New Hampshire Ave. N.W., Washington, D.C. 20009. Filed 4/9/82. Legislative interest — ". . .RARE II, HR 2477, HR 2354, and S 842."

NATIONAL WOMEN'S POLITICAL CAUCUS, 1411 K St. N.W., Washington, D.C. 20005. Filed for self 4/14/82. Legislative interest — ". . .HR 900, S 158, S 1741, S J Res 110 and H J Res 372 . . . family planning: oppose changes in Title X regulations . . . support the Women's Economic Equity Act, S 888 and HR 3117; support extension of the Voting Rights Act, HR 3112 and S 1992; opposed the Administration's proposed FY83 Budget." Lobbyist — Patricia A. Marks.

ONEIDA TRIBE OF WISCONSIN, Washington, D.C. Lobbyist — Sense Inc., 1010 Vermont Ave. N.W., Washington, D.C. 20005. Filed 4/14/82. Legislative interest — ". . .S 2084/HR 5494 ancient Indian land claims bill, Title V of the Older Americans Act and appropriations related to American Indian interests. . . ."

PUBLIC CITIZEN INC., 1346 Connecticut Ave. N.W., Washington, D.C. 20036. Filed for self 4/12/82. Legislative interest — "Public participation in federal agency proceedings; access to justice legislation; bills regarding attorneys' fees; congressional veto legislation and regulatory reform bills; auto safety legislation, transportation legislation; Freedom of Information Act; FTC authorization; CPSC authorization; product liability; used car rule; Export Trading Co.; campaign finance reform; beer bottlers; tax issues; telecommunications; legal services; social security; Foreign Corrupt Practices Act; Clinch River breeder reactor; synthetic fuels; nuclear waste; clean air; OSHA legislation, TRIS compensation; drug patent extension; food safety." Lobbyist — Joan Claybrook.

REPUBLICANS ABROAD, Washington, D.C. Lobbyist — Lois Burke Shepard, 8602 Hidden Hill Lane, Potomac, Md. 20854. Filed 4/8/82. Legislative interest — "HR 4449 - 'Social Security Alien and Foreign Resident Limitations Act of 1981.' "

SAVE OUR SECURITY, 1201 16th St. N.W., Washington, D.C. 20036. Filed for self 4/13/82. Legislative interest — "Support for legislation preserving status of social security system; opposition to cuts in benefits, changes in formula for computing benefits, changes in qualifications for entitlement to benefits." Lobbyist — William J. Driver.

THE WILDERNESS SOCIETY, 1901 Pennsylvania Ave. N.W., Washington, D.C. 20006. Filed for self 4/1/82. Legislative interest — ". . .issues relating to the public lands." Lobbyist — Edward M. Norton Jr. Filed for self 4/1/82. Legislative interest — "National forest issues." Lobbyist — Susan Alexander.

Corporations and Businesses

A & S TRANSPORTATION CO., 75 Jacobus Ave., South Kearny, N.J. 07032. Lobbyist — Blank, Rome, Comisky & McCauley, 1700 K St. N.W., Washington, D.C. 20006. Filed 4/23/82. Legislative interest — "Reauthorization and amendments to the Marine Protection, Research and Sanctuaries Act, 33 U.S.C. 1401 *et seq.*" Filed for self 4/23/82. Legislative interest — "Reauthorization and amendments to the Marine Protection, Research and Sanctuaries Act, 33 U.S.C. 1401 *et seq.*" Lobbyist — Richard F. Albers.

AETNA INSURANCE CO., Chicago, Ill. Lobbyist — Dennis M. Olsen, 485 E St., Idaho Falls, Idaho 83402. Filed 4/12/82. Legislative interest — "Introduction of legislation for congressional reference to Court of Claims on claims arising out of the failure of the Teton Dam in Idaho."

AIRCO INC., Montvale, N.J. Lobbyist — McNair, Glenn, Konduros, Corley, Singletary, Porter & Dibble, Bankers Trust Towers, Columbia, S.C. 29211. Filed 4/14/82. Legislative interest — "S 255."

AMERICAN BANKER'S INSURANCE COMPANY OF FLORIDA, Salt Lake City, Utah. Lobbyist — Dennis M. Olsen, 485 E St., Idaho Falls, Idaho 83402. Filed 4/12/82. Legislative interest — "Introduction of legislation for congressional reference to Court of Claims on claims arising out of the failure of the Teton Dam in Idaho."

AMERICAN CAN CO., Greenwich, Conn. Lobbyist — Ballard, Spahr, Andrews & Ingersoll, 1850 K St. N.W., Washington, D.C. 20006. Filed 4/20/82. Legislative interest — ". . .to preserve the present authority for use of IDB's."

AMERICAN METAL DETECTORS MANUFACTURERS INC., Garland, Texas. Lobbyist — John Russell Deane III, 1607 New Hampshire Ave. N.W., Washington, D.C. 20009. Filed 4/9/82. Legislative interest — ". . .legislation affecting the multiple use of public lands. . . ."

AMERICAN PRESIDENT LINES, Washington, D.C. Lobbyist — Patton, Boggs & Blow, 2550 M St. N.W., Washington, D.C. 20037. Filed 4/19/82. Legislative interest — "In favor of S 1682, the Merchant Marine Act of 1936, 46 U.S.C. 1101 *et seq.*"

GEORGE K. BAUM & CO., Kansas City, Mo. Lobbyist — Camp, Carmouche, Palmer, Barsh & Hunter, 2550 M St. N.W., Washington, D.C. 20037. Filed 4/16/82. Legislative interest — ". . .I.R.S. Code Section 103."

BLYTH EASTMAN PAINE WEBBER INC., New York, N.Y. Lobbyist — Camp, Carmouche, Palmer, Barsh & Hunter, 2550 M St. N.W., Washington, D.C. 20037. Filed 4/16/82. Legislative interest — ". . .I.R.S. Code Section 103."

BURLINGTON NORTHERN INC., 1111 Third Ave., Seattle, Wash. 98101. Filed for self 4/9/82. Legislative interest — "Legislation in any way affecting the transportation industry generally . . . natural resources legislation including land ownership and development, timber, forest products, coal, oil, gas and other minerals. . . ." Lobbyists — Catharine R. Batky, Trisha Bennett, 600 Maryland Ave. S.W., Washington, D.C. 20024.

CALIFORNIA NICKEL CORP., Palos Verdes, Calif. Lobbyist — Bracy, Williams & Co., 1730 Rhode Island Ave. N.W., Washington, D.C. 20036. Filed 4/12/82. Legislative interest — ". . .HR 5540 and S 1982. . . ."

CENTENNIAL INSURANCE CO., Seattle, Wash. Lobbyist — Dennis M. Olsen, 485 E St., Idaho Falls, Idaho 83402. Filed 4/12/82. Legislative interest — "Introduction of legislation for congressional reference to Court of Claims on claims arising out of the failure of the Teton Dam in Idaho."

CHAPMAN & CUTLER, Chicago, Ill. Lobbyist — Camp, Carmouche, Palmer, Barsh & Hunter, 2550 M St. N.W., Washington, D.C. 20037. Filed 4/16/82. Legislative interest — ". . .I.R.S. Code Section 103."

CHARTER OAK INSURANCE, Salt Lake City, Utah. Lobbyist — Dennis M. Olsen, 485 E St., Idaho Falls, Idaho 83402. Filed 4/12/82. Legislative interest — "Introduction of legislation for congressional reference to Court of Claims on claims arising out of the failure of the Teton Dam in Idaho."

CITIES SERVICE CO., Box 300, Tulsa, Okla. 74102. Filed for self 4/23/82. Legislative interest — "Corporate and energy taxation." Lobbyist — M. Kent Anderson.

CNA INSURANCE CO., Chicago, Ill. Lobbyist — Cook, Purcell, Hansen & Henderson, 1015 18th St. N.W., Washington, D.C. 20036. Filed 4/26/82. Legislative interest — ". . .support legislation mandating 'open season' for Federal Employees Health Benefits Program."

CONTROL DATA CORP., Minneapolis, Minn. Filed for self 4/12/82. Legislative interest — ". . .trade, regulatory agencies and taxation." Lobbyist — James J. O'Connell, 1201 Pennsylvania Ave. N.W., Washington, D.C. 20004.

CSC CLEARING CORP., New York, N.Y. Lobbyist — Barrett, Smith, Schapiro, Simon & Armstrong, 26 Broadway, New York, N.Y. 10004. Filed 4/16/82. Legislative interest — ". . .the Commodity Exchange Act, and the commodity broker provisions of the Bankruptcy Act. . . ."

CUMBERLAND SECURITIES, Knoxville, Tenn. Lobbyist — Camp, Carmouche, Palmer, Barsh & Hunter, 2550 M St. N.W., Washington, D.C. 20037. Filed 4/16/82. Legislative interest — ". . .I.R.S. Code Section 103."

DICKSTEIN, SHAPIRO & MORIN, 2101 L St. N.W., Washington, D.C. 20037. Filed for self 4/16/82. Legislative interest — "...health care." Lobbyist — Manuel D. Fierro.

EMPLOYEE OWNED AIRLINES, Leesburg, Va. Lobbyist — Bracy, Williams & Co., 1730 Rhode Island Ave. N.W., Washington, D.C. 20036. Filed 4/12/82. Legislative interest — "All legislation affecting the airline industry."

ENSERCH CORP., 300 S. Saint Paul St., Dallas, Texas. 75201. Filed for self 4/9/82. Legislative interest — "...natural gas decontrol, Foreign Corrupt Practices Act, Amendments to the Internal Revenue Code...." Lobbyist — Victoria V. Schaff, 1025 Connecticut Ave. N.W., Washington, D.C. 20036.

ENTEX INC., P.O. Box 2628, Houston, Texas 77001. Filed for self 4/12/82. Legislative interest — "Legislation of general interest to the gas industry." Lobbyist — Thomas J. Lee Jr.

ESSEX, Montgomery, Ala. Lobbyist — Camp, Carmouche, Palmer, Barsh & Hunter, 2550 M St. N.W., Washington, D.C. 20037. Filed 4/16/82. Legislative interest — "...I.R.S. Code Section 103."

EXXON CORP., New York, N.Y. Filed for self 4/13/82. Legislative interest — "...trade policy, export administration and export controls." Lobbyist — Alphonse DeRosso, 1899 L St. N.W., Washington, D.C. 20036.

FEDERAL HOME LOAN MORTGAGE CORP., Washington, D.C. Lobbyist — Thomas Ludlow Ashley, 1730 Pennsylvania Ave. N.W., Washington, D.C. 20006. Filed 4/12/82. (Former U.S. rep., D-Ohio, 1955-81.) Legislative interest — "HR 4787, to recapitalize and restructure the Mortgage Corporation...."

FLORISTS' MUTUAL INSURANCE CO., Edwardsville, Ill. Lobbyist — Dennis M. Olsen, 485 E St., Idaho Falls, Idaho 83402. Filed 4/12/82. Legislative interest — "Introduction of legislation for congressional reference to Court of Claims on claims arising out of the failure of the Teton Dam in Idaho."

FOREMOST INSURANCE CO., Grand Rapids, Mich. Lobbyist — Dennis M. Olsen, 485 E St., Idaho Falls, Idaho 83402. Filed 4/12/82. Legislative interest — "Introduction of legislation for congressional reference to Court of Claims on claims arising out of the failure of the Teton Dam in Idaho."

THE FRAZER LANIER CO., Montgomery, Ala. Lobbyist — Camp, Carmouche, Palmer, Barsh & Hunter, 2550 M St. N.W., Washington, D.C. 20037. Filed 4/16/82. Legislative interest — "...I.R.S. Code Section 103."

GATX CORP., Chicago, Ill. Lobbyist — Powell, Goldstein, Frazer & Murphy, 1110 Vermont Ave. N.W., Washington, D.C. 20005. Filed 4/14/82. Legislative interest — "...the corporate minimum tax."

GENERAL TELEPHONE & ELECTRONICS CORP., Stamford, Conn. Lobbyist — McNair, Glenn, Konduros, Corley, Singletary, Porter & Dibble, Bankers Trust Towers, Columbia, S.C. 29211. Filed 4/14/82. Legislative interest — "S 898...."

GENEVA PACIFIC CORP., Glenview, Ill. Lobbyist — National Counsel Associates Inc., 421 New Jersey Ave. S.E., Washington, D.C. 20003. Filed 4/9/82. Legislative interest — "Concerned with the development of Alaskan mineral resources and the procurement of land patents and roads...."

GEORGIA PACIFIC CORP., Portland, Ore. Lobbyist — McNair, Glenn, Konduros, Corley, Singletary, Porter & Dibble, Bankers Trust Towers, Columbia, S.C. 29211. Filed 4/14/82. Legislative interest — "S 995...."

GOLDMAN SACHS & CO., New York, N.Y. Lobbyist — Camp, Carmouche, Palmer, Barsh & Hunter, 2550 M St. N.W., Washington, D.C. 20037. Filed 4/16/82. Legislative interest — "...I.R.S. Code Section 103."

GPU SERVICE CORP., Parsippany, N.J. Lobbyist — Debevoise and Liberman, 1200 17th St. N.W., Washington, D.C. 20036. Filed 4/26/82. Legislative interest — "TMI 2 Cleanup."

GREAT AMERICAN INSURANCE CO., Spokane, Wash. Lobbyist — Dennis M. Olsen, 485 E St., Idaho Falls, Idaho 83402. Filed 4/12/82. Legislative interest — "Introduction of legislation for congressional reference to Court of Claims on claims arising out of the failure of the Teton Dam in Idaho."

HEINHOLD COMMODITIES INC., Chicago, Ill. Lobbyist — Sidley & Austin, One First National Plaza, Chicago, Ill.

60603. Filed 4/26/82. Legislative interest — "Tax legislation concerning bank forward contracts."

HUMANA INC., Louisville, Ky. Lobbyist — Bracy, Williams & Co., 1730 Rhode Island Ave. N.W., Washington, D.C. 20036. Filed 4/12/82. Legislative interest — Not specified.

INTELSAT, Washington, D.C. Lobbyist — Arent, Fox, Kintner, Plotkin & Kahn, 1815 H St. N.W., Washington, D.C. 20006. Filed 4/20/82. Legislative interest — "...HR 6550 ... S 1611...."

KIDDER, PEABODY, New York, N.Y. Lobbyist — Camp, Carmouche, Palmer, Barsh & Hunter, 2550 M St. N.W., Washington, D.C. 20037. Filed 4/16/82. Legislative interest — "...I.R.S. Code Section 103."

KING & SPAULDING, Atlanta, Ga. Lobbyist — Camp, Carmouche, Palmer, Barsh & Hunter, 2550 M St. N.W., Washington, D.C. 20037. Filed 4/16/82. Legislative interest — "...I.R.S. Code Section 103."

KLINE IRON & STEEL CO., Columbia, S.C. Lobbyist — McNair, Glenn, Konduros, Corley, Singletary, Porter & Dibble, Bankers Trust Towers, Columbia, S.C. 29211. Filed 4/16/82. Legislative interest — "HR 5599."

KWAJALEIN ATOLL CORP., Ebeye, Marshall Islands. Lobbyist — Cadwalader, Wickersham & Taft, 1333 New Hampshire Ave. N.W., Washington, D.C. 20036. Filed 4/9/82. Legislative interest — "...settlement of claims against the United States for past use of Kwajalein Atoll during 1944-1979 and with the prospective termination of the present trusteeship agreement regarding the trust Territory of the Pacific Islands."

LEBOEUF, LAMB, LEIBY & MACRAE, 1333 New Hampshire Ave. N.W., Washington, D.C. 20036. Filed for self 4/12/82. Legislative interest — "...43 U.S.C. subsection 1811, *et seq.*, HR 85, the Comprehensive Oil Pollution Liability and Compensation Act, S 681, the Oil Spill Liability and Compensation Act of 1981, HR 5735, the Occupational Health Hazards Compensation Act, and product liability tort reform." Lobbyist — Charles W. Havens III, L. Charles Landgraf.

LEGAL SERVICES CORP., 733 15th St. N.W., Washington, D.C. 20005. Filed for self 4/30/82. Legislative interest — Not specified. Lobbyists — Gerald M. Caplan, M. Dennis Daugherty.

LEHMAN BROTHERS, New York, N.Y. Lobbyist — Camp, Camouche, Palmer, Barsh & Hunter, 2550 M St. N.W., Washington, D.C. 20037. Filed 4/16/82. Legislative interest — "...I.R.S. Code Section 103."

LOCKHEED CORP., Washington, D.C. Lobbyist — C & B Associates, 1750 New York Ave. N.W., Washington, D.C. 20006. Filed 4/23/82. Legislative interest — "S 2248, Military Authorization Bill."

THE LONDON COMMODITY EXCHANGE CO. LTD., London, England. Lobbyist — John V. Rainbolt, 1800 K St. N.W., Washington, D.C. 20006. Filed 4/8/82. Legislative interest — "Legislation amending, or related to, the Commodity Exchange Act, as amended (7 U.S.C. 1, *et seq.*); S 2109, HR 5447."

THE LONDON GOLD FUTURES MARKET, London, England. Lobbyist — John V. Rainbolt, 1800 K St. N.W., Washington, D.C. 20006. Filed 4/8/82. Legislative interest — "Legislation amending, or related to, the Commodity Exchange Act, as amended (7 U.S.C. 1, *et seq.*); S 2109, HR 5447."

THE LONDON INTERNATIONAL FINANCIAL FUTURES EXCHANGE LTD., London, England. Lobbyist — John V. Rainbolt, 1800 K St. N.W., Washington, D.C. 20006. Filed 4/8/82. Legislative interest — "Legislation amending, or related to, the Commodity Exchange Act, as amended (7 U.S.C. 1, *et seq.*); S 2109, HR 5447."

MAGIC PANTRY FOODS INC., Ontario, Canada. Lobbyist — Rogers & Wells, 1666 K St. N.W., Washington, D.C. 20006. Filed 4/1/82. Legislative interest — "Department of Defense Appropriation Act, 1982."

MARCONI ELECTRONICS, Arlington, Va. Lobbyist — Van Fleet Associates Inc., 1341 G St. N.W., Washington, D.C. 20005. Filed 4/9/82. Legislative interest — Not specified.

MATSUSHITA ELECTRIC CORPORATION OF AMERICA, 1 Panasonic Way, Secaucus, N.J. Filed for self 4/12/82. Legislative interest — "Imports of consumer electronic

products." Lobbyists — Mike M. Masaoka, Patti A. Tilson, T. Albert Yamada, 900 17th St. N.W., Washington, D.C. 20006.

McDONALD & CO., Cleveland, Ohio. Lobbyist — Camp, Carmouche, Palmer, Barsh & Hunter, 2550 M St. N.W., Washington, D.C. 20037. Filed 4/16/82. Legislative interest — "...I.R.S. Code Section 103."

MICHIGAN CONSOLIDATED GAS CO., One Woodward Ave., Detroit, Mich. 48226. Filed for self 4/14/82. Legislative interest — "...energy, environment and regulatory issues." Lobbyist — William L. Johnson, 1050 17th St. N.W., Washington, D.C. 20036.

MINNEHOMA INSURANCE CO., Tulsa, Okla. Lobbyist — Dennis M. Olsen, 485 E St., Idaho Falls, Idaho 83402. Filed 4/12/82. Legislative interest — "Introduction of legislation for congressional reference to Court of Claims on claims arising out of the failure of the Teton Dam in Idaho."

MOLDOW DUST CONTROL INC., Greensboro, N.C. Lobbyist — Metzger, Shadyac & Schwarz, 1 Farragut Square South N.W., Washington, D.C. 20006. Filed 4/15/82. Legislative interest — "...in favor of the passage of HR 5927."

MOUNTAIN FIR LUMBER CO. INC., Salem, Ore. Lobbyist — Schwabe, Williamson, Wyatt, Moore & Roberts, 1000 Potomac St. N.W., Washington, D.C. 20007. Filed 4/12/82. (Former U.S. Rep. Robert B. Duncan, D-Ore., 1963-67, 1975-81, was listed as agent for this client.) Legislative interest — "Federal timber sales policies, including pricing and volumes."

NATIONAL FARMERS UNION PROPERTY AND CASUALTY INSURANCE CO., Denver, Colo. Lobbyist — Dennis M. Olsen, 485 E St., Idaho Falls, Idaho 83402. Filed 4/12/82. Legislative interest — "Introduction of legislation for congressional reference to Court of Claims on claims arising out of the failure of the Teton Dam in Idaho."

THE NATIONAL FOOTBALL LEAGUE, New York, N.Y. Lobbyist — Cook, Purcell, Hansen & Henderson, 1015 18th St. N.W., Washington, D.C. 20036. Filed 4/26/82. Legislative interest — "...clarification of the application of antitrust laws to professional sports leagues."

NIKE INTERNATIONAL LTD., Beaverton, Ore. Lobbyist — Bracy, Williams & Co, 1730 Rhode Island Ave. N.W., Washington, D.C. 20036. Filed 4/12/82. Legislative interest — "...legislation affecting shoe industry."

NORTH, HASKELL, SLAUGHTER, YOUNG AND LEWIS, Birmingham, Ala. Lobbyist — Camp, Carmouche, Palmer, Barsh & Hunter, 2550 M St. N.W., Washington, D.C. 20037. Filed 4/16/82. Legislative interest — "...I.R.S. Code Section 103."

PAUL, HASTINGS, JANOFSKY & WALKER, 1050 Thomas Jefferson St. N.W., Washington, D.C. 20007. Filed for self 4/8/82. Legislative interest — "Revision of the Clean Air Act; Taxation of the life insurance companies." Lobbyist — Fred B. Rooney (former U.S. rep., D-Pa., 1963-79).

PHILADELPHIA STOCK EXCHANGE INC., Philadelphia, Pa. Lobbyist — Cadwalader, Wickersham & Taft, 1333 New Hampshire Ave. N.W., Washington, D.C. 20036. Filed 4/8/82. Legislative interest — "...legislation designed to implement the jurisdictional accord announced by the Securities and Exchange Commission and the Commodity Futures Trading Commission ... including the Futures Trading Act of 1982, (S 2109 and HR 5447) and the Securities-Commodities Accord Amendments of 1982 (S 2260)...."

PRATT & WHITNEY AIRCRAFT GROUP, East Hartford, Conn. Lobbyist — Bracy, Williams & Co., 1730 Rhode Island Ave. N.W., Washington, D.C. 20036. Filed 4/12/82. Legislative interest — "All legislation relating to business activities and strategic and critical minerals policy, including HR 5540 and S 1982."

QUIXOTE CORP., Chicago, Ill. Lobbyist — Bracy, Williams & Co., 1730 Rhode Island Ave. N.W., Washington, D.C. 20036. Filed 4/12/82. Legislative interest — Not specified.

RAUSCHER, PIERCE, REFSNES, Dallas, Texas. Lobbyist — Camp, Carmouche, Palmer, Barsh & Hunter, 2550 M St. N.W., Washington, D.C. 20037. Filed 4/16/82. Legislative interest — "...I.R.S. Code Section 103."

RELIANCE GROUP INC., New York, N.Y. Lobbyist — Willkie, Farr & Gallagher, 818 Connecticut Ave. N.W., Washington, D.C. 20006. Filed 4/13/82. Legislative interest — "Financial Institutions Restructuring Act; Thrift Institutions Restructuring Act. S 1720, S 1703."

RYDER SYSTEMS INC., Miami, Fla. Lobbyist — Bregman, Abell & Kay, 1900 L St. N.W., Washington, D.C. 20036. Filed 4/8/82. Legislative interest — "...the corporate minimum tax...."

SOUTHERN COMPANY SERVICES INC., 1101 17th St. N.W., Washington, D.C. 20036. Filed for self 4/13/82. Legislative interest — "...environmental; transportation; plant siting and construction; power generation fuel; taxation and finance...." Lobbyists — Paul C. Bailey, W. Robert Worley.

SOUTHLAND ROYALTY CO., Fort Worth, Texas. Lobbyist — Akin, Gump, Strauss, Hauer & Feld, 1333 New Hampshire Ave. N.W., Washington, D.C. 20036. Filed 4/26/82. Legislative interest — "...legislation relating to the crude oil windfall profits tax, including but not limited to HR 6056, the Technical Corrections Act."

SOUTHWEST MARINE INC., San Diego, Calif. Lobbyist — Robert C. Wilson, 216 South Carolina Ave. S.E., Washington, D.C. 20003. Filed 4/9/82. (Former U.S. rep., R-Calif., 1953-81.) Legislative interest — "Ship repair."

STATE FARM INSURANCE CO., Salem, Ore. Lobbyist — Dennis M. Olsen, 485 E St., Idaho Falls, Idaho 83402. Filed 4/12/82. Legislative interest — "Introduction of legislation for congressional reference to Court of Claims on claims arising out of the failure of the Teton Dam in Idaho."

STERN, AGEE & LEACH, Birmingham, Ala. Lobbyist — Camp, Camouche, Palmer, Barsh & Hunter, 2550 M St. N.W., Washington, D.C. 20037. Filed 4/16/82. Legislative interest — "...I.R.S. Code Section 103."

TECHNOLOGY CENTER INC., Montgomeryville, Pa. Lobbyist — Christopher L. Davis, 1920 N St. N.W., Washington, D.C. 20036. Filed 4/7/82. Legislative interest — "...development assistance for small high-technology businesses."

TEXACO INC., Washington, D.C. Lobbyist — Camp, Carmouche, Palmer, Barsh & Hunter, 2550 M St. N.W., Washington, D.C. 20037. Filed 4/27/82. Legislative interest — "...legislation affecting the production, refining, processing and marketing of oil and natural gas...."

TORONTO STOCK EXCHANGE, Toronto, Ontario, Canada. Lobbyist — Proskauer, Rose, Goetz & Mendelsohn, 1150 Connecticut Ave. N.W., Washington, D.C. 20036. Filed 4/16/82. Legislative interest — "...S 2109 and HR 5447...."

TOSCO CORP., Boulder, Colo.; Los Angeles, Calif.; Washington, D.C. Lobbyist — Wexler and Associates Inc., 1616 H St. N.W., Washington, D.C. 20006. Filed 4/9/82. Legislative interest — "...legislation affecting the development of synthetic fuels programs, particularly with respect to oil shale...." Lobbyist — Sisk, Foley, Hultin & Driver, 2501 M St. N.W., Washington, D.C. 20037. Filed 4/14/82. Legislative interest — "...legislation to increase domestic production of energy (including S 725, S 750, and HR 2133) ... tax and other legislation to promote economic recovery...." Lobbyist — National Counsel Associates Inc., 421 New Jersey Ave. S.E., Washington, D.C. 20003. Filed 4/9/82. Legislative interest — "...synthetic fuel development."

TOYOTA MOTOR SALES U.S.A. INC., 919 18th St. N.W., Washington, D.C. 20006. Filed for self 4/12/82. Legislative interest — "Imports of automobiles and trucks." Lobbyist — Patti Tilson, 900 17th St. N.W., Washington, D.C. 20006.

TRAVELER'S INDEMNITY OF RHODE ISLAND, Salt Lake City, Utah. Lobbyist — Dennis M. Olsen, 485 E St., Idaho Falls, Idaho 83402. Filed 4/12/82. Legislative interest — "Introduction of legislation for congressional reference to Court of Claims on claims arising out of the failure of the Teton Dam in Idaho."

TRW INC., 23555 Euclid Ave., Cleveland, Ohio 44117. Filed for self 4/1/82. Legislative interest — "...taxes, pension, health insurance, trade, patent...." Lobbyist — William H. Birtcil Jr., 1000 Wilson Blvd., Arlington, Va. 22209.

TURNER BROADCASTING SYSTEM INC., Atlanta,

Ga. Lobbyist — Pepper, Hamilton & Scheetz, 1777 F St. N.W., Washington, D.C. 20006-5269. Filed 4/13/82. Legislative interest — "Legislation affecting the communications industry and copyright legislation affecting cable."

URANERZBERGBAU-GMBH, Bonn, West Germany. Lobbyist — Arent, Fox, Kintner, Plotkin & Kahn, 1815 H St. N.W., Washington, D.C. 20006. Filed 4/20/82. (Former U.S. Sen. John C. Culver, D-Iowa, 1975-81, House 1965-75, was listed as agent for this client.) Legislative interest — "Opposing section 206(e) of Senate version of HR 2330, which section may have the effect of restricting the importation of uranium into the United States for use in commercial nuclear power facilities."

WASHINGTON GAS LIGHT CO., 1100 H St. N.W., Washington, D.C. 20080. Filed for self 4/9/82. Legislative interest — Not specified. Lobbyist — Prudence H. Parks.

WHEAT FIRST SECURITIES INC., Richmond, Va. Lobbyist — Camp, Carmouche, Palmer, Barsh & Hunter, 2550 M St. N.W., Washington, D.C. 20037. Filed 4/16/82. Legislative interest — "...I.R.S. Code Section 103."

F. W. WOOLWORTH CO., New York, N.Y. Lobbyist — Silverstein and Mullens, 1776 K St. N.W., Washington, D.C. 20006. Filed 4/12/82. Legislative interest — "...the Administration's proposed corporate alternative minimum tax."

International Relations

GOVERNMENT OF ANTIGUA AND BARBUDA, St. John's, Antigua. Lobbyist — Finley, Kumble, Wagner, Heine, Underberg & Casey, 1120 Connecticut Ave. N.W., Washington, D.C. 20036. Filed 4/15/82. (Former U.S. Sen. Joseph D. Tydings, D-Md., 1965-71, was listed as agent for this client.) Legislative interest — "...international agreements and economic assistance programs; S 2237 and HR 5900, 'Caribbean Basin Economic Recovery Act'...."

ASOCIACION DE AMIGOS DEL PAIS, Guatemala City, Guatemala. Lobbyists — Patton, Boggs & Blow, 2550 M St. N.W., Washington, D.C. 20037. Filed 4/1/82. Legislative interest — "In favor of the Caribbean Basin Economic Recovery Act - HR 5900 and S 2237."

ASOCIACION DE AZUCAREROS DE GUATEMALA, Guatemala City, Guatemala. Lobbyist — Patton, Boggs & Blow, 2550 M St. N.W., Washington, D.C. 20037. Legislative interest — "In favor of the Caribbean Basin Economic Recovery Act - HR 5900 and S 2237."

Labor Groups

FOOD AND BEVERAGE TRADES DEPARTMENT, AFL-CIO, 815 16th St. N.W., Washington, D.C. 20006. Filed for self 4/16/82. Legislative interest — "...polygraphs ... national health insurance ... food stamps and child nutrition ... food labeling and safety ... FTC ... consumer protection ... ERA, national voting rights, FTC voting rights ... better nutrition for low-income citizens ... taxation of fringe benefits ... constitutional amendment requiring a balanced budget ... tobacco ... international trade ... minimum wage and youth subminimum wage ... plant closings ... successorship ... bottle bill ... tourism ... gasahol programs." Lobbyist — Edward J. Durkin.

INTERNATIONAL ASSOCIATION OF MACHINISTS AND AEROSPACE WORKERS, 1300 Connecticut Ave. N.W., Washington, D.C. 20036. Filed for self 4/15/82. Legislative interest — "...social security, national health, aid to the physically handicapped, labor relations, displaced people, energy...." Lobbyist — William J. Holayter.

NATIONAL ASSOCIATION OF GOVERNMENT EMPLOYEES, South Boston, Mass. Lobbyist — Cook, Purcell, Hansen & Henderson, 1015 18th St. N.W., Washington, D.C. 20036. Filed 4/26/82. Legislative interest — "...public employees health benefits programs."

NATIONAL EDUCATION ASSOCIATION, 1201 16th St. N.W., Washington, D.C. 20036. Filed for self 4/12/82. Legislative interest — "...HR 2504 ... H J Res 325 ... HR 1323 ... HR 72 ... HR 1454 ... H J Res 86 ... H J Res 91 ... HR 92 ... HR 394 ... HR 573 ... HR 802 ... HR 924 ... HR 985 ... S 181 ... HR 815 ... S 25 ... HR 1522 ... Voting Rights Act extension, social security issues, comprehensive elementary school guidance programs, Department of Education proposals, budget resolutions, truth in testing proposals, federal assistance programs, consolidation, school lunch issues, overseas schools, impact aid, Education Consolidation and Improvement Act, AWACs, El Salvador aid, Family Protection Act." Lobbyists — John A. Conway, Michael D. Edwards.

PENNSYLVANIA STATE EDUCATION ASSOCIATION, 400 N. Third St., Harrisburg, Pa. 17105. Filed for self 4/12/82. Legislative interest — "...Cabinet level Department of Education, federal collective bargaining rights, education for the handicapped, teacher training programs, higher education programs, appropriations for education, social security, tuition tax credits, federal funding of education." Lobbyist — Janet B. Figler.

State and Local Governments

GUADALUPE BLANCO RIVER AUTHORITY, Seguin, Texas. Lobbyist — Vinson & Elkins, 3300 First City Tower, Houston, Texas 77002. Filed 4/21/82. Legislative interest — "Tax legislation."

MONTGOMERY COUNTY INDUSTRIAL DEVELOPMENT CORP., Conroe, Texas. Lobbyist — Vinson & Elkins, 3300 First City Tower, Houston, Texas 77002. Filed 4/21/82. Legislative interest — "Tax legislation."

OFFICE OF STATES' WASHINGTON REPRESENTATIVE TO APPALACHIAN REGIONAL COMMISSION, Washington, D.C. Lobbyist — William H. Harsha & Associates Inc., P.O. Box 24157, Washington, D.C. 20024. Filed 4/8/82. (Former U.S. Rep. William H. Harsha, R-Ohio, 1961-81, was listed as agent for this client.) Legislative interest — Not specified.

OHIO ASSOCIATION OF COMMUNITY ACTION AGENCIES, Columbus, Ohio. Lobbyist — Taft, Stettinius & Hollister, 1800 Massachusetts Ave. N.W., Washington, D.C. 20036. Filed 4/12/82. (Former U.S. Sen. Robert A. Taft Jr., R-Ohio, 1971-77, was listed as agent for this client.) Legislative interest — "...matters relating to community service block grants in the 1983 budget and to the proposed Training for Jobs Act, S 2036 ... HR 5461, HR 5320."

PAPILLION, NEB., SCHOOL DISTRICT, Papillion, Neb. Lobbyist — John K. Green, 800 Nebraska Savings Building, Omaha, Neb. 68102. Filed 4/10/82. Legislative interest — "Continued funding for PL 874, 81st Congress (20 U.S.C. 238)."

PUERTO RICO HOUSE OF REPRESENTATIVES, San Juan, Puerto Rico. Lobbyist — Jose A. Ortiz Daliot, 1522 K St. N.W., Washington, D.C. 20005. Filed 4/21/82. Legislative interest — "...the Caribbean Basin Initiative, Food Stamps...." Lobbyist — Richard M. Millman, 1730 M St. N.W., Washington, D.C. 20036. Filed 4/12/82. Legislative interest — "HR 3982...."

CITY OF TUCSON, Tucson, Ariz. Lobbyist — Bracy, Williams & Co., 1730 Rhode Island Ave. N.W., Washington, D.C. 20036. Filed 4/12/82. Legislative interest — Not specified.

WEST VIRGINIA INDUSTRIAL DEVELOPMENT ASSOCIATION, Moorefield, W.Va. Lobbyist — Ballard, Spahr, Andrews & Ingersoll, 1850 K St. N.W., Washington, D.C. 20006. Filed 4/14/82. Legislative interest — "...to preserve the present authority for use of IDBs."

Trade Associations

AD HOC COMMITTEE OF MUTUAL FUND MANAGERS, 1750 Pennsylvania Ave. N.W., Washington, D.C. 20006. Filed for self 4/12/82. Legislative interest — "...Title 3 of Senate bill no. 1720...." Lobbyist — Daniel J. Pilliero II.

AMERICAN ADVERTISING FEDERATION, 1225 Connecticut Ave. N.W., Washington, D.C. 20036. Filed for self 4/14/82. Legislative interest — "...legislation that affects advertising agencies, advertisers and advertising media...." Lobbyist — Daniel L. Jaffe.

AMERICAN ASSOCIATION OF ORAL AND MAXILLOFACIAL SURGEONS, Chicago, Ill. Lobbyist — Covington & Burling, 1201 Pennsylvania Ave. N.W., Washington, D.C. 20044. Filed 4/20/82. Legislative interest — "Medicare amendments; PSRO legislation."

AMERICAN ASSOCIATION OF RETIRED PERSONS, 1909 K St. N.W., Washington, D.C. 20049. Filed for self 4/15/82. Legislative interest — "...improved social security and medicare/medicaid laws, Older Americans Act amendments, improved tax treatment of older Americans, improved nursing home standards, consumer protection legislation, employment of older workers, transportation of the elderly, no-fault insurance, housing for the elderly, national health insurance." Lobbyist — William K. Brunette.

AMERICAN BUS ASSOCIATION, Washington, D.C. Lobbyist — F/P Research Associates, 1700 K St. N.W., Washington, D.C. 20006. Filed 4/7/82. Legislative interest — "The Bus Regulatory Reform Act of 1981 - HR 3663, S 926, S 927."

AMERICAN DENTAL ASSOCIATION, 1101 17th St. N.W., Washington, D.C. 20036. Filed for self 4/4/82. Legislative interest — "...S 433, HR 850, HR 3722, S 1984, HR 3827, S 2142...." Lobbyist — Roy S. Bredder.

AMERICAN INSTITUTE OF MERCHANT SHIPPING, 1625 K St. N.W., Washington, D.C. 20006. Filed for self 4/13/82. Legislative interest — Not specified. Lobbyist — Ernest J. Corrado.

AMERICAN MINING CONGRESS, 1920 N St. N.W., Washington, D.C. 20036. Filed for self 4/12/82. Legislative interest — "Measures affecting mining such as income taxation, social security, public lands, monetary policy, mine safety, stockpiling, environmental quality control...." Lobbyist — Rae Cronmiller.

ASSOCIATED BUILDERS AND CONTRACTORS INC., 444 North Capitol St. N.W., Washington, D.C. 20001. Filed for self 4/16/82. Legislative interest — "...HR 48, HR 321, HR 1034, HR 1325, HR 1437 ... S 398, HR 283 ... S 351, S 496, HR 1603 ... S 613, HR 3047, HR 450 ... S 1080, HR 746 ... S 3 ... S 348...." Lobbyist — Michael M. Schoor.

THE ASSOCIATED GENERAL CONTRACTORS OF AMERICA, 1957 E St. N.W., Washington, D.C. 20006. Filed for self 4/8/82. Legislative interest — "...Davis-Bacon Repeal (HR 48)...." Lobbyist — G. Brockwel Baylin. Filed for self 4/8/82. Legislative interest — "Public Building Act (S 533)...." Lobbyist — Richard F. Lane.

ASSOCIATION OF AMERICAN RAILROADS, 1920 L St. N.W., Washington, D.C. 20036. Filed for self 4/14/82. Legislative interest — Not specified. Lobbyist — John Gonella, 412 First St. S.E., Washington, D.C. 20003.

ASSOCIATION OF NIGHT VISION MANUFACTURERS, Washington, D.C. Lobbyist — Parrish & Chambers Inc., 1300 N. 17th St., Arlington, Va. 22209. Filed 4/7/82. Legislative interest — "Any measures relating to government recoupment of non-recurring R and D costs."

BRICK INSTITUTE OF AMERICA, 1750 Old Meadow Road, McLean, Va. 22102. Filed for self 4/19/82. Legislative interest — "...legislation affecting the manufacturing of brick products, including energy, tax and housing legislation." Lobbyist — Margaret M. Morris, Joel B. Stronberg.

BUSINESS COUNCIL FOR IMPROVED TRANSPORT POLICIES, 1000 Connecticut Ave. N.W., Washington, D.C. 20036. Filed for self 4/28/82. Legislative interest — "...passage of the Motor Carrier Act of 1980...." Lobbyist — Jack Pearce.

THE BUSINESS ROUNDTABLE, 1828 L St. N.W., Washington, D.C. 20036. Filed for self 4/10/82. Legislative interest — "...proposals regarding the production and utilization of energy, proposals in the fields of taxation and antitrust...." Lobbyist — Samuel L. Maury.

COALITION OF SERVICE INDUSTRIES INC., Washington, D.C. Lobbyist — Akin, Gump, Strauss, Hauer & Feld, 1333 New Hampshire Ave. N.W., Washington, D.C. 20036. Filed 4/26/82. Legislative interest — "Hearings and legislation relating to strengthening the service industries status under U.S. international trade laws, including but not limited to S 2058, HR 5383, S 2094 and HR 5519."

THE CONSUMER BANKERS ASSOCIATION, 1300 N. 17th St., Arlington, Va. 22209. Filed for self 4/12/82. Legislative interest — "...HR 2501, S 1406 ... S 1720 ... S 2000, HR 4786...." Lobbyist — Marcia Z. Sullivan.

DESERT GRAPE GROWERS LEAGUE OF CALIFORNIA, Coachella, Calif. Lobbyist — Damrell, Damrell & Nelson, 911 13th St., Modesto, Calif. 95353. Filed 4/14/82. Legislative interest — "Hearings and any legislation relating to HR 1852 and S 505 (amendment to Agricultural Marketing Agreement Act)." Lobbyist — Akin, Gump, Strauss, Hauer & Feld, 1333 New Hampshire Ave. N.W., Washington, D.C. 20036. Filed 4/16/82. Legislative interest — "Hearings and any legislation relating to improving the quality of table grapes for marketing in the United States, including but not limited to S 505 and HR 1852."

THE EMPLOYERS COUNCIL ON FLEXIBLE COMPENSATION, 1700 Pennsylvania Ave. N.W., Washington, D.C. 20006. Filed for self 4/16/82. Legislative interest — "...legislation affecting flexible compensation for employees such as 26 U.S.C. subsection 125, 401(k)...." Lobbyist — Ivins, Phillips & Barker, 1700 Pennsylvania Ave. N.W., Washington, D.C. 20006. Filed 4/16/82. Legislative interest — "...legislation affecting flexible compensation for employees such as 26 U.S.C. subsections 125, 401(k), and health care cost containment measures...."

FARMERS FOR FAIRNESS, Camilla, Ga. Lobbyist — Shaw, Pittman, Potts & Trowbridge, 1800 M St. N.W., Washington, D.C. 20036. Filed 4/28/82. Legislative interest — "...section 702 ('National Poundage Quota and Farm Poundage Quota') of the Agriculture and Food Act of 1981 (7 U.S.C. 1281)...."

HOME RECORDING RIGHTS COALITION, Washington, D.C. Lobbyist — Cook, Purcell, Hansen & Henderson, 1015 18th St. N.W., Washington, D.C. 20036. Filed 4/26/82. Legislative interest — "...S 1758, HR 4808, HR 5488, HR 5709; opposes amendments nos. 1242 and 1331 to S 1758. Supports HR 4808, HR 5250, and S 1758."

INVESTMENT COMPANY INSTITUTE, 1775 K St. N.W., Washington, D.C. 20006. Lobbyist — Shaw, Pittman, Potts & Trowbridge, 1800 M St. N.W., Washington, D.C. 20036. Filed 4/15/82. Legislative interest — "S 1424 ... S 1427 ... S 1720 ... S 1888 ... HR 1916 ... HR 2591 ... HR 2916 ... HR 3058 ... HR 3097 ... HR 3230 ... HR 3456 ... HR 2980 ... HR 4049 ... HR 5004 ... HR 5053 ... HR 5699...." Filed for self 4/13/82. Legislative interest — "S 1424 ... S 1427 ... S 1720 ... S 1888 ... HR 1916 ... HR 2591 ... HR 2916 ... HR 3058 ... HR 3097 ... HR 3230 ... HR 3456 ... HR 2980 ... HR 4049 ... HR 5004 ... HR 5053 ... HR 5699...." Lobbyist — Mark J. Mackey.

NATIONAL ASSOCIATION OF ALCOHOLISM TREATMENT PROGRAMS INC., Irvine, Calif. Lobbyist — Perito, Duerk, Carlson & Pinco, 1140 Connecticut Ave. N.W., Washington, D.C. 20036. Legislative interest — "HR 5995, S 1989."

NATIONAL ASSOCIATION OF AMERICAN MINORITY CONTRACTORS AND CONSULTING ENGINEERS OF INDIAN ORIGIN, Sterling Heights, Mich. Lobbyist — David Vienna & Associates, 510 C St. N.E., Washington, D.C. 20002. Filed 4/8/82. Legislative interest — "Minority business economic development; Public Law 95-50; PL 96-302."

NATIONAL ASSOCIATION OF HOME BUILDERS OF THE UNITED STATES, 15th & M Sts. N.W., Washington, D.C. 20005. Filed for self 4/8/82. Legislative interest — Not specified. Lobbyists — Carole R. Carlin, Patricia K. Economos, Larry D. McBennett, Stephen J. Melman, Dale J. Wheeler.

NATIONAL ASSOCIATION OF MANUFACTURERS, 1776 F St. N.W., Washington, D.C. 20006. Filed for self 4/15/82. Legislative interest — "Budget and tax legislation; environmental legislation such as, but not limited to, HR 5252; economic development; and manpower legislation." Lobbyist — J. Lee Hamilton. Filed for self 4/9/82. Legislative interest — "...tax, budget, energy, regulatory, international labor, natural resources...." Lobbyist — Alexander B. Trowbridge.

NATIONAL ASSOCIATION OF PUBLIC TELEVISION STATIONS, 955 L'Enfant Plaza S.W., Washington, D.C. 20024. Filed for self 4/30/82. Legislative interest — "...appropri-

ations for the Corporation for Public Broadcasting (Labor-HEW appropriation bill) and for the Public Telecommunications Facilities Program (State, Justice, Commerce appropriation bill) and legislative amendments to the Communications Act of 1934 which affect public broadcasting." Lobbyist — Bruce L. Christensen.

NATIONAL ASSOCIATION OF SMALL BUSINESS INVESTMENT COMPANIES, 618 Washington Building, Washington, D.C. 20005. Filed for self 4/16/82. Legislative interest — Not specified. Lobbyist — L. Andrea Hatfield, Peter F. McNeish.

NATIONAL CABLE TELEVISION ASSOCIATION INC., 1724 Massachusetts Ave. N.W., Washington, D.C. 20036. Filed for self 4/13/82. Legislative interest — "Amendments to the Communications Act of 1934 and other legislation affecting cable television generally." Lobbyists — Michael Donaghue, Patrick C. Koch, Patrick L. Mellon.

NATIONAL COUNCIL FOR INDUSTRIAL INNOVATION, 1001 Connecticut Ave. N.W., Washington, D.C. 20036. Filed for self 4/30/82. Legislative interest — "S 881 ... HR 4326...." Lobbyist — Jere W. Glover.

NATIONAL FARM AND POWER EQUIPMENT DEALERS ASSOCIATION, St. Louis, Mo. Lobbyist — Neill & Mullenholz, 1100 17th St. N.W., Washington, D.C. 20036. Filed 4/2/82. Legislative interest — Not specified.

NATIONAL MACHINE TOOL BUILDERS' ASSOCIATION, 7901 Westpark Drive, McLean, Va. 22102. Filed for self 4/12/82. Legislative interest — "Tax, product liability, Eximbank, export control, and other legislation affecting the machine tool industry." Lobbyist — Carolyn Kim McCarthy.

THE NATIONAL PASSENGER TRAFFIC ASSOCIATION INC., New York, N.Y. Lobbyist — Baron/Canning and Co., Inc., 540 Madison Ave., New York, N.Y. 10022. Filed 4/22/82. (Former U.S. Rep. Seymour Halpern, R-N.Y., 1959-73, was listed as agent for this client.) Legislative interest — "...matters pertaining to the CAB, airline deregulation and sunset legislation."

NATIONAL RESTAURANT ASSOCIATION, 311 First St. N.W., Washington, D.C. 20001. Filed for self 4/1/82. Legislative interest — "...legislation involving small business, labor laws, wages and hours, taxation, consumer protection, food marketing, and economic stabilization." Lobbyist — Ann Cole.

NATIONAL RETIRED TEACHERS ASSOCIATION, 1909 K St. N.W., Washington, D.C. 20049. Filed for self 4/15/82. Legislative interest — "...improved social security and medicare/medicaid laws, Older Americans Act amendments, improved tax treatment of older Americans, improved nursing home standards, consumer protection legislation, employment of older workers, transportation of the elderly, no-fault insurance, housing for the elderly, national health insurance." Lobbyist — William K. Brunette.

NATIONAL TELEPHONE COOPERATIVES ASSOCIATION, 2626 Pennsylvania Ave. N.W., Washington, D.C. 20037. Filed for self 4/16/82. Legislative interest — "All legislation affecting the rural telephone program provided for in the Rural Electrification Act of 1936; all legislation affecting telecommunications and amendments to the Communications Act of 1934; all legislation affecting the Rural Telephone Bank Act of 1971...." Lobbyist — Kimberly Ann Neilsen.

NORTH CAROLINA PEANUT GROWERS, Rocky Mount, N.C. Lobbyist — Larry Meyers, 412 First St. S.E., Washington, D.C. 20003. Filed 4/16/82. Legislative interest — "General farm bill."

SENIOR EXECUTIVES ASSOCIATION, P.O. Box 7610, Benjamin Franklin Station, Washington, D.C. 20044. Filed for self 4/8/82. Legislative interest — "Legislation affecting pay, benefits, and job security of federal government SES and supergrade employees; affecting improvements in government management, efficiency and effectiveness; affecting the liability of government employees to suit...." Lobbyists — Blair G. Childs, Mary Hoyer.

SLURRY TRANSPORT ASSOCIATION, Washington, D.C. Lobbyist — Kirby & Gillick, 600 Maryland Ave. S.W., Washington, D.C. 20024. Filed 4/14/82. Legislative interest — "Supporting legislation designed to grant federal rights of eminent domain for the construction of a coal slurry pipeline." Lobbyist —

Van Ness, Feldman, Sutcliffe, Curtis & Levenberg, 1050 Thomas Jefferson St. N.W., Washington, D.C. 20007. Filed 4/10/82. Legislative interest — "General federal energy transportation issues, specifically the coal slurry pipeline legislation."

WASHINGTON PSYCHIATRIC SOCIETY, Washington, D.C. Lobbyist — C & B Associates, 1750 18th St. N.W., Washington, D.C. 20006. Filed 4/12/82. Legislative interest — "Health legislation dealing especially with mental health."

Miscellaneous

AMERICAN BUREAU OF COLLECTIONS INC., Buffalo, N.Y. Lobbyist — Christopher L. Davis, 1920 N St. N.W., Washington, D.C. 20036. Filed 4/7/82. Legislative interest — "Legislation pertaining to the collection of monies owed the federal government."

THOMAS E. BRYANT, Washington, D.C. Lobbyist — Gerald R. Connor, 6500 Wisconsin Ave., Chevy Chase, Md. 20815. Filed 4/30/82. Legislative interest — "Amendments to the Public Health Service Act; amendments to Title XVIII and XIX of the Social Security Act; amendments to tax law concerning nonprofit organizations."

CALIFORNIA STUDENT LOAN FINANCE CORP., Los Angeles, Calif. Lobbyist — Nossaman, Krueger & Marsh, 1140 19th St. N.W., Washington, D.C. 20036. Filed 4/14/82. Legislative interest — "Opposition to proposed changes in Internal Revenue Code affecting non-profit organizations issuing revenue bonds to purchase scholarship loan obligations."

HARRY GANDERSON, P.O. Box 2593, Washington, D.C. 20013 and P.O. Box 25899, Richmond, Va. 23260. Filed for self 4/18/82. Legislative interest — "...international trade and laws, and all foreign affairs related directly or indirectly to such."

ESTATE OF HELEN WODELL HALBACH, Union, N.J. Lobbyist — Hamel, Park, McCabe & Saunders, 888 16th St. N.W., Washington, D.C. 20006. Filed 4/28/82. Legislative interest — "...passage of S 1983 or HR 2583...."

May Registrations

Citizens' Groups

AMERICAN ISRAEL PUBLIC AFFAIRS COMMITTEE, 444 North Capitol St. N.W., Washington, D.C. 20001. Filed for self 5/19/82. Legislative interest — "Support Foreign Assistance authorization and appropriations legislation for FY 82, with full funding for Administration request for Israel, and resettlement funds for Soviet and Eastern European refugees in Israel. Support general legislation to maintain and strengthen the friendship between the United States and Israel." Lobbyist — Leslie Levy.

COALITION FOR AN EFFECTIVE ENERGY INVESTMENT TAX CREDIT, Washington, D.C. Lobbyist — Camp, Carmouche, Palmer, Barsh & Hunter, 2550 M St. N.W., Washington, D.C. 20037. Filed 5/24/82. Legislative interest — "Matters pertaining to the energy investment tax credit (Internal Revenue Code, Sections 46-48)."

CONSERVATIVES AGAINST LIBERAL LEGISLATION, 5707 Seminary Road, Bailey's Crossroads, Va. 22041. Filed for self 5/17/82. Legislative interest — "...to circumscribe major legislation designed to expand the power of the federal government and support legislation which will lessen the burden of government." Lobbyist — Patrick R. Curren.

FARMWORKER JUSTICE FUND INC., 806 15th St. N.W., Washington, D.C. 20005. Filed for self 5/26/82. Legislative interest — Not specified. Lobbyist — Mark S. Schacht.

INSTITUTE FOR PUBLIC REPRESENTATION, 600 New Jersey Ave. N.W., Washington, D.C. 20001. Filed for self 5/15/82. Legislative interest — "The Voting Rights of the Handicapped and the Elderly Act, S 2334, HR 6036...." Lobbyist — Karen Peltz Strauss.

SCENIC HUDSON INC., 9 Vassar St., Poughkeepsie, N.Y. 12601. Filed for self 5/11/82. Legislative interest — Not specified. Lobbyist — Klara B. Sauer.

UNION OF CONCERNED SCIENTISTS, 1384 Massachusetts Ave., Cambridge, Mass. 02238. Filed for self 5/24/82. Legislative interest — "Promotion of arms control, strategic arms limitation talks, reduced military spending. Opposition to specific arms programs (MX, B1-B)." Lobbyist — Charles A. Monfort, 1346 Connecticut Ave. N.W., Washington, D.C. 20036.

Corporations and Businesses

ALAMO RENT A CAR, Fort Lauderdale, Fla. Lobbyist — Fulbright & Jaworski, 1150 Connecticut Ave. N.W., Washington, D.C. 20036. Filed 5/26/82. Legislative interest — "Legislation affecting Title 26 of the U.S.C."

ALASKA RESOURCE ANALYSTS INC., P.O. Box 3576 ECB, Anchorage, Alaska 99501. Filed for self 5/24/82. Legislative interest — "Alaska lands legislation." Lobbyist — Art Kennedy.

AMERICAN STOCK EXCHANGE, New York, N.Y. Lobbyist — Kirkpatrick, Lockhart, Hill, Christopher & Phillips, 1900 M St. N.W., Washington, D.C. 20036. Filed 5/14/82. Legislative interest — "Legislation relating to CFTC/SEC jurisdictional accord. S 2260, S 2109, HR 5447, HR 6156."

ANCHOR NATIONAL LIFE INSURANCE CO., Phoenix, Ariz. Lobbyist — Covington & Burling, P.O. Box 7566, Washington, D.C. 20004. Filed 5/13/82. Legislative interest — "Federal tax legislation relating to annuity contracts."

BENEFICIAL CORP., Wilmington, Del. Lobbyist — Akin, Gump, Strauss, Hauer & Feld, 1333 New Hampshire Ave. N.W., Washington, D.C. 20036. Legislative interest — "Hearings and any legislation affecting financial institutions, including securities, tax, export trading and general banking powers."

BENENSON REALTY CO., New York, N.Y. Lobbyist — Wexler and Associates Inc., 1616 H St. N.W., Washington, D.C. 20006. Filed 5/21/82. Legislative interest — "Action by the House Public Works Committee and Senate Environment and Public Works Committee in regards to a lease at 1775 Pennsylvania Ave. N.W." Lobbyist — Williams & Connolly, 1000 Hill Building, Washington, D.C. 20006. Filed 5/20/82. Legislative interest — "Prospectus No. PDC 82010 - House Committee on Public Works - proposal to consolidate ICA facilities."

BOEING CO., Seattle, Wash. Lobbyist — Preston, Thorgrimson, Ellis & Holman, 1776 G St. N.W., Washington, D.C. 20006. Filed 5/25/82. (Former U.S. Rep. Lloyd Meeds, D-Wash., 1965-79, was listed as agent for this client.) Legislative interest — "Efforts to achieve adjustments in authorization for procurement of aircraft and to effect appropriations for same. HR 6030 and other legislation dealing with this subject matter."

BROWARD FEDERAL SAVINGS AND LOAN ASSOCIATION, Sunrise, Fla. Lobbyist — Avenel Associates Inc., P.O. Box 53131, Washington, D.C. 20009. Filed 5/3/82. Legislative interest — "HR 5731 - will favor if amended."

CAPITAL BANK, Miami, Fla. Lobbyist — Akin, Gump, Strauss, Hauer & Feld, 1333 New Hampshire Ave. N.W., Washington, D.C. 20036. Filed 5/3/82. Legislative interest — "Hearings and any related legislation affecting financial institutions, including securities, tax, export trading and general banking powers."

CBS INC., New York, N.Y. Lobbyist — Wilmer, Cutler & Pickering, 1666 K St. N.W., Washington, D.C. 20006. Filed 5/16/82. Legislative interest — "To promote passage of legislation to amend Title 17 of the United States Code with respect to home audio and video recording, including amendment No. 1333 to S 1758 and HR 5705."

CHESAPEAKE INDUSTRIES INC., 2111 Harbor Drive, Annapolis, Md. 21401. Filed for self 5/16/82. Legislative interest — "...the furthering of free enterprise...." Lobbyist — Floyd H. Gilkey.

CLAIBORNE GASOLINE CO., Dallas, Texas. Lobbyist — O'Connor & Hannan, 1919 Pennsylvania Ave. N.W., Washington, D.C. 20006. Filed 5/19/82. Legislative interest — "Lobbying and support of continuing the small refiners' exemption to the EPA lead phasedown regulations."

CONSUMERS POWER CO., 212 W. Michigan Ave., Jackson, Mich. 49201. Filed for self 5/24/82. Legislative interest — "...Clean Air Act Amendments, nuclear waste legislation, Public Utility Holding Company Act, outdoor gas lighting, natural gas deregulation." Lobbyist — John A. Howes, 1050 17th St. N.W., Washington, D.C. 20036.

CONTINENTAL AIRLINES, Los Angeles, Calif. Lobbyist — Akin, Gump, Strauss, Hauer & Feld, 1333 New Hampshire Ave. N.W., Washington, D.C. 20036. Filed for self 5/18/82. Legislative interest — "Tax legislation relating to airlines, including but not limited to safe harbor leasing tax legislation."

EASTERN MICROWAVE INC., Syracuse, N.Y. Lobbyist — Dow, Lohnes & Albertson, 1225 Connecticut Ave. N.W., Washington, D.C. 20036. Filed 5/12/82. Legislative interest — "General amendments to the Copyright Act, HR 5949...." Lobbyist — Gray and Co., 3255 Grace St. N.W., Washington, D.C. 20007. Filed 5/24/82. Legislative interest — "Including but not limited to copyright revision legislation."

ENERGY FUELS CORP., Denver, Colo. Lobbyist — Teno Roncalio, P.O. Box 1707, Cheyenne, Wyo. 82001. Filed 5/26/82. (Former U.S. rep., D-Wyo., 1965-67, 1971-78.) Legislative interest — "...HR 5603; a bill to withdraw national wilderness preservation system lands from operation of general mining and mineral leasing ... HR 5552, HR 5162, and similar bills directing the Secretary of the Interior to prepare and submit a State of the Parks Report to Congress."

EQUITABLE BANK, Dallas, Texas. Lobbyist — Akin, Gump, Strauss, Hauer & Feld, 1333 New Hampshire Ave. N.W., Washington, D.C. 20036. Filed 5/3/82. Legislative interest — "Hearings and any related legislation affecting financial institutions including securities, tax, export trading and general banking powers."

FACET CORP., Tulsa, Okla. Lobbyist — Chambers Associates, 1100 17th St. N.W., Washington, D.C. 20036. Filed 5/24/82. Legislative interest — "S 1835 amending Employment Retirement Income Security Act of 1974 (for)."

FLUOR CORP., Washington, D.C. Lobbyist — Bliss & Craft, 1050 Thomas Jefferson St. N.W., Washington, D.C. 20036. Filed 5/10/82. Legislative interest — "All legislation affecting the Alaska Natural Gas Pipeline and the issue of completion contract accounting."

FORD AEROSPACE AND COMMUNICATIONS CORP., Arlington, Va. Lobbyist — J. C. Steen, 406 First St. S.E., Washington, D.C. 20003. Filed 5/11/82. Legislative interest — "Defense authorization (HR 6030 and S 2248) and appropriation ... bills...."

GENERAL MOTORS CORP., Washington, D.C. Lobbyist — J. C. Steen, 406 First St. S.E., Washington, D.C. 20003. Filed 5/19/82. Legislative interest — "Defense authorization (HR 6030 and S 2248) and appropriation ... bills...."

GETTY OIL CO., 3810 Wilshire Blvd., Los Angeles, Calif. 90010. Filed for self 5/10/82. Legislative interest — "...coal slurry pipeline (HR 4230 - S 1844); natural gas (S 2074); cargo preference (S 1692); retail marketing divorcement (HR 1362); clean air (HR 5252); clean water; OCS leasing policy (HR 5252); lead phasedown; corporate minimum tax; product liability reform (HR 5214 & HR 5216); oil import fee." Lobbyist — Elvira J. Orly, 1701 Pennsylvania Ave. N.W., Washington, D.C. 20006.

HALLMARK CARDS INC., 25th & McGee, Kansas City, Mo. 64108. Lobbyist — Rae Forker Evans, 1201 Pennsylvania Ave. N.W., Washington, D.C. 20004. Filed 5/18/82. Legislative interest — "General legislative interest and postal and communications matters...." Filed for self 5/18/82. Legislative interest — "General legislative interest and postal and communication matters...." Lobbyist — Jane E. Greenbaum.

HARSCO CORP., Camp Hill, Pa. 17011. Filed for self 5/17/82. Legislative interest — Not specified. Lobbyist — Robert A. Haynos, 4711 Hunt Circle, Harrisburg, Pa. 17112.

HEMISPHERE NATIONAL BANK, Washington, D.C. Lobbyist — Akin, Gump, Strauss, Hauer & Feld, 1333 New Hampshire Ave. N.W., Washington, D.C. 20036. Filed 5/3/82. Legislative interest — "Hearings and any related legislation affecting financial institutions, including securities, tax, export trading

and general banking powers."

HUNTON & WILLIAMS, 1919 Pennsylvania Ave. N.W., Washington, D.C. 20036. Lobbyist — Pamela S. Aycock, 2601 Woodley Place N.W., Washington, D.C. 20008. Filed 5/7/82. Legislative interest — "To clarify the income tax treatment of amounts realized by certain regulated public utilities in settlement of damages under contracts for the purchase of fuels; the M.D.L. 235 Settlement Discounts Tax Act of 1981; S 1928 and HR 5147...."

IDEAL BASIC INDUSTRIES, Denver, Colo. Lobbyist — Charls E. Walker Associates Inc., 1730 Pennsylvania Ave. N.W., Washington, D.C. 20006. Filed 5/20/82. Legislative interest — "...may concern refundability of the investment tax credit, or items relating to taxation of leasing transactions."

INTERNATIONAL TITANIUM INC., Moses Lake, Wash. Lobbyist — Ullman Consultants Inc., 1000 Potomac St. N.W., Washington, D.C. 20007. Filed 5/27/82. (Former U.S. Rep. Al Ullman, D-Ore., 1957-81, was listed as agent for this client.) Legislative interest — "Appropriations affecting the National Defense Stockpile."

THE IRVINE CO., Newport Beach, Calif. Lobbyist — Latham, Watkins & Hills, 1333 New Hampshire Ave. N.W., Washington, D.C. 20036. Filed 5/10/82. Legislative interest — "Urgent Supplemental Appropriations Bill; housing and community development amendments. HR 5922...."

K-A CO., Kansas City, Mo. Lobbyist — Gardner, Carton & Douglas, 1875 I St. N.W., Washington, D.C. 20006. Filed 5/20/82. Legislative interest — "Legislation authorizing the exchange of U.S. government land to further industrial and business development in Kansas City, Missouri."

LAWYERS TITLE INSURANCE CORP., 6630 West Broad St., Richmond, Va. 23230. Lobbyist — Foley, Lardner, Hollabaugh & Jacobs, 1775 Pennsylvania Ave. N.W., Washington, D.C. 20006. Filed 5/25/82. Legislative interest — "...HR 6269 and related or successor legislation which would impose restrictions on controlled business arrangements incident to providing real estate settlement services." Filed for self 5/24/82. Legislative interest — "...proposed repeal of RESPA, Section 8." Lobbyists — Marvin C. Bowling Jr., Robert C. Dawson, William J. Rumsey, Billy F. Vaughn.

LONE STAR INDUSTRIES INC., Washington, D.C. Lobbyist — Charls E. Walker Associates Inc., 1730 Pennsylvania Ave. N.W., Washington, D.C. 20006. Filed 5/20/82. Legislative interest — "...may concern refundability of the investment tax credit or items relating to taxation of leasing transactions."

MARLINE OIL CORP., Washington, D.C. Lobbyist — Bliss & Craft, 1050 Thomas Jefferson St. N.W., Washington, D.C. 20006. Filed 5/10/82. Legislative interest — "All legislation dealing with the import of uranium."

MELAMINE CHEMICALS INC., Donaldsonville, La. Lobbyist — John C. Stone, P.O. Box 1300, McLean, Va. 22102. Filed 5/16/82. Legislative interest — "Legislation to increase duty on Melamine."

MID ATLANTIC NEPHROLOGY CENTER LTD., Washington, D.C. Lobbyist — Manatt, Phelps, Rothenberg & Tunney, 1200 New Hampshire Ave. N.W., Washington, D.C. 20036. Filed 5/16/82. (Former U.S. Rep. James C. Corman, D-Calif., 1961-81, was listed as agent for this client.) Legislative interest — "In opposition to HHS regulations concerning compensation for renal disease under Medicare...."

MISSISSIPPI CHEMICAL CORP., Yazoo City, Miss. Lobbyist — Jones, Day, Reavis & Pogue, 1735 I St. N.W., Washington, D.C. 20006. Filed 5/19/82. Legislative interest — "Legislation concerning natural gas sales contracts."

MORSE TYPEWRITER CO. INC., New York, N.Y. Lobbyist — Chwat/Weigend Associates, 226 Massachusetts Ave. N.E., Washington, D.C. 20002. Filed 5/18/82. Legislative interest — "...federal laws, policies, regulations and procedures regarding federal procurement and international trade of typewriters."

MOTOROLA INC., 1776 K St. N.W., Washington, D.C. 20006. Filed for self 5/10/82. Legislative interest — "HR 5008 and HR 5158, Telecommunications bills ... all 'reciprocity' trade legislation ... work sharing legislation ... HR 5332 and S 2256...." Lobbyist — Bruce C. Ladd Jr.

NATIONAL BROADCASTING CORP., Washington, D.C. Lobbyist — Robert G. Beckel, 609 G St. S.E., Washington, D.C. 20003. Filed 5/20/82. Legislative interest — Not specified.

NATIONAL SECURITIES CLEARING CORP., New York, N.Y. Lobbyist — Black, Manafort & Stone, 435 N. Lee St., Alexandria, Va. 22314. Filed 5/27/82. Legislative interest — "For legislation dealing with federal bankruptcy code, HR 4935."

NEW CHANNELS CORP., Washington, D.C. Lobbyist — Gray and Co., 3255 Grace St. N.W., Washington, D.C. 20007. Filed 5/24/82. Legislative interest — "...copyright legislation."

NEW YORK AIR, Flushing, N.Y. Lobbyist — Akin, Gump, Strauss, Hauer & Feld, 1333 New Hampshire Ave. N.W., Washington, D.C. 20036. Filed 5/18/82. Legislative interest — "Tax legislation relating to airlines, including but not limited to safe harbor leasing tax legislation."

O'BRIEN, FIERCE & EBERLE, Washington, D.C. Lobbyist — Pamela S. Aycock, 2601 Woodley Place N.W., Washington, D.C. 20008. Filed 5/7/82. Legislative interest — "To clarify the income tax treatment of amounts realized by certain regulated public utilities in settlement of damages under contracts for the purchase of fuels; the M.D.L. 235 Settlement Discounts Tax Act of 1981; S 1928 and HR 5147...."

OREGON METALLURGICAL CORP., Albany, Ore. Lobbyist — Ullman Consultants Inc., 1000 Potomac St. N.W, Washington, D.C. 20007. Filed 5/27/82. (Former U.S. Rep. Al Ullman, D-Ore., 1957-81, was listed as agent for this client.) Legislative interest — "Appropriations affecting the National Defense Stockpile."

PENNZOIL CO., Pennzoil Place, Box 2967, Houston, Texas 77001. Filed for self 5/11/82. Legislative interest — "Refining policy; deregulation of natural gas; end use controls; environmental matters; tax matters; international matters; public lands; and related matters." Lobbyist — Janice A. Fenberg, 1155 15th St. N.W., Washington, D.C. 20005.

PHILLIPS PETROLEUM CO., Bartlesville, Okla. 74004. Filed for self 5/26/82. Legislative interest — Not specified. Lobbyist — Earl F. David, 1825 K St. N.W., Washington, D.C. 20006.

THOMAS SAFRAN & ASSOCIATES, Los Angeles, Calif. Lobbyist — Latham, Watkins & Hills, 1333 New Hampshire Ave. N.W., Washington, D.C. 20036. Filed 5/10/82. Legislative interest — "Urgent Supplemental Appropriations Bill; housing and community development amendments. HR 5922."

SCOTT PAPER CO., Scott Plaza, Philadelphia, Pa. 19113. Filed for self 5/27/82. Legislative interest — "Income tax legislation." Lobbyist — Robert A. Ladig.

SHELL OIL CO., P.O. Box 2563, Houston, Texas 77001. Filed for self 5/27/82. Legislative interest — "...oil and gas production, chemicals, health, safety and the environment, taxation concerns, and employee/employer relations." Lobbyist — James E. Rich Jr., 1025 Connecticut Ave. N.W., Washington, D.C. 20036.

SOFREAVIA, Paris, France. Lobbyist — DGA International Inc., 1225 19th St. N.W., Washington, D.C. 20036. Filed 5/10/82. Legislative interest — Not specified.

SONY CORPORATION OF AMERICA, New York, N.Y. Lobbyist — Cornell, Pelcovits & Brenner, 1211 Connecticut Ave. N.W., Washington, D.C. 20036. Filed 5/17/82. Legislative interest — "...pending proposals to amend the copyright laws, title 17 of the United States Code, to exempt from copyright liability off-air recording by videotape recorders and/or establish a compulsory license fee or make other revisions of the copyright laws relating to such activities ... HR 4808, HR 5250, HR 4783, HR 5488, HR 5705, S 1758 (Amendment Nos. 1242, 1333)...."

TADIRAN ISRAEL ELECTRONICS INDUSTRIES LTD., New York, N.Y. Lobbyist — Kaplan, Russin & Vecchi, 1218 16th St. N.W., Washington, D.C. 20036. Filed 5/10/82. Legislative interest — "Amendments to the Department of Defense Authorization Bill for Fiscal Year 1983 relating to the limitation of procurement of FM, tactical voice communications system equipment outside the United States. S 2248."

TOYOTA MOTOR SALES U.S.A. INC., 2055 West 190th St., Torrance, Calif. 90509. Filed for self 5/13/82. Legislative interest — "Japan-U.S. trade and auto related legislation." Lobby-

ists — Phillip J. Broman, Hideaki Otaka, Yoshinori Usui, 919 18th St. N.W., Washington, D.C. 20006.

THE TRAVELERS INSURANCE CO., Hartford, Conn. Lobbyist — Vinson & Elkins, 1101 Connecticut Ave. N.W., Washington, D.C. 20036. Filed 5/26/82. Legislative interest — "...S 2353, HR 6045 (stopgap life insurance company taxation)."

UNION CAMP CORP., Washington, D.C. Lobbyist — Beveridge & Diamond, 1333 New Hampshire Ave. N.W., Washington, D.C. 20036. Filed 5/28/82. Legislative interest — "...the Clean Air Act."

UNION OIL COMPANY OF CALIFORNIA, 461 South Boylston St., Los Angeles, Calif. 90017. Filed for self 5/26/82. Legislative interest — "Clean Air Act amendments...." Lobbyist — Patricia M. O'Toole, 1100 Connecticut Ave. N.W., Washington, D.C. 20036.

UNITED SERVICES AUTOMOBILE ASSOCIATION, San Antonio, Texas. Lobbyist — Steponkus & Associates, 815 Connecticut Ave. N.W., Washington, D.C. 20006. Filed 5/13/82. Legislative interest — "Individual retirement accounts (IRAs) and auto safety appliances."

WAGNER & BAROODY, Washington, D.C. Lobbyist — R/A Associates, 1100 17th St. N.W., Washington, D.C. 20036. Filed 5/20/82. Legislative interest — "For retention of safe harbor leasing provision of Economic Recovery Act of 1981."

WARNER COMMUNICATIONS INC., New York, N.Y. Lobbyist — Bayh, Tabbert & Capehart, 1575 I St. N.W., Washington, D.C. 20005. Filed 5/20/82. Legislative interest — "HR 5705, S 1758, and related legislation." Lobbyist — Gray and Co., 3255 Grace St. N.W., Washington, D.C. 20007. Filed 5/20/82. Legislative interest — "...amendment 1333 to S 1758 and HR 5705."

WASTE MANAGEMENT INC., Oak Brook, Ill. Lobbyist — Johnson, Smith and Hibbard, P.O. Box 5524, Spartanburg, S.C. 29304. Filed 5/5/82. Legislative interest — "...oppose enactment of the Biaggi Ocean Incineration Amendment to HR 5723 or any similar amendments designed to preclude use of ocean incineration ships now in use or under construction by Waste Management."

WESTINGHOUSE ELECTRIC CORP., Washington, D.C. Lobbyist — Florida Business Associates, 2000 L St. N.W., Washington, D.C. 20036. Filed 5/24/82. Legislative interest — "...increased funding of mass transit in the House Transportation Appropriations bill and of transportation export programs through the Export-Import Bank in the House Foreign Operations Appropriations bill." Lobbyist — George Patten Resources Inc., 2000 L St. N.W., Washington, D.C. 20036. Filed 5/24/82. Legislative interest — "...increased funding of mass transit in the House Transportation Appropriations bill and of transportation export programs through the Export-Import Bank in the House Foreign Operations Appropriations bill."

Labor Groups

AMERICAN POSTAL WORKERS UNION, Washington, D.C. Lobbyist — Chambers Associates, 1100 17th St. N.W., Washington, D.C. 20036. Filed 5/24/82. Legislative interest — "Federal Employees Health Benefits Act, Federal Employees Compensation Act, Civil Service Retirement Act, concurrent budget resolutions, appropriations bills."

State and Local Governments

GOVERNMENT OF THE VIRGIN ISLANDS, St. Thomas, Virgin Islands. Lobbyist — Peabody, Lambert & Meyers, 1150 Connecticut Ave. N.W., Washington, D.C. 20036. Filed 5/26/82. Legislative interest — "...protecting Virgin Islands tariff and tax advantages vis-à-vis other Caribbean countries in the Caribbean Basin Initiatives (HR 5900), with particular reference to rum and business conventions ... promoting preferential tariff and tax treatment for Virgin Islands businesses, including HR 5985, HR 5758, and HR 2232."

STATE OF LOUISIANA, Baton Rouge, La. Lobbyists —

John C. McCarthy, John C. Stone, Box 1300, McLean, Va. 22102. Filed 5/16/82. Legislative interest — Not specified.

Trade Associations

AMERICAN BAKERS ASSOCIATION, Washington, D.C. Lobbyist — Lynn M. Daft, 1339 Wisconsin Ave. N.W., Washington, D.C. 20007. Filed 5/4/82. Legislative interest — "Amendments to the Food Stamp Act of 1977; S 2352...." Lobbyist — James H. Lake, 1200 New Hampshire Ave. N.W., Washington, D.C. 20036. Filed 5/11/82. Legislative interest — "Food stamp legislation."

AMERICAN COUNCIL FOR CAPITAL FORMATION, 1850 K St. N.W., Washington, D.C. 20006. Filed 5/20/82. Legislative interest — "...supports capital gains tax reductions for individuals and corporations; inventory accounting reform, including the delay and/or repeal of LIFO recapture provision of the Windfall Profit Tax Act of 1978; the Tax Limitation-Balanced Budget Constitutional Amendment (S Res 58, H Res 350) ... opposes proposals for a new corporate minimum income tax and repeal of the 'safe harbor' leasing provisions of the Economic Recovery Tax Act of 1981." Lobbyist — Margo Thorning.

AMERICAN COUNCIL OF LIFE INSURERS, Washington, D.C. Lobbyist — John P. Winburn, 1101 15th St. N.W., Washington, D.C. 20005. Filed 5/24/82. Legislative interest — "...legislation relating to taxation of life insurers."

AMERICAN HOME SEWING ASSOCIATION INC., New York, N.Y. Lobbyist — Chwat/Weigend Associates, 226 Massachusetts Ave. N.E., Washington, D.C. 20002. Filed 5/18/82. Legislative interest — "...legislation recognizing September 1982 as 'National Sewing Month,' and any federal laws, policies, regulations and procedures which involve the sewing industry and sewing consumers."

AMERICAN LOGISTICS ASSOCIATION, Falls Church, Va. Lobbyist — David Austern, 918 16th St. N.W., Washington, D.C. 20006. Filed 5/20/82. Legislative interest — "...military commissary and exchange funding authorization and appropriations for fiscal year 1983."

AMERICAN NUCLEAR ENERGY COUNCIL, 410 First St. S.E., Washington, D.C. 20003. Filed for self 5/3/82. Legislative interest — Not specified. Lobbyist — Mary Alice Cotter.

AMERICAN SUBCONTRACTORS ASSOCIATION INC., 8401 Corporate Drive, Landover, Md. 20785. Filed for self 5/24/82. Legislative interest — "HR 5022, S 1782 ... S 1131 ... HR 233 ... elimination of completed contract method of accounting...." Lobbyist — E. Colette Nelson.

ASSOCIATED BUILDERS AND CONTRACTORS INC., 444 North Capitol St. N.W., Washington, D.C. 20001. Filed for self 5/21/82. Legislative interest — "...HR 48, HR 321, HR 1034, HR 1325, HR 1437 ... S 398, HR 283 ... S 351, HR 1603 ... S 613, HR 3047, HR 450 ... unemployment compensation reform ... minority set-asides ... lobbying disclosure ... S 1080, HR 746 ... OSHA reform ... budget cuts (Administration proposals) ... tax legislation (Administration proposals) ... S 3 ... S 348...." Lobbyist — Judy L. Harris.

ASSOCIATION OF OIL PIPELINES, Washington, D.C. Lobbyist — Vinson & Elkins, 3300 First City Tower, Houston, Texas 77002. Filed 5/10/82. Legislative interest — "...S 1626 and HR 4488."

CIVIL PILOTS FOR REGULATORY REFORM, Austin, Texas. Lobbyist — Joseph, Powell, McDermott & Reiner, 1300 19th St. N.W., Washington, D.C. 20036. Filed 5/26/82. Legislative interest — "Legislation affecting licensing and certification of private and commercial pilots under the Federal Aviation Act of 1958, as amended. CPRR is specifically interested in the airman medical regulations contained in the Federal Aviation Regulations, 14 CFR, part 67."

COMMISSIONED OFFICERS ASSOCIATION OF THE PUBLIC HEALTH SERVICE, Washington, D.C. Lobbyist — Chambers Associates, 1100 17th St. N.W., Washington, D.C. 20036. Filed 5/24/82. Legislative interest — "Concurrrent Budget Resolutions, Labor, Health, Education, and Welfare Appropriations Bills."

CONSORTIUM OF SOCIAL SCIENCE ASSOCIATIONS, 1755 Massachusetts Ave. N.W., Washington, D.C. 20036. Filed for self 5/7/82. Legislative interest — "...HR 5919." Lobbyist — Philip Speser.

COUNCIL OF EUROPEAN & JAPANESE NATIONAL SHIPOWNERS' ASSOCIATION, London, England. Lobbyist — Kirlin, Campbell & Keating, 1150 Connecticut Ave. N.W., Washington, D.C. 20036. Filed 5/26/82. Legislative interest — "...legislation relating to liner transportation in international commerce."

FLORIDA BANKERS ASSOCIATION, Orlando, Fla. Lobbyist — George Patten Resources Inc., 2000 L St. N.W., Washington, D.C. 20036. Filed 5/20/82. Legislative interest — "...supports an extension of the moratorium on Interstate Trust Banking."

FOOD MARKETING INSTITUTE, Washington, D.C. Lobbyist — Nossaman, Krueger & Knox, 1140 19th St. N.W., Washington, D.C. 20036. Filed 5/13/82. Legislative interest — "...amendments to the Employee Retirement Income Security Act and Multiemployer Pension Plan Amendments Act...."

THE INSTITUTE OF ELECTRICAL AND ELECTRONICS ENGINEERS INC., New York, N.Y. Lobbyist — Nossaman, Krueger & Knox, 1140 19th St. N.W., Washington, D.C. 20036. Filed 5/28/82. Legislative interest — "Amendments to federal procurement statutes affecting engineers employed by contractors...."

MOTION PICTURE ASSOCIATION OF AMERICA INC., Washington, D.C. Lobbyist — Guild, Hagen & Clark Ltd., 102 Roff Way, Reno, Nev. 89505. Filed 5/18/82. Legislative interest — "...HR 4808, HR 5705 and S 1758."

NATIONAL ASSOCIATION OF INSURANCE BROKERS INC., 311 First St. N.W., Washington, D.C. 20001. Filed for self 5/21/82. Legislative interest — "HR 25, S 1182 ... S 294 ... HR 6114 ... S 1483." Lobbyist — Donald L. Jordan.

NATIONAL OFFICE MACHINE DEALERS ASSOCIATION, Wood Dale, Ill. Lobbyist — McNair, Glenn, Konduros, Corley, Singletary, Porter & Dibble, 1155 15th St. N.W., Washington, D.C. 20005. Filed 5/10/82. Legislative interest — "...S 1256...."

NATURAL GAS SUPPLY ASSOCIATION, 1025 Connecticut Ave. N.W., Washington, D.C. 20036. Filed for self 5/13/82. Legislative interest — "...Natural Gas Policy Act of 1978...." Lobbyist — Nicholas J. Bush.

PHARMACEUTICAL MANUFACTURERS ASSOCIATION, Washington, D.C. Lobbyist — Surrey & Morse, 1156 15th St. N.W., Washington, D.C. 20005. Filed 5/26/82. Legislative interest — "...passage of HR 1937, the Patent Term Restoration Act of 1982."

ROSES INC., 1152 Haslett Road, Haslett, Mich. 48840. Lobbyist — Daniel J. Edelman Inc., 1730 Pennsylvania Ave. N.W., Washington, D.C. 20006. Filed 5/20/82. Legislative interest — "To amend tariff schedules of the United States to align those rates on fresh cut roses to those imposed by the European Economic Community. S 2466; HR 6239...." Lobbyist — Eugene L. Stewart, 1001 Connecticut Ave. N.W., Washington, D.C. 20036. Filed 5/27/82. Legislative interest — "To amend tariff schedules of the United States to align those rates on fresh cut roses to those imposed by the European Economic Community. S 2466; HR 6239...." Filed for self 5/27/82. Legislative interest — "To amend tariff schedules of the United States to align those rates on fresh cut roses to those imposed by the European Economic Community. S 2466; HR 6239...." Lobbyist — James C. Krone.

SLURRY TRANSPORT ASSOCIATION, 490 L'Enfant Plaza S.W., Washington, D.C. 20024. Filed for self 5/13/82. Legislative interest — "HR 4230, the Coal Pipeline Act of 1982 ... S 1844." Lobbyist — George H. Eatman. Filed for self 5/14/82. Legislative interest — "HR 4230, the 'Coal Pipeline Act' ... S 1844, the 'Coal Distribution and Utilization Act'...." Lobbyist — Stuart D. Serkin.

VIRGIN ISLANDS TRADE AND ECONOMIC DEVELOPMENT INSTITUTE, Washington, D.C. Lobbyist — Peabody, Lambert & Meyers, 1150 Connecticut Ave. N.W., Washington, D.C. 20036. Filed 5/26/82. Legislative interest — "...protecting Virgin Islands tariff and tax advantages vis-à-vis other Caribbean countries in the Caribbean Basin Initiatives (HR 5900), with particular reference to rum and business conventions ... promoting preferential tariff and tax treatment for Virgin Islands businesses, including HR 5985, HR 5758, and HR 2232."

Miscellaneous

AMHERST COLLEGE, Amherst, Mass. Lobbyist — Ropes & Gray, 1200 New Hampshire Ave. N.W., Washington, D.C. 20036. Filed 5/25/82. Legislative interest — "Enactment of legislation relating to employment withholding tax liability of educational institutions for faculty housing...."

ARKANSAS 2000 INC., Russellville, Ark. Lobbyist — Thurman L. Boykin, 1799 Swann St. N.W., Washington, D.C. 20009. Filed 5/21/82. Legislative interest — "Transportation." Filed for self 5/21/82. Legislative interest — "Transportation." Lobbyist — James Harrell.

CALIFORNIA WESTSIDE FARMERS, Fresno, Calif. Lobbyists — Daniel A. Dutko, Larry Meyers, 412 First St. S.E., Washington, D.C. 20003. Filed 5/13/82. Legislative interest — "Reclamation Reform Act of 1982, HR 5539, S 1867."

CORRUGATED CONTAINER ANTITRUST LITIGATION MDL NO. 310, Houston, Texas. Lobbyist — Finley, Kumble, Wagner, Heine, Underberg & Casey, 1120 Connecticut Ave. N.W., Washington, D.C. 20036. Filed 5/14/82. (Former U.S. Sen. Joseph D. Tydings, D-Md., 1965-71, was listed as agent for this client.) Legislative interest — "S 995 — Amendment to Clayton Act, 15 U.S.C. 12 *et seq.*, new Section 41; HR 1242 — Amendment to Clayton Act, 15 U.S.C. 12 *et seq.*, new Section 41...."

PLYWOOD ANTITRUST LITIGATION MDL NO. 159, New Orleans, La. Lobbyist — Finley, Kumble, Wagner, Heine, Underberg & Casey, 1120 Connecticut Ave. N.W., Washington, D.C. 20036. Filed 5/14/82. (Former U.S. Sen Joseph D. Tydings, D-Md., 1965-71, was listed as agent for this client.) Legislative interest — "S 995 - Amendment to Clayton Act, 15 U.S.C. 12 *et seq.*, new Section 41; HR 1242 - Amendment to Clayton Act, 15 U.S.C. 12 *et seq.*, new Section 41...."

ROUNDTABLE ISSUES & ANSWERS, 1500 Wilson Blvd., Arlington, Va. 22209. Filed for self 5/12/82. Legislative interest — Not specified. Lobbyist — Barbara Joan DeFuria.

WELLESLEY COLLEGE, Wellesley, Mass. Lobbyist — Ropes & Gray, 1200 New Hampshire Ave. N.W., Washington, D.C. 20036. Filed 5/25/82. Legislative interest — "Enactment of legislation relating to employment withholding tax liability of educational institutions for faculty housing...."

WICHITA & AFFILIATED TRIBES, Anadarko, Okla. Lobbyist — Wilkinson, Cragun & Barker, 1735 New York Ave. N.W., Washington, D.C. 20006. Filed 5/11/82. Legislative interest — "Indian judgment distribution plan (Docket No. 375) and various bills dealing with royalty collection on Indian lands (*e.g.*, S 2300, HR 5121)."

June Registrations

Citizens' Groups

AMERICAN RIVERS CONSERVATION COUNCIL, Washington, D.C. Lobbyist — Beard and Associates, P.O. Box 2394, Columbia, Md. 21045. Filed 6/7/82. Legislative interest — "Appropriations for the National Wild and Scenic Rivers System in the Interior and Related Agencies appropriation bill for FY 1983."

CITIZENS FOR A NUCLEAR FREEZE, 324 4th St. N.E., Washington, D.C. 20002. Filed for self 6/14/82. Legislative interest — "S J Res 163 - favor (Nuclear Freeze Resolution). Conte-Markey Resolution ... favor." Lobbyist — Walton M. Chalmers II.

COMMITTEE FOR THE IMPROVEMENT OF THE TAX LAWS ON ANNUITY TAXATION INC., Washington, D.C. Lobbyist — Williams & Jensen, 1101 Connecticut Ave. N.W., Washington, D.C. 20036. Filed 6/30/82. Legislative interest — "Federal tax laws affecting the taxation of annuities."

COMMON CAUSE, 2030 M St. N.W., Washington, D.C. 20036. Filed for self 6/9/82. Legislative interest —"...supported specific legislation in the 97th Congress to reduce the dairy price supports and sugar loan program subsidies included in the farm bill (HR 3603, S 884) ... urged passage of a bill (S Res 20) providing for TV and radio coverage of Senate sessions and of bills (HR 18 and S 10) creating a Commission for More Effective Government ... opposing efforts to pass a constitutional amendment to balance the budget (S Res 58 and H J Res 10) as well as S 708, a bill to weaken the Foreign Corrupt Practices Act, and S 1730, a bill which would weaken the Freedom of Information Act ... working to reauthorize key provisions of the Voting Rights Act (S 1992) and opposing efforts to weaken the Clean Air Act ... worked to reduce the appropriation for the Tennessee-Tombigbee water project ... supported reauthorization of the Legal Services Corporation (S 393, HR 3480) and have supported adequate appropriations for it ... lobbied on behalf of the Federal Election Commission and opposed efforts to eliminate or reduce funding for the Commission ... opposed efforts to limit federal court jurisdiction in matters concerning abortion, busing and school prayer (S 1760, S 951, S 1647, S 158) ... supported legislation to provide for a review of tax expenditures in the budget process (S 193, HR 4882) ... supported the Special Prosecutor provision of the Ethics in Government Act of 1978...." Lobbyists — Stephen Hitchner, Susan Luipersbeck, Marcy Stephens, Jay Sherman.

CONSERVATIVES FOR IMMIGRATION REFORM INC., 227 Massachusetts Ave. N.E., Washington, D.C. 20002. Filed for self 6/14/82. Legislative interest — "Support effective enforcement of immigration laws and reforms such as employer sanctions. Oppose amnesty for illegal aliens." Lobbyist — Mary Connell Hedberg.

DISABLED AMERICAN VETERANS, Cold Spring, Ky. Lobbyist — Morgan, Lewis & Bockius, 1800 M St. N.W., Washington, D.C. 20036. Filed 6/14/82. Legislative interest — Not specified.

F.A.I.R. CONGRESSIONAL TASK FORCE, 2028 P St. N.W., Washington, D.C. 20036. Filed for self 6/18/82. Legislative interest — "S 2222/HR 6514, The Immigration Reform and Control Act (for)." Lobbyist — Mary Lou Tanton.

HAZARDOUS WASTE TREATMENT COUNCIL, Washington, D.C. Lobbyist — Zuckert, Scoutt & Rasenberger, 888 17th St. N.W., Washington, D.C. 20006. Legislative interest — "HR 6307, Resource Recovery Act Reauthorization."

MIDWEST ALLIANCE FOR INDUSTRIAL FINANCING AND RESTRUCTURING, 1520 Ohio Savings Plaza, Cleveland, Ohio 44114. Lobbyist — Benesch, Friedlander, Coplan & Aronoff, 1100 Citizens Building, Cleveland, Ohio 44114. Filed 6/28/82. Legislative interest — "...HR 6510 and HR 6468, both relating to proposed revisions to Section 168(f)(8) of the Internal Revenue Code. ...for HR 6510 and against HR 6468." Filed for self 6/28/82. Legislative interest — "...HR 6510 and HR 6468, both relating to proposed revisions to Section 168(f)(8) of the Internal Revenue Code. ...for HR 6510 and against HR 6468." Lobbyists — Stephen F. Botsford, Louis Nagy, John R. Wilson.

Corporations and Businesses

AMERICAN BROADCASTING CO. INC., New York, N.Y. Lobbyist — Timmons and Co. Inc., 1850 K St. N.W., Washington, D.C. 20006. Filed 6/21/82. Legislative interest — "...HR 5949, Cable Copyright Act; HR 5242, Broadcast Licensing Renewal and Deregulation Act; S 1629, Broadcast Deregulation Act of 1981; S 2172, Cable Telecommunications Act of 1982."

AMERICAN GENERAL LIFE INSURANCE CO., 2727 Allen Parkway, Houston, Texas 77001. Lobbyist — Hughes & Hill, 1000 Mercantile Dallas Building, Dallas, Texas 75201. Filed 6/11/82. Legislative interest — "...in favor of S 2353 and HR 6045, the 'Life Insurance Taxation Act of 1982.'" Filed for self 6/11/82.

Legislative interest — "...in favor of S 2353 and HR 6045, the 'Life Insurance Taxation Act of 1982.'" Lobbyist — James F. Janke.

AMERICAN NATIONAL INSURANCE CO., One Moody Plaza, Galveston, Texas 77550. Lobbyist — Hughes & Hill, 1000 Mercantile Dallas Building, Dallas, Texas 75201. Filed 6/11/82. Legislative interest — "...in favor of S 2353 and HR 6045, the 'Life Taxation Act of 1982.'" Filed for self 6/11/82. Legislative interest — "...in favor of S 2353 and HR 6045, the 'Life Taxation Act of 1982.'" Lobbyist — William K. Nicol.

AMERICAN TELEPHONE & TELEGRAPH CO., New York, N.Y. Lobbyist — Paul, Hastings, Janofsky & Walker, 1050 Thomas Jefferson St. N.W., Washington, D.C. 20007. Filed 6/17/82. Legislative interest — "Legislation affecting the communications industry."

ANHEUSER-BUSCH CO. INC., One Busch Place, St. Louis, Mo. 63118. Lobbyist — Timmons and Co. Inc., 1850 K St. N.W., Washington, D.C. 20006. Filed 6/25/82. Legislative interest — "...HR 3269 and S 1215, Malt Beverage Interbrand Competition Act and amendments to Economic Recovery Tax Act of 1981." Filed for self 6/14/82. Legislative interest — "...supports HR 3269 and S 1215 (Malt Beverage Interbrand Competition Act); supports HR 1808 (bill to amend the IRS Code of 1954); opposes S 709 and HR 2498 (Beverage Container Reuse and Recycling Act); opposes sections of HR 5602 and S 2211 (Trademark Operations of the United States Patent and Trademark Office)." Lobbyist — Stephen K. Lambright.

BALDWIN-UNITED CORP., Cincinnati, Ohio. Lobbyist — Morgan, Lewis & Bockius, 1800 M St. N.W., Washington, D.C. 20036. Filed 6/21/82. Legislative interest — "Legislation affecting the tax treatment of insurance and annuity products."

BELLINGHAM COLD STORAGE, Bellingham, Wash. Lobbyist — Preston, Thorgrimson, Ellis & Holman, 1776 G St. N.W., Washington, D.C. 20006. Filed 6/17/82. Legislative interest — "...governing international fisheries agreements pursuant to 16 U.S.C. subsection 1801 *et seq*."

BERENERGY CORP., Denver, Colo. Lobbyist — O'Connor & Hannan, 1919 Pennsylvania Ave. N.W., Washington, D.C. 20006. Filed 6/28/82. Legislative interest — "HR 6055/S 2350, sections 3(a) and (b)."

CBI INDUSTRIES INC., Oak Brook, Ill. Lobbyist — Hopkins & Sutter, 3 First National Plaza, Chicago, Ill. 60602. Filed 6/15/82. Legislative interest — Not specified.

CHRIS-CRAFT INDUSTRIES INC., New York, N.Y. Lobbyist — Paul, Weiss, Rifkind, Wharton & Garrison, 1714 Massachusetts Ave. N.W., Washington, D.C. 20036. Filed 6/24/82. Legislative interest — "HR 6056, Technical Corrections Bill, provisons relating to certain safe harbor leases before October 21, 1981, or similar provisions. In favor."

CITY NATIONAL BANK OF BEVERLY HILLS, CALIF., Beverly Hills, Calif. Lobbyist — Patton, Boggs & Blow, 2550 M St. N.W., Washington, D.C. 20037. Filed 6/23/82. Legislative interest — "...amendment to S 1720, Financial Institutions Restructuring and Services Act, to extend for two more years the period of time in which the bank has to divest itself of its real estate holdings."

COMMUNICATIONS SATELLITE CORP., Washington, D.C. Lobbyist — Crowell & Moring, 1100 Connecticut Ave. N.W., Washington, D.C. 20036. Filed 6/7/82. Legislative interest — "...amendments in connection with the partnership provisions of HR 6300."

CONGOLEUM CORP., Portsmouth, N.H. Lobbyist — Hopkins & Sutter, 3 First National Plaza, Chicago, Ill. 60602. Filed 6/15/82. Legislative interest — Not specified.

CONTINENTAL AIR LINES INC., Los Angeles, Calif. Lobbyist — Hughes, Hubbard & Reed, 1201 Pennsylvania Ave. N.W., Washington, D.C. 20004. Filed 6/10/82. Legislative interest — "...legislation affecting the airline industry."

CORAL PETROLEUM INC., Houston, Texas. Lobbyist — Dickstein, Shapiro, & Morin, 2101 L St. N.W., Washington, D.C. 20037. Filed 6/30/82. Legislative interest — "Energy taxes in administration's revenue raising proposals. S 2562 - DOE [Department of Energy] dismantlement legislation."

CORPORATION FOR GOVERNMENT ACTION INC., 1000 Potomac St. N.W., Washington, D.C. 20007. Filed for self 6/22/82. Legislative interest — "Proposals of Treasury Department to eliminate the completed contract method of accounting. Immigration Reform and Control Act of 1982. Agriculture reform legislation." Lobbyist — Ben Jarratt Brown.

CRINCO INVESTMENTS INC., El Paso, Texas. Lobbyist — O'Connor & Hannan, 1919 Pennsylvania Ave. N.W., Washington, D.C. 20006. Filed 6/28/82. Legislative interest — "Oil and gas tax legislation."

CSX CORP., Washington, D.C. Lobbyist — Reid & Priest, 1111 19th St. N.W., Washington, D.C. 20036. Filed 6/9/82. Legislative interest — "Revision of administration proposed tax increases of 1/26/82."

DELTA STEAMSHIP LINES INC., 1700 International Trade Mart, New Orleans, La. 70150. Filed for self 6/4/82. Legislative interest — "...Shipping Act, 1916 and amendments thereto ... Merchant Marine Acts of 1920 and 1936 and amendments thereto ... annual maritime authorizations." Lobbyist — J. William Charrier Jr.

E. F. HUTTON LIFE INSURANCE CO., La Jolla, Calif. Lobbyist — Patton, Boggs & Blow, 2550 M St. N.W., Washington, D.C. 20037. Filed 6/24/82. Legislative interest — "Legislation to revise the Life Insurance Company Income Tax Act of 1959, such as S 2353 and HR 6045."

ESTEE LAUDER INC., New York, N.Y. Lobbyist — Williams & Jensen, 1101 Connecticut Ave. N.W., Washington, D.C. 20036. Filed 6/14/82. Legislative interest — "Tax matters affecting the cosmetics industry."

FINLEY, KUMBLE, WAGNER, HEINE, UNDERBERG & CASEY, 1120 Connecticut Ave. N.W., Washington, D.C. 20036. Filed for self 6/30/82. Legislative interest — "HR 6410 - The Pension Equity Tax of 1982, against passage." Lobbyists — Robert J. Casey, Louis H. Diamond, Frank Ikard, Marc J. Scheineson.

FOREST CITY DILLON INC., Cleveland, Ohio. Lobbyist — Coan, Couture, Lyons & Moorhead, 1625 I St. N.W., Washington, D.C. 20006. Filed 6/18/82. Legislative interest — "Housing for elderly."

CARL M. FREEMAN ASSOCIATES INC., Potomac, Md. Lobbyist — C & B Associates Inc., 1750 New York Ave. N.W., Washington, D.C. 20006. Filed 6/10/82. Legislative interest — "Coastal Barrier Island Bill, HR 3252, S 1018."

GENERAL ELECTRIC CREDIT CORP., Stamford, Conn. Lobbyist — Williams & Jensen, 1101 Connecticut Ave. N.W., Washington, D.C. 20036. Filed 6/14/82. Legislative interest — "Tax matters affecting the leasing industry."

GILBANE BUILDING CO., Providence, R.I. Lobbyist — Dickstein, Shapiro & Morin, 2101 L St. N.W., Washington, D.C. 20037. Filed 6/30/82. Legislative interest — "Strategic Petroleum Reserves Phase III."

GLENDALE FEDERAL SAVINGS & LOAN ASSOCIATION, Glendale, Calif. Lobbyist — Hogan & Hartson, 815 Connecticut Ave. N.W., Washington, D.C. 20006. Filed 6/11/82. Legislative interest — "Legislation to provide increased powers for savings and loan association."

GRAHAM-WHITE MANUFACTURING CO., Salem, Va. Lobbyist — Cole & Corette, 1200 17th St. N.W., Washington, D.C. 20036. Filed 6/21/82. Legislative interest — "...HR 6055; S 2035; 26 U.S.C. subsection 1371 *et seq.*"

HOLIDAY INNS INC., Memphis, Tenn. Lobbyist — Talcott, McCabe and Bowser, 600 Maryland Ave. S.W., Washington, D.C. 20024. Filed 6/7/82. (Former U.S. Rep. Burt L. Talcott, R-Calif., 1963-77, was listed as agent for this client.) Legislative interest — "Standby Petroleum Allocation Act - S 1503 - oppose. United States Travel and Tourism Administration reauthorization - S 2261 - support."

HOLLYWOOD INC., Hollywood, Fla. Lobbyist — Sutherland, Asbill & Brennan, 1666 K St. N.W., Washington, D.C. 20006. Filed 6/10/82. Legislative interest — "Legislation pertaining to undeveloped coastal barriers, particularly S 1018 and HR 3252."

HUNT OIL CO., 2900 First National Bank Building, Dallas, Texas 75202. Lobbyist — Johnson & Swanson, 4700 First International Building, Dallas, Texas 75270. Filed 6/7/82. Legislative interest — "To seek modification of the 'At Risk Rules' contained in section 465 of the Internal Revenue Code." Filed for self 6/7/82. Legislative interest — "To seek modification of the 'At Risk Rules' contained in section 465 of the Internal Revenue Code." Lobbyist — James C. Oberwetter.

HVIDE SHIPPING INC., Fort Lauderdale, Fla. Lobbyist — Dickstein, Shapiro & Morin, 2101 L St. N.W., Washington, D.C. 20037. Filed 6/30/82. Legislative interest — "HR 4230 - Coal Slurry Pipeline - Coal Pipeline Act; S 1844 - Coal Distribution and Utilization Act."

INDECO INC., Jupiter, Fla. Lobbyist — Patton, Boggs & Blow, 2550 M St. N.W., Washington, D.C. 20037. Filed 6/24/82. Legislative interest — "Legislation relating to and possible amendments thereto coastal barriers."

ITT CORP., New York, N.Y. Lobbyist — Cohen and Uretz, 1775 K St. N.W., Washington, D.C. 20006. Filed 6/7/82. Legislative interest — "Tax legislation affecting the U.S. Virgin Islands, including HR 5985 and HR 5113."

JMB REALTY CORP., Chicago, Ill. Lobbyist — Manatt, Phelps, Rothenberg & Tunney, 1200 New Hampshire Ave. N.W., Washington, D.C. 20036. Filed 6/8/82. (Former U.S. Rep. James C. Corman, D-Calif., 1961-81, was listed as agent for this client.) Legislative interest — "In opposition of legislation relating to deductibility of interest and taxes during construction period."

KIMBERLY-CLARK CORP., 201 North Lake St., Neenah, Wis. 54956. Filed for self 6/1/82. Legislative interest — "...tax, the economy and budgetary matters, clean air, clean water, energy, labor, regulatory reform...." Lobbyist — Margaret K. Harding, 1000 Wilson Blvd., Arlington, Va. 22209.

LEASE MANAGEMENT CORP., Chicago, Ill. Lobbyist — Winston & Strawn, 2550 M St. N.W., Washington, D.C. 20037. Filed 6/9/82. Legislative interest — "Safe harbor leasing including HR 6468, HR 6510."

LOCKHEED CORP., Burbank, Calif. Lobbyist — Miller & Chevalier, 1700 Pennsylvania Ave. N.W., Washington, D.C. 20006. Filed 6/16/82. Legislative interest — "For enactment of FY 1983 Defense Authorization and Appropriation bills containing authorization and funding for the aquisition of C-5Bs in HR 6030 and S 2248." Lobbyist — Patton, Boggs & Blow, 2550 M St. N.W., Washington, D.C. 20037. Filed 6/22/82. Legislative interest — "HR 6030 Defense authorization bill in favor of the bill but opposed to amendment reducing or eliminating procurement of C-5B airlift aircraft."

LORD, BISSELL AND BROOK, Chicago, Ill. Lobbyist — O'Connor & Hannan, 1919 Pennsylvania Ave. N.W., Washington, D.C. 20006. Filed 6/28/82. Legislative interest — "Proposed tax legislation relating to ESOPs, Insurance Subchapter S."

MACCABEES MUTUAL LIFE INSURANCE CO., Southfield, Mich. Lobbyist — Sutherland, Asbill & Brennan, 1666 K St. N.W., Washington, D.C. 20006. Filed 6/8/82. Legislative interest — "...tax proposals affecting the life insurance industry."

M.A.N. TRUCK AND BUS CORP., Southfield, Mich. Lobbyist — Kemp, Klein, Endelman & Beer, 1320 19th St. N.W., Washington, D.C. 20036. Filed 6/18/82. Legislative interest — "Legislation involving 'Buy American' or 'local content' re buses and trucks."

MANAGEMENT INSIGHTS INC., Dallas, Texas. Lobbyist — Hopkins & Sutter, 3 First National Plaza, Chicago, Ill. 60602. Filed 6/15/82. Legislative interest — "...legislation dealing with targeted jobs tax credit and related areas."

MIDWEST TELEVISION INC., Champaign, Ill. Lobbyist — Covington & Burling, 1201 Pennsylvania Ave. N.W., Washington, D.C. 20044. Filed 6/28/82. Legislative interest — "Support of HR 6055 and S 2350 dealing with revisions to Subchapter S of the Internal Revenue Code."

MOBIL OIL CORP., New York, N.Y. Lobbyist — Nossaman, Krueger & Knox, 1140 19th St. N.W., Washington, D.C. 20036. Filed 6/16/82. Legislative interest — "...various amendments to the Internal Revenue Code and the Employee Retirement Income Security Act of 1974."

PADDOCK PUBLICATIONS INC., Arlington Heights, Ill. Lobbyist — O'Connor & Hannan, 1919 Pennsylvania Ave.

N.W., Washington, D.C. 20006. Filed 6/28/82. Legislative interest — "Proposed ESOP amendment."

J. ROYAL PARKER ASSOCIATES, Cherry Hill, N.J. Lobbyist — Porter, Wright, Morris & Arthur, 1133 15th St. N.W., Washington, D.C. 20005. Filed 6/9/82. Legislative interest — "Caribbean Basin Economic Recovery Act; HR 5900/S 2231. . . ."

PFIZER INC., New York, N.Y. Lobbyist — Williams & Jensen, 1101 Connecticut Ave. N.W., Washington, D.C. 20036. Filed 6/22/82. Legislative interest — Not specified.

PHILLIPS PETROLEUM CO., Phillips Building, Bartlesville, Okla. 70004. Filed for self 6/15/82. Legislative interest — "Legislation affecting integrated oil, gas, chemicals and energy industries." Lobbyists — Barbara J. Price, Patricia L. Roberts, 1825 K St. N.W., Washington, D.C. 20006.

REPUBLIC NATIONAL LIFE INSURANCE CO., 3988 N. Central Expressway, Dallas, Texas 75201. Lobbyist — Hughes & Hill, 1000 Mercantile Dallas Building, Dallas, Texas 75201. Filed 6/11/82. Legislative interest — ". . .in favor of S 2353 and HR 6045, the 'Life Insurance Taxation Act of 1982.'" Filed for self 6/11/82. Legislative interest — ". . .in favor of S 2353 and HR 6045, the 'Life Insurance Taxation Act of 1982.'" Lobbyist — Joseph E. Connell.

RSV MINING EQUIPMENT B.V., Rotterdam, The Netherlands. Lobbyist — Holland & Knight, 600 Maryland Ave. S.W., Washington, D.C. 20024. Filed 6/7/82. Legislative interest — "Tariff Reductions, Suspensions, and Extensions of Suspensions; HR 4566; Tariff Schedules of the United States, 19 U.S.C. subsection 1202(d). . . ."

RYDER SYSTEM INC., Miami, Fla. Lobbyist — Piper & Marbury, 888 16th St. N.W., Washington, D.C. 20006. Filed 6/17/82. Legislative interest — "To support legislation that facilitates equipment and other types of leasing transactions."

SEQUOIA VENTURES INC., San Francisco, Calif. Lobbyist — Morgan, Lewis, & Bockius, 1800 M St. N.W., Washington, D.C. 20036. Filed 6/24/82. Legislative interest — "HR 6055."

SERVICEMASTER INDUSTRIES INC., Downers Grove, Ill. Lobbyist — Talcott, McCabe and Bowser, 600 Maryland Ave. S.W., Washington, D.C. 20024. Filed 6/7/82. (Former U.S. Rep. Burt L. Talcott, R-Calif., 1963-77, was listed as agent for this client.) Legislative interest — Not specified.

SONY CORPORATION OF AMERICA, New York, N.Y. Lobbyist — Daniel J. Edelman Inc., 1730 Pennsylvania Ave. N.W., Washington, D.C. 20006. Filed 6/23/82. Legislative interest — "Amend Title XVII of the U.S. Code to exempt the private noncommercial recording of copyrighted works on video records from copyright infringement; HR 4808, HR 5705, S 1758."

STORER BROADCASTING CO., Washington, D.C. Lobbyist — Taft, Stettinius & Hollister, First National Bank Center, Cincinnati, Ohio 45202 and 1800 Massachusetts Ave. N.W., Washington, D.C. 20036. Filed 6/25/82. (Robert Taft Jr., R-Ohio, U.S. Senate 1971-76; U.S. House 1963-65, 1967-71, was listed as agent for this client.) Legislative interest — ". . .Federal Communications Act amendments proposed in HR 5008."

TUCSON ELECTRIC POWER CO., Tucson, Ariz. Lobbyist — Reid & Priest, 1111 19th St. N.W., Washington, D.C. 20036. Filed 6/8/82. Legislative interest — ". . .in support of income tax legislation which would provide a proper sharing of investment tax credits between the company and ratepayers (Internal Revenue Code section 46(f))."

UNION NAVIGATION CORP. LTD., Orlando, Fla. Lobbyist — Lawrence D. Johnson, 800 N. Highland Ave., Orlando, Fla. 32803. Filed 6/7/82. Legislative interest — "Foreign Investment in Real Property Tax Act of 1980 (FIRPTA) and subsequent related tax legislation and regulations. . . ."

U.S. AIR INC., Washington, D.C. Lobbyist — Piper & Marbury, 888 16th St. N.W., Washington, D.C. 20006. Filed 6/17/82. Legislative interest — "To support legislation that facilitates equipment and other types of leasing transactions."

VISA U.S.A. INC., 1620 I St. N.W., Washington, D.C. 20006. Filed for self 6/7/82. Legislative interest — "Legislation affecting the business of banking including S 1720, HR 2501 and S 2000."

WASTE MANAGEMENT INC., Washington, D.C. Lobbyist — State and Federal Associates, 1101 15th St. N.W., Washing-

ton, D.C. 20005. Filed 6/1/82. Legislative interest — "HR 5723 and matters relating to the ocean incineration of hazardous wastes."

WOODHOUSE DRAKE & CAREY INC., New York, N.Y. Lobbyist — Barnes, Richardson & Colburn, 1819 H St. N.W., Washington, D.C. 20006. Filed 6/24/82. Legislative interest — "Sugar support program."

WORLD BOOK LIFE INSURANCE CO., Chicago, Ill. Lobbyist — O'Connor & Hannan, 1919 Pennsylvania Ave. N.W., Washington, D.C. 20006. Filed 6/28/82. Legislative interest — "Proposed Annuity Tax changes."

International Relations

THE GOVERNMENT OF EL SALVADOR, San Salvador, El Salvador. Lobbyist — Neill and Co. Inc., 1100 17th St. N.W., Washington, D.C. 20036. Filed 6/21/82. Legislative interest — "Promoting the passage of the Administration's military and economic assistance program insofar as it may relate to the Government of El Salvador, including the foreign assistance authorization and appropriation bills."

State and Local Governments

CITY OF BATON ROUGE, Baton Rouge, La. Lobbyist — Jones & Winburn, 1101 15th St. N.W., Washington, D.C. 20005. Filed 6/8/82. Legislative interest — "To monitor legislative material affecting municipal and local governments."

CITY OF MINNEAPOLIS, Minneapolis, Minn. Lobbyist — Foley, Lardner, Hollabaugh & Jacobs, 1775 Pennsylvania Ave. N.W., Washington, D.C. 20006. Filed 6/9/82. Legislative interest — "Legislative matters affecting the City of Minneapolis, including but not limited to grant-in-aid and budget matters."

COMMONWEALTH OF PUERTO RICO, San Juan, Puerto Rico. Lobbyist — Gray and Co., 3255 Grace St. N.W., Washington, D.C. 20007. Filed 6/11/82. Legislative interest — Not specified.

MASSACHUSETTS BAY TRANSPORTATION AUTHORITY, Boston, Mass. Lobbyist — Wickerson-Ingram & Associates Inc., 1150 17th St. N.W., Washington, D.C. 20036. Filed 6/18/82. Legislative interest — "All legislation concerning the financing, operation and regulation of public mass transit."

METROPOLITAN TRANSPORTATION AUTHORITY, New York, N.Y. Lobbyist — Dickstein, Shapiro & Morin, 2101 L St. N.W., Washington, D.C. 20037. Filed 6/30/82. Legislative interest — "Safe harbor leasing; minimum tax preference item, 'lessors' safe harbor leasing benefits,' in administration's revenue raising proposals."

MINNEAPOLIS COMMUNITY DEVELOPMENT AGENCY, Minneapolis, Minn. Lobbyist — O'Connor & Hannan, 1919 Pennsylvania Ave. N.W., Washington, D.C. 20006. Filed 6/26/82. Legislative interest — "Proposed Industrial Development Bond Tax changes."

NORTHERN COLORADO WATER CONSERVANCY DISTRICT, Loveland, Colo. Lobbyist — Davis, Graham & Stubbs, 1920 N St. N.W., Washington, D.C. 20036. Filed 6/14/82. Legislative interest — "Support S 1867 and HR 5539 to amend the Reclamation Act of 1902."

PORT OF WILMINGTON, Wilmington, Del. Lobbyist — Ballard, Spahr, Andrews & Ingersoll, 1850 K St. N.W., Washington, D.C. 20006. Filed 6/18/82. Legislative interest — ". . .Port development legislation and user fees."

SOUTH JERSEY PORT CORP., Lobbyist — Ballard, Spahr, Andrews & Ingersoll, 1850 K St. N.W., Washington, D.C. 20006. Filed 6/18/82. Legislative interest — ". . .Port development legislation and user fees."

STATE OF ALASKA, Juneau, Alaska. Lobbyist — Van Ness, Feldman, Sutcliffe, Curtis & Levenberg, 1050 Thomas Jefferson St. N.W., Washington, D.C. 20001. Filed 6/4/82. Legislative interest — "In opposition to legislative attempts to limit traditional state taxing authority."

Trade Associations

AFFILIATED FOOD PROCESSORS INC., Santa Monica, Calif. Lobbyist — Barnett & Alagia, 1627 K St. N.W., Washington, D.C. 20006. Filed 6/10/82. Legislative interest — "Hearings and any related legislation concerning child nutrition and school food services."

AIR FREIGHT ASSOCIATION, Washington, D.C. Lobbyist — Akin, Gump, Strauss, Hauer & Feld, 1333 New Hampshire Ave. N.W., Washington, D.C. 20036. Filed 6/29/82. Legislative interest — "General aviation legislation."

AMERICAN ASSOCIATION OF EQUIPMENT LESSORS, 1300 N. 17th St., Arlington, Va. 22209. Lobbyist — Volpe, Boskey & Lyons, 918 16th St. N.W., Washington, D.C. 20006. Filed 6/10/82. Legislative interest — "...'safe harbor' leasing (HR 6468, HR 6510, etc.), tax technical corrections (HR 6056), minimum corporate tax (HR 5206), bankruptcy (S 863) and federal preemption of state usury laws (S 1720, HR 4603)." Lobbyist — Jones & Winburn, 1101 15th St. N.W., Washington, D.C. 20005. Filed 6/10/82. Legislative interest — "...'safe harbor' leasing (HR 6468, HR 6510, etc.), tax technical corrections (HR 6056), minimum corporate tax (HR 5206), bankruptcy (S 863) and federal preemption of state usury laws (S 1720, HR 4603)." Filed for self 6/10/82. Legislative interest — "...'safe harbor' leasing (HR 6468, HR 6510, etc.), tax technical corrections (HR 6056), minimum corporate tax (HR 5206), bankruptcy (S 863) and federal preemption of state usury laws (S 1720, HR 4603)." Lobbyist — Michael Fleming.

AMERICAN CLEAN WATER ASSOCIATION, 1341 G St. N.W., Washington, D.C. 20005. Filed for self 6/23/82. Legislative interest — "Clean Water Act, Safe Drinking Water Act...." Lobbyist — Larry Silverman.

AMERICAN COLLEGE OF MORTGAGE ATTORNEYS, Matairie, La. Lobbyist — Patton, Boggs & Blow, 2550 M St. N.W., Washington, D.C. 20037. Filed 6/24/82. Legislative interest — "Monitoring of Real Estate Settlement Procedures Act of 1974 and amendments thereto...."

AMERICAN COUNCIL FOR CAPITAL FORMATION, 1850 K St. N.W., Washington, D.C. 20006. Filed for self 6/25/82. Legislative interest — "...supports capital gains tax reductions for individuals and corporations; inventory accounting reform, including the delay and/or repeal of LIFO recapture procedure of the Windfall Profit Tax Act of 1978; the Tax Limitation-Balanced Budget Constitutional Amendment (S Res 58, H Res 350) ... opposes proposals for a new corporate minimum income tax and repeal of the 'safe harbor' leasing provisions of the Economic Recovery Tax Act of 1981." Lobbyist — Margo Thorning.

AMERICAN HOSPITAL ASSOCIATION, 840 N. Lake Shore Drive, Chicago, Ill. 60611. Filed for self 6/14/82. Legislative interest — Not specified. Lobbyist — Jack W. Owen, Richard Pollack, 444 N. Capitol St. N.W., Washington, D.C. 20001.

BOOK MANUFACTURERS' INSTITUTE INC., Stamford, Conn. Lobbyist — Loomis, Owen, Fellman & Howe, 2020 K St. N.W., Washington, D.C. 20006. Filed 6/25/82. Legislative interest — "S 1880, HR 6198, HR 3940 dealing with extension of manufacturing clause."

DAIRY FARMER DISTRIBUTORS OF AMERICA INC., Chittenango, N.Y. Lobbyist — Woodruff L. Caroll, 918 Onondaga Bank Building, Syracuse, N.Y. 13202. Filed 6/17/82. Legislative interest — "Food and Agriculture Act of 1981."

THE EMPLOYEE STOCK OWNERSHIP ASSOCIATION, Washington, D.C. Lobbyist — David P. Stang, 1629 K St. N.W., Washington, D.C. 20006. Filed 6/21/82. Legislative interest — "HR 6227, to amend the Internal Revenue Code of 1954 with respect to requirements to allow participants to direct how securities are voted in qualified plans."

HOME HEALTH SERVICES & STAFFING ASSOCIATION, Washington, D.C. Lobbyist — Dickstein, Shapiro & Morin, 2101 L St. N.W., Washington, D.C. 20037. Filed 6/30/82. Legislative interest — "HR 5180 and S 1958 - Medicare Hospice Care Coverage; HR 5531 and S 234 - Community Home Health Service Act of 1981; HR 4531, HR 4971, HR 5729, HR 5867 and S 2369 - independent contractors legislation; HR 6173, HR 6338 and S 2311 - health planning legislation."

INSTITUTO BRASILEIRO DO CAFE (BRAZILIAN COFFEE INSTITUTE), New York, N.Y. Lobbyist — Samuel E. Stavisky & Associates Inc., 1100 17th St. N.W., Washington, D.C. 20036. Filed 6/7/82. Legislative interest — "International Coffee Agreement Act of 1980 ... HR 6280 ... S 2540 ... approval of the legislation by both Houses."

INSURANCE ASSOCIATION OF CONNECTICUT, Hartford, Conn. Lobbyist — Theodore L. Jones, 3081 Teddy Drive, Baton Rouge, La. 70809. Filed 6/8/82. Legislative interest — "Legislation affecting insurance industry."

LEAF TOBACCO EXPORTERS ASSOCIATION, Raleigh, N.C. Lobbyist — Davis & McLeod, 499 S. Capitol St. S.W., Washington, D.C. 20003. Filed 6/18/82. Legislative interest — "...legislation to change to a tobacco price support program to make U.S. tobacco more competitive in the world market ... amending HR 6590, the No Net Cost Tobacco Program Act of 1982."

NATIONAL ASSOCIATION OF HOMES FOR CHILDREN, New York, N.Y. Lobbyist — Talcott, McCabe and Bowser, 600 Maryland Ave. S.W., Washington, D.C. 20024. Filed 6/7/82. (Former U.S. Rep. Burt L. Talcott, R-Calif., 1963-77, was listed as agent for this client.) Legislative interest — "Child Welfare Amendments - PL 96-272...."

NATIONAL ASSOCIATION OF REAL ESTATE INVESTMENT TRUSTS, Washington, D.C. Lobbyist — Fulbright & Jaworski, 1150 Connecticut Ave. N.W., Washington, D.C. 20036. Filed 6/24/82. Legislative interest — "Section 856 *et seq.* of the Internal Revenue Code, relating to taxation of REITs."

NATIONAL ASSOCIATION OF RETIRED FEDERAL EMPLOYEES, 1533 New Hampshire Ave. N.W., Washington, D.C. 20036. Filed for self 6/17/82. Legislative interest — "...all proposals affecting Federal civil service annuitants...." Lobbyist — L. J. Andolsek.

NATIONAL COALITION FOR PORT PROGRESS, Washington, D.C. Lobbyist — Patton, Boggs & Blow, 2550 M St. N.W., Washington, D.C. 20037. Filed 6/24/82. Legislative interest — "Legislation relating to port development, dredging, and federal funding of such activities."

NATIONAL OFFICE PRODUCTS ASSOCIATION, Alexandria, Va. Lobbyist — George H. Denison, 4837 Del Ray Ave., Washington, D.C. 20814. Filed 6/21/82. Legislative interest — Not specified.

NATIONAL PEANUT GROWERS GROUP, Gorman, Texas. Lobbyist — Larry D. Meyers, 412 First St. S.E., Washington, D.C. 20003. Filed 6/28/82. Legislative interest — "General Farm Bill."

NATIONAL RURAL ELECTRIC COOPERATIVE ASSOCIATION, 1800 Massachusetts Ave. N.W., Washington, D.C. 20036. Filed for self 6/7/82. Legislative interest — "...the Rural Electrification Act of 1936 as amended." Lobbyist — Arthur W. Hartmann.

PHARMACEUTICAL MANUFACTURERS ASSOCIATION, Washington, D.C. Lobbyist — Venable, Baetjer, Howard & Civiletti, 1301 Pennsylvania Ave. N.W., Washington, D.C. 20004. Filed 6/10/82. Legislative interest — "The Patent Term Restoration Act of 1981 - HR 1937 and HR 6444."

RECORDING INDUSTRY ASSOCIATION OF AMERICA INC., New York, N.Y. Lobbyist — Arnold & Porter, 1200 New Hampshire Ave. N.W., Washington, D.C. 20036. Filed 6/17/82. Legislative interest — "HR 4531, HR 4971, HR 5729, HR 5867, HR 6310, S 2369."

Miscellaneous

THE AHMANSON FOUNDATION, Los Angeles, Calif. Lobbyist — Arnold & Porter, 1200 New Hampshire Ave. N.W., Washington, D.C. 20036. Filed 6/16/82. Legislative interest — "...an extension of time for the divestiture of excess business holdings under section 4943 of the Internal Revenue Code of 1954."

AMERICAN COUNCIL OF INTERNATIONAL PERSONNEL INC., New York, N.Y. Lobbyist — Cornelius J. Leary,

2113 Countryside Drive, Silver Spring, Md. 20904. Filed 6/7/82. Legislative interest — "Immigration Reform and Control Act; S 2222 and HR 6514."

HOUSTON ENDOWMENT INC., Houston, Texas. Lobbyist — Williams & Jensen, 1101 Connecticut Ave. N.W., Washington, D.C. 20036. Filed 6/14/82. Legislative interest — "Tax matters affecting foundations."

RESTON ADVISER COMMITTEE, Reston, Va. Lobbyist — John G. Toth, 11935 Barrel Cooper Court, Reston, Va. 22091. Filed 6/29/82. Legislative interest — "For - HUD Housing Counseling Program - Mutual Mortgage Insurance Regulations, 24CFR 203.500-203.662 'Servicing Responsibilities' - Section 8-Sub. Housing Program/New Construction, Existing Housing, Public Housing, Handicapped Housing ... Against - Voucher Sub. Housing System."

H. H. TIFFANY, Waynesboro, Va. Lobbyist — Elwyn LaBauve Darden, 1224 S. George Mason Drive, Arlington, Va. 22204. Filed 6/4/82. Legislative interest — "...HR 5872 and S 2222, both in Title II, part B, dealing with 8 U.S.C. 1101-1182."

U.S. COMMITTEE FOR UNICEF, New York, N.Y. Lobbyist — Ballard, Spahr, Andrews & Ingersoll, 1850 K St. N.W., Washington, D.C. 20006. Filed 6/4/82. Legislative interest — "...level of U.S. voluntary contribution."

July Registrations

Citizens' Groups

THE AMERICAN LOBBY FOR PRESIDENT REAGAN'S BALANCED BUDGET AMENDMENT INC., 2307 Riviera Drive, Vienna, Va. 22180. Filed for self 7/26/82. Legislative interest — "Balanced Budget Amendment to the U.S. Constitution - for." Lobbyist — Andre E. LeTendre.

AMERICANS FOR THE NATIONAL DIVIDEND ACT INC., Rosslyn, Va. Lobbyist — Alcalde, Henderson & O'Bannon, 1901 N. Fort Myer Drive, Rosslyn, Va. 22209. Filed 7/9/82. Legislative interest — "General tax and capital formation legislation, particularly HR 5085 (for)."

CHUGACH NATIVES INC., Anchorage, Alaska. Lobbyist — Birch, Horton, Bittner and Monroe, 1140 Connecticut Ave. N.W., Washington, D.C. 20036. Filed 7/6/82. Legislative interest — "Public land issues."

CONGRESS WATCH, 215 Pennsylvania Ave. S.E., Washington, D.C. 20003. Filed for self 7/9/82. Legislative interest — "The Clinch River Breeder Reactor appropriations; Three Mile Island cleanup proposals." Lobbyist — Janet Hathaway.

MINIMUM TAX COALITION, Washington, D.C. Lobbyist — Gray and Co., 3255 Grace St. N.W., Washington, D.C. 20007. Filed 7/22/82. Legislative interest — "Including but not limited to amendments to HR 4961."

NATIONAL AUDUBON SOCIETY, 950 Third Ave., New York, N.Y. 10022. Filed for self 7/21/82. Legislative interest — "Clean Air Act, HR 5252 - not in favor. Other environmental legislation." Lobbyist — Carol M. Beim.

NATIONAL CAMPAIGN TO STOP THE MX, 711 G St. S.E., Washington, D.C. 20003. Filed for self 7/26/82. Legislative interest — "MX legislation, amendments to HR 6030 and later appropriations legislation." Lobbyist — April Moore.

NATIONAL COMMUNITY ACTION FOUNDATION, Washington, D.C. Lobbyist — Moss, McGee, Bellmon, Bradley, Ushio & Foley, 1740 N St. N.W., Washington, D.C. 20036. Filed 7/23/82. Legislative interest — "Community Services Block Grant Act, Budget Act, Labor/HEW appropriations."

NATIONAL RIGHT TO WORK COMMITTEE, 8001 Braddock Road, Springfield, Va. 22160. Filed for self 7/28/82. Legislative interest — "Legislative proposals related to compulsory unionism in private industry, farm labor, public sector employees ... Hobbs Act Amendment (Anti-Extortion Act) ... S 613, S 2189, HR 450 ... National Right to Work bill ... HR 2301 and S 1416 ... Student Right to Work bill ... HR 2300 and S 1416

... Seeking amendments to: S 1160, Urban Mass Transportation Act; S 1007, Food Stamps (restrain eligibility)." Lobbyist — Karl Gallant.

Corporations and Businesses

A. I. LEASING CORP., New York, N.Y. Lobbyist — Seward & Kissel, 919 18th St. N.W., Washington, D.C. 20006. Filed 7/1/82. Legislative interest — "Legislation regarding leasing tax benefits."

ALASKA NATIONAL BANK OF THE NORTH, Fairbanks, Alaska. Lobbyist — Birch, Horton, Bittner and Monroe, 1140 Connecticut Ave. N.W., Washington, D.C. 20036. Filed 7/6/82. Legislative interest — "...legislative matters relating to the savings and loan industry."

AMERICAN CYANAMID CO., One Cyanamid Plaza, Wayne, N.J. 07470. Filed for self 7/10/82. Legislative interest — "Natural Gas Deregulation, Clean Air Act, Clean Water Act, Safe Drinking Water Act, Resource Conservation and Recovery Act." Lobbyist — Juliane B. Harvey, 1575 I St. N.W., Washington, D.C. 20005.

AMERICAN GENERAL CORP., 2727 Allen Parkway, Houston, Texas 77001. Filed for self 7/23/82. Legislative interest — "Tax revenue relating to insurance - HR 4961, HR 6410, S 2353, HR 6045." Lobbyist — C. M. Schauerte.

AMERICAN MILITARY SALES, Woodbury, N.Y. Lobbyist — Robert Stewart Royer, 1025 Connecticut Ave. N.W., Washington, D.C. 20036. Filed 7/22/82. Legislative interest — "Legislation affecting the auto industry and other matters affecting overseas military sales group."

AMERICAN MOTORS CORP., Southfield, Mich. Lobbyist — Jones, Day, Reavis & Pogue, 1735 I St. N.W., Washington, D.C. 20006. Filed 7/21/82. Legislative interest — "...HR 4961, the Tax Equity and Fiscal Responsibility Act of 1982."

AMWAY CORP., 7575 East Fulton Road, Ada, Mich. 49355. Filed for self 7/13/82. Legislative interest — "...government regulation of manufacturing and distribution of products, environmental requirements, and taxation." Lobbyist — John C. Gartland, 1019 19th St. N.W., Washington, D.C. 20036.

BARKLEY COMPANY OF ARIZONA, Somerton, Ariz. Lobbyist — Miller & Chevalier, 1700 Pennsylvania Ave. N.W., Washington, D.C. 20006. Filed 7/21/82. Legislative interest — "...in support of S 2479 and HR 6407."

BEATRICE FOODS CO., Chicago, Ill. Lobbyist — Winston & Strawn, 2550 M St. N.W., Washington, D.C. 20037. Filed 7/29/82. Legislative interest — "Food and food-related issues; tax and regulatory issues of interest to diversified food company."

BLYTH EASTMAN PAINE WEBBER HEALTH CARE FUNDING INC., New York, N.Y. Lobbyist — O'Connor & Hannan, 1919 Pennsylvania Ave. N.W., Washington, D.C. 20006. Filed 7/9/82. Legislative interest — "...preserving the FHA sections 232/242 mortgage insurance programs for health care facilities."

CAPITAL HOLDING CORP., Louisville, Ky. Lobbyist — Miller & Chevalier, 1700 Pennsylvania Ave. N.W., Washington, D.C. 20006. Filed 7/22/82. Legislative interest — "...partial liquidation changes in HR 4961...."

CHRIS CRAFT INDUSTRIES INC., New York, N.Y. Lobbyist — Kaye, Scholer, Fierman, Hayes & Handler, 1575 I St. N.W., Washington, D.C. 20005. Filed 7/28/82. Legislative interest — "General interest in safe harbor leasing provisions of tax code, seeking clarification of provision of the 1981 amendments to the tax code. Specific interest in Tax Equity and Fiscal Responsibility Act of 1982, HR 4961."

CHRYSLER MILITARY SALES CORP., Woodbury, N.Y. Lobbyist — Robert Stewart Royer, 1025 Connecticut Ave. N.W., Washington, D.C. 20036. Filed 7/22/82. Legislative interest — "Legislation affecting the auto industry and other matters affecting overseas military sales group."

CITICORP, New York, N.Y. Lobbyist — Wilmer, Cutler & Pickering, 1666 K St. N.W., Washington, D.C. 20006. Filed 7/29/82. Legislative interest — "Possible oversight hearings concerning SEC enforcement activities."

COLT INDUSTRIES INC., New York, N.Y. Lobbyist — Paul, Weiss, Rifkind, Wharton & Garrison, 345 Park Ave., New York, N.Y. 10154. Filed 7/6/82. Legislative interest — "...supports the adoption of HR 5214."

DAMSON OIL CORP., Houston, Texas. Lobbyist — Gerard, Byler & Associates, 1100 17th St. N.W., Washington, D.C. 20036. Filed 7/24/82. Legislative interest — "Promote legislation (S 1894) to facilitate non-lease agreements between Indian tribes and energy firms."

DANVILLE RESOURCES INC., New York, N.Y. Lobbyist — Shea & Gould, 330 Madison Ave., New York, N.Y. 10017. Filed 7/9/82. Legislative interest — "In support of Domenici amendment compelling use of 80% U.S. uranium in all uranium products."

DOUGLAS OIL PURCHASING CORP., Mobile, Ala. Lobbyist — Daniel A. Dutko, 412 First St. S.E., Washington, D.C. 20003. Filed 7/6/82. Legislative interest — "Legislation concerning status of transactions of export sales under expired federal regulation."

DRESSER INDUSTRIES, Dallas, Texas. Lobbyist — Bracewell & Patterson, 1825 I St. N.W., Washington, D.C. 20006. Filed 7/12/82. Legislative interest — "Tax legislation and related matters."

THE DREYFUS CORP., New York, N.Y. Lobbyist — Zuckert, Scoutt & Rasenberger, 888 17th St. N.W., Washington, D.C. 20006. Filed 7/29/82. Legislative interest — "To modify provisions of the Safe Harbor Leasing sections of HR 4961."

ETHYL CORP., Washington, D.C. Lobbyist — Manatt, Phelps, Rothenberg & Tunney, 1200 New Hampshire Ave. N.W., Washington, D.C. 20036. Filed 7/21/82. (Former U.S. Rep. James C. Corman, D-Calif., 1961-81, was listed as agent for this client.) Legislative interest — "...changes in legislation dealing with acquisitions and mergers."

FEDERAL CARTRIDGE CORP., Minneapolis, Minn. Lobbyist — Baker & Hostetler, 818 Connecticut Ave. N.W., Washington, D.C. 20006. Filed 7/27/82. Legislative interest — "General legislative interest is in federal tax legislation; specific interest is in tax bill reported by Senate Finance Committee and to be acted on by Ways and Means Committee."

FEDERAL PAPER BOARD CO. INC., Montvale, N.J. Lobbyist — Charls E. Walker Associates Inc., 1730 Pennsylvania Ave. N.W., Washington, D.C. 20006. Filed 7/21/82. Legislative interest — "...may concern issues relating to taxation of leasing transactions."

FIRST FEDERAL SAVINGS AND LOAN ASSOCIATION, Anchorage, Alaska. Lobbyist — Birch, Horton, Bittner and Monroe, 1140 Connecticut Ave. N.W., Washington, D.C. 20036. Filed 7/6/82. Legislative interest — "...matters relating to the savings and loan industry."

THE FIRST NATIONAL BANK OF BOSTON, 100 Federal St., Boston, Mass. 02110. Filed for self 7/8/82. Legislative interest — "...ERISA, federal tax legislation and federal bankruptcy legislation." Lobbyist — Patti A. Stoll.

FLORISTS' TRANSWORLD DELIVERY, Southfield, Mich. Lobbyist — Hill and Knowlton Inc., 1201 Pennsylvania Ave. N.W., Washington, D.C. 20004. Filed 7/30/82. Legislative interest — "Legislation concerning imports on cut-flowers and Mothers-In-Law Day."

FLUOR CORP., 1627 K St. N.W., Washington, D.C. 20006. Filed for self 7/23/82. Legislative interest — "Energy-related bills, tax legislation, construction legislation, S 1844, HR 4230." Lobbyists — E. Joseph Hillings, Betty Hudson, Charles E. Southwick.

FORD, RIFF & BURGESS, Washington, D.C. Lobbyist — Robert Stewart Royer, 1025 Connecticut Ave. N.W., Washington, D.C. 20036. Filed 7/22/82. Legislative interest — Not specified.

FORUM COMMUNICATIONS, Seattle, Wash. Lobbyist — Parrish & Chambers Inc., 1300 N. 17th St., Arlington, Va. 22209. Filed 7/9/82. Legislative interest — "DOT authorization and appropriations legislation."

THE GADSDEN TIMES INC., Washington, D.C. Lobbyist — Williams & Connolly, 839 17th St. N.W., Washington, D.C. 20006. Filed 7/23/82. Legislative interest — "...a possible amendment to Internal Revenue Code."

GENEVA PACIFIC CORP., Glenview, Ill. Lobbyist — National Counsel Associates Inc., 421 New Jersey Ave. S.E., Washington, D.C. 20003. Filed 7/12/82. Legislative interest — "...the development of Alaskan mineral resources and the procurement of land pattens and roads...."

GOLDEN GATEWAY CENTER, San Francisco, Calif. Lobbyist — O'Connor & Hannan, 1919 Pennsylvania Ave. N.W., Washington, D.C. 20006. Filed 7/7/82. (Former U.S. Sen. Edward W. Brooke, R-Mass., 1967-79, was listed as agent for this client.) Legislative interest — "...housing legislation."

GOLDEN NUGGET INC., Las Vegas, Nev. Lobbyist — James E. Ritchie, 499 S. Capitol St. S.W., Washington, D.C. 20003. Filed 7/28/82. Legislative interest — "...HR 4961, 'Tax Equity and Fiscal Responsibility Act of 1982.'"

GOLDMAN SACHS & CO., New York, N.Y. Lobbyist — O'Connor & Hannan, 1919 Pennsylvania Ave. N.W., Washington, D.C. 20006. Filed 7/9/82. Legislative interest — "Legislation regarding preserving the FHA Sections 232/242 mortgage insurance programs for health care facilities." Lobbyist — Akin, Gump, Strauss, Hauer & Feld, 1333 New Hampshire Ave. N.W., Washington, D.C. 20036. Filed 7/26/82. Legislative interest — "...investment banking and taxes...."

GUARDIAN LIFE INSURANCE COMPANY OF AMERICA, New York, N.Y. Lobbyist — Arent, Fox, Kintner, Plotkin & Kahn, 1819 H St. N.W., Washington, D.C. 20006. Filed 7/21/82. Legislative interest — "Supporting sections of Parts I-IV of subtitle D of HR 4961, concerning taxation of life insurance companies and annuities, and certain amendments to HR 4961."

THE HANNA MINING CO., Cleveland, Ohio. Lobbyist — Jones, Day, Reavis & Pogue, 1735 I St. N.W., Washington, D.C. 20006. Filed 7/21/82. Legislative interest — "...HR 4961, 'The Tax Equity and Fiscal Responsibility Act of 1982.'"

HARLEY-DAVIDSON MILITARY SALES, Woodbury, N.Y. Lobbyist — Robert Stewart Royer, 1025 Connecticut Ave. N.W., Washington, D.C. 20036. Filed 7/22/82. Legislative interest — "Legislation affecting the auto industry and other matters affecting overseas military sales group."

HOGAN & CO. INC., Greenwich, Conn. Lobbyist — Rogers & Wells, 1666 K St. N.W., Washington, D.C. 20006. Filed 7/13/82. Legislative interest — "Legislation generally dealing with commodity trading and specifically HR 6056 (Technical Corrections Act of 1982)."

HOSPITAL CORPORATION OF AMERICA, Washington, D.C. Lobbyist — Shea & Gould, 330 Madison Ave., New York, N.Y. 10017. Filed 7/9/82. Legislative interest — "Section 189 of Internal Revenue Code."

HOUSTON NATURAL GAS CORP., Arlington, Va. Lobbyist — Bracewell & Patterson, 1825 I St. N.W., Washington, D.C. 20006. Filed 7/12/82. Legislative interest — "Tax legislation and related matters."

THE HOUSTON POST CO., Houston, Texas. Lobbyist — Fulbright & Jaworski, 1150 Connecticut Ave. N.W., Washington, D.C. 20036. Filed 7/29/82. Legislative interest — "Legislation affecting Title 26 of the U.S. Code."

ROY M. HUFFINGTON INC., First International Plaza, P.O. Box 4455, Houston, Texas 77210. Lobbyist — Davis, Polk & Wardwell, 1575 I St. N.W., Washington, D.C. 20005. Filed 7/28/82. Legislative interest — "...Tax Equity and Fiscal Responsibility Act of 1982...." Filed for self 7/28/82. Legislative interest — "...Tax Equity and Fiscal Responsibility Act of 1982...." Lobbyists — Lorne D. Bain, Roy M. Huffington, Roger W. Wallace.

INCO UNITED STATES INC., New York, N.Y. Lobbyist — Sullivan & Cromwell, 125 Broad St., New York, N.Y. 10004. Filed 7/10/82. Legislative interest — "Tax legislation affecting foreign corporations and their domestic subsidiaries."

INDEPENDENT VALLEY ENERGY CO., Houston, Texas. Lobbyist — Hansell, Post, Brandon & Dorsey, 1915 I St. N.W., Washington, D.C. 20006. Filed 7/26/82. Legislative interest — "Activities in connection with certain provisions of the Economic Recovery Tax Act of 1981."

INGERSOLL-RAND CO., Woodcliff Lake, N.J. Lobbyist — Clifford & Warnke, 815 Connecticut Ave. N.W., Washington, D.C. 20006. Filed 7/2/82. Legislative interest — "...amendments

of Export Administration Act of 1969 and Overseas Private Investment Corporation Act Amendments of 1981."

INTERMOUNTAIN HEALTH CARE, Salt Lake City, Utah. Lobbyist — Marian Troyer, 1242 D St. S.E., Washington, D.C. 20003. Filed 7/26/82. Legislative interest — "Health issues."

INTERNATIONAL BUSINESS MACHINES CORP., Old Orchard Road, Armonk, N.Y. 10504. Filed for self 7/2/82. Legislative interest — "...international trade and investment policy...." Lobbyist — Aaron W. Cross, 1801 K St. N.W., Washington, D.C. 20006.

INTERNATIONAL FUTURES EXCHANGE LTD., Hamilton, Bermuda. Lobbyist — Robert Stewart Royer, 1025 Connecticut Ave. N.W., Washington, D.C. 20036. Filed 7/22/82. Legislative interest — "CFTC reauthorization and other legislation that would affect foreign commodities exchanges."

INTERNATIONAL TELEPHONE & TELEGRAPH CORP., 320 Park Ave., New York, N.Y. 10022. Lobbyist — Jones, Day, Reavis & Pogue, 1735 I St. N.W., Washington, D.C. 20006. Filed 7/29/82. Legislative interest — "...HR 4961, 'The Equity and Fiscal Responsibility Act of 1982.'" Lobbyist — Charls E. Walker Associates Inc., 1730 Pennsylvania Ave. N.W., Washington, D.C. 20006. Filed 7/9/82. Legislative interest — "...may concern refundability of the investment tax credit, or items relating to taxation of leasing transactions." Filed for self 7/9/82. Legislative interest — "...matters which affect multi-product and services international company ... government regulation, capital formation, military and defense, miscellaneous tax matters...." Lobbyist — E. George Riedel, 1707 L St. N.W., Washington, D.C. 20036.

INTEX HOLDINGS (BERMUDA) LTD., Hamilton, Bermuda. Lobbyist — Robert Stewart Royer, 1025 Connecticut Ave. N.W., Washington, D.C. 20036. Filed 7/22/82. Legislative interest — "S 2109 and other legislation affecting commodity transactions."

JEFFERSON-PILOT CORP., Greensboro, N.C. Lobbyist — Scribner, Hall & Thompson, 1875 I St. N.W., Washington, D.C. 20006. Filed 7/28/82. Legislative interest — "...federal income tax of company and subsidiaries."

JOHNSON SCANSTAR, San Francisco, Calif. Lobbyist — Lillick, McHose & Charles, 21 Dupont Circle N.W., Washington, D.C. 20036. Filed 7/9/82. Legislative interest — "Shipping Act of 1981; Shipping Act Amendments of 1981, S 1593; HR 4374."

KAISER FOUNDATION HEALTH PLAN INC., 900 17th St. N.W., Washington, D.C. 20006. Filed for self 7/8/82. Legislative interest — "...legislation relating to organizing, providing, delivering, and paying for medical care and related subjects which might have an effect upon the operation of this business." Lobbyist — Richard B. Froh.

KERR-MCGEE CORP., 1625 K St. N.W., Washington, D.C. 20006. Filed for self 7/12/82. Legislative interest — "...energy-related legislation that may apply to the discovery, development and processing of natural resources." Lobbyists — Peter M. Frank, Pat I. Heth.

LIGGETT GROUP INC., Montvale, N.J. Lobbyist — Sullivan & Cromwell, 125 Broad St., New York, N.Y. 10004. Filed 7/13/82. Legislative interest — "Federal income tax legislation affecting distributions of property by corporations...."

LOCKHEED CORP., Burbank, Calif. Lobbyist — Thomas Ludlow Ashley, 1730 Pennsylvania Ave. N.W., Washington, D.C. 20006. Filed 7/8/82. (Former U.S. rep., D-Ohio, 1955-81.) Legislative interest — "Selection of Lockheed's C5-B for the new Air Force cargo transporter."

MARRIOTT CORP., Bethesda, Md. Lobbyist — Kaswell, Perazich & Watson, 1825 K St. N.W., Washington, D.C. 20006. Filed 7/14/82. Legislative interest — "...tax bills ... relates to partial liquidations section 189...."

MELLON BANK N.A. AND MELLON NATIONAL CORP., Mellon Square, Pittsburgh, Pa. 15230. Filed for self 7/31/82. Legislative interest — "All legislation affecting banks and bank holding companies. Export Trading Act, S 734 ... Financial Institutions Restructuring and Services Act of 1981, S 1720 ... Bankruptcy Improvement Act of 1981, S 2000 ... Tax Equity and Fiscal Responsibility Act, HR 4961...." Lobbyist — Harry R. Obley.

WILLIAM M. MERCER INC., New York, N.Y. Lobbyist — Peter Small & Associates Inc., 400 Madison Ave., New York, N.Y. 10017. Filed 7/6/82. Legislative interest — "Legislation impacting employee benefits and compensation, *e.g.*, income tax legislation, Social Security, executive compensation, etc."

MERRILL LYNCH WHITE WELD CAPITAL MARKETS GROUP, New York, N.Y. Lobbyist — O'Connor & Hannan, 1919 Pennsylvania Ave. N.W., Washington, D.C. 20006. Filed 7/9/82. Legislative interest — "Legislation regarding preserving the FHA Sections 232/242 mortgage insurance programs for health care facilities."

MICHIGAN TRADE EXCHANGE, Southfield, Mich. Lobbyist — Robert Stewart Royer, 1025 Connecticut Ave. N.W., Washington, D.C. 20036. Filed 7/22/82. Legislative interest — "Legislation regarding third-party record keeping and other matters affecting barter exchanges."

MORGAN STANLEY & CO. INC., New York, N.Y. Lobbyist — Robert Stewart Royer, 1025 Connecticut Ave. N.W., Washington, D.C. 20036. Filed 7/22/82. Legislative interest — Not specified.

NATIONAL CORPORATION FOR HOUSING PARTNERSHIPS, Washington, D.C. Lobbyist — Brownstein, Zeidman and Schomer, 1025 Connecticut Ave. N.W., Washington, D.C. 20036. Filed 7/9/82. Legislative interest — "All legislation affecting insured and subsidized housing development."

NORTON SIMON INC., New York, N.Y. Lobbyist — Akin, Gump, Strauss, Hauer & Feld, 1333 New Hampshire Ave. N.W., Washington, D.C. 20036. Filed 7/2/82. Legislative interest — "Hearings and any legislation relating to consumer products and services including tax legislation."

OVERSEAS MILITARY SALES GROUP, Woodbury, N.Y. Lobbyist — Robert Stewart Royer, 1025 Connecticut Ave. N.W., Washington, D.C. 20036. Filed 7/22/82. Legislative interest — "Legislation affecting the auto industry and other matters affecting overseas military sales group."

PALMER COMMUNICATIONS INC., Des Moines, Iowa. Lobbyist — Dow, Lohnes & Albertson, 1225 Connecticut Ave. N.W., Washington, D.C. 20036. Filed 7/12/82. Legislative interest — "Radio broadcasting to Cuba ... HR 5427; S 1853; 22 U.S.C. 2871."

PEABODY COAL CO., Washington, D.C. Lobbyist — Van Ness, Feldman, Sutcliffe, Curtis & Levenberg, 1050 Thomas Jefferson St. N.W., Washington, D.C. 20036. Filed 7/21/82. Legislative interest — "Clean Air Act amendments, specifically legislative proposals related to acid precipitation control."

PEARLSTINE, SALKIN, HARDIMAN & ROBINSON, Lansdale, Pa. Lobbyist — Kutak, Rock & Huie, 1101 Connecticut Ave. N.W., Washington, D.C. 20036. Filed 7/9/82. Legislative interest — "Preparation of legislative language to preserve state authority to determine jurisdiction for issuers of industrial development and general monitoring of developments."

PENNSYLVANIA SHIPBUILDING CO., Chester, Pa. Lobbyist — Butler, Binion, Rice, Cook & Knapp, 1747 Pennsylvania Ave. N.W., Washington, D.C. 20006. Filed 7/9/82. Legislative interest — "Defense authorization, defense appropriations."

PFIZER INC., New York, N.Y. Lobbyist — Jones, Day, Reavis & Pogue, 1735 I St. N.W., Washington, D.C. 20006. Filed 7/21/82. Legislative interest — "...HR 4961, 'The Tax Equity and Fiscal Responsibility Act of 1982.'"

PHIBRO-SALOMON INC., New York, N.Y. Lobbyist — Dewey, Ballantine, Bushby, Palmer & Wood, 1775 Pennsylvania Ave. N.W., Washington, D.C. 20006. Filed 7/22/82. Legislative interest — "...tax legislation."

PHILADELPHIA LIFE INSURANCE CO., Philadelphia, Pa. Lobbyist — Scribner, Hall & Thompson, 1875 I St. N.W., Washington, D.C. 20006. Filed 7/8/82. Legislative interest — "Proposed legislation with respect to acquisition and mergers of corporations."

PHILLIPS PETROLEUM CO., Bartlesville, Okla. Lobbyist — Clifford & Warnke, 815 Connecticut Ave. N.W., Washington, D.C. 20006. Filed 7/29/82. Legislative interest — "HR 4961, Tax Equity and Fiscal Responsibility Act of 1982."

PIZZA HUT INC., Wichita, Kan. Lobbyist — Miles &

Stockbridge, 1701 Pennsylvania Ave. N.W., Washington, D.C. 20006. Filed 7/10/82. Legislative interest — "All legislative matters relating to dairy price supports and tax reform."

PORTMAN PROPERTIES, Atlanta, Ga. Lobbyist — Hansell, Post, Brandon & Dorsey, 1915 I St. N.W., Washington, D.C. 20006. Filed 7/26/82. Legislative interest — "...in support of certain provisions of the Economic Recovery Tax Act of 1981."

PUBLIC WELFARE FOUNDATION INC., Washington, D.C. Lobbyist — Williams & Connolly, 839 17th St. N.W., Washington, D.C. 20006. Filed 7/23/82. Legislative interest — "...a possible amendment to Internal Revenue Code."

RADNOR CORP., P.O. Box 1308, Jupiter, Fla. 33458. Lobbyist — Blank, Rome, Comisky & McCauley, 1700 K St. N.W., Washington, D.C. 20006. Filed 7/7/82. Legislative interest — "S 1018, HR 3252, and related proposals addressing the development of undeveloped coastal barriers." Filed for self 7/12/82. Legislative interest — "S 1018, HR 3252, and related proposals addressing the development of undeveloped coastal barriers." Lobbyist — Stephen H. Osburn.

R. J. REYNOLDS INDUSTRIES INC., Winston-Salem, N.C. Lobbyist — Akin, Gump, Strauss, Hauer & Feld, 1333 New Hampshire Ave. N.W., Washington, D.C. 20036. Filed 7/26/82. Legislative interest — "Hearings and any legislation affecting tobacco interests generally."

SALOMON BROTHERS INC., New York, N.Y. Lobbyist — Cleary, Gottlieb, Steen & Hamilton, 1250 Connecticut Ave. N.W., Washington, D.C. 20036. Filed 7/7/82. Legislative interest — "Legislation concerning the Bankruptcy Tax Act of 1980 and related legislation (S 2688)."

SECURITY LIFE OF DENVER, Denver, Colo. Lobbyist — Paul, Hastings, Janofsky & Walker, 1050 Thomas Jefferson St. N.W., Washington, D.C. 20007. Filed 7/6/82. (Former U.S. Rep. Fred B. Rooney, D-Pa., 1963-79, was listed as agent for this client.) Legislative interest — "Taxation of the life insurance companies."

SEQUOIA VENTURES INC., San Francisco, Calif. Lobbyist — Thelen, Marrin, Johnson & Bridges, Two Embarcadero Center, San Francisco, Calif. 94111. Filed 7/10/82. Legislative interest — "HR 6055."

SHAKLEE CORP., San Francisco, Calif. Lobbyist — Gray and Co., 3255 Grace St. N.W., Washington, D.C. 20007. Filed 7/22/82. Legislative interest — "Including but not limited to HR 4961."

SHELL OIL CO., P.O. Box 2463, Houston, Texas 77001. Filed for self 7/30/82. Legislative interest — "...oil and gas production, chemicals, health, safety and the environment, taxation concerns, and employee/employer relations." Lobbyist — Philip C. Holladay, 1025 Connecticut Ave. N.W., Washington, D.C. 20036.

SOUTH HAMPTON INC., Silsbee, Texas. Lobbyist — Akin, Gump, Strauss, Hauer & Feld, 1333 New Hampshire Ave. N.W., Washington, D.C. 20036. Filed 7/9/82. Legislative interest — "Hearings and any energy legislation, including but not limited to the Federal Energy and Mineral Resource Act of 1982, S 2305."

THE SPARTANBURG HERALD & JOURNAL INC., Washington, D.C. Lobbyist — Williams & Connolly, 839 17th St. N.W., Washington, D.C. 20006. Filed 7/22/82. Legislative interest — "...a possible amendment to Internal Revenue Code."

J. P. STEVENS & CO. INC., 1185 Avenue of the Americas, New York, N.Y. 10036. Lobbyist — Skadden, Arps, Slate, Meagher & Flom, 919 Third Ave., New York, N.Y. 10022. Filed 7/22/82. Legislative interest — "Tax Equity and Fiscal Responsibility Act of 1982 (HR 4961), safe harbor leasing provisions." Filed for self 7/23/82. Legislative interest — "Tax Equity and Fiscal Responsibility Act of 1982 (HR 4961), safe harbor leasing provisions." Lobbyists — Douglas E. Buie, Leonard J. Conenna.

TECHNOLOGY FOR ENERGY CORP., 1200 New Hampshire Ave. N.W., Washington, D.C. 20036. Filed for self 7/26/82. Legislative interest — Not specified. Lobbyist — Michael J. McShane.

THE TUSCALOOSA NEWS INC., Washington, D.C. Lobbyist — Williams & Connolly, 839 17th St. N.W., Washington, D.C. 20006. Filed 7/23/82. Legislative interest — "...a possible amendment to Internal Revenue Code."

UNION CARBIDE CORP., Old Ridgebury Road, Danbury, Conn. 06817. Filed for self 7/7/82. Legislative interest — "...Clean Air Amendments (HR 5252, S 1706, S 1709, S 2027), Clean Water Amendments (HR 6670, S 2590), Safe Drinking Water Amendments (S 1866, S 2131, S 2576), Mine Safety and Health Amendments (HR 6548, S 1423), Animals in Research Act (HR 6245)." Lobbyist — Scott S. Cunningham, 1100 15th St. N.W., Washington, D.C. 20005.

UNITED DISTRIBUTION COS., 159 Town Hall Square, Falmouth, Mass. 02540. Filed for self 7/2/82. Legislative interest — "Amendments to the Natural Gas Policy Act; and amendments to the Natural Gas Act." Lobbyist — C. William Cooper.

UNITED STATES AUTOMOBILE ASSOCIATION, San Antonio, Texas. Lobbyist — Daniel J. Swillinger, 920 Pennsylvania Ave. S.E., Washington, D.C. 20003. Filed 7/21/82. Legislative interest — "HR 6426 (IRAs)."

VOLVO OF AMERICA CORP., Rockleigh, N.J. Lobbyist — Winston & Strawn, 2550 M St. N.W., Washington, D.C. 20037. Filed 7/31/82. Legislative interest — "Related or similar legislation that may have a substantial impact on U.S. free trade, including HR 5133, HR 6629, S 2300."

WESTINGHOUSE ELECTRIC CORP., Washington, D.C. Lobbyist — Parrish & Chambers Inc., 1300 N. 17th St., Arlington, Va. 22209. Filed 7/9/82. Legislative interest — "Surface Transportation Act of 1982; DOT appropriations; HR 6266...."

Labor Groups

AMERICAN FEDERATION OF LABOR-CONGRESS OF INDUSTRIAL ORGANIZATIONS, Washington, D.C. Lobbyist — Bregman, Abell & Kay, 1900 L St. N.W., Washington, D.C. 20036. Filed 7/12/82. Legislative interest — "All matters concerning the balanced budget amendment."

State and Local Governments

BROWARD COUNTY, FLA., Fort Lauderdale, Fla. Lobbyist — Butler, Binion, Rice, Cook & Knapp, 1747 Pennsylvania Ave. N.W., Washington, D.C. 20006. Filed 7/8/82. Legislative interest — "Airport development legislation."

CITY OF AKRON, OHIO, Akron, Ohio. Lobbyist — Robert Stewart Royer, 1025 Connecticut Ave. N.W., Washington, D.C. 20036. Filed 7/22/82. Legislative interest — "Matters relating to solid waste, to energy and others affecting the city of Akron."

COMMONWEALTH OF PUERTO RICO, San Juan, Puerto Rico. Lobbyist — Gray and Co., 3255 Grace St. N.W., Washington, D.C. 20007. Filed 7/22/82. Legislative interest — "Including but not limited to HR 4961."

METROPOLITAN TRANSPORTATION AUTHORITY, New York, N.Y. Lobbyist — Barrett, Smith, Schapiro, Simon & Armstrong, 26 Broadway, New York, N.Y. 10004. Filed 7/13/82. Legislative interest — "Various provisions of the Internal Revenue Code, including section 168."

MUNICIPAL SUBDISTRICT, NORTHERN COLORADO WATER CONSERVANCY DISTRICT, Loveland, Colo. Lobbyist — Davis, Graham & Stubbs, 1920 N St. N.W., Washington, D.C. 20036. Filed 7/9/82. Legislative interest — "Support for amendments to Clean Water Act to exempt dams from the Act's NPDES program; support S 1867 and HR 5539 to amend the Reclamation Act of 1902; support S 956 and oppose amendment requiring reimbursement; and urge reauthorization of Endangered Species Act to include protection of state water rights."

OAKLAND COLISEUM, Oakland, Calif. Lobbyist — Richard L. Sinnott & Co., 2021 K St. N.W., Washington, D.C. 20006. Filed 7/29/82. Legislative interest — "HR 6467, Major League Sports Community Protection Act of 1982."

PORT OF TACOMA, Tacoma, Wash. Lobbyist — Preston, Thorgrimson, Ellis & Holman, 1776 G St. N.W., Washington, D.C. 20006. Filed 7/12/82. Legislative interest — "Legislation concerning domestic shipping requirements."

PUERTO RICO FEDERAL AFFAIRS ADMINISTRA-TION, Washington, D.C. Lobbyist — Hamel, Park, McCabe, & Saunders, 888 16th St. N.W., Washington, D.C. 20006. Filed 7/28/82. Legislative interest — "...favors amendment to HR 4961."

Trade Associations

THE ADHERENCE GROUP INC., New York, N.Y. Lobbyist — Billig, Sher & Jones, 2033 K St. N.W., Washington, D.C. 20006. Filed 7/12/82. Legislative interest — "Shipping legislation; HR 4374 and S 1593."

AD HOC COMMITTEE FOR RESPONSIBLE TAX POLICY, 1750 Pennsylvania Ave. N.W., Washington, D.C. 20006. Filed for self 7/30/82. Legislative interest — "...against so-called flat-tax rate proposals and for the deductibility of 'investment interest.'" Lobbyist — Daniel J. Piliero II.

AIR LINE PILOTS ASSOCIATION, Washington, D.C. Lobbyist — William H. Harsha, 1102 Delf Drive, McLean, Va. 22101. Filed 7/9/82. (Former U.S. rep., R-Ohio, 1961-81.) Legislative interest — "War Risk Insurance; HR 5930."

AMERICAN CONSULTING ENGINEERS COUNCIL, 1015 15th St. N.W., Washington, D.C. 20005. Filed for self 7/8/82. Legislative interest — "Matters relating to public works; transportation; the environment; pollution control; housing; equal employment opportunity; public health and safety; economy and efficiency in government; and energy legislation." Lobbyist — Stacy Richards.

AMERICAN ELECTRONICS ASSOCIATION, Palo Alto, Calif. Lobbyist — Leva, Hawes, Symington, Martin & Oppenheimer, 815 Connecticut Ave. N.W., Washington, D.C. 20006. Filed 7/12/82. Legislative interest — "...pending amendments to the Clean Air Act, 42 U.S.C. section 9401 *et seq.*, particularly HR 5252."

AMERICAN HEALTH CARE ASSOCIATION, Washington, D.C. Lobbyist — Gardner, Carton & Douglas, 1875 I St. N.W., Washington, D.C. 20006. Filed 7/21/82. Legislative interest — "Tax and health legislation."

AMERICAN MEDICAL ASSOCIATION, 535 N. Dearborn St., Chicago, Ill. 60610. Filed for self 7/12/82. Legislative interest — "...all federal legislation of a health or medical nature." Lobbyist — Joe D. Miller.

AMERICAN OPTOMETRIC ASSOCIATION, 600 Maryland Ave. S.W., Washington, D.C. 20024. Filed for self 7/7/82. Legislative interest — Not specified. Lobbyists — Millicent Gorham, Jeffrey G. Mays.

AMERICAN PUBLIC HEALTH ASSOCIATION, 1015 15th St. N.W., Washington, D.C. 20005. Filed for self 7/8/82. Legislative interest — "...legislation which affects national health policy and which promotes effective public and private health and environmental health programming at federal, state and local levels." Lobbyist — Richard Gilbert.

THE AMERICAN PUBLIC TRANSIT ASSOCIATION, 1225 Connecticut Ave. N.W., Washington, D.C. 20036. Filed for self 7/6/82. Legislative interest — "...transit authorizing and appropriations legislation. HR 6211, S 2377, S 2367 (Mass Transit Act of 1982); HR 3663 (Bus Deregulation Act); S Con Res 92 (First Budget Resolution)." Lobbyist — Deborah K. Rudolph.

AMERICAN SOCIETY OF CIVIL ENGINEERS, New York, N.Y. Filed for self 7/9/82. Legislative interest — "...Clean Air Act, Clean Water Act, nuclear waste disposal, hazardous waste disposal." Lobbyist — Frank Dominic Musica, 1625 I St. N.W., Washington, D.C. 20006.

AMERICAN SOCIETY FOR GASTROINTESTINAL ENDOSCOPY, Thorofare, N.J. Lobbyist — John T. Grupenhoff, 10,000 Falls Road, Potomac, Md. 20854. Filed 7/12/82. Legislative interest — "Medicare/Medicaid/digestive diseases research/medical policy legislation."

AMERICAN SOYBEAN ASSOCIATION, 600 Maryland Ave. S.W., Washington, D.C. 20024. Filed for self 7/8/82. Legislative interest — "HR 5133, Fair Practices in Automotive Products Act, against; S 2357, to provide contract sanctity, for; HR 4627 and

S 1692, to facilitate port dredging and development, against." Lobbyist — Nancy E. Foster.

AMERICAN SUGARBEET GROWERS ASSOCIA-TION, 1156 15th St. N.W., Washington, D.C. 20005. Filed for self 7/6/82. Legislative interest — "General agriculture legislation." Lobbyist — Luther A. Markwart.

THE ASSOCIATED GENERAL CONTRACTORS OF AMERICA, 1957 E St. N.W., Washington, D.C. 20006. Filed for self 7/9/82. Legislative interest — "Public financing of congressional election proposals - against; increased limitations on PAC contributions or business election involvement - against." Lobbyist — Joan H. LaVor.

ASSOCIATION OF SPANISH FISHERMEN, Vigo, Spain. Lobbyist — Finley, Kumble, Wagner, Heine, Underberg & Casey, 1120 Connecticut Ave. N.W., Washington, D.C. 20036. Filed 7/21/82. Legislative interest — "...activities of the association members within U.S. coastal waters."

CALIFORNIA HOUSING COUNCIL, Sacramento, Calif. Lobbyist — Davis, Simpich & Siena, 1301 Pennsylvania Ave. N.W., Washington, D.C. 20004. Filed 7/27/82. Legislative interest — "For amendment to tax code to provide capital gains treatment for apartment owners on conversion to condominiums...."

CALIFORNIA WESTSIDE FARMERS, Washington, D.C. Lobbyist — James H. Lake, 1200 New Hampshire Ave. N.W., Washington, D.C. 20036. Filed 7/26/82. Legislative interest — "S 1867/Reclamation legislation."

CHAMBER OF COMMERCE OF THE UNITED STATES, 1615 H St. N.W., Washington, D.C. 20062. Filed for self 7/9/82. Legislative interest — Not specified. Lobbyists — Ronald D. Utt, Jeanne Morin.

COUPON BOND TAX COMMITTEE, Chicago, Ill. Lobbyist — Charls E. Walker Associates Inc., 1730 Pennsylvania Ave. N.W., Washington, D.C. 20006. Filed 7/21/82. Legislative interest — "...may concern issues relating to the tax treatment of stripping of interest coupons from bonds."

DESIGN PROFESSIONS GROUP, Washington, D.C. Lobbyist — Hogan & Hartson, 815 Connecticut Ave. N.W., Washington, D.C. 20006. Filed 7/12/82. Legislative interest — "...legislation affecting the treatment of the learned professions under the antitrust laws."

EDISON ELECTRIC INSTITUTE, 1111 19th St. N.W., Washington, D.C. 20036. Filed for self 7/6/82. Legislative interest — "Oil and gas legislation." Lobbyist — Elizabeth LeMond.

HAWAIIAN SUGAR PLANTERS' ASSOCIATION, P.O. Box 1057, Aiea, Hawaii. Filed for self 7/29/82. Legislative interest — "The Food and Agriculture Act and all other legislation affecting the sugar industry in Hawaii." Lobbyist — Eiler C. Ravnholt, 729 Investment Building, Washington, D.C. 20005.

HEALTH INSURANCE ASSOCIATION OF AMER-ICA, Washington, D.C. Lobbyist — Gray and Co., 3255 Grace St. N.W., Washington, D.C. 20007. Filed 7/22/82. Legislative interest — "Including but not limited to amendments to HR 4961."

INSURANCE ECONOMICS SOCIETY OF AMERICA, Washington, D.C. Lobbyist — O'Connor & Hannan, 1919 Pennsylvania Ave. N.W., Washington, D.C. 20006. Filed 7/7/82. Legislative interest — "...the Social Security Act."

JEWELRY INDUSTRY COORDINATING COMMIT-TEE, Providence, R.I. Lobbyist — John M. Martin Jr., 6909 Fort Hunt Road, Alexandria, Va. 22307. Filed 7/9/82. Legislative interest — "Proposed excise tax on jewelry."

MID-CONTINENT OIL & GAS ASSOCIATION, 711 Adams Office Building, Tulsa, Okla. 74103. Filed for self 7/8/82. Legislative interest — Not specified. Lobbyist — Clifford M. Naeve, 1919 Pennsylvania Ave. N.W., Washington, D.C. 20006.

NATIONAL ASSOCIATION OF MANUFACTURERS, 1776 F St. N.W., Washington, D.C. 20006. Filed for self 7/9/82. Legislative interest — "...legislative proposals affecting corporate industrial relations, *i.e.*, Walsh-Healey, Workers' Compensation, Social Security, etc."

NATIONAL COUNCIL ON SYNTHETIC FUELS PRODUCTION, 1825 I St. N.W., Washington, D.C. 20006. Filed for self 7/6/82. Legislative interest — "Any legislation affecting the synthetic fuels industry (may concern tax, environmental and

consumer issues)...." Lobbyist — Joseph D. Keefer.

NATIONAL COUNCIL ON TEACHER RETIRE-MENT, Columbus, Ohio. Lobbyist — Adams, Duque & Hazeltine, 1920 N St. N.W., Washington, D.C. 20036. Filed 7/29/82. Legislative interest — "Opposition to federal regulation of state and local public pension funds. In opposition to S 2105, S 2106, HR 4928 and HR 4929."

NATIONAL HOSPICE EDUCATION PROJECT, Miami, Fla. Lobbyist — Hogan & Hartson, 815 Connecticut Ave. N.W., Washington, D.C. 20006. Filed 7/12/82. Legislative interest — "Bills to provide for coverage of hospice care under the Medicare program: HR 5180; S 1958."

NATIONAL INDEPENDENT DAIRY FOODS ASSO-CIATION, Washington, D.C. Lobbyist — Davis, Wright, Todd, Riese & Jones, 1050 Thomas Jefferson St. N.W., Washington, D.C. 20007. Filed 7/2/82. Legislative interest — "Antitrust jurisdiction of the Federal Trade Commission. S 2499 - Federal Trade Commission Amendments Act of 1982. Federal Trade Commission's authorizing legislation...."

NATIONAL OFFICE MACHINE DEALERS ASSOCI-ATION, Wood Dale, Ill. Lobbyist — McNair, Glenn, Konduros, Corley, Singletary, Porter & Dibble, 1155 15th St. N.W., Washington, D.C. 20005. Filed 7/13/82. Legislative interest — "S 1256, for."

NATIONAL SATELLITE CABLE ASSOCIATION, Birmingham, Mich. Lobbyist — Morris J. Amitay, 400 N. Capitol St. N.W., Washington, D.C. 20001. Filed 7/13/82. Legislative interest — "Telecommunications legislation (S 2172, HR 5158)."

NORTH CAROLINA FARM BUREAU, Raleigh, N.C. Lobbyist — Larry D. Meyers, 412 First St. S.E., Washington, D.C. 20003. Filed 7/8/82. Legislative interest — "Tobacco legislation."

PHARMACEUTICAL MANUFACTURERS ASSOCI-ATION, Washington, D.C. Lobbyist — Jones, Day, Reavis & Pogue, 1735 I St. N.W., Washington, D.C. 20006. Filed 7/29/82. Legislative interest — "...HR 4961, 'The Tax Equity and Fiscal Responsibility Act of 1982.'"

SECURITIES INDUSTRY ASSOCIATION, New York, N.Y. Lobbyist — Robert Stewart Royer, 1025 Connecticut Ave. N.W., Washington, D.C. 20036. Filed 7/22/82. Legislative interest — "HR 2828; S 1720...."

SYNTHETIC ORGANIC CHEMICAL MANUFAC-TURERS ASSOCIATION, Scarsdale, N.Y. Lobbyist — Cleary, Gottlieb, Steen & Hamilton, 1250 Connecticut Ave. N.W., Washington, D.C. 20036. Filed 7/9/82. Legislative interest — "Legislation concerning trade-related issues under the Trade Act of 1974, *e.g.*, HR 4761, and legislation to reauthorize the Resource Conservation and Recovery Act (HR 6302)."

THE TOBACCO INSTITUTE, Washington, D.C. Lobbyist — Gray and Co., 3255 Grace St. N.W., Washington, D.C. 20007. Filed 7/22/82. Legislative interest — "Including but not limited to amendments to HR 4961." Lobbyist — Zuckert, Scoutt & Rasenberger, 888 17th St. N.W., Washington, D.C. 20006. Filed 7/26/82. Legislative interest — "...opposes section 285 of HR 4961."

TRANSIT ADVERTISERS ASSOCIATION, New York, N.Y. Lobbyist — Epstein, Becker, Borsody and Green, 1140 19th St. N.W., Washington, D.C. 20036. Filed 7/6/82. Legislative interest —"Legislation affecting advertising generally and the District of Columbia lottery."

TRAVEL AND TOURISM GOVERNMENT AFFAIRS POLICY COUNCIL, 1899 L St. N.W., Washington, D.C. 20036. Filed for self 7/12/82. Legislative interest — "Visa waiver, HR 5872; USTTA authorization, HR 6258 and HR 2261; bus deregulation, HR 3663." Lobbyist — James E. Gaffigan.

Miscellaneous

AMERICAN COLLEGE OF NEUROPSYCHO-PHARMACOLOGY, Nashville, Tenn. Lobbyist — Perito, Duerk, Carlson & Pinco, 1140 Connecticut Ave. N.W., Washington, D.C. 20036. Filed 7/9/82. Legislative interest — "...Small Business Innovation Act; S 881, HR 4326...."

THE CATHOLIC UNIVERSITY OF AMERICA, Washington, D.C. Lobbyist — Schlossberg-Cassidy and Associates Inc., 955 L'Enfant Plaza S.W., Washington, D.C. 20024. Filed 7/21/82. Legislative interest — "Legislation relating to federal research, education and development programs."

COLUMBIA UNIVERSITY, New York, N.Y. Lobbyist — Schlossberg-Cassidy and Associates Inc., 955 L'Enfant Plaza S.W., Washington, D.C. 20024. Filed 7/21/82. Legislative interest — "Legislation relating to federal research, education and development programs."

DR. RALPH LANDAU, Northport, N.Y. Lobbyist — Jones, Day, Reavis & Pogue, 1735 I St. N.W., Washington, D.C. 20006. Filed 7/28/82. Legislative interest — "...HR 4961, 'The Tax Equity and Fiscal Responsibility Act of 1982.'"

TIMKEN FOUNDATION, Canton, Ohio. Lobbyist — Baker & Hostetler, 818 Connecticut Ave. N.W., Washington, D.C. 20006. Filed 7/27/82. Legislative interest — "...Federal Tax legislation...."

WESTERN FARMERS ELECTRIC COOPERATIVE, Anadarko, Okla. Lobbyist — Pierson, Ball & Dowd, 1200 18th St. N.W., Washington, D.C. 20036. Filed 7/30/82. Legislative interest — "Tax Equity and Fiscal Responsibility Act of 1982, HR 4961...."

August Registrations

Citizens' Groups

AFRICAN FRIENDS OF ISRAEL INC., 4801 Massachusetts Ave. N.W., Washington, D.C. 20016. Filed for self 8/5/82. Legislative interest — Not specified. Lobbyist — Rohulamin Quander.

CITIZEN/LABOR ENERGY COALITION, Washington, D.C. Lobbyist — Ed Rothschild, 2000 P St. N.W., Washington, D.C. 20036. Filed 8/16/82. Legislative interest — "...legislation that relates to . . . price controls on oil and gas, the formation of a public energy corporation, horizontal and vertical divestiture of the largest oil companies, the solar band and other conservation measures, adequate fuel assistance for low-income persons, a federal oil import authority, establishment of an office of Special Prosecutor to investigate pricing and supply violations and elimination of oil industry tax subsidies."

CITIZEN'S CHOICE INC., 1615 H St. N.W., Washington, D.C. 20062. Filed for self 8/26/82. Legislative interest — "S Res 58 to enact a balanced budget amendment (support); Taxpayer's Bill of Rights (support passage of some form of such legislation); Clean Air Act Reform (support); Omnibus Regulatory Reform (support); Alternatives to the present tax system (support); Independent Contractors Legislation (support passage of some form of such legislation)." Lobbyist — John C. Lynch.

COMMITTEE FOR CONSTITUTIONAL INTEGRITY, 1900 L St. N.W., Washington, D.C. 20036. Filed for self 8/11/82. Legislative interest — "All matters concerning the balanced budget amendment." Lobbyist — Linda Rogers-Kingsbury.

COMMON CAUSE, 2030 M St. N.W., Washington, D.C. 20036. Filed for self 8/12/82. Legislative interest — "...HR 4070 ... to limit the money candidates for federal office can receive from political action committees ... reduce the dairy price supports and sugar loan program subsidies included in the farm bill (HR 3603, S 884). ...urged passage of a bill (S Res 20) providing for TV and radio coverage of Senate sessions, and of bills (HR 18 and S 10) creating a Commission for More Effective Government. ...oppose efforts to pass a constitutional amendment to balance the budget (S J Res 58 and H J Res 10) as well as S 708, a bill to weaken the Foreign Corrupt Practices Act, and S 1730, a bill which would weaken the Freedom of Information Act. ...reauthorize key provisions of the Voting Rights Act (S 1992) and opposing efforts to weaken the Clean Air Act. ...reduce the appropriation for the Tennessee-Tombigbee water project. ...supported reauthorization of the Legal Services Corporation (S 393, HR 3480) and have

supported adequate appropriation for it. ...the Federal Election Commission and opposed efforts to eliminate or reduce funding for the Commission. ...opposed efforts to limit federal court jurisdiction in matters concerning abortion, busing and school prayer (S 1760, S 951, S 1647, S 158). ...supported legislation to provide for a review of tax expenditures in the budget process (S 193, HR 482). ..." Lobbyist — Karen Pollitz.

COUNCIL FOR TECHNOLOGICAL GROWTH, 1200 18th St. N.W., Washington, D.C. 20036. Filed for self 8/17/82. Legislative interest — "All measures affecting technology, research and development." Lobbyist — Ross Stovall.

COUPON BOND COMMITTEE, Washington, D.C. Lobbyist — Davis & McLeod, 499 S. Capitol St. S.W., Washington, D.C. 20003. Filed 8/20/82. Legislative interest — "Tax Equity and Fiscal Responsibility Act of 1982 ... HR 4691...."

THE CUBAN AMERICAN NATIONAL FOUNDATION, Washington, D.C. Lobbyist — Barnett & Alagia, 1627 K St. N.W., Washington, D.C. 20006. Filed 8/23/82. Legislative interest — "S 1853 regarding radio broadcasting to Cuba and related bills, for."

NATIONAL COALITION FOR A FREE CUBA, Washington, D.C. Lobbyist — Gray and Co., 3255 Grace St. N.W., Washington, D.C. 20007. Filed 8/12/82. Legislative interest — "Including but not limited to S 1853."

NATIONAL WOMEN'S POLITICAL CAUCUS, 1411 K St. N.W., Washington, D.C. 20005. Filed for self 8/16/82. Legislative interest — "...opposed to 'Federalism' Constitutional Amendment, S J Res 110, 'Human Life' bills, HR 900, S 158, S 1741, and S 2372 ... opposed to changes in Title X regulations ... opposed to Vocational/Adult education consolidation, S 2325 ... oppose block grants and cuts in domestic spending for FY 83." Lobbyist — Laurie A. Westley.

THE WILDERNESS SOCIETY, 1901 Pennsylvania Ave. N.W., Washington, D.C. 20006. Filed for self 8/2/82. Legislative interest — "Wilderness issues relating to the national parks." Lobbyist — James Norton. Filed for self 8/2/82. Legislative interest — "Wilderness issues relating to the public lands managed by the Bureau of Land Management." Lobbyist — Doug Pike. Filed for self 8/2/82. Legislative interest — "Wilderness related issues pertaining to Alaska and wildlife." Lobbyist — Jon Simms.

Corporations and Businesses

ALASKA LUMBER AND PULP CO./LOUISIANA PACIFIC OF KETCHIKAN (ALP/LPK), Juneau, Alaska. Lobbyist — Preston, Thorgrimson, Ellis & Holman, 1776 G St. N.W., Washington, D.C. 20006. Filed 8/3/82. (Former U.S. Rep. Lloyd Meeds, D-Wash., 1965-79, was listed as agent for this client.) Legislative interest — "Legislation affecting House Agriculture Committee budget year 1983 reconciliation and sections 705 and 706, PL 96-487."

ALLIANCE CAPITAL MANAGEMENT CORP., New York, N.Y. Lobbyist — Seward & Kissel, 919 18th St. N.W., Washington, D.C. 20006. Filed 8/20/82. Legislative interest — "CFTC-SEC accord legislation."

ALVIN NEDERLANDER ASSOCIATES INC., Lobbyist — The Keefe Co., 1625 Massachusetts Ave. N.W., Washington, D.C. 20036. Filed 8/4/82. Legislative interest — "...tax credit for theatrical productions."

AMERICAN EXPRESS CO., Washington, D.C. Lobbyist — Reid & Priest, 1111 19th St. N.W., Washington, D.C. 20036. Filed 8/20/82. Legislative interest — "Amendment to section 316 of HR 4961 as reported by the Senate Finance Committee."

AMERICAN GLOBAL LINES INC., New York, N.Y. Lobbyist — Whittlesey & O'Brien, 1607 New Hampshire Ave. N.W., Washington, D.C. 20009. Filed 8/13/82. Legislative interest — "HR 3191."

AMERICAN NATURAL RESOURCES CO., 1 Woodward Ave., Detroit, Mich. 48226. Filed for self 8/20/82. Legislative interest — "1982 tax bill, Clean Air Act amendments, Highway User's tax...." Lobbyist — Robert E. Moss, 1899 L St.

N.W., Washington, D.C. 20036.

AMERICAN TELEPHONE & TELEGRAPH CO., New York, N.Y. Lobbyist — C. G. Pete Milligan, 4360 N.E. Joe's Point, Stuart, Fla. 33494. Filed 8/4/82. Legislative interest — "...legislation affecting the communications industry, including corporate, financial and tax issues (*e.g.* HR 1524)."

AT-SEA INCINERATION INC., Port Newark, N.J. Lobbyist — Finley, Kumble, Wagner, Heine, Underberg & Casey, 1120 Connecticut Ave. N.W., Washington, D.C. 20036. Filed 8/12/82. (Former U.S. Sen. Joseph D. Tydings, D-Md., 1965-71 and former U.S. Rep. Frank N. Ikard, D-Texas, 1951-61, were listed as agents for this client.) Legislative interest — "...amendment to the Merchant Marine Act pertaining to the incineration of hazardous wastes at sea. HR 5723 and S 2336 would amend section 27 of the Merchant Marine Act of 1920, 46 U.S.C. section 883."

BACARDI CORP., San Juan, Puerto Rico. Lobbyist — Everett, Johnson & Breckinridge, 20 Exchange Place, New York, N.Y. 10005. Filed 8/9/82. Legislative interest — "...proposed amendments of section 926 of the Internal Revenue Code of 1954. HR 4961, section 218."

B. ALTMAN & CO., New York, N.Y. Lobbyist — Reid & Priest, 1111 19th St. N.W., Washington, D.C. 20036. Filed 8/20/82. Legislative interest — "Amendment to section 4943 of the Internal Revenue Code of 1954."

THE BOEING CO., Seattle, Wash. Lobbyist — Surrey & Morse, 1156 15th St. N.W., Washington, D.C. 20005. Filed 8/5/82. Legislative interest — "...HR 4961, The Tax and Fiscal Responsibility Act of 1982...."

BROWN & ROOT INC., Houston, Texas. Lobbyist — David P. Stang, 1629 K St. N.W., Washington, D.C. 20006. Filed 8/6/82. Legislative interest — "HR 4961, Tax Equity Act."

BROWN AND WILLIAMSON TOBACCO CORP., Louisville, Ky. Lobbyist — William H. Hecht, 499 S. Capitol St. S.W., Washington, D.C. 20003. Filed 8/16/82. Legislative interest — "...including, but not limited to: HR 4961." Lobbyist — Jones and Winburn, 1101 15th St. N.W., Washington, D.C. 20005. Filed 8/16/82. Legislative interest — "HR 4961 as it relates to the excise tax on cigarettes."

CHARTER BUSINESS SERVICES INC., Fort Lauderdale, Fla. Lobbyist — Paul Suplizio Associates, 5001 Seminary Road, Alexandria, Va. 22311. Filed 8/3/82. Legislative interest — "To support renewal of the targeted jobs tax credit provisions of the Internal Revenue Code. For S 2455, HR 6700 and HR 4961."

CHICAGO BOARD OPTIONS EXCHANGE INC., Chicago, Ill. Lobbyist — Schiff, Hardin & Waite, 1101 Connecticut Ave. N.W., Washington, D.C. 20036. Filed 8/3/82. Legislative interest — "Tax Equity and Fiscal Responsibility Act of 1982...."

CITIES SERVICE CO., Tulsa, Okla. Lobbyist — Akin, Gump, Strauss, Hauer & Feld, 1333 New Hampshire Ave. N.W., Washington, D.C. 20036. Filed 8/12/82. Legislative interest — "...any legislation affecting energy matters generally, including tax legislation, HR 4961, the 'Tax Equity and Fiscal Responsibility Act.'"

CITY INVESTING CO., New York, N.Y. Lobbyist — Patton, Boggs & Blow, 2550 M St. N.W., Washington, D.C. 20037. Filed 8/16/82. Legislative interest — "HR 4961, the Tax Equity and Fiscal Responsibility Act of 1982. In favor of certain provisions dealing with the taxation of pension funds."

THE CLOROX CO., P.O. Box 24305, Oakland, Calif. Filed for self 8/10/82. Legislative interest — "HR 4437, Daylight Savings Time; HR 1242, antitrust contribution; HR 4961, taxes; HR 6410, pensions; HR 6402, taxation of interstate commerce; S 1080, HR 746, HR 1776; regulatory reform; HR 6262, S 2266, Clean Air; S 1748, multi-employer pensions; S 1541, HR 4334, ERISA; HR 5203, S 2620, S 2621, environmental; S J Res 58, budget; S 2499, FTC; S 2631, HR 5214, product liability...." Lobbyist — Robert A. Ragland.

COMDISCO INC., Rosemont, Ill. Lobbyist — Bracewell & Patterson, 1825 I St. N.W., Washington, D.C. 20006. Filed 8/6/82. Legislative interest — "...amendments to the Internal Revenue Code."

CONTINENTAL AIR LINES, Los Angeles, Calif. Lobbyist — Van Ness, Feldman, Sutcliffe, Curtis & Levenberg, 1050

Thomas Jefferson St. N.W., Washington, D.C. 20007. Filed 8/10/82. Legislative interest — "HR 5930, the Aviation War Risk Insurance Bill: Against the inclusion of a provision that mandates certain labor protection provisions in certain transactions that are subject to CAB approval. HR 4961, the Tax Equity and Fiscal Responsibility Act of 1982: Against certain tax leasing provisions."

ELECTRONICS CORPORATION OF AMERICA, Cambridge, Mass. Lobbyist — Schlossberg-Cassidy and Associates Inc., 955 L'Enfant Plaza S.W., Washington, D.C. 20024. Filed 8/3/82. Legislative interest — "Legislative matters relating to taxation."

E G & G SYNFUELS INC., Washington, D.C. Lobbyist — Camp, Carmouche, Palmer, Barsh & Hunter, 2550 M St. N.W., Washington, D.C. 20037. Filed 8/5/82. Legislative interest — "Tax issues of relevance to synthetic fuels development in HR 4961."

FIRST NATIONAL BANK IN HARVEY, Chicago, Ill. Lobbyist — Tucker & Associates, 1015 18th St. N.W., Washington, D.C. 20036. Filed 8/13/82. Legislative interest — "...an amendment to section 237 of HR 4961 to change the effective date of the stripped bond rules from July 1, 1982, to the date of conference consideration of the amendment." Lobbyist — Wellford, Wegman, Krulwich, Gold and Hoff, 1015 18th St. N.W., Washington, D.C. 20036. Filed 8/13/82. Legislative interest — "...an amendment to section 237 of HR 4961 to change the effective date of the stripped bond rules from July 1, 1982, to the date of conference reconsideration of the amendment."

FLUOR CORP., Washington, D.C. Lobbyist — Patton, Boggs & Blow, 2550 M St. N.W., Washington, D.C. 20037. Filed 8/16/82. Legislative interest — "Legislation relating to the national distribution and utilization of coal such as S 1844 and HR 4230, The Coal Pipeline Act of 1981. In favor."

GENERAL ELECTRIC CO., Washington, D.C. Lobbyist — Nossaman, Krueger & Knox, 1140 19th St. N.W., Washington, D.C. 20036. Filed 8/6/82. Legislative interest — Not specified.

GOLDMAN SACHS & CO., New York, N.Y. Lobbyist — Groom & Nordberg, 1775 Pennsylvania Ave. N.W., Washington, D.C. 20006. Filed 8/17/82. Legislative interest — "Federal legislation affecting Title 26 of U.S.C."

GOULD INC., Rolling Meadows, Ill. Lobbyist — Kent & O'Connor Inc., 1919 Pennsylvania Ave. N.W., Washington, D.C. 20006. Filed 8/13/82. Legislative interest — "HR 5540 (for)...."

GROUP W CABLE, New York, N.Y. Lobbyist — Carl Robert Wagner, 2550 M St. N.W., Washington, D.C. 20036. Filed 8/3/82. Legislative interest — "...to amend Communications Act of 1934 - S 2172; Cable Copyright and Signal Carriage Act of 1982 - HR 5949."

HAWAIIAN SUGAR TRANSPORTATION CO., Aiea, Hawaii. Lobbyist — Donald C. Lubick, 1776 F St. N.W., Washington, D.C. 20006. Filed 8/13/82. Legislative interest — "...HR 4961 - transition rules on safe harbor leasing."

HILLCREST EQUITIES INC., Dallas, Texas. Lobbyist — Daniel A. Dutko, 412 First St. S.E., Washington, D.C. 20003. Filed 8/2/82. Legislative interest — "Treatment of stripped coupon bonds; specifically, effective date of legislation, HR 4961."

HORN & HARDART CO., New York, N.Y. Lobbyist — Califano, Ross & Heineman, 1575 I St. N.W., Washington, D.C. 20005. Filed 8/10/82. Legislative interest — "Bills to amend the Internal Revenue Code of 1954 with respect to the tax treatment of bond issuers and bond holders...."

ROY M. HUFFINGTON INC., Houston, Texas. Lobbyist — Charles E. Walker Associates Inc., 1730 Pennsylvania Ave. N.W., Washington, D.C. 20006. Filed 8/2/82. Legislative interest — "...may concern issues relating to taxation of leasing transactions."

ITALIAN AEROSPACE INDUSTRIES (U.S.A.) INC., 1235 Jefferson Davis Highway, Arlington, Va. 22202. Lobbyist — Marion L. Boswell, 6646 Madison-McLean Drive, McLean, Va. 22101. Filed 8/11/82. Legislative interest — "Legislation affecting aerospace products and programs including acquisition and regulation thereof." Filed for self 8/11/82. Legislative interest — "...legislation which concerns aerospace products, their acquisition, their use and their regulation." Lobbyist — Frank D. Moruzzi. Filed for self 8/11/82. Legislative interest — "Authoriza-

tion and appropriation bills relating to defense expenditures." Lobbyist — Vincent C. Hughes.

K & S ASSOCIATES INC., Perth Amboy, N.J. Lobbyist — Paul Suplizio Associates, 5001 Seminary Road, Alexandria, Va. 22311. Filed 8/3/82. Legislative interest — "To support renewal of the targeted jobs tax credit provisions of the Internal Revenue Code. For S 2455, HR 6700 and HR 4961."

M.A.N. TRUCK AND BUS CORP., Southfield, Mich. Lobbyist — Burch and Mandel, 1320 19th St. N.W., Washington, D.C. 20036. Filed 8/23/82. Legislative interest — "Legislation involving 'Buy American' or 'Local Content' re buses and trucks." Lobbyist — Cramer, Hoffman & Haber, 1320 19th St. N.W., Washington, D.C. 20036. Filed 8/4/82. (Former U.S. Rep. William C. Cramer, R-Fla., 1955-71, was listed as agent for this client.) Legislative interest — "Legislation involving 'Buy American' or 'Local Content' re buses and trucks."

MBT ASSOCIATES INC., 240 W. State St., Trenton, N.J. 08608. Filed for self 8/11/82. Legislative interest — "Tax reform, HR 4961, HR 6877, HR 6878 ... Tax Training Act, HR 5320, S 2036 ... banking legislation, S 2351, S 2352, S 1720, HR 6267 ... Surface Transportation Act ... HR 6211 ... housing, community development ... S 2607, HR 6296...." Lobbyists — Brendan T. Byrne, George John Keto, Marilyn Berry Thompson.

McGLEN ASSOCIATES, Fort Lee, N.J. Lobbyist — Paul E. Suplizio Associates, 5001 Seminary Road, Alexandria, Va. 22311. Filed 8/3/82. Legislative interest — "To support renewal of targeted jobs tax credit provisions of the Internal Revenue Code. For S 2455, HR 6700 and HR 4961."

NATIONAL CITY BANCORP., Minneapolis, Minn. Lobbyist — O'Connor & Hannan, 1919 Pennsylvania Ave. N.W., Washington, D.C. 20006. Filed 8/9/82. Legislative interest — "Effective date provisions of HR 4961, section 226."

NATIONAL FOOTBALL LEAGUE, New York, N.Y. Lobbyist — McNair, Glenn, Konduros, Corley, Singletary, Porter, & Dibble, 1155 15th St. N.W., Washington, D.C. 20005. Filed 8/20/82. Legislative interest — "...S 2784...."

THE NOKOTA CO., Bismarck, N.D. Lobbyist — Hamel, Park, McCabe & Saunders, 888 16th St. N.W., Washington, D.C. 20006. Filed 8/11/82. Legislative interest — "Amendment to HR 4961 to provide transition rule for energy projects commenced prior to July 1, 1982."

NORFOLK SOUTHERN, Washington, D.C. Lobbyist — Bricker & Eckler, 100 E. Broad St., Columbus, Ohio 43215. Filed 8/17/82. Legislative interest — "Coal slurry."

THE PERMANENTE MEDICAL GROUP INC., Oakland, Calif. Lobbyist — Caplin & Drysdale, 1101 17th St. N.W., Washington, D.C. 20036. Filed 8/9/82. Legislative interest — "...Tax Equity and Fiscal Responsibility Act of 1982 ... subtitle 'C', HR 4961, section 246-489 of bill ... generally support the bill." Lobbyist — McCutchen, Doyle, Brown & Emersen, 3 Embarcadero Center, San Francisco, Calif. 94111. Filed 8/9/82. Legislative interest — "...Tax Equity and Fiscal Responsibility Act of 1982 ... subtitle 'C', HR 4961, section 246-489 of bill ... generally support the bill."

PFIZER INC., Washington, D.C. Lobbyist — Reid & Priest, 1111 19th St. N.W., Washington, D.C. 20036. Filed 8/20/82. Legislative interest — "Amendment to section 3121 of the Internal Revenue Code of 1954."

REED ROBERTS HUMAN RESOURCE SERVICES, Clifton, N.J. Lobbyist — Paul Suplizio Associates, 5001 Seminary Road, Alexandria, Va. 22311. Filed 8/3/82. Legislative interest — "To support renewal of the targeted jobs tax credit provisions of the Internal Revenue Code. For S 2455, HR 6700 and HR 4961."

R. J. REYNOLDS TOBACCO CO., Winston-Salem, N.C. Lobbyist — Jones and Winburn, 1101 15th St. N.W., Washington, D.C. 20005. Filed 8/16/82. Legislative interest — "HR 4961 as it related to the excise tax on cigarettes."

ROLLINS INC., Atlanta, Ga. Lobbyist — Sutherland, Asbill & Brennan, 1666 K St. N.W., Washington, D.C. 20006. Filed 8/5/82. Legislative interest — "Matters regarding safe harbor leasing provisions of HR 4961."

THE ROSENBERG REAL ESTATE EQUITY FUND CORP., San Francisco, Calif. Lobbyist — Seward & Kissel, 919

18th St. N.W., Washington, D.C. 20006. Filed 8/24/82. Legislative interest — "HR 4961 and other tax and pension legislation."

SAVIN CORP., 420 Columbus Ave., Valhalla, N.Y. Filed for self 8/23/82. Legislative interest — "...Retail Dealers Agreement Act (HR 4009 and S 1256)...." Lobbyists — Roderick D. Marcoux, Robert Raffa.

SAVINGS BANK OF PUGET SOUND, Seattle, Wash. Lobbyist — Barnett, Yingling & Shay, 1090 Vermont Ave. N.W., Washington, D.C. 20005. Filed 8/25/82. Legislative interest — "Tax legislation affecting stock savings banks, HR 6941."

SECURITY LIFE OF DENVER, Denver, Colo. Lobbyist — Powell, Goldstein, Frazer & Murphy, 1110 Vermont Ave. N.W., Washington, D.C. 20005. Filed 8/6/82. Legislative interest — "HR 4961, Tax Equity and Fiscal Responsibility Act of 1982, section 257."

RICHARD L. SINNOTT & CO., Washington, D.C. Lobbyist — Gray and Co., 3255 Grace St. N.W., Washington, D.C. 20007. Filed 8/12/82. Legislative interest — "Including but not limited to legislation to provide a limited exemption from the antitrust laws for professional football."

SOUTHEASTERN RESEARCH INC., Columbia, S.C. Lobbyist — Paul Suplizio Associates, 5001 Seminary Road, Alexandria, Va. 22311. Filed 8/3/82. Legislative interest — "To support renewal of the targeted jobs tax credit provisions of the Internal Revenue Code. For S 2455, HR 6700 and HR 4961."

SQUIBB CORP., New York, N.Y. Lobbyist — Lee, Toomey & Kent, 1200 18th St. N.W., Washington, D.C. 20036. Filed 8/26/82. Legislative interest — "HR 4961."

STERLING DRUG INC., New York, N.Y. Lobbyist — Everett, Johnson & Breckinridge, 20 Exchange Place, New York, N.Y. 10005. Filed 8/24/82. Legislative interest — "...proposed amendments of section 936 of the Internal Revenue Code of 1954. HR 4961, section 218."

SUBURBAN CABLEVISION, East Orange, N.J. Lobbyist — Brown & Finn, 1920 N St. N.W., Washington, D.C. 20036. Filed 8/5/82. Legislative interest — "Legislation dealing with a rewrite of the Communications Act of 1934 as amended (HR 4225, S 2172)."

TEXAS AIR CORP., Houston, Texas. Lobbyist — Van Ness, Feldman, Sutcliffe, Curtis & Levenberg, 1050 Thomas Jefferson St. N.W., Washington, D.C. 20007. Filed 8/10/82. Legislative interest — "HR 5930, the Aviation War Risk Insurance Bill: Against the inclusion of a provision that mandates certain labor protection provisions in certain transactions that are subject to CAB approval. HR 4961, the Tax Equity and Fiscal Responsibility Act of 1982: Against certain tax leasing provisions."

U.S. TOBACCO CO., Greenwich, Conn. Lobbyist — William H. Hecht, 499 S. Capitol St. S.W., Washington, D.C. 20003. Filed 8/17/82. Legislative interest — Not specified.

VISA U.S.A. INC., San Mateo, Calif. Lobbyist — Seward & Kissel, 919 18th St. N.W., Washington, D.C. 20006. Filed 8/20/82. Legislative interest — "CFTC-SEC accord legislation."

WAYNE CABLEVISION, Taylor, Mich. Lobbyist — Brown & Finn, 1920 N St. N.W., Washington, D.C. 20036. Filed 8/5/82. Legislative interest — "Legislation dealing with a rewrite of the Communications Act of 1934 as amended (HR 4225, S 2172)."

WESTERN AIR LINES INC., Los Angeles, Calif. Lobbyist — Akin, Gump, Strauss, Hauer & Feld, 1333 New Hampshire Ave. N.W., Washington, D.C. 20036. Filed 8/12/82. Legislative interest — "Legislation to extend aviation insurance programs, including HR 5930."

WITKOWSKI, WEINER, McCAFFREY AND BRODSKY, Washington, D.C. Lobbyist — Thomas Ludlow Ashley, 1730 Pennsylvania Ave. N.W., Washington, D.C. 20006. Filed 8/18/82. (Former U.S. Rep., D-Ohio, 1955-81.) Legislative interest — "To defeat section 518 of HR 6296 or similar legislation which may be considered by Congress."

WRIGHT & McGILL CO., Denver, Colo. Lobbyist — Camp, Carmouche, Palmer, Barsh & Hunter, 2550 M St. N.W., Washington, D.C. 20037. Filed 8/12/82. Legislative interest — "Matters pertaining to excise taxes on fishing equipment under HR 4961."

International Relations

LEBANESE INFORMATION AND RESEARCH CENTER, Washington, D.C. Lobbyist — Hannaford International Inc., 905 16th St. N.W., Washington, D.C. 20006. Filed 8/4/82. Legislative interest — Not specified.

State and Local Governments

GALVESTON WHARVES OF THE CITY OF GALVESTON, Galveston, Texas. Lobbyist — Vinson & Elkins, 1101 Connecticut Ave. N.W., Washington, D.C. 20036. Filed 8/2/82. Legislative interest — "Tax legislation."

REGIONAL TRANSPORTATION AUTHORITY, Chicago, Ill. Lobbyist — Tucker & Associates, 1015 18th St. N.W., Washington, D.C. 20036. Filed 8/13/82. Legislative interest — "House and Senate bills relating to funding programs for urban mass transportation authorities; specifically programs under Department of Transportation UMTA and FRA...."

Trade Associations

AMERICAN BAKERS ASSOCIATION, Washington, D.C. Lobbyist — Lynn M. Daft, 1339 Wisconsin Ave. N.W., Washington, D.C. 20007. Filed 8/9/82. Legislative interest — "...debt ceiling bill...H J Res 520...Agricultural Act of 1949...support for amendment offered by Senators Tsongas and Quayle to reduce the price support for sugar."

AMERICAN FEDERATION OF INDEPENDENT BUSINESS, 469 James St., Syracuse, N.Y. 13203. Filed for self 8/24/82. Legislative interest — Not specified. Lobbyist — Raymond W. Ackerman.

AMERICAN LAND DEVELOPMENT ASSOCIATION, 1000 16th St. N.W., Washington, D.C. 20036. Filed for self 8/19/82. Legislative interest — "Tax, environmental, land use, and all other legislation affecting resort, recreational and residential development." Lobbyists — Lori A. Antolock, Thomas C. Franks.

THE AMERICAN SOCIETY OF MECHANICAL ENGINEERS, 345 E. 47th St., New York, N.Y. 10017. Filed for self 8/25/82. Legislative interest — "Codes and standards, consumer legislation, energy legislation, environmental legislation, metric conversion, occupational safety and health, transportation and mass transit and other areas that would affect the profession of mechanical engineers." Lobbyists — Jack M. Howell, M. Melissa Moore, 2029 K St. N.W., Washington, D.C. 20006.

ASSOCIATED SPECIALTY CONTRACTORS INC., Bethesda, Md. Lobbyist — Gibson, Dunn & Crutcher, 1776 G St. N.W., Washington, D.C. 20006. Filed 8/19/82. Legislative interest — "The Multiemployer Pension Plans Stabilization Act of 1982, S 1748...."

THE ASSOCIATION OF TRIAL LAWYERS OF AMERICA, 1050 31st St. N.W., Washington, D.C. 20007. Filed for self 8/3/82. Legislative interest — "Legislation relative to admiralty, automobile reparations, aviation, consumer protection, criminal law, the environment, health, the administration of justice, legal services, product liability and workers' compensation." Lobbyist — David W. Densford.

CONSORTIUM OF SOCIAL SCIENCE ASSOCIATIONS, 1755 Massachusetts Ave. N.W., Washington, D.C. 20036. Filed for self 8/9/82. Legislative interest — Not specified. Lobbyist — Helen Rauch.

COUNCIL OF AMERICAN-FLAG SHIP OPERATORS, Washington, D.C. Lobbyist — Bowman, Conner, Touhey & Thornton, 2828 Pennsylvania Ave. N.W., Washington, D.C. 20007. Filed 8/18/82. Legislative interest — "Tax Equity and Fiscal Responsibility Act of 1982, HR 4691...." Lobbyist — Preston, Thorgrimson, Ellis & Holman, 1776 G St. N.W., Washington, D.C. 20006. Filed 8/25/82. Legislative interest — "...S 1593, HR 4374 and all related legislation."

DAIRY FARMER DISTRIBUTORS OF AMERICA INC., Chittenango, N.Y. Lobbyist — Woodruff L. Carroll, 918

Onondaga Bank Building, Syracuse, N.Y. 13202. Filed 8/16/82. Legislative interest — "Food and Agriculture Act of 1981."

DIRECT SELLING ASSOCIATION, Washington, D.C. Lobbyist — Jones and Winburn, 1101 15th St. N.W., Washington, D.C. 20005. Filed 8/18/82. Legislative interest — "Lobbying on the tax bill; particularly as it related to the tax status of independent contractors."

GROCERY MANUFACTURERS OF AMERICA INC., 1010 Wisconsin Ave. N.W., Washington, D.C. 20007. Filed for self 8/17/82. Legislative interest — "All matters affecting the food industry." Lobbyist — Edward A. Merlis.

INDEPENDENT PETROLEUM ASSOCIATION OF THE MOUNTAIN STATES, Denver, Colo. Lobbyist — Daniel A. Dutko, 412 First St. S.E., Washington, D.C. 20003. Filed 8/24/82. Legislative interest — "General legislation dealing with independent oil and gas measures."

NATIONAL AGRICULTURAL CHEMICAL ASSOCIATION, Washington, D.C. Lobbyist — McKenna, Conner & Cuneo, 1575 I St. N.W., Washington, D.C. 20005. Filed 8/26/82. Legislative interest — ". . .amendments to the Federal Insecticide, Fungicide and Rodenticide Act, 7 U.S.C., section 136 . . . HR 5203, S 2620, S 2621. . . ."

NATIONAL ASSOCIATION OF PRIVATE PSYCHIATRIC HOSPITALS, 1319 F St. N.W., Washington, D.C. 20004. Filed for self 8/9/82. Legislative interest — "Issues affecting mental health, hospitals, manpower, and patients." Lobbyist — Michael Feinstein.

NATIONAL COMMERCIAL FINANCE CONFERENCE, 1 Penn Plaza, New York, N.Y. 10001. Filed for self 8/4/82. Legislative interest — "Pre-emption of state usury limits, S 1720, the 'Depository Institutions Amendments of 1982'; bankruptcy reform." Lobbyist — Sharon T. Portnoy.

NATIONAL FOREST PRODUCTS ASSOCIATION, 1619 Massachusetts Ave. N.W., Washington, D.C. 20036. Filed for self 8/25/82. Legislative interest — "Legislation directly or indirectly affecting the interest of the forest products industry including federal land management policies and environmental legislation with specific interest in FIFRA, TSCA, RCRA, the Clean Air Act and the Clean Water Act." Lobbyists — Robert A. Kirshner, Mark E. Rey, John A. Thorner.

NATIONAL MULTI HOUSING COUNCIL, 1150 17th St. N.W., Washington, D.C. 20036. Filed for self 8/11/82. Legislative interest — "Legislation affecting the financing, development, production and management of multifamily housing including condominium and cooperative conversion." Lobbyist — Susan Riley.

NATIONAL RESTAURANT ASSOCIATION, Washington, D.C. Lobbyist — Powell, Goldstein, Frazer & Murphy, 1110 Vermont Ave. N.W., Washington, D.C. 20005. Filed 8/5/82. Legislative interest — ". . .the Tax Equity and Fiscal Responsibility Act of 1982, HR 4961, section 210."

NATIONAL WHOLESALE DRUGGISTS' ASSOCIATION, P.O. Box 238, Alexandria, Va. 22313. Filed for self 8/3/82. Legislative interest — "Health issues." Lobbyist — Ronald J. Streck.

OIL INVESTMENT INSTITUTE, Washington, D.C. Lobbyist — David P. Stang, 1629 K St. N.W., Washington, D.C. 20006. Filed 8/3/82. Legislative interest — "HR 4961, Tax Equity and Fiscal Responsibility Act of 1982."

PENNAG INDUSTRIES ASSOCIATION, P.O. Box 329, Ephrata, Pa. 17522. Filed for self 8/23/82. Legislative interest — ". . .S 2357 - prohibit embargo of valid grain sales (favor); S 2410 - prohibit embargo prior to embargo date for valid contracts (favor)." Lobbyist — David Brubaker.

SUGAR USERS GROUP, Washington, D.C. Lobbyist — Bayh, Tabbert and Capehart, 1575 I St. N.W., Washington, D.C. 20005. Filed 8/6/82. Legislative interest — "Amendments to Agriculture Act of 1949. . . ." Lobbyist — Calmar Communications, 500 N. Dearborn St., Chicago, Ill. 60610. Filed 8/24/82. Legislative interest — "Amendments to Agriculture Act of 1949. . . ."

THE TOBACCO INSTITUTE, Washington, D.C. Lobbyist — Manatt, Phelps, Rothenberg & Tunney, 1200 New Hampshire Ave. N.W., Washington, D.C. 20036. Filed 8/23/82. (Former U.S.

Rep. James C. Corman, D-Calif., 1961-81, was listed as agent for this client.) Legislative interest — "To advocate changes dealing with the tobacco excise tax and the omnibus tax bill."

WEST TEXAS LAND & ROYALTY OWNERS ASSOCIATION, 4302 Airport Blvd., Austin, Texas 78722. Filed for self 8/4/82. Legislative interest — "Tax issues for royalty owners, natural gas legislation, windfall profits tax." Lobbyist — Don R. McCullough.

Miscellaneous

EUGENE BAKER, 2010 Colebrooke Drive, Temple Hills, Md. 20748. Filed for self 8/20/82. Legislative interest — "The Omnibus Regulatory Reform bill . . . Job Training Bill . . . Federal Employee Flexible and Compressed Work Schedule . . . Short Time Compensation Bill . . . The Small Business Administration Personnel Bill . . . an amendment to the Small Business Administration's 8(a) program. . . ."

BETZ COLLEGE, Cincinnati, Ohio, Lobbyist — Sachs, Greenebaum & Tayler, 1620 I St. N.W., Washington, D.C. 20006. Filed 8/23/82. Legislative interest — "Education legislation."

DRAUGHONS JUNIOR COLLEGE, Nashville, Tenn. Lobbyist — Sachs, Greenebaum & Tayler, 1620 I St. N.W., Washington, D.C. 20006. Filed 8/23/82. Legislative interest — "Education legislation."

INSTITUTE FOR PUBLIC REPRESENTATION, GEORGETOWN UNIVERSITY LAW CENTER, 600 New Jersey Ave. N.W., Washington, D.C. 20001. Filed for self 8/11/82. Legislative interest — ". . .communications legislation. . . ." Lobbyist — Wilhelmina Reuben Cooke.

LINDA E. KATZ, 3350 Huntley Square Drive, Temple Hills, Md. 20031. Filed for self 8/20/82. Legislative interest — Not specified.

WILLIAM STEVEN PALEOS, P.O. Box 57466-0466, Washington, D.C. 20037. Filed for self 8/16/82. Legislative interest — Not specified.

PHILLIPS COLLEGES, Gulfport, Miss. Lobbyist — Sachs, Greenebaum & Tayler, 1620 I St. N.W., Washington, D.C. 20006. Filed 8/23/82. Legislative interest — "Education legislation."

UNITED CHURCH OF CHRIST, New York, N.Y. Lobbyist — Beveridge & Diamond, 1333 New Hampshire Ave. N.W., Washington, D.C. 20036. Filed 8/18/82. Legislatve interest — "Fiscal 1983 budget."

September Registrations

Citizens' Groups

COMMON CAUSE, 2030 M St. N.W., Washington, D.C. 20036. Filed for self 9/22/82. Legislative interest — ". . .supports HR 4070, a bill introduced by Reps. Synar, Glickman, and Leach, to limit the money candidates for federal office can receive from political action committees . . . supported specific legislation in the 97th Congress to reduce the dairy price supports and sugar loan program subsidies included in the farm bill (HR 3603, S 884) . . . urged passage of a bill (S Res 20) providing for TV and radio coverage of Senate sessions, and of bills (HR 18 and S 10) creating a Commission for More Effective Government . . . opposing efforts to pass a constitutional amendment to balance the budget (S Res 58 and H J Res 10) as well as S 708, a bill to weaken the Foreign Corrupt Practices Act, and S 1730, a bill which would weaken the Freedom of Information Act . . . working to reauthorize key provisions of the Voting Rights Act (S 1992) and opposing efforts to weaken the Clean Air Act . . . worked to reduce the appropriation for the Tennessee-Tombigbee water project . . . supported reauthorization of the Legal Services Corporation (S 393, HR 3480) and have supported adequate appropriations for it . . . lobbied on behalf of the Federal Election Commission and opposed

efforts to eliminate or reduce funding for the Commission ... opposed efforts to limit federal court jurisdiction in matters concerning abortion, busing and school prayer (S 1760, S 951, S 1647, S 158) ... supported legislation to provide for a review of tax expenditures in the budget process (S 193, HR 4882) ... supported the Special Prosecutor provision of the Ethics in Government Act of 1978 as it stands but suggesting minor adjustments ... supported a strong budget process and has opposed specific FY83 budget proposals which do not adhere to important standards of equity and fairness." Lobbyist — D. Michal Freedman.

Corporations and Businesses

AGRISTORE SYSTEMS CO., Indianapolis, Ind. Lobbyist — Thurman L. Boykin, 2772 S. Randolph St., Arlington, Va. 22206. Filed 9/30/82. Legislative interest — Not specified.

AMERICAN STOCK EXCHANGE INC., New York, N.Y. Lobbyist — Akin, Gump, Strauss, Hauer & Feld, 1333 New Hampshire Ave. N.W., Washington, D.C. 20036. Filed 9/22/82. Legislative interest — "Hearings and any legislation relating to federal regulation of securities options trading including, but not limited to S 2260, 'Securities Commodities Accord Amendments of 1982'; S 2109, 'Futures Trading Act of 1982'; HR 5447, 'Futures Trading Act of 1982'; and HR 6156, legislation clarifying the jurisdiction of the SEC and the definition of security."

AMURCON CORP., Southfield, Mich. Lobbyist — Gnau, Carter, Jacobsen & Associates Inc., 1777 F St. N.W., Washington, D.C. 20006. Filed 9/29/82. Legislative interest — "General interest in housing."

BEAR, STEARNS & CO., New York, N.Y. Lobbyist — Cleary, Gottlieb, Steen & Hamilton, 1250 Connecticut Ave. N.W., Washington, D.C. 20036. Filed 9/28/82. Legislative interest — "Proposed bankruptcy legislation relating to repurchase agreements."

CAC ASSOCIATES, Muskegon, Mich. Lobbyist — Gnau, Carter, Jacobsen & Associates Inc., 1777 F St. N.W., Washington, D.C. 20006. Filed 9/29/82. Legislative interest — "Government loan guarantees to business."

R. J. CHAMBERS, Royal Oak, Mich. Lobbyist — Gnau, Carter, Jacobsen & Associates Inc., 1777 F St. N.W., Washington, D.C. 20006. Filed 9/29/82. Legislative interest — "Housing."

CHICAGO BOARD OPTIONS EXCHANGE, Chicago, Ill. Lobbyist — Patton, Boggs & Blow, 2550 M St. N.W., Washington, D.C. 20037. Filed 9/24/82. Legislative interest — "HR 1656, clarifying jurisdiction of the Securities and Exchange Commission. For the bill."

CLAVER, MATTHEWS SMITH & CO., Falls Church, Va. Lobbyist — David Cohen, 1322 Holly St. N.W., Washington, D.C. 20012. Filed 9/24/82. Legislative interest — "Legislation affecting postal subsidy formula by amending Omnibus Budget Reconciliation Act of 1981 and the Urgent Supplemental Appropriation for fiscal 1982 (HR 6685)."

CONTINENTAL INSURANCE COMPANIES, New York, N.Y. Lobbyist — Alston, Miller & Gaines, 35 Broad St., Atlanta, Ga. 30335. Filed 9/24/82. Legislative interest — "For passage of S 2631, the 'Product Liability Act.'"

DREYFUS CORP., New York, N.Y. Lobbyist — Stroock & Stroock & Lavan, 1150 17th St. N.W., Washington, D.C. 20036. Filed 9/24/82. Legislative interest — "In support of certain amendments to S 2879, the Omnibus Financial Reform legislation."

FIRSTMARK CORP., Buffalo, N.Y. Lobbyist — Covington & Burling, 1201 Pennsylvania Ave. N.W., Washington, D.C. 20044. Filed 9/23/82. Legislative interest — "Legislation related to the financial services industry, in particular legislation that affects the interests of industrial banks and industrial loan and investment companies, including the Depository Institutions Amendments of 1982, S 2879."

GRAND TRAVERSE DEVELOPMENT INC., Bloomfield Hills, Mich. Lobbyist — Gnau, Carter, Jacobsen & Associates Inc., 1777 F St. N.W., Washington, D.C. 20006. Filed 9/29/82. Legislative interest — "Farmers home loan guarantees, housing."

INTERNATIONAL TELEPHONE AND TELEGRAPH CORP., Washington, D.C. Lobbyist — Richard A. Bishop, 1616 H St. N.W., Washington, D.C. 20006. Filed 9/24/82. Legislative interest — Not specified.

LEHMAN COMMERCIAL PAPER INC., New York, N.Y. Lobbyist — Cleary, Gottlieb, Steen & Hamilton, 1250 Connecticut Ave. N.W., Washington, D.C. 20036. Legislative interest — "Proposed bankruptcy legislation relating to repurchase agreements."

ORMOND RE GROUP INC., Ormond Beach, Fla. Lobbyist — Stroock & Stroock & Lavan, 1150 17th St. N.W., Washington, D.C. 20036. Filed 9/24/82. Legislative interest — "In support of certain amendments to HR 6055 and S 2350 to revise the Subchapter S sections of the Internal Revenue Code of 1954."

POTTER INSTRUMENT CO. INC., Gonic, N.H. Lobbyist — Gnau, Carter, Jacobsen & Associates Inc., 1777 F St. N.W., Washington, D.C. 20006. Filed 9/29/82. Legislative interest — "Government business loan guarantees."

RCA CORP., New York, N.Y. Lobbyist — Powell, Goldstein, Frazer & Murphy, 1110 Vermont Ave. N.W., Washington, D.C. 20005. Filed 9/29/82. Legislative interest — "Tax legislative matters relating to safe harbor leasing transactions."

RJR INDUSTRIES INC., 2550 M St. N.W., Washington, D.C. 20037. Filed for self 9/28/82. Legislative interest — "Any legislation affecting the oil industry. (a) Crude oil pricing and transportation. (b) Fuels and energy: (1) shortages — rationing and allocation; (2) gasoline marketing; (3) energy conservation; (4) research and development; (5) oil shortages. (c) Natural gas. (d) Environmental — air, water, oil pollution. (e) Land use/public land use — OCS development. (f) Antitrust and monopoly. (g) Dealer day in court. (h) Tax legislation. (i) Tax reform." Lobbyist — J. Richard Hargis.

SANDERS CORP., Detroit, Mich. Lobbyist — Gnau, Carter, Jacobsen & Associates Inc., 1777 F St. N.W., Washington, D.C. 20006. Filed 9/29/82. Legislative interest — "Government business loan guarantees."

SAVINGS BANK OF PUGET SOUND, Seattle, Wash. Lobbyist — Thomas Ludlow Ashley, 1129 20th St. N.W., Washington, D.C. 20036. (Former U.S. rep., D-Ohio, 1955-81.) Filed 9/30/82. Legislative interest — "Legislation affecting stock savings banks, HR 6056."

URBAN REVITALIZATION INC., Detroit, Mich. Lobbyist — Gnau, Carter, Jacobsen & Associates Inc., 1777 F St. N.W., Washington, D.C. 20006. Filed 9/29/82. Legislative interest — "Housing, job training legislation."

UTOTEM INC., Cincinnati, Ohio. Lobbyist — Nossaman, Krueger & Knox, 1140 19th St. N.W., Washington, D.C. 20006. Filed 9/27/82. Legislative interest — "Amendments facilitating application of ERISA subsection 4204 to partial asset sales. ...In favor of."

WESTINGHOUSE CORP., 1801 K St. N.W., Washington, D.C. 20006. Filed for self 9/15/82. Legislative interest — Not specified. Lobbyist — Linda E. Katz.

State and Local Governments

CITY OF CAMDEN, Camden, N.J. Lobbyist — Krivit & Krivit, 101 Duddington Place S.E., Washington, D.C. 20003. Filed 9/3/82. Legislative interest — "Tax Equity and Fiscal Responsibility Act of 1982 ... HR 4961 and conference report [S Rept] 97-530 ... Section 287, relating to New Jersey general revenue sharing; Section 156(a)(iii) of the Senate Finance Committee bill ... For Section 287; Against Section 156(a)(iii) of the original bill."

MOVE DETROIT FORWARD FUND, Detroit, Mich. Lobbyist — Gnau, Carter, Jacobsen & Associates Inc., 1777 F St. N.W., Washington, D.C. 20006. Filed 9/29/82. Legislative interest — "Housing, job training, government business loan guarantees."

Trade Associations

AMERICAN SOCIETY OF MECHANICAL ENGINEERS, 345 E. 47th St., New York, N.Y. 10017. Filed for self

9/29/82. Legislative interest — Not specified. Lobbyists — Jack M. Howell, M. Melissa Moore, 2029 K St. N.W., Washington, D.C. 20006.

AMERICAN OSTEOPATHIC HOSPITAL ASSOCI-ATION, Arlington Heights, Ill. Lobbyist — Martin A. Wall, 1025 Vermont Ave. N.W., Washington, D.C. 20005. Filed 9/30/82. Legislative interest — "All legislation regarding Medicare/Medicaid programs; competition/consumer health promotion, health professions and other general hospital, health issues."

AMERICAN PETROLEUM INSTITUTE, 2101 L St. N.W., Washington, D.C. 20037. Filed for self 9/21/82. Legislative interest — "Legislation affecting the petroleum industry." Lobbyist — Wayne S. Ewing, P.O. Box 925, Harrisburg, Pa. 17108.

AMERICAN TRUCKING ASSOCIATIONS, Washington, D.C. Lobbyist — Stroock & Stroock & Lavan, 1150 17th St. N.W., Washington, D.C. 20036. Filed 9/24/82. Legislative interest — "Involved in the drafting of proposed legislation to amend certain provisions of the Employee Retirement Income Security Act of 1974 concerning multi-employer plans."

ARTPAC, Washington, D.C. Lobbyist — Patton, Boggs & Blow, 2550 M St. N.W., Washington, D.C. 20037. Filed 9/27/82. Legislative interest — "S 252 and HR 1524, Public Utility Tax Bill. Seeking amendment allowing fair market charitable deductions to creators."

COUNCIL OF AMERICAN-FLAG SHIP OPERATORS, 1625 K St. N.W., Washington, D.C. 20006. Filed for self 9/29/82. Legislative interest — "Miscellaneous matters relating to the Merchant Marine Act of 1926 as amended in 1970...." Lobbyist — Marla M. Donahue.

EDISON ELECTRIC INSTITUTE, 1111 19th St. N.W., Washington, D.C. 20036. Filed for self 9/22/82. Legislative interest — "Low-income energy assistance, telecommunications, residential conservation service, apartment conservation service and regulatory reform." Lobbyist — Susan T. Fritschler. Filed for self 9/22/82. Legislative interest — "Coal and transportation related issues." Lobbyist — Gregory S. Dole.

GENERIC PHARMACEUTICAL INDUSTRY ASSO-CIATION, 600 Third Ave., New York, N.Y. 10016. Filed for self 9/21/82. Legislative interest — "Matters of interest to the generic drug industry including patent extension (HR 6444, S 255)." Lobbyist — Judith W. Fensterer.

MECHANICAL CONTRACTORS ASSOCIATION OF AMERICA INC., Chevy Chase, Md. Lobbyist — Gibson, Dunn & Crutcher, 1776 G St. N.W., Washington, D.C. 20006. Filed 9/30/82. Legislative interest — "...the Multi-employer Pension Plans Stabilization Act of 1981 ... S 1748, S 2860 ... Amendments to 29 U.S.C. 1001 *et seq.* (ERISA) and 26 U.S.C. 1 *et seq.* (Internal Revenue Code) ... In favor of S 1748 and the thrust of S 2860."

NATIONAL CATTLEMEN'S ASSOCIATION, Englewood, Colo. Lobbyist — Davis & McLeod, 499 South Capitol St. S.E., Washington, D.C. 20003. Filed 9/28/82. Legislative interest — "...legislation which would affect the tax rules relating to the cattle industry. We have an interest in legislation such as HR 6055 which would affect tax rules relating to subchapter S corporations."

NATIONAL PEACH COUNCIL, P.O. Box 1085, Martinsburg, W.Va. 25401. Filed for self 9/24/82. Legislative interest — "Labor and immigration laws, wage and hour, tax laws, agricultural research budget, environmental law. Current interest focused on Migrant and Seasonal Agricultural Workers Protection Act (HR 7102 and S 2930) and the Immigration Reform and Control Act (HR 6514). We are for both bills." Lobbyist — Lillie E. Hoover.

PHARMACEUTICAL MANUFACTURERS ASSOCI-ATION, Washington, D.C. Lobbyist — Bayh, Tabbert & Capehart, 1575 I St. N.W., Washington, D.C. 20005. Filed 9/21/82. Legislative interest — "HR 6444 - Patent Term Extension and related matters."

TRANSPORTATION INSTITUTE, 923 15th St. N.W., Washington, D.C. 20005. Filed for self 9/22/82. Legislative interest — "General educational functions concerning maritime legislation." Lobbyist — Peter J. Luciano.

U.S. TUNA FOUNDATION, Washington, D.C. Lobbyist — Bracewell & Patterson, 1825 I St. N.W., Washington, D.C. 20006. Filed 9/24/82. Legislative interest — "Protect domestic tuna industry."

Miscellaneous

JOSEPH CANIZARO, New Orleans, La. Lobbyist — Camp, Carmouche, Palmer, Barsh & Hunter, 2550 M St. N.W., Washington, D.C. 20037. Filed 9/23/82. Legislative interest — "Technical Corrections Bill HR 6056 dealing with the alternative minimum tax."

ESTATE OF MABEL R. LADD, Bunker Hill, Ind. Lobbyist — McHale, Cook & Welch, 1122 Chamber of Commerce Building, Indianapolis, Ind. 46204. Filed 9/27/82. Legislative interest — "To obtain amendment of 26 U.S.C. subsection 2032A."

NORMAN B. TURE, 1100 Connecticut Ave. N.W., Washington, D.C. 20036. Filed for self 9/30/82. Legislative interest — "...those areas dealing with taxes and tax policy."

October Registrations

Citizens' Groups

AMERICANS FOR DEMOCRATIC ACTION, 1411 K St. N.W., Washington, D.C. 20005. Filed for self 10/5/82. Legislative interest — "...all matters relating to the foreign and defense policy of the United States...." Lobbyist — Gregory James Weaver.

CONFEDERATED SALISH AND KOOTENAI TRIBES OF THE FLATHEAD RESERVATION, Montana. Lobbyist — Baenen, Timme, De Reitzes & Middleton, 1049 30th St. N.W., Washington, D.C. 20007. Filed 10/28/82. Legislative interest — "...all legislative activity directly or indirectly affecting Indian affairs, including but not limited to tribal lands and natural resources, jurisdiction, taxation, health, education and welfare."

COUNCIL OF ENERGY RESOURCE TRIBES, 1140 Connecticut Ave. N.W., Washington, D.C. 20036. Filed for self 10/8/82. Legislative interest — "Energy issues affecting American Indian tribes." Lobbyists — Allison John Epperson, Robert J. Martin.

ENVIRONMENTAL POLICY INSTITUTE, 317 Pennsylvania Ave. S.E., Washington, D.C. 20003. Filed for self 10/25/82. Legislative interest — "All legislation concerning coal development and federal coal leasing." Lobbyists — Carol Freedman, Mark Squillace.

LEAGUE OF WOMEN VOTERS OF THE UNITED STATES, 1730 M St. N.W., Washington, D.C. 20036. Filed for self 10/13/82. Legislative interest — "...CETA reauthorization and budgeting; civil rights; day care; education; employment; food stamps; HUD authorizations and appropriations; unemployment compensation; vocational education ... legislation to rescind IRS regulations on private school non-profit status; tuition tax credits; anti-busing legislation ... international development banks; foreign economic development assistance; free flow in international trade/reduction of trade barriers ... Clean Air Act; Clean Water Act; energy conservation; sound land use legislation; Surface Mining Control and Reclamation Act; low-income energy assistance; environmental protection measures generally ... D.C. representation ... Voting Rights Act reauthorization ... urban mass transit; Economic Development Administration; CDBG/UDAG; general revenue sharing." Lobbyist — Mary E. Brooks.

MIDDLE INCOME LOBBY OF AMERICA, 359 Washington Ave., Oakmont, Pa. 15139. Filed for self 10/1/82. Legislative interest — "...laws affecting the middle income person in America." Lobbyist — Robert C. Lee.

NATIONAL COALITION FOR A FREE CUBA, Washington, D.C. Lobbyist — Gray and Co., 3255 Grace St. N.W., Washington, D.C. 20007. Filed 10/13/82. Legislative interest — "For S 1853."

NATIONAL RURAL HOUSING COALITION, 1016 16th St. N.W., Washington, D.C. 20036. Filed for self 10/27/82. Legislative interest — "Matters necessary to the provision of representation and legislative choice with respect to low-income housing and community development issues." Lobbyist — Leslie R. Strauss.

SHEE ATIKA INC., Sitka, Alaska. Lobbyist — Baenen, Timme, De Reitzes & Middleton, 1049 30th St. N.W., Washington, D.C. 20007. Filed 10/28/82. Legislative interest — "...all matters relating generally to Alaska, its lands and natural resources, the Alaska Native Claims Settlement Act, matters relating to Indians, Eskimos and Aleuts, generally."

SOLAR LOBBY, 1001 Connecticut Ave. N.W., Washington, D.C. 20036. Filed for self 10/13/82. Legislative interest — "For Solar and Conservation Bank. For Public Utility Regulatory Policies Act. Review of energy appropriations and tax issues." Lobbyist — Richard Munson.

U.S. COMMITTEE FOR UNICEF, 331 E. 38th St., New York, N.Y. 10016. Filed for self 10/12/82. Legislative interest — "...congressional support for UNICEF ... level of U.S. voluntary contribution." Lobbyist — Kimberly A. Gamble, 110 Maryland Ave. N.E., Washington, D.C. 20002.

UNITED STATES DEFENSE COMMITTEE, 3238 Wynford Drive, Fairfax, Va. 22031. Filed for self 10/4/82. Legislative interest — "...Defense Appropriations bill, HR 630...." Lobbyists — John R. Crane, Bradley D. Palmer.

Corporations and Businesses

AAI CORP., Baltimore, Md. Lobbyist — Lathrop, Koontz, 1140 Connecticut Ave. N.W., Washington, D.C. 20036. Filed 10/8/82. (Former U.S. Rep. Richard H. Ichord, D-Mo., 1961-81, was listed as agent for this client.) Legislative interest — "Legislative issues dealing with certain defense weapon systems."

AMERICAN SHIP BUILDING CO., Tampa, Fla. Lobbyist — Larkin, McCarthy, Noel & Falk, 1301 Pennsylvania Ave. N.W., Washington, D.C. 20004. Filed 10/10/82. Legislative interest — "Defense legislation."

AMERICAN TRADE AND FINANCE CO., 2001 Jefferson Davis Highway, Arlington, Va. 22002. Filed for self 10/12/82. Legislative interest — "General legislation dealing with international trade and U.S. defense authorizations/procurement/appropriation bills." Lobbyists — Henry J. Kuss Jr., Craig E. Musick.

ARMCO INC., 703 Curtis St., Middletown, Ohio 45043. Filed for self 10/7/82. Legislative interest — "Federal taxation ... Pension Equity Tax Act, HR 6410; Product Liability Act, S 2631; unemployment compensation; employee health." Lobbyist — Stephen B. Holland, 1747 Pennsylvania Ave. N.W., Washington, D.C. 20006.

ATARI INC., Sunnyvale, Calif. Lobbyist — Hogan & Hartson, 815 Connecticut Ave. N.W., Washington, D.C. 20006. Filed 10/12/82. Legislative interest — "Legislation generally affecting the tax treatment of its Puerto Rican subsidiary."

BENDIX CORP., Southfield, Mich. Lobbyist — Gray and Co., 3255 Grace St. N.W., Washington, D.C. 20007. Filed 10/13/82. Legislative interest — "Including but not limited to the Bendix-Martin Marietta merger."

THE BENENSON CAPITAL CO., New York, N.Y. Lobbyist — Cook, Purcell, Hansen & Henderson, 1015 18th St. N.W., Washington, D.C. 20036. Filed 10/9/82. Legislative interest — "Prospectus for lease on 1776 Pennsylvania Ave. N.W., Washington, D.C."

BETHLEHEM STEEL CORP., Bethlehem, Pa. 18016. Filed for self 10/14/82. Legislative interest — Not specified. Lobbyists — David A. Blair, John E. Bouchard, Kurt L. Malmgren, William E. Wickert Jr., Leonard B. Williams, 1000 16th St. N.W., Washington, D.C. 20036.

THE BLACK AND DECKER MANUFACTURING CO., Towson, Md. Lobbyist — Miles and Stockbridge, 1701 Pennsylvania Ave. N.W., Washington, D.C. 20006. Filed 10/14/82. Legislative interest — "All matters relating to product liability legislation."

BOEING COMPUTER SERVICES, 7980 Gallows Court, Vienna, Va. 22180. Filed for self 10/27/82. Legislative interest — "...federal procurement; federal contracting-out; domestic and international trade in services; domestic and international communications...." Lobbyist — William F. Harris.

CAYMAN TURTLE FARM LTD., Grand Cayman, British West Indies. Lobbyist — Orren Merren, 1000 Potomac St. N.W., Washington, D.C. 20007. Filed 10/12/82. Legislative interest — "Endangered Species Act; 16 U.S.C. sections 1531-1543."

CELERON, Lafayette, La. Lobbyist — Nancy Whorton George, 499 South Capitol St. S.W., Washington, D.C. 20003. Filed 10/12/82. Legislative interest — "...energy and tax."

CHAMPLIN PETROLEUM CO., Fort Worth, Texas. Lobbyist — Camp, Carmouche, Palmer, Barsh & Hunter, 2550 M St. N.W., Washington, D.C. 20037. Filed 10/21/82. Legislative interest — "...the taxation, production, transportation, refining, distribution and marketing of oil and natural gas...."

CHICAGO MERCANTILE EXCHANGE, Washington, D.C. Lobbyist — James H. Lake, 1200 New Hampshire Ave. N.W., Washington, D.C. 20036. Filed 10/9/82. Legislative interest — "CFTC Reauthorization, HR 5447."

THE CLOROX CO., P.O. Box 24305, Oakland, Calif. 94623. Filed for self 10/4/82. Legislative interest — "HR 4437, Daylight-Saving Time; HR 1242, Antitrust Contribution; HR 4961, Taxes; HR 6410, Pensions; HR 6402, Taxation of Interstate Commerce; S 1080, HR 746, HR 1776; Regulatory Reform; HR 5252, S 2266, Clean Air; S 1748, Multi-employer pensions; S 1541, HR 4334, ERISA; HR 5203, S 2620, S 2621, environmental; S J Res 58, budget; S 2499, FTC; S 2631, HR 5214, product liability...." Lobbyist — J. Phillip Halstead.

CONSOLIDATION COAL CO., 1800 Washington Road, Pittsburgh, Pa. 15241. Filed for self 10/5/82. Legislative interest — Not specified. Lobbyist — Thomas F. Hoffman, 1701 Pennsylvania Ave. N.W., Washington, D.C. 20006.

COURTNEY, McCAMANT & TURNEY, 1725 K St. N.W., Washington, D.C. 20006. Filed for self 10/7/82. Legislative interest — Not specified. Lobbyist — Virginia B. Bliss.

CRUISE AMERICA INC., Fort Lauderdale, Fla. Lobbyist — O'Neill and Haase, 1333 New Hampshire Ave. N.W., Washington, D.C. 20036. Filed 10/8/82. Legislative interest — "...enactment of S 3038."

DESERT GROUP INC., Las Vegas, Nev. Lobbyist — Shea & Gould, 330 Madison Ave., New York, N.Y. 10017. Filed 10/12/82. Legislative interest — "Section 214 Tax Equity and Fiscal Responsibility Act of 1982."

DIGITAL EQUIPMENT CORP., Maynard, Mass. Lobbyist — Hogan & Hartson, 815 Connecticut Ave. N.W., Washington, D.C. 20006. Filed 10/12/82. Legislative interest — "Legislation generally affecting the tax treatment of its Puerto Rican subsidiary."

ENERGY ABSORPTION SYSTEMS INC., Chicago, Ill. Lobbyist — Bracy Williams & Co., 1000 Connecticut Ave. N.W., Washington, D.C. 20036. Filed 10/9/82. Legislative interest — "General legislation affecting business, particularly transportation appropriations."

EXXON CORP., New York, N.Y. Lobbyist — Ullman Consultants Inc., 1000 Potomac St. N.W., Washington, D.C. 20007. Filed 10/13/82. (Former U.S. Rep. Al Ullman, D-Ore., 1957-81, was listed as agent for this client.) Legislative interest — "The tax treatment of Foreign oil extraction credits."

FAIRCHILD INDUSTRIES INC., Washington, D.C. Lobbyist — Richard M. Millman, 1730 M St. N.W., Washington, D.C. 20036. Filed 10/12/82. Legislative interest — "HR 63 and S 2248...."

FALCON JET CORP., Teterboro, N.J. Lobbyist — Diebold & Millonzi, 1920 N St. N.W., Washington, D.C. 20036. Filed 10/22/82. Legislative interest — "Legislation relating to the manufacture, sale, operation and maintenance of aircraft."

FEDERATION EMPLOYMENT AND GUIDANCE SERVICE, New York, N.Y. Lobbyists — Keith L. Baker, David M. F. Lambert, 1000 Potomac St. N.W., Washington, D.C. 20007. Filed 10/5/82. Legislative interest — "...a potential private relief bill...."

FIDELITY UNION LIFE, P.O. Box 500, Dallas, Texas 75221. Lobbyist — Hughes & Hill, 1000 Mercantile Dallas Building, Dallas, Texas 75201. Filed 10/11/82. Legislative interest — "To obtain legislation amending section 256 of HR 4961, the Tax Equity and Fiscal Responsibility Act of 1982." Filed for self 10/11/82. Legislative interest — "To obtain legislation amending section 256 of HR 4961, the Tax Equity and Fiscal Responsibility Act of 1982." Lobbyist — John C. Bower.

FILMS INC., Wilmette, Ill. Lobbyist — Roger Tilles, 1111 19th St. N.W., Washington, D.C. 20036. Filed 10/14/82. Legislative interest — ". . .especially, but not limited to copyright legislation, educational technology and educational funding."

FIRST NATIONAL BANK OF OMAHA, Omaha, Neb. Lobbyist — Kutak, Rock & Huie, 1101 Connecticut Ave. N.W., Washington, D.C. 20036. Filed 10/7/82. Legislative interest — "Monitoring HR 6267 as it affects section 23A of the Federal Reserve Act (12 U.S.C. 371c) and general monitoring of banking developments."

HAZELTINE CORP., Greenlawn, N.Y. Lobbyist — Heffernan & Moseman, 1875 I St. N.W., Washington, D.C. 20006. Filed 10/9/82. Legislative interest — "Support SEEK TALK advanced communications system in defense authorization legislation."

HEWLETT-PACKARD CO., Palo Alto, Calif. Lobbyist — Hogan & Hartson, 815 Connecticut Ave. N.W., Washington, D.C. 20006. Filed 10/12/82. Legislative interest — "Legislation affecting the tax treatment of its Puerto Rican subsidiary."

HILL ASSOCIATES, 8301 Fort Hunt Road, Alexandria, Va. 22308. Filed for self 10/25/82. Legislative interest — "Congressional liaison for health and human services." Lobbyist — Carl L. Rasak.

INDEPENDENT FEDERAL SAVINGS, Washington, D.C. Lobbyist — O'Connor & Hannan, 1919 Pennsylvania Ave. N.W., Washington, D.C. 20006. Filed 10/9/82. (Former U.S. Sen. Edward W. Brooke, R-Mass., 1967-79, was listed as agent for this client.) Legislative interest — "Monitor banking legislation."

INTEL CORP., Sunnyvale, Calif. Lobbyist — Hogan & Hartson, 815 Connecticut Ave. N.W., Washington, D.C. 20006. Filed 10/12/82. Legislative interest — "Legislation generally affecting the tax treatment of its Puerto Rican subsidiary."

INTER-REGIONAL FINANCIAL GROUP LEASING CO., Great Falls, Mont. Lobbyist — Heffernan & Moseman, 1875 I St. N.W., Washington, D.C. 20006. Filed 10/9/82. Legislative interest — "Support for continuation of safe harbor leasing provisions of HR 4961 - Tax Equity and Fiscal Responsibility Act of 1982."

INTERMEDICS, Freeport, Texas. Lobbyist — Camp, Carmouche, Palmer, Barsh & Hunter, 2550 M St. N.W., Washington, D.C. 20037. Filed 10/1/82. Legislative interest — "Proposed legislation dealing with Medicare cost reimbursement policy."

JACOBS ENGINEERING GROUP INC., Pasadena, Calif. Lobbyist — Van Ness, Feldman, Sutcliffe, Curtis & Levenberg, 1050 Thomas Jefferson St. N.W., Washington, D.C. 20007. Filed 10/12/82. Legislative interest — "Legislation affecting Remedial Action Program under the Uranium Mill Tailings Radiation Control Act of 1978."

LAKE OSWEGO CORP., Lake Oswego, Ore. Lobbyist — Schwabe, Williamson, Wyatt, Moore & Roberts, 1000 Potomac St. N.W., Washington, D.C. 20007. Filed 10/15/82. (Former U.S. Rep. Robert B. Duncan, D-Ore., 1963-67, 1975-81, was listed as agent for this client.) Legislative interest — "S 1573/HR 6657, legislation to exempt Lake Oswego's hydroelectric plant from part I of the Federal Power Act and section 408 of the Renewable Energy Resources Act of 1980."

LIBERTY FINANCIAL, Bakersfield, Calif. Lobbyist — James E. Ritchie, 499 South Capitol St. S.W., Washington, D.C. 20003. Filed 10/12/82. Legislative interest — ". . .HR 6056 - 'Technical Corrections Act of 1982.' "

MARINE CONSTRUCTION & DESIGN CO., Seattle, Wash. Lobbyist — Bogle & Gates, 1575 I St. N.W., Washington, D.C. 20005. Filed 10/18/82. Legislative interest — ". . .FY83-84 budget. . . ."

MARLINE OIL CORP., Washington, D.C. Lobbyist —

Bliss & Craft, 1050 Thomas Jefferson St. N.W., Washington, D.C. 20007. Filed 10/14/82. Legislative interest — "All legislation dealing with the importation of uranium."

MEDAL DISTILLED PRODUCTS INC., Beverly Hills, Calif. Lobbyist — Silverstein and Mullens, 1776 K St. N.W., Washington, D.C. 20006. Filed 10/13/82. Legislative interest — "HR 4961 - PL 97-248, (Tax Equity and Fiscal Responsibility Act of 1982)."

MERCK & CO., Rahway, N.J. Lobbyist — Blum & Nash, 1015 18th St. N.W., Washington, D.C. 20036. Filed 10/15/82. Legislative interest — "Clean Air Act and Patent Term Restoration."

NATIONAL BASKETBALL ASSOCIATION, New York, N.Y. Lobbyist — Bayh, Tabbert & Capehart, 1575 I St. N.W., Washington, D.C. 20005. Filed 10/26/82. Legislative interest — "HR 5949 Cable Television Copyright Act Amendments."

NATIONAL FOOTBALL LEAGUE, New York, N.Y. Lobbyist — Richard L. Sinnott & Co., 2021 K St. N.W., Washington, D.C. 20006. Filed 10/9/82. Legislative interest — "HR 6467 and S 2784, the Major League Sports Community Protection Act of 1982."

NEW CHANNELS CORP., Washington, D.C. Lobbyist — Gray and Co., 3255 Grace St. N.W., Washington, D.C. 20007. Filed 10/13/82. Legislative interest — "For HR 5949."

NIEDERMEYER-MARTIN CO., Portland, Ore. Lobbyist — Schwabe, Williamson, Wyatt, Moore & Roberts, 1000 Potomac St. N.W., Washington, D.C. 20007. Filed 10/15/82. (Former U.S. Rep. Robert B. Duncan, D-Ore., 1963-67, 1975-81, was listed as agent for this client.) Legislative interest — "Inclusion of Douglas Fir and creosote-treated poles and piling in Rural Electrification Administration and Agency for International Development specifications."

NORTH ALABAMA COAL GASIFICATION CONSORTIUM, New York, N.Y. Lobbyist — Webster & Sheffield, 1200 New Hampshire Ave. N.W., Washington, D.C. 20036. Filed 10/8/82. Legislative interest — ". . .amendment to Technical Corrections Act of 1982 related to long-term commitments for energy property."

OCCIDENTAL PETROLEUM CORP., Los Angeles, Calif. Lobbyist — Camp, Carmouche, Palmer, Barsh & Hunter, 2550 M St. N.W., Washington, D.C. 20037. Filed 10/12/82. Legislative interest — ". . .safe harbor leasing, foreign tax credits and corporate tax preference provisions of tax legislation."

RONALD C. PADDOCK AND CO., 5151 E. Broadway, Tucson, Ariz. 85711. Filed for self 10/15/82. Legislative interest — ". . .statutes and bills relating to telecommunications and medical electronics related to hospital health care." Lobbyist — Ronald C. Paddock.

PENINSULA AIRWAYS INC., Anchorage, Alaska. Lobbyist — Butler, Binion, Rice, Cook & Knapp, 1747 Pennsylvania Ave. N.W., Washington, D.C. 20006. Filed 10/12/82. Legislative interest — "Department of Transportation Appropriations FY 1983, HR 7019."

PHILLIP MORRIS INC., Washington, D.C. Lobbyist — Shea & Gould, 330 Madison Ave., New York, N.Y. 10017. Filed 10/12/82. Legislative interest — "Excise taxes."

PIASECKI AIRCRAFT CORP., Philadelphia, Pa. Lobbyist — Schwabe, Williamson, Wyatt, Moore & Roberts, 1000 Potomac St. N.W., Washington, D.C. 20007. Filed 10/15/82. (Former U.S. Rep. Robert B. Duncan, D-Ore., 1963-67, 1975-81, was listed as agent for this client.) Legislative interest — "Interior appropriations funding for Heli-Stat."

POST-NEWSWEEK STATIONS INC., Washington, D.C. Lobbyist — Covington & Burling, 1201 Pennsylvania Ave. N.W., Washington, D.C. 20044. Filed 10/6/82. Legislative interest — "Proposals for changing the standards and procedures applicable to comparative television renewal proceedings. . . ."

QUIXOTE CORP., Chicago, Ill. Lobbyist — Gray and Co., 3255 Grace St. N.W., Washington, D.C. 20007. Filed 10/13/82. Legislative interest — "Including but not limited to highway safety issues."

REMCO ENTERPRISES INC., Houston, Texas. Lobbyist — Brownstein, Zeidman and Schomer, 1025 Connecticut Ave.

N.W., Washington, D.C. 20036. Filed 10/13/82. Legislative interest — "All legislation affecting truth-in-lending; particularly regulations M and Z."

ST. JOE MINERALS CORP., 250 Park Ave., New York, N.Y. 10017. Filed for self 10/8/82. Legislative interest — "All measures affecting mining, manufacturing and oil and gas production such as income taxation, tariff and trade legislation, stockpiling, foreign investments in U.S. natural resources, public lands, and environmental and safety regulations." Lobbyist — Robert E. Carlstrom Jr., 1730 Rhode Island Ave. N.W., Washington, D.C. 20036.

SAN DIEGO GAS AND ELECTRIC CO., 101 Ash St., San Diego, Calif. 92101. Filed for self 10/8/82. Legislative interest — "Legislation of concern to the utility industry, specifically; HR 7187, HR 6500, S 1885, and HR 6897." Lobbyist — Marian Hall-Crawford, 316 Pennsylvania Ave. S.E., Washington, D.C. 20003.

SAVIN CORP., Valhalla, N.Y. Lobbyist — Rivkin, Sherman and Levy, 900 17th St. N.W., Washington, D.C. 20006. Filed 10/8/82. Legislative interest — "...bills affecting the relationship between office equipment manufacturers and dealers. Specific legislative interests include the 'Retail Dealers Agreement Act,' HR 7106; S 1256...."

RICHARD L. SINNOTT AND CO., Washington, D.C. Lobbyist — Gray and Co., 3255 Grace St. N.W., Washington, D.C. 20007. Filed 10/13/82. Legislative interest — "...to provide a limited exemption from the antitrust laws for professional football."

SQUIBB CORP., New York, N.Y. Lobbyist — Shea & Gould, 330 Madison Ave., New York, N.Y. 10017. Filed 10/12/82. Legislative interest — "...taxation policy toward possession corporations."

STEWART ENVIRONMENTAL, New York, N.Y. Lobbyist — Finley, Kumble, Wagner, Heine, Underberg & Casey, 1120 Connecticut Ave. N.W., Washington, D.C. 20036. Filed 10/22/82. Legislative interest — " 'Export of Hazardous Waste Control Act of 1981,' S 622; opposed."

STROMBERG-CARLSON CORP., Orlando, Fla. Lobbyist — Pepper, Hamilton, & Scheetz, 1777 F St. N.W., Washington, D.C. 20006. Filed 10/14/82. Legislative interest — "Legislation affecting the communications industry, HR 5158; S 898."

SUPERIOR FARMING CO., 1725 K St. N.W., Washington, D.C. 20006. Filed for self 10/15/82. Legislative interest — "Natural gas deregulation; the president's tax program; federal royalties collection; tribal mineral resources; Wilderness Protection Act; windfall profits tax; offshore leasing; reclamation issue." Lobbyist — David P. Prosperi.

THE SUPERIOR OIL CO., 1725 K St. N.W., Washington, D.C. 20006. Filed for self 10/15/82. Legislative interest — "Natural gas deregulation; the president's tax program; federal royalties collection; tribal mineral resources; Wilderness Protection Act; windfall profits tax; offshore leasing; reclamation issue." Lobbyist — David P. Prosperi.

THE TERSON CO. INC., Chicago, Ill. Lobbyist — Winston & Strawn, 2550 M St. N.W., Washington, D.C. 20037. Filed 10/4/82. Legislative interest — "Pension-related legislation; legislation affecting the food industry generally."

THUNDERBIRD FINANCIAL CORP., Shawnee, Okla. Lobbyist — Williams & Jensen, 1101 Connecticut Ave. N.W., Washington, D.C. 20036. Filed 10/4/82. Legislative interest — "Banking legislation of interest particularly S 2879 and HR 6267."

THYSSEN NORDSEEWERKE GMBH, Emden, West Germany. Lobbyist — Gray and Co., 3255 Grace St. N.W., Washington, D.C. 20007. Filed 10/18/82. Legislative interest — "Including but not limited to interesting the U.S. government in purchasing German-built diesel-electric submarine."

TRW INC., Redondo Beach, Calif. Lobbyist — Crowell & Moring, 1100 Connecticut Ave. N.W., Washington, D.C. 20036. Filed 10/23/82. Legislative interest — "Legislation relating to contribution and indemnification for government contractors."

UNITED TECHNOLOGIES COMMUNICATIONS CO., St. Louis, Mo. Lobbyist — Pepper, Hamilton & Scheetz, 1777 F St. N.W., Washington, D.C. 20006. Filed 10/14/82. Legislative interest — "Legislation affecting the communications industry, S 898; HR 5158."

NANCY WALLACE INC., 5003 Fort Sumner Drive, Bethesda, Md. 20816. Filed for self 10/12/82. Legislative interest — "...Marine Mammal Protection Act (for); Endangered Species Act (for) ... constitutional amendment, ERA (for)." Lobbyist — Nancy Wallace.

International Relations

PORTFOLIO OF AGRICULTURE, LANDS AND NATURAL RESOURCES, Grand Cayman, British West Indies. Lobbyist — Orren Merren, 1000 Potomac St. N.W., Washington, D.C. 20007. Filed 10/12/82. Legislative interest — "Endangered Species Act; 16 U.S.C. sections 1531-1543."

Labor Groups

INDUSTRIAL UNION DEPARTMENT, AFL-CIO, 815 16th St. N.W., Washington, D.C. 20006. Filed for self 10/20/82. Legislative interest — "...bills affecting workers such as: trade, OSHA, pension and employment legislation." Lobbyist — Judy Scott.

MIDWEST PENSION FUND OF CENTRAL STATES JOINT BOARD — AFL-CIO, Chicago, Ill. Lobbyist — Winston & Strawn, 2550 M St. N.W., Washington, D.C. 20037. Filed 10/4/82. Legislative interest — "Legislation affecting pension funds."

Trade Associations

AMERICAN BUSINESS CONFERENCE INC., 1025 Connecticut Ave. N.W., Washington, D.C. 20036. Filed for self 10/15/82. Legislative interest — "...tax and regulatory reform legislation for high-growth, mid-range business organizations...." Lobbyist — Dorothy J. Drummer.

THE AMERICAN INSTITUTE OF ARCHITECTS, 1735 New York Ave. N.W., Washington, D.C. 20006. Filed for self 10/8/82. Legislative interest — Not specified. Lobbyist — Albert C. Eisenberg.

AMERICAN PETROLEUM INSTITUTE, 2101 L St. N.W., Washington, D.C. 20037. Filed for self 10/21/82. Legislative interest — Not specified. Lobbyist — Rosemary L. Wilson, 300 Northern Federal Building, St. Paul, Minn. 55102.

AMERICAN SHRIMPBOAT ASSOCIATION, Tampa, Fla. Lobbyist — Bogle & Gates, 1575 I St. N.W., Washington, D.C. 20005. Filed 10/18/82. Legislative interest — "...FY 83-84 budget (for); Shrimp Promotion Act (against)...."

AMERICAN SOCIETY OF ASSOCIATION EXECUTIVES, 1575 I St. N.W., Washington, D.C. 20005. Filed for self 10/8/82. Legislative interest — "...taxation of association income; postal rates for non-profit mailers, and association liability for voluntary standards."

AMERICAN TEXTILE MACHINERY ASSOCIATION, Falls Church, Va. Lobbyist — Collier, Shannon, Rill & Scott, 1055 Thomas Jefferson St. N.W., Washington, D.C. 20007. Filed 10/27/82. Legislative interest — "...matters affecting the textile machinery industry ... legislation that affects small business exporters."

ASSOCIATED GENERAL CONTRACTORS, 1957 E St. N.W., Washington, D.C. 20006. Filed for self 10/8/82. Legislative interest — "ERISA (S 1514) - support in part." Lobbyist — Stephen R. Lindauer.

ASSOCIATION OF DATA PROCESSING SERVICE ORGANIZATIONS INC., Arlington, Va. Lobbyist — Squire, Sanders & Dempsey, 1201 Pennsylvania Ave. N.W., Washington, D.C. 20004. Filed 10/28/82. Legislative interest — "Revisions to the Communications Act of 1934; other matters affecting domestic and international telecommunications services and facilities, international trade in data processing services, the government's organizational structure concerned with U.S.-international telecommunications and information policy."

CHAMBER OF COMMERCE OF THE UNITED STATES, 1615 H St. N.W., Washington, D.C. Filed for self 10/13/82. Legislative interest — Not specified. Lobbyist — Karen D. Alexander.

FEDERATION OF JAPAN SALMON FISHERIES COOPERATIVE ASSOCIATION, Tokyo, Japan. Lobbyist — McDermott, Will & Emery, 1850 K St. N.W., Washington, D.C. 20006. Filed 10/12/82. Legislative interest — "...North Pacific Fisheries Act, Magnuson Fishery Conservation and Management Act, Marine Mammal Protection Act...."

FOOD MARKETING INSTITUTE, 1750 K St. N.W., Washington, D.C. 20006. Filed 10/12/82. Legislative interest — "...the farm bill and other general agricultural legislation." Lobbyist — Nancy Foster.

INDEPENDENT DATA COMMUNICATIONS MANUFACTURERS ASSOCIATION INC., Washington, D.C. Lobbyist — Squire, Sanders & Dempsey, 1201 Pennsylvania Ave. N.W., Washington, D.C. 20004. Filed 10/28/82. Legislative interest — "Revisions to the Communications Act of 1934 and other matters affecting competition among manufacturers of data communications equipment."

INVESTMENT COMPANY INSTITUTE, 1775 K St. N.W., Washington, D.C. 20006. Filed for self 10/12/82. Legislative interest — "S 1424, amend the Investment Company Act - oppose; S 1427, State and Local Government Financing Reform Act of 1981 - oppose; S 1541, a bill to amend ERISA - may favor amendment; S 1720, to enhance the competitiveness of depository institutions - oppose; S 1888, to amend the Internal Revenue Code - oppose; S 2536, to amend the Securities Acts of 1933 and 1934 and the Investment Company Act of 1940 - oppose; HR 1916, Financial Industry Equity Act - oppose; HR 2591, Federal Reserve Act Amendments of 1981 - oppose; HR 2916, to amend the Federal Reserve Act - oppose; HR 3058, to amend the Federal Reserve Act - oppose; HR 3097, to amend the Federal Reserve Act - oppose; HR 3230, to amend the Federal Reserve Act - oppose; HR 3456, to amend the Investment Company Act - oppose; HR 2980, to amend the Federal Reserve Act - oppose; HR 4049, to amend the Glass-Steagall Act - oppose; HR 5004, to amend the Internal Revenue Code - oppose; HR 5053, to amend the Internal Revenue Code - support; HR 5699, to amend the Internal Revenue Code - support; HR 6124, to extend the Credit Control Act - oppose; HR 6410, to amend the Internal Revenue Code - oppose." Lobbyist — Catherine L. Heron.

MANUFACTURED HOUSING INSTITUTE, Arlington, Va. Lobbyist — Jerry C. Connors, 3321 Stephenson Place N.W., Washington, D.C. 20015. Filed 10/21/82. Legislative interest — "General interest in housing legislation, specifically mobile and modular."

MILK INDUSTRY FOUNDATION, Washington, D.C. Lobbyist — O'Neill and Haase, 1333 New Hampshire Ave. N.W., Washington, D.C. 20036. Filed 10/25/82. Legislative interest — "Agriculture Appropriations bill."

NATIONAL ASSOCIATION OF BEVERAGE IMPORTERS, 1025 Vermont Ave. N.W., Washington, D.C. 20005. Filed for self 10/21/82. Legislative interest — Not specified. Lobbyist — Thomas E. O'Neill.

NATIONAL ASSOCIATION OF INDEPENDENT COLLEGES AND UNIVERSITIES, 1717 Massachusetts Ave. N.W., Washington, D.C. 20036. Filed for self 10/12/82. Legislative interest — "...including but not limited to reauthorization of the Higher Education Act of 1965, tax, budget and appropriations legislation." Lobbyist — Kathleen L. Curry.

NATIONAL BANKERS ASSOCIATION, Washington, D.C. Lobbyist — Moss, McGee and Bellmon, 1740 N St. N.W., Washington, D.C. 20036. Filed 10/15/82. Legislative interest — "PL 95-507."

NATIONAL CABLE TELEVISION ASSOCIATION INC., 1724 Massachusetts Ave. N.W., Washington, D.C. 20036. Filed for self 10/12/82. Legislative interest — "Amendments to the Communications Act of 1934 and other legislation affecting cable television generally." Lobbyist — Kim Hetherington.

NATIONAL COUNCIL OF FARMER COOPERATIVES, 1800 Massachusetts Ave. N.W., Washington, D.C.

Filed for self 10/12/82. Legislative interest — Not specified. Lobbyist — David T. Crow. Filed for self 10/12/82. Legislative interest — "HR 6995, S 2499, FTC reauthorization, for." Lobbyist — Gary D. Myers.

OHIO VALLEY IMPROVEMENT ASSOCIATION INC., Cincinnati, Ohio. Lobbyist — Cook, Purcell, Hansen & Henderson, 1015 18th St. N.W., Washington, D.C. 20036. Filed 10/8/82. Legislative interest — "...authorize and fund navigation improvements on Ohio and Monongahela rivers."

PHARMACEUTICAL MANUFACTURING ASSOCIATION, Washington, D.C. Lobbyist — Preston, Thorgrimson, Ellis & Holman, 1776 G St. N.W., Washington, D.C. 20006. Filed 10/13/82. (Former U.S. Rep. Lloyd Meeds, D-Wash., 1965-79, was listed as agent for this client.) Legislative interest — "...HR 6444...."

PRIVATE TRUCK COUNCIL OF AMERICA INC., 1101 17th St. N.W., Washington, D.C. 20036. Filed for self 10/12/82. Legislative interest — "...'the Motor Carrier Act of 1980' and pending legislation in truck safety, sizes and weight, and highway funding matters." Lobbyist — Joseph M. Normandy III.

TENNESSEE RAILROAD ASSOCIATION, 916 Nashville Trust Building, Nashville, Tenn. 37201. Filed for self 10/28/82. Legislative interest — Not specified. Lobbyist — Tom Benson.

TRANSPORTATION INSTITUTE, Washington, D.C. Lobbyist — Lipsen, Hamberger, Whitten and Hamberger, 1725 DeSales St. N.W., Washington, D.C. 20036. Filed 10/15/82. Legislative interest — "...maritime industry."

TUNA RESEARCH FOUNDATION INC., Washington, D.C. Lobbyist — McDermott, Will & Emery, 1850 K St. N.W., Washington, D.C. 20036. Filed 10/12/82. Legislative interest — "...Marine Mammal Protection Act, Fishery Conservation and Management Act, Fishery Conservation Zone Transition Act, Fisherman's Protective Act, Tuna Conventions Act...."

WASHINGTON INDEPENDENT WRITERS INC., 525 National Press Building, Washington, D.C. 20045. Filed for self 10/27/82. Legislative interest — "...S 2044, a proposed amendment to the Copyright Act, 17 U.S.C. section 101 *et seq....*" Lobbyists — Ronald L. Goldfarb, Ronald A. Schechter.

WEST MEXICO VEGETABLE DISTRIBUTORS ASSOCIATION, Nogales, Ariz. Lobbyist — Jennifer L. Smith, 900 17th St. N.W., Washington, D.C. 20006. Filed 10/6/82. Legislative interest — "Imports of fresh fruits and vegetables."

WESTERN RIVER GUIDES ASSOCIATION, Salt Lake City, Utah. Lobbyist — Brown, Roady, Bonvillian & Gold, 1300 19th St. N.W., Washington, D.C. 20036. Filed 10/8/82. Legislative interest — "...a draft proposal by the U.S. Forest Service that addresses policies concerning river use. No bills have been introduced. Statutes involved: 16 U.S.C. section 20 *et. seq.*, 16 U.S.C. section 471a, 16 U.S.C. section 1271 *et. seq.*, and 43 U.S.C. section 1701 *et. seq.*"

WINE AND SPIRITS WHOLESALERS OF AMERICA, Washington, D.C. Lobbyist — O'Connor & Hannan, 1919 Pennsylvania Ave. N.W., Washington, D.C. 20006. Filed 10/9/82. (Former U.S. Sen. Edward W. Brooke, R-Mass., 1967-79, was listed as agent for this client.) Legislative interest — Not specified.

Miscellaneous

WILLIAM P. KING, 8475 Coral Way, Miami, Fla. 33155. Filed for self 10/23/82. Legislative interest — Not specified.

NATIONAL CENTER FOR APPROPRIATE TECHNOLOGY, Butte, Mont. Lobbyist — Moss, McGee & Bellmon, 1740 N St. N.W., Washington, D.C. 20036. Filed 10/15/82. Legislative interest — "Labor/HHS/Appropriations Act, Community Services Block Grant Act."

NATIONAL VOLUNTARY PROFESSIONAL SOCIETY, Washington, D.C. Lobbyist — Philip R. Crossmann, 1735 New York Ave. N.W., Washington, D.C. 20006. Filed 10/8/82. Legislative interest — Not specified.

GEORGE E. O'CONNOR, 600 New Hampshire Ave. N.W., Washington, D.C. 20037. Filed for self 10/6/82. Legislative interest

— "Life insurance company income tax of 1959 - PL 88-69. Legislation and regulation affecting life, health insurance and annuities."

PLAINTIFF CLASS, CORRUGATED CONTAINER ANTITRUST LITIGATION, MDL NO. 310, Houston, Texas. Lobbyist — Findley, Kumble, Wagner, Heine, Underberg & Casey, 1120 Connecticut Ave. N.W., Washington, D.C. 20036. Filed 10/19/82. Legislative interest — "S 995 - amendment to Clayton Act, 15 U.S.C. 12 *et. seq.*, new Section 41; HR 1242 - Amendment to Clayton Act, 15 U.S.C. 12 *et. seq.*, new section 41. Against both bills."

PLAINTIFF CLASS, PLYWOOD ANTITRUST LITI- GATION, MDL NO. 159, New Orleans, La. Lobbyist — Findley, Kumble, Wagner, Heine, Underberg & Casey, 1120 Connecticut Ave. N.W., Washington, D.C. 20036. Filed 10/19/82. Legislative interest — "S 995 - amendment to Clayton Act, 15 U.S.C. 12 *et. seq.*, new Section 41; HR 1242 - Amendment to Clayton Act, 15 U.S.C. 12 *et. seq.*, new section 41. Against both bills."

THE SOCIETY FOR AMERICAN ARCHAEOLOGY, San Antonio, Texas. Lobbyist — Philip Speser, 5070 MacArthur Blvd. N.W., Washington, D.C. 20016. Filed 10/9/82. Legislative interest — "Convention on Cultural Properties Implementation Act, Abandoned Historic Shipwrecks Act; S 1723, HR 132. . . ." ∎

Lobby Registration Index

A

A & S Transportation Co. - 22-D
AAI Corp. - 48-D
Abadie & Hudson
　Coastal Corp. - 7-D
Abercrombie, Alvin L. - 7-D
Abraham, Georgia - 9-D
Ackerman, Raymond W. - 44-D
Adams County - 16-D
Adams, Duque & Hazeltine
　National Council on Teacher Retirement - 41-D
Ad Hoc Committee for Responsible Tax Policy - 40-D
Ad Hoc Committee of Mutual Fund Managers - 25-D
Adherence Group Inc. - 40-D
Advance Publications Inc. - 10-D
Advanced Fuel Systems Inc. - 10-D
Aerospace Industries Association of America - 19-D
Aetna Insurance Co - 22-D
Affiliated Food Processors Inc. - 35-D
African Friends of Israel Inc. - 41-D
Agrigenetics Corp. - 17-D
Agristore Systems Co. - 46-D
Ahmanson Foundation - 35-D
A.I. Leasing Corp. - 36-D
Ailsworth, Herbert Allen - 15-D
Air Freight Association - 35-D
Air Line Pilots Association - 40-D
Air Transport Association of America - 5-D
Airco Inc. - 17-D, 22-D
Aisenberg, Michael A. - 14-D
A-K Associates Inc.
　California Air Tanker Operators Association - 20-D
Akin, Gump, Strauss, Hauer & Feld
　Air Freight Association - 35-D
　American Stock Exchange Inc. - 46-D
　Beneficial Corp. - 28-D
　Capital Bank - 28-D
　Cities Service Co. - 42-D
　Coalition of Service Industries Inc. - 26-D
　Continental Airlines - 28-D
　Desert Grape Growers League of California - 28-D
　Equitable Bank - 28-D
　Hemisphere National Bank - 28-D
　Marlex Petroleum Inc. - 18-D
　Motion Picture Association of America Inc. - 6-D
　National Football League - 15-D
　New York Air - 29-D
　Norton Simon Inc. - 38-D
　R.J. Reynolds Industries Inc. - 39-D
　South Hampton Inc. - 39-D

Southland Royalty Co. - 24-D
Western Air Lines Inc. - 44-D
Akron, Ohio, City of - 39-D
Alabama Power Co. - 14-D
Alamo Rent A Car - 28-D
Alarm Device Manufacturing Co. - 17-D
Alaska Lumber and Pulp Co./ Louisiana Pacific of Ketchikan (ALP/LPK) - 42-D
Alaska National Bank of the North - 36-D
Alaska Resource Analysts Inc. - 28-D
Alaska, State of - 8-D, 34-D
Alaska State Senate, Transportation Committee - 5-D
Albers, Richard F. - 22-D
Alcalde, Henderson & O'Bannon
　Americans for the National Dividend Act Inc. - 36-D
Alcorn, Bakewell & Smith
　Helen Wodell Halbach Estate - 21-D
Alexander, Karen D. - 51-D
Alexander, Susan - 22-D
Allder, Jeff Samuel - 9-D
Allen, Robert G. - 20-D
Allen, William M. - 3-D
Alliance Capital Management Corp. - 42-D
Alliance for Justice - 13-D
Alliance of Third Class Non-Profit Mailers - 17-D
Alliance to Save Energy - 3-D, 21-D
Alston, Miller & Gaines
　Continental Insurance Companies - 46-D
Alvin Nederlander Associates Inc. - 42-D
AM General Corp. - 14-D, 17-D
Amalgamated Transit Union - 5-D, 8-D
American Advertising Federation - 25-D
American Association of Equipment Lessors - 20-D, 35-D
American Association of Homes for the Aging - 16-D
American Association of Oral and Maxillofacial Surgeons - 26-D
American Association of Retired Persons - 8-D, 11-D, 20-D, 26-D
American Association of School Administrators - 11-D
American Bakers Association - 30-D, 44-D
American Bankers Insurance Company - 22-D
American Bar Association - 16-D
American Broadcasting Co. Inc. - 32-D
American Bureau of Collections Inc. - 27-D

American Bus Association - 26-D
American Business Conference - 16-D, 50-D
American Can Company - 22-D
American Cancer Society - 9-D
American Clean Water Association - 35-D
American College of Mortgage Attorneys - 35-D
American College of Neuropsychopharmacology - 6-D, 41-D
American College of Nurse-Midwives - 6-D
American Congress on Surveying & Mapping - 16-D
American Consulting Engineers Council - 40-D
American Council for Capital Formation - 30-D, 35-D
American Council of International Personnel Inc. - 35-D
American Council of Life Insurance Inc. - 5-D, 20-D
American Council of Life Insurers - 30-D
American Cyanamid Co. - 14-D, 36-D
American Dental Association - 26-D
American Land Development Association - 44-D
American Electronics Association - 20-D, 40-D
American Express Co. - 3-D, 17-D, 42-D
American Federation of Independent Business - 44-D
American Federation of Labor-Congress of Industrial Organizations - 39-D
American Federation of Musicians - 19-D
American Federation of State, County and Municipal Employees (AFL-CIO) - 19-D
American Feed Manufacturers Association - 16-D
American Friends of Kiryat Sanz Laniado Hospital - 13-D
American Fur Industry Inc. - 12-D
American General Corp. - 36-D
American General Life Insurance Co. - 32-D
American Global Lines Inc. - 42-D
American Group Practice Association - 12-D
American Guild of Authors and Composers - 19-D
American Health Care Association - 40-D
American Health Planning Association - 5-D
American Hoechst Corp. - 17-D

American Home Sewing Association Inc. - 30-D
American Hospital Association - 5-D, 8-D, 12-D, 35-D
American Institute of Architects - 50-D
American Institute of Merchant Shipping - 26-D
American Israel Public Affairs Committee - 27-D
American Legion - 9-D
American Lobby for President Reagan's Balanced Budget Amendment Inc. - 36-D
American Logistics Association - 30-D
American Maritime Association - 5-D, 8-D
American Medical Association - 40-D
American Metal Detectors Manufacturers Inc. - 22-D
American Mining Congress - 26-D
American Motors Corp. - 36-D
American National Insurance Co. - 32-D
American Natural Resources Co. - 42-D
American Nuclear Energy Council - 5-D, 30-D
American Optometric Association - 40-D
American Osteopathic Hospital Association - 47-D
American Petroleum Institute - 5-D, 12-D, 16-D, 47-D, 50-D
American Postal Workers Union - 30-D
American President Lines - 14-D, 22-D
American Public Health Association - 21-D, 40-D
American Public Transit Association - 40-D
American Rivers Conservation Council - 7-D, 9-D, 31-D
American Samoa - 8-D
American Ship Building Co. - 48-D
American Shrimpboat Association - 50-D
American Society for Gastrointestinal Endoscopy - 40-D
American Society of Association Executives - 5-D, 16-D, 50-D
American Society of Civil Engineers - 40-D
American Society of Mechanical Engineers - 44-D, 46-D
American Society of Photogrammetry - 16-D
American Soybean Association - 40-D
American Stock Exchange Inc. - 28-D, 46-D
American Subcontractors Association - 5-D, 30-D

American Sugarbeet Growers Association - 40-D

American Telephone & Telegraph Co. - 32-D, 42-D

American Textile Machinery Association - 50-D

American Trade and Finance Co. - 48-D

American Truck Dealers - 20-D

American Trucking Associations - 8-D, 47-D

American Tunaboat Association - 5-D

American Waterways Operators Inc. - 12-D

American Wood Preservers Institute - 8-D

Americans for Democratic Action - 47-D

Americans for the National Dividend Act Inc. - 36-D

Amherst College - 31-D

Amitay, Morris J. - 41-D

Amurcon Corp. - 46-D

Amway Corp. - 36-D

Anchor National Life Insurance Co. - 28-D

Anderson, Hibey, Nauheim & Blair
Bay Area Rapid Transit District - 5-D
Communication Industries Association of Japan - 16-D
Metropolitan Atlanta Rapid Transit Authority - 5-D
Morgan Guaranty Trust Company of New York - 7-D

Anderson, M. Kent - 22-D

Andolsek, L.J. - 35-D

Andresen, Jack O. - 8-D, 12-D

Andrews & Kurth
Space Services Inc. - 19-D

Anheuser-Busch Co. Inc. - 10-D, 32-D

Antolock, Lori A. - 44-D

Apple Computer Corp. - 14-D

Arab Republic of Egypt - 11-D

Arent, Fox, Kintner, Plotkin & Kahn
Central States Southeast and Southwest Areas Health and Welfare and Pension Funds - 21-D
Guardian Life Insurance Company of America - 37-D
Intelsat - 23-D
Uranerzbergbau-GMBH - 25-D

Arkansas 2000 Inc. - 31-D

Arnold & Porter
Ahmanson Foundation - 35-D
Building and Construction Trades Department (AFL-CIO) - 19-D
Federation Suisse des Associations de Fabricants D'Horlogerie - 20-D
London Gold Futures Market - 18-D
London International Financial Futures Exchange Ltd. - 18-D
Metal Market & Exchange Company Ltd. - 18-D
Recording Industry Association of America Inc. - 35-D

ARMCO Inc. - 48-D

Aron, Nan - 13-D

Artpac - 47-D

ASARCO - 7-D

Asbestos Compensation Coalition - 21-D

Ashley, Thomas Ludlow - 7-D, 8-D, 23-D, 38-D, 44-D, 46-D

Associated Builders and Contractors - 16-D, 26-D, 30-D

Associated General Contractors of America - 8-D, 12-D, 26-D, 40-D, 50-D

Associated Specialty Contractors Inc. - 44-D

Association for Equal Access to Natural Gas Markets and Supplies - 5-D

Association of American Railroads - 12-D, 26-D

Association of Data Processing Service Organizations Inc. - 50-D

Association of Executive Recruiting Consultants Inc. - 12-D

Association of Night Vision Manufacturers - 26-D

Association of Oil Pipelines - 30-D

Association of Spanish Fishermen - 40-D

Association of Trial Lawyers of America - 8-D, 44-D

Atari Inc. - 48-D

At-Sea Incineration Inc. - 42-D

Attaway, Fritz - 12-D

Austern, David - 30-D

Austin, Claudia Mansfield - 11-D

Automotive Dismantlers and Recyclers Association - 8-D

Avenel Associates Inc.
Broward Federal Savings and Loan Association - 28-D

Aycock, Pamela S. - 29-D

B

B. Altman & Co. - 42-D

Bacardi Corp. - 42-D

Baenen, Timme, De Reitzes & Middleton
Confederated Salish and Kootenai Tribes of the Flathead Reservation - 47-D
Shee Atika Inc. - 48-D

Bailey, Paul C. - 24-D

Bain, Lorne D. - 37-D

Baker & Hostetler
Federal Cartridge Corp. - 37-D
Timken Foundation - 41-D

Baker & McKenzie
Daily Express Inc. - 14-D
Geosource Inc. - 14-D

Baker, Eugene - 45-D

Baker, Keith L. - 48-D

Baldwin-United Corp. - 32-D

Ball, W. Allen - 18-D

Ballard, Spahr, Andrews & Ingersoll
American Can Co. - 22-D
Delaware River Port Authority - 8-D
Philadelphia Port Corp. - 8-D
Port of Wilmington - 34-D
South Jersey Port Corp. - 34-D
U.S. Committee for UNICEF - 36-D
West Virginia Industrial Development Association - 25-D

Banneker Associates - 3-D

Baraff, Koerner, Olender & Hochberg
National Basketball Association - 15-D
North American Soccer League - 15-D

Baretta Corp. - 3-D

Barkley Company of Arizona - 36-D

Barnes, Richardson & Colburn
United States Cantaloupe Growers & Importers Association - 13-D
Woodhouse Drake & Carey Inc. - 34-D

Barnett & Alagia
Affiliated Food Processors Inc. - 35-D
Asbestos Compensation Coalition - 21-D
Cuban American National Foundation - 42-D
National Milk Producers Federation - 20-D

Barnett, Yingling & Shay
Savings Bank of Puget Sound - 44-D

Baron/Canning and Co. Inc.
Embassy of India - 8-D
National Passenger Traffic Association Inc. - 27-D

Barrett, Smith, Schapiro, Simon & Armstrong
CSC Clearing Corp. - 22-D

Metropolitan Transportation Authority - 39-D

Barrison, Harvey - 18-D

Batky, Catharine R. - 22-D

Baton Rouge, City of - 34-D

Baum, George K. & Co. - 22-D

Bay Area Rapid Transit District - 5-D

Bayh, Tabbert & Capehart
American Cancer Society - 9-D
National Basketball Association - 49-D
Pharmaceutical Manufacturers Association - 47-D
Sugar Users Group - 45-D
Warner Communications Inc. - 30-D

Baylin, G. Brockwel - 26-D

Bear, Stearns & Co. - 46-D

Beard and Associates
American Rivers Conservation Council - 31-D
Seneca and Associates - 15-D

Beatrice Foods Co. - 36-D

Beatty & McNamee
Boeing Co. - 10-D

Bechtel Power Corp. - 14-D

Beckel, Finchem, Torricelli & Associates Inc.
Registration - 17-D
Westinghouse Electric Corp. - 19-D

Beckel, Robert G. - 17-D, 29-D

Beim, Carol M. - 36-D

Belcher Towing Co. - 17-D

Bellingham Cold Storage - 32-D

Belridge Capital Corp. - 14-D

Belz Institute of Israel - 17-D

Bendix Corp. - 48-D

Beneficial Corp. - 28-D

Beneficial Management Corporation of America - 14-D

Benenson Capital Co. - 48-D

Benenson Realty Co. - 28-D

Bennett, Trisha - 22-D

Benson, Tom - 51-D

Berenergy Corp. - 32-D

Beretta Corp. - 3-D, 7-D

Berlin, Frank Brett - 3-D

Bernier, Robert E. - 17-D

Besson, Frank S. III - 17-D

Bethlehem Steel Co. - 48-D

Betz College - 45-D

Beute, William M. - 21-D

Beveridge & Diamond
Dow Chemical Co. - 17-D
Union Camp Corp. - 30-D
United Church of Christ - 45-D

Billig, Sher & Jones
Adherence Group Inc. - 40-D
Alaska State Senate, Transportation Committee - 5-D

Birch, Horton, Bittner and Monroe
Alaska National Bank of the North - 36-D
First Federal Savings and Loan Association - 37-D
Government Research & Development Corp. - 14-D
Highly Enterprise Corp. - 10-D
St. George Tanaq Corp. - 11-D

Bird, Bonnie G. - 12-D

Birtcil, William H. Jr. - 24-D

Bishop, H. Radford - 6-D

Bishop, Richard A. - 46-D

Black, Manafort & Stone
National Securities Clearing Corp. - 29-D

Black and Decker Manufacturing Co. - 48-D

Blaine, Barbara S. - 16-D

Blair, David A. - 48-D

Blank, Rome, Comisky & McCauley
A & S Transportation Co. - 22-D
Radnor Corp. - 39-D

Bliss & Craft

Fluor Corp. - 28-D

Marline Oil Corp. 49-D

Bliss, Richard W. - 7-D, 8-D

Bliss, Virginia B. - 48-D

Block, Ellen - 13-D

Blum & Nash
Merck & Co. - 49-D

Blyth Eastman Paine Webber Inc. - 22-D

Blyth Eastman Paine Webber Health Care Funding Inc. - 36-D

Boasberg, Klores, Feldesman & Tucker
Committee for Farmworker Programs - 15-D

Boeing Co. - 10-D, 28-D, 42-D, 48-D

Bogle & Gates
American Shrimpboat Association - 50-D
Marine Construction and Design Co. - 49-D

Book Manufacturers' Institute Inc. - 35-D

Borens, Robert N. - 14-D

Boswell, Marion L. - 43-D

Botsford, Stephen F. - 32-D

Bouchard, John E. - 48-D

Bower, John C. - 49-D

Bowling, Marvin C. Jr. - 29-D

Boykin, Thurman S. - 31-D, 46-D

Bracewell & Patterson
Comdisco Inc. - 42-D
Dresser Industries - 37-D
Houston Natural Gas Corp. - 37-D
U.S. Tuna Foundation - 47-D

Bracy, Williams & Co.
California Nickel Corp. - 22-D
City of Tucson - 25-D
Employee Owned Airlines - 23-D
Energy Absorption Systems Inc. - 48-D
Humana Inc. - 23-D
Nike International Ltd. - 24-D
Pratt & Whitney Aircraft Group - 24-D
Quixote Corp. - 24-D

Bredder, Roy S. - 26-D

Bregman, Abell & Kay
American Federation of Labor-Congress of Industrial Organizations - 39-D
Consolidated Freightway Corp. - 10-D
Roadway Express Inc. - 11-D
Ryder Systems Inc. - 24-D

Brick Institute of America - 26-D

Bricker & Eckler
Norfolk Southern - 43-D

Brickey, Carolyn - 13-D

Broman, Phillip J. - 30-D

Brooke, Edward W. - 37-D, 49-D, 51-D

Brooks, Mary E. - 47-D

Broward County, Fla. - 39-D

Broward Federal Savings and Loan Association - 28-D

Brown & Finn
Suburban Cablevision - 44-D
Wayne Cablevision - 44-D

Brown & Roady
Kansas City Southern Railway - 4-D
Metropolitan Transit Authority - 19-D
Western River Guides Association - 51-D

Brown & Root Inc. - 42-D

Brown and Williamson Tobacco Corp. - 42-D

Brown, Ben Jarratt - 33-D

Brown, Dennis E. - 6-D

Brown, Ellen B. - 16-D

Brown, Garry E. - 11-D

Brown, James F. - 5-D

Brown, Terrance J., Associates
Eastern Band of Cherokee Indians - 13-D
Red Lake Band of Chippewa Indians - 13-D

Lawyers Title Insurance Corp. - 29-D

Food and Beverage Trades Department, AFL-CIO - 25-D

Food Marketing Institute - 16-D, 31-D, 51-D

Food Research and Action Center - 13-D

Foothills Pipe Lines (Yukon) Ltd. - 4-D

Ford Aerospace and Communications Corp. - 28-D

Ford Motor Co. - 4-D

Ford, Riff & Burgess - 37-D

Foremost Insurance Co. - 23-D

Forest City Dillon Inc. - 33-D

Forum Communications - 37-D

Foster, Nancy 40-D, 51-D

Fox, Eric R. - 14-D

F/P Research Associates
American Bus Association - 26-D
Slurry Transport Association - 21-D

Francis Associates Ltd.
Continental Airline Employees Association - 5-D
National Education Association - 5-D

Frank, Peter M. - 38-D

Franks, Thomas C. - 44-D

Franz, Charles W. - 10-D

Frazer Lanier Co. - 23-D

Freedman, Carol - 47-D

Freedman, D. Michael - 46-D

Freeman, Carl M., Associates - 7-D, 33-D

Fried, Frank, Harris, Shriver & Kampelman
Agrigenetics Corp. - 17-D

Friends of the Columbia Gorge - 13-D

Fritschler, Susan T. - 47-D

Froh, Richard B. - 38-D

Fruitdale Telephone Co. - 14-D

Fulbright & Jaworski
Alamo Rent A Car - 28-D
Crystal Oil Co. - 3-D
Houston Post Co., The - 37-D
National Association of Real Estate Investment Trusts - 35-D

Fur Conservation Institute of America - 12-D

G

Gabor, Mark P. - 5-D

Gadsden Times Inc. - 37-D

Gaffigan, James E. - 41-D

Gallagher, Linda P. - 3-D

Gallant, Karl - 36-D

Galveston Wharves of the City of Galveston - 44-D

Gamble, Kimberly A. - 48-D

Ganderson, Harry - 27-D

Garabedian, Michael N. - 17-D

Gardner, Carton & Douglas
American Health Care Association - 40-D
K-A Co. - 29-D
Midcon Corp. - 10-D

Gartland, John C. - 36-D

Garvey, Schubert, Adams & Barer
Cominco American Inc. - 3-D
Japan Fisheries Association - 16-D

Gatti, Louis - 10-D

Gatx Corp. - 18-D, 23-D

Gatx Terminals Corp. - 14-D

General Dynamics Corp. - 10-D

General Electric Co. - 43-D

General Electric Credit Corp. - 33-D

General Motors Corp. - 4-D, 28-D

General Public Utilities Corp. - 10-D, 18-D

General Telephone and Electronics Corp. - 10-D, 23-D

Generic Pharmaceutical Industry Association - 47-D

Geneva Pacific Corp. - 23-D, 37-D

George, Nancy Whorton - 48-D

George Washington University Student Association - 3-D

Georgia Agricultural Commodity Commission for Peanuts - 16-D

Georgia Pacific Corp. - 23-D

Geosource Inc. - 14-D

Gerard, Byler & Associates
Damson Oil Corp. - 37-D

Gerber Products Co. - 7-D

Gerson, Llewellyn H. - 5-D

Getty Oil Co. - 14-D, 28-D

GHK Companies - 4-D

Gibson, Dunn & Crutcher
Associated Specialty Contractors Inc. - 44-D
Mechanical Contractors Association of America Inc. - 47-D

Gibson, John A. C. - 5-D

Gilbane Building Co. - 33-D

Gilbert, Richard - 40-D

Giles, John - 12-D

Gilkey, Floyd H. - 28-D

Ginsburg, Feldman, Wail and Bress
Belcher Towing Co. - 17-D

Glass Packaging Institute - 6-D

Glendale Federal Savings & Loan Association - 33-D

Global Exploration & Development Corp. - 4-D

Glover, Jere W. - 27-D

Gnau, Carter, Jacobsen & Associates Inc.
Amurcon Corp. - 46-D
CAC Associates - 46-D
Grand Traverse Development Inc. - 46-D
Move Detroit Forward Fund - 46-D
Potter Instrument Co. Inc. - 46-D
R.J. Chambers - 46-D
Sanders Corp. - 46-D
Urban Revitalization Inc. - 46-D

Goldberg, Stephen M. - 10-D

Golden Gateway Center - 37-D

Golden Nugget Inc. - 37-D

Goldfarb, Ronald L. - 51-D

Goldman Sachs & Co. - 23-D, 37-D, 43-D

Gonella, John - 26-D

Goodyear Tire and Rubber Co. - 14-D

Gorham, Millicent - 40-D

Gorman, James M. - 18-D

Gould Inc. - 43-D

Government Guaranteed Loan Committee, Public Securities Association - 20-D

Government of Antigua and Barbuda - 25-D

Government of Nicaragua - 5-D

Government of the Virgin Islands - 30-D

Government Research & Development Corp. - 14-D

GPU Service Corp. - 23-D

Graeper-Van Noy-Wagner Inc. - 10-D

Graham-White Manufacturing Co. - 33-D

Grand Traverse Development Inc. - 46-D

Graul, Michael R. - 5-D

Graves, E.M. & Co. Inc. - 14-D

Gray & Co.
American Maritime Association - 5-D, 8-D
American Trucking Associations - 8-D
ASARCO - 7-D
Banneker Associates - 3-D
Bendix Corp. - 48-D
Beretta Corp. - 3-D, 7-D
Commonwealth of Puerto Rico - 34-D, 39-D

Council of State Housing Agencies - 5-D

Health Insurance Association of America - 9-D, 40-D

HTB Corp. - 7-D

Minimum Tax Coalition - 13-D, 36-D

National Association of Home Builders - 9-D

National Coalition for a Free Cuba - 42-D, 47-D

New Channels Corp. - 29-D, 49-D

Republic Airlines - 4-D

Quixote Corp. - 49-D

Richard L. Sinnott & Co. - 44-D, 50-D

Shaklee Corp. - 39-D

Thyssen Nordseewerke GMBH - 50-D

Tobacco Institute, The - 41-D

Warner Communications/Franklin Mint - 8-D, 15-D

Warner Communications Inc. - 30-D

Great American Insurance Co. - 23-D

Green, John K. - 25-D

Greenbaum, Jane E. - 28-D

Greene, Calvin Reginald Jr. - 20-D

Greenstein, Robert - 21-D

Grocery Manufacturers of America - 16-D, 20-D, 45-D

Groom & Nordberg
Goldman Sachs & Co. - 43-D

Group W Cable - 43-D

Grupenhoff, John T. - 40-D

Guadalupe Blanco River Authority - 25-D

Guam Airport Authority - 5-D

Guardian Life Insurance Company of America - 37-D

Guild, Hagen & Clark Ltd.
Motion Picture Association of America Inc. - 31-D

Guthrie, Ned H. - 19-D

H

Hagan, Thomas M. - 14-D

Halbach, Helen Wodell, Estate of - 27-D

Hale and Dorr
GHK Companies - 4-D
Seneca County - 16-D
Town of Mashpee - 16-D

Hall-Crawford, Marion - 50-D

Hallmark Cards Inc. - 18-D, 28-D

Halpern, Seymour - 8-D, 27-D

Halstead, J. Phillip - 48-D

Hamel, Park, McCabe & Saunders
Graeper-Van Noy-Wagner Inc. - 10-D
Helen Wodell Halbach Estate - 27-D
Nokota Co. - 43-D
Puerto Rico Federal Affairs Administration - 40-D
Tandy Corp. - 19-D

Hammer, Amy - 3-D

Hampshire Energy - 10-D

Hanczor, Theresa Rose - 3-D

Handgun Control Inc. - 9-D

Hanley, Edward R. - 17-D

Hanley, James M. - 17-D

Hanna Mining Co. - 37-D

Hannaford Co. Inc.
Fireman's Fund Insurance Companies - 7-D

Hannaford International Inc.
Lebanese Information and Research Center - 44-D

Hansell, Post, Brandon & Dorsey
Independent Valley Energy Co. - 37-D
Portman Properties - 39-D
Rockwell International Corp. - 4-D

Harding, Margaret K. - 33-D

Hardy, Eugene J. - 7-D

Hargis, J. Richard - 46-D

Harley, William G. - 12-D

Harley-Davidson Military Sales - 37-D

Harman, Charles E. Jr. - 12-D

Harrel, James - 31-D

Harris, Allen - 6-D

Harris Communications Inc.
Alarm Device Manufacturing Co. - 17-D

Harris, Judy L. - 30-D

Harris, William F. - 48-D

Harsco Corp. - 28-D

Harsha, William H., & Associates
Air Line Pilots Association - 40-D
Office of States' Washington Representative to Appalachian Regional Commission - 25-D

Hart, Lynn S. - 5-D

Hartmann, Arthur W. - 35-D

Harvey, Juliane B. - 36-D

Hatfield, L. Andrea - 27-D

Hathaway, Janet - 36-D

Havens, Charles W. III - 23-D

Hawaiian Sugar Planters' Association - 16-D, 40-D

Hawaiian Sugar Transportation Co. - 43-D

Hayes Inc. - 18-D

Haynos, Robert A. - 28-D

Hazardous Waste Treatment Council - 32-D

Hazeltine Corp. - 49-D

Health Insurance Association of America - 9-D, 40-D

Hecht, William H. - 42-D, 44-D

Hedberg, Mary Connell - 32-D

Hedlund, James B. - 12-D

Heffernan & Moseman
Hazeltine Corp. - 49-D
Inter-regional Financial Group Leasing Co. - 49-D

Heinhold Commodities Inc. - 23-D

Helen Keller National Center - 13-D

Helen Wodell Halbach Estate - 21-D

Help Inc. - 13-D

Hemisphere National Bank - 28-D

Heron, Catherine L. - 51-D

Hervey, Fred - 17-D

Heth, Pat I. - 38-D

Hetherington, Kim - 51-D

Hewlett-Packard Co. - 49-D

Higgins, Lawrence P. - 20-D

Highly Enterprise Corp. - 10-D

Hilderley, Clifton T. Jr. - 19-D

Hill and Knowlton Inc.
Florists' Transworld Delivery - 37-D

Hill Associates - 49-D

Hillcrest Equities Inc. - 43-D

Hillings, E. Joseph - 37-D

Hillsdale County Railway Co. - 4-D, 7-D

Hiram Walker & Sons Inc. - 10-D

Hitchner, Stephen - 32-D

Hoffheimer & Johnson
Helen Keller National Center - 13-D

Hoffheimer, Lawrence S. - 16-D

Hoffman, Thomas F. - 48-D

Hoffmann, F. Nordy, and Associates Inc.
EPIC - 11-D
Marine Engineers Beneficial Association - 11-D
Page Airways - 11-D
Westinghouse Electric Corp. - 11-D

Hogan & Co. Inc. - 37-D

Hogan & Hartson
Atari Inc. - 48-D
Design Professions Group - 40-D
Digital Equipment Corp. - 48-D
Glendale Federal Savings & Loan Association - 33-D
Hewlett-Packard Co. - 49-D
Intel Corp. - 49-D
National Hospice Education Project - 41-D

Hogg, James F. - 17-D
Holayter, William J. - 25-D
Holiday Inns Inc. - 33-D
Holladay, Philip C. - 39-D
Holland, Stephen B. - 48-D
Holland & Knight
  RSV Mining Equipment B.V. - 34-D
Hollywood Inc. - 33-D
Home Health Services & Staffing Association - 35-D
Home Recording Rights Coalition - 16-D, 20-D, 26-D
Hoover, Lillie E. - 47-D
Hope, Judith Richards - 18-D
Hopkins & Sutter
  CBI Industries Inc. - 32-D
  Congoleum Corp. - 32-D
  Management Insights Inc. - 33-D
Horn & Hardart Co. - 43-D
Hospital Corporation of America - 37-D
Houston Endowment Inc. - 36-D
Houston Natural Gas Corp. - 18-D, 37-D
Houston Post Co. - 37-D
Howell, Jack M. - 44-D, 47-D
Howes, John A. - 28-D
Hoyer, Mary - 27-D
HTB Corp. - 7-D
Hudson, Betty - 37-D
Hudson, Creyke, Koehler & Tacke
  James P. Purvis - 9-D
Hudson Securities Inc. - 4-D
Huffington, Roy M. Inc. - 37-D, 43-D
Hughes & Hill
  American General Life Insurance Co. - 32-D
  American National Insurance Co. - 32-D
  Fidelity Union Life - 49-D
  Republic National Life Insurance Co. - 34-D
Hughes, Hubbard & Reed
  Continental Air Lines Inc. - 32-D
Hughes, Vincent C. - 43-D
Humana Inc. - 23-D
Hunt Inc. - 33-D
Hunt, James H. - 3-D
Hunter, J. Robert - 3-D
Hunton & Williams - 29-D
Hutchinson, Robert E. - 17-D
Hvide Shipping Inc. - 33-D
Hyde, Isabel E. - 14-D

I

Ichord, Richard H. - 48-D
Ideal Basic Industries - 29-D
IFG Leasing Co. - 18-D
Ikard, Frank - 33-D, 42-D
Illinois Bell Telephone Co. - 14-D
Inco United States Inc. - 37-D
Indeco Inc. - 33-D
Independent Data Communications Manufacturers Association Inc. - 51-D
Independent Federal Savings - 49-D
Independent Gas Producers Committee - 20-D
Independent Petroleum Association of the Mountain States - 45-D
Independent Valley Energy Co. - 37-D
Index - 4-D
India, Embassy of - 8-D
Industrial Union Department, AFL-CIO - 50-D
Industrial Union of Marine & Ship-building Workers of America, AFL-CIO Local 9 - 8-D
Inexco Oil Co. - 10-D
Ingersoll-Rand Co. - 37-D
Inland Steel Corp. - 14-D
Institute for Public Representation - 27-D

Institute for Public Representation, Georgetown University Law Center - 45-D
Institute of Electrical and Electronics Engineers Inc., The - 31-D
Instituto Brasileiro do Cafe (Brazilian Coffee Institute) - 35-D
Insurance Association of Connecticut - 35-D
Insurance Economic Society of America - 40-D
Intel Corp. - 49-D
Intelsat - 23-D
Intermedics - 49-D
Intermountain Health Care - 38-D
International Association of Drilling Contractors - 20-D
International Association of Machinists and Aerospace Workers - 25-D
International Business Machines Corp. - 10-D, 38-D
International District Heating Association - 16-D
International Futures Exchange (Bermuda) Ltd. - 18-D, 38-D
International Telephone & Telegraph Corp. - 38-D, 46-D
International Titanium Inc. - 29-D
Inter-Regional Financial Group Leasing - 49-D
Intex Holdings (Bermuda) Ltd. - 18-D, 38-D
Investment Company Institute - 12-D, 26-D, 51-D
Irvine Co., The - 29-D
Italian Aerospace Industries (U.S.A.) Inc. - 43-D
ITT Corp. - 33-D
Ivins, Phillips & Barker
  Employers Council on Flexible Compensation - 26-D

J

Jacobs Engineering Group Inc. - 49-D
Jacques Borel Enterprises Inc. - 10-D
Jaffe, Daniel L. - 25-D
James M. Hanley and Associates
  Alliance of Third Class Non-profit Mailers - 17-D
Janke, James F. - 32-D
Japan Fisheries Association - 16-D
Jarmin, Gary L. - 7-D
Jeffers, Patricia A. - 16-D
Jefferson-Pilot Corp. - 38-D
Jensen, Sanders & McConnell
  Carma-Sandling Group - 14-D
  Santa Ana River Flood Protection Agency - 11-D
Jessick, Nancy H. - 10-D
Jewelry Industry Coordinating Committee - 40-D
JMB Realty Corp. - 33-D
John Adams Associates - 14-D
Johnson & Swanson
  Hunt Oil Co. - 33-D
Johnson, Alfred E. - 10-D
Johnson, Carl T. - 3-D
Johnson, Larry W. - 13-D
Johnson Scandar - 38-D
Johnson, Smith and Hibbard
  Milliken & Co. - 8-D, 10-D
  Waste Management Inc. - 30-D
Johnson, William L. - 24-D
Johnston, T. Glenn - 11-D
Joint Task Force on Federal Financial Assistance for Law Students - 21-D
Joint Trawlers (North America) Ltd. - 10-D
Jolly, Mary Karen - 7-D
Jones, Day, Reavis & Pogue
  American Motors Corp. - 36-D

Hanna Mining Co., The - 37-D
International Telephone & Telegraph Corp. - 38-D
Landau, Dr. Ralph - 41-D
Marathon Oil Co. - 4-D
Mississippi Chemical Corp. - 29-D
Pfizer Inc. - 38-D
Pharmaceutical Manufacturers Association - 41-D
Jones & Winburn
  American Association of Equipment Lessors - 20-D, 35-D
  Brown and Williamson Tobacco Corp. - 42-D
  City of Baton Rouge - 34-D
  Direct Selling Association - 45-D
  R.J. Reynolds Tobacco Co. - 43-D
Jones, Theodore L. - 35-D
Jordan, Donald L. - 31-D
Joseph, Powell, McDermott & Reiner
  Civil Pilots for Regulatory Reform - 30-D
Journal Co. - 18-D

K

K-A Co. - 29-D
K & S Associates Inc. - 43-D
Kaiser Foundation Health Plan Inc. - 38-D
Kansas City Southern Railway - 4-D
Kaplan, Russin & Vecchi
  Tadiran Israel Electronics Industries Ltd. - 29-D
Kaswell, Perazich & Watson
  Marriott Corp. - 38-D
Katz, Linda E. - 45-D, 46-D
Kaye, Scholer, Fierman, Hayes & Handler
  Chris Craft Industries Inc. - 36-D
Keating, Richard F. - 10-D
Keefe Co., The - 42-D
Keefer, Joseph D. - 41-D
Kemp, Klein, Endelman & Beer
  M.A.N. Truck and Bus Corp. - 33-D
Kennedy, Art - 28-D
Kennedy, Michael E. - 8-D, 12-D
Kent and O'Connor Inc
  Gould Inc. - 43-D
  Motor Carrier Lawyers Association - 20-D
Kent, Phil - 21-D
Kerr-McGee Corp. - 38-D
Keto, George John - 43-D
Kiawah Island Co. - 18-D
Kidder, Peabody - 23-D
Kiefer & Morrison
  American Fur Industry Inc. - 12-D
  Fur Conservation Institute of America - 12-D
Kilgore & Kilgore Inc.
  Deminex U.S. Oil Co. - 10-D, 17-D
  Texasgulf Inc. - 19-D
Kimberly-Clark Corp. - 33-D
King, William P. - 51-D
King and Spaulding - 23-D
Kinney, Frank J. - 12-D
Kirkpatrick, Lockhart, Hill, Christopher & Phillips
  American Stock Exchange - 28-D
  Council of State Housing Agencies - 11-D
  Grocery Manufacturers of America - 16-D
  Southern Shipbuilding Corp. - 15-D
Kirlin, Campbell & Keating
  Council of European & Japanese National Shipowners' Association - 31-D
Kirshner, Robert A. - 45-D
Klasky, Terrence H. - 3-D, 4-D, 6-D
Kline Iron & Steel Co. - 23-D
Knoder, C. Eugene - 7-D

Koch, Patrick C. - 27-D
Kominers, Fort, Schlefer & Boyer
  Committee for Title XI Vessel Financing - 12-D
Kopp, Eugene P. - 8-D
Kopperud, Steven L. - 16-D
Kostmayer, Peter H. - 14-D
Koteen & Burt
  CSL Energy Controls Inc. - 3-D
Krajewski, Thomas G. - 5-D
Krivit & Krivit
  City of Camden - 46-D
Krone, James C. - 31-D
Kunofsky, Judith - 13-D
Kushan, E. J. - 8-D
Kuss, Henry J. - 48-D
Kutak, Rock & Huie
  First National Bank of Omaha - 49-D
  Hayes Inc. - 18-D
  Pearlstine, Salkin, Hardiman & Robinson - 38-D
Kwajalein Atoll Corp. - 23-D

L

Lacopo, John D. - 10-D
Ladd, Bruce C. Jr. - 29-D
Ladd, Mabel R., Estate of - 47-D
Ladig, Robert A. - 29-D
Lake, James H. - 9-D, 30-D, 40-D, 48-D
Lake Oswego Corp. - 49-D
Lambert, David M.F. - 48-D
Lambright, Stephen K. - 32-D
Landau, Ralph - 41-D
Landgraf, Charles - 23-D
Lane, Richard F. - 26-D
Larkin, McCarthy, Noel & Falk
  American Ship Building Co. - 48-D
Latham, Watkins & Hills
  Irvine Co., The - 29-D
  Safran, Thomas & Associates - 29-D
  Wilshire Terrace Cooperative Housing Corp. - 8-D
Lathrop, Koontz
  AAI Corp. - 48-D
Lavin, V. Michele - 3-D
LaVor, Joan H. - 40-D
Lawyers Title Insurance Corp. - 29-D
Leaf Tobacco Exporters Association - 35-D
Leaffer Co. Inc., The - 18-D
League of Women Voters of the United States - 47-D
Lear Siegler Inc. - 10-D
Leary, Cornelius J. - 35-D
Lease Management Corp. - 33-D
Lebanese Information and Research Center - 44-D
Leboeuf, Lamb, Leiby & Macrae
  Registration - 23-D
Lee, Robert C. - 47-D
Lee, Thomas J. Jr. - 23-D
Lee, Toomey & Kent
  Squibb Corp. - 44-D
Legal Services Corp. - 23-D
Lehman Brothers - 23-D
Lehman Commercial Paper Inc. - 46-D
Leighton, Conklin, Lemov, Jacobs & Buckley
  National Bulk Vendors Association - 20-D
LeMond, Elizabeth - 40-D
Leonard, Betty Jane - 19-D
LeTendre, Andre E. - 36-D
Leva, Hawes, Symington, Martin & Oppenheimer
  American Electronics Association - 40-D
  Sony Corporation of America - 19-D
Levy, Leslie - 27-D
Lewis, Stuart A. - 15-D
Liberty Financial - 49-D

National Association of Real Estate Developers - 20-D
National Association of Real Estate Investment Trusts - 35-D
National Association of Realtors - 6-D, 9- D, 16-D
National Association of Retired Federal Employees - 35-D
National Association of Small Business Investment Companies - 27-D
National Association of Truck Stop Operators 9-D
National Audubon Society - 3-D, 7-D, 36-D
National Bankers Association - 51-D
National Barrel & Drum Association - 6-D
National Basketball Association - 15-D, 49-D
National Broadcasting Corp. - 29-D
National Bulk Vendors Association - 20-D
National Business and Economic Freedom Council - 7-D
National Cable Television Association - 12-D, 27-D, 51-D
National Campaign to Stop the MX - 36-D
National Cattlemen's Association - 47-D
National Center for Appropriate Technology - 51-D
National City Bancorp. - 43-D
National Coal Consumers Alliance - 12-D
National Coalition for a Free Cuba - 42-D, 47-D
National Coalition for Port Progress - 35-D
National Coalition of Telecommunications Users and Providers - 20-D
National Coalition to Ban Handguns - 21-D
National Commercial Finance Conference - 45-D
National Community Action Foundation - 36-D
National Conservative Political Action Committee - 7-D
National Consumer Cooperative Bank - 18-D
National Corporation for Housing Partnerships - 38-D
National Council for Industrial Innovation - 20-D, 27-D
National Council of Farmer Cooperatives - 51-D
National Council on Synthetic Fuels Production - 40-D
National Council on Teacher Retirement - 41-D
National Counsel Associates Inc.
  Geneva Pacific Corp. - 23-D, 37-D
  Tosco Corp. - 24-D
National Education Association - 5-D, 25-D
National Farm and Power Equipment Dealers Association - 27-D
National Farmers Union Property and Casualty Insurance Co. - 24-D
National Federation of Federal Employees - 11-D
National Fertilizer Solutions Association - 6-D
National Football League - 11-D, 15-D, 24-D, 43-D, 49-D
National Forest Products Association - 20-D, 45-D
National Frozen Food Association - 12-D
National Gypsum Co. - 15-D
National Health Care Financing Association - 6-D

National Home Furnishings Association - 12-D
National Hospice Education Project - 41-D
National Independent Dairy Foods Association - 41-D
National Insurance Consumer Organization - 3-D
National Machine Tool Builders' Association - 27-D
National Milk Producers Federation - 20-D
National Multi Housing Council - 20-D, 45-D
National Music Publishers Association Inc. - 9-D, 20-D
National Ocean Industries Association - 12-D
National Office Machine Dealers Association - 31-D, 41-D
National Office Products Association - 35-D
National Outdoor Coalition - 22-D
National Passenger Traffic Association - 20-D, 27-D
National Peach Council - 47-D
National Peanut Growers Group - 35-D
National Public Radio - 13-D
National Restaurant Association - 6-D, 27-D, 45-D
National Retail Merchants Association - 6-D
National Retired Teachers Association - 8-D, 11-D, 20-D, 27-D
National Rifle Association of America - 7-D, 9-D
National Right to Work Committee - 3-D, 36-D
National Rural Electric Cooperative Association - 35-D
National Rural Housing Coalition - 48-D
National Satellite Cable Association - 41-D
National Securities Clearing Corp. - 29-D
National Skeet Shooting Association - 13-D
National Steel Corp. - 15-D
National Tax Limitation Committee - 3-D, 17-D
National Telephone Cooperatives Association - 27-D
National Treasury Employees Union - 15-D
National Utility Contractors Association - 12-D
National Venture Capital Association - 20-D
National Voluntary Professional Society - 51-D
National Wholesale Druggists' Association - 45-D
National Women's Political Caucus - 22-D, 42-D
Nationwide Mutual Insurance Co. - 7-D
Natural Gas Supply Association - 6-D, 31-D
Nature Conservancy - 13-D
Neece, Cator & Associates Inc.
  Government Guaranteed Loan Committee, Public Securities Association - 20-D
  National Association of Real Estate Developers - 20-D
  National Venture Capital Association - 20-D
  Small Business Development Center Directors Association - 21-D
  Small Business United - 21-D
  Southeastern Lumber Manufacturers Association - 21-D

Neely, C.B. Jr. - 14-D
Neill and Co. Inc.
  Arab Republic of Egypt - 11-D
  Government of El Salvador - 34-D
Neill & Mullenholz
  National Farm and Power Equipment Dealers Association - 27-D
Neilsen, Kimberly Ann - 27-D
Nelson, E. Colette - 30-D
Nestlerode, Mal - 12-D
New Channels Corp. - 29-D, 49-D
New York Air - 29-D
New York Shipping Association Inc. - 20-D
Nicol, William K. - 32-D
Niedermeyer-Martin Co. - 49-D
Nike International Ltd. - 24-D
Nippon Electric Co. Ltd. - 11-D
Nokota Co. - 43-D
Norfolk Southern - 43-D
Normandy, Joseph M. III - 51-D
North Alabama Coal Gasification Consortium - 49-D
North American Soccer League - 15-D
North Carolina Farm Bureau - 41-D
North Carolina Peanut Growers - 27-D
North, Haskell, Slaughter, Young and Lewis - 24-D
Northern Colorado Water Conservancy District - 24-D
Northwest Pipeline Corp. - 15-D
Norton, Edward M. Jr. - 22-D
Norton, James - 22-D
Norton, Joe M. - 20-D
Norton Simon Inc. - 38-D
Nossaman, Krueger & Knox
  Food Marketing Institute - 31-D
  General Electric Co. - 43-D
  Institute of Electrical and Electronics Engineers Inc., The - 31-D
  Utotum Inc. - 46-D
Nossaman, Krueger & Marsh
  California Student Loan Finance Corp. - 27-D
  Joint Trawlers (North America) Ltd. - 10-D
  Mission Resources - 4-D
  Mobil Oil Corp. - 33-D
  Renewable Energy Institute - 3-D
Northwest Alaskan Pipeline Co. - 7-D

O

Oakland Coliseum - 39-D
Oakland County Department of Public Works - 5-D
Obey, Harry R. - 38-D
O'Brien, Fierce & Eberle
  American Electronics Association - 20-D
  Committee for Title XI Vessel Financing - 16-D
  Lobby Registration - 29-D
  Utility Group, The - 9-D
Occidental Petroleum Corp. - 49-D
O'Connell, James J. - 22-D
O'Connor, George E. - 51-D
O'Connor & Hannan
  Berenergy Corp. - 32-D
  Blyth Eastman Paine Webber Health Care Funding Inc. - 36-D
  Claiborne Gasoline Co. - 28-D
  Competitive Telecommunications Coalition - 16-D
  Crinco Investments Inc. - 33-D
  Golden Gateway Center - 37-D
  Goldman Sachs & Co. - 37-D
  Independent Federal Savings - 49-D
  Insurance Economics Society of America - 40-D
  Lord, Bissell and Brook - 33-D
  Merrill Lynch White Weld Capital Markets Group - 38-D

Minneapolis Community Development Agency - 34-D
National City Bancorp. - 43-D
Paddock Publications Inc. - 33-D
Wine and Spirits Wholesalers of America - 51-D
World Book Life Insurance Co. - 34-D
Office of States' Washington Representative to Appalachian Regional Commission - 25-D
Oglethorpe Power Corp. - 18-D
Ohio Association of Community Action Agencies - 25-D
Ohio Valley Improvement Association Inc. - 51-D
Oil Investment Institute - 45-D
Olsen, Dennis M. - 22-D, 23-D, 24-D
Olszewski, Alan M.- 9-D
O'Melveny & Myers
  Air Transport Association of America - 5-D
Oneida Tribe of Wisconsin - 22-D
O'Neill and Haase
  Cruise America Inc. - 48-D
  Glass Packaging Institute - 6-D
  Milk Industry Foundation - 51-D
  Panhandle Producing Co. - 4-D
  Sugar Users Group - 6-D
O'Neill, Kathleen A. - 20-D
O'Neill, Thomas E. - 51-D
Oregon Metallurgical Corp. - 29-D
Organization of Heater Manufacturers - 9-D, 13-D
Orly, Elvira J. - 28-D
Ormond Re Group Inc. - 46-D
Osburn, Stephen H. - 39-D
Osick, John J. - 9-D
Otaka, Hideaki - 30-D
O'Toole, Patricia M. - 30-D
Overseas Military Sales Group - 38-D
Owen, Jack W. - 35-D

P

Paabo, R. Ray - 11-D
Pacific Westbound Conference - 6-D
Paddock Publications Inc. - 33-D
Paddock, Ronald C. - 49-D
Page Airways - 11-D
Palatiello, John M. - 16-D
Palmer, Bradley D. - 48-D
Palmer Communications Inc. - 11-D, 38-D
Panhandle Producing Co. - 4-D
Papillion, Neb., School District - 25-D
Parker, J. Royal, Associates - 34-D
Parks, Prudence H. - 25-D
Parrish & Chambers Inc.
  Association of Night Vision Manufacturers - 26-D
  Forum Communications - 37-D
  Westinghouse Electric Corp. - 39-D
Patriots Foundation Inc. - 3-D
Patten, George Resources Inc.
  Florida Bankers Association - 31-D
  Westinghouse Electric Corp. - 30-D
Patton, Boggs & Blow
  American College of Mortgage Attorneys - 35-D
  American Express Co. - 17-D
  American President Lines - 22-D
  Artpac - 47-D
  Asociacion de Amigos del Pais - 25-D
  Asociacion de Azucareros de Guatemala - 25-D
  Burlington Northern Inc. - 17-D
  Chicago Board Options Exchange - 46-D
  City Investing Co. - 42-D
  City National Bank of Beverly Hills, Calif. - 32-D

E.F. Hutton Life Insurance Co. - 33-D
Energy Research Corp. - 18-D
Fluor Corp. - 43-D
Indeco Inc. - 33-D
Lockheed Corp. - 33-D
National Coalition for Port Progress - 35-D
Rockwell International Corp. - 4-D
Paul, Hastings, Janofsky & Walker
  AM General Inc. - 14-D
  American Telephone & Telegraph Co. - 32-D
  Registration - 24-D
  Security Life of Denver - 11-D, 39-D
Paul, Weiss, Rifkind, Wharton & Garrison
  Chris-Craft Industries Inc. - 32-D
  Colt Industries Inc. - 37-D
  Nippon Electric Co. Ltd. - 11-D
Peabody Coal Co. - 38-D
Peabody, Lambert & Meyers
  Government of the Virgin Islands - 30-D
  Virgin Islands Trade and Economic Development Institute - 31-D
  Yamaha Motor Co. Ltd. - 4-D
Pearce, Jack - 26-D
Pearlstine, Salkin, Hardiman & Robinson - 38-D
Pearson, James B. - 10-D
  National Conservative Political Action Committee - 7-D
Pelican Terminal Co. - 4-D
Pelton, Robert S. - 13-D
Peltz, Elin - 16-D
Peninsula Airways Inc. - 49-D
Pennag Industries Association - 45-D
Pennsylvania State Education Association - 25-D
Pennsylvania Shipbuilding Co. - 38-D
Pennzoil Co. - 29-D
Pepper, Hamilton & Scheetz
  Direct Broadcast Satellite Corp. - 10-D
  General Dynamics Corp. - 10-D
  Stromberg-Carlson Corp. - 50-D
  Turner Broadcasting System Inc. - 24-D
  United Technologies Communications Co. - 50-D
Perito, Duerk, Carlson & Pinco
  American College of Neuropsycho-Pharmacology - 6-D, 41-D
  National Association of Alcoholism Treatment Programs Inc. - 26-D
Perkins, Coie, Stone, Olsen & Williams
  General Public Utilities Corp. - 18-D
Perley, Ernest Michael - 11-D
Permanente Medical Group Inc. - 43-D
Permar, Mark - 18-D
Perry, Richard J. - 9D
Peter Small & Associates - 38-D
Peterson, Geoffrey G. - 12-D
Peterson, Lars E. - 16-D
Petrillo, Joseph J. - 6-D
Petro-Lewis Corp. - 7-D, 18-D
Pfizer Inc. - 34-D, 38-D, 43-D
Pharmaceutical Manufacturers Association - 16-D, 21-D, 31-D, 35-D, 41-D, 47-D
Phibro-Salomon Inc. - 38-D
Philadelphia Life Insurance Co. - 38-D
Philadelphia Port Corp. - 8-D
Philadelphia Stock Exchange Inc. - 24-D
Phillip Morris Inc. - 49-D
Phillips Colleges - 45-D
Phillips, George C. Jr. - 21-D
Phillips Petroleum Co. - 29-D, 34-D, 38-D
Piasecki Aircraft Corp. - 49-D
Pierson, Ball & Dowd
  International Futures Exchange (Bermuda) Ltd. - 18-D
  Intex Holdings (Bermuda) Ltd. - 18-D

National Music Publishers Association - 20-D
Pharmaceutical Manufacturers Association - 21-D
Western Farmers Electric Cooperative - 41-D
Pilliero, Daniel J. II - 25-D, 40-D
Piper & Marbury
  Ryder System Inc. - 34-D
  U.S. Air Inc. - 34-D
Pizza Hut Inc. - 38-D
Plaintiff Class, Corrugated Container Antitrust Litigation, MDL No.310 - 52-D
Plaintiff Class, Plywood Antitrust Litigation, MDL No. 159 - 52-D
Planned Parenthood of New York City Inc. - 9-D
Plywood Antitrust Litigation MDL No. 159 - 52-D
Podhorzer, Michael - 13-D
Pollack, Richard - 35-D
Pollitz, Karen - 42-D
Port of Tacoma - 39-D
Port of Wilmington - 34-D
Porter, Carol Alice - 13-D
Porter, Wright, Morris & Arthur
  Coalition for Environmental-Energy Balance - 9-D
  J. Royal Parker Associates - 34-D
Portfolio of Agriculture, Land and Natural Resouces - 50-D
Portman Properties - 39-D
Portnoy, Sharon T. - 45-D
Post-Newsweek Stations Inc. - 49-D
Potlatch Corp. - 18-D
Potter Instrument Co. Inc. - 46-D
Powell, Goldstein, Frazer & Murphy
  Association of Executive Recruiting Consultants Inc. - 12-D
  Coalition for Employment Through Exports - 20-D
  Federal National Mortgage Association - 18-D
  Gatx Corp. - 23-D
  Government of Nicaragua - 5-D
  Jacques Borel Enterprises Inc. - 10-D
  National Association of Real Estate Developers - 20-D
  National Council for Industrial Innovation - 20-D
  National Restaurant Association - 45-D
  RCA Corp. - 46-D
  Security Life of Denver - 44-D
  St. Vincent's Medical Center of Richmond - 4-D
Pratt & Whitney Aircraft Group - 24-D
Preston, Thorgrimson, Ellis & Holman
  Alaska Lumber and Pulp Co./Louisiana Pacific of Ketchikan (ALP/LPK) - 42-D
  American President Lines - 14-D
  Bellingham Cold Storage - 32-D
  Boeing Co. - 28-D
  Council of American-Flag Ship Operators - 44-D
  Pharmaceutical Manufacturing Association - 51-D
  Port of Tacoma - 39-D
Price & Glover
  Service Station Dealers of America - 17-D
Price, Barbara J. - 34-D
Private Truck Council of America Inc. - 51-D
Proctor & Gamble Co., The - 15-D
Proskauer, Rose, Goetz & Mendelsohn
  Toronto Stock Exchange - 24-D
Prosperi, David P. - 50-D
Public Citizen Inc. - 7-D, 22-D
Public Health Hospital Preservation and Development Authority - 9-D
Public Welfare Foundation Inc. - 39-D

Publicker Industries Inc. - 15-D
Puerto Rico Federal Affairs Administration - 19-D, 40-D
Puerto Rico House of Representatives - 25-D
Purvis, James P. - 9-D

Q, R

Quander, Rohulamin - 41-D
Quixote Corp. - 24-D, 49-D

R/A Associates
  Wagner & Baroody - 30-D
Radnor Corp. - 39-D
Raffa, Robert - 44-D
Ragland, Robert A. - 42-D
Rainbolt, John V. - 18-D, 23-D
Rasak, Carl L. - 49-D
Rauch, Helen - 44-D
Rauscher, Pierce, Refsnes - 24-D
Ravnholt, Eiler C. - 40-D
RCA Corp. - 46-D
Reardon, Dennis M. - 15-D
Reaves, John David - 16-D
Recording Industry Association of America Inc. - 35-D
Recording Industry of America Inc. - 16-D
Red Lake Band of Chippewa Indians - 13-D
Reduce Our Debt Foundation - 17-D
Reed, Jo - 11-D
Reed Roberts Human Resource Services - 43-D
Reeping, Pauline B. - 20-D
Refrigerated Transport Inc. - 15-D
Regional Transportation Authority - 44-D
Reid & Priest
  American Express Co. - 42-D
  B. Altman & Co. - 42-D
  CSX Corp. - 33-D
  Pfizer Inc. - 43-D
  Tucson Electric Power Co. - 34-D
Reid, Michael W. - 21-D
Reinecke, Wolfgang - 17-D
Reliance Group Inc. - 24-D
Remco Enterprises Inc. - 49-D
Rendon Co., The - 18-D
Rendon, John W. Jr. - 18-D
Renewable Energy Institute - 3-D
Republic Airlines - 4-D
Republic National Life Insurance Co. - 34-D
Republic of Indonesia - 19-D
Republic Steel Corp. - 15-D
Republicans Abroad - 22-D
Reston Advisor Committee - 36-D
Rey, Mark E. - 45-D
R.J. Reynolds Industries Inc. - 39-D, 43-D
Rice, Lois D. - 17-D
Rich, James E. Jr. - 29-D
Richard L. Sinnott & Co. - 50-D
  National Football League - 49-D
Richards, Stacy - 40-D
Riedel, E. George - 38-D
Riley, Susan - 45-D
Rinn, R. Scott - 5-D
Risso, Robin - 20-D
Ritchie, James E. - 37-D, 49-D
Rivkin, Sherman and Levy
  Savin Corp. - 50-D
  Toyota Motors Co. Ltd. - 15-D
RJR Industries Inc. - 46-D
Roadway Express Inc. - 11-D, 15-D
Roberts, Patricia L. - 34-D
Robbins, Elizabeth Jane - 8-D, 9-D
Robinson, Kenneth Michael - 6-D
Robinson, Tom - 7-D

Rockwell International Corp. - 4-D
Rogers & Cowan Inc. - 11-D
Rogers & Wells
  Desert Palace Inc. - 17-D
  Hogan & Co. Inc. - 37-D
  Magic Pantry Foods Inc. - 23-D
  Merrill Lynch & Co. - 15-D
  Merrill Lynch Commodities Inc. - 18-D
  National Coal Consumers Alliance - 12-D
Rogers-Kingsbury, Linda - 41-D
Rogol, Martin H. - 20-D
Rohm & Haas Co. - 4-D
Roisman, Reno & Cavanaugh
  Council of Large Public Housing Authorities - 9-D
Rollins Inc. - 43-D
Ronald C. Paddock & Co. - 49-D
Roncalio, Teno - 28-D
Rooney, Fred B. - 24-D, 39-D
Ropes & Gray
  Amherst College - 31-D
  Dow Corning Co. - 17-D
  Wellesley College - 31-D
Roseman, Louise L. - 15-D
Rosenberg Real Estate Equity Fund Corp. - 43-D
Roses Inc. - 31-D
Ross, Joe - 9-D
Rothschild, Ed - 41-D
Roundtable Issues and Answers - 31-D
Rowan Companies Inc. - 18-D
Rowland, Kevin - 20-D
Royal Hawaiian Cruises Inc. - 4-D
Roybal, Michael - 5-D
Royer, Robert Stewart - 36-D, 37-D, 38-D, 39-D, 41-D
RSV Mining Equipment B.V. - 34-D
Rubber Manufacturers Association - 13-D
Rudolph, Deborah K. - 40-D
Rule of Law Committee - 6-D
Rumsey, William J. - 29-D
Rupert, Clarke - 22-D
Ryan, Frank T. - 13-D
Ryan, John G. - 15-D
Ryder Systems Inc. - 24-D, 34-D

S

St. George Tanaq Corp. - 11-D
St. Joe Minerals Corp. - 7-D, 50-D
St. Vincent's Medical Center of Richmond - 4-D
Sachs, Greenebaum & Taylor
  Betz College - 45-D
  Draughons Junior College - 45-D
  Phillips Colleges - 45-D
Safran, Thomas & Associates - 29-D
Saft America Inc. - 15-D
Salomon Brothers Inc. - 39-D
Salt Institute - 9-D
Sample, V. Alaric Jr. - 7-D
San Diego Gas and Electric Co. - 50-D
Sanders Corp. - 46-D
Sandford, Charles W. - 14-D
Sandoz Inc. - 15-D
Santa Ana River Flood Protection Agency - 11-D
Santa Fe Industries Inc. - 11-D
Santarelli, Donald E. - 4-D
Sauer, Klara B. - 28-D
Save Our Security - 22-D
Savin Corp. - 44-D, 50-D
Savings Bank of Puget Sound - 44-D, 46-D
Scenic Hudson Inc. - 28-D
Schacht, Mark S. - 27-D
Schaff, Victoria V. - 23-D
Schauerte, C.M. - 36-D
Schechter, Ronald A. - 51-D

PRESIDENTIAL MESSAGES

CQ

Reagan's State of the Union Address

Following is the Congressional Record *text of President Reagan's State of the Union address to a joint session of Congress Jan. 26.*

THE PRESIDENT: Mr. Speaker, Mr. President, distinguished Members of the Congress, honored guests, and fellow citizens.

Today marks my first State of the Union address to you, a constitutional duty as old as our Republic itself.

President Washington began this tradition in 1790 after reminding the Nation that the destiny of self-government and the preservation of the sacred fire of liberty is "finally staked on the experiment entrusted to the hands of the American people." For our friends in the press, who place a high premium on accuracy, let me say: I did not actually hear George Washington say that, but it is a matter of historic record.

But from this podium, Winston Churchill asked the free world to stand together against the onslaught of aggression. Franklin Delano Roosevelt spoke of a day of infamy and summoned a nation to arms. Douglas MacArthur made an unforgettable farewell to a country he had loved and served so well. Dwight Eisenhower reminded us that peace was purchased only at the price of strength and John F. Kennedy spoke of the burden and glory that is freedom.

When I visited this Chamber last year as a newcomer to Washington, critical of past policies which I believe had failed, I proposed a new spirit of partnership between this Congress and this administration and between Washington and our State and local governments.

In forging this new partnership for America we could achieve the oldest hopes of our Republic — prosperity for our Nation, peace for the world, and the blessings of individual liberty for our children and, someday, for all of humanity.

It is my duty to report to you tonight on the progress that we have made in our relations with other nations, on the foundation we have carefully laid for our economic recovery and, finally, on a bold and spirited initiative that I believe can change the face of American Government and make it again the servant of the people.

The Economy - Past and Present

Seldom have the stakes been higher for America. What we do and say here will make all the difference to autoworkers in Detroit, lumberjacks in the Northwest, steelworkers in Steubenville who are in the unemployment lines, the black teenagers in Newark and Chicago, to hard-pressed farmers and small businessmen, and to millions of everyday Americans who harbor the simple wish of a safe and financially secure future for their children.

To understand the state of the Union, we must look not only at where we are and where we are going but where we have been. The situation at this time last year was truly ominous.

The last decade has seen a series of recessions. There was a recession in 1970, another in 1974, and again in the spring of 1980. Each time, unemployment increased and inflation soon turned up again. We coined the word "stagflation" to describe this.

Government's response to these recessions was to pump up the money supply and increase spending.

In the last 6 months of 1980, as an example, the money supply increased at the fastest rate in postwar history — 13 percent. Inflation remained in double digits and government spending increased at an annual rate of 17 percent. Interest rates reached a staggering 21½ percent. There were 8 million unemployed.

Late in 1981, we sank into the present recession, largely because continued high interest rates hurt the auto industry and construction. There was a drop in productivity and the already high unemployment increased.

This time, however, things are different. We have an economic program in place completely different from the artificial quick-fixes of the past. It calls for a reduction of the rate of increase in government spending, and already that rate has been cut nearly in half. But reduced spending alone is not enough. We have just implemented the first and smallest phase of a 3-year tax rate reduction plan designed to stimulate the economy and create jobs.

Already interest rates are down to 15¾ percent, but they must still go lower. Inflation is down from 12.4 to 8.9 percent, and for the month of December it was running at an annualized rate of 5.2 percent.

If we had not acted as we did, things would be far worse for all Americans than they are today. [Applause.]

Inflation, taxes and interest rates would all be higher.

An Era of American Renewal

A year ago, Americans' faith in their governmental process was steadily declining. Six out of ten Americans were saying they were pessimistic about their future.

A new kind of defeatism was heard. Some said our domestic problems were uncontrollable, that we had to learn to live with the seemingly endless cycle of high inflation and high unemployment.

There were also pessimistic predictions about the relationship between our administration and this Congress. It was said we could never work together. Well, those predictions were wrong.

The record is clear, and I believe history will remember this as an era of American renewal; remember this administration

as an administration of change, and remember this Congress as a Congress of destiny.

Together, we not only cut the increase in Government spending nearly in half, we brought about the largest tax reductions and the most sweeping changes in our tax structure since the beginning of this century. And because we indexed future taxes to the rate of inflation, we took away Government's built-in profit on inflation and its hidden incentive to grow larger at the expense of American workers.

Together, after 50 years of taking power away from the hands of the people in their States and local communities, we have started returning power and resources to them.

Together, we have cut the growth of new Federal regulations nearly in half. In 1981, there were 23,000 fewer pages in the *Federal Register*, which lists new regulations, than there were in 1980. [Applause.] By deregulating oil, we have come closer to achieving energy independence and helped bring down the costs of gasoline and heating fuel.

Together, we have created an effective Federal strike force to combat waste and fraud in Government. In just 6 months it has saved the taxpayers more than $2 billion — and it is only getting started.

Together, we have begun to mobilize the private sector — not to duplicate wasteful and discredited Government programs, but to bring thousands of Americans into a volunteer effort to help solve many of America's social problems.

Together, we have begun to restore that margin of military safety that insures peace. Our country's uniform is being worn once again with pride. [Applause.]

Together, we have made a New Beginning, but we have only begun.

Continued Recovery

No one pretends that the way ahead will be easy. In my Inaugural Address last year, I warned that the "ills we suffer have come upon us over several decades. They will not go away in days, weeks or months, but they will go away * * * because we as Americans have the capacity now, as we've had in the past, to do whatever needs to be done to preserve this last and greatest bastion of freedom." [Applause.]

The economy will face difficult moments in the months ahead. But, the program for economic recovery that is in place will pull the economy out of its slump and put us on the road to prosperity and stable growth by the latter half of this year.

That is why I can report to you tonight that in the near future the state of the Union and the economy will be better — much better — if we summon the strength to continue on the course we have charted.

And so the question: If the fundamentals are in place, what now?

Two things. First, we must understand what is happening at the moment to the economy. Our current problems are not the product of the recovery program that is only just now getting under way, as some would have you believe; they are the inheritance of decades of tax and tax, spend and spend.

Second, because our economic problems are deeply rooted and will not respond to quick political fixes we must stick to our carefully integrated plan for recovery. And that plan is based on four commonsense fundamentals: continued reduction of the growth in Federal spending; preserving the individual and business tax reductions that will stimulate saving and investment; removing unnecessary Federal regulations to spur productivity; and maintaining a healthy dollar and a stable monetary policy — the latter a responsibility of the Federal Reserve System.

The only alternative being offered to this economic program is a return to the policies that gave us a trillion dollar debt, runaway inflation, runaway interest rates and unemployment.

The doubters would have us turn back the clock with tax increases that would offset the personal tax rate reductions already passed by this Congress.

Raise present taxes to cut future deficits, they tell us. Well, I don't believe we should buy that argument. There are too many imponderables for anyone to predict deficits or surpluses several years ahead with any degree of accuracy. The budget in place when I took office had been projected as balanced. It turned out to have one of the biggest deficits in history. Another example of the imponderables that can make deficit projections highly questionable: A change of only one percentage point in unemployment can alter a deficit up or down by some $25 billion.

As it now stands, our forecasts, which we are required by law to make will show major deficits, starting at less than $100 billion and declining, but still too high.

More important, we are making progress with the three keys to reducing deficits: economic growth, lower interest rates, and spending control. The policies we have in place will reduce the deficit steadily, surely and, in time, completely.

Taxes

Higher taxes would not mean lower deficits. If they did, how would we explain that tax revenues more than doubled just since 1976, yet in that same 6-year period we ran the largest series of deficits in our history? In 1980, tax revenues increased by $54 billion, and in 1980 we had one of our all-time biggest deficits.

Raising taxes won't balance the budget. It will encourage more Government spending and less private investment. Raising taxes will slow economic growth, reduce production, and destroy future jobs, making it more difficult for those without jobs to find them and more likely that those who now have jobs could lose them.

So I will not ask you to try to balance the budget on the backs of the American taxpayers. [Applause.]

I will seek no tax increases this year and I have no intention of retreating from our basic program of tax relief. [Applause.]

I promised the American people to bring their tax rates down and to keep them down, to provide them incentives to rebuild our economy, to save, to invest in America's future. I will stand by my word. Tonight I am urging the American people: Seize these new opportunities to produce, to save, to invest, and together we will make this economy a mighty engine of freedom, hope and prosperity again. [Applause.]

Federal Budget

Now, the budget deficit this year will exceed our earlier expectations. The recession did that. It lowered revenues and increased costs. To some extent, we are also victims of our own success. We have brought inflation down faster than we thought we could. [Applause.]

And in doing this, we have deprived Government of those hidden revenues that occur when inflation pushes people into higher income tax brackets. And the continued high interest rates last year cost the Government about $5 billion more than anticipated.

We must cut out more nonessential Government spending and root out more waste, and we will continue our efforts to reduce the number of employees in the Federal work force by 75,000.

The budget plan I submit to you on February 8 will realize major savings by dismantling the Departments of Energy and Education, and by eliminating ineffective subsidies for business. We will continue to redirect our resources to our two highest budget priorities — a strong national defense to keep America free and at peace, and a reliable safety net of social programs for those who have contributed and those who are in need.

Entitlement Programs

Contrary to some of the wild charges you may have heard, this Administration has not and will not turn its back on America's elderly or America's poor. [Applause.]

Under the new budget, funding for social insurance programs will be more than double the amount spent only 6 years ago.

But it would be foolish to pretend that these or any programs cannot be made more efficient and economical.

The entitlement programs that make up our safety net for the truly needy have worthy goals and many deserving recipients. We will protect them. But there is only one way to see to it that these programs really help those whom they were designed to help, and that is to bring their spiraling costs under control.

Today we face the absurd situation of a Federal budget with three-quarters of its expenditures routinely referred to as "un-controllable" — and a large part of this goes to entitlement programs.

Committee after committee of this Congress has heard witness after witness describe many of these programs as poorly administered and rife with waste and fraud. Virtually every American who shops in a local supermarket is aware of the daily abuses that take place in the food stamp program — which has grown by 16,000 persons in the last 15 years. Another example is medicare and medicaid — programs with worthy goals but whose costs have increased from $11.2 billion to almost $60 billion, more than five times as much, in just 10 years.

Waste and fraud are serious problems. Back in 1980, Federal investigators testified before one of your committees that "corruption has permeated virtually every area of the Medicare and Medicaid health care industry." One official said many of the people who are cheating the system were "very confident that nothing was going to happen to them."

Well, something is going to happen. Not only the taxpayers are defrauded — the people with real dependency on these programs are deprived of what they need because available resources are going not to the needy but to the greedy.

The time has come to control the uncontrollable.

In August we made a start. I signed a bill to reduce the growth of these programs by $44 billion over the next 3 years, while at the same time preserving essential services for the truly needy. Shortly you will receive from me a message on further reforms we intend to install — some new, but others long recommended by your own congressional committees. I ask you to help make these savings for the American taxpayer.

The savings we propose in entitlement programs will total some $63 billion over 4 years and will, without affecting social security, go a long way toward bringing Federal spending under control.

But don't be fooled by those who proclaim that spending cuts will deprive the elderly, the needy and the helpless. The Federal Government will still subsidize 95 million meals every day. That is one out of seven of all the meals served in America. Head Start, senior nutrition programs, and child welfare programs will not be cut from the levels we proposed last year. More than one-half billion dollars has been proposed for minority business assistance. And research at the National Institutes of Health will be increased by over $100 million. While meeting all these needs, we intend to plug unwarranted tax loopholes and strengthen the law which requires all large corporations to pay a minimum tax. [Applause.]

I am confident the economic program we have put into operation will protect the needy while it triggers a recovery that will benefit all Americans. It will stimulate the economy, result in increased savings and provide capital for expansion, mortgages

for homebuilding, and jobs for the unemployed.

The New Federalism

Now that the essentials of that program are in place, our next major undertaking must be a program, just as bold, just as innovative, to make government again accountable to the people, to make our system of federalism work again.

Our citizens feel they have lost control of even the most basic decisions made about the essential services of government, such as schools, welfare, roads, and even garbage collection. They are right.

A maze of interlocking jurisdictions and levels of government confronts average citizens in trying to solve even the simplest of problems. They do not know where to turn for answers, who to hold accountable, who to praise, who to blame, who to vote for or against.

The main reason for this is the overpowering growth of Federal grants-in-aid programs during the past few decades.

In 1960, the Federal Government had 132 categorical grant programs, costing $7 billion. When I took office, there were approximately 500, costing nearly $100 billion — 13 programs for energy conservation, 36 for pollution control, 66 for social services, 90 for education. And here, in the Congress, it takes at least 166 committees just to try to keep track of them.

You know and I know that neither the President nor the Congress can properly oversee this jungle of grants-in-aid; indeed, the growth of these grants has led to a distortion in the vital functions of government. As one Democratic Governor put it recently: The national government should be worrying about "arms controls, not potholes." [Applause.]

The growth in these Federal programs has, in the words of one intergovernmental commission, made the Federal Government "more pervasive, more intrusive, more unmanageable, more ineffective, more costly, and above all more unaccountable."

Let us solve this problem with a single bold stroke — the return of some $47 billion in Federal programs to State and local government, together with the means to finance them and a transition period of nearly 10 years to avoid unnecessary disruption.

I will shortly send the Congress a message describing this program. I want to emphasize, however, that its full details will have been worked out only after close consultation with congressional, State, and local officials.

Starting in fiscal 1984, the Federal Government will assume full responsibility for the cost of the rapidly growing Medicaid program to go along with its existing responsibility for Medicare. As part of a financially equal swap, the States will simultaneously take full responsibility for aid to families with dependent children and food stamps. (Applause.)

This will make welfare less costly and more responsive to genuine need because it

will be designed and administered closer to the grassroots and the people it serves.

In 1984, the Federal Government will apply the full proceeds from certain excise taxes to a grassroots trust fund that will belong, in fair shares, to the 50 States. The total amount flowing into this fund will be $28 billion a year.

Over the next four years, the States can use this money in either of two ways. If they want to continue receiving Federal grants in such areas as transportation, education and social services, they can use their trust fund money to pay for the grants or, to the extent they choose to forgo the Federal grant programs, they can use their trust fund money on their own, for those or other purposes. There will be a mandatory passthrough of part of these funds to local governments.

By 1988, the States will be in complete control of over 40 Federal grant programs. The trust fund will start to phase out, eventually to disappear, and the excise taxes will be turned over to the States. They can then preserve, lower or raise taxes on their own and fund and manage these programs as they see fit.

In a single stroke, we will be accomplishing a realignment that will end cumbersome administration and spiraling costs at the Federal level while we insure these programs will be more responsive to both the people they are meant to help and the people who pay for them.

Urban Enterprise Zones

Hand in hand with this program to strengthen the discretion and flexibility of State and local governments, we are proposing legislation for an experimental effort to improve and develop our depressed urban areas in the 1980's and 1990's. This legislation will permit States and localities to apply to the Federal Government for designation as urban enterprise zones. A broad range of special economic incentives in the zones will help attract new business, new jobs, new opportunity to America's inner cities and rural towns. Some will say our mission is to save free enterprise. I say we must free enterprise so that, together, we can save America. [Applause.]

Some will also say our States and local communities are not up to the challenge of a new and creative partnership. That might have been true 20 years ago before reforms like reapportionment and the Voting Rights Act, the 10-year extension of which I strongly support. It is no longer true today. This Administration has faith in State and local governments and the constitutional balance envisioned by the Founding Fathers. We also believe in the integrity, decency and sound good sense of grassroots Americans.

Private Sector Initiatives Task Force

Our faith in the American people is reflected in another major endeavor. Our private sector initiatives task force is seeking out successful community models of school, church, business, union, foundation

and civic programs that help community needs. Such groups are almost invariably far more efficient than government in running social programs.

We are not asking them to replace discarded and often discredited Government programs dollar for dollar, service for service. We just want to help them perform the good works they choose, and help others to profit by their example. Three hundred eighty-five thousand corporations and private organizations are already working on social programs ranging from drug rehabilitation to job training, and thousands more Americans have written us asking how they can help. The volunteer spirit is still alive and well in America. [Applause.]

Other Concerns

Our Nation's long journey toward civil rights for all our citizens — once a source of discord, now a source of pride — must continue with no backsliding or slowing down. We must and shall see that those basic laws that guarantee equal rights are preserved and, when necessary, strengthened. Our concern for equal rights for women is firm and unshakable. We launched a new Task Force on Legal Equity for Women, and a Fifty-States Project that will examine State laws for discriminatory language. And for the first time in our history a woman sits on the highest court in the land. [Applause.]

So, too, the problem of crime — one as real and deadly serious as any in America today — demands that we seek transformation of our legal system, which overly protects the rights of criminals while it leaves society and the innocent victims of crime without justice.

We look forward to the enactment of a responsible Clean Air Act to increase jobs while continuing to improve the quality of our air. We are encouraged by the bipartisan initiative of the House and are hopeful of further progress as the Senate continues its deliberations.

Foreign Policy

So far I have concentrated largely on domestic matters. To view the state of the Union in perspective, we must not ignore the rest of the world. There is not time tonight for a lengthy treatment of foreign policy — a subject I intend to address in detail in the near future. A few words, however, are in order on the progress we have made over the past year re-establishing respect for our Nation around the globe and some of the challenges and goals we will approach in the year ahead.

At Ottawa and Cancún, I met with leaders of the major industrial powers and developing nations. Some of those I met were a little surprised that I did not apologize for America's wealth. Instead I spoke of the strength of the free marketplace system and how that system could help them realize their aspirations for economic development and political freedom. I believe lasting friendships were made and the foundation was laid for future cooperation.

In the vital region of the Caribbean Basin, we are developing a program of aid, trade and investment incentives to promote self-sustaining growth and a better, more secure life for our neighbors to the south. Toward those who would export terrorism and subversion in the Caribbean and elsewhere, especially Cuba and Libya, we will act with firmness.

Our foreign policy is a policy of strength, fairness and balance. By restoring America's military credibility, by pursuing peace at the negotiating table wherever both sides are willing to sit down in good faith, and by regaining the respect of America's allies and adversaries alike, we have strengthened our country's position as a force for peace and progress in the world.

Poland

When action is called for, we are taking it. Our sanctions against the military dictatorship that has attempted to crush human rights in Poland — and against the Soviet regime behind that military dictatorship — clearly demonstrated to the world that America will not conduct "business as usual" with the forces of oppression. [Applause.]

If the events in Poland continue to deteriorate, further measures will follow.

Let me also note that private American groups have taken the lead in making January 30 a day of solidarity with the people of Poland — so, too, the European Parliament has called for March 21 to be an international day of support for Afghanistan. I urge all peace-loving peoples to join together on those days, to raise their voices, to speak and pray for freedom.

National Security

Meantime, we are working for reduction of arms and military activities. As I announced in my address to the Nation last November 18, we have proposed to the Soviet Union a far-reaching agenda for mutual reduction of military forces and have already initiated negotiations with them in Geneva on intermediate range nuclear forces.

In these talks, it is essential that we negotiate from a position of strength. There must be a real incentive for the Soviets to take these talks seriously. This requires that we rebuild our defenses.

In the last decade, while we sought the moderation of Soviet power through a process of restraint and accommodation, the Soviets engaged in an unrelenting build-up of their military forces.

The protection of our national security has required that we undertake a substantial program to enhance our military forces.

We have not neglected to strengthen our traditional alliances in Europe and Asia, or to develop key relationships with our partners in the Middle East and other countries.

Building a more peaceful world requires a sound strategy and the national resolve to back it up. When radical forces threaten our friends, when economic misfortune creates conditions of instability, when strategically vital parts of the world fall under the shadow of Soviet power, our response can make the difference between peaceful change or disorder and violence. That is why we have laid such stress not only on our own defense, but on our vital foreign assistance program. Your recent passage of the foreign assistance act sent a signal to the world that America will not shrink from making the investments necessary for both peace and security. Our foreign policy must be rooted in realism, not naivete or self-delusion.

A recognition of what the Soviet empire is about is the starting point. Winston Churchill, in negotiating with the Soviets, observed that they respect only strength and resolve in their dealings with other nations.

That is why we have moved to reconstruct our national defenses. We intend to keep the peace — we will also keep our freedom. [Applause.]

We have made pledges of a new frankness in our public statements and worldwide broadcasts. In the face of a climate of falsehood and misinformation, we have promised the world a season of truth — the truth of our great civilized ideas: individual liberty, representative government, the rule of law under God.

We have never needed walls or mine fields or barbwire to keep our people in. Nor do we declare martial law to keep our people from voting for the kind of government they want.

Everyday Heroes in America

Yes, we have our problems. Yes, we are in a time of recession. And it is true, there is no quick fix, as I said, to instantly end the tragic pain of unemployment. But we will end it. The process has already begun and we will see its effect as the year goes on.

We speak with pride and admiration of that little band of Americans who overcame insuperable odds to set this Nation on course 200 years ago. But our glory did not end with them — Americans ever since have emulated their deeds.

We don't have to turn to our history books for heroes. They are all around us. One who sits among you here tonight epitomized that heroism at the end of the longest imprisonment ever inflicted on men of our Armed Forces. Who will ever forget that night when we waited for television to bring us the scene of that first plane landing at Clark Field in the Philippines — bringing our POWs home? The plane door opened and Jeremiah Denton came slowly down the ramp. He caught sight of our flag, saluted, and said, "God bless America," and then thanked us for bringing him home. [Applause.]

Just 2 weeks ago, in the midst of a terrible tragedy on the Potomac, we saw again the spirit of American heroism at its finest, the heroism of dedicated rescue workers saving crash victims from icy waters. We saw the heroism of one of our young Government employees, Lenny Skutnik, who, when he saw a woman lose her grip on the helicopter line, dived into the water and dragged her to safety. [Applause.]

And then there are countless quiet, everyday heroes of American life — parents who sacrifice long and hard so their children will know a better life than they have known; church and civic volunteers who help to feed, clothe, nurse and teach the needy; millions who have made our Nation, and our Nation's destiny, so very special — unsung heroes who may not have realized their own dreams themselves but who then reinvest those dreams in their children.

Don't let anyone tell you that America's best days are behind her, that the American spirit has been vanquished. We have seen it triumph too often in our lives to stop believing in it now. [Applause.]

One hundred and twenty years ago, the greatest of all our Presidents delivered his second state of the Union message in this Chamber. "We cannot escape history," Abraham Lincoln warned. "We of this Congress and this administration will be remembered in spite of ourselves." The "trial through which we pass will light us down in honor or dishonor to the last generation."

That President and the Congress did not fail the American people. Together, they weathered the storm and preserved the Union.

Let it be said of us that we, too, did not fail; that we, too, worked together to bring America through difficult times. Let us so conduct ourselves that two centuries from now, another Congress and another President, meeting in this Chamber as we are meeting, will speak of us with pride, saying that we met the test and preserved for them in their day the sacred flame of liberty — this last, best hope of man on Earth.

God bless you, and thank you.

[Applause, the Members rising.] ∎

President's Budget Message

Following is the text of President Reagan's budget message to Congress Feb. 8.

TO THE CONGRESS OF
THE UNITED STATES:

One year ago, in my first address to the country, I went before the American people to report on the condition of our economy. It was not a happy occasion.

Inflation, interest, and unemployment rates were at painfully high levels, while real growth, job creation, new investment, personal savings, and productivity gains had virtually ceased. Our economy was staggering under the burden of excessive

tax rates, double-digit inflation, runaway Government spending, counter-productive regulations, and uneven money supply growth. The economy, I declared, was in the "worst mess" in half a century.

To our great good fortune, there were many in the Congress who understood the nature of our difficulties and who rose with us to meet the challenge. Fundamental and long-overdue remedies were proposed and put in place. Together, we enacted the biggest spending and tax reductions in history. Counter-productive regulations have been swept away, and the Federal Reserve has taken action to bring excessive monetary growth under control.

The first year of the 97th Congress will be remembered for its decisive action to hold down spending and cut tax rates. Today, the question before us is whether the second year of this Congress will bring forward equal determination, courage, and wisdom. Clearly, there is a great deal more to be done.

Some seek instant relief from the economic problems we face. There is no such panacea. Our program began October 1, and it cannot solve in 4 months problems that have been building for more than 4 decades. All the quick fixes tried in the past not only failed to solve but actually aggravated our economic difficulties. They simply ensured a new cycle of boom and bust, of exaggerated hopes and eventual disappointment.

We did not promise the American people a miracle. We did promise them progress, and progress they will get.

Our goal was and remains economic recovery — the return of non-inflationary and sustained prosperity. We seek a larger economic pie to provide all Americans more jobs, more after-tax income, and a better life. Quick fixes won't get us there.

What will get us there is firm resolve and unwavering adherence to the four fundamentals of our economic recovery program that I outlined to the Congress 1 year ago:

● Reducing personal and business taxes to stimulate saving, investment, work effort, and productivity.

● Reducing the growth of overall Federal spending by eliminating Federal activities that overstep the proper sphere of Federal Government responsibilities.

● Reducing the Federal regulatory burden in areas where the Federal Government intrudes unnecessarily into our private lives or interferes unnecessarily with the efficient conduct of private business or of State or local government.

● Supporting a moderate and steady monetary policy, to bring inflation under control.

At the same time, I have proposed strengthening the Nation's defenses, to restore our margin of safety and counter the Soviet military buildup.

Congressional response to these proposals has been positive and gratifying. While much remains to be done, we have made a good beginning.

The Nation's fiscal policy is now firmly embarked on a new, sound, and sustainable course. For the first time in 2 decades, the destructive pattern of runaway spending, rising tax rates, and expanding budgetary commitments has been slowed, and with the cooperation of the Congress this year, will finally be broken.

● Where the growth rate of spending had soared to 17.4% in 1980, it is now declining dramatically — to 10.4% this year, and, under the budget I am submitting, to 4.5% next year.

● Where budget growth totaled $166 billion from 1979 to 1981, spending will rise by only 60% of that amount from 1981 to 1983, despite cost-of-living adjustments and the needed defense buildup.

● After having reached 23% of GNP in 1981, the Federal Government's claim on our economy will steadily recede — to 22% in 1983 and to below 20% by 1987.

● After a decade of tax-flation in which fiscal and monetary excess fueled the unrelenting rise of prices and the automatic increase of taxes, significant tax rate reductions have been enacted. A permanent safeguard against bracket creep and Government profiteering on inflation — income tax indexing — has also been created.

● Where Government had passively tolerated the swift, continuous growth of automatic entitlements and had actively shortchanged the national security, a long-overdue reordering of priorities has begun, entitlement growth is being checked, and the restoration of our defenses is underway.

This dramatic progress in reordering fiscal policy has been paralleled by a similar redirection of monetary policy. The excessive, unsustainable, and eventually ruinous growth of money and credit of the past decade has been curbed. The inflation spiral has been broken. The growth of prices is slowing down. Peoples' savings are beginning to flow out of unproductive speculation, tangible assets, and other inflation hedges back into the Nation's financial arteries where they will be available to power economic recovery, more jobs, and growing incomes and opportunities.

In short, we are putting the false prosperity of overspending, easy credit, depreciating money, and financial excess behind us. A solid foundation has been laid for a sound dollar, sustained real economic growth, lasting financial stability, and non-inflationary prosperity for all Americans.

We are also moving to shackle the regulatory juggernaut that burdened production, consumed jobs, and diminished productivity growth. During the past year no significant new regulatory statutes were enacted and few major new regulations were imposed. Additions to the *Federal Register* declined by 23,000 pages. Benefit-cost analysis was made mandatory for regulations. Dozens of existing regulations were reviewed, modified, or eliminated. Without taking into account billions of dollars of savings from regulations never formally proposed because of the changed climate our program has created, quantifiable one-time cost savings of over $3 billion and recurring annual savings of nearly $2 billion have been realized. And the effort has just begun.

A Year of Historic Achievement

These remarkable achievements are the cornerstones of our national economic recovery program. They far exceed anything that the skeptics and critics ever dreamed possible just 1 year ago. They occurred because the executive and legislative branches of our Government joined together to respond to the mandate of the American people and overcome the impediments that had paralyzed Washington for a decade. Together, we have launched a process of reform and change that can transform the course of events.

The Economic Recovery Tax Act of 1981 is the largest, most comprehensive, and most constructive tax bill ever adopted. With the cooperation of the Congress and support of the public, it was enacted in just 5 months. It addressed and substantially remedied most of the tax system's shortcomings and disincentives that had accumulated over decades — distortions that were imposing an increasingly heavy toll on investment, economic growth, and job creation.

● The penalty tax rate on investment income has been eliminated. By dropping the top rate from 70 to 50%, the attractiveness of tax shelters will be re-

The Budget Totals

(in billions of dollars)

	1981 Actual	1982 Estimate	1983 Estimate	1984 Estimate	1985 Estimate
Budget receipts	599.3	626.8	666.1	723.0	796.6
Budget outlays	657.2	725.3	757.6	805.9	868.5
Surplus or deficit (−)	−57.9	−98.6	−91.5	−82.9	−71.9
Budget authority	718.4	765.5	801.9	858.0	943.5

duced and the incentives for productive investment in stocks, bonds, new business ventures, and other financial assets will be increased. Our Nation's capital will again flow to the growth of business and jobs rather than to the vendors of protection from punitive taxation.

● Marginal tax rates have been significantly lowered for the first time in two decades. The 23% across-the-board rate reduction will mean $183 billion in lower taxes for individuals over the first 3 years. The financial reward for savings, work effort, and new production will stop diminishing and start rising once again.

● Powerful new incentives for savings have been established. Beginning this year, 50 million workers will be eligible for the first time to set aside tax-free up to $2,000 per year for Individual Retirement Accounts. The annual limit for existing Keogh and IRA investors will also be raised. By sharply altering the incentives for saving as opposed to consumption, a huge new flow of current income will be channeled toward restoring our productivity and lifting our national savings rate from last place in the industrial world.

● The taxation of phantom corporate profits has also been significantly curtailed. The new accelerated cost recovery system will shorten depreciation periods to 5 years for machinery and 15 years for structures. This will permit fuller recovery of asset costs, a more valid accounting of taxable profits, and a reasonable after-tax return on investments for the first time in years. By eliminating the drastic under-depreciation provided in previous tax law, after-tax business cash flow will be increased by $10½ billion this year and $211 billion over the next 6 years. This growing stream of funds for modernization, new machinery, new technology, new products, and new plants will revive our lagging productivity, restore our competitiveness in world markets, and spur the steady growth of jobs, production, and real incomes.

● The confiscatory taxing of estates and inheritances has been halted as well. By raising the exemption to $600,000, by lowering the rate to 50%, and by removing the limits on the marital deduction, 99.7% of all estates will eventually be exempt from estate taxation. Hard-working American farmers, small businessmen, investors, and workers can once again be confident that the sweat, sacrifices, and accumulations of a lifetime will belong to their heirs rather than their Government.

● Government profiteering on inflation has been abolished. Beginning in 1985, the individual income tax brackets, the zero-bracket amount, and the personal exemption will be corrected annually for inflation. Bracket creep will never again systematically plunder the rewards for production and effort. Government will never again use inflation to take a rising share of the people's income without a vote of their representatives.

The past year's achievements on spending control and the reestablishment of budgetary discipline are no less impressive than the sweeping tax changes. For the first time ever, the Congress activated its central budgetary machinery and overcame the spending impulses of its fragmented parts. The Omnibus Budget Reconciliation Act of 1981 was a watershed in fiscal history — a giant step toward the restoration of fiscal discipline. By the accounting of its own Congressional Budget Office, spending will be $35 billion lower this year and about $130 billion lower over the next 3 years due to just one bill passed in only 5 months after having been considered by 30 different committees, a bill that reduced, reformed or eliminated hundreds of programs. The growth of budgetary outlays is at last being brought in line with the growth of the tax base and the national income. Excess spending commitments, unnecessary programs and overlapping activities were meaningfully addressed in the Reconciliation Act for the first time in decades.

● As a result of congressional action in 1981, the growth of entitlements will be reduced by $41 billion during the next 3 years. For the first time, eligibility standards for food stamps and student loans have been tightened. Unemployment benefits have been targeted to States where they are needed. Subsidies for non-needy students have been reduced in the school lunch program. Abuses of the Medicaid, nutrition, and AFDC programs have been curtailed, saving $14.4 billion over the next 3 years. Overly generous and unaffordable twice-a-year cost-of-living adjustments for Federal retirees have been eliminated. The "uncontrollables" are being brought under control, and benefits have been retargeted where they are most needed.

● Dozens of ineffective or counter-productive programs have been eliminated or reduced. The $4 billion make-work CETA public sector jobs program was abolished. Extravagant dairy subsidies have been cut substantially. The ineffective $700 million Economic Development Administration is being phased out. The Community Services Administration has been eliminated. An unnecessary $2 billion in Government subsidies for new energy supplies and technologies has been cut. The excessively-funded impact aid program was substantially scaled back. In short, a long-overdue housecleaning of excess budgetary commitments was accomplished.

● Inappropriate Federal subsidies have been withdrawn. Legislation to return Conrail to the private sector has been enacted. The National Consumer Cooperative Bank has been privatized. Subsidies to the auto industry for new technology demonstrations have been eliminated. Operating subsidies to local mass transit systems are being phased out. Subsidies to exporters have been sharply curtailed. Subsidized disaster loans to financially viable businesses have been eliminated.

● A major stride toward rationalizing the structure, reducing the cost, and increasing State and local flexibility in the Nation's $91 billion grant-in-aid system has been enacted. Fifty-seven narrow, redtape-ridden categorical grants programs have been replaced with 9 block grants. The pages of regulation imposed on State and local governments have been reduced from over 300 to 6, while the cost to the Federal budget has been reduced.

● Total funding for nondefense discretionary programs has been reduced. After continuous growth for two decades, the budget cost of these programs will actually decline from $137 billion in 1981 to $130 billion in 1982.

● An impressive start at reducing fraud, waste, abuse, and unnecessary Government overhead was made. The President's Council on Integrity and Efficiency, established to coordinate a Government-wide attack on fraud and waste, saved $2 billion in the last 6 months of 1981 alone. A comprehensive effort to collect $33 billion in delinquent debts has been launched and will recover $1.5 billion in 1982 and $4.0 billion in 1983. These estimates include recoveries of delinquent taxes due to the Internal Revenue Service. Federal nondefense employment has been reduced by 35,000 since January 1981. The cost of Government travel, publications, and consultants has been reduced substantially.

At the same time that the Congress joined in these long-overdue efforts to pare back the size of the Federal budget and slow its momentum of growth, it has fully supported our ambitious but essential plan to rebuild our national defense. A year ago every component of military strength was flashing warning lights of neglect, under-investment, and deteriorating capability. Today, health is being restored.

● Pervasive deficiencies in readiness — including too many units not ready for combat, too many weapons systems out of commission, too few people with critical combat skills, and too few planes and ships fully capable of their missions — are being corrected. Funds for operations and maintenance, including training and aircraft flying hours, have been boosted. Backlogs of combat equipment needing repair are being eliminated. Adequate supplies of spare parts necessary to support high operating rates for training, as well as to provide war reserves, are being purchased.

● The serious inadequacy in pay and benefits that threatened the all-volunteer force, caused an exodus of skilled personnel, and sapped morale throughout the armed services has been corrected. Last year's 14.3% pay increase has improved recruit quality, boosted reenlistment rates, stopped the drain of critical skills, and contributed to the dramatic revival of morale in our military services. End-strength goals are now being exceeded. In addition, the percentage of recruits with higher test scores has risen in the past year.

● Critical investments in conventional and strategic force modernization are now moving rapidly forward. A new bomber for early deployment and an advanced (Stealth) bomber for the 1990's have been

approved to retain our capability to penetrate Soviet air defenses. Development of a new, larger, and more accurate MX missile to preserve our land-based deterrent is proceeding. A 5-year shipbuilding program including 133 new ships and a total investment of $96 billion — double the 5-year program of the previous administration — has been launched. Rapid production of new combat systems including the M-1 Abrams tank, the AV-8B Marine Corps attack aircraft and the F/A-18 Navy tactical fighter have been approved. Improvements in our airlift and sealift forces to transport equipment and soldiers rapidly to counter military aggression anywhere in the world, are moving forward.

No Time to Retreat

These achievements of the first year truly constitute a new beginning. In every major dimension of national strength and well-being we have launched the redirection of policy that was so desperately needed and so long overdue. We are ending the destructive inflation and the financial disorder built up over a decade. We have removed the yoke of over-taxation from our workers and our business enterprises. We have begun to dismantle the regulatory straitjacket that impeded our commerce and sapped our prosperity. And we have reversed the dangerous erosion of our military capabilities.

The task before us now is a different one, but no less crucial. Our task is to persevere; to stay the course; to shun retreat; to weather the temporary dislocations and pressures that must inevitably accompany the restoration of national economic, fiscal, and military health.

The correction of previous fiscal and monetary excesses has come too late to avert an unwelcome, painful, albeit temporary business slump. In the months ahead there will be temptation to resort to pump-priming and spending stimulus programs. Such efforts have failed in the past, are not needed now, and must be resisted at every turn. Our program for permanent economic recovery is already in place. Artificial stimulants will undermine that program, not reinforce it.

Likewise, previous excesses in money and credit growth have resulted in financial strain in many regions and sectors of our national economy. The adjustment to lower inflation and a more moderate money and credit policy did not come soon enough to avoid interest rates and unemployment far higher than we would like, and that we are working to reduce. But these effects are temporary. They cannot be remedied by a return to rapid, unsustainable expansion of Federal spending and money growth, which would drive inflation and interest rates to new highs. Our hard-won gains in reducing inflation must be preserved and extended — because permanent reduction of interest rates and unemployment is impossible if the fight against inflation is abandoned, just when it is being won.

Similarly, our budget deficits will be large because of the current recession, and because it is impossible in a short period of time to correct the mistakes of decades. But our incentive-minded tax policy and our security-based defense programs are right and necessary for long-run peace and prosperity, and must not be tampered with in a vain attempt to cure deficits in the short-run. The answer to deficits is economic growth and indefatigable efforts to control spending and borrowing. These principles we dare not abandon.

The Deficit Problem: Its Origins

Despite the new course we have charted and the gains we have achieved, the voices of doubt, retreat and rejection are beginning to rise. They conveniently forget that the present business slump was not caused by our program but is the result of the accumulated burdens of past policy errors, which we have taken action to redress. They fail to comprehend that our spending cuts and tax reductions were not designed to redistribute the output of a stagnant economy, but to revive the economy's growth and to increase its size — for the jobless as well as the affluent, for those who aspire to get ahead as well as those who have already arrived.

Increasingly, the larger budget deficits that we unavoidably face are offered as evidence that our entire course should be recharted. The matter of budget deficits, therefore, must be addressed squarely. We must fully comprehend why they have grown from our original projections, why they may remain with us for some time to come, what dangers they pose if not vigorously combatted and what steps we can and must take to steadily reduce their size and drain on our available savings.

Our original plan called for a balanced budget in 1984. Balance is no longer achievable in 1984, but the factors that have postponed its realization are neither permanent nor cause for abandoning the goal of eventually living within our means.

In the near term, the most important setback to our budgetary timetable is the recession now underway. During 1982, receipts will decline by $31 billion and outlays rise by $8 billion due to the fall-off of business activity and the increase of unemployment-related payments. This factor alone accounts for nearly all of the difference between the $45 billion 1982 deficit we projected last year and our current estimate of $98.6 billion.

While the recession will end before this fiscal year is over, its budgetary impact will spill over for many years into the future. It will take time for the unemployment rate to come down and safety net payments to diminish. The growth of receipts will recover, but not at the levels previously projected. This will add billions to deficits for 1983 and 1984.

The second major factor widening the deficit projection is interest payments on our trillion dollar debt. Here we are being penalized doubly for the misguided policies of the past.

The discredited philosophy of spend and spend, borrow and borrow, saddled us with a permanent debt burden of staggering dimensions. This year's interest payment of $83 billion exceeds the size of the entire Federal budget as recently as 1958.

In addition, past fiscal, monetary, and credit excesses have resulted in temporarily high interest rates — rates that will come down, but only as inflation abates, private and public financing practices adjust, and long-term confidence rebuilds. Since market confidence has been so badly shaken by runaway inflation and interest rates in the past 3 years, it is apparent that interest rates over the next several years will fall less rapidly than we had originally anticipated. Between the huge inherited base of national debt, the high interest rates, and the large prospective additions to the national debt in the next several years, our total debt service costs will rise substantially.

Interest payments on the debt will exceed our original projections by $18 billion in 1982, $32 billion in 1983, and $182 billion over 1982-86 taken as a whole. The interest rate/debt service factor, then, constitutes a major source of the setback to our budget timetable. But let us be clear about its origins: it arises primarily from a legacy of past excesses, not from a shortfall in our current budget control efforts, nor from a flaw in our overall program.

The third and most important factor contributing to the growth in deficit projections is quite simply the ironic by-product of our rapid and decisive success in bringing down the rate of inflation. Our economic forecast last February projected a 9.5% inflation rate in calendar year 1981 and a further decline to 7.7% in 1982. This projection was scorned by many as too rosy just 1 year ago. Yet the actual inflation rate in 1981 turned out to be lower than our projection, and the inflation decline this year and next year almost certainly will exceed our earlier projections.

This is welcome news to every American and we have adjusted our inflation forecast accordingly. But lower rates of price increase also mean lower inflation components in wages and incomes and a reduced flow of inflation-swollen tax receipts to the Treasury.

This point is not merely academic. Over the next 5 years, our forecast projects a 9.9% average rate of growth in nominal GNP reflecting a steady fall of inflation to about 4½% by 1987. If nominal GNP growth were just 2% higher each year, reflecting a continuation of higher inflation, Federal receipts would be enlarged by the staggering sum of $353 billion over the 5 years. On paper, at least, the budget would be nearly balanced in 1987 rather than more than $50 billion in deficit.

But if the last decade offers any lesson, it is that we cannot inflate our way to budget balance. Indeed, every budget from 1975 forward projected a balanced budget 2 years into the future and growing surpluses

in the out-years. Not one of these surpluses materialized for a very compelling reason: the monetary excesses needed to finance inflationary growth of wages and incomes are the enemy of savings, investment, real economic growth, and fundamental business confidence and financial stability. They lead to the kind of pervasive economic breakdown that we experienced during 1979-81 — a breakdown that swells Government spending, interrupts the flow of receipts, and causes prospective budgetary surpluses to vanish in a flow of red ink.

Thus, we cannot and will not pursue the will-o'-the-wisp of reflation nor the phantom of future budget surpluses premised on a continuance of high inflation.

Instead, we must recognize that for a period of time, success in our unyielding battle against inflation will appear to work against our goal of a balanced budget. Thus, while our current revenues will reflect the decline of inflation today, part of our current outlays will reflect the higher rates of inflation in years past. This is especially true in the case of some $249 billion in indexed programs. Generally, the inflation rate used to adjust indexed benefits lags a year or more behind the current payment period. During 1983, for example, an inflation rate of 6.5% is projected, but cost-of-living adjustments to social security and other program benefits will be 8.1% based largely on the actual inflation experience of 1981. Much the same is true of the $96.4 billion in debt service for 1983. Some part of that will reflect the higher cost of debt securities issued in 1980-82 when inflation and interest rates will have been higher than is now projected for 1983.

Thus, the conquest of inflation will contribute to budgetary imbalance for some years to come. But these deficits will prove manageable if we understand why we have them and redouble our efforts to reduce them.

The final factor contributing to the worsening of the deficit outlook is that all of the budget savings we had planned for last year were not actually achieved. Most importantly, our plan to ensure the short- and long-run solvency of social security was discarded by the Congress. In an effort to eliminate partisanship and facilitate movement toward a constructive solution, our reform proposal has been withdrawn in favor of a bipartisan commission charged with developing a plan to rescue the social security system by next fall. I am confident that the commission will do just that, but in the meanwhile our outlay projections must be increased by $6 billion in 1983 and $18 billion for 1987.

Likewise, the Congress failed to adopt all of the reforms we proposed for medicaid, guaranteed student loans, food stamps and other entitlements. Without further action, about $4 billion would be added to the 1983 deficit in these areas alone. While major and unprecedented action was taken to curb the growth of entitlements last year, the shortfall is still substantial. Entitlement reforms not acted upon by the Congress last year will add nearly $20 billion to the deficit over the next 3 years. When this is combined with substantial added outlays for farm subsidies and for discretionary programs that were not reformed, it is clear that the task of budget control is far from complete.

The Budget Deficit in Perspective

Taken together, the effects of recession, higher interest rates, declining inflation, and incomplete congressional action will mean high, continuing, and troublesome Federal budget deficits. Constant vigilance and relentless efforts to pare back future spending and borrowing will be imperative to ensure that they are not permitted to worsen and add further pressure to financial markets and interest rates.

Nevertheless, three features of these high deficit numbers must not be lost sight of even as we seek eventually to eliminate them.

First, even the 1982 deficit of $98.6 billion is not unprecedented in the context of a recession and recovery cycle. Relative to the present size of the U.S. economy, the budget deficit would have been $94 billion for 1975, followed by deficits of $139 billion, $91 billion and $97 billion in the next 3 years, respectively.

Second, these deficits reflect the excess spending commitments of past rather than new spending programs with potential to grow in the future. That means that by remaining firm in our efforts to reduce waste and excess, reform entitlements, reduce low priority spending, and gradually return domestic programs back to State and local governments, the gap between spending subject to firm fiscal discipline and revenues being lifted by steady economic expansion will gradually diminish.

Finally, the share of GNP taken in taxes will be substantially lower and the incentives for savings markedly stronger. This expansion of the total savings supply will increase our capacity to absorb deficits and give us additional time to work toward their elimination.

$239 Billion Deficit Reduction Plan

The prospect of high deficits during the transition to strong economic growth and low inflation contains a profound warning: any relaxation of our budget control efforts, any backsliding to spending politics as usual, any retreat to time-worn excuses about "uncontrollables" — that results in spending growth significantly above our projections, will mean a serious threat to the progress of our entire economic recovery program. There is precious little margin for shirking or diluting the task the American people have charged us with. That task is nothing less than a constant, comprehensive, ceaseless search for ways to reduce the size of Government and the future growth of its spending.

The 1983 budget I am presenting to the Congress faithfully adheres to that mandate. If all proposed measures are adopted, the prospective deficit will be reduced by $56 billion next year, $84 billion in 1984, and $99 billion in 1985. In short, the budget this year represents much more than simply a tabulation of accounts or a compilation of spending decisions, large and small. Instead, it represents a far-reaching, resourceful, and integrated blueprint for reducing the prospective deficit by $239 billion over the next 3 years. It is a bold action plan that, if faithfully implemented, can cut the prospective deficits over that period by nearly 50%.

Our plan for deficit reduction consists of five parts. It addresses each area of the budget where actions to reduce the gap between spending and revenues are possible and desirable.

The first area concerns nonsocial security entitlements. Despite the heartening progress we made toward reform last year, the cost of these automatic spending programs will rise to $201 billion in 1983 without further action. This figure compares to only $119 billion in 1979.

Thus, our 1983 budget proposals continue the objective set out previously: to reduce the swift growth of automatic entitlements while preserving benefits for the truly needy. If acted upon fully by the Congress, these new reform measures will save $12 billion next year and $52 billion over the next 3 years. They include new steps to tighten eligibility, reduce errors and abuse and curtail unwarranted benefits in the welfare, medical, and nutrition programs. The explosive growth of medical programs — 16.7% per year since 1978 — will be contained with tighter reimbursement standards for providers, modest copayment requirements for medicaid beneficiaries, and, later in the year, a comprehensive plan to reform the health care reimbursement system and provide new cost control incentives for all participants. We have also proposed measures to target guaranteed student loans better to those with financial need and to limit the cost growth of Federal military and civilian retirement programs.

Nevertheless, let me be clear on this point. Our administration has not and will not turn its back on our elderly or needy citizens. Under our new budget, funding for social insurance programs will be more than double the amount spent only 6 years ago. For example, the Federal Government will subsidize 95 million meals every day. That is one of every seven of all meals served in America. Headstart, senior nutrition programs, and child welfare programs will not be cut from the levels we proposed last year.

The second component of our deficit reduction plan covers domestic discretionary and other programs for purposes ranging from agricultural research to housing subsidies and manpower training. Our proposed savings here total $14 billion next year and $76 billion over the next 3 years.

These savings measures involve two essential principles. First, where programs are unnecessary, can be better targeted or

can be significantly streamlined, we have proposed substantial reductions. Our proposals to convert the fragmented and wasteful CETA training program to a block grant, to target low-income energy assistance to the colder States where it is needed, to combine the WIC program with the child and maternal health block grant, and to further reduce subsidies to business for energy technology development and commercialization are all examples of this principle.

The other principle governing discretionary programs is that we have generally not provided inflation allowances for them. This will provide a powerful incentive to reduce overhead, waste, and low-priority activities and ensure that the money we spend for many worthwhile purposes in the areas of education, transportation, community development, and research is utilized in the most efficient and productive manner possible. Our deficit problem is simply too severe to permit business as usual to continue any longer.

The third component of the deficit reduction program involves user fees, or more appropriately, the recovery of costs borne by the taxpayers generally, but that predominantly benefit a limited group of businesses, communities or individuals. Total savings would amount to $2.5 billion in 1983 and $10 billion over the next 3 years.

While the Congress made great strides on most of our proposed budget cuts last year, the user fees proposals were a noticeable and disappointing departure from this pattern. The case for action now is even stronger than it was last year. With sacrifices required of almost every beneficiary of Federal programs, it is simply inexcusable and intolerable that yacht owners escape without paying even a small part of the Coast Guard services; or that commercial and general aviation are not paying the cost of the air traffic control system that ensures their safety; or that ship and barge operators do not pay a fair share of the costs of waterways maintained by the Federal Government. Our user fee package corrects these and similar shortcomings in current budget policy and will contribute signifcantly toward reducing the deficit.

The fourth part of the plan is aimed at the executive branch and the most inexcusable of all forms of spending: lax management, the toleration of fraud and abuse, the failure to recover debts owed the Government or to dispose of properties it does not need, and outdated, inefficient, procurement practices.

Our fiscal plan has always assumed that our new management would take hold, and that savings would be possible in areas we have simply never looked at before. After 1 year, our new management team has indeed taken hold, the results to date have been impressive, and our plans for future savings are bold and far-reaching. All told, these efforts will reduce the budget deficit by $20 billion next year and $68 billion over the next 3 years.

We will collect the debts we are owed

and the taxes we are due. New legislation will be needed in some cases, but much of these savings will flow from tighter, more aggressive management throughout executive branch agencies.

Likewise, we will move systematically to reduce the vast Federal holdings of surplus land and real property. It is estimated that the Federal Government owns approximately 775 million acres, and 405,000 buildings, covering about 2.6 billion square feet. Some of this real property is not in use and would be of greater value to society if transferred to the private sector. During the next 3 years we will save $9 billion by shedding these unnecessary properties while fully protecting and preserving our national parks, forests, wildernesses and scenic areas.

Our management efforts will also be directed toward the more cost-effective procurement of the goods and services required by the Federal Government. The changes we seek will increase competition for the Government's business, reduce and simplify paperwork and regulations, and develop better standards for our procurement processes and personnel. Over time these efforts will yield large outyear savings not included in the budget totals.

Finally, our emphasis thus far has been on reducing excessive tax rates and shrinking the Government's take from the paychecks of workers and the profits of business. On that principle we will not waver. But that does not mean unintended loopholes should go uncorrected, that obsolete tax incentives should be continued, or that profitable business should not contribute at least some minimum fair share to the cost of financing Government. Thus, our deficit reduction plan includes $34 billion over the next 3 years in additional receipts from new initiatives in these areas.

About one-third of this total is attributable to our proposal to strengthen the minimum corporate tax, and a substantial share of the other tax revisions will also affect business. In every case, these measures involve the collection of a tax that is owed now or that was intended by the Congress, or elimination of incentives that are no longer needed due to the sweeping reform of business taxation contained in the Economic Recovery Act of 1981.

These new proposals will have no adverse impact on our economic recovery program, are fair and equitable, and will contribute significantly to the reduction of future deficits.

Continuing the Restoration of National Defense

Our 1983 budget plan continues the effort begun last year to strengthen our military posture in four primary areas: strategic forces, combat readiness, force mobility, and general purpose forces.

A thorough 8-month review of U.S. strategic forces and objectives preceded my decision this past October to strengthen our strategic forces. The review found that the relative imbalance with the Soviet

Union will be at its worst in the mid-1980's and hence needs to be addressed quickly. It also concluded that the multiple protective structure basing proposal for MX did not provide long-term survivability since the Soviets could counter it (at about the same cost) by simply deploying more warheads.

In addition, our review pointed to serious deficiencies in force survivability, endurance, and the capability to exercise command and control during nuclear war. Current communications and warning systems were found to be vulnerable to severe disruption from an attack of very modest scale.

The 1983 budget funds programs to correct these deficiencies. The 1983 strategic program of $23.1 billion, an increase of $6.9 billion over 1982, provides for both near-term improvements and longer-term programs. These initiatives include:

● Early deployment of cruise missiles on existing bombers and attack submarines.

● Acquisition of a new bomber (the B-1B) and development of advanced technology (Stealth) bomber for deployment in the 1990's to provide a continued capability to penetrate Soviet defenses.

● Development and procurement of a new, larger, and more accurate land-based missile, the MX.

● Continued deployment of Trident ballistic missile submarines to strengthen the sea-based leg of our strategic deterrent.

Longer-term programs include: development of a survivable deployment plan for the MX missile, development of a new submarine-launched ballistic missile, continued improvements in the survivability of warning and communications systems, and improvements in strategic defenses against both bomber and missile attacks.

The 1983 budget provides $114.3 billion in operations and military personnel costs, an increase of over $13 billion from the 1982 level to improve the combat readiness of our forces.

Today a major conflict involving the United States could occur without adequate time to upgrade U.S. force readiness. Our concerns with military readiness reflect both the long lead time required to procure sophisticated equipment (both parts and finished equipment) and past failures to provide adequate peacetime support for combat units. We cannot wait for a period of rising tensions before bringing forces up to combat readiness.

My program will continue to bolster combat readiness by increasing training, operating rates, and equipment support. There will be increased aircraft flying hours and supply inventories. In addition, backlogs of combat equipment and real property awaiting maintenance will be reduced. Also, the 1983 budget will provide levels of military compensation that will improve the readiness and capability of the All Volunteer Force.

Current U.S. mobility forces cannot move the required combat or combat support units fast enough to counter effectively military aggression in Europe, Korea

or in the Southwest Asia/Persian Gulf region. For example, at present only a small light combat force could be moved rapidly to the Southwest Asia region. Major mobility shortages include wide-body military cargo aircraft; fast logistics ships; and prepositioned ships and associated support equipment. Elimination of these shortages is an essential first step toward improving U.S. military capability during the first 30 days after the beginning of a crisis.

The 1983 budget provides $4.4 billion for:

● Initial procurement of a fleet of improved C-5 cargo aircraft, and additional KC-10A tanker/cargo aircraft that will double our wide-bodied military airlift capability by the 1990's.

● Continued upgrading of existing C-5A aircraft to extend their effectiveness beyond the year 2000.

● Conversion of four additional fast logistic ships that will provide the capability to move heavy combat forces rapidly.

● Chartering a fleet of supply ships that can be stationed with equipment and supplies in Southwest Asia to reduce the time required for deployment of heavy forces.

In the last decade, the Soviet Union introduced large quantities of highly capable, new-generation tactical equipment including combat ships, tanks and aircraft, which must be countered by modernized U.S. forces. Also, the traditional U.S. superiority in system quality has been considerably narrowed, making Soviet quantitative advantages more serious. The Soviet military force buildup has increased the risk that they may rely on military power to support their foreign policy goals. For the U.S. to maintain, in concert with our allies, sufficient conventional forces to deter potential aggression, our forces must be provided with adequate numbers of new, modern tactical equipment.

My 1983 budget includes $106.2 billion for general purpose forces (including both operations and investment), an $18 billion increase over 1982. A key initiative is an expanded shipbuilding program. The United States, dependent on open seas for commerce and military resupply, must have the naval capability to maintain control of vital sea lands. While our naval forces have declined from the mid-1960's, the Soviets have in existence or under construction eight new classes of submarines and eight new classes of major surface warships, including nuclear-powered cruisers and new aircraft carriers.

The budget provides an $18.6 billion shipbuilding program including full funding for two nuclear-powered aircraft carriers, to be constructed during 1983-87. Other ships included in my 1983 program are three large cruisers equipped with an advanced air defense system; two nuclear-powered attack submarines; two frigates for convoy protection and four mine countermeasure ships to improve fleet capability to operate in mined waters. My longer term objective is to increase the deployable battle force from 513 ships in 1982 to over 600 by the end of the decade.

In addition, the budget provides for increased production of ground and tactical air force weapons. Production rates will be increased for a variety of new systems such as the M-1 Abrams tank, light armored vehicles, and the AV-8B Marine corps attack aircraft.

All of this will be done with a major reform of the acquisition process and vastly improved management of defense operations, which will save $51 billion by 1987. In a continuing fight against fraud, waste, and inefficiency, the Secretary of Defense has appointed an Assistant for Review and Oversight and a Council on Integrity and Management Improvement.

Revitalization of American Federalism

The Constitution provides clear distinctions between the roles of the Federal Government and of the States and localities. In their wisdom, our founding fathers provided for considerable flexibility so that in following centuries these responsibilities could be adapted to new conditions. But in recent years we have not adapted well to new conditions. We have created confusion as to who is responsible for what. During the past 20 years, what had been a classic division of functions between the Federal Government and the States and localities has become a confused mess. Traditional understandings about the roles of each level of government have been violated.

Governments at all levels have had and will continue to face various problems. But, as Governor of California, I learned that a problem in one part of the country does not automatically mean that we need a new Federal program in all 50 States. Yet that is what has happened.

In 1964, total Federal grants to State and local governments were $10 billion. By 1980, total Federal grants to States and localities exceeded $90 billion, meaning that 18% of Federal tax receipts were being passed through to States and localities for one reason or another. However, these funds were not passed through entirely benignly. Attached to them were Federal rules, mandates, and requirements. This massive Federal grantmaking system has distorted State and local decisions and usurped State and local functions.

I propose that over the coming years we clean up this mess. I am proposing a major effort to restore American federalism. This transition over nearly 10 years will give States and localities the time they need to plan for themselves when and how to meet State and local needs that are now being met with Federal Government funds. My proposal will also make available to the States and localities the tax resources that would otherwise fund these programs by the Federal Government.

In coming weeks, we will have intensive discussions with local and State officials, the Congress, and many others to hammer out a proposal I will soon send to the Congress. Essentially, I believe the Federal Government should assume full responsibility for the medicaid program which assures adequate health care for the poor. In contrast, financial assistance to the poor is a legitimate responsibility of States and localities. I am proposing, therefore, that the aid to families with dependent children (AFDC) and food stamp programs be turned over to the States. This swap will clarify responsibilities substantially because these programs will become the clear responsibility of one level of government or another. That responsibility is now mixed.

In addition, I propose that more than 40 current grant-in-aid programs costing the Federal Government about $30 billion a year be turned back to the States and localities, along with the funds to pay for them. During the period 1984-87, these programs will be funded by a specially designated set of taxes to be used exclusively for financing this transition program. These taxes will be deposited in a fund that will belong to the States. Each State will be able to make its own decision on how rapidly to phase out the turnback programs. This is because each State will have two options: it may use its share of the federalism trust fund to reimburse Federal agencies for continuing to carry out turnback programs, or it may ask that the programs be terminated and then use the funds directly for whatever purposes it desires.

Beginning in 1987, the federalism trust fund will gradually be dissolved and the tax sources themselves will be made available to the States.

The key to this program is that the States and localities make the critical choices. They have the time to make them in an orderly way. A major sorting out of Federal, State and local responsibilities will occur, and the Federal presence and intervention in State and local affairs will gradually diminish.

Conclusion

While some administration proposals have been turned down, turned aside, or compromised by the Congress, the overall assessment of the past year's action on the budget is heartening. Cooperation, support, goodwill, and a genuine sense of national purpose have enabled us to make significant progress in setting the Federal Government's affairs in order and America on the road to economic recovery.

I urge the Congress to approach the new, or renewed, proposals in this budget in the same spirit and with the same goodwill as it did my proposals of a year ago. Much has been accomplished. This budget proposes that more be done.

The proposals set forth in this budget will not be accepted readily. They are a second challenging installment of a politically difficult, yet necessary, program. In their specifics, these proposals will undoubtedly be altered by the Congress. The general direction we must travel, however, is clear. I urge the Congress to weigh these budget proposals thoughtfully, and to join

me, and my administration, in a constructive effort to curb the growth of Federal spending and to provide for the Nation's security. We must, in the end, roll up our sleeves, face our responsibilities squarely, and persevere at the unending task of setting, and keeping, the Nation's affairs in order.

RONALD REAGAN

February 8, 1982 ∎

Reagan's Economic Report

Following is the text of President Reagan's Economic Report sent to Congress Feb. 10.

TO THE CONGRESS OF
THE UNITED STATES:

In the year just ended, the first decisive steps were taken toward a fundamental reorientation of the role of the Federal Government in our economy — a reorientation that will mean more jobs, more opportunity, and more freedom for all Americans. This long overdue redirection is designed to foster the energy, creativity, and ambition of the American people so that they can create better lives for themselves, their families, and the communities in which they live. Equally important, this redirection puts the economy on the path of less inflationary but more rapid economic growth.

My economic program is based on the fundamental precept that government must respect, protect, and enhance the freedom and integrity of the individual. Economic policy must seek to create a climate that encourages the development of private institutions conducive to individual responsibility and initiative. People should be encouraged to go about their daily lives with the right and the responsibility for determining their own activities, status, and achievements.

This *Report* reviews the condition of the American economy as it was inherited by this Administration. It describes the policies which have been adopted to reverse the debilitating trends of the past, and which will lead to recovery in 1982 and sustained, noninflationary growth in the years to follow. And, finally, this *Report* explains the impact these policies will have on the economic well-being of all Americans in the years to come.

The Legacy of the Past

For several decades, an ever-larger role for the Federal Government and, more recently, inflation have sapped the economic vitality of the Nation.

In the 1960s Federal spending averaged 19.5 percent of the Nation's output. In the 1970s it rose to 20.9 percent, and in 1980 it reached 22.5 percent. The burden of tax revenues showed a similar pattern, with increasingly high tax rates stifling individual initiative and distorting the flow of saving and investment.

The substantially expanded role of the Federal Government has been far deeper and broader than even the growing burden of spending and taxing would suggest. Over the past decade the government has spun a vast web of regulations that intrude into almost every aspect of every American's working day. This regulatory web adversely affects the productivity of our Nation's businesses, farms, educational institutions, State and local governments, and the operations of the Federal Government itself. That lessened productivity growth, in turn, increases the costs of the goods and services we buy from each other. And those regulations raise the cost of government at all levels and the taxes we pay to support it.

Consider also the tragic record of inflation — that unlegislated tax on everyone's income — which causes high interest rates and discourages saving and investment. During the 1960s, the average yearly increase in the consumer price index was 2.3 percent. In the 1970s the rate more than doubled to 7.1 percent; and in the first year of the 1980s it soared to 13.5 percent. We simply cannot blame crop failures and oil price increases for our basic inflation problem. The continuous, underlying cause was poor government policy.

The combination of these two factors — ever higher rates of inflation and ever greater intrusion by the Federal Government into the Nation's economic life — have played a major part in a fundamental deterioration in the performance of our economy. In the 1960s productivity in the American economy grew at an annual rate of 2.9 percent; in the 1970s productivity growth slowed by nearly one-half, to 1.5 percent. Real gross national product per capita grew at an annual rate of 2.8 percent in the 1960s compared to 2.1 percent in the 1970s. This deterioration in our economic performance has been accompanied by inadequate growth in employment opportunities for our Nation's growing work force.

Reversing the trends of the past is not an easy task. I never thought or stated it would be. The damage that has been inflicted on our economy was done by imprudent and inappropriate policies over a period of many years; we cannot realistically expect to undo it all in a few short months. But during the past year we have made a substantial beginning.

Policies for the 1980s

Upon coming into office, my Administration set out to design and carry out a long-run economic program that would decisively reverse the trends of the past, and make growth and prosperity the norm, rather than the exception for the American economy. To that end, my first and foremost objective has been to improve the performance of the economy by reducing the role of the Federal Government in all its many dimensions. This involves a commitment to reduce Federal spending and taxing as a share of gross national product. It means a commitment to reduce progressively the size of the Federal deficit. It involves a substantial reform of Federal regulation, eliminating it where possible and simplifying it where appropriate. It means eschewing the stop-and-go economic policies of the past which, with their short-term focus, only added to our long-run economic ills. A reduced role for the Federal Government means an enhanced role for State and local governments. A wide range of Federal activities can be more appropriately and efficiently carried out by the States. I am proposing in my *Budget Message* a major shift in this direction. This shift will eliminate the "freight charge" imposed by the Federal Government on the taxpayers' money when it is sent to Washington and then doled out again. It will permit a substantial reduction in Federal employment involved in administering these programs. Transfers of programs will permit public sector activities to be more closely tailored to the needs and desires of the electorate, bringing taxing and spending decisions closer to the people. Furthermore, as a result of last year's Economic Recovery Tax Act, Federal taxation as a share of national income will be substantially reduced, providing States and localities with an expanded tax base so that they can finance those transferred programs they wish to continue. That tax base will be further increased later in this decade, as Federal excise taxes are phased out.

These initiatives follow some common sense approaches to making government more efficient and responsive:

● We should leave to private initiative all the functions that individuals can perform privately.

● We should use the level of government closest to the community involved for all the public functions it can handle. This principle includes encouraging intergovernmental arrangements among the State and local communities.

● Federal Government action should be reserved for those needed functions that only the national government can undertake.

The accompanying report from my Council of Economic Advisers develops the basis for these guidelines more fully.

To carry out these policies for the 1980s, my Administration has put into place a series of fundamental and far-reaching changes in Federal Government spending, taxing, and regulatory policy, and we have made clear our support for a monetary policy that will steadily bring down inflation.

Slowing the Growth of
Government Spending

Last February I promised to bring a halt to the rapid growth of Federal spend-

ing. To that end, I made budget control the cutting edge of my program for economic recovery. Thanks to the cooperation of the Congress and the American people, we have taken a major step forward in accomplishing this objective, although much more remains to be done.

The Congress approved rescissions in the fiscal 1981 budget of $12.1 billion, by far the largest amount ever cut from the budget through this procedure. Spending for fiscal 1982 was subsequently reduced by another $35 billion. The Omnibus Budget Reconciliation Act of 1981 also cut $95 billion from the next 2 fiscal years, measured against previous spending trends. Many of these cuts in so-called "uncontrollable" programs were carried out by substantive changes in authorizing legislation, demonstrating that we can bring government spending under control — if only we have the will. These spending cuts have been made without damaging the programs that many of our truly needy Americans depend upon. Indeed, my program will continue to increase the funds, before and after allowing for inflation, that such programs receive in the future.

In this undertaking to bring spending under control, I have made a conscious effort to ensure that the Federal Government fully discharges its duty to provide all Americans with the needed services and protections that only a national government can provide. Chief among these is a strong national defense, a vital function which had been allowed to deteriorate dangerously in previous years.

As a result of my program, Federal Government spending growth has been cut drastically — from nearly 14 percent annually in the 3 fiscal years ending last September to an estimated 7 percent over the next 3 years — at the same time that we are rebuilding our national defense capabilities.

We must redouble our efforts to control the growth in spending. We face high, continuing, and troublesome deficits. Although these deficits are undesirably high, they will not jeopardize the economic recovery. We must understand the reasons behind the deficits now facing us: recession, lower inflation, and higher interest rates than anticipated. Although my original timetable for a balanced budget is no longer achievable, the factors which have postponed it do not mean we are abandoning the goal of living within our means. The appropriate ways to reducing the deficit will be working in our favor in 1982 and beyond: economic growth, lower interest rates, and spending control.

Reducing Tax Burdens

We often hear it said that we work the first few months of the year for the government and then we start to work for ourselves. But that is backwards. In fact, the first part of the year we work for ourselves. We begin working for the government only when our income reaches taxable levels. After that, the more we earn, the more we

work for the government, until rising tax rates on each dollar of extra income discourage many people from further work effort or from further saving and investment.

As a result of passage of the historic Economic Recovery Tax Act of 1981, we have set in place a fundamental reorientation of our tax laws. Rather than using the tax system to redistribute existing income, we have significantly restructured it to encourage people to work, save, and invest more. Across-the-board cuts in individual income tax rates phased-in over 3 years and the indexing of tax brackets in subsequent years will help put an end to making inflation profitable for the Federal Government. The reduction in marginal rates for all taxpayers, making Individual Retirement Accounts available to all workers, cutting the top tax bracket from 70 percent to 50 percent, and reduction of the "marriage penalty" will have a powerful impact on the incentives for all Americans to work, save, and invest.

These changes are moving us away from a tax system which has encouraged individuals to borrow and spend to one in which saving and investment will be more fully rewarded.

To spur further business investment and productivity growth, the new tax law provides faster write-offs for capital investment and a restructured investment tax credit. Research and development expenditures are encouraged with a new tax credit. Small business tax rates have been reduced.

Regulatory Reform

My commitment to regulatory reform was made clear in one of my very first acts in office, when I accelerated the decontrol of crude oil prices and eliminated the cumbersome crude oil entitlements system. Only skeptics of the free market system are surprised by the results. For the first time in 10 years, crude oil production in the continental United States has begun to rise. Prices and availability are now determined by the forces of the market, not dictated by Washington. And, helped by world supply and demand developments, oil and gasoline prices have been falling, rather than rising.

I have established, by Executive order, a process whereby all executive agency regulatory activity is subject to close and sensitive monitoring by the Executive Office of the President. During the first year of my Administration, 2,893 regulations have been subjected to Executive Office review. The number of pages in the *Federal Register*, the daily publication that contains a record of the Federal Government's official regulatory actions, has fallen by over one-quarter after increasing steadily for a decade.

But the full impact of this program cannot be found in easy-to-measure actions by the Federal Government. It is taking place outside of Washington, in large and small businesses, in State and local govern-

ments, and in our schools and hospitals where the full benefits of regulatory reform are being felt. The redirection of work and effort away from trying to cope with or anticipate Federal regulation toward more productive pursuits is how regulatory reform will make its greatest impact in raising productivity and reducing costs.

Controlling Money Growth

Monetary policy is carried out by the independent Federal Reserve System. I have made clear my support for a policy of gradual and less volatile reduction in the growth of the money supply. Such a policy will ensure that inflationary pressures will continue to decline without impairing the operation of our financial markets as they mobilize savings and direct them to their most productive uses. It will also ensure that high interest rates, with their large inflation premiums, will no longer pose a threat to the well-being of our housing and motor vehicle industries, to small business and farmers, and to all who rely upon the use of credit in their daily activities. In addition, reduced monetary volatility will strengthen confidence in monetary policy and help lower interest rates.

The International Aspects of the Program

The poor performance of the American economy over the past decade and more has had its impact on our position in the world economy. Concern about the dollar was evidenced by a prolonged period of decline in its value on foreign exchange markets. A decline in our competitiveness in many world markets reflected, in part, problems of productivity at home.

A strengthened domestic economy will mean a faster growing market for our trading partners and greater competitiveness for American exports abroad. At the same time it will mean that the dollar should increase in its attractiveness as the primary international trading currency, and thus provide more stability to world trade and finance.

I see an expansion of the international trading system as the chief instrument for economic growth in many of the less developed countries as well as an important factor in our own future and that of the world's other major industrial nations. To this end, I reaffirm my Administration's commitment to free trade. International cooperation is particularly vital, however, in confronting the challenge of increased protectionism both at home and abroad. My Administration will work closely with other nations toward reducing trade barriers on an even-handed basis.

I am sensitive to the fact that American domestic economic policies can have significant impacts on our trading partners and on the entire system of world trade and finance. But it is important for all concerned that the United States pursue economic policies that focus on our long-run problems, and lead to sustained and vigorous growth at home. In this way the

United States will continue to be a constructive force in the world economy.

1981: Building for the Future

In 1981 not only were the far-reaching policies needed for the remainder of the 1980s developed and put into place, their first positive results also began to be felt.

The most significant result was the contribution these policies made to a substantial reduction in inflation, bringing badly needed relief from inflationary pressures to every American. For example, in 1980 the consumer price index rose 13.5 percent for the year as a whole; in 1981 that rate of increase was reduced substantially, to 10.4 percent. This moderation in the rate of price increases meant that inflation, "the cruelest tax," was taking less away from individual savings and taking less out of every working American's paycheck.

There are other, more indirect but equally important benefits that flow from a reduction in inflation. The historically high level of interest rates of recent years was a direct reflection of high rates of actual and expected inflation. As the events of this past year suggested, only a reduction in inflationary pressures will lead to substantial, lasting reductions in interest rates.

In the 6 months preceding this Administration's taking office, interest rates had risen rapidly, reflecting excessively fast monetary growth. Since late last summer, however, short- and long-term interest rates have, on average, moved down somewhat in response to anti-inflationary economic policies.

Unfortunately, the high and volatile money growth of the past, and the high inflation and high interest rates which accompanied it, were instrumental in bringing about the poor and highly uneven economic performance of 1980 and 1981,

culminating in a sharp fall in output and a rise in unemployment in the latter months of 1981.

This Administration views the current recession with concern. I am convinced that our policies, now that they are in place, are the appropriate response to our current difficulties and will provide the basis for a vigorous economic recovery this year. It is of the greatest importance that we avoid a return to the stop-and-go policies of the past. The private sector works best when the Federal Government intervenes least. The Federal Government's task is to construct a sound, stable, long-term framework in which the private sector is the key engine to growth, employment, and rising living standards.

The policies of the past have failed. They failed because they did not provide the environment in which American energy, entrepreneurship, and talent can best be put to work. Instead of being a successful promoter of economic growth and individual freedom, government became the enemy of growth and an intruder on individual initiative and freedom. My program — a careful combination of reducing incentive-stifling taxes, slowing the growth of Federal spending and regulations, and a gradually slowing expansion of the money supply — seeks to create a new environment in which the strengths of America can be put to work for the benefit of us all. That environment will be an America in which honest work is no longer discouraged by ever-rising prices and tax rates, a country that looks forward to the future not with uncertainty but with the confidence that infused our forefathers.

RONALD REAGAN

February 10, 1982 ∎

Message on Caribbean Basin

Following is the Congressional Record *text of President Reagan's March 17 message to Congress on economic cooperation for the Caribbean Basin.*

TO THE CONGRESS OF
THE UNITED STATES:

On February 24, before the Organization of American States, I outlined a major new program for economic cooperation for the Caribbean Basin. Today I am transmitting this plan to the Congress for its action.

The economic, political and security challenges in the Caribbean Basin are formidable. Our neighbors need time to develop representative and responsive institutions, which are the guarantors of the democracy and justice that freedom's foes seek to stamp out. They also need the opportunity to achieve economic progress and improve their standard of living. Finally,

they need the means to defend themselves against attempts by externally-supported minorities to impose an alien, hostile and unworkable system upon them by force. The alternative is further expansion of political violence from the extreme left and the extreme right, resulting in the imposition of dictatorships and — inevitably — more economic decline, and more human suffering and dislocation.

Today, I seek from the Congress the means to address the economic aspect of the challenge in the Caribbean Basin — the underlying economic crisis which provides the opportunities which extremist and violent minorities exploit.

The crisis facing most of the Basin countries is real and acute. Deteriorating trade opportunities, worldwide recession, mounting debt burdens, growing unemployment and deep-seated structural problems are having a catastrophic impact throughout the region. This economic di-

saster is consuming our neighbors' money reserves and credit, forcing thousands of people to emigrate, and shaking even the most established democracies.

This is not a crisis we can afford to ignore. The people of the Caribbean Basin are our neighbors. Their well-being and security are in our own vital interest. Events occurring in the Caribbean Basin can affect our lives in profound and dramatic ways. The migrants in our midst are a vivid reminder of the closeness of this problem to all of us.

The program I am presenting to Congress today is integrated and designed to improve the lives of the peoples of the Caribbean Basin by enabling them to earn their own way to a better future. It builds on the principles of integrating aid, self-help and participation in trade and investment which I emphasized at the Cancún Summit last October. It is a different kind of assistance program for developing countries, based on principles and practices which are uniquely American and which we know have worked in the past. It will help revitalize the economies of this strategically critical region by attacking the underlying causes of economic stagnation. Most significantly, it helps expand economic opportunities for the people of the Caribbean Basin to make possible the achievement of a lasting political and social tranquility based on freedom and justice.

I want to emphasize that this program is not an end in itself. What we seek in the final analysis is to help the people in the Basin build for themselves a better life, not just economically but across the full spectrum of human needs and aspirations. History, and particularly the history of this Hemisphere, has shown that a pluralistic society with strong, free private institutions — churches, free trade unions, businesses, professional and other voluntary associations, and an independent press — is our best hope in moving toward that ultimate goal.

Our development program takes this into account; it will encourage progress in the beneficiary countries toward reasonable workplace conditions and opportunities for workers to associate freely and bargain collectively.

The United States has been developing this program in close consultation with the countries of the region and with other donor countries. Last July, we joined with Canada, Mexico and Venezuela to launch a multilateral action program for the region. It was agreed that each country would develop its own program but within a multilateral consultative framework. Mexico and Venezuela are operating an oil facility for the Caribbean Basin. Canada is more than doubling its aid. The program I am presenting today is our contribution.

We have worked carefully with both government officials and the private sector in the Basin countries to assess their needs and their own priorities. We have also consulted with other potential donors, including Colombia, as well as multilateral devel-

opment institutions. This program is part of an overall coordinated effort by countries within and outside the region. Its structure will insure not only that our own actions will be effective, but that their impact will be multiplied by the efforts of many others.

The program is based on integrated and mutually-reinforcing measures in the fields of trade, investment and financial assistance:

● Its centerpiece is the offer of one-way free trade. I am requesting authority to eliminate duties on all imports from the Basin except textiles and apparel items subject to textile agreements. The only other limitation will be for sugar; as long as a sugar price support program is in effect, duty-free imports of sugar will be permitted only up to specified ceilings. Safeguards will be available to U.S. industries seriously injured by increased Basin imports. Rules of origin will be liberal to encourage investment but will require a minimum amount of local content (25 percent). I will designate beneficiary countries taking into account such factors as the countries' self-help policies.

● I am proposing an extension of the 10 percent tax credit that now applies only to domestic investment to new equity investments in qualifying Caribbean Basin countries. A country would qualify for the benefit for a period of five years by entering into a bilateral executive agreement with the U.S. to exchange information for tax administration purposes.

● I am requesting a supplemental appropriation for the FY 1982 foreign assistance program in the amount of $350 million in emergency economic assistance. This assistance will help make possible financing of critical imports for the private sector in Basin countries experiencing a severe credit crunch. I expect to allocate the emergency supplemental in the region as follows:

El Salvador: $128 million. El Salvador's economy is in desperate straits. The insurgents have used every tactic of terrorism to try to destroy it. El Salvador desperately needs as much assistance to stimulate production and employment as we can prudently provide while also helping other countries of the region.

Costa Rica: $70 million. Costa Rica has a long tradition of democracy which is now being tested by the turmoil of its economy. Once Costa Rica has embarked on a recovery plan, it will need significant assistance to succeed in restoring investor confidence and credit to its hard-hit private sector.

Honduras: $35 million. The poorest country in the Central American region, Honduras faces severe balance of payments constraints, spawned primarily from falling prices of major exports and rising import costs.

Jamaica: $50 million. Jamaica's recovery is under way but continued success is still heavily dependent on further quick-disbursing assistance to overcome a shortage of foreign exchange for raw materials and spare parts.

Dominican Republic: $40 million. The Dominican Republic is attempting to adjust to drastically-reduced economic activity brought on primarily by falling prices of its major export crop (sugar) and heavy dependence on imported oil. Critical economic reforms must take place in a difficult political climate as elections grow near. Once the free trade provisions go into effect, the Dominican Republic will also receive as a result of the duty-free quota for its sugar exports immediate benefits going beyond the $40 million indicated here.

Eastern Caribbean: $10 million. Economic stagnation has dried up investment and strangled development in these island mini-states where unemployment is a particular problem, especially among youths.

Belize: $10 million. Newly-independent Belize faces a perilous economic situation brought on by falling sugar prices and stagnant growth. Belize needs short-term assistance as a bridge to the development of its own considerable natural resources.

Haiti: $5 million. Illegal immigration from Haiti is spurred by stagnant economic activity and a credit-starved private sector in a country already desperately poor.

Latin American Regional/American Institute for Labor Development (AIFLD): $2 million. Free labor movements, assisted by our small AIFLD programs, can be the underpinning of a healthy private sector and its ability to expand and grow, leading the region to stable social and economic progress.

In a separate action I am also requesting action on the economic assistance program for FY 1983. This includes $664 million in economic assistance for the Caribbean Basin. This program will be directed largely into longer-term programs aimed at removing basic impediments to growth. Although not a part of the legislation which I am transmitting today, the FY 1983 aid request is an integral part of our overall program for the Caribbean Basin. We cannot think of this program as a one-time injection of U.S. interest and effort. If it is to succeed it must be a sustained commitment over a number of years. I strongly urge the Congress to approve this request in full.

In addition to these legislative requests, I am directing the following actions, which are within the discretion of the Executive Branch:

● We will extend more favorable treatment to Caribbean Basin textile and apparel exports within the context of our overall textile policy.

● We will seek to negotiate bilateral investment treaties with interested countries.

● We will work with multilateral development banks and the private sector to develop insurance facilities to supplement OPIC's political risk insurance coverage for U.S. investors.

● The U.S. Export-Import Bank will expand protection, where its lending criteria allow, for short-term credit from U.S. banks, as well as local commercial banks, to Caribbean Basin private sectors for critical imports.

● With the governments and private sectors of interested countries, we will develop private sector strategies for each country. These strategies will coordinate and focus development efforts of local business, U.S. firms, private voluntary organizations, the U.S. Government, and Puerto Rico and the Virgin Islands. The strategies will seek new investment and employment opportunities and will also seek to remove impediments to growth including lack of marketing skills, trained manpower, poor regional transport, and inadequate infrastructure.

Puerto Rico and the U.S. Virgin Islands have a long-standing special relationship with the United States. Their development must be enhanced by our policy toward the rest of the region. We have consulted closely with Puerto Rico and the Virgin Islands about the Caribbean Basin Initiative and the legislation I am requesting today will reflect Puerto Rican and Virgin Island interests in many important ways.

● The Accelerated Cost Recovery System (ACRS) and the Investment Tax Credit (ITC) will be extended to property used by companies operating in Puerto Rico and the U.S. Virgin Islands. Similar benefits will be available to other U.S. possessions.

● Excise taxes on all imported rum will be transferred to Puerto Rico and the Virgin Islands.

● Inputs into Caribbean Basin production from Puerto Rico and the U.S. Virgin Islands will be considered domestic inputs from Caribbean Basin countries for purposes of the rules of origin.

● Industries in Puerto Rico and the Virgin Islands will have access to the same safeguards provisions as mainland industries.

In addition, we will support proposed legislation which will permit products from the Virgin Islands whose foreign content does not exceed 70 percent to receive duty-free treatment. At present the maximum foreign content permitted is 50 percent.

To further the integrated agricultural development of the Caribbean Basin, we will make greater use of the agricultural and forestry research, extension and training facilities of the Federal Government and those of Puerto Rico and the United States Virgin Islands, especially the tropical agricultural research facility at Mayaguez, Puerto Rico.

All these elements in the Caribbean Basin program are inextricably linked together, and to the fundamental objective of helping our neighbors help themselves. A key principle of the program is to encourage a more productive, competitive and dynamic private sector, and thereby provide the jobs, goods and services which the people of the Basin need for a better life for themselves and their children. All the elements of this program are designed to help establish the conditions under which a free and competitive private sector can flourish.

Most countries in the Basin already recognize that they must reform many of their economic policies and structures in profound and sometimes painful ways in order to take advantage of the new economic opportunities of this program. We — the United States and other outside donors — can offer assistance and support, but only the people in the Basin themselves can make this program work.

Some of the benefits of this program will take considerable time to mature; others are designed to have an immediate effect. But the challenge is already upon us; the time to begin is now. I urge the Congress to act with maximum speed.

I also urge the Congress to consider very carefully any changes in this program. The actions in trade, aid and investment are inter-related. Each supports the other, so that together they comprise a real spur toward the entrepreneurial dynamism which the area so badly needs. A significant weakening in any of them could undermine the whole program. In the Caribbean Basin, we seek above all to support those values and principles that shape the proud heritage of this Nation and this Hemisphere. With the help of this Congress, we shall see these values not only survive but triumph in a Caribbean Basin which is a community of peace, freedom and prosperity. ∎

Petroleum Allocation Veto

Following is the White House text of President Reagan's March 20 message accompanying his veto of S 1503, authorizing the president to allocate petroleum supplies in a severe shortage. It was Reagan's third veto of a public bill during the 97th Congress.

TO THE HOUSE OF
REPRESENTATIVES:

Although I appreciate the good faith efforts of the sponsors of this legislation, I am returning without my approval S. 1503, the "Standby Petroleum Allocation Act of 1982."

While I am sympathetic to the assertion that this bill responds to an understandable concern that our nation must prepare against the possible disruption of energy supplies, this legislation grew from an assumption, which has been demonstrated to be invalid, that giving the Federal Government the power to allocate and set prices will result in an equitable and orderly response to a supply interruption. We can all still recall that sincere efforts to allow bureaucratic allocation of fuel supplies actually harmed our citizens and economy, adding to inequity and turmoil. Further, the threat of such controls will discourage the very steps that are needed to provide real protection against such emergencies.

The Act would require the promulgation of standby petroleum allocation and price controls, including a specific program for the sharing of crude oil among refiners at controlled prices. Those controls could be imposed in the event of future petroleum supply shortages, subject to Congressional approval. The Act would also require the Federal Government to continue extensive and burdensome data collection even when the regulations were not in effect.

Today I have ample powers to take the steps necessary to protect national security, meet our treaty obligations and assure essential public health and safety functions. The supplies in the Strategic Petroleum Reserve and significant production in the National Petroleum Reserve also ensure that petroleum for truly essential needs will be available. What I do not have, do not want and do not need is general power to reimpose on all Americans another web of price controls and mandatory allocations.

We must recognize that an interruption of a significant portion of foreign energy supplies, whether because of armed strife, human choice or natural disaster, will involve real costs to the United States and the world. Proper preparation beforehand, and free trade among our citizens afterward, can mitigate these costs, but no magic federal plan can simply make them go away. Controls can only shift losses from one set of Americans to others, with vast

dislocation and loss of efficiency along the way. This was very amply demonstrated during the supply interruptions of 1973-74 and 1978-79. Those interruptions precipitated much higher oil prices, but they did not cause gas lines and shortages. It took government to do that.

The bill could be counterproductive to our preparedness efforts. In the event of a supply interruption, the best protection will be stockpiling and plans for switching to less costly ways to achieve our goals. This bill would discourage self-protective measures, because it tells the public that those measures will be nullified by government allocations and controls or that such measures are unnecessary because the government will guarantee them low-priced energy in the event of any disruption.

The current world oil situation, with declining prices and ample supplies, provides the best opportunity for future preparedness. This is why the Administration continues to add to the Strategic Petroleum Reserve as fast as permanent storage becomes available. By the end of this year we will have nearly tripled the size of the Reserve in two years. All citizens who are concerned about the possibility of shortages and higher prices in the future should use the current opportunity to prepare in ways that are appropriate to their situation.

This legislation does contain one important feature, which should be adopted immediately as a separate Act. Since 1974 the United States has participated with other countries in the International Energy Agency, in an effort to improve our effectiveness in combatting international energy problems. A coordinated response to any international oil supply disruption through the IEA requires cooperation by private American oil companies in ways that are not possible absent statutory authorization. This authorization, contained in Section 252 of the Energy Policy and Conservation Act, has been extended routinely since its enactment in 1975. The most recent extension expires on April 1st of this year. This authority should again be extended, and H.R. 5789 and S. 1937 are now pending in Congress for this purpose.

RONALD REAGAN

The White House
March 20, 1982 ∎

Message to Congress on Enterprise Zones

Following is the Congressional Record *text of President Reagan's March 23 message to Congress on enterprise zones.*

TO THE CONGRESS OF
THE UNITED STATES:

I am transmitting to the Congress today legislation entitled, "The Enterprise

Zone Tax Act of 1982." This legislation authorizes the establishment of an Enterprise Zone program, which is an experimental, free market-oriented program for dealing with the severe problems of our Nation's economically-depressed areas.

In my January 26 State of the Union message, I indicated that we would propose legislation for a new effort to review the decaying areas of America's inner cities

and rural towns. We have now completed work on this new effort and it is embodied in the proposed "Enterprise Zone Tax Act." Therefore, I am requesting today that the bill be referred to the appropriate committees and I urge its early enactment.

The Enterprise Zone concept is based on utilizing the market to solve urban problems, relying primarily on private sector institutions. The idea is to create a

productive, free market environment in economically-depressed areas by reducing taxes, regulations and other government burdens on economic activity. The removal of these burdens will create and expand economic opportunity within the zone areas, allowing private sector firms and entrepreneurs to create jobs — particularly for disadvantaged workers — and expand economic activity.

Enterprise Zones are based on an entirely fresh approach for promoting economic growth in the inner cities. The old approach relied on heavy government subsidies and central planning. A prime example was the Model Cities Program of the 1960's, which concentrated government programs, subsidies and regulations in specific, depressed urban areas. The Enterprise Zone approach would remove government barriers freeing individuals to create, produce and earn their own wages and profits. In its basic thrust, Enterprise Zones are the direct opposite of the Model Cities Program of the 1960's.

Enterprise Zones will not require appropriations at the Federal level, except for necessary administrative expenses. States and cities will still have the option of allocating discretionary Federal funds for their Enterprise Zones if they desire, or to appropriate additional funds of their own for such zones.

Enterprise Zones must be more than just a Federal initiative. State and local contributions to these zones will be critically important in the selection of the zones, and probably determine whether individual zones succeed or fail. In the spirit of our new policy of Federalism, State and local governments will have broad flexibility to develop the contributions to their zones most suitable to local conditions and preferences.

The Enterprise Zone program includes four basic elements:

First, tax reduction at the Federal, State and local levels to lessen this obvious burden on economic activity.

Second, regulatory relief at the Federal, State and local levels to reduce burdens which can be equally costly.

Third, new efforts to improve local services, including experimentation with private alternatives to provide those services. Eliminating inefficiencies of monopolized government services and increasing reliance on the private sector are key parts of the overall Enterprise Zone theme. Experience has shown that these efforts can save taxpayers substantial sums while significantly improving services at the same time.

Finally, involvement in the program by neighborhood organizations. These organizations can contribute much to the improvement of Enterprise Zone neighborhoods. They can also help to ensure that local residents participate in the economic success of the zones.

By combining all these elements we will create the right environment to help revive our Nation's economically-depressed areas.

Title I of the Act describes the program structure and how the zones will be established.

The initial designation and establishment of each zone will depend on local leadership and initiative. To obtain the Federal incentives for Enterprise Zones, State and local governments must first nominate the zones within the eligible areas as defined by the Federal legislation.

These areas will include all areas in UDAG-eligible jurisdictions which have recently experienced significant unemployment, poverty or population loss. Based on these criteria, there will be more than 2,000 cities, rural areas and Indian reservations with Enterprise Zone eligible areas.

The Secretary of HUD will be authorized to designate up to 25 zones in each of three years for the application of the Federal incentives. The actual numbers designated will depend on the number and quality of the applications.

The Enterprise Zone program is, thus, a potential source of economic assistance to distressed areas of all types, shapes and sizes, all across the country. Rural areas as well as large urban areas will be eligible to become Enterprise Zones.

After State and local nomination, these governments will apply to the Secretary of HUD for Federal designation to allow the Federal incentives to apply to their zones.

Federal designation of nominated zones will not be automatic or routine. Rather, the Secretary will evaluate the various applications on a competitive basis, choosing the best applications for the limited number of Federal designations available each year. A key criterion in this competitive process will be the nature and strength of the State and local incentives to be contributed to the zones, consistent with the overall Enterprise Zone theme of creating an open market environment by removing government burdens. Other important factors will also be considered.

In evaluating State and local contribution packages, the Federal Government will be highly flexible. For example, the Secretary of HUD will not insist upon any particular item of tax or regulatory relief. A weakness of incentives in one area, such as tax relief, could be offset by greater strength in another area, such as regulatory relief. It should be remembered, however, that the incentive packages will be competitively evaluated against each other.

Each Enterprise Zone will last for the period chosen by the nominating State and local governments. The Federal incentives will apply to an approved zone for this entire period, up to a maximum of 20 years plus a 4-year, phase-out period.

The Federal Tax Incentives of the Enterprise Zone Program —

Title II of the Act describes the Federal tax incentives to apply within Enterprise Zones, which include:

● a 3- or 5-percent investment tax credit for capital investments in personal property in an Enterprise Zone;

● a 10-percent tax credit for the construction or rehabilitation of commercial, industrial or rental housing structures within a zone;

● a 10-percent tax credit to employers for payroll paid to qualified zone employees in excess of payroll paid to such employees in the year prior to zone designation, with a maximum credit of $1,500 per worker;

● a special, strengthened tax credit to employers for wages paid to qualified zone employees who were disadvantaged individuals when hired, with the credit equal to 50 percent of wages in each of the first 3 years of employment, and declining by 10 percentage points in each year after that;

● a 5-percent tax credit, up to $450 per worker to qualified zone employees for wages earned in zone employment;

● the elimination of capital gains taxes for qualified property within Enterprise Zones;

● the designation of suitable Enterprise Zone areas as Foreign Trade Zones, providing relief from tariffs and import duties for goods subsequently exported to other countries;

● the continued availability of Industrial Development Bonds to small business in Enterprise Zones, even if the availability of such bonds is terminated elsewhere; and,

● the extension of the operating loss carry-over period for Enterprise Zone businesses, and permission for Enterprise Zone tax credits to be carried over for this period as well.

The Federal tax reductions applying to Enterprise Zones will be substantial. They will include reductions for employers, employees, entrepreneurs and investors. They will include incentives for capital investment, for hiring workers, particularly disadvantaged workers, for increasing work effort, and for starting and building up new businesses. They will include reductions in corporate income taxes, individual incomes taxes and capital gains taxes.

The Treasury Department estimates that with this tax package the designation of 10 to 25 zones in the first year of the program will result in $124-$310 million in lost Federal tax revenues for that year. The cost of the program will increase in future years as additional zones are designated and as zone activity increases.

Federal Regulatory Relief —

Title III of the Act describes the Federal regulatory relief to apply within Enterprise Zones. Under these provisions, State and local governments will be authorized to request relief for their approved zones from any Federal regulation, unless it would directly violate a requirement imposed by statute. Federal regulatory bodies will be authorized to weigh these requests under Congressionally-mandated standards, and to relax these regulations when it is in the public interest to do so, given the goals of the Enterprise Zone program.

This special authority would expressly not apply, however, to any regulations to carry out a statute or Executive Order de-

signed to protect any person against discrimination because of race, color, religion, sex, marital status, national origin, age or handicap. It would also expressly not cover any regulation whose relaxation would likely present a significant risk to the public safety, including environmental pollution. The minimum wage law would not be covered by this authority because it is specifically imposed and spelled out by statute.

It should be emphasized that there will be no authority for any Federal regulatory relief within an Enterprise Zone without a request for such relief from both the State and local governments governing the zone.

While these Federal incentives are substantial, strong State and local contributions to the zones will be necessary for the program to succeed.

These contributions can be from each of the four basic categories noted earlier: tax relief; regulatory relief; improved local services; and neighborhood organizations. More traditional urban efforts, such as job training, minority business assistance or infrastructure grants, can also be contributed

to the zone.

Consistent with the Administration's policy of Federalism, the Federal Government will not dictate to State and local governments what they must contribute to the zones. The program is designed for creative and innovative experiments by State and local governments within the zone areas. The program retains the flexibility for these governments to tailor their contributions to suit local needs and preferences.

The State and local contributions to the zones need not be costly. Regulatory relief, service improvements through privatization, and private sector involvement all entail no budgetary cost.

Even the cost of State and local tax relief should be modest because of the weak economic activity currently existing in potential Enterprise Zone areas. If the program is successful in stimulating new economic activity, these losses will be substantially offset by increased revenues from the new activity, State and local expenditures would be reduced as individuals who formerly received government aid are employed in the zone.

The legislation we advance today is based on the path-breaking work of many Members from both sides of the aisle who offered Enterprise Zone bills in prior sessions of Congress. We commend these efforts and anticipate that these innovative individuals will work for early, bipartisan passage of this legislation.

More than government expenditures and subsidies, residents of economically-depressed areas need opportunities. This is the focus of the Enterprise Zone program. The program will identify and remove government barriers to entrepreneurs who can create jobs and economic growth. It will spark the latent talents and abilities already in existence in our Nation's most depressed areas. This bold, new concept deserves to be given a chance to work. As I said in my State of the Union Address, some will say our mission is to save free enterprise, but, I say that with your help, we must free enterprise so that together we can save America.

RONALD REAGAN

The White House,
March 23, 1982 ∎

Reagan Speech on the Federal Budget

Following is the White House text of President Reagan's televised address as delivered April 29.

Good evening. My fellow Americans, you know the most important goal that all of us share tonight is economic recovery — to see our factories reopening their gates, to see the unemployed returned to their jobs and every American enjoy the fruits of prosperity.

To get our economy moving again, it's imperative that we enact a federal budget that will bring down deficits and bring down interest rates. I had hoped that when I addressed you tonight, it would be to give you the details of a bipartisan agreement on a budget and revenue plan for 1983.

As you know, yesterday marked the end of a long series of discussions to help reach such an agreement. They ended, despite our best efforts to achieve a fair compromise. But before I discuss these talks and our plans for the future, let me give the background that led up to them.

In our budget proposal, we had continued the process we started last year of trying to get control of runaway government spending. Deficits over the last few decades have been literally built into the federal structure. The rate of increase in spending was 17 percent when we took office. There's no way that government can pay for increases at that rate without gigantic tax increases each year or borrowing and adding to the national debt.

Now, this latter course has been followed for so many years that we now have a trillion dollar debt. To give you some idea of how much a trillion is, if we started

paying off the debt at a billion dollars a year, it would take a thousand years to wipe it out.

Now, if I may, let me take you back a little to 1977. When the previous administration took office, inflation was 4.8 percent. It rose steadily and in 1979 and '80 we had two years of back-to-back double-digit inflation. Unemployment started to increase and by 1980 we were in a recession with nearly eight million unemployed, inflation at 12.4 percent and interest rates at 21½ percent. As those interest rates continued, home construction and automobiles were hard hit because few could afford to take out a mortgage or buy a car on time. Unemployment continued to increase. The 1981 budget was already in place when our administration began, and while we managed to effect several billions of dollars savings during the balance of the fiscal year, there was nothing we could do but set our sights on the 1982 budget, which would be our first.

We had to reduce the built-in rate of increase. At the same time, we had to reduce the share of the people's earnings that government was taking in taxes. Now, this may sound strange in view of the increased spending and it was contrary to the philosophy of the Democratic leadership. But high taxes, destroying incentive, had contributed to reduced productivity and a reduction in savings, which left us without the capital we needed for industrial expansion.

And because government always finds a need for whatever money it gets, the cost of government continued to go up. Between 1976 and 1981, federal tax revenues in-

creased by $300 billion. Deficits ran $318 billion. There was no way we could get the rate of spending down to where it should be in one year. But our economic recovery program did manage to reduce the rate of increase in spending to nearly half of what it had been.

We also proposed a three-year program of tax rate reduction for individuals and for business. You helped us get both the reductions in spending and the tax reductions by letting your elected representatives know you wanted them.

During the debate on our economic program, we stated many times that there would have to be a second installment of budget reductions in 1983. That built-in automatic spending increase I spoke of would otherwise give us a budget of $827 billion in '83, $918 billion in 1984 and more than a trillion in 1985.

What is our situation now and how well have we done with our economic recovery program? Well, we're still in a recession and unemployment has continued to go up, particularly in those areas affected by the troubles of the automobile and construction industries.

Farmers, too, are hurt by the high interest rates. They borrow to plant and pay back at harvest, but that doesn't work when interest rates remain at too high a level. It is true, however, that those rates are down about a fifth from that high of 21½ percent. But they must come down some more and they have every reason to because that 12.4 percent inflation rate we inherited has been running at only 3.2 percent for the last six months. And last month, for the first time in 17 years, it

dropped below zero. Prices actually went down.

Now, with all of this in mind, we introduced a budget for 1983 of $758 billion, lower than the built-in spending by a considerable amount. Still, it represented an increase over the '82 budget of $32 billion.

Nevertheless, there were outraged screams of protest and you were led to believe that we were actually proposing less spending than the present level. There's been an insistent drumbeat, aided by special interest groups charging that our budget would deprive the needy, the handicapped and the elderly of the necessities of life.

I'm sure many of these people were sincere, well intentioned, but also misinformed. Our original budget proposal would have funded 95 million meals a day for the needy, provided medical care for 47 million Americans, subsidized housing for about 10 million people. In addition, there would be seven million loans and grants for college students, of which there are 11 million full time. Social Security, which was $122 billion in 1980, will be $188 billion in 1983.

But the drumbeat was too loud. Many in Congress criticized that budget and demanded that we send up a new one.

Well, we worked many months with the Cabinet on the one we submitted and believed it could fulfill government's responsibility for those who, through no fault of their own, had to depend on their fellow citizens for help.

Besides, I felt that some workable alternative to ours should have been suggested by our critics so we could begin arriving at a consensus.

As the talk grew of stalemate, I asked my Chief-of-Staff, Jim Baker, to contact the Congressional leadership of both Houses, and see if some means couldn't be agreed upon in which the matter could be discussed with the idea of finding an area of agreement. A bipartisan arrangement was made whereby the Senate had five representatives, the House of Representatives had seven, and the Administration had five. This group, which began to be called the "Gang of 17," held its first meeting on April 1st, and its 13th and last the day before yesterday, April 27th. The rule they followed was that nothing was binding on Speaker O'Neill, Senate Majority Leader Howard Baker, or myself. They would simply see if they could find enough agreement that actual negotiations seemed possible and practical. I, in turn, had told our representatives the areas I felt were non-negotiable. They were that any changes in defense spending must not interfere with or delay our rebuilding of national security, and that spending must be significantly reduced, and that our tax reductions, adopted last year, must be preserved.

I received regular progress reports and was greatly encouraged. The "Gang of 17" worked long, hard hours, and deliberated in good faith. What they were doing couldn't really be called negotiation. That

would come later. Speaker O'Neill referred to it once as "dialoguery." Well, the projected deficits for the next three years continued to increase as the lower inflation rate reduced estimated revenues. Continued unemployment, which costs government about 25 billion dollars for every added one percentage point, took its toll. And the persistent high interest rates added to the cost of government borrowing. While I don't believe in the accuracy of long-range projections, we're required to acknowledge them in our budgeting. They stand at $182 billion for 1983, $216 billion in '84, and $233 billion in 1985 if we do nothing about reducing spending. Not only must those deficits be reduced, they must show a decline over the next three years, not an increase. Our goal must be a balanced budget. And our budget would have set us on that road. But, apparently, there was no meeting of the minds. There's no question but that a difference in philosophy exists. While the Democratic leadership lamented about the deficit facing us, committees in the House of Representatives controlled by them were recommending increases above and beyond our proposed budget of more than $50 billion dollars in higher spending.

Apparently the philosophical difference between us is that they want more and more spending and more and more taxes. I believe we should have less spending, less taxes, and more prosperity.

There hasn't been too much opportunity in the last 40 years to see what our philosophy can do. But we know what theirs can do. The longest sustained inflation in history, the highest interest rates in a hundred years, eight recessions since World War II, and a trillion dollar debt. The day before yesterday, Jim Baker told me the group had decided they could come no closer to agreement than they were and there would be no more meetings. So I called Speaker O'Neill and suggested we meet to take up where the "Gang of 17" had left off. That meeting took place for more than three hours yesterday. The work-sheets of the committee showed that on our side our non-defense spending cuts had been reduced to about 60 percent of what we had originally proposed. There were some areas such as estimated savings from improved management practices which had been accepted. On the Democratic side they had expressed a willingness to accept some cuts which they thought were a concession on their part inasmuch as they had not wanted any budget reductions except in defense.

On revenues we had originally proposed about $13 billion for next year, most of which could be obtained through changes in tax regulations. Some regulations have been regulated or interpreted in such a way as to provide tax advantages which were never intended.

The group was discussing a figure of $25 billion which meant actually increasing some taxes or passing new ones. Now that figure would not have required eliminating

or reducing the tax cuts in our economic recovery program. Still the $25 billion figure was almost double our original proposal.

In yesterday afternoon's meeting on Capitol Hill, Speaker O'Neill, Senator Howard Baker, myself, and five of the "Gang of 17" participated. As I say, the figures on which the group had found some agreement were far from those we had proposed in February. But I decided against trying to start the negotiations on the basis of that original budget. The most essential thing is to send a message to the money market that we, Democrats and Republicans alike, can agree on reducing the deficit and continuing to hold down inflation. Actually the "Gang of 17" had come very close in their deliberations, and I was encouraged to believe that we could arrive at a settlement.

Our original cuts totalled $101 billion. I can't make a big enough mark to show you, but they were rejected — believe me. Our own representatives from the Congress proposed compromising at $60 billion. Their counterparts from the Democratic side of the aisle proposed $35 billion. In our meeting yesterday, which went on for more than three hours, our compromise of $60 billion was rejected. Now my pen is working. And then I swallowed hard and volunteered to split the difference between our $60 billion and their $35 billion and settle for $48 billion, and that was rejected. The meeting was over.

Now on this chart the red line is where we go in the next three years with regard to deficits if there is no compromise. It will reach a deficit of $233 billion in 1985 alone and as you can see, the line is still going up. And so will interest rates. The blue line is where we go if we settle on a reasonable compromise — steadily down to a deficit by 1985 of only $44 billion. And you can see that a balanced budget is not far distant. And this blue line will, I'm convinced, start interest rates down from the moment there is agreement on the compromise.

It is essential that we have a prompt resolution of this budget debate. It is, of course, up to the Congress to act now. But I'll do everything I can to help in getting a prompt settlement.

If American workers can show the statesmanship they've shown in redrawing their contracts to restrain their own wages to help in this time of recession, surely we in Washington can show some statesmanship, too.

I'm convinced we're in the trough, as it's called, of this recession and that we'll begin to see recovery in the second half of the year. There will be political pressure from some to turn on the printing presses and flood us with paper money. Well, that's been done before, and the answer is always the same — a flush feeling for about five minutes, then more inflation leading toward a plunge into an even worse recession.

There is another road that leads to permanent recovery. It begins with a responsible budget now.

In the coming days, I will do everything I can to help the Congress achieve this vital goal. And you can help, too, by letting your representatives know that you think this is no time for "politics as usual"; that you, too, want an end to runaway taxes, spending, government debt and high interest rates.

Tomorrow I will meet with Republican members of the "Gang of 17" to forge the beginnings of an acceptable budget initiative. On Monday I will meet with the full Republican leadership and with members of the Senate and House Budget Committees. I will also consult with responsible members of the Democratic Party in the Congress to make this a truly bipartisan effort in the national interest.

But our efforts must not stop there. Once we've achieved a balanced budget — and we will — I want to ensure that we keep it for many long years after I've left office. And there's only one way to do that.

So tonight I am asking the Congress to pass as soon as possible a constitutional amendment to require balanced federal budgets. This amendment will, of course, have to be ratified by three-fourths of the states. But I'm confident that the grassroots support for a balanced budget amendment is out there and will carry the day against the special interests.

Most Americans understand the need for a balanced budget and most Americans have seen how difficult it is for the Congress to withstand the pressures for more spending. This amendment will force government to stay within the limit of its revenues. Government will have to do what each of us does with our own family budgets — spend no more than we can afford.

Only a constitutional amendment will do the job. We've tried the carrot, and it failed. With the stick of a balanced budget amendment, we can stop government squandering, overtaxing ways, and save our

economy. Time and again the American people — you — have worked wonders that have astounded the world. We've done it in war and peace, in good times and bad because we're a people who care and who know how to pull together — family by family, community by community, coast to coast, to change things for the better.

The success story of America is neighbor helping neighbor. So, tonight I ask for your help, your voice, at this turning point. So often in history great causes have been won or lost at the last moment because one side or the other lacked that last reserve of character and stamina, of faith and fortitude, to see the way through to success. Make your voice heard. Let your representatives know that you support the kind of fair, effective approach I have outlined for you tonight. Let them know you stand behind our recovery program.

You did it once, you can do it again. Thank you and God bless you. ∎

Reagan Address on East-West Relations

Following is the White House text of President Reagan's May 9 speech as delivered at the Eureka College commencement ceremony, in Eureka, Ill.

THE PRESIDENT: Thank you very much. President Gilbert, Trustees, Administration, and Faculty, students and the friends of Eureka College and particularly those whose day this is — the graduating class of '82 — (applause) — Dan, you said the 25th and now the 50th. Do you mind if I try for the 75th? (Applause.)

But it goes without saying that this is a very special day for you who are graduating. Would you forgive me if I say it's a very special day for me also? Over the years since I sat where you, the graduating class of 1982, are now sitting, I've returned to the campus many times, always with great pleasure and warm nostalgia. Now, it just isn't true that I only came back this time to clean out my gym locker. (Laughter.)

On one of those occasions, as you've been told, I addressed the graduating class here, " 'neath the elms," and was awarded an honorary degree. At that time I informed those assembled that while I was grateful for the honor, it added to a feeling of guilt I've been nursing for 25 years, because I always figured that first degree they give me was honorary. (Laughter.)

Now, if it's true that tradition is the glue holding civilization together, then Eureka has made its contribution to that effort. Yes, it is a small college in a small community. It's no impersonal, assembly-line diploma mill. As the years pass, if you have let yourselves absorb the spirit and tradition of this place, you'll find the four years you've spent here living in your mem-

ory as a rich and important part of your life.

Oh, you'll have some regrets along with the happy memories. I let football and other extracurricular activities eat into my study time with the result that my grade average was closer to the C level required for eligibility than it was to straight A's. And even now I wonder what I might have accomplished if I'd studied harder. (Laughter.) (Applause.)

Now, I know there are differences between the Eureka College of 1932 and the Eureka of 1982, but I'm also sure that in many ways — important ways — Eureka remains the same. For one thing, it's impossible for you now to believe what I've said about things being the same. We who preceded you understand that very well, because when we were here we thought old grads who came back only after five years — not 50 — couldn't understand what our life was like and what had taken place and changed. So take my word for it. As the years go by, you'll be amazed at how fresh the memory of these years will remain in your mind; how easily you can relive the very emotions that you experienced.

The Class of '32 has no yearbook to record our final days on the campus. The Class of '33 didn't put out a *Prism* because of the hardships of that great Depression era. The faculty sometimes went for months on end without pay. And yet this school made it possible for young men and women, myself included, to get an education even though we were totally without funds, our families destitute victims of the Depression.

Yes, this place is deep in my heart. Everything that has been good in my life began here. (Applause.)

Graduation Day is called "Commencement" and properly so because it is both a

recognition of completion and a beginning. And I would like, seriously, to talk to you about this new phase — the society in which you're now going to take your place as full-time participants. You're no longer observers. You will be called upon to make decisions and express your views on global events because those events will affect your lives.

I've spoken of similarities, and the 1980's like the 1930's may be one of those — a crucial juncture in history that will determine the direction of the future.

In about a month I will meet in Europe with the leaders of nations who are our closest friends and allies. At Versailles, leaders of the industrial powers of the world will seek better ways to meet today's economic challenges. In Bonn, I will join my colleagues from the Atlantic Alliance nations to renew those ties which have been the foundation of Western, free-world defense for 37 years. There will also be meetings in Rome and London.

Now, these meetings are significant for a simple but very important reason. Our own nation's fate is directly linked to that of our sister democracies in Western Europe. The values for which America and all democratic nations stand represent the culmination of Western culture. Andrei Sakharov, the distinguished Nobel Laureate and courageous Soviet human rights advocate, has written in a message smuggled to freedom, "I believe in Western man. I have faith in his mind which is practical and efficient and, at the same time, aspires to great goals. I have faith in his good intentions and in his decisiveness."

This glorious tradition requires a partnership to preserve and protect it. Only as partners can we hope to achieve the goal of a peaceful community of nations. Only as partners can we defend the values of de-

mocracy and human dignity that we hold so dear.

There is a single, major issue in our partnership which will underlie the discussions that I will have with the European leaders: the future of Western relations with the Soviet Union. How should we deal with the Soviet Union in the years ahead? What framework should guide our conduct and our policies toward it? And what can we realistically expect from a world power of such deep fears, hostilities, and external ambitions?

I believe the unity of the West is the foundation for any successful relationship with the East. Without Western unity, we'll squander our energies in bickering while the Soviets continue as they please. With unity, we have the strength to moderate Soviet behavior. We've done so in the past and we can do so again.

Our challenge is to establish a framework in which sound East-West relations will endure. I'm optimistic that we can build a more constructive relationship with the Soviet Union. To do so, however, we must understand the nature of the Soviet system and the lessons of the past.

The Soviet Union is a huge empire ruled by an elite that holds all power and all privilege. They hold it tightly because, as we've seen in Poland, they fear what might happen if even the smallest amount of control slips from their grasp. They fear the infectiousness of even a little freedom and because of this in many ways their system has failed. The Soviet empire is faltering because it is rigid — centralized control has destroyed incentives for innovation, efficiency and individual achievement. Spiritually, there is a sense of malaise and resentment.

But in the midst of social and economic problems, the Soviet dictatorship has forged the largest armed force in the world. It has done so by preempting the human needs of its people, and, in the end, this course will undermine the foundations of the Soviet system. Harry Truman was right when he said of the Soviets that, "When you try to conquer other people or extend yourself over vast areas you cannot win in the long run."

Yet Soviet aggressiveness has grown as Soviet military power has increased. To compensate, we must learn from the lessons of the past. When the West has stood unified and firm, the Soviet Union has taken heed. For 35 years Western Europe has lived free despite the shadow of Soviet military might. Through unity, you'll remember from your modern history courses, the West secured the withdrawal of occupation forces from Austria and the recognition of its rights in Berlin.

Other Western policies have not been successful. East-West trade was expanded in the hope of providing incentives for Soviet restraint, but the Soviets exploited the benefits of trade without moderating their behavior. Despite a decade of ambitious arms control efforts, the Soviet buildup continues. And despite its signature of the

Helsinki agreements on human rights, the Soviet Union has not relaxed its hold on its own people or those of Western[1] Europe.

During the 1970's some of us forgot the warning of President Kennedy who said that the Soviets "have offered to trade us an apple for an orchard. We don't do that in this country." But we came perilously close to doing just that.

If East-West relations in the detente era in Europe have yielded disappointment, detente outside of Europe has yielded a severe disillusionment for those who expected a moderation of Soviet behavior. The Soviet Union continues to support Vietnam in its occupation of Kampuchea and its massive military presence in Laos. It is engaged in a war of aggression against Afghanistan. Soviet proxy forces have brought instability and conflict to Africa and Central America.

We are now approaching an extremely important phase in East-West relations as the current Soviet leadership is succeeded by a new generation. Both the current and the new Soviet leadership should realize aggressive policies will meet a firm Western response. On the other hand, a Soviet leadership devoted to improving its people's lives, rather than expanding its armed conquests, will find a sympathetic partner in the West. The West will respond with expanded trade and other forms of cooperation. But all of this depends on Soviet actions. Standing in the Athenian marketplace 2,000 years ago, Demosthenes said: "What sane man would let another man's words rather than his deeds proclaim who is at peace and who is at war with him?"

Peace is not the absence of conflict, but the ability to cope with conflict by peaceful means. I believe we can cope. I believe that the West can fashion a realistic, durable policy that will protect our interests and keep the peace, not just for this generation, but for your children and your grandchildren. (Applause.)

I believe such a policy consists of five points: military balance, economic security, regional stability, arms reductions, and dialogue. Now, these are the means by which we can seek peace with the Soviet Union in the years ahead. Today, I want to set this five-point program to guide the future of our East-West relations, set it out for all to hear and see.

First, a sound East-West military balance is absolutely essential. Last week NATO published a comprehensive comparison of its forces with those of the Warsaw Pact. Its message is clear. During the past decade, the Soviet Union has built up its forces across the board. During that same period, the defense expenditures of the United States declined in real terms. The United States has already undertaken steps to recover from that decade of neglect. And I should add that the expenditures of our European allies have increased slowly but steadily, something we often fail to recognize here at home.

The second point on which we must

reach consensus with our allies deals with economic security. Consultations are under way among Western nations on the transfer of militarily significant technology and the extension of financial credits to the East as well as on the question of energy dependence on the East, that energy dependence of Europe. We recognize that some of our allies economic requirements are distinct from our own. But the Soviets must not have access to Western technology with military applications, and we must not subsidize the Soviet economy. The Soviet Union must make the difficult choices brought on by its military budgets and economic shortcomings.

The third element is regional stability with peaceful change. Last year in a speech in Philadelphia and in the Summit meetings at Cancún, I outlined the basic American plan to assist the developing world. These principles for economic development remain the foundation of our approach. They represent no threat to the Soviet Union. Yet in many areas of the developing world we find that Soviet arms and Soviet-supported troops are attempting to destabilize societies and extend Moscow's influence.

High on our agenda must be progress toward peace in Afghanistan. The United States is prepared to engage in a serious effort to negotiate an end to the conflict caused by the Soviet invasion of that country. We are ready to cooperate in an international effort to resolve this problem, to secure a full Soviet withdrawal from Afghanistan, and to ensure self-determination for the Afghan people.

In southern Africa, working closely with our Western allies and the African states, we've made real progress toward independence for Namibia. These negotiations, if successful, will result in peaceful and secure conditions throughout southern Africa. The simultaneous withdrawal of Cuban forces from Angola is essential to achieving Namibian independence, as well as creating long-range prospects for peace in the region.

Central America also has become a dangerous point of tension in East-West relations. The Soviet Union cannot escape responsibility for the violence and suffering in the region caused by its support for Cuban activities in Central America and its accelerated transfer of advanced military equipment to Cuba.

However, it was in Western Europe — or Eastern Europe, I should say — that the hopes of the 1970's were greatest, and it is there that they have been the most bitterly disappointed. There was hope that the people of Poland could develop a freer society. But the Soviet Union has refused to allow the people of Poland to decide their own fate, just as it refused to allow the people of Hungary to decide theirs in 1956, or the people of Czechoslovakia in 1968.

If martial law in Poland is lifted, if all the political prisoners are released, and if a dialogue is restored with the Solidarity Union, the United States is prepared to

join in a program of economic support. Water cannons and clubs against the Polish people are hardly the kind of dialogue that gives us hope. It is up to the Soviets and their client regimes to show good faith by concrete actions.

The fourth point is arms reduction. I know that this weighs heavily on many of your minds. In our 1931 *Prism*, we quoted Carl Sandburg, who in his own beautiful way quoted the Mother Prairie, saying, "Have you seen a red sunset drip over one of my cornfields, the shore of night stars, the wave lines of dawn up a wheat valley?" What an idyllic scene that paints in our minds — and what a nightmarish prospect that a huge mushroom cloud might someday destroy such beauty. My duty as President is to ensure that the ultimate nightmare never occurs, that the prairies and the cities and the people who inhabit them remain free and untouched by nuclear conflict.

I wish more than anything there were a simple policy that would eliminate that nuclear danger. But there are only difficult policy choices through which we can achieve a stable nuclear balance at the lowest possible level.

I do not doubt that the Soviet people, and, yes, the Soviet leaders have an overriding interest in preventing the use of nuclear weapons. The Soviet Union within the memory of its leaders has known the devastation of total conventional war and knows that nuclear war would be even more calamitous. Yet, so far, the Soviet Union has used arms control negotiations primarily as an instrument to restrict U.S. defense programs and, in conjunction with their own arms buildup, a means to enhance Soviet power and prestige.

Unfortunately, for some time suspicions have grown that the Soviet Union has not been living up to its obligations under existing arms control treaties. There is conclusive evidence the Soviet Union has provided toxins to the Laotians and Vietnamese for use against defenseless villagers in Southeast Asia. And the Soviets themselves are employing chemical weapons on the freedom fighters in Afghanistan.

We must establish firm criteria for arms control in the 1980's if we're to secure genuine and lasting restraint on Soviet military programs throughout arms control. We must seek agreements which are verifiable, equitable, and militarily significant. Agreements that provide only the appearance of arms control breed dangerous illusions.

Last November, I committed the United States to seek significant reductions on nuclear and conventional forces. In Geneva, we have since proposed limits on U.S. and Soviet intermediate-range missiles, including the complete elimination of the most threatening systems on both sides.

In Vienna, we're negotiating, together with our allies, for reductions of conventional forces in Europe. In the 40-nation Committee on Disarmament, the United

Nations[2] seeks a total ban on all chemical weapons.

Since the first days of my administration, we've been working on our approach to the crucial issue of strategic arms and the control and negotiations for control of those arms with the Soviet Union. The study and analysis required has been complex and difficult. It had to be undertaken deliberately, thoroughly, and correctly. We've laid a solid basis for these negotiations. We're consulting with Congressional leaders and with our allies, and we are now ready to proceed.

The main threat to peace posed by nuclear weapons today is the growing instability of the nuclear balance. This is due to the increasingly destructive potential of the massive Soviet buildup in its ballistic missile force.

Therefore, our goal is to enhance deterrence and achieve stability through significant reductions in the most destabilizing nuclear systems, ballistic missiles, and especially the giant intercontinental ballistic missiles, while maintaining a nuclear capability sufficient to deter conflict, to underwrite our national security and to meet our commitment to allies and friends.

For the immediate future, I'm asking my START, and START really means, we've given up on SALT, START means, "Strategic Arms Reduction Talks," and that negotiating team to propose to their Soviet counterparts a practical, phased reduction plan. The focus of our efforts will be, reduce significantly the most destabilizing systems, the ballistic missiles, the number of warheads they carry and their overall destructive potential.

At the first phase, or the end of the first phase of START, I expect ballistic missile warheads, the most serious threat we face, to be reduced to equal levels, equal ceilings, at least a third below the current levels. To enhance stability, I would ask that no more than half of those warheads be land-based. I hope that these warhead reductions as well as significant reductions in missiles themselves could be achieved as rapidly as possible.

In a second phase, we'll seek to achieve an equal ceiling on other elements of our strategic nuclear forces including limits on the ballistic missile throwweight at less than current American levels. In both phases, we shall insist on verification procedures to insure compliance with the agreement.

This, I might say, will be the twentieth time that we have sought such negotiations with the Soviet Union since World War II.

The monumental task of reducing and reshaping our strategic forces to enhance stability will take many years of concentrated effort. But I believe that it will be possible to reduce the risks of war by removing the instabilities that now exist and by dismantling the nuclear menace. (Applause.)

I have written to President Brezhnev and directed Secretary Haig to approach the Soviet government concerning the initi-

ation of formal negotiations on the reduction of strategic nuclear arms, START, at the earliest opportunity. We hope negotiations will begin by the end of June.

We will negotiate seriously, in good faith and carefully consider all proposals made by the Soviet Union. If they approach these negotiations in the same spirit, I'm confident that together we can achieve an agreement of enduring value that reduces the number of nuclear weapons, halts the growth in strategic forces and opens the way to even more far-reaching steps in the future. (Applause.)

I hope the Commencement today will also mark the commencement of a new era, in both senses of the word a new start toward a more peaceful and secure world.

The fifth and final point I propose for East-West relations is dialogue. I've always believed that people's problems can be solved when people talk to each other instead of about each other. And I've already expressed my own desire to meet with President Brezhnev in New York next month. If this can't be done, I'd hope we could arrange a future meeting where positive results can be anticipated. And when we sit down, I'll tell President Brezhnev that the United States is ready to build a new understanding based upon the principles I've outlined today. I'll tell him that his government and his people have nothing to fear from the United States. The free nations living at peace in the world community can vouch for the fact that we seek only harmony. And I'll ask President Brezhnev why our two nations can't practice mutual restraint. Why can't our peoples enjoy the benefits that would flow from real cooperation? Why can't we reduce the number of horrendous weapons?

Perhaps I should also speak to him of this school and these graduates who are leaving it today — of your hopes for the future, of your deep desire for peace, and yet your strong commitment to defend your values if threatened. Perhaps if he someday could attend such a ceremony as this, he'd better understand America. In the only system he knows, you would be here by the decision of government and on this day the government representatives would be here telling most, if not all of you, where you were going to report to work tomorrow.

But as we go to Europe for the talks and as we proceed in the important challenges facing this country, I want you to know that I will be thinking of you and of Eureka and what you represent. In one of my yearbooks, I remember reading that, "The work of the prairie is to be the soil for the growth of a strong western culture." I believe Eureka is fulfilling that work. You, the members of the 1982 graduating class, are this year's harvest.

I spoke of the difference between our two countries. I try to follow the humor of the Russian people. We don't hear much about the Russian people. We hear about the Russian leaders. But you can learn a lot because they do have a sense of humor and

you can learn from the jokes they're telling. And one of the most recent jokes I found kind of — well, personally interesting. Maybe you might — tell you something about your country. The joke they tell is that an American and a Russian were arguing about the differences between our two countries. And the American said, "Look. In my country I can walk into the Oval Office, I can hit the desk with my fist, and say, 'President Reagan, I don't like the way you are governing the United States.'" And the Russian said, "I can do that." The American said, "What?" He says "I can walk into the Kremlin, into Brezhnev's office. I can pound Brezhnev's desk and I can say, 'Mr. President, I don't like the way

Ronald Reagan is governing the United States.'" (Laughter.) (Applause.)

Eureka as an institution and you as individuals are sustaining the best of Western man's ideals. As a fellow graduate and in the office I hold, I'll do my best to uphold these same ideals. To the Class of '82, congratulations and God bless you. (Applause.)

[1] *The White House transcript indicated President Reagan intended to say "Eastern."*

[2] *The White House transcript indicated President Reagan intended to say "United States."* ∎

Southern Arizona Water Rights Veto

Following is the White House text of President Reagan's June 1 message accompanying his veto of HR 5118, to provide water to the Papago Tribe of Arizona. It was Reagan's fourth veto of a public bill during the 97th Congress.

TO THE HOUSE OF
REPRESENTATIVES:

I return herewith, without my approval, H.R. 5118, the proposed "Southern Arizona Water Rights Settlement Act of 1982." I take this action with sincere disappointment. I am well aware of the hard work of the Arizona Congressional leaders that went into the development and passage of this legislation. I also understand their desire to resolve the litigation that has hung over the head of the City of Tucson and the many private parties involved for the past seven years.

I strongly believe that the most appropriate means of resolving Indian water rights disputes is through negotiated settlement and legislation if it is needed to implement any such settlement. However, H.R. 5118 is a negotiated settlement with a serious flaw. The United States Government was never a party to the negotiations that led to the development of this proposal. This settlement was negotiated among the Tribe, the City of Tucson, the State of Arizona, the affected commercial interests and other defendants with assistance from the Arizona Congressional delegation. The result of this negotiation was that the United States Government, which was absent from the negotiation table, would bear almost the entire financial burden of the settlement at a potential initial cost of $112 million and a potential annual cost of approximately $5 million.

I cannot support this resolution of litigation on behalf of the Papago Tribe by the United States Government. I can only in good conscience approve legislation intended to implement a settlement if the United States has been a major party in the negotiations and if the contribution by

the defendants in the litigation involved is significant.

I pledge the full cooperation of my Administration to the States and local governments that are facing the difficult task of equitably resolving Indian water rights suits. I cannot, however, pledge the Federal Treasury as a panacea for this problem.

H.R. 5118 is a multi-million dollar bailout of local public and commercial interests at the expense of Federal taxpayers throughout the nation. It is a prime example of serious misuse of Federal funds. It asks the Federal Government to pay the settlement share of the mining companies and other local water users whose share should more properly be borne by the defendants themselves.

I therefore must return this legislation to you without my approval. I will only approve legislation that implements a true negotiated settlement. Such a settlement is one in which all parties that are making contributions or concessions have agreed to those contributions or concessions at the negotiating table. I look forward to receiving such legislation from the Congress. I am asking the Secretary of the Interior to coordinate participation by my Administration in any such negotiations.

RONALD REAGAN

The White House
June 1, 1982 ∎

Supplemental Veto HR 5922

Following is the White House text of President Reagan's June 24 message accompanying his veto of HR 5922, to provide fiscal year 1982 supplemental appropriations and subsidies of home mortgage interest rates. It was Reagan's fifth veto of a public bill during the 97th Congress.

TO THE HOUSE OF
REPRESENTATIVES:

Today I am returning to the House of Representatives, without my approval, H.R. 5922, an act providing supplemental appropriations for several Federal programs in urgent need of additional funds in Fiscal Year 1982. Unfortunately, in addition to providing the urgent supplemental appropriations requested by the Administration, the Congress has added other unrequested, non-urgent funds that would increase the 1983 deficit by $1.3 billion and would add at least $5 billion to Federal spending in the next few years. The bill also establishes a housing subsidy program that sets a bad precedent for other Federal programs. For these reasons, I cannot approve this legislation. I urge the Congress to act quickly to send me a clean bill for signature containing only those items urgently needed to continue 1982 activities.

I share the heartfelt Congressional concerns about the particular problems confronting the housing industry. But we will not promote a housing recovery by going even deeper in debt. More red ink spending will only make the housing recession worse.

It is my belief this bill will do little to increase construction of new housing; most of the aid will go for homes that would be built and purchased anyway. The bill does not increase available financing, but shifts funds to housing that would otherwise be used by, and create jobs in, other sectors of the economy. My concern also is that the bill would add to the Federal deficit and generate upward pressures on interest rates — aggravating the very situation it seeks to help.

Furthermore, we cannot justify singling out one industry for special relief. The recession and high interest rates have created hardship and unemployment for farmers, small businesses, the thrift industry, automobile manufacturers and dealers and many others. This Government must convince a skeptical country — the business community, taxpayers, investors and workers — that lasting recovery is a fundamental commitment that will not be derailed by a return to excessive Federal spending and borrowing.

My Administration has taken a number of steps to remove tax, regulatory and administrative burdens on housing finance and construction. We have proposed legislation to extend Federal Housing Administration insurance to a number of innovative mortgage financing instruments to encourage private market use of these flexible instruments. We have removed regulatory restrictions limiting the use of pension funds in mortgage credit markets. We have provided an additional $3.4 billion of subsidized housing funds in 1982 to allow up to 70,000 additional units of new rental housing for low income households to begin construction this summer. We are revising our regulations on the use of tax exempt financing for housing to allow states and localities to use this financing vehicle to the

full extent authorized by the Congress.

More fundamentally, we have established a long-term program designed to provide incentives and to create conditions for sustained non-inflationary economic recovery. That recovery is getting underway. Housing permits have risen in six of the last seven months and are now 31 percent above their October low. Housing starts rose by 22 percent in May and are 27 percent above their October low. The key to sustaining this upturn is lower interest rates. This, in turn, depends on public confidence that the Congress will control Federal spending and reduce Federal deficits — thus leaving an adequate supply of funds for housing and business investment.

In addition to the housing proposal, there are several other provisions in this act that I urge the Congress to delete. The urgent supplemental legislation is the first significant spending measure in this session of Congress. It is essential that this act be a clear example of the willingness of the Congress to join with me in holding the line and establishing meaningful control over all Federal spending programs. I must ask that supplemental appropriations in excess of the proposals I have indicated to be urgent requests be pared back to the maximum extent feasible. Some of these unrequested supplemental funds include:

• $150 million for the GNMA special assistance function ("tandem") program;
• $62 million for the postal service;
• $58 million for the WIN program; and
• other unrequested funds for Federal aid to highways, flood control programs of the Corps of Engineers, and a number of smaller HHS programs.

The bill also includes several undesirable language provisions restricting, in varying degrees, the Executive Branch from exercising its authority to allocate funds appropriated by Congress. The most notable among these are:

• language mandating the modernization of 5,073 public housing units, extending the time period for completion of the construction of certain HUD subsidized housing projects to 24 months, and precluding HUD from applying cost containment procedures to such projects.
• language mandating minimum spending levels for certain NASA programs that will severely disrupt two important scientific missions and lead to the waste of more than $150 million; and
• language mandating new construction on starts for the Soil Conservation Service.

Therefore, I am returning H.R. 5922 without approval and urge the Congress to enact immediately a 1982 supplemental appropriations bill that addresses only those items I have indicated need urgent attention and excludes these objectionable additions. I look forward to prompt Congressional action on a revised bill which will assure continuity in the operations of Federal agencies and be consistent with continued progress toward economic recovery.

RONALD REAGAN

The White House
June 24, 1982 ∎

Supplemental Veto HR 6682

Following is the White House text of President Reagan's June 25 message accompanying his veto of HR 6682, to provide fiscal year 1982 supplemental appropriations. It was Reagan's sixth veto of a public bill during the 97th Congress.

TO THE HOUSE OF
REPRESENTATIVES:

Today, I have the extremely disappointing task of again returning to the Congress, without my signature, a bill providing supplemental appropriations for several Federal programs in need of additional funds in Fiscal Year 1982. I use the word "again" because H.R. 6682, like its predecessor H.R. 5922, contains excessive and unrequested budget authority totalling nearly $1 billion. For this reason, I cannot approve this legislation.

A key to lasting economic recovery is to bring interest rates down and keep them down. We can only do that by convincing skeptical markets that this Government has the will to control Federal spending and borrowing across the board. The American people need deeds, not just promises, to be convinced deficits will be reduced.

I regret that this revised urgent supplemental still does not do the job. Therefore, I am returning H.R. 6682 without approval and urge the Congress to enact immediately a 1982 supplemental appropriations bill that addresses only those items I have indicated need urgent attention. Again, I look forward to prompt Congressional action on a revised bill that will assure continuity in the operations of Federal agencies and be consistent with continued progress toward economic recovery.

RONALD REAGAN

The White House
June 25, 1982 ∎

Copyright Bill Veto

Following is the White House text of President Reagan's July 8 message accompanying his veto of HR 6198, to extend until 1986 a provision in copyright law providing copyright protection for books and periodicals written in English only if they are printed in the United States. It was Reagan's seventh veto of a public bill during the 97th Congress.

TO THE HOUSE OF
REPRESENTATIVES:

I am returning without my approval H.R. 6198, a bill that would extend for four years the "manufacturing clause" of the U.S. copyright law that expired on June 30, 1982.

The manufacturing clause requires that many printed materials be printed in the United States in order to enjoy copyright protection. The clause was written into law nearly a century ago, in an effort to strengthen our relatively new printing industry by limiting foreign competition. However, the "infant industry" justification for protecting our printing industry is no longer valid; our industry is now one of the most modern and efficient in the world.

During the recent Tokyo Round of Multilateral Trade Negotiations, our trading partners objected to the manufacturing clause as inconsistent with our international obligations. Extension of the clause, as provided in H.R. 6198, could result in increased international trade tensions that could endanger American jobs. I would further note that if the printing or publishing industry believes itself injured, or threatened by injury, due to the expiration of the manufacturing clause, it has the option of requesting relief under the Trade Act.

My Administration has placed a very high priority on strengthening free trade, and we are energetically seeking to remove artificial foreign barriers to American exports. We are confident that our free enterprise system will enable American products to face foreign competition in our own open market and to do well in markets overseas, provided our access to those markets is not blocked by protectionist barriers that distort international competition. Given the importance of our efforts to remove foreign trade barriers, it would be self-defeating to extend an artificial barrier of our own. For these reasons, I cannot approve H.R. 6198.

RONALD REAGAN

The White House
July 8, 1982 ∎

Supplemental Veto HR 6863

Following is the White House text of President Reagan's Aug. 28 message accompanying his veto of HR 6863, to provide fiscal year 1982 supplemental appropriations. It was Reagan's eighth veto of a public bill during the 97th Congress.

TO THE HOUSE OF
REPRESENTATIVES:

A week ago, the Congress passed important legislation to reduce deficits through tax reform. I worked hard to help win that passage — and at the same time

stressed that if we are to keep deficits down we must also keep Federal spending down. We can only do this if the Congress resists the temptation to slide back into old spendthrift habits. I will use every means in my power, including the veto, to prevent that from happening.

Accordingly, today I am returning to the House of Representatives, without my signature, the bill H.R. 6863, making supplemental appropriations for Federal programs and agencies for fiscal year 1982.

I do not take this step lightly. Delay in the adoption of this legislation poses serious problems for the Department of Defense and other Federal agencies in meeting prior commitments, including payroll, that are funded by this bill. In addition, the bill contains funds for important new programs, such as the Caribbean Basin Initiative, for which funds are needed prior to the beginning of the next fiscal year.

But this bill would bust the budget by nearly a billion dollars. It provides an unacceptable total of $918 million in unrequested and unwarranted increases in domestic spending programs. We have seen a positive reaction to last week's Congressional action in the Nation's securities markets and other areas. It is founded in large measure on a growing conviction that this Government has finally developed the will to set its fiscal house in order. This legislation flies in the face of that conviction. Unless amended to restrict its scope to only those funds that are urgently needed, it will undermine the confidence crucial to continued reductions in deficits and interest rates which we must achieve for sustained economic growth.

Increases in domestic spending include $367 million in funding for items contained in the urgent supplemental I vetoed in June that were subsequently deleted from the urgent supplemental bill I signed in July. Also restored is $892 million in funding that was cut by the Congress last fall.

This simply is not tolerable in the face of triple-digit deficits, and I cannot endorse these unwarranted spending increases.

While the enrolled bill includes $918 million in unrequested domestic increases, it provides only $0.5 billion of the $2.6 billion defense program supplementals I requested, a reduction of 82 percent. The enrolled bill fails to provide required funding in virtually every major defense program — military personnel (reduced 52 percent), operation and maintenance (reduced 93 percent), procurement (reduced 86 percent), and military construction (reduced 77 percent).

The bill also unnecessarily restricts the Executive Branch from exercising its authority to allocate funds appropriated by the Congress. Most notable among these are provisions that would:

• prevent the planned consolidation of the Office of the Inspector General into the Department of the Treasury and thereby block improvements in administrative effectiveness and efficiency;

• require the expenditure of $1.75 billion in unexpended balances in 1982 for the Section 8 housing program. The Administration would achieve similar purposes by using budget authority available from program deobligations, rather than new appropriations;

• require the Department of Energy to maintain specified employment levels that are unnecessary for the effective management of the Department;

• require a minimum staffing level for the Railroad Retirement Board, blocking savings that could be achieved through improved management and administrative consolidation;

• direct 1982 Energy and Water funds be made available for a specific project (Tug Fork, West Virginia), that is expected to cost over $1 billion before it is completed; and

• extend, through 1983, the restrictions

on the President's ability to deal with the Polish debt problem.

For these reasons, I am returning H.R. 6863 without approval. I urge the Congress to enact immediately a 1982 supplemental appropriations bill that does not contain excessive and unwarranted spending increases for domestic programs and that provides an acceptable balance of supplemental funding for those programs requiring additional money in fiscal year 1982.

Certain important provisions of the bill must be preserved, notably funding for the Caribbean Basin Initiative. This funding is designed to resolve an unprecedented economic crisis that affects a strategic region located at our doorstep. I hope the Congress will review and modify country funding levels to bring them closer in line with the Administration's original request. The Congress has also provided $50 million for special Lebanon emergency relief. This humanitarian assistance is essential for thousands of Lebanese civilians requiring aid. The funds provided for security assistance, while less than I requested, will help demonstrate that countries in pivotal regions of the world can count on American support when they need it. I strongly urge the Congress to continue to include these essential programs as they work on an acceptable alternative.

To bring the sustained recovery we all want we must not only rewrite this measure; we must also press forward in an all-out attack on wasteful and unnecessary spending. I look forward to prompt Congressional action on a revised bill that will assure continuity in the operations of Federal agencies and be consistent with continued progress toward economic recovery.

RONALD REAGAN

The White House
August 28, 1982

Reagan Speech on the Middle East

Following is the White House text of President Reagan's Sept. 1 address as delivered on the Middle East.

THE PRESIDENT: My fellow Americans, today has been a day that can make us proud. It marks the end of the successful evacuation of the PLO from Beirut, Lebanon. This peaceful step could never have been taken without the good offices of the United States and especially the truly heroic work of a great American diplomat, Ambassador Philip Habib. Thanks to his efforts I am happy to announce that the U.S. Marine contingent helping supervise the evacuation has accomplished its mission. Our young men should be out of Lebanon within two weeks. They, too, have served the cause of peace with distinction and we can all be very proud of them.

But the situation in Lebanon is only part of the overall problem of conflict in the Middle East. So over the past two weeks while events in Beirut dominated the front page, America was engaged in a quiet, behind-the-scenes effort to lay the groundwork for a broader peace in the region. For once, there were no premature leaks as U.S. diplomatic missions traveled to Mideast capitals and I met here at home with a wide range of experts to map out an American peace initiative for the long-suffering peoples of the Middle East — Arab and Israeli alike. It seemed to me that with the agreement in Lebanon we had an opportunity for a more far-reaching peace effort in the region and I was determined to seize that moment.

In the words of the scriptures, the time had come to follow after the things which

make for peace. Tonight, I want to report to you the steps we have taken and the prospects they can open up for a just and lasting peace in the Middle East.

America has long been committed to bringing peace to this troubled region. For more than a generation, successive United States administrations have endeavored to develop a fair and workable process that could lead to a true and lasting Arab-Israeli peace. Our involvement in the search for Mideast peace is not a matter of preference, it is a moral imperative. The strategic importance of the region to the United States is well known, but our policy is motivated by more than strategic interests. We also have an irreversible commitment to the survival and territorial integrity of friendly states. Nor can we ignore the fact that the well-being of much of the world's

economy is tied to stability in the strife-torn Middle East. Finally, our traditional humanitarian concerns dictated a continuing effort to peacefully resolve the conflict.

When our administration assumed office in January of 1981 I decided that the general framework for our Middle East policy should follow the broad guidelines laid down by my predecessors. There were two basic issues we had to address. First, there was a strategic threat to the region posed by the Soviet Union and its surrogates, best demonstrated by the brutal war in Afghanistan, and, second, the peace process between Israel and its Arab neighbors.

With regard to the Soviet threat, we have strengthened our efforts to develop with our friends and allies a joint policy to deter the Soviets and their surrogates from further expansion in the region, and, if necessary, to defend against it.

With respect to the Arab-Israeli conflict, we have embraced the Camp David framework as the only way to proceed. We have also recognized, however, solving the Arab-Israeli conflict in and of itself cannot assure peace throughout a region as vast and troubled as the Middle East.

Our first objective under the Camp David process was to ensure the successful fulfillment of the Egyptian-Israeli Peace Treaty. This was achieved with the peaceful return of the Sinai to Egypt in April, 1982. To accomplish this, we worked hard with our Egyptian and Israeli friends, and eventually, with other friendly countries to create the multinational force which now operates in the Sinai.

Throughout this period of difficult and time consuming negotiations we never lost sight of the next step of Camp David — autonomy talks to pave the way for permitting the Palestinian people to exercise their legitimate rights. However, owing to the tragic assassination of President Sadat and other crises in the area, it was not until January, 1982 that we were able to make a major effort to renew these talks.

Secretary of State Haig and Ambassador Fairbanks made three visits to Israel and Egypt early this year to pursue the autonomy talks. Considerable progress was made in developing the basic outline of an American approach which was to be presented to Egypt and Israel after April.

The successful completion of Israel's withdrawal from Sinai and the courage shown on this occasion by Prime Minister Begin and President Mubarak in living up to their agreements convinced me the time had come for a new American policy to try to bridge the remaining differences between Egypt and Israel on the autonomy process. So, in May, I called for specific measures and a timetable for consultations with the governments of Egypt and Israel on the next step in the peace process. However, before this effort could be launched, the conflict in Lebanon pre-empted our effort.

The autonomy talks were, basically, put on hold while we sought to untangle the parties in Lebanon and still the guns of

war. The Lebanon war, tragic as it was, has left us with a new opportunity for Middle East peace. We must seize it now, and bring peace to this troubled area so vital to world stability while there is still time. It was with this strong conviction that over a month ago, before the present negotiations in Beirut had been completed, I directed Secretary of State Shultz to again review our policy, and to consult a wide range of outstanding Americans on the best ways to strengthen chances for peace in the Middle East. We have consulted with many of the officials who were historically involved in the process, with members of the Congress, and with individuals from the private sector. And I have held extensive consultations with my own advisors on the principals I will outline to you tonight.

The evacuation of the PLO from Beirut is now complete. And we can now help the Lebanese to rebuild their war-torn country. We owe it to ourselves, and to posterity, to move quickly to build upon this achievement. A stable and revived Lebanon is essential to all our hopes for peace in the region. The people of Lebanon deserve the best efforts of the international community to turn the nightmares of the past several years into a new dawn of hope.

But the opportunities for peace in the Middle East do not begin and end in Lebanon. As we help Lebanon rebuild, we must also move to resolve the root causes of conflict between Arabs and Israelis. The war in Lebanon has demonstrated many things, but two consequences are key to the peace process. First, the military losses of the PLO have not diminished the yearning of the Palestinian people for a just solution of their claims; and second, while Israel's military successes in Lebanon have demonstrated that its armed forces are second to none in the region, they alone cannot bring just and lasting peace to Israel and her neighbors. The question now is how to reconcile Israel's legitimate security concerns with the legitimate rights of the Palestinians. And that answer can only come at the negotiating table. Each party must recognize that the outcome must be acceptable to all and that true peace will require compromises by all.

So, tonight I'm calling for a fresh start. This is the moment for all those directly concerned to get involved — or lend their support — to a workable basis for peace. The Camp David agreement remains the foundation of our policy. Its language provides all parties with the leeway they need for successful negotiations.

I call on Israel to make clear that the security for which she yearns can only be achieved through genuine peace, a peace requiring magnanimity, vision and courage.

I call on the Palestinian people to recognize that their own political aspirations are inextricably bound to recognition of Israel's right to a secure future.

And I call on the Arab states to accept the reality of Israel — and the reality that peace and justice are to be gained only through hard, fair, direct negotiation. In

making these calls upon others, I recognize that the United States has a special responsibility. No other nation is in the position to deal with the key parties to the conflict on the basis of trust and reliability.

The time has come for a new realism on the part of all the people of the Middle East. The State of Israel is an accomplished fact; it deserves unchallenged legitimacy within the community of nations. But Israel's legitimacy has thus far been recognized by too few countries and has been denied by every Arab state except Egypt. Israel exists; it has a right to exist in peace behind secure and defensible borders; and it has a right to demand of its neighbors that they recognize those facts.

I have personally followed and supported Israel's heroic struggle for survival, ever since the founding of the State of Israel 34 years ago. In the pre-1967 borders Israel was barely ten miles wide at its narrowest point. The bulk of Israel's population lived within artillery range of hostile Arab armies. I am not about to ask Israel to live that way again.

The war in Lebanon has demonstrated another reality in the region. The departure of the Palestinians from Beirut dramatizes more than ever the homelessness of the Palestinian people. Palestinians feel strongly that their cause is more than a question of refugees. I agree. The Camp David agreements recognized that fact when it spoke of the legitimate rights of the Palestinian people and their just requirements. For peace to endure it must involve all those who have been most deeply affected by the conflict. Only through broader participation in the peace process, most immediately by Jordan and by the Palestinians, will Israel be able to rest confident in the knowledge that its security and integrity will be respected by its neighbors. Only through the process of negotiation can all the nations of the Middle East achieve a secure peace.

These, then, are our general goals. What are the specific new American positions and why are we taking them? In the Camp David talks thus far both Israel and Egypt have felt free to express openly their views as to what the outcome should be. Understandably their views have differed on many points. The United States has thus far sought to play the role of mediator. We have avoided public comment on the key issues. We have always recognized and continue to recognize that only the voluntary agreement of those parties most directly involved in the conflict can provide an enduring solution.

But it has become evident to me that some clearer sense of America's position on the key issues is necessary to encourage wider support for the peace process. First, as outlined in the Camp David Accords, there must be a period of time during which the Palestinian inhabitants of the West Bank and Gaza will have full autonomy over their own affairs. Due consideration must be given to the principle of self-government by the inhabitants of the

territory and the legitimate security concerns of the parties involved.

The proof is in the five-year period of transition which would begin after free elections for a self-governing Palestinian authority to prove to the Palestinians that they could run their own affairs, and that such Palestinian autonomy poses no threat to Israel's security. The United States will not support the use of any additional land for the purpose of settlement during the transitional period. Indeed, the immediate adoption of a settlement freeze by Israel, more than any other action, could create the confidence needed for wider participation in these talks. Further settlement activity is in no way necessary for the security of Israel and only diminishes the confidence of the Arabs that a final outcome can be freely and fairly negotiated.

I want to make the American position clearly understood. The purpose of this transitional period is the peaceful and orderly transfer of authority from Israel to the Palestinian inhabitants of the West Bank and Gaza. At the same time, such a transfer must not interfere with Israel's security requirements.

Beyond the transition period, as we look to the future of the West Bank and Gaza, it is clear to me that peace cannot be achieved by the formation of an independent Palestinian state in those territories, nor is it achievable on the basis of Israeli sovereignty or permanent control over the West Bank and Gaza. So the United States will not support the establishment of an independent Palestinian state in the West Bank and Gaza. And we will not support annexation or permanent control by Israel.

There is, however, another way to peace. The final status of these lands must, of course, be reached through the give and take of negotiations. But it is the firm view of the United States that self-government by the Palestinians of the West Bank and Gaza in association with Jordan offers the best chance for a durable, just, and lasting peace. We base our approach squarely on the principle that the Arab-Israeli conflict should be resolved through negotiations involving an exchange of territory for peace.

This exchange is enshrined in United Nations Security Council Resolution 242, which is, in turn, incorporated in all its parts in the Camp David Agreement. U.N. Resolution 242 remains wholly valid as the foundation stone of America's Middle East peace effort. It is the United States' position that, in return for peace, the withdrawal provision of Resolution 242 applies to all fronts, including the West Bank and Gaza. When the border is negotiated between Jordan and Israel, our view on the extent to which Israel should be asked to give up territory will be heavily affected by the extent of true peace and normalization, and the security arrangement offered in return.

Finally, we remain convinced that Jerusalem must remain undivided. But its final status should be decided through negotiation. In the course of the negotiations

to come, the United States will support positions that seem to us fair and reasonable compromises and likely to promote a sound agreement. We will also put forward our own detailed proposals when we believe that they can be helpful. And, make no mistake, the United States will oppose any proposal from any party and at any point in the negotiating process that threatens the security of Israel. America's commitment to the security of Israel is ironclad. And I might add, so is mine.

During the past few days, our Ambassadors in Israel, Egypt, Jordan, and Saudi Arabia have presented to their host governments the proposals, in full detail, that I have outlined here today. Now, I am convinced that these proposals can bring justice, bring security, and bring durability to an Arab-Israeli peace. The United States will stand by these principles with total dedication. They are fully consistent with Israel's security requirements and the aspirations of the Palestinians. We will work hard to broaden participation at the peace table as envisaged by the Camp David Accords. And I fervently hope that the Palestinians and Jordan, with the support of their Arab colleagues, will accept this opportunity.

Tragic turmoil in the Middle East runs back to the dawn of history. In our modern day, conflict after conflict has taken its brutal toll there. In an age of nuclear challenge and economic interdependence, such conflicts are a threat to all the people of the world, not just the Middle East itself. It

is time for us all — in the Middle East and around the world — to call a halt to conflict, hatred and prejudice. It's time for us all to launch a common effort for reconstruction, peace and progress.

It has often been said — and regrettably too often been true — that the story of the search for peace and justice in the Middle East is a tragedy of opportunities missed. In the aftermath of the settlement in Lebanon, we now face an opportunity for a broader peace. This time we must not let it slip from our grasp. We must look beyond the difficulties and obstacles of the present and move with a fairness and resolve toward a brighter future. We owe it to ourselves — and to posterity — to do no less. For if we miss this chance to make a fresh start, we may look back on this moment from some later vantage point and realize how much that failure cost us all.

These, then, are the principles upon which American policy toward the Arab-Israeli conflict will be based. I have made a personal commitment to see that they endure and, God willing, that they will come to be seen by all reasonable, compassionate people as fair, achievable, and in the interests of all who wish to see peace in the Middle East. Tonight, on the eve of what can be a dawning of new hope for the people of the troubled Middle East — and for all the world's people who dream of a just and peaceful future — I ask you, my fellow Americans, for your support and your prayers in this great undertaking. Thank you and God bless you. ∎

Message on Crime Legislation

Following is the White House text of President Reagan's Sept. 13 message to Congress proposing legislation to reform the criminal justice system.

TO THE CONGRESS OF
THE UNITED STATES:

I am herewith transmitting proposed legislation entitled the Criminal Justice Reform Act of 1982. This Act — plus other proposals now pending in Congress — would strengthen society's defenses against the continuing and pervasive menace of crime.

Crime is clearly one of the most serious problems we face today. Crime — and the fear of crime — affect the lives of most Americans. Government's inability to deal effectively with crime diminishes the public's confidence in our system of government as a whole. Last year alone, one out of every three households in the country fell victim to some form of serious crime. By 1981, according to one survey, nearly eight out of ten Americans did not believe that our system of law enforcement discouraged people from committing crimes — a fifty percent increase in just the last fifteen

years. As the threat of crime has become clearer to all Americans, so too has the need for improving our defenses against crime. As my Attorney General said only a few weeks ago:

> "In recent years, through actions by the courts and inaction by Congress, an imbalance has arisen in the scales of justice. The criminal justice system has tilted too decidedly in favor of the rights of the criminal and against the rights of society."

It is time to restore the balance — and to make the law work to protect decent, law-abiding citizens.

To protect the rights of law-abiding citizens, the Administration has previously announced its strong support for a comprehensive law enforcement measure, the Violent Crime and Drug Enforcement Improvements Act of 1982, introduced in the Congress as S. 2572 and H.R. 6497. That important legislative initiative addresses many of our most pressing needs: bail reform, victim-witness protection, strengthened drug penalties, protection of federal officials, sentencing reform, expanded criminal forfeiture, donation of surplus federal property to State and local govern-

ments for needed correctional facilities, and a series of miscellaneous improvements in federal criminal laws.

The attached legislative proposal that I am now submitting would reform three additional areas of federal law affecting the criminal justice system. First, it would limit the insanity defense so that only those who did not have the mental state which is an element of their crime would escape responsibility for their acts. Second, the proposal would reform the exclusionary rule to prevent the suppression of evidence seized by an officer acting in the reasonable, good faith belief that his actions complied with law. Although the argument for

retaining the exclusionary rule in any form is, at best, tenuous, this proposal eliminates application of the rule in those cases in which it most clearly has no deterrent effect. Finally, the bill would reform federal habeas corpus review of State adjudications to ensure greater deference to full and fair State judicial proceedings and to limit the time within which habeas corpus proceedings may be initiated. Habeas corpus reform would conserve scarce federal and State judicial and prosecutorial resources.

This new proposal and the Violent Crime and Drug Enforcement Improvements Act of 1982 represent a legislative

program to protect all our citizens. These are not partisan initiatives. They are far too important to the Nation's well-being. In my view, they provide the basis for a renewed effort against the menace of crime. They will help restore the balance between the forces of law and the forces of lawlessness. I join with all Americans in urging the Congress to give both these legislative proposals its immediate attention and to begin the process of reclaiming our communities from criminals.

RONALD REAGAN

The White House
September 13, 1982   ∎

Multinational Force to Re-enter Lebanon

Following is the White House text of President Reagan's Sept. 20 announcement to send U.S. Marines back into Lebanon.

THE PRESIDENT: My fellow Americans, the scenes that the whole world witnessed this past weekend were among the most heartrending in the long nightmare of Lebanon's agony. Millions of us have seen pictures of the Palestinian victims of this tragedy. There is little that words can add. But there are actions we can and must take to bring that nightmare to an end.

It is not enough for us to view this as some remote event in which we ourselves are not involved. For our friends in Lebanon and Israel, for our friends in Europe and elsewhere in the Middle East, and for us as Americans, this tragedy, horrible as it is, reminds us of the absolute imperative of bringing peace to that troubled country and region. By working for peace in the Middle East, we serve the cause of world peace, and the future of mankind.

For the criminals who did this deed no punishment is enough to remove the blot of their crime. But for the rest of us, there are things that we can learn and things that we must do. The people of Lebanon must have learned that the cycle of massacre upon massacre must end. Children are not avenged by the murder of other children. Israel must have learned that there is no way it can impose its own solutions on hatreds as deep and bitter as those that produced this tragedy. If it seeks to do so, it will only sink more deeply into the quagmire that looms before it. Those outsiders who have fed the flames of civil war in Lebanon for so many years need to learn that the fire will consume them too if it is not put out. And we must all rededicate ourselves to the cause of peace. I re-emphasize my call for early progress to solve the Palestinian issue and repeat the U.S. proposals which are now even more urgent.

For now is not the time for talk alone. Now is a time for action. To act together to restore peace to Beirut; to help a stable

government emerge that can restore peace and independence to all of Lebanon; and to bring a just and lasting resolution to the conflict between Israel and its Arab neighbors, one that satisfies the legitimate rights of the Palestinians who are all too often its victims.

Our basic objectives in Lebanon have not changed, for they are the objectives of the government and the people of Lebanon themselves. First and foremost, we seek the restoration of a strong and stable central government in that country, brought into being by orderly constitutional processes. Lebanon elected a new president two short weeks ago only to see him murdered even before he could assume his office. This week a distressed Lebanon will again be electing a new president. May God grant him safety as well as the wisdom and courage to lead his country into a new and happier era.

The international community has an obligation to assist the government of Lebanon in reasserting authority over all its territory. Foreign forces and armed factions have too long obstructed the legitimate role of the government of Lebanon's security forces. We must pave the way for withdrawal of foreign forces.

The place to begin this task is in Beirut. The Lebanese government must be permitted to restore internal security in its capital. It cannot do this if foreign forces remain in or near Beirut. With this goal in mind, I have consulted with our French and Italian allies. We have agreed to form a new multinational force, similar to the one which served so well last month, with the mission of enabling the Lebanese government to resume full sovereignty over its capital, the essential precondition for extending its control over the entire country.

The Lebanese government, with the support of its people, requested this help. For this multinational force to succeed, it is essential that Israel withdraw from Beirut. With the expected cooperation of all parties, the multinational force will return to Beirut for a limited period of time. Its purpose is not to act as a police force but to

make it possible for the lawful authorities of Lebanon to discharge those duties for themselves.

Secretary Shultz, on my behalf, has also reiterated our views to the government of Israel through its Ambassador in Washington. Unless Israel moves quickly and courageously to withdraw, it will find itself ever more deeply involved in problems that are not its own and which it cannot solve.

The participation of American forces in Beirut will again be for a limited period. But I've concluded there is no alternative to their returning to Lebanon if that country is to have a chance to stand on its own feet.

Peace in Beirut is only a first step. Together with the people of Lebanon, we seek the removal of all foreign military forces from that country. The departure of all foreign forces at the request of the Lebanese authorities has been widely endorsed by Arab as well as other states. Israel and Syria have both indicated that they have no territorial ambitions in Lebanon and are prepared to withdraw. It is now urgent that specific arrangements for withdrawal of all foreign forces be agreed upon. This must happen very soon. The legitimate security concerns of neighboring states, including particularly the safety of Israel's northern population, must be provided for. But this is not a difficult task if the political will is there. The Lebanese people must be allowed to chart their own future. They must rely solely on Lebanese armed forces who are willing and able to bring security to their country. They must be allowed to do so, and the sooner the better.

Ambassador Draper, who has been in close consultation with the parties concerned in Lebanon, will remain in the area to work for the full implementation of our proposal. Ambassador Habib will join him, will represent me at the inauguration of the new President of Lebanon and will consult with the leaders in the area. He will return promptly to Washington to report to me.

Early in the summer our government met its responsibility to help resolve a severe crisis and to relieve the Lebanese peo-

ple of the crushing burden. We succeeded. Recent events have produced new problems and we must again assume our responsibility. I am especially anxious to end the agony of Lebanon because it is both right and in our national interest. But I am also determined to press ahead on the broader effort to achieve peace between Israel and its Arab neighbors. The events in Beirut of last week have served only to reinforce my conviction that such a peace is desperately needed and that the initiative we undertook on September 1st is the right way to proceed. We will not be discouraged or deterred in our efforts to seek peace in Lebanon and a just and lasting peace throughout the Middle East.

All of us must learn the appropriate lessons from this tragedy and assume the responsibilities that it imposes upon us. We owe it to ourselves and to our children. The whole world will be a safer place when this region which has known so much trouble can begin to know peace instead. Both our purpose and our actions are peaceful and we are taking them in a spirit of international cooperation.

So tonight I ask for your prayers and your support as our country continues its vital role as a leader for world peace, the role that all of us as Americans can be proud of. Thank you and God bless you.■

Contract Disputes Veto

Following is the White House text of President Reagan's Oct. 15 message accompanying his veto of HR 1371, making amendments to the Contract Disputes Act of 1978. It was Reagan's ninth veto of a public bill during the 97th Congress.

I am returning without my approval H.R. 1371, a bill "To amend section 12 of the Contract Disputes Act of 1978."

H.R. 1371 would require the Federal Government to pay interest to contractors on claims in excess of $50,000 without regard to the date the claims are certified, as now required by section 6(c) of the Contract Disputes Act. The bill would also require the Secretary of the Treasury to determine interest rates to be paid contractors, taking into account the rates of interest on current commercial loans maturing in approximately five years.

The payment of interest by the Government on contractual claims has a long history. Traditionally, the Government's sovereign immunity has barred interest payments unless the terms of a specific statute or contract required it. Among other reforms suggested by the Commission on Government Procurement in 1972 was a recommendation that the Federal Government pay interest on contractual claims. As a result of this recommendation, Congress passed the Contract Disputes Act of 1978.

I have no objection to the language in H.R. 1371 concerning the way in which interest rates on contractual claims against the Government are determined. I strongly object, however, to other language in the bill that would amend the Contract Disputes Act to require that interest on a claim run from the time a claim is submitted without regard to the date of certification of the contractor's claim. This provision is inconsistent with the purpose of the certification requirement of the Contract Disputes Act. That requirement is intended to discourage the submission of inflated claims against the Government by requiring contractors to certify that their claims are made in good faith and are accurate and complete to the best of their knowledge.

By permitting interest to run from the date a claim is submitted, instead of from the date of certification, as current law provides, H.R. 1371 could result in a large increase in Governmental obligations without any corresponding benefits to the claims resolution process so carefully established in the Contract Disputes Act. For this reason, and considering that there have been no hearings or studies conducted addressing the need for such a substantial departure from existing law, I find the bill unacceptable.

RONALD REAGAN

The White House
October 15, 1982   ■

Environmental Research Act Veto

Following is the White House text of President Reagan's Oct. 22 message accompanying his veto of S 2577, to authorize research and development programs of the Environmental Protection Agency. It was Reagan's 10th veto of a public bill during the 97th Congress.

TO THE SENATE OF
THE UNITED STATES:

I am returning without my signature S. 2577, the "Environmental Research, Development and Demonstration Act of 1983."

It should be understood that my disapproval of this legislation will in no way interfere with the conduct of any of the research programs of the Environmental Protection Agency. Pursuant to the Department of Housing and Urban Development — Independent Agencies Appropriations Act of 1983, which I signed into law on September 30, 1982, EPA will spend $220.8 million on its research activities in fiscal year 1983. The appropriations authorized for research in 1983 are 10 percent higher than in 1982, reflecting this Administration's commitment to putting environmental regulation on the soundest possible scientific footing.

While S. 2577 is unacceptable as a whole, I want to commend Congressman Cooper Evans of Iowa for contributing to this bill an amendment to authorize the Senior Environmental Assistance Program. Congressman Evans' amendment provides the authority for EPA to continue promoting meaningful employment opportunities for older Americans in Federal, State, and local agencies, as they accomplish important short-term environmental protection projects. The amendment is based on a highly successful demonstration project carried out by EPA in conjunction with the Administration on Aging and the Department of Labor. I believe the amendment would further this Administration's goals of providing productive, meaningful employment to older workers, and providing the benefits of a cleaner, safer environment to future generations.

Nevertheless, enactment of S. 2577 would represent a major step backward in achieving the goal of assuring that our vitally important environmental research programs reflect the best judgment of the scientific community, unhampered by partisan or interest group politics.

S. 2577 would mandate that the EPA Science Advisory Board membership include representatives from "States, industry, labor, academia, consumers, and the general public." This requirement runs counter to the basic premise of modern scientific thought as an objective undertaking in which the views of special interests have no role. The purpose of the Science Advisory Board is to apply the universally accepted principles of scientific peer review to the research conclusions that will form the basis for EPA regulations, a function that must remain above interest group politics.

In addition, under the statutes governing actual promulgation of EPA rules, the Administrator is obligated to seek public comment from any and all interested parties and to weigh such comment in shaping final rules. That is the stage of the rulemaking process at which involvement of special interest viewpoints is appropriate, not the earlier stage of developing a sound scientific understanding of the research findings that may be relevant to a particular rulemaking or class of rules.

Environmental regulation involves scientific, political, social, and economic judgments. The laws mandating protection of our air, water, and land against harmful pollution reflect this necessity to balance a wide range of factors. But for the entire

regulatory process to function effectively, it must have as its starting point an objectively developed review of the state of scientific knowledge. The Science Advisory Board is vital to the preparation of this objective scientific review; to require that the Board become a political entity, with representatives from various special interests, would completely undermine the use of scientific knowledge in EPA rulemaking.

The maintenance of a free, essentially self-governing scientific research community is one of the great strengths of our Nation. To undermine this tradition by requiring that the scientists appointed to the EPA Science Advisory Board wear the label of "industry" or "labor" or "consumer" is a modern-day version of Lysenkoism to which I must strongly object.

In addition to imposing these new requirements on the procedures for selecting the EPA Science Advisory Board, S. 2577 contains a number of other objectionable features. It authorizes spending that is $46.4 million above the previously enacted appropriation bill; it mandates an increase in the proportion of funds devoted to basic research from 15 percent to 20 percent, which will take funds away from high-priority research needed for the support of regulatory proceedings; it mandates a duplicative and wasteful effort to create another national environmental monitoring network; and it mandates a number of research activities that are inconsistent with the previously enacted appropriation.

For these reasons, I am returning S. 2577 without my signature.

RONALD REAGAN

The White House
October 22, 1982   ∎

Reagan Speech on Nuclear Arms Control

Following is the White House text of President Reagan's Nov. 22 address as delivered on nuclear arms control and production and deployment of the MX missile.

THE PRESIDENT: Good evening. The week before last was an especially moving one here in Washington. The Vietnam veterans finally came home once and for all to America's heart. They were welcomed with tears, with pride and with a monument to their great sacrifice. Many of their names, like those of our Republic's greatest citizens, are now engraved in stone in this city that belongs to all of us. On behalf of the nation, let me again thank the Vietnam veterans from the bottom of my heart for their courageous service to America.

Seeing those moving scenes, I know mothers of a new generation must have worried about their children and about peace. And that's what I would like to talk to you about tonight — the future of our children in a world where peace is made uneasy by the presence of nuclear weapons.

A year ago, I said the time was right to move forward on arms control. I outlined several proposals and said nothing would have a higher priority in this administration. Now, a year later, I want to report on those proposals and on other efforts we're making to ensure the safety of our children's future.

The prevention of conflict and the reduction of weapons are the most important public issues of our time. Yet, on no other issue are there more misconceptions and misunderstandings. You, the American people, deserve an explanation from your government on what our policy is on these issues. Too often, the experts have been content to discuss grandiose strategies among themselves, and cloud the public debate in technicalities no one can understand. The result is that many Americans have become frightened and, let me say, fear of the unknown is entirely understandable. Unfortunately, much of the information emerging in this debate bears little semblance to the facts.

To begin, let's go back to what the world was like at the end of World War II. The United States was the only undamaged industrial power in the world. Our military power was at its peak, and we alone had the atomic weapon. But we didn't use this wealth and this power to bully. We used it to rebuild. We raised up the war-ravaged economies, including the economies of those who had fought against us. At first, the peace of the world was unthreatened, because we alone were left with any real power, and we were using it for the good of our fellow man. Any potential enemy was deterred from aggression because the cost would have far outweighted the gain.

As the Soviets' power grew, we still managed to maintain the peace.

The United States had established a system of alliances with NATO as the centerpiece. In addition, we grew even more respected as a world leader with a strong economy and deeply-held moral values.

With our commitment to help shape a better world, the United States also pursued, and always pursued every diplomatic channel for peace. And for at least 30 years after World War II, the United States still continued to possess a large military advantage over the Soviet Union. Our strength deterred, that is, prevented, aggression against us.

This nation's military objective has always been to maintain peace by preventing war. This is neither a Democratic nor a Republican policy. It's supported by our allies. And most important of all, it's worked for nearly 40 years.

What do we mean when we speak of "nuclear deterrents"? Certainly, we don't want such weapons for their own sake. We don't desire excessive forces or what some people have called "overkill." Basically, it's a matter of others knowing that starting a conflict would be more costly to them than anything they might hope to gain.

And, yes, it is sadly ironic that in these modern times, it still takes weapons to prevent war. I wish it did not.

We desire peace. But peace is a goal, not a policy. Lasting peace is what we hope for at the end of our journey. It doesn't describe the steps we must take nor the paths we should follow to reach that goal.

I intend to search for peace along two parallel paths: deterrents and arms reductions. I believe these are the only paths that offer any real hope for an enduring peace.

And let me say I believe that if we follow prudent policies, the risk of nuclear conflict will be reduced.

Certainly the United States will never use its forces except in response to attack. Through the years, Soviet leaders have also expressed a sober view of nuclear war. And if we maintain a strong deterrent, they are exceedingly unlikely to launch an attack.

Now, while the policy of deterrents has stood the test of time, the things we must do in order to maintain deterrents have changed. You often hear that the United States and the Soviet Union are in an arms race. Well, the truth is that while the Soviet Union has raced, we have not. As you can see from this blue U.S. line in constant dollars, our defense spending in the 1960s went up because of Vietnam. And then it went downward through much of the 1970s.

And now follow the red line, which is Soviet spending. It's gone up and up and up. In spite of a stagnating Soviet economy, Soviet leaders invest 12 to 14 percent of their country's gross national product in military spending. Two to three times the level we invest.

I might add that the defense share of our United States federal budget has gone way down, too. Watch the blue line again. In 1962, when John Kennedy was President, 46 percent, almost half of the federal budget, went to our national defense. In recent years, about one quarter of our budget has gone to defense, while the share for social programs has nearly doubled. And most of our defense budget is spent on people, not weapons.

The combination of the Soviets spending more and the United States spending proportionately less changed the military balance, and weakened our deterrent.

Today, in virtually every measure of

military power, the Soviet Union enjoys a decided advantage. This chart shows the changes in the total number of intercontinental missiles and bombers. You will see that in 1962 and in 1972, the United States' forces remained about the same — even dropping some by 1982. But take a look now at the Soviet side. In 1962, at the time of the Cuban Missile Crisis, the Soviets could not compare with us in terms of strength. In 1972, when we signed the SALT I Treaty, we were nearly equal. But in 1982 — well, that red, Soviet bar stretching above the blue, American bar tells the story.

I could show you chart after chart where there is a great deal of red and a much lesser amount of U.S. blue. For example, the Soviet Union has deployed a third more land-based intercontinental ballistic missiles than we have. Believe it or not, we froze our number in 1965, and have deployed no additional missiles since then. The Soviet Union put to sea 60 new ballistic missile submarines in the last 15 years. Until last year, we had not commissioned one in that same period. The Soviet Union has built over 200 modern backfire bombers, and is building 30 more a year. For 20 years, the United States has deployed no new strategic bombers. Many of our B-52 bombers are now older than the pilots who fly them.

The Soviet Union now has 600 of the missiles considered most threatening by both sides — the intermediate-range missiles based on land. We have none. The United States withdrew its intermediate-range land-based missiles from Europe almost 20 years ago.

The world has, also, witnessed unprecedented growth in the area of Soviet conventional forces. The Soviets far exceed us in the number of tanks, artillery pieces, aircraft, and ships they produce every year. What is more, when I arrived in this office, I learned that in our own forces we had planes that could not fly and ships that could not leave port mainly for lack of spare parts and crew members.

The Soviet military buildup must not be ignored. We have recognized the problem. And, together with our allies, we have begun to correct the imbalance. Look at this chart of projected, real defense spending for the next several years. Here is the Soviet line. Let us assume the Soviets rate of spending remains at the level they have followed since the 1960s. The blue line is the United States. If my defense proposals are passed, it will still take five years before we come close to the Soviet level. Yet, the modernization of our strategic and conventional forces will assure that deterrence works and peace prevails.

Our deployed nuclear forces were built before the age of microcircuits. It is not right to ask our young men and women in uniform to maintain and operate such antiques. Many have already given their lives in missile explosions and aircraft accidents caused by the old age of their equipment. We must replace and modernize our forces.

And that is why I decided to proceed with the production and deployment of the new ICBM known as the MX. Three earlier Presidents worked to develop this missile.

Based on the best advice that I could get I concluded that the MX is the right missile at the right time. On the other hand, when I arrived in office I felt the proposal on where and how to base the missile simply cost too much in terms of money and the impact on our citizens' lives. I have concluded, however, it is absolutely essential that we proceed to produce this missile and that we base it in a series of closely based silos at Warren Air Force Base near Cheyenne, Wyoming. This plan requires only half as many missiles as the earlier plan and will fit in an area of only twenty square miles. It is the product of around-the-clock research that has been underway since I directed a search for a better, cheaper way.

I urge the members of Congress who must pass this plan to listen and examine the facts before they come to their own conclusion. Some may question what modernizing our military has to do with peace. Well, as I explained earlier, a secure force keeps others from threatening us and that keeps the peace. Just as important, it also increases the prospects of reaching significant arms reductions with the Soviets, and that is what we really want.

The United States wants deep cuts in the world's arsenal of weapons, but unless we demonstrate the will to rebuild our strength and restore the military balance, the Soviets, since they are so far ahead, have little incentive to negotiate with us. Let me repeat that point because it goes to the heart of our policies. Unless we demonstrate the will to rebuild our strength, the Soviets have little incentive to negotiate. If we had not begun to modernize, the Soviet negotiators would know we had nothing to bargain with except talk. They would know that we were bluffing without a good hand because they know what cards we hold just as we know what is in their hand.

You may recall that in 1969 the Soviets did not want to negotiate a treaty banning anti-ballistic missiles. It was only after our Senate narrowly voted to fund an anti-ballistic missile program that the Soviets agreed to negotiate. We then reached an agreement. We also know that one-sided arms control does not work. We have tried time and time again to set an example by cutting our own forces in the hope that the Soviets would do likewise. The result has always been that they keep building.

I believe that our strategy for peace will succeed. Never before has the United States proposed such a comprehensive program of nuclear arms control. Never in our history have we engaged in so many negotiations with the Soviets to reduce nuclear arms and to find a stable peace. What we are saying to them is this: We will modernize our military in order to keep the balance for peace, but wouldn't it be better if we both simply reduced our arsenals to a much lower level?

Let me begin with the negotiations on the intermediate-range nuclear forces that are currently underway in Geneva. As I said earlier, the most threatening of these forces are the land-based missiles which the Soviet Union now has aimed at Europe, the Middle East, and Asia.

This chart shows the number of warheads on these Soviet missiles. In 1972 there were 600. The United States was at zero. In 1977 there were 600. The United States was still at zero. Then the Soviets began deploying powerful new missiles with three warheads and a reach of thousands of miles — the SS-20. Since then the bar has gone through the roof — the Soviets have added a missile with three warheads every week. Still you see no United States blue on the chart. Although the Soviet leaders earlier this year declared they had frozen deployment of this dangerous missile, they have in fact continued deployment.

Last year, on November 18th, I proposed the total, global elimination of all these missiles. I proposed that the United States would deploy no comparable missiles which are scheduled for late 1983 if the Soviet Union would dismantle theirs. We would follow agreement on the land-based missiles with limits on other intermediate-range systems.

The European governments strongly support our initiative. The Soviet Union has thus far shown little inclination to take this major step to zero levels. Yet I believe and I am hoping that, as the talks proceed and as we approach the scheduled placement of our new systems in Europe, the Soviet leaders will see the benefits of such a far-reaching agreement.

This summer we also began negotiations on Strategic Arms Reductions, the proposal we call START. Here we're talking about intercontinental missiles — the weapons with a longer range than the intermediate-range ones I was just discussing. We are negotiating on the basis of deep reductions. I proposed in May that we cut the number of warheads on these missiles to an equal number, roughly one-third below current levels. I also proposed that we cut the number of missiles themselves to an equal number, about half the current U.S. level. Our proposals would eliminate some 4,700 warheads and 2,250 missiles. I think that would be quite a service to mankind.

This chart shows the current level of United States ballistic missiles, both land- and sea-based. This is the Soviet level. We intend to convince the Soviets it would be in their own best interest to reduce these missiles. Look at the reduced numbers both sides would have under our proposal — quite a dramatic change. We also seek to reduce the total destructive power of these missiles and other elements of United States and Soviet strategic forces.

In 1977, when the last administration proposed more limited reductions, the Soviet Union refused even to discuss them. This time their reaction has been quite different. Their opening position is a seri-

ous one, and even though it doesn't meet our objective of deep reductions, there's no question we're heading in the right direction. One reason for this change is clear. The Soviet Union knows that we are now serious about our own strategic programs and that they must be prepared to negotiate in earnest.

We also have other important arms control efforts underway. In the talks in Vienna on Mutual and Balanced Force Reductions, we've proposed cuts in military personnel to a far lower and equal level. And in the 40-nation Committee on Disarmament in Geneva, we're working to develop effective limitations on nuclear testing and chemical weapons. The whole world remains outraged by the Soviets' and their allies' use of biological and chemical weapons against defenseless people in Afghanistan, Cambodia, and Laos. This experience makes ironclad verification all the more essential for arms control.

There is, of course, much more that needs to be done. In an age when intercontinental missiles can span half the globe in less than half an hour, it's crucial that Soviet and American leaders have a clear understanding of each other's capabilities and intentions.

Last June in Berlin, and again at the United Nations Special Session on Disarmament, I vowed that the United States would make every effort to reduce the risks of accident and misunderstanding and thus to strengthen mutual confidence between the United States and the Soviet Union. Since then, we've been actively studying detailed measures to implement this Berlin initiative.

Today I would like to announce some of the measures which I have proposed in a special letter just sent to the Soviet leadership and which I have instructed our ambassadors in Geneva to discuss with their Soviet counterparts. They include but also go beyond some of the suggestions I made in Berlin.

The first of these measures involves advance notification of all United States and Soviet test launches of intercontinental ballistic missiles. We will also seek Soviet agreement on notification of all sea-launched ballistic missiles as well as intermediate-range land-based ballistic missiles of the type we're currently negotiating. This would remove surprise and uncertainty at the sudden appearance of such missiles on the warning screens of the two countries.

In another area of potential misunderstanding, we propose to the Soviets that we provide each other with advance notification of our major military exercises. Here again, our objective is to reduce the surprise and uncertainty surrounding otherwise sudden moves by either side.

These sorts of measures are designed to deal with the immediate issues of miscalculation in time of crisis. But there are deeper, longer-term problems as well. In order to clear away some of the mutual ignorance and suspicion between our two

countries, I will propose that we both engage in a broad-ranging exchange of basic data about our nuclear forces. I am instructing our ambassadors at the negotiations on both strategic and intermediate forces to seek Soviet agreement on an expanded exchange of information. The more one side knows about what the other side is doing, the less room there is for surprise and miscalculation.

Probably everyone has heard of the so-called Hotline, which enables me to communicate directly with the Soviet leadership in the event of a crisis. The existing Hotline is dependable and rapid — with both ground and satellite links. But because it's so important, I've also directed that we carefully examine any possible improvements to the existing Hotline system.

Now, although we've begun negotiations on these many proposals, this doesn't mean we've exhausted all the initiatives that could help to reduce the risk of accidental conflict. We'll leave no opportunity unexplored, and we'll consult closely with Senators Nunn, Jackson, and Warner, and other Members of the Congress who have made important suggestions in this field.

We are also making strenuous efforts to prevent the spread of nuclear weapons to additional countries. It would be tragic if we succeeded in reducing existing arsenals only to have new threats emerge in other areas of the world.

Earlier I spoke of America's contributions to peace following World War II, of all we did to promote peace and prosperity for our fellow man. Well, we're still those same people. We still seek peace above all else.

I want to remind our own citizens and those around the world of this tradition of American good will because I am concerned about the effects the nuclear fear is having on our people. The most upsetting letters I receive are from schoolchildren who write to me as a class assignment. It's evident they've discussed the most nightmarish aspects of a nuclear holocaust in their classrooms. Their letters are often full of terror. Well, this should not be so.

The philosopher, Spinoza, said, "Peace is a virtue, a state of mind, a disposition for benevolence, confidence, justice." Well, those are the qualities we want our children to inherit, not fear. They must grow up confident if they're to meet the challenges of tomorrow as we will meet the challenges of today.

I began these remarks speaking of our children. I want to close on the same theme. Our children should not grow up frightened. They should not fear the future. We're working to make it peaceful and free. I believe their future can be the brightest, most exciting of any generation. We must reassure them and let them know that their parents and the leaders of this world are seeking, above all else, to keep them safe and at peace. I consider this to be a sacred trust.

My fellow Americans, on this Thanksgiving, when we have so much to be grate-

ful for, let us give special thanks for our peace, our freedom and our good people.

I've always believed that this land was set aside in an uncommon way, that a divine plan placed this great continent between the oceans to be found by a people from every corner of the earth who had a special love of faith, freedom and peace.

Let us reaffirm America's destiny of goodness and good will. Let us work for peace; and as we do, let us remember the lines of the famous old hymn "Oh, God of Love, Oh, King of Peace, make wars throughout the world to cease."

Thank you. Good night and God bless you.   ■

Indian Colleges Veto

Following is the White House text of President Reagan's Jan. 3 memorandum of disapproval (pocket veto) on S 2623, authorizing federal assistance to the nation's 18 tribally controlled Indian community colleges. It was Reagan's 11th veto of a public bill during the 97th Congress.

I am withholding my approval of S 2623, which would amend the Tribally Controlled Community Colleges Assistance Act of 1978 and extend its authorities through 1987.

I am taking this action with reluctance, because my Administration is deeply committed to providing educational opportunities for American Indians. Education is critical to economic betterment for all elements of our society. It is an equally important aspect of increasing self-determination for American Indians. I support fully the intent of S 2623 to improve existing Indian community college programs. My Administration is dedicated to furthering this goal. The bill which is before me, however, includes a number of provisions that are unacceptable and that do not contribute to enhancement of Indian education.

Foremost among the unacceptable provisions of this bill is section 2, which would declare the Federal government's support of tribal community colleges to be a part of its trust responsibility toward Indian tribes. College level Indian education has never been characterized in law or treaty as a trust responsibility of the Federal government, and to do so now would potentially create legal obligations and entitlements that are not clearly intended or understood. Such a declaration is wholly unnecessary to the continuation of a successful program of Federal assistance to tribally controlled community colleges.

Although the conference report on S 2623 suggests that "Federal policy (on Indian education) should be clear and unequivocal," the enrolled bill is highly ambiguous as to the nature and extent of this new policy of trust responsibility. S 2623 imposes what the conference report itself

admits is a "very general" trust responsibility. However, neither the bill nor the report makes any attempt to define the nature or extent of that responsibility, except to suggest — in nonbinding report language — some concepts that are *not* intended. This vague nonstatutory language could be interpreted by the courts in a variety of ways. It could be read as establishing a trust relationship that creates an absolute responsibility to provide assistance to tribal colleges and Indian students regardless of need, and it could establish a highly undesirable precedent for making all Indian social service programs a part of the Federal government's "very general" trust responsibility.

Finally, section 2 would also provide that grants could be used for the improvement and expansion of physical facilities. When the program of assistance to tribally controlled community colleges was originally conceived, the Congress contemplated use of existing community facilities. To begin a major new building program when there are so many other competing tribal needs would be duplicative, unwarranted, and ill-advised under current economic conditions. Funds provided through the Bureau of Indian Affairs for the tribally controlled community colleges assistance program are for program support only, and should remain so.

Another unacceptable provision is in section 14(b) of this bill, which would subject regulations issued by the Secretary of the Interior under the program to an unconstitutional legislative veto device presently found in section 431 of the General Education Provisions Act. The Attorney General has advised me, and I agree, that two Houses of Congress cannot bind the Executive Branch by passing a concurrent resolution that is not presented to me for approval or veto. Such a provision unconstitutionally encroaches on the principle of separation of powers that is at the foundation of our government.

In addition to these strong objections, I also have serious reservations about a number of other provisions of the bill, which would significantly increase Federal expenditures in a time that demands fiscal restraint. Those reservations have been explained in reports and testimony of the Department of the Interior on the bill.

The authorities in the Tribally Controlled Community Colleges Assistance Act are not scheduled to expire until September 30, 1984, under current law. Accordingly, there will be no interruption of our current successful program activities as a result of my disapproval of S 2623. It is my hope that Congress will reconsider legislation extending the Act early in the next session and enact a bill which both advances the program's objectives and meets the Administration's objections to S 2623.

RONALD REAGAN

The White House
January 3, 1983 ∎

Silver Dealers Veto

Following is the White House text of President Reagan's Jan. 4 memorandum of disapproval (pocket veto) on HR 5858, authorizing payment to three silver dealers for losses incurred after the Treasury Department stopped selling silver in 1967. It was Reagan's first veto of a private bill during the 97th Congress.

I am withholding my approval of HR 5858, a bill for the relief of three silver dealers who suffered business losses as a result of their short market positions resulting from a decision by the Department of the Treasury to terminate the sale of Government-owned silver on May 18, 1967, without honoring the dealers' telephonic requests made that day to purchase almost seven million ounces of silver.

These claims were the subject of very extensive proceedings before the former United States Court of Claims, which on May 18, 1967, held that no legally binding contracts to purchase the silver had been established by these claimants, because the claimants (1) were clearly on notice that the Treasury's involvement in the silver market was altogether inseparable from monetary policy, (2) had reason to expect that Treasury would abandon the marketplace just as soon as doing so would serve monetary policy, and (3) knew that Government silver sales would end soon in view of the published reports that Treasury's supply of silver was being rapidly depleted. (*Primary Metal & Mineral Corp. v. United States,* 556 F.2d 507 (Ct.Cl. 1997).)

In parallel proceedings before a trial commissioner of the same court pursuant to a Congressional Reference proceeding under 28 U.S.C. Sections 1494 and 2509 (1970), the trial commissioner had earlier found that the same dealers had valid breach of contract claims, even though he, too, found that they were well aware of the potential for a sudden termination of the sales program. After the court had rejected his analysis, he nevertheless concluded that the claimants had "equitable" claims sufficient to justify private relief legislation merely because (in his opinion) the Court of Claims was wrong in disagreeing with his legal theory. In its report to the Congress, a review panel of three trial commissioners, without explaining its reasoning, stated that it agreed with this unprecedented rationale for the existence of an equitable claim against the Government.

To permit the silver dealers covered by HR 5858 to recover over $3.3 million without any findings that they received inequitable treatment from the Government, in the face of the unappealed holding of the Court of Claims that they had no legal claims against the Treasury, would establish an undesirable precedent for payment of a host of claims to claimants who may have encountered hardships due to busi-

ness decisions made with full awareness of the risks that a change in a Government property disposal program might entail. No doubt many similarly situated individuals have had their expectations frustrated in the past by similar program changes. To single out these three claimants for special relief would be unjust to the others, while payment to all for frustrated expectations would result in an unacceptable interference with the Government's ability to decisively and expeditiously respond to developments affecting vital national policies. For these reasons I find the bill unacceptable.

RONALD REAGAN

The White House
January 4, 1983 ∎

Education Bill Veto

Following is the White House text of President Reagan's Jan. 12 memorandum of disapproval (pocket veto) on HR 7336, making amendments to the Education Consolidation and Improvement Act of 1981. It was Reagan's 12th veto of a public bill during the 97th Congress.

I am withholding my approval of HR 7336, which would make certain amendments intended to improve the implementation of the Education Consolidation and Improvement Act of 1981.

I continue to support the objectives of both Chapter 1 and Chapter 2 of the Education Consolidation and Improvement Act. However, I cannot approve HR 7336 because the bill makes substantive changes to the Education Consolidation and Improvement Act that are unacceptable, as well as amendments to the legislative veto provision of the General Education Provisions Act that I believe to be an unwarranted intrusion on the Executive branch's constitutional authority.

Among the unacceptable provisions is section 17(a)(1), which would declare the Federal government's assistance to disadvantaged Indian students under ECIA Chapter 1 to be a part of its trust responsibility toward Indian tribes. This provision is the same as one included in S 2623, the Tribally Controlled Community College Assistance Act Amendments, from which I recently withheld my approval. The provision of Federal education assistance to Indian students is not characterized in law or treaty as a trust responsibility, and has not been held by the courts to be so. As I noted in my Memorandum of Disapproval on S 2623, to declare the provision of education to Indian students a trust responsibility would potentially create legal obligations and entitlements that are not clearly intended or understood. This provision of HR 7336 is unnecessary to the administra-

tion of the Chapter 1 program.

Also unacceptable is section 16(b) of HR 7336, which would make certain amendments to a two-House legislative veto device presently contained in section 431 of the General Education Provisions Act. The Attorney General has advised me, and I agree, that two Houses of Congress cannot bind the Executive branch by passing a concurrent resolution that is not presented to me for approval or veto.

Another objectionable provision of HR 7336, section 1, would require continuation under Chapter 1 of the definition of a currently migratory child that was in use under the antecedent Title I program. This requirement would prevent the Administration from focusing the limited resources available for migrant services under Chapter 1 on those children whose education is actually interrupted as a result of their migrant status.

Other amendments in the bill relating to the Education Consolidation and Improvement Act could be construed to reinstate requirements and procedures contrary to the intent of the Act to provide greater authority and flexibility for State and local educational agencies.

My disapproval of HR 7336 in no way reflects upon the efforts of the author of this bill, Representative William Goodling, of Pennsylvania. Mr. Goodling worked closely with the Department of Education to clarify specific weaknesses in the Education Consolidation and Improvement Act and to reflect that effort in the House report language. Despite his efforts, there are substantive provisions in HR 7336 that do not eliminate the ambiguities in the language of the existing ECIA and seem to restore undesirable complexity to the administration of ECIA programs.

Although the bill would make several desirable changes to the Education Consolidation and Improvement Act, the objectionable provisions far outweigh any of its benefits.

For these reasons, I cannot approve the bill.

RONALD REAGAN

The White House
January 12, 1983 ∎

Wilderness Bill Veto

Following is the White House text of President Reagan's Jan. 14 memorandum of disapproval (pocket veto) on HR 9, designating federal wilderness areas in Florida. It was Reagan's 13th veto of a public bill during the 97th Congress.

After careful consideration, I have determined, for the reasons stated below, to withhold my approval of HR 9. I regret that this action is necessary, because I sup-port the designation of additions to the National Wilderness Preservation System in the State of Florida, as recommended by the Administration and set forth in this bill. My Administration has proposed almost two million acres of land for designation as wilderness and the unique natural habitat designated in HR 9 would be particularly valuable additions to the national wilderness system.

Although HR 9 is intended to resolve an issue that has been in contention during three prior Administrations, it does so in a way that is unnecessarily costly to the Federal taxpayer. Because of administrative actions taken earlier this week by the Secretary of the Interior, my disapproval of this legislation will not have the effect of permitting phosphate mining to proceed in the Osceola National Forest. I do not object to legislative efforts to preclude phosphate mining in the Osceola National Forest. I do object, however, to the provisions of this bill that would vest previously contingent property rights in certain mining companies. This could require the Federal government to pay those mining companies as much as $200 million for those property rights — rights that, absent this legislation, might not otherwise have existed.

Specifically, this bill attempts to convey to several mining companies the rights to, and value from, 41 preference right lease applications for deposits of phosphates underlying the Osceola National Forest. Under present law, these mining companies are entitled to these mining leases only if the Secretary of the Interior determines that the phosphate deposits underlying this land are valuable deposits. HR 9 would establish property rights to the leases in specific companies by requiring the Secretary of the Interior, and ultimately the courts, to judge the lease applications without reference to the cost of compliance with current applicable statutory and regulatory requirements for environmental protection. Such requirements include those established under the National Environmental Policy Act, the Clean Water Act, and the Clean Air Act. Hence, under this legislation, the determination of whether these phosphate deposits are "valuable" would not take into consideration the cost of returning the Osceola National Forest lands to their natural state as required by current law.

This Administration is opposed to a policy of conveying interests in public resources by waiving applicable statutory requirements that are designed to protect the environment.

Moreover, having required the mineral rights to be conveyed to the companies by the Secretary of the Interior, this bill would then prohibit mining on the leases and require the Federal government to purchase the conveyed lease rights back from the companies. Thus, the bill would, in effect, force Federal purchase of rights that under current law would remain in Federal ownership in the first place.

Analyses available to the Department of the Interior indicate that no current technology is capable of returning the mined lands to the reclamation standards required by current Federal laws and regulations. The Department of the Interior is faced with an administrative record regarding restoration that demonstrates that the applicant mining companies cannot meet the valuable deposit test required by current law for lease issuance. Consequently, the Secretary of the Interior has advised me that, based on that administrative record, mining should not now take place in the Osceola National Forest, and that he has rejected the preference right lease applications.

However, because HR 9 specifies a less strenuous standard than current law, the lease applicants would most likely be found to have met the valuable deposit test were this measure to become law. The Department of the Interior would then have to determine the fair market value of the interests and extend monetary credits to the lease applicants. Further, though the bill provides that the fair market value is to be determined by taking into account all environmental laws, any Secretarial action valuing these leases in a way adverse to the applicants' expectations would likely result in costly litigation, and the possible recovery in the United States Claims Court of payments to these companies for loss of their "rights" in public resources to which they would not be entitled absent this litigation.

The administrative decision process, necessary under current law to resolve this issue, is being brought to conclusion under my Administration. To the extent that further litigation is entered into on this issue, it should be decided under current law applicable to all similar cases.

RONALD REAGAN

The White House
January 14, 1983 ∎

Anti-Crime Bill Veto

Following is the White House text of President Reagan's Jan. 14 memorandum of disapproval (pocket veto) on HR 3963, an anti-crime bill package. It was Reagan's 14th veto of a public bill during the 97th Congress.

I am withholding my approval of HR 3963, a bill concerning criminal law matters, because its disadvantages far outweigh any intended benefits.

In late September 1982, the Senate overwhelmingly approved a major crime bill by a vote of 95 to 1. That measure, the Violent Crime and Drug Enforcement Improvements Act of 1982 (S 2572), would have resulted in urgently needed reforms in Federal bail laws to put an end to our "revolving door" system of justice, compre-

hensive reforms in Federal forfeiture laws to strip away the enormous assets and profits of narcotics traffickers and organized crime syndicates, and sweeping sentencing reforms to insure more uniform, determinate prison sentences for those convicted of Federal crimes. That major crime bill also contained other criminal law reforms. I strongly supported the principal elements of the Violent Crime and Drug Enforcement Improvements Act, especially the bail, sentencing, and forfeiture provisions.

The House of Representatives failed to approve this measure. It adopted a miscellaneous assortment of criminal justice proposals, HR 3963, which was approved in the waning hours of the 97th Congress. Although some elements of the House-initiated bill are good, other provisions are misguided or seriously flawed, possibly even unconstitutional. While its provisions on forfeiture of criminal assets and profits fall short of what the Administration proposed, they are clearly desirable. Had they been presented to me as a separate measure, I would have been pleased to give my approval. But HR 3963 does not deal with bail reform, nor does it address sentencing reform. Both are subjects long overdue for congressional action.

In addition to its failure to address some of the most serious problems facing Federal law enforcement, this "mini-crime bill" would in several respects hamper existing enforcement activity. I am particularly concerned about its adverse impact on our efforts to combat drug abuse.

The Act would create a drug director and a new bureaucracy within the Executive Branch with the power to coordinate and direct all domestic and international Federal drug efforts, including law enforcement operations. The creation of another layer of bureaucracy within the Executive Branch would produce friction, disrupt effective law enforcement, and could threaten the integrity of criminal investigations and prosecutions — the very opposite of what its proponents apparently intend.

The seriousness of this threat is underscored by the overwhelming opposition to this provision by the Federal law enforcement community as well as by such groups as the International Association of Chiefs of Police and the National Association of Attorneys General. The so-called "drug Czar" provision was enacted hastily without thoughtful debate and without benefit of any hearings. Although its aim — with which I am in full agreement — is to promote coordination, this can be and is being achieved through existing administrative structures.

Upon taking office, I directed the Attorney General and other senior officials of the Administration to improve the coordination and efficiency of Federal law enforcement efforts, with particular emphasis on drug-related crime. This has been accomplished through the establishment of the Cabinet Council on Legal Policy, which is chaired by the Attorney General and whose membership includes all Cabinet officers with responsibility for narcotics law enforcement. Working through the Cabinet Council, the White House Office on Drug Policy is an integral part of the process by which a comprehensive and coordinated narcotics enforcement policy is carried out.

I am pleased with the results of this process, which last Fall led to the creation of a nationwide task force effort to combat organized crime and narcotics trafficking. The war on crime and drugs does not need more bureaucracy in Washington. It does need more action in the field, and that is where my Administration will focus its efforts.

HR 3963 would also authorize the Federal prosecution of an armed robber or burglar who has twice been convicted in State court. This provision includes an unworkable and possibly unconstitutional restraint upon federal prosecutions in this area, by allowing a State or local prosecutor to veto any Federal prosecution under his or her authority, even if the Attorney General had approved the prosecution. Such a restraint on Federal prosecutorial discretion and the delegation of Executive responsibility it entails raise grave constitutional and practical concerns. It would, for example, surely increase friction among Federal, State, and local prosecutors at a time when we are doing so much to decrease it.

Other provisions of HR 3963 are also defective. For example, the provision that expands Federal jurisdiction whenever food, drugs, or other products are tampered with, an expansion that I strongly support, was drafted to include tampering that occurs in an injured consumer's own home. It also fails to distinguish between tampering that results in injury and tampering that results in death. These are, however, essentially technical matters which might have been overcome but for the press of time in the closing days of Congress. I share the widespread public desire for new legislation on tampering and will work with the new Congress to produce an acceptable bill on that subject.

My Administration has proposed significant legislation to strengthen law enforcement and restore the balance between the forces of law and the forces of crime. Changes in sentencing, bail laws, the exclusionary rule, the insanity defense, and other substantive reforms in criminal law were not passed by the 97th Congress. Such reforms, if enacted, could make a real difference in the quality of justice in this country.

It would have given me great pleasure to be able to approve substantive criminal justice legislation. I completely support some of the features of HR 3963, such as the Federal Intelligence Personnel Protection Act. Others I agree with in principle. But the disadvantages of this bill greatly outweigh its benefits. I look forward to approving legislation that does not contain the serious detriments of the present bill, and my Administration will work closely with Chairman Thurmond and Chairman Rodino to secure passage of substantive criminal justice reforms.

RONALD REAGAN

The White House
January 14, 1983

PUBLIC LAWS

Public Laws, 97th Congress, 2nd Session

PL 97-146 (H J Res 382) Permit the broadcasting in the United States of the International Communication Agency film "Let Poland Be Poland: A Day of Solidarity With the People of Poland." ZABLOCKI, D-Wis. — 1/25/82 — House passed Jan. 27. Senate passed Jan. 28. President signed Jan. 30, 1982.

PL 97-147 (H J Res 389) Make urgent supplemental appropriations for the fiscal year ending Sept. 30, 1982, for the Department of Agriculture and the Commodity Credit Corporation, and provide reimbursement for net realized losses. WHITTEN, D-Miss. — 1/29/82 — House Appropriations reported Feb. 4 (H Rept 97-424). House passed Feb. 9. Senate passed, amended, Feb. 10. House agreed to Senate amendment Feb. 10. President signed Feb. 15, 1982.

PL 97-148 (H J Res 391) Make urgent supplemental appropriations for the fiscal year ending Sept. 30, 1982, for the Department of Labor and the Employment and Training Administration, provide grants to states for unemployment insurance and employment services, and advances to the Unemployment Trust Fund and other funds. WHITTEN, D-Miss. — 1/29/82 — House Appropriations reported Feb. 4 (H Rept 97-425). House passed Feb. 9. Senate passed Feb. 10. President signed Feb. 22, 1982.

PL 97-149 (S J Res 134) Designate 1982 as the "National Year of Disabled Persons." ARMSTRONG, R-Colo. — 12/10/81 — Senate Judiciary reported Dec. 15. Senate passed Dec. 16. House Post Office and Civil Service discharged. House passed Feb. 10, 1982. President signed Feb. 26, 1982.

PL 97-150 (S J Res 122) Designate the week of Feb. 28-March 6, 1982, as "National Construction Industry Week." BAKER, R-Tenn. — 11/9/81 — Senate Judiciary reported Dec. 3. Senate passed Dec. 4. House Post Office and Civil Service discharged. House passed Feb. 10, 1982. President signed March 1, 1982.

PL 97-151 (S J Res 142) Designate March 21, 1982, as "Afghanistan Day," commemorating the struggle of the people of Afghanistan against the occupation of their country by Soviet forces. SPECTER, R-Pa. — 2/2/82 — Senate Judiciary reported March 2. Senate passed March 3. House passed March 4. President signed March 10, 1982.

PL 97-152 (HR 5021) Extend the date for submission to Congress of the report of the Commission on Wartime Relocation and Internment of Civilians. MATSUI, D-Calif. — 11/18/81 — House Judiciary reported Dec. 10 (H Rept 97-378). House passed Dec. 15. Senate Judiciary discharged. Senate passed Feb. 25, 1982. President signed March 16, 1982.

PL 97-153 (S J Res 91) Designate the month of July 1982 as "National Peach Month." THURMOND, R-S.C. — 6/11/81 — Senate Judiciary reported June 24. Senate passed June 25. House Post Office and Civil Service discharged. House passed, amended, Feb. 10, 1982. Senate agreed to House amendments March 2. President signed March 16, 1982.

PL 97-154 (S J Res 105) Authorize and request the president to designate the month of October 1982 as "National P.T.A. Membership Month." LAXALT, R-Nev. — 7/31/81 — Senate Judiciary reported Sept. 15. Senate passed Sept. 16. House Post Office and Civil Service discharged. House passed, amended, Feb. 10. Senate agreed to House amendments March 2. President signed March 16, 1982.

PL 97-155 (HR 4625) Provide for the review and transfer of certain works of art to West Germany. WHITE, D-Texas — 9/29/81 — House Armed Services reported Oct. 27 (H Rept 97-298). House passed, under suspension of the rules, Nov. 4. Senate Armed Services reported Dec. 10 (S Rept 97-291). Senate passed, amended, Feb. 25, 1982. House agreed to Senate amendments March 2. President signed March 17, 1982.

PL 97-156 (S J Res 148) Designate March 18, 1982, as "National Agriculture Day." HELMS, R-N.C. — 2/24/82 — Senate Judiciary reported March 2. Senate passed March 4. House passed March 11. President signed March 18, 1982.

PL 97-157 (H J Res 373) Express the sense of Congress that the government of the Soviet Union should respect the rights of its citizens to practice religion and to emigrate. SCHROEDER, D-Colo. — 12/10/81 — House passed, under suspension of the rules, March 2, 1982. Senate passed March 4. President signed March 22, 1982.

PL 97-158 (H J Res 348) Provide for the awarding of a special gold medal to Queen Beatrix of the Netherlands in recognition of the 1982 bicentennial anniversary of diplomatic and trade relations between the Netherlands and the United States. VANDER JAGT, R-Mich. — 10/26/81 — House passed, under suspension of the rules, March 2, 1982. Senate passed March 4. President signed March 22, 1982.

PL 97-159 (S 2166) Provide for distribution within the United States of the International Communication Agency slide show entitled "Montana: The People Speak." BAUCUS, D-Mont. — 3/3/82 — Senate Foreign Relations reported March 10. Senate passed March 15. House

passed, under suspension of the rules, March 23. President signed March 24, 1982.

PL 97-160 (S 2254) Temporarily extend the authority to conduct experiments in flexible and compressed schedules under the Federal Employees Flexible and Compressed Work Schedules Act of 1978. STEVENS, R-Alaska — 3/22/82 — Senate passed March 22. House passed, under suspension of the rules, March 26. President signed March 26, 1982.

PL 97-161 (H J Res 409) Make further continuing appropriations for fiscal year 1982. WHITTEN, D-Miss. — 2/24/82 — House Appropriations reported March 23 (H Rept 97-465). House passed March 24. Senate passed March 31. President signed March 31, 1982.

PL 97-162 (S 892) Provide for continued authority of the Federal Grant and Cooperative Agreement Act and renew the authority of the Office of Management and Budget to exempt individual transactions and programs from the requirements of the act. ROTH, R-Del. — 4/7/81 — Senate Governmental Affairs reported Aug. 13 (S Rept 97-180). Senate passed Sept. 22. House Government Operations discharged. House passed March 23, 1982. President signed April 1, 1982.

PL 97-163 (S 1937) Extend the expiration date of section 252 of the Energy Policy and Conservation Act. McCLURE, R-Idaho — 12/10/81 — Senate Judiciary and Energy and Natural Resources discharged. Senate passed March 31, 1982. House passed April 1. President signed April 1, 1982.

PL 97-164 (HR 4482) Establish a U.S. Court of Appeals for the Federal Circuit and establish a U.S. Claims Court. KASTENMEIER, D-Wis. — 9/15/81 — House Judiciary reported Nov. 4 (H Rept 97-312). House passed, under suspension of the rules, Nov. 18. Senate passed, amended, Dec. 8. House agreed to Senate amendment with an amendment March 9, 1982. Senate agreed to House amendment March 22. President signed April 2, 1982.

PL 97-165 (H J Res 272) Authorize and request the president to designate April 4-10, 1982, as "National Medic Alert Week." COELHO, D-Calif. — 6/2/81 — House Post Office and Civil Service discharged. House passed March 11, 1982. Senate Judiciary discharged. Senate passed March 30. President signed April 3, 1982.

PL 97-166 (H J Res 447) Authorize and request the president to designate April 4, 1982, as "National Day of Reflection." KEMP, R-N.Y. — 3/29/82 — House Post Office and Civil Service discharged. House passed March 30. Senate Judiciary discharged. Senate passed March 31. President signed April 3, 1982.

PL 97-167 (H J Res 435) Designate April 12, 1982, as "American Salute to Cabanatuan Prisoner of War Memorial Day." McCOLLUM, R-Fla. — 3/11/82 — House Post Office and Civil Service discharged. House passed April 1. Senate passed April 1. President signed April 6, 1982.

PL 97-168 (S 634) Authorize the exchange of certain lands in Idaho and Wyoming. McCLURE, R-Idaho — 3/5/81 — Senate Energy and Natural Resources reported Aug. 27 (S Rept 97-182). Senate passed Sept. 22. House Interior and Insular Affairs reported March 2, 1982 (H Rept 97-439). House passed, amended, March 16. Senate agreed to House amendments March 25. President signed April 6, 1982.

PL 97-169 (S J Res 102) Authorize and request the president to designate the month of April 1982 as "Parliamentary Emphasis Month." BAKER, R-Tenn. — 7/29/81 — Senate passed July 29. House Post Office and Civil Service discharged. House passed April 1, 1982. President signed April 6, 1982.

PL 97-170 (H J Res 410) Designate April 19, 1982, as "Dutch-American Friendship Day." ALEXANDER, D-Ark. — 2/24/82 — House Post Office and Civil Service discharged. House passed March 30. Senate passed March 31. President signed April 12, 1982.

PL 97-171 (S 2333) Permit an officer or employee of the U.S. government, injured during an assassination attempt, to receive contributions from charitable organizations. ROTH, R-Del. — 4/1/82 — Senate passed April 1. House passed April 1. President signed April 13, 1982.

PL 97-172 (S J Res 67) Designate the week of April 19-26, 1982, as "National Nurse-Midwifery Week." INOUYE, D-Hawaii — 4/8/81 — Senate Judiciary reported Sept. 23. Senate passed Sept. 25. House Post Office and Civil Service discharged. House passed April 1, 1982. President signed April 16, 1982.

PL 97-173 (H J Res 448) Designate April 25-May 2, 1982, as "Jewish Heritage Week." ADDABBO, D-N.Y. — 3/30/82 — House Post Office and Civil Service discharged. House passed April 22. Senate passed April 22. President signed April 28, 1982.

PL 97-174 (S 266) Implement procedures and guidelines for the interagency sharing of health resources between the Department of Defense and the Veterans Administration. PERCY, R-Ill. — 1/27/81 — Senate Governmental Affairs reported June 15 (S Rept 97-137). Senate Veterans' Affairs reported Sept. 29 (S Rept 97-196). Senate passed Oct. 27. House passed, amended, Nov. 4. Senate agreed to House

amendments with amendments April 1, 1982. House agreed to Senate amendments April 20. President signed May 4, 1982.

PL 97-175 (S 2373) Change the name of the landing strip at White Sands missile range in the State of New Mexico to "White Sands Space Harbor." SCHMITT, R-N.M. — 4/15/82 — Senate passed April 15. House Armed Services discharged. House passed April 27. President signed May 11, 1982.

PL 97-176 (S 2244) Give effect to the Protocol amending the Convention for the Preservation of the Halibut Fishery of the Northern Pacific Ocean and Bering Sea. PACKWOOD, R-Ore. — 3/22/82 — Senate Commerce, Science and Transportation reported March 22 (S Rept 97-323). Senate passed April 22. House Merchant Marine and Fisheries discharged. House passed May 4. President signed May 17, 1982.

PL 97-177 (S 1131) Require the federal government to pay interest on late payments to contractors. DANFORTH, R-Mo. — 1/6/81 — Senate Governmental Affairs reported Dec. 14 (S Rept 97-302). Senate passed Dec. 15. House Government Operations discharged. House passed, amended, March 23, 1982. Senate agreed to House amendments May 11. President signed May 21, 1982.

PL 97-178 (H J Res 412) Designate May 20, 1982, as "Amelia Earhart Day." JEFFRIES, R-Kan. — 2/24/82 — House Post Office and Civil Service discharged. House passed May 18. Senate passed May 19. President signed May 21, 1982.

PL 97-179 (HR 2863) Provide for the sale at public auction of certain lands in the Tahoe National Forest known as Blythe Arena. CHAPPIE, R-Calif. — 3/25/81 — House Interior and Insular Affairs reported Dec. 4 (H Rept 97-359). House passed Dec. 15. Senate Energy and Natural Resources reported April 28, 1982 (S Rept 97-367). Senate passed May 10. President signed May 24, 1982.

PL 97-180 (S 691) Increase the penalties for criminal infringement of a copyright involving the reproduction or distribution of phonograph records, motion pictures or audiovisual works. THURMOND, R-S.C. — 3/12/81 — Senate Judiciary reported Nov. 18 (S Rept 97-274). Senate passed Dec. 1. House Judiciary discharged. House passed May 10, 1982. President signed May 24, 1982.

PL 97-181 (H J Res 361) Grant official recognition to the international ballet competition held in Jackson, Miss. DOWDY, D-Miss. — 10/12/81 — House Post Office and Civil Service discharged. House passed March 11, 1982. Senate Labor and Human Resources discharged. Senate passed May 5. President signed May 24, 1982.

PL 97-182 (S J Res 170) Designate the week of Nov. 7-14, 1982, as "National Hospice Week." RANDOLPH, D-W.Va. — 3/18/82 — Senate Judiciary reported March 30. Senate passed April 1. House Post Office and Civil Service discharged. House passed May 11. President signed May 24, 1982.

PL 97-183 (S J Res 145) Designate the week beginning June 13, 1982, as "National Orchestra Week." HEINZ, R-Pa. — 2/10/82 — Senate Judiciary reported March 2. Senate passed March 4. House Post Office and Civil Service discharged. House passed May 11. President signed May 24, 1982.

PL 97-184 (S 146) Authorize secretary of the interior to assist in the preservation of historic Camden, S.C. THURMOND, R-S.C. — 1/19/81 — Senate Energy and Natural Resources reported Oct. 7 (S Rept 97-207). Senate passed Oct. 21. House Interior and Insular Affairs reported March 15, 1982 (H Rept 97-459). House passed May 11. President signed May 24, 1982.

PL 97-185 (HR 6038) Extend the authority of the secretary of housing and urban development to enter into contracts to provide mortgage assistance payments for lower income families. GONZALEZ, D-Texas — 4/1/82 — House passed, under suspension of the rules, April 20. Senate passed May 12. President signed May 24, 1982.

PL 97-186 (S 1611) Provide for completion of the planned International Diplomatic Center within the federally owned Bureau of Standards site in Washington, D.C. PERCY, R-Ill. — 9/11/81 — Senate Foreign Relations reported Nov. 30 (S Rept 97-281). Senate passed April 29, 1982. House passed May 13. President signed May 25, 1982.

PL 97-187 (S J Res 53) Designate Sept. 5, 1982, as "Working Mothers' Day." KASSEBAUM, R-Kan. — 3/23/81 — Senate Judiciary reported July 30. Senate passed July 31. House Post Office and Civil Service discharged. House passed, amended, May 11, 1982. Senate agreed to House amendments May 19. President signed June 1, 1982.

PL 97-188 (S J Res 59) Designate the square dance as the national folk dance of the United States for 1982 and 1983. BYRD, D-W.Va. — 3/30/81 — Senate Judiciary discharged. Senate passed Sept. 23. House Post Office and Civil Service discharged. House passed, amended, May 11, 1982. Senate agreed to House amendment May 19. President signed June 1, 1982.

PL 97-189 (S J Res 160) Designate July 9, 1982, and April 9, 1983, as "National P.O.W./M.I.A. Recognition Day." HAYAKAWA, R-Calif. — 3/8/82 — Senate Judiciary reported April 29. Senate passed May 5. House Post Office and Civil Service discharged. House passed,

amended, May 11. Senate agreed to House amendments May 19. President signed June 1, 1982.

PL 97-190 (S 2575) Extend the expiration date of section 252 of the Energy Policy and Conservation Act until July 1, 1982. McCLURE, R-Idaho — 5/26/82 — Senate Energy and Natural Resources discharged. Senate passed May 27. House passed May 28. President signed June 1, 1982.

PL 97-191 (S 2535) Regulate the operation of foreign fish processing vessels within state waters. STEVENS, R-Alaska — 5/17/82 — Senate passed May 17. House Merchant Marine and Fisheries discharged. House passed, amended, May 25. Senate agreed to House amendments May 27. President signed June 1, 1982.

PL 97-192 (HR 4769) Grant a federal charter to the American Council of Learned Societies. SIMON, D-Ill. — 10/15/81 — House Judiciary reported Oct. 22 (H Rept 97-285). House passed, under suspension of the rules, Oct 26. Senate Judiciary reported May 14, 1982 (S Rept 97-395). Senate passed May 24. President signed June 1, 1982.

PL 97-193 (S J Res 149) Designate the week of June 6-12, 1982, as "National Child Abuse Prevention Week." METZENBAUM, D-Ohio — 2/23/82 — Senate Judiciary reported March 10. Senate passed March 15. House Post Office and Civil Service discharged. House passed June 3. President signed June 15, 1982.

PL 97-194 (S J Res 131) Designate the week of June 7-13, 1982, as "National Theatre Week." EXON, D-Neb. — 12/2/81 — Senate Judiciary reported April 29, 1982. Senate passed May 5. House Post Office and Civil Service discharged. House passed June 3. President signed June 16, 1982.

PL 97-195 (S 1808) Establish the position of under secretary of commerce for economic affairs in the Department of Commerce. PACKWOOD, R-Ore. — 11/4/81 — Senate Commerce, Science and Transportation reported Dec. 11. Senate passed Dec. 15. House passed, amended, May 11, 1982. Senate agreed to House amendment May 27. President signed June 16, 1982.

PL 97-196 (S J Res 201) Authorize and request the president to issue a proclamation for the observance of "Baltic Freedom Day." RIEGLE, D-Mich. — 6/9/82 — Senate passed June 9. House passed June 14. President signed June 18, 1982.

PL 97-197 (S 896) Designate the control tower at Memphis International Airport, Tennessee, as the "Omlie Tower." BAKER, R-Tenn. — 4/7/81 — Senate Commerce, Science and Transportation reported April 30. Senate passed May 4. House Public Works and Transportation discharged. House passed June 7, 1982. President signed June 21, 1982.

PL 97-198 (S J Res 140) Designate Feb. 11, 1983, as "National Inventor's Day." MATHIAS, R-Md. — 1/28/82 — Senate Judiciary reported March 10. Senate passed March 15. House passed June 3. President signed June 21, 1982.

PL 97-199 (HR 6132) Adjust the rate of interest paid on funds of the Smithsonian Institution deposited with the U.S. Treasury. BOLAND, D-Mass. — 4/21/82 — House Administration reported May 6 (H Rept 97-503). House passed, under suspension of the rules, May 10. Senate Rules and Administration reported May 26 (S Rept 97-438). Senate passed June 9. President signed June 22, 1982.

PL 97-200 (HR 4) Establish criminal penalties for the disclosure of classified information identifying an individual engaged in foreign intelligence activities for the U.S. government. BOLAND, D-Mass. — 1/5/81 — House Intelligence reported Sept. 10 (H Rept 97-221). House passed Sept. 23. Senate passed, amended, March 18, 1982. House agreed to conference report June 3 (H Rept 97-580). Senate agreed to conference report June 10. President signed June 23, 1982.

PL 97-201 (HR 5432) Authorize the presentation on behalf of the Congress of a specially struck gold medal to Admiral Hyman George Rickover. STRATTON, D-N.Y. — 2/3/82 — House passed, under suspension of the rules, April 27. Senate passed June 9. President signed June 23, 1982.

PL 97-202 (HR 5566) Authorize funds for services necessary to the nonperforming arts functions of the John F. Kennedy Center for the Performing Arts. HOWARD, D-N.J. — 2/23/82 — House Public Works and Transportation reported May 17 (H Rept 97-531). House passed June 3. Senate passed June 9. President signed June 24, 1982.

PL 97-203 (HR 5659) Authorize funds to the Board of Regents of the Smithsonian Institution to construct a building for the Museum of African Art and a Center for Eastern Art. BOLAND, D-Mass. — 3/2/82 — House Public Works and Transportation reported May 17 (H Rept 97-534). House passed June 3. Senate passed June 9. President signed June 24, 1982.

PL 97-204 (H J Res 519) Temporarily increase the public debt limit by $743,100,000,000 until Sept. 30, 1982. NO SPONSOR — 6/23/82 — House passed June 23. Senate passed June 23. President signed June 28, 1982.

PL 97-205 (HR 3112) Extend certain provisions of the Voting Rights Act of 1965. RODINO, D-N.J. — 4/7/81 — House Judiciary reported Sept.

15 (H Rept 97-227). House passed Oct. 5. Senate passed, amended, June 18, 1982. House agreed to Senate amendment June 23. President signed June 29, 1982.

PL 97-206 (HR 3863) Amend the Poultry Products Inspection Act to increase the number of turkeys which may be slaughtered and processed without inspection under such Act. MARLENEE, R-Mont. — 6/9/81 — House Agriculture reported May 27, 1982 (H Rept 97-589). House passed, under suspension of the rules, June 14. Senate passed June 21. President signed June 30, 1982.

PL 97-207 (HR 4569) Designate the United States Post Office Building in Hartford, Conn., as the "William R. Cotter Federal Building." McKINNEY, R-Conn. — 9/23/81 — House Public Works and Transportation reported Nov. 12 (H Rept 97-323). House passed Nov. 16. Senate Governmental Affairs reported June 18, 1982 (S Rept 97-477). Senate passed June 24. President signed June 30, 1982.

PL 97-208 (HR 6631) Authorize funds for the relief, rehabilitation and reconstruction needs of the people of Lebanon. GEJDENSON, D-Conn. — 6/17/82 — House Foreign Affairs reported June 23 (H Rept 97-622). House passed June 23. Senate passed June 24. President signed June 30, 1982.

PL 97-209 (H J Res 230) Declare that Dr. Semyon Gluzman should be released from prison in the Soviet Union and be allowed to emigrate to Israel. GREEN, R-N.Y. — 4/9/81 — House passed, under suspension of the rules, May 4, 1982. Senate Foreign Relations reported June 16. Senate passed June 21. President signed June 30, 1982.

PL 97-210 (H J Res 518) Designate the week commencing with the fourth Monday in June 1982 as "National NCO/Petty Officer Week." SPENCE, R-S.C. — 6/23/82 — House Post Office and Civil Service discharged. House passed June 24. Senate passed June 24. President signed June 30, 1982.

PL 97-211 (S 1519) Designate certain national wildlife refuge lands in Florida as the Florida Keys Wilderness. TSONGAS, D-Mass. — 7/27/81 — Senate Energy and Natural Resources reported May 3, 1982 (S Rept 97-377). Senate passed May 10. House Interior and Insular Affairs reported June 7 (H Rept 97-599). House passed June 21. President signed June 30, 1982.

PL 97-212 (HR 3816) Revise the administration of the Fishermen's Contingency Fund. BREAUX, D-La. — 6/4/81 — House Merchant Marine and Fisheries reported Dec. 3 (H Rept 97-354). House passed, under suspension of the rules, Dec. 15. Senate Commerce, Science and Transportation reported June 23, 1982. Senate passed, amended, June 23. House agreed to Senate amendments with amendments June 24. Senate agreed to House amendments June 29. President signed June 30, 1982.

PL 97-213 (HR 4903) Grant the consent of Congress to the compact between Mississippi and Louisiana that establishes a commission to study the feasibility of rapid rail transit service between the two states. WHITTEN, D-Miss. — 11/4/81 — House Judiciary reported May 21, 1982 (H Rept 97-584). House passed June 7. Senate Judiciary reported June 23. Senate passed June 24. President signed June 30, 1982.

PL 97-214 (HR 6451) Revise certain provisions of the law relating to military construction and military family housing. BRINKLEY, D-Ga. — 5/20/82 — House Armed Services reported June 17 (H Rept 97-612). House passed, under suspension of the rules, June 21. Senate passed June 30. President signed July 12, 1982.

PL 97-215 (HR 6198) Extend the manufacturing clause of the Copyright Law of 1976 until July 1986. KASTENMEIER, D-Wis. — 4/28/82 — House Judiciary reported May 19 (H Rept 97-575, Part I). House Ways and Means reported June 10 (H Rept 97-575, Part II). House passed, under suspension of the rules, June 15. Senate passed June 30. President vetoed July 8. House passed, over presidential veto, July 13. Senate passed, over presidential veto, July 13. Became public law without presidential approval July 13, 1982.

PL 97-216 (HR 6685) Appropriate urgent supplemental funds for fiscal year ending Sept. 30, 1982, for the federal government. WHITTEN, D-Miss. — 6/24/82 — House passed June 24. Senate passed, amended, June 29. Conference report filed in House July 14 (H Rept 97-632). House receded and concurred with an amendment in Senate amendment July 15. Senate agreed to conference report July 15. Senate agreed to House amendment to Senate amendment July 15. President signed July 18, 1982.

PL 97-217 (S 2651) Extend expiration date of section 252 of the Energy Policy and Conservation Act, which provides a limited antitrust defense for U.S. oil companies participating in the international energy program. McCLURE, R-Idaho — 6/17/82 — Senate Energy and Natural Resources discharged. Senate passed June 24. House passed July 15. President signed July 19, 1982.

PL 97-218 (HR 6590) Provide for the operation of the tobacco support and production adjustment program in such a manner as to result in no net cost to taxpayers and limiting increases in the support price of tobacco. ROSE, D-N.C. — 6/15/82 — House Agriculture reported

June 18 (H Rept 97-613). House passed, under suspension of the rules, June 21. Senate Agriculture, Nutrition and Forestry reported June 24. Senate passed, amended, July 14. House agreed to Senate amendments July 15. President signed July 20, 1982.

PL 97-219 (S 881) Stimulate technological innovation and increase economic productivity by using business more effectively in federal research and development programs. RUDMAN, R-N.H. — 4/7/81 — Senate Small Business reported Sept. 25 (S Rept 97-194). Senate passed Dec. 8. House passed, amended, June 23, 1982. Senate agreed to House amendment June 29. President signed July 22, 1982.

PL 97-220 (S 1230) Authorize the minting of special coins commemorating the 1984 Olympic games in Los Angeles. CRANSTON, D-Calif. — 5/20/81 — Senate Banking, Housing and Urban Affairs reported Oct. 30 (S Rept 97-264). Senate passed Dec. 9. House Banking, Finance and Urban Affairs reported May 17, 1982 (H Rept 97-554). House passed, amended, May 20. Senate agreed to House amendment July 1. President signed July 22, 1982.

PL 97-221 (S 2240) Authorize federal agencies to use flexible and compressed employee work schedules. STEVENS, R-Alaska — 3/18/82 — Senate Governmental Affairs reported April 28 (S Rept 97-365). Senate passed June 30. House passed, under suspension of the rules, July 12. President signed July 23, 1982.

PL 97-222 (HR 4935) Amend Title II, U.S. Code to correct technical errors and to clarify and make substantive changes, with respect to securities and commodities. RODINO, D-N.J. — 11/10/81 — House Judiciary reported Jan. 25, 1982 (H Rept 97-420). House passed, under suspension of the rules, Feb. 9. Senate Judiciary discharged. Senate passed July 13. President signed July 27, 1982.

PL 97-223 (H J Res 225) Designate the week of June 5-11, 1983, as "Management Week in America." BROWN, R-Ohio — 4/7/81 — House Post Office and Civil Service discharged. House passed June 3, 1982. Senate passed July 13. President signed July 27, 1982.

PL 97-224 (S J Res 95) Authorize the construction of the Franklin D. Roosevelt Memorial in the District of Columbia. HATFIELD, R-Ore. — 7/8/81 — Senate Rules and Administration reported Feb. 8, 1982 (S Rept 97-311). Senate passed March 8. House Administration discharged. House passed July 14. President signed July 28, 1982.

PL 97-225 (H J Res 444) Authorize and request the president to designate Aug. 14, 1982, as "National Navaho Code Talkers Day." RUDD, R-Ariz. — 3/18/82 — House Post Office and Civil Service discharged. House passed May 18. Senate Judiciary discharged. Senate passed July 13. President signed July 28, 1982.

PL 97-226 (HR 4688) Amend the Military Personnel and Civilian Employees' Claims Act of 1964, increasing from $15,000 to $25,000 the maximum amount the United States may pay in settlement of a claim under section 3 of the act. DANIELSON, D-Calif. — 10/5/81 — House Judiciary reported March 8, 1982 (H Rept 97-452). House passed, under suspension of the rules, March 18. Senate Judiciary discharged. Senate passed July 16. President signed July 28, 1982.

PL 97-227 (HR 6663) Delay the effective date of proposed amendments to rule 4 of the Federal Rules of Civil Procedure. EDWARDS, D-Calif. — 6/23/82 — House Judiciary reported July 23 (H Rept 97-662). House passed, under suspension of the rules, July 26. Senate passed July 28. President signed Aug. 2, 1982.

PL 97-228 (H J Res 526) Authorize and request the president to issue a proclamation designating the week of Aug. 1-7, 1982, as "National Purple Heart Week." SOLOMON, R-N.Y. — 6/23/82 — House Post Office and Civil Service discharged. House passed June 24. Senate Judiciary discharged. Senate passed July 28. President signed Aug. 2, 1982.

PL 97-229 (S 2332) Extend until Aug. 1, 1983, the expiration date of section 252 of the Energy Policy and Conservation Act, which provides a limited antitrust defense for U.S. oil companies participating in the international energy program. McCLURE, R-Idaho — 4/1/82 — Senate Energy and Natural Resources reported May 13 (S Rept 97-393). Senate passed May 26. House passed, amended, June 23. House agreed to conference report July 29 (H Rept 97-663). Senate agreed to conference report July 30. President signed Aug. 3, 1982.

PL 97-230 (S 2706) Modify the bar membership requirements for U.S. magistrates. STEVENS, R-Alaska — 6/30/82 — Senate passed June 30. House Judiciary discharged. House passed July 23. President signed Aug. 6, 1982.

PL 97-231 (S 2317) Grant a federal charter to the National Federation of Music Clubs. COCHRAN, R-Miss. — 3/31/82 — Senate Judiciary reported May 14 (S Rept 97-394). Senate passed May 24. House Judiciary reported July 20 (H Rept 97-644). House passed, amended, under suspension of the rules, July 20. Senate agreed to House amendments July 27. President signed Aug. 9, 1982.

PL 97-232 (S 2218) Provide for the development and improvement of the recreation facilities at Gateway National Recreation Area, in New York City, and for the utilization of its energy resources. D'AMATO, R-N.Y. — 3/16/82 — Senate Energy and Natural Resources reported

May 28 (S Rept 97-455). Senate passed June 9. House Interior and Insular Affairs reported June 14 (H Rept 97-677). House passed, under suspension of the rules, Aug. 2. President signed Aug. 9, 1982.

PL 97-233 (H J Res 494) Amend the requirements for presidential certifications of conditions in El Salvador. STUDDS, D-Mass. — 5/25/82 — House passed, under suspension of the rules, July 13. Senate Foreign Relations reported July 20. Senate passed July 27. President signed Aug. 10, 1982.

PL 97-234 (HR 5380) Grant a federal charter to the American Ex-Prisoners of War. MOORHEAD, R-Calif. — 1/27/82 — House Judiciary reported July 20 (H Rept 97-643). House passed, under suspension of the rules, July 20. Senate Judiciary discharged. Senate passed July 28. President signed Aug. 10, 1982.

PL 97-235 (S J Res 190) Designate the week of Nov. 21-27, 1982, as "National Family Week." BURDICK, D-N.D. — 4/21/82 — Senate Judiciary reported May 25. Senate passed May 26. House Post Office and Civil Service discharged. House passed Aug. 5. President signed Aug. 16, 1982.

PL 97-236 (S J Res 183) Designate the week of Oct. 19-25, 1982, as "Lupus Awareness Week." SPECTER, R-Pa. — 4/1/82 — Senate Judiciary reported June 23. Senate passed June 24. House Post Office and Civil Service discharged. House passed Aug. 5. President signed Aug. 17, 1982.

PL 97-237 (H J Res 541) Congratulate the National Aeronautics and Space Administration and all persons involved in the successful completion of the test flight phase of the space shuttle program. HAWKINS, D-Calif. — 7/20/82 — House passed July 26. Senate passed, amended, Aug. 4. House agreed to Senate amendments Aug. 10. President signed Aug. 20, 1982.

PL 97-238 (S 2154) Require the secretary of agriculture to convey a revisionary interest held by the United States in certain lands located in Christian County, Ky., to the Shy Flat Tabernacle Cemetery Inc., Christian County, Ky. FORD, D-Ky. — 3/2/82 — Senate Agriculture, Nutrition and Forestry reported April 19 (S Rept 97-333). Senate passed May 5. House Agriculture discharged. House passed Aug. 9. President signed Aug. 20, 1982.

PL 97-239 (H J Res 516) Provide for the designation of April 17-23, 1983, as "National Coin Week." ANNUNZIO, D-Ill. — 6/22/82 — House Judiciary discharged. House passed Aug. 5. Senate Judiciary discharged. Senate passed Aug. 12. President signed Aug. 20, 1982.

PL 97-240 (S J Res 123) Designate the week of Nov. 7-13, 1982, as "National Disabled Veterans Week." HAYAKAWA, R-Calif. — 11/10/81 — Senate Judiciary reported Dec. 3. Senate passed Dec. 11. House Post Office and Civil Service discharged. House passed Aug. 5, 1982. President signed Aug. 20, 1982.

PL 97-241 (S 1193) Authorize funds for fiscal years 1982-83 for the Department of State, the International Communication Agency and the Board for International Broadcasting; and authorize funds for fiscal year 1982 for the Arms Control and Disarmament Agency. PERCY, R-Ill. — 5/18/81 — Senate Foreign Relations reported May 15 (S Rept 97-71). Senate passed June 18. House passed, amended, Oct. 29. Senate agreed to conference report Aug. 9, 1982 (H Rept 97-693). House agreed to conference report Aug. 11. President signed Aug. 24, 1982.

PL 97-242 (S 2073) Repeal outdated size and weight limitations imposed on the U.S. Postal Service. STEVENS, R-Alaska — 2/8/82 — Senate Governmental Affairs reported June 18. Senate passed July 29. House Post Office and Civil Service discharged. House passed Aug. 12. President signed Aug. 24, 1982.

PL 97-243 (HR 6530) Provide for the redevelopment of the Mount St. Helens Volcanic Area in the state of Washington. BONKER, D-Wash. — 6/3/82 — House Interior and Insular Affairs reported July 15 (H Rept 97-636, Part I). House Agriculture reported July 15 (H Rept 97-636, Part II). House passed, under suspension of the rules, July 19. Senate passed, amended, July 21. Senate agreed to conference report Aug. 13 (H Rept 97-748). House agreed to conference report Aug. 17. President signed Aug. 26, 1982.

PL 97-244 (HR 2160) Revise certain provisions of the Potato Research and Promotion Act to change the formula used by the National Potato Promotion Board to assess potato producers. PANETTA, D-Calif. — 2/25/81 — House Agriculture reported March 5, 1982 (H Rept 97-446). House passed, under suspension of the rules, March 9. Senate Agriculture, Nutrition and Forestry reported April 19 (S Rept 97-334). Senate passed, amended, May 5. House disagreed to Senate amendments July 26. Senate receded from its amendments Aug. 12. President signed Aug. 26, 1982.

PL 97-245 (HR 6033) Authorize the secretary of the interior to enter into an agreement with the Association for the Preservation of Historic Congressional Cemetery to assist in the preservation of the Congressional Cemetery, in Washington, D.C. BOGGS, D-La. — 4/1/82 — House Interior and Insular Affairs reported July 27 (H Rept 97-667). House passed, under suspension of the rules, Aug. 2. Senate

passed Aug. 13. President signed Aug. 26, 1982.

PL 97-246 (HR 4647) Award special congressional gold medals to Fred Waring, the widow of Joe Louis, and Louis L'Amour. GAYDOS, D-Pa. — 9/30/81 — House passed, under suspension of the rules, Aug. 2, 1982. Senate passed Aug. 12. President signed Aug. 26, 1982.

PL 97-247 (HR 6260) Authorize funds through fiscal year 1985 and supplemental funds for the fiscal year ending Sept. 30, 1982, for the Patent and Trademark Office, and establish a schedule of patent fees. KASTENMEIER, D-Wis. — 5/4/82 — House Judiciary reported May 17 (H Rept 97-542). House passed, under suspension of the rules, June 8. Senate Judiciary reported July 6. Senate passed Aug. 12. President signed Aug. 27, 1982.

PL 97-248 (HR 4961) Make miscellaneous changes in the tax laws. STARK, D-Calif. — 11/13/81 — House Ways and Means reported Dec. 14 (H Rept 97-404). House passed, under suspension of the rules, Dec. 15. Senate Finance reported July 12, 1982 (S Rept 97-494). Senate passed, amended, July 23. House agreed to conference report Aug. 19 (H Rept 97-760). Senate agreed to conference report Aug. 19. President signed Sept. 3, 1982.

PL 97-249 (HR 6732) Amend the International Safe Container Act. JONES, D-N.C. — 7/12/82 — House Merchant Marine and Fisheries reported Aug. 12 (H Rept 97-737). House passed, under suspension of the rules, Aug. 17. Senate Commerce, Science and Transportation discharged. Senate passed Aug. 20. President signed Sept. 8, 1982.

PL 97-250 (S 1119) Revise the boundary of Crater Lake National Park, in Oregon. HATFIELD, R-Ore. — 5/6/81 — Senate Energy and Natural Resources reported Oct. 7 (S Rept 97-205). Senate passed Oct. 21. House Interior and Insular Affairs reported Dec. 10 (H Rept 97-383). House passed, amended, under suspension of the rules, Dec. 15. Senate agreed to House amendment Aug. 19, 1982. President signed Sept. 8, 1982.

PL 97-251 (HR 6350) Authorize funds for the Veterans Administration health professional scholarship program. MONTGOMERY, D-Miss. — 5/11/82 — House Veterans' Affairs reported May 17 (H Rept 97-543). House passed, under suspension of the rules, June 15. Senate passed, amended, June 21. House agreed to Senate amendments with amendments Aug. 19. Senate agreed to House amendments Aug. 20. President signed Sept. 8, 1982.

PL 97-252 (S 2248) Authorize funds for fiscal year 1983 and supplemental funds for the fiscal year ending Sept. 30, 1982, for military procurement programs of the Department of Defense. TOWER, R-Texas — 3/22/82 — Senate Armed Services reported April 13 (S Rept 97-330). Senate passed May 14. House passed, amended, July 29. Senate agreed to conference report Aug. 17 (H Rept 97-749). House agreed to conference report Aug. 18. President signed Sept. 8, 1982.

PL 97-253 (HR 6955) Provide for reconciliation pursuant to section 2 of the first concurrent resolution on the budget for fiscal year 1983, as mandated in S Con Res 92; revise the congressional budget for the federal government for fiscal years 1983-85; and revise the congressional budget for the federal government for the fiscal year ending Sept. 30, 1982. JONES, D-Okla. — 8/10/82 — House passed Aug. 10. Senate passed, amended, Aug. 11. House recommitted conference report Aug. 17 (H Rept 97-750). House agreed to conference report Aug. 18 (H Rept 97-759). Senate agreed to conference report Aug. 18. President signed Sept. 8, 1982.

PL 97-254 (HR 6409) Provide for U.S. participation in the 1984 Louisiana World Exposition to be held in New Orleans. BOGGS, D-La. — 5/19/82 — House Foreign Affairs reported July 19 (H Rept 97-639). House passed, under suspension of the rules, July 19. Senate Foreign Relations reported Aug. 13 (S Rept 97-525). Senate passed, amended, Aug. 19. House agreed to Senate amendment Aug. 19. President signed Sept. 8, 1982.

PL 97-255 (HR 1526) Require each federal agency to submit an annual report to the president on the adequacy of its internal accounting and administrative control systems. BROOKS, D-Texas — 2/2/81 — House Government Operations reported May 14 (H Rept 97-38). House passed, under suspension of the rules, May 18. Senate passed, amended, Aug. 4, 1982. House agreed to Senate amendment Aug. 19. President signed Sept. 8, 1982.

PL 97-256 (HR 3345) Make technical and conforming changes in patent and trademark laws and in the civil rights of institutionalized persons. RODINO, D-N.J. — 4/30/81 — House Judiciary reported Dec. 11 (H Rept 97-389). House passed, under suspension of the rules, March 18, 1982. Senate Judiciary discharged. Senate passed Aug. 20. President signed Sept. 8, 1982.

PL 97-257 (HR 6863) Appropriate supplemental funds for the fiscal year ending Sept. 30, 1982, for the federal government. WHITTEN, D-Miss. — 7/27/82 — House Appropriations reported July 27 (H Rept 97-673). House passed July 29. Senate Appropriations reported Aug. 3 (S Rept 97-516). Senate passed, amended, Aug. 11. House agreed to conference report Aug. 18 (H Rept 97-747). Senate agreed to conference report Aug. 20. President vetoed Aug. 28. House passed over

presidential veto Sept. 9. Senate passed over presidential veto Sept. 10. Became public law without presidential approval Sept. 10, 1982.

PL 97-258 (HR 6128) Revise, codify and enact without substantive change certain general and permanent laws related to money and finance, as Title 31, U.S. Code, "Money and Finance." RODINO, D-N.J. — 4/21/82 — House Judiciary reported July 21 (H Rept 97-651). House passed, under suspension of the rules, Aug. 9. Senate Judiciary discharged. Senate passed Aug. 20. President signed Sept. 12, 1982.

PL 97-259 (HR 3239) Amend the Communications Act of 1934 to authorize appropriations for the administration of such act. WIRTH, D-Colo. — 4/10/81 — House Energy and Commerce reported May 19 (H Rept 97-84). House passed, under suspension of the rules, June 9. Senate passed, amended, Aug. 18, 1982. Senate agreed to conference report Aug. 19 (H Rept 97-765). House agreed to conference report Aug. 19. President signed Sept. 12, 1982.

PL 97-260 (S J Res 194) Provide for the appointment of Nancy Hanks as a citizen regent of the Board of Regents of the Smithsonian Institution. GOLDWATER, R-Ariz. — 5/4/82 — Senate Rules and Administration reported May 26 (S Rept 97-434). Senate passed June 9. House Administration reported Aug. 17 (H Rept 97-753). House passed Sept. 13. President signed Sept. 18, 1982.

PL 97-261 (HR 3663) Revise the regulation of motor carriers of passengers. ANDERSON, D-Calif. — 5/21/81 — House Public Works and Transportation reported Nov. 17 (H Rept 97-334). House passed March 19. Senate Commerce, Science and Transportation reported May 20, 1982 (S Rept 97-411). Senate passed, amended, June 30. House agreed to conference report Aug. 19 (H Rept 97-780). Senate agreed to conference report Aug. 20. President signed Sept. 20, 1982.

PL 97-262 (S J Res 250) Provide for the solution of the single outstanding issue in the railway labor-management dispute. HATCH, R-Utah — 9/21/82 — Senate passed Sept. 21. House passed Sept. 22. President signed Sept. 22, 1982.

PL 97-263 (HR 1710) Authorize the use of the frank for official mail sent by the Law Revision Counsel of the U.S. House of Representatives. FORD, D-Mich. — 2/5/81 — House Post Office and Civil Service reported Nov. 5 (H Rept 97-314). House passed Nov. 16. Senate Governmental Affairs reported Aug. 10, 1982. Senate passed Sept. 14. President signed Sept. 24, 1982.

PL 97-264 (S 2582) Provide for an increase in the amount of interest paid on the money of the Oliver Wendell Holmes Devise Fund deposited with the U.S. Treasury. MATHIAS, R-Md. — 5/26/82 — Senate Rules and Administration reported May 26 (S Rept 97-431). Senate passed June 9. House Administration reported Aug. 17 (H Rept 97-752). House passed Sept. 13. President signed Sept. 24, 1982.

PL 97-265 (S J Res 186) Designate the week of Sept. 19-25, 1982, as "National Cystic Fibrosis Week." DOLE, R-Kan. — 4/1/82 — Senate Judiciary reported April 14. Senate passed April 20. House Post Office and Civil Service discharged. House passed Sept. 21. President signed Sept. 24, 1982.

PL 97-266 (S J Res 205) Designate September 1982 as "National Sewing Month." EAST, R-N.C. — 6/24/82 — Senate Judiciary discharged. Senate passed Sept. 14. House Post Office and Civil Service discharged. House passed Sept. 21. President signed Sept. 24, 1982.

PL 97-267 (S 923) Establish pretrial services in each federal district to assist judicial officers in making pretrial release decisions and to supervise and monitor conditions of pretrial release. BIDEN, D-Del. — 4/8/81 — Senate Judiciary reported May 15 (S Rept 97-77). Senate passed June 18. House passed, amended, May 11, 1982. Senate agreed to conference report Aug. 20 (H Rept 97-792). House agreed to conference report Sept. 15. President signed Sept. 27, 1982.

PL 97-268 (HR 3620) Provide for the transfer of certain federal property to the city of Hoboken, N.J. GUARINI, D-N.J. — 5/19/81 — House Merchant Marine and Fisheries reported Jan. 29 (H Rept 97-421). House passed, under suspension of the rules, March 18, 1982. Senate Governmental Affairs reported Aug. 11 (S Rept 97-521). Senate passed, amended, Aug. 19. House agreed to Senate amendments Sept. 14. President signed Sept. 27, 1982.

PL 97-269 (HR 6068) Authorize appropriations for fiscal year 1983 for the intelligence community staff and the Central Intelligence Agency Retirement and Disability System, and authorize supplemental funds for the fiscal year ending Sept. 30, 1982, for the intelligence community. BOLAND, D-Mass. — 4/5/82 — House Intelligence reported April 26 (H Rept 97-486, Part I). House Armed Services reported May 6 (H Rept 97-486, Part II). House passed May 19. Senate passed, amended, June 30. House agreed to conference report Sept. 8 (H Rept 97-779). Senate agreed to conference report Sept. 10. President signed Sept. 27, 1982.

PL 97-270 (H J Res 520) Provide for a temporary increase in the public debt. WRIGHT, D-Texas — 6/23/82 — House passed June 23. Senate Finance reported Aug. 11. Senate passed Sept. 23. President signed Sept. 30, 1982.

PL 97-271 (HR 3517) Authorize the granting of permanent residence status to certain non-immigrant aliens residing in the Virgin Islands. DE LUGO, D-Virgin Islands — 5/12/81 — House Judiciary reported Oct. 29 (H Rept 97-307). House passed, under suspension of the rules, Nov. 4. Senate Judiciary reported Aug. 18, 1982 (S Rept 97-529). Senate passed, amended, Aug. 20. House agreed to Senate amendment Sept. 8. President signed Sept. 30, 1982.

PL 97-272 (HR 6956) Appropriate funds for fiscal year 1983 for the Department of Housing and Urban Development and certain independent agencies. BOLAND, D-Mass. — 8/10/82 — House Appropriations reported Aug. 10 (H Rept 97-720). House passed Sept. 15. Senate Appropriations reported Sept. 16 (S Rept 97-549). Senate passed, amended, Sept. 24. House agreed to conference report Sept. 29 (H Rept 97-891). House receded and concurred in Senate amendments Sept. 29. House receded and concurred in Senate amendments with amendments Sept. 29. Senate agreed to conference report Sept. 29. Senate agreed to House amendments to Senate amendments. President signed Sept. 30, 1982.

PL 97-273 (HR 4347) Provide for the development of the WEB Rural Water Development Project in South Dakota, and for studies within the Pick-Sloan Missouri River Basin. ROBERTS, R-S.D. — 7/30/81 — House Interior and Insular Affairs reported May 17, 1982 (H Rept 97-524, Part I). House Agriculture reported May 17 (H Rept 97-524, Part II). House passed, under suspension of the rules, June 8. Senate Energy and Natural Resources reported Aug. 2 (S Rept 97-514). Senate passed, amended, Aug. 19. House agreed to Senate amendment Sept. 23. President signed Sept. 30, 1982.

PL 97-274 (HR 7065) Amend the Community Services Block Grant Act to clarify the authority of the secretary of health and human services to designate community action agencies for certain community action programs administered by the secretary. MATSUI, D-Calif. — 9/8/82 — House passed, under suspension of the rules, Sept. 20. Senate passed Sept. 24. President signed Sept. 30, 1982.

PL 97-275 (S 1628) Provide that the Emergency Fund Act of 1948 be available for all projects governed by federal reclamation acts. McCLURE, R-Idaho — 9/16/81 — Senate Energy and Natural Resources reported April 27, 1982 (S Rept 97-363). Senate passed May 10. House Interior and Insular Affairs reported Aug. 19 (H Rept 97-769). House passed Sept. 20. President signed Oct. 1, 1982.

PL 97-276 (H J Res 599) Make continuing appropriations through Dec. 17, 1982, for programs of the federal government, and appropriate funds for fiscal year 1983 for the legislative branch. WHITTEN, D-Miss. — 9/16/82 — House Appropriations reported Sept. 16 (H Rept 97-834). House passed Sept. 22. Senate Appropriations reported Sept. 23 (S Rept 97-581). Senate passed, amended, Sept. 29. House agreed to conference report Oct. 1 (H Rept 97-914). House receded and concurred in Senate amendments Oct. 1. House receded and concurred in Senate amendments with amendments Oct. 1. Senate agreed to conference report Oct. 1. Senate agreed to House amendments to Senate amendments Oct. 1. President signed Oct. 2, 1982.

PL 97-277 (H J Res 496) Designate the week beginning Nov. 21, 1982, as "National Alzheimer's Disease Week." LOWERY, R-Calif. — 5/27/82 — House Post Office and Civil Service discharged. House passed Sept. 21. Senate passed Sept. 24. President signed Oct. 4, 1982.

PL 97-278 (HR 5288) Grant the consent of Congress to the agreement between the states of New Hampshire and Vermont providing for the construction and operation of facilities for the processing or disposal of solid waste. GREGG, R-N.H. — 12/16/81 — House Judiciary reported Aug. 11, 1982 (H Rept 97-724). House passed Aug. 16. Senate passed Sept. 20. President signed Oct. 4, 1982.

PL 97-279 (S J Res 193) Designate the week of Nov. 7-13, 1982, as "National Respiratory Therapy Week." KASSEBAUM, R-Kan. — 4/27/82 — Senate Judiciary reported June 23. Senate passed June 24. House Post Office and Civil Service discharged. House passed Sept. 21. President signed Oct. 4, 1982.

PL 97-280 (S J Res 165) Proclaim 1983 as the "Year of the Bible." ARMSTRONG, R-Colo. — 3/15/82 — Senate Judiciary reported March 30. Senate passed March 31. House Post Office and Civil Service discharged. House passed Sept. 21. President signed Oct. 4, 1982.

PL 97-281 (H J Res 568) Designate Oct. 5, 1982, as "Dr. Robert H. Goddard Day." EARLY, D-Mass. — 8/11/82 — House Post Office and Civil Service discharged. House passed Sept. 21. Senate Judiciary discharged. Senate passed Oct. 1. President signed Oct. 5, 1982.

PL 97-282 (S J Res 174) Designate Oct. 16, 1982, as "World Food Day." LEAHY, D-Vt. — 3/24/82 — Senate Judiciary reported Sept. 14. Senate passed Sept. 15. House Post Office and Civil Service discharged. House passed Sept. 21. President signed Oct. 5, 1982.

PL 97-283 (S 2405) Provide for certain lands in New Mexico to be included in the Cibola National Forest System and in the existing Sandia Wilderness. DOMENICI, R-N.M. — 4/21/82 — Senate Energy and Natural Resources reported Sept. 9 (S Rept 97-539). Senate passed Sept. 17. House passed Sept. 23. President signed Oct. 5, 1982.

PL 97-284 (H J Res 486) Designate the period Oct. 3-9, 1982, as "National Schoolbus Safety Week of 1982." HOWARD, D-N.J. — 5/13/82 — House Post Office and Civil Service discharged. House passed Sept. 21. Senate Judiciary discharged. Senate passed Oct. 1. President signed Oct. 5, 1982.

PL 97-285 (S 907) Include Cabinet officers under the provisions of the U.S. Code relating to assassination, kidnapping and assault. THURMOND, R-S.C. — 4/8/81 — Senate Judiciary reported March 10, 1982 (S Rept 97-320). Senate passed May 5. House Judiciary reported Sept. 14 (H Rept 97-803). House passed, amended, under suspension of the rules, Sept. 14. Senate agreed to House amendment Sept. 22. President signed Oct. 6, 1982.

PL 97-286 (S 2271) Authorize funds for fiscal year 1983 for the National Bureau of Standards. PACKWOOD, R-Ore. — 3/24/82 — Senate Commerce, Science and Transportation reported April 21 (S Rept 97-337). Senate passed April 29. House passed, amended, May 19. Senate agreed to House amendment with amendments Aug. 12. House agreed to Senate amendments Sept. 22. President signed Oct. 6, 1982.

PL 97-287 (HR 3589) Authorize the exchange of certain land held by the Navajo tribe and the Bureau of Land Management. SKEEN, R-N.M. — 5/13/81 — House Interior and Insular Affairs reported June 21, 1982 (H Rept 97-616). House passed July 19. Senate passed, amended, Aug. 20. House agreed to Senate amendment Sept. 23. President signed Oct. 6, 1982.

PL 97-288 (HR 5081) Declare that the United States holds in trust certain land in Nevada for the Washoe tribe of Nevada and California. SANTINI, D-Nev. — 11/20/81 — House Interior and Insular Affairs reported June 7, 1982 (H Rept 97-598). House passed July 19. Senate passed, amended, Aug. 19. House agreed to Senate amendment Sept. 23. President signed Oct. 6, 1982.

PL 97-289 (H J Res 612) Provide for the temporary extension of certain insurance programs relating to housing and community development. GONZALEZ, D-Texas — 9/28/82 — House Banking, Finance and Urban Affairs discharged. House passed Sept. 29. Senate passed Oct. 1. President signed Oct. 6, 1982.

PL 97-290 (S 734) Promote the formation of U.S. export trading companies to expand export participation by small U.S. companies. HEINZ, R-Pa. — 3/19/81 — Senate Banking, Housing and Urban Affairs reported March 18 (S Rept 97-27). Senate passed April 8. House Banking, Finance and Urban Affairs, House Foreign Affairs and House Judiciary discharged. House passed, amended, July 27, 1982. Senate agreed to conference report Oct. 1 (H Rept 97-924). House agreed to conference report Oct. 1. President signed Oct. 8, 1982.

PL 97-291 (S 2420) Provide protection to victims and witnesses of crimes. HEINZ, R-Pa. — 4/22/82 — Senate Judiciary reported Aug. 19 (S Rept 97-532). Senate passed Sept. 14. House Judiciary discharged. House passed, amended, Sept. 30. Senate agreed to House amendments with amendment Oct. 1. House agreed to Senate amendment Oct. 1. President signed Oct. 12, 1982.

PL 97-292 (HR 6976) Establish a national clearinghouse to facilitate the location of missing children. SIMON, D-Ill. — 8/11/82 — House Judiciary reported Sept. 16 (H Rept 97-820). House passed, under suspension of the rules, Sept. 20. Senate Judiciary discharged. Senate passed, amended, Sept. 28. House agreed to conference report Sept. 30 (H Rept 97-911). Senate agreed to conference report Oct. 1. President signed Oct. 12, 1982.

PL 97-293 (S 1409) Authorize the enlargement of the Buffalo Bill Dam and Reservoir in Wyoming, increase limitations of federal reclamation laws, and provide for the resolution of the Papago Indian water issues. WALLOP, R-Wyo. — 6/23/81 — Senate Energy and Natural Resources reported May 26, 1982 (S Rept 97-420). Senate passed June 22. House Interior and Insular Affairs discharged. House passed, amended, Aug. 17. Senate agreed to House amendment with amendment Aug. 20. Senate agreed to conference report Sept. 24 (H Rept 97-855). House agreed to conference report Sept. 29. President signed Oct. 12, 1982.

PL 97-294 (S J Res 239) Designate Oct. 16, 1982, as "National Newspaper Carrier Appreciation Day." WARNER, R-Va. — 9/9/82 — Senate Judiciary reported Sept. 14. Senate passed Sept. 15. House Post Office and Civil Service discharged. House passed Sept. 29. President signed Oct. 12, 1982.

PL 97-295 (HR 4623) Codify without substantive changes recent laws concerning the Armed Forces, the Coast Guard, military pay and allowances, and veterans. RODINO, D-N.J. — 9/29/81 — House Judiciary reported Dec. 11 (H Rept 97-388). House, passed, under suspension of the rules, July 19, 1982. Senate Judiciary discharged. Senate passed, amended, Sept. 24. House agreed to Senate amendments Sept. 28. President signed Oct. 12, 1982.

PL 97-296 (HR 5154) Amend title 5, U.S. Code, providing training opportunities for employees under the Office of the Architect of the Capitol and the Botanic Garden. PATTERSON, D-Calif. — 12/9/81 — House Judiciary reported Aug. 19, 1982 (H Rept 97-778). House

passed, under suspension of the rules, Sept. 20. Senate passed Sept. 29. President signed Oct. 12, 1982.

PL 97-297 (HR 6168) Amend title 18, U.S. Code, providing a criminal penalty for threats against former presidents, major presidential candidates, and certain other persons protected by the Secret Service. S. HALL, D-Texas — 4/27/82 — House Judiciary reported Aug. 11 (H Rept 97-725). House passed Aug. 16. Senate Judiciary discharged. Senate passed Sept. 28. President signed Oct. 12, 1982.

PL 97-298 (HR 6454) Clarify the applicability of offenses involving explosives and fire. HUGHES, D-N.J. — 5/20/82 — House Judiciary reported July 28 (H Rept 97-678). House passed, under suspension of the rules, Aug. 2. Senate passed, amended, Sept. 22. House agreed to Senate amendments Sept. 28. President signed Oct. 12, 1982.

PL 97-299 (H J Res 207) Provide for the placement of a plaque at the U.S. Marine Corps War Memorial honoring Joseph Rosenthal, the photographer of the scene depicted by the memorial. J. BURTON, D-Calif. — 3/12/81 — House Interior and Insular Affairs reported July 29 (H Rept 97-206). House passed Aug. 4. Senate Energy and Natural Resources reported Sept. 20, 1982 (S Rept 97-559). Senate passed Sept. 29. President signed Oct. 12, 1982.

PL 97-300 (S 2036) Provide for state and local employment training assistance. QUAYLE, R-Ind. — 2/2/82 — Senate Labor and Human Resources reported May 28 (S Rept 97-469). Senate passed July 1. House passed, amended, Aug. 4. Senate agreed to conference report Sept. 30 (H Rept 97-889). House agreed to conference report Oct. 1. President signed Oct. 13, 1982.

PL 97-301 (S 2852) Authorize funds for fiscal years 1983-84 for student loan assistance programs and provide for an exception under federal priority for recovering monies owed the Student Loan Marketing Association. HATCH, R-Utah — 8/18/82 — Senate Labor and Human Resources reported Sept. 9 (S Rept 97-538). Senate passed Sept. 16. House passed, amended, Sept. 22. Senate agreed to conference report Sept. 27 (H Rept 97-887). Senate receded from its disagreement to House amendment Sept. 27. House agreed to conference report Sept. 29. President signed Oct. 13, 1982.

PL 97-302 (HR 3881) Provide for the release of reversionary and mineral interests of the United States conveyed to the Arkansas Forestry Commission. ANTHONY, D-Ark. — 6/11/81 — House Agriculture reported March 5, 1982 (H Rept 97-447, Part I). House Interior and Insular Affairs reported April 27 (H Rept 97-447, Part II). House passed May 17. Senate Energy and Natural Resources discharged. Senate Agriculture, Nutrition and Forestry reported Sept. 22 (S Rept 97-570). Senate passed Sept. 29. President signed Oct. 13, 1982.

PL 97-303 (HR 6156) Resolve jurisdictional questions involving the Securities and Exchange Commission and the Commodity Futures Trading Commission over the developing markets in futures and options on financial instruments. WIRTH, D-Colo. — 4/22/82 — House Energy and Commerce reported June 24 (H Rept 97-626, Part I). House Agriculture reported July 30 (H Rept 97-626, Part II). House passed Sept. 23. Senate passed Oct. 1. President signed Oct. 13, 1982.

PL 97-304 (HR 6133) Authorize funds for fiscal years 1983-85 to provide protection for endangered species of plants and animals. BREAUX, D-La. — 4/21/82 — House Merchant Marine and Fisheries reported May 17 (H Rept 97-567, Part I). House Foreign Affairs discharged. House passed, under suspension of the rules, June 8. Senate passed, amended, June 9. Senate agreed to conference report Sept. 20 (H Rept 97-835). House agreed to conference report Sept. 30. President signed Oct. 13, 1982.

PL 97-305 (S 188) Authorize the conveyance of certain lands in the Gallatin National Forest to a named individual upon payment of the fair market value. MELCHER, D-Mont. — 1/21/81 — Senate Energy and Natural Resources reported Oct. 7 (S Rept 97-206). Senate passed Oct. 21. House Interior and Insular Affairs reported Sept. 30, 1982 (H Rept 97-905). House passed Sept. 30. President signed Oct. 14, 1982.

PL 97-306 (HR 6782) Increase the rates of disability compensation for disabled veterans, increase the rates of dependency and indemnity compensation for surviving spouses and children of disabled veterans, discontinue duplicative payment to certain veterans, increase the level of disability required for the payment of dependent allowances, provide for cost-saving improvements in veterans' programs, and improve certain aspects of the Veterans Administration educational benefits program and the Department of Labor veterans' employment programs. APPLEGATE, D-Ohio — 7/19/82 — House Veterans' Affairs reported July 23 (H Rept 97-660). House passed, under suspension of the rules, July 27. Senate passed, amended, Sept. 24. House agreed to Senate amendment with amendment Sept. 28. Senate agreed to House amendment Sept. 29. President signed Oct. 14, 1982.

PL 97-307 (S 2874) Credit entrance fees for the migratory-bird hunting and conservation stamp contest to the account that pays for the administration of the contest. CHAFEE, R-R.I. — 8/20/82 — Senate passed Aug. 20. House passed Sept. 30. President signed Oct. 14, 1982.

PL 97-308 (HR 4468) Authorize the secretary of the Treasury to estab-

lish zones of protection for certain persons protected by the Secret Service. DANIELSON, D-Calif. — 9/14/81 — House Judiciary reported March 8, 1982 (H Rept 97-451). House passed, under suspension of the rules, March 18. Senate Judiciary discharged. Senate passed Oct. 1. President signed Oct. 14, 1982.

PL 97-309 (HR 5930) Extend the authority of the secretary of transportation to provide certain aviation insurance and reinsurance. MINETA, D-Calif. — 3/23/82 — House Public Works and Transportation reported May 17 (H Rept 97-519). House passed, under suspension of the rules, June 2. Senate Commerce, Science and Transportation discharged. Senate passed, amended, June 21. Senate agreed to conference report Sept. 30 (H Rept 97-864). House agreed to conference report Sept. 30. President signed Oct. 14, 1982.

PL 97-310 (HR 7293) Authorize funds for certain activities of the Wolf Trap Foundation for the Performing Arts. WOLF, R-Va. — 10/1/82 — House Interior and Insular Affairs discharged. House passed Oct. 2. Senate passed Oct. 2. President signed Oct. 14, 1982.

PL 97-311 (HR 6422) Provide for the release of reversionary interest of the United States conveyed to the state of Connecticut. GEJDENSON, D-Conn. — 5/19/82 — House Agriculture reported Aug. 19 (H Rept 97-773). House passed, under suspension of the rules, Sept. 13. Senate Agriculture, Nutrition and Forestry reported Sept. 22 (S Rept 97-571). Senate passed Sept. 29. President signed Oct. 14, 1982.

PL 97-312 (HR 2035) Authorize Department of Agriculture employees engaged in animal disease control work to carry firearms in the performance of their official duties. KAZEN, D-Texas — 2/24/81 — House Agriculture reported May 13, 1982 (H Rept 97-515). House passed, under suspension of the rules, May 18. Senate Agriculture, Nutrition and Forestry reported Sept. 22 (S Rept 97-569). Senate passed, amended, Sept. 29. House agreed to Senate amendments Sept. 30. President signed Oct. 14, 1982.

PL 97-313 (HR 5658) Provide elementary and secondary assistance grants to assist in the teaching of citizenship principles. BENNETT, D-Fla. — 3/2/82 — House Education and Labor reported Sept. 9 (H Rept 97-798). House passed, under suspension of the rules, Sept. 14. Senate passed Oct. 1. President signed Oct. 14, 1982.

PL 97-314 (HR 5941) Designate the building known as the Federal Building and United States Courthouse in Greenville, S.C., as the "Clement F. Haynsworth Jr. Federal Building," the building known as the Quincy Post Office in Quincy, Mass., as the "James A. Burke Post Office," and the United States Post Office Building in Portsmouth, Ohio, as the "William H. Harsha United States Post Office Building." CAMPBELL, R-S.C. — 3/24/82 — House Public Works and Transportation reported Sept. 23 (H Rept 97-866). House passed Sept. 29. Senate Governmental Affairs discharged. Senate passed Oct. 1. President signed Oct. 14, 1982.

PL 97-315 (H J Res 588) Designate the month of October 1982 as "Head Start Awareness Month." ROGERS, R-Ky. — 8/19/82 — House Post Office and Civil Service discharged. House passed Sept. 29. Senate passed Oct. 1. President signed Oct. 14, 1982.

PL 97-316 (S J Res 113) Designate the week of Nov. 28-Dec. 4, 1982, as "National Home Health Care Week." HATCH, R-Utah — 10/6/81 — Senate Judiciary reported Oct. 27. Senate passed Oct. 30. House Post Office and Civil Service discharged. House passed, amended, Sept. 21, 1982. Senate agreed to House amendments Oct. 1. President signed Oct. 14, 1982.

PL 97-317 (S J Res 197) Designate the week of Oct. 17-23, 1982, as "Myasthenia Gravis Awareness Week." METZENBAUM, D-Ohio — 5/10/82 — Senate Judiciary reported May 18. Senate passed May 19. House Post Office and Civil Service discharged. House passed Sept. 30. President signed Oct. 14, 1982.

PL 97-318 (S J Res 235) Proclaim March 21, 1983, as "National Agriculture Day." HELMS, R-N.C. — 8/19/82 — Senate Judiciary reported Sept. 14. Senate passed Sept. 15. House Post Office and Civil Service discharged. House passed Sept. 30. President signed Oct. 14, 1982.

PL 97-319 (S J Res 249) Designate the month of October 1982 as "National Spinal Cord Injury Month." KENNEDY, D-Mass. — 9/20/82 — Senate passed Oct. 1. House passed Oct. 2. President signed Oct. 14, 1982.

PL 97-320 (HR 6267) Assist the thrift industry by providing net worth assistance to savings institutions and additional flexibility to their federal regulatory agencies. ST GERMAIN, D-R.I. — 5/4/82 — House Banking, Finance and Urban Affairs reported May 17 (H Rept 97-550). House passed May 20. Senate Banking, Housing and Urban Affairs discharged. Senate passed, amended, Sept. 24. Senate agreed to conference report Sept. 30 (H Rept 97-899). House agreed to conference report Oct. 1. President signed Oct. 15, 1982.

PL 97-321 (S 2586) Authorize funds for fiscal year 1983 for military construction programs of the Department of Defense. THURMOND, R-S.C. — 5/27/82 — Senate Armed Services reported May 27 (S Rept 97-440). Senate passed June 30. House passed, amended, Aug. 11.

Senate agreed to conference report Sept 28 (H Rept 97-880). House agreed to conference report Sept. 29. President signed Oct. 15, 1982.

PL 97-322 (S 2252) Authorize funds for fiscal years 1983-84 for the U.S. Coast Guard, Department of Transportation. STEVENS, R-Alaska — 3/22/82 — Senate Commerce, Science and Transportation reported April 26 (S Rept 97-361). Senate passed May 5. House passed, amended, July 15. Senate agreed to House amendment with amendment Sept 27. House agreed to Senate amendment Sept. 29. President signed Oct. 15, 1982.

PL 97-323 (HR 6968) Appropriate funds for fiscal year 1983 for military construction programs of the Department of Defense. GINN, D-Ga. — 8/11/82 — House Appropriations reported Aug. 11 (H Rept 97-726). House passed Aug. 19. Senate Appropriations reported Sept. 22 (S Rept 97-572). Senate passed, amended, Sept. 27. House agreed to conference report Oct. 1 (H Rept 97-913). Senate agreed to conference report Oct. 1. President signed Oct. 15, 1982.

PL 97-324 (HR 5890) Authorize funds for fiscal year 1983 for the National Aeronautics and Space Administration. FUQUA, D-Fla. — 3/18/82 — House Science and Technology reported May 5 (H Rept 97-502). House passed May 13. Senate Commerce, Science and Transportation discharged. Senate passed, amended, June 9. Senate agreed to conference report Sept. 30 (H Rept 97-897). House agreed to conference report Oct. 1. President signed Oct. 15, 1982.

PL 97-325 (HR 6164) Authorize the secretary of agriculture to implement the Agreement on the International Carriage of Perishable Foodstuffs and on the Special Equipment to be Used for Such Carriage (ATP). DE LA GARZA, D-Texas — 4/27/82 — House Agriculture reported May 14 (H Rept 97-516). House passed, under suspension of the rules, May 18. Senate passed, amended, Sept. 29. House agreed to Senate amendment Sept. 30. President signed Oct. 15, 1982.

PL 97-326 (S 2386) Provide for the establishment of a system to collect and report data on the geographic distribution of federal funds for each year by state, county and city area. SASSER, D-Tenn. — 4/15/82 — Senate Governmental Affairs reported May 28 (S Rept 97-473). Senate passed July 29. House Government Operations discharged. House passed, amended, Sept. 28. Senate agreed to House amendment Oct. 1. President signed Oct. 15, 1982.

PL 97-327 (S 2574) Extend authorizations for the federal aid highway program. SYMMS, R-Idaho — 5/26/82 — Senate Environment and Public Works reported May 26 (S Rept 97-421). Senate passed Oct. 1. House passed, amended, Oct. 1. Senate agreed to House amendment Oct. 1. President signed Oct. 15, 1982.

PL 97-328 (HR 6276) Amend the District of Columbia Self Government and Governmental Reorganization Act to allow the issuance of revenue bonds to finance college and university programs that provide student educational loans. DYMALLY, D-Calif. — 5/5/82 — House District of Columbia reported July 15 (H Rept 97-634). House passed Aug. 9. Senate Governmental Affairs reported Sept. 28. Senate passed Oct. 1. President signed Oct. 15, 1982.

PL 97-329 (S 2436) Designate the Mary McLeod Bethune Council House in Washington, D.C., as a national historic site. WARNER, R-Va. — 4/27/82 — Senate Energy and Natural Resources reported Aug. 19 (S Rept 97-534). Senate passed Sept. 22. House passed Sept. 30. President signed Oct. 15, 1982.

PL 97-330 (HR 4476) Authorize funds through fiscal year 1986 for the Administrative Conference of the United States. DANIELSON, D-Calif. — 9/15/81 — House Judiciary reported May 12, 1982 (H Rept 97-511). House passed, under suspension of the rules, June 14. Senate Judiciary reported Sept. 9. Senate passed Oct. 1. President signed Oct. 15, 1982.

PL 97-331 (HR 6273) Authorize funds for fiscal years 1983-85 for programs of the National Traffic and Motor Vehicle Safety Act and the Motor Vehicle Information and Cost Savings Act. WIRTH, D-Colo. — 5/5/82 — House Energy and Commerce reported May 19 (H Rept 97-576). House passed, under suspension of the rules, June 14. Senate Commerce, Science and Transportation reported July 27 (S Rept 97-505). Senate passed Oct. 1. President signed Oct. 15, 1982.

PL 97-332 (HR 2528) Authorize any federal department or agency to order from another department or agency any material or service such other agency can obtain by contract. BROOKS, D-Texas — 3/17/81 — House Government Operations reported March 11, 1982 (H Rept 97-456). House passed, under suspension of the rules, March 23. Senate Governmental Affairs reported Sept. 24. Senate passed Oct. 1. President signed Oct. 15, 1982.

PL 97-333 (HR 1486) Establish the Protection Island National Wildlife Refuge in the state of Washington. BONKER, D-Wash. — 1/29/81 — House Merchant Marine and Fisheries reported Dec. 14 (H Rept 97-403). House passed, under suspension of the rules, Dec. 15. Senate Energy and Natural Resources reported May 26, 1982 (S Rept 97-426). Senate passed, amended, June 9. House agreed to Senate amendments Sept. 30. President signed Oct. 15, 1982.

PL 97-334 (S 2457) Provide for an increase in the funding level for the

federal payment to the government of the District of Columbia. MATHIAS, R-Md. — 4/29/82 — Senate Governmental Affairs reported May 28 (S Rept 97-471). Senate passed June 21. House passed, amended, Aug. 12. Senate agreed to conference report Oct. 1 (H Rept 97-931). House agreed to conference report Oct. 2. President signed Oct. 15, 1982.

PL 97-335 (S 1777) Establish a permanent boundary for the portion of Acadia National Park that lies within the town of Isle au Haut, Maine. MITCHELL, D-Maine — 10/27/81 — Senate Energy and Natural Resources reported May 26, 1982 (S Rept 97-425). Senate passed June 10. House Interior and Insular Affairs discharged. House passed Sept. 30. President signed Oct. 15, 1982.

PL 97-336 (S 2375) Extend for one year the Defense Production Act, providing availability of authorities necessary to continue improvement in U.S. ability to mobilize resources in times of national emergency. SCHMITT, R-N.M. — 4/15/82 — Senate Banking, Housing and Urban Affairs reported May 21 (S Rept 97-412). Senate passed Oct. 1. House passed, amended, Oct. 2. Senate agreed to House amendments Oct. 2. President signed Oct. 15, 1982.

PL 97-337 (HR 3278) Provide sizing criteria for the construction of military medical facilities. HOLT, R-Md. — 4/28/81 — House Armed Services reported Sept. 23, 1982 (H Rept 97-857). House passed, under suspension of the rules, Sept. 28. Senate Armed Services discharged. Senate passed Oct. 1. President signed Oct. 15, 1982.

PL 97-338 (HR 6188) Authorize the secretary of the interior to engage in a special study to assist the state of Nebraska in establishing water resource development priorities in the Platte River Basin. BEREUTER, R-Neb. — 4/28/82 — House Interior and Insular Affairs reported Aug. 10 (H Rept 97-713). House passed, under suspension of the rules, Aug. 16. Senate Energy and Natural Resources reported Sept. 20 (S Rept 97-562). Senate passed Oct. 1. President signed Oct. 15, 1982.

PL 97-339 (HR 3467) Authorize funds for the U.S. Arms Control and Disarmament Agency. ZABLOCKI, D-Wis. — 5/6/81 — House Foreign Affairs reported May 19 (H Rept 97-55). House passed, under suspension of the rules, June 8. Senate Foreign Relations reported May 26, 1982 (S Rept 97-430). Senate passed, amended, Oct. 1. House agreed to Senate amendment Oct. 1. President signed Oct. 15, 1982.

PL 97-340 (HR 1281) Provide for the conveyance of certain lands in Alaska. YOUNG, R-Alaska — 1/23/81 — House Interior and Insular Affairs reported Dec. 4 (H Rept 97-357). House passed Dec. 15. Senate Energy and Natural Resources reported Sept. 20, 1982 (S Rept 97-560). Senate passed Oct. 1. President signed Oct. 15, 1982.

PL 97-341 (S 1872) Extend the period of grazing privileges afforded to privately owned lands within the Capitol Reed National Park in Utah. GARN, R-Utah — 11/19/81 — Senate Energy and Natural Resources reported May 27, 1982 (S Rept 97-448). Senate passed June 9. House Interior and Insular Affairs reported Sept. 16 (H Rept 97-823). House passed, amended, under suspension of the rules, Sept. 20. Senate agreed to House amendments with amendments Sept. 30. House agreed to Senate amendments Sept. 30. President signed Oct. 15, 1982.

PL 97-342 (HR 7115) Authorize the transfer of certain naval vessels to certain foreign governments. PRICE, D-Ill. — 9/15/82 — House Armed Services reported Sept. 21 (H Rept 97-843, Part I). House Foreign Affairs reported Sept. 23 (H Rept 97-843, Part II). House passed, under suspension of the rules, Sept. 28. Senate Foreign Relations discharged. Senate passed Oct. 1. President signed Oct. 15, 1982.

PL 97-343 (S J Res 241) Designate the week of Dec. 12-18, 1982, as "National Drunk and Drugged Driving Awareness Week." HUMPHREY, R-N.H. — 9/10/82 — Senate Judiciary reported Sept. 14. Senate passed Sept. 15. House Post Office and Civil Service discharged. House passed Sept. 30. President signed Oct. 15, 1982.

PL 97-344 (S 478) Provide for the partition or sale of certain restricted Indian lands in the state of Kansas. DOLE, R-Kan. — 2/16/81 — Senate Indian Affairs reported May 15 (S Rept 97-107). Senate passed May 21. House Interior and Insular Affairs reported Nov. 18 (H Rept 97-341). House passed, amended, Dec. 15. Senate agreed to House amendment Oct. 1, 1982. President signed Oct. 15, 1982.

PL 97-345 (S 1573) Restore Lake Oswego, Ore., as a non-navigable water of the United States. HATFIELD, R-Ore. — 7/31/81 — Senate Energy and Natural Resources reported May 11, 1982 (S Rept 97-387). Senate passed May 19. House Energy and Commerce reported Sept. 29 (H Rept 97-893). House passed, amended, Sept. 30. Senate agreed to House amendment Oct. 1. President signed Oct. 15, 1982.

PL 97-346 (HR 5145) Amend title 5, U.S. Code, to provide training opportunities for employees under the Office of the Architect of the Capitol and the Botanic Garden. FORD, D-Mich. — 12/9/81 — House Post Office and Civil Service reported March 25, 1982 (H Rept 97-473). House passed, under suspension of the rules, May 11. Senate Governmental Affairs discharged. Senate passed, amended, Sept. 29. House agreed to Senate amendments Oct. 1. President signed Oct. 15, 1982.

PL 97-347 (HR 5662) Extend the authority and appropriations for certain programs under the Fish and Wildlife Act of 1956. BREAUX, D-La. — 3/2/82 — House Merchant Marine and Fisheries reported May 13 (H Rept 97-514). House passed, under suspension of the rules, June 8. Senate Environment and Public Works discharged. Senate passed Oct. 1. President signed Oct. 18, 1982.

PL 97-348 (S 1018) Prohibit the federal government from funding commercial and residential growth on undeveloped barrier beaches and islands. CHAFEE, R-R.I. — 4/28/81 — Senate Environment and Public Works reported May 26, 1982 (S Rept 97-419). Senate passed Sept. 23. House passed, amended, Sept. 28. Senate agreed to conference report Oct. 1 (H Rept 97-928). House agreed to conference report Oct. 2. President signed Oct. 18, 1982.

PL 97-349 (S J Res 261) Designate the week of Oct. 24-31, 1982, as "National Housing Week." BAKER, R-Tenn. — 10/1/82 — Senate passed Oct. 1. House passed Oct. 2. President signed Oct. 18, 1982.

PL 97-350 (S 1210) Authorize funds for fiscal year 1982 for the Council on Environmental Quality. GORTON, R-Wash. — 5/18/81 — Senate Environment and Public Works reported May 15 (S Rept 97-116). Senate passed June 2. House passed, amended, Sept. 22. Senate agreed to House amendments with amendments June 14, 1982. House agreed to Senate amendments with an amendment Sept. 30. Senate agreed to House amendment Oct. 1. President signed Oct. 18, 1982.

PL 97-351 (HR 5228) Amend title 18, U.S. Code, to implement the Convention on the Physical Protection of Nuclear Material. HUGHES, D-N.J. — 12/15/81 — House Judiciary reported June 24, 1982 (H Rept 97-624). House passed, under suspension of the rules, July 20. Senate Judiciary discharged. Senate passed, amended, Sept. 14. House disagreed to Senate amendments Sept. 28. House agreed to Senate amendments with amendments Sept. 28. Senate agreed to House amendments Oct. 1. Senate receded from its amendments Oct. 1. President signed Oct. 18, 1982.

PL 97-352 (HR 6865) Suppress unfair and fraudulent practices in the marketing of fresh and frozen fruits and vegetables in interstate and foreign commerce. DE LA GARZA, D-Texas — 7/27/82 — House Agriculture reported Sept. 26 (H Rept 97-876). House passed, under suspension of the rules, Sept. 28. Senate Agriculture, Nutrition and Forestry discharged. Senate passed Oct. 2. President signed Oct. 18, 1982.

PL 97-353 (S J Res 257) Designate the month of November 1982 as "National Diabetes Month." WEICKER, R-Conn. — 9/29/82 — Senate Judiciary discharged. Senate passed Oct. 1. House passed Oct. 2. President signed Oct. 19, 1982.

PL 97-354 (HR 6055) Allow taxpayers to choose to conduct their business in corporate or noncorporate form based solely upon business reasons. ROSTENKOWSKI, D-Ill. — 4/1/82 — House Ways and Means reported Sept. 16 (H Rept 97-826). House passed, under suspension of the rules, Sept. 20. Senate Finance reported Sept. 29 (S Rept 97-640). Senate passed, amended, Sept. 30. House agreed to Senate amendments Oct. 1. President signed Oct. 19, 1982.

PL 97-355 (S J Res 262) Designate the month of November 1982 as "National Christmas Seal Month." BYRD, D-W.Va. — 10/1/82 — Senate passed Oct. 1. House passed Oct. 2. President signed Oct. 19, 1982.

PL 97-356 (HR 6029) Provide for the secretary of the interior to acquire from the state of Indiana certain lands by exchange at the Indiana Dunes National Lakeshore. BENJAMIN, D-Ind. — 4/1/81 — House Interior and Insular Affairs reported Aug. 10, 1982 (H Rept 97-710). House passed Aug. 16. Senate Energy and Natural Resources reported Sept. 20 (S Rept 97-561). Senate passed Oct. 2. President signed Oct. 19, 1982.

PL 97-357 (HR 5139) Modify provisions of the revised Organic Act of the Virgin Islands and provide certain other authorities affecting the territories and possessions of the United States. WON PAT, D-Guam — 12/8/81 — House Interior and Insular Affairs reported Dec. 11 (H Rept 97-387). House passed Dec. 11. Senate Energy and Natural Resources reported April 29, 1982 (S Rept 97-372). Senate passed, amended, May 10. House agreed to Senate amendment with an amendment Sept. 9. Senate agreed to House amendment with amendments Sept. 30. House agreed to Senate amendments Oct. 1. President signed Oct. 19, 1982.

PL 97-358 (HR 6142) Require the Commodity Credit Corporation to dispose of government-owned stocks of agricultural commodities. BEDELL, D-Iowa — 4/22/82 — House Agriculture reported Sept. 26 (H Rept 97-874). House passed, under suspension of the rules, Sept. 28. Senate Agriculture, Nutrition and Forestry discharged. Senate passed Oct. 1. President signed Oct. 21, 1982.

PL 97-359 (S 1698) Amend the Immigration and Nationality Act to provide preferential treatment in the admission of certain children of United States armed forces personnel. DENTON, R-Ala. — 10/1/81 — Senate Judiciary reported Sept. 23, 1982. Senate passed Sept. 28. House passed, amended, Oct. 1. Senate agreed to House amendments

Oct. 1. President signed Oct. 22, 1982.

PL 97-360 (HR 4828) Set aside certain surplus vessels for use by private non-profit organizations in providing health and other humanitarian services to developing countries. MITCHELL, D-Md. — 10/22/81 — House Merchant Marine and Fisheries reported Aug. 12, 1982 (H Rept 97-734). House passed, under suspension of the rules, Aug. 17. Senate Commerce, Science and Transportation discharged. Senate passed Oct. 1. President signed Oct. 22, 1982.

PL 97-361 (HR 3787) Amend sections 10 and 11 of PL 91-479, an act to establish in the state of Michigan the Sleeping Bear Dunes National Lakeshore. BROOMFIELD, R-Mich. — 6/4/81 — House Interior and Insular Affairs reported Sept. 28, 1982 (H Rept 97-882). House passed, under suspension of the rules, Sept. 29. Senate passed, amended, Oct. 1. House agreed to Senate amendments Oct. 2. President signed Oct. 22, 1982.

PL 97-362 (HR 4717) Amend the effective date provisions of section 403(b)(3) of the Windfall Profit Tax Act of 1980 to further defer the effective date of certain provisions providing for the recognition of income of LIFO inventory amounts. JENKINS, D-Ga. — 10/7/81 — House Ways and Means reported Dec. 14 (H Rept 97-405). House passed, under suspension of the rules, Dec. 15. Senate passed, amended, Dec. 16. House agreed to Senate amendment with an amendment March 16, 1982. House agreed to conference report Oct. 1 (H Rept 97-929). Senate agreed to conference report Oct. 1. President signed Oct. 25, 1982.

PL 97-363 (HR 5879) Amend the Immigration and Nationality Act to extend for three years the authorization for refugee assistance programs and to make certain improvements in the operation of the program. RODINO, D-N.J. — 4/17/82 — House Judiciary reported May 17 (H Rept 97-541). House passed June 22. Senate Judiciary reported Sept. 29 (S Rept 97-638). Senate passed Oct. 1. President signed Oct. 25, 1982.

PL 97-364 (HR 6170) Amend title 23, U.S. Code, to encourage the establishment by states of effective alcohol traffic safety programs and to require the secretary of transportation to assist state driver licensing officials in exchanging information regarding the motor vehicle driving records of certain individuals. HOWARD, D-N.J. — 4/27/82 — House Public Works and Transportation reported Sept. 23 (H Rept 97-867). House passed, under suspension of the rules, Sept. 29. Senate passed Oct. 1. President signed Oct. 25, 1982.

PL 97-365 (HR 4613) Increase the efficiency of government-wide efforts to collect debts owed the United States and to provide additional procedures for the collection of debts owed the United States. CONABLE, R-N.Y. — 9/29/81 — House Ways and Means reported April 29, 1982 (H Rept 97-496). House passed, under suspension of the rules, May 5. Senate passed, amended, Sept. 28. House agreed to Senate amendment with amendments Sept 30. Senate agreed to House amendments Oct. 2. President signed Oct. 25, 1982.

PL 97-366 (HR 4441) Amend title 17, U.S. Code, to require that registration fees be paid to the Copyright Office when registration applications are filed. RODINO, D-N.J. — 9/9/81 — House Judiciary reported April 29, 1982 (H Rept 97-494). House passed, under suspension of the rules, May 10. Senate Judiciary reported June 23. Senate passed, amended, June 30. Senate agreed to conference report Oct. 1 (H Rept 97-930). House agreed to conference report Oct. 2. President signed Oct. 25, 1982.

PL 97-367 (HR 7292) Establish a White House Conference on Productivity. LaFALCE, D-N.Y. — 10/1/82 — House Banking, Finance and Urban Affairs discharged. House passed Oct. 2. Senate passed Oct. 2. President signed Oct. 25, 1982.

PL 97-368 (H J Res 595) Designate Dec. 11, 1982, as "Fiorello H. La Guardia Memorial Day." BIAGGI, D-N.Y. — 9/16/82 — House Post Office and Civil Service discharged. House passed Sept. 30. Senate Judiciary discharged. Senate passed Dec. 10. President signed Dec. 17, 1982.

PL 97-369 (HR 7019) Appropriate funds for the fiscal year ending Sept. 30, 1983, for the Department of Transportation and related agencies. BENJAMIN, D-Ind. — 8/19/82 — House Appropriations reported Aug. 19 (H Rept 97-783). House passed Sept. 21. Senate Appropriations reported Sept. 22 (S Rept 97-567). Senate passed, amended, Dec. 2. House agreed to conference report Dec. 16 (H Rept 97-960). Senate agreed to conference report Dec. 16. President signed Dec. 18, 1982.

PL 97-370 (HR 7072) Appropriate funds for the fiscal year ending Sept. 30, 1983, for agriculture, rural development and related agencies. WHITTEN, D-Miss. — 9/9/82 — House Appropriations reported Sept. 9 (H Rept 97-800). House passed Sept. 21. Senate Appropriations reported Sept. 22 (S Rept 97-566). Senate passed, amended, Sept. 28. House agreed to conference report Dec. 15 (H Rept 97-957). Senate agreed to conference report Dec. 15. President signed Dec. 18, 1982.

PL 97-371 (HR 6403) Provide for the use and distribution of funds to the Wyandot tribe of Indians in docket 139 before the Indian Claims Commission and docket 141 before the U.S. Court of Claims. UDALL, D-Ariz. — 5/18/82 — House Interior and Insular Affairs reported Sept. 16 (H Rept 97-819). House passed Sept. 29. Senate Indian Affairs discharged. Senate passed Dec. 8. President signed Dec. 20, 1982.

PL 97-372 (HR 5795) Provide for the use and distribution of the funds awarded to the Shawnee tribe of Indians in dockets 64, 335 and 338 by the Indian Claims Commission and docket 64-A by the U.S. Court of Claims. McCURDY, D-Okla. — 3/10/82 — House Interior and Insular Affairs reported Sept. 16 (H Rept 97-817). House passed Sept. 29. Senate Indian Affairs discharged. Senate passed Dec. 8. President signed Dec. 20, 1982.

PL 97-373 (S 2177) Amend title III of the Colorado River Basin Project Act to provide for the inclusion of ordinary fluctuations in costs for the construction of distribution and drainage facilities for non-Indian lands. DeCONCINI, D-Ariz. — 3/8/82 — Senate Energy and Natural Resources reported May 12 (S Rept 97-389). Senate passed May 19. House Interior and Insular Affairs reported Aug. 19 (H Rept 97-776, Part I). House Interior and Insular Affairs further reported Sept. 14 (H Rept 97-776, Part II). House passed, amended, Sept. 30. Senate agreed to House amendments with an amendment Dec. 8. House agreed to Senate amendment Dec. 9. President signed Dec. 20, 1982.

PL 97-374 (S 764) Provide for protection of the John Sack Cabin in the Targhee National Forest, Idaho. McCLURE, R-Idaho — 3/23/81 — Senate Energy and Natural Resources reported Aug. 27 (S Rept 97-184). Senate passed Sept. 22. House Interior and Insular Affairs discharged. House passed Dec. 10, 1982. President signed Dec. 20, 1982.

PL 97-375 (HR 6005) Discontinue or amend certain requirements for agency reports to Congress. BROOKS, D-Texas — 3/31/82 — House Government Operations reported Sept. 14 (H Rept 97-804). House passed, under suspension of the rules, Sept. 20. Senate Governmental Affairs discharged. Senate passed Dec. 8. President signed Dec. 21, 1982.

PL 97-376 (HR 5553) Provide for the use and disposition of Miami Indians judgment funds in dockets 124-b and 254 before the U.S. Court of Claims. UDALL, D-Ariz. — 2/22/82 — House Interior and Insular Affairs reported Sept. 16 (H Rept 97-815). House passed Sept. 29. Senate Indian Affairs discharged. Senate passed Dec. 8. President signed Dec. 21, 1982.

PL 97-377 (H J Res 631) Make further continuing appropriations for fiscal year 1983. WHITTEN, D-Miss. — 12/10/82 — House Appropriations reported Dec. 10 (H Rept 97-959). House passed Dec. 14. Senate Appropriations reported Dec. 15. Senate passed, amended, Dec. 19. House agreed to conference report Dec. 20 (H Rept 97-980). Senate agreed to conference report Dec. 20. President signed Dec. 21, 1982.

PL 97-378 (HR 7144) Appropriate funds for the fiscal year ending Sept. 30, 1983, for the government of the District of Columbia and other activities chargeable in whole or in part against the revenues of the district. DIXON, D-Calif. — 9/21/82 — House Appropriations reported Sept. 21 (H Rept 97-849). House passed Sept. 30. Senate passed, amended, Dec. 7. House agreed to conference report Dec. 17 (H Rept 97-972). Senate agreed to conference report Dec. 18. President signed Dec. 22, 1982.

PL 97-379 (HR 6417) Amend PL 96-432 to include certain sidewalks and contiguous areas within the definition of the U.S. Capitol grounds. FARY, D-Ill. — 5/19/82 — House Public Works and Transportation reported June 23 (H Rept 97-623). House passed, under suspension of the rules, July 12. Senate Rules and Administration reported Oct. 1 (S Rept 97-651). Senate passed Dec. 10. President signed Dec. 22, 1982.

PL 97-380 (S 1444) Authorize the administrator of General Services to donate to a state or local government certain federal personal property loaned to the government for civil defense use. THURMOND, R-S.C. — 7/8/81 — Senate Governmental Affairs reported Sept. 29, 1982. Senate passed Oct. 1. House passed Dec. 13. President signed Dec. 22, 1982.

PL 97-381 (S 1681) Designate the southern Nevada water project, in Clark County, Nev., as the "Robert B. Griffin Water Project." CANNON, D-Nev. — 9/29/81 — Senate Energy and Natural Resources discharged. Senate passed April 1. House Interior and Insular Affairs discharged. House passed Dec. 13. President signed Dec. 22, 1982.

PL 97-382 (S 1894) Permit Indian tribes to enter into certain agreements for the disposition of tribal mineral resources. MELCHER, D-Mont. — 11/30/81 — Senate Indian Affairs reported June 10, 1982 (S Rept 97-472). Senate passed June 30. House Interior and Insular Affairs reported Aug. 13 (H Rept 97-746). House passed, amended, under suspension of the rules, Aug. 17. Senate agreed to House amendment with amendments Dec. 8. House agreed to Senate amendments Dec. 10. President signed Dec. 22, 1982.

PL 97-383 (S 2034) Designate the lock and dam known as the Jones Bluff Lock and Dam, located on the Alabama River, as the "Robert F. Henry Lock and Dam." HEFLIN, D-Ala. — 1/29/82 — Senate Envi-

ronment and Public Works reported May 25 (S Rept 97-416). Senate passed June 30. House Public Works and Transportation discharged. House passed Dec. 13. President signed Dec. 22, 1982.

PL 97-384 (S 2710) Establish a wilderness area in the Hoosier National Forest, Ind. LUGAR, R-Ind. — 7/1/82 — Senate Energy and Natural Resources reported Sept. 20 (S Rept 97-557). Senate passed Oct. 2. House Interior and Insular Affairs reported Dec. 9 (H Rept 97-948, Part I). House passed, under suspension of the rules, Dec. 13. President signed Dec. 22, 1982.

PL 97-385 (HR 2329) Confer jurisdiction on certain courts of the United States to hear and render judgments in connection with certain claims of the Cherokee Nation of Oklahoma. SYNAR, D-Okla. — 3/4/81 — House Judiciary reported March 8, 1982 (H Rept 97-453, Part I). House passed July 23. Senate Judiciary reported Dec. 8. Senate passed Dec. 10. President signed Dec. 23, 1982.

PL 97-386 (HR 4364) Declare that the United States shall hold in trust for the Pascua Yaqui tribe of Arizona certain land in Pima County, Ariz. UDALL, D-Ariz. — 7/31/81 — House Interior and Insular Affairs reported Nov. 20 (H Rept 97-347). House passed Dec. 15. Senate Indian Affairs reported Oct. 1, 1982 (S Rept 97-657). Senate passed, amended, Dec. 3. House agreed to Senate amendments Dec. 10. President signed Dec. 23, 1982.

PL 97-387 (S 2611) Amend the Peace Corps Act to set a new minimum monthly adjustment allowance for volunteer leaders of the Peace Corps. PERCY, R-Ill. — 6/9/82 — Senate Foreign Relations reported Dec. 7. Senate passed Dec. 16. House passed Dec. 17. President signed Dec. 23, 1982.

PL 97-388 (S 3073) Provide for the distribution within the United States of the United States Information Agency film entitled "Dumas Malone: A Journey with Mr. Jefferson." WARNER, R-Va. — 12/3/82 — Senate Foreign Relations reported Dec. 8. Senate passed Dec. 16. House Foreign Affairs discharged. House passed Dec. 17. President signed Dec. 23, 1982.

PL 97-389 (HR 3942) Amend the Commercial Fisheries Research and Development Act of 1964 to encourage cooperation among the states to facilitate research on and development of commercial fishery resources. BREAUX, D-La. — 6/17/81 — House Merchant Marine and Fisheries reported Oct. 27 (H Rept 97-295). House passed, under suspension of the rules, Nov. 4. Senate Commerce, Science and Transportation discharged. Senate passed, amended, Dec. 10, 1982. House agreed to Senate amendment Dec. 10. President signed Dec. 29, 1982.

PL 97-390 (HR 6204) Amend title 28, U.S. Code, and related statutes with respect to the appointment and jurisdiction of the Supreme Court Police. RODINO, D-N.J. — 4/28/82 — House Judiciary reported Aug. 10 (H Rept 97-704). House passed Aug. 16. Senate passed, amended, Oct. 1. House agreed to Senate amendment Dec. 13. President signed Dec. 29, 1982.

PL 97-391 (HR 6588) Provide for federal recognition of the Cow Creek band of the Umpqua tribe of Indians and institute for the tribe those federal services provided to Indians who are recognized by the federal government and who receive such services because of the federal trust responsibility. WEAVER, D-Ore. — 6/14/82 — House Interior and Insular Affairs reported Sept. 23 (H Rept 97-862). House passed Dec. 6. Senate Indian Affairs discharged. Senate passed Dec. 17. President signed Dec. 29, 1982.

PL 97-392 (HR 6758) Authorize the sale of defense articles, defense services and unclassified defense service publications to United States companies for incorporation into end items to be sold to friendly foreign countries. GOODLING, R-Pa. — 7/14/82 — House Foreign Affairs reported. House passed, under suspension of the rules, July 19. Senate Foreign Relations reported Sept. 24 (S Rept 97-586). Senate passed, amended, Oct. 1. House agreed to Senate amendments Dec. 13. President signed Dec. 29, 1982.

PL 97-393 (S 816) Amend the Clayton Act to limit the circumstances under which foreign governments may sue for violations of the antitrust laws. THURMOND, R-S.C. — 3/26/81 — Senate Judiciary reported May 15 (S Rept 97-98). Senate passed July 9. House Judiciary discharged. House passed, amended, under suspension of the rules, Dec. 13, 1982. Senate agreed to House amendments Dec. 16. President signed Dec. 29, 1982.

PL 97-394 (HR 7356) Appropriate funds for the fiscal year ending Sept. 30, 1983, for the Department of the Interior and related agencies. YATES, D-Ill. — 12/2/82 — House Appropriations reported Dec. 2 (H Rept 97-942). House passed Dec. 3. Senate Appropriations reported Dec. 8. Senate passed, amended, Dec. 14. House agreed to conference report Dec. 18 (H Rept 97-978). Senate agreed to conference report Dec. 19. President signed Dec. 30, 1982.

PL 97-395 (S 823) Provide for the payment of losses incurred as a result of the ban on the use of the chemical Tris in apparel, fabric, yarn or fiber. THURMOND, R-S.C. — 3/27/81 — Senate Judiciary reported June 3 (S Rept 97-130). Senate passed June 18. House Judiciary discharged. House passed, amended, under suspension of the rules,

Dec. 13, 1982. Senate agreed to House amendment Dec. 14. President signed Dec. 30, 1982.

PL 97-396 (HR 1952) Authorize appropriations for fiscal years 1982-84 for certain conservation programs on military reservations and public lands. BREAUX, D-La. — 2/19/81 — House Merchant Marine and Fisheries reported May 18 (H Rept 97-49). House passed, under suspension of the rules, Sept. 21. Senate Environment and Public Works reported May 25, 1982 (S Rept 97-413). Senate passed, amended, June 9. House passed Senate amendments with an amendment Sept. 30. Senate agreed to House amendment with amendments Dec. 16. House agreed to Senate amendments Dec. 17. President signed Dec. 31, 1982.

PL 97-397 (HR 5204) Authorize and direct the secretary of the interior to accept certain lands for the benefit of the Sycuan band of Mission Indians. BURGENER, R-Calif. — 12/14/81 — House Interior and Insular Affairs reported Sept. 14, 1982 (H Rept 97-805). House passed Sept. 20. Senate Indian Affairs discharged. Senate passed Dec. 17. President signed Dec. 31, 1982.

PL 97-398 (HR 6946) Amend title 18, U.S. Code, to provide penalties for certain false identification related crimes. HUGHES, D-N.J. — 8/5/82 — House Judiciary reported Sept. 10 (H Rept 97-802). House passed, under suspension of the rules, Sept. 14. Senate passed, amended, Oct. 1. House agreed to conference report Dec. 17 (H Rept 97-975). Senate agreed to conference report Dec. 19. President signed Dec. 31, 1982.

PL 97-399 (HR 7155) Settle certain Indian land claims within the state of Florida. FASCELL, D-Fla. — 9/21/82 — House Interior and Insular Affairs reported Nov. 30 (H Rept 97-938). House passed Dec. 6. Senate Indian Affairs discharged. Senate passed Dec. 17. President signed Dec. 31, 1982.

PL 97-400 (HR 7377) Designate the Lakeview Lake project, in Mountain Creek, Texas, as the "Joe Pool Lake." WRIGHT, D-Texas — 12/7/82 — House Public Works and Transportation discharged. House passed Dec. 7. Senate passed Dec. 19. President signed Dec. 31, 1982.

PL 97-401 (S 187) Authorize the secretary of the interior to convey certain lands near Miles City, Mont., and to remove reversionary provisions of prior conveyances. MELCHER, D-Mont. — 1/21/81 — Senate Energy and Natural Resources reported Aug. 27 (S Rept 97-181). Senate passed Sept. 22. House Interior and Insular Affairs reported Sept. 30, 1982 (H Rept 97-904). House passed, amended, Sept. 30. Senate agreed to House amendment Dec. 17. President signed Dec. 31, 1982.

PL 97-402 (S 1340) Provide for the use and distribution of funds awarded the Clallam Indian tribe, in the state of Washington, by the Indian Claims Commission in docket 134. GORTON, R-Wash. — 6/8/81 — Senate Indian Affairs reported Oct. 1, 1982 (S Rept 97-654). Senate passed Dec. 3. House Interior and Insular Affairs discharged. House passed Dec. 17. President signed Dec. 31, 1982.

PL 97-403 (S 1735) Provide for the use and distribution of funds awarded the Pembina Chippewa Indians in dockets 113, 191, 221 and 246 of the U.S. Court of Claims. ANDREWS, R-N.D. — 10/14/81 — Senate Indian Affairs reported Oct. 1, 1982 (S Rept 97-655). Senate passed Dec. 3. House passed, amended, Dec. 6. Senate agreed to House amendment Dec. 16. President signed Dec. 31, 1982.

PL 97-404 (S 3113) Make certain minor and technical amendments to the Job Training Partnership Act. QUAYLE, R-Ind. — 12/16/82 — Senate passed Dec. 17. House Education and Labor discharged. House passed Dec. 18. President signed Dec. 31, 1982.

PL 97-405 (S 625) Revise the boundary of Voyageurs National Park in the state of Minnesota. DURENBERGER, R-Minn. — 3/5/81 — Senate Energy and Natural Resources reported May 26, 1982 (S Rept 97-423). Senate passed June 10. House Interior and Insular Affairs discharged. House passed, amended, Sept. 29. Senate agreed to House amendment with amendments Oct. 1. House agreed to Senate amendments with an amendment Dec. 14. Senate agreed to House amendment Dec. 17. President signed Jan. 3, 1983.

PL 97-406 (S 1501) Provide for the conveyance to the University of Alaska all right, title and interest of the United States in approximately 76 acres of land in Alaska. STEVENS, R-Alaska — 7/17/81 — Senate Energy and Natural Resources reported April 28, 1982 (S Rept 97-370). Senate passed May 10. House Interior and Insular Affairs reported Dec. 10 (H Rept 97-952). House passed, amended, under suspension of the rules, Dec. 14. Senate disagreed to House amendment Dec. 19. House receded from its amendment Dec. 20. President signed Jan. 3, 1983.

PL 97-407 (S 1965) Designate as components of the National Wilderness Preservation System certain lands known as the Paddy Creek Wilderness Area in the Mark Twain National Forest, Mo. EAGLETON, D-Mo. — 12/15/81 — Senate Energy and Natural Resources reported Sept. 20, 1982 (S Rept 97-554). Senate passed Oct. 2. House Interior and Insular Affairs reported Dec. 9 (H Rept 97-949, Part I). House Agriculture discharged. House passed, amended, Dec. 16. Senate agreed to House amendment Dec. 19. President signed Jan. 3, 1983.

PL 97-408 (S 1986) Provide for the use and distribution of funds

awarded the Blackfeet, Gros Ventre and Assiniboine Indian tribes, in Montana. MELCHER, D-Mont. — 12/16/81 — Senate Indian Affairs reported July 6, 1982 (S Rept 97-492). Senate passed Aug. 19. House Interior and Insular Affairs reported Sept. 8 (H Rept 97-935). House passed, amended, Dec. 6. Senate agreed to House amendments with an amendment Dec. 16. House agreed to Senate amendment Dec. 17. President signed Jan. 3, 1983.

PL 97-409 (S 2059) Revise the special prosecutor provisions of the Ethics in Government Act of 1978 to insure independent investigation of high-ranking federal officials and to remove inequities in the present law. COHEN, R-Maine — 2/3/82 — Senate Governmental Affairs reported July 14 (S Rept 97-496). Senate passed Aug. 12. House Judiciary discharged. House passed, amended, under suspension of the rules, Dec. 13. Senate agreed to House amendments Dec. 17. President signed Jan. 3, 1983.

PL 97-410 (S 2355) Provide adequate telephone service to persons with impaired hearing. CANNON, D-Nev. — 4/1/82 — Senate Commerce, Science and Transportation reported July 23 (S Rept 97-503). Senate passed Aug. 18. House Energy and Commerce reported Sept. 28 (H Rept 97-888). House passed, amended, under suspension of the rules, Dec. 13. Senate agreed to House amendments with an amendment Dec. 17. House agreed to Senate amendment Dec. 18. President signed Jan. 3, 1983.

PL 97-411 (S 2955) Establish the Cheaha Wilderness in Talladega National Forest, Ala. DENTON, R-Ala. — 9/24/82 — Senate Energy and Natural Resources reported Dec. 13. Senate passed Dec. 19. House passed Dec. 20. President signed Jan. 3, 1983.

PL 97-412 (S 3103) Provide that participation fees, which the President's Commission on Executive Exchange may impose for private sector participation in its Executive Exchange Program, shall be collected and credited to the fund, and shall be available for the costs of education and related travel of exchanged executives, for printing, and in such amounts as may be specified in appropriations acts for entertainment expenses. STEVENS, R-Alaska — 12/15/82 — Senate passed Dec. 15. House passed Dec. 20. President signed Jan. 3, 1983.

PL 97-413 (S J Res 270) Designate 1983 as the Bicentennial of Air and Space Flight. MATHIAS, R-Md. — 12/7/82 — Senate passed Dec. 7. House Post Office and Civil Service discharged. House passed Dec. 20. President signed Jan. 3, 1983.

PL 97-414 (HR 5238) Amend the Federal Food, Drug and Cosmetic Act to facilitate the development of drugs for rare diseases and conditions. WAXMAN, D-Calif. — 12/15/81 — House Energy and Commerce reported Sept. 17, 1982 (H Rept 97-840, Part I). House passed, under suspension of the rules, Sept. 28. Senate Labor and Human Resources discharged. Senate passed, amended, Oct. 1. House agreed to Senate amendment with an amendment Dec. 14. Senate agreed to House amendment Dec. 17. President signed Jan. 4, 1983.

PL 97-415 (HR 2330) Authorize appropriations for fiscal years 1982-83 for the Nuclear Regulatory Commission in accordance with section 261 of the Atomic Energy Act of 1954, as amended, and section 305 of the Energy Reorganization Act of 1974, as amended. UDALL, D-Ariz. — 3/4/81 — House Interior and Insular Affairs reported April 10 (H Rept 97-22, Part I). House Science and Technology discharged. House Energy and Commerce reported June 9 (H Rept 97-22, Part II). House passed Nov. 5. Senate passed, amended, March 30, 1982. Senate agreed to conference report Oct. 1 (H Rept 97-884). House rejected conference report Dec. 2. House receded and concurred in Senate amendment with an amendment Dec. 2. Senate agreed to House amendment Dec. 17. President signed Jan. 4, 1983.

PL 97-416 (HR 6120) Reauthorize the Deep Seabed Hard Minerals Resources Act for fiscal years 1983-85. JONES, D-N.C. — 4/20/82 — House Merchant Marine and Fisheries reported May 17 (H Rept 97-522, Part I). House Interior and Insular Affairs reported May 17 (H Rept 97-522, Part II). House Foreign Affairs reported May 17 (H Rept 97-522, Part III). House passed, under suspension of the rules, Dec. 13. Senate Energy and Natural Resources discharged. Senate passed Dec. 19. President signed Jan. 4, 1983.

PL 97-417 (HR 6804) Provide subsistence allowances for members of the Coast Guard officer candidate program. STUDDS, D-Mass. — 7/20/82 — House Merchant Marine and Fisheries reported Aug. 23 (H Rept 97-789). House passed, under suspension of the rules, Sept. 14. Senate passed Dec. 17. President signed Jan. 4, 1983.

PL 97-418 (HR 6254) Amend title 3, U.S. Code, to clarify the function of the United States Secret Service uniformed division with respect to certain foreign diplomatic missions in the United States. FERRARO, D-N.Y. — 5/3/82 — House Public Works and Transportation reported May 17 (H Rept 97-533). House passed June 15. Senate Finance discharged. Senate passed Dec. 19. President signed Jan. 4, 1983.

PL 97-419 (S J Res 258) Authorize and request the president to designate the month of December 1982 as "National Close-Captioned Television Month." WEICKER, R-Conn. — 9/29/82 — Senate Judiciary discharged. Senate passed Dec. 3. House Post Office and Civil Service

discharged. House passed Dec. 20. President signed Jan. 4, 1983.

PL 97-420 (H J Res 619) Designate Jan. 17, 1983, as "Public Employees Appreciation Day." HOYER, D-Md. — 9/30/82 — House Post Office and Civil Service discharged. House passed Dec. 17. Senate Judiciary discharged. Senate passed Dec. 21. President signed Jan. 4, 1983.

PL 97-421 (H J Res 630) Commemorate the 150th anniversary of the founding of Greene County, Mo. TAYLOR, R-Mo. — 12/10/82 — House Post Office and Civil Service discharged. House passed Dec. 17. Senate Judiciary discharged. Senate passed Dec. 23. President signed Jan. 4, 1983.

PL 97-422 (HR 7420) Name the fish hatchery at the Warm Springs Dam component of the Russian River, Dry Creek, Calif., as the "Don H. Clausen Fish Hatchery." WRIGHT, D-Texas — 12/14/82 — House Public Works and Transportation discharged. House passed Dec. 17. Senate Environment and Public Works discharged. Senate passed Dec. 21. President signed Jan. 4, 1983.

PL 97-423 (HR 7406) Designate a certain federal building in Springfield, Ill., as the "Paul Findley Building." MICHEL, R-Ill. — 12/10/82 — House Public Works and Transportation discharged. House passed Dec. 17. Senate Environment and Public Works discharged. Senate passed Dec. 21. President signed Jan. 4, 1983.

PL 97-424 (HR 6211) Authorize appropriations through the fiscal year ending Sept. 30, 1989, to improve the nation's highway system and to restructure the current taxes that go into the highway trust fund. ANDERSON, D-Calif. — 4/29/82 — House Public Works and Transportation reported May 17 (H Rept 97-555). House passed Dec. 7. Senate Finance reported Dec. 9. Senate passed, amended, Dec. 21. House agreed to conference report Dec. 21 (H Rept 97-987). Senate agreed to conference report Dec. 23. President signed Jan. 6, 1983.

PL 97-425 (HR 3809) Provide for the development of repositories for the disposal of high-level radioactive waste and spent nuclear fuel and to establish a program of research development and demonstration regarding the disposal of high-level radioactive waste and spent nuclear fuel. UDALL, D-Ariz. — 6/4/81 — House Interior and Insular Affairs reported April 27, 1982 (H Rept 97-491, Part I). House Armed Services reported July 16 (H Rept 97-491, Part II). House Judiciary discharged. House Merchant Marine and Fisheries discharged. House passed Dec. 2. Senate passed, amended, Dec. 20. House agreed to Senate amendment Dec. 20. President signed Jan. 7, 1983.

PL 97-426 (HR 2475) Provide for the withdrawal of certain lands from the operation of the general public lands laws to protect the watershed supplying water to Los Angeles. SHUMWAY, R-Calif. — 3/11/81 — House Interior and Insular Affairs reported Dec. 4 (H Rept 97-358). House passed Dec. 15. Senate Energy and Natural Resources reported April 28, 1982 (S Rept 97-371). Senate passed, amended, May 10. House agreed to Senate amendment Sept. 13. House disagreed to Senate amendments Sept. 13. Senate receded from its amendments Dec. 19. President signed Jan. 8, 1983.

PL 97-427 (HR 7423) Recognize the organization known as Former Members of Congress. S. HALL, D-Texas — 12/15/82 — House passed Dec. 17. Senate passed Dec. 19. President signed Jan. 8, 1983.

PL 97-428 (HR 4001) Provide for an exchange of certain land in New Mexico held in trust by the U.S. for the Navajo Indian tribe. SKEEN, R-N.M. — 6/23/81 — House Interior and Insular Affairs reported Nov. 20 (H Rept 97-346). House passed Dec. 15. Senate Indian Affairs reported Sept. 29, 1982. Senate passed, amended, Dec. 17. House agreed to Senate amendments Dec. 20. President signed Jan. 8, 1983.

PL 97-429 (HR 4496) Clarify the citizenship status of the Texas Band of Kickapoo Indians, provide for a reservation for the Texas Band of Kickapoo, and provide those services and benefits furnished to American Indian tribes and individuals. KAZEN, D-Texas — 9/16/81 — House Interior and Insular Affairs reported Sept. 23, 1982 (H Rept 97-858). House passed Sept. 29. Senate Indian Affairs reported Dec. 15 (S Rept 97-684). Senate passed, amended, Dec. 21. House agreed to Senate amendment Dec. 21. President signed Jan. 8, 1983.

PL 97-430 (HR 5027) Designate the U.S. Post Office and Courthouse in Norfolk, Va., as the "Walter E. Hoffman United States Courthouse." WHITEHURST, R-Va. — 11/18/81 — House Public Works and Transportation discharged. House passed Dec. 17, 1982. Senate Governmental Affairs discharged. Senate passed Dec. 23. President signed Jan. 8, 1983.

PL 97-431 (HR 4568) Direct the secretary of the interior to release certain conditions in a patent for land transferred to the city of Albuquerque, N.M., and provide for the exchange of land between the city and named individuals. LUJAN, R-N.M. — 9/23/81 — House Interior and Insular Affairs reported July 15, 1982 (H Rept 97-635). House passed Aug. 2. Senate Energy and Natural Resources discharged. Senate passed Dec. 23. President signed Jan. 8, 1983.

PL 97-432 (HR 5456) Amend the Plant Quarantine Act of 1912 to eliminate specified public hearing requirements. WAMPLER, R-Va. — 2/3/82 — House Agriculture reported Sept. 26 (H Rept 97-873). House passed, under suspension of the rules, Sept. 28. Senate Agricul-

ture, Nutrition and Forestry discharged. Senate passed Dec. 21. President signed Jan. 8, 1983.

PL 97-433 (HR 7316) Establish the National Park System Visitor Facilities Fund. LUJAN, R-N.M. — 11/29/82 — House Interior and Insular Affairs reported Dec. 10 (H Rept 97-953). House passed Dec. 10. Senate passed Dec. 21. President signed Jan. 8, 1983.

PL 97-434 (HR 5916) Declare that certain federal lands be held in trust for the Ramah Band of the Navajo tribe. SKEEN, R-N.M. — 3/22/82 — House Interior and Insular Affairs reported Sept. 16 (H Rept 97-816). House passed Sept. 29. Senate Indian Affairs discharged. Senate passed Dec. 21. President signed Jan. 8, 1983.

PL 97-435 (HR 6419) Direct the secretary of the interior to release certain conditions contained in a patent concerning certain land conveyed by the U.S. to Eastern Washington University and enable the university to sell or exchange those lands in order to acquire other lands more suitable for educational or recreational purposes. FOLEY, D-Wash. — 5/19/82 — House Interior and Insular Affairs reported Aug. 10 (H Rept 97-709). House passed Aug. 16. Senate Energy and Natural Resources reported Dec. 13. Senate passed Dec. 19. President signed Jan. 8, 1983.

PL 97-436 (HR 6243) Provide for the distribution of funds awarded the Confederated Tribes of the Warm Springs Reservation, in Oregon, by the Indian Claims Commission. SMITH, R-Ore. — 4/29/82 — House Interior and Insular Affairs reported Nov. 30 (H Rept 97-936). House passed Dec. 6. Senate Indian Affairs discharged. Senate passed Dec. 21. President signed Jan. 8, 1983.

PL 97-437 (HR 6519) Provide for student internships at the Internal Revenue Service. SCHROEDER, D-Colo. — 5/27/82 — House passed, under suspension of the rules, Dec. 13. Senate Governmental Affairs discharged. Senate passed Dec. 23. President signed Jan. 8, 1983.

PL 97-438 (HR 7143) Amend the Foreign Assistance Act of 1961 to extend for an additional year the Agricultural and Productive Credit and Self-Help Community Development Programs. ZABLOCKI, D-Wis. — 9/21/82 — House passed, under suspension of the rules, Sept. 28. Senate Foreign Relations discharged. Senate passed Dec. 21. President signed Jan. 8, 1983.

PL 97-439 (HR 7005) Amend the Federal Seed Act regarding lawn and turf seed mixture labeling and importation. FAZIO, D-Calif. — 8/18/82 — House Agriculture reported Sept. 26 (H Rept 97-877). House passed, under suspension of the rules, Sept. 28. Senate Agriculture, Nutrition and Forestry discharged. Senate passed Dec. 21. President signed Jan. 8, 1983.

PL 97-440 (HR 7159) Allow modifications of certain effluent limitations relating to biochemical oxygen demand and pH with regard to two pulp mills in California. CLAUSEN, R-Calif. — 9/22/82 — House Public Works and Transportation reported Sept. 23 (H Rept 97-868). House passed, under suspension of the rules, Sept. 29. Senate Environment and Public Works reported Dec. 16 (S Rept 97-686). Senate passed, amended, Dec. 19. House agreed to Senate amendment Dec. 20. President signed Jan. 8, 1983.

PL 97-441 (S J Res 101) Request the president to designate the week of Oct. 17-23, 1983, as "National High School Activities Week." DOLE, R-Kan. — 7/28/81 — Senate Judiciary reported Sept. 15. Senate passed Sept. 16. House Post Office and Civil Service discharged. House passed, amended, Sept. 21, 1982. Senate agreed to House amendment Dec. 16. President signed Jan. 8, 1983.

PL 97-442 (S J Res 240) Authorize and request the president to designate the week of Jan. 16-22, 1983, as "National Jaycee Week." BOREN, D-Okla. — 9/10/82 — Senate Judiciary discharged. Senate passed Dec. 8, 1982. House Post Office and Civil Service discharged. House passed Dec. 21. President signed Jan. 8, 1983.

PL 97-443 (S J Res 264) Designate the week of March 13-19, 1983, as "National Children and Television Week." HEINZ, R-Pa. — 10/1/82 — Senate Judiciary discharged. Senate passed Dec. 3. House Post Office and Civil Service discharged. House passed Dec. 21. President signed Jan. 8, 1983.

PL 97-444 (HR 5447) Authorize funds for the Commodity Futures Trading Commission. JONES, D-Tenn. — 2/3/82 — House Agriculture reported May 17 (H Rept 97-565, Part I). House Energy and Commerce reported June 21 (H Rept 97-565, Part II). House passed Sept. 23. Senate passed, amended, Oct. 1. Senate agreed to conference report Dec. 15 (H Rept 97-964). House agreed to conference report Dec. 16. President signed Jan. 12, 1983.

PL 97-445 (H J Res 459) Authorize the president to proclaim May 13, 1983, as "American Indian Day." FIEDLER, R-Calif. — 4/20/82 — House Post Office and Civil Service discharged. House passed Dec. 17. Senate Judiciary discharged. Senate passed Dec. 21. President signed Jan. 12, 1983.

PL 97-446 (HR 4566) Revise the tariff treatment of various articles. GIBBONS, D-Fla. — 9/23/81 — House Ways and Means reported Sept. 25 (H Rept 97-257). House passed, under suspension of the rules, Oct. 13. Senate Finance reported Sept. 21, 1982 (S Rept 97-564).

Senate passed, amended, Dec. 19. House agreed to conference report Dec. 21 (H Rept 97-989). Senate agreed to conference report Dec. 22. President signed Jan. 12, 1983.

PL 97-447 (HR 4491) Exempt the U.S. Capitol Historical Society from certain taxes. CONABLE, R-N.Y. — 9/16/81 — House Judiciary reported March 5, 1982 (H Rept 97-445). House passed, under suspension of the rules, Dec. 13. Senate Governmental Affairs discharged. Senate passed Dec. 21. President signed Jan. 12, 1983.

PL 97-448 (HR 6056) Make technical corrections relating to the Economic Recovery Tax Act (PL 97-34), the Crude Oil Windfall Profit Tax Act (PL 96-223) and the Installment Sales Revision Act (PL 96-471). ROSTENKOWSKI, D-Ill. — 4/1/82 — House Ways and Means reported Sept. 8 (H Rept 97-794). House passed, under suspension of the rules, Sept. 14. Senate Finance reported Sept. 27 (S Rept 97-592). Senate passed, amended, Sept. 30. House agreed to conference report Dec. 21 (H Rept 97-986). Senate agreed to conference report Dec. 22. President signed Jan. 12, 1983.

PL 97-449 (HR 6993) Revise, codify and enact without substantive change certain general and permanent laws related to transportation as subtitle I and chapter 31 of subtitle II of title 49, U.S. Code, "Transportation." RODINO, D-N.J. — 8/16/82 — House passed, under suspension of the rules, Dec. 13. Senate Judiciary discharged. Senate passed Dec. 19. President signed Jan. 12, 1983.

PL 97-450 (HR 5029) Designate the federal building in Fresno, Calif., as the "B. F. Sisk Federal Building." COELHO, D-Calif. — 11/18/81 — House Public Works and Transportation discharged. House passed Dec. 17, 1982. Senate Environment and Public Works discharged. Senate passed Dec. 21. President signed Jan. 12, 1983.

PL 97-451 (HR 5121) Ensure that all energy and mineral resources originating on public lands and on the Outer Continental Shelf are accounted for under the direction of the secretary of the interior. MARKEY, D-Mass. — 12/7/81 — House Interior and Insular Affairs reported Sept. 23, 1982 (H Rept 97-859). House passed, under suspension of the rules, Sept. 29. Senate Energy and Natural Resources discharged. Senate passed, amended, Dec. 6. House agreed to Senate amendments with an amendment Dec. 13. Senate agreed to House amendment with an amendment Dec. 16. House agreed to Senate amendment with an amendment Dec. 18. Senate disagreed to House amendment Dec. 21. House receded from its amendment Dec. 21. President signed Jan. 12, 1983.

PL 97-452 (HR 7378) Codify without substantive change recent laws related to money and finance and improve the U.S. Code. RODINO, D-N.J. — 12/7/82 — House passed, under suspension of the rules, Dec. 13. Senate Judiciary discharged. Senate passed Dec. 19. President signed Jan. 12, 1983.

PL 97-453 (HR 5002) Improve fishery conservation and management. BREAUX, D-La. — 11/17/81 — House Merchant Marine and Fisheries reported May 17, 1982 (H Rept 97-549). House passed Dec. 16. Senate passed, amended, Dec. 17. House agreed to conference report Dec. 20 (H Rept 97-982). Senate agreed to conference report Dec. 21. President signed Jan. 12, 1983.

PL 97-454 (HR 7410) Amend title 13, U.S. Code, to transfer responsibility for the quarterly financial report from the Federal Trade Commission to the secretary of commerce. GARCIA, D-N.Y. — 12/13/82 — House Post Office and Civil Service discharged. House passed Dec. 17. Senate passed Dec. 23. President signed Jan. 12, 1983.

PL 97-455 (HR 7093) Reduce the rate of certain taxes paid to the Virgin Islands on Virgin Islands source income. DE LUGO, D-Virgin Islands — 9/14/82 — House Ways and Means reported Sept. 16 (H Rept 97-833). House passed, under suspension of the rules, Sept. 20. Senate Finance reported Oct. 1 (S Rept 97-648). Senate passed, amended, Dec. 3. House agreed to conference report Dec. 21 (H Rept 97-985). Senate agreed to conference report Dec. 21. President signed Jan. 12, 1983.

PL 97-456 (HR 6094) Authorize funds for fiscal year 1983 for the U.S. International Trade Commission, U.S. Trade Representative and the U.S. Customs Service, Department of the Treasury. GIBBONS, D-Fla. — 4/6/82 — House Ways and Means reported April 29 (H Rept 97-497). House passed June 16. Senate passed, amended, Sept. 30. House agreed to conference report Dec. 21 (H Rept 97-988). Senate agreed to conference report Dec. 22. President signed Jan. 12, 1983.

PL 97-457 (S J Res 271) Make technical corrections in certain banking and related statutes. GARN, R-Utah — 12/13/82 — Senate Banking, Housing and Urban Affairs reported Dec. 16. Senate passed Dec. 16. House passed, amended, Dec. 21. Senate agreed to House amendments Dec. 21. President signed Jan. 12, 1983.

PL 97-458 (HR 3731) Provide for the use or distribution of certain judgment funds awarded by the Indain Claims Commission of the Court of Claims. UDALL, D-Ariz. — 5/28/81 — House Interior and Insular Affairs reported Nov. 18 (H Rept 97-340). House passed Dec. 15. Senate Indian Affairs reported Oct. 1, 1982 (S Rept 97-658). Senate passed, amended, Dec. 19. House agreed to Senate amendments Dec.

20. President signed Jan. 12, 1983.

PL 97-459 (S 503) Provide for the purchase, sale and exchange of lands by the Devils Lake Sioux Indian tribe of the Devils Lake Sioux Reservation, N.D. BURDICK, D-N.D. — 2/19/81 — Senate Indian Affairs reported July 28, 1982 (S Rept 97-507). Senate passed Aug. 20. House Interior and Insular Affairs reported Sept. 30 (H Rept 97-908). House passed, amended, Dec. 6. Senate agreed to House amendments with amendments Dec. 19. House agreed to Senate amendments Dec. 20. President signed Jan. 12, 1983.

PL 97-460 (S 1540) Revise the boundaries of the Saratoga National Park, N.Y. MOYNIHAN, D-N.Y. — 7/29/81 — Senate Energy and Natural Resources reported May 26, 1982 (S Rept 97-424). Senate passed June 10. House Interior and Insular Affairs reported Oct. 1 (H Rept 97-926). House passed, amended, Oct. 2. Senate agreed to House amendment Dec. 21. President signed Jan. 12, 1983.

PL 97-461 (HR 6679) Authorize civil penalties for violations of various laws for preventing the introduction and dissemination of livestock and poultry diseases, plant diseases and plant pests. WAMPLER, R-Va. — 6/23/82 — House Agriculture reported Sept. 26 (H Rept 97-875). House passed, under suspension of the rules, Sept. 28. Senate Agriculture, Nutrition and Forestry discharged. Senate passed Dec. 21. President signed Jan. 12, 1983.

PL 97-462 (HR 7154) Amend the Federal Rules of Civil Procedure to authorize the service of a summons and complaint by first class mail. EDWARDS, D-Calif. — 9/21/82 — House Judiciary discharged. House passed Dec. 15. Senate Judiciary discharged. Senate passed, amended, Dec. 19. House agreed to Senate amendment with an amendment Dec. 20. Senate agreed to House amendment Dec. 21. President signed Jan. 12, 1983.

PL 97-463 (S 2863) Extend federal employees compensation benefits to all federal jurors, provide the awarding of attorney fees for court-appointed attorneys and expand the method of serving jury summons. GRASSLEY, R-Iowa — 8/19/82 — Senate Judiciary reported Dec. 8 (S Rept 97-674). Senate passed Dec. 21. House passed Dec. 21. President signed Jan. 12, 1983.

PL 97-464 (S 2273) Authorize funds for fiscal year 1983 for programs of the Earthquake Hazards Reduction Act. SCHMITT, R-N.M. — 3/24/82 — Senate Commerce, Science and Transportation reported April 20 (S Rept 97-336). Senate passed April 29. House passed, amended, Sept. 14. Senate agreed to House amendments with amendments Oct. 1. House agreed to Senate amendments with an amendment Oct. 1. Senate agreed to House amendment Dec. 17. President signed Jan. 12, 1983.

PL 97-465 (S 705) Authorize the conveyance of certain National Forest System lands when determined to be in the public interest. DOMENICI, R-N.M. — 3/12/81 — Senate Agriculture, Nutrition and Forestry reported April 19, 1982 (S Rept 97-332). Senate Energy and Natural Resources reported July 1 (S Rept 97-490). Senate passed Aug. 19. House Agriculture discharged. House Interior and Insular Affairs discharged. House passed Dec. 21. President signed 12, 1983.

PL 97-466 (HR 5161) Designate certain lands in the Monongahela National Forest, W.Va., as wilderness and designate management of certain lands for uses other than wilderness. BENEDICT, R-W.Va. — 12/10/81 — House Interior and Insular Affairs reported May 17, 1982 (H Rept 97-561, Part I). House Agriculture discharged. House passed, under suspension of the rules, June 14. Senate Energy and Natural Resources reported Dec. 13. Senate passed, amended, Dec. 18. House agreed to Senate amendment with an amendment Dec. 20. Senate agreed to House amendment Dec. 21. President signed Jan. 13, 1983.

PL 97-467 (HR 6538) Designate the federal building in Lima, Ohio, as the "Tennyson Guyer Federal Building." OXLEY, R-Ohio — 6/7/82 — House Public Works and Transportation discharged. House passed Dec. 17. Senate Environment and Public Works discharged. Senate passed Dec. 21. President signed Jan. 14, 1983.

PL 97-468 (HR 3420) Authorize funds for fiscal years 1982-83 for the National Gas Pipeline Safety Act and the Hazardous Liquid Pipeline Safety Act. ANDERSON, D-Calif. — 5/5/81 — House Public Works and Transportation reported May 19 (H Rept 97-89, Part I). House Energy and Commerce reported May 19 (H Rept 97-89, Part II). House passed, under suspension of the rules, June 1. Senate passed, amended, July 17. House agreed to Senate amendments with an amendment Dec. 20, 1982. Senate agreed to House amendment with amendments Dec. 21. House agreed to Senate amendments Dec. 21. President signed Jan. 14, 1983.

PL 97-469 (H J Res 635) Establish the dates for submission by the president of the Budget Message and Economic Report to Congress. WRIGHT, D-Texas — 12/20/82 — House passed Dec. 20. Senate passed Dec. 21. President signed Jan. 14, 1983.

PL 97-470 (HR 7102) Provide for the protection of migrant and seasonal agricultural workers and for the registration of contractors of migrant and seasonal agricultural labor. MILLER, D-Calif. — 9/14/82 — House Education and Labor reported Sept. 28 (H Rept 97-885). House passed, under suspension of the rules, Sept. 29. Senate passed, amended, Dec. 19. House agreed to Senate amendment Dec. 20. President signed Jan. 14, 1983.

PL 97-471 (S 3105) Modify the judicial district of the state of West Virginia. BYRD, D-W.Va. — 12/15/82 — Senate passed Dec. 16. House passed Dec. 20. President signed Jan. 14, 1983.

PL 97-472 (S J Res 260) Designate Jan. 1-Dec. 31, 1983, as the "Tricentennial Anniversary Year of German Settlement in America." HEINZ, R-Pa. — 10/1/82 — Senate passed Oct. 1. House Post Office and Civil Service discharged. House passed, amended, Dec. 17. Senate agreed to House amendment Dec. 19. President signed Jan. 14, 1983.

PL 97-473 (HR 5470) Insure periodic payments for damages received on account of personal injuries. JACOBS, D-Ind. — 2/8/82 — House Ways and Means reported Sept. 16 (H Rept 97-832). House passed, under suspension of the rules, Sept. 20. Senate Finance reported Oct. 1 (S Rept 97-646). Senate passed, amended, Oct. 1. House agreed to conference report Dec. 21 (H Rept 97-984). Senate agreed to conference report Dec. 22. President signed Jan. 14, 1983. ■

SENATE ROLL-CALL VOTES

CQ Senate Votes 1 - 3

Corresponding to Congressional Record Votes 1, 2, 3

	1	2	3
ALABAMA			
Denton	Y	Y	Y
Heflin	Y	N	Y
ALASKA			
Murkowski	Y	Y	Y
Stevens	Y	Y	Y
ARIZONA			
Goldwater	?	?	?
DeConcini	Y	Y	Y
ARKANSAS			
Bumpers	Y	N	Y
Pryor	Y	Y	Y
CALIFORNIA			
Hayakawa	?	Y	Y
Cranston	Y	N	Y
COLORADO			
Armstrong	Y	Y	Y
Hart	Y	N	Y
CONNECTICUT			
Weicker	?	N	Y
Dodd	Y	N	Y
DELAWARE			
Roth	Y	Y	Y
Biden	?	Y	Y
FLORIDA			
Hawkins	?	+	+
Chiles	Y	Y	Y
GEORGIA			
Mattingly	Y	Y	Y
Nunn	Y	Y	Y
HAWAII			
Inouye	Y	N	Y
Matsunaga	Y	N	Y
IDAHO			
McClure	Y	Y	Y
Symms	?	Y	Y
ILLINOIS			
Percy	Y	N	Y
Dixon	Y	N	Y
INDIANA			
Lugar	Y	Y	Y
Quayle	N	Y	Y
IOWA			
Grassley	Y	Y	Y
Jepsen	Y	Y	Y
KANSAS			
Dole	Y	Y	Y
Kassebaum	Y	Y	Y
KENTUCKY			
Ford	Y	Y	Y
Huddleston	Y	Y	N
LOUISIANA			
Johnston	Y	Y	Y
Long	Y	Y	Y
MAINE			
Cohen	?	N	Y
Mitchell	Y	N	Y
MARYLAND			
Mathias	Y	N	Y
Sarbanes	Y	N	Y
MASSACHUSETTS			
Kennedy	Y	N	Y
Tsongas	Y	N	Y
MICHIGAN			
Levin	Y	N	Y
Riegle	Y	N	Y
MINNESOTA			
Boschwitz	Y	N	Y
Durenberger	Y	N	Y
MISSISSIPPI			
Cochran	Y	Y	Y
Stennis	Y	Y	Y
MISSOURI			
Danforth	Y	Y	Y
Eagleton	Y	N	Y
MONTANA			
Baucus	?	N	Y
Melcher	Y	Y	Y
NEBRASKA			
Exon	Y	Y	Y
Zorinsky	Y	Y	Y
NEVADA			
Laxalt	Y	Y	Y
Cannon	?	Y	Y
NEW HAMPSHIRE			
Humphrey	Y	N	Y
Rudman	Y	N	Y
NEW JERSEY			
Bradley	?	N	Y
Williams	?	?	?
NEW MEXICO			
Domenici	Y	Y	Y
Schmitt	Y	Y	Y
NEW YORK			
D'Amato	Y	Y	Y
Moynihan	Y	N	Y
NORTH CAROLINA			
East	Y	Y	Y
Helms	Y	Y	Y
NORTH DAKOTA			
Andrews	Y	Y	Y
Burdick	Y	N	Y
OHIO			
Glenn	?	N	Y
Metzenbaum	Y	N	Y
OKLAHOMA			
Nickles	Y	Y	Y
Boren	Y	Y	Y
OREGON			
Hatfield	Y	N	Y
Packwood	Y	N	Y
PENNSYLVANIA			
Heinz	Y	N	Y
Specter	Y	N	Y
RHODE ISLAND			
Chafee	Y	N	Y
Pell	Y	N	Y
SOUTH CAROLINA			
Thurmond	Y	Y	Y
Hollings	Y	Y	Y
SOUTH DAKOTA			
Abdnor	Y	Y	Y
Pressler	Y	Y	Y
TENNESSEE			
Baker	Y	?	#
Sasser	Y	Y	Y
TEXAS			
Tower	Y	Y	X
Bentsen	Y	Y	Y
UTAH			
Garn	Y	Y	Y
Hatch	Y	Y	Y
VERMONT			
Stafford	Y	N	Y
Leahy	Y	N	Y
VIRGINIA			
Warner	Y	Y	Y
Byrd*	Y	Y	Y
WASHINGTON			
Gorton	Y	Y	Y
Jackson	Y	N	Y
WEST VIRGINIA			
Byrd	Y	Y	Y
Randolph	Y	Y	N
WISCONSIN			
Kasten	Y	Y	Y
Proxmire	N	Y	N
WYOMING			
Simpson	Y	Y	Y
Wallop	Y	Y	Y

KEY

Y Voted for (yea).
\# Paired for.
\+ Announced for.
N Voted against (nay).
X Paired against.
- Announced against.
P Voted "present".
C Voted "present" to avoid possible conflict of interest.
? Did not vote or otherwise make a position known.

Democrats   *Republicans*

ND - Northern Democrats   SD - Southern Democrats (Southern states - Ala., Ark., Fla., Ga., Ky., La., Miss., N.C., Okla., S.C., Tenn., Texas, Va.)

*Byrd elected as an independent.

1. S Res 20. Broadcast of Senate Proceedings. Baker, R-Tenn., motion to instruct the sergeant-at-arms to request the attendance of absent senators. Motion agreed to 86-2: R 46-1; D 40-1 (ND 25-1, SD 15-0), Feb. 2, 1982.

2. S 951. Department of Justice Authorization, Fiscal 1982. Helms, R-N.C.-Johnston, D-La., amendment to prevent the Department of Justice from bringing any legal action that could lead directly or indirectly to court-ordered busing; bar federal courts from ordering busing except in narrowly defined circumstances; and allow the attorney general to reopen existing busing orders imposed in violation of the standards set out in the amendment. Adopted 58-38: R 36-14; D 22-24 (ND 9-22, SD 13-2), Feb. 4, 1982.

3. S Res 20. Broadcast of Senate Proceedings. Baker, R-Tenn., motion to proceed to the consideration of the resolution to instruct the Senate Committee on Rules and Administration to provide for continuous television and radio coverage of Senate proceedings. Motion agreed to 92-3: R 49-0; D 43-3 (ND 29-2, SD 14-1), Feb. 4, 1982.

	4	5	6	7	8	9	10
ALABAMA							
Denton	Y	Y	?	Y	Y	Y	Y
Heflin	Y	N	Y	N	Y	N	Y
ALASKA							
Murkowski	Y	Y	Y	Y	Y	Y	Y
Stevens	Y	Y	N	Y	Y	Y	Y
ARIZONA							
Goldwater	N	Y	N	N	Y	Y	Y
DeConcini	Y	Y	Y	Y	Y	Y	Y
ARKANSAS							
Bumpers	N	N	N	Y	Y	N	N
Pryor	Y	Y	N	Y	Y	Y	Y
CALIFORNIA							
Hayakawa	Y	Y	N	Y	Y	Y	Y
Cranston	N	N	N	Y	Y	N	N
COLORADO							
Armstrong	Y	Y	Y	N	Y	Y	Y
Hart	N	N	N	Y	Y	N	N
CONNECTICUT							
Weicker	N	Y	Y	Y	Y	N	Y
Dodd	N	N	?	+	+	?	?
DELAWARE							
Roth	Y	Y	N	Y	Y	Y	Y
Biden	Y	Y	N	Y	Y	Y	N
FLORIDA							
Hawkins	?	?	?	#	+	?	+
Chiles	Y	Y	Y	Y	Y	Y	Y
GEORGIA							
Mattingly	Y	Y	Y	N	Y	Y	Y
Nunn	Y	Y	Y	Y	Y	Y	Y
HAWAII							
Inouye	N	N	Y	Y	Y	N	N
Matsunaga	N	N	N	Y	Y	N	N
IDAHO							
McClure	Y	Y	N	N	Y	Y	Y
Symms	Y	Y	Y	N	Y	Y	Y
ILLINOIS							
Percy	N	N	N	Y	Y	Y	Y
Dixon	Y	N	N	Y	Y	N	Y
INDIANA							
Lugar	Y	Y	N	Y	Y	Y	Y
Quayle	Y	Y	Y	Y	Y	Y	Y

	4	5	6	7	8	9	10
IOWA							
Grassley	?	?	N	Y	Y	Y	Y
Jepsen	Y	Y	N	Y	Y	Y	Y
KANSAS							
Dole	Y	Y	N	Y	Y	?	?
Kassebaum	Y	Y	N	Y	Y	Y	Y
KENTUCKY							
Ford	Y	Y	N	Y	Y	Y	Y
Huddleston	Y	Y	N	Y	Y	Y	Y
LOUISIANA							
Johnston	Y	Y	Y	Y	Y	Y	Y
Long	Y	Y	N	Y	Y	Y	Y
MAINE							
Cohen	N	N	Y	Y	Y	N	N
Mitchell	N	N	Y	Y	Y	N	N
MARYLAND							
Mathias	N	N	N	Y	Y	N	N
Sarbanes	N	N	Y	Y	Y	N	N
MASSACHUSETTS							
Kennedy	N	N	Y	Y	Y	N	N
Tsongas	N	N	N	Y	Y	N	N
MICHIGAN							
Levin	N	N	Y	Y	Y	N	Y
Riegle	N	N	Y	Y	Y	Y	N
MINNESOTA							
Boschwitz	N	N	N	Y	Y	N	N
Durenberger	N	N	N	Y	Y	Y	N
MISSISSIPPI							
Cochran	Y	Y	N	Y	Y	?	?
Stennis	Y	Y	N	Y	Y	Y	Y
MISSOURI							
Danforth	Y	Y	N	Y	Y	Y	Y
Eagleton	N	N	Y	Y	Y	N	N
MONTANA							
Baucus	N	N	N	Y	Y	N	N
Melcher	Y	Y	N	Y	Y	Y	Y
NEBRASKA							
Exon	Y	Y	N	Y	Y	Y	Y
Zorinsky	Y	Y	N	Y	Y	Y	Y
NEVADA							
Laxalt	Y	Y	N	Y	Y	Y	Y
Cannon	Y	Y	Y	Y	Y	Y	Y

	4	5	6	7	8	9	10
NEW HAMPSHIRE							
Humphrey	Y	N	Y	Y	Y	N	N
Rudman	N	N	N	Y	Y	N	N
NEW JERSEY							
Bradley	N	N	Y	Y	Y	N	N
Williams	?	?	?	+	+	?	?
NEW MEXICO							
Domenici	Y	Y	N	Y	Y	Y	Y
Schmitt	Y	Y	N	Y	Y	Y	Y
NEW YORK							
D'Amato	Y	Y	Y	Y	Y	?	?
Moynihan	N	N	Y	Y	Y	N	Y
NORTH CAROLINA							
East	Y	Y	Y	Y	Y	Y	Y
Helms	Y	Y	Y	N	Y	Y	Y
NORTH DAKOTA							
Andrews	Y	Y	N	Y	Y	Y	Y
Burdick	Y	N	N	Y	Y	N	Y
OHIO							
Glenn	?	?	?	?	?	?	?
Metzenbaum	N	N	N	Y	Y	?	?
OKLAHOMA							
Nickles	Y	Y	Y	N	Y	Y	Y
Boren	Y	Y	N	Y	Y	Y	Y
OREGON							
Hatfield	N	N	-	X	+	-	?
Packwood	N	N	Y	Y	Y	N	N
PENNSYLVANIA							
Heinz	N	N	Y	Y	Y	?	?
Specter	N	N	Y	Y	Y	N	N
RHODE ISLAND							
Chafee	N	N	N	Y	Y	N	N
Pell	Y	N	N	Y	Y	N	N
SOUTH CAROLINA							
Thurmond	Y	Y	N	Y	Y	Y	Y
Hollings	Y	Y	Y	Y	Y	Y	Y
SOUTH DAKOTA							
Abdnor	Y	Y	N	Y	Y	Y	Y
Pressler	N	Y	Y	Y	Y	Y	Y
TENNESSEE							
Baker	Y	Y	N	Y	Y	Y	Y
Sasser	Y	Y	Y	Y	Y	Y	Y

	4	5	6	7	8	9	10
TEXAS							
Tower	Y	Y	N	Y	Y	Y	Y
Bentsen	Y	Y	Y	Y	Y	Y	Y
UTAH							
Garn	Y	Y	N	Y	Y	Y	Y
Hatch	Y	Y	Y	Y	Y	Y	Y
VERMONT							
Stafford	N	N	N	Y	Y	N	N
Leahy	N	N	N	Y	Y	N	N
VIRGINIA							
Warner	Y	Y	N	Y	Y	Y	Y
Byrd*	Y	Y	N	Y	N	Y	Y
WASHINGTON							
Gorton	Y	Y	N	Y	Y	Y	Y
Jackson	Y	N	Y	Y	Y	N	N
WEST VIRGINIA							
Byrd	Y	Y	N	Y	Y	Y	Y
Randolph	Y	Y	Y	Y	Y	Y	Y
WISCONSIN							
Kasten	Y	Y	N	Y	Y	Y	Y
Proxmire	Y	Y	N	Y	Y	N	Y
WYOMING							
Simpson	Y	Y	N	Y	Y	Y	Y
Wallop	Y	Y	N	Y	Y	Y	Y

KEY

- **Y** Voted for (yea).
- **#** Paired for.
- **+** Announced for.
- **N** Voted against (nay).
- **X** Paired against.
- **-** Announced against.
- **P** Voted "present".
- **C** Voted "present" to avoid possible conflict of interest.
- **?** Did not vote or otherwise make a position known.

Democrats *Republicans*

ND - Northern Democrats   SD - Southern Democrats (Southern states - Ala., Ark., Fla., Ga., Ky., La., Miss., N.C., Okla., S.C., Tenn., Texas, Va.)   *Byrd elected as an independent.

4. S 951. Department of Justice Authorization, Fiscal 1982. Johnston, D-La., motion to invoke cloture (thus limiting debate) on the bill to authorize fiscal 1982 funds for the Department of Justice. Motion agreed to 63-33: R 36-15; D 27-18 (ND 13-17, SD 14-1), Feb. 9, 1982. A three-fifths majority vote (60) of the total Senate is required to invoke cloture.

5. S 951. Department of Justice Authorization, Fiscal 1982. Helms, R-N.C., motion to table (kill) the first committee amendment increasing to $50.2 million from $37.65 million expenditures authorized for administration, with up to $12.6 million earmarked for drug enforcement grants to state and local law enforcement agencies. Motion agreed to 60-36: R 38-13; D 22-23 (ND 9-21, SD 13-2), Feb. 9, 1982.

6. H J Res 389. Fiscal 1982 Supplemental Appropriations/Commodity Credit Corporation. Moynihan, D-N.Y., amendment to prohibit the Commodity Credit Corporation from honoring its guarantees of commercial loans to Poland in the absence of a declaration by Poland's creditors that Poland was in default on such loans, unless the president had given Congress a monthly report explaining how the national security interests of the United States had been served by honoring guarantees of Polish debts in the absence of a declaration of default. Rejected 39-55: R 18-32; D 21-23 (ND 14-15, SD 7-8), Feb. 10, 1982.

7. H J Res 389. Fiscal 1982 Supplemental Appropriations/Commodity Credit Corporation. Kennedy, D-Mass., amendment to add to the joint resolution an appropriation of $123 million for the Department of Health and Human Services to fund low-income energy assistance. Adopted 85-10: R 44-7; D 41-3 (ND 28-1, SD 13-2), Feb. 10, 1982.

8. H J Res 391. Fiscal 1982 Supplemental Appropriations/Unemployment Compensation. Passage of the joint resolution to provide a fiscal 1982 supplemental appropriation of $2,293,490,000 for the unemployment insurance program and the U.S. Employment Service. Passed (thus cleared for the president) 95-0: R 51-0; D 44-0 (ND 29-0, SD 15-0), Feb. 10, 1982. The president had requested $2,290,490,000.

9. S 951. Department of Justice Authorization, Fiscal 1982. Weicker, R-Conn., motion to table (kill) the Helms, R-N.C., motion to reconsider the vote by which the first committee amendment *(see vote 5, above)* was laid on the table. Motion agreed to 60-30: R 37-10; D 23-20 (ND 10-18, SD 13-2), Feb. 10, 1982.

10. S 951. Department of Justice Authorization, Fiscal 1982. Johnston, D-La., motion to table (kill) the second committee amendment increasing from $127.1 million to $176.7 million funding authorized for civil and criminal prosecutions. Motion agreed to 63-27: R 37-10; D 26-17 (ND 12-16, SD 14-1), Feb. 10, 1982.

	11	12	13
ALABAMA			
Denton	Y	Y	Y
Heflin	Y	Y	?
ALASKA			
Murkowski	Y	Y	Y
Stevens	Y	Y	Y
ARIZONA			
Goldwater	?	Y	?
DeConcini	Y	Y	Y
ARKANSAS			
Bumpers	N	Y	N
Pryor	Y	Y	Y
CALIFORNIA			
Hayakawa	Y	Y	?
Cranston	N	X	N
COLORADO			
Armstrong	Y	Y	Y
Hart	N	N	N
CONNECTICUT			
Weicker	N	N	N
Dodd	N	N	N
DELAWARE			
Roth	Y	Y	Y
Biden	?	?	Y
FLORIDA			
Hawkins	+	+	?
Chiles	Y	Y	Y
GEORGIA			
Mattingly	Y	Y	Y
Nunn	Y	Y	Y
HAWAII			
Inouye	X	N	Y
Matsunaga	?	?	Y
IDAHO			
McClure	?	?	?
Symms	Y	Y	Y
ILLINOIS			
Percy	Y	Y	Y
Dixon	Y	Y	Y
INDIANA			
Lugar	Y	Y	Y
Quayle	Y	Y	Y
IOWA			
Grassley	Y	Y	Y
Jepsen	Y	Y	Y
KANSAS			
Dole	?	?	?
Kassebaum	Y	Y	Y
KENTUCKY			
Ford	Y	Y	Y
Huddleston	Y	Y	Y
LOUISIANA			
Johnston	Y	Y	Y
Long	Y	Y	Y
MAINE			
Cohen	N	N	N
Mitchell	N	N	N
MARYLAND			
Mathias	N	N	N
Sarbanes	N	N	N
MASSACHUSETTS			
Kennedy	N	Y	N
Tsongas	N	N	N
MICHIGAN			
Levin	N	N	N
Riegle	N	N	N
MINNESOTA			
Boschwitz	N	N	N
Durenberger	N	N	N
MISSISSIPPI			
Cochran	Y	Y	Y
Stennis	Y	Y	Y
MISSOURI			
Danforth	Y	Y	Y
Eagleton	N	N	Y
MONTANA			
Baucus	N	N	N
Melcher	Y	Y	Y
NEBRASKA			
Exon	Y	Y	Y
Zorinsky	Y	Y	Y
NEVADA			
Laxalt	Y	Y	?
Cannon	Y	Y	Y
NEW HAMPSHIRE			
Humphrey	N	Y	Y
Rudman	N	N	N
NEW JERSEY			
Bradley	N	N	N
Williams	?	?	?
NEW MEXICO			
Domenici	Y	Y	Y
Schmitt	Y	Y	Y
NEW YORK			
D'Amato	Y	Y	Y
Moynihan	N	N	N
NORTH CAROLINA			
East	Y	Y	Y
Helms	Y	Y	Y
NORTH DAKOTA			
Andrews	Y	Y	Y
Burdick	Y	Y	Y
OHIO			
Glenn	?	?	?
Metzenbaum	N	N	N
OKLAHOMA			
Nickles	Y	Y	Y
Boren	Y	Y	Y
OREGON			
Hatfield	?	?	?
Packwood	N	N	N
PENNSYLVANIA			
Heinz	N	Y	N
Specter	N	Y	Y
RHODE ISLAND			
Chafee	N	N	N
Pell	N	N	?
SOUTH CAROLINA			
Thurmond	Y	Y	Y
Hollings	Y	Y	Y
SOUTH DAKOTA			
Abdnor	Y	Y	Y
Pressler	Y	Y	Y
TENNESSEE			
Baker	Y	Y	Y
Sasser	#	#	+
TEXAS			
Tower	Y	Y	Y
Bentsen	Y	Y	Y
UTAH			
Garn	Y	Y	Y
Hatch	Y	Y	Y
VERMONT			
Stafford	N	N	N
Leahy	N	N	?
VIRGINIA			
Warner	Y	Y	Y
Byrd*	Y	Y	Y
WASHINGTON			
Gorton	Y	Y	Y
Jackson	N	N	Y
WEST VIRGINIA			
Byrd	Y	Y	Y
Randolph	Y	Y	Y
WISCONSIN			
Kasten	Y	Y	Y
Proxmire	Y	Y	Y
WYOMING			
Simpson	Y	Y	Y
Wallop	Y	Y	Y

KEY

Y   Voted for (yea).
\#   Paired for.
\+   Announced for.
N   Voted against (nay).
X   Paired against.
-   Announced against.
P   Voted "present".
C   Voted "present" to avoid possible conflict of interest.
?   Did not vote or otherwise make a position known.

Democrats   *Republicans*

ND - Northern Democrats   SD - Southern Democrats (Southern states - Ala., Ark., Fla., Ga., Ky., La., Miss., N.C., Okla., S.C., Tenn., Texas, Va.)

* Byrd elected as an independent.

11. S 951. Department of Justice Authorization, Fiscal 1982. Johnston, D-La., motion to table (kill) the Weicker, R-Conn., motion to reconsider the vote by which the second committee amendment was laid on the table *(see vote 10, p. 3-S)*. Motion agreed to 59-30: R 36-12; D 23-18 (ND 10-17, SD 13-1), Feb. 11, 1982.

12. S 951. Department of Justice Authorization, Fiscal 1982. Judgment of the Senate affirming the chair's ruling that the third committee amendment to require that $49.56 million of the funding authorized in the bill be allotted to the department's antitrust division was non-germane. Ruling of the chair upheld 65-25: R 40-9; D 25-16 (ND 11-16, SD 14-0), Feb. 11, 1982.

13. S 951. Department of Justice Authorization, Fiscal 1982. Johnston, D-La., motion to table (kill) the fourth committee amendment to make a technical re-numbering change in the bill. Motion agreed to 63-24: R 36-10; D 27-14 (ND 15-13, SD 12-1), Feb. 11, 1982.

	14	15	16	17	18	19	20	21
ALABAMA								
Denton	Y	Y	Y	Y	Y	Y	Y	N
Heflin	Y	Y	Y	Y	N	Y	Y	Y
ALASKA								
Murkowski	Y	Y	Y	Y	Y	Y	Y	Y
Stevens	Y	Y	Y	Y	Y	Y	Y	N
ARIZONA								
Goldwater	N	N	N	N	Y	N	N	N
DeConcini	Y	Y	Y	Y	Y	Y	Y	Y
ARKANSAS								
Bumpers	Y	Y	Y	Y	N	Y	Y	Y
Pryor	Y	Y	Y	Y	Y	Y	Y	Y
CALIFORNIA								
Hayakawa	Y	Y	Y	N	Y	Y	Y	N
Cranston	Y	Y	Y	N	Y	Y	Y	Y
COLORADO								
Armstrong	Y	Y	Y	Y	Y	Y	Y	N
Hart	Y	Y	Y	N	Y	Y	Y	Y
CONNECTICUT								
Weicker	N	N	N	N	Y	N	N	N
Dodd	Y	Y	?	?	N	Y	Y	Y
DELAWARE								
Roth	Y	Y	Y	Y	Y	Y	Y	Y
Biden	Y	Y	Y	Y	Y	Y	N	N
FLORIDA								
Hawkins	?	?	?	?	Y	Y	Y	N
Chiles	Y	Y	Y	Y	Y	Y	Y	Y
GEORGIA								
Mattingly	Y	Y	Y	Y	Y	Y	Y	N
Nunn	Y	Y	Y	Y	Y	Y	Y	Y
HAWAII								
Inouye	Y	Y	?	?	?	?	?	?
Matsunaga	Y	Y	?	N	Y	N	Y	?
IDAHO								
McClure	?	?	Y	Y	Y	Y	Y	N
Symms	Y	Y	Y	Y	Y	Y	Y	N
ILLINOIS								
Percy	Y	Y	?	?	N	Y	Y	Y
Dixon	Y	Y	Y	Y	Y	Y	Y	Y
INDIANA								
Lugar	Y	Y	Y	Y	Y	Y	Y	N
Quayle	N	N	N	N	Y	N	N	N
IOWA								
Grassley	Y	Y	Y	Y	Y	Y	Y	N
Jepsen	Y	Y	Y	Y	Y	Y	Y	N
KANSAS								
Dole	Y	Y	Y	Y	Y	Y	Y	N
Kassebaum	Y	Y	Y	Y	Y	Y	Y	N
KENTUCKY								
Ford	Y	Y	Y	Y	Y	Y	Y	Y
Huddleston	Y	Y	Y	Y	Y	Y	Y	Y
LOUISIANA								
Johnston	Y	Y	Y	Y	Y	Y	Y	N
Long	Y	Y	Y	?	Y	Y	Y	Y
MAINE								
Cohen	Y	Y	Y	Y	N	Y	Y	Y
Mitchell	Y	Y	Y	Y	N	Y	Y	Y
MARYLAND								
Mathias	?	?	?	?	?	?	?	?
Sarbanes	Y	Y	Y	Y	N	Y	Y	Y
MASSACHUSETTS								
Kennedy	Y	Y	Y	Y	N	Y	Y	Y
Tsongas	Y	Y	?	Y	N	Y	Y	Y
MICHIGAN								
Levin	Y	Y	Y	Y	N	Y	Y	Y
Riegle	Y	Y	Y	Y	N	Y	?	?
MINNESOTA								
Boschwitz	Y	N	N	N	N	N	N	Y
Durenberger	?	?	?	Y	N	Y	Y	Y
MISSISSIPPI								
Cochran	Y	Y	?	?	?	?	?	?
Stennis	?	Y	Y	Y	Y	Y	Y	?
MISSOURI								
Danforth	?	?	Y	Y	Y	Y	Y	N
Eagleton	Y	Y	Y	Y	N	Y	Y	Y
MONTANA								
Baucus	Y	Y	Y	Y	N	Y	Y	Y
Melcher	Y	Y	Y	Y	N	Y	Y	Y
NEBRASKA								
Exon	Y	Y	Y	Y	N	Y	Y	Y
Zorinsky	Y	Y	Y	Y	Y	Y	Y	N
NEVADA								
Laxalt	Y	Y	Y	Y	Y	Y	Y	N
Cannon	Y	Y	Y	Y	Y	Y	Y	Y
NEW HAMPSHIRE								
Humphrey	Y	Y	Y	Y	Y	Y	Y	N
Rudman	Y	Y	Y	Y	Y	Y	Y	N
NEW JERSEY								
Bradley	Y	Y	Y	Y	N	Y	Y	Y
Williams	?	?	?	?	?	?	?	?
NEW MEXICO								
Domenici	Y	?	Y	Y	Y	Y	N	N
Schmitt	Y	Y	Y	Y	Y	Y	Y	N
NEW YORK								
D'Amato	Y	Y	Y	Y	Y	Y	Y	N
Moynihan	Y	Y	Y	N	Y	Y	Y	Y
NORTH CAROLINA								
East	Y	Y	N	N	Y	N	N	N
Helms	Y	Y	N	N	Y	Y	Y	N
NORTH DAKOTA								
Andrews	Y	Y	Y	Y	Y	Y	Y	Y
Burdick	?	?	Y	Y	N	Y	Y	Y
OHIO								
Glenn	Y	Y	Y	Y	N	Y	Y	Y
Metzenbaum	Y	Y	Y	Y	N	Y	Y	Y
OKLAHOMA								
Nickles	Y	Y	Y	Y	Y	Y	Y	N
Boren	Y	Y	Y	Y	N	Y	Y	Y
OREGON								
Hatfield	?	?	Y	Y	N	Y	Y	?
Packwood	Y	Y	?	?	Y	Y	Y	Y
PENNSYLVANIA								
Heinz	Y	Y	Y	Y	Y	Y	Y	N
Specter	Y	Y	Y	Y	Y	Y	Y	Y
RHODE ISLAND								
Chafee	?	?	?	?	?	?	?	?
Pell	Y	Y	Y	Y	N	Y	Y	Y
SOUTH CAROLINA								
Thurmond	?	?	?	?	+	?	?	?
Hollings	Y	Y	Y	Y	Y	Y	Y	Y
SOUTH DAKOTA								
Abdnor	Y	Y	Y	Y	Y	Y	Y	N
Pressler	Y	Y	Y	Y	Y	Y	Y	N
TENNESSEE								
Baker	Y	Y	Y	Y	Y	Y	Y	N
Sasser	Y	Y	Y	Y	Y	Y	Y	N
TEXAS								
Tower	?	?	Y	Y	Y	Y	Y	N
Bentsen	Y	Y	Y	Y	Y	Y	Y	Y
UTAH								
Garn	Y	Y	Y	N	Y	Y	N	N
Hatch	Y	Y	Y	Y	Y	Y	Y	N
VERMONT								
Stafford	Y	Y	Y	Y	N	Y	Y	N
Leahy	Y	Y	Y	Y	N	Y	Y	Y
VIRGINIA								
Warner	N	N	N	N	Y	N	N	N
Byrd*	Y	Y	Y	Y	Y	Y	Y	N
WASHINGTON								
Gorton	Y	Y	Y	Y	Y	Y	Y	N
Jackson	Y	Y	Y	Y	Y	Y	Y	N
WEST VIRGINIA								
Byrd	Y	Y	Y	Y	Y	Y	Y	N
Randolph	Y	Y	Y	Y	Y	Y	Y	Y
WISCONSIN								
Kasten	Y	Y	Y	Y	Y	Y	Y	N
Proxmire	N	N	N	N	Y	N	N	N
WYOMING								
Simpson	Y	Y	Y	Y	?	Y	Y	N
Wallop	Y	Y	Y	Y	Y	Y	Y	N

KEY

Y Voted for (yea).
\# Paired for.
+ Announced for.
N Voted against (nay).
X Paired against.
– Announced against.
P Voted "present".
C Voted "present" to avoid possible conflict of interest.
? Did not vote or otherwise make a position known.

Democrats *Republicans*

ND - Northern Democrats   SD - Southern Democrats (Southern states - Ala., Ark., Fla., Ga., Ky., La., Miss., N.C., Okla., S.C., Tenn., Texas, Va.)   *Byrd elected as an independent.*

14. S 951. Department of Justice Authorization, Fiscal 1982. Baker, R-Tenn., motion to instruct the sergeant-at-arms to request the attendance of absent senators. Motion agreed to 83-5: R 40-4; D 43-1 (ND 29-1, SD 14-0), Feb. 23, 1982.

15. S 951. Department of Justice Authorization, Fiscal 1982. Baker, R-Tenn., motion to instruct the sergeant-at-arms to request the attendance of absent senators. Motion agreed to 82-6: R 38-5; D 44-1 (ND 29-1, SD 15-0), Feb. 23, 1982.

16. S 951. Department of Justice Authorization, Fiscal 1982. Baker, R-Tenn., motion to instruct the sergeant-at-arms to invite the attendance of absent senators. Motion agreed to 79-8: R 38-7; D 41-1 (ND 26-1, SD 15-0), Feb. 24, 1982.

17. S 951. Department of Justice Authorization, Fiscal 1982. Johnston, D-La., motion to instruct the sergeant-at-arms to request the attendance of absent senators. Motion agreed to 78-10: R 37-9; D 41-1 (ND 27-1, SD 14-0), Feb. 24, 1982.

18. S 951. Department of Justice Authorization, Fiscal 1982. Judgment of the Senate affirming the chair's ruling that the Gorton, R-Wash., amendment to prohibit state and federal courts or agencies from implementing plans requiring student assignment by race was germane. Ruling of the chair upheld 63-30: R 42-6; D 21-24 (ND 9-21, SD 12-3), Feb. 24, 1982.

19. S 951. Department of Justice Authorization, Fiscal 1982. Baker, R-Tenn., motion to instruct the sergeant-at-arms to compel the attendance of absent senators. Motion agreed to 87-7: R 43-6; D 44-1 (ND 29-1, SD 15-0), Feb. 24, 1982.

20. S 951. Department of Justice Authorization, Fiscal 1982. Baker, R-Tenn., motion to instruct the sergeant-at-arms to compel the attendance of absent senators. Motion agreed to 82-11: R 41-8; D 41-3 (ND 26-3, SD 15-0), Feb. 24, 1982.

21. S 951. Department of Justice Authorization, Fiscal 1982. Exon, D-Neb., motion to table (kill) the Gorton, R-Wash., amendment to prohibit state and federal courts or agencies from implementing plans requiring student assignment by race. Motion rejected 40-51: R 6-42; D 34-9 (ND 23-6, SD 11-3), Feb. 24, 1982.

KEY

- Y Voted for (yea).
- # Paired for.
- + Announced for.
- N Voted against (nay).
- X Paired against.
- - Announced against.
- P Voted "present".
- C Voted "present" to avoid possible conflict of interest.
- ? Did not vote or otherwise make a position known.

Democrats   *Republicans*

	22	23	24	25	26	27	28	29
ALABAMA								
Denton	Y	N	Y	Y	Y	Y	Y	Y
Heflin	N	N	Y	Y	Y	Y	Y	N
ALASKA								
Murkowski	Y	Y	Y	Y	Y	Y	Y	Y
Stevens	Y	Y	Y	Y	Y	Y	Y	Y
ARIZONA								
Goldwater	Y	Y	N	Y	N	N	Y	Y
DeConcini	Y	Y	Y	Y	Y	Y	Y	Y
ARKANSAS								
Bumpers	N	N	Y	N	N	Y	N	N
Pryor	N	N	Y	Y	Y	Y	Y	Y
CALIFORNIA								
Hayakawa	Y	Y	N	Y	N	Y	N	Y
Cranston	N	N	Y	N	N	Y	N	N
COLORADO								
Armstrong	Y	Y	Y	Y	Y	Y	Y	Y
Hart	N	N	Y	N	N	?	N	?
CONNECTICUT								
Weicker	N	N	N	N	N	N	N	N
Dodd	N	N	Y	N	N	Y	N	Y
DELAWARE								
Roth	Y	Y	Y	Y	Y	Y	Y	Y
Biden	Y	N	Y	Y	Y	Y	Y	Y
FLORIDA								
Hawkins	Y	Y	Y	Y	N	Y	Y	Y
Chiles	N	N	Y	Y	N	Y	Y	Y
GEORGIA								
Mattingly	Y	Y	Y	Y	Y	Y	Y	Y
Nunn	N	N	Y	Y	Y	Y	Y	Y
HAWAII								
Inouye	?	?	?	?	?	?	?	?
Matsunaga	N	?	Y	N	N	Y	N	N
IDAHO								
McClure	Y	Y	N	Y	Y	N	Y	Y
Symms	Y	Y	Y	Y	Y	Y	Y	Y
ILLINOIS								
Percy	N	N	Y	Y	Y	Y	Y	Y
Dixon	N	N	Y	Y	Y	Y	Y	Y
INDIANA								
Lugar	Y	Y	Y	Y	Y	Y	Y	Y
Quayle	Y	Y	N	Y	Y	N	Y	Y

	22	23	24	25	26	27	28	29
IOWA								
Grassley	Y	Y	Y	Y	Y	Y	Y	Y
Jepsen	Y	Y	Y	Y	Y	Y	Y	Y
KANSAS								
Dole	Y	Y	Y	Y	Y	Y	Y	Y
Kassebaum	Y	Y	Y	Y	Y	Y	Y	Y
KENTUCKY								
Ford	N	N	Y	Y	Y	Y	Y	Y
Huddleston	N	N	Y	Y	Y	Y	Y	Y
LOUISIANA								
Johnston	Y	N	Y	Y	Y	Y	Y	Y
Long	N	N	N	Y	Y	Y	Y	Y
MAINE								
Cohen	N	N	Y	N	N	Y	N	N
Mitchell	N	N	Y	N	N	Y	N	N
MARYLAND								
Mathias	?	N	Y	N	N	Y	N	N
Sarbanes	N	?	?	?	?	?	?	?
MASSACHUSETTS								
Kennedy	N	N	Y	N	N	Y	N	N
Tsongas	N	N	Y	N	N	Y	N	Y
MICHIGAN								
Levin	N	N	Y	N	N	Y	N	N
Riegle	?	?	?	?	?	Y	N	N
MINNESOTA								
Boschwitz	N	N	N	N	N	Y	N	N
Durenberger	N	N	Y	N	N	Y	N	N
MISSISSIPPI								
Cochran	?	?	?	?	?	?	?	?
Stennis	N	N	Y	Y	Y	?	?	?
MISSOURI								
Danforth	Y	Y	Y	Y	Y	Y	Y	Y
Eagleton	N	N	Y	N	N	Y	Y	Y
MONTANA								
Baucus	N	N	Y	N	N	Y	N	N
Melcher	N	N	Y	Y	Y	Y	Y	Y
NEBRASKA								
Exon	N	N	Y	Y	Y	Y	N	Y
Zorinsky	Y	Y	Y	Y	Y	Y	Y	Y
NEVADA								
Laxalt	Y	Y	?	?	?	?	?	?
Cannon	N	N	Y	Y	Y	Y	Y	Y

	22	23	24	25	26	27	28	29
NEW HAMPSHIRE								
Humphrey	Y	Y	Y	Y	Y	Y	Y	Y
Rudman	Y	Y	Y	Y	Y	Y	Y	Y
NEW JERSEY								
Bradley	N	N	Y	N	N	Y	N	N
Williams	?	?	?	?	?	?	?	?
NEW MEXICO								
Domenici	Y	Y	Y	Y	Y	Y	Y	Y
Schmitt	Y	Y	Y	Y	Y	Y	Y	Y
NEW YORK								
D'Amato	Y	Y	Y	Y	Y	Y	Y	Y
Moynihan	N	N	Y	N	N	Y	Y	N
NORTH CAROLINA								
East	Y	N	N	Y	Y	Y	Y	Y
Helms	Y	N	Y	Y	Y	Y	Y	Y
NORTH DAKOTA								
Andrews	Y	Y	Y	Y	Y	Y	Y	Y
Burdick	N	N	Y	Y	Y	Y	Y	Y
OHIO								
Glenn	N	N	Y	N	N	Y	Y	N
Metzenbaum	N	N	Y	N	N	Y	N	N
OKLAHOMA								
Nickles	Y	Y	Y	Y	Y	Y	Y	Y
Boren	N	N	Y	Y	Y	Y	Y	Y
OREGON								
Hatfield	?	?	Y	N	Y	N	N	N
Packwood	N	N	Y	Y	N	N	N	N
PENNSYLVANIA								
Heinz	Y	Y	Y	N	N	Y	N	N
Specter	N	N	Y	Y	Y	Y	Y	N
RHODE ISLAND								
Chafee	?	?	Y	N	N	Y	N	N
Pell	N	N	Y	N	N	Y	Y	N
SOUTH CAROLINA								
Thurmond	?	+	?	+	+	?	?	?
Hollings	N	N	Y	Y	Y	Y	Y	Y
SOUTH DAKOTA								
Abdnor	Y	Y	Y	Y	Y	Y	Y	Y
Pressler	Y	Y	Y	N	Y	Y	Y	Y
TENNESSEE								
Baker	Y	Y	Y	Y	Y	Y	Y	Y
Sasser	Y	Y	Y	Y	Y	Y	Y	Y

	22	23	24	25	26	27	28	29
TEXAS								
Tower	Y	N	Y	Y	Y	Y	Y	Y
Bentsen	N	N	Y	Y	Y	Y	Y	Y
UTAH								
Garn	Y	N	Y	Y	Y	Y	Y	Y
Hatch	Y	Y	Y	Y	Y	Y	Y	Y
VERMONT								
Stafford	N	N	Y	N	N	Y	N	N
Leahy	N	N	Y	N	Y	N	Y	N
VIRGINIA								
Warner	Y	Y	N	Y	Y	N	Y	Y
Byrd*	Y	Y	Y	Y	Y	Y	Y	Y
WASHINGTON								
Gorton	Y	Y	Y	Y	Y	Y	Y	Y
Jackson	Y	Y	Y	Y	N	Y	Y	Y
WEST VIRGINIA								
Byrd	Y	Y	Y	Y	Y	Y	Y	Y
Randolph	N	N	Y	Y	Y	Y	Y	Y
WISCONSIN								
Kasten	Y	Y	Y	Y	Y	Y	Y	Y
Proxmire	Y	Y	N	Y	N	Y	N	Y
WYOMING								
Simpson	Y	Y	Y	Y	Y	Y	Y	Y
Wallop	Y	Y	Y	Y	Y	Y	Y	Y

ND - Northern Democrats   SD - Southern Democrats (Southern states - Ala., Ark., Fla., Ga., Ky., La., Miss., N.C., Okla., S.C., Tenn., Texas, Va.)   * Byrd elected as an independent.

22. S 951. Department of Justice Authorization, Fiscal 1982. Baker, R-Tenn., motion to table (kill) the Weicker, R-Conn., motion to reconsider the vote by which the Exon, D-Neb., motion to table was rejected (see vote 21, p. 5-S). Motion agreed to 49-43: R 40-8; D 9-35 (ND 6-23, SD 3-12), Feb. 24, 1982.

23. S 951. Department of Justice Authorization, Fiscal 1982. Gorton, R-Wash., amendment to bar any state or federal court, agency or department from implementing any student assignment plan based on race. Rejected 42-49: R 35-14; D 7-35 (ND 5-22, SD 2-13), Feb. 24, 1982.

24. S 951. Department of Justice Authorization, Fiscal 1982. Baker, R-Tenn., motion to instruct the sergeant-at-arms to compel the attendance of absent senators. Motion agreed to 83-10: R 42-8; D 41-2 (ND 27-1, SD 14-1), Feb. 24, 1982.

25. S 951. Department of Justice Authorization, Fiscal 1982. Judgment of the Senate affirming the chair's ruling that the Johnston, D-La., amendment to bar federal courts from ordering busing for racial balance, and to authorize programs for the Department of Justice was germane. Ruling of the chair upheld 66-27: R 39-11; D 27-16 (ND 13-15, SD 14-1), Feb. 24, 1982.

26. S 951. Department of Justice Authorization, Fiscal 1982. Johnston, D-La., motion to table (kill) the Weicker, R-Conn., amendment concerning compensation for Drug Enforcement Administration informers. Motion agreed to 62-31: R 38-12; D 24-19 (ND 11-17, SD 13-2), Feb. 24, 1982.

27. S 951. Department of Justice Authorization, Fiscal 1982. Baker, R-Tenn., motion to instruct the sergeant-at-arms to compel the attendance of absent senators. Motion agreed to 85-7: R 44-6; D 41-1 (ND 27-1, SD 14-0), Feb. 24, 1982.

28. S 951. Department of Justice Authorization, Fiscal 1982. Baker, R-Tenn., motion to table (kill) the Metzenbaum, D-Ohio, appeal of the chair's ruling that a quorum call was not in order. Motion agreed to 69-23: R 40-10; D 29-13 (ND 16-12, SD 13-1), Feb. 24, 1982.

29. S 951. Department of Justice Authorization, Fiscal 1982. Baker, R-Tenn., motion to table (kill) the Weicker, R-Conn., appeal of the chair's ruling that the Weicker amendment concerning program evaluations by the attorney general was not germane. Motion agreed to 65-28: R 39-11; D 26-17 (ND 14-15, SD 12-2), Feb. 24, 1982.

	30	31	32	33	34	35	36	37
ALABAMA								
Denton	Y	Y	N	Y	Y	Y	N	Y
Heflin	Y	Y	N	Y	Y	Y	Y	Y
ALASKA								
Murkowski	Y	Y	N	Y	Y	Y	Y	Y
Stevens	Y	Y	N	Y	Y	Y	Y	Y
ARIZONA								
Goldwater	?	?	?	?	?	?	N	N
DeConcini	Y	Y	N	Y	Y	Y	Y	Y
ARKANSAS								
Bumpers	N	N	Y	N	N	N	Y	Y
Pryor	Y	Y	N	Y	Y	Y	Y	Y
CALIFORNIA								
Hayakawa	Y	Y	N	Y	Y	Y	N	N
Cranston	N	N	Y	N	N	N	Y	Y
COLORADO								
Armstrong	Y	Y	N	Y	Y	Y	Y	Y
Hart	N	N	Y	N	N	N	Y	Y
CONNECTICUT								
Weicker	N	N	Y	N	N	N	N	N
Dodd	N	Y	Y	N	N	N	Y	Y
DELAWARE								
Roth	Y	Y	N	Y	Y	Y	Y	Y
Biden	Y	Y	N	Y	Y	Y	Y	N
FLORIDA								
Hawkins	Y	Y	N	Y	Y	Y	Y	Y
Chiles	Y	Y	N	Y	Y	Y	Y	Y
GEORGIA								
Mattingly	Y	Y	N	Y	Y	Y	Y	Y
Nunn	Y	Y	N	Y	Y	Y	Y	Y
HAWAII								
Inouye	?	?	?	?	?	?	?	?
Matsunaga	N	N	Y	N	N	N	Y	Y
IDAHO								
McClure	Y	Y	N	Y	Y	Y	Y	Y
Symms	Y	Y	N	Y	Y	Y	Y	Y
ILLINOIS								
Percy	Y	Y	N	Y	Y	Y	Y	Y
Dixon	Y	Y	Y	Y	Y	Y	Y	Y
INDIANA								
Lugar	Y	Y	N	Y	Y	Y	Y	Y
Quayle	Y	Y	N	Y	Y	Y	N	N

	30	31	32	33	34	35	36	37
IOWA								
Grassley	Y	Y	N	Y	Y	Y	Y	Y
Jepsen	Y	Y	N	Y	Y	Y	Y	Y
KANSAS								
Dole	Y	Y	N	Y	Y	Y	Y	Y
Kassebaum	Y	Y	?	Y	Y	Y	?	Y
KENTUCKY								
Ford	Y	Y	N	Y	Y	Y	Y	Y
Huddleston	Y	Y	N	Y	Y	Y	Y	Y
LOUISIANA								
Johnston	Y	Y	N	Y	Y	Y	Y	Y
Long	Y	Y	N	Y	Y	Y	Y	Y
MAINE								
Cohen	N	N	Y	N	N	N	Y	Y
Mitchell	N	N	Y	N	N	N	Y	Y
MARYLAND								
Mathias	N	N	Y	N	N	N	Y	Y
Sarbanes	?	?	?	?	?	?	Y	Y
MASSACHUSETTS								
Kennedy	N	N	Y	N	N	N	Y	Y
Tsongas	Y	Y	Y	N	N	N	Y	Y
MICHIGAN								
Levin	N	N	Y	N	N	N	Y	Y
Riegle	N	N	Y	N	N	N	Y	Y
MINNESOTA								
Boschwitz	N	N	Y	N	N	N	Y	Y
Durenberger	N	N	Y	N	N	N	Y	Y
MISSISSIPPI								
Cochran	?	?	?	?	?	?	?	?
Stennis	?	?	?	?	?	Y	Y	Y
MISSOURI								
Danforth	Y	Y	N	Y	Y	Y	Y	Y
Eagleton	Y	Y	Y	Y	Y	Y	Y	Y
MONTANA								
Baucus	N	N	Y	N	N	N	Y	Y
Melcher	Y	Y	N	Y	Y	Y	Y	Y
NEBRASKA								
Exon	Y	Y	N	Y	Y	Y	?	Y
Zorinsky	Y	Y	N	Y	Y	Y	Y	Y
NEVADA								
Laxalt	?	?	?	?	?	?	Y	Y
Cannon	Y	Y	N	Y	Y	Y	Y	Y

	30	31	32	33	34	35	36	37
NEW HAMPSHIRE								
Humphrey	Y	Y	N	Y	Y	Y	Y	Y
Rudman	Y	Y	N	Y	Y	Y	Y	Y
NEW JERSEY								
Bradley	N	N	Y	N	N	N	Y	Y
Williams	?	?	?	?	?	?	?	?
NEW MEXICO								
Domenici	Y	Y	N	Y	Y	Y	Y	Y
Schmitt	Y	Y	N	Y	Y	Y	Y	Y
NEW YORK								
D'Amato	Y	Y	N	Y	Y	Y	Y	Y
Moynihan	Y	Y	Y	N	Y	Y	Y	Y
NORTH CAROLINA								
East	Y	Y	N	Y	Y	Y	?	N
Helms	Y	Y	N	Y	Y	Y	Y	Y
NORTH DAKOTA								
Andrews	Y	Y	N	Y	Y	Y	Y	Y
Burdick	Y	Y	N	Y	Y	Y	Y	Y
OHIO								
Glenn	N	N	Y	N	N	N	Y	Y
Metzenbaum	N	N	Y	N	N	N	Y	Y
OKLAHOMA								
Nickles	Y	Y	N	Y	Y	Y	Y	Y
Boren	Y	Y	N	Y	Y	Y	Y	N
OREGON								
Hatfield	N	N	Y	N	N	N	Y	Y
Packwood	N	N	Y	N	N	N	Y	Y
PENNSYLVANIA								
Heinz	N	N	Y	N	N	N	Y	?
Specter	Y	Y	Y	Y	Y	Y	Y	Y
RHODE ISLAND								
Chafee	N	N	Y	N	N	N	Y	Y
Pell	N	N	Y	N	N	N	Y	Y
SOUTH CAROLINA								
Thurmond	?	?	-	?	?	?	?	?
Hollings	Y	Y	N	Y	Y	Y	Y	Y
SOUTH DAKOTA								
Abdnor	Y	Y	N	Y	Y	Y	Y	Y
Pressler	Y	Y	N	Y	?	?	Y	Y
TENNESSEE								
Baker	Y	Y	N	Y	Y	Y	?	?
Sasser	Y	Y	N	Y	Y	Y	Y	Y

KEY

Y Voted for (yea).
\# Paired for.
\+ Announced for.
N Voted against (nay).
X Paired against.
- Announced against.
P Voted ''present''.
C Voted ''present'' to avoid possible conflict of interest.
? Did not vote or otherwise make a position known.

Democrats   *Republicans*

	30	31	32	33	34	35	36	37
TEXAS								
Tower	Y	Y	N	Y	Y	Y	?	Y
Bentsen	Y	Y	N	Y	Y	Y	Y	Y
UTAH								
Garn	Y	Y	N	Y	Y	Y	N	Y
Hatch	Y	Y	N	Y	Y	Y	Y	Y
VERMONT								
Stafford	N	?	?	?	?	?	Y	Y
Leahy	N	N	Y	N	N	N	Y	Y
VIRGINIA								
Warner	Y	Y	N	Y	Y	Y	N	N
Byrd*	Y	Y	N	Y	Y	Y	Y	Y
WASHINGTON								
Gorton	Y	Y	N	Y	Y	Y	Y	Y
Jackson	Y	Y	N	Y	Y	Y	Y	Y
WEST VIRGINIA								
Byrd	Y	Y	N	Y	Y	Y	Y	Y
Randolph	Y	Y	N	Y	Y	Y	Y	Y
WISCONSIN								
Kasten	Y	Y	N	Y	Y	Y	Y	Y
Proxmire	Y	Y	N	Y	Y	Y	N	N
WYOMING								
Simpson	Y	Y	N	Y	Y	Y	Y	Y
Wallop	Y	Y	N	Y	Y	Y	Y	Y

ND - Northern Democrats   SD - Southern Democrats (Southern states - Ala., Ark., Fla., Ga., Ky., La., Miss., N.C., Okla., S.C., Tenn., Texas, Va.)   *Byrd elected as an independent.

30. S 951. Department of Justice Authorization, Fiscal 1982. Baker, R-Tenn., motion to table (kill) the Weicker, R-Conn., appeal of the chair's ruling that the Weicker amendment concerning program evaluations by the attorney general was not germane. Motion agreed to 67-25: R 39-10; D 28-15 (ND 15-14, SD 13-1), Feb. 24, 1982.

31. S 951. Department of Justice Authorization, Fiscal 1982. Baker, R-Tenn., motion to table (kill) the Weicker, R-Conn., appeal of the chair's ruling that the Weicker amendment concerning program evaluations by the attorney general was not in order. Motion agreed to 68-23: R 39-9; D 29-14 (ND 16-13, SD 13-1), Feb. 24, 1982.

32. S 951. Department of Justice Authorization, Fiscal 1982. Weicker, R-Conn., motion to table (kill) the bill to authorize fiscal 1982 funds for the Department of Justice. Motion rejected 30-60: R 11-36; D 19-24 (ND 18-11, SD 1-13), in the session which began Feb. 24, 1982.

33. S 951. Department of Justice Authorization, Fiscal 1982. Baker, R-Tenn., motion to table (kill) the Weicker, R-Conn., appeal of the chair's ruling that the Weicker amendment concerning program evaluations by the attorney general was dilatory and thus not in order. Motion agreed to 65-26: R 39-9; D 26-17 (ND 13-16, SD 13-1), in the session which began Feb. 24, 1982.

34. S 951. Department of Justice Authorization, Fiscal 1982. Baker, R-Tenn., motion to table (kill) the Weicker, R-Conn., appeal of the chair's ruling that the Weicker amendment relating to travel expenses for Justice officials was dilatory and thus not in order. Motion agreed to 65-25: R 38-9; D 27-16 (ND 14-15, SD 13-1), in the session which began Feb. 24, 1982.

35. S 951. Department of Justice Authorization, Fiscal 1982. Baker, R-Tenn., motion to table (kill) the Weicker, R-Conn., appeal of the chair's ruling that the Weicker amendment concerning Justice personnel costs was dilatory and thus not in order. Motion agreed to 65-25: R 38-9; D 27-16 (ND 14-15, SD 13-1), in the session which began Feb. 24, 1982.

36. S 951. Department of Justice Authorization, Fiscal 1982. Stevens, R-Alaska, motion to instruct the sergeant-at-arms to compel the attendance of absent senators. Motion agreed to 83-8: R 40-7; D 43-1 (ND 28-1, SD 15-0), Feb. 25, 1982.

37. S 951. Department of Justice Authorization, Fiscal 1982. Stevens, R-Alaska, motion to instruct the sergeant-at-arms to request the attendance of absent senators. Motion agreed to 85-9: R 43-6; D 42-3 (ND 28-2, SD 14-1), Feb. 25, 1982.

	38	39	40	41	42
ALABAMA					
Denton	Y	Y	Y	Y	Y
Heflin	Y	Y	Y	Y	Y
ALASKA					
Murkowski	Y	Y	Y	Y	Y
Stevens	Y	Y	Y	Y	Y
ARIZONA					
Goldwater	Y	N	Y	?	Y
DeConcini	Y	Y	Y	Y	Y
ARKANSAS					
Bumpers	Y	N	Y	Y	Y
Pryor	Y	Y	Y	Y	Y
CALIFORNIA					
Hayakawa	Y	Y	Y	Y	Y
Cranston	Y	N	N	Y	Y
COLORADO					
Armstrong	Y	Y	Y	Y	N
Hart	Y	N	Y	Y	Y
CONNECTICUT					
Weicker	N	N	Y	Y	Y
Dodd	N	N	Y	Y	Y
DELAWARE					
Roth	Y	Y	Y	Y	Y
Biden	Y	Y	Y	Y	+
FLORIDA					
Hawkins	+	+	Y	Y	Y
Chiles	Y	Y	Y	Y	Y
GEORGIA					
Mattingly	Y	Y	Y	Y	N
Nunn	Y	Y	Y	Y	Y
HAWAII					
Inouye	Y	Y	Y	Y	Y
Matsunaga	N	N	Y	Y	Y
IDAHO					
McClure	Y	Y	Y	Y	Y
Symms	Y	Y	Y	Y	Y
ILLINOIS					
Percy	N	N	Y	Y	N
Dixon	Y	N	Y	Y	Y
INDIANA					
Lugar	Y	Y	Y	Y	Y
Quayle	Y	Y	Y	Y	N

	38	39	40	41	42
IOWA					
Grassley	Y	Y	Y	Y	Y
Jepsen	Y	Y	Y	Y	Y
KANSAS					
Dole	Y	Y	Y	Y	Y
Kassebaum	N	Y	Y	Y	Y
KENTUCKY					
Ford	Y	Y	Y	Y	Y
Huddleston	Y	Y	Y	Y	Y
LOUISIANA					
Johnston	Y	Y	N	Y	Y
Long	Y	Y	N	Y	Y
MAINE					
Cohen	N	N	Y	Y	Y
Mitchell	N	N	Y	Y	Y
MARYLAND					
Mathias	N	N	Y	Y	Y
Sarbanes	Y	N	Y	Y	Y
MASSACHUSETTS					
Kennedy	N	N	N	Y	Y
Tsongas	N	N	N	Y	Y
MICHIGAN					
Levin	Y	N	Y	Y	Y
Riegle	Y	N	N	Y	Y
MINNESOTA					
Boschwitz	N	N	Y	Y	+
Durenberger	N	N	Y	Y	Y
MISSISSIPPI					
Cochran	Y	Y	Y	Y	Y
Stennis	Y	Y	Y	Y	Y
MISSOURI					
Danforth	Y	Y	Y	Y	Y
Eagleton	Y	N	N	Y	Y
MONTANA					
Baucus	Y	N	Y	Y	Y
Melcher	Y	Y	Y	Y	Y
NEBRASKA					
Exon	Y	Y	Y	Y	Y
Zorinsky	Y	Y	Y	Y	Y
NEVADA					
Laxalt	Y	Y	Y	Y	Y
Cannon	Y	Y	Y	Y	Y

	38	39	40	41	42
NEW HAMPSHIRE					
Humphrey	Y	N	Y	Y	N
Rudman	N	Y	Y	Y	Y
NEW JERSEY					
Bradley	N	N	Y	Y	N
Williams	Y	N	Y	Y	Y
NEW MEXICO					
Domenici	Y	Y	Y	Y	Y
Schmitt	?	?	?	?	?
NEW YORK					
D'Amato	Y	Y	Y	Y	Y
Moynihan	Y	N	Y	Y	Y
NORTH CAROLINA					
East	Y	Y	Y	Y	Y
Helms	Y	Y	N	Y	Y
NORTH DAKOTA					
Andrews	Y	Y	Y	Y	Y
Burdick	Y	N	Y	Y	Y
OHIO					
Glenn	N	N	Y	Y	Y
Metzenbaum	N	N	N	Y	Y
OKLAHOMA					
Nickles	Y	Y	Y	Y	N
Boren	Y	Y	Y	Y	Y
OREGON					
Hatfield	N	N	Y	Y	Y
Packwood	N	N	Y	Y	Y
PENNSYLVANIA					
Heinz	Y	Y	Y	Y	Y
Specter	N	N	Y	Y	Y
RHODE ISLAND					
Chafee	N	N	Y	Y	Y
Pell	N	N	Y	Y	Y
SOUTH CAROLINA					
Thurmond	+	+	+	+	+
Hollings	Y	Y	Y	Y	Y
SOUTH DAKOTA					
Abdnor	Y	Y	Y	Y	Y
Pressler	Y	Y	Y	Y	Y
TENNESSEE					
Baker	Y	Y	Y	Y	Y
Sasser	Y	Y	Y	Y	Y

KEY

Y	Voted for (yea).
#	Paired for.
+	Announced for.
N	Voted against (nay).
X	Paired against.
-	Announced against.
P	Voted "present".
C	Voted "present" to avoid possible conflict of interest.
?	Did not vote or otherwise make a position known.

Democrats   *Republicans*

	38	39	40	41	42
TEXAS					
Tower	Y	Y	Y	Y	Y
Bentsen	Y	Y	Y	Y	Y
UTAH					
Garn	Y	Y	Y	Y	Y
Hatch	Y	Y	Y	Y	Y
VERMONT					
Stafford	?	?	?	?	?
Leahy	N	N	N	Y	Y
VIRGINIA					
Warner	Y	Y	Y	Y	Y
Byrd*	Y	Y	Y	Y	Y
WASHINGTON					
Gorton	Y	N	Y	Y	Y
Jackson	Y	N	Y	Y	Y
WEST VIRGINIA					
Byrd	Y	Y	N	Y	Y
Randolph	Y	Y	Y	Y	Y
WISCONSIN					
Kasten	Y	Y	Y	Y	Y
Proxmire	Y	N	N	Y	Y
WYOMING					
Simpson	+	+	+	+	+
Wallop	?	?	?	+	?

ND - Northern Democrats   SD - Southern Democrats (Southern states - Ala., Ark., Fla., Ga., Ky., La., Miss., N.C., Okla., S.C., Tenn., Texas, Va.)   *Byrd elected as an independent.

38. S 951. Department of Justice Authorization, Fiscal 1982. Heflin, D-Ala., amendment to allow the Department of Justice to participate in legal proceedings to remove or reduce the requirement of busing in existing court orders. Adopted 72-22: R 35-12; D 37-10 (ND 22-10, SD 15-0), March 2, 1982.

39. S 951. Department of Justice Authorization, Fiscal 1982. Passage of the bill to authorize funds for Department of Justice programs; to bar federal courts from ordering students bused more than five miles or 15 minutes from their homes; and to bar the Department of Justice from participating in busing litigation unless it is to reduce or remove busing requirements from existing court orders. Passed 57-37: R 34-13; D 23-24 (ND 9-23, SD 14-1), March 2, 1982.

40. Theberge Nomination. Confirmation of President Reagan's nomination of James Daniel Theberge to be U.S. ambassador to Chile. Confirmed 83-12: R 47-1; D 36-11 (ND 23-9, SD 13-2), March 2, 1982. A "yea" was a vote supporting the president's position.

41. S Res 330. Martial Law in Poland. Adoption of the resolution to call for the release by Poland's military government of Lech Walesa, leader of the Polish independent trade union federation Solidarity, held in detention since the imposition of martial law in that nation Dec. 13, 1981. Adopted 94-0: R 47-0; D 47-0 (ND 32-0, SD 15-0), March 2, 1982.

42. S 1503. Standby Petroleum Allocation Act. Adoption of the conference report on the bill to authorize the president to allocate petroleum supplies in a severe shortage. Adopted 86-7: R 41-6; D 45-1 (ND 30-1, SD 15-0), March 2, 1982. A "nay" was a vote supporting the president's position.

	43	44	45		43	44	45		43	44	45
ALABAMA				**IOWA**				**NEW HAMPSHIRE**			
Denton	Y	Y	Y	*Grassley*	Y	Y	Y	*Humphrey*	Y	Y	Y
Heflin	Y	Y	Y	*Jepsen*	Y	Y	Y	*Rudman*	Y	Y	Y
ALASKA				**KANSAS**				**NEW JERSEY**			
Murkowski	Y	Y	Y	*Dole*	Y	Y	Y	Bradley	Y	Y	Y
Stevens	Y	Y	Y	*Kassebaum*	Y	Y	?	Williams	?	Y	Y
ARIZONA				**KENTUCKY**				**NEW MEXICO**			
Goldwater	Y	N	?	Ford	Y	Y	Y	*Domenici*	Y	Y	Y
DeConcini	Y	Y	Y	Huddleston	Y	Y	Y	*Schmitt*	?	Y	Y
ARKANSAS				**LOUISIANA**				**NEW YORK**			
Bumpers	Y	Y	Y	Johnston	Y	Y	Y	*D'Amato*	Y	Y	Y
Pryor	Y	Y	Y	Long	Y	Y	Y	Moynihan	Y	Y	Y
CALIFORNIA				**MAINE**				**NORTH CAROLINA**			
Hayakawa	Y	Y	Y	*Cohen*	Y	Y	Y	*East*	Y	Y	Y
Cranston	Y	Y	Y	Mitchell	Y	Y	Y	*Helms*	Y	Y	Y
COLORADO				**MARYLAND**				**NORTH DAKOTA**			
Armstrong	Y	Y	Y	*Mathias*	Y	Y	Y	*Andrews*	Y	Y	Y
Hart	Y	Y	Y	Sarbanes	Y	Y	Y	Burdick	Y	Y	Y
CONNECTICUT				**MASSACHUSETTS**				**OHIO**			
Weicker	Y	Y	Y	Kennedy	Y	Y	Y	Glenn	Y	Y	Y
Dodd	Y	Y	Y	Tsongas	Y	Y	Y	Metzenbaum	Y	Y	Y
DELAWARE				**MICHIGAN**				**OKLAHOMA**			
Roth	Y	Y	Y	Levin	Y	Y	Y	*Nickles*	Y	Y	Y
Biden	Y	Y	Y	Riegle	Y	Y	Y	Boren	Y	Y	Y
FLORIDA				**MINNESOTA**				**OREGON**			
Hawkins	Y	Y	Y	*Boschwitz*	Y	Y	Y	*Hatfield*	Y	Y	Y
Chiles	Y	Y	Y	*Durenberger*	Y	Y	Y	*Packwood*	Y	Y	Y
GEORGIA				**MISSISSIPPI**				**PENNSYLVANIA**			
Mattingly	Y	Y	Y	*Cochran*	Y	Y	Y	*Heinz*	Y	Y	Y
Nunn	Y	Y	Y	Stennis	Y	Y	Y	*Specter*	Y	Y	Y
HAWAII				**MISSOURI**				**RHODE ISLAND**			
Inouye	Y	Y	Y	*Danforth*	Y	Y	Y	*Chafee*	Y	Y	Y
Matsunaga	Y	Y	Y	Eagleton	Y	Y	?	Pell	Y	Y	Y
IDAHO				**MONTANA**				**SOUTH CAROLINA**			
McClure	Y	Y	Y	Baucus	Y	Y	Y	*Thurmond*	+	?	?
Symms	?	Y	Y	Melcher	Y	Y	Y	Hollings	Y	Y	Y
ILLINOIS				**NEBRASKA**				**SOUTH DAKOTA**			
Percy	Y	Y	Y	Exon	Y	Y	Y	*Abdnor*	Y	Y	Y
Dixon	Y	Y	Y	Zorinsky	Y	Y	Y	*Pressler*	Y	Y	Y
INDIANA				**NEVADA**				**TENNESSEE**			
Lugar	Y	Y	Y	*Laxalt*	Y	Y	Y	*Baker*	Y	Y	Y
Quayle	Y	N	N	Cannon	Y	Y	Y	Sasser	Y	Y	Y

	43	44	45
TEXAS			
Tower	Y	Y	Y
Bentsen	Y	Y	?
UTAH			
Garn	Y	Y	Y
Hatch	Y	Y	Y
VERMONT			
Stafford	Y	Y	Y
Leahy	Y	Y	Y
VIRGINIA			
Warner	Y	Y	Y
Byrd*	Y	Y	Y
WASHINGTON			
Gorton	Y	Y	Y
Jackson	Y	Y	Y
WEST VIRGINIA			
Byrd	Y	Y	Y
Randolph	Y	Y	Y
WISCONSIN			
Kasten	Y	Y	Y
Proxmire	Y	Y	N
WYOMING			
Simpson	Y	?	?
Wallop	Y	Y	Y

ND - Northern Democrats   SD - Southern Democrats (Southern states - Ala., Ark., Fla., Ga., Ky., La., Miss., N.C., Okla., S.C., Tenn., Texas, Va.)

*Byrd elected as an independent.

43. S J Res 142. Afghanistan Day. Passage of the joint resolution to request the president to proclaim March 21, 1982, as "Afghanistan Day" to commemorate the struggle of the people of Afghanistan against the occupation of their country by Soviet forces. Passed 96-0: R 50-0; D 46-0 (ND 31-0, SD 15-0), March 3, 1982.

44. S Res 204. Harrison A. Williams Jr. Expulsion. Baker, R-Tenn., motion to instruct the sergeant-at-arms to compel the attendance of absent senators. Motion agreed to 96-2: R 49-2; D 47-0 (ND 32-0, SD 15-0), March 4, 1982.

45. S Res 204. Harrison A. Williams Jr. Expulsion. Baker, R-Tenn., motion to instruct the sergeant-at-arms to compel the attendance of absent senators. Motion agreed to 92-2: R 48-1; D 44-1 (ND 30-1, SD 14-0), March 4, 1982.

	46	47	48	49	50	51
ALABAMA						
Denton	Y	Y	Y	Y	Y	Y
Heflin	Y	Y	Y	Y	Y	Y
ALASKA						
Murkowski	Y	Y	Y	Y	Y	Y
Stevens	Y	Y	Y	Y	Y	Y
ARIZONA						
Goldwater	N	?	N	N	N	N
DeConcini	Y	Y	Y	Y	Y	Y
ARKANSAS						
Bumpers	Y	Y	Y	Y	Y	Y
Pryor	Y	Y	Y	Y	Y	Y
CALIFORNIA						
Hayakawa	Y	Y	Y	Y	Y	Y
Cranston	Y	Y	Y	Y	Y	Y
COLORADO						
Armstrong	Y	Y	Y	Y	Y	Y
Hart	Y	Y	Y	Y	Y	Y
CONNECTICUT						
Weicker	Y	Y	Y	Y	Y	Y
Dodd	?	?	Y	Y	Y	Y
DELAWARE						
Roth	Y	Y	Y	Y	Y	Y
Biden	Y	Y	Y	Y	Y	Y
FLORIDA						
Hawkins	Y	Y	Y	Y	Y	Y
Chiles	Y	Y	Y	Y	Y	Y
GEORGIA						
Mattingly	Y	Y	Y	Y	Y	Y
Nunn	Y	Y	Y	Y	Y	Y
HAWAII						
Inouye	Y	Y	Y	Y	Y	Y
Matsunaga	Y	Y	Y	Y	Y	Y
IDAHO						
McClure	Y	Y	Y	Y	Y	Y
Symms	Y	Y	Y	Y	Y	Y
ILLINOIS						
Percy	Y	Y	Y	Y	Y	Y
Dixon	Y	Y	Y	Y	Y	Y
INDIANA						
Lugar	Y	Y	Y	Y	Y	Y
Quayle	N	N	N	N	N	N

	46	47	48	49	50	51
IOWA						
Grassley	Y	Y	Y	Y	?	Y
Jepsen	?	Y	Y	Y	Y	Y
KANSAS						
Dole	Y	Y	Y	Y	?	Y
Kassebaum	Y	Y	Y	?	?	Y
KENTUCKY						
Ford	Y	Y	Y	Y	Y	Y
Huddleston	?	?	Y	Y	Y	Y
LOUISIANA						
Johnston	Y	Y	N	?	Y	Y
Long	Y	N	N	Y	N	N
MAINE						
Cohen	Y	Y	Y	Y	Y	Y
Mitchell	?	?	Y	Y	Y	Y
MARYLAND						
Mathias	Y	Y	Y	Y	Y	Y
Sarbanes	Y	Y	Y	Y	?	Y
MASSACHUSETTS						
Kennedy	Y	Y	Y	Y	Y	Y
Tsongas	Y	Y	Y	Y	Y	Y
MICHIGAN						
Levin	Y	Y	Y	Y	Y	Y
Riegle	?	?	Y	Y	Y	Y
MINNESOTA						
Boschwitz	Y	Y	Y	Y	Y	Y
Durenberger	?	?	Y	Y	Y	Y
MISSISSIPPI						
Cochran	Y	Y	Y	Y	Y	Y
Stennis	Y	Y	Y	Y	Y	Y
MISSOURI						
Danforth	Y	Y	Y	Y	Y	Y
Eagleton	Y	Y	Y	Y	Y	Y
MONTANA						
Baucus	Y	Y	Y	Y	Y	Y
Melcher	Y	Y	Y	Y	Y	Y
NEBRASKA						
Exon	Y	Y	Y	Y	Y	Y
Zorinsky	Y	Y	Y	?	?	?
NEVADA						
Laxalt	Y	Y	Y	Y	Y	Y
Cannon	Y	Y	Y	Y	Y	Y

	46	47	48	49	50	51
NEW HAMPSHIRE						
Humphrey	Y	Y	Y	Y	Y	Y
Rudman	Y	Y	Y	Y	Y	Y
NEW JERSEY						
Bradley	Y	Y	Y	Y	Y	Y
Williams	Y	Y	Y	Y	Y	Y
NEW MEXICO						
Domenici	Y	Y	Y	Y	Y	Y
Schmitt	Y	Y	Y	Y	Y	Y
NEW YORK						
D'Amato	?	?	Y	Y	Y	Y
Moynihan	Y	Y	Y	Y	Y	Y
NORTH CAROLINA						
East	Y	Y	Y	Y	Y	Y
Helms	Y	Y	Y	Y	Y	Y
NORTH DAKOTA						
Andrews	Y	Y	Y	Y	Y	Y
Burdick	Y	Y	Y	Y	Y	Y
OHIO						
Glenn	Y	Y	Y	Y	Y	Y
Metzenbaum	Y	Y	Y	Y	Y	Y
OKLAHOMA						
Nickles	Y	Y	Y	Y	Y	Y
Boren	Y	Y	Y	Y	Y	Y
OREGON						
Hatfield	Y	Y	Y	Y	Y	Y
Packwood	Y	Y	Y	Y	Y	Y
PENNSYLVANIA						
Heinz	Y	Y	Y	Y	Y	Y
Specter	Y	Y	Y	Y	Y	Y
RHODE ISLAND						
Chafee	Y	Y	Y	Y	Y	Y
Pell	Y	Y	Y	Y	Y	Y
SOUTH CAROLINA						
Thurmond	Y	Y	Y	Y	?	Y
Hollings	Y	Y	Y	Y	Y	Y
SOUTH DAKOTA						
Abdnor	Y	Y	Y	Y	Y	Y
Pressler	Y	Y	Y	Y	Y	Y
TENNESSEE						
Baker	Y	Y	Y	Y	Y	Y
Sasser	Y	Y	Y	Y	Y	Y

	46	47	48	49	50	51
TEXAS						
Tower	Y	Y	Y	?	Y	Y
Bentsen	Y	Y	Y	Y	Y	Y
UTAH						
Garn	Y	Y	Y	Y	Y	Y
Hatch	Y	Y	?	Y	Y	Y
VERMONT						
Stafford	Y	Y	Y	Y	Y	Y
Leahy	Y	Y	Y	Y	Y	Y
VIRGINIA						
Warner	Y	Y	Y	Y	Y	Y
Byrd*	Y	Y	Y	Y	Y	Y
WASHINGTON						
Gorton	Y	Y	Y	Y	Y	Y
Jackson	Y	Y	Y	Y	Y	Y
WEST VIRGINIA						
Byrd	Y	Y	Y	Y	Y	Y
Randolph	Y	Y	Y	Y	Y	Y
WISCONSIN						
Kasten	Y	Y	Y	Y	Y	Y
Proxmire	N	N	N	N	N	N
WYOMING						
Simpson	Y	Y	Y	Y	Y	Y
Wallop	Y	Y	Y	Y	Y	Y

KEY

Y Voted for (yea).
\# Paired for.
\+ Announced for.
N Voted against (nay).
X Paired against.
- Announced against.
P Voted "present".
C Voted "present" to avoid possible conflict of interest.
? Did not vote or otherwise make a position known.

Democrats   *Republicans*

ND - Northern Democrats   SD - Southern Democrats (Southern states - Ala., Ark., Fla., Ga., Ky., La., Miss., N.C., Okla., S.C., Tenn., Texas, Va.)   * Byrd elected as an independent.

---

46. S Res 204. Harrison A. Williams Jr. Expulsion. Baker, R-Tenn., motion to instruct the sergeant-at-arms to require the attendance of absent senators. Motion agreed to 90-3: R 48-2; D 42-1 (ND 28-1, SD 14-0), March 8, 1982.

47. S Res 204. Harrison A. Williams Jr. Expulsion. Baker, R-Tenn., motion to instruct the sergeant-at-arms to compel the attendance of absent senators. Motion agreed to 90-3: R 49-1; D 41-2 (ND 28-1, SD 13-1), March 8, 1982.

48. S Res 204. Harrison A. Williams Jr. Expulsion. Baker, R-Tenn., motion to instruct the sergeant-at-arms to compel the attendance of absent senators. Motion agreed to 94-5: R 50-2; D 44-3 (ND 31-1, SD 13-2), March 9, 1982.

49. S Res 204. Harrison A. Williams Jr. Expulsion. Stevens, R-Alaska, motion to instruct the sergeant-at-arms to compel the attendance of absent senators. Motion agreed to 93-3: R 49-2; D 44-1 (ND 30-1, SD 14-0), March 10, 1982.

50. S Res 204. Harrison A. Williams Jr. Expulsion. Baker, R-Tenn., motion to instruct the sergeant-at-arms to compel the attendance of absent senators. Motion agreed to 90-4: R 47-2; D 43-2 (ND 29-1, SD 14-1), March 10, 1982.

51. S Res 204. Harrison A. Williams Jr. Expulsion. Baker, R-Tenn., motion to instruct the sergeant-at-arms to compel the attendance of absent senators. Motion agreed to 95-4: R 51-2; D 44-2 (ND 30-1, SD 14-1), March 10, 1982.

	52		52		52
ALABAMA		**IOWA**		**NEW HAMPSHIRE**	
Denton	Y	*Grassley*	Y	*Humphrey*	Y
Heflin	Y	*Jepsen*	Y	*Rudman*	Y
ALASKA		**KANSAS**		**NEW JERSEY**	
Murkowski	Y	*Dole*	Y	Bradley	Y
Stevens	Y	*Kassebaum*	Y	Williams	Y
ARIZONA		**KENTUCKY**		**NEW MEXICO**	
Goldwater	N	Ford	Y	*Domenici*	Y
DeConcini	Y	Huddleston	Y	*Schmitt*	Y
ARKANSAS		**LOUISIANA**		**NEW YORK**	
Bumpers	Y	Johnston	Y	*D'Amato*	Y
Pryor	Y	Long	Y	Moynihan	Y
CALIFORNIA		**MAINE**		**NORTH CAROLINA**	
Hayakawa	Y	*Cohen*	Y	*East*	Y
Cranston	Y	Mitchell	Y	*Helms*	Y
COLORADO		**MARYLAND**		**NORTH DAKOTA**	
Armstrong	Y	*Mathias*	Y	*Andrews*	Y
Hart	Y	Sarbanes	Y	Burdick	Y
CONNECTICUT		**MASSACHUSETTS**		**OHIO**	
Weicker	Y	Kennedy	Y	Glenn	Y
Dodd	Y	Tsongas	Y	Metzenbaum	Y
DELAWARE		**MICHIGAN**		**OKLAHOMA**	
Roth	Y	Levin	Y	*Nickles*	Y
Biden	Y	Riegle	Y	Boren	Y
FLORIDA		**MINNESOTA**		**OREGON**	
Hawkins	Y	*Boschwitz*	Y	*Hatfield*	Y
Chiles	Y	*Durenberger*	Y	*Packwood*	Y
GEORGIA		**MISSISSIPPI**		**PENNSYLVANIA**	
Mattingly	Y	*Cochran*	Y	*Heinz*	Y
Nunn	Y	Stennis	Y	*Specter*	Y
HAWAII		**MISSOURI**		**RHODE ISLAND**	
Inouye	Y	*Danforth*	Y	*Chafee*	Y
Matsunaga	Y	Eagleton	Y	Pell	Y
IDAHO		**MONTANA**		**SOUTH CAROLINA**	
McClure	Y	Baucus	Y	*Thurmond*	Y
Symms	Y	Melcher	Y	Hollings	Y
ILLINOIS		**NEBRASKA**		**SOUTH DAKOTA**	
Percy	Y	Exon	Y	*Abdnor*	Y
Dixon	Y	Zorinsky	Y	*Pressler*	Y
INDIANA		**NEVADA**		**TENNESSEE**	
Lugar	Y	*Laxalt*	Y	*Baker*	Y
Quayle	N	Cannon	Y	Sasser	Y

KEY

Y	Voted for (yea).
#	Paired for.
+	Announced for.
N	Voted against (nay).
X	Paired against.
-	Announced against.
P	Voted "present".
C	Voted "present" to avoid possible conflict of interest.
?	Did not vote or otherwise make a position known.

Democrats *Republicans*

	52
TEXAS	
Tower	Y
Bentsen	Y
UTAH	
Garn	Y
Hatch	Y
VERMONT	
Stafford	Y
Leahy	Y
VIRGINIA	
Warner	Y
Byrd*	Y
WASHINGTON	
Gorton	Y
Jackson	Y
WEST VIRGINIA	
Byrd	Y
Randolph	Y
WISCONSIN	
Kasten	Y
Proxmire	N
WYOMING	
Simpson	Y
Wallop	Y

ND - Northern Democrats   SD - Southern Democrats (Southern states - Ala., Ark., Fla., Ga., Ky., La., Miss., N.C., Okla., S.C., Tenn., Texas, Va.)

*Byrd elected as an independent.

52. S Res 204. Harrison A. Williams Jr. Expulsion. Baker, R-Tenn., motion to instruct the sergeant-at-arms to require the attendance of absent senators. Motion agreed to 97-3: R 51-2; D 46-1 (ND 31-1, SD 15-0), March 11, 1982.

	53 54 55 56		53 54 55 56		53 54 55 56	KEY
ALABAMA		**IOWA**		**NEW HAMPSHIRE**		Y Voted for (yea).
Denton	Y N Y Y	*Grassley*	Y N Y Y	*Humphrey*	Y N Y Y	# Paired for.
Heflin	Y N Y Y	*Jepsen*	Y N Y Y	*Rudman*	Y N Y Y	+ Announced for.
ALASKA		**KANSAS**		**NEW JERSEY**		N Voted against (nay).
Murkowski	Y N Y Y	*Dole*	Y N Y Y	Bradley	N Y N Y	X Paired against.
Stevens	Y N Y Y	*Kassebaum*	Y N Y Y	Vacancy **		- Announced against.
ARIZONA		**KENTUCKY**		**NEW MEXICO**		P Voted "present".
Goldwater	Y N Y Y	Ford	N Y Y Y	*Domenici*	Y N Y Y	C Voted "present" to avoid possible conflict of interest.
DeConcini	N Y Y Y	Huddleston	N Y Y Y	*Schmitt*	Y N Y ?	? Did not vote or otherwise make a position known.
ARKANSAS		**LOUISIANA**		**NEW YORK**		
Bumpers	Y N Y Y	Johnston	Y N Y Y	*D'Amato*	? N Y Y	*Democrats Republicans*
Pryor	Y N Y Y	Long	Y ? ? ?	Moynihan	N Y N Y	
CALIFORNIA		**MAINE**		**NORTH CAROLINA**		
Hayakawa	Y N Y Y	*Cohen*	N Y Y Y	*East*	Y N Y Y	
Cranston	N Y N Y	Mitchell	N Y Y Y	*Helms*	Y N Y Y	
COLORADO		**MARYLAND**		**NORTH DAKOTA**		
Armstrong	Y N Y Y	*Mathias*	N ? ? ?	*Andrews*	Y N Y Y	
Hart	N Y N Y	Sarbanes	N Y Y Y	Burdick	Y N Y Y	
CONNECTICUT		**MASSACHUSETTS**		**OHIO**		53 54 55 56
Weicker	N Y Y Y	Kennedy	N Y Y Y	Glenn	Y N Y Y	
Dodd	N Y Y Y	Tsongas	N Y Y Y	Metzenbaum	N Y Y Y	**TEXAS**
DELAWARE		**MICHIGAN**		**OKLAHOMA**		*Tower* Y N Y Y
Roth	N Y Y Y	Levin	N Y Y ?	*Nickles*	Y N Y Y	Bentsen N N N Y
Biden	N Y N Y	Riegle	N Y Y Y	Boren	Y N Y Y	**UTAH**
FLORIDA		**MINNESOTA**		**OREGON**		*Garn* Y N Y Y
Hawkins	Y N Y Y	*Boschwitz*	Y N Y Y	*Hatfield*	N Y Y Y	*Hatch* Y N Y Y
Chiles	Y N Y Y	*Durenberger*	Y N Y Y-	*Packwood*	N Y Y Y	**VERMONT**
GEORGIA		**MISSISSIPPI**		**PENNSYLVANIA**		*Stafford* N Y Y Y
Mattingly	Y N Y Y	*Cochran*	Y N Y Y	*Heinz*	Y N Y Y	Leahy N Y Y Y
Nunn	Y N Y Y	Stennis	Y N Y Y	*Specter*	N Y Y Y	**VIRGINIA**
HAWAII		**MISSOURI**		**RHODE ISLAND**		*Warner* Y N Y Y
Inouye	N N Y Y	*Danforth*	Y N Y Y	*Chafee*	Y N Y Y	Byrd* Y N Y Y
Matsunaga	N Y Y Y	Eagleton	N Y Y Y	Pell	? N Y Y	**WASHINGTON**
IDAHO		**MONTANA**		**SOUTH CAROLINA**		*Gorton* N Y Y Y
McClure	Y N Y Y	Baucus	N Y Y Y	*Thurmond*	Y N Y Y	Jackson Y N Y Y
Symms	Y N Y Y	Melcher	N Y Y Y	Hollings	? Y Y Y	**WEST VIRGINIA**
ILLINOIS		**NEBRASKA**		**SOUTH DAKOTA**		Byrd N Y Y Y
Percy	Y N Y Y	Exon	N Y Y Y	*Abdnor*	Y N Y Y	Randolph N Y Y Y
Dixon	N N Y Y	Zorinsky	Y N Y Y	*Pressler*	? Y N Y	**WISCONSIN**
INDIANA		**NEVADA**		**TENNESSEE**		*Kasten* Y N Y Y
Lugar	Y N Y Y	*Laxalt*	Y N Y Y	*Baker*	Y N Y Y	Proxmire N Y Y Y
Quayle	N Y Y Y	Cannon	? ? ? +	Sasser	N Y Y Y	**WYOMING**
						Simpson Y N Y Y
						Wallop Y N Y Y

ND - Northern Democrats   SD - Southern Democrats (Southern states - Ala., Ark., Fla., Ga., Ky., La., Miss., N.C., Okla., S.C., Tenn., Texas, Va.)

*Byrd elected as an independent.
** Sen. Harrison A. Williams Jr., D-N.J., resigned March 11, 1982. The last vote for which he was eligible was CQ vote 52.

53. S 391. Intelligence Identities Protection Act. Chafee, R-R.I., amendment to provide that private persons can be convicted of criminally exposing U.S. secret agents if they had "reason to believe" their acts would harm U.S. intelligence, as opposed to having an "intent" to harm U.S. intelligence. Adopted 55-39: R 41-10; D 14-29 (ND 4-25, SD 10-4), March 17, 1982. A "yea" was a vote supporting the president's position.

54. S 391. Intelligence Identities Protection Act. Bradley, D-N.J., amendment to narrow the definition of "pattern of activities" intended to identify and expose covert intelligence agents, for which a person could be prosecuted under the bill. The amendment would have required that "the main direction" of the pattern of activities "must be to identify and expose covert agents." Rejected 37-59: R 10-42; D 27-17 (ND 23-7, SD 4-10), March 18, 1982.

55. HR 4. Intelligence Identities Protection Act. Passage of the bill to make it a felony to publicly expose the identities of U.S. covert intelligence officers, agents, informants and sources. Passed 90-6: R 51-1; D 39-5 (ND 25-5, SD 14-0), March 18, 1982. A "yea" was a vote supporting the president's position.

56. S Res 344. Importation of Libyan Oil. Adoption of the resolution stating the sense of the Senate in support of the president's decision to prohibit future imports of oil from Libya. Adopted 94-0: R 51-0; D 43-0 (ND 29-0, SD 14-0), March 18, 1982.

	57 58 59 60 61 62 63		57 58 59 60 61 62 63		57 58 59 60 61 62 63	KEY
ALABAMA		**IOWA**		**NEW HAMPSHIRE**		Y Voted for (yea).
Denton	N Y N Y Y Y N	*Grassley*	N Y N Y Y Y Y	*Humphrey*	N Y N Y Y Y N	# Paired for.
Heflin	N Y N N Y Y N	*Jepsen*	N Y N Y Y Y Y	*Rudman*	N Y Y Y Y Y Y	+ Announced for.
ALASKA		**KANSAS**		**NEW JERSEY**		N Voted against (nay).
Murkowski	N Y N Y Y Y N	*Dole*	N Y N Y Y Y N	Bradley	N Y Y Y Y Y N	X Paired against.
Stevens	N Y N Y Y Y N	*Kassebaum*	Y N N Y Y Y N	Vacancy		- Announced against.
ARIZONA		**KENTUCKY**		**NEW MEXICO**		P Voted "present".
Goldwater	N Y N Y ? Y N	Ford	Y N Y Y Y Y Y	*Domenici*	N Y N Y Y Y Y	C Voted "present" to avoid possi-
DeConcini	N Y N Y Y Y Y	Huddleston	N Y Y Y Y Y Y	*Schmitt*	N Y N Y Y Y N	ble conflict of interest.
ARKANSAS		**LOUISIANA**		**NEW YORK**		? Did not vote or otherwise make a
Bumpers	# X N Y ? Y Y	Johnston	N Y N Y Y Y Y	*D'Amato*	N Y ? Y Y Y N	position known.
Pryor	N Y Y Y Y Y Y	Long	? ? ? ? ? ? ?	Moynihan	N Y Y Y Y Y +	
CALIFORNIA		**MAINE**		**NORTH CAROLINA**		Democrats *Republicans*
Hayakawa	N Y N N Y Y N	*Cohen*	N Y Y Y Y Y Y	*East*	N Y N Y Y Y N	
Cranston	N Y Y Y Y Y Y	Mitchell	N Y N Y Y Y Y	*Helms*	N Y N Y Y Y N	
COLORADO		**MARYLAND**		**NORTH DAKOTA**		57 58 59 60 61 62 63
Armstrong	N Y N Y Y Y N	*Mathias*	Y N Y N Y Y N	Andrews	N Y ? Y Y Y Y	
Hart	Y N N Y Y Y Y	Sarbanes	Y N Y N Y Y Y	Burdick	N Y Y Y Y Y Y	
CONNECTICUT		**MASSACHUSETTS**		**OHIO**		**TEXAS**
Weicker	Y N N Y Y Y Y	Kennedy	Y N Y Y Y Y Y	Glenn	N Y Y Y Y Y Y	*Tower*	N Y N Y Y Y N
Dodd	N Y Y N Y Y Y	Tsongas	Y N Y Y Y Y Y	Metzenbaum	Y N Y Y Y Y Y	Bentsen	N Y N Y Y Y N
DELAWARE		**MICHIGAN**		**OKLAHOMA**		**UTAH**
Roth	? Y N Y Y Y Y	Levin	N Y Y Y Y Y Y	*Nickles*	N Y N Y Y Y N	*Garn*	N Y N Y Y Y Y
Biden	Y N N Y Y Y Y	Riegle	X # ? Y Y Y Y	Boren	N Y N Y Y Y N	*Hatch*	N Y N Y Y Y N
FLORIDA		**MINNESOTA**		**OREGON**		**VERMONT**
Hawkins	N Y N Y Y Y Y	*Boschwitz*	N Y N Y Y Y N	*Hatfield*	Y N N Y Y Y Y	*Stafford*	N N N Y Y Y N
Chiles	N Y N Y Y Y Y	*Durenberger*	N Y Y Y Y Y Y	*Packwood*	N N N Y Y Y N	Leahy	Y N N Y Y Y Y
GEORGIA		**MISSISSIPPI**		**PENNSYLVANIA**		**VIRGINIA**
Mattingly	N Y N Y Y Y N	*Cochran*	N Y N ? ? ? ?	Heinz	Y N ? Y Y Y N	*Warner*	N Y N Y Y Y N
Nunn	N Y N Y Y Y Y	Stennis	Y N N Y Y Y Y	*Specter*	N Y N Y Y Y N	Byrd*	N Y N Y Y Y Y
HAWAII		**MISSOURI**		**RHODE ISLAND**		**WASHINGTON**
Inouye	N Y Y ? ? ? ?	*Danforth*	Y N Y Y Y Y Y	*Chafee*	Y N N ? ? ? Y	*Gorton*	Y N Y Y Y Y Y
Matsunaga	N Y Y N ? Y Y	Eagleton	Y N Y Y Y Y Y	Pell	+ - + N Y Y	Jackson	Y N Y Y Y Y Y
IDAHO		**MONTANA**		**SOUTH CAROLINA**		**WEST VIRGINIA**
McClure	N Y N Y Y Y Y	Baucus	N Y N Y Y Y Y	*Thurmond*	N Y N Y Y Y N	Byrd	N Y N Y Y Y Y
Symms	N Y N Y Y Y Y	Melcher	N Y N Y Y Y Y	Hollings	Y N Y Y Y Y Y	Randolph	Y N Y Y Y Y Y
ILLINOIS		**NEBRASKA**		**SOUTH DAKOTA**		**WISCONSIN**
Percy	Y N N Y Y Y N	Exon	N Y N Y Y Y Y	*Abdnor*	N Y N N Y Y N	*Kasten*	N Y N Y Y Y N
Dixon	N Y N Y Y Y Y	Zorinsky	N Y N Y Y Y Y	*Pressler*	N Y N N Y Y N	Proxmire	Y N Y Y Y Y Y
INDIANA		**NEVADA**		**TENNESSEE**		**WYOMING**
Lugar	N Y N Y Y Y N	*Laxalt*	N Y N Y Y Y N	*Baker*	N Y N Y Y Y N	*Simpson*	N Y N Y Y Y N
Quayle	N Y N Y Y Y N	Cannon	+ - ? ? ? + +	Sasser	N Y N Y Y Y Y	*Wallop*	N Y N Y Y Y N

ND - Northern Democrats   SD - Southern Democrats (Southern states - Ala., Ark., Fla., Ga., Ky., La., Miss., N.C., Okla., S.C., Tenn., Texas, Va.)   *Byrd elected as an independent.

57. S 1080. Regulatory Reform Act. Danforth, R-Mo., motion to table (kill) the Schmitt, R-N.M., amendment to give Congress a two-house legislative veto over federal agency regulations. Motion rejected 23-70: R 9-43; D 14-27 (ND 11-17, SD 3-10), March 23, 1982. A "yea" was a vote supporting the president's position.

58. S 1080. Regulatory Reform Act. Schmitt, R-N.M., amendment to give Congress a two-house legislative veto over federal agency regulations. Adopted 69-25: R 42-11; D 27-14 (ND 17-11, SD 10-3), March 23, 1982. A "nay" was a vote supporting the president's position.

59. S 1080. Regulatory Reform Act. Eagleton, D-Mo., amendment to prevent judicial review of an agency's designation of whether a rule is "major" under the test that it must have a $100 million annual impact on the economy. Rejected 27-65: R 6-44; D 21-21 (ND 17-11, SD 4-10), March 23, 1982. A "nay" was a vote supporting the president's position.

60. S 1080. Regulatory Reform Act. Laxalt, R-Nev., motion to table (kill) the Pressler, R-S.D., amendment to exempt federal buildings containing U.S. court facilities from regulations on the acquisition of products and services needed by the government. Motion agreed to 85-9: R 47-4; D 38-5 (ND 25-4, SD 13-1), March 24, 1982.

61. S 1080. Regulatory Reform Act. Levin, D-Mich., amendment to require that changes in proposed regulations resulting from Office of Management and Budget intervention be noted by the affected agency in the public rule-making file. Adopted 92-0: R 50-0; D 42-0 (ND 29-0, SD 13-0), March 24, 1982.

62. S 1080. Regulatory Reform Act. Passage of the bill to modify federal regulatory procedures by requiring federal agencies to analyze the costs and benefits of rules, and altering the role of Congress, the president and the courts in the federal rule-making process. Passed 94-0: R 51-0; D 43-0 (ND 29-0, SD 14-0), March 24, 1982. A "yea" was a vote supporting the president's position.

63. S 1503. Standby Petroleum Allocation Act. Passage, over President Reagan's March 20 veto, of the bill to authorize the president to allocate petroleum supplies in a severe shortage. Rejected 58-36: R 20-32; D 38-4 (ND 27-1, SD 11-3), March 24, 1982. A two-thirds majority of those present and voting (63 in this case) of both houses is required to override a veto. A "nay" was a vote supporting the president's position.

CQ Senate Votes 64 - 71

Corresponding to Congressional Record Votes 64, 65, 66, 67, 68, 69, 70, 71

	64	65	66	67	68	69	70	71
ALABAMA								
Denton	N	Y	N	Y	N	N	Y	Y
Heflin	N	Y	N	N	N	N	N	Y
ALASKA								
Murkowski	Y	Y	N	Y	N	Y	Y	Y
Stevens	Y	Y	Y	Y	Y	Y	Y	Y
ARIZONA								
Goldwater	N	Y	Y	N	?	?	?	N
DeConcini	Y	Y	N	N	N	N	Y	Y
ARKANSAS								
Bumpers	Y	Y	N	N	N	N	N	Y
Pryor	Y	Y	N	N	N	N	Y	Y
CALIFORNIA								
Hayakawa	Y	Y	Y	Y	Y	Y	Y	Y
Cranston	Y	Y	Y	N	Y	Y	Y	Y
COLORADO								
Armstrong	Y	Y	N	N	N	N	N	Y
Hart	Y	Y	N	N	N	N	Y	Y
CONNECTICUT								
Weicker	Y	Y	N	Y	N	Y	N	Y
Dodd	Y	Y	Y	Y	Y	Y	Y	Y
DELAWARE								
Roth	Y	Y	N	N	Y	N	Y	Y
Biden	Y	Y	N	N	N	Y	N	Y
FLORIDA								
Hawkins	Y	Y	N	N	Y	N	N	Y
Chiles	Y	Y	N	N	N	N	Y	Y
GEORGIA								
Mattingly	Y	Y	N	Y	N	Y	Y	Y
Nunn	Y	Y	N	N	N	Y	Y	Y
HAWAII								
Inouye	Y	Y	Y	Y	N	Y	Y	Y
Matsunaga	Y	Y	N	Y	N	N	N	?
IDAHO								
McClure	Y	Y	Y	Y	N	N	N	Y
Symms	Y	Y	Y	Y	N	N	N	Y
ILLINOIS								
Percy	Y	Y	N	N	N	N	N	Y
Dixon	Y	Y	N	N	N	N	Y	Y
INDIANA								
Lugar	Y	Y	N	Y	N	N	Y	Y
Quayle	Y	Y	N	Y	N	N	N	N

	64	65	66	67	68	69	70	71
IOWA								
Grassley	Y	Y	N	N	N	N	N	Y
Jepsen	Y	Y	N	N	N	N	N	Y
KANSAS								
Dole	Y	Y	Y	Y	Y	Y	Y	Y
Kassebaum	Y	Y	N	N	N	N	Y	?
KENTUCKY								
Ford	Y	Y	N	N	N	N	N	Y
Huddleston	Y	Y	N	Y	N	Y	Y	Y
LOUISIANA								
Johnston	Y	Y	N	N	N	N	N	Y
Long	Y	Y	N	N	N	N	N	N
MAINE								
Cohen	Y	Y	N	N	N	N	Y	Y
Mitchell	Y	Y	N	N	N	N	Y	Y
MARYLAND								
Mathias	Y	Y	N	N	N	N	N	Y
Sarbanes	Y	Y	N	N	N	N	Y	?
MASSACHUSETTS								
Kennedy	Y	Y	N	N	N	N	Y	Y
Tsongas	Y	Y	Y	Y	N	Y	Y	Y
MICHIGAN								
Levin	Y	Y	N	N	N	N	Y	Y
Riegle	Y	Y	-	-	?	N	Y	Y
MINNESOTA								
Boschwitz	Y	Y	N	N	Y	N	N	Y
Durenberger	Y	Y	N	N	N	N	N	Y
MISSISSIPPI								
Cochran	Y	Y	N	Y	N	N	N	Y
Stennis	Y	Y	N	N	N	N	N	Y
MISSOURI								
Danforth	Y	Y	N	N	N	N	N	Y
Eagleton	Y	Y	N	N	N	N	N	Y
MONTANA								
Baucus	Y	Y	N	Y	N	Y	Y	Y
Melcher	Y	Y	N	N	N	N	Y	Y
NEBRASKA								
Exon	Y	Y	N	N	N	N	N	Y
Zorinsky	Y	Y	N	N	N	N	N	Y
NEVADA								
Laxalt	Y	Y	Y	Y	Y	Y	N	Y
Cannon	Y	Y	N	N	N	Y	Y	Y

	64	65	66	67	68	69	70	71
NEW HAMPSHIRE								
Humphrey	Y	Y	N	Y	N	Y	Y	Y
Rudman	Y	Y	Y	Y	N	Y	Y	Y
NEW JERSEY								
Bradley	Y	Y	N	N	N	N	N	Y
Vacancy								
NEW MEXICO								
Domenici	Y	Y	N	N	N	Y	N	Y
Schmitt	?	+	?	?	?	N	Y	Y
NEW YORK								
D'Amato	Y	Y	N	Y	Y	Y	N	Y
Moynihan	Y	Y	N	N	Y	Y	Y	Y
NORTH CAROLINA								
East	N	Y	N	N	N	N	N	Y
Helms	N	Y	N	Y	N	Y	N	Y
NORTH DAKOTA								
Andrews	Y	Y	N	Y	Y	N	Y	Y
Burdick	Y	Y	N	N	N	N	Y	Y
OHIO								
Glenn	Y	Y	N	N	N	N	N	Y
Metzenbaum	Y	Y	N	N	N	N	N	Y
OKLAHOMA								
Nickles	N	Y	N	N	N	Y	N	Y
Boren	Y	Y	N	N	N	N	Y	Y
OREGON								
Hatfield	Y	Y	Y	N	N	N	N	Y
Packwood	Y	Y	Y	Y	Y	N	N	Y
PENNSYLVANIA								
Heinz	Y	Y	N	N	N	N	Y	Y
Specter	Y	Y	N	Y	N	N	N	Y
RHODE ISLAND								
Chafee	Y	Y	N	Y	N	N	N	Y
Pell	Y	Y	N	N	N	N	N	Y
SOUTH CAROLINA								
Thurmond	N	Y	N	N	N	N	N	Y
Hollings	Y	Y	Y	Y	N	N	N	Y
SOUTH DAKOTA								
Abdnor	Y	Y	N	N	N	Y	Y	Y
Pressler	Y	Y	N	N	N	N	Y	Y
TENNESSEE								
Baker	Y	Y	Y	Y	Y	Y	Y	Y
Sasser	Y	Y	N	N	N	N	Y	Y

KEY

Y Voted for (yea).
\# Paired for.
\+ Announced for.
N Voted against (nay).
X Paired against.
- Announced against.
P Voted "present".
C Voted "present" to avoid possible conflict of interest.
? Did not vote or otherwise make a position known.

Democrats   *Republicans*

	64	65	66	67	68	69	70	71
TEXAS								
Tower	N	Y	Y	Y	N	Y	N	Y
Bentsen	?	?	N	N	N	N	N	Y
UTAH								
Garn	N	Y	Y	Y	Y	Y	Y	Y
Hatch	Y	Y	N	N	N	N	N	Y
VERMONT								
Stafford	Y	Y	N	Y	N	N	Y	Y
Leahy	Y	Y	N	N	N	N	N	Y
VIRGINIA								
Warner	Y	Y	N	Y	N	N	Y	Y
Byrd*	Y	Y	N	N	N	N	N	Y
WASHINGTON								
Gorton	Y	Y	N	Y	N	Y	Y	Y
Jackson	Y	Y	N	N	N	N	N	Y
WEST VIRGINIA								
Byrd	Y	Y	N	Y	N	N	Y	Y
Randolph	Y	Y	N	N	N	N	N	Y
WISCONSIN								
Kasten	Y	Y	N	N	N	N	N	Y
Proxmire	Y	Y	N	N	N	N	N	Y
WYOMING								
Simpson	Y	Y	N	Y	N	Y	Y	Y
Wallop	Y	Y	Y	Y	Y	Y	Y	Y

ND - Northern Democrats   SD - Southern Democrats (Southern states - Ala., Ark., Fla., Ga., Ky., La., Miss., N.C., Okla., S.C., Tenn., Texas, Va.)   *Byrd elected as an independent.*

64. S 1207. Nuclear Regulatory Commission Authorization. Hart, D-Colo., amendment to prohibit the government from making nuclear weapons from fuel that has been burned by civilian nuclear power plants. Adopted 88-9: R 44-8; D 44-1 (ND 31-0, SD 13-1), March 30, 1982. A "nay" was a vote supporting the president's position.

65. HR 2330. Nuclear Regulatory Commission Authorization. Passage of the bill to authorize $485 million in fiscal 1982 and $530 million in fiscal 1983 for the Nuclear Regulatory Commission. Passed 97-0: R 52-0; D 45-0 (ND 31-0, SD 14-0), March 30, 1982.

66. H J Res 409. Continuing Appropriations, Fiscal 1982. Baker, R-Tenn., motion to table (kill) the Armstrong, R-Colo., amendment to restore the previous $3,000 limit on federal income tax deductions members of Congress may take for Washington, D.C., living expenses, repealing provisions allowing greater deductions that Congress had passed in 1981. Motion rejected 20-77: R 15-37; D 5-40 (ND 4-26, SD 1-14), March 30, 1982.

67. H J Res 409. Continuing Appropriations, Fiscal 1982. Specter, R-Pa., amendment, to the Armstrong, R-Colo., amendment (see vote 66, above), to eliminate tax code provisions that allow members of Congress to deduct living expenses without substantiation of such expenses. Rejected 37-60: R 28-24; D 9-36 (ND 7-23, SD 2-13), March 30, 1982.

68. H J Res 409. Continuing Appropriations, Fiscal 1982. Stevens, R-Alaska, amendment (offered on behalf of Dole, R-Kan.), to the Armstrong, R-Colo., amendment (see vote 66, above), to repeal tax code provisions that allow state legislators to deduct travel expenses away from home. Rejected 17-79: R 15-36; D 2-43 (ND 2-28, SD 0-15), March 30, 1982.

69. H J Res 409. Continuing Appropriations, Fiscal 1982. Stevens, R-Alaska, amendment, to the Armstrong, R-Colo., amendment (see vote 66, above), to limit any tax reduction due to deductions for Washington, D.C., living expenses in any taxable year to no more than $5,000 per member of Congress, and to require each member to insert copies of his federal tax returns in the *Congressional Record* each year. Rejected 24-74: R 16-36; D 8-38 (ND 7-24, SD 1-14), March 30, 1982.

70. H J Res 409. Continuing Appropriations, Fiscal 1982. Tsongas, D-Mass., amendment, to the Armstrong, R-Colo., amendment (see vote 66, above), to require each member of Congress to insert copies of his federal tax returns in the *Congressional Record* each year. Adopted 55-43: R 24-28; D 31-15 (ND 24-7, SD 7-8), March 30, 1982.

71. H J Res 409. Continuing Appropriations, Fiscal 1982. Baker, R-Tenn., motion to instruct the sergeant-at-arms to require the attendance of absent senators. Motion agreed to 92-4: R 49-3; D 43-1 (ND 29-0, SD 14-1), March 31, 1982.

	72 73 74 75 76		72 73 74 75 76		72 73 74 75 76
ALABAMA		**IOWA**		**NEW HAMPSHIRE**	
Denton	Y Y Y Y Y	Grassley	Y Y N Y N	Humphrey	Y Y N N Y
Heflin	Y Y N Y N	Jepsen	Y Y N Y N	Rudman	Y N Y Y Y
ALASKA		**KANSAS**		**NEW JERSEY**	
Murkowski	Y N Y Y Y	Dole	Y N Y Y Y	Bradley	Y Y N N N
Stevens	Y N Y Y Y	Kassebaum	Y Y N Y N	Vacancy	
ARIZONA		**KENTUCKY**		**NEW MEXICO**	
Goldwater	N N Y N Y	Ford	Y Y N Y N	Domenici	Y Y N Y N
DeConcini	Y Y N Y N	Huddleston	Y N Y N Y	Schmitt	Y Y N Y N
ARKANSAS		**LOUISIANA**		**NEW YORK**	
Bumpers	Y Y N N N	Johnston	N N Y Y Y	D'Amato	Y N Y Y Y
Pryor	Y Y N Y N	Long	N N N Y N	Moynihan	Y N N Y N
CALIFORNIA		**MAINE**		**NORTH CAROLINA**	
Hayakawa	Y N Y Y Y	Cohen	Y Y N N N	East	Y Y N N N
Cranston	Y N Y Y Y	Mitchell	Y Y N N N	Helms	Y Y N Y N
COLORADO		**MARYLAND**		**NORTH DAKOTA**	
Armstrong	Y Y N N N	Mathias	Y Y N N N	Andrews	Y N N Y N
Hart	Y Y N N N	Sarbanes	Y Y N Y N	Burdick	Y Y N Y N
CONNECTICUT		**MASSACHUSETTS**		**OHIO**	
Weicker	N N Y Y N	Kennedy	Y Y N N N	Glenn	Y N Y N Y
Dodd	Y N Y N Y	Tsongas	Y N Y N Y	Metzenbaum	Y Y N Y N
DELAWARE		**MICHIGAN**		**OKLAHOMA**	
Roth	Y Y N N N	Levin	Y Y N N N	Nickles	Y Y N Y N
Biden	Y N N N N	Riegle	Y Y N Y N	Boren	Y Y N Y N
FLORIDA		**MINNESOTA**		**OREGON**	
Hawkins	Y Y N Y N	Boschwitz	Y N Y N Y	Hatfield	Y N Y N Y
Chiles	Y Y N Y N	Durenberger	Y Y N N N	Packwood	Y N Y N Y
GEORGIA		**MISSISSIPPI**		**PENNSYLVANIA**	
Mattingly	Y Y N Y N	Cochran	Y N Y Y Y	Heinz	Y Y N N N
Nunn	Y Y ? Y N	Stennis	Y N N N N	Specter	Y Y N N N
HAWAII		**MISSOURI**		**RHODE ISLAND**	
Inouye	Y N Y Y Y	Danforth	Y Y N Y N	Chafee	Y N N N N
Matsunaga	Y N Y N Y	Eagleton	Y Y N Y N	Pell	Y Y N N N
IDAHO		**MONTANA**		**SOUTH CAROLINA**	
McClure	Y N Y N Y	Baucus	Y Y N Y N	Thurmond	Y Y Y Y N
Symms	Y N Y N Y	Melcher	Y Y N Y N	Hollings	Y N Y N Y
ILLINOIS		**NEBRASKA**		**SOUTH DAKOTA**	
Percy	Y N N N N	Exon	Y Y N N N	Abdnor	Y Y N Y N
Dixon	Y N N N N	Zorinsky	Y Y N Y N	Pressler	Y Y N Y N
INDIANA		**NEVADA**		**TENNESSEE**	
Lugar	Y Y N N N	Laxalt	Y N Y Y Y	Baker	Y N Y Y Y
Quayle	N N Y Y Y	Cannon	Y Y N Y N	Sasser	Y Y N Y N

KEY

Y Voted for (yea).
\# Paired for.
\+ Announced for.
N Voted against (nay).
X Paired against.
\- Announced against.
P Voted "present".
C Voted "present" to avoid possible conflict of interest.
? Did not vote or otherwise make a position known.

Democrats   *Republicans*

	72 73 74 75 76
TEXAS	
Tower	Y N Y Y Y
Bentsen	Y Y N Y N
UTAH	
Garn	Y N Y Y Y
Hatch	Y Y N Y N
VERMONT	
Stafford	? ? ? Y N
Leahy	Y N N Y N
VIRGINIA	
Warner	Y Y N Y N
Byrd*	Y Y N Y N
WASHINGTON	
Gorton	Y N Y N Y
Jackson	Y Y N Y N
WEST VIRGINIA	
Byrd	Y N N Y N
Randolph	Y Y N Y N
WISCONSIN	
Kasten	Y Y N Y N
Proxmire	Y Y N Y N
WYOMING	
Simpson	Y N N Y N
Wallop	Y N Y Y Y

ND - Northern Democrats   SD - Southern Democrats (Southern states - Ala., Ark., Fla., Ga., Ky., La., Miss., N.C., Okla., S.C., Tenn., Texas, Va.)

* Byrd elected as an independent.

72. H J Res 409. Continuing Appropriations, Fiscal 1982. Baker, R-Tenn., motion to instruct the sergeant-at-arms to compel the attendance of absent senators. Motion agreed to 93-5: R 49-3; D 44-2 (ND 31-0, SD 13-2), March 31, 1982.

73. H J Res 409. Continuing Appropriations, Fiscal 1982. Judgment of the Senate whether the Armstrong, R-Colo., amendment *(see vote 66, p. 14-S)* was germane. Ruled germane 57-41: R 27-25; D 30-16 (ND 20-11, SD 10-5), March 31, 1982.

74. H J Res 409. Continuing Appropriations, Fiscal 1982. Hatfield, R-Ore., motion to table (kill) the Armstrong, R-Colo., amendment *(see vote 66, p. 14-S)*. Motion rejected 32-65: R 23-29; D 9-36 (ND 6-25, SD 3-11), March 31, 1982.

75. H J Res 409. Continuing Appropriations, Fiscal 1982. Stevens, R-Alaska, amendment, to the Armstrong, R-Colo., amendment *(see vote 66, p. 14-S)*, to reduce the salaries of members of Congress by 10 percent. Adopted 63-36: R 34-19; D 29-17 (ND 18-13, SD 11-4), March 31, 1982.

76. H J Res 409. Continuing Appropriations, Fiscal 1982. Hatfield, R-Ore., motion to table (kill) the Armstrong, R-Colo., amendment *(see vote 66, p. 14-S)*, as amended. Motion rejected 31-68: R 22-31; D 9-37 (ND 6-25, SD 3-12), March 31, 1982.

	77 78 79		77 78 79		77 78 79	KEY
ALABAMA		**IOWA**		**NEW HAMPSHIRE**		**Y** Voted for (yea).
Denton	Y Y Y	*Grassley*	N N N	*Humphrey*	Y Y N	**#** Paired for.
Heflin	N N N	*Jepsen*	N N Y	*Rudman*	Y Y Y	**+** Announced for.
ALASKA		**KANSAS**		**NEW JERSEY**		**N** Voted against (nay).
Murkowski	Y Y Y	*Dole*	Y Y Y	Bradley	N N Y	**X** Paired against.
Stevens	Y Y Y	*Kassebaum*	N N Y	Vacancy		**-** Announced against.
ARIZONA		**KENTUCKY**		**NEW MEXICO**		**P** Voted "present".
Goldwater	Y Y Y	Ford	N N Y	*Domenici*	N Y Y	**C** Voted "present" to avoid possi-
DeConcini	N N Y	Huddleston	Y Y Y	*Schmitt*	N Y Y	ble conflict of interest.
ARKANSAS		**LOUISIANA**		**NEW YORK**		**?** Did not vote or otherwise make a
Bumpers	N N Y	Johnston	Y Y Y	*D'Amato*	Y Y Y	position known.
Pryor	N N Y	Long	Y Y Y	Moynihan	N N N	
CALIFORNIA		**MAINE**		**NORTH CAROLINA**		Democrats *Republicans*
Hayakawa	Y Y Y	*Cohen*	N N N	*East*	N N N	
Cranston	Y Y Y	Mitchell	N N N	*Helms*	N N N	
COLORADO		**MARYLAND**		**NORTH DAKOTA**		77 78 79
Armstrong	N N N	*Mathias*	N N Y	*Andrews*	Y N Y	
Hart	N Y Y	Sarbanes	N N Y	Burdick	N N Y	
CONNECTICUT		**MASSACHUSETTS**		**OHIO**		**TEXAS**
Weicker	Y Y Y	Kennedy	N N N	Glenn	Y Y Y	*Tower* Y Y Y
Dodd	Y Y Y	Tsongas	Y Y Y	Metzenbaum	N N N	Bentsen Y N Y
DELAWARE		**MICHIGAN**		**OKLAHOMA**		**UTAH**
Roth	N N Y	Levin	N N Y	*Nickles*	N N Y	*Garn* Y Y Y
Biden	Y Y Y	Riegle	N N Y	Boren	N N Y	*Hatch* N N N
FLORIDA		**MINNESOTA**		**OREGON**		**VERMONT**
Hawkins	N Y Y	*Boschwitz*	Y Y Y	*Hatfield*	Y Y Y	*Stafford* Y Y Y
Chiles	N N Y	*Durenberger*	N N Y	*Packwood*	Y Y Y	Leahy Y Y Y
GEORGIA		**MISSISSIPPI**		**PENNSYLVANIA**		**VIRGINIA**
Mattingly	Y Y Y	*Cochran*	Y Y Y	*Heinz*	N N Y	*Warner* Y Y Y
Nunn	N N Y	Stennis	Y Y Y	*Specter*	Y Y Y	Byrd* N N Y
HAWAII		**MISSOURI**		**RHODE ISLAND**		**WASHINGTON**
Inouye	Y Y Y	*Danforth*	Y Y Y	*Chafee*	Y Y Y	*Gorton* Y Y Y
Matsunaga	Y Y Y	Eagleton	N N N	Pell	Y Y Y	Jackson N N Y
IDAHO		**MONTANA**		**SOUTH CAROLINA**		**WEST VIRGINIA**
McClure	Y Y Y	Baucus	N N Y	*Thurmond*	Y Y Y	Byrd N N Y
Symms	Y Y N	Melcher	N N Y	Hollings	Y Y Y	Randolph N N Y
ILLINOIS		**NEBRASKA**		**SOUTH DAKOTA**		**WISCONSIN**
Percy	Y Y Y	Exon	Y N N	*Abdnor*	Y Y Y	*Kasten* N N N
Dixon	Y Y Y	Zorinsky	N N N	*Pressler*	N N N	Proxmire N N N
INDIANA		**NEVADA**		**TENNESSEE**		**WYOMING**
Lugar	N N Y	*Laxalt*	Y Y Y	*Baker*	Y Y Y	*Simpson* Y Y Y
Quayle	Y Y Y	Cannon	N N N	Sasser	N N Y	*Wallop* Y Y Y

ND - Northern Democrats   SD - Southern Democrats (Southern states - Ala., Ark., Fla., Ga., Ky., La., Miss., N.C., Okla., S.C., Tenn., Texas, Va.)   *Byrd elected as an independent.*

77. H J Res 409. Continuing Appropriations, Fiscal 1982. Judgment of the Senate affirming the chair's ruling that the Armstrong, R-Colo., amendment *(see vote 66, p. 14-S)* was out of order because it constituted legislation on an appropriations bill. Ruling of the chair upheld 51-48: R 34-19; D 17-29 (ND 11-20, SD 6-9), March 31, 1982.

78. H J Res 409. Continuing Appropriations, Fiscal 1982. Baker, R-Tenn., motion to table (kill) the Exon, D-Neb., motion to reconsider the vote *(see vote 77, above)* by which the Senate upheld the chair's ruling that the Armstrong, R-Colo., amendment *(see vote 66, p. 14-S)* was out of order. Motion agreed to 52-47: R 36-17; D 16-30 (ND 11-20, SD 5-10), March 31, 1982.

79. H J Res 409. Continuing Appropriations, Fiscal 1982. Passage of the joint resolution to provide funding through Sept. 30, 1982, for government agencies whose regular fiscal 1982 appropriations bills had not been enacted. Passed (thus cleared for the president) 81-18: R 43-10; D 38-8 (ND 24-7, SD 14-1), March 31, 1982.

	80		80		80		KEY
ALABAMA		**IOWA**		**NEW HAMPSHIRE**			Y Voted for (yea).
Denton	-	*Grassley*	N	*Humphrey*	N		# Paired for.
Heflin	N	*Jepsen*	N	*Rudman*	N		+ Announced for.
ALASKA		**KANSAS**		**NEW JERSEY**			N Voted against (nay).
Murkowski	?	*Dole*	N	Bradley	Y		X Paired against.
Stevens	?	*Kassebaum*	Y	Vacancy			- Announced against.
ARIZONA		**KENTUCKY**		**NEW MEXICO**			P Voted "present".
Goldwater	?	Ford	Y	*Domenici*	N		C Voted "present" to avoid possi-
DeConcini	-	Huddleston	Y	*Schmitt*	N		ble conflict of interest.
ARKANSAS		**LOUISIANA**		**NEW YORK**			? Did not vote or otherwise make a
Bumpers	Y	Johnston	Y	*D'Amato*	N		position known.
Pryor	N	Long	Y	Moynihan	Y		
CALIFORNIA		**MAINE**		**NORTH CAROLINA**			Democrats *Republicans*
Hayakawa	Y	*Cohen*	?	*East*	N		
Cranston	Y	Mitchell	?	*Helms*	N		
COLORADO		**MARYLAND**		**NORTH DAKOTA**				80
Armstrong	N	*Mathias*	Y	*Andrews*	N		
Hart	Y	Sarbanes	Y	Burdick	N		
CONNECTICUT		**MASSACHUSETTS**		**OHIO**			**TEXAS**	
Weicker	Y	Kennedy	Y	Glenn	Y		*Tower*	Y
Dodd	Y	Tsongas	?	Metzenbaum	Y		Bentsen	N
DELAWARE		**MICHIGAN**		**OKLAHOMA**			**UTAH**	
Roth	N	Levin	Y	*Nickles*	N		*Garn*	N
Biden	Y	Riegle	-	Boren	N		*Hatch*	N
FLORIDA		**MINNESOTA**		**OREGON**			**VERMONT**	
Hawkins	-	*Boschwitz*	Y	*Hatfield*	Y		*Stafford*	?
Chiles	?	*Durenberger*	Y	*Packwood*	?		Leahy	?
GEORGIA		**MISSISSIPPI**		**PENNSYLVANIA**			**VIRGINIA**	
Mattingly	N	*Cochran*	N	*Heinz*	N		*Warner*	N
Nunn	?	Stennis	Y	*Specter*	N		Byrd*	Y
HAWAII		**MISSOURI**		**RHODE ISLAND**			**WASHINGTON**	
Inouye	Y	*Danforth*	Y	*Chafee*	Y		*Gorton*	Y
Matsunaga	Y	Eagleton	Y	Pell	Y		Jackson	N
IDAHO		**MONTANA**		**SOUTH CAROLINA**			**WEST VIRGINIA**	
McClure	N	Baucus	?	*Thurmond*	N		Byrd	Y
Symms	N	Melcher	?	Hollings	N		Randolph	N
ILLINOIS		**NEBRASKA**		**SOUTH DAKOTA**			**WISCONSIN**	
Percy	Y	Exon	Y	*Abdnor*	N		*Kasten*	-
Dixon	Y	Zorinsky	N	*Pressler*	N		Proxmire	Y
INDIANA		**NEVADA**		**TENNESSEE**			**WYOMING**	
Lugar	Y	*Laxalt*	N	*Baker*	Y		*Simpson*	N
Quayle	Y	Cannon	?	Sasser	N		*Wallop*	N

ND - Northern Democrats   SD - Southern Democrats (Southern states - Ala., Ark., Fla., Ga., Ky., La., Miss., N.C., Okla., S.C., Tenn., Texas, Va.)   *Byrd elected as an independent.*

80. S Res 20. Broadcast of Senate Proceedings. Percy, R-Ill., motion to table (kill) the Symms, R-Idaho, amendment stating the sense of the Senate that the United States is determined to use force if necessary to stop Cuba from aggression or subversion in the Western Hemisphere or from acquiring or using external military support to endanger the United States, and will support "the aspirations of the Cuban people for self-determination." Motion agreed to 41-39: R 15-29; D 26-10 (ND 19-4, SD 7-6), April 14, 1982. A "yea" was a vote supporting the president's position.

	81 82 83		81 82 83		81 82 83	KEY
ALABAMA		**IOWA**		**NEW HAMPSHIRE**		Y Voted for (yea).
Denton	N N Y	*Grassley*	Y N Y	*Humphrey*	N N Y	# Paired for.
Heflin	Y Y Y	*Jepsen*	Y N ?	*Rudman*	Y N Y	+ Announced for.
ALASKA		**KANSAS**		**NEW JERSEY**		N Voted against (nay).
Murkowski	Y N Y	*Dole*	N N Y	*Brady***	Y N Y	X Paired against.
Stevens	Y N Y	*Kassebaum*	Y N Y	Bradley	N Y Y	- Announced against.
ARIZONA		**KENTUCKY**		**NEW MEXICO**		P Voted "present".
Goldwater	N N Y	Ford	N Y Y	*Domenici*	N N Y	C Voted "present" to avoid possi-
DeConcini	Y Y Y	Huddleston	N Y Y	*Schmitt*	Y N Y	ble conflict of interest.
ARKANSAS		**LOUISIANA**		**NEW YORK**		? Did not vote or otherwise make a
Bumpers	Y Y Y	Johnston	N Y Y	*D'Amato*	N N ?	position known.
Pryor	N Y Y	Long	N Y Y	Moynihan	Y Y Y	
CALIFORNIA		**MAINE**		**NORTH CAROLINA**		*Democrats* ***Republicans***
Hayakawa	Y N Y	*Cohen*	Y N Y	*East*	N N Y	
Cranston	N Y Y	Mitchell	Y Y Y	*Helms*	N N Y	
COLORADO		**MARYLAND**		**NORTH DAKOTA**		81 82 83
Armstrong	Y N ?	*Mathias*	Y N Y	*Andrews*	Y N Y	
Hart	N Y Y	Sarbanes	N Y Y	Burdick	N Y Y	
CONNECTICUT		**MASSACHUSETTS**		**OHIO**		**TEXAS**
Weicker	Y N Y	Kennedy	N Y Y	Glenn	N Y Y	*Tower* N N Y
Dodd	N Y Y	Tsongas	? ? Y	Metzenbaum	Y Y Y	Bentsen N Y Y
DELAWARE		**MICHIGAN**		**OKLAHOMA**		**UTAH**
Roth	Y N Y	Levin	N Y Y	*Nickles*	Y N Y	*Garn* Y N Y
Biden	N Y Y	Riegle	N Y Y	Boren	N Y Y	*Hatch* Y N Y
FLORIDA		**MINNESOTA**		**OREGON**		**VERMONT**
Hawkins	Y N Y	*Boschwitz*	N N Y	*Hatfield*	Y N Y	*Stafford* N N Y
Chiles	Y Y Y	*Durenberger*	N N Y	*Packwood*	Y N Y	Leahy N Y Y
GEORGIA		**MISSISSIPPI**		**PENNSYLVANIA**		**VIRGINIA**
Mattingly	N N Y	*Cochran*	Y N +	*Heinz*	Y N Y	*Warner* N N Y
Nunn	N Y Y	Stennis	N Y Y	*Specter*	Y N Y	Byrd* N Y Y
HAWAII		**MISSOURI**		**RHODE ISLAND**		**WASHINGTON**
Inouye	N Y Y	*Danforth*	? ? Y	*Chafee*	Y N Y	*Gorton* Y N Y
Matsunaga	N Y Y	Eagleton	N Y Y	Pell	Y Y Y	Jackson N Y Y
IDAHO		**MONTANA**		**SOUTH CAROLINA**		**WEST VIRGINIA**
McClure	Y N Y	Baucus	N Y Y	*Thurmond*	Y N Y	Byrd N Y Y
Symms	Y N Y	Melcher	Y Y Y	Hollings	N Y Y	Randolph N Y Y
ILLINOIS		**NEBRASKA**		**SOUTH DAKOTA**		**WISCONSIN**
Percy	Y N Y	Exon	N Y Y	*Abdnor*	Y N Y	*Kasten* Y N Y
Dixon	N Y Y	Zorinsky	N Y Y	*Pressler*	Y ? Y	Proxmire N Y Y
INDIANA		**NEVADA**		**TENNESSEE**		**WYOMING**
Lugar	Y N Y	*Laxalt*	N N N	*Baker*	Y N Y	*Simpson* N Y Y
Quayle	Y N Y	Cannon	N Y Y	Sasser	Y Y Y	*Wallop* Y N Y

ND - Northern Democrats   SD - Southern Democrats (Southern states - Ala., Ark., Fla., Ga., Ky., La., Miss., N.C., Okla., S.C., Tenn., Texas, Va.)

* Byrd elected as an independent.
** Sen. Nicholas F. Brady, R-N.J., was sworn in April 20, 1982. The first vote for which he was eligible was CQ vote 81.

81. S Res 20. Broadcast of Senate Proceedings. Baker, R-Tenn., motion to invoke cloture (thus limiting debate) on S Res 20, a resolution to direct the Committee on Rules and Administration to provide for continuous television and radio coverage of Senate proceedings in a manner to be determined by the committee. Motion rejected 47-51: R 37-16; D 10-35 (ND 6-24, SD 4-11), April 20, 1982. A three-fifths majority vote (60) of the total Senate is required to invoke cloture.

82. S Res 20. Broadcast of Senate Proceedings. Randolph, D-W.Va., amendment to amend the standing rules of the Senate to require senators to vote from their assigned desks. Rejected 46-51: R 1-51; D 45-0 (ND 30-0, SD 15-0), April 20, 1982.

83. S Res 20. Broadcast of Senate Proceedings. Baker, R-Tenn., amendment to require the Committee on Rules and Administration to report back to the Senate within 60 days of the adoption of S Res 20 a second resolution containing all regulations and rules changes needed to carry out television and/or radio coverage of Senate proceedings, to delay the effective date of S Res 20 until the Senate's adoption of the second resolution, and to delete from S Res 20 the requirement that the broadcast coverage be continuous. Adopted 95-1: R 49-1; D 46-0 (ND 31-0, SD 15-0), April 21, 1982. (S Res 20 subsequently was adopted by voice vote.)

	84	85	86	87	88	89	90	91
ALABAMA								
Denton	N	N	?	?	?	?	?	?
Heflin	N	N	Y	Y	Y	?	N	Y
ALASKA								
Murkowski	Y	Y	Y	Y	Y	Y	Y	Y
Stevens	Y	N	Y	Y	Y	Y	Y	Y
ARIZONA								
Goldwater	Y	Y	Y	Y	Y	N	Y	N
DeConcini	?	?	N	N	N	N	Y	Y
ARKANSAS								
Bumpers	Y	Y	N	N	N	N	Y	Y
Pryor	Y	N	?	N	N	N	N	Y
CALIFORNIA								
Hayakawa	Y	Y	Y	Y	Y	Y	Y	Y
Cranston	N	Y	?	?	N	N	N	Y
COLORADO								
Armstrong	N	Y	N	N	Y	Y	Y	Y
Hart	N	Y	Y	Y	Y	Y	Y	Y
CONNECTICUT								
Weicker	N	N	?	?	Y	Y	Y	Y
Dodd	N	N	Y	Y	Y	Y	Y	Y
DELAWARE								
Roth	N	N	Y	N	N	N	Y	Y
Biden	Y	?	Y	N	N	N	N	Y
FLORIDA								
Hawkins	N	N	Y	N	N	Y	Y	Y
Chiles	N	N	Y	Y	Y	Y	Y	Y
GEORGIA								
Mattingly	Y	N	Y	Y	Y	Y	Y	Y
Nunn	N	N	Y	N	Y	N	Y	Y
HAWAII								
Inouye	?	?	?	N	N	N	N	Y
Matsunaga	?	Y	?	N	N	N	N	Y
IDAHO								
McClure	N	N	Y	Y	Y	Y	Y	Y
Symms	N	?	Y	Y	Y	Y	Y	Y
ILLINOIS								
Percy	Y	N	Y	N	N	N	Y	Y
Dixon	Y	Y	Y	N	N	Y	Y	Y
INDIANA								
Lugar	Y	N	Y	N	Y	N	Y	Y
Quayle	Y	Y	Y	Y	N	N	Y	Y

	84	85	86	87	88	89	90	91
IOWA								
Grassley	N	N	Y	N	N	N	Y	Y
Jepsen	?	?	Y	Y	N	N	Y	Y
KANSAS								
Dole	Y	Y	N	N	Y	Y	N	Y
Kassebaum	N	Y	Y	Y	N	N	Y	Y
KENTUCKY								
Ford	N	Y	Y	N	Y	Y	?	?
Huddleston	N	N	Y	Y	Y	Y	Y	?
LOUISIANA								
Johnston	N	N	Y	Y	Y	Y	N	N
Long	Y	Y	Y	Y	?	?	?	?
MAINE								
Cohen	Y	Y	Y	N	N	N	Y	Y
Mitchell	N	Y	Y	N	N	N	Y	Y
MARYLAND								
Mathias	N	Y	Y	Y	Y	Y	Y	Y
Sarbanes	N	Y	?	?	N	N	Y	Y
MASSACHUSETTS								
Kennedy	N	Y	N	N	N	N	N	Y
Tsongas	N	N	Y	Y	N	N	N	Y
MICHIGAN								
Levin	N	Y	N	N	N	N	Y	Y
Riegle	N	Y	N	N	N	N	Y	Y
MINNESOTA								
Boschwitz	Y	N	N	N	N	N	N	Y
Durenberger	N	N	?	?	?	?	?	?
MISSISSIPPI								
Cochran	N	N	N	N	Y	Y	N	N
Stennis	N	Y	N	N	Y	Y	N	N
MISSOURI								
Danforth	?	?	Y	Y	Y	Y	Y	Y
Eagleton	N	Y	Y	Y	N	N	Y	?
MONTANA								
Baucus	N	N	N	N	?	N	Y	Y
Melcher	N	N	N	N	-	-	?	?
NEBRASKA								
Exon	Y	Y	Y	N	Y	Y	Y	Y
Zorinsky	Y	Y	Y	N	Y	Y	Y	Y
NEVADA								
Laxalt	Y	N	Y	N	N	N	N	Y
Cannon	N	Y	N	N	N	N	N	Y

	84	85	86	87	88	89	90	91
NEW HAMPSHIRE								
Humphrey	N	Y	N	N	N	N	Y	Y
Rudman	Y	Y	Y	Y	N	N	Y	Y
NEW JERSEY								
Brady	Y	N	Y	Y	Y	Y	Y	Y
Bradley	N	Y	Y	N	Y	Y	Y	Y
NEW MEXICO								
Domenici	Y	N	Y	Y	Y	Y	Y	Y
Schmitt	?	N	Y	Y	Y	Y	?	?
NEW YORK								
D'Amato	Y	Y	Y	Y	Y	N	N	Y
Moynihan	Y	Y	Y	Y	Y	N	Y	Y
NORTH CAROLINA								
East	N	N	Y	Y	Y	Y	Y	Y
Helms	N	N	Y	Y	Y	Y	Y	Y
NORTH DAKOTA								
Andrews	Y	Y	Y	Y	Y	N	Y	Y
Burdick	N	Y	Y	N	Y	Y	N	Y
OHIO								
Glenn	Y	N	Y	N	Y	N	Y	N
Metzenbaum	N	Y	N	?	?	?	Y	Y
OKLAHOMA								
Nickles	N	N	Y	Y	Y	Y	Y	Y
Boren	Y	?	Y	Y	Y	Y	N	Y
OREGON								
Hatfield	+	+	#	+	?	?	?	?
Packwood	Y	N	Y	N	N	Y	Y	Y
PENNSYLVANIA								
Heinz	?	Y	Y	Y	Y	Y	Y	Y
Specter	Y	N	Y	Y	N	?	Y	Y
RHODE ISLAND								
Chafee	Y	Y	Y	N	N	Y	Y	Y
Pell	Y	Y	Y	N	N	Y	Y	Y
SOUTH CAROLINA								
Thurmond	Y	Y	Y	N	N	Y	Y	Y
Hollings	Y	Y	Y	N	N	Y	Y	Y
SOUTH DAKOTA								
Abdnor	Y	N	Y	Y	?	?	?	?
Pressler	Y	N	Y	N	Y	Y	Y	Y
TENNESSEE								
Baker	Y	N	?	+	?	?	?	?
Sasser	Y	Y	Y	Y	Y	Y	N	N

	84	85	86	87	88	89	90	91
TEXAS								
Tower	Y	N	Y	Y	Y	Y	Y	Y
Bentsen	N	Y	Y	Y	Y	Y	Y	Y
UTAH								
Garn	N	N	N	N	N	Y	N	Y
Hatch	Y	N	N	N	N	N	N	Y
VERMONT								
Stafford	Y	Y	Y	Y	Y	Y	Y	Y
Leahy	N	Y	N	N	N	N	Y	Y
VIRGINIA								
Warner	Y	Y	Y	Y	Y	Y	Y	Y
Byrd*	Y	Y	Y	Y	N	N	Y	Y
WASHINGTON								
Gorton	Y	Y	Y	Y	Y	Y	Y	Y
Jackson	N	Y	Y	Y	Y	Y	N	Y
WEST VIRGINIA								
Byrd	N	Y	N	Y	N	Y	N	Y
Randolph	Y	N	Y	Y	N	Y	N	N
WISCONSIN								
Kasten	N	N	X	N	Y	N	Y	Y
Proxmire	N	Y	N	N	N	N	N	Y
WYOMING								
Simpson	Y	N	Y	Y	Y	Y	Y	Y
Wallop	?	N	Y	Y	?	?	?	?

KEY

Y	Voted for (yea).
#	Paired for.
+	Announced for.
N	Voted against (nay).
X	Paired against.
-	Announced against.
P	Voted "present".
C	Voted "present" to avoid possible conflict of interest.
?	Did not vote or otherwise make a position known.

Democrats *Republicans*

ND - Northern Democrats   SD - Southern Democrats (Southern states - Ala., Ark., Fla., Ga., Ky., La., Miss., N.C., Okla., S.C., Tenn., Texas, Va.)   * Byrd elected as an independent.

84. S 1630. Criminal Code Reform Act of 1981. Thurmond, R-S.C., motion to invoke cloture (thus limiting debate) on the motion to proceed to consideration of S 1630, a bill to revise federal criminal laws. Motion rejected 45-46: R 30-18; D 15-28 (ND 8-20, SD 7-8), April 27, 1982. A three-fifths majority vote (60) of the total Senate is required to invoke cloture.

85. S 854. Foreign Missions Act of 1982. Mathias, R-Md., amendment to delete provisions to establish a joint federal-local District of Columbia Foreign Missions Commission to govern zoning of foreign missions and to give the State Department overriding authority to determine where foreign missions can locate in the United States. The Mathias amendment substituted a requirement that state and local authorities give "substantial weight" to recommendations by the secretary of state or the director of the State Department Office of Foreign Missions. Adopted 49-43: R 19-31; D 30-12 (ND 22-6, SD 8-6), April 27, 1982.

86. S 1662. National Nuclear Waste Policy Act. McClure, R-Idaho, motion to table (kill) the Proxmire, D-Wis., amendment to allow states to veto a decision by the federal government to put a nuclear waste repository in a state. Motion agreed to 70-19: R 41-7; D 29-12 (ND 17-10, SD 12-2), April 29, 1982.

87. S 1662. National Nuclear Waste Policy Act. McClure, R-Idaho, motion to table (kill) the Cannon, D-Nev., amendment to allow states to block a decision by the federal government to put a nuclear waste repository in a state unless both the House and Senate passed a resolution overriding the state. Motion agreed to 52-40: R 34-15; D 18-25 (ND 9-19, SD 9-6), April 29, 1982.

88. S 1662. National Nuclear Waste Policy Act. Johnston, D-La., motion to table (kill) the Thurmond, R-S.C., amendment to delete the section of the bill that would allow the federal government to provide temporary storage for burned fuel from nuclear power plants. Motion agreed to 47-43: R 28-20; D 19-23 (ND 10-18, SD 9-5), April 29, 1982.

89. S 1662. National Nuclear Waste Policy Act. Johnston, D-La., motion to table (kill) the Moynihan, D-N.Y., motion to reconsider the vote by which the Thurmond, R-S.C., amendment was tabled (see vote 88, above). Motion agreed to 46-43: R 28-19; D 18-24 (ND 10-19, SD 8-5), April 29, 1982.

90. S 1662. National Nuclear Waste Policy Act. McClure, R-Idaho, motion to table (kill) the Stennis, D-Miss., amendment to delay the initial selection of a site for a nuclear waste repository until after a national survey of potential sites was completed. Motion agreed to 63-27: R 39-8; D 24-19 (ND 17-13, SD 7-6), April 29, 1982. A "yea" was a vote supporting the president's position.

91. S 1662. National Nuclear Waste Policy Act. McClure, R-Idaho, motion to table (kill) the Cochran, R-Miss., amendment to require that of the first three sites initially considered for a waste repository, one must be in a granite formation. The effect of the amendment would have been to delay the selection of the first three sites. Motion agreed to 83-5: R 46-1; D 37-4 (ND 28-1, SD 9-3), April 29, 1982. A "yea" was a vote supporting the president's position.

	92	93	94	95	96	97	98	99
ALABAMA								
Denton	?	+	Y	N	N	Y	Y	Y
Heflin	Y	Y	N	Y	Y	N	Y	Y
ALASKA								
Murkowski	Y	Y	Y	N	N	Y	N	Y
Stevens	Y	Y	Y	N	N	Y	N	Y
ARIZONA								
Goldwater	?	+	Y	N	N	Y	Y	Y
DeConcini	Y	Y	?	+	+	N	N	Y
ARKANSAS								
Bumpers	?	?	N	Y	Y	N	N	Y
Pryor	?	?	N	Y	Y	N	N	Y
CALIFORNIA								
Hayakawa	?	?	Y	N	N	Y	Y	Y
Cranston	Y	Y	?	?	?	N	N	Y
COLORADO								
Armstrong	?	?	Y	N	N	Y	N	Y
Hart	Y	Y	N	Y	Y	N	N	Y
CONNECTICUT								
Weicker	Y	Y	N	Y	Y	N	N	Y
Dodd	Y	Y	N	Y	Y	-	Y	Y
DELAWARE								
Roth	Y	Y	N	Y	Y	N	Y	Y
Biden	Y	?	N	Y	Y	N	N	Y
FLORIDA								
Hawkins	Y	Y	Y	N	N	-	?	?
Chiles	Y	?	Y	Y	Y	N	N	Y
GEORGIA								
Mattingly	Y	Y	Y	N	N	Y	N	Y
Nunn	Y	Y	Y	Y	N	Y	N	Y
HAWAII								
Inouye	Y	Y	Y	Y	Y	N	N	Y
Matsunaga	Y	Y	N	Y	Y	N	-	Y
IDAHO								
McClure	Y	Y	Y	N	N	Y	Y	Y
Symms	Y	Y	Y	N	N	Y	Y	Y
ILLINOIS								
Percy	Y	N	Y	Y	Y	Y	Y	Y
Dixon	Y	N	N	Y	Y	N	N	Y
INDIANA								
Lugar	Y	Y	Y	N	N	Y	Y	Y
Quayle	Y	Y	Y	N	N	Y	N	Y
IOWA								
Grassley	Y	Y	Y	N	N	Y	N	Y
Jepsen	Y	Y	Y	N	N	Y	Y	Y
KANSAS								
Dole	Y	Y	Y	N	N	Y	Y	Y
Kassebaum	Y	Y	Y	N	N	Y	Y	Y
KENTUCKY								
Ford	?	?	N	Y	Y	N	N	Y
Huddleston	?	?	Y	Y	Y	N	N	Y
LOUISIANA								
Johnston	Y	Y	Y	Y	Y	N	N	Y
Long	?	?	Y	Y	Y	?	Y	Y
MAINE								
Cohen	Y	Y	Y	Y	Y	Y	Y	Y
Mitchell	Y	Y	N	Y	Y	N	N	Y
MARYLAND								
Mathias	Y	Y	N	Y	Y	Y	?	Y
Sarbanes	Y	Y	N	Y	Y	N	?	Y
MASSACHUSETTS								
Kennedy	Y	Y	Y	Y	Y	N	N	Y
Tsongas	Y	Y	Y	Y	Y	N	N	Y
MICHIGAN								
Levin	Y	N	Y	Y	Y	N	N	Y
Riegle	Y	N	N	Y	Y	N	N	Y
MINNESOTA								
Boschwitz	Y	Y	Y	N	N	Y	N	Y
Durenberger	?	?	N	N	N	Y	N	Y
MISSISSIPPI								
Cochran	Y	N	Y	Y	Y	Y	Y	Y
Stennis	Y	N	Y	Y	Y	Y	Y	Y
MISSOURI								
Danforth	Y	Y	Y	N	N	Y	N	Y
Eagleton	?	?	N	Y	Y	N	N	Y
MONTANA								
Baucus	Y	Y	N	Y	Y	N	N	Y
Melcher	?	X	N	Y	Y	N	N	Y
NEBRASKA								
Exon	Y	Y	N	Y	Y	N	?	Y
Zorinsky	Y	Y	N	Y	Y	N	N	Y
NEVADA								
Laxalt	Y	Y	Y	N	N	Y	N	Y
Cannon	Y	Y	N	Y	Y	N	N	Y
NEW HAMPSHIRE								
Humphrey	Y	Y	Y	N	N	Y	Y	Y
Rudman	Y	Y	Y	N	N	Y	N	Y
NEW JERSEY								
Brady	?	?	Y	N	N	Y	Y	Y
Bradley	Y	Y	N	Y	Y	N	N	Y
NEW MEXICO								
Domenici	Y	Y	Y	N	N	Y	N	Y
Schmitt	?	?	Y	N	N	Y	N	Y
NEW YORK								
D'Amato	Y	Y	Y	N	N	Y	N	Y
Moynihan	Y	Y	Y	Y	Y	N	N	Y
NORTH CAROLINA								
East	?	+	Y	N	N	Y	Y	Y
Helms	N	Y	Y	N	N	Y	Y	Y
NORTH DAKOTA								
Andrews	Y	Y	Y	N	N	Y	N	Y
Burdick	Y	Y	N	Y	Y	N	N	Y
OHIO								
Glenn	Y	Y	Y	N	N	N	Y	Y
Metzenbaum	Y	N	Y	Y	N	Y	N	Y
OKLAHOMA								
Nickles	Y	Y	Y	N	N	Y	N	Y
Boren	Y	Y	Y	Y	N	N	N	Y
OREGON								
Hatfield	?	?	Y	N	N	Y	N	Y
Packwood	Y	Y	Y	N	N	Y	N	Y
PENNSYLVANIA								
Heinz	Y	Y	Y	Y	Y	Y	N	Y
Specter	Y	N	Y	Y	Y	N	Y	Y
RHODE ISLAND								
Chafee	Y	Y	Y	Y	Y	Y	Y	Y
Pell	Y	N	Y	Y	Y	N	+	Y
SOUTH CAROLINA								
Thurmond	Y	Y	Y	N	N	Y	N	Y
Hollings	Y	N	N	Y	Y	N	Y	Y
SOUTH DAKOTA								
Abdnor	?	?	Y	N	N	Y	N	Y
Pressler	Y	Y	Y	N	N	?	N	Y
TENNESSEE								
Baker	?	+	Y	N	N	Y	Y	Y
Sasser	+	#	N	Y	Y	-	N	Y
TEXAS								
Tower	Y	Y	Y	N	N	Y	Y	Y
Bentsen	Y	Y	Y	Y	Y	N	N	Y
UTAH								
Garn	Y	Y	Y	N	N	Y	N	Y
Hatch	Y	Y	Y	N	N	Y	Y	Y
VERMONT								
Stafford	Y	Y	N	Y	N	Y	N	Y
Leahy	Y	N	N	Y	Y	N	N	Y
VIRGINIA								
Warner	Y	Y	Y	N	N	Y	N	Y
Byrd*	Y	Y	Y	N	N	N	N	Y
WASHINGTON								
Gorton	Y	Y	Y	N	N	Y	N	Y
Jackson	Y	Y	N	Y	Y	N	N	Y
WEST VIRGINIA								
Byrd	Y	Y	N	Y	Y	N	N	Y
Randolph	Y	Y	N	Y	Y	N	N	Y
WISCONSIN								
Kasten	Y	Y	Y	N	N	?	Y	Y
Proxmire	Y	N	N	N	N	N	N	Y
WYOMING								
Simpson	Y	Y	Y	N	N	Y	?	Y
Wallop	?	?	?	?	?	Y	N	Y

KEY

Y	Voted for (yea).
#	Paired for.
+	Announced for.
N	Voted against (nay).
X	Paired against.
-	Announced against.
P	Voted "present".
C	Voted "present" to avoid possible conflict of interest.
?	Did not vote or otherwise make a position known.

Democrats   *Republicans*

ND - Northern Democrats   SD - Southern Democrats (Southern states - Ala., Ark., Fla., Ga., Ky., La., Miss., N.C., Okla., S.C., Tenn., Texas, Va.)   * Byrd elected as an independent.

92. S Res 382. Falkland Islands. Adoption of the resolution to declare that the United States "cannot stand neutral" in the dispute between Britain and Argentina over the Falkland Islands. While recognizing "the right of the United Kingdom and all other nations" to self-defense, the resolution said the United States should "further all efforts" to "achieve full withdrawal of Argentine forces from the Falkland Islands." Adopted 79-1: R 41-1; D 38-0 (ND 29-0, SD 9-0), April 29, 1982.

93. S 1662. National Nuclear Waste Policy Act. Passage of the bill to establish a federal program for the interim storage and eventual permanent disposal of highly radioactive nuclear waste. Passed 69-9: R 40-2; D 29-7 (ND 23-5, SD 6-2), April 29, 1982. A "yea" was a vote supporting the president's position.

94. S 2248. Department of Defense Authorization, Fiscal 1983. Quayle, R-Ind., amendment to prohibit transfer from the Department of Defense to the Department of Education of the schools for dependents of Department of Defense personnel. Adopted 59-38: R 46-7; D 13-31 (ND 5-24, SD 8-7), May 6, 1982.

95. S 2248. Department of Defense Authorization, Fiscal 1983. Mitchell, D-Maine, amendment to prohibit contracting out to civilian firms firefighting or base security jobs at military facilities. Adopted 50-47: R 9-44; D 41-3 (ND 27-2, SD 14-1), May 6, 1982.

96. S 2248. Department of Defense Authorization, Fiscal 1983. Metzenbaum, D-Ohio, motion to table (kill) the Mitchell, D-Maine, motion to reconsider the vote by which the Mitchell amendment (see vote 95, above) was adopted. Motion agreed to 50-47: R 9-44; D 41-3 (ND 27-2, SD 14-1), May 6, 1982.

97. S 2248. Department of Defense Authorization, Fiscal 1983/Social Security. Baker, R-Tenn., motion to table (kill) the Moynihan, D-N.Y., amendment to reject the May 5 action of the Senate Budget Committee calling for a $40 billion deficit reduction for fiscal 1983-85 from changes in the Social Security program. Motion agreed to 51-44: R 49-3; D 2-41 (ND 0-30, SD 2-11), May 11, 1982. (The tabling motion took with it the Byrd, D-W.Va., substitute to the Moynihan amendment, which would have added language declaring that Congress should take no action on Social Security until it considered the recommendations of the National Commission on Social Security Reform.)

98. S 2248. Department of Defense Authorization, Fiscal 1983. Percy, R-Ill., motion to table (kill) the Specter, R-Pa., amendment, as modified, stating the sense of Congress that the president should request a summit meeting with leaders of the Soviet Union to discuss the control of nuclear arms. Motion rejected 32-60: R 25-25; D 7-35 (ND 2-25, SD 5-10), May 12, 1982. A "yea" was a vote supporting the president's position.

99. S 2248. Department of Defense Authorization, Fiscal 1983. Tower, R-Texas, motion to recommit the bill to the Armed Services Committee with instructions to make $2.379 billion in reductions, as proposed earlier by the committee. Motion agreed to 99-0: R 53-0; D 46-0 (ND 31-0, SD 15-0), May 12, 1982.

	100	101	102	103	104	105	106	107
ALABAMA								
Denton	Y	Y	Y	Y	N	Y	N	N
Heflin	N	Y	Y	N	Y	Y	?	N
ALASKA								
Murkowski	Y	Y	Y	Y	N	Y	N	Y
Stevens	Y	Y	Y	Y	N	Y	N	Y
ARIZONA								
Goldwater	Y	N	N	Y	N	Y	N	N
DeConcini	N	Y	Y	N	Y	Y	N	Y
ARKANSAS								
Bumpers	N	Y	Y	N	Y	Y	N	Y
Pryor	N	Y	Y	N	Y	Y	N	Y
CALIFORNIA								
Hayakawa	Y	Y	Y	Y	N	Y	Y	N
Cranston	N	Y	Y	N	Y	Y	Y	N
COLORADO								
Armstrong	Y	Y	Y	Y	N	Y	N	N
Hart	N	Y	Y	N	Y	Y	N	Y
CONNECTICUT								
Weicker	N	Y	Y	N	N	Y	N	Y
Dodd	N	Y	Y	N	Y	Y	Y	N
DELAWARE								
Roth	N	Y	Y	Y	N	Y	N	Y
Biden	N	Y	Y	N	Y	Y	Y	N
FLORIDA								
Hawkins	N	Y	Y	N	Y	N	N	Y
Chiles	N	Y	Y	N	Y	Y	Y	N
GEORGIA								
Mattingly	Y	Y	Y	Y	N	Y	N	Y
Nunn	N	N	Y	Y	N	Y	Y	N
HAWAII								
Inouye	N	Y	Y	N	Y	Y	Y	N
Matsunaga	N	Y	Y	N	Y	Y	N	Y
IDAHO								
McClure	Y	Y	Y	Y	N	Y	Y	N
Symms	Y	Y	Y	Y	N	Y	N	?
ILLINOIS								
Percy	Y	Y	Y	Y	N	N	N	N
Dixon	N	Y	Y	N	Y	N	N	N
INDIANA								
Lugar	Y	Y	Y	Y	N	Y	N	N
Quayle	Y	Y	Y	Y	N	Y	N	Y
IOWA								
Grassley	Y	Y	Y	Y	N	Y	N	Y
Jepsen	Y	Y	Y	Y	N	Y	N	N
KANSAS								
Dole	Y	Y	Y	Y	N	Y	N	Y
Kassebaum	Y	Y	Y	Y	N	Y	N	Y
KENTUCKY								
Ford	N	Y	Y	N	Y	Y	Y	N
Huddleston	N	Y	Y	N	Y	Y	N	N
LOUISIANA								
Johnston	N	Y	Y	?	?	?	?	N
Long	Y	N	Y	N	Y	Y	Y	Y
MAINE								
Cohen	Y	Y	Y	Y	N	Y	N	N
Mitchell	N	Y	Y	N	Y	Y	Y	N
MARYLAND								
Mathias	Y	Y	Y	N	N	Y	N	?
Sarbanes	N	Y	Y	N	Y	Y	Y	N
MASSACHUSETTS								
Kennedy	N	Y	Y	N	Y	Y	Y	N
Tsongas	N	Y	Y	N	Y	Y	Y	N
MICHIGAN								
Levin	N	Y	Y	N	Y	Y	Y	N
Riegle	N	Y	Y	N	Y	Y	Y	N
MINNESOTA								
Boschwitz	Y	Y	Y	Y	N	Y	Y	N
Durenberger	Y	Y	Y	?	?	?	N	Y
MISSISSIPPI								
Cochran	Y	Y	Y	Y	N	Y	N	Y
Stennis	Y	N	N	N	Y	Y	Y	N
MISSOURI								
Danforth	Y	Y	Y	N	N	Y	N	N
Eagleton	N	Y	Y	N	Y	Y	Y	N
MONTANA								
Baucus	N	Y	Y	N	Y	Y	Y	N
Melcher	N	Y	Y	N	Y	Y	N	Y
NEBRASKA								
Exon	N	Y	Y	N	Y	Y	Y	N
Zorinsky	N	Y	Y	N	Y	Y	Y	N
NEVADA								
Laxalt	Y	Y	Y	Y	N	Y	N	N
Cannon	N	Y	Y	N	Y	Y	Y	N
NEW HAMPSHIRE								
Humphrey	Y	Y	Y	Y	N	Y	Y	N
Rudman	Y	Y	Y	Y	N	Y	N	Y
NEW JERSEY								
Brady	Y	Y	Y	Y	N	Y	N	N
Bradley	N	Y	Y	N	Y	Y	N	N
NEW MEXICO								
Domenici	Y	Y	Y	?	N	Y	N	Y
Schmitt	Y	Y	Y	?	N	Y	N	Y
NEW YORK								
D'Amato	Y	Y	Y	Y	N	Y	N	Y
Moynihan	N	N	Y	N	Y	Y	N	Y
NORTH CAROLINA								
East	Y	Y	N	Y	N	Y	N	N
Helms	Y	Y	Y	Y	N	Y	N	N
NORTH DAKOTA								
Andrews	Y	Y	Y	Y	N	Y	N	Y
Burdick	N	Y	Y	N	Y	N	N	Y
OHIO								
Glenn	N	Y	Y	N	Y	Y	Y	N
Metzenbaum	?	?	?	?	?	?	?	?
OKLAHOMA								
Nickles	Y	Y	Y	Y	N	Y	N	N
Boren	N	Y	Y	N	Y	Y	Y	N
OREGON								
Hatfield	Y	Y	Y	Y	N	Y	N	Y
Packwood	Y	Y	Y	Y	N	Y	N	Y
PENNSYLVANIA								
Heinz	Y	Y	Y	Y	N	Y	N	Y
Specter	Y	Y	Y	Y	N	Y	N	Y
RHODE ISLAND								
Chafee	Y	Y	Y	Y	N	Y	?	?
Pell	N	Y	Y	N	Y	Y	N	Y
SOUTH CAROLINA								
Thurmond	Y	Y	N	Y	N	Y	Y	N
Hollings	Y	N	Y	?	?	?	?	?
SOUTH DAKOTA								
Abdnor	Y	Y	Y	Y	N	Y	N	Y
Pressler	N	Y	Y	?	?	?	?	?
TENNESSEE								
Baker	Y	Y	Y	Y	N	Y	N	N
Sasser	N	Y	Y	N	Y	Y	Y	N
TEXAS								
Tower	Y	N	N	Y	N	Y	Y	N
Bentsen	N	Y	Y	N	Y	Y	Y	N
UTAH								
Garn	Y	Y	Y	Y	N	Y	N	N
Hatch	?	?	+	?	?	?	?	?
VERMONT								
Stafford	Y	Y	Y	?	?	Y	N	N
Leahy	N	Y	Y	N	Y	Y	Y	N
VIRGINIA								
Warner	Y	Y	Y	Y	N	Y	N	Y
Byrd*	Y	Y	Y	N	Y	Y	Y	N
WASHINGTON								
Gorton	Y	Y	Y	Y	N	Y	N	N
Jackson	N	Y	Y	N	Y	N	Y	N
WEST VIRGINIA								
Byrd	N	Y	Y	N	Y	Y	Y	N
Randolph	N	Y	Y	N	Y	Y	N	Y
WISCONSIN								
Kasten	Y	Y	Y	Y	N	N	N	N
Proxmire	N	Y	Y	N	Y	N	Y	N
WYOMING								
Simpson	Y	Y	Y	Y	N	Y	N	Y
Wallop	Y	Y	Y	Y	N	Y	N	Y

KEY

- Y Voted for (yea).
- # Paired for.
- + Announced for.
- N Voted against (nay).
- X Paired against.
- - Announced against.
- P Voted "present".
- C Voted "present" to avoid possible conflict of interest.
- ? Did not vote or otherwise make a position known.

Democrats *Republicans*

ND - Northern Democrats   SD - Southern Democrats (Southern states - Ala., Ark., Fla., Ga., Ky., La., Miss., N.C., Okla., S.C., Tenn., Texas, Va.)   *Byrd elected as an independent.

100. S 2248. Department of Defense Authorization, Fiscal 1983/Social Security. Baker, R-Tenn., motion to table (kill) the Baucus, D-Mont., amendment to direct the secretary of defense to make expenditures only to the extent funds are available and in amounts that have been appropriated. Motion agreed to 53-45: R 49-4; D 4-41 (ND 0-30, SD 4-11), May 12, 1982. (The tabling motion took with it the Byrd, D-W.Va., substitute to reject the Budget Committee's May 5 action calling for a $40 billion savings in Social Security for fiscal 1983-85.)

101. S 2248. Department of Defense Authorization, Fiscal 1983/Social Security. Baker, R-Tenn., substitute to the Dole, R-Kan., amendment and the Dole amendment (considered en bloc) to declare that the scheduled 7.4 percent Social Security cost-of-living increase would be paid on July 1, that the Senate would renew its commitment to preserve Social Security, and that no action would be taken that was not absolutely necessary to keep the system solvent. The Baker substitute added language declaring that Congress would await the recommendations of the National Commission on Social Security Reform before making changes to the system. Adopted 91-7: R 51-2; D 40-5 (ND 29-1, SD 11-4), May 12, 1982.

102. S 2248. Department of Defense Authorization, Fiscal 1983. Specter, R-Pa., amendment, as modified by the Tower, R-Texas, amendment, to commend President Reagan for his desire to meet with the president of the Soviet Union; to state that such a meeting should be "an essential step" in efforts to achieve "significant, balanced and verifiable reductions" in nuclear arms; and to request the president of the Soviet Union to respond favorably to an invitation to such a summit meeting. Adopted 92-6: R 48-5; D 44-1 (ND 30-0, SD 14-1), May 12, 1982.

103. S 2248. Department of Defense Authorization, Fiscal 1983. Roth, R-Del., motion to table (kill) the Bentsen, D-Texas, amendment to the Roth, R-Del., amendment to establish an office of inspector general in the Department of Defense. The Bentsen amendment gave the inspector general greater independence from the secretary of defense than did the Roth amendment. Motion rejected 45-46: R 44-4; D 1-42 (ND 0-30, SD 1-12), May 12, 1982. (The Bentsen amendment subsequently was tabled by voice vote. The Roth amendment subsequently was adopted (see vote 105, below).)

104. S 2248. Department of Defense Authorization, Fiscal 1983. Bentsen, D-Texas, motion to table (kill) the Baker, R-Tenn., motion to reconsider the vote by which the Roth, R-Del., motion was rejected (see vote 103, above). The purpose of the Bentsen motion was to keep alive the Bentsen amendment to establish an office of inspector general in the Department of Defense. Motion rejected 42-51: R 0-50; D 42-1 (ND 30-0, SD 12-1), May 12, 1982. (The Bentsen amendment subsequently was tabled by voice vote.)

105. S 2248. Department of Defense Authorization, Fiscal 1983. Roth, R-Del., amendment to establish an office of inspector general in the Department of Defense. Adopted 94-0: R 51-0; D 43-0 (ND 30-0, SD 13-0), May 12, 1982.

106. S 2248. Department of Defense Authorization, Fiscal 1983. Exon, D-Neb., motion to table (kill) the Dole, R-Kan., amendment to eliminate $80 million in fiscal 1983 for retention, operation and maintenance of Titan II intercontinental ballistic missiles. Motion rejected 32-61: R 8-43; D 24-18 (ND 15-15, SD 9-3), May 12, 1982. (The Dole amendment subsequently was rejected (see vote 107, below).)

107. S 2248. Department of Defense Authorization, Fiscal 1983. Dole, R-Kan., amendment to eliminate $80 million in fiscal 1983 for retention, operation and maintenance of Titan II intercontinental ballistic missiles. Rejected 40-54: R 24-26; D 16-28 (ND 13-17, SD 3-11), May 12, 1982.

	108	109	110	111	112
ALABAMA					
Denton	Y	Y	N	Y	Y
Heflin	Y	N	Y	Y	Y
ALASKA					
Murkowski	Y	N	Y	Y	Y
Stevens	Y	N	Y	Y	Y
ARIZONA					
Goldwater	Y	Y	N	N	Y
DeConcini	Y	N	Y	Y	Y
ARKANSAS					
Bumpers	Y	N	Y	N	N
Pryor	Y	N	Y	N	N
CALIFORNIA					
Hayakawa	Y	N	Y	Y	Y
Cranston	Y	Y	N	N	N
COLORADO					
Armstrong	?	N	N	Y	Y
Hart	Y	Y	N	N	N
CONNECTICUT					
Weicker	Y	N	N	Y	Y
Dodd	Y	N	Y	N	N
DELAWARE					
Roth	Y	Y	N	Y	Y
Biden	?	Y	N	Y	N
FLORIDA					
Hawkins	Y	N	Y	Y	Y
Chiles	Y	Y	N	Y	Y
GEORGIA					
Mattingly	Y	Y	N	Y	Y
Nunn	Y	Y	N	Y	Y
HAWAII					
Inouye	Y	N	Y	Y	Y
Matsunaga	?	N	Y	N	N
IDAHO					
McClure	Y	N	Y	N	?
Symms	Y	N	Y	Y	Y
ILLINOIS					
Percy	Y	Y	N	Y	Y
Dixon	Y	N	+	+	+
INDIANA					
Lugar	Y	N	Y	Y	Y
Quayle	Y	N	N	Y	Y

	108	109	110	111	112
IOWA					
Grassley	N	Y	N	Y	Y
Jepsen	Y	Y	N	Y	Y
KANSAS					
Dole	Y	N	Y	N	Y
Kassebaum	?	N	Y	N	Y
KENTUCKY					
Ford	Y	N	Y	N	N
Huddleston	?	Y	N	N	N
LOUISIANA					
Johnston	Y	Y	N	Y	Y
Long	Y	Y	N	Y	Y
MAINE					
Cohen	Y	Y	N	Y	Y
Mitchell	Y	N	Y	Y	Y
MARYLAND					
Mathias	Y	N	Y	N	Y
Sarbanes	?	N	?	?	?
MASSACHUSETTS					
Kennedy	?	N	Y	N	N
Tsongas	Y	Y	N	?	?
MICHIGAN					
Levin	Y	Y	N	N	N
Riegle	Y	N	N	N	N
MINNESOTA					
Boschwitz	Y	N	Y	Y	Y
Durenberger	Y	N	Y	Y	Y
MISSISSIPPI					
Cochran	Y	Y	N	Y	Y
Stennis	Y	Y	N	Y	Y
MISSOURI					
Danforth	Y	N	Y	Y	?
Eagleton	Y	N	Y	N	N
MONTANA					
Baucus	Y	Y	N	N	N
Melcher	Y	N	Y	N	N
NEBRASKA					
Exon	Y	Y	N	N	Y
Zorinsky	Y	Y	N	Y	Y
NEVADA					
Laxalt	?	Y	N	Y	Y
Cannon	Y	N	Y	?	?

	108	109	110	111	112
NEW HAMPSHIRE					
Humphrey	Y	Y	N	Y	Y
Rudman	Y	N	Y	Y	Y
NEW JERSEY					
Brady	Y	N	Y	Y	?
Bradley	Y	Y	N	N	Y
NEW MEXICO					
Domenici	Y	N	Y	Y	Y
Schmitt	Y	N	Y	Y	Y
NEW YORK					
D'Amato	Y	N	Y	Y	Y
Moynihan	?	N	Y	N	Y
NORTH CAROLINA					
East	Y	Y	N	Y	Y
Helms	Y	Y	N	Y	Y
NORTH DAKOTA					
Andrews	Y	N	Y	Y	Y
Burdick	Y	N	Y	N	Y
OHIO					
Glenn	Y	Y	N	Y	Y
Metzenbaum	Y	N	Y	N	Y
OKLAHOMA					
Nickles	Y	Y	N	Y	Y
Boren	Y	Y	N	Y	Y
OREGON					
Hatfield	Y	N	Y	N	Y
Packwood	Y	N	Y	Y	Y
PENNSYLVANIA					
Heinz	?	N	Y	Y	Y
Specter	Y	N	Y	Y	Y
RHODE ISLAND					
Chafee	Y	N	Y	N	N
Pell	?	N	Y	N	N
SOUTH CAROLINA					
Thurmond	Y	Y	N	Y	Y
Hollings	?	?	?	?	?
SOUTH DAKOTA					
Abdnor	Y	N	Y	Y	Y
Pressler	Y	N	Y	Y	Y
TENNESSEE					
Baker	Y	Y	N	Y	Y
Sasser	Y	Y	N	Y	Y

	108	109	110	111	112
TEXAS					
Tower	Y	Y	N	Y	Y
Bentsen	Y	N	Y	Y	Y
UTAH					
Garn	Y	Y	N	Y	Y
Hatch	Y	Y	N	Y	Y
VERMONT					
Stafford	Y	N	Y	N	Y
Leahy	Y	N	Y	N	N
VIRGINIA					
Warner	Y	N	Y	Y	Y
Byrd*	Y	Y	N	Y	Y
WASHINGTON					
Gorton	Y	N	Y	N	Y
Jackson	Y	N	Y	Y	Y
WEST VIRGINIA					
Byrd	Y	N	N	Y	Y
Randolph	Y	N	Y	N	Y
WISCONSIN					
Kasten	Y	Y	N	Y	Y
Proxmire	Y	N	Y	N	N
WYOMING					
Simpson	Y	N	Y	Y	Y
Wallop	Y	N	Y	Y	?

KEY

Y Voted for (yea).
Paired for.
+ Announced for.
N Voted against (nay).
X Paired against.
- Announced against.
P Voted "present".
C Voted "present" to avoid possible conflict of interest.
? Did not vote or otherwise make a position known.

Democrats *Republicans*

ND - Northern Democrats   SD - Southern Democrats (Southern states - Ala., Ark., Fla., Ga., Ky., La., Miss., N.C., Okla., S.C., Tenn., Texas, Va.)

*Byrd elected as an independent.

108. S 2248. Department of Defense Authorization, Fiscal 1983. Roth, R-Del., amendment expressing the sense of Congress that the member countries of NATO must pool their resources more effectively for their common defense. Adopted 87-1: R 49-1; D 38-0 (ND 25-0, SD 13-0), May 13, 1982.

109. S 2248. Department of Defense Authorization, Fiscal 1983. Baker, R-Tenn., motion to table (kill) the Jackson, D-Wash., amendment to purchase wide-body jetliners from U.S. airlines instead of newly manufactured C-5 transport planes. Motion rejected 39-60: R 20-34; D 19-26 (ND 10-21, SD 9-5), May 13, 1982. A "yea" was a vote supporting the president's position. (The Jackson amendment and a substantially identical Gorton, R-Wash., substitute amendment subsequently were adopted by voice vote.)

110. S 2248. Department of Defense Authorization, Fiscal 1983. Dole, R-Kan., motion to table (kill) the Mattingly, R-Ga., amendment to require that funds to acquire wide-body jetliners (see vote 109, above) be used to lease and modify the

planes for the Civil Reserve Air Fleet, rather than to purchase them. Motion agreed to 53-44: R 31-23; D 22-21 (ND 17-12, SD 5-9), May 13, 1982. A "nay" was a vote supporting the president's position. (The Mattingly amendment was a substitute for a substantially identical Nunn, D-Ga., amendment. The Nunn amendment subsequently was withdrawn.)

111. S 2248. Department of Defense Authorization, Fiscal 1983. Tower, R-Texas, motion to table (kill) the Hart, D-Colo., amendment to delete authorization for one of two *Nimitz*-class nuclear-powered aircraft carriers included in the bill. Motion agreed to 63-32: R 45-9; D 18-23 (ND 8-19, SD 10-4), May 13, 1982. A "yea" was a vote supporting the president's position.

112. S 2248. Department of Defense Authorization, Fiscal 1983. Tower, R-Texas, motion to table (kill) the Hart, D-Colo., amendment to delete authorization for one *Nimitz*-class nuclear-powered aircraft carrier and add authorization for two smaller aircraft carriers. Motion agreed to 72-19: R 49-1; D 23-18 (ND 13-14, SD 10-4), May 13, 1982. A "yea" was a vote supporting the president's position.

	113	114	115	116	117	118	119	120
ALABAMA								
Denton	Y	Y	N	Y	Y	Y	Y	Y
Heflin	Y	Y	Y	N	N	Y	Y	Y
ALASKA								
Murkowski	Y	N	Y	Y	Y	Y	Y	Y
Stevens	Y	N	Y	N	N	Y	Y	Y
ARIZONA								
Goldwater	Y	N	N	Y	Y	Y	Y	Y
DeConcini	Y	Y	Y	N	N	N	Y	Y
ARKANSAS								
Bumpers	N	N	N	N	N	Y	Y	Y
Pryor	N	N	N	Y	N	N	Y	Y
CALIFORNIA								
Hayakawa	N	Y	N	Y	Y	Y	Y	Y
Cranston	N	Y	Y	Y	Y	N	Y	Y
COLORADO								
Armstrong	Y	N	N	Y	Y	Y	Y	Y
Hart	N	Y	Y	Y	Y	N	Y	N
CONNECTICUT								
Weicker	N	N	N	N	N	N	Y	Y
Dodd	N	Y	Y	Y	Y	N	Y	Y
DELAWARE								
Roth	Y	N	N	Y	Y	N	Y	Y
Biden	Y	Y	Y	N	N	N	Y	Y
FLORIDA								
Hawkins	Y	N	Y	Y	Y	?	?	?
Chiles	Y	N	N	Y	Y	N	Y	Y
GEORGIA								
Mattingly	Y	N	N	Y	Y	Y	Y	Y
Nunn	Y	N	?	Y	Y	Y	Y	Y
HAWAII								
Inouye	N	Y	Y	N	N	N	?	?
Matsunaga	N	Y	Y	N	N	N	Y	Y
IDAHO								
McClure	?	?	?	?	?	?	?	?
Symms	Y	N	N	Y	Y	Y	Y	Y
ILLINOIS								
Percy	Y	Y	Y	Y	Y	N	Y	Y
Dixon	?	+	+	-	-	#	+	+
INDIANA								
Lugar	Y	Y	Y	Y	Y	Y	Y	Y
Quayle	Y	Y	Y	Y	Y	Y	Y	Y
IOWA								
Grassley	Y	N	N	Y	Y	N	Y	Y
Jepsen	Y	N	N	Y	Y	Y	Y	Y
KANSAS								
Dole	Y	Y	Y	Y	Y	Y	Y	Y
Kassebaum	Y	N	N	Y	Y	N	Y	N
KENTUCKY								
Ford	Y	Y	Y	N	N	N	Y	Y
Huddleston	Y	N	N	N	N	N	N	Y
LOUISIANA								
Johnston	N	N	N	Y	Y	Y	Y	Y
Long	Y	N	N	Y	Y	Y	Y	Y
MAINE								
Cohen	Y	Y	Y	Y	Y	Y	Y	Y
Mitchell	N	Y	Y	Y	Y	N	Y	Y
MARYLAND								
Mathias	N	Y	Y	Y	Y	N	Y	Y
Sarbanes	?	?	?	?	?	?	?	?
MASSACHUSETTS								
Kennedy	N	Y	Y	?	?	X	?	?
Tsongas	?	?	?	Y	Y	N	Y	N
MICHIGAN								
Levin	N	Y	Y	N	N	N	Y	N
Riegle	N	+	Y	N	N	N	Y	Y
MINNESOTA								
Boschwitz	Y	Y	Y	Y	Y	Y	Y	Y
Durenberger	Y	Y	Y	N	N	N	?	?
MISSISSIPPI								
Cochran	Y	N	N	Y	Y	N	Y	Y
Stennis	Y	N	N	Y	Y	Y	Y	Y
MISSOURI								
Danforth	Y	N	N	Y	Y	N	Y	Y
Eagleton	N	Y	Y	N	N	N	Y	Y
MONTANA								
Baucus	N	Y	Y	N	N	N	Y	N
Melcher	N	Y	Y	N	N	N	Y	Y
NEBRASKA								
Exon	Y	N	N	N	N	Y	Y	Y
Zorinsky	Y	N	N	N	N	Y	Y	Y
NEVADA								
Laxalt	Y	N	N	Y	Y	Y	Y	Y
Cannon	?	N	N	N	N	Y	Y	Y
NEW HAMPSHIRE								
Humphrey	Y	N	N	Y	Y	Y	Y	Y
Rudman	Y	Y	Y	N	N	Y	Y	Y
NEW JERSEY								
Brady	Y	Y	Y	N	Y	Y	Y	Y
Bradley	N	Y	Y	Y	N	N	Y	Y
NEW MEXICO								
Domenici	Y	N	Y	Y	Y	Y	Y	Y
Schmitt	Y	N	Y	Y	Y	Y	Y	Y
NEW YORK								
D'Amato	Y	Y	Y	N	Y	Y	Y	Y
Moynihan	N	Y	Y	Y	N	N	Y	Y
NORTH CAROLINA								
East	Y	N	N	Y	Y	Y	Y	Y
Helms	Y	N	N	Y	Y	Y	Y	Y
NORTH DAKOTA								
Andrews	Y	N	Y	N	N	N	Y	Y
Burdick	N	Y	Y	N	N	N	Y	Y
OHIO								
Glenn	N	Y	Y	N	N	Y	Y	Y
Metzenbaum	N	Y	Y	N	N	Y	Y	Y
OKLAHOMA								
Nickles	Y	N	N	Y	Y	Y	Y	Y
Boren	Y	N	N	N	N	N	Y	Y
OREGON								
Hatfield	N	Y	Y	Y	N	N	Y	N
Packwood	Y	N	Y	Y	Y	N	Y	Y
PENNSYLVANIA								
Heinz	Y	Y	Y	N	N	N	Y	Y
Specter	N	Y	Y	N	N	N	Y	Y
RHODE ISLAND								
Chafee	Y	Y	Y	Y	Y	N	Y	Y
Pell	N	Y	Y	Y	N	N	Y	Y
SOUTH CAROLINA								
Thurmond	Y	N	N	Y	Y	Y	Y	Y
Hollings	?	?	?	?	?	?	?	?
SOUTH DAKOTA								
Abdnor	Y	N	N	N	N	Y	Y	Y
Pressler	Y	N	N	Y	Y	Y	Y	Y
TENNESSEE								
Baker	Y	Y	Y	Y	Y	Y	Y	Y
Sasser	Y	Y	Y	N	N	Y	Y	Y
TEXAS								
Tower	Y	N	N	Y	Y	Y	Y	Y
Bentsen	Y	N	N	N	N	Y	Y	Y
UTAH								
Garn	Y	N	N	Y	Y	Y	Y	Y
Hatch	Y	N	N	Y	Y	Y	Y	Y
VERMONT								
Stafford	Y	Y	Y	Y	Y	N	Y	Y
Leahy	N	Y	Y	Y	Y	N	Y	Y
VIRGINIA								
Warner	Y	N	N	Y	Y	Y	Y	Y
Byrd*	Y	N	?	Y	Y	Y	Y	Y
WASHINGTON								
Gorton	Y	N	N	Y	Y	Y	Y	Y
Jackson	Y	Y	Y	N	N	Y	Y	Y
WEST VIRGINIA								
Byrd	Y	Y	Y	N	N	Y	Y	Y
Randolph	N	Y	Y	N	N	Y	Y	Y
WISCONSIN								
Kasten	Y	N	N	Y	Y	Y	Y	Y
Proxmire	N	N	N	Y	Y	N	Y	N
WYOMING								
Simpson	Y	N	N	Y	Y	Y	Y	Y
Wallop	Y	N	N	Y	Y	Y	Y	Y

KEY

Y Voted for (yea).
Paired for.
+ Announced for.
N Voted against (nay).
X Paired against.
- Announced against.
P Voted "present".
C Voted "present" to avoid possible conflict of interest.
? Did not vote or otherwise make a position known.

Democrats *Republicans*

ND - Northern Democrats   SD - Southern Democrats (Southern states - Ala., Ark., Fla., Ga., Ky., La., Miss., N.C., Okla., S.C., Tenn., Texas, Va.)   *Byrd elected as an independent.

113. S 2248. Department of Defense Authorization, Fiscal 1983. Warner, R-Va., motion to table (kill) the Glenn, D-Ohio, amendment to delete $1,734,300 for research and development of the MX missile, to prohibit use of funds in the bill for research and development on the MX, and to authorize up to $565 million for research and development of a new intercontinental missile system that would be capable of surviving an attack and delivering a devastating counterattack. Motion agreed to 65-29: R 48-5; D 17-24 (ND 6-21, SD 11-3), May 13, 1982. A "yea" was a vote supporting the president's position.

114. S 2248. Department of Defense Authorization, Fiscal 1983. Moynihan, D-N.Y., amendment to direct the secretary of defense to continue a test program that allowed a limited waiver of the so-called "Maybank amendment," thus permitting the preferential awarding of contracts to firms located in labor surplus areas, as long as the price differential on each such contract did not exceed 2 percent and the total value of such contracts did not exceed $3 billion. Rejected 45-49: R 19-34; D 26-15 (ND 23-4, SD 3-11), May 13, 1982.

115. S 2248. Department of Defense Authorization, Fiscal 1983. Moynihan, D-N.Y., amendment to direct the secretary of defense to continue a test program allowing waivers of the "Maybank amendment," thus permitting the preferential awarding of contracts to firms in labor surplus areas, if the price differential on each contract did not exceed 1.5 percent and the total value of such contracts did not exceed $3 billion. Adopted 48-45: R 21-32; D 27-13 (ND 24-4, SD 3-9), May 13, 1982.

116. S 2248. Department of Defense Authorization, Fiscal 1983. Tower, R-Texas, motion to table (kill) the Heinz, R-Pa., amendment to restore a prohibition of most Department of Defense purchases of foreign-made specialty metals or chemical warfare protective clothing. Motion agreed to 59-36: R 43-10; D 16-26 (ND 9-19, SD 7-7), in the session which began May 13, 1982. A "yea" was a vote supporting the president's position.

117. S 2248. Department of Defense Authorization, Fiscal 1983. Tower, R-Texas, motion to table (kill) the Byrd, D-W.Va., amendment to prohibit Department of Defense purchases of foreign-made specialty metals or chemical warfare protective clothing, unless such purchases were required by agreements with foreign nations or were needed to standardize NATO equipment. Motion agreed to 56-39: R 43-10; D 13-29 (ND 7-21, SD 6-8), in the session which began May 13, 1982. A "yea" was a vote supporting the president's position.

118. S 2248. Department of Defense Authorization, Fiscal 1983. Tower, R-Texas, motion to table (kill) the Hart, D-Colo., amendment to delete from the bill $54 million for the production of binary chemical weapons and to earmark $54 million in the bill to buy equipment and materials to defend against chemical weapons. Motion agreed to 49-45: R 35-17; D 14-28 (ND 6-22, SD 8-6), in the session which began May 13, 1982. A "yea" was a vote supporting the president's position.

119. S 2248. Department of Defense Authorization, Fiscal 1983. Hatfield, R-Ore., amendment to prohibit the use of funds in the bill to produce binary chemical weapons unless the president certified to Congress that the United States would not engage in live chemical or bacteriological agent testing on human beings; that one existing unitary chemical weapon shell would be destroyed for each binary shell produced; and that the number of new shells would not exceed the requirement for U.S. stocks, unless one or more NATO nations agreed to accept the binary chemical weapons. Adopted 92-0: R 51-0; D 41-0 (ND 27-0, SD 14-0), in the session which began May 13, 1982.

120. S 2248. Department of Defense Authorization, Fiscal 1983. Passage of the bill to authorize $177,397,810,000 for Department of Defense research, procurement and operations in fiscal year 1983, and making a supplemental authorization of $731,400,000 for fiscal year 1982. Passed 84-8: R 49-2; D 35-6 (ND 21-6, SD 14-0), in the session which began May 13, 1982.

CQ Senate Votes 121 - 128

Corresponding to Congressional Record Votes 121, 122, 123, 124, 125, 126, 127, 128

	121	122	123	124	125	126	127	128
ALABAMA								
Denton	Y	Y	N	?	Y	N	N	N
Heflin	Y	Y	Y	N	Y	Y	N	Y
ALASKA								
Murkowski	Y	Y	N	N	Y	N	N	N
Stevens	Y	Y	N	N	Y	N	N	Y
ARIZONA								
Goldwater	?	?	N	N	Y	X	N	Y
DeConcini	Y	Y	N	N	Y	Y	N	Y
ARKANSAS								
Bumpers	Y	Y	Y	N	N	Y	Y	N
Pryor	+	?	Y	N	N	Y	Y	N
CALIFORNIA								
Hayakawa	Y	Y	N	N	Y	N	N	N
Cranston	N	Y	Y	N	N	Y	Y	N
COLORADO								
Armstrong	Y	Y	N	N	Y	N	N	N
Hart	N	Y	Y	Y	N	Y	Y	N
CONNECTICUT								
Weicker	N	N	Y	N	N	Y	?	N
Dodd	N	?	Y	Y	N	Y	Y	N
DELAWARE								
Roth	Y	Y	N	N	Y	N	N	Y
Biden	N	Y	Y	N	N	Y	Y	N
FLORIDA								
Hawkins	N	Y	N	N	Y	N	Y	N
Chiles	Y	Y	Y	N	Y	Y	Y	N
GEORGIA								
Mattingly	Y	Y	N	N	Y	N	N	N
Nunn	Y	Y	N	N	Y	Y	N	N
HAWAII								
Inouye	Y	Y	Y	?	?	Y	Y	N
Matsunaga	+	Y	Y	Y	N	Y	?	N
IDAHO								
McClure	Y	Y	N	N	Y	N	N	N
Symms	Y	Y	N	N	Y	N	N	Y
ILLINOIS								
Percy	?	Y	N	N	N	N	N	N
Dixon	Y	Y	Y	N	N	Y	N	N
INDIANA								
Lugar	N	Y	N	N	Y	N	N	N
Quayle	Y	N	N	N	Y	N	N	N
IOWA								
Grassley	Y	Y	N	N	N	N	N	Y
Jepsen	Y	Y	N	N	Y	N	N	N
KANSAS								
Dole	Y	?	N	N	N	N	N	N
Kassebaum	Y	Y	N	N	N	N	N	N
KENTUCKY								
Ford	Y	Y	Y	N	Y	N	Y	Y
Huddleston	Y	Y	Y	N	Y	Y	Y	N
LOUISIANA								
Johnston	Y	Y	Y	N	Y	Y	N	N
Long	N	N	Y	N	Y	Y	N	Y
MAINE								
Cohen	N	Y	N	N	Y	N	Y	N
Mitchell	N	Y	Y	N	N	Y	Y	N
MARYLAND								
Mathias	N	Y	N	N	N	Y	N	N
Sarbanes	N	?	Y	Y	N	Y	Y	N
MASSACHUSETTS								
Kennedy	N	Y	Y	Y	N	Y	Y	N
Tsongas	N	Y	Y	N	N	Y	Y	N
MICHIGAN								
Levin	Y	Y	Y	Y	N	Y	Y	N
Riegle	Y	Y	Y	Y	N	Y	Y	N
MINNESOTA								
Boschwitz	Y	Y	N	N	Y	N	N	N
Durenberger	N	Y	N	N	N	N	Y	N
MISSISSIPPI								
Cochran	Y	Y	N	N	Y	N	N	N
Stennis	Y	Y	?	N	Y	Y	Y	Y
MISSOURI								
Danforth	N	Y	N	N	Y	N	N	N
Eagleton	Y	?	Y	Y	N	Y	Y	N
MONTANA								
Baucus	Y	Y	Y	N	N	Y	Y	Y
Melcher	Y	Y	Y	Y	N	Y	Y	Y
NEBRASKA								
Exon	Y	Y	N	N	Y	Y	Y	Y
Zorinsky	Y	Y	N	N	Y	N	N	Y
NEVADA								
Laxalt	Y	Y	N	N	Y	N	N	N
Cannon	Y	Y	Y	N	N	Y	N	Y
NEW HAMPSHIRE								
Humphrey	Y	Y	N	N	Y	N	N	Y
Rudman	Y	Y	N	N	Y	N	N	N
NEW JERSEY								
Brady	Y	Y	N	N	Y	N	N	N
Bradley	N	Y	Y	Y	N	Y	Y	N
NEW MEXICO								
Domenici	Y	Y	N	N	Y	N	N	N
Schmitt	Y	Y	N	N	Y	N	N	N
NEW YORK								
D'Amato	Y	Y	N	N	Y	N	Y	N
Moynihan	N	Y	Y	Y	N	Y	Y	N
NORTH CAROLINA								
East	Y	Y	N	N	Y	N	N	N
Helms	Y	Y	N	N	Y	N	N	Y
NORTH DAKOTA								
Andrews	Y	Y	N	N	N	N	N	N
Burdick	Y	Y	Y	N	N	Y	Y	Y
OHIO								
Glenn	Y	Y	Y	N	Y	Y	Y	Y
Metzenbaum	N	Y	Y	Y	N	Y	Y	Y
OKLAHOMA								
Nickles	Y	Y	N	N	Y	N	N	Y
Boren	Y	Y	N	N	N	N	N	Y
OREGON								
Hatfield	Y	Y	N	N	N	N	N	Y
Packwood	N	Y	N	N	N	N	N	N
PENNSYLVANIA								
Heinz	N	Y	N	N	X	#	N	N
Specter	N	Y	N	N	N	N	N	N
RHODE ISLAND								
Chafee	N	Y	N	N	N	N	N	N
Pell	N	Y	Y	N	N	Y	Y	N
SOUTH CAROLINA								
Thurmond	Y	Y	N	N	Y	N	N	N
Hollings	Y	Y	Y	N	Y	Y	Y	N
SOUTH DAKOTA								
Abdnor	Y	Y	N	N	Y	N	N	N
Pressler	Y	Y	N	N	N	N	N	Y
TENNESSEE								
Baker	Y	Y	N	N	#	N	N	N
Sasser	Y	Y	Y	N	Y	Y	Y	N
TEXAS								
Tower	Y	Y	N	N	Y	N	N	N
Bentsen	Y	Y	Y	N	Y	Y	Y	N
UTAH								
Garn	Y	Y	N	N	Y	N	N	N
Hatch	Y	Y	N	N	Y	N	N	N
VERMONT								
Stafford	Y	Y	N	N	Y	N	N	N
Leahy	Y	Y	Y	N	N	Y	Y	Y
VIRGINIA								
Warner	Y	N	N	N	Y	N	N	N
Byrd*	Y	Y	N	N	Y	N	N	Y
WASHINGTON								
Gorton	N	Y	N	N	Y	N	N	N
Jackson	N	Y	Y	Y	N	Y	N	N
WEST VIRGINIA								
Byrd	Y	Y	Y	N	Y	Y	Y	N
Randolph	Y	Y	Y	Y	N	Y	Y	Y
WISCONSIN								
Kasten	Y	Y	N	N	Y	N	N	N
Proxmire	N	N	N	N	N	N	N	N
WYOMING								
Simpson	Y	Y	N	N	Y	N	N	N
Wallop	Y	Y	N	N	Y	N	N	N

KEY

Y Voted for (yea).
\# Paired for.
\+ Announced for.
N Voted against (nay).
X Paired against.
\- Announced against.
P Voted "present".
C Voted "present" to avoid possible conflict of interest.
? Did not vote or otherwise make a position known.

Democrats *Republicans*

ND - Northern Democrats   SD - Southern Democrats (Southern states - Ala., Ark., Fla., Ga., Ky., La., Miss., N.C., Okla., S.C., Tenn., Texas, Va.)   * Byrd elected as an independent.

---

121. S Con Res 60. Disapproval of Federal Trade Commission Used-Car Rule. Adoption of the concurrent resolution to disapprove a proposed Federal Trade Commission rule to require used-car dealers to inform customers of major known defects in used automobiles. Adopted 69-27: R 40-12; D 29-15 (ND 16-14, SD 13-1), May 18, 1982.

122. S Con Res 92. First Budget Resolution, Fiscal 1983. Baker, R-Tenn., motion to instruct the sergeant-at-arms to require the attendance of absent senators. Motion agreed to 89-5: R 49-3; D 40-2 (ND 27-1, SD 13-1), May 19, 1982.

123. S Con Res 92. First Budget Resolution, Fiscal 1983. Moynihan, D-N.Y., amendment to increase budget authority by $1.8 billion and outlays by $9.6 billion in fiscal 1983-85 to accommodate restoration of funding for Medicare and Medicaid. Rejected 39-60: R 1-53; D 38-7 (ND 27-4, SD 11-3), May 19, 1982.

124. S Con Res 92. First Budget Resolution, Fiscal 1983. Kennedy, D-Mass., amendment to increase budget authority by $2.5 billion in fiscal 1982-83 and outlays by $2.5 billion in fiscal 1982-84 to accommodate funding for targeted jobs programs in areas of high unemployment. Rejected 14-84: R 0-53; D 14-31 (ND 14-16, SD 0-15), May 19, 1982.

125. S Con Res 92. First Budget Resolution, Fiscal 1983. Baker, R-Tenn., motion to table (kill) the Kassebaum, R-Kan., amendment to reduce defense programs by $35.3 billion in budget authority and $13.9 billion in outlays in fiscal 1983-85. Motion agreed to 53-44: R 38-14; D 15-30 (ND 5-25, SD 10-5), May 19, 1982.

126. S Con Res 92. First Budget Resolution, Fiscal 1983. Bradley, D-N.J., amendment to increase revenues by $2.1 billion, budget authority by $3.7 billion and outlays by $2.1 billion in fiscal 1983-85 to accommodate restoration of funding for various education programs. Rejected 44-54: R 2-50; D 42-4 (ND 29-2, SD 13-2), May 19, 1982.

127. S Con Res 92. First Budget Resolution, Fiscal 1983. Leahy, D-Vt., amendment to increase budget authority by $1.2 billion and outlays by $600 million in fiscal 1983-85 to accommodate increased funding for environmental protection and toxic dump cleanup programs of the Environmental Protection Agency. Rejected 38-60: R 5-48; D 33-12 (ND 25-5, SD 8-7), May 20, 1982.

128. S Con Res 92. First Budget Resolution, Fiscal 1983. Melcher, D-Mont., amendment to reduce budget authority by $15 billion and outlays by $7 billion in fiscal 1982-85 by cutting funding for foreign aid programs. Rejected 27-73: R 11-43; D 16-30 (ND 9-22, SD 7-8), May 20, 1982.

Corresponding to Congressional Record Votes 129, 130, 131, 132, 133, 134, 135, 136

KEY

- Y Voted for (yea).
- # Paired for.
- + Announced for.
- N Voted against (nay).
- X Paired against.
- - Announced against.
- P Voted "present".
- C Voted "present" to avoid possible conflict of interest.
- ? Did not vote or otherwise make a position known.

Democrats **Republicans**

Senator	129	130	131	132	133	134	135	136
ALABAMA								
Denton	N	Y	Y	N	N	N	N	Y
Heflin	Y	N	N	N	Y	Y	Y	N
ALASKA								
Murkowski	N	Y	Y	N	N	N	N	Y
Stevens	N	Y	N	N	N	N	N	Y
ARIZONA								
Goldwater	N	Y	Y	N	N	N	N	Y
DeConcini	Y	N	N	N	Y	Y	Y	N
ARKANSAS								
Bumpers	Y	N	N	Y	Y	Y	Y	N
Pryor	Y	N	N	Y	Y	Y	Y	N
CALIFORNIA								
Hayakawa	N	Y	Y	N	N	N	N	Y
Cranston	Y	N	N	Y	Y	Y	Y	N
COLORADO								
Armstrong	N	Y	Y	N	N	N	N	Y
Hart	N	N	N	Y	Y	Y	Y	N
CONNECTICUT								
Weicker	Y	N	N	Y	N	Y	Y	Y
Dodd	?	N	N	Y	Y	Y	Y	N
DELAWARE								
Roth	N	Y	N	N	N	N	Y	Y
Biden	Y	N	N	Y	N	Y	Y	N
FLORIDA								
Hawkins	N	Y	N	N	N	Y	Y	Y
Chiles	Y	N	N	N	Y	Y	Y	N
GEORGIA								
Mattingly	N	Y	Y	N	N	N	N	Y
Nunn	Y	N	N	Y	Y	Y	Y	N
HAWAII								
Inouye	Y	N	N	Y	Y	Y	Y	N
Matsunaga	Y	N	N	Y	Y	Y	Y	N
IDAHO								
McClure	N	Y	Y	N	N	N	N	Y
Symms	N	Y	Y	N	N	N	N	Y
ILLINOIS								
Percy	N	Y	N	N	N	N	Y	Y
Dixon	Y	N	N	Y	Y	Y	Y	N
INDIANA								
Lugar	N	Y	N	N	N	N	N	Y
Quayle	N	Y	N	N	N	N	N	Y
IOWA								
Grassley	N	Y	N	N	N	N	N	Y
Jepsen	N	Y	N	N	N	N	N	Y
KANSAS								
Dole	N	Y	N	N	N	N	N	Y
Kassebaum	N	Y	N	N	N	N	Y	Y
KENTUCKY								
Ford	Y	N	N	N	Y	Y	Y	N
Huddleston	Y	N	N	N	Y	Y	Y	N
LOUISIANA								
Johnston	Y	N	N	Y	N	Y	Y	N
Long	Y	Y	N	N	N	Y	Y	N
MAINE								
Cohen	N	Y	N	N	N	N	N	Y
Mitchell	Y	N	N	N	Y	Y	Y	N
MARYLAND								
Mathias	Y	N	N	Y	N	N	Y	Y
Sarbanes	Y	N	N	Y	Y	Y	Y	N
MASSACHUSETTS								
Kennedy	Y	N	N	Y	?	Y	Y	N
Tsongas	Y	N	N	Y	Y	Y	Y	N
MICHIGAN								
Levin	Y	N	N	Y	Y	Y	Y	N
Riegle	Y	N	N	N	Y	Y	Y	N
MINNESOTA								
Boschwitz	N	Y	N	N	N	N	N	Y
Durenberger	Y	N	N	N	N	N	N	Y
MISSISSIPPI								
Cochran	N	Y	N	N	N	N	N	Y
Stennis	Y	N	N	N	N	Y	Y	N
MISSOURI								
Danforth	N	Y	N	N	N	N	N	Y
Eagleton	Y	N	N	Y	Y	Y	Y	N
MONTANA								
Baucus	Y	N	N	N	Y	Y	Y	N
Melcher	Y	N	N	N	Y	Y	Y	N
NEBRASKA								
Exon	Y	N	N	Y	Y	Y	Y	N
Zorinsky	Y	N	Y	N	N	Y	Y	N
NEW HAMPSHIRE								
Humphrey	N	Y	Y	N	N	N	N	Y
Rudman	N	Y	N	N	N	N	N	Y
NEW JERSEY								
Brady	N	Y	N	N	N	N	N	Y
Bradley	Y	N	N	Y	Y	Y	Y	N
NEW MEXICO								
Domenici	N	Y	N	N	N	N	N	Y
Schmitt	N	Y	N	N	N	N	N	Y
NEW YORK								
D'Amato	N	Y	Y	N	N	N	N	Y
Moynihan	Y	N	N	N	N	Y	Y	N
NORTH CAROLINA								
East	N	Y	Y	N	N	N	N	Y
Helms	N	Y	Y	N	N	N	N	Y
NORTH DAKOTA								
Andrews	Y	Y	N	Y	N	N	Y	Y
Burdick	Y	N	N	Y	Y	Y	Y	N
OHIO								
Glenn	Y	N	N	Y	Y	Y	Y	N
Metzenbaum	Y	N	N	Y	Y	Y	Y	N
OKLAHOMA								
Nickles	N	Y	Y	N	N	N	N	Y
Boren	N	N	N	Y	Y	Y	Y	N
OREGON								
Hatfield	N	Y	N	N	-	-	-	+
Packwood	N	Y	N	Y	N	N	N	Y
PENNSYLVANIA								
Heinz	Y	N	N	N	N	N	Y	Y
Specter	N	Y	N	Y	N	Y	Y	Y
RHODE ISLAND								
Chafee	Y	N	N	N	N	N	N	Y
Pell	Y	N	N	Y	Y	Y	Y	N
SOUTH CAROLINA								
Thurmond	N	Y	Y	N	N	N	N	Y
Hollings	Y	N	N	Y	Y	Y	Y	Y
SOUTH DAKOTA								
Abdnor	N	Y	N	N	N	N	N	Y
Pressler	N	Y	N	N	N	N	N	Y
TENNESSEE								
Baker	N	Y	N	N	N	N	N	Y
Sasser	Y	N	N	Y	Y	Y	Y	N
TEXAS								
Tower	N	Y	N	N	N	N	N	Y
Bentsen	Y	N	N	N	N	Y	Y	N
UTAH								
Garn	N	Y	N	N	N	N	N	Y
Hatch	N	Y	N	N	N	N	Y	Y
VERMONT								
Stafford	Y	N	N	N	N	N	Y	Y
Leahy	Y	N	N	Y	Y	Y	Y	N
VIRGINIA								
Warner	N	Y	N	N	N	N	N	Y
Byrd*	N	Y	N	N	N	N	N	Y
WASHINGTON								
Gorton	N	Y	N	N	N	N	N	Y
Jackson	Y	N	N	Y	Y	Y	Y	N
WEST VIRGINIA								
Byrd	Y	N	N	N	Y	Y	Y	N
Randolph	Y	N	N	Y	Y	Y	Y	N
WISCONSIN								
Kasten	N	Y	Y	N	N	N	Y	Y
Proxmire	N	Y	Y	N	N	N	Y	N
WYOMING								
Simpson	N	Y	N	N	N	N	N	Y
Wallop	N	Y	N	N	N	N	N	Y

ND - Northern Democrats SD - Southern Democrats (Southern states - Ala., Ark., Fla., Ga., Ky., La., Miss., N.C., Okla., S.C., Tenn., Texas, Va.) *Byrd elected as an independent.

129. S Con Res 92. First Budget Resolution, Fiscal 1983. Hart, D-Colo., amendment to increase budget authority by $1.8 billion and outlays by $916 million in fiscal 1983-85 to accommodate additional funding for compensatory education programs. Rejected 48-51: R 7-47; D 41-4 (ND 28-2, SD 13-2), May 20, 1982.

130. S Con Res 92. First Budget Resolution, Fiscal 1983. Domenici, R-N.M., motion to table (kill) the Domenici motion to reconsider the vote by which the Hart, D-Colo., amendment was rejected *(see vote 129, above).* Motion agreed to 51-49: R 48-6; D 3-43 (ND 1-30, SD 2-13), May 20, 1982.

131. S Con Res 92. First Budget Resolution, Fiscal 1983. Helms, R-N.C., amendment to reduce revenue increases in fiscal 1983-85 to $6 billion from $107.2 billion and make compensating pro-rata cuts in non-defense spending. Rejected 17-83: R 15-39; D 2-44 (ND 2-29, SD 0-15), May 20, 1982.

132. S Con Res 92. First Budget Resolution, Fiscal 1983. Hollings, D-S.C., amendment to increase revenues by $76.3 billion in fiscal 1983-85 by repealing the scheduled July 1983 individual income tax cut. Rejected 32-68: R 5-49; D 27-19 (ND 21-10, SD 6-9), May 20, 1982.

133. S Con Res 92. First Budget Resolution, Fiscal 1983. Byrd, D-W.Va., amendment to express the sense of the Senate that the Finance Committee should defer the 1983 individual income tax cut or eliminate it and substitute a "fiscally prudent tax cut which distributes benefits fairly to all working and middle-income Americans." Rejected 35-63: R 0-53; D 35-10 (ND 25-5, SD 10-5), May 20, 1982.

134. S Con Res 92. First Budget Resolution, Fiscal 1983. Chiles, D-Fla., amendment to increase budget authority by $3.3 billion and outlays by $3.1 billion in fiscal 1983-85 to accommodate full cost-of-living adjustments (COLAs) for veterans' pensions and compensation benefits, fund veterans' hospitals and clinics at the administration's request level, and require only $150 million in legislative savings in veterans' programs annually, as recommended by the Veterans' Affairs Committee. Rejected 46-53: R 2-51; D 44-2 (ND 30-1, SD 14-1), May 20, 1982.

135. S Con Res 92. First Budget Resolution, Fiscal 1983. Sasser, D-Tenn., motion to table (kill) the Jepsen, R-Iowa, amendment, to the Sasser amendment *(see vote 139, p. 26-S),* to remove funding for full cost-of-living adjustments (COLAs) for railroad retirees and for maintenance of the Railroad Retirement Board and its field offices. Motion agreed to 58-41: R 13-40; D 45-1 (ND 31-0, SD 14-1), May 20, 1982.

136. S Con Res 92. First Budget Resolution, Fiscal 1983. Baker, R-Tenn., motion that the Senate stand in recess until 9 a.m. May 21. Motion agreed to 55-44: R 53-0; D 2-44 (ND 0-31, SD 2-13), in the session which began May 20, 1982.

CQ Senate Votes 137 - 144

Corresponding to Congressional Record Votes 137, 138, 139, 140, 141, 142, 143, 144

KEY

- Y Voted for (yea).
- # Paired for.
- + Announced for.
- N Voted against (nay).
- X Paired against.
- - Announced against.
- P Voted "present".
- C Voted "present" to avoid possible conflict of interest.
- ? Did not vote or otherwise make a position known.

Democrats Republicans

	137	138	139	140	141	142	143	144
ALABAMA								
Denton	?	N	N	Y	N	C	N	Y
Heflin	N	Y	Y	N	N	N	Y	N
ALASKA								
Murkowski	N	N	N	Y	N	Y	N	Y
Stevens	N	N	N	Y	N	Y	N	Y
ARIZONA								
Goldwater	N	N	N	Y	N	Y	N	Y
DeConcini	Y	Y	Y	N	Y	N	Y	N
ARKANSAS								
Bumpers	Y	Y	Y	N	Y	N	Y	N
Pryor	Y	Y	Y	N	Y	N	Y	N
CALIFORNIA								
Hayakawa	N	N	N	Y	N	Y	N	Y
Cranston	Y	Y	Y	N	Y	N	Y	N
COLORADO								
Armstrong	N	N	N	Y	N	Y	N	Y
Hart	Y	Y	Y	N	Y	N	Y	N
CONNECTICUT								
Weicker	Y	Y	Y	N	N	N	N	N
Dodd	Y	Y	Y	N	Y	Y	Y	N
DELAWARE								
Roth	N	Y	Y	Y	N	Y	N	Y
Biden	Y	Y	Y	N	Y	N	Y	N
FLORIDA								
Hawkins	N	Y	Y	Y	Y	Y	N	N
Chiles	Y	Y	Y	Y	N	Y	N	Y
GEORGIA								
Mattingly	?	N	N	Y	N	Y	N	Y
Nunn	Y	Y	Y	N	N	N	Y	N
HAWAII								
Inouye	Y	Y	Y	N	Y	N	Y	N
Matsunaga	?	Y	Y	N	Y	N	Y	N
IDAHO								
McClure	N	N	N	Y	N	Y	N	Y
Symms	N	N	N	Y	N	Y	N	Y
ILLINOIS								
Percy	N	N	Y	N	Y	N	Y	N
Dixon	Y	Y	Y	N	N	N	Y	N
INDIANA								
Lugar	N	N	N	Y	N	Y	N	Y
Quayle	N	N	N	Y	N	Y	N	Y
IOWA								
Grassley	N	N	N	Y	N	Y	N	Y
Jepsen	N	N	N	Y	N	Y	N	Y
KANSAS								
Dole	N	N	N	Y	N	Y	N	Y
Kassebaum	N	N	Y	Y	N	Y	N	Y
KENTUCKY								
Ford	Y	Y	Y	N	Y	N	Y	N
Huddleston	+	?	+	X	+	?	?	?
LOUISIANA								
Johnston	Y	Y	Y	#	N	Y	Y	N
Long	Y	Y	Y	Y	Y	Y	Y	N
MAINE								
Cohen	N	N	N	Y	Y	Y	N	Y
Mitchell	Y	Y	Y	N	Y	N	Y	N
MARYLAND								
Mathias	Y	Y	Y	Y	Y	N	N	Y
Sarbanes	Y	Y	Y	N	Y	N	Y	N
MASSACHUSETTS								
Kennedy	Y	Y	Y	N	Y	N	Y	N
Tsongas	Y	Y	Y	N	Y	N	Y	N
MICHIGAN								
Levin	Y	Y	Y	N	Y	N	Y	N
Riegle	Y	Y	Y	N	Y	N	Y	N
MINNESOTA								
Boschwitz	N	N	N	Y	N	Y	N	Y
Durenberger	Y	Y	Y	N	Y	Y	N	Y
MISSISSIPPI								
Cochran	N	N	N	Y	N	Y	N	Y
Stennis	Y	Y	N	N	N	Y	Y	N
MISSOURI								
Danforth	N	N	N	Y	N	Y	N	Y
Eagleton	Y	Y	Y	N	Y	N	Y	N
MONTANA								
Baucus	Y	Y	Y	N	Y	N	Y	N
Melcher	Y	Y	Y	X	#	X	+	-
NEBRASKA								
Exon	Y	Y	Y	Y	Y	Y	Y	N
Zorinsky	Y	Y	Y	Y	N	N	Y	N
NEVADA								
Laxalt	N	N	N	Y	N	Y	N	Y
Cannon	Y	Y	Y	N	Y	N	Y	N
NEW HAMPSHIRE								
Humphrey	N	N	N	Y	N	Y	N	Y
Rudman	N	N	N	Y	N	Y	N	Y
NEW JERSEY								
Brady	N	N	N	Y	N	Y	?	Y
Bradley	Y	Y	Y	N	Y	N	Y	N
NEW MEXICO								
Domenici	N	N	N	Y	N	Y	N	Y
Schmitt	?	?	?	?	?	?	?	?
NEW YORK								
D'Amato	N	N	Y	Y	Y	Y	N	Y
Moynihan	Y	Y	Y	N	Y	N	Y	N
NORTH CAROLINA								
East	N	N	N	Y	N	Y	N	Y
Helms	N	N	N	Y	N	Y	N	Y
NORTH DAKOTA								
Andrews	N	Y	Y	Y	N	Y	N	N
Burdick	Y	Y	Y	N	Y	N	Y	N
OHIO								
Glenn	Y	Y	Y	N	Y	N	Y	N
Metzenbaum	Y	Y	Y	N	Y	N	Y	N
OKLAHOMA								
Nickles	N	N	N	Y	N	Y	N	Y
Boren	N	Y	Y	#	X	N	Y	N
OREGON								
Hatfield	-	-	-	+	-	-	-	#
Packwood	N	N	N	N	N	Y	N	Y
PENNSYLVANIA								
Heinz	N	Y	Y	N	Y	N	N	Y
Specter	N	Y	Y	N	N	Y	N	Y
RHODE ISLAND								
Chafee	Y	N	N	N	N	N	N	Y
Pell	Y	Y	Y	N	Y	N	Y	N
SOUTH CAROLINA								
Thurmond	N	N	N	Y	N	Y	N	Y
Hollings	Y	Y	Y	N	Y	Y	Y	N
SOUTH DAKOTA								
Abdnor	N	N	N	Y	N	N	N	Y
Pressler	N	Y	Y	Y	?	?	?	?
TENNESSEE								
Baker	N	N	N	Y	N	Y	N	Y
Sasser	Y	Y	Y	N	Y	N	Y	N
TEXAS								
Tower	N	N	N	Y	N	Y	N	Y
Bentsen	N	Y	Y	Y	N	Y	Y	N
UTAH								
Garn	N	N	N	Y	N	Y	N	Y
Hatch	N	N	Y	N	Y	N	Y	Y
VERMONT								
Stafford	Y	N	Y	Y	Y	Y	N	X
Leahy	Y	Y	Y	N	Y	N	Y	N
VIRGINIA								
Warner	N	N	N	Y	N	Y	N	Y
Byrd*	N	N	N	Y	N	#	N	Y
WASHINGTON								
Gorton	N	N	N	Y	N	Y	N	Y
Jackson	Y	Y	Y	N	Y	N	Y	N
WEST VIRGINIA								
Byrd	Y	Y	Y	N	Y	N	Y	N
Randolph	Y	Y	Y	N	Y	N	Y	N
WISCONSIN								
Kasten	N	N	N	Y	N	Y	N	Y
Proxmire	N	Y	Y	N	N	N	Y	N
WYOMING								
Simpson	N	N	N	Y	N	Y	N	Y
Wallop	N	N	N	Y	N	Y	N	Y

ND - Northern Democrats   SD - Southern Democrats (Southern states - Ala., Ark., Fla., Ga., Ky., La., Miss., N.C., Okla., S.C., Tenn., Texas, Va.)   *Byrd elected as an independent.

137. S Con Res 92. First Budget Resolution, Fiscal 1983. Hollings, D-S.C., amendment to increase budget authority and outlays by $350 million in fiscal 1983-85 to maintain current funding levels for the special supplemental food program for women, infants and children. Rejected 44-50: R 5-45; D 39-5 (ND 29-1, SD 10-4), May 21, 1982.

138. S Con Res 92. First Budget Resolution, Fiscal 1983. Sasser, D-Tenn., motion to table (kill) the Domenici, R-N.M., substitute, to the Sasser amendment *(see vote 139, below)*, to provide sufficient funding to accommodate cost-of-living adjustments (COLAs) of 7.4 percent in 1982 and 4 percent in 1983 and 1984 for railroad retirees, as well as dual benefits provided under 1974 railroad retirement legislation (PL 93-445). Motion agreed to 53-44: R 9-43; D 44-1 (ND 31-0, SD 13-1), May 21, 1982.

139. S Con Res 92. First Budget Resolution, Fiscal 1983. Sasser, D-Tenn., amendment to increase outlays by $1.7 billion in fiscal 1982-85 to accommodate cost-of-living adjustments (COLAs) for railroad retirees of 7.4 percent in fiscal 1982 and 1983 and at the level of the Consumer Price Index in fiscal 1984 and 1985, to accommodate full funding of dual benefits under PL 93-445, and of Railroad Retirement Board field offices. Adopted 57-40: R 14-38; D 43-2 (ND 31-0, SD 12-2), May 21, 1982.

140. S Con Res 92. First Budget Resolution, Fiscal 1983. Dole, R-Kan., motion to table (kill) the Byrd, D-W.Va., amendment to increase budget authority and outlays by $1.1 billion to accommodate a 13-week extension of unemployment benefits in states suffering high unemployment. Motion agreed to 52-42: R 46-6; D 6-36 (ND 2-28, SD 4-8), May 21, 1982.

141. S Con Res 92. First Budget Resolution, Fiscal 1983. Moynihan, D-N.Y., amendment to increase budget authority by $400 million in fiscal 1983-85 and outlays by $100 million in fiscal 1985 to accommodate additional funding for cleanup of hazardous waste sites, as recommended by the Environment and Public Works Committee. Rejected 41-53: R 7-44; D 34-9 (ND 27-3, SD 7-6), May 21, 1982.

142. S Con Res 92. First Budget Resolution, Fiscal 1983. Domenici, R-N.M., motion to table (kill) the Hawkins, R-Fla., amendment to increase budget authority and outlays for income security programs by $2.2 billion in fiscal 1983-85 to accommodate 4 percent cost-of-living adjustments (COLAs) for military and civilian retirees in each of those years, with offsetting cuts in defense programs. Motion agreed to 51-42: R 44-6; D 7-36 (ND 2-28, SD 5-8), May 21, 1982.

143. S Con Res 92. First Budget Resolution, Fiscal 1983. DeConcini, D-Ariz., amendment to increase savings anticipated from improved debt collection and reduction of waste, fraud and abuse by $6.6 billion in fiscal 1983-85. Rejected 43-51: R 0-50; D 43-1 (ND 30-0, SD 13-1), May 21, 1982.

144. S Con Res 92. First Budget Resolution, Fiscal 1983. Simpson, R-Wyo., motion to table (kill) the DeConcini, D-Ariz., amendment to provide sufficient funding for veterans' programs to accommodate a 7.4 percent cost-of-living adjustment (COLA) for all disabled veterans in fiscal 1983 and increases consistent with Social Security increases in fiscal 1984-85. Motion agreed to 49-45: R 47-3; D 2-42 (ND 1-29, SD 1-13), May 21, 1982.

KEY

Y Voted for (yea).
\# Paired for.
\+ Announced for.
N Voted against (nay).
X Paired against.
\- Announced against.
P Voted "present".
C Voted "present" to avoid possible conflict of interest.
? Did not vote or otherwise make a position known.

Democrats   *Republicans*

	145	146	147	148	149	150	151	152
ALABAMA								
Denton	N	Y	Y	N	Y	Y	Y	Y
Heflin	Y	N	N	N	N	Y	N	Y
ALASKA								
Murkowski	N	Y	Y	N	Y	Y	Y	Y
Stevens	?	?	?	?	?	?	?	?
ARIZONA								
Goldwater	N	Y	N	Y	N	Y	Y	Y
DeConcini	?	?	?	?	?	?	?	?
ARKANSAS								
Bumpers	N	N	N	Y	N	Y	N	N
Pryor	N	N	N	Y	N	Y	N	N
CALIFORNIA								
Hayakawa	N	Y	Y	N	Y	Y	Y	Y
Cranston	Y	N	Y	Y	N	Y	N	N
COLORADO								
Armstrong	N	Y	N	Y	N	Y	Y	Y
Hart	Y	N	Y	N	N	Y	N	N
CONNECTICUT								
Weicker	N	N	Y	Y	Y	Y	Y	N
Dodd	Y	N	Y	Y	N	Y	N	N
DELAWARE								
Roth	N	Y	Y	N	Y	Y	Y	Y
Biden	N	N	Y	Y	N	Y	N	N
FLORIDA								
Hawkins	N	Y	Y	N	Y	Y	N	Y
Chiles	Y	N	N	Y	N	N	N	Y
GEORGIA								
Mattingly	N	Y	N	N	Y	Y	Y	Y
Nunn	N	N	N	Y	N	N	N	Y
HAWAII								
Inouye	Y	N	Y	Y	N	Y	N	N
Matsunaga	Y	N	Y	N	Y	Y	N	N
IDAHO								
McClure	N	Y	N	N	Y	N	Y	Y
Symms	N	Y	N	N	Y	N	Y	Y
ILLINOIS								
Percy	N	Y	Y	N	Y	Y	Y	Y
Dixon	Y	N	N	N	N	Y	N	Y
INDIANA								
Lugar	N	Y	Y	N	Y	Y	Y	Y
Quayle	N	Y	Y	N	Y	N	Y	Y

	145	146	147	148	149	150	151	152
IOWA								
Grassley	N	Y	N	N	Y	Y	Y	Y
Jepsen	N	Y	Y	N	Y	Y	Y	Y
KANSAS								
Dole	N	Y	Y	N	Y	Y	Y	Y
Kassebaum	N	Y	Y	N	Y	N	Y	Y
KENTUCKY								
Ford	Y	N	N	Y	N	Y	N	N
Huddleston	?	?	?	?	?	?	?	?
LOUISIANA								
Johnston	Y	N	Y	Y	N	N	N	N
Long	Y	N	N	N	Y	N	N	Y
MAINE								
Cohen	N	Y	Y	N	Y	N	Y	Y
Mitchell	Y	N	N	Y	Y	Y	N	N
MARYLAND								
Mathias	N	N	Y	Y	Y	Y	N	Y
Sarbanes	Y	N	Y	N	Y	N	N	N
MASSACHUSETTS								
Kennedy	Y	N	Y	N	Y	N	N	N
Tsongas	Y	N	Y	N	Y	N	N	N
MICHIGAN								
Levin	Y	N	N	N	Y	N	N	N
Riegle	Y	N	Y	N	N	Y	N	N
MINNESOTA								
Boschwitz	N	Y	Y	N	Y	N	Y	Y
Durenberger	?	?	?	?	?	?	?	?
MISSISSIPPI								
Cochran	N	Y	Y	N	Y	Y	Y	Y
Stennis	N	N	N	Y	Y	Y	N	Y
MISSOURI								
Danforth	N	N	Y	N	Y	Y	Y	Y
Eagleton	Y	N	N	Y	N	Y	N	N
MONTANA								
Baucus	N	N	Y	N	Y	Y	N	N
Melcher	+	?	-	?	?	?	-	?
NEBRASKA								
Exon	Y	N	N	N	N	N	N	Y
Zorinsky	Y	Y	N	N	Y	Y	N	Y
NEVADA								
Laxalt	N	Y	Y	N	Y	Y	Y	Y
Cannon	Y	N	N	Y	N	Y	N	N

	145	146	147	148	149	150	151	152
NEW HAMPSHIRE								
Humphrey	N	Y	Y	N	Y	Y	Y	Y
Rudman	N	Y	Y	N	Y	N	Y	Y
NEW JERSEY								
Brady	N	Y	Y	N	Y	N	Y	Y
Bradley	Y	N	Y	Y	Y	Y	N	N
NEW MEXICO								
Domenici	N	Y	Y	N	Y	Y	Y	Y
Schmitt	?	?	?	?	?	?	?	?
NEW YORK								
D'Amato	N	N	Y	N	Y	Y	Y	Y
Moynihan	Y	N	Y	N	Y	Y	N	N
NORTH CAROLINA								
East	N	Y	Y	N	Y	Y	Y	Y
Helms	N	Y	N	N	Y	Y	Y	Y
NORTH DAKOTA								
Andrews	Y	Y	Y	Y	Y	N	Y	Y
Burdick	Y	N	N	Y	N	Y	N	N
OHIO								
Glenn	N	N	Y	Y	N	Y	N	Y
Metzenbaum	Y	N	Y	N	Y	N	N	N
OKLAHOMA								
Nickles	N	Y	N	Y	N	Y	N	Y
Boren	N	N	N	N	Y	N	N	Y
OREGON								
Hatfield	-	+	-	-	+	-	#	-
Packwood	Y	N	Y	N	Y	N	Y	Y
PENNSYLVANIA								
Heinz	N	Y	Y	?	Y	Y	X	Y
Specter	N	Y	Y	N	Y	Y	Y	Y
RHODE ISLAND								
Chafee	N	N	Y	Y	Y	Y	Y	N
Pell	Y	N	Y	N	Y	N	N	N
SOUTH CAROLINA								
Thurmond	N	Y	Y	N	Y	Y	Y	Y
Hollings	Y	N	N	N	Y	N	N	N
SOUTH DAKOTA								
Abdnor	N	Y	N	N	Y	Y	Y	Y
Pressler	?	?	?	?	?	?	?	?
TENNESSEE								
Baker	N	Y	Y	N	Y	Y	Y	Y
Sasser	Y	N	N	Y	N	Y	N	N

	145	146	147	148	149	150	151	152
TEXAS								
Tower	N	Y	Y	N	Y	Y	Y	Y
Bentsen	Y	N	N	N	Y	N	N	Y
UTAH								
Garn	N	Y	Y	N	Y	Y	Y	Y
Hatch	N	Y	Y	N	Y	Y	Y	Y
VERMONT								
Stafford	N	Y	Y	?	?	?	?	?
Leahy	N	N	N	Y	N	Y	N	Y
VIRGINIA								
Warner	N	Y	N	Y	Y	Y	Y	Y
Byrd*	C	N	N	Y	Y	N	Y	Y
WASHINGTON								
Gorton	N	N	Y	N	Y	N	Y	Y
Jackson	Y	N	Y	Y	Y	Y	N	N
WEST VIRGINIA								
Byrd	Y	N	Y	N	Y	N	N	N
Randolph	Y	N	N	Y	N	Y	N	N
WISCONSIN								
Kasten	N	Y	Y	N	Y	Y	Y	Y
Proxmire	N	N	N	N	Y	Y	Y	N
WYOMING								
Simpson	N	Y	Y	N	Y	Y	Y	Y
Wallop	N	Y	Y	Y	Y	Y	Y	Y

ND - Northern Democrats   SD - Southern Democrats (Southern states - Ala., Ark., Fla., Ga., Ky., La., Miss., N.C., Okla., S.C., Tenn., Texas, Va.)

* Byrd elected as an independent.

145. S Con Res 92. First Budget Resolution, Fiscal 1983. Moynihan, D-N.Y., amendment to increase budget authority and outlays by $300 million in fiscal 1983-85 to accommodate restoration of third-class mailing subsidies. Rejected 34-57: R 2-47; D 32-10 (ND 24-5, SD 8-5), May 21, 1982.

146. S Con Res 92. First Budget Resolution, Fiscal 19\3. Mattingly, R-Ga., amendment to express the sense of the Ser ite that if actual revenue levels for a year exceed those specified in the resolution, revenue levels for the following year should be cor spondingly decreased. Rejected 43-49: R 42-7; D 1-42 (ND 1-28, S \0-14), May 21, 1982.

147. S Con Res 92. First Budget Resolution, Fiscal 1983. Baker, R-Tenn., motion to table (kill) the Dixon, D-Ill., amendment to reduce outlays for foreign aid programs by $2.4 billion in fiscal 1983-85 in order to maintain foreign aid at the fiscal 1982 level. Motion agreed to 60-32: R 41-8; D 19-24 (ND 18-11, SD 1-13), May 21, 1982.

148. S Con Res 92. First Budget Resolution, Fiscal 1983. Eagleton, D-Mo., amendment to express the sense of the Senate that the Finance Committee should report a bill repealing the indexing provisions of the 1981 tax cut legislation. Rejected 34-56: R 5-42; D 29-14 (ND 19-10, SD 10-4), May 21, 1982.

149. S Con Res 92. First Budget Resolution, Fiscal 1983. Baker, R-Tenn., motion to table (kill) the Chiles, D-Fla., motion to recommit the bill to the Budget Committee with instructions to permit alternative spending cuts or tax packages to be offered as amendments to reconciliation savings legislation, provided such amendments are not predominantly non-budgetary in nature. Motion agreed to 61-30: R 48-0; D 13-30 (ND 8-21, SD 5-9), May 21, 1982.

150. S Con Res 92. First Budget Resolution, Fiscal 1983. Baker, R-Tenn., motion to table (kill) the Johnston, D-La., amendment to balance the budget by fiscal 1985 through additional revenue increases of $39 billion and spending cuts of $66.6 billion. Motion agreed to 70-21: R 36-12; D 34-9 (ND 28-1, SD 6-8), May 21, 1982.

151. S Con Res 92. First Budget Resolution, Fiscal 1983. Baker, R-Tenn., motion to table (kill) the Riegle, D-Mich., amendment to provide sufficient funding to accommodate cost-of-living adjustments (COLAs) for federal civilian and military retirees of 6.6 percent in fiscal 1983 and 4 percent in fiscal 1984 and 1985. Motion agreed to 47-43: R 45-2; D 2-41 (ND 1-28, SD 1-13), May 21, 1982.

152. S Con Res 92. First Budget Resolution, Fiscal 1983. Baker, R-Tenn., motion to table (kill) the Riegle, D-Mich., amendment to reduce defense outlays by $18.9 billion in fiscal 1983-85, transfer $14 billion to four domestic programs and allocate the remainder to deficit reduction. Motion agreed to 61-30: R 46-2; D 15-28 (ND 5-24, SD 10-4), May 21, 1982.

	153	154	155	156	157	158	159	160
ALABAMA								
Denton	Y	N	Y	Y	Y	Y	Y	Y
Heflin	Y	N	Y	Y	Y	N	Y	Y
ALASKA								
Murkowski	Y	N	Y	N	Y	Y	?	Y
Stevens	?	N	Y	Y	Y	N	Y	Y
ARIZONA								
Goldwater	Y	N	N	Y	N	Y	N	Y
DeConcini	-	Y	Y	Y	Y	N	Y	Y
ARKANSAS								
Bumpers	N	Y	N	Y	Y	N	Y	Y
Pryor	N	Y	N	Y	Y	N	Y	Y
CALIFORNIA								
Hayakawa	Y	?	?	?	?	?	Y	Y
Cranston	N	Y	N	Y	Y	N	Y	Y
COLORADO								
Armstrong	Y	N	Y	N	Y	Y	Y	Y
Hart	N	Y	N	Y	Y	Y	Y	Y
CONNECTICUT								
Weicker	N	Y	N	Y	Y	N	N	Y
Dodd	N	Y	N	Y	Y	?	Y	Y
DELAWARE								
Roth	Y	N	Y	N	N	Y	Y	Y
Biden	N	Y	N	Y	Y	N	Y	Y
FLORIDA								
Hawkins	Y	N	Y	N	Y	N	Y	Y
Chiles	N	Y	Y	Y	Y	N	Y	Y
GEORGIA								
Mattingly	Y	N	Y	N	Y	Y	Y	Y
Nunn	N	Y	Y	Y	Y	N	Y	Y
HAWAII								
Inouye	N	Y	N	Y	Y	N	Y	Y
Matsunaga	N	Y	N	Y	Y	N	Y	Y
IDAHO								
McClure	Y	N	N	Y	N	Y	Y	N
Symms	Y	N	N	Y	N	Y	Y	Y
ILLINOIS								
Percy	Y	+	?	?	+	?	Y	+
Dixon	N	N	N	Y	Y	N	Y	Y
INDIANA								
Lugar	Y	N	Y	Y	Y	N	Y	Y
Quayle	Y	N	Y	Y	Y	N	N	Y

	153	154	155	156	157	158	159	160
IOWA								
Grassley	Y	N	Y	Y	N	N	Y	Y
Jepsen	Y	N	Y	Y	N	N	Y	Y
KANSAS								
Dole	Y	N	Y	Y	N	Y	Y	Y
Kassebaum	Y	N	Y	Y	Y	Y	Y	Y
KENTUCKY								
Ford	N	Y	N	Y	Y	N	Y	Y
Huddleston	N	Y	N	Y	Y	N	Y	Y
LOUISIANA								
Johnston	N	Y	N	Y	Y	Y	Y	Y
Long	N	Y	N	Y	Y	N	Y	Y
MAINE								
Cohen	Y	Y	N	Y	Y	N	Y	Y
Mitchell	N	Y	N	Y	Y	N	Y	Y
MARYLAND								
Mathias	Y	Y	N	Y	Y	N	Y	Y
Sarbanes	N	Y	N	Y	Y	N	Y	Y
MASSACHUSETTS								
Kennedy	N	Y	N	Y	Y	N	Y	Y
Tsongas	N	?	N	Y	Y	N	Y	Y
MICHIGAN								
Levin	N	Y	N	Y	Y	N	Y	Y
Riegle	N	Y	N	Y	Y	N	Y	Y
MINNESOTA								
Boschwitz	Y	N	Y	Y	Y	N	Y	Y
Durenberger	?	Y	N	Y	Y	N	Y	Y
MISSISSIPPI								
Cochran	Y	N	Y	Y	Y	N	Y	Y
Stennis	Y	N	Y	Y	Y	N	Y	Y
MISSOURI								
Danforth	Y	N	N	Y	N	N	Y	Y
Eagleton	N	Y	N	Y	Y	N	Y	Y
MONTANA								
Baucus	N	Y	N	Y	Y	N	Y	Y
Melcher	-	+	?	+	+	-	?	Y
NEBRASKA								
Exon	N	Y	Y	Y	Y	N	Y	Y
Zorinsky	Y	N	N	Y	N	N	Y	Y
NEVADA								
Laxalt	Y	N	Y	Y	N	N	Y	Y
Cannon	N	?	?	+	?	-	?	Y

	153	154	155	156	157	158	159	160
NEW HAMPSHIRE								
Humphrey	Y	N	Y	Y	N	Y	Y	Y
Rudman	Y	N	Y	Y	N	Y	Y	Y
NEW JERSEY								
Brady	Y	N	Y	Y	Y	?	Y	Y
Bradley	N	Y	N	Y	Y	N	?	Y
NEW MEXICO								
Domenici	Y	N	Y	Y	Y	Y	Y	Y
Schmitt	+	N	Y	Y	Y	N	?	?
NEW YORK								
D'Amato	Y	Y	Y	Y	Y	N	Y	Y
Moynihan	N	Y	N	Y	Y	N	Y	Y
NORTH CAROLINA								
East	Y	N	Y	N	N	N	Y	Y
Helms	N	N	Y	N	N	N	Y	N
NORTH DAKOTA								
Andrews	Y	N	N	Y	N	Y	Y	Y
Burdick	N	Y	N	Y	Y	N	Y	Y
OHIO								
Glenn	N	Y	N	Y	N	N	Y	Y
Metzenbaum	N	Y	N	Y	N	Y	Y	Y
OKLAHOMA								
Nickles	Y	N	N	N	Y	Y	Y	Y
Boren	N	Y	Y	Y	Y	N	Y	Y
OREGON								
Hatfield	+	N	Y	Y	Y	N	Y	Y
Packwood	Y	N	Y	Y	Y	N	Y	Y
PENNSYLVANIA								
Heinz	Y	Y	N	Y	Y	N	Y	Y
Specter	Y	Y	N	Y	Y	Y	Y	Y
RHODE ISLAND								
Chafee	Y	Y	Y	Y	Y	N	Y	?
Pell	N	Y	N	Y	Y	N	Y	Y
SOUTH CAROLINA								
Thurmond	Y	N	Y	Y	N	Y	Y	Y
Hollings	N	Y	N	Y	Y	N	Y	Y
SOUTH DAKOTA								
Abdnor	Y	N	Y	Y	N	Y	Y	Y
Pressler	?	N	N	Y	Y	N	Y	Y
TENNESSEE								
Baker	Y	N	Y	Y	Y	Y	Y	Y
Sasser	N	Y	N	Y	Y	N	Y	Y

	153	154	155	156	157	158	159	160
TEXAS								
Tower	Y	?	?	?	?	?	Y	Y
Bentsen	N	Y	N	Y	Y	N	Y	Y
UTAH								
Garn	Y	N	Y	Y	Y	N	Y	Y
Hatch	Y	N	Y	Y	Y	N	Y	Y
VERMONT								
Stafford	+	Y	N	Y	Y	N	Y	Y
Leahy	N	Y	N	Y	Y	N	Y	Y
VIRGINIA								
Warner	Y	N	N	Y	Y	N	Y	Y
Byrd*	N	N	Y	N	Y	N	Y	Y
WASHINGTON								
Gorton	Y	N	Y	Y	Y	N	Y	Y
Jackson	N	Y	N	Y	Y	N	Y	Y
WEST VIRGINIA								
Byrd	N	Y	N	Y	Y	N	Y	Y
Randolph	N	Y	N	Y	Y	N	Y	Y
WISCONSIN								
Kasten	Y	N	Y	Y	Y	N	Y	Y
Proxmire	N	N	Y	Y	N	N	N	Y
WYOMING								
Simpson	Y	N	Y	Y	Y	Y	Y	Y
Wallop	Y	N	Y	Y	N	Y	Y	Y

KEY

Y Voted for (yea).
Paired for.
+ Announced for.
N Voted against (nay).
X Paired against.
- Announced against.
P Voted "present".
C Voted "present" to avoid possible conflict of interest.
? Did not vote or otherwise make a position known.

Democrats   *Republicans*

ND - Northern Democrats   SD - Southern Democrats (Southern states - Ala., Ark., Fla., Ga., Ky., La., Miss., N.C., Okla., S.C., Tenn., Texas, Va.)   *Byrd elected as an independent.

153. S Con Res 92. First Budget Resolution, Fiscal 1983. Adoption of the concurrent resolution to set budget targets for the fiscal year ending Sept. 30, 1983, as follows: budget authority, $835.7 billion; outlays, $784.3 billion; revenues, $668.4 billion; and deficit, $115.9 billion. The resolution also set preliminary goals for fiscal 1984-85, revised binding budget levels for fiscal 1982 and included reconciliation instructions requiring Senate and House committees to recommend legislative savings to meet the budget targets. Adopted 49-43: R 46-2; D 3-41 (ND 1-28, SD 2-13), May 21, 1982.

154. HR 5922. Urgent Supplemental Appropriations, Fiscal 1982. Dixon, D-Ill., amendment to provide an additional $76,842,000 to the Department of Health and Human Services for the work incentive (WIN) program, which provides employment, training and social services to help welfare recipients move into jobs in the private sector. Rejected 46-48: R 9-42; D 37-6 (ND 25-3, SD 12-3), May 26, 1982. (A modified version of the amendment subsequently was adopted (*see vote 157, below*).)

155. S 2332. Energy Emergency Preparedness. Domenici, R-N.M., amendment to require the Strategic Petroleum Reserve to be filled at a rate of 208,000 barrels of oil daily, instead of the 300,000-barrel-a-day rate in the bill. Rejected 44-51: R 36-15; D 8-36 (ND 3-26, SD 5-10), May 26, 1982. A "yea" was a vote supporting the president's position.

156. S 2332. Energy Emergency Preparedness. Passage of the bill to extend antitrust defense for oil companies sharing information with the International Energy Agency, to require the president to write contingency plans for handling oil shortages and to set a minimum fill rate for the Strategic Petroleum Reserve. Passed 88-7: R 45-6; D 43-1 (ND 29-0, SD 14-1), May 26, 1982.

157. HR 5922. Urgent Supplemental Appropriations, Fiscal 1982. Dixon, D-Ill., amendment to provide an additional $38,400,000 to the Department of Health and Human Services for the work incentive (WIN) program. Adopted 76-19: R 35-16; D 41-3 (ND 27-2, SD 14-1), May 26, 1982.

158. HR 5922. Urgent Supplemental Appropriations, Fiscal 1982. Baker, R-Tenn., motion to table (kill) the Lugar, R-Ind., amendment to provide $5,120,000,000 to the Department of Housing and Urban Development for mortgage interest rate subsidy payments to help middle- and lower-income families buy new homes. Motion rejected 23-70: R 20-30; D 3-40 (ND 1-27, SD 2-13), May 26, 1982. A "yea" was a vote supporting the president's position. (The Lugar amendment subsequently was adopted by a vote of 69-23 (*see vote 167, p. 29-S*).)

159. HR 5922. Urgent Supplemental Appropriations, Fiscal 1982. Baker, R-Tenn., motion to instruct the sergeant-at-arms to require the attendance of absent senators. Motion agreed to 91-4: R 49-3; D 42-1 (ND 27-1, SD 15-0), May 27, 1982.

160. HR 5922. Urgent Supplemental Appropriations, Fiscal 1982. Baker, R-Tenn., motion to invoke cloture (thus limiting debate) on the bill to provide $6.3 billion in new spending and to rescind $7.6 billion in previously appropriated funds, for a net spending reduction of $1.2 billion in fiscal 1982. Motion agreed to 95-2: R 49-2; D 46-0 (ND 31-0, SD 15-0), May 27, 1982. A three-fifths majority vote (60) of the total Senate is required to invoke cloture.

Corresponding to Congressional Record Votes 161, 162, 163, 164, 165, 166, 167, 168

KEY

Y	Voted for (yea).
#	Paired for.
+	Announced for.
N	Voted against (nay).
X	Paired against.
-	Announced against.
P	Voted "present".
C	Voted "present" to avoid possible conflict of interest.
?	Did not vote or otherwise make a position known.

Democrats *Republicans*

Name	161	162	163	164	165	166	167	168
ALABAMA								
Denton	Y	?	?	?	?	?	?	?
Heflin	Y	Y	Y	Y	Y	N	Y	N
ALASKA								
Murkowski	Y	Y	N	Y	N	Y	N	Y
Stevens	Y	Y	N	Y	X	Y	Y	Y
ARIZONA								
Goldwater	Y	N	Y	Y	N	Y	N	N
DeConcini	Y	Y	Y	N	Y	N	Y	Y
ARKANSAS								
Bumpers	Y	Y	Y	Y	Y	Y	Y	Y
Pryor	Y	Y	Y	Y	Y	Y	Y	Y
CALIFORNIA								
Hayakawa	Y	Y	X	Y	N	Y	N	N
Cranston	Y	N	Y	N	Y	N	Y	Y
COLORADO								
Armstrong	Y	Y	Y	Y	N	Y	N	N
Hart	Y	Y	Y	N	N	?	N	Y
CONNECTICUT								
Weicker	Y	Y	Y	N	Y	Y	Y	Y
Dodd	Y	Y	N	N	Y	N	Y	Y
DELAWARE								
Roth	Y	Y	Y	Y	N	Y	N	N
Biden	Y	Y	Y	N	Y	Y	Y	Y
FLORIDA								
Hawkins	Y	Y	Y	Y	Y	Y	Y	Y
Chiles	Y	Y	Y	Y	Y	Y	Y	Y
GEORGIA								
Mattingly	Y	Y	N	N	N	Y	N	N
Nunn	Y	Y	Y	N	Y	Y	Y	Y
HAWAII								
Inouye	?	?	?	?	?	?	?	?
Matsunaga	Y	Y	Y	N	Y	N	Y	Y
IDAHO								
McClure	Y	Y	N	Y	N	Y	N	Y
Symms	Y	Y	N	Y	N	Y	N	N
ILLINOIS								
Percy	+	?	?	-	?	?	?	-
Dixon	Y	Y	Y	N	Y	N	Y	Y
INDIANA								
Lugar	Y	Y	Y	N	Y	N	N	N
Quayle	Y	Y	Y	Y	Y	Y	Y	Y
IOWA								
Grassley	Y	Y	Y	Y	N	Y	Y	N
Jepsen	Y	Y	Y	Y	Y	Y	Y	Y
KANSAS								
Dole	Y	Y	N	Y	N	Y	N	N
Kassebaum	Y	Y	Y	?	N	Y	N	Y
KENTUCKY								
Ford	Y	Y	N	Y	Y	Y	Y	Y
Huddleston	Y	Y	Y	N	Y	Y	Y	Y
LOUISIANA								
Johnston	Y	Y	Y	Y	X	Y	N	Y
Long	Y	Y	Y	Y	Y	Y	Y	Y
MAINE								
Cohen	Y	Y	Y	N	Y	N	Y	N
Mitchell	Y	Y	Y	N	Y	N	Y	Y
MARYLAND								
Mathias	Y	N	Y	N	Y	Y	Y	Y
Sarbanes	Y	Y	Y	N	Y	N	Y	Y
MASSACHUSETTS								
Kennedy	Y	Y	Y	N	Y	N	Y	Y
Tsongas	Y	Y	Y	?	Y	N	Y	Y
MICHIGAN								
Levin	Y	Y	Y	N	Y	N	Y	Y
Riegle	Y	Y	Y	N	Y	N	Y	Y
MINNESOTA								
Boschwitz	Y	Y	Y	Y	Y	Y	Y	Y
Durenberger	Y	?	#	-	#	?	+	+
MISSISSIPPI								
Cochran	Y	Y	N	Y	Y	Y	Y	Y
Stennis	Y	Y	Y	Y	Y	Y	Y	Y
MISSOURI								
Danforth	Y	N	Y	Y	Y	Y	Y	Y
Eagleton	Y	Y	Y	N	Y	N	Y	Y
MONTANA								
Baucus	Y	Y	Y	Y	N	Y	N	Y
Melcher	Y	Y	Y	Y	N	Y	Y	Y
NEBRASKA								
Exon	Y	Y	Y	Y	N	Y	N	Y
Zorinsky	Y	Y	Y	Y	Y	Y	Y	Y
NEVADA								
Laxalt	Y	Y	N	Y	N	Y	Y	Y
Cannon	+	?	+	?	#	?	+	?
NEW HAMPSHIRE								
Humphrey	Y	Y	N	Y	N	Y	N	N
Rudman	Y	N	N	N	Y	Y	Y	Y
NEW JERSEY								
Brady	Y	Y	N	N	N	Y	N	Y
Bradley	Y	Y	Y	N	Y	Y	Y	Y
NEW MEXICO								
Domenici	Y	?	Y	Y	N	Y	N	N
Schmitt	?	?	?	?	?	?	?	?
NEW YORK								
D'Amato	Y	Y	Y	Y	N	Y	?	Y
Moynihan	Y	Y	Y	N	Y	N	Y	Y
NORTH CAROLINA								
East	Y	Y	Y	Y	N	Y	N	N
Helms	Y	Y	Y	Y	N	Y	Y	N
NORTH DAKOTA								
Andrews	Y	Y	Y	Y	Y	Y	Y	Y
Burdick	Y	Y	Y	Y	Y	N	Y	Y
OHIO								
Glenn	Y	Y	Y	N	Y	?	Y	Y
Metzenbaum	Y	Y	Y	N	Y	N	Y	Y
OKLAHOMA								
Nickles	Y	Y	Y	N	Y	N	N	N
Boren	Y	Y	Y	Y	Y	Y	Y	Y
OREGON								
Hatfield	Y	N	N	Y	N	Y	Y	Y
Packwood	Y	N	Y	Y	Y	Y	Y	Y
PENNSYLVANIA								
Heinz	Y	Y	Y	N	Y	N	Y	Y
Specter	Y	Y	N	N	Y	Y	Y	Y
RHODE ISLAND								
Chafee	Y	N	N	N	Y	Y	Y	Y
Pell	Y	Y	Y	N	+	?	+	+
SOUTH CAROLINA								
Thurmond	Y	Y	Y	Y	N	Y	Y	Y
Hollings	Y	Y	Y	Y	N	Y	Y	Y
SOUTH DAKOTA								
Abdnor	Y	Y	Y	Y	Y	Y	Y	Y
Pressler	Y	Y	Y	-	+	+	+	+
TENNESSEE								
Baker	Y	N	N	N	N	Y	N	Y
Sasser	Y	Y	Y	N	Y	N	Y	Y
TEXAS								
Tower	Y	N	N	Y	N	Y	Y	N
Bentsen	Y	Y	Y	?	Y	Y	Y	Y
UTAH								
Garn	Y	Y	N	Y	Y	Y	Y	Y
Hatch	Y	Y	Y	Y	Y	Y	Y	Y
VERMONT								
Stafford	Y	N	Y	N	Y	Y	Y	Y
Leahy	Y	Y	Y	N	Y	N	Y	Y
VIRGINIA								
Warner	Y	Y	Y	Y	N	Y	N	N
Byrd*	Y	Y	Y	N	Y	N	N	N
WASHINGTON								
Gorton	Y	Y	Y	Y	N	Y	N	Y
Jackson	Y	Y	Y	Y	N	Y	N	Y
WEST VIRGINIA								
Byrd	Y	Y	Y	N	Y	N	Y	Y
Randolph	Y	Y	N	Y	N	Y	N	Y
WISCONSIN								
Kasten	Y	Y	Y	N	Y	N	Y	Y
Proxmire	Y	Y	Y	N	Y	N	Y	N
WYOMING								
Simpson	Y	Y	N	Y	N	Y	N	Y
Wallop	Y	Y	N	Y	N	Y	N	N

ND - Northern Democrats　　SD - Southern Democrats (Southern states - Ala., Ark., Fla., Ga., Ky., La., Miss., N.C., Okla., S.C., Tenn., Texas, Va.)　　*Byrd elected as an independent.

161. S Con Res 96. Nuclear Export Controls. Adoption of the concurrent resolution to reaffirm S Res 179 and H Res 177 regarding nuclear export controls and to declare that the president should seek at the June 4-6 economic summit conference at Versailles, France, and by other routes to reach agreement among all nuclear supplier nations that they would export nuclear fuel, equipment and technology only to those non-nuclear weapon states that had accepted full-scope safeguards of the International Atomic Energy Agency. Adopted 96-0: R 52-0; D 44-0 (ND 29-0, SD 15-0), May 27, 1982.

162. HR 5922. Urgent Supplemental Appropriations, Fiscal 1982. Kasten, R-Wis., amendment to the provision of the bill prohibiting payments under loans guaranteed by the U.S. government to the government of Poland unless Poland was declared to be in default or the president declared that such payments were in the national interest. The amendment clarified procedures by which the president would certify to Congress that the loan payments were in the national interest. Adopted 83-10: R 40-9; D 43-1 (ND 28-1, SD 15-0), May 27, 1982.

163. HR 5922. Urgent Supplemental Appropriations, Fiscal 1982. Proxmire, D-Wis., amendment to limit business-related tax deductions claimed by individual members of Congress to $3,000 a year, beginning in 1982. Adopted 70-23: R 28-21; D 42-2 (ND 28-1, SD 14-1), May 27, 1982.

164. HR 5922. Urgent Supplemental Appropriations, Fiscal 1982. Bumpers, D-Ark., amendment to delete the section of the bill transferring jurisdiction for the inspection of surface mining of clay, sand and gravel, stone and colloidal phosphate to the Mine Safety and Health Administration from the Occupational Safety and Health Administration. Adopted 52-38: R 35-13; D 17-25 (ND 6-22, SD 11-3), May 27, 1982.

165. HR 5922. Urgent Supplemental Appropriations, Fiscal 1982. Lugar, R-Ind., motion to suspend the rules in order to allow the Lugar amendment, providing $5.1 billion in subsidies of home mortgage interest rates, to be added to the bill. Motion agreed to 63-27: R 23-25; D 40-2 (ND 27-1, SD 13-1), May 27, 1982. A two-thirds majority of those present and voting (60 in this case) is required to suspend the rules.

166. HR 5922. Urgent Supplemental Appropriations, Fiscal 1982. Judgment of the Senate affirming the chair's ruling that the Riegle, D-Mich., amendment, to establish a new, $500 million loan program for homeowners who were in arrears on their mortgages, was not germane and therefore out of order. Ruling of the chair upheld 64-25: R 48-0; D 16-25 (ND 4-22, SD 12-3), May 27, 1982.

167. HR 5922. Urgent Supplemental Appropriations, Fiscal 1982. Lugar, R-Ind., amendment to establish a new subsidy program to provide mortgages at below-market interest rates for buyers of new homes. The amendment contained a fiscal 1982 appropriation of $5.1 billion. Adopted 69-23: R 29-20; D 40-3 (ND 27-1, SD 13-2), May 27, 1982. A "nay" was a vote supporting the president's position.

168. HR 5922. Urgent Supplemental Appropriations, Fiscal 1982. Passage of the bill to provide $10,534,524,300 in new budget authority and $7,564,604,165 in rescissions for fiscal 1982. Passed 73-19: R 33-16; D 40-3 (ND 27-1, SD 13-2), May 27, 1982.

	169 170		169 170		169 170	KEY
ALABAMA		**IOWA**		**NEW HAMPSHIRE**		Y Voted for (yea).
Denton	Y Y	*Grassley*	Y Y	*Humphrey*	Y Y	# Paired for.
Heflin	Y Y	*Jepsen*	? ?	*Rudman*	Y Y	+ Announced for.
ALASKA		**KANSAS**		**NEW JERSEY**		N Voted against (nay).
Murkowski	? ?	*Dole*	Y Y	*Brady*	Y Y	X Paired against.
Stevens	Y Y	*Kassebaum*	Y Y	Bradley	Y Y	- Announced against.
ARIZONA		**KENTUCKY**		**NEW MEXICO**		P Voted "present".
Goldwater	Y Y	Ford	Y Y	*Domenici*	Y Y	C Voted "present" to avoid possi-
DeConcini	Y ?	Huddleston	Y Y	*Schmitt*	Y ?	ble conflict of interest.
ARKANSAS		**LOUISIANA**		**NEW YORK**		? Did not vote or otherwise make a
Bumpers	Y ?	Johnston	Y Y	*D'Amato*	Y Y	position known.
Pryor	Y Y	Long	Y Y	Moynihan	Y N	
CALIFORNIA		**MAINE**		**NORTH CAROLINA**		Democrats *Republicans*
Hayakawa	Y Y	*Cohen*	Y Y	*East*	Y Y	
Cranston	Y X	Mitchell	? ?	*Helms*	Y Y	
COLORADO		**MARYLAND**		**NORTH DAKOTA**		169 170
Armstrong	Y Y	*Mathias*	Y N	*Andrews*	Y Y	
Hart	Y N	Sarbanes	Y Y	Burdick	Y Y	
CONNECTICUT		**MASSACHUSETTS**		**OHIO**		**TEXAS**	
Weicker	Y Y	Kennedy	Y Y	Glenn	Y Y	*Tower*	Y Y
Dodd	Y Y	Tsongas	Y Y	Metzenbaum	Y Y	Bentsen	Y Y
DELAWARE		**MICHIGAN**		**OKLAHOMA**		**UTAH**	
Roth	Y ?	Levin	Y Y	*Nickles*	Y Y	*Garn*	Y Y
Biden	? N	Riegle	Y Y	Boren	Y Y	*Hatch*	Y Y
FLORIDA		**MINNESOTA**		**OREGON**		**VERMONT**	
Hawkins	+ +	*Boschwitz*	Y Y	*Hatfield*	Y Y	*Stafford*	Y ?
Chiles	Y Y	*Durenberger*	Y Y	*Packwood*	+ +	Leahy	Y Y
GEORGIA		**MISSISSIPPI**		**PENNSYLVANIA**		**VIRGINIA**	
Mattingly	Y Y	*Cochran*	Y Y	*Heinz*	Y Y	*Warner*	Y Y
Nunn	Y Y	Stennis	Y Y	*Specter*	Y Y	Byrd*	Y Y
HAWAII		**MISSOURI**		**RHODE ISLAND**		**WASHINGTON**	
Inouye	Y Y	*Danforth*	Y Y	*Chafee*	Y Y	*Gorton*	Y Y
Matsunaga	Y ?	Eagleton	Y Y	Pell	Y Y	Jackson	Y Y
IDAHO		**MONTANA**		**SOUTH CAROLINA**		**WEST VIRGINIA**	
McClure	Y Y	Baucus	Y Y	*Thurmond*	Y Y	Byrd	Y Y
Symms	Y Y	Melcher	Y Y	Hollings	Y Y	Randolph	Y Y
ILLINOIS		**NEBRASKA**		**SOUTH DAKOTA**		**WISCONSIN**	
Percy	Y Y	Exon	Y Y	*Abdnor*	Y Y	*Kasten*	Y Y
Dixon	Y Y	Zorinsky	N Y	*Pressler*	+ ?	Proxmire	Y Y
INDIANA		**NEVADA**		**TENNESSEE**		**WYOMING**	
Lugar	Y Y	*Laxalt*	Y Y	*Baker*	? ?	*Simpson*	Y Y
Quayle	Y Y	Cannon	Y Y	Sasser	Y #	*Wallop*	Y Y

ND - Northern Democrats   SD - Southern Democrats (Southern states - Ala., Ark., Fla., Ga., Ky., La., Miss., N.C., Okla., S.C., Tenn., Texas, Va.)   *Byrd elected as an independent.*

169. HR 5432. Admiral Rickover Gold Medal. Passage of the bill to authorize the presentation on behalf of Congress of a specially struck gold medal to retired Admiral Hyman G. Rickover. Passed 91-1: R 48-0; D 43-1 (ND 28-1, SD 15-0), June 9, 1982.

170. HR 4. Intelligence Identities Protection Act. Adoption of the conference report on the bill to make it a felony to publicly expose the identities of U.S. covert intelligence officers, agents, informants and sources. Adopted 81-4: R 44-1; D 37-3 (ND 24-3, SD 13-0), June 10, 1982. A "yea" was a vote supporting the president's position.

	171	172	173	174	175	176	177
ALABAMA							
Denton	Y	N	Y	Y	Y	Y	N
Heflin	Y	Y	Y	Y	N	N	N
ALASKA							
Murkowski	?	Y	Y	Y	N	N	N
Stevens	Y	Y	Y	Y	N	N	?
ARIZONA							
Goldwater	Y	Y	?	Y	N	N	N
DeConcini	Y	Y	Y	Y	N	N	N
ARKANSAS							
Bumpers	Y	Y	Y	Y	N	N	N
Pryor	Y	Y	Y	Y	N	N	N
CALIFORNIA							
Hayakawa	Y	Y	Y	Y	Y	N	N
Cranston	?	Y	Y	Y	N	N	N
COLORADO							
Armstrong	Y	Y	Y	Y	Y	Y	N
Hart	?	Y	Y	Y	N	?	N
CONNECTICUT							
Weicker	Y	Y	N	Y	N	N	N
Dodd	?	Y	Y	Y	N	N	N
DELAWARE							
Roth	Y	Y	Y	Y	N	N	N
Biden	?	Y	Y	Y	?	?	?
FLORIDA							
Hawkins	+	Y	Y	Y	N	Y	N
Chiles	Y	Y	?	Y	N	N	N
GEORGIA							
Mattingly	Y	Y	Y	Y	N	N	N
Nunn	Y	Y	Y	Y	N	N	N
HAWAII							
Inouye	Y	Y	Y	Y	N	N	N
Matsunaga	Y	Y	?	Y	N	N	N
IDAHO							
McClure	Y	N	Y	Y	Y	?	?
Symms	Y	N	Y	Y	Y	Y	N
ILLINOIS							
Percy	Y	+	?	Y	N	N	N
Dixon	Y	Y	Y	Y	N	N	N
INDIANA							
Lugar	Y	Y	Y	Y	N	N	N
Quayle	Y	Y	N	Y	N	N	N
IOWA							
Grassley	Y	Y	Y	Y	N	N	N
Jepsen	Y	Y	?	Y	N	N	N
KANSAS							
Dole	Y	Y	Y	Y	N	N	N
Kassebaum	?	Y	Y	Y	N	N	N
KENTUCKY							
Ford	Y	Y	Y	Y	N	N	N
Huddleston	Y	Y	Y	Y	N	N	N
LOUISIANA							
Johnston	Y	?	?	Y	N	N	N
Long	Y	Y	N	Y	N	N	N
MAINE							
Cohen	Y	Y	Y	Y	N	N	N
Mitchell	?	Y	Y	Y	N	N	N
MARYLAND							
Mathias	Y	Y	Y	Y	N	N	N
Sarbanes	?	Y	Y	Y	N	N	N
MASSACHUSETTS							
Kennedy	Y	Y	Y	Y	N	N	N
Tsongas	Y	+	Y	Y	N	N	N
MICHIGAN							
Levin	?	Y	?	Y	N	N	N
Riegle	?	Y	Y	Y	N	N	N
MINNESOTA							
Boschwitz	Y	Y	Y	Y	N	N	N
Durenberger	Y	Y	Y	Y	N	N	N
MISSISSIPPI							
Cochran	Y	Y	Y	Y	N	N	N
Stennis	Y	N	Y	Y	N	N	N
MISSOURI							
Danforth	Y	Y	Y	Y	N	N	N
Eagleton	Y	Y	Y	?	N	N	N
MONTANA							
Baucus	Y	Y	Y	Y	N	N	N
Melcher	Y	Y	Y	Y	N	N	N
NEBRASKA							
Exon	Y	Y	Y	?	?	?	?
Zorinsky	Y	Y	Y	Y	N	N	N
NEVADA							
Laxalt	Y	Y	Y	Y	Y	Y	N
Cannon	Y	Y	Y	Y	N	N	N
NEW HAMPSHIRE							
Humphrey	Y	Y	Y	Y	Y	N	N
Rudman	Y	Y	Y	Y	N	N	N
NEW JERSEY							
Brady	?	Y	Y	Y	N	N	N
Bradley	?	Y	Y	Y	N	N	N
NEW MEXICO							
Domenici	Y	Y	?	Y	N	N	N
Schmitt	?	Y	Y	Y	N	N	N
NEW YORK							
D'Amato	Y	Y	Y	Y	N	N	N
Moynihan	Y	Y	Y	Y	N	N	N
NORTH CAROLINA							
East	Y	N	Y	Y	Y	Y	N
Helms	Y	N	Y	Y	Y	Y	N
NORTH DAKOTA							
Andrews	Y	Y	Y	Y	N	N	N
Burdick	+	+	?	+	-	-	-
OHIO							
Glenn	Y	+	?	Y	N	N	N
Metzenbaum	Y	Y	Y	Y	N	N	N
OKLAHOMA							
Nickles	Y	Y	Y	Y	N	Y	N
Boren	?	Y	Y	Y	N	N	N
OREGON							
Hatfield	Y	Y	Y	Y	N	N	N
Packwood	Y	Y	Y	Y	N	N	N
PENNSYLVANIA							
Heinz	?	Y	Y	Y	N	N	N
Specter	Y	Y	Y	Y	N	N	Y
RHODE ISLAND							
Chafee	Y	Y	Y	Y	N	N	N
Pell	+	Y	Y	Y	N	N	N
SOUTH CAROLINA							
Thurmond	Y	Y	Y	Y	Y	Y	N
Hollings	?	Y	Y	Y	N	N	N
SOUTH DAKOTA							
Abdnor	Y	Y	Y	Y	N	Y	N
Pressler	Y	Y	Y	Y	N	N	N
TENNESSEE							
Baker	Y	Y	?	Y	N	N	N
Sasser	+	Y	Y	Y	N	N	N
TEXAS							
Tower	Y	?	?	Y	Y	Y	N
Bentsen	?	Y	Y	Y	N	N	N
UTAH							
Garn	Y	Y	Y	Y	Y	Y	N
Hatch	Y	Y	Y	Y	Y	Y	N
VERMONT							
Stafford	?	Y	Y	Y	N	N	N
Leahy	?	Y	Y	Y	N	N	N
VIRGINIA							
Warner	Y	N	Y	Y	Y	N	N
Byrd*	Y	N	Y	Y	Y	Y	N
WASHINGTON							
Gorton	Y	Y	Y	Y	N	N	N
Jackson	Y	Y	Y	Y	N	N	N
WEST VIRGINIA							
Byrd	Y	Y	Y	Y	N	N	N
Randolph	Y	Y	Y	Y	N	N	N
WISCONSIN							
Kasten	?	Y	Y	Y	N	N	N
Proxmire	Y	Y	N	Y	N	N	N
WYOMING							
Simpson	Y	Y	?	Y	N	N	N
Wallop	Y	Y	Y	Y	Y	Y	N

KEY

Y   Voted for (yea).
\#   Paired for.
+   Announced for.
N   Voted against (nay).
X   Paired against.
-   Announced against.
P   Voted "present".
C   Voted "present" to avoid possible conflict of interest.
?   Did not vote or otherwise make a position known.

Democrats   *Republicans*

ND - Northern Democrats   SD - Southern Democrats (Southern states - Ala., Ark., Fla., Ga., Ky., La., Miss., N.C., Okla., S.C., Tenn., Texas, Va.)   *Byrd elected as an independent.

171. S 1210. Environmental Quality Improvement. Gorton, R-Wash., motion that the Senate concur in the House amendments to the bill to reauthorize the Council on Environmental Quality at $44,000 annually for fiscal 1982-1984, with the Gorton amendment to bar oil and gas leasing in the Seattle-Tacoma, Wash., watershed in Mount Baker-Snoqualmie National Forest. Motion agreed to 76-0: R 46-0; D 30-0 (ND 19-0, SD 11-0), June 14, 1982.

172. S 1992. Voting Rights Act Extension. Baker, R-Tenn., motion to invoke cloture (thus limiting debate) on the Baker motion to proceed to the consideration of the bill to extend for 25 years Section Five, the major enforcement provision of the 1965 Voting Rights Act. Motion agreed to 86-8: R 46-6; D 40-2 (ND 28-0, SD 12-2), June 15, 1982. A three-fifths majority vote (60) of the total Senate is required to invoke cloture.

173. S 1992. Voting Rights Act Extension. Stevens, R-Alaska, motion to instruct the sergeant-at-arms to compel the attendance of absent senators. Motion agreed to 83-4: R 45-2; D 38-2 (ND 26-1, SD 12-1), June 16, 1982.

174. S 1992. Voting Rights Act Extension. Stevens, R-Alaska, motion (offered on behalf of Baker, R-Tenn.) to proceed to consideration of S 1992, a bill to extend for 25 years Section Five, the major enforcement provision of the 1965 Voting Rights Act. Motion agreed to 97-0: R 54-0; D 43-0 (ND 28-0, SD 15-0), June 17, 1982.

175. S 1992. Voting Rights Act Extension. East, R-N.C., amendment to delete a provision allowing certain voting rights violations to be proved by showing that an election procedure results in discrimination. Rejected 16-81: R 15-39; D 1-42 (ND 0-28, SD 1-14), June 17, 1982.

176. S 1992. Voting Rights Act Extension. East, R-N.C., amendment to bar a federal judge from requiring proportional representation or quotas as a remedy for voting rights violations. Rejected 14-81: R 13-40; D 1-41 (ND 0-27, SD 1-14), June 17, 1982.

177. S 1992. Voting Rights Act Extension. Helms, R-N.C., amendment to allow a federal judge to require proportional representation or quotas as a remedy for voting rights violations. Rejected 1-94: R 1-51; D 0-43 (ND 0-28, SD 0-15), June 17, 1982.

CQ Senate Votes 178 - 185
Corresponding to Congressional Record Votes 178, 179, 180, 181, 182, 183, 184, 185

	178	179	180	181	182	183	184	185
ALABAMA								
Denton	Y	Y	Y	?	?	Y	Y	Y
Heflin	Y	Y	Y	Y	N	Y	Y	Y
ALASKA								
Murkowski	N	N	Y	Y	?	N	Y	N
Stevens	N	N	Y	Y	Y	N	N	N
ARIZONA								
Goldwater	N	N	Y	?	Y	Y	Y	Y
DeConcini	N	N	N	N	N	N	N	N
ARKANSAS								
Bumpers	N	N	N	N	N	N	Y	N
Pryor	N	N	N	N	?	N	Y	N
CALIFORNIA								
Hayakawa	Y	N	Y	Y	Y	Y	Y	Y
Cranston	N	N	N	N	N	N	N	N
COLORADO								
Armstrong	Y	N	Y	?	Y	N	N	N
Hart	N	N	N	N	N	N	N	N
CONNECTICUT								
Weicker	N	N	N	N	N	N	N	N
Dodd	N	N	N	N	N	N	N	N
DELAWARE								
Roth	N	N	N	N	N	N	N	N
Biden	?	?	?	?	N	N	N	N
FLORIDA								
Hawkins	N	N	Y	N	N	N	Y	N
Chiles	Y	N	N	N	N	N	Y	N
GEORGIA								
Mattingly	Y	N	Y	Y	Y	Y	Y	N
Nunn	Y	Y	Y	Y	N	Y	Y	N
HAWAII								
Inouye	N	N	N	N	N	N	Y	N
Matsunaga	N	N	N	N	-	-	-	N
IDAHO								
McClure	Y	Y	Y	Y	Y	Y	Y	Y
Symms	Y	Y	Y	Y	Y	Y	Y	Y
ILLINOIS								
Percy	N	N	N	N	?	N	N	N
Dixon	N	N	N	N	N	N	N	N
INDIANA								
Lugar	Y	N	Y	N	?	?	?	?
Quayle	N	N	Y	N	Y	N	N	N

	178	179	180	181	182	183	184	185
IOWA								
Grassley	N	N	N	N	N	N	N	N
Jepsen	N	N	N	N	N	N	N	N
KANSAS								
Dole	N	N	N	N	N	N	N	N
Kassebaum	N	N	N	N	N	N	N	?
KENTUCKY								
Ford	N	N	N	N	N	N	N	N
Huddleston	N	N	N	Y	N	Y	N	N
LOUISIANA								
Johnston	Y	N	N	Y	N	N	Y	N
Long	Y	N	N	Y	Y	N	Y	N
MAINE								
Cohen	N	N	N	Y	N	Y	N	N
Mitchell	N	N	N	N	N	N	N	N
MARYLAND								
Mathias	N	N	N	N	N	N	N	N
Sarbanes	N	N	N	N	N	N	N	N
MASSACHUSETTS								
Kennedy	N	N	N	N	N	N	N	N
Tsongas	N	N	N	N	N	N	N	N
MICHIGAN								
Levin	N	N	N	N	N	N	N	N
Riegle	N	N	N	N	N	N	N	N
MINNESOTA								
Boschwitz	N	N	N	N	N	N	N	N
Durenberger	N	N	N	N	N	N	N	N
MISSISSIPPI								
Cochran	Y	Y	Y	Y	Y	Y	Y	Y
Stennis	Y	Y	Y	Y	N	Y	Y	Y
MISSOURI								
Danforth	N	N	N	?	?	?	?	?
Eagleton	N	N	N	N	N	N	N	N
MONTANA								
Baucus	Y	N	N	N	N	N	N	N
Melcher	N	N	N	N	N	N	N	N
NEBRASKA								
Exon	?	?	?	?	?	?	?	?
Zorinsky	Y	N	N	N	Y	N	Y	N
NEVADA								
Laxalt	Y	Y	Y	?	?	N	Y	Y
Cannon	N	N	N	N	N	N	N	N

	178	179	180	181	182	183	184	185
NEW HAMPSHIRE								
Humphrey	Y	Y	Y	Y	Y	N	Y	Y
Rudman	N	N	Y	Y	Y	N	N	N
NEW JERSEY								
Brady	N	N	Y	Y	Y	N	N	N
Bradley	N	N	N	N	N	N	N	N
NEW MEXICO								
Domenici	N	N	N	N	?	?	Y	N
Schmitt	N	N	Y	N	N	N	N	N
NEW YORK								
D'Amato	N	N	Y	N	N	Y	N	N
Moynihan	N	N	N	?	N	N	N	N
NORTH CAROLINA								
East	Y	Y	Y	Y	Y	Y	Y	Y
Helms	Y	Y	Y	Y	Y	Y	Y	Y
NORTH DAKOTA								
Andrews	N	N	Y	Y	Y	N	N	N
Burdick	-	-	?	?	-	-	-	-
OHIO								
Glenn	N	N	N	N	?	?	?	?
Metzenbaum	N	N	N	N	N	N	N	N
OKLAHOMA								
Nickles	Y	Y	Y	Y	Y	N	Y	Y
Boren	N	N	N	N	N	N	N	?
OREGON								
Hatfield	N	N	N	N	Y	N	N	N
Packwood	N	N	N	Y	N	N	N	N
PENNSYLVANIA								
Heinz	N	N	N	N	N	N	N	N
Specter	N	N	Y	N	N	N	N	N
RHODE ISLAND								
Chafee	N	N	N	N	N	N	N	N
Pell	N	N	N	Y	Y	N	N	N
SOUTH CAROLINA								
Thurmond	Y	Y	Y	Y	Y	Y	Y	Y
Hollings	N	N	N	N	N	N	N	N
SOUTH DAKOTA								
Abdnor	Y	N	Y	Y	Y	Y	Y	Y
Pressler	?	N	Y	Y	Y	N	N	N
TENNESSEE								
Baker	N	N	Y	N	Y	N	Y	N
Sasser	N	N	N	N	N	N	Y	N

	178	179	180	181	182	183	184	185
TEXAS								
Tower	Y	Y	Y	Y	?	?	Y	Y
Bentsen	Y	N	N	N	N	N	Y	N
UTAH								
Garn	Y	Y	Y	Y	Y	N	Y	Y
Hatch	Y	Y	Y	Y	Y	N	Y	Y
VERMONT								
Stafford	N	N	N	N	N	N	N	N
Leahy	N	N	N	N	N	N	N	N
VIRGINIA								
Warner	Y	Y	Y	Y	Y	Y	Y	Y
Byrd*	Y	Y	Y	Y	Y	Y	Y	Y
WASHINGTON								
Gorton	N	N	N	N	N	N	N	N
Jackson	N	N	N	N	N	N	N	N
WEST VIRGINIA								
Byrd	N	N	N	N	N	N	N	N
Randolph	Y	N	N	N	N	N	N	N
WISCONSIN								
Kasten	N	N	Y	Y	Y	N	N	N
Proxmire	N	N	N	N	N	N	N	N
WYOMING								
Simpson	N	N	N	?	?	?	N	N
Wallop	Y	Y	Y	?	?	?	?	?

ND - Northern Democrats   SD - Southern Democrats (Southern states - Ala., Ark., Fla., Ga., Ky., La., Miss., N.C., Okla., S.C., Tenn., Texas, Va.)   *Byrd elected as an independent.*

178. S 1992. Voting Rights Act Extension. East, R-N.C., amendment to allow suits under Section Five of the 1965 Voting Rights Act, the pre-clearance enforcement provision, to be heard in local federal courts rather than the District of Columbia. Rejected 31-65: R 20-33; D 11-32 (ND 3-25, SD 8-7), June 17, 1982.

179. S 1992. Voting Rights Act Extension. East, R-N.C., amendment to ease provisions allowing covered jurisdictions to bail out from coverage of Section Five of the Voting Rights Act. Rejected 19-78: R 15-39; D 4-39 (ND 0-28, SD 4-11), June 17, 1982.

180. S 1992. Voting Rights Act Extension. Stevens, R-Alaska, amendment to incorporate into the bailout provisions of Section Five the "results" test included in Section Two of the act. Rejected 38-59: R 34-20; D 4-39 (ND 0-28, SD 4-11), June 17, 1982.

181. S 1992. Voting Rights Act Extension. Stevens, R-Alaska, amendment to allow states to bail out from coverage of Section Five of the Voting Rights Act regardless of whether their individual counties or municipalities are eligible to bail out. Rejected 32-58: R 25-23; D 7-35 (ND 1-26, SD 6-9), June 17, 1982.

182. S 1992. Voting Rights Act Extension. Hayakawa, R-Calif., amendment to repeal provisions requiring bilingual election materials in certain areas of the country. Rejected 32-54: R 27-18; D 5-36 (ND 2-25, SD 3-11), June 18, 1982.

183. S 1992. Voting Rights Act Extension. Cochran, R-Miss., amendment to include all states under Section Five of the Voting Rights Act, requiring them to get Department of Justice approval for any election law changes. Rejected 16-74: R 12-36; D 4-38 (ND 0-27, SD 4-11), June 18, 1982.

184. S 1992. Voting Rights Act Extension. Nunn, D-Ga., amendment to reduce the time allowed for the Department of Justice to object to a proposed election law change after the department has requested additional information. Rejected 38-55: R 23-28; D 15-27 (ND 3-24, SD 12-3), June 18, 1982.

185. S 1992. Voting Rights Act Extension. Denton, R-Ala., amendment to ease provisions allowing jurisdictions covered by Section Five of the Voting Rights Act to bail out from coverage. Rejected 19-73: R 16-34; D 3-39 (ND 0-28, SD 3-11), June 18, 1982.

	186	187	188	189	190	191	192	193
ALABAMA								
Denton	Y	Y	Y	Y	N	Y	Y	N
Heflin	N	Y	N	N	Y	N	Y	Y
ALASKA								
Murkowski	+	Y	N	N	Y	Y	Y	N
Stevens	Y	Y	N	Y	Y	Y	Y	N
ARIZONA								
Goldwater	Y	N	?	?	+	Y	N	N
DeConcini	N	N	N	N	Y	N	N	N
ARKANSAS								
Bumpers	N	N	N	N	Y	Y	Y	N
Pryor	N	N	N	N	Y	Y	N	N
CALIFORNIA								
Hayakawa	Y	Y	Y	Y	N	Y	Y	N
Cranston	N	N	N	N	Y	Y	N	Y
COLORADO								
Armstrong	N	Y	Y	N	Y	Y	Y	N
Hart	N	N	N	N	Y	Y	N	Y
CONNECTICUT								
Weicker	N	N	N	N	Y	N	N	Y
Dodd	N	N	N	N	Y	Y	N	N
DELAWARE								
Roth	N	N	N	N	Y	Y	Y	N
Biden	N	N	N	N	Y	Y	N	+
FLORIDA								
Hawkins	N	N	N	N	Y	N	Y	Y
Chiles	N	N	N	N	Y	N	N	Y
GEORGIA								
Mattingly	N	N	N	N	Y	Y	Y	N
Nunn	N	Y	N	N	Y	Y	N	Y
HAWAII								
Inouye	N	N	N	N	Y	Y	N	Y
Matsunaga	N	N	N	N	Y	N	N	?
IDAHO								
McClure	Y	Y	Y	Y	N	Y	Y	N
Symms	Y	Y	Y	Y	N	Y	Y	N
ILLINOIS								
Percy	N	N	N	N	Y	Y	Y	N
Dixon	N	N	N	N	Y	Y	N	N
INDIANA								
Lugar	?	?	?	?	+	Y	Y	N
Quayle	N	Y	N	N	Y	Y	Y	N
IOWA								
Grassley	N	N	N	N	Y	N	Y	N
Jepsen	N	N	N	N	Y	Y	Y	N
KANSAS								
Dole	N	N	N	N	Y	Y	Y	N
Kassebaum	N	N	N	N	Y	Y	Y	N
KENTUCKY								
Ford	N	N	N	N	Y	N	N	Y
Huddleston	N	N	N	N	Y	Y	N	Y
LOUISIANA								
Johnston	Y	Y	N	N	Y	N	Y	N
Long	Y	Y	N	N	Y	N	N	Y
MAINE								
Cohen	N	N	N	N	Y	Y	Y	N
Mitchell	N	N	N	N	Y	N	N	N
MARYLAND								
Mathias	N	N	N	N	Y	Y	N	N
Sarbanes	N	N	N	N	Y	N	N	Y
MASSACHUSETTS								
Kennedy	N	N	N	N	Y	N	N	Y
Tsongas	N	N	N	N	Y	Y	N	Y
MICHIGAN								
Levin	N	N	N	N	Y	N	N	Y
Riegle	N	N	N	N	Y	N	N	N
MINNESOTA								
Boschwitz	N	N	N	N	Y	Y	Y	N
Durenberger	N	N	N	N	Y	?	Y	N
MISSISSIPPI								
Cochran	N	Y	N	Y	Y	Y	Y	N
Stennis	N	Y	Y	N	Y	Y	Y	N
MISSOURI								
Danforth	?	?	?	?	+	N	Y	N
Eagleton	N	N	N	N	Y	N	?	Y
MONTANA								
Baucus	N	N	N	N	Y	Y	N	N
Melcher	N	N	N	N	Y	N	N	Y
NEBRASKA								
Exon	?	?	?	?	?	?	N	N	Y
Zorinsky	N	Y	N	N	Y	N	Y	N
NEVADA								
Laxalt	Y	Y	Y	N	Y	Y	Y	N
Cannon	N	N	N	N	Y	-	-	?
NEW HAMPSHIRE								
Humphrey	Y	Y	N	Y	N	Y	Y	N
Rudman	Y	Y	N	Y	N	Y	Y	Y
NEW JERSEY								
Brady	Y	N	N	N	Y	?	?	N
Bradley	N	N	N	N	Y	N	N	Y
NEW MEXICO								
Domenici	N	N	N	N	Y	Y	Y	N
Schmitt	Y	N	N	N	Y	N	Y	N
NEW YORK								
D'Amato	Y	N	N	N	Y	Y	Y	N
Moynihan	N	N	N	N	Y	N	N	Y
NORTH CAROLINA								
East	Y	Y	Y	Y	N	N	Y	N
Helms	Y	Y	Y	Y	N	N	N	N
NORTH DAKOTA								
Andrews	?	N	N	N	Y	Y	Y	N
Burdick	-	-	-	-	+	N	N	Y
OHIO								
Glenn	?	?	?	?	+	Y	N	Y
Metzenbaum	N	N	N	N	Y	N	N	Y
OKLAHOMA								
Nickles	Y	Y	N	Y	N	Y	N	Y
Boren	N	N	N	N	Y	N	N	N
OREGON								
Hatfield	N	N	N	N	Y	Y	Y	N
Packwood	N	N	N	N	Y	Y	?	N
PENNSYLVANIA								
Heinz	N	N	N	N	Y	Y	Y	N
Specter	N	N	N	N	Y	Y	Y	Y
RHODE ISLAND								
Chafee	N	N	N	N	Y	Y	Y	N
Pell	Y	N	N	N	Y	N	N	Y
SOUTH CAROLINA								
Thurmond	Y	Y	Y	N	Y	Y	Y	N
Hollings	N	N	N	N	Y	Y	N	Y
SOUTH DAKOTA								
Abdnor	Y	Y	N	N	Y	?	Y	N
Pressler	Y	N	N	N	Y	N	Y	N
TENNESSEE								
Baker	Y	N	N	N	Y	Y	Y	N
Sasser	N	N	N	N	Y	N	N	Y
TEXAS								
Tower	Y	Y	Y	Y	Y	Y	Y	N
Bentsen	N	N	N	N	Y	N	N	N
UTAH								
Garn	Y	Y	N	Y	Y	Y	Y	N
Hatch	Y	Y	N	Y	Y	Y	Y	N
VERMONT								
Stafford	N	N	N	N	Y	Y	Y	N
Leahy	N	N	N	N	Y	N	N	Y
VIRGINIA								
Warner	Y	Y	N	N	Y	N	Y	N
Byrd*	Y	Y	Y	N	N	?	N	N
WASHINGTON								
Gorton	N	N	N	N	Y	Y	Y	N
Jackson	N	N	N	N	Y	N	N	Y
WEST VIRGINIA								
Byrd	N	N	N	N	Y	N	N	N
Randolph	Y	N	N	N	Y	N	N	Y
WISCONSIN								
Kasten	N	N	N	N	Y	Y	Y	N
Proxmire	N	N	N	N	Y	N	N	N
WYOMING								
Simpson	N	N	N	N	Y	N	Y	N
Wallop	?	?	?	?	?	N	Y	N

KEY

Y Voted for (yea).
\# Paired for.
\+ Announced for.
N Voted against (nay).
X Paired against.
- Announced against.
P Voted "present".
C Voted "present" to avoid possible conflict of interest.
? Did not vote or otherwise make a position known.

Democrats   *Republicans*

ND - Northern Democrats   SD - Southern Democrats (Southern states - Ala., Ark., Fla., Ga., Ky., La., Miss., N.C., Okla., S.C., Tenn., Texas, Va.)   *Byrd elected as an independent.

186. S 1992. Voting Rights Act Extension. Stevens, R-Alaska, amendment to make it easier for Alaska to bail out from coverage of Section Five of the Voting Rights Act. Rejected 28-64: R 23-26; D 5-38 (ND 2-26, SD 3-12), June 18, 1982.

187. S 1992. Voting Rights Act Extension. Thurmond, R-S.C., amendment to extend Section Five of the Voting Rights Act for 15 years rather than 25 years. Rejected 28-66: R 21-30; D 7-36 (ND 1-27, SD 6-9), June 18, 1982.

188. S 1992. Voting Rights Act Extension. Helms, R-N.C., amendment to exempt 40 counties in North Carolina from coverage under Section Five of the Voting Rights Act. Rejected 12-81: R 10-40; D 2-41 (ND 0-28, SD 2-13), June 18, 1982.

189. S 1992. Voting Rights Act Extension. Helms, R-N.C., amendment to bring under Section Five of the Voting Rights Act any state with a black voter registration of less than 43.7 percent and to exempt from coverage any state with a black registration greater than 60 percent. Rejected 12-81: R 12-38; D 0-43 (ND 0-28, SD 0-15), June 18, 1982.

190. HR 3112. Voting Rights Act Extension. Passage of the bill to extend for 25 years Section Five, the pre-clearance enforcement provision, of the 1965 Voting Rights Act and to make it easier to prove certain voting rights violations in federal court.

Passed 85-8: R 43-7; D 42-1 (ND 28-0, SD 14-1), June 18, 1982. A "yea" was a vote supporting the president's position.

191. HR 5922. Urgent Supplemental Appropriations, Fiscal 1982. Hatfield, R-Ore., motion that the Senate disagree with a House amendment, to limit annual outside income earned by members of Congress to 30 percent of their annual congressional salaries, to the conference report on the bill. Motion agreed to 54-41: R 38-13; D 16-28 (ND 9-21, SD 7-7), June 22, 1982.

192. S Con Res 92. First Budget Resolution, Fiscal 1983. Adoption of the conference report on the resolution, reported in technical disagreement, to set budget targets for the fiscal year ending Sept. 30, 1983. Adopted 51-45: R 48-4; D 3-41 (ND 1-28, SD 2-13), June 22, 1982.

193. S Con Res 92. First Budget Resolution, Fiscal 1983. Chiles, D-Fla., motion to approve the substitute resolution, agreed to by Senate-House conferees but reported in technical disagreement, with an amendment to provide an additional $150 million in fiscal 1983 outlays for federal law enforcement agencies. Motion rejected 33-64: R 4-50; D 29-14 (ND 20-8, SD 9-6), June 23, 1982.

	194 195 196 197 198		194 195 196 197 198		194 195 196 197 198	KEY
ALABAMA		**IOWA**		**NEW HAMPSHIRE**		Y Voted for (yea).
Denton	Y N N Y Y	*Grassley*	Y N N Y N	*Humphrey*	Y Y Y N N	# Paired for.
Heflin	Y N N Y N	*Jepsen*	Y N N Y N	*Rudman*	Y ? N Y Y	+ Announced for.
ALASKA		**KANSAS**		**NEW JERSEY**		N Voted against (nay).
Murkowski	Y N N N Y	*Dole*	Y Y Y N Y	*Brady*	Y Y Y N ?	X Paired against.
Stevens	Y Y Y Y Y	*Kassebaum*	Y N Y N Y	Bradley	N N N Y N	- Announced against.
ARIZONA		**KENTUCKY**		**NEW MEXICO**		P Voted "present".
Goldwater	Y Y Y N ?	Ford	N N N Y N	*Domenici*	Y N N Y N	C Voted "present" to avoid possible conflict of interest.
DeConcini	N N N Y N	Huddleston	N N N Y N	*Schmitt*	Y N N Y Y	? Did not vote or otherwise make a position known.
ARKANSAS		**LOUISIANA**		**NEW YORK**		
Bumpers	N N N Y ?	Johnston	N N Y N ?	*D'Amato*	Y N N Y Y	Democrats *Republicans*
Pryor	N N N Y ?	Long	N N Y Y Y	Moynihan	N N N Y N	
CALIFORNIA		**MAINE**		**NORTH CAROLINA**		
Hayakawa	Y Y Y N Y	*Cohen*	Y N Y N Y	*East*	Y N Y N Y	194 195 196 197 198
Cranston	N Y N Y ?	Mitchell	N N N Y N	*Helms*	N N Y Y N	
COLORADO		**MARYLAND**		**NORTH DAKOTA**		
Armstrong	Y N Y N N	*Mathias*	N N N Y Y	*Andrews*	Y N N Y Y	**TEXAS**	
Hart	N N Y N N	Sarbanes	N N N Y N	Burdick	N N N Y Y	*Tower*	Y Y Y N Y
CONNECTICUT		**MASSACHUSETTS**		**OHIO**		Bentsen	N N N Y Y
Weicker	N N N Y Y	Kennedy	N N N Y N	Glenn	N N N Y N	**UTAH**	
Dodd	N Y N Y N	Tsongas	N N N Y N	Metzenbaum	N N N Y N	*Garn*	Y Y N Y Y
DELAWARE		**MICHIGAN**		**OKLAHOMA**		*Hatch*	Y N N ? ?
Roth	Y N Y N Y	Levin	N N N Y Y	*Nickles*	Y N Y N N	**VERMONT**	
Biden	N N N Y N	Riegle	N N N Y N	Boren	N N N Y N	*Stafford*	Y N N Y ?
FLORIDA		**MINNESOTA**		**OREGON**		Leahy	N N N Y N
Hawkins	Y N N Y Y	*Boschwitz*	Y N N Y Y	*Hatfield*	Y Y Y N Y	**VIRGINIA**	
Chiles	N N N Y N	*Durenberger*	Y N N Y Y	*Packwood*	Y Y N Y Y	*Warner*	Y N Y N Y
GEORGIA		**MISSISSIPPI**		**PENNSYLVANIA**		Byrd*	N N Y N N
Mattingly	Y N Y N N	*Cochran*	Y Y Y Y Y	*Heinz*	Y N N ? ?	**WASHINGTON**	
Nunn	N N N Y N	Stennis	Y N Y Y Y	*Specter*	Y N N Y Y	*Gorton*	Y Y Y Y Y
HAWAII		**MISSOURI**		**RHODE ISLAND**		Jackson	N N N Y Y
Inouye	N Y N Y N	*Danforth*	Y N N Y Y	*Chafee*	Y N N Y Y	**WEST VIRGINIA**	
Matsunaga	N Y N Y N	Eagleton	N N N Y Y	Pell	N N N Y Y	Byrd	N N N Y N
IDAHO		**MONTANA**		**SOUTH CAROLINA**		Randolph	N N N Y N
McClure	Y Y Y N Y	Baucus	N N N Y N	*Thurmond*	Y N Y N Y	**WISCONSIN**	
Symms	Y Y Y N N	Melcher	N N N Y N	Hollings	N N N Y N	*Kasten*	Y N N Y Y
ILLINOIS		**NEBRASKA**		**SOUTH DAKOTA**		Proxmire	N N N Y N
Percy	Y Y Y N Y	Exon	N N N Y N	*Abdnor*	Y N N Y Y	**WYOMING**	
Dixon	N N N Y N	Zorinsky	Y N N Y N	*Pressler*	Y N N Y Y	*Simpson*	Y ? Y N Y
INDIANA		**NEVADA**		**TENNESSEE**		*Wallop*	Y N Y N Y
Lugar	Y N N Y Y	*Laxalt*	Y Y Y Y Y	*Baker*	Y Y Y N Y		
Quayle	Y N N Y Y	Cannon	- - - + -	Sasser	N N N Y N		

ND - Northern Democrats   SD - Southern Democrats (Southern states - Ala., Ark., Fla., Ga., Ky., La., Miss., N.C., Okla., S.C., Tenn., Texas, Va.)   *Byrd elected as an independent.*

194. S Con Res 92. First Budget Resolution, Fiscal 1983. Domenici, R-N.M., motion to approve the substitute resolution, agreed to by House-Senate conferees but reported in technical disagreement, to set budget targets for the fiscal year ending Sept. 30, 1983, as follows: budget authority, $822.39 billion; outlays, $769.8 billion; revenues, $665.9 billion; deficit, $103.9 billion. The resolution also set preliminary goals for fiscal 1984-85, revised budget levels for fiscal 1982 and included reconciliation instructions requiring House and Senate committees to recommend legislative savings to meet the budget targets. Motion agreed to 54-45: R 51-3; D 3-42 (ND 1-29, SD 2-13), June 23, 1982.

195. HR 6645. Urgent Supplemental Appropriations, Fiscal 1982. Hatfield, R-Ore., motion to table (kill) the Proxmire, D-Wis., amendment to limit business-related tax deductions for living expenses claimed by individual members of Congress to $3,000 a year, beginning in 1982. Motion rejected 21-76: R 17-35; D 4-41 (ND 4-26, SD 0-15), June 23, 1982.

196. HR 6645. Urgent Supplemental Appropriations, Fiscal 1982. Judgment of the Senate affirming the chair's ruling that the Lugar, R-Ind., amendment to provide $3 billion for subsidies of home mortgage interest rates was out of order because it constituted legislation on an appropriations bill. Ruling of the chair rejected 33-66: R 28-26; D 5-40 (ND 1-29, SD 4-11), June 23, 1982. The Lugar amendment subsequently was adopted *(see vote 197, below)*.

197. HR 6645. Urgent Supplemental Appropriations, Fiscal 1982. Lugar, R-Ind., amendment to the Proxmire, D-Wis., amendment *(see vote 195, above)* to provide $3 billion for subsidies of home mortgage interest rates. Adopted 70-27: R 28-24; D 42-3 (ND 29-1, SD 13-2), June 23, 1982.

198. H J Res 519. Temporary Debt Limit Increase. Passage of the joint resolution to increase the temporary limit in the public debt to $1.143 trillion through Sept. 30, 1982. Passed (and thus cleared for the president) 49-41: R 41-8; D 8-33 (ND 5-24, SD 3-9), June 23, 1982. A "yea" was a vote supporting the president's position.

	199		199		199	KEY
ALABAMA		**IOWA**		**NEW HAMPSHIRE**		Y Voted for (yea).
Denton	N	*Grassley*	N	*Humphrey*	N	# Paired for.
Heflin	Y	*Jepsen*	N	*Rudman*	N	+ Announced for.
ALASKA		**KANSAS**		**NEW JERSEY**		N Voted against (nay).
Murkowski	Y	*Dole*	N	*Brady*	N	X Paired against.
Stevens	?	*Kassebaum*	N	Bradley	Y	- Announced against.
ARIZONA		**KENTUCKY**		**NEW MEXICO**		P Voted "present".
Goldwater	N	Ford	Y	*Domenici*	N	C Voted "present" to avoid possi-
DeConcini	Y	Huddleston	Y	*Schmitt*	Y	ble conflict of interest.
ARKANSAS		**LOUISIANA**		**NEW YORK**		? Did not vote or otherwise make a
Bumpers	?	Johnston	?	*D'Amato*	Y	position known.
Pryor	Y	Long	Y	Moynihan	Y	
CALIFORNIA		**MAINE**		**NORTH CAROLINA**		Democrats *Republicans*
Hayakawa	N	*Cohen*	Y	*East*	N	
Cranston	?	Mitchell	Y	*Helms*	N	
COLORADO		**MARYLAND**		**NORTH DAKOTA**		199
Armstrong	N	*Mathias*	Y	*Andrews*	Y	
Hart	?	Sarbanes	Y	Burdick	Y	
CONNECTICUT		**MASSACHUSETTS**		**OHIO**		**TEXAS**
Weicker	Y	Kennedy	?	Glenn	?	*Tower* Y
Dodd	Y	Tsongas	Y	Metzenbaum	?	Bentsen Y
DELAWARE		**MICHIGAN**		**OKLAHOMA**		**UTAH**
Roth	Y	Levin	Y	*Nickles*	N	*Garn* N
Biden	Y	Riegle	Y	Boren	Y	*Hatch* ?
FLORIDA		**MINNESOTA**		**OREGON**		**VERMONT**
Hawkins	Y	*Boschwitz*	N	*Hatfield*	Y	*Stafford* Y
Chiles	Y	*Durenberger*	Y	*Packwood*	Y	Leahy Y
GEORGIA		**MISSISSIPPI**		**PENNSYLVANIA**		**VIRGINIA**
Mattingly	N	*Cochran*	Y	*Heinz*	#	*Warner* N
Nunn	N	Stennis	Y	*Specter*	Y	Byrd* N
HAWAII		**MISSOURI**		**RHODE ISLAND**		**WASHINGTON**
Inouye	Y	*Danforth*	Y	*Chafee*	Y	*Gorton* Y
Matsunaga	Y	Eagleton	Y	Pell	Y	Jackson Y
IDAHO		**MONTANA**		**SOUTH CAROLINA**		**WEST VIRGINIA**
McClure	?	Baucus	Y	*Thurmond*	N	Byrd Y
Symms	?	Melcher	Y	Hollings	Y	Randolph Y
ILLINOIS		**NEBRASKA**		**SOUTH DAKOTA**		**WISCONSIN**
Percy	N	Exon	Y	*Abdnor*	Y	*Kasten* N
Dixon	Y	Zorinsky	Y	*Pressler*	Y	Proxmire N
INDIANA		**NEVADA**		**TENNESSEE**		**WYOMING**
Lugar	Y	*Laxalt*	Y	*Baker*	X	*Simpson* N
Quayle	Y	Cannon	+	Sasser	Y	*Wallop* ?

ND - Northern Democrats   SD - Southern Democrats (Southern states - Ala., Ark., Fla., Ga., Ky., La., Miss., N.C., Okla., S.C., Tenn., Texas, Va.)   *Byrd elected as an independent.

199. HR 6682. Urgent Supplemental Appropriations, Fiscal 1982. Passage of the bill to provide supplemental appropriations of $5,924,835,000 and to rescind previous appropriations of $5,678,120,000. Passed 59-26: R 24-23; D 35-3 (ND 24-1, SD 11-2), June 24, 1982. The president had requested $4,579,679,000 in new budget authority and $7,750,269,165 in rescissions.

KEY

- Y — Voted for (yea).
- # — Paired for.
- + — Announced for.
- N — Voted against (nay).
- X — Paired against.
- - — Announced against.
- P — Voted "present".
- C — Voted "present" to avoid possible conflict of interest.
- ? — Did not vote or otherwise make a position known.

Italic = Democrats; Regular = Republicans

	200	201	202	203	204	205
ALABAMA						
Denton	Y	Y	?	+	?	?
Heflin	Y	N	Y	Y	Y	Y
ALASKA						
Murkowski	Y	Y	Y	Y	Y	Y
Stevens	Y	Y	Y	Y	Y	Y
ARIZONA						
Goldwater	Y	Y	N	Y	?	Y
DeConcini	Y	N	Y	Y	Y	Y
ARKANSAS						
Bumpers	N	N	Y	Y	Y	Y
Pryor	Y	N	N	Y	N	Y
CALIFORNIA						
Hayakawa	+	+	-	+	+	+
Cranston	N	N	Y	Y	?	?
COLORADO						
Armstrong	Y	Y	N	Y	Y	Y
Hart	N	Y	Y	Y	N	Y
CONNECTICUT						
Weicker	N	N	Y	Y	Y	Y
Dodd	N	N	Y	Y	N	Y
DELAWARE						
Roth	Y	Y	N	Y	N	Y
Biden	N	N	Y	Y	N	Y
FLORIDA						
Hawkins	?	?	N	Y	Y	Y
Chiles	N	N	N	Y	Y	Y
GEORGIA						
Mattingly	+	+	-	+	+	+
Nunn	Y	N	Y	Y	Y	Y
HAWAII						
Inouye	N	N	Y	Y	N	Y
Matsunaga	N	N	N	Y	Y	Y
IDAHO						
McClure	Y	Y	N	Y	Y	Y
Symms	Y	Y	N	Y	Y	Y
ILLINOIS						
Percy	Y	Y	N	Y	Y	Y
Dixon	Y	N	Y	Y	Y	Y
INDIANA						
Lugar	Y	N	N	Y	Y	Y
Quayle	Y	Y	N	Y	Y	Y

	200	201	202	203	204	205
IOWA						
Grassley	Y	Y	N	Y	Y	Y
Jepsen	Y	Y	N	Y	Y	Y
KANSAS						
Dole	Y	Y	N	Y	Y	Y
Kassebaum	Y	Y	?	Y	Y	Y
KENTUCKY						
Ford	N	N	Y	Y	N	Y
Huddleston	N	N	Y	Y	N	Y
LOUISIANA						
Johnston	Y	Y	Y	Y	Y	?
Long	N	Y	Y	Y	Y	Y
MAINE						
Cohen	N	Y	N	Y	Y	Y
Mitchell	N	N	Y	Y	N	Y
MARYLAND						
Mathias	N	Y	Y	Y	Y	Y
Sarbanes	N	N	Y	Y	N	Y
MASSACHUSETTS						
Kennedy	N	N	Y	Y	Y	N
Tsongas	?	?	?	?	N	Y
MICHIGAN						
Levin	N	N	Y	Y	Y	Y
Riegle	N	N	Y	Y	N	Y
MINNESOTA						
Boschwitz	Y	Y	N	Y	Y	Y
Durenberger	N	Y	Y	Y	Y	Y
MISSISSIPPI						
Cochran	Y	Y	N	Y	Y	Y
Stennis	Y	Y	N	Y	Y	Y
MISSOURI						
Danforth	Y	Y	N	Y	Y	Y
Eagleton	N	N	Y	Y	N	Y
MONTANA						
Baucus	N	N	Y	Y	N	Y
Melcher	N	N	Y	Y	?	?
NEBRASKA						
Exon	Y	N	N	Y	Y	Y
Zorinsky	Y	N	Y	N	Y	Y
NEVADA						
Laxalt	Y	Y	N	Y	Y	Y
Cannon	N	N	Y	Y	N	Y

	200	201	202	203	204	205
NEW HAMPSHIRE						
Humphrey	Y	Y	N	Y	Y	Y
Rudman	Y	Y	N	N	Y	Y
NEW JERSEY						
Brady	Y	Y	N	Y	Y	Y
Bradley	N	N	Y	Y	N	Y
NEW MEXICO						
Domenici	Y	Y	N	Y	Y	Y
Schmitt	Y	Y	N	Y	Y	Y
NEW YORK						
D'Amato	Y	Y	N	Y	Y	Y
Moynihan	N	N	Y	Y	Y	Y
NORTH CAROLINA						
East	Y	Y	N	Y	Y	Y
Helms	Y	Y	N	Y	Y	Y
NORTH DAKOTA						
Andrews	Y	Y	N	Y	Y	Y
Burdick	N	N	Y	Y	N	Y
OHIO						
Glenn	N	N	Y	Y	Y	Y
Metzenbaum	?	?	Y	Y	N	Y
OKLAHOMA						
Nickles	Y	Y	N	Y	Y	Y
Boren	Y	N	Y	Y	Y	Y
OREGON						
Hatfield	Y	Y	N	Y	N	N
Packwood	Y	N	Y	Y	Y	Y
PENNSYLVANIA						
Heinz	N	N	Y	Y	Y	Y
Specter	N	Y	Y	Y	Y	Y
RHODE ISLAND						
Chafee	Y	Y	Y	Y	N	Y
Pell	N	N	Y	Y	N	Y
SOUTH CAROLINA						
Thurmond	Y	Y	N	Y	Y	Y
Hollings	N	N	Y	Y	Y	Y
SOUTH DAKOTA						
Abdnor	Y	Y	N	Y	Y	Y
Pressler	?	?	N	Y	Y	Y
TENNESSEE						
Baker	Y	Y	N	Y	Y	Y
Sasser	N	N	Y	Y	N	Y

	200	201	202	203	204	205
TEXAS						
Tower	Y	Y	N	N	Y	Y
Bentsen	N	N	N	Y	Y	Y
UTAH						
Garn	Y	Y	N	Y	Y	Y
Hatch	Y	Y	N	Y	Y	Y
VERMONT						
Stafford	?	?	Y	?	Y	Y
Leahy	Y	N	Y	Y	Y	Y
VIRGINIA						
Warner	Y	Y	Y	Y	Y	Y
Byrd*	Y	Y	N	Y	Y	Y
WASHINGTON						
Gorton	Y	Y	N	Y	Y	Y
Jackson	N	N	Y	Y	Y	Y
WEST VIRGINIA						
Byrd	N	N	Y	Y	N	Y
Randolph	N	N	Y	Y	N	Y
WISCONSIN						
Kasten	Y	N	N	Y	Y	Y
Proxmire	Y	N	Y	N	Y	Y
WYOMING						
Simpson	+	+	N	Y	Y	Y
Wallop	Y	Y	N	Y	Y	Y

ND - Northern Democrats SD - Southern Democrats (Southern states - Ala., Ark., Fla., Ga., Ky., La., Miss., N.C., Okla., S.C., Tenn., Texas, Va.) *Byrd elected as an independent.

200. HR 6685. Urgent Supplemental Appropriations, Fiscal 1982. Hatfield, R-Ore., motion to table (kill) the Kennedy, D-Mass., amendment to provide an additional $63 million for summer youth employment programs. Motion agreed to 55-37: R 42-6; D 13-31 (ND 6-23, SD 7-8), June 29, 1982.

201. HR 6685. Urgent Supplemental Appropriations, Fiscal 1982. Hatfield, R-Ore., motion to table (kill) the Riegle, D-Mich., amendment to provide $3 billion for subsidies of home mortgage interest rates. Motion agreed to 48-44: R 43-5; D 5-39 (ND 1-28, SD 4-11), June 29, 1982. A "yea" was a vote supporting the president's position.

202. S 2240. Federal Flexible and Compressed Work Schedules. Stevens, R-Alaska, motion to table (kill) the Armstrong, R-Colo., amendment to permit federal contractors the option of instituting flexible work schedules. Motion agreed to 49-46: R 12-38; D 37-8 (ND 27-3, SD 10-5), June 30, 1982. A "nay" was a vote supporting the president's position.

203. S 2240. Federal Flexible and Compressed Work Schedules. Passage of the bill to authorize federal agencies to use flexible and compressed employee work schedules. Passed 93-2: R 48-2; D 45-0 (ND 30-0, SD 15-0), June 30, 1982. A "yea" was a vote supporting the president's position.

204. S 2586. Military Construction Authorization, Fiscal 1983. Tower, R-Texas, motion to table (kill) the Pell, D-R.I., amendment to bar the use of funds in the bill for airfield improvement projects in Honduras. (The bill contained $21 million for such projects.) Motion agreed to 65-29: R 47-3; D 18-26 (ND 7-22, SD 11-4), June 30, 1982. A "nay" was a vote supporting the president's position.

205. S 2586. Military Construction Authorization, Fiscal 1983. Passage of the bill to authorize $6,435,506,000 for military construction projects of the Department of Defense. Passed 93-1: R 50-1; D 43-0 (ND 29-0, SD 14-0), June 30, 1982.

	206	207	208
ALABAMA			
Denton	?	Y	Y
Heflin	Y	Y	Y
ALASKA			
Murkowski	Y	Y	Y
Stevens	Y	Y	Y
ARIZONA			
Goldwater	Y	Y	N
DeConcini	Y	Y	Y
ARKANSAS			
Bumpers	Y	Y	Y
Pryor	Y	Y	Y
CALIFORNIA			
Hayakawa	+	+	+
Cranston	?	?	?
COLORADO			
Armstrong	Y	Y	Y
Hart	Y	Y	Y
CONNECTICUT			
Weicker	Y	Y	?
Dodd	Y	Y	Y
DELAWARE			
Roth	Y	Y	Y
Biden	Y	Y	Y
FLORIDA			
Hawkins	Y	Y	Y
Chiles	Y	Y	Y
GEORGIA			
Mattingly	+	+	+
Nunn	Y	Y	Y
HAWAII			
Inouye	Y	Y	Y
Matsunaga	Y	Y	Y
IDAHO			
McClure	N	Y	N
Symms	Y	Y	N
ILLINOIS			
Percy	Y	Y	Y
Dixon	Y	Y	Y
INDIANA			
Lugar	Y	Y	Y
Quayle	Y	Y	Y

	206	207	208
IOWA			
Grassley	Y	Y	Y
Jepsen	Y	Y	Y
KANSAS			
Dole	Y	Y	Y
Kassebaum	Y	?	Y
KENTUCKY			
Ford	Y	Y	Y
Huddleston	Y	Y	Y
LOUISIANA			
Johnston	Y	Y	Y
Long	Y	Y	Y
MAINE			
Cohen	N	Y	Y
Mitchell	N	Y	Y
MARYLAND			
Mathias	Y	Y	Y
Sarbanes	Y	Y	Y
MASSACHUSETTS			
Kennedy	Y	Y	Y
Tsongas	Y	Y	Y
MICHIGAN			
Levin	Y	Y	Y
Riegle	Y	Y	Y
MINNESOTA			
Boschwitz	Y	Y	Y
Durenberger	Y	Y	Y
MISSISSIPPI			
Cochran	Y	Y	Y
Stennis	Y	Y	Y
MISSOURI			
Danforth	Y	Y	Y
Eagleton	Y	Y	Y
MONTANA			
Baucus	N	Y	Y
Melcher	?	+	+
NEBRASKA			
Exon	Y	Y	Y
Zorinsky	Y	Y	Y
NEVADA			
Laxalt	Y	Y	Y
Cannon	Y	Y	Y

	206	207	208
NEW HAMPSHIRE			
Humphrey	Y	Y	Y
Rudman	Y	Y	Y
NEW JERSEY			
Brady	Y	Y	Y
Bradley	Y	Y	Y
NEW MEXICO			
Domenici	Y	Y	Y
Schmitt	Y	Y	Y
NEW YORK			
D'Amato	Y	Y	Y
Moynihan	Y	Y	Y
NORTH CAROLINA			
East	Y	Y	N
Helms	Y	Y	N
NORTH DAKOTA			
Andrews	N	Y	Y
Burdick	Y	Y	Y
OHIO			
Glenn	Y	Y	Y
Metzenbaum	Y	Y	Y
OKLAHOMA			
Nickles	Y	Y	N
Boren	Y	Y	Y
OREGON			
Hatfield	Y	Y	Y
Packwood	Y	Y	Y
PENNSYLVANIA			
Heinz	Y	Y	Y
Specter	Y	Y	Y
RHODE ISLAND			
Chafee	Y	Y	Y
Pell	Y	Y	Y
SOUTH CAROLINA			
Thurmond	Y	Y	Y
Hollings	Y	Y	Y
SOUTH DAKOTA			
Abdnor	N	Y	Y
Pressler	N	Y	Y
TENNESSEE			
Baker	Y	Y	Y
Sasser	Y	Y	Y

KEY

Y Voted for (yea).
\# Paired for.
+ Announced for.
N Voted against (nay).
X Paired against.
- Announced against.
P Voted "present".
C Voted "present" to avoid possible conflict of interest.
? Did not vote or otherwise make a position known.

Democrats   *Republicans*

	206	207	208
TEXAS			
Tower	Y	Y	Y
Bentsen	Y	Y	Y
UTAH			
Garn	Y	Y	Y
Hatch	Y	Y	Y
VERMONT			
Stafford	Y	Y	Y
Leahy	Y	Y	Y
VIRGINIA			
Warner	N	Y	Y
Byrd*	Y	Y	Y
WASHINGTON			
Gorton	Y	Y	Y
Jackson	Y	Y	Y
WEST VIRGINIA			
Byrd	N	Y	Y
Randolph	N	Y	Y
WISCONSIN			
Kasten	Y	Y	Y
Proxmire	Y	Y	Y
WYOMING			
Simpson	Y	Y	Y
Wallop	Y	Y	Y

ND - Northern Democrats   SD - Southern Democrats (Southern states - Ala., Ark., Fla., Ga., Ky., La., Miss., N.C., Okla., S.C., Tenn., Texas, Va.)   *Byrd elected as an independent.

206. HR 3663. Bus Regulatory Reform. Passage of the bill to reduce government regulation of the intercity bus industry. Passed 85-10: R 45-6; D 40-4 (ND 25-4, SD 15-0), June 30, 1982. A "yea" was a vote supporting the president's position.

207. S 2036. Job Training. Passage of the bill to establish a new job training program to replace the expiring Comprehensive Employment and Training Act (CETA). Passed 95-0: R 51-0; D 44-0 (ND 29-0, SD 15-0), July 1, 1982.

208. S Res 340. Community Service Employment for the Elderly. Adoption of the resolution expressing the sense of the Senate in opposition to termination of the community service employment for older Americans program. Adopted 89-6: R 45-6; D 44-0 (ND 29-0, SD 15-0), July 1, 1982.

	209	210	211	212	213
ALABAMA					
Denton	N	Y	Y	Y	Y
Heflin	Y	Y	Y	Y	Y
ALASKA					
Murkowski	?	?	?	?	?
Stevens	Y	Y	Y	Y	Y
ARIZONA					
Goldwater	N	Y	Y	Y	Y
DeConcini	Y	N	Y	N	Y
ARKANSAS					
Bumpers	Y	N	N	N	N
Pryor	Y	?	?	?	?
CALIFORNIA					
Hayakawa	Y	Y	Y	Y	Y
Cranston	Y	Y	N	Y	Y
COLORADO					
Armstrong	Y	Y	Y	Y	Y
Hart	Y	Y	Y	N	Y
CONNECTICUT					
Weicker	Y	N	Y	?	?
Dodd	Y	N	N	N	N
DELAWARE					
Roth	Y	N	Y	N	Y
Biden	Y	N	N	N	N
FLORIDA					
Hawkins	?	Y	Y	Y	Y
Chiles	Y	Y	N	Y	Y
GEORGIA					
Mattingly	Y	Y	Y	Y	Y
Nunn	Y	Y	Y	Y	Y
HAWAII					
Inouye	Y	Y	N	Y	Y
Matsunaga	Y	Y	N	Y	Y
IDAHO					
McClure	N	Y	Y	Y	Y
Symms	N	Y	Y	Y	Y
ILLINOIS					
Percy	Y	N	Y	N	Y
Dixon	Y	N	Y	N	Y
INDIANA					
Lugar	Y	Y	Y	N	Y
Quayle	Y	N	Y	N	Y

	209	210	211	212	213
IOWA					
Grassley	Y	Y	Y	Y	Y
Jepsen	Y	Y	Y	N	Y
KANSAS					
Dole	N	Y	Y	Y	Y
Kassebaum	Y	N	Y	Y	Y
KENTUCKY					
Ford	Y	Y	N	Y	Y
Huddleston	Y	Y	Y	Y	Y
LOUISIANA					
Johnston	Y	Y	Y	Y	Y
Long	Y	Y	Y	Y	+
MAINE					
Cohen	Y	N	Y	N	Y
Mitchell	Y	N	N	N	Y
MARYLAND					
Mathias	N	N	Y	N	N
Sarbanes	Y	Y	N	Y	Y
MASSACHUSETTS					
Kennedy	Y	Y	N	N	Y
Tsongas	Y	N	N	N	N
MICHIGAN					
Levin	Y	N	N	N	Y
Riegle	+	N	N	N	N
MINNESOTA					
Boschwitz	Y	Y	Y	Y	Y
Durenberger	Y	N	Y	N	Y
MISSISSIPPI					
Cochran	Y	Y	Y	Y	Y
Stennis	Y	Y	Y	Y	Y
MISSOURI					
Danforth	Y	N	Y	N	Y
Eagleton	Y	N	N	N	Y
MONTANA					
Baucus	Y	Y	N	N	Y
Melcher	Y	Y	N	Y	Y
NEBRASKA					
Exon	Y	Y	N	N	Y
Zorinsky	Y	Y	Y	N	Y
NEVADA					
Laxalt	?	Y	Y	Y	Y
Cannon	Y	N	Y	N	N

	209	210	211	212	213
NEW HAMPSHIRE					
Humphrey	N	N	Y	N	N
Rudman	Y	Y	Y	Y	Y
NEW JERSEY					
Brady	Y	Y	Y	Y	?
Bradley	Y	N	N	N	N
NEW MEXICO					
Domenici	Y	Y	Y	Y	Y
Schmitt	Y	Y	Y	Y	Y
NEW YORK					
D'Amato	Y	N	Y	N	N
Moynihan	Y	N	N	N	N
NORTH CAROLINA					
East	Y	Y	Y	Y	Y
Helms	Y	Y	Y	Y	Y
NORTH DAKOTA					
Andrews	?	Y	Y	Y	Y
Burdick	Y	Y	Y	Y	Y
OHIO					
Glenn	Y	?	?	?	?
Metzenbaum	Y	N	N	N	N
OKLAHOMA					
Nickles	N	N	Y	N	Y
Boren	Y	Y	N	Y	Y
OREGON					
Hatfield	?	N	Y	N	Y
Packwood	Y	N	Y	N	Y
PENNSYLVANIA					
Heinz	Y	N	Y	N	N
Specter	Y	N	Y	N	Y
RHODE ISLAND					
Chafee	Y	N	Y	N	Y
Pell	Y	N	Y	N	Y
SOUTH CAROLINA					
Thurmond	Y	Y	Y	Y	Y
Hollings	Y	Y	Y	Y	Y
SOUTH DAKOTA					
Abdnor	?	Y	Y	Y	Y
Pressler	N	Y	Y	Y	Y
TENNESSEE					
Baker	Y	Y	Y	Y	Y
Sasser	Y	Y	N	Y	Y

KEY

Y	Voted for (yea).
#	Paired for.
+	Announced for.
N	Voted against (nay).
X	Paired against.
-	Announced against.
P	Voted "present".
C	Voted "present" to avoid possible conflict of interest.
?	Did not vote or otherwise make a position known.

Democrats   *Republicans*

	209	210	211	212	213
TEXAS					
Tower	Y	Y	Y	Y	Y
Bentsen	Y	N	Y	Y	Y
UTAH					
Garn	Y	N	Y	N	N
Hatch	Y	N	Y	N	N
VERMONT					
Stafford	Y	?	?	Y	N
Leahy	Y	N	N	N	Y
VIRGINIA					
Warner	Y	Y	Y	Y	Y
Byrd*	Y	Y	Y	Y	Y
WASHINGTON					
Gorton	Y	Y	N	Y	Y
Jackson	Y	N	Y	N	N
WEST VIRGINIA					
Byrd	Y	Y	Y	Y	Y
Randolph	Y	N	Y	N	Y
WISCONSIN					
Kasten	Y	N	Y	N	Y
Proxmire	Y	N	N	N	N
WYOMING					
Simpson	Y	Y	Y	N	Y
Wallop	Y	Y	Y	N	Y

ND - Northern Democrats   SD - Southern Democrats (Southern states - Ala., Ark., Fla., Ga., Ky., La., Miss., N.C., Okla., S.C., Tenn., Texas, Va.)

Byrd elected as an independent.

209. HR 6198. Copyright Manufacturing Clause Protection Act. Passage, over President Reagan's July 8 veto, of the bill to extend for four years the "manufacturing clause" in U.S. copyright law, which requires that English language books and periodicals by U.S. authors be printed and bound in the United States or Canada to receive full copyright protection. Passed 84-9: R 39-9; D 45-0 (ND 30-0, SD 15-0), July 13, 1982. A two-thirds majority of those present and voting (62 in this case) of both houses is required to override a veto. A "nay" was a vote supporting the president's position.

210. HR 6590. Tobacco Program Revisions. Baker, R-Tenn., motion to table (kill) the Eagleton, D-Mo., amendment to give the secretary of agriculture discretion to set price support loan levels for tobacco grades in surplus supply, beginning in 1983. Loan levels could not drop below 1981 levels. Motion agreed to 56-40: R 32-20; D 24-20 (ND 12-18, SD 12-2), July 14, 1982.

211. Stearns Nomination. Confirmation of President Reagan's nomination of James G. Stearns of Nevada to be a director of the Securities Investor Protection Corp. Confirmed 70-26: R 52-0; D 18-26 (ND 9-21, SD 9-5), July 14, 1982. A "yea" was a vote supporting the president's position.

212. HR 6590. Tobacco Program Revisions. Baker, R-Tenn., motion to table (kill) the Eagleton, D-Mo., amendment to authorize tobacco price support loans through 1985 (thus ending permanent authorization for these loans). Motion agreed to 49-47: R 29-23; D 20-24 (ND 7-23, SD 13-1), July 14, 1982.

213. HR 6590. Tobacco Program Revisions. Passage of the bill to require tobacco producers to repay program losses to the federal government and to make certain other revisions in the program. Passed 77-17: R 44-7; D 33-10 (ND 21-9, SD 12-1), July 14, 1982.

	214	215	216	217	218		214	215	216	217	218		214	215	216	217	218
ALABAMA						**IOWA**						**NEW HAMPSHIRE**					
Denton	Y	N	Y	N	Y	*Grassley*	N	Y	Y	N	Y	*Humphrey*	N	N	Y	Y	Y
Heflin	Y	N	Y	Y	Y	*Jepsen*	Y	Y	Y	N	N	*Rudman*	Y	Y	Y	Y	Y
ALASKA						**KANSAS**						**NEW JERSEY**					
Murkowski	?	?	?	?	?	*Dole*	Y	N	Y	N	Y	*Brady*	Y	N	Y	N	Y
Stevens	Y	N	Y	N	Y	*Kassebaum*	Y	N	Y	N	Y	Bradley	Y	Y	Y	Y	N
ARIZONA						**KENTUCKY**						**NEW MEXICO**					
Goldwater	Y	N	Y	N	?	Ford	Y	N	Y	N	Y	*Domenici*	Y	N	Y	N	Y
DeConcini	Y	N	Y	Y	Y	Huddleston	Y	N	Y	Y	Y	*Schmitt*	Y	N	Y	N	Y
ARKANSAS						**LOUISIANA**						**NEW YORK**					
Bumpers	Y	Y	Y	Y	N	Johnston	Y	N	Y	N	Y	*D'Amato*	Y	N	Y	N	Y
Pryor	?	?	?	?	?	Long	Y	N	Y	Y	Y	Moynihan	Y	Y	Y	Y	N
CALIFORNIA						**MAINE**						**NORTH CAROLINA**					
Hayakawa	Y	N	Y	N	Y	*Cohen*	Y	Y	Y	Y	N	*East*	N	N	Y	N	Y
Cranston	Y	N	Y	N	Y	Mitchell	Y	Y	Y	Y	N	*Helms*	N	N	Y	N	Y
COLORADO						**MARYLAND**						**NORTH DAKOTA**					
Armstrong	N	N	Y	N	Y	*Mathias*	Y	N	Y	Y	Y	*Andrews*	Y	N	Y	N	Y
Hart	Y	Y	Y	N	N	Sarbanes	Y	Y·	Y	Y	N	Burdick	Y	N	Y	N	Y
CONNECTICUT						**MASSACHUSETTS**						**OHIO**					
Weicker	?	?	?	?	?	Kennedy	Y	Y	Y	Y	N	Glenn	Y	Y	Y	N	N
Dodd	Y	Y	Y	Y	N	Tsongas	Y	Y	Y	Y	N	Metzenbaum	Y	Y	Y	Y	N
DELAWARE						**MICHIGAN**						**OKLAHOMA**					
Roth	Y	Y	Y	Y	N	Levin	Y	Y	Y	Y	N	*Nickles*	Y	N	Y	N	N
Biden	Y	Y	Y	Y	N	Riegle	Y	Y	Y	Y	N	Boren	Y	N	Y	N	Y
FLORIDA						**MINNESOTA**						**OREGON**					
Hawkins	Y	N	Y	N	Y	*Boschwitz*	Y	Y	Y	N	Y	*Hatfield*	Y	Y	Y	N	N
Chiles	Y	Y	Y	Y	N	*Durenberger*	Y	Y	Y	N	N	*Packwood*	Y	N	Y	N	Y
GEORGIA						**MISSISSIPPI**						**PENNSYLVANIA**					
Mattingly	Y	N	Y	N	Y	*Cochran*	Y	N	Y	N	Y	*Heinz*	Y	Y	Y	Y	N
Nunn	Y	Y	Y	Y	N	Stennis	Y	N	Y	N	Y	*Specter*	Y	Y	Y	N	N
HAWAII						**MISSOURI**						**RHODE ISLAND**					
Inouye	Y	N	Y	Y	Y	*Danforth*	Y	Y	Y	Y	N	*Chafee*	Y	Y	Y	N	N
Matsunaga	Y	N	Y	Y	Y	Eagleton	Y	Y	Y	Y	N	Pell	Y	Y	Y	Y	N
IDAHO						**MONTANA**						**SOUTH CAROLINA**					
McClure	Y	N	Y	N	Y	Baucus	Y	N	Y	N	Y	*Thurmond*	Y	N	Y	N	Y
Symms	Y	N	Y	N	Y	Melcher	Y	N	Y	N	Y	Hollings	Y	N	Y	Y	N
ILLINOIS						**NEBRASKA**						**SOUTH DAKOTA**					
Percy	N	Y	Y	N	N	Exon	Y	N	Y	N	N	*Abdnor*	Y	N	Y	N	Y
Dixon	Y	Y	Y	Y	N	Zorinsky	Y	N	Y	N	N	*Pressler*	Y	N	Y	N	+
INDIANA						**NEVADA**						**TENNESSEE**					
Lugar	Y	Y	Y	Y	N	*Laxalt*	Y	N	Y	N	Y	*Baker*	Y	N	Y	N	Y
Quayle	Y	Y	Y	N	N	Cannon	Y	N	Y	Y	Y	Sasser	Y	N	Y	Y	Y

KEY

Y Voted for (yea).
\# Paired for.
\+ Announced for.
N Voted against (nay).
X Paired against.
\- Announced against.
P Voted "present".
C Voted "present" to avoid possible conflict of interest.
? Did not vote or otherwise make a position known.

Democrats   *Republicans*

	214	215	216	217	218
TEXAS					
Tower	Y	N	Y	N	Y
Bentsen	Y	N	Y	N	Y
UTAH					
Garn	Y	N	Y	N	Y
Hatch	Y	N	Y	N	Y
VERMONT					
Stafford	Y	Y	Y	N	Y
Leahy	Y	Y	Y	Y	N
VIRGINIA					
Warner	Y	N	Y	N	Y
Byrd*	Y	Y	Y	Y	N
WASHINGTON					
Gorton	Y	N	Y	N	Y
Jackson	Y	N	Y	Y	Y
WEST VIRGINIA					
Byrd	Y	N	Y	N	Y
Randolph	Y	N	Y	N	Y
WISCONSIN					
Kasten	Y	Y	Y	Y	N
Proxmire	Y	Y	Y	Y	N
WYOMING					
Simpson	Y	N	Y	N	Y
Wallop	Y	N	Y	N	Y

ND - Northern Democrats   SD - Southern Democrats (Southern states - Ala., Ark., Fla., Ga., Ky., La., Miss., N.C., Okla., S.C., Tenn., Texas, Va.)   *Byrd elected as an independent.*

214. HR 6685. Urgent Supplemental Appropriations, Fiscal 1982. Hatfield, R-Ore., motion that the Senate agree to the House amendment, embodying the conference agreement on the bill, to provide $5,448,452,000 in new budget authority and $5,849,120,000 in rescissions. Motion agreed to (thus cleared for the president) 91-6: R 46-6; D 45-0 (ND 31-0, SD 14-0), July 15, 1982. The president requested $4,543,371,000 in new budget authority and $7,750,269,165 in rescissions.

215. S 1867. Reclamation Law Amendments. Lugar, R-Ind., amendment to permit reclamation water service at existing rates to an individual farm of up to 320 acres, to permit water service at half a rate set by a new "full-cost" formula for additional farm acreage between 320 acres and 960 acres, and to permit water service to farm acreage exceeding 960 acres at the new "full-cost" rate. Rejected 39-58: R 17-35, D 22-23 (ND 18-13, SD 4-10), July 15, 1982.

216. Shultz Nomination. Confirmation of President Reagan's nomination of George P. Shultz of California as secretary of state. Confirmed 97-0: R 52-0; D 45-0 (ND 31-0, SD 14-0), July 15, 1982. A "yea" was a vote supporting the president's position.

217. S 1867. Reclamation Law Amendments. Bumpers, D-Ark., amendment to require competitive bidding for all leases of public land for oil and gas exploration. Rejected 39-58: R 9-43, D 30-15 (ND 21-10, SD 9-5), July 15, 1982. A "nay" was a vote supporting the president's position.

218. S 1867. Reclamation Law Amendments. Wallop, R-Wyo., motion to table (kill) the Proxmire, D-Wis., amendment to permit reclamation water service at existing rates to an individual farm of up to 960 acres, and to permit water service to farm acreage exceeding 960 acres at a new, "full-cost" rate. Motion agreed to 56-39: R 36-14; D 20-25 (ND 11-20, SD 9-5), July 15, 1982.

KEY

- Y Voted for (yea).
- # Paired for.
- + Announced for.
- N Voted against (nay).
- X Paired against.
- - Announced against.
- P Voted "present".
- C Voted "present" to avoid possible conflict of interest.
- ? Did not vote or otherwise make a position known.

Democrats   Republicans

	219	220	221	222	223	224	225	226
ALABAMA								
Denton	Y	N	Y	Y	N	Y	Y	N
Heflin	?	?	?	?	?	?	?	?
ALASKA								
Murkowski	?	?	?	?	?	?	?	?
Stevens	Y	N	Y	Y	N	Y	Y	N
ARIZONA								
Goldwater	Y	N	Y	Y	N	Y	Y	N
DeConcini	Y	N	Y	Y	N	Y	Y	N
ARKANSAS								
Bumpers	?	?	?	?	?	?	?	?
Pryor	Y	N	Y	Y	N	Y	Y	N
CALIFORNIA								
Hayakawa	?	-	?	?	+	?	?	?
Cranston	Y	N	Y	Y	Y	Y	N	N
COLORADO								
Armstrong	Y	N	Y	Y	N	Y	Y	N
Hart	Y	Y	Y	N	Y	N	Y	N
CONNECTICUT								
Weicker	?	?	?	?	?	?	?	?
Dodd	Y	Y	?	?	?	?	?	?
DELAWARE								
Roth	Y	N	Y	Y	Y	Y	Y	N
Biden	?	?	Y	N	Y	N	N	Y
FLORIDA								
Hawkins	Y	N	Y	Y	N	Y	Y	N
Chiles	Y	Y	Y	Y	Y	Y	N	N
GEORGIA								
Mattingly	Y	N	Y	Y	N	Y	Y	N
Nunn	Y	Y	Y	?	Y	Y	N	N
HAWAII								
Inouye	?	Y	Y	Y	Y	Y	N	N
Matsunaga	?	N	Y	Y	N	Y	Y	N
IDAHO								
McClure	Y	N	Y	Y	N	Y	Y	N
Symms	Y	N	Y	Y	N	Y	Y	N
ILLINOIS								
Percy	?	-	?	?	#	?	?	-
Dixon	Y	Y	Y	Y	Y	Y	N	N
INDIANA								
Lugar	Y	N	Y	Y	Y	Y	Y	N
Quayle	N	N	N	N	Y	N	Y	N

	219	220	221	222	223	224	225	226
IOWA								
Grassley	Y	N	Y	Y	Y	Y	Y	N
Jepsen	Y	N	Y	Y	Y	?	?	?
KANSAS								
Dole	Y	N	Y	Y	N	Y	Y	N
Kassebaum	Y	N	Y	Y	N	?	Y	N
KENTUCKY								
Ford	Y	N	Y	Y	N	Y	Y	N
Huddleston	Y	Y	Y	Y	N	Y	Y	N
LOUISIANA								
Johnston	N	N	Y	Y	N	N	Y	N
Long	Y	N	Y	Y	N	N	N	N
MAINE								
Cohen	Y	N	Y	Y	Y	Y	N	N
Mitchell	Y	Y	Y	Y	Y	Y	N	N
MARYLAND								
Mathias	Y	N	Y	Y	Y	Y	N	N
Sarbanes	?	?	?	?	?	Y	N	N
MASSACHUSETTS								
Kennedy	Y	Y	Y	Y	Y	?	N	Y
Tsongas	Y	Y	Y	Y	Y	Y	N	N
MICHIGAN								
Levin	Y	Y	Y	Y	Y	?	N	#
Riegle	Y	Y	?	?	?	?	?	+
MINNESOTA								
Boschwitz	?	?	?	?	?	?	?	?
Durenberger	Y	N	Y	Y	Y	Y	N	N
MISSISSIPPI								
Cochran	Y	N	Y	Y	N	Y	Y	N
Stennis	Y	N	Y	Y	N	?	Y	N
MISSOURI								
Danforth	Y	N	Y	Y	N	Y	Y	N
Eagleton	Y	#	Y	Y	Y	Y	N	N
MONTANA								
Baucus	Y	N	Y	Y	N	Y	Y	N
Melcher	Y	N	Y	Y	N	Y	Y	N
NEBRASKA								
Exon	Y	Y	Y	Y	#	Y	N	N
Zorinsky	Y	Y	Y	Y	N	Y	Y	N
NEVADA								
Laxalt	Y	N	Y	Y	N	Y	Y	N
Cannon	?	X	?	?	X	?	?	X

	219	220	221	222	223	224	225	226
NEW HAMPSHIRE								
Humphrey	Y	N	Y	Y	N	Y	Y	N
Rudman	Y	N	Y	Y	N	Y	Y	N
NEW JERSEY								
Brady	Y	N	Y	Y	N	Y	Y	N
Bradley	Y	Y	Y	Y	Y	Y	N	N
NEW MEXICO								
Domenici	Y	N	Y	Y	N	Y	Y	N
Schmitt	Y	N	Y	?	X	?	?	-
NEW YORK								
D'Amato	Y	N	Y	Y	Y	Y	Y	N
Moynihan	Y	Y	Y	Y	Y	Y	N	Y
NORTH CAROLINA								
East	Y	N	Y	Y	N	Y	Y	N
Helms	Y	N	Y	Y	N	Y	Y	N
NORTH DAKOTA								
Andrews	Y	N	Y	Y	N	Y	Y	N
Burdick	Y	Y	Y	Y	Y	Y	N	N
OHIO								
Glenn	Y	N	?	Y	N	Y	N	N
Metzenbaum	Y	Y	Y	Y	Y	Y	N	Y
OKLAHOMA								
Nickles	Y	N	Y	Y	N	Y	Y	N
Boren	Y	N	Y	N	N	Y	Y	N
OREGON								
Hatfield	Y	N	Y	Y	N	Y	Y	N
Packwood	Y	N	Y	Y	N	Y	Y	N
PENNSYLVANIA								
Heinz	?	?	?	?	?	?	?	?
Specter	Y	N	Y	Y	Y	Y	N	N
RHODE ISLAND								
Chafee	Y	N	Y	Y	Y	Y	N	N
Pell	Y	Y	Y	Y	Y	Y	N	Y
SOUTH CAROLINA								
Thurmond	+	N	Y	N	Y	N	Y	N
Hollings	Y	Y	Y	N	Y	Y	Y	?
SOUTH DAKOTA								
Abdnor	Y	N	Y	Y	N	Y	Y	?
Pressler	+	-	+	+	-	+	+	-
TENNESSEE								
Baker	Y	N	Y	?	N	Y	Y	N
Sasser	Y	N	Y	Y	N	Y	Y	N

	219	220	221	222	223	224	225	226
TEXAS								
Tower	Y	N	Y	Y	N	Y	Y	N
Bentsen	Y	N	Y	Y	N	Y	Y	N
UTAH								
Garn	N	N	N	N	N	N	Y	N
Hatch	Y	N	Y	Y	N	Y	Y	N
VERMONT								
Stafford	Y	N	Y	Y	Y	Y	Y	?
Leahy	Y	Y	Y	Y	Y	Y	N	Y
VIRGINIA								
Warner	Y	N	?	?	?	?	?	N
Byrd*	Y	N	N	Y	N	N	Y	N
WASHINGTON								
Gorton	Y	N	Y	Y	N	Y	Y	N
Jackson	Y	N	Y	Y	N	Y	Y	N
WEST VIRGINIA								
Byrd	Y	N	Y	Y	N	Y	Y	N
Randolph	Y	N	Y	Y	N	Y	Y	N
WISCONSIN								
Kasten	Y	N	Y	Y	N	Y	Y	N
Proxmire	N	Y	N	N	Y	N	N	Y
WYOMING								
Simpson	Y	N	Y	Y	N	Y	Y	N
Wallop	Y	N	Y	Y	N	Y	Y	N

ND - Northern Democrats   SD - Southern Democrats (Southern states - Ala., Ark., Fla., Ga., Ky., La., Miss., N.C., Okla., S.C., Tenn., Texas, Va.)   *Byrd elected as an independent.

219. S 1867. Reclamation Law Amendments. Baker, R-Tenn., motion to instruct the sergeant-at-arms to compel the attendance of absent senators. Motion agreed to 81-4: R 44-2; D 37-2 (ND 25-1, SD 12-1), July 16, 1982.

220. S 1867. Reclamation Law Amendments. Exon, D-Neb., amendment to restrict to a total of 960 acres of owned and/or leased land, the size of individual farms that may receive irrigation water from federal reclamation projects. Rejected 22-65: R 0-47; D 22-18 (ND 18-9, SD 4-9), July 16, 1982.

221. S 1867. Reclamation Law Amendments. Baker, R-Tenn., motion to instruct the sergeant-at-arms to compel the attendance of absent senators. Motion agreed to 82-4: R 44-2; D 38-2 (ND 26-1, SD 12-1), July 16, 1982.

222. S 1867. Reclamation Law Amendments. McClure, R-Idaho, motion to instruct the sergeant-at-arms to compel the attendance of absent senators. Motion agreed to 78-5: R 42-2; D 36-3 (ND 25-2, SD 11-1), July 16, 1982.

223. S 1867. Reclamation Law Amendments. Moynihan, D-N.Y., amendment to require that farms larger than 960 acres pay the "full cost," according to a formula, for irrigation of the additional acreage with water from reclamation projects, and to require certain studies, with recommendations for administrative or legislative actions to apply cost-recovery provisions to agricultural irrigation and conservation services of Army Corps of Engineers water projects. Rejected 29-55: R 12-33; D 17-22 (ND 16-10, SD 1-12), July 16, 1982.

224. S 1867. Reclamation Law Amendments. Baker, R-Tenn., motion to instruct the sergeant-at-arms to compel the attendance of absent senators. Motion agreed to 74-7: R 41-2; D 33-5 (ND 24-2, SD 9-3), July 16, 1982.

225. S 1867. Reclamation Law Amendments. Baker, R-Tenn., motion to table (kill) the Wallop, R-Wyo., motion to reconsider the vote by which the Moynihan, D-N.Y., amendment was rejected *(see vote 223, above)*. Motion agreed to 61-34: R 40-4; D 21-20 (ND 10-18, SD 11-2), July 16, 1982.

226. S 1867. Reclamation Law Amendments. Metzenbaum, D-Ohio, amendment to delete from the bill a section that repealed the reclamation law residency requirement, in effect leaving intact a requirement that farmers wishing to receive irrigation water from reclamation projects must live on or within 50 miles of the irrigated farm. Rejected 7-75: R 0-43; D 7-32 (ND 7-20, SD 0-12), July 16, 1982.

	227	228	229	230	231	232	233	234
ALABAMA								
Denton	Y	Y	Y	Y	N	Y	N	N
Heflin	?	?	Y	N	Y	Y	Y	Y
ALASKA								
Murkowski	?	?	Y	Y	N	Y	N	N
Stevens	Y	Y	Y	Y	N	Y	N	N
ARIZONA								
Goldwater	N	Y	N	N	N	Y	Y	N
DeConcini	Y	Y	Y	N	Y	Y	Y	Y
ARKANSAS								
Bumpers	?	?	Y	N	Y	Y	Y	Y
Pryor	Y	Y	Y	N	Y	Y	N	Y
CALIFORNIA								
Hayakawa	?	+	Y	Y	N	Y	N	N
Cranston	Y	Y	Y	N	Y	Y	Y	Y
COLORADO								
Armstrong	Y	Y	Y	N	Y	N	N	N
Hart	Y	Y	Y	N	Y	Y	Y	Y
CONNECTICUT								
Weicker	?	?	N	Y	N	Y	N	Y
Dodd	?	?	Y	N	Y	N	Y	N
DELAWARE								
Roth	Y	N	Y	Y	N	N	N	N
Biden	Y	N	Y	N	Y	Y	N	N
FLORIDA								
Hawkins	+	+	Y	Y	N	Y	N	N
Chiles	?	?	?	?	?	Y	Y	Y
GEORGIA								
Mattingly	Y	Y	Y	Y	N	Y	N	Y
Nunn	Y	Y	Y	N	Y	Y	Y	Y
HAWAII								
Inouye	Y	Y	Y	N	Y	Y	N	+
Matsunaga	Y	Y	Y	N	Y	Y	Y	Y
IDAHO								
McClure	Y	Y	Y	N	Y	N	Y	N
Symms	Y	Y	Y	Y	N	Y	N	N
ILLINOIS								
Percy	+	+	Y	N	Y	N	N	N
Dixon	Y	N	Y	N	Y	Y	Y	Y
INDIANA								
Lugar	Y	Y	Y	N	Y	N	N	N
Quayle	Y	Y	N	Y	N	Y	N	N

	227	228	229	230	231	232	233	234
IOWA								
Grassley	Y	Y	Y	Y	N	Y	N	N
Jepsen	?	?	Y	Y	N	Y	Y	N
KANSAS								
Dole	Y	Y	Y	Y	N	Y	N	N
Kassebaum	?	?	Y	Y	N	Y	N	N
KENTUCKY								
Ford	Y	Y	Y	N	Y	Y	Y	Y
Huddleston	Y	Y	Y	N	Y	N	Y	Y
LOUISIANA								
Johnston	Y	Y	N	N	Y	Y	Y	Y
Long	Y	Y	Y	N	Y	Y	N	Y
MAINE								
Cohen	?	X	Y	Y	N	Y	Y	N
Mitchell	?	?	Y	Y	Y	Y	Y	Y
MARYLAND								
Mathias	Y	X	Y	Y	N	Y	N	N
Sarbanes	Y	N	Y	N	Y	Y	Y	Y
MASSACHUSETTS								
Kennedy	+	+	?	N	Y	N	Y	N
Tsongas	Y	N	Y	N	Y	N	Y	N
MICHIGAN								
Levin	Y	N	Y	N	Y	Y	Y	Y
Riegle	+	X	Y	N	Y	Y	Y	Y
MINNESOTA								
Boschwitz	?	?	Y	Y	N	Y	N	N
Durenberger	+	+	Y	Y	N	Y	N	N
MISSISSIPPI								
Cochran	?	?	Y	Y	N	Y	N	N
Stennis	?	?	Y	N	Y	N	Y	Y
MISSOURI								
Danforth	Y	Y	Y	Y	N	Y	N	N
Eagleton	Y	Y	Y	N	Y	Y	Y	Y
MONTANA								
Baucus	Y	Y	Y	N	Y	Y	Y	Y
Melcher	+	#	?	?	?	?	?	Y
NEBRASKA								
Exon	?	?	Y	N	Y	Y	Y	Y
Zorinsky	Y	N	Y	N	Y	Y	Y	Y
NEVADA								
Laxalt	N	Y	Y	Y	N	Y	Y	N
Cannon	+	#	Y	N	Y	N	Y	Y

	227	228	229	230	231	232	233	234
NEW HAMPSHIRE								
Humphrey	Y	Y	Y	Y	N	Y	N	N
Rudman	Y	Y	Y	Y	N	Y	N	N
NEW JERSEY								
Brady	Y	#	Y	Y	N	Y	N	N
Bradley	Y	N	Y	N	Y	Y	N	N
NEW MEXICO								
Domenici	Y	Y	Y	Y	N	Y	N	N
Schmitt	+	#	Y	Y	N	Y	N	
NEW YORK								
D'Amato	+	+	?	Y	N	Y	N	N
Moynihan	N	N	Y	N	Y	Y	Y	Y
NORTH CAROLINA								
East	Y	Y	Y	Y	N	Y	N	Y
Helms	Y	Y	Y	Y	N	Y	N	Y
NORTH DAKOTA								
Andrews	?	?	Y	Y	N	Y	N	N
Burdick	?	?	Y	N	Y	Y	Y	Y
OHIO								
Glenn	Y	Y	Y	N	Y	Y	Y	Y
Metzenbaum	Y	N	Y	N	Y	Y	Y	Y
OKLAHOMA								
Nickles	?	+	Y	Y	N	Y	N	N
Boren	?	?	Y	N	Y	N	Y	N
OREGON								
Hatfield	Y	Y	Y	N	Y	N	N	Y
Packwood	Y	Y	Y	Y	N	Y	N	N
PENNSYLVANIA								
Heinz	?	?	Y	Y	N	Y	N	N
Specter	Y	N	Y	Y	N	Y	N	N
RHODE ISLAND								
Chafee	Y	Y	Y	Y	N	Y	N	N
Pell	Y	Y	Y	N	Y	Y	Y	Y
SOUTH CAROLINA								
Thurmond	Y	Y	Y	Y	N	Y	N	N
Hollings	?	?	Y	N	Y	N	Y	Y
SOUTH DAKOTA								
Abdnor	?	?	Y	Y	N	Y	N	N
Pressler	+	+	Y	Y	N	Y	N	N
TENNESSEE								
Baker	Y	Y	Y	Y	N	Y	N	N
Sasser	+	+	Y	N	Y	Y	Y	Y

	227	228	229	230	231	232	233	234
TEXAS								
Tower	Y	Y	Y	Y	N	Y	N	N
Bentsen	Y	Y	Y	N	Y	Y	Y	Y
UTAH								
Garn	N	Y	Y	Y	N	Y	N	Y
Hatch	N	Y	Y	Y	N	Y	N	N
VERMONT								
Stafford	?	?	Y	Y	N	Y	N	N
Leahy	Y	X	Y	N	Y	Y	Y	Y
VIRGINIA								
Warner	Y	Y	Y	Y	N	Y	N	N
Byrd*	?	?	Y	N	Y	N	N	N
WASHINGTON								
Gorton	Y	Y	Y	Y	N	Y	N	N
Jackson	Y	Y	Y	N	Y	Y	Y	Y
WEST VIRGINIA								
Byrd	Y	Y	Y	N	Y	Y	Y	Y
Randolph	Y	Y	?	-	+	+	+	Y
WISCONSIN								
Kasten	Y	N	Y	N	Y	N	N	N
Proxmire	Y	N	N	N	Y	N	N	Y
WYOMING								
Simpson	Y	Y	Y	N	Y	N	N	N
Wallop	Y	Y	Y	N	Y	N	N	N

ND - Northern Democrats   SD - Southern Democrats (Southern states - Ala., Ark., Fla., Ga., Ky., La., Miss., N.C., Okla., S.C., Tenn., Texas, Va.)   *Byrd elected as an independent.*

227. S 1867. Reclamation Law Amendments. Wallop, R-Wyo.-Metzenbaum, D-Ohio, amendment to change the bill's formula for calculating certain costs for irrigation water from reclamation projects, to restrict to 1,280 acres the size of an individual farm that may receive irrigation water at existing rates, and to make certain other changes. Adopted 60-5: R 31-4; D 29-1 (ND 22-1, SD 7-0), July 16, 1982.

228. HR 5539. Reclamation Law Amen~ ~ents. Passage of the bill to increase acreage limitations for farms irrigated by water from reclamation projects, to raise the price for some of that water, and to make other changes in federal reclamation laws. Passed 49-13: R 30-3; D 19-10 (ND 12-10, SD 7-0), July 16, 1982.

229. HR 4961. Budget Reconciliation Tax Increases/Spending Cuts. Baker, R-Tenn., motion to instruct the sergeant-at-arms to require the attendance of absent senators. Motion agreed to 90-5: R 50-3; D 40-2 (ND 27-1, SD 13-1), July 20, 1982.

230. HR 4961. Budget Reconciliation Tax Increases/Spending Cuts. Judgment of the Senate affirming the chair's ruling that the Packwood, R-Ore., amendment to authorize $20 billion in spending from the Airport and Airway Trust Fund over five years was germane. Ruling of the chair upheld 53-44: R 53-1; D 0-43 (ND 0-29, SD 0-14), July 20, 1982. (The Packwood amendment subsequently was adopted (see vote 232, below).)

231. HR 4961. Budget Reconciliation Tax Increases/Spending Cuts. Byrd, D-W.Va., motion to recommit the bill to the Finance Committee with instructions to report the

bill back to the Senate with title IV deleted. Title IV was substantially identical to the Packwood, R-Ore., amendment, which was proposed as a substitute (see vote 232, below). Motion rejected 43-54: R 0-54; D 43-0 (ND 29-0, SD 14-0), July 20, 1982.

232. HR 4961. Budget Reconciliation Tax Increases/Spending Cuts. Packwood, R-Ore., amendment to authorize $20 billion in spending from the Airport and Airway Trust Fund over five years. The amendment was proposed as a substitute for substantially identical provisions in the bill. Adopted 93-5: R 54-0; D 39-5 (ND 27-2, SD 12-3), July 20, 1982.

233. HR 4961. Budget Reconciliation Tax Increases/Spending Cuts. Cannon, D-Nev., amendment to require that 12- and 14-cent-a-gallon aviation fuel fees for general aviation included in the bill be reduced to 8.5 cents a gallon during any fiscal year in which the Airport and Airway Trust Fund begins the year with an unobligated surplus of $500 million or more. Rejected 44-54: R 12-42; D 32-12 (ND 21-8, SD 11-4), July 20, 1982.

234. HR 4961. Budget Reconciliation Tax Increases/Spending Cuts. Bradley, D-N.J., amendment to defer until the federal budget is balanced the tax cuts scheduled under current law in 1983 for high-income persons; eliminate from the bill increases in telephone, tobacco and unemployment insurance taxes; eliminate the bill's restrictions on casualty deductions and soften its restrictions on medical deductions; and restore some cuts the bill would make in Medicare spending by raising costs for beneficiaries. Rejected 45-54: R 2-52; D 43-2 (ND 29-1, SD 14-1), July 21, 1982.

KEY

- Y — Voted for (yea).
- # — Paired for.
- + — Announced for.
- N — Voted against (nay).
- X — Paired against.
- - — Announced against.
- P — Voted "present".
- C — Voted "present" to avoid possible conflict of interest.
- ? — Did not vote or otherwise make a position known.

Democrats   *Republicans*

	235	236	237	238	239	240	241	242
ALABAMA								
Denton	N	Y	N	N	N	Y	N	-
Heflin	Y	Y	Y	Y	N	Y	Y	Y
ALASKA								
Murkowski	N	Y	N	N	Y	N	N	N
Stevens	N	Y	N	N	N	Y	N	N
ARIZONA								
Goldwater	N	Y	N	N	Y	N	N	N
DeConcini	Y	Y	Y	X	Y	Y	Y	Y
ARKANSAS								
Bumpers	Y	Y	Y	N	Y	N	Y	N
Pryor	Y	Y	Y	Y	Y	Y	N	N
CALIFORNIA								
Hayakawa	N	Y	N	N	Y	N	Y	N
Cranston	Y	Y	Y	Y	Y	Y	N	N
COLORADO								
Armstrong	N	Y	N	N	N	N	N	N
Hart	Y	Y	Y	N	Y	N	N	N
CONNECTICUT								
Weicker	Y	Y	Y	N	Y	N	N	N
Dodd	Y	Y	Y	N	Y	N	Y	N
DELAWARE								
Roth	N	Y	N	N	Y	N	N	N
Biden	Y	Y	Y	N	Y	N	Y	Y
FLORIDA								
Hawkins	Y	Y	Y	N	N	N	Y	Y
Chiles	Y	Y	Y	N	Y	Y	N	N
GEORGIA								
Mattingly	N	Y	N	Y	Y	Y	N	N
Nunn	N	Y	Y	Y	N	Y	N	N
HAWAII								
Inouye	+	+	+	?	?	?	?	?
Matsunaga	Y	Y	Y	Y	Y	Y	N	N
IDAHO								
McClure	N	Y	N	N	N	N	N	N
Symms	N	Y	N	N	Y	N	N	N
ILLINOIS								
Percy	N	Y	N	N	Y	N	Y	N
Dixon	Y	Y	Y	N	Y	Y	N	N
INDIANA								
Lugar	N	Y	N	N	Y	Y	N	N
Quayle	N	Y	N	N	Y	Y	N	N
IOWA								
Grassley	N	Y	N	N	Y	Y	N	N
Jepsen	N	Y	N	N	Y	N	N	Y
KANSAS								
Dole	N	Y	N	N	Y	Y	N	N
Kassebaum	N	Y	N	N	Y	Y	N	N
KENTUCKY								
Ford	Y	Y	Y	Y	Y	Y	Y	Y
Huddleston	Y	Y	Y	Y	Y	Y	Y	N
LOUISIANA								
Johnston	Y	Y	Y	N	Y	N	N	N
Long	N	Y	Y	Y	Y	Y	N	N
MAINE								
Cohen	Y	Y	Y	N	N	Y	N	N
Mitchell	Y	Y	Y	Y	Y	Y	Y	N
MARYLAND								
Mathias	Y	Y	N	N	Y	N	N	N
Sarbanes	Y	Y	Y	N	Y	Y	Y	N
MASSACHUSETTS								
Kennedy	Y	Y	Y	N	Y	-	+	?
Tsongas	Y	Y	Y	N	Y	N	Y	N
MICHIGAN								
Levin	Y	Y	Y	N	Y	N	N	N
Riegle	Y	Y	Y	N	Y	Y	Y	Y
MINNESOTA								
Boschwitz	N	Y	N	N	Y	N	Y	N
Durenberger	N	Y	N	Y	N	Y	N	Y
MISSISSIPPI								
Cochran	N	Y	N	N	Y	Y	N	N
Stennis	N	Y	Y	Y	Y	Y	N	N
MISSOURI								
Danforth	N	Y	N	N	Y	N	N	N
Eagleton	Y	Y	Y	N	Y	Y	N	N
MONTANA								
Baucus	Y	Y	Y	N	Y	Y	N	N
Melcher	Y	Y	Y	N	Y	Y	N	?
NEBRASKA								
Exon	Y	Y	Y	Y	Y	Y	N	N
Zorinsky	Y	Y	Y	Y	Y	Y	N	N
NEVADA								
Laxalt	N	Y	N	N	Y	Y	N	N
Cannon	Y	Y	Y	N	Y	N	Y	N
NEW HAMPSHIRE								
Humphrey	N	Y	N	N	Y	Y	N	N
Rudman	N	Y	N	N	N	Y	N	N
NEW JERSEY								
Brady	N	Y	N	N	Y	N	N	Y
Bradley	Y	Y	Y	Y	Y	Y	Y	N
NEW MEXICO								
Domenici	N	Y	N	N	Y	N	N	N
Schmitt	N	Y	Y	N	Y	N	N	Y
NEW YORK								
D'Amato	N	Y	N	N	Y	N	N	Y
Moynihan	Y	Y	Y	N	Y	N	Y	N
NORTH CAROLINA								
East	N	Y	N	Y	N	Y	N	N
Helms	N	N	Y	N	Y	N	Y	Y
NORTH DAKOTA								
Andrews	N	Y	N	N	Y	N	N	N
Burdick	Y	Y	Y	N	Y	N	N	N
OHIO								
Glenn	Y	Y	Y	N	Y	N	N	N
Metzenbaum	Y	Y	N	+	?	?	?	?
OKLAHOMA								
Nickles	N	Y	N	N	N	Y	N	N
Boren	N	Y	Y	N	Y	N	N	N
OREGON								
Hatfield	N	Y	N	N	Y	N	N	N
Packwood	Y	Y	N	N	Y	N	?	N
PENNSYLVANIA								
Heinz	N	Y	N	N	Y	N	N	N
Specter	N	Y	N	N	N	N	N	N
RHODE ISLAND								
Chafee	Y	Y	N	N	Y	N	N	N
Pell	Y	Y	Y	N	Y	N	Y	N
SOUTH CAROLINA								
Thurmond	N	Y	N	Y	N	Y	N	Y
Hollings	Y	Y	Y	#	?	Y	Y	N
SOUTH DAKOTA								
Abdnor	N	Y	N	N	Y	N	N	N
Pressler	Y	Y	N	N	Y	N	Y	N
TENNESSEE								
Baker	N	Y	N	N	Y	Y	N	N
Sasser	Y	Y	Y	Y	Y	Y	Y	Y
TEXAS								
Tower	N	Y	Y	N	N	Y	N	N
Bentsen	N	Y	Y	N	Y	N	N	Y
UTAH								
Garn	N	Y	N	N	Y	N	N	N
Hatch	N	Y	N	N	Y	N	N	N
VERMONT								
Stafford	Y	Y	N	N	Y	Y	N	N
Leahy	Y	Y	Y	Y	Y	Y	Y	N
VIRGINIA								
Warner	N	Y	Y	N	Y	N	N	N
Byrd*	N	Y	Y	Y	Y	N	N	N
WASHINGTON								
Gorton	N	Y	N	N	Y	N	N	N
Jackson	Y	Y	Y	N	Y	N	Y	N
WEST VIRGINIA								
Byrd	Y	Y	Y	Y	Y	N	N	Y
Randolph	Y	Y	Y	Y	Y	Y	N	Y
WISCONSIN								
Kasten	N	Y	N	N	N	N	N	N
Proxmire	N	Y	N	N	Y	N	Y	N
WYOMING								
Simpson	N	Y	N	N	Y	N	N	N
Wallop	N	Y	N	N	N	Y	N	N

ND - Northern Democrats   SD - Southern Democrats (Southern states - Ala., Ark., Fla., Ga., Ky., La., Miss., N.C., Okla., S.C., Tenn., Texas, Va.)

Byrd elected as an independent.

235. HR 4961. Budget Reconciliation Tax Increases/Spending Cuts. Baucus, D-Mont., amendment to strike sections of the bill dealing with Medicare and providing for home health copayments, indexing of part B deductibles, and maintaining the part B premiums as a constant percentage of costs. Rejected 46-53: R 8-46; D 38-7 (ND 29-1, SD 9-6), July 21, 1982.

236. HR 4961. Budget Reconciliation Tax Increases/Spending Cuts. Durenberger, R-Minn., amendment to delete increases in Medicare part B deductibles in 1983 and provide gradual increases in 1984 and 1985; to provide for some copayment for home health care starting with the 20th visit; and to repeal after three years the provision holding the part B premium at a constant percentage of costs. Adopted 99-0: R 54-0; D 45-0 (ND 30-0, SD 15-0), July 21, 1982.

237. HR 4961. Budget Reconciliation Tax Increases/Spending Cuts. Bentsen, D-Texas, amendment to strike the section of the bill increasing the federal unemployment tax from .7 percent of the first $6,000 of wages to .8 percent of the first $7,000 in wages. Rejected 48-51: R 5-49; D 43-2 (ND 28-2, SD 15-0), July 21, 1982.

238. HR 4961. Budget Reconciliation Tax Increases/Spending Cuts. Ford, D-Ky., amendment to delete a provision to double the federal excise tax on cigarettes from 8 cents to 16 cents a package. Rejected 24-72: R 6-48; D 18-24 (ND 9-19, SD 9-5), July 22, 1982.

239. HR 4961. Budget Reconciliation Tax Increases/Spending Cuts. Judgment of the Senate affirming the chair's ruling that the Thurmond, R-S.C., amendment to strike the provision doubling the excise tax on cigarettes and substituting it with a 50 percent increase in the excise tax on cigarettes to 12 cents per package and a $3.30 increase in the current $10.50 per gallon excise tax on distilled liquors was non-germane. Ruling of the chair upheld 79-18: R 38-16; D 41-2 (ND 29-0, SD 12-2), July 22, 1982.

240. HR 4961. Budget Reconciliation Tax Increases/Spending Cuts. Helms, R-N.C., amendment to repeal the provisions doubling the excise tax on cigarettes on Sept. 30, 1985. Adopted 60-37: R 33-21; D 27-16 (ND 15-13, SD 12-3), July 22, 1982.

241. HR 4961. Budget Reconciliation Tax Increases/Spending Cuts. Eagleton, D-Mo., amendment to strike the provision calling for an increase in the telephone excise tax of $2.8 billion for fiscal years 1983-85 and to further cut back tax breaks for intangible oil and gas drilling costs. Rejected 24-72: R 3-50; D 21-22 (ND 16-12, SD 5-10), July 22, 1982.

242. HR 4961. Budget Reconciliation Tax Increases/Spending Cuts. Mattingly, R-Ga., amendment to delete two provisions which would repeal new accelerated depreciation benefits for businesses for 1985-86 and to limit the amount of tax liability that can be offset by the investment tax credit. Rejected 23-72: R 14-39; D 9-33 (ND 5-22, SD 4-11), July 22, 1982.

State / Senator	243	244	245	246	247	248	249	250
ALABAMA								
Denton	+	N	N	Y	N	N	N	Y
Heflin	Y	N	N	Y	Y	Y	N	Y
ALASKA								
Murkowski	Y	N	N	Y	N	N	Y	Y
Stevens	Y	N	N	Y	N	N	Y	Y
ARIZONA								
Goldwater	Y	?	?	?	+	?	?	?
DeConcini	Y	N	Y	Y	Y	Y	N	Y
ARKANSAS								
Bumpers	Y	Y	N	Y	Y	N	N	Y
Pryor	Y	Y	Y	Y	Y	Y	N	Y
CALIFORNIA								
Hayakawa	N	Y	N	Y	N	N	N	Y
Cranston	N	Y	Y	Y	N	Y	N	Y
COLORADO								
Armstrong	Y	N	N	Y	N	N	N	Y
Hart	N	Y	Y	Y	Y	Y	N	Y
CONNECTICUT								
Weicker	Y	N	?	?	+	?	?	?
Dodd	N	Y	Y	Y	N	Y	N	?
DELAWARE								
Roth	Y	N	N	Y	N	N	Y	Y
Biden	N	Y	Y	Y	Y	Y	Y	N
FLORIDA								
Hawkins	Y	?	N	Y	Y	N	Y	Y
Chiles	Y	N	Y	Y	Y	Y	N	Y
GEORGIA								
Mattingly	Y	N	N	Y	N	Y	N	Y
Nunn	Y	Y	Y	Y	Y	Y	N	Y
HAWAII								
Inouye	?	?	+	+	+	?	?	+
Matsunaga	N	Y	Y	Y	Y	Y	N	Y
IDAHO								
McClure	Y	N	N	Y	N	N	N	Y
Symms	Y	N	N	Y	N	N	N	Y
ILLINOIS								
Percy	Y	N	N	Y	N	Y	N	Y
Dixon	Y	N	Y	Y	Y	Y	N	Y
INDIANA								
Lugar	N	Y	N	Y	N	N	N	Y
Quayle	Y	N	N	Y	N	N	N	Y
IOWA								
Grassley	Y	N	N	Y	N	N	N	N
Jepsen	Y	N	N	Y	Y	N	Y	N
KANSAS								
Dole	Y	N	N	Y	N	N	N	N
Kassebaum	N	Y	N	Y	N	N	N	Y
KENTUCKY								
Ford	Y	N	Y	Y	Y	Y	N	Y
Huddleston	N	Y	Y	Y	Y	Y	N	Y
LOUISIANA								
Johnston	Y	N	Y	Y	Y	N	N	Y
Long	Y	N	N	Y	N	N	N	Y
MAINE								
Cohen	Y	N	Y	Y	N	Y	N	Y
Mitchell	N	Y	Y	Y	Y	Y	Y	N
MARYLAND								
Mathias	N	Y	N	Y	N	N	N	Y
Sarbanes	N	Y	Y	Y	Y	Y	N	Y
MASSACHUSETTS								
Kennedy	-	+	Y	Y	N	Y	N	N
Tsongas	N	Y	Y	Y	Y	Y	N	N
MICHIGAN								
Levin	N	Y	Y	Y	Y	Y	N	N
Riegle	N	Y	Y	Y	Y	Y	N	N
MINNESOTA								
Boschwitz	N	Y	N	Y	N	N	N	Y
Durenberger	Y	N	N	Y	N	N	N	N
MISSISSIPPI								
Cochran	Y	N	N	Y	N	N	N	Y
Stennis	N	Y	Y	Y	Y	N	N	Y
MISSOURI								
Danforth	Y	N	N	Y	N	N	N	Y
Eagleton	N	Y	?	Y	Y	Y	N	N
MONTANA								
Baucus	N	Y	Y	Y	Y	Y	N	Y
Melcher	Y	N	Y	Y	Y	Y	N	Y
NEBRASKA								
Exon	N	Y	Y	Y	Y	Y	N	Y
Zorinsky	Y	N	N	Y	Y	Y	N	Y
NEVADA								
Laxalt	Y	N	N	Y	N	N	N	Y
Cannon	Y	N	Y	Y	Y	Y	N	Y
NEW HAMPSHIRE								
Humphrey	Y	N	N	Y	N	N	N	Y
Rudman	Y	N	N	Y	N	N	N	Y
NEW JERSEY								
Brady	Y	N	N	Y	N	N	Y	Y
Bradley	Y	N	Y	Y	N	Y	Y	N
NEW MEXICO								
Domenici	Y	N	N	Y	N	N	N	Y
Schmitt	Y	N	N	Y	Y	N	Y	N
NEW YORK								
D'Amato	Y	N	N	Y	N	N	N	Y
Moynihan	Y	N	Y	Y	Y	Y	N	Y
NORTH CAROLINA								
East	Y	N	N	Y	N	N	N	Y
Helms	Y	N	N	Y	N	N	N	Y
NORTH DAKOTA								
Andrews	Y	N	N	Y	N	N	N	Y
Burdick	N	Y	Y	Y	Y	Y	N	Y
OHIO								
Glenn	N	Y	Y	Y	Y	Y	N	Y
Metzenbaum	?	Y	Y	Y	N	Y	N	N
OKLAHOMA								
Nickles	Y	N	N	Y	N	N	N	Y
Boren	Y	N	Y	Y	Y	Y	N	Y
OREGON								
Hatfield	Y	N	N	Y	N	N	N	Y
Packwood	Y	N	N	Y	N	Y	Y	Y
PENNSYLVANIA								
Heinz	N	Y	N	Y	N	Y	N	Y
Specter	Y	N	Y	N	Y	N	Y	N
RHODE ISLAND								
Chafee	N	Y	N	Y	Y	Y	Y	Y
Pell	N	Y	Y	Y	N	Y	N	N
SOUTH CAROLINA								
Thurmond	Y	N	N	Y	N	N	N	Y
Hollings	N	Y	Y	Y	Y	Y	N	Y
SOUTH DAKOTA								
Abdnor	Y	N	N	Y	N	N	N	Y
Pressler	Y	N	N	Y	Y	N	N	N
TENNESSEE								
Baker	Y	N	N	Y	N	N	N	Y
Sasser	N	Y	Y	Y	Y	Y	N	Y
TEXAS								
Tower	Y	N	N	Y	N	N	N	Y
Bentsen	Y	N	Y	Y	Y	N	N	Y
UTAH								
Garn	Y	N	N	Y	N	N	N	Y
Hatch	Y	N	N	Y	N	Y	N	Y
VERMONT								
Stafford	N	N	N	Y	N	N	N	Y
Leahy	N	Y	Y	Y	Y	Y	N	Y
VIRGINIA								
Warner	Y	N	N	Y	N	N	N	Y
Byrd*	Y	N	N	Y	N	N	N	Y
WASHINGTON								
Gorton	Y	N	N	Y	N	N	N	Y
Jackson	N	Y	Y	Y	Y	Y	N	Y
WEST VIRGINIA								
Byrd	N	Y	Y	Y	Y	Y	N	Y
Randolph	N	Y	Y	Y	Y	Y	N	Y
WISCONSIN								
Kasten	Y	N	N	Y	N	Y	N	Y
Proxmire	Y	N	Y	Y	Y	Y	Y	N
WYOMING								
Simpson	Y	N	N	Y	N	N	N	Y
Wallop	Y	N	N	Y	N	N	N	Y

KEY

- Y Voted for (yea).
- # Paired for.
- + Announced for.
- N Voted against (nay).
- X Paired against.
- - Announced against.
- P Voted "present".
- C Voted "present" to avoid possible conflict of interest.
- ? Did not vote or otherwise make a position known.

Democrats *Republicans*

ND - Northern Democrats   SD - Southern Democrats (Southern states - Ala., Ark., Fla., Ga., Ky., La., Miss., N.C., Okla., S.C., Tenn., Texas, Va.)   *Byrd elected as an independent.*

243. HR 4961. Budget Reconciliation Tax Increases/Spending Cuts. Armstrong, R-Colo., amendment to index the value of assets subject to capital gains taxes to reflect inflation, beginning in 1985. Adopted 64-32: R 45-8; D 19-24 (ND 8-20, SD 11-4), July 22, 1982.

244. HR 4961. Budget Reconciliation Tax Increases/Spending Cuts. Bumpers, D-Ark., motion to reconsider the vote by which the Armstrong, R-Colo., amendment *(see vote 243, above)* was adopted. Motion rejected 35-61: R 7-45; D 28-16 (ND 21-8, SD 7-8), July 22, 1982.

245. HR 4961. Budget Reconciliation Tax Increases/Spending Cuts. Mitchell, D-Maine, amendment to replace the 10 percent across-the-board individual income tax cuts scheduled for July 1982 and 1983 with cuts skewed to benefit those earning less than $50,000 a year. Rejected 43-53: R 3-49; D 40-4 (ND 28-1, SD 12-3), July 22, 1982. A "nay" was a vote supporting the president's position.

246. HR 4961. Budget Reconciliation Tax Increases/Spending Cuts. Nickles, R-Okla., amendment to increase from $10 to $100 the maximum amount of interest and/or dividends an individual can receive in one year and still be exempt from new withholding requirements. Adopted 97-0: R 52-0; D 45-0 (ND 30-0, SD 15-0), July 22, 1982.

247. HR 4961. Budget Reconciliation Tax Increases/Spending Cuts. Kasten, R-Wis., amendment to replace a provision requiring 10 percent withholding of interest and dividends with tougher requirements for the reporting of such income to the Internal Revenue Service. Rejected 48-49: R 10-42; D 38-7 (ND 23-7, SD 15-0), July 22, 1982. A "nay" was a vote supporting the president's position.

248. HR 4961. Budget Reconciliation Tax Increases/Spending Cuts. Metzenbaum, D-Ohio, amendment to prohibit proposed increases in Federal Unemployment Tax Act (FUTA) taxes until a program is enacted to allow 13 additional weeks of extended unemployment benefits. Rejected 48-49: R 8-44; D 40-5 (ND 30-0, SD 10-5), July 22, 1982.

249. HR 4961. Budget Reconciliation Tax Increases/Spending Cuts. Stevens, R-Alaska, motion to table (kill) the Dodd, D-Conn., amendment to limit a proposed minimum tax on individuals by restricting taxation of interest from tax-exempt obligations to tax-exempt industrial development bonds and mortgage subsidy bonds. Motion rejected 16-81: R 12-40; D 4-41 (ND 4-26, SD 0-15), July 22, 1982. (The Dodd amendment subsequently was adopted by voice vote.)

250. HR 4961. Budget Reconciliation Tax Increases/Spending Cuts. Stevens, R-Alaska, amendment to exclude the Alaska Natural Gas Transportation System from a provision requiring firms to amortize over 10 years interest and taxes incurred in the construction of non-residential real property. Adopted 80-16: R 46-6; D 34-10 (ND 19-10, SD 15-0), in the session which began July 22, 1982.

	251	252	253	254	255	256	257	258
ALABAMA								
Denton	Y	N	Y	N	N	Y	Y	Y
Heflin	Y	Y	N	Y	Y	Y	N	Y
ALASKA								
Murkowski	Y	Y	N	N	N	Y	Y	Y
Stevens	Y	Y	Y	N	N	Y	Y	Y
ARIZONA								
Goldwater	?	?	?	?	?	?	-	Y
DeConcini	Y	Y	N	Y	Y	N	N	Y
ARKANSAS								
Bumpers	N	Y	Y	Y	Y	N	N	Y
Pryor	Y	Y	Y	Y	Y	N	N	Y
CALIFORNIA								
Hayakawa	N	N	N	N	N	Y	Y	Y
Cranston	N	Y	Y	Y	Y	N	N	Y
COLORADO								
Armstrong	N	N	Y	N	N	Y	Y	Y
Hart	N	Y	Y	Y	Y	Y	N	Y
CONNECTICUT								
Weicker	?	?	?	?	?	?	-	Y
Dodd	Y	Y	Y	Y	Y	N	N	Y
DELAWARE								
Roth	Y	N	Y	N	N	Y	Y	Y
Biden	N	Y	Y	Y	Y	N	N	Y
FLORIDA								
Hawkins	Y	Y	N	Y	N	N	N	Y
Chiles	N	Y	N	Y	Y	N	N	Y
GEORGIA								
Mattingly	Y	Y	N	N	N	Y	N	Y
Nunn	Y	Y	Y	Y	Y	Y	N	Y
HAWAII								
Inouye	+	#	?	?	?	?	-	Y
Matsunaga	Y	Y	N	Y	Y	N	N	Y
IDAHO								
McClure	N	N	N	N	N	Y	Y	Y
Symms	N	N	N	N	N	Y	Y	N
ILLINOIS								
Percy	Y	N	N	N	Y	Y	N	Y
Dixon	Y	Y	N	Y	Y	N	N	Y
INDIANA								
Lugar	N	N	Y	N	N	Y	Y	Y
Quayle	N	N	Y	N	N	Y	Y	Y
IOWA								
Grassley	N	N	N	N	N	Y	Y	Y
Jepsen	Y	Y	N	N	N	N	Y	Y
KANSAS								
Dole	N	N	N	N	N	Y	Y	Y
Kassebaum	N	Y	N	N	Y	Y	Y	Y
KENTUCKY								
Ford	Y	Y	Y	Y	Y	N	N	Y
Huddleston	Y	Y	N	Y	Y	N	N	Y
LOUISIANA								
Johnston	Y	Y	N	Y	Y	N	N	Y
Long	Y	Y	N	Y	N	N	N	Y
MAINE								
Cohen	Y	N	N	N	Y	Y	Y	Y
Mitchell	Y	Y	N	Y	Y	N	N	Y
MARYLAND								
Mathias	N	N	N	N	Y	N	Y	Y
Sarbanes	N	Y	Y	Y	Y	N	N	Y
MASSACHUSETTS								
Kennedy	Y	Y	N	Y	Y	Y	N	Y
Tsongas	Y	Y	Y	Y	Y	Y	N	?
MICHIGAN								
Levin	Y	Y	N	Y	Y	N	N	Y
Riegle	Y	Y	N	Y	Y	N	N	Y
MINNESOTA								
Boschwitz	N	Y	N	N	N	N	Y	Y
Durenberger	N	Y	N	N	N	Y	Y	Y
MISSISSIPPI								
Cochran	Y	Y	N	Y	Y	Y	Y	Y
Stennis	Y	Y	Y	N	N	N	N	Y
MISSOURI								
Danforth	N	N	N	N	N	Y	Y	Y
Eagleton	Y	Y	Y	Y	Y	N	N	Y
MONTANA								
Baucus	Y	Y	Y	Y	Y	Y	N	Y
Melcher	Y	Y	N	Y	Y	N	N	Y
NEBRASKA								
Exon	Y	Y	N	Y	Y	N	N	Y
Zorinsky	Y	Y	N	Y	Y	N	N	Y
NEVADA								
Laxalt	Y	Y	N	N	N	Y	Y	Y
Cannon	Y	Y	N	Y	Y	N	N	+
NEW HAMPSHIRE								
Humphrey	N	Y	N	N	N	Y	Y	Y
Rudman	N	N	N	N	N	Y	Y	Y
NEW JERSEY								
Brady	N	N	N	N	N	Y	Y	Y
Bradley	N	Y	N	Y	Y	N	N	Y
NEW MEXICO								
Domenici	N	N	N	N	N	Y	Y	Y
Schmitt	Y	Y	N	Y	N	N	Y	Y
NEW YORK								
D'Amato	Y	Y	N	N	N	Y	Y	Y
Moynihan	N	Y	N	Y	Y	N	N	Y
NORTH CAROLINA								
East	Y	Y	N	N	N	Y	Y	N
Helms	Y	Y	Y	N	N	Y	Y	P
NORTH DAKOTA								
Andrews	Y	Y	N	N	N	Y	Y	Y
Burdick	Y	Y	N	Y	Y	N	N	Y
OHIO								
Glenn	Y	Y	N	Y	N	N	N	Y
Metzenbaum	N	Y	Y	Y	Y	N	N	Y
OKLAHOMA								
Nickles	N	Y	N	Y	Y	Y	Y	Y
Boren	N	X	Y	Y	Y	N	N	Y
OREGON								
Hatfield	N	N	Y	N	N	Y	Y	Y
Packwood	N	N	N	N	N	Y	Y	Y
PENNSYLVANIA								
Heinz	N	?	N	N	N	Y	Y	Y
Specter	Y	Y	N	Y	Y	Y	Y	Y
RHODE ISLAND								
Chafee	N	N	N	N	N	Y	Y	Y
Pell	N	Y	Y	Y	Y	N	N	Y
SOUTH CAROLINA								
Thurmond	Y	Y	N	N	N	Y	Y	Y
Hollings	Y	Y	Y	Y	Y	N	N	Y
SOUTH DAKOTA								
Abdnor	Y	Y	N	N	N	Y	Y	Y
Pressler	Y	Y	N	N	N	Y	Y	Y
TENNESSEE								
Baker	Y	N	N	N	N	Y	Y	Y
Sasser	Y	Y	Y	Y	Y	N	N	Y
TEXAS								
Tower	N	N	N	N	N	Y	Y	Y
Bentsen	Y	Y	N	Y	N	N	N	Y
UTAH								
Garn	Y	Y	N	N	N	Y	Y	Y
Hatch	Y	Y	N	N	N	Y	Y	Y
VERMONT								
Stafford	Y	Y	N	Y	N	N	N	Y
Leahy	Y	Y	Y	Y	Y	N	N	Y
VIRGINIA								
Warner	Y	Y	N	N	N	Y	Y	Y
Byrd*	N	Y	N	N	N	Y	N	Y
WASHINGTON								
Gorton	N	N	N	N	N	Y	Y	Y
Jackson	Y	Y	N	Y	N	N	N	Y
WEST VIRGINIA								
Byrd	Y	Y	N	Y	N	N	N	Y
Randolph	Y	Y	N	Y	Y	N	N	Y
WISCONSIN								
Kasten	Y	Y	N	N	N	Y	Y	Y
Proxmire	N	Y	Y	Y	Y	Y	N	Y
WYOMING								
Simpson	N	N	Y	N	N	Y	Y	Y
Wallop	N	N	N	N	N	Y	Y	Y

KEY

Y Voted for (yea).
Paired for.
+ Announced for.
N Voted against (nay).
X Paired against.
- Announced against.
P Voted "present".
C Voted "present" to avoid possible conflict of interest.
? Did not vote or otherwise make a position known.

Democrats *Republicans*

ND - Northern Democrats   SD - Southern Democrats (Southern states - Ala., Ark., Fla., Ga., Ky., La., Miss., N.C., Okla., S.C., Tenn., Texas, Va.)   *Byrd elected as an independent.

251. HR 4961. Budget Reconciliation Tax Increases/Spending Cuts. D'Amato, R-N.Y., amendment to delete from the proposed minimum tax on individuals the interest from tax-exempt industrial development bonds and mortgage subsidy bonds, which were not exempted by adoption of the Dodd, D-Conn., amendment *(see vote 249, p. 43-S)*. Adopted 58-39: R 26-26; D 32-13 (ND 21-9, SD 11-4), in the session which began July 22, 1982.

252. HR 4961. Budget Reconciliation Tax Increases/Spending Cuts. Pryor, D-Ark., amendment to delete a provision requiring employers to report estimated employee tip income to the Internal Revenue Service. Adopted 70-25: R 26-25; D 44-0 (ND 30-0, SD 14-0), in the session which began July 22, 1982.

253. HR 4961. Budget Reconciliation Tax Increases/Spending Cuts. Baucus, D-Mont., amendment to repeal "safe-harbor" leasing provisions of the 1981 tax cut law (PL 97-34), which allowed firms to sell unused tax breaks to firms that could use them to offset tax liability. Rejected 31-66: R 10-42; D 21-24 (ND 12-18, SD 9-6), in the session which began July 22, 1982.

254. HR 4961. Budget Reconciliation Tax Increases/Spending Cuts. Metzenbaum, D-Ohio, amendment to delete a provision lowering from $150 to $100 the maximum deduction for health insurance premiums and another provision to increase the floor on unreimbursed medical deductions from 3 percent to 7 percent of adjusted gross income. Rejected 46-51: R 4-48; D 42-3 (ND 30-0, SD 12-3), in the session which began July 22, 1982.

255. HR 4961. Budget Reconciliation Tax Increases/Spending Cuts. Hart, D-Colo., amendment to delete a provision allowing a business expense deduction for payments made to foreign officials, if the payments are legal under the Foreign Corrupt Practices Act. Rejected 46-51: R 5-47; D 41-4 (ND 30-0, SD 11-4), in the session which began July 22, 1982.

256. HR 4961. Budget Reconciliation Tax Increases/Spending Cuts. Dole, R-Kan., amendment on behalf of the Finance Committee to allow deductions for only 50 percent of business meal and entertainment expenses, except while on travel away from home. Adopted 57-40: R 46-6; D 11-34 (ND 8-22, SD 3-12), in the session which began July 22, 1982.

257. HR 4961. Budget Reconciliation Tax Increases/Spending Cuts. Passage of the bill to increase taxes $99 billion for fiscal years 1983-85 and to cut welfare, Medicare and Medicaid spending $17 billion for the same three years, in compliance with reconciliation instructions in the fiscal 1983 budget resolution (S Con Res 92). Passed 50-47: R 49-3; D 1-44 (ND 0-30, SD 1-14), in the session which began July 22, 1982.

258. H J Res 494. Presidential Certification on El Salvador. Passage of the joint resolution conditioning further U.S. aid to El Salvador on the president's certification to Congress that El Salvador was making "good faith efforts" to investigate and to bring to justice those responsible for the murders of six U.S. citizens in 1980 and 1981. The president also would have to certify that El Salvador was taking "all reasonable steps" to investigate the disappearance of journalist John Sullivan in 1981. Passed 95-2: R 51-2; D 44-0 (ND 29-0, SD 15-0), July 27, 1982.

	259	260	261	262	263	264	265
ALABAMA							
Denton	N	N	Y	-	-	N	N
Heflin	Y	N	Y	N	N	N	Y
ALASKA							
Murkowski	N	N	Y	N	N	N	N
Stevens	N	N	Y	N	N	N	N
ARIZONA							
Goldwater	N	N	Y	N	N	N	N
DeConcini	N	N	Y	N	N	N	N
ARKANSAS							
Bumpers	Y	Y	Y	N	Y	Y	Y
Pryor	Y	?	?	N	N	N	Y
CALIFORNIA							
Hayakawa	N	N	Y	N	N	N	N
Cranston	Y	Y	Y	Y	Y	Y	Y
COLORADO							
Armstrong	N	N	Y	?	N	N	N
Hart	Y	Y	Y	Y	Y	Y	Y
CONNECTICUT							
Weicker	Y	N	Y	N	Y	Y	Y
Dodd	Y	Y	Y	N	Y	Y	Y
DELAWARE							
Roth	N	N	Y	N	N	N	N
Biden	Y	Y	Y	Y	Y	Y	Y
FLORIDA							
Hawkins	N	N	Y	N	N	N	N
Chiles	N	N	Y	N	N	N	N
GEORGIA							
Mattingly	N	N	Y	N	N	N	N
Nunn	N	N	Y	N	N	N	Y
HAWAII							
Inouye	Y	Y	Y	Y	Y	Y	Y
Matsunaga	Y	Y	Y	?	Y	Y	Y
IDAHO							
McClure	N	N	Y	N	N	N	Y
Symms	N	N	Y	N	N	N	N
ILLINOIS							
Percy	N	N	Y	N	Y	N	N
Dixon	Y	N	Y	N	Y	Y	Y
INDIANA							
Lugar	N	N	Y	N	N	N	N
Quayle	N	N	Y	N	N	N	N

	259	260	261	262	263	264	265
IOWA							
Grassley	N	N	Y	N	N	N	N
Jepsen	N	N	Y	N	N	N	?
KANSAS							
Dole	N	N	Y	N	N	N	N
Kassebaum	N	N	Y	N	N	N	N
KENTUCKY							
Ford	Y	Y	Y	N	Y	N	Y
Huddleston	Y	N	Y	Y	Y	Y	Y
LOUISIANA							
Johnston	Y	N	Y	N	N	N	Y
Long	Y	N	Y	N	N	N	Y
MAINE							
Cohen	N	N	Y	N	N	N	N
Mitchell	Y	Y	Y	N	Y	Y	Y
MARYLAND							
Mathias	Y	N	Y	Y	Y	Y	Y
Sarbanes	Y	Y	Y	Y	Y	Y	Y
MASSACHUSETTS							
Kennedy	Y	Y	Y	N	Y	Y	Y
Tsongas	?	?	?	?	?	?	?
MICHIGAN							
Levin	Y	Y	Y	Y	Y	Y	Y
Riegle	Y	Y	Y	Y	Y	Y	Y
MINNESOTA							
Boschwitz	N	N	Y	N	N	N	N
Durenberger	N	N	Y	?	?	?	N
MISSISSIPPI							
Cochran	N	N	Y	N	N	N	N
Stennis	Y	N	Y	N	N	N	Y
MISSOURI							
Danforth	N	N	Y	N	N	N	N
Eagleton	Y	Y	Y	Y	Y	Y	Y
MONTANA							
Baucus	Y	Y	Y	N	Y	Y	Y
Melcher	N	N	Y	N	N	N	N
NEBRASKA							
Exon	Y	N	Y	N	N	N	Y
Zorinsky	Y	N	Y	N	N	N	N
NEVADA							
Laxalt	N	N	Y	N	N	N	N
Cannon	+	?	?	?	?	?	?

	259	260	261	262	263	264	265
NEW HAMPSHIRE							
Humphrey	N	N	Y	N	N	N	N
Rudman	N	N	Y	N	N	N	N
NEW JERSEY							
Brady	N	N	Y	N	N	N	N
Bradley	Y	Y	Y	N	Y	Y	Y
NEW MEXICO							
Domenici	N	N	Y	N	N	N	N
Schmitt	N	N	Y	N	N	N	N
NEW YORK							
D'Amato	N	N	Y	N	N	N	?
Moynihan	Y	Y	Y	Y	Y	Y	Y
NORTH CAROLINA							
East	N	N	Y	N	N	N	N
Helms	N	N	Y	N	N	N	N
NORTH DAKOTA							
Andrews	N	N	Y	N	N	N	N
Burdick	Y	Y	Y	N	N	Y	Y
OHIO							
Glenn	Y	N	Y	N	?	Y	Y
Metzenbaum	Y	Y	Y	N	Y	Y	Y
OKLAHOMA							
Nickles	Y	N	Y	N	N	N	N
Boren	Y	N	Y	N	N	N	N
OREGON							
Hatfield	N	N	Y	N	Y	N	N
Packwood	N	N	Y	N	N	N	N
PENNSYLVANIA							
Heinz	N	N	Y	N	N	N	N
Specter	N	N	Y	N	Y	N	N
RHODE ISLAND							
Chafee	Y	N	Y	N	Y	Y	Y
Pell	Y	Y	Y	N	Y	Y	Y
SOUTH CAROLINA							
Thurmond	N	N	Y	N	N	N	N
Hollings	Y	N	Y	N	N	Y	N
SOUTH DAKOTA							
Abdnor	N	N	Y	N	N	N	N
Pressler	N	N	Y	N	N	N	N
TENNESSEE							
Baker	N	N	Y	N	N	N	N
Sasser	Y	N	Y	N	Y	N	Y

KEY

Y	Voted for (yea).
#	Paired for.
+	Announced for.
N	Voted against (nay).
X	Paired against.
-	Announced against.
P	Voted "present".
C	Voted "present" to avoid possible conflict of interest.
?	Did not vote or otherwise make a position known.

Democrats	*Republicans*

	259	260	261	262	263	264	265
TEXAS							
Tower	N	N	Y	N	N	N	N
Bentsen	Y	N	Y	N	N	N	Y
UTAH							
Garn	N	N	Y	N	N	N	N
Hatch	N	N	Y	N	N	N	N
VERMONT							
Stafford	N	N	Y	N	N	Y	N
Leahy	Y	Y	Y	Y	Y	Y	Y
VIRGINIA							
Warner	N	N	Y	N	N	N	N
Byrd*	Y	N	Y	N	N	N	N
WASHINGTON							
Gorton	N	N	Y	N	N	N	N
Jackson	Y	N	Y	Y	Y	Y	Y
WEST VIRGINIA							
Byrd	Y	Y	Y	N	Y	Y	Y
Randolph	Y	Y	Y	Y	Y	Y	Y
WISCONSIN							
Kasten	N	N	Y	N	N	N	N
Proxmire	Y	N	Y	N	N	N	Y
WYOMING							
Simpson	N	N	Y	N	N	N	N
Wallop	Y	N	Y	N	N	N	N

ND - Northern Democrats   SD - Southern Democrats (Southern states - Ala., Ark., Fla., Ga., Ky., La., Miss., N.C., Okla., S.C., Tenn., Texas, Va.)   *Byrd elected as an independent.*

259. S J Res 58. Balanced Budget/Tax Limitation Amendment. Ford, D-Ky., amendment to require the president to submit a balanced budget to Congress. Rejected 45-53: R 5-49; D 40-4 (ND 27-2, SD 13-2), July 27, 1982. A "nay" was a vote supporting the president's position.

260. S J Res 58. Balanced Budget/Tax Limitation Amendment. Cranston, D-Calif., amendment to the Domenici, R-N.M., amendment, to make clear the president does not have the authority to impound funds to enforce the balanced budget amendment. Rejected 23-74: R 0-54; D 23-20 (ND 21-8, SD 2-12), July 27, 1982. A "nay" was a vote supporting the president's position.

261. S J Res 58. Balanced Budget/Tax Limitation Amendment. Domenici, R-N.M., amendment to make clear that neither Congress nor the president is given new authority with respect to the federal budget, that Congress can enact legislation to implement the balanced budget amendment, and to broaden the base period for measuring national income. Adopted 97-0: R 54-0; D 43-0 (ND 29-0, SD 14-0), July 27, 1982. A "nay" was a vote supporting the president's position.

262. S J Res 58. Balanced Budget/Tax Limitation Amendment. Moynihan, D-N.Y., amendment to specify an algebraic formula for determining national income. Rejected 13-81: R 1-50; D 12-31 (ND 11-17, SD 1-14), July 28, 1982. A "nay" was a vote supporting the president's position.

263. S J Res 58. Balanced Budget/Tax Limitation Amendment. Cranston, D-Calif., amendment to allow deficit spending during a national emergency declared either by the president or Congress. Rejected 34-61: R 8-44; D 26-17 (ND 22-6, SD 4-11), July 28, 1982. A "nay" was a vote supporting the president's position.

264. S J Res 58. Balanced Budget/Tax Limitation Amendment. Dixon, D-Ill., amendment to allow deficit spending during an economic emergency. Rejected 30-67: R 3-50; D 27-17 (ND 24-5, SD 3-12), July 28, 1982. A "nay" was a vote supporting the president's position.

265. S J Res 58. Balanced Budget/Tax Limitation Amendment. Ford, D-Ky., amendment to allow the president to send Congress a budget calling for deficit spending so long as he submits a detailed statement explaining the reasons for the deficit. Rejected 43-53: R 4-48; D 39-5 (ND 26-3, SD 13-2), July 28, 1982. A "nay" was a vote supporting the president's position.

	266	267	268	269	270	271
ALABAMA						
Denton	N	?	N	N	N	N
Heflin	N	N	N	N	N	N
ALASKA						
Murkowski	N	N	N	N	N	Y
Stevens	N	?	N	N	N	Y
ARIZONA						
Goldwater	N	N	N	N	N	N
DeConcini	N	N	N	N	N	N
ARKANSAS						
Bumpers	Y	Y	Y	Y	Y	Y
Pryor	N	N	N	N	N	N
CALIFORNIA						
Hayakawa	N	N	N	N	N	N
Cranston	Y	Y	Y	Y	Y	Y
COLORADO						
Armstrong	N	N	N	N	N	Y
Hart	Y	Y	Y	Y	Y	N
CONNECTICUT						
Weicker	Y	Y	Y	Y	Y	Y
Dodd	Y	Y	Y	Y	Y	Y
DELAWARE						
Roth	Y	N	N	N	N	Y
Biden	Y	Y	Y	Y	N	Y
FLORIDA						
Hawkins	Y	N	N	N	N	N
Chiles	N	N	N	N	N	N
GEORGIA						
Mattingly	N	N	N	N	N	N
Nunn	N	N	N	N	N	Y
HAWAII						
Inouye	Y	Y	Y	Y	Y	N
Matsunaga	Y	Y	Y	Y	Y	Y
IDAHO						
McClure	N	N	N	N	N	?
Symms	N	N	N	N	N	N
ILLINOIS						
Percy	N	N	N	N	N	Y
Dixon	Y	N	N	N	Y	Y
INDIANA						
Lugar	N	N	N	N	N	Y
Quayle	N	N	N	N	N	Y

	266	267	268	269	270	271
IOWA						
Grassley	N	N	N	N	N	N
Jepsen	N	N	N	N	N	Y
KANSAS						
Dole	N	N	N	N	N	Y
Kassebaum	N	N	N	N	N	Y
KENTUCKY						
Ford	Y	N	N	X	Y	Y
Huddleston	Y	N	Y	Y	Y	N
LOUISIANA						
Johnston	N	N	N	N	N	Y
Long	N	N	Y	Y	Y	Y
MAINE						
Cohen	N	N	N	N	N	Y
Mitchell	Y	N	N	N	Y	Y
MARYLAND						
Mathias	N	N	N	N	N	Y
Sarbanes	Y	Y	Y	Y	Y	?
MASSACHUSETTS						
Kennedy	Y	Y	Y	Y	Y	N
Tsongas	?	?	?	?	?	N
MICHIGAN						
Levin	Y	Y	Y	Y	Y	Y
Riegle	Y	Y	Y	Y	Y	N
MINNESOTA						
Boschwitz	N	N	N	N	N	N
Durenberger	Y	N	N	N	N	N
MISSISSIPPI						
Cochran	N	N	N	N	N	N
Stennis	N	N	N	N	N	N
MISSOURI						
Danforth	N	N	N	N	N	Y
Eagleton	Y	Y	Y	Y	Y	Y
MONTANA						
Baucus	Y	N	N	N	N	Y
Melcher	N	N	N	N	N	N
NEBRASKA						
Exon	N	?	X	N	N	N
Zorinsky	N	N	N	N	N	N
NEVADA						
Laxalt	N	?	?	?	N	N
Cannon	?	?	?	?	?	?

	266	267	268	269	270	271
NEW HAMPSHIRE						
Humphrey	N	N	N	N	N	Y
Rudman	N	N	N	N	N	Y
NEW JERSEY						
Brady	N	N	N	N	N	Y
Bradley	Y	Y	Y	Y	Y	Y
NEW MEXICO						
Domenici	N	N	N	N	N	N
Schmitt	N	N	N	N	N	N
NEW YORK						
D'Amato	Y	N	N	N	N	N
Moynihan	Y	Y	Y	Y	Y	Y
NORTH CAROLINA						
East	N	N	N	N	N	N
Helms	N	N	N	N	N	N
NORTH DAKOTA						
Andrews	N	N	N	N	N	N
Burdick	Y	N	Y	N	Y	N
OHIO						
Glenn	Y	Y	Y	Y	Y	N
Metzenbaum	Y	Y	#	#	#	?
OKLAHOMA						
Nickles	N	N	N	N	N	N
Boren	N	N	N	N	X	N
OREGON						
Hatfield	Y	N	N	N	N	Y
Packwood	Y	N	N	N	N	N
PENNSYLVANIA						
Heinz	N	Y	Y	Y	Y	Y
Specter	Y	Y	Y	Y	Y	Y
RHODE ISLAND						
Chafee	Y	Y	Y	Y	Y	Y
Pell	Y	Y	Y	Y	Y	Y
SOUTH CAROLINA						
Thurmond	N	N	N	N	N	N
Hollings	N	N	Y	Y	Y	Y
SOUTH DAKOTA						
Abdnor	N	N	N	N	N	N
Pressler	Y	N	N	N	N	Y
TENNESSEE						
Baker	N	N	N	N	N	N
Sasser	Y	N	N	N	Y	N

KEY

Y	Voted for (yea).
#	Paired for.
+	Announced for.
N	Voted against (nay).
X	Paired against.
-	Announced against.
P	Voted "present".
C	Voted "present" to avoid possible conflict of interest.
?	Did not vote or otherwise make a position known.

Democrats   *Republicans*

	266	267	268	269	270	271
TEXAS						
Tower	N	?	?	N	N	N
Bentsen	N	N	N	N	N	N
UTAH						
Garn	N	N	N	N	N	N
Hatch	N	N	N	N	N	N
VERMONT						
Stafford	N	N	Y	N	Y	N
Leahy	Y	Y	Y	Y	Y	N
VIRGINIA						
Warner	N	N	N	N	N	N
Byrd*	N	N	N	N	N	N
WASHINGTON						
Gorton	N	N	N	N	N	Y
Jackson	Y	Y	Y	Y	Y	Y
WEST VIRGINIA						
Byrd	Y	Y	Y	Y	Y	N
Randolph	Y	Y	Y	Y	Y	Y
WISCONSIN						
Kasten	N	N	N	N	N	Y
Proxmire	Y	N	N	N	N	N
WYOMING						
Simpson	N	N	N	N	N	N
Wallop	N	N	N	N	N	Y

ND - Northern Democrats   SD - Southern Democrats (Southern states - Ala., Ark., Fla., Ga., Ky., La., Miss., N.C., Okla., S.C., Tenn., Texas, Va.)   *Byrd elected as an independent.*

266. S J Res 58. Balanced Budget/Tax Limitation Amendment. Moynihan, D-N.Y., amendment to bar any budget that calls for cuts in Social Security entitlement benefits. Rejected 39-59: R 10-44; D 29-15 (ND 25-4, SD 4-11), July 29, 1982. A "nay" was a vote supporting the president's position.

267. S J Res 58. Balanced Budget/Tax Limitation Amendment. Leahy, D-Vt., amendment to allow deficit spending when necessary to prevent unemployment from exceeding 10 percent or 11 million unemployed, whichever is greater. Rejected 25-68: R 4-46; D 21-22 (ND 20-8, SD 1-14), July 29, 1982. A "nay" was a vote supporting the president's position.

268. S J Res 58. Balanced Budget/Tax Limitation Amendment. Leahy, D-Vt., amendment to allow deficit spending when necessary to prevent unemployment from exceeding 16 percent or 17.6 million, whichever is greater. Rejected 29-65: R 5-47; D 24-18 (ND 20-7, SD 4-11), July 29, 1982. A "nay" was a vote supporting the president's position.

269. S J Res 58. Balanced Budget/Tax Limitation Amendment. Leahy, D-Vt., amendment to allow deficit spending when necessary to prevent unemployment from exceeding 20 percent or 22 million, whichever is greater. Rejected 29-66: R 5-48; D 24-18 (ND 20-8, SD 4-10), July 29, 1982. A "nay" was a vote supporting the president's position.

270. S J Res 58. Balanced Budget/Tax Limitation Amendment. Leahy, D-Vt., amendment to allow deficit spending in case of a depression. Rejected 30-66: R 4-50; D 26-16 (ND 20-8, SD 6-8), July 29, 1982. A "nay" was a vote supporting the president's position.

271. S J Res 58. Balanced Budget/Tax Limitation Amendment. Gorton, R-Wash.-Rudman, R-N.H., amendment to clarify and restrict the authority of the federal judiciary to interpret the amendment. Rejected 45-51: R 27-26; D 18-25 (ND 12-16, SD 6-9), July 29, 1982. A "nay" was a vote supporting the president's position.

	272 273 274 275 276 277 278 279		272 273 274 275 276 277 278 279		272 273 274 275 276 277 278 279	KEY
ALABAMA		**IOWA**		**NEW HAMPSHIRE**		Y Voted for (yea).
Denton	N N N N N N Y N	Grassley	N N N N N N Y N	Humphrey	N N N N Y N N N	# Paired for.
Heflin	N N N Y N N Y N	Jepsen	N N N N N Y N N	Rudman	N Y N N N Y N N	+ Announced for.
ALASKA		**KANSAS**		**NEW JERSEY**		N Voted against (nay).
Murkowski	N N N N N N Y N	Dole	N N N N N N Y N	Brady	N N N N N Y N N	X Paired against.
Stevens	? ? ? ? ? ? + ? ?	Kassebaum	N Y N N N Y N N	Bradley	Y Y N Y Y N N N	- Announced against.
ARIZONA		**KENTUCKY**		**NEW MEXICO**		P Voted "present".
Goldwater	N N N N N N Y N	Ford	Y Y N Y N Y N N	Domenici	N N N N N N Y N	C Voted "present" to avoid possible conflict of interest.
DeConcini	N N N N N N Y N	Huddleston	N N N Y N Y N N	Schmitt	N N N N N N Y N	
ARKANSAS		**LOUISIANA**		**NEW YORK**		? Did not vote or otherwise make a position known.
Bumpers	Y Y N N N Y N N	Johnston	N N N Y N N N N	D'Amato	N N N N N N Y N	
Pryor	N N N Y N N Y N	Long	N N N Y N N N N	Moynihan	Y Y Y Y Y Y N N	
CALIFORNIA		**MAINE**		**NORTH CAROLINA**		**Democrats** *Republicans*
Hayakawa	N N N N N N Y N	Cohen	N Y N N N N N N	East	N N N N N N Y N	
Cranston	Y Y Y Y Y N N N	Mitchell	Y Y N Y N Y N N	Helms	N N N N N N Y N	
COLORADO		**MARYLAND**		**NORTH DAKOTA**		
Armstrong	N N N N N N Y N	Mathias	Y Y N Y N Y N N	Andrews	N N N Y N Y N N	
Hart	? ? ? ? ? Y N N	Sarbanes	Y Y Y Y Y Y N N	Burdick	N N N Y N Y N N	
CONNECTICUT		**MASSACHUSETTS**		**OHIO**		**TEXAS**
Weicker	? ? ? ? ? ? ? ?	Kennedy	Y Y Y Y Y Y N N	Glenn	? ? ? ? ? ? ? ?	Tower	N N N N N N Y N
Dodd	Y Y Y Y N N N N	Tsongas	Y Y Y Y Y N N N	Metzenbaum	Y Y N Y N Y N N	Bentsen	N N N Y N Y N N
DELAWARE		**MICHIGAN**		**OKLAHOMA**		**UTAH**
Roth	N N N N N N Y N	Levin	Y Y N Y N Y N N	Nickles	N N N N N N Y N	Garn	N N N N N N Y N
Biden	Y Y N Y N Y N N	Riegle	Y N N Y N Y N N	Boren	N N N N N N Y N	Hatch	N N N N N N Y N
FLORIDA		**MINNESOTA**		**OREGON**		**VERMONT**
Hawkins	N N N N N N Y N	Boschwitz	N Y N N N N Y N	Hatfield	N N N N N N Y N	Stafford	N N N N N N Y N
Chiles	N N N N N Y N N	Durenberger	N N N N N N Y N	Packwood	N N N N N N Y N	Leahy	Y Y N Y Y Y N N
GEORGIA		**MISSISSIPPI**		**PENNSYLVANIA**		**VIRGINIA**
Mattingly	N N N N N N Y N	Cochran	N N N N N N Y N	Heinz	N N N N N N Y N	Warner	N N N N N N Y N
Nunn	N N N N N Y N N	Stennis	N N N ? ? N Y N	Specter	Y Y N N N N N N	Byrd*	N N N N N Y N N
HAWAII		**MISSOURI**		**RHODE ISLAND**		**WASHINGTON**
Inouye	Y Y Y Y Y Y N N	Danforth	? ? ? ? ? ? ? ?	Chafee	N N N N Y N N N	Gorton	Y N N N N N Y N
Matsunaga	Y Y Y Y Y N Y N	Eagleton	Y Y Y Y Y N N N	Pell	Y Y Y Y Y Y N N	Jackson	Y Y Y Y Y Y N N
IDAHO		**MONTANA**		**SOUTH CAROLINA**		**WEST VIRGINIA**
McClure	N N N N N N Y N	Baucus	Y Y N N N Y N N	Thurmond	N N N N N N Y N	Byrd	N N Y Y Y Y N N
Symms	N N N N N N Y N	Melcher	N N N N N N Y N	Hollings	N N N Y N Y N N	Randolph	Y Y N Y Y Y N N
ILLINOIS		**NEBRASKA**		**SOUTH DAKOTA**		**WISCONSIN**
Percy	N N N N N N Y N	Exon	N N N Y N Y N N	Abdnor	N N N N N N Y N	Kasten	N N N N N N Y N
Dixon	N N N Y N N N N	Zorinsky	N N N Y N Y N N	Pressler	N N N N N N Y N	Proxmire	N N N N N N Y N
INDIANA		**NEVADA**		**TENNESSEE**		**WYOMING**
Lugar	N N N N N N Y N	Laxalt	N N N N N N Y N	Baker	N N N N N Y N N	Simpson	N N N N N Y N N
Quayle	N N N N N N Y N	Cannon	N N N Y N Y N N	Sasser	N N N Y N Y N N	Wallop	N N N N N N Y N

ND - Northern Democrats   SD - Southern Democrats (Southern states - Ala., Ark., Fla., Ga., Ky., La., Miss., N.C., Okla., S.C., Tenn., Texas, Va.)   *Byrd elected as an independent.

272. S J Res 58. Balanced Budget/Tax Limitation Amendment. Dodd, D-Conn., amendment to freeze current spending levels by statute and to require that new revenue be raised to equal any new spending for federal programs. Rejected 25-70: R 3-48; D 22-22 (ND 20-9, SD 2-13), Aug. 3, 1982. A "nay" was a vote supporting the president's position.

273. S J Res 58. Balanced Budget/Tax Limitation Amendment. Mathias, R-Md.-Baucus, D-Mont., amendment to make provisions of S J Res 58 statutory rather than a constitutional amendment. Rejected 28-67: R 7-44; D 21-23 (ND 19-10, SD 2-13), Aug. 3, 1982. A "nay" was a vote supporting the president's position.

274. S J Res 58. Balanced Budget/Tax Limitation Amendment. Moynihan, D-N.Y., amendment to allow total outlays to exceed total receipts by the same percent as national defense outlays increased over the previous year. Rejected 12-83: R 0-51; D 12-32 (ND 12-17, SD 0-15), Aug. 3, 1982. A "nay" was a vote supporting the president's position.

275. S J Res 58. Balanced Budget/Tax Limitation Amendment. Cranston, D-Calif., amendment to require the president to submit a balanced budget to Congress that states its underlying monetary policy and to require Congress in adopting a budget to state the underlying monetary policy. Rejected 36-58: R 2-49; D 34-9 (ND 25-4, SD 9-5), Aug. 3, 1982. A "nay" was a vote supporting the president's position.

276. S J Res 58. Balanced Budget/Tax Limitation Amendment. Cranston, D-Calif., amendment to delete the provision allowing deficit spending by a three-fifths majority of Congress, thus allowing deficit spending under normal rules, which would require only a simple majority. Rejected 18-76: R 1-50; D 17-26 (ND 17-12, SD 0-14), Aug. 3, 1982. A "nay" was a vote supporting the president's position.

277. S J Res 58. Balanced Budget/Tax Limitation Amendment. Armstrong, R-Colo.-Boren, D-Okla., amendment to freeze the debt ceiling at the time S J Res 58 takes effect and to require a three-fifths vote of Congress to increase the debt ceiling. Adopted 51-45: R 20-31; D 31-14 (ND 19-11, SD 12-3), Aug. 3, 1982. A "nay" was a vote supporting the president's position.

278. S J Res 58. Balanced Budget/Tax Limitation Amendment. Baker, R-Tenn., motion to reconsider the vote by which the Armstrong, R-Colo.-Boren, D-Okla., amendment was adopted *(see vote 277, above)*. Motion rejected 40-56: R 32-19; D 8-37 (ND 4-26, SD 4-11), Aug. 3, 1982. A "nay" was a vote supporting the president's position.

279. S J Res 58. Balanced Budget/Tax Limitation Amendment. Cohen, R-Maine, amendment to give federal courts jurisdiction to hear cases under the amendment and to allow any person to bring a lawsuit for "appropriate redress" under the amendment. Rejected 0-96: R 0-51; D 0-45 (ND 0-30, SD 0-15), Aug. 3, 1982. A "nay" was a vote supporting the president's position.

KEY

- Y Voted for (yea).
- # Paired for.
- + Announced for.
- N Voted against (nay).
- X Paired against.
- - Announced against.
- P Voted "present".
- C Voted "present" to avoid possible conflict of interest.
- ? Did not vote or otherwise make a position known.

Democrats   *Republicans*

	280	281	282	283	284	285	286	287
ALABAMA								
Denton	N	N	N	N	Y	N	N	N
Heflin	Y	N	N	N	Y	N	N	N
ALASKA								
Murkowski	N	N	N	N	N	N	N	N
Stevens	N	N	N	N	N	N	N	N
ARIZONA								
Goldwater	N	N	N	N	?	?	?	N
DeConcini	N	N	N	N	N	N	N	N
ARKANSAS								
Bumpers	Y	Y	Y	Y	Y	Y	N	N
Pryor	Y	Y	N	N	Y	N	Y	N
CALIFORNIA								
Hayakawa	N	N	N	N	N	N	N	N
Cranston	Y	Y	Y	Y	Y	Y	Y	Y
COLORADO								
Armstrong	N	N	N	N	N	N	N	N
Hart	Y	Y	Y	Y	Y	N	N	N
CONNECTICUT								
Weicker	N	N	N	Y	Y	Y	N	Y
Dodd	Y	Y	Y	Y	Y	N	N	N
DELAWARE								
Roth	N	N	N	N	N	N	N	N
Biden	Y	N	N	Y	Y	Y	Y	Y
FLORIDA								
Hawkins	N	N	N	N	N	N	N	Y
Chiles	Y	N	N	Y	Y	N	N	N
GEORGIA								
Mattingly	N	N	N	N	N	N	N	N
Nunn	Y	N	N	N	N	N	N	N
HAWAII								
Inouye	Y	Y	Y	Y	Y	Y	Y	Y
Matsunaga	Y	Y	Y	Y	Y	Y	Y	Y
IDAHO								
McClure	N	N	N	N	N	N	N	N
Symms	N	N	N	N	N	N	N	N
ILLINOIS								
Percy	N	N	N	N	N	N	N	N
Dixon	Y	N	N	Y	Y	N	N	N
INDIANA								
Lugar	N	N	N	N	N	N	N	N
Quayle	N	N	N	N	N	N	N	N

	280	281	282	283	284	285	286	287
IOWA								
Grassley	N	N	N	N	N	N	N	N
Jepsen	N	N	N	N	N	N	N	N
KANSAS								
Dole	N	N	N	N	N	N	N	N
Kassebaum	N	N	N	N	N	N	N	N
KENTUCKY								
Ford	Y	Y	Y	N	Y	Y	Y	Y
Huddleston	Y	N	N	Y	Y	Y	N	N
LOUISIANA								
Johnston	Y	N	N	Y	Y	N	?	N
Long	Y	N	N	Y	N	Y	?	N
MAINE								
Cohen	N	N	Y	N	Y	N	N	N
Mitchell	Y	Y	Y	N	Y	Y	N	N
MARYLAND								
Mathias	Y	Y	N	Y	N	Y	N	Y
Sarbanes	Y	Y	Y	Y	Y	Y	N	Y
MASSACHUSETTS								
Kennedy	Y	Y	Y	Y	Y	Y	N	Y
Tsongas	Y	Y	Y	Y	Y	Y	Y	N
MICHIGAN								
Levin	Y	Y	Y	Y	Y	Y	N	Y
Riegle	Y	Y	Y	Y	Y	Y	N	Y
MINNESOTA								
Boschwitz	N	N	N	N	N	N	N	N
Durenberger	?	?	?	?	?	?	?	N
MISSISSIPPI								
Cochran	N	N	N	N	N	N	N	N
Stennis	N	N	N	N	Y	N	N	N
MISSOURI								
Danforth	?	N	N	N	N	N	N	N
Eagleton	Y	Y	Y	Y	Y	Y	Y	Y
MONTANA								
Baucus	Y	N	N	Y	N	N	N	N
Melcher	N	N	N	N	N	N	N	N
NEBRASKA								
Exon	Y	N	N	Y	N	N	N	N
Zorinsky	Y	N	N	N	Y	N	N	N
NEVADA								
Laxalt	N	N	N	N	N	N	N	N
Cannon	Y	N	N	Y	Y	Y	N	Y

	280	281	282	283	284	285	286	287
NEW HAMPSHIRE								
Humphrey	N	N	N	N	N	N	N	N
Rudman	N	N	N	N	N	N	N	N
NEW JERSEY								
Brady	N	?	?	?	N	N	N	N
Bradley	Y	Y	Y	Y	Y	Y	N	Y
NEW MEXICO								
Domenici	N	N	N	N	N	N	N	N
Schmitt	N	N	N	N	N	N	N	N
NEW YORK								
D'Amato	N	N	N	N	N	N	N	N
Moynihan	Y	Y	Y	Y	Y	Y	N	Y
NORTH CAROLINA								
East	N	N	N	N	N	N	N	N
Helms	N	N	N	N	N	N	N	N
NORTH DAKOTA								
Andrews	Y	N	N	N	N	N	N	N
Burdick	Y	N	N	Y	N	N	N	Y
OHIO								
Glenn	?	?	?	?	Y	N	N	Y
Metzenbaum	Y	Y	Y	Y	Y	Y	N	Y
OKLAHOMA								
Nickles	N	N	N	N	N	N	N	N
Boren	Y	N	N	N	N	N	N	N
OREGON								
Hatfield	N	N	N	N	N	N	N	N
Packwood	N	N	N	N	N	N	N	N
PENNSYLVANIA								
Heinz	Y	N	?	Y	Y	Y	N	N
Specter	Y	N	N	Y	Y	Y	N	Y
RHODE ISLAND								
Chafee	N	N	N	Y	N	N	N	N
Pell	Y	Y	Y	Y	Y	Y	N	Y
SOUTH CAROLINA								
Thurmond	N	N	N	N	N	N	N	N
Hollings	Y	Y	N	Y	Y	Y	N	N
SOUTH DAKOTA								
Abdnor	N	N	N	N	N	N	N	N
Pressler	N	N	N	N	N	N	N	N
TENNESSEE								
Baker	N	N	N	N	N	N	N	N
Sasser	Y	N	Y	Y	Y	Y	N	Y

	280	281	282	283	284	285	286	287
TEXAS								
Tower	N	N	N	N	Y	N	N	N
Bentsen	Y	N	N	N	Y	N	Y	N
UTAH								
Garn	N	N	?	N	N	N	N	N
Hatch	N	N	N	N	N	N	N	N
VERMONT								
Stafford	N	N	N	N	N	?	?	Y
Leahy	Y	Y	Y	N	Y	N	N	N
VIRGINIA								
Warner	N	N	N	N	N	N	N	N
Byrd*	N	N	N	N	N	N	N	N
WASHINGTON								
Gorton	N	N	N	N	N	N	N	N
Jackson	Y	Y	Y	Y	Y	Y	Y	Y
WEST VIRGINIA								
Byrd	Y	N	N	Y	Y	N	N	Y
Randolph	Y	Y	Y	Y	Y	Y	Y	Y
WISCONSIN								
Kasten	N	N	N	N	N	N	N	N
Proxmire	Y	N	N	N	N	N	N	N
WYOMING								
Simpson	N	N	N	N	N	N	N	N
Wallop	N	N	N	N	N	N	N	N

ND - Northern Democrats   SD - Southern Democrats (Southern states - Ala., Ark., Fla., Ga., Ky., La., Miss., N.C., Okla., S.C., Tenn., Texas, Va.)   *Byrd elected as an independent.

280. S J Res 58. Balanced Budget/Tax Limitation Amendment. Exon, D-Neb., amendment to require the president to send Congress a recommended statement of receipts and outlays, and if outlays are greater than receipts, the president must explain why. Rejected 45-52: R 4-48; D 41-4 (ND 28-2, SD 13-2), Aug. 3, 1982. A "nay" was a vote supporting the president's position.

281. S J Res 58. Balanced Budget/Tax Limitation Amendment. Hart, D-Colo., amendment to require Congress, by statute, to adopt a balanced capital budget covering such things as construction, education and research, and a balanced operating budget. Deficit spending would be allowed to ensure national security or during a depression. Rejected 23-74: R 1-51; D 22-23 (ND 19-11, SD 3-12), Aug. 3, 1982. A "nay" was a vote supporting the president's position.

282. S J Res 58. Balanced Budget/Tax Limitation Amendment. Tsongas, D-Mass., amendment to require the president to submit a balanced budget, and if not, to send Congress recommendations for balancing the budget. Rejected 23-72: R 1-49; D 22-23 (ND 19-11, SD 3-12), Aug. 3, 1982. A "nay" was a vote supporting the president's position.

283. S J Res 58. Balanced Budget/Tax Limitation Amendment. Levin, D-Mich., amendment to allow deficit spending by majority vote if Congress, by a three-fifths vote, declares a national emergency. Rejected 37-60: R 5-47; D 32-13 (ND 24-6, SD 8-7), Aug. 3, 1982. A "nay" was a vote supporting the president's position.

284. S J Res 58. Balanced Budget/Tax Limitation Amendment. Heflin, D-Ala., amendment to allow deficit spending to meet an "unforeseen and imminent threat to the national security." Rejected 47-51: R 8-44; D 39-7 (ND 27-4, SD 12-3), Aug. 3, 1982. A "nay" was a vote supporting the president's position.

285. S J Res 58. Balanced Budget/Tax Limitation Amendment. Bumpers, D-Ark., amendment including the provisions of S J Res 58 and adding three elements — requiring the president to submit a balanced budget; allowing deficit spending after Congress, by majority vote, declares an economic emergency; and restricting federal courts' powers to handle cases under the amendment. Rejected 32-65: R 6-45; D 26-20 (ND 17-14, SD 9-6), Aug. 3, 1982. A "nay" was a vote supporting the president's position.

286. S J Res 58. Balanced Budget/Tax Limitation Amendment. Biden, D-Del., amendment to restrict the growth of federal outlays for a fiscal year to the rate of increase in the gross national product in the last calendar year before the fiscal year. This provision could be waived by a three-fifths vote of Congress or if Congress or the president declares a national emergency. Rejected 10-85: R 0-51; D 10-34 (ND 9-22, SD 1-12), Aug. 3, 1982. A "nay" was a vote supporting the president's position.

287. S J Res 58. Balanced Budget/Tax Limitation Amendment. Cranston, D-Calif., amendment to exempt Social Security and veterans benefits from a balanced budget requirement and to allow a waiver if Congress or the president declares a national emergency. Rejected 27-73: R 5-49; D 22-24 (ND 20-11, SD 2-13), Aug. 4, 1982. A "nay" was a vote supporting the president's position.

KEY

Y Voted for (yea).
\# Paired for.
\+ Announced for.
N Voted against (nay).
X Paired against.
\- Announced against.
P Voted "present".
C Voted "present" to avoid possible conflict of interest.
? Did not vote or otherwise make a position known.

Democrats *Republicans*

	288	289	290	291	292	293	294	295
ALABAMA								
Denton	Y	N	N	Y	N	N	Y	Y
Heflin	Y	Y	Y	Y	Y	Y	N	N
ALASKA								
Murkowski	Y	N	N	Y	N	N	N	Y
Stevens	Y	N	N	Y	N	Y	N	N
ARIZONA								
Goldwater	Y	N	N	N	N	N	N	Y
DeConcini	Y	Y	Y	Y	Y	Y	N	N
ARKANSAS								
Bumpers	N	Y	Y	Y	Y	Y	N	N
Pryor	Y	Y	Y	Y	Y	Y	N	N
CALIFORNIA								
Hayakawa	Y	N	N	Y	N	N	N	Y
Cranston	N	Y	Y	Y	Y	Y	N	N
COLORADO								
Armstrong	Y	N	N	Y	N	N	C	Y
Hart	N	Y	Y	Y	Y	Y	N	N
CONNECTICUT								
Weicker	N	Y	Y	Y	Y	Y	N	N
Dodd	N	Y	N	Y	Y	?	N	N
DELAWARE								
Roth	Y	N	N	Y	N	N	N	Y
Biden	N	Y	Y	Y	Y	N	N	Y
FLORIDA								
Hawkins	Y	Y	N	Y	N	N	Y	Y
Chiles	Y	Y	Y	Y	Y	N	Y	N
GEORGIA								
Mattingly	Y	N	N	N	N	N	N	Y
Nunn	Y	N	N	Y	N	Y	N	N
HAWAII								
Inouye	N	Y	Y	Y	Y	Y	N	N
Matsunaga	N	Y	Y	Y	Y	Y	N	N
IDAHO								
McClure	Y	N	N	N	N	Y	Y	Y
Symms	Y	N	N	N	N	N	Y	Y
ILLINOIS								
Percy	Y	N	N	Y	N	N	Y	Y
Dixon	Y	Y	Y	Y	Y	N	N	N
INDIANA								
Lugar	Y	N	N	Y	N	Y	N	N
Quayle	Y	N	N	Y	N	N	N	N

	288	289	290	291	292	293	294	295
IOWA								
Grassley	Y	N	N	Y	N	Y	Y	N
Jepsen	Y	N	N	Y	Y	Y	Y	N
KANSAS								
Dole	Y	N	N	Y	N	Y	Y	Y
Kassebaum	N	N	N	Y	N	Y	N	N
KENTUCKY								
Ford	N	Y	Y	Y	N	Y	N	N
Huddleston	Y	Y	Y	Y	Y	Y	N	N
LOUISIANA								
Johnston	Y	N	N	N	N	Y	N	N
Long	Y	N	Y	N	N	Y	Y	N
MAINE								
Cohen	N	N	N	Y	N	Y	N	Y
Mitchell	N	Y	Y	Y	Y	N	N	N
MARYLAND								
Mathias	N	Y	N	Y	Y	Y	N	Y
Sarbanes	N	Y	Y	Y	Y	Y	N	N
MASSACHUSETTS								
Kennedy	N	Y	Y	Y	Y	Y	N	N
Tsongas	N	Y	Y	Y	Y	Y	N	N
MICHIGAN								
Levin	N	Y	Y	Y	Y	Y	N	N
Riegle	N	Y	Y	Y	Y	Y	N	N
MINNESOTA								
Boschwitz	Y	N	N	Y	N	Y	Y	N
Durenberger	Y	N	N	Y	N	Y	Y	N
MISSISSIPPI								
Cochran	Y	N	N	N	N	Y	N	Y
Stennis	Y	?	?	?	?	?	?	?
MISSOURI								
Danforth	Y	N	N	Y	N	Y	N	N
Eagleton	N	Y	Y	Y	Y	Y	N	N
MONTANA								
Baucus	N	Y	N	Y	N	Y	N	N
Melcher	Y	Y	Y	Y	Y	Y	Y	N
NEBRASKA								
Exon	Y	Y	Y	Y	N	Y	N	N
Zorinsky	Y	Y	Y	Y	N	Y	N	N
NEVADA								
Laxalt	Y	N	N	Y	N	N	Y	Y
Cannon	Y	Y	Y	Y	Y	N	N	N

	288	289	290	291	292	293	294	295
NEW HAMPSHIRE								
Humphrey	Y	N	N	N	N	N	Y	N
Rudman	Y	N	N	Y	N	N	N	Y
NEW JERSEY								
Brady	Y	N	N	Y	N	N	Y	N
Bradley	N	Y	Y	Y	Y	N	N	N
NEW MEXICO								
Domenici	Y	N	N	Y	N	N	N	N
Schmitt	Y	N	N	N	N	N	N	N
NEW YORK								
D'Amato	Y	N	N	Y	Y	Y	N	Y
Moynihan	N	Y	Y	Y	Y	Y	N	N
NORTH CAROLINA								
East	Y	N	N	N	N	Y	Y	N
Helms	Y	N	N	N	N	N	Y	Y
NORTH DAKOTA								
Andrews	Y	Y	N	Y	N	Y	N	N
Burdick	Y	Y	Y	Y	Y	Y	N	N
OHIO								
Glenn	N	Y	?	?	?	Y	N	N
Metzenbaum	N	Y	Y	Y	Y	Y	N	N
OKLAHOMA								
Nickles	Y	N	N	N	N	Y	Y	N
Boren	Y	N	Y	N	N	Y	N	N
OREGON								
Hatfield	Y	N	N	Y	N	N	N	Y
Packwood	Y	N	N	Y	N	N	N	Y
PENNSYLVANIA								
Heinz	N	Y	N	Y	Y	Y	N	Y
Specter	Y	Y	N	Y	Y	Y	Y	Y
RHODE ISLAND								
Chafee	N	N	N	Y	N	N	N	Y
Pell	N	Y	Y	Y	Y	N	N	N
SOUTH CAROLINA								
Thurmond	Y	N	N	Y	N	Y	Y	Y
Hollings	Y	N	Y	Y	Y	Y	N	N
SOUTH DAKOTA								
Abdnor	Y	N	N	N	N	Y	N	N
Pressler	Y	Y	N	Y	N	Y	N	N
TENNESSEE								
Baker	Y	N	?	?	?	N	Y	Y
Sasser	Y	Y	Y	Y	Y	Y	N	N

	288	289	290	291	292	293	294	295
TEXAS								
Tower	Y	N	N	Y	N	Y	N	Y
Bentsen	Y	Y	Y	Y	N	Y	Y	N
UTAH								
Garn	Y	N	N	Y	N	N	Y	Y
Hatch	Y	N	N	Y	N	Y	Y	Y
VERMONT								
Stafford	Y	Y	N	Y	Y	Y	N	Y
Leahy	N	Y	Y	Y	Y	Y	N	N
VIRGINIA								
Warner	Y	Y	N	Y	N	Y	N	N
Byrd*	Y	N	N	N	N	N	N	N
WASHINGTON								
Gorton	N	N	N	Y	N	Y	N	N
Jackson	N	Y	Y	Y	Y	Y	N	N
WEST VIRGINIA								
Byrd	Y	Y	Y	Y	Y	Y	N	N
Randolph	N	Y	Y	Y	Y	Y	N	N
WISCONSIN								
Kasten	Y	N	N	Y	N	Y	Y	Y
Proxmire	Y	N	N	Y	N	Y	N	N
WYOMING								
Simpson	Y	N	N	Y	N	N	N	Y
Wallop	Y	N	N	Y	N	Y	N	N

ND - Northern Democrats   SD - Southern Democrats (Southern states - Ala., Ark., Fla., Ga., Ky., La., Miss., N.C., Okla., S.C., Tenn., Texas, Va.)   *Byrd elected as an independent.

288. S J Res 58. Balanced Budget/Tax Limitation Amendment. Passage of the joint resolution to propose an amendment to the Constitution to require a balanced budget at the beginning of each fiscal year unless a three-fifths majority of Congress agreed to deficit spending. The amendment could be waived during the time of a declared war. Passed 69-31: R 47-7; D 22-24 (ND 9-22, SD 13-2), Aug. 4, 1982. A two-thirds majority of those present and voting (67 in this case) of both houses is required for passage of a joint resolution proposing an amendment to the Constitution. A "yea" was a vote supporting the president's position.

289. S 2774. Omnibus Reconciliation Act. Riegle, D-Mich., amendment to delete provisions that would impose a 4 percent cap on cost-of-living adjustments for federal and military retirees but retain the cap for members of Congress who retire after the date of the bill's enactment. Rejected 48-51: R 10-44; D 38-7 (ND 30-1, SD 8-6), Aug. 4, 1982.

290. S 2774. Omnibus Reconciliation Act. Mitchell, D-Maine, amendment to delete provisions that would impose a user fee on Veterans Administration home loan guarantees. Rejected 38-59: R 1-52; D 37-7 (ND 27-3, SD 10-4), Aug. 5, 1982.

291. S 2774. Omnibus Reconciliation Act. Metzenbaum, D-Ohio, amendment to express the sense of the Senate that conferees on the Tax Equity and Fiscal Responsibility Act (HR 4961) shall provide up to 13 weeks of additional unemployment benefits and ease restrictions on unemployment benefits enacted in 1981. Adopted 84-13: R 43-10; D 41-3 (ND 30-0, SD 11-3), Aug. 5, 1982.

292. S 2774. Omnibus Reconciliation Act. Kennedy, D-Mass., amendment to strike provisions that phase out by April 1985 college benefits for dependents of veterans with non-service connected disabilities. Rejected 40-57: R 7-46; D 33-11 (ND 26-4, SD 7-7), Aug. 5, 1982.

293. S 2774. Omnibus Reconciliation Act. Cochran, R-Miss., motion to table (kill) the Hawkins, R-Fla., amendment to lower the dairy price support level from the current level of $13.10 per hundredweight to $12.60 per hundredweight on the date of enactment and to $12.00 per hundredweight on Jan. 1, 1983. Motion agreed to 65-33: R 29-25; D 36-8 (ND 24-6, SD 12-2), Aug. 5, 1982.

294. S 2774. Omnibus Reconciliation Act. East, R-N.C., amendment to strike provisions that would reduce the size of the Federal Communications Commission from seven to five members. Rejected 27-71: R 23-30; D 4-41 (ND 1-30, SD 3-11), Aug. 5, 1982.

295. S 2774. Omnibus Reconciliation Act. Helms, R-N.C., motion to table (kill) the Boren, D-Okla., amendment to set up a program to pay farmers for not growing wheat, corn and feed grains. Motion rejected 33-66: R 32-22; D 1-44 (ND 1-30, SD 0-14), Aug. 5, 1982. (The Boren amendment subsequently was adopted by voice vote.)

	296	297	298	299	300	301
ALABAMA						
Denton	Y	N	Y	Y	N	Y
Heflin	N	Y	N	Y	N	Y
ALASKA						
Murkowski	Y	N	Y	Y	Y	Y
Stevens	Y	N	Y	Y	Y	Y
ARIZONA						
Goldwater	Y	N	Y	Y	Y	N
DeConcini	N	Y	N	Y	N	Y
ARKANSAS						
Bumpers	Y	Y	N	N	N	Y
Pryor	Y	Y	N	N	N	Y
CALIFORNIA						
Hayakawa	Y	N	Y	N	Y	Y
Cranston	N	Y	N	N	Y	Y
COLORADO						
Armstrong	Y	N	Y	Y	Y	Y
Hart	N	Y	N	N	N	Y
CONNECTICUT						
Weicker	N	N	Y	N	N	Y
Dodd	N	Y	N	?	Y	Y
DELAWARE						
Roth	Y	N	Y	Y	N	?
Biden	N	N	Y	Y	N	Y
FLORIDA						
Hawkins	Y	N	Y	N	N	Y
Chiles	N	Y	Y	Y	Y	Y
GEORGIA						
Mattingly	Y	N	Y	Y	Y	Y
Nunn	N	Y	N	Y	N	Y
HAWAII						
Inouye	N	Y	N	N	N	Y
Matsunaga	N	Y	N	N	Y	Y
IDAHO						
McClure	Y	N	Y	Y	Y	N
Symms	Y	N	Y	Y	Y	N
ILLINOIS						
Percy	Y	N	Y	Y	Y	Y
Dixon	N	N	Y	N	N	Y
INDIANA						
Lugar	N	N	Y	Y	Y	Y
Quayle	N	N	Y	Y	Y	Y

	296	297	298	299	300	301
IOWA						
Grassley	N	N	N	Y	N	Y
Jepsen	N	N	Y	Y	Y	Y
KANSAS						
Dole	Y	N	Y	Y	Y	Y
Kassebaum	N	N	Y	Y	Y	Y
KENTUCKY						
Ford	N	Y	N	Y	Y	Y
Huddleston	N	Y	N	Y	Y	Y
LOUISIANA						
Johnston	Y	Y	N	Y	Y	Y
Long	Y	Y	N	Y	Y	Y
MAINE						
Cohen	?	?	?	?	N	Y
Mitchell	N	N	Y	N	N	Y
MARYLAND						
Mathias	Y	N	Y	Y	?	?
Sarbanes	N	Y	N	N	N	Y
MASSACHUSETTS						
Kennedy	N	Y	N	N	N	Y
Tsongas	N	Y	N	Y	N	Y
MICHIGAN						
Levin	N	Y	N	N	N	Y
Riegle	N	Y	N	N	N	Y
MINNESOTA						
Boschwitz	N	Y	N	Y	N	Y
Durenberger	N	Y	N	Y	N	Y
MISSISSIPPI						
Cochran	Y	Y	N	Y	Y	Y
Stennis	?	?	?	?	Y	Y
MISSOURI						
Danforth	N	Y	N	Y	N	Y
Eagleton	N	Y	N	N	N	Y
MONTANA						
Baucus	N	Y	N	Y	Y	Y
Melcher	N	Y	N	Y	Y	Y
NEBRASKA						
Exon	N	Y	N	Y	N	Y
Zorinsky	N	Y	N	Y	N	Y
NEVADA						
Laxalt	Y	N	Y	Y	Y	Y
Cannon	N	Y	N	N	Y	Y

	296	297	298	299	300	301
NEW HAMPSHIRE						
Humphrey	N	N	Y	Y	N	Y
Rudman	Y	N	Y	Y	Y	Y
NEW JERSEY						
Brady	N	N	Y	?	Y	Y
Bradley	N	N	Y	N	Y	N
NEW MEXICO						
Domenici	N	N	Y	Y	Y	Y
Schmitt	N	N	Y	Y	Y	Y
NEW YORK						
D'Amato	Y	N	N	Y	Y	Y
Moynihan	N	Y	N	N	N	Y
NORTH CAROLINA						
East	Y	N	Y	Y	Y	N
Helms	Y	N	Y	Y	Y	Y
NORTH DAKOTA						
Andrews	N	Y	N	Y	Y	Y
Burdick	N	Y	N	Y	N	Y
OHIO						
Glenn	N	Y	N	N	Y	Y
Metzenbaum	N	Y	N	N	N	Y
OKLAHOMA						
Nickles	N	N	Y	N	Y	Y
Boren	N	Y	N	Y	N	Y
OREGON						
Hatfield	Y	N	Y	Y	N	Y
Packwood	Y	N	Y	Y	Y	Y
PENNSYLVANIA						
Heinz	Y	Y	N	Y	?	Y
Specter	Y	N	Y	Y	Y	Y
RHODE ISLAND						
Chafee	Y	N	Y	N	Y	Y
Pell	N	N	Y	Y	Y	Y
SOUTH CAROLINA						
Thurmond	Y	N	Y	Y	Y	Y
Hollings	N	Y	N	Y	Y	Y
SOUTH DAKOTA						
Abdnor	N	Y	N	Y	N	Y
Pressler	N	Y	N	Y	N	Y
TENNESSEE						
Baker	N	N	Y	Y	Y	?
Sasser	N	Y	N	Y	N	Y

	296	297	298	299	300	301
TEXAS						
Tower	Y	N	?	Y	Y	Y
Bentsen	N	Y	Y	Y	N	Y
UTAH						
Garn	Y	N	Y	Y	Y	Y
Hatch	Y	N	Y	Y	N	Y
VERMONT						
Stafford	Y	Y	N	Y	N	Y
Leahy	N	Y	N	Y	Y	Y
VIRGINIA						
Warner	Y	N	Y	Y	N	Y
Byrd*	N	N	Y	Y	N	Y
WASHINGTON						
Gorton	N	N	Y	Y	Y	Y
Jackson	N	Y	N	N	N	Y
WEST VIRGINIA						
Byrd	N	Y	N	N	N	Y
Randolph	N	Y	N	N	N	Y
WISCONSIN						
Kasten	Y	Y	N	Y	N	Y
Proxmire	N	Y	N	Y	N	Y
WYOMING						
Simpson	Y	N	Y	Y	N	Y
Wallop	Y	N	Y	Y	N	Y

ND - Northern Democrats   SD - Southern Democrats (Southern states - Ala., Ark., Fla., Ga., Ky., La., Miss., N.C., Okla., S.C., Tenn., Texas, Va.)

Byrd elected as an independent.

296. S 2774. Omnibus Reconciliation Act. Helms, R-N.C., substitute, to the Boren, D-Okla., amendment, to require a 5 percent paid land diversion on 1983 crops of wheat, feed grains and rice. Rejected 38-60: R 34-19; D 4-41 (ND 0-31, SD 4-10), Aug. 5, 1982. (The Boren amendment, to require the secretary of agriculture to offer a combination paid diversion/acreage reduction program for wheat, corn and feed grains, subsequently was adopted by voice vote.)

297. S 2774. Omnibus Reconciliation Act. Huddleston, D-Ky., motion to table (kill) the Hayakawa, R-Calif., amendment *(see vote 298, below)* to modify the dairy price support program so as to increase the price support level as production declines. Motion rejected 49-49: R 10-43; D 39-6 (ND 26-5, SD 13-1), Aug. 5, 1982.

298. S 2774. Omnibus Reconciliation Act. Hayakawa, R-Calif., amendment to modify the dairy price support program so as to increase the price support level as production declines. Rejected 48-49: R 40-12; D 8-37 (ND 5-26, SD 3-11), Aug. 5, 1982.

299. S 2774. Omnibus Reconciliation Act. Passage of the bill to reduce projected spending by $2.5 billion in outlays in fiscal 1983 and a total of $12.6 billion in outlays over fiscal years 1983-85 in compliance with reconciliation instructions in the fiscal 1983 budget resolution (S Con Res 92). Passed 72-24: R 49-3; D 23-21 (ND 11-19, SD 12-2), Aug. 5, 1982.

300. HR 6863. Supplemental Appropriations, Fiscal 1982. Hatfield, R-Ore., motion to table (kill) the Proxmire, D-Wis., appeal of the chair's ruling that the Proxmire amendment to delete $736,400 for a third gymnasium for senators in a nearly completed new Senate office building was out of order. Motion agreed to 50-48: R 32-20; D 18-28 (ND 11-20, SD 7-8), Aug. 10, 1982.

301. HR 6863. Supplemental Appropriations, Fiscal 1982. Weicker, R-Conn., amendment expressing the sense of Congress that proposed Reagan administration changes in regulations on educating handicapped children should not become effective until after Congress has an opportunity to vote down the rules, either in a post-election session in 1982 or at the beginning of 1983. Adopted 93-4: R 47-4; D 46-0 (ND 31-0, SD 15-0), Aug. 10, 1982.

	302 303 304 305 306 307 308 309		302 303 304 305 306 307 308 309		302 303 304 305 306 307 308 309	KEY
ALABAMA		**IOWA**		**NEW HAMPSHIRE**		Y Voted for (yea).
Denton	Y N Y N Y Y N Y	Grassley	Y N Y N Y Y N Y	Humphrey	Y N Y N Y Y N N	# Paired for.
Heflin	N Y Y N Y Y N Y	Jepsen	Y N Y N Y Y N Y	Rudman	Y N Y N Y Y N Y	+ Announced for.
ALASKA		**KANSAS**		**NEW JERSEY**		N Voted against (nay).
Murkowski	Y N Y N Y Y N Y	Dole	Y N Y N Y Y N Y	Brady	Y N Y N Y N N ?	X Paired against.
Stevens	Y N Y N Y Y N Y	Kassebaum	Y N Y N Y N Y Y	Bradley	N Y N N N N Y Y	− Announced against.
ARIZONA		**KENTUCKY**		**NEW MEXICO**		P Voted "present".
Goldwater	Y N Y N Y Y N Y	Ford	N Y N Y N N Y Y	Domenici	Y N Y N Y Y N Y	C Voted "present" to avoid possi-
DeConcini	N Y ? N Y Y N Y	Huddleston	N Y N Y ? N Y Y	Schmitt	Y N Y N Y Y N Y	ble conflict of interest.
ARKANSAS		**LOUISIANA**		**NEW YORK**		? Did not vote or otherwise make a
Bumpers	N Y N Y N N Y Y	Johnston	N Y N Y N Y N Y	D'Amato	Y N Y N Y Y N Y	position known.
Pryor	N Y N N N N Y Y	Long	N Y N Y Y Y N Y	Moynihan	N Y N Y N N Y Y	
CALIFORNIA		**MAINE**		**NORTH CAROLINA**		Democrats *Republicans*
Hayakawa	Y N Y N Y Y N Y	Cohen	Y N Y N Y Y N Y	East	Y N Y N Y Y N Y	
Cranston	N Y N Y N N Y Y	Mitchell	N Y N N Y N Y Y	Helms	Y N Y N Y Y N N	
COLORADO		**MARYLAND**		**NORTH DAKOTA**		
Armstrong	Y N Y N Y Y N Y	Mathias	? ? ? ? N N Y Y	Andrews	Y N Y N Y Y N Y	302 303 304 305 306 307 308 309
Hart	N Y N ? N N Y Y	Sarbanes	N Y ? ? ? N Y Y	Burdick	N Y N N Y Y N Y	
CONNECTICUT		**MASSACHUSETTS**		**OHIO**		**TEXAS**	
Weicker	Y N Y Y N N Y Y	Kennedy	N Y N N Y N Y Y	Glenn	N Y N N N N Y Y	Tower	Y N Y N Y Y N Y
Dodd	N Y N Y ? N Y Y	Tsongas	N Y N Y N N Y Y	Metzenbaum	N Y N N N N Y Y	Bentsen	N Y N N Y Y N Y
DELAWARE		**MICHIGAN**		**OKLAHOMA**		**UTAH**	
Roth	Y N N N ? ? ? Y	Levin	N + − + Y N Y Y	Nickles	Y N Y N Y Y N Y	Garn	Y N Y N Y Y N Y
Biden	N Y N Y N N Y Y	Riegle	N ? − + N N Y Y	Boren	N Y N N Y N Y Y	Hatch	Y N Y N Y Y N Y
FLORIDA		**MINNESOTA**		**OREGON**		**VERMONT**	
Hawkins	Y N Y N Y Y N Y	Boschwitz	Y N Y N Y Y N Y	Hatfield	Y N Y N N N Y Y	Stafford	N N Y N N Y N Y
Chiles	N Y N N Y Y N Y	Durenberger	Y N Y Y N N Y Y	Packwood	Y N Y N N N Y Y	Leahy	N Y N Y N N Y Y
GEORGIA		**MISSISSIPPI**		**PENNSYLVANIA**		**VIRGINIA**	
Mattingly	Y N Y N Y Y N Y	Cochran	Y N Y N Y Y N Y	Heinz	Y N Y N Y N Y Y	Warner	Y N Y N Y Y N Y
Nunn	N ? Y N Y N Y Y	Stennis	N Y N Y Y N Y Y	Specter	Y N Y N Y N Y Y	Byrd*	N Y N N Y N Y N
HAWAII		**MISSOURI**		**RHODE ISLAND**		**WASHINGTON**	
Inouye	Y N Y Y N N Y Y	Danforth	Y N Y N Y Y N Y	Chafee	Y N Y N Y N Y Y	Gorton	Y N Y N Y N Y Y
Matsunaga	N Y N Y N N Y Y	Eagleton	N Y N Y N N Y Y	Pell	N Y N N Y N Y Y	Jackson	N Y N Y Y N Y Y
IDAHO		**MONTANA**		**SOUTH CAROLINA**		**WEST VIRGINIA**	
McClure	Y N Y N Y Y N Y	Baucus	N Y N Y N N N Y	Thurmond	Y N Y N Y Y N Y	Byrd	N Y N N N Y N Y
Symms	Y N Y N Y Y N Y	Melcher	N Y N N Y N Y Y	Hollings	N Y N N Y N Y Y	Randolph	N Y N N Y Y N Y
ILLINOIS		**NEBRASKA**		**SOUTH DAKOTA**		**WISCONSIN**	
Percy	Y N Y Y N N Y Y	Exon	N Y N Y N Y N Y	Abdnor	Y N Y N Y Y N Y	Kasten	Y N Y N Y N N Y
Dixon	N Y N Y N N Y Y	Zorinsky	N Y N N Y N Y Y	Pressler	Y N Y N Y Y N Y	Proxmire	N Y N Y N N Y Y
INDIANA		**NEVADA**		**TENNESSEE**		**WYOMING**	
Lugar	Y N Y N Y Y N Y	Laxalt	Y N Y N Y Y N Y	Baker	Y N Y N Y N N Y	Simpson	Y N Y N Y N N Y
Quayle	Y N Y N Y Y N Y	Cannon	N Y N N Y N Y Y	Sasser	N Y N N Y N Y Y	Wallop	Y N Y N Y Y N Y

ND - Northern Democrats   SD - Southern Democrats (Southern states - Ala., Ark., Fla., Ga., Ky., La., Miss., N.C., Okla., S.C., Tenn., Texas, Va.)   *Byrd elected as an independent.*

302. HR 6863. Supplemental Appropriations, Fiscal 1982. Judgment of the Senate whether the Appropriations Committee amendment to fund the president's Caribbean Basin Initiative was germane and could remain in the bill. Ruled germane 53-46: R 52-1; D 1-45 (ND 1-30, SD 0-15), Aug. 10, 1982.

303. HR 6863. Supplemental Appropriations, Fiscal 1982. Leahy, D-Vt., amendment to delete approximately $600 million for foreign economic and military aid. Rejected 42-54: R 0-53; D 42-1 (ND 28-1, SD 14-0), Aug. 10, 1982. A "nay" was a vote supporting the president's position.

304. HR 6863. Supplemental Appropriations, Fiscal 1982. Kasten, R-Wis., motion to table (kill) the Dodd, D-Conn., amendment to reduce by one-half funding for the president's Caribbean Basin Initiative. Motion agreed to 55-40: R 52-1; D 3-39 (ND 1-26, SD 2-13), Aug. 10, 1982. A "yea" was a vote supporting the president's position.

305. HR 6863. Supplemental Appropriations, Fiscal 1982. Percy, R-Ill., motion to table (kill) the Symms, R-Idaho, amendment to declare it U.S. policy to block Cuban expansionism by whatever means necessary, including military force. Motion rejected 30-65: R 8-45; D 22-20 (ND 16-11, SD 6-9), Aug. 10, 1982. A "nay" was a vote supporting the president's position.

306. HR 6863. Supplemental Appropriations, Fiscal 1982. Symms, R-Idaho, amendment to state that it would be U.S. policy to oppose Cuban expansionism in the Western Hemisphere by any means necessary, including the use of force; to prevent the creation of an externally supported military capability in Cuba that could endanger U.S. security; and to support "the aspirations of the Cuban people for self-determination." Adopted 68-28: R 45-8; D 23-20 (ND 12-17, SD 11-3), Aug. 11, 1982. A "yea" was a vote supporting the president's position.

307. HR 6863. Supplemental Appropriations, Fiscal 1982. Helms, R-N.C., motion to table (kill) the Percy, R-Ill., amendment to replace the Symms, R-Idaho, amendment on U.S. policy toward Cuba (see vote 306, above) with less forceful language. Motion rejected 48-51: R 38-15; D 10-36 (ND 5-26, SD 5-10), Aug. 11, 1982.

308. HR 6863. Supplemental Appropriations, Fiscal 1982. Percy, R-Ill., amendment to replace the Symms, R-Idaho, amendment (see vote 306, above) with less forceful language. Rejected 47-52: R 12-41; D 35-11 (ND 26-5, SD 9-6), Aug. 11, 1982.

309. HR 6863. Supplemental Appropriations, Fiscal 1982. Schmitt, R-N.M., amendment to provide "such funds as may be necessary" for extended unemployment benefits expected to be authorized by Congress later in August. Adopted 96-3: R 51-2; D 45-1 (ND 31-0, SD 14-1), Aug. 11, 1982.

	310	311	312	313	314	315	316	317
ALABAMA								
Denton	Y	Y	N	N	N	Y	Y	Y
Heflin	Y	Y	N	Y	Y	Y	Y	Y
ALASKA								
Murkowski	Y	Y	N	N	N	N	Y	N
Stevens	Y	Y	N	N	N	N	Y	N
ARIZONA								
Goldwater	Y	N	N	N	N	N	Y	N
DeConcini	Y	Y	N	Y	Y	N	N	Y
ARKANSAS								
Bumpers	N	Y	Y	Y	Y	N	Y	Y
Pryor	Y	Y	N	N	N	N	Y	Y
CALIFORNIA								
Hayakawa	Y	Y	Y	N	N	N	Y	N
Cranston	N	Y	Y	Y	Y	N	N	N
COLORADO								
Armstrong	N	Y	N	N	N	Y	Y	Y
Hart	N	Y	Y	Y	Y	N	N	N
CONNECTICUT								
Weicker	N	Y	Y	Y	Y	N	Y	N
Dodd	N	Y	Y	Y	Y	N	N	N
DELAWARE								
Roth	Y	Y	N	N	N	N	Y	Y
Biden	N	Y	Y	Y	Y	N	Y	N
FLORIDA								
Hawkins	Y	Y	N	N	N	N	Y	Y
Chiles	Y	Y	N	N	Y	N	Y	Y
GEORGIA								
Mattingly	Y	Y	N	N	N	N	Y	#
Nunn	N	Y	N	N	N	N	Y	Y
HAWAII								
Inouye	Y	Y	Y	Y	Y	N	N	N
Matsunaga	Y	Y	Y	Y	Y	N	Y	N
IDAHO								
McClure	N	Y	N	N	N	Y	Y	N
Symms	N	Y	N	N	N	Y	Y	N
ILLINOIS								
Percy	N	Y	N	Y	Y	Y	N	Y
Dixon	N	Y	Y	Y	Y	N	N	N
INDIANA								
Lugar	N	Y	N	N	N	N	Y	N
Quayle	Y	Y	N	N	N	N	Y	N
IOWA								
Grassley	N	Y	N	N	N	N	Y	Y
Jepsen	Y	Y	N	N	N	Y	Y	N
KANSAS								
Dole	Y	Y	N	N	N	N	Y	N
Kassebaum	Y	Y	N	N	N	N	Y	Y
KENTUCKY								
Ford	Y	Y	N	N	Y	Y	N	Y
Huddleston	Y	Y	N	N	N	N	Y	Y
LOUISIANA								
Johnston	Y	Y	N	N	N	N	Y	Y
Long	N	Y	N	N	N	Y	Y	Y
MAINE								
Cohen	Y	Y	N	N	N	Y	Y	Y
Mitchell	N	Y	Y	Y	Y	N	Y	N
MARYLAND								
Mathias	Y	Y	N	N	N	N	Y	N
Sarbanes	N	Y	Y	Y	Y	N	N	N
MASSACHUSETTS								
Kennedy	N	Y	Y	Y	Y	N	N	N
Tsongas	N	Y	Y	Y	Y	N	N	N
MICHIGAN								
Levin	N	Y	Y	Y	Y	N	N	N
Riegle	N	Y	Y	Y	Y	N	Y	N
MINNESOTA								
Boschwitz	N	Y	Y	Y	Y	N	Y	N
Durenberger	Y	Y	N	N	N	N	Y	N
MISSISSIPPI								
Cochran	Y	Y	N	N	N	N	Y	Y
Stennis	N	Y	N	N	N	N	Y	Y
MISSOURI								
Danforth	Y	Y	N	N	N	N	Y	N
Eagleton	N	Y	Y	Y	Y	N	Y	N
MONTANA								
Baucus	Y	Y	N	N	N	N	Y	N
Melcher	Y	Y	Y	Y	Y	N	Y	N
NEBRASKA								
Exon	N	Y	N	N	Y	Y	Y	N
Zorinsky	N	Y	N	N	N	Y	N	Y
NEVADA								
Laxalt	Y	Y	N	N	N	N	Y	N
Cannon	Y	Y	Y	Y	Y	N	Y	Y
NEW HAMPSHIRE								
Humphrey	N	Y	N	N	N	Y	Y	Y
Rudman	Y	Y	N	N	N	N	Y	Y
NEW JERSEY								
Brady	?	?	N	N	N	N	Y	N
Bradley	N	Y	Y	Y	Y	N	Y	N
NEW MEXICO								
Domenici	Y	Y	N	N	Y	N	Y	N
Schmitt	Y	Y	N	N	N	N	Y	N
NEW YORK								
D'Amato	Y	Y	Y	Y	Y	N	Y	N
Moynihan	N	Y	Y	Y	Y	N	N	N
NORTH CAROLINA								
East	Y	N	N	N	N	Y	Y	Y
Helms	Y	Y	N	N	N	Y	Y	Y
NORTH DAKOTA								
Andrews	Y	Y	N	N	N	N	Y	N
Burdick	N	Y	N	N	N	N	Y	N
OHIO								
Glenn	N	Y	Y	Y	Y	N	Y	N
Metzenbaum	N	Y	Y	Y	Y	N	N	N
OKLAHOMA								
Nickles	N	Y	N	N	N	Y	Y	N
Boren	Y	Y	N	Y	N	Y	Y	Y
OREGON								
Hatfield	N	Y	N	N	N	N	Y	X
Packwood	Y	Y	N	N	N	N	Y	N
PENNSYLVANIA								
Heinz	Y	Y	N	Y	Y	N	Y	N
Specter	Y	Y	Y	Y	Y	N	N	N
RHODE ISLAND								
Chafee	N	Y	Y	Y	Y	N	Y	N
Pell	N	Y	Y	Y	Y	N	Y	N
SOUTH CAROLINA								
Thurmond	Y	Y	N	N	N	N	Y	N
Hollings	N	Y	N	N	Y	N	Y	N
SOUTH DAKOTA								
Abdnor	Y	Y	N	N	N	N	Y	N
Pressler	Y	Y	N	N	N	?	Y	Y
TENNESSEE								
Baker	Y	Y	N	N	N	N	Y	N
Sasser	Y	Y	N	N	N	N	Y	Y
TEXAS								
Tower	N	Y	N	N	N	N	Y	N
Bentsen	N	Y	N	Y	N	Y	N	Y
UTAH								
Garn	Y	Y	N	N	N	N	Y	N
Hatch	Y	Y	N	N	N	N	Y	N
VERMONT								
Stafford	Y	Y	N	N	N	N	Y	N
Leahy	N	Y	Y	Y	Y	N	Y	N
VIRGINIA								
Warner	N	Y	N	N	N	N	Y	Y
Byrd*	N	Y	N	N	N	Y	Y	Y
WASHINGTON								
Gorton	Y	Y	N	N	N	N	Y	N
Jackson	Y	Y	N	Y	Y	N	Y	N
WEST VIRGINIA								
Byrd	Y	Y	N	Y	Y	N	Y	Y
Randolph	Y	Y	N	N	N	N	Y	Y
WISCONSIN								
Kasten	Y	Y	N	Y	Y	N	Y	N
Proxmire	N	Y	Y	N	N	N	Y	N
WYOMING								
Simpson	Y	Y	N	N	N	N	Y	N
Wallop	N	Y	N	N	N	N	Y	Y

KEY

Y Voted for (yea).
\# Paired for.
+ Announced for.
N Voted against (nay).
X Paired against.
- Announced against.
P Voted "present".
C Voted "present" to avoid possible conflict of interest.
? Did not vote or otherwise make a position known.

Democrats *Republicans*

ND - Northern Democrats   SD - Southern Democrats (Southern states - Ala., Ark., Fla., Ga., Ky., La., Miss., N.C., Okla., S.C., Tenn., Texas, Va.)   *Byrd elected as an independent.

310. HR 6863. Supplemental Appropriations, Fiscal 1982. Schmitt, R-N.M., amendment to provide that proceeds from the sale of materials in the National Defense Stockpile be used to purchase copper, mined and smelted in the United States after July 31, 1982, for the stockpile. Adopted 55-44: R 38-15; D 17-29 (ND 9-22, SD 8-7), Aug. 11, 1982.

311. HR 6863. Supplemental Appropriations, Fiscal 1982. Bumpers, D-Ark., amendment to make clear that nothing in the bill changes or affects any standards or procedures established by the National Security Act of 1947, the Foreign Assistance Act of 1961 or the War Powers Resolution of 1973, and that the bill does not constitute authorization for the use of U.S. military forces. The amendment was aimed at the Symms, R-Idaho, amendment *(see vote 306, p. 51-S)*. Adopted 97-2: R 51-2; D 46-0 (ND 31-0, SD 15-0), Aug. 11, 1982.

312. S 2222. Immigration Reform and Control Act. Kennedy, D-Mass., amendment to restore current law by deleting a provision in the bill that would reduce the number of available family reunification visas by the number of immediate relatives of U.S. citizens admitted in the previous fiscal year. Rejected 30-70: R 6-48; D 24-22 (ND 23-8, SD 1-14), Aug. 12, 1982. A "nay" was a vote supporting the president's position.

313. S 2222. Immigration Reform and Control Act. Kennedy, D-Mass., amendment to restore current law by giving a visa preference for adult unmarried sons and daughters of permanent residents. Rejected 37-63: R 8-46; D 29-17 (ND 25-6, SD 4-11), Aug. 12, 1982. A "nay" was a vote supporting the president's position.

314. S 2222. Immigration Reform and Control Act. Kennedy, D-Mass., amendment to restore current law by giving a visa preference to unmarried brothers and sisters of certain U.S. citizens. Rejected 41-59: R 9-45; D 32-14 (ND 26-5, SD 6-9), Aug. 12, 1982. A "nay" was a vote supporting the president's position.

315. S 2222. Immigration Reform and Control Act. Helms, R-N.C., amendment to delete provisions granting amnesty to illegal aliens already in the United States who meet certain conditions. Rejected 17-82: R 10-43; D 7-39 (ND 2-29, SD 5-10), Aug. 12, 1982. A "nay" was a vote supporting the president's position.

316. S 2222. Immigration Reform and Control Act. Grassley, R-Iowa, amendment to move from Jan. 1, 1978, to Jan. 1, 1977, the date by which illegal aliens must have entered the United States to gain immediate eligibility to become permanent residents. The amendment also bars these permanent residents from obtaining federal benefits for three years. The amendment would move from Jan. 1, 1982, to Jan. 1, 1980, the date by which aliens had to enter the United States to qualify as temporary residents. It requires these temporary residents to wait three years before applying to become permanent residents. Finally, the amendment establishes a block grant program to reimburse states for costs associated with the aliens. Adopted 84-16: R 52-2; D 32-14 (ND 18-13, SD 14-1), Aug. 12, 1982. A "yea" was a vote supporting the president's position.

317. S 2222. Immigration Reform and Control Act. Huddleston, D-Ky., amendment to include refugee admissions within the annual immigration cap of 425,000. In the past, refugee admissions have not been part of quotas for immigrants, who come to the United States voluntarily, as opposed to refugees, who are fleeing persecution in their homelands. Rejected 35-63: R 17-35; D 18-28 (ND 5-26, SD 13-2), Aug. 12, 1982. A "nay" was a vote supporting the president's position.

	318	319	320	321	322	323	324	325
ALABAMA								
Denton	Y	N	N	N	Y	N	N	Y
Heflin	Y	N	N	N	Y	N	N	Y
ALASKA								
Murkowski	Y	?	?	?	?	N	N	N
Stevens	Y	N	Y	N	N	N	N	N
ARIZONA								
Goldwater	Y	N	N	N	N	Y	N	N
DeConcini	N	N	N	N	Y	N	Y	Y
ARKANSAS								
Bumpers	Y	N	N	N	Y	N	Y	Y
Pryor	Y	N	N	N	Y	N	Y	Y
CALIFORNIA								
Hayakawa	Y	?	Y	N	N	Y	Y	Y
Cranston	N	Y	N	Y	N	N	Y	N
COLORADO								
Armstrong	Y	N	Y	N	N	Y	Y	Y
Hart	N	Y	N	Y	Y	N	Y	N
CONNECTICUT								
Weicker	N	?	?	?	?	N	N	N
Dodd	N	Y	Y	N	?	N	Y	Y
DELAWARE								
Roth	Y	N	Y	N	Y	N	Y	Y
Biden	N	Y	Y	N	N	N	Y	Y
FLORIDA								
Hawkins	Y	N	Y	N	N	Y	N	Y
Chiles	N	N	Y	N	Y	N	Y	Y
GEORGIA								
Mattingly	Y	N	Y	N	N	N	N	Y
Nunn	Y	N	N	N	Y	N	N	Y
HAWAII								
Inouye	N	Y	N	Y	Y	N	N	Y
Matsunaga	N	N	N	Y	N	N	N	Y
IDAHO								
McClure	Y	N	Y	Y	Y	Y	Y	Y
Symms	?	N	Y	Y	N	Y	Y	Y
ILLINOIS								
Percy	Y	Y	N	N	N	N	N	Y
Dixon	N	Y	N	Y	N	Y	Y	Y
INDIANA								
Lugar	Y	N	N	N	N	N	N	Y
Quayle	Y	N	Y	N	N	N	N	Y
IOWA								
Grassley	Y	N	N	N	Y	N	N	N
Jepsen	Y	N	Y	N	N	N	Y	Y
KANSAS								
Dole	N	-	N	N	N	N	N	Y
Kassebaum	Y	N	Y	N	N	N	N	Y
KENTUCKY								
Ford	Y	N	N	N	Y	?	?	?
Huddleston	Y	N	N	N	Y	N	N	Y
LOUISIANA								
Johnston	Y	Y	N	N	Y	N	N	Y
Long	Y	Y	N	N	Y	N	N	Y
MAINE								
Cohen	Y	Y	Y	N	?	N	N	Y
Mitchell	N	Y	Y	Y	Y	N	N	Y
MARYLAND								
Mathias	N	?	?	?	?	N	N	N
Sarbanes	N	Y	Y	N	N	N	Y	Y
MASSACHUSETTS								
Kennedy	N	Y	N	Y	N	N	Y	N
Tsongas	N	Y	N	Y	N	N	Y	N
MICHIGAN								
Levin	N	Y	N	N	Y	N	N	Y
Riegle	N	Y	Y	Y	Y	N	Y	N
MINNESOTA								
Boschwitz	Y	N	Y	N	N	Y	Y	Y
Durenberger	N	N	N	N	N	N	N	N
MISSISSIPPI								
Cochran	N	N	N	N	N	N	N	N
Stennis	Y	N	N	N	Y	N	Y	Y
MISSOURI								
Danforth	Y	Y	N	N	N	N	N	Y
Eagleton	N	N	N	N	Y	N	N	Y
MONTANA								
Baucus	N	N	N	N	N	N	N	Y
Melcher	N	N	?	N	N	N	N	Y
NEBRASKA								
Exon	Y	N	Y	Y	Y	N	Y	Y
Zorinsky	Y	N	Y	N	Y	N	Y	Y
NEVADA								
Laxalt	Y	N	N	N	N	Y	Y	Y
Cannon	N	?	?	?	?	N	Y	Y
NEW HAMPSHIRE								
Humphrey	C	N	Y	N	N	N	N	Y
Rudman	Y	N	N	Y	N	Y	N	Y
NEW JERSEY								
Brady	Y	N	N	N	?	N	N	N
Bradley	Y	Y	Y	N	N	N	Y	Y
NEW MEXICO								
Domenici	Y	N	N	N	N	N	N	Y
Schmitt	Y	?	?	?	?	Y	Y	N
NEW YORK								
D'Amato	N	N	Y	Y	Y	N	Y	Y
Moynihan	N	Y	Y	N	Y	N	Y	Y
NORTH CAROLINA								
East	Y	N	Y	N	Y	N	Y	Y
Helms	Y	N	N	N	Y	Y	Y	Y
NORTH DAKOTA								
Andrews	N	N	N	N	N	N	N	Y
Burdick	N	N	N	N	N	N	N	Y
OHIO								
Glenn	Y	Y	N	Y	N	Y	N	N
Metzenbaum	N	Y	N	Y	N	N	Y	Y
OKLAHOMA								
Nickles	Y	N	Y	Y	Y	N	Y	Y
Boren	Y	N	Y	Y	Y	Y	Y	Y
OREGON								
Hatfield	?	-	-	-	-	Y	Y	Y
Packwood	N	N	N	N	N	N	N	Y
PENNSYLVANIA								
Heinz	N	Y	Y	Y	N	N	N	Y
Specter	N	Y	Y	Y	N	N	N	N
RHODE ISLAND								
Chafee	Y	Y	N	Y	Y	N	Y	N
Pell	Y	Y	Y	Y	N	N	N	Y
SOUTH CAROLINA								
Thurmond	Y	N	N	N	N	N	N	Y
Hollings	Y	N	N	N	?	N	Y	Y
SOUTH DAKOTA								
Abdnor	Y	N	Y	N	N	N	N	Y
Pressler	N	N	N	N	Y	Y	Y	Y
TENNESSEE								
Baker	Y	N	N	N	N	N	N	N
Sasser	N	Y	Y	N	Y	N	N	Y

	318	319	320	321	322	323	324	325
TEXAS								
Tower	Y	N	N	N	N	Y	Y	N
Bentsen	N	N	N	?	?	N	Y	Y
UTAH								
Garn	Y	N	N	N	N	Y	Y	Y
Hatch	Y	?	?	?	?	Y	Y	Y
VERMONT								
Stafford	N	N	N	N	?	N	N	Y
Leahy	Y	N	N	N	N	N	N	Y
VIRGINIA								
Warner	Y	N	N	N	N	Y	N	Y
Byrd*	Y	N	N	N	Y	N	Y	Y
WASHINGTON								
Gorton	Y	N	N	N	N	N	N	Y
Jackson	N	Y	Y	N	Y	N	Y	Y
WEST VIRGINIA								
Byrd	N	N	Y	N	N	N	N	Y
Randolph	Y	N	N	N	Y	N	N	Y
WISCONSIN								
Kasten	Y	N	Y	N	N	Y	N	Y
Proxmire	Y	Y	N	N	N	N	N	Y
WYOMING								
Simpson	Y	N	N	N	N	N	N	N
Wallop	Y	?	?	?	?	N	Y	Y

KEY

Y	Voted for (yea).
#	Paired for.
+	Announced for.
N	Voted against (nay).
X	Paired against.
-	Announced against.
P	Voted "present".
C	Voted "present" to avoid possible conflict of interest.
?	Did not vote or otherwise make a position known.

Democrats   *Republicans*

ND - Northern Democrats   SD - Southern Democrats (Southern states - Ala., Ark., Fla., Ga., Ky., La., Miss., N.C., Okla., S.C., Tenn., Texas, Va.)   *Byrd elected as an independent.*

318. HR 5930. Aviation Insurance Program. Judgment of the Senate affirming the chair's ruling that a point of order can be made against the conference report because new material beyond the scope of the conference was added. Ruling of the chair upheld (thus recommitting the bill to conference) 59-38: R 39-12; D 20-26 (ND 8-23, SD 12-3), Aug. 12, 1982.

319. S 2222. Immigration Reform and Control Act. Kennedy, D-Mass., amendment to delete provisions that would revise and expand the existing temporary worker program. Rejected 28-62: R 6-39; D 22-23 (ND 19-11, SD 3-12), Aug. 13, 1982. A "nay" was a vote supporting the president's position.

320. S 2222. Immigration Reform and Control Act. D'Amato, R-N.Y., amendment to allow U.S. citizens to bring in brothers and sisters who have legally applied for and been given visas to enter the United States ahead of relatives of present illegal aliens who would be granted permanent resident status under S 2222. Rejected 38-53: R 22-25; D 16-28 (ND 13-16, SD 3-12), Aug. 13, 1982. A "nay" was a vote supporting the president's position.

321. S 2222. Immigration Reform and Control Act. Kennedy, D-Mass., amendment to terminate employer sanctions after three years unless the president certifies such sanctions have not resulted in discrimination. Rejected 22-69: R 8-39; D 14-30 (ND 13-17, SD 1-13), Aug. 13, 1982. A "nay" was a vote supporting the president's position.

322. S 2222. Immigration Reform and Control Act. Bumpers, D-Ark., amendment to require the president, except in "emergency" situations, to notify Congress if he wants to admit more than 75,000 refugees to the United States in a year and to give Congress 30 days in which to disapprove such a proposal. Rejected 41-45: R 13-31; D 28-14 (ND 15-14, SD 13-0), Aug. 13, 1982. A "nay" was a vote supporting the president's position.

323. S 2222. Immigration Reform and Control Act. Hayakawa, R-Calif., amendment to create a Mexican guest worker program that would allow Mexican workers to stay in the United States up to 180 days. Rejected 16-83: R 15-39; D 1-44 (ND 0-31, SD 1-13), Aug. 17, 1982. A "nay" was a vote supporting the president's position.

324. S 2222. Immigration Reform and Control Act. Hayakawa, R-Calif., amendment to require officers of the Immigration and Naturalization Service to have a warrant before entering a farm or other agricultural operation. Rejected 46-53: R 22-32; D 24-21 (ND 16-15, SD 8-6), Aug. 17, 1982. A "nay" was a vote supporting the president's position.

325. S 2222. Immigration Reform and Control Act. Hayakawa, R-Calif., amendment to express the sense of the Congress that English be declared the official language of the United States. Adopted 78-21: R 37-17; D 41-4 (ND 27-4, SD 14-0), Aug. 17, 1982. A "nay" was a vote supporting the president's position.

	326	327	328	329	330	331	332	333
ALABAMA								
Denton	N	N	Y	Y	Y	Y	Y	Y
Heflin	Y	Y	Y	N	Y	Y	Y	Y
ALASKA								
Murkowski	Y	N	N	Y	Y	Y	Y	Y
Stevens	Y	Y	N	Y	Y	Y	Y	Y
ARIZONA								
Goldwater	N	Y	Y	Y	Y	Y	Y	N
DeConcini	N	N	N	N	Y	Y	Y	Y
ARKANSAS								
Bumpers	Y	N	Y	Y	Y	N	N	Y
Pryor	Y	Y	N	Y	Y	N	Y	Y
CALIFORNIA								
Hayakawa	Y	Y	Y	N	Y	Y	?	Y
Cranston	Y	N	N	N	Y	Y	N	Y
COLORADO								
Armstrong	N	N	Y	N	Y	Y	Y	?
Hart	Y	N	N	N	N	N	N	Y
CONNECTICUT								
Weicker	Y	N	Y	Y	Y	Y	Y	N
Dodd	Y	N	Y	Y	Y	Y	N	Y
DELAWARE								
Roth	Y	N	N	Y	Y	Y	?	N
Biden	Y	N	Y	Y	Y	Y	N	Y
FLORIDA								
Hawkins	N	N	N	Y	Y	Y	Y	Y
Chiles	N	N	N	Y	Y	Y	Y	Y
GEORGIA								
Mattingly	Y	N	N	Y	Y	Y	Y	Y
Nunn	N	N	N	Y	Y	Y	Y	Y
HAWAII								
Inouye	Y	N	N	Y	Y	Y	N	N
Matsunaga	Y	N	N	Y	Y	N	N	?
IDAHO								
McClure	N	Y	N	N	Y	N	Y	N
Symms	N	Y	N	N	Y	Y	Y	Y
ILLINOIS								
Percy	Y	N	N	Y	Y	Y	Y	Y
Dixon	Y	N	N	Y	Y	Y	?	?
INDIANA								
Lugar	Y	N	N	Y	Y	Y	Y	Y
Quayle	Y	N	N	Y	Y	Y	Y	N

	326	327	328	329	330	331	332	333
IOWA								
Grassley	N	N	N	Y	Y	Y	Y	Y
Jepsen	N	Y	N	Y	Y	Y	Y	Y
KANSAS								
Dole	Y	Y	N	Y	Y	Y	Y	Y
Kassebaum	Y	N	N	Y	N	Y	N	Y
KENTUCKY								
Ford	?	?	?	?	?	?	?	Y
Huddleston	Y	N	Y	Y	Y	Y	N	Y
LOUISIANA								
Johnston	N	N	Y	Y	Y	Y	Y	N
Long	N	N	Y	Y	Y	Y	Y	N
MAINE								
Cohen	N	N	Y	N	Y	Y	N	Y
Mitchell	Y	N	N	N	Y	Y	N	Y
MARYLAND								
Mathias	Y	N	Y	Y	Y	N	Y	Y
Sarbanes	Y	N	Y	Y	Y	Y	Y	Y
MASSACHUSETTS								
Kennedy	Y	N	N	N	Y	N	N	Y
Tsongas	Y	N	N	Y	Y	N	Y	Y
MICHIGAN								
Levin	Y	N	N	Y	Y	N	N	Y
Riegle	Y	N	N	Y	N	Y	N	Y
MINNESOTA								
Boschwitz	Y	N	Y	Y	Y	Y	Y	Y
Durenberger	Y	N	N	Y	N	Y	N	Y
MISSISSIPPI								
Cochran	N	N	Y	Y	Y	Y	Y	Y
Stennis	N	N	Y	Y	Y	Y	Y	Y
MISSOURI								
Danforth	Y	N	N	Y	Y	Y	Y	Y
Eagleton	Y	N	N	Y	Y	Y	Y	Y
MONTANA								
Baucus	Y	N	N	Y	N	N	N	Y
Melcher	Y	N	N	Y	N	Y	N	Y
NEBRASKA								
Exon	N	N	N	Y	N	Y	N	Y
Zorinsky	N	N	N	Y	N	Y	Y	Y
NEVADA								
Laxalt	Y	N	N	Y	Y	Y	Y	Y
Cannon	N	N	Y	Y	Y	Y	Y	Y

	326	327	328	329	330	331	332	333
NEW HAMPSHIRE								
Humphrey	N	N	Y	N	Y	Y	Y	Y
Rudman	N	N	Y	Y	Y	Y	Y	Y
NEW JERSEY								
Brady	Y	N	N	Y	Y	Y	Y	Y
Bradley	Y	N	Y	Y	Y	Y	Y	Y
NEW MEXICO								
Domenici	Y	Y	N	N	Y	Y	Y	Y
Schmitt	Y	Y	N	N	Y	N	Y	Y
NEW YORK								
D'Amato	Y	N	Y	Y	Y	Y	Y	Y
Moynihan	Y	N	Y	Y	Y	Y	Y	Y
NORTH CAROLINA								
East	N	N	Y	N	Y	Y	Y	Y
Helms	N	Y	Y	N	Y	Y	Y	Y
NORTH DAKOTA								
Andrews	Y	N	Y	Y	Y	Y	Y	Y
Burdick	Y	Y	Y	Y	Y	Y	Y	Y
OHIO								
Glenn	Y	N	Y	Y	Y	Y	N	Y
Metzenbaum	Y	N	Y	Y	Y	N	Y	Y
OKLAHOMA								
Nickles	N	N	Y	Y	Y	Y	Y	Y
Boren	Y	N	Y	Y	Y	Y	Y	Y
OREGON								
Hatfield	Y	N	N	Y	N	Y	Y	Y
Packwood	Y	N	Y	Y	Y	Y	Y	Y
PENNSYLVANIA								
Heinz	Y	N	Y	Y	Y	Y	Y	Y
Specter	Y	N	Y	Y	Y	Y	Y	Y
RHODE ISLAND								
Chafee	Y	N	Y	Y	Y	Y	Y	Y
Pell	Y	N	N	Y	Y	N	Y	Y
SOUTH CAROLINA								
Thurmond	N	Y	Y	Y	Y	Y	Y	Y
Hollings	Y	N	Y	Y	Y	Y	N	Y
SOUTH DAKOTA								
Abdnor	Y	N	Y	Y	Y	Y	Y	Y
Pressler	N	N	Y	Y	Y	N	Y	Y
TENNESSEE								
Baker	N	N	N	Y	Y	Y	Y	Y
Sasser	N	N	Y	Y	Y	Y	+	?

	326	327	328	329	330	331	332	333
TEXAS								
Tower	Y	Y	N	N	Y	Y	Y	Y
Bentsen	N	N	N	Y	Y	Y	Y	Y
UTAH								
Garn	Y	N	N	Y	Y	Y	Y	Y
Hatch	Y	N	N	Y	Y	Y	Y	Y
VERMONT								
Stafford	Y	N	N	Y	Y	Y	Y	Y
Leahy	Y	N	N	Y	Y	Y	Y	Y
VIRGINIA								
Warner	N	N	N	Y	Y	Y	Y	Y
Byrd*	N	Y	Y	Y	Y	Y	Y	Y
WASHINGTON								
Gorton	Y	N	Y	Y	Y	Y	Y	Y
Jackson	Y	N	Y	Y	Y	Y	N	Y
WEST VIRGINIA								
Byrd	N	N	Y	Y	Y	Y	Y	Y
Randolph	N	N	N	Y	Y	Y	Y	Y
WISCONSIN								
Kasten	N	N	Y	Y	Y	Y	Y	Y
Proxmire	Y	N	N	Y	Y	N	Y	N
WYOMING								
Simpson	Y	N	N	Y	+	+	+	?
Wallop	N	N	N	Y	Y	Y	Y	Y

KEY

- Y Voted for (yea).
- # Paired for.
- + Announced for.
- N Voted against (nay).
- X Paired against.
- - Announced against.
- P Voted "present".
- C Voted "present" to avoid possible conflict of interest.
- ? Did not vote or otherwise make a position known.

Democrats   *Republicans*

ND - Northern Democrats   SD - Southern Democrats (Southern states - Ala., Ark., Fla., Ga., Ky., La., Miss., N.C., Okla., S.C., Tenn., Texas, Va.)   *Byrd elected as an independent.*

---

326. S 2222. Immigration Reform and Control Act. Simpson, R-Wyo., motion to table (kill) the Helms, R-N.C., amendment to establish a congressional policy that states have the right not to provide free public schooling and other benefits to illegal aliens. Motion agreed to 64-35: R 33-21; D 31-14 (ND 25-6, SD 6-8), Aug. 17, 1982.

327. S 2222. Immigration Reform and Control Act. Tower, R-Texas, amendment to ease provisions imposing sanctions against employers who hire, recruit or refer for employment illegal aliens by requiring "willful" action on the part of an employer and creating an affirmative defense to an alleged violation if the employer used a standard form to verify an employee's work eligibility. Rejected 14-85: R 12-42; D 2-43 (ND 0-31, SD 2-12), Aug. 17, 1982. A "nay" was a vote supporting the president's position.

328. S 2222. Immigration Reform and Control Act. Boschwitz, R-Minn.-Huddleston, D-Ky., amendment to prevent Canada and Mexico from transferring unused visas from one to the other. Rejected 38-61: R 20-34; D 18-27 (ND 8-23, SD 10-4), Aug. 17, 1982. A "nay" was a vote supporting the president's position.

329. S 2222. Immigration Reform and Control Act. Passage of the bill to revise immigration laws by establishing sanctions against employers who knowingly hire illegal aliens, granting amnesty to certain aliens already in the United States, putting a yearly cap on legal immigration, providing a temporary worker program primarily for the agricultural industry, and streamlining procedures for asylum, deportation and exclusion cases. Passed 80-19: R 43-11; D 37-8 (ND 24-7, SD 13-1), Aug. 17, 1982. A "yea" was a vote supporting the president's position.

330. H J Res 520. Temporary Debt Limit Increase. Baker, R-Tenn., amendment to block further spending on a planned gymnasium in the new Hart Senate Office Building and to close an existing gym in the Dirksen Senate Office Building. Adopted 98-0: R 53-0; D 45-0 (ND 31-0, SD 14-0), Aug. 17, 1982.

331. S 2248. Department of Defense Authorizations, Fiscal 1983. Adoption of the conference report on the bill to authorize $177,867,548,000 for Defense Department programs in fiscal year 1983. Adopted 77-21: R 47-6; D 30-15 (ND 18-13, SD 12-2), Aug. 17, 1982.

332. H J Res 520. Temporary Debt Limit Increase. Dole, R-Kan., substitute, to make technical changes in a previous Dole amendment, to reduce to six months from one year the length of time an investment must be held to qualify for long-term capital gains tax rates. Adopted 77-17: R 49-2; D 28-15 (ND 18-12, SD 10-3), Aug. 17, 1982. (The Dole amendment, as amended, subsequently was adopted by voice vote.)

333. H J Res 520. Temporary Debt Limit Increase. Baker, R-Tenn., motion to instruct the sergeant-at-arms to require the attendance of absent senators. Motion agreed to 88-7: R 48-4; D 40-3 (ND 28-1, D 12-2), Aug. 18, 1982.

	334	335	336	337
ALABAMA				
Denton	Y	Y	N	Y
Heflin	N	Y	N	N
ALASKA				
Murkowski	Y	Y	Y	Y
Stevens	N	Y	Y	Y
ARIZONA				
Goldwater	N	N	Y	N
DeConcini	Y	Y	Y	N
ARKANSAS				
Bumpers	N	N	N	N
Pryor	N	N	N	N
CALIFORNIA				
Hayakawa	N	Y	Y	Y
Cranston	N	N	Y	Y
COLORADO				
Armstrong	Y	Y	Y	Y
Hart	N	N	Y	Y
CONNECTICUT				
Weicker	N	N	Y	N
Dodd	N	N	Y	Y
DELAWARE				
Roth	Y	Y	Y	Y
Biden	N	Y	Y	N
FLORIDA				
Hawkins	Y	N	Y	N
Chiles	N	?	?	?
GEORGIA				
Mattingly	Y	Y	Y	N
Nunn	N	Y	Y	N
HAWAII				
Inouye	N	N	Y	N
Matsunaga	?	N	Y	Y
IDAHO				
McClure	Y	Y	N	Y
Symms	Y	Y	Y	Y
ILLINOIS				
Percy	Y	Y	Y	Y
Dixon	N	Y	N	N
INDIANA				
Lugar	Y	Y	Y	Y
Quayle	Y	Y	Y	Y

	334	335	336	337
IOWA				
Grassley	Y	Y	Y	Y
Jepsen	Y	N	Y	Y
KANSAS				
Dole	Y	Y	Y	Y
Kassebaum	N	Y	Y	Y
KENTUCKY				
Ford	Y	N	Y	N
Huddleston	N	Y	N	N
LOUISIANA				
Johnston	Y	Y	?	N
Long	Y	Y	Y	N
MAINE				
Cohen	N	Y	Y	Y
Mitchell	N	N	N	N
MARYLAND				
Mathias	N	N	Y	Y
Sarbanes	N	N	N	N
MASSACHUSETTS				
Kennedy	N	N	Y	Y
Tsongas	N	N	Y	Y
MICHIGAN				
Levin	N	Y	N	N
Riegle	N	N	N	N
MINNESOTA				
Boschwitz	N	Y	Y	Y
Durenberger	N	N	Y	Y
MISSISSIPPI				
Cochran	N	Y	Y	Y
Stennis	Y	Y	Y	N
MISSOURI				
Danforth	N	Y	Y	Y
Eagleton	N	N	N	N
MONTANA				
Baucus	N	Y	Y	Y
Melcher	N	N	N	N
NEBRASKA				
Exon	Y	Y	N	N
Zorinsky	Y	N	N	N
NEVADA				
Laxalt	Y	Y	Y	Y
Cannon	N	N	N	N

	334	335	336	337
NEW HAMPSHIRE				
Humphrey	Y	Y	N	N
Rudman	N	Y	Y	Y
NEW JERSEY				
Brady	N	Y	Y	Y
Bradley	N	Y	Y	Y
NEW MEXICO				
Domenici	Y	Y	Y	Y
Schmitt	N	Y	Y	N
NEW YORK				
D'Amato	Y	Y	Y	Y
Moynihan	N	N	Y	N
NORTH CAROLINA				
East	Y	Y	N	N
Helms	Y	Y	N	N
NORTH DAKOTA				
Andrews	N	Y	Y	Y
Burdick	N	N	N	N
OHIO				
Glenn	N	Y	N	N
Metzenbaum	N	N	Y	N
OKLAHOMA				
Nickles	Y	Y	Y	N
Boren	N	Y	N	N
OREGON				
Hatfield	N	Y	Y	Y
Packwood	N	Y	Y	Y
PENNSYLVANIA				
Heinz	N	Y	Y	Y
Specter	N	Y	Y	Y
RHODE ISLAND				
Chafee	N	Y	Y	Y
Pell	N	Y	Y	Y
SOUTH CAROLINA				
Thurmond	Y	Y	?	Y
Hollings	N	N	N	N
SOUTH DAKOTA				
Abdnor	Y	Y	Y	Y
Pressler	Y	Y	Y	Y
TENNESSEE				
Baker	N	Y	Y	Y
Sasser	?	N	N	N

KEY

Y	Voted for (yea).
#	Paired for.
+	Announced for.
N	Voted against (nay).
X	Paired against.
-	Announced against.
P	Voted ''present''.
C	Voted ''present'' to avoid possible conflict of interest.
?	Did not vote or otherwise make a position known.

Democrats   *Republicans*

	334	335	336	337
TEXAS				
Tower	N	Y	Y	Y
Bentsen	N	Y	Y	N
UTAH				
Garn	Y	Y	Y	Y
Hatch	Y	Y	Y	Y
VERMONT				
Stafford	N	Y	?	Y
Leahy	N	Y	Y	N
VIRGINIA				
Warner	Y	Y	?	N
Byrd*	Y	Y	Y	N
WASHINGTON				
Gorton	N	Y	Y	Y
Jackson	N	N	Y	N
WEST VIRGINIA				
Byrd	N	N	N	N
Randolph	Y	N	N	N
WISCONSIN				
Kasten	Y	Y	N	N
Proxmire	Y	N	N	N
WYOMING				
Simpson	?	Y	Y	Y
Wallop	N	Y	Y	Y

ND - Northern Democrats   SD - Southern Democrats (Southern states - Ala., Ark., Fla., Ga., Ky., La., Miss., N.C., Okla., S.C., Tenn., Texas, Va.)   *Byrd elected as an independent.*

334. H J Res 520. Temporary Debt Limit Increase. Helms, R-N.C., motion to table (kill) the Weicker, R-Conn., amendment to make clear that the Justice Department can enforce the Constitution and to make clear that nothing in the debt ceiling bill should be interpreted to modify or diminish the authority of the federal courts to fully enforce the Constitution. Rejected 38-59: R 28-25; D 10-34 (ND 5-25, SD 5-9), Aug. 18, 1982.

335. HR 6955. Omnibus Reconciliation Act of 1982. Adoption of the conference report on the bill to reduce the federal budget for fiscal years 1983, 1984 and 1985 by approximately $13.3 billion. Adopted 67-32: R 48-6; D 19-26 (ND 10-21, SD 9-5), Aug. 18, 1982. A "yea" was a vote supporting the president's position.

336. HR 4961. Budget Reconciliation Tax Increases/Spending Cuts. Judgment of the Senate affirming the chair's ruling rejecting the East, R-N.C., point of order that the conference report on the bill contained certain provisions that were not germane. Ruling of the chair upheld 68-27: R 45-6; D 23-21 (ND 17-14, SD 6-7), Aug. 19, 1982.

337. HR 4961. Budget Reconciliation Tax Increases/Spending Cuts. Adoption of the conference report on the bill to increase revenues by $98.3 billion in fiscal 1983-85 and reduce projected spending by $17.5 billion in fiscal 1983-85 in compliance with the fiscal 1983 budget resolution. Adopted (thus cleared for the president) 52-47: R 43-11; D 9-36 (ND 9-22, SD 0-14), Aug. 19, 1982. A "yea" was a vote supporting the president's position.

	338	339			338	339			338	339		**KEY**
ALABAMA				**IOWA**				**NEW HAMPSHIRE**				Y Voted for (yea).
Denton	Y	N		*Grassley*	Y	N		*Humphrey*	Y	N		# Paired for.
Heflin	Y	Y		*Jepsen*	Y	N		*Rudman*	Y	N		+ Announced for.
ALASKA				**KANSAS**				**NEW JERSEY**				N Voted against (nay).
Murkowski	Y	N		*Dole*	Y	N		*Brady*	Y	N		X Paired against.
Stevens	Y	N		*Kassebaum*	Y	N		Bradley	Y	Y		- Announced against.
ARIZONA				**KENTUCKY**				**NEW MEXICO**				P Voted "present".
Goldwater	Y	?		Ford	Y	Y		*Domenici*	Y	N		C Voted "present" to avoid possible conflict of interest.
DeConcini	Y	?		Huddleston	Y	Y		*Schmitt*	Y	N		
ARKANSAS				**LOUISIANA**				**NEW YORK**				? Did not vote or otherwise make a position known.
Bumpers	P	Y		Johnston	Y	Y		*D'Amato*	Y	N		
Pryor	Y	Y		Long	Y	N		Moynihan	Y	Y		Democrats *Republicans*
CALIFORNIA				**MAINE**				**NORTH CAROLINA**				
Hayakawa	Y	N		*Cohen*	N	N		*East*	Y	N		
Cranston	?	?		Mitchell	N	Y		*Helms*	Y	N		
COLORADO				**MARYLAND**				**NORTH DAKOTA**				
Armstrong	Y	N		*Mathias*	Y	Y		*Andrews*	Y	N		
Hart	Y	Y		Sarbanes	Y	Y		Burdick	Y	Y		

	338	339

	338	339			338	339			338	339			338	339
CONNECTICUT				**MASSACHUSETTS**				**OHIO**				**TEXAS**		
Weicker	Y	Y		Kennedy	Y	Y		Glenn	Y	Y		*Tower*	Y	N
Dodd	Y	Y		Tsongas	Y	Y		Metzenbaum	Y	Y		Bentsen	?	?
DELAWARE				**MICHIGAN**				**OKLAHOMA**				**UTAH**		
Roth	Y	N		Levin	Y	Y		*Nickles*	Y	N		*Garn*	Y	N
Biden	?	?		Riegle	Y	Y		Boren	Y	Y		*Hatch*	Y	N
FLORIDA				**MINNESOTA**				**OREGON**				**VERMONT**		
Hawkins	Y	N		*Boschwitz*	N	N		*Hatfield*	Y	N		*Stafford*	Y	N
Chiles	?	?		*Durenberger*	Y	?		*Packwood*	Y	N		Leahy	Y	Y
GEORGIA				**MISSISSIPPI**				**PENNSYLVANIA**				**VIRGINIA**		
Mattingly	Y	N		*Cochran*	Y	N		*Heinz*	Y	Y		*Warner*	Y	N
Nunn	Y	N		Stennis	Y	Y		*Specter*	Y	Y		Byrd*	Y	N
HAWAII				**MISSOURI**				**RHODE ISLAND**				**WASHINGTON**		
Inouye	Y	Y		*Danforth*	Y	N		*Chafee*	Y	Y		*Gorton*	Y	N
Matsunaga	Y	Y		Eagleton	Y	Y		Pell	Y	Y		Jackson	Y	Y
IDAHO				**MONTANA**				**SOUTH CAROLINA**				**WEST VIRGINIA**		
McClure	?	?		Baucus	N	Y		*Thurmond*	Y	N		Byrd	N	Y
Symms	?	N		Melcher	N	Y		Hollings	Y	Y		Randolph	N	Y
ILLINOIS				**NEBRASKA**				**SOUTH DAKOTA**				**WISCONSIN**		
Percy	Y	N		Exon	Y	Y		*Abdnor*	?	?		*Kasten*	Y	N
Dixon	Y	Y		Zorinsky	Y	Y		*Pressler*	N	?		Proxmire	Y	N
INDIANA				**NEVADA**				**TENNESSEE**				**WYOMING**		
Lugar	Y	N		*Laxalt*	Y	N		*Baker*	Y	N		*Simpson*	Y	N
Quayle	Y	N		Cannon	Y	Y		Sasser	Y	Y		*Wallop*	Y	?

ND - Northern Democrats   SD - Southern Democrats (Southern states - Ala., Ark., Fla., Ga., Ky., La., Miss., N.C., Okla., S.C., Tenn., Texas, Va.)   *Byrd elected as an independent.*

338. HR 3663. Bus Regulatory Reform. Adoption of the conference report on the bill to ease government regulation of the intercity bus industry. Adopted 84-8: R 48-3; D 36-5 (ND 24-5, SD 12-0), Aug. 20, 1982. A "yea" was a vote supporting the president's position.

339. HR 6863. Supplemental Appropriations, Fiscal 1982. Levin, D-Mich., amendment to extend until October 1982 the deadline for enrolling in college in order to qualify for student benefits under the Social Security Act, and to provide that uncashed Social Security checks be returned to the Social Security trust fund rather than to the Treasury's general fund. The student benefits, for children of deceased or disabled Social Security recipients, had been terminated May 1 by the 1981 budget reconciliation act (PL 97-35). Rejected 42-47: R 5-43; D 37-4 (ND 27-1, SD 10-3), Aug. 20, 1982. A "nay" was a vote supporting the president's position.

	340 341		340 341		340 341
ALABAMA		**IOWA**		**NEW HAMPSHIRE**	
Denton	Y N	*Grassley*	Y Y	*Humphrey*	Y N
Heflin	Y N	*Jepsen*	Y Y	*Rudman*	N Y
ALASKA		**KANSAS**		**NEW JERSEY**	
Murkowski	Y N	*Dole*	? N	*Brady*	N N
Stevens	N N	*Kassebaum*	+ N	Bradley	N Y
ARIZONA		**KENTUCKY**		**NEW MEXICO**	
Goldwater	? N	Ford	Y Y	*Domenici*	Y Y
DeConcini	Y Y	Huddleston	Y Y	*Schmitt*	? #
ARKANSAS		**LOUISIANA**		**NEW YORK**	
Bumpers	N Y	Johnston	Y N	*D'Amato*	Y Y
Pryor	N Y	Long	N N	Moynihan	N Y
CALIFORNIA		**MAINE**		**NORTH CAROLINA**	
Hayakawa	N N	*Cohen*	N Y	*East*	Y N
Cranston	N Y	Mitchell	N Y	*Helms*	Y N
COLORADO		**MARYLAND**		**NORTH DAKOTA**	
Armstrong	Y N	*Mathias*	N Y	*Andrews*	N Y
Hart	N Y	Sarbanes	N Y	Burdick	N Y
CONNECTICUT		**MASSACHUSETTS**		**OHIO**	
Weicker	N Y	Kennedy	N Y	Glenn	N Y
Dodd	N Y	Tsongas	N Y	Metzenbaum	N Y
DELAWARE		**MICHIGAN**		**OKLAHOMA**	
Roth	Y Y	Levin	N Y	*Nickles*	Y N
Biden	Y Y	Riegle	N Y	Boren	N Y
FLORIDA		**MINNESOTA**		**OREGON**	
Hawkins	Y Y	*Boschwitz*	Y N	*Hatfield*	+ Y
Chiles	N Y	*Durenberger*	Y Y	*Packwood*	N Y
GEORGIA		**MISSISSIPPI**		**PENNSYLVANIA**	
Mattingly	Y N	*Cochran*	Y ?	*Heinz*	N Y
Nunn	Y Y	Stennis	N #	*Specter*	N ?
HAWAII		**MISSOURI**		**RHODE ISLAND**	
Inouye	N Y	*Danforth*	Y Y	*Chafee*	N Y
Matsunaga	- Y	Eagleton	Y Y	Pell	Y Y
IDAHO		**MONTANA**		**SOUTH CAROLINA**	
McClure	? ?	Baucus	N Y	*Thurmond*	Y N
Symms	Y N	Melcher	? Y	Hollings	N +
ILLINOIS		**NEBRASKA**		**SOUTH DAKOTA**	
Percy	N N	Exon	Y Y	*Abdnor*	Y Y
Dixon	N Y	Zorinsky	Y Y	*Pressler*	Y Y
INDIANA		**NEVADA**		**TENNESSEE**	
Lugar	Y ?	Laxalt	? N	*Baker*	Y N
Quayle	Y ?	Cannon	? Y	Sasser	Y Y

KEY

Y   Voted for (yea).
Paired for.
+   Announced for.
N   Voted against (nay).
X   Paired against.
-   Announced against.
P   Voted "present".
C   Voted "present" to avoid possible conflict of interest.
?   Did not vote or otherwise make a position known.

Democrats   *Republicans*

	340 341
TEXAS	
Tower	N X
Bentsen	N ?
UTAH	
Garn	Y N
Hatch	? N
VERMONT	
Stafford	N Y
Leahy	N Y
VIRGINIA	
Warner	N N
Byrd*	N N
WASHINGTON	
Gorton	N Y
Jackson	N Y
WEST VIRGINIA	
Byrd	N Y
Randolph	Y Y
WISCONSIN	
Kasten	Y N
Proxmire	Y Y
WYOMING	
Simpson	N N
Wallop	? N

ND - Northern Democrats   SD - Southern Democrats (Southern states - Ala., Ark., Fla., Ga., Ky., La., Miss., N.C., Okla., S.C., Tenn., Texas, Va.)   *Byrd elected as an independent.

340. H J Res 520. Temporary Debt Limit Increase. Baker, R-Tenn., motion to invoke cloture (thus limiting debate) on the Helms, R-N.C., amendment designed to ban abortion, which was an amendment to the Helms amendment (stripping the Supreme Court of jurisdiction to review any case involving voluntary prayers in public schools) to the committee version of the bill. Motion rejected 41-47: R 27-18; D 14-29 (ND 8-20, SD 6-9), Sept. 9, 1982. A three-fifths majority vote (60) of the total Senate is required to invoke cloture.

341. HR 6863. Supplemental Appropriations, Fiscal 1982. Passage, over President Reagan's Aug. 28 veto, of the bill to appropriate $14,578,111,924 in new fiscal 1982 budget authority for federal military and civilian pay raises, commodity credit programs, defense and other programs, and to rescind $400,846,000 in previously appropriated funds. Passed (thus enacted into law) 60-30: R 21-26; D 39-4 (ND 31-0, SD 8-4), Sept. 10, 1982. A two-thirds majority of those present and voting (60 in this case) of both houses is required to override a veto. A "nay" was a vote supporting the president's position. (The House voted to override the veto the previous day *(see vote 299, p. 90-H).)*

CQ Senate Votes 342 - 344

Corresponding to Congressional Record Votes 342, 343, 344

	342 343 344		342 343 344		342 343 344	KEY
ALABAMA		**IOWA**		**NEW HAMPSHIRE**		Y Voted for (yea).
Denton	Y Y N	*Grassley*	Y Y N	*Humphrey*	Y Y N	# Paired for.
Heflin	Y Y N	*Jepsen*	Y Y N	*Rudman*	N N Y	+ Announced for.
ALASKA		**KANSAS**		**NEW JERSEY**		N Voted against (nay).
Murkowski	Y Y N	*Dole*	Y Y N	*Brady*	N N Y	X Paired against.
Stevens	N N Y	*Kassebaum*	Y Y Y	Bradley	? N Y	- Announced against.
ARIZONA		**KENTUCKY**		**NEW MEXICO**		P Voted "present".
Goldwater	? N N	Ford	Y Y N	*Domenici*	Y Y N	C Voted "present" to avoid possible conflict of interest.
DeConcini	Y Y N	Huddleston	Y Y N	*Schmitt*	? N Y	
ARKANSAS		**LOUISIANA**		**NEW YORK**		? Did not vote or otherwise make a position known.
Bumpers	? N Y	Johnston	Y + -	*D'Amato*	Y Y N	
Pryor	? N Y	Long	N N N	Moynihan	N N Y	Democrats *Republicans*

CALIFORNIA		**MAINE**		**NORTH CAROLINA**			342 343 344
Hayakawa	N N Y	*Cohen*	N N Y	*East*	Y Y N		
Cranston	? N Y	Mitchell	N N Y	*Helms*	Y Y N		
COLORADO		**MARYLAND**		**NORTH DAKOTA**		**TEXAS**	
Armstrong	Y Y N	*Mathias*	N N Y	Andrews	N N N	*Tower*	N N Y
Hart	N N Y	Sarbanes	N N Y	Burdick	N N Y	Bentsen	? N Y
CONNECTICUT		**MASSACHUSETTS**		**OHIO**		**UTAH**	
Weicker	N N Y	Kennedy	X N Y	Glenn	N ? +	*Garn*	Y Y N
Dodd	N N Y	Tsongas	N N Y	Metzenbaum	N N Y	*Hatch*	Y Y N
DELAWARE		**MICHIGAN**		**OKLAHOMA**		**VERMONT**	
Roth	Y Y Y	Levin	N N Y	*Nickles*	Y Y N	*Stafford*	? ? #
Biden	? Y N	Riegle	- N Y	Boren	N X ?	Leahy	N N Y
FLORIDA		**MINNESOTA**		**OREGON**		**VIRGINIA**	
Hawkins	Y Y N	*Boschwitz*	Y Y N	*Hatfield*	Y Y N	*Warner*	Y Y N
Chiles	? Y N	*Durenberger*	Y Y N	*Packwood*	N N Y	Byrd*	N Y Y
GEORGIA		**MISSISSIPPI**		**PENNSYLVANIA**		**WASHINGTON**	
Mattingly	Y Y N	*Cochran*	Y Y N	*Heinz*	? N +	*Gorton*	N N Y
Nunn	Y Y Y	Stennis	N Y N	*Specter*	N N Y	Jackson	N N Y
HAWAII		**MISSOURI**		**RHODE ISLAND**		**WEST VIRGINIA**	
Inouye	? N Y	*Danforth*	? Y N	*Chafee*	N N Y	Byrd	N N Y
Matsunaga	N N Y	Eagleton	Y Y N	Pell	# Y Y	Randolph	Y Y N
IDAHO		**MONTANA**		**SOUTH CAROLINA**		**WISCONSIN**	
McClure	Y Y N	Baucus	N N Y	*Thurmond*	Y Y N	*Kasten*	Y Y N
Symms	Y Y N	Melcher	? Y Y	Hollings	N N Y	Proxmire	Y Y N
ILLINOIS		**NEBRASKA**		**SOUTH DAKOTA**		**WYOMING**	
Percy	? N Y	Exon	Y # N	*Abdnor*	Y Y N	*Simpson*	N N Y
Dixon	N N Y	Zorinsky	Y Y N	*Pressler*	Y Y N	*Wallop*	? N Y
INDIANA		**NEVADA**		**TENNESSEE**			
Lugar	Y Y N	*Laxalt*	Y Y N	*Baker*	Y Y X		
Quayle	Y Y N	Cannon	? ? ?	Sasser	Y Y Y		

ND - Northern Democrats   SD - Southern Democrats (Southern states - Ala., Ark., Fla., Ga., Ky., La., Miss., N.C., Okla., S.C., Tenn., Texas, Va.)   *Byrd elected as an independent.*

342. H J Res 520. Temporary Debt Limit Increase. Helms, R-N.C., motion to invoke cloture (thus limiting debate) on the Helms amendment designed to ban abortion, which was an amendment to the Helms amendment (stripping the Supreme Court of jurisdiction to review any case involving voluntary prayers in public schools) to the committee version of the bill. Motion rejected 45-35: R 33-14; D 12-21 (ND 6-16, SD 6-5), Sept. 13, 1982. A three-fifths majority vote (60) of the total Senate is required to invoke cloture.

343. H J Res 520. Temporary Debt Limit Increase. Helms, R-N.C., motion to invoke cloture (thus limiting debate) on the Helms amendment designed to ban abortion, which was an amendment to the Helms amendment (stripping the Supreme Court of jurisdiction to review any case involving voluntary prayers in public schools) to the committee version of the bill. Motion rejected 50-44: R 34-19; D 16-25 (ND 8-20, SD 8-5), Sept. 15, 1982. A three-fifths majority vote (60) of the total Senate is required to invoke cloture.

344. H J Res 520. Temporary Debt Limit Increase. Hayakawa, R-Calif., motion to table (kill) the Helms, R-N.C., amendment designed to ban abortion, which was an amendment to the Helms amendment (stripping the Supreme Court of jurisdiction to review any case involving voluntary prayers in public schools) to the committee version of the bill. Motion agreed to 47-46: R 18-33; D 29-13 (ND 22-7, SD 7-6), Sept. 15, 1982.

KEY

- Y Voted for (yea).
- # Paired for.
- + Announced for.
- N Voted against (nay).
- X Paired against.
- − Announced against.
- P Voted "present".
- C Voted "present" to avoid possible conflict of interest.
- ? Did not vote or otherwise make a position known.

Democrats   *Republicans*

	345	346	347	348
ALABAMA				
Denton	Y	Y	Y	N
Heflin	Y	Y	Y	N
ALASKA				
Murkowski	Y	Y	Y	N
Stevens	Y	Y	Y	N
ARIZONA				
Goldwater	N	N	N	Y
DeConcini	?	Y	Y	N
ARKANSAS				
Bumpers	−	N	N	Y
Pryor	N	N	N	Y
CALIFORNIA				
Hayakawa	N	N	N	Y
Cranston	N	N	N	Y
COLORADO				
Armstrong	Y	Y	Y	N
Hart	N	N	N	Y
CONNECTICUT				
Weicker	N	N	N	Y
Dodd	N	N	N	Y
DELAWARE				
Roth	Y	Y	Y	N
Biden	N	N	N	Y
FLORIDA				
Hawkins	Y	Y	Y	N
Chiles	N	Y	Y	Y
GEORGIA				
Mattingly	Y	Y	Y	N
Nunn	Y	Y	Y	N
HAWAII				
Inouye	N	N	N	Y
Matsunaga	N	N	N	Y
IDAHO				
McClure	?	Y	Y	N
Symms	Y	Y	Y	N
ILLINOIS				
Percy	N	N	N	Y
Dixon	N	N	N	Y
INDIANA				
Lugar	Y	Y	Y	N
Quayle	Y	Y	Y	N
IOWA				
Grassley	Y	Y	Y	N
Jepsen	Y	Y	Y	N
KANSAS				
Dole	Y	Y	Y	N
Kassebaum	Y	Y	Y	Y
KENTUCKY				
Ford	Y	Y	Y	N
Huddleston	Y	Y	Y	N
LOUISIANA				
Johnston	Y	Y	Y	N
Long	Y	Y	Y	N
MAINE				
Cohen	N	N	N	Y
Mitchell	N	N	N	Y
MARYLAND				
Mathias	N	N	N	Y
Sarbanes	N	N	N	Y
MASSACHUSETTS				
Kennedy	N	N	N	Y
Tsongas	N	N	N	Y
MICHIGAN				
Levin	N	N	N	Y
Riegle	N	N	N	Y
MINNESOTA				
Boschwitz	N	N	N	Y
Durenberger	?	N	N	Y
MISSISSIPPI				
Cochran	Y	Y	Y	N
Stennis	?	N	Y	N
MISSOURI				
Danforth	?	N	N	Y
Eagleton	N	N	N	Y
MONTANA				
Baucus	N	N	N	Y
Melcher	?	N	N	Y
NEBRASKA				
Exon	Y	Y	Y	N
Zorinsky	Y	Y	Y	N
NEVADA				
Laxalt	Y	Y	Y	N
Cannon	Y	Y	Y	N
NEW HAMPSHIRE				
Humphrey	Y	Y	Y	N
Rudman	N	N	N	Y
NEW JERSEY				
Brady	?	N	N	Y
Bradley	N	N	N	Y
NEW MEXICO				
Domenici	Y	Y	Y	N
Schmitt	Y	Y	Y	N
NEW YORK				
D'Amato	Y	Y	Y	N
Moynihan	N	N	N	Y
NORTH CAROLINA				
East	Y	Y	Y	N
Helms	Y	Y	Y	N
NORTH DAKOTA				
Andrews	N	N	N	N
Burdick	−	N	N	Y
OHIO				
Glenn	N	N	N	Y
Metzenbaum	N	N	N	Y
OKLAHOMA				
Nickles	Y	Y	Y	N
Boren	Y	Y	Y	N
OREGON				
Hatfield	N	N	N	Y
Packwood	N	N	N	Y
PENNSYLVANIA				
Heinz	N	N	N	Y
Specter	N	N	N	Y
RHODE ISLAND				
Chafee	N	N	N	Y
Pell	Y	Y	Y	Y
SOUTH CAROLINA				
Thurmond	Y	Y	Y	N
Hollings	N	N	N	Y
SOUTH DAKOTA				
Abdnor	Y	Y	Y	N
Pressler	Y	Y	Y	N
TENNESSEE				
Baker	Y	Y	Y	N
Sasser	Y	Y	Y	N
TEXAS				
Tower	Y	Y	Y	N
Bentsen	Y	Y	Y	N
UTAH				
Garn	Y	Y	Y	N
Hatch	Y	Y	Y	N
VERMONT				
Stafford	?	N	N	Y
Leahy	N	N	N	Y
VIRGINIA				
Warner	Y	Y	Y	N
Byrd*	Y	Y	Y	N
WASHINGTON				
Gorton	Y	N	N	Y
Jackson	N	N	N	Y
WEST VIRGINIA				
Byrd	N	N	N	N
Randolph	Y	Y	Y	N
WISCONSIN				
Kasten	Y	Y	Y	N
Proxmire	Y	Y	Y	N
WYOMING				
Simpson	Y	Y	Y	N
Wallop	?	Y	Y	N

ND - Northern Democrats   SD - Southern Democrats (Southern states - Ala., Ark., Fla., Ga., Ky., La., Miss., N.C., Okla., S.C., Tenn., Texas, Va.)   * Byrd elected as an independent.

345. H J Res 520. Temporary Debt Limit Increase. Helms, R-N.C., motion to invoke cloture (thus limiting debate) on the Helms amendment, barring the federal courts, including the Supreme Court, from hearing "voluntary" school prayer cases, to the Finance Committee version of the bill. Motion rejected 50-39: R 34-14; D 16-25 (ND 6-22, SD 10-3), Sept. 20, 1982. A three-fifths majority vote (60) of the total Senate is required to invoke cloture.

346. H J Res 520. Temporary Debt Limit Increase. Helms, R-N.C., motion to invoke cloture (thus limiting debate) on the Helms amendment, barring the federal courts, including the Supreme Court, from hearing "voluntary" school prayer cases, to the Finance Committee version of the bill. Motion rejected 53-47: R 35-19; D 18-28 (ND 7-24, SD 11-4), Sept. 21, 1982. A three-fifths majority vote (60) of the total Senate is required to invoke cloture.

347. H J Res 520. Temporary Dept Increase. Helms, R-N.C., motion to invoke cloture (thus limiting debate) on the Helms amendment, barring the federal courts, including the Supreme Court, from hearing "voluntary" school prayer cases, to the Finance Committee version of the bill. Motion rejected 54-46: R 35-19; D 19-27 (ND 7-24, SD 12-3), Sept. 22, 1982. A three-fifths majority vote (60) of the total Senate is required to invoke cloture.

348. H J Res 520. Temporary Debt Limit Increase. Goldwater, R-Ariz., motion to table (kill) the Helms, R-N.C., amendment, barring the federal courts, including the Supreme Court, from hearing "voluntary" school prayer cases, to the Finance Committee version of the bill. Motion rejected 47-53: R 19-35; D 28-18 (ND 24-7, SD 4-11), Sept. 22, 1982.

	349	350	351	352	353	354
ALABAMA						
Denton	Y	N	Y	N	N	Y
Heflin	Y	N	Y	N	?	N
ALASKA						
Murkowski	Y	N	Y	Y	Y	Y
Stevens	Y	N	Y	Y	Y	Y
ARIZONA						
Goldwater	N	Y	N	Y	X	N
DeConcini	Y	N	Y	Y	Y	N
ARKANSAS						
Bumpers	N	Y	Y	Y	N	N
Pryor	N	Y	Y	Y	N	N
CALIFORNIA						
Hayakawa	N	Y	Y	Y	Y	Y
Cranston	N	Y	Y	Y	Y	Y
COLORADO						
Armstrong	Y	N	Y	N	Y	N
Hart	N	Y	Y	Y	Y	N
CONNECTICUT						
Weicker	N	Y	?	?	?	?
Dodd	?	?	?	+	?	?
DELAWARE						
Roth	Y	N	Y	N	N	Y
Biden	N	Y	Y	Y	Y	N
FLORIDA						
Hawkins	Y	N	Y	Y	Y	N
Chiles	Y	Y	Y	Y	Y	N
GEORGIA						
Mattingly	Y	N	Y	N	N	N
Nunn	?	N	Y	N	N	N
HAWAII						
Inouye	N	Y	Y	Y	Y	Y
Matsunaga	N	Y	Y	Y	Y	Y
IDAHO						
McClure	Y	N	Y	Y	Y	N
Symms	Y	N	Y	N	Y	N
ILLINOIS						
Percy	N	Y	Y	Y	N	Y
Dixon	N	Y	Y	Y	Y	?
INDIANA						
Lugar	Y	N	Y	Y	N	Y
Quayle	Y	Y	N	Y	N	Y

	349	350	351	352	353	354
IOWA						
Grassley	Y	N	Y	N	Y	N
Jepsen	Y	N	Y	N	Y	N
KANSAS						
Dole	Y	N	Y	Y	Y	Y
Kassebaum	Y	Y	Y	Y	Y	Y
KENTUCKY						
Ford	Y	N	Y	N	Y	N
Huddleston	Y	N	Y	Y	Y	N
LOUISIANA						
Johnston	Y	N	N	Y	Y	Y
Long	Y	N	Y	Y	Y	Y
MAINE						
Cohen	N	Y	Y	Y	N	Y
Mitchell	N	Y	Y	Y	N	N
MARYLAND						
Mathias	N	Y	Y	Y	Y	Y
Sarbanes	N	Y	Y	Y	Y	N
MASSACHUSETTS						
Kennedy	N	Y	Y	Y	Y	Y
Tsongas	N	Y	Y	Y	N	Y
MICHIGAN						
Levin	N	Y	Y	Y	Y	Y
Riegle	N	Y	Y	Y	Y	N
MINNESOTA						
Boschwitz	N	Y	Y	Y	Y	Y
Durenberger	N	Y	Y	Y	Y	Y
MISSISSIPPI						
Cochran	Y	N	Y	Y	Y	Y
Stennis	Y	N	Y	Y	Y	Y
MISSOURI						
Danforth	N	Y	Y	Y	Y	Y
Eagleton	N	Y	Y	Y	N	Y
MONTANA						
Baucus	N	Y	Y	Y	Y	N
Melcher	N	Y	Y	?	?	-
NEBRASKA						
Exon	Y	N	Y	Y	Y	N
Zorinsky	Y	N	Y	N	Y	N
NEVADA						
Laxalt	Y	N	Y	Y	Y	Y
Cannon	Y	N	Y	N	Y	N

	349	350	351	352	353	354
NEW HAMPSHIRE						
Humphrey	Y	Y	Y	Y	N	N
Rudman	N	Y	Y	Y	?	?
NEW JERSEY						
Brady	N	Y	Y	Y	N	Y
Bradley	N	Y	Y	Y	N	Y
NEW MEXICO						
Domenici	Y	N	Y	Y	Y	Y
Schmitt	Y	N	Y	Y	N	Y
NEW YORK						
D'Amato	Y	N	Y	Y	N	Y
Moynihan	N	Y	?	#	?	?
NORTH CAROLINA						
East	Y	N	Y	N	Y	N
Helms	Y	N	Y	N	Y	N
NORTH DAKOTA						
Andrews	N	Y	Y	Y	Y	Y
Burdick	N	Y	Y	Y	Y	Y
OHIO						
Glenn	N	Y	Y	Y	Y	N
Metzenbaum	N	Y	Y	Y	Y	N
OKLAHOMA						
Nickles	Y	N	Y	Y	N	N
Boren	Y	N	Y	Y	Y	N
OREGON						
Hatfield	N	Y	Y	Y	Y	Y
Packwood	N	Y	Y	Y	Y	Y
PENNSYLVANIA						
Heinz	N	Y	Y	Y	N	Y
Specter	N	Y	Y	Y	N	Y
RHODE ISLAND						
Chafee	N	Y	Y	Y	N	Y
Pell	Y	Y	Y	Y	N	#
SOUTH CAROLINA						
Thurmond	Y	N	Y	Y	Y	Y
Hollings	N	Y	Y	Y	Y	N
SOUTH DAKOTA						
Abdnor	Y	N	Y	N	Y	Y
Pressler	Y	N	Y	N	Y	N
TENNESSEE						
Baker	Y	Y	Y	Y	Y	Y
Sasser	Y	N	Y	X	+	X

KEY

- **Y** Voted for (yea).
- **#** Paired for.
- **+** Announced for.
- **N** Voted against (nay).
- **X** Paired against.
- **−** Announced against.
- **P** Voted "present".
- **C** Voted "present" to avoid possible conflict of interest.
- **?** Did not vote or otherwise make a position known.

Democrats   *Republicans*

	349	350	351	352	353	354
TEXAS						
Tower	Y	Y	Y	Y	Y	Y
Bentsen	Y	N	Y	N	Y	Y
UTAH						
Garn	Y	N	Y	Y	N	Y
Hatch	Y	N	Y	Y	N	Y
VERMONT						
Stafford	N	Y	Y	Y	N	Y
Leahy	N	Y	Y	Y	N	N
VIRGINIA						
Warner	Y	N	Y	Y	Y	N
Byrd*	Y	N	Y	N	N	N
WASHINGTON						
Gorton	N	Y	Y	Y	Y	Y
Jackson	N	Y	Y	Y	Y	Y
WEST VIRGINIA						
Byrd	N	N	Y	Y	N	N
Randolph	Y	N	Y	Y	N	N
WISCONSIN						
Kasten	Y	N	Y	Y	N	Y
Proxmire	Y	N	N	Y	N	N
WYOMING						
Simpson	Y	N	Y	Y	Y	N
Wallop	Y	N	Y	Y	#	?

ND - Northern Democrats   SD - Southern Democrats (Southern states - Ala., Ark., Fla., Ga., Ky., La., Miss., N.C., Okla., S.C., Tenn., Texas, Va.)   *Byrd elected as an independent.*

349. H J Res 520. Temporary Debt Limit Increase. Helms, R-N.C., motion to invoke cloture (thus limiting debate) on the Helms amendment, barring federal courts, including the Supreme Court, from handling "voluntary" school prayer cases, to the Finance Committee version of the bill. Motion rejected 53-45: R 35-19; D 18-26 (ND 7-23, SD 11-3), Sept. 23, 1982. A three-fifths majority vote (60) of the total Senate is required to invoke cloture.

350. H J Res 520. Temporary Debt Limit Increase. Goldwater, R-Ariz., motion to table (kill) the Helms, R-N.C., motion to recommit the Finance Committee substitute to that committee with instructions to send it back to the Senate after incorporating the Helms amendment to bar the federal courts, including the Supreme Court, from handling "voluntary" school prayer cases. Motion agreed to 51-48: R 24-30; D 27-18 (ND 23-7, SD 4-11), Sept. 23, 1982.

351. H J Res 520. Temporary Debt Limit Increase. Baker, R-Tenn., motion to instruct the sergeant-at-arms to require the attendance of absent senators. Motion agreed to 93-4: R 51-2; D 42-2 (ND 28-1, SD 14-1), Sept. 23, 1982.

352. H J Res 520. Temporary Debt Limit Increase. Baker, R-Tenn., motion to recommit the Finance Committee substitute to that committee with instructions to send it back to the Senate stripped of all amendments. Motion agreed to 79-16: R 43-10; D 36-6 (ND 26-2, SD 10-4), Sept. 23, 1982.

353. H J Res 520. Temporary Debt Limit Increase. Dole, R-Kan., motion to table (kill) the Quayle, R-Ind., amendment to lower sugar price supports for the 1982 crop year from 17 cents a pound to 14 cents. Motion agreed to 60-31: R 31-19; D 29-12 (ND 20-8, SD 9-4), Sept. 23, 1982.

354. H J Res 520. Temporary Debt Limit Increase. Passage of the joint resolution increasing the temporary federal debt limit to $1.29 trillion and extending the limit through Sept. 30, 1983. Passed 50-41: R 36-15; D 14-26 (ND 10-16, SD 4-10), Sept. 23, 1982.

	355	356	357	358	359	360	361	362
ALABAMA								
Denton	Y	Y	Y	Y	Y	Y	N	Y
Heflin	Y	Y	N	N	Y	N	Y	N
ALASKA								
Murkowski	Y	Y	Y	N	Y	Y	N	Y
Stevens	Y	Y	Y	Y	Y	Y	N	Y
ARIZONA								
Goldwater	Y	Y	Y	Y	Y	Y	N	Y
DeConcini	?	?	?	?	Y	Y	Y	N
ARKANSAS								
Bumpers	Y	N	Y	Y	Y	Y	Y	N
Pryor	Y	N	Y	Y	Y	N	Y	N
CALIFORNIA								
Hayakawa	?	?	?	?	Y	Y	N	Y
Cranston	Y	N	Y	Y	Y	N	Y	N
COLORADO								
Armstrong	Y	Y	N	Y	Y	Y	N	Y
Hart	Y	N	N	Y	Y	Y	Y	N
CONNECTICUT								
Weicker	Y	Y	Y	?	N	Y	N	Y
Dodd	?	-	?	?	Y	N	Y	N
DELAWARE								
Roth	?	?	?	Y	Y	Y	N	N
Biden	Y	-	?	Y	Y	N	Y	N
FLORIDA								
Hawkins	Y	N	Y	Y	Y	Y	N	Y
Chiles	Y	N	Y	Y	Y	Y	N	N
GEORGIA								
Mattingly	Y	Y	Y	+	Y	Y	N	Y
Nunn	Y	Y	Y	Y	Y	N	Y	N
HAWAII								
Inouye	Y	N	Y	Y	Y	Y	N	Y
Matsunaga	?	?	Y	Y	Y	N	Y	N
IDAHO								
McClure	Y	Y	Y	Y	Y	Y	N	Y
Symms	+	Y	N	?	Y	Y	N	Y
ILLINOIS								
Percy	Y	Y	Y	Y	Y	Y	N	Y
Dixon	+	Y	Y	Y	Y	N	Y	N
INDIANA								
Lugar	Y	Y	N	Y	Y	Y	N	Y
Quayle	Y	Y	Y	Y	Y	Y	N	Y
IOWA								
Grassley	Y	Y	Y	Y	Y	Y	Y	N
Jepsen	Y	Y	Y	Y	Y	Y	Y	N
KANSAS								
Dole	Y	Y	Y	N	Y	N	N	Y
Kassebaum	Y	Y	?	Y	Y	Y	Y	N
KENTUCKY								
Ford	Y	N	Y	Y	Y	N	Y	N
Huddleston	Y	Y	Y	Y	Y	N	Y	N
LOUISIANA								
Johnston	Y	N	Y	Y	Y	Y	Y	N
Long	Y	N	Y	N	Y	Y	Y	N
MAINE								
Cohen	Y	N	Y	Y	Y	N	N	Y
Mitchell	Y	N	Y	Y	Y	Y	N	N
MARYLAND								
Mathias	?	?	?	?	N	Y	N	Y
Sarbanes	Y	N	Y	Y	Y	Y	Y	N
MASSACHUSETTS								
Kennedy	?	?	?	?	Y	Y	Y	N
Tsongas	Y	N	Y	Y	Y	Y	Y	N
MICHIGAN								
Levin	Y	N	Y	Y	Y	Y	Y	N
Riegle	Y	N	Y	Y	Y	Y	Y	N
MINNESOTA								
Boschwitz	Y	N	Y	Y	Y	Y	N	Y
Durenberger	Y	N	+	?	Y	Y	Y	N
MISSISSIPPI								
Cochran	Y	Y	Y	Y	Y	N	N	Y
Stennis	?	?	Y	Y	Y	N	Y	N
MISSOURI								
Danforth	?	?	?	?	Y	Y	N	N
Eagleton	Y	N	Y	Y	Y	N	Y	N
MONTANA								
Baucus	Y	N	Y	Y	Y	N	Y	N
Melcher	?	?	?	?	Y	Y	Y	N
NEBRASKA								
Exon	?	N	Y	N	Y	Y	Y	N
Zorinsky	Y	Y	N	Y	Y	Y	Y	N
NEVADA								
Laxalt	Y	Y	Y	Y	Y	N	N	Y
Cannon	+	-	+	?	Y	Y	N	N
NEW HAMPSHIRE								
Humphrey	Y	Y	N	Y	Y	Y	N	Y
Rudman	Y	N	Y	Y	Y	Y	N	Y
NEW JERSEY								
Brady	Y	N	Y	Y	Y	Y	N	?
Bradley	Y	N	Y	N	Y	Y	Y	N
NEW MEXICO								
Domenici	Y	Y	Y	Y	Y	Y	N	N
Schmitt	Y	N	Y	Y	Y	Y	Y	N
NEW YORK								
D'Amato	Y	N	Y	Y	Y	Y	N	Y
Moynihan	Y	N	Y	Y	Y	Y	Y	N
NORTH CAROLINA								
East	Y	Y	N	Y	Y	N	N	Y
Helms	Y	Y	N	Y	Y	Y	N	Y
NORTH DAKOTA								
Andrews	Y	Y	Y	?	Y	N	Y	N
Burdick	Y	N	Y	Y	Y	Y	Y	N
OHIO								
Glenn	Y	N	Y	Y	Y	N	Y	N
Metzenbaum	Y	N	Y	?	Y	Y	N	Y
OKLAHOMA								
Nickles	Y	Y	N	N	Y	Y	Y	N
Boren	Y	Y	Y	N	?	?	?	?
OREGON								
Hatfield	Y	Y	Y	+	Y	Y	N	Y
Packwood	Y	Y	Y	Y	Y	Y	N	Y
PENNSYLVANIA								
Heinz	Y	N	Y	Y	?	?	?	?
Specter	Y	N	Y	Y	N	N	N	Y
RHODE ISLAND								
Chafee	Y	N	Y	Y	Y	Y	N	Y
Pell	Y	N	Y	Y	Y	Y	N	Y
SOUTH CAROLINA								
Thurmond	Y	Y	Y	Y	Y	N	N	N
Hollings	N	Y	Y	Y	Y	Y	Y	N
SOUTH DAKOTA								
Abdnor	Y	Y	Y	Y	Y	N	Y	N
Pressler	?	Y	Y	Y	Y	Y	Y	N
TENNESSEE								
Baker	Y	Y	Y	?	Y	N	N	Y
Sasser	+	-	+	?	Y	N	Y	N
TEXAS								
Tower	Y	Y	Y	Y	Y	N	N	N
Bentsen	?	?	?	?	Y	Y	Y	N
UTAH								
Garn	Y	Y	Y	Y	Y	Y	N	Y
Hatch	Y	Y	Y	Y	Y	Y	Y	Y
VERMONT								
Stafford	Y	N	Y	?	Y	Y	N	Y
Leahy	Y	N	Y	Y	Y	Y	Y	N
VIRGINIA								
Warner	Y	Y	Y	Y	Y	Y	N	Y
Byrd*	Y	Y	N	?	Y	Y	N	Y
WASHINGTON								
Gorton	Y	N	Y	Y	Y	Y	N	Y
Jackson	Y	N	Y	Y	Y	N	Y	N
WEST VIRGINIA								
Byrd	Y	N	Y	Y	Y	Y	N	Y
Randolph	Y	N	Y	Y	Y	Y	Y	N
WISCONSIN								
Kasten	Y	Y	Y	Y	Y	Y	N	N
Proxmire	Y	Y	N	N	Y	Y	N	Y
WYOMING								
Simpson	+	+	+	?	Y	Y	N	Y
Wallop	?	?	?	?	Y	Y	N	N

KEY

Y Voted for (yea).
Paired for.
+ Announced for.
N Voted against (nay).
X Paired against.
- Announced against.
P Voted "present".
C Voted "present" to avoid possible conflict of interest.
? Did not vote or otherwise make a position known.

Democrats   *Republicans*

ND - Northern Democrats   SD - Southern Democrats (Southern states - Ala., Ark., Fla., Ga., Ky., La., Miss., N.C., Okla., S.C., Tenn., Texas, Va.)   *Byrd elected as an independent.*

355. HR 6956. Department of Housing and Urban Development Appropriations, Fiscal 1983. Armstrong, R-Colo., amendment to state the sense of the Senate that the State Department should investigate reports that the Soviet Union is using slave labor to build the trans-Siberian pipeline. Adopted 80-1: R 46-0; D 34-1 (ND 23-0, SD 11-1), Sept. 24, 1982.

356. HR 6956. Department of Housing and Urban Development Appropriations, Fiscal 1983. Garn, R-Utah, motion to table (kill) the Moynihan, D-N.Y., amendment to add $39.3 million for Environmental Protection Agency research and development and $30 million to the hazardous wastes cleanup superfund. Motion agreed to 44-40: R 35-13; D 9-27 (ND 3-21, SD 6-6), Sept. 24, 1982.

357. HR 6956. Department of Housing and Urban Development Appropriations, Fiscal 1983. Passage of the bill to appropriate $47,503,877,200 in fiscal 1983 for the Department of Housing and Urban Development and 17 independent agencies. Passed 73-11: R 39-7; D 34-4 (ND 23-2, SD 11-2), Sept. 24, 1982. The president had requested $41,400,675,000 for the programs covered by the bill.

358. S 2879. Depository Institutions Amendments. Garn, R-Utah, motion to table (kill) the Boren, D-Okla., amendment to make federal savings and loan associations and federal savings and loan banks subject to the same conditions for opening new branches that are applicable to national banks in the same state. Motion agreed to 67-11: R 38-3; D 29-8 (ND 20-5, SD 9-3), Sept. 24, 1982.

359. HR 4613. Debt Collection Act of 1982. Passage of the bill to make it easier for the federal government to collect billions of dollars owed to it in delinquent taxes and overdue loans. Passed 96-2: R 51-2; D 45-0 (ND 31-0, SD 14-0), Sept. 28, 1982.

360. HR 7072. Agriculture Appropriations, Fiscal 1983. Armstrong, R-Colo., amendment to deny eligibility for price support, crop insurance and other federal farm programs to farmers who cultivate highly erodible land as classified by the Agriculture Department's Soil Conservation Service land capability classification system. Adopted 69-29: R 41-12; D 28-17 (ND 21-10, SD 7-7), Sept. 28, 1982.

361. HR 7072. Agriculture Appropriations, Fiscal 1983. Zorinsky, D-Neb., amendment to require that federal payments to farmers for on-farm storage of grain in the farmer-held reserve be made at rates equal to those paid to commercial grain storage facilities. Rejected 48-50: R 10-43; D 38-7 (ND 26-5, SD 12-2), Sept. 28, 1982.

362. HR 7072. Agriculture Appropriations, Fiscal 1983. Cochran, R-Miss., motion to table (kill) the Huddleston, D-Ky., amendment to extend the economic emergency loan program through fiscal 1983, provide $600 million for the loans and to provide for one-year deferrals of Farmers Home Administration farm loan repayments in certain circumstances. Motion rejected 37-60: R 34-18; D 3-42 (ND 2-29, SD 1-13), Sept. 28, 1982. A "nay" was a vote supporting the president's position.

CQ Senate Votes 363 - 369

Corresponding to Congressional Record Votes 363, 364, 365, 366, 367, 368, 369

	363	364	365	366	367	368	369
ALABAMA							
Denton	Y	Y	N	N	Y	N	N
Heflin	N	Y	N	Y	N	Y	Y
ALASKA							
Murkowski	N	Y	N	N	Y	Y	N
Stevens	N	Y	N	N	Y	Y	N
ARIZONA							
Goldwater	N	Y	Y	N	Y	N	N
DeConcini	N	Y	Y	Y	N	Y	Y
ARKANSAS							
Bumpers	N	Y	Y	Y	N	Y	Y
Pryor	N	Y	Y	Y	N	Y	Y
CALIFORNIA							
Hayakawa	N	Y	N	N	Y	N	Y
Cranston	N	Y	Y	Y	N	Y	Y
COLORADO							
Armstrong	N	N	Y	N	Y	N	N
Hart	Y	Y	Y	Y	N	Y	Y
CONNECTICUT							
Weicker	N	Y	N	Y	N	Y	Y
Dodd	N	Y	Y	Y	N	Y	Y
DELAWARE							
Roth	N	N	Y	N	Y	Y	Y
Biden	N	Y	Y	Y	N	Y	Y
FLORIDA							
Hawkins	N	N	Y	N	Y	N	Y
Chiles	Y	Y	Y	N	Y	Y	Y
GEORGIA							
Mattingly	N	Y	N	N	Y	N	N
Nunn	Y	Y	Y	Y	N	Y	Y
HAWAII							
Inouye	Y	Y	N	Y	N	Y	Y
Matsunaga	N	Y	?	Y	N	Y	Y
IDAHO							
McClure	Y	Y	N	N	Y	N	N
Symms	N	N	N	N	Y	N	N
ILLINOIS							
Percy	Y	N	Y	N	Y	Y	Y
Dixon	Y	Y	Y	Y	N	Y	Y
INDIANA							
Lugar	N	Y	Y	Y	N	Y	N
Quayle	N	Y	Y	N	Y	N	N
IOWA							
Grassley	N	Y	N	N	Y	N	N
Jepsen	N	Y	Y	N	Y	N	N
KANSAS							
Dole	N	Y	N	N	Y	N	Y
Kassebaum	N	Y	Y	N	Y	Y	Y
KENTUCKY							
Ford	Y	Y	N	Y	N	Y	Y
Huddleston	Y	Y	N	Y	N	Y	Y
LOUISIANA							
Johnston	N	Y	N	Y	N	Y	Y
Long	Y	Y	N	X	?	Y	Y
MAINE							
Cohen	Y	Y	Y	N	Y	N	Y
Mitchell	Y	Y	Y	Y	N	Y	Y
MARYLAND							
Mathias	N	N	N	Y	N	Y	Y
Sarbanes	N	Y	Y	Y	N	Y	Y
MASSACHUSETTS							
Kennedy	N	Y	+	#	-	+	Y
Tsongas	N	Y	Y	Y	N	Y	Y
MICHIGAN							
Levin	N	Y	Y	Y	N	Y	Y
Riegle	N	Y	Y	Y	N	Y	+
MINNESOTA							
Boschwitz	N	Y	Y	N	Y	N	Y
Durenberger	N	Y	Y	Y	N	Y	Y
MISSISSIPPI							
Cochran	Y	Y	N	N	Y	N	Y
Stennis	Y	Y	N	Y	N	Y	Y
MISSOURI							
Danforth	N	Y	N	Y	N	Y	Y
Eagleton	N	Y	Y	Y	N	Y	Y
MONTANA							
Baucus	N	Y	+	Y	N	Y	Y
Melcher	N	Y	Y	Y	N	Y	Y
NEBRASKA							
Exon	N	Y	Y	Y	N	Y	Y
Zorinsky	N	Y	N	N	Y	Y	Y
NEVADA							
Laxalt	N	Y	N	N	Y	N	N
Cannon	Y	Y	N	Y	N	Y	Y
NEW HAMPSHIRE							
Humphrey	Y	N	Y	N	Y	N	N
Rudman	N	Y	Y	N	Y	N	N
NEW JERSEY							
Brady	N	Y	N	N	Y	Y	N
Bradley	Y	Y	Y	Y	N	Y	Y
NEW MEXICO							
Domenici	Y	Y	N	N	Y	N	N
Schmitt	N	Y	N	N	Y	N	Y
NEW YORK							
D'Amato	N	Y	N	N	Y	Y	Y
Moynihan	N	Y	Y	Y	N	Y	Y
NORTH CAROLINA							
East	N	N	N	N	Y	N	N
Helms	N	N	N	N	Y	N	N
NORTH DAKOTA							
Andrews	N	Y	N	N	Y	N	Y
Burdick	N	Y	N	Y	N	Y	Y
OHIO							
Glenn	Y	Y	Y	Y	N	Y	Y
Metzenbaum	Y	Y	Y	Y	N	Y	Y
OKLAHOMA							
Nickles	N	N	Y	N	Y	N	N
Boren	?	?	N	Y	N	Y	Y
OREGON							
Hatfield	Y	Y	Y	N	Y	N	Y
Packwood	Y	Y	N	Y	N	Y	Y
PENNSYLVANIA							
Heinz	?	?	N	Y	N	Y	Y
Specter	N	Y	N	Y	N	Y	Y
RHODE ISLAND							
Chafee	Y	Y	Y	Y	N	Y	Y
Pell	Y	N	Y	N	Y	Y	Y
SOUTH CAROLINA							
Thurmond	N	Y	N	Y	N	Y	N
Hollings	Y	Y	Y	N	Y	N	Y
SOUTH DAKOTA							
Abdnor	N	Y	N	Y	N	Y	N
Pressler	N	Y	N	Y	N	Y	Y
TENNESSEE							
Baker	Y	Y	N	Y	N	Y	N
Sasser	N	Y	N	Y	N	Y	Y
TEXAS							
Tower	N	Y	N	N	Y	N	N
Bentsen	N	Y	Y	Y	N	Y	Y
UTAH							
Garn	N	Y	N	N	Y	N	N
Hatch	N	Y	N	N	Y	N	Y
VERMONT							
Stafford	N	Y	Y	Y	N	Y	Y
Leahy	N	Y	Y	Y	N	Y	Y
VIRGINIA							
Warner	N	Y	N	Y	N	Y	Y
Byrd*	Y	N	Y	N	Y	N	Y
WASHINGTON							
Gorton	N	N	N	N	Y	N	N
Jackson	N	Y	N	Y	N	Y	Y
WEST VIRGINIA							
Byrd	N	Y	Y	Y	N	Y	Y
Randolph	N	Y	Y	Y	N	Y	Y
WISCONSIN							
Kasten	N	Y	N	Y	N	Y	N
Proxmire	N	N	Y	Y	N	Y	Y
WYOMING							
Simpson	N	Y	N	N	Y	N	N
Wallop	N	Y	N	N	Y	N	Y

KEY

Y Voted for (yea).
\# Paired for.
\+ Announced for.
N Voted against (nay).
X Paired against.
- Announced against.
P Voted "present".
C Voted "present" to avoid possible conflict of interest.
? Did not vote or otherwise make a position known.

Democrats *Republicans*

ND - Northern Democrats   SD - Southern Democrats (Southern states - Ala., Ark., Fla., Ga., Ky., La., Miss., N.C., Okla., S.C., Tenn., Texas, Va.)   *Byrd elected as an independent.

---

363. HR 7072. Agriculture Appropriations, Fiscal 1983. Cochran, R-Miss., motion to table (kill) the Hayakawa, R-Calif., amendment to revise federal standards for solids content of fresh milk. Motion rejected 28-70: R 11-42; D 17-28 (ND 9-22, SD 8-6), Sept. 28, 1982.

364. HR 7072. Agriculture Appropriations, Fiscal 1983. Passage of the bill to appropriate $25,155,989,000 in new budget authority for fiscal 1983 for the Agriculture Department and related agencies. Passed 84-14: R 42-11; D 42-3 (ND 29-2, SD 13-1), Sept. 28, 1982. The president had requested $23,083,665,000.

365. H J Res 599. Continuing Appropriations, Fiscal 1983. Humphrey, R-N.H., amendment to bar use of funds provided by the joint resolution for the Clinch River breeder reactor project. Rejected 48-49: R 18-36; D 30-13 (ND 23-5, SD 7-8), Sept. 29, 1982. A "nay" was a vote supporting the president's position.

366. H J Res 599. Continuing Appropriations, Fiscal 1983. Metzenbaum, D-Ohio, amendment, to the Metzenbaum amendment, to liberalize unemployment benefits by 1) suspending, until the national unemployment rate declines to 8.7 percent, provisions of the 1981 reconciliation legislation (PL 97-35) that excluded persons who had exhausted their regular unemployment benefits from calculations used to trigger extended benefits; 2) suspending provisions of PL 97-35 that altered the formula used to trigger extended benefits; and 3) terminating the supplemental unemployment benefits program enacted by Congress in 1982 (PL

97-248) only when unemployment drops below 8.7 percent. Rejected 47-51: R 7-47; D 40-4 (ND 28-2, SD 12-2), Sept. 29, 1982. (The amendment made clarifying changes in the original Metzenbaum amendment, which subsequently was rejected by voice vote.) A "nay" was a vote supporting the president's position.

367. H J Res 599. Continuing Appropriations, Fiscal 1983. Dole, R-Kan., motion to table (kill) the Baker, R-Tenn., motion to reconsider the vote by which the Metzenbaum, D-Ohio, amendment was rejected *(see vote 366, above)*. Motion agreed to 50-48: R 47-7; D 3-41 (ND 1-29, SD 2-12), Sept. 29, 1982.

368. H J Res 599. Continuing Appropriations, Fiscal 1983. Hatfield, R-Ore., motion to table (kill) the Helms, R-N.C., amendment to require the Federal Election Commission to prepare and implement regulations to enforce court decisions barring use by labor organizations for political purposes of union dues or other money required as a condition of employment. Motion agreed to 62-37: R 18-36; D 44-1 (ND 30-0, SD 14-1), Sept. 29, 1982.

369. H J Res 599. Continuing Appropriations, Fiscal 1983. Moynihan, D-N.Y., amendment, as amended by the Bumpers, D-Ark., amendment, to state the sense of the Senate that Congress should reject any proposal to impose a "means" test on eligibility or benefits under the Medicare program. (The Bumpers amendment, adopted by voice vote, stated the sense of the Senate that the president should proclaim Oct. 10, 1982, as "National Peace Day.") Adopted 70-29: R 25-29; D 45-0 (ND 30-0, SD 15-0), Sept. 29, 1982.

	370	371	372	373	374	375	376
ALABAMA							
Denton	?	-	?	?	+	+	?
Heflin	Y	Y	N	N	Y	Y	Y
ALASKA							
Murkowski	Y	Y	Y	Y	Y	Y	Y
Stevens	Y	Y	Y	Y	Y	Y	Y
ARIZONA							
Goldwater	Y	N	Y	N	Y	Y	Y
DeConcini	Y	Y	Y	Y	Y	Y	Y
ARKANSAS							
Bumpers	N	Y	N	Y	Y	Y	Y
Pryor	N	N	Y	Y	Y	Y	Y
CALIFORNIA							
Hayakawa	Y	N	Y	Y	Y	Y	Y
Cranston	N	Y	N	N	Y	Y	Y
COLORADO							
Armstrong	Y	N	Y	N	Y	Y	Y
Hart	N	Y	N	N	Y	Y	Y
CONNECTICUT							
Weicker	N	Y	N	Y	Y	Y	Y
Dodd	N	Y	N	N	?	?	?
DELAWARE							
Roth	Y	N	Y	N	Y	Y	Y
Biden	N	Y	N	N	Y	Y	Y
FLORIDA							
Hawkins	Y	N	Y	Y	Y	Y	Y
Chiles	N	Y	Y	Y	Y	Y	Y
GEORGIA							
Mattingly	Y	N	Y	Y	Y	Y	Y
Nunn	N	N	Y	Y	Y	Y	Y
HAWAII							
Inouye	N	Y	N	Y	Y	Y	Y
Matsunaga	N	Y	N	Y	?	?	?
IDAHO							
McClure	Y	Y	Y	Y	Y	Y	Y
Symms	Y	N	Y	N	Y	Y	Y
ILLINOIS							
Percy	+	?	?	?	Y	Y	Y
Dixon	N	Y	N	Y	Y	Y	Y
INDIANA							
Lugar	Y	N	Y	Y	Y	Y	Y
Quayle	N	N	Y	Y	Y	Y	Y
IOWA							
Grassley	Y	N	Y	Y	Y	Y	Y
Jepsen	Y	N	Y	Y	Y	Y	Y
KANSAS							
Dole	Y	N	Y	Y	Y	Y	Y
Kassebaum	N	N	Y	Y	Y	Y	Y
KENTUCKY							
Ford	N	Y	N	Y	Y	Y	Y
Huddleston	N	Y	N	Y	Y	Y	Y
LOUISIANA							
Johnston	N	Y	Y	Y	Y	Y	Y
Long	Y	Y	Y	Y	Y	?	?
MAINE							
Cohen	Y	N	Y	Y	Y	Y	Y
Mitchell	N	Y	N	Y	Y	Y	Y
MARYLAND							
Mathias	N	Y	Y	Y	Y	Y	Y
Sarbanes	N	Y	N	Y	Y	Y	Y
MASSACHUSETTS							
Kennedy	-	Y	N	N	Y	Y	Y
Tsongas	N	Y	N	Y	Y	Y	Y
MICHIGAN							
Levin	N	Y	N	N	Y	Y	Y
Riegle	?	#	-	N	Y	Y	Y
MINNESOTA							
Boschwitz	Y	N	Y	Y	Y	Y	Y
Durenberger	N	Y	N	Y	Y	Y	Y
MISSISSIPPI							
Cochran	Y	N	Y	Y	Y	Y	Y
Stennis	Y	N	Y	Y	Y	Y	Y
MISSOURI							
Danforth	N	Y	Y	Y	Y	Y	Y
Eagleton	N	Y	N	Y	Y	Y	Y
MONTANA							
Baucus	N	Y	N	N	Y	Y	Y
Melcher	N	Y	N	Y	Y	Y	Y
NEBRASKA							
Exon	N	X	Y	Y	Y	Y	Y
Zorinsky	Y	N	Y	Y	Y	Y	Y
NEVADA							
Laxalt	Y	N	Y	Y	Y	Y	Y
Cannon	Y	Y	N	Y	Y	Y	Y
NEW HAMPSHIRE							
Humphrey	Y	N	Y	Y	Y	Y	Y
Rudman	Y	N	Y	Y	Y	Y	Y
NEW JERSEY							
Brady	Y	N	Y	Y	Y	Y	Y
Bradley	N	Y	N	N	Y	Y	Y
NEW MEXICO							
Domenici	Y	N	Y	Y	Y	Y	Y
Schmitt	Y	N	Y	Y	Y	Y	Y
NEW YORK							
D'Amato	Y	Y	Y	Y	Y	Y	Y
Moynihan	N	Y	N	N	Y	Y	Y
NORTH CAROLINA							
East	Y	N	Y	N	Y	Y	N
Helms	Y	N	Y	N	Y	Y	Y
NORTH DAKOTA							
Andrews	N	Y	Y	Y	Y	Y	Y
Burdick	N	Y	N	Y	Y	Y	Y
OHIO							
Glenn	N	Y	N	Y	Y	Y	Y
Metzenbaum	N	Y	N	N	Y	Y	Y
OKLAHOMA							
Nickles	Y	N	Y	N	Y	Y	Y
Boren	N	N	Y	N	Y	Y	+
OREGON							
Hatfield	N	Y	Y	Y	Y	Y	Y
Packwood	Y	Y	Y	Y	Y	Y	Y
PENNSYLVANIA							
Heinz	N	Y	N	Y	Y	Y	Y
Specter	N	Y	N	Y	Y	Y	Y
RHODE ISLAND							
Chafee	N	Y	N	Y	Y	Y	Y
Pell	N	Y	N	N	Y	Y	Y
SOUTH CAROLINA							
Thurmond	Y	N	Y	Y	Y	Y	Y
Hollings	N	Y	Y	N	Y	Y	Y
SOUTH DAKOTA							
Abdnor	Y	N	Y	Y	Y	Y	Y
Pressler	Y	N	Y	Y	Y	Y	Y
TENNESSEE							
Baker	Y	N	Y	Y	Y	Y	Y
Sasser	Y	Y	N	Y	Y	Y	Y
TEXAS							
Tower	Y	N	Y	Y	Y	?	?
Bentsen	Y	N	Y	Y	Y	Y	Y
UTAH							
Garn	Y	N	Y	Y	Y	Y	Y
Hatch	Y	N	Y	Y	Y	Y	Y
VERMONT							
Stafford	N	Y	Y	Y	Y	Y	Y
Leahy	N	Y	N	N	Y	Y	Y
VIRGINIA							
Warner	Y	N	Y	Y	Y	Y	Y
Byrd*	N	N	Y	N	Y	Y	Y
WASHINGTON							
Gorton	Y	N	Y	Y	Y	Y	Y
Jackson	Y	Y	N	Y	Y	Y	Y
WEST VIRGINIA							
Byrd	Y	Y	N	Y	Y	Y	Y
Randolph	N	Y	N	Y	Y	Y	Y
WISCONSIN							
Kasten	Y	N	Y	Y	Y	Y	Y
Proxmire	N	Y	N	N	Y	Y	Y
WYOMING							
Simpson	Y	N	Y	Y	Y	Y	Y
Wallop	Y	N	Y	Y	Y	Y	Y

KEY

Y Voted for (yea).
\# Paired for.
+ Announced for.
N Voted against (nay).
X Paired against.
- Announced against.
P Voted "present".
C Voted "present" to avoid possible conflict of interest.
? Did not vote or otherwise make a position known.

Democrats   *Republicans*

ND - Northern Democrats   SD - Southern Democrats (Southern states - Ala., Ark., Fla., Ga., Ky., La., Miss., N.C., Okla., S.C., Tenn., Texas, Va.)   *Byrd elected as an independent.*

370. H J Res 599. Continuing Appropriations, Fiscal 1983. Baker, R-Tenn., motion to table (kill) the Hollings, D-S.C., amendment to prohibit use of funds in the resolution for procurement of MX missiles until Congress had approved a plan for the basing mode of the system. Motion agreed to 50-46: R 40-12; D 10-34 (ND 5-24, SD 5-10), Sept. 29, 1982. A "yea" was a vote supporting the president's position.

371. H J Res 599. Continuing Appropriations, Fiscal 1983. Hatfield, R-Ore., motion to table (kill) the Nickles, R-Okla., amendment, to the Kennedy, D-Mass., amendment *(see vote 372, below)*, to establish in law certain regulatory changes proposed by the Labor Department, but blocked by court order, in the Davis-Bacon prevailing wage law; the provisions would increase the minimum size of federal contracts affected by the law to $100,000 from $2,000, and make certain changes in the way local prevailing wages were calculated, for example by barring use of urban wage scales in rural areas. Motion agreed to 52-44: R 15-37; D 37-7 (ND 28-1, SD 9-6), Sept. 29, 1982. A "nay" was a vote supporting the president's position.

372. H J Res 599. Continuing Appropriations, Fiscal 1983. Goldwater, R-Ariz., motion to table (kill) the Kennedy, D-Mass., amendment to establish a new federal public works program, funded at an amount equal to 5 percent of annual federal unemployment compensation costs, to provide jobs to the unemployed. Motion agreed to 60-37: R 47-5; D 13-32 (ND 3-27, SD 10-5), Sept. 29, 1982. A "yea" was a vote supporting the president's position.

373. H J Res 599. Continuing Appropriations, Fiscal 1983. Passage of the joint resolution to provide continued funding, through Dec. 22, 1982, for government agencies whose regular fiscal 1983 appropriations bills had not been enacted. Passed 72-26: R 45-7; D 27-19 (ND 16-15, SD 11-4), Sept. 29, 1982.

374. Treaties. Adoption of the resolutions of ratification for the following treaties: **97-2,** Protocol to the Agreement on the Importation of Educational, Scientific and Cultural Materials; **97-18,** Convention Between the United States and Mexico for the Recovery and Return of Stolen or Embezzled Vehicles and Aircraft; **Exec N, 92th Cong, 2nd Sess,** International Convention on Tonnage Measurements of Ships, 1969; **97-25,** Convention for the Conservation of Salmon in the North Atlantic Ocean; and **97-26,** Tax Convention with the Republic of Austria. Adopted en bloc 97-0: R 53-0; D 44-0 (ND 29-0, SD 15-0), Sept. 30, 1982. A two-thirds majority of those present and voting (65 in this case) is required for adoption of resolutions of ratification.

375. S 2036. Job Training. Adoption of the conference report on the bill to establish a new program, replacing the expired Comprehensive Employment and Training Act, of grants to states and local governments for providing skill training and other employment-related assistance to economically disadvantaged youths and adults. Adopted 95-0: R 52-0; D 43-0 (ND 29-0, SD 14-0), Sept. 30, 1982. A "yea" was a vote supporting the president's position.

376. S 1688. Armed Career Criminal Act. Passage of the bill to authorize prosecution in federal court of anyone using a firearm to commit or attempt to commit robbery or burglary if that person has two prior convictions for such offenses, and to provide a minimum mandatory sentence of 15 years in prison. Passed 93-1: R 51-1; D 42-0 (ND 29-0, SD 13-0), Sept. 30, 1982.

KEY

Y	Voted for (yea).
#	Paired for.
+	Announced for.
N	Voted against (nay).
X	Paired against.
-	Announced against.
P	Voted "present".
C	Voted "present" to avoid possible conflict of interest.
?	Did not vote or otherwise make a position known.

Democrats *Republicans*

	377	378	379	380	381	382	383
ALABAMA							
Denton	N	N	Y	Y	N	Y	Y
Heflin	Y	N	Y	Y	N	Y	Y
ALASKA							
Murkowski	N	Y	Y	N	Y	Y	N
Stevens	N	N	Y	N	Y	Y	N
ARIZONA							
Goldwater	N	N	Y	?	N	Y	N
DeConcini	Y	N	Y	Y	N	Y	?
ARKANSAS							
Bumpers	Y	N	Y	N	Y	Y	Y
Pryor	Y	Y	Y	Y	N	Y	Y
CALIFORNIA							
Hayakawa	N	N	Y	Y	Y	Y	Y
Cranston	Y	Y	Y	Y	N	Y	Y
COLORADO							
Armstrong	N	Y	Y	N	N	Y	N
Hart	Y	Y	Y	Y	N	Y	Y
CONNECTICUT							
Weicker	Y	Y	Y	?	?	?	?
Dodd	?	?	?	?	?	?	?
DELAWARE							
Roth	Y	N	Y	Y	N	Y	N
Biden	Y	Y	Y	Y	Y	Y	N
FLORIDA							
Hawkins	Y	N	Y	N	N	Y	Y
Chiles	Y	N	Y	N	N	Y	N
GEORGIA							
Mattingly	Y	N	Y	N	Y	Y	N
Nunn	Y	N	Y	Y	N	Y	Y
HAWAII							
Inouye	Y	N	Y	N	N	Y	Y
Matsunaga	?	?	?	?	?	?	?
IDAHO							
McClure	Y	N	Y	N	N	Y	Y
Symms	N	N	Y	N	N	Y	Y
ILLINOIS							
Percy	N	N	Y	N	N	Y	N
Dixon	Y	N	Y	N	N	Y	N
INDIANA							
Lugar	N	N	Y	N	Y	Y	Y
Quayle	N	N	Y	Y	Y	Y	Y
IOWA							
Grassley	N	N	Y	N	N	Y	Y
Jepsen	N	N	Y	N	N	Y	N
KANSAS							
Dole	N	Y	Y	N	Y	Y	N
Kassebaum	Y	N	Y	N	N	Y	N
KENTUCKY							
Ford	Y	N	Y	Y	N	Y	Y
Huddleston	Y	N	Y	Y	N	Y	Y
LOUISIANA							
Johnston	Y	Y	Y	N	N	Y	?
Long	Y	Y	Y	Y	N	Y	Y
MAINE							
Cohen	Y	N	Y	N	N	Y	Y
Mitchell	Y	Y	Y	N	N	Y	Y
MARYLAND							
Mathias	N	Y	N	Y	N	Y	Y
Sarbanes	Y	N	Y	Y	N	Y	N
MASSACHUSETTS							
Kennedy	Y	Y	Y	?	?	?	?
Tsongas	Y	N	Y	Y	N	?	N
MICHIGAN							
Levin	Y	Y	Y	Y	Y	Y	Y
Riegle	Y	Y	Y	Y	N	Y	+
MINNESOTA							
Boschwitz	N	Y	Y	N	N	Y	N
Durenberger	Y	Y	Y	N	N	Y	?
MISSISSIPPI							
Cochran	N	N	Y	N	N	Y	N
Stennis	Y	N	Y	Y	N	Y	Y
MISSOURI							
Danforth	?	?	?	Y	N	Y	Y
Eagleton	Y	N	Y	Y	N	Y	Y
MONTANA							
Baucus	Y	Y	Y	N	N	Y	Y
Melcher	Y	Y	Y	?	-	+	+
NEBRASKA							
Exon	Y	N	Y	N	N	Y	Y
Zorinsky	Y	N	Y	N	Y	Y	Y
NEVADA							
Laxalt	N	N	Y	Y	Y	Y	Y
Cannon	Y	N	Y	N	N	Y	Y
NEW HAMPSHIRE							
Humphrey	N	N	Y	Y	Y	Y	N
Rudman	N	Y	Y	Y	Y	Y	N
NEW JERSEY							
Brady	N	N	Y	Y	N	?	N
Bradley	Y	N	Y	Y	N	Y	Y
NEW MEXICO							
Domenici	Y	N	Y	Y	N	Y	Y
Schmitt	Y	N	Y	Y	Y	Y	N
NEW YORK							
D'Amato	Y	N	Y	N	N	Y	N
Moynihan	Y	N	Y	N	Y	N	N
NORTH CAROLINA							
East	N	N	Y	N	N	Y	Y
Helms	N	N	Y	N	N	Y	Y
NORTH DAKOTA							
Andrews	N	Y	Y	N	N	Y	Y
Burdick	Y	Y	Y	N	N	Y	Y
OHIO							
Glenn	Y	N	Y	N	N	Y	Y
Metzenbaum	Y	N	Y	N	Y	N	N
OKLAHOMA							
Nickles	N	N	Y	N	Y	Y	N
Boren	?	?	?	?	-	?	?
OREGON							
Hatfield	Y	Y	Y	N	N	Y	Y
Packwood	Y	Y	Y	N	N	Y	N
PENNSYLVANIA							
Heinz	Y	N	Y	N	Y	N	N
Specter	Y	Y	Y	N	Y	Y	Y
RHODE ISLAND							
Chafee	Y	Y	Y	Y	Y	Y	Y
Pell	Y	Y	Y	Y	Y	Y	Y
SOUTH CAROLINA							
Thurmond	N	N	Y	Y	Y	Y	Y
Hollings	Y	N	Y	Y	N	Y	?
SOUTH DAKOTA							
Abdnor	N	N	Y	N	Y	Y	Y
Pressler	N	N	Y	N	N	Y	Y
TENNESSEE							
Baker	N	Y	Y	Y	Y	Y	N
Sasser	Y	N	Y	N	N	Y	Y

	377	378	379	380	381	382	383
TEXAS							
Tower	N	N	Y	N	N	Y	N
Bentsen	Y	N	Y	?	?	?	?
UTAH							
Garn	Y	Y	Y	Y	N	Y	Y
Hatch	Y	N	Y	N	Y	N	N
VERMONT							
Stafford	Y	Y	Y	Y	N	Y	?
Leahy	Y	Y	Y	Y	N	Y	Y
VIRGINIA							
Warner	Y	N	Y	N	Y	N	Y
Byrd*	Y	N	Y	N	Y	N	Y
WASHINGTON							
Gorton	N	Y	Y	N	Y	Y	N
Jackson	Y	N	Y	N	N	Y	Y
WEST VIRGINIA							
Byrd	Y	N	Y	N	Y	N	Y
Randolph	Y	N	Y	Y	Y	Y	Y
WISCONSIN							
Kasten	N	N	Y	N	N	Y	N
Proxmire	Y	N	Y	Y	Y	Y	N
WYOMING							
Simpson	N	N	Y	N	N	Y	Y
Wallop	N	N	Y	N	N	Y	Y

ND - Northern Democrats   SD - Southern Democrats (Southern states - Ala., Ark., Fla., Ga., Ky., La., Miss., N.C., Okla., S.C., Tenn., Texas, Va.)   *Byrd elected as an independent.*

---

377. S 2572. Violent Crime and Drug Enforcement Act. DeConcini, D-Ariz., amendment to create a White House office to coordinate drug enforcement operations and policy. Adopted 63-33: R 20-33; D 43-0 (ND 29-0, SD 14-0), Sept. 30, 1982.

378. S 2572. Violent Crime and Drug Enforcement Act. Specter, R-Pa., amendment to reduce from 90 days to 60 days the time in which federal prosecutors must bring to trial persons jailed prior to trial. Rejected 32-64: R 17-36; D 15-28 (ND 12-17, SD 3-11), Sept. 30, 1982.

379. S 2572. Violent Crime and Drug Enforcement Act. Passage of the bill to authorize preventive detention; establish new sentencing guidelines providing for fixed sentences and no parole; require mandatory minimum sentences for crimes committed with a gun; and to set increased penalties for drug traffickers. Passed 95-1: R 52-1; D 43-0 (ND 29-0, SD 14-0), Sept. 30, 1982.

380. S 2574. Federal Highway Authorizations. Eagleton, D-Mo., substitute to the Andrews, R-N.D., amendment, to allow a state to permit trucks up to 102 inches wide on Interstate and other federal-aid highways. Adopted 47-45: R 21-31; D 26-14 (ND 16-11, SD 10-3), Oct. 1, 1982. (The Andrews amendment to require states to permit 102-inch wide trucks on Interstate and federal-aid highways, as amended, subsequently was adopted by voice vote.)

381. S 2109. Futures Trading Act of 1982. Roth, R-Del., amendment to provide for fees on futures and options transactions, and to authorize the Commodity Futures Trading Commission to reduce or suspend the fees in certain circumstances. Rejected 27-66: R 21-32; D 6-34 (ND 6-21, SD 0-13), Oct. 1, 1982. A "yea" was a vote supporting the president's position.

382. HR 6156. Securities and Exchange Commission Jurisdiction. Passage of the bill to revise federal securities laws to affirm a jurisdictional agreement between the Securities and Exchange Commission and the Commodity Futures Trading Commission. Passed 91-0: R 52-0; D 39-0 (ND 26-0, SD 13-0), Oct. 1, 1982.

383. S 2375. Defense Production Act. McClure, R-Idaho, amendment to terminate the bill's extension of the Defense Production Act of 1950 on Dec. 31, 1982. Adopted 49-37: R 22-29; D 27-8 (ND 17-7, SD 10-1), Oct. 1, 1982.

	384	385	386	387	388	389
ALABAMA						
Denton	Y	Y	N	N	?	?
Heflin	Y	Y	Y	Y	Y	N
ALASKA						
Murkowski	Y	Y	Y	Y	Y	N
Stevens	Y	Y	Y	Y	Y	N
ARIZONA						
Goldwater	?	?	?	?	?	?
DeConcini	Y	Y	Y	Y	Y	Y
ARKANSAS						
Bumpers	Y	Y	Y	?	?	?
Pryor	?	Y	N	N	N	Y
CALIFORNIA						
Hayakawa	Y	Y	N	N	N	Y
Cranston	N	Y	N	N	N	Y
COLORADO						
Armstrong	Y	?	Y	Y	Y	N
Hart	?	?	?	?	?	?
CONNECTICUT						
Weicker	N	N	N	N	N	N
Dodd	N	Y	N	N	N	N
DELAWARE						
Roth	Y	Y	Y	Y	N	Y
Biden	?	Y	Y	Y	N	Y
FLORIDA						
Hawkins	Y	Y	Y	Y	Y	N
Chiles	Y	Y	N	N	Y	N
GEORGIA						
Mattingly	Y	Y	Y	Y	Y	N
Nunn	Y	Y	Y	Y	Y	Y
HAWAII						
Inouye	N	Y	N	N	Y	N
Matsunaga	N	Y	N	N	Y	N
IDAHO						
McClure	Y	Y	N	N	Y	N
Symms	Y	Y	N	N	Y	N
ILLINOIS						
Percy	Y	Y	N	N	Y	N
Dixon	Y	Y	N	N	Y	N
INDIANA						
Lugar	Y	Y	Y	Y	Y	N
Quayle	Y	N	Y	Y	Y	N
IOWA						
Grassley	Y	Y	Y	Y	Y	N
Jepsen	?	Y	Y	Y	Y	N
KANSAS						
Dole	Y	Y	N	N	N	Y
Kassebaum	Y	Y	N	Y	Y	Y
KENTUCKY						
Ford	Y	Y	Y	Y	Y	N
Huddleston	?	Y	Y	Y	Y	N
LOUISIANA						
Johnston	Y	Y	N	N	Y	N
Long	Y	Y	N	N	Y	N
MAINE						
Cohen	N	Y	N	N	Y	N
Mitchell	Y	Y	N	N	Y	N
MARYLAND						
Mathias	?	Y	Y	Y	Y	Y
Sarbanes	?	Y	Y	Y	Y	Y
MASSACHUSETTS						
Kennedy	?	Y	N	N	N	Y
Tsongas	?	Y	N	N	N	Y
MICHIGAN						
Levin	Y	Y	N	N	Y	N
Riegle	Y	Y	N	N	Y	N
MINNESOTA						
Boschwitz	Y	Y	N	N	Y	N
Durenberger	N	Y	N	Y	Y	N
MISSISSIPPI						
Cochran	?	Y	Y	Y	Y	N
Stennis	N	Y	N	N	Y	N
MISSOURI						
Danforth	Y	Y	N	N	N	Y
Eagleton	N	Y	N	N	N	Y
MONTANA						
Baucus	N	Y	N	N	Y	N
Melcher	Y	Y	N	N	Y	N
NEBRASKA						
Exon	N	Y	N	N	Y	N
Zorinsky	N	Y	N	N	Y	N
NEVADA						
Laxalt	Y	Y	Y	Y	Y	N
Cannon	?	Y	N	N	Y	N
NEW HAMPSHIRE						
Humphrey	N	Y	N	N	N	N
Rudman	N	Y	N	N	N	N
NEW JERSEY						
Brady	Y	Y	Y	Y	N	Y
Bradley	N	Y	N	N	N	Y
NEW MEXICO						
Domenici	Y	?	?	?	?	?
Schmitt	Y	Y	Y	Y	N	Y
NEW YORK						
D'Amato	Y	Y	N	N	Y	N
Moynihan	N	Y	N	N	Y	Y
NORTH CAROLINA						
East	Y	Y	N	N	Y	N
Helms	Y	Y	N	Y	Y	N
NORTH DAKOTA						
Andrews	Y	Y	N	N	Y	N
Burdick	N	Y	N	N	Y	N
OHIO						
Glenn	Y	Y	Y	Y	Y	N
Metzenbaum	N	Y	N	N	Y	N
OKLAHOMA						
Nickles	Y	Y	N	N	Y	N
Boren	Y	Y	N	N	Y	N
OREGON						
Hatfield	Y	Y	Y	Y	Y	N
Packwood	Y	Y	Y	Y	Y	N
PENNSYLVANIA						
Heinz	Y	Y	N	N	N	Y
Specter	Y	Y	N	N	Y	N
RHODE ISLAND						
Chafee	Y	Y	N	N	N	Y
Pell	Y	Y	Y	Y	N	Y
SOUTH CAROLINA						
Thurmond	Y	Y	Y	Y	Y	N
Hollings	?	?	?	?	?	?
SOUTH DAKOTA						
Abdnor	Y	Y	N	N	Y	N
Pressler	Y	Y	Y	Y	Y	N
TENNESSEE						
Baker	Y	Y	Y	Y	Y	?
Sasser	Y	Y	Y	Y	Y	N
TEXAS						
Tower	Y	?	Y	Y	Y	N
Bentsen	Y	Y	N	N	N	Y
UTAH						
Garn	Y	Y	Y	Y	N	Y
Hatch	Y	Y	Y	Y	Y	Y
VERMONT						
Stafford	N	Y	N	N	N	Y
Leahy	Y	Y	N	N	N	Y
VIRGINIA						
Warner	Y	Y	N	Y	Y	Y
Byrd*	Y	Y	N	Y	Y	Y
WASHINGTON						
Gorton	Y	Y	N	N	Y	N
Jackson	Y	Y	N	N	Y	N
WEST VIRGINIA						
Byrd	Y	Y	Y	Y	Y	N
Randolph	Y	Y	Y	Y	N	Y
WISCONSIN						
Kasten	Y	Y	N	N	Y	N
Proxmire	N	N	N	N	N	Y
WYOMING						
Simpson	Y	Y	Y	Y	Y	N
Wallop	Y	Y	Y	Y	Y	N

KEY

Y Voted for (yea).
\# Paired for.
+ Announced for.
N Voted against (nay).
X Paired against.
- Announced against.
P Voted "present".
C Voted "present" to avoid possible conflict of interest.
? Did not vote or otherwise make a position known.

Democrats   *Republicans*

ND - Northern Democrats   SD - Southern Democrats (Southern states - Ala., Ark., Fla., Ga., Ky., La., Miss., N.C., Okla., S.C., Tenn., Texas, Va.)   *Byrd elected as an independent.*

384. S 995. Antitrust Equal Enforcement Act. Baker, R-Tenn., motion that the Senate proceed to consideration of the bill to allow damages to be apportioned among those found liable for price fixing in antitrust suits and to permit reduction of total damages in proportion to a settling defendant's share of the liability. Motion agreed to 67-20: R 44-6; D 23-14 (ND 12-13, SD 11-1), Nov. 30, 1982.

385. S 995. Antitrust Equal Enforcement Act. Baker, R-Tenn., motion to instruct the sergeant-at-arms to require the attendance of absent senators. Motion agreed to 91-3: R 48-2; D 43-1 (ND 29-1, SD 14-0), Dec. 2, 1982.

386. S 995. Antitrust Equal Enforcement Act. Thurmond, R-S.C., motion to invoke cloture (thus limiting debate) on the Judiciary Committee amendment to the bill, which would allow application to pending cases of provisions in the bill permitting reduction of total damages in proportion to a settling defendant's share of the liability in price-fixing cases. Motion rejected 38-58: R 25-27; D 13-31 (ND 7-23, SD 6-8), Dec. 2, 1982. A three-fifths majority vote (60) of the total Senate is required to invoke cloture.

387. S 995. Antitrust Equal Enforcement Act. Thurmond, R-S.C., motion to invoke cloture (thus limiting debate) on the bill to allow damages to be apportioned among those found liable for price fixing in antitrust suits and to permit reduction of total damages in proportion to a settling defendant's share of the liability. All provisions would apply to cases initiated after enactment. Motion rejected 44-51: R 31-21; D 13-30 (ND 7-23, SD 6-7), Dec. 2, 1982. A three-fifths majority vote (60) of the total Senate is required to invoke cloture.

388. HR 7019. Transportation Appropriations, Fiscal 1983. Judgment of the Senate whether the Appropriations Committee amendment to require states to allow 102-inch-wide trucks on the highways in order to receive funds under the bill was germane. Ruled germane 67-27: R 38-13; D 29-14 (ND 18-12, SD 11-2), Dec. 2, 1982.

389. HR 7019. Transportation Appropriations, Fiscal 1983. Eagleton, D-Mo., amendment to strike a provision of the bill that would require states to allow 102-inch-wide trucks on the highways in order to receive funds under the bill. Rejected 31-62: R 13-37; D 18-25 (ND 14-16, SD 4-9), Dec. 2, 1982.

	390	391	392		390	391	392		390	391	392
ALABAMA				**IOWA**				**NEW HAMPSHIRE**			
Denton	Y	Y	N	*Grassley*	Y	Y	N	*Humphrey*	Y	Y	N
Heflin	?	Y	N	*Jepsen*	Y	Y	Y	*Rudman*	Y	Y	Y
ALASKA				**KANSAS**				**NEW JERSEY**			
Murkowski	Y	Y	Y	*Dole*	Y	Y	N	*Brady*	Y	Y	N
Stevens	Y	Y	Y	*Kassebaum*	Y	Y	N	*Bradley*	Y	Y	N
ARIZONA				**KENTUCKY**				**NEW MEXICO**			
Goldwater	?	?	?	Ford	Y	Y	N	*Domenici*	?	Y	N
DeConcini	Y	Y	Y	Huddleston	Y	Y	N	*Schmitt*	Y	Y	Y
ARKANSAS				**LOUISIANA**				**NEW YORK**			
Bumpers	?	Y	Y	Johnston	?	Y	Y	*D'Amato*	Y	Y	Y
Pryor	Y	Y	?	Long	N	Y	Y	Moynihan	Y	Y	Y
CALIFORNIA				**MAINE**				**NORTH CAROLINA**			
Hayakawa	Y	Y	N	*Cohen*	Y	Y	Y	*East*	Y	Y	Y
Cranston	?	Y	N	Mitchell	?	Y	N	*Helms*	N	Y	N
COLORADO				**MARYLAND**				**NORTH DAKOTA**			
Armstrong	Y	Y	N	*Mathias*	?	Y	Y	*Andrews*	Y	Y	Y
Hart	?	Y	N	Sarbanes	Y	Y	Y	Burdick	Y	Y	Y
CONNECTICUT				**MASSACHUSETTS**				**OHIO**			
Weicker	Y	Y	Y	Kennedy	Y	Y	N	Glenn	Y	?	?
Dodd	?	Y	N	Tsongas	?	Y	N	Metzenbaum	Y	Y	Y
DELAWARE				**MICHIGAN**				**OKLAHOMA**			
Roth	?	Y	N	Levin	Y	Y	N	*Nickles*	Y	Y	N
Biden	+	Y	N	Riegle	+	Y	N	Boren	Y	Y	N
FLORIDA				**MINNESOTA**				**OREGON**			
Hawkins	Y	Y	?	*Boschwitz*	Y	Y	Y	*Hatfield*	Y	Y	N
Chiles	Y	Y	Y	*Durenberger*	Y	Y	N	*Packwood*	Y	Y	Y
GEORGIA				**MISSISSIPPI**				**PENNSYLVANIA**			
Mattingly	Y	Y	Y	*Cochran*	Y	Y	Y	*Heinz*	?	Y	N
Nunn	?	Y	N	Stennis	Y	Y	Y	*Specter*	Y	Y	N
HAWAII				**MISSOURI**				**RHODE ISLAND**			
Inouye	Y	?	?	*Danforth*	Y	Y	N	*Chafee*	Y	Y	N
Matsunaga	?	Y	Y	Eagleton	?	Y	N	Pell	+	Y	N
IDAHO				**MONTANA**				**SOUTH CAROLINA**			
McClure	Y	Y	Y	Baucus	Y	Y	N	*Thurmond*	Y	Y	Y
Symms	?	Y	N	Melcher	Y	Y	N	Hollings	Y	Y	N
ILLINOIS				**NEBRASKA**				**SOUTH DAKOTA**			
Percy	+	Y	Y	Exon	Y	Y	N	*Abdnor*	Y	Y	Y
Dixon	+	Y	N	Zorinsky	N	Y	N	*Pressler*	Y	Y	Y
INDIANA				**NEVADA**				**TENNESSEE**			
Lugar	Y	Y	N	*Laxalt*	Y	Y	Y	*Baker*	Y	Y	N
Quayle	?	Y	Y	Cannon	Y	Y	N	Sasser	Y	Y	Y

KEY

- Y   Voted for (yea).
- #   Paired for.
- +   Announced for.
- N   Voted against (nay).
- X   Paired against.
- -   Announced against.
- P   Voted "present".
- C   Voted "present" to avoid possible conflict of interest.
- ?   Did not vote or otherwise make a position known.

Democrats   *Republicans*

	390	391	392
TEXAS			
Tower	Y	Y	Y
Bentsen	?	Y	N
UTAH			
Garn	Y	Y	N
Hatch	Y	+	-
VERMONT			
Stafford	?	Y	Y
Leahy	Y	Y	Y
VIRGINIA			
Warner	Y	Y	Y
Byrd*	N	Y	N
WASHINGTON			
Gorton	Y	Y	N
Jackson	Y	Y	Y
WEST VIRGINIA			
Byrd	Y	Y	N
Randolph	Y	Y	Y
WISCONSIN			
Kasten	Y	Y	Y
Proxmire	Y	Y	N
WYOMING			
Simpson	Y	Y	N
Wallop	?	Y	N

ND - Northern Democrats   SD - Southern Democrats (Southern states - Ala., Ark., Fla., Ga., Ky., La., Miss., N.C., Okla., S.C., Tenn., Texas, Va.)   *Byrd elected as an independent.*

390. HR 7093. Virgin Islands Tax Reduction/Disability Insurance. Passage of the bill to allow the Virgin Islands to reduce taxes on certain investment income earned from sources within the Virgin Islands and paid to individuals in the United States; to provide disability insurance payments and Medicare coverage to individuals appealing their termination from the disability rolls before Oct. 1, 1983, and to make other changes in the disability review process. Passed 70-4: R 43-1; D 27-3 (ND 19-1, SD 8-2), Dec. 3, 1982.

391. S Res 501. Polish Solidarity Day. Adoption of the resolution to urge the president to declare Dec. 12 as a national day of solidarity with and prayer for the Polish people. Dec. 12 was the eve of the first anniversary of the declaration of martial law in Poland. Adopted 96-0: R 52-0; D 44-0 (ND 29-0, SD 15-0), Dec. 7, 1982.

392. HR 7144. District of Columbia Appropriations, Fiscal 1983. Leahy, D-Vt.-D'Amato, R-N.Y., substitute to prohibit use of the Washington Convention Center for any professional concert, athletic event or similar entertainment activity unless such activity is incidental to a convention at the center or the event is for educational or charitable purposes. Rejected 40-54: R 25-26; D 15-28 (ND 9-20, SD 6-8), Dec. 7, 1982.

	393	394	395
ALABAMA			
Denton	Y	Y	Y
Heflin	N	Y	Y
ALASKA			
Murkowski	Y	Y	Y
Stevens	Y	Y	Y
ARIZONA			
Goldwater	?	?	?
DeConcini	N	Y	Y
ARKANSAS			
Bumpers	Y	Y	Y
Pryor	?	N	Y
CALIFORNIA			
Hayakawa	Y	Y	Y
Cranston	Y	N	N
COLORADO			
Armstrong	N	Y	Y
Hart	Y	?	?
CONNECTICUT			
Weicker	?	?	?
Dodd	Y	N	Y
DELAWARE			
Roth	Y	Y	Y
Biden	Y	Y	Y
FLORIDA			
Hawkins	Y	Y	Y
Chiles	Y	Y	Y
GEORGIA			
Mattingly	Y	Y	Y
Nunn	Y	Y	Y
HAWAII			
Inouye	?	?	?
Matsunaga	Y	N	Y
IDAHO			
McClure	Y	Y	Y
Symms	N	Y	Y
ILLINOIS			
Percy	?	+	+
Dixon	Y	N	Y
INDIANA			
Lugar	Y	Y	Y
Quayle	N	Y	Y
IOWA			
Grassley	N	Y	Y
Jepsen	N	Y	Y
KANSAS			
Dole	N	Y	Y
Kassebaum	Y	Y	Y
KENTUCKY			
Ford	Y	Y	Y
Huddleston	Y	Y	Y
LOUISIANA			
Johnston	Y	Y	Y
Long	Y	Y	Y
MAINE			
Cohen	Y	Y	Y
Mitchell	Y	Y	Y
MARYLAND			
Mathias	Y	Y	Y
Sarbanes	Y	N	N
MASSACHUSETTS			
Kennedy	Y	N	N
Tsongas	Y	Y	N
MICHIGAN			
Levin	Y	N	N
Riegle	Y	N	N
MINNESOTA			
Boschwitz	Y	Y	Y
Durenberger	Y	Y	Y
MISSISSIPPI			
Cochran	Y	Y	Y
Stennis	N	Y	Y
MISSOURI			
Danforth	Y	Y	Y
Eagleton	Y	Y	Y
MONTANA			
Baucus	Y	N	N
Melcher	Y	N	Y
NEBRASKA			
Exon	Y	Y	Y
Zorinsky	N	Y	Y
NEVADA			
Laxalt	N	Y	Y
Cannon	Y	N	Y
NEW HAMPSHIRE			
Humphrey	Y	Y	Y
Rudman	Y	Y	Y
NEW JERSEY			
Brady	Y	Y	Y
Bradley	Y	Y	Y
NEW MEXICO			
Domenici	Y	Y	Y
Schmitt	Y	Y	Y
NEW YORK			
D'Amato	Y	Y	Y
Moynihan	Y	Y	Y
NORTH CAROLINA			
East	N	Y	Y
Helms	N	Y	Y
NORTH DAKOTA			
Andrews	Y	Y	Y
Burdick	Y	N	Y
OHIO			
Glenn	?	Y	Y
Metzenbaum	Y	N	Y
OKLAHOMA			
Nickles	N	Y	Y
Boren	Y	Y	Y
OREGON			
Hatfield	Y	Y	Y
Packwood	Y	Y	Y
PENNSYLVANIA			
Heinz	Y	Y	Y
Specter	N	Y	Y
RHODE ISLAND			
Chafee	Y	Y	Y
Pell	Y	Y	Y
SOUTH CAROLINA			
Thurmond	Y	Y	Y
Hollings	Y	Y	Y
SOUTH DAKOTA			
Abdnor	Y	Y	Y
Pressler	N	Y	Y
TENNESSEE			
Baker	Y	Y	Y
Sasser	Y	N	Y
TEXAS			
Tower	N	Y	Y
Bentsen	Y	Y	Y
UTAH			
Garn	Y	Y	Y
Hatch	+	Y	Y
VERMONT			
Stafford	Y	Y	Y
Leahy	Y	Y	N
VIRGINIA			
Warner	N	Y	Y
Byrd*	N	Y	?
WASHINGTON			
Gorton	Y	Y	Y
Jackson	Y	N	Y
WEST VIRGINIA			
Byrd	Y	N	Y
Randolph	Y	Y	Y
WISCONSIN			
Kasten	N	Y	Y
Proxmire	N	N	Y
WYOMING			
Simpson	Y	Y	Y
Wallop	N	Y	Y

KEY

Y Voted for (yea).
\# Paired for.
\+ Announced for.
N Voted against (nay).
X Paired against.
- Announced against.
P Voted "present".
C Voted "present" to avoid possible conflict of interest.
? Did not vote or otherwise make a position known.

Democrats *Republicans*

ND - Northern Democrats   SD - Southern Democrats (Southern states - Ala., Ark., Fla., Ga., Ky., La., Miss., N.C., Okla., S.C., Tenn., Texas, Va.)

*Byrd elected as an independent.

393. HR 7144. District of Columbia Appropriations, Fiscal 1983. Passage of the bill to appropriate $573,000,000 in federal funds and $2,007,309,900 in local revenues for the District of Columbia in fiscal 1983. Passed 71-22: R 34-16; D 37-6 (ND 26-3, SD 11-3), Dec. 7, 1982. The president had requested $579,870,000 in federal funds and $2,005,949,400 in local revenues.

394. Feldstein Nomination. Confirmation of President Reagan's nomination of Martin S. Feldstein of Massachusetts to be a member of the Council of Economic Advisers. Confirmed 77-18: R 51-0; D 26-18 (ND 13-16, SD 13-2), Dec. 8, 1982. A "yea" was a vote supporting the president's position.

395. Hodel Nomination. Confirmation of President Reagan's nomination of Donald P. Hodel of Oregon to be secretary of energy. Confirmed 86-8: R 51-0; D 35-8 (ND 21-8, SD 14-0), Dec. 8, 1982. A "yea" was a vote supporting the president's position.

	396	397	398	399	400	401	402	403
ALABAMA								
Denton	Y	Y	Y	Y	N	N	N	N
Heflin	Y	Y	Y	Y	N	Y	N	Y
ALASKA								
Murkowski	Y	Y	Y	Y	N	Y	N	N
Stevens	Y	Y	Y	Y	N	Y	N	?
ARIZONA								
Goldwater	?	?	?	?	?	#	?	?
DeConcini	?	Y	Y	Y	?	-	?	?
ARKANSAS								
Bumpers	Y	Y	Y	Y	Y	N	Y	Y
Pryor	Y	N	Y	Y	Y	Y	Y	Y
CALIFORNIA								
Hayakawa	Y	Y	Y	Y	N	Y	N	N
Cranston	Y	?	?	?	Y	Y	Y	Y
COLORADO								
Armstrong	Y	Y	?	Y	N	Y	N	N
Hart	Y	Y	?	?	?	Y	Y	Y
CONNECTICUT								
Weicker	Y	Y	N	N	N	N	N	N
Dodd	Y	?	Y	Y	Y	Y	Y	Y
DELAWARE								
Roth	Y	Y	Y	Y	N	Y	N	N
Biden	?	Y	Y	Y	Y	N	Y	Y
FLORIDA								
Hawkins	?	Y	Y	Y	N	N	N	N
Chiles	Y	Y	Y	Y	Y	N	Y	Y
GEORGIA								
Mattingly	Y	Y	Y	Y	N	N	N	N
Nunn	Y	Y	Y	Y	Y	N	N	Y
HAWAII								
Inouye	Y	?	?	?	Y	Y	Y	Y
Matsunaga	?	?	?	?	Y	X	Y	Y
IDAHO								
McClure	Y	Y	Y	Y	N	Y	N	N
Symms	Y	?	?	?	N	Y	N	N
ILLINOIS								
Percy	Y	Y	Y	Y	N	Y	N	N
Dixon	Y	Y	Y	Y	Y	Y	Y	N
INDIANA								
Lugar	Y	Y	Y	Y	N	Y	N	N
Quayle	Y	Y	N	N	N	Y	N	N
IOWA								
Grassley	Y	Y	Y	Y	N	N	N	N
Jepsen	Y	Y	Y	Y	N	Y	N	N
KANSAS								
Dole	Y	Y	Y	Y	N	Y	N	N
Kassebaum	Y	Y	Y	Y	N	Y	N	N
KENTUCKY								
Ford	Y	Y	Y	Y	Y	N	Y	Y
Huddleston	Y	Y	Y	Y	N	Y	N	Y
LOUISIANA								
Johnston	?	Y	Y	Y	Y	#	Y	Y
Long	Y	Y	N	N	Y	N	Y	Y
MAINE								
Cohen	Y	Y	Y	Y	N	Y	N	N
Mitchell	Y	Y	Y	Y	Y	N	Y	Y
MARYLAND								
Mathias	Y	?	?	?	?	#	?	?
Sarbanes	Y	Y	?	?	Y	N	Y	Y
MASSACHUSETTS								
Kennedy	Y	Y	Y	Y	N	Y	N	Y
Tsongas	?	Y	Y	Y	Y	Y	Y	Y
MICHIGAN								
Levin	N	N	Y	?	Y	N	Y	Y
Riegle	Y	Y	Y	Y	N	Y	N	Y
MINNESOTA								
Boschwitz	Y	Y	Y	Y	N	Y	N	N
Durenberger	Y	Y	Y	Y	N	Y	N	N
MISSISSIPPI								
Cochran	Y	Y	Y	Y	N	N	N	N
Stennis	Y	Y	Y	Y	N	Y	N	Y
MISSOURI								
Danforth	?	Y	Y	Y	Y	N	Y	Y
Eagleton	Y	Y	Y	Y	N	Y	N	Y
MONTANA								
Baucus	Y	Y	Y	Y	N	Y	N	Y
Melcher	Y	Y	Y	Y	N	Y	N	Y
NEBRASKA								
Exon	N	N	Y	Y	Y	N	Y	Y
Zorinsky	N	N	Y	Y	Y	N	Y	N
NEVADA								
Laxalt	Y	Y	Y	Y	N	Y	N	N
Cannon	Y	?	?	?	Y	N	Y	Y
NEW HAMPSHIRE								
Humphrey	N	N	Y	Y	Y	Y	N	N
Rudman	Y	Y	Y	Y	N	Y	N	N
NEW JERSEY								
Brady	Y	Y	?	?	N	Y	N	N
Bradley	Y	?	?	Y	Y	N	Y	Y
NEW MEXICO								
Domenici	Y	Y	Y	Y	N	Y	N	N
Schmitt	Y	Y	Y	Y	N	X	N	N
NEW YORK								
D'Amato	Y	Y	Y	Y	N	Y	N	N
Moynihan	Y	?	Y	Y	?	?	Y	?
NORTH CAROLINA								
East	N	N	Y	N	N	N	N	N
Helms	N	N	Y	N	N	N	N	N
NORTH DAKOTA								
Andrews	Y	?	?	?	N	N	N	N
Burdick	Y	Y	Y	Y	N	N	Y	Y
OHIO								
Glenn	?	Y	Y	Y	Y	Y	Y	Y
Metzenbaum	Y	Y	Y	Y	Y	N	Y	Y
OKLAHOMA								
Nickles	N	N	Y	Y	N	N	N	N
Boren	N	N	N	N	Y	N	Y	N
OREGON								
Hatfield	Y	Y	Y	Y	N	Y	N	N
Packwood	Y	Y	Y	Y	Y	Y	Y	Y
PENNSYLVANIA								
Heinz	Y	?	?	?	N	Y	N	N
Specter	Y	Y	Y	Y	N	Y	N	N
RHODE ISLAND								
Chafee	Y	Y	Y	Y	N	Y	N	N
Pell	Y	Y	Y	Y	N	Y	N	Y
SOUTH CAROLINA								
Thurmond	Y	Y	Y	Y	N	Y	N	N
Hollings	Y	N	Y	Y	Y	Y	Y	Y
SOUTH DAKOTA								
Abdnor	Y	Y	Y	Y	N	N	N	N
Pressler	Y	Y	Y	N	N	N	N	N
TENNESSEE								
Baker	Y	Y	Y	Y	N	Y	N	N
Sasser	Y	Y	Y	Y	Y	X	Y	Y
TEXAS								
Tower	Y	Y	Y	Y	N	Y	N	N
Bentsen	?	Y	Y	Y	Y	Y	Y	Y
UTAH								
Garn	Y	Y	N	N	Y	N	N	N
Hatch	N	N	Y	N	Y	N	N	N
VERMONT								
Stafford	Y	Y	Y	Y	N	Y	N	N
Leahy	Y	Y	Y	Y	Y	Y	Y	Y
VIRGINIA								
Warner	Y	Y	Y	Y	N	Y	N	N
Byrd*	Y	Y	N	Y	N	Y	N	Y
WASHINGTON								
Gorton	Y	Y	Y	Y	N	Y	N	N
Jackson	Y	Y	Y	Y	Y	N	Y	Y
WEST VIRGINIA								
Byrd	Y	Y	Y	Y	N	Y	N	Y
Randolph	Y	Y	Y	Y	Y	Y	Y	Y
WISCONSIN								
Kasten	Y	Y	Y	Y	N	N	N	N
Proxmire	N	N	N	N	Y	N	Y	Y
WYOMING								
Simpson	Y	Y	Y	Y	N	Y	N	?
Wallop	?	N	Y	Y	N	Y	N	N

KEY

Y Voted for (yea).
\# Paired for.
\+ Announced for.
N Voted against (nay).
X Paired against.
- Announced against.
P Voted "present".
C Voted "present" to avoid possible conflict of interest.
? Did not vote or otherwise make a position known.

Democrats *Republicans*

ND - Northern Democrats   SD - Southern Democrats (Southern states - Ala., Ark., Fla., Ga., Ky., La., Miss., N.C., Okla., S.C., Tenn., Texas, Va.)

Byrd elected as an independent.

396. HR 6211. Transportation Assistance Act of 1982. Baker, R-Tenn., motion to table (kill) the Nickles, R-0kla., motion to postpone the Baker motion to proceed to consideration of the bill to authorize highway and transit funding and to raise highway taxes. Motion agreed to 79-10: R 45-5; D 34-5 (ND 22-4, SD 12-1), Dec. 10, 1982.

397. HR 6211. Transportation Assistance Act of 1982. Baker, R-Tenn., motion to invoke cloture (thus limiting debate) on the Baker motion to proceed to consideration of the bill to authorize highway and transit funding and increase highway taxes. Motion agreed to 75-13: R 43-6; D 32-7 (ND 20-4, SD 12-3), Dec. 13, 1982. A three-fifths majority vote (60) of the total Senate is required to invoke cloture.

398. HR 6211. Transportation Assistance Act of 1982. Baker, R-Tenn., motion to instruct the sergeant-at-arms to request the attendance of absent senators. Motion agreed to 79-7: R 44-3; D 35-4 (ND 23-1, SD 12-3), Dec. 13, 1982.

399. HR 6211. Transportation Assistance Act of 1982. Baker, R-Tenn., motion to instruct the sergeant-at-arms to request the attendance of absent senators. Motion agreed to 81-6: R 45-3; D 36-3 (ND 23-1, SD 13-2), Dec. 13, 1982.

400. HR 7356. Interior Appropriations, Fiscal 1983. Bumpers, D-Ark., amendment to strike from the bill $2.13 million for the Bureau of Land Management's coal leasing program in order to prevent two 1983 sales of some 2.7 billion tons of coal. Rejected 47-48: R 6-46; D 41-2 (ND 27-1, SD 14-1), Dec. 14, 1982.

401. S Res 512. Outside Income of Senators. Adoption of the resolution to abolish the limit in the Senate rules on the total income senators may receive from outside sources, including money for speeches and articles. Adopted 54-38: R 39-12; D 15-26 (ND 9-19, SD 6-7), Dec. 14, 1982.

402. HR 6211. Transportation Assistance Act of 1982/Jobs/Tax Cut. Byrd, D-W.Va., amendment to establish a job creation and extended unemployment compensation program costing $5.3 billion in fiscal 1983; delay the scheduled July 1983 income tax cut for upper-income taxpayers; and eliminate the 5-cent-a-gallon gasoline tax increase contained in the bill. Rejected 44-53: R 1-51; D 43-2 (ND 30-0, SD 13-2), Dec. 14, 1982. A "nay" was a vote supporting the president's position.

403. HR 6211. Transportation Assistance Act of 1982/Tax Cut. Bentsen, D-Texas, amendment to advance the effective date of the 1983 income tax cut to April 1, from July 1, and to defer 5 percent of the cut until there is no deficit in the annual federal budget. Rejected 40-54: R 1-49; D 39-5 (ND 26-3, SD 13-2), Dec. 14, 1982.

	404	405	406	407	408
ALABAMA					
Denton	N	Y	Y	Y	N
Heflin	N	N	Y	Y	N
ALASKA					
Murkowski	Y	Y	Y	Y	Y
Stevens	Y	Y	Y	Y	Y
ARIZONA					
Goldwater	?	?	?	?	?
DeConcini	?	?	?	?	N
ARKANSAS					
Bumpers	Y	N	N	Y	N
Pryor	Y	Y	Y	Y	N
CALIFORNIA					
Hayakawa	Y	N	Y	Y	Y
Cranston	Y	N	N	Y	N
COLORADO					
Armstrong	Y	Y	Y	Y	Y
Hart	Y	Y	Y	Y	Y
CONNECTICUT					
Weicker	Y	?	?	?	Y
Dodd	Y	N	N	Y	N
DELAWARE					
Roth	N	Y	Y	Y	Y
Biden	Y	N	N	Y	N
FLORIDA					
Hawkins	Y	N	N	Y	Y
Chiles	Y	Y	Y	Y	Y
GEORGIA					
Mattingly	Y	Y	Y	Y	Y
Nunn	?	Y	Y	Y	Y
HAWAII					
Inouye	Y	Y	Y	Y	N
Matsunaga	Y	?	N	Y	Y
IDAHO					
McClure	Y	Y	Y	Y	Y
Symms	Y	Y	Y	Y	Y
ILLINOIS					
Percy	Y	Y	Y	Y	Y
Dixon	Y	N	N	Y	N
INDIANA					
Lugar	Y	Y	Y	Y	N
Quayle	Y	Y	Y	Y	Y
IOWA					
Grassley	N	N	N	Y	N
Jepsen	Y	N	N	Y	Y
KANSAS					
Dole	Y	N	N	Y	Y
Kassebaum	Y	N	N	Y	Y
KENTUCKY					
Ford	Y	Y	Y	Y	N
Huddleston	Y	Y	Y	Y	N
LOUISIANA					
Johnston	Y	Y	Y	Y	Y
Long	Y	Y	Y	N	N
MAINE					
Cohen	Y	Y	Y	Y	Y
Mitchell	Y	Y	Y	Y	N
MARYLAND					
Mathias	?	?	?	?	?
Sarbanes	Y	N	N	Y	N
MASSACHUSETTS					
Kennedy	Y	N	N	Y	N
Tsongas	Y	N	N	Y	N
MICHIGAN					
Levin	Y	N	N	Y	N
Riegle	Y	N	N	Y	N
MINNESOTA					
Boschwitz	Y	N	Y	Y	N
Durenberger	+	N	Y	Y	N
MISSISSIPPI					
Cochran	Y	Y	Y	Y	Y
Stennis	Y	Y	Y	?	N
MISSOURI					
Danforth	Y	N	N	Y	Y
Eagleton	N	N	N	Y	N
MONTANA					
Baucus	Y	Y	Y	Y	Y
Melcher	Y	Y	Y	Y	N
NEBRASKA					
Exon	Y	N	N	Y	Y
Zorinsky	?	N	N	Y	N
NEVADA					
Laxalt	Y	Y	Y	Y	Y
Cannon	Y	Y	Y	Y	N
NEW HAMPSHIRE					
Humphrey	Y	N	N	Y	Y
Rudman	Y	N	N	Y	Y
NEW JERSEY					
Brady	Y	Y	Y	Y	Y
Bradley	Y	N	Y	Y	Y
NEW MEXICO					
Domenici	Y	Y	Y	Y	Y
Schmitt	Y	Y	Y	Y	Y
NEW YORK					
D'Amato	Y	N	N	Y	N
Moynihan	?	?	?	?	N
NORTH CAROLINA					
East	Y	Y	Y	Y	Y
Helms	N	Y	Y	Y	Y
NORTH DAKOTA					
Andrews	Y	N	N	Y	N
Burdick	Y	Y	Y	Y	Y
OHIO					
Glenn	Y	Y	Y	Y	N
Metzenbaum	Y	N	N	Y	N
OKLAHOMA					
Nickles	N	Y	Y	N	Y
Boren	Y	Y	Y	N	N
OREGON					
Hatfield	Y	N	N	Y	Y
Packwood	Y	Y	Y	Y	Y
PENNSYLVANIA					
Heinz	Y	N	N	Y	N
Specter	Y	N	N	Y	N
RHODE ISLAND					
Chafee	Y	N	Y	Y	Y
Pell	Y	N	N	Y	N
SOUTH CAROLINA					
Thurmond	Y	Y	Y	Y	Y
Hollings	Y	Y	Y	Y	N
SOUTH DAKOTA					
Abdnor	Y	N	Y	Y	Y
Pressler	Y	N	Y	Y	N
TENNESSEE					
Baker	Y	Y	Y	Y	Y
Sasser	Y	N	N	Y	N
TEXAS					
Tower	Y	Y	Y	Y	Y
Bentsen	Y	Y	Y	Y	N
UTAH					
Garn	Y	Y	Y	Y	Y
Hatch	Y	Y	Y	?	N
VERMONT					
Stafford	Y	Y	Y	Y	Y
Leahy	Y	Y	Y	Y	N
VIRGINIA					
Warner	Y	Y	Y	Y	Y
Byrd*	N	Y	Y	Y	Y
WASHINGTON					
Gorton	Y	Y	Y	Y	Y
Jackson	Y	Y	Y	Y	Y
WEST VIRGINIA					
Byrd	Y	Y	N	Y	N
Randolph	Y	Y	Y	Y	Y
WISCONSIN					
Kasten	Y	N	N	Y	N
Proxmire	N	N	N	Y	N
WYOMING					
Simpson	Y	Y	Y	Y	N
Wallop	Y	Y	Y	Y	N

KEY

- **Y** Voted for (yea).
- **#** Paired for.
- **+** Announced for.
- **N** Voted against (nay).
- **X** Paired against.
- **-** Announced against.
- **P** Voted "present".
- **C** Voted "present" to avoid possible conflict of interest.
- **?** Did not vote or otherwise make a position known.

Democrats   *Republicans*

ND - Northern Democrats   SD - Southern Democrats (Southern states - Ala., Ark., Fla., Ga., Ky., La., Miss., N.C., Okla., S.C., Tenn., Texas, Va.)

* Byrd elected as an independent.

404. HR 7356. Interior Appropriations, Fiscal 1983. Passage of the bill to appropriate $7,391,607,000 in new budget authority in fiscal 1983 for the Department of Interior and certain related agencies. Passed 84-9: R 46-5; D 38-4 (ND 26-2, SD 12-2), Dec. 14, 1982. The president had requested $6,576,960,000.

405. HR 6211. Transportation Assistance Act of 1982/Natural Gas. Baker, R-Tenn., motion to table (kill) division I of the Kassebaum, R-Kan., amendment to authorize the Federal Energy Regulatory Commission to allow natural gas pipelines to modify their contractual obligations to buy higher cost gas when lower cost gas is available. Motion agreed to 56-38: R 31-20; D 25-18 (ND 13-15, SD 12-3), Dec. 14, 1982.

406. HR 6211. Transportation Assistance Act of 1982/Natural Gas. Baker, R-Tenn., motion to table (kill) division II of the Kassebaum, R-Kan., amendment to freeze the wellhead price of natural gas at Oct. 1 levels for a two-year period.

Motion agreed to 62-33: R 37-14; D 25-19 (ND 12-17, SD 13-2), in the session which began Dec. 14, 1982.

407. S Res 515. Natural Gas Price Relief. Adoption of the resolution expressing the sense of the Senate that the Federal Energy Regulatory Commission should immediately take whatever actions it could to seek relief for natural gas consumers from rapidly rising gas prices, that gas pipeline companies attempt to renegotiate the portions of their contracts that required them to buy high-cost gas when lower-cost gas was available, and that available federal energy assistance funds be provided on an expedited basis for low-income consumers of natural gas. Adopted 90-3: R 49-1; D 41-2 (ND 29-0, SD 12-2), in the session which began Dec. 14, 1982.

408. HR 6211. Transportation Assistance Act of 1982/Buy American. Baker, R-Tenn., motion to table (kill) the Metzenbaum, D-Ohio, amendment to require that only steel and cement manufactured in the United States be used in construction and repair of highways and bridges. Motion agreed to 51-47: R 39-13; D 12-34 (ND 8-23, SD 4-11), Dec. 15, 1982.

KEY

- Y Voted for (yea).
- # Paired for.
- + Announced for.
- N Voted against (nay).
- X Paired against.
- - Announced against.
- P Voted "present".
- C Voted "present" to avoid possible conflict of interest.
- ? Did not vote or otherwise make a position known.

Democrats   *Republicans*

	409	410	411	412	413	414	415	416
ALABAMA								
Denton	N	N	Y	N	N	N	Y	Y
Heflin	N	N	N	N	N	N	Y	Y
ALASKA								
Murkowski	N	Y	Y	Y	N	N	Y	Y
Stevens	N	Y	Y	Y	N	N	Y	Y
ARIZONA								
Goldwater	?	?	?	?	?	?	?	?
DeConcini	N	?	N	Y	Y	N	Y	Y
ARKANSAS								
Bumpers	N	N	N	N	N	N	Y	Y
Pryor	N	N	N	N	N	N	Y	Y
CALIFORNIA								
Hayakawa	N	Y	Y	N	N	N	Y	Y
Cranston	?	?	N	N	N	N	Y	Y
COLORADO								
Armstrong	N	N	Y	N	N	N	N	N
Hart	N	Y	N	N	N	N	Y	Y
CONNECTICUT								
Weicker	?	?	N	N	N	N	Y	Y
Dodd	N	N	N	N	N	N	Y	Y
DELAWARE								
Roth	N	?	Y	Y	N	N	Y	Y
Biden	N	N	N	N	N	N	Y	Y
FLORIDA								
Hawkins	N	Y	Y	Y	N	N	Y	Y
Chiles	N	N	N	Y	N	N	Y	Y
GEORGIA								
Mattingly	N	N	Y	Y	N	N	Y	Y
Nunn	N	N	N	N	N	N	Y	Y
HAWAII								
Inouye	N	N	N	N	N	N	Y	Y
Matsunaga	N	N	?	N	N	N	Y	Y
IDAHO								
McClure	N	Y	Y	Y	N	N	N	Y
Symms	N	Y	Y	Y	N	N	N	Y
ILLINOIS								
Percy	N	Y	N	Y	N	N	Y	Y
Dixon	N	N	N	N	N	N	Y	Y
INDIANA								
Lugar	Y	N	N	Y	N	N	Y	Y
Quayle	Y	Y	N	Y	N	N	Y	Y
IOWA								
Grassley	N	Y	Y	N	N	N	Y	Y
Jepsen	N	Y	Y	Y	N	N	Y	Y
KANSAS								
Dole	Y	Y	Y	Y	N	N	Y	Y
Kassebaum	N	N	Y	Y	N	N	Y	Y
KENTUCKY								
Ford	N	N	N	N	N	N	Y	Y
Huddleston	N	N	N	N	N	N	Y	Y
LOUISIANA								
Johnston	N	?	N	N	N	N	Y	Y
Long	N	N	N	N	N	N	Y	Y
MAINE								
Cohen	N	N	Y	N	N	N	Y	Y
Mitchell	N	N	N	N	N	N	Y	Y
MARYLAND								
Mathias	N	Y	N	Y	N	N	?	?
Sarbanes	Y	N	N	N	N	N	Y	Y
MASSACHUSETTS								
Kennedy	Y	?	N	N	N	N	Y	Y
Tsongas	Y	N	N	N	N	N	Y	Y
MICHIGAN								
Levin	Y	N	N	N	N	N	Y	Y
Riegle	Y	N	N	N	N	N	Y	Y
MINNESOTA								
Boschwitz	N	N	Y	N	N	N	Y	Y
Durenberger	N	Y	Y	Y	N	N	Y	Y
MISSISSIPPI								
Cochran	N	Y	Y	N	N	N	Y	Y
Stennis	?	?	N	N	N	N	Y	Y
MISSOURI								
Danforth	N	Y	Y	N	N	N	Y	Y
Eagleton	?	?	N	N	N	N	Y	Y
MONTANA								
Baucus	N	Y	N	N	N	N	Y	Y
Melcher	N	Y	N	N	N	N	Y	Y
NEBRASKA								
Exon	#	?	Y	N	N	N	Y	Y
Zorinsky	Y	N	Y	N	N	Y	N	Y
NEVADA								
Laxalt	N	Y	Y	Y	N	N	Y	Y
Cannon	N	N	N	N	N	N	Y	Y
NEW HAMPSHIRE								
Humphrey	Y	Y	Y	N	N	N	N	N
Rudman	N	Y	Y	Y	N	N	Y	Y
NEW JERSEY								
Brady	N	Y	Y	N	N	N	Y	Y
Bradley	N	Y	N	N	N	N	Y	Y
NEW MEXICO								
Domenici	N	Y	Y	Y	N	N	Y	Y
Schmitt	N	Y	Y	Y	N	N	Y	Y
NEW YORK								
D'Amato	N	Y	Y	N	N	N	Y	Y
Moynihan	X	?	N	N	N	N	Y	Y
NORTH CAROLINA								
East	N	N	Y	N	N	Y	N	Y
Helms	N	N	Y	N	N	Y	N	Y
NORTH DAKOTA								
Andrews	N	Y	N	N	N	N	Y	Y
Burdick	N	Y	N	N	N	N	Y	Y
OHIO								
Glenn	+	?	?	?	?	?	?	?
Metzenbaum	Y	N	N	N	N	N	Y	Y
OKLAHOMA								
Nickles	N	N	Y	N	N	Y	N	N
Boren	N	Y	N	N	N	N	Y	Y
OREGON								
Hatfield	N	Y	Y	Y	N	N	Y	Y
Packwood	N	?	N	Y	N	N	Y	Y
PENNSYLVANIA								
Heinz	Y	Y	N	Y	N	?	?	Y
Specter	Y	N	N	N	N	N	Y	Y
RHODE ISLAND								
Chafee	N	Y	N	Y	N	N	Y	Y
Pell	Y	Y	N	Y	N	N	Y	Y
SOUTH CAROLINA								
Thurmond	N	Y	Y	Y	N	N	Y	Y
Hollings	N	N	N	N	N	N	Y	Y
SOUTH DAKOTA								
Abdnor	N	Y	Y	Y	N	N	Y	Y
Pressler	N	N	Y	N	N	N	Y	Y
TENNESSEE								
Baker	N	Y	Y	Y	N	N	Y	Y
Sasser	Y	N	N	Y	N	N	Y	Y
TEXAS								
Tower	N	Y	Y	Y	N	N	Y	Y
Bentsen	N	Y	N	Y	N	N	Y	Y
UTAH								
Garn	N	Y	Y	Y	N	N	Y	Y
Hatch	?	?	Y	N	N	N	Y	Y
VERMONT								
Stafford	N	Y	Y	Y	N	N	Y	Y
Leahy	N	Y	N	N	N	N	Y	Y
VIRGINIA								
Warner	N	Y	Y	Y	N	N	Y	Y
Byrd*	N	?	Y	Y	N	Y	N	N
WASHINGTON								
Gorton	N	Y	Y	Y	N	N	Y	Y
Jackson	N	N	N	N	N	N	Y	Y
WEST VIRGINIA								
Byrd	N	N	N	N	N	N	Y	Y
Randolph	N	Y	N	Y	Y	N	Y	Y
WISCONSIN								
Kasten	Y	Y	Y	N	N	N	Y	Y
Proxmire	Y	Y	N	N	N	N	N	Y
WYOMING								
Simpson	N	Y	Y	Y	N	N	Y	Y
Wallop	N	Y	Y	Y	N	N	Y	Y

ND - Northern Democrats   SD - Southern Democrats (Southern states - Ala., Ark., Fla., Ga., Ky., La., Miss., N.C., Okla., S.C., Tenn., Texas, Va.)   *Byrd elected as an independent.

409. HR 6211. Transportation Assistance Act of 1982. Tsongas, D-Mass., amendment to transfer $16 billion from the bill's authorization for new Interstate Highway construction to Interstate and bridge repair. Rejected 17-74: R 7-44; D 10-30 (ND 9-17, SD 1-13), Dec. 15, 1982.

410. HR 6211. Transportation Assistance Act of 1982. Baker, R-Tenn., motion to table (kill) the Pryor, D-Ark., amendment to eliminate the increase in non-fuel truck taxes and to maintain current gross weight, length and width limitations for vehicles using the Interstate System. Motion agreed to 48-37: R 37-12; D 11-25 (ND 9-15, SD 2-10), Dec. 15, 1982.

411. HR 6211. Transportation Assistance Act of 1982. Dole, R-Kan., motion to table (kill) the Levin, D-Mich., amendment to provide for an additional two to five weeks of federal supplemental unemployment compensation. Motion rejected 47-50: R 44-9; D 3-41 (ND 2-27, SD 1-14), Dec. 16, 1982.

412. HR 6211. Transportation Assistance Act of 1982. Baker, R-Tenn., motion to invoke cloture (thus limiting debate) on the Baker substitute for the bill to authorize funds for highway and transit programs and to increase gasoline and other highway taxes. Motion rejected 48-50: R 41-12; D 7-38 (ND 3-27, SD 4-11), Dec. 16, 1982. A three-fifths majority vote (60) of the total Senate is required to invoke cloture.

413. HR 6211. Transportation Assistance Act of 1982. Baker, R-Tenn., motion to invoke cloture (thus limiting debate) on the bill to authorize funds for highway and transit programs and to increase gasoline and other highway taxes. Motion rejected 5-93: R 1-52; D 4-41 (ND 3-27, SD 1-14), Dec. 16, 1982. A three-fifths majority vote (60) of the total Senate is required to invoke cloture.

414. HR 6211. Transportation Assistance Act of 1982. Humphrey, R-N.H., motion to table (kill) the Domenici, R-N.M., motion *(see vote 415, below)* to waive provisions of the Congressional Budget Act (PL 93-344) that would bar consideration of the Dole, R-Kan., amendment *(see vote 416, below)*. Motion rejected 5-92: R 3-49; D 2-43 (ND 1-29, SD 1-14), Dec. 16, 1982.

415. HR 6211. Transportation Assistance Act of 1982. Domenici, R-N.M., motion to waive provisions of the Congressional Budget Act (PL 93-344) that would bar consideration of the Dole, R-Kan., amendment *(see vote 416, below)* because it would breach the budget levels set in the fiscal 1983 budget resolution (S Con Res 92). Motion agreed to 87-9: R 44-7; D 43-2 (ND 29-1, SD 14-1), Dec. 16, 1982.

416. HR 6211. Transportation Assistance Act of 1982. Dole, R-Kan., amendment to provide for an additional two to six weeks of federal supplemental unemployment compensation. Adopted 93-4: R 49-3; D 44-1 (ND 30-0, SD 14-1), Dec. 16, 1982.

	417 418 419 420 421 422 423 424		417 418 419 420 421 422 423 424		417 418 419 420 421 422 423 424	KEY
ALABAMA		**IOWA**		**NEW HAMPSHIRE**		Y Voted for (yea).
Denton	Y N Y Y Y Y N N	*Grassley*	Y N Y Y N Y N N	*Humphrey*	Y Y Y Y Y N N Y	# Paired for.
Heflin	Y N Y Y N Y Y N	*Jepsen*	Y Y Y Y Y Y N N	*Rudman*	Y Y Y Y Y Y N Y	+ Announced for.
ALASKA		**KANSAS**		**NEW JERSEY**		N Voted against (nay).
Murkowski	Y Y Y Y Y Y N Y	*Dole*	Y Y Y Y Y Y N Y	*Brady*	? Y Y Y Y Y N Y	X Paired against.
Stevens	Y Y Y Y Y Y N N	*Kassebaum*	Y N Y N Y N N Y	Bradley	Y Y N N Y N Y Y	- Announced against.
ARIZONA		**KENTUCKY**		**NEW MEXICO**		P Voted "present".
Goldwater	? ? ? ? ? # ? ?	Ford	Y Y Y N Y N N N	*Domenici*	Y N Y Y Y Y N N	C Voted "present" to avoid possi-
DeConcini	Y Y Y Y N N N N	Huddleston	Y Y Y N Y Y N N	*Schmitt*	Y N Y Y Y Y N N	ble conflict of interest.
ARKANSAS		**LOUISIANA**		**NEW YORK**		? Did not vote or otherwise make a
Bumpers	Y Y N N Y N Y Y	Johnston	Y Y Y Y Y Y N N	*D'Amato*	Y Y Y Y Y Y N Y	position known.
Pryor	Y N N N N N Y Y	Long	Y N Y Y Y Y N ?	Moynihan	Y Y N Y N Y N N	
CALIFORNIA		**MAINE**		**NORTH CAROLINA**		Democrats *Republicans*
Hayakawa	N N Y Y Y Y N Y	*Cohen*	Y Y Y Y Y N N Y	*East*	Y Y Y N Y N N N	
Cranston	Y Y N N Y N Y Y	Mitchell	Y Y N N Y N Y Y	*Helms*	Y N Y N Y N N N	
COLORADO		**MARYLAND**		**NORTH DAKOTA**		
Armstrong	Y Y N N Y N Y Y	*Mathias*	Y Y N N Y N N Y	*Andrews*	Y Y N Y Y Y N Y	417 418 419 420 421 422 423 424
Hart	Y Y N N Y N N Y	Sarbanes	Y Y N N Y N N Y	Burdick	Y N Y N Y Y Y Y	
CONNECTICUT		**MASSACHUSETTS**		**OHIO**		**TEXAS**
Weicker	Y Y N N Y Y N Y	Kennedy	Y Y N N Y N Y Y	Glenn	? ? ? ? ? - ? ?	*Tower*	Y N Y Y Y Y N N
Dodd	Y Y N N Y N Y Y	Tsongas	Y Y N N Y N N N	Metzenbaum	Y Y N N Y N Y Y	Bentsen	Y N Y Y N N N N
DELAWARE		**MICHIGAN**		**OKLAHOMA**		**UTAH**
Roth	Y N Y Y Y Y N N	Levin	Y Y N N N N Y Y	*Nickles*	Y N Y N Y N N N	*Garn*	Y N Y Y N Y N N
Biden	Y Y Y N Y N Y Y	Riegle	Y Y N N Y N Y Y	Boren	Y N Y N Y Y N Y	*Hatch*	Y N Y Y Y Y - -
FLORIDA		**MINNESOTA**		**OREGON**		**VERMONT**
Hawkins	Y Y Y Y Y Y N Y	*Boschwitz*	Y Y Y Y Y N N Y	*Hatfield*	Y N Y N Y X N Y	*Stafford*	Y Y Y N Y N N Y
Chiles	Y Y Y Y Y N N Y	*Durenberger*	Y Y N Y Y N N Y	*Packwood*	Y Y N Y N N N Y	Leahy	Y N N N Y N Y Y
GEORGIA		**MISSISSIPPI**		**PENNSYLVANIA**		**VIRGINIA**
Mattingly	Y N Y Y Y N Y N	*Cochran*	Y N Y Y Y Y N N	*Heinz*	Y Y N Y N Y N N	*Warner*	Y N Y Y Y Y N Y
Nunn	Y Y Y Y N N N Y	Stennis	Y N Y Y Y Y N N	*Specter*	Y Y N Y Y N Y Y	Byrd*	Y N Y Y N N N N
HAWAII		**MISSOURI**		**RHODE ISLAND**		**WASHINGTON**
Inouye	Y Y N N Y N N N	*Danforth*	Y Y Y Y Y N N Y	*Chafee*	Y N N N Y N N Y	*Gorton*	Y Y Y Y Y N N Y
Matsunaga	Y Y N N Y N Y N	Eagleton	Y Y N N Y N N N	Pell	Y Y N N Y N N Y	Jackson	Y Y Y Y Y Y Y Y
IDAHO		**MONTANA**		**SOUTH CAROLINA**		**WEST VIRGINIA**
McClure	Y N Y Y Y Y N N	Baucus	Y Y N N N N N Y	*Thurmond*	Y N Y Y Y Y N Y	Byrd	Y N Y Y N Y N Y
Symms	Y Y Y Y Y Y N N	Melcher	Y N N N Y N N N	Hollings	Y N Y N Y N N N	Randolph	Y N Y N Y N Y N
ILLINOIS		**NEBRASKA**		**SOUTH DAKOTA**		**WISCONSIN**
Percy	Y N N Y Y N N Y	Exon	Y N Y Y N N Y N	*Abdnor*	Y N Y Y Y Y N N	*Kasten*	Y Y Y Y Y Y N N
Dixon	Y Y Y N N Y Y Y	Zorinsky	Y N Y Y N Y Y N	*Pressler*	Y Y N Y Y Y N N	Proxmire	Y N N N N N Y Y
INDIANA		**NEVADA**		**TENNESSEE**		**WYOMING**
Lugar	Y Y Y Y Y N Y N	*Laxalt*	Y N Y Y Y Y N N	*Baker*	Y N Y Y Y Y N Y	*Simpson*	Y Y Y Y Y Y N N
Quayle	Y Y Y Y Y N N Y	Cannon	Y N Y Y N Y N Y	Sasser	Y Y N N Y Y Y N	*Wallop*	Y N Y Y Y Y N N

ND - Northern Democrats   SD - Southern Democrats (Southern states - Ala., Ark., Fla., Ga., Ky., La., Miss., N.C., Okla., S.C., Tenn., Texas, Va.)   *Byrd elected as an independent.

417. HR 6211. Transportation Assistance Act of 1982. Boschwitz, R-Minn., amendment to the Baker, R-Tenn., substitute, to reduce heavy-truck taxes from the substitute's level of $1,600 for an 80,000-pound truck to $1,200, and to make other changes in truck taxes. Adopted 96-1: R 51-1; D 45-0 (ND 30-0, SD 15-0), Dec. 16, 1982.

418. H J Res 631. Continuing Appropriations, Fiscal 1983/Foreign Aid. Appropriations Committee amendment to provide $11.5 billion for foreign aid programs in fiscal 1983. Adopted 57-41: R 29-24; D 28-17 (ND 21-9, SD 7-8), Dec. 16, 1982.

419. H J Res 631. Continuing Appropriations, Fiscal 1983/MX Missile. Hatfield, R-Ore., motion to table (kill) the Cranston, D-Calif., motion to recommit the bill to the Appropriations Committee with instructions to report it back with an amendment cutting $988 million for procurement of the MX missile, and providing that no funds in the bill be used for work on the so-called "dense pack" missile basing mode. Motion agreed to 70-28: R 48-5; D 22-23 (ND 10-20, SD 12-3), in the session which began Dec. 16, 1982. A "yea" was a vote supporting the president's position.

420. H J Res 631. Continuing Appropriations, Fiscal 1983/MX Missile. Jackson, D-Wash., amendment to bar the use of funds in the bill for procurement of the MX missile until Congress by concurrent resolution had approved a basing mode for it; set out procedures for congressional consideration of the concurrent resolution, and required the president to submit a detailed report on basing mode options to Congress by March 1, 1983. Adopted 56-42: R 41-12; D 15-30 (ND 6-24, SD 9-6), in the session which began Dec. 16, 1982. A "yea" was a vote supporting the president's position.

421. H J Res 631. Continuing Appropriations, Fiscal 1983. Appropriations Committee amendment to set funding levels for the departments of Labor, Health and Human Services and Education, and related agencies, at the level in the version of the fiscal 1983 appropriations bill for those departments (HR 7205) reported by the committee Dec. 8. Adopted 78-20: R 47-6; D 31-14 (ND 22-8, SD 9-6), in the session which began Dec. 16, 1982.

422. H J Res 631. Continuing Appropriations, Fiscal 1983/Clinch River. Appropriations Committee amendment to drop the House-approved provision in the bill eliminating construction funds for the Clinch River (Tenn.) nuclear breeder reactor. Adopted 49-48: R 38-14; D 11-34 (ND 4-26, SD 7-8), in the session which began Dec. 16, 1982. A "yea" was a vote supporting the president's position.

423. H J Res 631. Continuing Appropriations, Fiscal 1983. Pryor, D-Ark., amendment to change the termination date of funding authority in the joint resolution to June 1, 1983, from Sept. 30, 1983. Rejected 24-73: R 0-52; D 24-21 (ND 19-11, SD 5-10), in the session which began Dec. 16, 1982.

424. H J Res 631. Continuing Appropriations, Fiscal 1983/Federal Trade Commission. Rudman, R-N.H., motion to table (kill) the McClure, R-Idaho, amendment to bar the use of funds by the Federal Trade Commission to investigate or make rules relating to the medical or other professions that were licensed and regulated by the states. Motion agreed to 59-37: R 31-21; D 28-16 (ND 23-7, SD 5-9), in the session which began Dec. 16, 1982. A "yea" was a vote supporting the president's position.

KEY

Y	Voted for (yea).
#	Paired for.
+	Announced for.
N	Voted against (nay).
X	Paired against.
-	Announced against.
P	Voted "present".
C	Voted "present" to avoid possible conflict of interest.
?	Did not vote or otherwise make a position known.

Democrats   Republicans

Senator	425	426	427	428	429	430	431	432
ALABAMA								
Denton	N	N	Y	Y	Y	Y	Y	N
Heflin	N	N	Y	N	Y	Y	Y	Y
ALASKA								
Murkowski	N	N	Y	Y	N	N	N	Y
Stevens	Y	Y	Y	Y	N	N	N	Y
ARIZONA								
Goldwater	?	?	?	?	?	?	?	?
DeConcini	N	N	Y	N	Y	N	Y	Y
ARKANSAS								
Bumpers	Y	Y	N	N	N	N	Y	Y
Pryor	Y	Y	N	N	N	N	Y	N
CALIFORNIA								
Hayakawa	Y	Y	Y	N	Y	N	N	N
Cranston	Y	Y	N	N	N	N	N	Y
COLORADO								
Armstrong	N	N	Y	Y	N	Y	N	N
Hart	Y	Y	N	N	N	N	Y	Y
CONNECTICUT								
Weicker	Y	Y	Y	Y	N	Y	N	Y
Dodd	Y	Y	N	N	N	Y	N	Y
DELAWARE								
Roth	N	N	Y	Y	N	N	N	Y
Biden	N	N	N	N	N	Y	N	Y
FLORIDA								
Hawkins	N	N	Y	Y	N	N	N	Y
Chiles	Y	Y	Y	N	N	N	Y	Y
GEORGIA								
Mattingly	N	N	Y	Y	N	N	N	Y
Nunn	Y	Y	Y	N	Y	N	Y	Y
HAWAII								
Inouye	Y	Y	N	N	N	N	N	Y
Matsunaga	Y	Y	N	N	N	N	N	Y
IDAHO								
McClure	N	N	Y	Y	N	Y	N	Y
Symms	N	N	Y	Y	N	Y	N	N
ILLINOIS								
Percy	Y	Y	Y	Y	N	N	N	Y
Dixon	N	N	N	N	N	N	Y	Y
INDIANA								
Lugar	N	N	Y	Y	N	N	N	Y
Quayle	N	N	Y	Y	N	N	N	Y
IOWA								
Grassley	N	N	Y	Y	Y	N	N	Y
Jepsen	N	N	Y	Y	N	N	N	Y
KANSAS								
Dole	N	N	Y	Y	Y	N	N	Y
Kassebaum	Y	Y	Y	N	?	N	N	Y
KENTUCKY								
Ford	N	N	Y	N	N	N	Y	Y
Huddleston	N	N	Y	N	N	N	N	Y
LOUISIANA								
Johnston	N	N	Y	N	N	Y	Y	N
Long	N	N	N	N	N	Y	Y	N
MAINE								
Cohen	Y	Y	N	N	Y	N	N	Y
Mitchell	N	N	N	N	Y	Y	Y	N
MARYLAND								
Mathias	Y	#	?	?	?	?	?	?
Sarbanes	Y	Y	N	N	N	Y	N	Y
MASSACHUSETTS								
Kennedy	Y	Y	N	N	N	Y	N	Y
Tsongas	Y	Y	N	N	N	Y	N	Y
MICHIGAN								
Levin	Y	Y	N	N	N	N	N	Y
Riegle	Y	Y	N	N	N	Y	N	Y
MINNESOTA								
Boschwitz	N	N	Y	N	Y	N	Y	Y
Durenberger	N	-	?	?	?	N	Y	Y
MISSISSIPPI								
Cochran	Y	Y	Y	N	Y	N	Y	N
Stennis	N	N	Y	N	N	N	Y	N
MISSOURI								
Danforth	N	N	Y	N	N	N	N	Y
Eagleton	N	N	N	N	N	N	N	Y
MONTANA								
Baucus	Y	Y	N	N	Y	N	Y	N
Melcher	N	N	N	N	N	N	Y	Y
NEBRASKA								
Exon	N	N	Y	N	Y	N	Y	N
Zorinsky	N	N	Y	Y	Y	N	Y	N
NEVADA								
Laxalt	N	N	Y	Y	N	Y	N	Y
Cannon	N	N	N	N	Y	N	Y	Y
NEW HAMPSHIRE								
Humphrey	N	N	Y	N	Y	N	Y	N
Rudman	Y	Y	Y	N	Y	N	Y	Y
NEW JERSEY								
Brady	Y	Y	?	Y	N	N	N	Y
Bradley	Y	Y	N	N	N	Y	N	Y
NEW MEXICO								
Domenici	N	N	Y	N	Y	N	Y	N
Schmitt	Y	Y	Y	Y	N	Y	Y	?
NEW YORK								
D'Amato	N	N	Y	Y	Y	N	N	Y
Moynihan	Y	Y	N	N	Y	?	N	Y
NORTH CAROLINA								
East	N	N	Y	N	Y	N	N	Y
Helms	N	N	Y	Y	Y	Y	N	N
NORTH DAKOTA								
Andrews	N	N	Y	Y	N	Y	N	Y
Burdick	Y	Y	N	N	Y	N	Y	Y
OHIO								
Glenn	?	?	?	?	?	?	?	?
Metzenbaum	Y	Y	Y	N	N	N	N	Y
OKLAHOMA								
Nickles	N	N	Y	Y	N	Y	N	Y
Boren	N	N	Y	N	Y	Y	Y	N
OREGON								
Hatfield	Y	Y	Y	N	Y	N	N	Y
Packwood	Y	Y	Y	Y	N	N	N	Y
PENNSYLVANIA								
Heinz	Y	Y	Y	N	N	N	N	Y
Specter	Y	Y	Y	N	N	N	N	Y
RHODE ISLAND								
Chafee	Y	Y	Y	N	N	N	N	Y
Pell	Y	Y	N	N	N	N	N	Y
SOUTH CAROLINA								
Thurmond	N	N	Y	Y	N	Y	N	N
Hollings	Y	Y	N	N	N	Y	Y	Y
SOUTH DAKOTA								
Abdnor	N	N	Y	Y	N	N	N	Y
Pressler	N	N	Y	N	N	N	Y	Y
TENNESSEE								
Baker	N	Y	Y	Y	N	Y	N	Y
Sasser	Y	Y	N	N	?	N	N	Y
TEXAS								
Tower	Y	Y	Y	Y	N	Y	Y	N
Bentsen	Y	Y	Y	N	N	Y	Y	N
UTAH								
Garn	N	N	Y	Y	N	N	N	Y
Hatch	-	X	+	-	-	-	-	+
VERMONT								
Stafford	Y	Y	Y	Y	N	N	N	Y
Leahy	Y	Y	N	N	N	N	N	Y
VIRGINIA								
Warner	Y	Y	Y	Y	N	N	N	Y
Byrd*	Y	Y	Y	Y	N	N	N	Y
WASHINGTON								
Gorton	Y	Y	Y	Y	N	N	N	Y
Jackson	Y	Y	N	N	N	N	N	Y
WEST VIRGINIA								
Byrd	Y	Y	N	N	N	N	Y	Y
Randolph	N	N	N	N	N	N	Y	Y
WISCONSIN								
Kasten	N	N	Y	Y	N	N	N	Y
Proxmire	N	N	Y	Y	N	N	N	Y
WYOMING								
Simpson	Y	Y	Y	N	N	N	Y	N
Wallop	Y	Y	Y	Y	N	N	Y	Y

ND - Northern Democrats   SD - Southern Democrats (Southern states - Ala., Ark., Fla., Ga., Ky., La., Miss., N.C., Okla., S.C., Tenn., Texas, Va.)   * Byrd elected as an independent.

425. H J Res 631. Continuing Appropriations, Fiscal 1983/Abortion. Appropriations Committee amendment to eliminate the prohibition in the joint resolution against the use of funds to pay for abortions under federal employee health insurance policies, except when needed to save the life of the mother. Adopted 49-48: R 22-30; D 27-18 (ND 19-11, SD 8-7), in the session which began Dec. 16, 1982. A "nay" was a vote supporting the president's position.

426. H J Res 631. Continuing Appropriations, Fiscal 1983/Abortion. Packwood, R-Ore., motion to table (kill) the Hatfield, R-Ore., motion to reconsider the vote by which the Appropriations Committee amendment on abortion funding (see vote 425, above) was adopted. Motion agreed to 50-45: R 23-27; D 27-18 (ND 19-11, SD 8-7), in the session which began Dec. 16, 1982.

427. H J Res 631. Continuing Appropriations, Fiscal 1983/Housing. Appropriations Committee amendment to delete the House-passed provision appropriating $1 billion for the community development block grant program of the Department of Housing and Urban Development. Adopted 62-32: R 48-1; D 14-31 (ND 4-26, SD 10-5), in the session which began Dec. 16, 1982.

428. H J Res 631. Continuing Appropriations, Fiscal 1983. Appropriations Committee amendment to delete the House-passed provision appropriating $50 million for the Federal Emergency Management Agency, to be given to the United Way of America for distribution to local charitable groups providing emergency food and shelter to the homeless. Rejected 43-52: R 40-10; D 3-42 (ND 2-28, SD 1-14), in the session which began Dec. 16, 1982.

429. H J Res 631. Continuing Appropriations, Fiscal 1983. Moynihan, D-N.Y., amendment to cut funds for congressional staffs by 10 percent. Rejected 25-68: R 12-37; D 13-31 (ND 10-20, SD 3-11), in the session which began Dec. 16, 1982.

430. H J Res 631. Continuing Appropriations, Fiscal 1983. Weicker, R-Conn., motion to table (kill) the Warner, R-Va., amendment to provide $200 million to states for use in low-income energy assistance and weatherization programs. Motion rejected 38-57: R 22-29; D 16-28 (ND 9-20, SD 7-8), in the session which began Dec. 16, 1982. (The Warner amendment subsequently was adopted (see vote 432, below).)

431. H J Res 631. Continuing Appropriations, Fiscal 1983. Johnston, D-La., amendment to the Warner, R-Va., amendment (see vote 432, below), to include each state's natural gas consumption, as well as its petroleum consumption, in the calculation used to allocate funds to state low-income energy programs. Rejected 40-56: R 16-35; D 24-21 (ND 12-18, SD 12-3), in the session which began Dec. 16, 1982.

432. H J Res 631. Continuing Appropriations, Fiscal 1983. Warner, R-Va., amendment to provide $200 million to states for use in low-income energy assistance and weatherization programs. The money would come out of funds already collected from violators of petroleum pricing and allocation rules and would be distributed on the basis of each state's past share of national petroleum consumption. In addition, the amendment directed the Energy Department to distribute to the states any additional funds collected from violators on which there were no outstanding claims. Adopted 76-19: R 40-10; D 36-9 (ND 27-3, SD 9-6), in the session which began Dec. 16, 1982.

	433	434	435	436	437	438	439	440
ALABAMA								
Denton	Y	Y	Y	Y	Y	Y	N	N
Heflin	Y	N	Y	Y	Y	Y	N	Y
ALASKA								
Murkowski	Y	Y	N	Y	N	Y	Y	Y
Stevens	Y	Y	Y	Y	N	Y	Y	Y
ARIZONA								
Goldwater	?	?	?	?	?	?	#	?
DeConcini	Y	N	Y	Y	Y	Y	N	?
ARKANSAS								
Bumpers	Y	N	N	N	Y	N	N	Y
Pryor	Y	N	N	N	Y	N	N	Y
CALIFORNIA								
Hayakawa	Y	Y	Y	Y	?	Y	Y	N
Cranston	Y	N	N	N	Y	N	?	?
COLORADO								
Armstrong	Y	Y	Y	Y	Y	Y	N	?
Hart	Y	N	Y	N	Y	N	N	Y
CONNECTICUT								
Weicker	Y	N	Y	Y	N	Y	N	Y
Dodd	Y	N	Y	N	Y	Y	N	?
DELAWARE								
Roth	Y	Y	N	Y	Y	N	N	Y
Biden	Y	N	N	N	Y	Y	N	Y
FLORIDA								
Hawkins	Y	Y	Y	Y	Y	Y	N	?
Chiles	Y	Y	Y	Y	Y	Y	N	N
GEORGIA								
Mattingly	Y	Y	Y	Y	Y	Y	N	Y
Nunn	Y	Y	Y	Y	Y	Y	N	Y
HAWAII								
Inouye	Y	N	Y	Y	N	N	?	Y
Matsunaga	Y	N	N	N	Y	N	N	?
IDAHO								
McClure	Y	Y	Y	N	Y	Y	N	N
Symms	Y	Y	Y	Y	Y	Y	N	N
ILLINOIS								
Percy	Y	Y	Y	Y	Y	N	N	Y
Dixon	Y	N	N	Y	Y	Y	N	Y
INDIANA								
Lugar	Y	Y	Y	Y	Y	Y	N	Y
Quayle	Y	Y	Y	Y	Y	Y	Y	Y

	433	434	435	436	437	438	439	440
IOWA								
Grassley	Y	Y	N	Y	Y	Y	N	Y
Jepsen	Y	Y	N	Y	Y	Y	N	Y
KANSAS								
Dole	Y	Y	Y	Y	N	Y	Y	Y
Kassebaum	Y	Y	N	N	Y	Y	N	Y
KENTUCKY								
Ford	Y	N	N	N	Y	N	N	Y
Huddleston	Y	N	?	Y	Y	N	N	Y
LOUISIANA								
Johnston	Y	N	Y	Y	Y	Y	N	Y
Long	Y	N	Y	N	Y	N	Y	Y
MAINE								
Cohen	Y	N	Y	Y	Y	Y	N	Y
Mitchell	Y	N	N	Y	Y	N	N	Y
MARYLAND								
Mathias	?	?	-	?	N	Y	Y	Y
Sarbanes	Y	N	N	N	Y	N	N	Y
MASSACHUSETTS								
Kennedy	Y	N	N	N	Y	?	Y	Y
Tsongas	Y	N	N	N	Y	N	N	Y
MICHIGAN								
Levin	Y	N	N	N	Y	N	N	Y
Riegle	Y	N	N	N	Y	N	N	Y
MINNESOTA								
Boschwitz	Y	Y	N	Y	Y	Y	N	Y
Durenberger	Y	Y	N	Y	Y	Y	N	Y
MISSISSIPPI								
Cochran	Y	N	Y	Y	Y	Y	N	Y
Stennis	Y	N	Y	N	Y	N	Y	?
MISSOURI								
Danforth	Y	Y	N	Y	Y	Y	N	Y
Eagleton	Y	N	N	N	Y	N	N	Y
MONTANA								
Baucus	Y	N	N	N	Y	N	N	Y
Melcher	Y	N	N	N	N	N	N	Y
NEBRASKA								
Exon	Y	Y	Y	N	Y	Y	N	Y
Zorinsky	Y	Y	Y	Y	Y	Y	N	Y
NEVADA								
Laxalt	Y	Y	Y	Y	Y	Y	Y	Y
Cannon	Y	N	Y	Y	Y	Y	N	Y

	433	434	435	436	437	438	439	440
NEW HAMPSHIRE								
Humphrey	Y	Y	Y	Y	Y	Y	N	Y
Rudman	Y	N	Y	N	Y	Y	Y	Y
NEW JERSEY								
Brady	Y	Y	Y	Y	Y	Y	Y	Y
Bradley	Y	N	N	N	Y	N	N	Y
NEW MEXICO								
Domenici	Y	Y	Y	Y	N	Y	N	Y
Schmitt	?	N	Y	Y	N	Y	X	Y
NEW YORK								
D'Amato	Y	N	N	Y	Y	Y	Y	Y
Moynihan	Y	N	N	N	Y	N	Y	Y
NORTH CAROLINA								
East	Y	Y	Y	Y	Y	Y	N	N
Helms	Y	Y	Y	Y	Y	Y	N	N
NORTH DAKOTA								
Andrews	Y	N	Y	N	Y	N	Y	Y
Burdick	Y	N	N	N	Y	N	N	Y
OHIO								
Glenn	?	?	Y	Y	Y	Y	N	Y
Metzenbaum	Y	N	N	N	Y	N	N	Y
OKLAHOMA								
Nickles	Y	Y	N	Y	Y	Y	N	N
Boren	Y	Y	N	Y	Y	N	N	Y
OREGON								
Hatfield	N	N	Y	N	N	Y	Y	Y
Packwood	Y	N	N	Y	Y	Y	Y	Y
PENNSYLVANIA								
Heinz	Y	N	N	Y	N	Y	Y	?
Specter	Y	N	N	Y	Y	Y	N	Y
RHODE ISLAND								
Chafee	Y	N	N	N	Y	Y	Y	Y
Pell	Y	N	N	N	Y	N	Y	Y
SOUTH CAROLINA								
Thurmond	Y	Y	Y	Y	Y	Y	N	Y
Hollings	Y	N	N	Y	N	N	N	Y
SOUTH DAKOTA								
Abdnor	Y	Y	Y	Y	N	Y	N	Y
Pressler	Y	N	Y	N	Y	N	Y	Y
TENNESSEE								
Baker	Y	Y	Y	Y	Y	Y	Y	Y
Sasser	Y	N	N	Y	N	N	N	Y

KEY

Y	Voted for (yea).
#	Paired for.
+	Announced for.
N	Voted against (nay).
X	Paired against.
-	Announced against.
P	Voted "present".
C	Voted "present" to avoid possible conflict of interest.
?	Did not vote or otherwise make a position known.

Democrats *Republicans*

	433	434	435	436	437	438	439	440
TEXAS								
Tower	Y	Y	Y	Y	Y	Y	Y	Y
Bentsen	Y	N	Y	Y	Y	?	Y	Y
UTAH								
Garn	Y	Y	Y	N	Y	N	Y	Y
Hatch	+	Y	Y	Y	Y	N	N	N
VERMONT								
Stafford	Y	Y	N	N	N	Y	Y	Y
Leahy	Y	N	N	N	Y	N	N	Y
VIRGINIA								
Warner	Y	Y	Y	Y	Y	Y	N	Y
Byrd*	Y	Y	N	Y	Y	N	N	N
WASHINGTON								
Gorton	Y	Y	N	N	Y	Y	Y	Y
Jackson	Y	N	Y	Y	Y	Y	N	+
WEST VIRGINIA								
Byrd	Y	N	Y	Y	Y	N	N	Y
Randolph	Y	N	Y	N	Y	Y	N	Y
WISCONSIN								
Kasten	Y	Y	Y	N	Y	N	Y	Y
Proxmire	Y	Y	N	N	N	N	Y	N
WYOMING								
Simpson	Y	Y	N	Y	N	Y	Y	N
Wallop	Y	?	Y	Y	N	Y	N	Y

ND - Northern Democrats   SD - Southern Democrats (Southern states - Ala., Ark., Fla., Ga., Ky., La., Miss., N.C., Okla., S.C., Tenn., Texas, Va.)   *Byrd elected as an independent.*

433. H J Res 631. Continuing Appropriations, Fiscal 1983. Quayle, R-Ind., amendment to provide payments equivalent to certain Social Security benefits, eliminated by the 1981 budget reconciliation act (PL 97-35), to widows and children of members of the armed forces who died in service or as a result of service-related disabilities. Adopted 94-1: R 49-1; D 45-0 (ND 30-0, SD 15-0), in the session which began Dec. 16, 1982. A "yea" was a vote supporting the president's position.

434. H J Res 631. Continuing Appropriations, Fiscal 1983. Domenici, R-N.M., amendment to delete the section of the joint resolution providing $1.2 billion for public works jobs. Rejected 46-50: R 39-12; D 7-38 (ND 3-27, SD 4-11), in the session which began Dec. 16, 1982. A "yea" was a vote supporting the president's position.

435. H J Res 631. Continuing Appropriations, Fiscal 1983. Stevens, R-Alaska, motion to table (kill) the Gorton, R-Wash., amendment to reduce Defense Department spending, other than for operations and maintenance, by 3.3 percent. Motion agreed to 52-45: R 34-18; D 18-27 (ND 11-20, SD 7-7), in the session which began Dec. 16, 1982.

436. H J Res 631. Continuing Appropriations, Fiscal 1983. Rudman, R-N.H., motion to table (kill) the Levin, D-Mich.-Hart, D-Colo., amendment to increase funds for maintenance of Navy aircraft by eliminating funds for building one nuclear-powered aircraft carrier. Motion agreed to 67-31: R 46-6; D 21-25

(ND 9-22, SD 12-3), in the session which began Dec. 16, 1982. A "yea" was a vote supporting the president's position.

437. H J Res 631. Continuing Appropriations, Fiscal 1983. Cohen, R-Maine, amendment to allow the use of funds to turn the Rapid Deployment Joint Task Force into a major military command concentrating on the Persian Gulf region, by deleting a prohibition in the joint resolution against such action. Adopted 73-25: R 34-18; D 39-7 (ND 28-3, SD 11-4), in the session which began Dec. 16, 1982.

438. H J Res 631. Continuing Appropriations, Fiscal 1983. Rudman, R-N.H., motion to table (kill) the Pryor, D-Ark., amendment to eliminate funds for the Maverick anti-tank missile. Motion agreed to 70-27: R 51-2; D 19-25 (ND 12-18, SD 7-7), in the session which began Dec. 16, 1982.

439. H J Res 631. Continuing Appropriations, Fiscal 1983. Stevens, R-Alaska, motion to table (kill) the Exon, D-Neb., amendment to freeze salaries of members of Congress at their existing level. Motion rejected 24-71: R 20-32; D 4-39 (ND 3-26, SD 1-13), in the session which began Dec. 16, 1982. (The Exon amendment subsequently was ruled out of order as being legislation on an appropriations bill.)

440. H J Res 631. Continuing Appropriations, Fiscal 1983. Danforth, R-Mo., amendment to provide an additional $200 million for the low-income energy assistance program. Adopted 80-11: R 42-8; D 38-3 (ND 25-1, SD 13-2), Dec. 18, 1982.

KEY

- Y Voted for (yea).
- # Paired for.
- + Announced for.
- N Voted against (nay).
- X Paired against.
- - Announced against.
- P Voted "present".
- C Voted "present" to avoid possible conflict of interest.
- ? Did not vote or otherwise make a position known.

Democrats **Republicans**

	441	442	443	444	445	446	447	448
ALABAMA								
Denton	Y	N	Y	Y	Y	Y	Y	N
Heflin	Y	N	Y	Y	N	N	N	N
ALASKA								
Murkowski	Y	Y	Y	Y	Y	Y	Y	N
Stevens	Y	Y	Y	Y	Y	Y	Y	N
ARIZONA								
Goldwater	?	?	?	?	?	?	?	?
DeConcini	Y	N	Y	Y	N	N	Y	X
ARKANSAS								
Bumpers	N	Y	Y	Y	N	N	Y	Y
Pryor	Y	N	Y	Y	N	N	Y	Y
CALIFORNIA								
Hayakawa	Y	Y	Y	Y	Y	Y	Y	N
Cranston	?	?	?	?	?	?	?	?
COLORADO								
Armstrong	Y	N	?	Y	Y	Y	N	N
Hart	N	Y	Y	Y	?	N	Y	Y
CONNECTICUT								
Weicker	N	Y	Y	Y	N	Y	Y	Y
Dodd	N	N	Y	Y	N	?	#	#
DELAWARE								
Roth	Y	N	Y	Y	N	N	Y	Y
Biden	N	Y	Y	Y	N	N	N	Y
FLORIDA								
Hawkins	Y	N	Y	Y	Y	Y	N	N
Chiles	Y	N	Y	Y	N	N	Y	Y
GEORGIA								
Mattingly	Y	Y	Y	Y	Y	Y	Y	N
Nunn	Y	Y	Y	Y	N	N	Y	N
HAWAII								
Inouye	N	N	Y	Y	N	N	Y	Y
Matsunaga	N	N	Y	Y	N	N	Y	Y
IDAHO								
McClure	Y	Y	Y	Y	Y	Y	Y	N
Symms	Y	N	Y	N	Y	Y	N	N
ILLINOIS								
Percy	Y	N	Y	Y	N	N	Y	Y
Dixon	N	N	Y	Y	N	N	Y	Y
INDIANA								
Lugar	Y	Y	Y	N	Y	Y	Y	N
Quayle	Y	Y	Y	Y	Y	Y	Y	N

	441	442	443	444	445	446	447	448
IOWA								
Grassley	Y	N	Y	Y	Y	Y	N	N
Jepsen	Y	N	Y	Y	Y	Y	Y	N
KANSAS								
Dole	Y	N	Y	N	Y	Y	Y	N
Kassebaum	N	Y	Y	N	Y	Y	Y	Y
KENTUCKY								
Ford	Y	N	Y	Y	N	N	Y	Y
Huddleston	Y	N	Y	Y	N	N	Y	Y
LOUISIANA								
Johnston	Y	N	Y	Y	N	N	Y	N
Long	Y	N	Y	Y	N	Y	N	Y
MAINE								
Cohen	Y	Y	Y	Y	Y	Y	N	N
Mitchell	N	Y	Y	Y	N	N	N	Y
MARYLAND								
Mathias	N	Y	?	Y	N	N	Y	Y
Sarbanes	N	N	Y	Y	N	N	Y	Y
MASSACHUSETTS								
Kennedy	-	?	Y	Y	?	?	?	?
Tsongas	N	N	Y	Y	N	N	Y	Y
MICHIGAN								
Levin	N	N	Y	Y	N	N	Y	Y
Riegle	N	N	Y	Y	N	N	Y	Y
MINNESOTA								
Boschwitz	N	Y	Y	Y	Y	Y	Y	Y
Durenberger	N	Y	Y	N	N	N	Y	Y
MISSISSIPPI								
Cochran	Y	N	Y	Y	Y	Y	Y	N
Stennis	Y	Y	Y	Y	N	N	Y	Y
MISSOURI								
Danforth	Y	Y	Y	Y	Y	Y	Y	Y
Eagleton	N	N	Y	Y	N	N	Y	Y
MONTANA								
Baucus	N	Y	Y	Y	N	N	N	Y
Melcher	N	Y	Y	Y	N	N	X	N
NEBRASKA								
Exon	Y	N	Y	Y	N	N	N	N
Zorinsky	Y	N	Y	Y	N	N	N	N
NEVADA								
Laxalt	Y	N	Y	Y	Y	Y	Y	N
Cannon	N	Y	Y	Y	N	N	N	?

	441	442	443	444	445	446	447	448
NEW HAMPSHIRE								
Humphrey	Y	N	Y	Y	Y	Y	N	N
Rudman	Y	Y	Y	Y	Y	Y	Y	Y
NEW JERSEY								
Brady	?	Y	Y	Y	Y	Y	Y	N
Bradley	N	N	Y	Y	N	N	N	Y
NEW MEXICO								
Domenici	Y	Y	Y	Y	Y	Y	Y	N
Schmitt	Y	Y	Y	Y	Y	Y	Y	N
NEW YORK								
D'Amato	Y	N	Y	Y	N	N	Y	N
Moynihan	N	N	Y	Y	N	N	Y	Y
NORTH CAROLINA								
East	Y	N	Y	Y	Y	Y	N	N
Helms	Y	N	Y	N	Y	Y	N	N
NORTH DAKOTA								
Andrews	Y	N	Y	Y	Y	Y	Y	Y
Burdick	N	N	Y	Y	N	N	N	N
OHIO								
Glenn	N	Y	Y	Y	N	?	?	?
Metzenbaum	N	N	Y	Y	N	N	Y	Y
OKLAHOMA								
Nickles	Y	Y	Y	Y	Y	Y	N	N
Boren	Y	N	Y	Y	N	N	N	N
OREGON								
Hatfield	Y	Y	Y	Y	Y	Y	Y	Y
Packwood	Y	N	Y	Y	Y	Y	Y	Y
PENNSYLVANIA								
Heinz	?	?	?	?	-	?	?	?
Specter	N	Y	Y	Y	N	N	N	Y
RHODE ISLAND								
Chafee	N	Y	Y	Y	Y	Y	Y	Y
Pell	N	-	+	+	?	?	-	+
SOUTH CAROLINA								
Thurmond	Y	Y	Y	Y	Y	Y	N	N
Hollings	Y	N	Y	Y	N	N	N	N
SOUTH DAKOTA								
Abdnor	Y	N	Y	Y	Y	Y	N	N
Pressler	N	Y	Y	Y	Y	Y	N	N
TENNESSEE								
Baker	Y	Y	Y	N	Y	Y	Y	Y
Sasser	N	Y	Y	Y	N	N	Y	Y

	441	442	443	444	445	446	447	448
TEXAS								
Tower	Y	Y	Y	N	Y	Y	Y	Y
Bentsen	Y	N	Y	Y	N	N	Y	N
UTAH								
Garn	Y	Y	Y	Y	Y	Y	N	N
Hatch	Y	Y	Y	N	Y	Y	N	N
VERMONT								
Stafford	N	Y	Y	Y	Y	Y	Y	Y
Leahy	N	N	Y	Y	N	N	N	Y
VIRGINIA								
Warner	Y	Y	Y	Y	Y	Y	Y	N
Byrd*	Y	Y	Y	Y	Y	Y	Y	N
WASHINGTON								
Gorton	N	Y	Y	Y	Y	Y	Y	Y
Jackson	+	+	+	+	-	-	+	+
WEST VIRGINIA								
Byrd	N	N	Y	Y	N	N	Y	N
Randolph	N	Y	Y	Y	N	N	N	N
WISCONSIN								
Kasten	Y	Y	Y	N	Y	Y	N	N
Proxmire	N	Y	Y	Y	N	N	Y	Y
WYOMING								
Simpson	N	Y	Y	Y	Y	Y	Y	Y
Wallop	Y	Y	Y	Y	Y	Y	Y	N

ND - Northern Democrats SD - Southern Democrats (Southern states - Ala., Ark., Fla., Ga., Ky., La., Miss., N.C., Okla., S.C., Tenn., Texas, Va.) *Byrd elected as an independent.*

441. H J Res 631. Continuing Appropriations, Fiscal 1983. Helms, R-N.C., motion to table (kill) the Dodd, D-Conn., amendment to bar the use of funds, after Jan. 20, 1983, to support irregular or paramilitary forces in Central America. Motion agreed to 56-38: R 40-11; D 16-27 (ND 3-25, SD 13-2), Dec. 18, 1982. A "yea" was a vote supporting the president's position.

442. H J Res 631. Continuing Appropriations, Fiscal 1983. Warner, R-Va., motion to table (kill) the Dixon, D-Ill.-Percy, R-Ill., amendment to delay funds for the purchase of aerial reconnaissance cameras for Navy aircraft from a German company. The amendment was intended to assist an Illinois firm that also sought to sell such a camera. Motion agreed to 48-46: R 34-18; D 14-28 (ND 9-18, SD 5-10), Dec. 18, 1982.

443. H J Res 631. Continuing Appropriations, Fiscal 1983. Boren, D-Okla., amendment to call on the Federal Reserve to take such actions as necessary to achieve and maintain interest rates low enough to generate economic growth and thereby reduce the nation's unemployment level. Adopted 93-0: R 50-0; D 43-0 (ND 28-0, SD 15-0), Dec. 18, 1982.

444. H J Res 631. Continuing Appropriations, Fiscal 1983. Glenn, D-Ohio, amendment to allow the sale or transfer of sensitive military equipment, materials or technology to a country only if the president established procedures to ensure that that country did not in turn transmit it to a communist country or to a country that received arms from a communist country. Adopted 85-10: R 42-10; D 43-0 (ND 28-0, SD 15-0), Dec. 18, 1982.

445. H J Res 631. Continuing Appropriations, Fiscal 1983. Dole, R-Kan., motion to table (kill) the Ford, D-Ky., amendment to make unemployed railroad workers with less than 10 years of experience eligible for supplemental unemployment insurance benefits. Motion agreed to 47-46: R 45-7; D 2-39 (ND 0-26, SD 2-13), Dec. 18, 1982.

446. H J Res 631. Continuing Appropriations, Fiscal 1983. Ford, D-Ky., motion to table (kill) the Hatfield, R-Ore., motion to reconsider the vote by which the Dole, R-Kan., motion to table the Ford amendment was agreed to (see vote 445, above). Motion agreed to 47-45: R 46-6; D 1-39 (ND 0-25, SD 1-14), Dec. 18, 1982.

447. H J Res 631. Continuing Appropriations, Fiscal 1983. Baker, R-Tenn., motion to table (kill) the Helms, R-N.C., appeal of the ruling of the chair that a Helms amendment freezing congressional salaries until the federal budget was balanced and the federal debt was below $1 trillion was out of order as legislation on an appropriations bill. Motion agreed to 62-29: R 36-16; D 26-13 (ND 15-9, SD 11-4), Dec. 18, 1982.

448. H J Res 631. Continuing Appropriations, Fiscal 1983. Hatfield, R-Ore., motion to table (kill) the Helms, R-N.C., amendment to bar the use of funds to implement the United Nations Convention on the Law of the Sea. Motion agreed to 46-44: R 19-33; D 27-11 (ND 18-5, SD 9-6), Dec. 18, 1982.

	449	450	451	452	453	454	455	456
ALABAMA								
Denton	N	N	N	Y	N	Y	N	N
Heflin	N	N	N	Y	Y	N	N	Y
ALASKA								
Murkowski	N	N	Y	Y	Y	Y	Y	Y
Stevens	N	Y	Y	Y	Y	Y	Y	Y
ARIZONA								
Goldwater	?	?	?	?	?	?	?	?
DeConcini	N	N	N	Y	N	N	N	N
ARKANSAS								
Bumpers	Y	Y	Y	Y	Y	N	Y	N
Pryor	N	Y	N	Y	N	N	N	N
CALIFORNIA								
Hayakawa	Y	N	N	Y	N	Y	Y	Y
Cranston	?	?	?	?	?	?	?	?
COLORADO								
Armstrong	N	N	N	Y	N	Y	N	N
Hart	Y	Y	Y	Y	Y	N	Y	Y
CONNECTICUT								
Weicker	Y	Y	Y	Y	Y	Y	Y	Y
Dodd	#	?	N	Y	Y	N	N	Y
DELAWARE								
Roth	N	Y	N	Y	N	Y	Y	Y
Biden	Y	Y	Y	Y	Y	N	N	Y
FLORIDA								
Hawkins	N	Y	Y	Y	N	Y	Y	Y
Chiles	Y	Y	Y	Y	N	N	Y	Y
GEORGIA								
Mattingly	N	Y	N	Y	N	Y	Y	Y
Nunn	N	Y	N	Y	N	N	N	Y
HAWAII								
Inouye	Y	Y	Y	Y	Y	N	Y	N
Matsunaga	Y	Y	?	Y	Y	N	Y	N
IDAHO								
McClure	N	N	Y	N	Y	N	Y	N
Symms	N	N	N	Y	N	Y	N	N
ILLINOIS								
Percy	Y	Y	Y	Y	Y	Y	Y	Y
Dixon	N	Y	N	Y	Y	N	N	Y
INDIANA								
Lugar	Y	Y	Y	Y	N	Y	Y	Y
Quayle	N	Y	Y	Y	N	Y	Y	Y
IOWA								
Grassley	N	N	N	Y	N	Y	N	N
Jepsen	N	N	Y	Y	N	Y	N	N
KANSAS								
Dole	N	Y	Y	Y	N	Y	Y	Y
Kassebaum	Y	Y	Y	Y	N	Y	Y	Y
KENTUCKY								
Ford	N	Y	Y	Y	N	Y	N	Y
Huddleston	Y	?	Y	Y	Y	N	Y	N
LOUISIANA								
Johnston	N	N	Y	Y	Y	N	Y	Y
Long	N	N	Y	Y	Y	N	Y	N
MAINE								
Cohen	Y	Y	Y	Y	N	N	N	N
Mitchell	Y	Y	N	Y	Y	N	N	N
MARYLAND								
Mathias	Y	Y	Y	Y	Y	Y	Y	Y
Sarbanes	Y	Y	Y	Y	N	N	Y	Y
MASSACHUSETTS								
Kennedy	?	?	Y	Y	Y	N	N	Y
Tsongas	Y	Y	Y	Y	Y	N	Y	Y
MICHIGAN								
Levin	Y	Y	N	Y	Y	N	N	Y
Riegle	Y	Y	Y	Y	Y	N	N	Y
MINNESOTA								
Boschwitz	Y	Y	Y	Y	N	Y	Y	Y
Durenberger	Y	Y	Y	Y	Y	Y	Y	Y
MISSISSIPPI								
Cochran	N	Y	Y	Y	N	Y	Y	N
Stennis	N	Y	Y	Y	N	Y	Y	Y
MISSOURI								
Danforth	Y	Y	Y	Y	Y	Y	Y	Y
Eagleton	Y	Y	N	Y	Y	N	N	Y
MONTANA								
Baucus	N	Y	N	Y	Y	N	N	N
Melcher	N	Y	Y	Y	Y	Y	Y	N
NEBRASKA								
Exon	N	Y	N	Y	N	N	N	N
Zorinsky	N	Y	N	Y	N	Y	N	N
NEVADA								
Laxalt	N	N	N	Y	N	Y	Y	N
Cannon	?	?	Y	?	?	?	N	N
NEW HAMPSHIRE								
Humphrey	N	N	N	N	N	N	N	Y
Rudman	Y	Y	Y	Y	N	Y	Y	Y
NEW JERSEY								
Brady	Y	Y	Y	Y	N	Y	Y	Y
Bradley	Y	Y	Y	Y	Y	N	N	Y
NEW MEXICO								
Domenici	N	Y	Y	Y	N	Y	Y	Y
Schmitt	Y	N	Y	Y	N	Y	Y	Y
NEW YORK								
D'Amato	Y	Y	Y	Y	Y	Y	Y	Y
Moynihan	Y	Y	Y	Y	Y	N	N	Y
NORTH CAROLINA								
East	N	N	N	N	N	N	N	N
Helms	N	N	N	N	N	Y	N	N
NORTH DAKOTA								
Andrews	N	N	Y	Y	Y	N	Y	N
Burdick	N	Y	Y	Y	N	Y	N	Y
OHIO								
Glenn	?	?	Y	Y	Y	N	N	Y
Metzenbaum	Y	Y	Y	Y	N	N	Y	Y
OKLAHOMA								
Nickles	N	N	N	N	N	Y	N	Y
Boren	X	Y	N	Y	N	N	N	N
OREGON								
Hatfield	Y	Y	Y	Y	N	Y	Y	N
Packwood	Y	Y	Y	Y	Y	Y	Y	Y
PENNSYLVANIA								
Heinz	?	?	+	?	?	?	?	?
Specter	Y	Y	Y	Y	N	N	Y	Y
RHODE ISLAND								
Chafee	Y	Y	Y	Y	Y	Y	Y	Y
Pell	+	+	-	+	+	-	N	Y
SOUTH CAROLINA								
Thurmond	N	N	Y	N	Y	N	N	N
Hollings	Y	Y	Y	Y	N	Y	Y	Y
SOUTH DAKOTA								
Abdnor	N	N	Y	N	Y	N	Y	N
Pressler	N	N	Y	N	Y	Y	N	N
TENNESSEE								
Baker	Y	Y	Y	Y	Y	Y	Y	Y
Sasser	Y	Y	N	Y	Y	N	N	N
TEXAS								
Tower	Y	N	Y	Y	N	Y	N	N
Bentsen	Y	Y	Y	Y	Y	?	Y	N
UTAH								
Garn	N	N	Y	Y	Y	N	Y	Y
Hatch	N	N	Y	Y	N	?	N	Y
VERMONT								
Stafford	Y	Y	Y	Y	Y	Y	Y	Y
Leahy	Y	Y	Y	Y	N	Y	N	N
VIRGINIA								
Warner	N	N	N	Y	N	Y	Y	Y
Byrd*	N	N	N	Y	N	Y	N	Y
WASHINGTON								
Gorton	Y	Y	Y	Y	N	Y	Y	Y
Jackson	+	+	+	+	+	-	.	+
WEST VIRGINIA								
Byrd	N	Y	Y	Y	N	Y	N	Y
Randolph	N	N	Y	Y	N	Y	N	Y
WISCONSIN								
Kasten	Y	Y	N	Y	N	Y	N	Y
Proxmire	N	Y	N	N	Y	N	Y	N
WYOMING								
Simpson	Y	N	Y	Y	N	Y	N	N
Wallop	N	N	N	Y	N	Y	N	N

KEY

Y Voted for (yea).
\# Paired for.
\+ Announced for.
N Voted against (nay).
X Paired against.
- Announced against.
P Voted "present".
C Voted "present" to avoid possible conflict of interest.
? Did not vote or otherwise make a position known.

Democrats   *Republicans*

ND · Northern Democrats   SD · Southern Democrats (Southern states - Ala., Ark., Fla., Ga., Ky., La., Miss., N.C., Okla., S.C., Tenn., Texas, Va.)   *Byrd elected as an independent.*

---

449. H J Res 631. Continuing Appropriations, Fiscal 1983. Hatfield, R-Ore., motion to table (kill) the Helms, R-N.C., amendment to limit to $700 million the appropriation for the International Development Association. Motion rejected 44-46: R 24-28; D 20-18 (ND 14-10, SD 6-8), Dec. 18, 1982. (The Helms amendment subsequently was adopted by voice vote.)

450. H J Res 631. Continuing Appropriations, Fiscal 1983. Moynihan, D-N.Y., motion to table (kill) the Helms, R-N.C., amendment to bar the use of funds by the Internal Revenue Service to deny tax-exempt status to private, religious schools. Motion agreed to 61-29: R 29-23; D 32-6 (ND 22-2, SD 10-4), Dec. 18, 1982.

451. H J Res 631. Continuing Appropriations, Fiscal 1983. Passage of the joint resolution to provide funding, through Sept. 30, 1983, for government agencies whose regular fiscal 1983 appropriations bills had not been enacted, and to provide $1.2 billion for jobs programs. Passed 63-31: R 37-15; D 26-16 (ND 17-10, SD 9-6), Dec. 19, 1982.

452. HR 6211. Transportation Assistance Act of 1982. Baker, R-Tenn., motion to invoke cloture (thus limiting debate) on the Baker substitute to the bill to authorize highways and transit funds and increase highway taxes. Motion agreed to 89-5: R 48-4; D 41-1 (ND 26-1, SD 15-0), Dec. 19, 1982. A three-fifths majority vote (60) of the total Senate is required to invoke cloture.

453. HR 6211. Transportation Assistance Act of 1982. Stafford, R-Vt., motion to table (kill) the Nickles, R-Okla., amendment to the Baker, R-Tenn., substitute, to remove the section of the bill relating to the Davis-Bacon Act requirement that an area's prevailing wage rate be paid on federal highway projects. Motion agreed to 48-46: R 15-37; D 33-9 (ND 25-2, SD 8-7), Dec. 19, 1982.

454. HR 6211. Transportation Assistance Act of 1982. Dole, R-Kan., motion to table (kill) the Riegle, D-Mich., amendment to the Baker, R-Tenn., substitute, to exempt families earning $10,000 or less a year from the gasoline tax increase. Motion agreed to 50-42: R 47-4; D 3-38 (ND 2-25, SD 1-13), Dec. 19, 1982.

455. H J Res 631. Continuing Appropriations, Fiscal 1983. Adoption of the conference report on the joint resolution providing funding, through Sept. 30, 1983, for government agencies whose regular fiscal 1983 appropriations bills had not been enacted. Adopted 55-41: R 37-15; D 18-26 (ND 9-20, SD 9-6), Dec. 20, 1982.

456. HR 6211. Transportation Assistance Act of 1982. Garn, R-Utah, motion to table (kill) the Bumpers, D-Ark., amendment to the Baker, R-Tenn., substitute, to require that every state receive 85 percent of the transit revenues derived from 1-cent-a-gallon of the gas tax increase that its motorists pay. Motion agreed to 52-44: R 30-22; D 22-22 (ND 15-14, SD 7-8), Dec. 20, 1982.

KEY

Y	Voted for (yea).	
#	Paired for.	
+	Announced for.	
N	Voted against (nay).	
X	Paired against.	
-	Announced against.	
P	Voted "present".	
C	Voted "present" to avoid possible conflict of interest.	
?	Did not vote or otherwise make a position known.	

Democrats   *Republicans*

	457	458	459	460	461	462	463
ALABAMA							
Denton	N	N	Y	Y	Y	Y	N
Heflin	N	N	Y	Y	Y	Y	N
ALASKA							
Murkowski	Y	Y	Y	Y	Y	Y	Y
Stevens	Y	Y	Y	Y	Y	Y	Y
ARIZONA							
Goldwater	?	?	?	?	?	?	?
DeConcini	Y	N	Y	Y	Y	Y	Y
ARKANSAS							
Bumpers	N	Y	Y	?	Y	Y	N
Pryor	N	N	Y	Y	Y	Y	N
CALIFORNIA							
Hayakawa	Y	Y	Y	Y	Y	Y	Y
Cranston	?	?	?	?	?	?	?
COLORADO							
Armstrong	Y	N	N	N	Y	N	N
Hart	Y	Y	Y	?	Y	Y	Y
CONNECTICUT							
Weicker	Y	Y	Y	Y	Y	Y	Y
Dodd	Y	Y	Y	Y	Y	Y	Y
DELAWARE							
Roth	Y	Y	Y	Y	Y	Y	Y
Biden	N	Y	Y	Y	Y	Y	N
FLORIDA							
Hawkins	Y	Y	Y	Y	Y	Y	Y
Chiles	Y	Y	Y	Y	Y	Y	Y
GEORGIA							
Mattingly	Y	N	N	Y	Y	Y	N
Nunn	Y	N	Y	Y	Y	Y	N
HAWAII							
Inouye	N	Y	Y	Y	Y	Y	Y
Matsunaga	Y	Y	Y	Y	Y	Y	Y
IDAHO							
McClure	Y	Y	Y	N	N	N	Y
Symms	Y	Y	Y	Y	Y	Y	Y
ILLINOIS							
Percy	Y	Y	Y	Y	N	N	Y
Dixon	Y	Y	Y	Y	Y	Y	Y
INDIANA							
Lugar	Y	Y	Y	Y	Y	Y	Y
Quayle	Y	Y	Y	Y	Y	Y	Y
IOWA							
Grassley	Y	N	Y	Y	Y	Y	Y
Jepsen	Y	Y	Y	Y	Y	Y	Y
KANSAS							
Dole	Y	Y	Y	Y	Y	Y	Y
Kassebaum	Y	Y	Y	Y	Y	Y	Y
KENTUCKY							
Ford	N	N	N	Y	Y	Y	N
Huddleston	Y	Y	Y	Y	Y	Y	Y
LOUISIANA							
Johnston	N	N	Y	Y	Y	Y	N
Long	Y	Y	Y	Y	Y	Y	Y
MAINE							
Cohen	Y	Y	Y	Y	Y	Y	N
Mitchell	N	Y	Y	Y	Y	Y	N
MARYLAND							
Mathias	Y	Y	Y	Y	Y	Y	Y
Sarbanes	N	Y	Y	Y	Y	Y	N
MASSACHUSETTS							
Kennedy	N	Y	Y	Y	Y	Y	-
Tsongas	Y	Y	Y	Y	Y	Y	Y
MICHIGAN							
Levin	Y	Y	Y	Y	Y	Y	Y
Riegle	Y	Y	Y	Y	Y	Y	N
MINNESOTA							
Boschwitz	Y	Y	Y	Y	Y	Y	Y
Durenberger	Y	Y	Y	Y	Y	Y	Y
MISSISSIPPI							
Cochran	Y	Y	Y	Y	Y	Y	N
Stennis	Y	Y	Y	Y	Y	Y	Y
MISSOURI							
Danforth	Y	Y	Y	Y	Y	Y	Y
Eagleton	N	Y	Y	Y	Y	Y	N
MONTANA							
Baucus	Y	Y	Y	Y	Y	Y	Y
Melcher	Y	Y	Y	Y	Y	Y	Y
NEBRASKA							
Exon	Y	N	N	Y	Y	Y	N
Zorinsky	Y	N	N	Y	Y	Y	N
NEVADA							
Laxalt	Y	Y	Y	Y	Y	Y	Y
Cannon	N	Y	Y	Y	N	N	?
NEW HAMPSHIRE							
Humphrey	Y	N	N	N	N	N	N
Rudman	Y	Y	Y	Y	Y	Y	Y
NEW JERSEY							
Brady	Y	Y	Y	Y	Y	Y	Y
Bradley	N	Y	Y	Y	Y	Y	N
NEW MEXICO							
Domenici	Y	Y	Y	Y	Y	Y	Y
Schmitt	Y	Y	Y	Y	Y	Y	Y
NEW YORK							
D'Amato	Y	Y	Y	Y	Y	Y	Y
Moynihan	Y	Y	Y	Y	Y	Y	?
NORTH CAROLINA							
East	N	N	N	N	N	N	N
Helms	N	N	N	N	N	N	N
NORTH DAKOTA							
Andrews	Y	Y	Y	Y	Y	Y	Y
Burdick	Y	Y	Y	Y	Y	Y	Y
OHIO							
Glenn	Y	Y	Y	Y	Y	Y	Y
Metzenbaum	N	Y	Y	Y	Y	Y	N
OKLAHOMA							
Nickles	Y	N	N	N	N	N	N
Boren	N	N	N	Y	Y	Y	N
OREGON							
Hatfield	?	?	?	?	?	?	?
Packwood	Y	Y	Y	Y	Y	Y	Y
PENNSYLVANIA							
Heinz	+	?	?	?	?	?	?
Specter	Y	Y	Y	Y	Y	Y	Y
RHODE ISLAND							
Chafee	Y	Y	Y	Y	Y	Y	Y
Pell	Y	Y	Y	Y	Y	Y	Y
SOUTH CAROLINA							
Thurmond	Y	Y	Y	Y	Y	Y	Y
Hollings	N	Y	N	Y	Y	Y	?
SOUTH DAKOTA							
Abdnor	Y	Y	Y	Y	Y	Y	Y
Pressler	Y	Y	N	Y	Y	Y	Y
TENNESSEE							
Baker	Y	Y	Y	Y	Y	Y	Y
Sasser	N	Y	N	Y	Y	Y	N
TEXAS							
Tower	Y	Y	Y	Y	Y	Y	N
Bentsen	Y	Y	Y	Y	Y	Y	Y
UTAH							
Garn	Y	Y	Y	Y	Y	Y	N
Hatch	Y	N	Y	Y	N	Y	-
VERMONT							
Stafford	Y	Y	Y	Y	Y	Y	Y
Leahy	Y	Y	Y	Y	Y	Y	Y
VIRGINIA							
Warner	Y	N	Y	Y	Y	Y	Y
Byrd*	Y	N	Y	Y	Y	Y	Y
WASHINGTON							
Gorton	Y	Y	Y	Y	Y	Y	Y
Jackson	+	+	+	+	+	+	+
WEST VIRGINIA							
Byrd	N	Y	Y	Y	Y	Y	N
Randolph	Y	Y	Y	Y	Y	Y	Y
WISCONSIN							
Kasten	N	N	Y	Y	Y	Y	N
Proxmire	N	N	N	N	N	N	N
WYOMING							
Simpson	Y	Y	Y	Y	Y	Y	N
Wallop	N	Y	Y	Y	Y	Y	N

ND - Northern Democrats   SD - Southern Democrats (Southern states - Ala., Ark., Fla., Ga., Ky., La., Miss., N.C., Okla., S.C., Tenn., Texas, Va.)   *Byrd elected as an independent.*

457. HR 6211. Transportation Assistance Act of 1982. Baker, R-Tenn., substitute for the bill to authorize approximately $70 billion for highways through fiscal 1987 and approximately $12 billion for transit through fiscal 1985, and increase highway taxes. Adopted 71-24: R 46-5; D 25-19 (ND 18-11, SD 7-8), Dec. 20, 1982. (The original bill, subsequently adopted as amended, included only highway tax increases.) A "yea" was a vote supporting the president's position.

458. HR 6211. Transportation Assistance Act of 1982. Baker, R-Tenn., motion to table (kill) the Helms, R-N.C., point of order against the bill to authorize highway and transit funding and increase highway taxes because it violated a law (PL 95-435) that prohibits federal expenditures from exceeding revenues. Motion agreed to 73-22: R 40-11; D 33-11 (ND 25-4, SD 8-7), Dec. 20, 1982.

459. HR 6211. Transportation Assistance Act of 1982. Baker, R-Tenn., motion to waive provisions of the Congressional Budget Act (PL 93-344) that would bar consideration of the bill to authorize highway and transit funding and increase highway taxes. Motion agreed to 81-14: R 44-7; D 37-7 (ND 26-3, SD 11-4), Dec. 20, 1982.

460. HR 6211. Transportation Assistance Act of 1982. Baker, R-Tenn., motion to proceed to the Baker motion to reconsider the vote by which the Baker motion to invoke cloture on the bill to authorize highway and transit funding and increase highway taxes was rejected. Motion agreed to 86-7: R 45-6; D 41-1 (ND 27-1, SD 14-0), Dec. 20, 1982.

461. HR 6211. Transportation Assistance Act of 1982. Baker, R-Tenn., motion to reconsider the Baker motion to invoke cloture on the bill to authorize highway and transit funding and increase highway taxes. Motion agreed to 87-8: R 45-6; D 42-2 (ND 27-2, SD 15-0), Dec. 20, 1982.

462. HR 6211. Transportation Assistance Act of 1982. Baker, R-Tenn., motion to invoke cloture (thus limiting debate) on the bill to authorize highway and transit funding and increase highway taxes. Motion agreed to 87-8: R 45-6; D 42-2 (ND 27-2, SD 15-0), Dec. 20, 1982. A three-fifths majority vote (60) of the total Senate is required to invoke cloture.

463. HR 6211. Transportation Assistance Act of 1982. Passage of the bill to authorize approximately $70 billion for highways through fiscal 1987 and approximately $12 billion for transit through fiscal 1985, and increase gasoline and other highway taxes. Passed 56-34: R 35-15; D 21-19 (ND 14-12, SD 7-7), in the session which began Dec. 20, 1982. A "yea" was a vote supporting the president's position.

	464	465			464	465			464	465
ALABAMA			**IOWA**			**NEW HAMPSHIRE**		
Denton	+	X	*Grassley*	Y	Y	*Humphrey*	?	?
Heflin	Y	N	*Jepsen*	Y	Y	*Rudman*	Y	Y
ALASKA			**KANSAS**			**NEW JERSEY**		
Murkowski	?	#	*Dole*	Y	Y	*Brady*	Y	Y
Stevens	Y	Y	*Kassebaum*	?	?	Bradley	Y	Y
ARIZONA			**KENTUCKY**			**NEW MEXICO**		
Goldwater	Y	N	Ford	Y	N	*Domenici*	Y	Y
DeConcini	Y	Y	Huddleston	Y	Y	*Schmitt*	Y	Y
ARKANSAS			**LOUISIANA**			**NEW YORK**		
Bumpers	?	?	Johnston	Y	N	*D'Amato*	Y	Y
Pryor	Y	N	Long	Y	Y	Moynihan	Y	Y
CALIFORNIA			**MAINE**			**NORTH CAROLINA**		
Hayakawa	Y	Y	*Cohen*	Y	N	*East*	N	N
Cranston	Y	Y	Mitchell	Y	N	*Helms*	N	N
COLORADO			**MARYLAND**			**NORTH DAKOTA**		
Armstrong	Y	N	*Mathias*	Y	Y	*Andrews*	Y	Y
Hart	Y	Y	Sarbanes	Y	N	Burdick	Y	Y
CONNECTICUT			**MASSACHUSETTS**			**OHIO**		
Weicker	Y	Y	Kennedy	Y	N	Glenn	+	#
Dodd	Y	Y	Tsongas	Y	Y	Metzenbaum	Y	N
DELAWARE			**MICHIGAN**			**OKLAHOMA**		
Roth	Y	Y	Levin	Y	Y	*Nickles*	N	N
Biden	?	?	Riegle	Y	X	Boren	Y	N
FLORIDA			**MINNESOTA**			**OREGON**		
Hawkins	Y	N	*Boschwitz*	Y	Y	*Hatfield*	Y	Y
Chiles	Y	Y	*Durenberger*	Y	Y	*Packwood*	Y	Y
GEORGIA			**MISSISSIPPI**			**PENNSYLVANIA**		
Mattingly	Y	N	*Cochran*	Y	N	*Heinz*	Y	Y
Nunn	Y	N	Stennis	Y	Y	*Specter*	Y	Y
HAWAII			**MISSOURI**			**RHODE ISLAND**		
Inouye	Y	N	*Danforth*	Y	Y	*Chafee*	Y	Y
Matsunaga	#	Y	Eagleton	Y	N	Pell	Y	Y
IDAHO			**MONTANA**			**SOUTH CAROLINA**		
McClure	Y	N	Baucus	X	X	*Thurmond*	Y	Y
Symms	Y	Y	Melcher	Y	N	Hollings	?	?
ILLINOIS			**NEBRASKA**			**SOUTH DAKOTA**		
Percy	Y	Y	Exon	N	N	*Abdnor*	Y	Y
Dixon	Y	Y	Zorinsky	?	?	*Pressler*	Y	Y
INDIANA			**NEVADA**			**TENNESSEE**		
Lugar	Y	Y	*Laxalt*	Y	Y	*Baker*	Y	Y
Quayle	Y	Y	Cannon	?	?	Sasser	?	N

	464	465
TEXAS		
Tower	Y	N
Bentsen	Y	Y
UTAH		
Garn	Y	N
Hatch	Y	N
VERMONT		
Stafford	Y	Y
Leahy	Y	Y
VIRGINIA		
Warner	Y	Y
Byrd*	Y	Y
WASHINGTON		
Gorton	Y	Y
Jackson	+	#
WEST VIRGINIA		
Byrd	Y	N
Randolph	Y	Y
WISCONSIN		
Kasten	Y	N
Proxmire	N	N
WYOMING		
Simpson	Y	N
Wallop	Y	N

KEY

Y Voted for (yea).
Paired for.
+ Announced for.
N Voted against (nay).
X Paired against.
- Announced against.
P Voted "present".
C Voted "present" to avoid possible conflict of interest.
? Did not vote or otherwise make a position known.

Democrats *Republicans*

ND - Northern Democrats   SD - Southern Democrats (Southern states - Ala., Ark., Fla., Ga., Ky., La., Miss., N.C., Okla., S.C., Tenn., Texas, Va.)

Byrd elected as an independent.

464. HR 6211. Transportation Assistance Act of 1982. Baker, R-Tenn., motion to invoke cloture (thus limiting debate) on the conference report on the bill to authorize $71.3 billion over four years for highway construction and repairs and mass transit, and to increase gasoline and other highway taxes. Motion agreed to 81-5: R 47-3; D 34-2 (ND 22-2, SD 12-0), Dec. 23, 1982. A three-fifths majority vote (60) of the total Senate is required to invoke cloture. A "yea" was a vote supporting the president's position.

465. HR 6211. Transportation Assistance Act of 1982. Adoption of the conference report on the bill to authorize $71.3 billion over four years for highway construction and repairs and mass transit, and to increase gasoline and other highway taxes. Adopted 54-33: R 34-16; D 20-17 (ND 14-10, SD 6-7), Dec. 23, 1982. A "yea" was a vote supporting the president's position.

HOUSE ROLL-CALL VOTES

CQ

1. H J Res 389/H J Res 391. Fiscal 1982 Supplemental Appropriations/Commodity Credit Corporation and Fiscal 1982 Supplemental Appropriations/Unemployment Compensation. Adoption of the rule (H Res 355) providing for House floor consideration of H J Res 389, to appropriate $5,000,000,000 in supplemental fiscal 1982 funding for the Commodity Credit Corporation, and consideration of H J Res 391, to appropriate $2.3 billion in supplemental fiscal 1982 funding for unemployment compensation and state employment services. Adopted 329-72: R 109-63; D 220-9 (ND 150-3, SD 70-6), Feb. 9, 1982.

2. H J Res 389. Fiscal 1982 Supplemental Appropriations/Commodity Credit Corporation. Lewis, R-Calif., motion to recommit the joint resolution to the Appropriations Committee, with instructions to add language prohibiting use of funds in the act for payment on guaranteed loans to Poland. Motion rejected 152-256: R 91-85; D 61-171 (ND 26-130, SD 35-41), Feb. 9, 1982.

3. H J Res 389. Fiscal 1982 Supplemental Appropriations/Commodity Credit Corporation. Passage of the joint resolution to provide a fiscal 1982 supplemental appropriation of $5,000,000,000 for the Commodity Credit Corporation to repay funds borrowed from the Treasury by the corporation in fiscal years 1980, 1981 and in the first quarter of fiscal year 1982. Passed 320-86: R 121-54; D 199-32 (ND 134-23, SD 65-9), Feb. 9, 1982. The president had requested $5,000,000,000.

4. H J Res 392. Fiscal 1982 Supplemental Appropriations/Low-income Energy Assistance. Passage of the joint resolution to provide a supplemental appropriation of $123,000,000 for low-income energy assistance payments, bringing fiscal 1982 appropriations for the program to the full authorization level of $1.875 billion. The resolution was modified by a Broyhill, R-N.C., amendment prohibiting use of the money for any purpose other than low-income energy aid and requiring that it be spent before May 31, 1982, to prevent its use for payment of air-conditioning bills. Passed 342-62: R 129-47; D 213-15 (ND 154-1, SD 59-14), Feb. 9, 1982. A "nay" was a vote supporting the president's position.

5. H J Res 391. Fiscal 1982 Supplemental Appropriations/Unemployment Compensation. Passage of the joint resolution to provide a fiscal 1982 supplemental appropriation of $2,293,490,000 for the unemployment insurance program and the U.S. Employment Service. Passed 398-3: R 173-2; D 225-1 (ND 153-0, SD 72-1), Feb. 9, 1982. The president had requested $2,290,490,000.

6. HR 4481. Justice Assistance Act. Passage of the bill to amend the Omnibus Crime Control and Safe Streets Act of 1968 to create an Office of Justice Assistance within the Justice Department and to authorize $170 million in 50-50 matching grants to the states in fiscal 1983 to aid in fighting crime. Passed 289-73: R 92-63; D 197-10 (ND 137-2, SD 60-8), Feb. 10, 1982. A "nay" was a vote supporting the president's position.

7. H J Res 389. Fiscal 1982 Supplemental Appropriations/Commodity Credit Corporation. Whitten, D-Miss., motion to concur in the Senate amendment to add an appropriation of $123,000,000 for the Department of Health and Human Services in fiscal 1982 for low-income energy assistance, to be available only until May 31, 1982, to the bill appropriating $5,000,000,000 in supplemental fiscal 1982 funding for the Commodity Credit Corporation. Motion agreed to 264-62: R 85-51; D 179-11 (ND 124-2, SD 55-9), Feb. 10, 1982.

KEY

Y	Voted for (yea).
#	Paired for.
+	Announced for.
N	Voted against (nay).
X	Paired against.
-	Announced against.
P	Voted "present".
C	Voted "present" to avoid possible conflict of interest.
?	Did not vote or otherwise make a position known.

Democrats *Republicans*

	1	2	3	4	5	6	7
ALABAMA							
1 *Edwards*	Y	N	Y	Y	Y	?	?
2 *Dickinson*	?	?	?	?	?	Y	?
3 Nichols	Y	Y	Y	Y	Y	Y	Y
4 Bevill	Y	Y	Y	Y	Y	Y	Y
5 Flippo	Y	Y	Y	Y	Y	?	?
6 *Smith*	N	Y	N	N	Y	N	?
7 Shelby	Y	Y	N	N	Y	N	N
ALASKA							
AL *Young*	N	Y	Y	Y	Y	Y	Y
ARIZONA							
1 *Rhodes*	Y	N	N	Y	Y	Y	Y
2 Udall	Y	N	Y	Y	Y	Y	Y
3 Stump	N	Y	N	Y	N	N	N
4 *Rudd*	N	Y	Y	Y	Y	N	?
ARKANSAS							
1 Alexander	Y	N	Y	Y	Y	Y	Y
2 *Bethune*	Y	Y	Y	Y	Y	N	Y
3 *Hammerschmidt*	Y	N	Y	Y	Y	N	N
4 Anthony	Y	N	Y	Y	Y	Y	Y
CALIFORNIA							
1 *Chappie*	Y	Y	Y	Y	Y	Y	Y
2 *Clausen*	Y	Y	Y	Y	Y	Y	Y
3 Matsui	Y	N	Y	Y	Y	Y	Y
4 Fazio	Y	N	Y	Y	Y	Y	Y
5 Burton, J.	Y	Y	Y	Y	Y	Y	?
6 Burton, P.	Y	N	Y	Y	Y	Y	Y
7 Miller	Y	N	Y	Y	Y	Y	Y
8 Dellums	?	N	N	Y	Y	Y	Y
9 Stark	Y	N	Y	Y	Y	Y	Y
10 Edwards	Y	N	Y	Y	Y	Y	Y
11 Lantos	Y	N	Y	Y	Y	Y	Y
12 *McCloskey*	?	?	?	?	?	?	?
13 Mineta	Y	N	Y	Y	Y	Y	Y
14 *Shumway*	N	Y	N	N	Y	N	N
15 Coelho	Y	N	Y	Y	Y	Y	Y
16 Panetta	Y	N	Y	Y	Y	Y	Y
17 *Pashayan*	Y	Y	Y	Y	Y	N	Y
18 *Thomas*	N	Y	Y	N	Y	N	N
19 *Lagomarsino*	Y	N	Y	N	Y	N	N
20 *Goldwater*	?	?	?	?	?	?	?
21 *Fiedler*	N	Y	N	Y	Y	N	N
22 *Moorhead*	N	Y	N	N	Y	N	N
23 Beilenson	Y	N	Y	Y	Y	Y	Y
24 Waxman	Y	N	Y	Y	Y	Y	Y
25 Roybal	Y	N	Y	Y	Y	?	?
26 *Rousselot*	N	Y	N	N	Y	N	N
27 *Dornan*	?	?	?	?	?	?	?
28 Dixon	Y	N	Y	Y	Y	Y	Y
29 Hawkins	Y	N	Y	Y	Y	Y	Y
30 Danielson	Y	N	Y	Y	Y	Y	Y
31 Dymally	?	?	?	?	?	?	?
32 Anderson	Y	Y	N	Y	Y	Y	Y
33 *Grisham*	N	N	N	N	Y	N	?
34 *Lungren*	N	Y	N	Y	N	N	N
35 *Dreier*	N	Y	N	Y	Y	N	Y
36 Brown	Y	?	?	?	?	Y	Y
37 *Lewis*	N	Y	Y	Y	Y	Y	Y
38 Patterson	Y	N	Y	Y	Y	Y	Y
39 *Dannemeyer*	N	Y	N	N	Y	N	N
40 *Badham*	N	Y	N	Y	?	?	?
41 *Lowery*	N	N	Y	N	Y	N	N
42 *Hunter*	Y	Y	Y	Y	Y	N	N
43 *Burgener*	N	N	Y	N	Y	Y	?
COLORADO							
1 Schroeder	Y	Y	Y	Y	Y	Y	Y
2 Wirth	Y	N	Y	Y	Y	Y	Y
3 Kogovsek	Y	N	Y	Y	Y	Y	Y
4 *Brown*	N	Y	N	N	Y	N	N

	1	2	3	4	5	6	7
5 *Kramer*	N	Y	N	Y	Y	?	?
CONNECTICUT							
1 Kennelly *	Y	N	Y	Y	Y	Y	Y
2 Gejdenson	Y	N	Y	Y	Y	Y	Y
3 *DeNardis*	+	-	+	+	+	Y	Y
4 *McKinney*	?	?	?	?	?	?	?
5 Ratchford	Y	N	Y	Y	Y	Y	Y
6 Moffett	Y	N	Y	Y	Y	Y	?
DELAWARE							
AL *Evans*	Y	N	Y	Y	Y	Y	Y
FLORIDA							
1 Hutto	Y	N	Y	N	Y	Y	?
2 Fuqua	Y	Y	Y	N	Y	Y	N
3 Bennett	Y	Y	N	Y	Y	Y	N
4 Chappell	Y	?	?	?	?	Y	N
5 *McCollum*	N	N	N	N	Y	N	N
6 *Young*	Y	N	Y	Y	Y	Y	Y
7 Gibbons	?	?	?	?	?	?	?
8 Ireland	Y	N	Y	N	Y	Y	Y
9 Nelson	Y	Y	Y	N	Y	Y	N
10 *Bafalis*	Y	Y	Y	N	Y	Y	N
11 Mica	Y	N	Y	Y	Y	Y	Y
12 *Shaw*	Y	N	Y	N	Y	Y	N
13 Lehman	Y	N	Y	Y	Y	Y	Y
14 Pepper	Y	N	Y	Y	Y	Y	Y
15 Fascell	Y	N	Y	Y	Y	Y	Y
GEORGIA							
1 Ginn	Y	N	Y	Y	Y	Y	Y
2 Hatcher	Y	N	Y	Y	Y	Y	Y
3 Brinkley	Y	Y	Y	Y	Y	?	?
4 Levitas	N	Y	N	Y	Y	Y	Y
5 Fowler	Y	Y	N	Y	Y	Y	Y
6 *Gingrich*	Y	Y	Y	Y	Y	Y	N
7 McDonald	N	N	N	N	N	N	N
8 Evans	N	N	Y	Y	Y	Y	Y
9 Jenkins	Y	Y	Y	Y	Y	Y	Y
10 Barnard	Y	N	Y	Y	Y	Y	?
HAWAII							
1 Heftel	?	N	Y	Y	Y	?	?
2 Akaka	Y	N	Y	Y	Y	Y	Y
IDAHO							
1 *Craig*	Y	Y	N	N	Y	N	?
2 *Hansen*	N	Y	N	N	Y	N	N
ILLINOIS							
1 Washington	Y	N	Y	Y	Y	Y	Y
2 Savage	Y	N	Y	Y	Y	Y	Y
3 Russo	Y	N	Y	Y	Y	?	?
4 *Derwinski*	N	Y	N	Y	Y	?	?
5 Fary	Y	N	Y	Y	Y	Y	Y
6 *Hyde*	Y	Y	Y	Y	Y	N	Y
7 Collins	Y	N	N	Y	Y	Y	Y
8 Rostenkowski	Y	N	Y	Y	Y	Y	Y
9 Yates	Y	N	Y	Y	Y	?	?
10 *Porter*	Y	N	N	Y	Y	Y	Y
11 Annunzio	Y	N	Y	Y	Y	Y	Y
12 *Crane, P.*	N	Y	N	N	N	N	N
13 *McClory*	Y	N	Y	Y	Y	Y	Y
14 *Erlenborn*	?	?	?	?	?	?	?
15 *Corcoran*	Y	Y	N	Y	Y	Y	Y
16 *Martin*	Y	N	Y	Y	Y	Y	Y
17 *O'Brien*	Y	N	N	Y	Y	?	?
18 *Michel*	Y	N	Y	Y	Y	N	N
19 *Railsback*	Y	N	?	Y	Y	Y	Y
20 *Findley*	Y	N	Y	Y	Y	?	Y
21 *Madigan*	Y	N	Y	Y	Y	Y	Y
22 *Crane, D.*	N	Y	N	Y	?	?	?
23 Price	Y	N	Y	Y	Y	Y	Y
24 Simon	Y	N	Y	Y	Y	Y	Y
INDIANA							
1 Benjamin	Y	Y	Y	Y	Y	Y	Y
2 Fithian	Y	Y	Y	Y	Y	Y	Y
3 *Hiler*	?	?	?	Y	Y	N	Y
4 *Coats*	+	-	+	Y	Y	N	Y
5 *Hillis*	Y	N	Y	Y	Y	Y	?
6 *Evans*	Y	N	Y	Y	Y	Y	Y
7 *Myers*	Y	N	Y	Y	Y	Y	Y
8 *Deckard*	Y	N	Y	Y	Y	Y	Y
9 Hamilton	Y	N	Y	Y	Y	Y	Y
10 Sharp	Y	Y	Y	Y	Y	Y	Y
11 Jacobs	Y	N	Y	Y	Y	?	?
IOWA							
1 *Leach*	Y	N	Y	Y	Y	Y	Y
2 *Tauke*	Y	Y	Y	Y	Y	?	?
3 *Evans*	Y	N	Y	Y	Y	Y	Y
4 Smith	Y	N	Y	Y	Y	Y	Y
5 Harkin	Y	N	Y	Y	Y	?	?
6 Bedell	Y	N	Y	Y	Y	Y	Y

ND - Northern Democrats SD - Southern Democrats

	1	2	3	4	5	6	7
KANSAS							
1 ***Roberts***	Y	N	Y	Y	Y	Y	Y
2 ***Jeffries***	?	?	?	?	?	?	?
3 ***Winn***	N	N	Y	Y	Y	Y	Y
4 Glickman	Y	N	Y	Y	Y	Y	Y
5 ***Whittaker***	Y	N	Y	Y	Y	Y	Y
KENTUCKY							
1 Hubbard	N	Y	Y	Y	Y	?	?
2 Natcher	Y	N	Y	Y	Y	Y	Y
3 Mazzoli	Y	Y	Y	+	+	+	+
4 ***Snyder***	N	Y	N	Y	Y	N	N
5 ***Rogers***	Y	N	Y	Y	Y	Y	?
6 ***Hopkins***	Y	Y	Y	Y	Y	Y	Y
7 Perkins	Y	N	?	Y	Y	Y	Y
LOUISIANA							
1 ***Livingston***	Y	Y	Y	N	Y	Y	N
2 Boggs	?	N	Y	Y	Y	Y	Y
3 Tauzin	Y	N	Y	N	Y	?	?
4 Roemer	Y	Y	N	N	Y	Y	N
5 Huckaby	Y	N	Y	N	Y	Y	Y
6 ***Moore***	N	N	Y	N	Y	Y	Y
7 Breaux	?	?	?	?	Y	Y	Y
8 Long	Y	N	Y	Y	Y	Y	Y
MAINE							
1 ***Emery***	Y	Y	Y	Y	Y	?	Y
2 ***Snowe***	Y	Y	Y	Y	Y	Y	Y
MARYLAND							
1 Dyson	Y	N	Y	Y	Y	Y	Y
2 Long	Y	Y	N	Y	Y	Y	Y
3 Mikulski	Y	N	Y	Y	Y	Y	Y
4 ***Holt***	N	N	Y	Y	Y	N	Y
5 Hoyer	Y	N	Y	Y	Y	Y	Y
6 Byron	Y	N	Y	Y	Y	Y	Y
7 Mitchell	Y	N	N	Y	Y	Y	Y
8 Barnes	Y	N	Y	Y	Y	Y	Y
MASSACHUSETTS							
1 ***Conte***	Y	N	Y	Y	Y	Y	Y
2 Boland	?	N	Y	Y	?	Y	Y
3 Early	?	?	?	?	?	?	?
4 Frank	Y	N	N	Y	Y	Y	Y
5 Shannon	Y	N	Y	Y	Y	Y	Y
6 Mavroules	Y	N	Y	Y	Y	?	?
7 Markey	Y	N	Y	Y	Y	Y	?
8 O'Neill							
9 Moakley	Y	N	Y	Y	Y	?	?
10 ***Heckler***	Y	N	N	Y	Y	Y	Y
11 Donnelly	Y	N	Y	Y	Y	Y	Y
12 Studds	Y	N	Y	Y	Y	Y	Y
MICHIGAN							
1 Conyers	Y	N	N	Y	Y	Y	Y
2 ***Pursell***	?	?	?	?	?	?	?
3 Wolpe	Y	N	Y	Y	Y	Y	Y
4 ***Siljander***	?	N	Y	Y	Y	N	N
5 ***Sawyer***	Y	N	Y	Y	Y	Y	Y
6 ***Dunn***	Y	N	Y	Y	Y	Y	Y
7 Kildee	Y	N	Y	Y	Y	Y	Y
8 Traxler	Y	N	Y	Y	Y	Y	Y
9 ***Vander Jagt***	Y	N	Y	Y	Y	Y	Y
10 Albosta	Y	N	Y	Y	Y	Y	?
11 ***Davis***	?	Y	Y	Y	Y	Y	?
12 Bonior	Y	N	Y	Y	Y	Y	Y
13 Crockett	Y	N	N	Y	Y	Y	Y
14 Hertel	Y	Y	N	Y	Y	Y	Y
15 Ford	Y	N	Y	Y	Y	?	Y
16 Dingell	Y	N	Y	Y	Y	Y	Y
17 Brodhead	Y	Y	N	Y	Y	Y	N
18 Blanchard	Y	N	Y	Y	Y	Y	Y
19 ***Broomfield***	Y	N	Y	?	?	Y	?
MINNESOTA							
1 ***Erdahl***	Y	Y	Y	Y	Y	Y	Y
2 ***Hagedorn***	Y	Y	Y	Y	Y	N	?
3 ***Frenzel***	Y	N	Y	N	Y	N	N
4 Vento	?	N	Y	Y	Y	Y	Y
5 Sabo	Y	N	Y	Y	Y	Y	?
6 ***Weber***	N	Y	Y	Y	Y	N	Y
7 ***Stangeland***	N	Y	Y	Y	Y	Y	Y
8 Oberstar	Y	N	Y	Y	Y	Y	Y
MISSISSIPPI							
1 Whitten	Y	N	Y	Y	Y	Y	Y
2 Bowen	Y	N	Y	Y	Y	Y	Y
3 Montgomery	Y	N	Y	Y	Y	Y	Y
4 Dowdy	Y	N	Y	Y	Y	Y	Y
5 ***Lott***	N	N	Y	N	Y	N	N
MISSOURI							
1 Clay	N	N	N	Y	Y	Y	Y
2 Young	Y	N	Y	Y	Y	?	?
3 Gephardt	Y	Y	Y	Y	Y	Y	Y
4 Skelton	Y	Y	Y	Y	Y	?	?
5 Bolling	Y	N	Y	Y	Y	?	?
6 ***Coleman***	Y	Y	Y	Y	Y	Y	Y
7 ***Taylor***	N	Y	Y	Y	Y	N	N
8 ***Bailey***	N	Y	Y	N	Y	N	N
9 Volkmer	Y	Y	Y	Y	Y	Y	Y
10 ***Emerson***	N	Y	Y	Y	Y	Y	Y
MONTANA							
1 Williams	Y	N	Y	?	?	Y	?
2 ***Marlenee***	Y	N	Y	Y	Y	?	?
NEBRASKA							
1 ***Bereuter***	Y	N	Y	Y	Y	N	Y
2 ***Daub***	Y	N	Y	Y	Y	Y	Y
3 ***Smith***	Y	N	Y	Y	Y	Y	Y
NEVADA							
AL Santini	?	?	?	?	?	?	?
NEW HAMPSHIRE							
1 D'Amours	Y	Y	Y	Y	Y	Y	Y
2 ***Gregg***	N	N	Y	Y	Y	Y	Y
NEW JERSEY							
1 Florio	Y	N	Y	Y	Y	Y	Y
2 Hughes	Y	N	N	Y	Y	Y	Y
3 Howard	Y	N	Y	Y	Y	Y	Y
4 ***Smith***	Y	Y	Y	Y	Y	Y	Y
5 ***Fenwick***	Y	Y	N	Y	Y	Y	Y
6 ***Forsythe***	Y	N	Y	Y	Y	Y	Y
7 ***Roukema***	Y	N	Y	Y	Y	Y	?
8 Roe	Y	N	Y	Y	Y	Y	Y
9 ***Hollenbeck***	Y	N	Y	Y	Y	Y	Y
10 Rodino	Y	N	Y	Y	Y	Y	Y
11 Minish	Y	N	Y	Y	Y	Y	Y
12 ***Rinaldo***	Y	N	N	Y	Y	Y	Y
13 ***Courter***	Y	Y	Y	Y	Y	Y	Y
14 Guarini	Y	N	Y	Y	Y	Y	Y
15 Dwyer	Y	N	Y	Y	Y	Y	Y
NEW MEXICO							
1 ***Lujan***	N	Y	N	Y	Y	Y	Y
2 ***Skeen***	N	N	Y	Y	Y	N	N
NEW YORK							
1 ***Carney***	N	Y	N	Y	Y	N	Y
2 Downey	Y	N	Y	Y	Y	Y	Y
3 ***Carman***	N	Y	N	Y	Y	?	?
4 ***Lent***	Y	Y	N	Y	Y	?	?
5 ***McGrath***	Y	Y	N	Y	Y	?	?
6 ***LeBoutillier***	Y	Y	N	Y	Y	?	?
7 Addabbo	Y	N	Y	Y	Y	Y	?
8 Rosenthal	Y	N	N	Y	Y	Y	Y
9 Ferraro	Y	N	Y	+	+	Y	Y
10 Biaggi	?	?	?	?	?	?	?
11 Scheuer	Y	Y	Y	Y	Y	Y	Y
12 Chisholm	Y	N	Y	Y	Y	Y	Y
13 Solarz	Y	N	Y	Y	Y	Y	Y
14 Richmond	Y	N	Y	Y	Y	Y	?
15 Zeferetti	Y	N	Y	Y	Y	Y	Y
16 Schumer	Y	N	Y	Y	Y	Y	Y
17 ***Molinari***	N	Y	Y	Y	Y	Y	Y
18 ***Green***	Y	N	Y	Y	Y	?	Y
19 Rangel	Y	N	N	Y	Y	Y	Y
20 Weiss	N	N	N	Y	Y	Y	Y
21 Garcia	Y	N	Y	Y	Y	Y	Y
22 Bingham	Y	N	Y	Y	Y	Y	Y
23 Peyser	Y	N	N	Y	?	?	Y
24 Ottinger	Y	Y	Y	Y	Y	Y	Y
25 ***Fish***	Y	N	Y	Y	Y	?	?
26 ***Gilman***	Y	Y	N	Y	Y	Y	Y
27 McHugh	Y	N	Y	Y	Y	Y	Y
28 Stratton	Y	N	Y	Y	Y	Y	Y
29 ***Solomon***	N	Y	N	Y	Y	Y	?
30 ***Martin***	Y	N	Y	Y	Y	Y	Y
31 ***Mitchell***	N	N	Y	Y	Y	?	?
32 ***Wortley***	Y	N	Y	Y	Y	Y	Y
33 ***Lee***	Y	Y	N	Y	Y	N	Y
34 ***Horton***	?	?	?	?	?	?	?
35 ***Conable***	Y	N	Y	Y	Y	N	N
36 LaFalce	Y	N	Y	Y	Y	Y	Y
37 Nowak	Y	N	Y	Y	Y	Y	Y
38 ***Kemp***	Y	Y	N	Y	Y	N	Y
39 Lundine	Y	N	Y	Y	Y	Y	Y
NORTH CAROLINA							
1 Jones	Y	N	Y	Y	Y	Y	?
2 Fountain	Y	Y	Y	Y	Y	Y	Y
3 Whitley	Y	Y	Y	Y	Y	Y	Y
4 Andrews	Y	N	Y	Y	Y	Y	Y
5 Neal	Y	Y	Y	Y	Y	Y	Y
6 ***Johnston***	N	Y	N	N	Y	N	N
7 Rose	Y	N	Y	?	?	?	?
8 Hefner	Y	Y	Y	Y	Y	Y	Y
9 ***Martin***	Y	Y	Y	Y	Y	Y	Y
10 ***Broyhill***	Y	Y	N	Y	Y	N	N
11 ***Hendon***	Y	Y	N	Y	Y	?	?
NORTH DAKOTA							
AL Dorgan	Y	Y	Y	Y	Y	N	Y
OHIO							
1 ***Gradison***	Y	N	N	Y	Y	Y	N
2 Luken	Y	N	Y	Y	Y	Y	Y
3 Hall	Y	Y	Y	Y	Y	Y	?
4 ***Oxley***	Y	N	Y	Y	Y	Y	Y
5 ***Latta***	Y	N	Y	Y	Y	N	?
6 ***McEwen***	Y	Y	Y	Y	Y	Y	?
7 ***Brown***	?	?	?	?	?	?	?
8 ***Kindness***	N	N	Y	Y	Y	?	Y
9 ***Weber***	Y	N	Y	Y	Y	N	?
10 ***Miller***	Y	Y	N	N	Y	Y	N
11 ***Stanton***	Y	N	Y	Y	Y	Y	Y
12 Shamansky	Y	N	Y	Y	Y	Y	Y
13 Pease	Y	Y	Y	Y	Y	Y	Y
14 Seiberling	Y	N	Y	Y	Y	Y	Y
15 ***Wylie***	N	N	N	Y	Y	N	?
16 ***Regula***	Y	N	Y	Y	Y	?	?
17 ***Ashbrook***	?	Y	N	Y	Y	?	?
18 Applegate	Y	?	Y	Y	Y	Y	Y
19 ***Williams***	Y	N	Y	Y	Y	Y	Y
20 Oakar	Y	N	Y	Y	Y	Y	Y
21 Stokes	Y	N	N	Y	Y	Y	Y
22 Eckart	Y	Y	Y	Y	Y	Y	Y
23 Mottl	Y	Y	N	Y	Y	Y	?
OKLAHOMA							
1 Jones	Y	Y	Y	Y	Y	N	Y
2 Synar	Y	N	Y	Y	Y	N	Y
3 Watkins	Y	Y	Y	Y	Y	N	Y
4 McCurdy	Y	Y	Y	Y	Y	N	Y
5 ***Edwards***	N	Y	Y	N	Y	N	Y
6 English	Y	Y	Y	N	Y	N	Y
OREGON							
1 AuCoin	Y	Y	Y	Y	Y	?	Y
2 ***Smith***	N	Y	N	N	Y	N	N
3 Wyden	Y	N	Y	Y	Y	Y	Y
4 Weaver	?	?	?	?	?	?	?
PENNSYLVANIA							
1 Foglietta	Y	N	Y	Y	Y	Y	Y
2 Gray	Y	N	Y	Y	Y	Y	Y
3 Smith	Y	N	Y	Y	Y	Y	Y
4 ***Dougherty***	Y	N	Y	Y	Y	Y	Y
5 ***Schulze***	Y	Y	N	Y	Y	N	N
6 Yatron	Y	Y	Y	Y	Y	Y	?
7 Edgar	Y	N	Y	Y	Y	Y	Y
8 ***Coyne, J.***	Y	Y	N	Y	Y	Y	Y
9 ***Shuster***	N	Y	Y	N	Y	?	?
10 ***McDade***	Y	N	Y	Y	Y	Y	Y
11 ***Nelligan***	Y	Y	Y	Y	Y	Y	Y
12 Murtha	Y	Y	Y	Y	Y	?	?
13 ***Coughlin***	Y	N	Y	Y	Y	Y	Y
14 Coyne, W.	Y	N	Y	Y	Y	Y	Y
15 ***Ritter***	N	Y	N	Y	Y	Y	N
16 ***Walker***	N	Y	N	N	Y	Y	N
17 Ertel	Y	N	Y	Y	Y	Y	Y
18 Walgren	Y	Y	N	Y	Y	Y	?
19 ***Goodling***	Y	N	N	Y	Y	Y	Y
20 Gaydos	Y	N	Y	Y	Y	Y	Y
21 Bailey	Y	N	Y	Y	Y	Y	Y
22 Murphy	Y	N	N	Y	Y	Y	Y
23 ***Clinger***	Y	N	Y	Y	Y	Y	Y
24 ***Marks***	Y	N	Y	?	?	?	?
25 ***Atkinson***	Y	N	Y	Y	Y	N	Y
RHODE ISLAND							
1 St Germain	Y	N	Y	Y	Y	?	?
2 ***Schneider***	Y	N	N	Y	Y	Y	Y
SOUTH CAROLINA							
1 ***Hartnett***	Y	Y	Y	N	Y	Y	N
2 ***Spence***	?	N	Y	N	Y	Y	?
3 Derrick	Y	Y	Y	?	?	Y	Y
4 ***Campbell***	?	?	?	N	Y	N	N
5 Holland	Y	N	Y	Y	Y	Y	Y
6 ***Napier***	Y	Y	Y	Y	Y	?	?
SOUTH DAKOTA							
1 Daschle	Y	N	Y	Y	Y	?	?
2 ***Roberts***	N	N	Y	Y	Y	N	Y
TENNESSEE							
1 ***Quillen***	Y	N	Y	Y	Y	Y	?
2 ***Duncan***	Y	Y	Y	Y	Y	Y	?
3 Bouquard	Y	Y	Y	Y	Y	Y	Y
4 Gore	Y	N	Y	Y	Y	Y	Y
5 Boner	Y	N	Y	Y	Y	?	?
6 ***Beard***	Y	Y	Y	Y	Y	?	?
7 Jones	Y	N	Y	Y	Y	Y	Y
8 Ford	Y	N	N	Y	Y	Y	Y
TEXAS							
1 Hall, S.	Y	Y	Y	Y	Y	Y	Y
2 Wilson	Y	Y	Y	Y	?	Y	Y
3 ***Collins***	N	Y	N	N	Y	N	N
4 Hall, R.	Y	Y	Y	N	Y	Y	Y
5 Mattox	Y	N	Y	Y	Y	Y	Y
6 Gramm	N	Y	N	N	Y	N	N
7 ***Archer***	N	Y	N	N	Y	N	N
8 ***Fields***	N	Y	Y	N	Y	N	N
9 Brooks	Y	N	Y	Y	Y	Y	Y
10 Pickle	Y	N	Y	Y	Y	Y	?
11 Leath	Y	Y	Y	Y	Y	Y	Y
12 Wright	Y	N	Y	Y	Y	Y	Y
13 Hightower	Y	Y	Y	Y	Y	?	Y
14 Patman	Y	Y	N	Y	Y	?	Y
15 de la Garza	Y	N	Y	Y	Y	Y	Y
16 White	Y	N	Y	Y	Y	Y	Y
17 Stenholm	Y	Y	Y	Y	Y	Y	Y
18 Leland	Y	N	Y	Y	Y	Y	?
19 Hance	Y	Y	Y	N	Y	Y	Y
20 Gonzalez	Y	N	Y	Y	Y	Y	Y
21 ***Loeffler***	Y	N	Y	N	Y	N	N
22 ***Paul***	N	Y	N	N	N	N	N
23 Kazen	Y	N	Y	Y	Y	Y	Y
24 Frost	Y	Y	Y	Y	Y	Y	Y
UTAH							
1 ***Hansen***	N	N	Y	N	Y	N	N
2 ***Marriott***	Y	N	Y	Y	Y	Y	Y
VERMONT							
AL ***Jeffords***	Y	N	Y	Y	Y	?	?
VIRGINIA							
1 ***Trible***	Y	N	Y	Y	Y	Y	Y
2 ***Whitehurst***	Y	N	Y	Y	Y	Y	?
3 ***Bliley***	N	Y	N	Y	Y	N	N
4 ***Daniel, R.***	N	N	Y	N	Y	N	N
5 Daniel, D.	N	N	?	N	Y	?	?
6 ***Butler***	N	N	Y	Y	Y	?	?
7 ***Robinson***	N	N	Y	N	Y	N	N
8 ***Parris***	N	Y	N	N	Y	Y	Y
9 ***Wampler***	?	?	?	?	?	?	?
10 ***Wolf***	Y	Y	Y	Y	Y	Y	Y
WASHINGTON							
1 ***Pritchard***	N	N	Y	Y	Y	Y	Y
2 Swift	?	N	Y	Y	Y	Y	?
3 Bonker	Y	N	Y	Y	Y	Y	Y
4 ***Morrison***	Y	N	Y	Y	Y	Y	Y
5 Foley	Y	N	Y	Y	Y	?	?
6 Dicks	Y	N	Y	Y	Y	Y	Y
7 Lowry	Y	N	Y	Y	Y	Y	Y
WEST VIRGINIA							
1 Mollohan	Y	N	Y	Y	Y	Y	?
2 ***Benedict***	Y	Y	Y	Y	Y	Y	Y
3 ***Staton***	Y	N	Y	Y	Y	Y	Y
4 Rahall	Y	N	Y	Y	Y	Y	Y
WISCONSIN							
1 Aspin	Y	N	Y	Y	Y	?	Y
2 Kastenmeier	Y	N	Y	Y	Y	Y	Y
3 ***Gunderson***	Y	N	Y	Y	Y	Y	Y
4 Zablocki	Y	N	Y	Y	Y	Y	Y
5 Reuss	Y	N	Y	Y	Y	Y	Y
6 ***Petri***	N	Y	Y	Y	Y	N	Y
7 Obey	Y	N	Y	Y	Y	Y	Y
8 ***Roth***	Y	Y	N	N	Y	Y	N
9 ***Sensenbrenner***	N	Y	N	Y	Y	N	Y
WYOMING							
AL ***Cheney***	?	?	?	?	?	N	N

**Rep. Barbara B. Kennelly, D-Conn., was sworn in Jan. 25, 1982. The first vote for which she was eligible was CQ vote 1.*

Southern states - Ala., Ark., Fla., Ga., Ky., La., Miss., N.C., Okla., S.C., Tenn., Texas, Va.

KEY

Y   Voted for (yea).
Paired for.
+   Announced for.
N   Voted against (nay).
X   Paired against.
-   Announced against.
P   Voted "present".
C   Voted "present" to avoid possible conflict of interest.
?   Did not vote or otherwise make a position known.

Democrats   *Republicans*

8. Procedural Motion. Walker, R-Pa., motion to approve the House *Journal* of Monday, March 1. Motion agreed to 342-15: R 155-8; D 187-7 (ND 123-7, SD 64-0), March 2, 1982.

9. H Con Res 226. El Salvador Elections. Barnes, D-Md., motion to suspend the rules and adopt the concurrent resolution expressing the sense of the Congress that the president should press for unconditional discussions among the major political factions in El Salvador in order to guarantee a safe and stable environment for free and open democratic elections. Motion agreed to 396-3: R 175-2; D 221-1 (ND 149-0, SD 72-1), March 2, 1982. A two-thirds majority of those present and voting (266 in this case) is required for adoption under suspension of the rules.

10. H J Res 373. Soviet Human Rights. Bonker, D-Wash., motion to suspend the rules and pass the joint resolution expressing the sense of the Congress that the president should take actions to express to the government of the Soviet Union the message that it should comply with its obligations under international agreements to respect the rights of its citizens to practice their religions and to emigrate, and should stop "harassments, arrests and trials" of members of its Jewish community and allow Jews who wish to emigrate to do so. Motion agreed to 387-0: R 170-0; D 217-0 (ND 146-0, SD 71-0), March 2, 1982. A two-thirds majority of those present and voting (258 in this case) is required for passage under suspension of the rules.

11. HR 5366. Federal Flexible and Compressed Work Schedules. Ferraro, D-N.Y., motion to suspend the rules and pass the bill to provide permanent authority for federal agencies to establish flexible employee work schedules as an alternative to the traditional 8-hour day. Motion rejected 255-142: R 64-113; D 191-29 (ND 140-7, SD 51-22), March 2, 1982. A two-thirds majority of those present and voting (265 in this case) is required for passage under suspension of the rules. A "nay" was a vote supporting the president's position.

12. Procedural Motion. Badham, R-Calif., motion to approve the House *Journal* of Tuesday, March 2. Motion agreed to 355-15: R 165-8; D 190-7 (ND 122-7, SD 68-0), March 3, 1982.

13. S 1503. Standby Petroleum Allocation Act. Adoption of the conference report on the bill to authorize the president to allocate petroleum supplies during a severe oil shortage. Adopted (thus cleared for the president) 246-144: R 56-121; D 190-23 (ND 139-5, SD 51-18), March 3, 1982. A "nay" was a vote supporting the president's position.

14. HR 5118. Southern Arizona Water Rights. Adoption of the rule (H Res 357) providing for House floor consideration of the bill to provide water to the Papago Tribe of Arizona. Adopted 374-1: R 174-1; D 200-0 (ND 134-0, SD 66-0), March 3, 1982.

15. Procedural Motion. Hagedorn, R-Minn., motion to approve the House *Journal* of Wednesday, March 3. Motion agreed to 336-13: R 160-6; D 176-7 (ND 113-7, SD 63-0), March 4, 1982.

	8	9	10	11	12	13	14	15
ALABAMA								
1 *Edwards*	Y	Y	Y	Y	Y	N	Y	Y
2 *Dickinson*	N	Y	Y	N	Y	?	?	Y
3 Nichols	Y	Y	Y	Y	Y	N	Y	Y
4 Bevill	Y	Y	Y	Y	Y	Y	Y	Y
5 Flippo	Y	Y	Y	Y	Y	N	Y	Y
6 *Smith*	Y	Y	Y	N	Y	N	Y	Y
7 Shelby	Y	Y	Y	Y	Y	N	Y	Y
ALASKA								
AL *Young*	?	Y	Y	Y	N	N	Y	?
ARIZONA								
1 *Rhodes*	Y	Y	Y	Y	Y	N	Y	Y
2 Udall	Y	Y	Y	Y	Y	Y	Y	Y
3 *Stump*	Y	Y	Y	N	Y	N	Y	Y
4 *Rudd*	Y	N	Y	N	Y	N	Y	Y
ARKANSAS								
1 Alexander	Y	Y	Y	Y	Y	Y	Y	Y
2 *Bethune*	?	?	?	?	Y	?	?	?
3 *Hammerschmidt*	Y	Y	Y	N	Y	N	Y	Y
4 Anthony	Y	Y	Y	Y	Y	Y	Y	Y
CALIFORNIA								
1 *Chappie*	Y	Y	Y	N	Y	Y	Y	?
2 *Clausen*	?	Y	Y	Y	Y	N	Y	Y
3 Matsui	Y	Y	Y	Y	Y	Y	Y	Y
4 Fazio	Y	Y	Y	Y	Y	Y	Y	Y
5 Burton, J.	?	?	?	?	?	?	?	?
6 Burton, P.	?	?	?	?	?	?	?	?
7 Miller	Y	Y	Y	Y	Y	Y	Y	Y
8 Dellums	?	Y	Y	Y	?	Y	Y	Y
9 Stark	Y	Y	Y	Y	Y	Y	Y	Y
10 Edwards	Y	Y	Y	Y	Y	Y	Y	?
11 Lantos	Y	Y	Y	Y	Y	Y	Y	Y
12 *McCloskey*	Y	Y	Y	Y	?	N	Y	?
13 Mineta	Y	Y	Y	Y	Y	Y	Y	Y
14 *Shumway*	Y	Y	Y	N	Y	N	Y	Y
15 Coelho	?	Y	Y	Y	Y	?	?	?
16 Panetta	Y	Y	Y	N	Y	Y	Y	Y
17 *Pashayan*	Y	Y	Y	N	Y	N	Y	Y
18 *Thomas*	Y	Y	Y	N	Y	N	Y	Y
19 *Lagomarsino*	Y	Y	Y	N	Y	N	Y	Y
20 *Goldwater*	?	?	?	?	Y	N	Y	Y
21 *Fiedler*	Y	Y	Y	Y	Y	N	Y	Y
22 *Moorhead*	Y	Y	Y	N	Y	N	Y	Y
23 Beilenson	Y	Y	Y	Y	Y	Y	Y	Y
24 Waxman	Y	Y	Y	Y	Y	Y	Y	Y
25 Roybal	?	Y	Y	Y	Y	Y	?	Y
26 *Rousselot*	Y	Y	Y	N	Y	N	Y	Y
27 *Dornan*	?	?	?	?	Y	N	Y	Y
28 Dixon	Y	Y	Y	Y	Y	Y	Y	?
29 Hawkins	Y	Y	Y	Y	Y	Y	Y	N
30 Danielson	Y	Y	Y	Y	?	Y	Y	Y
31 Dymally	Y	Y	Y	Y	Y	Y	Y	Y
32 Anderson	Y	Y	Y	Y	Y	N	Y	Y
33 *Grisham*	Y	Y	Y	N	Y	N	Y	Y
34 *Lungren*	Y	Y	Y	N	Y	N	Y	Y
35 *Dreier*	Y	Y	Y	N	Y	N	Y	Y
36 Brown	Y	Y	Y	Y	?	Y	Y	?
37 *Lewis*	Y	Y	Y	Y	Y	N	Y	Y
38 Patterson	Y	Y	Y	N	Y	N	Y	?
39 *Dannemeyer*	Y	Y	Y	N	Y	N	Y	Y
40 *Badham*	Y	?	?	?	Y	N	Y	Y
41 *Lowery*	Y	Y	Y	N	Y	N	Y	Y
42 *Hunter*	Y	Y	Y	Y	N	Y	Y	Y
43 *Burgener*	?	Y	Y	N	Y	N	?	Y
COLORADO								
1 Schroeder	N	Y	Y	Y	N	Y	N	N
2 Wirth	Y	Y	Y	Y	Y	Y	Y	Y
3 Kogovsek	Y	Y	Y	Y	Y	Y	Y	Y
4 *Brown*	Y	Y	Y	N	Y	N	Y	Y

	8	9	10	11	12	13	14	15
5 *Kramer*	Y	Y	Y	N	Y	N	Y	Y
CONNECTICUT								
1 Kennelly	?	Y	Y	Y	Y	Y	Y	Y
2 Gejdenson	N	Y	Y	Y	N	Y	Y	N
3 *DeNardis*	?	Y	?	Y	Y	Y	Y	Y
4 *McKinney*	Y	Y	Y	Y	Y	Y	Y	Y
5 Ratchford	Y	Y	Y	Y	Y	Y	Y	Y
6 Moffett	?	?	?	?	Y	Y	Y	Y
DELAWARE								
AL *Evans*	Y	Y	Y	N	Y	Y	Y	Y
FLORIDA								
1 Hutto	?	Y	Y	Y	Y	N	Y	?
2 Fuqua	Y	Y	Y	Y	?	?	?	Y
3 Bennett	Y	Y	Y	Y	Y	Y	Y	Y
4 Chappell	Y	Y	Y	N	Y	N	Y	Y
5 *McCollum*	Y	Y	Y	N	Y	N	Y	?
6 *Young*	Y	Y	Y	N	Y	N	Y	Y
7 Gibbons	Y	Y	Y	N	N	Y	Y	Y
8 Ireland	Y	Y	Y	N	?	Y	Y	Y
9 Nelson	Y	Y	Y	Y	Y	Y	Y	Y
10 *Bafalis*	Y	Y	Y	N	Y	N	Y	Y
11 Mica	Y	Y	Y	Y	?	?	?	?
12 *Shaw*	Y	Y	Y	N	Y	N	Y	Y
13 Lehman	Y	Y	Y	Y	Y	Y	Y	Y
14 Pepper	Y	Y	Y	Y	Y	Y	+	?
15 Fascell	?	Y	Y	Y	Y	Y	Y	Y
GEORGIA								
1 Ginn	Y	Y	Y	Y	Y	Y	Y	Y
2 Hatcher	Y	Y	Y	N	Y	Y	?	?
3 Brinkley	Y	Y	Y	Y	Y	Y	Y	Y
4 Levitas	Y	Y	Y	N	Y	Y	Y	Y
5 Fowler	?	?	?	?	?	?	?	?
6 *Gingrich*	Y	Y	Y	N	Y	N	Y	Y
7 McDonald	Y	Y	Y	N	Y	N	Y	Y
8 Evans	Y	Y	Y	Y	Y	N	Y	Y
9 Jenkins	Y	Y	Y	Y	Y	Y	Y	Y
10 Barnard	Y	Y	Y	N	Y	N	Y	Y
HAWAII								
1 Heftel	Y	Y	Y	Y	Y	Y	Y	Y
2 Akaka	?	Y	Y	Y	Y	Y	Y	Y
IDAHO								
1 *Craig*	Y	Y	Y	N	Y	N	Y	Y
2 *Hansen*	Y	Y	Y	N	Y	N	Y	Y
ILLINOIS								
1 Washington	Y	Y	Y	Y	?	Y	Y	?
2 Savage	?	Y	Y	Y	?	Y	?	?
3 Russo	Y	Y	Y	Y	Y	Y	Y	Y
4 *Derwinski*	?	?	?	?	?	Y	?	?
5 Fary	?	?	?	?	?	#	Y	?
6 *Hyde*	Y	Y	Y	N	Y	N	Y	Y
7 Collins	?	?	?	?	Y	Y	?	?
8 Rostenkowski	?	?	?	?	?	?	?	?
9 Yates	N	Y	Y	Y	Y	Y	Y	Y
10 *Porter*	Y	Y	Y	Y	Y	N	Y	Y
11 Annunzio	Y	Y	Y	Y	Y	Y	Y	Y
12 *Crane, P.*	Y	Y	Y	N	Y	N	N	Y
13 *McClory*	Y	Y	Y	N	Y	N	Y	Y
14 *Erlenborn*	?	?	?	?	?	?	?	?
15 *Corcoran*	Y	Y	Y	N	Y	N	Y	Y
16 *Martin*	Y	Y	?	Y	Y	Y	?	Y
17 *O'Brien*	Y	Y	Y	N	?	?	?	?
18 *Michel*	?	Y	Y	Y	N	Y	Y	Y
19 *Railsback*	Y	Y	?	Y	Y	Y	Y	Y
20 *Findley*	Y	Y	Y	N	Y	Y	Y	Y
21 *Madigan*	Y	Y	Y	N	Y	N	Y	Y
22 *Crane, D.*	?	Y	Y	N	Y	N	Y	Y
23 Price	Y	Y	Y	Y	?	?	?	?
24 Simon	Y	Y	Y	Y	?	Y	Y	?
INDIANA								
1 Benjamin	Y	Y	Y	Y	Y	Y	Y	Y
2 Fithian	Y	Y	Y	N	Y	Y	Y	Y
3 *Hiler*	Y	Y	Y	N	Y	N	Y	Y
4 *Coats*	Y	Y	Y	N	Y	N	Y	Y
5 *Hillis*	Y	Y	Y	Y	Y	Y	Y	Y
6 Evans	Y	Y	Y	Y	Y	Y	Y	Y
7 *Myers*	Y	Y	Y	N	Y	N	Y	Y
8 *Deckard*	Y	Y	Y	N	Y	N	Y	Y
9 Hamilton	Y	Y	Y	Y	Y	Y	Y	Y
10 Sharp	Y	Y	Y	Y	Y	Y	Y	?
11 Jacobs	N	Y	Y	Y	N	Y	Y	N
IOWA								
1 *Leach*	Y	Y	Y	Y	Y	Y	Y	?
2 *Tauke*	Y	Y	Y	Y	Y	Y	Y	Y
3 *Evans*	?	Y	Y	Y	N	Y	Y	?
4 Smith	Y	Y	Y	Y	Y	Y	Y	Y
5 Harkin	N	Y	Y	Y	N	Y	Y	N
6 Bedell	Y	Y	Y	Y	Y	Y	Y	Y

ND - Northern Democrats   SD - Southern Democrats

Corresponding to Congressional Record Votes 9, 10, 11, 12, 13, 14, 15, 16

	8	9	10	11	12	13	14	15
KANSAS								
1 ***Roberts***	Y	Y	Y	N	Y	Y	Y	Y
2 ***Jeffries***	Y	Y	Y	N	Y	N	Y	Y
3 ***Winn***	Y	Y	Y	N	Y	N	Y	Y
4 Glickman	Y	Y	Y	Y	Y	Y	?	Y
5 ***Whittaker***	Y	Y	Y	N	Y	Y	Y	Y
KENTUCKY								
1 Hubbard	Y	Y	Y	N	Y	N	Y	Y
2 Natcher	Y	Y	Y	Y	Y	Y	Y	Y
3 Mazzoli	Y	Y	Y	Y	Y	Y	Y	?
4 ***Snyder***	Y	Y	Y	N	Y	N	Y	Y
5 ***Rogers***	Y	Y	Y	N	Y	Y	Y	Y
6 ***Hopkins***	Y	Y	Y	N	?	Y	Y	Y
7 Perkins	Y	Y	Y	Y	Y	Y	Y	Y
LOUISIANA								
1 ***Livingston***	Y	Y	Y	N	Y	N	Y	Y
2 Boggs	Y	Y	Y	Y	Y	Y	Y	?
3 Tauzin	Y	Y	Y	Y	Y	Y	Y	Y
4 Roemer	Y	Y	Y	N	Y	N	Y	Y
5 Huckaby	Y	Y	Y	Y	?	?	?	?
6 ***Moore***	Y	Y	Y	Y	Y	N	Y	Y
7 Breaux	Y	Y	Y	Y	Y	N	Y	Y
8 Long	?	Y	Y	Y	Y	Y	?	Y
MAINE								
1 ***Emery***	Y	Y	Y	Y	Y	Y	Y	Y
2 ***Snowe***	Y	Y	Y	Y	Y	Y	Y	Y
MARYLAND								
1 Dyson	Y	Y	Y	Y	Y	N	Y	Y
2 Long	?	Y	Y	Y	Y	Y	?	Y
3 Mikulski	Y	Y	Y	Y	Y	Y	Y	Y
4 ***Holt***	Y	Y	Y	Y	?	X	?	?
5 Hoyer	Y	Y	Y	Y	Y	Y	Y	?
6 Byron	Y	Y	Y	Y	Y	N	Y	Y
7 Mitchell	N	Y	Y	Y	N	Y	Y	?
8 Barnes	Y	Y	Y	Y	N	Y	Y	N
MASSACHUSETTS								
1 ***Conte***	Y	Y	Y	N	Y	Y	Y	Y
2 Boland	Y	Y	Y	Y	Y	Y	Y	Y
3 Early	?	Y	Y	Y	Y	Y	Y	Y
4 Frank	Y	Y	Y	Y	Y	Y	Y	Y
5 Shannon	Y	Y	Y	Y	Y	Y	Y	Y
6 Mavroules	Y	Y	Y	Y	Y	Y	Y	Y
7 Markey	Y	Y	Y	Y	Y	Y	Y	Y
8 O'Neill								
9 Moakley	Y	Y	Y	Y	Y	Y	Y	Y
10 ***Heckler***	Y	Y	Y	Y	?	Y	Y	Y
11 Donnelly	Y	Y	Y	Y	Y	Y	Y	Y
12 Studds	Y	Y	Y	Y	Y	Y	Y	Y
MICHIGAN								
1 Conyers	?	Y	?	Y	Y	Y	?	Y
2 ***Pursell***	?	Y	Y	Y	Y	Y	Y	Y
3 Wolpe	Y	Y	Y	Y	Y	Y	Y	Y
4 ***Siljander***	Y	Y	Y	N	Y	N	Y	Y
5 ***Sawyer***	Y	Y	Y	N	Y	Y	Y	Y
6 ***Dunn***	Y	Y	Y	Y	Y	Y	Y	Y
7 Kildee	Y	Y	Y	Y	Y	Y	Y	Y
8 Traxler	Y	Y	Y	Y	?	Y	Y	Y
9 ***Vander Jagt***	Y	Y	Y	Y	Y	N	Y	Y
10 Albosta	Y	Y	Y	Y	Y	Y	Y	Y
11 ***Davis***	?	Y	Y	Y	Y	N	Y	Y
12 Bonior	Y	Y	Y	Y	Y	Y	?	?
13 Crockett	Y	Y	?	Y	?	Y	?	?
14 Hertel	Y	Y	Y	Y	Y	Y	Y	Y
15 Ford	?	Y	Y	Y	?	Y	Y	?
16 Dingell	Y	Y	Y	Y	Y	Y	Y	Y
17 Brodhead	Y	Y	Y	Y	Y	Y	Y	Y
18 Blanchard	Y	Y	Y	Y	Y	?	?	?
19 ***Broomfield***	Y	Y	Y	N	Y	N	Y	Y
MINNESOTA								
1 ***Erdahl***	?	?	?	?	?	?	?	?
2 ***Hagedorn***	?	?	?	?	Y	Y	Y	Y
3 ***Frenzel***	Y	Y	Y	N	Y	N	Y	Y
4 Vento	Y	Y	Y	Y	Y	Y	Y	Y
5 Sabo	N	Y	Y	Y	N	Y	Y	N
6 ***Weber***	N	Y	Y	N	N	Y	Y	N
7 ***Stangeland***	Y	Y	Y	N	Y	Y	?	?
8 Oberstar	Y	Y	Y	Y	Y	Y	Y	-
MISSISSIPPI								
1 Whitten	Y	Y	Y	Y	Y	Y	Y	Y
2 Bowen	Y	Y	Y	Y	Y	Y	Y	Y
3 Montgomery	Y	Y	Y	N	Y	N	Y	Y
4 Dowdy	Y	Y	Y	Y	Y	Y	Y	Y
5 ***Lott***	Y	Y	Y	N	Y	N	Y	Y
MISSOURI								
1 Clay	?	Y	Y	Y	?	Y	Y	?
2 Young	Y	Y	Y	N	Y	Y	?	Y
3 Gephardt	Y	Y	Y	Y	Y	Y	Y	Y
4 Skelton	?	?	?	?	?	?	?	Y
5 Bolling	Y	Y	Y	Y	Y	Y	Y	Y
6 ***Coleman***	Y	Y	Y	N	Y	Y	Y	Y
7 ***Taylor***	Y	Y	Y	Y	Y	N	Y	Y
8 ***Bailey***	Y	Y	Y	Y	Y	Y	Y	Y
9 Volkmer	Y	Y	Y	Y	Y	Y	Y	Y
10 ***Emerson***	Y	Y	Y	N	N	Y	Y	Y
MONTANA								
1 Williams	Y	Y	Y	Y	?	Y	Y	Y
2 ***Marlenee***	Y	Y	Y	N	Y	Y	Y	Y
NEBRASKA								
1 ***Bereuter***	Y	Y	Y	N	Y	Y	Y	Y
2 ***Daub***	Y	Y	Y	N	Y	Y	Y	Y
3 ***Smith***	Y	Y	Y	N	Y	Y	Y	Y
NEVADA								
AL Santini	?	?	?	?	?	?	?	?
NEW HAMPSHIRE								
1 D'Amours	Y	Y	Y	Y	?	Y	Y	Y
2 ***Gregg***	?	Y	Y	N	Y	N	Y	Y
NEW JERSEY								
1 Florio	Y	Y	Y	Y	Y	Y	?	?
2 Hughes	Y	Y	Y	Y	Y	Y	Y	Y
3 Howard	Y	Y	Y	Y	Y	Y	Y	Y
4 ***Smith***	Y	Y	Y	Y	Y	N	Y	Y
5 ***Fenwick***	Y	Y	Y	Y	Y	N	Y	?
6 ***Forsythe***	?	Y	Y	N	N	N	Y	N
7 ***Roukema***	Y	Y	Y	N	?	Y	Y	Y
8 Roe	Y	Y	Y	Y	Y	Y	Y	Y
9 ***Hollenbeck***	Y	Y	Y	Y	Y	Y	Y	Y
10 Rodino	?	Y	Y	Y	Y	Y	Y	Y
11 Minish	Y	Y	Y	Y	Y	Y	Y	Y
12 ***Rinaldo***	?	Y	Y	Y	Y	N	Y	Y
13 ***Courter***	Y	Y	Y	Y	Y	N	Y	Y
14 Guarini	Y	Y	Y	Y	Y	Y	Y	Y
15 Dwyer	Y	Y	Y	Y	?	?	?	?
NEW MEXICO								
1 ***Lujan***	Y	Y	Y	N	Y	Y	Y	Y
2 ***Skeen***	Y	Y	Y	N	Y	Y	Y	Y
NEW YORK								
1 ***Carney***	Y	Y	Y	Y	Y	N	Y	Y
2 Downey	?	?	?	?	?	?	?	?
3 ***Carman***	Y	Y	Y	N	Y	N	Y	Y
4 ***Lent***	Y	Y	Y	Y	Y	N	Y	Y
5 ***McGrath***	Y	Y	Y	N	Y	N	Y	Y
6 ***LeBoutillier***	N	Y	Y	N	?	N	Y	Y
7 Addabbo	Y	Y	Y	Y	Y	Y	Y	Y
8 Rosenthal	Y	Y	Y	Y	Y	Y	Y	Y
9 Ferraro	Y	Y	Y	Y	Y	Y	Y	Y
10 Biaggi	?	?	?	?	?	#	?	?
11 Scheuer	?	Y	?	Y	?	Y	Y	Y
12 Chisholm	?	Y	Y	Y	?	Y	Y	?
13 Solarz	Y	Y	Y	Y	Y	Y	Y	Y
14 Richmond	Y	Y	Y	Y	Y	Y	Y	?
15 Zeferetti	Y	Y	Y	Y	?	?	?	?
16 Schumer	Y	Y	Y	Y	Y	Y	Y	Y
17 ***Molinari***	Y	Y	Y	Y	Y	Y	Y	Y
18 ***Green***	Y	Y	Y	Y	Y	N	Y	Y
19 Rangel	Y	Y	Y	Y	?	Y	Y	Y
20 Weiss	Y	Y	Y	Y	Y	Y	Y	Y
21 Garcia	Y	Y	Y	Y	Y	Y	Y	?
22 Bingham	Y	Y	Y	Y	Y	Y	Y	?
23 Peyser	Y	Y	Y	Y	?	Y	Y	Y
24 Ottinger	Y	Y	Y	Y	P	Y	Y	P
25 ***Fish***	?	Y	Y	Y	Y	Y	Y	?
26 ***Gilman***	Y	Y	Y	Y	Y	Y	Y	Y
27 McHugh	?	?	?	?	?	?	?	?
28 Stratton	Y	Y	Y	Y	Y	Y	Y	Y
29 ***Solomon***	Y	Y	+	N	Y	Y	Y	Y
30 ***Martin***	Y	Y	Y	Y	Y	Y	Y	Y
31 ***Mitchell***	Y	Y	Y	N	Y	Y	Y	Y
32 ***Wortley***	Y	Y	Y	N	Y	Y	Y	Y
33 ***Lee***	?	?	?	?	Y	Y	Y	Y
34 ***Horton***	Y	Y	Y	Y	Y	Y	Y	Y
35 ***Conable***	Y	?	?	?	Y	N	Y	Y
36 LaFalce	Y	Y	Y	Y	Y	Y	Y	?
37 Nowak	Y	Y	Y	Y	Y	Y	Y	Y
38 ***Kemp***	Y	Y	Y	Y	Y	N	Y	Y
39 Lundine	Y	Y	Y	Y	Y	Y	Y	?
NORTH CAROLINA								
1 Jones	?	Y	Y	Y	?	?	?	?
2 Fountain	Y	Y	Y	N	Y	Y	Y	Y
3 Whitley	Y	Y	?	Y	Y	Y	Y	Y
4 Andrews	?	?	?	?	Y	Y	Y	Y
5 Neal	Y	Y	Y	Y	Y	Y	Y	?
6 ***Johnston***	Y	Y	Y	N	Y	N	Y	Y
7 Rose	Y	Y	Y	Y	Y	?	?	Y
8 Hefner	Y	Y	Y	Y	Y	Y	Y	Y
9 ***Martin***	Y	Y	Y	N	Y	N	Y	Y
10 ***Broyhill***	Y	Y	Y	N	Y	N	Y	Y
11 ***Hendon***	Y	Y	Y	N	Y	N	Y	Y
NORTH DAKOTA								
AL Dorgan	Y	Y	Y	Y	Y	Y	Y	Y
OHIO								
1 ***Gradison***	Y	Y	Y	Y	Y	N	Y	Y
2 Luken	Y	Y	Y	Y	Y	Y	Y	Y
3 Hall	Y	Y	Y	Y	Y	Y	Y	Y
4 ***Oxley***	?	Y	Y	N	Y	N	Y	Y
5 ***Latta***	Y	Y	Y	N	Y	N	Y	Y
6 ***McEwen***	Y	Y	Y	N	Y	N	Y	Y
7 ***Brown***	Y	Y	Y	N	Y	N	Y	Y
8 ***Kindness***	Y	Y	Y	N	Y	N	Y	Y
9 ***Weber***	Y	Y	Y	N	Y	N	Y	Y
10 ***Miller***	N	Y	Y	N	N	N	Y	N
11 ***Stanton***	Y	Y	Y	Y	Y	N	Y	Y
12 Shamansky	Y	Y	Y	Y	Y	Y	Y	Y
13 Pease	Y	Y	Y	?	Y	Y	Y	Y
14 Seiberling	?	Y	Y	Y	Y	Y	Y	Y
15 ***Wylie***	Y	Y	Y	N	Y	N	Y	Y
16 ***Regula***	Y	Y	Y	Y	Y	N	Y	Y
17 ***Ashbrook***	Y	Y	Y	N	Y	?	?	?
18 Applegate	?	Y	Y	Y	?	N	Y	?
19 ***Williams***	Y	Y	Y	Y	Y	N	Y	?
20 Oakar	Y	Y	Y	Y	Y	Y	Y	Y
21 Stokes	Y	Y	Y	Y	Y	Y	Y	?
22 Eckart	Y	Y	Y	Y	Y	Y	Y	Y
23 Mottl	Y	Y	Y	Y	Y	Y	Y	Y
OKLAHOMA								
1 Jones	?	Y	Y	Y	Y	Y	Y	Y
2 Synar	?	Y	Y	Y	Y	Y	Y	Y
3 Watkins	Y	Y	Y	N	Y	Y	Y	Y
4 McCurdy	Y	Y	Y	Y	Y	N	Y	?
5 ***Edwards***	?	?	?	?	?	?	?	?
6 English	Y	Y	Y	N	Y	Y	Y	Y
OREGON								
1 AuCoin	Y	Y	Y	Y	Y	Y	Y	Y
2 ***Smith***	Y	Y	Y	N	Y	N	Y	?
3 Wyden	Y	Y	Y	Y	Y	Y	Y	Y
4 Weaver	Y	Y	Y	Y	Y	Y	Y	Y
PENNSYLVANIA								
1 Foglietta	?	?	?	?	Y	Y	Y	?
2 Gray	Y	Y	Y	Y	Y	Y	Y	Y
3 Smith	Y	Y	Y	Y	Y	Y	Y	Y
4 ***Dougherty***	Y	Y	Y	Y	Y	Y	Y	Y
5 ***Schulze***	Y	Y	Y	N	Y	N	Y	Y
6 Yatron	Y	Y	Y	Y	Y	Y	Y	Y
7 Edgar	Y	Y	Y	Y	Y	?	?	Y
8 ***Coyne, J.***	Y	Y	Y	N	Y	N	Y	?
9 ***Shuster***	Y	Y	Y	Y	Y	N	Y	Y
10 ***McDade***	+	+	+	+	+	+	+	+
11 ***Nelligan***	Y	Y	Y	N	Y	Y	Y	Y
12 Murtha	?	Y	Y	N	?	?	?	Y
13 ***Coughlin***	N	Y	Y	N	Y	N	Y	Y
14 Coyne, W.	Y	Y	Y	Y	Y	Y	Y	Y
15 ***Ritter***	Y	Y	Y	N	Y	N	Y	Y
16 ***Walker***	N	Y	Y	N	N	N	Y	N
17 Ertel	Y	Y	Y	Y	Y	Y	Y	Y
18 Walgren	Y	Y	Y	Y	Y	?	Y	Y
19 ***Goodling***	N	Y	Y	N	?	N	Y	N
20 Gaydos	Y	Y	Y	Y	Y	Y	Y	?
21 Bailey	Y	Y	Y	Y	Y	Y	Y	Y
22 Murphy	Y	Y	Y	Y	Y	Y	Y	Y
23 ***Clinger***	Y	Y	+	N	Y	N	Y	Y
24 ***Marks***	?	Y	Y	Y	Y	Y	?	?
25 ***Atkinson***	Y	Y	Y	Y	Y	N	Y	Y
RHODE ISLAND								
1 St Germain	?	Y	Y	Y	Y	Y	Y	Y
2 ***Schneider***	Y	Y	?	Y	Y	Y	Y	Y
SOUTH CAROLINA								
1 ***Hartnett***	?	Y	Y	N	Y	Y	Y	Y
2 ***Spence***	Y	Y	Y	N	Y	N	Y	Y
3 Derrick	?	Y	Y	Y	Y	Y	Y	Y
4 ***Campbell***	?	?	?	?	?	X	?	Y
5 Holland	Y	Y	Y	Y	?	Y	Y	Y
6 ***Napier***	Y	Y	Y	Y	Y	Y	Y	Y
SOUTH DAKOTA								
1 Daschle	Y	Y	Y	Y	Y	Y	Y	Y
2 ***Roberts***	Y	Y	?	N	Y	Y	Y	Y
TENNESSEE								
1 ***Quillen***	Y	Y	Y	N	Y	N	Y	Y
2 ***Duncan***	Y	Y	Y	N	Y	N	Y	Y
3 Bouquard	Y	Y	Y	N	Y	Y	Y	Y
4 Gore	Y	Y	Y	Y	Y	Y	Y	Y
5 Boner	Y	Y	Y	Y	Y	Y	Y	Y
6 ***Beard***	Y	Y	Y	N	Y	N	Y	Y
7 Jones	Y	Y	Y	Y	Y	Y	Y	?
8 Ford	Y	Y	Y	Y	Y	Y	Y	Y
TEXAS								
1 Hall, S.	Y	Y	Y	N	Y	Y	Y	Y
2 Wilson	?	Y	Y	Y	Y	Y	Y	Y
3 ***Collins***	Y	Y	Y	N	Y	N	Y	Y
4 Hall, R.	?	Y	?	N	Y	Y	Y	Y
5 Mattox	?	?	?	?	?	#	?	?
6 Gramm	Y	Y	Y	N	Y	N	Y	Y
7 ***Archer***	Y	Y	Y	N	Y	N	Y	Y
8 ***Fields***	Y	Y	Y	N	Y	N	Y	Y
9 Brooks	?	?	?	?	?	?	?	Y
10 Pickle	Y	Y	Y	Y	Y	Y	Y	Y
11 Leath	Y	Y	Y	N	Y	N	Y	Y
12 Wright	Y	Y	Y	Y	Y	Y	Y	Y
13 Hightower	Y	Y	Y	N	Y	Y	Y	Y
14 Patman	Y	Y	Y	Y	Y	N	Y	Y
15 de la Garza	Y	Y	Y	Y	?	X	?	?
16 White	Y	Y	Y	N	Y	Y	Y	Y
17 Stenholm	Y	Y	Y	N	Y	Y	Y	Y
18 Leland	?	?	?	?	?	?	?	?
19 Hance	?	?	?	?	Y	Y	Y	?
20 Gonzalez	Y	N	Y	Y	Y	Y	Y	Y
21 ***Loeffler***	Y	Y	Y	N	Y	N	Y	Y
22 ***Paul***	Y	N	Y	N	Y	N	Y	Y
23 Kazen	Y	Y	Y	Y	Y	Y	Y	Y
24 Frost	Y	Y	Y	Y	Y	Y	Y	Y
UTAH								
1 ***Hansen***	Y	Y	Y	N	Y	N	Y	Y
2 ***Marriott***	Y	Y	Y	Y	Y	N	Y	Y
VERMONT								
AL ***Jeffords***	Y	?	?	?	?	?	?	?
VIRGINIA								
1 ***Trible***	Y	Y	Y	Y	?	?	?	Y
2 ***Whitehurst***	Y	Y	Y	Y	Y	N	Y	Y
3 ***Bliley***	Y	Y	Y	N	Y	N	Y	Y
4 ***Daniel, R.***	Y	Y	Y	Y	Y	N	Y	Y
5 Daniel, D.	Y	Y	Y	N	Y	N	Y	Y
6 ***Butler***	N	Y	Y	N	N	N	Y	N
7 ***Robinson***	Y	Y	Y	N	Y	N	Y	Y
8 ***Parris***	Y	Y	Y	Y	Y	Y	Y	?
9 ***Wampler***	Y	Y	Y	N	Y	Y	Y	Y
10 ***Wolf***	Y	Y	Y	Y	Y	N	Y	Y
WASHINGTON								
1 ***Pritchard***	Y	Y	Y	Y	?	?	?	?
2 Swift	?	Y	Y	+	Y	Y	Y	Y
3 Bonker	Y	Y	Y	Y	Y	Y	Y	Y
4 ***Morrison***	Y	Y	Y	N	Y	N	Y	Y
5 Foley	Y	Y	Y	Y	Y	Y	Y	Y
6 Dicks	Y	Y	Y	Y	Y	Y	Y	Y
7 Lowry	?	?	?	?	?	?	?	?
WEST VIRGINIA								
1 Mollohan	Y	Y	Y	N	Y	Y	?	Y
2 ***Benedict***	Y	Y	Y	N	Y	+	Y	Y
3 ***Staton***	Y	Y	Y	N	Y	N	Y	Y
4 Rahall	Y	Y	Y	Y	?	Y	Y	?
WISCONSIN								
1 Aspin	Y	Y	Y	N	Y	Y	Y	Y
2 Kastenmeier	Y	Y	Y	Y	Y	Y	Y	Y
3 ***Gunderson***	Y	Y	Y	Y	Y	Y	Y	Y
4 Zablocki	Y	Y	Y	Y	Y	Y	Y	Y
5 Reuss	Y	Y	Y	Y	Y	Y	Y	Y
6 ***Petri***	Y	Y	Y	Y	Y	N	Y	Y
7 Obey	?	?	?	?	?	?	?	?
8 ***Roth***	Y	Y	Y	N	Y	N	Y	Y
9 ***Sensenbrenner***	Y	Y	Y	N	Y	N	Y	Y
WYOMING								
AL ***Cheney***	?	?	?	?	Y	N	Y	Y

Southern states - Ala., Ark., Fla., Ga., Ky., La., Miss., N.C., Okla., S.C., Tenn., Texas, Va.

KEY

Y Voted for (yea).
\# Paired for.
\+ Announced for.
N Voted against (nay).
X Paired against.
- Announced against.
P Voted "present".
C Voted "present" to avoid possible conflict of interest.
? Did not vote or otherwise make a position known.

Democrats *Republicans*

16. HR 5118. Southern Arizona Water Rights. Udall, D-Ariz., motion that the House resolve itself into the Committee of the Whole for consideration of the bill to provide water to the Papago Tribe of Arizona. Motion agreed to 359-0: R 167-0; D 192-0 (ND 132-0, SD 60-0), March 4, 1982.

17. HR 5118. Southern Arizona Water Rights. Passage of the bill to provide water to the Papago Tribe of Arizona. Passed 311-50: R 133-37; D 178-13 (ND 127-4, SD 51-9), March 4, 1982.

18. S J Res 142. Afghanistan Day. Passage of the joint resolution to request the president to proclaim March 21, 1982, as "Afghanistan Day" to commemorate the struggle of the people of Afghanistan against the occupation of their country by Soviet forces. Passed 346-0: R 161-0; D 185-0 (ND 126-0, SD 59-0), March 4, 1982.

19. Procedural Motion. Hagedorn, R-Minn., motion to approve the House *Journal* of Monday, March 8. Motion agreed to 340-17: R 156-10; D 184-7 (ND 121-6, SD 63-1), March 9, 1982.

20. HR 2160. Potato Research and Promotion. De la Garza, D-Texas, motion to suspend the rules and pass the bill to authorize an increase in the producer assessment for research and promotion activities by the National Potato Promotion Board and to authorize certain other changes in the potato research and promotion program. (The changes must also be approved by potato producers in a referendum.) Motion agreed to 361-8: R 166-3; D 195-5 (ND 130-3, SD 65-2), March 9, 1982. A two-thirds majority of those present and voting (246 in this case) is required for passage under suspension of the rules. A "yea" was a vote supporting the president's position.

21. Procedural Motion. Coyne, R-Pa., motion to approve the House *Journal* of Tuesday, March 9. Motion agreed to 371-16: R 165-8; D 206-8 (ND 133-7, SD 73-1), March 10, 1982.

	16	17	18	19	20	21
ALABAMA						
1 *Edwards*	?	Y	Y	?	?	Y
2 *Dickinson*	Y	N	Y	Y	Y	N
3 Nichols	Y	Y	Y	Y	Y	Y
4 Bevill	Y	Y	Y	Y	Y	Y
5 Flippo	Y	Y	Y	Y	Y	Y
6 *Smith*	Y	N	Y	Y	Y	Y
7 Shelby	?	?	?	?	Y	Y
ALASKA						
AL *Young*	?	?	?	N	Y	Y
ARIZONA						
1 *Rhodes*	Y	Y	Y	Y	Y	Y
2 Udall	Y	Y	Y	Y	Y	Y
3 *Stump*	Y	N	Y	Y	Y	Y
4 *Rudd*	Y	Y	Y	Y	Y	Y
ARKANSAS						
1 Alexander	Y	Y	?	Y	Y	Y
2 *Bethune*	?	?	?	?	?	Y
3 *Hammerschmidt*	Y	Y	Y	Y	Y	Y
4 Anthony	Y	Y	Y	Y	Y	Y
CALIFORNIA						
1 *Chappie*	Y	Y	Y	Y	Y	Y
2 *Clausen*	Y	Y	?	Y	Y	Y
3 Matsui	Y	Y	Y	Y	Y	Y
4 Fazio	Y	Y	Y	Y	Y	Y
5 Burton, J.	?	?	?	Y	Y	Y
6 Burton, P.	?	?	?	?	?	?
7 Miller	Y	Y	Y	Y	N	Y
8 Dellums	Y	Y	Y	?	?	?
9 Stark	Y	Y	Y	Y	Y	Y
10 Edwards	?	?	?	Y	Y	Y
11 Lantos	Y	Y	Y	?	?	Y
12 *McCloskey*	?	?	?	Y	Y	Y
13 Mineta	Y	Y	Y	Y	Y	Y
14 *Shumway*	Y	Y	Y	Y	Y	Y
15 Coelho	?	?	?	Y	Y	Y
16 Panetta	Y	Y	Y	Y	Y	Y
17 *Pashayan*	Y	Y	Y	Y	Y	Y
18 *Thomas*	Y	Y	Y	?	?	Y
19 *Lagomarsino*	Y	Y	Y	Y	Y	Y
20 *Goldwater*	?	Y	Y	?	?	?
21 *Fiedler*	Y	Y	Y	Y	Y	Y
22 *Moorhead*	Y	Y	Y	Y	Y	Y
23 Beilenson	Y	Y	Y	Y	Y	Y
24 Waxman	Y	Y	?	Y	Y	Y
25 Roybal	Y	Y	Y	Y	Y	Y
26 *Rousselot*	Y	Y	Y	Y	Y	N
27 *Dornan*	Y	Y	Y	?	?	Y
28 Dixon	Y	Y	Y	?	?	Y
29 Hawkins	Y	Y	Y	N	Y	N
30 Danielson *	Y	Y	Y	?		
31 Dymally	Y	Y	Y	Y	Y	Y
32 Anderson	Y	Y	Y	Y	Y	Y
33 *Grisham*	Y	N	Y	Y	Y	Y
34 *Lungren*	Y	Y	Y	Y	Y	Y
35 *Dreier*	Y	N	Y	Y	N	Y
36 Brown	Y	Y	Y	?	Y	?
37 *Lewis*	Y	Y	Y	Y	Y	Y
38 Patterson	?	?	?	Y	Y	Y
39 *Dannemeyer*	Y	Y	Y	Y	N	Y
40 *Badham*	Y	Y	Y	Y	Y	Y
41 *Lowery*	Y	Y	Y	Y	Y	Y
42 *Hunter*	Y	Y	Y	Y	Y	Y
43 *Burgener*	Y	Y	Y	Y	Y	Y
COLORADO						
1 Schroeder	Y	Y	Y	N	Y	N
2 Wirth	Y	Y	Y	Y	Y	Y
3 Kogovsek	Y	Y	Y	Y	Y	Y
4 *Brown*	Y	N	Y	Y	Y	Y

	16	17	18	19	20	21
5 *Kramer*	Y	Y	Y	Y	Y	Y
CONNECTICUT						
1 Kennelly	Y	Y	Y	?	Y	Y
2 Gejdenson	Y	Y	Y	N	Y	N
3 *DeNardis*	Y	Y	Y	?	Y	Y
4 *McKinney*	Y	Y	Y	Y	?	Y
5 Ratchford	Y	Y	Y	Y	Y	Y
6 Moffett	Y	Y	Y	Y	Y	Y
DELAWARE						
AL *Evans*	Y	Y	Y	Y	Y	Y
FLORIDA						
1 Hutto	?	?	?	Y	Y	Y
2 Fuqua	Y	Y	Y	Y	Y	Y
3 Bennett	Y	Y	Y	Y	N	Y
4 Chappell	Y	?	?	Y	Y	Y
5 *McCollum*	?	?	?	Y	Y	Y
6 *Young*	Y	Y	Y	Y	Y	Y
7 Gibbons	Y	Y	Y	Y	Y	Y
8 Ireland	Y	Y	Y	?	?	Y
9 Nelson	Y	Y	Y	Y	Y	Y
10 *Bafalis*	Y	Y	Y	Y	Y	Y
11 Mica	?	?	?	Y	Y	Y
12 *Shaw*	Y	Y	Y	Y	Y	Y
13 Lehman	Y	Y	Y	Y	Y	Y
14 Pepper	+	+	+	Y	Y	Y
15 Fascell	Y	Y	Y	Y	Y	Y
GEORGIA						
1 Ginn	Y	Y	?	?	?	Y
2 Hatcher	?	?	?	Y	Y	Y
3 Brinkley	Y	Y	Y	Y	Y	Y
4 Levitas	Y	N	Y	Y	Y	Y
5 Fowler	?	?	?	Y	Y	Y
6 *Gingrich*	?	Y	Y	Y	Y	Y
7 McDonald	Y	N	Y	N	Y	N
8 Evans	Y	Y	Y	Y	Y	Y
9 Jenkins	Y	Y	Y	Y	Y	Y
10 Barnard	Y	Y	Y	Y	Y	
HAWAII						
1 Heftel	Y	Y	Y	Y	Y	Y
2 Akaka	Y	Y	Y	Y	Y	Y
IDAHO						
1 *Craig*	Y	Y	Y	Y	Y	Y
2 *Hansen*	Y	Y	Y	Y	Y	Y
ILLINOIS						
1 Washington	Y	Y	Y	?	?	Y
2 Savage	?	Y	Y	?	?	?
3 Russo	Y	Y	Y	Y	Y	Y
4 *Derwinski*	?	?	?	?	?	?
5 Fary	?	?	?	?	?	?
6 *Hyde*	Y	N	Y	Y	Y	Y
7 Collins	Y	Y	Y	Y	?	Y
8 Rostenkowski	?	?	?	Y	Y	Y
9 Yates	Y	N	Y	?	?	Y
10 *Porter*	Y	Y	Y	Y	Y	Y
11 Annunzio	Y	Y	Y	Y	Y	Y
12 *Crane, P.*	Y	N	?	Y	Y	Y
13 *McClory*	Y	N	Y	Y	Y	Y
14 *Erlenborn*	?	?	?	?	?	?
15 *Corcoran*	Y	N	+	Y	Y	Y
16 *Martin*	Y	Y	Y	Y	Y	Y
17 *O'Brien*	?	?	?	?	?	?
18 *Michel*	Y	Y	Y	Y	Y	Y
19 *Railsback*	Y	Y	Y	Y	Y	Y
20 *Findley*	Y	Y	Y	Y	Y	Y
21 *Madigan*	Y	Y	?	Y	Y	Y
22 *Crane, D.*	Y	N	?	Y	Y	Y
23 Price	?	?	?	Y	Y	Y
24 Simon	Y	Y	Y	Y	Y	Y
INDIANA						
1 Benjamin	Y	Y	Y	Y	Y	Y
2 Fithian	Y	Y	Y	Y	Y	Y
3 *Hiler*	Y	Y	Y	Y	Y	Y
4 *Coats*	Y	Y	Y	Y	Y	Y
5 *Hillis*	Y	Y	Y	Y	Y	Y
6 Evans	Y	?	?	Y	Y	?
7 *Myers*	Y	Y	Y	Y	Y	Y
8 *Deckard*	Y	Y	Y	Y	Y	Y
9 Hamilton	Y	Y	Y	Y	Y	Y
10 Sharp	Y	Y	Y	Y	Y	Y
11 Jacobs	Y	Y	Y	N	Y	N
IOWA						
1 *Leach*	Y	Y	Y	Y	Y	Y
2 *Tauke*	Y	N	Y	Y	Y	Y
3 *Evans*	Y	Y	Y	?	Y	N
4 Smith	Y	Y	Y	Y	Y	Y
5 Harkin	Y	Y	Y	N	Y	?
6 Bedell	Y	Y	Y	Y	Y	Y

ND - Northern Democrats   SD - Southern Democrats

	16	17	18	19	20	21
KANSAS						
1 ***Roberts***	Y	Y	Y	?	?	Y
2 ***Jeffries***	Y	N	Y	Y	Y	Y
3 ***Winn***	Y	Y	Y	Y	Y	Y
4 Glickman	Y	Y	Y	Y	Y	Y
5 ***Whittaker***	Y	N	Y	Y	Y	Y
KENTUCKY						
1 Hubbard	Y	Y	Y	?	?	?
2 Natcher	Y	Y	Y	Y	Y	Y
3 Mazzoli	?	?	?	Y	Y	Y
4 ***Snyder***	Y	Y	Y	Y	Y	Y
5 ***Rogers***	Y	Y	Y	Y	Y	?
6 ***Hopkins***	Y	Y	Y	Y	Y	Y
7 Perkins	Y	Y	Y	Y	Y	Y
LOUISIANA						
1 ***Livingston***	Y	Y	Y	Y	Y	Y
2 Boggs	?	?	?	Y	Y	Y
3 Tauzin	Y	Y	Y	Y	Y	Y
4 Roemer	Y	N	Y	N	Y	N
5 Huckaby	?	?	?	Y	Y	Y
6 ***Moore***	Y	Y	Y	Y	Y	Y
7 Breaux	Y	Y	Y	Y	Y	Y
8 Long	Y	Y	Y	Y	Y	Y
MAINE						
1 ***Emery***	Y	Y	Y	Y	Y	Y
2 ***Snowe***	Y	Y	Y	Y	Y	Y
MARYLAND						
1 Dyson	Y	Y	Y	Y	Y	Y
2 Long	Y	Y	?	Y	Y	Y
3 Mikulski	Y	Y	Y	Y	Y	Y
4 ***Holt***	?	?	?	Y	Y	Y
5 Hoyer	Y	Y	Y	Y	Y	Y
6 Byron	Y	Y	Y	Y	Y	Y
7 Mitchell	?	?	?	N	Y	N
8 Barnes	Y	Y	Y	Y	Y	N
MASSACHUSETTS						
1 ***Conte***	Y	Y	Y	Y	Y	Y
2 Boland	Y	?	Y	Y	Y	Y
3 Early	Y	Y	Y	Y	Y	?
4 Frank	Y	Y	Y	Y	Y	Y
5 Shannon	Y	Y	Y	Y	Y	Y
6 Mavroules	Y	Y	Y	Y	Y	Y
7 Markey	Y	Y	Y	Y	Y	Y
8 O'Neill						
9 Moakley	?	?	?	Y	Y	Y
10 ***Heckler***	Y	Y	?	Y	Y	Y
11 Donnelly	Y	Y	Y	Y	Y	Y
12 Studds	Y	Y	Y	Y	Y	Y
MICHIGAN						
1 Conyers	Y	Y	?	Y	Y	Y
2 ***Pursell***	Y	Y	Y	Y	Y	Y
3 Wolpe	Y	Y	Y	Y	Y	Y
4 ***Siljander***	Y	Y	Y	Y	Y	Y
5 ***Sawyer***	Y	Y	Y	Y	Y	Y
6 ***Dunn***	Y	Y	Y	Y	Y	Y
7 Kildee	Y	Y	Y	Y	Y	Y
8 Traxler	Y	Y	Y	Y	Y	Y
9 ***Vander Jagt***	Y	Y	Y	Y	Y	Y
10 Albosta	Y	Y	Y	Y	Y	Y
11 ***Davis***	Y	?	?	Y	Y	Y
12 Bonior	Y	Y	Y	Y	Y	Y
13 Crockett	?	Y	?	?	Y	?
14 Hertel	Y	Y	Y	Y	Y	Y
15 Ford	Y	Y	Y	?	Y	Y
16 Dingell	Y	?	Y	Y	Y	Y
17 Brodhead	Y	Y	Y	Y	Y	Y
18 Blanchard	?	?	?	?	Y	Y
19 ***Broomfield***	Y	Y	Y	Y	?	Y
MINNESOTA						
1 ***Erdahl***	?	?	?	?	?	Y
2 ***Hagedorn***	Y	Y	Y	Y	Y	Y
3 ***Frenzel***	Y	N	Y	Y	Y	Y
4 Vento	Y	Y	Y	Y	?	Y
5 Sabo	Y	Y	Y	?	?	N
6 ***Weber***	Y	Y	Y	N	Y	N
7 ***Stangeland***	?	?	?	?	?	Y
8 Oberstar	-	-	Y	Y	?	Y
MISSISSIPPI						
1 Whitten	?	Y	Y	?	Y	?
2 Bowen	Y	Y	Y	Y	Y	Y
3 Montgomery	?	Y	Y	Y	Y	Y
4 Dowdy	Y	Y	Y	Y	?	Y
5 ***Lott***	Y	Y	Y	Y	Y	Y
MISSOURI						
1 Clay	?	Y	Y	?	Y	N
2 Young	Y	Y	Y	Y	Y	Y
3 Gephardt	Y	Y	Y	Y	Y	Y
4 Skelton	Y	Y	Y	Y	Y	Y
5 Bolling	Y	Y	Y	?	Y	?
6 ***Coleman***	Y	Y	Y	Y	Y	Y
7 ***Taylor***	Y	Y	Y	Y	Y	Y
8 ***Bailey***	Y	Y	Y	Y	Y	Y
9 Volkmer	Y	Y	Y	Y	Y	Y
10 ***Emerson***	Y	Y	Y	N	Y	N
MONTANA						
1 Williams	Y	Y	Y	Y	Y	?
2 ***Marlenee***	Y	Y	Y	?	?	Y
NEBRASKA						
1 ***Bereuter***	Y	Y	Y	Y	Y	Y
2 ***Daub***	Y	Y	Y	Y	Y	Y
3 ***Smith***	Y	Y	Y	Y	Y	Y
NEVADA						
AL Santini	?	?	?	Y	Y	Y
NEW HAMPSHIRE						
1 D'Amours	Y	Y	Y	Y	Y	Y
2 ***Gregg***	Y	Y	Y	Y	Y	Y
NEW JERSEY						
1 Florio	?	?	?	Y	Y	Y
2 Hughes	Y	Y	Y	Y	Y	Y
3 Howard	Y	Y	Y	?	?	Y
4 ***Smith***	Y	Y	Y	Y	Y	Y
5 ***Fenwick***	Y	N	Y	?	+	?
6 ***Forsythe***	?	N	Y	N	Y	N
7 ***Roukema***	Y	N	+	Y	Y	Y
8 Roe	Y	Y	Y	Y	Y	Y
9 ***Hollenbeck***	Y	Y	Y	Y	Y	Y
10 Rodino	Y	Y	Y	?	?	Y
11 Minish	Y	Y	Y	Y	Y	Y
12 ***Rinaldo***	Y	Y	Y	Y	Y	Y
13 ***Courter***	Y	N	Y	Y	Y	Y
14 Guarini	Y	?	?	Y	Y	Y
15 Dwyer	?	?	?	Y	Y	Y
NEW MEXICO						
1 ***Lujan***	Y	Y	Y	Y	Y	Y
2 ***Skeen***	Y	Y	Y	Y	Y	Y
NEW YORK						
1 ***Carney***	Y	Y	Y	Y	Y	Y
2 Downey	?	?	?	?	?	Y
3 ***Carman***	Y	N	Y	Y	Y	?
4 ***Lent***	Y	Y	Y	Y	Y	Y
5 ***McGrath***	Y	Y	Y	Y	Y	Y
6 ***LeBoutillier***	Y	Y	Y	N	Y	Y
7 Addabbo	?	Y	?	Y	Y	Y
8 Rosenthal	Y	Y	Y	Y	Y	Y
9 Ferraro	Y	Y	Y	Y	Y	Y
10 Biaggi	?	?	?	Y	Y	Y
11 Scheuer	Y	?	?	Y	Y	Y
12 Chisholm	?	Y	Y	?	Y	?
13 Solarz	Y	Y	Y	Y	Y	Y
14 Richmond	?	?	?	Y	Y	?
15 Zeferetti	?	?	?	Y	Y	Y
16 Schumer	Y	Y	Y	Y	Y	Y
17 ***Molinari***	Y	Y	Y	Y	Y	Y
18 ***Green***	Y	Y	Y	Y	Y	Y
19 Rangel	Y	Y	?	Y	Y	Y
20 Weiss	Y	Y	Y	Y	Y	Y
21 Garcia	Y	Y	Y	?	?	Y
22 Bingham	?	Y	Y	Y	Y	Y
23 Peyser	Y	Y	Y	Y	Y	Y
24 Ottinger	Y	Y	Y	P	N	P
25 ***Fish***	?	?	?	Y	Y	?
26 ***Gilman***	Y	Y	Y	Y	Y	Y
27 McHugh	?	?	?	?	?	Y
28 Stratton	Y	N	Y	Y	Y	Y
29 ***Solomon***	Y	N	Y	Y	Y	Y
30 ***Martin***	Y	Y	Y	Y	Y	Y
31 ***Mitchell***	Y	Y	Y	Y	Y	Y
32 ***Wortley***	Y	Y	Y	Y	Y	Y
33 ***Lee***	Y	Y	Y	Y	Y	Y
34 ***Horton***	Y	Y	Y	Y	Y	Y
35 ***Conable***	Y	N	Y	Y	Y	Y
36 LaFalce	Y	?	Y	Y	Y	Y
37 Nowak	Y	Y	Y	Y	Y	Y
38 ***Kemp***	Y	Y	?	Y	Y	Y
39 Lundine	Y	Y	Y	?	?	Y
NORTH CAROLINA						
1 Jones	Y	Y	Y	?	?	Y
2 Fountain	Y	N	Y	Y	Y	Y
3 Whitley	Y	Y	?	?	?	Y
4 Andrews	Y	N	Y	Y	Y	Y
5 Neal	?	Y	Y	?	?	Y
6 ***Johnston***	Y	N	Y	Y	Y	Y
7 Rose	Y	Y	Y	?	?	?
8 Hefner	Y	Y	Y	Y	Y	Y
9 ***Martin***	Y	N	?	Y	Y	Y
10 ***Broyhill***	Y	N	Y	Y	Y	Y
11 ***Hendon***	Y	Y	Y	N	Y	Y
NORTH DAKOTA						
AL Dorgan	Y	Y	Y	Y	+	Y
OHIO						
1 ***Gradison***	Y	Y	Y	Y	Y	Y
2 Luken	Y	Y	Y	Y	Y	Y
3 Hall	Y	Y	Y	?	Y	Y
4 ***Oxley***	Y	N	Y	Y	Y	Y
5 ***Latta***	Y	Y	Y	Y	Y	Y
6 ***McEwen***	Y	Y	Y	Y	Y	Y
7 ***Brown***	Y	N	Y	?	?	?
8 ***Kindness***	Y	Y	Y	Y	Y	Y
9 ***Weber***	Y	N	Y	?	Y	Y
10 ***Miller***	Y	N	Y	N	Y	N
11 ***Stanton***	Y	Y	Y	Y	Y	Y
12 Shamansky	Y	Y	Y	Y	Y	Y
13 Pease	Y	Y	Y	Y	Y	Y
14 Seiberling	Y	Y	Y	Y	Y	Y
15 ***Wylie***	Y	Y	Y	Y	Y	Y
16 ***Regula***	Y	Y	Y	Y	Y	Y
17 ***Ashbrook***	?	?	?	?	?	?
18 Applegate	Y	Y	Y	?	Y	?
19 ***Williams***	?	?	?	Y	Y	Y
20 Oakar	Y	Y	Y	Y	Y	Y
21 Stokes	?	?	?	Y	Y	Y
22 Eckart	Y	Y	Y	Y	Y	Y
23 Mottl	Y	N	Y	Y	N	Y
OKLAHOMA						
1 Jones	Y	Y	Y	Y	Y	Y
2 Synar	Y	Y	Y	Y	Y	Y
3 Watkins	Y	Y	Y	Y	Y	Y
4 McCurdy	?	?	?	Y	Y	Y
5 ***Edwards***	?	?	?	?	?	?
6 English	Y	Y	Y	Y	Y	Y
OREGON						
1 AuCoin	Y	Y	Y	?	?	Y
2 ***Smith***	?	?	?	Y	Y	Y
3 Wyden	Y	Y	Y	Y	Y	Y
4 Weaver	Y	Y	Y	Y	Y	Y
PENNSYLVANIA						
1 Foglietta	?	?	?	?	?	?
2 Gray	Y	Y	?	?	Y	Y
3 Smith	Y	Y	Y	Y	Y	Y
4 ***Dougherty***	Y	Y	Y	Y	?	Y
5 ***Schulze***	Y	Y	Y	Y	Y	Y
6 Yatron	Y	Y	Y	Y	Y	Y
7 Edgar	Y	Y	Y	Y	Y	Y
8 ***Coyne, J.***	Y	Y	Y	Y	Y	Y
9 ***Shuster***	Y	Y	Y	Y	Y	Y
10 ***McDade***	+	+	+	+	+	+
11 ***Nelligan***	Y	N	Y	Y	Y	Y
12 Murtha	?	?	?	Y	Y	Y
13 ***Coughlin***	Y	Y	Y	Y	Y	Y
14 Coyne, W.	Y	Y	Y	Y	Y	Y
15 ***Ritter***	Y	N	Y	Y	Y	Y
16 ***Walker***	Y	Y	Y	N	Y	N
17 Ertel	Y	Y	?	?	?	?
18 Walgren	Y	Y	Y	Y	Y	Y
19 ***Goodling***	Y	Y	Y	N	Y	?
20 Gaydos	Y	Y	Y	Y	Y	Y
21 Bailey	Y	Y	Y	Y	Y	Y
22 Murphy	Y	Y	Y	Y	Y	Y
23 ***Clinger***	Y	Y	Y	Y	Y	Y
24 ***Marks***	?	?	?	?	?	?
25 ***Atkinson***	Y	Y	Y	Y	Y	Y
RHODE ISLAND						
1 St Germain	Y	?	?	Y	Y	Y
2 ***Schneider***	Y	Y	Y	Y	Y	Y
SOUTH CAROLINA						
1 ***Hartnett***	Y	Y	?	Y	Y	Y
2 ***Spence***	Y	Y	Y	Y	Y	Y
3 Derrick	Y	?	?	?	?	Y
4 ***Campbell***	Y	Y	Y	Y	Y	Y
5 Holland	Y	Y	Y	Y	Y	Y
6 ***Napier***	?	Y	Y	?	?	Y
SOUTH DAKOTA						
1 Daschle	Y	Y	Y	Y	Y	Y
2 ***Roberts***	Y	Y	Y	Y	Y	Y
TENNESSEE						
1 ***Quillen***	Y	Y	?	Y	Y	Y
2 ***Duncan***	Y	Y	Y	Y	Y	Y
3 Bouquard	Y	Y	Y	Y	Y	Y
4 Gore	Y	Y	Y	Y	Y	Y
5 Boner	Y	Y	Y	Y	Y	Y
6 ***Beard***	?	?	Y	Y	Y	?
7 Jones	?	?	?	?	Y	Y
8 Ford	Y	?	Y	Y	Y	Y
TEXAS						
1 Hall, S.	Y	Y	Y	Y	Y	Y
2 Wilson	Y	?	Y	?	?	Y
3 ***Collins***	Y	N	Y	Y	Y	Y
4 Hall, R.	Y	Y	Y	Y	Y	Y
5 Mattox	?	?	?	?	?	?
6 Gramm	Y	N	Y	Y	Y	Y
7 ***Archer***	Y	N	Y	Y	Y	Y
8 ***Fields***	Y	N	Y	Y	Y	Y
9 Brooks	Y	Y	Y	?	?	?
10 Pickle	Y	Y	Y	Y	Y	Y
11 Leath	Y	N	Y	Y	Y	Y
12 Wright	Y	Y	Y	Y	Y	Y
13 Hightower	Y	Y	Y	Y	Y	Y
14 Patman	Y	Y	Y	Y	Y	Y
15 de la Garza	?	?	?	Y	Y	Y
16 White	Y	Y	Y	Y	Y	Y
17 Stenholm	Y	N	Y	Y	Y	Y
18 Leland	?	?	?	Y	Y	Y
19 Hance	?	?	?	Y	Y	Y
20 Gonzalez	?	Y	Y	Y	Y	Y
21 ***Loeffler***	Y	Y	Y	Y	Y	Y
22 ***Paul***	Y	N	Y	Y	N	Y
23 Kazen	Y	Y	Y	Y	Y	Y
24 Frost	Y	Y	Y	Y	Y	Y
UTAH						
1 ***Hansen***	Y	Y	Y	?	Y	Y
2 ***Marriott***	Y	Y	Y	Y	Y	Y
VERMONT						
AL ***Jeffords***	?	?	?	Y	Y	Y
VIRGINIA						
1 ***Trible***	Y	Y	Y	Y	Y	Y
2 ***Whitehurst***	Y	Y	Y	Y	Y	Y
3 ***Bliley***	Y	N	Y	Y	Y	Y
4 ***Daniel, R.***	Y	N	Y	Y	Y	Y
5 Daniel, D.	Y	N	Y	Y	Y	Y
6 ***Butler***	Y	Y	Y	N	Y	Y
7 ***Robinson***	Y	N	Y	Y	Y	Y
8 ***Parris***	Y	Y	Y	Y	Y	Y
9 ***Wampler***	Y	Y	Y	?	Y	Y
10 ***Wolf***	Y	Y	Y	Y	Y	Y
WASHINGTON						
1 ***Pritchard***	?	?	?	Y	Y	Y
2 Swift	Y	Y	Y	Y	Y	Y
3 Bonker	Y	Y	Y	Y	Y	Y
4 ***Morrison***	Y	Y	Y	Y	Y	Y
5 Foley	Y	Y	Y	Y	?	Y
6 Dicks	Y	Y	Y	Y	Y	Y
7 Lowry	?	?	?	?	?	Y
WEST VIRGINIA						
1 Mollohan	Y	Y	Y	?	?	?
2 ***Benedict***	Y	Y	Y	Y	Y	Y
3 ***Staton***	Y	Y	Y	Y	Y	Y
4 Rahall	Y	Y	?	Y	Y	Y
WISCONSIN						
1 Aspin	Y	Y	Y	Y	Y	Y
2 Kastenmeier	Y	Y	Y	Y	Y	Y
3 ***Gunderson***	Y	Y	Y	Y	Y	Y
4 Zablocki	Y	Y	Y	Y	?	Y
5 Reuss	Y	Y	Y	Y	Y	Y
6 ***Petri***	Y	Y	Y	?	?	Y
7 Obey	?	?	?	?	?	Y
8 ***Roth***	Y	Y	Y	Y	Y	Y
9 ***Sensenbrenner***	Y	Y	Y	Y	Y	Y
WYOMING						
AL ***Cheney***	Y	Y	Y	Y	Y	Y

**Rep. George E. Danielson, D-Calif., resigned March 9, 1982. The last vote for which he was eligible was CQ vote 19.*

Southern states - Ala., Ark., Fla., Ga., Ky., La., Miss., N.C., Okla., S.C., Tenn., Texas, Va.

22. Procedural Motion. Gregg, R-N.H., motion to approve the House *Journal* of Wednesday, March 17. Motion agreed to 337-17: R 149-9; D 188-8 (ND 122-7, SD 66-1), March 18, 1982.

23. HR 3620. Hoboken Pier Properties. Jones, D-N.C., motion to suspend the rules and pass the bill to sell pier terminals owned by the federal government to the city of Hoboken, N.J., at a negotiated price that may be less than fair market value. Motion agreed to 336-43: R 128-36; D 208-7 (ND 143-3, SD 65-4), March 18, 1982. A two-thirds majority of those present and voting (254 in this case) is required for passage under suspension of the rules.

24. HR 4468. Secret Service Zones of Protection. Synar, D-Okla., motion to suspend the rules and pass the bill to clarify the authority of the Secret Service to protect persons, including the vice president and his family, officially designated presidential and vice presidential candidates and their spouses, and visiting heads of state. The bill also increased penalties for violating a Secret Service "zone of protection" around a protected person. Motion agreed to 379-1: R 167-0; D 212-1 (ND 143-1, SD 69-0), March 18, 1982. A two-thirds majority of those present and voting (254 in this case) is required for passage under suspension of the rules.

25. HR 4688. Military Personnel and Civilian Employees Claims Act Amendments. Synar, D-Okla., motion to suspend the rules and pass the bill to increase from $15,000 to $25,000 the maximum settlement the U.S. must pay for personal property losses related to the service of military and civilian employees. Motion agreed to 370-11: R 160-8; D 210-3 (ND 142-2, SD 68-1), March 18, 1982. A two-thirds majority of those present and voting (255 in this case) is required for passage under suspension of the rules.

26. HR 3345. Patent and Trade Mark Laws and Civil Rights of Institutionalized Persons Act. Synar, D-Okla., motion to suspend the rules and pass the bill to make technical changes in the patent and trademark laws and in the Civil Rights of Institutionalized Persons Act (PL 96-247). Motion agreed to 382-0: R 170-0; D 212-0 (ND 145-0, SD 67-0), March 18, 1982. A two-thirds majority of those present and voting (256 in this case) is required for passage under suspension of the rules.

27. HR 2329. Cherokee Nation of Oklahoma. Synar, D-Okla., motion to suspend the rules and pass the bill to waive the statute of limitations applicable to two claims that three Indian nations in Oklahoma have against the United States government. Motion rejected 174-215: R 13-158; D 161-57 (ND 123-25, SD 38-32), March 18, 1982. A two-thirds majority of those present and voting (260 in this case) is required for passage under suspension of the rules.

28. H Con Res 290. Federally Insured Deposits. St Germain, D-R.I., motion to suspend the rules and adopt the concurrent resolution to reaffirm that savings deposits up to the statutorily prescribed amount — currently $100,000 — in federally insured depository institutions are backed by the full faith and credit of the United States. Motion agreed to 382-7: R 165-6; D 217-1 (ND 148-0, SD 69-1), March 18, 1982. A two-thirds majority of those present and voting (260 in this case) is required for adoption under suspension of the rules.

KEY

Y	Voted for (yea).
#	Paired for.
+	Announced for.
N	Voted against (nay).
X	Paired against.
-	Announced against.
P	Voted "present".
C	Voted "present" to avoid possible conflict of interest.
?	Did not vote or otherwise make a position known.

Democrats *Republicans*

	22	23	24	25	26	27	28
ALABAMA							
1 *Edwards*	Y	Y	Y	Y	Y	Y	Y
2 *Dickinson*	N	N	Y	Y	Y	N	Y
3 Nichols	Y	Y	Y	Y	Y	N	Y
4 Bevill	Y	Y	Y	Y	Y	Y	Y
5 Flippo	?	?	?	?	?	?	?
6 *Smith*	Y	Y	Y	Y	Y	N	Y
7 Shelby	Y	Y	Y	Y	Y	N	Y
ALASKA							
AL *Young*	?	?	?	?	?	?	?
ARIZONA							
1 *Rhodes*	Y	Y	Y	Y	Y	N	Y
2 Udall	?	Y	Y	Y	Y	Y	Y
3 *Stump*	Y	N	Y	Y	Y	Y	Y
4 *Rudd*	Y	Y	Y	Y	Y	N	Y
ARKANSAS							
1 Alexander	Y	Y	Y	Y	Y	Y	Y
2 *Bethune*	Y	Y	Y	Y	Y	N	Y
3 *Hammerschmidt*	Y	N	Y	Y	Y	N	Y
4 Anthony	Y	Y	Y	Y	Y	Y	Y
CALIFORNIA							
1 *Chappie*	Y	Y	Y	?	Y	N	Y
2 *Clausen*	Y	Y	Y	?	Y	Y	Y
3 Matsui	Y	Y	Y	Y	Y	Y	Y
4 Fazio	Y	Y	Y	Y	Y	Y	Y
5 Burton, J.	N	Y	Y	Y	Y	Y	Y
6 Burton, P.	Y	Y	Y	Y	Y	Y	Y
7 Miller	?	?	?	?	?	#	?
8 Dellums	Y	Y	?	?	?	#	?
9 Stark	Y	Y	Y	Y	Y	Y	Y
10 Edwards	Y	Y	Y	Y	Y	Y	Y
11 Lantos	?	?	?	?	?	?	?
12 *McCloskey*	?	?	?	?	?	?	?
13 Mineta	Y	Y	Y	Y	Y	Y	Y
14 *Shumway*	Y	N	Y	Y	Y	N	Y
15 Coelho	Y	Y	Y	Y	Y	N	Y
16 Panetta	Y	Y	Y	Y	Y	Y	Y
17 *Pashayan*	Y	Y	Y	Y	Y	N	Y
18 *Thomas*	Y	Y	Y	Y	Y	N	Y
19 *Lagomarsino*	Y	Y	Y	Y	Y	N	Y
20 *Goldwater*	?	?	?	?	?	?	?
21 *Fiedler*	Y	Y	Y	Y	Y	N	Y
22 *Moorhead*	Y	Y	Y	Y	Y	N	Y
23 Beilenson	Y	Y	Y	Y	Y	Y	Y
24 Waxman	Y	Y	Y	Y	Y	Y	Y
25 Roybal	Y	Y	Y	Y	Y	Y	Y
26 *Rousselot*	?	?	?	?	?	?	?
27 *Dornan*	?	?	?	?	?	?	?
28 Dixon	?	?	?	?	?	?	?
29 Hawkins	?	?	?	?	?	?	?
30 Vacancy							
31 Dymally	Y	Y	Y	Y	Y	Y	Y
32 Anderson	Y	Y	Y	Y	Y	Y	Y
33 Grisham	Y	N	Y	Y	Y	N	Y
34 *Lungren*	?	+	Y	Y	Y	Y	Y
35 *Dreier*	Y	N	Y	Y	Y	N	Y
36 Brown	Y	Y	Y	Y	Y	Y	Y
37 *Lewis*	?	?	?	?	?	X	?
38 Patterson	?	Y	Y	Y	Y	Y	Y
39 *Dannemeyer*	Y	N	Y	Y	Y	N	Y
40 *Badham*	Y	Y	Y	Y	Y	N	Y
41 *Lowery*	?	?	?	Y	Y	N	Y
42 *Hunter*	Y	Y	Y	Y	Y	N	Y
43 *Burgener*	Y	Y	Y	Y	Y	N	Y
COLORADO							
1 Schroeder	N	Y	Y	Y	Y	Y	Y
2 Wirth	Y	Y	Y	Y	Y	Y	Y
3 Kogovsek	Y	Y	Y	Y	Y	Y	Y
4 *Brown*	Y	Y	Y	N	Y	N	Y

	22	23	24	25	26	27	28
5 *Kramer*	Y	N	Y	Y	Y	N	Y
CONNECTICUT							
1 Kennelly	Y	Y	Y	Y	Y	Y	Y
2 Gejdenson	N	Y	Y	Y	Y	Y	Y
3 *DeNardis*	?	?	?	?	?	?	?
4 *McKinney*	Y	Y	Y	Y	Y	N	Y
5 Ratchford	Y	Y	Y	Y	Y	Y	Y
6 Moffett	P	Y	Y	Y	Y	Y	Y
DELAWARE							
AL *Evans*	Y	Y	Y	Y	Y	N	Y
FLORIDA							
1 Hutto	Y	Y	Y	Y	Y	N	Y
2 Fuqua	Y	Y	Y	Y	Y	N	Y
3 Bennett	Y	Y	Y	Y	Y	Y	Y
4 Chappell	Y	Y	Y	Y	Y	N	Y
5 *McCollum*	Y	N	Y	Y	Y	N	Y
6 *Young*	?	?	?	?	?	?	?
7 Gibbons	Y	Y	Y	Y	Y	Y	Y
8 Ireland	Y	Y	Y	Y	Y	N	Y
9 Nelson	Y	Y	Y	Y	Y	Y	Y
10 *Bafalis*	Y	Y	Y	Y	Y	N	Y
11 Mica	Y	Y	Y	Y	Y	Y	Y
12 *Shaw*	Y	N	Y	Y	Y	N	Y
13 Lehman	Y	Y	Y	Y	Y	Y	Y
14 Pepper	Y	Y	Y	Y	Y	Y	Y
15 Fascell	Y	Y	Y	Y	Y	Y	Y
GEORGIA							
1 Ginn	?	?	?	?	?	?	?
2 Hatcher	Y	Y	Y	Y	Y	N	Y
3 Brinkley	Y	Y	Y	Y	Y	N	Y
4 Levitas	Y	Y	Y	Y	Y	Y	Y
5 Fowler	Y	Y	Y	Y	Y	Y	Y
6 *Gingrich*	Y	Y	Y	Y	Y	N	Y
7 McDonald	Y	N	Y	Y	Y	N	N
8 Evans	Y	Y	Y	Y	Y	Y	Y
9 Jenkins	Y	Y	Y	Y	Y	?	Y
10 Barnard	Y	Y	Y	Y	Y	N	Y
HAWAII							
1 Heftel	?	?	?	?	?	?	?
2 Akaka	Y	Y	Y	Y	Y	Y	Y
IDAHO							
1 *Craig*	Y	N	Y	N	Y	N	Y
2 *Hansen*	Y	N	Y	N	Y	N	Y
ILLINOIS							
1 Washington	Y	Y	Y	Y	Y	Y	Y
2 Savage	?	?	?	?	?	?	?
3 Russo	Y	Y	Y	Y	Y	Y	Y
4 *Derwinski*	Y	Y	Y	Y	Y	N	Y
5 Fary	?	?	?	?	?	#	?
6 *Hyde*	Y	Y	Y	Y	Y	N	Y
7 Collins	Y	Y	Y	Y	Y	Y	Y
8 Rostenkowski	Y	Y	Y	Y	Y	Y	Y
9 Yates	Y	Y	Y	Y	Y	Y	Y
10 *Porter*	Y	Y	Y	Y	Y	Y	Y
11 Annunzio	Y	Y	Y	Y	Y	Y	Y
12 *Crane, P.*	Y	N	Y	Y	Y	N	N
13 *McClory*	Y	Y	Y	Y	Y	N	Y
14 Erlenborn	?	?	?	?	?	?	?
15 *Corcoran*	+	+	Y	Y	Y	N	Y
16 *Martin*	Y	Y	Y	Y	Y	N	Y
17 O'Brien	?	?	?	?	?	?	?
18 *Michel*	Y	Y	Y	Y	Y	N	Y
19 *Railsback*	Y	Y	Y	Y	Y	N	Y
20 *Findley*	Y	Y	Y	Y	Y	N	Y
21 *Madigan*	Y	Y	Y	Y	Y	N	Y
22 *Crane, D.*	?	Y	Y	Y	Y	N	N
23 Price	Y	Y	Y	Y	Y	Y	Y
24 Simon	Y	Y	Y	Y	Y	Y	Y
INDIANA							
1 Benjamin	Y	Y	Y	Y	Y	N	Y
2 Fithian	Y	Y	Y	Y	Y	N	Y
3 *Hiler*	Y	Y	Y	Y	Y	N	Y
4 *Coats*	Y	Y	Y	Y	Y	N	Y
5 *Hillis*	Y	Y	Y	Y	Y	N	Y
6 *Evans*	?	?	?	?	?	?	?
7 *Myers*	Y	Y	Y	Y	Y	N	Y
8 *Deckard*	Y	Y	Y	Y	Y	Y	Y
9 Hamilton	Y	Y	Y	Y	Y	Y	Y
10 Sharp	Y	Y	Y	Y	Y	Y	Y
11 Jacobs	?	?	?	?	?	?	?
IOWA							
1 *Leach*	Y	Y	Y	Y	Y	Y	Y
2 *Tauke*	Y	Y	Y	Y	Y	N	Y
3 *Evans*	N	Y	N	Y	Y	Y	Y
4 Smith	?	Y	Y	Y	Y	Y	Y
5 Harkin	N	Y	Y	Y	Y	Y	Y
6 Bedell	Y	Y	Y	N	Y	Y	Y

ND - Northern Democrats   SD - Southern Democrats

	22	23	24	25	26	27	28
KANSAS							
1 ***Roberts***	Y	N	Y	Y	Y	N	Y
2 ***Jeffries***	Y	N	Y	Y	Y	N	N
3 ***Winn***	Y	N	Y	Y	Y	N	Y
4 Glickman	Y	Y	Y	Y	Y	Y	Y
5 ***Whittaker***	Y	N	Y	Y	Y	N	Y
KENTUCKY							
1 Hubbard	Y	Y	Y	Y	Y	N	Y
2 Natcher	Y	Y	Y	Y	Y	N	Y
3 Mazzoli	Y	Y	Y	Y	Y	Y	Y
4 ***Snyder***	Y	N	Y	Y	Y	N	Y
5 ***Rogers***	Y	Y	Y	N	Y	N	Y
6 ***Hopkins***	Y	N	Y	Y	Y	N	Y
7 Perkins	Y	Y	Y	Y	Y	Y	Y
LOUISIANA							
1 ***Livingston***	Y	Y	Y	Y	Y	N	Y
2 Boggs	?	Y	Y	Y	Y	Y	Y
3 Tauzin	Y	Y	Y	Y	Y	Y	Y
4 Roemer	N	N	Y	N	Y	N	Y
5 Huckaby	Y	Y	Y	Y	Y	Y	Y
6 ***Moore***	Y	N	Y	Y	Y	N	Y
7 Breaux	Y	Y	Y	Y	Y	N	Y
8 Long	Y	Y	Y	Y	Y	Y	Y
MAINE							
1 ***Emery***	Y	Y	Y	Y	Y	N	Y
2 ***Snowe***	Y	Y	Y	Y	Y	N	Y
MARYLAND							
1 Dyson	Y	Y	Y	Y	Y	N	Y
2 Long	Y	Y	Y	?	Y	Y	Y
3 Mikulski	Y	Y	Y	Y	Y	Y	Y
4 ***Holt***	Y	Y	Y	Y	Y	N	Y
5 Hoyer	?	Y	Y	Y	Y	Y	Y
6 Byron	Y	Y	Y	Y	Y	N	Y
7 Mitchell	N	Y	Y	Y	Y	Y	Y
8 Barnes	N	Y	Y	Y	Y	Y	Y
MASSACHUSETTS							
1 ***Conte***	Y	Y	Y	Y	Y	N	Y
2 Boland	Y	Y	Y	Y	Y	Y	Y
3 Early	Y	Y	Y	Y	Y	Y	Y
4 Frank	Y	Y	Y	Y	Y	Y	Y
5 Shannon	Y	Y	Y	Y	Y	Y	Y
6 Mavroules	Y	Y	Y	Y	Y	Y	Y
7 Markey	Y	Y	Y	Y	Y	Y	Y
8 O'Neill							
9 Moakley	Y	Y	Y	Y	Y	Y	Y
10 ***Heckler***	?	#	+	+	+	-	+
11 Donnelly	Y	Y	Y	Y	Y	Y	Y
12 Studds	Y	Y	Y	Y	Y	Y	Y
MICHIGAN							
1 Conyers	Y	Y	Y	Y	Y	Y	Y
2 ***Pursell***	?	?	?	?	?	?	?
3 Wolpe	Y	Y	Y	Y	Y	Y	Y
4 ***Siljander***	Y	Y	Y	Y	Y	N	Y
5 ***Sawyer***	Y	Y	Y	Y	Y	N	Y
6 ***Dunn***	Y	Y	Y	Y	Y	N	Y
7 Kildee	Y	Y	Y	Y	Y	Y	Y
8 Traxler	Y	Y	Y	Y	Y	Y	Y
9 ***Vander Jagt***	Y	Y	Y	Y	Y	N	Y
10 Albosta	Y	Y	Y	Y	Y	Y	Y
11 ***Davis***	Y	Y	Y	Y	Y	Y	Y
12 Bonior	Y	Y	Y	Y	Y	Y	Y
13 Crockett	?	?	?	?	?	?	?
14 Hertel	Y	Y	Y	Y	Y	Y	Y
15 Ford	?	?	?	?	?	Y	Y
16 Dingell	Y	Y	Y	Y	Y	Y	Y
17 Brodhead	Y	Y	Y	Y	Y	Y	Y
18 Blanchard	Y	Y	Y	Y	Y	Y	Y
19 ***Broomfield***	Y	Y	Y	Y	Y	N	Y
MINNESOTA							
1 ***Erdahl***	Y	Y	Y	Y	Y	N	Y
2 ***Hagedorn***	Y	N	Y	Y	Y	N	Y
3 ***Frenzel***	Y	Y	Y	Y	Y	N	Y
4 Vento	Y	Y	Y	Y	Y	Y	Y
5 Sabo	N	Y	Y	Y	Y	Y	Y
6 ***Weber***	N	N	Y	Y	Y	N	Y
7 ***Stangeland***	Y	N	Y	Y	Y	N	Y
8 Oberstar	Y	Y	Y	Y	Y	Y	Y
MISSISSIPPI							
1 Whitten	?	Y	Y	Y	Y	Y	Y
2 Bowen	Y	Y	Y	Y	Y	Y	Y
3 Montgomery	Y	Y	Y	Y	Y	N	Y
4 Dowdy	?	?	?	Y	Y	N	Y
5 ***Lott***	?	N	Y	Y	Y	N	Y
MISSOURI							
1 Clay	?	Y	Y	Y	Y	Y	Y
2 Young	Y	Y	Y	Y	Y	N	Y
3 Gephardt	Y	Y	Y	Y	Y	Y	Y
4 Skelton	Y	N	Y	Y	Y	N	Y
5 Bolling	Y	Y	Y	Y	Y	Y	Y
6 ***Coleman***	Y	Y	Y	Y	Y	Y	Y
7 ***Taylor***	Y	N	Y	Y	Y	N	Y
8 ***Bailey***	Y	N	Y	Y	Y	N	Y
9 Volkmer	Y	Y	Y	Y	Y	Y	Y
10 ***Emerson***	N	N	Y	Y	Y	N	Y
MONTANA							
1 Williams	?	?	?	?	?	Y	Y
2 ***Marlenee***	Y	Y	Y	Y	Y	N	Y
NEBRASKA							
1 ***Bereuter***	Y	Y	Y	Y	Y	N	Y
2 ***Daub***	Y	Y	Y	Y	Y	N	Y
3 ***Smith***	Y	Y	Y	Y	Y	N	Y
NEVADA							
AL Santini	?	?	?	?	Y	N	Y
NEW HAMPSHIRE							
1 D'Amours	Y	Y	Y	Y	Y	Y	Y
2 ***Gregg***	Y	N	Y	Y	Y	N	Y
NEW JERSEY							
1 Florio	Y	Y	?	Y	Y	Y	Y
2 Hughes	Y	Y	Y	Y	Y	Y	Y
3 Howard	Y	Y	Y	Y	Y	Y	Y
4 ***Smith***	Y	Y	Y	Y	Y	N	Y
5 ***Fenwick***	?	#	+	+	+	-	+
6 ***Forsythe***	N	Y	Y	Y	Y	N	Y
7 ***Roukema***	Y	Y	Y	Y	Y	N	Y
8 Roe	Y	Y	Y	Y	Y	Y	Y
9 ***Hollenbeck***	Y	Y	Y	Y	Y	N	Y
10 Rodino	?	+	+	+	+	+	+
11 Minish	Y	Y	Y	Y	Y	Y	Y
12 ***Rinaldo***	Y	Y	Y	Y	Y	N	Y
13 ***Courter***	Y	Y	Y	Y	Y	N	Y
14 Guarini	Y	Y	Y	Y	Y	Y	Y
15 Dwyer	Y	Y	Y	Y	Y	Y	Y
NEW MEXICO							
1 ***Lujan***	Y	Y	Y	Y	Y	N	Y
2 ***Skeen***	Y	Y	Y	Y	Y	N	Y
NEW YORK							
1 ***Carney***	Y	Y	Y	Y	Y	N	Y
2 Downey	Y	Y	Y	Y	Y	Y	Y
3 ***Carman***	?	Y	Y	Y	Y	N	Y
4 ***Lent***	Y	Y	Y	Y	Y	N	Y
5 ***McGrath***	Y	Y	Y	Y	Y	N	Y
6 ***LeBoutillier***	?	Y	Y	Y	Y	N	Y
7 Addabbo	?	?	?	?	?	X	?
8 Rosenthal	Y	Y	Y	Y	Y	N	Y
9 Ferraro	Y	Y	Y	Y	Y	Y	Y
10 Biaggi	Y	Y	Y	Y	Y	Y	Y
11 Scheuer	Y	Y	Y	Y	Y	Y	Y
12 Chisholm	?	Y	Y	Y	Y	Y	Y
13 Solarz	Y	Y	Y	Y	Y	Y	Y
14 Richmond	Y	Y	Y	Y	Y	Y	Y
15 Zeferetti	Y	Y	Y	Y	Y	N	Y
16 Schumer	Y	Y	Y	Y	Y	Y	Y
17 ***Molinari***	Y	Y	Y	Y	Y	N	Y
18 ***Green***	Y	Y	Y	Y	Y	N	N
19 Rangel	Y	Y	Y	Y	Y	Y	Y
20 Weiss	?	Y	Y	Y	Y	Y	Y
21 Garcia	Y	Y	Y	Y	Y	Y	Y
22 Bingham	Y	Y	Y	Y	Y	Y	Y
23 Peyser	Y	Y	Y	Y	Y	Y	Y
24 Ottinger	P	Y	Y	Y	Y	Y	Y
25 ***Fish***	Y	Y	Y	Y	Y	N	Y
26 ***Gilman***	Y	Y	Y	Y	Y	N	Y
27 McHugh	Y	Y	Y	Y	Y	Y	Y
28 Stratton	Y	Y	Y	Y	Y	N	Y
29 ***Solomon***	Y	N	Y	Y	Y	N	Y
30 ***Martin***	Y	Y	Y	Y	Y	N	Y
31 ***Mitchell***	Y	Y	Y	Y	Y	N	Y
32 ***Wortley***	?	?	?	?	?	?	?
33 ***Lee***	Y	Y	Y	Y	Y	N	Y
34 ***Horton***	Y	Y	Y	Y	Y	N	Y
35 ***Conable***	?	?	Y	Y	Y	N	Y
36 LaFalce	Y	Y	Y	Y	Y	Y	Y
37 Nowak	Y	Y	Y	Y	Y	Y	Y
38 ***Kemp***	Y	Y	Y	Y	Y	N	Y
39 Lundine	Y	Y	Y	Y	Y	Y	Y
NORTH CAROLINA							
1 Jones	Y	Y	Y	Y	Y	Y	Y
2 Fountain	?	?	?	?	?	?	?
3 Whitley	Y	Y	Y	Y	Y	N	Y
4 Andrews	Y	Y	Y	Y	Y	N	Y
5 Neal	?	?	?	?	?	?	?
6 ***Johnston***	Y	Y	Y	N	Y	N	Y
7 Rose	?	?	?	?	?	?	?
8 Hefner	Y	Y	Y	Y	Y	Y	Y
9 ***Martin***	Y	Y	Y	Y	Y	N	Y
10 ***Broyhill***	Y	Y	Y	Y	Y	N	Y
11 ***Hendon***	Y	Y	Y	Y	Y	N	Y
NORTH DAKOTA							
AL Dorgan	Y	Y	Y	Y	?	Y	Y
OHIO							
1 ***Gradison***	Y	N	Y	Y	Y	N	Y
2 Luken	?	Y	Y	Y	Y	Y	Y
3 Hall	?	?	?	?	?	?	?
4 ***Oxley***	Y	Y	Y	Y	Y	N	Y
5 ***Latta***	?	?	?	?	?	?	?
6 ***McEwen***	Y	Y	Y	Y	Y	N	Y
7 ***Brown***	?	?	?	?	?	?	?
8 ***Kindness***	Y	Y	Y	Y	Y	N	Y
9 ***Weber***	Y	Y	Y	Y	Y	N	Y
10 ***Miller***	N	N	Y	Y	Y	N	Y
11 ***Stanton***	Y	Y	Y	Y	Y	N	Y
12 Shamansky	Y	Y	Y	Y	Y	Y	Y
13 Pease	Y	Y	Y	Y	Y	Y	Y
14 Seiberling	Y	Y	Y	Y	Y	Y	Y
15 ***Wylie***	Y	Y	Y	Y	Y	N	Y
16 ***Regula***	Y	Y	Y	Y	Y	N	Y
17 ***Ashbrook***	?	?	?	?	?	?	?
18 Applegate	?	Y	Y	Y	Y	N	Y
19 ***Williams***	Y	Y	Y	Y	Y	N	Y
20 Oakar	Y	Y	Y	Y	Y	N	Y
21 Stokes	Y	Y	Y	Y	Y	Y	Y
22 Eckart	Y	Y	Y	Y	Y	Y	Y
23 Mottl	Y	N	Y	N	Y	N	Y
OKLAHOMA							
1 Jones	Y	Y	Y	Y	Y	Y	Y
2 Synar	Y	Y	Y	Y	Y	Y	Y
3 Watkins	Y	Y	Y	Y	Y	Y	Y
4 McCurdy	Y	Y	Y	Y	Y	Y	Y
5 ***Edwards***	N	N	Y	Y	Y	Y	Y
6 English	Y	Y	Y	Y	Y	Y	Y
OREGON							
1 AuCoin	?	Y	Y	Y	Y	N	Y
2 ***Smith***	Y	N	Y	N	Y	N	Y
3 Wyden	Y	Y	Y	Y	Y	N	Y
4 Weaver	Y	Y	Y	Y	Y	N	Y
PENNSYLVANIA							
1 Foglietta	?	Y	Y	Y	Y	Y	Y
2 Gray	Y	Y	Y	Y	Y	Y	Y
3 Smith	Y	Y	Y	Y	Y	Y	Y
4 ***Dougherty***	?	Y	Y	Y	Y	N	Y
5 ***Schulze***	Y	Y	Y	Y	Y	N	Y
6 Yatron	Y	Y	Y	Y	Y	N	Y
7 Edgar	Y	Y	Y	Y	Y	Y	Y
8 ***Coyne, J.***	Y	Y	Y	Y	Y	N	Y
9 ***Shuster***	Y	Y	Y	Y	Y	N	Y
10 ***McDade***	+	+	+	+	+	-	+
11 ***Nelligan***	Y	Y	Y	Y	Y	N	Y
12 Murtha	?	Y	Y	Y	Y	Y	Y
13 ***Coughlin***	?	?	?	?	?	?	?
14 Coyne, W.	Y	Y	Y	Y	Y	Y	Y
15 ***Ritter***	Y	Y	Y	Y	Y	N	Y
16 ***Walker***	N	N	Y	Y	Y	N	Y
17 Ertel	Y	Y	Y	Y	Y	Y	Y
18 Walgren	Y	Y	Y	Y	Y	Y	Y
19 ***Goodling***	N	Y	Y	Y	Y	N	Y
20 Gaydos	Y	Y	Y	Y	Y	N	Y
21 Bailey	Y	Y	Y	Y	Y	Y	Y
22 Murphy	Y	Y	N	Y	Y	N	Y
23 ***Clinger***	Y	Y	Y	Y	Y	N	Y
24 ***Marks***	Y	Y	?	Y	Y	Y	Y
25 ***Atkinson***	?	?	?	?	?	?	?
RHODE ISLAND							
1 St Germain	Y	Y	Y	Y	Y	N	Y
2 ***Schneider***	+	X	+	+	+	Y	Y
SOUTH CAROLINA							
1 ***Hartnett***	Y	Y	Y	Y	Y	N	Y
2 ***Spence***	Y	Y	Y	Y	Y	N	Y
3 Derrick	Y	Y	Y	Y	Y	Y	Y
4 ***Campbell***	Y	Y	Y	Y	Y	N	Y
5 Holland	Y	Y	Y	Y	Y	Y	Y
6 ***Napier***	Y	Y	Y	Y	Y	N	Y
SOUTH DAKOTA							
1 Daschle	Y	Y	Y	Y	Y	Y	Y
2 ***Roberts***	?	?	?	?	?	?	?
TENNESSEE							
1 ***Quillen***	Y	Y	Y	Y	Y	N	Y
2 ***Duncan***	Y	Y	Y	Y	Y	N	Y
3 Bouquard	Y	Y	Y	Y	Y	N	Y
4 Gore	Y	Y	Y	Y	Y	Y	Y
5 Boner	Y	Y	Y	Y	Y	N	Y
6 ***Beard***	Y	Y	Y	Y	Y	N	Y
7 Jones	Y	Y	Y	Y	Y	N	Y
8 Ford	?	?	?	?	?	#	?
TEXAS							
1 Hall, S.	Y	Y	Y	Y	Y	N	Y
2 Wilson	?	Y	Y	Y	Y	Y	Y
3 ***Collins***	Y	N	Y	Y	Y	N	Y
4 Hall, R.	Y	N	Y	?	?	N	Y
5 Mattox	Y	Y	Y	Y	Y	Y	Y
6 Gramm	Y	Y	Y	Y	Y	N	Y
7 ***Archer***	Y	N	Y	Y	Y	N	Y
8 ***Fields***	Y	N	Y	Y	Y	N	Y
9 Brooks	?	?	?	?	?	?	?
10 Pickle	Y	Y	Y	Y	Y	N	Y
11 Leath	Y	Y	Y	Y	Y	N	Y
12 Wright	Y	Y	Y	Y	Y	Y	Y
13 Hightower	Y	Y	Y	Y	Y	Y	Y
14 Patman	Y	N	Y	Y	Y	N	Y
15 de la Garza	?	?	?	?	?	?	?
16 White	Y	Y	Y	Y	Y	Y	Y
17 Stenholm	Y	Y	Y	Y	?	N	Y
18 Leland	Y	Y	Y	Y	Y	Y	Y
19 Hance	Y	Y	Y	Y	Y	N	Y
20 Gonzalez	Y	P	P	P	P	P	P
21 ***Loeffler***	Y	Y	Y	Y	Y	Y	Y
22 ***Paul***	Y	Y	Y	Y	Y	N	N
23 Kazen	Y	Y	Y	Y	Y	N	Y
24 Frost	Y	Y	Y	Y	Y	Y	Y
UTAH							
1 ***Hansen***	Y	Y	Y	N	Y	N	Y
2 ***Marriott***	Y	Y	Y	Y	Y	N	Y
VERMONT							
AL ***Jeffords***	?	Y	Y	Y	Y	N	N
VIRGINIA							
1 ***Trible***	Y	Y	Y	Y	Y	N	Y
2 ***Whitehurst***	Y	Y	Y	Y	Y	N	Y
3 ***Bliley***	Y	Y	Y	Y	Y	N	Y
4 ***Daniel, R.***	Y	Y	Y	Y	Y	N	Y
5 Daniel, D.	Y	Y	Y	Y	Y	N	Y
6 ***Butler***	?	?	Y	Y	Y	N	Y
7 ***Robinson***	Y	Y	Y	Y	Y	N	Y
8 ***Parris***	?	?	?	Y	Y	N	Y
9 ***Wampler***	Y	Y	Y	Y	Y	N	Y
10 ***Wolf***	Y	Y	Y	Y	Y	N	Y
WASHINGTON							
1 ***Pritchard***	Y	Y	Y	Y	Y	N	Y
2 Swift	Y	Y	Y	Y	Y	N	Y
3 Bonker	?	Y	Y	Y	Y	N	Y
4 ***Morrison***	Y	Y	Y	Y	Y	N	Y
5 Foley	Y	Y	Y	Y	Y	N	Y
6 Dicks	Y	Y	Y	Y	Y	N	Y
7 Lowry	Y	Y	Y	Y	Y	Y	Y
WEST VIRGINIA							
1 Mollohan	Y	Y	Y	Y	Y	Y	Y
2 ***Benedict***	Y	Y	Y	Y	Y	N	Y
3 ***Staton***	Y	Y	Y	Y	Y	N	Y
4 Rahall	Y	Y	Y	Y	Y	Y	Y
WISCONSIN							
1 Aspin	P	Y	Y	Y	Y	Y	Y
2 Kastenmeier	?	Y	Y	Y	Y	Y	Y
3 ***Gunderson***	Y	Y	Y	Y	Y	N	Y
4 Zablocki	Y	Y	Y	Y	Y	Y	Y
5 Reuss	Y	Y	Y	Y	Y	Y	Y
6 ***Petri***	Y	Y	Y	Y	Y	N	Y
7 Obey	Y	Y	Y	Y	Y	Y	Y
8 ***Roth***	Y	Y	Y	Y	Y	N	Y
9 ***Sensenbrenner***	Y	Y	Y	Y	Y	N	Y
WYOMING							
AL ***Cheney***	Y	N	Y	Y	Y	N	Y

Southern states - Ala., Ark., Fla., Ga., Ky., La., Miss., N.C., Okla., S.C., Tenn., Texas, Va.

29. Procedural Motion. Gregg, R-N.H., motion to approve the House *Journal* of Monday, March 22. Motion agreed to 345-17: R 153-11; D 192-6 (ND 125-5, SD 67-1), March 23, 1982.

30. H Con Res 100. Russian Refugees. Leach, R-Iowa, demand for a second on the Bonker, D-Wash., motion to suspend the rules and adopt the concurrent resolution expressing the sense of the Congress that the president should take such steps as necessary to ensure that the Chmykhalov and Vashchenko families, who sought refuge in the U.S. Embassy in Moscow on June 27, 1978, in hopes of emigrating from the Soviet Union, be permitted to reside in the embassy until the Soviet Union permits them to emigrate. Second ordered 373-1: R 162-0; D 211-1 (ND 139-1, SD 72-0), March 23, 1982. The Bonker motion subsequently was agreed to by voice vote.

31. HR 5014. Gateway National Recreation Area. Seiberling, D-Ohio, motion to suspend the rules and pass the bill to extend for 10 years the life of the Gateway National Recreation Area Advisory Commission, which expires Oct. 27, 1982. Motion agreed to 368-30: R 149-22; D 219-8 (ND 150-2, SD 69-6), March 23, 1982. A two-thirds majority of those present and voting (266 in this case) is required for passage under suspension of the rules.

32. HR 4750. Roosevelt Memorial. Seiberling, D-Ohio, motion to suspend the rules and pass the bill to authorize a study for the establishment of a Franklin D. Roosevelt living memorial in Warm Springs, Ga. Motion agreed to 288-107: R 70-99; D 218-8 (ND 146-6, SD 72-2), March 23, 1982. A two-thirds majority of those present and voting (264 in this case) is required for passage under suspension of the rules. A "nay" was a vote supporting the president's position.

33. S 146. Historic Preservation for Camden, S.C. Seiberling, D-Ohio, motion to suspend the rules and pass the bill to authorize the interior secretary to enter into cooperative agreements to assist in the historic preservation of Camden, S.C. Motion rejected 243-152: R 39-129; D 204-23 (ND 136-17, SD 68-6), March 23, 1982. A two-thirds majority of those present and voting (264 in this case) is required for passage under suspension of the rules.

34. S 2166. Distribution of the Slide Show "Montana." Zablocki, D-Wis., motion to suspend the rules and pass the bill to authorize the International Communication Agency to distribute within the United States a slide show entitled "Montana: The People Speak." Motion agreed to 388-11: R 164-7; D 224-4 (ND 149-3, SD 75-1), March 23, 1982. A two-thirds majority of those present and voting (266 in this case) is required for passage under suspension of the rules.

35. HR 4709. Prompt Payment Act. Brooks, D-Texas, motion to suspend the rules and pass the bill to require the federal government to pay interest on overdue payments for property or services. Motion agreed to 396-0: R 168-0; D 228-0 (ND 153-0, SD 75-0), March 23, 1982. A two-thirds majority of those present and voting (264 in this case) is required for passage under suspension of the rules. A "yea" was a vote supporting the president's position.

36. HR 2528. Economy Act Amendments. Brooks, D-Texas, motion to suspend the rules and pass the bill to provide that all departments and agencies may obtain material and services from other agencies by contract. Motion agreed to 356-43: R 169-2; D 187-41 (ND 116-36, SD 71-5), March 23, 1982. A two-thirds majority of those present and voting (266 in this case) is required for passage under suspension of the rules. A "yea" was a vote supporting the president's position.

KEY

Y	Voted for (yea).
#	Paired for.
+	Announced for.
N	Voted against (nay).
X	Paired against.
-	Announced against.
P	Voted "present".
C	Voted "present" to avoid possible conflict of interest.
?	Did not vote or otherwise make a position known.

Democrats *Republicans*

	29	30	31	32	33	34	35	36
ALABAMA								
1 *Edwards*	Y	Y	Y	Y	Y	Y	Y	Y
2 *Dickinson*	?	?	Y	Y	Y	Y	Y	Y
3 Nichols	Y	Y	Y	Y	Y	Y	Y	Y
4 Bevill	Y	Y	Y	Y	Y	Y	Y	Y
5 Flippo	Y	Y	Y	Y	Y	Y	Y	Y
6 *Smith*	Y	Y	Y	N	N	Y	Y	Y
7 Shelby	Y	Y	Y	Y	Y	Y	Y	Y
ALASKA								
AL *Young*	?	?	Y	N	Y	Y	Y	Y
ARIZONA								
1 *Rhodes*	?	?	?	?	?	?	?	?
2 Udall	Y	Y	Y	Y	Y	Y	Y	Y
3 *Stump*	Y	Y	N	N	N	Y	N	Y
4 *Rudd*	Y	Y	Y	N	N	Y	Y	Y
ARKANSAS								
1 Alexander	Y	Y	Y	Y	Y	Y	Y	Y
2 *Bethune*	Y	Y	Y	N	Y	Y	?	Y
3 *Hammerschmidt*	Y	Y	Y	N	Y	Y	Y	Y
4 Anthony	Y	Y	Y	Y	Y	Y	Y	Y
CALIFORNIA								
1 *Chappie*	Y	Y	Y	N	N	Y	Y	Y
2 *Clausen*	Y	Y	Y	N	Y	Y	Y	Y
3 Matsui	Y	Y	Y	Y	Y	Y	Y	N
4 Fazio	Y	Y	Y	Y	Y	Y	Y	N
5 Burton, J.	?	?	?	?	?	?	?	?
6 Burton, P.	Y	Y	Y	Y	Y	Y	Y	N
7 Miller	?	Y	Y	Y	Y	Y	Y	N
8 Dellums	Y	Y	Y	Y	Y	Y	Y	N
9 Stark	Y	Y	Y	Y	Y	Y	Y	N
10 Edwards	?	Y	Y	Y	Y	Y	Y	N
11 Lantos	Y	Y	Y	Y	Y	Y	Y	Y
12 *McCloskey*	?	?	?	?	?	?	?	?
13 Mineta	Y	Y	Y	Y	Y	Y	Y	Y
14 *Shumway*	Y	Y	Y	N	N	Y	Y	Y
15 Coelho	Y	Y	Y	Y	Y	Y	Y	Y
16 Panetta	Y	Y	Y	Y	Y	Y	Y	Y
17 *Pashayan*	?	?	?	?	?	?	?	?
18 *Thomas*	Y	Y	Y	N	N	Y	Y	Y
19 *Lagomarsino*	Y	Y	Y	N	Y	Y	Y	Y
20 *Goldwater*	Y	Y	Y	N	Y	Y	Y	Y
21 *Fiedler*	Y	Y	Y	N	Y	Y	Y	Y
22 *Moorhead*	Y	Y	Y	N	N	Y	Y	Y
23 Beilenson	Y	Y	Y	Y	Y	Y	Y	N
24 Waxman	Y	Y	Y	Y	Y	Y	Y	Y
25 Roybal	Y	Y	Y	Y	Y	Y	Y	Y
26 *Rousselot*	Y	Y	N	Y	N	Y	Y	Y
27 *Dornan*	?	?	?	?	?	?	?	?
28 Dixon	Y	Y	Y	Y	Y	Y	Y	Y
29 Hawkins	Y	Y	Y	Y	Y	Y	Y	N
30 Vacancy								
31 *Dymally*	Y	Y	Y	Y	Y	Y	Y	N
32 Anderson	Y	Y	Y	Y	Y	Y	Y	Y
33 *Grisham*	Y	Y	Y	N	N	Y	Y	Y
34 *Lungren*	Y	Y	Y	N	N	Y	Y	Y
35 *Dreier*	Y	Y	N	N	N	Y	Y	Y
36 Brown	Y	Y	Y	Y	Y	Y	Y	Y
37 *Lewis*	Y	Y	Y	Y	N	Y	Y	Y
38 Patterson	?	Y	Y	Y	Y	Y	Y	Y
39 *Dannemeyer*	Y	N	N	N	N	Y	Y	Y
40 *Badham*	?	?	?	?	?	?	?	?
41 *Lowery*	Y	Y	Y	N	N	Y	Y	Y
42 *Hunter*	Y	Y	Y	N	N	Y	Y	Y
43 *Burgener*	Y	Y	Y	N	N	Y	Y	Y
COLORADO								
1 Schroeder	N	Y	Y	Y	Y	Y	Y	Y
2 Wirth	Y	Y	Y	Y	Y	Y	Y	Y
3 Kogovsek	Y	Y	Y	Y	Y	Y	Y	Y
4 *Brown*	Y	Y	N	N	N	N	Y	Y

	29	30	31	32	33	34	35	36
5 *Kramer*	Y	Y	Y	Y	N	Y	Y	Y
CONNECTICUT								
1 Kennelly	Y	Y	Y	Y	Y	Y	Y	Y
2 Gejdenson	?	?	?	?	?	?	?	?
3 *DeNardis*	Y	Y	Y	Y	Y	Y	Y	Y
4 *McKinney*	Y	?	Y	Y	N	Y	Y	Y
5 Ratchford	Y	Y	Y	Y	Y	Y	Y	Y
6 Moffett	Y	Y	Y	Y	Y	Y	Y	Y
DELAWARE								
AL *Evans*	Y	Y	Y	Y	Y	Y	Y	Y
FLORIDA								
1 Hutto	Y	Y	Y	Y	Y	Y	Y	Y
2 Fuqua	Y	Y	Y	Y	Y	Y	Y	Y
3 Bennett	Y	Y	Y	Y	Y	Y	Y	N
4 Chappell	Y	Y	Y	Y	Y	Y	Y	Y
5 *McCollum*	?	?	?	?	X	?	?	?
6 *Young*	Y	Y	Y	N	Y	Y	Y	Y
7 Gibbons	Y	Y	Y	Y	Y	Y	Y	Y
8 Nelson	?	Y	Y	Y	Y	Y	Y	Y
9 *Bafalis*	Y	Y	Y	Y	Y	Y	Y	Y
10 *Bafalis*	Y	Y	Y	Y	Y	Y	Y	Y
11 Mica	Y	Y	Y	Y	Y	Y	Y	Y
12 *Shaw*	Y	Y	Y	N	Y	Y	Y	Y
13 Lehman	Y	Y	Y	Y	Y	Y	Y	Y
14 Pepper	Y	Y	Y	Y	Y	Y	Y	Y
15 Fascell	?	Y	Y	?	Y	Y	?	Y
GEORGIA								
1 Ginn	?	?	Y	Y	Y	Y	Y	Y
2 Hatcher	Y	Y	Y	Y	Y	Y	Y	Y
3 Brinkley	Y	Y	Y	Y	Y	Y	Y	Y
4 Levitas	Y	Y	Y	Y	Y	Y	Y	Y
5 Fowler	Y	Y	Y	Y	Y	Y	Y	Y
6 *Gingrich*	Y	Y	Y	N	Y	Y	Y	Y
7 McDonald	Y	N	N	N	N	N	N	Y
8 Evans	Y	N	Y	Y	Y	Y	Y	Y
9 Jenkins	Y	Y	Y	Y	Y	Y	Y	Y
10 Barnard	Y	Y	Y	Y	Y	Y	Y	Y
HAWAII								
1 Heftel	?	Y	Y	Y	Y	Y	Y	Y
2 Akaka	Y	Y	Y	Y	Y	Y	Y	Y
IDAHO								
1 *Craig*	Y	Y	Y	N	N	Y	Y	Y
2 *Hansen*	Y	N	N	N	N	Y	Y	Y
ILLINOIS								
1 Washington	Y	Y	Y	Y	Y	Y	Y	N
2 Savage	?	?	Y	Y	Y	Y	Y	Y
3 Russo	?	?	?	?	?	?	?	?
4 *Derwinski*	Y	Y	Y	?	Y	Y	Y	Y
5 Fary	?	?	Y	Y	Y	Y	Y	Y
6 *Hyde*	?	Y	Y	Y	Y	Y	Y	Y
7 Collins	Y	Y	Y	Y	Y	Y	Y	Y
8 Rostenkowski	?	?	?	?	?	?	?	?
9 Yates	Y	Y	Y	Y	Y	Y	Y	N
10 *Porter*	Y	Y	Y	Y	Y	Y	Y	Y
11 Annunzio	Y	Y	Y	Y	Y	Y	Y	Y
12 *Crane, P.*	Y	Y	N	N	N	Y	Y	Y
13 *McClory*	Y	Y	Y	Y	Y	Y	Y	Y
14 *Erlenborn*	Y	Y	Y	N	N	Y	Y	Y
15 *Corcoran*	Y	Y	Y	N	N	Y	Y	Y
16 *Martin*	Y	N	Y	N	N	Y	Y	Y
17 *O'Brien*	Y	Y	Y	Y	Y	Y	Y	Y
18 *Michel*	Y	Y	Y	N	N	Y	Y	Y
19 *Railsback*	Y	Y	Y	N	Y	Y	Y	Y
20 *Findley*	Y	Y	Y	Y	N	Y	Y	Y
21 *Madigan*	Y	?	Y	Y	Y	Y	Y	Y
22 *Crane, D.*	Y	N	N	N	N	Y	Y	Y
23 Price	Y	Y	Y	Y	Y	Y	Y	Y
24 Simon	Y	Y	Y	Y	Y	Y	Y	Y
INDIANA								
1 Benjamin	Y	Y	Y	Y	Y	Y	Y	Y
2 Fithian	Y	Y	Y	Y	N	Y	Y	Y
3 *Hiler*	Y	Y	Y	N	N	Y	Y	Y
4 *Coats*	Y	N	N	N	N	Y	Y	Y
5 *Hillis*	Y	?	Y	N	Y	Y	Y	Y
6 Evans	?	?	?	?	?	?	?	?
7 *Myers*	Y	Y	Y	N	N	Y	Y	Y
8 *Deckard*	Y	Y	Y	N	N	Y	Y	Y
9 Hamilton	Y	Y	Y	Y	Y	Y	Y	Y
10 Sharp	Y	Y	Y	Y	Y	Y	Y	Y
11 Jacobs	N	Y	Y	N	N	Y	Y	Y
IOWA								
1 Leach	?	Y	Y	Y	Y	Y	Y	Y
2 Tauke	Y	Y	Y	N	Y	Y	Y	Y
3 Evans	N	Y	Y	N	N	Y	Y	Y
4 Smith	Y	Y	Y	Y	?	Y	Y	Y
5 Harkin	?	Y	Y	Y	Y	Y	Y	Y
6 Bedell	Y	Y	Y	N	N	Y	Y	Y

ND - Northern Democrats   SD - Southern Democrats

Corresponding to Congressional Record Votes 30, 31, 32, 33, 34, 35, 36, 37

	29	30	31	32	33	34	35	36
KANSAS								
1 ***Roberts***	Y	Y	Y	N	N	Y	Y	Y
2 ***Jeffries***	Y	Y	N	N	N	N	Y	Y
3 ***Winn***	Y	Y	Y	N	N	Y	Y	Y
4 Glickman	Y	Y	Y	N	N	Y	Y	Y
5 ***Whittaker***	Y	Y	Y	N	N	Y	Y	Y
KENTUCKY								
1 Hubbard	Y	Y	Y	Y	Y	Y	Y	Y
2 Natcher	Y	Y	Y	Y	Y	Y	Y	Y
3 Mazzoli	Y	Y	Y	Y	Y	Y	Y	Y
4 ***Snyder***	Y	Y	Y	Y	N	Y	Y	Y
5 ***Rogers***	Y	Y	Y	Y	Y	Y	Y	Y
6 ***Hopkins***	Y	Y	Y	N	N	Y	Y	Y
7 Perkins	Y	Y	Y	Y	Y	Y	Y	Y
LOUISIANA								
1 ***Livingston***	Y	Y	Y	N	N	Y	?	Y
2 Boggs	?	?	?	?	#	?	?	?
3 Tauzin	Y	Y	Y	Y	N	Y	Y	Y
4 Roemer	N	Y	Y	N	Y	Y	Y	Y
5 Huckaby	Y	Y	Y	Y	Y	Y	Y	Y
6 ***Moore***	Y	Y	Y	N	N	Y	Y	Y
7 Breaux	Y	Y	Y	Y	Y	Y	Y	Y
8 Long	Y	Y	Y	Y	Y	Y	Y	Y
MAINE								
1 ***Emery***	?	?	?	?	?	?	?	?
2 ***Snowe***	Y	Y	Y	Y	N	Y	Y	Y
MARYLAND								
1 Dyson	Y	Y	Y	N	Y	Y	Y	N
2 Long	Y	Y	Y	Y	N	Y	Y	Y
3 Mikulski	Y	Y	Y	Y	Y	Y	Y	N
4 ***Holt***	N	Y	Y	N	Y	Y	Y	Y
5 Hoyer	Y	Y	Y	Y	Y	Y	Y	N
6 Byron	Y	Y	Y	N	Y	Y	Y	Y
7 Mitchell	N	Y	Y	Y	Y	Y	Y	N
8 Barnes	N	Y	Y	Y	Y	Y	Y	N
MASSACHUSETTS								
1 ***Conte***	Y	Y	Y	Y	N	Y	Y	Y
2 Boland	Y	Y	Y	Y	Y	Y	Y	Y
3 Early	Y	Y	Y	Y	Y	Y	Y	Y
4 Frank	Y	Y	Y	Y	Y	Y	Y	Y
5 Shannon	Y	Y	Y	Y	Y	Y	Y	N
6 Mavroules	Y	Y	Y	Y	Y	Y	Y	Y
7 Markey	Y	Y	Y	Y	Y	Y	Y	N
8 O'Neill								
9 Moakley	Y	Y	Y	Y	Y	Y	Y	?
10 ***Heckler***	Y	Y	Y	Y	N	Y	Y	Y
11 Donnelly	Y	Y	Y	Y	Y	Y	Y	Y
12 Studds	Y	Y	Y	Y	Y	Y	Y	N
MICHIGAN								
1 Conyers	Y	Y	Y	Y	Y	Y	Y	Y
2 ***Pursell***	?	Y	?	?	?	?	?	?
3 Wolpe	Y	Y	Y	Y	Y	Y	Y	N
4 ***Siljander***	Y	Y	Y	N	N	Y	Y	Y
5 ***Sawyer***	Y	?	Y	N	N	Y	Y	Y
6 ***Dunn***	Y	Y	Y	N	N	Y	Y	Y
7 Kildee	Y	Y	Y	Y	Y	Y	Y	Y
8 Traxler	Y	Y	Y	Y	Y	Y	Y	Y
9 ***Vander Jagt***	Y	Y	Y	Y	Y	Y	Y	Y
10 Albosta	Y	Y	Y	Y	Y	Y	Y	Y
11 ***Davis***	Y	Y	Y	Y	Y	Y	Y	Y
12 Bonior	Y	Y	Y	Y	Y	Y	Y	Y
13 Crockett	?	N	Y	Y	Y	Y	Y	Y
14 Hertel	Y	Y	Y	Y	Y	Y	Y	Y
15 Ford	?	Y	Y	Y	Y	Y	Y	N
16 Dingell	Y	Y	Y	Y	Y	Y	Y	Y
17 Brodhead	Y	Y	N	Y	Y	Y	Y	Y
18 Blanchard	Y	Y	Y	Y	Y	Y	Y	Y
19 ***Broomfield***	Y	Y	Y	Y	Y	Y	Y	Y
MINNESOTA								
1 ***Erdahl***	Y	Y	Y	Y	Y	Y	Y	Y
2 ***Hagedorn***	Y	Y	Y	N	N	Y	Y	Y
3 ***Frenzel***	Y	Y	Y	N	N	Y	Y	Y
4 Vento	Y	Y	Y	Y	Y	Y	Y	N
5 Sabo	N	Y	Y	Y	Y	Y	Y	Y
6 ***Weber***	N	Y	N	N	N	N	Y	Y
7 ***Stangeland***	?	?	Y	N	N	Y	Y	Y
8 Oberstar	Y	Y	Y	Y	Y	Y	Y	Y
MISSISSIPPI								
1 Whitten	Y	Y	Y	Y	Y	Y	Y	Y
2 Bowen	Y	Y	Y	Y	Y	Y	Y	Y
3 Montgomery	Y	?	Y	Y	Y	Y	Y	Y
4 Dowdy	Y	Y	Y	Y	Y	Y	Y	Y
5 ***Lott***	Y	Y	Y	Y	Y	Y	Y	Y
MISSOURI								
1 Clay	?	?	Y	Y	Y	Y	Y	N
2 Young	Y	Y	Y	Y	Y	Y	Y	Y
3 Gephardt	Y	Y	Y	Y	Y	Y	Y	Y
4 Skelton	Y	Y	Y	Y	N	Y	Y	Y
5 Bolling	Y	Y	Y	Y	Y	Y	Y	Y
6 ***Coleman***	Y	?	Y	N	N	Y	Y	Y
7 ***Taylor***	Y	Y	Y	N	N	Y	Y	Y
8 ***Bailey***	?	?	?	?	X	?	?	?
9 Volkmer	Y	Y	Y	Y	Y	Y	Y	Y
10 ***Emerson***	N	Y	N	N	N	Y	Y	Y
MONTANA								
1 Williams	?	Y	Y	Y	Y	Y	Y	Y
2 ***Marlenee***	Y	Y	Y	Y	N	Y	Y	Y
NEBRASKA								
1 ***Bereuter***	Y	Y	Y	N	N	Y	Y	Y
2 ***Daub***	Y	Y	Y	N	N	Y	Y	Y
3 ***Smith***	Y	Y	Y	N	N	Y	Y	Y
NEVADA								
AL Santini	Y	Y	Y	Y	N	Y	Y	Y
NEW HAMPSHIRE								
1 D'Amours	?	?	Y	Y	N	Y	Y	Y
2 ***Gregg***	Y	Y	Y	N	N	Y	Y	Y
NEW JERSEY								
1 Florio	Y	?	Y	Y	Y	Y	Y	Y
2 Hughes	Y	Y	Y	Y	Y	Y	Y	Y
3 Howard	Y	Y	Y	Y	Y	Y	Y	Y
4 ***Smith***	Y	Y	Y	Y	Y	Y	Y	Y
5 ***Fenwick***	Y	Y	Y	Y	N	Y	Y	Y
6 ***Forsythe***	?	Y	Y	N	N	Y	?	Y
7 ***Roukema***	?	+	-	-	-	+	+	+
8 Roe	Y	Y	Y	Y	Y	Y	Y	Y
9 ***Hollenbeck***	Y	Y	Y	N	N	Y	Y	Y
10 Rodino	?	Y	Y	Y	Y	Y	Y	Y
11 Minish	Y	Y	Y	Y	Y	Y	Y	Y
12 ***Rinaldo***	Y	Y	Y	N	N	Y	Y	Y
13 ***Courter***	?	Y	Y	N	N	Y	Y	Y
14 Guarini	?	?	Y	Y	Y	Y	Y	Y
15 Dwyer	Y	Y	Y	Y	Y	Y	Y	Y
NEW MEXICO								
1 ***Lujan***	Y	Y	Y	N	Y	Y	Y	Y
2 ***Skeen***	Y	Y	Y	N	N	Y	Y	Y
NEW YORK								
1 ***Carney***	Y	Y	Y	N	N	Y	Y	Y
2 Downey	?	Y	Y	Y	Y	Y	Y	Y
3 ***Carman***	Y	Y	Y	N	N	Y	Y	Y
4 ***Lent***	Y	+	+	+	+	+	+	+
5 ***McGrath***	Y	Y	Y	Y	N	Y	Y	Y
6 ***LeBoutillier***	?	?	?	?	?	?	?	?
7 Addabbo	Y	Y	Y	Y	Y	Y	Y	Y
8 Rosenthal	?	Y	Y	Y	Y	Y	Y	Y
9 Ferraro	Y	Y	Y	Y	Y	Y	Y	N
10 Biaggi	?	Y	Y	Y	Y	Y	Y	Y
11 Scheuer	Y	Y	Y	Y	Y	Y	Y	Y
12 Chisholm	?	?	Y	Y	Y	Y	Y	Y
13 Solarz	Y	Y	Y	Y	Y	Y	Y	Y
14 Richmond	?	Y	Y	Y	Y	Y	Y	Y
15 Zeferetti	Y	Y	Y	Y	Y	Y	Y	Y
16 Schumer	Y	Y	Y	Y	Y	Y	Y	N
17 ***Molinari***	Y	?	?	?	?	?	?	?
18 ***Green***	Y	?	?	?	?	?	?	?
19 Rangel	Y	Y	Y	Y	Y	Y	Y	Y
20 Weiss	Y	Y	Y	Y	Y	Y	Y	N
21 Garcia	Y	Y	Y	Y	Y	Y	Y	Y
22 Bingham	Y	Y	Y	Y	Y	Y	Y	Y
23 Peyser	Y	Y	Y	Y	Y	Y	Y	Y
24 Ottinger	P	Y	Y	Y	Y	Y	Y	N
25 ***Fish***	Y	Y	Y	Y	Y	Y	Y	Y
26 ***Gilman***	Y	Y	Y	Y	N	Y	Y	Y
27 McHugh	Y	Y	?	?	Y	Y	Y	N
28 Stratton	Y	Y	Y	Y	N	Y	Y	N
29 ***Solomon***	Y	Y	Y	N	N	Y	Y	Y
30 ***Martin***	Y	Y	Y	Y	Y	Y	Y	Y
31 ***Mitchell***	Y	Y	Y	Y	N	Y	Y	Y
32 ***Wortley***	Y	Y	Y	Y	?	Y	Y	Y
33 ***Lee***	Y	Y	Y	Y	N	N	Y	Y
34 ***Horton***	Y	Y	Y	?	N	Y	Y	Y
35 ***Conable***	Y	Y	Y	N	N	N	Y	Y
36 LaFalce	Y	?	Y	Y	Y	Y	Y	Y
37 Nowak	?	?	Y	Y	Y	Y	Y	Y
38 ***Kemp***	Y	Y	Y	Y	?	Y	Y	Y
39 Lundine	Y	Y	Y	Y	Y	N	Y	Y
NORTH CAROLINA								
1 Jones	Y	Y	Y	Y	Y	Y	Y	N
2 Fountain	Y	Y	Y	Y	#	Y	Y	Y
3 Whitley	Y	Y	Y	Y	Y	Y	Y	N
4 Andrews	Y	Y	Y	Y	Y	Y	Y	Y
5 Neal	?	?	?	?	#	?	?	?
6 ***Johnston***	N	Y	N	N	Y	Y	Y	Y
7 Rose	Y	Y	Y	Y	Y	Y	Y	Y
8 Hefner	?	Y	Y	Y	Y	Y	Y	Y
9 ***Martin***	Y	Y	Y	N	Y	Y	Y	Y
10 ***Broyhill***	Y	Y	Y	N	N	Y	Y	Y
11 ***Hendon***	?	?	?	?	?	?	?	?
NORTH DAKOTA								
AL Dorgan	Y	Y	Y	Y	N	Y	Y	Y
OHIO								
1 ***Gradison***	Y	Y	Y	N	N	Y	Y	Y
2 Luken	Y	Y	Y	Y	Y	Y	Y	Y
3 Hall	Y	?	Y	Y	Y	Y	Y	Y
4 ***Oxley***	Y	Y	Y	N	N	Y	Y	Y
5 ***Latta***	Y	Y	Y	Y	Y	Y	Y	Y
6 ***McEwen***	Y	Y	Y	Y	N	Y	Y	Y
7 ***Brown***	?	?	?	?	?	?	?	?
8 ***Kindness***	?	?	?	?	?	?	?	?
9 ***Weber***	Y	Y	Y	N	N	Y	Y	Y
10 ***Miller***	N	Y	Y	N	N	Y	Y	Y
11 ***Stanton***	Y	Y	Y	Y	N	Y	Y	Y
12 Shamansky	Y	Y	Y	Y	Y	Y	Y	Y
13 Pease	Y	Y	Y	Y	Y	Y	Y	Y
14 Seiberling	Y	Y	Y	Y	Y	Y	Y	Y
15 ***Wylie***	?	Y	Y	Y	N	Y	Y	Y
16 ***Regula***	Y	Y	Y	Y	N	Y	Y	Y
17 ***Ashbrook***	Y	Y	Y	?	?	?	?	?
18 Applegate	Y	Y	Y	Y	N	Y	Y	Y
19 ***Williams***	Y	Y	Y	Y	Y	Y	Y	Y
20 Oakar	Y	?	Y	Y	Y	Y	Y	N
21 Stokes	Y	Y	Y	Y	Y	Y	Y	Y
22 Eckart	?	?	?	?	?	?	?	?
23 Mottl	Y	Y	Y	Y	N	Y	Y	N
OKLAHOMA								
1 Jones	?	Y	Y	Y	Y	Y	Y	Y
2 Synar	Y	Y	Y	Y	Y	Y	Y	Y
3 Watkins	Y	Y	Y	Y	Y	Y	Y	Y
4 McCurdy	?	?	?	?	?	Y	Y	Y
5 ***Edwards***	N	Y	N	N	N	Y	Y	Y
6 English	Y	Y	Y	Y	Y	Y	Y	Y
OREGON								
1 AuCoin	Y	Y	Y	Y	Y	Y	Y	Y
2 ***Smith***	Y	Y	N	N	N	Y	Y	Y
3 Wyden	Y	Y	Y	Y	Y	Y	Y	Y
4 Weaver	Y	Y	Y	Y	Y	Y	Y	Y
PENNSYLVANIA								
1 Foglietta	?	?	?	?	?	?	?	?
2 Gray	?	Y	Y	Y	Y	Y	Y	N
3 Smith	Y	Y	Y	Y	Y	Y	Y	Y
4 ***Dougherty***	?	?	?	?	?	?	?	?
5 ***Schulze***	Y	Y	Y	N	N	Y	Y	Y
6 Yatron	Y	Y	Y	Y	Y	Y	Y	Y
7 Edgar	Y	Y	Y	Y	Y	Y	Y	Y
8 ***Coyne, J.***	Y	Y	Y	N	Y	Y	Y	Y
9 ***Shuster***	Y	Y	Y	N	N	Y	Y	Y
10 ***McDade***	+	+	+	+	-	+	+	+
11 ***Nelligan***	Y	Y	Y	Y	N	Y	Y	Y
12 Murtha	Y	?	?	?	?	?	?	?
13 ***Coughlin***	N	Y	Y	N	N	Y	Y	Y
14 Coyne, W.	Y	Y	Y	Y	Y	Y	Y	Y
15 ***Ritter***	Y	Y	Y	N	N	Y	Y	Y
16 ***Walker***	N	?	N	N	N	Y	Y	Y
17 Ertel	?	?	?	?	?	?	?	?
18 Walgren	Y	Y	Y	Y	N	Y	Y	Y
19 ***Goodling***	N	Y	Y	Y	N	Y	Y	Y
20 Gaydos	Y	Y	Y	Y	Y	Y	Y	Y
21 Bailey	Y	Y	Y	Y	Y	Y	Y	Y
22 Murphy	Y	Y	Y	Y	Y	Y	Y	Y
23 ***Clinger***	Y	Y	Y	N	Y	Y	Y	Y
24 ***Marks***	?	?	?	?	?	?	?	?
25 ***Atkinson***	?	?	Y	Y	Y	Y	Y	Y
RHODE ISLAND								
1 St Germain	Y	Y	Y	Y	N	Y	Y	Y
2 ***Schneider***	Y	Y	Y	Y	N	Y	Y	Y
SOUTH CAROLINA								
1 ***Hartnett***	Y	Y	Y	N	Y	Y	Y	N
2 ***Spence***	Y	Y	Y	N	Y	Y	Y	Y
3 Derrick	?	?	?	?	#	?	?	?
4 ***Campbell***	Y	Y	Y	N	Y	Y	Y	Y
5 Holland	Y	Y	Y	Y	Y	Y	Y	Y
6 ***Napier***	Y	Y	Y	Y	Y	Y	Y	Y
SOUTH DAKOTA								
1 Daschle	Y	Y	Y	Y	N	Y	Y	Y
2 ***Roberts***	Y	Y	N	N	N	Y	Y	Y
TENNESSEE								
1 ***Quillen***	Y	Y	Y	N	Y	Y	Y	Y
2 ***Duncan***	Y	Y	Y	N	Y	Y	Y	Y
3 Bouquard	Y	Y	Y	Y	Y	Y	Y	Y
4 Gore	Y	Y	Y	Y	Y	Y	Y	Y
5 Boner	Y	Y	Y	Y	N	Y	Y	Y
6 ***Beard***	Y	Y	Y	N	N	Y	Y	Y
7 Jones	Y	Y	Y	Y	Y	Y	Y	Y
8 Ford	Y	Y	Y	Y	Y	Y	Y	Y
TEXAS								
1 Hall, S.	Y	Y	Y	Y	N	Y	Y	Y
2 Wilson	Y	Y	Y	Y	Y	Y	Y	Y
3 ***Collins***	Y	Y	N	N	N	Y	Y	Y
4 Hall, R.	Y	Y	Y	Y	N	Y	Y	Y
5 Mattox	?	Y	Y	Y	Y	Y	Y	Y
6 Gramm	Y	Y	N	Y	N	Y	Y	Y
7 ***Archer***	Y	Y	N	N	N	Y	Y	Y
8 ***Fields***	Y	Y	N	N	N	Y	Y	Y
9 Brooks	Y	Y	Y	Y	Y	Y	Y	Y
10 Pickle	Y	Y	Y	Y	Y	Y	Y	Y
11 Leath	Y	Y	N	Y	Y	Y	Y	Y
12 Wright	Y	Y	Y	Y	Y	Y	Y	Y
13 Hightower	Y	Y	Y	Y	Y	Y	Y	Y
14 Patman	Y	Y	Y	Y	Y	Y	Y	Y
15 de la Garza	Y	Y	Y	Y	Y	Y	Y	Y
16 White	Y	Y	Y	Y	Y	Y	Y	N
17 Stenholm	Y	Y	N	Y	Y	Y	Y	Y
18 Leland	?	Y	Y	Y	Y	Y	Y	Y
19 Hance	Y	Y	N	Y	Y	Y	Y	Y
20 Gonzalez	Y	Y	Y	Y	Y	Y	Y	Y
21 ***Loeffler***	Y	Y	N	N	N	Y	Y	Y
22 ***Paul***	Y	Y	N	N	N	N	Y	N
23 Kazen	Y	Y	Y	Y	Y	Y	Y	Y
24 Frost	Y	Y	Y	Y	Y	Y	Y	Y
UTAH								
1 ***Hansen***	?	Y	?	N	N	Y	Y	Y
2 ***Marriott***	Y	Y	Y	N	N	Y	Y	Y
VERMONT								
AL ***Jeffords***	Y	Y	Y	N	N	Y	Y	Y
VIRGINIA								
1 ***Trible***	Y	Y	Y	?	N	Y	Y	Y
2 ***Whitehurst***	Y	Y	Y	N	N	Y	Y	Y
3 ***Bliley***	Y	Y	Y	N	N	Y	Y	Y
4 ***Daniel, R.***	Y	Y	Y	N	N	Y	Y	Y
5 Daniel, D.	Y	?	Y	Y	Y	Y	Y	N
6 ***Butler***	N	Y	Y	N	Y	Y	Y	Y
7 ***Robinson***	Y	Y	Y	N	N	Y	Y	Y
8 ***Parris***	Y	Y	Y	Y	N	Y	Y	Y
9 ***Wampler***	Y	Y	Y	Y	Y	Y	Y	Y
10 ***Wolf***	Y	Y	Y	Y	Y	Y	Y	Y
WASHINGTON								
1 ***Pritchard***	Y	Y	Y	Y	N	Y	Y	Y
2 Swift	?	Y	Y	Y	Y	Y	Y	Y
3 Bonker	Y	Y	Y	Y	Y	Y	Y	Y
4 ***Morrison***	Y	?	Y	Y	N	Y	Y	Y
5 Foley	Y	Y	Y	Y	Y	Y	Y	Y
6 Dicks	Y	Y	Y	Y	Y	Y	Y	N
7 Lowry	Y	Y	Y	Y	Y	Y	Y	N
WEST VIRGINIA								
1 Mollohan	Y	?	Y	Y	Y	Y	Y	Y
2 ***Benedict***	Y	Y	Y	Y	N	Y	Y	Y
3 ***Staton***	Y	Y	Y	N	Y	Y	Y	Y
4 Rahall	Y	Y	Y	Y	Y	Y	Y	Y
WISCONSIN								
1 Aspin	Y	Y	Y	Y	Y	Y	Y	Y
2 Kastenmeier	?	Y	Y	Y	Y	Y	Y	N
3 ***Gunderson***	Y	Y	Y	N	N	Y	Y	Y
4 Zablocki	Y	Y	Y	Y	Y	Y	Y	Y
5 Reuss	Y	Y	Y	Y	Y	Y	Y	Y
6 ***Petri***	Y	Y	Y	Y	N	N	Y	Y
7 Obey	Y	?	Y	Y	Y	N	Y	Y
8 ***Roth***	Y	Y	Y	Y	N	Y	Y	Y
9 ***Sensenbrenner***	Y	Y	Y	N	N	Y	Y	Y
WYOMING								
AL ***Cheney***	Y	Y	Y	N	N	Y	Y	Y

Southern states - Ala., Ark., Fla., Ga., Ky., La., Miss., N.C., Okla., S.C., Tenn., Texas, Va.

37. HR 5708. National Housing Act Extension. Gonzalez, D-Texas, motion to suspend the rules and pass the bill to extend through fiscal 1982 the Section 235 program of mortgage assistance for low-income home buyers. Motion agreed to 341-54: R 124-45; D 217-9 (ND 148-3, SD 69-6), March 23, 1982. A two-thirds majority of those present and voting (264 in this case) is required for passage under suspension of the rules.

38. S 2254. Federal Flexible and Compressed Work Schedules. Ferraro, D-N.Y., motion to suspend the rules and pass the bill to extend for four months flexible work schedules for federal employees. Motion agreed to (thus cleared for the president) 361-33: R 145-24; D 216-9 (ND 148-1, SD 68-8), March 23, 1982. A two-thirds majority of those present and voting (263 in this case) is required for passage under suspension of the rules.

39. Procedural Motion. Walker, R-Pa., motion to approve the House *Journal* of Tuesday, March 23. Motion agreed to 367-25: R 162-15; D 205-10 (ND 135-9, SD 70-1), March 24, 1982.

40. H J Res 409. Continuing Appropriations, Fiscal 1982. Passage of the joint resolution to provide funding through Sept. 30, 1982, for government agencies whose regular fiscal 1982 appropriations bills had not been enacted. Passed 299-103: R 118-57; D 181-46 (ND 125-29, SD 56-17), March 24, 1982.

	37	38	39	40
ALABAMA				
1 *Edwards*	Y	Y	Y	Y
2 *Dickinson*	Y	Y	N	Y
3 Nichols	Y	Y	?	Y
4 Bevill	Y	Y	Y	Y
5 Flippo	Y	Y	Y	Y
6 *Smith*	Y	Y	Y	N
7 Shelby	Y	Y	Y	N
ALASKA				
AL *Young*	Y	Y	N	Y
ARIZONA				
1 *Rhodes*	?	?	?	?
2 Udall	Y	Y	Y	Y
3 Stump	N	N	N	N
4 *Rudd*	N	N	Y	Y
ARKANSAS				
1 Alexander	Y	Y	Y	Y
2 *Bethune*	Y	Y	Y	Y
3 *Hammerschmidt*	Y	Y	Y	Y
4 Anthony	Y	Y	Y	Y
CALIFORNIA				
1 *Chappie*	Y	Y	Y	N
2 *Clausen*	Y	Y	Y	Y
3 Matsui	Y	Y	Y	Y
4 Fazio	Y	Y	Y	Y
5 Burton, J.	?	?	?	?
6 Burton, P.	Y	Y	Y	N
7 Miller	Y	Y	Y	Y
8 Dellums	Y	Y	Y	N
9 Stark	Y	Y	?	Y
10 Edwards	Y	Y	Y	N
11 Lantos	Y	Y	Y	?
12 *McCloskey*	?	?	Y	Y
13 Mineta	Y	Y	Y	Y
14 *Shumway*	N	Y	N	N
15 Coelho	Y	Y	Y	Y
16 Panetta	Y	Y	Y	Y
17 *Pashayan*	?	?	?	?
18 *Thomas*	N	Y	Y	N
19 *Lagomarsino*	Y	Y	Y	N
20 *Goldwater*	Y	Y	?	?
21 *Fiedler*	Y	Y	Y	N
22 *Moorhead*	N	Y	Y	N
23 Beilenson	Y	Y	Y	Y
24 Waxman	Y	Y	Y	Y
25 Roybal	Y	Y	Y	Y
26 *Rousselot*	N	Y	N	N
27 *Dornan*	?	?	Y	Y
28 Dixon	Y	Y	Y	Y
29 Hawkins	Y	Y	N	Y
30 Vacancy				
31 Dymally	Y	Y	Y	Y
32 Anderson	Y	Y	Y	Y
33 *Grisham*	Y	Y	Y	N
34 *Lungren*	N	Y	Y	N
35 *Dreier*	N	Y	N	N
36 Brown	Y	Y	Y	Y
37 *Lewis*	N	Y	Y	N
38 Patterson	Y	Y	Y	Y
39 *Dannemeyer*	N	Y	Y	N
40 *Badham*	?	?	?	N
41 *Lowery*	Y	Y	Y	N
42 *Hunter*	Y	Y	Y	Y
43 *Burgener*	N	Y	Y	Y
COLORADO				
1 Schroeder	Y	Y	N	N
2 Wirth	Y	Y	Y	Y
3 Kogovsek	Y	Y	Y	Y
4 *Brown*	Y	Y	N	N

	37	38	39	40
5 *Kramer*	Y	Y	Y	N
CONNECTICUT				
1 Kennelly	Y	Y	Y	Y
2 Gejdenson	?	?	N	Y
3 *DeNardis*	Y	Y	Y	Y
4 *McKinney*	Y	Y	?	?
5 Ratchford	Y	Y	Y	Y
6 Moffett	Y	Y	Y	Y
DELAWARE				
AL *Evans*	Y	Y	Y	Y
FLORIDA				
1 Hutto	Y	Y	Y	Y
2 Fuqua	Y	Y	Y	Y
3 Bennett	Y	Y	Y	Y
4 Chappell	Y	N	Y	Y
5 *McCollum*	?	?	Y	N
6 *Young*	Y	Y	Y	Y
7 Gibbons	Y	N	Y	Y
8 Ireland	Y	Y	Y	Y
9 Nelson	Y	Y	Y	N
10 *Bafalis*	Y	Y	?	?
11 Mica	Y	Y	Y	Y
12 *Shaw*	Y	Y	Y	Y
13 Lehman	Y	Y	Y	?
14 Pepper	Y	Y	Y	Y
15 Fascell	Y	Y	Y	Y
GEORGIA				
1 Ginn	Y	Y	?	?
2 Hatcher	Y	Y	Y	Y
3 Brinkley	Y	Y	Y	Y
4 Levitas	Y	Y	Y	Y
5 Fowler	Y	Y	?	Y
6 *Gingrich*	Y	Y	Y	N
7 McDonald	N	Y	Y	N
8 Evans	Y	Y	Y	N
9 Jenkins	Y	Y	Y	N
10 Barnard	Y	Y	Y	Y
HAWAII				
1 Heftel	Y	Y	Y	N
2 Akaka	Y	Y	Y	Y
IDAHO				
1 *Craig*	N	Y	Y	N
2 *Hansen*	N	Y	?	N
ILLINOIS				
1 Washington	Y	Y	Y	N
2 Savage	Y	Y	?	N
3 Russo	?	?	?	X
4 *Derwinski*	N	Y	Y	N
5 Fary	Y	Y	Y	Y
6 *Hyde*	N	Y	Y	N
7 Collins	Y	Y	Y	N
8 Rostenkowski	?	?	?	?
9 Yates	Y	Y	Y	Y
10 *Porter*	Y	Y	Y	N
11 Annunzio	Y	Y	Y	Y
12 *Crane, P.*	N	Y	Y	X
13 *McClory*	N	Y	Y	N
14 *Erlenborn*	N	Y	Y	N
15 *Corcoran*	N	Y	Y	Y
16 *Martin*	N	Y	Y	N
17 O'Brien	Y	Y	?	?
18 *Michel*	N	Y	Y	N
19 *Railsback*	Y	Y	Y	Y
20 *Findley*	Y	Y	Y	Y
21 *Madigan*	Y	Y	Y	Y
22 *Crane, D.*	N	N	Y	N
23 Price	Y	Y	Y	Y
24 Simon	Y	Y	Y	Y
INDIANA				
1 Benjamin	Y	Y	Y	Y
2 Fithian	Y	Y	Y	N
3 *Hiler*	Y	Y	Y	N
4 *Coats*	Y	Y	Y	N
5 *Hillis*	N	N	Y	Y
6 Evans	?	?	Y	Y
7 *Myers*	N	N	Y	?
8 *Deckard*	Y	Y	Y	Y
9 Hamilton	Y	Y	Y	N
10 Sharp	Y	Y	Y	Y
11 Jacobs	Y	Y	N	Y
IOWA				
1 *Leach*	Y	Y	Y	Y
2 *Tauke*	Y	Y	Y	Y
3 *Evans*	Y	Y	N	Y
4 Smith	Y	Y	Y	Y
5 Harkin	Y	Y	N	Y
6 Bedell	Y	Y	?	+

ND - Northern Democrats   SD - Southern Democrats

	37	38	39	40
KANSAS				
1 *Roberts*	Y	Y	Y	N
2 *Jeffries*	N	Y	Y	Y
3 *Winn*	Y	Y	Y	Y
4 Glickman	Y	Y	Y	Y
5 *Whittaker*	Y	Y	Y	Y
KENTUCKY				
1 Hubbard	Y	N	N	Y
2 Natcher	Y	Y	Y	Y
3 Mazzoli	Y	Y	Y	Y
4 *Snyder*	N	N	Y	N
5 *Rogers*	Y	N	Y	Y
6 *Hopkins*	Y	N	Y	Y
7 Perkins	Y	Y	Y	Y
LOUISIANA				
1 *Livingston*	Y	Y	Y	Y
2 Boggs	?	?	?	?
3 Tauzin	Y	Y	Y	Y
4 Roemer	N	N	N	N
5 Huckaby	Y	Y	Y	Y
6 *Moore*	Y	Y	Y	Y
7 Breaux	Y	Y	?	?
8 Long	Y	Y	Y	Y
MAINE				
1 *Emery*	?	?	Y	Y
2 *Snowe*	Y	Y	Y	Y
MARYLAND				
1 Dyson	Y	Y	Y	N
2 Long	?	Y	Y	Y
3 Mikulski	Y	Y	Y	Y
4 *Holt*	Y	Y	N	Y
5 Hoyer	Y	?	Y	N
6 Byron	Y	Y	Y	Y
7 Mitchell	Y	Y	N	Y
8 Barnes	Y	Y	N	N
MASSACHUSETTS				
1 *Conte*	Y	Y	Y	Y
2 Boland	Y	Y	?	?
3 Early	Y	?	Y	Y
4 Frank	Y	Y	Y	N
5 Shannon	Y	Y	Y	Y
6 Mavroules	Y	Y	Y	Y
7 Markey	Y	Y	Y	Y
8 O'Neill				
9 *Moakley*	?	?	Y	Y
10 *Heckler*	Y	Y	Y	Y
11 Donnelly	Y	Y	Y	Y
12 Studds	Y	Y	Y	Y
MICHIGAN				
1 Conyers	Y	Y	Y	N
2 *Pursell*	?	?	Y	N
3 Wolpe	Y	Y	Y	Y
4 *Siljander*	Y	Y	Y	N
5 *Sawyer*	Y	Y	Y	Y
6 *Dunn*	Y	Y	Y	Y
7 Kildee	Y	Y	Y	N
8 Traxler	Y	Y	Y	Y
9 *Vander Jagt*	Y	Y	Y	Y
10 Albosta	Y	Y	Y	N
11 *Davis*	Y	Y	Y	N
12 Bonior	Y	Y	Y	Y
13 Crockett	Y	Y	?	Y
14 Hertel	Y	Y	Y	N
15 Ford	Y	Y	Y	Y
16 Dingell	Y	Y	Y	Y
17 Brodhead	Y	Y	Y	Y
18 Blanchard	Y	Y	Y	Y
19 *Broomfield*	Y	Y	Y	N
MINNESOTA				
1 *Erdahl*	Y	Y	Y	Y
2 *Hagedorn*	Y	Y	Y	Y
3 *Frenzel*	?	+	Y	Y
4 Vento	Y	Y	Y	Y
5 Sabo	Y	Y	Y	Y
6 *Weber*	Y	Y	N	N
7 *Stangeland*	N	Y	Y	Y
8 Oberstar	Y	Y	Y	Y
MISSISSIPPI				
1 Whitten	Y	Y	Y	Y
2 Bowen	Y	Y	Y	Y
3 Montgomery	N	N	Y	N
4 Dowdy	Y	Y	Y	Y
5 *Lott*	Y	Y	Y	Y
MISSOURI				
1 Clay	Y	Y	N	Y
2 Young	Y	Y	Y	Y
3 Gephardt	Y	Y	Y	Y

	37	38	39	40
4 Skelton	Y	Y	Y	N
5 Bolling	Y	Y	?	Y
6 Coleman	Y	Y	Y	Y
7 Taylor	N	Y	Y	Y
8 Bailey	?	?	Y	Y
9 Volkmer	Y	Y	Y	N
10 *Emerson*	Y	Y	N	N
MONTANA				
1 Williams	Y	Y	Y	Y
2 *Marlenee*	Y	Y	Y	N
NEBRASKA				
1 *Bereuter*	Y	Y	Y	Y
2 *Daub*	Y	Y	Y	Y
3 *Smith*	Y	Y	Y	Y
NEVADA				
AL Santini	Y	Y	Y	N
NEW HAMPSHIRE				
1 D'Amours	Y	Y	Y	Y
2 *Gregg*	N	N	Y	N
NEW JERSEY				
1 Florio	Y	Y	Y	Y
2 Hughes	Y	Y	Y	N
3 Howard	Y	Y	Y	Y
4 *Smith*	Y	Y	Y	Y
5 Fenwick	Y	Y	Y	Y
6 Forsythe	Y	N	N	N
7 Roukema	+	+	Y	Y
8 Roe	Y	Y	Y	Y
9 *Hollenbeck*	Y	Y	Y	N
10 Rodino	Y	Y	Y	Y
11 Minish	Y	Y	Y	Y
12 *Rinaldo*	Y	Y	Y	Y
13 *Courter*	Y	Y	Y	Y
14 Guarini	Y	Y	Y	Y
15 Dwyer	Y	Y	Y	Y
NEW MEXICO				
1 *Lujan*	Y	Y	Y	Y
2 *Skeen*	Y	Y	Y	Y
NEW YORK				
1 *Carney*	Y	Y	Y	Y
2 Downey	Y	Y	Y	Y
3 *Carman*	N	Y	Y	?
4 *Lent*	+	+	Y	Y
5 McGrath	Y	Y	Y	Y
6 *LeBoutillier*	?	?	?	?
7 Addabbo	Y	Y	Y	Y
8 Rosenthal	Y	Y	Y	Y
9 Ferraro	Y	Y	Y	Y
10 Biaggi	Y	Y	Y	Y
11 Scheuer	Y	Y	Y	Y
12 Chisholm	Y	Y	Y	?
13 Solarz	Y	Y	Y	Y
14 Richmond	Y	Y	?	Y
15 Zeferetti	Y	Y	Y	Y
16 Schumer	Y	Y	Y	Y
17 *Molinari*	?	?	Y	Y
18 *Green*	?	?	Y	N
19 Rangel	N	?	Y	Y
20 Weiss	Y	Y	Y	N
21 Garcia	Y	Y	Y	Y
22 Bingham	Y	Y	Y	Y
23 Peyser	Y	Y	Y	Y
24 Ottinger	Y	Y	P	Y
25 *Fish*	Y	Y	Y	Y
26 *Gilman*	Y	Y	Y	Y
27 McHugh	Y	Y	Y	Y
28 Stratton	Y	Y	Y	Y
29 *Solomon*	Y	Y	Y	N
30 *Martin*	Y	Y	Y	Y
31 *Mitchell*	Y	Y	Y	Y
32 *Wortley*	Y	Y	Y	Y
33 *Lee*	Y	Y	Y	Y
34 *Horton*	Y	Y	Y	N
35 *Conable*	Y	Y	Y	Y
36 LaFalce	Y	Y	Y	Y
37 Nowak	Y	Y	Y	Y
38 *Kemp*	Y	Y	Y	Y
39 Lundine	Y	Y	Y	Y
NORTH CAROLINA				
1 Jones	Y	Y	Y	Y
2 Fountain	Y	Y	Y	Y
3 Whitley	Y	Y	Y	Y
4 Andrews	Y	Y	Y	Y
5 Neal	?	?	?	#
6 *Johnston*	N	N	N	N
7 Rose	Y	Y	Y	Y
8 Hefner	Y	Y	Y	Y

	37	38	39	40
9 *Martin*	Y	Y	Y	N
10 *Broyhill*	N	N	Y	Y
11 *Hendon*	?	?	?	?
NORTH DAKOTA				
AL Dorgan	Y	Y	Y	Y
OHIO				
1 *Gradison*	Y	Y	Y	Y
2 Luken	Y	Y	Y	Y
3 Hall	Y	Y	Y	Y
4 *Oxley*	N	Y	Y	Y
5 *Latta*	N	N	Y	N
6 *McEwen*	N	Y	Y	Y
7 *Brown*	?	?	?	?
8 *Kindness*	?	?	Y	Y
9 *Weber*	Y	Y	Y	Y
10 *Miller*	N	N	N	Y
11 *Stanton*	Y	Y	?	?
12 Shamansky	Y	Y	Y	Y
13 Pease	Y	Y	Y	?
14 Seiberling	Y	Y	Y	Y
15 *Wylie*	Y	Y	Y	N
16 *Regula*	Y	Y	Y	Y
17 *Ashbrook*	?	?	Y	N
18 Applegate	Y	Y	?	N
19 *Williams*	Y	Y	Y	Y
20 Oakar	Y	Y	Y	Y
21 Stokes	Y	Y	Y	Y
22 Eckart	?	?	Y	N
23 Mottl	N	Y	Y	N
OKLAHOMA				
1 Jones	Y	Y	Y	Y
2 Synar	Y	Y	Y	Y
3 Watkins	Y	Y	Y	Y
4 McCurdy	Y	Y	Y	N
5 *Edwards*	N	Y	Y	N
6 English	Y	N	Y	N
OREGON				
1 AuCoin	Y	Y	?	N
2 *Smith*	N	N	Y	N
3 Wyden	Y	Y	Y	N
4 Weaver	Y	Y	Y	N
PENNSYLVANIA				
1 Foglietta	?	?	?	?
2 Gray	Y	Y	Y	Y
3 Smith	Y	Y	Y	Y
4 *Dougherty*	?	?	Y	Y
5 *Schulze*	?	?	?	#
6 Yatron	Y	Y	Y	Y
7 Edgar	Y	Y	Y	?
8 *Coyne, J.*	Y	N	Y	Y
9 *Shuster*	N	Y	N	N
10 McDade	+	+	+	+
11 *Nelligan*	Y	Y	Y	Y
12 Murtha	?	?	Y	Y
13 *Coughlin*	Y	N	Y	Y
14 Coyne, W.	Y	Y	Y	Y
15 *Ritter*	Y	Y	Y	Y
16 *Walker*	N	N	N	N
17 Ertel	?	?	Y	Y
18 Walgren	Y	Y	Y	Y
19 *Goodling*	Y	Y	N	Y
20 Gaydos	Y	Y	?	Y
21 Bailey	Y	Y	Y	Y
22 Murphy	Y	Y	Y	Y
23 *Clinger*	Y	Y	Y	Y
24 *Marks*	?	?	Y	?
25 Atkinson	Y	Y	Y	Y
RHODE ISLAND				
1 St Germain	Y	Y	Y	Y
2 *Schneider*	Y	Y	Y	Y
SOUTH CAROLINA				
1 *Hartnett*	Y	N	Y	Y
2 *Spence*	Y	Y	Y	Y
3 Derrick	?	?	Y	Y
4 *Campbell*	Y	Y	Y	Y
5 Holland	Y	Y	Y	Y
6 *Napier*	Y	Y	Y	Y
SOUTH DAKOTA				
1 Daschle	Y	Y	Y	Y
2 *Roberts*	Y	Y	Y	N
TENNESSEE				
1 *Quillen*	Y	Y	Y	Y
2 *Duncan*	Y	Y	Y	Y
3 Bouquard	Y	Y	Y	Y
4 Gore	Y	Y	Y	Y
5 Boner	Y	Y	Y	Y
6 Beard	Y	Y	Y	Y

	37	38	39	40
7 Jones	Y	Y	Y	Y
8 Ford	Y	Y	Y	Y
TEXAS				
1 Hall, S.	Y	N	Y	N
2 Wilson	Y	Y	Y	Y
3 *Collins*	N	N	Y	N
4 Hall, R.	?	Y	Y	N
5 Mattox	Y	Y	Y	Y
6 *Gramm*	N	Y	Y	N
7 *Archer*	N	Y	Y	N
8 *Fields*	N	N	Y	N
9 Brooks	Y	Y	?	?
10 Pickle	Y	Y	Y	Y
11 Leath	N	N	Y	Y
12 Wright	Y	Y	Y	Y
13 Hightower	Y	Y	Y	Y
14 Patman	Y	Y	Y	N
15 de la Garza	Y	Y	Y	Y
16 White	Y	Y	Y	Y
17 Stenholm	N	Y	Y	N
18 Leland	Y	Y	?	N
19 Hance	Y	Y	Y	Y
20 Gonzalez	Y	Y	Y	Y
21 *Loeffler*	Y	Y	Y	Y
22 *Paul*	N	N	Y	N
23 Kazen	Y	Y	Y	Y
24 Frost	Y	Y	Y	Y
UTAH				
1 *Hansen*	N	Y	Y	N
2 *Marriott*	Y	Y	Y	Y
VERMONT				
AL *Jeffords*	Y	Y	Y	Y
VIRGINIA				
1 *Trible*	Y	Y	Y	Y
2 *Whitehurst*	Y	Y	Y	Y
3 *Bliley*	Y	Y	Y	Y
4 *Daniel, R.*	Y	Y	Y	Y
5 Daniel, D.	Y	Y	Y	Y
6 *Butler*	Y	Y	N	Y
7 *Robinson*	Y	Y	Y	Y
8 *Parris*	Y	Y	Y	Y
9 *Wampler*	Y	Y	?	?
10 *Wolf*	Y	Y	Y	Y
WASHINGTON				
1 *Pritchard*	Y	Y	Y	Y
2 Swift	Y	Y	Y	Y
3 Bonker	Y	Y	Y	Y
4 *Morrison*	Y	Y	Y	Y
5 Foley	Y	Y	Y	Y
6 Dicks	Y	Y	Y	Y
7 Lowry	Y	Y	Y	Y
WEST VIRGINIA				
1 Mollohan	Y	Y	Y	Y
2 *Benedict*	Y	Y	Y	Y
3 Staton	Y	N	Y	Y
4 Rahall	Y	Y	Y	Y
WISCONSIN				
1 Aspin	Y	Y	Y	Y
2 Kastenmeier	Y	Y	Y	Y
3 *Gunderson*	Y	Y	Y	Y
4 Zablocki	Y	Y	Y	Y
5 Reuss	Y	Y	Y	Y
6 *Petri*	Y	Y	Y	Y
7 Obey	Y	Y	?	Y
8 Roth	Y	N	Y	Y
9 Sensenbrenner	Y	N	Y	Y
WYOMING				
AL *Cheney*	N	Y	Y	Y

Southern states - Ala., Ark., Fla., Ga., Ky., La., Miss., N.C., Okla., S.C., Tenn., Texas, Va.

41. Procedural Motion. Edwards, D-Calif., motion to approve the House *Journal* of Monday, March 29. Motion agreed to 332-22: R 152-11; D 180-11 (ND 123-10, SD 57-1), March 30, 1982.

42. H Res 413. House Chaplain. Adoption of the resolution to state the House's belief that its establishment of a chaplaincy is an appropriate and constitutional exercise of its powers, to express its concern over the March 9 decision of a three-judge panel of the U.S. Appeals Court for the District of Columbia in the case of *Jon Garth Murray et al v. Angela Marie Buchanan et al*, and to instruct counsel for the House and its chaplain to petition the full appeals court for an *en banc* hearing in order to seek dismissal of that case. Adopted 388-0: R 172-0; D 216-0 (ND 151-0, SD 65-0), March 30, 1982.

43. H J Res 410. Dutch-American Friendship Day. Passage of the joint resolution to designate April 19, 1982, as Dutch-American Friendship Day. Passed 379-1: R 172-0; D 207-1 (ND 142-1, SD 65-0), March 30, 1982.

44. H J Res 447. National Day of Reflection. Passage of the joint resolution to authorize and request the president to issue a proclamation designating April 4, 1982, as the National Day of Reflection. Passed 387-3: R 174-1; D 213-2 (ND 147-2, SD 66-0), March 30, 1982.

45. Procedural Motion. Walker, R-Pa., motion to approve the House *Journal* of Tuesday, March 30. Motion agreed to 377-24: R 162-14; D 215-10 (ND 140-8, SD 75-2), March 31, 1982.

46. H Res 378. House Committee Funds. House Administration Committee substitute amendment to authorize expenditures from the House contingent fund for calendar year 1982 of a total of $39,605,273 for investigations and studies to be conducted by the 23 House committees other than the Budget and Appropriations committees and for computer services. Adopted 416-0: R 181-0; D 235-0 (ND 159-0, SD 76-0), March 31, 1982.

47. H Res 378. House Committee Funds. Beard, R-Tenn., motion to recommit the resolution to the House Administration Committee without instructions. Motion rejected 148-270: R 132-49; D 16-221 (ND 6-154, SD 10-67), March 31, 1982.

48. H Res 378. House Committee Funds. Adoption of the resolution to authorize expenditures from the House contingent fund for calendar year 1982 of a total of $39,605,273 for investigations and studies to be conducted by the 23 House committees other than the Budget and Appropriations committees and for computer services. Adopted 282-132: R 62-116; D 220-16 (ND 152-7, SD 68-9), March 31, 1982.

KEY

- Y Voted for (yea).
- # Paired for.
- + Announced for.
- N Voted against (nay).
- X Paired against.
- − Announced against.
- P Voted "present".
- C Voted "present" to avoid possible conflict of interest.
- ? Did not vote or otherwise make a position known.

Democrats   *Republicans*

	41	42	43	44	45	46	47	48
ALABAMA								
1 Edwards	Y	Y	Y	Y	Y	Y	N	Y
2 Dickinson	Y	Y	Y	Y	N	Y	N	Y
3 Nichols	Y	Y	Y	Y	Y	Y	N	Y
4 Bevill	Y	Y	Y	Y	Y	Y	N	Y
5 Flippo	?	?	?	?	Y	Y	N	Y
6 Smith	Y	Y	Y	Y	Y	Y	Y	N
7 Shelby	Y	Y	Y	Y	Y	Y	N	Y
ALASKA								
AL Young	N	Y	Y	Y	Y	Y	N	Y
ARIZONA								
1 Rhodes	Y	Y	Y	Y	Y	Y	N	Y
2 Udall	Y	Y	Y	Y	Y	Y	N	Y
3 Stump	Y	Y	Y	Y	Y	Y	Y	N
4 Rudd	Y	Y	Y	Y	Y	Y	Y	Y
ARKANSAS								
1 Alexander	Y	Y	Y	Y	Y	Y	N	Y
2 Bethune	Y	Y	Y	Y	?	Y	N	Y
3 Hammerschmidt	Y	Y	?	Y	Y	Y	N	Y
4 Anthony	Y	Y	Y	Y	Y	Y	N	N
CALIFORNIA								
1 Chappie	Y	Y	Y	Y	Y	Y	N	N
2 Clausen	Y	Y	Y	Y	Y	Y	N	Y
3 Matsui	Y	Y	Y	Y	Y	Y	N	Y
4 Fazio	Y	Y	Y	Y	Y	Y	N	Y
5 Burton, J.	?	?	?	?	?	?	X	#
6 Burton, P.	?	?	?	?	Y	Y	N	Y
7 Miller	Y	Y	Y	Y	Y	Y	N	Y
8 Dellums	?	Y	Y	Y	?	Y	N	Y
9 Stark	Y	Y	Y	Y	Y	Y	N	Y
10 Edwards	Y	Y	Y	Y	Y	Y	N	Y
11 Lantos	Y	Y	Y	Y	Y	Y	N	Y
12 McCloskey	?	Y	Y	Y	?	?	?	?
13 Mineta	Y	Y	Y	Y	Y	Y	N	Y
14 Shumway	Y	Y	Y	N	Y	Y	Y	N
15 Coelho	Y	Y	Y	Y	Y	Y	N	Y
16 Panetta	Y	Y	Y	Y	Y	Y	N	Y
17 Pashayan	Y	Y	Y	Y	Y	Y	Y	N
18 Thomas	Y	Y	Y	Y	Y	Y	N	Y
19 Lagomarsino	Y	Y	Y	Y	Y	Y	N	Y
20 Goldwater	?	?	?	?	?	?	?	?
21 Fiedler	Y	Y	Y	Y	Y	Y	N	Y
22 Moorhead	Y	Y	Y	Y	Y	Y	N	Y
23 Beilenson	Y	Y	Y	Y	Y	Y	N	Y
24 Waxman	Y	Y	?	Y	Y	Y	N	Y
25 Roybal	Y	Y	Y	Y	Y	Y	N	Y
26 Rousselot	?	?	Y	N	Y	Y	N	Y
27 Dornan	Y	Y	Y	Y	Y	?	?	X
28 Dixon	Y	Y	?	Y	Y	Y	N	Y
29 Hawkins	Y	Y	?	Y	Y	Y	N	Y
30 Vacancy								
31 Dymally	Y	Y	Y	Y	Y	Y	N	Y
32 Anderson	Y	Y	Y	Y	Y	Y	N	Y
33 Grisham	Y	Y	Y	Y	Y	Y	Y	N
34 Lungren	Y	Y	Y	Y	Y	Y	Y	N
35 Dreier	Y	Y	Y	Y	Y	Y	Y	N
36 Brown	?	Y	Y	Y	?	Y	N	Y
37 Lewis	Y	Y	Y	Y	Y	Y	Y	Y
38 Patterson	Y	Y	Y	Y	Y	Y	N	Y
39 Dannemeyer	Y	Y	Y	Y	Y	Y	N	Y
40 Badham	?	?	?	?	?	?	?	#
41 Lowery	?	?	?	?	Y	Y	N	Y
42 Hunter	Y	Y	Y	Y	Y	Y	N	Y
43 Burgener	?	?	?	?	?	?	?	?
COLORADO								
1 Schroeder	N	Y	Y	Y	N	Y	N	N
2 Wirth	Y	Y	Y	Y	Y	Y	N	Y
3 Kogovsek	Y	Y	?	Y	Y	Y	N	Y
4 Brown	Y	Y	Y	N	Y	N	Y	N

	41	42	43	44	45	46	47	48
5 Kramer	Y	Y	Y	Y	Y	Y	Y	N
CONNECTICUT								
1 Kennelly	Y	Y	Y	Y	Y	Y	N	Y
2 Gejdenson	N	Y	Y	Y	Y	Y	N	Y
3 DeNardis	Y	Y	Y	Y	Y	Y	N	N
4 McKinney	Y	?	Y	Y	Y	Y	N	Y
5 Ratchford	Y	Y	Y	Y	Y	Y	N	Y
6 Moffett	?	Y	Y	Y	?	Y	N	Y
DELAWARE								
AL Evans	Y	Y	Y	Y	Y	Y	Y	N
FLORIDA								
1 Hutto	Y	Y	Y	Y	Y	Y	N	Y
2 Fuqua	?	?	?	?	Y	Y	N	Y
3 Bennett	Y	Y	Y	Y	Y	Y	N	Y
4 Chappell	Y	Y	Y	Y	Y	Y	N	Y
5 McCollum	Y	Y	Y	Y	Y	Y	Y	N
6 Young	Y	Y	Y	Y	Y	N	Y	N
7 Gibbons	Y	Y	Y	Y	Y	Y	N	Y
8 Ireland	Y	Y	Y	?	Y	Y	N	Y
9 Nelson	+	+	+	Y	Y	N	Y	
10 Bafalis	Y	Y	Y	Y	Y	N	N	N
11 Mica	Y	Y	Y	Y	Y	Y	N	Y
12 Shaw	Y	Y	Y	Y	Y	Y	N	N
13 Lehman	?	Y	Y	Y	Y	Y	N	Y
14 Pepper	+	Y	Y	Y	Y	Y	N	Y
15 Fascell	Y	Y	Y	Y	Y	Y	N	Y
GEORGIA								
1 Ginn	?	?	?	?	Y	Y	N	Y
2 Hatcher	Y	Y	Y	Y	Y	Y	N	Y
3 Brinkley	Y	Y	Y	Y	Y	Y	N	Y
4 Levitas	Y	Y	Y	Y	Y	Y	N	Y
5 Fowler	Y	Y	Y	Y	Y	Y	N	Y
6 Gingrich	Y	Y	Y	Y	Y	Y	N	Y
7 McDonald	Y	Y	Y	Y	Y	N	Y	N
8 Evans	Y	Y	Y	Y	Y	Y	N	Y
9 Jenkins	?	?	?	?	Y	Y	N	Y
10 Barnard	Y	Y	Y	Y	Y	Y	N	Y
HAWAII								
1 Heftel	Y	Y	Y	Y	Y	Y	N	Y
2 Akaka	Y	Y	Y	Y	Y	Y	N	Y
IDAHO								
1 Craig	Y	Y	Y	Y	Y	Y	Y	N
2 Hansen	Y	Y	Y	Y	Y	Y	Y	N
ILLINOIS								
1 Washington	Y	Y	Y	Y	Y	Y	N	Y
2 Savage	?	Y	Y	Y	?	Y	N	Y
3 Russo	Y	Y	?	Y	Y	Y	N	Y
4 Derwinski	?	Y	Y	Y	Y	Y	N	Y
5 Fary	Y	Y	Y	Y	Y	Y	N	Y
6 Hyde	Y	Y	Y	Y	Y	Y	N	Y
7 Collins	Y	Y	Y	Y	Y	Y	N	Y
8 Rostenkowski	Y	Y	Y	Y	Y	Y	N	Y
9 Yates	Y	Y	Y	N	Y	N	Y	
10 Porter	Y	Y	Y	Y	Y	Y	N	Y
11 Annunzio	?	?	?	?	Y	Y	N	Y
12 Crane, P.	?	?	?	?	?	?	?	X
13 McClory	Y	Y	Y	Y	Y	Y	N	Y
14 Erlenborn	Y	Y	Y	Y	Y	Y	N	Y
15 Corcoran	Y	Y	Y	Y	Y	Y	N	Y
16 Martin	Y	Y	Y	Y	Y	Y	N	Y
17 O'Brien	Y	Y	Y	Y	Y	Y	N	Y
18 Michel	Y	Y	Y	Y	Y	Y	N	Y
19 Railsback	Y	Y	?	?	?	Y	N	Y
20 Findley	Y	Y	Y	Y	Y	Y	N	Y
21 Madigan	?	Y	Y	Y	Y	Y	N	Y
22 Crane, D.	Y	Y	Y	Y	Y	Y	N	Y
23 Price	Y	Y	Y	Y	Y	Y	N	Y
24 Simon	Y	Y	Y	Y	Y	Y	N	Y
INDIANA								
1 Benjamin	Y	Y	Y	Y	Y	Y	N	Y
2 Fithian	Y	Y	Y	Y	Y	Y	N	Y
3 Hiler	?	Y	Y	Y	Y	Y	N	Y
4 Coats	Y	Y	Y	Y	Y	Y	N	Y
5 Hillis	Y	Y	Y	Y	Y	Y	Y	Y
6 Evans	?	?	?	?	Y	Y	N	Y
7 Myers	Y	Y	Y	Y	Y	Y	N	Y
8 Deckard	Y	Y	Y	Y	Y	Y	N	Y
9 Hamilton	Y	Y	Y	Y	Y	Y	N	Y
10 Sharp	N	Y	Y	Y	Y	Y	N	Y
11 Jacobs	N	Y	Y	N	Y	N	N	N
IOWA								
1 Leach	Y	Y	Y	Y	Y	Y	Y	N
2 Tauke	Y	Y	Y	Y	Y	Y	Y	N
3 Evans	N	Y	Y	Y	N	Y	N	Y
4 Smith	Y	Y	Y	Y	Y	Y	N	Y
5 Harkin	N	Y	Y	N	Y	N	Y	
6 Bedell	Y	Y	Y	Y	Y	Y	N	Y

ND - Northern Democrats   SD - Southern Democrats

Corresponding to Congressional Record Votes 42, 43, 44, 45, 46, 47, 48, 49

	41	42	43	44	45	46	47	48
KANSAS								
1 *Roberts*	Y	Y	Y	Y	?	Y	Y	N
2 *Jeffries*	Y	Y	Y	Y	Y	Y	Y	N
3 *Winn*	Y	Y	Y	Y	Y	Y	Y	N
4 Glickman	Y	Y	Y	Y	Y	Y	N	Y
5 *Whittaker*	Y	Y	Y	Y	Y	Y	Y	N
KENTUCKY								
1 Hubbard	Y	Y	Y	Y	Y	Y	N	N
2 Natcher	Y	Y	Y	Y	Y	Y	N	Y
3 Mazzoli	Y	Y	Y	Y	Y	Y	N	Y
4 *Snyder*	Y	Y	Y	Y	Y	Y	N	Y
5 *Rogers*	Y	Y	Y	Y	Y	Y	Y	N
6 *Hopkins*	Y	Y	Y	Y	Y	Y	Y	N
7 Perkins	Y	Y	Y	Y	Y	Y	N	Y
LOUISIANA								
1 *Livingston*	?	?	?	?	Y	Y	Y	Y
2 Boggs	Y	Y	Y	Y	Y	Y	N	Y
3 Tauzin	Y	Y	Y	Y	Y	Y	Y	Y
4 Roemer	N	Y	Y	Y	N	Y	Y	N
5 Huckaby	Y	Y	Y	Y	Y	Y	N	Y
6 *Moore*	Y	Y	Y	Y	Y	Y	Y	N
7 Breaux	Y	Y	Y	Y	Y	?	?	?
8 Long	Y	Y	Y	Y	Y	Y	N	Y
MAINE								
1 *Emery*	Y	Y	Y	Y	Y	Y	Y	N
2 *Snowe*	Y	Y	Y	Y	Y	Y	Y	N
MARYLAND								
1 Dyson	Y	Y	Y	Y	Y	Y	N	Y
2 Long	Y	Y	Y	Y	Y	Y	N	Y
3 Mikulski	Y	Y	Y	Y	Y	Y	N	Y
4 *Holt*	N	Y	Y	Y	Y	Y	Y	N
5 Hoyer	Y	Y	Y	Y	Y	Y	N	Y
6 Byron	Y	Y	Y	Y	Y	Y	N	Y
7 Mitchell	N	Y	Y	Y	N	Y	N	Y
8 Barnes	N	Y	Y	Y	N	Y	N	Y
MASSACHUSETTS								
1 *Conte*	Y	Y	Y	Y	Y	Y	Y	N
2 Boland	?	?	?	?	Y	Y	N	Y
3 Early	Y	Y	Y	Y	?	Y	N	Y
4 Frank	Y	Y	Y	Y	Y	Y	N	Y
5 Shannon	Y	Y	Y	Y	Y	Y	N	Y
6 Mavroules	?	Y	Y	Y	?	Y	N	Y
7 Markey	Y	Y	Y	Y	Y	?	N	Y
8 O'Neill								
9 Moakley	Y	Y	Y	Y	Y	Y	N	Y
10 *Heckler*	Y	Y	Y	Y	Y	Y	Y	N
11 Donnelly	?	Y	Y	Y	Y	Y	N	Y
12 Studds	Y	Y	Y	Y	Y	Y	N	Y
MICHIGAN								
1 Conyers	?	P	Y	N	Y	Y	N	Y
2 *Pursell*	?	Y	Y	Y	Y	Y	N	Y
3 Wolpe	Y	Y	Y	Y	Y	Y	N	Y
4 *Siljander*	Y	Y	Y	Y	Y	Y	Y	N
5 *Sawyer*	Y	Y	Y	Y	Y	Y	Y	Y
6 *Dunn*	?	Y	Y	Y	Y	Y	Y	N
7 Kildee	Y	Y	Y	Y	Y	Y	N	Y
8 Traxler	Y	Y	Y	Y	Y	Y	N	Y
9 *Vander Jagt*	Y	Y	Y	Y	Y	Y	Y	Y
10 Albosta	Y	Y	Y	Y	Y	Y	N	Y
11 *Davis*	Y	Y	Y	Y	?	Y	Y	Y
12 Bonior	Y	Y	Y	Y	Y	Y	N	Y
13 Crockett	?	?	?	Y	?	Y	N	Y
14 Hertel	Y	Y	Y	Y	Y	Y	N	Y
15 Ford	Y	Y	Y	Y	Y	Y	N	Y
16 Dingell	?	Y	Y	Y	Y	Y	N	Y
17 Brodhead	Y	Y	Y	Y	Y	Y	N	Y
18 Blanchard	?	Y	Y	Y	Y	Y	N	Y
19 *Broomfield*	Y	Y	Y	Y	Y	Y	N	Y
MINNESOTA								
1 *Erdahl*	Y	Y	Y	Y	Y	Y	N	Y
2 *Hagedorn*	Y	Y	Y	Y	Y	Y	N	Y
3 *Frenzel*	Y	Y	Y	Y	Y	Y	N	Y
4 Vento	Y	Y	Y	Y	Y	Y	N	Y
5 Sabo	N	Y	Y	Y	N	Y	N	Y
6 *Weber*	N	Y	Y	Y	N	Y	Y	N
7 *Stangeland*	Y	Y	Y	Y	Y	Y	Y	N
8 Oberstar	Y	Y	Y	Y	Y	Y	N	Y
MISSISSIPPI								
1 Whitten	Y	Y	Y	Y	Y	Y	N	Y
2 Bowen	Y	Y	Y	Y	Y	Y	N	Y
3 Montgomery	Y	Y	Y	Y	Y	Y	N	Y
4 Dowdy	Y	Y	Y	Y	Y	Y	N	Y
5 *Lott*	Y	Y	Y	Y	Y	Y	N	Y
MISSOURI								
1 Clay	N	Y	Y	Y	N	Y	N	Y
2 Young	Y	Y	Y	Y	Y	Y	N	Y
3 Gephardt	Y	Y	?	Y	Y	Y	N	Y
4 Skelton	Y	Y	Y	Y	Y	Y	Y	N
5 Bolling	Y	Y	?	?	Y	Y	N	Y
6 *Coleman*	Y	Y	Y	Y	Y	Y	Y	N
7 *Taylor*	Y	Y	Y	Y	Y	Y	N	N
8 *Bailey*	Y	Y	Y	Y	Y	Y	Y	N
9 Volkmer	Y	Y	Y	Y	Y	Y	N	N
10 *Emerson*	N	Y	Y	Y	N	Y	Y	N
MONTANA								
1 Williams	?	Y	Y	?	Y	Y	N	Y
2 *Marlenee*	Y	Y	Y	Y	Y	Y	N	Y
NEBRASKA								
1 *Bereuter*	Y	Y	Y	Y	Y	Y	Y	N
2 *Daub*	Y	Y	Y	Y	Y	Y	Y	N
3 *Smith*	Y	Y	Y	Y	Y	Y	Y	N
NEVADA								
AL Santini	Y	Y	?	?	Y	Y	Y	N
NEW HAMPSHIRE								
1 D'Amours	Y	Y	Y	Y	?	Y	N	Y
2 *Gregg*	Y	Y	Y	Y	Y	Y	Y	N
NEW JERSEY								
1 Florio	Y	Y	Y	Y	Y	Y	N	Y
2 Hughes	Y	Y	Y	Y	Y	Y	N	Y
3 Howard	Y	Y	Y	Y	Y	Y	N	Y
4 *Smith*	Y	Y	Y	Y	Y	Y	N	Y
5 *Fenwick*	?	Y	Y	Y	Y	Y	Y	N
6 *Forsythe*	N	Y	Y	Y	N	Y	N	Y
7 *Roukema*	Y	Y	Y	Y	Y	Y	Y	N
8 Roe	Y	Y	Y	Y	Y	Y	N	Y
9 *Hollenbeck*	?	Y	Y	Y	Y	?	N	Y
10 Rodino	Y	Y	Y	Y	Y	Y	N	Y
11 Minish	Y	Y	Y	Y	Y	Y	N	Y
12 *Rinaldo*	Y	Y	Y	Y	Y	Y	N	Y
13 *Courter*	Y	Y	Y	Y	Y	Y	Y	N
14 Guarini	Y	Y	Y	Y	Y	Y	N	Y
15 Dwyer	Y	?	Y	Y	Y	Y	N	Y
NEW MEXICO								
1 *Lujan*	?	?	?	?	Y	Y	Y	N
2 *Skeen*	?	?	Y	Y	Y	Y	Y	N
NEW YORK								
1 *Carney*	Y	Y	Y	Y	Y	Y	Y	Y
2 Downey	Y	Y	Y	Y	Y	Y	N	Y
3 *Carman*	Y	Y	Y	Y	Y	Y	Y	N
4 *Lent*	Y	Y	Y	Y	Y	Y	Y	?
5 *McGrath*	Y	Y	Y	Y	Y	Y	Y	N
6 *LeBoutillier*	?	?	?	?	?	?	?	?
7 Addabbo	Y	Y	Y	Y	Y	Y	N	Y
8 Rosenthal	Y	Y	Y	Y	Y	Y	N	Y
9 Ferraro	Y	Y	Y	Y	Y	Y	N	Y
10 Biaggi	?	Y	Y	Y	?	?	X	#
11 Scheuer	Y	Y	Y	Y	Y	Y	N	Y
12 Chisholm	Y	Y	Y	Y	?	Y	N	Y
13 Solarz	Y	Y	Y	Y	Y	Y	N	Y
14 Richmond	Y	Y	Y	Y	Y	Y	N	Y
15 Zeferetti	Y	Y	Y	Y	Y	Y	N	Y
16 Schumer	Y	Y	Y	Y	Y	Y	N	Y
17 *Molinari*	Y	Y	Y	Y	Y	Y	N	Y
18 *Green*	Y	Y	Y	Y	Y	Y	Y	Y
19 Rangel	Y	Y	Y	Y	Y	Y	N	Y
20 Weiss	Y	Y	Y	Y	Y	Y	N	Y
21 Garcia	?	?	?	?	Y	Y	N	Y
22 Bingham	Y	Y	Y	Y	Y	Y	N	Y
23 Peyser	Y	Y	Y	Y	Y	Y	N	Y
24 Ottinger	P	Y	Y	Y	P	Y	N	Y
25 *Fish*	Y	Y	?	?	Y	Y	Y	Y
26 *Gilman*	?	?	Y	Y	Y	Y	Y	N
27 McHugh	?	Y	Y	Y	Y	Y	N	Y
28 Stratton	Y	Y	Y	Y	Y	Y	N	Y
29 *Solomon*	Y	Y	Y	Y	Y	Y	Y	N
30 *Martin*	Y	Y	Y	Y	Y	Y	Y	Y
31 *Mitchell*	Y	Y	Y	Y	Y	Y	Y	N
32 *Wortley*	Y	Y	Y	Y	Y	Y	N	Y
33 *Lee*	Y	Y	Y	Y	Y	Y	Y	N
34 *Horton*	Y	Y	Y	Y	Y	Y	N	Y
35 *Conable*	Y	Y	Y	Y	Y	Y	Y	Y
36 LaFalce	Y	Y	?	Y	Y	Y	N	Y
37 Nowak	?	Y	Y	Y	Y	Y	N	Y
38 *Kemp*	Y	Y	Y	Y	Y	Y	#	N
39 Lundine	?	Y	Y	?	Y	Y	N	Y
NORTH CAROLINA								
1 Jones	Y	Y	?	?	Y	Y	N	Y
2 Fountain	Y	Y	Y	Y	Y	Y	N	Y
3 Whitley	Y	Y	Y	Y	Y	Y	N	Y
4 Andrews	?	?	?	?	Y	Y	N	Y
5 Neal	Y	Y	Y	Y	Y	Y	N	Y
6 *Johnston*	N	Y	Y	Y	N	Y	Y	N
7 Rose	?	Y	Y	Y	Y	Y	N	Y
8 Hefner	?	?	?	?	Y	Y	N	Y
9 *Martin*	Y	Y	Y	Y	Y	Y	Y	N
10 *Broyhill*	Y	Y	Y	Y	Y	Y	N	Y
11 *Hendon*	Y	Y	Y	Y	Y	Y	Y	N
NORTH DAKOTA								
AL Dorgan	Y	Y	Y	Y	Y	Y	N	Y
OHIO								
1 *Gradison*	Y	Y	Y	Y	Y	Y	Y	N
2 Luken	Y	Y	Y	Y	Y	Y	N	Y
3 Hall	?	Y	?	Y	Y	Y	N	Y
4 *Oxley*	Y	Y	Y	Y	Y	Y	Y	N
5 *Latta*	Y	Y	Y	Y	Y	Y	Y	N
6 *McEwen*	Y	Y	Y	Y	Y	Y	Y	N
7 *Brown*	?	?	?	?	?	?	?	?
8 *Kindness*	Y	Y	Y	Y	Y	Y	Y	N
9 *Weber*	Y	Y	Y	Y	?	Y	Y	N
10 *Miller*	N	Y	Y	Y	N	Y	Y	N
11 *Stanton*	Y	Y	Y	Y	Y	Y	N	Y
12 Shamansky	Y	Y	Y	Y	Y	Y	N	Y
13 Pease	Y	Y	Y	Y	Y	Y	N	Y
14 Seiberling	Y	Y	Y	Y	Y	Y	N	Y
15 *Wylie*	Y	Y	Y	Y	Y	Y	Y	N
16 *Regula*	Y	Y	Y	Y	Y	Y	N	Y
17 *Ashbrook*	?	?	?	?	?	?	#	X
18 Applegate	Y	Y	?	?	?	Y	N	Y
19 *Williams*	Y	Y	Y	Y	Y	Y	N	Y
20 Oakar	Y	Y	Y	Y	Y	Y	N	Y
21 Stokes	?	Y	Y	Y	?	Y	N	Y
22 Eckart	Y	Y	Y	Y	Y	Y	N	Y
23 Mottl	Y	Y	Y	Y	Y	Y	Y	N
OKLAHOMA								
1 Jones	Y	Y	Y	Y	Y	Y	N	Y
2 Synar	Y	Y	Y	Y	Y	Y	N	Y
3 Watkins	?	?	?	?	Y	Y	N	Y
4 McCurdy	?	?	?	Y	Y	Y	N	Y
5 *Edwards*	N	Y	Y	Y	Y	Y	Y	N
6 English	Y	Y	Y	Y	Y	Y	N	Y
OREGON								
1 AuCoin	N	Y	Y	Y	Y	Y	N	Y
2 *Smith*	?	?	?	?	Y	Y	Y	N
3 Wyden	Y	Y	Y	Y	Y	Y	N	Y
4 Weaver	Y	Y	Y	Y	Y	Y	N	Y
PENNSYLVANIA								
1 Foglietta	?	Y	Y	Y	Y	Y	N	?
2 Gray	Y	Y	Y	Y	Y	Y	N	Y
3 Smith	Y	Y	Y	Y	Y	Y	N	Y
4 *Dougherty*	Y	Y	Y	Y	Y	Y	N	Y
5 *Schulze*	Y	Y	Y	Y	Y	Y	Y	Y
6 Yatron	Y	Y	Y	Y	Y	Y	N	Y
7 Edgar	Y	Y	Y	Y	Y	Y	N	Y
8 *Coyne, J.*	Y	Y	Y	Y	Y	Y	Y	N
9 *Shuster*	Y	Y	Y	Y	Y	Y	Y	N
10 *McDade*	+	+	+	+	+	+	-	+
11 *Nelligan*	Y	Y	Y	Y	Y	Y	Y	N
12 Murtha	?	?	?	?	Y	Y	N	Y
13 *Coughlin*	N	Y	Y	Y	N	Y	Y	N
14 Coyne, W.	Y	Y	Y	Y	Y	Y	N	Y
15 *Ritter*	Y	Y	Y	Y	Y	Y	Y	N
16 *Walker*	N	Y	Y	Y	N	Y	Y	N
17 Ertel	Y	Y	Y	Y	Y	Y	N	Y
18 Walgren	Y	Y	Y	Y	Y	Y	N	Y
19 *Goodling*	?	?	?	?	N	Y	Y	N
20 Gaydos	Y	Y	Y	Y	Y	Y	N	Y
21 Bailey	Y	Y	Y	Y	Y	Y	N	Y
22 Murphy	Y	Y	Y	Y	Y	Y	N	Y
23 *Clinger*	Y	Y	Y	Y	Y	Y	N	Y
24 *Marks*	?	?	?	?	?	Y	N	?
25 *Atkinson*	Y	Y	Y	Y	Y	Y	Y	N
RHODE ISLAND								
1 St Germain	?	Y	Y	Y	Y	Y	N	Y
2 *Schneider*	Y	Y	Y	Y	Y	Y	Y	N
SOUTH CAROLINA								
1 *Hartnett*	Y	Y	Y	Y	Y	Y	Y	N
2 *Spence*	Y	Y	Y	Y	Y	Y	Y	N
3 Derrick	?	Y	Y	Y	?	Y	N	Y
4 *Campbell*	Y	Y	Y	Y	Y	Y	Y	Y
5 Holland	?	?	?	?	Y	Y	N	Y
6 *Napier*	Y	Y	Y	Y	Y	Y	Y	N
SOUTH DAKOTA								
1 Daschle	Y	Y	Y	Y	Y	Y	N	Y
2 *Roberts*	Y	Y	Y	Y	N	Y	Y	N
TENNESSEE								
1 *Quillen*	Y	Y	Y	Y	Y	Y	N	Y
2 *Duncan*	Y	Y	Y	Y	Y	Y	N	Y
3 Bouquard	Y	Y	Y	Y	Y	Y	N	Y
4 Gore	Y	Y	Y	Y	N	Y	N	Y
5 Boner	?	?	?	?	Y	Y	N	Y
6 *Beard*	Y	Y	Y	Y	Y	Y	Y	N
7 Jones	?	Y	Y	Y	Y	Y	N	Y
8 Ford	Y	Y	Y	Y	Y	?	N	Y
TEXAS								
1 Hall, S.	Y	Y	Y	Y	Y	Y	Y	N
2 Wilson	?	?	?	Y	Y	Y	N	Y
3 *Collins*	Y	Y	Y	Y	Y	Y	Y	N
4 Hall, R.	Y	Y	Y	Y	Y	Y	Y	N
5 Mattox	?	?	?	?	?	?	?	?
6 Gramm	Y	Y	Y	Y	Y	Y	Y	N
7 *Archer*	Y	Y	Y	Y	Y	Y	Y	N
8 *Fields*	?	Y	Y	Y	Y	Y	Y	N
9 Brooks	Y	Y	Y	Y	Y	Y	N	Y
10 Pickle	Y	+	Y	Y	Y	Y	N	Y
11 Leath	?	Y	Y	Y	Y	Y	N	Y
12 Wright	Y	Y	Y	Y	Y	Y	N	Y
13 Hightower	Y	Y	Y	Y	Y	Y	Y	Y
14 Patman	Y	Y	Y	Y	Y	Y	N	Y
15 de la Garza	Y	Y	Y	Y	Y	Y	N	Y
16 White	Y	Y	Y	Y	Y	Y	N	Y
17 Stenholm	Y	Y	Y	Y	Y	Y	Y	N
18 Leland	?	?	?	?	Y	Y	N	Y
19 Hance	?	Y	Y	Y	Y	Y	N	Y
20 Gonzalez	Y	Y	Y	Y	Y	Y	N	Y
21 *Loeffler*	Y	Y	Y	Y	Y	Y	Y	N
22 *Paul*	Y	Y	Y	Y	Y	Y	Y	N
23 Kazen	Y	Y	Y	Y	Y	Y	Y	Y
24 Frost	Y	Y	Y	Y	Y	Y	N	Y
UTAH								
1 *Hansen*	?	Y	Y	Y	Y	Y	Y	N
2 *Marriott*	Y	Y	Y	Y	Y	Y	Y	N
VERMONT								
AL *Jeffords*	?	?	?	Y	Y	Y	N	Y
VIRGINIA								
1 *Trible*	Y	Y	Y	Y	Y	Y	Y	N
2 *Whitehurst*	Y	Y	Y	Y	Y	Y	Y	N
3 *Bliley*	Y	Y	Y	Y	Y	Y	Y	N
4 *Daniel, R.*	Y	Y	Y	Y	Y	Y	Y	N
5 Daniel, D.	Y	Y	Y	Y	Y	Y	N	Y
6 *Butler*	?	?	?	?	N	Y	N	Y
7 *Robinson*	Y	Y	Y	Y	Y	Y	Y	Y
8 *Parris*	?	Y	Y	Y	Y	Y	Y	N
9 *Wampler*	Y	Y	Y	Y	Y	Y	N	Y
10 *Wolf*	Y	Y	Y	Y	Y	Y	Y	N
WASHINGTON								
1 *Pritchard*	Y	Y	Y	Y	Y	Y	N	Y
2 Swift	Y	Y	Y	Y	Y	Y	N	Y
3 Bonker	?	Y	Y	Y	Y	Y	N	Y
4 *Morrison*	Y	Y	Y	Y	Y	Y	N	Y
5 Foley	Y	Y	Y	Y	Y	Y	N	Y
6 Dicks	Y	Y	Y	Y	Y	Y	N	Y
7 Lowry	Y	Y	Y	Y	Y	Y	N	Y
WEST VIRGINIA								
1 Mollohan	Y	?	Y	Y	Y	Y	N	Y
2 *Benedict*	Y	Y	?	Y	Y	Y	Y	N
3 *Staton*	Y	Y	Y	Y	Y	Y	N	N
4 Rahall	Y	Y	Y	Y	Y	Y	N	Y
WISCONSIN								
1 Aspin	Y	Y	Y	Y	Y	Y	N	Y
2 Kastenmeier	?	Y	Y	Y	Y	Y	N	Y
3 *Gunderson*	Y	Y	Y	Y	Y	Y	Y	N
4 Zablocki	Y	Y	Y	Y	Y	Y	N	Y
5 Reuss	Y	Y	Y	Y	Y	Y	N	Y
6 *Petri*	Y	Y	Y	Y	Y	Y	Y	N
7 Obey	Y	Y	N	N	Y	Y	N	Y
8 *Roth*	Y	Y	Y	Y	Y	Y	Y	N
9 *Sensenbrenner*	Y	Y	Y	Y	Y	Y	Y	N
WYOMING								
AL *Cheney*	Y	Y	Y	Y	Y	Y	Y	N

Southern states - Ala., Ark., Fla., Ga., Ky., La., Miss., N.C., Okla., S.C., Tenn., Texas, Va.

KEY

Y Voted for (yea).
Paired for.
+ Announced for.
N Voted against (nay).
X Paired against.
- Announced against.
P Voted ''present''.
C Voted ''present'' to avoid possible conflict of interest.
? Did not vote or otherwise make a position known.

Democrats *Republicans*

49. S Con Res 78. Easter Recess. Adoption of the concurrent resolution to provide for an adjournment of the Senate from the close of business on April 1 or 2 until noon on April 13, and for an adjournment of the House from the close of business on April 6 until noon on April 20. Adopted 209-173: R 20-150; D 189-23 (ND 128-13, SD 61-10), April 1, 1982.

50. HR 5789. International Energy Agency Antitrust Exemption Extension. Sharp, D-Ind., substitute amendment to limit to 60 days the extension of a provision of the 1975 Energy Policy and Conservation Act (PL 94-163) that provides oil companies with a limited antitrust defense in sharing supply information with the International Energy Agency. Adopted 211-163: R 22-144; D 189-19 (ND 133-5, SD 56-14), April 1, 1982.

51. HR 5789. International Energy Agency Antitrust Exemption Extension. Passage of the bill to extend for 60 days, until June 1, 1982, the provision of PL 94-163 that gives oil companies a limited antitrust defense so they can share supply information with the International Energy Agency. Passed 374-3: R 163-3; D 211-0 (ND 140-0, SD 71-0), April 1, 1982. A "yea" was a vote supporting the president's position. The House subsequently passed by voice vote an identical Senate bill, S 1937, clearing that measure for the president.

	49	50	51
ALABAMA			
1 *Edwards*	Y	N	Y
2 *Dickinson*	Y	N	Y
3 Nichols	Y	Y	Y
4 Bevill	Y	Y	Y
5 Flippo	Y	Y	Y
6 *Smith*	N	N	Y
7 Shelby	Y	Y	Y
ALASKA			
AL *Young*	Y	N	Y
ARIZONA			
1 *Rhodes*	N	N	Y
2 Udall	Y	Y	Y
3 *Stump*	N	N	Y
4 *Rudd*	?	?	?
ARKANSAS			
1 Alexander	Y	Y	Y
2 *Bethune*	N	Y	Y
3 *Hammerschmidt*	N	N	Y
4 Anthony	Y	Y	Y
CALIFORNIA			
1 *Chappie*	N	N	Y
2 *Clausen*	N	N	Y
3 Matsui	Y	Y	Y
4 Fazio	Y	Y	Y
5 Burton, J.	?	?	?
6 Burton, P.	Y	Y	Y
7 Miller	Y	Y	Y
8 Dellums	Y	Y	Y
9 Stark	Y	Y	Y
10 Edwards	Y	Y	Y
11 Lantos	Y	Y	Y
12 *McCloskey*	?	?	?
13 Mineta	Y	Y	Y
14 *Shumway*	N	N	Y
15 Coelho	Y	Y	Y
16 Panetta	Y	Y	Y
17 *Pashayan*	N	N	Y
18 *Thomas*	N	N	Y
19 *Lagomarsino*	N	N	Y
20 *Goldwater*	?	?	?
21 *Fiedler*	N	N	Y
22 *Moorhead*	N	N	Y
23 Beilenson	Y	Y	Y
24 Waxman	Y	?	?
25 Roybal	Y	Y	Y
26 *Rousselot*	N	N	Y
27 *Dornan*	?	?	?
28 Dixon	Y	Y	Y
29 Hawkins	Y	Y	Y
30 Vacancy			
31 Dymally	?	?	?
32 Anderson	N	N	Y
33 *Grisham*	?	?	?
34 *Lungren*	N	N	Y
35 *Dreier*	N	N	Y
36 Brown	Y	Y	Y
37 *Lewis*	N	N	Y
38 Patterson	Y	Y	Y
39 *Dannemeyer*	?	?	?
40 *Badham*	?	?	?
41 *Lowery*	?	N	Y
42 *Hunter*	N	N	Y
43 *Burgener*	?	?	?
COLORADO			
1 Schroeder	N	Y	Y
2 Wirth	Y	Y	Y
3 Kogovsek	Y	Y	Y
4 *Brown*	N	Y	N

	49	50	51
5 *Kramer*	N	N	Y
CONNECTICUT			
1 Kennelly	Y	Y	Y
2 Gejdenson	?	Y	Y
3 *DeNardis*	-	+	Y
4 *McKinney*	N	N	Y
5 Ratchford	Y	Y	Y
6 Moffett	Y	Y	Y
DELAWARE			
AL *Evans*	N	N	Y
FLORIDA			
1 Hutto	Y	N	Y
2 Fuqua	Y	Y	Y
3 Bennett	Y	Y	Y
4 Chappell	Y	Y	Y
5 *McCollum*	N	N	Y
6 *Young*	N	N	Y
7 Gibbons	Y	Y	Y
8 Ireland	Y	N	Y
9 Nelson	N	Y	Y
10 *Bafalis*	N	N	Y
11 Mica	Y	Y	Y
12 *Shaw*	N	N	Y
13 Lehman	Y	Y	Y
14 Pepper	Y	Y	Y
15 Fascell	Y	Y	Y
GEORGIA			
1 Ginn	Y	?	?
2 Hatcher	Y	Y	Y
3 Brinkley	Y	Y	Y
4 Levitas	N	Y	Y
5 Fowler	Y	Y	Y
6 *Gingrich*	N	N	Y
7 McDonald	Y	N	Y
8 Evans	?	Y	Y
9 Jenkins	?	?	?
10 Barnard	Y	N	Y
HAWAII			
1 Heftel	Y	Y	Y
2 Akaka	Y	Y	Y
IDAHO			
1 *Craig*	N	N	Y
2 *Hansen*	N	N	Y
ILLINOIS			
1 Washington	Y	Y	Y
2 Savage	?	?	?
3 Russo	Y	Y	Y
4 *Derwinski*	?	?	?
5 Fary	Y	Y	Y
6 *Hyde*	N	N	Y
7 Collins	Y	Y	Y
8 Rostenkowski	Y	Y	Y
9 Yates	Y	?	?
10 *Porter*	N	N	Y
11 Annunzio	Y	Y	Y
12 *Crane, P.*	?	?	?
13 *McClory*	N	N	Y
14 *Erlenborn*	N	N	Y
15 *Corcoran*	N	N	Y
16 *Martin*	?	?	?
17 O'Brien	N	N	Y
18 *Michel*	Y	N	Y
19 *Railsback*	N	N	Y
20 *Findley*	N	?	Y
21 *Madigan*	N	N	Y
22 *Crane, D.*	Y	N	Y
23 Price	Y	Y	Y
24 Simon	?	?	?
INDIANA			
1 Benjamin	Y	Y	Y
2 Fithian	Y	Y	Y
3 *Hiler*	N	N	Y
4 *Coats*	N	N	Y
5 *Hillis*	Y	N	Y
6 Evans	Y	Y	Y
7 *Myers*	Y	N	Y
8 *Deckard*	N	N	Y
9 Hamilton	Y	Y	Y
10 Sharp	-	Y	Y
11 Jacobs	?	Y	Y
IOWA			
1 *Leach*	N	Y	Y
2 *Tauke*	N	N	Y
3 *Evans*	N	Y	Y
4 Smith	Y	Y	Y
5 Harkin	Y	Y	Y
6 Bedell	Y	Y	?

ND - Northern Democrats   SD - Southern Democrats

	49 50 51		49 50 51		49 50 51		49 50 51
KANSAS		4 Skelton	? ? ?	9 Martin	N N Y	7 Jones	Y Y Y
1 Roberts	? N Y	5 Bolling	Y ? Y	10 Broyhill	N N N	8 Ford	Y Y Y
2 Jeffries	N N Y	6 Coleman	N N Y	11 Hendon	N N Y	**TEXAS**	
3 Winn	Y N Y	7 Taylor	N N Y	**NORTH DAKOTA**		1 Hall, S.	Y N Y
4 Glickman	Y Y Y	8 Bailey	N N Y	AL Dorgan	Y Y Y	2 Wilson	Y Y Y
5 Whittaker	N N Y	9 Volkmer	Y Y Y	**OHIO**		3 Collins	N N Y
KENTUCKY		10 Emerson	N N Y	1 Gradison	N N Y	4 Hall, R.	N N Y
1 Hubbard	N Y Y	**MONTANA**		2 Luken	Y Y Y	5 Mattox	? ? ?
2 Natcher	Y Y Y	1 Williams	N Y Y	3 Hall	Y Y Y	6 Gramm	N N Y
3 Mazzoli	Y Y Y	2 Marlenee	? ? ?	4 Oxley	N N Y	7 Archer	N N Y
4 Snyder	Y Y Y	**NEBRASKA**		5 Latta	N N Y	8 Fields	N N Y
5 Rogers	N N Y	1 Bereuter	N N Y	6 McEwen	N N Y	9 Brooks	? ? ?
6 Hopkins	N Y Y	2 Daub	N N Y	7 Brown	N N Y	10 Pickle	Y Y Y
7 Perkins	Y Y Y	3 Smith	N N Y	8 Kindness	N N Y	11 Leath	Y N Y
LOUISIANA		**NEVADA**		9 Weber	N N Y	12 Wright	Y Y Y
1 Livingston	N N Y	AL Santini	Y Y Y	10 Miller	N N Y	13 Hightower	Y Y Y
2 Boggs	Y Y Y	**NEW HAMPSHIRE**		11 Stanton	N ? ?	14 Patman	N Y Y
3 Tauzin	N Y Y	1 D'Amours	? ? ?	12 Shamansky	Y Y Y	15 de la Garza	Y Y Y
4 Roemer	N N Y	2 Gregg	N Y Y	13 Pease	Y Y Y	16 White	Y N Y
5 Huckaby	? ? ?	**NEW JERSEY**		14 Seiberling	Y Y Y	17 Stenholm	Y N Y
6 Moore	N N Y	1 Florio	Y Y Y	15 Wylie	N N Y	18 Leland	Y Y Y
7 Breaux	? ? ?	2 Hughes	N Y Y	16 Regula	Y N Y	19 Hance	Y Y Y
8 Long	Y Y Y	3 Howard	Y Y Y	17 Ashbrook	? ? ?	20 Gonzalez	Y Y Y
MAINE		4 Smith	N N Y	18 Applegate	Y Y Y	21 Loeffler	N N Y
1 Emery	N Y Y	5 Fenwick	N ? Y	19 Williams	N N Y	22 Paul	N N Y
2 Snowe	N Y Y	6 Forsythe	Y N Y	20 Oakar	Y Y Y	23 Kazen	Y Y Y
MARYLAND		7 Roukema	Y Y Y	21 Stokes	Y Y Y	24 Frost	Y Y Y
1 Dyson	Y N Y	8 Roe	Y Y Y	22 Eckart	Y Y Y	**UTAH**	
2 Long	N Y Y	9 Hollenbeck	N N Y	23 Mottl	N Y Y	1 Hansen	N N Y
3 Mikulski	Y Y Y	10 Rodino	Y Y Y	**OKLAHOMA**		2 Marriott	Y N Y
4 Holt	Y N Y	11 Minish	Y Y Y	1 Jones	? Y Y	**VERMONT**	
5 Hoyer	Y Y Y	12 Rinaldo	N N Y	2 Synar	Y Y Y	AL Jeffords	N Y Y
6 Byron	Y N Y	13 Courter	N N Y	3 Watkins	Y Y Y	**VIRGINIA**	
7 Mitchell	Y Y Y	14 Guarini	Y Y ?	4 McCurdy	Y ? Y	1 Trible	N N ?
8 Barnes	Y Y Y	15 Dwyer	Y Y Y	5 Edwards	? N Y	2 Whitehurst	Y N Y
MASSACHUSETTS		**NEW MEXICO**		6 English	Y Y Y	3 Bliley	N N Y
1 Conte	N Y Y	1 Lujan	N N Y	**OREGON**		4 Daniel, R.	N N Y
2 Boland	Y Y Y	2 Skeen	N N Y	1 AuCoin	N ? Y	5 Daniel, D.	Y N Y
3 Early	Y Y Y	**NEW YORK**		2 Smith	N N Y	6 Butler	N N N
4 Frank	Y Y Y	1 Carney	N N Y	3 Wyden	Y Y Y	7 Robinson	N N Y
5 Shannon	Y Y Y	2 Downey	Y Y Y	4 Weaver	? ? ?	8 Parris	N N ?
6 Mavroules	Y Y Y	3 Carman	N N Y	**PENNSYLVANIA**		9 Wampler	N N Y
7 Markey	? Y Y	4 Lent	N N Y	1 Foglietta	? ? ?	10 Wolf	N N Y
8 O'Neill		5 McGrath	N N Y	2 Gray	Y Y Y	**WASHINGTON**	
9 Moakley	Y Y Y	6 LeBoutillier	? ? ?	3 Smith	? ? ?	1 Pritchard	N ? Y
10 Heckler	N Y Y	7 Addabbo	Y Y Y	4 Dougherty	Y Y Y	2 Swift	Y Y Y
11 Donnelly	Y Y Y	8 Rosenthal	Y Y Y	5 Schulze	N N Y	3 Bonker	Y Y Y
12 Studds	Y Y Y	9 Ferraro	? Y Y	6 Yatron	N Y Y	4 Morrison	N Y Y
MICHIGAN		10 Biaggi	? ? ?	7 Edgar	N Y Y	5 Foley	Y ? Y
1 Conyers	? ? Y	11 Scheuer	Y Y Y	8 Coyne, J.	N Y Y	6 Dicks	Y Y Y
2 Pursell	N Y Y	12 Chisholm	Y Y Y	9 Shuster	N N Y	7 Lowry	Y Y Y
3 Wolpe	Y Y Y	13 Solarz	Y Y Y	10 McDade	- - +	**WEST VIRGINIA**	
4 Siljander	N ? ?	14 Richmond	Y Y Y	11 Nelligan	N N Y	1 Mollohan	? N Y
5 Sawyer	Y N Y	15 Zeferetti	? ? ?	12 Murtha	Y Y Y	2 Benedict	N N Y
6 Dunn	N N Y	16 Schumer	? ? ?	13 Coughlin	N N Y	3 Staton	N N Y
7 Kildee	Y Y Y	17 Molinari	N N ?	14 Coyne, W.	Y Y Y	4 Rahall	Y Y Y
8 Traxler	Y ? Y	18 Green	N N Y	15 Ritter	N N Y	**WISCONSIN**	
9 Vander Jagt	N N Y	19 Rangel	Y Y Y	16 Walker	N N Y	1 Aspin	Y Y Y
10 Albosta	Y Y Y	20 Weiss	Y Y Y	17 Ertel	Y Y Y	2 Kastenmeier	Y Y Y
11 Davis	Y Y Y	21 Garcia	Y ? ?	18 Walgren	Y Y Y	3 Gunderson	N N Y
12 Bonior	Y Y Y	22 Bingham	Y Y Y	19 Goodling	N N Y	4 Zablocki	Y Y Y
13 Crockett	? ? ?	23 Peyser	Y ? ?	20 Gaydos	Y Y Y	5 Reuss	Y Y Y
14 Hertel	Y Y Y	24 Ottinger	Y Y Y	21 Bailey	Y Y Y	6 Petri	N N Y
15 Ford	Y Y Y	25 Fish	N N Y	22 Murphy	Y ? ?	7 Obey	Y Y Y
16 Dingell	Y Y Y	26 Gilman	N N ?	23 Clinger	N N Y	8 Roth	N N Y
17 Brodhead	Y Y Y	27 McHugh	? Y Y	24 Marks	? ? ?	9 Sensenbrenner	N N Y
18 Blanchard	Y Y Y	28 Stratton	N N Y	25 Atkinson	N N Y	**WYOMING**	
19 Broomfield	N N Y	29 Solomon	N N Y	**RHODE ISLAND**		AL Cheney	N N Y
MINNESOTA		30 Martin	N Y Y	1 St Germain	Y ? ?		
1 Erdahl	N N Y	31 Mitchell	N Y Y	2 Schneider	N Y Y		
2 Hagedorn	N N Y	32 Wortley	N ? Y	**SOUTH CAROLINA**			
3 Frenzel	N N Y	33 Lee	N N Y	1 Hartnett	N N Y		
4 Vento	Y Y Y	34 Horton	? ? ?	2 Spence	N N Y		
5 Sabo	Y Y Y	35 Conable	N N Y	3 Derrick	Y Y Y		
6 Weber	N N Y	36 LaFalce	Y Y Y	4 Campbell	N N Y		
7 Stangeland	N N Y	37 Nowak	N Y Y	5 Holland	Y Y Y		
8 Oberstar	Y Y Y	38 Kemp	N Y Y	6 Napier	? ? ?		
MISSISSIPPI		39 Lundine	Y Y Y	**SOUTH DAKOTA**			
1 Whitten	Y N Y	**NORTH CAROLINA**		1 Daschle	N Y Y		
2 Bowen	Y Y Y	1 Jones	Y Y Y	2 Roberts	N N Y		
3 Montgomery	Y N Y	2 Fountain	Y Y Y	**TENNESSEE**			
4 Dowdy	N Y Y	3 Whitley	Y ? ?	1 Quillen	Y ? ?		
5 Lott	N N Y	4 Andrews	Y Y Y	2 Duncan	N N ?		
MISSOURI		5 Neal	N Y Y	3 Bouquard	Y Y Y		
1 Clay	Y Y Y	6 Johnston	N N Y	4 Gore	Y Y Y		
2 Young	Y Y Y	7 Rose	? ? ?	5 Boner	Y Y Y		
3 Gephardt	Y Y Y	8 Hefner	Y Y Y	6 Beard	N N Y		

Southern states - Ala., Ark., Fla., Ga., Ky., La., Miss., N.C., Okla., S.C., Tenn., Texas, Va.

KEY

Y Voted for (yea).
Paired for.
+ Announced for.
N Voted against (nay).
X Paired against.
- Announced against.
P Voted "present".
C Voted "present" to avoid possible conflict of interest.
? Did not vote or otherwise make a position known.

Democrats   *Republicans*

52. HR 3208. Reclamation Safety of Dams Act. Adoption of the rule (H Res 438) providing for House floor consideration of the bill to increase from $100 million to $650 million the authorization for repairs to federally built dams. Adopted 343-5: R 152-3; D 191-2 (ND 134-1, SD 57-1), April 29, 1982.

53. HR 3208. Reclamation Safety of Dams Act. Solomon, R-N.Y., amendment to require local beneficiaries of federal irrigation dams to share in the cost of repairs authorized under the bill. Adopted 212-140: R 105-57; D 107-83 (ND 90-41, SD 17-42), April 29, 1982.

54. HR 3208. Reclamation Safety of Dams Act. Passage of the bill to amend the Reclamation Safety of Dams Act of 1978 to increase from $100 million to $650 million the authorization for repairs to federally built dams and to require those who benefit from the dams to share in the repair costs. Passed 335-9: R 154-5; D 181-4 (ND 126-3, SD 55-1), April 29, 1982.

55. HR 4613. Debt Collection Act of 1982. Rostenkowski, D-Ill., motion to suspend the rules and pass the bill to increase the efficiency of government debt collection. Motion agreed to 402-3: R 176-1; D 226-2 (ND 151-2, SD 75-0), May 5, 1982. A two-thirds majority of those present and voting (271 in this case) is required for passage under suspension of the rules.

56. HR 5539. Reclamation Law Amendments. Adoption of the rule (H Res 449) providing for House floor consideration of the bill to amend the law governing farmers' use of irrigation water from federal reclamation projects. Adopted 393-5: R 172-2; D 221-3 (ND 147-3, SD 74-0), May 5, 1982.

57. Procedural Motion. Levitas, D-Ga., motion to approve the House *Journal* of Wednesday, May 5. Motion agreed to 352-15: R 159-5; D 193-10 (ND 125-9, SD 68-1), May 6, 1982.

58. HR 5922. Urgent Supplemental Appropriations, Fiscal 1982. Lott, R-Miss., motion to order the previous question (thus ending debate and the possibility of amendment) on the rule (H Res 415) providing for House floor consideration of the bill to provide $4,868,934,000 in net new budget authority for fiscal 1982. Motion agreed to 240-158: R 32-145; D 208-13 (ND 144-6, SD 64-7), May 6, 1982. The effect of the vote was to foreclose a Republican-sponsored $1-billion assistance program for the housing industry.

59. HR 5922. Urgent Supplemental Appropriations, Fiscal 1982. Adoption of the rule (H Res 415) providing for House floor consideration of the bill to provide $4,868,934,000 in net new budget authority for fiscal 1982 and waiving points of order against certain provisions. Adopted 338-54: R 127-50; D 211-4 (ND 143-2, SD 68-2), May 6, 1982.

	52	53	54	55	56	57	58	59
ALABAMA								
1 Edwards	?	?	?	Y	?	?	N	N
2 *Dickinson*	Y	N	Y	N	N	Y	N	N
3 Nichols	Y	N	Y	Y	Y	Y	Y	Y
4 Bevill	Y	N	Y	Y	Y	Y	Y	Y
5 Flippo	?	?	?	Y	Y	Y	Y	Y
6 *Smith*	Y	N	Y	Y	Y	Y	N	N
7 Shelby	Y	N	Y	Y	Y	Y	Y	Y
ALASKA								
AL *Young*	?	N	Y	?	?	?	N	Y
ARIZONA								
1 *Rhodes*	Y	N	Y	?	Y	Y	Y	Y
2 Udall	Y	N	Y	Y	Y	Y	Y	Y
3 Stump	Y	N	Y	Y	Y	Y	N	N
4 *Rudd*	Y	N	Y	Y	Y	Y	Y	Y
ARKANSAS								
1 Alexander	Y	N	?	Y	Y	Y	Y	Y
2 *Bethune*	Y	N	Y	Y	Y	Y	N	Y
3 *Hammerschmidt*	?	?	?	Y	Y	Y	N	Y
4 Anthony	Y	X	?	Y	Y	Y	Y	Y
CALIFORNIA								
1 *Chappie*	Y	N	Y	Y	Y	Y	N	Y
2 *Clausen*	Y	N	Y	Y	Y	Y	N	Y
3 Matsui	Y	N	Y	Y	Y	Y	Y	Y
4 Fazio	Y	N	Y	Y	Y	Y	Y	Y
5 Burton, J.	Y	N	Y	?	?	?	?	?
6 Burton, P.	?	?	?	Y	Y	Y	Y	Y
7 Miller	Y	Y	Y	Y	?	Y	Y	Y
8 Dellums	Y	Y	Y	Y	?	Y	Y	Y
9 Stark	Y	Y	Y	Y	Y	Y	Y	Y
10 Edwards	Y	Y	Y	Y	Y	Y	Y	Y
11 Lantos	Y	N	Y	Y	Y	Y	Y	Y
12 *McCloskey*	?	?	?	Y	Y	Y	Y	Y
13 Mineta	Y	Y	Y	Y	Y	Y	Y	Y
14 *Shumway*	Y	N	Y	Y	Y	Y	N	N
15 Coelho	Y	?	Y	Y	Y	Y	Y	Y
16 Panetta	Y	N	Y	Y	Y	?	Y	Y
17 *Pashayan*	Y	N	Y	Y	Y	Y	Y	Y
18 Thomas	Y	N	Y	Y	Y	N	N	N
19 *Lagomarsino*	Y	Y	Y	Y	Y	Y	N	Y
20 *Goldwater*	?	?	?	?	?	?	?	?
21 *Fiedler*	?	?	+	Y	Y	Y	Y	Y
22 *Moorhead*	Y	N	Y	Y	Y	Y	N	N
23 Beilenson	Y	Y	Y	Y	Y	Y	Y	Y
24 Waxman	Y	Y	Y	Y	?	Y	Y	Y
25 Roybal	Y	N	Y	Y	Y	?	Y	Y
26 *Rousselot*	Y	N	Y	Y	Y	Y	N	N
27 *Dornan*	?	?	?	?	Y	N	N	N
28 Dixon	Y	N	Y	Y	Y	Y	Y	Y
29 Hawkins	?	#	?	Y	Y	Y	Y	Y
30 Vacancy								
31 Dymally	Y	N	Y	Y	Y	Y	Y	Y
32 Anderson	Y	Y	Y	Y	Y	Y	Y	Y
33 *Grisham*	?	?	?	?	?	?	?	?
34 *Lungren*	Y	Y	Y	Y	Y	Y	N	Y
35 *Dreier*	?	?	?	Y	Y	?	?	?
36 Brown	Y	N	Y	Y	Y	Y	Y	Y
37 *Lewis*	?	N	Y	Y	Y	Y	N	Y
38 Patterson	Y	N	?	Y	Y	Y	Y	Y
39 *Dannemeyer*	Y	Y	Y	Y	Y	Y	N	N
40 *Badham*	?	?	?	Y	Y	N	N	N
41 *Lowery*	Y	Y	Y	Y	Y	Y	N	Y
42 *Hunter*	Y	N	Y	Y	Y	N	N	Y
43 *Burgener*	?	?	?	Y	Y	Y	N	Y
COLORADO								
1 Schroeder	Y	Y	Y	Y	Y	N	Y	N
2 Wirth	Y	N	Y	Y	Y	Y	N	Y
3 Kogovsek	Y	N	Y	Y	Y	Y	Y	Y
4 *Brown*	N	N	Y	Y	N	Y	N	N

	52	53	54	55	56	57	58	59
5 *Kramer*	Y	N	Y	Y	Y	Y	N	N
CONNECTICUT								
1 Kennelly	Y	Y	?	Y	Y	Y	Y	Y
2 Gejdenson	Y	N	Y	Y	Y	N	Y	Y
3 *DeNardis*	+	#	+	Y	Y	Y	N	Y
4 *McKinney*	Y	Y	Y	Y	Y	Y	Y	Y
5 Ratchford	Y	Y	Y	Y	Y	Y	Y	Y
6 Moffett	Y	Y	Y	Y	Y	Y	Y	Y
DELAWARE								
AL Evans	Y	Y	Y	Y	Y	Y	N	Y
FLORIDA								
1 Hutto	Y	Y	Y	Y	Y	Y	Y	Y
2 Fuqua	Y	N	Y	Y	Y	Y	Y	Y
3 Bennett	Y	N	Y	Y	Y	Y	Y	Y
4 Chappell	Y	N	Y	Y	Y	Y	Y	Y
5 *McCollum*	Y	Y	Y	Y	Y	Y	N	N
6 *Young*	Y	Y	Y	Y	Y	N	Y	N
7 Gibbons	Y	Y	Y	Y	Y	?	Y	Y
8 Ireland	Y	N	Y	Y	Y	Y	Y	Y
9 Nelson	Y	Y	Y	Y	Y	Y	?	Y
10 *Bafalis*	Y	Y	Y	Y	Y	Y	N	?
11 Mica	Y	Y	Y	Y	Y	Y	Y	Y
12 *Shaw*	Y	Y	Y	Y	Y	Y	Y	Y
13 Lehman	Y	Y	Y	Y	Y	Y	Y	Y
14 Pepper	Y	Y	Y	Y	Y	Y	Y	Y
15 Fascell	Y	N	Y	Y	Y	Y	Y	Y
GEORGIA								
1 Ginn	?	?	?	?	?	?	?	?
2 Hatcher	Y	N	Y	Y	Y	?	?	?
3 Brinkley	Y	Y	Y	Y	Y	Y	Y	Y
4 Levitas	Y	Y	Y	Y	Y	Y	Y	Y
5 Fowler	Y	Y	Y	Y	Y	Y	Y	Y
6 *Gingrich*	Y	Y	Y	Y	Y	Y	N	N
7 McDonald	N	Y	N	Y	?	N	N	N
8 Evans	Y	N	?	Y	Y	Y	Y	Y
9 Jenkins	Y	Y	Y	Y	Y	Y	Y	Y
10 Barnard	?	?	?	Y	Y	Y	?	?
HAWAII								
1 Heftel	?	?	?	Y	Y	Y	Y	Y
2 Akaka	?	?	?	Y	Y	?	Y	Y
IDAHO								
1 *Craig*	?	?	?	Y	Y	Y	N	N
2 *Hansen*	Y	N	Y	Y	Y	Y	N	N
ILLINOIS								
1 Washington	Y	Y	Y	Y	Y	?	Y	Y
2 Savage	Y	N	Y	P	Y	?	Y	Y
3 Russo	Y	Y	N	Y	Y	Y	Y	Y
4 *Derwinski*	?	#	Y	?	?	?	?	?
5 Fary	Y	N	Y	Y	Y	Y	Y	Y
6 *Hyde*	Y	Y	Y	Y	Y	Y	N	Y
7 Collins	?	#	Y	Y	Y	Y	Y	Y
8 Rostenkowski	Y	Y	Y	Y	Y	Y	Y	Y
9 Yates	Y	Y	Y	N	N	Y	Y	Y
10 *Porter*	Y	Y	Y	Y	Y	Y	N	Y
11 Annunzio	Y	N	Y	Y	Y	Y	Y	Y
12 *Crane, P.*	N	Y	N	Y	Y	?	N	N
13 *McClory*	Y	Y	Y	Y	Y	Y	Y	Y
14 *Erlenborn*	Y	Y	Y	Y	Y	Y	N	Y
15 *Corcoran*	Y	Y	Y	Y	Y	Y	N	Y
16 *Martin*	Y	Y	Y	Y	Y	?	N	Y
17 O'Brien	Y	Y	Y	Y	Y	?	N	Y
18 *Michel*	Y	N	Y	?	?	?	?	Y
19 *Railsback*	Y	?	?	Y	Y	Y	N	Y
20 *Findley*	Y	?	?	Y	Y	Y	N	Y
21 *Madigan*	Y	N	Y	Y	Y	Y	N	N
22 *Crane, D.*	N	Y	N	Y	Y	N	N	N
23 Price	Y	N	Y	Y	Y	Y	Y	Y
24 Simon	?	?	?	Y	Y	Y	Y	Y
INDIANA								
1 Benjamin	Y	Y	Y	?	?	Y	Y	Y
2 Fithian	Y	Y	Y	Y	Y	Y	Y	Y
3 *Hiler*	Y	Y	Y	Y	Y	Y	N	Y
4 *Coats*	Y	Y	Y	Y	Y	Y	N	Y
5 *Hillis*	Y	Y	Y	Y	Y	Y	N	Y
6 Evans	?	?	?	?	?	?	?	?
7 *Myers*	Y	N	Y	Y	Y	Y	N	Y
8 *Deckard*	Y	Y	Y	Y	Y	N	N	N
9 Hamilton	Y	Y	Y	Y	Y	Y	Y	Y
10 Sharp	Y	Y	?	Y	Y	Y	Y	Y
11 Jacobs	?	?	?	Y	Y	N	N	Y
IOWA								
1 *Leach*	Y	Y	?	Y	Y	Y	N	Y
2 *Tauke*	Y	Y	Y	Y	Y	Y	N	Y
3 *Evans*	Y	Y	Y	Y	Y	?	?	?
4 Smith	Y	Y	Y	Y	Y	Y	Y	Y
5 Harkin	Y	Y	Y	Y	Y	N	Y	Y
6 Bedell	Y	?	?	Y	Y	Y	Y	Y

ND - Northern Democrats   SD - Southern Democrats

	52	53	54	55	56	57	58	59
KANSAS								
1 ***Roberts***	Y	Y	Y	Y	Y	Y	Y	Y
2 ***Jeffries***	Y	Y	Y	Y	Y	Y	N	N
3 ***Winn***	Y	Y	Y	Y	Y	Y	N	Y
4 Glickman	Y	Y	Y	Y	Y	Y	Y	Y
5 ***Whittaker***	Y	Y	Y	Y	Y	Y	N	Y
KENTUCKY								
1 Hubbard	Y	N	Y	Y	Y	Y	Y	Y
2 Natcher	Y	N	Y	Y	Y	Y	Y	Y
3 Mazzoli	+	+	+	Y	Y	Y	Y	Y
4 ***Snyder***	?	X	?	Y	Y	Y	N	N
5 ***Rogers***	Y	N	Y	Y	Y	Y	N	Y
6 ***Hopkins***	Y	N	Y	Y	Y	Y	N	N
7 Perkins	Y	N	Y	Y	Y	Y	Y	Y
LOUISIANA								
1 ***Livingston***	?	N	Y	Y	?	Y	Y	Y
2 Boggs	Y	Y	Y	Y	Y	Y	Y	Y
3 Tauzin	Y	N	?	+	Y	Y	Y	Y
4 Roemer	?	Y	Y	Y	Y	N	Y	Y
5 Huckaby	Y	N	Y	Y	Y	Y	N	Y
6 ***Moore***	Y	N	Y	Y	Y	Y	N	N
7 Breaux	?	N	Y	Y	Y	Y	Y	Y
8 Long	Y	Y	Y	Y	Y	Y	Y	Y
MAINE								
1 ***Emery***	Y	Y	Y	Y	Y	Y	N	Y
2 ***Snowe***	Y	Y	Y	Y	Y	Y	N	Y
MARYLAND								
1 Dyson	Y	Y	Y	Y	Y	Y	Y	Y
2 Long	Y	Y	Y	Y	Y	Y	Y	Y
3 Mikulski	?	Y	Y	Y	Y	Y	Y	Y
4 ***Holt***	Y	Y	Y	Y	Y	Y	N	N
5 Hoyer	Y	Y	Y	Y	Y	Y	Y	Y
6 Byron	Y	Y	Y	Y	Y	Y	Y	Y
7 Mitchell	Y	Y	Y	Y	Y	N	Y	Y
8 Barnes	Y	Y	Y	Y	Y	N	Y	Y
MASSACHUSETTS								
1 ***Conte***	Y	Y	Y	Y	Y	Y	Y	Y
2 Boland	?	?	?	Y	Y	Y	Y	Y
3 Early	Y	Y	Y	Y	Y	?	Y	Y
4 Frank	Y	Y	Y	Y	Y	?	?	?
5 Shannon	Y	Y	Y	Y	Y	Y	Y	Y
6 Mavroules	Y	Y	Y	Y	Y	Y	Y	Y
7 Markey	Y	?	Y	Y	Y	Y	Y	Y
8 O'Neill								
9 Moakley	?	?	?	Y	Y	Y	Y	Y
10 ***Heckler***	Y	Y	N	Y	Y	Y	N	Y
11 Donnelly	Y	Y	Y	Y	Y	?	?	?
12 Studds	Y	Y	Y	Y	Y	Y	Y	Y
MICHIGAN								
1 Conyers	Y	Y	Y	N	Y	Y	Y	Y
2 ***Pursell***	Y	Y	Y	Y	Y	Y	N	Y
3 Wolpe	Y	Y	Y	Y	Y	Y	N	Y
4 ***Siljander***	Y	Y	Y	Y	Y	?	?	?
5 ***Sawyer***	Y	Y	Y	Y	Y	Y	Y	Y
6 ***Dunn***	Y	Y	Y	Y	Y	Y	N	Y
7 Kildee	Y	Y	Y	Y	N	Y	Y	Y
8 Traxler	Y	?	Y	Y	Y	Y	N	Y
9 ***Vander Jagt***	Y	Y	Y	Y	Y	?	?	?
10 Albosta	Y	Y	Y	Y	Y	Y	Y	Y
11 ***Davis***	Y	Y	Y	Y	Y	Y	N	Y
12 Bonior	Y	Y	?	Y	Y	Y	Y	Y
13 Crockett	?	N	Y	Y	Y	Y	Y	Y
14 Hertel	Y	Y	Y	Y	Y	Y	Y	Y
15 Ford	Y	Y	Y	Y	Y	?	Y	Y
16 Dingell	Y	Y	Y	Y	Y	Y	Y	Y
17 Brodhead	Y	Y	Y	Y	Y	Y	Y	Y
18 Blanchard	Y	Y	Y	?	?	Y	Y	Y
19 ***Broomfield***	Y	N	Y	Y	Y	Y	Y	Y
MINNESOTA								
1 ***Erdahl***	Y	Y	Y	Y	Y	Y	N	N
2 ***Hagedorn***	?	?	?	Y	Y	Y	N	N
3 ***Frenzel***	Y	Y	Y	Y	Y	Y	N	N
4 Vento	Y	Y	Y	Y	Y	Y	Y	Y
5 Sabo	Y	N	Y	Y	Y	N	Y	Y
6 ***Weber***	Y	Y	Y	Y	Y	Y	?	?
7 ***Stangeland***	Y	N	Y	Y	Y	Y	N	N
8 Oberstar	Y	Y	Y	Y	Y	Y	Y	?
MISSISSIPPI								
1 Whitten	Y	N	Y	Y	Y	Y	Y	Y
2 Bowen	Y	N	Y	Y	Y	Y	Y	Y
3 Montgomery	Y	N	Y	Y	Y	Y	Y	Y
4 Dowdy	Y	N	Y	Y	Y	Y	Y	?
5 ***Lott***	Y	Y	Y	Y	Y	?	Y	Y
MISSOURI								
1 Clay	Y	?	?	Y	Y	N	Y	?
2 Young	Y	N	Y	Y	Y	Y	Y	?
3 Gephardt	Y	Y	Y	Y	Y	Y	Y	Y

	52	53	54	55	56	57	58	59
4 Skelton	Y	N	Y	Y	Y	Y	Y	Y
5 Bolling	?	?	Y	Y	Y	?	Y	Y
6 ***Coleman***	Y	N	Y	Y	Y	Y	N	Y
7 ***Taylor***	Y	N	Y	Y	Y	Y	N	Y
8 ***Bailey***	?	X	?	Y	Y	Y	N	N
9 Volkmer	Y	Y	Y	Y	Y	Y	Y	Y
10 ***Emerson***	Y	N	Y	Y	Y	Y	N	Y
MONTANA								
1 Williams	Y	N	Y	Y	Y	?	Y	Y
2 ***Marlenee***	Y	N	Y	Y	Y	Y	N	Y
NEBRASKA								
1 ***Bereuter***	Y	N	Y	Y	Y	Y	N	Y
2 ***Daub***	Y	Y	Y	Y	Y	Y	N	Y
3 ***Smith***	Y	N	Y	Y	Y	Y	Y	Y
NEVADA								
AL Santini	Y	N	Y	Y	Y	?	?	?
NEW HAMPSHIRE								
1 D'Amours	Y	Y	Y	Y	Y	Y	Y	Y
2 ***Gregg***	?	Y	Y	Y	Y	Y	N	N
NEW JERSEY								
1 Florio	Y	Y	?	Y	Y	Y	Y	Y
2 Hughes	Y	Y	N	Y	Y	Y	Y	Y
3 Howard	?	?	?	Y	Y	Y	Y	Y
4 ***Smith***	Y	Y	Y	Y	Y	Y	N	N
5 ***Fenwick***	Y	Y	Y	Y	Y	Y	N	Y
6 ***Forsythe***	Y	Y	Y	Y	Y	N	N	N
7 ***Roukema***	Y	Y	Y	Y	Y	Y	Y	Y
8 Roe	?	?	?	Y	Y	Y	Y	Y
9 ***Hollenbeck***	Y	Y	Y	Y	Y	Y	N	Y
10 Rodino	Y	Y	Y	Y	Y	Y	Y	Y
11 Minish	Y	Y	Y	Y	Y	Y	Y	Y
12 ***Rinaldo***	Y	Y	Y	Y	Y	Y	Y	Y
13 ***Courter***	Y	Y	Y	?	?	?	N	Y
14 Guarini	Y	Y	Y	Y	Y	Y	Y	Y
15 Dwyer	Y	Y	Y	Y	Y	Y	Y	Y
NEW MEXICO								
1 ***Lujan***	?	?	?	Y	Y	Y	N	N
2 ***Skeen***	Y	N	Y	Y	Y	Y	N	Y
NEW YORK								
1 ***Carney***	Y	Y	Y	Y	Y	Y	N	Y
2 Downey	Y	Y	?	Y	Y	Y	Y	Y
3 ***Carman***	Y	Y	Y	Y	Y	Y	N	Y
4 ***Lent***	Y	Y	Y	Y	Y	Y	N	Y
5 ***McGrath***	Y	Y	Y	Y	Y	Y	N	Y
6 ***LeBoutillier***	Y	Y	Y	Y	Y	Y	N	Y
7 Addabbo	Y	Y	Y	Y	Y	Y	Y	Y
8 Rosenthal	Y	Y	Y	Y	Y	Y	Y	Y
9 Ferraro	?	?	Y	Y	Y	Y	Y	Y
10 Biaggi	?	?	?	Y	?	?	?	?
11 Scheuer	Y	Y	Y	Y	Y	Y	Y	Y
12 Chisholm	Y	#	?	Y	Y	?	?	?
13 Solarz	Y	Y	Y	Y	Y	Y	Y	Y
14 Richmond	Y	Y	Y	Y	Y	Y	Y	Y
15 Zeferetti	Y	?	Y	Y	Y	Y	Y	Y
16 Schumer	Y	Y	Y	Y	Y	Y	Y	Y
17 ***Molinari***	?	N	Y	?	Y	Y	N	Y
18 ***Green***	Y	Y	Y	Y	Y	Y	Y	Y
19 Rangel	Y	Y	Y	Y	Y	?	Y	?
20 Weiss	Y	Y	Y	N	Y	Y	Y	Y
21 Garcia	Y	Y	Y	Y	Y	?	Y	Y
22 Bingham	Y	Y	Y	Y	Y	Y	Y	Y
23 Peyser	Y	Y	Y	Y	Y	Y	Y	Y
24 Ottinger	Y	Y	Y	Y	Y	?	Y	Y
25 ***Fish***	?	?	?	?	?	Y	N	Y
26 ***Gilman***	Y	Y	Y	Y	Y	Y	N	Y
27 McHugh	Y	Y	Y	Y	Y	Y	Y	Y
28 Stratton	Y	Y	Y	Y	Y	Y	Y	Y
29 ***Solomon***	Y	Y	Y	Y	Y	Y	N	Y
30 ***Martin***	Y	Y	?	Y	Y	Y	N	Y
31 ***Mitchell***	Y	Y	Y	Y	Y	Y	N	Y
32 ***Wortley***	Y	Y	Y	Y	Y	Y	N	Y
33 ***Lee***	Y	Y	Y	Y	Y	Y	N	Y
34 ***Horton***	?	Y	Y	Y	Y	Y	N	Y
35 ***Conable***	?	#	?	Y	Y	?	Y	Y
36 LaFalce	?	?	?	Y	Y	Y	Y	Y
37 Nowak	Y	Y	Y	Y	Y	Y	Y	Y
38 ***Kemp***	Y	Y	Y	Y	Y	?	?	?
39 Lundine	Y	Y	Y	Y	Y	Y	Y	Y
NORTH CAROLINA								
1 Jones	?	?	?	Y	Y	?	Y	Y
2 Fountain	?	Y	Y	Y	Y	Y	Y	Y
3 Whitley	Y	?	?	Y	Y	Y	Y	Y
4 Andrews	?	?	?	Y	Y	Y	N	Y
5 Neal	Y	N	Y	Y	Y	Y	N	Y
6 ***Johnston***	Y	Y	N	Y	Y	Y	N	N
7 Rose	Y	N	Y	Y	?	?	Y	?
8 Hefner	?	?	?	Y	Y	Y	Y	Y

	52	53	54	55	56	57	58	59
9 ***Martin***	?	Y	Y	Y	Y	Y	N	Y
10 ***Broyhill***	Y	Y	Y	Y	Y	Y	N	N
11 ***Hendon***	?	?	?	Y	Y	Y	N	Y
NORTH DAKOTA								
AL Dorgan	Y	N	Y	Y	Y	Y	Y	Y
OHIO								
1 ***Gradison***	Y	Y	Y	Y	Y	Y	N	Y
2 Luken	Y	N	Y	Y	Y	Y	Y	Y
3 Hall	Y	Y	Y	Y	Y	Y	Y	Y
4 ***Oxley***	?	?	?	Y	Y	Y	Y	Y
5 ***Latta***	Y	Y	Y	Y	Y	?	N	Y
6 ***McEwen***	Y	Y	Y	Y	Y	Y	N	Y
7 ***Brown***	?	?	?	?	?	?	N	Y
8 ***Kindness***	Y	Y	Y	?	Y	Y	Y	Y
9 ***Weber***	Y	Y	Y	Y	Y	Y	N	N
10 ***Miller***	Y	Y	Y	Y	Y	N	N	Y
11 ***Stanton***	?	?	?	?	?	?	?	?
12 Shamansky	?	?	?	Y	Y	Y	Y	Y
13 Pease	Y	Y	Y	Y	Y	Y	Y	Y
14 Seiberling	Y	Y	Y	Y	?	Y	Y	Y
15 ***Wylie***	Y	Y	Y	Y	Y	Y	Y	Y
16 ***Regula***	Y	Y	Y	Y	Y	Y	N	Y
17 Vacancy*								
18 Applegate	Y	Y	Y	Y	Y	Y	Y	Y
19 ***Williams***	Y	Y	Y	Y	Y	?	?	Y
20 Oakar	Y	Y	Y	Y	Y	Y	Y	Y
21 Stokes	Y	Y	Y	Y	Y	Y	Y	Y
22 Eckart	Y	Y	Y	Y	Y	Y	Y	Y
23 Mottl	Y	Y	Y	Y	Y	Y	Y	Y
OKLAHOMA								
1 Jones	Y	N	Y	Y	Y	Y	Y	Y
2 Synar	Y	N	Y	Y	Y	Y	Y	Y
3 Watkins	?	?	?	Y	Y	Y	Y	Y
4 McCurdy	?	?	?	Y	Y	Y	Y	Y
5 ***Edwards***	Y	N	Y	Y	Y	Y	Y	Y
6 English	Y	N	Y	Y	Y	Y	Y	Y
OREGON								
1 AuCoin	?	?	?	?	?	?	?	?
2 ***Smith***	Y	N	Y	Y	Y	Y	N	N
3 Wyden	Y	N	Y	Y	Y	Y	Y	Y
4 Weaver	Y	Y	Y	Y	Y	Y	N	Y
PENNSYLVANIA								
1 Foglietta	?	?	?	?	?	?	?	?
2 Gray	?	#	?	Y	Y	Y	Y	Y
3 Smith	Y	N	Y	?	?	?	?	?
4 ***Dougherty***	Y	Y	Y	Y	Y	Y	?	?
5 ***Schulze***	Y	Y	Y	Y	Y	Y	N	Y
6 Yatron	?	?	Y	Y	Y	Y	Y	Y
7 Edgar	N	Y	Y	Y	N	Y	Y	Y
8 ***Coyne, J.***	Y	Y	Y	?	?	?	?	?
9 ***Shuster***	Y	Y	Y	Y	Y	Y	N	N
10 ***McDade***	Y	Y	Y	Y	Y	Y	Y	Y
11 ***Nelligan***	Y	Y	Y	Y	Y	Y	N	Y
12 Murtha	?	?	?	?	?	?	?	?
13 ***Coughlin***	Y	Y	Y	Y	Y	Y	N	N
14 Coyne, W.	Y	N	Y	Y	Y	Y	Y	Y
15 ***Ritter***	Y	Y	Y	Y	Y	Y	N	Y
16 ***Walker***	Y	Y	Y	Y	Y	N	N	N
17 Ertel	?	?	?	Y	?	?	?	?
18 Walgren	Y	Y	Y	Y	Y	Y	Y	Y
19 ***Goodling***	Y	Y	Y	Y	Y	N	N	N
20 Gaydos	Y	N	Y	Y	Y	Y	Y	Y
21 Bailey	Y	N	Y	Y	Y	Y	Y	Y
22 Murphy	Y	N	Y	Y	Y	Y	Y	Y
23 ***Clinger***	Y	N	Y	Y	Y	Y	Y	Y
24 ***Marks***	?	?	?	?	?	?	?	?
25 ***Atkinson***	Y	Y	Y	Y	Y	Y	N	Y
RHODE ISLAND								
1 St Germain	Y	Y	Y	Y	Y	Y	Y	Y
2 ***Schneider***	Y	Y	Y	Y	Y	Y	N	Y
SOUTH CAROLINA								
1 ***Hartnett***	Y	Y	Y	?	?	?	N	Y
2 ***Spence***	Y	Y	Y	Y	Y	Y	N	Y
3 Derrick	Y	Y	Y	Y	Y	Y	Y	Y
4 ***Campbell***	Y	Y	Y	Y	Y	Y	N	Y
5 Holland	Y	Y	Y	Y	?	Y	Y	Y
6 ***Napier***	Y	N	Y	Y	Y	Y	N	Y
SOUTH DAKOTA								
1 Daschle	Y	N	Y	Y	Y	Y	Y	Y
2 ***Roberts***	Y	N	Y	Y	Y	Y	Y	Y
TENNESSEE								
1 ***Quillen***	Y	X	?	Y	Y	Y	N	Y
2 ***Duncan***	Y	N	Y	Y	Y	Y	N	Y
3 Bouquard	?	X	?	Y	Y	Y	Y	Y
4 Gore	Y	N	Y	Y	Y	Y	Y	Y
5 Boner	?	?	?	Y	Y	?	?	?
6 ***Beard***	Y	N	Y	Y	Y	Y	N	Y

	52	53	54	55	56	57	58	59
7 Jones	?	?	?	Y	Y	?	?	?
8 Ford	Y	N	Y	Y	Y	Y	Y	Y
TEXAS								
1 Hall, S.	?	?	?	Y	Y	Y	Y	Y
2 Wilson	Y	?	?	?	?	?	?	?
3 ***Collins***	?	?	?	Y	Y	Y	N	N
4 Hall, R.	Y	N	Y	Y	Y	Y	N	Y
5 Mattox	?	X	?	Y	Y	?	?	?
6 Gramm	?	?	?	Y	Y	Y	Y	Y
7 ***Archer***	Y	Y	Y	Y	Y	Y	N	N
8 ***Fields***	Y	Y	Y	Y	Y	Y	N	N
9 Brooks	?	?	?	Y	Y	Y	Y	Y
10 Pickle	Y	N	Y	Y	Y	Y	Y	Y
11 Leath	Y	N	Y	Y	Y	Y	Y	Y
12 Wright	Y	N	Y	Y	Y	Y	Y	Y
13 Hightower	Y	N	Y	Y	Y	Y	Y	Y
14 Patman	Y	N	Y	Y	Y	Y	Y	Y
15 de la Garza	Y	N	Y	Y	Y	Y	Y	Y
16 White	Y	N	Y	Y	Y	Y	Y	Y
17 Stenholm	Y	N	Y	Y	Y	Y	Y	Y
18 Leland	?	X	?	Y	Y	Y	Y	Y
19 Hance	Y	N	Y	?	?	Y	Y	Y
20 Gonzalez	?	N	Y	Y	Y	Y	Y	Y
21 ***Loeffler***	Y	N	Y	Y	Y	Y	N	Y
22 ***Paul***	Y	Y	N	N	Y	Y	N	N
23 Kazen	Y	N	Y	Y	Y	Y	N	Y
24 Frost	Y	N	Y	Y	Y	Y	Y	Y
UTAH								
1 ***Hansen***	Y	N	Y	Y	Y	Y	N	Y
2 ***Marriott***	Y	N	Y	Y	Y	Y	N	Y
VERMONT								
AL ***Jeffords***	Y	Y	Y	Y	Y	Y	N	Y
VIRGINIA								
1 ***Trible***	?	?	?	Y	Y	?	N	Y
2 ***Whitehurst***	Y	N	Y	Y	Y	Y	Y	Y
3 ***Bliley***	Y	N	Y	Y	Y	Y	N	Y
4 ***Daniel, R.***	Y	N	Y	Y	Y	Y	N	Y
5 Daniel, D.	Y	N	Y	Y	Y	Y	N	N
6 ***Butler***	?	N	Y	Y	Y	Y	N	N
7 ***Robinson***	Y	N	Y	Y	Y	Y	Y	Y
8 ***Parris***	Y	N	Y	Y	Y	Y	N	Y
9 ***Wampler***	Y	N	Y	Y	Y	Y	N	Y
10 ***Wolf***	Y	N	Y	Y	Y	Y	N	Y
WASHINGTON								
1 ***Pritchard***	Y	Y	Y	Y	Y	Y	N	Y
2 Swift	Y	N	Y	Y	Y	Y	Y	Y
3 Bonker	Y	N	?	Y	Y	Y	Y	Y
4 ***Morrison***	?	?	?	Y	?	Y	N	N
5 Foley	?	N	Y	Y	Y	Y	Y	Y
6 Dicks	Y	N	Y	Y	Y	Y	Y	Y
7 Lowry	Y	N	Y	Y	Y	Y	Y	Y
WEST VIRGINIA								
1 Mollohan	Y	N	Y	Y	Y	?	Y	Y
2 ***Benedict***	Y	N	Y	Y	Y	?	N	Y
3 ***Staton***	Y	N	Y	Y	Y	Y	N	Y
4 Rahall	Y	N	Y	Y	Y	Y	Y	Y
WISCONSIN								
1 Aspin	Y	Y	Y	Y	Y	?	Y	?
2 Kastenmeier	Y	Y	Y	Y	Y	Y	Y	Y
3 ***Gunderson***	Y	N	Y	Y	Y	Y	N	Y
4 Zablocki	Y	N	Y	Y	Y	Y	Y	Y
5 Reuss	?	?	?	Y	Y	Y	Y	Y
6 ***Petri***	Y	Y	Y	Y	Y	?	N	N
7 Obey	Y	Y	N	Y	Y	Y	Y	Y
8 ***Roth***	Y	Y	Y	Y	Y	Y	N	Y
9 ***Sensenbrenner***	Y	Y	Y	Y	Y	Y	N	Y
WYOMING								
AL ***Cheney***	?	N	Y	Y	Y	?	Y	Y

** Rep. John M. Ashbrook, R-Ohio, died April 24, 1982. The last vote for which he was eligible was CQ vote 51.*

Southern states - Ala., Ark., Fla., Ga., Ky., La., Miss., N.C., Okla., S.C., Tenn., Texas, Va.

60. HR 5539. Reclamation Law Amendments. Kildee, D-Mich., amendment to make corporations numbering 18 persons or more who use irrigation water from federal reclamation projects pay "full cost" for all such water, according to a new formula in the bill. (The committee bill had permitted a lower-cost water rate for up to 960 acres of irrigated land owned by such corporations.) Adopted 220-160: R 81-92; D 139-68 (ND 114-27, SD 25-41), May 6, 1982.

61. HR 5539. Reclamation Law Amendments. Passage of the bill to amend the law governing farmers' use of irrigation water from federal reclamation projects. Passed 228-117: R 108-43; D 120-74 (ND 58-69, SD 62-5), May 6, 1982. A "yea" was a vote supporting the president's position.

62. Procedural Motion. Whittaker, R-Kan., motion to approve the House *Journal* of Monday, May 10. Motion agreed to 351-24: R 153-12; D 198-12 (ND 132-11, SD 66-1), May 11, 1982.

63. HR 6294. Housing Assistance Authorization. St Germain, D-R.I., motion to suspend the rules and pass the bill to provide a supplemental authorization to stimulate sales and production of single-family housing. Motion agreed to 349-55: R 135-43; D 214-12 (ND 149-4, SD 65-8), May 11, 1982. A two-thirds majority of those present and voting (270 in this case) is required for passage under suspension of the rules.

64. HR 3481. Pretrial Services Act of 1981. Passage of the bill to expand 10 demonstration programs providing federal judges pretrial services for determining a defendant's eligibility for bail. Passed 369-30: R 152-27; D 217-3 (ND 147-1, SD 70-2), May 11, 1982.

65. HR 861. National Trails System Act. Passage of the bill to amend the National Trails System Act by designating three new national scenic trails and authorizing study of six additional routes. Passed 389-6: R 170-5; D 219-1 (ND 147-0, SD 72-1), May 11, 1982.

66. H Con Res 322. United Nations and Israel. Fascell, D-Fla., motion to suspend the rules and adopt the concurrent resolution stating the sense of the Congress that if Israel is illegally expelled from, or denied its credentials to, the United Nations General Assembly or any specialized U.N. agency, the United States should suspend its participation in the General Assembly and withhold its assessed contribution to the U.N. or the specialized agency in question. Motion agreed to 401-3: R 182-0; D 219-3 (ND 147-3, SD 72-0), May 12, 1982. A two-thirds majority of those present and voting (270 in this case) is required for adoption under suspension of the rules.

67. HR 5922. Urgent Supplemental Appropriations, Fiscal 1982. Whitten, D-Miss., motion that the House resolve itself into the Committee of the Whole for consideration of the bill to provide $4,868,934,000 in net new budget authority for fiscal 1982. Motion agreed to 385-12: R 168-11; D 217-1 (ND 147-0, SD 70-1), May 12, 1982.

KEY

Y Voted for (yea).
\# Paired for.
+ Announced for.
N Voted against (nay).
X Paired against.
- Announced against.
P Voted "present".
C Voted "present" to avoid possible conflict of interest.
? Did not vote or otherwise make a position known.

Democrats   *Republicans*

Member	60	61	62	63	64	65	66	67
ALABAMA								
1 *Edwards*	N	Y	Y	Y	Y	Y	Y	Y
2 *Dickinson*	N	Y	?	?	?	?	Y	Y
3 Nichols	N	Y	Y	N	Y	Y	Y	Y
4 Bevill	N	Y	Y	Y	Y	Y	Y	Y
5 Flippo	N	Y	Y	Y	Y	Y	?	Y
6 *Smith*	Y	Y	Y	Y	Y	N	Y	Y
7 Shelby	N	Y	Y	Y	Y	Y	Y	Y
ALASKA								
AL *Young*	N	Y	Y	Y	Y	Y	Y	Y
ARIZONA								
1 *Rhodes*	?	#	?	?	Y	Y	Y	Y
2 Udall	N	Y	?	Y	Y	Y	Y	Y
3 *Stump*	N	Y	N	Y	N	Y	Y	Y
4 *Rudd*	N	Y	?	N	N	Y	Y	Y
ARKANSAS								
1 Alexander	N	Y	Y	Y	Y	Y	Y	Y
2 *Bethune*	N	Y	N	Y	Y	Y	Y	Y
3 *Hammerschmidt*	N	Y	Y	Y	Y	Y	Y	Y
4 Anthony	N	?	?	Y	Y	Y	Y	Y
CALIFORNIA								
1 *Chappie*	N	Y	Y	Y	Y	Y	Y	Y
2 *Clausen*	N	Y	Y	Y	Y	Y	Y	Y
3 Matsui	N	Y	Y	Y	Y	Y	Y	Y
4 Fazio	N	Y	Y	Y	Y	Y	Y	Y
5 Burton, J.	?	?	?	?	?	?	?	?
6 Burton, P.	Y	N	Y	Y	Y	Y	Y	Y
7 Miller	Y	Y	Y	Y	Y	Y	Y	Y
8 Dellums	Y	N	Y	Y	Y	Y	Y	Y
9 Stark	Y	X	?	Y	Y	Y	Y	Y
10 Edwards	Y	N	Y	Y	Y	Y	Y	Y
11 Lantos	Y	Y	Y	Y	Y	Y	Y	Y
12 *McCloskey*	N	Y	Y	N	Y	Y	Y	?
13 Mineta	N	Y	Y	Y	Y	Y	Y	Y
14 *Shumway*	N	?	Y	N	Y	Y	Y	Y
15 Coelho	N	Y	Y	Y	Y	Y	Y	Y
16 Panetta	N	Y	Y	Y	Y	Y	Y	Y
17 *Pashayan*	N	Y	Y	Y	Y	Y	Y	Y
18 *Thomas*	N	Y	Y	Y	Y	Y	Y	Y
19 *Lagomarsino*	N	Y	Y	Y	Y	Y	Y	Y
20 *Goldwater*	?	?	?	?	?	?	?	?
21 *Fiedler*	N	Y	Y	Y	Y	Y	Y	Y
22 *Moorhead*	N	Y	N	Y	Y	Y	Y	Y
23 Beilenson	Y	Y	Y	Y	Y	Y	Y	Y
24 Waxman	Y	N	Y	Y	Y	Y	Y	Y
25 Roybal	Y	N	Y	Y	Y	Y	Y	Y
26 *Rousselot*	?	Y	?	Y	Y	Y	Y	Y
27 *Dornan*	N	Y	N	Y	Y	Y	Y	Y
28 Dixon	N	Y	Y	?	Y	Y	Y	Y
29 Hawkins	N	Y	N	Y	Y	Y	?	Y
30 Vacancy								
31 Dymally	Y	Y	Y	Y	Y	Y	?	?
32 Anderson	N	Y	Y	Y	Y	Y	Y	Y
33 *Grisham*	?	?	?	?	?	?	?	?
34 *Lungren*	N	Y	N	Y	Y	Y	Y	Y
35 *Dreier*	?	#	?	?	?	?	?	?
36 Brown	N	Y	Y	Y	Y	Y	?	Y
37 *Lewis*	N	Y	Y	Y	Y	Y	Y	Y
38 Patterson	Y	Y	Y	Y	Y	Y	Y	Y
39 *Dannemeyer*	Y	Y	Y	N	Y	Y	Y	N
40 *Badham*	N	Y	Y	N	Y	Y	Y	Y
41 *Lowery*	N	Y	Y	Y	Y	Y	Y	Y
42 *Hunter*	N	Y	Y	N	Y	Y	Y	Y
43 *Burgener*	N	Y	?	?	?	?	Y	Y
COLORADO								
1 Schroeder	Y	Y	N	N	Y	Y	Y	Y
2 Wirth	Y	N	Y	Y	Y	Y	Y	Y
3 Kogovsek	N	Y	Y	Y	Y	Y	Y	Y
4 *Brown*	Y	Y	Y	N	N	Y	Y	N

Member	60	61	62	63	64	65	66	67
5 *Kramer*	N	Y	Y	Y	N	Y	Y	Y
CONNECTICUT								
1 Kennelly	Y	N	Y	Y	Y	Y	Y	Y
2 Gejdenson	Y	Y	N	Y	Y	Y	Y	Y
3 *DeNardis*	Y	?	?	Y	Y	Y	Y	Y
4 *McKinney*	Y	?	Y	Y	Y	Y	Y	Y
5 Ratchford	Y	Y	Y	Y	Y	Y	Y	Y
6 Moffett	Y	N	?	Y	Y	Y	Y	?
DELAWARE								
AL *Evans*	Y	?	Y	N	Y	Y	Y	Y
FLORIDA								
1 Hutto	?	Y	Y	Y	Y	Y	Y	Y
2 Fuqua	Y	Y	Y	Y	Y	Y	Y	?
3 Bennett	Y	Y	Y	Y	Y	Y	Y	Y
4 Chappell	Y	Y	?	?	Y	Y	Y	Y
5 *McCollum*	N	Y	Y	Y	Y	Y	Y	Y
6 *Young*	N	Y	Y	Y	Y	Y	Y	Y
7 Gibbons	Y	Y	Y	N	Y	Y	Y	?
8 Ireland	Y	N	?	?	?	?	?	Y
9 Nelson	N	Y	Y	Y	Y	Y	Y	Y
10 *Bafalis*	?	?	Y	Y	Y	Y	Y	Y
11 Mica	Y	Y	Y	Y	Y	Y	Y	Y
12 *Shaw*	N	Y	Y	Y	Y	Y	Y	Y
13 Lehman	Y	N	Y	Y	Y	Y	Y	Y
14 Pepper	N	Y	?	?	?	Y	Y	Y
15 Fascell	N	Y	Y	Y	Y	Y	Y	Y
GEORGIA								
1 Ginn	?	?	?	?	?	?	?	?
2 Hatcher	?	?	Y	Y	?	Y	Y	Y
3 Brinkley	N	Y	Y	Y	Y	Y	Y	Y
4 Levitas	Y	N	Y	Y	Y	Y	Y	Y
5 Fowler	N	Y	Y	Y	Y	Y	Y	Y
6 *Gingrich*	Y	N	?	?	?	?	Y	Y
7 McDonald	Y	Y	Y	N	N	N	Y	N
8 Evans	?	#	Y	Y	Y	Y	Y	Y
9 Jenkins	Y	Y	Y	Y	Y	Y	Y	Y
10 Barnard	?	?	Y	Y	Y	Y	?	Y
HAWAII								
1 Heftel	Y	Y	Y	Y	Y	?	?	?
2 Akaka	Y	Y	Y	Y	Y	Y	Y	Y
IDAHO								
1 *Craig*	N	Y	Y	Y	N	Y	Y	Y
2 *Hansen*	N	Y	Y	N	N	Y	Y	Y
ILLINOIS								
1 Washington	Y	N	Y	Y	Y	Y	Y	Y
2 Savage	Y	?	?	Y	Y	Y	N	Y
3 Russo	Y	N	?	Y	Y	Y	Y	Y
4 *Derwinski*	?	?	Y	Y	Y	Y	Y	Y
5 Fary	Y	Y	Y	Y	Y	Y	Y	Y
6 *Hyde*	N	?	Y	Y	Y	Y	Y	Y
7 Collins	Y	N	Y	Y	Y	Y	?	Y
8 Rostenkowski	?	?	Y	Y	Y	Y	Y	Y
9 Yates	Y	N	N	Y	Y	Y	Y	Y
10 *Porter*	N	Y	Y	Y	Y	Y	Y	Y
11 Annunzio	Y	Y	Y	Y	Y	Y	Y	Y
12 *Crane, P.*	N	Y	?	N	N	N	Y	Y
13 *McClory*	N	?	?	Y	Y	Y	Y	Y
14 *Erlenborn*	N	Y	Y	Y	Y	Y	Y	Y
15 *Corcoran*	N	Y	Y	N	+	+	Y	Y
16 *Martin*	N	N	Y	Y	Y	Y	Y	Y
17 *O'Brien*	N	?	Y	Y	Y	Y	Y	Y
18 *Michel*	N	?	Y	N	Y	Y	Y	Y
19 *Railsback*	Y	Y	Y	Y	Y	Y	Y	Y
20 *Findley*	Y	N	?	Y	Y	Y	Y	Y
21 *Madigan*	Y	N	Y	Y	Y	Y	Y	Y
22 *Crane, D.*	N	Y	Y	N	N	N	Y	Y
23 Price	Y	Y	Y	?	Y	Y	Y	Y
24 Simon	?	Y	Y	Y	Y	Y	Y	Y
INDIANA								
1 Benjamin	Y	Y	Y	Y	Y	Y	Y	Y
2 Fithian	Y	N	Y	Y	Y	Y	Y	Y
3 *Hiler*	Y	Y	Y	Y	Y	Y	Y	Y
4 *Coats*	Y	Y	Y	Y	Y	Y	Y	Y
5 *Hillis*	N	Y	Y	Y	Y	Y	Y	Y
6 Evans	?	?	?	?	?	?	Y	Y
7 *Myers*	N	Y	Y	Y	Y	Y	Y	Y
8 *Deckard*	Y	N	Y	Y	Y	Y	Y	?
9 Hamilton	Y	N	Y	Y	Y	Y	Y	Y
10 Sharp	Y	N	Y	Y	Y	Y	Y	Y
11 Jacobs	Y	N	N	Y	?	Y	Y	Y
IOWA								
1 *Leach*	Y	?	?	Y	Y	Y	Y	Y
2 *Tauke*	Y	Y	Y	Y	Y	Y	Y	Y
3 *Evans*	?	?	N	Y	Y	Y	?	Y
4 Smith	Y	?	Y	Y	Y	Y	Y	Y
5 Harkin	Y	N	N	Y	?	Y	Y	Y
6 Bedell	Y	Y	Y	Y	Y	Y	Y	Y

ND - Northern Democrats   SD - Southern Democrats

Corresponding to Congressional Record Votes 63, 64, 65, 66, 67, 68, 69, 70

	60	61	62	63	64	65	66	67
KANSAS								
1 ***Roberts***	N	Y	Y	Y	Y	Y	Y	Y
2 ***Jeffries***	N	Y	Y	N	N	Y	Y	N
3 ***Winn***	N	Y	Y	Y	Y	Y	Y	Y
4 Glickman	N	Y	Y	Y	Y	Y	Y	Y
5 ***Whittaker***	N	Y	Y	Y	Y	Y	Y	Y
KENTUCKY								
1 Hubbard	N	Y	Y	Y	Y	Y	Y	Y
2 Natcher	Y	Y	Y	Y	Y	Y	Y	Y
3 Mazzoli	N	Y	Y	Y	Y	Y	Y	Y
4 ***Snyder***	N	Y	Y	N	Y	Y	Y	Y
5 ***Rogers***	Y	Y	Y	Y	Y	Y	Y	Y
6 ***Hopkins***	N	Y	Y	Y	Y	Y	Y	Y
7 Perkins	Y	Y	Y	Y	Y	Y	Y	Y
LOUISIANA								
1 ***Livingston***	N	Y	Y	N	Y	Y	Y	Y
2 Boggs	N	Y	Y	Y	?	Y	Y	Y
3 Tauzin	N	Y	Y	Y	Y	Y	Y	Y
4 Roemer	Y	Y	N	Y	Y	Y	Y	Y
5 Huckaby	N	Y	Y	Y	Y	Y	Y	Y
6 ***Moore***	N	Y	Y	Y	Y	Y	Y	Y
7 Breaux	N	Y	Y	Y	Y	Y	Y	Y
8 Long	N	Y	Y	Y	Y	Y	Y	Y
MAINE								
1 ***Emery***	Y	X	Y	Y	Y	Y	Y	Y
2 ***Snowe***	Y	?	Y	Y	Y	Y	Y	Y
MARYLAND								
1 Dyson	Y	Y	Y	Y	Y	Y	Y	Y
2 Long	Y	Y	Y	N	Y	Y	Y	Y
3 Mikulski	Y	N	Y	Y	Y	Y	Y	Y
4 ***Holt***	N	Y	N	N	N	Y	Y	N
5 Hoyer	Y	Y	Y	Y	Y	Y	Y	Y
6 Byron	Y	Y	Y	Y	Y	Y	Y	Y
7 Mitchell	Y	Y	N	Y	Y	Y	Y	Y
8 Barnes	Y	N	N	Y	Y	Y	Y	Y
MASSACHUSETTS								
1 ***Conte***	Y	Y	Y	Y	Y	Y	Y	Y
2 Boland	Y	Y	Y	Y	Y	Y	Y	Y
3 Early	Y	?	Y	N	Y	Y	Y	Y
4 Frank	#	?	Y	Y	Y	Y	?	?
5 Shannon	Y	?	Y	Y	Y	Y	Y	Y
6 Mavroules	Y	N	Y	Y	Y	Y	Y	Y
7 Markey	Y	N	Y	Y	Y	Y	Y	Y
8 O'Neill								
9 Moakley	Y	Y	Y	Y	Y	Y	Y	Y
10 ***Heckler***	Y	N	Y	Y	Y	Y	Y	?
11 Donnelly	?	?	Y	N	Y	Y	Y	Y
12 Studds	Y	N	Y	Y	Y	Y	Y	Y
MICHIGAN								
1 Conyers	Y	N	Y	Y	Y	Y	N	Y
2 ***Pursell***	Y	?	?	Y	Y	Y	Y	Y
3 Wolpe	Y	N	Y	Y	Y	Y	Y	Y
4 ***Siljander***	?	?	Y	Y	Y	Y	Y	Y
5 ***Sawyer***	Y	N	Y	Y	Y	Y	Y	Y
6 ***Dunn***	Y	N	?	Y	Y	Y	Y	Y
7 Kildee	Y	N	Y	Y	Y	Y	Y	Y
8 Traxler	Y	N	?	Y	Y	Y	Y	Y
9 ***Vander Jagt***	?	?	Y	Y	Y	Y	?	Y
10 Albosta	Y	Y	?	?	?	?	Y	Y
11 ***Davis***	Y	Y	Y	Y	Y	Y	Y	Y
12 Bonior	?	N	Y	Y	?	?	Y	Y
13 Crockett	?	?	?	Y	Y	?	Y	?
14 Hertel	Y	N	Y	Y	Y	Y	Y	Y
15 Ford	Y	N	Y	Y	Y	Y	Y	Y
16 Dingell	Y	N	Y	Y	Y	Y	Y	Y
17 Brodhead	Y	N	Y	Y	Y	Y	Y	Y
18 Blanchard	Y	N	Y	Y	Y	Y	Y	Y
19 ***Broomfield***	N	Y	Y	Y	Y	Y	Y	Y
MINNESOTA								
1 ***Erdahl***	Y	Y	?	Y	Y	Y	Y	Y
2 ***Hagedorn***	Y	Y	Y	N	?	Y	Y	Y
3 ***Frenzel***	N	Y	Y	N	Y	Y	Y	N
4 Vento	Y	N	Y	Y	Y	Y	Y	Y
5 Sabo	Y	Y	N	Y	Y	Y	Y	Y
6 ***Weber***	Y	N	Y	Y	N	Y	Y	Y
7 ***Stangeland***	Y	Y	Y	Y	Y	Y	Y	Y
8 Oberstar	Y	N	Y	Y	Y	Y	Y	Y
MISSISSIPPI								
1 Whitten	N	Y	Y	Y	Y	?	Y	Y
2 Bowen	N	Y	Y	Y	Y	Y	Y	Y
3 Montgomery	N	Y	Y	Y	Y	Y	Y	Y
4 Dowdy	?	?	Y	Y	Y	Y	Y	Y
5 ***Lott***	N	?	Y	Y	Y	Y	Y	?
MISSOURI								
1 Clay	?	?	N	Y	Y	Y	Y	Y
2 Young	?	?	?	?	?	?	Y	Y
3 Gephardt	Y	Y	?	Y	Y	Y	Y	Y
4 Skelton	N	Y	Y	Y	Y	Y	Y	Y
5 Bolling	?	Y	Y	Y	Y	Y	Y	Y
6 ***Coleman***	N	Y	Y	Y	Y	Y	Y	Y
7 ***Taylor***	N	#	Y	N	N	Y	Y	Y
8 ***Bailey***	N	N	Y	Y	N	Y	Y	Y
9 Volkmer	Y	X	Y	Y	Y	Y	Y	Y
10 ***Emerson***	N	Y	N	Y	N	Y	Y	Y
MONTANA								
1 Williams	N	Y	Y	Y	Y	Y	Y	?
2 ***Marlenee***	N	Y	N	Y	Y	Y	Y	Y
NEBRASKA								
1 ***Bereuter***	Y	Y	?	?	?	?	Y	Y
2 ***Daub***	Y	Y	Y	Y	Y	Y	Y	Y
3 ***Smith***	Y	Y	Y	Y	Y	Y	Y	Y
NEVADA								
AL Santini	X	#	Y	Y	Y	Y	?	?
NEW HAMPSHIRE								
1 D'Amours	?	?	Y	Y	Y	Y	Y	Y
2 ***Gregg***	Y	N	Y	Y	Y	Y	Y	Y
NEW JERSEY								
1 Florio	Y	N	Y	Y	Y	Y	Y	Y
2 Hughes	Y	N	Y	Y	Y	Y	Y	Y
3 Howard	N	Y	Y	Y	Y	Y	Y	Y
4 ***Smith***	Y	Y	Y	Y	Y	Y	Y	Y
5 ***Fenwick***	Y	N	Y	N	Y	Y	Y	Y
6 ***Forsythe***	N	N	?	?	Y	Y	Y	Y
7 ***Roukema***	Y	N	Y	N	Y	Y	Y	Y
8 Roe	Y	Y	Y	Y	Y	Y	Y	Y
9 ***Hollenbeck***	Y	N	Y	Y	Y	Y	Y	Y
10 Rodino	Y	N	Y	Y	Y	Y	Y	Y
11 Minish	Y	Y	Y	Y	Y	Y	Y	Y
12 ***Rinaldo***	Y	N	Y	Y	Y	Y	Y	Y
13 ***Courter***	N	#	?	?	?	?	Y	Y
14 Guarini	Y	?	Y	Y	Y	Y	Y	Y
15 Dwyer	Y	Y	Y	Y	Y	Y	Y	Y
NEW MEXICO								
1 ***Lujan***	N	Y	Y	Y	N	Y	Y	Y
2 ***Skeen***	N	Y	Y	N	N	Y	Y	Y
NEW YORK								
1 ***Carney***	Y	Y	Y	Y	Y	Y	Y	Y
2 Downey	Y	N	Y	Y	Y	Y	Y	Y
3 ***Carman***	Y	Y	Y	Y	Y	Y	Y	Y
4 ***Lent***	Y	X	Y	Y	Y	Y	Y	Y
5 ***McGrath***	Y	N	?	Y	Y	Y	Y	Y
6 ***LeBoutillier***	Y	N	N	Y	Y	Y	Y	Y
7 Addabbo	Y	X	Y	Y	Y	Y	Y	Y
8 Rosenthal	Y	N	Y	Y	Y	Y	Y	Y
9 Ferraro	N	N	?	Y	Y	Y	Y	Y
10 Biaggi	?	?	Y	Y	Y	Y	Y	Y
11 Scheuer	Y	N	Y	Y	Y	Y	Y	Y
12 Chisholm	?	?	?	?	Y	Y	Y	?
13 Solarz	Y	N	Y	Y	?	?	Y	Y
14 Richmond	Y	?	Y	Y	Y	Y	?	?
15 Zeferetti	Y	X	Y	Y	Y	Y	Y	Y
16 Schumer	Y	N	Y	Y	Y	Y	Y	Y
17 ***Molinari***	Y	N	Y	Y	Y	Y	Y	Y
18 ***Green***	Y	X	Y	N	Y	Y	Y	Y
19 Rangel	Y	N	Y	Y	Y	Y	Y	Y
20 Weiss	Y	N	Y	Y	Y	Y	Y	Y
21 Garcia	Y	N	Y	Y	Y	Y	Y	Y
22 Bingham	Y	N	Y	Y	Y	Y	Y	Y
23 Peyser	?	?	Y	Y	Y	Y	Y	Y
24 Ottinger	Y	N	P	Y	Y	Y	Y	P
25 ***Fish***	Y	N	Y	Y	Y	Y	Y	Y
26 ***Gilman***	Y	N	Y	Y	Y	Y	Y	Y
27 McHugh	Y	N	Y	Y	Y	Y	Y	Y
28 Stratton	N	?	Y	Y	Y	Y	Y	Y
29 ***Solomon***	Y	N	N	Y	N	Y	Y	N
30 ***Martin***	Y	Y	Y	Y	Y	Y	Y	Y
31 ***Mitchell***	?	?	Y	Y	Y	Y	Y	Y
32 ***Wortley***	Y	Y	Y	Y	Y	Y	Y	Y
33 ***Lee***	Y	N	Y	Y	N	Y	Y	Y
34 ***Horton***	?	X	Y	Y	Y	Y	Y	Y
35 ***Conable***	N	N	Y	N	Y	?	Y	Y
36 LaFalce	Y	N	Y	Y	Y	Y	Y	Y
37 Nowak	Y	N	Y	Y	Y	Y	Y	Y
38 ***Kemp***	?	N	Y	N	Y	Y	Y	Y
39 Lundine	Y	N	Y	Y	Y	Y	Y	Y
NORTH CAROLINA								
1 Jones	?	Y	Y	Y	Y	Y	Y	Y
2 Fountain	N	Y	Y	Y	N	Y	Y	Y
3 Whitley	N	Y	Y	Y	Y	Y	Y	Y
4 Andrews	N	Y	Y	Y	Y	Y	Y	Y
5 Neal	Y	Y	Y	Y	Y	Y	Y	Y
6 ***Johnston***	Y	Y	N	N	N	Y	Y	N
7 Rose	?	?	Y	Y	Y	Y	Y	?
8 Hefner	N	Y	Y	Y	Y	Y	Y	Y
9 ***Martin***	N	N	Y	Y	Y	Y	Y	Y
10 ***Broyhill***	N	Y	Y	N	N	Y	Y	N
11 ***Hendon***	N	Y	Y	Y	N	Y	Y	Y
NORTH DAKOTA								
AL Dorgan	Y	N	Y	Y	Y	Y	Y	Y
OHIO								
1 ***Gradison***	N	Y	Y	N	N	Y	Y	Y
2 Luken	N	?	Y	Y	Y	Y	Y	Y
3 Hall	Y	N	Y	Y	Y	?	Y	Y
4 ***Oxley***	Y	N	Y	Y	Y	Y	Y	Y
5 ***Latta***	Y	Y	Y	N	Y	Y	Y	Y
6 ***McEwen***	Y	?	Y	Y	Y	Y	Y	Y
7 ***Brown***	Y	Y	?	?	Y	Y	?	?
8 ***Kindness***	N	Y	Y	Y	Y	Y	Y	Y
9 ***Weber***	Y	N	Y	Y	Y	Y	Y	Y
10 ***Miller***	Y	N	N	N	Y	Y	Y	Y
11 ***Stanton***	?	?	?	?	?	?	?	?
12 Shamansky	?	?	Y	Y	Y	Y	Y	Y
13 Pease	Y	N	?	Y	Y	Y	Y	Y
14 Seiberling	Y	?	Y	Y	Y	Y	Y	Y
15 ***Wylie***	N	Y	Y	Y	Y	Y	Y	Y
16 ***Regula***	Y	N	Y	Y	Y	Y	Y	Y
17 Vacancy								
18 Applegate	Y	N	?	Y	Y	Y	Y	?
19 ***Williams***	Y	Y	Y	Y	Y	Y	Y	Y
20 Oakar	Y	Y	Y	Y	Y	Y	Y	Y
21 Stokes	Y	Y	Y	Y	Y	Y	Y	Y
22 Eckart	Y	Y	Y	Y	Y	Y	Y	Y
23 Mottl	Y	N	Y	Y	Y	?	Y	Y
OKLAHOMA								
1 Jones	N	Y	Y	Y	Y	Y	Y	Y
2 Synar	N	Y	Y	Y	Y	Y	Y	Y
3 Watkins	Y	Y	?	Y	Y	Y	?	Y
4 McCurdy	Y	Y	Y	Y	Y	Y	Y	?
5 ***Edwards***	N	Y	Y	Y	Y	Y	Y	Y
6 English	Y	Y	Y	Y	Y	Y	Y	Y
OREGON								
1 AuCoin	?	?	Y	Y	Y	Y	Y	Y
2 ***Smith***	N	?	Y	Y	N	Y	Y	Y
3 Wyden	Y	N	Y	Y	Y	Y	Y	Y
4 Weaver	Y	N	Y	Y	Y	Y	Y	Y
PENNSYLVANIA								
1 Foglietta	?	?	?	?	?	?	?	?
2 Gray	Y	N	Y	Y	Y	Y	Y	Y
3 Smith	?	?	Y	Y	?	?	?	?
4 ***Dougherty***	?	N	Y	Y	Y	Y	Y	?
5 ***Schulze***	Y	X	Y	Y	Y	Y	Y	Y
6 Yatron	Y	N	Y	Y	Y	Y	Y	Y
7 Edgar	Y	N	N	Y	Y	?	Y	Y
8 ***Coyne, J.***	?	?	Y	Y	Y	Y	Y	Y
9 ***Shuster***	Y	Y	Y	Y	Y	Y	Y	Y
10 ***McDade***	Y	N	Y	Y	Y	Y	Y	Y
11 ***Nelligan***	Y	N	Y	Y	Y	Y	Y	Y
12 Murtha	?	?	?	?	?	?	Y	Y
13 ***Coughlin***	Y	N	N	Y	Y	?	Y	Y
14 Coyne, W.	N	Y	Y	Y	Y	Y	Y	Y
15 ***Ritter***	Y	N	Y	Y	Y	Y	Y	Y
16 ***Walker***	Y	N	N	N	Y	Y	Y	Y
17 Ertel	?	?	Y	Y	Y	Y	Y	Y
18 Walgren	N	N	Y	Y	Y	Y	Y	Y
19 ***Goodling***	Y	N	N	Y	Y	N	Y	Y
20 Gaydos	Y	?	Y	Y	Y	Y	Y	Y
21 Bailey	Y	Y	Y	Y	Y	Y	Y	Y
22 Murphy	Y	?	Y	Y	?	Y	Y	Y
23 ***Clinger***	Y	N	Y	N	Y	Y	Y	Y
24 ***Marks***	?	?	?	Y	Y	?	Y	?
25 ***Atkinson***	Y	N	Y	Y	Y	Y	Y	Y
RHODE ISLAND								
1 St Germain	Y	Y	Y	Y	Y	Y	Y	Y
2 ***Schneider***	Y	X	Y	Y	Y	Y	Y	Y
SOUTH CAROLINA								
1 ***Hartnett***	Y	Y	Y	Y	Y	Y	Y	Y
2 ***Spence***	N	Y	Y	Y	Y	Y	Y	Y
3 Derrick	Y	Y	?	Y	Y	Y	?	Y
4 ***Campbell***	N	Y	Y	Y	Y	Y	Y	Y
5 Holland	?	#	?	Y	Y	Y	Y	Y
6 ***Napier***	N	Y	Y	Y	Y	Y	Y	Y
SOUTH DAKOTA								
1 Daschle	Y	Y	Y	Y	Y	Y	?	Y
2 ***Roberts***	N	Y	?	Y	Y	Y	Y	Y
TENNESSEE								
1 ***Quillen***	N	Y	Y	Y	Y	Y	Y	Y
2 ***Duncan***	N	Y	Y	Y	Y	Y	Y	Y
3 Bouquard	N	Y	Y	Y	Y	Y	Y	Y
4 Gore	N	Y	Y	Y	Y	Y	Y	Y
5 Boner	?	?	Y	Y	Y	Y	Y	Y
6 ***Beard***	?	?	Y	Y	Y	Y	Y	Y
7 Jones	?	#	?	Y	Y	Y	Y	Y
8 Ford	Y	Y	Y	Y	Y	Y	Y	Y
TEXAS								
1 Hall, S.	N	Y	Y	Y	Y	Y	Y	Y
2 Wilson	?	?	?	?	?	?	Y	Y
3 ***Collins***	Y	Y	Y	N	N	Y	Y	N
4 Hall, R.	Y	Y	Y	Y	Y	Y	Y	Y
5 Mattox	?	?	?	?	?	?	?	?
6 Gramm	Y	Y	Y	N	Y	Y	Y	Y
7 ***Archer***	N	Y	Y	Y	Y	Y	Y	?
8 ***Fields***	Y	Y	Y	Y	N	Y	Y	Y
9 Brooks	N	Y	Y	Y	Y	Y	Y	Y
10 Pickle	N	Y	Y	Y	Y	Y	Y	Y
11 Leath	N	Y	Y	N	Y	Y	Y	Y
12 Wright	N	Y	Y	Y	Y	Y	Y	Y
13 Hightower	Y	Y	Y	Y	Y	Y	Y	Y
14 Patman	Y	Y	Y	Y	Y	Y	Y	Y
15 de la Garza	N	Y	Y	Y	Y	Y	Y	Y
16 White	N	Y	Y	Y	Y	Y	Y	Y
17 Stenholm	Y	Y	Y	N	Y	Y	?	?
18 Leland	N	Y	Y	Y	Y	Y	Y	Y
19 Hance	Y	N	Y	N	Y	Y	Y	Y
20 Gonzalez	N	Y	Y	Y	Y	Y	Y	Y
21 ***Loeffler***	N	Y	Y	Y	Y	Y	Y	Y
22 ***Paul***	Y	?	Y	N	N	N	Y	N
23 Kazen	N	Y	Y	Y	Y	Y	Y	Y
24 Frost	N	N	Y	Y	Y	Y	Y	Y
UTAH								
1 ***Hansen***	N	Y	?	Y	Y	Y	Y	Y
2 ***Marriott***	N	Y	?	+	+	+	Y	Y
VERMONT								
AL ***Jeffords***	Y	?	Y	Y	Y	Y	?	Y
VIRGINIA								
1 ***Trible***	N	#	Y	Y	Y	?	Y	Y
2 ***Whitehurst***	N	Y	Y	Y	Y	Y	Y	Y
3 ***Bliley***	N	Y	Y	Y	Y	Y	Y	Y
4 ***Daniel, R.***	N	Y	Y	Y	Y	Y	Y	Y
5 Daniel, D.	N	Y	?	Y	Y	Y	Y	?
6 ***Butler***	N	Y	N	N	Y	Y	Y	Y
7 ***Robinson***	N	Y	Y	Y	Y	Y	Y	Y
8 ***Parris***	Y	Y	Y	Y	Y	Y	Y	Y
9 ***Wampler***	N	Y	Y	Y	Y	Y	Y	Y
10 ***Wolf***	Y	Y	Y	Y	Y	Y	Y	Y
WASHINGTON								
1 ***Pritchard***	N	#	Y	Y	Y	Y	Y	Y
2 Swift	N	Y	Y	Y	Y	Y	Y	Y
3 Bonker	N	Y	Y	Y	Y	Y	Y	Y
4 ***Morrison***	N	Y	Y	Y	Y	Y	Y	Y
5 Foley	N	Y	Y	Y	Y	Y	Y	Y
6 Dicks	N	Y	Y	Y	Y	Y	Y	Y
7 Lowry	N	Y	Y	Y	?	?	Y	Y
WEST VIRGINIA								
1 Mollohan	N	Y	Y	Y	Y	Y	Y	Y
2 ***Benedict***	N	Y	Y	Y	Y	Y	+	Y
3 ***Staton***	N	Y	Y	Y	Y	Y	Y	Y
4 Rahall	Y	N	Y	Y	?	Y	Y	Y
WISCONSIN								
1 Aspin	?	?	Y	Y	Y	Y	Y	Y
2 Kastenmeier	Y	N	Y	Y	Y	Y	N	Y
3 ***Gunderson***	Y	N	Y	Y	N	Y	Y	Y
4 Zablocki	Y	Y	Y	Y	Y	Y	Y	Y
5 Reuss	Y	N	Y	Y	Y	Y	Y	Y
6 ***Petri***	Y	N	Y	Y	N	Y	Y	N
7 Obey	Y	N	Y	Y	Y	Y	Y	Y
8 ***Roth***	Y	N	Y	Y	Y	Y	Y	Y
9 ***Sensenbrenner***	Y	N	Y	Y	N	Y	Y	Y
WYOMING								
AL ***Cheney***	N	Y	Y	N	Y	Y	Y	Y

Southern states - Ala., Ark., Fla., Ga., Ky., La., Miss., N.C., Okla., S.C., Tenn., Texas, Va.

68. HR 5922. Urgent Supplemental Appropriations, Fiscal 1982. Boland, D-Mass., amendment to provide $1 billion to the Department of Housing and Urban Development for mortgage interest subsidy payments to home-buyers with family income not exceeding 130 percent of the median income for their area. Adopted 343-67: R 128-52; D 215-15 (ND 149-6, SD 66-9), May 12, 1982.

69. HR 5922. Urgent Supplemental Appropriations, Fiscal 1982. Walker, R-Pa., amendment to prohibit any expenditure of funds under the housing section of the bill if such expenditure would violate a 1978 law (PL 95-435) requiring that the federal budget be balanced. Rejected 132-276: R 114-66; D 18-210 (ND 4-149, SD 14-61), May 12, 1982.

70. HR 5922. Urgent Supplemental Appropriations, Fiscal 1982. Rousselot, R-Calif., amendment to continue under the Occupational Safety and Health Administration (OSHA) the authority to enforce safety standards on surface mining of stone, gravel, clay and phosphate, rather than transferring jurisdiction to the Mine Safety and Health Administration (MSHA) as provided in the bill. Rejected 186-220: R 132-46; D 54-174 (ND 9-143, SD 45-31), May 12, 1982.

71. Procedural Motion. Lungren, R-Calif., motion to approve the House *Journal* of Wednesday, May 12. Motion agreed to 293-73: R 103-60; D 190-13 (ND 124-10, SD 66-3), May 13, 1982.

72. HR 5890. NASA Authorization. Winn, R-Kan., amendment to reduce the aeronautics portion of the National Aeronautics and Space Administration authorization by $34.4 million. Rejected 169-204: R 134-33; D 35-171 (ND 19-120, SD 16-51), May 13, 1982.

73. HR 5890. NASA Authorization. Walker, R-Pa., amendment to bar the authorization of funds that would violate the law (PL 95-435) requiring a balanced budget. Rejected 121-248: R 99-70; D 22-178 (ND 11-120, SD 11-58), May 13, 1982.

74. HR 5890. NASA Authorization. Passage of the bill to authorize $6,647,300,000 in fiscal 1983 for National Aeronautics and Space Administration research and development. Passed 277-84: R 102-65; D 175-19 (ND 114-13, SD 61-6), May 13, 1982.

75. HR 6068. Intelligence Agencies Authorizations, Fiscal 1983. Passage of the bill to authorize secret amounts in fiscal 1983 for operations of U.S. intelligence agencies. Passed 357-23: R 168-1; D 189-22 (ND 121-21, SD 68-1), May 19, 1982.

KEY

Y Voted for (yea).
\# Paired for.
\+ Announced for.
N Voted against (nay).
X Paired against.
\- Announced against.
P Voted "present".
C Voted "present" to avoid possible conflict of interest.
? Did not vote or otherwise make a position known.

Democrats   *Republicans*

	68	69	70	71	72	73	74	75
ALABAMA								
1 *Edwards*	Y	N	Y	Y	Y	N	Y	Y
2 *Dickinson*	Y	N	Y	N	Y	N	Y	Y
3 Nichols	N	N	Y	?	?	?	?	Y
4 Bevill	Y	N	N	Y	N	N	Y	Y
5 Flippo	Y	N	Y	Y	N	N	Y	Y
6 *Smith*	Y	N	Y	N	Y	N	Y	Y
7 Shelby	Y	N	Y	N	Y	N	Y	Y
ALASKA								
AL *Young*	N	N	Y	?	Y	N	Y	Y
ARIZONA								
1 *Rhodes*	N	Y	Y	?	?	?	?	Y
2 Udall	Y	N	Y	Y	N	Y	N	Y
3 *Stump*	N	Y	Y	N	Y	Y	N	Y
4 *Rudd*	N	Y	Y	Y	Y	Y	?	Y
ARKANSAS								
1 Alexander	Y	N	Y	Y	N	N	Y	Y
2 *Bethune*	N	N	Y	N	Y	N	Y	Y
3 *Hammerschmidt*	Y	Y	Y	Y	Y	Y	Y	Y
4 Anthony	Y	N	Y	Y	N	N	Y	Y
CALIFORNIA								
1 *Chappie*	N	Y	Y	Y	Y	Y	Y	Y
2 *Clausen*	Y	N	Y	Y	Y	Y	Y	Y
3 Matsui	Y	N	N	Y	N	N	Y	Y
4 Fazio	Y	N	N	Y	N	N	Y	Y
5 Burton, J.	?	?	?	?	?	?	?	?
6 Burton, P.	Y	N	N	Y	N	N	Y	N
7 Miller	Y	N	N	Y	N	N	Y	N
8 Dellums	Y	N	N	?	N	N	Y	N
9 Stark	Y	N	N	?	N	Y	Y	N
10 Edwards	Y	N	N	Y	N	N	Y	Y
11 Lantos	Y	N	N	Y	N	N	Y	Y
12 *McCloskey*	?	?	?	?	?	?	?	Y
13 Mineta	Y	N	N	Y	N	N	Y	Y
14 *Shumway*	N	Y	Y	Y	Y	Y	N	Y
15 Coelho	Y	N	N	Y	N	N	Y	Y
16 Panetta	Y	N	Y	?	N	N	Y	Y
17 *Pashayan*	Y	Y	Y	Y	Y	Y	N	Y
18 *Thomas*	Y	Y	Y	N	Y	Y	Y	?
19 *Lagomarsino*	Y	Y	Y	Y	Y	Y	Y	Y
20 *Goldwater*	?	?	?	?	?	?	?	?
21 *Fiedler*	Y	Y	Y	N	N	Y	Y	Y
22 *Moorhead*	N	Y	Y	Y	Y	Y	Y	Y
23 Beilenson	N	N	N	N	N	N	Y	Y
24 Waxman	Y	N	N	Y	N	N	Y	Y
25 Roybal	Y	N	N	Y	N	N	Y	Y
26 *Rousselot*	N	Y	Y	N	Y	Y	Y	Y
27 *Dornan*	N	Y	Y	?	?	?	Y	?
28 Dixon	Y	N	N	Y	N	N	Y	Y
29 Hawkins	?	?	?	?	?	?	X	P
30 Vacancy								
31 Dymally	?	?	?	Y	N	N	Y	N
32 Anderson	Y	N	N	Y	N	?	?	Y
33 *Grisham*	?	?	?	?	?	?	?	?
34 *Lungren*	N	Y	Y	N	Y	Y	Y	Y
35 *Dreier*	?	?	?	?	?	?	?	?
36 Brown	Y	N	?	Y	N	N	Y	Y
37 *Lewis*	Y	Y	Y	N	N	Y	Y	Y
38 Patterson	Y	N	N	Y	N	N	Y	Y
39 *Dannemeyer*	N	Y	Y	Y	Y	Y	N	?
40 *Badham*	N	Y	Y	Y	Y	Y	N	?
41 *Lowery*	Y	Y	Y	Y	Y	Y	Y	Y
42 *Hunter*	N	Y	Y	Y	Y	Y	N	Y
43 *Burgener*	Y	Y	Y	Y	Y	N	N	?
COLORADO								
1 Schroeder	Y	N	N	N	N	N	N	N
2 Wirth	Y	N	N	Y	N	N	Y	+
3 Kogovsek	Y	N	N	Y	N	N	Y	Y
4 *Brown*	N	Y	Y	N	Y	N	Y	N
5 *Kramer*	N	Y	Y	N	Y	Y	Y	Y
CONNECTICUT								
1 Kennelly	Y	N	N	N	N	N	N	Y
2 Gejdenson	Y	N	N	N	N	N	N	Y
3 *DeNardis*	Y	N	N	?	N	N	Y	Y
4 *McKinney*	Y	N	N	Y	N	N	Y	Y
5 Ratchford	Y	N	N	Y	N	N	N	Y
6 Moffett	Y	N	N	?	N	N	?	?
DELAWARE								
AL *Evans*	Y	N	N	Y	N	N	Y	Y
FLORIDA								
1 Hutto	Y	N	Y	N	N	N	Y	Y
2 Fuqua	Y	N	Y	N	N	N	Y	Y
3 Bennett	Y	N	Y	N	N	N	Y	Y
4 Chappell	Y	N	Y	Y	?	N	Y	Y
5 *McCollum*	Y	Y	?	N	Y	Y	Y	Y
6 *Young*	Y	Y	Y	N	N	Y	Y	Y
7 Gibbons	N	N	Y	N	N	N	?	Y
8 Ireland	Y	Y	Y	N	N	N	Y	Y
9 Nelson	Y	N	Y	N	N	N	Y	Y
10 *Bafalis*	Y	Y	C	N	N	N	Y	?
11 Mica	Y	N	Y	N	N	N	Y	Y
12 *Shaw*	N	Y	?	?	Y	N	Y	Y
13 Lehman	Y	N	N	Y	N	N	Y	Y
14 Pepper	Y	N	N	Y	N	N	N	Y
15 Fascell	N	N	N	Y	N	N	N	Y
GEORGIA								
1 Ginn	?	?	?	?	?	?	?	?
2 Hatcher	Y	N	N	Y	N	N	?	Y
3 Brinkley	Y	N	Y	N	N	N	Y	Y
4 Levitas	Y	Y	N	Y	N	N	Y	Y
5 Fowler	Y	N	Y	N	N	N	Y	Y
6 *Gingrich*	Y	Y	Y	N	Y	Y	Y	N
7 McDonald	N	Y	Y	Y	Y	N	Y	Y
8 Evans	Y	N	N	?	?	?	?	Y
9 Jenkins	Y	Y	N	Y	N	Y	N	Y
10 Barnard	Y	Y	Y	Y	?	?	?	Y
HAWAII								
1 Heftel	?	?	?	?	N	Y	Y	Y
2 Akaka	Y	N	N	Y	N	N	Y	Y
IDAHO								
1 *Craig*	Y	Y	Y	Y	Y	Y	N	Y
2 *Hansen*	N	Y	Y	Y	Y	Y	N	Y
ILLINOIS								
1 Washington	Y	N	N	Y	N	Y	N	Y
2 Savage	Y	N	N	?	N	N	Y	?
3 Russo	Y	Y	N	Y	N	Y	Y	N
4 *Derwinski*	Y	Y	N	Y	N	Y	N	Y
5 Fary	Y	N	N	Y	N	N	Y	Y
6 *Hyde*	Y	N	N	Y	N	N	Y	Y
7 Collins	Y	N	N	Y	N	N	N	Y
8 Rostenkowski	Y	N	N	Y	N	N	Y	Y
9 Yates	Y	N	N	?	?	?	?	Y
10 *Porter*	Y	N	Y	Y	Y	Y	N	Y
11 Annunzio	Y	N	N	Y	N	N	Y	Y
12 *Crane, P.*	N	Y	Y	Y	Y	Y	N	Y
13 *McClory*	Y	Y	Y	Y	?	?	?	Y
14 *Erlenborn*	N	Y	Y	?	Y	Y	Y	Y
15 *Corcoran*	N	Y	Y	Y	Y	Y	Y	Y
16 *Martin*	N	Y	N	Y	Y	Y	Y	Y
17 *O'Brien*	Y	N	N	?	?	?	?	Y
18 *Michel*	N	Y	N	Y	N	Y	N	Y
19 *Railsback*	Y	N	Y	N	N	Y	Y	Y
20 Findley	Y	N	N	Y	N	N	Y	Y
21 *Madigan*	Y	Y	Y	Y	N	Y	Y	Y
22 *Crane, D.*	N	Y	Y	Y	Y	Y	N	Y
23 Price	Y	N	N	Y	N	N	Y	Y
24 Simon	Y	N	N	Y	N	N	Y	Y
INDIANA								
1 Benjamin	Y	Y	N	Y	N	N	Y	Y
2 Fithian	Y	N	N	Y	N	Y	N	Y
3 *Hiler*	Y	Y	Y	N	Y	Y	N	Y
4 *Coats*	Y	Y	N	N	N	Y	N	Y
5 *Hillis*	Y	Y	Y	N	Y	N	?	Y
6 Evans	Y	N	N	?	?	?	?	Y
7 *Myers*	Y	Y	Y	Y	N	N	Y	Y
8 *Deckard*	Y	N	Y	Y	N	Y	N	Y
9 Hamilton	Y	N	N	?	?	?	?	Y
10 Sharp	Y	N	N	Y	N	N	Y	Y
11 Jacobs	Y	Y	N	N	Y	Y	N	?
IOWA								
1 *Leach*	Y	N	Y	N	Y	N	Y	Y
2 *Tauke*	Y	N	Y	Y	N	N	Y	?
3 *Evans*	Y	N	Y	N	Y	N	Y	Y
4 Smith	Y	N	Y	Y	N	N	Y	Y
5 Harkin	Y	N	Y	N	?	?	?	Y
6 Bedell	Y	N	N	Y	N	N	Y	Y

ND · Northern Democrats   SD · Southern Democrats

Corresponding to Congressional Record Votes 71, 72, 73, 74, 76, 77, 78, 79

	68	69	70	71	72	73	74	75
KANSAS								
1 *Roberts*	N	Y	Y	N	Y	Y	N	Y
2 *Jeffries*	N	Y	Y	N	Y	Y	N	Y
3 *Winn*	Y	Y	Y	Y	Y	Y	Y	Y
4 Glickman	Y	N	N	Y	N	N	Y	Y
5 *Whittaker*	N	Y	Y	N	Y	Y	N	Y
KENTUCKY								
1 Hubbard	Y	N	Y	Y	?	?	?	?
2 Natcher	Y	Y	N	Y	Y	Y	Y	Y
3 Mazzoli	Y	N	N	Y	Y	N	Y	Y
4 *Snyder*	N	Y	Y	Y	Y	Y	Y	Y
5 *Rogers*	Y	N	N	Y	Y	N	Y	Y
6 *Hopkins*	Y	Y	N	N	Y	Y	Y	Y
7 Perkins	Y	N	N	Y	N	N	Y	Y
LOUISIANA								
1 *Livingston*	?	?	?	?	?	?	?	Y
2 Boggs	Y	N	Y	Y	N	N	Y	#
3 Tauzin	Y	N	Y	Y	Y	N	N	?
4 Roemer	N	N	Y	N	Y	Y	N	Y
5 Huckaby	Y	N	Y	Y	N	N	Y	?
6 *Moore*	Y	N	Y	Y	Y	N	Y	Y
7 Breaux	Y	?	Y	Y	N	N	Y	Y
8 Long	Y	N	Y	Y	N	N	Y	Y
MAINE								
1 *Emery*	Y	N	Y	Y	Y	N	Y	Y
2 *Snowe*	Y	N	Y	Y	Y	N	Y	Y
MARYLAND								
1 Dyson	Y	N	N	?	?	?	?	Y
2 Long	N	N	N	Y	N	N	Y	Y
3 Mikulski	?	?	?	Y	N	N	Y	Y
4 *Holt*	N	Y	Y	Y	N	N	Y	Y
5 Hoyer	Y	N	N	Y	N	N	Y	Y
6 Byron	Y	N	N	Y	Y	?	Y	Y
7 Mitchell	Y	N	N	N	N	N	N	N
8 Barnes	Y	N	N	N	N	N	Y	Y
MASSACHUSETTS								
1 *Conte*	Y	N	N	Y	Y	N	Y	Y
2 Boland	Y	N	N	Y	?	?	?	Y
3 Early	N	N	N	Y	N	?	?	Y
4 Frank	Y	N	N	Y	N	N	Y	Y
5 Shannon	Y	N	N	Y	N	N	Y	Y
6 Mavroules	Y	N	N	Y	N	?	?	Y
7 Markey	Y	N	N	Y	N	N	Y	Y
8 O'Neill								
9 Moakley	Y	N	N	Y	N	N	Y	Y
10 *Heckler*	Y	N	N	Y	N	N	Y	Y
11 Donnelly	N	N	N	Y	N	N	Y	Y
12 Studds	Y	N	N	Y	N	N	Y	Y
MICHIGAN								
1 Conyers	Y	N	N	Y	Y	N	Y	N
2 *Pursell*	Y	Y	Y	?	N	N	Y	Y
3 Wolpe	Y	N	N	Y	Y	N	Y	Y
4 *Siljander*	Y	Y	N	Y	Y	Y	N	Y
5 *Sawyer*	Y	N	Y	Y	Y	N	Y	Y
6 *Dunn*	Y	Y	Y	Y	Y	Y	N	Y
7 Kildee	Y	N	N	Y	N	N	Y	Y
8 Traxler	Y	N	N	Y	N	N	Y	Y
9 *Vander Jagt*	Y	Y	Y	Y	Y	Y	Y	Y
10 Albosta	Y	N	N	Y	N	N	Y	Y
11 *Davis*	Y	N	N	Y	N	N	Y	?
12 Bonior	Y	N	N	Y	N	Y	Y	Y
13 Crockett	Y	N	N	?	Y	?	?	N
14 Hertel	Y	N	N	Y	N	N	Y	Y
15 Ford	Y	N	N	Y	N	N	Y	Y
16 Dingell	Y	N	N	Y	N	N	Y	Y
17 Brodhead	Y	N	N	Y	N	Y	Y	Y
18 Blanchard	Y	N	N	Y	N	N	Y	Y
19 *Broomfield*	Y	Y	Y	Y	Y	Y	Y	Y
MINNESOTA								
1 *Erdahl*	Y	N	Y	Y	Y	N	N	?
2 *Hagedorn*	N	N	Y	N	Y	Y	N	Y
3 *Frenzel*	N	Y	Y	Y	Y	Y	N	Y
4 Vento	Y	N	N	Y	N	N	?	Y
5 Sabo	Y	N	N	Y	N	N	Y	Y
6 *Weber*	N	Y	Y	N	Y	N	N	Y
7 *Stangeland*	Y	N	Y	Y	Y	Y	N	Y
8 Oberstar	Y	N	N	Y	N	N	Y	Y
MISSISSIPPI								
1 Whitten	Y	N	N	Y	Y	N	Y	Y
2 Bowen	Y	N	N	Y	N	N	Y	?
3 Montgomery	Y	N	Y	Y	Y	?	?	Y
4 Dowdy	Y	N	N	Y	N	N	Y	Y
5 *Lott*	Y	Y	Y	N	Y	N	Y	Y
MISSOURI								
1 Clay	Y	N	N	?	N	N	Y	N
2 Young	Y	N	Y	Y	N	N	Y	Y
3 Gephardt	N	N	N	Y	N	N	Y	Y
4 Skelton	Y	N	Y	Y	?	?	?	?
5 Bolling	Y	N	N	?	N	Y	Y	Y
6 *Coleman*	Y	Y	Y	N	N	Y	Y	Y
7 *Taylor*	N	Y	Y	Y	?	Y	N	Y
8 *Bailey*	Y	Y	Y	N	Y	Y	N	Y
9 Volkmer	Y	N	N	Y	N	Y	Y	Y
10 *Emerson*	Y	Y	N	N	N	Y	N	Y
MONTANA								
1 Williams	Y	N	N	?	?	?	?	Y
2 *Marlenee*	Y	N	Y	Y	?	?	?	Y
NEBRASKA								
1 *Bereuter*	Y	N	Y	N	Y	N	N	Y
2 *Daub*	Y	Y	Y	N	Y	Y	N	Y
3 *Smith*	Y	Y	Y	N	Y	Y	N	Y
NEVADA								
AL Santini	Y	N	Y	Y	?	?	?	Y
NEW HAMPSHIRE								
1 D'Amours	Y	N	N	Y	Y	N	?	Y
2 *Gregg*	N	Y	Y	N	Y	Y	N	Y
NEW JERSEY								
1 Florio	Y	N	N	Y	N	N	Y	Y
2 Hughes	Y	N	N	Y	Y	N	N	Y
3 Howard	Y	N	N	Y	N	N	Y	Y
4 *Smith*	Y	N	N	Y	N	N	Y	Y
5 *Fenwick*	?	?	?	Y	?	?	Y	Y
6 *Forsythe*	Y	N	Y	?	Y	N	N	Y
7 *Roukema*	N	N	N	Y	Y	N	Y	Y
8 Roe	Y	N	N	Y	N	N	Y	Y
9 *Hollenbeck*	Y	N	N	N	N	N	Y	Y
10 Rodino	Y	N	N	Y	N	N	Y	N
11 Minish	Y	N	N	Y	N	N	Y	Y
12 *Rinaldo*	Y	N	N	Y	Y	N	Y	Y
13 *Courter*	Y	N	?	?	?	?	?	?
14 Guarini	Y	N	N	Y	N	?	?	Y
15 Dwyer	Y	N	N	Y	N	N	Y	Y
NEW MEXICO								
1 *Lujan*	Y	Y	Y	Y	Y	Y	Y	Y
2 *Skeen*	N	Y	Y	Y	Y	Y	Y	Y
NEW YORK								
1 *Carney*	Y	N	Y	N	Y	Y	Y	Y
2 Downey	Y	N	N	Y	N	N	Y	Y
3 *Carman*	Y	Y	Y	Y	Y	Y	Y	Y
4 *Lent*	Y	Y	N	Y	Y	N	Y	?
5 *McGrath*	Y	N	N	N	Y	Y	Y	Y
6 *LeBoutillier*	Y	Y	Y	Y	Y	N	N	Y
7 Addabbo	Y	N	N	Y	N	N	#	Y
8 Rosenthal	Y	N	N	Y	N	N	Y	Y
9 Ferraro	Y	N	N	Y	N	N	Y	Y
10 Biaggi	Y	N	N	Y	N	Y	Y	Y
11 Scheuer	Y	N	N	Y	N	N	Y	Y
12 Chisholm	Y	N	N	?	?	?	?	N
13 Solarz	Y	N	N	Y	N	N	Y	Y
14 Richmond	Y	N	N	Y	N	?	?	X
15 Zeferetti	Y	N	N	Y	N	N	Y	#
16 Schumer	Y	N	N	Y	N	N	N	Y
17 *Molinari*	Y	N	Y	Y	N	N	Y	Y
18 *Green*	N	N	N	Y	N	N	Y	Y
19 Rangel	Y	N	N	Y	N	?	?	N
20 Weiss	Y	N	N	?	Y	N	Y	N
21 Garcia	Y	N	N	Y	N	N	Y	N
22 Bingham	Y	N	N	Y	N	N	Y	Y
23 Peyser	Y	N	N	?	?	?	?	Y
24 Ottinger	Y	N	N	P	N	N	N	N
25 *Fish*	Y	N	Y	Y	Y	N	Y	Y
26 *Gilman*	Y	N	N	Y	Y	N	Y	Y
27 McHugh	Y	N	N	Y	N	N	Y	Y
28 Stratton	Y	N	Y	?	?	?	?	Y
29 *Solomon*	Y	Y	Y	N	Y	Y	N	Y
30 *Martin*	Y	Y	Y	Y	Y	Y	N	Y
31 *Mitchell*	Y	N	Y	?	Y	N	Y	Y
32 *Wortley*	Y	Y	Y	Y	Y	Y	Y	Y
33 *Lee*	Y	Y	Y	N	Y	Y	N	Y
34 *Horton*	Y	N	Y	Y	Y	N	Y	Y
35 *Conable*	N	N	Y	Y	Y	Y	N	Y
36 LaFalce	Y	?	?	?	?	?	?	Y
37 Nowak	Y	N	N	Y	N	?	Y	Y
38 *Kemp*	N	N	N	Y	Y	N	N	Y
39 Lundine	Y	N	N	Y	N	N	Y	?
NORTH CAROLINA								
1 Jones	Y	N	N	?	?	N	Y	Y
2 Fountain	Y	N	Y	N	Y	N	N	Y
3 Whitley	Y	N	Y	Y	Y	N	Y	Y
4 Andrews	Y	N	Y	?	N	?	Y	Y
5 Neal	?	?	?	?	?	?	?	Y
6 *Johnston*	N	Y	Y	N	Y	Y	N	Y
7 Rose	Y	N	N	?	?	?	?	Y
8 Hefner	Y	N	Y	?	N	N	Y	Y
9 *Martin*	Y	Y	Y	N	Y	N	N	?
10 *Broyhill*	N	Y	Y	Y	Y	N	N	Y
11 *Hendon*	Y	Y	Y	N	Y	Y	N	Y
NORTH DAKOTA								
AL Dorgan	Y	N	N	Y	N	N	N	Y
OHIO								
1 *Gradison*	N	Y	Y	Y	Y	Y	Y	Y
2 Luken	Y	N	N	Y	N	N	Y	Y
3 Hall	Y	N	N	Y	N	N	N	Y
4 *Oxley*	Y	Y	Y	Y	N	N	Y	Y
5 *Latta*	N	Y	N	Y	?	Y	N	Y
6 *McEwen*	Y	Y	N	Y	Y	Y	N	Y
7 *Brown*	?	?	?	?	?	?	?	?
8 *Kindness*	Y	N	Y	N	Y	N	N	Y
9 *Weber*	Y	N	N	Y	N	N	Y	Y
10 *Miller*	N	Y	Y	N	Y	Y	N	Y
11 *Stanton*	?	?	?	?	?	?	?	?
12 Shamansky	Y	N	N	Y	N	N	Y	Y
13 Pease	Y	N	N	Y	N	N	Y	Y
14 Seiberling	Y	N	N	Y	N	N	Y	N
15 *Wylie*	Y	Y	Y	Y	Y	N	N	Y
16 *Regula*	Y	N	N	Y	N	Y	Y	Y
17 Vacancy								
18 Applegate	Y	N	N	?	N	N	Y	Y
19 *Williams*	Y	N	N	Y	N	N	Y	Y
20 Oakar	Y	N	N	Y	N	N	Y	Y
21 Stokes	Y	N	N	Y	N	N	Y	N
22 Eckart	Y	N	N	Y	N	N	Y	Y
23 Mottl	Y	N	N	Y	N	N	Y	Y
OKLAHOMA								
1 Jones	Y	N	N	Y	N	N	Y	Y
2 Synar	Y	N	N	Y	N	N	Y	Y
3 Watkins	Y	N	Y	Y	N	N	Y	Y
4 McCurdy	Y	Y	Y	Y	?	N	Y	#
5 *Edwards*	Y	Y	Y	Y	Y	Y	Y	Y
6 English	Y	Y	Y	Y	N	N	Y	Y
OREGON								
1 AuCoin	Y	N	N	Y	N	N	N	?
2 *Smith*	Y	Y	Y	N	Y	Y	N	Y
3 Wyden	Y	N	N	Y	N	N	N	Y
4 Weaver	Y	N	N	Y	Y	?	?	?
PENNSYLVANIA								
1 Foglietta	?	?	?	?	?	?	?	?
2 Gray	Y	?	?	?	?	?	?	X
3 Smith	?	?	?	?	?	?	?	?
4 *Dougherty*	Y	N	N	Y	Y	N	?	?
5 *Schulze*	Y	Y	Y	Y	Y	Y	N	Y
6 Yatron	Y	N	N	Y	N	N	Y	Y
7 Edgar	Y	N	N	N	N	N	Y	N
8 *Coyne, J.*	Y	Y	N	Y	N	Y	Y	Y
9 *Shuster*	Y	Y	N	Y	Y	Y	N	Y
10 *McDade*	Y	N	N	N	Y	Y	Y	Y
11 *Nelligan*	Y	N	N	Y	Y	N	N	Y
12 Murtha	Y	N	N	?	?	?	?	?
13 *Coughlin*	Y	N	N	N	Y	N	Y	Y
14 Coyne, W.	Y	N	N	Y	N	N	Y	Y
15 *Ritter*	Y	Y	N	?	Y	Y	N	Y
16 *Walker*	N	Y	N	N	Y	N	Y	Y
17 Ertel	Y	N	N	?	?	?	?	?
18 Walgren	Y	N	N	Y	N	N	Y	Y
19 *Goodling*	N	Y	Y	N	Y	Y	N	Y
20 Gaydos	Y	N	N	Y	N	N	?	?
21 Bailey	Y	N	N	?	?	?	?	Y
22 Murphy	Y	N	N	Y	N	Y	Y	Y
23 *Clinger*	N	Y	Y	N	Y	Y	N	Y
24 *Marks*	Y	N	N	?	N	N	Y	Y
25 *Atkinson*	Y	Y	N	N	N	Y	Y	?
RHODE ISLAND								
1 St Germain	Y	N	N	Y	N	N	Y	Y
2 *Schneider*	+	-	-	+	+	-	+	Y
SOUTH CAROLINA								
1 *Hartnett*	N	Y	Y	N	Y	Y	N	Y
2 *Spence*	Y	Y	Y	Y	Y	Y	Y	Y
3 Derrick	Y	N	N	Y	N	N	Y	?
4 *Campbell*	?	?	?	?	?	?	?	Y
5 Holland	Y	N	N	Y	N	N	?	Y
6 *Napier*	Y	N	Y	Y	Y	Y	N	Y
SOUTH DAKOTA								
1 Daschle	Y	N	N	Y	Y	N	N	Y
2 *Roberts*	Y	Y	Y	N	Y	Y	N	Y
TENNESSEE								
1 *Quillen*	Y	N	Y	Y	?	?	?	Y
2 *Duncan*	Y	N	N	Y	N	N	Y	Y
3 Bouquard	Y	N	Y	Y	N	N	Y	Y
4 Gore	Y	N	N	Y	N	N	Y	Y
5 Boner	Y	N	N	Y	N	N	Y	Y
6 *Beard*	Y	N	Y	Y	Y	Y	N	Y
7 Jones	Y	N	Y	Y	N	N	Y	Y
8 Ford	?	N	N	Y	N	N	Y	Y
TEXAS								
1 Hall, S.	Y	N	Y	Y	Y	Y	Y	Y
2 Wilson	Y	N	N	Y	?	N	Y	Y
3 *Collins*	N	Y	Y	Y	Y	Y	Y	Y
4 Hall, R.	Y	N	Y	Y	N	Y	Y	Y
5 Mattox	?	?	?	Y	N	N	Y	?
6 Gramm	N	Y	Y	Y	Y	Y	N	Y
7 *Archer*	Y	Y	Y	N	Y	Y	Y	Y
8 *Fields*	Y	Y	Y	N	Y	Y	Y	Y
9 Brooks	Y	N	N	Y	N	N	Y	Y
10 Pickle	Y	Y	Y	N	Y	Y	Y	Y
11 Leath	N	N	Y	Y	N	N	Y	Y
12 Wright	Y	N	N	Y	N	N	Y	Y
13 Hightower	Y	N	Y	Y	?	?	?	Y
14 Patman	Y	N	Y	Y	Y	Y	Y	Y
15 de la Garza	Y	N	Y	Y	N	N	Y	Y
16 White	Y	N	Y	Y	N	N	Y	Y
17 Stenholm	N	Y	Y	N	Y	Y	N	Y
18 Leland	Y	N	N	?	N	N	Y	X
19 Hance	N	Y	N	Y	N	N	Y	Y
20 Gonzalez	Y	N	N	Y	N	N	Y	N
21 *Loeffler*	Y	Y	Y	N	Y	Y	N	Y
22 *Paul*	N	Y	Y	Y	Y	Y	N	N
23 Kazen	Y	N	Y	Y	Y	Y	Y	Y
24 Frost	Y	N	N	Y	N	N	Y	Y
UTAH								
1 *Hansen*	?	?	?	?	?	?	?	?
2 *Marriott*	Y	N	Y	Y	Y	N	Y	Y
VERMONT								
AL *Jeffords*	Y	N	Y	Y	?	?	?	Y
VIRGINIA								
1 *Trible*	Y	N	N	?	?	?	?	?
2 *Whitehurst*	Y	Y	Y	?	?	?	?	Y
3 *Bliley*	Y	Y	Y	?	Y	Y	Y	Y
4 *Daniel, R.*	Y	Y	Y	Y	Y	Y	Y	Y
5 Daniel, D.	Y	Y	Y	?	Y	Y	Y	Y
6 *Butler*	N	Y	Y	?	?	?	?	Y
7 *Robinson*	Y	Y	Y	Y	Y	Y	Y	Y
8 *Parris*	Y	Y	Y	Y	Y	Y	Y	Y
9 *Wampler*	Y	Y	N	Y	Y	Y	Y	Y
10 *Wolf*	Y	Y	Y	Y	Y	N	Y	Y
WASHINGTON								
1 *Pritchard*	Y	N	Y	Y	N	N	Y	Y
2 Swift	Y	N	N	Y	N	N	Y	?
3 Bonker	Y	N	N	Y	N	N	Y	Y
4 *Morrison*	Y	Y	N	Y	Y	Y	Y	Y
5 Foley	Y	N	N	Y	N	N	Y	Y
6 Dicks	Y	N	N	Y	N	N	Y	Y
7 Lowry	Y	N	N	Y	N	N	Y	N
WEST VIRGINIA								
1 Mollohan	Y	N	N	Y	N	N	Y	Y
2 *Benedict*	Y	Y	N	Y	Y	Y	Y	?
3 *Staton*	Y	Y	N	N	Y	Y	N	Y
4 Rahall	Y	N	N	Y	N	N	Y	Y
WISCONSIN								
1 Aspin	Y	N	N	Y	?	N	Y	Y
2 Kastenmeier	Y	N	N	Y	N	N	Y	Y
3 *Gunderson*	Y	Y	Y	N	Y	Y	N	Y
4 Zablocki	Y	N	N	Y	N	N	Y	Y
5 Reuss	Y	N	N	Y	N	N	Y	Y
6 *Petri*	N	Y	N	N	Y	N	Y	Y
7 Obey	Y	N	N	Y	N	N	Y	Y
8 *Roth*	Y	N	Y	Y	Y	Y	N	Y
9 *Sensenbrenner*	Y	Y	Y	N	Y	Y	N	Y
WYOMING								
AL *Cheney*	N	Y	Y	N	Y	N	N	Y

Southern states - Ala., Ark., Fla., Ga., Ky., La., Miss., N.C., Okla., S.C., Tenn., Texas, Va.

KEY

- **Y** Voted for (yea).
- **#** Paired for.
- **+** Announced for.
- **N** Voted against (nay).
- **X** Paired against.
- **-** Announced against.
- **P** Voted "present".
- **C** Voted "present" to avoid possible conflict of interest.
- **?** Did not vote or otherwise make a position known.

Democrats   *Republicans*

76. HR 5842. National Science Foundation Authorization. Winn, R-Kan., amendment to cut $30 million from the National Science Foundation authorization for fiscal 1983. Adopted 194-191: R 148-16; D 46-175 (ND 17-130, SD 29-45), May 19, 1982.

77. HR 5842. National Science Foundation Authorization. Walker, R-Pa., amendment to bar the authorization of funds that would violate the law (PL 95-435) requiring a balanced budget unless both houses of Congress have considered a constitutional amendment to require a balanced budget. Rejected 158-227: R 120-49; D 38-178 (ND 17-128, SD 21-50), May 19, 1982.

78. HR 5842. National Science Foundation Authorization. Winn, R-Kan., amendment to the Peyser, D-N.Y., substitute *(see vote 79, below),* to cut $30 million from the National Science Foundation authorization for fiscal 1983. Rejected 189-203: R 151-19; D 38-184 (ND 10-138, SD 28-46), May 19, 1982.

79. HR 5842. National Science Foundation Authorization. Peyser, D-N.Y., substitute to add $20 million for science and engineering education to the National Science Foundation authorization for fiscal 1983. Adopted 203-188: R 19-151; D 184-37 (ND 138-10, SD 46-27), May 19, 1982.

80. HR 5842. National Science Foundation Authorization. Passage of the bill to authorize $1,085,000,000 in fiscal 1982 and $1,089,481,000 in fiscal 1983 for the National Science Foundation. Passed 282-111: R 73-97; D 209-14 (ND 145-4, SD 64-10), May 19, 1982.

81. HR 5726. National Bureau of Standards Authorization. Fuqua, D-Fla., amendments to the Walker, R-Pa., amendments, to reduce the National Bureau of Standards authorization approved by the Science and Technology Committee by $6.228 million. Adopted 195-191: R 0-166; D 195-25 (ND 140-6, SD 55-19), May 19, 1982. (The Walker amendments would have cut $12.5 million from the authorization.)

82. HR 5726. National Bureau of Standards Authorization. Walker, R-Pa., motion to recommit the bill to the Science and Technology Committee. Motion rejected 193-193: R 163-3; D 30-190 (ND 7-139, SD 23-51), May 19, 1982.

83. HR 5726. National Bureau of Standards Authorization. Passage of the bill to authorize $117,800,000 for the National Bureau of Standards, $1,900,000 for the National Technical Information Service and $1,898,000 for the Office of Productivity, Technology and Innovation in fiscal 1983. Passed 249-131: R 43-118; D 206-13 (ND 143-4, SD 63-9), May 19, 1982.

	76	77	78	79	80	81	82	83
ALABAMA								
1 *Edwards*	N	N	N	Y	N	Y	N	Y
2 *Dickinson*	?	Y	Y	N	N	N	Y	?
3 Nichols	N	N	N	Y	Y	Y	N	Y
4 Bevill	N	N	N	Y	Y	Y	N	Y
5 Flippo	N	N	N	Y	Y	Y	N	Y
6 *Smith*	Y	Y	Y	N	Y	?	Y	N
7 Shelby	N	Y	N	Y	Y	Y	Y	Y
ALASKA								
AL *Young*	Y	Y	Y	N	Y	N	Y	Y
ARIZONA								
1 *Rhodes*	Y	N	Y	N	Y	N	Y	Y
2 Udall	N	N	N	Y	Y	Y	N	Y
3 *Stump*	Y	Y	Y	N	N	N	Y	N
4 *Rudd*	Y	Y	Y	N	N	N	Y	N
ARKANSAS								
1 Alexander	N	Y	N	Y	Y	Y	N	Y
2 *Bethune*	Y	N	Y	N	N	N	Y	N
3 *Hammerschmidt*	Y	Y	Y	N	N	N	Y	N
4 Anthony	Y	N	N	Y	Y	Y	N	Y
CALIFORNIA								
1 *Chappie*	Y	Y	Y	N	N	N	Y	N
2 *Clausen*	Y	Y	Y	N	Y	N	Y	N
3 Matsui	N	N	N	Y	Y	Y	N	Y
4 Fazio	N	N	N	Y	Y	Y	N	Y
5 Burton, J.	?	?	?	?	?	?	?	?
6 Burton, P.	N	N	N	Y	Y	Y	N	Y
7 Miller	N	N	N	Y	Y	Y	N	Y
8 Dellums	N	N	N	Y	Y	Y	N	Y
9 Stark	N	N	?	Y	Y	Y	N	Y
10 Edwards	N	N	N	Y	Y	Y	N	Y
11 Lantos	N	N	N	Y	Y	Y	N	Y
12 *McCloskey*	Y	N	Y	N	Y	?	?	?
13 Mineta	N	N	N	Y	Y	Y	N	Y
14 *Shumway*	Y	Y	Y	N	N	Y	N	N
15 Coelho	N	Y	N	Y	Y	Y	N	Y
16 Panetta	N	N	N	Y	Y	Y	N	Y
17 *Pashayan*	Y	Y	Y	N	N	N	Y	N
18 *Thomas*	#	?	?	X	X	?	#	X
19 *Lagomarsino*	Y	Y	Y	N	N	N	Y	N
20 *Goldwater*	?	?	?	?	?	?	?	?
21 *Fiedler*	Y	Y	Y	N	Y	N	Y	N
22 *Moorhead*	Y	Y	Y	N	N	N	Y	N
23 Beilenson	N	N	N	Y	Y	Y	N	Y
24 Waxman	N	N	N	Y	Y	Y	N	Y
25 Roybal	N	N	N	Y	Y	Y	N	Y
26 *Rousselot*	Y	?	Y	N	N	Y	N	N
27 *Dornan*	Y	Y	Y	N	N	?	#	?
28 Dixon	X	?	?	#	Y	?	X	?
29 Hawkins	N	N	N	Y	Y	Y	N	Y
30 Vacancy								
31 Dymally	N	N	N	Y	Y	Y	N	Y
32 Anderson	N	Y	N	Y	Y	Y	Y	Y
33 *Grisham*	?	?	?	?	?	?	?	?
34 *Lungren*	Y	Y	Y	N	N	N	Y	N
35 *Dreier*	#	?	?	X	?	?	?	?
36 Brown	N	N	N	Y	Y	Y	N	Y
37 *Lewis*	Y	Y	Y	N	N	N	Y	N
38 Patterson	N	N	N	Y	Y	Y	N	Y
39 *Dannemeyer*	Y	Y	Y	N	N	N	Y	N
40 *Badham*	?	?	?	?	?	?	?	?
41 *Lowery*	Y	Y	Y	N	Y	N	Y	N
42 *Hunter*	Y	Y	Y	N	N	N	Y	N
43 *Burgener*	?	?	?	X	?	?	?	?
COLORADO								
1 Schroeder	N	Y	N	Y	Y	Y	N	Y
2 Wirth	-	N	N	Y	Y	Y	N	Y
3 Kogovsek	Y	N	N	Y	Y	Y	N	Y
4 *Brown*	Y	Y	Y	N	Y	N	Y	N

	76	77	78	79	80	81	82	83
5 *Kramer*	Y	Y	Y	N	N	N	Y	N
CONNECTICUT								
1 Kennelly	N	N	N	Y	Y	Y	N	Y
2 Gejdenson	N	N	N	Y	Y	Y	N	Y
3 *DeNardis*	N	N	N	Y	Y	N	Y	N
4 *McKinney*	Y	N	Y	N	Y	N	Y	Y
5 Ratchford	Y	N	N	Y	Y	Y	N	Y
6 Moffett	N	N	N	Y	Y	Y	?	Y
DELAWARE								
AL *Evans*	Y	N	N	Y	N	Y	N	Y
FLORIDA								
1 Hutto	N	N	N	Y	Y	Y	N	Y
2 Fuqua	N	N	N	Y	Y	Y	N	?
3 Bennett	Y	N	N	Y	N	Y	N	Y
4 Chappell	N	N	N	Y	Y	Y	N	Y
5 *McCollum*	Y	Y	N	N	N	Y	Y	N
6 *Young*	Y	Y	Y	N	N	N	Y	Y
7 Gibbons	N	N	N	Y	Y	Y	N	Y
8 Ireland	N	N	N	Y	Y	Y	N	Y
9 Nelson	N	N	N	Y	Y	Y	N	Y
10 *Bafalis*	?	?	?	?	?	?	?	?
11 Mica	Y	N	N	Y	Y	Y	N	Y
12 *Shaw*	Y	Y	Y	N	N	N	Y	N
13 Lehman	N	N	N	Y	Y	Y	N	Y
14 Pepper	N	N	N	Y	Y	Y	N	Y
15 Fascell	N	N	N	Y	Y	Y	N	Y
GEORGIA								
1 Ginn	?	?	?	?	?	?	?	?
2 Hatcher	N	N	N	Y	Y	Y	N	Y
3 Brinkley	N	N	N	Y	Y	Y	N	Y
4 Levitas	Y	Y	Y	N	Y	Y	N	Y
5 Fowler	N	Y	Y	N	Y	Y	N	Y
6 *Gingrich*	N	Y	N	Y	Y	N	Y	N
7 McDonald	Y	Y	Y	N	N	N	Y	N
8 Evans	N	Y	N	Y	Y	Y	N	Y
9 Jenkins	N	Y	N	Y	Y	Y	N	Y
10 Barnard	N	N	N	Y	Y	Y	N	Y
HAWAII								
1 Heftel	N	N	N	Y	Y	Y	N	Y
2 Akaka	N	N	N	Y	Y	Y	N	Y
IDAHO								
1 *Craig*	Y	Y	Y	N	N	N	Y	N
2 *Hansen*	Y	Y	Y	N	N	N	Y	N
ILLINOIS								
1 Washington	N	N	N	Y	Y	Y	N	Y
2 Savage	N	?	N	Y	Y	Y	N	Y
3 Russo	N	N	N	Y	Y	Y	N	Y
4 *Derwinski*	Y	N	Y	N	N	N	Y	N
5 Fary	N	N	N	Y	Y	Y	N	Y
6 *Hyde*	Y	N	Y	N	N	N	Y	N
7 Collins	N	N	N	Y	Y	Y	N	Y
8 Rostenkowski	N	N	N	Y	Y	Y	N	Y
9 Yates	N	N	N	Y	Y	Y	N	Y
10 *Porter*	Y	N	N	Y	N	Y	N	Y
11 Annunzio	N	N	N	Y	Y	Y	N	Y
12 *Crane, P.*	#	?	?	X	X	?	#	X
13 *McClory*	Y	N	Y	N	N	N	Y	N
14 *Erlenborn*	Y	Y	Y	N	N	N	Y	N
15 *Corcoran*	Y	Y	Y	N	N	N	Y	N
16 *Martin*	Y	Y	Y	N	N	N	Y	N
17 *O'Brien*	Y	N	N	Y	N	N	Y	N
18 *Michel*	#	N	Y	N	N	N	Y	N
19 *Railsback*	Y	N	Y	N	Y	N	Y	N
20 *Findley*	Y	Y	Y	N	Y	?	#	Y
21 *Madigan*	Y	Y	Y	N	N	N	Y	N
22 *Crane, D.*	Y	Y	Y	N	N	N	Y	N
23 Price	N	N	N	Y	Y	Y	N	Y
24 Simon	N	N	N	Y	Y	Y	N	Y
INDIANA								
1 Benjamin	N	N	N	Y	Y	Y	N	Y
2 Fithian	N	Y	N	N	Y	Y	N	Y
3 *Hiler*	Y	Y	Y	N	N	N	Y	N
4 *Coats*	Y	Y	Y	N	N	N	Y	N
5 *Hillis*	Y	Y	Y	N	N	N	Y	N
6 Evans	N	N	N	Y	Y	Y	N	Y
7 *Myers*	Y	Y	Y	N	N	N	Y	N
8 *Deckard*	Y	Y	Y	?	N	Y	N	Y
9 Hamilton	N	Y	N	Y	Y	N	N	Y
10 Sharp	N	Y	N	Y	Y	N	N	Y
11 Jacobs	?	?	?	?	?	?	?	?
IOWA								
1 *Leach*	N	N	N	Y	#	N	Y	Y
2 *Tauke*	?	N	N	Y	N	Y	Y	N
3 *Evans*	N	N	Y	N	Y	N	Y	N
4 Smith	N	N	N	Y	Y	Y	N	Y
5 Harkin	N	N	N	Y	Y	Y	N	Y
6 Bedell	N	N	N	Y	Y	Y	N	Y

ND - Northern Democrats   SD - Southern Democrats

	76	77	78	79	80	81	82	83
KANSAS								
1 ***Roberts***	Y	Y	Y	N	N	N	Y	N
2 ***Jeffries***	Y	Y	Y	N	N	N	Y	N
3 ***Winn***	Y	Y	Y	N	Y	N	Y	N
4 Glickman	N	N	N	Y	Y	Y	N	Y
5 ***Whittaker***	Y	Y	Y	N	N	N	Y	N
KENTUCKY								
1 Hubbard	?	?	?	?	?	?	?	?
2 Natcher	Y	Y	Y	N	Y	N	N	Y
3 Mazzoli	N	N	N	Y	Y	Y	N	Y
4 ***Snyder***	Y	Y	Y	N	N	N	Y	N
5 ***Rogers***	Y	N	?	?	?	?	?	?
6 ***Hopkins***	Y	Y	Y	N	N	N	Y	N
7 Perkins	N	N	N	Y	Y	N	N	Y
LOUISIANA								
1 ***Livingston***	Y	Y	Y	N	N	N	Y	Y
2 Boggs	N	N	N	Y	Y	Y	N	Y
3 Tauzin	Y	Y	Y	N	Y	N	Y	Y
4 Roemer	Y	N	Y	N	Y	N	Y	Y
5 Huckaby	Y	Y	Y	N	Y	N	N	Y
6 ***Moore***	Y	N	Y	N	Y	N	Y	Y
7 Breaux	Y	N	N	Y	Y	Y	N	Y
8 Long	N	N	N	Y	Y	Y	N	Y
MAINE								
1 ***Emery***	Y	N	Y	N	Y	N	Y	Y
2 ***Snowe***	Y	Y	Y	N	Y	N	Y	Y
MARYLAND								
1 Dyson	Y	Y	Y	N	Y	Y	N	Y
2 Long	Y	N	N	?	Y	Y	N	Y
3 Mikulski	N	N	N	Y	Y	Y	N	Y
4 ***Holt***	Y	N	Y	N	Y	N	Y	Y
5 Hoyer	N	N	N	?	Y	Y	N	Y
6 Byron	Y	N	Y	N	Y	Y	N	Y
7 Mitchell	N	?	N	Y	Y	Y	N	Y
8 Barnes	N	N	N	Y	Y	Y	N	Y
MASSACHUSETTS								
1 ***Conte***	N	N	N	Y	Y	N	Y	Y
2 Boland	N	N	N	Y	Y	Y	N	Y
3 Early	N	N	N	Y	Y	Y	N	Y
4 Frank	N	N	N	Y	Y	Y	N	Y
5 Shannon	N	N	N	Y	Y	Y	N	Y
6 Mavroules	N	N	N	Y	Y	Y	N	Y
7 Markey	N	N	N	Y	Y	Y	N	Y
8 O'Neill								
9 Moakley	N	N	N	Y	Y	Y	N	Y
10 ***Heckler***	N	N	N	Y	Y	N	Y	Y
11 Donnelly	N	N	N	Y	Y	Y	N	Y
12 Studds	N	N	N	Y	Y	Y	N	Y
MICHIGAN								
1 Conyers	N	N	N	Y	Y	Y	N	Y
2 ***Pursell***	N	N	N	N	Y	N	Y	Y
3 Wolpe	N	N	N	Y	Y	Y	N	Y
4 ***Siljander***	Y	Y	Y	N	N	N	Y	N
5 ***Sawyer***	Y	N	Y	N	Y	N	Y	Y
6 ***Dunn***	N	Y	N	Y	Y	Y	Y	N
7 Kildee	N	N	N	Y	Y	Y	N	Y
8 Traxler	N	N	N	Y	Y	Y	N	Y
9 ***Vander Jagt***	Y	Y	Y	N	Y	N	Y	Y
10 Albosta	Y	N	N	Y	Y	Y	N	Y
11 ***Davis***	Y	N	N	N	Y	N	Y	Y
12 Bonior	N	N	N	Y	Y	Y	N	Y
13 Crockett	N	N	N	Y	Y	?	?	?
14 Hertel	N	N	N	Y	Y	Y	N	Y
15 Ford	N	N	N	Y	Y	Y	N	Y
16 Dingell	N	N	N	Y	Y	Y	N	Y
17 Brodhead	N	N	N	N	Y	Y	N	Y
18 Blanchard	N	N	N	Y	Y	Y	N	Y
19 ***Broomfield***	Y	Y	Y	N	Y	N	Y	N
MINNESOTA								
1 ***Erdahl***	?	?	?	?	?	?	?	?
2 ***Hagedorn***	Y	Y	Y	N	N	N	Y	N
3 ***Frenzel***	Y	N	Y	N	N	N	Y	N
4 Vento	N	N	N	Y	Y	Y	N	Y
5 Sabo	N	N	N	Y	Y	Y	N	Y
6 ***Weber***	Y	Y	Y	N	N	N	Y	N
7 ***Stangeland***	Y	Y	Y	N	N	N	Y	N
8 Oberstar	N	N	N	Y	Y	Y	N	Y
MISSISSIPPI								
1 Whitten	Y	N	Y	N	Y	N	Y	Y
2 Bowen	?	?	?	?	?	?	?	?
3 Montgomery	Y	N	Y	N	Y	N	Y	Y
4 Dowdy	Y	?	Y	Y	Y	Y	N	Y
5 ***Lott***	Y	N	Y	N	N	N	Y	N
MISSOURI								
1 Clay	N	N	N	Y	Y	Y	N	Y
2 Young	N	N	N	Y	Y	Y	N	Y
3 Gephardt	N	Y	N	Y	Y	Y	N	Y
4 Skelton	N	Y	N	Y	N	N	Y	N
5 Bolling	N	?	N	Y	?	Y	?	?
6 ***Coleman***	N	Y	N	Y	Y	N	Y	N
7 ***Taylor***	Y	Y	Y	N	N	N	Y	N
8 ***Bailey***	Y	Y	Y	N	Y	N	Y	N
9 Volkmer	N	Y	N	Y	Y	Y	N	Y
10 ***Emerson***	Y	Y	Y	N	N	N	Y	N
MONTANA								
1 Williams	N	N	N	Y	Y	Y	N	Y
2 ***Marlenee***	?	Y	Y	N	N	N	Y	N
NEBRASKA								
1 ***Bereuter***	Y	Y	Y	N	Y	N	Y	N
2 ***Daub***	Y	Y	Y	N	Y	N	Y	N
3 ***Smith***	Y	Y	Y	N	N	N	Y	N
NEVADA								
AL Santini	Y	Y	?	N	Y	Y	Y	Y
NEW HAMPSHIRE								
1 D'Amours	N	N	N	Y	Y	N	Y	Y
2 ***Gregg***	Y	Y	Y	N	N	N	Y	N
NEW JERSEY								
1 Florio	Y	N	N	Y	Y	Y	N	Y
2 Hughes	Y	N	Y	N	Y	Y	N	Y
3 Howard	N	N	N	Y	Y	Y	N	Y
4 ***Smith***	Y	Y	Y	N	Y	N	Y	Y
5 ***Fenwick***	Y	Y	Y	N	Y	?	?	#
6 ***Forsythe***	Y	N	Y	N	Y	N	Y	N
7 ***Roukema***	Y	N	Y	N	Y	N	Y	Y
8 Roe	N	P	N	Y	Y	Y	N	Y
9 ***Hollenbeck***	N	N	N	Y	Y	N	N	Y
10 Rodino	N	N	N	Y	Y	Y	N	Y
11 Minish	N	N	N	Y	Y	Y	N	Y
12 ***Rinaldo***	N	N	N	Y	Y	N	Y	Y
13 ***Courter***	?	?	?	?	#	?	?	#
14 Guarini	Y	N	N	Y	Y	Y	N	Y
15 Dwyer	Y	N	N	Y	Y	Y	N	Y
NEW MEXICO								
1 ***Lujan***	Y	Y	Y	N	N	N	Y	N
2 ***Skeen***	Y	Y	Y	N	Y	N	Y	N
NEW YORK								
1 ***Carney***	Y	Y	Y	N	Y	N	Y	N
2 Downey	N	Y	N	Y	Y	Y	N	Y
3 ***Carman***	Y	Y	Y	N	N	N	Y	N
4 ***Lent***	?	Y	Y	N	N	N	Y	N
5 ***McGrath***	Y	Y	Y	N	Y	N	Y	N
6 ***LeBoutillier***	Y	Y	Y	N	N	N	Y	N
7 Addabbo	Y	N	N	Y	Y	Y	N	Y
8 Rosenthal	N	N	N	Y	Y	Y	N	Y
9 Ferraro	N	N	N	Y	Y	?	?	?
10 Biaggi	N	N	N	Y	Y	Y	N	Y
11 Scheuer	N	N	N	Y	Y	Y	N	Y
12 Chisholm	N	N	N	Y	Y	?	N	Y
13 Solarz	N	N	N	Y	Y	Y	N	Y
14 Richmond	X	N	N	Y	Y	Y	N	Y
15 Zeferetti	?	?	?	#	#	?	X	#
16 Schumer	N	N	N	Y	Y	Y	N	Y
17 ***Molinari***	Y	Y	Y	N	Y	N	Y	N
18 ***Green***	N	N	N	Y	Y	N	Y	Y
19 Rangel	N	N	N	Y	Y	Y	N	Y
20 Weiss	N	N	N	Y	Y	Y	N	Y
21 Garcia	N	N	N	Y	Y	Y	N	Y
22 Bingham	N	?	N	Y	Y	Y	N	Y
23 Peyser	N	N	N	Y	Y	?	N	Y
24 Ottinger	N	N	N	Y	Y	Y	N	Y
25 ***Fish***	?	?	?	?	?	?	Y	Y
26 ***Gilman***	Y	N	Y	N	Y	N	Y	Y
27 McHugh	N	N	N	Y	Y	Y	N	Y
28 Stratton	Y	N	Y	Y	Y	Y	Y	Y
29 ***Solomon***	Y	Y	Y	N	N	N	Y	N
30 ***Martin***	Y	Y	Y	N	Y	N	Y	Y
31 ***Mitchell***	Y	N	Y	N	Y	N	Y	Y
32 ***Wortley***	Y	N	Y	N	N	N	Y	N
33 ***Lee***	Y	Y	Y	N	Y	N	Y	Y
34 ***Horton***	?	?	Y	N	Y	N	Y	Y
35 ***Conable***	Y	Y	Y	N	N	N	Y	N
36 LaFalce	N	N	N	Y	Y	Y	N	Y
37 Nowak	N	N	N	Y	Y	Y	N	Y
38 ***Kemp***	?	?	Y	N	N	N	Y	N
39 Lundine	?	?	?	?	?	?	?	?
NORTH CAROLINA								
1 Jones	N	N	N	N	Y	Y	N	Y
2 Fountain	Y	N	Y	N	Y	N	Y	Y
3 Whitley	Y	N	Y	N	Y	N	Y	Y
4 Andrews	N	N	N	Y	Y	Y	N	Y
5 Neal	N	N	N	Y	Y	Y	N	Y
6 ***Johnston***	Y	Y	?	N	N	N	Y	N
7 Rose	N	N	N	N	Y	Y	N	Y
8 Hefner	Y	N	Y	N	Y	Y	Y	Y
9 ***Martin***	?	?	?	?	?	?	?	?
10 ***Broyhill***	Y	Y	Y	N	N	N	Y	N
11 ***Hendon***	Y	Y	Y	N	N	N	Y	N
NORTH DAKOTA								
AL Dorgan	N	Y	N	Y	Y	Y	N	Y
OHIO								
1 ***Gradison***	Y	Y	Y	N	N	N	Y	N
2 Luken	N	N	N	Y	Y	Y	N	Y
3 Hall	Y	N	Y	N	Y	Y	N	N
4 ***Oxley***	Y	N	Y	N	N	N	Y	N
5 ***Latta***	Y	Y	Y	N	N	N	Y	N
6 ***McEwen***	Y	Y	Y	N	N	N	Y	N
7 ***Brown***	?	?	?	?	?	?	?	?
8 ***Kindness***	Y	Y	Y	N	N	N	Y	N
9 ***Weber***	Y	N	Y	Y	Y	N	Y	Y
10 ***Miller***	Y	Y	Y	N	N	N	Y	N
11 ***Stanton***	?	?	?	?	?	?	?	?
12 Shamansky	N	N	N	Y	Y	Y	N	Y
13 Pease	N	N	N	Y	Y	Y	N	Y
14 Seiberling	N	N	N	Y	Y	Y	N	Y
15 ***Wylie***	Y	Y	Y	N	Y	N	?	?
16 ***Regula***	Y	Y	Y	N	Y	N	Y	N
17 Vacancy								
18 Applegate	Y	N	Y	N	N	Y	Y	N
19 ***Williams***	N	N	Y	N	N	N	Y	Y
20 Oakar	N	N	N	Y	Y	Y	N	Y
21 Stokes	N	N	N	Y	Y	Y	N	Y
22 Eckart	N	N	N	Y	Y	Y	N	Y
23 Mottl	N	N	N	Y	Y	Y	N	Y
OKLAHOMA								
1 Jones	N	N	N	Y	Y	Y	N	Y
2 Synar	N	N	N	Y	Y	Y	N	Y
3 Watkins	N	Y	N	N	N	Y	N	Y
4 McCurdy	N	N	N	Y	Y	Y	N	Y
5 ***Edwards***	Y	Y	Y	N	N	N	?	?
6 English	Y	Y	Y	N	N	Y	N	Y
OREGON								
1 AuCoin	?	?	?	?	?	?	?	?
2 ***Smith***	Y	Y	Y	N	N	N	Y	N
3 Wyden	N	N	N	Y	Y	Y	N	Y
4 Weaver	?	?	?	?	?	?	?	?
PENNSYLVANIA								
1 Foglietta	?	?	?	?	?	?	?	?
2 Gray	X	?	?	#	?	?	X	?
3 Smith	?	?	?	?	?	?	?	?
4 ***Dougherty***	?	?	?	?	?	?	?	?
5 ***Schulze***	Y	Y	Y	N	N	N	Y	N
6 Yatron	N	Y	Y	Y	Y	Y	N	Y
7 Edgar	N	N	N	Y	Y	Y	N	Y
8 ***Coyne, J.***	Y	Y	Y	N	Y	N	Y	Y
9 ***Shuster***	Y	Y	Y	N	N	N	Y	N
10 ***McDade***	Y	N	Y	N	Y	N	Y	Y
11 ***Nelligan***	Y	N	Y	N	Y	N	Y	Y
12 Murtha	?	?	?	?	?	?	?	?
13 ***Coughlin***	Y	N	Y	N	Y	N	Y	Y
14 Coyne, W.	N	N	N	Y	Y	Y	N	Y
15 ***Ritter***	Y	Y	Y	N	N	N	N	Y
16 ***Walker***	Y	Y	Y	N	N	N	Y	N
17 Ertel	N	N	N	Y	Y	Y	N	Y
18 Walgren	N	N	N	Y	Y	Y	N	Y
19 ***Goodling***	Y	Y	Y	N	Y	N	Y	N
20 Gaydos	?	?	?	?	?	?	?	?
21 Bailey	N	N	N	Y	Y	Y	N	Y
22 Murphy	N	Y	Y	Y	Y	Y	N	Y
23 ***Clinger***	N	Y	N	Y	Y	N	Y	N
24 ***Marks***	?	?	?	?	?	?	?	?
25 ***Atkinson***	?	?	?	?	?	?	?	?
RHODE ISLAND								
1 St Germain	N	N	N	Y	Y	Y	N	Y
2 ***Schneider***	Y	N	N	Y	Y	N	N	Y
SOUTH CAROLINA								
1 ***Hartnett***	Y	Y	Y	N	N	N	Y	N
2 ***Spence***	Y	Y	Y	N	N	N	Y	?
3 Derrick	N	N	N	Y	Y	Y	N	Y
4 ***Campbell***	Y	Y	Y	N	N	N	Y	?
5 Holland	N	?	N	Y	Y	Y	Y	?
6 ***Napier***	Y	Y	Y	N	N	N	Y	?
SOUTH DAKOTA								
1 Daschle	N	Y	Y	N	Y	Y	N	Y
2 ***Roberts***	Y	Y	Y	N	N	N	Y	N
TENNESSEE								
1 ***Quillen***	Y	Y	Y	N	N	N	Y	N
2 ***Duncan***	Y	Y	N	Y	Y	Y	N	N
3 Bouquard	N	N	N	Y	Y	Y	N	Y
4 Gore	N	N	N	Y	Y	Y	N	Y
5 Boner	Y	N	Y	Y	Y	Y	N	Y
6 ***Beard***	Y	Y	Y	N	N	N	Y	N
7 Jones	Y	N	Y	N	N	Y	Y	N
8 Ford	N	N	N	Y	Y	Y	N	Y
TEXAS								
1 Hall, S.	Y	Y	Y	N	N	Y	N	Y
2 Wilson	N	?	N	Y	Y	Y	N	Y
3 ***Collins***	Y	Y	Y	N	N	N	Y	N
4 Hall, R.	N	N	N	Y	Y	Y	N	Y
5 Mattox	?	?	?	?	?	?	?	?
6 Gramm	Y	Y	Y	N	N	Y	Y	N
7 ***Archer***	?	Y	Y	N	N	N	Y	N
8 ***Fields***	Y	Y	Y	N	N	N	Y	N
9 Brooks	N	N	N	Y	Y	Y	N	Y
10 Pickle	N	Y	Y	Y	Y	Y	N	Y
11 Leath	Y	N	Y	N	N	Y	N	Y
12 Wright	N	N	N	Y	Y	Y	N	Y
13 Hightower	Y	N	Y	N	Y	N	Y	Y
14 Patman	Y	Y	Y	N	Y	N	Y	Y
15 de la Garza	Y	N	N	Y	Y	N	Y	Y
16 White	N	Y	N	Y	Y	Y	Y	Y
17 Stenholm	Y	Y	Y	N	N	N	Y	N
18 Leland	X	?	?	#	?	?	X	?
19 Hance	Y	Y	Y	Y	Y	N	N	N
20 Gonzalez	N	N	N	Y	Y	Y	N	Y
21 ***Loeffler***	Y	Y	Y	N	N	N	Y	N
22 ***Paul***	Y	Y	Y	N	N	N	Y	N
23 Kazen	Y	Y	Y	N	Y	N	Y	Y
24 Frost	N	N	N	?	Y	Y	N	Y
UTAH								
1 ***Hansen***	?	?	?	?	X	?	?	X
2 ***Marriott***	Y	N	Y	N	N	N	Y	N
VERMONT								
AL ***Jeffords***	N	N	N	Y	Y	N	Y	Y
VIRGINIA								
1 ***Trible***	?	?	?	?	?	?	?	?
2 ***Whitehurst***	Y	Y	Y	N	N	N	Y	N
3 ***Bliley***	Y	Y	Y	N	N	N	Y	N
4 ***Daniel, R.***	Y	Y	Y	N	N	N	Y	N
5 Daniel, D.	Y	Y	Y	N	N	N	Y	N
6 ***Butler***	Y	N	Y	N	N	N	Y	?
7 ***Robinson***	Y	Y	Y	N	N	N	Y	N
8 ***Parris***	Y	Y	Y	N	Y	N	Y	Y
9 ***Wampler***	Y	Y	Y	N	N	N	Y	N
10 ***Wolf***	Y	N	Y	N	Y	N	Y	Y
WASHINGTON								
1 ***Pritchard***	Y	N	Y	N	Y	N	Y	?
2 Swift	?	N	N	Y	Y	Y	N	Y
3 Bonker	N	N	N	Y	Y	Y	N	Y
4 ***Morrison***	Y	Y	Y	N	N	N	Y	N
5 Foley	N	N	N	Y	Y	Y	N	Y
6 Dicks	Y	N	N	Y	Y	Y	N	Y
7 Lowry	N	N	N	Y	Y	Y	N	Y
WEST VIRGINIA								
1 Mollohan	N	N	N	Y	Y	Y	N	Y
2 ***Benedict***	Y	Y	Y	Y	Y	N	Y	N
3 ***Staton***	Y	Y	Y	N	N	N	Y	N
4 Rahall	N	N	N	Y	Y	Y	N	Y
WISCONSIN								
1 Aspin	N	N	N	Y	Y	Y	N	Y
2 Kastenmeier	N	N	N	Y	Y	Y	N	Y
3 ***Gunderson***	Y	Y	Y	N	N	N	Y	N
4 Zablocki	N	N	N	Y	Y	N	N	Y
5 Reuss	N	N	N	Y	Y	Y	N	Y
6 ***Petri***	Y	Y	Y	N	Y	N	Y	N
7 Obey	N	N	N	Y	Y	Y	N	Y
8 ***Roth***	Y	Y	Y	N	N	N	Y	N
9 ***Sensenbrenner***	Y	Y	Y	N	N	N	Y	N
WYOMING								
AL ***Cheney***	Y	Y	Y	N	N	N	Y	N

Southern states - Ala., Ark., Fla., Ga., Ky., La., Miss., N.C., Okla., S.C., Tenn., Texas, Va.

84. S 1230. Olympic Coins. Annunzio, D-Ill., substitute to authorize the minting of three coins commemorating the 1984 Los Angeles Olympic Games to be sold domestically by the Treasury and overseas by a private marketing organization. Adopted 302-84: R 121-49; D 181-35 (ND 117-28, SD 64-7), May 20, 1982.

85. HR 6267. Net Worth Guarantee Act. Wylie, R-Ohio, substitute to authorize the Federal Savings and Loan Insurance Corporation to provide capital assistance to qualified lending institutions through the purchase of income capital certificates. Rejected 155-209: R 137-22; D 18-187 (ND 2-133, SD 16-54), May 20, 1982.

86. HR 6267. Net Worth Guarantee Act. Passage of the bill to revitalize the housing industry by setting up a Treasury fund to guarantee the net worth of qualified mortgage lending institutions. Passed 272-91: R 84-75; D 188-16 (ND 131-4, SD 57-12), May 20, 1982.

87. Procedural Motion. Solomon, R-N.Y., motion to approve the House *Journal* of Thursday, May 20. Motion agreed to 295-32: R 120-25; D 175-7 (ND 107-6, SD 68-1), May 21, 1982.

88. H Con Res 345. First Budget Resolution, Fiscal 1983. Jones, D-Okla., motion that the House resolve itself into the Committee of the Whole for consideration of the concurrent resolution to set budget targets for the fiscal year ending Sept. 30, 1983. Motion agreed to 342-0: R 149-0; D 193-0 (ND 123-0, SD 70-0), May 21, 1982.

89. Procedural Motion. Cheney, R-Wyo., motion to approve the House *Journal* of Friday, May 21. Motion agreed to 329-30: R 144-18; D 185-12 (ND 116-11, SD 69-1), May 24, 1982.

90. H Con Res 345. First Budget Resolution, Fiscal 1983. Miller, D-Calif., substitute, known as the "pay as you go" budget, to require that any increases in spending above fiscal 1982 levels be matched by offsetting revenue increases or spending cuts in other programs. The substitute would result in a $27.5 billion surplus in fiscal 1985, according to Congressional Budget Office estimates. Rejected 181-225: R 3-179; D 178-46 (ND 130-18, SD 48-28), May 24, 1982.

91. H Con Res 345. First Budget Resolution, Fiscal 1983. Obey, D-Wis., substitute to provide funding for emergency jobs programs while maintaining other domestic programs at real fiscal 1982 levels and increasing non-pay defense programs by 7 percent, and to scale back the tax cuts enacted in 1981. The substitute would result in a $1.3 billion deficit in fiscal 1985, according to Congressional Budget Office estimates. Rejected 152-268: R 8-176; D 144-92 (ND 133-26, SD 11-66), May 24, 1982.

KEY

Y Voted for (yea).
Paired for.
+ Announced for.
N Voted against (nay).
X Paired against.
- Announced against.
P Voted "present".
C Voted "present" to avoid possible conflict of interest.
? Did not vote or otherwise make a position known.

Democrats   *Republicans*

	84	85	86	87	88	89	90	91
ALABAMA								
1 Edwards	N	Y	Y	Y	Y	Y	N	N
2 *Dickinson*	Y	Y	Y	?	Y	N	N	N
3 Nichols	Y	Y	Y	Y	Y	Y	N	N
4 Bevill	Y	N	Y	Y	Y	Y	Y	N
5 Flippo	Y	N	Y	Y	Y	Y	Y	N
6 *Smith*	Y	Y	N	N	Y	N	N	N
7 Shelby	Y	Y	Y	?	Y	Y	N	N
ALASKA								
AL *Young*	Y	N	Y	?	?	N	N	N
ARIZONA								
1 *Rhodes*	Y	Y	N	Y	Y	Y	N	N
2 Udall	Y	N	Y	Y	Y	?	Y	Y
3 Stump	Y	Y	N	Y	Y	N	N	N
4 *Rudd*	Y	Y	N	Y	Y	Y	N	N
ARKANSAS								
1 Alexander	Y	N	Y	∨	Y	Y	Y	N
2 *Bethune*	?	Y	N	∨	Y	N	N	N
3 *Hammerschmidt*	N	N	Y	∨	Y	Y	N	N
4 Anthony	Y	?	?	∨	Y	Y	Y	N
CALIFORNIA								
1 *Chappie*	Y	Y	N	?	?	Y	N	N
2 *Clausen*	N	Y	Y	Y	Y	Y	N	N
3 Matsui	Y	N	Y	Y	Y	Y	Y	Y
4 Fazio	N	N	Y	Y	Y	Y	Y	Y
5 Burton, J.	?	?	?	?	?	?	?	?
6 Burton, P.	N	?	?	?	?	Y	Y	Y
7 Miller	Y	N	Y	Y	Y	Y	Y	N
8 Dellums	Y	N	Y	Y	Y	Y	Y	Y
9 Stark	Y	?	?	?	?	Y	Y	Y
10 Edwards	N	N	Y	Y	Y	Y	Y	Y
11 Lantos	Y	N	Y	Y	Y	Y	Y	Y
12 *McCloskey*	?	#	?	?	?	?	X	?
13 Mineta	Y	N	Y	Y	Y	Y	Y	Y
14 *Shumway*	N	Y	N	Y	Y	N	N	N
15 Coelho	N	?	?	?	Y	Y	Y	Y
16 Panetta	Y	N	Y	Y	Y	Y	Y	N
17 *Pashayan*	N	Y	N	Y	Y	Y	N	N
18 *Thomas*	?	#	?	?	?	Y	N	N
19 *Lagomarsino*	N	Y	N	Y	Y	Y	N	N
20 *Goldwater*	?	?	?	?	Y	Y	N	N
21 *Fiedler*	Y	Y	Y	N	Y	Y	N	?
22 *Moorhead*	N	N	Y	Y	Y	Y	N	N
23 Beilenson	Y	N	Y	Y	Y	Y	Y	Y
24 Waxman	N	N	Y	Y	Y	?	Y	Y
25 Roybal	Y	N	Y	Y	Y	Y	Y	Y
26 *Rousselot*	P	Y	N	N	Y	?	N	N
27 *Dornan*	?	?	X	?	?	Y	N	N
28 Dixon	N	?	?	?	?	Y	Y	Y
29 Hawkins	X	?	?	?	Y	Y	Y	Y
30 Vacancy								
31 Dymally	Y	N	Y	?	?	Y	Y	Y
32 Anderson	N	N	Y	Y	Y	Y	Y	N
33 Grisham	?	?	?	?	?	Y	N	N
34 Lungren	N	Y	N	Y	Y	Y	N	N
35 *Dreier*	?	?	?	?	Y	Y	N	N
36 Brown	Y	N	Y	Y	Y	Y	Y	Y
37 *Lewis*	Y	?	?	?	Y	N	N	N
38 Patterson	N	N	Y	?	Y	Y	Y	N
39 *Dannemeyer*	Y	Y	N	N	Y	N	N	N
40 *Badham*	?	?	?	?	Y	Y	N	N
41 *Lowery*	N	Y	Y	Y	Y	?	N	N
42 Hunter	N	Y	N	Y	Y	Y	N	N
43 *Burgener*	N	Y	N	Y	Y	Y	N	N
COLORADO								
1 Schroeder	Y	N	N	-	+	N	Y	Y
2 Wirth	Y	N	Y	Y	Y	Y	Y	Y
3 Kogovsek	N	N	Y	Y	Y	Y	Y	N
4 *Brown*	N	Y	N	N	Y	N	N	N

	84	85	86	87	88	89	90	91
5 *Kramer*	N	Y	N	Y	Y	Y	N	N
CONNECTICUT								
1 Kennelly	Y	N	Y	Y	Y	?	Y	Y
2 Gejdenson	N	N	Y	N	Y	N	Y	Y
3 *DeNardis*	Y	Y	Y	Y	Y	Y	Y	N
4 *McKinney*	N	Y	Y	?	?	?	N	N
5 Ratchford	Y	N	Y	?	Y	Y	Y	N
6 Moffett	?	?	?	?	?	?	#	Y
DELAWARE								
AL *Evans*	Y	Y	Y	Y	Y	Y	N	N
FLORIDA								
1 Hutto	Y	N	Y	Y	Y	Y	Y	N
2 Fuqua	Y	N	Y	Y	Y	Y	Y	N
3 Bennett	Y	N	Y	Y	Y	Y	Y	N
4 Chappell	Y	Y	Y	Y	Y	?	Y	N
5 *McCollum*	N	Y	Y	Y	Y	Y	N	N
6 *Young*	Y	C	C	Y	Y	Y	N	N
7 Gibbons	Y	Y	Y	Y	Y	Y	N	N
8 *Ireland*	?	?	?	?	Y	Y	N	N
9 *Nelson*	Y	N	Y	Y	Y	N	N	N
10 *Bafalis*	Y	Y	Y	?	Y	Y	N	N
11 Mica	Y	N	Y	Y	?	Y	N	N
12 *Shaw*	N	Y	Y	Y	Y	Y	N	N
13 Lehman	Y	N	Y	Y	Y	Y	Y	Y
14 Pepper	Y	N	Y	Y	Y	?	Y	Y
15 Fascell	Y	N	Y	Y	Y	Y	Y	Y
GEORGIA								
1 Ginn	?	?	?	?	?	Y	Y	N
2 Hatcher	?	?	?	?	?	Y	Y	N
3 Brinkley	Y	N	Y	Y	Y	Y	Y	N
4 Levitas	Y	N	N	Y	Y	Y	Y	N
5 Fowler	Y	N	Y	Y	Y	Y	Y	N
6 *Gingrich*	N	Y	N	Y	Y	Y	N	N
7 McDonald	Y	Y	N	Y	Y	Y	N	N
8 Evans	Y	N	Y	Y	Y	Y	Y	N
9 Jenkins	Y	N	N	Y	Y	Y	Y	N
10 Barnard	Y	N	Y	Y	?	Y	Y	N
HAWAII								
1 Heftel	Y	N	Y	Y	?	Y	Y	Y
2 Akaka	Y	N	Y	?	Y	Y	Y	Y
IDAHO								
1 *Craig*	Y	Y	N	?	?	Y	N	N
2 *Hansen*	N	Y	N	?	Y	Y	N	N
ILLINOIS								
1 Washington	Y	N	Y	N	Y	N	Y	Y
2 Savage	?	?	?	?	?	?	Y	Y
3 Russo	Y	N	Y	Y	Y	N	Y	N
4 *Derwinski*	Y	Y	Y	?	Y	N	N	N
5 Fary	Y	N	Y	Y	Y	Y	Y	Y
6 *Hyde*	Y	C	C	Y	Y	Y	X	?
7 Collins	Y	N	Y	?	?	Y	Y	Y
8 Rostenkowski	Y	N	Y	Y	Y	?	N	N
9 Yates	Y	N	Y	N	Y	N	Y	Y
10 *Porter*	Y	N	Y	Y	Y	Y	N	N
11 Annunzio	Y	N	Y	Y	Y	N	Y	N
12 *Crane, P.*	Y	Y	N	Y	Y	Y	N	N
13 *McClory*	Y	N	Y	Y	Y	Y	N	N
14 *Erlenborn*	Y	Y	N	?	Y	Y	N	N
15 *Corcoran*	Y	Y	Y	Y	Y	Y	N	N
16 *Martin*	Y	Y	Y	Y	Y	Y	N	N
17 *O'Brien*	Y	Y	Y	?	?	Y	N	N
18 *Michel*	Y	Y	N	Y	Y	Y	N	N
19 *Railsback*	Y	Y	Y	?	Y	Y	N	N
20 *Findley*	Y	Y	Y	Y	Y	Y	N	N
21 *Madigan*	Y	Y	Y	Y	Y	Y	N	N
22 *Crane, D.*	Y	Y	N	N	Y	N	N	N
23 Price	Y	N	Y	Y	Y	Y	Y	N
24 Simon	Y	N	Y	?	?	Y	Y	Y
INDIANA								
1 Benjamin	Y	N	Y	Y	Y	Y	Y	N
2 Fithian	Y	N	Y	Y	?	Y	Y	Y
3 *Hiler*	Y	Y	N	N	Y	Y	N	N
4 *Coats*	Y	N	N	Y	Y	N	N	N
5 *Hillis*	Y	Y	N	?	Y	Y	N	N
6 Evans	N	N	Y	?	Y	Y	Y	Y
7 *Myers*	Y	Y	N	Y	Y	Y	N	N
8 *Deckard*	Y	Y	Y	Y	Y	N	N	N
9 Hamilton	Y	N	Y	Y	Y	Y	Y	N
10 Sharp	Y	N	Y	Y	Y	Y	Y	N
11 Jacobs	?	?	?	?	?	N	Y	Y
IOWA								
1 *Leach*	Y	?	?	Y	Y	Y	N	N
2 *Tauke*	N	Y	N	Y	Y	Y	N	N
3 *Evans*	Y	Y	Y	Y	Y	Y	N	N
4 Smith	Y	N	Y	Y	Y	Y	Y	Y
5 Harkin	Y	N	Y	N	Y	N	Y	Y
6 Bedell	Y	N	Y	Y	Y	Y	Y	Y

ND - Northern Democrats   SD - Southern Democrats

Corresponding to Congressional Record Votes 90, 91, 92, 93, 94, 95, 96, 97

	84	85	86	87	88	89	90	91
KANSAS								
1 **Roberts**	Y	Y	Y	Y	Y	Y	N	N
2 **Jeffries**	Y	Y	N	Y	?	Y	N	N
3 **Winn**	Y	Y	Y	Y	Y	Y	N	N
4 Glickman	Y	N	Y	Y	Y	Y	Y	N
5 **Whittaker**	Y	Y	Y	Y	Y	Y	N	N
KENTUCKY								
1 Hubbard	N	N	Y	Y	Y	Y	N	N
2 Natcher	Y	N	Y	Y	Y	Y	Y	N
3 Mazzoli	Y	N	Y	Y	Y	Y	Y	N
4 **Snyder**	Y	Y	Y	Y	Y	Y	Y	N
5 **Rogers**	?	?	?	?	?	Y	N	N
6 **Hopkins**	Y	Y	N	Y	Y	Y	N	N
7 Perkins	Y	N	Y	Y	Y	Y	Y	Y
LOUISIANA								
1 **Livingston**	Y	Y	N	Y	Y	Y	N	N
2 Boggs	Y	X	?	Y	Y	?	Y	N
3 Tauzin	Y	Y	N	Y	Y	Y	N	N
4 Roemer	Y	Y	N	N	Y	N	N	N
5 Huckaby	Y	Y	Y	Y	?	?	Y	N
6 **Moore**	N	Y	N	Y	Y	Y	N	N
7 Breaux	Y	Y	Y	Y	Y	Y	?	N
8 Long	Y	N	Y	Y	Y	Y	Y	N
MAINE								
1 **Emery**	Y	Y	N	Y	Y	Y	N	N
2 **Snowe**	Y	N	Y	Y	Y	Y	N	N
MARYLAND								
1 Dyson	Y	N	Y	Y	Y	Y	N	Y
2 Long	Y	N	Y	Y	Y	?	Y	N
3 Mikulski	Y	N	Y	Y	Y	?	?	Y
4 **Holt**	N	#	#	Y	Y	Y	N	N
5 Hoyer	N	N	Y	Y	Y	Y	Y	Y
6 Byron	Y	N	Y	Y	Y	Y	N	N
7 Mitchell	Y	N	Y	N	Y	N	Y	Y
8 Barnes	Y	N	Y	N	Y	N	Y	Y
MASSACHUSETTS								
1 **Conte**	Y	N	Y	Y	Y	Y	N	N
2 Boland	N	N	Y	Y	Y	Y	Y	Y
3 Early	Y	N	Y	Y	Y	Y	Y	Y
4 Frank	N	N	Y	Y	Y	?	Y	Y
5 Shannon	N	N	Y	Y	Y	Y	Y	Y
6 Mavroules	Y	N	Y	?	Y	Y	Y	Y
7 Markey	N	N	Y	?	Y	Y	Y	Y
8 O'Neill								
9 Moakley	Y	N	Y	Y	Y	Y	Y	Y
10 **Heckler**	Y	N	Y	?	?	?	N	Y
11 Donnelly	Y	N	Y	Y	Y	?	Y	Y
12 Studds	N	N	Y	Y	Y	?	Y	Y
MICHIGAN								
1 Conyers	Y	N	Y	?	?	N	Y	Y
2 **Pursell**	?	?	#	?	?	Y	N	N
3 Wolpe	Y	N	Y	Y	Y	Y	Y	Y
4 **Siljander**	Y	Y	Y	?	?	Y	N	N
5 **Sawyer**	Y	Y	Y	Y	Y	Y	N	N
6 **Dunn**	Y	N	Y	Y	Y	Y	N	N
7 Kildee	Y	N	Y	Y	Y	Y	Y	Y
8 Traxler	Y	N	Y	?	Y	?	?	Y
9 **Vander Jagt**	N	Y	Y	Y	Y	?	X	N
10 Albosta	Y	N	Y	Y	Y	Y	Y	Y
11 **Davis**	Y	N	Y	?	?	Y	N	N
12 Bonior	Y	N	Y	Y	Y	Y	Y	Y
13 Crockett	?	?	?	?	?	?	Y	Y
14 Hertel	N	N	Y	Y	Y	Y	Y	Y
15 Ford	Y	N	Y	?	Y	?	Y	Y
16 Dingell	Y	N	Y	Y	Y	Y	Y	Y
17 Brodhead	Y	N	Y	Y	Y	?	?	Y
18 Blanchard	N	N	Y	?	?	?	Y	Y
19 **Broomfield**	Y	Y	Y	Y	Y	Y	N	N
MINNESOTA								
1 **Erdahl**	?	?	?	?	?	Y	N	N
2 **Hagedorn**	Y	Y	N	?	?	Y	N	N
3 **Frenzel**	Y	?	?	?	?	Y	N	N
4 Vento	Y	N	Y	Y	Y	Y	Y	Y
5 Sabo	Y	?	?	?	Y	N	Y	Y
6 **Weber**	Y	Y	N	Y	Y	Y	N	N
7 **Stangeland**	Y	Y	N	Y	Y	Y	N	N
8 Oberstar	Y	N	Y	Y	Y	Y	Y	Y
MISSISSIPPI								
1 Whitten	Y	N	Y	Y	Y	Y	Y	N
2 Bowen	Y	N	Y	Y	Y	Y	Y	Y
3 Montgomery	Y	Y	Y	Y	Y	Y	N	N
4 Dowdy	N	N	Y	?	?	Y	Y	Y
5 **Lott**	N	Y	N	Y	Y	Y	N	N
MISSOURI								
1 Clay	?	?	?	?	?	N	Y	Y
2 Young	Y	N	Y	Y	Y	?	Y	N
3 Gephardt	Y	N	Y	Y	Y	Y	N	N
4 Skelton	Y	N	Y	P	Y	Y	N	N
5 Bolling	?	?	?	Y	Y	Y	N	Y
6 **Coleman**	Y	Y	Y	?	?	Y	N	N
7 **Taylor**	Y	Y	N	Y	Y	?	N	N
8 **Bailey**	N	Y	Y	Y	Y	Y	N	N
9 Volkmer	Y	N	Y	Y	Y	Y	Y	N
10 **Emerson**	Y	Y	Y	N	Y	N	N	N
MONTANA								
1 Williams	Y	N	Y	?	P	Y	N	Y
2 **Marlenee**	N	Y	Y	Y	Y	Y	N	N
NEBRASKA								
1 **Bereuter**	N	Y	Y	Y	Y	Y	N	N
2 **Daub**	Y	Y	N	Y	Y	Y	N	N
3 **Smith**	Y	Y	N	Y	Y	Y	N	N
NEVADA								
AL Santini	?	?	?	Y	Y	Y	N	N
NEW HAMPSHIRE								
1 D'Amours	N	N	Y	Y	?	Y	Y	Y
2 **Gregg**	N	Y	N	N	Y	Y	N	N
NEW JERSEY								
1 Florio	Y	N	Y	Y	Y	Y	Y	Y
2 Hughes	Y	N	Y	Y	Y	Y	Y	Y
3 Howard	Y	N	Y	Y	Y	Y	Y	Y
4 **Smith**	Y	N	Y	Y	Y	Y	N	N
5 **Fenwick**	Y	#	?	?	?	?	N	?
6 **Forsythe**	N	Y	Y	N	?	N	N	N
7 **Roukema**	N	N	Y	Y	Y	Y	N	N
8 Roe	Y	N	Y	Y	Y	?	#	Y
9 **Hollenbeck**	Y	N	Y	Y	Y	Y	N	Y
10 Rodino	Y	N	Y	Y	Y	Y	Y	Y
11 Minish	Y	N	Y	Y	Y	Y	Y	Y
12 **Rinaldo**	Y	N	Y	Y	Y	?	N	Y
13 **Courter**	Y	Y	Y	Y	?	?	X	X
14 Guarini	Y	N	Y	Y	Y	Y	Y	Y
15 Dwyer	Y	N	Y	Y	Y	Y	Y	Y
NEW MEXICO								
1 **Lujan**	Y	Y	Y	Y	Y	Y	N	N
2 **Skeen**	N	Y	N	Y	Y	Y	N	N
NEW YORK								
1 **Carney**	Y	Y	Y	Y	Y	?	X	N
2 Downey	Y	N	Y	Y	Y	Y	Y	Y
3 **Carman**	Y	Y	Y	Y	Y	Y	N	N
4 **Lent**	Y	Y	Y	Y	Y	Y	N	N
5 **McGrath**	Y	Y	Y	Y	Y	Y	N	N
6 **LeBoutillier**	N	Y	Y	N	Y	N	N	N
7 Addabbo	Y	N	Y	Y	Y	?	Y	Y
8 Rosenthal	Y	N	Y	?	Y	Y	Y	Y
9 Ferraro	Y	N	Y	Y	Y	Y	Y	Y
10 Biaggi	Y	N	Y	Y	Y	?	#	Y
11 Scheuer	Y	N	Y	Y	Y	?	Y	Y
12 Chisholm	Y	N	Y	Y	Y	?	?	Y
13 Solarz	N	N	Y	Y	Y	Y	Y	Y
14 Richmond	Y	X	?	?	?	?	Y	Y
15 Zeferetti	#	?	?	?	?	Y	Y	Y
16 Schumer	N	N	Y	Y	Y	Y	N	Y
17 **Molinari**	Y	Y	Y	Y	Y	Y	N	N
18 **Green**	N	Y	Y	Y	Y	Y	N	N
19 Rangel	Y	N	Y	Y	Y	Y	Y	Y
20 Weiss	Y	N	Y	Y	Y	Y	N	Y
21 Garcia	Y	N	Y	?	?	?	#	Y
22 Bingham	?	N	Y	Y	Y	Y	Y	Y
23 Peyser	Y	?	?	Y	Y	Y	Y	Y
24 Ottinger	Y	N	Y	P	P	P	N	Y
25 **Fish**	Y	?	?	?	?	?	N	N
26 **Gilman**	Y	Y	Y	Y	Y	?	X	N
27 McHugh	Y	N	Y	?	Y	Y	?	Y
28 Stratton	Y	N	Y	Y	Y	Y	N	N
29 **Solomon**	Y	Y	Y	N	Y	N	N	N
30 **Martin**	N	Y	Y	Y	Y	Y	N	N
31 **Mitchell**	Y	Y	Y	?	?	Y	N	N
32 **Wortley**	N	N	Y	Y	Y	Y	N	N
33 **Lee**	Y	Y	Y	Y	Y	Y	N	N
34 **Horton**	Y	Y	Y	Y	Y	?	N	N
35 **Conable**	Y	Y	N	Y	Y	Y	N	N
36 LaFalce	Y	N	Y	Y	Y	Y	Y	Y
37 Nowak	Y	N	Y	Y	Y	Y	Y	Y
38 **Kemp**	N	Y	N	Y	Y	Y	?	N
39 Lundine	?	?	?	?	?	Y	Y	N
NORTH CAROLINA								
1 Jones	?	?	?	?	?	Y	Y	N
2 Fountain	Y	N	Y	Y	Y	Y	N	N
3 Whitley	Y	N	Y	Y	Y	Y	N	N
4 Andrews	Y	N	Y	Y	Y	Y	N	N
5 Neal	Y	N	Y	Y	Y	Y	N	?
6 **Johnston**	Y	Y	?	N	Y	N	N	N
7 Rose	Y	?	?	?	?	Y	Y	N
8 Hefner	Y	N	Y	Y	Y	Y	Y	N
9 **Martin**	Y	Y	N	Y	Y	?	N	N
10 **Broyhill**	Y	Y	N	Y	Y	Y	N	N
11 **Hendon**	Y	N	Y	N	Y	N	N	N
NORTH DAKOTA								
AL Dorgan	Y	N	Y	Y	Y	Y	Y	N
OHIO								
1 **Gradison**	Y	?	?	?	?	Y	N	N
2 Luken	N	N	Y	?	?	Y	Y	N
3 Hall	Y	Y	N	?	Y	Y	Y	N
4 **Oxley**	N	?	?	N	Y	Y	N	N
5 **Latta**	N	Y	N	N	Y	Y	N	N
6 **McEwen**	Y	Y	Y	Y	Y	Y	N	Y
7 **Brown**	?	?	?	?	?	?	?	?
8 **Kindness**	Y	Y	N	Y	Y	Y	N	N
9 **Weber**	Y	Y	N	Y	Y	Y	N	N
10 **Miller**	Y	Y	N	N	Y	N	N	N
11 **Stanton**	?	?	?	?	?	?	X	?
12 Shamansky	Y	N	Y	Y	Y	Y	Y	N
13 Pease	Y	N	Y	Y	Y	?	?	Y
14 Seiberling	Y	N	Y	Y	Y	Y	Y	Y
15 **Wylie**	N	Y	N	Y	Y	Y	N	N
16 **Regula**	N	Y	N	N	Y	Y	N	N
17 Vacancy								
18 Applegate	Y	N	N	?	?	?	Y	Y
19 **Williams**	Y	Y	Y	Y	Y	Y	N	Y
20 Oakar	N	N	Y	Y	Y	?	N	Y
21 Stokes	#	X	?	Y	Y	Y	?	Y
22 Eckart	Y	X	?	?	?	Y	Y	Y
23 Mottl	Y	?	?	?	?	?	#	Y
OKLAHOMA								
1 Jones	N	N	Y	Y	Y	Y	N	N
2 Synar	N	N	Y	Y	Y	Y	Y	N
3 Watkins	?	?	?	?	?	?	?	N
4 McCurdy	Y	N	Y	Y	Y	?	N	N
5 **Edwards**	?	?	?	Y	Y	Y	N	N
6 English	N	N	Y	Y	Y	Y	N	N
OREGON								
1 AuCoin	?	?	?	Y	Y	Y	Y	Y
2 **Smith**	Y	Y	N	N	Y	Y	N	N
3 Wyden	N	N	Y	Y	Y	Y	Y	Y
4 Weaver	?	?	?	?	?	Y	Y	Y
PENNSYLVANIA								
1 Foglietta	?	?	?	?	?	Y	Y	Y
2 Gray	N	N	Y	Y	Y	Y	Y	Y
3 Smith	X	?	?	?	?	Y	Y	Y
4 **Dougherty**	Y	N	Y	Y	Y	Y	N	N
5 **Schulze**	Y	Y	N	Y	Y	Y	N	N
6 Yatron	N	N	Y	Y	Y	Y	N	Y
7 Edgar	Y	N	Y	Y	Y	Y	Y	Y
8 **Coyne, J.**	P	Y	Y	Y	Y	Y	N	N
9 **Shuster**	Y	?	?	Y	Y	Y	N	N
10 **McDade**	Y	N	Y	Y	Y	Y	N	Y
11 **Nelligan**	Y	N	Y	Y	Y	Y	N	N
12 Murtha	Y	N	Y	Y	Y	Y	Y	Y
13 **Coughlin**	Y	?	?	N	Y	N	N	N
14 Coyne, W.	Y	N	Y	Y	Y	Y	Y	Y
15 **Ritter**	Y	Y	N	Y	Y	Y	N	N
16 **Walker**	N	Y	N	N	Y	N	N	N
17 Ertel	Y	N	Y	?	?	?	Y	Y
18 Walgren	Y	N	Y	Y	Y	Y	Y	Y
19 **Goodling**	Y	Y	N	N	Y	N	N	N
20 Gaydos	Y	N	Y	Y	Y	Y	Y	Y
21 Bailey	Y	N	Y	Y	Y	Y	Y	Y
22 Murphy	Y	?	?	?	?	?	?	?
23 **Clinger**	N	Y	Y	Y	+	+	N	N
24 **Marks**	?	?	?	?	?	?	N	N
25 **Atkinson**	Y	Y	Y	Y	Y	?	N	Y
RHODE ISLAND								
1 St Germain	N	N	Y	?	?	Y	Y	Y
2 **Schneider**	Y	N	Y	Y	Y	Y	N	Y
SOUTH CAROLINA								
1 **Hartnett**	N	Y	N	Y	Y	Y	N	N
2 **Spence**	Y	Y	Y	Y	Y	Y	N	N
3 Derrick	N	N	Y	Y	Y	Y	Y	N
4 **Campbell**	Y	Y	N	Y	Y	?	N	N
5 Holland	Y	N	?	Y	Y	Y	Y	N
6 **Napier**	Y	N	Y	Y	Y	Y	Y	N
SOUTH DAKOTA								
1 Daschle	Y	N	Y	Y	Y	Y	Y	Y
2 **Roberts**	N	Y	N	?	Y	N	N	N
TENNESSEE								
1 **Quillen**	N	?	?	Y	Y	Y	N	N
2 **Duncan**	Y	N	Y	Y	Y	Y	N	N
3 Bouquard	Y	N	Y	Y	Y	Y	N	N
4 Gore	Y	N	Y	Y	Y	Y	Y	Y
5 Boner	N	N	Y	Y	Y	Y	N	N
6 **Beard**	Y	N	Y	?	?	Y	N	N
7 Jones	Y	N	Y	Y	Y	?	#	N
8 Ford	Y	N	Y	?	Y	Y	Y	Y
TEXAS								
1 Hall, S.	Y	N	N	Y	Y	Y	Y	N
2 Wilson	?	Y	Y	Y	Y	Y	N	N
3 **Collins**	Y	?	X	?	?	Y	N	N
4 Hall, R.	Y	N	N	Y	Y	Y	N	N
5 Mattox	?	?	?	?	?	Y	Y	P
6 Gramm	Y	Y	N	Y	Y	Y	N	N
7 **Archer**	Y	?	N	Y	Y	Y	N	N
8 **Fields**	N	Y	N	N	Y	?	N	N
9 Brooks	Y	N	Y	Y	Y	Y	Y	N
10 Pickle	Y	N	Y	Y	Y	Y	Y	N
11 Leath	Y	Y	N	Y	Y	Y	N	N
12 Wright	?	N	Y	Y	Y	Y	Y	N
13 Hightower	Y	N	Y	Y	Y	?	Y	N
14 Patman	Y	N	Y	Y	Y	Y	Y	N
15 de la Garza	Y	N	Y	Y	Y	Y	Y	N
16 White	Y	Y	Y	Y	Y	Y	Y	N
17 Stenholm	Y	Y	N	Y	Y	Y	N	N
18 Leland	Y	N	Y	Y	Y	Y	N	Y
19 Hance	Y	N	N	Y	Y	Y	N	N
20 Gonzalez	Y	N	Y	Y	Y	Y	Y	N
21 **Loeffler**	Y	Y	N	Y	Y	?	N	N
22 **Paul**	Y	Y	N	Y	Y	?	N	N
23 Kazen	Y	N	Y	Y	Y	Y	Y	N
24 Frost	Y	N	Y	Y	Y	Y	Y	Y
UTAH								
1 **Hansen**	?	#	?	?	?	Y	N	N
2 **Marriott**	Y	Y	Y	Y	Y	Y	N	N
VERMONT								
AL **Jeffords**	N	Y	Y	Y	Y	Y	N	N
VIRGINIA								
1 **Trible**	?	?	?	?	?	?	N	N
2 **Whitehurst**	Y	Y	N	Y	Y	Y	N	N
3 **Bliley**	Y	Y	N	?	Y	Y	N	N
4 **Daniel, R.**	Y	Y	N	Y	Y	Y	N	N
5 Daniel, D.	Y	Y	N	Y	Y	Y	N	N
6 **Butler**	?	?	?	N	Y	N	N	N
7 **Robinson**	Y	Y	N	Y	Y	Y	N	N
8 **Parris**	N	Y	Y	Y	Y	Y	N	N
9 **Wampler**	Y	Y	Y	Y	Y	?	N	N
10 **Wolf**	Y	Y	Y	Y	Y	Y	N	N
WASHINGTON								
1 **Pritchard**	Y	Y	Y	Y	Y	Y	N	N
2 Swift	Y	N	Y	?	Y	Y	Y	Y
3 Bonker	Y	N	Y	Y	Y	Y	Y	Y
4 **Morrison**	Y	Y	Y	Y	Y	Y	N	N
5 Foley	Y	N	Y	Y	Y	Y	Y	N
6 Dicks	Y	N	Y	Y	Y	Y	Y	Y
7 Lowry	Y	N	Y	Y	Y	Y	Y	Y
WEST VIRGINIA								
1 Mollohan	Y	N	Y	Y	Y	?	Y	Y
2 **Benedict**	Y	Y	Y	?	?	Y	N	N
3 **Staton**	Y	Y	Y	Y	Y	Y	N	N
4 Rahall	Y	X	?	?	?	?	#	#
WISCONSIN								
1 Aspin	Y	N	Y	Y	Y	Y	Y	Y
2 Kastenmeier	Y	N	Y	Y	Y	Y	Y	Y
3 **Gunderson**	Y	Y	N	Y	Y	Y	N	N
4 Zablocki	Y	N	Y	Y	Y	Y	Y	Y
5 Reuss	Y	N	Y	Y	Y	Y	Y	Y
6 **Petri**	Y	Y	N	Y	Y	Y	N	N
7 Obey	Y	N	Y	Y	Y	Y	Y	Y
8 **Roth**	Y	Y	N	?	?	?	N	N
9 **Sensenbrenner**	N	Y	N	Y	Y	Y	N	N
WYOMING								
AL **Cheney**	N	Y	N	Y	Y	Y	N	N

Southern states - Ala., Ark., Fla., Ga., Ky., La., Miss., N.C., Okla., S.C., Tenn., Texas, Va.

92. H Con Res 345. First Budget Resolution, Fiscal 1983. Fauntroy, D-D.C., substitute, proposed by the Congressional Black Caucus, to make substantial increases above current policy levels in spending for non-defense programs, hold defense spending at fiscal 1982 levels, and increase revenues through extensive tax reforms. The substitute would result in an $18.7 billion surplus in fiscal 1985, according to Congressional Budget Office estimates. Rejected 86-322: R 0-177; D 86-145 (ND 78-79, SD 8-66), May 24, 1982.

93. Procedural Motion. Solomon, R-N.Y., motion to approve the House *Journal* of Monday, May 24. Motion agreed to 371-31: R 167-14; D 204-17 (ND 130-15, SD 74-2), May 25, 1982.

94. H Con Res 345. First Budget Resolution, Fiscal 1983. Rousselot, R-Calif., substitute to balance the budget in fiscal 1983-85 by making large cuts in non-defense programs while maintaining the three-year tax cut enacted in 1981. The substitute assumed higher revenues under current tax policy than projected by the Congressional Budget Office. Rejected 182-242: R 135-53; D 47-189 (ND 5-154, SD 42-35), May 25, 1982.

95. H Con Res 345. First Budget Resolution, Fiscal 1983. Pease, D-Ohio, amendment, to the Latta, R-Ohio, substitute, to express the sense of the House that Congress should close tax loopholes to the maximum extent possible as a way of raising revenues over the next three years. Rejected 68-342: R 7-176; D 61-166 (ND 58-93, SD 3-73), May 25, 1982.

96. H Con Res 345. First Budget Resolution, Fiscal 1983. Bonior, D-Mich., amendment, to the Aspin, D-Wis., substitute, to set a level for total tax expenditures of $273.1 billion. Rejected 164-246: R 30-155; D 134-91 (ND 118-34, SD 16-57), May 25, 1982.

97. H Con Res 345. First Budget Resolution, Fiscal 1983. Jones, D-Okla., amendment to the Latta, R-Ohio, substitute, to increase fiscal 1983 revenues by $7.5 billion and redistribute those funds to entitlement and domestic discretionary programs. Rejected 175-237: R 4-181; D 171-56 (ND 134-19, SD 37-37), May 25, 1982.

98. H Con Res 345. First Budget Resolution, Fiscal 1983. Martin, R-N.C., amendment, to the Jones, D-Okla., substitute, to reduce revenue levels by $10.8 billion. Rejected 178-237: R 163-21; D 15-216 (ND 2-153, SD 13-63), May 25, 1982.

99. Procedural Motion. Walker, R-Pa., motion to approve the House *Journal* of Tuesday, May 25. Motion agreed to 353-36: R 151-24; D 202-12 (ND 129-11, SD 73-1), May 26, 1982.

KEY

- Y Voted for (yea).
- # Paired for.
- + Announced for.
- N Voted against (nay).
- X Paired against.
- - Announced against.
- P Voted "present".
- C Voted "present" to avoid possible conflict of interest.
- ? Did not vote or otherwise make a position known.

Democrats *Republicans*

	92	93	94	95	96	97	98	99
ALABAMA								
1 Edwards	N	Y	Y	N	N	N	Y	?
2 Dickinson	N	Y	Y	N	N	N	Y	N
3 Nichols	N	Y	Y	N	N	N	N	?
4 Bevill	N	Y	Y	N	N	N	Y	Y
5 Flippo	N	Y	Y	N	N	N	N	Y
6 Smith	N	Y	Y	N	N	N	Y	Y
7 Shelby	N	Y	Y	N	N	N	Y	Y
ALASKA								
AL Young	N	N	Y	N	N	N	?	?
ARIZONA								
1 Rhodes	?	Y	Y	?	?	X	?	?
2 Udall	Y	Y	N	N	?	Y	N	Y
3 Stump	N	Y	Y	N	N	N	Y	Y
4 Rudd	N	Y	Y	N	N	N	Y	Y
ARKANSAS								
1 Alexander	N	Y	N	N	Y	Y	N	Y
2 Bethune	N	Y	Y	N	Y	N	Y	Y
3 Hammerschmidt	N	Y	Y	N	N	N	Y	Y
4 Anthony	N	Y	N	N	N	N	N	Y
CALIFORNIA								
1 Chappie	N	Y	Y	N	N	N	Y	Y
2 Clausen	N	Y	Y	N	N	N	Y	Y
3 Matsui	N	Y	N	N	N	Y	N	Y
4 Fazio	N	Y	N	N	N	Y	N	Y
5 Burton, J.	?	?	?	?	?	?	?	?
6 Burton, P.	Y	Y	N	N	Y	Y	N	Y
7 Miller	Y	Y	N	Y	Y	Y	N	Y
8 Dellums	Y	Y	N	Y	Y	Y	N	Y
9 Stark	Y	?	N	Y	N	Y	N	Y
10 Edwards	Y	Y	N	Y	Y	Y	N	Y
11 Lantos	N	Y	N	N	N	Y	N	Y
12 McCloskey	?	Y	Y	Y	Y	N	N	Y
13 Mineta	N	Y	N	N	N	Y	N	Y
14 Shumway	N	Y	Y	N	N	N	Y	Y
15 Coelho	N	Y	N	N	N	Y	N	Y
16 Panetta	N	Y	N	N	N	Y	N	Y
17 Pashayan	N	Y	Y	N	N	N	Y	Y
18 Thomas	N	Y	Y	N	N	N	Y	Y
19 Lagomarsino	N	Y	Y	N	N	N	Y	Y
20 Goldwater	?	Y	Y	N	N	N	Y	?
21 Fiedler	N	Y	Y	N	N	N	Y	Y
22 Moorhead	N	Y	Y	N	N	N	Y	Y
23 Beilenson	Y	Y	N	Y	N	Y	N	Y
24 Waxman	Y	Y	N	Y	Y	Y	N	?
25 Roybal	Y	Y	N	Y	Y	Y	N	Y
26 Rousselot	N	N	Y	N	N	N	Y	N
27 Dornan	N	Y	Y	N	N	N	Y	N
28 Dixon	#	?	?	#	?	?	?	?
29 Hawkins	Y	Y	N	Y	Y	Y	N	Y
30 Vacancy								
31 Dymally	Y	Y	N	N	Y	Y	N	?
32 Anderson	N	Y	N	Y	Y	Y	N	Y
33 Grisham	N	Y	Y	N	N	N	Y	Y
34 Lungren	N	Y	Y	N	N	N	Y	Y
35 Dreier	N	Y	Y	N	N	N	Y	N
36 Brown	Y	Y	N	Y	Y	Y	N	?
37 Lewis	N	Y	Y	N	N	N	Y	Y
38 Patterson	N	?	N	N	Y	Y	N	Y
39 Dannemeyer	N	Y	Y	N	N	N	Y	Y
40 Badham	N	Y	Y	N	N	N	Y	Y
41 Lowery	N	?	Y	N	N	N	Y	?
42 Hunter	N	Y	Y	N	N	N	Y	Y
43 Burgener	N	Y	Y	N	N	N	Y	Y
COLORADO								
1 Schroeder	Y	N	N	N	Y	Y	N	N
2 Wirth	N	Y	N	N	#	N	N	Y
3 Kogovsek	Y	Y	N	N	Y	N	N	Y
4 Brown	N	Y	Y	N	N	N	Y	N

	92	93	94	95	96	97	98	99
5 Kramer	N	Y	Y	N	N	N	N	Y
CONNECTICUT								
1 Kennelly	N	Y	N	N	Y	Y	N	Y
2 Gejdenson	N	N	N	Y	N	Y	Y	N
3 DeNardis	N	Y	N	N	N	N	Y	N
4 McKinney	N	Y	N	N	N	N	N	?
5 Ratchford	N	N	N	N	Y	Y	N	Y
6 Moffett	?	?	N	Y	Y	Y	N	Y
DELAWARE								
AL Evans	?	Y	N	N	Y	N	N	Y
FLORIDA								
1 Hutto	N	Y	Y	N	N	N	N	Y
2 Fuqua	N	Y	Y	N	N	N	N	Y
3 Bennett	N	Y	Y	N	N	N	N	Y
4 Chappell	N	Y	Y	N	N	N	N	Y
5 McCollum	N	Y	N	N	N	N	Y	Y
6 Young	N	Y	N	N	N	N	Y	Y
7 Gibbons	N	Y	Y	N	N	N	N	Y
8 Ireland	N	Y	Y	N	N	N	Y	Y
9 Nelson	N	Y	Y	N	N	Y	N	Y
10 Bafalis	N	Y	?	?	?	?	?	?
11 Mica	N	Y	N	N	N	N	N	Y
12 Shaw	N	Y	Y	N	N	N	Y	Y
13 Lehman	Y	Y	N	N	Y	N	N	Y
14 Pepper	Y	Y	N	N	Y	N	N	Y
15 Fascell	N	Y	N	N	Y	Y	N	Y
GEORGIA								
1 Ginn	?	Y	Y	?	?	?	?	Y
2 Hatcher	N	Y	Y	N	N	N	N	Y
3 Brinkley	N	Y	N	N	N	N	N	Y
4 Levitas	N	Y	N	N	N	N	N	Y
5 Fowler	Y	Y	N	N	N	N	N	Y
6 Gingrich	N	Y	Y	N	N	N	Y	Y
7 McDonald	N	Y	Y	N	N	N	N	Y
8 Evans	N	Y	Y	N	Y	N	N	Y
9 Jenkins	N	Y	N	N	N	N	N	Y
10 Barnard	N	Y	Y	N	N	N	N	Y
HAWAII								
1 Heftel	N	?	N	N	N	N	Y	N
2 Akaka	Y	Y	N	N	N	Y	N	Y
IDAHO								
1 Craig	N	Y	Y	N	N	N	Y	Y
2 Hansen	N	Y	Y	N	N	N	Y	Y
ILLINOIS								
1 Washington	Y	N	N	Y	Y	Y	N	N
2 Savage	Y	?	N	Y	Y	Y	N	?
3 Russo	N	Y	N	N	N	Y	N	Y
4 Derwinski	N	Y	Y	Y	N	Y	N	Y
5 Fary	N	Y	N	N	Y	N	N	Y
6 Hyde	N	Y	N	N	N	N	N	Y
7 Collins	Y	N	Y	N	Y	Y	N	Y
8 Rostenkowski	N	N	N	N	N	N	N	Y
9 Yates	Y	N	N	Y	Y	Y	N	Y
10 Porter	N	Y	N	Y	N	N	N	Y
11 Annunzio	N	Y	N	N	Y	N	N	Y
12 Crane, P.	N	Y	Y	N	N	N	Y	Y
13 McClory	N	Y	Y	N	N	N	N	Y
14 Erlenborn	N	Y	N	N	N	N	N	?
15 Corcoran	N	Y	N	N	N	N	Y	Y
16 Martin	N	Y	Y	N	N	N	Y	Y
17 O'Brien	N	?	Y	N	N	N	Y	Y
18 Michel	N	Y	N	N	N	N	N	Y
19 Railsback	?	Y	N	N	N	N	Y	Y
20 Findley	N	Y	N	Y	N	N	N	Y
21 Madigan	N	Y	N	N	N	N	N	Y
22 Crane, D.	N	Y	Y	N	N	N	Y	Y
23 Price	N	Y	N	Y	N	Y	N	Y
24 Simon	Y	Y	N	N	Y	?	N	Y
INDIANA								
1 Benjamin	Y	Y	N	N	Y	Y	N	N
2 Fithian	Y	Y	N	N	Y	Y	N	Y
3 Hiler	N	Y	Y	N	N	N	Y	N
4 Coats	N	Y	Y	N	N	N	Y	Y
5 Hillis	N	Y	N	N	N	N	Y	Y
6 Evans	N	Y	N	N	Y	N	N	Y
7 Myers	N	Y	Y	N	N	N	Y	Y
8 Deckard	N	Y	Y	N	N	N	Y	Y
9 Hamilton	N	Y	N	N	N	N	N	Y
10 Sharp	N	Y	N	N	N	N	N	Y
11 Jacobs	Y	N	N	Y	Y	N	N	N
IOWA								
1 Leach	N	Y	N	N	Y	Y	N	Y
2 Tauke	N	Y	N	N	N	N	N	Y
3 Evans	N	N	N	N	N	N	Y	N
4 Smith	N	Y	N	N	Y	N	N	Y
5 Harkin	N	N	N	Y	Y	N	N	Y
6 Bedell	N	Y	N	N	Y	Y	N	Y

ND - Northern Democrats   SD - Southern Democrats

	92	93	94	95	96	97	98	99
KANSAS								
1 **Roberts**	N	Y	Y	N	N	N	Y	Y
2 **Jeffries**	N	Y	Y	N	N	N	Y	Y
3 **Winn**	N	Y	Y	N	N	N	Y	Y
4 Glickman	N	Y	N	N	Y	N	N	Y
5 **Whittaker**	N	Y	Y	N	N	N	Y	Y
KENTUCKY								
1 Hubbard	N	Y	Y	N	N	Y	N	Y
2 Natcher	N	Y	N	N	N	N	N	Y
3 Mazzoli	-	Y	N	-	+	+	-	Y
4 **Snyder**	N	Y	Y	N	N	N	Y	Y
5 **Rogers**	N	Y	N	?	X	X	?	Y
6 **Hopkins**	N	Y	Y	N	N	N	Y	Y
7 Perkins	N	Y	N	N	N	Y	N	Y
LOUISIANA								
1 **Livingston**	N	Y	Y	N	N	N	Y	Y
2 Boggs	Y	Y	N	N	Y	Y	N	Y
3 Tauzin	N	Y	N	N	N	N	Y	Y
4 Roemer	N	N	Y	N	N	N	Y	N
5 Huckaby	N	Y	Y	N	N	N	N	Y
6 **Moore**	N	Y	Y	N	N	N	Y	Y
7 Breaux	N	Y	N	N	N	N	Y	Y
8 Long	N	Y	N	N	Y	Y	N	Y
MAINE								
1 **Emery**	N	Y	N	N	N	N	Y	Y
2 **Snowe**	N	Y	N	N	Y	N	N	Y
MARYLAND								
1 Dyson	N	Y	Y	N	N	N	N	Y
2 Long	N	?	N	Y	Y	Y	N	Y
3 Mikulski	N	Y	N	Y	Y	Y	N	Y
4 **Holt**	?	Y	Y	N	Y	N	Y	N
5 Hoyer	Y	Y	N	N	N	Y	N	Y
6 Byron	N	Y	Y	N	N	N	N	Y
7 Mitchell	Y	N	N	Y	Y	Y	N	?
8 Barnes	N	N	N	N	Y	Y	N	N
MASSACHUSETTS								
1 **Conte**	N	Y	N	N	Y	N	Y	Y
2 Boland	N	Y	N	N	Y	Y	N	Y
3 Early	Y	Y	N	Y	Y	Y	N	Y
4 Frank	Y	Y	N	N	Y	Y	N	Y
5 Shannon	Y	Y	N	Y	Y	Y	N	Y
6 Mavroules	Y	Y	N	N	Y	Y	N	Y
7 Markey	N	Y	N	N	Y	Y	N	?
8 O'Neill								
9 Moakley	Y	Y	N	Y	Y	Y	N	Y
10 **Heckler**	N	Y	N	N	Y	N	N	?
11 Donnelly	Y	Y	N	N	N	Y	N	Y
12 Studds	Y	Y	N	Y	Y	Y	N	Y
MICHIGAN								
1 Conyers	Y	N	N	Y	Y	Y	N	Y
2 **Pursell**	N	Y	N	N	Y	N	N	Y
3 Wolpe	Y	Y	N	Y	Y	Y	N	Y
4 **Siljander**	N	Y	Y	N	N	N	Y	Y
5 **Sawyer**	N	Y	Y	N	N	N	Y	Y
6 **Dunn**	N	Y	Y	N	N	N	Y	Y
7 Kildee	Y	Y	N	Y	Y	Y	N	Y
8 Traxler	N	Y	N	N	N	N	Y	Y
9 **Vander Jagt**	?	Y	Y	?	N	N	Y	Y
10 Albosta	N	Y	N	N	Y	Y	N	Y
11 **Davis**	N	Y	N	N	Y	N	N	Y
12 Bonior	Y	Y	N	Y	Y	Y	N	Y
13 Crockett	Y	?	N	?	Y	Y	N	?
14 Hertel	N	Y	N	Y	Y	Y	N	Y
15 Ford	Y	?	N	N	Y	Y	N	?
16 Dingell	N	Y	N	Y	Y	Y	N	Y
17 Brodhead	Y	Y	N	Y	Y	Y	N	Y
18 Blanchard	?	Y	N	N	Y	Y	N	Y
19 **Broomfield**	N	Y	Y	N	N	N	Y	Y
MINNESOTA								
1 **Erdahl**	N	Y	Y	N	N	N	Y	Y
2 **Hagedorn**	N	Y	Y	N	N	N	Y	Y
3 **Frenzel**	N	Y	Y	N	N	N	Y	Y
4 Vento	N	Y	N	Y	Y	Y	N	Y
5 Sabo	Y	N	N	Y	Y	Y	N	N
6 **Weber**	N	Y	Y	N	N	N	Y	Y
7 **Stangeland**	N	Y	Y	N	N	N	Y	Y
8 Oberstar	Y	Y	N	Y	Y	Y	N	Y
MISSISSIPPI								
1 Whitten	?	Y	N	N	N	N	N	Y
2 Bowen	N	Y	N	N	?	?	?	Y
3 Montgomery	N	Y	Y	N	N	N	Y	Y
4 Dowdy	N	Y	?	N	N	N	N	Y
5 **Lott**	N	Y	Y	N	N	N	Y	Y
MISSOURI								
1 Clay	Y	N	N	Y	Y	Y	N	N
2 Young	N	Y	N	N	Y	N	N	Y
3 Gephardt	N	Y	N	N	Y	N	N	Y
4 Skelton	N	Y	N	N	N	N	Y	Y
5 Bolling	Y	Y	N	?	Y	Y	N	?
6 **Coleman**	N	Y	N	N	N	N	Y	Y
7 **Taylor**	N	Y	Y	N	N	N	Y	Y
8 **Bailey**	N	Y	Y	N	N	N	Y	Y
9 Volkmer	N	Y	N	N	Y	N	N	Y
10 **Emerson**	N	N	Y	N	N	N	Y	N
MONTANA								
1 Williams	Y	Y	N	N	Y	Y	N	Y
2 **Marlenee**	N	Y	Y	N	N	N	Y	Y
NEBRASKA								
1 **Bereuter**	N	Y	Y	N	Y	N	Y	Y
2 **Daub**	N	Y	Y	N	Y	N	Y	Y
3 **Smith**	N	Y	Y	N	N	N	Y	Y
NEVADA								
AL Santini	N	Y	N	N	N	N	N	Y
NEW HAMPSHIRE								
1 D'Amours	N	Y	N	N	Y	N	N	Y
2 **Gregg**	N	Y	Y	N	N	N	Y	N
NEW JERSEY								
1 Florio	Y	Y	N	Y	Y	Y	N	Y
2 Hughes	N	Y	N	N	Y	N	N	Y
3 Howard	N	Y	N	N	Y	Y	N	Y
4 **Smith**	N	Y	N	N	Y	N	N	Y
5 **Fenwick**	?	Y	N	N	N	N	Y	?
6 **Forsythe**	N	N	Y	N	N	N	Y	N
7 **Roukema**	N	Y	N	N	N	N	N	Y
8 Roe	N	Y	N	N	Y	Y	N	Y
9 **Hollenbeck**	N	Y	N	?	N	Y	N	Y
10 Rodino	Y	Y	N	Y	Y	Y	N	Y
11 Minish	Y	Y	N	?	?	?	?	Y
12 **Rinaldo**	N	Y	N	N	Y	N	N	Y
13 **Courter**	X	?	N	N	N	N	Y	Y
14 Guarini	Y	Y	N	N	N	Y	N	Y
15 Dwyer	Y	Y	N	N	Y	Y	N	Y
NEW MEXICO								
1 **Lujan**	N	Y	Y	Y	Y	N	Y	Y
2 **Skeen**	N	Y	Y	N	N	N	Y	Y
NEW YORK								
1 **Carney**	N	Y	Y	N	N	N	Y	Y
2 Downey	Y	Y	N	N	N	Y	N	Y
3 **Carman**	N	Y	Y	N	N	N	Y	Y
4 **Lent**	N	Y	N	N	N	X	Y	Y
5 **McGrath**	N	Y	N	N	N	N	Y	P
6 **LeBoutillier**	N	N	Y	N	N	N	Y	N
7 Addabbo	Y	Y	N	Y	Y	Y	N	Y
8 Rosenthal	Y	Y	N	Y	Y	Y	N	Y
9 Ferraro	N	Y	N	N	Y	Y	N	Y
10 Biaggi	Y	Y	N	Y	Y	Y	N	Y
11 Scheuer	Y	Y	N	Y	Y	Y	N	Y
12 Chisholm	Y	?	N	?	X	?	?	?
13 Solarz	N	Y	N	Y	Y	Y	N	Y
14 Richmond	Y	?	N	?	#	#	?	Y
15 Zeferetti	N	Y	N	X	#	#	?	Y
16 Schumer	Y	Y	N	N	Y	Y	N	Y
17 **Molinari**	N	Y	N	N	N	N	Y	Y
18 **Green**	N	Y	N	N	N	N	N	Y
19 Rangel	Y	Y	N	N	N	Y	N	Y
20 Weiss	Y	Y	N	N	Y	Y	N	Y
21 Garcia	Y	Y	N	N	Y	Y	N	Y
22 Bingham	Y	Y	N	?	Y	Y	N	?
23 Peyser	N	Y	N	N	Y	Y	N	Y
24 Ottinger	Y	P	N	Y	Y	Y	N	P
25 **Fish**	N	Y	N	N	N	N	Y	Y
26 **Gilman**	N	Y	N	N	Y	N	Y	Y
27 McHugh	N	Y	N	N	Y	Y	N	Y
28 Stratton	N	Y	N	N	N	N	Y	Y
29 **Solomon**	N	N	Y	N	N	N	Y	N
30 **Martin**	N	Y	Y	N	N	N	Y	Y
31 **Mitchell**	N	?	N	N	N	Y	Y	Y
32 **Wortley**	N	Y	Y	N	N	N	Y	Y
33 **Lee**	N	N	Y	N	Y	N	Y	Y
34 **Horton**	?	Y	N	N	N	N	Y	Y
35 **Conable**	N	Y	N	N	N	N	Y	Y
36 LaFalce	N	Y	N	N	Y	Y	N	Y
37 Nowak	Y	Y	N	N	Y	Y	N	Y
38 **Kemp**	N	Y	N	N	N	N	Y	Y
39 Lundine	N	Y	N	N	Y	Y	N	Y
NORTH CAROLINA								
1 Jones	N	Y	N	Y	Y	Y	N	Y
2 Fountain	N	Y	Y	N	N	Y	N	?
3 Whitley	N	Y	Y	N	N	Y	N	Y
4 Andrews	N	Y	N	N	?	?	N	Y
5 Neal	?	Y	Y	N	N	Y	N	Y
6 **Johnston**	N	N	Y	?	?	X	?	N
7 Rose	N	Y	Y	N	N	Y	N	Y
8 Hefner	N	Y	Y	N	N	Y	N	?
9 **Martin**	N	Y	Y	N	N	N	Y	Y
10 **Broyhill**	N	?	Y	N	N	N	Y	Y
11 **Hendon**	?	N	Y	N	N	N	Y	N
NORTH DAKOTA								
AL Dorgan	N	Y	N	N	Y	N	N	Y
OHIO								
1 **Gradison**	N	Y	Y	N	N	N	Y	Y
2 Luken	N	Y	N	N	N	N	N	N
3 Hall	N	Y	N	N	?	Y	N	Y
4 **Oxley**	N	Y	Y	Y	N	N	Y	Y
5 **Latta**	N	Y	Y	N	N	N	Y	Y
6 **McEwen**	N	Y	Y	N	N	N	Y	Y
7 **Brown**	?	?	?	N	N	N	Y	Y
8 **Kindness**	N	Y	Y	N	N	N	Y	Y
9 **Weber**	N	Y	Y	N	N	N	Y	Y
10 **Miller**	N	N	Y	N	Y	N	Y	N
11 **Stanton**	?	?	?	?	?	?	?	?
12 Shamansky	N	Y	N	N	Y	Y	N	Y
13 Pease	N	Y	N	Y	Y	Y	N	Y
14 Seiberling	Y	Y	N	Y	Y	Y	N	Y
15 **Wylie**	N	Y	Y	N	Y	N	Y	Y
16 **Regula**	N	Y	N	N	N	N	Y	Y
17 Vacancy								
18 Applegate	N	?	N	N	N	N	N	?
19 **Williams**	N	Y	N	N	Y	N	N	Y
20 Oakar	Y	Y	N	Y	Y	Y	N	Y
21 Stokes	Y	N	N	Y	Y	Y	N	Y
22 Eckart	N	Y	N	Y	Y	Y	N	Y
23 Mottl	N	Y	N	Y	Y	Y	N	Y
OKLAHOMA								
1 Jones	N	Y	N	N	N	Y	N	Y
2 Synar	N	Y	N	N	Y	Y	N	Y
3 Watkins	N	Y	N	N	N	Y	N	Y
4 McCurdy	N	Y	N	N	N	N	N	Y
5 **Edwards**	N	Y	Y	N	N	N	Y	Y
6 English	N	Y	N	N	N	N	N	Y
OREGON								
1 AuCoin	N	?	N	N	Y	Y	N	Y
2 **Smith**	N	Y	Y	N	N	N	Y	N
3 Wyden	N	Y	N	N	N	Y	N	Y
4 Weaver	N	Y	N	Y	Y	Y	N	Y
PENNSYLVANIA								
1 Foglietta	Y	Y	N	Y	Y	Y	N	Y
2 Gray	Y	Y	N	Y	Y	Y	N	?
3 Smith	Y	Y	N	N	Y	Y	N	Y
4 **Dougherty**	N	Y	N	N	N	Y	N	Y
5 **Schulze**	N	Y	Y	N	N	N	Y	Y
6 Yatron	N	Y	N	N	Y	Y	N	Y
7 Edgar	Y	N	N	Y	Y	Y	N	Y
8 **Coyne, J.**	N	Y	Y	N	N	N	Y	Y
9 **Shuster**	N	Y	N	N	N	N	Y	Y
10 **McDade**	N	Y	N	N	Y	N	Y	Y
11 **Nelligan**	N	Y	N	N	N	N	Y	Y
12 Murtha	N	Y	N	N	Y	N	N	Y
13 **Coughlin**	N	N	N	N	N	N	Y	N
14 Coyne, W.	Y	Y	N	Y	Y	Y	N	Y
15 **Ritter**	N	Y	Y	N	N	N	Y	Y
16 **Walker**	N	N	Y	N	N	N	Y	N
17 Ertel	N	Y	N	N	Y	Y	N	Y
18 Walgren	N	Y	N	Y	Y	Y	N	?
19 **Goodling**	N	N	N	N	N	N	Y	N
20 Gaydos	N	Y	N	N	N	Y	N	Y
21 Bailey	Y	Y	N	N	Y	N	N	Y
22 Murphy	Y	Y	N	N	Y	Y	N	N
23 **Clinger**	N	Y	N	N	N	N	Y	Y
24 **Marks**	N	Y	N	Y	Y	Y	?	?
25 **Atkinson**	N	Y	N	N	N	N	Y	Y
RHODE ISLAND								
1 St Germain	Y	Y	N	Y	N	Y	N	Y
2 **Schneider**	N	Y	N	Y	Y	N	N	?
SOUTH CAROLINA								
1 **Hartnett**	N	Y	Y	N	N	N	Y	N
2 **Spence**	N	Y	Y	N	N	N	Y	Y
3 Derrick	N	?	N	N	N	N	Y	Y
4 **Campbell**	N	Y	Y	N	N	N	Y	Y
5 Holland	N	Y	Y	N	?	?	N	?
6 **Napier**	N	Y	Y	?	?	N	Y	?
SOUTH DAKOTA								
1 Daschle	N	Y	Y	N	Y	Y	N	Y
2 **Roberts**	N	Y	Y	N	N	N	Y	Y
TENNESSEE								
1 **Quillen**	N	Y	Y	N	N	N	Y	Y
2 **Duncan**	N	Y	Y	N	N	N	Y	Y
3 Bouquard	N	Y	Y	N	N	N	N	Y
4 Gore	N	Y	N	Y	Y	Y	N	Y
5 Boner	N	Y	N	N	N	Y	N	Y
6 **Beard**	N	Y	Y	N	N	N	Y	Y
7 Jones	N	Y	N	N	N	N	N	Y
8 Ford	#	?	?	#	?	Y	N	Y
TEXAS								
1 Hall, S.	N	Y	Y	N	N	N	N	Y
2 Wilson	N	Y	N	N	N	Y	N	Y
3 **Collins**	N	Y	Y	N	N	N	Y	Y
4 Hall, R.	N	Y	Y	N	N	N	Y	Y
5 Mattox	Y	Y	N	N	Y	Y	N	Y
6 Gramm	N	Y	Y	N	N	N	Y	Y
7 **Archer**	N	Y	Y	N	N	N	Y	Y
8 **Fields**	N	Y	Y	N	N	N	Y	N
9 Brooks	N	Y	N	N	N	N	N	Y
10 Pickle	N	Y	N	N	N	N	Y	Y
11 Leath	N	Y	Y	N	N	N	N	Y
12 Wright	N	Y	N	N	N	Y	N	Y
13 Hightower	N	Y	N	N	N	N	N	Y
14 Patman	N	Y	Y	N	N	N	N	Y
15 de la Garza	N	Y	N	N	Y	Y	N	Y
16 White	N	Y	Y	N	N	N	N	?
17 Stenholm	N	Y	Y	N	N	N	Y	Y
18 Leland	Y	Y	N	Y	Y	Y	N	Y
19 Hance	N	Y	Y	N	N	N	N	Y
20 Gonzalez	Y	N	N	N	N	Y	N	Y
21 **Loeffler**	N	Y	Y	N	N	N	Y	Y
22 **Paul**	N	Y	Y	N	N	N	Y	Y
23 Kazen	N	Y	Y	N	N	N	Y	Y
24 Frost	Y	?	N	N	Y	Y	N	Y
UTAH								
1 **Hansen**	N	Y	Y	N	N	N	Y	Y
2 **Marriott**	N	Y	Y	N	N	N	Y	Y
VERMONT								
AL **Jeffords**	N	Y	N	N	Y	N	N	Y
VIRGINIA								
1 **Trible**	?	?	Y	N	N	N	Y	Y
2 **Whitehurst**	N	Y	Y	N	N	N	Y	Y
3 **Bliley**	N	Y	Y	N	N	N	Y	Y
4 **Daniel, R.**	N	Y	Y	N	N	N	Y	Y
5 Daniel, D.	N	Y	Y	N	N	N	Y	Y
6 **Butler**	N	?	Y	N	N	N	N	N
7 **Robinson**	N	Y	Y	N	N	N	Y	Y
8 **Parris**	N	Y	Y	N	N	N	Y	Y
9 **Wampler**	N	Y	Y	N	N	N	Y	Y
10 **Wolf**	N	Y	Y	N	N	N	Y	Y
WASHINGTON								
1 **Pritchard**	N	?	N	N	N	N	N	Y
2 Swift	N	?	N	N	Y	Y	N	Y
3 Bonker	N	Y	N	N	Y	Y	N	?
4 **Morrison**	N	Y	Y	N	N	N	Y	Y
5 Foley	N	Y	N	?	Y	Y	N	Y
6 Dicks	N	Y	N	N	Y	Y	N	Y
7 Lowry	Y	Y	N	N	Y	Y	N	Y
WEST VIRGINIA								
1 Mollohan	N	Y	N	N	N	Y	N	Y
2 **Benedict**	N	Y	Y	N	N	N	Y	Y
3 **Staton**	N	Y	Y	N	N	N	Y	Y
4 Rahall	X	?	?	X	X	#	?	?
WISCONSIN								
1 Aspin	N	Y	N	Y	N	Y	N	Y
2 Kastenmeier	Y	Y	N	Y	Y	Y	N	Y
3 **Gunderson**	N	Y	N	N	N	N	Y	Y
4 Zablocki	N	Y	N	N	N	Y	N	Y
5 Reuss	Y	Y	N	Y	Y	Y	N	Y
6 **Petri**	N	Y	Y	N	Y	N	Y	Y
7 Obey	Y	Y	N	N	Y	Y	N	?
8 **Roth**	N	Y	Y	N	N	N	Y	Y
9 **Sensenbrenner**	N	Y	Y	N	N	N	Y	Y
WYOMING								
AL **Cheney**	N	Y	Y	N	N	N	Y	Y

Southern states - Ala., Ark., Fla., Ga., Ky., La., Miss., N.C., Okla., S.C., Tenn., Texas, Va.

KEY

Y	Voted for (yea).
#	Paired for.
+	Announced for.
N	Voted against (nay).
X	Paired against.
-	Announced against.
P	Voted "present".
C	Voted "present" to avoid possible conflict of interest.
?	Did not vote or otherwise make a position known.

Democrats *Republicans*

100. S Con Res 60. Disapproval of Federal Trade Commission Used-Car Rule. Dingell, D-Mich., motion to limit debate to two hours on the Federal Trade Commission used-car rule. Motion agreed to 317-92: R 154-26; D 163-66 (ND 93-59, SD 70-7), May 26, 1982.

101. S Con Res 60. Disapproval of Federal Trade Commission Used-Car Rule. Adoption of the concurrent resolution to disapprove the Federal Trade Commission rule to require used-car dealers to inform customers of major known defects in used automobiles. Adopted 286-133: R 167-18; D 119-115 (ND 50-108, SD 69-7), May 26, 1982.

102. H Con Res 345. First Budget Resolution, Fiscal 1983. Huckaby, D-La., amendment, to the Jones, D-Okla., substitute, to increase budget authority by $10.5 billion and outlays by $7.6 billion in fiscal 1983-85 and to reduce discretionary programs and entitlements by the same amounts. Rejected 83-339: R 12-175; D 71-164 (ND 14-143, SD 57-21), May 26, 1982.

103. H Con Res 345. First Budget Resolution, Fiscal 1983. Green, R-N.Y., amendment, to the Jones, D-Okla., substitute, to reduce defense budget authority by $16 billion and outlays by $4 billion annually in fiscal 1983-85 and to reduce revenues by $4 billion in each of those years. Rejected 125-295: R 43-143; D 82-152 (ND 79-78, SD 3-74), May 26, 1982.

104. H Con Res 345. First Budget Resolution, Fiscal 1983. Conyers, D-Mich., amendment, to the Jones, D-Okla., substitute, to reduce budget authority by $20.4 billion and outlays by $8 billion in fiscal 1983, reflecting a freeze on nuclear weapons testing, production and deployment. Rejected 28-383: R 1-184; D 27-199 (ND 25-126, SD 2-73), May 26, 1982.

105. H Con Res 345. First Budget Resolution, Fiscal 1983. Wylie, R-Ohio, amendment to the Latta, R-Ohio, substitute, to reduce fiscal 1983 defense outlays by $7.5 billion and increase revenues by $15 billion through enactment of luxury and excise taxes. Rejected 128-285: R 37-149; D 91-136 (ND 85-65, SD 6-71), May 26, 1982.

106. H Con Res 345. First Budget Resolution, Fiscal 1983. Simon, D-Ill., amendment, to the Latta, R-Ohio, Jones, D-Okla., and Aspin, D-Wis., substitutes, to increase budget authority by $1.85 billion in fiscal 1982-85 and outlays by $450 million in fiscal 1984-85 to accommodate additional funding for the Export-Import Bank direct loan program. Rejected 186-232: R 48-138; D 138-94 (ND 105-51, SD 33-43), May 26, 1982.

107. H Con Res 345. First Budget Resolution, Fiscal 1983. Simon, D-Ill., amendment, to the Jones, D-Okla., substitute, to increase budget authority by $668 million and outlays by $87 million for education programs in fiscal 1983, and to make corresponding reductions in the allowances function. Adopted 323-99: R 100-88; D 223-11 (ND 156-1, SD 67-10), May 26, 1982.

	100	101	102	103	104	105	106	107
ALABAMA								
1 *Edwards*	Y	Y	N	N	N	N	Y	N
2 *Dickinson*	Y	Y	N	N	N	N	N	N
3 Nichols	Y	Y	Y	N	N	N	N	Y
4 Bevill	Y	Y	Y	N	N	N	Y	Y
5 Flippo	Y	Y	Y	N	N	Y	Y	Y
6 *Smith*	Y	Y	N	N	N	N	N	N
7 Shelby	Y	Y	N	N	N	N	N	Y
ALASKA								
AL *Young*	Y	Y	N	N	N	N	N	Y
ARIZONA								
1 *Rhodes*	?	#	N	?	?	?	?	?
2 Udall	Y	N	N	?	N	Y	Y	Y
3 *Stump*	Y	Y	N	N	N	N	N	N
4 *Rudd*	Y	Y	N	N	N	N	N	N
ARKANSAS								
1 Alexander	Y	Y	Y	N	N	N	Y	Y
2 *Bethune*	Y	Y	N	N	N	N	N	N
3 *Hammerschmidt*	Y	Y	N	N	N	N	N	Y
4 Anthony	Y	Y	Y	N	N	N	N	Y
CALIFORNIA								
1 *Chappie*	Y	Y	N	Y	N	N	N	Y
2 *Clausen*	Y	Y	N	N	N	Y	Y	Y
3 Matsui	Y	Y	N	N	N	Y	Y	Y
4 Fazio	Y	Y	Y	N	N	Y	Y	Y
5 Burton, J.	?	?	?	?	?	?	?	?
6 Burton, P.	N	N	N	Y	Y	Y	Y	Y
7 Miller	N	N	N	Y	Y	Y	Y	Y
8 Dellums	N	N	N	Y	Y	Y	Y	Y
9 Stark	N	N	N	Y	N	Y	N	Y
10 Edwards	N	N	N	P	Y	Y	Y	Y
11 Lantos	Y	Y	N	N	N	Y	Y	Y
12 *McCloskey*	Y	Y	N	N	N	N	N	Y
13 Mineta	Y	Y	N	N	N	Y	Y	Y
14 *Shumway*	Y	Y	Y	N	N	N	N	N
15 Coelho	Y	Y	N	N	N	N	Y	Y
16 Panetta	Y	Y	N	N	N	Y	Y	Y
17 *Pashayan*	Y	Y	N	Y	N	N	Y	Y
18 *Thomas*	Y	Y	N	N	N	N	N	N
19 *Lagomarsino*	Y	Y	N	N	N	Y	Y	Y
20 *Goldwater*	N	Y	N	N	N	N	N	N
21 *Fiedler*	Y	Y	N	N	N	N	N	Y
22 *Moorhead*	Y	Y	N	N	N	N	N	N
23 Beilenson	Y	N	N	Y	N	Y	N	Y
24 Waxman	N	N	N	Y	N	Y	Y	Y
25 Royal	Y	N	Y	Y	N	Y	Y	Y
26 *Rousselot*	Y	Y	N	N	N	N	N	N
27 *Dornan*	N	Y	N	N	N	N	N	Y
28 Dixon	?	N	Y	N	Y	N	Y	Y
29 Hawkins	?	N	Y	N	?	Y	N	Y
30 Vacancy								
31 Dymally	N	Y	N	Y	Y	Y	Y	Y
32 Anderson	Y	Y	N	N	N	N	Y	Y
33 *Grisham*	Y	Y	N	N	N	N	N	N
34 Lungren	Y	Y	N	N	N	N	N	N
35 *Dreier*	Y	Y	N	N	N	N	N	N
36 Brown	N	N	N	Y	Y	Y	Y	Y
37 Lewis	N	Y	N	N	N	N	N	N
38 Patterson	Y	N	N	N	N	Y	Y	Y
39 *Dannemeyer*	Y	Y	N	N	N	N	N	N
40 *Badham*	Y	Y	?	N	N	N	N	N
41 *Lowery*	?	Y	N	N	N	N	Y	Y
42 *Hunter*	Y	Y	Y	N	N	N	N	N
43 *Burgener*	Y	Y	N	N	N	N	N	N
COLORADO								
1 Schroeder	N	N	N	Y	N	Y	N	Y
2 Wirth	N	N	N	N	N	N	N	Y
3 Kogovsek	Y	Y	N	N	N	Y	Y	Y
4 *Brown*	Y	Y	N	Y	N	Y	N	Y

	100	101	102	103	104	105	106	107
5 *Kramer*	Y	Y	N	N	N	N	N	N
CONNECTICUT								
1 Kennelly	N	N	N	N	N	Y	Y	Y
2 Gejdenson	N	N	N	N	N	Y	Y	Y
3 *DeNardis*	Y	Y	N	Y	N	Y	N	Y
4 *McKinney*	?	N	N	Y	N	Y	Y	Y
5 Ratchford	N	N	N	Y	N	N	Y	Y
6 Moffett	N	N	N	Y	N	N	Y	Y
DELAWARE								
AL *Evans*	Y	Y	N	N	N	N	Y	Y
FLORIDA								
1 Hutto	Y	Y	N	N	N	N	N	Y
2 Fuqua	Y	Y	Y	N	N	N	N	Y
3 Bennett	Y	Y	Y	N	N	Y	N	N
4 Chappell	Y	Y	Y	?	N	N	N	Y
5 *McCollum*	Y	Y	N	N	N	N	N	N
6 *Young*	N	Y	N	N	N	N	N	N
7 Gibbons	N	N	N	N	N	N	Y	Y
8 Ireland	Y	Y	N	N	N	N	N	Y
9 Nelson	Y	Y	Y	N	N	Y	Y	Y
10 *Bafalis*	?	?	N	N	N	N	N	N
11 Mica	Y	Y	N	N	N	N	N	Y
12 *Shaw*	N	N	N	N	N	N	N	N
13 Lehman	Y	C	N	N	N	Y	Y	Y
14 Pepper	Y	N	N	N	N	Y	Y	Y
15 Fascell	Y	Y	N	N	N	N	N	Y
GEORGIA								
1 Ginn	Y	Y	Y	N	N	N	N	Y
2 Hatcher	Y	Y	Y	N	N	N	N	Y
3 Brinkley	Y	Y	Y	N	Y	N	N	Y
4 Levitas	N	Y	N	N	N	Y	Y	Y
5 Fowler	Y	Y	N	N	N	N	N	Y
6 *Gingrich*	N	N	N	N	N	N	N	N
7 McDonald	N	Y	N	N	N	N	N	N
8 Evans	Y	Y	Y	N	N	N	N	Y
9 Jenkins	Y	Y	Y	N	N	N	N	Y
10 Barnard	Y	Y	Y	N	N	N	N	Y
HAWAII								
1 Heftel	Y	N	N	N	N	N	Y	N
2 Akaka	Y	N	N	N	N	N	N	Y
IDAHO								
1 *Craig*	Y	Y	N	N	N	N	N	N
2 *Hansen*	Y	Y	N	N	N	N	N	N
ILLINOIS								
1 Washington	N	N	N	Y	Y	Y	N	Y
2 Savage	?	N	Y	Y	Y	Y	Y	Y
3 Russo	Y	N	N	N	N	N	Y	Y
4 *Derwinski*	N	Y	N	N	N	Y	Y	N
5 Fary	Y	N	N	N	N	N	Y	Y
6 *Hyde*	Y	N	N	N	N	N	N	N
7 Collins	N	N	N	Y	N	Y	N	Y
8 Rostenkowski	Y	N	N	N	N	N	N	Y
9 Yates	N	N	N	Y	N	Y	Y	Y
10 *Porter*	N	Y	N	Y	N	Y	Y	Y
11 Annunzio	Y	N	N	N	N	N	Y	Y
12 *Crane, P.*	N	Y	N	N	N	X	X	N
13 *McClory*	Y	Y	N	N	N	N	N	N
14 *Erlenborn*	Y	Y	N	N	N	N	N	N
15 *Corcoran*	Y	Y	N	N	N	N	N	N
16 *Martin*	Y	Y	N	N	N	N	N	N
17 *O'Brien*	Y	Y	N	N	N	N	N	N
18 *Michel*	Y	Y	N	N	N	N	N	N
19 *Railsback*	Y	Y	N	Y	N	Y	?	Y
20 *Findley*	Y	Y	Y	N	Y	N	N	N
21 *Madigan*	Y	Y	N	N	N	N	N	N
22 *Crane, D.*	N	Y	N	N	N	N	N	N
23 Price	Y	N	Y	N	N	Y	N	Y
24 Simon	Y	Y	N	Y	N	Y	Y	Y
INDIANA								
1 Benjamin	Y	Y	N	N	N	Y	Y	Y
2 Fithian	Y	Y	Y	N	N	N	Y	Y
3 *Hiler*	Y	Y	N	N	N	N	N	N
4 *Coats*	Y	Y	N	N	N	N	N	N
5 *Hillis*	?	Y	N	N	N	N	N	Y
6 Evans	Y	Y	N	N	N	?	?	Y
7 *Myers*	Y	Y	N	N	N	N	N	N
8 *Deckard*	Y	Y	N	N	N	Y	N	Y
9 Hamilton	Y	Y	N	N	N	N	N	Y
10 Sharp	Y	N	N	N	N	Y	N	Y
11 Jacobs	N	Y	N	Y	P	Y	N	Y
IOWA								
1 *Leach*	Y	N	N	Y	N	N	Y	Y
2 *Tauke*	Y	Y	N	Y	N	N	Y	Y
3 *Evans*	Y	Y	N	N	N	N	N	Y
4 Smith	Y	N	N	N	N	Y	Y	Y
5 Harkin	N	N	N	N	N	Y	N	Y
6 Bedell	N	Y	N	Y	N	Y	Y	Y

ND - Northern Democrats   SD - Southern Democrats

	100	101	102	103	104	105	106	107
KANSAS								
1 ***Roberts***	Y	Y	N	N	N	N	Y	Y
2 ***Jeffries***	Y	Y	N	N	N	N	N	N
3 ***Winn***	Y	Y	N	N	N	N	Y	Y
4 Glickman	Y	N	N	N	N	Y	Y	Y
5 ***Whittaker***	Y	Y	N	N	N	N	Y	Y
KENTUCKY								
1 Hubbard	Y	Y	Y	N	N	N	Y	Y
2 Natcher	Y	Y	N	N	N	N	Y	Y
3 Mazzoli	Y	N	N	N	N	N	N	Y
4 ***Snyder***	Y	Y	N	N	N	N	N	N
5 ***Rogers***	Y	Y	N	N	N	N	N	Y
6 ***Hopkins***	Y	Y	N	Y	N	N	N	Y
7 Perkins	Y	Y	N	N	N	N	N	Y
LOUISIANA								
1 ***Livingston***	Y	Y	Y	N	N	N	N	N
2 Boggs	Y	Y	Y	N	X	N	Y	Y
3 Tauzin	Y	Y	Y	N	N	N	N	Y
4 Roemer	Y	Y	Y	N	N	N	N	N
5 Huckaby	Y	Y	Y	N	N	N	N	N
6 ***Moore***	N	Y	Y	N	N	N	N	N
7 Breaux	Y	Y	Y	N	N	N	N	Y
8 Long	?	Y	N	N	N	N	Y	Y
MAINE								
1 ***Emery***	N	N	N	N	N	N	N	Y
2 ***Snowe***	Y	N	N	N	N	N	N	Y
MARYLAND								
1 Dyson	Y	Y	Y	N	N	N	Y	Y
2 Long	Y	Y	N	N	N	N	N	Y
3 Mikulski	Y	N	N	Y	N	N	N	Y
4 ***Holt***	Y	Y	N	N	N	N	N	Y
5 Hoyer	Y	N	N	N	N	?	Y	Y
6 Byron	Y	Y	Y	N	N	N	Y	Y
7 Mitchell	N	N	N	Y	Y	Y	N	Y
8 Barnes	Y	N	N	N	N	N	Y	Y
MASSACHUSETTS								
1 ***Conte***	N	N	N	Y	N	Y	Y	Y
2 Boland	Y	N	N	Y	N	Y	Y	Y
3 Early	N	N	N	Y	N	Y	N	Y
4 Frank	N	N	N	Y	N	Y	Y	Y
5 Shannon	N	N	N	Y	N	Y	Y	Y
6 Mavroules	N	N	N	Y	N	N	Y	Y
7 Markey	N	N	N	Y	N	Y	N	Y
8 O'Neill								
9 Moakley	N	N	N	Y	N	N	Y	Y
10 ***Heckler***	N	N	N	Y	N	N	Y	Y
11 Donnelly	Y	N	N	N	N	N	N	Y
12 Studds	N	N	N	Y	N	Y	N	Y
MICHIGAN								
1 Conyers	N	N	N	Y	Y	Y	N	?
2 ***Pursell***	Y	Y	N	Y	N	Y	N	Y
3 Wolpe	Y	N	N	Y	N	Y	Y	Y
4 ***Siljander***	Y	Y	N	N	N	N	N	N
5 ***Sawyer***	Y	Y	N	N	N	N	N	N
6 ***Dunn***	Y	Y	N	Y	N	Y	N	Y
7 Kildee	N	N	N	Y	N	Y	Y	Y
8 Traxler	Y	Y	N	Y	N	Y	Y	Y
9 ***Vander Jagt***	Y	Y	N	N	N	N	Y	N
10 Albosta	Y	Y	N	N	N	Y	Y	Y
11 ***Davis***	Y	Y	N	N	N	N	N	Y
12 Bonior	N	N	N	Y	N	Y	N	Y
13 Crockett	N	N	N	Y	Y	Y	N	Y
14 Hertel	Y	N	N	N	N	N	Y	Y
15 Ford	Y	Y	N	N	N	Y	Y	Y
16 Dingell	Y	Y	N	N	N	Y	Y	Y
17 Brodhead	Y	N	N	Y	Y	Y	Y	Y
18 Blanchard	Y	Y	N	N	N	Y	Y	Y
19 ***Broomfield***	Y	Y	N	N	N	N	N	Y
MINNESOTA								
1 ***Erdahl***	Y	Y	N	Y	N	N	Y	Y
2 ***Hagedorn***	Y	Y	N	N	N	N	N	N
3 ***Frenzel***	Y	Y	N	N	N	N	Y	N
4 Vento	N	N	N	Y	N	Y	Y	Y
5 Sabo	Y	N	N	Y	N	Y	Y	Y
6 ***Weber***	Y	Y	N	Y	N	N	N	Y
7 ***Stangeland***	Y	Y	N	N	N	N	N	Y
8 Oberstar	Y	N	N	Y	N	Y	Y	Y
MISSISSIPPI								
1 Whitten	Y	Y	N	N	N	N	Y	Y
2 Bowen	Y	Y	Y	N	N	N	Y	Y
3 Montgomery	Y	Y	Y	N	N	N	N	N
4 Dowdy	Y	Y	Y	N	N	N	N	Y
5 ***Lott***	Y	Y	N	N	N	N	N	N
MISSOURI								
1 Clay	N	N	N	Y	Y	Y	Y	Y
2 Young	Y	Y	Y	N	N	N	Y	Y
3 Gephardt	Y	Y	Y	N	N	N	Y	Y

	100	101	102	103	104	105	106	107
4 Skelton	Y	Y	Y	N	N	N	N	Y
5 Bolling	Y	N	N	N	N	N	N	Y
6 ***Coleman***	Y	Y	N	N	N	N	N	Y
7 ***Taylor***	Y	Y	N	N	N	N	N	N
8 ***Bailey***	Y	Y	N	N	N	N	N	N
9 Volkmer	Y	Y	Y	N	N	Y	N	Y
10 ***Emerson***	Y	Y	N	N	N	N	N	Y
MONTANA								
1 Williams	Y	N	N	Y	N	N	Y	Y
2 ***Marlenee***	Y	Y	N	N	N	N	N	Y
NEBRASKA								
1 ***Bereuter***	C	C	N	Y	N	N	N	Y
2 ***Daub***	Y	Y	N	Y	N	N	N	Y
3 ***Smith***	Y	Y	N	Y	N	N	N	Y
NEVADA								
AL Santini	Y	Y	N	N	N	N	N	Y
NEW HAMPSHIRE								
1 D'Amours	Y	Y	N	N	N	Y	N	Y
2 ***Gregg***	Y	Y	N	Y	N	N	N	N
NEW JERSEY								
1 Florio	Y	N	N	Y	N	N	?	Y
2 Hughes	Y	Y	N	N	N	Y	N	Y
3 Howard	Y	N	N	Y	N	Y	Y	Y
4 ***Smith***	Y	N	N	Y	N	N	N	Y
5 ***Fenwick***	?	X	?	?	N	N	Y	Y
6 ***Forsythe***	Y	Y	N	Y	Y	N	Y	N
7 ***Roukema***	Y	Y	N	N	N	N	N	Y
8 Roe	Y	N	N	Y	N	N	N	Y
9 ***Hollenbeck***	N	N	N	Y	N	N	Y	Y
10 Rodino	N	N	N	Y	P	Y	N	Y
11 Minish	Y	N	N	Y	N	N	N	Y
12 ***Rinaldo***	N	Y	N	Y	N	N	Y	Y
13 ***Courter***	Y	Y	N	N	?	X	?	?
14 Guarini	Y	N	N	N	N	Y	Y	Y
15 Dwyer	N	N	N	N	N	Y	Y	Y
NEW MEXICO								
1 ***Lujan***	Y	Y	N	Y	N	Y	N	Y
2 ***Skeen***	Y	Y	N	N	N	N	N	N
NEW YORK								
1 ***Carney***	Y	Y	N	N	N	N	N	Y
2 Downey	N	N	N	N	N	N	Y	Y
3 ***Carman***	Y	Y	N	N	N	N	N	Y
4 ***Lent***	Y	Y	N	N	N	N	N	Y
5 ***McGrath***	Y	Y	N	N	N	N	N	Y
6 ***LeBoutillier***	Y	Y	N	N	N	N	N	Y
7 Addabbo	Y	N	N	Y	N	#	Y	Y
8 Rosenthal	N	N	N	Y	N	Y	Y	Y
9 Ferraro	N	N	N	N	N	Y	Y	Y
10 Biaggi	N	N	N	N	N	N	Y	Y
11 Scheuer	N	N	N	N	N	Y	Y	Y
12 Chisholm	?	X	?	?	#	#	X	?
13 Solarz	N	N	N	Y	N	N	Y	Y
14 Richmond	N	N	N	Y	Y	N	Y	Y
15 Zeferetti	Y	N	N	N	N	N	Y	Y
16 Schumer	N	N	N	Y	N	Y	N	Y
17 ***Molinari***	Y	Y	N	Y	N	N	Y	Y
18 ***Green***	Y	N	N	Y	N	N	Y	Y
19 Rangel	N	N	N	Y	Y	Y	N	Y
20 Weiss	N	N	N	Y	Y	Y	Y	Y
21 Garcia	N	N	N	Y	Y	Y	N	Y
22 Bingham	?	X	?	?	?	?	?	?
23 Peyser	N	N	N	Y	N	N	Y	Y
24 Ottinger	?	N	N	Y	N	Y	Y	Y
25 ***Fish***	N	Y	N	N	N	N	Y	Y
26 ***Gilman***	N	N	N	Y	N	N	N	Y
27 McHugh	Y	N	N	Y	N	Y	Y	Y
28 Stratton	Y	Y	Y	N	N	N	Y	Y
29 ***Solomon***	Y	Y	N	N	N	N	N	N
30 ***Martin***	Y	Y	N	N	N	N	N	N
31 ***Mitchell***	Y	Y	N	N	N	N	N	Y
32 ***Wortley***	Y	Y	N	N	N	Y	Y	Y
33 ***Lee***	Y	Y	N	N	N	Y	N	N
34 ***Horton***	Y	Y	N	N	N	N	Y	Y
35 ***Conable***	Y	Y	N	?	?	X	?	N
36 LaFalce	Y	N	N	Y	N	Y	N	Y
37 Nowak	Y	N	N	Y	N	Y	N	Y
38 ***Kemp***	Y	Y	N	N	N	N	N	N
39 Lundine	Y	N	N	Y	N	Y	Y	Y
NORTH CAROLINA								
1 Jones	Y	Y	Y	N	N	N	N	Y
2 Fountain	Y	Y	Y	N	N	N	N	Y
3 Whitley	Y	Y	Y	N	N	N	N	Y
4 Andrews	Y	Y	Y	N	?	N	N	Y
5 Neal	Y	Y	Y	N	N	N	Y	Y
6 ***Johnston***	Y	Y	N	N	N	N	N	N
7 Rose	Y	Y	N	N	N	N	Y	Y
8 Hefner	Y	Y	Y	N	N	N	N	Y

	100	101	102	103	104	105	106	107
9 ***Martin***	Y	Y	N	N	N	N	N	N
10 ***Broyhill***	Y	Y	N	N	N	N	N	N
11 ***Hendon***	Y	Y	Y	N	N	N	N	Y
NORTH DAKOTA								
AL Dorgan	Y	Y	N	N	N	Y	Y	Y
OHIO								
1 ***Gradison***	Y	N	N	Y	N	N	N	N
2 Luken	Y	Y	N	N	N	N	Y	Y
3 Hall	Y	Y	N	Y	N	N	N	Y
4 ***Oxley***	Y	Y	N	N	N	N	N	N
5 ***Latta***	Y	Y	N	N	N	N	N	N
6 ***McEwen***	Y	Y	N	N	N	N	N	N
7 ***Brown***	Y	Y	N	N	N	N	N	Y
8 ***Kindness***	Y	Y	N	N	N	Y	N	N
9 ***Weber***	Y	Y	N	N	N	Y	N	Y
10 ***Miller***	N	Y	N	Y	N	Y	N	N
11 ***Stanton***	?	?	?	?	?	?	?	?
12 Shamansky	Y	N	N	N	N	Y	Y	Y
13 Pease	Y	Y	N	Y	?	?	?	Y
14 Seiberling	N	Y	N	Y	N	Y	N	Y
15 ***Wylie***	Y	Y	N	Y	N	Y	N	Y
16 ***Regula***	N	Y	N	N	N	N	N	N
17 Vacancy								
18 Applegate	Y	Y	N	N	N	N	N	Y
19 ***Williams***	Y	Y	N	Y	N	Y	Y	Y
20 Oakar	N	N	N	N	N	N	Y	Y
21 Stokes	N	N	N	Y	Y	Y	N	Y
22 Eckart	N	Y	N	N	N	Y	Y	Y
23 Mottl	Y	N	N	N	N	N	N	Y
OKLAHOMA								
1 Jones	Y	Y	Y	N	N	N	N	Y
2 Synar	Y	Y	N	N	N	N	Y	Y
3 Watkins	Y	Y	Y	N	N	N	N	Y
4 McCurdy	Y	Y	Y	N	N	N	N	Y
5 ***Edwards***	N	Y	N	N	N	N	N	N
6 English	Y	Y	Y	N	N	N	N	Y
OREGON								
1 AuCoin	Y	N	N	N	Y	Y	Y	Y
2 ***Smith***	Y	Y	N	N	N	N	N	N
3 Wyden	N	N	N	Y	N	Y	Y	Y
4 Weaver	N	N	N	Y	Y	Y	N	Y
PENNSYLVANIA								
1 Foglietta	Y	N	N	Y	N	N	Y	Y
2 Gray	N	N	N	Y	Y	Y	Y	Y
3 Smith	Y	Y	N	N	N	N	N	Y
4 ***Dougherty***	Y	Y	N	N	N	N	Y	Y
5 ***Schulze***	Y	Y	Y	N	N	N	Y	N
6 Yatron	Y	Y	N	N	N	N	N	Y
7 Edgar	N	N	N	Y	N	Y	Y	Y
8 ***Coyne, J.***	Y	Y	N	Y	N	Y	Y	Y
9 ***Shuster***	Y	Y	N	N	N	N	Y	N
10 ***McDade***	Y	N	N	N	N	N	N	Y
11 ***Nelligan***	N	Y	N	N	N	N	N	Y
12 Murtha	Y	Y	Y	N	N	N	Y	Y
13 ***Coughlin***	N	N	N	?	N	Y	Y	Y
14 Coyne, W.	N	N	N	Y	N	N	Y	Y
15 ***Ritter***	Y	Y	N	Y	N	N	N	N
16 ***Walker***	Y	Y	N	N	N	N	N	Y
17 Ertel	N	Y	N	?	?	?	N	Y
18 Walgren	?	N	N	N	N	Y	Y	Y
19 ***Goodling***	Y	Y	N	N	N	Y	N	N
20 Gaydos	Y	N	N	N	N	N	Y	Y
21 Bailey	N	N	Y	N	N	N	Y	Y
22 Murphy	Y	Y	N	N	N	N	Y	Y
23 ***Clinger***	Y	Y	N	N	N	Y	N	Y
24 ***Marks***	?	Y	?	Y	N	Y	Y	Y
25 ***Atkinson***	Y	Y	N	N	N	Y	Y	Y
RHODE ISLAND								
1 St Germain	Y	N	N	N	N	?	Y	Y
2 ***Schneider***	Y	N	N	Y	N	Y	Y	Y
SOUTH CAROLINA								
1 ***Hartnett***	Y	Y	N	N	N	N	N	N
2 ***Spence***	Y	Y	Y	N	N	N	N	Y
3 Derrick	Y	Y	Y	N	N	N	?	Y
4 ***Campbell***	Y	Y	N	N	?	N	N	N
5 Holland	Y	#	Y	N	N	N	N	?
6 ***Napier***	?	Y	N	N	N	N	N	Y
SOUTH DAKOTA								
1 Daschle	Y	Y	N	N	?	?	Y	Y
2 ***Roberts***	Y	Y	N	N	N	N	N	N
TENNESSEE								
1 ***Quillen***	Y	Y	N	N	N	N	Y	Y
2 ***Duncan***	Y	Y	N	N	N	N	N	Y
3 Bouquard	Y	Y	Y	N	N	N	N	Y
4 Gore	N	N	N	N	N	N	Y	Y
5 Boner	Y	Y	N	N	N	?	#	Y
6 ***Beard***	Y	Y	N	N	N	N	N	N

	100	101	102	103	104	105	106	107
7 Jones	Y	Y	N	N	N	N	N	Y
8 Ford	Y	N	N	Y	Y	N	Y	Y
TEXAS								
1 Hall, S.	?	Y	Y	N	N	Y	N	N
2 Wilson	Y	Y	Y	N	N	N	Y	Y
3 ***Collins***	Y	Y	N	N	N	N	N	N
4 Hall, R.	Y	Y	Y	N	N	Y	N	Y
5 Mattox	Y	?	?	?	?	?	?	?
6 Gramm	Y	Y	Y	N	N	N	N	N
7 ***Archer***	Y	Y	N	N	N	N	N	N
8 ***Fields***	Y	Y	N	N	N	N	N	N
9 Brooks	Y	Y	N	N	N	N	N	Y
10 Pickle	N	Y	N	Y	N	N	N	Y
11 Leath	Y	Y	Y	N	N	N	N	N
12 Wright	Y	Y	Y	N	N	N	Y	Y
13 Hightower	Y	Y	N	N	N	N	N	Y
14 Patman	Y	Y	Y	N	N	N	Y	Y
15 de la Garza	Y	Y	Y	N	N	N	Y	Y
16 White	Y	Y	Y	N	N	N	N	Y
17 Stenholm	Y	Y	Y	N	N	N	N	N
18 Leland	N	N	N	Y	Y	Y	Y	Y
19 Hance	Y	Y	Y	N	N	Y	N	Y
20 Gonzalez	N	N	Y	N	P	N	N	Y
21 ***Loeffler***	Y	Y	N	N	N	N	N	N
22 ***Paul***	Y	Y	N	Y	P	N	N	N
23 Kazen	Y	Y	Y	N	N	N	N	Y
24 Frost	Y	Y	Y	N	N	N	Y	Y
UTAH								
1 ***Hansen***	Y	Y	N	N	N	N	N	N
2 ***Marriott***	Y	Y	N	N	N	N	Y	Y
VERMONT								
AL ***Jeffords***	Y	Y	N	Y	N	N	Y	Y
VIRGINIA								
1 ***Trible***	Y	Y	N	N	N	N	N	Y
2 ***Whitehurst***	Y	Y	N	N	N	N	N	Y
3 ***Bliley***	Y	Y	N	N	N	N	N	N
4 ***Daniel, R.***	Y	Y	N	N	N	N	N	N
5 Daniel, D.	Y	Y	N	N	N	N	N	N
6 ***Butler***	Y	Y	N	N	N	Y	N	N
7 ***Robinson***	Y	Y	N	N	N	N	N	N
8 ***Parris***	C	C	Y	N	N	N	Y	Y
9 ***Wampler***	Y	Y	N	N	N	N	N	Y
10 ***Wolf***	N	Y	N	N	N	N	N	Y
WASHINGTON								
1 ***Pritchard***	Y	N	N	N	N	Y	Y	Y
2 Swift	Y	Y	N	N	N	N	Y	Y
3 Bonker	Y	N	N	N	N	N	Y	Y
4 ***Morrison***	Y	Y	N	N	N	N	Y	Y
5 Foley	?	Y	Y	N	N	N	Y	Y
6 Dicks	Y	Y	?	N	N	N	Y	Y
7 Lowry	N	N	N	N	N	Y	Y	Y
WEST VIRGINIA								
1 Mollohan	Y	Y	Y	N	N	#	Y	?
2 ***Benedict***	Y	Y	N	N	N	N	N	N
3 ***Staton***	Y	Y	N	N	N	N	N	N
4 Rahall	?	#	?	N	Y	Y	N	Y
WISCONSIN								
1 Aspin	Y	N	N	N	N	N	N	Y
2 Kastenmeier	N	N	N	Y	Y	Y	N	Y
3 ***Gunderson***	Y	Y	N	N	N	Y	N	Y
4 Zablocki	Y	N	N	N	N	N	Y	Y
5 Reuss	Y	N	N	Y	Y	Y	Y	Y
6 ***Petri***	N	Y	N	Y	N	Y	N	Y
7 Obey	Y	N	N	Y	N	Y	N	Y
8 ***Roth***	N	Y	N	N	N	Y	Y	Y
9 ***Sensenbrenner***	Y	Y	N	Y	N	Y	N	Y
WYOMING								
AL ***Cheney***	Y	Y	N	N	N	N	N	N

Southern states - Ala., Ark., Fla., Ga., Ky., La., Miss., N.C., Okla., S.C., Tenn., Texas, Va.

<table>
<tr><th colspan="7">KEY</th></tr>
<tr><td>Y</td><td colspan="6">Voted for (yea).</td></tr>
<tr><td>#</td><td colspan="6">Paired for.</td></tr>
<tr><td>+</td><td colspan="6">Announced for.</td></tr>
<tr><td>N</td><td colspan="6">Voted against (nay).</td></tr>
<tr><td>X</td><td colspan="6">Paired against.</td></tr>
<tr><td>-</td><td colspan="6">Announced against.</td></tr>
<tr><td>P</td><td colspan="6">Voted "present".</td></tr>
<tr><td>C</td><td colspan="6">Voted "present" to avoid possible conflict of interest.</td></tr>
<tr><td>?</td><td colspan="6">Did not vote or otherwise make a position known.</td></tr>
<tr><td colspan="3">Democrats</td><td colspan="4">*Republicans*</td></tr>
</table>

108. H Con Res 345. First Budget Resolution, Fiscal 1983. Conte, R-Mass., amendment, to the Latta, R-Ohio, substitute, to increase budget authority by $1.7 billion and outlays by $837 million for education programs in fiscal 1983, and to make corresponding reductions in the allowances function. Adopted 343-72: R 128-57; D 215-15 (ND 148-6, SD 67-9), May 26, 1982.

109. Procedural Motion. Gregg, R-N.H., motion to approve the House *Journal* of Wednesday, May 26. Motion agreed to 322-55: R 135-36; D 187-19 (ND 121-15, SD 66-4), May 27, 1982.

110. H Con Res 345. First Budget Resolution, Fiscal 1983. Oakar, D-Ohio, amendment, to the Latta, R-Ohio, substitute, to increase budget authority by $400 million and outlays by $4.85 billion for health programs in fiscal 1983 to accommodate Medicare funding at current services levels, and to make corresponding reductions in defense programs. Adopted 228-196: R 64-125; D 164-71 (ND 136-20, SD 28-51), May 27, 1982.

111. H Con Res 345. First Budget Resolution, Fiscal 1983. Oakar, D-Ohio, amendment, to the Aspin, D-Wis., substitute, to increase budget authority by $200 million and outlays by $2.35 billion for health programs in fiscal 1983 to accommodate Medicare funding at current services levels, and to make corresponding reductions in defense programs. Adopted 328-94: R 143-44; D 185-50 (ND 135-22, SD 50-28), May 27, 1982.

112. H Con Res 345. First Budget Resolution, Fiscal 1983. Hoyer, D-Md., amendment, to the Latta, R-Ohio, Aspin, D-Wis., and Jones, D-Okla., substitutes, to increase fiscal 1983 budget authority and outlays by $1.15 billion to accommodate a 7 percent pay raise for federal employees, rather than 4 percent as assumed in the substitutes. Rejected 143-281: R 26-163; D 117-118 (ND 107-50, SD 10-68), May 27, 1982.

113. H Con Res 345. First Budget Resolution, Fiscal 1983. Hoyer, D-Md., amendment, to the Latta, R-Ohio, Aspin, D-Wis., and Jones, D-Okla., substitutes, to increase fiscal 1983 budget authority by $396 million and outlays by $398 million to accommodate a 5 percent pay raise for federal employees, rather than 4 percent as assumed in the substitutes. Adopted 259-159: R 64-123; D 195-36 (ND 144-9, SD 51-27), May 27, 1982.

	108	109	110	111	112	113
ALABAMA						
1 *Edwards*	?	?	N	Y	N	Y
2 *Dickinson*	Y	N	N	N	N	Y
3 Nichols	Y	Y	N	Y	N	Y
4 Bevill	Y	Y	Y	Y	N	Y
5 Flippo	Y	Y	Y	Y	N	Y
6 *Smith*	N	N	N	N	N	N
7 Shelby	Y	Y	N	N	N	Y
ALASKA						
AL *Young*	?	?	N	Y	Y	Y
ARIZONA						
1 *Rhodes*	?	?	?	?	?	?
2 Udall	Y	?	Y	Y	N	Y
3 *Stump*	N	Y	N	N	N	N
4 *Rudd*	N	Y	N	Y	N	N
ARKANSAS						
1 Alexander	Y	Y	N	N	N	Y
2 *Bethune*	N	Y	N	Y	N	Y
3 *Hammerschmidt*	Y	Y	N	Y	N	Y
4 Anthony	Y	Y	Y	Y	N	Y
CALIFORNIA						
1 *Chappie*	Y	?	N	Y	N	Y
2 *Clausen*	Y	Y	N	Y	N	Y
3 Matsui	Y	Y	Y	Y	Y	Y
4 Fazio	Y	Y	Y	N	Y	Y
5 Burton, J.	?	?	?	?	?	?
6 Burton, P.	Y	Y	Y	Y	Y	Y
7 Miller	Y	Y	Y	Y	Y	Y
8 Dellums	Y	Y	Y	Y	Y	Y
9 Stark	Y	Y	Y	Y	Y	Y
10 Edwards	Y	Y	Y	Y	N	Y
11 Lantos	Y	Y	Y	Y	Y	Y
12 *McCloskey*	Y	?	N	Y	N	N
13 Mineta	Y	Y	N	N	N	Y
14 *Shumway*	N	Y	N	N	N	N
15 Coelho	Y	Y	Y	Y	Y	Y
16 Panetta	Y	Y	N	N	N	N
17 *Pashayan*	Y	Y	Y	N	N	N
18 *Thomas*	Y	Y	N	Y	N	N
19 *Lagomarsino*	Y	Y	N	Y	N	Y
20 *Goldwater*	Y	?	Y	N	Y	Y
21 *Fiedler*	Y	Y	N	Y	N	Y
22 *Moorhead*	Y	Y	N	Y	N	N
23 Beilenson	N	Y	Y	N	Y	Y
24 Waxman	Y	Y	Y	N	Y	Y
25 Roybal	Y	Y	Y	Y	Y	Y
26 Rousselot	N	?	N	N	N	N
27 *Dornan*	Y	Y	N	Y	N	N
28 Dixon	Y	Y	Y	Y	Y	?
29 Hawkins	Y	N	Y	Y	Y	Y
30 Vacancy						
31 Dymally	Y	Y	Y	N	Y	Y
32 Anderson	Y	Y	Y	Y	N	Y
33 Grisham	N	Y	N	?	N	N
34 Lungren	N	N	N	N	N	Y
35 *Dreier*	N	N	N	N	N	N
36 Brown	Y	?	Y	N	Y	Y
37 *Lewis*	Y	N	N	Y	Y	N
38 Patterson	Y	Y	Y	Y	Y	Y
39 *Dannemeyer*	N	Y	N	N	N	N
40 *Badham*	N	N	N	Y	N	N
41 *Lowery*	Y	?	N	Y	N	N
42 *Hunter*	Y	Y	N	N	N	N
43 *Burgener*	Y	Y	N	N	N	N
COLORADO						
1 Schroeder	Y	N	Y	Y	Y	Y
2 Wirth	Y	Y	N	N	Y	Y
3 Kogovsek	Y	Y	Y	Y	N	Y
4 *Brown*	Y	N	Y	N	N	Y

	108	109	110	111	112	113
5 *Kramer*	N	Y	N	Y	N	N
CONNECTICUT						
1 Kennelly	Y	Y	Y	Y	Y	Y
2 Gejdenson	Y	?	Y	Y	Y	Y
3 *DeNardis*	Y	Y	Y	Y	N	Y
4 *McKinney*	Y	Y	Y	Y	N	Y
5 Ratchford	Y	Y	Y	Y	Y	Y
6 Moffett	Y	Y	Y	Y	Y	Y
DELAWARE						
AL *Evans*	Y	Y	Y	Y	N	Y
FLORIDA						
1 Hutto	Y	?	N	Y	N	Y
2 Fuqua	Y	Y	N	N	N	Y
3 Bennett	N	N	N	N	N	Y
4 Chappell	Y	Y	N	N	N	Y
5 *McCollum*	Y	N	N	Y	N	N
6 *Young*	Y	N	N	Y	N	Y
7 Gibbons	Y	?	N	N	N	N
8 Ireland	Y	Y	N	N	N	Y
9 Nelson	Y	Y	N	N	N	Y
10 *Bafalis*	Y	Y	N	Y	N	N
11 Mica	Y	Y	Y	Y	N	Y
12 *Shaw*	Y	Y	N	N	N	N
13 Lehman	Y	Y	Y	Y	Y	Y
14 Pepper	Y	Y	Y	Y	Y	Y
15 Fascell	Y	Y	Y	Y	N	Y
GEORGIA						
1 Ginn	Y	Y	N	Y	N	Y
2 Hatcher	Y	Y	N	N	N	Y
3 Brinkley	Y	Y	Y	Y	N	Y
4 Levitas	Y	Y	N	Y	N	Y
5 Fowler	Y	Y	N	N	N	Y
6 *Gingrich*	Y	Y	N	Y	N	Y
7 McDonald	N	Y	N	N	N	N
8 Evans	Y	?	N	Y	N	Y
9 Jenkins	Y	Y	N	N	N	Y
10 Barnard	Y	Y	N	Y	N	Y
HAWAII						
1 Heftel	Y	Y	Y	Y	Y	?
2 Akaka	Y	Y	Y	Y	Y	Y
IDAHO						
1 *Craig*	N	Y	N	N	N	N
2 *Hansen*	N	Y	N	N	N	N
ILLINOIS						
1 Washington	Y	N	Y	Y	Y	Y
2 Savage	Y	?	Y	Y	Y	Y
3 Russo	Y	Y	Y	N	Y	Y
4 *Derwinski*	N	N	N	N	N	N
5 Fary	Y	Y	Y	Y	Y	Y
6 *Hyde*	N	Y	N	N	N	N
7 Collins	Y	Y	Y	Y	Y	Y
8 Rostenkowski	Y	Y	Y	Y	N	N
9 Yates	Y	N	Y	Y	Y	Y
10 *Porter*	Y	Y	Y	Y	N	N
11 Annunzio	?	Y	Y	Y	Y	Y
12 *Crane, P.*	N	N	N	N	N	N
13 *McClory*	N	Y	N	N	N	N
14 *Erlenborn*	N	Y	N	N	N	N
15 *Corcoran*	Y	Y	N	N	N	N
16 *Martin*	N	Y	N	Y	N	N
17 *O'Brien*	Y	Y	Y	Y	N	N
18 *Michel*	N	Y	N	N	N	N
19 *Railsback*	Y	Y	Y	Y	N	Y
20 *Findley*	Y	Y	Y	Y	N	N
21 *Madigan*	Y	Y	N	N	N	N
22 *Crane, D.*	N	Y	N	N	N	N
23 Price	Y	Y	N	N	Y	Y
24 Simon	Y	Y	Y	Y	Y	Y
INDIANA						
1 Benjamin	Y	Y	Y	Y	N	Y
2 Fithian	Y	Y	Y	Y	Y	Y
3 *Hiler*	N	Y	N	N	N	N
4 *Coats*	Y	Y	N	Y	N	N
5 *Hillis*	Y	Y	N	N	N	N
6 Evans	Y	Y	Y	Y	Y	Y
7 *Myers*	Y	Y	N	N	N	N
8 *Deckard*	Y	Y	Y	Y	N	N
9 Hamilton	Y	Y	Y	Y	N	Y
10 Sharp	Y	N	Y	Y	N	Y
11 Jacobs	Y	N	Y	Y	N	Y
IOWA						
1 *Leach*	Y	?	Y	Y	N	Y
2 *Tauke*	Y	Y	N	N	N	N
3 *Evans*	Y	N	Y	N	N	N
4 Smith	Y	Y	Y	Y	Y	Y
5 Harkin	Y	N	Y	Y	Y	Y
6 Bedell	Y	Y	Y	N	N	N

ND - Northern Democrats   SD - Southern Democrats

Corresponding to Congressional Record Votes 114, 115, 116, 117, 118, 119

	108	109	110	111	112	113
KANSAS						
1 ***Roberts***	Y	N	N	N	N	N
2 ***Jeffries***	N	Y	N	N	N	N
3 ***Winn***	Y	Y	N	N	N	?
4 Glickman	Y	Y	N	N	N	N
5 ***Whittaker***	Y	Y	N	N	N	N
KENTUCKY						
1 Hubbard	Y	Y	N	Y	N	Y
2 Natcher	Y	Y	Y	Y	N	Y
3 Mazzoli	Y	Y	N	Y	N	N
4 ***Snyder***	N	Y	Y	Y	N	Y
5 ***Rogers***	Y	?	N	N	N	Y
6 ***Hopkins***	Y	Y	Y	Y	N	N
7 Perkins	Y	Y	Y	Y	Y	Y
LOUISIANA						
1 ***Livingston***	N	Y	N	Y	N	N
2 Boggs	?	Y	Y	Y	N	?
3 Tauzin	Y	Y	N	Y	N	Y
4 Roemer	Y	N	N	Y	N	N
5 Huckaby	N	Y	N	N	?	N
6 ***Moore***	N	Y	N	Y	N	N
7 Breaux	Y	N	N	Y	N	N
8 Long	Y	Y	Y	Y	N	Y
MAINE						
1 ***Emery***	Y	Y	Y	Y	N	N
2 ***Snowe***	Y	Y	Y	Y	N	N
MARYLAND						
1 Dyson	Y	Y	Y	Y	Y	Y
2 Long	Y	?	N	Y	N	Y
3 Mikulski	Y	Y	Y	Y	Y	Y
4 ***Holt***	N	N	Y	Y	Y	Y
5 Hoyer	N	Y	Y	Y	Y	Y
6 Byron	Y	Y	Y	Y	N	Y
7 Mitchell	Y	N	Y	Y	Y	Y
8 Barnes	Y	N	Y	Y	Y	Y
MASSACHUSETTS						
1 ***Conte***	Y	Y	Y	Y	N	N
2 Boland	Y	Y	Y	Y	N	Y
3 Early	Y	Y	Y	Y	N	Y
4 Frank	Y	Y	Y	Y	Y	Y
5 Shannon	Y	Y	Y	Y	Y	Y
6 Mavroules	Y	Y	Y	Y	Y	Y
7 Markey	Y	Y	Y	Y	Y	Y
8 O'Neill						
9 Moakley	Y	Y	Y	Y	Y	Y
10 ***Heckler***	Y	N	Y	Y	Y	Y
11 Donnelly	Y	?	N	N	Y	Y
12 Studds	Y	Y	Y	Y	Y	Y
MICHIGAN						
1 Conyers	?	N	Y	Y	Y	Y
2 ***Pursell***	Y	Y	Y	Y	N	N
3 Wolpe	Y	Y	Y	Y	Y	Y
4 ***Siljander***	N	Y	N	Y	N	N
5 ***Sawyer***	Y	Y	N	Y	N	N
6 ***Dunn***	Y	Y	N	Y	N	N
7 Kildee	Y	Y	Y	Y	Y	Y
8 Traxler	Y	?	Y	Y	Y	Y
9 ***Vander Jagt***	Y	?	N	Y	N	N
10 Albosta	Y	?	Y	Y	Y	Y
11 ***Davis***	Y	Y	Y	Y	Y	Y
12 Bonior	Y	Y	Y	Y	Y	Y
13 Crockett	Y	?	?	?	?	?
14 Hertel	Y	Y	Y	Y	N	Y
15 Ford	Y	?	Y	Y	Y	Y
16 Dingell	Y	Y	Y	Y	Y	Y
17 Brodhead	Y	Y	Y	Y	Y	Y
18 Blanchard	Y	Y	Y	Y	N	Y
19 ***Broomfield***	?	Y	N	Y	N	N
MINNESOTA						
1 ***Erdahl***	Y	Y	N	Y	N	N
2 ***Hagedorn***	Y	Y	N	Y	N	N
3 ***Frenzel***	Y	N	N	Y	N	N
4 Vento	Y	Y	Y	Y	Y	Y
5 Sabo	Y	N	Y	Y	Y	Y
6 ***Weber***	Y	Y	N	Y	N	N
7 ***Stangeland***	Y	Y	Y	Y	N	Y
8 Oberstar	Y	Y	Y	Y	Y	Y
MISSISSIPPI						
1 Whitten	Y	Y	Y	Y	N	N
2 Bowen	Y	Y	N	Y	N	Y
3 Montgomery	N	Y	N	Y	N	N
4 Dowdy	Y	Y	Y	Y	N	Y
5 ***Lott***	N	Y	N	Y	N	N
MISSOURI						
1 Clay	Y	?	Y	Y	Y	Y
2 Young	Y	Y	N	N	N	Y
3 Gephardt	Y	Y	N	N	N	N

	108	109	110	111	112	113
4 Skelton	Y	N	N	Y	N	Y
5 Bolling	Y	Y	Y	N	N	?
6 ***Coleman***	Y	N	Y	Y	N	N
7 ***Taylor***	Y	Y	N	Y	N	Y
8 ***Bailey***	Y	Y	N	Y	N	N
9 Volkmer	Y	Y	Y	Y	N	Y
10 ***Emerson***	Y	N	N	Y	N	N
MONTANA						
1 Williams	Y	Y	Y	Y	Y	Y
2 ***Marlenee***	Y	Y	Y	Y	N	Y
NEBRASKA						
1 ***Bereuter***	Y	Y	Y	Y	N	Y
2 ***Daub***	Y	Y	Y	Y	N	Y
3 ***Smith***	Y	Y	Y	Y	N	N
NEVADA						
AL Santini	Y	?	Y	Y	Y	Y
NEW HAMPSHIRE						
1 D'Amours	Y	Y	Y	Y	N	Y
2 ***Gregg***	Y	N	N	Y	N	N
NEW JERSEY						
1 Florio	?	Y	Y	Y	Y	Y
2 Hughes	Y	Y	Y	N	N	Y
3 Howard	Y	Y	Y	Y	Y	Y
4 ***Smith***	Y	Y	Y	Y	Y	Y
5 ***Fenwick***	Y	?	Y	Y	N	N
6 ***Forsythe***	N	N	Y	Y	N	N
7 ***Roukema***	Y	Y	Y	N	Y	Y
8 Roe	Y	Y	Y	Y	Y	Y
9 ***Hollenbeck***	Y	N	Y	Y	Y	Y
10 Rodino	Y	Y	Y	Y	Y	Y
11 Minish	Y	Y	Y	Y	Y	Y
12 ***Rinaldo***	Y	Y	Y	Y	Y	Y
13 ***Courter***	?	Y	Y	Y	Y	Y
14 Guarini	Y	Y	Y	Y	Y	Y
15 Dwyer	Y	Y	Y	Y	Y	Y
NEW MEXICO						
1 ***Lujan***	Y	Y	Y	Y	N	Y
2 ***Skeen***	Y	Y	N	N	N	Y
NEW YORK						
1 ***Carney***	Y	Y	N	Y	Y	Y
2 Downey	Y	Y	Y	Y	Y	Y
3 ***Carman***	Y	Y	N	Y	N	N
4 ***Lent***	Y	Y	Y	Y	Y	Y
5 ***McGrath***	Y	N	Y	Y	Y	Y
6 ***LeBoutillier***	Y	N	Y	Y	N	N
7 Addabbo	Y	Y	Y	Y	Y	Y
8 Rosenthal	?	?	?	?	?	Y
9 Ferraro	Y	Y	Y	Y	Y	Y
10 Biaggi	Y	Y	Y	Y	Y	Y
11 Scheuer	Y	Y	Y	Y	Y	Y
12 Chisholm	?	?	?	?	?	?
13 Solarz	Y	Y	Y	Y	Y	Y
14 Richmond	Y	?	Y	Y	Y	Y
15 Zeferetti	Y	Y	Y	Y	Y	Y
16 Schumer	Y	Y	Y	Y	Y	Y
17 ***Molinari***	Y	Y	Y	Y	N	Y
18 ***Green***	Y	Y	Y	Y	Y	Y
19 Rangel	Y	Y	Y	Y	Y	Y
20 Weiss	N	Y	Y	Y	Y	Y
21 Garcia	Y	?	?	Y	Y	Y
22 Bingham	?	?	?	?	?	?
23 Peyser	Y	Y	Y	Y	Y	Y
24 Ottinger	N	P	Y	Y	Y	Y
25 ***Fish***	Y	Y	Y	Y	Y	Y
26 ***Gilman***	Y	Y	Y	Y	Y	Y
27 McHugh	Y	?	Y	Y	Y	Y
28 Stratton	Y	Y	N	N	N	N
29 ***Solomon***	N	N	N	Y	N	N
30 ***Martin***	N	Y	N	Y	N	Y
31 ***Mitchell***	Y	Y	N	Y	N	Y
32 ***Wortley***	Y	Y	N	Y	N	N
33 ***Lee***	N	N	Y	Y	N	N
34 ***Horton***	Y	Y	Y	Y	N	Y
35 ***Conable***	N	Y	N	Y	N	N
36 LaFalce	Y	N	Y	Y	N	Y
37 Nowak	Y	Y	Y	Y	Y	Y
38 ***Kemp***	N	Y	N	Y	N	N
39 Lundine	Y	Y	Y	Y	N	Y
NORTH CAROLINA						
1 Jones	Y	Y	Y	Y	Y	Y
2 Fountain	Y	?	N	Y	N	N
3 Whitley	Y	Y	N	Y	N	Y
4 Andrews	Y	Y	N	Y	N	Y
5 Neal	Y	?	N	Y	N	Y
6 ***Johnston***	N	N	N	Y	N	N
7 Rose	Y	?	N	N	N	Y
8 Hefner	Y	Y	N	Y	N	Y

	108	109	110	111	112	113
9 ***Martin***	Y	Y	N	Y	N	N
10 ***Broyhill***	N	Y	N	N	N	N
11 ***Hendon***	Y	N	N	Y	N	N
NORTH DAKOTA						
AL Dorgan	Y	Y	Y	Y	N	Y
OHIO						
1 ***Gradison***	Y	Y	N	Y	N	N
2 Luken	Y	N	Y	Y	N	Y
3 Hall	Y	Y	Y	Y	N	Y
4 ***Oxley***	Y	Y	N	Y	N	Y
5 ***Latta***	Y	Y	N	Y	N	N
6 ***McEwen***	Y	Y	N	Y	Y	Y
7 ***Brown***	Y	Y	Y	Y	N	N
8 ***Kindness***	N	Y	N	Y	N	N
9 ***Weber***	Y	Y	Y	Y	N	N
10 ***Miller***	N	N	N	Y	N	N
11 ***Stanton***	?	?	?	?	?	?
12 Shamansky	Y	Y	Y	Y	N	Y
13 Pease	Y	Y	Y	Y	Y	Y
14 Seiberling	Y	?	Y	Y	Y	Y
15 ***Wylie***	Y	Y	Y	Y	N	N
16 ***Regula***	Y	Y	N	Y	N	N
17 Vacancy						
18 Applegate	Y	?	Y	Y	N	Y
19 ***Williams***	Y	Y	Y	Y	N	N
20 Oakar	Y	Y	Y	Y	Y	Y
21 Stokes	Y	Y	Y	Y	Y	Y
22 Eckart	Y	Y	Y	Y	Y	Y
23 Mottl	Y	Y	Y	Y	N	Y
OKLAHOMA						
1 Jones	Y	Y	N	N	N	N
2 Synar	Y	Y	N	N	N	N
3 Watkins	Y	?	N	N	N	N
4 McCurdy	Y	Y	N	N	N	Y
5 ***Edwards***	N	Y	N	N	N	N
6 English	Y	Y	N	N	N	N
OREGON						
1 AuCoin	Y	?	Y	Y	N	Y
2 ***Smith***	N	Y	N	N	N	N
3 Wyden	Y	Y	Y	Y	Y	Y
4 Weaver	Y	Y	Y	Y	N	Y
PENNSYLVANIA						
1 Foglietta	Y	Y	Y	Y	Y	Y
2 Gray	Y	Y	Y	Y	Y	Y
3 Smith	Y	?	Y	Y	Y	Y
4 ***Dougherty***	Y	?	Y	Y	Y	Y
5 ***Schulze***	Y	Y	N	Y	N	N
6 Yatron	Y	Y	Y	Y	N	Y
7 Edgar	Y	N	Y	Y	Y	Y
8 ***Coyne, J.***	Y	Y	N	Y	N	Y
9 ***Shuster***	N	Y	Y	Y	N	N
10 ***McDade***	Y	Y	Y	Y	Y	Y
11 ***Nelligan***	Y	Y	Y	Y	Y	Y
12 Murtha	Y	Y	N	N	Y	Y
13 ***Coughlin***	Y	N	N	Y	N	Y
14 Coyne, W.	Y	Y	Y	Y	Y	?
15 ***Ritter***	N	Y	Y	Y	N	N
16 ***Walker***	Y	N	N	Y	N	N
17 Ertel	Y	Y	Y	Y	Y	?
18 Walgren	N	Y	Y	Y	N	Y
19 ***Goodling***	Y	N	N	Y	Y	Y
20 Gaydos	Y	Y	Y	Y	N	Y
21 Bailey	Y	Y	N	Y	Y	Y
22 Murphy	Y	?	Y	Y	Y	Y
23 ***Clinger***	Y	Y	N	N	N	Y
24 ***Marks***	Y	?	Y	?	N	?
25 ***Atkinson***	Y	Y	Y	Y	N	Y
RHODE ISLAND						
1 St Germain	Y	Y	Y	Y	Y	Y
2 ***Schneider***	Y	Y	Y	N	N	Y
SOUTH CAROLINA						
1 ***Hartnett***	N	N	N	N	N	N
2 ***Spence***	Y	Y	N	Y	N	N
3 Derrick	Y	?	Y	Y	N	N
4 ***Campbell***	Y	?	N	Y	N	N
5 Holland	?	Y	Y	Y	N	N
6 ***Napier***	Y	N	N	Y	N	Y
SOUTH DAKOTA						
1 Daschle	Y	Y	Y	N	N	N
2 ***Roberts***	Y	Y	N	N	N	N
TENNESSEE						
1 ***Quillen***	Y	Y	Y	Y	N	N
2 ***Duncan***	Y	Y	Y	Y	N	Y
3 Bouquard	Y	Y	N	N	N	N
4 Gore	Y	Y	Y	Y	N	Y
5 Boner	Y	Y	Y	Y	Y	Y
6 ***Beard***	N	Y	N	N	N	N

	108	109	110	111	112	113
7 Jones	Y	Y	Y	N	N	N
8 Ford	Y	?	Y	Y	N	Y
TEXAS						
1 Hall, S.	N	N	N	Y	N	Y
2 Wilson	Y	Y	N	N	N	Y
3 ***Collins***	N	Y	N	N	N	N
4 Hall, R.	Y	Y	N	Y	N	Y
5 Mattox	?	Y	Y	Y	N	Y
6 Gramm	N	Y	N	Y	N	N
7 ***Archer***	N	Y	N	N	N	N
8 ***Fields***	N	N	N	N	N	N
9 Brooks	Y	Y	N	N	N	Y
10 Pickle	Y	Y	Y	N	N	N
11 Leath	N	Y	N	Y	N	N
12 Wright	Y	Y	N	N	Y	Y
13 Hightower	Y	Y	N	Y	N	N
14 Patman	Y	Y	N	N	N	N
15 de la Garza	Y	Y	Y	?	N	Y
16 White	Y	Y	N	Y	N	Y
17 Stenholm	N	N	N	Y	N	N
18 Leland	Y	Y	Y	Y	Y	Y
19 Hance	Y	Y	N	N	N	N
20 Gonzalez	Y	Y	Y	N	Y	Y
21 ***Loeffler***	N	Y	N	Y	N	N
22 ***Paul***	N	Y	N	N	N	N
23 Kazen	Y	Y	N	Y	Y	Y
24 Frost	Y	Y	Y	Y	N	Y
UTAH						
1 ***Hansen***	N	Y	N	N	N	Y
2 ***Marriott***	Y	Y	N	Y	N	Y
VERMONT						
AL ***Jeffords***	Y	?	Y	N	N	N
VIRGINIA						
1 ***Trible***	Y	?	N	Y	Y	Y
2 ***Whitehurst***	Y	Y	N	N	Y	Y
3 ***Bliley***	Y	Y	N	N	N	N
4 ***Daniel, R.***	N	Y	N	N	Y	Y
5 Daniel, D.	N	Y	N	N	N	N
6 ***Butler***	N	N	N	N	N	N
7 ***Robinson***	Y	Y	N	N	N	N
8 ***Parris***	N	Y	Y	Y	Y	Y
9 ***Wampler***	Y	Y	Y	Y	N	N
10 ***Wolf***	N	Y	Y	Y	Y	Y
WASHINGTON						
1 ***Pritchard***	Y	Y	N	N	N	N
2 Swift	Y	Y	N	Y	Y	Y
3 Bonker	Y	Y	N	N	N	Y
4 ***Morrison***	Y	?	N	Y	N	N
5 Foley	Y	Y	N	N	N	Y
6 Dicks	Y	Y	N	N	Y	Y
7 Lowry	Y	Y	Y	Y	N	Y
WEST VIRGINIA						
1 Mollohan	?	Y	Y	Y	N	Y
2 ***Benedict***	Y	Y	N	Y	N	N
3 ***Staton***	N	Y	N	Y	N	N
4 Rahall	Y	Y	Y	Y	Y	Y
WISCONSIN						
1 Aspin	Y	Y	N	N	N	N
2 Kastenmeier	Y	Y	Y	Y	Y	Y
3 ***Gunderson***	Y	?	Y	Y	N	N
4 Zablocki	Y	Y	Y	Y	N	Y
5 Reuss	Y	?	Y	Y	N	Y
6 ***Petri***	Y	Y	Y	Y	N	N
7 Obey	Y	Y	Y	Y	N	Y
8 ***Roth***	Y	Y	N	N	N	N
9 ***Sensenbrenner***	Y	N	N	Y	N	N
WYOMING						
AL ***Cheney***	N	Y	N	Y	N	N

Southern states - Ala., Ark., Fla., Ga., Ky., La., Miss., N.C., Okla., S.C., Tenn., Texas, Va.

114. H Con Res 345. First Budget Resolution, Fiscal 1983. Downey, D-N.Y., amendment, to the Latta, R-Ohio, and Jones, D-Okla., substitutes, to increase fiscal 1983 budget authority by $200 million and outlays by $500 million to accommodate removal of the 4 percent ceiling on cost-of-living adjustments (COLAs) for federal civilian and military retirees. Adopted 327-94: R 109-77; D 218-17 (ND 154-3, SD 64-14), May 27, 1982.

115. H Con Res 345. First Budget Resolution, Fiscal 1983. Hughes, D-N.J., amendment, to the Latta, R-Ohio, Aspin, D-Wis., and Jones, D-Okla., substitutes, to increase fiscal 1983 budget authority by $451 million and outlays by $501 million (above the Latta substitute) to accommodate funding at authorized levels for law enforcement activities. Rejected 152-264: R 32-155; D 120-109 (ND 93-61, SD 27-48), May 27, 1982.

116. H Con Res 345. First Budget Resolution, Fiscal 1983. Zeferetti, D-N.Y., amendment, to the Latta, R-Ohio, Aspin, D-Wis., and Jones, D-Okla., substitutes, to increase fiscal 1983 budget authority by $1.15 billion and outlays by $100 million (above the Latta substitute) to accommodate funding at the levels recommended by House authorizing committees for drug law enforcement agencies. Rejected 182-237: R 39-149; D 143-88 (ND 118-35, SD 25-53), May 27, 1982.

117. H Con Res 345. First Budget Resolution, Fiscal 1983. Perkins, D-Ky., amendment, to the Aspin, D-Wis., and Jones, D-Okla., substitutes, to strike reconciliation instructions directing the House Education and Labor Committee to reduce fiscal 1983 budget authority and outlays by $73 million through savings in the worker compensation program for federal civilian employees. Rejected 193-225: R 24-163; D 169-62 (ND 136-17, SD 33-45), May 27, 1982.

118. H Con Res 345. First Budget Resolution, Fiscal 1983. Weiss, D-N.Y., amendment, to the Latta, R-Ohio, substitute, to delete all reconciliation instructions requiring committees to report legislation making changes in programs within their jurisdictions to achieve specified savings targets. Rejected 60-357: R 1-186; D 59-171 (ND 53-100, SD 6-71), May 27, 1982.

119. H Con Res 345. First Budget Resolution, Fiscal 1983. Whitten, D-Miss., amendment, to the Jones, D-Okla., substitute, to delete provisions calling for deferred enrollment, until adoption of the second budget resolution, of any spending bill that exceeds the allocations provided under the first resolution. Adopted 212-205: R 39-148; D 173-57 (ND 122-31, SD 51-26), May 27, 1982.

120. H Con Res 345. First Budget Resolution, Fiscal 1983. Whitten, D-Miss., amendment, to the Latta, R-Ohio, substitute, to delete provisions calling for deferred enrollment, until adoption of the second budget resolution, of any spending bill that exceeds the allocations provided under the first resolution. Adopted 212-206: R 22-166; D 190-40 (ND 136-17, SD 54-23), May 27, 1982.

121. H Con Res 345. First Budget Resolution, Fiscal 1983. Latta, R-Ohio, substitute, as amended, to set budget targets for the fiscal year ending Sept. 30, 1983, as follows: budget authority, $805.8 billion; outlays, $769.4 billion; revenues, $665.9 billion; and deficit, $103.5 billion. Rejected 192-235: R 171-20; D 21-215 (ND 3-155, SD 18-60), May 27, 1982.

KEY

Y Voted for (yea).
Paired for.
+ Announced for.
N Voted against (nay).
X Paired against.
- Announced against.
P Voted "present".
C Voted "present" to avoid possible conflict of interest.
? Did not vote or otherwise make a position known.

Democrats *Republicans*

	114	115	116	117	118	119	120	121
ALABAMA								
1 Edwards	N	N	N	N	N	N	N	Y
2 Dickinson	N	N	N	N	N	N	N	Y
3 Nichols	Y	N	N	N	Y	Y	Y	Y
4 Bevill	Y	N	Y	N	Y	Y	Y	N
5 Flippo	Y	Y	N	Y	N	Y	Y	N
6 *Smith*	N	N	N	N	N	N	N	Y
7 Shelby	Y	Y	N	N	N	N	N	Y
ALASKA								
AL *Young*	Y	?	Y	Y	N	N	N	Y
ARIZONA								
1 *Rhodes*	?	?	?	?	?	?	?	Y
2 Udall	Y	N	N	Y	?	Y	Y	N
3 Stump	Y	N	N	N	N	N	N	Y
4 *Rudd*	N	N	N	N	N	Y	Y	Y
ARKANSAS								
1 Alexander	Y	N	N	Y	N	Y	Y	N
2 *Bethune*	Y	N	N	N	N	N	N	Y
3 *Hammerschmidt*	N	N	N	N	Y	N	Y	Y
4 Anthony	Y	N	Y	N	Y	N	Y	N
CALIFORNIA								
1 *Chappie*	Y	N	N	N	N	N	N	Y
2 *Clausen*	N	N	N	N	Y	N	Y	Y
3 Matsui	Y	N	Y	N	Y	Y	Y	N
4 Fazio	Y	N	Y	N	Y	Y	Y	N
5 Burton, J.	?	?	?	?	?	?	?	?
6 Burton, P.	Y	Y	Y	Y	N	Y	Y	N
7 Miller	Y	Y	Y	Y	N	Y	Y	N
8 Dellums	Y	Y	Y	Y	Y	Y	Y	N
9 Stark	Y	Y	Y	Y	Y	Y	?	N
10 Edwards	Y	N	Y	Y	Y	Y	Y	N
11 Lantos	Y	N	Y	N	Y	Y	N	N
12 *McCloskey*	N	N	N	N	N	N	N	Y
13 Mineta	Y	N	Y	Y	N	Y	Y	N
14 *Shumway*	N	N	N	N	N	N	N	Y
15 Coelho	Y	N	N	Y	N	Y	Y	N
16 Panetta	Y	N	N	N	N	N	N	N
17 *Pashayan*	Y	Y	N	N	N	N	N	Y
18 *Thomas*	N	N	N	N	N	N	N	Y
19 *Lagomarsino*	Y	N	N	N	N	N	N	Y
20 *Goldwater*	Y	N	N	N	N	N	N	Y
21 *Fiedler*	Y	N	N	N	N	N	N	Y
22 *Moorhead*	N	N	N	N	N	N	N	Y
23 Beilenson	Y	Y	Y	N	Y	Y	Y	N
24 Waxman	Y	Y	Y	Y	Y	Y	Y	N
25 Roybal	Y	Y	Y	Y	Y	Y	Y	N
26 *Rousselot*	N	N	N	N	N	N	N	Y
27 Dornan	N	N	Y	N	N	Y	N	Y
28 Dixon	Y	N	Y	N	Y	Y	Y	N
29 Hawkins	Y	Y	Y	Y	Y	Y	Y	N
30 Vacancy								
31 Dymally	Y	N	Y	Y	Y	Y	Y	N
32 Anderson	Y	Y	Y	Y	Y	Y	Y	N
33 Grisham	N	N	N	N	N	N	Y	Y
34 Lungren	Y	N	N	N	N	N	N	Y
35 *Dreier*	N	N	N	N	N	N	N	Y
36 Brown	Y	Y	Y	Y	Y	Y	Y	N
37 Lewis	Y	N	N	N	Y	N	Y	Y
38 Patterson	Y	Y	Y	N	Y	Y	Y	N
39 *Dannemeyer*	N	N	N	N	N	N	N	Y
40 *Badham*	N	N	N	N	N	N	N	Y
41 *Lowery*	Y	N	N	N	N	N	N	Y
42 *Hunter*	Y	N	N	N	N	N	N	Y
43 *Burgener*	N	N	N	N	N	N	N	Y
COLORADO								
1 Schroeder	Y	Y	N	Y	N	N	N	N
2 Wirth	Y	N	Y	N	Y	N	Y	N
3 Kogovsek	Y	N	Y	N	Y	N	Y	N
4 *Brown*	N	N	N	N	N	N	N	Y

	114	115	116	117	118	119	120	121
5 *Kramer*	Y	Y	N	N	N	N	N	Y
CONNECTICUT								
1 Kennelly	Y	Y	Y	N	Y	N	Y	N
2 Gejdenson	Y	Y	Y	Y	Y	Y	Y	N
3 *DeNardis*	Y	N	Y	N	N	N	N	Y
4 *McKinney*	N	N	N	N	?	N	N	Y
5 Ratchford	Y	N	Y	N	Y	Y	Y	N
6 Moffett	Y	Y	Y	N	Y	N	Y	N
DELAWARE								
AL *Evans*	Y	N	Y	N	N	N	N	Y
FLORIDA								
1 Hutto	Y	Y	Y	N	Y	Y	Y	Y
2 Fuqua	Y	Y	Y	N	N	Y	Y	N
3 Bennett	Y	Y	Y	N	Y	Y	Y	Y
4 Chappell	Y	N	N	N	Y	Y	Y	Y
5 *McCollum*	Y	N	N	N	N	N	N	Y
6 *Young*	Y	Y	N	N	N	N	N	Y
7 Gibbons	N	P	N	N	N	Y	Y	N
8 Ireland	Y	N	N	N	N	N	N	Y
9 Nelson	Y	Y	N	N	N	N	Y	N
10 *Bafalis*	Y	Y	Y	N	N	N	N	Y
11 Mica	Y	Y	Y	N	Y	N	Y	N
12 *Shaw*	Y	Y	N	N	N	N	N	Y
13 Lehman	Y	Y	Y	Y	Y	Y	Y	N
14 Pepper	Y	Y	Y	N	N	Y	Y	N
15 Fascell	Y	Y	Y	Y	Y	Y	Y	N
GEORGIA								
1 Ginn	Y	N	N	N	N	Y	Y	N
2 Hatcher	Y	Y	Y	N	Y	Y	Y	N
3 Brinkley	Y	Y	Y	N	Y	Y	Y	N
4 Levitas	Y	N	N	N	N	Y	Y	N
5 Fowler	Y	N	N	N	N	Y	Y	N
6 *Gingrich*	Y	N	N	N	N	N	N	Y
7 McDonald	N	N	N	N	N	Y	Y	Y
8 Evans	Y	Y	Y	Y	N	Y	Y	N
9 Jenkins	N	N	N	N	N	N	N	Y
10 Barnard	Y	N	N	N	N	N	N	Y
HAWAII								
1 Heftel	Y	N	Y	N	Y	N	Y	N
2 Akaka	Y	Y	Y	Y	N	Y	Y	N
IDAHO								
1 *Craig*	Y	N	N	N	N	N	N	Y
2 *Hansen*	N	N	N	N	N	N	N	Y
ILLINOIS								
1 Washington	Y	N	N	Y	Y	Y	Y	N
2 Savage	Y	N	N	Y	Y	Y	Y	N
3 Russo	Y	Y	Y	N	N	Y	Y	N
4 *Derwinski*	Y	N	N	N	N	N	N	Y
5 Fary	Y	Y	Y	N	Y	Y	Y	N
6 *Hyde*	Y	N	N	N	N	N	N	Y
7 Collins	Y	Y	Y	Y	Y	Y	Y	N
8 Rostenkowski	N	N	N	N	N	Y	Y	N
9 Yates	Y	Y	Y	Y	Y	Y	Y	N
10 *Porter*	N	N	N	N	N	N	N	Y
11 Annunzio	Y	Y	Y	Y	N	Y	Y	N
12 *Crane, P.*	N	N	N	N	N	N	N	Y
13 *McClory*	N	Y	N	N	N	N	N	Y
14 *Erlenborn*	N	N	N	N	N	N	N	Y
15 *Corcoran*	N	N	N	N	N	N	N	Y
16 *Martin*	N	N	N	N	N	N	N	Y
17 *O'Brien*	Y	N	N	N	N	N	N	Y
18 *Michel*	N	N	N	N	N	N	N	Y
19 *Railsback*	Y	Y	Y	N	Y	Y	Y	N
20 *Findley*	Y	N	N	N	N	N	N	Y
21 *Madigan*	Y	N	N	N	N	N	?	Y
22 *Crane, D.*	N	N	N	N	N	N	N	Y
23 Price	Y	Y	Y	Y	N	Y	Y	N
24 Simon	Y	Y	Y	Y	N	Y	Y	N
INDIANA								
1 Benjamin	Y	Y	Y	N	Y	Y	Y	N
2 Fithian	Y	Y	N	Y	N	Y	Y	N
3 *Hiler*	N	N	N	N	N	N	N	Y
4 *Coats*	N	N	N	N	N	N	N	Y
5 Hillis	Y	N	N	Y	N	Y	Y	N
6 Evans	Y	Y	Y	Y	N	Y	Y	N
7 *Myers*	Y	N	N	N	N	N	N	Y
8 *Deckard*	Y	N	Y	N	N	N	N	Y
9 Hamilton	Y	N	N	N	N	N	N	Y
10 Sharp	Y	N	Y	N	Y	N	N	N
11 Jacobs	Y	N	Y	N	N	N	N	N
IOWA								
1 Leach	N	N	N	N	N	N	N	Y
2 Tauke	N	N	N	N	N	N	N	Y
3 *Evans*	Y	N	N	N	N	N	N	Y
4 *Smith*	Y	Y	Y	Y	Y	Y	Y	N
5 Harkin	Y	N	N	N	N	N	N	N
6 Bedell	Y	Y	Y	N	Y	Y	Y	N

ND - Northern Democrats   SD - Southern Democrats

Corresponding to Congressional Record Votes 120, 121, 122, 123, 124, 125, 126, 127

	114	115	116	117	118	119	120	121
KANSAS								
1 ***Roberts***	N	N	N	N	N	N	N	Y
2 ***Jeffries***	Y	N	N	N	N	N	N	Y
3 ***Winn***	N	N	N	N	N	N	N	Y
4 Glickman	Y	N	N	Y	N	N	Y	N
5 ***Whittaker***	N	N	N	N	N	N	N	Y
KENTUCKY								
1 Hubbard	Y	N	N	Y	N	N	N	N
2 Natcher	Y	N	N	Y	N	Y	Y	N
3 Mazzoli	Y	N	N	Y	N	N	N	N
4 ***Snyder***	Y	N	N	N	N	Y	Y	N
5 ***Rogers***	Y	N	N	Y	N	N	Y	Y
6 ***Hopkins***	Y	N	N	N	N	N	Y	N
7 Perkins	Y	?	N	Y	N	Y	Y	N
LOUISIANA								
1 ***Livingston***	N	Y	N	N	N	Y	N	Y
2 Boggs	?	?	?	?	X	?	?	?
3 Tauzin	N	N	N	N	N	N	N	Y
4 Roemer	N	N	N	N	N	N	N	Y
5 Huckaby	N	N	N	N	N	Y	N	N
6 ***Moore***	N	N	N	N	N	N	N	Y
7 Breaux	N	N	N	N	N	Y	Y	Y
8 Long	Y	Y	Y	Y	?	Y	Y	N
MAINE								
1 ***Emery***	N	N	Y	N	N	N	N	Y
2 ***Snowe***	N	N	Y	N	N	N	N	Y
MARYLAND								
1 Dyson	Y	N	Y	Y	N	Y	Y	Y
2 Long	Y	Y	Y	N	N	Y	Y	N
3 Mikulski	Y	Y	Y	Y	Y	Y	Y	N
4 ***Holt***	Y	N	Y	N	N	N	N	Y
5 Hoyer	Y	Y	Y	?	?	Y	Y	N
6 Byron	Y	N	N	N	N	N	N	Y
7 Mitchell	Y	N	Y	Y	Y	Y	Y	N
8 Barnes	Y	Y	Y	Y	N	Y	Y	N
MASSACHUSETTS								
1 ***Conte***	N	N	N	N	N	Y	Y	Y
2 Boland	Y	N	N	Y	N	Y	Y	N
3 Early	Y	N	Y	Y	Y	Y	Y	N
4 Frank	Y	Y	Y	Y	Y	Y	Y	N
5 Shannon	Y	N	Y	Y	Y	Y	Y	N
6 Mavroules	Y	N	Y	Y	N	Y	Y	N
7 Markey	Y	Y	Y	Y	N	Y	Y	N
8 O'Neill								
9 Moakley	Y	N	Y	Y	N	Y	Y	N
10 ***Heckler***	Y	N	Y	Y	N	Y	Y	N
11 Donnelly	Y	N	Y	N	N	N	N	N
12 Studds	Y	Y	Y	Y	N	N	N	N
MICHIGAN								
1 Conyers	Y	N	?	?	Y	?	?	N
2 ***Pursell***	N	N	N	Y	N	Y	Y	Y
3 Wolpe	Y	N	Y	Y	N	N	N	N
4 ***Siljander***	N	N	N	N	N	N	N	Y
5 ***Sawyer***	N	Y	N	Y	N	N	N	Y
6 ***Dunn***	N	N	N	N	N	N	N	N
7 Kildee	Y	Y	Y	Y	Y	Y	Y	N
8 Traxler	Y	N	N	Y	N	Y	Y	N
9 ***Vander Jagt***	N	Y	Y	N	N	N	N	Y
10 Albosta	Y	N	N	Y	N	Y	Y	N
11 ***Davis***	Y	N	Y	Y	N	Y	Y	N
12 Bonior	Y	?	Y	Y	N	Y	Y	N
13 Crockett	?	?	?	?	#	?	?	?
14 Hertel	Y	Y	N	Y	N	Y	Y	N
15 Ford	Y	?	?	Y	?	Y	Y	N
16 Dingell	Y	N	Y	Y	Y	Y	Y	N
17 Brodhead	Y	Y	Y	Y	Y	Y	Y	N
18 Blanchard	Y	N	Y	Y	N	Y	Y	N
19 ***Broomfield***	N	N	Y	N	N	N	Y	Y
MINNESOTA								
1 ***Erdahl***	N	N	N	N	N	N	N	Y
2 ***Hagedorn***	N	Y	N	N	N	Y	N	Y
3 ***Frenzel***	N	N	N	N	N	N	N	Y
4 Vento	Y	Y	Y	Y	Y	Y	Y	N
5 Sabo	Y	N	Y	Y	N	Y	Y	N
6 ***Weber***	N	N	N	N	N	N	N	Y
7 ***Stangeland***	Y	N	N	N	N	Y	Y	Y
8 Oberstar	Y	N	Y	Y	Y	Y	Y	N
MISSISSIPPI								
1 Whitten	Y	Y	N	Y	Y	Y	Y	N
2 Bowen	Y	N	N	Y	N	Y	Y	N
3 Montgomery	Y	?	N	N	N	Y	N	Y
4 Dowdy	Y	N	N	Y	N	Y	Y	N
5 ***Lott***	Y	N	N	N	N	N	N	Y
MISSOURI								
1 Clay	Y	N	Y	Y	Y	Y	Y	N
2 Young	Y	N	Y	N	N	Y	Y	N
3 Gephardt	Y	Y	Y	N	N	N	Y	N
4 Skelton	Y	N	N	N	N	Y	Y	N
5 Bolling	Y	N	Y	Y	N	?	?	N
6 ***Coleman***	Y	Y	N	N	N	N	N	Y
7 ***Taylor***	Y	N	N	N	N	Y	N	Y
8 ***Bailey***	Y	N	N	N	N	N	N	Y
9 Volkmer	Y	N	N	Y	N	Y	Y	N
10 ***Emerson***	Y	N	N	N	N	N	N	Y
MONTANA								
1 Williams	Y	N	Y	Y	Y	N	Y	N
2 ***Marlenee***	Y	N	N	N	N	N	N	Y
NEBRASKA								
1 ***Bereuter***	Y	N	N	N	N	N	N	Y
2 ***Daub***	N	N	N	Y	N	N	N	Y
3 ***Smith***	N	N	N	N	N	Y	Y	Y
NEVADA								
AL Santini	Y	N	N	Y	N	N	N	N
NEW HAMPSHIRE								
1 D'Amours	Y	Y	Y	N	N	N	N	N
2 ***Gregg***	N	N	N	N	N	N	N	Y
NEW JERSEY								
1 Florio	Y	Y	Y	Y	Y	Y	Y	N
2 Hughes	Y	Y	Y	N	N	Y	Y	N
3 Howard	Y	Y	Y	Y	Y	Y	Y	N
4 ***Smith***	Y	Y	Y	Y	N	N	N	Y
5 ***Fenwick***	N	N	N	?	?	N	N	Y
6 ***Forsythe***	N	N	Y	N	N	N	N	Y
7 ***Roukema***	Y	N	N	N	N	N	N	Y
8 Roe	Y	Y	Y	Y	Y	Y	Y	N
9 ***Hollenbeck***	Y	N	Y	Y	N	Y	Y	N
10 Rodino	Y	Y	Y	Y	Y	Y	Y	N
11 Minish	Y	Y	Y	Y	Y	Y	Y	N
12 ***Rinaldo***	Y	Y	Y	Y	N	Y	Y	N
13 ***Courter***	Y	N	N	N	N	N	N	Y
14 Guarini	Y	Y	Y	Y	Y	Y	Y	N
15 Dwyer	Y	Y	Y	Y	Y	Y	Y	N
NEW MEXICO								
1 ***Lujan***	Y	N	N	N	N	N	N	Y
2 ***Skeen***	Y	N	N	N	N	N	N	Y
NEW YORK								
1 ***Carney***	Y	Y	Y	Y	N	N	N	Y
2 Downey	Y	Y	Y	Y	N	Y	Y	N
3 ***Carman***	N	N	N	N	N	N	N	Y
4 ***Lent***	Y	Y	Y	N	N	N	N	Y
5 ***McGrath***	Y	Y	Y	N	N	Y	N	Y
6 ***LeBoutillier***	Y	Y	Y	N	N	N	N	Y
7 Addabbo	Y	Y	Y	Y	Y	Y	Y	N
8 Rosenthal	Y	Y	Y	Y	Y	Y	Y	N
9 Ferraro	Y	Y	Y	Y	N	Y	Y	N
10 Biaggi	Y	Y	Y	Y	N	Y	Y	N
11 Scheuer	Y	Y	Y	Y	Y	Y	Y	N
12 Chisholm	?	?	?	?	#	?	?	?
13 Solarz	Y	Y	Y	Y	N	N	Y	N
14 Richmond	Y	Y	Y	Y	Y	Y	Y	N
15 Zeferetti	Y	Y	Y	Y	N	Y	Y	N
16 Schumer	Y	Y	Y	Y	Y	Y	Y	N
17 ***Molinari***	Y	Y	Y	Y	N	N	N	N
18 ***Green***	Y	Y	Y	N	N	N	N	N
19 Rangel	Y	Y	Y	Y	Y	Y	Y	N
20 Weiss	Y	Y	Y	Y	Y	Y	Y	N
21 Garcia	Y	Y	Y	Y	Y	Y	Y	N
22 Bingham	?	?	?	?	?	?	?	?
23 Peyser	Y	Y	Y	Y	N	?	Y	N
24 Ottinger	Y	Y	Y	Y	Y	Y	Y	N
25 ***Fish***	Y	Y	N	N	N	N	N	Y
26 ***Gilman***	Y	Y	Y	Y	N	N	N	N
27 McHugh	Y	N	N	Y	N	Y	Y	N
28 Stratton	N	N	Y	Y	Y	Y	N	N
29 ***Solomon***	?	N	N	N	N	N	N	Y
30 ***Martin***	Y	N	N	N	N	N	N	Y
31 ***Mitchell***	Y	N	N	Y	N	Y	Y	Y
32 ***Wortley***	Y	N	N	N	N	N	N	Y
33 ***Lee***	Y	Y	Y	N	N	N	N	Y
34 ***Horton***	Y	Y	N	N	N	N	N	Y
35 ***Conable***	N	N	N	N	N	N	N	Y
36 LaFalce	Y	N	Y	Y	N	N	N	N
37 Nowak	Y	Y	Y	Y	N	Y	Y	N
38 ***Kemp***	Y	N	N	N	N	N	N	Y
39 Lundine	Y	N	N	Y	N	N	N	N
NORTH CAROLINA								
1 Jones	Y	Y	Y	N	N	Y	Y	N
2 Fountain	N	N	N	N	N	N	N	N
3 Whitley	Y	N	N	N	N	Y	Y	N
4 Andrews	Y	N	N	Y	N	N	N	N
5 Neal	Y	N	N	Y	N	N	N	N
6 ***Johnston***	Y	N	N	N	N	N	N	Y
7 Rose	Y	N	N	Y	N	?	?	N
8 Hefner	Y	N	N	N	N	Y	Y	N
9 ***Martin***	Y	N	N	N	N	N	N	Y
10 ***Broyhill***	N	N	N	N	N	N	N	Y
11 ***Hendon***	Y	N	N	N	N	N	N	Y
NORTH DAKOTA								
AL Dorgan	Y	N	N	Y	N	N	Y	N
OHIO								
1 ***Gradison***	N	N	N	N	N	N	N	Y
2 Luken	Y	N	N	Y	N	Y	Y	N
3 Hall	Y	N	N	Y	N	?	Y	N
4 ***Oxley***	Y	N	N	N	N	N	N	Y
5 ***Latta***	?	N	N	N	N	N	N	Y
6 ***McEwen***	Y	Y	N	N	N	N	N	Y
7 ***Brown***	Y	N	N	N	N	N	N	Y
8 ***Kindness***	N	N	N	N	?	N	N	Y
9 ***Weber***	Y	N	N	N	N	N	N	Y
10 ***Miller***	N	N	N	N	N	Y	Y	Y
11 ***Stanton***	?	?	?	?	?	?	N	Y
12 Shamansky	Y	Y	N	N	N	Y	Y	N
13 Pease	Y	Y	Y	N	N	N	N	N
14 Seiberling	Y	Y	Y	Y	Y	Y	Y	N
15 ***Wylie***	N	Y	Y	N	N	N	N	Y
16 ***Regula***	Y	N	N	N	N	N	N	Y
17 Vacancy								
18 Applegate	Y	N	Y	Y	N	Y	Y	N
19 ***Williams***	Y	Y	N	N	N	Y	Y	N
20 Oakar	Y	Y	Y	Y	N	Y	Y	N
21 Stokes	Y	N	Y	Y	Y	Y	Y	N
22 Eckart	Y	Y	Y	Y	N	N	Y	N
23 Mottl	Y	Y	Y	Y	N	Y	Y	N
OKLAHOMA								
1 Jones	N	N	N	Y	N	N	N	N
2 Synar	Y	N	N	Y	N	N	N	N
3 Watkins	Y	N	N	N	N	Y	Y	N
4 McCurdy	Y	N	N	N	N	N	Y	Y
5 ***Edwards***	Y	N	N	N	N	Y	N	Y
6 English	Y	N	Y	N	N	N	N	N
OREGON								
1 AuCoin	Y	N	Y	Y	N	Y	Y	N
2 ***Smith***	N	N	N	N	N	N	N	N
3 Wyden	Y	Y	Y	Y	N	Y	Y	N
4 Weaver	Y	N	Y	Y	N	N	N	N
PENNSYLVANIA								
1 Foglietta	Y	Y	Y	Y	Y	Y	Y	N
2 Gray	Y	Y	Y	Y	Y	Y	Y	N
3 Smith	Y	Y	?	?	N	Y	Y	N
4 ***Dougherty***	Y	Y	Y	Y	N	N	N	N
5 ***Schulze***	N	N	N	N	N	N	N	Y
6 Yatron	Y	Y	Y	Y	N	Y	Y	N
7 Edgar	Y	Y	Y	Y	Y	N	Y	N
8 ***Coyne, J.***	Y	N	N	N	N	N	N	Y
9 ***Shuster***	Y	N	N	N	N	N	N	Y
10 ***McDade***	Y	N	N	Y	N	Y	Y	Y
11 ***Nelligan***	Y	N	N	Y	N	N	N	Y
12 Murtha	Y	Y	Y	N	N	Y	Y	N
13 ***Coughlin***	N	N	N	N	N	N	Y	Y
14 Coyne, W.	Y	Y	Y	Y	N	Y	Y	N
15 ***Ritter***	N	N	N	N	N	N	N	Y
16 ***Walker***	Y	N	N	N	N	N	N	Y
17 Ertel	?	?	?	?	N	Y	Y	N
18 Walgren	Y	Y	Y	Y	N	N	Y	N
19 ***Goodling***	Y	N	N	N	N	N	N	Y
20 Gaydos	Y	Y	Y	Y	N	Y	Y	N
21 Bailey	Y	Y	Y	Y	N	Y	Y	N
22 Murphy	Y	?	?	?	?	?	?	N
23 ***Clinger***	Y	N	N	N	N	N	N	Y
24 ***Marks***	?	?	Y	Y	Y	?	?	N
25 ***Atkinson***	Y	N	N	N	N	Y	Y	Y
RHODE ISLAND								
1 St Germain	Y	Y	Y	Y	Y	Y	Y	N
2 ***Schneider***	Y	N	Y	N	N	Y	Y	N
SOUTH CAROLINA								
1 ***Hartnett***	N	N	N	N	N	N	N	Y
2 ***Spence***	Y	Y	Y	N	N	Y	N	Y
3 Derrick	Y	Y	N	N	N	N	Y	N
4 ***Campbell***	Y	N	N	N	N	Y	N	Y
5 Holland	Y	N	N	N	N	Y	Y	N
6 ***Napier***	Y	Y	Y	N	N	Y	Y	Y
SOUTH DAKOTA								
1 Daschle	Y	N	Y	Y	X	Y	Y	N
2 ***Roberts***	N	N	N	N	N	N	N	Y
TENNESSEE								
1 ***Quillen***	Y	N	N	N	N	N	N	Y
2 ***Duncan***	Y	Y	N	N	N	N	N	Y
3 Bouquard	Y	Y	Y	Y	N	Y	Y	N
4 Gore	Y	N	N	Y	N	Y	Y	N
5 Boner	Y	N	N	Y	N	Y	Y	N
6 ***Beard***	N	N	N	N	N	N	N	Y
7 Jones	Y	N	N	N	N	Y	Y	N
8 Ford	Y	N	N	Y	Y	Y	Y	N
TEXAS								
1 Hall, S.	Y	Y	N	N	N	Y	N	Y
2 Wilson	Y	N	Y	N	N	Y	Y	N
3 ***Collins***	N	N	N	N	N	Y	N	Y
4 Hall, R.	Y	Y	N	N	N	Y	Y	Y
5 Mattox	Y	Y	Y	N	N	N	N	N
6 Gramm	N	N	N	N	N	N	N	Y
7 ***Archer***	N	N	N	N	N	N	N	Y
8 ***Fields***	N	N	N	N	N	N	N	Y
9 Brooks	Y	Y	Y	Y	N	Y	Y	N
10 Pickle	N	N	N	N	N	N	N	N
11 Leath	Y	N	N	N	N	N	N	Y
12 Wright	Y	Y	N	Y	N	N	Y	N
13 Hightower	Y	N	N	N	N	Y	Y	Y
14 Patman	Y	Y	Y	N	N	N	N	N
15 de la Garza	Y	N	Y	Y	N	Y	Y	N
16 White	Y	N	N	N	N	Y	Y	Y
17 Stenholm	N	N	N	N	N	N	N	Y
18 Leland	Y	Y	Y	Y	Y	Y	Y	N
19 Hance	N	N	N	N	N	N	N	N
20 Gonzalez	Y	Y	Y	Y	Y	Y	Y	N
21 ***Loeffler***	Y	N	N	N	N	Y	N	Y
22 ***Paul***	N	N	N	N	N	N	N	Y
23 Kazen	Y	N	Y	N	N	Y	Y	N
24 Frost	Y	N	N	Y	N	N	Y	N
UTAH								
1 ***Hansen***	N	N	N	N	N	N	N	Y
2 ***Marriott***	Y	N	N	N	N	N	N	Y
VERMONT								
AL ***Jeffords***	Y	N	N	N	N	N	N	N
VIRGINIA								
1 ***Trible***	Y	N	N	Y	N	N	N	Y
2 ***Whitehurst***	Y	N	N	N	N	N	N	Y
3 ***Bliley***	N	N	N	N	N	N	N	Y
4 ***Daniel, R.***	Y	N	N	N	N	N	N	Y
5 Daniel, D.	N	N	N	N	N	N	N	Y
6 ***Butler***	N	N	N	N	N	N	N	Y
7 ***Robinson***	N	N	N	N	N	N	N	Y
8 ***Parris***	Y	N	Y	Y	N	N	N	Y
9 ***Wampler***	Y	N	N	N	N	N	N	Y
10 ***Wolf***	Y	N	N	Y	N	N	N	Y
WASHINGTON								
1 ***Pritchard***	Y	N	N	N	N	N	N	Y
2 Swift	Y	N	Y	Y	N	Y	Y	N
3 Bonker	Y	N	Y	Y	N	Y	Y	N
4 ***Morrison***	Y	N	N	N	N	N	N	Y
5 Foley	Y	Y	N	Y	N	N	Y	N
6 Dicks	Y	Y	Y	Y	N	Y	Y	N
7 Lowry	Y	Y	Y	Y	N	N	N	N
WEST VIRGINIA								
1 Mollohan	Y	N	Y	Y	N	Y	Y	N
2 ***Benedict***	N	N	N	N	N	N	N	Y
3 ***Staton***	N	N	N	N	N	N	N	Y
4 Rahall	Y	Y	Y	Y	N	Y	Y	N
WISCONSIN								
1 Aspin	N	N	N	Y	N	N	Y	N
2 Kastenmeier	Y	Y	Y	Y	Y	Y	Y	N
3 ***Gunderson***	Y	N	N	N	N	N	N	Y
4 Zablocki	Y	Y	Y	Y	N	Y	Y	N
5 Reuss	Y	N	N	Y	N	Y	Y	N
6 ***Petri***	N	N	N	N	N	N	N	Y
7 Obey	Y	N	N	Y	N	Y	Y	N
8 ***Roth***	Y	N	?	N	N	N	N	Y
9 ***Sensenbrenner***	N	N	N	N	N	N	N	Y
WYOMING								
AL ***Cheney***	N	N	N	?	N	N	N	Y

Southern states - Ala., Ark., Fla., Ga., Ky., La., Miss., N.C., Okla., S.C., Tenn., Texas, Va.

KEY

Y Voted for (yea).
\# Paired for.
+ Announced for.
N Voted against (nay).
X Paired against.
- Announced against.
P Voted "present".
C Voted "present" to avoid possible conflict of interest.
? Did not vote or otherwise make a position known.

Democrats *Republicans*

122. H Con Res 345. First Budget Resolution, Fiscal 1983. Aspin, D-Wis., substitute, as amended, to set budget targets for the fiscal year ending Sept. 30, 1983, as follows: budget authority, $825.5 billion; outlays, $772.9 billion; revenues, $675.7 billion; and deficit, $97.2 billion. Rejected 137-289: R 29-161; D 108-128 (ND 90-68, SD 18-60), May 27, 1982.

123. H Con Res 345. First Budget Resolution, Fiscal 1983. Jones, D-Okla., substitute, as amended, to set budget targets for the fiscal year ending Sept. 30, 1983, as follows: budget authority, $828.9 billion; outlays, $781.7 billion; revenues, $676.7 billion; and deficit, $105.0 billion. Rejected 171-253: R 0-190; D 171-63 (ND 125-31, SD 46-32), in the session which began May 27, 1982.

124. H Con Res 345. First Budget Resolution, Fiscal 1983. Adoption of the concurrent resolution, as reported by the House Budget Committee, to set budget targets for the fiscal year ending Sept. 30, 1983, as follows: budget authority, $828 billion; outlays, $780.55 billion; revenues, $676.70 billion; and deficit, $103.85 billion. Rejected 159-265: R 6-184; D 153-81 (ND 104-52, SD 49-29), in the session which began May 27, 1982.

125. HR 4. Intelligence Identities Protection Act. Adoption of the conference report on the bill to make it a felony to publicly expose the identities of U.S. covert intelligence officers, agents, informants and sources. Adopted 315-32: R 159-0; D 156-32 (ND 94-31, SD 62-1), June 3, 1982. A "yea" was a vote supporting the president's position.

	122	123	124	125
ALABAMA				
1 *Edwards*	N	N	N	Y
2 *Dickinson*	N	N	N	?
3 Nichols	N	Y	Y	Y
4 Bevill	N	Y	Y	Y
5 Flippo	N	Y	Y	Y
6 *Smith*	N	N	N	Y
7 Shelby	N	N	Y	Y
ALASKA				
AL *Young*	N	N	N	Y
ARIZONA				
1 *Rhodes*	N	N	N	Y
2 Udall	N	Y	Y	Y
3 Stump	N	N	N	?
4 *Rudd*	N	N	N	Y
ARKANSAS				
1 Alexander	Y	Y	Y	Y
2 *Bethune*	N	N	N	Y
3 *Hammerschmidt*	N	N	N	Y
4 Anthony	Y	Y	Y	Y
CALIFORNIA				
1 *Chappie*	N	N	N	Y
2 *Clausen*	N	N	N	Y
3 Matsui	N	Y	Y	Y
4 Fazio	Y	Y	Y	?
5 Burton, J.	?	?	?	?
6 Burton, P.	N	N	N	N
7 Miller	N	Y	Y	N
8 Dellums	N	N	N	N
9 Stark	N	N	N	N
10 Edwards	N	Y	Y	N
11 Lantos	N	Y	Y	Y
12 *McCloskey*	Y	N	Y	?
13 Mineta	Y	Y	Y	Y
14 Shumway	N	N	N	Y
15 Coelho	Y	Y	Y	Y
16 Panetta	Y	Y	Y	Y
17 *Pashayan*	N	N	N	Y
18 *Thomas*	N	N	N	Y
19 *Lagomarsino*	N	N	N	Y
20 *Goldwater*	N	N	N	?
21 *Fiedler*	N	N	N	?
22 *Moorhead*	N	N	N	Y
23 Beilenson	Y	Y	Y	Y
24 Waxman	N	Y	N	?
25 Roybal	N	Y	Y	N
26 *Rousselot*	N	N	N	?
27 *Dornan*	N	N	N	?
28 Dixon	N	N	N	?
29 Hawkins	N	Y	Y	Y
30 Vacancy				
31 Dymally	N	N	N	X
32 Anderson	Y	Y	Y	Y
33 *Grisham*	N	N	N	?
34 *Lungren*	N	N	N	Y
35 *Dreier*	N	N	N	?
36 Brown	Y	Y	Y	Y
37 *Lewis*	N	N	N	Y
38 Patterson	Y	Y	Y	?
39 *Dannemeyer*	N	N	N	Y
40 *Badham*	N	N	N	Y
41 *Lowery*	N	N	N	Y
42 *Hunter*	N	N	N	Y
43 *Burgener*	N	N	N	?
COLORADO				
1 Schroeder	N	Y	Y	Y
2 Wirth	Y	Y	Y	Y
3 Kogovsek	Y	Y	Y	?
4 *Brown*	N	N	N	Y

	122	123	124	125
5 *Kramer*	N	N	N	Y
CONNECTICUT				
1 Kennelly	Y	Y	Y	N
2 Gejdenson	Y	Y	Y	N
3 *DeNardis*	Y	N	N	Y
4 *McKinney*	Y	N	N	?
5 Ratchford	Y	Y	N	Y
6 Moffett	Y	Y	N	?
DELAWARE				
AL *Evans*	Y	N	N	Y
FLORIDA				
1 Hutto	N	Y	Y	Y
2 Fuqua	N	Y	Y	Y
3 Bennett	N	N	Y	Y
4 Chappell	N	N	N	?
5 *McCollum*	N	N	N	Y
6 *Young*	N	N	N	Y
7 Gibbons	N	Y	Y	Y
8 Ireland	N	N	N	Y
9 Nelson	N	N	Y	Y
10 *Bafalis*	N	N	N	Y
11 Mica	N	Y	Y	Y
12 *Shaw*	N	N	N	Y
13 Lehman	N	Y	Y	N
14 Pepper	Y	Y	Y	Y
15 Fascell	Y	Y	Y	Y
GEORGIA				
1 Ginn	N	N	N	?
2 Hatcher	N	N	N	?
3 Brinkley	N	N	N	Y
4 Levitas	N	N	N	Y
5 Fowler	N	Y	Y	Y
6 *Gingrich*	N	N	N	Y
7 McDonald	N	N	N	Y
8 Evans	N	Y	Y	Y
9 Jenkins	N	N	N	?
10 Barnard	N	N	N	Y
HAWAII				
1 Heftel	Y	Y	Y	?
2 Akaka	Y	Y	Y	Y
IDAHO				
1 *Craig*	N	N	N	Y
2 *Hansen*	N	N	N	Y
ILLINOIS				
1 Washington	N	N	N	X
2 Savage	N	N	N	N
3 Russo	N	N	N	Y
4 *Derwinski*	N	N	N	Y
5 Fary	N	Y	Y	Y
6 *Hyde*	N	N	N	Y
7 Collins	N	N	N	Y
8 Rostenkowski	Y	Y	Y	N
9 Yates	N	Y	Y	N
10 *Porter*	Y	N	N	Y
11 Annunzio	N	Y	Y	Y
12 *Crane, P.*	N	N	N	Y
13 *McClory*	N	N	N	Y
14 *Erlenborn*	N	N	N	Y
15 *Corcoran*	N	N	N	Y
16 *Martin*	N	N	N	Y
17 *O'Brien*	Y	N	N	Y
18 *Michel*	N	N	N	Y
19 *Railsback*	Y	N	N	Y
20 *Findley*	Y	N	N	Y
21 *Madigan*	N	N	N	Y
22 *Crane, D.*	N	N	N	Y
23 Price	N	Y	Y	Y
24 Simon	Y	Y	Y	Y
INDIANA				
1 Benjamin	N	Y	Y	Y
2 Fithian	N	N	N	?
3 *Hiler*	N	N	N	Y
4 *Coats*	N	N	N	Y
5 *Hillis*	N	N	N	Y
6 Evans	Y	N	Y	Y
7 *Myers*	N	N	N	Y
8 *Deckard*	N	N	N	?
9 Hamilton	Y	N	Y	Y
10 Sharp	Y	Y	Y	Y
11 Jacobs	N	N	N	N
IOWA				
1 *Leach*	Y	N	N	Y
2 *Tauke*	Y	N	N	Y
3 *Evans*	Y	N	N	Y
4 Smith	N	N	N	Y
5 Harkin	N	N	N	Y
6 Bedell	Y	Y	Y	Y

ND - Northern Democrats   SD - Southern Democrats

	122	123	124	125
KANSAS				
1 Roberts	N	N	N	Y
2 Jeffries	N	N	N	Y
3 Winn	N	N	N	Y
4 Glickman	Y	Y	Y	Y
5 Whittaker	N	N	N	Y
KENTUCKY				
1 Hubbard	N	Y	N	Y
2 Natcher	N	Y	Y	Y
3 Mazzoli	Y	Y	Y	Y
4 Snyder	N	N	N	Y
5 Rogers	N	N	N	Y
6 Hopkins	N	N	N	Y
7 Perkins	N	Y	Y	Y
LOUISIANA				
1 Livingston	N	N	N	Y
2 Boggs	#	#	?	?
3 Tauzin	N	N	N	Y
4 Roemer	N	N	N	Y
5 Huckaby	N	N	N	?
6 Moore	N	N	N	Y
7 Breaux	N	N	N	Y
8 Long	Y	Y	Y	Y
MAINE				
1 Emery	N	N	N	Y
2 Snowe	N	N	N	Y
MARYLAND				
1 Dyson	Y	Y	Y	Y
2 Long	Y	Y	Y	Y
3 Mikulski	Y	Y	N	Y
4 Holt	N	N	N	Y
5 Hoyer	Y	Y	Y	?
6 Byron	N	N	N	Y
7 Mitchell	N	N	N	N
8 Barnes	Y	Y	Y	Y
MASSACHUSETTS				
1 Conte	N	N	Y	Y
2 Boland	Y	Y	Y	Y
3 Early	Y	Y	Y	Y
4 Frank	Y	Y	N	Y
5 Shannon	Y	Y	Y	Y
6 Mavroules	Y	Y	Y	Y
7 Markey	Y	Y	Y	Y
8 O'Neill				
9 Moakley	Y	Y	Y	Y
10 Heckler	Y	N	N	Y
11 Donnelly	Y	Y	Y	?
12 Studds	Y	Y	Y	Y
MICHIGAN				
1 Conyers	N	N	?	?
2 Pursell	N	N	N	Y
3 Wolpe	Y	Y	Y	N
4 Siljander	N	N	N	Y
5 Sawyer	N	N	N	Y
6 Dunn	N	N	N	Y
7 Kildee	N	Y	Y	N
8 Traxler	N	Y	Y	?
9 Vander Jagt	N	N	N	Y
10 Albosta	N	Y	Y	Y
11 Davis	Y	N	N	Y
12 Bonior	N	Y	Y	Y
13 Crockett	X	X	?	N
14 Hertel	Y	Y	Y	Y
15 Ford	N	Y	Y	Y
16 Dingell	Y	Y	Y	Y
17 Brodhead	Y	Y	Y	Y
18 Blanchard	Y	Y	Y	?
19 Broomfield	N	N	N	Y
MINNESOTA				
1 Erdahl	Y	N	N	?
2 Hagedorn	N	N	N	?
3 Frenzel	N	N	N	Y
4 Vento	Y	Y	Y	N
5 Sabo	Y	Y	Y	N
6 Weber	N	N	N	Y
7 Stangeland	N	N	N	Y
8 Oberstar	N	Y	Y	N
MISSISSIPPI				
1 Whitten	N	Y	Y	Y
2 Bowen	N	Y	Y	Y
3 Montgomery	N	N	N	Y
4 Dowdy	Y	Y	Y	?
5 Lott	N	N	N	Y
MISSOURI				
1 Clay	N	N	N	N
2 Young	N	N	N	Y
3 Gephardt	Y	Y	Y	Y
4 Skelton	N	N	N	Y
5 Bolling	Y	Y	Y	?
6 Coleman	N	N	N	Y
7 Taylor	N	N	N	?
8 Bailey	N	N	N	?
9 Volkmer	N	N	N	Y
10 Emerson	N	N	N	Y
MONTANA				
1 Williams	Y	Y	Y	Y
2 Marlenee	N	N	N	?
NEBRASKA				
1 Bereuter	Y	N	N	Y
2 Daub	N	N	N	Y
3 Smith	N	N	N	Y
NEVADA				
AL Santini	Y	N	N	?
NEW HAMPSHIRE				
1 D'Amours	N	N	N	?
2 Gregg	N	N	N	Y
NEW JERSEY				
1 Florio	Y	Y	Y	Y
2 Hughes	N	N	N	Y
3 Howard	Y	Y	Y	Y
4 Smith	Y	N	N	Y
5 Fenwick	N	N	N	Y
6 Forsythe	N	N	N	Y
7 Roukema	N	N	Y	Y
8 Roe	Y	Y	N	#
9 Hollenbeck	Y	N	N	Y
10 Rodino	N	Y	N	N
11 Minish	Y	Y	N	Y
12 Rinaldo	Y	N	N	Y
13 Courter	N	N	N	?
14 Guarini	Y	Y	N	#
15 Dwyer	Y	Y	Y	Y
NEW MEXICO				
1 Lujan	N	N	N	Y
2 Skeen	N	N	N	Y
NEW YORK				
1 Carney	N	N	N	Y
2 Downey	Y	Y	Y	Y
3 Carman	N	N	N	Y
4 Lent	N	N	N	Y
5 McGrath	N	N	N	Y
6 LeBoutillier	N	N	N	Y
7 Addabbo	Y	Y	N	#
8 Rosenthal	N	Y	N	?
9 Ferraro	Y	Y	N	Y
10 Biaggi	N	Y	N	Y
11 Scheuer	Y	Y	Y	Y
12 Chisholm	?	?	?	?
13 Solarz	N	Y	Y	Y
14 Richmond	Y	Y	X	X
15 Zeferetti	Y	Y	N	#
16 Schumer	N	Y	N	N
17 Molinari	N	N	N	?
18 Green	N	N	N	Y
19 Rangel	N	N	N	Y
20 Weiss	N	X	N	N
21 Garcia	N	N	N	N
22 Bingham	?	#	?	?
23 Peyser	Y	Y	Y	Y
24 Ottinger	Y	Y	Y	N
25 Fish	Y	N	N	?
26 Gilman	Y	N	N	Y
27 McHugh	Y	Y	Y	?
28 Stratton	N	Y	Y	Y
29 Solomon	N	N	N	Y
30 Martin	N	N	N	Y
31 Mitchell	N	N	N	?
32 Wortley	N	N	N	Y
33 Lee	N	N	N	Y
34 Horton	N	N	Y	Y
35 Conable	N	N	Y	Y
36 LaFalce	Y	Y	Y	Y
37 Nowak	Y	Y	Y	Y
38 Kemp	N	N	N	Y
39 Lundine	Y	Y	Y	Y
NORTH CAROLINA				
1 Jones	N	Y	Y	?
2 Fountain	N	N	N	Y
3 Whitley	N	N	N	Y
4 Andrews	N	Y	Y	Y
5 Neal	N	N	N	?
6 Johnston	N	N	N	Y
7 Rose	N	Y	Y	Y
8 Hefner	N	Y	N	Y
9 Martin	N	N	N	Y
10 Broyhill	N	N	N	Y
11 Hendon	N	N	N	Y
NORTH DAKOTA				
AL Dorgan	N	Y	Y	Y
OHIO				
1 Gradison	N	N	N	?
2 Luken	Y	Y	Y	Y
3 Hall	Y	Y	Y	Y
4 Oxley	N	N	N	Y
5 Latta	N	N	N	Y
6 McEwen	N	N	N	Y
7 Brown	N	N	N	?
8 Kindness	N	N	N	Y
9 Weber	N	N	N	Y
10 Miller	N	N	N	Y
11 Stanton	N	N	N	Y
12 Shamansky	N	Y	Y	Y
13 Pease	Y	Y	Y	N
14 Seiberling	Y	Y	Y	N
15 Wylie	N	N	N	Y
16 Regula	N	N	N	Y
17 Vacancy				
18 Applegate	N	N	N	Y
19 Williams	Y	N	N	Y
20 Oakar	Y	Y	N	Y
21 Stokes	N	N	N	?
22 Eckart	Y	Y	N	?
23 Mottl	Y	Y	N	?
OKLAHOMA				
1 Jones	Y	Y	Y	Y
2 Synar	Y	Y	Y	Y
3 Watkins	N	Y	Y	Y
4 McCurdy	N	N	Y	Y
5 Edwards	N	N	N	Y
6 English	N	N	N	Y
OREGON				
1 AuCoin	Y	Y	Y	Y
2 Smith	N	N	N	Y
3 Wyden	Y	Y	Y	Y
4 Weaver	N	Y	Y	N
PENNSYLVANIA				
1 Foglietta	Y	Y	Y	Y
2 Gray	N	N	N	N
3 Smith	N	Y	Y	?
4 Dougherty	N	N	Y	Y
5 Schulze	N	?	?	Y
6 Yatron	N	N	N	Y
7 Edgar	Y	Y	N	N
8 Coyne, J.	Y	N	Y	Y
9 Shuster	N	N	N	Y
10 McDade	Y	N	N	Y
11 Nelligan	N	N	N	Y
12 Murtha	N	Y	Y	Y
13 Coughlin	Y	N	N	Y
14 Coyne, W.	N	N	N	Y
15 Ritter	N	N	N	Y
16 Walker	N	N	N	Y
17 Ertel	Y	Y	Y	?
18 Walgren	Y	Y	Y	Y
19 Goodling	N	N	N	Y
20 Gaydos	N	Y	Y	Y
21 Bailey	N	Y	Y	Y
22 Murphy	N	?	?	?
23 Clinger	Y	N	N	Y
24 Marks	N	N	N	?
25 Atkinson	N	N	N	Y
RHODE ISLAND				
1 St Germain	Y	Y	Y	Y
2 Schneider	Y	N	N	Y
SOUTH CAROLINA				
1 Hartnett	N	N	N	Y
2 Spence	N	N	N	Y
3 Derrick	N	Y	Y	?
4 Campbell	N	N	N	?
5 Holland	N	Y	Y	Y
6 Napier	N	N	N	Y
SOUTH DAKOTA				
1 Daschle	N	Y	Y	?
2 Roberts	N	N	N	?
TENNESSEE				
1 Quillen	N	N	N	Y
2 Duncan	N	N	N	Y
3 Bouquard	Y	Y	Y	Y
4 Gore	Y	Y	Y	Y
5 Boner	Y	Y	Y	Y
6 Beard	?	N	N	?
7 Jones	Y	Y	Y	Y
8 Ford	N	Y	N	X
TEXAS				
1 Hall, S.	N	N	N	Y
2 Wilson	N	Y	Y	?
3 Collins	N	N	N	?
4 Hall, R.	N	N	N	Y
5 Mattox	N	N	Y	?
6 Gramm	N	N	N	Y
7 Archer	N	N	N	Y
8 Fields	N	N	N	Y
9 Brooks	Y	Y	Y	Y
10 Pickle	Y	Y	Y	Y
11 Leath	N	N	N	Y
12 Wright	Y	Y	Y	Y
13 Hightower	N	Y	Y	Y
14 Patman	N	Y	Y	Y
15 de la Garza	N	Y	Y	Y
16 White	N	Y	Y	?
17 Stenholm	N	N	N	Y
18 Leland	N	N	N	Y
19 Hance	N	N	N	Y
20 Gonzalez	Y	Y	Y	Y
21 Loeffler	N	N	N	Y
22 Paul	N	N	N	Y
23 Kazen	N	Y	Y	Y
24 Frost	Y	Y	Y	?
UTAH				
1 Hansen	N	N	N	Y
2 Marriott	N	N	N	?
VERMONT				
AL Jeffords	Y	N	Y	Y
VIRGINIA				
1 Trible	N	N	N	?
2 Whitehurst	N	N	N	Y
3 Bliley	N	N	N	Y
4 Daniel, R.	N	N	N	Y
5 Daniel, D.	N	N	N	Y
6 Butler	N	N	N	Y
7 Robinson	N	N	N	Y
8 Parris	N	N	N	Y
9 Wampler	N	N	N	Y
10 Wolf	N	N	N	Y
WASHINGTON				
1 Pritchard	Y	N	N	Y
2 Swift	Y	Y	Y	Y
3 Bonker	Y	Y	Y	Y
4 Morrison	N	N	N	Y
5 Foley	Y	Y	Y	Y
6 Dicks	N	Y	Y	?
7 Lowry	Y	Y	Y	Y
WEST VIRGINIA				
1 Mollohan	N	Y	Y	Y
2 Benedict	N	N	N	Y
3 Staton	N	N	N	Y
4 Rahall	Y	Y	Y	Y
WISCONSIN				
1 Aspin	Y	Y	Y	Y
2 Kastenmeier	Y	Y	N	N
3 Gunderson	N	N	N	Y
4 Zablocki	Y	Y	Y	Y
5 Reuss	N	Y	Y	N
6 Petri	Y	N	N	?
7 Obey	N	Y	Y	Y
8 Roth	N	N	N	Y
9 Sensenbrenner	N	N	N	Y
WYOMING				
AL Cheney	N	N	N	Y

Southern states · Ala., Ark., Fla., Ga., Ky., La., Miss., N.C., Okla., S.C., Tenn., Texas, Va.

126. Procedural Motion. Seiberling, D-Ohio, motion to approve the House *Journal* of Tuesday, June 8. Motion agreed to 340-25: R 145-17; D 195-8 (ND 123-7, SD 72-1), June 9, 1982.

127. HR 4861. American Conservation Corps. Seiberling, D-Ohio, motion to suspend the rules and pass the bill to establish an American Conservation Corps to employ youths aged 16-25 for conservation, rehabilitation and improvement projects on federal, state or Indian lands. Motion agreed to 291-102: R 74-96; D 217-6 (ND 144-1, SD 73-5), June 9, 1982. A two-thirds majority of those present and voting (262 in this case) is required for passage under suspension of the rules. A "nay" was a vote supporting the president's position.

128. HR 5922. Urgent Supplemental Appropriations, Fiscal 1982. Myers, R-Ind., motion to order the previous question (thus ending debate and the possibility of amendment) on the Myers motion to instruct the House conferees on the fiscal 1982 urgent supplemental appropriations bill to accept Senate amendments 50 (to delete the House-passed amendment repealing a provision of existing law to require a balanced federal budget by fiscal year 1981) and 62 (to restore a $3,000 annual limit on business-related income tax deductions by members of Congress), with an amendment to allow all business-related tax deductions, even in excess of $3,000, provided they were substantiated. Motion rejected 176-218: R 77-95; D 99-123 (ND 57-90, SD 42-33), June 9, 1982. A modified version of Myers' instructions subsequently was adopted *(see vote 130, below)*.

129. HR 5922. Urgent Supplemental Appropriations, Fiscal 1982. Schroeder, D-Colo., amendment to the Myers, R-Ind., motion *(see vote 128, above)*, to instruct conferees on the fiscal 1982 urgent supplemental appropriations bill to accept Senate amendments 50, relating to the balanced budget, and 62, restoring the $3,000 limit on business-related tax deductions claimed by members of Congress. Adopted 356-43: R 148-24; D 208-19 (ND 137-13, SD 71-6), June 9, 1982.

130. HR 5922. Urgent Supplemental Appropriations, Fiscal 1982. Myers, R-Ind., motion, as amended by the Schroeder, D-Colo., amendment *(see vote 129, above)*, to instruct the conferees on the fiscal 1982 urgent supplemental appropriations bill to accept Senate amendments 50 and 62. Motion agreed to 378-7: R 166-3; D 212-4 (ND 139-2, SD 73-2), June 9, 1982.

KEY

Y Voted for (yea).
\# Paired for.
+ Announced for.
N Voted against (nay).
X Paired against.
- Announced against.
P Voted "present".
C Voted "present" to avoid possible conflict of interest.
? Did not vote or otherwise make a position known.

Democrats   *Republicans*

	126	127	128	129	130
ALABAMA					
1 *Edwards*	Y	N	Y	N	Y
2 *Dickinson*	N	N	?	?	?
3 Nichols	?	Y	Y	Y	Y
4 Bevill	Y	Y	N	Y	Y
5 Flippo	Y	Y	Y	Y	Y
6 *Smith*	Y	N	N	Y	Y
7 Shelby	Y	Y	Y	Y	Y
ALASKA					
AL *Young*	?	Y	Y	?	N
ARIZONA					
1 *Rhodes*	Y	Y	?	?	Y
2 Udall	Y	Y	Y	Y	Y
3 *Stump*	Y	N	N	Y	Y
4 *Rudd*	Y	N	Y	Y	Y
ARKANSAS					
1 Alexander	Y	Y	Y	Y	Y
2 *Bethune*	Y	Y	N	Y	Y
3 *Hammerschmidt*	Y	Y	N	Y	Y
4 Anthony	Y	Y	N	Y	Y
CALIFORNIA					
1 *Chappie*	Y	N	Y	Y	Y
2 *Clausen*	Y	Y	Y	Y	Y
3 Matsui	Y	Y	N	Y	Y
4 Fazio	Y	Y	N	Y	Y
5 Burton, J.	?	?	?	?	?
6 Burton, P.	Y	Y	N	Y	Y
7 Miller	Y	Y	N	Y	Y
8 Dellums	Y	Y	N	Y	Y
9 Stark	Y	Y	N	Y	Y
10 Edwards	?	Y	N	Y	?
11 Lantos	?	Y	N	Y	Y
12 *McCloskey*	?	?	?	?	?
13 Mineta	?	Y	N	Y	Y
14 *Shumway*	Y	N	N	Y	Y
15 Coelho	Y	Y	N	Y	Y
16 Panetta	Y	Y	N	Y	Y
17 *Pashayan*	Y	Y	Y	Y	Y
18 *Thomas*	?	?	?	?	?
19 *Lagomarsino*	Y	Y	N	Y	Y
20 *Goldwater*	?	?	?	?	?
21 *Fiedler*	?	Y	N	Y	Y
22 *Moorhead*	Y	N	Y	Y	Y
23 Beilenson	Y	Y	N	Y	Y
24 Waxman	?	?	?	?	?
25 Roybal	Y	Y	Y	Y	Y
26 *Rousselot*	?	?	?	?	?
27 *Dornan*	?	?	?	?	?
28 Dixon	?	?	?	?	?
29 Hawkins	Y	?	Y	Y	?
30 Vacancy					
31 Dymally	?	?	?	?	?
32 Anderson	Y	Y	N	Y	Y
33 *Grisham*	?	?	?	?	?
34 *Lungren*	?	?	?	?	?
35 *Dreier*	?	?	?	?	?
36 Brown	?	?	?	?	?
37 *Lewis*	Y	N	Y	N	Y
38 Patterson	Y	Y	Y	Y	Y
39 *Dannemeyer*	Y	N	N	Y	Y
40 *Badham*	Y	N	Y	N	Y
41 *Lowery*	?	?	?	?	?
42 *Hunter*	Y	?	N	Y	Y
43 *Burgener*	?	?	?	?	?
COLORADO					
1 Schroeder	N	Y	N	Y	Y
2 Wirth	Y	Y	N	Y	Y
3 Kogovsek	Y	Y	N	Y	Y
4 *Brown*	N	N	N	Y	Y

	126	127	128	129	130
5 *Kramer*	Y	N	N	Y	Y
CONNECTICUT					
1 Kennelly	Y	Y	N	Y	Y
2 Gejdenson	N	Y	N	Y	Y
3 *DeNardis*	Y	?	N	Y	?
4 *McKinney*	Y	Y	N	Y	Y
5 Ratchford	Y	Y	N	Y	Y
6 Moffett	Y	Y	N	Y	Y
DELAWARE					
AL *Evans*	Y	Y	N	Y	Y
FLORIDA					
1 Hutto	Y	Y	N	Y	Y
2 Fuqua	Y	Y	N	Y	Y
3 Bennett	Y	Y	N	Y	Y
4 Chappell	Y	Y	Y	Y	Y
5 *McCollum*	Y	N	N	Y	Y
6 *Young*	Y	N	Y	N	Y
7 Gibbons	?	Y	Y	N	Y
8 Ireland	Y	Y	Y	Y	Y
9 Nelson	Y	Y	N	Y	Y
10 *Bafalis*	Y	N	N	Y	Y
11 Mica	Y	Y	N	Y	Y
12 *Shaw*	Y	N	Y	Y	Y
13 Lehman	Y	Y	N	Y	Y
14 Pepper	Y	Y	N	Y	Y
15 Fascell	Y	Y	N	Y	Y
GEORGIA					
1 Ginn	Y	Y	?	?	+
2 Hatcher	Y	Y	Y	Y	Y
3 Brinkley	Y	Y	Y	Y	Y
4 Levitas	Y	Y	N	Y	Y
5 Fowler	Y	Y	Y	Y	Y
6 *Gingrich*	Y	N	N	Y	Y
7 McDonald	Y	N	Y	Y	Y
8 Evans	Y	Y	Y	Y	Y
9 Jenkins	Y	Y	Y	Y	Y
10 Barnard	Y	Y	Y	Y	Y
HAWAII					
1 Heftel	?	?	Y	Y	Y
2 Akaka	Y	Y	Y	Y	Y
IDAHO					
1 *Craig*	Y	N	N	Y	?
2 *Hansen*	Y	N	Y	Y	Y
ILLINOIS					
1 Washington	N	Y	N	Y	Y
2 Savage	Y	Y	?	N	N
3 Russo	Y	Y	N	Y	Y
4 *Derwinski*	Y	N	Y	Y	?
5 Fary	?	?	?	?	?
6 *Hyde*	Y	N	Y	N	Y
7 Collins	Y	Y	Y	Y	Y
8 Rostenkowski	Y	Y	N	Y	Y
9 Yates	N	Y	N	Y	Y
10 *Porter*	Y	N	Y	N	Y
11 Annunzio	Y	Y	N	Y	Y
12 *Crane, P.*	Y	N	Y	N	?
13 *McClory*	Y	Y	N	Y	Y
14 *Erlenborn*	Y	N	Y	N	Y
15 *Corcoran*	Y	N	Y	N	Y
16 *Martin*	Y	N	N	Y	Y
17 *O'Brien*	Y	Y	Y	Y	Y
18 *Michel*	Y	N	Y	Y	Y
19 *Railsback*	Y	Y	Y	Y	Y
20 *Findley*	Y	Y	N	Y	Y
21 Madigan	P	Y	Y	Y	Y
22 *Crane, D.*	Y	N	Y	N	Y
23 Price	Y	Y	Y	Y	Y
24 Simon	?	?	?	Y	Y
INDIANA					
1 Benjamin	Y	Y	N	Y	Y
2 Fithian	Y	Y	N	Y	Y
3 *Hiler*	Y	N	N	Y	Y
4 *Coats*	Y	N	Y	Y	Y
5 *Hillis*	Y	N	Y	Y	Y
6 Evans	Y	Y	Y	Y	Y
7 *Myers*	Y	N	Y	N	Y
8 *Deckard*	Y	Y	N	Y	Y
9 Hamilton	Y	Y	N	Y	Y
10 Sharp	Y	Y	N	Y	Y
11 Jacobs	?	Y	N	Y	Y
IOWA					
1 *Leach*	Y	Y	N	Y	Y
2 *Tauke*	Y	Y	N	Y	Y
3 *Evans*	N	Y	N	Y	Y
4 Smith	Y	Y	Y	Y	Y
5 Harkin	N	Y	N	Y	Y
6 Bedell	Y	Y	N	Y	Y

ND - Northern Democrats   SD - Southern Democrats

	126	127	128	129	130
KANSAS					
1 Roberts	Y	N	N	Y	Y
2 Jeffries	Y	N	Y	N	Y
3 Winn	Y	N	Y	Y	Y
4 Glickman	Y	Y	N	Y	Y
5 Whittaker	Y	N	N	Y	Y
KENTUCKY					
1 Hubbard	Y	Y	N	Y	Y
2 Natcher	Y	Y	N	Y	Y
3 Mazzoli	Y	Y	N	Y	Y
4 Snyder	Y	Y	N	Y	Y
5 Rogers	Y	Y	Y	Y	Y
6 Hopkins	Y	Y	Y	Y	Y
7 Perkins	Y	Y	Y	Y	Y
LOUISIANA					
1 Livingston	Y	N	Y	N	Y
2 Boggs	Y	Y	Y	Y	Y
3 Tauzin	Y	Y	Y	Y	Y
4 Roemer	N	N	N	Y	Y
5 Huckaby	Y	Y	N	Y	Y
6 Moore	Y	N	Y	Y	Y
7 Breaux	Y	Y	Y	N	Y
8 Long	Y	Y	Y	Y	Y
MAINE					
1 Emery	Y	Y	N	Y	Y
2 Snowe	Y	Y	N	Y	Y
MARYLAND					
1 Dyson	Y	Y	N	Y	Y
2 Long	Y	Y	Y	Y	Y
3 Mikulski	Y	Y	Y	Y	Y
4 Holt	N	N	N	Y	Y
5 Hoyer	Y	Y	Y	Y	Y
6 Byron	Y	?	Y	Y	Y
7 Mitchell	?	Y	Y	Y	Y
8 Barnes	N	Y	Y	Y	Y
MASSACHUSETTS					
1 Conte	Y	Y	Y	N	N
2 Boland	Y	Y	N	Y	Y
3 Early	Y	Y	Y	N	Y
4 Frank	Y	Y	N	Y	Y
5 Shannon	Y	Y	Y	N	Y
6 Mavroules	Y	Y	Y	Y	Y
7 Markey	Y	Y	N	Y	Y
8 O'Neill					
9 Moakley	Y	Y	Y	Y	Y
10 Heckler	Y	Y	N	Y	Y
11 Donnelly	Y	Y	Y	Y	Y
12 Studds	Y	Y	Y	N	Y
MICHIGAN					
1 Conyers	?	?	?	?	?
2 Pursell	Y	Y	N	Y	Y
3 Wolpe	Y	Y	N	Y	Y
4 Siljander	Y	N	Y	N	Y
5 Sawyer	Y	Y	N	Y	Y
6 Dunn	Y	Y	N	Y	Y
7 Kildee	Y	Y	N	Y	Y
8 Traxler	Y	Y	N	Y	Y
9 Vander Jagt	Y	Y	N	N	Y
10 Albosta	Y	Y	N	Y	Y
11 Davis	Y	Y	N	Y	Y
12 Bonior	Y	Y	N	Y	Y
13 Crockett	?	Y	Y	N	?
14 Hertel	Y	Y	N	Y	Y
15 Ford	?	Y	Y	N	Y
16 Dingell	?	Y	Y	Y	?
17 Brodhead	Y	Y	Y	Y	Y
18 Blanchard	?	?	?	?	+
19 Broomfield	Y	Y	N	Y	Y
MINNESOTA					
1 Erdahl	Y	Y	N	Y	Y
2 Hagedorn	Y	N	Y	Y	Y
3 Frenzel	Y	N	Y	N	Y
4 Vento	Y	Y	N	Y	Y
5 Sabo	N	Y	N	Y	Y
6 Weber	Y	Y	N	Y	Y
7 Stangeland	Y	N	Y	Y	Y
8 Oberstar	Y	Y	N	Y	Y
MISSISSIPPI					
1 Whitten	Y	Y	N	Y	Y
2 Bowen	Y	Y	Y	Y	Y
3 Montgomery	Y	N	Y	Y	Y
4 Dowdy	Y	Y	N	Y	Y
5 Lott	Y	N	Y	Y	Y
MISSOURI					
1 Clay	?	Y	Y	Y	Y
2 Young	Y	Y	N	Y	Y
3 Gephardt	Y	Y	N	Y	Y
4 Skelton	Y	Y	N	Y	Y
5 Bolling	?	?	?	?	?
6 Coleman	Y	Y	N	N	Y
7 Taylor	Y	N	N	Y	Y
8 Bailey	Y	N	N	Y	?
9 Volkmer	Y	Y	N	Y	Y
10 Emerson	N	N	N	Y	?
MONTANA					
1 Williams	?	Y	Y	N	N
2 Marlenee	?	N	Y	Y	Y
NEBRASKA					
1 Bereuter	Y	Y	N	Y	Y
2 Daub	Y	N	Y	Y	Y
3 Smith	Y	N	N	Y	Y
NEVADA					
AL Santini	?	Y	N	Y	?
NEW HAMPSHIRE					
1 D'Amours	Y	Y	N	Y	Y
2 Gregg	Y	N	N	Y	Y
NEW JERSEY					
1 Florio	Y	Y	N	Y	Y
2 Hughes	Y	Y	Y	Y	Y
3 Howard	Y	Y	N	Y	Y
4 Smith	Y	Y	N	Y	Y
5 Fenwick	?	N	N	?	Y
6 Forsythe	N	N	N	Y	Y
7 Roukema	Y	N	N	Y	Y
8 Roe	Y	Y	N	Y	Y
9 Hollenbeck	Y	Y	N	Y	Y
10 Rodino	?	Y	Y	Y	?
11 Minish	Y	Y	N	Y	Y
12 Rinaldo	Y	Y	N	Y	Y
13 Courter	?	?	?	?	?
14 Guarini	?	?	?	?	?
15 Dwyer	Y	Y	N	Y	Y
NEW MEXICO					
1 Lujan	Y	?	Y	Y	Y
2 Skeen	Y	N	Y	Y	Y
NEW YORK					
1 Carney	Y	Y	Y	Y	Y
2 Downey	Y	Y	Y	Y	Y
3 Carman	Y	N	Y	N	Y
4 Lent	Y	Y	Y	Y	Y
5 McGrath	Y	Y	N	Y	Y
6 LeBoutillier	Y	Y	?	Y	Y
7 Addabbo	Y	Y	Y	Y	Y
8 Rosenthal	Y	Y	N	Y	Y
9 Ferraro	?	?	?	?	?
10 Biaggi	Y	Y	Y	Y	Y
11 Scheuer	Y	Y	Y	Y	Y
12 Chisholm	Y	Y	Y	Y	Y
13 Solarz	Y	Y	Y	Y	Y
14 Richmond	Y	Y	Y	Y	Y
15 Zeferetti	Y	Y	Y	Y	Y
16 Schumer	Y	Y	Y	Y	Y
17 Molinari	Y	Y	Y	Y	Y
18 Green	?	?	N	Y	Y
19 Rangel	Y	Y	Y	N	?
20 Weiss	Y	Y	Y	Y	Y
21 Garcia	?	Y	Y	Y	Y
22 Bingham	Y	Y	N	Y	Y
23 Peyser	Y	Y	Y	Y	Y
24 Ottinger	P	Y	Y	Y	Y
25 Fish	Y	Y	Y	Y	Y
26 Gilman	Y	Y	N	Y	Y
27 McHugh	Y	Y	N	Y	Y
28 Stratton	Y	Y	N	Y	Y
29 Solomon	N	N	N	Y	Y
30 Martin	Y	Y	Y	N	Y
31 Mitchell	?	Y	N	Y	Y
32 Wortley	Y	N	Y	Y	Y
33 Lee	Y	N	Y	Y	Y
34 Horton	Y	Y	N	Y	Y
35 Conable	Y	N	Y	Y	Y
36 LaFalce	Y	Y	Y	N	Y
37 Nowak	Y	Y	Y	Y	Y
38 Kemp	Y	N	Y	Y	Y
39 Lundine	Y	Y	Y	N	Y
NORTH CAROLINA					
1 Jones	Y	Y	Y	N	?
2 Fountain	?	Y	Y	Y	Y
3 Whitley	Y	N	N	Y	Y
4 Andrews	Y	Y	N	Y	?
5 Neal	Y	Y	Y	Y	Y
6 Johnston	N	N	Y	Y	Y
7 Rose	?	?	?	?	?
8 Hefner	Y	Y	Y	Y	Y
9 Martin	Y	N	Y	N	Y
10 Broyhill	Y	N	Y	Y	Y
11 Hendon	N	N	N	Y	Y
NORTH DAKOTA					
AL Dorgan	Y	Y	N	Y	Y
OHIO					
1 Gradison	Y	N	Y	Y	Y
2 Luken	Y	Y	Y	Y	Y
3 Hall	?	?	Y	Y	Y
4 Oxley	Y	?	Y	Y	Y
5 Latta	Y	N	N	Y	Y
6 McEwen	Y	Y	N	Y	Y
7 Brown	?	?	?	?	?
8 Kindness	Y	N	Y	N	Y
9 Weber	Y	Y	N	Y	Y
10 Miller	N	N	N	Y	Y
11 Stanton	?	?	?	?	?
12 Shamansky	Y	Y	N	Y	Y
13 Pease	Y	Y	N	Y	Y
14 Seiberling	Y	Y	N	Y	Y
15 Wylie	Y	Y	N	Y	Y
16 Regula	Y	Y	Y	Y	Y
17 Vacancy					
18 Applegate	Y	Y	Y	Y	Y
19 Williams	?	?	?	?	?
20 Oakar	Y	Y	N	Y	Y
21 Stokes	Y	Y	N	Y	Y
22 Eckart	Y	N	N	Y	Y
23 Mottl	Y	Y	N	Y	Y
OKLAHOMA					
1 Jones	Y	Y	N	N	Y
2 Synar	Y	Y	N	Y	Y
3 Watkins	Y	N	Y	Y	Y
4 McCurdy	Y	Y	N	Y	Y
5 Edwards	Y	N	N	Y	Y
6 English	Y	Y	N	Y	Y
OREGON					
1 AuCoin	?	Y	N	Y	?
2 Smith	N	N	Y	N	Y
3 Wyden	Y	Y	N	Y	Y
4 Weaver	Y	Y	N	Y	Y
PENNSYLVANIA					
1 Foglietta	Y	Y	N	Y	Y
2 Gray	Y	Y	Y	Y	Y
3 Smith	?	?	?	?	?
4 Dougherty	Y	Y	N	Y	Y
5 Schulze	Y	Y	Y	N	Y
6 Yatron	Y	Y	N	Y	Y
7 Edgar	Y	Y	N	Y	Y
8 Coyne, J.	Y	Y	N	Y	Y
9 Shuster	Y	Y	Y	Y	Y
10 McDade	?	Y	Y	N	Y
11 Nelligan	?	Y	N	Y	Y
12 Murtha	Y	Y	Y	N	Y
13 Coughlin	N	Y	N	Y	Y
14 Coyne, W.	Y	Y	N	Y	?
15 Ritter	?	N	N	Y	Y
16 Walker	N	N	N	Y	Y
17 Ertel	Y	Y	N	Y	Y
18 Walgren	Y	Y	N	Y	Y
19 Goodling	N	Y	N	Y	Y
20 Gaydos	Y	Y	N	Y	Y
21 Bailey	Y	Y	N	Y	Y
22 Murphy	Y	Y	N	Y	Y
23 Clinger	Y	Y	N	Y	Y
24 Marks	?	Y	Y	N	Y
25 Atkinson	?	Y	N	Y	Y
RHODE ISLAND					
1 St Germain	Y	Y	N	Y	Y
2 Schneider	Y	Y	N	Y	Y
SOUTH CAROLINA					
1 Hartnett	Y	N	Y	Y	Y
2 Spence	Y	Y	Y	Y	Y
3 Derrick	Y	?	?	Y	Y
4 Campbell	?	?	?	Y	Y
5 Holland	Y	Y	Y	Y	Y
6 Napier	Y	N	Y	Y	Y
SOUTH DAKOTA					
1 Daschle	Y	Y	N	Y	Y
2 Roberts	Y	N	N	Y	Y
TENNESSEE					
1 Quillen	Y	N	N	Y	Y
2 Duncan	?	N	N	Y	Y
3 Bouquard	Y	Y	N	Y	Y
4 Gore	Y	Y	N	Y	Y
5 Boner	Y	Y	N	Y	Y
6 Beard	Y	N	N	Y	Y
7 Jones	Y	Y	N	Y	Y
8 Ford	?	Y	N	Y	N
TEXAS					
1 Hall, S.	Y	Y	N	Y	Y
2 Wilson	?	Y	Y	Y	Y
3 Collins	Y	N	N	Y	Y
4 Hall, R.	Y	Y	Y	Y	Y
5 Mattox	Y	Y	Y	Y	Y
6 Gramm	Y	N	Y	Y	Y
7 Archer	Y	N	N	Y	Y
8 Fields	N	N	N	Y	Y
9 Brooks	Y	Y	Y	Y	Y
10 Pickle	Y	Y	Y	Y	Y
11 Leath	Y	Y	N	Y	Y
12 Wright	Y	Y	Y	Y	Y
13 Hightower	Y	Y	Y	Y	Y
14 Patman	Y	Y	Y	Y	Y
15 de la Garza	Y	Y	?	N	Y
16 White	Y	Y	Y	Y	Y
17 Stenholm	Y	Y	N	Y	Y
18 Leland	Y	Y	Y	Y	Y
19 Hance	Y	Y	Y	Y	Y
20 Gonzalez	Y	Y	Y	N	N
21 Loeffler	Y	N	N	Y	Y
22 Paul	Y	N	N	Y	Y
23 Kazen	Y	N	Y	Y	Y
24 Frost	Y	Y	N	Y	Y
UTAH					
1 Hansen	Y	N	Y	Y	Y
2 Marriott	Y	Y	Y	Y	Y
VERMONT					
AL Jeffords	Y	Y	Y	Y	Y
VIRGINIA					
1 Trible	?	?	?	?	?
2 Whitehurst	Y	N	Y	Y	Y
3 Bliley	Y	N	Y	Y	Y
4 Daniel, R.	Y	N	Y	Y	Y
5 Daniel, D.	Y	Y	Y	Y	Y
6 Butler	N	N	Y	N	N
7 Robinson	Y	N	Y	Y	Y
8 Parris	Y	N	N	Y	Y
9 Wampler	Y	Y	N	Y	Y
10 Wolf	Y	Y	N	Y	Y
WASHINGTON					
1 Pritchard	Y	Y	N	Y	Y
2 Swift	Y	Y	N	Y	Y
3 Bonker	Y	Y	N	Y	Y
4 Morrison	Y	Y	N	Y	Y
5 Foley	Y	Y	N	Y	Y
6 Dicks	Y	Y	N	Y	Y
7 Lowry	Y	Y	N	Y	Y
WEST VIRGINIA					
1 Mollohan	Y	Y	Y	Y	Y
2 Benedict	Y	N	Y	Y	Y
3 Staton	N	N	N	Y	Y
4 Rahall	Y	Y	Y	Y	Y
WISCONSIN					
1 Aspin	Y	Y	N	Y	Y
2 Kastenmeier	Y	Y	N	Y	Y
3 Gunderson	Y	N	N	Y	Y
4 Zablocki	Y	Y	N	Y	Y
5 Reuss	Y	Y	N	Y	Y
6 Petri	Y	Y	N	Y	Y
7 Obey	Y	Y	N	Y	Y
8 Roth	Y	Y	N	Y	Y
9 Sensenbrenner	Y	N	N	Y	Y
WYOMING					
AL Cheney	Y	N	Y	Y	Y

Southern states · Ala., Ark., Fla., Ga., Ky., La., Miss., N.C., Okla., S.C., Tenn., Texas, Va.

KEY

Y Voted for (yea).
\# Paired for.
\+ Announced for.
N Voted against (nay).
X Paired against.
- Announced against.
P Voted "present".
C Voted "present" to avoid possible conflict of interest.
? Did not vote or otherwise make a position known.

Democrats   *Republicans*

131. Procedural Motion. Solomon, R-N.Y., motion to approve the House *Journal* of Wednesday, June 9. Motion agreed to 352-32: R 160-20; D 192-12 (ND 125-10, SD 67-2), June 10, 1982.

132. H Con Res 352. First Budget Resolution, Fiscal 1983. Adoption of the rule (H Res 496) providing for House floor consideration of the first concurrent budget resolution to set budget targets for the fiscal year ending Sept. 30, 1983. Adopted 339-72: R 135-47; D 204-25 (ND 134-19, SD 70-6), June 10, 1982.

133. H Con Res 352. First Budget Resolution, Fiscal 1983. Jones, D-Okla., substitute to the Latta, R-Ohio, substitute, to set budget targets for the fiscal year ending Sept. 30, 1983, as follows: budget authority, $836.2 billion; outlays, $784.15 billion; revenues, $676.7 billion; and deficit, $107.45 billion. Rejected 202-225: R 3-186; D 199-39 (ND 148-12, SD 51-27), June 10, 1982.

134. H Con Res 352. First Budget Resolution, Fiscal 1983. Latta, R-Ohio, substitute for the president's fiscal 1983 budget submission, to set budget targets for the fiscal year ending Sept. 30, 1983, as follows: budget authority, $800.38 billion; outlays, $765.17 billion; revenues, $665.9 billion; and deficit, $99.27 billion. Adopted 220-207: R 174-15; D 46-192 (ND 9-151, SD 37-41), June 10, 1982.

135. H Con Res 352. First Budget Resolution, Fiscal 1983. Adoption of the first concurrent budget resolution to set budget targets for the fiscal year ending Sept. 30, 1983, as follows: budget authority, $800.38 billion; outlays, $765.17 billion; revenues, $665.9 billion, and deficit, $99.27 billion. The resolution also set preliminary goals for fiscal 1984-85, revised budget levels for fiscal 1982 and included reconciliation instructions requiring House and Senate committees to recommend legislative savings to meet the budget targets. Adopted 219-206: R 156-32; D 63-174 (ND 16-144, SD 47-30), June 10, 1982.

	131	132	133	134	135
ALABAMA					
1 Edwards	Y	Y	N	Y	Y
2 Dickinson	N	Y	N	Y	Y
3 Nichols	?	Y	N	Y	Y
4 Bevill	Y	Y	Y	N	Y
5 Flippo	Y	Y	Y	N	Y
6 Smith	Y	Y	N	Y	Y
7 Shelby	Y	Y	N	Y	Y
ALASKA					
AL Young	N	Y	N	Y	Y
ARIZONA					
1 Rhodes	Y	Y	N	Y	Y
2 Udall	Y	Y	Y	N	N
3 Stump	Y	Y	N	Y	Y
4 Rudd	Y	Y	N	Y	+
ARKANSAS					
1 Alexander	Y	Y	Y	N	Y
2 Bethune	Y	Y	N	Y	Y
3 Hammerschmidt	Y	Y	N	Y	Y
4 Anthony	Y	Y	Y	N	Y
CALIFORNIA					
1 Chappie	Y	N	N	Y	Y
2 Clausen	Y	Y	N	Y	Y
3 Matsui	?	Y	Y	N	N
4 Fazio	Y	Y	Y	N	N
5 Burton, J.	?	?	#	X	X
6 Burton, P.	Y	Y	Y	N	N
7 Miller	N	N	Y	N	N
8 Dellums	Y	Y	N	N	N
9 Stark	?	Y	Y	N	N
10 Edwards	Y	Y	Y	N	N
11 Lantos	Y	Y	Y	N	N
12 McCloskey	?	Y	N	Y	Y
13 Mineta	Y	Y	Y	N	N
14 Shumway	Y	Y	N	Y	Y
15 Coelho	Y	Y	Y	N	N
16 Panetta	Y	Y	Y	N	N
17 Pashayan	Y	Y	N	Y	Y
18 Thomas	Y	Y	N	Y	Y
19 Lagomarsino	Y	Y	N	Y	Y
20 Goldwater	?	?	X	#	#
21 Fiedler	Y	Y	N	Y	Y
22 Moorhead	Y	Y	N	Y	Y
23 Beilenson	?	Y	Y	N	N
24 Waxman	Y	Y	Y	N	N
25 Roybal	Y	Y	Y	N	N
26 Rousselot	?	?	N	Y	N
27 Dornan	?	?	?	?	?
28 Dixon	?	?	Y	N	N
29 Hawkins	?	Y	Y	N	N
30 Vacancy					
31 Dymally	Y	Y	Y	N	N
32 Anderson	Y	Y	Y	N	Y
33 Grisham	Y	N	N	Y	Y
34 Lungren	Y	Y	N	Y	Y
35 Dreier	Y	N	N	Y	Y
36 Brown	Y	Y	Y	N	N
37 Lewis	Y	Y	N	Y	Y
38 Patterson	?	Y	Y	N	N
39 Dannemeyer	Y	N	N	N	N
40 Badham	N	Y	N	Y	Y
41 Lowery	Y	Y	N	Y	Y
42 Hunter	Y	Y	N	Y	Y
43 Burgener	Y	Y	N	Y	Y
COLORADO					
1 Schroeder	N	N	Y	N	N
2 Wirth	Y	Y	Y	N	N
3 Kogovsek	Y	Y	Y	N	N
4 Brown	Y	N	N	Y	N

	131	132	133	134	135
5 Kramer	Y	N	N	Y	N
CONNECTICUT					
1 Kennelly	Y	Y	Y	N	N
2 Gejdenson	N	Y	Y	N	N
3 DeNardis	Y	N	N	N	N
4 McKinney	?	N	N	N	N
5 Ratchford	Y	Y	Y	N	N
6 Moffett	?	?	Y	N	N
DELAWARE					
AL Evans	Y	N	N	Y	Y
FLORIDA					
1 Hutto	Y	Y	N	Y	Y
2 Fuqua	Y	Y	N	Y	Y
3 Bennett	Y	N	N	N	N
4 Chappell	Y	Y	N	Y	Y
5 McCollum	Y	Y	N	Y	Y
6 Young	Y	Y	N	Y	Y
7 Gibbons	?	?	Y	Y	Y
8 Ireland	Y	Y	N	Y	Y
9 Nelson	Y	Y	Y	Y	Y
10 Bafalis	Y	Y	N	Y	Y
11 Mica	Y	Y	N	Y	N
12 Shaw	Y	Y	N	Y	Y
13 Lehman	Y	Y	Y	N	N
14 Pepper	Y	Y	Y	N	N
15 Fascell	Y	Y	N	N	N
GEORGIA					
1 Ginn	?	?	Y	Y	?
2 Hatcher	Y	Y	Y	Y	Y
3 Brinkley	Y	Y	N	Y	Y
4 Levitas	Y	N	N	Y	Y
5 Fowler	Y	Y	N	Y	N
6 Gingrich	Y	Y	N	Y	Y
7 McDonald	N	N	N	N	N
8 Evans	Y	N	Y	N	Y
9 Jenkins	Y	Y	Y	Y	Y
10 Barnard	Y	Y	N	Y	Y
HAWAII					
1 Heftel	Y	Y	Y	Y	Y
2 Akaka	Y	Y	Y	N	N
IDAHO					
1 Craig	Y	N	N	Y	N
2 Hansen	Y	N	N	Y	Y
ILLINOIS					
1 Washington	?	Y	Y	N	N
2 Savage	?	Y	N	N	N
3 Russo	Y	Y	N	N	N
4 Derwinski	Y	N	N	Y	Y
5 Fary	?	?	Y	N	N
6 Hyde	Y	Y	N	Y	Y
7 Collins	Y	Y	N	N	N
8 Rostenkowski	Y	Y	Y	N	N
9 Yates	N	Y	Y	N	N
10 Porter	Y	N	N	Y	Y
11 Annunzio	Y	Y	Y	N	N
12 Crane, P.	Y	N	N	Y	N
13 McClory	Y	Y	N	Y	Y
14 Erlenborn	Y	Y	N	Y	Y
15 Corcoran	Y	Y	N	Y	Y
16 Martin	Y	Y	N	Y	Y
17 O'Brien	Y	Y	N	Y	Y
18 Michel	Y	Y	N	Y	Y
19 Railsback	?	Y	N	Y	Y
20 Findley	Y	Y	N	Y	Y
21 Madigan	Y	Y	N	Y	Y
22 Crane, D.	Y	N	N	Y	N
23 Price	Y	Y	N	N	N
24 Simon	Y	Y	Y	N	N
INDIANA					
1 Benjamin	Y	Y	Y	N	N
2 Fithian	Y	Y	Y	N	N
3 Hiler	Y	Y	N	Y	Y
4 Coats	Y	Y	N	Y	Y
5 Hillis	Y	Y	N	Y	Y
6 Evans	Y	N	Y	N	N
7 Myers	Y	Y	N	Y	Y
8 Deckard	Y	Y	N	Y	Y
9 Hamilton	Y	Y	Y	Y	Y
10 Sharp	Y	N	N	N	N
11 Jacobs	N	N	Y	N	N
IOWA					
1 Leach	Y	N	N	Y	Y
2 Tauke	Y	N	Y	Y	Y
3 Evans	N	N	Y	Y	Y
4 Smith	Y	Y	N	N	N
5 Harkin	N	N	Y	N	N
6 Bedell	?	?	Y	N	Y

ND - Northern Democrats   SD - Southern Democrats

	131	132	133	134	135
KANSAS					
1 Roberts	Y	Y	N	Y	Y
2 Jeffries	Y	N	N	Y	N
3 Winn	Y	Y	N	Y	Y
4 Glickman	Y	Y	Y	N	Y
5 Whittaker	Y	Y	N	Y	Y
KENTUCKY					
1 Hubbard	Y	Y	Y	N	N
2 Natcher	Y	Y	Y	N	N
3 Mazzoli	Y	Y	Y	N	Y
4 Snyder	Y	N	N	Y	N
5 Rogers	Y	Y	N	Y	Y
6 Hopkins	Y	N	N	Y	N
7 Perkins	?	Y	Y	Y	N
LOUISIANA					
1 Livingston	Y	Y	N	Y	Y
2 Boggs	Y	Y	Y	N	N
3 Tauzin	Y	Y	N	Y	N
4 Roemer	N	Y	N	Y	Y
5 Huckaby	Y	Y	N	Y	Y
6 Moore	Y	Y	N	Y	Y
7 Breaux	Y	Y	N	Y	Y
8 Long	Y	Y	Y	N	N
MAINE					
1 Emery	Y	Y	N	Y	Y
2 Snowe	Y	Y	N	Y	Y
MARYLAND					
1 Dyson	Y	Y	N	Y	Y
2 Long	Y	Y	Y	N	N
3 Mikulski	Y	N	Y	N	N
4 Holt	N	Y	N	Y	Y
5 Hoyer	Y	Y	Y	N	N
6 Byron	Y	Y	N	Y	N
7 Mitchell	N	Y	Y	N	N
8 Barnes	N	Y	Y	N	N
MASSACHUSETTS					
1 Conte	Y	Y	N	Y	Y
2 Boland	Y	Y	Y	N	N
3 Early	Y	N	Y	N	N
4 Frank	Y	N	Y	N	N
5 Shannon	Y	Y	Y	N	N
6 Mavroules	?	N	Y	N	N
7 Markey	Y	Y	Y	N	N
8 O'Neill					
9 Moakley	?	Y	Y	N	N
10 Heckler	Y	N	N	N	N
11 Donnelly	Y	Y	Y	N	N
12 Studds	Y	Y	Y	N	N
MICHIGAN					
1 Conyers	Y	N	N	N	N
2 Pursell	Y	Y	N	Y	Y
3 Wolpe	Y	Y	Y	N	N
4 Siljander	Y	Y	N	Y	Y
5 Sawyer	Y	Y	N	Y	Y
6 Dunn	Y	P	N	Y	Y
7 Kildee	Y	Y	Y	N	N
8 Traxler	Y	Y	Y	N	N
9 Vander Jagt	Y	Y	Y	N	Y
10 Albosta	Y	Y	Y	Y	Y
11 Davis	Y	Y	Y	Y	Y
12 Bonior	Y	Y	Y	N	N
13 Crockett	Y	Y	Y	N	N
14 Hertel	Y	Y	Y	N	N
15 Ford	?	Y	Y	N	N
16 Dingell	Y	Y	Y	N	N
17 Brodhead	Y	Y	Y	N	N
18 Blanchard	Y	Y	Y	N	N
19 Broomfield	Y	Y	N	Y	Y
MINNESOTA					
1 Erdahl	Y	N	N	Y	Y
2 Hagedorn	Y	N	N	Y	Y
3 Frenzel	Y	Y	N	Y	Y
4 Vento	Y	N	Y	N	N
5 Sabo	N	Y	Y	N	N
6 Weber	Y	N	N	Y	Y
7 Stangeland	Y	N	N	Y	Y
8 Oberstar	Y	Y	Y	N	N
MISSISSIPPI					
1 Whitten	Y	Y	Y	N	N
2 Bowen	Y	Y	Y	N	N
3 Montgomery	Y	Y	N	Y	N
4 Dowdy	Y	Y	Y	N	N
5 Lott	Y	Y	N	Y	Y
MISSOURI					
1 Clay	N	Y	Y	N	N
2 Young	Y	Y	Y	Y	Y
3 Gephardt	?	Y	Y	Y	Y

	131	132	133	134	135
4 Skelton	Y	Y	N	Y	Y
5 Bolling	?	?	?	?	?
6 Coleman	Y	Y	N	Y	Y
7 Taylor	Y	Y	N	Y	Y
8 Bailey	Y	Y	N	Y	Y
9 Volkmer	Y	Y	Y	Y	N
10 Emerson	N	N	N	Y	Y
MONTANA					
1 Williams	Y	Y	Y	N	Y
2 Marlenee	Y	N	N	Y	Y
NEBRASKA					
1 Bereuter	Y	Y	N	Y	Y
2 Daub	Y	N	N	Y	Y
3 Smith	Y	Y	N	Y	Y
NEVADA					
AL Santini	Y	Y	N	N	N
NEW HAMPSHIRE					
1 D'Amours	Y	Y	N	N	N
2 Gregg	Y	Y	N	Y	Y
NEW JERSEY					
1 Florio	Y	Y	Y	N	N
2 Hughes	Y	N	Y	N	N
3 Howard	Y	Y	Y	N	N
4 Smith	Y	N	N	N	N
5 Fenwick	Y	N	Y	N	Y
6 Forsythe	N	Y	N	Y	Y
7 Roukema	Y	Y	N	Y	Y
8 Roe	Y	Y	Y	N	N
9 Hollenbeck	Y	N	N	Y	N
10 Rodino	Y	Y	Y	N	N
11 Minish	Y	Y	Y	N	N
12 Rinaldo	Y	N	N	N	N
13 Courter	Y	N	N	Y	Y
14 Guarini	Y	Y	Y	N	N
15 Dwyer	Y	Y	Y	Y	N
NEW MEXICO					
1 Lujan	Y	N	N	Y	N
2 Skeen	Y	Y	N	Y	Y
NEW YORK					
1 Carney	Y	Y	N	Y	Y
2 Downey	Y	Y	Y	N	N
3 Carman	Y	Y	N	Y	N
4 Lent	Y	Y	N	Y	Y
5 McGrath	N	Y	N	Y	Y
6 LeBoutillier	N	N	Y	N	Y
7 Addabbo	Y	Y	Y	N	N
8 Rosenthal	Y	Y	Y	N	N
9 Ferraro	Y	Y	Y	N	N
10 Biaggi	Y	?	Y	N	N
11 Scheuer	?	Y	Y	N	N
12 Chisholm	?	Y	Y	N	N
13 Solarz	Y	Y	Y	N	N
14 Richmond	?	Y	Y	N	N
15 Zeferetti	Y	Y	Y	N	N
16 Schumer	Y	N	Y	N	N
17 Molinari	Y	Y	N	Y	N
18 Green	Y	Y	N	N	N
19 Rangel	Y	?	Y	N	N
20 Weiss	?	?	Y	N	N
21 Garcia	?	?	Y	N	N
22 Bingham	Y	Y	Y	N	N
23 Peyser	Y	Y	Y	N	N
24 Ottinger	P	Y	Y	N	N
25 Fish	?	?	N	Y	Y
26 Gilman	Y	N	N	Y	N
27 McHugh	Y	Y	Y	N	N
28 Stratton	?	?	Y	Y	N
29 Solomon	N	N	N	Y	Y
30 Martin	Y	Y	N	Y	Y
31 Mitchell	Y	N	Y	N	Y
32 Wortley	Y	Y	N	Y	Y
33 Lee	Y	Y	N	Y	Y
34 Horton	Y	Y	N	Y	Y
35 Conable	Y	Y	N	Y	Y
36 LaFalce	Y	N	Y	N	N
37 Nowak	Y	Y	Y	N	N
38 Kemp	Y	Y	Y	N	N
39 Lundine	Y	Y	Y	N	Y
NORTH CAROLINA					
1 Jones	?	Y	Y	N	Y
2 Fountain	?	Y	Y	Y	Y
3 Whitley	Y	Y	Y	N	N
4 Andrews	Y	Y	Y	N	N
5 Neal	?	N	N	N	N
6 Johnston	N	Y	N	Y	N
7 Rose	Y	Y	Y	N	N
8 Hefner	Y	Y	Y	N	Y

	131	132	133	134	135
9 Martin	Y	Y	N	Y	Y
10 Broyhill	Y	Y	N	Y	Y
11 Hendon	Y	Y	N	Y	Y
NORTH DAKOTA					
AL Dorgan	Y	N	Y	N	N
OHIO					
1 Gradison	?	?	N	Y	Y
2 Luken	Y	N	N	Y	N
3 Hall	?	Y	Y	N	N
4 Oxley	Y	Y	N	Y	Y
5 Latta	Y	Y	N	Y	Y
6 McEwen	Y	Y	N	Y	Y
7 Brown	Y	Y	N	Y	Y
8 Kindness	Y	Y	N	Y	Y
9 Weber	?	?	N	Y	Y
10 Miller	N	Y	N	Y	Y
11 Stanton	Y	Y	N	Y	Y
12 Shamansky	Y	Y	Y	N	N
13 Pease	Y	Y	Y	N	N
14 Seiberling	Y	Y	Y	N	N
15 Wylie	Y	Y	N	Y	Y
16 Regula	Y	Y	N	Y	Y
17 Vacancy					
18 Applegate	?	Y	N	N	N
19 Williams	Y	Y	N	Y	Y
20 Oakar	Y	N	N	N	N
21 Stokes	Y	Y	Y	N	N
22 Eckart	Y	Y	Y	N	N
23 Mottl	Y	Y	Y	N	N
OKLAHOMA					
1 Jones	N	Y	N	Y	Y
2 Synar	Y	Y	N	Y	N
3 Watkins	Y	Y	N	Y	N
4 McCurdy	Y	Y	N	Y	Y
5 Edwards	Y	N	N	Y	N
6 English	Y	Y	N	N	N
OREGON					
1 AuCoin	Y	Y	Y	N	N
2 Smith	N	N	N	Y	Y
3 Wyden	Y	Y	Y	N	N
4 Weaver	Y	N	Y	N	N
PENNSYLVANIA					
1 Foglietta	Y	Y	Y	N	N
2 Gray	Y	Y	Y	N	N
3 Smith	Y	Y	Y	N	N
4 Dougherty	Y	Y	N	Y	N
5 Schulze	Y	Y	N	Y	Y
6 Yatron	Y	Y	Y	N	N
7 Edgar	Y	Y	Y	N	N
8 Coyne, J.	?	?	N	Y	Y
9 Shuster	Y	Y	N	Y	Y
10 McDade	Y	Y	N	Y	Y
11 Nelligan	Y	N	N	Y	Y
12 Murtha	Y	Y	Y	N	N
13 Coughlin	Y	N	N	Y	Y
14 Coyne, W.	Y	Y	Y	N	N
15 Ritter	Y	Y	N	Y	Y
16 Walker	N	N	N	Y	Y
17 Ertel	Y	Y	Y	N	N
18 Walgren	Y	Y	Y	N	N
19 Goodling	N	Y	N	Y	Y
20 Gaydos	Y	Y	Y	N	N
21 Bailey	Y	Y	Y	N	N
22 Murphy	Y	Y	Y	N	N
23 Clinger	Y	Y	N	Y	N
24 Marks	?	?	N	N	N
25 Atkinson	Y	Y	N	Y	Y
RHODE ISLAND					
1 St Germain	Y	Y	Y	N	N
2 Schneider	Y	N	N	N	N
SOUTH CAROLINA					
1 Hartnett	N	N	N	Y	Y
2 Spence	Y	Y	N	Y	N
3 Derrick	?	Y	Y	N	N
4 Campbell	Y	Y	N	Y	Y
5 Holland	?	?	?	?	?
6 Napier	Y	N	N	Y	Y
SOUTH DAKOTA					
1 Daschle	Y	Y	Y	N	N
2 Roberts	Y	Y	N	Y	Y
TENNESSEE					
1 Quillen	Y	Y	N	Y	Y
2 Duncan	Y	Y	N	Y	Y
3 Bouquard	Y	Y	Y	N	N
4 Gore	Y	Y	N	Y	N
5 Boner	Y	Y	Y	N	N
6 Beard	Y	Y	N	Y	Y

	131	132	133	134	135
7 Jones	Y	Y	Y	Y	Y
8 Ford	Y	Y	Y	N	N
TEXAS					
1 Hall, S.	Y	Y	N	Y	Y
2 Wilson	Y	Y	N	Y	Y
3 Collins	Y	Y	N	Y	N
4 Hall, R.	Y	Y	N	Y	Y
5 Mattox	Y	N	N	Y	N
6 Gramm	Y	Y	N	Y	Y
7 Archer	Y	Y	N	Y	N
8 Fields	N	Y	N	Y	N
9 Brooks	Y	Y	Y	N	N
10 Pickle	Y	Y	Y	N	N
11 Leath	Y	Y	N	Y	N
12 Wright	Y	Y	Y	N	N
13 Hightower	Y	Y	Y	N	N
14 Patman	Y	Y	Y	Y	Y
15 de la Garza	Y	Y	Y	N	N
16 White	Y	Y	N	Y	N
17 Stenholm	Y	Y	N	Y	N
18 Leland	?	?	Y	N	N
19 Hance	Y	Y	Y	Y	Y
20 Gonzalez	Y	Y	Y	N	N
21 Loeffler	Y	Y	N	Y	Y
22 Paul	Y	Y	N	Y	N
23 Kazen	Y	Y	Y	N	N
24 Frost	Y	Y	Y	N	N
UTAH					
1 Hansen	Y	Y	N	Y	Y
2 Marriott	Y	Y	N	Y	Y
VERMONT					
AL Jeffords	Y	N	N	N	N
VIRGINIA					
1 Trible	Y	Y	N	Y	Y
2 Whitehurst	Y	Y	N	Y	Y
3 Bliley	Y	Y	N	Y	Y
4 Daniel, R.	Y	Y	N	Y	Y
5 Daniel, D.	Y	Y	N	Y	Y
6 Butler	N	Y	N	Y	Y
7 Robinson	Y	Y	N	Y	Y
8 Parris	Y	Y	N	Y	Y
9 Wampler	Y	Y	N	Y	Y
10 Wolf	Y	Y	N	Y	Y
WASHINGTON					
1 Pritchard	Y	Y	N	Y	Y
2 Swift	Y	Y	Y	N	N
3 Bonker	Y	Y	Y	N	N
4 Morrison	Y	Y	N	Y	Y
5 Foley	Y	Y	Y	N	N
6 Dicks	?	Y	Y	N	N
7 Lowry	Y	Y	Y	N	N
WEST VIRGINIA					
1 Mollohan	Y	Y	Y	N	N
2 Benedict	Y	Y	N	Y	Y
3 Staton	N	N	Y	N	Y
4 Rahall	Y	Y	Y	N	N
WISCONSIN					
1 Aspin	Y	Y	N	Y	Y
2 Kastenmeier	Y	Y	Y	N	N
3 Gunderson	Y	Y	N	Y	Y
4 Zablocki	Y	Y	N	Y	N
5 Reuss	?	Y	Y	N	N
6 Petri	Y	Y	N	Y	Y
7 Obey	Y	Y	N	N	N
8 Roth	Y	Y	N	Y	Y
9 Sensenbrenner	Y	N	N	N	N
WYOMING					
AL Cheney	Y	Y	N	Y	Y

Southern states - Ala., Ark., Fla., Ga., Ky., La., Miss., N.C., Okla., S.C., Tenn., Texas, Va.

136. HR 6198. Copyright Manufacturing Clause Protection Act. Kastenmeier, D-Wis., motion to suspend the rules and pass the bill to extend until 1986 a provision in copyright law providing copyright protection for books and periodicals written in English only if they are printed in the United States. Motion agreed to 339-47: R 134-40; D 205-7 (ND 138-3, SD 67-4), June 15, 1982. A two-thirds majority of those present and voting (259 in this case) is required for passage under suspension of the rules.

137. HR 6350. Veterans Administration Health Care. Montgomery, D-Miss., motion to suspend the rules and pass the bill to permit Veterans Administration (VA) nurses who work two 12-hour regularly scheduled shifts over a weekend to be considered as having worked a full workweek; to extend until Sept. 30, 1983, the authority of the VA administrator to contract out medical services and hospital care for veterans in Puerto Rico and the Virgin Islands; and to extend through Sept. 30, 1985, a program of grants to states for the construction and alteration of state veterans' homes. Motion agreed to 390-0: R 180-0; D 210-0 (ND 139-0, SD 71-0), June 15, 1982. A two-thirds majority of those present and voting (260 in this case) is required for passage under suspension of the rules.

138. HR 6254. Protection of Foreign Missions. Passage of the bill to increase to $7 million, from $3.5 million, the amount to be reimbursed to state and local governments in fiscal 1983 for their expenses in protecting foreign diplomatic missions. The bill also authorized reimbursements to state and local governments for protection of motorcades and visits by foreign dignitaries and authorized $17.7 million in reimbursements for expenses incurred prior to Oct. 1, 1982. Passed 218-177: R 62-119; D 156-58 (ND 118-24, SD 38-34), June 15, 1982.

139. Procedural Motion. Walker, R-Pa., motion to approve the House *Journal* of Tuesday, June 15. Motion agreed to 347-23: R 156-15; D 191-8 (ND 119-7, SD 72-1), June 16, 1982.

140. HR 5922. Urgent Supplemental Appropriations, Fiscal 1982. Adoption of the rule (H Res 502) waiving points of order against the conference report on the bill to provide supplemental appropriations of $8,924,835,000 for fiscal 1982 and to rescind previous appropriations of $5,678,120,000. Adopted 257-155: R 41-142; D 216-13 (ND 147-6, SD 69-7), June 16, 1982.

141. HR 5922. Urgent Supplemental Appropriations, Fiscal 1982. Whitten, D-Miss., motion that the House concur in a Senate amendment, with an amendment, to rescind fiscal 1982 budget authority of $4,098,640,000 for annual contributions for assisted housing and $1,579,480,000 for the rent supplement program. Motion agreed to 312-96: R 175-7; D 137-89 (ND 68-83, SD 69-6), June 16, 1982.

142. HR 5922. Urgent Supplemental Appropriations, Fiscal 1982. Whitten, D-Miss., motion that the House concur in a Senate amendment to rescind $3,340,000 of fiscal 1982 contract authority in the rent supplement program. Motion agreed to 299-104: R 172-6; D 127-98 (ND 60-90, SD 67-8), June 16, 1982.

143. HR 5922. Urgent Supplemental Appropriations, Fiscal 1982. Fazio, D-Calif., motion that the House concur in a Senate amendment to establish a $3,000 annual limit on business-related tax deductions for Washington, D.C., living expenses claimed by individual members of Congress, with an amendment to limit annual outside income earned by members of Congress to 30 percent of their annual congressional salaries. Motion agreed to 381-29: R 169-13; D 212-16 (ND 141-11, SD 71-5), June 16, 1982.

KEY

Y	Voted for (yea).
#	Paired for.
+	Announced for.
N	Voted against (nay).
X	Paired against.
-	Announced against.
P	Voted "present".
C	Voted "present" to avoid possible conflict of interest.
?	Did not vote or otherwise make a position known.

Democrats *Republicans*

	136	137	138	139	140	141	142	143
ALABAMA								
1 *Edwards*	Y	Y	Y	Y	N	Y	Y	Y
2 *Dickinson*	Y	Y	Y	N	N	Y	Y	Y
3 Nichols	Y	Y	Y	Y	Y	Y	Y	Y
4 Bevill	Y	Y	Y	Y	Y	Y	Y	Y
5 Flippo	Y	Y	Y	Y	Y	Y	Y	Y
6 *Smith*	?	?	?	?	X	?	?	?
7 Shelby	Y	Y	N	Y	Y	N	Y	Y
ALASKA								
AL *Young*	Y	Y	N	?	N	Y	Y	Y
ARIZONA								
1 *Rhodes*	Y	Y	Y	N	Y	Y	Y	Y
2 Udall	Y	Y	Y	Y	Y	Y	Y	Y
3 *Stump*	N	Y	N	Y	N	Y	Y	Y
4 *Rudd*	Y	Y	N	Y	N	Y	Y	Y
ARKANSAS								
1 Alexander	Y	Y	Y	Y	Y	Y	Y	Y
2 *Bethune*	Y	Y	N	Y	N	Y	Y	Y
3 *Hammerschmidt*	Y	Y	N	Y	Y	Y	Y	Y
4 Anthony	Y	Y	N	?	Y	Y	Y	Y
CALIFORNIA								
1 *Chappie*	?	?	N	Y	N	Y	Y	Y
2 *Clausen*	Y	Y	Y	N	Y	Y	Y	Y
3 Matsui	Y	Y	Y	Y	Y	Y	N	Y
4 Fazio	Y	Y	Y	Y	Y	Y	Y	Y
5 Burton, J.	?	?	?	?	#	X	X	?
6 Burton, P.	Y	Y	Y	Y	Y	N	N	N
7 Miller	Y	Y	Y	Y	N	N	N	Y
8 Dellums	Y	Y	Y	?	N	N	N	Y
9 Stark	Y	Y	Y	Y	N	?	?	Y
10 Edwards	Y	?	?	?	N	N	Y	Y
11 Lantos	?	?	?	Y	Y	Y	Y	Y
12 *McCloskey*	Y	Y	Y	Y	N	Y	Y	N
13 Mineta	Y	Y	Y	Y	N	N	N	Y
14 Shumway	N	Y	N	Y	N	Y	Y	N
15 Coelho	Y	Y	N	Y	Y	Y	Y	Y
16 Panetta	Y	Y	Y	N	N	Y	Y	Y
17 *Pashayan*	Y	Y	N	Y	N	Y	Y	Y
18 *Thomas*	N	Y	Y	N	Y	N	Y	Y
19 *Lagomarsino*	N	Y	N	Y	N	Y	Y	Y
20 *Goldwater*	?	?	?	?	X	?	?	?
21 *Fiedler*	Y	Y	Y	Y	N	Y	Y	Y
22 *Moorhead*	Y	Y	N	Y	N	Y	Y	Y
23 Beilenson	N	Y	Y	Y	Y	Y	N	Y
24 Waxman	Y	Y	Y	Y	N	N	N	?
25 Roybal	Y	Y	Y	Y	Y	Y	Y	Y
26 *Rousselot*	Y	Y	N	Y	N	Y	Y	Y
27 *Dornan*	?	Y	Y	Y	N	Y	Y	Y
28 Dixon	Y	Y	Y	Y	Y	Y	Y	Y
29 Hawkins	Y	Y	?	N	Y	N	N	Y
30 Vacancy								
31 Dymally	Y	Y	Y	Y	Y	Y	N	N
32 Anderson	Y	Y	N	Y	Y	Y	Y	Y
33 *Grisham*	Y	Y	N	Y	N	Y	Y	Y
34 Lungren	N	Y	N	?	N	Y	Y	Y
35 *Dreier*	N	Y	N	N	N	Y	Y	Y
36 Brown	?	?	?	?	Y	Y	Y	Y
37 Lewis	Y	Y	Y	N	N	Y	Y	Y
38 Patterson	Y	Y	Y	Y	Y	Y	Y	Y
39 *Dannemeyer*	N	Y	N	Y	N	Y	Y	Y
40 *Badham*	N	Y	N	Y	N	Y	Y	Y
41 *Lowery*	Y	Y	Y	Y	N	Y	Y	Y
42 *Hunter*	Y	Y	Y	N	N	Y	Y	Y
43 *Burgener*	N	Y	N	Y	N	Y	Y	Y
COLORADO								
1 Schroeder	Y	Y	N	N	Y	Y	Y	N
2 Wirth	Y	Y	Y	Y	Y	Y	Y	Y
3 Kogovsek	Y	Y	Y	Y	Y	Y	Y	Y
4 *Brown*	N	Y	N	N	N	Y	Y	N

	136	137	138	139	140	141	142	143
5 *Kramer*	Y	Y	Y	N	Y	Y	Y	Y
CONNECTICUT								
1 Kennelly	Y	Y	Y	N	N	Y	N	Y
2 Gejdenson	Y	Y	Y	N	Y	N	Y	N
3 *DeNardis*	Y	Y	Y	Y	Y	Y	Y	Y
4 *McKinney*	Y	Y	Y	#	Y	Y	Y	Y
5 Ratchford	Y	Y	Y	Y	N	N	Y	Y
6 Moffett	?	?	?	?	Y	N	N	Y
DELAWARE								
AL *Evans*	Y	Y	Y	N	Y	Y	Y	Y
FLORIDA								
1 Hutto	Y	Y	N	Y	Y	Y	Y	Y
2 Fuqua	Y	Y	N	Y	Y	Y	Y	Y
3 Bennett	Y	Y	Y	Y	N	Y	Y	Y
4 Chappell	Y	Y	N	Y	Y	Y	Y	Y
5 *McCollum*	Y	Y	N	Y	N	Y	Y	Y
6 *Young*	Y	Y	N	Y	N	Y	Y	Y
7 Gibbons	Y	Y	Y	N	Y	Y	Y	Y
8 Ireland	Y	Y	N	Y	N	Y	Y	Y
9 Nelson	Y	Y	N	Y	Y	Y	Y	Y
10 *Bafalis*	Y	Y	N	Y	N	Y	Y	Y
11 Mica	Y	Y	Y	Y	Y	Y	Y	Y
12 *Shaw*	Y	Y	N	Y	N	Y	Y	Y
13 Lehman	Y	Y	Y	Y	Y	N	N	N
14 Pepper	Y	Y	Y	Y	N	N	N	Y
15 Fascell	Y	Y	Y	Y	Y	N	Y	N
GEORGIA								
1 Ginn	?	?	?	?	?	?	?	?
2 Hatcher	?	?	Y	Y	Y	Y	Y	Y
3 Brinkley	Y	Y	Y	Y	Y	Y	Y	Y
4 Levitas	Y	Y	Y	Y	Y	Y	Y	Y
5 Fowler	Y	Y	Y	Y	Y	Y	N	N
6 *Gingrich*	Y	N	N	Y	N	Y	?	Y
7 *McDonald*	N	N	N	N	N	Y	Y	Y
8 Evans	Y	N	Y	Y	Y	Y	Y	Y
9 Jenkins	Y	Y	N	Y	Y	Y	Y	Y
10 Barnard	Y	N	Y	Y	Y	Y	Y	Y
HAWAII								
1 Heftel	Y	Y	?	?	Y	Y	Y	Y
2 Akaka	?	?	Y	Y	Y	N	N	Y
IDAHO								
1 *Craig*	Y	Y	N	Y	N	Y	N	Y
2 *Hansen*	N	Y	N	Y	N	Y	N	Y
ILLINOIS								
1 Washington	Y	Y	N	Y	N	N	N	Y
2 Savage	?	?	?	Y	N	N	N	Y
3 Russo	Y	Y	Y	Y	Y	Y	Y	Y
4 *Derwinski*	N	Y	N	Y	N	Y	Y	N
5 Fary	Y	Y	Y	Y	Y	Y	Y	Y
6 *Hyde*	Y	Y	Y	Y	N	Y	Y	N
7 Collins	Y	Y	Y	Y	N	N	N	Y
8 Rostenkowski	Y	Y	Y	N	N	N	N	Y
9 Yates	Y	Y	Y	Y	?	+	N	Y
10 *Porter*	Y	Y	Y	N	Y	N	Y	Y
11 Annunzio	Y	Y	Y	Y	N	Y	N	Y
12 *Crane, P.*	N	Y	N	N	N	Y	Y	N
13 *McClory*	Y	Y	Y	Y	N	Y	Y	Y
14 *Erlenborn*	N	Y	N	Y	N	Y	Y	N
15 *Corcoran*	Y	Y	N	Y	N	Y	Y	Y
16 *Martin*	Y	N	N	Y	N	Y	Y	Y
17 *O'Brien*	Y	Y	Y	Y	N	Y	Y	Y
18 *Michel*	Y	N	N	Y	N	Y	Y	?
19 *Railsback*	Y	Y	Y	Y	N	Y	Y	Y
20 *Findley*	N	Y	N	Y	Y	Y	N	Y
21 *Madigan*	?	Y	N	Y	N	Y	?	Y
22 *Crane, D.*	N	Y	N	Y	N	Y	Y	N
23 Price	Y	Y	Y	Y	Y	Y	Y	Y
24 Simon	?	?	?	Y	Y	N	N	Y
INDIANA								
1 Benjamin	Y	Y	Y	Y	Y	Y	Y	Y
2 Fithian	?	?	?	Y	Y	Y	Y	Y
3 *Hiler*	N	Y	N	Y	N	Y	Y	Y
4 *Coats*	N	Y	N	Y	N	Y	Y	Y
5 Hillis	Y	Y	N	Y	N	Y	Y	Y
6 Evans	?	?	?	Y	Y	Y	N	Y
7 *Myers*	Y	Y	N	Y	N	Y	Y	Y
8 *Deckard*	Y	Y	Y	Y	N	Y	Y	Y
9 Hamilton	Y	Y	Y	Y	Y	Y	Y	Y
10 Sharp	Y	Y	N	Y	N	Y	Y	Y
11 Jacobs	Y	Y	N	N	Y	N	N	Y
IOWA								
1 *Leach*	Y	Y	Y	?	N	Y	Y	Y
2 *Tauke*	N	Y	N	Y	Y	Y	Y	Y
3 *Evans*	Y	Y	N	N	N	Y	Y	Y
4 *Smith*	Y	Y	Y	Y	Y	Y	Y	Y
5 *Harkin*	Y	Y	N	Y	N	N	Y	Y
6 Bedell	Y	Y	Y	Y	Y	Y	Y	Y

ND - Northern Democrats   SD - Southern Democrats

	136	137	138	139	140	141	142	143
KANSAS								
1 **Roberts**	Y	Y	N	Y	N	Y	Y	Y
2 **Jeffries**	N	Y	N	Y	N	Y	Y	Y
3 **Winn**	Y	Y	N	Y	N	Y	Y	Y
4 Glickman	N	Y	N	Y	Y	Y	Y	Y
5 **Whittaker**	Y	Y	N	Y	N	Y	Y	Y
KENTUCKY								
1 Hubbard	Y	Y	N	Y	Y	Y	Y	Y
2 Natcher	Y	Y	Y	Y	Y	Y	Y	Y
3 Mazzoli	Y	Y	Y	Y	Y	Y	Y	Y
4 **Snyder**	Y	Y	N	Y	N	Y	Y	Y
5 **Rogers**	Y	Y	N	Y	N	Y	Y	Y
6 **Hopkins**	Y	Y	N	Y	N	Y	Y	Y
7 Perkins	Y	Y	Y	Y	Y	Y	Y	Y
LOUISIANA								
1 **Livingston**	N	Y	Y	Y	N	Y	Y	Y
2 Boggs	Y	Y	Y	?	Y	Y	Y	Y
3 Tauzin	Y	Y	N	Y	Y	Y	Y	Y
4 Roemer	N	Y	N	N	N	Y	Y	Y
5 Huckaby	Y	Y	Y	Y	Y	Y	Y	Y
6 **Moore**	N	Y	N	Y	N	Y	Y	Y
7 Breaux	Y	Y	N	Y	Y	Y	Y	Y
8 Long	Y	Y	Y	Y	Y	?	Y	Y
MAINE								
1 **Emery**	Y	Y	N	Y	Y	Y	Y	Y
2 **Snowe**	Y	Y	Y	Y	Y	Y	Y	Y
MARYLAND								
1 Dyson	Y	Y	N	Y	Y	Y	Y	Y
2 Long	Y	Y	Y	?	Y	Y	Y	Y
3 Mikulski	Y	Y	Y	?	Y	N	N	Y
4 **Holt**	Y	Y	?	N	N	Y	Y	N
5 Hoyer	Y	Y	Y	Y	Y	N	N	N
6 Byron	Y	Y	N	?	Y	Y	Y	Y
7 Mitchell	Y	Y	Y	?	Y	N	?	Y
8 Barnes	Y	Y	Y	N	Y	N	N	Y
MASSACHUSETTS								
1 **Conte**	?	?	?	Y	Y	Y	Y	Y
2 Boland	Y	?	Y	Y	Y	Y	Y	N
3 Early	Y	Y	Y	Y	Y	Y	Y	N
4 Frank	?	?	Y	Y	Y	N	N	N
5 Shannon	Y	Y	Y	Y	Y	N	N	Y
6 Mavroules	Y	Y	?	Y	Y	N	N	Y
7 Markey	Y	Y	Y	Y	Y	N	N	Y
8 O'Neill								
9 Moakley	Y	Y	Y	Y	Y	Y	Y	Y
10 **Heckler**	Y	Y	Y	Y	Y	N	N	Y
11 Donnelly	Y	Y	Y	Y	Y	N	N	Y
12 Studds	Y	Y	Y	Y	Y	N	N	Y
MICHIGAN								
1 Conyers	Y	Y	Y	Y	Y	N	N	Y
2 **Pursell**	?	?	?	Y	Y	Y	Y	Y
3 Wolpe	Y	Y	Y	Y	Y	N	N	Y
4 **Siljander**	N	Y	N	Y	N	Y	Y	Y
5 **Sawyer**	Y	Y	Y	Y	Y	Y	Y	Y
6 **Dunn**	Y	Y	Y	Y	Y	Y	Y	Y
7 Kildee	Y	Y	Y	Y	Y	N	N	Y
8 Traxler	Y	Y	Y	Y	Y	Y	N	Y
9 **Vander Jagt**	N	Y	N	Y	N	Y	Y	Y
10 Albosta	Y	Y	Y	Y	Y	Y	Y	Y
11 **Davis**	Y	Y	N	Y	Y	Y	Y	Y
12 Bonior	Y	Y	Y	Y	Y	N	N	Y
13 Crockett	Y	Y	Y	?	Y	N	N	Y
14 Hertel	?	?	?	Y	Y	N	N	Y
15 Ford	Y	Y	Y	?	Y	N	?	Y
16 Dingell	Y	Y	Y	Y	Y	N	N	Y
17 Brodhead	Y	Y	Y	Y	Y	N	N	Y
18 Blanchard	?	?	?	Y	Y	N	N	Y
19 **Broomfield**	?	?	?	?	?	?	?	?
MINNESOTA								
1 **Erdahl**	Y	Y	Y	Y	N	Y	Y	Y
2 **Hagedorn**	Y	Y	Y	Y	N	Y	Y	Y
3 **Frenzel**	N	Y	N	Y	N	Y	Y	Y
4 Vento	Y	Y	Y	Y	Y	N	N	Y
5 Sabo	Y	Y	Y	Y	Y	N	N	Y
6 **Weber**	N	Y	N	Y	N	Y	Y	Y
7 **Stangeland**	Y	Y	Y	Y	N	Y	Y	Y
8 Oberstar	Y	Y	Y	Y	Y	N	N	Y
MISSISSIPPI								
1 Whitten	Y	Y	N	Y	Y	Y	Y	Y
2 Bowen	Y	Y	Y	Y	Y	Y	Y	Y
3 Montgomery	Y	Y	N	Y	Y	Y	Y	Y
4 Dowdy	?	?	?	?	#	?	?	?
5 **Lott**	Y	Y	N	Y	N	Y	Y	Y
MISSOURI								
1 Clay	?	?	?	?	?	?	?	?
2 Young	Y	Y	Y	Y	Y	Y	Y	Y
3 Gephardt	?	Y	N	?	N	Y	Y	Y

	136	137	138	139	140	141	142	143
4 Skelton	Y	Y	N	?	Y	Y	Y	Y
5 Bolling	?	?	?	?	?	?	?	?
6 **Coleman**	Y	Y	Y	Y	N	Y	Y	Y
7 **Taylor**	Y	Y	N	Y	N	Y	Y	Y
8 **Bailey**	?	?	?	?	N	Y	Y	N
9 Volkmer	Y	Y	N	Y	Y	Y	Y	Y
10 **Emerson**	Y	Y	N	N	N	Y	Y	Y
MONTANA								
1 Williams	Y	Y	N	Y	Y	N	N	Y
2 **Marlenee**	Y	Y	N	Y	N	Y	Y	Y
NEBRASKA								
1 **Bereuter**	Y	Y	N	Y	N	Y	Y	Y
2 **Daub**	Y	Y	N	Y	N	Y	Y	Y
3 **Smith**	Y	Y	N	Y	Y	Y	Y	Y
NEVADA								
AL Santini	?	?	?	?	Y	Y	N	Y
NEW HAMPSHIRE								
1 D'Amours	?	?	?	?	Y	Y	Y	Y
2 **Gregg**	Y	Y	N	Y	N	Y	Y	Y
NEW JERSEY								
1 Florio	Y	Y	Y	Y	Y	Y	Y	Y
2 Hughes	Y	Y	Y	Y	Y	Y	Y	Y
3 Howard	Y	Y	Y	Y	Y	N	N	Y
4 **Smith**	Y	Y	Y	Y	Y	N	N	Y
5 **Fenwick**	Y	Y	N	Y	Y	Y	Y	Y
6 **Forsythe**	N	Y	Y	N	N	Y	Y	Y
7 **Roukema**	Y	Y	Y	Y	Y	Y	Y	Y
8 Roe	Y	Y	Y	Y	Y	N	N	Y
9 **Hollenbeck**	Y	Y	Y	Y	Y	N	N	Y
10 Rodino	Y	Y	Y	Y	Y	N	N	Y
11 Minish	Y	Y	Y	Y	Y	N	N	Y
12 **Rinaldo**	Y	Y	Y	Y	Y	N	N	Y
13 **Courter**	Y	Y	N	Y	N	Y	Y	Y
14 Guarini	Y	Y	Y	Y	Y	N	N	Y
15 Dwyer	Y	Y	Y	Y	Y	Y	Y	Y
NEW MEXICO								
1 **Lujan**	Y	Y	N	Y	N	Y	Y	Y
2 **Skeen**	Y	Y	N	Y	N	Y	Y	Y
NEW YORK								
1 **Carney**	Y	Y	Y	Y	N	Y	Y	Y
2 Downey	Y	?	Y	Y	Y	Y	Y	Y
3 **Carman**	Y	Y	Y	Y	N	Y	Y	Y
4 **Lent**	Y	Y	Y	Y	N	Y	Y	Y
5 **McGrath**	Y	Y	Y	Y	N	Y	Y	Y
6 **LeBoutillier**	N	Y	Y	Y	N	Y	Y	Y
7 Addabbo	Y	Y	Y	?	Y	N	N	Y
8 Rosenthal	Y	Y	Y	Y	Y	N	N	Y
9 Ferraro	Y	Y	Y	Y	Y	N	N	Y
10 Biaggi	Y	Y	Y	Y	Y	N	N	Y
11 Scheuer	?	?	?	?	?	?	?	?
12 Chisholm	Y	Y	Y	?	Y	?	N	Y
13 Solarz	Y	Y	Y	Y	Y	N	N	Y
14 Richmond	Y	Y	?	Y	Y	N	N	Y
15 Zeferetti	Y	Y	Y	Y	Y	N	N	Y
16 Schumer	Y	Y	Y	?	Y	N	N	Y
17 **Molinari**	Y	Y	Y	?	N	Y	Y	Y
18 **Green**	Y	Y	Y	Y	Y	N	N	Y
19 Rangel	Y	Y	Y	?	Y	N	N	Y
20 Weiss	Y	Y	Y	?	Y	N	N	Y
21 Garcia	Y	Y	Y	Y	Y	N	N	Y
22 Bingham	Y	Y	Y	?	Y	N	N	Y
23 Peyser	Y	Y	Y	Y	Y	N	N	Y
24 Ottinger	Y	Y	Y	P	Y	N	N	Y
25 **Fish**	Y	Y	Y	?	N	Y	Y	Y
26 **Gilman**	Y	Y	Y	Y	Y	Y	N	N
27 McHugh	Y	Y	Y	?	Y	Y	Y	Y
28 Stratton	Y	Y	Y	?	?	?	?	?
29 **Solomon**	Y	Y	Y	N	N	Y	Y	Y
30 **Martin**	Y	Y	Y	Y	N	Y	Y	Y
31 **Mitchell**	Y	Y	Y	Y	N	Y	Y	Y
32 **Wortley**	Y	Y	Y	Y	Y	Y	Y	Y
33 **Lee**	N	Y	N	Y	Y	Y	Y	Y
34 **Horton**	Y	Y	Y	Y	Y	?	?	Y
35 **Conable**	N	Y	Y	?	X	?	?	Y
36 LaFalce	Y	Y	Y	Y	Y	Y	N	Y
37 Nowak	Y	Y	Y	Y	Y	Y	N	Y
38 **Kemp**	N	Y	Y	Y	N	Y	Y	Y
39 Lundine	Y	Y	Y	Y	Y	Y	Y	Y
NORTH CAROLINA								
1 Jones	Y	Y	Y	Y	Y	Y	Y	Y
2 Fountain	Y	Y	Y	?	Y	Y	Y	Y
3 Whitley	Y	Y	Y	Y	Y	Y	Y	Y
4 Andrews	Y	Y	?	Y	Y	Y	Y	Y
5 Neal	Y	Y	Y	Y	Y	Y	Y	Y
6 **Johnston**	C	Y	N	Y	N	Y	Y	Y
7 Rose	Y	Y	Y	Y	Y	Y	Y	Y
8 Hefner	Y	Y	Y	Y	Y	Y	Y	Y

	136	137	138	139	140	141	142	143
9 **Martin**	Y	Y	N	Y	N	Y	Y	Y
10 **Broyhill**	Y	Y	N	Y	N	?	?	Y
11 **Hendon**	Y	Y	N	Y	Y	Y	Y	Y
NORTH DAKOTA								
AL Dorgan	Y	Y	Y	Y	Y	Y	Y	Y
OHIO								
1 **Gradison**	N	Y	N	Y	N	Y	Y	Y
2 Luken	Y	Y	Y	Y	Y	N	N	Y
3 Hall	Y	Y	Y	Y	Y	Y	Y	Y
4 **Oxley**	Y	Y	N	Y	N	Y	Y	Y
5 **Latta**	Y	Y	N	Y	N	Y	Y	Y
6 **McEwen**	Y	Y	N	Y	N	Y	Y	Y
7 **Brown**	C	Y	?	?	?	?	?	?
8 **Kindness**	Y	Y	N	Y	N	Y	Y	Y
9 **Weber**	Y	Y	N	Y	N	Y	Y	Y
10 **Miller**	Y	Y	N	N	N	Y	Y	Y
11 **Stanton**	Y	Y	Y	Y	N	Y	Y	Y
12 Shamansky	Y	Y	Y	Y	Y	Y	Y	N
13 Pease	Y	Y	Y	Y	Y	Y	Y	Y
14 Seiberling	Y	Y	Y	Y	Y	?	N	Y
15 **Wylie**	Y	Y	N	Y	Y	Y	Y	N
16 **Regula**	Y	Y	N	Y	Y	Y	Y	Y
17 Vacancy								
18 Applegate	Y	Y	N	?	Y	Y	Y	Y
19 **Williams**	Y	Y	Y	Y	N	N	Y	Y
20 Oakar	Y	Y	Y	Y	Y	N	N	Y
21 Stokes	Y	Y	Y	Y	Y	N	N	Y
22 Eckart	Y	Y	Y	Y	Y	N	Y	Y
23 Mottl	Y	Y	N	Y	Y	Y	Y	Y
OKLAHOMA								
1 Jones	Y	Y	N	Y	Y	Y	Y	Y
2 Synar	Y	Y	Y	Y	Y	Y	Y	Y
3 Watkins	?	?	N	Y	Y	Y	Y	Y
4 McCurdy	Y	Y	N	Y	N	Y	Y	Y
5 **Edwards**	N	Y	N	?	N	Y	Y	Y
6 English	Y	Y	N	Y	N	Y	Y	Y
OREGON								
1 AuCoin	?	?	?	?	#	#	#	?
2 **Smith**	N	Y	N	Y	N	Y	Y	Y
3 Wyden	Y	Y	N	Y	Y	N	N	Y
4 Weaver	Y	Y	N	Y	Y	Y	N	Y
PENNSYLVANIA								
1 Foglietta	Y	Y	Y	Y	Y	N	N	Y
2 Gray	Y	Y	Y	Y	Y	N	N	Y
3 Smith	Y	Y	Y	Y	Y	Y	N	Y
4 **Dougherty**	Y	Y	Y	Y	Y	Y	Y	Y
5 **Schulze**	Y	Y	N	Y	Y	Y	Y	Y
6 Yatron	Y	Y	Y	Y	Y	Y	N	Y
7 Edgar	Y	Y	Y	Y	Y	N	N	Y
8 **Coyne, J.**	?	?	?	?	N	Y	Y	Y
9 **Shuster**	Y	Y	Y	Y	N	Y	Y	Y
10 **McDade**	Y	Y	Y	?	Y	Y	Y	Y
11 **Nelligan**	Y	Y	N	?	N	Y	Y	Y
12 Murtha	Y	Y	Y	Y	Y	Y	Y	Y
13 **Coughlin**	Y	Y	N	N	N	Y	Y	Y
14 Coyne, W.	Y	Y	Y	Y	Y	N	N	Y
15 **Ritter**	Y	Y	N	Y	N	Y	Y	Y
16 **Walker**	Y	Y	N	N	N	Y	Y	Y
17 Ertel	Y	Y	Y	?	?	?	?	?
18 Walgren	Y	Y	Y	Y	Y	Y	Y	Y
19 **Goodling**	Y	Y	N	N	N	?	?	?
20 Gaydos	Y	Y	N	?	Y	N	N	Y
21 Bailey	Y	Y	Y	Y	Y	Y	N	Y
22 Murphy	Y	Y	N	Y	Y	N	N	Y
23 **Clinger**	N	Y	Y	Y	N	Y	Y	Y
24 **Marks**	?	?	?	?	?	Y	Y	?
25 **Atkinson**	Y	Y	Y	Y	Y	Y	Y	Y
RHODE ISLAND								
1 St Germain	Y	Y	Y	Y	Y	N	N	Y
2 **Schneider**	Y	Y	Y	Y	Y	Y	Y	Y
SOUTH CAROLINA								
1 **Hartnett**	N	Y	N	N	N	Y	Y	Y
2 **Spence**	Y	Y	N	Y	N	Y	?	Y
3 Derrick	?	?	Y	?	Y	Y	N	Y
4 **Campbell**	?	Y	N	Y	N	Y	Y	Y
5 Holland	Y	Y	Y	Y	Y	Y	Y	?
6 **Napier**	Y	Y	Y	Y	Y	Y	Y	Y
SOUTH DAKOTA								
1 Daschle	Y	Y	Y	Y	Y	Y	Y	Y
2 **Roberts**	N	Y	N	Y	N	Y	Y	Y
TENNESSEE								
1 **Quillen**	Y	Y	N	Y	N	Y	Y	N
2 **Duncan**	Y	Y	N	Y	Y	Y	Y	Y
3 Bouquard	Y	Y	N	Y	Y	Y	Y	Y
4 Gore	Y	Y	Y	Y	Y	Y	Y	Y
5 Boner	Y	Y	N	Y	Y	Y	Y	Y
6 **Beard**	Y	Y	N	Y	N	Y	Y	Y

	136	137	138	139	140	141	142	143
7 Jones	?	?	?	?	Y	Y	Y	Y
8 Ford	Y	Y	Y	Y	Y	N	N	Y
TEXAS								
1 Hall, S.	Y	Y	N	Y	Y	Y	Y	Y
2 Wilson	Y	Y	?	Y	Y	?	?	Y
3 **Collins**	Y	Y	N	?	X	?	?	?
4 Hall, R.	Y	Y	N	Y	Y	Y	Y	Y
5 Mattox	?	?	?	Y	Y	Y	Y	Y
6 Gramm	N	Y	N	Y	N	Y	Y	Y
7 **Archer**	N	Y	N	Y	N	Y	Y	Y
8 **Fields**	N	Y	N	N	N	Y	Y	Y
9 Brooks	Y	Y	Y	Y	Y	Y	Y	Y
10 Pickle	Y	Y	N	Y	Y	Y	Y	N
11 Leath	N	Y	N	Y	Y	Y	Y	Y
12 Wright	Y	Y	Y	Y	Y	Y	?	Y
13 Hightower	Y	Y	Y	Y	Y	Y	Y	Y
14 Patman	Y	Y	N	Y	Y	Y	Y	Y
15 de la Garza	Y	Y	Y	Y	Y	Y	Y	Y
16 White	Y	Y	Y	Y	Y	Y	Y	Y
17 Stenholm	Y	Y	N	Y	Y	Y	Y	Y
18 Leland	Y	Y	Y	Y	Y	N	N	Y
19 Hance	Y	Y	N	Y	Y	Y	Y	Y
20 Gonzalez	Y	Y	N	Y	N	N	N	N
21 **Loeffler**	N	Y	N	Y	N	Y	Y	Y
22 **Paul**	N	Y	N	Y	N	Y	Y	Y
23 Kazen	Y	Y	N	Y	Y	Y	Y	N
24 Frost	?	?	Y	Y	Y	Y	N	Y
UTAH								
1 **Hansen**	Y	Y	N	Y	N	Y	Y	Y
2 **Marriott**	Y	Y	N	Y	N	Y	Y	Y
VERMONT								
AL **Jeffords**	Y	Y	Y	Y	N	Y	Y	Y
VIRGINIA								
1 **Trible**	?	?	N	Y	Y	Y	Y	Y
2 **Whitehurst**	Y	Y	N	Y	N	Y	Y	Y
3 **Bliley**	Y	Y	N	Y	N	Y	Y	Y
4 **Daniel, R.**	Y	Y	N	Y	N	Y	Y	Y
5 Daniel, D.	Y	Y	N	Y	Y	Y	Y	Y
6 **Butler**	Y	Y	N	N	N	Y	?	Y
7 **Robinson**	Y	Y	N	Y	N	Y	Y	Y
8 **Parris**	Y	Y	N	Y	Y	Y	Y	Y
9 **Wampler**	?	?	N	Y	N	Y	Y	Y
10 **Wolf**	Y	Y	N	Y	Y	Y	Y	Y
WASHINGTON								
1 **Pritchard**	Y	Y	Y	Y	N	Y	Y	Y
2 Swift	Y	Y	Y	Y	Y	Y	Y	Y
3 Bonker	Y	Y	Y	Y	Y	Y	Y	Y
4 **Morrison**	?	Y	N	Y	N	Y	Y	Y
5 Foley	Y	Y	Y	Y	Y	Y	Y	Y
6 Dicks	Y	Y	Y	Y	Y	Y	Y	Y
7 Lowry	Y	Y	Y	Y	Y	N	N	Y
WEST VIRGINIA								
1 Mollohan	?	?	Y	?	Y	Y	Y	Y
2 **Benedict**	Y	Y	N	Y	N	Y	Y	?
3 **Staton**	Y	Y	N	?	N	Y	Y	Y
4 Rahall	Y	Y	Y	Y	Y	Y	Y	?
WISCONSIN								
1 Aspin	Y	Y	Y	Y	Y	Y	Y	Y
2 Kastenmeier	Y	Y	Y	Y	Y	N	N	Y
3 **Gunderson**	Y	Y	N	Y	N	Y	Y	Y
4 Zablocki	?	?	?	?	?	?	?	?
5 Reuss	Y	Y	Y	Y	Y	Y	N	Y
6 **Petri**	Y	Y	N	Y	N	Y	Y	Y
7 Obey	Y	Y	N	Y	N	Y	Y	Y
8 **Roth**	Y	Y	Y	Y	Y	Y	Y	Y
9 **Sensenbrenner**	Y	Y	N	Y	N	Y	Y	Y
WYOMING								
AL **Cheney**	N	Y	N	Y	N	Y	Y	Y

Southern states - Ala., Ark., Fla., Ga., Ky., La., Miss., N.C., Okla., S.C., Tenn., Texas, Va.

KEY

Y   Voted for (yea).
\#   Paired for.
+   Announced for.
N   Voted against (nay).
X   Paired against.
-   Announced against.
P   Voted "present".
C   Voted "present" to avoid possible conflict of interest.
?   Did not vote or otherwise make a position known.

Democrats   *Republicans*

144. HR 6094. International Trade Commission Authorization. Ways and Means Committee amendment to remove the $25,000 cap on overtime pay for U.S. Customs Service employees. Adopted 220-178: R 35-142; D 185-36 (ND 128-18, SD 57-18), June 16, 1982.

145. HR 6094. International Trade Commission Authorization. Passage of the bill to authorize appropriations for fiscal year 1983 of $19,737,000 for the U.S. International Trade Commission, $568,801,000 for the U.S. Customs Service and $10,100,000 for the Office of the U.S. Trade Representative. Passed 337-67: R 127-54; D 210-13 (ND 142-5, SD 68-8), June 16, 1982.

146. Procedural Motion. Corcoran, R-Ill., motion to approve the House *Journal* of Wednesday, June 16. Motion agreed to 338-29: R 151-18; D 187-11 (ND 119-9, SD 68-2), June 17, 1982.

147. HR 5879. Refugee Assistance Act Amendments. Adoption of the rule (H Res 499) providing for House floor consideration of the bill to reauthorize programs that reimburse states for cash, social services and medical assistance to refugees. Adopted 388-3: R 174-1; D 214-2 (ND 140-2, SD 74-0), June 17, 1982.

148. HR 4326. Small Business Innovation Development Act. Adoption of the rule (H Res 501) providing for House floor consideration of the bill to strengthen the role of small firms in federally funded research and development. Adopted 388-6: R 173-4; D 215-2 (ND 141-2, SD 74-0), June 17, 1982.

149. HR 4326. Small Business Innovation Development Act. LaFalce, D-N.Y., motion that the House resolve itself into the Committee of the Whole for consideration of the bill to strengthen the role of small firms in federally funded research and development. Motion agreed to 383-5: R 171-2; D 212-3 (ND 137-3, SD 75-0), June 17, 1982.

150. HR 4326. Small Business Innovation Development Act. McDonald, D-Ga., amendments to exempt the Department of Defense and the Department of Energy atomic energy defense programs from the provisions of the bill. Rejected 80-295: R 44-122; D 36-173 (ND 15-122, SD 21-51), June 17, 1982.

151. HR 4326. Small Business Innovation Development Act. Waxman, D-Calif., amendment to exempt all health-related research conducted under the Department of Health and Human Services from the scope of the bill. Rejected 164-193: R 69-93; D 95-100 (ND 66-62, SD 29-38), June 17, 1982.

	144	145	146	147	148	149	150	151
ALABAMA								
1 *Edwards*	Y	Y	Y	Y	Y	Y	N	Y
2 *Dickinson*	N	Y	N	N	Y	?	Y	Y
3 Nichols	Y	Y	Y	Y	Y	Y	Y	Y
4 Bevill	Y	Y	Y	Y	Y	Y	N	Y
5 Flippo	Y	Y	Y	Y	Y	Y	N	Y
6 *Smith*	?	?	Y	Y	Y	Y	Y	Y
7 Shelby	Y	Y	Y	Y	Y	Y	Y	?
ALASKA								
AL *Young*	N	Y	Y	Y	Y	Y	N	N
ARIZONA								
1 *Rhodes*	N	Y	Y	Y	Y	Y	Y	Y
2 Udall	Y	Y	Y	Y	Y	?	N	Y
3 *Stump*	N	N	Y	Y	Y	Y	Y	N
4 *Rudd*	N	N	Y	Y	Y	Y	\#	\#
ARKANSAS								
1 Alexander	Y	Y	Y	Y	Y	Y	N	N
2 *Bethune*	N	Y	Y	Y	Y	Y	N	N
3 *Hammerschmidt*	N	Y	Y	Y	Y	Y	N	N
4 Anthony	Y	Y	Y	Y	Y	Y	N	N
CALIFORNIA								
1 *Chappie*	N	Y	Y	Y	Y	Y	N	N
2 *Clausen*	Y	Y	Y	Y	Y	Y	N	N
3 Matsui	Y	Y	Y	Y	Y	Y	N	Y
4 Fazio	Y	Y	Y	Y	Y	Y	N	Y
5 Burton, J.	?	?	?	?	Y	Y	?	?
6 Burton, P.	Y	Y	Y	Y	Y	N	N	?
7 Miller	Y	Y	Y	Y	Y	N	N	N
8 Dellums	Y	Y	Y	Y	Y	N	N	N
9 Stark	Y	Y	Y	Y	Y	N	N	?
10 Edwards	Y	Y	Y	Y	Y	Y	N	N
11 Lantos	Y	Y	Y	Y	Y	Y	Y	Y
12 *McCloskey*	N	Y	?	Y	N	N	Y	Y
13 Mineta	Y	Y	Y	Y	Y	Y	N	Y
14 *Shumway*	N	N	Y	Y	Y	Y	Y	Y
15 Coelho	Y	Y	Y	Y	Y	Y	N	Y
16 Panetta	N	Y	Y	Y	Y	Y	?	?
17 *Pashayan*	N	N	Y	Y	Y	Y	N	N
18 *Thomas*	N	Y	Y	Y	Y	Y	N	N
19 *Lagomarsino*	N	Y	Y	Y	Y	Y	N	N
20 *Goldwater*	?	?	?	?	?	?	?	?
21 *Fiedler*	N	Y	?	Y	Y	Y	N	N
22 *Moorhead*	N	N	Y	Y	Y	Y	N	N
23 Beilenson	Y	Y	Y	Y	Y	Y	N	Y
24 Waxman	Y	Y	Y	Y	Y	Y	Y	Y
25 Roybal	Y	Y	Y	Y	?	Y	N	Y
26 *Rousselot*	N	Y	N	Y	Y	Y	N	N
27 *Dornan*	N	Y	?	Y	Y	Y	N	N
28 Dixon	Y	Y	?	Y	Y	Y	N	X
29 Hawkins	Y	Y	Y	Y	Y	Y	N	N
30 Vacancy								
31 Dymally	Y	Y	Y	Y	Y	Y	N	P
32 Anderson	Y	Y	Y	Y	Y	Y	N	Y
33 *Grisham*	N	N	Y	Y	Y	Y	?	?
34 *Lungren*	N	Y	Y	Y	Y	N	N	N
35 *Dreier*	N	N	Y	Y	Y	Y	N	N
36 Brown	Y	Y	Y	Y	Y	Y	N	?
37 *Lewis*	Y	Y	Y	Y	Y	Y	N	N
38 Patterson	Y	Y	Y	Y	Y	N	Y	Y
39 *Dannemeyer*	N	N	Y	Y	Y	Y	N	N
40 *Badham*	N	Y	Y	Y	Y	Y	Y	?
41 *Lowery*	N	Y	?	Y	Y	Y	N	N
42 *Hunter*	N	Y	Y	Y	Y	?	Y	?
43 *Burgener*	N	Y	Y	Y	Y	Y	\#	?
COLORADO								
1 Schroeder	Y	Y	N	Y	Y	Y	N	Y
2 Wirth	Y	Y	Y	Y	Y	N	N	N
3 Kogovsek	Y	Y	?	?	?	?	N	N
4 *Brown*	N	N	Y	Y	Y	N	N	Y

	144	145	146	147	148	149	150	151
5 *Kramer*	N	Y	Y	Y	Y	Y	N	N
CONNECTICUT								
1 Kennelly	Y	Y	Y	Y	Y	Y	N	Y
2 Gejdenson	?	?	N	Y	Y	Y	N	N
3 *DeNardis*	N	Y	Y	Y	Y	Y	N	?
4 *McKinney*	N	Y	Y	Y	Y	?	N	N
5 Ratchford	Y	Y	Y	Y	Y	Y	N	N
6 Moffett	?	?	?	?	?	?	?	?
DELAWARE								
AL *Evans*	N	Y	Y	Y	Y	Y	N	Y
FLORIDA								
1 Hutto	Y	Y	Y	Y	Y	Y	Y	Y
2 Fuqua	Y	Y	Y	Y	Y	Y	Y	Y
3 Bennett	N	Y	Y	Y	Y	Y	N	Y
4 Chappell	Y	Y	Y	Y	Y	Y	N	Y
5 *McCollum*	N	Y	Y	Y	Y	Y	N	N
6 *Young*	N	Y	Y	Y	Y	Y	N	N
7 Gibbons	Y	Y	Y	Y	Y	Y	?	?
8 Ireland	Y	Y	Y	Y	Y	Y	N	N
9 Nelson	Y	Y	Y	Y	Y	Y	Y	Y
10 *Bafalis*	N	Y	Y	Y	Y	Y	N	?
11 Mica	Y	Y	Y	Y	Y	Y	N	N
12 *Shaw*	N	Y	Y	Y	Y	Y	N	N
13 Lehman	Y	Y	Y	Y	Y	Y	N	Y
14 Pepper	Y	Y	Y	Y	Y	Y	N	Y
15 Fascell	Y	Y	Y	Y	Y	Y	N	N
GEORGIA								
1 Ginn	?	?	?	?	?	?	?	?
2 Hatcher	N	Y	Y	Y	Y	Y	Y	?
3 Brinkley	N	Y	Y	Y	Y	Y	Y	?
4 Levitas	Y	Y	Y	Y	Y	N	Y	Y
5 Fowler	Y	Y	Y	Y	Y	Y	N	Y
6 *Gingrich*	Y	Y	Y	Y	Y	N	N	N
7 McDonald	N	N	Y	Y	Y	Y	Y	N
8 Evans	Y	Y	Y	Y	Y	Y	N	Y
9 Jenkins	N	Y	?	?	?	?	?	?
10 Barnard	Y	Y	Y	Y	Y	Y	Y	?
HAWAII								
1 Heftel	Y	Y	?	Y	Y	Y	N	Y
2 Akaka	Y	Y	Y	Y	Y	Y	N	N
IDAHO								
1 *Craig*	N	N	Y	Y	Y	Y	?	?
2 *Hansen*	N	N	Y	?	?	?	Y	N
ILLINOIS								
1 Washington	Y	Y	N	Y	Y	Y	N	N
2 Savage	Y	Y	?	?	?	N	N	N
3 Russo	Y	Y	Y	Y	Y	Y	N	Y
4 *Derwinski*	Y	N	Y	Y	Y	Y	N	N
5 Fary	Y	Y	Y	Y	Y	Y	Y	N
6 *Hyde*	N	Y	Y	Y	Y	Y	Y	Y
7 Collins	Y	Y	Y	Y	Y	Y	N	N
8 Rostenkowski	Y	Y	Y	Y	Y	Y	N	Y
9 Yates	Y	N	Y	Y	Y	Y	N	Y
10 *Porter*	N	Y	Y	Y	Y	Y	N	Y
11 Annunzio	Y	Y	Y	Y	Y	Y	N	Y
12 *Crane, P.*	N	N	Y	Y	Y	Y	N	Y
13 *McClory*	N	Y	Y	Y	Y	Y	N	Y
14 *Erlenborn*	?	?	?	?	?	?	?	?
15 *Corcoran*	N	Y	Y	Y	Y	Y	Y	Y
16 *Martin*	N	N	Y	Y	Y	Y	N	N
17 *O'Brien*	N	Y	Y	Y	Y	Y	Y	Y
18 *Michel*	N	N	Y	Y	Y	Y	N	N
19 *Railsback*	N	N	Y	Y	Y	Y	N	Y
20 *Findley*	N	Y	Y	Y	Y	Y	N	N
21 *Madigan*	N	N	?	?	Y	Y	Y	Y
22 *Crane, D.*	N	N	Y	Y	Y	Y	Y	N
23 Price	Y	Y	Y	Y	Y	Y	N	Y
24 Simon	Y	Y	?	Y	?	Y	N	Y
INDIANA								
1 Benjamin	Y	Y	Y	Y	Y	Y	N	Y
2 Fithian	N	Y	?	Y	Y	Y	N	N
3 *Hiler*	N	Y	N	Y	Y	N	N	N
4 *Coats*	N	Y	Y	Y	Y	Y	N	N
5 *Hillis*	N	Y	Y	Y	Y	Y	?	N
6 Evans	Y	Y	?	?	?	?	?	?
7 *Myers*	N	Y	Y	Y	Y	Y	Y	Y
8 *Deckard*	N	Y	Y	Y	Y	Y	N	N
9 Hamilton	N	Y	Y	Y	Y	Y	N	Y
10 Sharp	N	Y	Y	Y	Y	Y	N	Y
11 Jacobs	Y	Y	?	Y	Y	Y	N	Y
IOWA								
1 *Leach*	N	Y	Y	Y	Y	Y	N	Y
2 *Tauke*	N	Y	Y	Y	Y	Y	N	Y
3 *Evans*	N	Y	N	Y	Y	Y	N	Y
4 Smith	Y	Y	Y	Y	Y	Y	N	Y
5 Harkin	Y	Y	N	Y	Y	Y	?	?
6 Bedell	N	Y	Y	Y	Y	Y	N	N

ND - Northern Democrats   SD - Southern Democrats

Corresponding to Congressional Record Votes 151, 152, 153, 154, 155, 156, 157, 158

	144	145	146	147	148	149	150	151
KANSAS								
1 ***Roberts***	N	N	Y	Y	Y	Y	N	N
2 ***Jeffries***	N	N	Y	Y	Y	Y	N	N
3 ***Winn***	N	N	Y	Y	Y	Y	N	N
4 Glickman	N	Y	Y	Y	Y	Y	N	N
5 ***Whittaker***	N	N	Y	Y	Y	Y	N	Y
KENTUCKY								
1 Hubbard	N	N	Y	Y	Y	Y	N	N
2 Natcher	N	Y	Y	Y	Y	Y	N	N
3 Mazzoli	N	Y	Y	Y	Y	Y	N	N
4 ***Snyder***	N	N	Y	Y	Y	Y	Y	Y
5 ***Rogers***	N	Y	Y	Y	Y	Y	N	Y
6 ***Hopkins***	N	Y	Y	Y	Y	Y	Y	Y
7 Perkins	Y	Y	Y	Y	Y	Y	N	Y
LOUISIANA								
1 ***Livingston***	Y	Y	Y	Y	Y	Y	N	Y
2 Boggs	Y	Y	Y	Y	Y	Y	N	Y
3 Tauzin	Y	Y	Y	Y	Y	Y	N	N
4 Roemer	Y	N	N	Y	Y	Y	N	N
5 Huckaby	Y	Y	Y	Y	Y	Y	N	?
6 ***Moore***	N	Y	Y	Y	Y	Y	Y	Y
7 Breaux	Y	Y	Y	Y	?	Y	N	N
8 Long	Y	Y	Y	Y	Y	Y	N	Y
MAINE								
1 ***Emery***	N	Y	Y	Y	Y	Y	N	Y
2 ***Snowe***	Y	Y	Y	Y	Y	Y	N	N
MARYLAND								
1 Dyson	Y	Y	?	Y	Y	Y	N	Y
2 Long	Y	Y	?	Y	Y	Y	N	Y
3 Mikulski	Y	Y	Y	Y	Y	Y	N	Y
4 ***Holt***	Y	Y	Y	Y	Y	Y	Y	Y
5 Hoyer	Y	Y	Y	Y	Y	Y	N	Y
6 Byron	Y	Y	Y	Y	Y	Y	Y	Y
7 Mitchell	?	?	N	Y	Y	Y	N	N
8 Barnes	Y	Y	N	Y	Y	Y	N	Y
MASSACHUSETTS								
1 ***Conte***	Y	Y	Y	Y	Y	Y	N	N
2 Boland	Y	Y	Y	Y	Y	?	N	N
3 Early	Y	Y	Y	Y	Y	Y	Y	Y
4 Frank	Y	?	Y	Y	Y	Y	N	N
5 Shannon	Y	Y	Y	Y	Y	N	Y	Y
6 Mavroules	Y	Y	Y	Y	?	Y	N	Y
7 Markey	Y	Y	Y	Y	Y	Y	N	N
8 O'Neill								
9 Moakley	Y	Y	Y	Y	Y	Y	N	N
10 ***Heckler***	Y	Y	?	Y	Y	Y	N	N
11 Donnelly	Y	Y	Y	Y	Y	Y	N	N
12 Studds	Y	Y	Y	Y	Y	Y	N	N
MICHIGAN								
1 Conyers	Y	Y	Y	N	N	N	N	Y
2 ***Pursell***	N	Y	Y	Y	Y	Y	?	?
3 Wolpe	N	Y	Y	Y	Y	Y	N	N
4 ***Siljander***	N	N	Y	Y	Y	Y	N	N
5 ***Sawyer***	N	Y	Y	Y	Y	Y	N	N
6 ***Dunn***	N	Y	Y	Y	Y	Y	N	N
7 Kildee	Y	Y	Y	Y	Y	Y	N	N
8 Traxler	Y	Y	Y	Y	Y	Y	N	N
9 ***Vander Jagt***	?	?	Y	Y	Y	Y	N	N
10 Albosta	Y	Y	Y	Y	Y	Y	N	Y
11 ***Davis***	Y	Y	Y	Y	Y	Y	Y	Y
12 Bonior	Y	Y	Y	Y	Y	Y	?	N
13 Crockett	?	?	?	Y	Y	Y	N	N
14 Hertel	Y	Y	Y	Y	Y	Y	N	Y
15 Ford	Y	Y	?	Y	Y	Y	N	Y
16 Dingell	Y	Y	Y	N	N	N	Y	Y
17 Brodhead	Y	Y	Y	Y	Y	Y	N	Y
18 Blanchard	?	Y	?	?	?	?	?	?
19 ***Broomfield***	?	?	?	?	?	?	?	Y
MINNESOTA								
1 ***Erdahl***	N	Y	Y	Y	Y	Y	N	Y
2 ***Hagedorn***	N	Y	Y	Y	Y	Y	?	N
3 ***Frenzel***	N	Y	Y	Y	Y	Y	N	X
4 Vento	Y	Y	Y	Y	Y	Y	N	N
5 Sabo	Y	Y	N	Y	Y	Y	N	Y
6 ***Weber***	N	N	Y	Y	Y	Y	N	X
7 ***Stangeland***	N	Y	Y	Y	Y	Y	N	N
8 Oberstar	Y	Y	Y	Y	Y	Y	N	N
MISSISSIPPI								
1 Whitten	N	Y	?	Y	Y	Y	N	N
2 Bowen	Y	Y	Y	Y	Y	Y	N	N
3 Montgomery	N	N	Y	Y	Y	Y	Y	N
4 Dowdy	?	?	?	?	?	?	?	?
5 ***Lott***	N	Y	?	?	Y	Y	N	N
MISSOURI								
1 Clay	?	?	?	?	?	?	?	?
2 Young	Y	Y	Y	Y	Y	Y	N	Y
3 Gephardt	Y	Y	Y	Y	Y	Y	N	Y

	144	145	146	147	148	149	150	151
4 Skelton	Y	Y	Y	Y	Y	?	X	X
5 Bolling	?	?	?	?	?	?	?	?
6 ***Coleman***	Y	Y	Y	Y	Y	Y	N	Y
7 ***Taylor***	N	N	Y	Y	N	Y	Y	Y
8 ***Bailey***	N	N	N	Y	Y	Y	?	?
9 Volkmer	N	N	Y	Y	Y	Y	N	Y
10 ***Emerson***	N	N	N	Y	N	Y	N	N
MONTANA								
1 Williams	Y	Y	Y	Y	Y	?	N	N
2 ***Marlenee***	N	N	Y	Y	Y	Y	N	?
NEBRASKA								
1 ***Bereuter***	N	Y	Y	Y	Y	Y	N	N
2 ***Daub***	N	Y	Y	Y	Y	Y	N	N
3 ***Smith***	N	Y	Y	Y	Y	Y	N	N
NEVADA								
AL Santini	N	Y	?	Y	Y	Y	?	?
NEW HAMPSHIRE								
1 D'Amours	N	Y	Y	Y	Y	Y	N	N
2 ***Gregg***	N	N	Y	Y	Y	?	N	?
NEW JERSEY								
1 Florio	Y	Y	Y	Y	Y	Y	N	?
2 Hughes	Y	Y	Y	Y	Y	Y	N	N
3 Howard	Y	Y	Y	Y	Y	Y	N	N
4 ***Smith***	N	Y	Y	Y	Y	Y	N	N
5 ***Fenwick***	-	Y	Y	Y	Y	Y	N	N
6 ***Forsythe***	N	Y	N	Y	Y	Y	N	N
7 ***Roukema***	N	Y	Y	Y	Y	Y	?	#
8 Roe	Y	Y	Y	Y	Y	Y	N	N
9 ***Hollenbeck***	Y	Y	Y	Y	Y	Y	?	Y
10 Rodino	Y	Y	Y	Y	Y	Y	N	Y
11 Minish	Y	Y	Y	Y	Y	Y	N	Y
12 ***Rinaldo***	Y	Y	Y	Y	Y	Y	N	Y
13 ***Courter***	N	Y	Y	?	Y	Y	N	N
14 Guarini	Y	Y	Y	Y	Y	Y	N	N
15 Dwyer	Y	Y	Y	Y	Y	Y	N	Y
NEW MEXICO								
1 ***Lujan***	N	N	Y	Y	Y	Y	N	N
2 ***Skeen***	N	N	Y	Y	Y	Y	N	N
NEW YORK								
1 ***Carney***	Y	Y	?	?	?	?	#	#
2 Downey	Y	Y	Y	Y	Y	Y	N	N
3 ***Carman***	Y	Y	Y	Y	Y	Y	N	N
4 ***Lent***	Y	Y	Y	Y	Y	Y	N	Y
5 ***McGrath***	?	Y	Y	Y	Y	Y	N	N
6 ***LeBoutillier***	N	?	N	Y	Y	Y	N	N
7 Addabbo	Y	Y	Y	Y	Y	Y	N	X
8 Rosenthal	Y	Y	Y	Y	Y	Y	?	?
9 Ferraro	Y	Y	Y	Y	Y	Y	N	Y
10 Biaggi	Y	Y	?	?	?	?	?	#
11 Scheuer	?	?	?	?	?	Y	N	Y
12 Chisholm	Y	Y	?	?	?	?	?	?
13 Solarz	Y	Y	Y	Y	Y	Y	Y	N
14 Richmond	?	Y	?	?	?	?	X	?
15 Zeferetti	Y	Y	Y	Y	Y	Y	N	#
16 Schumer	Y	Y	Y	Y	Y	Y	N	Y
17 ***Molinari***	Y	Y	Y	Y	Y	Y	N	N
18 ***Green***	N	Y	Y	Y	Y	Y	N	N
19 Rangel	Y	Y	Y	Y	Y	Y	N	X
20 Weiss	Y	Y	Y	Y	Y	Y	N	N
21 Garcia	Y	Y	?	Y	Y	Y	N	Y
22 Bingham	Y	Y	Y	Y	Y	Y	N	N
23 Peyser	?	?	Y	Y	Y	Y	N	?
24 Ottinger	Y	Y	P	Y	Y	Y	N	Y
25 ***Fish***	N	Y	Y	Y	Y	Y	X	Y
26 ***Gilman***	Y	Y	Y	Y	Y	Y	N	Y
27 McHugh	Y	Y	Y	Y	Y	Y	N	Y
28 Stratton	?	?	?	?	?	?	#	?
29 ***Solomon***	N	N	N	Y	Y	Y	Y	N
30 ***Martin***	Y	Y	Y	Y	Y	Y	N	N
31 ***Mitchell***	N	Y	Y	Y	Y	Y	?	?
32 ***Wortley***	Y	Y	Y	Y	Y	Y	N	N
33 ***Lee***	N	N	Y	Y	Y	Y	N	N
34 ***Horton***	Y	Y	Y	Y	Y	Y	N	Y
35 ***Conable***	N	Y	Y	Y	Y	Y	N	Y
36 LaFalce	Y	Y	Y	Y	Y	Y	N	N
37 Nowak	Y	Y	Y	Y	Y	Y	N	N
38 ***Kemp***	Y	Y	?	?	?	?	?	?
39 Lundine	N	Y	Y	Y	Y	Y	N	N
NORTH CAROLINA								
1 Jones	Y	Y	?	Y	Y	Y	N	N
2 Fountain	N	Y	?	Y	Y	Y	N	Y
3 Whitley	Y	Y	Y	Y	Y	Y	N	N
4 Andrews	Y	Y	Y	Y	Y	Y	Y	Y
5 Neal	N	Y	Y	Y	Y	Y	N	Y
6 ***Johnston***	N	N	N	Y	Y	N	Y	N
7 Rose	Y	Y	Y	Y	Y	Y	N	Y
8 Hefner	?	Y	Y	Y	Y	Y	N	N

	144	145	146	147	148	149	150	151
9 ***Martin***	N	Y	Y	Y	Y	Y	N	Y
10 ***Broyhill***	N	N	Y	Y	Y	Y	N	Y
11 ***Hendon***	N	N	N	Y	Y	Y	N	Y
NORTH DAKOTA								
AL Dorgan	Y	Y	Y	Y	Y	Y	N	N
OHIO								
1 ***Gradison***	Y	Y	Y	Y	Y	Y	N	Y
2 Luken	Y	N	?	?	?	?	?	?
3 Hall	Y	Y	Y	?	Y	?	N	N
4 ***Oxley***	Y	Y	Y	Y	Y	Y	N	N
5 ***Latta***	N	Y	Y	Y	Y	Y	Y	N
6 ***McEwen***	Y	Y	Y	Y	Y	?	N	Y
7 ***Brown***	?	?	?	?	?	?	?	?
8 ***Kindness***	N	N	Y	Y	Y	Y	Y	Y
9 ***Weber***	Y	Y	Y	Y	Y	Y	N	N
10 ***Miller***	N	Y	?	Y	Y	Y	Y	Y
11 ***Stanton***	N	Y	Y	Y	Y	Y	N	N
12 Shamansky	N	Y	Y	Y	Y	Y	N	?
13 Pease	N	Y	Y	Y	Y	Y	N	Y
14 Seiberling	Y	Y	Y	Y	Y	Y	N	N
15 ***Wylie***	N	N	Y	Y	Y	Y	N	?
16 ***Regula***	N	Y	Y	Y	Y	Y	N	N
17 Vacancy								
18 Applegate	Y	Y	?	Y	Y	Y	N	Y
19 ***Williams***	N	Y	Y	Y	Y	Y	N	N
20 Oakar	Y	Y	Y	Y	Y	Y	N	Y
21 Stokes	Y	Y	Y	Y	Y	Y	N	N
22 Eckart	Y	Y	Y	Y	Y	Y	N	N
23 Mottl	N	N	Y	Y	Y	Y	?	Y
OKLAHOMA								
1 Jones	N	Y	Y	Y	Y	Y	Y	N
2 Synar	Y	Y	Y	Y	Y	Y	N	N
3 Watkins	N	N	Y	?	Y	Y	Y	N
4 McCurdy	Y	Y	Y	Y	Y	Y	Y	N
5 ***Edwards***	N	N	?	?	?	?	?	?
6 English	N	Y	Y	Y	Y	Y	Y	N
OREGON								
1 AuCoin	?	?	?	?	?	?	X	#
2 ***Smith***	N	N	N	Y	Y	Y	Y	?
3 Wyden	Y	Y	Y	Y	Y	Y	N	Y
4 Weaver	Y	N	Y	Y	Y	Y	N	Y
PENNSYLVANIA								
1 Foglietta	Y	Y	Y	Y	Y	Y	N	Y
2 Gray	Y	Y	Y	Y	Y	Y	N	N
3 Smith	N	Y	?	?	?	?	?	?
4 ***Dougherty***	Y	Y	Y	Y	Y	Y	Y	Y
5 ***Schulze***	N	Y	?	?	?	?	?	X
6 Yatron	Y	Y	Y	Y	Y	Y	N	Y
7 Edgar	Y	Y	N	Y	Y	Y	?	?
8 ***Coyne, J.***	?	?	?	?	?	?	N	N
9 ***Shuster***	N	Y	Y	Y	Y	Y	N	N
10 ***McDade***	Y	Y	Y	Y	Y	Y	N	N
11 ***Nelligan***	N	Y	Y	Y	Y	Y	?	N
12 Murtha	Y	Y	Y	Y	Y	?	Y	?
13 ***Coughlin***	N	Y	Y	Y	Y	Y	N	Y
14 Coyne, W.	Y	Y	Y	Y	Y	Y	N	Y
15 ***Ritter***	N	N	Y	Y	Y	Y	N	N
16 ***Walker***	N	N	N	Y	Y	Y	N	N
17 Ertel	?	?	?	?	?	?	?	?
18 Walgren	Y	Y	Y	Y	Y	Y	N	Y
19 ***Goodling***	+	+	N	Y	?	Y	N	N
20 Gaydos	Y	Y	Y	Y	Y	Y	N	Y
21 Bailey	Y	Y	Y	Y	Y	Y	N	N
22 Murphy	N	Y	?	Y	Y	Y	Y	Y
23 ***Clinger***	N	Y	Y	Y	Y	Y	Y	Y
24 ***Marks***	?	Y	?	?	?	?	?	?
25 ***Atkinson***	Y	Y	?	Y	Y	Y	N	Y
RHODE ISLAND								
1 St Germain	Y	Y	Y	Y	Y	Y	N	Y
2 ***Schneider***	N	Y	Y	Y	Y	Y	N	Y
SOUTH CAROLINA								
1 ***Hartnett***	?	Y	N	Y	Y	Y	Y	Y
2 ***Spence***	N	Y	Y	Y	Y	Y	Y	Y
3 Derrick	N	Y	Y	Y	Y	Y	N	N
4 ***Campbell***	N	Y	Y	Y	Y	Y	N	N
5 Holland	?	?	?	?	?	?	?	?
6 ***Napier***	N	Y	Y	Y	Y	Y	Y	N
SOUTH DAKOTA								
1 Daschle	Y	Y	Y	Y	Y	Y	N	N
2 ***Roberts***	N	Y	Y	Y	Y	Y	N	N
TENNESSEE								
1 ***Quillen***	N	N	Y	Y	N	Y	Y	Y
2 ***Duncan***	N	Y	Y	Y	Y	Y	Y	N
3 Bouquard	N	Y	Y	Y	Y	Y	Y	Y
4 Gore	Y	Y	Y	Y	Y	Y	N	N
5 Boner	Y	Y	Y	Y	Y	Y	N	N
6 ***Beard***	N	Y	?	?	?	?	#	#

	144	145	146	147	148	149	150	151
7 Jones	Y	Y	Y	Y	Y	Y	N	N
8 Ford	Y	Y	Y	Y	Y	Y	N	N
TEXAS								
1 Hall, S.	Y	Y	Y	Y	Y	Y	Y	Y
2 Wilson	Y	Y	?	Y	Y	Y	N	Y
3 ***Collins***	?	?	?	?	?	?	X	X
4 Hall, R.	Y	Y	Y	Y	Y	Y	N	Y
5 Mattox	Y	Y	Y	Y	Y	Y	N	N
6 Gramm	Y	N	Y	Y	Y	Y	Y	Y
7 ***Archer***	N	N	Y	Y	Y	Y	N	N
8 ***Fields***	Y	N	N	Y	Y	Y	N	N
9 Brooks	Y	Y	Y	Y	Y	Y	N	Y
10 Pickle	Y	Y	Y	Y	Y	Y	N	Y
11 Leath	Y	Y	Y	Y	Y	Y	?	?
12 Wright	Y	Y	Y	Y	Y	Y	N	Y
13 Hightower	Y	Y	Y	Y	Y	Y	N	N
14 Patman	Y	Y	Y	Y	Y	Y	N	N
15 de la Garza	Y	Y	Y	Y	Y	Y	N	?
16 White	Y	Y	Y	Y	Y	Y	Y	N
17 Stenholm	Y	N	N	Y	Y	Y	N	N
18 Leland	Y	Y	?	Y	Y	Y	N	N
19 Hance	Y	Y	Y	Y	Y	Y	N	Y
20 Gonzalez	Y	Y	Y	Y	Y	Y	N	N
21 ***Loeffler***	Y	N	Y	Y	Y	Y	N	N
22 ***Paul***	N	N	Y	Y	Y	Y	N	N
23 Kazen	Y	Y	Y	Y	Y	Y	N	N
24 Frost	Y	Y	Y	Y	Y	Y	N	Y
UTAH								
1 ***Hansen***	N	N	N	Y	Y	Y	Y	N
2 ***Marriott***	N	Y	Y	Y	Y	Y	N	N
VERMONT								
AL ***Jeffords***	Y	Y	Y	Y	Y	Y	?	?
VIRGINIA								
1 ***Trible***	?	Y	Y	Y	Y	Y	Y	N
2 ***Whitehurst***	N	Y	Y	Y	Y	Y	Y	Y
3 ***Bliley***	N	N	Y	Y	Y	Y	Y	Y
4 ***Daniel, R.***	N	N	Y	Y	Y	Y	Y	Y
5 Daniel, D.	N	N	Y	Y	Y	Y	Y	Y
6 ***Butler***	N	N	N	Y	Y	Y	N	Y
7 ***Robinson***	N	N	Y	Y	Y	Y	Y	N
8 ***Parris***	Y	Y	Y	Y	Y	Y	N	Y
9 ***Wampler***	N	Y	Y	Y	Y	Y	Y	Y
10 ***Wolf***	Y	Y	Y	Y	Y	Y	N	N
WASHINGTON								
1 ***Pritchard***	N	Y	Y	Y	Y	Y	N	Y
2 Swift	Y	Y	Y	Y	Y	Y	N	Y
3 Bonker	Y	Y	Y	Y	Y	Y	N	N
4 ***Morrison***	N	Y	Y	Y	Y	Y	N	Y
5 Foley	Y	Y	Y	Y	Y	Y	N	Y
6 Dicks	Y	Y	Y	Y	Y	Y	N	N
7 Lowry	Y	Y	Y	Y	Y	Y	N	Y
WEST VIRGINIA								
1 Mollohan	Y	Y	?	Y	Y	Y	Y	#
2 ***Benedict***	N	Y	Y	Y	Y	Y	N	Y
3 ***Staton***	N	Y	Y	Y	Y	Y	N	N
4 Rahall	?	?	Y	Y	Y	Y	N	Y
WISCONSIN								
1 Aspin	Y	Y	?	Y	Y	Y	N	N
2 Kastenmeier	Y	Y	Y	Y	Y	Y	N	N
3 ***Gunderson***	N	N	Y	Y	Y	Y	N	N
4 Zablocki	?	?	?	?	?	?	?	N
5 Reuss	N	Y	Y	Y	Y	Y	?	N
6 ***Petri***	N	Y	Y	Y	Y	Y	N	N
7 Obey	Y	Y	Y	Y	Y	Y	?	?
8 ***Roth***	N	Y	Y	Y	Y	Y	N	N
9 ***Sensenbrenner***	N	N	Y	Y	Y	Y	Y	Y
WYOMING								
AL ***Cheney***	N	N	Y	Y	Y	Y	Y	Y

Southern states - Ala., Ark., Fla., Ga., Ky., La., Miss., N.C., Okla., S.C., Tenn., Texas, Va.

152. Procedural Motion. Emerson, R-Mo., motion to approve the House *Journal* of Monday, June 21. Motion agreed to 361-26: R 162-13; D 199-13 (ND 128-12, SD 71-1), June 22, 1982.

153. S Con Res 92. First Budget Resolution, Fiscal 1983. Jones, D-Okla., motion to approve the substitute resolution, agreed to by Senate-House conferees but reported in technical disagreement, to set budget targets for the fiscal year ending Sept. 30, 1983, as follows: budget authority, $822.39 billion; outlays, $769.8 billion; revenues, $665.9 billion; deficit, $103.9 billion. The resolution also set preliminary goals for fiscal 1984-85, revised budget levels for fiscal 1982 and included reconciliation instructions requiring House and Senate committees to recommend legislative savings to meet the budget targets. Motion agreed to 210-208: R 156-32; D 54-176 (ND 14-141, SD 40-35), June 22, 1982.

154. HR 5879. Refugee Assistance Act Reauthorization. Passage of the bill to reauthorize for one year refugee assistance programs established in 1980 and to place new conditions on refugee eligibility for public assistance. Passed 357-58: R 162-25; D 195-33 (ND 135-19, SD 60-14), June 22, 1982.

155. HR 4326. Small Business Innovation Development Act. Fuqua, D-Fla., amendment to eliminate the mandatory set-asides and require certain federal agencies to reserve a portion of their research and development budgets for small firms, while allowing Congress to decide through the authorization and appropriations process the actual amount spent on small businesses. Rejected 118-290: R 37-143; D 81-147 (ND 48-104, SD 33-43), June 22, 1982.

156. HR 4326. Small Business Innovation Development Act. O'Brien, R-Ill., amendment to exempt the National Institutes of Health from the set-aside provisions of the bill. Rejected 169-228: R 66-113; D 103-115 (ND 69-75, SD 34-40), June 22, 1982.

157. Procedural Motion. Corcoran, R-Ill., motion to approve the House *Journal* of Tuesday, June 22. Motion agreed to 340-34: R 156-18; D 184-16 (ND 115-14, SD 69-2), June 23, 1982.

158. HR 4326. Small Business Innovation Development Act. LaFalce, D-N.Y, motion that the House resolve itself into the Committee of the Whole for consideration of the bill to strengthen the role of small, innovative firms in federally funded research and development. Motion agreed to 389-2: R 177-0; D 212-2 (ND 140-2, SD 72-0), June 23, 1982.

159. HR 4326. Small Business Innovation Development Act. Passage of the bill to strengthen the role of small, innovative firms in federally funded research and development. Passed 353-57: R 158-27; D 195-30 (ND 129-21, SD 66-9), June 23, 1982.

KEY

Y	Voted for (yea).
#	Paired for.
+	Announced for.
N	Voted against (nay).
X	Paired against.
-	Announced against.
P	Voted "present".
C	Voted "present" to avoid possible conflict of interest.
?	Did not vote or otherwise make a position known.

Democrats **Republicans**

	152	153	154	155	156	157	158	159
ALABAMA								
1 Edwards	Y	Y	Y	N	Y	Y	Y	N
2 Dickinson	N	Y	Y	Y	Y	N	Y	N
3 Nichols	Y	Y	Y	Y	Y	Y	Y	Y
4 Bevill	Y	Y	Y	N	N	Y	Y	Y
5 Flippo	Y	Y	Y	Y	Y	Y	Y	Y
6 Smith	Y	Y	N	N	N	Y	Y	Y
7 Shelby	Y	Y	N	N	Y	Y	Y	Y
ALASKA								
AL Young	N	Y	Y	?	N	N	Y	Y
ARIZONA								
1 Rhodes	?	#	?	?	?	?	?	?
2 Udall	Y	N	Y	Y	?	Y	Y	Y
3 Stump	Y	Y	N	Y	Y	Y	Y	N
4 Rudd	Y	Y	Y	N	N	Y	Y	N
ARKANSAS								
1 Alexander	Y	N	Y	N	Y	Y	Y	Y
2 Bethune	Y	Y	Y	N	N	?	Y	Y
3 Hammerschmidt	Y	Y	Y	N	N	Y	Y	Y
4 Anthony	Y	Y	Y	N	Y	Y	?	Y
CALIFORNIA								
1 Chappie	Y	N	Y	Y	N	Y	Y	Y
2 Clausen	Y	Y	Y	N	N	Y	Y	Y
3 Matsui	Y	N	Y	Y	Y	Y	Y	Y
4 Fazio	Y	N	Y	Y	Y	Y	Y	N
5 Burton, J.	Y	N	Y	N	?	?	Y	Y
6 Burton, P.	Y	N	Y	N	Y	?	Y	Y
7 Miller	Y	N	Y	N	?	Y	Y	Y
8 Dellums	Y	N	N	N	N	Y	Y	Y
9 Stark	Y	N	Y	N	Y	Y	Y	Y
10 Edwards	Y	N	Y	N	Y	Y	Y	Y
11 Lantos	Y	N	Y	Y	Y	Y	Y	N
12 McCloskey	?	Y	Y	Y	Y	Y	Y	N
13 Mineta	Y	N	Y	Y	Y	Y	Y	N
14 Shumway	Y	Y	Y	Y	Y	Y	Y	N
15 Coelho	Y	N	Y	Y	Y	Y	Y	Y
16 Panetta	Y	Y	N	Y	Y	Y	Y	?
17 Pashayan	Y	Y	Y	N	N	Y	Y	Y
18 Thomas	Y	Y	Y	N	N	Y	Y	N
19 Lagomarsino	Y	Y	Y	N	Y	Y	Y	Y
20 Goldwater	?	Y	Y	N	?	Y	Y	Y
21 Fiedler	Y	Y	N	N	Y	Y	Y	Y
22 Moorhead	Y	Y	Y	N	N	Y	Y	Y
23 Beilenson	Y	N	Y	Y	Y	Y	Y	N
24 Waxman	Y	N	Y	Y	Y	Y	Y	N
25 Roybal	Y	N	Y	N	Y	Y	Y	Y
26 Rousselot	Y	N	Y	N	N	?	Y	Y
27 Dornan	Y	Y	Y	N	N	Y	Y	Y
28 Dixon	Y	N	Y	N	Y	Y	Y	Y
29 Hawkins	Y	N	N	N	N	Y	Y	Y
30 Vacancy								
31 Dymally	Y	N	Y	N	Y	Y	Y	Y
32 Anderson	Y	N	Y	N	Y	Y	Y	Y
33 Grisham	Y	N	N	Y	?	Y	Y	Y
34 Lungren	Y	Y	Y	N	Y	Y	Y	Y
35 Dreier	Y	Y	Y	N	N	N	Y	Y
36 Brown	?	N	Y	Y	Y	N	Y	N
37 Lewis	Y	Y	Y	N	N	Y	Y	Y
38 Patterson	Y	N	Y	Y	Y	Y	Y	Y
39 Dannemeyer	Y	N	Y	N	N	Y	N	Y
40 Badham	?	Y	Y	Y	N	Y	Y	N
41 Lowery	Y	Y	Y	N	Y	Y	Y	Y
42 Hunter	Y	Y	Y	N	Y	Y	Y	Y
43 Burgener	Y	Y	Y	Y	Y	Y	?	N
COLORADO								
1 Schroeder	N	N	Y	N	Y	N	Y	Y
2 Wirth	Y	N	Y	N	Y	N	Y	Y
3 Kogovsek	Y	N	N	N	Y	Y	Y	Y
4 Brown	Y	N	N	N	Y	Y	Y	Y

	152	153	154	155	156	157	158	159
5 Kramer	Y	N	Y	N	N	Y	Y	Y
CONNECTICUT								
1 Kennelly	?	N	Y	N	Y	Y	Y	Y
2 Gejdenson	N	N	Y	N	N	N	Y	Y
3 DeNardis	Y	Y	N	N	N	Y	?	+
4 McKinney	Y	Y	Y	N	N	Y	?	?
5 Ratchford	Y	N	Y	N	Y	N	Y	Y
6 Moffett	?	N	Y	N	Y	?	Y	Y
DELAWARE								
AL Evans	Y	Y	Y	N	Y	Y	Y	Y
FLORIDA								
1 Hutto	Y	Y	Y	Y	Y	Y	Y	Y
2 Fuqua	Y	Y	Y	Y	Y	Y	Y	N
3 Bennett	Y	Y	Y	Y	N	Y	Y	Y
4 Chappell	Y	Y	Y	Y	N	?	Y	Y
5 McCollum	Y	Y	Y	N	N	Y	Y	Y
6 Young	Y	Y	Y	N	N	Y	Y	Y
7 Gibbons	Y	Y	Y	Y	Y	?	?	Y
8 Ireland	Y	Y	Y	N	N	Y	Y	Y
9 Nelson	Y	Y	Y	Y	Y	Y	Y	Y
10 Bafalis	?	?	?	?	?	?	?	?
11 Mica	Y	N	Y	N	N	Y	Y	Y
12 Shaw	Y	Y	Y	N	N	Y	Y	Y
13 Lehman	Y	N	Y	N	Y	Y	Y	Y
14 Pepper	Y	N	Y	Y	Y	Y	Y	Y
15 Fascell	Y	N	Y	?	Y	Y	Y	Y
GEORGIA								
1 Ginn	?	#	?	?	?	?	?	?
2 Hatcher	Y	Y	Y	N	N	Y	Y	Y
3 Brinkley	Y	N	Y	N	Y	Y	Y	Y
4 Levitas	Y	N	N	N	Y	Y	Y	Y
5 Fowler	Y	Y	Y	N	N	Y	Y	Y
6 Gingrich	Y	Y	Y	N	N	Y	Y	Y
7 McDonald	Y	N	N	Y	N	N	Y	N
8 Evans	Y	Y	Y	N	N	Y	Y	Y
9 Jenkins	Y	Y	Y	N	Y	Y	Y	Y
10 Barnard	Y	Y	Y	?	Y	Y	Y	Y
HAWAII								
1 Heftel	Y	Y	Y	N	Y	N	Y	Y
2 Akaka	Y	N	Y	N	N	Y	Y	Y
IDAHO								
1 Craig	Y	N	N	N	N	Y	Y	Y
2 Hansen	?	Y	N	N	N	Y	Y	N
ILLINOIS								
1 Washington	N	N	N	N	Y	N	Y	Y
2 Savage	?	N	N	N	N	?	?	Y
3 Russo	Y	N	Y	N	Y	Y	Y	Y
4 Derwinski	Y	Y	Y	N	N	N	Y	Y
5 Fary	Y	N	Y	N	N	Y	Y	Y
6 Hyde	Y	Y	Y	N	N	Y	Y	Y
7 Collins	Y	N	N	N	N	Y	Y	Y
8 Rostenkowski	Y	N	Y	N	Y	Y	Y	Y
9 Yates	N	N	Y	?	N	Y	N	Y
10 Porter	Y	Y	Y	N	Y	Y	Y	Y
11 Annunzio	Y	N	Y	N	N	Y	Y	Y
12 Crane, P.	Y	N	Y	N	Y	Y	Y	N
13 McClory	Y	Y	Y	Y	Y	Y	?	Y
14 Erlenborn	?	#	?	?	?	Y	Y	N
15 Corcoran	Y	Y	Y	N	Y	Y	Y	Y
16 Martin	Y	Y	Y	N	N	Y	Y	Y
17 O'Brien	Y	Y	Y	Y	Y	Y	Y	Y
18 Michel	Y	Y	Y	N	N	Y	?	Y
19 Railsback	Y	Y	Y	N	N	Y	Y	Y
20 Findley	Y	Y	Y	N	N	Y	Y	Y
21 Madigan	Y	Y	Y	N	N	Y	Y	Y
22 Crane, D.	Y	N	Y	N	Y	Y	Y	N
23 Price	Y	N	Y	Y	Y	Y	Y	Y
24 Simon	Y	X	Y	Y	?	Y	Y	Y
INDIANA								
1 Benjamin	Y	N	Y	N	N	Y	Y	Y
2 Fithian	?	?	?	?	?	?	?	?
3 Hiler	Y	Y	Y	N	N	Y	Y	Y
4 Coats	Y	Y	Y	N	N	Y	Y	Y
5 Hillis	Y	Y	Y	N	N	Y	Y	Y
6 Evans	Y	N	Y	N	N	Y	Y	Y
7 Myers	Y	Y	Y	N	Y	Y	Y	Y
8 Deckard	Y	Y	Y	N	N	Y	Y	Y
9 Hamilton	Y	Y	Y	Y	Y	Y	Y	Y
10 Sharp	Y	N	Y	N	Y	Y	Y	Y
11 Jacobs	N	N	Y	Y	Y	N	Y	N
IOWA								
1 Leach	Y	Y	Y	N	Y	Y	Y	Y
2 Tauke	Y	Y	Y	N	Y	Y	Y	Y
3 Evans	N	Y	Y	N	Y	N	Y	Y
4 Smith	Y	N	Y	N	N	P	Y	Y
5 Harkin	N	N	Y	N	N	?	Y	Y
6 Bedell	Y	Y	Y	N	N	Y	Y	Y

Corresponding to Congressional Record Votes 159, 161, 162, 163, 164, 165, 166, 167

	152	153	154	155	156	157	158	159
KANSAS								
1 ***Roberts***	Y	Y	Y	N	N	Y	Y	Y
2 ***Jeffries***	Y	N	N	Y	N	Y	Y	Y
3 ***Winn***	Y	Y	Y	N	N	Y	Y	Y
4 Glickman	Y	Y	Y	Y	N	?	Y	Y
5 ***Whittaker***	Y	Y	Y	N	Y	Y	Y	Y
KENTUCKY								
1 Hubbard	Y	N	Y	N	Y	Y	Y	N
2 Natcher	Y	N	Y	N	N	Y	Y	Y
3 Mazzoli	Y	N	Y	N	N	Y	?	Y
4 ***Snyder***	Y	N	Y	N	N	Y	Y	Y
5 ***Rogers***	Y	Y	Y	N	N	Y	Y	Y
6 ***Hopkins***	Y	N	Y	N	Y	Y	Y	N
7 Perkins	Y	N	Y	N	N	Y	Y	Y
LOUISIANA								
1 ***Livingston***	?	Y	Y	N	Y	Y	Y	Y
2 Boggs	Y	N	Y	N	Y	Y	Y	Y
3 Tauzin	Y	Y	Y	N	N	Y	Y	Y
4 Roemer	N	Y	N	N	N	N	Y	Y
5 Huckaby	Y	Y	Y	N	N	Y	Y	Y
6 ***Moore***	Y	Y	N	Y	Y	Y	Y	N
7 Breaux	Y	Y	Y	N	N	Y	Y	Y
8 Long	?	N	Y	N	Y	Y	Y	Y
MAINE								
1 ***Emery***	Y	Y	Y	N	Y	Y	Y	Y
2 ***Snowe***	Y	Y	Y	N	N	Y	Y	Y
MARYLAND								
1 Dyson	?	#	?	?	?	?	?	?
2 Long	Y	N	Y	Y	N	Y	Y	Y
3 Mikulski	?	X	?	?	?	?	Y	Y
4 ***Holt***	Y	Y	Y	N	Y	Y	Y	Y
5 Hoyer	Y	N	Y	N	Y	Y	Y	Y
6 Byron	Y	Y	Y	N	N	?	Y	Y
7 Mitchell	N	N	N	N	N	N	Y	Y
8 Barnes	N	N	Y	N	Y	N	Y	Y
MASSACHUSETTS								
1 ***Conte***	Y	Y	Y	N	N	Y	Y	Y
2 Boland	?	N	Y	N	Y	+	+	+
3 Early	Y	N	Y	Y	Y	Y	Y	N
4 Frank	Y	N	Y	N	N	Y	Y	Y
5 Shannon	Y	N	Y	Y	Y	Y	Y	N
6 Mavroules	Y	N	Y	N	N	Y	Y	Y
7 Markey	Y	N	Y	N	N	Y	Y	Y
8 O'Neill								
9 Moakley	Y	N	Y	N	N	Y	Y	Y
10 ***Heckler***	Y	N	Y	N	N	Y	Y	Y
11 Donnelly	?	X	Y	N	Y	Y	Y	Y
12 Studds	Y	N	Y	N	N	Y	Y	Y
MICHIGAN								
1 Conyers	Y	N	N	Y	Y	Y	Y	N
2 ***Pursell***	Y	Y	Y	N	Y	Y	Y	Y
3 Wolpe	Y	N	Y	N	N	N	Y	Y
4 ***Siljander***	Y	Y	Y	N	N	?	?	?
5 ***Sawyer***	Y	Y	Y	N	N	Y	Y	Y
6 ***Dunn***	Y	Y	Y	N	N	Y	Y	Y
7 Kildee	Y	N	Y	N	N	Y	Y	Y
8 Traxler	Y	N	Y	N	N	?	Y	Y
9 ***Vander Jagt***	Y	Y	Y	?	N	Y	Y	Y
10 Albosta	Y	N	Y	N	Y	Y	Y	Y
11 ***Davis***	Y	N	Y	N	N	Y	Y	Y
12 Bonior	Y	N	?	?	N	?	Y	Y
13 Crockett	?	X	N	N	Y	?	Y	Y
14 Hertel	Y	N	Y	N	N	Y	Y	Y
15 Ford	?	N	Y	Y	Y	?	?	Y
16 Dingell	Y	N	Y	Y	Y	Y	?	N
17 Brodhead	Y	N	Y	Y	Y	Y	Y	Y
18 Blanchard	Y	N	?	?	?	?	?	?
19 ***Broomfield***	Y	Y	Y	N	N	Y	Y	Y
MINNESOTA								
1 ***Erdahl***	Y	Y	Y	N	Y	Y	Y	Y
2 ***Hagedorn***	Y	Y	Y	N	N	Y	Y	Y
3 ***Frenzel***	Y	Y	Y	N	Y	Y	?	Y
4 Vento	N	N	Y	N	Y	N	Y	Y
5 Sabo	N	N	Y	Y	Y	N	Y	N
6 ***Weber***	Y	Y	Y	N	N	N	Y	Y
7 ***Stangeland***	Y	Y	Y	N	N	Y	Y	Y
8 Oberstar	Y	N	Y	N	N	Y	Y	Y
MISSISSIPPI								
1 Whitten	Y	N	Y	Y	Y	Y	Y	Y
2 Bowen	?	?	?	Y	Y	Y	Y	Y
3 Montgomery	Y	Y	Y	Y	N	Y	Y	?
4 Dowdy	?	?	?	?	N	Y	Y	Y
5 ***Lott***	Y	Y	Y	N	N	Y	Y	Y
MISSOURI								
1 Clay	N	N	Y	N	N	?	?	?
2 Young	Y	Y	Y	Y	N	Y	Y	Y
3 Gephardt	Y	Y	Y	N	Y	Y	Y	N
4 Skelton	Y	Y	Y	N	N	Y	Y	Y
5 Bolling	?	?	?	?	?	?	?	?
6 ***Coleman***	Y	Y	Y	N	Y	Y	Y	Y
7 ***Taylor***	Y	Y	Y	N	Y	Y	Y	N
8 ***Bailey***	Y	Y	Y	N	Y	Y	Y	Y
9 Volkmer	Y	N	Y	Y	Y	Y	Y	Y
10 ***Emerson***	N	Y	Y	N	N	N	Y	Y
MONTANA								
1 Williams	?	N	Y	N	N	Y	Y	Y
2 ***Marlenee***	Y	Y	N	N	N	Y	Y	Y
NEBRASKA								
1 ***Bereuter***	Y	Y	Y	N	N	Y	Y	Y
2 ***Daub***	Y	Y	Y	N	N	Y	Y	Y
3 ***Smith***	Y	Y	Y	N	N	Y	Y	Y
NEVADA								
AL Santini	Y	N	N	N	N	?	Y	Y
NEW HAMPSHIRE								
1 D'Amours	Y	N	Y	N	N	Y	Y	Y
2 ***Gregg***	Y	Y	Y	N	N	Y	Y	Y
NEW JERSEY								
1 Florio	Y	N	Y	N	Y	Y	?	Y
2 Hughes	Y	N	Y	N	N	Y	Y	Y
3 Howard	Y	N	Y	N	N	Y	Y	Y
4 ***Smith***	Y	N	Y	N	?	Y	Y	Y
5 ***Fenwick***	Y	Y	Y	N	N	Y	Y	Y
6 ***Forsythe***	?	Y	Y	N	?	N	Y	Y
7 ***Roukema***	Y	Y	Y	Y	Y	Y	Y	Y
8 Roe	Y	N	Y	N	N	Y	Y	Y
9 ***Hollenbeck***	Y	N	Y	N	Y	Y	Y	Y
10 Rodino	Y	N	Y	Y	Y	Y	Y	Y
11 Minish	Y	N	Y	N	?	Y	Y	Y
12 ***Rinaldo***	Y	N	Y	Y	?	?	Y	Y
13 ***Courter***	Y	Y	Y	N	N	Y	Y	Y
14 Guarini	Y	N	Y	N	N	Y	Y	Y
15 Dwyer	Y	N	Y	Y	Y	Y	Y	Y
NEW MEXICO								
1 ***Lujan***	Y	Y	Y	N	N	Y	Y	Y
2 ***Skeen***	Y	Y	Y	N	N	Y	Y	Y
NEW YORK								
1 ***Carney***	Y	Y	Y	Y	N	Y	Y	Y
2 Downey	Y	N	Y	N	N	Y	Y	Y
3 ***Carman***	Y	Y	Y	N	N	Y	Y	Y
4 ***Lent***	Y	Y	Y	N	N	Y	Y	Y
5 ***McGrath***	N	Y	Y	N	N	Y	?	Y
6 ***LeBoutillier***	Y	N	Y	N	Y	N	Y	Y
7 Addabbo	Y	N	Y	N	N	Y	Y	Y
8 Rosenthal	Y	N	Y	N	Y	?	?	Y
9 Ferraro	Y	N	Y	N	?	Y	Y	Y
10 Biaggi	?	N	Y	Y	Y	Y	Y	Y
11 Scheuer	Y	N	Y	Y	Y	Y	Y	N
12 Chisholm	?	N	N	?	?	?	?	Y
13 Solarz	Y	N	Y	Y	?	Y	Y	Y
14 Richmond	Y	N	Y	?	N	?	?	Y
15 Zeferetti	Y	N	Y	N	N	Y	Y	Y
16 Schumer	?	N	N	N	Y	?	?	?
17 ***Molinari***	Y	Y	Y	N	N	Y	Y	Y
18 ***Green***	Y	N	Y	N	N	?	Y	Y
19 Rangel	Y	N	N	N	Y	Y	Y	Y
20 Weiss	Y	N	N	N	N	+	+	+
21 Garcia	?	N	?	?	?	?	?	?
22 Bingham	Y	N	Y	Y	Y	Y	Y	Y
23 Peyser	Y	N	Y	?	?	Y	Y	Y
24 Ottinger	P	N	Y	Y	Y	P	P	Y
25 ***Fish***	Y	Y	Y	N	Y	Y	Y	Y
26 ***Gilman***	Y	N	Y	N	Y	Y	Y	Y
27 McHugh	Y	N	Y	Y	N	?	Y	Y
28 Stratton	Y	Y	Y	Y	Y	Y	N	N
29 ***Solomon***	N	N	Y	Y	N	N	?	Y
30 ***Martin***	Y	Y	Y	?	?	Y	Y	Y
31 ***Mitchell***	Y	Y	Y	N	Y	Y	Y	Y
32 ***Wortley***	N	Y	Y	Y	Y	Y	Y	Y
33 ***Lee***	Y	N	Y	N	N	Y	Y	Y
34 ***Horton***	Y	Y	Y	N	Y	Y	Y	Y
35 ***Conable***	Y	Y	Y	N	Y	Y	Y	Y
36 LaFalce	Y	N	Y	N	N	?	Y	Y
37 Nowak	Y	N	Y	N	N	Y	Y	Y
38 ***Kemp***	Y	N	Y	N	N	?	Y	Y
39 Lundine	Y	Y	Y	N	N	Y	Y	Y
NORTH CAROLINA								
1 Jones	Y	Y	Y	Y	N	Y	Y	Y
2 Fountain	Y	Y	Y	Y	Y	?	Y	N
3 Whitley	Y	N	Y	N	N	Y	Y	Y
4 Andrews	Y	N	Y	Y	Y	Y	Y	N
5 Neal	Y	N	Y	N	Y	Y	Y	Y
6 ***Johnston***	N	Y	N	N	N	N	Y	Y
7 Rose	?	Y	Y	N	N	?	Y	Y
8 Hefner	Y	Y	Y	N	N	Y	Y	Y
9 ***Martin***	Y	Y	N	Y	Y	?	Y	N
10 ***Broyhill***	Y	Y	?	?	Y	Y	Y	Y
11 ***Hendon***	Y	Y	N	N	Y	Y	Y	Y
NORTH DAKOTA								
AL Dorgan	Y	N	Y	N	N	Y	Y	Y
OHIO								
1 ***Gradison***	Y	Y	Y	Y	Y	Y	Y	N
2 Luken	Y	N	Y	N	N	Y	Y	Y
3 Hall	Y	N	Y	N	N	Y	Y	Y
4 ***Oxley***	Y	Y	Y	N	N	Y	Y	Y
5 ***Latta***	Y	Y	N	N	N	Y	Y	Y
6 ***McEwen***	Y	Y	Y	N	N	Y	Y	Y
7 ***Brown***	Y	Y	Y	?	?	?	?	?
8 ***Kindness***	Y	Y	Y	Y	N	Y	Y	Y
9 ***Weber***	Y	Y	Y	N	N	Y	Y	Y
10 ***Miller***	N	Y	N	Y	Y	N	Y	Y
11 ***Stanton***	Y	Y	Y	N	N	Y	Y	Y
12 Shamansky	Y	N	Y	N	N	Y	Y	Y
13 Pease	Y	N	Y	N	Y	Y	?	Y
14 Seiberling	?	N	Y	N	N	Y	Y	Y
15 ***Wylie***	Y	Y	Y	N	Y	Y	Y	Y
16 ***Regula***	Y	Y	Y	N	N	Y	Y	Y
17 Vacancy								
18 Applegate	?	N	?	N	Y	?	Y	Y
19 ***Williams***	Y	Y	Y	N	N	Y	Y	Y
20 Oakar	Y	N	Y	N	N	Y	Y	Y
21 Stokes	Y	N	N	N	N	Y	Y	Y
22 Eckart	Y	N	Y	N	N	Y	Y	Y
23 Mottl	Y	N	N	Y	Y	Y	Y	Y
OKLAHOMA								
1 Jones	Y	Y	Y	Y	Y	Y	Y	Y
2 Synar	Y	N	Y	N	N	Y	Y	Y
3 Watkins	Y	N	Y	N	N	Y	Y	Y
4 McCurdy	Y	Y	Y	Y	N	Y	Y	Y
5 ***Edwards***	?	N	Y	Y	N	Y	Y	Y
6 English	Y	N	Y	N	N	Y	Y	Y
OREGON								
1 AuCoin	Y	N	Y	N	Y	?	Y	Y
2 ***Smith***	Y	Y	N	N	N	Y	Y	Y
3 Wyden	Y	N	Y	N	Y	Y	Y	Y
4 Weaver	Y	N	Y	N	N	Y	Y	Y
PENNSYLVANIA								
1 Foglietta	Y	N	Y	N	Y	Y	Y	Y
2 Gray	Y	N	N	N	N	Y	Y	Y
3 Smith	Y	N	Y	N	N	?	Y	Y
4 ***Dougherty***	Y	Y	Y	Y	Y	?	Y	N
5 ***Schulze***	Y	Y	Y	N	N	Y	Y	Y
6 Yatron	Y	N	Y	N	N	Y	Y	Y
7 Edgar	N	N	Y	N	N	Y	Y	Y
8 ***Coyne, J.***	Y	Y	Y	N	N	Y	Y	Y
9 ***Shuster***	Y	Y	Y	N	N	Y	Y	Y
10 ***McDade***	?	Y	Y	N	N	?	Y	Y
11 ***Nelligan***	Y	Y	Y	N	N	Y	Y	Y
12 Murtha	Y	N	Y	Y	N	Y	Y	Y
13 ***Coughlin***	N	Y	Y	N	N	N	Y	?
14 Coyne, W.	Y	N	Y	Y	Y	Y	Y	N
15 ***Ritter***	Y	Y	Y	N	N	Y	Y	Y
16 ***Walker***	N	Y	Y	N	N	N	Y	Y
17 Ertel	?	N	Y	N	?	?	?	?
18 Walgren	Y	N	Y	Y	Y	Y	Y	Y
19 ***Goodling***	N	Y	Y	N	N	N	Y	Y
20 Gaydos	Y	N	Y	Y	Y	Y	Y	Y
21 Bailey	Y	Y	Y	N	Y	Y	Y	Y
22 Murphy	Y	N	N	Y	N	N	Y	Y
23 ***Clinger***	Y	Y	Y	Y	Y	Y	Y	Y
24 ***Marks***	?	N	Y	?	?	?	?	Y
25 ***Atkinson***	Y	Y	Y	N	Y	Y	Y	Y
RHODE ISLAND								
1 St Germain	Y	N	Y	N	N	Y	Y	Y
2 ***Schneider***	Y	N	Y	N	Y	?	Y	Y
SOUTH CAROLINA								
1 ***Hartnett***	Y	Y	N	N	N	Y	?	Y
2 ***Spence***	Y	Y	Y	N	Y	Y	Y	Y
3 Derrick	?	N	Y	N	N	?	Y	Y
4 ***Campbell***	Y	Y	Y	N	N	Y	Y	Y
5 Holland	Y	Y	Y	N	?	?	?	?
6 ***Napier***	Y	Y	Y	N	N	Y	Y	Y
SOUTH DAKOTA								
1 Daschle	Y	N	Y	N	N	Y	Y	Y
2 ***Roberts***	?	Y	Y	N	N	?	Y	Y
TENNESSEE								
1 ***Quillen***	Y	Y	N	Y	Y	Y	Y	N
2 ***Duncan***	Y	Y	Y	N	N	Y	Y	Y
3 Bouquard	Y	N	N	Y	Y	Y	Y	N
4 Gore	Y	N	Y	N	N	Y	Y	Y
5 Boner	Y	N	N	N	Y	Y	Y	Y
6 ***Beard***	Y	Y	N	Y	N	Y	Y	Y
7 Jones	Y	N	N	N	N	Y	Y	Y
8 Ford	Y	N	N	N	N	Y	Y	Y
TEXAS								
1 Hall, S.	Y	Y	Y	N	N	Y	Y	Y
2 Wilson	?	?	?	?	?	?	?	?
3 ***Collins***	Y	N	N	N	N	Y	Y	Y
4 Hall, R.	Y	Y	Y	Y	Y	Y	Y	Y
5 Mattox	Y	N	Y	N	N	Y	Y	Y
6 Gramm	Y	Y	N	Y	Y	Y	Y	N
7 ***Archer***	?	N	N	N	N	Y	Y	Y
8 ***Fields***	N	Y	N	N	N	N	Y	Y
9 Brooks	Y	N	Y	Y	Y	Y	Y	N
10 Pickle	Y	Y	Y	Y	Y	Y	Y	Y
11 Leath	Y	Y	N	Y	Y	Y	Y	Y
12 Wright	Y	N	Y	N	Y	Y	Y	Y
13 Hightower	Y	Y	Y	N	N	Y	Y	Y
14 Patman	Y	Y	Y	N	N	Y	Y	Y
15 de la Garza	Y	N	Y	Y	Y	Y	Y	Y
16 White	Y	Y	Y	Y	N	N	Y	Y
17 Stenholm	Y	Y	N	N	N	Y	Y	Y
18 Leland	Y	N	N	N	Y	Y	Y	Y
19 Hance	Y	Y	N	Y	Y	Y	Y	Y
20 Gonzalez	Y	N	P	Y	N	Y	Y	Y
21 ***Loeffler***	Y	Y	N	N	N	Y	Y	Y
22 ***Paul***	Y	N	N	N	N	Y	Y	N
23 Kazen	Y	N	Y	N	N	Y	Y	Y
24 Frost	Y	N	N	N	Y	Y	Y	Y
UTAH								
1 ***Hansen***	Y	Y	N	N	N	Y	Y	Y
2 ***Marriott***	Y	Y	Y	N	N	Y	Y	Y
VERMONT								
AL ***Jeffords***	Y	Y	Y	N	Y	Y	Y	Y
VIRGINIA								
1 ***Trible***	Y	Y	Y	N	Y	Y	Y	Y
2 ***Whitehurst***	Y	Y	Y	Y	Y	Y	Y	N
3 ***Bliley***	Y	Y	Y	Y	?	Y	Y	N
4 ***Daniel, R.***	Y	Y	Y	Y	Y	Y	Y	Y
5 Daniel, D.	Y	Y	Y	Y	N	Y	?	N
6 ***Butler***	?	Y	Y	Y	Y	N	Y	N
7 ***Robinson***	Y	Y	Y	Y	N	Y	Y	N
8 ***Parris***	Y	Y	Y	Y	Y	Y	Y	Y
9 ***Wampler***	Y	Y	Y	Y	Y	Y	Y	N
10 ***Wolf***	Y	Y	Y	N	N	Y	Y	Y
WASHINGTON								
1 ***Pritchard***	Y	Y	Y	?	Y	Y	Y	Y
2 Swift	Y	N	Y	Y	Y	Y	N	Y
3 Bonker	Y	N	Y	N	N	Y	Y	Y
4 ***Morrison***	Y	Y	Y	N	Y	Y	Y	Y
5 Foley	Y	N	Y	Y	Y	Y	Y	Y
6 Dicks	Y	N	Y	N	Y	Y	Y	Y
7 Lowry	Y	N	Y	Y	Y	N	Y	Y
WEST VIRGINIA								
1 Mollohan	Y	N	Y	N	?	?	?	?
2 ***Benedict***	Y	Y	Y	N	Y	Y	Y	Y
3 ***Staton***	Y	Y	Y	N	N	Y	Y	Y
4 Rahall	Y	N	Y	N	Y	Y	Y	Y
WISCONSIN								
1 Aspin	Y	Y	Y	Y	N	Y	Y	N
2 Kastenmeier	Y	N	N	Y	Y	Y	Y	Y
3 ***Gunderson***	Y	Y	Y	N	N	Y	Y	Y
4 Zablocki	Y	N	Y	N	N	Y	Y	Y
5 Reuss	Y	N	Y	N	N	Y	Y	Y
6 ***Petri***	Y	N	Y	N	N	Y	Y	Y
7 Obey	Y	N	Y	Y	Y	Y	Y	N
8 ***Roth***	?	N	Y	N	N	Y	Y	Y
9 ***Sensenbrenner***	Y	N	Y	Y	Y	Y	Y	N
WYOMING								
AL ***Cheney***	Y	Y	N	N	Y	Y	Y	N

Southern states - Ala., Ark., Fla., Ga., Ky., La., Miss., N.C., Okla., S.C., Tenn., Texas, Va.

160. HR 6631. Relief for Lebanon. Passage of the bill to authorize $50 million in emergency aid to relieve suffering in Lebanon resulting from the June 6 invasion by Israel. Passed 334-70: R 136-44; D 198-26 (ND 143-7, SD 55-19), June 23, 1982. A "yea" was a vote supporting the president's position.

161. S Con Res 98. Thailand's Bicentennial. Adoption of the resolution to congratulate Thailand on the Rattanakosin Bicentennial, the 200th year of the Charki Dynasty. Adopted 398-1: R 182-1; D 216-0 (ND 144-0, SD 72-0), June 23, 1982.

162. HR 6337. Energy Emergency Preparedness. Marks, R-Pa., amendment to require the president to fill the Strategic Petroleum Reserve at the rate of 200,000 barrels of petroleum products per day until the reserve has reached the level of 750 million barrels, and to require that at least 140 million barrels be stored in new steel tanks. Rejected 110-282: R 46-134; D 64-148 (ND 53-88, SD 11-60), June 23, 1982. A "nay" was a vote supporting the president's position.

163. HR 6337. Energy Emergency Preparedness. Passage of the bill to set a minimum fill rate for the Strategic Petroleum Reserve of 200,000 barrels of petroleum products per day until the reserve has reached the level of 500 million barrels of oil, to extend until June 30, 1985, the immunity from antitrust laws granted oil companies that share information with the International Energy Agency, and to require the president to report to Congress on various aspects of the administration's plans for dealing with an energy emergency. Passed 396-3: R 181-3; D 215-0 (ND 143-0, SD 72-0), June 23, 1982.

164. Procedural Motion. Gregg, R-N.H., motion to approve the House *Journal* of Wednesday, June 23. Motion agreed to 331-34: R 151-24; D 180-10 (ND 120-9, SD 60-1), June 24, 1982.

165. HR 5922. Urgent Supplemental Appropriations, Fiscal 1982. Passage, over President Reagan's June 24 veto, of the bill to provide supplemental appropriations of $8,924,835,000 and to rescind previous appropriations of $5,678,120,000. Rejected 253-151: R 53-131; D 200-20 (ND 148-1, SD 52-19), June 24, 1982. A two-thirds majority of those present and voting (270 in this case) of both houses is required to override a veto. A "nay" was a vote supporting the president's position.

166. HR 6682. Urgent Supplemental Appropriations, Fiscal 1982. Passage of the bill to provide supplemental appropriations of $5,924,835,000 and to rescind previous appropriations of $5,678,120,000. Passed 267-106: R 86-87; D 181-19 (ND 127-6, SD 54-13), June 24, 1982. The president had requested $4,579,679,000 in new budget authority and $7,750,269,165 in rescissions.

167. HR 6685. Urgent Supplemental Appropriations, Fiscal 1982. Passage of the bill to provide supplemental appropriations of $4,524,123,000 and to rescind previous appropriations of $4,098,640,000. Passed 342-25: R 153-18; D 189-7 (ND 125-5, SD 64-2), June 24, 1982. The president had requested $4,579,679,000 in new budget authority and $7,750,269,165 in rescissions.

KEY

Y Voted for (yea).
Paired for.
+ Announced for.
N Voted against (nay).
X Paired against.
- Announced against.
P Voted "present".
C Voted "present" to avoid possible conflict of interest.
? Did not vote or otherwise make a position known.

Democrats **Republicans**

	160	161	162	163	164	165	166	167
ALABAMA								
1 Edwards	Y	Y	N	Y	Y	N	N	Y
2 Dickinson	Y	Y	N	Y	N	N	?	?
3 Nichols	Y	?	Y	Y	Y	Y	Y	Y
4 Bevill	Y	Y	N	Y	Y	Y	Y	Y
5 Flippo	N	Y	Y	Y	Y	Y	Y	Y
6 Smith	N	Y	Y	N	N	N	N	Y
7 Shelby	N	Y	Y	Y	?	Y	Y	Y
ALASKA								
AL Young	N	Y	?	?	?	?	#	?
ARIZONA								
1 Rhodes	?	?	?	?	?	X	X	?
2 Udall	Y	Y	N	Y	Y	Y	Y	Y
3 Stump	N	Y	N	Y	?	?	?	?
4 Rudd	N	Y	N	Y	Y	N	N	Y
ARKANSAS								
1 Alexander	Y	Y	?	?	?	Y	Y	Y
2 Bethune	N	Y	Y	N	Y	N	N	Y
3 Hammerschmidt	N	Y	N	Y	Y	Y	N	Y
4 Anthony	Y	Y	N	Y	Y	Y	?	?
CALIFORNIA								
1 Chappie	Y	Y	N	Y	Y	N	N	Y
2 Clausen	Y	Y	N	Y	Y	Y	Y	Y
3 Matsui	Y	Y	N	Y	Y	Y	Y	Y
4 Fazio	Y	Y	N	Y	Y	Y	Y	Y
5 Burton, J.	?	?	?	?	?	Y	?	?
6 Burton, P.	Y	Y	N	Y	Y	Y	Y	Y
7 Miller	Y	Y	N	Y	Y	Y	Y	Y
8 Dellums	Y	Y	N	Y	?	Y	Y	Y
9 Stark	Y	Y	N	Y	Y	Y	Y	Y
10 Edwards	Y	Y	N	Y	?	Y	Y	Y
11 Lantos	Y	Y	N	Y	Y	Y	Y	Y
12 McCloskey	Y	Y	N	Y	Y	N	N	Y
13 Mineta	Y	Y	N	Y	Y	Y	Y	Y
14 Shumway	N	Y	N	Y	Y	N	N	Y
15 Coelho	Y	Y	N	Y	Y	Y	Y	?
16 Panetta	Y	Y	N	Y	Y	Y	Y	Y
17 Pashayan	Y	Y	N	Y	Y	N	N	Y
18 Thomas	Y	Y	N	Y	Y	N	N	Y
19 Lagomarsino	Y	Y	N	Y	Y	N	N	Y
20 Goldwater	N	Y	?	Y	?	N	X	?
21 Fiedler	Y	Y	N	Y	Y	Y	Y	Y
22 Moorhead	N	Y	N	Y	Y	N	N	Y
23 Beilenson	Y	Y	N	Y	Y	Y	Y	Y
24 Waxman	Y	Y	Y	Y	Y	Y	?	Y
25 Roybal	Y	Y	N	Y	Y	Y	Y	Y
26 Rousselot	?	Y	?	?	N	N	N	Y
27 Dornan	Y	Y	N	N	N	N	N	Y
28 Dixon	Y	Y	N	Y	Y	Y	Y	Y
29 Hawkins	Y	Y	N	Y	Y	Y	Y	Y
30 Vacancy								
31 Dymally	Y	Y	N	Y	Y	Y	Y	Y
32 Anderson	Y	Y	N	Y	Y	Y	N	Y
33 Grisham	?	Y	Y	Y	Y	X	?	?
34 Lungren	Y	Y	N	Y	Y	N	N	Y
35 Dreier	N	Y	N	Y	N	N	N	Y
36 Brown	Y	?	?	N	Y	Y	Y	Y
37 Lewis	?	Y	N	Y	Y	N	N	Y
38 Patterson	Y	Y	N	Y	Y	N	Y	Y
39 Dannemeyer	N	Y	N	N	N	N	N	Y
40 Badham	Y	Y	N	Y	Y	N	N	Y
41 Lowery	Y	Y	N	Y	?	N	N	Y
42 Hunter	Y	Y	N	Y	Y	N	N	Y
43 Burgener	Y	Y	N	Y	Y	N	N	Y
COLORADO								
1 Schroeder	Y	Y	N	Y	N	Y	Y	N
2 Wirth	Y	Y	N	Y	Y	Y	Y	Y
3 Kogovsek	Y	Y	N	Y	Y	Y	Y	Y
4 Brown	N	Y	N	N	Y	N	Y	Y

	160	161	162	163	164	165	166	167
5 Kramer	Y	Y	N	Y	Y	Y	Y	Y
CONNECTICUT								
1 Kennelly	Y	Y	Y	Y	Y	Y	Y	Y
2 Gejdenson	Y	Y	N	Y	N	Y	Y	Y
3 DeNardis	Y	Y	Y	Y	Y	Y	Y	Y
4 McKinney	Y	Y	N	Y	?	Y	Y	Y
5 Ratchford	Y	Y	N	Y	N	Y	Y	Y
6 Moffett	Y	?	?	?	?	#	?	?
DELAWARE								
AL Evans	Y	Y	N	Y	Y	N	Y	Y
FLORIDA								
1 Hutto	Y	Y	N	Y	?	?	Y	Y
2 Fuqua	Y	Y	N	Y	Y	N	Y	Y
3 Bennett	Y	Y	N	Y	Y	N	N	Y
4 Chappell	Y	Y	N	Y	?	N	N	Y
5 McCollum	?	?	N	Y	Y	N	N	Y
6 Young	Y	Y	N	Y	Y	N	N	Y
7 Gibbons	N	Y	?	Y	Y	N	N	Y
8 Ireland	Y	Y	N	Y	?	N	N	Y
9 Nelson	Y	Y	N	Y	Y	Y	-	-
10 Bafalis	Y	Y	N	Y	Y	N	N	Y
11 Mica	Y	Y	N	Y	P	Y	Y	Y
12 Shaw	Y	Y	N	Y	Y	N	Y	Y
13 Lehman	Y	Y	N	Y	?	Y	Y	Y
14 Pepper	Y	Y	Y	Y	Y	Y	Y	Y
15 Fascell	Y	Y	N	Y	Y	Y	Y	Y
GEORGIA								
1 Ginn	?	?	?	?	?	?	?	?
2 Hatcher	N	?	?	?	?	?	Y	Y
3 Brinkley	Y	Y	N	Y	Y	Y	Y	Y
4 Levitas	Y	Y	N	Y	Y	Y	Y	Y
5 Fowler	Y	Y	N	Y	Y	Y	Y	Y
6 Gingrich	N	Y	N	Y	Y	N	Y	Y
7 McDonald	N	Y	N	Y	N	N	N	N
8 Evans	Y	Y	N	Y	?	N	Y	Y
9 Jenkins	Y	Y	N	Y	Y	Y	Y	Y
10 Barnard	N	Y	?	?	?	?	?	?
HAWAII								
1 Heftel	N	Y	N	Y	?	Y	N	Y
2 Akaka	N	Y	N	Y	Y	Y	Y	Y
IDAHO								
1 Craig	N	Y	N	Y	Y	N	N	Y
2 Hansen	N	Y	N	Y	Y	N	N	Y
ILLINOIS								
1 Washington	Y	Y	Y	Y	?	Y	Y	Y
2 Savage	Y	P	N	Y	Y	?	?	?
3 Russo	Y	Y	Y	Y	Y	Y	Y	Y
4 Derwinski	Y	Y	N	Y	Y	N	?	?
5 Fary	Y	Y	N	Y	Y	Y	Y	Y
6 Hyde	Y	Y	N	Y	Y	N	N	Y
7 Collins	Y	Y	N	Y	Y	Y	Y	Y
8 Rostenkowski	Y	Y	N	Y	Y	Y	Y	Y
9 Yates	Y	Y	N	Y	Y	Y	Y	Y
10 Porter	Y	Y	?	Y	Y	N	N	Y
11 Annunzio	Y	Y	N	Y	Y	Y	Y	Y
12 Crane, P.	N	Y	N	N	Y	N	N	N
13 McClory	Y	Y	N	Y	N	Y	N	Y
14 Erlenborn	Y	Y	Y	Y	Y	N	N	Y
15 Corcoran	Y	Y	N	Y	Y	N	#	+
16 Martin	Y	Y	Y	Y	?	N	N	Y
17 O'Brien	Y	Y	Y	Y	Y	Y	Y	Y
18 Michel	Y	Y	N	Y	Y	N	N	Y
19 Railsback	Y	Y	Y	Y	Y	N	N	Y
20 Findley	Y	Y	Y	Y	?	Y	Y	Y
21 Madigan	Y	Y	Y	Y	Y	Y	Y	Y
22 Crane, D.	N	Y	N	Y	N	N	N	N
23 Price	Y	Y	N	Y	Y	Y	Y	Y
24 Simon	Y	Y	N	Y	Y	Y	Y	Y
INDIANA								
1 Benjamin	Y	Y	N	Y	Y	Y	Y	Y
2 Fithian	?	?	?	?	Y	Y	Y	Y
3 Hiler	Y	Y	N	Y	N	Y	N	Y
4 Coats	Y	Y	N	Y	N	N	N	Y
5 Hillis	Y	Y	Y	Y	Y	N	N	Y
6 Evans	Y	Y	Y	?	Y	Y	Y	Y
7 Myers	Y	Y	N	Y	Y	N	N	Y
8 Deckard	Y	Y	N	Y	Y	N	N	Y
9 Hamilton	Y	Y	N	Y	Y	Y	Y	Y
10 Sharp	Y	Y	N	Y	Y	Y	?	Y
11 Jacobs	Y	Y	N	Y	N	Y	Y	Y
IOWA								
1 Leach	Y	Y	N	Y	?	Y	Y	Y
2 Tauke	Y	Y	N	Y	Y	Y	Y	?
3 Evans	Y	Y	N	Y	N	N	Y	Y
4 Smith	Y	Y	N	Y	Y	Y	Y	Y
5 Harkin	Y	Y	N	Y	N	Y	Y	?
6 Bedell	Y	Y	N	Y	Y	Y	Y	Y

ND - Northern Democrats   SD - Southern Democrats

Corresponding to Congressional Record Votes 168, 169, 171, 172, 173, 174, 175, 176

	160	161	162	163	164	165	166	167
KANSAS								
1 ***Roberts***	N	Y	N	Y	Y	N	N	Y
2 ***Jeffries***	N	Y	N	Y	Y	N	N	Y
3 ***Winn***	Y	Y	N	Y	?	Y	Y	Y
4 Glickman	Y	Y	N	Y	Y	Y	Y	Y
5 ***Whittaker***	Y	Y	N	Y	Y	N	Y	Y
KENTUCKY								
1 Hubbard	N	Y	Y	Y	Y	Y	N	Y
2 Natcher	Y	Y	Y	Y	Y	Y	Y	Y
3 Mazzoli	Y	Y	N	Y	Y	Y	Y	Y
4 ***Snyder***	Y	Y	N	Y	Y	N	N	Y
5 ***Rogers***	Y	Y	N	Y	Y	N	Y	Y
6 ***Hopkins***	N	Y	N	Y	Y	Y	Y	Y
7 Perkins	Y	Y	Y	Y	Y	Y	Y	Y
LOUISIANA								
1 ***Livingston***	N	Y	N	Y	Y	N	Y	Y
2 Boggs	Y	Y	N	Y	Y	Y	Y	Y
3 Tauzin	N	Y	N	Y	Y	Y	N	Y
4 Roemer	N	Y	N	Y	N	N	N	Y
5 Huckaby	Y	Y	N	Y	Y	Y	Y	Y
6 ***Moore***	N	Y	N	Y	Y	N	N	Y
7 Breaux	Y	Y	N	Y	Y	N	Y	Y
8 Long	Y	Y	N	Y	Y	Y	Y	Y
MAINE								
1 ***Emery***	Y	Y	Y	Y	Y	Y	Y	Y
2 ***Snowe***	Y	Y	N	Y	Y	Y	Y	N
MARYLAND								
1 Dyson	?	?	?	?	?	Y	Y	Y
2 Long	Y	Y	Y	Y	?	Y	Y	Y
3 Mikulski	Y	Y	Y	Y	Y	Y	Y	Y
4 ***Holt***	Y	Y	N	Y	Y	N	N	Y
5 Hoyer	Y	Y	N	Y	N	Y	Y	Y
6 Byron	Y	Y	N	Y	Y	Y	Y	Y
7 Mitchell	Y	P	Y	Y	?	Y	?	?
8 Barnes	Y	Y	N	Y	N	Y	Y	Y
MASSACHUSETTS								
1 ***Conte***	Y	Y	N	Y	Y	N	Y	N
2 Boland	+	+	+	+	Y	Y	Y	Y
3 Early	Y	Y	N	Y	Y	Y	Y	Y
4 Frank	Y	Y	Y	Y	Y	Y	Y	?
5 Shannon	Y	Y	N	Y	Y	Y	Y	Y
6 Mavroules	Y	Y	N	Y	Y	Y	Y	Y
7 Markey	Y	Y	N	Y	Y	Y	Y	Y
8 O'Neill								
9 Moakley	Y	Y	Y	Y	Y	Y	Y	?
10 ***Heckler***	Y	Y	Y	Y	Y	Y	Y	N
11 Donnelly	Y	Y	N	Y	Y	Y	Y	Y
12 Studds	Y	Y	N	Y	Y	Y	Y	Y
MICHIGAN								
1 Conyers	Y	Y	N	Y	?	Y	Y	N
2 ***Pursell***	Y	Y	Y	Y	Y	N	Y	N
3 Wolpe	Y	Y	N	Y	Y	Y	Y	Y
4 ***Siljander***	?	?	?	?	?	?	?	?
5 ***Sawyer***	Y	Y	N	Y	Y	N	Y	Y
6 ***Dunn***	N	Y	Y	Y	Y	Y	Y	Y
7 Kildee	Y	Y	N	Y	Y	Y	Y	Y
8 Traxler	Y	Y	Y	?	Y	Y	?	?
9 ***Vander Jagt***	?	Y	N	Y	Y	Y	Y	Y
10 Albosta	Y	Y	Y	Y	Y	Y	Y	Y
11 ***Davis***	N	Y	Y	Y	Y	Y	Y	Y
12 Bonior	Y	Y	?	Y	Y	Y	Y	Y
13 Crockett	Y	?	Y	Y	?	?	?	?
14 Hertel	Y	Y	Y	Y	Y	Y	Y	Y
15 Ford	Y	Y	Y	Y	?	Y	Y	Y
16 Dingell	Y	?	N	Y	Y	Y	?	?
17 Brodhead	Y	Y	N	Y	Y	Y	N	N
18 Blanchard	?	?	?	?	?	?	?	?
19 ***Broomfield***	Y	Y	Y	Y	Y	Y	N	N
MINNESOTA								
1 ***Erdahl***	Y	Y	N	Y	Y	N	Y	Y
2 ***Hagedorn***	Y	Y	N	Y	Y	N	N	Y
3 ***Frenzel***	Y	Y	N	Y	Y	N	N	Y
4 Vento	Y	Y	N	Y	Y	Y	Y	Y
5 Sabo	Y	Y	Y	Y	N	Y	Y	Y
6 ***Weber***	Y	Y	N	Y	Y	N	N	Y
7 ***Stangeland***	?	Y	?	Y	Y	N	Y	Y
8 Oberstar	Y	Y	Y	Y	Y	Y	Y	Y
MISSISSIPPI								
1 Whitten	N	Y	N	Y	Y	Y	Y	Y
2 Bowen	?	Y	N	Y	Y	Y	Y	Y
3 Montgomery	N	Y	N	Y	Y	N	N	Y
4 Dowdy	Y	Y	N	Y	Y	Y	Y	Y
5 ***Lott***	Y	Y	N	Y	Y	N	N	Y
MISSOURI								
1 Clay	?	?	?	?	?	?	?	?
2 Young	N	Y	N	Y	Y	Y	Y	Y
3 Gephardt	N	Y	?	Y	Y	Y	Y	Y

	160	161	162	163	164	165	166	167
4 Skelton	N	Y	Y	Y	Y	Y	Y	Y
5 Bolling	?	?	?	?	?	?	?	?
6 ***Coleman***	Y	Y	N	Y	Y	Y	Y	Y
7 ***Taylor***	Y	Y	N	Y	Y	N	N	Y
8 ***Bailey***	N	Y	N	Y	Y	N	N	Y
9 Volkmer	N	Y	N	Y	Y	Y	Y	Y
10 ***Emerson***	N	Y	N	Y	N	N	Y	Y
MONTANA								
1 Williams	Y	Y	N	Y	Y	Y	Y	Y
2 ***Marlenee***	N	N	N	Y	Y	#	?	?
NEBRASKA								
1 ***Bereuter***	Y	Y	N	Y	Y	N	Y	Y
2 ***Daub***	Y	Y	N	Y	N	N	Y	Y
3 ***Smith***	Y	Y	N	Y	Y	N	Y	Y
NEVADA								
AL Santini	Y	Y	?	Y	?	Y	?	?
NEW HAMPSHIRE								
1 D'Amours	Y	Y	Y	Y	Y	Y	Y	Y
2 ***Gregg***	Y	Y	N	Y	Y	N	N	Y
NEW JERSEY								
1 Florio	Y	Y	Y	Y	Y	Y	Y	Y
2 Hughes	Y	Y	N	Y	Y	N	Y	Y
3 Howard	Y	Y	N	Y	Y	Y	Y	Y
4 ***Smith***	Y	Y	Y	Y	Y	Y	Y	Y
5 ***Fenwick***	Y	Y	N	Y	Y	N	Y	N
6 ***Forsythe***	Y	Y	N	Y	?	N	N	Y
7 ***Roukema***	Y	Y	N	Y	Y	N	Y	N
8 Roe	Y	Y	Y	Y	Y	Y	Y	Y
9 ***Hollenbeck***	Y	Y	Y	Y	Y	Y	Y	Y
10 Rodino	Y	Y	Y	Y	?	Y	Y	Y
11 Minish	Y	Y	N	Y	Y	Y	Y	Y
12 ***Rinaldo***	Y	Y	Y	Y	Y	Y	Y	Y
13 ***Courter***	Y	Y	Y	Y	Y	N	Y	Y
14 Guarini	Y	Y	N	Y	Y	Y	Y	Y
15 Dwyer	Y	Y	Y	Y	Y	Y	Y	Y
NEW MEXICO								
1 ***Lujan***	Y	Y	N	Y	Y	N	N	Y
2 ***Skeen***	Y	Y	N	Y	Y	N	N	Y
NEW YORK								
1 ***Carney***	Y	Y	N	Y	Y	N	Y	Y
2 Downey	Y	Y	N	Y	Y	Y	Y	Y
3 ***Carman***	Y	Y	N	Y	Y	N	N	Y
4 ***Lent***	Y	?	N	Y	Y	N	Y	Y
5 ***McGrath***	Y	Y	N	Y	N	N	Y	Y
6 ***LeBoutillier***	Y	Y	N	Y	N	N	N	Y
7 Addabbo	Y	Y	N	Y	?	Y	?	?
8 Rosenthal	Y	Y	N	Y	Y	Y	Y	Y
9 Ferraro	Y	Y	N	Y	Y	Y	Y	Y
10 Biaggi	Y	Y	Y	Y	Y	Y	?	?
11 Scheuer	Y	Y	N	Y	Y	Y	Y	Y
12 Chisholm	Y	Y	?	Y	?	Y	Y	Y
13 Solarz	Y	Y	Y	Y	?	Y	Y	Y
14 Richmond	Y	Y	N	Y	?	Y	?	?
15 Zeferetti	Y	Y	N	Y	Y	Y	?	?
16 Schumer	?	?	X	?	?	?	?	?
17 ***Molinari***	Y	Y	N	Y	?	?	?	?
18 ***Green***	Y	Y	N	Y	Y	N	Y	Y
19 Rangel	Y	Y	N	Y	Y	Y	Y	Y
20 Weiss	+	+	+	+	Y	Y	Y	Y
21 Garcia	Y	Y	N	Y	?	?	?	?
22 Bingham	Y	Y	N	Y	Y	Y	Y	Y
23 Peyser	Y	Y	?	?	Y	Y	Y	Y
24 Ottinger	Y	Y	Y	?	P	Y	Y	Y
25 ***Fish***	Y	Y	Y	Y	Y	Y	Y	Y
26 ***Gilman***	Y	Y	Y	Y	Y	Y	Y	N
27 McHugh	Y	Y	N	Y	Y	Y	Y	Y
28 Stratton	Y	Y	Y	Y	Y	Y	Y	?
29 ***Solomon***	N	Y	Y	Y	N	N	N	Y
30 ***Martin***	?	Y	Y	Y	Y	N	?	?
31 ***Mitchell***	Y	Y	Y	Y	Y	Y	Y	N
32 ***Wortley***	Y	Y	N	Y	Y	N	Y	Y
33 ***Lee***	Y	Y	N	Y	Y	N	Y	Y
34 ***Horton***	Y	?	N	Y	Y	Y	Y	N
35 ***Conable***	Y	Y	N	Y	Y	N	N	Y
36 LaFalce	Y	Y	N	Y	Y	Y	Y	Y
37 Nowak	Y	Y	Y	Y	Y	Y	?	?
38 ***Kemp***	Y	Y	?	Y	?	N	N	Y
39 Lundine	Y	Y	Y	Y	Y	Y	?	?
NORTH CAROLINA								
1 Jones	?	?	?	?	?	?	?	?
2 Fountain	Y	Y	N	Y	?	Y	Y	Y
3 Whitley	Y	Y	N	Y	Y	Y	?	?
4 Andrews	Y	Y	N	Y	Y	Y	Y	Y
5 Neal	Y	Y	N	Y	Y	Y	Y	Y
6 ***Johnston***	?	?	N	Y	N	N	X	?
7 Rose	Y	Y	N	Y	?	Y	Y	Y
8 Hefner	Y	Y	N	Y	Y	Y	Y	Y

	160	161	162	163	164	165	166	167
9 ***Martin***	N	Y	N	Y	Y	N	N	Y
10 ***Broyhill***	Y	Y	N	Y	Y	N	N	Y
11 ***Hendon***	N	Y	N	Y	Y	Y	Y	Y
NORTH DAKOTA								
AL Dorgan	Y	Y	N	Y	?	Y	Y	Y
OHIO								
1 ***Gradison***	Y	Y	N	Y	Y	N	N	Y
2 Luken	Y	Y	Y	Y	Y	Y	N	N
3 Hall	Y	Y	N	Y	Y	Y	Y	Y
4 ***Oxley***	Y	Y	N	Y	Y	N	N	Y
5 ***Latta***	N	Y	N	Y	Y	N	N	Y
6 ***McEwen***	Y	Y	Y	Y	Y	N	N	Y
7 ***Brown***	?	?	?	?	?	?	?	?
8 ***Kindness***	N	Y	Y	Y	Y	N	N	Y
9 ***Weber***	Y	Y	N	Y	Y	N	Y	Y
10 ***Miller***	N	Y	Y	Y	N	N	Y	Y
11 ***Stanton***	Y	Y	Y	Y	Y	N	Y	Y
12 Shamansky	Y	Y	N	Y	Y	Y	Y	Y
13 Pease	Y	Y	N	Y	Y	Y	Y	Y
14 Seiberling	Y	Y	Y	Y	Y	Y	Y	Y
15 ***Wylie***	Y	Y	N	Y	Y	N	Y	Y
16 ***Regula***	Y	Y	N	Y	Y	N	Y	Y
17 Vacancy								
18 Applegate	Y	Y	Y	Y	?	Y	Y	Y
19 ***Williams***	Y	Y	Y	Y	Y	Y	Y	Y
20 Oakar	Y	Y	Y	Y	Y	Y	Y	Y
21 Stokes	Y	Y	Y	Y	Y	Y	Y	Y
22 Eckart	Y	Y	Y	Y	Y	Y	Y	Y
23 Mottl	Y	Y	Y	Y	Y	Y	#	?
OKLAHOMA								
1 Jones	Y	Y	N	Y	Y	Y	Y	Y
2 Synar	Y	Y	N	Y	Y	Y	Y	?
3 Watkins	Y	Y	N	Y	Y	Y	Y	Y
4 McCurdy	Y	Y	N	Y	Y	N	Y	Y
5 ***Edwards***	Y	Y	N	Y	Y	N	N	Y
6 English	Y	?	N	Y	Y	N	Y	Y
OREGON								
1 AuCoin	Y	Y	N	Y	Y	Y	Y	N
2 ***Smith***	N	Y	N	Y	N	Y	N	N
3 Wyden	Y	Y	N	Y	Y	Y	Y	Y
4 Weaver	Y	Y	N	Y	Y	Y	Y	Y
PENNSYLVANIA								
1 Foglietta	Y	Y	N	Y	Y	Y	Y	Y
2 Gray	Y	Y	N	Y	?	?	?	?
3 Smith	Y	Y	Y	Y	Y	Y	Y	Y
4 ***Dougherty***	Y	Y	Y	?	Y	Y	Y	N
5 ***Schulze***	Y	Y	Y	Y	Y	Y	N	?
6 Yatron	Y	Y	Y	Y	Y	Y	?	?
7 Edgar	Y	Y	?	?	?	+	?	?
8 ***Coyne, J.***	Y	Y	Y	Y	Y	Y	Y	Y
9 ***Shuster***	N	Y	N	Y	Y	N	N	Y
10 ***McDade***	Y	Y	Y	Y	Y	Y	#	?
11 ***Nelligan***	Y	Y	?	?	Y	Y	Y	Y
12 Murtha	Y	Y	Y	Y	Y	Y	Y	Y
13 ***Coughlin***	Y	Y	Y	Y	N	N	N	Y
14 Coyne, W.	Y	?	?	?	Y	Y	Y	Y
15 ***Ritter***	Y	Y	Y	Y	Y	N	N	Y
16 ***Walker***	Y	Y	Y	Y	N	N	Y	Y
17 Ertel	?	?	?	?	?	?	N	N
18 Walgren	Y	Y	Y	Y	Y	Y	Y	Y
19 ***Goodling***	Y	Y	Y	Y	N	N	N	Y
20 Gaydos	Y	Y	Y	Y	Y	Y	Y	Y
21 Bailey	Y	Y	Y	Y	Y	Y	Y	Y
22 Murphy	Y	Y	Y	Y	Y	Y	Y	Y
23 ***Clinger***	Y	Y	Y	Y	Y	N	Y	N
24 ***Marks***	Y	Y	Y	Y	Y	Y	?	?
25 ***Atkinson***	Y	Y	Y	Y	Y	Y	Y	Y
RHODE ISLAND								
1 St Germain	Y	Y	N	Y	Y	Y	Y	Y
2 ***Schneider***	Y	Y	Y	Y	Y	Y	Y	Y
SOUTH CAROLINA								
1 ***Hartnett***	N	Y	N	Y	N	N	N	Y
2 ***Spence***	Y	Y	N	Y	Y	N	N	Y
3 Derrick	N	Y	N	Y	?	Y	Y	Y
4 ***Campbell***	Y	Y	N	Y	Y	N	N	Y
5 Holland	?	?	?	?	?	?	?	?
6 ***Napier***	Y	Y	?	Y	Y	Y	Y	Y
SOUTH DAKOTA								
1 Daschle	Y	Y	N	Y	Y	Y	Y	Y
2 ***Roberts***	N	Y	N	Y	N	N	Y	Y
TENNESSEE								
1 ***Quillen***	Y	Y	Y	Y	Y	N	?	?
2 ***Duncan***	Y	Y	N	Y	Y	Y	Y	Y
3 Bouquard	N	Y	N	Y	Y	Y	Y	Y
4 Gore	Y	Y	N	Y	Y	Y	Y	Y
5 Boner	N	Y	N	Y	Y	?	?	?
6 ***Beard***	N	Y	N	Y	Y	N	Y	Y

	160	161	162	163	164	165	166	167
7 Jones	N	Y	N	Y	Y	Y	Y	Y
8 Ford	Y	Y	N	Y	?	Y	Y	Y
TEXAS								
1 Hall, S.	Y	Y	Y	Y	Y	Y	Y	Y
2 Wilson	?	?	?	?	?	?	?	?
3 ***Collins***	N	Y	N	Y	Y	N	N	N
4 Hall, R.	N	Y	N	Y	Y	Y	Y	Y
5 Mattox	Y	Y	N	Y	Y	Y	Y	Y
6 Gramm	N	Y	N	Y	Y	N	N	Y
7 ***Archer***	N	Y	N	Y	N	N	N	Y
8 ***Fields***	N	Y	Y	Y	N	N	Y	Y
9 Brooks	Y	Y	N	Y	Y	Y	Y	Y
10 Pickle	Y	Y	N	Y	Y	N	Y	Y
11 Leath	Y	Y	N	Y	Y	N	?	?
12 Wright	Y	Y	N	Y	Y	Y	Y	Y
13 Hightower	Y	Y	N	Y	Y	Y	Y	Y
14 Patman	N	Y	N	Y	Y	Y	Y	Y
15 de la Garza	Y	Y	N	Y	Y	Y	Y	Y
16 White	Y	Y	N	Y	Y	Y	Y	Y
17 Stenholm	Y	Y	N	Y	Y	N	N	Y
18 Leland	Y	Y	N	Y	Y	Y	Y	Y
19 Hance	Y	Y	N	Y	Y	N	Y	Y
20 Gonzalez	Y	Y	Y	Y	Y	N	N	N
21 ***Loeffler***	Y	Y	N	Y	Y	N	N	Y
22 ***Paul***	N	Y	N	N	Y	N	N	N
23 Kazen	Y	Y	N	Y	Y	Y	Y	Y
24 Frost	Y	Y	Y	Y	Y	Y	Y	Y
UTAH								
1 ***Hansen***	N	Y	N	Y	Y	N	Y	Y
2 ***Marriott***	Y	Y	N	Y	Y	Y	Y	Y
VERMONT								
AL ***Jeffords***	Y	Y	Y	Y	Y	N	Y	N
VIRGINIA								
1 ***Trible***	Y	Y	N	Y	Y	Y	Y	Y
2 ***Whitehurst***	Y	Y	N	Y	Y	Y	Y	Y
3 ***Bliley***	Y	Y	N	Y	Y	N	N	Y
4 ***Daniel, R.***	Y	Y	N	Y	Y	N	N	Y
5 Daniel, D.	Y	Y	N	Y	Y	N	N	Y
6 ***Butler***	Y	Y	N	Y	N	N	N	Y
7 ***Robinson***	Y	Y	N	Y	Y	N	N	Y
8 ***Parris***	Y	Y	N	Y	Y	Y	Y	Y
9 ***Wampler***	Y	?	N	Y	Y	Y	Y	Y
10 ***Wolf***	Y	Y	N	Y	Y	Y	Y	Y
WASHINGTON								
1 ***Pritchard***	Y	Y	N	Y	Y	Y	Y	Y
2 Swift	Y	Y	N	Y	Y	Y	Y	Y
3 Bonker	Y	Y	N	Y	Y	Y	?	?
4 ***Morrison***	Y	Y	N	Y	Y	Y	Y	Y
5 Foley	Y	Y	N	Y	Y	Y	Y	Y
6 Dicks	?	?	?	?	Y	Y	Y	Y
7 Lowry	Y	Y	N	Y	Y	Y	?	?
WEST VIRGINIA								
1 Mollohan	?	?	#	?	?	?	?	?
2 ***Benedict***	Y	Y	Y	Y	?	?	?	?
3 ***Staton***	Y	Y	N	Y	Y	Y	N	Y
4 Rahall	Y	Y	Y	Y	Y	Y	Y	Y
WISCONSIN								
1 Aspin	Y	Y	N	Y	Y	Y	Y	Y
2 Kastenmeier	Y	Y	N	Y	Y	Y	Y	Y
3 ***Gunderson***	Y	Y	N	Y	Y	Y	Y	Y
4 Zablocki	Y	Y	Y	Y	Y	Y	Y	Y
5 Reuss	Y	Y	N	Y	Y	Y	Y	Y
6 ***Petri***	N	Y	N	Y	Y	N	Y	Y
7 Obey	Y	Y	Y	Y	Y	Y	Y	Y
8 ***Roth***	Y	Y	N	Y	Y	Y	Y	Y
9 ***Sensenbrenner***	Y	Y	Y	Y	Y	N	Y	Y
WYOMING								
AL ***Cheney***	N	Y	N	Y	Y	N	?	?

Southern states - Ala., Ark., Fla., Ga., Ky., La., Miss., N.C., Okla., S.C., Tenn., Texas, Va.

168. Procedural Motion. Walker, R-Pa., motion to approve the House *Journal* of Monday, July 12. Motion agreed to 363-25: R 162-15; D 201-10 (ND 133-8, SD 68-2), July 13, 1982.

169. HR 6198. Copyright Manufacturing Clause Protection Act. Passage, over President Reagan's July 8 veto, of the bill to extend for four years the "manufacturing clause" in U.S. copyright law, which requires that English language books and periodicals by U.S. authors be printed and bound in the United States or Canada to receive full copyright protection. Passed 324-86: R 111-73; D 213-13 (ND 150-4, SD 63-9), July 13, 1982. A two-thirds majority of those present and voting (275 in this case) of both houses is required to override a veto. A "nay" was a vote supporting the president's position.

170. HR 6682. Urgent Supplemental Appropriations, Fiscal 1982. Passage, over President Reagan's June 25 veto, of the bill to provide supplemental appropriations of $5,924,835,000 and to rescind previous appropriations of $5,678,120,000. Rejected 242-169: R 39-146; D 203-23 (ND 150-2, SD 53-21), July 13, 1982. A two-thirds majority of those present and voting (274 in this case) of both houses is required to override a veto. A "nay" was a vote supporting the president's position.

171. H Res 518. House Ethics Investigation. Wright, D-Texas, motion to suspend the rules and adopt the resolution to authorize the House Committee on Standards of Official Conduct to investigate allegations of improper sexual conduct or illegal drug use by members, House officers or employees, particularly House pages. Motion agreed to 407-1: R 185-0; D 222-1 (ND 150-0, SD 72-1), July 13, 1982. A two-thirds majority of those present and voting (272 in this case) is required for adoption under suspension of the rules.

172. H J Res 494. El Salvador Aid Conditions. Barnes, D-Md., motion to suspend the rules and pass the joint resolution conditioning further U.S. aid to El Salvador on the president's certification to Congress that El Salvador was making "good faith efforts" to investigate and to bring to justice those responsible for the murders of six U.S. citizens in 1980 and 1981. The president also would have to certify that El Salvador was taking "all reasonable steps" to investigate the disappearance of journalist John Sullivan in 1981. Motion agreed to 399-1: R 181-1; D 218-0 (ND 146-0, SD 72-0), July 13, 1982. A two-thirds majority of those present and voting (267 in this case) is required for passage under suspension of the rules.

173. H J Res 400. Roosevelt Memorial. Walker, R-Pa., amendment to prohibit expenditure of funds authorized under the bill except in the context of a balanced federal budget. Rejected 158-247: R 125-54; D 33-193 (ND 12-141, SD 21-52), July 14, 1982.

174. H J Res 400. Roosevelt Memorial. Passage of the joint resolution to authorize the expenditure of such sums as may be necessary to construct a memorial to the late President Franklin Delano Roosevelt in West Potomac Park in Washington, D.C. Passed 254-151: R 66-116; D 188-35 (ND 134-16, SD 54-19), July 14, 1982.

KEY

- Y Voted for (yea).
- # Paired for.
- + Announced for.
- N Voted against (nay).
- X Paired against.
- − Announced against.
- P Voted "present".
- C Voted "present" to avoid possible conflict of interest.
- ? Did not vote or otherwise make a position known.

Democrats *Republicans*

	168	169	170	171	172	173	174
ALABAMA							
1 *Edwards*	Y	Y	N	Y	Y	N	N
2 *Dickinson*	N	N	N	Y	?	N	Y
3 Nichols	Y	Y	Y	Y	Y	N	Y
4 Bevill	Y	Y	Y	Y	Y	N	Y
5 Flippo	Y	Y	Y	Y	Y	N	Y
6 *Smith*	Y	N	N	Y	Y	Y	N
7 Shelby	Y	N	N	Y	Y	Y	Y
ALASKA							
AL *Young*	N	Y	N	Y	Y	Y	N
ARIZONA							
1 *Rhodes*	Y	N	N	Y	Y	N	Y
2 Udall	Y	Y	Y	Y	Y	N	Y
3 *Stump*	Y	N	N	Y	Y	Y	N
4 *Rudd*	Y	Y	N	Y	Y	Y	N
ARKANSAS							
1 Alexander	Y	Y	Y	Y	Y	N	Y
2 *Bethune*	Y	N	N	Y	Y	N	Y
3 *Hammerschmidt*	Y	N	N	Y	Y	Y	Y
4 Anthony	Y	Y	Y	Y	Y	N	Y
CALIFORNIA							
1 *Chappie*	Y	N	N	Y	Y	Y	N
2 *Clausen*	Y	N	N	Y	Y	Y	Y
3 Matsui	Y	Y	Y	Y	Y	N	Y
4 Fazio	Y	Y	Y	Y	Y	N	Y
5 Burton, J.	?	?	?	?	?	N	Y
6 Burton, P.	Y	Y	Y	Y	Y	N	Y
7 Miller	Y	Y	Y	Y	Y	N	Y
8 Dellums	Y	Y	Y	Y	Y	?	?
9 Stark	Y	Y	Y	Y	Y	N	Y
10 Edwards	Y	Y	Y	Y	?	N	Y
11 Lantos	Y	Y	Y	Y	Y	N	Y
12 *McCloskey*	Y	N	N	Y	Y	?	?
13 Mineta	Y	Y	Y	Y	Y	N	Y
14 *Shumway*	Y	N	N	Y	Y	Y	N
15 Coelho	Y	Y	Y	Y	Y	N	Y
16 Panetta	Y	Y	Y	Y	Y	N	Y
17 *Pashayan*	Y	N	Y	Y	Y	Y	N
18 *Thomas*	Y	N	N	Y	Y	Y	N
19 *Lagomarsino*	Y	N	N	Y	Y	Y	N
20 *Goldwater*	?	N	X	Y	Y	?	N
21 *Fiedler*	Y	N	Y	Y	Y	N	N
22 *Moorhead*	Y	N	N	Y	Y	Y	N
23 Beilenson	Y	N	Y	Y	Y	N	Y
24 Waxman	Y	Y	Y	Y	Y	N	?
25 Roybal	Y	Y	Y	Y	Y	N	Y
26 *Rousselot*	?	?	?	?	?	Y	N
27 *Dornan*	Y	N	N	Y	Y	Y	N
28 Dixon	Y	Y	Y	Y	Y	N	Y
29 Hawkins	Y	Y	Y	Y	Y	N	Y
30 Vacancy							
31 Dymally	Y	Y	Y	Y	Y	N	Y
32 Anderson	Y	Y	Y	Y	Y	N	Y
33 *Grisham*	Y	N	N	Y	Y	Y	N
34 *Lungren*	Y	N	N	Y	Y	Y	N
35 *Dreier*	N	N	N	Y	Y	Y	N
36 Brown	Y	Y	Y	Y	Y	N	Y
37 *Lewis*	Y	N	N	Y	Y	Y	N
38 Patterson	Y	Y	Y	Y	?	N	Y
39 *Dannemeyer*	N	N	N	Y	Y	Y	N
40 *Badham*	Y	N	N	Y	Y	Y	N
41 *Lowery*	Y	Y	N	Y	Y	Y	Y
42 *Hunter*	Y	N	N	Y	Y	Y	N
43 *Burgener*	Y	N	N	Y	Y	Y	N
COLORADO							
1 Schroeder	N	Y	Y	Y	Y	N	Y
2 Wirth	Y	Y	Y	Y	Y	N	Y
3 Kogovsek	Y	Y	Y	Y	Y	N	Y
4 *Brown*	Y	N	N	Y	Y	Y	N
5 *Kramer*	Y	Y	Y	Y	Y	Y	Y
CONNECTICUT							
1 Kennelly	Y	Y	Y	Y	Y	N	Y
2 Gejdenson	N	Y	Y	Y	Y	N	Y
3 *DeNardis*	?	Y	Y	Y	Y	N	Y
4 *McKinney*	?	Y	Y	Y	Y	N	Y
5 Ratchford	Y	Y	Y	Y	Y	N	Y
6 Moffett	?	Y	Y	Y	?	?	?
DELAWARE							
AL *Evans*	Y	Y	N	Y	Y	Y	N
FLORIDA							
1 Hutto	Y	Y	Y	Y	Y	N	Y
2 Fuqua	Y	Y	Y	Y	Y	N	Y
3 Bennett	Y	Y	N	Y	Y	Y	N
4 Chappell	?	?	?	?	?	N	Y
5 *McCollum*	Y	Y	N	Y	Y	Y	N
6 *Young*	Y	N	N	Y	Y	?	N
7 Gibbons	Y	N	N	Y	Y	N	Y
8 Ireland	Y	?	N	Y	Y	?	?
9 Nelson	Y	Y	Y	Y	Y	N	N
10 *Bafalis*	Y	N	N	Y	Y	Y	N
11 Mica	Y	Y	Y	Y	Y	N	Y
12 *Shaw*	Y	N	Y	Y	Y	Y	N
13 Lehman	Y	Y	Y	Y	Y	N	Y
14 Pepper	Y	Y	Y	Y	Y	N	Y
15 Fascell	?	Y	Y	Y	Y	N	Y
GEORGIA							
1 Ginn	?	?	?	?	?	?	?
2 Hatcher	Y	Y	Y	Y	Y	N	N
3 Brinkley	Y	Y	Y	Y	Y	N	Y
4 Levitas	Y	Y	Y	Y	Y	Y	Y
5 Fowler	Y	Y	Y	Y	Y	N	Y
6 *Gingrich*	Y	N	N	Y	Y	Y	N
7 McDonald	Y	N	N	Y	Y	Y	N
8 Evans	Y	Y	Y	Y	Y	N	Y
9 Jenkins	Y	Y	Y	Y	Y	Y	Y
10 Barnard	Y	N	Y	Y	Y	Y	Y
HAWAII							
1 Heftel	Y	Y	Y	Y	Y	N	Y
2 Akaka	Y	Y	Y	Y	Y	N	Y
IDAHO							
1 *Craig*	Y	N	N	Y	Y	Y	N
2 *Hansen*	Y	N	N	Y	Y	Y	N
ILLINOIS							
1 Washington	N	Y	Y	Y	Y	N	Y
2 Savage	?	Y	Y	Y	Y	?	?
3 Russo	Y	Y	Y	Y	Y	N	Y
4 *Derwinski*	Y	N	N	Y	Y	Y	N
5 Fary	Y	Y	Y	Y	Y	N	Y
6 *Hyde*	Y	N	N	Y	Y	N	N
7 Collins	Y	Y	Y	Y	Y	N	Y
8 Rostenkowski	Y	Y	Y	Y	Y	N	Y
9 Yates	N	Y	Y	Y	?	N	Y
10 *Porter*	Y	N	Y	Y	Y	N	Y
11 Annunzio	Y	Y	Y	Y	Y	N	Y
12 *Crane, P.*	Y	N	N	Y	Y	#	X
13 *McClory*	Y	N	N	Y	Y	N	Y
14 *Erlenborn*	Y	N	N	Y	Y	Y	N
15 *Corcoran*	Y	N	Y	Y	Y	Y	N
16 *Martin*	Y	N	Y	Y	Y	N	Y
17 *O'Brien*	Y	N	Y	Y	Y	N	N
18 *Michel*	Y	N	N	Y	Y	Y	N
19 *Railsback*	Y	N	Y	Y	Y	N	?
20 *Findley*	Y	N	Y	Y	Y	N	?
21 *Madigan*	Y	N	N	Y	Y	N	Y
22 *Crane, D.*	Y	N	Y	Y	Y	N	Y
23 Price	Y	Y	Y	Y	Y	N	Y
24 Simon	Y	Y	Y	Y	Y	N	Y
INDIANA							
1 Benjamin	Y	Y	Y	Y	Y	N	Y
2 Fithian	Y	Y	Y	Y	Y	Y	Y
3 *Hiler*	Y	N	N	Y	Y	Y	N
4 *Coats*	Y	N	N	Y	Y	Y	N
5 *Hillis*	Y	Y	Y	Y	Y	N	Y
6 Evans	Y	Y	Y	Y	Y	?	Y
7 *Myers*	Y	N	Y	Y	Y	N	Y
8 *Deckard*	Y	Y	?	?	?	?	?
9 Hamilton	Y	Y	Y	Y	Y	N	Y
10 Sharp	Y	Y	Y	Y	Y	N	Y
11 Jacobs	N	Y	Y	Y	Y	Y	N
IOWA							
1 *Leach*	Y	Y	Y	Y	Y	N	Y
2 *Tauke*	Y	N	Y	Y	Y	N	Y
3 *Evans*	N	Y	N	Y	Y	Y	N
4 Smith	Y	Y	Y	Y	Y	N	Y
5 Harkin	N	Y	Y	Y	Y	N	Y
6 Bedell	Y	Y	Y	Y	Y	N	N

ND - Northern Democrats   SD - Southern Democrats

Corresponding to Congressional Record Votes 177, 178, 179, 180, 181, 182, 183

	168	169	170	171	172	173	174
KANSAS							
1 ***Roberts***	Y	N	N	Y	Y	Y	N
2 ***Jeffries***	Y	N	N	Y	Y	Y	N
3 ***Winn***	Y	N	N	Y	Y	Y	N
4 Glickman	Y	N	Y	Y	Y	N	N
5 ***Whittaker***	Y	N	N	Y	Y	Y	N
KENTUCKY							
1 Hubbard	Y	Y	Y	Y	Y	N	Y
2 Natcher	Y	Y	Y	Y	Y	N	Y
3 Mazzoli	Y	Y	Y	Y	Y	N	Y
4 ***Snyder***	Y	Y	N	Y	Y	Y	N
5 ***Rogers***	Y	Y	N	Y	Y	Y	N
6 ***Hopkins***	Y	Y	N	Y	Y	Y	N
7 Perkins	Y	Y	Y	Y	Y	N	Y
LOUISIANA							
1 ***Livingston***	Y	N	N	Y	Y	Y	N
2 Boggs	Y	Y	Y	Y	Y	N	Y
3 Tauzin	Y	Y	N	Y	Y	Y	N
4 Roemer	N	Y	N	Y	Y	Y	N
5 Huckaby	Y	N	Y	Y	Y	Y	Y
6 ***Moore***	Y	N	N	Y	Y	N	N
7 Breaux	Y	N	N	Y	Y	Y	N
8 Long	Y	Y	Y	Y	Y	N	Y
MAINE							
1 ***Emery***	Y	Y	Y	Y	Y	N	N
2 ***Snowe***	Y	Y	Y	Y	Y	N	Y
MARYLAND							
1 Dyson	Y	Y	N	Y	Y	Y	Y
2 Long	Y	Y	Y	Y	Y	Y	N
3 Mikulski	Y	Y	Y	Y	Y	N	N
4 ***Holt***	?	?	N	Y	Y	Y	N
5 Hoyer	Y	Y	Y	Y	Y	N	Y
6 Byron	Y	Y	Y	Y	Y	N	N
7 Mitchell	?	Y	Y	Y	Y	N	Y
8 Barnes	N	Y	Y	Y	Y	N	Y
MASSACHUSETTS							
1 ***Conte***	Y	Y	Y	Y	Y	N	Y
2 Boland	?	Y	Y	Y	Y	N	Y
3 Early	Y	Y	Y	Y	Y	N	Y
4 Frank	Y	Y	Y	Y	Y	N	Y
5 Shannon	Y	Y	Y	Y	Y	N	Y
6 Mavroules	Y	Y	Y	Y	Y	N	Y
7 Markey	Y	Y	?	Y	Y	N	Y
8 O'Neill							
9 Moakley	Y	Y	Y	Y	Y	N	Y
10 ***Heckler***	Y	Y	Y	Y	Y	N	Y
11 Donnelly	Y	Y	Y	Y	Y	N	Y
12 Studds	Y	Y	Y	Y	Y	N	Y
MICHIGAN							
1 Conyers	?	Y	Y	Y	Y	N	Y
2 ***Pursell***	Y	N	Y	Y	Y	N	Y
3 Wolpe	Y	Y	Y	Y	Y	N	Y
4 ***Siljander***	Y	N	N	Y	Y	?	?
5 ***Sawyer***	Y	Y	N	Y	Y	N	Y
6 ***Dunn***	Y	Y	Y	Y	Y	Y	N
7 Kildee	Y	Y	Y	Y	Y	N	Y
8 Traxler	?	?	?	?	?	N	Y
9 ***Vander Jagt***	Y	N	N	Y	Y	N	Y
10 Albosta	Y	Y	Y	Y	Y	N	Y
11 ***Davis***	Y	Y	Y	Y	Y	Y	N
12 Bonior	Y	Y	Y	Y	Y	Y	Y
13 Crockett	?	Y	Y	Y	Y	N	Y
14 Hertel	Y	Y	Y	Y	Y	N	Y
15 Ford	?	Y	Y	Y	Y	N	Y
16 Dingell	Y	Y	Y	?	Y	N	Y
17 Brodhead	Y	Y	Y	Y	Y	N	Y
18 Blanchard	?	?	?	?	?	?	?
19 ***Broomfield***	Y	N	N	Y	Y	N	Y
MINNESOTA							
1 ***Erdahl***	Y	Y	N	Y	Y	N	Y
2 ***Hagedorn***	Y	Y	N	Y	Y	Y	N
3 ***Frenzel***	Y	N	N	Y	Y	N	N
4 Vento	Y	Y	Y	Y	Y	N	Y
5 Sabo	N	Y	Y	Y	Y	N	Y
6 ***Weber***	Y	N	N	Y	Y	Y	N
7 ***Stangeland***	Y	N	N	Y	Y	?	N
8 Oberstar	Y	Y	Y	Y	Y	N	Y
MISSISSIPPI							
1 Whitten	Y	Y	Y	Y	Y	N	Y
2 Bowen	Y	Y	Y	Y	Y	N	Y
3 Montgomery	Y	Y	N	Y	Y	Y	N
4 Dowdy	Y	Y	Y	Y	Y	N	Y
5 ***Lott***	?	N	N	Y	Y	Y	N
MISSOURI							
1 Clay	?	?	?	?	?	?	?
2 Young	Y	Y	?	?	?	?	?
3 Gephardt	Y	Y	?	Y	Y	N	Y

	168	169	170	171	172	173	174
4 Skelton	Y	Y	Y	Y	Y	Y	Y
5 Bolling	?	Y	Y	Y	?	N	Y
6 ***Coleman***	Y	Y	N	Y	Y	Y	Y
7 ***Taylor***	Y	Y	N	Y	Y	Y	N
8 ***Bailey***	Y	N	N	Y	Y	Y	N
9 Volkmer	Y	Y	Y	Y	Y	Y	N
10 ***Emerson***	N	Y	N	Y	Y	Y	N
MONTANA							
1 Williams	Y	Y	Y	Y	Y	N	Y
2 ***Marlenee***	?	?	?	?	?	Y	N
NEBRASKA							
1 ***Bereuter***	Y	Y	Y	Y	Y	Y	N
2 ***Daub***	Y	Y	N	Y	Y	Y	N
3 ***Smith***	Y	N	N	Y	Y	Y	N
NEVADA							
AL Santini	?	?	Y	Y	Y	Y	N
NEW HAMPSHIRE							
1 D'Amours	Y	Y	Y	Y	Y	N	Y
2 ***Gregg***	Y	Y	N	Y	Y	Y	N
NEW JERSEY							
1 Florio	Y	Y	Y	Y	Y	N	Y
2 Hughes	Y	Y	Y	Y	Y	N	Y
3 Howard	Y	Y	Y	Y	Y	N	Y
4 ***Smith***	Y	Y	Y	Y	Y	N	Y
5 ***Fenwick***	Y	Y	Y	Y	Y	Y	N
6 ***Forsythe***	N	N	N	Y	Y	Y	N
7 ***Roukema***	Y	Y	N	Y	Y	N	N
8 Roe	Y	Y	Y	Y	Y	N	Y
9 ***Hollenbeck***	Y	Y	Y	Y	Y	N	Y
10 Rodino	Y	Y	Y	Y	Y	N	Y
11 Minish	Y	Y	Y	Y	Y	N	Y
12 ***Rinaldo***	Y	Y	Y	Y	Y	N	Y
13 ***Courter***	Y	Y	N	Y	Y	Y	N
14 Guarini	Y	Y	Y	Y	Y	N	?
15 Dwyer	Y	Y	Y	Y	Y	N	Y
NEW MEXICO							
1 ***Lujan***	Y	Y	N	Y	Y	Y	N
2 ***Skeen***	Y	Y	N	Y	Y	Y	N
NEW YORK							
1 ***Carney***	Y	Y	N	Y	Y	Y	N
2 Downey	Y	Y	Y	Y	Y	N	Y
3 ***Carman***	Y	Y	N	Y	Y	Y	N
4 ***Lent***	Y	Y	N	Y	Y	N	Y
5 ***McGrath***	Y	Y	N	Y	Y	Y	N
6 ***LeBoutillier***	?	N	N	Y	Y	Y	N
7 Addabbo	Y	Y	Y	Y	Y	N	Y
8 Rosenthal	Y	Y	Y	Y	Y	N	Y
9 Ferraro	Y	Y	Y	Y	Y	N	Y
10 Biaggi	Y	Y	Y	Y	Y	N	Y
11 Scheuer	Y	Y	Y	Y	Y	N	Y
12 Chisholm	?	Y	Y	Y	Y	?	Y
13 Solarz	Y	Y	Y	Y	Y	N	Y
14 Richmond	Y	Y	Y	Y	Y	N	Y
15 Zeferetti	Y	Y	Y	Y	Y	N	Y
16 Schumer	Y	Y	Y	Y	Y	N	Y
17 ***Molinari***	?	?	?	?	?	?	?
18 ***Green***	Y	Y	Y	Y	Y	N	Y
19 Rangel	Y	Y	Y	Y	Y	N	?
20 Weiss	Y	Y	Y	Y	Y	N	Y
21 Garcia	?	Y	Y	Y	Y	N	Y
22 Bingham	Y	Y	Y	Y	Y	N	Y
23 Peyser	Y	Y	Y	Y	Y	N	Y
24 Ottinger	P	Y	Y	Y	Y	N	Y
25 ***Fish***	Y	Y	Y	Y	Y	N	Y
26 ***Gilman***	Y	Y	Y	Y	Y	N	Y
27 McHugh	Y	Y	Y	Y	Y	N	Y
28 Stratton	Y	Y	Y	Y	Y	N	Y
29 ***Solomon***	N	Y	N	Y	Y	Y	N
30 ***Martin***	?	Y	N	Y	?	Y	N
31 ***Mitchell***	Y	Y	Y	Y	Y	N	Y
32 ***Wortley***	Y	C	N	Y	Y	Y	Y
33 ***Lee***	Y	N	N	Y	Y	Y	N
34 ***Horton***	Y	Y	Y	Y	Y	N	Y
35 ***Conable***	Y	N	N	Y	Y	N	Y
36 LaFalce	Y	Y	Y	Y	Y	?	?
37 Nowak	?	Y	Y	Y	?	N	Y
38 ***Kemp***	Y	N	N	Y	Y	N	Y
39 Lundine	Y	Y	Y	Y	Y	N	Y
NORTH CAROLINA							
1 Jones	Y	Y	Y	Y	Y	N	Y
2 Fountain	?	Y	Y	Y	Y	X	#
3 Whitley	Y	Y	Y	Y	Y	N	Y
4 Andrews	?	?	?	?	?	?	?
5 Neal	Y	Y	Y	Y	Y	N	Y
6 ***Johnston***	N	C	N	Y	Y	Y	N
7 Rose	Y	Y	Y	Y	Y	N	Y
8 Hefner	Y	Y	Y	Y	Y	N	Y

	168	169	170	171	172	173	174
9 ***Martin***	?	N	N	Y	Y	Y	N
10 ***Broyhill***	Y	Y	N	Y	Y	Y	N
11 ***Hendon***	Y	Y	N	Y	Y	Y	N
NORTH DAKOTA							
AL Dorgan	Y	Y	Y	Y	Y	N	Y
OHIO							
1 ***Gradison***	Y	N	N	Y	Y	Y	N
2 Luken	Y	Y	Y	Y	Y	N	?
3 Hall	Y	Y	Y	Y	Y	N	Y
4 ***Oxley***	Y	Y	N	Y	Y	Y	N
5 ***Latta***	Y	N	N	Y	Y	Y	N
6 ***McEwen***	Y	Y	N	Y	Y	Y	N
7 ***Brown***	?	?	?	?	?	?	?
8 ***Kindness***	Y	Y	N	Y	Y	Y	N
9 ***Weber***	Y	Y	N	Y	Y	Y	Y
10 ***Miller***	N	Y	N	Y	Y	Y	N
11 ***Stanton***	Y	N	N	Y	Y	N	Y
12 Shamansky	Y	Y	Y	Y	Y	N	Y
13 Pease	Y	Y	Y	Y	Y	N	N
14 Seiberling	Y	Y	Y	Y	Y	N	N
15 ***Wylie***	Y	Y	Y	Y	Y	N	Y
16 ***Regula***	Y	Y	Y	Y	Y	N	Y
17 ***Ashbrook****	Y	Y	N	Y	Y	Y	N
18 Applegate	?	Y	Y	Y	Y	N	Y
19 ***Williams***	Y	Y	Y	Y	Y	N	Y
20 Oakar	Y	Y	Y	Y	Y	N	Y
21 Stokes	Y	Y	Y	Y	Y	N	Y
22 Eckart	Y	Y	Y	Y	Y	N	Y
23 Mottl	Y	Y	Y	Y	Y	N	Y
OKLAHOMA							
1 Jones	Y	N	N	Y	Y	N	N
2 Synar	Y	Y	Y	Y	Y	N	Y
3 Watkins	Y	Y	Y	Y	Y	Y	N
4 McCurdy	Y	Y	N	Y	Y	N	N
5 ***Edwards***	Y	N	N	Y	Y	Y	N
6 English	Y	Y	N	Y	Y	Y	N
OREGON							
1 AuCoin	Y	Y	Y	?	?	N	Y
2 ***Smith***	Y	N	N	Y	Y	Y	N
3 Wyden	Y	Y	Y	Y	Y	N	Y
4 Weaver	Y	Y	Y	Y	Y	N	Y
PENNSYLVANIA							
1 Foglietta	?	?	#	?	?	N	Y
2 Gray	Y	Y	Y	Y	Y	N	Y
3 Smith	Y	Y	Y	?	?	N	Y
4 ***Dougherty***	Y	Y	Y	Y	Y	N	Y
5 ***Schulze***	Y	Y	Y	Y	Y	Y	Y
6 Yatron	Y	Y	Y	Y	Y	N	Y
7 Edgar	Y	Y	Y	Y	Y	N	N
8 ***Coyne, J.***	Y	Y	N	Y	Y	N	N
9 ***Shuster***	Y	Y	N	Y	Y	Y	N
10 ***McDade***	Y	Y	Y	Y	Y	N	Y
11 ***Nelligan***	Y	Y	Y	Y	Y	N	Y
12 Murtha	Y	Y	Y	Y	Y	N	Y
13 ***Coughlin***	N	Y	N	Y	Y	Y	N
14 Coyne, W.	Y	Y	Y	Y	Y	N	Y
15 ***Ritter***	Y	Y	N	Y	Y	N	Y
16 ***Walker***	N	Y	N	Y	Y	Y	N
17 Ertel	?	?	?	?	?	N	Y
18 Walgren	Y	Y	Y	Y	Y	Y	N
19 ***Goodling***	N	Y	N	Y	Y	Y	N
20 Gaydos	Y	Y	Y	Y	Y	N	Y
21 Bailey	Y	Y	Y	Y	Y	N	Y
22 Murphy	Y	Y	Y	Y	Y	N	Y
23 ***Clinger***	Y	N	Y	Y	Y	N	Y
24 ***Marks***	?	N	Y	Y	?	?	Y
25 ***Atkinson***	Y	Y	Y	Y	Y	N	Y
RHODE ISLAND							
1 St Germain	Y	Y	Y	Y	Y	N	Y
2 ***Schneider***	Y	Y	Y	Y	Y	Y	Y
SOUTH CAROLINA							
1 ***Hartnett***	Y	Y	N	Y	Y	Y	N
2 ***Spence***	Y	Y	N	Y	Y	Y	N
3 Derrick	?	Y	Y	Y	Y	N	Y
4 ***Campbell***	Y	Y	N	Y	Y	Y	N
5 Holland	Y	Y	Y	Y	Y	N	Y
6 ***Napier***	Y	Y	N	Y	Y	Y	Y
SOUTH DAKOTA							
1 Daschle	Y	Y	Y	Y	Y	N	Y
2 ***Roberts***	+	-	-	+	+	+	-
TENNESSEE							
1 ***Quillen***	Y	Y	N	Y	Y	Y	N
2 ***Duncan***	Y	N	N	Y	Y	Y	N
3 Bouquard	Y	Y	Y	Y	Y	N	Y
4 Gore	Y	Y	Y	Y	Y	N	Y
5 Boner	?	?	Y	Y	Y	N	Y
6 ***Beard***	Y	Y	N	Y	Y	?	?

	168	169	170	171	172	173	174
7 Jones	?	?	#	?	?	?	?
8 Ford	Y	Y	Y	Y	Y	N	Y
TEXAS							
1 Hall, S.	Y	Y	N	+	+	Y	N
2 Wilson	Y	Y	N	Y	Y	N	Y
3 ***Collins***	Y	N	N	Y	Y	Y	N
4 Hall, R.	Y	Y	Y	Y	Y	Y	N
5 Mattox	Y	Y	Y	Y	Y	N	Y
6 Gramm	Y	N	N	Y	Y	Y	N
7 ***Archer***	Y	N	N	Y	Y	Y	N
8 ***Fields***	N	N	N	Y	Y	Y	N
9 Brooks	Y	Y	Y	Y	Y	N	Y
10 Pickle	Y	Y	N	Y	Y	N	Y
11 Leath	Y	N	N	Y	Y	Y	N
12 Wright	Y	Y	Y	Y	?	N	Y
13 Hightower	Y	Y	Y	Y	Y	Y	Y
14 Patman	Y	N	N	Y	Y	Y	Y
15 de la Garza	Y	Y	Y	Y	Y	N	Y
16 White	Y	Y	Y	Y	Y	Y	Y
17 Stenholm	N	Y	N	Y	Y	?	?
18 Leland	?	?	?	?	?	N	Y
19 Hance	Y	Y	Y	Y	Y	Y	N
20 Gonzalez	Y	Y	Y	N	Y	N	Y
21 ***Loeffler***	Y	N	N	Y	Y	Y	N
22 ***Paul***	Y	N	N	Y	N	Y	N
23 Kazen	Y	Y	Y	Y	Y	N	N
24 Frost	Y	Y	Y	Y	Y	N	Y
UTAH							
1 ***Hansen***	Y	Y	N	Y	Y	Y	N
2 ***Marriott***	Y	Y	N	Y	Y	Y	N
VERMONT							
AL ***Jeffords***	?	Y	Y	Y	Y	N	Y
VIRGINIA							
1 ***Trible***	Y	Y	N	Y	Y	Y	Y
2 ***Whitehurst***	Y	Y	N	Y	Y	Y	N
3 ***Bliley***	Y	Y	N	Y	Y	Y	N
4 ***Daniel, R.***	Y	Y	N	Y	Y	Y	N
5 Daniel, D.	Y	Y	N	Y	Y	N	Y
6 ***Butler***	N	Y	N	Y	Y	Y	N
7 ***Robinson***	Y	Y	N	Y	Y	Y	N
8 ***Parris***	Y	Y	Y	Y	Y	Y	Y
9 ***Wampler***	Y	Y	Y	?	?	N	Y
10 ***Wolf***	Y	Y	Y	Y	Y	N	Y
WASHINGTON							
1 ***Pritchard***	Y	N	N	Y	Y	N	Y
2 Swift	Y	Y	Y	Y	Y	N	Y
3 Bonker	?	?	?	+	?	N	Y
4 ***Morrison***	Y	N	N	Y	Y	Y	Y
5 Foley	Y	Y	Y	Y	Y	N	Y
6 Dicks	Y	Y	Y	Y	Y	N	Y
7 Lowry	Y	N	Y	Y	Y	N	Y
WEST VIRGINIA							
1 Mollohan	Y	Y	Y	Y	Y	N	Y
2 ***Benedict***	Y	Y	N	Y	Y	?	?
3 ***Staton***	Y	Y	N	Y	Y	Y	N
4 Rahall	Y	Y	Y	Y	Y	N	Y
WISCONSIN							
1 Aspin	Y	Y	Y	Y	Y	N	Y
2 Kastenmeier	Y	Y	Y	Y	Y	N	Y
3 ***Gunderson***	Y	Y	N	Y	Y	Y	N
4 Zablocki	Y	Y	Y	?	?	N	Y
5 Reuss	Y	Y	Y	Y	Y	N	Y
6 ***Petri***	Y	Y	N	Y	Y	Y	Y
7 Obey	Y	Y	Y	Y	Y	N	Y
8 ***Roth***	Y	Y	N	Y	Y	Y	Y
9 ***Sensenbrenner***	Y	Y	N	Y	Y	Y	N
WYOMING							
AL ***Cheney***	Y	N	N	Y	Y	Y	N

** Rep. Jean Ashbrook, R-Ohio, was sworn in July 12, 1982. The first vote for which she was eligible was CQ vote 168.*

Southern states - Ala., Ark., Fla., Ga., Ky., La., Miss., N.C., Okla., S.C., Tenn., Texas, Va.

	175	176	177	178
KEY				

Y Voted for (yea).
\# Paired for.
+ Announced for.
N Voted against (nay).
X Paired against.
- Announced against.
P Voted "present".
C Voted "present" to avoid possible conflict of interest.
? Did not vote or otherwise make a position known.

Democrats *Republicans*

175. Procedural Motion. Corcoran, R-Ill., motion to approve the House *Journal* of Wednesday, July 14. Motion agreed to 334-27: R 145-16; D 189-11 (ND 128-9, SD 61-2), July 15, 1982.

176. HR 6685. Urgent Supplemental Appropriations, Fiscal 1982. Whitten, D-Miss., motion that the House agree to the Senate amendment, with an amendment, embodying the conference report on the bill, to provide $5,448,452,000 in new budget authority and $5,849,120,000 in rescissions. Motion agreed to 389-13: R 173-7; D 216-6 (ND 148-2, SD 68-4), July 15, 1982. The president requested $4,543,371,000 in new budget authority and $7,750,269,165 in rescissions.

177. HR 5617. Coast Guard Authorization. Adoption of the rule (H Res 520) providing for House floor consideration of the bill to authorize appropriations for Coast Guard activities in fiscal 1983 and 1984. Adopted 394-1: R 178-0; D 216-1 (ND 145-1, SD 71-0), July 15, 1982.

178. HR 5617. Coast Guard Authorization. Passage of the bill to authorize $2.55 billion in fiscal 1983 and $2.759 billion in fiscal 1984 for Coast Guard activities. Passed 348-25: R 135-22; D 213-3 (ND 145-2, SD 68-1), July 15, 1982.

	175	176	177	178
ALABAMA				
1 *Edwards*	Y	Y	Y	Y
2 *Dickinson*	N	Y	Y	Y
3 Nichols	Y	Y	Y	Y
4 Bevill	Y	Y	Y	Y
5 Flippo	Y	Y	Y	Y
6 *Smith*	Y	Y	Y	Y
7 Shelby	?	Y	Y	Y
ALASKA				
AL *Young*	N	Y	?	Y
ARIZONA				
1 *Rhodes*	Y	Y	Y	Y
2 Udall	Y	?	?	Y
3 *Stump*	?	?	?	Y
4 *Rudd*	Y	Y	Y	Y
ARKANSAS				
1 Alexander	Y	Y	Y	Y
2 *Bethune*	?	Y	Y	Y
3 *Hammerschmidt*	?	Y	Y	Y
4 Anthony	?	Y	Y	Y
CALIFORNIA				
1 *Chappie*	?	?	?	?
2 *Clausen*	Y	Y	Y	Y
3 Matsui	Y	Y	Y	Y
4 Fazio	Y	?	?	Y
5 Burton, J.	Y	Y	Y	Y
6 Burton, P.	Y	Y	Y	Y
7 Miller	?	?	?	Y
8 Dellums	Y	Y	Y	Y
9 Stark	Y	Y	Y	Y
10 Edwards	Y	Y	Y	Y
11 Lantos	Y	Y	Y	Y
12 *McCloskey*	Y	Y	Y	?
13 Mineta	Y	Y	Y	Y
14 Shumway	Y	Y	Y	Y
15 Coelho	Y	?	?	Y
16 Panetta	Y	Y	Y	Y
17 *Pashayan*	Y	Y	Y	Y
18 *Thomas*	N	Y	Y	?
19 *Lagomarsino*	Y	Y	Y	Y
20 *Goldwater*	?	Y	Y	Y
21 *Fiedler*	Y	Y	Y	Y
22 *Moorhead*	Y	Y	Y	Y
23 Beilenson	Y	Y	Y	Y
24 Waxman	Y	Y	Y	Y
25 Roybal	Y	Y	Y	Y
26 *Rousselot*	Y	Y	Y	Y
27 *Dornan*	Y	Y	Y	Y
28 Dixon	?	Y	Y	Y
29 Hawkins	Y	N	Y	Y
30 Martinez*		Y	Y	Y
31 Dymally	?	Y	Y	Y
32 Anderson	Y	Y	Y	Y
33 *Grisham*	Y	N	Y	Y
34 *Lungren*	Y	Y	Y	Y
35 *Dreier*	N	Y	Y	Y
36 Brown	Y	Y	Y	Y
37 *Lewis*	?	Y	Y	Y
38 Patterson	Y	Y	Y	Y
39 *Dannemeyer*	Y	Y	Y	N
40 *Badham*	Y	Y	Y	N
41 *Lowery*	Y	Y	Y	Y
42 *Hunter*	Y	Y	Y	Y
43 *Burgener*	Y	Y	Y	Y
COLORADO				
1 Schroeder	N	Y	Y	N
2 Wirth	Y	Y	Y	Y
3 Kogovsek	Y	Y	Y	Y
4 *Brown*	Y	Y	Y	N

	175	176	177	178
5 *Kramer*	Y	Y	Y	N
CONNECTICUT				
1 Kennelly	Y	Y	Y	Y
2 Gejdenson	N	Y	Y	Y
3 *DeNardis*	?	Y	Y	Y
4 *McKinney*	Y	Y	Y	Y
5 Ratchford	Y	Y	Y	Y
6 Moffett	?	?	?	?
DELAWARE				
AL *Evans*	Y	Y	Y	Y
FLORIDA				
1 Hutto	Y	Y	Y	Y
2 Fuqua	Y	?	?	?
3 Bennett	Y	Y	Y	Y
4 Chappell	Y	Y	Y	Y
5 *McCollum*	Y	Y	Y	Y
6 *Young*	Y	Y	Y	Y
7 Gibbons	Y	Y	Y	Y
8 Ireland	Y	Y	Y	Y
9 Nelson	Y	Y	Y	Y
10 *Bafalis*	Y	Y	Y	Y
11 Mica	Y	Y	Y	Y
12 *Shaw*	Y	Y	Y	Y
13 Lehman	Y	Y	Y	Y
14 Pepper	Y	Y	Y	Y
15 Fascell	Y	Y	Y	Y
GEORGIA				
1 Ginn	?	?	?	?
2 Hatcher	Y	Y	Y	Y
3 Brinkley	Y	Y	Y	Y
4 Levitas	Y	Y	Y	Y
5 Fowler	Y	Y	Y	Y
6 *Gingrich*	?	Y	Y	Y
7 McDonald	Y	N	Y	Y
8 Evans	Y	Y	Y	Y
9 Jenkins	Y	Y	Y	Y
10 Barnard	Y	Y	Y	Y
HAWAII				
1 Heftel	Y	Y	Y	Y
2 Akaka	Y	Y	Y	Y
IDAHO				
1 *Craig*	Y	Y	Y	N
2 *Hansen*	Y	Y	Y	Y
ILLINOIS				
1 Washington	?	Y	Y	Y
2 Savage	?	Y	N	?
3 Russo	?	?	?	?
4 *Derwinski*	Y	Y	Y	Y
5 Fary	Y	Y	Y	Y
6 *Hyde*	Y	Y	Y	Y
7 Collins	Y	Y	Y	Y
8 Rostenkowski	Y	Y	Y	Y
9 Yates	N	Y	Y	Y
10 *Porter*	?	Y	Y	Y
11 Annunzio	Y	Y	Y	Y
12 *Crane, P.*	Y	N	Y	Y
13 *McClory*	Y	Y	Y	Y
14 *Erlenborn*	?	Y	Y	Y
15 *Corcoran*	Y	Y	Y	Y
16 *Martin*	Y	Y	Y	N
17 *O'Brien*	Y	Y	Y	Y
18 *Michel*	Y	Y	Y	?
19 *Railsback*	Y	Y	Y	?
20 *Findley*	Y	Y	Y	?
21 *Madigan*	Y	Y	Y	?
22 *Crane, D.*	Y	N	Y	Y
23 Price	Y	Y	Y	Y
24 Simon	Y	Y	Y	Y
INDIANA				
1 Benjamin	Y	Y	Y	Y
2 Fithian	Y	Y	Y	Y
3 *Hiler*	Y	Y	Y	N
4 *Coats*	Y	Y	Y	Y
5 *Hillis*	?	?	?	?
6 Evans	?	?	?	?
7 *Myers*	Y	Y	Y	Y
8 *Deckard*	?	?	?	?
9 Hamilton	Y	Y	Y	Y
10 Sharp	Y	Y	Y	Y
11 Jacobs	N	Y	Y	Y
IOWA				
1 *Leach*	?	Y	Y	Y
2 *Tauke*	Y	Y	Y	Y
3 *Evans*	N	Y	Y	?
4 Smith	Y	Y	Y	Y
5 Harkin	N	Y	Y	Y
6 Bedell	Y	Y	Y	Y

ND - Northern Democrats   SD - Southern Democrats

	175	176	177	178
KANSAS				
1 Roberts	Y	Y	Y	?
2 Jeffries	?	N	Y	Y
3 Winn	Y	Y	Y	Y
4 Glickman	Y	Y	Y	Y
5 Whittaker	Y	Y	Y	Y
KENTUCKY				
1 Hubbard	?	?	?	?
2 Natcher	Y	Y	Y	Y
3 Mazzoli	Y	Y	Y	Y
4 Snyder	Y	Y	Y	Y
5 Rogers	Y	Y	Y	Y
6 Hopkins	Y	Y	Y	?
7 Perkins	Y	Y	Y	Y
LOUISIANA				
1 Livingston	?	Y	Y	Y
2 Boggs	?	Y	Y	Y
3 Tauzin	Y	Y	Y	Y
4 Roemer	N	N	Y	Y
5 Huckaby	?	Y	Y	Y
6 Moore	Y	Y	Y	Y
7 Breaux	?	?	?	?
8 Long	Y	Y	Y	Y
MAINE				
1 Emery	Y	Y	Y	Y
2 Snowe	Y	Y	Y	Y
MARYLAND				
1 Dyson	Y	Y	Y	Y
2 Long	?	Y	Y	Y
3 Mikulski	Y	Y	Y	Y
4 Holt	Y	Y	Y	Y
5 Hoyer	Y	Y	Y	Y
6 Byron	?	Y	Y	Y
7 Mitchell	N	Y	Y	Y
8 Barnes	?	Y	Y	?
MASSACHUSETTS				
1 Conte	Y	Y	Y	Y
2 Boland	Y	Y	Y	?
3 Early	Y	Y	Y	Y
4 Frank	Y	Y	Y	Y
5 Shannon	?	Y	Y	Y
6 Mavroules	Y	Y	Y	Y
7 Markey	Y	Y	Y	Y
8 O'Neill				
9 Moakley	Y	Y	Y	Y
10 Heckler	?	?	?	?
11 Donnelly	Y	Y	Y	Y
12 Studds	Y	Y	Y	Y
MICHIGAN				
1 Conyers	Y	Y	Y	?
2 Pursell	Y	Y	Y	Y
3 Wolpe	N	Y	Y	Y
4 Siljander	?	?	?	?
5 Sawyer	Y	Y	Y	Y
6 Dunn	Y	Y	Y	N
7 Kildee	Y	Y	Y	Y
8 Traxler	Y	Y	Y	Y
9 Vander Jagt	Y	Y	Y	Y
10 Albosta	Y	Y	Y	Y
11 Davis	?	Y	Y	Y
12 Bonior	Y	Y	Y	Y
13 Crockett	?	N	Y	Y
14 Hertel	Y	Y	Y	Y
15 Ford	Y	Y	?	Y
16 Dingell	Y	Y	Y	Y
17 Brodhead	Y	Y	Y	Y
18 Blanchard	?	?	?	?
19 Broomfield	Y	Y	Y	Y
MINNESOTA				
1 Erdahl	Y	Y	Y	Y
2 Hagedorn	Y	Y	Y	?
3 Frenzel	Y	N	Y	N
4 Vento	Y	Y	Y	Y
5 Sabo	N	Y	Y	Y
6 Weber	Y	Y	Y	N
7 Stangeland	Y	Y	Y	Y
8 Oberstar	Y	Y	Y	Y
MISSISSIPPI				
1 Whitten	Y	Y	Y	Y
2 Bowen	?	Y	Y	?
3 Montgomery	Y	Y	Y	Y
4 Dowdy	Y	Y	Y	Y
5 Lott	Y	Y	Y	?
MISSOURI				
1 Clay	N	Y	Y	Y
2 Young	?	?	?	?
3 Gephardt	Y	Y	Y	Y

	175	176	177	178
4 Skelton	Y	Y	Y	Y
5 Bolling	Y	Y	Y	Y
6 Coleman	Y	Y	Y	?
7 Taylor	Y	Y	Y	Y
8 Bailey	Y	Y	Y	N
9 Volkmer	Y	Y	Y	Y
10 Emerson	N	Y	Y	?
MONTANA				
1 Williams	Y	Y	?	Y
2 Marlenee	?	Y	Y	?
NEBRASKA				
1 Bereuter	Y	Y	Y	N
2 Daub	Y	Y	Y	N
3 Smith	Y	Y	Y	N
NEVADA				
AL Santini	Y	Y	Y	Y
NEW HAMPSHIRE				
1 D'Amours	Y	Y	?	Y
2 Gregg	N	Y	Y	Y
NEW JERSEY				
1 Florio	Y	Y	Y	Y
2 Hughes	Y	Y	Y	Y
3 Howard	Y	Y	Y	Y
4 Smith	Y	Y	Y	Y
5 Fenwick	Y	Y	Y	Y
6 Forsythe	N	Y	Y	Y
7 Roukema	Y	Y	Y	Y
8 Roe	Y	Y	Y	Y
9 Hollenbeck	Y	Y	Y	Y
10 Rodino	Y	Y	Y	Y
11 Minish	Y	Y	Y	Y
12 Rinaldo	Y	Y	Y	Y
13 Courter	Y	Y	Y	Y
14 Guarini	?	Y	Y	Y
15 Dwyer	Y	Y	Y	Y
NEW MEXICO				
1 Lujan	Y	Y	Y	N
2 Skeen	Y	Y	Y	?
NEW YORK				
1 Carney	Y	Y	Y	Y
2 Downey	Y	Y	Y	Y
3 Carman	Y	Y	Y	Y
4 Lent	Y	Y	Y	Y
5 McGrath	Y	Y	Y	Y
6 LeBoutillier	N	Y	Y	Y
7 Addabbo	Y	Y	Y	Y
8 Rosenthal	Y	Y	Y	Y
9 Ferraro	Y	Y	Y	Y
10 Biaggi	?	?	?	?
11 Scheuer	Y	Y	Y	?
12 Chisholm	?	Y	Y	Y
13 Solarz	Y	Y	Y	Y
14 Richmond	?	Y	Y	Y
15 Zeferetti	Y	Y	Y	Y
16 Schumer	Y	Y	Y	Y
17 Molinari	?	Y	Y	Y
18 Green	Y	Y	Y	Y
19 Rangel	Y	Y	Y	Y
20 Weiss	Y	Y	Y	Y
21 Garcia	Y	Y	Y	Y
22 Bingham	Y	Y	Y	Y
23 Peyser	Y	Y	Y	Y
24 Ottinger	?	Y	Y	Y
25 Fish	Y	Y	Y	Y
26 Gilman	Y	Y	Y	Y
27 McHugh	Y	Y	Y	Y
28 Stratton	Y	Y	Y	Y
29 Solomon	?	?	?	?
30 Martin	Y	Y	Y	Y
31 Mitchell	Y	Y	Y	?
32 Wortley	Y	Y	Y	Y
33 Lee	Y	Y	Y	Y
34 Horton	?	Y	Y	Y
35 Conable	Y	Y	Y	N
36 LaFalce	Y	Y	Y	Y
37 Nowak	Y	Y	Y	Y
38 Kemp	?	Y	Y	Y
39 Lundine	Y	Y	Y	Y
NORTH CAROLINA				
1 Jones	Y	Y	Y	Y
2 Fountain	?	Y	Y	Y
3 Whitley	Y	Y	Y	Y
4 Andrews	?	?	?	Y
5 Neal	?	Y	Y	Y
6 Johnston	N	N	Y	Y
7 Rose	Y	Y	Y	Y
8 Hefner	?	?	?	?

	175	176	177	178
9 Martin	Y	Y	Y	Y
10 Broyhill	Y	Y	Y	Y
11 Hendon	Y	Y	Y	Y
NORTH DAKOTA				
AL Dorgan	Y	Y	Y	Y
OHIO				
1 Gradison	Y	Y	Y	Y
2 Luken	Y	Y	Y	Y
3 Hall	Y	Y	Y	Y
4 Oxley	Y	Y	Y	Y
5 Latta	?	?	?	?
6 McEwen	Y	Y	Y	Y
7 Brown	?	?	?	?
8 Kindness	Y	Y	Y	Y
9 Weber	Y	Y	Y	Y
10 Miller	N	Y	Y	Y
11 Stanton	Y	Y	Y	?
12 Shamansky	Y	Y	Y	Y
13 Pease	Y	Y	Y	Y
14 Seiberling	Y	Y	Y	Y
15 Wylie	Y	Y	Y	Y
16 Regula	Y	Y	Y	Y
17 Ashbrook	Y	Y	Y	N
18 Applegate	?	Y	Y	Y
19 Williams	Y	Y	Y	Y
20 Oakar	Y	Y	Y	Y
21 Stokes	?	Y	Y	Y
22 Eckart	Y	Y	Y	Y
23 Mottl	Y	Y	Y	Y
OKLAHOMA				
1 Jones	Y	Y	Y	Y
2 Synar	Y	Y	Y	Y
3 Watkins	Y	Y	Y	Y
4 McCurdy	Y	Y	Y	Y
5 Edwards	?	?	?	?
6 English	Y	Y	Y	?
OREGON				
1 AuCoin	Y	Y	Y	Y
2 Smith	?	?	?	?
3 Wyden	Y	Y	Y	Y
4 Weaver	Y	Y	Y	Y
PENNSYLVANIA				
1 Foglietta	Y	Y	Y	Y
2 Gray	Y	Y	Y	Y
3 Smith	Y	Y	Y	Y
4 Dougherty	Y	Y	Y	Y
5 Schulze	Y	Y	Y	Y
6 Yatron	Y	Y	Y	Y
7 Edgar	Y	Y	Y	Y
8 Coyne, J.	Y	Y	Y	Y
9 Shuster	Y	Y	Y	Y
10 McDade	Y	Y	Y	Y
11 Nelligan	Y	Y	Y	Y
12 Murtha	Y	Y	Y	Y
13 Coughlin	N	Y	Y	Y
14 Coyne, W.	Y	Y	Y	Y
15 Ritter	Y	Y	Y	Y
16 Walker	N	Y	Y	N
17 Ertel	Y	?	Y	?
18 Walgren	Y	Y	Y	Y
19 Goodling	N	Y	Y	Y
20 Gaydos	Y	Y	Y	Y
21 Bailey	Y	Y	Y	Y
22 Murphy	Y	Y	Y	Y
23 Clinger	Y	Y	Y	Y
24 Marks	?	Y	Y	Y
25 Atkinson	Y	Y	Y	Y
RHODE ISLAND				
1 St Germain	Y	Y	?	Y
2 Schneider	?	?	?	Y
SOUTH CAROLINA				
1 Hartnett	Y	Y	Y	Y
2 Spence	Y	Y	Y	Y
3 Derrick	Y	Y	Y	Y
4 Campbell	Y	Y	Y	Y
5 Holland	Y	Y	?	Y
6 Napier	?	Y	Y	Y
SOUTH DAKOTA				
1 Daschle	Y	Y	Y	Y
2 Roberts	Y	Y	Y	?
TENNESSEE				
1 Quillen	Y	Y	Y	Y
2 Duncan	Y	Y	Y	Y
3 Bouquard	Y	Y	Y	Y
4 Gore	Y	Y	Y	Y
5 Boner	Y	Y	Y	Y
6 Beard	?	?	?	?

	175	176	177	178
7 Jones	?	?	?	?
8 Ford	Y	Y	Y	Y
TEXAS				
1 Hall, S.	Y	Y	Y	Y
2 Wilson	Y	Y	Y	?
3 Collins	Y	Y	Y	N
4 Hall, R.	Y	Y	Y	Y
5 Mattox	Y	Y	Y	Y
6 Gramm	Y	N	Y	N
7 Archer	Y	Y	Y	Y
8 Fields	N	Y	Y	Y
9 Brooks	Y	Y	Y	Y
10 Pickle	Y	Y	Y	Y
11 Leath	Y	Y	Y	Y
12 Wright	Y	Y	Y	Y
13 Hightower	Y	Y	Y	Y
14 Patman	Y	Y	Y	Y
15 de la Garza	?	Y	Y	Y
16 White	Y	Y	Y	Y
17 Stenholm	N	Y	Y	Y
18 Leland	Y	Y	Y	Y
19 Hance	Y	Y	Y	Y
20 Gonzalez	?	N	Y	Y
21 Loeffler	Y	Y	Y	Y
22 Paul	Y	N	Y	N
23 Kazen	Y	Y	Y	Y
24 Frost	Y	Y	Y	Y
UTAH				
1 Hansen	?	Y	Y	N
2 Marriott	Y	Y	Y	Y
VERMONT				
AL Jeffords	Y	Y	Y	?
VIRGINIA				
1 Trible	Y	Y	Y	?
2 Whitehurst	Y	Y	Y	Y
3 Bliley	Y	Y	Y	Y
4 Daniel, R.	Y	Y	Y	Y
5 Daniel, D.	Y	Y	Y	Y
6 Butler	N	Y	Y	Y
7 Robinson	Y	Y	Y	Y
8 Parris	Y	Y	Y	Y
9 Wampler	Y	Y	Y	Y
10 Wolf	Y	Y	Y	Y
WASHINGTON				
1 Pritchard	Y	Y	Y	Y
2 Swift	Y	Y	?	Y
3 Bonker	Y	Y	Y	Y
4 Morrison	Y	Y	Y	Y
5 Foley	Y	Y	Y	Y
6 Dicks	Y	Y	Y	Y
7 Lowry	Y	Y	Y	Y
WEST VIRGINIA				
1 Mollohan	?	?	Y	Y
2 Benedict	?	Y	Y	Y
3 Staton	Y	Y	Y	Y
4 Rahall	Y	Y	Y	Y
WISCONSIN				
1 Aspin	Y	Y	Y	Y
2 Kastenmeier	Y	Y	Y	Y
3 Gunderson	Y	Y	Y	+
4 Zablocki	Y	Y	Y	Y
5 Reuss	Y	Y	Y	Y
6 Petri	Y	Y	Y	?
7 Obey	Y	Y	Y	Y
8 Roth	Y	Y	Y	Y
9 Sensenbrenner	Y	Y	Y	Y
WYOMING				
AL Cheney	Y	Y	Y	N

*Rep. Matthew G. "Marty" Martinez, D-Calif., was sworn in July 15, 1982. The first vote for which he was eligible was CQ vote 176.

Southern states - Ala., Ark., Fla., Ga., Ky., La., Miss., N.C., Okla., S.C., Tenn., Texas, Va.

179. H Con Res 278. Older Americans Employment.
Andrews, D-N.C., motion to suspend the rules and adopt the concurrent resolution to express the sense of Congress in support of maintaining current employment levels in the community service employment for older Americans program. Motion agreed to 407-4: R 180-3; D 227-1 (ND 154-0, SD 73-1), July 20, 1982. A two-thirds majority of those present and voting (274 in this case) is required for adoption under suspension of the rules.

180. HR 5228. Physical Protection of Nuclear Materials.
Hughes, D-N.J., motion to suspend the rules and pass the bill to make it a federal crime to unlawfully obtain nuclear materials and use them to terrorize or harm individuals. Motion agreed to 396-9: R 174-7; D 222-2 (ND 151-1, SD 71-1), July 20, 1982. A two-thirds majority of those present and voting (271 in this case) is required for passage under suspension of the rules.

181. HR 6258. International Travel Act Authorization.
Florio, D-N.J., motion to suspend the rules and pass the bill to authorize $10 million in fiscal 1983 for the U.S. Travel and Tourism Administration. Motion rejected 241-167: R 79-103; D 162-64 (ND 123-29, SD 39-35), July 20, 1982. A two-thirds majority of those present and voting (272 in this case) is required for passage under suspension of the rules.

182. H Con Res 310. Cyprus Dispute.
Hamilton, D-Ind., motion to suspend the rules and adopt the concurrent resolution stating the sense of Congress that the president should consider appointing a personal representative to seek an end to the dispute over Cyprus between Greece and Turkey, should urge Turkey to take steps to withdraw its forces from Cyprus and should support United Nations efforts to end the dispute. Motion agreed to 405-6: R 181-3; D 224-3 (ND 152-2, SD 72-1) July 20, 1982. A two-thirds majority of those present and voting (274 in this case) is required for adoption under suspension of the rules.

183. HR 6030. Defense Department Authorizations, Fiscal 1983.
Bennett, D-Fla., amendment to delete from the bill $699 million for one Trident missile-firing submarine. Adopted 344-65: R 154-31; D 190-34 (ND 121-30, SD 69-4), July 20, 1982.

184. HR 6030. Defense Department Authorizations, Fiscal 1983.
Stratton, D-N.Y., amendment to delete from the bill $2.07 billion for various Army, Navy and Air Force procurement programs. Adopted 406-6: R 185-1; D 221-5 (ND 149-5, SD 72-0), July 20, 1982.

185. HR 6030. Defense Department Authorizations, Fiscal 1983.
Daniel, D-Va., amendment to delete from the bill $398.5 million for various operations and maintenance programs. Adopted 386-19: R 179-3; D 207-16 (ND 134-15, SD 73-1), July 20, 1982.

186. HR 6030. Defense Department Authorizations, Fiscal 1983.
Dellums, D-Calif., amendment to reduce the bill by $50.9 billion and prohibit procurement of MX, Pershing II or cruise missiles, B-1 bombers and nuclear-powered aircraft carriers. Rejected 55-348: R 3-178; D 52-170 (ND 49-100, SD 3-70), July 20, 1982. A "nay" was a vote supporting the president's position.

KEY	
Y	Voted for (yea).
#	Paired for.
+	Announced for.
N	Voted against (nay).
X	Paired against.
-	Announced against.
P	Voted "present".
C	Voted "present" to avoid possible conflict of interest.
?	Did not vote or otherwise make a position known.

Democrats *Republicans*

	179	180	181	182	183	184	185	186
ALABAMA								
1 Edwards	Y	Y	Y	Y	Y	Y	Y	N
2 Dickinson	Y	Y	Y	Y	Y	Y	Y	N
3 Nichols	Y	Y	N	Y	Y	Y	Y	N
4 Bevill	Y	Y	N	Y	Y	Y	Y	N
5 Flippo	Y	Y	N	Y	Y	Y	Y	N
6 Smith	Y	Y	N	Y	Y	Y	Y	N
7 Shelby	Y	Y	N	Y	N	Y	Y	N
ALASKA								
AL Young	Y	Y	Y	Y	?	Y	Y	N
ARIZONA								
1 Rhodes	Y	Y	Y	Y	N	Y	Y	N
2 Udall	Y	Y	N	Y	Y	Y	Y	N
3 Stump	Y	Y	N	Y	Y	Y	Y	N
4 Rudd	Y	Y	N	Y	Y	Y	Y	N
ARKANSAS								
1 Alexander	Y	Y	Y	Y	N	?	Y	?
2 Bethune	Y	?	N	Y	Y	Y	?	N
3 Hammerschmidt	Y	Y	N	Y	Y	Y	Y	N
4 Anthony	Y	Y	Y	Y	Y	Y	Y	N
CALIFORNIA								
1 Chappie	Y	Y	N	Y	Y	Y	Y	N
2 Clausen	Y	Y	Y	Y	Y	Y	Y	N
3 Matsui	Y	Y	Y	Y	Y	Y	Y	N
4 Fazio	Y	Y	Y	Y	N	Y	Y	N
5 Burton, J.	?	?	?	?	?	?	?	?
6 Burton, P.	Y	Y	Y	Y	Y	Y	Y	Y
7 Miller	Y	Y	Y	Y	N	Y	Y	Y
8 Dellums	Y	Y	Y	Y	Y	Y	Y	Y
9 Stark	Y	Y	Y	Y	Y	Y	N	Y
10 Edwards	Y	Y	Y	Y	Y	Y	Y	Y
11 Lantos	Y	Y	Y	Y	Y	Y	Y	N
12 McCloskey	Y	Y	N	Y	Y	Y	Y	N
13 Mineta	Y	Y	Y	Y	N	Y	N	N
14 Shumway	Y	Y	N	Y	Y	Y	Y	N
15 Coelho	Y	Y	Y	Y	Y	Y	Y	N
16 Panetta	Y	Y	Y	Y	N	Y	Y	N
17 Pashayan	Y	Y	N	Y	Y	Y	Y	N
18 Thomas	Y	Y	N	Y	Y	Y	Y	N
19 Lagomarsino	Y	Y	Y	Y	Y	Y	Y	N
20 Goldwater	Y	Y	N	Y	Y	Y	Y	Y
21 Fiedler	Y	Y	N	Y	Y	Y	Y	N
22 Moorhead	Y	Y	N	Y	Y	Y	Y	N
23 Beilenson	Y	Y	N	Y	N	Y	Y	Y
24 Waxman	Y	Y	Y	Y	Y	Y	Y	N
25 Roybal	Y	Y	Y	Y	Y	Y	Y	Y
26 Rousselot	?	?	?	?	?	?	?	?
27 Dornan	Y	Y	N	Y	Y	Y	Y	N
28 Dixon	Y	Y	Y	Y	Y	Y	Y	Y
29 Hawkins	Y	Y	Y	Y	Y	Y	Y	?
30 Martinez	Y	Y	Y	Y	Y	Y	Y	N
31 Dymally	Y	Y	Y	Y	Y	Y	Y	Y
32 Anderson	Y	Y	Y	Y	Y	Y	Y	N
33 Grisham	Y	Y	N	N	Y	Y	Y	N
34 Lungren	Y	Y	N	Y	Y	Y	Y	N
35 Dreier	Y	Y	N	Y	Y	Y	Y	N
36 Brown	Y	Y	Y	Y	Y	?	?	N
37 Lewis	Y	Y	N	Y	Y	Y	Y	N
38 Patterson	Y	Y	Y	Y	Y	Y	Y	N
39 Dannemeyer	Y	Y	N	Y	Y	Y	Y	N
40 Badham	Y	Y	Y	Y	Y	Y	Y	N
41 Lowery	Y	Y	Y	Y	N	Y	Y	N
42 Hunter	Y	Y	Y	Y	N	Y	Y	N
43 Burgener	Y	Y	N	Y	Y	Y	Y	?
COLORADO								
1 Schroeder	Y	Y	N	Y	Y	Y	N	Y
2 Wirth	Y	Y	Y	Y	Y	Y	N	N
3 Kogovsek	Y	Y	Y	Y	Y	Y	Y	N
4 Brown	Y	Y	N	Y	Y	Y	Y	N

	179	180	181	182	183	184	185	186
5 Kramer	Y	Y	Y	Y	N	Y	Y	N
CONNECTICUT								
1 Kennelly	Y	Y	N	Y	N	N	Y	N
2 Gejdenson	Y	Y	N	Y	N	N	N	N
3 DeNardis	Y	Y	N	Y	Y	Y	Y	N
4 McKinney	Y	Y	Y	Y	N	Y	Y	Y
5 Ratchford	Y	Y	N	Y	N	Y	Y	N
6 Moffett	Y	Y	?	Y	N	N	N	N
DELAWARE								
AL Evans	Y	Y	Y	Y	Y	Y	Y	?
FLORIDA								
1 Hutto	Y	Y	Y	Y	Y	Y	Y	N
2 Fuqua	Y	Y	Y	Y	Y	Y	Y	N
3 Bennett	Y	Y	N	Y	Y	Y	Y	N
4 Chappell	?	?	?	?	X	?	?	X
5 McCollum	Y	Y	N	Y	Y	Y	Y	N
6 Young	Y	Y	Y	Y	Y	Y	Y	N
7 Gibbons	Y	Y	Y	Y	Y	Y	Y	N
8 Ireland	Y	Y	N	Y	Y	Y	Y	N
9 Nelson	Y	Y	Y	Y	Y	Y	Y	N
10 Bafalis	Y	Y	Y	Y	Y	Y	Y	N
11 Mica	Y	Y	Y	Y	Y	Y	Y	N
12 Shaw	Y	Y	Y	Y	Y	Y	Y	N
13 Lehman	Y	Y	Y	Y	Y	Y	Y	Y
14 Pepper	Y	Y	Y	Y	Y	Y	Y	N
15 Fascell	Y	Y	Y	Y	Y	Y	Y	N
GEORGIA								
1 Ginn	Y	Y	Y	Y	Y	Y	Y	N
2 Hatcher	Y	Y	N	Y	Y	Y	Y	N
3 Brinkley	Y	Y	Y	Y	Y	Y	Y	N
4 Levitas	Y	Y	N	Y	Y	Y	Y	N
5 Fowler	Y	Y	Y	Y	Y	Y	N	N
6 Gingrich	Y	Y	Y	Y	Y	Y	Y	N
7 McDonald	N	N	N	Y	Y	Y	Y	N
8 Evans	Y	Y	Y	Y	Y	Y	Y	N
9 Jenkins	Y	Y	Y	Y	Y	Y	Y	N
10 Barnard	Y	Y	Y	Y	Y	Y	Y	N
HAWAII								
1 Heftel	Y	Y	Y	Y	Y	Y	?	N
2 Akaka	?	?	?	?	#	?	?	X
IDAHO								
1 Craig	Y	Y	N	Y	Y	Y	Y	N
2 Hansen	Y	Y	N	Y	Y	Y	Y	N
ILLINOIS								
1 Washington	Y	Y	Y	Y	Y	Y	Y	Y
2 Savage	Y	Y	Y	Y	Y	Y	Y	Y
3 Russo	Y	Y	Y	Y	N	Y	Y	N
4 Derwinski	Y	Y	N	Y	Y	Y	Y	N
5 Fary	Y	Y	Y	Y	Y	Y	Y	N
6 Hyde	Y	Y	N	Y	Y	Y	Y	N
7 Collins	Y	Y	Y	Y	Y	Y	Y	#
8 Rostenkowski	Y	Y	Y	Y	Y	Y	Y	N
9 Yates	Y	Y	N	Y	Y	Y	?	Y
10 Porter	Y	Y	N	Y	Y	Y	Y	N
11 Annunzio	Y	Y	Y	Y	Y	Y	Y	N
12 Crane, P.	N	N	N	N	Y	N	Y	N
13 McClory	Y	Y	N	Y	Y	Y	Y	N
14 Erlenborn	Y	Y	N	Y	Y	Y	Y	N
15 Corcoran	Y	Y	N	Y	Y	Y	Y	N
16 Martin	Y	Y	N	Y	Y	Y	Y	N
17 O'Brien	Y	Y	N	Y	N	Y	Y	N
18 Michel	Y	Y	N	Y	Y	Y	Y	N
19 Railsback	Y	Y	Y	Y	Y	Y	Y	N
20 Findley	Y	Y	?	N	Y	Y	Y	N
21 Madigan	Y	Y	Y	Y	Y	Y	Y	N
22 Crane, D.	?	N	N	Y	N	Y	Y	N
23 Price	Y	Y	Y	Y	Y	Y	Y	N
24 Simon	Y	Y	Y	Y	Y	Y	N	N
INDIANA								
1 Benjamin	Y	Y	Y	Y	Y	Y	Y	N
2 Fithian	?	?	?	?	?	Y	Y	N
3 Hiler	Y	Y	N	Y	N	Y	Y	N
4 Coats	Y	Y	N	Y	N	Y	Y	N
5 Hillis	Y	Y	N	Y	Y	Y	Y	N
6 Evans	Y	Y	Y	Y	Y	Y	Y	N
7 Myers	Y	Y	N	Y	Y	Y	Y	N
8 Deckard	Y	Y	N	Y	Y	Y	Y	N
9 Hamilton	Y	Y	Y	Y	Y	Y	Y	N
10 Sharp	Y	Y	N	Y	Y	Y	Y	N
11 Jacobs	Y	Y	N	Y	Y	Y	Y	N
IOWA								
1 Leach	Y	Y	Y	Y	Y	Y	Y	N
2 Tauke	Y	Y	Y	Y	Y	Y	Y	N
3 Evans	Y	Y	N	Y	Y	Y	N	N
4 Smith	Y	Y	N	Y	Y	Y	Y	Y
5 Harkin	Y	N	Y	Y	Y	Y	Y	Y
6 Bedell	Y	Y	Y	Y	Y	Y	Y	Y

ND - Northern Democrats   SD - Southern Democrats

Corresponding to Congressional Record Votes 188, 189, 190, 191, 192, 193, 194, 195

	179	180	181	182	183	184	185	186
KANSAS								
1 ***Roberts***	Y	Y	N	Y	Y	Y	Y	N
2 ***Jeffries***	Y	Y	N	Y	N	Y	Y	N
3 ***Winn***	Y	Y	N	Y	Y	Y	Y	N
4 Glickman	Y	Y	N	Y	Y	Y	Y	N
5 ***Whittaker***	Y	Y	N	Y	Y	Y	Y	N
KENTUCKY								
1 Hubbard	Y	Y	Y	Y	Y	Y	Y	N
2 Natcher	Y	Y	N	Y	Y	Y	Y	N
3 Mazzoli	Y	Y	N	Y	?	Y	Y	N
4 ***Snyder***	Y	Y	N	Y	Y	Y	Y	N
5 ***Rogers***	Y	Y	Y	Y	Y	Y	Y	N
6 ***Hopkins***	Y	Y	N	Y	Y	Y	Y	N
7 Perkins	Y	Y	Y	Y	Y	Y	Y	N
LOUISIANA								
1 ***Livingston***	Y	Y	N	Y	Y	Y	Y	N
2 Boggs	Y	Y	Y	Y	Y	Y	Y	N
3 Tauzin	Y	Y	N	Y	Y	Y	Y	N
4 Roemer	Y	Y	N	Y	Y	Y	Y	N
5 Huckaby	Y	Y	N	Y	N	Y	Y	N
6 ***Moore***	Y	Y	N	Y	Y	Y	Y	N
7 Breaux	Y	Y	N	Y	Y	Y	Y	N
8 Long	Y	Y	Y	Y	Y	Y	Y	N
MAINE								
1 ***Emery***	Y	Y	Y	Y	Y	Y	Y	N
2 ***Snowe***	Y	Y	Y	Y	Y	Y	Y	N
MARYLAND								
1 Dyson	Y	Y	Y	Y	Y	Y	Y	N
2 Long	Y	Y	N	Y	N	Y	Y	N
3 Mikulski	Y	Y	Y	Y	Y	Y	Y	N
4 ***Holt***	Y	Y	N	Y	Y	Y	Y	N
5 Hoyer	Y	Y	Y	Y	Y	Y	Y	N
6 Byron	Y	Y	Y	Y	Y	Y	Y	N
7 Mitchell	Y	Y	Y	Y	Y	Y	Y	#
8 Barnes	Y	Y	Y	Y	Y	Y	Y	N
MASSACHUSETTS								
1 ***Conte***	Y	Y	Y	Y	Y	Y	Y	N
2 Boland	Y	?	Y	Y	Y	Y	Y	N
3 Early	Y	Y	Y	Y	Y	Y	Y	N
4 Frank	Y	Y	Y	Y	Y	Y	Y	Y
5 Shannon	Y	Y	Y	Y	Y	Y	Y	N
6 Mavroules	Y	Y	Y	Y	Y	Y	Y	N
7 Markey	Y	Y	Y	Y	Y	Y	Y	Y
8 O'Neill								
9 Moakley	Y	Y	Y	Y	Y	Y	Y	N
10 ***Heckler***	Y	Y	Y	Y	N	Y	Y	N
11 Donnelly	Y	Y	Y	Y	N	Y	Y	Y
12 Studds	Y	Y	Y	Y	N	Y	N	Y
MICHIGAN								
1 Conyers	Y	Y	Y	N	Y	Y	Y	Y
2 ***Pursell***	Y	?	?	Y	Y	Y	Y	N
3 Wolpe	Y	Y	N	Y	N	Y	Y	Y
4 ***Siljander***	Y	Y	Y	Y	N	Y	Y	N
5 ***Sawyer***	Y	Y	Y	Y	Y	Y	Y	N
6 ***Dunn***	Y	Y	N	Y	Y	Y	Y	N
7 Kildee	Y	Y	Y	Y	Y	Y	Y	N
8 Traxler	Y	Y	Y	Y	Y	Y	Y	N
9 ***Vander Jagt***	Y	Y	Y	Y	Y	Y	Y	?
10 Albosta	?	?	?	?	?	?	?	?
11 ***Davis***	Y	Y	Y	Y	Y	Y	Y	N
12 Bonior	Y	Y	Y	Y	Y	Y	Y	Y
13 Crockett	Y	Y	Y	Y	?	Y	Y	Y
14 Hertel	Y	Y	N	Y	Y	Y	N	N
15 Ford	Y	Y	?	Y	N	Y	N	N
16 Dingell	Y	Y	Y	Y	N	Y	N	N
17 Brodhead	Y	Y	Y	Y	Y	Y	Y	Y
18 Blanchard	?	?	?	?	?	?	?	?
19 ***Broomfield***	Y	Y	Y	Y	Y	Y	Y	N
MINNESOTA								
1 ***Erdahl***	Y	Y	Y	Y	Y	Y	Y	N
2 ***Hagedorn***	?	?	?	?	Y	Y	Y	N
3 ***Frenzel***	Y	Y	N	Y	Y	Y	Y	N
4 Vento	Y	Y	Y	Y	N	Y	Y	N
5 Sabo	Y	Y	N	Y	N	Y	N	Y
6 ***Weber***	Y	Y	N	Y	Y	Y	Y	N
7 ***Stangeland***	Y	Y	Y	Y	Y	Y	Y	N
8 Oberstar	Y	Y	Y	Y	N	Y	N	Y
MISSISSIPPI								
1 Whitten	Y	Y	N	Y	Y	Y	Y	N
2 Bowen	?	?	?	?	?	?	?	?
3 Montgomery	Y	Y	N	Y	Y	Y	Y	N
4 Dowdy	Y	?	Y	Y	Y	Y	Y	N
5 ***Lott***	Y	Y	Y	Y	Y	Y	Y	N
MISSOURI								
1 Clay	?	?	?	?	?	?	?	?
2 Young	Y	Y	Y	Y	?	Y	Y	N
3 Gephardt	Y	Y	N	Y	Y	Y	Y	N
4 Skelton	Y	Y	Y	Y	Y	Y	Y	N
5 Bolling	Y	Y	Y	Y	?	?	?	?
6 ***Coleman***	Y	Y	Y	Y	Y	Y	Y	N
7 ***Taylor***	Y	Y	N	Y	Y	Y	Y	N
8 ***Bailey***	Y	Y	N	Y	Y	Y	Y	N
9 Volkmer	Y	Y	N	Y	Y	Y	Y	N
10 ***Emerson***	Y	Y	N	Y	Y	Y	Y	N
MONTANA								
1 Williams	Y	Y	Y	Y	N	Y	Y	N
2 ***Marlenee***	Y	Y	Y	Y	Y	Y	Y	N
NEBRASKA								
1 ***Bereuter***	Y	Y	N	Y	Y	Y	Y	N
2 ***Daub***	Y	Y	N	Y	Y	Y	Y	N
3 ***Smith***	Y	Y	N	Y	Y	Y	Y	N
NEVADA								
AL Santini	Y	Y	Y	Y	Y	N	Y	N
NEW HAMPSHIRE								
1 D'Amours	Y	Y	Y	Y	Y	Y	Y	N
2 ***Gregg***	Y	Y	N	Y	Y	Y	Y	N
NEW JERSEY								
1 Florio	Y	Y	Y	Y	N	Y	Y	N
2 Hughes	Y	Y	Y	Y	N	Y	Y	N
3 Howard	Y	Y	Y	Y	Y	Y	Y	N
4 ***Smith***	Y	Y	Y	Y	Y	Y	Y	N
5 ***Fenwick***	Y	Y	N	Y	Y	Y	Y	N
6 ***Forsythe***	Y	Y	N	Y	Y	Y	Y	Y
7 ***Roukema***	Y	Y	N	Y	Y	Y	Y	N
8 Roe	Y	Y	Y	Y	Y	Y	Y	N
9 ***Hollenbeck***	Y	Y	Y	Y	Y	Y	Y	N
10 Rodino	Y	Y	Y	Y	Y	Y	Y	Y
11 Minish	Y	Y	Y	Y	Y	Y	Y	N
12 ***Rinaldo***	Y	Y	Y	Y	Y	Y	Y	N
13 ***Courter***	Y	Y	Y	Y	N	Y	Y	N
14 Guarini	Y	Y	Y	Y	Y	Y	Y	N
15 Dwyer	Y	Y	Y	Y	Y	Y	Y	N
NEW MEXICO								
1 ***Lujan***	Y	Y	N	Y	Y	Y	?	N
2 ***Skeen***	Y	Y	N	Y	Y	Y	Y	N
NEW YORK								
1 ***Carney***	Y	Y	Y	Y	Y	Y	Y	N
2 Downey	Y	Y	Y	Y	N	N	Y	N
3 ***Carman***	Y	Y	Y	Y	Y	Y	Y	N
4 ***Lent***	Y	Y	Y	Y	N	Y	?	N
5 ***McGrath***	Y	Y	Y	Y	Y	Y	Y	N
6 ***LeBoutillier***	?	?	?	?	Y	Y	Y	N
7 Addabbo	Y	Y	Y	Y	Y	Y	Y	Y
8 Rosenthal	Y	Y	Y	Y	Y	Y	Y	Y
9 Ferraro	Y	Y	Y	Y	Y	Y	Y	N
10 Biaggi	+	?	?	+	?	Y	Y	Y
11 Scheuer	Y	Y	Y	Y	Y	Y	Y	N
12 Chisholm	Y	Y	Y	Y	?	?	?	Y
13 Solarz	Y	Y	Y	N	N	Y	Y	N
14 Richmond	Y	Y	Y	Y	Y	Y	Y	#
15 Zeferetti	Y	Y	Y	Y	N	Y	Y	N
16 Schumer	+	+	+	+	?	Y	Y	Y
17 ***Molinari***	Y	Y	Y	Y	N	Y	Y	N
18 ***Green***	?	?	?	?	?	Y	N	N
19 Rangel	?	?	?	?	Y	Y	Y	Y
20 Weiss	Y	Y	Y	Y	Y	Y	Y	Y
21 Garcia	Y	Y	Y	Y	Y	Y	Y	Y
22 Bingham	Y	Y	N	Y	Y	Y	Y	Y
23 Peyser	Y	Y	Y	Y	Y	Y	?	?
24 Ottinger	Y	Y	Y	Y	N	Y	Y	Y
25 ***Fish***	Y	Y	Y	Y	Y	Y	Y	N
26 ***Gilman***	Y	Y	Y	Y	Y	Y	Y	N
27 McHugh	Y	Y	Y	Y	Y	Y	Y	N
28 Stratton	Y	Y	Y	Y	Y	Y	Y	N
29 ***Solomon***	?	?	?	?	?	?	?	?
30 ***Martin***	Y	Y	Y	Y	?	?	?	?
31 ***Mitchell***	Y	Y	Y	Y	N	Y	Y	N
32 ***Wortley***	Y	Y	Y	Y	Y	Y	Y	N
33 ***Lee***	Y	Y	Y	Y	N	Y	Y	N
34 ***Horton***	Y	Y	Y	Y	Y	Y	?	N
35 ***Conable***	Y	Y	N	Y	N	Y	Y	N
36 LaFalce	Y	Y	Y	Y	Y	Y	Y	N
37 Nowak	Y	Y	Y	Y	Y	Y	Y	N
38 ***Kemp***	Y	?	Y	Y	N	N	N	N
39 Lundine	Y	Y	Y	Y	Y	Y	Y	?
NORTH CAROLINA								
1 Jones	Y	Y	Y	Y	Y	Y	Y	N
2 Fountain	Y	Y	N	?	Y	Y	Y	N
3 Whitley	Y	Y	N	Y	Y	Y	Y	N
4 Andrews	Y	Y	N	Y	Y	Y	Y	N
5 Neal	Y	Y	N	Y	Y	Y	Y	N
6 ***Johnston***	Y	Y	N	Y	Y	Y	Y	N
7 Pose	?	?	?	?	?	?	?	?
8 Hefner	Y	Y	Y	Y	Y	Y	Y	N
9 ***Martin***	Y	Y	N	Y	Y	Y	Y	N
10 ***Broyhill***	Y	Y	N	Y	Y	Y	Y	N
11 ***Hendon***	Y	Y	Y	Y	N	Y	Y	N
NORTH DAKOTA								
AL Dorgan	Y	Y	Y	Y	Y	Y	Y	N
OHIO								
1 ***Gradison***	Y	Y	N	Y	Y	Y	Y	N
2 Luken	Y	Y	Y	Y	Y	Y	?	N
3 Hall	Y	Y	N	Y	Y	Y	Y	N
4 ***Oxley***	Y	Y	N	Y	Y	Y	Y	N
5 ***Latta***	Y	Y	N	Y	Y	Y	Y	N
6 ***McEwen***	Y	Y	N	Y	Y	Y	Y	N
7 ***Brown***	?	?	?	?	?	?	?	?
8 ***Kindness***	Y	N	N	Y	Y	Y	Y	N
9 ***Weber***	Y	Y	N	Y	Y	Y	Y	N
10 ***Miller***	Y	Y	N	Y	Y	Y	Y	N
11 ***Stanton***	Y	Y	N	Y	Y	Y	?	?
12 Shamansky	Y	Y	Y	Y	Y	Y	Y	N
13 Pease	Y	Y	N	Y	Y	Y	Y	N
14 Seiberling	Y	Y	N	Y	Y	Y	Y	Y
15 ***Wylie***	Y	Y	N	Y	Y	Y	Y	N
16 ***Regula***	Y	Y	N	Y	Y	Y	Y	N
17 ***Ashbrook***	N	N	N	Y	Y	Y	Y	N
18 Applegate	Y	Y	Y	Y	N	Y	Y	N
19 ***Williams***	Y	Y	N	Y	Y	Y	Y	N
20 Oakar	Y	Y	Y	Y	Y	Y	Y	N
21 Stokes	Y	Y	Y	Y	Y	Y	Y	Y
22 Eckart	Y	Y	N	Y	Y	Y	N	N
23 Mottl	Y	Y	Y	Y	Y	Y	Y	N
OKLAHOMA								
1 Jones	Y	Y	N	Y	Y	Y	Y	N
2 Synar	Y	Y	Y	Y	Y	Y	Y	N
3 Watkins	Y	Y	Y	Y	Y	Y	Y	N
4 McCurdy	Y	Y	N	Y	Y	Y	Y	N
5 ***Edwards***	Y	Y	N	Y	Y	Y	Y	N
6 English	Y	Y	N	Y	Y	Y	Y	N
OREGON								
1 AuCoin	Y	?	Y	Y	Y	Y	Y	Y
2 ***Smith***	Y	Y	N	Y	Y	Y	Y	N
3 Wyden	Y	Y	Y	Y	Y	Y	Y	Y
4 Weaver	Y	Y	Y	Y	Y	Y	Y	Y
PENNSYLVANIA								
1 Foglietta	Y	Y	Y	Y	Y	Y	Y	N
2 Gray	Y	Y	Y	Y	Y	Y	Y	Y
3 Smith	Y	Y	Y	Y	Y	Y	Y	N
4 ***Dougherty***	Y	Y	Y	Y	Y	Y	Y	N
5 ***Schulze***	Y	Y	N	Y	N	Y	Y	N
6 Yatron	Y	Y	Y	Y	Y	Y	Y	N
7 Edgar	Y	Y	N	Y	Y	Y	Y	Y
8 ***Coyne, J.***	?	?	?	?	?	?	?	?
9 ***Shuster***	Y	Y	Y	Y	Y	Y	Y	N
10 ***McDade***	Y	Y	Y	Y	Y	Y	Y	N
11 ***Nelligan***	Y	Y	Y	Y	Y	Y	Y	N
12 Murtha	Y	Y	Y	Y	N	Y	Y	N
13 ***Coughlin***	Y	Y	N	Y	Y	Y	Y	N
14 Coyne, W.	Y	Y	Y	Y	Y	Y	Y	Y
15 ***Ritter***	Y	Y	N	Y	Y	Y	Y	N
16 ***Walker***	Y	Y	N	Y	Y	Y	Y	N
17 Ertel	Y	Y	Y	Y	Y	Y	Y	N
18 Walgren	Y	Y	Y	Y	Y	Y	Y	N
19 ***Goodling***	Y	Y	N	Y	Y	?	Y	N
20 Gaydos	Y	Y	Y	Y	Y	Y	Y	N
21 Bailey	Y	Y	Y	Y	N	?	?	?
22 Murphy	Y	Y	Y	Y	Y	Y	Y	N
23 ***Clinger***	Y	Y	N	Y	Y	Y	Y	N
24 ***Marks***	Y	Y	Y	Y	Y	Y	Y	?
25 ***Atkinson***	Y	Y	N	Y	N	Y	Y	N
RHODE ISLAND								
1 St Germain	Y	Y	N	Y	N	Y	Y	N
2 ***Schneider***	Y	Y	Y	Y	N	Y	Y	N
SOUTH CAROLINA								
1 ***Hartnett***	Y	Y	N	Y	N	Y	Y	N
2 ***Spence***	Y	Y	Y	Y	Y	Y	Y	N
3 Derrick	Y	Y	Y	Y	Y	Y	Y	N
4 ***Campbell***	Y	Y	Y	Y	Y	Y	Y	N
5 Holland	Y	Y	Y	Y	Y	?	Y	N
6 ***Napier***	Y	Y	Y	Y	Y	Y	Y	N
SOUTH DAKOTA								
1 Daschle	Y	Y	Y	Y	Y	Y	Y	N
2 ***Roberts***	Y	Y	Y	Y	Y	Y	Y	N
TENNESSEE								
1 ***Quillen***	Y	Y	Y	Y	N	Y	Y	N
2 ***Duncan***	Y	Y	Y	Y	Y	Y	Y	N
3 Bouquard	Y	Y	Y	Y	Y	Y	Y	N
4 Gore	Y	Y	Y	Y	Y	Y	Y	N
5 Boner	Y	Y	Y	Y	Y	Y	Y	N
6 ***Beard***	Y	Y	N	Y	Y	Y	Y	N
7 Jones	?	?	?	?	?	?	?	X
8 Ford	Y	Y	Y	Y	Y	Y	Y	Y
TEXAS								
1 Hall, S.	Y	Y	N	Y	Y	Y	Y	N
2 Wilson	Y	Y	Y	Y	N	Y	Y	N
3 ***Collins***	Y	Y	N	Y	Y	Y	Y	N
4 Hall, R.	Y	Y	Y	Y	Y	Y	Y	N
5 Mattox	Y	Y	N	Y	Y	Y	Y	N
6 Gramm	Y	Y	N	Y	Y	Y	Y	N
7 ***Archer***	Y	Y	N	Y	Y	Y	Y	N
8 ***Fields***	Y	Y	N	Y	Y	Y	Y	N
9 Brooks	Y	Y	N	Y	Y	Y	Y	N
10 Pickle	Y	Y	Y	Y	Y	Y	Y	N
11 Leath	Y	Y	N	Y	Y	Y	Y	N
12 Wright	Y	Y	Y	Y	Y	Y	Y	N
13 Hightower	Y	Y	N	Y	Y	Y	Y	N
14 Patman	Y	Y	N	Y	Y	Y	Y	N
15 de la Garza	?	?	?	?	?	?	?	?
16 White	Y	Y	N	Y	Y	Y	Y	N
17 Stenholm	Y	Y	N	Y	Y	Y	Y	N
18 Leland	Y	Y	Y	Y	Y	Y	Y	Y
19 Hance	Y	Y	N	Y	Y	Y	Y	N
20 Gonzalez	Y	P	Y	Y	Y	Y	Y	N
21 ***Loeffler***	Y	Y	N	Y	Y	Y	Y	N
22 ***Paul***	N	N	N	N	Y	Y	Y	N
23 Kazen	Y	Y	Y	Y	Y	Y	Y	N
24 Frost	Y	Y	Y	Y	Y	Y	Y	N
UTAH								
1 ***Hansen***	Y	Y	N	Y	Y	Y	Y	N
2 ***Marriott***	Y	Y	Y	Y	Y	Y	Y	N
VERMONT								
AL ***Jeffords***	Y	Y	Y	Y	Y	Y	Y	N
VIRGINIA								
1 ***Trible***	?	?	?	?	Y	Y	Y	?
2 ***Whitehurst***	Y	Y	N	Y	Y	Y	Y	N
3 ***Bliley***	Y	Y	N	Y	Y	Y	Y	N
4 ***Daniel, R.***	Y	Y	N	Y	Y	Y	Y	N
5 Daniel, D.	Y	Y	N	Y	Y	Y	Y	N
6 ***Butler***	Y	Y	N	Y	Y	Y	Y	N
7 ***Robinson***	Y	Y	N	Y	Y	Y	Y	N
8 ***Parris***	Y	Y	Y	Y	Y	Y	?	N
9 ***Wampler***	Y	Y	Y	Y	Y	Y	Y	N
10 ***Wolf***	Y	Y	Y	Y	Y	Y	Y	N
WASHINGTON								
1 ***Pritchard***	Y	Y	Y	Y	Y	Y	Y	N
2 Swift	Y	Y	Y	Y	Y	Y	Y	N
3 Bonker	Y	Y	Y	Y	Y	Y	Y	Y
4 ***Morrison***	Y	Y	Y	Y	Y	Y	Y	N
5 Foley	Y	Y	Y	Y	Y	Y	Y	N
6 Dicks	Y	Y	Y	Y	Y	Y	Y	N
7 Lowry	Y	Y	Y	Y	Y	Y	Y	Y
WEST VIRGINIA								
1 Mollohan	Y	Y	Y	Y	Y	Y	?	?
2 ***Benedict***	Y	Y	Y	Y	Y	Y	Y	N
3 ***Staton***	Y	Y	Y	Y	Y	Y	Y	N
4 Rahall	Y	Y	Y	Y	Y	Y	Y	N
WISCONSIN								
1 Aspin	Y	Y	N	Y	Y	Y	Y	N
2 Kastenmeier	Y	Y	Y	Y	Y	Y	Y	Y
3 ***Gunderson***	Y	Y	N	Y	N	Y	Y	N
4 Zablocki	Y	Y	Y	Y	Y	Y	Y	N
5 Reuss	Y	Y	Y	Y	Y	Y	Y	Y
6 ***Petri***	Y	N	N	Y	Y	Y	Y	N
7 Obey	Y	Y	N	Y	Y	Y	N	N
8 ***Roth***	Y	Y	Y	Y	Y	Y	Y	N
9 ***Sensenbrenner***	Y	N	N	Y	Y	Y	Y	N
WYOMING								
AL ***Cheney***	Y	Y	N	Y	N	Y	Y	N

Southern states - Ala., Ark., Fla., Ga., Ky., La., Miss., N.C., Okla., S.C., Tenn., Texas, Va.

KEY

Y Voted for (yea).
Paired for.
+ Announced for.
N Voted against (nay).
X Paired against.
- Announced against.
P Voted "present".
C Voted "present" to avoid possible conflict of interest.
? Did not vote or otherwise make a position known.

Democrats   *Republicans*

187. Procedural Motion. Weber, R-Minn., motion to approve the House *Journal* of Tuesday, July 20. Motion agreed to 358-26: R 167-14; D 191-12 (ND 126-11, SD 65-1), July 21, 1982.

188. HR 6030. Defense Department Authorizations, Fiscal 1983. Stratton, D-N.Y., substitute for the Mavroules, D-Mass., amendment, to authorize $1,141,900,000 for the MX intercontinental missile; the $259,900,000 of that amount for MX basing and deployment could not be obligated until the 30 days after the president notified the Congress that a basing mode had been selected. The Mavroules amendment would have deleted the $1,141,900,000 for procurement of MX Missiles. Adopted 212-209: R 142-45; D 70-164 (ND 18-141, SD 52-23), July 21, 1982. A "yea" was a vote supporting the president's position. (The Mavroules amendment, as amended by the Stratton substitute, subsequently was adopted by voice vote.)

189. HR 6030. Defense Department Authorizations, Fiscal 1983. Badham, R-Calif., substitute for the Dicks, D-Wash., amendment, to prohibit use of any funds in the bill for purchase of new strategic airlift aircraft for the Air Force, except for the KC-10 aircraft. The Dicks amendment prohibited use of funds in the bill to purchase additional C-5 aircraft and authorized $350,000,000 for procurement instead of the "most cost-effective" commercial wide-body aircraft. Rejected 74-344: R 30-156; D 44-188 (ND 41-117, SD 3-71), July 21, 1982. (The Dicks amendment subsequently was rejected *(see vote 190, below)*.)

190. HR 6030. Defense Department Authorizations, Fiscal 1983. Dicks, D-Wash., amendment to prohibit use of funds in the bill to purchase additional C-5 aircraft and to authorize $350,000,000 for procurement instead of the "most cost-effective" commercial wide-body aircraft. The intent of the amendment was to require the Air Force to buy Boeing 747 aircraft. Rejected 127-289: R 37-148; D 90-141 (ND 82-75, SD 8-66), July 21, 1982. A "nay" was a vote supporting the president's position.

191. HR 6030. Defense Department Authorizations, Fiscal 1983. Dellums, D-Calif., amendment to delete from the bill $498,300,000 for procurement of Pershing II ballistic missiles. Rejected 74-311: R 6-167; D 68-144 (ND 65-78, SD 3-66), July 21, 1982. A "nay" was a vote supporting the president's position.

	187	188	189	190	191
ALABAMA					
1 Edwards	Y	Y	N	Y	?
2 Dickinson	Y	Y	N	N	N
3 Nichols	Y	Y	N	N	?
4 Bevill	Y	Y	N	N	N
5 Flippo	Y	Y	N	N	N
6 *Smith*	Y	Y	N	N	N
7 Shelby	Y	Y	N	N	N
ALASKA					
AL *Young*	N	Y	N	Y	?
ARIZONA					
1 *Rhodes*	Y	Y	N	Y	?
2 Udall	Y	N	N	Y	N
3 *Stump*	Y	Y	N	N	N
4 *Rudd*	Y	Y	N	Y	N
ARKANSAS					
1 Alexander	Y	N	N	Y	N
2 *Bethune*	Y	Y	N	N	N
3 *Hammerschmidt*	Y	Y	N	N	N
4 Anthony	Y	N	N	N	N
CALIFORNIA					
1 *Chappie*	Y	Y	N	N	N
2 *Clausen*	Y	Y	Y	N	N
3 Matsui	Y	Y	N	N	N
4 Fazio	Y	Y	Y	Y	N
5 Burton, J.	?	?	?	?	?
6 Burton, P.	Y	N	Y	Y	Y
7 Miller	Y	N	Y	Y	Y
8 Dellums	?	N	Y	Y	Y
9 Stark	Y	N	Y	Y	?
10 Edwards	Y	N	N	N	Y
11 Lantos	Y	N	N	N	N
12 *McCloskey*	?	Y	Y	N	?
13 Mineta	Y	N	N	N	N
14 *Shumway*	Y	Y	N	N	N
15 Coelho	Y	N	N	N	N
16 Panetta	Y	N	N	N	Y
17 *Pashayan*	Y	Y	Y	N	N
18 *Thomas*	Y	Y	Y	N	N
19 *Lagomarsino*	Y	Y	N	N	N
20 *Goldwater*	?	Y	N	N	N
21 *Fiedler*	Y	Y	N	N	N
22 *Moorhead*	Y	Y	N	N	N
23 Beilenson	N	N	N	N	Y
24 Waxman	Y	N	N	N	Y
25 Roybal	Y	N	Y	Y	Y
26 *Rousselot*	Y	Y	N	N	N
27 *Dornan*	Y	Y	Y	N	N
28 Dixon	Y	N	N	N	?
29 Hawkins	N	N	N	N	N
30 Martinez	?	Y	N	?	N
31 Dymally	Y	N	Y	Y	N
32 Anderson	Y	N	Y	Y	N
33 Grisham	Y	Y	Y	Y	N
34 *Lungren*	Y	Y	Y	N	N
35 *Dreier*	N	Y	N	N	N
36 Brown	?	N	N	N	?
37 *Lewis*	Y	Y	Y	N	N
38 Patterson	Y	N	N	Y	N
39 *Dannemeyer*	Y	Y	Y	Y	N
40 *Badham*	Y	Y	N	N	N
41 *Lowery*	Y	Y	N	N	N
42 *Hunter*	Y	Y	N	N	N
43 *Burgener*	?	#	?	?	?
COLORADO					
1 Schroeder	N	N	Y	Y	Y
2 Wirth	Y	N	Y	Y	N
3 Kogovsek	Y	N	N	Y	N
4 *Brown*	Y	Y	Y	Y	N

	187	188	189	190	191
5 *Kramer*	Y	Y	N	N	N
CONNECTICUT					
1 Kennelly	Y	N	N	Y	Y
2 Gejdenson	N	N	N	Y	Y
3 *DeNardis*	Y	N	N	Y	Y
4 *McKinney*	Y	X	Y	Y	Y
5 Ratchford	Y	N	N	Y	N
6 Moffett	?	N	?	#	#
DELAWARE					
AL *Evans*	Y	Y	N	N	N
FLORIDA					
1 Hutto	Y	Y	N	N	N
2 Fuqua	Y	N	N	N	N
3 Bennett	Y	N	N	N	N
4 Chappell	Y	Y	N	N	N
5 *McCollum*	Y	Y	N	N	N
6 *Young*	Y	Y	N	N	N
7 Gibbons	Y	Y	N	N	N
8 Ireland	Y	Y	N	N	?
9 Nelson	Y	N	N	N	N
10 *Bafalis*	Y	Y	N	N	N
11 Mica	Y	Y	N	N	N
12 *Shaw*	Y	Y	N	N	N
13 Lehman	Y	N	N	Y	Y
14 Pepper	?	N	N	N	N
15 Fascell	Y	N	N	N	N
GEORGIA					
1 Ginn	Y	Y	N	N	?
2 Hatcher	Y	N	N	N	N
3 Brinkley	Y	Y	N	N	N
4 Levitas	Y	Y	N	N	N
5 Fowler	?	N	N	N	N
6 *Gingrich*	Y	Y	N	N	N
7 McDonald	Y	Y	N	N	N
8 Evans	Y	N	N	N	N
9 Jenkins	Y	Y	N	N	N
10 Barnard	Y	Y	N	N	N
HAWAII					
1 Heftel	Y	N	N	N	N
2 Akaka	Y	N	N	Y	N
IDAHO					
1 *Craig*	Y	Y	N	N	N
2 *Hansen*	Y	Y	N	N	?
ILLINOIS					
1 Washington	N	N	Y	Y	Y
2 Savage	?	N	Y	Y	Y
3 Russo	Y	N	N	Y	Y
4 *Derwinski*	Y	Y	N	N	?
5 Fary	Y	N	N	N	N
6 *Hyde*	Y	N	Y	N	N
7 Collins	Y	N	Y	Y	Y
8 Rostenkowski	Y	N	N	N	N
9 Yates	?	N	Y	Y	N
10 *Porter*	Y	N	N	N	N
11 Annunzio	Y	N	N	N	N
12 *Crane, P.*	Y	N	N	N	N
13 *McClory*	Y	Y	N	N	N
14 *Erlenborn*	Y	N	N	N	N
15 *Corcoran*	Y	Y	N	N	N
16 *Martin*	Y	Y	N	N	N
17 *O'Brien*	Y	N	N	N	N
18 *Michel*	Y	Y	N	N	N
19 *Railsback*	Y	N	N	N	N
20 *Findley*	Y	N	Y	Y	N
21 *Madigan*	Y	Y	N	N	?
22 *Crane, D.*	Y	Y	N	N	N
23 Price	Y	N	N	N	N
24 Simon	?	N	Y	Y	N
INDIANA					
1 Benjamin	Y	N	N	N	N
2 Fithian	Y	N	N	N	N
3 *Hiler*	N	Y	N	N	N
4 *Coats*	Y	N	N	N	N
5 *Hillis*	Y	Y	N	N	N
6 Evans	Y	N	N	N	N
7 *Myers*	Y	N	N	N	N
8 *Deckard*	Y	N	N	N	N
9 Hamilton	Y	N	N	N	N
10 Sharp	Y	N	N	Y	N
11 Jacobs	N	N	Y	N	N
IOWA					
1 *Leach*	Y	N	N	Y	N
2 *Tauke*	Y	N	N	Y	N
3 *Evans*	N	N	N	N	N
4 Smith	Y	N	N	Y	N
5 Harkin	N	N	Y	Y	Y
6 Bedell	Y	N	N	Y	Y

ND - Northern Democrats   SD - Southern Democrats

Corresponding to Congressional Record Votes 196, 197, 198, 199, 200

Member	187	188	189	190	191
KANSAS					
1 Roberts	Y	N	N	Y	N
2 Jeffries	?	Y	N	Y	N
3 Winn	Y	N	N	Y	N
4 Glickman	Y	N	N	Y	Y
5 Whittaker	Y	N	N	Y	N
KENTUCKY					
1 Hubbard	Y	Y	N	N	N
2 Natcher	Y	Y	N	N	N
3 Mazzoli	Y	N	N	N	N
4 Snyder	Y	Y	N	N	N
5 Rogers	Y	Y	N	N	N
6 Hopkins	Y	Y	N	N	N
7 Perkins	Y	Y	N	N	N
LOUISIANA					
1 Livingston	Y	Y	N	C	N
2 Boggs	Y	N	N	N	N
3 Tauzin	?	#	?	?	N
4 Roemer	N	N	N	N	N
5 Huckaby	Y	Y	?	?	?
6 Moore	Y	Y	N	N	N
7 Breaux	Y	Y	N	Y	N
8 Long	?	N	N	Y	N
MAINE					
1 Emery	Y	Y	N	N	N
2 Snowe	Y	N	N	Y	N
MARYLAND					
1 Dyson	Y	N	N	N	N
2 Long	Y	N	N	N	Y
3 Mikulski	?	N	Y	Y	Y
4 Holt	Y	Y	N	N	N
5 Hoyer	Y	N	N	N	N
6 Byron	Y	N	N	N	N
7 Mitchell	N	N	Y	Y	Y
8 Barnes	N	N	Y	N	N
MASSACHUSETTS					
1 Conte	Y	N	N	N	N
2 Boland	?	N	N	Y	N
3 Early	Y	N	N	N	N
4 Frank	Y	N	N	N	Y
5 Shannon	Y	N	N	N	Y
6 Mavroules	Y	N	N	N	N
7 Markey	Y	N	N	N	Y
8 O'Neill					
9 Moakley	Y	N	N	N	N
10 Heckler	Y	N	N	N	Y
11 Donnelly	Y	N	N	N	Y
12 Studds	Y	N	N	N	Y
MICHIGAN					
1 Conyers	Y	N	Y	Y	Y
2 Pursell	Y	N	N	N	?
3 Wolpe	Y	N	N	N	Y
4 Siljander	Y	Y	N	N	N
5 Sawyer	Y	Y	N	N	N
6 Dunn	Y	N	N	N	N
7 Kildee	Y	N	N	N	Y
8 Traxler	Y	N	N	N	?
9 Vander Jagt	Y	Y	N	N	N
10 Albosta	Y	N	N	Y	N
11 Davis	Y	Y	N	N	N
12 Bonior	Y	N	Y	N	Y
13 Crockett	Y	N	Y	Y	Y
14 Hertel	Y	N	N	N	N
15 Ford	Y	N	N	Y	N
16 Dingell	Y	N	Y	N	N
17 Brodhead	Y	N	Y	Y	?
18 Blanchard	?	X	?	?	?
19 Broomfield	Y	Y	N	N	N
MINNESOTA					
1 Erdahl	Y	N	Y	N	N
2 Hagedorn	Y	N	N	N	N
3 Frenzel	?	N	Y	Y	N
4 Vento	Y	N	N	N	N
5 Sabo	N	N	Y	N	Y
6 Weber	Y	Y	Y	Y	N
7 Stangeland	Y	N	N	N	N
8 Oberstar	Y	N	N	N	Y
MISSISSIPPI					
1 Whitten	?	Y	N	N	N
2 Bowen	?	?	?	?	?
3 Montgomery	Y	Y	N	N	N
4 Dowdy	Y	Y	N	N	N
5 Lott	Y	Y	N	N	N
MISSOURI					
1 Clay	?	X	?	?	#
2 Young	?	N	Y	N	Y
3 Gephardt	Y	Y	Y	Y	N
4 Skelton	Y	Y	Y	Y	N
5 Bolling	?	N	?	?	?
6 Coleman	Y	Y	N	N	N
7 Taylor	Y	Y	Y	Y	N
8 Bailey	Y	Y	N	N	N
9 Volkmer	Y	N	Y	Y	N
10 Emerson	N	N	Y	Y	N
MONTANA					
1 Williams	Y	N	N	N	Y
2 Marlenee	Y	Y	N	N	N
NEBRASKA					
1 Bereuter	Y	Y	N	N	N
2 Daub	Y	Y	N	N	N
3 Smith	Y	N	N	N	N
NEVADA					
AL Santini	Y	N	N	N	N
NEW HAMPSHIRE					
1 D'Amours	Y	N	N	Y	N
2 Gregg	Y	N	N	N	N
NEW JERSEY					
1 Florio	Y	N	N	Y	N
2 Hughes	Y	N	N	N	N
3 Howard	Y	N	Y	Y	N
4 Smith	Y	N	N	N	N
5 Fenwick	Y	N	Y	N	N
6 Forsythe	N	N	Y	N	Y
7 Roukema	Y	N	Y	N	N
8 Roe	Y	N	N	N	?
9 Hollenbeck	Y	N	N	Y	N
10 Rodino	?	N	Y	Y	Y
11 Minish	Y	N	N	N	N
12 Rinaldo	?	N	N	N	N
13 Courter	Y	Y	N	N	N
14 Guarini	Y	N	N	Y	N
15 Dwyer	Y	N	N	Y	N
NEW MEXICO					
1 Lujan	Y	Y	N	N	N
2 Skeen	Y	Y	N	N	N
NEW YORK					
1 Carney	Y	Y	N	N	N
2 Downey	Y	N	N	Y	Y
3 Carman	Y	Y	N	N	N
4 Lent	Y	Y	N	N	N
5 McGrath	Y	Y	N	N	N
6 LeBoutillier	N	Y	N	N	N
7 Addabbo	Y	N	N	N	Y
8 Rosenthal	?	X	N	N	Y
9 Ferraro	Y	N	N	N	N
10 Biaggi	Y	N	N	N	?
11 Scheuer	?	N	N	Y	N
12 Chisholm	?	N	N	N	Y
13 Solarz	Y	N	N	N	N
14 Richmond	?	N	Y	Y	?
15 Zeferetti	?	N	N	Y	N
16 Schumer	Y	N	N	Y	N
17 Molinari	Y	N	N	N	N
18 Green	Y	N	N	N	N
19 Rangel	Y	N	N	N	Y
20 Weiss	Y	N	Y	Y	Y
21 Garcia	Y	N	Y	N	Y
22 Bingham	Y	N	N	Y	?
23 Peyser	Y	N	N	Y	N
24 Ottinger	P	N	N	Y	Y
25 Fish	Y	Y	N	N	N
26 Gilman	Y	Y	N	N	N
27 McHugh	Y	N	N	N	N
28 Stratton	Y	Y	N	N	N
29 Solomon	?	#	?	?	?
30 Martin	?	Y	N	N	N
31 Mitchell	Y	Y	N	N	N
32 Wortley	Y	Y	N	N	N
33 Lee	Y	Y	N	N	N
34 Horton	Y	N	N	N	N
35 Conable	Y	Y	N	N	N
36 LaFalce	Y	N	N	N	N
37 Nowak	Y	N	N	Y	N
38 Kemp	Y	N	N	N	N
39 Lundine	Y	N	N	N	Y
NORTH CAROLINA					
1 Jones	?	N	N	N	N
2 Fountain	?	Y	N	N	?
3 Whitley	Y	Y	N	N	N
4 Andrews	Y	N	N	N	N
5 Neal	Y	N	N	N	N
6 Johnston	N	Y	N	N	N
7 Rose	?	Y	N	Y	N
8 Hefner	Y	Y	N	N	N
9 Martin	Y	Y	N	N	N
10 Broyhill	Y	Y	N	N	N
11 Hendon	Y	Y	N	N	N
NORTH DAKOTA					
AL Dorgan	Y	N	N	N	N
OHIO					
1 Gradison	Y	Y	N	N	N
2 Luken	Y	Y	N	N	N
3 Hall	Y	N	N	N	N
4 Oxley	Y	Y	N	N	N
5 Latta	Y	Y	N	N	N
6 McEwen	Y	Y	N	N	N
7 Brown	?	?	?	?	?
8 Kindness	Y	Y	N	N	N
9 Weber	Y	Y	N	N	N
10 Miller	N	Y	N	N	N
11 Stanton	Y	Y	N	N	?
12 Shamansky	Y	N	N	N	?
13 Pease	Y	N	Y	Y	N
14 Seiberling	Y	N	Y	Y	Y
15 Wylie	Y	Y	N	N	N
16 Regula	Y	Y	N	N	N
17 Ashbrook	Y	Y	N	N	N
18 Applegate	?	N	N	N	N
19 Williams	?	Y	N	N	N
20 Oakar	Y	N	N	N	N
21 Stokes	Y	N	N	Y	Y
22 Eckart	Y	N	N	Y	N
23 Mottl	Y	Y	N	N	N
OKLAHOMA					
1 Jones	Y	N	Y	N	N
2 Synar	Y	N	Y	N	N
3 Watkins	Y	N	N	N	N
4 McCurdy	Y	Y	N	N	N
5 Edwards	Y	Y	N	N	N
6 English	Y	Y	N	N	N
OREGON					
1 AuCoin	Y	N	N	Y	Y
2 Smith	Y	Y	Y	Y	N
3 Wyden	Y	N	N	Y	Y
4 Weaver	Y	N	Y	Y	Y
PENNSYLVANIA					
1 Foglietta	Y	N	N	Y	Y
2 Gray	?	N	Y	Y	Y
3 Smith	?	Y	N	N	N
4 Dougherty	Y	Y	?	?	?
5 Schulze	Y	N	Y	N	N
6 Yatron	Y	Y	N	Y	N
7 Edgar	Y	N	Y	Y	Y
8 Coyne, J.	Y	N	N	N	N
9 Shuster	Y	Y	N	N	?
10 McDade	Y	Y	N	N	N
11 Nelligan	Y	Y	N	N	N
12 Murtha	?	Y	N	N	N
13 Coughlin	N	N	N	Y	N
14 Coyne, W.	Y	N	N	Y	N
15 Ritter	Y	Y	N	N	N
16 Walker	N	Y	Y	N	N
17 Ertel	?	N	N	Y	?
18 Walgren	Y	N	N	Y	Y
19 Goodling	N	N	N	N	N
20 Gaydos	Y	N	N	N	N
21 Bailey	Y	Y	N	N	N
22 Murphy	N	N	N	Y	N
23 Clinger	Y	N	N	N	N
24 Marks	?	?	?	?	?
25 Atkinson	N	Y	N	N	N
RHODE ISLAND					
1 St Germain	Y	N	N	N	N
2 Schneider	Y	N	N	N	Y
SOUTH CAROLINA					
1 Hartnett	Y	Y	N	N	N
2 Spence	Y	Y	N	N	N
3 Derrick	?	Y	N	N	N
4 Campbell	Y	Y	N	N	N
5 Holland	Y	Y	N	N	N
6 Napier	Y	Y	N	N	N
SOUTH DAKOTA					
1 Daschle	Y	N	N	Y	N
2 Roberts	Y	Y	N	N	N
TENNESSEE					
1 Quillen	Y	Y	N	N	N
2 Duncan	Y	Y	N	N	N
3 Bouquard	Y	Y	N	N	N
4 Gore	Y	N	N	N	N
5 Boner	Y	Y	N	N	?
6 Beard	Y	Y	N	N	N
7 Jones	?	#	?	X	X
8 Ford	?	N	N	Y	Y
TEXAS					
1 Hall, S.	Y	Y	N	N	N
2 Wilson	Y	Y	N	N	N
3 Collins	Y	Y	N	N	N
4 Hall, R.	Y	Y	N	N	N
5 Mattox	Y	N	N	N	N
6 Gramm	Y	Y	N	N	N
7 Archer	Y	Y	Y	Y	N
8 Fields	N	Y	N	N	N
9 Brooks	Y	N	N	N	N
10 Pickle	Y	N	N	N	N
11 Leath	Y	N	N	N	N
12 Wright	Y	Y	N	N	N
13 Hightower	Y	N	N	N	N
14 Patman	Y	N	N	N	N
15 de la Garza	?	?	?	?	?
16 White	Y	Y	N	N	N
17 Stenholm	Y	N	N	N	N
18 Leland	Y	N	Y	Y	Y
19 Hance	Y	Y	N	N	N
20 Gonzalez	Y	Y	N	N	N
21 Loeffler	Y	N	N	N	N
22 Paul	Y	N	Y	Y	Y
23 Kazen	Y	Y	N	N	N
24 Frost	Y	N	N	Y	?
UTAH					
1 Hansen	Y	Y	N	N	N
2 Marriott	Y	Y	N	N	N
VERMONT					
AL Jeffords	Y	N	N	N	N
VIRGINIA					
1 Trible	Y	Y	?	?	?
2 Whitehurst	Y	Y	N	N	?
3 Bliley	Y	Y	N	N	N
4 Daniel, R.	Y	Y	N	N	N
5 Daniel, D.	Y	N	N	N	N
6 Butler	Y	Y	Y	Y	N
7 Robinson	Y	Y	N	N	N
8 Parris	Y	Y	N	N	N
9 Wampler	Y	Y	N	N	N
10 Wolf	Y	Y	N	Y	N
WASHINGTON					
1 Pritchard	Y	N	Y	Y	?
2 Swift	Y	N	N	Y	Y
3 Bonker	Y	N	N	Y	N
4 Morrison	Y	Y	N	N	N
5 Foley	Y	N	N	Y	?
6 Dicks	Y	N	N	Y	?
7 Lowry	Y	N	Y	Y	Y
WEST VIRGINIA					
1 Mollohan	Y	Y	N	N	X
2 Benedict	Y	Y	N	N	N
3 Staton	Y	Y	N	N	N
4 Rahall	Y	N	N	N	?
WISCONSIN					
1 Aspin	Y	N	N	N	N
2 Kastenmeier	Y	N	N	Y	Y
3 Gunderson	Y	N	N	N	N
4 Zablocki	Y	N	N	N	N
5 Reuss	Y	N	N	N	Y
6 Petri	Y	N	Y	Y	N
7 Obey	Y	N	Y	N	N
8 Roth	Y	Y	N	N	N
9 Sensenbrenner	Y	Y	N	N	N
WYOMING					
AL Cheney	Y	Y	N	N	N

Southern states - Ala., Ark., Fla., Ga., Ky., La., Miss., N.C., Okla., S.C., Tenn., Texas, Va.

KEY

Y Voted for (yea).
Paired for.
+ Announced for.
N Voted against (nay).
X Paired against.
- Announced against.
P Voted "present".
C Voted "present" to avoid possible conflict of interest.
? Did not vote or otherwise make a position known.

Democrats *Republicans*

192. HR 6030. Defense Department Authorizations, Fiscal 1983. Price, D-Ill., motion that the House resolve itself into the Committee of the Whole for further consideration of the bill to authorize fiscal 1983 appropriations for the Defense Department. Motion agreed to 388-1: R 178-0; D 210-1 (ND 144-1, SD 66-0), July 22, 1982.

193. HR 6030. Defense Department Authorizations, Fiscal 1983. Bethune, R-Ark., amendment to the Zablocki, D-Wis., amendment (*see vote 195, below*), to prohibit the use of any authorized funds for procurement of binary chemical munitions or production equipment for such weapons. Adopted 232-181: R 76-108; D 156-73 (ND 132-25, SD 24-48), July 22, 1982. A "nay" was a vote supporting the president's position.

194. HR 6030. Defense Department Authorizations, Fiscal 1983. Courter, R-N.J., substitute for the Zablocki, D-Wis., amendment (*see vote 195, below*), to ban the production of binary munitions unless one existing chemical weapon were destroyed for each new binary weapon built. Rejected 192-225: R 112-72; D 80-153 (ND 27-132, SD 53-21), July 22, 1982. A "yea" was a vote supporting the president's position.

195. HR 6030. Defense Department Authorizations, Fiscal 1983. Zablocki, D-Wis., amendment to delete $54 million earmarked for procurement of binary chemical munitions and barring the use of any authorized funds for that program. Adopted 251-159: R 81-101; D 170-58 (ND 140-15, SD 30-43), July 22, 1982. A "nay" was a vote supporting the president's position.

196. HR 6030. Defense Department Authorizations, Fiscal 1983. Dellums, D-Calif., amendment to delete $4.03 billion for procurement of the B-1 bomber. Rejected 142-257: R 24-153; D 118-104 (ND 108-43, SD 10-61), July 22, 1982. A "nay" was a vote supporting the president's position.

197. HR 6030. Defense Department Authorizations, Fiscal 1983. Dellums, D-Calif., amendment to delete $6.87 billion for two nuclear-powered aircraft carriers. Rejected 83-303: R 20-156; D 63-147 (ND 59-80, SD 4-67), July 22, 1982. A "nay" was a vote supporting the president's position.

198. HR 6030. Defense Department Authorizations, Fiscal 1983. Conyers, D-Mich., amendment to delete $10.5 billion for nuclear weapons authorizations. Rejected 21-355: R 1-169; D 20-186 (ND 19-118, SD 1-68), July 22, 1982. A "nay" was a vote supporting the president's position.

	192	193	194	195	196	197	198
ALABAMA							
1 *Edwards*	Y	N	Y	N	N	N	N
2 *Dickinson*	Y	N	Y	N	N	N	N
3 Nichols	Y	N	Y	N	N	N	N
4 Bevill	Y	N	Y	N	N	N	N
5 Flippo	Y	N	Y	N	N	N	N
6 *Smith*	Y	N	Y	N	N	N	N
7 Shelby	Y	N	Y	N	N	N	N
ALASKA							
AL *Young*	?	N	Y	N	N	N	N
ARIZONA							
1 *Rhodes*	?	?	?	?	?	?	?
2 Udall	Y	Y	N	Y	Y	N	N
3 Stump	Y	N	Y	N	N	N	N
4 *Rudd*	?	N	Y	N	N	N	N
ARKANSAS							
1 Alexander	Y	N	Y	N	N	N	N
2 *Bethune*	Y	Y	N	Y	N	N	N
3 *Hammerschmidt*	Y	N	Y	N	N	N	N
4 Anthony	Y	N	Y	N	N	N	N
CALIFORNIA							
1 *Chappie*	Y	?	?	?	?	?	?
2 *Clausen*	Y	Y	N	Y	N	N	N
3 Matsui	Y	Y	N	Y	N	N	N
4 Fazio	Y	N	Y	Y	Y	N	N
5 Burton, J.	?	?	?	?	?	?	?
6 Burton, P.	Y	Y	N	Y	Y	Y	N
7 Miller	Y	Y	N	Y	Y	Y	N
8 Dellums	Y	Y	N	Y	Y	Y	Y
9 Stark	Y	Y	N	Y	Y	?	?
10 Edwards	Y	Y	N	Y	Y	Y	Y
11 Lantos	Y	Y	N	Y	Y	Y	N
12 *McCloskey*	Y	Y	N	Y	Y	Y	N
13 Mineta	Y	Y	N	Y	Y	Y	N
14 *Shumway*	Y	N	Y	N	?	?	?
15 Coelho	Y	Y	N	Y	N	N	N
16 Panetta	Y	Y	N	Y	Y	Y	N
17 *Pashayan*	Y	N	Y	N	N	N	N
18 *Thomas*	Y	N	Y	N	N	N	N
19 *Lagomarsino*	Y	N	Y	N	N	N	N
20 *Goldwater*	?	N	Y	N	?	N	N
21 *Fiedler*	Y	N	Y	N	N	N	N
22 *Moorhead*	Y	N	Y	N	N	N	N
23 Beilenson	Y	Y	N	#	#	?	N
24 Waxman	Y	Y	N	Y	Y	Y	N
25 Roybal	Y	Y	N	Y	Y	Y	Y
26 *Rousselot*	Y	N	Y	?	N	N	N
27 Dornan	Y	N	Y	N	N	N	?
28 Dixon	Y	Y	N	?	N	Y	?
29 Hawkins	Y	Y	N	Y	N	N	N
30 Martinez	Y	Y	N	Y	N	N	N
31 Dymally	Y	Y	N	Y	N	#	?
32 Anderson	Y	N	Y	N	N	N	N
33 *Grisham*	Y	N	Y	N	N	?	?
34 *Lungren*	Y	N	Y	N	N	N	N
35 *Dreier*	Y	N	Y	N	N	N	N
36 Brown	?	Y	N	Y	N	?	?
37 *Lewis*	Y	N	Y	N	N	N	N
38 Patterson	Y	?	N	Y	N	Y	N
39 *Dannemeyer*	Y	N	Y	N	N	N	N
40 *Badham*	Y	N	Y	N	N	N	N
41 *Lowery*	?	N	Y	N	N	N	N
42 *Hunter*	Y	N	Y	N	N	N	N
43 *Burgener*	?	?	?	?	?	?	?
COLORADO							
1 Schroeder	Y	Y	N	Y	Y	Y	N
2 Wirth	Y	Y	N	Y	Y	Y	Y
3 Kogovsek	Y	Y	N	Y	Y	Y	N
4 *Brown*	Y	Y	N	Y	Y	Y	N

	192	193	194	195	196	197	198
5 *Kramer*	Y	N	Y	N	N	N	N
CONNECTICUT							
1 Kennelly	Y	Y	N	Y	Y	N	N
2 Gejdenson	Y	Y	N	Y	Y	N	N
3 *DeNardis*	Y	Y	N	Y	Y	N	N
4 *McKinney*	Y	Y	N	Y	Y	N	N
5 Ratchford	Y	Y	N	Y	Y	N	N
6 Moffett	?	Y	N	Y	#	#	?
DELAWARE							
AL *Evans*	Y	Y	N	Y	N	N	N
FLORIDA							
1 Hutto	Y	N	Y	N	N	N	N
2 Fuqua	Y	N	Y	N	N	N	N
3 Bennett	Y	N	Y	N	N	N	N
4 Chappell	Y	N	Y	N	N	N	N
5 *McCollum*	Y	N	Y	N	N	N	N
6 *Young*	Y	N	Y	N	N	N	N
7 Gibbons	Y	N	Y	N	Y	N	N
8 Ireland	Y	N	Y	N	N	N	?
9 Nelson	Y	N	Y	N	N	N	N
10 *Bafalis*	Y	N	Y	N	N	N	N
11 Mica	Y	Y	N	Y	N	N	N
12 *Shaw*	Y	N	Y	N	N	N	N
13 Lehman	Y	Y	N	Y	Y	Y	N
14 Pepper	+	+	-	?	X	N	N
15 Fascell	Y	Y	N	Y	Y	Y	N
GEORGIA							
1 Ginn	?	?	?	?	?	?	?
2 Hatcher	Y	N	Y	?	?	?	?
3 Brinkley	Y	N	Y	N	N	N	N
4 Levitas	Y	N	Y	N	N	N	N
5 Fowler	Y	Y	N	Y	Y	N	N
6 *Gingrich*	?	N	Y	N	N	N	N
7 McDonald	Y	N	Y	N	N	N	N
8 Evans	?	N	Y	N	N	N	N
9 Jenkins	Y	Y	N	Y	N	N	N
10 Barnard	Y	N	Y	N	N	N	N
HAWAII							
1 Heftel	?	N	Y	P	N	N	N
2 Akaka	Y	N	Y	N	Y	N	N
IDAHO							
1 *Craig*	Y	Y	N	Y	N	N	N
2 *Hansen*	Y	N	Y	N	N	N	N
ILLINOIS							
1 Washington	Y	Y	N	Y	Y	Y	Y
2 Savage	?	Y	N	Y	Y	Y	Y
3 Russo	Y	Y	N	Y	Y	Y	N
4 *Derwinski*	Y	N	Y	N	N	N	N
5 Fary	Y	N	Y	N	N	N	N
6 *Hyde*	Y	N	Y	N	?	?	?
7 Collins	Y	Y	N	Y	#	Y	Y
8 Rostenkowski	Y	Y	Y	Y	N	N	N
9 Yates	Y	Y	N	Y	Y	Y	Y
10 *Porter*	Y	N	Y	N	N	N	N
11 Annunzio	Y	Y	N	Y	N	N	N
12 *Crane, P.*	Y	N	N	N	N	N	N
13 *McClory*	Y	Y	N	Y	?	?	?
14 *Erlenborn*	Y	N	Y	N	N	N	N
15 *Corcoran*	Y	N	Y	N	N	N	N
16 *Martin*	Y	Y	N	Y	N	Y	N
17 O'Brien	Y	N	Y	N	X	X	?
18 *Michel*	Y	N	Y	N	N	N	N
19 *Railsback*	Y	Y	N	Y	N	N	?
20 *Findley*	Y	Y	N	Y	Y	N	N
21 *Madigan*	Y	N	Y	N	N	N	N
22 *Crane, D.*	Y	N	N	N	N	N	N
23 Price	Y	Y	N	Y	N	N	N
24 Simon	Y	Y	N	Y	?	?	?
INDIANA							
1 Benjamin	Y	N	Y	N	Y	Y	N
2 Fithian	Y	Y	N	Y	Y	N	?
3 *Hiler*	Y	N	Y	N	N	N	N
4 *Coats*	Y	N	Y	N	N	N	N
5 *Hillis*	Y	Y	N	Y	N	N	N
6 Evans	Y	Y	Y	Y	Y	Y	N
7 *Myers*	Y	N	Y	N	N	N	N
8 *Deckard*	Y	N	Y	N	N	N	N
9 Hamilton	Y	Y	N	Y	Y	N	N
10 Sharp	Y	Y	N	Y	Y	Y	N
11 Jacobs	Y	Y	N	Y	Y	Y	N
IOWA							
1 *Leach*	Y	Y	N	Y	Y	Y	N
2 *Tauke*	Y	Y	N	Y	Y	Y	N
3 *Evans*	Y	N	Y	N	N	N	N
4 Smith	?	Y	N	Y	Y	Y	Y
5 Harkin	Y	N	Y	N	Y	Y	Y
6 Bedell	Y	Y	N	Y	Y	Y	N

ND - Northern Democrats SD - Southern Democrats

Corresponding to Congressional Record Votes 201, 202, 203, 204, 206, 207, 208

	192	193	194	195	196	197	198
KANSAS							
1 ***Roberts***	Y	Y	N	Y	N	N	N
2 ***Jeffries***	Y	N	Y	N	N	N	?
3 ***Winn***	Y	N	Y	N	N	N	N
4 Glickman	Y	Y	N	Y	N	Y	N
5 ***Whittaker***	Y	Y	N	Y	N	Y	N
KENTUCKY							
1 Hubbard	Y	N	Y	N	N	N	?
2 Natcher	Y	Y	N	Y	N	N	N
3 Mazzoli	Y	Y	N	Y	Y	N	N
4 ***Snyder***	Y	N	Y	N	N	N	N
5 ***Rogers***	Y	N	Y	N	N	N	N
6 ***Hopkins***	Y	Y	N	Y	N	N	N
7 Perkins	Y	Y	N	Y	N	N	N
LOUISIANA							
1 ***Livingston***	Y	N	Y	N	N	N	N
2 Boggs	Y	Y	Y	Y	N	N	N
3 Tauzin	Y	N	Y	N	N	N	N
4 Roemer	Y	N	Y	N	N	N	N
5 Huckaby	?	?	Y	N	N	N	N
6 ***Moore***	Y	N	Y	N	N	N	N
7 Breaux	Y	N	?	?	N	N	N
8 Long	?	Y	Y	Y	N	N	N
MAINE							
1 ***Emery***	Y	Y	N	Y	N	N	N
2 ***Snowe***	Y	Y	N	Y	N	N	N
MARYLAND							
1 Dyson	Y	N	Y	N	N	N	N
2 Long	Y	Y	N	Y	N	N	N
3 Mikulski	?	Y	N	Y	Y	N	N
4 ***Holt***	Y	N	Y	N	N	N	N
5 Hoyer	Y	Y	N	Y	N	N	?
6 Byron	Y	N	Y	N	N	N	N
7 Mitchell	N	Y	N	Y	Y	?	Y
8 Barnes	Y	+	-	+	#	?	?
MASSACHUSETTS							
1 ***Conte***	Y	Y	N	Y	Y	N	N
2 Boland	Y	Y	N	Y	Y	N	N
3 Early	Y	Y	N	Y	Y	Y	N
4 Frank	Y	Y	N	Y	Y	N	N
5 Shannon	?	Y	N	Y	Y	Y	N
6 Mavroules	Y	Y	N	Y	Y	?	?
7 Markey	Y	Y	N	Y	Y	?	?
8 O'Neill							
9 Moakley	Y	Y	N	?	#	?	?
10 ***Heckler***	Y	Y	N	Y	Y	N	N
11 Donnelly	Y	Y	N	Y	Y	N	N
12 Studds	Y	Y	N	Y	Y	Y	N
MICHIGAN							
1 Conyers	Y	Y	N	Y	Y	Y	Y
2 ***Pursell***	Y	Y	N	Y	Y	N	N
3 Wolpe	Y	Y	N	Y	Y	Y	N
4 ***Siljander***	Y	N	Y	N	N	N	N
5 ***Sawyer***	Y	N	N	N	N	N	N
6 ***Dunn***	Y	Y	N	Y	N	N	N
7 Kildee	Y	Y	N	Y	Y	Y	N
8 Traxler	Y	Y	N	Y	Y	N	N
9 ***Vander Jagt***	Y	Y	N	Y	N	?	?
10 Albosta	Y	Y	N	Y	Y	N	N
11 ***Davis***	Y	N	Y	N	N	N	N
12 Bonior	Y	Y	N	Y	Y	?	N
13 Crockett	Y	Y	N	Y	Y	Y	Y
14 Hertel	Y	Y	N	Y	Y	N	N
15 Ford	?	Y	N	?	Y	Y	N
16 Dingell	?	N	Y	N	Y	Y	N
17 Brodhead	Y	Y	N	Y	Y	N	N
18 Blanchard	Y	Y	N	Y	Y	N	N
19 ***Broomfield***	Y	Y	Y	Y	N	N	?
MINNESOTA							
1 ***Erdahl***	Y	Y	N	Y	Y	Y	N
2 ***Hagedorn***	Y	N	Y	N	N	Y	N
3 ***Frenzel***	Y	Y	N	Y	N	Y	N
4 Vento	Y	Y	N	Y	Y	Y	N
5 Sabo	Y	Y	N	Y	Y	Y	Y
6 ***Weber***	Y	Y	N	Y	Y	Y	N
7 ***Stangeland***	Y	N	Y	N	N	Y	N
8 Oberstar	Y	Y	N	Y	Y	Y	N
MISSISSIPPI							
1 Whitten	Y	Y	N	Y	N	Y	N
2 Bowen	?	?	?	?	?	?	?
3 Montgomery	Y	N	Y	N	N	N	N
4 Dowdy	Y	?	Y	N	?	?	?
5 ***Lott***	Y	N	Y	N	N	N	N
MISSOURI							
1 Clay	?	?	?	?	#	#	?
2 Young	Y	N	Y	N	X	?	?
3 Gephardt	Y	N	Y	N	N	N	N
4 Skelton	Y	N	Y	N	N	N	N
5 Bolling	Y	N	Y	N	?	?	?
6 ***Coleman***	Y	?	?	?	X	X	?
7 ***Taylor***	Y	N	Y	N	N	N	N
8 ***Bailey***	Y	Y	N	Y	N	N	N
9 Volkmer	Y	N	Y	Y	N	N	N
10 ***Emerson***	Y	?	?	?	X	X	?
MONTANA							
1 Williams	Y	Y	N	Y	Y	N	N
2 ***Marlenee***	Y	N	Y	Y	N	N	N
NEBRASKA							
1 ***Bereuter***	Y	Y	N	Y	N	N	N
2 ***Daub***	?	Y	N	Y	N	N	N
3 ***Smith***	Y	Y	N	Y	N	N	N
NEVADA							
AL Santini	Y	?	?	?	?	?	?
NEW HAMPSHIRE							
1 D'Amours	Y	Y	N	Y	Y	N	N
2 ***Gregg***	Y	Y	N	Y	N	Y	N
NEW JERSEY							
1 Florio	Y	Y	N	Y	Y	Y	N
2 Hughes	Y	Y	N	Y	Y	N	N
3 Howard	Y	Y	N	Y	Y	Y	N
4 ***Smith***	Y	Y	N	Y	N	N	N
5 ***Fenwick***	Y	Y	N	Y	Y	Y	N
6 ***Forsythe***	Y	Y	N	Y	Y	Y	Y
7 ***Roukema***	Y	Y	N	Y	N	N	N
8 Roe	Y	Y	N	Y	Y	N	N
9 ***Hollenbeck***	Y	Y	N	Y	Y	N	N
10 Rodino	Y	Y	N	Y	Y	Y	N
11 Minish	Y	Y	N	Y	Y	N	N
12 ***Rinaldo***	Y	Y	N	Y	N	N	N
13 ***Courter***	Y	N	Y	N	N	N	N
14 Guarini	Y	Y	N	Y	Y	N	N
15 Dwyer	Y	Y	N	Y	Y	N	N
NEW MEXICO							
1 ***Lujan***	Y	N	Y	N	N	N	N
2 ***Skeen***	Y	N	Y	N	N	N	N
NEW YORK							
1 ***Carney***	Y	N	Y	N	N	N	N
2 Downey	Y	Y	N	Y	Y	N	N
3 ***Carman***	Y	N	N	N	N	N	N
4 ***Lent***	Y	N	Y	N	N	N	N
5 ***McGrath***	Y	Y	N	Y	N	N	N
6 ***LeBoutillier***	?	N	Y	N	N	N	N
7 Addabbo	Y	Y	N	Y	Y	?	?
8 Rosenthal	?	Y	N	Y	Y	Y	N
9 Ferraro	Y	Y	N	Y	Y	N	N
10 Biaggi	Y	Y	N	Y	Y	N	N
11 Scheuer	Y	Y	N	Y	Y	N	N
12 Chisholm	?	?	N	Y	Y	?	?
13 Solarz	Y	Y	N	Y	Y	N	N
14 Richmond	?	Y	N	Y	Y	#	?
15 Zeferetti	Y	Y	N	Y	N	N	N
16 Schumer	Y	Y	N	Y	Y	Y	N
17 ***Molinari***	Y	Y	N	Y	N	N	N
18 ***Green***	Y	Y	N	Y	Y	Y	N
19 Rangel	Y	Y	N	Y	Y	Y	Y
20 Weiss	Y	Y	N	Y	Y	Y	Y
21 Garcia	Y	Y	N	Y	Y	Y	Y
22 Bingham	Y	Y	N	Y	Y	Y	N
23 Peyser	Y	Y	N	Y	Y	N	N
24 Ottinger	P	Y	N	Y	Y	Y	N
25 ***Fish***	Y	Y	N	Y	N	N	N
26 ***Gilman***	Y	N	Y	Y	N	N	N
27 McHugh	Y	Y	N	Y	Y	N	N
28 Stratton	Y	N	Y	N	N	N	N
29 ***Solomon***	?	?	?	?	?	?	?
30 ***Martin***	Y	N	Y	N	N	N	?
31 ***Mitchell***	Y	N	Y	N	N	N	N
32 ***Wortley***	Y	Y	Y	Y	N	N	N
33 ***Lee***	Y	Y	N	Y	N	N	N
34 ***Horton***	Y	Y	N	Y	Y	N	N
35 ***Conable***	Y	Y	Y	N	N	Y	N
36 LaFalce	Y	Y	N	Y	Y	N	N
37 Nowak	Y	Y	N	Y	Y	Y	N
38 ***Kemp***	?	N	Y	N	N	N	N
39 Lundine	Y	Y	N	Y	Y	N	N
NORTH CAROLINA							
1 Jones	Y	N	Y	Y	N	N	N
2 Fountain	?	N	Y	N	N	N	N
3 Whitley	Y	N	Y	N	N	N	N
4 Andrews	Y	Y	Y	Y	N	N	N
5 Neal	Y	N	Y	Y	N	N	N
6 ***Johnston***	Y	N	Y	N	N	N	N
7 Rose	Y	Y	N	Y	N	N	N
8 Hefner	Y	N	Y	Y	N	X	?
9 ***Martin***	Y	Y	N	Y	N	N	N
10 ***Broyhill***	Y	Y	Y	Y	N	Y	N
11 ***Hendon***	Y	N	Y	N	N	N	N
NORTH DAKOTA							
AL Dorgan	Y	Y	N	Y	Y	N	N
OHIO							
1 ***Gradison***	Y	N	Y	Y	N	N	N
2 Luken	Y	Y	N	Y	N	N	N
3 Hall	Y	Y	N	Y	N	Y	N
4 ***Oxley***	Y	N	N	Y	N	N	N
5 ***Latta***	Y	N	Y	N	N	N	N
6 ***McEwen***	Y	Y	N	Y	N	N	N
7 ***Brown***	?	?	?	?	?	?	?
8 ***Kindness***	?	N	Y	N	N	N	N
9 ***Weber***	Y	Y	N	Y	N	N	N
10 ***Miller***	Y	N	Y	N	N	N	N
11 ***Stanton***	Y	Y	Y	Y	?	?	?
12 Shamansky	Y	Y	N	Y	N	N	N
13 Pease	Y	Y	N	Y	Y	Y	N
14 Seiberling	Y	Y	N	Y	Y	Y	Y
15 ***Wylie***	Y	Y	Y	Y	?	?	?
16 ***Regula***	Y	Y	N	Y	N	N	N
17 ***Ashbrook***	Y	N	Y	N	N	N	N
18 Applegate	?	N	Y	Y	N	N	N
19 ***Williams***	Y	Y	N	Y	N	N	N
20 Oakar	Y	Y	N	Y	N	Y	N
21 Stokes	Y	Y	N	Y	Y	Y	Y
22 Eckart	Y	Y	N	Y	N	N	N
23 Mottl	Y	N	Y	N	?	?	?
OKLAHOMA							
1 Jones	?	Y	N	Y	N	N	N
2 Synar	Y	Y	N	Y	N	N	N
3 Watkins	Y	N	Y	N	?	?	?
4 McCurdy	Y	Y	N	Y	N	N	N
5 ***Edwards***	Y	Y	N	Y	N	N	N
6 English	Y	N	Y	N	N	N	N
OREGON							
1 AuCoin	Y	Y	N	Y	Y	Y	N
2 ***Smith***	Y	N	Y	N	N	N	N
3 Wyden	Y	Y	N	Y	Y	Y	N
4 Weaver	Y	Y	N	Y	Y	Y	Y
PENNSYLVANIA							
1 Foglietta	Y	Y	N	Y	Y	Y	N
2 Gray	Y	Y	N	Y	Y	#	?
3 Smith	Y	Y	N	Y	N	N	?
4 ***Dougherty***	Y	N	Y	N	N	N	N
5 ***Schulze***	Y	N	Y	N	N	N	N
6 Yatron	Y	Y	N	Y	N	N	N
7 Edgar	Y	Y	N	Y	Y	Y	N
8 ***Coyne, J.***	Y	Y	Y	Y	N	N	N
9 ***Shuster***	Y	Y	N	Y	N	N	N
10 ***McDade***	Y	Y	N	Y	N	N	N
11 ***Nelligan***	Y	N	Y	N	N	N	N
12 Murtha	Y	N	Y	N	N	N	N
13 ***Coughlin***	Y	Y	N	Y	N	N	N
14 Coyne, W.	?	Y	N	Y	Y	Y	N
15 ***Ritter***	Y	N	Y	N	N	N	N
16 ***Walker***	Y	Y	N	Y	N	N	N
17 Ertel	?	Y	N	Y	Y	?	?
18 Walgren	Y	Y	N	Y	Y	N	N
19 ***Goodling***	Y	Y	N	Y	N	N	?
20 Gaydos	Y	N	N	Y	N	N	N
21 Bailey	Y	N	Y	N	N	N	N
22 Murphy	Y	N	Y	Y	N	N	N
23 ***Clinger***	Y	N	Y	N	N	N	N
24 ***Marks***	?	?	?	?	?	?	?
25 ***Atkinson***	Y	N	Y	N	N	N	N
RHODE ISLAND							
1 St Germain	Y	Y	N	Y	Y	N	N
2 ***Schneider***	Y	Y	N	Y	Y	N	N
SOUTH CAROLINA							
1 ***Hartnett***	Y	N	Y	N	N	N	N
2 ***Spence***	Y	N	Y	N	N	N	N
3 Derrick	Y	Y	N	Y	Y	N	N
4 ***Campbell***	Y	N	Y	N	N	N	N
5 Holland	Y	N	Y	N	N	N	N
6 ***Napier***	Y	N	Y	N	N	N	N
SOUTH DAKOTA							
1 Daschle	Y	Y	N	Y	N	N	N
2 ***Roberts***	Y	Y	N	Y	N	N	N
TENNESSEE							
1 ***Quillen***	Y	N	Y	N	N	N	N
2 ***Duncan***	Y	N	Y	N	N	N	N
3 Bouquard	Y	N	Y	N	N	N	N
4 Gore	Y	N	Y	Y	Y	N	N
5 Boner	?	N	Y	N	N	N	N
6 ***Beard***	Y	N	Y	N	N	N	N
7 Jones	?	?	?	?	X	X	?
8 Ford	?	Y	N	Y	Y	Y	N
TEXAS							
1 Hall, S.	?	Y	N	Y	N	N	N
2 Wilson	?	?	Y	N	?	?	?
3 ***Collins***	Y	N	Y	N	N	N	N
4 Hall, R.	Y	N	Y	N	N	N	N
5 Mattox	Y	Y	N	Y	N	Y	N
6 Gramm	Y	N	Y	N	N	N	N
7 ***Archer***	Y	N	Y	N	N	N	N
8 ***Fields***	Y	N	Y	N	N	N	N
9 Brooks	Y	N	Y	N	Y	N	N
10 Pickle	Y	N	N	Y	N	N	N
11 Leath	Y	N	Y	N	N	N	N
12 Wright	Y	N	Y	Y	N	N	N
13 Hightower	Y	Y	N	Y	N	N	N
14 Patman	Y	N	Y	N	N	N	N
15 de la Garza	Y	N	Y	N	N	N	N
16 White	Y	N	Y	N	N	N	N
17 Stenholm	Y	N	Y	N	N	N	N
18 Leland	Y	Y	N	Y	Y	Y	Y
19 Hance	Y	N	Y	N	N	N	N
20 Gonzalez	Y	Y	N	Y	N	N	N
21 ***Loeffler***	Y	N	Y	N	N	N	N
22 ***Paul***	Y	Y	N	Y	Y	Y	N
23 Kazen	Y	N	Y	N	N	N	N
24 Frost	Y	Y	Y	Y	N	N	N
UTAH							
1 ***Hansen***	Y	N	Y	N	N	N	N
2 ***Marriott***	Y	N	Y	N	N	N	N
VERMONT							
AL ***Jeffords***	Y	Y	N	Y	Y	N	N
VIRGINIA							
1 ***Trible***	Y	N	Y	N	N	N	N
2 ***Whitehurst***	Y	N	Y	N	N	N	N
3 ***Bliley***	Y	N	Y	N	N	N	N
4 ***Daniel, R.***	Y	N	Y	N	N	N	N
5 Daniel, D.	Y	N	Y	N	N	N	N
6 ***Butler***	Y	N	Y	N	N	N	N
7 ***Robinson***	Y	N	Y	N	N	N	N
8 ***Parris***	Y	Y	N	Y	N	N	N
9 ***Wampler***	Y	N	Y	N	N	N	N
10 ***Wolf***	Y	N	Y	N	N	N	N
WASHINGTON							
1 ***Pritchard***	Y	Y	N	Y	Y	N	N
2 Swift	Y	Y	N	Y	Y	N	N
3 Bonker	Y	Y	N	Y	Y	N	N
4 ***Morrison***	Y	N	Y	N	N	N	N
5 Foley	Y	Y	N	Y	N	N	N
6 Dicks	Y	N	Y	Y	N	N	N
7 Lowry	Y	Y	N	Y	Y	Y	N
WEST VIRGINIA							
1 Mollohan	Y	N	Y	N	N	X	?
2 ***Benedict***	Y	Y	N	Y	N	N	N
3 ***Staton***	Y	N	Y	N	N	N	N
4 Rahall	Y	Y	N	Y	Y	Y	N
WISCONSIN							
1 Aspin	Y	Y	N	Y	Y	N	N
2 Kastenmeier	Y	Y	N	Y	Y	Y	Y
3 ***Gunderson***	Y	Y	N	Y	Y	N	N
4 Zablocki	Y	Y	N	Y	N	N	N
5 Reuss	Y	Y	N	Y	Y	N	N
6 ***Petri***	Y	N	Y	N	Y	Y	N
7 Obey	Y	Y	N	Y	Y	Y	N
8 ***Roth***	Y	Y	N	Y	N	Y	N
9 ***Sensenbrenner***	Y	Y	N	Y	N	Y	N
WYOMING							
AL ***Cheney***	Y	N	Y	N	N	N	N

Southern states - Ala., Ark., Fla., Ga., Ky., La., Miss., N.C., Okla., S.C., Tenn., Texas, Va.

199. HR 2329. Cherokee Nations of Oklahoma. Passage of the bill to waive the statue of limitations and grant jurisdiction to the Court of Claims or U.S. District Court for the Eastern District of Oklahoma to resolve two longstanding compensation claims of the Cherokee, Choctaw and Chickasaw Indian Nation of Oklahoma. Passed 293-26: R 122-21; D 171-5 (ND 117-1, SD 54-4), July 23, 1982.

200. HR 2643. Airport and Airway System. Frost, D-Texas, motion to order the previous question (thus ending debate and the possibility of amendment) on the rule (H Res 489) providing for House floor consideration of the bill. Motion rejected 135-178: R 16-131; D 119-47 (ND 94-17, SD 25-30), July 23, 1982.

201. HR 5203. Federal Insecticide, Fungicide and Rodenticide Act. Adoption of the rule (H Res 528) providing for House floor consideration of the bill to revise the Federal Insecticide, Fungicide and Rodenticide Act and authorize funds for federal pesticide programs for fiscal years 1983 and 1984. Adopted 301-2: R 142-0; D 159-2 (ND 106-1, SD 53-1), July 23, 1982.

202. HR 5427. Radio Marti. Adoption of the rule (H Res 529) providing for House floor consideration of the bill to authorize the establishment of a radio to broadcast to Cuba. Adopted 254-22: R 123-5; D 131-17 (ND 80-15, SD 51-2), July 23, 1982.

203. HR 5427. Radio Marti. Fascell, D-Fla., motion that the House resolve itself into the Committee of the Whole for consideration of the bill to authorize the establishment of a radio to broadcast to Cuba. Motion agreed to 239-8: R 108-5; D 131-3 (ND 85-3, SD 46-0), July 23, 1982.

204. Procedural Motion. Walker, R-Pa., motion to approve the House *Journal* of Monday, July 26. Motion agreed to 355-25: R 163-14; D 192-11 (ND 130-10, SD 62-1), July 27, 1982.

205. HR 6782. Veterans' Disability Compensation Amendments. Montgomery, D-Miss., motion to suspend the rules and pass the bill to award a 7.4 percent cost-of-living increase to veterans and their survivors for service-connected disability compensation, and to achieve budget savings from veterans' programs of $169.7 million in fiscal 1983, $185.9 million in fiscal 1984 and $195 million in fiscal 1985. Motion agreed to 400-0: R 180-0; D 220-0 (ND 150-0, SD 70-0), July 27, 1982. A two-thirds majority of those present and voting (267 in this case) is required for passage under suspension of the rules. A "yea" was a vote supporting the president's position.

206. Procedural Motion. Carman, R-N.Y., motion to approve the House *Journal* of Tuesday, July 27. Motion agreed to 346-28: R 163-16; D 183-12 (ND 120-11, SD 63-1), July 28, 1982.

KEY						
Y Voted for (yea).						
# Paired for.						
+ Announced for.						
N Voted against (nay).						
X Paired against.						
- Announced against.						
P Voted "present".						
C Voted "present" to avoid possible conflict of interest.						
? Did not vote or otherwise make a position known.						

Democrats *Republicans*

	199	200	201	202	203	204	205	206
ALABAMA								
1 *Edwards*	Y	N	Y	?	?	Y	Y	Y
2 *Dickinson*	Y	N	Y	Y	Y	N	Y	N
3 Nichols	?	?	?	?	?	Y	Y	Y
4 Bevill	Y	N	Y	Y	Y	Y	Y	Y
5 Flippo	Y	N	Y	Y	Y	Y	Y	Y
6 *Smith*	N	N	Y	Y	Y	Y	Y	Y
7 Shelby	N	N	Y	Y	Y	Y	Y	Y
ALASKA								
AL *Young*	?	N	Y	N	N	?	Y	?
ARIZONA								
1 *Rhodes*	?	?	?	?	?	?	Y	Y
2 Udall	Y	Y	Y	Y	Y	Y	Y	Y
3 Stump	?	?	?	?	?	Y	Y	Y
4 *Rudd*	?	X	?	?	?	Y	Y	Y
ARKANSAS								
1 Alexander	Y	Y	Y	Y	Y	Y	Y	Y
2 *Bethune*	N	N	Y	Y	Y	Y	Y	Y
3 *Hammerschmidt*	Y	N	Y	?	?	Y	Y	Y
4 Anthony	Y	Y	Y	Y	Y	Y	Y	Y
CALIFORNIA								
1 *Chappie*	?	X	?	?	?	Y	Y	Y
2 *Clausen*	Y	N	Y	Y	?	Y	Y	Y
3 Matsui	Y	Y	Y	Y	Y	Y	Y	Y
4 Fazio	?	#	?	?	?	Y	Y	Y
5 Burton, J.	?	?	?	?	?	?	?	Y
6 Burton, P.	?	?	?	?	?	?	?	Y
7 Miller	Y	Y	Y	N	N	Y	Y	Y
8 Dellums	Y	Y	?	X	?	Y	Y	?
9 Stark	Y	Y	Y	Y	Y	Y	Y	Y
10 Edwards	Y	Y	Y	N	Y	Y	Y	Y
11 Lantos	Y	Y	Y	Y	Y	Y	Y	Y
12 *McCloskey*	?	?	?	?	?	?	?	?
13 Mineta	Y	Y	Y	Y	Y	Y	Y	Y
14 *Shumway*	?	?	?	?	?	Y	Y	Y
15 Coelho	?	?	?	?	?	Y	Y	Y
16 Panetta	Y	Y	Y	Y	Y	Y	Y	Y
17 *Pashayan*	Y	N	Y	Y	Y	Y	Y	Y
18 *Thomas*	?	?	?	?	?	Y	Y	Y
19 *Lagomarsino*	Y	N	Y	Y	Y	Y	Y	Y
20 *Goldwater*	?	?	?	?	?	Y	Y	Y
21 *Fiedler*	Y	N	Y	Y	Y	Y	Y	Y
22 *Moorhead*	Y	N	Y	Y	Y	Y	Y	Y
23 Beilenson	?	?	?	?	?	Y	Y	Y
24 Waxman	Y	Y	Y	Y	Y	Y	Y	Y
25 Roybal	Y	Y	Y	Y	Y	Y	Y	Y
26 *Rousselot*	?	X	?	?	?	Y	Y	Y
27 *Dornan*	?	?	?	?	?	?	?	?
28 Dixon	Y	Y	Y	Y	Y	Y	Y	Y
29 Hawkins	Y	#	Y	Y	?	N	Y	Y
30 Martinez	Y	Y	Y	Y	Y	Y	Y	Y
31 Dymally	?	#	?	?	?	?	?	?
32 Anderson	Y	N	Y	Y	Y	Y	Y	Y
33 *Grisham*	N	N	Y	Y	Y	Y	Y	Y
34 *Lungren*	Y	Y	Y	Y	Y	?	Y	Y
35 *Dreier*	Y	N	Y	Y	Y	Y	Y	Y
36 Brown	Y	Y	Y	?	?	?	Y	?
37 *Lewis*	Y	N	Y	Y	Y	Y	Y	Y
38 Patterson	Y	Y	Y	Y	Y	Y	Y	Y
39 *Dannemeyer*	Y	N	Y	Y	Y	Y	?	Y
40 *Badham*	?	?	?	?	?	Y	Y	Y
41 *Lowery*	Y	X	?	?	?	Y	Y	Y
42 *Hunter*	Y	N	Y	Y	Y	Y	Y	Y
43 *Burgener*	?	?	?	?	?	Y	Y	Y
COLORADO								
1 Schroeder	Y	N	Y	Y	Y	N	Y	N
2 Wirth	Y	Y	Y	Y	Y	Y	Y	Y
3 Kogovsek	Y	Y	Y	Y	?	Y	Y	Y
4 *Brown*	Y	N	Y	Y	Y	Y	Y	Y

	199	200	201	202	203	204	205	206
5 *Kramer*	?	?	?	?	?	Y	Y	Y
CONNECTICUT								
1 Kennelly	Y	Y	Y	?	?	Y	Y	Y
2 Gejdenson	Y	Y	Y	?	?	N	Y	N
3 *DeNardis*	?	X	?	?	?	?	Y	?
4 *McKinney*	?	X	?	?	?	?	Y	?
5 Ratchford	Y	Y	Y	Y	Y	Y	Y	N
6 Moffett	?	?	?	?	?	?	?	?
DELAWARE								
AL *Evans*	Y	N	Y	Y	Y	Y	Y	Y
FLORIDA								
1 Hutto	Y	Y	Y	Y	Y	Y	Y	Y
2 Fuqua	?	?	?	?	?	Y	Y	Y
3 Bennett	Y	Y	Y	Y	Y	Y	Y	Y
4 Chappell	Y	Y	Y	Y	?	Y	Y	Y
5 *McCollum*	N	N	Y	Y	Y	Y	Y	Y
6 *Young*	?	X	?	?	?	Y	Y	Y
7 Gibbons	Y	Y	Y	Y	Y	Y	Y	Y
8 Ireland	?	N	Y	?	?	?	Y	?
9 Nelson	+	#	+	#	+	Y	Y	Y
10 *Bafalis*	?	?	?	?	?	Y	Y	Y
11 Mica	Y	Y	Y	Y	Y	Y	Y	Y
12 *Shaw*	Y	N	Y	Y	Y	Y	Y	Y
13 Lehman	Y	Y	Y	Y	Y	Y	Y	Y
14 Pepper	Y	Y	Y	Y	?	?	?	?
15 Fascell	Y	Y	Y	Y	Y	Y	Y	Y
GEORGIA								
1 Ginn	?	?	?	?	?	?	?	Y
2 Hatcher	?	?	?	?	?	Y	Y	Y
3 Brinkley	Y	N	Y	Y	Y	Y	Y	Y
4 Levitas	?	?	?	?	?	?	?	?
5 Fowler	Y	Y	Y	Y	Y	Y	Y	Y
6 *Gingrich*	Y	N	Y	Y	Y	Y	Y	Y
7 McDonald	N	N	N	Y	Y	Y	Y	?
8 Evans	?	?	?	?	?	?	?	?
9 Jenkins	Y	Y	Y	Y	Y	Y	Y	Y
10 Barnard	?	?	?	?	?	Y	Y	Y
HAWAII								
1 Heftel	Y	Y	Y	Y	Y	Y	Y	Y
2 Akaka	Y	Y	Y	Y	Y	Y	Y	Y
IDAHO								
1 *Craig*	?	?	?	?	?	Y	Y	Y
2 *Hansen*	N	N	Y	Y	Y	Y	?	Y
ILLINOIS								
1 Washington	Y	Y	Y	N	Y	N	Y	N
2 Savage	?	?	?	?	?	Y	?	?
3 Russo	Y	Y	Y	Y	Y	Y	Y	Y
4 *Derwinski*	Y	N	Y	Y	?	Y	Y	Y
5 Fary	Y	Y	Y	Y	Y	Y	Y	Y
6 *Hyde*	?	X	?	?	?	Y	Y	Y
7 Collins	Y	#	?	X	?	?	?	?
8 Rostenkowski	Y	Y	Y	?	?	Y	Y	Y
9 Yates	Y	Y	N	Y	Y	Y	Y	Y
10 *Porter*	Y	Y	Y	?	?	Y	Y	Y
11 Annunzio	Y	Y	Y	Y	Y	Y	Y	Y
12 *Crane, P.*	N	N	Y	Y	Y	Y	Y	Y
13 *McClory*	?	?	?	?	?	Y	Y	Y
14 *Erlenborn*	?	?	?	?	?	Y	Y	Y
15 *Corcoran*	Y	N	Y	Y	Y	Y	Y	Y
16 *Martin*	Y	N	Y	Y	Y	Y	Y	Y
17 *O'Brien*	?	?	?	?	?	?	Y	Y
18 *Michel*	Y	Y	Y	Y	Y	Y	Y	Y
19 *Railsback*	?	?	?	?	?	Y	Y	Y
20 *Findley*	?	?	?	?	?	Y	Y	Y
21 *Madigan*	?	N	Y	Y	Y	Y	Y	Y
22 *Crane, D.*	N	N	Y	?	?	?	?	Y
23 Price	Y	Y	Y	Y	Y	Y	Y	Y
24 Simon	?	?	?	?	?	Y	Y	Y
INDIANA								
1 Benjamin	Y	Y	Y	Y	Y	Y	Y	Y
2 Fithian	?	?	?	?	?	Y	Y	Y
3 *Hiler*	Y	N	Y	Y	Y	?	Y	Y
4 *Coats*	Y	N	Y	Y	Y	Y	Y	Y
5 *Hillis*	Y	N	Y	Y	Y	Y	Y	Y
6 Evans	?	?	?	?	?	Y	Y	Y
7 *Myers*	Y	N	?	?	?	Y	Y	Y
8 *Deckard*	Y	N	Y	Y	Y	Y	Y	Y
9 Hamilton	Y	N	?	?	?	Y	Y	Y
10 Sharp	Y	N	Y	Y	?	Y	Y	Y
11 Jacobs	Y	N	Y	N	Y	N	Y	N
IOWA								
1 *Leach*	Y	N	Y	N	Y	Y	Y	Y
2 *Tauke*	Y	Y	Y	N	Y	Y	Y	Y
3 *Evans*	Y	N	Y	N	N	N	Y	Y
4 *Smith*	Y	N	Y	N	Y	Y	Y	Y
5 Harkin	Y	N	Y	?	?	N	Y	N
6 Bedell	Y	N	Y	N	Y	Y	Y	N

ND - Northern Democrats   SD - Southern Democrats

	199	200	201	202	203	204	205	206
KANSAS								
1 ***Roberts***	Y	N	Y	Y	Y	Y	Y	Y
2 ***Jeffries***	Y	N	?	Y	?	?	Y	?
3 ***Winn***	Y	N	Y	Y	Y	Y	Y	Y
4 Glickman	Y	N	Y	Y	Y	Y	Y	Y
5 ***Whittaker***	Y	N	Y	Y	Y	Y	Y	Y
KENTUCKY								
1 Hubbard	?	?	?	?	?	Y	Y	?
2 Natcher	Y	Y	Y	Y	Y	Y	Y	Y
3 Mazzoli	Y	N	Y	Y	Y	Y	Y	Y
4 ***Snyder***	Y	N	Y	Y	Y	Y	Y	Y
5 ***Rogers***	Y	N	Y	Y	Y	Y	Y	Y
6 ***Hopkins***	?	?	?	?	?	?	Y	N
7 Perkins	Y	N	Y	Y	?	Y	Y	Y
LOUISIANA								
1 ***Livingston***	Y	N	Y	Y	Y	Y	Y	Y
2 Boggs	Y	#	?	?	?	Y	Y	Y
3 Tauzin	Y	N	Y	Y	Y	Y	Y	Y
4 Roemer	Y	N	Y	Y	Y	N	Y	N
5 Huckaby	Y	N	Y	Y	Y	Y	Y	Y
6 ***Moore***	Y	N	Y	Y	Y	Y	Y	Y
7 Breaux	?	?	?	?	?	Y	Y	Y
8 Long	Y	Y	Y	Y	Y	Y	Y	?
MAINE								
1 ***Emery***	?	?	?	?	?	Y	Y	Y
2 ***Snowe***	Y	N	Y	Y	?	Y	Y	Y
MARYLAND								
1 Dyson	Y	Y	Y	Y	Y	Y	Y	Y
2 Long	?	?	?	?	?	?	Y	Y
3 Mikulski	Y	Y	Y	Y	Y	Y	Y	Y
4 ***Holt***	Y	N	Y	Y	Y	N	Y	Y
5 Hoyer	Y	N	Y	Y	Y	Y	Y	Y
6 Byron	Y	Y	Y	Y	Y	Y	Y	?
7 Mitchell	Y	Y	Y	N	?	N	Y	?
8 Barnes	?	?	?	?	?	N	Y	N
MASSACHUSETTS								
1 ***Conte***	Y	Y	Y	Y	Y	Y	Y	Y
2 Boland	Y	?	?	?	?	?	Y	?
3 Early	?	?	?	?	?	Y	Y	Y
4 Frank	Y	Y	Y	Y	Y	Y	Y	Y
5 Shannon	Y	Y	Y	Y	Y	Y	Y	Y
6 Mavroules	?	?	?	?	?	Y	Y	Y
7 Markey	Y	Y	Y	Y	Y	Y	Y	Y
8 O'Neill								
9 Moakley	?	?	?	?	?	Y	Y	Y
10 ***Heckler***	Y	N	Y	Y	?	Y	Y	?
11 Donnelly	Y	Y	?	?	?	Y	Y	Y
12 Studds	Y	Y	Y	?	?	?	Y	Y
MICHIGAN								
1 Conyers	?	?	?	?	?	Y	Y	Y
2 ***Pursell***	?	?	?	?	?	Y	Y	Y
3 Wolpe	Y	?	?	?	?	Y	Y	Y
4 ***Siljander***	?	X	?	?	?	?	?	?
5 ***Sawyer***	Y	N	Y	Y	Y	Y	Y	Y
6 ***Dunn***	?	?	?	?	?	Y	Y	Y
7 Kildee	Y	Y	Y	N	Y	Y	Y	Y
8 Traxler	Y	Y	Y	Y	Y	Y	Y	Y
9 ***Vander Jagt***	Y	Y	Y	Y	Y	Y	Y	Y
10 Albosta	?	?	?	?	?	Y	Y	Y
11 ***Davis***	Y	N	Y	?	?	Y	Y	Y
12 Bonior	?	#	?	?	?	?	?	?
13 Crockett	?	?	?	?	?	?	?	?
14 Hertel	?	?	?	?	?	?	Y	Y
15 Ford	Y	Y	Y	Y	Y	Y	Y	?
16 Dingell	?	Y	?	Y	Y	Y	Y	Y
17 Brodhead	?	?	?	?	?	Y	Y	Y
18 Blanchard	Y	Y	Y	Y	Y	?	?	?
19 ***Broomfield***	?	?	?	?	?	Y	Y	Y
MINNESOTA								
1 ***Erdahl***	Y	N	Y	Y	Y	Y	Y	Y
2 ***Hagedorn***	Y	N	Y	Y	Y	Y	Y	Y
3 ***Frenzel***	Y	N	Y	Y	?	Y	Y	Y
4 Vento	Y	Y	Y	Y	Y	Y	Y	N
5 Sabo	Y	Y	Y	N	N	N	Y	N
6 ***Weber***	Y	N	?	?	?	Y	?	?
7 ***Stangeland***	Y	N	Y	Y	Y	Y	Y	Y
8 Oberstar	Y	Y	Y	Y	Y	Y	Y	N
MISSISSIPPI								
1 Whitten	Y	N	Y	Y	Y	Y	Y	Y
2 Bowen	?	?	?	?	?	Y	Y	Y
3 Montgomery	?	?	?	?	?	Y	Y	Y
4 Dowdy	?	?	?	?	?	Y	Y	Y
5 ***Lott***	Y	Y	Y	Y	?	Y	Y	Y
MISSOURI								
1 Clay	?	#	?	?	?	?	?	?
2 Young	?	?	?	?	?	Y	Y	Y
3 Gephardt	Y	Y	Y	Y	Y	Y	Y	Y
4 Skelton	?	?	?	?	?	Y	Y	Y
5 Bolling	?	?	?	?	?	?	?	?
6 ***Coleman***	?	N	Y	Y	Y	Y	Y	Y
7 ***Taylor***	Y	N	Y	Y	Y	Y	Y	Y
8 ***Bailey***	?	X	?	?	?	Y	Y	Y
9 Volkmer	Y	N	Y	Y	Y	Y	Y	Y
10 ***Emerson***	?	N	Y	Y	N	N	Y	N
MONTANA								
1 Williams	?	?	?	?	?	?	Y	?
2 ***Marlenee***	Y	N	?	?	?	Y	Y	Y
NEBRASKA								
1 ***Bereuter***	Y	N	Y	Y	Y	Y	Y	Y
2 ***Daub***	Y	N	Y	N	Y	Y	Y	Y
3 ***Smith***	Y	N	Y	Y	Y	Y	Y	Y
NEVADA								
AL Santini	?	?	?	?	?	Y	Y	?
NEW HAMPSHIRE								
1 D'Amours	Y	N	Y	Y	?	Y	Y	Y
2 ***Gregg***	Y	N	Y	?	?	Y	Y	Y
NEW JERSEY								
1 Florio	?	#	?	#	?	Y	Y	Y
2 Hughes	Y	Y	Y	?	?	Y	Y	Y
3 Howard	Y	Y	Y	Y	Y	Y	Y	Y
4 ***Smith***	Y	N	Y	Y	Y	Y	Y	Y
5 ***Fenwick***	?	Y	Y	?	Y	Y	Y	Y
6 ***Forsythe***	Y	N	Y	Y	Y	N	Y	N
7 ***Roukema***	Y	N	Y	?	?	Y	Y	Y
8 Roe	Y	Y	Y	Y	Y	Y	Y	Y
9 ***Hollenbeck***	?	X	?	?	?	Y	Y	Y
10 Rodino	Y	Y	Y	Y	Y	Y	Y	Y
11 Minish	Y	Y	Y	Y	Y	Y	Y	Y
12 ***Rinaldo***	Y	N	Y	Y	Y	Y	Y	Y
13 ***Courter***	Y	N	Y	Y	Y	Y	Y	Y
14 Guarini	Y	Y	Y	Y	Y	Y	Y	Y
15 Dwyer	Y	Y	Y	?	?	Y	Y	Y
NEW MEXICO								
1 ***Lujan***	Y	N	Y	Y	Y	Y	Y	Y
2 ***Skeen***	Y	N	?	Y	Y	Y	Y	Y
NEW YORK								
1 ***Carney***	Y	N	Y	Y	Y	Y	Y	Y
2 Downey	Y	Y	Y	N	Y	Y	Y	Y
3 ***Carman***	Y	N	Y	Y	Y	Y	Y	Y
4 ***Lent***	Y	N	Y	Y	Y	Y	Y	Y
5 ***McGrath***	N	N	Y	Y	Y	Y	Y	Y
6 ***LeBoutillier***	Y	N	Y	Y	?	N	Y	N
7 Addabbo	?	#	?	?	?	Y	Y	?
8 Rosenthal	Y	Y	Y	Y	Y	Y	Y	?
9 Ferraro	Y	Y	Y	Y	Y	Y	Y	Y
10 Biaggi	?	?	?	?	?	?	?	?
11 Scheuer	Y	Y	Y	Y	Y	Y	Y	Y
12 Chisholm	?	#	?	?	?	?	Y	?
13 Solarz	Y	Y	Y	Y	Y	Y	Y	Y
14 Richmond	?	#	?	?	?	Y	Y	Y
15 Zeferetti	?	#	?	?	?	Y	Y	Y
16 Schumer	Y	Y	Y	N	Y	Y	Y	Y
17 ***Molinari***	Y	N	Y	Y	Y	Y	Y	Y
18 ***Green***	Y	N	Y	Y	Y	Y	Y	Y
19 Rangel	Y	Y	Y	N	Y	Y	Y	Y
20 Weiss	Y	Y	Y	N	?	Y	Y	Y
21 Garcia	Y	Y	Y	Y	Y	?	Y	Y
22 Bingham	Y	Y	Y	Y	Y	Y	Y	Y
23 Peyser	Y	Y	?	?	?	Y	Y	Y
24 Ottinger	Y	Y	Y	Y	P	P	Y	P
25 ***Fish***	?	X	?	?	?	Y	Y	Y
26 ***Gilman***	Y	N	Y	Y	Y	Y	Y	Y
27 McHugh	Y	Y	Y	Y	Y	Y	Y	?
28 Stratton	Y	N	Y	Y	Y	Y	Y	Y
29 ***Solomon***	?	X	?	?	?	N	Y	Y
30 ***Martin***	?	X	?	?	?	Y	Y	Y
31 ***Mitchell***	?	X	?	?	?	Y	Y	Y
32 ***Wortley***	N	N	Y	Y	N	Y	Y	Y
33 ***Lee***	N	N	Y	Y	Y	Y	Y	Y
34 ***Horton***	Y	N	Y	Y	?	?	Y	Y
35 ***Conable***	Y	Y	Y	Y	Y	Y	Y	Y
36 LaFalce	Y	Y	Y	Y	Y	Y	Y	Y
37 Nowak	Y	Y	Y	Y	Y	Y	Y	Y
38 ***Kemp***	Y	N	Y	Y	Y	Y	Y	Y
39 Lundine	Y	Y	Y	?	?	Y	Y	Y
NORTH CAROLINA								
1 Jones	Y	Y	Y	Y	?	?	Y	Y
2 Fountain	Y	N	Y	Y	Y	?	?	?
3 Whitley	Y	N	Y	Y	Y	Y	Y	Y
4 Andrews	Y	N	?	Y	Y	Y	Y	?
5 Neal	Y	N	Y	Y	Y	Y	Y	Y
6 ***Johnston***	N	N	Y	Y	N	N	Y	N
7 Rose	Y	N	Y	Y	Y	Y	Y	?
8 Hefner	?	?	?	?	?	Y	Y	Y
9 ***Martin***	Y	N	Y	Y	Y	Y	Y	Y
10 ***Broyhill***	Y	N	Y	Y	Y	Y	Y	Y
11 ***Hendon***	Y	N	Y	Y	Y	Y	Y	Y
NORTH DAKOTA								
AL Dorgan	Y	-	+	+	+	Y	Y	Y
OHIO								
1 ***Gradison***	Y	N	Y	Y	Y	Y	Y	Y
2 Luken	Y	Y	Y	Y	Y	Y	Y	?
3 Hall	Y	Y	Y	?	Y	Y	Y	?
4 ***Oxley***	Y	N	Y	?	?	Y	Y	Y
5 ***Latta***	Y	N	Y	Y	Y	Y	Y	Y
6 ***McEwen***	Y	N	Y	?	?	N	Y	Y
7 ***Brown***	?	?	?	?	?	?	?	?
8 ***Kindness***	Y	N	Y	?	?	Y	Y	Y
9 ***Weber***	Y	N	Y	Y	Y	Y	Y	Y
10 ***Miller***	Y	N	Y	Y	Y	N	Y	N
11 ***Stanton***	?	?	?	?	?	Y	Y	N
12 Shamansky	Y	N	Y	Y	Y	Y	Y	Y
13 Pease	Y	Y	Y	Y	Y	Y	Y	Y
14 Seiberling	Y	?	Y	N	N	Y	Y	Y
15 ***Wylie***	Y	N	Y	Y	Y	Y	Y	Y
16 ***Regula***	Y	N	Y	Y	Y	Y	Y	Y
17 ***Ashbrook***	N	N	Y	Y	Y	Y	Y	Y
18 Applegate	Y	Y	?	?	?	Y	Y	Y
19 ***Williams***	Y	N	Y	Y	Y	Y	Y	Y
20 Oakar	?	?	?	?	?	?	?	?
21 Stokes	Y	Y	Y	N	?	Y	Y	Y
22 Eckart	Y	Y	Y	Y	Y	Y	Y	Y
23 Mottl	?	?	?	?	?	Y	Y	Y
OKLAHOMA								
1 Jones	Y	Y	Y	Y	Y	Y	Y	Y
2 Synar	Y	N	Y	Y	?	Y	Y	Y
3 Watkins	?	?	?	?	?	Y	Y	Y
4 McCurdy	Y	N	Y	Y	Y	Y	Y	Y
5 ***Edwards***	Y	N	Y	Y	Y	?	Y	Y
6 English	Y	N	Y	Y	Y	?	Y	Y
OREGON								
1 AuCoin	Y	Y	Y	?	Y	Y	Y	Y
2 ***Smith***	?	?	?	?	?	Y	Y	Y
3 Wyden	?	?	?	?	?	Y	Y	Y
4 Weaver	Y	Y	Y	Y	Y	Y	Y	Y
PENNSYLVANIA								
1 Foglietta	Y	Y	Y	Y	Y	Y	Y	Y
2 Gray	?	#	?	?	?	Y	Y	Y
3 Smith	?	?	?	?	?	Y	Y	?
4 ***Dougherty***	Y	Y	Y	Y	Y	Y	?	?
5 ***Schulze***	Y	N	Y	Y	Y	Y	Y	Y
6 Yatron	Y	?	?	Y	?	Y	Y	Y
7 Edgar	?	?	?	?	?	Y	Y	Y
8 ***Coyne, J.***	N	N	Y	?	?	Y	Y	Y
9 ***Shuster***	?	?	?	?	?	Y	Y	Y
10 ***McDade***	Y	Y	Y	Y	Y	Y	Y	?
11 ***Nelligan***	Y	Y	Y	Y	Y	Y	Y	Y
12 Murtha	Y	?	?	?	?	Y	Y	Y
13 ***Coughlin***	Y	Y	Y	Y	Y	Y	Y	N
14 Coyne, W.	Y	Y	Y	Y	Y	Y	Y	Y
15 ***Ritter***	N	N	Y	Y	Y	Y	Y	Y
16 ***Walker***	Y	N	Y	Y	Y	N	Y	N
17 Ertel	?	?	?	?	?	?	Y	Y
18 Walgren	Y	N	Y	Y	Y	Y	Y	Y
19 ***Goodling***	Y	N	Y	Y	?	N	Y	N
20 Gaydos	Y	Y	Y	Y	Y	Y	Y	Y
21 Bailey	Y	Y	Y	Y	Y	Y	Y	Y
22 Murphy	Y	Y	Y	Y	Y	N	Y	Y
23 ***Clinger***	Y	N	Y	Y	Y	Y	Y	Y
24 ***Marks***	?	?	?	?	?	?	?	?
25 ***Atkinson***	?	?	?	?	?	Y	Y	Y
RHODE ISLAND								
1 St Germain	Y	Y	Y	?	?	Y	Y	Y
2 ***Schneider***	Y	N	Y	Y	Y	Y	Y	Y
SOUTH CAROLINA								
1 ***Hartnett***	N	N	Y	Y	?	Y	Y	Y
2 ***Spence***	Y	N	Y	Y	Y	Y	Y	Y
3 Derrick	Y	Y	Y	Y	Y	?	Y	Y
4 ***Campbell***	Y	N	Y	Y	Y	Y	Y	Y
5 Holland	Y	?	?	Y	?	?	Y	Y
6 ***Napier***	?	X	?	?	?	Y	Y	Y
SOUTH DAKOTA								
1 Daschle	Y	N	Y	Y	Y	Y	Y	Y
2 ***Roberts***	N	N	Y	Y	Y	Y	Y	Y
TENNESSEE								
1 ***Quillen***	Y	Y	Y	?	?	Y	Y	Y
2 ***Duncan***	Y	N	Y	Y	Y	Y	Y	Y
3 Bouquard	Y	N	Y	?	?	Y	Y	Y
4 Gore	Y	Y	Y	Y	Y	Y	Y	Y
5 Boner	Y	Y	Y	N	Y	Y	Y	Y
6 ***Beard***	Y	?	?	?	?	Y	Y	Y
7 Jones	?	?	?	?	?	?	?	?
8 Ford	?	?	?	?	?	?	?	?
TEXAS								
1 Hall, S.	Y	?	?	?	?	?	Y	Y
2 Wilson	?	?	?	?	?	Y	Y	?
3 ***Collins***	Y	N	Y	Y	Y	Y	Y	Y
4 Hall, R.	Y	N	Y	?	?	Y	Y	Y
5 Mattox	Y	Y	Y	Y	Y	Y	Y	Y
6 Gramm	N	Y	Y	Y	?	Y	Y	Y
7 ***Archer***	N	N	Y	Y	Y	Y	Y	Y
8 ***Fields***	Y	N	Y	Y	Y	N	Y	N
9 Brooks	Y	N	Y	Y	Y	?	Y	Y
10 Pickle	Y	Y	Y	Y	Y	Y	Y	Y
11 Leath	?	?	?	?	?	?	?	?
12 Wright	Y	?	Y	Y	Y	Y	Y	Y
13 Hightower	Y	N	Y	Y	Y	Y	Y	Y
14 Patman	N	N	Y	Y	Y	Y	Y	Y
15 de la Garza	Y	Y	Y	Y	Y	Y	Y	Y
16 White	?	?	?	?	?	Y	Y	Y
17 Stenholm	Y	N	Y	Y	Y	Y	Y	Y
18 Leland	Y	Y	Y	N	Y	?	?	?
19 Hance	Y	Y	Y	Y	?	Y	Y	Y
20 Gonzalez	Y	N	P	P	Y	Y	Y	Y
21 ***Loeffler***	Y	N	Y	Y	Y	Y	Y	Y
22 ***Paul***	N	N	Y	Y	Y	Y	Y	Y
23 Kazen	Y	N	Y	Y	Y	Y	Y	Y
24 Frost	Y	Y	Y	Y	Y	Y	Y	Y
UTAH								
1 ***Hansen***	N	N	Y	Y	Y	Y	Y	Y
2 ***Marriott***	Y	N	Y	+	+	Y	Y	Y
VERMONT								
AL ***Jeffords***	Y	N	Y	?	?	Y	Y	Y
VIRGINIA								
1 ***Trible***	?	?	?	?	?	Y	Y	Y
2 ***Whitehurst***	?	X	?	?	?	Y	Y	Y
3 ***Bliley***	Y	N	Y	Y	Y	Y	Y	Y
4 ***Daniel, R.***	Y	N	Y	Y	Y	Y	Y	Y
5 Daniel, D.	Y	N	Y	Y	?	Y	Y	Y
6 ***Butler***	Y	N	Y	?	Y	N	Y	N
7 ***Robinson***	Y	N	Y	Y	Y	Y	Y	Y
8 ***Parris***	Y	N	Y	Y	Y	Y	Y	Y
9 ***Wampler***	Y	N	Y	Y	?	Y	Y	Y
10 ***Wolf***	Y	N	Y	Y	Y	Y	Y	Y
WASHINGTON								
1 ***Pritchard***	Y	N	Y	?	?	Y	Y	Y
2 Swift	N	Y	Y	Y	Y	Y	Y	Y
3 Bonker	Y	N	Y	Y	Y	Y	Y	Y
4 ***Morrison***	Y	N	Y	Y	?	Y	Y	Y
5 Foley	Y	Y	Y	Y	Y	Y	Y	Y
6 Dicks	Y	Y	Y	Y	Y	Y	Y	Y
7 Lowry	Y	Y	Y	Y	Y	Y	Y	Y
WEST VIRGINIA								
1 Mollohan	?	#	?	?	?	Y	Y	Y
2 ***Benedict***	Y	N	Y	Y	Y	Y	Y	Y
3 ***Staton***	N	N	Y	Y	Y	Y	?	Y
4 Rahall	?	#	?	?	?	?	?	?
WISCONSIN								
1 Aspin	Y	Y	Y	Y	Y	Y	Y	Y
2 Kastenmeier	Y	Y	Y	N	Y	Y	Y	Y
3 ***Gunderson***	Y	N	Y	Y	Y	Y	Y	Y
4 Zablocki	Y	Y	Y	Y	Y	Y	Y	Y
5 Reuss	Y	Y	Y	?	?	Y	Y	Y
6 ***Petri***	Y	N	Y	Y	Y	Y	Y	Y
7 Obey	Y	Y	Y	Y	Y	Y	Y	Y
8 ***Roth***	N	N	Y	Y	Y	Y	Y	Y
9 ***Sensenbrenner***	Y	N	Y	Y	Y	Y	Y	Y
WYOMING								
AL ***Cheney***	Y	Y	Y	Y	Y	Y	Y	?

Southern states - Ala., Ark., Fla., Ga., Ky., La., Miss., N.C., Okla., S.C., Tenn., Texas, Va.

207. HR 6862. Civil Service Reconciliation. Adoption of the rule (H Res 536) providing for House floor consideration of the bill to reduce federal pension spending. Adopted 240-170: R 30-156; D 210-14 (ND 151-2, SD 59-12), July 28, 1982.

208. HR 6030. Defense Department Authorizations, Fiscal 1983. Hance, D-Texas, amendment to the Schroeder, D-Colo., amendment, as amended by the Nichols, D-Ala., amendment, to allow state courts, in states that treat marital property as community property, to decide whether to include armed service members' military pensions and military benefits in the property to be divided by a divorce settlement. Adopted 332-74: R 131-54; D 201-20 (ND 140-10, SD 61-10), July 28, 1982. (The Schroeder amendment, as amended, subsequently was adopted by voice vote.)

209. HR 6030. Defense Department Authorizations, Fiscal 1983. Stratton, D-N.Y., amendment to extend for one year a test policy allowing the Pentagon to pay a premium price in order to purchase certain goods from firms in areas of high unemployment. This waiver of the so-called Maybank amendment was to apply to contracts of the Defense Logistics Agency for routine commercial supplies, excluding weapons and petroleum, worth a total of $5 billion. Adopted 237-170: R 97-86; D 140-84 (ND 134-16, SD 6-68), July 28, 1982.

210. HR 6030. Defense Department Authorizations, Fiscal 1983. Simon, D-Ill., substitute, as amended by the Bennett, D-Fla., amendment, for the Solomon, R-N.Y., amendment, to prohibit federal education assistance to any young man who did not comply with the law requiring registration with the Selective Service System. The original Simon amendment would have exempted from the prohibition anyone informing the Selective Service in writing that he had religious or moral objections to registration. Rejected 161-241: R 39-141; D 122-100 (ND 104-45, SD 18-55), July 28, 1982. (The Solomon amendment, as amended, subsequently was adopted (see vote 211, below).)

211. HR 6030. Defense Department Authorizations, Fiscal 1983. Solomon, R-N.Y., amendment, as amended, to prohibit federal education assistance to any young man who did not comply with the law requiring registration with the Selective Service System. Adopted 303-95: R 161-18; D 142-77 (ND 72-74, SD 70-3), July 28, 1982.

212. HR 4961. Budget Reconciliation Tax Increases/Spending Cuts. Rostenkowski, D-Ill., motion to table (kill) the Rousselot, R-Calif., privileged resolution (H Res 541) directing the House to return the Senate-passed bill to the Senate with a message challenging the constitutionality of the measure. Motion agreed to 229-169: R 32-147; D 197-22 (ND 137-9, SD 60-13), July 28, 1982.

213. HR 4961. Budget Reconciliation Tax Increases/Spending Cuts. Rostenkowski, D-Ill., motion to disagree to the Senate amendments to the bill and to agree to a conference requested by the Senate. Motion agreed to 208-197: R 44-137; D 164-60 (ND 116-35, SD 48-25), July 28, 1982.

214. HR 4961. Budget Reconciliation Tax Increases/Spending Cuts. Conable, R-N.Y., motion to instruct the conferees to insist that the conference agreement reach the revenue-raising and spending-reduction targets included in the first fiscal 1983 budget resolution (S Con Res 92). Motion agreed to 299-89: R 144-33; D 155-56 (ND 97-45, SD 58-11), July 28, 1982.

KEY	
Y	Voted for (yea).
#	Paired for.
+	Announced for.
N	Voted against (nay).
X	Paired against.
-	Announced against.
P	Voted "present".
C	Voted "present" to avoid possible conflict of interest.
?	Did not vote or otherwise make a position known.

Democrats *Republicans*

	207	208	209	210	211	212	213	214
ALABAMA								
1 *Edwards*	N	Y	N	N	Y	Y	Y	Y
2 *Dickinson*	N	N	N	Y	N	N	N	Y
3 Nichols	Y	N	N	N	Y	Y	Y	?
4 Bevill	Y	N	N	N	Y	N	N	Y
5 Flippo	Y	N	N	N	N	N	N	Y
6 *Smith*	N	N	N	N	Y	N	N	Y
7 Shelby	Y	Y	N	N	Y	N	N	Y
ALASKA								
AL *Young*	Y	Y	N	?	?	Y	Y	Y
ARIZONA								
1 *Rhodes*	N	Y	N	N	Y	Y	Y	Y
2 Udall	Y	Y	Y	N	Y	Y	Y	Y
3 Stump	N	N	N	N	N	N	N	Y
4 *Rudd*	N	N	N	N	N	N	N	Y
ARKANSAS								
1 Alexander	Y	Y	Y	Y	Y	Y	Y	Y
2 *Bethune*	N	Y	N	N	Y	N	N	Y
3 *Hammerschmidt*	N	N	N	N	Y	N	N	Y
4 Anthony	Y	Y	N	Y	Y	Y	Y	Y
CALIFORNIA								
1 *Chappie*	N	N	N	N	Y	N	N	Y
2 *Clausen*	N	Y	Y	Y	Y	N	N	Y
3 Matsui	Y	Y	Y	N	Y	Y	Y	Y
4 Fazio	Y	Y	Y	Y	Y	Y	Y	Y
5 Burton, J.	Y	Y	Y	N	N	?	?	?
6 Burton, P.	Y	Y	Y	N	Y	Y	N	Y
7 Miller	Y	Y	?	Y	N	Y	Y	Y
8 Dellums	Y	Y	Y	N	N	Y	N	Y
9 Stark	Y	Y	?	N	Y	Y	Y	?
10 Edwards	Y	Y	N	Y	N	?	Y	N
11 Lantos	Y	Y	Y	N	Y	Y	Y	Y
12 *McCloskey*	?	?	?	?	?	?	?	?
13 Mineta	Y	Y	Y	N	Y	Y	Y	Y
14 *Shumway*	N	Y	N	N	Y	N	N	N
15 Coelho	Y	Y	Y	N	Y	Y	Y	Y
16 Panetta	Y	Y	Y	N	Y	Y	Y	Y
17 *Pashayan*	N	N	N	N	N	N	N	Y
18 *Thomas*	N	Y	N	N	Y	N	N	Y
19 *Lagomarsino*	N	Y	N	N	Y	N	N	Y
20 *Goldwater*	N	Y	N	N	N	N	N	Y
21 *Fiedler*	N	N	N	Y	N	N	N	Y
22 *Moorhead*	N	Y	N	N	Y	N	N	Y
23 Beilenson	Y	Y	Y	N	Y	Y	Y	N
24 Waxman	Y	Y	Y	N	Y	Y	Y	N
25 Roybal	Y	Y	Y	N	Y	Y	Y	N
26 *Rousselot*	N	Y	N	N	Y	N	N	N
27 *Dornan*	?	?	?	?	?	?	?	?
28 Dixon	Y	Y	Y	Y	Y	Y	Y	Y
29 Hawkins	Y	Y	Y	Y	Y	Y	Y	N
30 Martinez	Y	Y	Y	N	Y	Y	Y	Y
31 Dymally	?	?	?	?	?	?	?	?
32 Anderson	Y	Y	Y	Y	Y	Y	Y	Y
33 *Grisham*	N	Y	N	N	Y	N	N	Y
34 Lungren	N	Y	N	N	Y	N	N	N
35 *Dreier*	N	Y	N	N	N	N	N	Y
36 Brown	Y	Y	Y	Y	N	Y	Y	Y
37 Lewis	N	?	N	N	Y	N	N	Y
38 Patterson	Y	Y	N	Y	N	Y	Y	Y
39 *Dannemeyer*	N	Y	N	N	N	N	N	N
40 *Badham*	N	Y	N	N	Y	N	N	?
41 *Lowery*	N	Y	N	N	Y	N	N	Y
42 *Hunter*	N	Y	N	N	Y	N	N	Y
43 *Burgener*	N	Y	N	N	Y	Y	Y	Y
COLORADO								
1 Schroeder	Y	Y	N	Y	N	Y	Y	N
2 Wirth	Y	Y	Y	N	Y	Y	Y	Y
3 Kogovsek	Y	Y	N	Y	Y	Y	Y	Y
4 *Brown*	N	Y	N	N	Y	N	N	Y

	207	208	209	210	211	212	213	214
5 *Kramer*	Y	Y	N	N	Y	N	N	Y
CONNECTICUT								
1 Kennelly	Y	Y	Y	N	Y	Y	Y	Y
2 Gejdenson	Y	Y	Y	Y	N	Y	Y	Y
3 *DeNardis*	N	Y	Y	N	Y	N	N	Y
4 *McKinney*	N	Y	Y	Y	N	Y	N	Y
5 Ratchford	Y	Y	Y	N	Y	N	Y	Y
6 Moffett	?	?	?	?	X	?	?	?
DELAWARE								
AL *Evans*	N	Y	Y	N	Y	N	N	Y
FLORIDA								
1 Hutto	Y	Y	N	N	Y	Y	N	Y
2 Fuqua	Y	Y	N	Y	Y	Y	N	Y
3 Bennett	N	N	N	Y	Y	Y	Y	Y
4 Chappell	Y	N	N	Y	Y	Y	N	Y
5 *McCollum*	N	Y	N	N	Y	N	N	Y
6 *Young*	N	N	N	N	N	N	N	N
7 Gibbons	Y	Y	N	N	Y	Y	Y	?
8 Nelson	N	Y	N	Y	Y	Y	Y	Y
9 Nelson	Y	Y	N	N	Y	Y	Y	Y
10 *Bafalis*	?	?	?	?	?	?	?	?
11 Mica	Y	Y	N	N	Y	Y	Y	Y
12 *Shaw*	N	Y	N	N	Y	N	N	N
13 Lehman	Y	Y	Y	Y	Y	Y	Y	Y
14 Pepper	?	?	?	?	?	?	?	?
15 Fascell	Y	Y	N	Y	Y	Y	Y	Y
GEORGIA								
1 Ginn	Y	?	?	?	?	?	?	?
2 Hatcher	Y	Y	N	Y	Y	Y	Y	Y
3 Brinkley	Y	N	N	N	Y	Y	Y	Y
4 Levitas	Y	Y	N	N	Y	N	N	Y
5 Fowler	Y	Y	N	Y	Y	Y	Y	Y
6 *Gingrich*	N	Y	N	N	Y	N	N	Y
7 McDonald	N	N	N	N	N	N	N	N
8 Evans	?	?	N	N	Y	N	N	Y
9 Jenkins	Y	Y	N	Y	Y	Y	Y	Y
10 Barnard	Y	Y	N	Y	Y	Y	N	Y
HAWAII								
1 Heftel	Y	Y	Y	N	Y	Y	Y	Y
2 Akaka	Y	Y	Y	Y	Y	Y	Y	N
IDAHO								
1 *Craig*	N	Y	N	N	Y	N	N	N
2 *Hansen*	N	Y	N	N	Y	N	N	Y
ILLINOIS								
1 Washington	Y	Y	Y	N	N	Y	N	Y
2 Savage	Y	?	Y	N	N	Y	Y	N
3 Russo	Y	Y	Y	Y	Y	Y	Y	Y
4 *Derwinski*	N	Y	N	Y	Y	Y	Y	Y
5 Fary	Y	Y	Y	Y	Y	Y	Y	Y
6 *Hyde*	N	Y	N	N	Y	N	N	Y
7 Collins	Y	Y	N	N	Y	Y	Y	Y
8 Rostenkowski	Y	N	Y	Y	Y	Y	Y	Y
9 Yates	Y	?	?	?	?	?	?	?
10 *Porter*	N	Y	Y	Y	N	N	N	Y
11 Annunzio	Y	Y	Y	Y	Y	Y	Y	Y
12 *Crane, P.*	N	N	N	N	N	N	N	N
13 *McClory*	N	Y	N	Y	Y	Y	Y	Y
14 *Erlenborn*	N	Y	N	N	Y	N	N	Y
15 *Corcoran*	N	Y	N	N	Y	N	N	Y
16 *Martin*	N	Y	N	Y	N	N	N	?
17 *O'Brien*	N	N	Y	?	?	?	#	?
18 *Michel*	N	N	Y	N	Y	Y	Y	Y
19 *Railsback*	N	N	Y	Y	Y	Y	Y	Y
20 *Findley*	N	Y	Y	Y	N	Y	N	Y
21 *Madigan*	N	N	Y	Y	N	N	N	Y
22 *Crane, D.*	N	N	N	N	N	N	N	N
23 Price	Y	N	Y	Y	Y	Y	Y	Y
24 Simon	Y	Y	Y	N	Y	Y	Y	Y
INDIANA								
1 Benjamin	Y	Y	Y	Y	Y	Y	Y	Y
2 Fithian	Y	Y	Y	Y	Y	Y	N	N
3 *Hiler*	N	Y	Y	N	Y	N	N	Y
4 *Coats*	N	Y	Y	N	Y	N	N	Y
5 *Hillis*	N	N	Y	N	Y	N	N	Y
6 Evans	Y	Y	Y	N	Y	N	N	N
7 *Myers*	N	N	Y	N	N	N	N	Y
8 *Deckard*	Y	Y	Y	Y	N	N	N	Y
9 Hamilton	Y	Y	Y	N	Y	Y	Y	Y
10 Sharp	Y	Y	Y	Y	N	Y	Y	Y
11 Jacobs	Y	Y	Y	Y	Y	Y	N	Y
IOWA								
1 *Leach*	N	Y	Y	N	N	N	N	Y
2 *Tauke*	N	Y	Y	Y	Y	N	N	Y
3 *Evans*	N	Y	Y	N	N	N	N	Y
4 *Smith*	Y	Y	Y	Y	Y	Y	Y	Y
5 Harkin	Y	Y	Y	N	N	Y	Y	N
6 Bedell	Y	Y	Y	Y	Y	Y	Y	Y

ND - Northern Democrats   SD - Southern Democrats

Corresponding to Congressional Record Votes 218, 219, 220, 221, 222, 223, 224, 225

	207	208	209	210	211	212	213	214
KANSAS								
1 ***Roberts***	N	Y	N	N	Y	N	N	Y
2 ***Jeffries***	N	N	N	N	Y	N	N	Y
3 ***Winn***	N	N	Y	N	Y	N	N	Y
4 Glickman	Y	Y	N	Y	Y	Y	Y	Y
5 ***Whittaker***	N	N	Y	Y	Y	N	N	Y
KENTUCKY								
1 Hubbard	?	?	N	N	Y	N	N	N
2 Natcher	Y	Y	Y	Y	Y	Y	N	N
3 Mazzoli	Y	Y	Y	Y	N	Y	Y	Y
4 ***Snyder***	N	N	N	N	Y	N	N	N
5 ***Rogers***	N	Y	N	N	Y	N	N	Y
6 ***Hopkins***	N	Y	N	N	Y	N	N	N
7 Perkins	Y	Y	Y	Y	Y	N	N	N
LOUISIANA								
1 ***Livingston***	N	Y	N	-	+	-	N	Y
2 Boggs	Y	Y	N	N	Y	Y	Y	?
3 Tauzin	N	Y	N	N	Y	Y	N	Y
4 Roemer	N	Y	N	N	Y	Y	Y	Y
5 Huckaby	N	Y	N	N	Y	Y	Y	Y
6 ***Moore***	N	Y	N	N	Y	N	N	Y
7 Breaux	N	Y	N	N	Y	Y	Y	Y
8 Long	Y	Y	N	N	Y	Y	Y	Y
MAINE								
1 ***Emery***	N	N	Y	N	Y	Y	Y	Y
2 ***Snowe***	N	Y	Y	Y	Y	N	Y	Y
MARYLAND								
1 Dyson	Y	Y	Y	N	Y	Y	Y	Y
2 Long	Y	N	Y	N	Y	Y	Y	Y
3 Mikulski	Y	Y	Y	Y	Y	Y	Y	N
4 ***Holt***	Y	N	N	N	Y	N	N	Y
5 Hoyer	Y	Y	Y	Y	N	Y	Y	N
6 Byron	Y	N	Y	N	Y	Y	Y	Y
7 Mitchell	Y	Y	Y	?	?	?	?	?
8 Barnes	Y	Y	Y	Y	N	Y	N	Y
MASSACHUSETTS								
1 ***Conte***	N	Y	Y	Y	N	Y	Y	Y
2 Boland	Y	?	Y	N	Y	Y	Y	Y
3 Early	Y	Y	Y	?	?	?	?	?
4 Frank	Y	Y	Y	Y	N	Y	N	N
5 Shannon	Y	Y	Y	N	N	Y	N	N
6 Mavroules	Y	Y	Y	N	N	Y	Y	Y
7 Markey	Y	Y	Y	Y	N	Y	Y	Y
8 O'Neill								
9 Moakley	Y	Y	Y	N	Y	Y	Y	Y
10 ***Heckler***	Y	Y	Y	Y	N	N	N	N
11 Donnelly	Y	Y	Y	N	Y	Y	Y	Y
12 Studds	Y	Y	Y	Y	N	N	N	N
MICHIGAN								
1 Conyers	Y	Y	N	Y	N	Y	Y	Y
2 ***Pursell***	N	Y	Y	Y	N	N	Y	Y
3 Wolpe	Y	Y	Y	Y	N	Y	Y	N
4 ***Siljander***	?	?	?	?	?	?	?	?
5 ***Sawyer***	N	Y	Y	N	Y	N	N	Y
6 ***Dunn***	N	N	Y	N	Y	N	N	Y
7 Kildee	Y	Y	Y	Y	N	N	N	N
8 Traxler	Y	Y	Y	Y	Y	Y	Y	Y
9 ***Vander Jagt***	N	Y	Y	N	Y	Y	Y	Y
10 Albosta	Y	Y	Y	N	Y	Y	Y	Y
11 ***Davis***	Y	Y	Y	N	Y	N	N	Y
12 Bonior	?	?	?	?	?	?	?	?
13 Crockett	Y	Y	Y	Y	N	Y	Y	?
14 Hertel	Y	Y	Y	N	Y	?	Y	Y
15 Ford	Y	Y	Y	Y	N	Y	Y	N
16 Dingell	Y	N	Y	Y	Y	Y	Y	N
17 Brodhead	Y	Y	Y	Y	N	Y	Y	Y
18 Blanchard	?	?	?	?	?	?	?	?
19 ***Broomfield***	N	N	Y	N	Y	N	N	Y
MINNESOTA								
1 ***Erdahl***	N	Y	Y	Y	N	N	N	Y
2 ***Hagedorn***	N	Y	Y	N	Y	N	N	Y
3 ***Frenzel***	N	Y	N	N	Y	Y	Y	Y
4 Vento	Y	Y	Y	Y	Y	Y	Y	N
5 Sabo	Y	Y	Y	Y	N	Y	Y	N
6 ***Weber***	N	Y	Y	N	Y	N	N	Y
7 ***Stangeland***	N	Y	?	N	Y	N	N	Y
8 Oberstar	Y	Y	Y	Y	Y	Y	Y	N
MISSISSIPPI								
1 Whitten	Y	Y	N	Y	Y	Y	N	N
2 Bowen	Y	N	N	Y	Y	Y	Y	Y
3 Montgomery	N	N	N	N	Y	Y	Y	Y
4 Dowdy	Y	Y	N	?	?	?	?	?
5 ***Lott***	N	Y	N	N	Y	Y	Y	Y
MISSOURI								
1 Clay	?	?	?	?	?	?	?	?
2 Young	Y	Y	N	N	Y	Y	Y	Y
3 Gephardt	Y	Y	Y	N	Y	Y	Y	Y
4 Skelton	Y	N	N	N	Y	Y	N	Y
5 Bolling	Y	Y	?	?	?	Y	Y	Y
6 ***Coleman***	N	N	Y	N	Y	Y	N	Y
7 ***Taylor***	N	N	N	N	Y	N	N	Y
8 ***Bailey***	N	N	Y	N	Y	N	N	N
9 Volkmer	Y	Y	N	Y	Y	Y	N	Y
10 ***Emerson***	N	N	N	N	Y	N	N	Y
MONTANA								
1 Williams	Y	Y	Y	N	N	N	N	N
2 ***Marlenee***	N	N	Y	N	Y	N	N	Y
NEBRASKA								
1 ***Bereuter***	N	Y	N	N	Y	N	N	Y
2 ***Daub***	N	Y	Y	N	Y	N	N	Y
3 ***Smith***	N	Y	N	N	Y	N	N	Y
NEVADA								
AL Santini	Y	Y	N	N	Y	N	N	Y
NEW HAMPSHIRE								
1 D'Amours	Y	Y	Y	N	Y	N	N	N
2 ***Gregg***	N	N	N	Y	Y	N	N	Y
NEW JERSEY								
1 Florio	Y	Y	Y	Y	N	Y	N	Y
2 Hughes	Y	Y	Y	Y	Y	Y	N	Y
3 Howard	Y	Y	Y	Y	N	Y	Y	Y
4 ***Smith***	Y	Y	Y	N	Y	N	N	N
5 ***Fenwick***	N	Y	Y	Y	Y	N	N	Y
6 ***Forsythe***	N	Y	Y	Y	N	Y	Y	Y
7 ***Roukema***	N	Y	Y	Y	Y	N	N	Y
8 Roe	Y	Y	Y	Y	Y	Y	N	Y
9 ***Hollenbeck***	Y	Y	Y	Y	N	N	N	N
10 Rodino	Y	Y	Y	Y	N	Y	Y	N
11 Minish	Y	Y	Y	Y	Y	Y	Y	Y
12 ***Rinaldo***	Y	Y	Y	Y	Y	N	N	N
13 ***Courter***	Y	Y	Y	N	Y	N	N	N
14 Guarini	Y	Y	Y	Y	Y	Y	Y	Y
15 Dwyer	Y	Y	Y	Y	N	Y	Y	Y
NEW MEXICO								
1 ***Lujan***	N	Y	N	Y	Y	N	N	Y
2 ***Skeen***	N	Y	N	N	Y	N	N	Y
NEW YORK								
1 ***Carney***	Y	Y	Y	N	Y	N	N	N
2 Downey	Y	Y	Y	Y	N	Y	Y	Y
3 ***Carman***	N	N	Y	N	Y	N	N	Y
4 ***Lent***	Y	N	Y	N	Y	N	N	Y
5 ***McGrath***	Y	Y	Y	N	Y	N	N	N
6 ***LeBoutillier***	Y	Y	Y	N	Y	N	N	Y
7 Addabbo	Y	Y	Y	Y	N	Y	Y	Y
8 Rosenthal	Y	Y	Y	Y	N	Y	Y	Y
9 Ferraro	Y	Y	Y	Y	N	Y	Y	Y
10 Biaggi	?	?	?	?	?	?	Y	Y
11 Scheuer	Y	Y	Y	Y	N	Y	Y	N
12 Chisholm	Y	Y	Y	Y	N	Y	Y	Y
13 Solarz	Y	Y	Y	N	N	Y	Y	N
14 Richmond	Y	Y	Y	Y	N	Y	Y	?
15 Zeferetti	Y	Y	Y	?	+	Y	Y	Y
16 Schumer	Y	Y	Y	Y	N	Y	Y	N
17 ***Molinari***	Y	Y	Y	N	Y	N	N	Y
18 ***Green***	N	Y	Y	Y	N	N	N	N
19 Rangel	Y	Y	Y	Y	N	Y	Y	Y
20 Weiss	Y	Y	Y	Y	N	+	Y	N
21 Garcia	Y	Y	Y	Y	N	Y	Y	Y
22 Bingham	Y	Y	Y	Y	N	Y	Y	?
23 Peyser	Y	Y	Y	Y	N	Y	Y	Y
24 Ottinger	Y	Y	Y	Y	N	Y	N	N
25 ***Fish***	N	Y	Y	Y	Y	?	Y	?
26 ***Gilman***	Y	Y	Y	Y	Y	N	N	N
27 McHugh	Y	Y	Y	Y	Y	Y	N	Y
28 Stratton	Y	N	Y	N	Y	Y	Y	Y
29 ***Solomon***	N	N	Y	N	Y	N	N	N
30 ***Martin***	N	N	Y	N	Y	N	N	Y
31 ***Mitchell***	Y	N	Y	N	Y	N	N	Y
32 ***Wortley***	N	Y	Y	N	Y	N	N	Y
33 ***Lee***	N	N	Y	?	?	-	-	-
34 ***Horton***	Y	N	Y	N	Y	N	N	Y
35 ***Conable***	N	Y	Y	N	Y	Y	Y	Y
36 LaFalce	N	Y	Y	Y	Y	Y	N	N
37 Nowak	Y	Y	Y	Y	Y	Y	N	N
38 ***Kemp***	N	Y	Y	N	Y	N	N	N
39 Lundine	Y	Y	Y	N	N	Y	Y	?
NORTH CAROLINA								
1 Jones	Y	Y	N	N	Y	N	Y	Y
2 Fountain	?	Y	N	N	Y	N	N	N
3 Whitley	Y	Y	N	N	Y	Y	Y	Y
4 Andrews	Y	Y	N	N	Y	N	N	Y
5 Neal	Y	Y	N	N	Y	N	N	Y
6 ***Johnston***	N	Y	N	N	Y	N	N	N
7 Rose	Y	Y	N	N	Y	Y	Y	Y
8 Hefner	Y	Y	N	N	Y	N	Y	Y
9 ***Martin***	N	N	N	N	Y	N	N	Y
10 ***Broyhill***	N	Y	N	N	Y	Y	Y	Y
11 ***Hendon***	Y	N	N	N	Y	N	N	Y
NORTH DAKOTA								
AL Dorgan	Y	Y	Y	N	Y	Y	Y	N
OHIO								
1 ***Gradison***	N	Y	N	N	Y	N	N	Y
2 Luken	Y	Y	Y	Y	Y	Y	Y	?
3 Hall	Y	Y	Y	Y	Y	Y	N	Y
4 ***Oxley***	N	N	Y	N	Y	Y	N	Y
5 ***Latta***	N	Y	Y	N	Y	N	Y	Y
6 ***McEwen***	N	N	Y	Y	?	N	N	Y
7 ***Brown***	?	?	?	?	?	?	?	?
8 ***Kindness***	N	Y	Y	N	Y	N	N	Y
9 ***Weber***	N	Y	Y	N	N	N	N	Y
10 ***Miller***	N	Y	Y	N	Y	Y	Y	Y
11 ***Stanton***	N	N	Y	N	Y	Y	Y	Y
12 Shamansky	Y	Y	Y	Y	Y	Y	Y	Y
13 Pease	Y	Y	Y	Y	Y	Y	Y	N
14 Seiberling	Y	Y	Y	N	N	Y	Y	N
15 ***Wylie***	N	N	Y	N	Y	N	N	N
16 ***Regula***	N	Y	Y	N	Y	Y	Y	Y
17 ***Ashbrook***	N	N	Y	N	Y	N	N	N
18 Applegate	Y	Y	Y	N	Y	Y	Y	Y
19 ***Williams***	N	Y	Y	N	Y	N	N	?
20 Oakar	?	?	?	?	?	?	?	?
21 Stokes	Y	Y	Y	N	N	Y	Y	?
22 Eckart	Y	Y	Y	Y	Y	Y	N	N
23 Mottl	Y	Y	Y	N	Y	Y	N	Y
OKLAHOMA								
1 Jones	Y	Y	N	Y	Y	Y	Y	Y
2 Synar	Y	Y	N	Y	Y	Y	N	Y
3 Watkins	Y	Y	N	N	Y	Y	Y	Y
4 McCurdy	Y	Y	N	N	Y	Y	N	Y
5 ***Edwards***	N	Y	N	N	Y	Y	Y	Y
6 English	Y	Y	N	N	Y	Y	N	Y
OREGON								
1 AuCoin	Y	Y	Y	Y	Y	Y	Y	Y
2 ***Smith***	N	Y	N	N	Y	N	N	N
3 Wyden	Y	Y	Y	Y	N	Y	Y	Y
4 Weaver	Y	Y	Y	Y	N	Y	Y	Y
PENNSYLVANIA								
1 Foglietta	Y	Y	Y	Y	N	Y	Y	Y
2 Gray	Y	Y	Y	N	N	Y	Y	Y
3 Smith	?	?	?	?	#	?	?	?
4 ***Dougherty***	Y	Y	Y	N	Y	Y	Y	Y
5 ***Schulze***	Y	Y	Y	Y	Y	N	N	Y
6 Yatron	Y	Y	Y	N	Y	Y	N	Y
7 Edgar	Y	Y	Y	Y	N	Y	N	N
8 ***Coyne, J.***	Y	Y	Y	Y	Y	N	N	Y
9 ***Shuster***	Y	Y	Y	N	Y	N	N	N
10 ***McDade***	N	N	Y	Y	Y	Y	Y	Y
11 ***Nelligan***	Y	Y	Y	N	Y	N	N	Y
12 Murtha	Y	N	Y	N	Y	Y	Y	?
13 ***Coughlin***	N	Y	Y	Y	N	Y	Y	Y
14 Coyne, W.	?	Y	Y	Y	N	Y	Y	Y
15 ***Ritter***	N	N	Y	Y	Y	N	N	Y
16 ***Walker***	N	Y	Y	N	Y	N	N	N
17 Ertel	Y	Y	Y	Y	Y	N	N	Y
18 Walgren	Y	Y	Y	Y	Y	Y	Y	Y
19 ***Goodling***	N	Y	Y	N	Y	N	N	Y
20 Gaydos	Y	?	Y	N	Y	Y	Y	Y
21 Bailey	Y	Y	Y	N	Y	Y	Y	Y
22 Murphy	Y	Y	Y	N	Y	Y	Y	Y
23 ***Clinger***	N	Y	Y	N	Y	N	N	Y
24 ***Marks***	?	?	?	?	?	?	?	?
25 ***Atkinson***	N	Y	Y	Y	N	Y	Y	Y
RHODE ISLAND								
1 St Germain	Y	Y	Y	Y	Y	Y	N	Y
2 ***Schneider***	Y	Y	Y	Y	N	Y	Y	Y
SOUTH CAROLINA								
1 ***Hartnett***	N	N	N	N	Y	N	Y	Y
2 ***Spence***	N	Y	N	N	Y	N	N	Y
3 Derrick	Y	Y	N	N	Y	Y	Y	?
4 ***Campbell***	N	Y	N	N	Y	N	N	Y
5 Holland	Y	Y	N	N	Y	Y	Y	Y
6 ***Napier***	N	Y	N	N	Y	N	N	N
SOUTH DAKOTA								
1 Daschle	Y	Y	Y	Y	Y	Y	N	Y
2 ***Roberts***	N	Y	N	N	Y	N	N	Y
TENNESSEE								
1 ***Quillen***	N	N	N	N	Y	Y	Y	Y
2 ***Duncan***	N	N	N	N	Y	Y	Y	Y
3 Bouquard	Y	Y	N	N	Y	Y	N	Y
4 Gore	Y	Y	N	N	Y	Y	Y	Y
5 Boner	Y	Y	N	N	Y	Y	N	Y
6 ***Beard***	N	Y	N	N	Y	?	X	?
7 Jones	?	?	?	?	?	?	?	?
8 Ford	?	?	?	?	?	?	?	?
TEXAS								
1 Hall, S.	Y	Y	N	N	Y	Y	N	Y
2 Wilson	?	?	N	N	Y	Y	Y	Y
3 ***Collins***	N	Y	N	?	?	?	?	?
4 Hall, R.	Y	Y	N	N	Y	N	N	N
5 Mattox	Y	Y	N	Y	Y	Y	Y	Y
6 Gramm	N	Y	N	N	Y	Y	Y	Y
7 ***Archer***	N	Y	N	N	Y	N	Y	?
8 ***Fields***	N	Y	N	N	Y	N	N	Y
9 Brooks	Y	Y	N	Y	Y	Y	Y	N
10 Pickle	Y	Y	N	Y	Y	Y	Y	Y
11 Leath	?	?	?	?	?	?	?	?
12 Wright	Y	Y	N	Y	Y	Y	Y	Y
13 Hightower	Y	Y	N	N	Y	Y	Y	Y
14 Patman	Y	Y	N	N	Y	Y	Y	Y
15 de la Garza	Y	Y	N	N	Y	Y	Y	Y
16 White	N	Y	N	N	Y	Y	Y	Y
17 Stenholm	N	Y	N	N	Y	Y	Y	Y
18 Leland	Y	Y	Y	N	N	Y	Y	N
19 Hance	Y	Y	N	N	Y	Y	Y	Y
20 Gonzalez	Y	Y	N	N	N	Y	N	N
21 ***Loeffler***	N	Y	N	N	Y	Y	Y	Y
22 ***Paul***	N	Y	N	Y	N	N	N	N
23 Kazen	Y	Y	N	N	Y	Y	N	N
24 Frost	Y	Y	N	N	Y	Y	Y	Y
UTAH								
1 ***Hansen***	N	Y	N	?	?	?	?	?
2 ***Marriott***	N	Y	Y	N	Y	N	N	Y
VERMONT								
AL ***Jeffords***	N	Y	Y	Y	N	Y	Y	Y
VIRGINIA								
1 ***Trible***	Y	Y	N	N	Y	N	N	Y
2 ***Whitehurst***	Y	Y	N	N	Y	N	N	Y
3 ***Bliley***	N	Y	N	N	Y	N	N	Y
4 ***Daniel, R.***	Y	N	N	N	Y	N	N	Y
5 Daniel, D.	N	N	N	N	Y	Y	Y	Y
6 ***Butler***	N	N	N	N	Y	N	Y	Y
7 ***Robinson***	N	N	N	N	Y	N	N	Y
8 ***Parris***	Y	Y	N	N	Y	N	N	N
9 ***Wampler***	N	N	?	N	Y	N	N	Y
10 ***Wolf***	Y	Y	N	N	Y	N	N	Y
WASHINGTON								
1 ***Pritchard***	N	Y	Y	N	Y	N	Y	Y
2 Swift	Y	Y	Y	Y	Y	Y	Y	Y
3 Bonker	Y	Y	Y	Y	Y	Y	Y	Y
4 ***Morrison***	N	Y	Y	N	Y	N	Y	Y
5 Foley	Y	Y	N	Y	?	?	Y	Y
6 Dicks	Y	N	N	N	Y	Y	Y	Y
7 Lowry	Y	Y	Y	Y	N	Y	Y	?
WEST VIRGINIA								
1 Mollohan	Y	Y	Y	Y	Y	Y	Y	Y
2 ***Benedict***	N	Y	Y	N	Y	N	Y	Y
3 ***Staton***	N	N	N	N	Y	N	N	N
4 Rahall	?	?	?	?	?	?	?	?
WISCONSIN								
1 Aspin	Y	Y	N	Y	Y	Y	Y	Y
2 Kastenmeier	Y	Y	Y	N	N	N	N	N
3 ***Gunderson***	N	N	+	Y	Y	N	N	Y
4 Zablocki	Y	Y	Y	N	Y	Y	Y	Y
5 Reuss	Y	Y	Y	Y	-	Y	Y	Y
6 ***Petri***	N	Y	Y	N	Y	N	N	Y
7 Obey	Y	Y	Y	Y	Y	Y	Y	Y
8 ***Roth***	N	N	N	N	Y	N	N	Y
9 ***Sensenbrenner***	N	Y	Y	Y	N	N	N	Y
WYOMING								
AL ***Cheney***	N	Y	N	N	Y	Y	Y	Y

Southern states - Ala., Ark., Fla., Ga., Ky., La., Miss., N.C., Okla., S.C., Tenn., Texas, Va.

KEY

Y   Voted for (yea).
\#   Paired for.
\+   Announced for.
N   Voted against (nay).
X   Paired against.
\-   Announced against.
P   Voted ''present''.
C   Voted ''present'' to avoid possible conflict of interest.
?   Did not vote or otherwise make a position known.

Democrats   *Republicans*

215. HR 6030. Defense Department Authorizations, Fiscal 1983. Markey, D-Mass., amendment to reduce the authorization for civil defense programs by $108 million. Rejected 163-240: R 35-145; D 128-95 (ND 118-33, SD 10-62), July 29, 1982. A "nay" was a vote supporting the president's position.

216. HR 6030. Defense Department Authorizations, Fiscal 1983. Downey, D-N.Y., amendment to delete $336.7 million for development of the Trident II submarine-launched missile and $26 million to modify Trident submarines to carry the Trident II missiles and to add $26 million for development of the Axe nonnuclear missile. Rejected 89-312: R 5-178; D 84-134 (ND 82-67, SD 2-67), July 29, 1982. A "nay" was a vote supporting the president's position.

217. HR 6030. Defense Department Authorizations, Fiscal 1983. Schroeder, D-Colo., amendment to reduce by 50 percent the number of U.S. military personnel stationed overseas over a four-year period. Rejected 87-314: R 20-161; D 67-153 (ND 62-87, SD 5-66), July 29, 1982. A "nay" was a vote supporting the president's position.

218. HR 6863. Supplemental Appropriations, Fiscal 1982. Passage of the bill to provide net new budget authority of $13,755,299,924 for federal employee pay raises, commodity credit programs, defense and other programs, and to limit outside earned income of members of Congress to 30 percent of their congressional salaries. Passed 282-111: R 103-73; D 179-38 (ND 133-15, SD 46-23), July 29, 1982. The president had requested net new budget authority of $15,702,932,000.

	215	216	217	218
ALABAMA				
1 *Edwards*	N	N	N	Y
2 *Dickinson*	N	N	N	N
3 Nichols	N	N	N	N
4 Bevill	N	N	N	Y
5 Flippo	N	N	N	Y
6 *Smith*	N	N	N	N
7 Shelby	N	N	N	N
ALASKA				
AL *Young*	N	N	N	?
ARIZONA				
1 *Rhodes*	N	N	N	Y
2 Udall	Y	Y	N	Y
3 *Stump*	N	N	N	N
4 *Rudd*	N	N	N	Y
ARKANSAS				
1 Alexander	Y	N	N	Y
2 *Bethune*	N	N	N	Y
3 *Hammerschmidt*	N	N	N	Y
4 Anthony	N	?	?	?
CALIFORNIA				
1 *Chappie*	N	N	N	Y
2 *Clausen*	N	N	N	Y
3 Matsui	Y	Y	N	Y
4 Fazio	Y	N	Y	Y
5 Burton, J.	Y	Y	Y	N
6 Burton, P.	Y	Y	N	Y
7 Miller	Y	Y	Y	Y
8 Dellums	Y	Y	Y	Y
9 Stark	Y	?	?	Y
10 Edwards	Y	Y	Y	Y
11 Lantos	Y	N	N	Y
12 *McCloskey*	?	?	?	?
13 Mineta	Y	N	N	Y
14 *Shumway*	N	N	N	N
15 Coelho	N	N	N	Y
16 Panetta	Y	N	N	Y
17 *Pashayan*	N	N	N	?
18 *Thomas*	N	N	N	N
19 *Lagomarsino*	N	N	N	N
20 *Goldwater*	N	N	N	N
21 *Fiedler*	N	N	N	Y
22 *Moorhead*	N	N	N	N
23 Beilenson	Y	Y	N	Y
24 Waxman	Y	Y	N	Y
25 Roybal	Y	Y	Y	Y
26 *Rousselot*	N	N	N	N
27 *Dornan*	?	?	?	?
28 Dixon	Y	Y	Y	Y
29 Hawkins	Y	N	Y	Y
30 Martinez	Y	Y	N	Y
31 Dymally	\#	?	\#	?
32 Anderson	N	N	N	N
33 Grisham	N	N	N	?
34 *Lungren*	N	N	N	N
35 *Dreier*	N	N	N	N
36 Brown	Y	?	Y	Y
37 *Lewis*	N	N	N	N
38 Patterson	Y	N	N	N
39 *Dannemeyer*	N	N	N	N
40 *Badham*	N	N	N	N
41 *Lowery*	N	N	N	N
42 *Hunter*	N	N	N	N
43 *Burgener*	N	N	N	Y
COLORADO				
1 Schroeder	Y	Y	Y	N
2 Wirth	Y	Y	N	Y
3 Kogovsek	Y	Y	N	Y
4 *Brown*	N	N	Y	N

	215	216	217	218
5 *Kramer*	N	N	N	N
CONNECTICUT				
1 Kennelly	Y	Y	N	Y
2 Gejdenson	Y	Y	N	Y
3 *DeNardis*	Y	N	N	Y
4 *McKinney*	Y	N	N	Y
5 Ratchford	Y	Y	N	Y
6 Moffett	\#	\#	?	?
DELAWARE				
AL *Evans*	N	N	N	N
FLORIDA				
1 Hutto	N	N	N	Y
2 Fuqua	N	N	?	?
3 Bennett	N	N	N	N
4 Chappell	N	N	N	Y
5 *McCollum*	N	N	N	N
6 *Young*	N	N	N	N
7 Gibbons	Y	N	N	N
8 Ireland	?	?	?	N
9 Nelson	N	N	N	Y
10 *Bafalis*	?	?	?	?
11 Mica	N	N	N	Y
12 *Shaw*	N	N	N	Y
13 Lehman	Y	Y	Y	Y
14 Pepper	X	X	X	?
15 Fascell	Y	N	N	Y
GEORGIA				
1 Ginn	?	?	?	?
2 Hatcher	N	?	N	?
3 Brinkley	N	N	N	Y
4 Levitas	N	N	N	N
5 Fowler	N	?	N	Y
6 *Gingrich*	N	N	N	N
7 McDonald	N	N	N	N
8 Evans	N	N	N	N
9 Jenkins	N	N	Y	N
10 Barnard	N	N	N	N
HAWAII				
1 Heftel	Y	Y	N	Y
2 Akaka	N	N	N	Y
IDAHO				
1 *Craig*	N	N	N	N
2 *Hansen*	N	N	N	N
ILLINOIS				
1 Washington	Y	Y	Y	Y
2 Savage	?	?	Y	Y
3 Russo	Y	Y	Y	Y
4 *Derwinski*	N	N	?	N
5 Fary	N	N	N	Y
6 *Hyde*	N	N	N	Y
7 Collins	Y	Y	Y	Y
8 Rostenkowski	Y	Y	Y	Y
9 Yates	?	?	?	?
10 *Porter*	Y	N	N	Y
11 Annunzio	Y	N	N	Y
12 *Crane, P.*	N	N	N	N
13 *McClory*	N	N	N	Y
14 *Erlenborn*	N	N	N	N
15 *Corcoran*	N	N	N	N
16 *Martin*	Y	N	Y	Y
17 *O'Brien*	?	N	N	Y
18 *Michel*	N	N	N	Y
19 *Railsback*	N	N	Y	Y
20 *Findley*	Y	N	N	Y
21 *Madigan*	N	N	N	Y
22 *Crane, D.*	N	N	N	N
23 Price	N	N	N	Y
24 Simon	Y	N	N	Y
INDIANA				
1 Benjamin	N	Y	Y	Y
2 Fithian	Y	N	N	Y
3 *Hiler*	N	N	Y	N
4 *Coats*	N	N	Y	N
5 *Hillis*	N	N	N	Y
6 Evans	N	Y	N	Y
7 *Myers*	N	N	N	N
8 *Deckard*	Y	N	N	N
9 Hamilton	N	N	N	Y
10 Sharp	Y	N	N	Y
11 Jacobs	Y	Y	Y	Y
IOWA				
1 *Leach*	Y	N	N	Y
2 *Tauke*	Y	N	N	Y
3 *Evans*	Y	N	N	Y
4 Smith	Y	N	N	Y
5 Harkin	Y	Y	Y	Y
6 Bedell	Y	Y	N	Y

ND - Northern Democrats   SD - Southern Democrats

	215	216	217	218
KANSAS				
1 Roberts	N	N	N	N
2 Jeffries	N	N	N	N
3 Winn	N	N	N	Y
4 Glickman	Y	N	N	N
5 Whittaker	N	N	N	N
KENTUCKY				
1 Hubbard	N	N	N	N
2 Natcher	N	N	N	Y
3 Mazzoli	N	N	N	Y
4 Snyder	N	N	N	N
5 Rogers	N	N	N	Y
6 Hopkins	N	N	N	Y
7 Perkins	N	N	N	Y
LOUISIANA				
1 Livingston	N	N	N	Y
2 Boggs	N	N	N	Y
3 Tauzin	N	N	N	N
4 Roemer	N	N	N	N
5 Huckaby	N	N	Y	N
6 Moore	N	N	N	N
7 Breaux	N	N	N	Y
8 Long	N	N	N	Y
MAINE				
1 Emery	N	N	N	Y
2 Snowe	Y	N	N	Y
MARYLAND				
1 Dyson	N	N	N	Y
2 Long	Y	N	N	Y
3 Mikulski	Y	N	N	Y
4 Holt	N	N	N	N
5 Hoyer	N	N	N	Y
6 Byron	N	N	N	Y
7 Mitchell	Y	Y	N	Y
8 Barnes	Y	N	N	Y
MASSACHUSETTS				
1 Conte	Y	N	N	Y
2 Boland	Y	N	N	Y
3 Early	?	?	?	Y
4 Frank	Y	Y	Y	Y
5 Shannon	Y	Y	Y	Y
6 Mavroules	Y	N	N	Y
7 Markey	Y	Y	N	Y
8 O'Neill				
9 Moakley	Y	Y	N	Y
10 Heckler	Y	Y	N	Y
11 Donnelly	Y	Y	Y	Y
12 Studds	Y	Y	N	Y
MICHIGAN				
1 Conyers	Y	Y	Y	Y
2 Pursell	Y	N	N	Y
3 Wolpe	Y	Y	Y	Y
4 Siljander	?	?	?	?
5 Sawyer	N	N	N	Y
6 Dunn	Y	N	N	Y
7 Kildee	N	Y	N	Y
8 Traxler	Y	N	N	Y
9 Vander Jagt	Y	N	N	Y
10 Albosta	Y	N	N	Y
11 Davis	N	N	N	Y
12 Bonior	X	#	X	?
13 Crockett	Y	Y	Y	Y
14 Hertel	Y	N	N	Y
15 Ford	Y	Y	Y	Y
16 Dingell	Y	N	N	Y
17 Brodhead	Y	Y	Y	Y
18 Blanchard	?	?	?	?
19 Broomfield	N	N	N	N
MINNESOTA				
1 Erdahl	Y	N	N	N
2 Hagedorn	N	N	Y	N
3 Frenzel	Y	N	N	N
4 Vento	Y	Y	N	Y
5 Sabo	Y	Y	N	Y
6 Weber	N	N	Y	N
7 Stangeland	N	N	N	N
8 Oberstar	Y	Y	N	Y
MISSISSIPPI				
1 Whitten	N	N	N	Y
2 Bowen	N	N	N	Y
3 Montgomery	N	N	N	N
4 Dowdy	?	?	?	?
5 Lott	N	N	N	?
MISSOURI				
1 Clay	#	?	#	?
2 Young	N	N	N	N
3 Gephardt	N	Y	Y	Y

	215	216	217	218
4 Skelton	N	N	N	N
5 Bolling	N	Y	?	?
6 Coleman	N	N	N	N
7 Taylor	N	N	N	N
8 Bailey	N	N	N	N
9 Volkmer	N	N	Y	N
10 Emerson	N	N	N	N
MONTANA				
1 Williams	N	Y	N	Y
2 Marlenee	N	N	N	Y
NEBRASKA				
1 Bereuter	N	N	N	Y
2 Daub	N	N	N	Y
3 Smith	N	N	N	Y
NEVADA				
AL Santini	N	N	N	Y
NEW HAMPSHIRE				
1 D'Amours	Y	N	N	Y
2 Gregg	Y	N	Y	N
NEW JERSEY				
1 Florio	Y	N	N	Y
2 Hughes	N	N	Y	N
3 Howard	Y	Y	Y	Y
4 Smith	N	N	N	Y
5 Fenwick	N	N	N	Y
6 Forsythe	Y	Y	Y	Y
7 Roukema	Y	N	N	Y
8 Roe	N	N	N	Y
9 Hollenbeck	Y	N	N	Y
10 Rodino	Y	Y	Y	Y
11 Minish	Y	N	N	Y
12 Rinaldo	N	N	N	Y
13 Courter	N	N	N	Y
14 Guarini	Y	N	N	Y
15 Dwyer	Y	N	N	Y
NEW MEXICO				
1 Lujan	N	N	Y	Y
2 Skeen	N	N	N	?
NEW YORK				
1 Carney	N	N	N	N
2 Downey	Y	Y	N	N
3 Carman	N	N	N	Y
4 Lent	N	N	N	Y
5 McGrath	N	N	N	Y
6 LeBoutillier	N	N	N	Y
7 Addabbo	Y	N	Y	Y
8 Rosenthal	Y	Y	Y	Y
9 Ferraro	Y	N	N	Y
10 Biaggi	Y	N	N	Y
11 Scheuer	Y	Y	Y	Y
12 Chisholm	Y	Y	Y	?
13 Solarz	Y	Y	N	Y
14 Richmond	Y	Y	Y	?
15 Zeferetti	Y	N	N	Y
16 Schumer	Y	Y	Y	Y
17 Molinari	N	N	N	Y
18 Green	Y	N	N	Y
19 Rangel	Y	Y	Y	Y
20 Weiss	Y	Y	Y	Y
21 Garcia	Y	Y	Y	Y
22 Bingham	Y	Y	Y	Y
23 Peyser	Y	N	N	Y
24 Ottinger	Y	Y	Y	Y
25 Fish	N	N	N	Y
26 Gilman	N	N	N	Y
27 McHugh	Y	Y	N	Y
28 Stratton	N	N	N	Y
29 Solomon	N	N	N	Y
30 Martin	N	N	N	Y
31 Mitchell	N	N	N	Y
32 Wortley	N	N	N	N
33 Lee	N	N	N	N
34 Horton	N	N	N	Y
35 Conable	Y	N	N	Y
36 LaFalce	Y	N	N	Y
37 Nowak	Y	Y	N	Y
38 Kemp	N	N	N	N
39 Lundine	Y	Y	Y	Y
NORTH CAROLINA				
1 Jones	Y	N	N	Y
2 Fountain	N	N	N	N
3 Whitley	N	N	N	Y
4 Andrews	N	N	N	Y
5 Neal	N	N	N	Y
6 Johnston	N	N	N	N
7 Rose	Y	N	N	Y
8 Hefner	N	N	N	Y

	215	216	217	218
9 Martin	N	N	N	N
10 Broyhill	N	N	N	N
11 Hendon	N	N	N	N
NORTH DAKOTA				
AL Dorgan	Y	Y	Y	Y
OHIO				
1 Gradison	Y	N	N	N
2 Luken	Y	N	N	N
3 Hall	Y	N	N	N
4 Oxley	N	N	N	N
5 Latta	N	N	N	N
6 McEwen	N	N	Y	N
7 Brown	?	?	?	?
8 Kindness	?	N	N	N
9 Weber	N	N	N	N
10 Miller	N	N	Y	N
11 Stanton	N	N	N	Y
12 Shamansky	Y	N	N	Y
13 Pease	Y	N	N	Y
14 Seiberling	Y	Y	Y	Y
15 Wylie	N	N	N	N
16 Regula	N	N	N	Y
17 Ashbrook	N	N	N	N
18 Applegate	N	N	Y	Y
19 Williams	N	N	N	Y
20 Oakar	?	?	?	?
21 Stokes	Y	Y	Y	Y
22 Eckart	N	Y	N	Y
23 Mottl	Y	N	Y	Y
OKLAHOMA				
1 Jones	N	N	N	Y
2 Synar	Y	N	N	Y
3 Watkins	N	N	N	Y
4 McCurdy	N	N	N	Y
5 Edwards	N	N	N	N
6 English	N	N	N	Y
OREGON				
1 AuCoin	Y	Y	Y	Y
2 Smith	?	?	?	?
3 Wyden	Y	Y	Y	Y
4 Weaver	Y	Y	Y	N
PENNSYLVANIA				
1 Foglietta	Y	N	N	Y
2 Gray	Y	Y	Y	?
3 Smith	X	X	X	?
4 Dougherty	N	N	N	Y
5 Schulze	N	N	N	Y
6 Yatron	N	N	N	Y
7 Edgar	Y	Y	Y	Y
8 Coyne, J.	Y	N	Y	N
9 Shuster	N	N	N	N
10 McDade	N	N	N	Y
11 Nelligan	N	N	N	Y
12 Murtha	N	N	N	Y
13 Coughlin	N	N	N	Y
14 Coyne, W.	Y	Y	N	Y
15 Ritter	N	N	N	Y
16 Walker	N	N	N	N
17 Ertel	?	?	?	?
18 Walgren	Y	Y	N	Y
19 Goodling	N	N	N	N
20 Gaydos	N	N	Y	Y
21 Bailey	N	N	N	Y
22 Murphy	N	N	Y	Y
23 Clinger	Y	N	N	Y
24 Marks	?	N	?	Y
25 Atkinson	N	N	Y	Y
RHODE ISLAND				
1 St Germain	Y	N	N	Y
2 Schneider	Y	Y	N	Y
SOUTH CAROLINA				
1 Hartnett	N	N	N	N
2 Spence	N	N	N	Y
3 Derrick	N	N	N	Y
4 Campbell	N	N	N	N
5 Holland	N	N	N	Y
6 Napier	N	N	N	Y
SOUTH DAKOTA				
1 Daschle	Y	Y	N	Y
2 Roberts	N	N	N	Y
TENNESSEE				
1 Quillen	N	N	N	Y
2 Duncan	N	N	N	Y
3 Bouquard	N	N	N	Y
4 Gore	N	N	N	Y
5 Boner	N	N	N	?
6 Beard	?	?	?	?

	215	216	217	218
7 Jones	?	X	X	?
8 Ford	#	#	#	?
TEXAS				
1 Hall, S.	N	N	N	N
2 Wilson	N	?	N	N
3 Collins	?	?	?	?
4 Hall, R.	N	N	N	N
5 Mattox	Y	N	Y	N
6 Gramm	N	N	N	N
7 Archer	N	N	N	N
8 Fields	N	N	N	N
9 Brooks	N	N	N	Y
10 Pickle	N	N	N	Y
11 Leath	?	N	N	N
12 Wright	N	N	N	?
13 Hightower	N	N	N	Y
14 Patman	N	N	N	Y
15 de la Garza	N	N	N	Y
16 White	N	N	N	Y
17 Stenholm	N	N	N	Y
18 Leland	Y	Y	Y	Y
19 Hance	N	N	N	Y
20 Gonzalez	N	N	N	Y
21 Loeffler	N	N	N	N
22 Paul	Y	N	Y	N
23 Kazen	N	N	N	Y
24 Frost	Y	N	N	Y
UTAH				
1 Hansen	?	?	?	?
2 Marriott	N	N	N	?
VERMONT				
AL Jeffords	Y	N	N	Y
VIRGINIA				
1 Trible	N	N	N	Y
2 Whitehurst	N	N	N	Y
3 Bliley	N	N	N	Y
4 Daniel, R.	N	N	N	N
5 Daniel, D.	N	N	N	N
6 Butler	N	N	N	Y
7 Robinson	N	N	N	Y
8 Parris	N	N	N	Y
9 Wampler	N	N	N	Y
10 Wolf	N	N	N	Y
WASHINGTON				
1 Pritchard	Y	Y	N	Y
2 Swift	N	N	N	Y
3 Bonker	N	Y	Y	Y
4 Morrison	N	N	N	Y
5 Foley	Y	N	?	Y
6 Dicks	Y	N	N	Y
7 Lowry	Y	Y	Y	Y
WEST VIRGINIA				
1 Mollohan	N	N	N	Y
2 Benedict	N	N	N	Y
3 Staton	N	N	N	Y
4 Rahall	X	?	#	?
WISCONSIN				
1 Aspin	Y	N	N	Y
2 Kastenmeier	Y	Y	Y	Y
3 Gunderson	Y	N	N	Y
4 Zablocki	N	N	N	Y
5 Reuss	Y	Y	N	?
6 Petri	Y	N	Y	N
7 Obey	Y	Y	N	N
8 Roth	N	N	N	Y
9 Sensenbrenner	Y	N	N	?
WYOMING				
AL Cheney	N	N	N	N

Southern states - Ala., Ark., Fla., Ga., Ky., La., Miss., N.C., Okla., S.C., Tenn., Texas, Va.

219. HR 6030. Defense Department Authorizations, Fiscal 1983. Glickman, D-Kan., substitute for the Schroeder, D-Colo., amendment, to limit the total obligation or expenditure of funds authorized by the bill to $175,300,000,000 — a reduction of 1 percent from the amount in the bill as previously amended by the House. The Schroeder amendment would have made a reduction of 5 percent. Adopted 238-136: R 90-75; D 148-61 (ND 122-22, SD 26-39), July 29, 1982. (The Schroeder amendment, as amended, subsequently was adopted (see vote 220, below).) A "nay" was a vote supporting the president's position.

220. HR 6030. Defense Department Authorizations, Fiscal 1983. Schroeder, D-Colo., amendment, as amended, to limit the total obligation or expenditure of funds authorized by the bill to $175,300,000,000 — a reduction of 1 percent from the amount in the bill as previously amended by the House. Adopted 235-135: R 90-73; D 145-62 (ND 119-22, SD 26-40), July 29, 1982. A "nay" was a vote supporting the president's position.

221. HR 6030. Defense Department Authorizations, Fiscal 1983. Passage of the bill to authorize $177,066,100,000 (with total obligations and expenditures limited to $175,300,000,000) in fiscal year 1983 for procurement, operations and management, and research and development programs of the Defense Department. Passed 290-73: R 145-16; D 145-57 (ND 84-55, SD 61-2), July 29, 1982.

222. Procedural Motion. Fields, R-Texas, motion to approve the House *Journal* of Monday, Aug. 2. Motion agreed to 333-25: R 151-12; D 182-13 (ND 118-12, SD 64-1), Aug. 3, 1982.

223. S 2248. Defense Department Authorizations, Fiscal 1983. Price, D-Ill., motion to close the conference committee meetings on the bill during consideration of national security matters. Motion agreed to 372-0: R 169-0; D 203-0 (ND 135-0, SD 68-0), Aug. 3, 1982.

224. HR 6862. Civil Service Reconciliation. Derwinski, R-Ill., motion to recommit the bill to the Post Office and Civil Service Committee to make reductions as ordered by the first budget resolution (S Con Res 92) for fiscal year 1983. Motion rejected 160-236: R 140-39; D 20-197 (ND 2-143, SD 18-54), Aug. 3, 1982.

225. HR 6862. Civil Service Reconciliation. Passage of the bill to reduce budget authority and outlays under certain civil service programs pursuant to the first budget resolution (S Con Res 92) for fiscal year 1983. Passed 268-128: R 69-110; D 199-18 (ND 141-4, SD 58-14), Aug. 3, 1982.

226. HR 5427. Radio Marti. Fascell, D-Fla., motion that the House resolve itself into the Committee of the Whole for consideration of the bill to authorize establishment of a radio station to broadcast to Cuba. Motion agreed to 361-20: R 167-5; D 194-15 (ND 126-13, SD 68-2), Aug. 3, 1982.

KEY

Y	Voted for (yea).
#	Paired for.
+	Announced for.
N	Voted against (nay).
X	Paired against.
-	Announced against.
P	Voted "present".
C	Voted "present" to avoid possible conflict of interest.
?	Did not vote or otherwise make a position known.

Democrats *Republicans*

	219	220	221	222	223	224	225	226
ALABAMA								
1 *Edwards*	N	N	Y	?	?	Y	N	Y
2 *Dickinson*	N	N	Y	N	Y	Y	N	Y
3 Nichols	N	N	?	Y	Y	Y	Y	Y
4 Bevill	N	N	Y	?	?	N	Y	Y
5 Flippo	?	?	?	?	Y	N	Y	Y
6 *Smith*	N	N	Y	Y	Y	Y	N	Y
7 Shelby	N	N	Y	Y	Y	N	Y	N
ALASKA								
AL *Young*	?	?	?	?	?	?	?	?
ARIZONA								
1 *Rhodes*	N	?	?	Y	Y	Y	N	Y
2 Udall	Y	Y	Y	Y	Y	N	Y	Y
3 *Stump*	N	N	Y	Y	Y	Y	N	Y
4 *Rudd*	N	N	Y	Y	Y	Y	N	Y
ARKANSAS								
1 Alexander	N	N	Y	Y	Y	N	Y	Y
2 *Bethune*	Y	Y	Y	Y	Y	Y	N	Y
3 *Hammerschmidt*	?	?	?	Y	Y	Y	N	Y
4 Anthony	?	?	?	Y	Y	N	Y	Y
CALIFORNIA								
1 *Chappie*	N	N	Y	Y	Y	Y	N	Y
2 *Clausen*	?	?	?	Y	Y	N	Y	Y
3 Matsui	Y	Y	Y	Y	Y	N	Y	Y
4 Fazio	Y	Y	Y	Y	Y	N	Y	Y
5 Burton, J.	?	?	?	?	?	?	?	?
6 Burton, P.	Y	Y	N	Y	Y	N	Y	Y
7 Miller	Y	Y	N	Y	N	Y	N	Y
8 Dellums	Y	Y	N	Y	N	Y	N	N
9 Stark	Y	Y	N	Y	N	N	Y	Y
10 Edwards	Y	Y	N	Y	Y	N	Y	Y
11 Lantos	Y	Y	Y	Y	N	Y	N	Y
12 *McCloskey*	?	?	?	Y	Y	Y	N	Y
13 Mineta	Y	Y	N	Y	N	Y	N	Y
14 Shumway	N	N	Y	Y	Y	Y	N	Y
15 Coelho	Y	Y	Y	Y	Y	N	Y	Y
16 Panetta	Y	Y	Y	Y	Y	N	Y	Y
17 *Pashayan*	?	?	?	Y	Y	Y	N	Y
18 *Thomas*	N	N	Y	Y	Y	Y	N	Y
19 *Lagomarsino*	N	N	Y	Y	Y	Y	N	Y
20 *Goldwater*	N	N	Y	?	Y	Y	N	?
21 *Fiedler*	N	N	Y	Y	Y	Y	N	N
22 *Moorhead*	N	N	Y	Y	Y	Y	N	Y
23 Beilenson	Y	Y	N	Y	N	N	Y	Y
24 Waxman	Y	Y	N	Y	N	N	Y	Y
25 Roybal	Y	Y	N	Y	N	N	Y	Y
26 *Rousselot*	Y	N	?	Y	Y	Y	N	Y
27 *Dornan*	?	?	?	?	?	#	X	?
28 Dixon	?	?	?	Y	Y	N	Y	?
29 Hawkins	Y	Y	Y	Y	N	Y	N	Y
30 Martinez	Y	Y	Y	Y	N	N	Y	Y
31 Dymally	?	?	?	P	Y	N	Y	Y
32 Anderson	Y	Y	Y	Y	Y	N	Y	Y
33 *Grisham*	?	?	?	Y	Y	N	Y	Y
34 Lungren	N	N	Y	Y	Y	Y	N	Y
35 *Dreier*	Y	Y	Y	Y	Y	Y	N	Y
36 Brown	Y	Y	N	Y	N	N	Y	Y
37 Lewis	N	N	Y	N	Y	Y	N	Y
38 Patterson	Y	Y	Y	Y	N	N	Y	Y
39 *Dannemeyer*	Y	Y	Y	Y	Y	Y	N	Y
40 *Badham*	N	N	Y	Y	Y	Y	N	Y
41 *Lowery*	N	N	Y	Y	Y	Y	N	Y
42 *Hunter*	N	N	Y	?	?	?	?	?
43 *Burgener*	N	N	Y	Y	Y	Y	N	Y
COLORADO								
1 Schroeder	Y	Y	N	N	Y	N	Y	Y
2 Wirth	Y	Y	N	Y	N	N	Y	Y
3 Kogovsek	Y	Y	Y	Y	Y	N	Y	Y
4 *Brown*	Y	Y	N	Y	Y	Y	N	Y

	219	220	221	222	223	224	225	226
5 *Kramer*	N	N	Y	Y	Y	N	Y	Y
CONNECTICUT								
1 Kennelly	Y	Y	Y	N	Y	N	Y	Y
2 Gejdenson	Y	Y	Y	N	Y	N	Y	Y
3 *DeNardis*	Y	Y	Y	?	?	?	?	?
4 *McKinney*	Y	Y	N	?	?	Y	N	Y
5 Ratchford	Y	Y	Y	Y	N	Y	Y	Y
6 Moffett	?	?	X	?	?	?	?	?
DELAWARE								
AL *Evans*	Y	Y	Y	Y	Y	Y	Y	Y
FLORIDA								
1 Hutto	N	N	Y	Y	Y	N	Y	Y
2 Fuqua	?	?	#	Y	Y	N	Y	Y
3 Bennett	N	N	Y	Y	Y	N	Y	Y
4 Chappell	N	N	Y	Y	Y	N	Y	Y
5 *McCollum*	Y	Y	Y	Y	Y	Y	N	Y
6 *Young*	N	N	Y	Y	Y	Y	N	Y
7 Gibbons	?	?	?	Y	Y	N	Y	Y
8 Ireland	Y	Y	?	Y	Y	Y	Y	Y
9 Nelson	N	N	Y	Y	N	Y	Y	Y
10 *Bafalis*	?	?	?	?	?	?	?	?
11 Mica	Y	Y	Y	Y	Y	N	Y	Y
12 *Shaw*	Y	Y	Y	Y	Y	N	Y	Y
13 Lehman	Y	Y	N	Y	N	Y	Y	Y
14 Pepper	?	?	#	Y	Y	N	Y	Y
15 Fascell	Y	Y	Y	Y	Y	N	Y	Y
GEORGIA								
1 Ginn	?	?	?	?	?	?	?	?
2 Hatcher	?	?	?	?	?	?	?	?
3 Brinkley	N	N	Y	Y	Y	N	Y	Y
4 Levitas	Y	Y	Y	Y	Y	N	Y	Y
5 Fowler	Y	Y	Y	?	?	?	?	?
6 *Gingrich*	N	N	Y	Y	Y	N	Y	Y
7 McDonald	N	N	Y	Y	Y	Y	N	Y
8 Evans	Y	Y	Y	Y	Y	N	Y	Y
9 Jenkins	N	N	Y	Y	Y	N	Y	Y
10 Barnard	N	N	Y	Y	Y	N	Y	Y
HAWAII								
1 Heftel	Y	?	Y	Y	Y	N	Y	Y
2 Akaka	N	N	Y	Y	Y	N	Y	Y
IDAHO								
1 *Craig*	Y	Y	Y	Y	Y	Y	N	Y
2 *Hansen*	N	N	Y	?	?	#	X	Y
ILLINOIS								
1 Washington	Y	Y	N	?	?	?	?	?
2 Savage	Y	Y	N	?	?	?	?	?
3 Russo	Y	Y	N	Y	N	Y	Y	Y
4 *Derwinski*	N	N	Y	Y	Y	Y	N	Y
5 Fary	N	N	Y	N	Y	N	Y	Y
6 *Hyde*	N	N	Y	Y	Y	Y	N	Y
7 Collins	Y	Y	N	Y	N	N	Y	Y
8 Rostenkowski	Y	Y	N	Y	N	Y	Y	Y
9 Yates	?	?	?	?	?	N	Y	Y
10 *Porter*	Y	Y	Y	Y	Y	Y	N	Y
11 Annunzio	N	N	Y	Y	N	Y	Y	Y
12 *Crane, P.*	N	N	Y	Y	Y	Y	N	Y
13 *McClory*	N	N	Y	Y	Y	N	Y	Y
14 *Erlenborn*	Y	Y	Y	Y	Y	Y	N	Y
15 *Corcoran*	N	N	Y	Y	Y	N	Y	Y
16 *Martin*	Y	Y	Y	Y	Y	N	Y	Y
17 *O'Brien*	N	N	Y	?	?	X	#	Y
18 *Michel*	N	N	Y	Y	Y	N	Y	Y
19 *Railsback*	Y	Y	Y	Y	Y	Y	Y	?
20 *Findley*	Y	Y	Y	Y	Y	Y	Y	Y
21 *Madigan*	N	N	Y	Y	Y	N	Y	Y
22 *Crane, D.*	N	N	Y	Y	Y	Y	N	Y
23 Price	N	N	Y	Y	Y	N	Y	Y
24 Simon	Y	Y	Y	?	?	?	?	?
INDIANA								
1 Benjamin	Y	Y	Y	Y	Y	N	Y	Y
2 Fithian	Y	Y	Y	Y	N	Y	Y	Y
3 *Hiler*	Y	Y	Y	Y	Y	Y	N	Y
4 *Coats*	Y	Y	Y	Y	Y	Y	N	Y
5 *Hillis*	N	N	Y	Y	Y	N	Y	Y
6 Evans	?	?	?	Y	Y	N	Y	Y
7 *Myers*	Y	Y	Y	Y	Y	Y	N	Y
8 *Deckard*	Y	Y	Y	Y	Y	Y	N	Y
9 Hamilton	Y	Y	Y	Y	Y	N	Y	Y
10 Sharp	Y	Y	Y	Y	N	Y	Y	Y
11 Jacobs	Y	Y	?	N	Y	N	Y	Y
IOWA								
1 *Leach*	Y	Y	N	Y	Y	Y	Y	N
2 *Tauke*	Y	Y	N	Y	Y	Y	Y	N
3 *Evans*	Y	Y	N	N	Y	Y	Y	Y
4 *Smith*	Y	Y	N	Y	Y	N	Y	Y
5 *Harkin*	Y	Y	N	Y	N	Y	Y	Y
6 Bedell	Y	Y	N	Y	Y	N	Y	N

ND - Northern Democrats   SD - Southern Democrats

Corresponding to Congressional Record Votes 230, 231, 232, 233, 234, 235, 236, 237

	219	220	221	222	223	224	225	226
KANSAS								
1 ***Roberts***	Y	Y	Y	Y	Y	Y	N	Y
2 ***Jeffries***	N	N	Y	Y	Y	Y	N	Y
3 ***Winn***	?	?	?	Y	Y	Y	Y	Y
4 Glickman	Y	Y	Y	Y	Y	N	Y	Y
5 ***Whittaker***	Y	Y	Y	?	?	Y	N	Y
KENTUCKY								
1 Hubbard	Y	Y	Y	Y	Y	N	Y	Y
2 Natcher	N	N	Y	Y	Y	N	Y	Y
3 Mazzoli	Y	Y	Y	Y	Y	N	N	Y
4 ***Snyder***	Y	Y	Y	Y	Y	N	Y	Y
5 ***Rogers***	N	N	Y	Y	Y	N	Y	Y
6 ***Hopkins***	Y	Y	Y	Y	Y	N	Y	Y
7 Perkins	Y	Y	Y	Y	Y	N	Y	Y
LOUISIANA								
1 ***Livingston***	N	N	Y	Y	Y	Y	N	Y
2 Boggs	N	N	Y	Y	Y	N	Y	Y
3 Tauzin	N	N	Y	Y	Y	Y	N	Y
4 Roemer	N	N	Y	N	Y	Y	N	Y
5 Huckaby	Y	Y	Y	Y	Y	N	Y	Y
6 ***Moore***	Y	Y	Y	Y	Y	Y	Y	Y
7 Breaux	N	N	Y	Y	Y	Y	N	Y
8 Long	Y	Y	Y	Y	Y	N	Y	Y
MAINE								
1 ***Emery***	N	N	Y	Y	Y	Y	Y	Y
2 ***Snowe***	Y	Y	Y	Y	Y	Y	Y	Y
MARYLAND								
1 Dyson	N	N	Y	Y	Y	N	Y	Y
2 Long	N	N	Y	Y	Y	N	Y	Y
3 Mikulski	Y	Y	N	Y	Y	N	Y	Y
4 ***Holt***	?	?	?	N	Y	N	Y	Y
5 Hoyer	Y	Y	Y	?	Y	N	Y	Y
6 Byron	N	N	Y	?	?	N	Y	Y
7 Mitchell	Y	Y	N	N	Y	N	Y	N
8 Barnes	Y	Y	Y	N	Y	N	Y	Y
MASSACHUSETTS								
1 ***Conte***	N	Y	Y	Y	Y	Y	Y	Y
2 Boland	Y	Y	Y	Y	Y	N	Y	Y
3 Early	N	N	N	?	Y	N	Y	Y
4 Frank	Y	Y	N	Y	Y	N	Y	Y
5 Shannon	N	N	N	Y	Y	N	Y	Y
6 Mavroules	N	N	Y	Y	Y	N	Y	Y
7 Markey	Y	Y	N	Y	Y	N	Y	Y
8 O'Neill								
9 Moakley	Y	Y	N	Y	Y	N	Y	Y
10 ***Heckler***	Y	Y	Y	Y	Y	N	Y	Y
11 Donnelly	Y	Y	N	Y	Y	N	Y	Y
12 Studds	Y	Y	N	Y	Y	N	Y	Y
MICHIGAN								
1 Conyers	Y	Y	N	?	?	?	?	?
2 ***Pursell***	Y	Y	N	?	?	Y	Y	Y
3 Wolpe	Y	Y	N	Y	Y	N	Y	N
4 ***Siljander***	?	?	?	?	?	?	?	?
5 ***Sawyer***	N	Y	Y	Y	Y	Y	Y	Y
6 ***Dunn***	Y	Y	Y	Y	Y	Y	Y	Y
7 Kildee	Y	Y	Y	Y	Y	N	Y	Y
8 Traxler	Y	Y	Y	Y	Y	N	Y	Y
9 ***Vander Jagt***	N	Y	Y	Y	Y	Y	N	Y
10 Albosta	Y	Y	Y	Y	Y	N	Y	Y
11 ***Davis***	Y	Y	Y	Y	Y	N	Y	Y
12 Bonior	?	?	-	Y	Y	N	Y	Y
13 Crockett	Y	Y	N	?	?	?	?	?
14 Hertel	Y	Y	Y	?	?	?	?	?
15 Ford	Y	Y	#	Y	Y	N	Y	?
16 Dingell	Y	Y	Y	Y	Y	N	Y	Y
17 Brodhead	Y	Y	Y	Y	Y	N	Y	Y
18 Blanchard	?	#	?	?	?	?	?	?
19 ***Broomfield***	N	Y	Y	Y	Y	Y	Y	Y
MINNESOTA								
1 ***Erdahl***	Y	Y	N	Y	Y	Y	N	Y
2 ***Hagedorn***	Y	Y	Y	Y	Y	Y	N	Y
3 ***Frenzel***	Y	Y	N	Y	Y	Y	N	Y
4 Vento	Y	Y	N	Y	Y	N	Y	Y
5 Sabo	Y	Y	N	N	Y	N	Y	Y
6 ***Weber***	Y	Y	N	Y	Y	Y	N	Y
7 ***Stangeland***	Y	Y	Y	?	Y	Y	N	Y
8 Oberstar	Y	Y	N	N	?	N	Y	Y
MISSISSIPPI								
1 Whitten	N	N	Y	Y	Y	N	Y	Y
2 Bowen	?	N	Y	Y	Y	N	Y	Y
3 Montgomery	N	N	Y	Y	Y	Y	N	Y
4 Dowdy	?	?	?	Y	Y	N	Y	Y
5 ***Lott***	?	?	?	Y	Y	Y	N	Y
MISSOURI								
1 Clay	?	?	X	?	?	?	?	?
2 Young	N	N	?	?	?	?	?	?
3 Gephardt	Y	Y	Y	?	?	N	N	Y
4 Skelton	N	N	Y	?	?	N	Y	N
5 Bolling	?	?	?	?	?	?	?	?
6 ***Coleman***	Y	Y	Y	Y	Y	Y	N	Y
7 ***Taylor***	N	N	Y	Y	Y	Y	N	Y
8 ***Bailey***	N	N	Y	Y	Y	Y	N	Y
9 Volkmer	Y	Y	?	Y	Y	N	Y	Y
10 ***Emerson***	Y	Y	Y	?	Y	Y	N	Y
MONTANA								
1 Williams	Y	Y	N	?	Y	N	Y	Y
2 ***Marlenee***	Y	Y	Y	Y	Y	Y	Y	Y
NEBRASKA								
1 ***Bereuter***	Y	Y	Y	Y	Y	Y	N	Y
2 ***Daub***	Y	Y	Y	Y	Y	N	Y	N
3 ***Smith***	Y	Y	Y	Y	Y	Y	N	Y
NEVADA								
AL Santini	Y	?	Y	?	?	N	Y	Y
NEW HAMPSHIRE								
1 D'Amours	Y	?	?	Y	Y	N	Y	Y
2 ***Gregg***	Y	Y	Y	Y	Y	Y	N	Y
NEW JERSEY								
1 Florio	Y	Y	N	Y	Y	N	Y	Y
2 Hughes	Y	Y	Y	Y	Y	N	Y	Y
3 Howard	N	N	Y	Y	Y	N	Y	Y
4 ***Smith***	Y	Y	Y	Y	Y	N	Y	Y
5 ***Fenwick***	Y	Y	Y	Y	Y	Y	Y	Y
6 ***Forsythe***	Y	Y	N	?	Y	N	Y	?
7 ***Roukema***	Y	Y	Y	Y	Y	Y	Y	Y
8 Roe	Y	Y	Y	Y	Y	N	Y	Y
9 ***Hollenbeck***	Y	Y	N	Y	Y	N	Y	Y
10 Rodino	Y	Y	N	Y	Y	N	Y	Y
11 Minish	Y	Y	Y	Y	Y	N	Y	Y
12 ***Rinaldo***	Y	Y	Y	Y	Y	N	Y	Y
13 ***Courter***	Y	Y	Y	Y	Y	N	Y	Y
14 Guarini	Y	Y	Y	Y	Y	N	Y	Y
15 Dwyer	Y	Y	Y	Y	Y	N	Y	Y
NEW MEXICO								
1 ***Lujan***	Y	Y	Y	Y	Y	Y	Y	Y
2 ***Skeen***	?	?	?	Y	Y	Y	N	Y
NEW YORK								
1 ***Carney***	N	N	Y	Y	Y	N	Y	Y
2 Downey	Y	Y	Y	Y	Y	N	Y	Y
3 ***Carman***	?	N	Y	Y	Y	Y	N	Y
4 ***Lent***	N	N	Y	Y	Y	N	Y	Y
5 ***McGrath***	N	N	Y	Y	Y	N	Y	Y
6 ***LeBoutillier***	N	N	Y	N	Y	N	Y	?
7 Addabbo	Y	Y	Y	?	?	N	Y	Y
8 Rosenthal	Y	Y	N	?	?	?	?	?
9 Ferraro	Y	Y	Y	Y	Y	N	Y	Y
10 Biaggi	Y	Y	Y	Y	Y	N	Y	Y
11 Scheuer	Y	Y	Y	Y	Y	N	Y	Y
12 Chisholm	?	?	X	?	?	N	Y	Y
13 Solarz	Y	Y	Y	Y	Y	N	Y	Y
14 Richmond	?	?	X	?	?	N	Y	Y
15 Zeferetti	N	N	Y	Y	Y	N	Y	Y
16 Schumer	Y	Y	Y	Y	Y	N	Y	Y
17 ***Molinari***	N	N	Y	Y	Y	N	Y	Y
18 ***Green***	Y	Y	Y	Y	Y	N	Y	Y
19 Rangel	Y	Y	N	Y	Y	N	Y	Y
20 Weiss	Y	Y	N	Y	Y	N	Y	N
21 Garcia	Y	Y	N	Y	Y	N	Y	Y
22 Bingham	Y	Y	N	Y	Y	N	Y	?
23 Peyser	Y	Y	Y	Y	Y	N	Y	Y
24 Ottinger	Y	Y	N	P	Y	N	Y	N
25 ***Fish***	Y	Y	Y	Y	Y	Y	N	Y
26 ***Gilman***	Y	Y	Y	Y	Y	N	Y	Y
27 McHugh	N	N	Y	Y	Y	N	Y	Y
28 Stratton	N	N	Y	Y	Y	Y	N	Y
29 ***Solomon***	N	N	Y	Y	Y	Y	N	Y
30 ***Martin***	?	?	?	?	?	Y	N	Y
31 ***Mitchell***	?	?	?	Y	Y	N	Y	Y
32 ***Wortley***	Y	Y	Y	Y	Y	Y	N	Y
33 ***Lee***	Y	Y	Y	Y	Y	Y	N	Y
34 ***Horton***	Y	Y	Y	?	Y	N	Y	Y
35 ***Conable***	Y	Y	Y	Y	Y	Y	N	Y
36 LaFalce	Y	Y	N	Y	Y	N	Y	Y
37 Nowak	Y	Y	Y	Y	Y	N	Y	Y
38 ***Kemp***	N	N	Y	Y	?	Y	N	Y
39 Lundine	?	?	Y	Y	Y	N	N	Y
NORTH CAROLINA								
1 Jones	N	Y	Y	Y	Y	N	Y	Y
2 Fountain	Y	Y	Y	Y	Y	Y	N	Y
3 Whitley	N	N	Y	Y	Y	N	Y	Y
4 Andrews	Y	Y	Y	?	Y	N	Y	Y
5 Neal	Y	Y	Y	Y	Y	N	Y	Y
6 ***Johnston***	Y	N	?	N	Y	Y	N	N
7 Rose	Y	Y	Y	Y	Y	N	Y	Y
8 Hefner	Y	Y	Y	Y	Y	N	Y	Y
9 ***Martin***	Y	Y	Y	Y	?	Y	N	Y
10 ***Broyhill***	Y	Y	Y	Y	Y	Y	N	Y
11 ***Hendon***	N	N	Y	Y	Y	N	Y	Y
NORTH DAKOTA								
AL Dorgan	Y	Y	Y	Y	Y	N	Y	Y
OHIO								
1 ***Gradison***	N	N	Y	Y	Y	Y	N	Y
2 Luken	Y	Y	Y	N	Y	N	Y	N
3 Hall	Y	Y	Y	?	?	?	?	?
4 ***Oxley***	Y	N	Y	?	Y	Y	N	Y
5 ***Latta***	N	N	Y	Y	Y	Y	N	Y
6 ***McEwen***	Y	Y	Y	Y	Y	Y	N	Y
7 ***Brown***	?	?	?	?	?	?	?	?
8 ***Kindness***	Y	N	Y	Y	Y	Y	N	Y
9 ***Weber***	N	N	Y	Y	Y	Y	N	Y
10 ***Miller***	Y	Y	Y	N	Y	Y	N	Y
11 ***Stanton***	N	?	Y	Y	Y	Y	N	Y
12 Shamansky	Y	Y	Y	Y	Y	N	Y	N
13 Pease	Y	Y	Y	Y	Y	N	Y	Y
14 Seiberling	Y	Y	N	Y	Y	N	Y	Y
15 ***Wylie***	Y	Y	Y	Y	Y	Y	N	Y
16 ***Regula***	Y	Y	Y	Y	Y	Y	N	Y
17 ***Ashbrook***	N	N	Y	Y	Y	Y	N	Y
18 Applegate	Y	Y	Y	Y	Y	N	Y	?
19 ***Williams***	Y	Y	?	?	?	X	#	?
20 Oakar	?	?	?	Y	Y	N	Y	Y
21 Stokes	Y	Y	N	?	?	N	Y	Y
22 Eckart	Y	Y	Y	Y	Y	N	Y	Y
23 Mottl	Y	Y	?	Y	Y	N	Y	Y
OKLAHOMA								
1 Jones	Y	N	Y	Y	Y	N	Y	Y
2 Synar	Y	Y	Y	Y	Y	N	Y	Y
3 Watkins	Y	N	Y	?	?	N	Y	Y
4 McCurdy	N	N	Y	Y	Y	N	Y	Y
5 ***Edwards***	N	N	Y	Y	Y	Y	N	Y
6 English	N	N	Y	?	?	N	Y	Y
OREGON								
1 AuCoin	Y	Y	N	?	?	?	?	?
2 ***Smith***	?	?	?	Y	Y	Y	N	Y
3 Wyden	Y	Y	N	Y	Y	N	Y	Y
4 Weaver	Y	Y	N	Y	Y	N	Y	Y
PENNSYLVANIA								
1 Foglietta	Y	Y	Y	Y	Y	N	Y	Y
2 Gray	?	?	?	?	Y	N	Y	Y
3 Smith	?	X	#	Y	Y	N	Y	Y
4 ***Dougherty***	N	N	Y	Y	Y	N	Y	Y
5 ***Schulze***	Y	Y	Y	Y	Y	Y	Y	Y
6 Yatron	Y	Y	Y	Y	Y	N	Y	Y
7 Edgar	Y	Y	N	N	Y	N	Y	Y
8 ***Coyne, J.***	Y	Y	N	Y	Y	N	Y	Y
9 ***Shuster***	Y	Y	Y	Y	Y	Y	N	Y
10 ***McDade***	Y	Y	Y	Y	Y	N	Y	Y
11 ***Nelligan***	N	N	Y	Y	Y	N	Y	Y
12 Murtha	N	N	Y	Y	Y	N	Y	Y
13 ***Coughlin***	Y	Y	Y	N	Y	Y	N	?
14 Coyne, W.	Y	Y	Y	Y	Y	N	Y	Y
15 ***Ritter***	Y	Y	Y	Y	Y	Y	N	Y
16 ***Walker***	Y	Y	Y	N	Y	Y	N	Y
17 Ertel	?	?	?	?	?	?	?	?
18 Walgren	Y	Y	N	Y	Y	N	Y	Y
19 ***Goodling***	Y	Y	Y	N	Y	Y	N	?
20 Gaydos	N	N	Y	Y	Y	N	Y	Y
21 Bailey	N	N	Y	Y	Y	N	Y	Y
22 Murphy	Y	Y	Y	N	Y	N	Y	Y
23 ***Clinger***	Y	Y	Y	Y	Y	Y	Y	Y
24 ***Marks***	?	?	N	?	?	?	?	?
25 ***Atkinson***	Y	Y	Y	N	Y	Y	Y	Y
RHODE ISLAND								
1 St Germain	Y	Y	Y	Y	Y	N	Y	Y
2 ***Schneider***	Y	Y	Y	Y	Y	N	Y	Y
SOUTH CAROLINA								
1 ***Hartnett***	N	?	?	Y	Y	Y	N	Y
2 ***Spence***	N	N	Y	Y	Y	Y	Y	Y
3 Derrick	Y	Y	Y	?	?	N	Y	Y
4 ***Campbell***	N	N	+	?	?	Y	N	Y
5 Holland	N	N	?	Y	Y	Y	N	Y
6 ***Napier***	N	N	Y	?	?	N	Y	Y
SOUTH DAKOTA								
1 Daschle	Y	Y	Y	?	?	-	+	?
2 ***Roberts***	Y	Y	Y	Y	Y	Y	N	Y
TENNESSEE								
1 ***Quillen***	N	N	Y	Y	Y	Y	Y	Y
2 ***Duncan***	N	N	Y	Y	Y	Y	Y	Y
3 Bouquard	N	N	Y	Y	Y	N	Y	Y
4 Gore	Y	Y	Y	Y	Y	N	Y	Y
5 Boner	?	?	?	?	Y	N	Y	Y
6 ***Beard***	?	?	?	?	?	?	?	?
7 Jones	?	?	#	?	?	?	?	?
8 Ford	?	?	-	?	?	?	?	?
TEXAS								
1 Hall, S.	N	N	Y	Y	Y	Y	Y	Y
2 Wilson	N	N	Y	Y	Y	N	Y	Y
3 ***Collins***	?	?	?	Y	Y	Y	N	Y
4 Hall, R.	N	N	Y	Y	Y	N	Y	Y
5 Mattox	?	?	#	Y	Y	N	Y	Y
6 Gramm	N	N	Y	Y	Y	Y	N	Y
7 ***Archer***	N	N	Y	Y	Y	Y	N	Y
8 ***Fields***	N	N	Y	N	Y	Y	N	Y
9 Brooks	N	N	Y	Y	Y	N	Y	Y
10 Pickle	Y	Y	Y	Y	Y	N	Y	Y
11 Leath	N	N	Y	Y	Y	N	Y	Y
12 Wright	?	?	?	Y	Y	N	Y	Y
13 Hightower	N	N	Y	Y	Y	N	Y	N
14 Patman	N	N	Y	Y	Y	N	Y	Y
15 de la Garza	N	Y	Y	Y	Y	N	Y	Y
16 White	N	N	Y	Y	Y	N	Y	Y
17 Stenholm	N	N	Y	?	?	?	?	?
18 Leland	Y	Y	N	?	?	?	?	?
19 Hance	Y	Y	Y	Y	Y	Y	Y	Y
20 Gonzalez	N	N	Y	Y	Y	N	Y	N
21 ***Loeffler***	N	N	Y	Y	Y	Y	N	Y
22 ***Paul***	Y	Y	N	Y	Y	Y	N	Y
23 Kazen	N	N	Y	Y	Y	N	Y	Y
24 Frost	Y	Y	Y	Y	Y	N	Y	?
UTAH								
1 ***Hansen***	?	?	?	Y	Y	Y	N	Y
2 ***Marriott***	?	?	?	Y	Y	Y	N	Y
VERMONT								
AL ***Jeffords***	Y	Y	Y	Y	Y	Y	Y	Y
VIRGINIA								
1 ***Trible***	?	?	?	Y	Y	N	Y	Y
2 ***Whitehurst***	N	N	Y	Y	Y	N	Y	Y
3 ***Bliley***	N	N	Y	Y	Y	Y	N	Y
4 ***Daniel, R.***	N	N	Y	Y	Y	N	Y	Y
5 Daniel, D.	N	N	Y	Y	Y	Y	N	?
6 ***Butler***	?	?	?	Y	Y	Y	N	Y
7 ***Robinson***	N	N	Y	Y	Y	Y	N	Y
8 ***Parris***	N	N	Y	Y	Y	N	Y	Y
9 ***Wampler***	Y	Y	Y	Y	Y	Y	Y	Y
10 ***Wolf***	Y	Y	Y	Y	Y	N	Y	Y
WASHINGTON								
1 ***Pritchard***	Y	Y	N	?	?	?	?	?
2 Swift	Y	Y	Y	Y	Y	N	Y	Y
3 Bonker	Y	Y	N	Y	Y	N	Y	Y
4 ***Morrison***	Y	Y	Y	Y	Y	Y	Y	Y
5 Foley	Y	Y	Y	Y	Y	N	Y	Y
6 Dicks	Y	Y	Y	Y	Y	N	Y	Y
7 Lowry	Y	Y	N	N	Y	N	Y	Y
WEST VIRGINIA								
1 Mollohan	N	N	Y	Y	?	?	?	?
2 ***Benedict***	N	N	Y	Y	Y	Y	Y	Y
3 ***Staton***	N	N	Y	Y	Y	Y	N	Y
4 Rahall	?	?	X	Y	Y	N	Y	Y
WISCONSIN								
1 Aspin	Y	Y	Y	Y	Y	N	Y	Y
2 Kastenmeier	Y	Y	N	Y	Y	N	Y	N
3 ***Gunderson***	Y	Y	N	Y	Y	Y	N	Y
4 Zablocki	Y	Y	Y	Y	Y	N	Y	Y
5 Reuss	?	?	X	Y	Y	N	Y	Y
6 ***Petri***	Y	Y	Y	Y	Y	Y	N	Y
7 Obey	N	N	N	?	Y	N	Y	Y
8 ***Roth***	?	?	?	?	?	Y	N	Y
9 ***Sensenbrenner***	?	?	?	Y	Y	Y	N	Y
WYOMING								
AL ***Cheney***	N	N	Y	Y	Y	Y	N	Y

Southern states - Ala., Ark., Fla., Ga., Ky., La., Miss., N.C., Okla., S.C., Tenn., Texas, Va.

227. HR 5427. Radio Marti. Smith, D-Iowa, amendment to the Energy and Commerce Committee amendment, to direct the Federal Communications Commission to assign a frequency for the radio station that would broadcast to Cuba, if the station was to operate on the AM band. The Energy and Commerce Committee amendment had given that responsibility to the assistant secretary of commerce for communications and information. Rejected 136-244: R 19-156; D 117-88 (ND 93-42, SD 24-46), Aug. 3, 1982.

228. HR 756. Federal Police and Firefighters Death Benefits. Miller, D-Calif., motion to suspend the rules and pass the bill to provide a $50,000 death benefit to dependents of federal law enforcement officers and firefighters killed in the line of duty. Motion agreed to 327-82: R 107-76; D 220-6 (ND 148-3, SD 72-3), Aug. 4, 1982. A two-thirds majority of those present and voting (273 in this case) is required for passage under suspension of the rules. A "nay" was a vote supporting the president's position.

229. HR 6011. Alabama Wilderness. Seiberling, D-Ohio, motion to suspend the rules and pass the bill to add approximately 28,500 acres to the Sipsey Wilderness in the Bankhead National Forest and designate a new 6,780-acre Cheaha Wilderness in the Talladega National Forest. Motion agreed to 349-59: R 129-54; D 220-5 (ND 148-2, SD 72-3), Aug. 4, 1982. A two-thirds majority of those present and voting (272 in this case) is required for passage under suspension of the rules.

230. HR 5320. Job Training. Erlenborn, R-Ill., amendment to increase the authority of state governments and locally based private industry councils in planning job training programs. Rejected 185-219: R 157-18; D 28-201 (ND 2-152, SD 26-49), Aug. 4, 1982.

231. HR 5320. Job Training. Roberts, R-S.D., amendment to prohibit use of funds to pay labor unions for training programs for migrant farm workers. Rejected 87-308: R 71-99; D 16-209 (ND 1-150, SD 15-59), Aug. 4, 1982.

232. HR 5320. Job Training. Johnston, R-N.C., motion to recommit the bill to the Education and Labor Committee, with instructions to report it back with the Erlenborn, R-Ill., amendment *(see vote 230, above)* relating to state and private industry council authority. Rejected 189-218: R 167-17; D 22-201 (ND 1-150, SD 21-51), Aug. 4, 1982.

233. HR 5320. Job Training. Passage of the bill to provide a permanent, open-ended authorization for a new program of assistance to local job skill training programs, and to authorize $650 million for the Job Corps in fiscal 1983, with open-ended funding in subsequent years. Passed 356-52: R 143-41; D 213-11 (ND 151-1, SD 62-10), Aug. 4, 1982.

KEY

Y Voted for (yea).
\# Paired for.
+ Announced for.
N Voted against (nay).
X Paired against.
- Announced against.
P Voted "present".
C Voted "present" to avoid possible conflict of interest.
? Did not vote or otherwise make a position known.

Democrats   *Republicans*

Member	227	228	229	230	231	232	233
ALABAMA							
1 *Edwards*	N	N	Y	?	?	Y	Y
2 *Dickinson*	N	Y	Y	Y	N	Y	Y
3 Nichols	Y	Y	Y	N	Y	N	Y
4 Bevill	Y	Y	N	N	N	N	Y
5 Flippo	Y	Y	Y	N	N	N	Y
6 *Smith*	N	N	Y	N	Y	N	Y
7 Shelby	N	Y	Y	Y	Y	Y	Y
ALASKA							
AL *Young*	?	Y	N	Y	N	Y	Y
ARIZONA							
1 *Rhodes*	N	?	?	?	?	#	?
2 Udall	Y	Y	N	N	N	N	Y
3 *Stump*	N	N	N	Y	Y	Y	N
4 *Rudd*	N	N	N	Y	N	Y	N
ARKANSAS							
1 Alexander							
2 *Bethune*	N	Y	Y	Y	N	Y	Y
3 *Hammerschmidt*	N	Y	Y	Y	N	Y	Y
4 Anthony	N	Y	N	N	N	N	Y
CALIFORNIA							
1 *Chappie*	N	Y	Y	Y	N	Y	Y
2 *Clausen*	N	Y	Y	Y	N	Y	Y
3 Matsui	Y	Y	Y	N	N	N	Y
4 Fazio	Y	Y	Y	N	N	N	Y
5 Burton, J.	?	Y	Y	N	N	N	Y
6 Burton, P.	Y	Y	Y	N	N	N	Y
7 Miller	Y	Y	Y	N	N	N	Y
8 Dellums	Y	Y	Y	N	N	N	Y
9 Stark	Y	Y	Y	X	N	N	Y
10 Edwards	Y	Y	Y	N	N	N	Y
11 Lantos	Y	Y	Y	N	N	N	Y
12 *McCloskey*	N	Y	Y	?	?	#	?
13 Mineta	N	Y	Y	N	N	N	Y
14 *Shumway*	N	N	Y	N	Y	Y	Y
15 Coelho	N	Y	Y	N	N	N	Y
16 Panetta	Y	Y	Y	N	N	N	Y
17 *Pashayan*	N	Y	Y	N	N	N	Y
18 *Thomas*	N	Y	N	Y	Y	Y	Y
19 *Lagomarsino*	N	Y	Y	Y	N	Y	Y
20 *Goldwater*	N	Y	Y	Y	?	Y	N
21 *Fiedler*	Y	Y	Y	N	N	N	Y
22 *Moorhead*	N	Y	Y	Y	Y	Y	Y
23 Beilenson	Y	N	Y	N	N	N	Y
24 Waxman	Y	Y	Y	N	N	N	Y
25 Roybal	Y	Y	Y	N	N	N	Y
26 *Rousselot*	N	Y	N	Y	Y	Y	Y
27 *Dornan*	?	?	?	?	?	#	?
28 Dixon	Y	Y	Y	N	N	N	Y
29 Hawkins	Y	Y	Y	N	N	N	Y
30 Martinez	Y	Y	Y	N	N	N	Y
31 Dymally	Y	Y	Y	N	N	N	Y
32 Anderson	N	Y	N	N	N	N	Y
33 Grisham	N	Y	N	?	Y	Y	N
34 *Lungren*	N	Y	N	Y	N	Y	Y
35 *Dreier*	N	N	N	Y	Y	Y	N
36 Brown	Y	Y	Y	N	N	N	Y
37 *Lewis*	N	Y	Y	Y	N	Y	Y
38 Patterson	N	Y	Y	N	Y	N	Y
39 *Dannemeyer*	N	N	N	Y	Y	Y	N
40 *Badham*	N	N	N	Y	Y	Y	N
41 *Lowery*	N	Y	?	Y	Y	Y	Y
42 *Hunter*	?	Y	Y	Y	Y	Y	N
43 *Burgener*	N	N	Y	Y	?	Y	N
COLORADO							
1 Schroeder	Y	Y	Y	N	N	?	?
2 Wirth	Y	Y	Y	N	N	N	Y
3 Kogovsek	Y	Y	Y	N	N	N	Y
4 *Brown*	N	N	Y	Y	Y	Y	N
5 *Kramer*	N	N	N	N	N	N	Y
CONNECTICUT							
1 Kennelly	N	Y	Y	N	N	N	Y
2 Gejdenson	?	Y	Y	N	N	N	Y
3 *DeNardis*	Y	Y	Y	Y	N	N	Y
4 *McKinney*	Y	Y	Y	Y	N	N	Y
5 Ratchford	Y	Y	Y	N	N	N	Y
6 Moffett	?	?	?	N	N	N	Y
DELAWARE							
AL *Evans*	N	Y	Y	Y	?	Y	Y
FLORIDA							
1 Hutto	N	Y	Y	N	N	N	Y
2 Fuqua	N	Y	Y	N	N	?	?
3 Bennett	N	Y	N	N	N	N	Y
4 Chappell	N	Y	Y	#	?	?	?
5 *McCollum*	N	Y	Y	Y	Y	Y	Y
6 *Young*	N	Y	Y	Y	Y	Y	N
7 Gibbons	N	Y	Y	N	N	N	Y
8 *Ireland*	N	?	?	Y	?	?	?
9 Nelson	N	Y	Y	N	N	N	Y
10 *Bafalis*	?	?	?	?	?	?	?
11 Mica	N	Y	Y	N	N	N	Y
12 *Shaw*	N	Y	Y	N	Y	N	Y
13 Lehman	N	Y	Y	N	N	N	Y
14 Pepper	N	Y	Y	N	N	N	Y
15 Fascell	N	Y	Y	N	N	N	Y
GEORGIA							
1 Ginn	?	?	?	?	?	?	?
2 Hatcher	?	Y	N	N	N	N	Y
3 Brinkley	Y	Y	Y	Y	N	N	Y
4 Levitas	Y	Y	Y	Y	N	N	Y
5 Fowler	?	Y	Y	N	N	N	Y
6 *Gingrich*	N	Y	Y	N	Y	N	Y
7 McDonald	N	N	N	Y	Y	Y	N
8 Evans	Y	Y	Y	N	N	N	Y
9 Jenkins	N	Y	Y	N	Y	N	Y
10 Barnard	N	Y	N	Y	N	Y	N
HAWAII							
1 Heftel	N	Y	Y	N	N	N	Y
2 Akaka	N	Y	Y	N	N	N	Y
IDAHO							
1 *Craig*	N	N	N	Y	N	Y	Y
2 *Hansen*	?	N	N	Y	Y	Y	N
ILLINOIS							
1 Washington	?	Y	Y	N	N	N	Y
2 Savage	?	Y	Y	N	N	N	Y
3 Russo	N	Y	Y	N	N	N	Y
4 *Derwinski*	N	N	N	Y	Y	Y	Y
5 Fary	N	Y	Y	N	N	N	Y
6 *Hyde*	N	Y	Y	N	Y	N	Y
7 Collins	Y	Y	Y	N	N	N	Y
8 Rostenkowski	N	Y	N	?	N	Y	?
9 Yates	?	Y	Y	X	?	?	?
10 *Porter*	N	Y	Y	N	N	N	Y
11 Annunzio	N	Y	Y	N	N	N	Y
12 *Crane, P.*	N	N	N	Y	N	Y	N
13 *McClory*	N	N	Y	Y	Y	Y	Y
14 *Erlenborn*	N	N	N	Y	Y	Y	Y
15 *Corcoran*	N	N	Y	Y	N	Y	Y
16 *Martin*	Y	Y	Y	N	N	N	Y
17 *O'Brien*	?	Y	Y	N	N	N	Y
18 *Michel*	N	?	Y	#	?	Y	Y
19 *Railsback*	Y	Y	Y	?	Y	Y	Y
20 Findley	N	Y	Y	N	N	N	Y
21 *Madigan*	?	Y	Y	?	Y	Y	Y
22 *Crane, D.*	N	N	N	Y	N	Y	N
23 Price	N	Y	Y	N	N	?	?
24 Simon	Y	Y	Y	N	N	N	Y
INDIANA							
1 Benjamin	Y	Y	Y	N	N	N	Y
2 Fithian	N	Y	Y	N	N	N	Y
3 *Hiler*	N	N	Y	N	Y	N	Y
4 *Coats*	N	N	Y	N	N	N	Y
5 *Hillis*	N	Y	Y	Y	Y	Y	Y
6 Evans	Y	Y	Y	N	N	N	Y
7 *Myers*	N	Y	Y	Y	Y	Y	Y
8 *Deckard*	N	Y	N	Y	N	Y	Y
9 Hamilton	N	Y	Y	N	N	N	Y
10 Sharp	N	Y	Y	N	N	N	Y
11 Jacobs	Y	Y	Y	N	N	N	Y
IOWA							
1 *Leach*	Y	Y	Y	Y	N	Y	Y
2 *Tauke*	N	Y	Y	N	N	N	Y
3 Evans	N	Y	N	Y	N	N	Y
4 Smith	Y	Y	Y	N	N	N	Y
5 Harkin	Y	Y	Y	?	?	?	?
6 Bedell	Y	Y	Y	N	N	N	Y

ND - Northern Democrats   SD - Southern Democrats

	227	228	229	230	231	232	233
KANSAS							
1 **Roberts**	N	N	Y	Y	Y	Y	N
2 **Jeffries**	N	N	N	Y	Y	Y	N
3 **Winn**	N	Y	?	Y	N	Y	Y
4 Glickman	Y	Y	Y	N	N	N	Y
5 **Whittaker**	N	N	Y	Y	N	Y	Y
KENTUCKY							
1 Hubbard	N	Y	Y	Y	N	Y	Y
2 Natcher	Y	Y	Y	N	N	N	Y
3 Mazzoli	Y	Y	Y	N	N	N	Y
4 **Snyder**	N	Y	Y	Y	Y	Y	N
5 **Rogers**	N	N	Y	Y	N	Y	Y
6 **Hopkins**	N	Y	N	Y	N	Y	Y
7 Perkins	Y	Y	Y	N	N	N	Y
LOUISIANA							
1 **Livingston**	N	Y	Y	Y	N	Y	Y
2 Boggs	Y	Y	Y	N	N	N	Y
3 Tauzin	N	Y	Y	Y	N	Y	Y
4 Roemer	Y	Y	Y	Y	N	Y	N
5 Huckaby	Y	Y	Y	N	N	N	Y
6 **Moore**	P	Y	Y	Y	N	Y	Y
7 Breaux	N	Y	Y	Y	N	N	Y
8 Long	N	Y	Y	N	N	N	Y
MAINE							
1 **Emery**	N	Y	Y	Y	N	Y	Y
2 **Snowe**	N	Y	Y	Y	N	Y	Y
MARYLAND							
1 Dyson	N	Y	Y	N	N	N	Y
2 Long	Y	Y	?	N	N	N	Y
3 Mikulski	N	Y	Y	N	N	N	Y
4 **Holt**	N	Y	Y	Y	Y	Y	Y
5 Hoyer	N	Y	Y	N	N	N	Y
6 Byron	?	Y	Y	N	N	N	Y
7 Mitchell	?	Y	Y	N	N	N	Y
8 Barnes	N	Y	Y	N	N	N	Y
MASSACHUSETTS							
1 **Conte**	?	Y	Y	N	N	N	Y
2 Boland	Y	Y	Y	N	N	?	Y
3 Early	?	Y	Y	N	N	N	Y
4 Frank	N	Y	Y	N	N	N	Y
5 Shannon	?	Y	?	?	?	?	?
6 Mavroules	N	Y	Y	N	N	N	Y
7 Markey	Y	Y	Y	N	N	N	Y
8 O'Neill							
9 Moakley	?	Y	Y	N	N	N	Y
10 **Heckler**	N	Y	?	N	N	N	Y
11 Donnelly	N	Y	Y	N	N	N	Y
12 Studds	Y	Y	Y	N	N	N	Y
MICHIGAN							
1 Conyers	?	?	?	X	?	?	?
2 **Pursell**	N	Y	Y	Y	N	Y	Y
3 Wolpe	Y	Y	Y	N	N	N	Y
4 **Siljander**	?	Y	N	Y	N	Y	Y
5 **Sawyer**	N	Y	Y	Y	N	Y	Y
6 **Dunn**	Y	N	Y	Y	Y	Y	Y
7 Kildee	Y	Y	Y	N	N	N	Y
8 Traxler	Y	Y	Y	N	N	N	Y
9 **Vander Jagt**	N	Y	Y	Y	?	Y	Y
10 Albosta	Y	Y	Y	N	N	N	Y
11 **Davis**	N	Y	Y	N	N	N	Y
12 Bonior	Y	Y	Y	N	N	N	Y
13 Crockett	?	Y	Y	N	N	N	Y
14 Hertel	?	Y	Y	N	N	N	Y
15 Ford	?	?	?	N	N	N	Y
16 Dingell	Y	Y	Y	N	N	N	Y
17 Brodhead	Y	Y	Y	N	N	N	Y
18 Blanchard	?	Y	Y	N	N	?	?
19 **Broomfield**	N	?	Y	Y	Y	Y	Y
MINNESOTA							
1 **Erdahl**	N	N	Y	Y	Y	Y	Y
2 **Hagedorn**	N	N	Y	Y	Y	Y	Y
3 **Frenzel**	N	N	N	Y	Y	Y	Y
4 Vento	Y	Y	Y	N	N	N	Y
5 Sabo	Y	Y	Y	N	N	N	Y
6 **Weber**	N	N	Y	Y	Y	Y	N
7 **Stangeland**	N	N	Y	Y	Y	Y	Y
8 Oberstar	Y	Y	Y	N	N	N	Y
MISSISSIPPI							
1 Whitten	?	Y	Y	N	N	N	Y
2 Bowen	N	Y	Y	N	N	N	Y
3 Montgomery	N	Y	Y	Y	Y	Y	N
4 Dowdy	N	Y	Y	N	N	N	Y
5 **Lott**	N	Y	Y	#	?	Y	N
MISSOURI							
1 Clay	?	?	?	X	?	N	Y
2 Young	?	Y	Y	N	N	N	Y
3 Gephardt	N	Y	Y	N	N	N	Y
4 Skelton	Y	Y	Y	N	N	?	?
5 Bolling	?	N	Y	N	?	N	Y
6 **Coleman**	N	N	Y	Y	Y	Y	Y
7 **Taylor**	N	Y	Y	Y	Y	Y	N
8 **Bailey**	N	N	N	Y	Y	Y	Y
9 Volkmer	Y	Y	Y	N	N	N	Y
10 **Emerson**	N	Y	Y	Y	Y	Y	Y
MONTANA							
1 Williams	Y	Y	Y	N	N	N	Y
2 **Marlenee**	N	Y	Y	Y	Y	Y	Y
NEBRASKA							
1 **Bereuter**	N	N	Y	Y	N	Y	Y
2 **Daub**	Y	N	Y	Y	N	Y	Y
3 **Smith**	Y	N	Y	Y	N	Y	Y
NEVADA							
AL Santini	N	?	?	N	N	N	Y
NEW HAMPSHIRE							
1 D'Amours	N	Y	Y	N	?	N	Y
2 **Gregg**	N	N	Y	Y	Y	Y	N
NEW JERSEY							
1 Florio	N	Y	Y	Y	N	N	Y
2 Hughes	Y	Y	Y	N	N	N	Y
3 Howard	Y	Y	Y	N	N	N	Y
4 **Smith**	N	Y	Y	Y	N	Y	Y
5 **Fenwick**	N	Y	Y	Y	N	Y	Y
6 **Forsythe**	N	Y	Y	Y	Y	Y	Y
7 **Roukema**	Y	N	Y	Y	N	Y	Y
8 Roe	N	Y	Y	N	N	N	Y
9 **Hollenbeck**	N	Y	Y	N	N	N	Y
10 Rodino	N	Y	Y	N	N	N	Y
11 Minish	Y	Y	Y	N	N	N	Y
12 **Rinaldo**	N	Y	Y	N	N	N	Y
13 **Courter**	N	N	N	Y	N	Y	Y
14 Guarini	N	Y	Y	N	N	N	Y
15 Dwyer	Y	Y	Y	N	N	N	Y
NEW MEXICO							
1 **Lujan**	N	Y	Y	Y	N	Y	Y
2 **Skeen**	N	Y	Y	Y	Y	Y	N
NEW YORK							
1 **Carney**	N	?	Y	Y	N	Y	Y
2 Downey	Y	Y	Y	N	N	N	Y
3 **Carman**	N	Y	N	Y	N	Y	Y
4 **Lent**	N	Y	N	Y	N	Y	Y
5 **McGrath**	N	Y	N	Y	N	Y	Y
6 **LeBoutillier**	N	Y	Y	Y	N	Y	Y
7 Addabbo	Y	Y	Y	N	N	N	Y
8 Rosenthal	?	?	?	?	?	X	?
9 Ferraro	Y	Y	Y	N	N	N	Y
10 Biaggi	N	Y	Y	N	N	N	Y
11 Scheuer	Y	Y	Y	N	N	N	Y
12 Chisholm	Y	Y	Y	X	N	N	Y
13 Solarz	Y	Y	Y	N	N	N	Y
14 Richmond	Y	?	?	N	?	X	?
15 Zeferetti	Y	Y	Y	N	N	N	Y
16 Schumer	Y	Y	Y	N	N	N	Y
17 **Molinari**	N	Y	Y	Y	N	Y	Y
18 **Green**	N	Y	Y	N	N	N	Y
19 Rangel	Y	Y	Y	N	N	N	Y
20 Weiss	Y	Y	Y	N	N	N	Y
21 Garcia	?	?	?	N	?	N	Y
22 Bingham	Y	Y	Y	N	N	N	Y
23 Peyser	Y	Y	Y	N	N	N	Y
24 Ottinger	?	Y	Y	N	N	N	Y
25 **Fish**	N	Y	Y	Y	N	Y	Y
26 **Gilman**	N	Y	Y	Y	N	Y	Y
27 McHugh	Y	Y	Y	N	N	N	Y
28 Stratton	N	?	Y	N	N	N	Y
29 **Solomon**	N	Y	N	Y	Y	Y	Y
30 **Martin**	N	Y	Y	Y	Y	Y	Y
31 **Mitchell**	N	Y	Y	Y	N	Y	Y
32 **Wortley**	N	N	Y	Y	N	Y	Y
33 **Lee**	N	N	N	Y	N	Y	Y
34 **Horton**	N	Y	Y	N	N	N	Y
35 **Conable**	N	N	N	#	?	Y	Y
36 LaFalce	Y	Y	Y	N	N	N	Y
37 Nowak	Y	Y	Y	N	N	N	Y
38 **Kemp**	N	Y	N	?	?	Y	Y
39 Lundine	Y	Y	Y	N	N	N	Y
NORTH CAROLINA							
1 Jones	Y	Y	Y	N	N	N	Y
2 Fountain	N	N	Y	Y	N	Y	Y
3 Whitley	N	Y	Y	N	Y	N	Y
4 Andrews	N	Y	Y	N	N	N	Y
5 Neal	N	Y	Y	N	N	N	Y
6 **Johnston**	N	N	N	Y	Y	Y	N
7 Rose	N	Y	Y	N	Y	N	Y
8 Hefner	C	Y	Y	N	N	N	Y
9 **Martin**	N	N	Y	Y	N	Y	Y
10 **Broyhill**	N	N	Y	N	Y	Y	Y
11 **Hendon**	N	Y	Y	Y	N	Y	N
NORTH DAKOTA							
AL Dorgan	N	Y	Y	N	N	N	Y
OHIO							
1 **Gradison**	N	N	Y	Y	Y	Y	Y
2 Luken	Y	Y	Y	N	N	N	Y
3 Hall	?	?	?	?	?	?	?
4 **Oxley**	N	N	N	Y	N	Y	Y
5 **Latta**	N	N	N	#	?	Y	Y
6 **McEwen**	N	N	Y	Y	Y	Y	Y
7 **Brown**	?	?	?	?	?	?	?
8 **Kindness**	N	N	N	Y	Y	Y	Y
9 **Weber**	N	N	Y	Y	N	Y	Y
10 **Miller**	Y	N	Y	Y	Y	Y	Y
11 **Stanton**	?	N	Y	Y	N	Y	Y
12 Shamansky	Y	Y	Y	N	N	N	Y
13 Pease	Y	Y	Y	N	N	N	Y
14 Seiberling	Y	Y	Y	N	N	N	Y
15 **Wylie**	N	Y	Y	Y	N	Y	Y
16 **Regula**	N	N	Y	Y	N	Y	Y
17 **Ashbrook**	N	N	N	Y	Y	Y	Y
18 Applegate	N	Y	Y	N	N	N	Y
19 **Williams**	?	Y	Y	?	?	X	?
20 Oakar	Y	Y	Y	N	N	N	Y
21 Stokes	Y	Y	Y	N	N	N	Y
22 Eckart	Y	Y	Y	N	N	N	Y
23 Mottl	Y	Y	Y	N	N	N	Y
OKLAHOMA							
1 Jones	Y	Y	Y	N	N	N	Y
2 Synar	Y	Y	Y	N	N	N	Y
3 Watkins	Y	Y	Y	N	N	N	Y
4 McCurdy	Y	Y	Y	Y	N	Y	Y
5 **Edwards**	Y	Y	N	Y	N	Y	N
6 English	Y	Y	Y	Y	N	Y	Y
OREGON							
1 AuCoin	?	?	?	N	N	N	Y
2 **Smith**	N	N	N	Y	Y	Y	N
3 Wyden	Y	Y	Y	N	N	N	Y
4 Weaver	Y	Y	Y	N	N	N	Y
PENNSYLVANIA							
1 Foglietta	N	Y	Y	N	N	N	Y
2 Gray	Y	Y	Y	N	N	N	Y
3 Smith	?	Y	Y	N	N	N	Y
4 **Dougherty**	N	Y	Y	N	N	Y	Y
5 **Schulze**	N	Y	Y	Y	N	Y	Y
6 Yatron	N	Y	Y	N	N	N	Y
7 Edgar	Y	Y	Y	N	N	N	Y
8 **Coyne, J.**	N	Y	Y	Y	N	Y	Y
9 **Shuster**	Y	Y	N	Y	Y	Y	N
10 **McDade**	N	Y	Y	N	N	N	Y
11 **Nelligan**	N	Y	Y	N	N	N	Y
12 Murtha	N	Y	Y	N	N	N	Y
13 **Coughlin**	N	Y	Y	Y	N	Y	Y
14 Coyne, W.	N	Y	Y	N	N	N	Y
15 **Ritter**	N	N	N	Y	N	Y	Y
16 **Walker**	N	N	N	Y	N	Y	Y
17 Ertel	?	?	?	N	N	N	Y
18 Walgren	Y	Y	Y	N	N	N	Y
19 **Goodling**	N	Y	N	Y	N	Y	Y
20 Gaydos	Y	Y	Y	N	N	N	Y
21 Bailey	N	Y	Y	N	N	N	Y
22 Murphy	Y	Y	Y	N	N	N	Y
23 **Clinger**	N	Y	Y	Y	N	Y	Y
24 **Marks**	?	?	?	?	?	?	?
25 **Atkinson**	N	N	N	Y	N	Y	Y
RHODE ISLAND							
1 St Germain	N	Y	Y	N	N	N	Y
2 **Schneider**	Y	Y	Y	Y	N	N	Y
SOUTH CAROLINA							
1 **Hartnett**	N	N	N	Y	Y	Y	N
2 **Spence**	N	Y	Y	Y	Y	Y	Y
3 Derrick	Y	Y	Y	N	N	N	Y
4 **Campbell**	N	Y	Y	Y	Y	Y	Y
5 Holland	N	Y	Y	N	N	Y	Y
6 **Napier**	Y	Y	Y	N	Y	Y	Y
SOUTH DAKOTA							
1 Daschle	?	Y	Y	N	N	N	Y
2 **Roberts**	N	N	N	Y	Y	Y	N
TENNESSEE							
1 **Quillen**	N	N	Y	#	?	Y	Y
2 **Duncan**	N	Y	Y	Y	N	Y	Y
3 Bouquard	Y	Y	Y	N	N	N	Y
4 Gore	N	Y	Y	N	N	N	Y
5 Boner	Y	Y	Y	N	N	N	Y
6 **Beard**	?	?	?	?	?	?	?
7 Jones	?	?	?	X	?	?	?
8 Ford	?	?	?	X	?	?	?
TEXAS							
1 Hall, S.	N	Y	Y	Y	Y	Y	N
2 Wilson	N	Y	Y	Y	N	Y	Y
3 **Collins**	Y	N	N	Y	Y	Y	N
4 Hall, R.	N	Y	Y	Y	N	Y	Y
5 Mattox	Y	Y	Y	N	N	N	Y
6 Gramm	N	Y	Y	Y	Y	Y	N
7 **Archer**	?	N	Y	Y	Y	Y	N
8 **Fields**	N	N	N	Y	Y	Y	N
9 Brooks	N	Y	Y	N	N	N	Y
10 Pickle	N	Y	Y	N	N	N	Y
11 Leath	N	Y	Y	Y	Y	Y	N
12 Wright	N	Y	Y	N	N	N	Y
13 Hightower	Y	Y	Y	N	Y	?	?
14 Patman	N	Y	Y	Y	Y	Y	Y
15 de la Garza	N	Y	Y	N	N	N	Y
16 White	N	Y	Y	Y	N	Y	Y
17 Stenholm	?	Y	Y	Y	Y	Y	N
18 Leland	?	Y	Y	N	N	N	Y
19 Hance	N	Y	Y	Y	Y	Y	N
20 Gonzalez	Y	Y	Y	N	N	N	Y
21 **Loeffler**	N	Y	N	Y	Y	Y	N
22 **Paul**	N	N	N	Y	Y	Y	N
23 Kazen	N	Y	Y	Y	N	N	Y
24 Frost	N	Y	Y	N	N	N	Y
UTAH							
1 **Hansen**	Y	N	Y	Y	Y	Y	Y
2 **Marriott**	N	Y	Y	Y	Y	Y	Y
VERMONT							
AL **Jeffords**	N	N	Y	Y	N	Y	Y
VIRGINIA							
1 **Trible**	N	Y	Y	Y	Y	Y	Y
2 **Whitehurst**	N	Y	Y	Y	Y	Y	N
3 **Bliley**	N	N	Y	Y	Y	Y	Y
4 **Daniel, R.**	N	Y	N	Y	Y	Y	N
5 Daniel, D.	N	N	N	Y	Y	Y	N
6 **Butler**	N	N	N	Y	Y	Y	N
7 **Robinson**	N	N	N	Y	Y	Y	N
8 **Parris**	N	Y	Y	Y	Y	Y	Y
9 **Wampler**	N	Y	Y	N	N	N	Y
10 **Wolf**	N	Y	Y	Y	Y	Y	Y
WASHINGTON							
1 **Pritchard**	?	Y	Y	Y	N	Y	Y
2 Swift	Y	Y	Y	N	N	N	Y
3 Bonker	Y	Y	Y	N	N	N	Y
4 **Morrison**	N	N	Y	Y	Y	Y	Y
5 Foley	Y	Y	Y	N	N	N	Y
6 Dicks	Y	Y	Y	N	N	N	Y
7 Lowry	Y	Y	Y	N	N	N	Y
WEST VIRGINIA							
1 Mollohan	?	Y	Y	N	N	N	Y
2 **Benedict**	N	N	Y	Y	Y	Y	Y
3 **Staton**	N	Y	N	Y	N	Y	Y
4 Rahall	Y	Y	Y	N	N	N	Y
WISCONSIN							
1 Aspin	Y	Y	Y	N	N	N	Y
2 Kastenmeier	Y	Y	Y	N	N	N	Y
3 **Gunderson**	N	N	Y	Y	N	Y	Y
4 Zablocki	N	Y	Y	N	N	N	Y
5 Reuss	Y	Y	Y	N	N	N	Y
6 **Petri**	N	N	Y	Y	N	Y	Y
7 Obey	Y	Y	Y	N	N	N	Y
8 **Roth**	N	Y	Y	Y	N	Y	Y
9 **Sensenbrenner**	N	N	Y	Y	Y	Y	N
WYOMING							
AL **Cheney**	N	N	N	#	?	Y	N

Southern states - Ala., Ark., Fla., Ga., Ky., La., Miss., N.C., Okla., S.C., Tenn., Texas, Va.

KEY		
Y	Voted for (yea).	
#	Paired for.	
+	Announced for.	
N	Voted against (nay).	
X	Paired against.	
-	Announced against.	
P	Voted "present".	
C	Voted "present" to avoid possible conflict of interest.	
?	Did not vote or otherwise make a position known.	

Democrats *Republicans*

	234	235
ALABAMA		
1 *Edwards*	Y	Y
2 *Dickinson*	N	Y
3 Nichols	?	Y
4 Bevill	Y	Y
5 Flippo	Y	N
6 *Smith*	Y	Y
7 Shelby	?	Y
ALASKA		
AL *Young*	?	Y
ARIZONA		
1 *Rhodes*	?	?
2 Udall	?	Y
3 Stump	Y	Y
4 *Rudd*	Y	Y
ARKANSAS		
1 Alexander	Y	Y
2 *Bethune*	Y	Y
3 *Hammerschmidt*	Y	Y
4 Anthony	Y	Y
CALIFORNIA		
1 *Chappie*	Y	Y
2 *Clausen*	Y	Y
3 Matsui	Y	N
4 Fazio	?	Y
5 Burton, J.	?	N
6 Burton, P.	Y	N
7 Miller	N	N
8 Dellums	Y	N
9 Stark	Y	N
10 Edwards	Y	N
11 Lantos	Y	Y
12 *McCloskey*	?	Y
13 Mineta	Y	Y
14 *Shumway*	Y	Y
15 Coelho	Y	Y
16 Panetta	Y	Y
17 *Pashayan*	Y	Y
18 *Thomas*	Y	Y
19 *Lagomarsino*	Y	Y
20 *Goldwater*	?	?
21 *Fiedler*	Y	Y
22 *Moorhead*	Y	Y
23 Beilenson	Y	N
24 Waxman	Y	N
25 Roybal	Y	N
26 *Rousselot*	Y	Y
27 *Dornan*	?	?
28 Dixon	Y	N
29 Hawkins	Y	N
30 Martinez	Y	Y
31 Dymally	Y	N
32 Anderson	Y	Y
33 *Grisham*	Y	Y
34 *Lungren*	Y	Y
35 *Dreier*	N	Y
36 Brown	Y	Y
37 *Lewis*	Y	Y
38 Patterson	Y	N
39 *Dannemeyer*	Y	Y
40 *Badham*	N	Y
41 *Lowery*	Y	Y
42 *Hunter*	?	Y
43 *Burgener*	Y	Y
COLORADO		
1 Schroeder	N	N
2 Wirth	Y	Y
3 Kogovsek	Y	Y
4 *Brown*	Y	Y

	234	235
5 *Kramer*	Y	Y
CONNECTICUT		
1 Kennelly	Y	Y
2 Gejdenson	N	N
3 *DeNardis*	?	Y
4 *McKinney*	?	Y
5 Ratchford	Y	Y
6 Moffett	?	N
DELAWARE		
AL *Evans*	?	?
FLORIDA		
1 Hutto	Y	Y
2 Fuqua	?	?
3 Bennett	Y	Y
4 Chappell	?	#
5 *McCollum*	Y	Y
6 *Young*	Y	Y
7 Gibbons	?	Y
8 Ireland	?	Y
9 Nelson	Y	Y
10 *Bafalis*	?	?
11 Mica	Y	Y
12 *Shaw*	Y	Y
13 Lehman	Y	N
14 Pepper	Y	Y
15 Fascell	Y	Y
GEORGIA		
1 Ginn	?	?
2 Hatcher	Y	?
3 Brinkley	Y	N
4 Levitas	Y	Y
5 Fowler	Y	Y
6 *Gingrich*	?	Y
7 McDonald	Y	Y
8 Evans	Y	N
9 Jenkins	Y	N
10 Barnard	Y	Y
HAWAII		
1 Heftel	Y	Y
2 Akaka	?	Y
IDAHO		
1 *Craig*	Y	Y
2 *Hansen*	Y	Y
ILLINOIS		
1 Washington	N	N
2 Savage	?	N
3 Russo	Y	Y
4 *Derwinski*	Y	Y
5 Fary	Y	Y
6 *Hyde*	Y	Y
7 Collins	Y	Y
8 Rostenkowski	Y	Y
9 Yates	?	Y
10 *Porter*	Y	Y
11 Annunzio	Y	Y
12 *Crane, P.*	?	Y
13 *McClory*	?	Y
14 Erlenborn	Y	Y
15 *Corcoran*	Y	Y
16 *Martin*	Y	Y
17 O'Brien	Y	Y
18 *Michel*	Y	Y
19 *Railsback*	Y	Y
20 *Findley*	Y	Y
21 *Madigan*	?	Y
22 *Crane, D.*	Y	Y
23 Price	Y	Y
24 Simon	Y	Y
INDIANA		
1 Benjamin	Y	Y
2 Fithian	Y	Y
3 *Hiler*	N	Y
4 *Coats*	Y	Y
5 *Hillis*	Y	Y
6 Evans	Y	Y
7 *Myers*	Y	Y
8 *Deckard*	?	Y
9 Hamilton	Y	Y
10 Sharp	Y	Y
11 Jacobs	N	N
IOWA		
1 *Leach*	Y	Y
2 *Tauke*	Y	Y
3 *Evans*	N	Y
4 Smith	Y	Y
5 Harkin	?	?
6 Bedell	Y	Y

234. Procedural Motion. Lent, R-N.Y., motion to approve the House *Journal* of Wednesday, Aug. 4. Motion agreed to 336-27: R 150-15; D 186-12 (ND 123-11, SD 63-1), Aug. 5, 1982.

235. HR 6812. Banking Reconciliation. Stanton, R-Ohio, substitute to provide for advance payment of Federal Housing Administration mortgage insurance premiums, and to authorize $50.165 million for expenditures of mints and assay offices in fiscal year 1983. Adopted 337-69: R 180-2; D 157-67 (ND 103-51, SD 54-16), Aug. 5, 1982.

ND - Northern Democrats   SD - Southern Democrats

	234	235
KANSAS		
1 *Roberts*	Y	Y
2 *Jeffries*	?	Y
3 *Winn*	Y	Y
4 Glickman	Y	Y
5 *Whittaker*	Y	Y
KENTUCKY		
1 Hubbard	Y	Y
2 Natcher	Y	Y
3 Mazzoli	Y	Y
4 *Snyder*	Y	Y
5 *Rogers*	Y	Y
6 *Hopkins*	Y	Y
7 Perkins	Y	Y
LOUISIANA		
1 *Livingston*	Y	Y
2 Boggs	?	Y
3 Tauzin	Y	N
4 Roemer	N	N
5 Huckaby	Y	N
6 *Moore*	Y	Y
7 Breaux	Y	Y
8 Long	Y	Y
MAINE		
1 *Emery*	Y	Y
2 *Snowe*	Y	Y
MARYLAND		
1 Dyson	Y	Y
2 Long	?	Y
3 Mikulski	Y	Y
4 *Holt*	Y	Y
5 Hoyer	Y	Y
6 Byron	?	Y
7 Mitchell	N	N
8 Barnes	N	Y
MASSACHUSETTS		
1 *Conte*	Y	Y
2 Boland	Y	Y
3 Early	Y	N
4 Frank	Y	N
5 Shannon	?	N
6 Mavroules	Y	Y
7 Markey	Y	Y
8 O'Neill		
9 Moakley	Y	Y
10 *Heckler*	Y	Y
11 Donnelly	Y	Y
12 Studds	Y	N
MICHIGAN		
1 Conyers	?	X
2 *Pursell*	Y	Y
3 Wolpe	?	Y
4 *Siljander*	Y	Y
5 *Sawyer*	Y	Y
6 *Dunn*	Y	Y
7 Kildee	Y	N
8 Traxler	Y	Y
9 *Vander Jagt*	Y	Y
10 Albosta	Y	Y
11 *Davis*	Y	Y
12 Bonior	Y	N
13 Crockett	?	N
14 Hertel	Y	N
15 Ford	Y	Y
16 Dingell	?	Y
17 Brodhead	Y	N
18 Blanchard	?	?
19 *Broomfield*	Y	Y
MINNESOTA		
1 *Erdahl*	Y	Y
2 *Hagedorn*	Y	Y
3 *Frenzel*	Y	Y
4 Vento	Y	N
5 Sabo	N	N
6 *Weber*	?	Y
7 *Stangeland*	Y	Y
8 Oberstar	N	Y
MISSISSIPPI		
1 Whitten	Y	Y
2 Bowen	Y	Y
3 Montgomery	Y	Y
4 Dowdy	Y	N
5 *Lott*	Y	Y
MISSOURI		
1 Clay	N	N
2 Young	Y	Y
3 Gephardt	Y	Y

	234	235
4 Skelton	?	?
5 Bolling	?	?
6 *Coleman*	Y	Y
7 *Taylor*	Y	Y
8 *Bailey*	Y	Y
9 Volkmer	Y	Y
10 *Emerson*	N	Y
MONTANA		
1 Williams	Y	Y
2 *Marlenee*	Y	Y
NEBRASKA		
1 *Bereuter*	Y	Y
2 *Daub*	Y	Y
3 *Smith*	Y	Y
NEVADA		
AL Santini	?	Y
NEW HAMPSHIRE		
1 D'Amours	Y	Y
2 *Gregg*	Y	Y
NEW JERSEY		
1 Florio	Y	N
2 Hughes	Y	Y
3 Howard	Y	Y
4 *Smith*	Y	Y
5 *Fenwick*	Y	Y
6 *Forsythe*	?	Y
7 *Roukema*	Y	Y
8 Roe	Y	N
9 *Hollenbeck*	?	Y
10 Rodino	?	Y
11 Minish	Y	Y
12 *Rinaldo*	Y	N
13 *Courter*	Y	Y
14 Guarini	Y	Y
15 Dwyer	Y	Y
NEW MEXICO		
1 *Lujan*	Y	Y
2 *Skeen*	Y	Y
NEW YORK		
1 *Carney*	Y	Y
2 Downey	Y	N
3 *Carman*	Y	Y
4 *Lent*	Y	Y
5 *McGrath*	Y	Y
6 *LeBoutillier*	N	Y
7 Addabbo	Y	Y
8 Rosenthal	?	?
9 Ferraro	Y	Y
10 Biaggi	Y	Y
11 Scheuer	Y	C
12 Chisholm	?	N
13 Solarz	Y	Y
14 Richmond	?	?
15 Zeferetti	Y	Y
16 Schumer	Y	Y
17 *Molinari*	Y	Y
18 *Green*	Y	Y
19 Rangel	Y	N
20 Weiss	Y	Y
21 Garcia	?	Y
22 Bingham	Y	N
23 Peyser	Y	Y
24 Ottinger	P	N
25 *Fish*	Y	Y
26 *Gilman*	?	Y
27 McHugh	Y	Y
28 Stratton	Y	Y
29 *Solomon*	Y	Y
30 *Martin*	Y	Y
31 *Mitchell*	?	Y
32 *Wortley*	Y	Y
33 *Lee*	Y	N
34 *Horton*	Y	Y
35 *Conable*	Y	Y
36 LaFalce	Y	N
37 Nowak	Y	N
38 *Kemp*	?	Y
39 Lundine	Y	Y
NORTH CAROLINA		
1 Jones	Y	Y
2 Fountain	?	Y
3 Whitley	Y	Y
4 Andrews	Y	N
5 Neal	Y	?
6 *Johnston*	N	Y
7 Rose	Y	Y
8 Hefner	Y	Y

	234	235
9 *Martin*	Y	Y
10 *Broyhill*	Y	Y
11 *Hendon*	N	Y
NORTH DAKOTA		
AL Dorgan	Y	Y
OHIO		
1 *Gradison*	Y	Y
2 Luken	N	Y
3 Hall	Y	N
4 *Oxley*	Y	Y
5 *Latta*	Y	Y
6 *McEwen*	Y	Y
7 *Brown*	?	?
8 *Kindness*	Y	Y
9 *Weber*	Y	Y
10 *Miller*	N	Y
11 *Stanton*	Y	Y
12 Shamansky	Y	Y
13 Pease	Y	Y
14 Seiberling	Y	N
15 *Wylie*	Y	Y
16 *Regula*	Y	Y
17 *Ashbrook*	Y	Y
18 Applegate	?	Y
19 *Williams*	Y	Y
20 Oakar	Y	Y
21 Stokes	Y	N
22 Eckart	Y	Y
23 *Mottl*	?	Y
OKLAHOMA		
1 Jones	Y	Y
2 Synar	Y	Y
3 Watkins	Y	Y
4 McCurdy	Y	Y
5 *Edwards*	Y	Y
6 English	Y	Y
OREGON		
1 AuCoin	Y	Y
2 *Smith*	Y	Y
3 Wyden	Y	Y
4 Weaver	Y	Y
PENNSYLVANIA		
1 Foglietta	Y	N
2 Gray	Y	N
3 Smith	Y	Y
4 *Dougherty*	Y	Y
5 *Schulze*	Y	Y
6 Yatron	Y	Y
7 Edgar	Y	N
8 *Coyne, J.*	?	?
9 *Shuster*	Y	Y
10 *McDade*	?	?
11 *Nelligan*	Y	Y
12 Murtha	Y	Y
13 *Coughlin*	N	Y
14 Coyne, W.	Y	Y
15 *Ritter*	Y	Y
16 *Walker*	?	Y
17 *Ertel*	?	?
18 Walgren	?	Y
19 *Goodling*	N	Y
20 Gaydos	Y	Y
21 Bailey	Y	Y
22 Murphy	Y	Y
23 *Clinger*	Y	Y
24 *Marks*	?	Y
25 Atkinson	N	Y
RHODE ISLAND		
1 St Germain	Y	Y
2 *Schneider*	Y	Y
SOUTH CAROLINA		
1 *Hartnett*	Y	Y
2 *Spence*	Y	Y
3 Derrick	Y	Y
4 *Campbell*	Y	Y
5 Holland	?	?
6 *Napier*	Y	Y
SOUTH DAKOTA		
1 Daschle	Y	Y
2 *Roberts*	Y	Y
TENNESSEE		
1 *Quillen*	Y	Y
2 *Duncan*	Y	Y
3 Bouquard	?	#
4 Gore	Y	Y
5 Boner	Y	Y
6 *Beard*	?	?

	234	235
7 Jones	?	?
8 Ford	?	X
TEXAS		
1 Hall, S.	Y	Y
2 Wilson	Y	Y
3 *Collins*	Y	Y
4 Hall, R.	Y	N
5 Mattox	Y	N
6 *Gramm*	Y	Y
7 *Archer*	Y	Y
8 *Fields*	N	Y
9 Brooks	Y	Y
10 Pickle	Y	Y
11 Leath	Y	Y
12 Wright	Y	N
13 Hightower	Y	Y
14 Patman	Y	Y
15 de la Garza	?	Y
16 White	Y	Y
17 Stenholm	Y	Y
18 Leland	Y	N
19 Hance	Y	N
20 Gonzalez	Y	Y
21 *Loeffler*	Y	Y
22 *Paul*	Y	Y
23 Kazen	Y	Y
24 Frost	?	N
UTAH		
1 *Hansen*	Y	Y
2 *Marriott*	Y	Y
VERMONT		
AL *Jeffords*	Y	Y
VIRGINIA		
1 *Trible*	Y	Y
2 *Whitehurst*	Y	Y
3 *Bliley*	Y	Y
4 *Daniel, R.*	Y	Y
5 Daniel, D.	Y	Y
6 *Butler*	N	Y
7 *Robinson*	Y	Y
8 *Parris*	Y	Y
9 *Wampler*	Y	Y
10 *Wolf*	Y	Y
WASHINGTON		
1 *Pritchard*	Y	Y
2 Swift	Y	Y
3 Bonker	Y	Y
4 *Morrison*	Y	Y
5 Foley	Y	Y
6 Dicks	Y	Y
7 Lowry	Y	Y
WEST VIRGINIA		
1 Mollohan	Y	N
2 *Benedict*	Y	Y
3 *Staton*	Y	Y
4 Rahall	Y	Y
WISCONSIN		
1 Aspin	Y	Y
2 Kastenmeier	Y	N
3 *Gunderson*	Y	Y
4 Zablocki	Y	Y
5 Reuss	Y	Y
6 *Petri*	Y	Y
7 Obey	Y	N
8 *Roth*	Y	Y
9 *Sensenbrenner*	Y	Y
WYOMING		
AL *Cheney*	Y	Y

Southern states - Ala., Ark., Fla., Ga., Ky., La., Miss., N.C., Okla., S.C., Tenn., Texas, Va.

KEY

Y Voted for (yea).
\# Paired for.
\+ Announced for.
N Voted against (nay).
X Paired against.
\- Announced against.
P Voted "present".
C Voted "present" to avoid possible conflict of interest.
? Did not vote or otherwise make a position known.

Democrats *Republicans*

236. H J Res 521. Nuclear Arms Freeze. Porter, R-Ill., amendment stating that a nuclear arms freeze was sought, not as an end in itself, but as the first step toward nuclear arms reductions by the United States and the Soviet Union. Adopted 323-84: R 116-64; D 207-20 (ND 152-7, SD 55-13), Aug. 5, 1982.

237. H J Res 521. Nuclear Arms Freeze. Broomfield, R-Mich., substitute to call for a nuclear weapons freeze by the United States and the Soviet Union at equal and substantially reduced levels. Adopted 204-202: R 151-27; D 53-175 (ND 11-149, SD 42-26), Aug. 5, 1982. A "yea" was a vote supporting the president's position. (As reported, the resolution had called for the United States and the Soviet Union to decide when and how to implement an immediate freeze on nuclear arms.)

238. H J Res 521. Nuclear Arms Freeze. Paul, R-Texas, motion to recommit to the Foreign Affairs Committee the joint resolution, as amended, to call for a nuclear weapons freeze by the United States and the Soviet Union at equal and substantially reduced levels. Rejected 175-229: R 23-155; D 152-74 (ND 137-21, SD 15-53), Aug. 5, 1982.

239. H J Res 521. Nuclear Arms Freeze. Passage of the joint resolution to call for a nuclear weapons freeze by the United States and the Soviet Union at equal and substantially reduced levels. Passed 273-125: R 163-15; D 110-110 (ND 50-103, SD 60-7), Aug. 5, 1982.

240. Procedural Motion. Hunter, R-Calif., motion to approve the House *Journal* of Monday, Aug. 9. Motion agreed to 287-25: R 128-14; D 159-11 (ND 102-10, SD 57-1), Aug. 10, 1982.

241. H Con Res 388. Education Regulations Disapproval. Perkins, D-Ky., motion to suspend the rules and adopt the concurrent resolution to disapprove Education Department regulations affecting the title I program of aid to disadvantaged children and elementary and secondary education block grant programs. Motion agreed to 363-0: R 164-0; D 199-0 (ND 134-0, SD 65-0), Aug. 10, 1982. A two-thirds majority of those present and voting (242 in this case) is required for adoption under suspension of the rules.

242. HR 6892. Agriculture Reconciliation. Adoption of the rule (H Res 551) providing for House floor consideration of the bill to revise dairy, grain and food stamp programs to meet budget reconciliation targets. Adopted 230-156: R 35-140; D 195-16 (ND 132-11, SD 63-5), Aug. 10, 1982.

243. HR 6892. Agriculture Reconciliation. De la Garza, D-Texas, motion that the House resolve itself into the Committee of the Whole for consideration of the bill to revise dairy, grain and food stamp programs to meet budget reconciliation targets. Motion agreed to 362-9: R 166-7; D 196-2 (ND 129-1, SD 67-1), Aug. 10, 1982.

	236	237	238	239	240	241	242	243
ALABAMA								
1 *Edwards*	Y	Y	N	Y	?	Y	N	Y
2 *Dickinson*	N	Y	N	N	Y	N	Y	Y
3 Nichols	N	Y	N	Y	?	Y	Y	Y
4 Bevill	N	Y	N	Y	?	?	Y	Y
5 Flippo	Y	Y	N	Y	?	?	?	?
6 *Smith*	N	Y	N	Y	Y	N	Y	Y
7 Shelby	N	Y	N	Y	Y	Y	Y	Y
ALASKA								
AL *Young*	Y	Y	N	Y	?	Y	Y	Y
ARIZONA								
1 *Rhodes*	N	Y	N	Y	?	Y	N	Y
2 Udall	Y	N	Y	N	?	Y	Y	Y
3 *Stump*	N	Y	N	Y	?	Y	N	Y
4 *Rudd*	N	Y	N	Y	Y	Y	N	Y
ARKANSAS								
1 Alexander	Y	N	Y	Y	Y	Y	Y	Y
2 *Bethune*	Y	Y	N	Y	Y	Y	Y	Y
3 *Hammerschmidt*	Y	Y	N	Y	Y	Y	Y	Y
4 Anthony	Y	N	N	Y	Y	?	Y	Y
CALIFORNIA								
1 *Chappie*	Y	Y	N	Y	Y	Y	N	Y
2 *Clausen*	Y	Y	N	Y	Y	Y	N	Y
3 Matsui	Y	N	Y	N	Y	Y	Y	Y
4 Fazio	Y	N	Y	N	Y	Y	Y	Y
5 Burton, J.	Y	N	Y	N	?	?	?	?
6 Burton, P.	Y	N	Y	N	Y	Y	Y	Y
7 Miller	Y	N	Y	N	Y	Y	Y	Y
8 Dellums	Y	N	Y	N	?	?	Y	Y
9 Stark	Y	N	Y	N	Y	Y	Y	Y
10 Edwards	Y	N	Y	N	Y	Y	Y	Y
11 Lantos	Y	N	Y	N	?	Y	Y	Y
12 *McCloskey*	Y	N	N	Y	?	?	?	?
13 Mineta	Y	N	Y	N	Y	Y	Y	Y
14 *Shumway*	N	Y	N	Y	Y	Y	N	N
15 Coelho	Y	N	Y	N	Y	Y	Y	Y
16 Panetta	Y	N	Y	N	Y	Y	Y	Y
17 *Pashayan*	Y	Y	?	?	Y	Y	Y	Y
18 *Thomas*	N	Y	N	Y	Y	Y	N	Y
19 *Lagomarsino*	Y	Y	N	Y	Y	Y	N	Y
20 *Goldwater*	?	?	?	?	?	?	?	?
21 *Fiedler*	Y	Y	N	Y	Y	Y	Y	?
22 *Moorhead*	N	Y	N	Y	Y	Y	N	Y
23 Beilenson	Y	N	Y	N	?	Y	Y	Y
24 Waxman	Y	N	Y	N	Y	Y	Y	Y
25 Roybal	Y	N	Y	N	Y	Y	Y	Y
26 *Rousselot*	N	Y	N	Y	N	Y	N	Y
27 *Dornan*	?	?	?	?	?	?	?	?
28 Dixon	Y	N	Y	N	?	Y	Y	Y
29 Hawkins	Y	N	Y	N	?	?	?	?
30 Martinez	Y	N	Y	N	Y	Y	Y	Y
31 Dymally	Y	N	Y	N	Y	Y	Y	Y
32 Anderson	Y	N	Y	N	Y	Y	Y	Y
33 Grisham	Y	Y	N	Y	?	?	?	?
34 *Lungren*	N	Y	N	Y	Y	Y	N	N
35 *Dreier*	N	Y	N	Y	Y	Y	N	N
36 Brown	Y	N	Y	N	Y	Y	Y	Y
37 *Lewis*	Y	Y	N	Y	Y	Y	N	N
38 Patterson	Y	N	Y	N	Y	Y	Y	Y
39 *Dannemeyer*	N	Y	N	Y	Y	N	N	Y
40 *Badham*	Y	Y	N	Y	Y	Y	N	Y
41 *Lowery*	Y	Y	N	Y	Y	Y	N	Y
42 *Hunter*	N	Y	N	Y	Y	Y	N	Y
43 *Burgener*	N	Y	N	Y	?	Y	N	Y
COLORADO								
1 Schroeder	Y	N	Y	N	N	Y	Y	Y
2 Wirth	Y	N	Y	N	Y	Y	Y	Y
3 Kogovsek	Y	N	Y	N	Y	Y	Y	Y
4 Brown	Y	Y	N	Y	Y	Y	N	Y

	236	237	238	239	240	241	242	243
5 *Kramer*	Y	Y	N	Y	Y	Y	N	Y
CONNECTICUT								
1 Kennelly	Y	N	Y	N	Y	Y	Y	Y
2 Gejdenson	Y	N	Y	N	Y	Y	Y	Y
3 *DeNardis*	Y	N	Y	N	Y	Y	N	?
4 *McKinney*	Y	N	Y	N	?	?	N	?
5 Ratchford	Y	N	Y	N	Y	Y	Y	Y
6 Moffett	Y	N	Y	N	?	?	?	?
DELAWARE								
AL *Evans*	Y	N	Y	Y	?	Y	N	Y
FLORIDA								
1 Hutto	N	Y	N	Y	Y	Y	Y	Y
2 Fuqua	?	?	?	?	?	Y	Y	Y
3 Bennett	Y	Y	N	Y	Y	Y	N	Y
4 Chappell	Y	Y	N	Y	?	?	?	?
5 *McCollum*	Y	Y	N	Y	?	Y	N	Y
6 *Young*	Y	Y	N	Y	Y	Y	N	Y
7 Gibbons	Y	N	N	Y	Y	Y	Y	Y
8 Ireland	?	Y	N	Y	?	?	Y	Y
9 Nelson	Y	Y	N	Y	?	Y	Y	Y
10 *Bafalis*	?	?	?	?	?	?	?	?
11 Mica	Y	N	Y	Y	?	Y	Y	Y
12 *Shaw*	Y	Y	N	Y	Y	Y	N	Y
13 Lehman	Y	N	Y	N	Y	Y	Y	Y
14 Pepper	Y	N	Y	N	Y	Y	Y	Y
15 Fascell	Y	N	Y	N	Y	Y	Y	Y
GEORGIA								
1 Ginn	?	?	?	?	?	?	?	?
2 Hatcher	Y	Y	N	Y	?	Y	Y	Y
3 Brinkley	Y	Y	N	Y	Y	Y	Y	Y
4 Levitas	Y	Y	Y	Y	Y	Y	N	Y
5 Fowler	Y	N	Y	N	Y	Y	Y	Y
6 *Gingrich*	Y	Y	N	Y	Y	Y	N	Y
7 McDonald	N	N	N	N	Y	Y	N	N
8 Evans	Y	Y	N	Y	?	?	?	?
9 Jenkins	Y	Y	N	Y	?	?	?	?
10 Barnard	Y	Y	N	Y	Y	Y	Y	Y
HAWAII								
1 Heftel	Y	N	Y	N	Y	?	?	Y
2 Akaka	Y	N	Y	N	?	?	?	?
IDAHO								
1 *Craig*	N	Y	N	Y	Y	Y	N	Y
2 *Hansen*	N	Y	N	Y	Y	Y	N	Y
ILLINOIS								
1 Washington	Y	N	Y	N	N	Y	Y	Y
2 Savage	Y	N	Y	N	?	Y	?	?
3 Russo	Y	N	Y	N	Y	Y	Y	Y
4 *Derwinski*	N	Y	N	Y	Y	Y	N	Y
5 Fary	Y	N	Y	N	Y	Y	Y	Y
6 *Hyde*	N	Y	N	Y	Y	Y	N	Y
7 Collins	Y	N	Y	N	Y	Y	Y	Y
8 Rostenkowski	Y	N	Y	N	Y	Y	Y	Y
9 Yates	Y	N	Y	N	?	Y	Y	Y
10 *Porter*	Y	N	Y	N	Y	Y	N	Y
11 Annunzio	Y	N	Y	N	Y	Y	Y	Y
12 *Crane, P.*	N	Y	N	N	Y	Y	N	Y
13 *McClory*	?	?	?	?	?	?	?	?
14 *Erlenborn*	N	Y	N	Y	Y	Y	N	Y
15 *Corcoran*	N	Y	N	Y	Y	Y	N	Y
16 *Martin*	Y	N	Y	Y	Y	Y	Y	Y
17 O'Brien	Y	N	Y	N	Y	Y	N	Y
18 *Michel*	N	Y	N	Y	?	Y	N	Y
19 *Railsback*	?	X	?	?	?	?	?	?
20 *Findley*	Y	N	Y	Y	Y	Y	N	Y
21 *Madigan*	N	Y	?	?	Y	Y	N	Y
22 *Crane, D.*	N	Y	N	N	N	Y	N	Y
23 Price	Y	N	Y	N	Y	Y	Y	Y
24 Simon	Y	N	Y	N	Y	Y	Y	Y
INDIANA								
1 Benjamin	Y	N	Y	N	Y	Y	Y	Y
2 Fithian	Y	N	Y	N	Y	Y	Y	Y
3 *Hiler*	Y	Y	N	Y	Y	Y	N	Y
4 *Coats*	Y	Y	N	Y	Y	Y	N	Y
5 *Hillis*	N	Y	N	Y	Y	Y	N	Y
6 Evans	Y	?	?	Y	Y	Y	Y	Y
7 *Myers*	N	Y	N	Y	Y	Y	?	Y
8 *Deckard*	Y	Y	N	Y	Y	Y	?	Y
9 Hamilton	Y	N	Y	Y	Y	Y	Y	Y
10 Sharp	Y	N	Y	Y	Y	Y	Y	Y
11 Jacobs	Y	N	Y	Y	?	Y	N	Y
IOWA								
1 *Leach*	Y	N	Y	N	Y	Y	Y	Y
2 *Tauke*	Y	N	N	Y	Y	Y	N	Y
3 *Evans*	Y	N	Y	N	Y	Y	N	Y
4 Smith	Y	N	Y	N	Y	Y	Y	Y
5 Harkin	Y	N	Y	N	N	Y	Y	?
6 Bedell	Y	N	Y	N	Y	Y	Y	Y

ND - Northern Democrats   SD - Southern Democrats

	236	237	238	239	240	241	242	243
KANSAS								
1 ***Roberts***	Y	Y	N	Y	Y	Y	N	Y
2 ***Jeffries***	N	Y	N	N	?	?	N	Y
3 ***Winn***	Y	Y	N	Y	Y	Y	N	Y
4 Glickman	Y	N	Y	N	Y	Y	Y	Y
5 ***Whittaker***	Y	Y	N	Y	Y	Y	N	Y
KENTUCKY								
1 Hubbard	Y	Y	N	Y	Y	Y	Y	Y
2 Natcher	Y	N	N	Y	Y	Y	Y	Y
3 Mazzoli	Y	N	N	Y	Y	Y	Y	Y
4 ***Snyder***	Y	Y	N	Y	Y	Y	N	Y
5 ***Rogers***	Y	Y	N	Y	Y	Y	N	Y
6 ***Hopkins***	Y	Y	N	Y	Y	Y	Y	Y
7 Perkins	Y	N	N	Y	Y	Y	Y	Y
LOUISIANA								
1 ***Livingston***	N	Y	N	Y	Y	Y	Y	Y
2 Boggs	Y	N	N	Y	Y	Y	Y	Y
3 Tauzin	Y	Y	N	Y	Y	Y	Y	Y
4 Roemer	Y	Y	N	Y	N	Y	Y	Y
5 Huckaby	Y	Y	N	Y	Y	Y	Y	Y
6 ***Moore***	N	Y	N	Y	Y	Y	N	Y
7 Breaux	N	Y	N	Y	Y	Y	Y	Y
8 Long	?	?	?	?	Y	Y	Y	Y
MAINE								
1 ***Emery***	N	Y	N	Y	Y	Y	Y	Y
2 ***Snowe***	Y	N	Y	Y	Y	Y	N	Y
MARYLAND								
1 Dyson	N	Y	N	Y	Y	Y	Y	Y
2 Long	Y	N	N	Y	Y	Y	Y	?
3 Mikulski	Y	N	Y	N	Y	Y	Y	Y
4 ***Holt***	N	Y	N	Y	Y	Y	N	Y
5 Hoyer	Y	N	Y	N	Y	Y	Y	Y
6 Byron	N	Y	N	Y	?	Y	Y	Y
7 Mitchell	Y	N	Y	N	N	Y	Y	Y
8 Barnes	Y	N	Y	N	N	Y	Y	Y
MASSACHUSETTS								
1 ***Conte***	Y	N	Y	N	?	Y	N	Y
2 Boland	Y	N	Y	N	Y	Y	Y	Y
3 Early	Y	N	Y	N	Y	Y	Y	Y
4 Frank	Y	N	Y	N	Y	Y	N	Y
5 Shannon	Y	N	Y	N	?	?	Y	Y
6 Mavroules	Y	N	Y	N	Y	Y	Y	?
7 Markey	Y	N	Y	N	?	Y	Y	Y
8 O'Neill		N						
9 Moakley	Y	N	Y	N	Y	Y	Y	Y
10 ***Heckler***	Y	N	Y	N	Y	Y	N	Y
11 Donnelly	Y	N	Y	N	Y	Y	Y	Y
12 Studds	Y	N	Y	N	Y	Y	Y	Y
MICHIGAN								
1 Conyers	N	N	Y	N	?	?	?	?
2 ***Pursell***	Y	N	Y	Y	?	?	?	?
3 Wolpe	Y	N	Y	N	Y	Y	Y	Y
4 ***Siljander***	N	Y	N	Y	?	?	?	?
5 ***Sawyer***	Y	Y	N	Y	Y	Y	N	Y
6 ***Dunn***	Y	Y	N	Y	?	?	N	Y
7 Kildee	Y	N	Y	N	Y	Y	Y	Y
8 Traxler	Y	N	Y	Y	?	?	?	?
9 ***Vander Jagt***	Y	Y	N	Y	?	Y	N	Y
10 Albosta	Y	N	Y	Y	Y	Y	Y	Y
11 ***Davis***	Y	Y	N	Y	?	?	?	?
12 Bonior	Y	N	Y	N	?	?	?	?
13 Crockett	Y	N	Y	N	?	?	?	?
14 Hertel	Y	N	Y	?	?	?	?	?
15 Ford	Y	N	Y	?	?	?	?	?
16 Dingell	Y	N	Y	Y	Y	Y	Y	Y
17 Brodhead	Y	N	Y	N	?	?	?	?
18 Blanchard	Y	N	Y	Y	?	?	?	?
19 ***Broomfield***	N	Y	N	Y	Y	Y	N	Y
MINNESOTA								
1 ***Erdahl***	Y	N	Y	Y	?	?	N	Y
2 ***Hagedorn***	Y	Y	N	Y	Y	Y	N	Y
3 ***Frenzel***	Y	Y	N	Y	Y	Y	N	Y
4 Vento	Y	N	Y	N	?	?	Y	Y
5 Sabo	Y	N	Y	N	N	Y	Y	Y
6 ***Weber***	Y	Y	N	Y	Y	Y	Y	Y
7 ***Stangeland***	Y	Y	N	Y	?	Y	Y	Y
8 Oberstar	Y	N	Y	N	P	Y	N	Y
MISSISSIPPI								
1 Whitten	?	?	?	?	Y	Y	Y	Y
2 Bowen	Y	N	Y	Y	?	Y	Y	Y
3 Montgomery	N	Y	N	Y	Y	Y	Y	Y
4 Dowdy	Y	N	Y	Y	Y	Y	Y	Y
5 ***Lott***	N	Y	N	Y	?	Y	N	Y
MISSOURI								
1 Clay	Y	N	Y	N	N	Y	Y	Y
2 Young	Y	N	N	Y	?	?	?	?
3 Gephardt	Y	N	N	Y	Y	Y	Y	?
4 Skelton	?	?	?	?	Y	Y	Y	?
5 Bolling	?	?	?	?	?	Y	Y	?
6 ***Coleman***	Y	Y	N	Y	Y	Y	Y	Y
7 ***Taylor***	Y	Y	N	Y	Y	Y	Y	Y
8 ***Bailey***	Y	Y	N	Y	N	Y	Y	Y
9 Volkmer	Y	N	N	Y	?	Y	Y	Y
10 ***Emerson***	Y	Y	N	Y	N	Y	Y	Y
MONTANA								
1 Williams	Y	N	Y	N	?	Y	Y	Y
2 ***Marlenee***	Y	Y	N	Y	?	?	N	Y
NEBRASKA								
1 ***Bereuter***	Y	Y	N	Y	Y	Y	Y	Y
2 ***Daub***	Y	Y	N	Y	Y	Y	Y	Y
3 ***Smith***	Y	Y	N	Y	Y	Y	Y	Y
NEVADA								
AL Santini	Y	Y	N	Y	?	?	?	?
NEW HAMPSHIRE								
1 D'Amours	Y	N	Y	Y	Y	Y	Y	Y
2 ***Gregg***	Y	N	N	Y	Y	Y	N	Y
NEW JERSEY								
1 Florio	Y	N	Y	N	Y	Y	Y	Y
2 Hughes	Y	N	Y	Y	Y	Y	N	Y
3 Howard	Y	N	Y	N	Y	Y	Y	Y
4 ***Smith***	Y	N	Y	Y	Y	Y	N	Y
5 ***Fenwick***	Y	N	Y	N	?	Y	N	Y
6 ***Forsythe***	N	Y	N	Y	?	Y	N	Y
7 ***Roukema***	Y	N	Y	N	Y	Y	N	Y
8 Roe	Y	N	Y	N	Y	Y	Y	Y
9 ***Hollenbeck***	Y	N	Y	N	Y	Y	N	Y
10 Rodino	Y	N	Y	N	Y	Y	Y	Y
11 Minish	Y	N	Y	N	Y	Y	Y	Y
12 ***Rinaldo***	Y	N	Y	Y	?	?	Y	Y
13 ***Courter***	Y	Y	N	Y	Y	Y	N	Y
14 Guarini	Y	N	Y	N	Y	Y	Y	Y
15 Dwyer	Y	N	Y	N	Y	Y	Y	Y
NEW MEXICO								
1 ***Lujan***	?	#	?	?	Y	Y	N	Y
2 ***Skeen***	N	Y	N	Y	Y	Y	Y	Y
NEW YORK								
1 ***Carney***	N	Y	N	Y	?	?	?	?
2 Downey	Y	N	Y	N	Y	Y	Y	Y
3 ***Carman***	Y	Y	N	Y	Y	Y	N	Y
4 ***Lent***	?	Y	N	Y	Y	Y	N	Y
5 ***McGrath***	Y	-	+	+	Y	Y	N	Y
6 ***LeBoutillier***	Y	Y	N	Y	?	?	?	?
7 Addabbo	Y	N	Y	?	Y	Y	Y	?
8 Rosenthal	?	X	?	?	?	?	?	?
9 Ferraro	Y	N	Y	?	?	Y	Y	Y
10 Biaggi	Y	N	Y	N	?	?	?	?
11 Scheuer	Y	N	Y	N	Y	Y	Y	Y
12 Chisholm	Y	N	Y	N	?	Y	Y	?
13 Solarz	Y	N	Y	N	Y	Y	Y	Y
14 Richmond	Y	N	?	?	?	?	Y	Y
15 Zeferetti	Y	N	Y	?	Y	Y	Y	?
16 Schumer	Y	N	Y	N	Y	Y	Y	Y
17 ***Molinari***	Y	Y	N	Y	Y	Y	N	Y
18 ***Green***	Y	N	Y	N	?	Y	N	Y
19 Rangel	Y	N	Y	N	Y	Y	Y	Y
20 Weiss	Y	N	Y	N	?	Y	Y	?
21 Garcia	Y	N	Y	N	?	?	Y	Y
22 Bingham	Y	N	Y	N	Y	Y	Y	Y
23 Peyser	Y	N	Y	N	Y	Y	Y	Y
24 Ottinger	Y	N	Y	N	P	Y	Y	Y
25 ***Fish***	Y	Y	N	Y	Y	Y	N	Y
26 ***Gilman***	N	Y	N	Y	?	Y	N	Y
27 McHugh	Y	N	Y	N	?	Y	Y	Y
28 Stratton	N	Y	N	Y	Y	Y	Y	Y
29 ***Solomon***	N	Y	N	Y	Y	Y	N	N
30 ***Martin***	Y	Y	N	Y	?	?	N	Y
31 ***Mitchell***	Y	Y	N	Y	Y	Y	N	Y
32 ***Wortley***	Y	Y	N	Y	Y	Y	N	Y
33 ***Lee***	Y	Y	N	Y	?	Y	N	Y
34 ***Horton***	Y	N	N	Y	Y	Y	N	Y
35 ***Conable***	Y	Y	N	Y	?	Y	N	N
36 LaFalce	Y	N	Y	Y	Y	Y	N	Y
37 Nowak	Y	N	Y	Y	Y	Y	N	Y
38 ***Kemp***	N	Y	N	Y	?	?	N	Y
39 Lundine	Y	N	Y	N	Y	Y	Y	Y
NORTH CAROLINA								
1 Jones	Y	Y	N	Y	Y	Y	Y	Y
2 Fountain	N	Y	N	Y	Y	Y	Y	Y
3 Whitley	Y	Y	N	?	Y	Y	Y	Y
4 Andrews	?	?	?	?	?	?	?	Y
5 Neal	Y	N	Y	Y	?	?	?	?
6 ***Johnston***	N	Y	N	Y	N	Y	N	Y
7 Rose	Y	N	Y	Y	?	?	?	?
8 Hefner	Y	Y	N	Y	Y	Y	Y	Y
9 ***Martin***	Y	Y	N	Y	Y	Y	N	Y
10 ***Broyhill***	Y	Y	N	Y	Y	Y	N	Y
11 ***Hendon***	N	Y	N	Y	Y	Y	N	Y
NORTH DAKOTA								
AL Dorgan	Y	N	Y	N	Y	Y	Y	Y
OHIO								
1 ***Gradison***	Y	Y	N	Y	Y	Y	N	Y
2 Luken	Y	N	Y	N	N	Y	Y	N
3 Hall	?	N	Y	N	Y	Y	Y	Y
4 ***Oxley***	Y	Y	N	Y	Y	Y	N	Y
5 ***Latta***	Y	Y	N	Y	N	Y	N	Y
6 ***McEwen***	Y	Y	N	Y	Y	Y	N	Y
7 ***Brown***	?	?	?	?	?	?	?	?
8 ***Kindness***	N	Y	N	Y	Y	Y	N	Y
9 ***Weber***	Y	Y	N	Y	Y	Y	N	Y
10 ***Miller***	Y	Y	N	Y	N	Y	Y	Y
11 ***Stanton***	Y	Y	N	Y	Y	Y	?	Y
12 Shamansky	Y	N	Y	Y	Y	Y	Y	Y
13 Pease	Y	N	Y	N	Y	Y	Y	Y
14 Seiberling	Y	N	Y	N	?	Y	Y	?
15 ***Wylie***	?	?	?	?	Y	Y	N	Y
16 ***Regula***	Y	Y	N	Y	Y	Y	N	Y
17 ***Ashbrook***	N	Y	N	Y	Y	Y	N	Y
18 Applegate	Y	N	N	Y	?	?	Y	?
19 ***Williams***	Y	Y	N	Y	Y	Y	N	Y
20 Oakar	Y	N	Y	N	Y	Y	Y	Y
21 Stokes	Y	N	Y	N	?	Y	Y	Y
22 Eckart	Y	N	Y	N	Y	Y	Y	Y
23 Mottl	Y	N	N	N	Y	Y	Y	Y
OKLAHOMA								
1 Jones	Y	N	N	Y	Y	Y	Y	Y
2 Synar	+	-	-	+	Y	Y	Y	Y
3 Watkins	Y	N	N	Y	?	?	?	?
4 McCurdy	Y	Y	N	Y	Y	Y	Y	Y
5 ***Edwards***	N	Y	N	Y	?	Y	N	Y
6 English	Y	Y	N	Y	Y	Y	Y	Y
OREGON								
1 AuCoin	Y	N	Y	N	?	?	?	?
2 ***Smith***	N	Y	N	Y	Y	Y	N	Y
3 Wyden	Y	N	Y	N	Y	Y	Y	Y
4 Weaver	Y	N	Y	N	Y	Y	Y	Y
PENNSYLVANIA								
1 Foglietta	Y	N	Y	N	Y	Y	Y	Y
2 Gray	Y	N	Y	N	Y	Y	Y	Y
3 Smith	Y	Y	N	Y	Y	Y	Y	Y
4 ***Dougherty***	N	Y	N	Y	?	?	Y	Y
5 ***Schulze***	Y	#	N	Y	Y	Y	N	Y
6 Yatron	Y	N	Y	Y	?	?	Y	Y
7 Edgar	Y	N	Y	N	Y	Y	Y	Y
8 ***Coyne, J.***	Y	Y	N	Y	Y	Y	N	Y
9 ***Shuster***	Y	Y	N	Y	Y	Y	N	Y
10 ***McDade***	?	#	?	?	?	Y	N	Y
11 ***Nelligan***	N	Y	N	Y	Y	Y	N	Y
12 Murtha	Y	Y	N	Y	Y	Y	Y	Y
13 ***Coughlin***	Y	Y	N	Y	N	Y	N	Y
14 Coyne, W.	Y	N	N	N	Y	Y	Y	Y
15 ***Ritter***	Y	Y	N	Y	Y	Y	N	Y
16 ***Walker***	N	Y	N	Y	N	Y	N	Y
17 Ertel	Y	N	Y	Y	?	?	?	?
18 Walgren	Y	N	Y	N	?	?	N	Y
19 ***Goodling***	Y	P	Y	Y	N	Y	N	Y
20 Gaydos	N	Y	N	Y	?	Y	Y	?
21 Bailey	N	Y	N	Y	Y	Y	Y	Y
22 Murphy	Y	N	N	Y	N	Y	Y	Y
23 ***Clinger***	Y	Y	N	Y	Y	Y	Y	Y
24 ***Marks***	N	Y	N	Y	?	?	?	?
25 ***Atkinson***	N	Y	N	Y	N	Y	N	Y
RHODE ISLAND								
1 St Germain	Y	N	Y	N	Y	Y	Y	Y
2 ***Schneider***	Y	N	Y	N	Y	Y	Y	Y
SOUTH CAROLINA								
1 ***Hartnett***	Y	Y	N	N	Y	Y	N	Y
2 ***Spence***	N	Y	N	Y	Y	Y	Y	Y
3 Derrick	Y	N	N	Y	Y	Y	?	?
4 ***Campbell***	Y	Y	N	Y	Y	Y	Y	Y
5 Holland	?	?	?	?	?	Y	Y	Y
6 ***Napier***	N	Y	N	Y	Y	Y	Y	Y
SOUTH DAKOTA								
1 Daschle	Y	N	Y	Y	?	Y	Y	Y
2 ***Roberts***	N	Y	N	Y	Y	Y	Y	Y
TENNESSEE								
1 ***Quillen***	N	Y	N	Y	?	Y	Y	Y
2 ***Duncan***	N	Y	N	Y	Y	Y	Y	Y
3 Bouquard	?	?	?	?	Y	Y	Y	Y
4 Gore	Y	N	Y	Y	Y	Y	Y	Y
5 Boner	Y	N	Y	Y	?	?	Y	Y
6 ***Beard***	?	?	?	?	?	?	Y	Y
7 Jones	?	?	?	?	Y	Y	Y	Y
8 Ford	?	X	?	?	?	?	Y	Y
TEXAS								
1 Hall, S.	N	Y	N	Y	Y	Y	Y	Y
2 Wilson	Y	Y	N	Y	Y	Y	?	?
3 ***Collins***	?	?	?	?	Y	Y	N	Y
4 Hall, R.	N	Y	N	Y	Y	Y	Y	Y
5 Mattox	Y	?	?	?	Y	Y	Y	Y
6 Gramm	N	Y	N	Y	Y	Y	N	Y
7 ***Archer***	N	Y	N	Y	Y	Y	N	Y
8 ***Fields***	N	Y	N	Y	N	Y	N	Y
9 Brooks	Y	N	Y	Y	Y	Y	Y	Y
10 Pickle	Y	Y	N	Y	Y	Y	Y	Y
11 Leath	N	Y	N	Y	Y	Y	Y	Y
12 Wright	Y	N	N	Y	Y	Y	Y	Y
13 Hightower	Y	Y	N	Y	Y	Y	Y	Y
14 Patman	Y	Y	N	Y	Y	Y	Y	Y
15 de la Garza	Y	Y	N	Y	Y	Y	Y	Y
16 White	Y	Y	N	Y	?	Y	Y	Y
17 Stenholm	Y	Y	N	Y	Y	Y	Y	Y
18 Leland	Y	N	Y	N	Y	Y	Y	Y
19 Hance	Y	Y	N	Y	Y	Y	Y	Y
20 Gonzalez	Y	N	Y	N	Y	Y	Y	Y
21 ***Loeffler***	N	Y	N	Y	Y	Y	N	Y
22 ***Paul***	N	Y	Y	N	Y	Y	N	Y
23 Kazen	Y	Y	N	Y	Y	Y	Y	Y
24 Frost	Y	N	N	Y	Y	Y	Y	Y
UTAH								
1 ***Hansen***	N	Y	N	Y	Y	Y	N	Y
2 ***Marriott***	Y	Y	N	Y	Y	Y	N	Y
VERMONT								
AL ***Jeffords***	Y	N	Y	Y	Y	Y	N	Y
VIRGINIA								
1 ***Trible***	Y	Y	N	Y	Y	Y	N	Y
2 ***Whitehurst***	N	Y	N	Y	Y	Y	N	?
3 ***Bliley***	Y	Y	N	Y	Y	Y	N	Y
4 ***Daniel, R.***	N	Y	N	Y	?	?	N	Y
5 Daniel, D.	N	Y	N	Y	?	Y	N	Y
6 ***Butler***	N	Y	Y	Y	N	Y	Y	Y
7 ***Robinson***	Y	Y	N	Y	Y	Y	N	Y
8 ***Parris***	Y	Y	N	Y	Y	Y	N	Y
9 ***Wampler***	Y	Y	N	Y	Y	Y	Y	Y
10 ***Wolf***	Y	Y	N	Y	?	?	?	?
WASHINGTON								
1 ***Pritchard***	Y	N	Y	Y	Y	Y	N	Y
2 Swift	Y	N	Y	Y	Y	Y	Y	Y
3 Bonker	Y	N	Y	Y	?	?	?	?
4 ***Morrison***	Y	Y	N	Y	Y	Y	Y	Y
5 Foley	Y	N	Y	Y	Y	Y	Y	Y
6 Dicks	Y	N	Y	Y	Y	Y	Y	Y
7 Lowry	Y	N	Y	Y	Y	Y	Y	Y
WEST VIRGINIA								
1 Mollohan	Y	Y	N	Y	Y	Y	Y	Y
2 ***Benedict***	Y	Y	N	Y	Y	Y	Y	Y
3 ***Staton***	Y	Y	N	Y	Y	Y	N	Y
4 Rahall	Y	N	Y	N	Y	Y	Y	Y
WISCONSIN								
1 Aspin	Y	N	Y	Y	Y	Y	Y	Y
2 Kastenmeier	Y	N	Y	N	Y	Y	Y	Y
3 ***Gunderson***	Y	N	N	Y	Y	Y	N	Y
4 Zablocki	Y	N	Y	Y	Y	Y	Y	Y
5 Reuss	Y	N	Y	Y	Y	Y	Y	Y
6 ***Petri***	Y	Y	N	Y	Y	Y	N	Y
7 Obey	Y	N	Y	Y	Y	Y	Y	Y
8 ***Roth***	Y	Y	N	Y	?	Y	N	Y
9 ***Sensenbrenner***	Y	Y	N	Y	Y	Y	N	Y
WYOMING								
AL ***Cheney***	N	Y	N	Y	?	Y	N	Y

Southern states - Ala., Ark., Fla., Ga., Ky., La., Miss., N.C., Okla., S.C., Tenn., Texas, Va.

244. HR 6892. Agriculture Reconciliation. Wampler, R-Va., substitute to revise the food stamp sections of the bill. Rejected 181-210: R 144-31; D 37-179 (ND 8-136, SD 29-43), Aug. 10, 1982.

245. HR 6892. Agriculture Reconciliation. Latta, R-Ohio, motion to recommit the bill to the Agriculture Committee with instructions to make reductions in programs within its jurisdiction in accordance with budget reconciliation requirements and to submit the reductions to the House Budget Committee. Motion rejected 145-245: R 133-43; D 12-202 (ND 7-136, SD 5-66), Aug. 10, 1982.

246. HR 6892. Agriculture Reconciliation. Passage of the bill to revise dairy, grain and food stamp programs to meet budget reconciliation targets. Passed 268-121: R 68-107; D 200-14 (ND 133-10, SD 67-4), Aug. 10, 1982. A "nay" was a vote supporting the president's position.

247. HR 5427. Radio Marti. Harkin, D-Iowa, amendment, to the Energy and Commerce Committee amendment, to authorize the Board for International Broadcasting to prepare material for broadcast to Cuba and to buy time on commercial radio stations to broadcast that material. Rejected 78-284: R 8-143; D 70-141 (ND 62-80, SD 8-61), Aug. 10, 1982. (The Energy and Commerce Committee amendment, which authorized the establishment of a radio station to broadcast to Cuba, subsequently was adopted by voice vote.)

248. HR 5427. Radio Marti. Tauke, R-Iowa, amendment, to the Energy and Commerce Committee amendment, to prohibit the Board for International Broadcasting from broadcasting to Cuba on or near a radio frequency allocated for non-governmental use. Rejected 109-277: R 19-157; D 90-120 (ND 77-63, SD 13-57), Aug. 10, 1982. (The Energy and Commerce Committee amendment, which authorized the assistant secretary of commerce for communications and information to select a frequency for a radio station to broadcast to Cuba, subsequently was adopted by voice vote.)

249. HR 5427. Radio Marti. Leach, R-Iowa, substitute, for the Energy and Commerce Committee amendment, to require the Board for International Broadcasting, in broadcasting to Cuba, to use the Voice of America's Marathon, Fla., facility and assigned radio frequency. Rejected 109-271: R 21-150; D 88-121 (ND 76-65, SD 12-56), Aug. 10, 1982. (The Energy and Commerce Committee amendment, which authorized the assistant secretary of commerce for communications and information to select a frequency for a radio station to broadcast to Cuba, subsequently was adopted by voice vote.)

250. HR 5427. Radio Marti. Passage of the bill to authorize the establishment, under the supervision of the Board for International Broadcasting, of a radio station to broadcast to Cuba, and authorize $7.5 million in fiscal 1983 for construction and operation of the station. Passed 250-134: R 141-32; D 109-102 (ND 54-86, SD 55-16), Aug. 10, 1982.

KEY

Y	Voted for (yea).
#	Paired for.
+	Announced for.
N	Voted against (nay).
X	Paired against.
-	Announced against.
P	Voted "present".
C	Voted "present" to avoid possible conflict of interest.
?	Did not vote or otherwise make a position known.

Democrats   *Republicans*

	244	245	246	247	248	249	250
ALABAMA							
1 *Edwards*	Y	Y	N	N	N	N	Y
2 *Dickinson*	Y	Y	Y	N	N	N	Y
3 Nichols	Y	N	Y	N	N	?	Y
4 Bevill	Y	N	Y	N	N	N	Y
5 Flippo	?	?	?	?	?	?	?
6 *Smith*	Y	Y	N	N	N	N	Y
7 Shelby	Y	N	Y	N	N	N	Y
ALASKA							
AL *Young*	N	N	Y	?	N	N	Y
ARIZONA							
1 *Rhodes*	Y	Y	Y	?	N	N	?
2 Udall	N	N	Y	N	N	N	Y
3 *Stump*	Y	Y	N	N	N	N	Y
4 *Rudd*	Y	Y	N	N	N	N	Y
ARKANSAS							
1 Alexander	N	N	Y	N	N	N	Y
2 *Bethune*	Y	N	Y	N	N	N	Y
3 *Hammerschmidt*	Y	Y	N	N	N	N	Y
4 Anthony	N	N	Y	N	N	N	N
CALIFORNIA							
1 *Chappie*	Y	Y	N	N	N	N	Y
2 *Clausen*	Y	Y	Y	N	N	N	Y
3 Matsui	N	?	Y	N	Y	N	Y
4 Fazio	N	N	Y	N	Y	N	Y
5 Burton, J.	?	?	?	?	?	?	?
6 Burton, P.	N	N	Y	Y	Y	Y	N
7 Miller	N	Y	Y	Y	Y	Y	N
8 Dellums	N	N	Y	Y	Y	Y	N
9 Stark	N	N	Y	Y	Y	Y	N
10 Edwards	N	N	Y	Y	Y	Y	N
11 Lantos	N	N	Y	N	N	N	Y
12 *McCloskey*	?	Y	N	Y	N	Y	Y
13 Mineta	N	N	Y	N	?	N	N
14 *Shumway*	Y	Y	N	N	N	N	Y
15 Coelho	N	N	Y	N	N	N	Y
16 Panetta	N	N	Y	N	N	N	Y
17 *Pashayan*	Y	Y	N	N	N	N	Y
18 *Thomas*	Y	Y	N	N	N	N	Y
19 *Lagomarsino*	Y	Y	N	N	N	N	Y
20 *Goldwater*	#	#	?	?	?	?	?
21 *Fiedler*	Y	Y	N	N	N	N	Y
22 *Moorhead*	Y	Y	N	N	N	N	Y
23 Beilenson	N	N	Y	N	Y	N	N
24 Waxman	N	N	Y	N	Y	Y	Y
25 Roybal	N	N	Y	Y	Y	Y	N
26 *Rousselot*	Y	Y	N	N	N	?	Y
27 Dornan	#	#	?	?	?	?	?
28 Dixon	N	N	Y	N	Y	Y	N
29 Hawkins	X	X	?	?	?	?	X
30 Martinez	N	N	Y	Y	Y	Y	N
31 Dymally	N	N	Y	Y	Y	Y	N
32 Anderson	N	N	N	N	N	N	Y
33 *Grisham*	#	#	?	?	?	?	?
34 *Lungren*	Y	Y	N	N	N	N	Y
35 *Dreier*	Y	Y	N	N	N	N	Y
36 Brown	N	N	Y	Y	Y	Y	N
37 *Lewis*	Y	Y	N	N	N	N	Y
38 Patterson	Y	N	Y	N	N	N	Y
39 *Dannemeyer*	Y	Y	N	N	N	N	Y
40 *Badham*	Y	Y	N	N	N	N	Y
41 *Lowery*	Y	Y	N	N	N	N	Y
42 *Hunter*	Y	Y	N	N	N	N	Y
43 *Burgener*	Y	Y	N	N	N	N	Y
COLORADO							
1 Schroeder	N	N	Y	Y	Y	Y	N
2 Wirth	N	N	Y	Y	Y	Y	N
3 Kogovsek	N	N	Y	Y	N	N	Y
4 *Brown*	Y	Y	N	N	N	N	Y
5 *Kramer*	Y	Y	N	N	N	N	Y
CONNECTICUT							
1 Kennelly	N	N	Y	N	N	N	Y
2 Gejdenson	N	N	Y	Y	Y	Y	N
3 *DeNardis*	N	N	N	N	N	N	N
4 *McKinney*	N	Y	N	?	N	N	Y
5 Ratchford	N	N	Y	Y	Y	Y	N
6 Moffett	X	X	?	?	?	?	?
DELAWARE							
AL *Evans*	Y	Y	Y	?	N	N	Y
FLORIDA							
1 Hutto	Y	N	Y	N	N	N	Y
2 Fuqua	Y	N	Y	N	N	N	Y
3 Bennett	Y	Y	N	N	N	N	Y
4 Chappell	?	?	?	?	?	?	?
5 *McCollum*	Y	Y	N	N	N	N	Y
6 *Young*	Y	Y	N	N	N	N	Y
7 Gibbons	Y	Y	N	N	N	N	Y
8 Ireland	Y	Y	N	N	N	N	Y
9 Nelson	Y	N	Y	N	N	N	Y
10 *Bafalis*	?	?	?	?	?	?	?
11 Mica	N	N	Y	N	N	N	Y
12 *Shaw*	Y	Y	N	N	N	N	Y
13 Lehman	N	N	Y	N	N	N	Y
14 Pepper	N	N	Y	N	N	N	Y
15 Fascell	N	N	Y	N	N	N	Y
GEORGIA							
1 Ginn	?	?	?	?	?	?	?
2 Hatcher	N	N	Y	N	N	N	Y
3 Brinkley	N	N	Y	N	N	N	Y
4 Levitas	N	N	Y	N	Y	N	Y
5 Fowler	N	N	Y	N	N	N	Y
6 *Gingrich*	Y	Y	N	N	N	?	Y
7 McDonald	Y	Y	N	N	N	N	Y
8 Evans	N	N	Y	?	?	N	Y
9 Jenkins	?	?	?	?	?	?	Y
10 Barnard	Y	N	?	N	N	N	Y
HAWAII							
1 Heftel	Y	N	Y	N	N	N	Y
2 Akaka	X	X	#	?	?	?	#
IDAHO							
1 *Craig*	Y	Y	N	N	N	N	Y
2 *Hansen*	Y	Y	N	N	N	N	Y
ILLINOIS							
1 Washington	N	N	Y	Y	Y	Y	N
2 Savage	N	N	Y	Y	Y	Y	N
3 Russo	N	N	Y	N	N	N	Y
4 *Derwinski*	Y	Y	N	N	N	N	Y
5 Fary	N	N	Y	N	N	N	Y
6 *Hyde*	Y	Y	N	N	N	N	Y
7 Collins	N	N	Y	Y	Y	Y	N
8 Rostenkowski	N	N	Y	N	N	N	Y
9 Yates	N	N	Y	N	?	?	?
10 *Porter*	Y	?	?	?	N	N	Y
11 Annunzio	N	N	Y	N	N	N	Y
12 *Crane, P.*	Y	Y	N	N	N	N	Y
13 *McClory*	?	?	?	?	?	N	Y
14 *Erlenborn*	Y	Y	N	N	N	N	Y
15 *Corcoran*	Y	Y	N	N	N	N	Y
16 *Martin*	Y	Y	N	N	Y	N	Y
17 *O'Brien*	Y	Y	N	?	N	N	Y
18 *Michel*	Y	Y	N	?	N	N	Y
19 *Railsback*	?	?	?	?	?	Y	N
20 *Findley*	Y	Y	N	N	N	N	Y
21 *Madigan*	#	Y	N	N	N	N	Y
22 *Crane, D.*	Y	Y	N	N	N	N	Y
23 Price	N	N	Y	N	N	N	Y
24 Simon	N	N	Y	N	Y	N	Y
INDIANA							
1 Benjamin	N	N	Y	Y	Y	Y	Y
2 Fithian	N	N	Y	Y	Y	Y	Y
3 *Hiler*	Y	Y	N	?	N	N	Y
4 *Coats*	Y	Y	N	N	N	N	Y
5 *Hillis*	Y	Y	N	?	N	?	N
6 Evans	N	N	Y	N	N	N	Y
7 *Myers*	Y	Y	N	N	N	N	Y
8 *Deckard*	Y	Y	N	Y	N	N	Y
9 Hamilton	N	N	Y	N	N	N	Y
10 Sharp	?	?	?	N	Y	N	Y
11 Jacobs	N	N	Y	N	Y	Y	Y
IOWA							
1 *Leach*	N	N	Y	Y	Y	Y	N
2 *Tauke*	N	Y	Y	Y	Y	Y	N
3 *Evans*	Y	N	Y	Y	Y	N	Y
4 Smith	N	N	N	N	N	N	N
5 Harkin	N	N	Y	Y	Y	Y	N
6 Bedell	N	N	Y	Y	Y	Y	N

ND - Northern Democrats   SD - Southern Democrats

	244	245	246	247	248	249	250
KANSAS							
1 ***Roberts***	Y	N	Y	N	N	N	Y
2 ***Jeffries***	#	Y	N	N	N	?	#
3 ***Winn***	Y	N	Y	N	N	N	Y
4 Glickman	N	N	Y	N	N	N	Y
5 ***Whittaker***	Y	N	Y	?	N	N	Y
KENTUCKY							
1 Hubbard	N	N	Y	N	N	N	Y
2 Natcher	N	N	Y	N	Y	Y	N
3 Mazzoli	N	N	Y	N	Y	Y	N
4 ***Snyder***	Y	Y	Y	N	N	N	Y
5 ***Rogers***	Y	Y	Y	N	N	N	Y
6 ***Hopkins***	Y	Y	N	N	N	N	N
7 Perkins	N	N	Y	N	N	Y	N
LOUISIANA							
1 ***Livingston***	Y	Y	N	N	N	N	Y
2 Boggs	N	N	Y	N	N	N	Y
3 Tauzin	Y	N	Y	N	Y	Y	Y
4 Roemer	Y	N	N	Y	Y	Y	N
5 Huckaby	N	N	Y	N	N	N	Y
6 ***Moore***	Y	Y	N	N	N	N	Y
7 Breaux	Y	N	Y	N	N	N	Y
8 Long	N	N	Y	N	N	N	Y
MAINE							
1 ***Emery***	Y	Y	Y	?	N	N	Y
2 ***Snowe***	N	N	Y	N	N	N	Y
MARYLAND							
1 Dyson	N	N	Y	N	N	N	N
2 Long	N	N	N	Y	N	N	N
3 Mikulski	N	N	Y	N	N	N	Y
4 ***Holt***	Y	Y	N	N	N	N	Y
5 Hoyer	N	N	Y	N	N	N	Y
6 Byron	N	Y	Y	N	N	N	N
7 Mitchell	N	N	Y	Y	Y	Y	N
8 Barnes	N	N	Y	N	N	N	Y
MASSACHUSETTS							
1 ***Conte***	N	Y	N	N	N	N	N
2 Boland	N	N	Y	N	N	N	Y
3 Early	N	N	Y	N	N	N	Y
4 Frank	N	Y	N	N	N	N	Y
5 Shannon	N	N	Y	Y	Y	Y	N
6 Mavroules	N	N	Y	N	N	N	Y
7 Markey	N	N	Y	Y	Y	Y	N
8 O'Neill							
9 Moakley	?	N	Y	N	N	N	Y
10 ***Heckler***	N	N	Y	N	N	N	Y
11 Donnelly	N	N	Y	N	N	N	Y
12 Studds	N	N	Y	Y	Y	Y	N
MICHIGAN							
1 Conyers	X	?	?	?	?	?	X
2 ***Pursell***	?	?	?	?	?	?	?
3 Wolpe	N	N	Y	Y	Y	Y	N
4 ***Siljander***	#	#	?	?	?	?	?
5 ***Sawyer***	Y	Y	Y	?	N	N	Y
6 ***Dunn***	Y	Y	N	N	N	Y	N
7 Kildee	N	N	Y	Y	Y	Y	N
8 Traxler	?	?	?	?	?	?	?
9 ***Vander Jagt***	#	Y	Y	N	N	?	Y
10 Albosta	N	N	Y	Y	Y	Y	N
11 ***Davis***	?	?	?	?	?	?	?
12 Bonior	?	?	?	?	?	?	?
13 Crockett	X	X	?	?	?	?	?
14 Hertel	?	?	?	?	?	?	?
15 Ford	X	X	?	?	?	?	X
16 Dingell	N	N	Y	Y	Y	Y	N
17 Brodhead	?	?	?	?	?	?	?
18 Blanchard	?	?	?	?	?	?	?
19 ***Broomfield***	Y	Y	N	N	N	?	Y
MINNESOTA							
1 ***Erdahl***	N	N	Y	N	N	Y	Y
2 ***Hagedorn***	Y	N	Y	N	N	Y	Y
3 ***Frenzel***	Y	Y	N	?	N	N	Y
4 Vento	N	N	Y	Y	Y	Y	N
5 Sabo	N	N	Y	Y	Y	Y	N
6 ***Weber***	Y	N	Y	?	N	N	Y
7 ***Stangeland***	Y	N	Y	N	N	N	Y
8 Oberstar	N	N	N	Y	Y	Y	N
MISSISSIPPI							
1 Whitten	N	N	Y	N	?	?	?
2 Bowen	N	N	Y	N	N	N	Y
3 Montgomery	Y	N	Y	N	N	N	Y
4 Dowdy	N	N	Y	Y	Y	N	Y
5 ***Lott***	Y	Y	N	?	N	N	Y
MISSOURI							
1 Clay	N	N	Y	Y	Y	?	N
2 Young	?	?	?	?	N	Y	N
3 Gephardt	Y	N	Y	N	N	N	Y

	244	245	246	247	248	249	250
4 Skelton	Y	N	Y	N	N	N	Y
5 Bolling	N	N	Y	?	?	?	?
6 ***Coleman***	Y	Y	Y	N	N	N	Y
7 ***Taylor***	Y	Y	Y	N	N	N	Y
8 ***Bailey***	Y	Y	Y	N	N	N	N
9 Volkmer	Y	N	Y	N	N	Y	N
10 ***Emerson***	Y	N	Y	N	N	N	N
MONTANA							
1 Williams	N	N	Y	Y	Y	Y	N
2 ***Marlenee***	Y	N	Y	N	N	N	N
NEBRASKA							
1 ***Bereuter***	Y	N	Y	?	N	N	N
2 ***Daub***	Y	N	Y	?	Y	Y	N
3 ***Smith***	Y	N	Y	N	Y	Y	N
NEVADA							
AL Santini	X	?	X	?	?	?	#
NEW HAMPSHIRE							
1 D'Amours	N	N	Y	N	Y	N	Y
2 ***Gregg***	Y	Y	N	N	N	N	Y
NEW JERSEY							
1 Florio	N	N	Y	N	N	N	Y
2 Hughes	N	Y	N	N	N	N	N
3 Howard	N	N	Y	N	Y	N	N
4 ***Smith***	N	N	Y	N	N	N	Y
5 ***Fenwick***	N	N	N	N	N	?	Y
6 ***Forsythe***	Y	Y	N	N	N	N	Y
7 ***Roukema***	Y	Y	N	?	Y	N	N
8 Roe	N	N	Y	N	N	N	Y
9 ***Hollenbeck***	N	N	Y	N	N	N	N
10 Rodino	N	N	Y	N	N	N	Y
11 Minish	N	N	Y	N	N	N	Y
12 ***Rinaldo***	N	N	Y	N	N	N	Y
13 ***Courter***	Y	Y	N	N	N	N	Y
14 Guarini	N	N	Y	N	N	N	Y
15 Dwyer	N	N	Y	N	Y	N	Y
NEW MEXICO							
1 ***Lujan***	Y	Y	N	N	N	N	Y
2 ***Skeen***	Y	Y	N	?	N	N	Y
NEW YORK							
1 ***Carney***	?	#	?	?	?	?	?
2 Downey	N	N	Y	Y	Y	Y	N
3 ***Carman***	N	Y	N	N	N	N	Y
4 ***Lent***	N	Y	N	N	N	N	Y
5 ***McGrath***	N	Y	N	N	N	N	Y
6 ***LeBoutillier***	Y	Y	N	N	N	N	Y
7 Addabbo	N	N	Y	N	N	N	N
8 Rosenthal	X	X	?	?	?	?	?
9 Ferraro	N	N	Y	Y	N	Y	Y
10 Biaggi	N	N	Y	N	N	N	Y
11 Scheuer	N	N	Y	N	Y	N	N
12 Chisholm	N	N	Y	N	?	?	N
13 Solarz	N	N	Y	N	Y	Y	N
14 Richmond	N	N	Y	?	?	?	X
15 Zeferetti	N	N	Y	N	N	N	?
16 Schumer	N	N	Y	Y	Y	Y	N
17 ***Molinari***	Y	Y	N	N	N	N	Y
18 ***Green***	N	N	N	N	Y	Y	N
19 Rangel	N	N	Y	N	N	Y	N
20 Weiss	N	N	Y	N	Y	Y	N
21 Garcia	N	N	Y	N	Y	Y	N
22 Bingham	N	N	Y	Y	Y	Y	N
23 Peyser	N	N	?	N	N	N	Y
24 Ottinger	N	N	Y	Y	Y	Y	N
25 ***Fish***	N	N	Y	N	Y	Y	?
26 ***Gilman***	N	N	N	N	N	N	Y
27 McHugh	N	N	Y	Y	Y	N	N
28 Stratton	N	N	Y	N	N	N	Y
29 ***Solomon***	Y	Y	N	N	N	N	Y
30 ***Martin***	Y	Y	N	N	N	N	Y
31 ***Mitchell***	N	N	Y	N	N	N	Y
32 ***Wortley***	Y	Y	N	N	N	N	Y
33 ***Lee***	Y	Y	N	N	N	N	Y
34 ***Horton***	N	N	Y	N	N	N	Y
35 ***Conable***	Y	Y	N	N	N	Y	Y
36 LaFalce	N	N	Y	Y	Y	Y	N
37 Nowak	N	N	Y	N	Y	Y	N
38 ***Kemp***	Y	Y	N	N	N	N	Y
39 Lundine	N	N	Y	Y	Y	Y	N
NORTH CAROLINA							
1 Jones	N	?	?	?	?	?	?
2 Fountain	Y	N	Y	N	N	N	Y
3 Whitley	Y	N	Y	N	N	N	Y
4 Andrews	Y	N	Y	N	N	N	Y
5 Neal	?	?	?	?	?	?	?
6 ***Johnston***	Y	Y	N	N	Y	N	N
7 Rose	?	?	?	?	?	?	?
8 Hefner	Y	N	Y	C	C	C	C

	244	245	246	247	248	249	250
9 ***Martin***	Y	Y	N	?	N	N	Y
10 ***Broyhill***	Y	Y	N	N	N	N	Y
11 ***Hendon***	Y	Y	N	N	Y	N	N
NORTH DAKOTA							
AL Dorgan	N	N	Y	Y	Y	Y	N
OHIO							
1 ***Gradison***	Y	Y	N	N	N	N	Y
2 Luken	N	N	Y	N	Y	Y	N
3 Hall	N	Y	N	N	Y	Y	N
4 ***Oxley***	Y	#	?	?	N	N	Y
5 ***Latta***	Y	Y	N	N	N	N	Y
6 ***McEwen***	N	Y	N	N	N	N	Y
7 ***Brown***	?	?	?	?	?	?	?
8 ***Kindness***	Y	Y	Y	N	N	N	Y
9 ***Weber***	Y	Y	N	N	N	N	Y
10 ***Miller***	Y	Y	N	N	N	N	N
11 ***Stanton***	Y	Y	Y	?	?	?	#
12 Shamansky	N	N	Y	Y	Y	Y	N
13 Pease	N	N	Y	Y	Y	N	N
14 Seiberling	N	N	Y	Y	Y	Y	N
15 ***Wylie***	N	Y	?	?	?	?	?
16 ***Regula***	Y	Y	N	N	N	N	Y
17 ***Ashbrook***	Y	Y	N	N	N	N	Y
18 Applegate	N	N	Y	N	N	N	Y
19 ***Williams***	N	N	Y	N	N	N	N
20 Oakar	N	N	Y	Y	N	Y	Y
21 Stokes	N	N	Y	Y	Y	N	N
22 Eckart	N	N	Y	N	N	N	N
23 Mottl	Y	Y	N	Y	Y	Y	N
OKLAHOMA							
1 Jones	N	N	Y	N	N	Y	N
2 Synar	N	N	Y	Y	Y	Y	N
3 Watkins	N	N	Y	N	N	N	N
4 McCurdy	N	N	Y	N	N	N	N
5 ***Edwards***	Y	Y	Y	N	Y	N	N
6 English	N	N	Y	N	N	N	N
OREGON							
1 AuCoin	?	X	?	?	?	?	X
2 ***Smith***	Y	Y	N	N	N	N	Y
3 Wyden	N	N	Y	N	Y	Y	N
4 Weaver	N	N	Y	N	Y	Y	N
PENNSYLVANIA							
1 Foglietta	N	N	Y	N	N	N	Y
2 Gray	N	N	Y	Y	Y	Y	N
3 Smith	N	N	Y	N	N	N	Y
4 ***Dougherty***	N	N	Y	?	N	N	Y
5 ***Schulze***	Y	Y	Y	N	N	N	Y
6 Yatron	N	N	Y	N	N	N	Y
7 Edgar	N	N	Y	Y	Y	Y	N
8 ***Coyne, J.***	N	Y	N	N	N	N	Y
9 ***Shuster***	Y	Y	N	N	N	N	N
10 ***McDade***	Y	Y	Y	?	N	N	Y
11 ***Nelligan***	Y	Y	Y	N	N	N	Y
12 Murtha	N	N	Y	N	N	N	Y
13 ***Coughlin***	Y	Y	N	N	N	N	Y
14 Coyne, W.	N	N	Y	N	Y	N	Y
15 ***Ritter***	Y	Y	N	?	N	N	Y
16 ***Walker***	Y	Y	N	N	N	N	Y
17 Ertel	N	N	Y	N	N	N	Y
18 Walgren	Y	N	Y	?	N	Y	?
19 ***Goodling***	Y	Y	Y	N	N	N	N
20 Gaydos	N	N	Y	?	N	Y	N
21 Bailey	N	N	Y	N	N	N	Y
22 Murphy	N	N	Y	N	N	N	Y
23 ***Clinger***	Y	N	Y	-	N	N	Y
24 ***Marks***	?	?	?	?	?	?	?
25 ***Atkinson***	N	Y	N	N	N	N	Y
RHODE ISLAND							
1 St Germain	N	N	Y	N	N	N	Y
2 ***Schneider***	N	N	Y	?	Y	Y	N
SOUTH CAROLINA							
1 ***Hartnett***	Y	Y	N	N	N	N	?
2 ***Spence***	Y	Y	Y	N	N	N	Y
3 Derrick	Y	N	Y	N	N	N	Y
4 ***Campbell***	Y	Y	Y	N	N	N	Y
5 Holland	N	N	Y	N	N	N	Y
6 ***Napier***	Y	N	Y	N	N	N	#
SOUTH DAKOTA							
1 Daschle	N	N	Y	Y	Y	Y	N
2 ***Roberts***	Y	N	Y	Y	Y	N	N
TENNESSEE							
1 ***Quillen***	Y	N	Y	N	N	N	Y
2 ***Duncan***	Y	N	Y	N	N	N	Y
3 Bouquard	Y	N	Y	N	N	N	Y
4 Gore	N	N	Y	N	N	N	Y
5 Boner	N	N	Y	N	N	N	N
6 ***Beard***	Y	Y	N	N	N	N	Y

	244	245	246	247	248	249	250
7 Jones	N	N	Y	Y	Y	Y	N
8 Ford	N	N	Y	N	Y	Y	Y
TEXAS							
1 Hall, S.	Y	N	Y	Y	N	Y	Y
2 Wilson	?	?	Y	?	N	N	?
3 ***Collins***	Y	Y	N	N	Y	Y	Y
4 Hall, R.	Y	N	Y	N	N	N	Y
5 Mattox	N	N	Y	N	N	N	Y
6 Gramm	Y	N	Y	N	N	N	Y
7 ***Archer***	Y	Y	N	N	N	N	Y
8 ***Fields***	Y	Y	N	N	N	N	Y
9 Brooks	N	N	Y	N	N	N	Y
10 Pickle	N	N	Y	N	N	N	Y
11 Leath	Y	N	Y	N	N	N	Y
12 Wright	N	N	Y	N	N	N	Y
13 Hightower	N	N	Y	Y	Y	Y	Y
14 Patman	Y	N	Y	N	N	N	Y
15 de la Garza	N	N	Y	N	N	N	Y
16 White	N	N	Y	N	N	N	Y
17 Stenholm	Y	N	Y	N	N	N	Y
18 Leland	N	N	Y	Y	Y	Y	N
19 Hance	N	N	Y	N	N	N	Y
20 Gonzalez	N	N	Y	Y	Y	P	N
21 ***Loeffler***	Y	Y	Y	N	N	N	Y
22 ***Paul***	Y	Y	N	Y	N	Y	N
23 Kazen	N	N	Y	N	N	N	Y
24 Frost	N	N	Y	N	Y	N	N
UTAH							
1 ***Hansen***	Y	Y	N	N	N	N	Y
2 ***Marriott***	N	Y	N	N	N	N	Y
VERMONT							
AL ***Jeffords***	N	N	Y	N	N	N	Y
VIRGINIA							
1 ***Trible***	Y	Y	Y	N	N	?	?
2 ***Whitehurst***	Y	Y	Y	N	N	N	Y
3 ***Bliley***	Y	Y	N	N	N	N	Y
4 ***Daniel, R.***	Y	Y	Y	N	N	N	Y
5 Daniel, D.	Y	Y	Y	N	N	N	Y
6 ***Butler***	Y	?	?	?	N	N	N
7 ***Robinson***	Y	Y	Y	N	N	N	Y
8 ***Parris***	Y	Y	N	N	Y	N	N
9 ***Wampler***	Y	N	Y	N	N	N	Y
10 ***Wolf***	#	#	?	?	?	?	?
WASHINGTON							
1 ***Pritchard***	Y	N	Y	Y	Y	Y	Y
2 Swift	N	N	Y	Y	Y	Y	N
3 Bonker	?	?	?	?	?	?	?
4 ***Morrison***	Y	Y	Y	N	N	Y	Y
5 Foley	N	N	Y	Y	Y	Y	?
6 Dicks	N	?	?	N	Y	Y	N
7 Lowry	N	N	Y	Y	Y	Y	N
WEST VIRGINIA							
1 Mollohan	N	N	Y	N	N	N	Y
2 ***Benedict***	N	Y	N	N	N	N	Y
3 ***Staton***	Y	Y	N	N	N	N	Y
4 Rahall	N	N	Y	Y	C	C	C
WISCONSIN							
1 Aspin	N	N	Y	Y	N	N	Y
2 Kastenmeier	N	N	Y	Y	Y	Y	N
3 ***Gunderson***	Y	Y	N	N	N	N	Y
4 Zablocki	N	N	Y	N	N	N	Y
5 Reuss	N	N	Y	Y	Y	Y	N
6 ***Petri***	Y	N	N	Y	N	N	Y
7 Obey	N	N	N	Y	N	Y	N
8 ***Roth***	Y	N	Y	N	N	N	Y
9 ***Sensenbrenner***	Y	N	Y	N	N	N	Y
WYOMING							
AL ***Cheney***	Y	Y	N	N	N	N	Y

Southern states - Ala., Ark., Fla., Ga., Ky., La., Miss., N.C., Okla., S.C., Tenn., Texas, Va.

251. Procedural Motion. Miller, D-Calif., motion to approve the House *Journal* of Tuesday, Aug. 10. Motion agreed to 337-26: R 149-12; D 188-14 (ND 122-11, SD 66-3), Aug. 11, 1982.

252. HR 5203. Federal Insecticide, Fungicide and Rodenticide Act. Harkin, D-Iowa, amendment to eliminate a section setting deadlines for state pesticide regulatory decisions, and permitting the administrator of the Environmental Protection Agency to overrule certain state requests for pesticide data from manufacturers. Adopted 250-154: R 72-107; D 178-47 (ND 135-16, SD 43-31), Aug. 11, 1982.

253. HR 5203. Federal Insecticide, Fungicide and Rodenticide Act. Passage of the bill to amend federal pesticide law and to authorize funds for pesticide programs for fiscal years 1983 and 1984. Passed 352-56: R 135-46; D 217-10 (ND 147-4, SD 70-6), Aug. 11, 1982. A "nay" was a vote supporting the president's position.

254. HR 6214. Military Construction Authorizations, Fiscal 1983. Eckart, D-Ohio, amendment to direct the secretary of defense to withhold the fiscal 1983 U.S. contribution to the NATO Infrastructure (common construction account) if he determined that any three NATO member nations failed in fiscal 1983 to meet their pledge to increase military spending by 3 percent over fiscal 1982. Rejected 151-245: R 64-114; D 87-131 (ND 75-71, SD 12-60), Aug. 11, 1982. A "nay" was a vote supporting the president's position.

255. HR 6214. Military Construction Authorizations, Fiscal 1983. Harkin, D-Iowa, amendment to prohibit obligation or expenditure of funds authorized by the bill to improve, construct or expand any temporary or permanent airfield in Honduras. Rejected 109-280: R 11-163; D 98-117 (ND 93-51, SD 5-66), Aug. 11, 1982. A "nay" was a vote supporting the president's position.

256. HR 6214. Military Construction Authorizations, Fiscal 1983. Passage of the bill to authorize $7,515,167,000 for military construction programs in fiscal year 1983. Passed 332-57: R 164-5; D 168-52 (ND 95-51, SD 73-1), Aug. 11, 1982.

257. Procedural Motion. Miller, D-Calif., motion to approve the House *Journal* of Wednesday, Aug. 11. Motion agreed to 344-27: R 153-16; D 191-11 (ND 123-10, SD 68-1), Aug. 12, 1982.

258. HR 6542. Wilderness Protection Act. Young, R-Alaska, amendment to permit surface use of explosives for seismic exploration for minerals in designated wilderness areas. Rejected 115-281: R 90-85; D 25-196 (ND 1-146, SD 24-50), Aug. 12, 1982.

KEY

Y Voted for (yea).
Paired for.
+ Announced for.
N Voted against (nay).
X Paired against.
- Announced against.
P Voted "present".
C Voted "present" to avoid possible conflict of interest.
? Did not vote or otherwise make a position known.

Democrats *Republicans*

	251	252	253	254	255	256	257	258
ALABAMA								
1 Edwards	Y	N	Y	N	N	Y	Y	Y
2 Dickinson	Y	N	Y	N	N	Y	N	Y
3 Nichols	Y	N	Y	N	N	Y	?	?
4 Bevill	Y	Y	Y	N	N	Y	Y	Y
5 Flippo	?	N	Y	N	N	Y	Y	N
6 *Smith*	Y	N	Y	N	?	?	Y	Y
7 Shelby	Y	N	Y	N	N	Y	Y	Y
ALASKA								
AL *Young*	?	Y	Y	N	N	Y	N	Y
ARIZONA								
1 *Rhodes*	Y	N	Y	?	?	?	Y	Y
2 Udall	Y	Y	Y	Y	Y	Y	Y	N
3 *Stump*	Y	N	N	N	N	N	Y	Y
4 *Rudd*	Y	N	Y	N	N	Y	Y	Y
ARKANSAS								
1 Alexander	Y	Y	Y	Y	N	Y	N	Y
2 *Bethune*	Y	Y	N	N	N	Y	?	N
3 *Hammerschmidt*	?	Y	Y	N	N	Y	Y	N
4 Anthony	Y	Y	Y	N	?	Y	?	N
CALIFORNIA								
1 *Chappie*	Y	N	Y	?	?	Y	Y	Y
2 *Clausen*	Y	Y	Y	N	N	Y	Y	N
3 Matsui	Y	Y	Y	N	Y	Y	?	N
4 Fazio	Y	Y	Y	N	Y	Y	Y	N
5 Burton, J.	?	?	?	?	?	?	?	?
6 Burton, P.	Y	Y	Y	N	Y	Y	Y	N
7 Miller	Y	Y	N	Y	N	Y	N	N
8 Dellums	Y	Y	Y	Y	Y	N	?	N
9 Stark	Y	Y	Y	N	Y	N	Y	N
10 Edwards	Y	Y	Y	N	Y	Y	N	N
11 Lantos	Y	Y	Y	N	Y	Y	Y	N
12 *McCloskey*	?	Y	Y	N	N	Y	?	?
13 Mineta	Y	Y	Y	Y	Y	Y	N	N
14 *Shumway*	Y	N	N	N	N	Y	Y	Y
15 Coelho	Y	N	Y	N	Y	Y	Y	N
16 Panetta	Y	Y	Y	Y	N	Y	Y	N
17 *Pashayan*	Y	N	Y	N	N	Y	Y	Y
18 Thomas	Y	N	Y	N	N	Y	Y	Y
19 *Lagomarsino*	Y	N	Y	N	N	Y	Y	Y
20 *Goldwater*	?	?	?	?	?	?	?	?
21 *Fiedler*	Y	N	Y	N	N	Y	Y	Y
22 *Moorhead*	Y	N	Y	N	X	?	Y	Y
23 Beilenson	Y	Y	Y	N	Y	N	Y	N
24 Waxman	Y	Y	Y	N	Y	N	Y	N
25 Roybal	Y	Y	Y	Y	Y	N	N	N
26 *Rousselot*	Y	N	Y	N	N	Y	?	Y
27 *Dornan*	?	?	?	?	?	?	?	?
28 Dixon	?	Y	Y	Y	Y	Y	?	?
29 Hawkins	Y	Y	Y	N	Y	Y	Y	N
30 Martinez	Y	Y	Y	N	Y	Y	Y	N
31 Dymally	Y	Y	Y	N	Y	Y	?	N
32 Anderson	Y	Y	Y	N	Y	Y	Y	N
33 *Grisham*	?	N	N	N	N	Y	Y	Y
34 *Lungren*	Y	N	N	N	N	N	Y	Y
35 *Dreier*	Y	N	N	N	N	Y	N	Y
36 Brown	Y	Y	Y	?	?	?	?	?
37 *Lewis*	?	N	N	N	N	Y	Y	Y
38 Patterson	Y	Y	Y	N	Y	Y	Y	N
39 *Dannemeyer*	Y	N	N	N	N	Y	Y	Y
40 *Badham*	Y	N	N	N	N	Y	Y	Y
41 *Lowery*	Y	N	Y	N	N	Y	Y	N
42 *Hunter*	Y	N	N	N	N	Y	Y	Y
43 *Burgener*	Y	N	?	?	?	?	?	?
COLORADO								
1 Schroeder	N	Y	Y	Y	Y	N	N	N
2 Wirth	+	Y	?	N	Y	N	Y	N
3 Kogovsek	Y	Y	Y	N	Y	Y	Y	N
4 *Brown*	Y	N	N	Y	N	Y	N	Y

	251	252	253	254	255	256	257	258
5 *Kramer*	Y	Y	N	N	N	Y	Y	Y
CONNECTICUT								
1 Kennelly	Y	Y	Y	N	Y	Y	Y	N
2 Gejdenson	N	Y	Y	N	Y	Y	N	N
3 *DeNardis*	Y	Y	Y	Y	N	Y	Y	N
4 *McKinney*	Y	N	Y	N	N	Y	?	N
5 Ratchford	Y	Y	Y	Y	Y	Y	Y	N
6 Moffett	?	?	?	?	#	X	?	?
DELAWARE								
AL *Evans*	Y	?	Y	N	N	Y	Y	N
FLORIDA								
1 Hutto	?	?	Y	N	N	Y	?	N
2 Fuqua	Y	Y	Y	N	N	Y	Y	N
3 Bennett	Y	Y	Y	N	Y	Y	Y	N
4 Chappell	Y	Y	Y	N	N	Y	Y	N
5 *McCollum*	Y	N	Y	N	N	Y	Y	N
6 *Young*	Y	Y	Y	N	N	Y	Y	N
7 Gibbons	Y	N	Y	N	N	Y	Y	?
8 Ireland	?	Y	?	?	?	Y	?	?
9 Nelson	Y	Y	Y	N	N	Y	Y	N
10 *Bafalis*	?	?	?	?	?	?	?	?
11 Mica	Y	N	Y	N	N	Y	Y	N
12 *Shaw*	Y	N	Y	N	N	Y	Y	N
13 Lehman	Y	Y	Y	N	Y	Y	Y	N
14 Pepper	Y	Y	Y	N	N	Y	Y	N
15 Fascell	Y	Y	Y	N	N	Y	Y	N
GEORGIA								
1 Ginn	?	?	?	?	?	?	?	?
2 Hatcher	Y	Y	Y	N	N	Y	Y	N
3 Brinkley	Y	N	Y	N	N	Y	Y	N
4 Levitas	Y	Y	Y	N	N	Y	Y	N
5 Fowler	Y	Y	Y	N	N	Y	Y	N
6 *Gingrich*	Y	Y	Y	N	?	?	Y	N
7 McDonald	Y	N	N	N	N	Y	Y	Y
8 Evans	Y	Y	Y	N	N	Y	Y	Y
9 Jenkins	?	Y	Y	Y	N	Y	Y	N
10 Barnard	Y	Y	Y	N	N	Y	Y	N
HAWAII								
1 Heftel	?	Y	Y	N	N	Y	?	N
2 Akaka	?	Y	Y	N	N	Y	Y	N
IDAHO								
1 *Craig*	Y	N	N	Y	N	Y	Y	Y
2 *Hansen*	Y	N	N	N	N	Y	Y	Y
ILLINOIS								
1 Washington	?	Y	Y	Y	Y	N	N	N
2 Savage	?	Y	Y	Y	?	?	?	?
3 Russo	Y	Y	Y	N	N	Y	N	N
4 *Derwinski*	N	N	Y	N	N	Y	N	Y
5 Fary	Y	Y	Y	N	N	Y	Y	N
6 *Hyde*	Y	N	Y	N	N	Y	Y	N
7 Collins	Y	Y	Y	N	Y	Y	Y	N
8 Rostenkowski	Y	Y	Y	N	N	Y	Y	N
9 Yates	?	Y	?	?	?	Y	Y	N
10 *Porter*	Y	Y	Y	N	N	Y	Y	N
11 Annunzio	Y	#	#	X	N	Y	Y	N
12 *Crane, P.*	Y	N	N	N	N	Y	Y	Y
13 *McClory*	Y	N	Y	N	N	Y	Y	?
14 *Erlenborn*	Y	N	N	N	Y	Y	Y	N
15 *Corcoran*	Y	N	Y	N	N	Y	Y	N
16 *Martin*	Y	Y	Y	N	N	Y	Y	N
17 *O'Brien*	Y	?	Y	N	Y	N	Y	N
18 *Michel*	Y	N	N	N	N	#	Y	?
19 *Railsback*	Y	N	N	N	N	Y	Y	N
20 *Findley*	Y	N	N	Y	Y	Y	N	N
21 *Madigan*	Y	N	Y	N	N	Y	Y	N
22 *Crane, D.*	Y	N	N	N	N	Y	Y	Y
23 Price	Y	Y	Y	?	?	?	Y	N
24 Simon	Y	Y	Y	N	Y	Y	Y	N
INDIANA								
1 Benjamin	Y	N	Y	N	N	Y	Y	N
2 Fithian	Y	N	Y	?	?	?	?	?
3 *Hiler*	N	Y	N	Y	N	Y	Y	Y
4 *Coats*	N	Y	Y	N	Y	N	Y	Y
5 *Hillis*	Y	N	Y	N	N	Y	Y	N
6 Evans	Y	N	Y	Y	?	?	Y	N
7 *Myers*	Y	N	N	N	N	Y	Y	Y
8 *Deckard*	Y	Y	Y	Y	N	Y	Y	N
9 Hamilton	Y	Y	Y	Y	N	Y	Y	N
10 Sharp	N	Y	Y	Y	Y	Y	Y	N
11 Jacobs	N	Y	Y	Y	Y	Y	Y	N
IOWA								
1 *Leach*	Y	Y	Y	N	Y	Y	Y	N
2 *Tauke*	Y	Y	Y	N	N	Y	Y	N
3 *Evans*	N	N	Y	N	Y	N	N	N
4 Smith	Y	Y	Y	N	Y	Y	Y	N
5 Harkin	N	Y	Y	N	Y	N	?	N
6 Bedell	Y	Y	Y	N	Y	N	Y	N

ND - Northern Democrats   SD - Southern Democrats

Corresponding to Congressional Record Votes 263, 264, 265, 266, 267, 268, 269, 270

	251	252	253	254	255	256	257	258
KANSAS								
1 ***Roberts***	Y	N	Y	Y	N	Y	N	Y
2 ***Jeffries***	?	N	N	N	?	?	?	Y
3 ***Winn***	Y	N	Y	N	N	Y	Y	Y
4 Glickman	Y	Y	Y	N	N	Y	Y	N
5 ***Whittaker***	Y	N	Y	Y	N	Y	Y	Y
KENTUCKY								
1 Hubbard	Y	Y	Y	N	N	Y	Y	N
2 Natcher	Y	Y	Y	N	N	Y	Y	N
3 Mazzoli	Y	Y	Y	N	N	Y	Y	N
4 ***Snyder***	Y	Y	Y	Y	Y	Y	Y	N
5 ***Rogers***	Y	N	Y	N	N	Y	Y	N
6 ***Hopkins***	Y	N	Y	N	N	Y	Y	N
7 Perkins	Y	Y	Y	N	N	Y	Y	N
LOUISIANA								
1 ***Livingston***	Y	Y	Y	N	N	Y	Y	Y
2 Boggs	Y	Y	Y	N	?	Y	?	N
3 Tauzin	Y	N	Y	Y	N	Y	Y	Y
4 Roemer	N	Y	Y	Y	N	Y	N	N
5 Huckaby	Y	Y	Y	?	N	Y	Y	Y
6 ***Moore***	Y	Y	Y	Y	N	Y	Y	Y
7 Breaux	Y	N	Y	?	?	#	Y	Y
8 Long	Y	N	Y	N	N	Y	Y	N
MAINE								
1 ***Emery***	Y	Y	Y	Y	N	Y	Y	N
2 ***Snowe***	Y	Y	Y	Y	N	Y	Y	N
MARYLAND								
1 Dyson	Y	Y	Y	N	N	Y	Y	N
2 Long	Y	Y	Y	N	Y	Y	Y	N
3 Mikulski	?	Y	Y	Y	Y	N	Y	N
4 ***Holt***	Y	N	N	N	N	Y	N	Y
5 Hoyer	Y	Y	Y	N	N	Y	Y	N
6 Byron	Y	N	Y	N	N	Y	?	N
7 Mitchell	N	Y	Y	Y	Y	N	N	N
8 Barnes	N	Y	Y	Y	Y	Y	N	N
MASSACHUSETTS								
1 ***Conte***	Y	Y	Y	N	Y	Y	Y	N
2 Boland	Y	Y	Y	N	N	Y	Y	N
3 Early	Y	Y	Y	Y	Y	N	?	N
4 Frank	Y	Y	Y	N	Y	N	Y	N
5 Shannon	Y	Y	Y	N	Y	N	Y	N
6 Mavroules	Y	Y	Y	N	Y	Y	Y	N
7 Markey	Y	Y	Y	Y	Y	N	Y	N
8 O'Neill								
9 Moakley	Y	Y	Y	N	N	Y	Y	N
10 ***Heckler***	Y	Y	Y	N	Y	Y	Y	?
11 Donnelly	?	Y	Y	Y	N	Y	Y	N
12 Studds	Y	Y	Y	N	Y	N	Y	N
MICHIGAN								
1 Conyers	?	X	X	?	?	?	?	?
2 ***Pursell***	?	Y	Y	Y	N	?	Y	N
3 Wolpe	Y	Y	Y	Y	Y	Y	Y	N
4 ***Siljander***	?	?	?	?	?	?	?	?
5 ***Sawyer***	Y	Y	Y	Y	N	Y	Y	N
6 ***Dunn***	Y	N	Y	Y	N	Y	Y	N
7 Kildee	Y	Y	Y	Y	Y	N	Y	N
8 Traxler	?	Y	Y	Y	Y	Y	Y	N
9 ***Vander Jagt***	Y	N	Y	Y	N	Y	Y	N
10 Albosta	Y	N	Y	Y	Y	Y	Y	N
11 ***Davis***	?	Y	Y	N	N	Y	?	N
12 Bonior	?	Y	Y	?	Y	N	Y	N
13 Crockett	?	?	?	?	?	?	?	?
14 Hertel	?	Y	Y	Y	Y	N	Y	N
15 Ford	?	Y	Y	Y	?	Y	Y	N
16 Dingell	Y	Y	Y	N	N	Y	Y	?
17 Brodhead	?	Y	Y	Y	Y	N	Y	N
18 Blanchard	?	?	?	?	?	?	?	?
19 ***Broomfield***	Y	N	Y	N	N	Y	Y	?
MINNESOTA								
1 ***Erdahl***	Y	N	Y	Y	N	Y	Y	N
2 ***Hagedorn***	Y	N	Y	N	N	Y	Y	Y
3 ***Frenzel***	Y	N	Y	N	N	Y	Y	N
4 Vento	Y	Y	Y	Y	Y	N	Y	N
5 Sabo	N	Y	Y	N	Y	N	N	N
6 ***Weber***	Y	Y	Y	Y	N	Y	Y	N
7 ***Stangeland***	Y	N	?	?	X	?	Y	Y
8 Oberstar	P	Y	Y	Y	Y	N	P	N
MISSISSIPPI								
1 Whitten	Y	Y	Y	N	N	Y	Y	Y
2 Bowen	Y	N	Y	N	N	Y	Y	Y
3 Montgomery	Y	Y	Y	N	N	Y	Y	Y
4 Dowdy	Y	Y	Y	N	N	Y	Y	N
5 ***Lott***	Y	N	N	Y	N	Y	Y	Y
MISSOURI								
1 Clay	N	Y	Y	Y	Y	N	N	N
2 Young	Y	N	Y	N	N	Y	Y	N
3 Gephardt	Y	N	Y	Y	N	Y	Y	N

	251	252	253	254	255	256	257	258
4 Skelton	Y	N	Y	N	N	Y	Y	N
5 Bolling	?	Y	Y	?	?	?	?	?
6 ***Coleman***	Y	N	Y	Y	N	?	Y	N
7 ***Taylor***	Y	Y	Y	N	N	Y	Y	Y
8 ***Bailey***	Y	N	Y	Y	N	Y	Y	Y
9 Volkmer	Y	N	Y	N	N	Y	Y	N
10 ***Emerson***	?	N	Y	N	N	Y	N	Y
MONTANA								
1 Williams	Y	Y	Y	N	Y	Y	Y	N
2 ***Marlenee***	?	?	?	?	N	Y	Y	Y
NEBRASKA								
1 ***Bereuter***	Y	Y	Y	N	N	Y	Y	Y
2 ***Daub***	Y	Y	Y	N	N	Y	Y	N
3 ***Smith***	Y	Y	Y	N	N	Y	Y	Y
NEVADA								
AL Santini	?	Y	Y	Y	N	Y	?	N
NEW HAMPSHIRE								
1 D'Amours	Y	Y	Y	Y	N	Y	Y	N
2 ***Gregg***	?	Y	N	Y	N	Y	Y	N
NEW JERSEY								
1 Florio	Y	Y	Y	Y	Y	N	Y	N
2 Hughes	Y	Y	Y	N	N	N	Y	N
3 Howard	Y	Y	Y	Y	Y	Y	Y	N
4 ***Smith***	Y	Y	Y	Y	N	Y	Y	N
5 ***Fenwick***	Y	Y	Y	N	N	N	Y	N
6 ***Forsythe***	N	N	Y	Y	Y	N	N	Y
7 ***Roukema***	Y	Y	Y	N	N	Y	Y	N
8 Roe	Y	Y	Y	Y	N	Y	Y	N
9 ***Hollenbeck***	Y	Y	Y	Y	N	Y	?	N
10 Rodino	Y	Y	Y	Y	Y	Y	Y	N
11 Minish	Y	Y	Y	Y	N	Y	Y	N
12 ***Rinaldo***	Y	Y	Y	Y	N	Y	?	N
13 ***Courter***	?	Y	Y	N	N	Y	Y	N
14 Guarini	Y	Y	Y	N	Y	Y	Y	N
15 Dwyer	Y	Y	Y	Y	N	Y	Y	N
NEW MEXICO								
1 ***Lujan***	Y	N	N	N	N	Y	Y	Y
2 ***Skeen***	Y	N	N	N	N	Y	Y	Y
NEW YORK								
1 ***Carney***	?	Y	Y	N	N	Y	Y	N
2 Downey	Y	Y	N	N	Y	N	Y	N
3 ***Carman***	Y	Y	Y	N	N	Y	Y	Y
4 ***Lent***	Y	Y	Y	N	N	Y	Y	N
5 ***McGrath***	Y	Y	Y	Y	N	Y	Y	N
6 ***LeBoutillier***	N	Y	Y	Y	N	Y	N	Y
7 Addabbo	Y	Y	Y	?	N	Y	Y	N
8 Rosenthal	?	?	?	?	#	X	?	?
9 Ferraro	Y	Y	Y	Y	N	Y	+	-
10 Biaggi	Y	?	Y	Y	N	Y	Y	N
11 Scheuer	Y	Y	Y	N	Y	Y	Y	N
12 Chisholm	?	?	Y	Y	Y	N	?	N
13 Solarz	Y	Y	Y	N	Y	Y	Y	N
14 Richmond	?	?	?	?	?	X	?	?
15 Zeferetti	Y	Y	Y	Y	N	Y	Y	N
16 Schumer	Y	Y	Y	N	Y	Y	Y	N
17 ***Molinari***	Y	Y	Y	Y	N	Y	Y	Y
18 ***Green***	Y	Y	Y	N	N	Y	Y	N
19 Rangel	Y	Y	Y	Y	Y	N	Y	N
20 Weiss	Y	Y	Y	N	Y	N	Y	N
21 Garcia	Y	Y	Y	N	Y	N	Y	N
22 Bingham	Y	Y	Y	N	Y	N	Y	N
23 Peyser	Y	Y	Y	Y	Y	Y	Y	N
24 Ottinger	P	Y	Y	Y	Y	N	?	N
25 ***Fish***	?	?	?	?	?	?	Y	N
26 ***Gilman***	Y	Y	Y	N	N	Y	Y	N
27 McHugh	Y	Y	Y	N	Y	Y	Y	N
28 Stratton	Y	N	Y	N	N	Y	Y	N
29 ***Solomon***	N	N	Y	N	N	Y	Y	Y
30 ***Martin***	Y	Y	Y	N	N	Y	Y	Y
31 ***Mitchell***	Y	Y	Y	N	N	Y	Y	N
32 ***Wortley***	Y	N	Y	N	N	Y	Y	N
33 ***Lee***	Y	N	Y	N	N	Y	Y	N
34 ***Horton***	Y	?	Y	N	N	Y	Y	N
35 ***Conable***	Y	N	Y	N	N	Y	Y	N
36 LaFalce	Y	Y	Y	N	Y	N	Y	N
37 Nowak	Y	Y	Y	Y	Y	N	Y	N
38 ***Kemp***	Y	Y	Y	N	N	Y	Y	Y
39 Lundine	Y	Y	Y	Y	?	N	Y	N
NORTH CAROLINA								
1 Jones	?	?	?	?	?	#	?	?
2 Fountain	?	Y	Y	N	N	Y	?	Y
3 Whitley	Y	N	Y	N	N	Y	Y	N
4 Andrews	Y	Y	Y	N	N	?	Y	N
5 Neal	Y	Y	Y	N	N	Y	Y	N
6 ***Johnston***	N	N	N	N	N	Y	N	Y
7 Rose	N	Y	Y	N	N	Y	Y	N
8 Hefner	Y	N	Y	N	N	Y	Y	N

	251	252	253	254	255	256	257	258
9 ***Martin***	Y	N	Y	N	N	Y	Y	Y
10 ***Broyhill***	Y	N	Y	N	N	Y	Y	Y
11 ***Hendon***	Y	N	N	N	N	Y	Y	N
NORTH DAKOTA								
AL Dorgan	Y	Y	Y	Y	Y	Y	N	N
OHIO								
1 ***Gradison***	Y	Y	Y	N	N	Y	Y	N
2 Luken	N	N	Y	Y	Y	Y	N	N
3 Hall	Y	Y	Y	Y	Y	Y	Y	N
4 ***Oxley***	Y	Y	N	N	N	Y	Y	Y
5 ***Latta***	Y	Y	N	N	N	Y	Y	?
6 ***McEwen***	Y	Y	N	Y	N	Y	Y	N
7 ***Brown***	?	?	?	?	?	?	?	?
8 ***Kindness***	Y	N	N	Y	N	Y	Y	Y
9 ***Weber***	Y	Y	N	N	N	Y	Y	Y
10 ***Miller***	N	Y	Y	Y	N	Y	?	?
11 ***Stanton***	Y	Y	Y	?	?	?	?	Y
12 Shamansky	Y	Y	Y	N	Y	Y	Y	N
13 Pease	Y	Y	Y	Y	Y	Y	Y	N
14 Seiberling	Y	Y	Y	N	Y	N	Y	N
15 ***Wylie***	Y	Y	Y	Y	N	Y	Y	?
16 ***Regula***	Y	Y	Y	Y	N	Y	Y	N
17 ***Ashbrook***	Y	N	N	N	N	Y	Y	Y
18 Applegate	?	Y	Y	Y	N	Y	?	N
19 ***Williams***	Y	Y	Y	Y	N	Y	Y	Y
20 Oakar	Y	Y	Y	Y	Y	Y	Y	N
21 Stokes	Y	Y	?	#	?	X	?	?
22 Eckart	Y	Y	Y	Y	Y	N	Y	N
23 Mottl	Y	Y	N	Y	N	Y	Y	N
OKLAHOMA								
1 Jones	Y	N	Y	Y	N	Y	Y	N
2 Synar	Y	Y	Y	Y	N	Y	Y	N
3 Watkins	Y	N	Y	N	N	Y	Y	Y
4 McCurdy	Y	N	Y	N	N	Y	Y	N
5 ***Edwards***	Y	N	Y	N	N	Y	?	Y
6 English	Y	N	Y	N	N	Y	Y	Y
OREGON								
1 AuCoin	?	?	?	Y	Y	Y	Y	N
2 ***Smith***	Y	N	N	Y	N	Y	Y	Y
3 Wyden	Y	Y	Y	Y	Y	N	Y	N
4 Weaver	Y	Y	Y	?	?	?	Y	N
PENNSYLVANIA								
1 Foglietta	Y	Y	Y	N	Y	N	Y	N
2 Gray	Y	Y	Y	Y	Y	N	Y	N
3 Smith	Y	Y	Y	N	N	Y	?	N
4 ***Dougherty***	Y	N	Y	N	N	Y	Y	N
5 ***Schulze***	Y	N	Y	Y	N	Y	Y	Y
6 Yatron	Y	Y	Y	Y	N	Y	Y	N
7 Edgar	Y	Y	Y	N	Y	N	Y	N
8 ***Coyne, J.***	?	N	Y	Y	N	Y	Y	N
9 ***Shuster***	Y	N	N	Y	N	Y	Y	Y
10 ***McDade***	Y	Y	Y	N	N	#	?	N
11 ***Nelligan***	Y	Y	Y	N	N	Y	Y	Y
12 Murtha	?	N	Y	N	N	Y	Y	N
13 ***Coughlin***	N	Y	Y	Y	N	Y	N	N
14 Coyne, W.	Y	Y	Y	N	N	Y	Y	N
15 ***Ritter***	Y	N	N	Y	N	Y	Y	Y
16 ***Walker***	N	N	Y	Y	N	Y	N	Y
17 Ertel	?	?	?	?	?	?	?	?
18 Walgren	Y	Y	Y	N	Y	N	Y	N
19 ***Goodling***	N	N	N	Y	N	Y	N	N
20 Gaydos	Y	N	Y	Y	N	Y	Y	N
21 Bailey	Y	Y	Y	N	N	Y	Y	N
22 Murphy	N	Y	Y	N	Y	Y	Y	N
23 ***Clinger***	Y	Y	Y	Y	N	Y	Y	N
24 ***Marks***	?	?	Y	Y	Y	Y	?	N
25 ***Atkinson***	Y	Y	N	N	N	Y	Y	N
RHODE ISLAND								
1 St Germain	Y	Y	Y	Y	N	Y	Y	N
2 ***Schneider***	Y	Y	Y	Y	Y	Y	Y	N
SOUTH CAROLINA								
1 ***Hartnett***	?	N	Y	N	N	Y	Y	Y
2 ***Spence***	Y	N	Y	N	N	Y	Y	Y
3 Derrick	Y	Y	Y	Y	N	Y	Y	N
4 ***Campbell***	?	N	Y	N	N	Y	Y	Y
5 Holland	Y	N	Y	?	?	?	Y	N
6 ***Napier***	?	N	Y	N	N	Y	Y	Y
SOUTH DAKOTA								
1 Daschle	Y	Y	Y	Y	Y	Y	Y	N
2 ***Roberts***	Y	N	Y	N	N	Y	Y	Y
TENNESSEE								
1 ***Quillen***	Y	N	Y	N	N	Y	Y	?
2 ***Duncan***	Y	N	Y	N	N	?	Y	N
3 Bouquard	Y	N	Y	N	N	Y	Y	Y
4 Gore	Y	Y	Y	N	N	Y	Y	N
5 Boner	Y	Y	Y	N	N	Y	Y	N
6 ***Beard***	Y	N	N	N	N	Y	Y	N

	251	252	253	254	255	256	257	258
7 Jones	Y	Y	Y	N	N	Y	Y	N
8 Ford	?	Y	Y	Y	Y	Y	Y	N
TEXAS								
1 Hall, S.	Y	N	Y	N	N	Y	Y	Y
2 Wilson	?	?	Y	?	N	Y	Y	Y
3 ***Collins***	Y	N	?	?	?	?	?	?
4 Hall, R.	Y	N	N	Y	N	Y	Y	Y
5 Mattox	N	Y	Y	Y	Y	Y	Y	N
6 Gramm	Y	N	N	N	N	Y	Y	Y
7 ***Archer***	Y	N	N	Y	N	Y	Y	Y
8 ***Fields***	?	N	N	Y	N	Y	N	Y
9 Brooks	?	Y	Y	N	N	Y	Y	N
10 Pickle	Y	Y	Y	N	N	Y	Y	Y
11 Leath	Y	N	N	N	N	Y	?	Y
12 Wright	Y	N	Y	N	N	Y	Y	N
13 Hightower	Y	N	Y	N	N	Y	Y	Y
14 Patman	Y	N	Y	N	N	Y	Y	Y
15 de la Garza	Y	N	Y	N	N	Y	Y	N
16 White	Y	N	Y	N	N	Y	Y	N
17 Stenholm	Y	N	N	Y	N	Y	Y	Y
18 Leland	Y	Y	Y	N	Y	N	Y	N
19 Hance	Y	Y	Y	Y	N	Y	Y	N
20 Gonzalez	Y	Y	Y	N	P	Y	Y	N
21 ***Loeffler***	?	N	N	N	N	Y	Y	Y
22 ***Paul***	Y	N	N	Y	Y	N	Y	Y
23 Kazen	Y	N	Y	N	N	Y	Y	Y
24 Frost	Y	?	Y	N	N	Y	Y	N
UTAH								
1 ***Hansen***	Y	N	N	Y	N	Y	Y	Y
2 ***Marriott***	Y	Y	Y	N	N	Y	Y	Y
VERMONT								
AL ***Jeffords***	Y	Y	Y	Y	Y	N	Y	N
VIRGINIA								
1 ***Trible***	Y	N	Y	N	N	Y	Y	N
2 ***Whitehurst***	Y	N	Y	N	N	Y	Y	Y
3 ***Bliley***	Y	N	Y	N	N	Y	Y	Y
4 ***Daniel, R.***	Y	N	Y	N	N	Y	Y	Y
5 Daniel, D.	Y	N	N	N	N	Y	Y	Y
6 ***Butler***	?	N	Y	N	N	Y	?	Y
7 ***Robinson***	Y	N	Y	N	?	Y	Y	Y
8 ***Parris***	Y	N	Y	?	N	Y	Y	N
9 ***Wampler***	Y	N	Y	N	N	Y	Y	Y
10 ***Wolf***	?	?	?	?	?	?	Y	N
WASHINGTON								
1 ***Pritchard***	Y	?	Y	N	N	Y	Y	N
2 Swift	Y	Y	Y	Y	Y	Y	Y	N
3 Bonker	Y	Y	Y	N	Y	Y	?	N
4 ***Morrison***	Y	N	Y	N	N	Y	Y	N
5 Foley	Y	N	Y	N	N	Y	Y	N
6 Dicks	Y	Y	Y	N	N	Y	Y	N
7 Lowry	Y	Y	Y	N	Y	Y	Y	N
WEST VIRGINIA								
1 Mollohan	Y	Y	Y	N	N	Y	Y	N
2 ***Benedict***	?	N	Y	Y	N	Y	Y	Y
3 ***Staton***	Y	N	N	N	N	Y	Y	Y
4 Rahall	Y	Y	Y	Y	Y	N	Y	N
WISCONSIN								
1 Aspin	Y	Y	Y	N	N	Y	Y	N
2 Kastenmeier	Y	Y	Y	N	Y	N	Y	N
3 ***Gunderson***	Y	N	Y	Y	N	Y	Y	N
4 Zablocki	Y	Y	Y	N	N	Y	Y	N
5 Reuss	Y	Y	Y	N	Y	N	Y	N
6 ***Petri***	Y	Y	Y	N	N	Y	Y	N
7 Obey	Y	Y	Y	Y	Y	N	Y	N
8 ***Roth***	?	N	Y	N	N	Y	Y	N
9 ***Sensenbrenner***	Y	Y	Y	N	N	Y	Y	N
WYOMING								
AL ***Cheney***	?	N	N	N	N	Y	Y	Y

Southern states - Ala., Ark., Fla., Ga., Ky., La., Miss., N.C., Okla., S.C., Tenn., Texas, Va.

259. HR 6542. Wilderness Protection Act. Passage of the bill to withdraw permanently designated federal wilderness areas from oil, gas and some mineral leasing and to provide temporary withdrawal of lands that are candidates for future designation as wilderness. Passed 340-58: R 128-47; D 212-11 (ND 147-1, SD 65-10), Aug. 12, 1982.

260. HR 5595. Federal Payment to the District of Columbia. Parris, R-Va., amendment to earmark $14.3 million of the funds authorized by the bill to eliminate deficits in the D.C. teachers', police officers' and firefighters' retirement fund. Adopted 221-181: R 162-13; D 59-168 (ND 23-129, SD 36-39), Aug. 12, 1982.

261. HR 5595. Federal Payment to the District of Columbia. Passage of the bill to authorize $361 million in federal funds as the annual federal payment for the District of Columbia for fiscal 1983. Passed 279-122: R 99-78; D 180-44 (ND 140-11, SD 40-33), Aug. 12, 1982.

262. HR 6100. National Development Investment Act. Hagedorn, R-Minn., amendment to exempt projects funded with Economic Development Administration grants from wage requirements of the Davis-Bacon Act if the bid of the contractor awarded the grant is 10 percent less than the next lowest bid. Rejected 140-237: R 102-63; D 38-174 (ND 3-137, SD 35-37), Aug. 12, 1982.

263. HR 6100. National Development Investment Act. Passage of the bill to revise the Public Works and Economic Development Act of 1965, authorize fiscal 1983-85 funding for economic development programs in distressed areas, and authorize funding to complete the Appalachian regional development program by fiscal 1987 and the Appalachian highway system by fiscal 1990. Passed 281-95: R 83-83; D 198-12 (ND 136-2, SD 62-10), Aug. 12, 1982. A "nay" was a vote supporting the president's position.

264. Procedural Motion. Rahall, D-W.Va., motion to approve the House *Journal* of Thursday, Aug. 12. Motion agreed to 312-28: R 144-16; D 168-12 (ND 115-10, SD 53-2), Aug. 13, 1982.

265. HR 6957. State, Justice, Commerce Appropriations, Fiscal 1983. Zeferetti, D-N.Y., motion to order the previous question on the State, Justice, Commerce appropriations bill, thus ending debate and the possibility of amendment on the rule (H Res 560). Motion rejected 144-208: R 11-146; D 133-62 (ND 115-17, SD 18-45), Aug. 13, 1982.

266. HR 6957. State, Justice, Commerce Appropriations, Fiscal 1983. Lott, R-Miss., motion to table (kill) the Zeferetti, D-N.Y., motion to refer the rule (H Res 560) on the State, Justice, Commerce appropriations bill back to the Rules Committee. Motion rejected 173-179: R 148-8; D 25-171 (ND 3-130, SD 22-41), Aug. 13, 1982.

KEY

Y	Voted for (yea).
#	Paired for.
+	Announced for.
N	Voted against (nay).
X	Paired against.
-	Announced against.
P	Voted "present".
C	Voted "present" to avoid possible conflict of interest.
?	Did not vote or otherwise make a position known.

Democrats   *Republicans*

	259	260	261	262	263	264	265	266
ALABAMA								
1 *Edwards*	?	N	Y	N	N	?	N	Y
2 *Dickinson*	N	Y	N	Y	N	N	N	Y
3 Nichols	?	?	?	?	?	?	?	?
4 Bevill	Y	Y	N	Y	Y	N	Y	N
5 Flippo	Y	Y	N	N	Y	?	N	N
6 *Smith*	N	Y	N	Y	N	N	N	Y
7 Shelby	Y	Y	N	N	Y	?	Y	Y
ALASKA								
AL *Young*	N	?	?	?	?	?	?	?
ARIZONA								
1 *Rhodes*	Y	N	Y	?	?	Y	N	Y
2 Udall	Y	N	Y	?	?	Y	Y	N
3 *Stump*	N	Y	N	Y	N	Y	N	Y
4 *Rudd*	N	Y	N	Y	N	Y	N	Y
ARKANSAS								
1 Alexander	Y	N	Y	N	Y	Y	Y	N
2 *Bethune*	Y	Y	Y	Y	N	Y	N	Y
3 *Hammerschmidt*	Y	Y	N	Y	Y	Y	N	Y
4 Anthony	Y	N	N	Y	Y	?	N	N
CALIFORNIA								
1 *Chappie*	Y	Y	Y	N	Y	N	N	Y
2 *Clausen*	Y	Y	Y	N	Y	N	N	Y
3 Matsui	Y	N	Y	N	Y	Y	Y	N
4 Fazio	Y	N	Y	N	Y	Y	Y	N
5 Burton, J.	?	?	?	?	?	?	?	?
6 Burton, P.	Y	N	Y	N	Y	Y	Y	N
7 Miller	Y	N	Y	N	Y	Y	Y	N
8 Dellums	Y	N	Y	N	Y	Y	Y	N
9 Stark	Y	N	Y	N	Y	Y	Y	N
10 Edwards	Y	N	Y	N	Y	Y	Y	N
11 Lantos	Y	N	Y	N	Y	Y	Y	N
12 *McCloskey*	?	?	?	?	?	?	?	?
13 Mineta	Y	N	Y	N	Y	Y	Y	N
14 *Shumway*	Y	Y	N	?	?	?	?	?
15 Coelho	?	N	Y	N	Y	Y	Y	N
16 Panetta	Y	N	Y	N	Y	Y	Y	N
17 *Pashayan*	Y	Y	N	N	Y	N	N	Y
18 *Thomas*	Y	Y	Y	N	Y	N	N	Y
19 *Lagomarsino*	Y	N	N	N	Y	Y	N	Y
20 *Goldwater*	Y	Y	Y	N	?	N	N	Y
21 *Fiedler*	Y	Y	Y	N	N	Y	N	Y
22 *Moorhead*	N	Y	N	Y	N	Y	N	Y
23 Beilenson	Y	N	Y	N	Y	Y	Y	N
24 Waxman	Y	N	Y	N	Y	Y	Y	N
25 Roybal	Y	N	Y	N	Y	Y	Y	N
26 *Rousselot*	N	Y	N	Y	N	Y	?	?
27 *Dornan*	?	?	?	?	?	?	?	?
28 Dixon	Y	N	Y	N	Y	Y	?	?
29 Hawkins	Y	N	Y	N	Y	Y	Y	N
30 Martinez	Y	N	Y	N	Y	Y	Y	N
31 Dymally	Y	N	Y	N	Y	Y	Y	N
32 Anderson	Y	N	Y	N	Y	Y	Y	N
33 Grisham	Y	Y	N	Y	N	Y	?	Y
34 *Lungren*	N	Y	Y	N	N	Y	N	Y
35 *Dreier*	N	Y	N	Y	N	N	N	Y
36 Brown	?	?	?	?	?	?	?	?
37 *Lewis*	Y	Y	Y	N	N	Y	N	Y
38 Patterson	Y	N	Y	N	Y	Y	Y	N
39 *Dannemeyer*	N	Y	N	Y	N	Y	N	Y
40 *Badham*	N	Y	N	Y	N	Y	?	?
41 *Lowery*	Y	Y	Y	N	Y	N	Y	N
42 *Hunter*	N	Y	?	N	Y	N	Y	N
43 *Burgener*	?	?	?	?	?	?	?	?
COLORADO								
1 Schroeder	Y	N	Y	N	Y	N	N	N
2 Wirth	Y	N	Y	?	?	Y	Y	N
3 Kogovsek	Y	N	Y	N	Y	Y	?	?
4 *Brown*	Y	Y	N	Y	N	N	N	Y

	259	260	261	262	263	264	265	266
5 *Kramer*	Y	Y	N	Y	N	Y	?	?
CONNECTICUT								
1 Kennelly	Y	N	Y	N	Y	Y	Y	N
2 Gejdenson	Y	N	Y	N	Y	N	Y	N
3 *DeNardis*	Y	Y	Y	N	Y	Y	Y	N
4 *McKinney*	Y	N	Y	N	Y	Y	N	?
5 Ratchford	Y	N	Y	N	Y	?	?	?
6 Moffett	?	?	?	?	?	?	?	?
DELAWARE								
AL *Evans*	Y	Y	Y	N	Y	Y	N	Y
FLORIDA								
1 Hutto	Y	Y	N	Y	Y	Y	N	Y
2 Fuqua	Y	Y	Y	Y	Y	Y	N	Y
3 Bennett	N	N	N	N	Y	Y	N	Y
4 Chappell	Y	N	N	Y	Y	?	?	?
5 *McCollum*	Y	Y	Y	N	Y	N	Y	N
6 *Young*	Y	Y	Y	N	Y	N	Y	N
7 Gibbons	Y	N	Y	Y	N	?	Y	N
8 *Ireland*	?	?	?	?	?	?	?	?
9 *Nelson*	Y	N	N	Y	Y	Y	N	N
10 *Bafalis*	?	?	?	?	?	?	?	?
11 Mica	Y	Y	N	Y	Y	Y	N	N
12 *Shaw*	Y	Y	Y	Y	Y	Y	N	N
13 Lehman	Y	N	Y	?	?	?	?	?
14 Pepper	Y	N	Y	N	Y	Y	Y	N
15 Fascell	Y	N	Y	N	Y	Y	Y	N
GEORGIA								
1 Ginn	?	?	?	?	?	?	?	?
2 Hatcher	Y	N	N	N	Y	Y	N	N
3 Brinkley	Y	Y	Y	N	Y	Y	Y	N
4 Levitas	Y	N	Y	N	Y	Y	Y	N
5 Fowler	Y	N	Y	N	Y	Y	?	?
6 *Gingrich*	Y	Y	Y	Y	N	Y	N	Y
7 McDonald	N	Y	N	Y	N	Y	N	Y
8 Evans	Y	N	?	N	Y	?	?	?
9 Jenkins	Y	Y	Y	N	Y	Y	Y	N
10 Barnard	Y	Y	N	Y	Y	?	N	N
HAWAII								
1 Heftel	Y	N	Y	N	Y	?	?	?
2 Akaka	Y	Y	Y	N	Y	Y	Y	?
IDAHO								
1 *Craig*	N	Y	Y	#	X	?	?	?
2 *Hansen*	N	Y	N	Y	N	?	N	Y
ILLINOIS								
1 Washington	Y	N	Y	N	Y	N	Y	N
2 Savage	?	N	Y	N	Y	?	?	?
3 Russo	Y	N	Y	N	Y	Y	Y	N
4 *Derwinski*	N	Y	N	N	N	N	N	Y
5 Fary	Y	N	Y	N	Y	Y	Y	N
6 *Hyde*	Y	N	Y	N	Y	Y	Y	N
7 Collins	Y	N	Y	N	Y	Y	Y	N
8 Rostenkowski	Y	N	Y	N	Y	Y	Y	N
9 Yates	Y	N	?	?	Y	Y	Y	N
10 *Porter*	Y	Y	Y	Y	N	Y	Y	N
11 Annunzio	Y	N	Y	N	Y	Y	Y	N
12 *Crane, P.*	N	Y	N	N	N	Y	N	Y
13 *McClory*	?	Y	Y	N	Y	N	Y	N
14 *Erlenborn*	?	Y	Y	N	Y	N	Y	N
15 *Corcoran*	Y	Y	Y	N	Y	Y	N	Y
16 *Martin*	Y	Y	N	N	Y	N	Y	N
17 *O'Brien*	Y	Y	Y	N	Y	Y	Y	N
18 *Michel*	?	?	Y	N	N	Y	N	Y
19 *Railsback*	Y	?	Y	N	Y	N	Y	?
20 *Findley*	Y	Y	Y	N	N	Y	N	Y
21 *Madigan*	Y	Y	?	N	Y	N	N	Y
22 *Crane, D.*	N	Y	N	Y	N	?	?	?
23 Price	Y	N	Y	N	Y	Y	Y	N
24 Simon	Y	N	Y	N	Y	Y	Y	N
INDIANA								
1 Benjamin	Y	N	Y	N	Y	Y	Y	N
2 Fithian	?	?	?	?	?	?	?	?
3 *Hiler*	Y	Y	N	Y	N	Y	N	Y
4 *Coats*	Y	Y	N	Y	N	Y	N	Y
5 *Hillis*	N	Y	N	Y	Y	?	?	?
6 Evans	Y	N	Y	N	Y	Y	Y	N
7 *Myers*	Y	Y	Y	N	Y	Y	N	Y
8 *Deckard*	Y	Y	Y	Y	N	Y	N	Y
9 Hamilton	Y	N	Y	N	Y	Y	Y	N
10 Sharp	Y	N	Y	N	Y	Y	Y	N
11 Jacobs	Y	N	Y	N	N	N	N	N
IOWA								
1 *Leach*	Y	Y	N	N	Y	Y	Y	N
2 *Tauke*	Y	Y	N	Y	Y	Y	N	Y
3 *Evans*	Y	Y	N	Y	Y	Y	N	Y
4 Smith	Y	N	Y	N	Y	Y	Y	N
5 Harkin	Y	N	Y	N	Y	Y	Y	N
6 Bedell	Y	N	Y	?	?	?	?	?

	259	260	261	262	263	264	265	266
KANSAS								
1 ***Roberts***	Y	Y	N	Y	N	N	?	?
2 ***Jeffries***	N	Y	N	Y	N	Y	N	Y
3 ***Winn***	Y	Y	Y	Y	N	Y	N	Y
4 Glickman	Y	Y	Y	N	Y	Y	Y	N
5 ***Whittaker***	Y	Y	N	Y	N	Y	N	Y
KENTUCKY								
1 Hubbard	Y	N	Y	N	Y	Y	N	N
2 Natcher	Y	N	Y	N	Y	Y	N	N
3 Mazzoli	Y	N	Y	N	Y	Y	N	Y
4 ***Snyder***	N	Y	N	Y	N	Y	N	Y
5 ***Rogers***	Y	Y	Y	Y	Y	Y	N	Y
6 ***Hopkins***	Y	Y	Y	Y	N	Y	N	Y
7 Perkins	Y	N	Y	N	Y	Y	Y	N
LOUISIANA								
1 ***Livingston***	N	Y	Y	Y	N	Y	N	Y
2 Boggs	Y	N	Y	N	Y	?	Y	N
3 Tauzin	Y	Y	Y	Y	Y	Y	N	Y
4 Roemer	Y	Y	Y	Y	N	N	N	Y
5 Huckaby	Y	Y	Y	?	?	?	?	?
6 ***Moore***	N	Y	N	Y	N	Y	N	Y
7 Breaux	Y	Y	Y	Y	Y	?	?	?
8 Long	Y	Y	Y	N	Y	Y	Y	N
MAINE								
1 ***Emery***	Y	Y	Y	Y	Y	?	?	?
2 ***Snowe***	Y	Y	Y	Y	Y	Y	N	Y
MARYLAND								
1 Dyson	Y	N	Y	N	N	Y	N	N
2 Long	Y	N	Y	Y	Y	?	N	N
3 Mikulski	Y	N	Y	N	Y	?	Y	N
4 ***Holt***	Y	Y	Y	Y	N	Y	N	Y
5 Hoyer	Y	N	Y	N	?	Y	Y	N
6 Byron	Y	Y	N	Y	Y	Y	N	Y
7 Mitchell	Y	N	Y	X	#	N	Y	N
8 Barnes	Y	Y	Y	N	Y	N	Y	N
MASSACHUSETTS								
1 ***Conte***	Y	Y	Y	N	Y	Y	N	Y
2 Boland	Y	N	Y	N	Y	Y	Y	N
3 Early	Y	N	Y	N	Y	Y	Y	N
4 Frank	Y	N	Y	N	Y	?	?	?
5 Shannon	Y	N	Y	N	Y	Y	?	N
6 Mavroules	Y	N	Y	N	Y	Y	Y	N
7 Markey	Y	N	Y	N	Y	N	Y	N
8 O'Neill								
9 Moakley	Y	N	Y	N	Y	Y	Y	N
10 ***Heckler***	Y	N	Y	N	Y	?	?	?
11 Donnelly	Y	N	Y	N	Y	Y	Y	N
12 Studds	Y	N	Y	N	Y	Y	Y	N
MICHIGAN								
1 Conyers	?	?	?	?	?	?	?	N
2 ***Pursell***	Y	Y	Y	?	?	?	?	?
3 Wolpe	Y	N	Y	N	Y	Y	N	N
4 ***Siljander***	?	?	?	?	?	?	?	?
5 ***Sawyer***	Y	Y	Y	N	Y	Y	?	Y
6 ***Dunn***	Y	Y	Y	Y	Y	Y	N	Y
7 Kildee	Y	N	Y	N	Y	Y	Y	N
8 Traxler	Y	Y	Y	N	Y	Y	Y	N
9 ***Vander Jagt***	Y	Y	Y	N	Y	Y	N	Y
10 Albosta	Y	Y	N	N	Y	Y	N	N
11 ***Davis***	N	Y	Y	N	Y	Y	?	Y
12 Bonior	Y	N	Y	N	Y	Y	Y	N
13 Crockett	?	?	?	?	?	Y	Y	N
14 Hertel	Y	Y	N	N	Y	Y	N	N
15 Ford	Y	N	Y	N	Y	?	Y	N
16 Dingell	Y	Y	N	N	Y	Y	Y	N
17 Brodhead	Y	N	Y	N	Y	Y	Y	N
18 Blanchard	?	Y	Y	N	Y	Y	Y	N
19 ***Broomfield***	?	Y	N	?	?	Y	N	Y
MINNESOTA								
1 ***Erdahl***	+	?	?	Y	Y	Y	?	Y
2 ***Hagedorn***	Y	Y	Y	Y	Y	Y	N	Y
3 ***Frenzel***	Y	Y	Y	#	X	?	?	?
4 Vento	Y	N	?	N	Y	Y	Y	N
5 Sabo	Y	N	Y	N	Y	N	Y	N
6 ***Weber***	Y	Y	N	Y	N	Y	N	Y
7 ***Stangeland***	N	Y	Y	Y	Y	Y	N	Y
8 Oberstar	Y	N	Y	N	Y	P	Y	N
MISSISSIPPI								
1 Whitten	Y	N	Y	Y	Y	Y	N	N
2 Bowen	Y	N	Y	N	Y	Y	N	N
3 Montgomery	N	Y	N	Y	Y	Y	N	N
4 Dowdy	Y	N	Y	N	Y	Y	N	N
5 ***Lott***	Y	Y	N	N	Y	Y	N	Y
MISSOURI								
1 Clay	Y	N	Y	?	?	?	?	?
2 Young	Y	N	Y	N	Y	?	?	?
3 Gephardt	Y	N	Y	N	Y	Y	Y	N
4 Skelton	Y	N	N	N	Y	Y	N	?
5 Bolling	?	N	?	N	?	?	?	?
6 ***Coleman***	Y	Y	N	Y	Y	Y	N	Y
7 ***Taylor***	Y	Y	N	N	Y	Y	N	Y
8 ***Bailey***	N	Y	N	Y	N	Y	N	Y
9 Volkmer	Y	N	N	N	Y	Y	N	N
10 ***Emerson***	Y	Y	N	Y	Y	N	N	Y
MONTANA								
1 Williams	Y	Y	Y	N	Y	Y	Y	N
2 ***Marlenee***	N	Y	N	N	Y	Y	N	Y
NEBRASKA								
1 ***Bereuter***	Y	Y	Y	Y	Y	Y	N	Y
2 ***Daub***	Y	Y	N	Y	N	Y	N	Y
3 ***Smith***	Y	Y	N	Y	N	Y	N	Y
NEVADA								
AL Santini	Y	Y	N	?	?	?	?	?
NEW HAMPSHIRE								
1 D'Amours	Y	N	Y	N	Y	Y	Y	N
2 ***Gregg***	Y	Y	N	Y	N	Y	N	Y
NEW JERSEY								
1 Florio	Y	Y	Y	N	Y	Y	Y	N
2 Hughes	Y	N	Y	N	Y	Y	Y	N
3 Howard	Y	N	Y	N	Y	Y	Y	N
4 ***Smith***	Y	Y	Y	N	Y	Y	N	Y
5 ***Fenwick***	Y	Y	?	N	Y	?	?	?
6 ***Forsythe***	N	Y	Y	Y	N	?	N	Y
7 ***Roukema***	Y	Y	Y	Y	N	?	?	?
8 Roe	Y	Y	Y	N	Y	Y	Y	N
9 ***Hollenbeck***	Y	N	Y	N	Y	Y	Y	N
10 Rodino	Y	N	Y	N	Y	Y	Y	N
11 Minish	Y	N	Y	N	Y	Y	Y	N
12 ***Rinaldo***	Y	Y	Y	?	?	Y	Y	N
13 ***Courter***	Y	Y	N	?	?	Y	N	Y
14 Guarini	Y	N	Y	N	Y	Y	Y	N
15 Dwyer	Y	N	Y	N	Y	Y	Y	N
NEW MEXICO								
1 ***Lujan***	Y	Y	Y	Y	Y	?	?	?
2 ***Skeen***	N	Y	Y	Y	N	Y	N	Y
NEW YORK								
1 ***Carney***	Y	Y	Y	N	Y	Y	N	Y
2 Downey	Y	N	Y	N	Y	Y	Y	N
3 ***Carman***	N	Y	Y	N	N	Y	N	Y
4 ***Lent***	Y	Y	Y	N	Y	Y	N	Y
5 ***McGrath***	Y	Y	N	N	Y	Y	N	Y
6 ***LeBoutillier***	Y	Y	N	N	Y	Y	N	Y
7 Addabbo	?	N	Y	N	Y	Y	Y	N
8 Rosenthal	?	?	?	?	?	?	?	?
9 Ferraro	+	-	+	-	+	Y	Y	N
10 Biaggi	Y	Y	Y	N	Y	Y	Y	N
11 Scheuer	Y	Y	Y	N	Y	Y	Y	N
12 Chisholm	Y	N	Y	?	?	?	?	?
13 Solarz	Y	N	Y	N	Y	Y	Y	N
14 Richmond	?	?	?	?	?	?	Y	N
15 Zeferetti	Y	Y	Y	N	Y	Y	Y	N
16 Schumer	Y	N	Y	N	Y	Y	Y	N
17 ***Molinari***	N	Y	Y	Y	Y	Y	N	Y
18 ***Green***	Y	N	Y	N	Y	Y	Y	N
19 Rangel	Y	N	Y	X	Y	Y	Y	N
20 Weiss	Y	N	Y	N	Y	Y	Y	N
21 Garcia	Y	N	Y	X	#	?	?	?
22 Bingham	Y	N	Y	N	?	Y	Y	N
23 Peyser	Y	N	Y	N	Y	Y	Y	N
24 Ottinger	Y	N	Y	N	Y	?	Y	N
25 ***Fish***	Y	Y	Y	N	Y	Y	N	Y
26 ***Gilman***	Y	Y	Y	N	Y	Y	N	Y
27 McHugh	Y	N	Y	N	Y	Y	Y	N
28 Stratton	Y	Y	Y	N	Y	Y	Y	N
29 ***Solomon***	Y	Y	N	?	Y	Y	N	Y
30 ***Martin***	Y	Y	N	N	Y	Y	N	Y
31 ***Mitchell***	Y	Y	Y	N	Y	Y	N	Y
32 ***Wortley***	Y	Y	Y	Y	Y	Y	N	Y
33 ***Lee***	Y	Y	Y	N	Y	Y	N	Y
34 ***Horton***	Y	Y	Y	N	Y	Y	N	Y
35 ***Conable***	Y	Y	Y	N	N	Y	N	Y
36 LaFalce	Y	N	Y	N	Y	Y	Y	N
37 Nowak	Y	N	Y	N	Y	Y	Y	N
38 ***Kemp***	Y	Y	Y	N	N	Y	N	Y
39 Lundine	Y	N	Y	N	Y	?	?	?
NORTH CAROLINA								
1 Jones	?	?	?	?	?	?	?	?
2 Fountain	Y	Y	N	Y	N	?	N	Y
3 Whitley	Y	N	N	Y	Y	Y	N	N
4 Andrews	Y	N	Y	Y	Y	?	?	?
5 Neal	Y	Y	N	Y	Y	Y	N	Y
6 ***Johnston***	Y	Y	N	Y	N	N	N	Y
7 Rose	Y	N	Y	Y	Y	Y	N	N
8 Hefner	Y	N	N	Y	Y	Y	N	N
9 ***Martin***	Y	Y	N	Y	N	Y	N	Y
10 ***Broyhill***	Y	Y	N	Y	N	Y	N	Y
11 ***Hendon***	Y	Y	N	Y	Y	Y	N	Y
NORTH DAKOTA								
AL Dorgan	Y	N	Y	N	Y	Y	N	N
OHIO								
1 ***Gradison***	Y	N	Y	N	Y	?	?	?
2 Luken	Y	N	Y	?	?	?	?	?
3 Hall	Y	N	Y	?	?	?	?	?
4 ***Oxley***	N	Y	Y	Y	N	Y	N	Y
5 ***Latta***	?	N	N	Y	N	Y	N	Y
6 ***McEwen***	Y	Y	N	Y	Y	?	?	?
7 ***Brown***	?	?	?	?	?	?	?	?
8 ***Kindness***	N	Y	Y	Y	N	Y	N	Y
9 ***Weber***	Y	Y	Y	N	N	Y	N	Y
10 ***Miller***	?	?	?	Y	Y	N	Y	?
11 ***Stanton***	Y	Y	Y	?	?	?	?	?
12 Shamansky	Y	N	Y	N	Y	?	?	?
13 Pease	Y	N	Y	N	Y	Y	Y	N
14 Seiberling	Y	N	Y	N	Y	?	Y	N
15 ***Wylie***	?	Y	Y	N	N	Y	N	Y
16 ***Regula***	Y	Y	Y	N	Y	Y	N	Y
17 ***Ashbrook***	N	Y	N	Y	N	Y	N	Y
18 Applegate	Y	Y	Y	N	Y	?	?	?
19 ***Williams***	Y	N	Y	N	Y	Y	N	Y
20 Oakar	Y	N	Y	N	Y	?	?	?
21 Stokes	Y	N	Y	N	Y	Y	Y	N
22 Eckart	Y	Y	Y	N	Y	Y	Y	N
23 Mottl	Y	Y	Y	N	Y	Y	N	N
OKLAHOMA								
1 Jones	Y	N	N	Y	Y	Y	N	N
2 Synar	N	N	Y	N	Y	Y	N	N
3 Watkins	Y	Y	N	Y	Y	?	?	?
4 McCurdy	Y	Y	N	?	?	?	?	?
5 ***Edwards***	N	Y	N	Y	N	Y	N	Y
6 English	Y	Y	N	Y	N	Y	N	Y
OREGON								
1 AuCoin	Y	N	Y	N	Y	?	N	N
2 ***Smith***	N	Y	Y	Y	N	?	?	?
3 Wyden	Y	N	Y	N	Y	Y	Y	N
4 Weaver	Y	N	N	?	?	?	?	N
PENNSYLVANIA								
1 Foglietta	Y	N	Y	N	Y	Y	Y	N
2 Gray	Y	N	Y	N	Y	Y	Y	?
3 Smith	Y	N	Y	N	Y	?	?	?
4 ***Dougherty***	Y	?	?	N	Y	Y	N	Y
5 ***Schulze***	Y	Y	Y	Y	Y	Y	N	Y
6 Yatron	Y	Y	Y	N	Y	Y	Y	N
7 Edgar	Y	N	Y	N	Y	Y	Y	N
8 ***Coyne, J.***	Y	Y	N	N	Y	Y	N	Y
9 ***Shuster***	N	Y	N	Y	Y	Y	N	Y
10 ***McDade***	Y	N	Y	N	Y	Y	N	Y
11 ***Nelligan***	Y	Y	N	N	Y	Y	N	Y
12 Murtha	Y	N	Y	N	Y	Y	Y	N
13 ***Coughlin***	Y	?	Y	N	N	N	N	Y
14 Coyne, W.	Y	N	Y	N	Y	Y	Y	N
15 ***Ritter***	Y	Y	N	N	Y	Y	N	Y
16 ***Walker***	Y	Y	N	Y	N	N	N	Y
17 Ertel	?	?	?	?	?	?	?	?
18 Walgren	Y	N	Y	N	Y	Y	Y	N
19 ***Goodling***	Y	Y	N	Y	Y	N	N	Y
20 Gaydos	Y	Y	Y	N	Y	Y	Y	N
21 Bailey	Y	N	Y	N	Y	Y	Y	N
22 Murphy	Y	N	Y	N	Y	N	Y	N
23 ***Clinger***	Y	-	Y	N	Y	Y	N	Y
24 ***Marks***	?	?	?	N	Y	?	Y	?
25 ***Atkinson***	Y	Y	Y	N	Y	N	N	Y
RHODE ISLAND								
1 St Germain	Y	N	Y	N	Y	Y	Y	N
2 ***Schneider***	Y	Y	Y	?	?	Y	Y	N
SOUTH CAROLINA								
1 ***Hartnett***	N	Y	N	Y	N	Y	N	Y
2 ***Spence***	Y	Y	N	Y	Y	Y	N	Y
3 Derrick	Y	N	Y	Y	Y	Y	Y	N
4 ***Campbell***	Y	Y	N	?	?	Y	N	Y
5 Holland	Y	Y	Y	N	Y	?	?	?
6 ***Napier***	Y	?	Y	Y	Y	Y	N	Y
SOUTH DAKOTA								
1 Daschle	Y	N	N	N	Y	?	N	N
2 ***Roberts***	N	Y	N	Y	N	Y	N	Y
TENNESSEE								
1 ***Quillen***	N	Y	N	N	Y	Y	Y	?
2 ***Duncan***	Y	Y	Y	Y	Y	Y	N	Y
3 Bouquard	Y	Y	N	N	Y	Y	N	Y
4 Gore	Y	N	Y	N	Y	Y	Y	N
5 Boner	Y	Y	Y	N	Y	Y	N	Y
6 ***Beard***	Y	Y	N	Y	Y	Y	N	Y
7 Jones	Y	N	N	N	Y	Y	N	N
8 Ford	Y	N	Y	N	Y	?	Y	N
TEXAS								
1 Hall, S.	N	Y	N	Y	Y	Y	N	N
2 Wilson	Y	N	Y	N	N	?	N	N
3 ***Collins***	?	?	?	?	?	Y	N	Y
4 Hall, R.	N	Y	N	Y	Y	N	N	Y
5 Mattox	Y	N	N	N	Y	?	?	?
6 Gramm	N	Y	N	Y	N	Y	N	Y
7 ***Archer***	N	Y	N	Y	N	Y	N	Y
8 ***Fields***	N	Y	N	Y	N	N	N	Y
9 Brooks	Y	Y	N	N	Y	?	?	?
10 Pickle	Y	N	?	N	Y	Y	N	Y
11 Leath	N	Y	N	Y	Y	Y	N	Y
12 Wright	Y	N	Y	N	Y	Y	Y	N
13 Hightower	Y	Y	Y	Y	Y	Y	Y	N
14 Patman	N	Y	N	N	Y	Y	N	N
15 de la Garza	Y	N	Y	N	Y	Y	N	N
16 White	Y	Y	Y	Y	Y	Y	N	Y
17 Stenholm	N	Y	N	Y	N	Y	N	Y
18 Leland	Y	N	Y	N	Y	Y	Y	N
19 Hance	Y	Y	N	Y	N	Y	Y	N
20 Gonzalez	Y	N	Y	N	Y	Y	Y	N
21 ***Loeffler***	N	Y	N	Y	N	Y	N	Y
22 ***Paul***	N	Y	N	Y	N	Y	N	Y
23 Kazen	Y	Y	Y	Y	Y	Y	N	Y
24 Frost	Y	N	Y	N	Y	Y	Y	N
UTAH								
1 ***Hansen***	Y	Y	N	?	?	?	?	?
2 ***Marriott***	Y	Y	Y	?	?	?	?	?
VERMONT								
AL ***Jeffords***	Y	N	Y	N	Y	Y	Y	N
VIRGINIA								
1 ***Trible***	Y	Y	Y	#	?	?	?	?
2 ***Whitehurst***	Y	Y	Y	?	?	Y	N	Y
3 ***Bliley***	Y	Y	Y	Y	N	Y	N	Y
4 ***Daniel, R.***	Y	Y	N	?	?	Y	N	Y
5 Daniel, D.	N	Y	N	Y	N	Y	N	Y
6 ***Butler***	N	Y	Y	Y	N	N	N	Y
7 ***Robinson***	N	Y	N	Y	N	Y	N	Y
8 ***Parris***	Y	Y	Y	Y	N	Y	N	Y
9 ***Wampler***	N	Y	Y	Y	Y	Y	N	Y
10 ***Wolf***	Y	Y	Y	Y	Y	Y	N	Y
WASHINGTON								
1 ***Pritchard***	Y	N	Y	N	Y	Y	N	Y
2 Swift	Y	N	Y	N	Y	Y	Y	N
3 Bonker	Y	N	Y	N	Y	?	?	?
4 ***Morrison***	Y	Y	Y	N	Y	Y	N	Y
5 Foley	Y	N	Y	N	Y	Y	Y	N
6 Dicks	Y	N	Y	N	Y	Y	Y	N
7 Lowry	Y	N	Y	N	Y	Y	Y	N
WEST VIRGINIA								
1 Mollohan	Y	N	Y	N	Y	Y	?	N
2 ***Benedict***	N	Y	Y	N	Y	Y	N	Y
3 ***Staton***	N	Y	Y	N	N	Y	N	Y
4 Rahall	Y	N	Y	N	Y	Y	Y	N
WISCONSIN								
1 Aspin	Y	N	Y	N	Y	?	Y	N
2 Kastenmeier	Y	N	Y	N	Y	Y	Y	N
3 ***Gunderson***	Y	Y	N	N	N	Y	N	Y
4 Zablocki	Y	N	Y	N	Y	Y	Y	N
5 Reuss	Y	N	Y	N	Y	Y	Y	N
6 ***Petri***	Y	Y	N	N	N	Y	N	Y
7 Obey	Y	P	N	N	Y	Y	Y	N
8 ***Roth***	Y	Y	Y	?	?	?	?	?
9 ***Sensenbrenner***	Y	Y	N	Y	N	Y	N	Y
WYOMING								
AL ***Cheney***	Y	Y	N	Y	N	?	?	?

Southern states - Ala., Ark., Fla., Ga., Ky., La., Miss., N.C., Okla., S.C., Tenn., Texas, Va.

267. HR 6957. State, Justice, Commerce Appropriations, Fiscal 1983. Zeferetti, D-N.Y., motion to order the previous question (thus ending debate and the possibility of amendment) on the Zeferetti motion to refer H Res 560, waiving certain points of order against the bill, to the Rules Committee. Motion agreed to 183-170: R 8-149; D 175-21 (ND 130-4, SD 45-17), Aug. 13, 1982.

268. HR 1489. Puerto Rican Passenger Service. Jones, D-N.C., motion to suspend the rules and pass the bill to allow the transportation of passengers between Puerto Rico and U.S. ports on foreign-flag vessels when U.S.-flag ships are not available. Motion agreed to 387-0: R 176-0; D 211-0 (ND 147-0, SD 64-0), Aug. 17, 1982. A two-thirds majority of those present and voting (258 in this case) is required for passage under suspension of the rules.

269. HR 5618. Organic Farming Act of 1982. Weaver, D-Ore., motion to suspend the rules and pass the bill to establish pilot projects on organic farming and to disseminate information on organic farming through the cooperative agricultural extension service and volunteers. Motion rejected 189-198: R 34-142; D 155-56 (ND 127-20, SD 28-36), Aug. 17, 1982. A two-thirds majority of those present and voting (259 in this case) is required for passage under suspension of the rules.

270. HR 6323. Environmental Protection Agency Research Authorization, Fiscal 1983-84. Fuqua, D-Fla., amendment to the Carney, R-N.Y., substitute, to reduce the fiscal 1983 authorization level for Environmental Protection Agency research and development to $277.9 million from $296.8 million, instead of $225.5 million as proposed by Carney, and to authorize $291 million in fiscal 1984. Adopted 244-153: R 45-131; D 199-22 (ND 147-4, SD 52-18), Aug. 17, 1982.

271. HR 6323. Environmental Protection Agency Research Authorization, Fiscal 1983-84. Carney, R-N.Y., substitute, as amended by the Fuqua, D-Fla., amendment (see vote 270, above), to reduce the fiscal 1983 authorization for Environmental Protection Agency research and development to $277.9 million from $296.8 million, and to reduce the fiscal 1984 authorization to $291 million from $310.9 million. Adopted 394-7: R 177-0; D 217-7 (ND 144-7, SD 73-0), Aug. 17, 1982.

272. HR 6323. Environmental Protection Agency Research Authorization, Fiscal 1983-84. Passage of the bill to authorize $277.9 million for Environmental Protection Agency research and development in fiscal 1983 and $291 million in fiscal 1984. Passed 314-92: R 104-75; D 210-17 (ND 149-5, SD 61-12), Aug. 17, 1982.

273. HR 6324. National Oceanic and Atmospheric Administration Authorization, Fiscal 1983-84. Passage of the bill to authorize $542.8 million in fiscal 1983 and $575.3 million in fiscal 1984 for the atmospheric, climatic and ocean pollution activities of the National Oceanic and Atmospheric Administration. Passed 340-65: R 121-58; D 219-7 (ND 150-4, SD 69-3), Aug. 17, 1982. A "nay" was a vote supporting the president's position.

274. HR 6955. Omnibus Reconciliation Act of 1982. Derwinski, R-Ill., motion to recommit to the conference committee the bill to reduce federal spending for fiscal 1983-1985. Motion agreed to 266-145: R 145-40; D 121-105 (ND 74-79, SD 47-26), Aug. 17, 1982.

KEY

Y	Voted for (yea).
#	Paired for.
+	Announced for.
N	Voted against (nay).
X	Paired against.
-	Announced against.
P	Voted "present".
C	Voted "present" to avoid possible conflict of interest.
?	Did not vote or otherwise make a position known.

Democrats *Republicans*

	267	268	269	270	271	272	273	274
ALABAMA								
1 *Edwards*	N	Y	N	N	Y	Y	Y	N
2 *Dickinson*	N	Y	N	N	Y	Y	Y	N
3 Nichols	?	Y	N	N	Y	Y	Y	Y
4 Bevill	Y	Y	N	Y	Y	Y	Y	Y
5 Flippo	Y	Y	Y	Y	Y	Y	Y	Y
6 *Smith*	N	?	X	?	?	?	Y	Y
7 Shelby	N	Y	N	Y	N	Y	Y	?
ALASKA								
AL *Young*	?	?	?	?	?	?	?	?
ARIZONA								
1 *Rhodes*	N	Y	N	?	?	Y	Y	N
2 Udall	Y	Y	Y	Y	?	Y	Y	N
3 *Stump*	N	Y	N	N	Y	N	N	Y
4 *Rudd*	N	Y	N	N	Y	N	N	Y
ARKANSAS								
1 Alexander	Y	Y	N	Y	Y	Y	Y	Y
2 *Bethune*	N	Y	N	N	Y	N	N	Y
3 *Hammerschmidt*	N	Y	N	N	Y	N	N	Y
4 Anthony	Y	Y	N	Y	Y	Y	Y	Y
CALIFORNIA								
1 *Chappie*	N	Y	N	N	Y	N	Y	Y
2 *Clausen*	N	Y	Y	N	Y	Y	Y	Y
3 Matsui	Y	Y	Y	Y	Y	Y	Y	N
4 Fazio	Y	Y	Y	Y	Y	Y	Y	N
5 Burton, J.	?	?	#	?	?	?	?	?
6 Burton, P.	Y	Y	Y	Y	N	Y	Y	N
7 Miller	Y	Y	Y	Y	Y	Y	Y	N
8 Dellums	Y	Y	Y	Y	Y	Y	Y	N
9 Stark	Y	Y	Y	Y	Y	Y	Y	N
10 Edwards	Y	Y	Y	Y	Y	Y	Y	N
11 Lantos	Y	Y	Y	Y	Y	Y	Y	Y
12 *McCloskey*	?	Y	N	N	Y	?	Y	N
13 Mineta	Y	Y	Y	Y	Y	Y	Y	N
14 *Shumway*	?	Y	N	N	Y	N	N	N
15 Coelho	Y	Y	Y	Y	Y	Y	Y	N
16 Panetta	Y	Y	Y	Y	Y	Y	Y	N
17 Pashayan	N	Y	N	N	Y	N	Y	N
18 *Thomas*	N	Y	N	N	Y	N	Y	N
19 *Lagomarsino*	N	Y	N	N	Y	N	?	Y
20 *Goldwater*	N	?	?	?	?	?	Y	N
21 *Fiedler*	N	Y	N	N	Y	Y	Y	Y
22 *Moorhead*	N	Y	N	N	Y	N	N	Y
23 Beilenson	Y	Y	Y	Y	Y	Y	Y	N
24 Waxman	Y	Y	Y	Y	Y	Y	Y	N
25 Roybal	Y	Y	Y	Y	Y	Y	Y	N
26 *Rousselot*	?	Y	N	N	Y	N	N	N
27 *Dornan*	?	Y	N	N	Y	N	Y	?
28 Dixon	?	Y	Y	Y	Y	Y	Y	N
29 Hawkins	Y	?	#	?	Y	Y	Y	N
30 Martinez	Y	Y	Y	Y	Y	Y	Y	N
31 Dymally	Y	Y	Y	Y	Y	Y	Y	N
32 Anderson	Y	Y	N	Y	Y	Y	Y	Y
33 Grisham	N	Y	N	Y	N	Y	N	Y
34 *Lungren*	N	Y	N	N	Y	N	N	N
35 *Dreier*	N	Y	N	N	Y	N	N	Y
36 Brown	?	Y	Y	Y	Y	Y	Y	N
37 *Lewis*	N	Y	N	N	Y	N	Y	N
38 Patterson	Y	Y	N	Y	Y	Y	Y	N
39 *Dannemeyer*	N	Y	N	N	Y	N	N	Y
40 *Badham*	?	Y	N	N	?	?	Y	N
41 *Lowery*	N	Y	N	N	Y	Y	Y	Y
42 *Hunter*	N	Y	N	N	Y	N	N	Y
43 *Burgener*	?	Y	N	N	Y	N	N	N
COLORADO								
1 Schroeder	Y	Y	Y	Y	Y	Y	Y	Y
2 Wirth	Y	Y	Y	Y	Y	Y	Y	Y
3 Kogovsek	?	Y	Y	Y	Y	Y	Y	Y
4 *Brown*	N	Y	N	N	Y	N	N	Y

	267	268	269	270	271	272	273	274
5 *Kramer*	?	Y	N	N	Y	N	N	Y
CONNECTICUT								
1 Kennelly	Y	Y	Y	Y	Y	Y	Y	Y
2 Gejdenson	Y	?	Y	Y	Y	Y	Y	Y
3 *DeNardis*	Y	Y	Y	Y	Y	Y	Y	Y
4 *McKinney*	?	Y	N	?	Y	Y	Y	N
5 Ratchford	Y	Y	N	Y	Y	Y	Y	Y
6 Moffett	?	?	?	?	?	?	?	?
DELAWARE								
AL *Evans*	N	Y	N	Y	Y	Y	Y	Y
FLORIDA								
1 Hutto	N	Y	Y	Y	Y	Y	Y	Y
2 Fuqua	N	Y	Y	Y	Y	Y	Y	Y
3 Bennett	Y	Y	N	Y	Y	Y	Y	Y
4 Chappell	?	Y	N	Y	Y	Y	Y	Y
5 *McCollum*	N	Y	N	N	Y	Y	Y	Y
6 *Young*	N	Y	?	N	Y	N	Y	Y
7 Gibbons	Y	Y	N	Y	Y	Y	Y	N
8 *Ireland*	?	?	?	?	?	?	?	?
9 Nelson	Y	Y	N	Y	Y	Y	Y	Y
10 *Bafalis*	?	?	?	?	?	?	?	?
11 Mica	Y	Y	Y	Y	Y	Y	Y	Y
12 *Shaw*	N	Y	N	N	Y	Y	Y	Y
13 Lehman	?	Y	Y	Y	Y	Y	Y	N
14 Pepper	Y	Y	Y	Y	Y	Y	Y	Y
15 Fascell	Y	Y	N	Y	Y	Y	Y	Y
GEORGIA								
1 Ginn	?	?	?	?	?	?	?	?
2 Hatcher	Y	?	?	?	Y	Y	Y	Y
3 Brinkley	Y	Y	Y	Y	Y	Y	Y	N
4 Levitas	N	Y	N	Y	Y	Y	Y	Y
5 Fowler	?	?	?	?	Y	Y	Y	Y
6 *Gingrich*	N	Y	Y	Y	Y	Y	Y	Y
7 McDonald	N	Y	N	N	Y	N	N	Y
8 Evans	?	?	?	?	?	?	?	Y
9 Jenkins	Y	Y	N	Y	N	Y	N	Y
10 Barnard	Y	Y	N	Y	Y	Y	Y	Y
HAWAII								
1 Heftel	?	?	?	?	?	?	?	?
2 Akaka	?	Y	N	Y	Y	Y	Y	N
IDAHO								
1 *Craig*	?	Y	N	N	Y	N	Y	Y
2 *Hansen*	N	Y	N	N	Y	N	N	Y
ILLINOIS								
1 Washington	Y	?	#	Y	Y	Y	Y	N
2 Savage	?	Y	Y	Y	Y	Y	Y	N
3 Russo	Y	Y	Y	Y	Y	Y	Y	N
4 *Derwinski*	N	Y	N	N	Y	N	Y	N
5 Fary	Y	Y	N	Y	N	Y	Y	N
6 *Hyde*	N	Y	N	N	Y	N	N	Y
7 Collins	Y	Y	Y	Y	Y	Y	Y	N
8 Rostenkowski	Y	Y	Y	Y	Y	Y	Y	N
9 Yates	Y	Y	Y	Y	Y	Y	Y	N
10 *Porter*	N	Y	Y	Y	Y	Y	Y	N
11 Annunzio	Y	Y	Y	Y	Y	Y	Y	N
12 *Crane, P.*	N	Y	N	N	N	N	N	Y
13 *McClory*	Y	Y	Y	Y	Y	Y	Y	Y
14 *Erlenborn*	N	Y	N	N	Y	N	N	N
15 *Corcoran*	-	Y	N	N	Y	N	N	Y
16 *Martin*	N	Y	N	N	Y	N	N	Y
17 *O'Brien*	N	Y	N	N	Y	Y	Y	N
18 *Michel*	N	Y	N	N	Y	N	N	Y
19 *Railsback*	?	Y	N	Y	Y	Y	Y	N
20 *Findley*	N	Y	N	Y	Y	Y	Y	N
21 *Madigan*	N	Y	N	N	Y	N	N	Y
22 *Crane, D.*	?	?	X	N	Y	N	N	Y
24 Simon	Y	?	Y	Y	Y	Y	Y	N
INDIANA								
1 Benjamin	Y	Y	N	Y	Y	Y	Y	Y
2 Fithian	?	Y	Y	Y	Y	Y	Y	Y
3 *Hiler*	N	Y	N	N	Y	N	N	Y
4 *Coats*	-	Y	N	N	Y	N	Y	Y
5 *Hillis*	?	Y	N	N	Y	Y	Y	Y
6 Evans	Y	Y	Y	Y	Y	Y	Y	Y
7 *Myers*	N	Y	N	N	Y	N	N	Y
8 *Deckard*	N	Y	Y	Y	Y	Y	Y	N
9 Hamilton	N	Y	Y	Y	Y	Y	Y	N
10 Sharp	Y	Y	Y	Y	Y	Y	Y	Y
11 Jacobs	N	Y	Y	Y	Y	Y	Y	Y
IOWA								
1 Leach	Y	Y	Y	Y	Y	Y	Y	Y
2 Tauke	N	Y	Y	Y	Y	Y	N	Y
3 Evans	N	Y	Y	Y	Y	Y	Y	Y
4 Smith	Y	Y	Y	Y	Y	Y	Y	Y
5 Harkin	Y	Y	Y	Y	Y	Y	Y	Y
6 Bedell	?	Y	Y	Y	Y	Y	Y	Y

ND - Northern Democrats   SD - Southern Democrats

Corresponding to Congressional Record Votes 279, 281, 282, 283, 284, 285, 286, 287

	267	268	269	270	271	272	273	274
KANSAS								
1 ***Roberts***	N	Y	N	N	Y	N	Y	Y
2 ***Jeffries***	N	Y	N	N	Y	N	N	Y
3 ***Winn***	N	Y	N	N	Y	N	N	Y
4 Glickman	Y	Y	Y	Y	Y	Y	Y	Y
5 ***Whittaker***	N	Y	N	N	Y	Y	N	Y
KENTUCKY								
1 Hubbard	Y	Y	N	N	Y	N	Y	Y
2 Natcher	Y	Y	Y	Y	Y	Y	Y	Y
3 Mazzoli	Y	Y	N	Y	Y	Y	Y	N
4 ***Snyder***	N	Y	N	N	Y	N	Y	Y
5 ***Rogers***	N	Y	N	N	Y	Y	Y	N
6 ***Hopkins***	N	Y	N	N	Y	Y	Y	Y
7 Perkins	Y	Y	N	Y	Y	Y	Y	N
LOUISIANA								
1 ***Livingston***	N	Y	N	N	?	N	?	N
2 Boggs	Y	Y	Y	Y	Y	Y	Y	Y
3 Tauzin	N	Y	N	N	Y	N	Y	Y
4 Roemer	N	Y	N	N	Y	N	N	Y
5 Huckaby	?	Y	Y	N	Y	Y	Y	Y
6 ***Moore***	N	Y	N	N	Y	N	N	Y
7 Breaux	?	?	?	?	?	?	?	?
8 Long	Y	?	?	Y	Y	Y	Y	Y
MAINE								
1 ***Emery***	?	?	#	?	?	?	?	?
2 ***Snowe***	N	Y	N	Y	Y	Y	Y	Y
MARYLAND								
1 Dyson	Y	Y	Y	Y	Y	Y	Y	Y
2 Long	Y	Y	Y	Y	Y	Y	Y	Y
3 Mikulski	Y	Y	Y	Y	Y	Y	Y	Y
4 ***Holt***	N	Y	N	?	?	?	?	?
5 Hoyer	Y	Y	Y	Y	Y	Y	Y	N
6 Byron	Y	Y	N	N	Y	N	Y	Y
7 Mitchell	Y	Y	Y	Y	Y	Y	Y	N
8 Barnes	Y	Y	Y	Y	Y	Y	Y	N
MASSACHUSETTS								
1 ***Conte***	N	Y	N	Y	Y	Y	Y	N
2 Boland	?	Y	Y	Y	Y	Y	Y	Y
3 Early	Y	Y	Y	Y	Y	Y	Y	N
4 Frank	?	Y	Y	Y	Y	Y	Y	Y
5 Shannon	Y	Y	Y	Y	Y	Y	Y	N
6 Mavroules	Y	Y	Y	Y	Y	Y	Y	Y
7 Markey	Y	Y	Y	Y	Y	Y	Y	Y
8 O'Neill								
9 Moakley	Y	Y	Y	Y	Y	Y	Y	N
10 ***Heckler***	?	Y	Y	Y	Y	Y	Y	Y
11 Donnelly	Y	Y	Y	Y	Y	Y	Y	N
12 Studds	Y	Y	Y	Y	Y	Y	Y	Y
MICHIGAN								
1 Conyers	Y	Y	Y	N	N	N	N	N
2 ***Pursell***	?	?	?	N	Y	Y	Y	N
3 Wolpe	Y	Y	Y	Y	Y	Y	Y	Y
4 ***Siljander***	?	Y	N	N	Y	N	N	Y
5 ***Sawyer***	N	Y	Y	N	Y	Y	Y	Y
6 ***Dunn***	N	Y	N	N	Y	Y	Y	Y
7 Kildee	Y	Y	Y	Y	Y	Y	Y	Y
8 Traxler	Y	Y	Y	Y	Y	Y	Y	Y
9 ***Vander Jagt***	N	?	?	N	Y	Y	Y	Y
10 Albosta	Y	Y	Y	Y	Y	Y	Y	Y
11 ***Davis***	N	Y	Y	Y	Y	Y	Y	Y
12 Bonior	Y	Y	Y	Y	Y	Y	Y	Y
13 Crockett	Y	Y	Y	Y	?	Y	Y	N
14 Hertel	Y	Y	Y	Y	Y	Y	Y	N
15 Ford	Y	Y	Y	Y	Y	Y	Y	N
16 Dingell	Y	Y	Y	Y	Y	Y	Y	N
17 Brodhead	Y	Y	Y	Y	Y	Y	Y	N
18 Blanchard	Y	Y	Y	Y	Y	Y	Y	Y
19 ***Broomfield***	N	Y	N	N	Y	Y	Y	Y
MINNESOTA								
1 ***Erdahl***	N	Y	N	Y	Y	Y	Y	Y
2 ***Hagedorn***	N	Y	Y	N	Y	N	N	Y
3 ***Frenzel***	?	Y	N	N	Y	Y	N	N
4 Vento	Y	?	?	Y	Y	Y	Y	N
5 Sabo	Y	Y	Y	Y	Y	Y	Y	N
6 ***Weber***	N	Y	N	Y	Y	Y	N	Y
7 ***Stangeland***	N	Y	Y	N	Y	Y	Y	Y
8 Oberstar	Y	Y	Y	Y	Y	Y	Y	N
MISSISSIPPI								
1 Whitten	Y	?	?	?	?	?	?	?
2 Bowen	Y	Y	Y	Y	Y	Y	Y	N
3 Montgomery	Y	Y	N	N	Y	N	Y	N
4 Dowdy	Y	?	?	Y	Y	Y	Y	N
5 ***Lott***	N	Y	N	N	Y	N	Y	N
MISSOURI								
1 Clay	?	Y	Y	Y	Y	Y	Y	N
2 Young	?	Y	Y	Y	Y	Y	Y	Y
3 Gephardt	Y	Y	Y	Y	Y	Y	Y	Y

	267	268	269	270	271	272	273	274
4 Skelton	?	Y	Y	Y	Y	N	Y	Y
5 Bolling	?	Y	Y	?	?	Y	Y	N
6 ***Coleman***	N	?	?	?	?	?	?	?
7 ***Taylor***	N	Y	N	N	Y	N	Y	Y
8 ***Bailey***	N	Y	N	N	Y	N	Y	Y
9 Volkmer	N	Y	Y	Y	Y	Y	Y	Y
10 ***Emerson***	N	Y	N	N	Y	N	Y	Y
MONTANA								
1 Williams	Y	+	+	+	+	+	+	+
2 ***Marlenee***	N	Y	N	N	Y	N	N	Y
NEBRASKA								
1 ***Bereuter***	N	Y	Y	Y	Y	Y	Y	Y
2 ***Daub***	N	Y	N	N	Y	Y	Y	Y
3 ***Smith***	N	Y	N	N	Y	Y	Y	Y
NEVADA								
AL Santini	?	Y	N	Y	Y	Y	Y	Y
NEW HAMPSHIRE								
1 D'Amours	Y	?	?	?	?	?	?	?
2 ***Gregg***	N	Y	N	Y	Y	Y	N	Y
NEW JERSEY								
1 Florio	Y	Y	Y	Y	Y	Y	Y	Y
2 Hughes	Y	Y	Y	Y	Y	Y	Y	Y
3 Howard	Y	Y	Y	Y	Y	Y	Y	N
4 ***Smith***	N	Y	Y	Y	Y	Y	Y	Y
5 ***Fenwick***	?	Y	Y	Y	Y	Y	?	Y
6 ***Forsythe***	N	Y	N	N	Y	Y	Y	N
7 ***Roukema***	?	Y	N	Y	Y	Y	Y	Y
8 Roe	Y	Y	Y	Y	Y	Y	Y	Y
9 ***Hollenbeck***	Y	Y	Y	Y	Y	Y	Y	Y
10 Rodino	Y	Y	Y	Y	Y	Y	Y	N
11 Minish	Y	Y	Y	Y	Y	Y	Y	Y
12 ***Rinaldo***	Y	Y	N	Y	Y	Y	Y	Y
13 ***Courter***	N	Y	N	Y	Y	?	Y	Y
14 Guarini	Y	Y	Y	Y	Y	Y	Y	Y
15 Dwyer	Y	Y	Y	Y	Y	Y	Y	Y
NEW MEXICO								
1 ***Lujan***	?	Y	N	N	Y	N	Y	Y
2 ***Skeen***	N	Y	N	N	Y	N	N	Y
NEW YORK								
1 ***Carney***	N	Y	N	N	Y	Y	Y	Y
2 Downey	Y	Y	Y	Y	Y	Y	Y	N
3 ***Carman***	N	Y	N	N	Y	N	Y	Y
4 ***Lent***	N	Y	N	Y	Y	Y	Y	Y
5 ***McGrath***	N	Y	N	Y	Y	Y	Y	Y
6 ***LeBoutillier***	N	Y	N	N	Y	Y	?	Y
7 Addabbo	Y	Y	Y	Y	Y	Y	Y	N
8 Rosenthal	?	?	?	?	?	?	?	?
9 Ferraro	Y	Y	Y	Y	Y	Y	Y	N
10 Biaggi	Y	Y	Y	Y	Y	Y	Y	N
11 Scheuer	Y	Y	Y	Y	Y	Y	Y	N
12 Chisholm	?	Y	Y	Y	Y	Y	Y	?
13 Solarz	Y	Y	Y	Y	N	Y	Y	N
14 Richmond	Y	?	#	Y	Y	Y	Y	N
15 Zeferetti	Y	Y	Y	Y	Y	Y	Y	N
16 Schumer	Y	Y	Y	Y	Y	Y	Y	N
17 ***Molinari***	N	Y	Y	Y	Y	Y	Y	Y
18 ***Green***	Y	Y	Y	Y	Y	Y	Y	N
19 Rangel	Y	Y	Y	Y	Y	Y	Y	N
20 Weiss	Y	Y	Y	Y	N	Y	Y	N
21 Garcia	?	Y	Y	Y	Y	Y	Y	N
22 Bingham	Y	Y	Y	Y	N	Y	Y	N
23 Peyser	Y	Y	Y	Y	Y	Y	Y	N
24 Ottinger	Y	Y	Y	Y	N	Y	Y	Y
25 ***Fish***	N	Y	N	Y	Y	Y	Y	Y
26 ***Gilman***	N	Y	Y	?	Y	Y	Y	Y
27 McHugh	Y	Y	Y	Y	Y	Y	Y	Y
28 Stratton	Y	Y	N	Y	Y	Y	Y	N
29 ***Solomon***	N	Y	N	Y	Y	Y	N	Y
30 ***Martin***	N	Y	N	Y	Y	Y	N	Y
31 ***Mitchell***	N	Y	Y	Y	Y	Y	Y	Y
32 ***Wortley***	N	Y	N	N	Y	N	N	Y
33 ***Lee***	N	Y	N	N	Y	N	N	Y
34 ***Horton***	N	Y	Y	Y	Y	Y	Y	N
35 ***Conable***	N	Y	N	N	Y	N	N	Y
36 LaFalce	Y	Y	N	Y	Y	Y	Y	Y
37 Nowak	Y	Y	Y	Y	Y	Y	Y	N
38 ***Kemp***	N	Y	N	N	Y	N	N	Y
39 Lundine	?	Y	Y	Y	Y	Y	Y	N
NORTH CAROLINA								
1 Jones	?	Y	Y	Y	Y	Y	Y	N
2 Fountain	N	?	Y	Y	Y	Y	Y	N
3 Whitley	Y	Y	N	Y	Y	Y	Y	Y
4 Andrews	?	?	?	Y	Y	Y	Y	Y
5 Neal	N	?	?	?	?	?	?	?
6 ***Johnston***	N	Y	N	N	Y	N	N	Y
7 Rose	?	Y	Y	Y	Y	Y	Y	Y
8 Hefner	Y	Y	Y	Y	Y	Y	Y	Y

	267	268	269	270	271	272	273	274
9 ***Martin***	N	Y	N	N	Y	Y	Y	Y
10 ***Broyhill***	N	?	X	?	?	?	?	?
11 ***Hendon***	N	Y	N	N	Y	N	Y	Y
NORTH DAKOTA								
AL Dorgan	Y	+	+	Y	Y	Y	Y	Y
OHIO								
1 ***Gradison***	?	Y	N	N	Y	Y	Y	Y
2 Luken	?	Y	N	Y	Y	Y	Y	Y
3 Hall	?	Y	Y	Y	Y	Y	Y	N
4 ***Oxley***	N	Y	N	N	Y	N	Y	Y
5 ***Latta***	N	Y	N	N	Y	N	N	Y
6 ***McEwen***	?	Y	N	N	Y	Y	N	Y
7 ***Brown***	?	?	?	?	?	?	?	?
8 ***Kindness***	N	Y	N	N	Y	N	N	Y
9 ***Weber***	N	Y	N	N	Y	N	N	Y
10 ***Miller***	N	Y	N	N	Y	N	Y	Y
11 ***Stanton***	?	Y	N	N	Y	Y	?	N
12 Shamansky	Y	Y	Y	Y	Y	Y	Y	Y
13 Pease	Y	Y	Y	Y	Y	Y	Y	Y
14 Seiberling	Y	Y	Y	Y	Y	Y	Y	Y
15 ***Wylie***	N	Y	Y	N	Y	Y	Y	N
16 ***Regula***	N	Y	N	N	Y	Y	Y	Y
17 ***Ashbrook***	N	Y	N	N	Y	N	N	Y
18 Applegate	?	Y	N	N	Y	N	N	Y
19 ***Williams***	N	Y	N	N	Y	Y	Y	Y
20 Oakar	?	Y	Y	Y	Y	Y	Y	Y
21 Stokes	Y	Y	Y	Y	Y	Y	Y	N
22 Eckart	Y	Y	Y	Y	Y	Y	Y	Y
23 Mottl	Y	Y	N	Y	Y	Y	Y	Y
OKLAHOMA								
1 Jones	Y	Y	N	Y	Y	Y	Y	N
2 Synar	Y	Y	Y	Y	Y	Y	Y	Y
3 Watkins	?	?	?	Y	Y	Y	Y	Y
4 McCurdy	?	Y	Y	Y	Y	Y	Y	Y
5 ***Edwards***	N	?	?	?	?	?	N	Y
6 English	Y	?	?	Y	Y	Y	Y	Y
OREGON								
1 AuCoin	Y	Y	Y	Y	Y	Y	Y	Y
2 ***Smith***	?	Y	N	N	Y	N	N	Y
3 Wyden	Y	Y	Y	Y	Y	Y	Y	Y
4 Weaver	Y	Y	Y	Y	Y	Y	Y	Y
PENNSYLVANIA								
1 Foglietta	Y	Y	Y	Y	Y	Y	Y	Y
2 Gray	Y	Y	Y	Y	Y	Y	Y	N
3 Smith	?	Y	Y	Y	Y	Y	Y	N
4 ***Dougherty***	N	?	?	Y	Y	Y	Y	N
5 ***Schulze***	N	?	N	Y	Y	Y	Y	Y
6 Yatron	Y	?	?	?	?	?	?	?
7 Edgar	Y	Y	Y	Y	Y	Y	Y	Y
8 ***Coyne, J.***	N	Y	Y	?	Y	Y	Y	Y
9 ***Shuster***	N	Y	N	N	Y	N	N	Y
10 ***McDade***	N	Y	Y	Y	Y	Y	Y	N
11 ***Nelligan***	N	Y	Y	Y	Y	Y	Y	Y
12 Murtha	Y	Y	N	Y	Y	Y	Y	N
13 ***Coughlin***	N	Y	N	Y	Y	Y	Y	N
14 Coyne, W.	Y	Y	Y	Y	Y	Y	Y	Y
15 ***Ritter***	N	Y	Y	Y	Y	Y	Y	Y
16 ***Walker***	N	Y	N	N	Y	N	N	Y
17 Ertel	?	?	?	?	?	?	?	?
18 Walgren	Y	Y	N	Y	Y	Y	Y	Y
19 ***Goodling***	N	Y	Y	N	Y	N	N	Y
20 Gaydos	Y	Y	Y	Y	Y	Y	Y	Y
21 Bailey	Y	Y	N	Y	Y	Y	Y	Y
22 Murphy	Y	Y	Y	Y	Y	Y	N	Y
23 ***Clinger***	N	Y	N	Y	Y	Y	Y	Y
24 ***Marks***	?	Y	Y	?	?	Y	?	N
25 ***Atkinson***	N	Y	N	N	Y	N	Y	Y
RHODE ISLAND								
1 St Germain	Y	Y	Y	Y	Y	Y	Y	Y
2 ***Schneider***	Y	Y	Y	Y	Y	Y	Y	Y
SOUTH CAROLINA								
1 ***Hartnett***	N	Y	N	N	Y	N	Y	N
2 ***Spence***	N	Y	N	N	Y	Y	Y	Y
3 Derrick	Y	Y	N	?	Y	Y	Y	Y
4 ***Campbell***	N	Y	N	N	Y	N	Y	Y
5 Holland	?	Y	Y	?	Y	Y	Y	N
6 ***Napier***	N	Y	Y	N	Y	Y	Y	Y
SOUTH DAKOTA								
1 Daschle	Y	Y	Y	Y	Y	Y	Y	Y
2 ***Roberts***	N	Y	N	N	Y	N	Y	Y
TENNESSEE								
1 ***Quillen***	N	Y	N	N	Y	N	Y	Y
2 ***Duncan***	N	Y	N	N	Y	Y	Y	Y
3 Bouquard	N	Y	N	Y	Y	Y	Y	Y
4 Gore	Y	Y	Y	Y	Y	Y	Y	N
5 Boner	Y	Y	N	Y	Y	Y	?	Y
6 ***Beard***	N	Y	N	N	Y	Y	Y	Y

	267	268	269	270	271	272	273	274
7 Jones	Y	Y	N	Y	Y	Y	Y	Y
8 Ford	Y	Y	Y	Y	Y	Y	Y	N
TEXAS								
1 Hall, S.	N	Y	Y	N	Y	Y	Y	Y
2 Wilson	Y	Y	Y	Y	Y	Y	Y	N
3 ***Collins***	N	Y	N	N	Y	N	N	Y
4 Hall, R.	N	Y	N	N	Y	N	Y	Y
5 Mattox	?	?	?	Y	Y	Y	Y	N
6 Gramm	N	Y	N	N	Y	N	N	Y
7 ***Archer***	N	Y	N	N	Y	N	N	Y
8 ***Fields***	N	Y	N	N	Y	N	Y	Y
9 Brooks	?	Y	Y	Y	Y	Y	Y	N
10 Pickle	Y	Y	N	Y	Y	Y	Y	Y
11 Leath	N	Y	N	N	Y	N	Y	N
12 Wright	Y	Y	Y	Y	Y	Y	Y	N
13 Hightower	Y	Y	Y	N	Y	Y	Y	Y
14 Patman	Y	Y	N	N	Y	Y	Y	Y
15 de la Garza	Y	Y	Y	Y	Y	Y	Y	N
16 White	N	Y	N	Y	Y	Y	Y	N
17 Stenholm	N	Y	N	N	Y	N	Y	Y
18 Leland	Y	Y	Y	Y	Y	Y	Y	N
19 Hance	Y	Y	N	N	Y	N	Y	Y
20 Gonzalez	Y	Y	P	Y	Y	Y	Y	Y
21 ***Loeffler***	N	Y	N	N	Y	N	N	Y
22 ***Paul***	N	?	?	?	?	N	N	Y
23 Kazen	Y	Y	N	N	Y	Y	Y	Y
24 Frost	Y	Y	N	Y	Y	Y	Y	N
UTAH								
1 ***Hansen***	?	Y	N	N	Y	N	N	Y
2 ***Marriott***	?	Y	N	N	Y	Y	Y	Y
VERMONT								
AL ***Jeffords***	Y	Y	Y	Y	Y	Y	Y	Y
VIRGINIA								
1 ***Trible***	?	Y	N	N	Y	N	Y	Y
2 ***Whitehurst***	N	Y	N	N	Y	N	Y	Y
3 ***Bliley***	N	Y	N	N	Y	N	Y	Y
4 ***Daniel, R.***	N	Y	N	N	Y	N	Y	Y
5 Daniel, D.	N	Y	N	N	Y	N	Y	N
6 ***Butler***	N	Y	N	N	Y	N	Y	N
7 ***Robinson***	N	Y	N	N	Y	N	Y	Y
8 ***Parris***	N	Y	N	Y	Y	Y	Y	Y
9 ***Wampler***	N	Y	N	N	Y	Y	Y	Y
10 ***Wolf***	N	Y	N	Y	Y	Y	Y	N
WASHINGTON								
1 ***Pritchard***	N	Y	N	N	Y	Y	Y	N
2 Swift	Y	Y	N	Y	Y	Y	Y	Y
3 Bonker	?	Y	Y	Y	Y	Y	Y	N
4 ***Morrison***	N	Y	N	N	Y	Y	Y	N
5 Foley	Y	Y	Y	Y	Y	Y	Y	N
6 Dicks	Y	Y	Y	Y	Y	Y	Y	Y
7 Lowry	Y	Y	Y	Y	Y	Y	Y	N
WEST VIRGINIA								
1 Mollohan	Y	Y	N	Y	Y	Y	Y	N
2 ***Benedict***	N	Y	N	N	Y	Y	Y	Y
3 ***Staton***	N	Y	N	N	Y	Y	N	Y
4 Rahall	Y	?	#	?	?	?	?	?
WISCONSIN								
1 Aspin	Y	Y	Y	Y	Y	Y	Y	N
2 Kastenmeier	Y	Y	Y	Y	Y	Y	Y	Y
3 ***Gunderson***	N	Y	N	Y	Y	Y	Y	Y
4 Zablocki	Y	Y	Y	Y	Y	Y	Y	N
5 Reuss	Y	Y	Y	Y	Y	Y	Y	Y
6 ***Petri***	N	Y	N	Y	N	Y	Y	Y
7 Obey	Y	Y	Y	Y	Y	Y	Y	N
8 ***Roth***	?	?	?	N	Y	Y	Y	Y
9 ***Sensenbrenner***	N	Y	N	N	Y	N	Y	Y
WYOMING								
AL ***Cheney***	?	Y	N	N	Y	N	N	Y

Southern states - Ala., Ark., Fla., Ga., Ky., La., Miss., N.C., Okla., S.C., Tenn., Texas, Va.

275. HR 6530. Mount St. Helens National Volcanic Monument. Adoption of the conference report on the bill to create a 110,000-acre national monument in the area of Washington state devastated by the May 18, 1980, volcanic eruption of Mount St. Helens. Adopted 393-8: R 169-7; D 224-1 (ND 151-0, SD 73-1), Aug. 17, 1982.

276. Procedural Motion. Waxman, D-Calif., motion to approve the House *Journal* of Tuesday, Aug. 17. Motion agreed to 353-37: R 160-18; D 193-19 (ND 130-15, SD 63-4), Aug. 18, 1982.

277. HR 6955. Omnibus Reconciliation Act of 1982. Adoption of the conference report on the bill to reduce the federal budget for fiscal years 1983, 1984 and 1985 by approximately $13.3 billion. Adopted 243-176: R 152-34; D 91-142 (ND 48-110, SD 43-32), Aug. 18, 1982. A "yea" was a vote supporting the president's position.

278. HR 5540. Defense Industrial Base Revitalization Act. Blanchard, D-Mich., motion that the House resolve itself into the Commitee of the Whole for consideration of the bill to provide financial incentives to defense-related industries. Motion agreed to 357-8: R 139-5; D 218-3 (ND 146-3, SD 72-0), Aug. 18, 1982.

279. HR 5540. Defense Industrial Base Revitalization Act. Perkins, D-Ky., amendment to prohibit use of funds authorized under the bill unless the funds were attributed to budget functions or allocations other than those for the departments of Education and Labor or for any programs under the jurisdiction of congressional committees responsible for education and labor programs. Adopted 242-180: R 52-134; D 190-46 (ND 149-10, SD 41-36), Aug. 18, 1982.

280. HR 6863. Supplemental Appropriations, Fiscal 1982. Adoption of the conference report on the bill to appropriate $14,578,111,924 in new fiscal 1982 budget authority for federal military and civilian employee pay raises, commodity credit programs, defense and other programs, and to rescind $400,846,000 in previously appropriated funds. Adopted 348-67: R 130-49; D 218-18 (ND 156-3, SD 62-15), Aug. 18, 1982. The president had requested spending of $16,343,043,000 and rescissions totaling $286,859,000.

281. HR 6863. Supplemental Appropriations, Fiscal 1982. Long, D-Md., motion that the House recede from its disagreement and concur with a Senate amendment to appropriate $350 million for President Reagan's Caribbean Basin Initiative. Motion agreed to 281-129: R 132-48; D 149-81 (ND 108-47, SD 41-34), Aug. 18, 1982. A "yea" was a vote supporting the president's position.

282. HR 6863. Supplemental Appropriations, Fiscal 1982. Long, D-Md., motion that the House recede from its disagreement and concur with a Senate amendment to provide funds for Military Assistance Program (MAP) grants, with an amendment to provide $2 million in new budget authority and to reprogram $25 million in already appropriated funds as follows: $10 million for Honduras, $5 million for Somalia, $2 million for Costa Rica and $10 million for Portugal. The principal effects of the amendment were to eliminate $20 million in military aid to El Salvador and halve the amount given to Somalia. Motion agreed to 237-175: R 146-35; D 91-140 (ND 42-114, SD 49-26), Aug. 18, 1982.

KEY

Y	Voted for (yea).
#	Paired for.
+	Announced for.
N	Voted against (nay).
X	Paired against.
-	Announced against.
P	Voted "present".
C	Voted "present" to avoid possible conflict of interest.
?	Did not vote or otherwise make a position known.

Democrats   *Republicans*

	275	276	277	278	279	280	281	282
ALABAMA								
1 *Edwards*	Y	Y	Y	?	N	Y	Y	Y
2 *Dickinson*	Y	N	Y	N	Y	N	Y	N
3 Nichols	Y	Y	N	Y	N	Y	N	Y
4 Bevill	Y	Y	N	Y	N	Y	Y	Y
5 Flippo	Y	Y	N	Y	N	Y	Y	Y
6 *Smith*	Y	Y	Y	Y	N	N	Y	Y
7 Shelby	Y	Y	Y	Y	N	Y	N	Y
ALASKA								
AL *Young*	?	?	N	Y	N	Y	N	Y
ARIZONA								
1 *Rhodes*	Y	Y	Y	Y	N	Y	Y	Y
2 Udall	Y	N	Y	Y	Y	Y	Y	N
3 *Stump*	Y	Y	Y	Y	N	N	N	Y
4 *Rudd*	Y	Y	Y	Y	N	Y	Y	Y
ARKANSAS								
1 Alexander	Y	Y	Y	Y	Y	Y	Y	Y
2 *Bethune*	Y	Y	Y	Y	N	Y	N	N
3 *Hammerschmidt*	Y	Y	Y	Y	N	Y	N	Y
4 Anthony	Y	Y	Y	Y	Y	Y	Y	N
CALIFORNIA								
1 *Chappie*	Y	Y	Y	Y	N	Y	N	Y
2 *Clausen*	Y	?	Y	Y	Y	Y	Y	Y
3 Matsui	Y	Y	N	Y	Y	Y	Y	Y
4 Fazio	Y	Y	N	Y	Y	Y	Y	Y
5 Burton, J.	?	?	?	Y	Y	?	?	?
6 Burton, P.	Y	Y	N	Y	Y	Y	N	N
7 Miller	Y	Y	N	Y	Y	Y	N	N
8 Dellums	Y	N	N	?	Y	N	Y	N
9 Stark	Y	Y	N	Y	?	N	Y	N
10 Edwards	Y	Y	N	Y	Y	Y	Y	Y
11 Lantos	Y	Y	N	Y	Y	Y	N	N
12 *McCloskey*	Y	Y	Y	?	Y	Y	Y	Y
13 Mineta	Y	Y	N	Y	Y	Y	Y	Y
14 *Shumway*	Y	Y	Y	Y	N	N	N	Y
15 Coelho	Y	Y	Y	Y	Y	Y	Y	N
16 Panetta	Y	Y	Y	Y	Y	Y	Y	Y
17 Pashayan	Y	Y	Y	Y	N	?	N	Y
18 Thomas	Y	Y	Y	Y	N	Y	Y	Y
19 *Lagomarsino*	Y	Y	Y	Y	N	Y	Y	Y
20 *Goldwater*	?	?	#	?	N	Y	?	?
21 *Fiedler*	Y	Y	Y	Y	N	Y	Y	Y
22 *Moorhead*	Y	Y	Y	Y	N	N	N	Y
23 Beilenson	Y	N	Y	Y	Y	Y	Y	N
24 Waxman	Y	Y	N	Y	Y	Y	Y	N
25 Roybal	Y	Y	N	Y	Y	Y	Y	Y
26 *Rousselot*	?	Y	Y	Y	N	N	Y	Y
27 *Dornan*	Y	Y	Y	?	N	Y	Y	Y
28 Dixon	Y	Y	Y	Y	Y	Y	Y	Y
29 Hawkins	Y	Y	Y	Y	Y	Y	Y	N
30 Martinez	Y	Y	N	Y	Y	Y	Y	N
31 Dymally	Y	Y	N	Y	Y	Y	Y	N
32 Anderson	Y	Y	Y	Y	Y	Y	Y	N
33 Grisham	Y	Y	Y	Y	N	N	Y	Y
34 *Lungren*	N	Y	Y	Y	N	Y	Y	Y
35 *Dreier*	N	N	Y	N	N	N	N	Y
36 Brown	Y	Y	N	Y	Y	Y	Y	N
37 *Lewis*	Y	Y	Y	Y	N	N	Y	Y
38 Patterson	Y	N	Y	Y	Y	N	N	N
39 *Dannemeyer*	Y	Y	N	Y	N	N	N	Y
40 *Badham*	Y	Y	Y	Y	N	N	Y	Y
41 *Lowery*	Y	Y	Y	?	N	Y	Y	Y
42 *Hunter*	Y	Y	Y	Y	N	N	Y	Y
43 *Burgener*	Y	Y	Y	?	N	Y	Y	Y
COLORADO								
1 Schroeder	Y	N	N	Y	Y	Y	Y	N
2 Wirth	Y	Y	N	Y	Y	Y	Y	N
3 Kogovsek	Y	Y	N	Y	Y	Y	N	N
4 *Brown*	Y	N	Y	Y	Y	X	N	N
5 *Kramer*	Y	Y	Y	?	N	Y	N	N
CONNECTICUT								
1 Kennelly	Y	Y	N	Y	Y	Y	Y	N
2 Gejdenson	Y	N	N	Y	Y	Y	Y	N
3 *DeNardis*	Y	Y	Y	Y	Y	Y	Y	Y
4 *McKinney*	Y	Y	Y	Y	Y	Y	Y	Y
5 Ratchford	Y	Y	N	Y	Y	Y	Y	N
6 Moffett	?	?	X	?	?	?	?	?
DELAWARE								
AL *Evans*	Y	Y	Y	?	Y	Y	Y	?
FLORIDA								
1 Hutto	Y	Y	N	Y	N	Y	Y	Y
2 Fuqua	Y	Y	Y	Y	Y	Y	Y	Y
3 Bennett	Y	Y	Y	Y	N	N	N	Y
4 Chappell	Y	?	#	Y	?	?	?	?
5 *McCollum*	Y	Y	Y	?	N	Y	Y	Y
6 *Young*	Y	?	?	Y	N	Y	Y	Y
7 Gibbons	Y	Y	Y	Y	N	Y	Y	Y
8 Ireland	?	?	?	Y	N	Y	?	?
9 Nelson	Y	Y	N	Y	N	Y	Y	Y
10 *Bafalis*	?	?	?	?	?	?	?	?
11 Mica	Y	Y	Y	Y	Y	Y	Y	Y
12 *Shaw*	Y	Y	Y	Y	N	Y	Y	Y
13 Lehman	Y	Y	Y	?	Y	Y	Y	Y
14 Pepper	Y	?	N	Y	Y	Y	Y	Y
15 Fascell	Y	Y	Y	Y	Y	Y	Y	Y
GEORGIA								
1 Ginn	?	?	?	?	?	?	?	?
2 Hatcher	Y	Y	Y	Y	Y	Y	N	N
3 Brinkley	Y	Y	N	Y	N	Y	Y	Y
4 Levitas	Y	Y	Y	Y	Y	Y	Y	Y
5 Fowler	Y	Y	Y	Y	Y	Y	Y	Y
6 *Gingrich*	Y	Y	Y	Y	N	N	Y	Y
7 McDonald	N	Y	N	Y	N	N	N	Y
8 Evans	Y	?	N	Y	Y	Y	Y	Y
9 Jenkins	Y	Y	Y	Y	N	Y	N	N
10 Barnard	Y	Y	Y	Y	N	Y	N	Y
HAWAII								
1 Heftel	?	?	?	?	?	?	?	?
2 Akaka	Y	Y	N	Y	N	Y	Y	Y
IDAHO								
1 *Craig*	Y	Y	Y	?	N	N	Y	Y
2 *Hansen*	Y	Y	Y	?	N	N	Y	Y
ILLINOIS								
1 Washington	Y	N	N	Y	Y	Y	N	N
2 Savage	Y	?	N	?	Y	Y	N	N
3 Russo	Y	Y	Y	Y	Y	Y	N	N
4 *Derwinski*	Y	N	Y	N	N	Y	Y	Y
5 Fary	Y	Y	Y	Y	Y	Y	Y	Y
6 *Hyde*	Y	Y	?	N	Y	Y	Y	Y
7 Collins	Y	Y	N	Y	Y	Y	Y	N
8 Rostenkowski	Y	Y	Y	Y	Y	Y	Y	N
9 Yates	?	N	N	Y	Y	Y	Y	N
10 *Porter*	Y	Y	Y	Y	Y	Y	Y	Y
11 Annunzio	Y	Y	Y	Y	Y	Y	Y	Y
12 *Crane, P.*	N	Y	Y	Y	N	N	N	Y
13 *McClory*	Y	Y	Y	Y	N	N	Y	Y
14 *Erlenborn*	Y	Y	Y	Y	N	N	Y	Y
15 *Corcoran*	Y	Y	Y	+	N	N	Y	Y
16 *Martin*	Y	Y	Y	Y	N	Y	N	N
17 *O'Brien*	Y	Y	Y	Y	?	?	?	?
18 *Michel*	Y	Y	Y	?	N	N	?	Y
19 *Railsback*	Y	Y	Y	Y	N	Y	N	N
20 *Findley*	Y	Y	Y	Y	N	Y	Y	Y
21 Madigan	Y	N	Y	N	N	?	?	?
22 *Crane, D.*	Y	Y	Y	Y	N	N	Y	Y
23 Price	Y	Y	Y	Y	N	Y	Y	Y
24 Simon	Y	Y	Y	Y	Y	Y	Y	Y
INDIANA								
1 Benjamin	Y	Y	Y	Y	Y	Y	N	N
2 Fithian	Y	Y	N	Y	Y	Y	Y	N
3 *Hiler*	Y	Y	Y	?	N	Y	Y	Y
4 *Coats*	Y	Y	Y	Y	N	Y	Y	Y
5 *Hillis*	Y	Y	Y	?	Y	Y	Y	Y
6 Evans	Y	Y	Y	Y	Y	Y	Y	N
7 *Myers*	Y	Y	N	Y	N	Y	Y	Y
8 *Deckard*	Y	Y	Y	Y	N	Y	Y	Y
9 Hamilton	Y	Y	Y	Y	Y	Y	Y	N
10 Sharp	Y	Y	Y	Y	Y	Y	Y	N
11 Jacobs	Y	N	Y	Y	Y	Y	Y	N
IOWA								
1 *Leach*	Y	?	Y	Y	Y	Y	Y	N
2 *Tauke*	Y	Y	N	Y	Y	Y	Y	N
3 *Evans*	Y	N	N	Y	Y	Y	Y	N
4 Smith	Y	Y	N	Y	Y	Y	Y	N
5 Harkin	Y	N	N	Y	Y	Y	Y	N
6 Bedell	Y	N	Y	Y	Y	Y	Y	N

ND - Northern Democrats   SD - Southern Democrats

	275	276	277	278	279	280	281	282
KANSAS								
1 ***Roberts***	Y	N	Y	?	N	Y	N	Y
2 ***Jeffries***	Y	Y	Y	Y	N	Y	N	Y
3 ***Winn***	Y	Y	Y	Y	N	Y	Y	Y
4 Glickman	Y	Y	Y	Y	Y	Y	Y	N
5 ***Whittaker***	Y	Y	Y	Y	N	Y	N	Y
KENTUCKY								
1 Hubbard	Y	?	N	Y	Y	N	N	Y
2 Natcher	Y	Y	Y	Y	Y	Y	Y	Y
3 Mazzoli	Y	Y	Y	Y	Y	Y	Y	N
4 ***Snyder***	Y	Y	Y	Y	Y	N	N	Y
5 ***Rogers***	Y	N	Y	Y	Y	Y	Y	Y
6 ***Hopkins***	Y	Y	Y	Y	Y	Y	N	Y
7 Perkins	Y	Y	Y	Y	Y	Y	Y	N
LOUISIANA								
1 ***Livingston***	?	Y	Y	Y	N	Y	Y	Y
2 Boggs	Y	Y	N	Y	Y	Y	Y	Y
3 Tauzin	Y	Y	Y	Y	N	Y	N	N
4 Roemer	Y	N	Y	Y	N	N	N	N
5 Huckaby	Y	Y	Y	Y	N	Y	Y	Y
6 ***Moore***	Y	Y	Y	Y	N	N	Y	Y
7 Breaux	?	Y	Y	Y	N	Y	N	N
8 Long	Y	Y	Y	Y	Y	Y	Y	N
MAINE								
1 ***Emery***	?	Y	Y	Y	N	Y	N	N
2 ***Snowe***	Y	Y	Y	Y	Y	Y	Y	N
MARYLAND								
1 Dyson	Y	Y	N	Y	N	Y	N	Y
2 Long	Y	Y	Y	Y	Y	Y	Y	Y
3 Mikulski	Y	Y	N	Y	Y	Y	N	N
4 ***Holt***	?	?	X	?	?	?	?	?
5 Hoyer	Y	Y	N	?	Y	Y	Y	N
6 Byron	Y	?	N	Y	N	Y	N	Y
7 Mitchell	Y	N	N	N	Y	Y	Y	N
8 Barnes	Y	N	N	Y	Y	Y	Y	N
MASSACHUSETTS								
1 ***Conte***	Y	Y	N	?	Y	Y	Y	N
2 Boland	Y	Y	Y	?	Y	Y	Y	Y
3 Early	Y	Y	Y	?	Y	Y	N	N
4 Frank	Y	Y	N	Y	Y	Y	N	N
5 Shannon	Y	Y	N	Y	Y	Y	N	N
6 Mavroules	Y	Y	N	Y	N	Y	Y	Y
7 Markey	Y	N	N	Y	Y	Y	Y	N
8 O'Neill								
9 Moakley	Y	Y	Y	Y	Y	Y	Y	Y
10 ***Heckler***	Y	Y	N	Y	Y	Y	N	N
11 Donnelly	Y	Y	Y	N	Y	Y	N	Y
12 Studds	Y	Y	N	Y	Y	Y	Y	N
MICHIGAN								
1 Conyers	?	Y	N	Y	Y	Y	N	N
2 ***Pursell***	Y	Y	Y	Y	Y	Y	Y	Y
3 Wolpe	Y	N	N	Y	Y	Y	Y	N
4 ***Siljander***	Y	Y	Y	?	N	Y	N	Y
5 ***Sawyer***	Y	Y	Y	Y	N	Y	Y	Y
6 ***Dunn***	Y	Y	Y	Y	Y	Y	N	N
7 Kildee	Y	Y	N	Y	Y	Y	Y	N
8 Traxler	Y	Y	N	Y	Y	Y	N	N
9 ***Vander Jagt***	Y	Y	Y	?	N	Y	Y	Y
10 Albosta	Y	Y	N	Y	Y	Y	N	N
11 ***Davis***	Y	Y	N	Y	Y	Y	Y	Y
12 Bonior	?	Y	N	Y	Y	Y	Y	N
13 Crockett	Y	Y	N	?	Y	Y	N	N
14 Hertel	Y	Y	N	Y	Y	Y	N	Y
15 Ford	Y	Y	N	Y	Y	Y	N	N
16 Dingell	Y	Y	Y	Y	Y	Y	Y	N
17 Brodhead	Y	Y	N	Y	Y	Y	N	N
18 Blanchard	Y	Y	N	Y	Y	Y	N	N
19 ***Broomfield***	?	Y	Y	Y	N	Y	Y	Y
MINNESOTA								
1 ***Erdahl***	Y	Y	Y	Y	Y	Y	Y	Y
2 ***Hagedorn***	Y	Y	Y	?	N	N	Y	Y
3 ***Frenzel***	Y	Y	Y	N	N	N	Y	Y
4 Vento	Y	Y	N	Y	Y	Y	N	N
5 Sabo	Y	N	Y	Y	Y	Y	Y	N
6 ***Weber***	Y	Y	Y	?	N	Y	Y	Y
7 ***Stangeland***	Y	Y	Y	Y	Y	Y	Y	Y
8 Oberstar	Y	?	N	?	Y	Y	Y	N
MISSISSIPPI								
1 Whitten	?	?	?	?	Y	Y	N	N
2 Bowen	Y	Y	Y	Y	N	Y	Y	Y
3 Montgomery	Y	Y	Y	Y	N	N	?	Y
4 Dowdy	Y	Y	N	Y	Y	Y	N	N
5 ***Lott***	Y	Y	Y	?	N	N	?	Y
MISSOURI								
1 Clay	Y	N	N	Y	Y	Y	Y	N
2 Young	Y	Y	Y	Y	Y	Y	Y	N
3 Gephardt	Y	Y	Y	Y	Y	Y	Y	N
4 Skelton	Y	Y	Y	Y	N	Y	N	N
5 Bolling	Y	?	Y	Y	Y	Y	?	?
6 ***Coleman***	?	N	Y	Y	Y	Y	Y	Y
7 ***Taylor***	Y	Y	Y	Y	N	N	N	Y
8 ***Bailey***	Y	Y	Y	Y	N	Y	N	N
9 Volkmer	Y	Y	Y	Y	Y	?	?	?
10 ***Emerson***	Y	N	Y	Y	N	Y	N	N
MONTANA								
1 Williams	+	Y	N	Y	Y	Y	Y	N
2 ***Marlenee***	N	Y	Y	?	N	N	N	N
NEBRASKA								
1 ***Bereuter***	Y	Y	Y	Y	N	Y	Y	Y
2 ***Daub***	Y	Y	Y	?	N	Y	Y	Y
3 ***Smith***	Y	Y	Y	Y	N	Y	N	Y
NEVADA								
AL Santini	Y	?	N	Y	Y	Y	Y	Y
NEW HAMPSHIRE								
1 D'Amours	?	Y	Y	Y	Y	Y	N	Y
2 ***Gregg***	Y	Y	Y	?	N	N	Y	Y
NEW JERSEY								
1 Florio	Y	Y	N	Y	Y	Y	Y	N
2 Hughes	Y	Y	N	Y	Y	N	N	N
3 Howard	Y	Y	N	Y	Y	Y	Y	N
4 ***Smith***	Y	Y	N	Y	Y	Y	Y	Y
5 ***Fenwick***	Y	Y	Y	Y	Y	Y	Y	Y
6 ***Forsythe***	Y	N	Y	?	Y	Y	Y	N
7 ***Roukema***	Y	Y	Y	?	Y	Y	N	Y
8 Roe	Y	Y	N	Y	Y	Y	Y	N
9 ***Hollenbeck***	Y	?	N	Y	Y	Y	Y	N
10 Rodino	Y	Y	N	Y	Y	Y	Y	N
11 Minish	Y	Y	N	Y	Y	Y	Y	Y
12 ***Rinaldo***	Y	Y	N	Y	Y	Y	Y	Y
13 ***Courter***	Y	Y	Y	Y	N	#	Y	Y
14 Guarini	Y	Y	N	Y	Y	Y	Y	Y
15 Dwyer	Y	Y	N	Y	Y	Y	Y	Y
NEW MEXICO								
1 ***Lujan***	Y	Y	Y	Y	N	Y	Y	N
2 ***Skeen***	Y	Y	Y	Y	N	Y	Y	Y
NEW YORK								
1 ***Carney***	Y	Y	Y	?	N	Y	Y	Y
2 Downey	Y	Y	N	Y	Y	Y	Y	N
3 ***Carman***	Y	Y	Y	Y	N	Y	Y	Y
4 ***Lent***	Y	Y	N	?	N	Y	Y	Y
5 ***McGrath***	Y	Y	N	Y	N	Y	Y	Y
6 ***LeBoutillier***	Y	?	Y	?	N	Y	Y	Y
7 Addabbo	Y	Y	N	Y	Y	Y	Y	Y
8 Rosenthal	?	?	X	?	Y	Y	?	?
9 Ferraro	Y	Y	N	Y	Y	Y	Y	N
10 Biaggi	Y	Y	N	Y	Y	Y	Y	Y
11 Scheuer	Y	Y	N	Y	Y	Y	Y	Y
12 Chisholm	Y	?	N	?	Y	Y	Y	N
13 Solarz	Y	Y	N	Y	Y	Y	Y	Y
14 Richmond	Y	?	N	Y	Y	Y	Y	N
15 Zeferetti	Y	Y	N	Y	Y	Y	Y	Y
16 Schumer	Y	Y	N	Y	Y	Y	Y	N
17 ***Molinari***	Y	Y	Y	Y	N	Y	Y	Y
18 ***Green***	Y	Y	N	Y	Y	Y	Y	Y
19 Rangel	Y	Y	N	Y	Y	Y	Y	N
20 Weiss	Y	Y	N	Y	Y	Y	Y	N
21 Garcia	Y	?	N	Y	Y	Y	Y	N
22 Bingham	Y	Y	Y	Y	Y	Y	Y	N
23 Peyser	Y	Y	N	Y	Y	Y	Y	N
24 Ottinger	Y	P	N	P	Y	Y	Y	N
25 ***Fish***	Y	Y	N	Y	?	?	Y	Y
26 ***Gilman***	?	Y	N	Y	Y	Y	Y	Y
27 McHugh	Y	Y	N	Y	Y	Y	Y	N
28 Stratton	Y	Y	Y	Y	N	Y	Y	Y
29 ***Solomon***	Y	Y	Y	Y	N	Y	N	Y
30 ***Martin***	Y	Y	Y	?	N	Y	Y	Y
31 ***Mitchell***	Y	Y	N	Y	N	?	Y	Y
32 ***Wortley***	Y	Y	Y	Y	Y	Y	Y	N
33 ***Lee***	Y	Y	Y	Y	N	Y	Y	N
34 ***Horton***	Y	Y	N	Y	Y	Y	Y	N
35 ***Conable***	Y	Y	Y	Y	N	Y	Y	Y
36 LaFalce	Y	Y	N	?	Y	Y	Y	Y
37 Nowak	Y	Y	N	Y	Y	Y	Y	N
38 ***Kemp***	Y	Y	Y	?	N	Y	Y	Y
39 Lundine	Y	Y	Y	Y	Y	Y	Y	N
NORTH CAROLINA								
1 Jones	Y	Y	Y	Y	N	Y	N	Y
2 Fountain	Y	N	Y	Y	N	Y	N	Y
3 Whitley	Y	Y	Y	Y	N	Y	N	Y
4 Andrews	Y	Y	Y	Y	Y	Y	N	Y
5 Neal	?	?	?	Y	N	Y	N	N
6 ***Johnston***	Y	N	Y	N	N	N	N	Y
7 Rose	Y	Y	N	?	Y	Y	N	Y
8 Hefner	Y	Y	Y	Y	Y	Y	N	N
9 ***Martin***	Y	Y	Y	?	N	Y	Y	Y
10 ***Broyhill***	?	Y	Y	Y	N	N	N	Y
11 ***Hendon***	Y	Y	Y	Y	N	Y	N	N
NORTH DAKOTA								
AL Dorgan	Y	Y	N	Y	Y	Y	N	N
OHIO								
1 ***Gradison***	Y	Y	Y	Y	Y	Y	Y	Y
2 Luken	Y	N	N	Y	Y	Y	Y	Y
3 Hall	?	Y	Y	Y	Y	N	N	N
4 ***Oxley***	Y	Y	Y	Y	N	Y	Y	Y
5 ***Latta***	Y	Y	Y	Y	N	N	Y	Y
6 ***McEwen***	Y	Y	Y	Y	N	Y	N	Y
7 ***Brown***	?	?	?	?	?	?	?	?
8 ***Kindness***	Y	Y	Y	?	N	N	N	N
9 ***Weber***	Y	Y	Y	Y	N	?	Y	Y
10 ***Miller***	Y	N	Y	Y	Y	Y	N	N
11 ***Stanton***	?	Y	#	Y	?	?	?	?
12 Shamansky	Y	Y	N	Y	Y	Y	Y	N
13 Pease	Y	Y	N	Y	Y	Y	Y	N
14 Seiberling	Y	Y	N	Y	Y	Y	Y	N
15 ***Wylie***	?	Y	Y	Y	Y	Y	Y	Y
16 ***Regula***	Y	Y	Y	Y	N	Y	Y	Y
17 ***Ashbrook***	N	Y	N	Y	N	N	N	Y
18 Applegate	Y	?	N	?	N	Y	N	N
19 ***Williams***	Y	Y	Y	Y	Y	Y	Y	N
20 Oakar	Y	Y	N	Y	Y	Y	N	N
21 Stokes	Y	Y	N	Y	Y	Y	Y	N
22 Eckart	Y	Y	N	Y	Y	Y	N	N
23 Mottl	Y	Y	N	Y	Y	Y	N	N
OKLAHOMA								
1 Jones	Y	Y	Y	Y	Y	Y	N	Y
2 Synar	Y	Y	N	Y	Y	Y	Y	N
3 Watkins	Y	Y	N	Y	Y	Y	N	N
4 McCurdy	Y	Y	N	Y	N	Y	Y	Y
5 ***Edwards***	N	Y	Y	?	N	N	Y	Y
6 English	Y	Y	N	Y	Y	Y	N	Y
OREGON								
1 AuCoin	Y	Y	Y	Y	Y	Y	N	N
2 ***Smith***	Y	Y	Y	Y	N	N	N	Y
3 Wyden	Y	Y	N	Y	Y	Y	N	N
4 Weaver	Y	Y	N	Y	Y	Y	N	N
PENNSYLVANIA								
1 Foglietta	Y	Y	N	Y	Y	Y	Y	N
2 Gray	Y	Y	N	Y	Y	Y	Y	N
3 Smith	Y	?	Y	Y	Y	Y	Y	Y
4 ***Dougherty***	Y	?	N	Y	N	Y	Y	Y
5 ***Schulze***	Y	?	Y	Y	N	Y	Y	Y
6 Yatron	?	Y	N	Y	Y	Y	N	Y
7 Edgar	Y	Y	N	Y	?	Y	Y	N
8 ***Coyne, J.***	Y	Y	N	Y	N	Y	Y	N
9 ***Shuster***	Y	Y	Y	Y	N	N	?	?
10 ***McDade***	Y	Y	N	Y	Y	Y	Y	Y
11 ***Nelligan***	Y	Y	N	Y	N	Y	Y	Y
12 Murtha	Y	Y	Y	Y	Y	Y	N	Y
13 ***Coughlin***	Y	N	Y	Y	Y	Y	Y	Y
14 Coyne, W.	Y	Y	Y	Y	Y	Y	Y	N
15 ***Ritter***	Y	Y	Y	Y	N	Y	N	N
16 ***Walker***	Y	N	Y	Y	N	N	N	Y
17 Ertel	Y	Y	N	Y	Y	Y	Y	?
18 Walgren	Y	Y	Y	Y	Y	Y	Y	N
19 ***Goodling***	Y	N	Y	Y	Y	Y	Y	N
20 Gaydos	Y	Y	N	Y	Y	Y	Y	N
21 Bailey	Y	Y	N	Y	Y	Y	Y	Y
22 Murphy	Y	Y	N	Y	Y	Y	N	N
23 ***Clinger***	Y	Y	Y	Y	N	Y	Y	Y
24 ***Marks***	?	?	Y	?	Y	?	?	?
25 ***Atkinson***	?	Y	N	Y	N	N	N	N
RHODE ISLAND								
1 St Germain	Y	?	N	Y	Y	Y	N	N
2 ***Schneider***	Y	Y	N	Y	Y	Y	Y	N
SOUTH CAROLINA								
1 ***Hartnett***	Y	Y	N	?	N	N	N	Y
2 ***Spence***	Y	Y	Y	Y	N	N	Y	Y
3 Derrick	Y	Y	Y	Y	N	Y	Y	Y
4 ***Campbell***	Y	Y	Y	Y	N	Y	Y	Y
5 Holland	Y	Y	Y	?	Y	Y	Y	?
6 ***Napier***	Y	Y	N	Y	N	Y	N	Y
SOUTH DAKOTA								
1 Daschle	Y	Y	Y	Y	Y	Y	N	N
2 ***Roberts***	Y	Y	Y	Y	N	Y	N	Y
TENNESSEE								
1 ***Quillen***	Y	Y	Y	Y	N	Y	N	N
2 ***Duncan***	Y	Y	Y	Y	N	Y	Y	Y
3 Bouquard	Y	Y	N	Y	N	N	N	Y
4 Gore	Y	N	N	Y	Y	Y	Y	Y
5 Boner	Y	Y	N	Y	Y	Y	N	N
6 ***Beard***	Y	Y	Y	Y	N	Y	?	?
7 Jones	Y	N	Y	Y	Y	N	N	Y
8 Ford	Y	?	N	Y	Y	Y	Y	N
TEXAS								
1 Hall, S.	Y	Y	N	Y	N	N	N	N
2 Wilson	Y	Y	Y	Y	N	Y	Y	Y
3 ***Collins***	Y	Y	Y	Y	N	N	N	N
4 Hall, R.	Y	Y	N	Y	N	N	N	N
5 Mattox	Y	Y	N	Y	Y	Y	N	N
6 Gramm	Y	Y	Y	Y	N	N	N	Y
7 ***Archer***	Y	Y	Y	?	N	N	Y	Y
8 ***Fields***	Y	N	Y	?	N	N	Y	Y
9 Brooks	Y	?	Y	Y	Y	Y	N	N
10 Pickle	Y	Y	Y	Y	Y	Y	Y	Y
11 Leath	Y	Y	N	Y	N	N	N	Y
12 Wright	Y	Y	N	Y	Y	Y	Y	Y
13 Hightower	Y	Y	Y	Y	Y	Y	Y	Y
14 Patman	Y	Y	N	Y	N	N	N	N
15 de la Garza	Y	Y	Y	Y	Y	Y	Y	Y
16 White	Y	Y	N	Y	N	Y	Y	Y
17 Stenholm	Y	Y	Y	Y	N	N	N	Y
18 Leland	Y	?	N	Y	Y	Y	N	N
19 Hance	Y	Y	N	Y	N	N	Y	Y
20 Gonzalez	Y	Y	N	Y	Y	Y	Y	N
21 ***Loeffler***	Y	Y	Y	?	N	N	Y	Y
22 ***Paul***	N	Y	Y	Y	N	N	N	N
23 Kazen	Y	Y	N	Y	Y	Y	Y	Y
24 Frost	Y	Y	N	Y	Y	Y	Y	Y
UTAH								
1 ***Hansen***	Y	Y	Y	Y	N	N	Y	Y
2 ***Marriott***	Y	Y	Y	Y	N	Y	Y	Y
VERMONT								
AL ***Jeffords***	Y	Y	N	Y	Y	Y	Y	Y
VIRGINIA								
1 ***Trible***	Y	?	?	Y	N	Y	Y	Y
2 ***Whitehurst***	Y	Y	Y	Y	N	Y	Y	Y
3 ***Bliley***	Y	Y	Y	Y	N	Y	Y	Y
4 ***Daniel, R.***	Y	Y	Y	Y	N	Y	Y	Y
5 Daniel, D.	Y	?	Y	Y	N	Y	Y	Y
6 ***Butler***	Y	N	Y	Y	N	Y	Y	Y
7 ***Robinson***	Y	Y	Y	?	N	Y	Y	Y
8 ***Parris***	Y	Y	N	Y	N	Y	Y	Y
9 ***Wampler***	Y	Y	Y	?	N	Y	Y	Y
10 ***Wolf***	Y	Y	N	Y	N	Y	Y	Y
WASHINGTON								
1 ***Pritchard***	Y	Y	Y	Y	Y	Y	Y	Y
2 Swift	Y	Y	Y	Y	Y	Y	Y	N
3 Bonker	Y	Y	Y	Y	Y	Y	N	N
4 ***Morrison***	Y	Y	Y	Y	N	Y	Y	Y
5 Foley	Y	Y	Y	Y	Y	Y	?	Y
6 Dicks	Y	Y	N	Y	Y	Y	Y	Y
7 Lowry	Y	Y	N	Y	Y	Y	Y	N
WEST VIRGINIA								
1 Mollohan	Y	?	?	Y	N	Y	Y	Y
2 ***Benedict***	Y	Y	Y	Y	N	Y	N	Y
3 ***Staton***	Y	Y	Y	Y	N	Y	Y	Y
4 Rahall	?	Y	N	Y	Y	Y	Y	N
WISCONSIN								
1 Aspin	Y	?	?	Y	Y	Y	Y	Y
2 Kastenmeier	Y	Y	N	Y	Y	Y	N	N
3 ***Gunderson***	Y	Y	N	Y	Y	Y	Y	Y
4 Zablocki	Y	Y	N	Y	Y	Y	Y	Y
5 Reuss	Y	Y	Y	Y	Y	Y	Y	N
6 ***Petri***	Y	Y	N	Y	Y	Y	Y	Y
7 Obey	Y	Y	N	Y	Y	Y	Y	Y
8 ***Roth***	Y	Y	N	Y	N	Y	Y	Y
9 ***Sensenbrenner***	Y	Y	N	Y	N	N	N	N
WYOMING								
AL ***Cheney***	Y	Y	Y	?	N	N	Y	Y

Southern states - Ala., Ark., Fla., Ga., Ky., La., Miss., N.C., Okla., S.C., Tenn., Texas, Va.

283. HR 6863. Supplemental Appropriations, Fiscal 1982. Rudd, R-Ariz., motion that the House agree to a Senate amendment to help the U.S. copper industry by requiring that all proceeds from sales of material in the government's national defense stockpile between July 31, 1982, and Oct. 1, 1983, be used to purchase copper, mined and smelted in the United States after July 31, 1982, for the stockpile. Motion rejected 62-339: R 29-144; D 33-195 (ND 26-127, SD 7-68), Aug. 18, 1982. A "nay" was a vote supporting the president's position.

284. S 2248. Department of Defense Authorizations, Fiscal 1983. Adoption of the conference report on the bill to authorize $177,867,548,000 for Defense Department programs in fiscal year 1983. Adopted 251-148: R 129-48; D 122-100 (ND 58-92, SD 64-8), Aug. 18, 1982.

285. Procedural Motion. Petri, R-Wis., motion to approve the House *Journal* of Wednesday, Aug. 18. Motion agreed to 366-27: R 165-13; D 201-14 (ND 129-13, SD 72-1), Aug. 19, 1982.

286. HR 4961. Budget Reconciliation Tax Increases/Spending Cuts. Rostenkowski, D-Ill., motion to table (kill) the Rousselot, R-Calif., resolution (H Res 571) to return HR 4961 to the Senate with a message that the Senate amendments and conference actions were not in accord with the Constitution and were an infringement on the privileges of the House. Motion agreed to 268-144: R 82-101; D 186-43 (ND 132-21, SD 54-22), Aug. 19, 1982.

287. HR 4961. Budget Reconciliation Tax Increases/Spending Cuts. Bolling, D-Mo., motion to order the previous question (thus ending debate and the possibility of amendment) on the rule (H Res 569) providing for House floor consideration of the conference report on the bill. Motion agreed to 220-210: R 75-116; D 145-94 (ND 97-64, SD 48-30), Aug. 19, 1982.

288. HR 4961. Budget Reconciliation Tax Increases/Spending Cuts. Adoption of the rule (H Res 569) providing for House floor consideration of the conference report on the bill to raise revenues by $98.3 billion in fiscal 1983-85 and reduce projected spending by $17.5 billion in fiscal 1983-85 in compliance with the fiscal 1983 budget resolution. Adopted 253-176: R 88-102; D 165-74 (ND 112-49, SD 53-25), Aug. 19, 1982.

289. HR 4961. Budget Reconciliation Tax Increases/Spending Cuts. Adoption of the conference report on the bill to raise revenues by $98.3 billion in fiscal 1983-85 and reduce projected spending by $17.5 billion in fiscal 1983-85 in compliance with the fiscal 1983 budget resolution. Adopted 226-207: R 103-89; D 123-118 (ND 93-69, SD 30-49), Aug. 19, 1982. A "yea" was a vote supporting the president's position.

KEY

Y	Voted for (yea).
#	Paired for.
+	Announced for.
N	Voted against (nay).
X	Paired against.
-	Announced against.
P	Voted "present".
C	Voted "present" to avoid possible conflict of interest.
?	Did not vote or otherwise make a position known.

Democrats **Republicans**

	283	284	285	286	287	288	289
ALABAMA							
1 Edwards	N	Y	Y	Y	Y	Y	Y
2 *Dickinson*	N	Y	N	?	Y	N	N
3 Nichols	N	Y	Y	Y	Y	Y	N
4 Bevill	N	Y	Y	Y	Y	Y	N
5 Flippo	N	Y	Y	Y	Y	Y	N
6 *Smith*	N	Y	N	N	N	N	N
7 Shelby	N	Y	?	N	Y	N	N
ALASKA							
AL *Young*	Y	Y	?	N	N	N	N
ARIZONA							
1 *Rhodes*	Y	?	Y	Y	Y	Y	Y
2 Udall	Y	Y	Y	Y	Y	N	N
3 *Stump*	Y	Y	Y	N	N	N	N
4 *Rudd*	Y	Y	Y	N	N	N	Y
ARKANSAS							
1 Alexander	Y	Y	Y	Y	Y	Y	N
2 *Bethune*	N	N	Y	N	N	N	N
3 *Hammerschmidt*	Y	Y	Y	N	N	Y	N
4 Anthony	N	N	Y	Y	Y	Y	Y
CALIFORNIA							
1 *Chappie*	N	Y	N	Y	N	Y	Y
2 *Clausen*	Y	Y	Y	N	N	N	N
3 Matsui	N	Y	Y	Y	Y	Y	Y
4 Fazio	N	Y	Y	Y	Y	Y	Y
5 Burton, J.	?	X	?	?	Y	Y	N
6 Burton, P.	N	N	Y	Y	Y	Y	Y
7 Miller	N	N	Y	Y	Y	Y	Y
8 Dellums	N	N	?	?	Y	Y	Y
9 Stark	N	N	?	Y	Y	Y	Y
10 Edwards	N	N	Y	Y	Y	Y	Y
11 Lantos	N	Y	Y	Y	Y	Y	N
12 *McCloskey*	N	N	?	N	Y	Y	Y
13 Mineta	N	N	Y	Y	Y	Y	Y
14 *Shumway*	N	Y	Y	N	N	N	N
15 Coelho	N	N	Y	Y	Y	Y	Y
16 Panetta	N	N	Y	Y	Y	Y	Y
17 *Pashayan*	N	N	?	N	N	N	Y
18 *Thomas*	N	Y	Y	N	Y	Y	Y
19 *Lagomarsino*	N	Y	Y	N	N	N	N
20 *Goldwater*	?	?	?	?	N	Y	Y
21 *Fiedler*	N	Y	Y	N	N	Y	N
22 *Moorhead*	Y	Y	Y	N	Y	N	N
23 Beilenson	N	N	Y	Y	Y	Y	Y
24 Waxman	N	N	Y	Y	Y	Y	Y
25 Roybal	N	N	Y	Y	Y	Y	Y
26 *Rousselot*	Y	Y	Y	N	N	N	N
27 *Dornan*	N	Y	Y	N	N	Y	Y
28 Dixon	N	N	Y	Y	Y	Y	Y
29 Hawkins	N	N	Y	Y	Y	N	Y
30 Martinez	N	N	Y	Y	N	N	N
31 Dymally	N	N	Y	Y	Y	Y	Y
32 Anderson	N	Y	Y	N	Y	N	N
33 *Grisham*	N	N	Y	Y	Y	Y	Y
34 *Lungren*	N	Y	Y	N	N	N	N
35 *Dreier*	N	Y	Y	N	N	N	N
36 Brown	N	N	?	Y	N	N	Y
37 *Lewis*	N	Y	Y	N	N	N	N
38 Patterson	N	Y	N	Y	N	N	N
39 *Dannemeyer*	N	Y	Y	N	Y	N	N
40 *Badham*	Y	Y	Y	Y	Y	Y	Y
41 *Lowery*	N	Y	Y	N	N	N	N
42 *Hunter*	N	Y	Y	Y	Y	Y	Y
43 *Burgener*	Y	Y	Y	Y	Y	Y	Y
COLORADO							
1 Schroeder	Y	N	N	Y	N	N	N
2 Wirth	N	N	Y	Y	Y	Y	Y
3 Kogovsek	Y	Y	Y	Y	Y	Y	Y
4 *Brown*	N	N	N	N	N	N	N

	283	284	285	286	287	288	289
5 *Kramer*	N	Y	Y	N	N	N	N
CONNECTICUT							
1 Kennelly	N	Y	Y	N	Y	Y	Y
2 Gejdenson	N	Y	N	Y	N	Y	Y
3 *DeNardis*	N	N	Y	Y	N	Y	Y
4 *McKinney*	N	N	?	Y	N	N	Y
5 Ratchford	Y	Y	Y	Y	Y	Y	N
6 Moffett	?	X	?	?	Y	Y	Y
DELAWARE							
AL *Evans*	N	Y	?	Y	N	Y	Y
FLORIDA							
1 Hutto	N	Y	Y	N	N	N	N
2 Fuqua	N	Y	Y	Y	N	N	N
3 Bennett	N	Y	Y	Y	N	N	N
4 Chappell	?	?	?	?	?	?	N
5 *McCollum*	N	Y	Y	N	N	N	N
6 *Young*	N	Y	Y	N	Y	N	Y
7 Gibbons	N	Y	Y	Y	Y	Y	Y
8 Ireland	N	Y	Y	Y	Y	Y	Y
9 Nelson	N	Y	Y	Y	Y	Y	Y
10 *Bafalis*	?	?	?	?	?	?	Y
11 Mica	N	Y	Y	Y	Y	Y	Y
12 *Shaw*	N	Y	Y	N	N	N	N
13 Lehman	N	N	Y	Y	Y	Y	Y
14 Pepper	N	Y	Y	Y	Y	Y	Y
15 Fascell	N	Y	Y	Y	Y	Y	Y
GEORGIA							
1 Ginn	?	?	Y	N	N	N	N
2 Hatcher	N	Y	Y	N	N	N	N
3 Brinkley	N	Y	Y	Y	N	N	N
4 Levitas	N	Y	N	Y	N	N	N
5 Fowler	N	Y	Y	Y	Y	Y	Y
6 *Gingrich*	N	Y	N	N	N	N	N
7 McDonald	N	Y	N	N	N	N	N
8 Evans	N	Y	N	N	N	N	N
9 Jenkins	Y	Y	Y	Y	N	N	N
10 Barnard	N	Y	Y	N	Y	N	N
HAWAII							
1 Heftel	?	?	?	?	Y	Y	Y
2 Akaka	N	Y	?	Y	Y	Y	Y
IDAHO							
1 *Craig*	N	Y	Y	N	Y	N	N
2 *Hansen*	N	Y	Y	N	Y	N	N
ILLINOIS							
1 Washington	N	N	Y	N	N	N	N
2 Savage	N	N	?	?	N	N	N
3 Russo	Y	N	Y	Y	Y	Y	Y
4 *Derwinski*	Y	Y	Y	Y	Y	Y	Y
5 Fary	N	Y	Y	Y	Y	Y	Y
6 *Hyde*	N	Y	N	Y	N	Y	N
7 Collins	N	N	Y	N	N	N	Y
8 Rostenkowski	Y	Y	Y	Y	Y	Y	Y
9 Yates	N	?	N	Y	Y	Y	Y
10 *Porter*	?	N	Y	N	N	N	Y
11 Annunzio	N	Y	Y	Y	Y	Y	Y
12 *Crane, P.*	N	Y	N	N	N	N	N
13 *McClory*	N	Y	Y	Y	Y	Y	Y
14 *Erlenborn*	N	Y	Y	Y	Y	Y	Y
15 *Corcoran*	N	Y	+	-	N	N	N
16 *Martin*	N	N	Y	Y	Y	Y	Y
17 *O'Brien*	?	#	Y	Y	Y	Y	Y
18 *Michel*	?	?	Y	Y	Y	Y	Y
19 *Railsback*	?	?	Y	Y	Y	Y	Y
20 *Findley*	N	N	Y	Y	Y	Y	Y
21 *Madigan*	?	?	Y	Y	Y	Y	Y
22 *Crane, D.*	N	Y	N	N	N	N	N
23 Price	N	Y	Y	Y	Y	Y	Y
24 Simon	N	N	Y	Y	Y	Y	Y
INDIANA							
1 Benjamin	N	N	Y	Y	Y	Y	Y
2 Fithian	N	N	Y	N	N	N	N
3 *Hiler*	N	Y	Y	N	Y	N	N
4 *Coats*	Y	N	Y	Y	Y	Y	Y
5 *Hillis*	N	Y	Y	Y	Y	Y	Y
6 Evans	N	Y	Y	N	N	N	N
7 *Myers*	N	Y	Y	N	N	N	N
8 *Deckard*	N	Y	Y	N	N	N	N
9 Hamilton	N	Y	Y	N	N	Y	Y
10 Sharp	N	Y	Y	Y	N	N	N
11 Jacobs	N	Y	N	N	N	N	N
IOWA							
1 *Leach*	N	N	Y	N	N	Y	Y
2 *Tauke*	N	N	Y	Y	N	N	Y
3 *Evans*	N	N	N	Y	N	N	Y
4 Smith	N	N	Y	N	N	N	Y
5 Harkin	N	N	N	Y	N	N	Y
6 Bedell	N	N	Y	N	N	N	Y

ND - Northern Democrats   SD - Southern Democrats

	283	284	285	286	287	288	289
KANSAS							
1 ***Roberts***	N	N	Y	Y	N	N	Y
2 ***Jeffries***	N	Y	Y	N	N	N	N
3 ***Winn***	N	Y	Y	Y	N	Y	N
4 Glickman	N	N	Y	Y	Y	Y	Y
5 ***Whittaker***	N	Y	Y	N	N	N	N
KENTUCKY							
1 Hubbard	N	N	Y	N	N	N	N
2 Natcher	Y	Y	Y	N	N	N	N
3 Mazzoli	N	Y	Y	Y	Y	Y	N
4 ***Snyder***	N	Y	Y	N	N	N	N
5 ***Rogers***	N	Y	Y	N	N	N	N
6 ***Hopkins***	N	Y	Y	N	N	N	N
7 Perkins	N	Y	Y	Y	N	N	N
LOUISIANA							
1 ***Livingston***	N	Y	Y	N	Y	Y	Y
2 Boggs	Y	Y	Y	Y	Y	Y	Y
3 Tauzin	N	Y	Y	N	Y	Y	N
4 Roemer	N	Y	N	Y	Y	Y	Y
5 Huckaby	N	?	Y	Y	Y	Y	Y
6 ***Moore***	N	Y	Y	N	Y	N	N
7 Breaux	N	?	Y	Y	Y	Y	Y
8 Long	N	Y	Y	Y	Y	Y	Y
MAINE							
1 ***Emery***	N	Y	Y	Y	N	Y	Y
2 ***Snowe***	N	N	Y	Y	N	N	Y
MARYLAND							
1 Dyson	N	Y	?	Y	Y	Y	N
2 Long	N	Y	Y	Y	Y	Y	Y
3 Mikulski	N	Y	Y	Y	N	N	N
4 ***Holt***	?	#	?	?	N	N	Y
5 Hoyer	N	Y	Y	Y	Y	Y	N
6 Byron	N	Y	?	Y	Y	Y	Y
7 Mitchell	N	N	N	Y	N	Y	N
8 Barnes	N	Y	N	Y	Y	Y	N
MASSACHUSETTS							
1 ***Conte***	Y	N	Y	Y	N	Y	Y
2 Boland	Y	Y	Y	Y	Y	Y	Y
3 Early	N	N	Y	Y	Y	?	Y
4 Frank	N	N	Y	N	N	N	N
5 Shannon	N	N	Y	Y	Y	Y	Y
6 Mavroules	Y	Y	Y	Y	N	N	N
7 Markey	N	N	N	Y	Y	Y	Y
8 O'Neill							
9 Moakley	Y	N	Y	Y	Y	Y	Y
10 ***Heckler***	Y	N	Y	N	N	N	N
11 Donnelly	Y	N	Y	Y	Y	Y	Y
12 Studds	N	N	Y	N	N	Y	N
MICHIGAN							
1 Conyers	N	N	Y	Y	Y	Y	Y
2 ***Pursell***	N	N	Y	Y	Y	Y	Y
3 Wolpe	N	N	Y	Y	Y	Y	Y
4 ***Siljander***	N	Y	Y	N	N	N	N
5 ***Sawyer***	N	Y	Y	Y	Y	Y	Y
6 ***Dunn***	?	Y	Y	Y	Y	Y	Y
7 Kildee	N	N	Y	N	N	N	Y
8 Traxler	N	N	Y	Y	Y	Y	N
9 ***Vander Jagt***	?	?	Y	Y	Y	Y	Y
10 Albosta	N	N	Y	N	Y	Y	N
11 ***Davis***	Y	Y	Y	Y	N	Y	Y
12 Bonior	N	N	Y	Y	Y	Y	Y
13 Crockett	N	N	Y	N	Y	Y	N
14 Hertel	N	N	Y	Y	N	N	N
15 Ford	N	?	Y	Y	Y	Y	Y
16 Dingell	N	Y	Y	Y	Y	Y	Y
17 Brodhead	?	N	Y	Y	Y	Y	Y
18 Blanchard	?	N	Y	Y	Y	Y	N
19 ***Broomfield***	N	Y	Y	Y	Y	Y	Y
MINNESOTA							
1 ***Erdahl***	N	N	Y	Y	N	Y	Y
2 ***Hagedorn***	N	Y	Y	N	N	N	N
3 ***Frenzel***	N	N	Y	Y	Y	Y	Y
4 Vento	N	N	Y	Y	Y	Y	Y
5 Sabo	N	N	N	Y	Y	Y	Y
6 ***Weber***	N	N	Y	N	N	N	N
7 ***Stangeland***	Y	N	Y	N	N	N	N
8 Oberstar	N	N	P	Y	Y	Y	Y
MISSISSIPPI							
1 Whitten	N	?	Y	N	N	Y	N
2 Bowen	N	Y	?	?	Y	Y	Y
3 Montgomery	N	Y	Y	Y	Y	Y	Y
4 Dowdy	N	Y	Y	N	N	N	N
5 ***Lott***	Y	Y	Y	Y	Y	Y	Y
MISSOURI							
1 Clay	N	N	N	Y	N	N	N
2 Young	N	Y	Y	Y	Y	Y	Y
3 Gephardt	Y	Y	Y	Y	Y	Y	Y
4 Skelton	N	Y	Y	N	N	N	N
5 Bolling	?	?	Y	Y	Y	Y	Y
6 ***Coleman***	N	Y	Y	Y	N	Y	Y
7 ***Taylor***	Y	Y	Y	N	N	N	N
8 ***Bailey***	N	Y	Y	N	N	N	N
9 Volkmer	?	?	?	Y	N	N	N
10 ***Emerson***	N	Y	N	N	N	N	N
MONTANA							
1 Williams	Y	N	?	N	N	N	Y
2 ***Marlenee***	N	Y	Y	N	N	N	Y
NEBRASKA							
1 ***Bereuter***	N	N	Y	Y	N	N	Y
2 ***Daub***	N	Y	Y	N	N	N	N
3 ***Smith***	N	N	Y	Y	Y	Y	Y
NEVADA							
AL Santini	Y	Y	?	N	N	N	N
NEW HAMPSHIRE							
1 D'Amours	N	N	Y	Y	N	N	N
2 ***Gregg***	N	Y	Y	N	N	N	Y
NEW JERSEY							
1 Florio	N	N	Y	Y	N	N	N
2 Hughes	N	N	Y	N	N	N	Y
3 Howard	N	Y	Y	Y	N	Y	N
4 ***Smith***	N	Y	Y	N	N	N	N
5 ***Fenwick***	N	N	Y	Y	Y	Y	Y
6 ***Forsythe***	N	N	N	Y	N	Y	Y
7 ***Roukema***	N	N	Y	Y	N	Y	Y
8 Roe	N	Y	Y	Y	N	N	N
9 ***Hollenbeck***	?	N	Y	Y	N	N	Y
10 Rodino	N	N	Y	Y	N	Y	Y
11 Minish	N	Y	Y	Y	N	Y	N
12 ***Rinaldo***	N	Y	Y	N	N	N	N
13 ***Courter***	N	Y	Y	Y	N	N	Y
14 Guarini	N	N	Y	Y	Y	Y	Y
15 Dwyer	N	Y	Y	Y	Y	Y	Y
NEW MEXICO							
1 ***Lujan***	Y	Y	Y	Y	N	N	Y
2 ***Skeen***	Y	Y	Y	N	Y	Y	Y
NEW YORK							
1 ***Carney***	N	Y	Y	N	N	N	N
2 Downey	N	N	Y	Y	Y	Y	Y
3 ***Carman***	N	?	Y	Y	N	N	Y
4 ***Lent***	N	Y	Y	N	N	?	Y
5 ***McGrath***	N	Y	Y	N	N	N	N
6 ***LeBoutillier***	N	Y	Y	N	N	N	N
7 Addabbo	N	N	Y	Y	N	N	N
8 Rosenthal	?	?	?	?	Y	Y	Y
9 Ferraro	N	Y	Y	Y	Y	Y	N
10 Biaggi	N	Y	Y	Y	N	Y	Y
11 Scheuer	N	N	Y	Y	Y	Y	+
12 Chisholm	?	N	?	?	Y	N	N
13 Solarz	N	N	Y	Y	Y	Y	Y
14 Richmond	N	X	Y	Y	Y	Y	Y
15 Zeferetti	N	Y	Y	Y	N	N	N
16 Schumer	N	N	Y	Y	N	Y	Y
17 ***Molinari***	N	Y	Y	Y	N	N	N
18 ***Green***	N	N	Y	Y	N	N	Y
19 Rangel	N	N	Y	Y	Y	Y	Y
20 Weiss	N	N	Y	Y	Y	N	Y
21 Garcia	N	N	Y	Y	Y	Y	N
22 Bingham	N	N	Y	?	Y	Y	Y
23 Peyser	N	N	Y	Y	N	N	N
24 Ottinger	N	N	P	N	N	N	N
25 ***Fish***	N	Y	Y	Y	N	Y	Y
26 ***Gilman***	N	Y	Y	N	N	N	N
27 McHugh	N	N	Y	Y	Y	Y	Y
28 Stratton	N	Y	Y	N	Y	Y	N
29 ***Solomon***	N	Y	N	N	N	N	N
30 ***Martin***	N	Y	Y	Y	N	N	Y
31 ***Mitchell***	?	Y	Y	Y	Y	Y	Y
32 ***Wortley***	N	Y	Y	N	N	N	N
33 ***Lee***	N	N	Y	N	N	N	N
34 ***Horton***	?	Y	Y	Y	Y	Y	Y
35 ***Conable***	?	N	Y	Y	Y	Y	Y
36 LaFalce	N	N	Y	N	?	Y	Y
37 Nowak	N	N	Y	Y	N	N	Y
38 ***Kemp***	N	?	Y	N	N	N	N
39 Lundine	N	N	Y	Y	Y	Y	N
NORTH CAROLINA							
1 Jones	N	?	?	Y	N	N	N
2 Fountain	N	Y	?	?	N	N	N
3 Whitley	N	Y	Y	N	N	N	N
4 Andrews	N	Y	Y	N	N	N	N
5 Neal	N	Y	Y	N	N	N	N
6 ***Johnston***	N	Y	N	N	N	N	N
7 Rose	N	Y	Y	Y	N	N	N
8 Hefner	N	Y	Y	N	N	N	N
9 ***Martin***	N	Y	Y	N	Y	N	N
10 ***Broyhill***	N	N	Y	Y	Y	Y	Y
11 ***Hendon***	N	Y	Y	N	N	N	N
NORTH DAKOTA							
AL Dorgan	Y	N	Y	Y	N	N	Y
OHIO							
1 ***Gradison***	N	Y	Y	Y	Y	Y	Y
2 Luken	Y	?	N	Y	N	N	N
3 Hall	Y	?	Y	Y	Y	Y	Y
4 ***Oxley***	N	Y	Y	Y	Y	Y	Y
5 ***Latta***	N	Y	Y	Y	Y	Y	Y
6 ***McEwen***	N	Y	Y	Y	N	Y	N
7 ***Brown***	?	?	?	?	Y	Y	Y
8 ***Kindness***	N	Y	Y	N	N	N	N
9 ***Weber***	N	Y	Y	Y	Y	Y	Y
10 ***Miller***	N	Y	N	N	N	N	N
11 ***Stanton***	?	?	Y	Y	Y	Y	Y
12 Shamansky	N	Y	Y	Y	N	Y	Y
13 Pease	N	N	Y	Y	Y	Y	Y
14 Seiberling	Y	N	Y	Y	N	Y	Y
15 ***Wylie***	N	N	Y	Y	Y	Y	Y
16 ***Regula***	N	N	Y	Y	Y	Y	Y
17 ***Ashbrook***	N	Y	Y	N	N	N	N
18 Applegate	N	Y	?	Y	N	N	N
19 ***Williams***	N	Y	Y	Y	N	N	Y
20 Oakar	Y	Y	Y	N	N	N	N
21 Stokes	N	N	Y	Y	Y	Y	N
22 Eckart	N	N	Y	Y	Y	Y	N
23 Mottl	Y	Y	Y	N	Y	Y	N
OKLAHOMA							
1 Jones	N	N	Y	Y	Y	N	N
2 Synar	N	Y	Y	Y	N	N	N
3 Watkins	N	Y	Y	Y	Y	Y	N
4 McCurdy	N	Y	Y	Y	N	N	N
5 ***Edwards***	N	Y	Y	Y	Y	N	N
6 English	N	Y	Y	Y	N	N	N
OREGON							
1 AuCoin	N	N	Y	Y	Y	?	N
2 ***Smith***	N	Y	Y	N	N	N	N
3 Wyden	N	N	Y	Y	Y	Y	N
4 Weaver	Y		Y	Y	Y	Y	Y
PENNSYLVANIA							
1 Foglietta	N	Y	Y	Y	N	N	Y
2 Gray	N	N	Y	Y	Y	Y	N
3 Smith	N	Y	Y	Y	N	N	Y
4 ***Dougherty***	N	Y	Y	Y	Y	Y	Y
5 ***Schulze***	N	Y	Y	N	N	N	N
6 Yatron	N	Y	Y	N	N	N	N
7 Edgar	N	N	Y	Y	Y	Y	Y
8 ***Coyne, J.***	N	N	Y	N	N	N	N
9 ***Shuster***	?	Y	Y	N	N	N	N
10 ***McDade***	N	Y	Y	Y	Y	Y	Y
11 ***Nelligan***	N	Y	Y	Y	N	N	Y
12 Murtha	N	Y	Y	Y	Y	Y	Y
13 ***Coughlin***	N	N	N	Y	Y	Y	Y
14 Coyne, W.	N	Y	Y	Y	Y	Y	Y
15 ***Ritter***	N	N	Y	N	N	N	N
16 ***Walker***	N	Y	N	N	Y	N	N
17 Ertel	?	?	?	?	N	N	Y
18 Walgren	N	N	?	Y	N	N	N
19 ***Goodling***	N	N	N	N	Y	Y	Y
20 Gaydos	Y	Y	Y	Y	N	Y	N
21 Bailey	N	Y	Y	Y	Y	Y	N
22 Murphy	Y	N	Y	Y	N	N	N
23 ***Clinger***	N	N	Y	Y	Y	Y	Y
24 ***Marks***	?	?	?	Y	N	Y	Y
25 ***Atkinson***	Y	N	?	?	Y	Y	Y
RHODE ISLAND							
1 St Germain	Y	Y	Y	Y	N	Y	Y
2 ***Schneider***	N	N	Y	Y	N	Y	Y
SOUTH CAROLINA							
1 ***Hartnett***	N	Y	Y	N	Y	N	Y
2 ***Spence***	Y	Y	Y	N	N	N	N
3 Derrick	N	Y	Y	Y	Y	Y	N
4 ***Campbell***	N	Y	Y	N	Y	Y	N
5 Holland	N	Y	Y	Y	Y	Y	Y
6 ***Napier***	N	Y	Y	N	N	N	N
SOUTH DAKOTA							
1 Daschle	Y	Y	Y	Y	N	Y	N
2 ***Roberts***	N	N	?	N	N	N	N
TENNESSEE							
1 ***Quillen***	Y	Y	Y	Y	Y	Y	Y
2 ***Duncan***	Y	Y	Y	?	Y	N	N
3 Bouquard	N	Y	Y	N	N	N	N
4 Gore	N	Y	Y	Y	Y	Y	Y
5 Boner	N	Y	Y	Y	Y	Y	N
6 ***Beard***	?	#	?	?	N	N	N
7 Jones	N	Y	Y	Y	N	N	N
8 Ford	N	Y	Y	Y	N	Y	Y
TEXAS							
1 Hall, S.	N	Y	Y	N	Y	Y	N
2 Wilson	?	?	?	Y	Y	Y	Y
3 ***Collins***	Y	Y	Y	N	Y	N	N
4 Hall, R.	N	N	Y	N	N	N	N
5 Mattox	Y	N	Y	Y	Y	Y	N
6 Gramm	?	N	Y	Y	Y	Y	Y
7 ***Archer***	Y	Y	Y	N	Y	Y	N
8 ***Fields***	N	Y	N	N	Y	Y	N
9 Brooks	N	Y	Y	Y	Y	Y	N
10 Pickle	N	Y	Y	Y	Y	Y	Y
11 Leath	Y	Y	Y	Y	Y	Y	Y
12 Wright	N	Y	Y	Y	Y	Y	Y
13 Hightower	N	Y	Y	Y	Y	Y	Y
14 Patman	N	Y	Y	N	N	N	N
15 de la Garza	N	Y	Y	Y	Y	Y	N
16 White	Y	Y	Y	Y	Y	Y	Y
17 Stenholm	N	Y	Y	N	Y	Y	N
18 Leland	N	N	Y	Y	Y	Y	Y
19 Hance	N	Y	Y	Y	Y	Y	Y
20 Gonzalez	N	Y	Y	N	N	Y	N
21 ***Loeffler***	Y	Y	Y	Y	N	Y	N
22 ***Paul***	N	?	Y	N	N	N	N
23 Kazen	N	Y	Y	N	N	Y	N
24 Frost	N	Y	Y	Y	Y	Y	Y
UTAH							
1 ***Hansen***	N	Y	Y	N	N	Y	N
2 ***Marriott***	Y	Y	Y	Y	N	Y	Y
VERMONT							
AL ***Jeffords***	N	N	Y	Y	Y	Y	Y
VIRGINIA							
1 ***Trible***	N	Y	Y	N	N	N	N
2 ***Whitehurst***	N	Y	Y	Y	Y	Y	Y
3 ***Bliley***	N	Y	Y	N	N	N	N
4 ***Daniel, R.***	N	Y	Y	N	N	N	N
5 Daniel, D.	N	Y	Y	Y	Y	Y	N
6 ***Butler***	Y	Y	N	Y	Y	Y	Y
7 ***Robinson***	N	Y	Y	N	N	N	N
8 ***Parris***	N	Y	Y	N	N	N	N
9 ***Wampler***	N	Y	Y	N	N	N	N
10 ***Wolf***	N	Y	Y	N	N	N	N
WASHINGTON							
1 ***Pritchard***	N	N	Y	Y	Y	Y	Y
2 Swift	N	N	Y	Y	N	Y	Y
3 Bonker	N	N	Y	Y	N	Y	N
4 ***Morrison***	N	Y	Y	N	Y	Y	Y
5 Foley	N	Y	Y	Y	Y	Y	Y
6 Dicks	Y	Y	Y	Y	Y	Y	Y
7 Lowry	N	N	Y	Y	Y	Y	Y
WEST VIRGINIA							
1 Mollohan	N	Y	Y	Y	Y	Y	N
2 ***Benedict***	N	Y	Y	Y	Y	Y	Y
3 ***Staton***	N	Y	Y	N	Y	Y	N
4 Rahall	Y	N	?	?	?	Y	Y
WISCONSIN							
1 Aspin	N	N	Y	Y	N	Y	Y
2 Kastenmeier	N	N	Y	Y	N	N	Y
3 ***Gunderson***	N	N	Y	N	N	N	Y
4 Zablocki	N	Y	Y	Y	Y	Y	Y
5 Reuss	N	N	Y	Y	Y	Y	Y
6 ***Petri***	N	N	Y	Y	N	Y	Y
7 Obey	N	N	Y	Y	Y	Y	Y
8 ***Roth***	N	Y	Y	N	N	Y	N
9 ***Sensenbrenner***	N	N	Y	N	N	N	N
WYOMING							
AL ***Cheney***	Y	Y	Y	Y	Y	Y	Y

Southern states - Ala., Ark., Fla., Ga., Ky., La., Miss., N.C., Okla., S.C., Tenn., Texas, Va.

KEY

Y Voted for (yea).
\# Paired for.
\+ Announced for.
N Voted against (nay).
X Paired against.
- Announced against.
P Voted "present".
C Voted "present" to avoid possible conflict of interest.
? Did not vote or otherwise make a position known.

Democrats   *Republicans*

	290	291
ALABAMA		
1 *Edwards*	N	Y
2 *Dickinson*	N	Y
3 Nichols	N	Y
4 Bevill	N	Y
5 Flippo	?	?
6 *Smith*	N	Y
7 Shelby	N	Y
ALASKA		
AL *Young*	?	?
ARIZONA		
1 *Rhodes*	N	Y
2 Udall	N	Y
3 *Stump*	N	Y
4 *Rudd*	N	?
ARKANSAS		
1 Alexander	N	Y
2 *Bethune*	?	Y
3 *Hammerschmidt*	N	Y
4 Anthony	N	Y
CALIFORNIA		
1 *Chappie*	N	Y
2 *Clausen*	N	Y
3 Matsui	N	Y
4 Fazio	N	Y
5 Burton, J.	?	?
6 Burton, P.	N	Y
7 Miller	N	Y
8 Dellums	Y	N
9 Stark	Y	Y
10 Edwards	?	?
11 Lantos	N	Y
12 *McCloskey*	N	?
13 Mineta	N	Y
14 *Shumway*	N	Y
15 Coelho	N	Y
16 Panetta	N	Y
17 *Pashayan*	N	Y
18 *Thomas*	?	?
19 *Lagomarsino*	N	Y
20 *Goldwater*	N	Y
21 *Fiedler*	N	Y
22 *Moorhead*	N	Y
23 Beilenson	N	Y
24 Waxman	N	Y
25 Roybal	Y	N
26 *Rousselot*	N	Y
27 *Dornan*	N	Y
28 Dixon	N	Y
29 Hawkins	N	Y
30 Martinez	N	Y
31 Dymally	Y	N
32 Anderson	N	Y
33 *Grisham*	N	Y
34 *Lungren*	N	Y
35 *Dreier*	N	Y
36 Brown	?	?
37 *Lewis*	N	Y
38 Patterson	N	Y
39 *Dannemeyer*	N	Y
40 *Badham*	N	Y
41 *Lowery*	?	Y
42 *Hunter*	N	Y
43 *Burgener*	N	Y
COLORADO		
1 Schroeder	Y	N
2 Wirth	N	N
3 Kogovsek	N	Y
4 *Brown*	Y	N

	290	291
5 *Kramer*	N	Y
CONNECTICUT		
1 Kennelly	N	Y
2 Gejdenson	N	Y
3 *DeNardis*	N	Y
4 *McKinney*	N	Y
5 Ratchford	N	Y
6 Moffett	?	?
DELAWARE		
AL *Evans*	N	Y
FLORIDA		
1 Hutto	N	Y
2 Fuqua	?	?
3 Bennett	N	Y
4 Chappell	N	Y
5 *McCollum*	N	Y
6 *Young*	?	?
7 Gibbons	N	Y
8 Ireland	N	?
9 Nelson	-	+
10 *Bafalis*	?	Y
11 Mica	?	Y
12 *Shaw*	N	Y
13 Lehman	Y	Y
14 Pepper	N	Y
15 Fascell	N	Y
GEORGIA		
1 Ginn	N	Y
2 Hatcher	N	Y
3 Brinkley	N	Y
4 Levitas	N	Y
5 Fowler	?	Y
6 *Gingrich*	N	Y
7 McDonald	N	Y
8 Evans	?	Y
9 Jenkins	?	?
10 Barnard	N	Y
HAWAII		
1 Heftel	N	Y
2 Akaka	N	Y
IDAHO		
1 *Craig*	N	Y
2 *Hansen*	N	Y
ILLINOIS		
1 Washington	Y	N
2 Savage	Y	N
3 Russo	N	N
4 *Derwinski*	N	Y
5 Fary	N	Y
6 *Hyde*	?	?
7 Collins	Y	N
8 Rostenkowski	N	Y
9 Yates	?	?
10 *Porter*	N	Y
11 Annunzio	N	Y
12 *Crane, P.*	N	Y
13 *McClory*	N	Y
14 *Erlenborn*	?	?
15 *Corcoran*	N	Y
16 *Martin*	Y	Y
17 *O'Brien*	N	Y
18 *Michel*	N	Y
19 *Railsback*	N	Y
20 *Findley*	N	Y
21 *Madigan*	?	Y
22 *Crane, D.*	N	Y
23 Price	N	Y
24 Simon	N	Y
INDIANA		
1 Benjamin	N	Y
2 Fithian	?	?
3 *Hiler*	N	Y
4 *Coats*	N	Y
5 *Hillis*	N	?
6 Evans	N	Y
7 *Myers*	N	Y
8 *Deckard*	N	Y
9 Hamilton	N	Y
10 Sharp	N	Y
11 Jacobs	N	Y
IOWA		
1 *Leach*	N	Y
2 *Tauke*	N	Y
3 *Evans*	N	Y
4 Smith	N	Y
5 Harkin	Y	N
6 Bedell	N	N

290. HR 6968. Military Construction Appropriations, Fiscal 1983. Obey, D-Wis., amendment to reduce the sum appropriated for each account, activity or project in the bill by 30.8 percent. Rejected 34-322: R 5-157; D 29-165 (ND 27-103, SD 2-62), Aug. 19, 1982. A "nay" was a vote supporting the president's position.

291. HR 6968. Military Construction Appropriations, Fiscal 1983. Passage of the bill to appropriate $7,000,249,000 for military construction and family housing projects in fiscal 1983. Passed 325-31: R 154-5; D 171-26 (ND 107-25, SD 64-1), Aug. 19, 1982. The president had requested $8,211,827,000.

ND - Northern Democrats   SD - Southern Democrats

	290 291			290 291			290 291			290 291
KANSAS			4 Skelton	N Y		9 *Martin*	N Y		7 Jones	N Y
1 *Roberts*	N Y		5 Bolling	? ?		10 *Broyhill*	N Y		8 Ford	N Y
2 *Jeffries*	N Y		6 *Coleman*	N Y		11 *Hendon*	N Y		**TEXAS**	
3 *Winn*	? ?		7 *Taylor*	N Y		**NORTH DAKOTA**			1 Hall, S.	N Y
4 Glickman	N Y		8 *Bailey*	N Y		AL Dorgan	N Y		2 Wilson	? ?
5 *Whittaker*	N Y		9 Volkmer	N Y		**OHIO**			3 *Collins*	? ?
KENTUCKY			10 *Emerson*	N Y		1 *Gradison*	N Y		4 Hall, R.	N Y
1 Hubbard	N Y		**MONTANA**			2 Luken	N Y		5 *Mattox*	? ?
2 Natcher	N Y		1 Williams	N Y		3 Hall	N Y		6 Gramm	N Y
3 Mazzoli	N Y		2 *Marlenee*	N Y		4 *Oxley*	N Y		7 *Archer*	N Y
4 *Snyder*	N Y		**NEBRASKA**			5 *Latta*	? ?		8 *Fields*	N Y
5 *Rogers*	N Y		1 *Bereuter*	N Y		6 *McEwen*	? ?		9 Brooks	N Y
6 *Hopkins*	N Y		2 *Daub*	N Y		7 *Brown*	? ?		10 Pickle	N Y
7 *Perkins*	N Y		3 *Smith*	N Y		8 *Kindness*	N Y		11 Leath	N Y
LOUISIANA			**NEVADA**			9 *Weber*	N Y		12 Wright	? ?
1 *Livingston*	N Y		AL Santini	N Y		10 *Miller*	Y N		13 Hightower	N Y
2 Boggs	N Y		**NEW HAMPSHIRE**			11 *Stanton*	? ?		14 Patman	N Y
3 Tauzin	N Y		1 D'Amours	N Y		12 Shamansky	N ?		15 de la Garza	N Y
4 Roemer	N Y		2 *Gregg*	N ?		13 Pease	N Y		16 White	N Y
5 Huckaby	N Y		**NEW JERSEY**			14 Seiberling	Y N		17 Stenholm	N Y
6 *Moore*	N Y		1 Florio	N Y		15 *Wylie*	N Y		18 Leland	Y N
7 Breaux	N Y		2 Hughes	N Y		16 *Regula*	N Y		19 Hance	N Y
8 Long	N Y		3 Howard	N Y		17 *Ashbrook*	N Y		20 Gonzalez	N Y
MAINE			4 Smith	N Y		18 Applegate	? ?		21 *Loeffler*	N Y
1 *Emery*	N Y		5 Fenwick	? ?		19 *Williams*	N Y		22 *Paul*	Y N
2 *Snowe*	N Y		6 *Forsythe*	Y N		20 Oakar	N Y		23 Kazen	N Y
MARYLAND			7 *Roukema*	N Y		21 Stokes	N Y		24 Frost	N Y
1 Dyson	N Y		8 Roe	? ?		22 Eckart	N Y		**UTAH**	
2 Long	N Y		9 *Hollenbeck*	N Y		23 *Mottl*	? ?		1 *Hansen*	N Y
3 Mikulski	? ?		10 Rodino	Y Y		**OKLAHOMA**			2 *Marriott*	N Y
4 *Holt*	? ?		11 Minish	N Y		1 Jones	N Y		**VERMONT**	
5 Hoyer	N Y		12 *Rinaldo*	N Y		2 Synar	N Y		AL *Jeffords*	? ?
6 Byron	N Y		13 *Courter*	? ?		3 Watkins	N Y		**VIRGINIA**	
7 Mitchell	Y N		14 Guarini	N Y		4 McCurdy	N Y		1 *Trible*	? ?
8 Barnes	N Y		15 Dwyer	N Y		5 *Edwards*	N Y		2 *Whitehurst*	? ?
MASSACHUSETTS			**NEW MEXICO**			6 English	N Y		3 *Bliley*	N Y
1 *Conte*	N Y		1 *Lujan*	N Y		**OREGON**			4 *Daniel, R.*	N Y
2 Boland	? ?		2 *Skeen*	N Y		1 AuCoin	N N		5 Daniel, D.	N Y
3 Early	? ?		**NEW YORK**			2 *Smith*	N Y		6 *Butler*	N Y
4 Frank	N Y		1 *Carney*	N Y		3 Wyden	N Y		7 *Robinson*	N Y
5 Shannon	? ?		2 Downey	N N		4 Weaver	Y N		8 *Parris*	N Y
6 Mavroules	N Y		3 *Carman*	N Y		**PENNSYLVANIA**			9 *Wampler*	? ?
7 Markey	N Y		4 *Lent*	N ?		1 Foglietta	N Y		10 *Wolf*	N Y
8 O'Neill			5 *McGrath*	N Y		2 Gray	N Y		**WASHINGTON**	
9 Moakley	N Y		6 *LeBoutillier*	N Y		3 Smith	? ?		1 *Pritchard*	N Y
10 *Heckler*	N Y		7 Addabbo	N Y		4 *Dougherty*	N Y		2 Swift	N Y
11 Donnelly	N Y		8 Rosenthal	? ?		5 *Schulze*	N Y		3 Bonker	N Y
12 Studds	? ?		9 Ferraro	N Y		6 Yatron	N Y		4 *Morrison*	N Y
MICHIGAN			10 Biaggi	? ?		7 Edgar	Y Y		5 Foley	? Y
1 Conyers	? ?		11 Scheuer	N Y		8 *Coyne, J.*	N Y		6 Dicks	N Y
2 *Pursell*	N Y		12 Chisholm	? ?		9 *Shuster*	N Y		7 Lowry	N Y
3 Wolpe	N Y		13 Solarz	? ?		10 *McDade*	N Y		**WEST VIRGINIA**	
4 *Siljander*	N Y		14 Richmond	? ?		11 *Nelligan*	N Y		1 Mollohan	N Y
5 *Sawyer*	N Y		15 Zeferetti	N Y		12 Murtha	N Y		2 *Benedict*	N Y
6 *Dunn*	? ?		16 Schumer	N Y		13 *Coughlin*	N N		3 *Staton*	N Y
7 Kildee	N Y		17 *Molinari*	N Y		14 Coyne, W.	N Y		4 Rahall	Y N
8 Traxler	? ?		18 *Green*	N Y		15 *Ritter*	N Y		**WISCONSIN**	
9 *Vander Jagt*	N Y		19 Rangel	Y N		16 *Walker*	N Y		1 Aspin	Y Y
10 Albosta	Y Y		20 Weiss	Y Y		17 Ertel	? ?		2 Kastenmeier	Y N
11 *Davis*	? ?		21 Garcia	Y N		18 Walgren	? ?		3 *Gunderson*	N Y
12 Bonior	Y Y		22 Bingham	? ?		19 *Goodling*	N Y		4 Zablocki	Y Y
13 Crockett	? N		23 Peyser	N Y		20 Gaydos	N Y		5 Reuss	Y N
14 Hertel	N Y		24 Ottinger	N N		21 Bailey	N Y		6 Petri	N Y
15 Ford	N Y		25 *Fish*	N Y		22 Murphy	Y N		7 Obey	Y Y
16 Dingell	N Y		26 *Gilman*	N Y		23 *Clinger*	N Y		8 *Roth*	N Y
17 Brodhead	? Y		27 McHugh	N Y		24 *Marks*	? ?		9 *Sensenbrenner*	? ?
18 Blanchard	? ?		28 Stratton	N Y		25 Atkinson	N Y		**WYOMING**	
19 *Broomfield*	N Y		29 *Solomon*	N Y		**RHODE ISLAND**			AL *Cheney*	N Y
MINNESOTA			30 *Martin*	N Y		1 St Germain	N Y			
1 *Erdahl*	N Y		31 *Mitchell*	? ?		2 Schneider	N Y			
2 *Hagedorn*	N Y		32 *Wortley*	N Y		**SOUTH CAROLINA**				
3 *Frenzel*	N Y		33 *Lee*	N Y		1 *Hartnett*	? ?			
4 Vento	N Y		34 *Horton*	? ?		2 *Spence*	N Y			
5 Sabo	N Y		35 *Conable*	N Y		3 Derrick	N Y			
6 *Weber*	N Y		36 LaFalce	N N		4 *Campbell*	N Y			
7 *Stangeland*	N Y		37 Nowak	? ?		5 Holland	? ?			
8 Oberstar	N Y		38 *Kemp*	N ?		6 *Napier*	N Y			
MISSISSIPPI			39 Lundine	? ?		**SOUTH DAKOTA**				
1 Whitten	N Y		**NORTH CAROLINA**			1 Daschle	N Y			
2 Bowen	N Y		1 Jones	N ?		2 *Roberts*	N Y			
3 Montgomery	N Y		2 Fountain	? Y		**TENNESSEE**				
4 Dowdy	N Y		3 Whitley	N Y		1 *Quillen*	N Y			
5 *Lott*	N Y		4 Andrews	N Y		2 *Duncan*	N Y			
MISSOURI			5 Neal	N Y		3 Bouquard	N Y			
1 Clay	? ?		6 *Johnston*	N ?		4 Gore	? ?			
2 Young	N Y		7 Rose	? ?		5 Boner	? ?			
3 Gephardt	Y Y		8 Hefner	N Y		6 *Beard*	? ?			

Southern states - Ala., Ark., Fla., Ga., Ky., La., Miss., N.C., Okla., S.C., Tenn., Texas, Va.

KEY

Y	Voted for (yea).
#	Paired for.
+	Announced for.
N	Voted against (nay).
X	Paired against.
-	Announced against.
P	Voted "present".
C	Voted "present" to avoid possible conflict of interest.
?	Did not vote or otherwise make a position known.

Democrats *Republicans*

292. Procedural Motion. Walker, R-Pa., motion to approve the House *Journal* of Thursday, Aug. 19. Motion agreed to 268-17: R 121-9; D 147-8 (ND 93-6, SD 54-2), Sept. 8, 1982.

293. HR 6307. Resource Conservation and Recovery Act Reauthorization. Gramm, D-Texas, amendment, to the Florio, D-N.J., substitute, to strike provisions that apply the law's regulations to small-quantity generators of hazardous waste, and to require the Environmental Protection Agency to study the advisability of applying regulations to such operations. Rejected 148-183: R 103-44; D 45-139 (ND 10-118, SD 35-21), Sept. 8, 1982. (The Florio substitute, to make technical and clarifying changes in the bill, subsequently was adopted by voice vote.)

294. HR 6307. Resource Conservation and Recovery Act Reauthorization. Dannemeyer, R-Calif., amendment, to the Florio, D-N.J., substitute, to strike language preserving the rights of private individuals to sue under federal common law. Rejected 85-255: R 66-87; D 19-168 (ND 2-120, SD 17-48), Sept. 8, 1982. (The Florio substitute, to make technical and clarifying changes in the bill, subsequently was adopted by voice vote.)

295. HR 6307. Resource Conservation and Recovery Act Reauthorization. Passage of the bill to expand and tighten the act's regulation of hazardous wastes and to authorize appropriations of $105.5 million in fiscal 1983 and $111.5 million in fiscal 1984. Passed 317-32: R 131-24; D 186-8 (ND 129-0, SD 57-8), Sept. 8, 1982.

	292	293	294	295
ALABAMA				
1 *Edwards*	Y	Y	N	Y
2 *Dickinson*	?	Y	Y	N
3 Nichols	Y	Y	N	Y
4 Bevill	?	?	?	?
5 Flippo	Y	Y	Y	Y
6 *Smith*	?	Y	Y	N
7 Shelby	?	?	Y	Y
ALASKA				
AL *Young*	?	?	?	?
ARIZONA				
1 *Rhodes*	Y	Y	N	Y
2 Udall	Y	?	N	Y
3 *Stump*	?	?	?	?
4 *Rudd*	?	#	?	?
ARKANSAS				
1 Alexander	Y	N	N	Y
2 *Bethune*	Y	Y	N	Y
3 *Hammerschmidt*	Y	Y	Y	Y
4 Anthony	?	?	?	?
CALIFORNIA				
1 *Chappie*	?	#	#	?
2 *Clausen*	Y	N	Y	N
3 Matsui	Y	N	N	Y
4 Fazio	Y	N	?	Y
5 Burton, J.	?	?	?	?
6 Burton, P.	Y	N	N	Y
7 Miller	?	?	?	?
8 Dellums	?	N	N	Y
9 Stark	Y	N	N	Y
10 Edwards	Y	N	N	Y
11 Lantos	Y	N	N	Y
12 *McCloskey*	?	?	?	?
13 Mineta	Y	N	N	Y
14 *Shumway*	?	?	?	?
15 Coelho	Y	N	N	Y
16 Panetta	Y	N	N	Y
17 *Pashayan*	?	?	?	?
18 *Thomas*	Y	Y	Y	Y
19 *Lagomarsino*	Y	Y	N	Y
20 *Goldwater*	?	#	Y	?
21 *Fiedler*	Y	Y	N	Y
22 *Moorhead*	Y	Y	Y	Y
23 Beilenson	Y	N	N	Y
24 Waxman	Y	N	N	Y
25 Roybal	Y	N	N	Y
26 *Rousselot*	Y	Y	Y	Y
27 *Dornan*	Y	Y	N	Y
28 Dixon	Y	N	N	Y
29 Hawkins	Y	N	N	Y
30 Martinez	?	N	N	Y
31 Dymally	P	N	N	Y
32 Anderson	?	Y	N	Y
33 Grisham	?	?	?	?
34 *Lungren*	Y	Y	Y	N
35 *Dreier*	Y	Y	Y	Y
36 Brown	Y	N	N	Y
37 *Lewis*	Y	Y	Y	Y
38 Patterson	Y	N	N	Y
39 *Dannemeyer*	Y	Y	Y	N
40 *Badham*	Y	Y	Y	N
41 *Lowery*	Y	Y	Y	Y
42 *Hunter*	Y	Y	N	Y
43 *Burgener*	Y	Y	Y	N
COLORADO				
1 Schroeder	N	N	N	Y
2 Wirth	Y	N	N	Y
3 Kogovsek	?	#	?	?
4 *Brown*	Y	Y	N	Y

	292	293	294	295
5 *Kramer*	Y	Y	N	Y
CONNECTICUT				
1 Kennelly	?	N	N	Y
2 Gejdenson	?	N	N	Y
3 *DeNardis*	?	N	N	Y
4 *McKinney*	?	N	N	Y
5 Ratchford	Y	N	N	Y
6 Moffett	?	X	?	?
DELAWARE				
AL *Evans*	Y	N	N	Y
FLORIDA				
1 Hutto	Y	Y	N	Y
2 Fuqua	?	Y	N	Y
3 Bennett	Y	Y	N	Y
4 Chappell	?	?	?	?
5 *McCollum*	Y	Y	N	Y
6 *Young*	Y	Y	Y	Y
7 Gibbons	Y	?	N	Y
8 Ireland	N	Y	N	N
9 Nelson	Y	N	N	Y
10 *Bafalis*	?	?	?	?
11 Mica	?	?	?	?
12 *Shaw*	Y	Y	N	Y
13 Lehman	?	?	?	?
14 Pepper	Y	X	-	+
15 Fascell	Y	N	N	Y
GEORGIA				
1 Ginn	Y	N	N	Y
2 Hatcher	Y	Y	N	Y
3 Brinkley	Y	Y	N	Y
4 Levitas	Y	N	N	Y
5 Fowler	Y	N	N	Y
6 *Gingrich*	Y	N	N	Y
7 McDonald	Y	Y	Y	N
8 Evans	?	?	?	?
9 Jenkins	?	N	Y	N
10 Barnard	?	?	?	?
HAWAII				
1 Heftel	Y	N	N	Y
2 Akaka	Y	N	N	Y
IDAHO				
1 *Craig*	?	#	X	Y
2 *Hansen*	?	?	?	?
ILLINOIS				
1 Washington	?	?	?	?
2 Savage	?	N	N	Y
3 Russo	Y	N	N	Y
4 *Derwinski*	Y	Y	Y	N
5 Fary	Y	N	N	Y
6 *Hyde*	Y	Y	Y	Y
7 Collins	Y	N	N	Y
8 Rostenkowski	Y	N	N	Y
9 Yates	Y	N	N	Y
10 *Porter*	Y	N	N	Y
11 Annunzio	Y	N	N	Y
12 *Crane, P.*	?	#	#	?
13 *McClory*	Y	N	N	Y
14 *Erlenborn*	?	?	?	?
15 *Corcoran*	Y	Y	Y	Y
16 *Martin*	?	N	N	Y
17 *O'Brien*	?	Y	N	Y
18 *Michel*	Y	Y	N	Y
19 *Railsback*	Y	N	N	Y
20 *Findley*	?	?	?	Y
21 *Madigan*	Y	N	N	Y
22 *Crane, D.*	?	Y	Y	N
23 Price	Y	N	N	Y
24 Simon	Y	N	N	Y
INDIANA				
1 Vacancy*				
2 Fithian	Y	N	N	Y
3 *Hiler*	Y	N	N	Y
4 *Coats*	Y	N	N	Y
5 *Hillis*	Y	N	Y	Y
6 Evans	?	N	N	Y
7 *Myers*	Y	Y	Y	Y
8 *Deckard*	?	N	N	Y
9 Hamilton	Y	N	N	Y
10 Sharp	Y	N	N	Y
11 Jacobs	N	N	N	Y
IOWA				
1 *Leach*	Y	N	N	Y
2 *Tauke*	?	Y	N	Y
3 *Evans*	N	N	N	Y
4 Smith	?	?	?	?
5 Harkin	?	N	N	Y
6 Bedell	Y	N	N	Y

	292	293	294	295
KANSAS				
1 Roberts	?	?	?	?
2 Jeffries	?	?	?	?
3 Winn	?	?	?	?
4 Glickman	?	?	?	?
5 Whittaker	?	?	?	?
KENTUCKY				
1 Hubbard	Y	?	Y	Y
2 Natcher	Y	N	N	Y
3 Mazzoli	Y	N	N	Y
4 Snyder	Y	Y	Y	Y
5 Rogers	Y	Y	?	Y
6 Hopkins	Y	Y	N	Y
7 Perkins	Y	N	N	Y
LOUISIANA				
1 Livingston	Y	Y	Y	Y
2 Boggs	?	Y	N	Y
3 Tauzin	Y	Y	N	Y
4 Roemer	N	Y	Y	Y
5 Huckaby	Y	Y	N	Y
6 Moore	Y	Y	Y	Y
7 Breaux	?	?	?	?
8 Long	?	Y	N	Y
MAINE				
1 Emery	?	N	N	Y
2 Snowe	Y	N	N	Y
MARYLAND				
1 Dyson	Y	Y	N	Y
2 Long	Y	N	N	Y
3 Mikulski	Y	N	N	Y
4 Holt	?	Y	N	Y
5 Hoyer	Y	N	N	Y
6 Byron	Y	Y	Y	Y
7 Mitchell	?	?	N	Y
8 Barnes	N	N	N	Y
MASSACHUSETTS				
1 Conte	Y	N	N	Y
2 Boland	?	N	N	Y
3 Early	?	?	?	Y
4 Frank	Y	N	N	Y
5 Shannon	Y	N	N	?
6 Mavroules	?	?	?	?
7 Markey	N	N	N	Y
8 O'Neill				
9 Moakley	Y	N	N	Y
10 Heckler	Y	N	N	Y
11 Donnelly	?	?	?	?
12 Studds	Y	N	N	Y
MICHIGAN				
1 Conyers	?	?	?	?
2 Pursell	?	?	X	?
3 Wolpe	Y	N	N	Y
4 Siljander	?	Y	Y	Y
5 Sawyer	?	?	?	?
6 Dunn	Y	Y	N	Y
7 Kildee	Y	N	N	Y
8 Traxler	Y	N	N	Y
9 Vander Jagt	Y	Y	Y	Y
10 Albosta	Y	N	N	Y
11 Davis	?	?	?	?
12 Bonior	P	N	N	Y
13 Crockett	?	N	N	Y
14 Hertel	?	N	N	Y
15 Ford	?	N	N	Y
16 Dingell	?	N	N	Y
17 Brodhead	Y	N	N	Y
18 Blanchard	?	?	?	?
19 Broomfield	P	Y	N	Y
MINNESOTA				
1 Erdahl	?	Y	N	Y
2 Hagedorn	Y	Y	N	Y
3 Frenzel	Y	Y	N	Y
4 Vento	?	?	?	?
5 Sabo	?	?	?	?
6 Weber	Y	N	N	Y
7 Stangeland	Y	Y	Y	Y
8 Oberstar	+	-	-	+
MISSISSIPPI				
1 Whitten	Y	Y	?	Y
2 Bowen	Y	Y	Y	Y
3 Montgomery	Y	Y	Y	Y
4 Dowdy	?	N	N	Y
5 Lott	?	Y	?	N
MISSOURI				
1 Clay	N	N	N	Y
2 Young	Y	Y	Y	Y
3 Gephardt	?	?	?	?

	292	293	294	295
4 Skelton	Y	Y	N	Y
5 Bolling	?	N	?	Y
6 Coleman	Y	N	N	Y
7 Taylor	Y	Y	Y	Y
8 Bailey	Y	Y	N	N
9 Volkmer	Y	Y	N	Y
10 Emerson	N	Y	Y	Y
MONTANA				
1 Williams	?	N	?	?
2 Marlenee	?	?	?	?
NEBRASKA				
1 Bereuter	?	Y	N	Y
2 Daub	Y	Y	Y	Y
3 Smith	Y	Y	Y	Y
NEVADA				
AL Santini	?	?	?	?
NEW HAMPSHIRE				
1 D'Amours	Y	N	?	?
2 Gregg	?	?	?	?
NEW JERSEY				
1 Florio	?	N	N	Y
2 Hughes	Y	N	N	Y
3 Howard	Y	N	N	Y
4 Smith	Y	N	N	Y
5 Fenwick	Y	N	N	?
6 Forsythe	N	Y	N	Y
7 Roukema	Y	N	N	Y
8 Roe	Y	N	N	Y
9 Hollenbeck	Y	N	N	Y
10 Rodino	?	X	?	?
11 Minish	Y	N	N	Y
12 Rinaldo	Y	?	N	Y
13 Courter	Y	N	N	Y
14 Guarini	Y	N	N	Y
15 Dwyer	Y	N	N	Y
NEW MEXICO				
1 Lujan	Y	Y	N	Y
2 Skeen	Y	Y	Y	N
NEW YORK				
1 Carney	Y	Y	N	Y
2 Downey	Y	N	N	Y
3 Carman	Y	Y	Y	N
4 Lent	?	N	Y	Y
5 McGrath	Y	Y	N	Y
6 LeBoutillier	?	Y	Y	Y
7 Addabbo	?	X	?	?
8 Rosenthal	Y	N	N	Y
9 Ferraro	Y	N	N	Y
10 Biaggi	?	?	?	?
11 Scheuer	Y	N	?	Y
12 Chisholm	?	N	?	Y
13 Solarz	Y	N	N	Y
14 Vacancy**				
15 Zeferetti	?	N	N	Y
16 Schumer	?	X	?	?
17 Molinari	Y	N	N	Y
18 Green	Y	N	N	Y
19 Rangel	?	N	N	Y
20 Weiss	?	X	?	?
21 Garcia	?	?	?	?
22 Bingham	?	N	N	Y
23 Peyser	?	?	?	?
24 Ottinger	P	N	N	Y
25 Fish	Y	N	N	Y
26 Gilman	Y	N	N	Y
27 McHugh	Y	N	N	Y
28 Stratton	Y	N	N	Y
29 Solomon	Y	?	Y	Y
30 Martin	Y	N	N	Y
31 Mitchell	Y	N	N	Y
32 Wortley	Y	?	N	Y
33 Lee	?	+	-	+
34 Horton	Y	N	N	Y
35 Conable	Y	?	N	Y
36 LaFalce	Y	N	N	Y
37 Nowak	Y	N	N	Y
38 Kemp	?	N	N	Y
39 Lundine	Y	Y	N	Y
NORTH CAROLINA				
1 Jones	Y	Y	N	Y
2 Fountain	?	Y	N	Y
3 Whitley	Y	Y	N	Y
4 Andrews	?	N	N	Y
5 Neal	Y	N	N	Y
6 Johnston	N	Y	N	Y
7 Rose	Y	N	N	Y
8 Hefner	Y	Y	N	Y

	292	293	294	295
9 Martin	Y	Y	N	Y
10 Broyhill	Y	Y	Y	Y
11 Hendon	?	#	?	?
NORTH DAKOTA				
AL Dorgan	Y	N	N	Y
OHIO				
1 Gradison	Y	Y	N	Y
2 Luken	N	N	N	Y
3 Hall	Y	N	N	Y
4 Oxley	Y	Y	N	Y
5 Latta	Y	Y	N	Y
6 McEwen	Y	Y	N	Y
7 Brown	?	?	?	?
8 Kindness	Y	N	N	Y
9 Weber	Y	N	Y	Y
10 Miller	N	Y	N	N
11 Stanton	Y	Y	N	Y
12 Shamansky	Y	N	N	Y
13 Pease	Y	N	N	Y
14 Seiberling	Y	N	N	Y
15 Wylie	Y	N	N	Y
16 Regula	Y	N	N	Y
17 Ashbrook	Y	Y	Y	N
18 Applegate	Y	Y	N	Y
19 Williams	Y	N	N	Y
20 Oakar	Y	N	N	Y
21 Stokes	Y	N	N	Y
22 Eckart	Y	N	N	Y
23 Mottl	Y	N	N	Y
OKLAHOMA				
1 Jones	Y	Y	N	Y
2 Synar	Y	Y	N	Y
3 Watkins	Y	Y	N	Y
4 McCurdy	Y	Y	N	Y
5 Edwards	Y	Y	N	Y
6 English	Y	Y	N	Y
OREGON				
1 AuCoin	Y	N	N	Y
2 Smith	N	Y	Y	N
3 Wyden	Y	N	N	Y
4 Weaver	?	?	?	?
PENNSYLVANIA				
1 Foglietta	?	X	?	?
2 Gray	?	X	?	?
3 Smith	Y	N	N	Y
4 Dougherty	?	?	?	?
5 Schulze	Y	?	N	Y
6 Yatron	Y	N	N	Y
7 Edgar	Y	N	?	Y
8 Coyne, J.	Y	C	N	Y
9 Shuster	Y	Y	Y	Y
10 McDade	Y	N	N	Y
11 Nelligan	?	?	?	?
12 Murtha	?	N	N	Y
13 Coughlin	?	N	N	Y
14 Coyne, W.	Y	N	N	Y
15 Ritter	Y	Y	Y	Y
16 Walker	N	Y	N	Y
17 Ertel	?	?	?	?
18 Walgren	Y	N	N	Y
19 Goodling	N	N	N	Y
20 Gaydos	Y	N	N	Y
21 Bailey	?	N	N	Y
22 Murphy	Y	N	N	Y
23 Clinger	Y	Y	N	Y
24 Marks	?	?	N	Y
25 Atkinson	?	?	N	Y
RHODE ISLAND				
1 St Germain	Y	N	N	Y
2 Schneider	Y	N	N	Y
SOUTH CAROLINA				
1 Hartnett	Y	Y	Y	N
2 Spence	?	Y	Y	Y
3 Derrick	?	?	N	?
4 Campbell	Y	Y	Y	Y
5 Holland	Y	N	N	Y
6 Napier	?	?	?	?
SOUTH DAKOTA				
1 Daschle	?	N	N	Y
2 Roberts	?	Y	Y	Y
TENNESSEE				
1 Quillen	Y	Y	Y	Y
2 Duncan	Y	Y	N	Y
3 Bouquard	Y	Y	N	Y
4 Gore	Y	N	N	Y
5 Boner	Y	N	N	Y
6 Beard	?	?	?	?

	292	293	294	295
7 Jones	Y	N	N	Y
8 Ford	Y	N	N	Y
TEXAS				
1 Hall, S.	Y	Y	Y	N
2 Wilson	Y	?	Y	Y
3 Collins	?	?	?	?
4 Hall, R.	Y	Y	Y	N
5 Mattox	?	?	?	?
6 Gramm	Y	Y	Y	N
7 Archer	Y	Y	Y	N
8 Fields	?	Y	Y	N
9 Brooks	Y	N	N	Y
10 Pickle	Y	?	N	Y
11 Leath	Y	Y	Y	N
12 Wright	?	?	N	Y
13 Hightower	Y	Y	Y	Y
14 Patman	?	?	Y	Y
15 de la Garza	?	?	?	?
16 White	?	?	?	?
17 Stenholm	Y	Y	N	N
18 Leland	?	?	?	?
19 Hance	Y	?	Y	N
20 Gonzalez	Y	N	N	Y
21 Loeffler	?	Y	Y	N
22 Paul	?	Y	Y	N
23 Kazen	Y	Y	N	Y
24 Frost	Y	N	N	Y
UTAH				
1 Hansen	Y	Y	Y	N
2 Marriott	?	?	?	?
VERMONT				
AL Jeffords	Y	N	N	Y
VIRGINIA				
1 Trible	Y	?	?	?
2 Whitehurst	?	?	?	?
3 Bliley	Y	Y	Y	N
4 Daniel, R.	Y	Y	Y	Y
5 Daniel, D.	Y	Y	Y	Y
6 Butler	N	?	?	?
7 Robinson	Y	Y	Y	Y
8 Parris	Y	Y	Y	Y
9 Wampler	Y	Y	Y	Y
10 Wolf	Y	Y	N	Y
WASHINGTON				
1 Pritchard	?	?	?	?
2 Swift	Y	N	N	Y
3 Bonker	?	?	?	?
4 Morrison	Y	Y	Y	Y
5 Foley	?	N	N	Y
6 Dicks	Y	N	N	Y
7 Lowry	Y	N	N	Y
WEST VIRGINIA				
1 Mollohan	Y	Y	N	Y
2 Benedict	Y	Y	Y	Y
3 Staton	Y	Y	Y	Y
4 Rahall	?	Y	N	Y
WISCONSIN				
1 Aspin	?	N	?	N
2 Kastenmeier	Y	N	N	Y
3 Gunderson	Y	Y	Y	Y
4 Zablocki	?	?	?	?
5 Reuss	Y	N	N	Y
6 Petri	?	Y	Y	Y
7 Obey	Y	N	N	Y
8 Roth	Y	Y	Y	Y
9 Sensenbrenner	Y	Y	Y	N
WYOMING				
AL Cheney	Y	#	?	?

*Rep. Adam Benjamin Jr., D-Ind., was found dead Sept. 7, 1982. The last vote for which he was eligible was CQ vote 291.

**Rep. Fred Richmond, D-N.Y., resigned Aug. 25, 1982. The last vote for which he was eligible was CQ vote 291.

Southern states - Ala., Ark., Fla., Ga., Ky., La., Miss., N.C., Okla., S.C., Tenn., Texas, Va.

296. Procedural Motion. Porter, R-Ill., motion to approve the House *Journal* of Wednesday, Sept. 8. Motion agreed to 344-20: R 158-11; D 186-9 (ND 118-8, SD 68-1), Sept. 9, 1982.

297. HR 5831. Farm Credit Limits. De la Garza, D-Texas, motion that the House resolve itself into the Committee of the Whole for consideration of the bill to authorize lending limits for fiscal years 1983-85 for Farmers Home Administration programs and to revise certain loan programs. Motion agreed to 381-0: R 173-0; D 208-0 (ND 136-0, SD 72-0), Sept. 9, 1982.

298. HR 5831. Farm Credit Limits. Passage of the bill to authorize lending limits for fiscal years 1983-85 for Farmers Home Administration programs, to revise certain loan programs and to extend the economic emergency loan program through fiscal 1983. Passed 372-39: R 148-34; D 224-5 (ND 151-3, SD 73-2), Sept. 9, 1982. A "nay" was a vote supporting the president's position.

299. HR 6863. Supplemental Appropriations, Fiscal 1982. Passage, over President Reagan's Aug. 28 veto, of the bill to appropriate $14,578,111,924 in new fiscal 1982 budget authority for federal military and civilian pay raises, commodity credit programs, defense and other programs, and to rescind $400,846,000 in previously appropriated funds. Passed 301-117: R 81-104; D 220-13 (ND 157-1, SD 63-12), Sept. 9, 1982. A two-thirds majority of those present and voting (279 in this case) of both houses is required to override a veto. A "nay" was a vote supporting the president's position. (The Senate also voted to override the veto (*see vote 341, p. 57-S*), so the bill was enacted.)

300. HR 6666. James Madison Memorial Building Authorization. Adoption of the rule (H Res 556) providing for House floor consideration of the bill to increase the construction authorization for the Library of Congress James Madison Memorial Building. Adopted 365-21: R 153-20; D 212-1 (ND 140-0, SD 72-1), Sept. 9, 1982.

301. HR 6666. James Madison Memorial Building Authorization. Fary, D-Ill., motion that the House resolve itself into the Committee of the Whole for consideration of the bill to increase the construction authorization for the Library of Congress James Madison Memorial Building. Motion agreed to 343-12: R 151-11; D 192-1 (ND 124-0, SD 68-1), Sept. 9, 1982.

302. HR 6666. James Madison Memorial Building Authorization. Passage of the bill to increase from $130,675,000 to $138,815,000 the construction authorization for the Library of Congress James Madison Memorial Building, amending PL 89-260. Passed 188-186: R 38-134; D 150-52 (ND 103-28, SD 47-24), Sept. 9, 1982.

KEY

Y	Voted for (yea).
#	Paired for.
+	Announced for.
N	Voted against (nay).
X	Paired against.
-	Announced against.
P	Voted "present".
C	Voted "present" to avoid possible conflict of interest.
?	Did not vote or otherwise make a position known.

Democrats **Republicans**

	296	297	298	299	300	301	302
ALABAMA							
1 *Edwards*	Y	Y	Y	Y	Y	Y	Y
2 *Dickinson*	N	Y	Y	N	N	Y	N
3 Nichols	?	?	?	?	?	?	?
4 Bevill	Y	Y	Y	Y	Y	Y	Y
5 Flippo	Y	Y	Y	Y	Y	Y	Y
6 *Smith*	Y	Y	N	N	Y	?	N
7 Shelby	Y	Y	Y	Y	Y	Y	N
ALASKA							
AL *Young*	?	?	?	#	?	?	?
ARIZONA							
1 *Rhodes*	Y	Y	Y	Y	?	Y	Y
2 Udall	Y	Y	Y	Y	Y	Y	Y
3 *Stump*	?	?	?	?	?	?	?
4 *Rudd*	?	?	?	?	?	?	?
ARKANSAS							
1 Alexander	Y	Y	Y	Y	Y	Y	Y
2 *Bethune*	Y	Y	N	N	Y	Y	N
3 *Hammerschmidt*	Y	Y	Y	Y	Y	Y	N
4 Anthony	Y	Y	Y	Y	Y	Y	Y
CALIFORNIA							
1 *Chappie*	Y	Y	Y	Y	Y	Y	N
2 *Clausen*	Y	Y	Y	Y	Y	Y	Y
3 Matsui	Y	Y	Y	Y	Y	Y	Y
4 Fazio	Y	Y	Y	Y	Y	Y	Y
5 Burton, J.	Y	?	?	Y	?	?	?
6 Burton, P.	Y	Y	Y	Y	Y	Y	Y
7 Miller	Y	Y	Y	Y	Y	Y	Y
8 Dellums	?	Y	Y	Y	Y	Y	Y
9 Stark	Y	Y	Y	Y	?	?	?
10 Edwards	Y	Y	Y	Y	Y	Y	Y
11 Lantos	Y	Y	Y	Y	Y	Y	Y
12 *McCloskey*	?	Y	Y	N	?	?	Y
13 Mineta	Y	Y	Y	Y	Y	Y	Y
14 *Shumway*	Y	Y	N	N	Y	Y	N
15 Coelho	Y	Y	Y	Y	Y	Y	Y
16 Panetta	Y	Y	Y	Y	Y	Y	N
17 *Pashayan*	Y	Y	Y	N	Y	Y	N
18 *Thomas*	Y	Y	N	Y	N	?	?
19 *Lagomarsino*	Y	Y	Y	N	Y	?	?
20 *Goldwater*	?	?	?	N	?	?	?
21 *Fiedler*	Y	Y	Y	N	Y	?	N
22 *Moorhead*	Y	Y	Y	N	Y	Y	N
23 Beilenson	?	Y	Y	Y	?	?	?
24 Waxman	Y	Y	Y	Y	Y	Y	Y
25 Roybal	Y	P	Y	Y	Y	?	?
26 *Rousselot*	Y	Y	N	N	Y	Y	N
27 *Dornan*	Y	Y	N	N	Y	Y	N
28 Dixon	Y	Y	Y	Y	Y	Y	Y
29 Hawkins	?	Y	Y	Y	Y	Y	Y
30 Martinez	Y	Y	Y	Y	Y	Y	Y
31 Dymally	?	Y	Y	Y	Y	?	?
32 Anderson	Y	Y	Y	Y	Y	Y	?
33 *Grisham*	?	Y	N	N	Y	Y	N
34 *Lungren*	Y	Y	N	N	Y	Y	N
35 *Dreier*	Y	Y	N	N	Y	Y	N
36 Brown	Y	Y	Y	Y	Y	Y	Y
37 *Lewis*	Y	Y	Y	N	Y	Y	Y
38 Patterson	Y	Y	Y	Y	Y	Y	N
39 *Dannemeyer*	Y	Y	N	N	Y	Y	N
40 *Badham*	Y	Y	N	N	N	N	N
41 *Lowery*	Y	?	Y	N	Y	Y	N
42 *Hunter*	Y	?	Y	N	Y	Y	N
43 *Burgener*	Y	Y	N	N	Y	Y	N
COLORADO							
1 Schroeder	?	?	?	?	?	?	?
2 Wirth	Y	Y	Y	Y	Y	Y	Y
3 Kogovsek	Y	Y	Y	Y	Y	?	?
4 *Brown*	Y	Y	N	N	N	Y	N

	296	297	298	299	300	301	302
5 *Kramer*	Y	Y	N	N	Y	Y	N
CONNECTICUT							
1 Kennelly	Y	Y	Y	Y	Y	Y	Y
2 Gejdenson	N	Y	Y	Y	Y	Y	Y
3 *DeNardis*	Y	?	Y	Y	Y	Y	Y
4 *McKinney*	Y	?	Y	Y	Y	?	Y
5 Ratchford	Y	Y	Y	Y	Y	Y	Y
6 Moffett	?	?	Y	Y	?	?	Y
DELAWARE							
AL *Evans*	Y	Y	Y	Y	Y	Y	N
FLORIDA							
1 Hutto	Y	Y	Y	Y	Y	Y	Y
2 Fuqua	Y	Y	Y	Y	Y	Y	Y
3 Bennett	Y	Y	Y	N	Y	Y	Y
4 Chappell	?	Y	Y	Y	Y	Y	Y
5 *McCollum*	Y	Y	N	Y	Y	?	N
6 *Young*	Y	Y	N	Y	Y	Y	N
7 Gibbons	?	Y	Y	Y	Y	Y	Y
8 Ireland	Y	?	Y	N	?	?	?
9 Nelson	Y	Y	Y	Y	Y	Y	N
10 *Bafalis*	?	?	?	?	?	?	?
11 Mica	Y	Y	Y	Y	Y	Y	N
12 *Shaw*	Y	Y	Y	Y	Y	Y	N
13 Lehman	Y	Y	Y	Y	Y	Y	Y
14 Pepper	?	Y	Y	Y	Y	Y	Y
15 Fascell	Y	Y	Y	Y	Y	Y	Y
GEORGIA							
1 Ginn	Y	Y	Y	Y	Y	Y	Y
2 Hatcher	Y	Y	Y	Y	Y	?	Y
3 Brinkley	Y	Y	Y	Y	Y	Y	Y
4 Levitas	Y	Y	Y	Y	Y	Y	N
5 Fowler	Y	Y	Y	Y	Y	Y	Y
6 *Gingrich*	Y	Y	Y	N	Y	Y	N
7 McDonald	Y	N	N	N	N	N	N
8 Evans	?	?	?	?	?	?	?
9 Jenkins	Y	Y	Y	Y	Y	Y	Y
10 Barnard	Y	Y	Y	Y	Y	Y	Y
HAWAII							
1 Heftel	?	Y	Y	Y	Y	Y	Y
2 Akaka	Y	Y	Y	Y	Y	Y	Y
IDAHO							
1 *Craig*	Y	Y	N	N	Y	Y	N
2 *Hansen*	Y	Y	N	N	Y	Y	N
ILLINOIS							
1 Washington	N	Y	Y	Y	Y	Y	Y
2 Savage	?	?	Y	Y	Y	Y	Y
3 Russo	Y	N	Y	Y	Y	Y	Y
4 *Derwinski*	?	Y	Y	N	Y	Y	N
5 Fary	Y	Y	Y	Y	Y	Y	Y
6 *Hyde*	Y	N	N	N	Y	N	N
7 Collins	Y	Y	Y	Y	Y	Y	Y
8 Rostenkowski	Y	Y	Y	Y	Y	Y	Y
9 Yates	Y	Y	Y	Y	Y	Y	Y
10 *Porter*	Y	Y	Y	N	Y	Y	N
11 Annunzio	Y	Y	Y	Y	Y	Y	Y
12 *Crane, P.*	Y	N	N	N	Y	N	N
13 *McClory*	Y	Y	N	N	Y	N	N
14 *Erlenborn*	?	?	?	Y	Y	Y	Y
15 *Corcoran*	Y	Y	Y	N	Y	Y	N
16 *Martin*	Y	Y	Y	N	N	Y	N
17 *O'Brien*	Y	Y	Y	Y	Y	?	?
18 *Michel*	Y	Y	Y	N	Y	Y	N
19 *Railsback*	Y	Y	?	Y	Y	Y	Y
20 *Findley*	Y	Y	Y	N	Y	Y	N
21 *Madigan*	Y	Y	N	Y	Y	Y	N
22 *Crane, D.*	Y	Y	N	N	Y	Y	N
23 Price	Y	Y	Y	Y	Y	Y	Y
24 Simon	?	Y	Y	Y	Y	Y	Y
INDIANA							
1 Vacancy							
2 Fithian	Y	Y	Y	Y	Y	Y	Y
3 *Hiler*	Y	Y	N	N	N	Y	N
4 *Coats*	Y	Y	Y	Y	Y	Y	Y
5 *Hillis*	Y	Y	Y	Y	Y	Y	Y
6 Evans	Y	Y	Y	Y	Y	Y	Y
7 *Myers*	Y	Y	Y	Y	Y	Y	Y
8 *Deckard*	Y	Y	N	N	Y	Y	N
9 Hamilton	Y	Y	Y	Y	Y	Y	Y
10 Sharp	Y	Y	Y	Y	Y	Y	Y
11 Jacobs	N	?	Y	Y	Y	Y	Y
IOWA							
1 *Leach*	Y	Y	Y	Y	Y	Y	Y
2 *Tauke*	Y	Y	Y	Y	Y	Y	N
3 *Evans*	N	Y	Y	Y	Y	Y	N
4 Smith	?	?	Y	Y	Y	Y	Y
5 Harkin	N	Y	Y	Y	Y	Y	N
6 Bedell	Y	Y	Y	Y	Y	?	N

ND - Northern Democrats   SD - Southern Democrats

	296	297	298	299	300	301	302
KANSAS							
1 ***Roberts***	Y	Y	Y	N	Y	Y	N
2 ***Jeffries***	?	?	N	N	N	N	N
3 ***Winn***	?	Y	Y	N	Y	Y	N
4 Glickman	Y	Y	Y	Y	Y	Y	N
5 ***Whittaker***	Y	Y	Y	N	Y	Y	N
KENTUCKY							
1 Hubbard	Y	Y	Y	N	Y	Y	N
2 Natcher	Y	Y	Y	Y	Y	Y	Y
3 Mazzoli	Y	Y	Y	Y	Y	Y	Y
4 ***Snyder***	Y	Y	Y	N	Y	Y	N
5 ***Rogers***	Y	Y	Y	Y	Y	Y	N
6 ***Hopkins***	Y	Y	Y	Y	Y	Y	N
7 Perkins	Y	Y	Y	Y	Y	Y	Y
LOUISIANA							
1 ***Livingston***	Y	Y	Y	N	Y	?	N
2 Boggs	Y	Y	Y	Y	Y	Y	?
3 Tauzin	Y	Y	Y	N	Y	Y	N
4 Roemer	N	Y	Y	N	Y	Y	N
5 Huckaby	Y	Y	Y	Y	Y	Y	N
6 ***Moore***	Y	Y	Y	N	Y	Y	N
7 Breaux	?	Y	Y	Y	Y	Y	Y
8 Long	Y	Y	Y	Y	Y	Y	Y
MAINE							
1 ***Emery***	Y	Y	Y	Y	?	?	?
2 ***Snowe***	Y	Y	Y	Y	Y	Y	N
MARYLAND							
1 Dyson	?	Y	Y	Y	Y	Y	N
2 Long	Y	Y	N	Y	Y	?	Y
3 Mikulski	Y	Y	Y	Y	Y	Y	Y
4 ***Holt***	N	Y	N	Y	Y	Y	N
5 Hoyer	Y	Y	Y	Y	Y	Y	Y
6 Byron	P	Y	Y	Y	Y	Y	N
7 Mitchell	N	?	Y	Y	?	?	?
8 Barnes	Y	Y	Y	Y	Y	Y	Y
MASSACHUSETTS							
1 ***Conte***	Y	Y	Y	Y	Y	Y	N
2 Boland	Y	Y	Y	Y	Y	Y	Y
3 Early	Y	Y	Y	Y	Y	Y	Y
4 Frank	Y	Y	Y	Y	Y	Y	?
5 Shannon	Y	Y	Y	Y	Y	?	Y
6 Mavroules	Y	Y	Y	Y	Y	Y	Y
7 Markey	Y	Y	Y	Y	Y	Y	Y
8 O'Neill				Y			
9 Moakley	Y	Y	Y	Y	Y	Y	Y
10 ***Heckler***	?	Y	N	Y	Y	Y	N
11 Donnelly	Y	Y	Y	Y	Y	Y	Y
12 Studds	Y	Y	Y	Y	Y	Y	Y
MICHIGAN							
1 Conyers	Y	Y	Y	Y	Y	?	?
2 ***Pursell***	Y	Y	Y	Y	Y	Y	N
3 Wolpe	Y	Y	Y	Y	Y	Y	N
4 ***Siljander***	?	Y	Y	N	Y	Y	N
5 ***Sawyer***	Y	Y	Y	N	Y	Y	N
6 ***Dunn***	Y	Y	Y	Y	Y	Y	N
7 Kildee	Y	Y	Y	Y	Y	Y	Y
8 Traxler	Y	Y	Y	Y	Y	Y	?
9 ***Vander Jagt***	Y	Y	Y	Y	Y	Y	N
10 Albosta	Y	Y	Y	Y	Y	?	Y
11 ***Davis***	Y	Y	Y	Y	Y	Y	Y
12 Bonior	Y	Y	Y	Y	Y	Y	Y
13 Crockett	?	?	Y	Y	?	?	?
14 Hertel	Y	Y	Y	Y	Y	?	Y
15 Ford	?	?	Y	Y	Y	Y	Y
16 Dingell	Y	Y	Y	Y	Y	Y	Y
17 Brodhead	Y	?	Y	Y	Y	Y	Y
18 Blanchard	?	?	Y	Y	Y	Y	Y
19 ***Broomfield***	?	Y	Y	N	Y	Y	N
MINNESOTA							
1 ***Erdahl***	Y	Y	Y	Y	Y	Y	N
2 ***Hagedorn***	Y	Y	Y	N	Y	Y	N
3 ***Frenzel***	Y	Y	Y	N	N	N	N
4 Vento	Y	Y	Y	Y	Y	Y	N
5 Sabo	N	Y	Y	Y	Y	Y	Y
6 ***Weber***	Y	Y	Y	N	N	N	N
7 ***Stangeland***	Y	Y	Y	Y	Y	Y	Y
8 Oberstar	P	Y	Y	Y	Y	Y	Y
MISSISSIPPI							
1 Whitten	Y	Y	Y	Y	Y	Y	Y
2 Bowen	Y	?	?	?	?	?	?
3 Montgomery	Y	Y	Y	N	Y	Y	N
4 Dowdy	Y	?	Y	Y	Y	Y	N
5 ***Lott***	Y	Y	Y	N	Y	Y	N
MISSOURI							
1 Clay	?	Y	Y	Y	Y	Y	Y
2 Young	Y	Y	Y	Y	Y	Y	Y
3 Gephardt	Y	Y	Y	Y	Y	Y	Y

	296	297	298	299	300	301	302
4 Skelton	Y	Y	Y	Y	Y	Y	N
5 Bolling	Y	?	?	Y	?	?	?
6 ***Coleman***	Y	Y	Y	Y	Y	Y	Y
7 ***Taylor***	Y	Y	Y	N	Y	Y	N
8 ***Bailey***	Y	Y	Y	N	Y	Y	N
9 Volkmer	Y	Y	Y	Y	Y	Y	N
10 ***Emerson***	N	Y	Y	Y	N	N	N
MONTANA							
1 Williams	Y	Y	Y	Y	?	?	?
2 ***Marlenee***	Y	Y	Y	N	N	N	N
NEBRASKA							
1 ***Bereuter***	Y	Y	Y	Y	Y	Y	N
2 ***Daub***	Y	Y	Y	N	Y	Y	N
3 ***Smith***	Y	Y	Y	Y	Y	Y	N
NEVADA							
AL Santini	?	Y	Y	Y	?	Y	N
NEW HAMPSHIRE							
1 D'Amours	Y	Y	Y	Y	Y	Y	N
2 ***Gregg***	Y	Y	N	N	N	Y	N
NEW JERSEY							
1 Florio	Y	Y	Y	Y	Y	Y	Y
2 Hughes	Y	Y	Y	Y	Y	Y	Y
3 Howard	Y	Y	Y	Y	Y	Y	Y
4 ***Smith***	Y	Y	Y	Y	Y	Y	Y
5 ***Fenwick***	Y	Y	Y	Y	Y	Y	Y
6 ***Forsythe***	N	?	Y	N	?	?	Y
7 ***Roukema***	Y	Y	Y	Y	Y	Y	N
8 Roe	?	Y	Y	Y	Y	Y	Y
9 ***Hollenbeck***	Y	Y	Y	Y	Y	Y	Y
10 Rodino	Y	Y	Y	Y	Y	Y	Y
11 Minish	Y	Y	Y	Y	Y	Y	Y
12 ***Rinaldo***	Y	Y	Y	Y	Y	Y	Y
13 ***Courter***	Y	Y	Y	N	Y	Y	N
14 Guarini	Y	Y	Y	Y	Y	Y	Y
15 Dwyer	Y	Y	Y	Y	Y	Y	Y
NEW MEXICO							
1 ***Lujan***	Y	Y	Y	N	Y	Y	Y
2 ***Skeen***	Y	Y	Y	N	Y	Y	N
NEW YORK							
1 ***Carney***	Y	Y	N	N	Y	Y	N
2 Downey	Y	Y	Y	Y	Y	Y	Y
3 ***Carman***	Y	Y	N	N	Y	Y	N
4 ***Lent***	Y	Y	Y	Y	Y	Y	?
5 ***McGrath***	Y	Y	N	Y	Y	Y	N
6 ***LeBoutillier***	Y	Y	N	Y	Y	Y	N
7 Addabbo	?	?	Y	Y	?	?	?
8 Rosenthal	?	?	Y	Y	?	?	?
9 Ferraro	Y	Y	Y	Y	Y	Y	Y
10 Biaggi	Y	Y	Y	Y	?	?	?
11 Scheuer	Y	?	Y	Y	Y	Y	Y
12 Chisholm	?	?	Y	Y	?	?	Y
13 Solarz	Y	Y	Y	Y	Y	Y	Y
14 Vacancy							
15 Zeferetti	Y	Y	Y	Y	?	?	?
16 Schumer	?	?	?	?	?	?	?
17 ***Molinari***	Y	Y	Y	Y	Y	Y	N
18 ***Green***	Y	Y	Y	Y	Y	Y	N
19 Rangel	?	Y	Y	Y	?	?	?
20 Weiss	?	?	?	?	?	?	?
21 Garcia	Y	Y	Y	Y	Y	Y	Y
22 Bingham	?	?	Y	Y	Y	Y	Y
23 Peyser	Y	Y	Y	Y	Y	Y	N
24 Ottinger	P	P	Y	Y	Y	Y	Y
25 ***Fish***	Y	Y	Y	Y	Y	Y	Y
26 ***Gilman***	Y	Y	Y	Y	Y	Y	N
27 McHugh	Y	Y	Y	Y	Y	Y	Y
28 Stratton	Y	Y	Y	Y	Y	Y	Y
29 ***Solomon***	Y	Y	Y	N	N	N	N
30 ***Martin***	Y	Y	Y	Y	Y	Y	?
31 ***Mitchell***	Y	Y	Y	Y	Y	Y	N
32 ***Wortley***	Y	Y	Y	Y	Y	Y	N
33 ***Lee***	Y	Y	Y	Y	Y	Y	Y
34 ***Horton***	P	Y	Y	Y	Y	Y	Y
35 ***Conable***	Y	Y	N	Y	Y	Y	N
36 LaFalce	Y	Y	Y	Y	Y	Y	Y
37 Nowak	Y	Y	Y	Y	Y	Y	Y
38 ***Kemp***	Y	Y	Y	N	Y	?	Y
39 Lundine	?	Y	Y	Y	Y	Y	N
NORTH CAROLINA							
1 Jones	Y	Y	Y	Y	Y	Y	Y
2 Fountain	?	Y	Y	Y	?	?	N
3 Whitley	Y	Y	Y	Y	Y	Y	N
4 Andrews	Y	Y	Y	Y	Y	Y	Y
5 Neal	Y	Y	Y	Y	Y	Y	N
6 ***Johnston***	N	Y	Y	N	N	N	N
7 Rose	Y	Y	Y	Y	Y	Y	Y
8 Hefner	Y	Y	Y	Y	Y	Y	N

	296	297	298	299	300	301	302
9 ***Martin***	Y	Y	Y	N	Y	Y	N
10 ***Broyhill***	Y	Y	Y	N	Y	Y	N
11 ***Hendon***	N	Y	Y	Y	Y	N	N
NORTH DAKOTA							
AL Dorgan	Y	Y	Y	Y	Y	Y	N
OHIO							
1 ***Gradison***	Y	Y	Y	N	Y	Y	Y
2 Luken	N	Y	Y	Y	?	?	?
3 Hall	?	Y	Y	N	Y	Y	Y
4 ***Oxley***	Y	Y	Y	N	Y	Y	N
5 ***Latta***	Y	Y	Y	N	N	N	N
6 ***McEwen***	Y	Y	Y	N	Y	Y	N
7 ***Brown***	?	?	?	?	?	?	?
8 ***Kindness***	Y	Y	Y	N	Y	?	N
9 ***Weber***	Y	Y	N	Y	Y	Y	N
10 ***Miller***	N	Y	Y	N	Y	Y	N
11 ***Stanton***	Y	?	?	N	?	?	Y
12 Shamansky	Y	Y	Y	Y	Y	?	?
13 Pease	Y	Y	Y	Y	Y	?	Y
14 Seiberling	Y	Y	?	Y	Y	Y	Y
15 ***Wylie***	Y	Y	Y	N	?	?	?
16 ***Regula***	Y	Y	Y	Y	Y	Y	N
17 ***Ashbrook***	Y	Y	Y	N	N	Y	N
18 Applegate	?	?	Y	Y	Y	?	Y
19 ***Williams***	Y	Y	Y	Y	Y	Y	N
20 Oakar	Y	Y	Y	Y	Y	Y	N
21 Stokes	Y	Y	Y	Y	Y	Y	Y
22 Eckart	Y	Y	Y	Y	Y	Y	N
23 Mottl	Y	Y	N	Y	Y	Y	Y
OKLAHOMA							
1 Jones	Y	Y	Y	Y	Y	Y	Y
2 Synar	Y	Y	Y	Y	Y	Y	Y
3 Watkins	Y	Y	Y	Y	Y	Y	Y
4 McCurdy	Y	Y	Y	Y	Y	Y	N
5 ***Edwards***	Y	Y	Y	N	Y	Y	N
6 English	Y	Y	Y	Y	Y	Y	N
OREGON							
1 AuCoin	Y	Y	Y	Y	Y	Y	Y
2 ***Smith***	Y	Y	N	N	Y	Y	N
3 Wyden	Y	Y	Y	Y	Y	Y	N
4 Weaver	Y	Y	Y	Y	Y	Y	N
PENNSYLVANIA							
1 Foglietta	Y	Y	Y	Y	Y	Y	Y
2 Gray	?	Y	Y	Y	Y	Y	Y
3 Smith	Y	Y	Y	Y	?	?	?
4 ***Dougherty***	?	?	Y	Y	Y	Y	?
5 ***Schulze***	Y	Y	Y	Y	Y	Y	Y
6 Yatron	Y	Y	Y	Y	?	?	?
7 Edgar	Y	Y	Y	Y	Y	?	?
8 ***Coyne, J.***	?	Y	Y	Y	Y	Y	Y
9 ***Shuster***	Y	Y	Y	Y	N	Y	Y
10 ***McDade***	Y	Y	Y	Y	Y	Y	Y
11 ***Nelligan***	Y	Y	Y	Y	Y	Y	Y
12 Murtha	Y	Y	Y	Y	Y	Y	?
13 ***Coughlin***	Y	Y	N	Y	Y	Y	N
14 Coyne, W.	Y	Y	Y	Y	Y	Y	Y
15 ***Ritter***	Y	Y	N	N	Y	Y	N
16 ***Walker***	N	Y	Y	N	N	N	N
17 Ertel	?	Y	Y	Y	Y	?	?
18 Walgren	?	Y	Y	Y	Y	Y	Y
19 ***Goodling***	N	?	Y	Y	Y	Y	N
20 Gaydos	Y	Y	Y	Y	Y	?	N
21 Bailey	Y	Y	Y	Y	Y	Y	Y
22 Murphy	N	Y	Y	Y	Y	Y	N
23 ***Clinger***	Y	Y	Y	Y	Y	Y	Y
24 ***Marks***	?	?	Y	Y	?	?	?
25 ***Atkinson***	Y	Y	Y	N	Y	Y	N
RHODE ISLAND							
1 St Germain	Y	Y	Y	Y	Y	Y	Y
2 ***Schneider***	Y	Y	Y	Y	Y	Y	Y
SOUTH CAROLINA							
1 ***Hartnett***	Y	Y	Y	N	Y	Y	N
2 ***Spence***	Y	Y	Y	N	?	Y	N
3 Derrick	Y	Y	Y	Y	Y	Y	N
4 ***Campbell***	Y	Y	Y	N	Y	Y	N
5 Holland	Y	Y	Y	Y	Y	Y	Y
6 ***Napier***	Y	Y	Y	N	Y	Y	N
SOUTH DAKOTA							
1 Daschle	Y	Y	Y	Y	Y	Y	N
2 ***Roberts***	Y	Y	Y	Y	?	?	?
TENNESSEE							
1 ***Quillen***	Y	Y	Y	N	Y	Y	N
2 ***Duncan***	Y	Y	Y	Y	Y	Y	N
3 Bouquard	Y	Y	Y	Y	Y	Y	Y
4 Gore	Y	Y	Y	Y	Y	Y	Y
5 Boner	Y	Y	Y	Y	Y	Y	Y
6 ***Beard***	?	?	Y	Y	Y	Y	N

	296	297	298	299	300	301	302
7 Jones	Y	Y	Y	Y	Y	Y	Y
8 Ford	Y	Y	Y	Y	Y	Y	Y
TEXAS							
1 Hall, S.	Y	Y	Y	N	Y	Y	Y
2 Wilson	Y	Y	Y	Y	Y	Y	Y
3 ***Collins***	?	?	?	X	?	?	?
4 Hall, R.	Y	Y	Y	N	Y	Y	Y
5 Mattox	?	?	?	#	?	?	?
6 Gramm	Y	Y	N	N	Y	Y	N
7 ***Archer***	Y	Y	N	N	Y	Y	N
8 ***Fields***	Y	Y	Y	N	?	?	?
9 Brooks	Y	Y	Y	Y	Y	Y	Y
10 Pickle	Y	Y	Y	Y	Y	Y	Y
11 Leath	Y	Y	Y	Y	Y	Y	Y
12 Wright	Y	?	Y	Y	Y	?	Y
13 Hightower	Y	Y	Y	Y	Y	Y	Y
14 Patman	Y	Y	Y	N	Y	?	Y
15 de la Garza	Y	Y	Y	Y	Y	Y	?
16 White	?	Y	Y	Y	Y	Y	Y
17 Stenholm	Y	Y	Y	N	Y	Y	N
18 Leland	Y	Y	Y	Y	Y	Y	Y
19 Hance	Y	Y	Y	Y	Y	Y	N
20 Gonzalez	Y	Y	Y	Y	Y	Y	Y
21 ***Loeffler***	Y	Y	Y	N	Y	Y	N
22 ***Paul***	Y	Y	N	N	N	Y	N
23 Kazen	Y	Y	Y	Y	Y	Y	N
24 Frost	Y	Y	Y	Y	Y	Y	Y
UTAH							
1 ***Hansen***	Y	Y	N	N	Y	?	?
2 ***Marriott***	?	?	?	?	?	?	?
VERMONT							
AL ***Jeffords***	Y	Y	Y	Y	Y	?	N
VIRGINIA							
1 ***Trible***	Y	Y	Y	N	Y	?	?
2 ***Whitehurst***	Y	Y	Y	N	Y	Y	N
3 ***Bliley***	Y	Y	Y	N	Y	?	N
4 ***Daniel, R.***	Y	Y	Y	N	Y	Y	N
5 Daniel, D.	P	Y	Y	Y	Y	?	N
6 ***Butler***	N	Y	N	N	Y	Y	N
7 ***Robinson***	Y	Y	Y	Y	Y	Y	N
8 ***Parris***	?	Y	Y	Y	Y	Y	Y
9 ***Wampler***	Y	Y	Y	Y	Y	Y	Y
10 ***Wolf***	Y	Y	Y	Y	Y	Y	N
WASHINGTON							
1 ***Pritchard***	?	Y	N	Y	Y	Y	Y
2 Swift	Y	Y	Y	Y	Y	?	Y
3 Bonker	Y	Y	Y	Y	Y	Y	Y
4 ***Morrison***	Y	Y	Y	Y	Y	?	N
5 Foley	Y	Y	Y	Y	Y	Y	Y
6 Dicks	Y	Y	Y	Y	Y	Y	N
7 Lowry	Y	Y	Y	Y	Y	Y	Y
WEST VIRGINIA							
1 Mollohan	Y	Y	Y	Y	Y	Y	Y
2 ***Benedict***	Y	Y	Y	N	N	Y	N
3 ***Staton***	Y	Y	Y	N	Y	Y	N
4 Rahall	Y	Y	Y	Y	Y	Y	Y
WISCONSIN							
1 Aspin	Y	Y	Y	Y	Y	Y	Y
2 Kastenmeier	Y	Y	Y	Y	Y	Y	Y
3 ***Gunderson***	Y	Y	Y	Y	N	Y	N
4 Zablocki	?	?	Y	Y	Y	Y	Y
5 Reuss	Y	Y	Y	Y	Y	Y	Y
6 ***Petri***	Y	Y	Y	Y	Y	Y	N
7 Obey	Y	Y	Y	Y	Y	Y	Y
8 ***Roth***	Y	Y	Y	N	?	?	?
9 ***Sensenbrenner***	Y	Y	Y	N	Y	Y	N
WYOMING							
AL ***Cheney***	Y	Y	N	N	Y	Y	N

Southern states - Ala., Ark., Fla., Ga., Ky., La., Miss., N.C., Okla., S.C., Tenn., Texas, Va.

303. Procedural Motion. Petri, R-Wis., motion to approve the House *Journal* of Tuesday, Sept. 14. Motion agreed to 305-19: R 138-7; D 167-12 (ND 104-11, SD 63-1), Sept. 15, 1982.

304. HR 4374. Shipping Act. Jones, D-N.C., motion to suspend the rules and pass the bill to clarify the provision of antitrust immunity for activities by conferences of international ocean liner companies. Motion agreed to 350-33: R 159-9; D 191-24 (ND 126-18, SD 65-6), Sept. 15, 1982. A two-thirds majority of those present and voting (256 in this case) is required for passage under suspension of the rules. A "yea" was a vote supporting the president's position.

305. HR 6444. Patent Term Extension. Kastenmeier, D-Wis., motion to suspend the rules and pass the bill to extend the patent term of specified items that are subject to federal regulatory review. Motion rejected 250-132: R 149-18; D 101-114 (ND 43-101, SD 58-13), Sept. 15, 1982. A two-thirds majority of those present and voting (255 in this case) is required for passage under suspension of the rules.

306. HR 6813. Boat Safety Act. Studds, D-Mass., motion to suspend the rules and pass the bill to allow monies from the National Recreational Boating Safety and Facilities Improvement Fund to be appropriated without scoring it against, or subtracting from, the Transportation Department's budget authority for budget purposes. Motion rejected 250-137: R 64-108; D 186-29 (ND 137-7, SD 49-22), Sept. 15, 1982. A two-thirds majority of those present and voting (258 in this case) is required for passage under suspension of the rules. A "nay" was a vote supporting the president's position.

307. HR 6580. Sailing School Vessel Regulation. Studds, D-Mass., motion to suspend the rules and pass the bill to require the Coast Guard to develop marine safety regulations specially designed for sailing school vessels, operated by non-profit education institutions. Motion rejected 236-154: R 51-124; D 185-30 (ND 133-12, SD 52-18), Sept. 15, 1982. A two-thirds majority of those present and voting (260 in this case) is required for passage under suspension of the rules.

308. HR 6355. Technical Corrections in Health Laws. Waxman, D-Calif., motion to suspend the rules and pass the bill to make technical corrections in amendments made by the 1981 reconciliation bill (PL 97-35) to the Public Health Service Act, Consumer Product Safety Act, Poison Prevention Packaging Act and certain other laws, to authorize appropriations for the training of nurse anesthetists in fiscal 1983-84 and to transfer the National Institute for Occupational Safety and Health from the Centers for Disease Control to the National Institutes of Health. Motion rejected 227-165: R 55-121; D 172-44 (ND 138-7, SD 34-37), Sept. 15, 1982. A two-thirds majority of those present and voting (262 in this case) is required for passage under suspension of the rules.

309. S 923. Pretrial Services Act of 1982. Adoption of the conference report on the bill to expand 10 demonstration programs that provide pretrial services to federal judges to help them make bail decisions. Adopted 367-20: R 158-16; D 209-4 (ND 141-1, SD 68-3), Sept. 15, 1982.

310. HR 6956. Department of Housing and Urban Development Appropriations, Fiscal 1983. Boland, D-Mass., motion that the House resolve itself into the Committee of the Whole for consideration of the bill to provide fiscal 1983 appropriations for the Department of Housing and Urban Development and independent agencies. Motion agreed to 346-5: R 152-4; D 194-1 (ND 128-0, SD 66-1), Sept. 15, 1982.

KEY

Y	Voted for (yea).
#	Paired for.
+	Announced for.
N	Voted against (nay).
X	Paired against.
-	Announced against.
P	Voted "present".
C	Voted "present" to avoid possible conflict of interest.
?	Did not vote or otherwise make a position known.

Democrats   *Republicans*

	303	304	305	306	307	308	309	310
ALABAMA								
1 Edwards	?	Y	Y	Y	N	N	Y	Y
2 *Dickinson*	N	Y	N	N	N	N	N	?
3 Nichols	Y	Y	Y	Y	N	Y	N	?
4 Bevill	Y	Y	N	Y	N	Y	N	Y
5 Flippo	Y	Y	Y	Y	N	N	Y	Y
6 *Smith*	?	?	#	?	?	X	Y	Y
7 Shelby	Y	Y	Y	Y	N	N	Y	Y
ALASKA								
AL *Young*	?	?	#	#	?	?	?	?
ARIZONA								
1 *Rhodes*	?	Y	Y	N	Y	N	Y	Y
2 Udall	Y	Y	N	Y	Y	Y	?	?
3 *Stump*	Y	Y	Y	N	N	N	N	?
4 *Rudd*	Y	Y	Y	N	Y	N	Y	Y
ARKANSAS								
1 Alexander	Y	Y	Y	Y	N	N	Y	Y
2 *Bethune*	Y	Y	?	Y	N	N	Y	?
3 *Hammerschmidt*	Y	Y	Y	Y	N	N	Y	Y
4 Anthony	Y	Y	Y	N	Y	N	Y	Y
CALIFORNIA								
1 *Chappie*	Y	Y	N	N	N	N	Y	Y
2 *Clausen*	Y	Y	Y	N	N	Y	Y	Y
3 Matsui	Y	Y	N	Y	Y	Y	Y	Y
4 Fazio	Y	Y	N	Y	Y	Y	Y	Y
5 Burton, J.	?	?	?	?	?	?	?	?
6 Burton, P.	Y	Y	N	Y	Y	Y	Y	Y
7 Miller	Y	Y	N	Y	Y	Y	Y	Y
8 Dellums	?	Y	N	Y	Y	Y	Y	Y
9 Stark	Y	Y	N	Y	Y	Y	Y	Y
10 Edwards	Y	N	N	Y	Y	Y	Y	Y
11 Lantos	?	Y	N	Y	Y	Y	Y	Y
12 *McCloskey*	Y	Y	N	Y	Y	N	Y	Y
13 Mineta	Y	Y	N	Y	Y	Y	Y	Y
14 Shumway	Y	Y	N	Y	N	Y	Y	Y
15 Coelho	Y	Y	Y	Y	Y	Y	Y	Y
16 Panetta	Y	Y	N	Y	Y	Y	Y	Y
17 *Pashayan*	Y	Y	N	N	N	N	Y	Y
18 *Thomas*	?	?	#	X	?	X	?	?
19 *Lagomarsino*	Y	Y	N	N	N	Y	Y	Y
20 *Goldwater*	?	?	?	?	?	?	?	?
21 *Fiedler*	Y	Y	Y	N	N	N	Y	Y
22 *Moorhead*	Y	Y	Y	N	N	N	Y	Y
23 Beilenson	Y	N	N	Y	Y	Y	Y	Y
24 Waxman	?	Y	N	Y	Y	Y	Y	Y
25 Roybal	?	Y	N	?	Y	Y	Y	Y
26 Rousselot	Y	Y	Y	N	N	N	Y	Y
27 *Dornan*	Y	Y	N	N	N	N	Y	Y
28 Dixon	?	Y	N	Y	Y	Y	Y	Y
29 Hawkins	P	Y	N	Y	Y	Y	Y	Y
30 Martinez	?	Y	N	Y	Y	Y	Y	Y
31 Dymally	Y	Y	Y	Y	Y	Y	Y	Y
32 Anderson	Y	Y	N	Y	Y	Y	Y	Y
33 *Grisham*	Y	Y	N	N	N	N	Y	Y
34 *Lungren*	Y	Y	N	N	N	N	Y	?
35 *Dreier*	Y	Y	N	N	N	N	Y	Y
36 Brown	Y	Y	N	Y	Y	Y	Y	Y
37 Lewis	Y	Y	N	N	N	N	Y	Y
38 Patterson	Y	Y	N	Y	Y	Y	Y	Y
39 *Dannemeyer*	Y	Y	N	N	N	N	Y	Y
40 *Badham*	Y	Y	N	N	N	N	N	N
41 *Lowery*	Y	Y	Y	N	N	N	Y	Y
42 *Hunter*	Y	Y	N	N	N	N	Y	Y
43 *Burgener*	?	Y	N	N	N	N	Y	Y
COLORADO								
1 Schroeder	N	Y	N	Y	N	Y	N	Y
2 Wirth	Y	N	N	Y	Y	Y	Y	Y
3 Kogovsek	Y	Y	N	Y	N	Y	Y	Y
4 *Brown*	Y	Y	N	N	Y	N	Y	Y

	303	304	305	306	307	308	309	310
5 *Kramer*	Y	Y	Y	N	N	N	Y	Y
CONNECTICUT								
1 Kennelly	Y	Y	Y	Y	Y	Y	Y	Y
2 Gejdenson	N	Y	Y	Y	Y	Y	Y	Y
3 *DeNardis*	Y	Y	Y	Y	Y	Y	Y	?
4 *McKinney*	?	Y	Y	N	N	Y	Y	Y
5 Ratchford	Y	Y	Y	Y	Y	Y	Y	Y
6 Moffett	?	?	?	?	?	?	?	?
DELAWARE								
AL *Evans*	Y	Y	Y	Y	Y	Y	Y	Y
FLORIDA								
1 Hutto	Y	Y	Y	Y	N	Y	N	Y
2 Fuqua	?	Y	Y	N	Y	N	Y	Y
3 Bennett	Y	Y	Y	Y	N	Y	N	Y
4 Chappell	?	?	?	?	?	?	?	?
5 *McCollum*	Y	Y	N	N	N	N	Y	Y
6 *Young*	Y	Y	Y	N	N	N	Y	Y
7 Gibbons	Y	Y	N	N	N	Y	Y	Y
8 Ireland	?	Y	Y	Y	?	?	Y	Y
9 Nelson	Y	N	N	Y	Y	Y	Y	Y
10 *Bafalis*	?	?	?	?	?	?	?	?
11 Mica	Y	Y	N	Y	Y	Y	Y	Y
12 *Shaw*	Y	N	N	N	N	N	Y	Y
13 Lehman	Y	Y	Y	Y	Y	Y	Y	Y
14 Pepper	?	?	X	#	?	#	?	?
15 Fascell	Y	Y	N	Y	Y	Y	Y	Y
GEORGIA								
1 Ginn	?	Y	Y	Y	N	Y	Y	Y
2 Hatcher	Y	Y	Y	N	N	N	Y	Y
3 Brinkley	Y	Y	Y	Y	N	Y	Y	Y
4 Levitas	Y	Y	Y	Y	N	Y	Y	Y
5 Fowler	?	Y	Y	Y	N	Y	Y	Y
6 *Gingrich*	Y	Y	N	N	N	N	Y	Y
7 McDonald	Y	Y	Y	N	N	N	N	N
8 Evans	?	?	?	?	?	?	?	?
9 Jenkins	Y	Y	Y	N	N	Y	Y	Y
10 Barnard	Y	Y	Y	N	Y	N	Y	Y
HAWAII								
1 Heftel	Y	Y	N	Y	Y	Y	Y	Y
2 Akaka	?	?	X	#	#	#	?	?
IDAHO								
1 *Craig*	Y	Y	Y	N	N	N	Y	Y
2 *Hansen*	?	Y	Y	N	N	N	N	Y
ILLINOIS								
1 Washington	N	Y	N	Y	Y	Y	Y	Y
2 Savage	?	?	?	Y	Y	Y	Y	?
3 Russo	Y	Y	N	Y	Y	Y	Y	Y
4 *Derwinski*	Y	Y	N	N	N	Y	Y	Y
5 Fary	Y	Y	N	Y	Y	Y	Y	Y
6 *Hyde*	Y	Y	N	Y	N	N	Y	Y
7 Collins	P	Y	N	Y	Y	Y	Y	Y
8 Rostenkowski	Y	Y	N	Y	Y	N	Y	Y
9 Yates	N	N	N	Y	Y	Y	Y	Y
10 *Porter*	Y	Y	N	N	N	N	Y	Y
11 Annunzio	Y	N	N	Y	Y	Y	Y	Y
12 *Crane, P.*	Y	N	N	Y	N	N	N	Y
13 *McClory*	?	?	#	#	X	?	?	?
14 *Erlenborn*	Y	Y	N	N	N	N	Y	Y
15 *Corcoran*	Y	Y	Y	N	N	N	Y	Y
16 *Martin*	Y	Y	N	N	N	Y	Y	Y
17 *O'Brien*	Y	Y	N	N	N	Y	Y	?
18 *Michel*	Y	Y	Y	N	N	Y	Y	Y
19 *Railsback*	Y	Y	Y	Y	Y	Y	Y	Y
20 *Findley*	Y	Y	N	N	N	N	Y	Y
21 *Madigan*	Y	Y	Y	Y	N	Y	Y	Y
22 *Crane, D.*	?	?	#	X	N	N	Y	Y
23 Price	Y	Y	N	Y	N	Y	Y	Y
24 Simon	Y	Y	N	Y	N	Y	Y	Y
INDIANA								
1 Vacancy								
2 Fithian	?	?	?	?	?	?	?	?
3 *Hiler*	Y	Y	Y	N	N	N	Y	?
4 *Coats*	Y	Y	Y	N	N	N	Y	Y
5 *Hillis*	?	?	?	?	?	?	?	?
6 Evans	?	?	?	?	?	?	?	?
7 *Myers*	Y	Y	N	N	Y	N	Y	Y
8 *Deckard*	Y	Y	Y	Y	N	Y	Y	Y
9 Hamilton	Y	Y	Y	N	N	Y	Y	Y
10 Sharp	Y	Y	N	Y	N	Y	Y	Y
11 Jacobs	N	Y	N	Y	Y	Y	Y	Y
IOWA								
1 Leach	?	N	N	N	N	Y	Y	Y
2 *Tauke*	Y	Y	Y	N	N	Y	Y	Y
3 Evans	N	Y	N	N	N	Y	Y	Y
4 Smith	Y	N	N	Y	N	Y	Y	Y
5 Harkin	N	N	N	Y	Y	Y	Y	Y
6 Bedell	Y	N	N	Y	N	Y	Y	Y

ND - Northern Democrats   SD - Southern Democrats

Corresponding to Congressional Record Votes 320, 321, 322, 323, 324, 325, 326, 327

	303	304	305	306	307	308	309	310
KANSAS								
1 **Roberts**	Y	Y	Y	N	N	N	Y	Y
2 **Jeffries**	Y	Y	Y	N	N	N	N	?
3 **Winn**	Y	Y	Y	N	N	N	Y	Y
4 Glickman	Y	N	N	Y	N	N	Y	Y
5 **Whittaker**	Y	Y	Y	N	N	N	Y	Y
KENTUCKY								
1 Hubbard	Y	Y	Y	Y	Y	N	Y	Y
2 Natcher	Y	Y	Y	N	Y	Y	Y	Y
3 Mazzoli	Y	N	Y	Y	Y	Y	Y	Y
4 **Snyder**	Y	Y	N	Y	N	N	Y	Y
5 **Rogers**	Y	Y	Y	N	N	N	Y	Y
6 **Hopkins**	Y	Y	N	N	Y	N	Y	Y
7 Perkins	Y	Y	Y	N	Y	Y	Y	Y
LOUISIANA								
1 **Livingston**	Y	Y	Y	Y	N	N	Y	Y
2 Boggs	Y	Y	N	Y	Y	Y	Y	?
3 Tauzin	Y	Y	Y	Y	Y	Y	Y	Y
4 Roemer	N	Y	N	Y	Y	N	Y	Y
5 Huckaby	Y	Y	N	Y	Y	N	Y	Y
6 **Moore**	Y	Y	Y	Y	N	Y	Y	Y
7 Breaux	Y	Y	Y	Y	Y	Y	Y	Y
8 Long	Y	Y	N	Y	Y	Y	Y	Y
MAINE								
1 **Emery**	Y	Y	Y	Y	Y	Y	Y	?
2 **Snowe**	Y	Y	N	Y	Y	Y	Y	Y
MARYLAND								
1 Dyson	?	Y	N	Y	Y	Y	Y	Y
2 Long	?	Y	N	Y	Y	Y	Y	Y
3 Mikulski	?	Y	N	Y	Y	Y	Y	Y
4 **Holt**	Y	Y	Y	N	Y	Y	Y	Y
5 Hoyer	Y	Y	N	Y	Y	?	Y	Y
6 Byron	?	?	?	?	?	?	Y	Y
7 Mitchell	N	Y	N	Y	?	#	Y	Y
8 Barnes	N	Y	N	Y	Y	Y	Y	Y
MASSACHUSETTS								
1 **Conte**	Y	Y	Y	N	Y	Y	Y	Y
2 Boland	Y	Y	Y	Y	Y	Y	Y	?
3 Early	Y	Y	N	Y	Y	Y	Y	Y
4 Frank	Y	Y	N	Y	Y	Y	Y	Y
5 Shannon	Y	Y	N	Y	Y	Y	Y	Y
6 Mavroules	?	Y	N	Y	Y	Y	Y	Y
7 Markey	?	Y	N	Y	Y	Y	Y	Y
8 O'Neill								
9 Moakley	Y	Y	N	Y	Y	Y	Y	Y
10 **Heckler**	?	Y	N	N	Y	Y	Y	Y
11 Donnelly	?	Y	N	Y	Y	Y	?	Y
12 Studds	Y	Y	N	Y	Y	Y	Y	Y
MICHIGAN								
1 Conyers	?	Y	N	Y	Y	Y	?	Y
2 **Pursell**	?	Y	Y	Y	N	Y	?	?
3 Wolpe	Y	Y	Y	Y	Y	Y	Y	Y
4 **Siljander**	Y	Y	Y	Y	N	N	Y	Y
5 **Sawyer**	Y	Y	Y	Y	Y	Y	Y	Y
6 **Dunn**	Y	Y	Y	N	Y	N	Y	Y
7 Kildee	Y	Y	N	Y	Y	Y	Y	Y
8 Traxler	Y	Y	N	Y	Y	Y	Y	Y
9 **Vander Jagt**	?	Y	Y	Y	N	Y	Y	Y
10 Albosta	Y	Y	Y	Y	N	Y	Y	Y
11 **Davis**	Y	Y	Y	Y	Y	Y	Y	Y
12 Bonior	Y	Y	N	Y	Y	Y	Y	Y
13 Crockett	?	N	N	Y	Y	Y	Y	?
14 Hertel	Y	Y	N	Y	Y	Y	Y	?
15 Ford	?	Y	N	Y	Y	Y	?	?
16 Dingell	Y	Y	Y	Y	Y	Y	Y	Y
17 Brodhead	Y	Y	N	Y	Y	Y	Y	Y
18 Blanchard	?	?	?	?	?	?	?	?
19 **Broomfield**	Y	Y	Y	Y	Y	N	Y	Y
MINNESOTA								
1 **Erdahl**	Y	Y	N	Y	N	Y	Y	Y
2 **Hagedorn**	Y	Y	Y	N	Y	N	Y	Y
3 **Frenzel**	Y	Y	Y	N	N	N	Y	Y
4 Vento	Y	Y	N	Y	Y	Y	Y	Y
5 Sabo	N	Y	N	Y	Y	Y	Y	?
6 **Weber**	Y	Y	Y	N	N	N	Y	Y
7 **Stangeland**	?	?	?	?	N	N	Y	Y
8 Oberstar	P	Y	N	Y	Y	Y	Y	Y
MISSISSIPPI								
1 Whitten	Y	Y	Y	N	Y	Y	Y	?
2 Bowen	Y	Y	Y	Y	Y	Y	Y	Y
3 Montgomery	Y	Y	Y	Y	Y	N	Y	Y
4 Dowdy	Y	Y	N	Y	Y	Y	Y	Y
5 **Lott**	?	Y	Y	Y	N	N	Y	Y
MISSOURI								
1 Clay	N	Y	N	Y	Y	Y	Y	?
2 Young	?	Y	Y	Y	Y	Y	Y	Y
3 Gephardt	Y	Y	Y	Y	N	Y	Y	Y
4 Skelton	?	?	?	?	?	N	Y	?
5 Bolling	?	Y	N	?	?	?	?	?
6 **Coleman**	Y	Y	Y	Y	Y	Y	Y	Y
7 **Taylor**	Y	Y	Y	N	N	N	N	Y
8 **Bailey**	Y	Y	Y	N	N	N	N	Y
9 Volkmer	Y	N	Y	Y	Y	Y	Y	Y
10 **Emerson**	?	Y	Y	N	N	N	N	Y
MONTANA								
1 Williams	Y	Y	N	N	Y	Y	?	?
2 **Marlenee**	Y	Y	Y	N	N	N	Y	Y
NEBRASKA								
1 **Bereuter**	Y	Y	N	N	N	N	Y	Y
2 **Daub**	Y	Y	Y	N	N	N	Y	Y
3 **Smith**	Y	Y	Y	N	N	N	Y	Y
NEVADA								
AL Santini	?	?	?	?	?	?	?	?
NEW HAMPSHIRE								
1 D'Amours	?	?	?	Y	Y	Y	Y	Y
2 **Gregg**	?	Y	Y	N	N	N	Y	Y
NEW JERSEY								
1 Florio	Y	Y	Y	Y	Y	Y	Y	Y
2 Hughes	Y	Y	Y	Y	Y	Y	Y	Y
3 Howard	Y	Y	N	Y	Y	Y	Y	Y
4 **Smith**	Y	Y	Y	Y	N	N	Y	Y
5 **Fenwick**	Y	Y	Y	Y	N	Y	Y	Y
6 **Forsythe**	?	#	#	#	#	?	?	?
7 **Roukema**	Y	Y	Y	Y	Y	Y	Y	?
8 Roe	Y	Y	Y	Y	Y	Y	Y	Y
9 **Hollenbeck**	Y	Y	Y	Y	Y	Y	Y	?
10 Rodino	Y	Y	Y	Y	Y	Y	Y	Y
11 Minish	Y	Y	Y	Y	Y	Y	Y	Y
12 **Rinaldo**	Y	Y	Y	Y	Y	Y	Y	Y
13 **Courter**	?	#	#	Y	Y	Y	Y	Y
14 Guarini	Y	Y	Y	Y	Y	Y	Y	Y
15 Dwyer	Y	Y	Y	Y	Y	Y	Y	Y
NEW MEXICO								
1 **Lujan**	Y	Y	Y	N	N	Y	Y	Y
2 **Skeen**	Y	Y	Y	N	N	N	Y	Y
NEW YORK								
1 **Carney**	?	?	?	Y	Y	Y	Y	Y
2 Downey	Y	Y	N	Y	Y	Y	Y	Y
3 **Carman**	?	Y	Y	Y	Y	N	Y	Y
4 **Lent**	Y	Y	Y	Y	Y	Y	Y	?
5 **McGrath**	Y	Y	Y	Y	Y	Y	Y	Y
6 **LeBoutillier**	Y	Y	Y	Y	Y	N	Y	?
7 Addabbo	?	Y	N	Y	Y	Y	Y	?
8 Rosenthal	?	Y	N	Y	Y	Y	?	Y
9 Ferraro	Y	Y	N	Y	Y	Y	Y	Y
10 Biaggi	Y	Y	Y	Y	Y	Y	Y	?
11 Scheuer	Y	N	Y	Y	Y	Y	Y	Y
12 Chisholm	?	Y	N	Y	Y	Y	Y	Y
13 Solarz	Y	Y	N	Y	Y	Y	Y	?
14 Vacancy								
15 Zeferetti	?	?	X	#	#	#	?	?
16 Schumer	Y	Y	N	Y	Y	Y	Y	Y
17 **Molinari**	Y	Y	N	Y	Y	N	Y	N
18 **Green**	Y	N	Y	N	Y	Y	Y	Y
19 Rangel	Y	Y	N	Y	Y	Y	Y	Y
20 Weiss	?	?	X	?	?	#	?	?
21 Garcia	?	Y	Y	Y	Y	Y	Y	Y
22 Bingham	?	N	Y	Y	Y	Y	Y	?
23 Peyser	Y	Y	N	Y	Y	Y	Y	Y
24 Ottinger	P	N	N	Y	Y	Y	Y	P
25 **Fish**	Y	Y	Y	N	Y	N	Y	Y
26 **Gilman**	Y	N	Y	N	Y	Y	?	?
27 McHugh	Y	Y	Y	Y	Y	Y	Y	Y
28 Stratton	Y	Y	Y	N	Y	N	Y	Y
29 **Solomon**	?	Y	Y	Y	N	N	Y	Y
30 **Martin**	Y	Y	Y	Y	N	N	Y	Y
31 **Mitchell**	?	Y	Y	Y	Y	Y	Y	Y
32 **Wortley**	Y	Y	Y	Y	N	N	Y	Y
33 **Lee**	?	?	?	?	?	?	?	?
34 **Horton**	Y	Y	Y	Y	Y	Y	Y	Y
35 **Conable**	?	Y	N	N	N	N	Y	Y
36 LaFalce	Y	Y	N	Y	Y	Y	Y	?
37 Nowak	?	Y	N	Y	Y	Y	Y	Y
38 **Kemp**	?	Y	Y	N	N	N	Y	?
39 Lundine	Y	Y	Y	Y	Y	Y	Y	Y
NORTH CAROLINA								
1 Jones	Y	Y	Y	Y	Y	Y	Y	Y
2 Fountain	?	?	?	?	?	?	?	?
3 Whitley	Y	Y	Y	Y	N	N	Y	Y
4 Andrews	Y	Y	Y	Y	Y	Y	Y	Y
5 Neal	Y	Y	Y	Y	Y	Y	Y	Y
6 **Johnston**	N	Y	Y	N	N	N	N	N
7 Rose	Y	Y	Y	Y	Y	N	Y	Y
8 Hefner	Y	Y	Y	Y	N	N	Y	Y
9 **Martin**	Y	Y	Y	N	N	Y	Y	?
10 **Broyhill**	Y	Y	Y	N	Y	N	Y	Y
11 **Hendon**	Y	Y	Y	N	N	N	N	?
NORTH DAKOTA								
AL Dorgan	Y	N	N	Y	N	Y	Y	Y
OHIO								
1 **Gradison**	Y	N	N	Y	N	Y	Y	Y
2 Luken	N	Y	Y	Y	Y	Y	Y	Y
3 Hall	Y	Y	N	Y	Y	Y	Y	?
4 **Oxley**	Y	Y	Y	N	N	N	Y	Y
5 **Latta**	?	Y	Y	N	N	N	Y	Y
6 **McEwen**	Y	Y	Y	N	N	N	Y	Y
7 **Brown**	?	?	?	?	?	?	?	?
8 **Kindness**	Y	N	Y	N	N	N	Y	Y
9 **Weber**	Y	Y	Y	Y	N	N	Y	Y
10 **Miller**	N	Y	Y	N	N	N	Y	Y
11 **Stanton**	?	?	?	?	?	?	?	?
12 Shamansky	Y	Y	Y	Y	Y	Y	Y	Y
13 Pease	Y	Y	N	Y	Y	Y	Y	Y
14 Seiberling	Y	N	N	Y	Y	Y	Y	Y
15 **Wylie**	?	Y	Y	N	N	Y	Y	Y
16 **Regula**	Y	Y	Y	Y	N	Y	Y	Y
17 **Ashbrook**	Y	Y	Y	N	Y	N	N	Y
18 Applegate	?	Y	N	N	N	Y	Y	Y
19 **Williams**	Y	Y	?	Y	Y	Y	Y	Y
20 Oakar	Y	Y	N	Y	Y	Y	Y	Y
21 Stokes	?	Y	N	Y	Y	Y	Y	Y
22 Eckart	Y	Y	N	Y	Y	Y	Y	Y
23 Mottl	Y	Y	N	N	N	Y	Y	Y
OKLAHOMA								
1 Jones	Y	Y	Y	N	N	N	Y	Y
2 Synar	Y	Y	Y	Y	Y	Y	Y	Y
3 Watkins	Y	Y	Y	N	N	N	Y	Y
4 McCurdy	Y	Y	Y	N	N	N	Y	Y
5 **Edwards**	?	Y	Y	N	N	N	Y	Y
6 English	Y	Y	Y	N	N	N	Y	Y
OREGON								
1 AuCoin	Y	Y	Y	Y	Y	Y	Y	Y
2 **Smith**	Y	Y	Y	N	N	N	?	?
3 Wyden	Y	Y	N	Y	Y	Y	Y	Y
4 Weaver	Y	Y	N	Y	Y	Y	Y	Y
PENNSYLVANIA								
1 Foglietta	Y	Y	N	Y	Y	Y	Y	Y
2 Gray	?	?	?	?	Y	Y	Y	Y
3 Smith	Y	Y	N	Y	Y	Y	Y	Y
4 **Dougherty**	?	?	?	?	Y	Y	Y	Y
5 **Schulze**	Y	Y	Y	N	N	N	Y	Y
6 Yatron	Y	Y	Y	Y	Y	Y	Y	Y
7 Edgar	Y	Y	Y	Y	Y	Y	Y	Y
8 **Coyne, J.**	Y	Y	Y	Y	Y	Y	Y	Y
9 **Shuster**	Y	Y	Y	Y	N	N	Y	Y
10 **McDade**	Y	Y	Y	N	Y	Y	Y	Y
11 **Nelligan**	Y	Y	Y	N	N	Y	Y	Y
12 Murtha	Y	Y	Y	Y	Y	Y	Y	?
13 **Coughlin**	?	Y	Y	N	N	N	Y	Y
14 Coyne, W.	Y	Y	N	Y	Y	Y	Y	Y
15 **Ritter**	?	?	#	N	N	Y	Y	Y
16 **Walker**	N	Y	Y	N	N	N	Y	Y
17 Ertel	?	?	?	?	?	?	?	?
18 Walgren	Y	Y	Y	Y	Y	Y	Y	Y
19 **Goodling**	N	Y	Y	N	N	N	Y	Y
20 Gaydos	Y	Y	N	Y	Y	Y	Y	Y
21 Bailey	Y	Y	N	Y	Y	Y	Y	Y
22 Murphy	Y	Y	Y	N	N	Y	Y	Y
23 **Clinger**	Y	Y	Y	N	N	Y	Y	Y
24 **Marks**	?	Y	Y	Y	Y	Y	Y	?
25 **Atkinson**	Y	Y	Y	N	N	N	Y	Y
RHODE ISLAND								
1 St Germain	Y	Y	N	Y	Y	Y	Y	Y
2 **Schneider**	+	X	Y	Y	Y	Y	Y	Y
SOUTH CAROLINA								
1 **Hartnett**	Y	?	?	N	N	N	Y	Y
2 **Spence**	Y	Y	Y	Y	N	N	Y	Y
3 Derrick	P	Y	Y	Y	Y	Y	+	?
4 **Campbell**	?	Y	Y	Y	N	N	Y	Y
5 Holland	Y	Y	Y	Y	Y	N	Y	Y
6 **Napier**	Y	Y	Y	Y	N	N	Y	Y
SOUTH DAKOTA								
1 Daschle	Y	N	N	Y	Y	Y	Y	Y
2 **Roberts**	?	?	?	?	?	?	Y	Y
TENNESSEE								
1 **Quillen**	Y	Y	Y	N	Y	Y	Y	Y
2 **Duncan**	Y	Y	Y	N	N	N	Y	Y
3 Bouquard	?	?	#	?	?	N	Y	Y
4 Gore	?	N	N	Y	Y	Y	Y	Y
5 Boner	Y	Y	Y	Y	Y	Y	Y	Y
6 **Beard**	Y	Y	Y	N	N	N	Y	?
7 Jones	Y	Y	Y	N	Y	Y	Y	Y
8 Ford	Y	Y	Y	Y	Y	Y	Y	Y
TEXAS								
1 Hall, S.	Y	Y	Y	N	Y	N	Y	Y
2 Wilson	Y	Y	Y	N	Y	Y	Y	Y
3 **Collins**	?	?	?	?	?	?	?	?
4 Hall, R.	Y	Y	Y	N	Y	N	Y	Y
5 Mattox	?	?	?	?	?	?	?	?
6 Gramm	Y	N	Y	N	N	N	N	Y
7 **Archer**	Y	Y	Y	N	N	N	Y	Y
8 **Fields**	N	Y	Y	N	Y	N	N	Y
9 Brooks	?	?	?	?	?	?	?	?
10 Pickle	?	?	?	?	?	?	?	?
11 Leath	Y	Y	Y	N	Y	N	N	Y
12 Wright	Y	Y	Y	Y	Y	Y	Y	Y
13 Hightower	Y	Y	Y	Y	Y	Y	Y	Y
14 Patman	Y	N	Y	N	Y	N	Y	Y
15 de la Garza	Y	Y	Y	Y	Y	Y	Y	Y
16 White	Y	Y	Y	Y	Y	N	Y	Y
17 Stenholm	Y	Y	Y	N	N	N	Y	Y
18 Leland	Y	Y	N	Y	Y	Y	Y	Y
19 Hance	Y	N	N	N	N	Y	Y	Y
20 Gonzalez	?	Y	N	N	Y	Y	Y	Y
21 **Loeffler**	Y	Y	Y	N	N	N	Y	Y
22 **Paul**	Y	N	Y	N	Y	N	N	N
23 Kazen	Y	N	Y	N	N	Y	Y	Y
24 Frost	Y	Y	Y	Y	Y	Y	Y	Y
UTAH								
1 **Hansen**	Y	Y	Y	N	N	N	Y	Y
2 **Marriott**	Y	Y	Y	N	N	N	Y	Y
VERMONT								
AL **Jeffords**	?	?	?	?	?	?	?	?
VIRGINIA								
1 **Trible**	Y	Y	Y	N	N	N	Y	Y
2 **Whitehurst**	Y	Y	Y	N	N	N	Y	Y
3 **Bliley**	Y	Y	Y	N	N	N	Y	Y
4 **Daniel, R.**	Y	Y	Y	N	N	N	Y	Y
5 Daniel, D.	Y	Y	Y	N	N	N	Y	?
6 **Butler**	?	?	#	X	X	X	?	?
7 **Robinson**	Y	Y	Y	N	N	N	?	Y
8 **Parris**	Y	Y	Y	N	N	Y	Y	Y
9 **Wampler**	Y	Y	Y	Y	N	N	Y	Y
10 **Wolf**	Y	Y	Y	Y	N	Y	Y	Y
WASHINGTON								
1 **Pritchard**	?	?	?	?	?	?	?	?
2 Swift	Y	Y	Y	Y	Y	Y	Y	Y
3 Bonker	Y	Y	N	Y	Y	Y	Y	Y
4 **Morrison**	Y	Y	Y	N	N	N	Y	Y
5 Foley	Y	Y	Y	Y	Y	Y	Y	Y
6 Dicks	Y	Y	N	Y	Y	Y	Y	Y
7 Lowry	Y	Y	N	Y	Y	Y	Y	Y
WEST VIRGINIA								
1 Mollohan	Y	Y	N	Y	Y	Y	Y	Y
2 **Benedict**	Y	Y	N	N	N	N	Y	Y
3 **Staton**	Y	Y	Y	Y	N	N	Y	Y
4 Rahall	Y	Y	N	N	N	Y	Y	Y
WISCONSIN								
1 Aspin	Y	Y	Y	Y	Y	Y	Y	Y
2 Kastenmeier	Y	N	Y	Y	Y	Y	Y	Y
3 **Gunderson**	Y	Y	Y	Y	Y	N	N	Y
4 Zablocki	?	?	?	?	?	?	?	?
5 Reuss	?	?	X	?	?	#	?	?
6 **Petri**	Y	N	Y	Y	Y	Y	Y	Y
7 Obey	Y	Y	N	Y	Y	Y	Y	Y
8 **Roth**	Y	Y	Y	Y	Y	Y	Y	?
9 **Sensenbrenner**	Y	N	Y	N	N	N	N	Y
WYOMING								
AL **Cheney**	Y	Y	Y	N	N	N	Y	Y

Southern states - Ala., Ark., Fla., Ga., Ky., La., Miss., N.C., Okla., S.C., Tenn., Texas, Va.

311. HR 6956. Department of Housing and Urban Development Appropriations, Fiscal 1983. Scheuer, D-N.Y., amendment to increase Environmental Protection Agency research and development funding by $25 million in fiscal 1983. Rejected 131-263: R 28-150; D 103-113 (ND 89-57, SD 14-56), Sept. 15, 1982.

312. HR 6956. Department of Housing and Urban Development Appropriations, Fiscal 1983. Flippo, D-Ala., amendment to delete $140 million for development of the National Aeronautics and Space Administration Centaur high energy upper stage space transportation system. Rejected 77-316: R 23-152; D 54-164 (ND 27-120, SD 27-44), Sept. 15, 1982.

313. HR 6956. Department of Housing and Urban Development Appropriations, Fiscal 1983. Walgren, D-Pa., amendment to bar the use of Environmental Protection Agency funds to implement a mandatory inspection and maintenance program for vehicle emissions. Adopted 200-184: R 121-48; D 79-136 (ND 34-113, SD 45-23), Sept. 15, 1982.

314. HR 6956. Department of Housing and Urban Development Appropriations, Fiscal 1983. Passage of the bill to appropriate $47,000,239,000 in fiscal 1983 for the Department of Housing and Urban Development and 17 independent agencies. Passed 343-38: R 139-28; D 204-10 (ND 144-2, SD 60-8), Sept. 15, 1982. A "yea" was a vote supporting the president's position. The president had requested $46,643,208,000 for the programs covered by the bill.

315. Procedural Motion. Bliley, R-Va., motion to approve the House *Journal* of Wednesday, Sept. 16. Motion agreed to 334-29: R 152-13; D 182-16 (ND 119-14, SD 63-2), Sept. 16, 1982.

316. H J Res 562. Urgent Supplemental, Fiscal 1982/Jobs Program. Adoption of the rule (H Res 582) providing for House floor consideration of the bill to authorize and appropriate $1 billion for public-service jobs. Adopted 221-176: R 5-173; D 216-3 (ND 150-1, SD 66-2), Sept. 16, 1982.

317. H J Res 562. Urgent Supplemental, Fiscal 1982/Jobs Program. Whitten, D-Miss., motion that the House resolve itself into the Committee of the Whole for consideration of the bill to authorize and appropriate $1 billion for public-service jobs. Motion agreed to 295-82: R 94-79; D 201-3 (ND 140-1, SD 61-2), Sept. 16, 1982.

318. H J Res 562. Urgent Supplemental, Fiscal 1982/Jobs Program. Martin, R-Ill., amendment to substitute for the bill's $1 billion authorization and appropriation for public-service jobs a $1.5 billion jobs program to be funded by transfer of budget authority from the Synthetic Fuels Corp. Rejected 152-243: R 141-33; D 11-210 (ND 4-146, SD 7-64), Sept. 16, 1982.

	311	312	313	314	315	316	317	318
ALABAMA								
1 *Edwards*	N	Y	Y	Y	Y	N	Y	N
2 *Dickinson*	N	N	Y	Y	N	N	?	Y
3 Nichols	N	Y	Y	Y	Y	Y	Y	N
4 Bevill	Y	Y	Y	Y	Y	Y	?	N
5 Flippo	Y	Y	Y	Y	Y	Y	Y	N
6 *Smith*	Y	Y	Y	Y	Y	N	N	Y
7 Shelby	N	Y	Y	Y	Y	Y	Y	N
ALASKA								
AL *Young*	?	?	?	?	?	?	?	\#
ARIZONA								
1 *Rhodes*	N	N	N	Y	Y	N	Y	Y
2 Udall	Y	N	Y	?	?	Y	Y	N
3 *Stump*	N	N	Y	Y	Y	N	N	N
4 *Rudd*	N	N	Y	Y	Y	N	N	N
ARKANSAS								
1 Alexander	N	N	Y	?	Y	Y	Y	N
2 *Bethune*	N	N	?	?	N	N	N	N
3 *Hammerschmidt*	N	N	Y	Y	Y	N	Y	Y
4 Anthony	N	N	Y	Y	?	Y	Y	N
CALIFORNIA								
1 *Chappie*	N	Y	Y	N	Y	N	Y	Y
2 *Clausen*	N	N	N	Y	Y	N	?	Y
3 Matsui	Y	Y	N	Y	Y	Y	Y	N
4 Fazio	N	Y	N	Y	Y	Y	Y	N
5 Burton, J.	?	?	?	?	?	?	?	?
6 *Burton, P.*	Y	Y	N	Y	Y	Y	Y	N
7 Miller	Y	N	N	Y	Y	Y	Y	N
8 Dellums	Y	N	N	Y	?	Y	Y	N
9 Stark	Y	Y	N	Y	Y	Y	Y	N
10 Edwards	Y	N	N	Y	Y	Y	Y	N
11 Lantos	N	N	N	Y	Y	Y	Y	N
12 *McCloskey*	N	N	N	Y	N	N	N	?
13 Mineta	Y	Y	N	Y	Y	Y	Y	N
14 Shumway	N	Y	N	Y	N	N	N	Y
15 Coelho	Y	Y	N	Y	Y	Y	Y	N
16 Panetta	N	N	N	Y	Y	Y	Y	N
17 *Pashayan*	N	N	Y	Y	N	Y	Y	Y
18 *Thomas*	?	\#	\#	?	?	?	?	\#
19 *Lagomarsino*	N	Y	Y	Y	N	N	N	Y
20 *Goldwater*	?	N	Y	Y	N	N	N	Y
21 *Fiedler*	N	Y	Y	N	Y	N	Y	Y
22 *Moorhead*	N	N	N	N	Y	N	N	\#
23 Beilenson	Y	N	N	Y	P	Y	Y	N
24 Waxman	Y	Y	N	Y	Y	Y	?	N
25 Roybal	Y	N	N	Y	Y	Y	Y	N
26 *Rousselot*	N	N	Y	Y	N	N	Y	Y
27 *Dornan*	N	N	Y	Y	N	N	N	Y
28 Dixon	\#	?	N	Y	?	Y	Y	N
29 Hawkins	Y	N	Y	Y	Y	Y	Y	N
30 Martinez	Y	N	N	Y	Y	Y	Y	N
31 Dymally	Y	N	N	Y	Y	Y	?	N
32 Anderson	N	Y	Y	Y	Y	Y	?	N
33 *Grisham*	?	N	Y	Y	Y	?	?	Y
34 *Lungren*	N	N	Y	Y	Y	N	N	Y
35 *Dreier*	N	N	N	N	N	N	N	Y
36 Brown	Y	N	N	Y	Y	Y	?	N
37 *Lewis*	Y	N	N	N	N	N	N	Y
38 Patterson	N	N	Y	Y	Y	Y	Y	N
39 *Dannemeyer*	N	N	Y	N	Y	N	N	Y
40 *Badham*	N	N	Y	N	Y	N	N	Y
41 *Lowery*	N	N	Y	?	Y	N	Y	Y
42 *Hunter*	N	N	Y	Y	N	N	Y	Y
43 *Burgener*	N	N	Y	?	Y	N	Y	Y
COLORADO								
1 Schroeder	Y	Y	N	N	N	Y	Y	N
2 Wirth	Y	N	N	Y	Y	Y	Y	N
3 Kogovsek	N	N	N	Y	Y	N	Y	N
4 *Brown*	N	N	N	N	Y	N	Y	Y

	311	312	313	314	315	316	317	318
5 *Kramer*	N	N	N	Y	Y	N	N	Y
CONNECTICUT								
1 Kennelly	N	N	N	Y	Y	Y	Y	N
2 Gejdenson	Y	N	N	Y	N	Y	Y	N
3 *DeNardis*	Y	N	N	Y	?	N	Y	Y
4 *McKinney*	Y	N	N	Y	?	N	?	Y
5 Ratchford	N	N	N	Y	Y	Y	Y	N
6 Moffett	?	N	N	Y	?	Y	?	N
DELAWARE								
AL *Evans*	N	N	N	Y	N	Y	N	Y
FLORIDA								
1 Hutto	N	N	Y	Y	Y	Y	Y	N
2 Fuqua	Y	Y	Y	Y	Y	Y	Y	N
3 Bennett	N	Y	N	N	Y	Y	Y	N
4 Chappell	?	?	?	?	?	?	?	N
5 *McCollum*	N	N	Y	Y	Y	N	N	N
6 *Young*	N	N	Y	Y	Y	N	Y	Y
7 Gibbons	Y	N	N	Y	?	?	?	N
8 Ireland	N	Y	Y	Y	?	?	?	N
9 Nelson	Y	N	Y	Y	Y	Y	Y	N
10 *Bafalis*	?	?	?	?	?	?	?	?
11 Mica	N	Y	N	Y	Y	Y	Y	N
12 *Shaw*	N	N	Y	Y	N	N	N	Y
13 Lehman	N	Y	C	Y	Y	Y	Y	N
14 Pepper	X	?	?	?	?	?	?	X
15 Fascell	N	Y	N	Y	Y	Y	Y	N
GEORGIA								
1 Ginn	N	Y	Y	Y	Y	Y	Y	N
2 Hatcher	N	Y	Y	Y	Y	Y	Y	N
3 Brinkley	N	N	N	Y	Y	Y	Y	N
4 Levitas	N	Y	N	Y	Y	Y	Y	N
5 Fowler	Y	N	N	Y	Y	Y	Y	N
6 *Gingrich*	Y	N	?	?	?	N	Y	Y
7 McDonald	N	N	Y	N	Y	N	N	Y
8 Evans	?	?	?	?	?	?	?	?
9 Jenkins	N	Y	Y	Y	Y	Y	Y	N
10 Barnard	N	Y	Y	Y	Y	Y	Y	N
HAWAII								
1 Heftel	N	Y	N	Y	?	Y	Y	N
2 Akaka	?	?	X	?	?	?	?	X
IDAHO								
1 *Craig*	N	N	N	Y	Y	N	Y	Y
2 *Hansen*	N	N	Y	N	Y	N	N	Y
ILLINOIS								
1 Washington	Y	N	N	Y	N	Y	Y	N
2 Savage	Y	?	N	Y	?	?	?	N
3 Russo	Y	Y	N	Y	Y	Y	Y	N
4 *Derwinski*	N	N	?	?	Y	N	?	Y
5 Fary	Y	N	N	Y	Y	Y	Y	N
6 *Hyde*	N	N	Y	Y	N	Y	N	Y
7 Collins	Y	N	N	Y	N	Y	Y	N
8 Rostenkowski	N	N	N	Y	Y	Y	Y	N
9 Yates	Y	N	N	Y	N	Y	Y	N
10 *Porter*	N	N	Y	Y	N	N	N	Y
11 Annunzio	N	N	Y	Y	Y	Y	Y	X
12 *Crane, P.*	N	N	Y	N	Y	N	N	Y
13 *McClory*	?	?	?	?	?	?	?	\#
14 *Erlenborn*	N	N	N	N	N	N	N	N
15 *Corcoran*	N	N	Y	Y	N	Y	Y	Y
16 *Martin*	N	N	Y	Y	N	N	Y	Y
17 *O'Brien*	N	N	Y	Y	Y	N	Y	N
18 *Michel*	N	N	Y	Y	N	?	N	Y
19 *Railsback*	N	N	N	Y	N	Y	Y	Y
20 *Findley*	N	N	Y	Y	N	Y	N	Y
21 *Madigan*	N	N	Y	Y	N	Y	?	?
22 *Crane, D.*	N	N	Y	N	Y	N	N	Y
23 Price	N	N	N	Y	Y	Y	Y	?
24 Simon	Y	N	?	?	Y	?	?	X
INDIANA								
1 Vacancy								
2 Fithian	?	?	?	?	?	Y	Y	N
3 *Hiler*	N	N	Y	Y	N	Y	N	N
4 *Coats*	N	N	Y	Y	N	Y	N	Y
5 *Hillis*	N	N	Y	Y	N	Y	N	Y
6 Evans	N	N	Y	Y	Y	Y	N	Y
7 *Myers*	N	N	Y	Y	N	Y	N	Y
8 *Deckard*	Y	N	Y	Y	N	Y	N	?
9 Hamilton	N	N	Y	Y	Y	Y	Y	N
10 Sharp	Y	N	Y	Y	Y	Y	Y	N
11 Jacobs	N	N	N	Y	N	Y	Y	N
IOWA								
1 *Leach*	Y	N	N	Y	Y	N	Y	Y
2 *Tauke*	Y	N	?	?	N	Y	N	\#
3 *Evans*	Y	N	N	Y	N	N	Y	Y
4 Smith	Y	N	N	Y	Y	Y	Y	N
5 Harkin	Y	N	Y	N	Y	Y	Y	N
6 Bedell	Y	N	N	Y	N	Y	Y	N

ND - Northern Democrats   SD - Southern Democrats

	311	312	313	314	315	316	317	318
KANSAS								
1 ***Roberts***	N	Y	Y	Y	Y	N	N	Y
2 ***Jeffries***	N	N	Y	N	?	N	N	Y
3 ***Winn***	N	Y	Y	Y	Y	N	Y	Y
4 Glickman	N	Y	N	Y	Y	Y	Y	N
5 ***Whittaker***	N	Y	Y	Y	Y	N	N	Y
KENTUCKY								
1 Hubbard	N	Y	Y	N	Y	Y	Y	N
2 Natcher	N	N	Y	Y	Y	Y	Y	N
3 Mazzoli	N	N	N	Y	Y	Y	Y	N
4 ***Snyder***	N	Y	Y	Y	Y	N	Y	?
5 ***Rogers***	N	N	Y	Y	Y	N	Y	Y
6 ***Hopkins***	N	Y	Y	Y	Y	N	Y	Y
7 Perkins	Y	N	Y	Y	Y	Y	Y	N
LOUISIANA								
1 ***Livingston***	N	N	N	Y	N	N	N	Y
2 Boggs	N	N	N	Y	Y	Y	Y	N
3 Tauzin	N	N	Y	Y	Y	Y	Y	Y
4 Roemer	N	Y	N	N	N	Y	Y	Y
5 Huckaby	N	Y	N	Y	Y	Y	Y	N
6 ***Moore***	N	Y	Y	Y	Y	N	Y	Y
7 Breaux	N	Y	Y	Y	Y	Y	Y	Y
8 Long	N	N	N	Y	Y	Y	Y	N
MAINE								
1 ***Emery***	Y	N	N	Y	Y	N	Y	Y
2 ***Snowe***	N	Y	N	Y	Y	N	Y	Y
MARYLAND								
1 Dyson	Y	N	Y	Y	Y	Y	Y	N
2 Long	Y	N	N	Y	Y	Y	Y	N
3 Mikulski	Y	N	Y	Y	Y	Y	Y	N
4 ***Holt***	Y	N	?	?	N	N	N	Y
5 Hoyer	Y	N	N	Y	Y	Y	Y	N
6 Byron	N	N	Y	Y	?	Y	Y	N
7 Mitchell	?	N	N	Y	N	Y	Y	Y
8 Barnes	Y	N	N	Y	Y	Y	Y	N
MASSACHUSETTS								
1 ***Conte***	N	N	N	Y	Y	N	Y	N
2 Boland	N	N	N	Y	Y	Y	Y	N
3 Early	N	N	N	Y	Y	Y	Y	N
4 Frank	Y	N	N	Y	Y	Y	Y	N
5 Shannon	N	N	N	Y	Y	Y	Y	N
6 Mavroules	N	N	N	Y	Y	Y	Y	N
7 Markey	N	N	N	Y	N	Y	Y	N
8 O'Neill								
9 Moakley	Y	N	N	Y	Y	Y	Y	N
10 ***Heckler***	Y	N	N	Y	?	Y	Y	N
11 Donnelly	N	N	N	Y	Y	Y	Y	N
12 Studds	Y	N	N	Y	Y	Y	Y	N
MICHIGAN								
1 Conyers	Y	N	N	Y	Y	?	Y	N
2 ***Pursell***	N	N	Y	Y	Y	N	Y	Y
3 Wolpe	Y	N	N	Y	Y	Y	Y	N
4 ***Siljander***	N	N	Y	Y	Y	N	N	Y
5 ***Sawyer***	N	N	Y	Y	Y	N	Y	N
6 ***Dunn***	N	N	Y	Y	Y	?	Y	Y
7 Kildee	Y	N	N	Y	Y	Y	Y	N
8 Traxler	N	N	N	Y	Y	Y	Y	N
9 ***Vander Jagt***	N	N	Y	Y	Y	N	Y	Y
10 Albosta	N	N	Y	Y	Y	Y	Y	N
11 ***Davis***	N	N	Y	Y	Y	N	Y	Y
12 Bonior	Y	N	N	Y	Y	Y	Y	N
13 Crockett	Y	N	N	Y	Y	Y	?	N
14 Hertel	Y	N	Y	Y	Y	Y	Y	N
15 Ford	Y	N	Y	Y	?	Y	Y	N
16 Dingell	Y	Y	Y	Y	?	Y	Y	N
17 Brodhead	Y	N	Y	Y	Y	Y	Y	N
18 Blanchard	?	?	?	?	?	?	?	?
19 ***Broomfield***	N	N	Y	Y	Y	N	N	Y
MINNESOTA								
1 ***Erdahl***	N	N	N	Y	Y	N	Y	Y
2 ***Hagedorn***	N	N	Y	Y	Y	N	N	Y
3 ***Frenzel***	N	N	Y	Y	Y	N	Y	Y
4 Vento	Y	N	N	Y	Y	Y	Y	N
5 Sabo	N	N	N	Y	N	Y	Y	N
6 ***Weber***	Y	N	N	Y	Y	N	N	Y
7 ***Stangeland***	N	?	Y	Y	Y	N	Y	Y
8 Oberstar	Y	Y	N	Y	P	Y	Y	N
MISSISSIPPI								
1 Whitten	N	N	Y	Y	Y	Y	Y	N
2 Bowen	N	N	Y	Y	Y	?	?	N
3 Montgomery	N	N	Y	Y	Y	Y	?	N
4 Dowdy	N	N	Y	Y	Y	Y	Y	N
5 ***Lott***	N	N	Y	Y	Y	N	N	Y
MISSOURI								
1 Clay	Y	N	N	Y	?	Y	?	N
2 Young	N	N	Y	Y	Y	Y	Y	N
3 Gephardt	N	Y	Y	Y	Y	Y	Y	N
4 Skelton	N	N	Y	Y	Y	Y	Y	N
5 Bolling	?	?	?	?	?	?	?	?
6 ***Coleman***	N	N	N	Y	Y	N	Y	Y
7 ***Taylor***	N	Y	Y	Y	Y	N	Y	Y
8 ***Bailey***	N	N	Y	Y	Y	N	N	Y
9 Volkmer	Y	Y	Y	Y	Y	Y	Y	N
10 ***Emerson***	N	Y	Y	Y	N	N	N	Y
MONTANA								
1 Williams	N	N	N	Y	Y	Y	Y	N
2 ***Marlenee***	N	N	Y	N	Y	N	N	?
NEBRASKA								
1 ***Bereuter***	N	N	Y	Y	Y	N	N	Y
2 ***Daub***	N	N	Y	Y	Y	N	N	Y
3 ***Smith***	N	N	Y	Y	Y	N	Y	Y
NEVADA								
AL Santini	?	?	?	?	?	?	?	?
NEW HAMPSHIRE								
1 D'Amours	?	N	N	Y	Y	Y	Y	N
2 ***Gregg***	N	N	N	Y	Y	N	Y	N
NEW JERSEY								
1 Florio	Y	N	N	Y	Y	Y	Y	N
2 Hughes	Y	N	N	Y	Y	Y	Y	N
3 Howard	Y	N	N	Y	Y	Y	Y	N
4 ***Smith***	Y	N	N	Y	Y	N	Y	Y
5 ***Fenwick***	Y	Y	N	Y	Y	N	Y	Y
6 ***Forsythe***	?	?	?	?	?	?	?	?
7 ***Roukema***	N	Y	N	Y	Y	N	Y	N
8 Roe	Y	Y	N	Y	Y	Y	Y	N
9 ***Hollenbeck***	Y	Y	N	Y	Y	Y	Y	N
10 Rodino	Y	N	N	Y	Y	Y	Y	N
11 Minish	Y	N	N	Y	Y	Y	Y	N
12 ***Rinaldo***	Y	Y	N	Y	Y	Y	Y	N
13 ***Courter***	Y	N	N	Y	Y	N	Y	Y
14 Guarini	Y	N	Y	Y	Y	Y	Y	N
15 Dwyer	Y	N	N	Y	Y	Y	Y	N
NEW MEXICO								
1 ***Lujan***	N	Y	N	Y	Y	N	Y	Y
2 ***Skeen***	N	N	Y	Y	Y	N	Y	N
NEW YORK								
1 ***Carney***	N	N	N	Y	Y	N	N	N
2 Downey	Y	Y	N	Y	Y	Y	Y	N
3 ***Carman***	N	N	Y	Y	Y	N	Y	Y
4 ***Lent***	Y	N	N	Y	Y	N	N	Y
5 ***McGrath***	Y	X	?	?	Y	N	Y	Y
6 ***LeBoutillier***	N	N	N	Y	?	N	N	N
7 Addabbo	Y	N	N	Y	Y	Y	Y	N
8 Rosenthal	Y	N	N	?	?	Y	Y	N
9 Ferraro	Y	N	N	Y	Y	Y	Y	N
10 Biaggi	N	Y	N	Y	Y	Y	Y	N
11 Scheuer	Y	Y	N	Y	Y	Y	Y	N
12 Chisholm	Y	?	?	Y	?	Y	?	N
13 Solarz	Y	N	N	Y	Y	Y	Y	N
14 Vacancy								
15 Zeferetti	#	X	X	?	Y	Y	Y	N
16 Schumer	N	N	N	Y	Y	Y	Y	N
17 ***Molinari***	Y	N	N	Y	Y	N	N	Y
18 ***Green***	N	N	N	Y	Y	N	N	N
19 Rangel	Y	N	N	Y	Y	Y	Y	N
20 Weiss	?	#	?	?	?	?	?	X
21 Garcia	N	N	N	Y	Y	Y	Y	N
22 Bingham	N	N	N	Y	Y	Y	Y	N
23 Peyser	Y	N	N	Y	Y	Y	Y	N
24 Ottinger	Y	N	N	Y	?	Y	P	Y
25 ***Fish***	N	N	N	Y	Y	N	Y	Y
26 ***Gilman***	?	?	?	?	Y	N	Y	N
27 McHugh	Y	N	N	Y	Y	Y	Y	N
28 Stratton	N	N	N	Y	Y	Y	Y	N
29 ***Solomon***	Y	N	N	N	Y	N	N	Y
30 ***Martin***	Y	N	N	Y	Y	N	N	Y
31 ***Mitchell***	N	N	N	Y	Y	N	N	N
32 ***Wortley***	N	N	?	?	Y	N	N	Y
33 ***Lee***	?	?	?	?	?	?	?	?
34 ***Horton***	N	N	N	Y	Y	N	Y	N
35 ***Conable***	N	N	Y	Y	Y	N	N	N
36 LaFalce	Y	N	N	Y	Y	Y	Y	N
37 Nowak	Y	N	N	Y	Y	Y	Y	N
38 ***Kemp***	N	N	Y	Y	Y	N	Y	Y
39 Lundine	N	N	N	Y	Y	Y	Y	N
NORTH CAROLINA								
1 Jones	N	Y	Y	Y	?	Y	Y	N
2 Fountain	?	?	?	?	?	?	?	?
3 Whitley	N	Y	?	?	Y	Y	Y	N
4 Andrews	Y	N	N	Y	Y	Y	Y	N
5 Neal	N	N	N	Y	Y	Y	Y	N
6 ***Johnston***	N	N	Y	N	N	N	N	#
7 Rose	N	N	N	Y	Y	Y	Y	X
8 Hefner	N	N	Y	Y	Y	Y	Y	N
9 ***Martin***	N	N	Y	Y	?	N	Y	Y
10 ***Broyhill***	N	N	Y	Y	?	N	N	Y
11 ***Hendon***	N	N	Y	Y	Y	N	?	N
NORTH DAKOTA								
AL Dorgan	N	N	N	Y	N	Y	Y	N
OHIO								
1 ***Gradison***	N	N	N	Y	Y	N	N	Y
2 Luken	Y	N	Y	Y	N	Y	Y	N
3 Hall	Y	N	N	Y	Y	Y	?	N
4 ***Oxley***	N	N	Y	Y	Y	N	N	N
5 ***Latta***	N	N	Y	N	Y	N	Y	Y
6 ***McEwen***	N	N	Y	Y	Y	N	N	Y
7 ***Brown***	?	?	?	?	Y	N	Y	Y
8 ***Kindness***	N	N	Y	N	Y	N	N	Y
9 ***Weber***	N	N	Y	Y	Y	N	Y	Y
10 ***Miller***	N	N	Y	Y	N	N	Y	Y
11 ***Stanton***	?	?	?	?	?	N	Y	Y
12 Shamansky	N	N	N	Y	Y	Y	Y	N
13 Pease	Y	N	N	Y	Y	Y	Y	N
14 Seiberling	Y	N	N	Y	Y	Y	Y	N
15 ***Wylie***	N	N	N	Y	Y	N	Y	N
16 ***Regula***	N	N	Y	Y	Y	N	Y	Y
17 ***Ashbrook***	N	N	Y	N	Y	N	N	Y
18 Applegate	N	N	Y	Y	Y	Y	Y	N
19 ***Williams***	N	N	Y	Y	Y	N	Y	Y
20 Oakar	Y	N	N	Y	Y	Y	Y	N
21 Stokes	Y	N	N	Y	?	Y	Y	N
22 Eckart	Y	N	N	Y	Y	Y	Y	N
23 Mottl	Y	N	N	Y	Y	Y	Y	N
OKLAHOMA								
1 Jones	N	Y	Y	Y	?	Y	Y	N
2 Synar	N	Y	N	Y	Y	Y	Y	N
3 Watkins	N	N	Y	Y	Y	Y	Y	N
4 McCurdy	N	N	Y	Y	?	?	?	?
5 ***Edwards***	N	N	Y	N	Y	N	Y	Y
6 English	N	N	Y	N	Y	Y	Y	N
OREGON								
1 AuCoin	N	N	N	Y	N	Y	Y	N
2 ***Smith***	N	N	Y	N	Y	N	N	Y
3 Wyden	Y	Y	N	Y	Y	Y	Y	N
4 Weaver	?	Y	N	Y	Y	Y	?	Y
PENNSYLVANIA								
1 Foglietta	Y	N	N	Y	Y	Y	Y	N
2 Gray	Y	N	?	?	Y	Y	Y	N
3 Smith	N	?	?	?	?	?	?	X
4 ***Dougherty***	N	N	Y	Y	?	N	Y	N
5 ***Schulze***	N	?	?	?	?	?	?	?
6 Yatron	N	N	Y	Y	Y	Y	Y	N
7 Edgar	Y	N	N	Y	Y	Y	Y	N
8 ***Coyne, J.***	N	N	Y	Y	Y	N	N	Y
9 ***Shuster***	N	N	Y	Y	Y	N	Y	Y
10 ***McDade***	N	N	Y	Y	?	N	Y	N
11 ***Nelligan***	N	N	Y	Y	Y	N	Y	Y
12 Murtha	N	N	Y	Y	Y	Y	Y	N
13 ***Coughlin***	N	N	Y	Y	N	N	Y	Y
14 Coyne, W.	N	N	N	Y	Y	Y	Y	N
15 ***Ritter***	N	N	Y	Y	Y	N	Y	Y
16 ***Walker***	N	Y	Y	N	N	N	N	Y
17 Ertel	?	?	?	?	?	Y	Y	N
18 Walgren	Y	Y	Y	Y	Y	Y	Y	N
19 ***Goodling***	N	Y	Y	Y	N	N	Y	N
20 Gaydos	N	N	Y	Y	?	Y	Y	N
21 Bailey	N	N	Y	Y	Y	Y	Y	N
22 Murphy	N	N	Y	Y	N	Y	Y	N
23 ***Clinger***	N	N	Y	Y	Y	N	Y	N
24 ***Marks***	?	?	?	?	?	?	?	N
25 ***Atkinson***	N	N	Y	Y	Y	N	N	Y
RHODE ISLAND								
1 St Germain	N	N	N	Y	Y	Y	Y	N
2 ***Schneider***	Y	N	N	Y	Y	Y	Y	Y
SOUTH CAROLINA								
1 ***Hartnett***	N	N	Y	Y	Y	N	N	Y
2 ***Spence***	N	N	Y	Y	Y	N	Y	Y
3 Derrick	Y	N	N	Y	Y	Y	Y	N
4 ***Campbell***	N	N	Y	Y	Y	N	N	Y
5 Holland	N	Y	Y	Y	?	Y	Y	N
6 ***Napier***	N	N	Y	Y	Y	N	Y	Y
SOUTH DAKOTA								
1 Daschle	N	N	Y	Y	Y	Y	Y	N
2 ***Roberts***	N	N	?	?	Y	N	N	Y
TENNESSEE								
1 ***Quillen***	N	N	Y	Y	Y	N	N	Y
2 ***Duncan***	N	N	Y	Y	Y	N	N	Y
3 Bouquard	Y	Y	Y	Y	Y	Y	Y	N
4 Gore	Y	N	N	Y	Y	Y	Y	N
5 Boner	N	?	#	?	Y	Y	Y	N
6 ***Beard***	N	N	Y	Y	?	?	?	#
7 Jones	N	N	Y	Y	Y	Y	Y	N
8 Ford	Y	N	N	Y	Y	Y	Y	N
TEXAS								
1 Hall, S.	N	N	Y	Y	Y	Y	Y	N
2 Wilson	N	N	Y	Y	Y	Y	Y	N
3 ***Collins***	N	N	Y	N	Y	N	Y	Y
4 Hall, R.	N	N	Y	Y	Y	Y	Y	N
5 Mattox	?	?	?	?	?	?	?	?
6 Gramm	N	N	Y	N	Y	N	N	Y
7 ***Archer***	N	N	Y	N	Y	N	N	Y
8 ***Fields***	N	N	Y	N	N	N	N	Y
9 Brooks	?	?	?	?	?	?	?	?
10 Pickle	?	?	?	?	?	?	?	?
11 Leath	?	Y	Y	Y	Y	Y	Y	N
12 Wright	N	N	Y	Y	Y	Y	Y	N
13 Hightower	N	N	Y	Y	Y	Y	Y	N
14 Patman	N	N	Y	Y	Y	Y	Y	N
15 de la Garza	N	N	Y	Y	Y	Y	Y	N
16 White	N	Y	Y	Y	Y	Y	Y	N
17 Stenholm	N	N	Y	N	N	Y	Y	N
18 Leland	Y	N	N	Y	Y	Y	?	N
19 Hance	N	N	?	?	Y	Y	?	N
20 Gonzalez	N	N	N	Y	Y	Y	Y	N
21 ***Loeffler***	N	N	Y	N	Y	N	N	Y
22 ***Paul***	N	N	Y	N	Y	N	N	Y
23 Kazen	N	N	Y	Y	Y	Y	Y	Y
24 Frost	Y	N	N	Y	Y	Y	Y	N
UTAH								
1 ***Hansen***	N	N	Y	Y	Y	N	N	N
2 ***Marriott***	N	N	Y	Y	Y	N	Y	N
VERMONT								
AL ***Jeffords***	Y	N	N	Y	Y	N	N	N
VIRGINIA								
1 ***Trible***	N	?	?	?	Y	N	N	Y
2 ***Whitehurst***	N	N	Y	Y	Y	N	N	Y
3 ***Bliley***	N	N	Y	Y	Y	N	N	Y
4 ***Daniel, R.***	N	N	Y	Y	Y	N	N	Y
5 Daniel, D.	?	N	Y	Y	Y	Y	Y	Y
6 ***Butler***	?	?	?	?	?	?	?	#
7 ***Robinson***	N	N	Y	Y	Y	N	N	Y
8 ***Parris***	N	N	N	Y	Y	N	N	Y
9 ***Wampler***	N	N	Y	Y	Y	Y	Y	Y
10 ***Wolf***	N	Y	N	Y	Y	N	N	Y
WASHINGTON								
1 ***Pritchard***	?	?	?	?	?	?	?	?
2 Swift	N	Y	N	Y	Y	Y	Y	N
3 Bonker	N	N	Y	Y	Y	Y	Y	N
4 ***Morrison***	N	N	Y	Y	Y	N	Y	Y
5 Foley	N	Y	Y	Y	Y	Y	Y	N
6 Dicks	N	Y	N	Y	Y	Y	Y	N
7 Lowry	Y	Y	N	Y	N	Y	Y	N
WEST VIRGINIA								
1 Mollohan	N	N	Y	Y	Y	Y	Y	N
2 ***Benedict***	N	?	?	?	?	N	Y	Y
3 ***Staton***	N	N	Y	Y	Y	N	Y	Y
4 Rahall	N	N	Y	Y	Y	Y	Y	N
WISCONSIN								
1 Aspin	Y	Y	Y	Y	Y	Y	Y	N
2 Kastenmeier	Y	Y	N	Y	Y	Y	Y	N
3 ***Gunderson***	Y	N	N	Y	Y	N	Y	Y
4 Zablocki	N	N	N	Y	Y	Y	Y	N
5 Reuss	X	?	?	?	?	?	?	X
6 ***Petri***	Y	N	Y	Y	Y	N	Y	N
7 Obey	Y	Y	N	Y	Y	Y	Y	N
8 ***Roth***	N	N	Y	Y	Y	N	Y	Y
9 ***Sensenbrenner***	Y	N	Y	N	Y	N	N	Y
WYOMING								
AL ***Cheney***	N	N	Y	N	Y	N	N	Y

Southern states - Ala., Ark., Fla., Ga., Ky., La., Miss., N.C., Okla., S.C., Tenn., Texas, Va.

319. H J Res 562. Urgent Supplemental, Fiscal 1982/Jobs Program. Passage of the joint resolution to authorize and appropriate fiscal 1982 funds for public-service jobs. Funding was set at 5 percent of the estimated cost of unemployment compensation for fiscal 1982, a formula that would call for appropriating $1.035 billion. Passed 223-169: R 32-141; D 191-28 (ND 144-5, SD 47-23), Sept. 16, 1982.

320. HR 5543. Ocean and Coastal Resources Management and Development Fund. Adoption of the rule (H Res 555) providing for House floor consideration of the bill to create a new fund to share with the states up to $300 million annually in federal revenues from offshore oil, gas and mineral leasing. Adopted 342-8: R 141-7; D 201-1 (ND 137-0, SD 64-1), Sept. 16, 1982.

321. HR 7019. Transportation Appropriations, Fiscal 1983. Coughlin, R-Pa., amendment to reduce certain transportation programs by a total of $320 million in fiscal 1983. Rejected 154-221: R 124-40; D 30-181 (ND 6-135, SD 24-46), Sept. 21, 1982. A "yea" was a vote supporting the president's position.

322. HR 7019. Transportation Appropriations, Fiscal 1983. Obey, D-Wis., amendment to reduce every appropriation in the legislation by 33.8 percent. Rejected 38-349: R 30-139; D 8-210 (ND 6-140, SD 2-70), Sept. 21, 1982.

323. HR 7019. Transportation Appropriations, Fiscal 1983. Passage of the bill to appropriate $11,199,399,919 in new budget authority for fiscal 1983 for the Transportation Department and related agencies. Passed 268-119: R 68-102; D 200-17 (ND 142-3, SD 58-14), Sept. 21, 1982. A "nay" was a vote supporting the president's position. The president had requested $10,396,811,919.

324. HR 7072. Agriculture Appropriations, Fiscal 1983. Walker, R-Pa., amendment to extend the food stamp appropriation to Sept. 30, 1983, instead of July 15, 1983, as provided in the bill. (The effect would have been to fund food stamps for two and one-half additional months without changing the amount of money provided by the bill.) Rejected 125-246: R 107-62; D 18-184 (ND 4-129, SD 14-55), Sept. 21, 1982.

325. HR 7072. Agriculture Appropriations, Fiscal 1983. Passage of the bill to appropriate $23,066,954,000 in new budget authority for fiscal 1983 for the Agriculture Department and related agencies. Passed 264-105: R 92-80; D 172-25 (ND 113-16, SD 59-9), Sept. 21, 1982. A "nay" was a vote supporting the president's position. The president had requested $23,083,665,000.

326. Procedural Motion. Foley, D-Wash., motion to dispense with Calendar Wednesday business of Sept. 22. (Calendar Wednesday is a seldom used and rarely successful procedure for bringing bills to the House floor without going through the Rules Committee. The Calendar Wednesday procedure is normally dispensed with by unanimous consent, but on Sept. 21, Walker, R-Pa., who wanted to bring certain bills to a floor vote, objected, which is why Foley made the motion.) Motion agreed to 226-79: R 76-74; D 150-5 (ND 101-3, SD 49-2), Sept. 21, 1982. A two-thirds majority of those present and voting (204 in this case) is required to suspend the rules.

KEY

Y	Voted for (yea).
#	Paired for.
+	Announced for.
N	Voted against (nay).
X	Paired against.
-	Announced against.
P	Voted "present".
C	Voted "present" to avoid possible conflict of interest.
?	Did not vote or otherwise make a position known.

Democrats   *Republicans*

	319	320	321	322	323	324	325	326
ALABAMA								
1 Edwards	N	Y	Y	N	Y	N	Y	Y
2 Dickinson	N	Y	Y	N	Y	N	Y	?
3 Nichols	Y	?	Y	N	Y	N	Y	?
4 Bevill	Y	Y	N	N	Y	N	Y	Y
5 Flippo	Y	Y	N	N	Y	N	Y	Y
6 Smith	N	Y	Y	N	Y	N	Y	N
7 Shelby	N	Y	N	N	Y	Y	Y	N
ALASKA								
AL Young	X	?	#	?	?	?	X	?
ARIZONA								
1 Rhodes	N	Y	Y	N	?	?	X	?
2 Udall	Y	Y	N	Y	N	?	Y	?
3 Stump	N	Y	Y	N	Y	N	Y	?
4 Rudd	N	Y	Y	N	N	Y	N	?
ARKANSAS								
1 Alexander	Y	Y	N	N	Y	N	Y	Y
2 Bethune	N	Y	Y	N	Y	N	Y	Y
3 Hammerschmidt	N	Y	N	N	Y	N	Y	Y
4 Anthony	Y	Y	N	N	Y	N	Y	Y
CALIFORNIA								
1 Chappie	N	Y	Y	N	N	Y	N	Y
2 Clausen	Y	Y	Y	Y	N	Y	?	Y
3 Matsui	Y	Y	N	N	Y	N	Y	Y
4 Fazio	Y	Y	N	N	Y	N	Y	Y
5 Burton, J.	#	?	Y	N	Y	?	?	?
6 Burton, P.	Y	Y	X	?	?	?	?	?
7 Miller	Y	Y	N	N	Y	N	Y	Y
8 Dellums	Y	Y	?	N	Y	N	Y	Y
9 Stark	Y	Y	?	N	Y	N	Y	?
10 Edwards	Y	Y	N	Y	?	?	?	
11 Lantos	Y	Y	#	?	?	?	?	?
12 McCloskey	?	?	#	N	N	N	?	?
13 Mineta	Y	Y	N	N	Y	N	Y	Y
14 Shumway	N	Y	Y	N	Y	N	N	N
15 Coelho	Y	Y	N	N	Y	N	Y	Y
16 Panetta	Y	Y	N	N	Y	N	?	Y
17 Pashayan	Y	Y	Y	N	Y	N	Y	Y
18 Thomas	X	?	Y	N	Y	N	N	N
19 Lagomarsino	N	Y	Y	N	N	Y	N	Y
20 Goldwater	N	Y	?	?	?	?	X	?
21 Fiedler	N	Y	Y	N	N	Y	N	N
22 Moorhead	X	?	Y	?	N	Y	N	N
23 Beilenson	Y	Y	N	N	Y	N	Y	Y
24 Waxman	Y	Y	N	N	Y	N	Y	?
25 Roybal	Y	Y	N	N	?	N	Y	Y
26 Rousselot	N	Y	Y	N	Y	N	N	N
27 Dornan	N	Y	Y	N	Y	N	N	N
28 Dixon	Y	Y	N	N	Y	N	Y	Y
29 Hawkins	Y	Y	N	N	Y	N	Y	?
30 Martinez	Y	Y	N	N	Y	N	Y	Y
31 Dymally	Y	Y	N	N	Y	N	Y	Y
32 Anderson	Y	Y	N	N	Y	N	Y	Y
33 Grisham	N	Y	?	?	?	?	?	?
34 Lungren	N	Y	Y	Y	N	Y	N	N
35 Dreier	N	Y	Y	Y	N	Y	N	N
36 Brown	Y	Y	N	N	Y	N	Y	Y
37 Lewis	N	?	Y	Y	N	Y	N	N
38 Patterson	N	Y	N	N	Y	N	N	N
39 Dannemeyer	N	Y	Y	Y	N	Y	N	N
40 Badham	N	Y	Y	N	N	Y	N	N
41 Lowery	N	Y	N	N	Y	N	Y	N
42 Hunter	N	Y	Y	N	N	Y	N	N
43 Burgener	N	Y	Y	N	N	?	X	Y
COLORADO								
1 Schroeder	Y	Y	Y	N	Y	N	N	?
2 Wirth	Y	Y	N	N	Y	N	Y	Y
3 Kogovsek	Y	Y	N	N	Y	N	Y	Y
4 Brown	N	Y	Y	Y	N	Y	N	N
5 Kramer	N	Y	N	N	Y	Y	N	N
CONNECTICUT								
1 Kennelly	Y	Y	N	N	Y	N	Y	?
2 Gejdenson	Y	Y	N	N	Y	N	Y	Y
3 DeNardis	Y	Y	N	N	Y	?	Y	Y
4 McKinney	Y	Y	N	N	Y	N	Y	Y
5 Ratchford	Y	Y	N	N	Y	N	Y	Y
6 Moffett	Y	?	X	?	?	?	?	?
DELAWARE								
AL Evans	N	Y	Y	N	Y	N	Y	?
FLORIDA								
1 Hutto	Y	Y	?	N	Y	N	Y	Y
2 Fuqua	Y	Y	N	N	Y	N	Y	Y
3 Bennett	Y	Y	Y	N	Y	N	N	Y
4 Chappell	Y	Y	?	?	?	?	?	?
5 McCollum	N	Y	N	N	N	N	N	N
6 Young	N	Y	Y	N	Y	N	Y	N
7 Gibbons	Y	Y	N	Y	Y	Y	Y	Y
8 Ireland	N	?	N	N	Y	N	?	?
9 Nelson	Y	Y	N	N	Y	N	Y	Y
10 Bafalis	?	?	?	?	?	?	?	?
11 Mica	Y	Y	N	N	Y	N	Y	Y
12 Shaw	N	Y	Y	N	Y	Y	N	Y
13 Lehman	Y	Y	N	N	Y	N	Y	Y
14 Pepper	#	?	N	N	Y	N	Y	Y
15 Fascell	Y	Y	N	N	Y	N	Y	Y
GEORGIA								
1 Ginn	N	Y	N	N	Y	N	Y	Y
2 Hatcher	Y	Y	N	N	Y	N	Y	Y
3 Brinkley	Y	Y	N	N	Y	N	Y	Y
4 Levitas	N	Y	N	N	Y	N	Y	Y
5 Fowler	Y	Y	N	N	Y	N	Y	Y
6 Gingrich	N	Y	Y	N	Y	N	N	N
7 McDonald	N	N	Y	N	Y	N	N	N
8 Evans	?	?	?	?	?	?	?	?
9 Jenkins	N	Y	Y	N	Y	N	Y	Y
10 Barnard	N	Y	N	N	Y	Y	Y	Y
HAWAII								
1 Heftel	Y	Y	Y	Y	Y	N	Y	Y
2 Akaka	#	?	N	N	Y	N	Y	Y
IDAHO								
1 Craig	N	Y	Y	N	N	Y	N	N
2 Hansen	N	N	Y	N	Y	N	N	N
ILLINOIS								
1 Washington	Y	?	?	?	?	?	?	?
2 Savage	Y	Y	?	?	?	?	?	?
3 Russo	Y	?	N	Y	N	N	N	Y
4 Derwinski	N	Y	?	?	?	?	X	?
5 Fary	Y	Y	N	N	Y	N	Y	Y
6 Hyde	N	?	Y	N	Y	N	Y	Y
7 Collins	Y	Y	N	N	Y	N	Y	Y
8 Rostenkowski	Y	Y	N	N	Y	?	Y	?
9 Yates	Y	Y	?	?	?	?	Y	Y
10 Porter	N	Y	Y	N	N	Y	N	?
11 Annunzio	#	?	N	N	Y	N	Y	?
12 Crane, P.	N	Y	Y	N	Y	N	N	N
13 McClory	X	?	Y	N	Y	N	N	N
14 Erlenborn	N	Y	Y	N	Y	N	N	N
15 Corcoran	N	Y	Y	N	N	Y	N	N
16 Martin	N	Y	N	N	Y	N	Y	N
17 O'Brien	Y	?	N	N	Y	N	Y	?
18 Michel	N	N	Y	N	Y	N	Y	N
19 Railsback	Y	Y	N	?	Y	N	Y	?
20 Findley	Y	Y	N	N	Y	N	Y	Y
21 Madigan	N	Y	N	N	Y	N	Y	N
22 Crane, D.	N	Y	Y	N	Y	N	N	N
23 Price	?	?	N	N	Y	N	Y	?
24 Simon	#	?	X	N	Y	N	Y	Y
INDIANA								
1 Vacancy								
2 Fithian	Y	?	?	?	?	?	?	?
3 Hiler	N	Y	Y	N	N	Y	N	N
4 Coats	N	Y	Y	N	N	Y	Y	N
5 Hillis	N	Y	Y	N	N	Y	N	Y
6 Evans	Y	Y	N	N	Y	N	Y	?
7 Myers	Y	Y	Y	N	N	N	Y	Y
8 Deckard	?	Y	N	N	?	N	Y	Y
9 Hamilton	Y	Y	N	N	?	N	Y	Y
10 Sharp	Y	Y	N	N	Y	N	Y	Y
11 Jacobs	Y	Y	N	N	Y	N	N	Y
IOWA								
1 Leach	Y	Y	N	N	Y	N	Y	Y
2 Tauke	X	?	N	N	Y	N	Y	Y
3 Evans	Y	Y	N	N	Y	N	Y	Y
4 Smith	Y	Y	N	N	Y	N	Y	Y
5 Harkin	Y	Y	?	N	Y	N	Y	Y
6 Bedell	N	Y	N	N	Y	N	Y	Y

ND - Northern Democrats   SD - Southern Democrats

Corresponding to Congressional Record Votes 339, 340, 342, 344, 345, 347, 348, 349

	319	320	321	322	323	324	325	326
KANSAS								
1 ***Roberts***	N	?	Y	N	N	Y	Y	N
2 ***Jeffries***	N	Y	Y	Y	N	Y	N	N
3 ***Winn***	N	Y	Y	N	N	Y	Y	N
4 Glickman	Y	Y	Y	N	Y	N	Y	Y
5 ***Whittaker***	N	Y	Y	N	N	N	Y	N
KENTUCKY								
1 Hubbard	Y	Y	Y	N	N	N	Y	Y
2 Natcher	Y	Y	N	N	Y	N	Y	Y
3 Mazzoli	Y	Y	N	N	Y	N	Y	Y
4 ***Snyder***	?	?	Y	N	N	Y	N	N
5 ***Rogers***	N	Y	Y	N	N	N	Y	Y
6 ***Hopkins***	N	Y	Y	N	N	N	Y	Y
7 Perkins	Y	Y	N	N	Y	N	Y	Y
LOUISIANA								
1 ***Livingston***	N	Y	Y	N	N	N	N	N
2 Boggs	Y	Y	N	N	Y	N	Y	Y
3 Tauzin	N	Y	Y	N	N	N	?	Y
4 Roemer	N	Y	Y	N	N	N	N	Y
5 Huckaby	Y	?	Y	N	N	N	Y	?
6 ***Moore***	N	Y	Y	N	N	N	N	N
7 Breaux	N	Y	Y	N	Y	?	?	?
8 Long	Y	Y	N	N	Y	?	?	?
MAINE								
1 ***Emery***	N	?	Y	?	?	Y	Y	Y
2 ***Snowe***	N	Y	Y	N	Y	N	Y	Y
MARYLAND								
1 Dyson	N	Y	N	N	Y	N	Y	Y
2 Long	Y	Y	N	Y	Y	N	Y	?
3 Mikulski	Y	?	N	N	Y	N	Y	Y
4 ***Holt***	N	Y	Y	?	?	Y	N	?
5 Hoyer	Y	Y	N	N	Y	?	?	?
6 Byron	N	Y	N	N	N	N	Y	Y
7 Mitchell	Y	Y	N	N	Y	N	Y	?
8 Barnes	Y	Y	N	N	Y	N	Y	Y
MASSACHUSETTS								
1 ***Conte***	N	Y	Y	N	Y	N	Y	Y
2 Boland	Y	Y	N	N	Y	N	Y	Y
3 Early	Y	Y	N	N	Y	N	Y	Y
4 Frank	Y	Y	N	N	Y	N	N	Y
5 Shannon	Y	Y	N	N	Y	N	Y	Y
6 Mavroules	Y	Y	N	N	Y	N	Y	Y
7 Markey	Y	Y	N	N	Y	N	?	Y
8 O'Neill								
9 Moakley	Y	Y	N	N	Y	?	?	?
10 ***Heckler***	Y	Y	N	N	Y	N	Y	Y
11 Donnelly	Y	Y	N	N	Y	N	Y	?
12 Studds	Y	Y	N	N	Y	N	Y	Y
MICHIGAN								
1 Conyers	Y	Y	N	N	Y	N	Y	Y
2 ***Pursell***	N	Y	Y	N	Y	N	Y	?
3 Wolpe	Y	Y	N	N	Y	N	Y	Y
4 ***Siljander***	N	Y	#	?	?	?	#	?
5 ***Sawyer***	N	Y	Y	N	Y	Y	Y	N
6 ***Dunn***	Y	Y	Y	N	Y	Y	Y	N
7 Kildee	Y	Y	N	N	Y	N	Y	Y
8 Traxler	Y	?	N	N	Y	N	Y	Y
9 ***Vander Jagt***	N	Y	Y	N	Y	Y	Y	?
10 Albosta	Y	Y	N	N	Y	N	Y	Y
11 ***Davis***	Y	Y	?	?	?	N	Y	Y
12 Bonior	Y	Y	N	N	Y	N	Y	Y
13 Crockett	Y	?	N	N	Y	N	Y	?
14 Hertel	Y	Y	N	N	Y	N	Y	Y
15 Ford	Y	Y	N	N	Y	N	Y	Y
16 Dingell	Y	Y	N	N	Y	N	Y	Y
17 Brodhead	Y	Y	N	N	Y	N	Y	Y
18 Blanchard	?	?	?	?	?	?	?	?
19 ***Broomfield***	N	Y	Y	Y	Y	Y	N	?
MINNESOTA								
1 ***Erdahl***	N	Y	Y	N	Y	N	Y	Y
2 ***Hagedorn***	N	?	Y	Y	N	Y	Y	?
3 ***Frenzel***	X	?	Y	N	N	Y	N	Y
4 Vento	Y	Y	N	N	Y	N	Y	?
5 Sabo	Y	Y	N	N	Y	N	Y	?
6 ***Weber***	N	?	Y	Y	N	Y	Y	Y
7 ***Stangeland***	N	?	Y	N	N	Y	Y	N
8 Oberstar	Y	Y	N	N	Y	N	Y	Y
MISSISSIPPI								
1 Whitten	Y	Y	N	N	Y	N	Y	?
2 Bowen	Y	Y	?	?	?	?	?	?
3 Montgomery	N	Y	Y	N	N	Y	Y	Y
4 Dowdy	Y	Y	?	?	?	?	?	?
5 ***Lott***	N	Y	Y	N	N	Y	N	N
MISSOURI								
1 Clay	Y	Y	N	N	Y	N	Y	?
2 Young	Y	Y	N	N	Y	N	Y	Y
3 Gephardt	Y	Y	N	Y	Y	N	Y	Y
4 Skelton	Y	Y	N	N	N	Y	Y	Y
5 Bolling	?	?	N	?	?	?	?	?
6 ***Coleman***	N	Y	?	N	Y	N	Y	N
7 ***Taylor***	N	N	Y	N	N	Y	Y	?
8 ***Bailey***	N	Y	Y	N	N	Y	Y	N
9 Volkmer	Y	Y	N	N	Y	N	Y	Y
10 ***Emerson***	N	N	Y	N	N	Y	Y	N
MONTANA								
1 Williams	Y	Y	N	N	Y	N	Y	?
2 ***Marlenee***	?	?	N	N	N	Y	Y	N
NEBRASKA								
1 ***Bereuter***	N	Y	Y	N	N	Y	Y	Y
2 ***Daub***	N	N	Y	N	N	Y	Y	Y
3 ***Smith***	N	Y	N	N	N	Y	Y	Y
NEVADA								
AL Santini	?	?	N	N	Y	Y	Y	?
NEW HAMPSHIRE								
1 D'Amours	Y	Y	Y	N	Y	N	Y	Y
2 ***Gregg***	N	Y	Y	?	N	Y	N	N
NEW JERSEY								
1 Florio	Y	Y	N	N	Y	?	?	?
2 Hughes	Y	Y	N	N	Y	N	N	Y
3 Howard	Y	Y	N	N	Y	N	Y	Y
4 ***Smith***	Y	Y	N	N	Y	N	Y	Y
5 ***Fenwick***	Y	Y	N	N	Y	N	Y	Y
6 ***Forsythe***	?	?	?	?	?	?	?	?
7 ***Roukema***	N	Y	Y	N	N	N	N	Y
8 Roe	Y	Y	N	N	Y	N	Y	Y
9 ***Hollenbeck***	Y	Y	N	N	Y	N	Y	Y
10 Rodino	Y	Y	N	N	Y	N	Y	Y
11 Minish	Y	Y	N	N	Y	N	Y	Y
12 ***Rinaldo***	Y	Y	?	?	?	?	?	?
13 ***Courter***	N	Y	N	N	Y	N	N	N
14 Guarini	Y	Y	N	N	Y	N	Y	Y
15 Dwyer	Y	Y	N	N	Y	N	Y	Y
NEW MEXICO								
1 ***Lujan***	N	Y	Y	Y	N	Y	N	Y
2 ***Skeen***	N	Y	Y	N	N	Y	Y	Y
NEW YORK								
1 ***Carney***	N	Y	Y	N	N	Y	Y	N
2 Downey	Y	Y	N	N	Y	N	Y	Y
3 ***Carman***	N	?	N	N	N	Y	N	N
4 ***Lent***	N	?	N	N	Y	N	N	Y
5 ***McGrath***	N	Y	N	N	Y	Y	N	Y
6 ***LeBoutillier***	N	Y	?	N	Y	Y	N	N
7 Addabbo	Y	Y	N	N	Y	?	#	?
8 Rosenthal	Y	?	N	N	Y	?	?	?
9 Ferraro	Y	Y	N	N	Y	N	Y	?
10 Biaggi	Y	Y	N	N	Y	N	Y	Y
11 Scheuer	Y	Y	N	N	Y	N	?	Y
12 Chisholm	Y	?	X	?	?	?	?	?
13 Solarz	Y	Y	N	N	Y	N	Y	Y
14 Vacancy								
15 Zeferetti	Y	Y	N	N	Y	N	Y	?
16 Schumer	Y	Y	N	N	Y	N	N	Y
17 ***Molinari***	N	Y	?	N	Y	N	N	Y
18 ***Green***	N	Y	N	N	Y	N	Y	Y
19 Rangel	Y	Y	N	N	Y	N	Y	?
20 Weiss	#	?	X	?	?	?	?	?
21 Garcia	Y	?	X	?	?	?	?	?
22 Bingham	Y	Y	N	N	Y	N	Y	?
23 Peyser	Y	Y	N	N	Y	N	N	Y
24 Ottinger	Y	Y	N	N	Y	N	N	Y
25 ***Fish***	Y	Y	N	N	Y	N	Y	Y
26 ***Gilman***	Y	Y	N	?	?	?	?	?
27 McHugh	Y	Y	N	N	Y	N	Y	Y
28 Stratton	Y	Y	?	?	?	?	?	?
29 ***Solomon***	N	Y	Y	N	N	Y	Y	N
30 ***Martin***	N	?	Y	N	N	N	Y	Y
31 ***Mitchell***	Y	?	N	N	Y	N	Y	Y
32 ***Wortley***	N	?	?	?	?	Y	Y	Y
33 ***Lee***	?	?	+	-	-	+	+	?
34 ***Horton***	N	Y	#	N	Y	N	Y	Y
35 ***Conable***	N	Y	Y	N	?	N	N	Y
36 LaFalce	Y	Y	N	N	Y	N	Y	Y
37 Nowak	Y	Y	N	N	Y	N	Y	Y
38 ***Kemp***	N	?	Y	N	N	?	?	?
39 Lundine	Y	?	?	N	Y	N	Y	?
NORTH CAROLINA								
1 Jones	Y	Y	N	N	Y	N	Y	?
2 Fountain	?	?	Y	N	Y	N	Y	Y
3 Whitley	Y	Y	Y	N	Y	N	Y	Y
4 Andrews	Y	Y	N	N	Y	N	Y	Y
5 Neal	Y	Y	Y	N	Y	N	Y	Y
6 ***Johnston***	X	?	Y	Y	N	Y	Y	?
7 Rose	#	?	N	N	Y	N	Y	?
8 Hefner	Y	Y	Y	N	Y	N	Y	?
9 ***Martin***	N	Y	Y	N	N	Y	N	N
10 ***Broyhill***	N	Y	Y	N	N	Y	N	Y
11 ***Hendon***	N	?	Y	Y	N	?	Y	N
NORTH DAKOTA								
AL Dorgan	Y	Y	N	N	Y	N	Y	Y
OHIO								
1 ***Gradison***	N	Y	Y	Y	N	N	N	Y
2 Luken	Y	Y	N	N	Y	N	N	Y
3 Hall	Y	Y	N	N	Y	N	Y	?
4 ***Oxley***	N	?	Y	N	N	?	#	?
5 ***Latta***	N	?	Y	N	N	Y	Y	Y
6 ***McEwen***	N	Y	Y	N	N	Y	Y	N
7 ***Brown***	Y	?	?	?	?	?	?	?
8 ***Kindness***	N	N	Y	N	N	Y	Y	?
9 ***Weber***	N	Y	Y	N	N	Y	N	Y
10 ***Miller***	N	Y	Y	Y	N	Y	N	N
11 ***Stanton***	N	?	?	?	?	?	?	?
12 Shamansky	Y	Y	N	N	Y	N	Y	Y
13 Pease	Y	Y	N	N	Y	N	Y	?
14 Seiberling	Y	Y	N	N	Y	N	Y	Y
15 ***Wylie***	N	?	N	N	Y	N	Y	Y
16 ***Regula***	N	Y	N	N	N	N	Y	Y
17 ***Ashbrook***	N	Y	#	Y	N	Y	N	N
18 Applegate	Y	Y	N	N	Y	N	Y	?
19 ***Williams***	Y	Y	N	N	Y	N	Y	?
20 Oakar	Y	Y	N	N	Y	N	Y	?
21 Stokes	Y	Y	N	N	Y	N	Y	Y
22 Eckart	Y	Y	N	N	Y	N	Y	Y
23 Mottl	Y	?	N	N	Y	Y	N	N
OKLAHOMA								
1 Jones	?	?	N	N	Y	N	Y	?
2 Synar	N	Y	N	N	Y	N	Y	?
3 Watkins	Y	Y	N	N	Y	N	Y	?
4 McCurdy	?	?	N	N	N	N	Y	?
5 ***Edwards***	N	Y	?	Y	N	N	Y	N
6 English	N	Y	N	Y	N	N	Y	?
OREGON								
1 AuCoin	Y	Y	N	N	Y	N	N	Y
2 ***Smith***	N	Y	Y	Y	N	Y	N	N
3 Wyden	Y	Y	N	N	Y	N	N	Y
4 Weaver	Y	Y	N	Y	Y	N	Y	Y
PENNSYLVANIA								
1 Foglietta	Y	Y	N	N	Y	N	Y	Y
2 Gray	Y	Y	N	N	Y	N	Y	?
3 Smith	#	?	N	N	Y	N	Y	?
4 ***Dougherty***	Y	Y	N	N	Y	N	Y	?
5 ***Schulze***	?	?	Y	N	N	Y	N	N
6 Yatron	Y	Y	N	N	Y	N	Y	Y
7 Edgar	Y	Y	N	N	Y	?	?	?
8 ***Coyne, J.***	Y	Y	Y	N	Y	N	N	Y
9 ***Shuster***	N	Y	?	N	Y	Y	N	N
10 ***McDade***	Y	Y	?	N	Y	N	Y	Y
11 ***Nelligan***	Y	Y	Y	N	Y	N	Y	Y
12 Murtha	Y	Y	N	N	Y	N	Y	Y
13 ***Coughlin***	N	Y	Y	N	Y	Y	N	N
14 Coyne, W.	Y	Y	N	N	Y	N	Y	Y
15 ***Ritter***	N	Y	Y	N	Y	Y	N	Y
16 ***Walker***	N	Y	Y	Y	N	Y	N	N
17 Ertel	Y	?	?	?	?	?	?	?
18 Walgren	Y	Y	?	N	Y	N	Y	Y
19 ***Goodling***	N	Y	Y	N	Y	Y	Y	N
20 Gaydos	Y	Y	N	N	Y	N	Y	Y
21 Bailey	Y	Y	N	N	Y	N	Y	Y
22 Murphy	Y	Y	N	N	Y	N	N	Y
23 ***Clinger***	N	Y	Y	N	Y	N	N	Y
24 ***Marks***	Y	?	?	?	Y	?	Y	?
25 ***Atkinson***	Y	Y	N	N	Y	Y	N	Y
RHODE ISLAND								
1 St Germain	Y	Y	N	N	Y	N	Y	Y
2 ***Schneider***	Y	?	N	N	Y	N	N	Y
SOUTH CAROLINA								
1 ***Hartnett***	N	Y	Y	N	N	Y	Y	N
2 ***Spence***	N	Y	Y	N	N	Y	Y	N
3 Derrick	Y	Y	?	N	Y	N	Y	?
4 ***Campbell***	N	Y	Y	N	N	Y	Y	N
5 Holland	Y	?	N	N	Y	N	Y	?
6 ***Napier***	Y	?	?	?	?	?	#	?
SOUTH DAKOTA								
1 Daschle	Y	Y	N	N	Y	N	Y	N
2 ***Roberts***	N	Y	Y	N	N	Y	Y	N
TENNESSEE								
1 ***Quillen***	N	Y	N	N	Y	Y	Y	Y
2 ***Duncan***	N	Y	?	N	Y	N	Y	Y
3 Bouquard	Y	Y	N	N	Y	N	Y	Y
4 Gore	Y	Y	N	N	Y	N	Y	Y
5 Boner	Y	Y	N	N	Y	N	Y	Y
6 ***Beard***	X	?	?	?	?	?	#	?
7 Jones	Y	Y	N	N	Y	N	Y	Y
8 Ford	Y	Y	N	N	Y	N	Y	Y
TEXAS								
1 Hall, S.	N	Y	Y	N	N	Y	Y	Y
2 Wilson	Y	Y	N	N	Y	N	?	?
3 ***Collins***	N	?	#	?	?	?	X	?
4 Hall, R.	N	Y	Y	N	Y	N	N	Y
5 Mattox	?	?	?	?	?	?	?	?
6 Gramm	N	Y	Y	N	N	Y	N	Y
7 ***Archer***	N	Y	Y	Y	N	Y	N	N
8 ***Fields***	N	Y	?	Y	N	Y	N	N
9 Brooks	?	?	N	?	?	?	?	?
10 Pickle	?	?	N	N	Y	N	Y	Y
11 Leath	N	Y	Y	N	N	Y	Y	Y
12 Wright	Y	Y	N	N	Y	?	Y	?
13 Hightower	N	?	N	N	Y	N	Y	Y
14 Patman	N	Y	Y	N	Y	N	Y	Y
15 de la Garza	Y	Y	?	?	?	?	?	?
16 White	N	Y	Y	N	Y	N	Y	Y
17 Stenholm	N	Y	Y	N	N	Y	N	Y
18 Leland	Y	Y	N	N	Y	N	Y	?
19 Hance	N	Y	Y	N	N	N	Y	Y
20 Gonzalez	Y	Y	N	N	Y	N	Y	Y
21 ***Loeffler***	N	Y	Y	N	N	Y	N	N
22 ***Paul***	?	?	Y	Y	N	Y	N	N
23 Kazen	Y	Y	Y	N	Y	N	Y	Y
24 Frost	Y	Y	N	N	Y	N	Y	Y
UTAH								
1 ***Hansen***	N	Y	Y	N	N	Y	Y	?
2 ***Marriott***	N	Y	Y	N	N	N	Y	N
VERMONT								
AL ***Jeffords***	N	Y	N	N	Y	N	Y	Y
VIRGINIA								
1 ***Trible***	N	Y	Y	N	Y	N	Y	Y
2 ***Whitehurst***	N	Y	Y	N	N	Y	Y	?
3 ***Bliley***	N	?	Y	N	N	N	N	Y
4 ***Daniel, R.***	N	Y	Y	N	N	Y	Y	Y
5 Daniel, D.	N	Y	#	N	N	Y	N	Y
6 ***Butler***	X	?	Y	N	Y	N	N	?
7 ***Robinson***	N	Y	Y	N	N	N	Y	Y
8 ***Parris***	N	Y	N	N	Y	N	Y	Y
9 ***Wampler***	N	?	N	N	Y	N	Y	Y
10 ***Wolf***	N	Y	N	N	Y	N	Y	Y
WASHINGTON								
1 ***Pritchard***	?	?	Y	N	Y	N	Y	?
2 Swift	Y	Y	N	N	Y	?	?	?
3 Bonker	Y	Y	N	N	Y	N	?	Y
4 ***Morrison***	N	Y	Y	N	Y	Y	Y	Y
5 Foley	Y	Y	N	N	Y	N	Y	Y
6 Dicks	Y	Y	N	N	Y	N	Y	Y
7 Lowry	Y	Y	N	N	Y	N	Y	Y
WEST VIRGINIA								
1 Mollohan	Y	Y	N	N	Y	?	#	?
2 ***Benedict***	Y	N	N	N	Y	N	N	Y
3 ***Staton***	Y	Y	N	N	Y	Y	N	N
4 Rahall	Y	Y	N	N	Y	N	Y	Y
WISCONSIN								
1 Aspin	Y	Y	N	Y	Y	N	?	Y
2 Kastenmeier	+	Y	N	N	Y	N	Y	?
3 ***Gunderson***	N	Y	Y	N	N	N	Y	Y
4 Zablocki	Y	Y	N	N	Y	N	?	Y
5 Reuss	#	?	N	N	Y	N	Y	Y
6 ***Petri***	N	Y	Y	N	Y	Y	Y	?
7 Obey	Y	Y	N	Y	Y	?	?	Y
8 ***Roth***	N	Y	Y	Y	N	Y	Y	N
9 ***Sensenbrenner***	N	Y	Y	Y	N	Y	N	N
WYOMING								
AL ***Cheney***	N	Y	Y	Y	N	Y	N	N

Southern states - Ala., Ark., Fla., Ga., Ky., La., Miss., N.C., Okla., S.C., Tenn., Texas, Va.

327. HR 3581. Foreign Corporation Taxation. Rostenkowski, D-Ill., motion to suspend the rules and pass the bill to allow shareholders of the Consolidated Foods Corp. to exempt from tax certain dividend income received by a foreign firm partly owned by the company. Motion rejected 113-274: R 37-142; D 76-132 (ND 52-85, SD 24-47), Sept. 22, 1982. A two-thirds majority of those present and voting (259 in this case) is required for passage under suspension of the rules.

328. HR 5573. Computer Equipment Contribution Act. Rostenkowski, D-Ill., motion to suspend the rules and pass the bill to allow computer companies to deduct up to twice their cost of computer equipment manufactured in 1983 and donated to primary and secondary schools. Motion agreed to 323-62: R 149-28; D 174-34 (ND 125-12, SD 49-22), Sept. 22, 1982. A two-thirds majority of those present and voting (257 in this case) is required for passage under suspension of the rules.

329. HR 6867. Miscellaneous Tariff Amendments. Rostenkowski, D-Ill., motion to suspend the rules and pass the bill to make miscellaneous tariff and trade changes, including the repeal of an embargo on the importation of mink and other furs from the People's Republic of China. Motion agreed to 267-125: R 110-69; D 157-56 (ND 101-41, SD 56-15), Sept. 22, 1982. A two-thirds majority of those present and voting (262 in this case) is required for passage under suspension of the rules.

330. HR 6317. Uniformed Services Pay Act. Montgomery, D-Miss., motion to suspend the rules and pass the bill to authorize a pay raise in fiscal 1983 for uniformed members of the armed services and to restrict the hiring of private contractors to perform Department of Defense services. Motion rejected 214-186: R 72-109; D 142-77 (ND 86-60, SD 56-17), Sept. 22, 1982. A two-thirds majority of those present and voting (267 in this case) is required for passage under suspension of the rules.

331. HR 7048. College Student Aid. Simon, D-Ill., motion to suspend the rules and pass the bill to require that the rules governing distribution of Pell grant awards to college students in the 1982-83 school year be used, with certain modifications, for the 1983-84 school year, and for the 1984-85 school year as well if the Education Department did not approve its own regulations by May 15, 1983; and to restore student aid grants to certain veterans. Motion agreed to 381-19: R 164-17; D 217-2 (ND 147-0, SD 70-2), Sept. 22, 1982. A two-thirds majority of those present and voting (267 in this case) is required for passage under suspension of the rules.

332. S J Res 250. Emergency Railroad Strike Legislation. Florio, D-N.J., substitute to prohibit further railroad strikes for 140 days and direct the Brotherhood of Locomotive Engineers to resume contract negotiations with railroad management. Rejected 37-361: R 10-168; D 27-193 (ND 20-128, SD 7-65), Sept. 22, 1982. A "nay" was a vote supporting the president's position.

333. S J Res 250. Emergency Railroad Strike Legislation. Passage of the joint resolution to end the railroad strike by the Brotherhood of Locomotive Engineers and impose the contract settlement recommended by the presidential Emergency Board barring strikes through June 30, 1984. Passed 383-17: R 173-6; D 210-11 (ND 138-9, SD 72-2), Sept. 22, 1982. A "yea" was a vote supporting the president's position.

KEY

- **Y** Voted for (yea).
- **#** Paired for.
- **+** Announced for.
- **N** Voted against (nay).
- **X** Paired against.
- **-** Announced against.
- **P** Voted "present".
- **C** Voted "present" to avoid possible conflict of interest.
- **?** Did not vote or otherwise make a position known.

Democrats   *Republicans*

	327	328	329	330	331	332	333
ALABAMA							
1 Edwards	N	Y	Y	Y	Y	N	Y
2 Dickinson	Y	Y	Y	Y	Y	N	Y
3 Nichols	N	Y	Y	Y	Y	N	Y
4 Bevill	N	Y	N	Y	Y	N	Y
5 Flippo	Y	Y	Y	Y	Y	N	Y
6 Smith	N	Y	N	N	Y	N	Y
7 Shelby	N	N	N	N	Y	N	Y
ALASKA							
AL Young	?	?	?	?	?	?	?
ARIZONA							
1 Rhodes	N	N	Y	Y	Y	N	Y
2 Udall	Y	N	Y	Y	Y	N	Y
3 Stump	N	N	Y	N	Y	N	Y
4 Rudd	N	N	Y	N	N	N	Y
ARKANSAS							
1 Alexander	Y	N	Y	N	Y	N	Y
2 Bethune	N	Y	Y	N	Y	Y	Y
3 Hammerschmidt	N	Y	N	Y	N	Y	N
4 Anthony	Y	Y	Y	Y	Y	N	Y
CALIFORNIA							
1 Chappie	Y	Y	N	N	Y	N	Y
2 Clausen	N	Y	Y	N	Y	N	Y
3 Matsui	Y	Y	Y	Y	Y	N	Y
4 Fazio	Y	Y	Y	Y	Y	N	Y
5 Burton, J.	?	?	?	?	?	?	?
6 Burton, P.	?	?	?	?	?	?	?
7 Miller	Y	Y	Y	N	Y	Y	Y
8 Dellums	N	Y	N	Y	Y	N	N
9 Stark	Y	Y	Y	Y	Y	N	Y
10 Edwards	N	Y	Y	Y	Y	N	Y
11 Lantos	?	?	?	Y	Y	N	Y
12 McCloskey	Y	Y	Y	Y	Y	?	Y
13 Mineta	Y	Y	Y	Y	Y	N	Y
14 Shumway	N	N	Y	N	N	N	Y
15 Coelho	Y	Y	Y	Y	Y	N	Y
16 Panetta	Y	Y	Y	Y	Y	N	Y
17 Pashayan	N	Y	N	N	Y	N	Y
18 Thomas	N	Y	N	N	Y	N	Y
19 Lagomarsino	N	Y	Y	Y	Y	N	Y
20 Goldwater	?	?	?	N	Y	N	Y
21 Fiedler	N	Y	Y	Y	Y	N	Y
22 Moorhead	Y	Y	Y	N	Y	N	Y
23 Beilenson	N	N	Y	Y	Y	N	Y
24 Waxman	Y	Y	Y	Y	Y	Y	Y
25 Roybal	N	Y	Y	Y	Y	N	Y
26 Rousselot	Y	Y	?	?	?	?	?
27 Dornan	Y	Y	N	Y	Y	N	Y
28 Dixon	Y	Y	Y	N	Y	N	Y
29 Hawkins	Y	Y	N	Y	Y	N	Y
30 Martinez	Y	Y	Y	Y	Y	N	Y
31 Dymally	N	Y	Y	N	Y	N	N
32 Anderson	N	Y	N	N	Y	N	Y
33 Grisham	?	?	?	?	?	?	?
34 Lungren	N	Y	N	N	N	N	Y
35 Dreier	N	N	N	N	N	N	Y
36 Brown	Y	Y	Y	Y	Y	N	Y
37 Lewis	N	Y	Y	N	Y	N	Y
38 Patterson	N	Y	N	N	Y	N	Y
39 Dannemeyer	N	Y	N	N	N	N	Y
40 Badham	N	N	Y	N	N	N	Y
41 Lowery	N	Y	Y	N	Y	N	Y
42 Hunter	Y	Y	N	Y	Y	N	Y
43 Burgener	N	Y	Y	N	N	N	Y
COLORADO							
1 Schroeder	N	Y	N	Y	Y	N	Y
2 Wirth	+	+	+	Y	Y	N	N
3 Kogovsek	N	Y	N	Y	Y	N	Y
4 Brown	N	Y	N	N	Y	Y	Y
5 Kramer	N	Y	N	Y	Y	N	Y
CONNECTICUT							
1 Kennelly	Y	Y	Y	Y	Y	N	Y
2 Gejdenson	N	Y	Y	Y	Y	N	Y
3 DeNardis	N	Y	N	Y	Y	N	Y
4 McKinney	N	Y	Y	N	Y	N	Y
5 Ratchford	Y	Y	Y	N	Y	N	Y
6 Moffett	?	?	?	?	?	?	?
DELAWARE							
AL Evans	N	Y	Y	N	Y	N	Y
FLORIDA							
1 Hutto	N	Y	Y	Y	Y	N	Y
2 Fuqua	N	Y	Y	Y	Y	N	Y
3 Bennett	N	Y	Y	N	Y	N	Y
4 Chappell	?	?	?	?	?	?	?
5 McCollum	N	Y	Y	N	Y	N	Y
6 Young	N	Y	Y	Y	Y	N	Y
7 Gibbons	Y	Y	Y	Y	Y	N	Y
8 Ireland	N	Y	N	Y	Y	N	Y
9 Nelson	N	Y	Y	N	Y	N	Y
10 Bafalis	?	?	?	?	?	?	?
11 Mica	N	Y	Y	Y	Y	N	Y
12 Shaw	N	N	Y	N	Y	N	Y
13 Lehman	Y	Y	Y	Y	Y	N	Y
14 Pepper	N	Y	Y	Y	Y	N	Y
15 Fascell	N	Y	Y	Y	Y	N	Y
GEORGIA							
1 Ginn	Y	Y	Y	Y	Y	N	Y
2 Hatcher	N	Y	Y	Y	Y	N	Y
3 Brinkley	Y	N	Y	N	Y	N	Y
4 Levitas	N	Y	N	Y	Y	N	Y
5 Fowler	Y	N	Y	Y	Y	N	Y
6 Gingrich	N	Y	Y	N	Y	N	Y
7 McDonald	N	N	N	Y	N	N	N
8 Evans	?	?	?	?	?	?	?
9 Jenkins	Y	Y	Y	Y	Y	N	Y
10 Barnard	N	Y	Y	Y	Y	N	Y
HAWAII							
1 Heftel	Y	Y	Y	Y	Y	N	Y
2 Akaka	Y	Y	Y	Y	Y	N	Y
IDAHO							
1 Craig	N	Y	N	Y	Y	N	Y
2 Hansen	Y	Y	N	Y	Y	N	+
ILLINOIS							
1 Washington	?	?	?	X	?	?	?
2 Savage	?	?	Y	N	Y	N	N
3 Russo	Y	Y	Y	Y	Y	N	Y
4 Derwinski	?	?	?	?	?	?	?
5 Fary	Y	Y	Y	Y	Y	N	Y
6 Hyde	Y	Y	Y	Y	Y	N	Y
7 Collins	N	Y	N	Y	Y	N	Y
8 Rostenkowski	?	?	?	?	?	N	Y
9 Yates	N	Y	N	Y	Y	N	Y
10 Porter	N	Y	N	Y	Y	N	Y
11 Annunzio	Y	Y	Y	Y	Y	N	Y
12 Crane, P.	Y	Y	N	N	N	N	Y
13 McClory	Y	N	N	N	Y	N	Y
14 Erlenborn	N	N	Y	N	N	N	Y
15 Corcoran	N	Y	N	N	Y	N	Y
16 Martin	Y	Y	Y	Y	Y	N	Y
17 O'Brien	Y	Y	Y	N	Y	N	Y
18 Michel	N	N	Y	N	Y	N	Y
19 Railsback	Y	Y	Y	Y	Y	N	?
20 Findley	Y	Y	N	N	Y	N	Y
21 Madigan	Y	Y	Y	Y	Y	N	Y
22 Crane, D.	Y	Y	N	N	N	N	Y
23 Price	N	Y	Y	Y	Y	N	Y
24 Simon	Y	Y	Y	Y	Y	Y	N
INDIANA							
1 Vacancy							
2 Fithian	?	?	?	?	?	?	?
3 Hiler	N	Y	Y	N	Y	N	Y
4 Coats	N	Y	Y	N	Y	N	Y
5 Hillis	N	Y	N	Y	Y	N	Y
6 Evans	N	Y	Y	N	Y	N	Y
7 Myers	Y	Y	N	Y	Y	N	Y
8 Deckard	N	Y	N	Y	Y	N	Y
9 Hamilton	N	Y	Y	N	Y	N	Y
10 Sharp	N	Y	N	Y	Y	N	Y
11 Jacobs	N	Y	N	Y	Y	N	Y
IOWA							
1 Leach	N	Y	Y	Y	Y	?	Y
2 Tauke	N	Y	N	Y	Y	N	Y
3 Evans	N	Y	N	N	Y	N	Y
4 Smith	N	Y	Y	N	Y	N	Y
5 Harkin	N	Y	Y	N	Y	N	Y
6 Bedell	N	N	Y	N	Y	N	Y

ND - Northern Democrats   SD - Southern Democrats

	327	328	329	330	331	332	333
KANSAS							
1 ***Roberts***	N	Y	N	N	Y	N	Y
2 ***Jeffries***	N	N	N	Y	N	N	Y
3 ***Winn***	N	Y	Y	Y	Y	N	Y
4 Glickman	N	Y	Y	N	Y	N	Y
5 ***Whittaker***	N	Y	Y	N	Y	N	Y
KENTUCKY							
1 Hubbard	Y	Y	Y	N	Y	N	Y
2 Natcher	N	Y	N	Y	Y	N	Y
3 Mazzoli	N	N	N	Y	Y	N	Y
4 ***Snyder***	N	Y	N	N	Y	N	Y
5 ***Rogers***	N	Y	N	N	Y	N	Y
6 ***Hopkins***	N	Y	N	N	Y	N	Y
7 Perkins	N	Y	N	Y	Y	Y	Y
LOUISIANA							
1 ***Livingston***	N	Y	Y	N	Y	N	Y
2 Boggs	Y	Y	Y	Y	?	N	Y
3 Tauzin	N	Y	N	N	Y	Y	Y
4 Roemer	N	Y	N	N	Y	Y	Y
5 Huckaby	N	Y	N	N	Y	?	Y
6 ***Moore***	Y	Y	Y	N	Y	N	Y
7 Breaux	?	?	?	?	?	?	Y
8 Long	Y	Y	Y	Y	Y	N	Y
MAINE							
1 ***Emery***	N	Y	Y	Y	Y	N	Y
2 ***Snowe***	N	Y	Y	N	Y	N	Y
MARYLAND							
1 Dyson	Y	Y	Y	Y	Y	N	Y
2 Long	N	Y	Y	Y	Y	N	Y
3 Mikulski	?	?	?	Y	Y	N	Y
4 ***Holt***	N	Y	Y	Y	Y	N	Y
5 Hoyer	Y	Y	Y	N	Y	N	Y
6 Byron	N	Y	Y	Y	Y	N	Y
7 Mitchell	Y	Y	N	N	Y	N	N
8 Barnes	Y	Y	Y	N	Y	N	Y
MASSACHUSETTS							
1 ***Conte***	N	Y	N	Y	Y	N	Y
2 Boland	Y	Y	Y	Y	Y	N	Y
3 Early	N	Y	Y	N	Y	N	Y
4 Frank	Y	Y	Y	Y	Y	N	Y
5 Shannon	Y	Y	Y	Y	Y	N	Y
6 Mavroules	Y	Y	Y	Y	Y	N	Y
7 Markey	N	?	Y	Y	Y	N	Y
8 O'Neill							
9 Moakley	Y	?	Y	Y	Y	N	Y
10 ***Heckler***	N	Y	Y	N	Y	N	Y
11 Donnelly	Y	Y	Y	N	Y	N	Y
12 Studds	N	Y	Y	N	Y	N	Y
MICHIGAN							
1 Conyers	?	?	N	N	Y	N	N
2 ***Pursell***	Y	Y	Y	N	Y	N	Y
3 Wolpe	N	Y	Y	N	Y	N	Y
4 ***Siljander***	N	Y	Y	N	Y	N	Y
5 ***Sawyer***	N	Y	Y	N	Y	N	Y
6 ***Dunn***	N	Y	Y	Y	Y	N	Y
7 Kildee	N	Y	N	Y	Y	N	Y
8 Traxler	N	Y	Y	N	Y	N	Y
9 ***Vander Jagt***	?	?	Y	Y	Y	N	Y
10 Albosta	N	Y	Y	N	Y	N	Y
11 ***Davis***	Y	Y	N	N	Y	N	Y
12 Bonior	N	N	Y	Y	Y	N	Y
13 Crockett	?	?	?	N	Y	N	?
14 Hertel	N	Y	Y	Y	Y	N	Y
15 Ford	Y	Y	Y	N	Y	N	Y
16 Dingell	Y	Y	Y	Y	Y	N	Y
17 Brodhead	Y	Y	Y	Y	Y	N	Y
18 Blanchard	?	?	?	?	?	?	?
19 ***Broomfield***	N	Y	N	N	Y	N	Y
MINNESOTA							
1 ***Erdahl***	N	Y	N	N	Y	?	Y
2 ***Hagedorn***	Y	Y	N	N	Y	N	Y
3 ***Frenzel***	Y	N	Y	N	Y	N	Y
4 Vento	N	Y	Y	N	Y	N	Y
5 Sabo	Y	N	Y	N	Y	N	Y
6 ***Weber***	N	Y	N	N	Y	N	Y
7 ***Stangeland***	N	N	N	N	Y	Y	Y
8 Oberstar	N	Y	N	N	Y	N	Y
MISSISSIPPI							
1 Whitten	N	Y	N	Y	Y	N	Y
2 Bowen	?	?	?	?	?	?	?
3 Montgomery	Y	Y	Y	Y	Y	N	Y
4 Dowdy	?	?	?	?	?	Y	Y
5 ***Lott***	N	?	Y	Y	Y	N	Y
MISSOURI							
1 Clay	N	Y	N	N	Y	N	N
2 Young	N	Y	Y	Y	Y	Y	Y
3 Gephardt	Y	Y	Y	Y	Y	Y	Y
4 Skelton	N	Y	N	Y	Y	N	Y
5 Bolling	?	Y	Y	?	?	?	?
6 ***Coleman***	N	Y	Y	N	Y	N	Y
7 ***Taylor***	N	Y	Y	N	Y	N	Y
8 ***Bailey***	N	Y	Y	Y	Y	N	Y
9 Volkmer	N	N	N	N	Y	Y	Y
10 ***Emerson***	N	Y	N	Y	Y	N	Y
MONTANA							
1 Williams	N	Y	Y	N	Y	Y	N
2 ***Marlenee***	N	Y	N	Y	N	Y	N
NEBRASKA							
1 ***Bereuter***	N	N	Y	N	Y	N	Y
2 ***Daub***	N	Y	N	N	Y	N	Y
3 ***Smith***	N	Y	N	N	Y	N	Y
NEVADA							
AL Santini	?	?	?	?	Y	N	Y
NEW HAMPSHIRE							
1 D'Amours	N	Y	N	N	Y	N	Y
2 ***Gregg***	N	Y	Y	N	Y	N	Y
NEW JERSEY							
1 Florio	N	Y	N	Y	Y	Y	Y
2 Hughes	N	Y	N	Y	Y	N	Y
3 Howard	N	Y	Y	Y	Y	N	Y
4 ***Smith***	N	Y	N	Y	Y	N	Y
5 ***Fenwick***	N	Y	Y	N	Y	N	Y
6 ***Forsythe***	?	?	?	?	?	?	?
7 ***Roukema***	N	Y	N	N	Y	N	Y
8 Roe	N	Y	Y	N	Y	N	Y
9 ***Hollenbeck***	N	Y	Y	N	Y	N	Y
10 Rodino	N	Y	N	N	Y	N	Y
11 Minish	N	Y	N	N	Y	N	Y
12 ***Rinaldo***	N	Y	N	N	Y	N	Y
13 ***Courter***	N	Y	Y	N	Y	N	Y
14 Guarini	?	Y	Y	Y	Y	N	Y
15 Dwyer	N	Y	N	Y	Y	N	Y
NEW MEXICO							
1 ***Lujan***	N	Y	Y	N	Y	N	Y
2 ***Skeen***	N	Y	N	Y	Y	N	Y
NEW YORK							
1 ***Carney***	N	N	N	Y	Y	N	Y
2 Downey	Y	Y	Y	N	Y	N	Y
3 ***Carman***	N	Y	N	Y	Y	N	Y
4 ***Lent***	N	Y	Y	N	Y	N	Y
5 ***McGrath***	N	Y	Y	N	Y	N	Y
6 ***LeBoutillier***	N	Y	Y	N	Y	N	Y
7 Addabbo	?	?	?	#	?	?	?
8 Rosenthal	N	Y	Y	Y	Y	N	Y
9 Ferraro	N	Y	Y	N	Y	N	Y
10 Biaggi	N	Y	Y	Y	Y	N	Y
11 Scheuer	N	Y	Y	Y	Y	N	Y
12 Chisholm	?	?	?	?	?	?	?
13 Solarz	N	Y	Y	Y	Y	N	Y
14 Vacancy							
15 Zeferetti	N	Y	Y	Y	Y	N	Y
16 Schumer	N	Y	N	N	Y	Y	Y
17 ***Molinari***	N	Y	Y	Y	Y	N	Y
18 ***Green***	N	N	Y	N	Y	N	Y
19 Rangel	N	Y	Y	N	Y	N	N
20 Weiss	?	?	?	?	?	?	?
21 Garcia	?	?	?	?	?	?	?
22 Bingham	N	Y	Y	Y	Y	N	Y
23 Peyser	N	Y	N	Y	Y	N	Y
24 Ottinger	N	Y	N	Y	Y	N	Y
25 ***Fish***	N	Y	N	Y	Y	N	Y
26 ***Gilman***	N	Y	N	Y	Y	N	Y
27 McHugh	N	Y	Y	N	Y	N	Y
28 Stratton	?	?	?	#	?	?	?
29 ***Solomon***	N	Y	N	Y	Y	N	Y
30 ***Martin***	N	Y	N	Y	Y	N	Y
31 ***Mitchell***	N	Y	Y	Y	Y	N	Y
32 ***Wortley***	N	Y	N	Y	Y	N	Y
33 ***Lee***	-	+	+	-	+	N	Y
34 ***Horton***	N	?	Y	Y	Y	N	Y
35 ***Conable***	Y	N	Y	N	Y	N	Y
36 LaFalce	Y	Y	Y	N	Y	N	Y
37 Nowak	Y	Y	Y	N	Y	N	Y
38 ***Kemp***	Y	Y	Y	N	Y	N	Y
39 Lundine	N	Y	Y	N	Y	N	Y
NORTH CAROLINA							
1 Jones	Y	Y	Y	Y	Y	N	Y
2 Fountain	N	N	Y	Y	Y	N	Y
3 Whitley	N	Y	Y	Y	Y	N	Y
4 Andrews	N	Y	Y	Y	Y	N	Y
5 Neal	N	Y	Y	Y	Y	N	Y
6 ***Johnston***	N	Y	Y	N	N	N	Y
7 Rose	?	?	?	Y	Y	N	Y
8 Hefner	N	Y	Y	N	Y	N	Y
9 ***Martin***	N	Y	Y	N	Y	N	Y
10 ***Broyhill***	N	Y	Y	N	N	N	Y
11 ***Hendon***	N	Y	Y	Y	Y	N	Y
NORTH DAKOTA							
AL Dorgan	N	N	N	N	Y	N	Y
OHIO							
1 ***Gradison***	N	N	Y	N	Y	Y	Y
2 Luken	N	Y	Y	N	Y	N	Y
3 Hall	Y	Y	N	Y	Y	N	Y
4 ***Oxley***	N	Y	Y	N	Y	N	Y
5 ***Latta***	N	Y	N	N	Y	N	Y
6 ***McEwen***	Y	N	N	Y	Y	N	Y
7 ***Brown***	?	?	?	?	?	?	?
8 ***Kindness***	N	N	N	N	Y	N	Y
9 ***Weber***	N	Y	Y	N	Y	N	Y
10 ***Miller***	N	Y	N	Y	Y	N	Y
11 ***Stanton***	?	?	?	?	?	?	?
12 Shamansky	Y	Y	Y	Y	Y	N	Y
13 Pease	Y	N	Y	N	Y	N	Y
14 Seiberling	N	Y	Y	Y	Y	Y	Y
15 ***Wylie***	N	Y	N	N	Y	N	Y
16 ***Regula***	N	N	N	Y	Y	N	Y
17 ***Ashbrook***	N	N	N	Y	N	N	N
18 Applegate	N	Y	N	N	Y	Y	Y
19 ***Williams***	N	Y	N	N	Y	N	Y
20 Oakar	N	Y	N	N	Y	N	Y
21 Stokes	Y	Y	Y	N	Y	N	Y
22 Eckart	N	Y	N	Y	Y	Y	Y
23 Mottl	Y	Y	N	N	Y	Y	Y
OKLAHOMA							
1 Jones	N	N	Y	N	Y	N	Y
2 Synar	N	Y	Y	Y	Y	Y	Y
3 Watkins	N	N	N	Y	Y	N	Y
4 McCurdy	N	Y	Y	Y	Y	N	Y
5 ***Edwards***	N	N	N	N	Y	N	Y
6 English	N	Y	Y	N	Y	N	Y
OREGON							
1 AuCoin	?	?	Y	Y	Y	N	Y
2 ***Smith***	N	Y	N	N	N	N	Y
3 Wyden	N	Y	Y	Y	Y	N	Y
4 Weaver	N	N	N	Y	Y	N	Y
PENNSYLVANIA							
1 Foglietta	N	Y	N	Y	Y	Y	Y
2 Gray	N	Y	Y	N	Y	N	Y
3 Smith	Y	Y	N	Y	Y	N	Y
4 ***Dougherty***	?	?	?	Y	Y	N	Y
5 ***Schulze***	Y	Y	Y	N	Y	N	Y
6 Yatron	N	Y	N	Y	Y	N	Y
7 Edgar	N	Y	Y	N	Y	N	Y
8 ***Coyne, J.***	N	Y	N	Y	Y	N	Y
9 ***Shuster***	N	Y	Y	N	Y	N	Y
10 ***McDade***	N	Y	Y	Y	Y	N	Y
11 ***Nelligan***	N	Y	Y	Y	Y	N	Y
12 Murtha	Y	Y	Y	Y	Y	N	Y
13 ***Coughlin***	N	Y	Y	N	Y	N	Y
14 Coyne, W.	Y	Y	Y	Y	Y	N	Y
15 ***Ritter***	N	Y	Y	N	Y	N	Y
16 ***Walker***	N	Y	Y	N	Y	N	Y
17 Ertel	?	?	?	?	?	?	?
18 Walgren	N	Y	Y	N	Y	Y	Y
19 ***Goodling***	Y	Y	Y	Y	Y	N	Y
20 Gaydos	Y	Y	N	Y	Y	Y	Y
21 Bailey	Y	Y	N	Y	Y	N	Y
22 Murphy	N	Y	N	Y	Y	N	Y
23 ***Clinger***	N	Y	Y	N	Y	N	Y
24 ***Marks***	N	N	Y	Y	Y	Y	N
25 ***Atkinson***	N	Y	N	Y	Y	N	Y
RHODE ISLAND							
1 St Germain	Y	Y	N	Y	Y	N	Y
2 ***Schneider***	N	Y	Y	Y	Y	+	+
SOUTH CAROLINA							
1 ***Hartnett***	N	Y	N	Y	N	N	Y
2 ***Spence***	N	Y	Y	Y	Y	N	Y
3 Derrick	N	Y	Y	N	Y	-	+
4 ***Campbell***	N	Y	Y	N	Y	N	Y
5 Holland	N	Y	Y	Y	Y	N	Y
6 ***Napier***	N	Y	Y	N	Y	Y	Y
SOUTH DAKOTA							
1 Daschle	?	?	?	Y	Y	N	Y
2 ***Roberts***	Y	Y	N	Y	Y	N	Y
TENNESSEE							
1 ***Quillen***	Y	N	Y	N	Y	N	Y
2 ***Duncan***	Y	Y	Y	Y	Y	N	Y
3 Bouquard	N	Y	Y	Y	Y	N	Y
4 Gore	N	Y	Y	Y	Y	N	Y
5 Boner	N	Y	N	Y	Y	N	Y
6 ***Beard***	N	Y	N	Y	Y	N	Y
7 Jones	N	Y	N	Y	Y	N	Y
8 Ford	Y	Y	Y	Y	Y	N	Y
TEXAS							
1 Hall, S.	N	N	Y	Y	Y	N	Y
2 Wilson	Y	Y	Y	Y	Y	N	Y
3 ***Collins***	?	?	?	?	?	?	?
4 Hall, R.	N	N	Y	Y	Y	N	Y
5 Mattox	?	?	?	?	?	?	?
6 Gramm	N	N	Y	N	N	N	Y
7 ***Archer***	Y	Y	Y	N	Y	N	Y
8 ***Fields***	N	Y	Y	N	Y	N	Y
9 Brooks	Y	N	Y	Y	Y	N	Y
10 Pickle	Y	Y	Y	Y	Y	N	Y
11 Leath	N	N	Y	Y	Y	N	Y
12 Wright	Y	N	Y	Y	Y	N	Y
13 Hightower	Y	Y	Y	Y	Y	N	Y
14 Patman	N	Y	Y	Y	Y	N	Y
15 de la Garza	N	N	Y	Y	Y	N	Y
16 White	Y	Y	Y	Y	Y	N	Y
17 Stenholm	N	N	Y	N	Y	N	Y
18 Leland	Y	Y	Y	N	Y	Y	N
19 Hance	Y	N	Y	Y	Y	N	Y
20 Gonzalez	P	?	P	Y	Y	Y	Y
21 ***Loeffler***	N	Y	Y	Y	Y	N	Y
22 ***Paul***	Y	Y	Y	Y	N	Y	N
23 Kazen	N	N	Y	Y	Y	N	Y
24 Frost	Y	N	Y	Y	Y	N	Y
UTAH							
1 ***Hansen***	N	Y	N	Y	N	N	Y
2 ***Marriott***	N	Y	N	N	Y	N	Y
VERMONT							
AL ***Jeffords***	N	Y	Y	N	Y	Y	Y
VIRGINIA							
1 ***Trible***	N	Y	Y	Y	Y	N	Y
2 ***Whitehurst***	N	Y	Y	Y	Y	N	Y
3 ***Bliley***	N	N	Y	Y	Y	N	Y
4 ***Daniel, R.***	N	Y	N	Y	Y	N	Y
5 Daniel, D.	N	N	Y	Y	Y	N	Y
6 ***Butler***	Y	Y	Y	Y	N	N	Y
7 ***Robinson***	N	N	Y	Y	Y	N	Y
8 ***Parris***	N	Y	Y	Y	Y	N	Y
9 ***Wampler***	Y	Y	Y	Y	Y	N	Y
10 ***Wolf***	N	Y	Y	N	Y	N	Y
WASHINGTON							
1 ***Pritchard***	N	Y	Y	Y	Y	N	Y
2 Swift	N	Y	N	Y	Y	N	Y
3 Bonker	N	Y	Y	Y	Y	N	Y
4 ***Morrison***	N	Y	Y	N	Y	N	Y
5 Foley	Y	Y	Y	Y	Y	N	Y
6 Dicks	N	Y	Y	Y	Y	N	Y
7 Lowry	N	N	Y	Y	Y	N	Y
WEST VIRGINIA							
1 Mollohan	N	Y	N	Y	Y	N	Y
2 ***Benedict***	Y	Y	N	Y	Y	N	Y
3 ***Staton***	?	?	?	?	?	?	?
4 Rahall	N	Y	Y	Y	Y	N	Y
WISCONSIN							
1 Aspin	N	Y	N	Y	Y	N	Y
2 Kastenmeier	N	Y	N	Y	Y	Y	Y
3 ***Gunderson***	N	N	N	Y	Y	N	Y
4 Zablocki	N	Y	N	Y	Y	N	Y
5 Reuss	Y	N	Y	Y	Y	Y	Y
6 ***Petri***	N	N	N	N	Y	Y	Y
7 Obey	N	Y	N	N	Y	Y	Y
8 ***Roth***	N	Y	N	N	Y	N	Y
9 ***Sensenbrenner***	N	N	N	N	Y	N	Y
WYOMING							
AL ***Cheney***	Y	Y	Y	N	Y	N	Y

Southern states - Ala., Ark., Fla., Ga., Ky., La., Miss., N.C., Okla., S.C., Tenn., Texas, Va.

KEY						334	335	336	337	338

KEY

Y Voted for (yea).
\# Paired for.
\+ Announced for.
N Voted against (nay).
X Paired against.
\- Announced against.
P Voted "present".
C Voted "present" to avoid possible conflict of interest.
? Did not vote or otherwise make a position known.

Democrats   *Republicans*

334. H J Res 599. Continuing Appropriations, Fiscal 1983. Adoption of the rule (H Res 596) providing for House floor consideration of the joint resolution to provide temporary funding for government agencies whose regular fiscal 1983 appropriations have not been enacted by Oct. 1. Adopted 280-120: R 87-91; D 193-29 (ND 123-24, SD 70-5), Sept. 22, 1982.

335. H J Res 599. Continuing Appropriations, Fiscal 1983. Conte, R-Mass., motion to recommit the joint resolution to the Appropriations Committee with instructions to change the expiration date from Feb. 28, 1983, to *sine die* adjournment of the 97th Congress. Motion rejected 188-215: R 168-13; D 20-202 (ND 14-134, SD 6-68), Sept. 22, 1982.

336. H J Res 599. Continuing Appropriations, Fiscal 1983. Passage of the joint resolution to provide temporary funding through Dec. 15 for government agencies whose regular fiscal 1983 appropriations have not been enacted by Oct. 1. Passed 242-161: R 89-92; D 153-69 (ND 96-52, SD 57-17), Sept. 22, 1982.

337. HR 6173. Health Planning Grants. Adoption of the rule (H Res 594) providing for House floor consideration of the bill to create a health planning block grant program and to authorize funds for fiscal 1983 and 1984 for the program. Adopted 380-7: R 169-5; D 211-2 (ND 138-1, SD 73-1), Sept. 22, 1982.

338. HR 6173. Health Planning Grants. Waxman, D-Calif., motion that the House resolve itself into the Committee of the Whole for consideration of the bill to create a health planning block grant program and to authorize funds for fiscal 1983 and 1984 for the program. Motion agreed to 346-11: R 158-9; D 188-2 (ND 121-1, SD 67-1), Sept. 22, 1982.

	334	335	336	337	338
ALABAMA					
1 *Edwards*	Y	Y	Y	Y	Y
2 Dickinson	N	Y	Y	Y	Y
3 Nichols	Y	N	Y	Y	Y
4 Bevill	Y	N	Y	Y	Y
5 Flippo	Y	N	Y	Y	Y
6 *Smith*	Y	N	Y	Y	Y
7 Shelby	Y	N	Y	Y	Y
ALASKA					
AL *Young*	?	?	?	?	?
ARIZONA					
1 *Rhodes*	Y	Y	Y	Y	?
2 Udall	Y	N	Y	?	?
3 Stump	N	Y	N	Y	Y
4 *Rudd*	Y	Y	Y	Y	Y
ARKANSAS					
1 Alexander	Y	N	Y	Y	Y
2 *Bethune*	N	Y	Y	Y	Y
3 *Hammerschmidt*	N	Y	Y	Y	Y
4 Anthony	Y	N	Y	Y	Y
CALIFORNIA					
1 *Chappie*	Y	Y	N	Y	Y
2 *Clausen*	N	Y	N	Y	Y
3 Matsui	Y	N	N	Y	Y
4 Fazio	Y	N	Y	Y	Y
5 Burton, J.	?	?	?	?	?
6 Burton, P.	?	?	?	?	?
7 Miller	N	N	N	?	Y
8 Dellums	N	N	N	Y	Y
9 Stark	N	N	Y	Y	Y
10 Edwards	Y	N	N	Y	Y
11 Lantos	Y	N	Y	Y	Y
12 *McCloskey*	N	Y	N	?	?
13 Mineta	Y	N	Y	Y	Y
14 *Shumway*	N	Y	N	Y	Y
15 Coelho	Y	N	Y	Y	Y
16 Panetta	Y	N	Y	Y	Y
17 *Pashayan*	N	Y	N	Y	Y
18 *Thomas*	Y	Y	N	Y	Y
19 *Lagomarsino*	N	Y	N	Y	Y
20 *Goldwater*	Y	Y	N	Y	?
21 *Fiedler*	Y	Y	Y	Y	N
22 *Moorhead*	N	Y	N	Y	Y
23 Beilenson	Y	N	Y	Y	Y
24 Waxman	Y	N	Y	Y	Y
25 Roybal	Y	N	Y	Y	Y
26 *Rousselot*	?	?	?	?	?
27 *Dornan*	Y	Y	N	Y	Y
28 Dixon	Y	N	Y	Y	Y
29 Hawkins	Y	N	Y	Y	Y
30 Martinez	Y	N	Y	Y	Y
31 Dymally	Y	N	Y	Y	Y
32 Anderson	Y	N	N	Y	Y
33 *Grisham*	?	?	?	?	?
34 *Lungren*	N	Y	N	Y	Y
35 *Dreier*	N	Y	N	Y	Y
36 Brown	Y	N	Y	Y	?
37 *Lewis*	Y	Y	N	Y	Y
38 Patterson	Y	Y	Y	Y	Y
39 *Dannemeyer*	N	Y	N	N	Y
40 *Badham*	N	Y	N	Y	Y
41 *Lowery*	N	Y	Y	Y	Y
42 *Hunter*	N	Y	N	Y	Y
43 *Burgener*	Y	Y	Y	Y	?
COLORADO					
1 Schroeder	N	N	N	Y	Y
2 Wirth	Y	N	Y	Y	Y
3 Kogovsek	Y	N	Y	Y	Y
4 *Brown*	N	Y	N	Y	Y

	334	335	336	337	338
5 *Kramer*	N	Y	Y	Y	Y
CONNECTICUT					
1 Kennelly	Y	N	Y	Y	Y
2 Gejdenson	Y	N	Y	Y	Y
3 *DeNardis*	N	N	Y	Y	?
4 *McKinney*	Y	Y	N	Y	Y
5 Ratchford	Y	N	Y	Y	Y
6 Moffett	?	?	?	?	?
DELAWARE					
AL *Evans*	N	Y	Y	Y	Y
FLORIDA					
1 Hutto	Y	N	Y	Y	Y
2 Fuqua	Y	N	Y	Y	?
3 Bennett	Y	N	Y	Y	Y
4 Chappell	?	?	?	?	?
5 *McCollum*	N	Y	N	Y	Y
6 *Young*	Y	Y	Y	Y	Y
7 Gibbons	Y	N	Y	Y	?
8 Ireland	Y	?	?	Y	Y
9 Nelson	Y	N	Y	Y	Y
10 *Bafalis*	?	?	?	?	?
11 Mica	Y	N	Y	Y	Y
12 *Shaw*	Y	Y	Y	Y	Y
13 Lehman	Y	N	Y	Y	Y
14 Pepper	Y	N	Y	Y	Y
15 Fascell	Y	N	N	Y	?
GEORGIA					
1 Ginn	Y	N	Y	Y	Y
2 Hatcher	Y	N	Y	Y	Y
3 Brinkley	Y	N	Y	Y	Y
4 Levitas	Y	N	N	Y	Y
5 Fowler	Y	N	Y	Y	Y
6 *Gingrich*	N	Y	N	Y	Y
7 McDonald	N	Y	N	N	N
8 Evans	?	?	?	?	?
9 Jenkins	Y	?	Y	Y	Y
10 Barnard	Y	N	Y	Y	Y
HAWAII					
1 Heftel	Y	N	Y	Y	Y
2 Akaka	Y	N	Y	Y	Y
IDAHO					
1 *Craig*	N	Y	N	Y	?
2 *Hansen*	Y	Y	N	Y	Y
ILLINOIS					
1 Washington	?	?	?	?	?
2 Savage	N	N	N	Y	?
3 Russo	Y	N	Y	Y	Y
4 *Derwinski*	?	?	?	?	?
5 Fary	Y	N	Y	Y	Y
6 *Hyde*	N	Y	N	Y	Y
7 Collins	Y	N	Y	Y	Y
8 Rostenkowski	Y	N	Y	Y	Y
9 Yates	Y	N	Y	Y	Y
10 *Porter*	N	Y	N	Y	Y
11 Annunzio	Y	N	Y	Y	Y
12 *Crane, P.*	N	Y	N	Y	Y
13 *McClory*	N	Y	N	Y	N
14 *Erlenborn*	Y	Y	Y	Y	Y
15 *Corcoran*	N	Y	N	Y	Y
16 *Martin*	N	Y	N	Y	Y
17 O'Brien	Y	Y	Y	Y	Y
18 *Michel*	Y	Y	Y	Y	Y
19 *Railsback*	N	Y	N	Y	Y
20 *Findley*	N	Y	N	Y	Y
21 *Madigan*	N	Y	N	Y	N
22 *Crane, D.*	N	Y	N	Y	Y
23 Price	Y	N	Y	Y	Y
24 Simon	Y	N	Y	Y	Y
INDIANA					
1 Vacancy					
2 Fithian	?	?	?	?	?
3 *Hiler*	N	Y	N	Y	N
4 *Coats*	N	Y	N	Y	Y
5 *Hillis*	Y	Y	Y	Y	?
6 Evans	Y	N	Y	Y	Y
7 *Myers*	Y	Y	Y	Y	Y
8 *Deckard*	N	Y	Y	?	?
9 Hamilton	N	N	N	Y	Y
10 Sharp	N	Y	N	Y	Y
11 Jacobs	N	N	N	Y	Y
IOWA					
1 *Leach*	Y	Y	N	Y	Y
2 *Tauke*	N	N	N	Y	Y
3 *Evans*	N	Y	N	Y	Y
4 Smith	Y	N	Y	Y	Y
5 Harkin	N	N	N	Y	Y
6 Bedell	N	N	N	Y	Y

ND - Northern Democrats   SD - Southern Democrats

Member	334	335	336	337	338
KANSAS					
1 Roberts	N	Y	Y	Y	Y
2 Jeffries	N	Y	N	Y	?
3 Winn	Y	Y	Y	Y	Y
4 Glickman	Y	Y	Y	Y	Y
5 Whittaker	Y	Y	Y	Y	Y
KENTUCKY					
1 Hubbard	Y	N	N	Y	Y
2 Natcher	Y	N	Y	Y	Y
3 Mazzoli	Y	N	Y	Y	Y
4 Snyder	N	Y	N	Y	Y
5 Rogers	Y	Y	Y	Y	Y
6 Hopkins	N	Y	Y	Y	Y
7 Perkins	Y	N	Y	Y	Y
LOUISIANA					
1 Livingston	Y	Y	Y	N	Y
2 Boggs	Y	N	Y	Y	Y
3 Tauzin	Y	N	N	Y	Y
4 Roemer	N	Y	N	Y	Y
5 Huckaby	Y	N	Y	Y	Y
6 Moore	N	Y	Y	Y	Y
7 Breaux	Y	N	Y	Y	Y
8 Long	Y	N	Y	Y	Y
MAINE					
1 Emery	N	Y	N	Y	Y
2 Snowe	Y	Y	N	Y	Y
MARYLAND					
1 Dyson	Y	Y	Y	Y	?
2 Long	Y	N	Y	Y	Y
3 Mikulski	Y	N	Y	Y	Y
4 Holt	Y	Y	Y	Y	N
5 Hoyer	Y	N	Y	Y	?
6 Byron	Y	N	Y	Y	Y
7 Mitchell	N	N	N	?	Y
8 Barnes	Y	Y	Y	Y	Y
MASSACHUSETTS					
1 Conte	Y	Y	N	Y	Y
2 Boland	Y	N	Y	Y	Y
3 Early	Y	N	Y	Y	Y
4 Frank	N	N	N	Y	Y
5 Shannon	Y	N	Y	Y	Y
6 Mavroules	Y	N	Y	Y	?
7 Markey	N	N	N	Y	?
8 O'Neill					
9 Moakley	Y	N	N	Y	Y
10 Heckler	N	Y	N	Y	Y
11 Donnelly	Y	N	Y	Y	Y
12 Studds	Y	N	N	Y	Y
MICHIGAN					
1 Conyers	N	N	N	Y	?
2 Pursell	Y	Y	Y	?	?
3 Wolpe	Y	N	N	Y	Y
4 Siljander	N	Y	Y	Y	Y
5 Sawyer	N	Y	Y	Y	Y
6 Dunn	N	Y	Y	Y	Y
7 Kildee	N	N	N	Y	Y
8 Traxler	Y	N	Y	Y	Y
9 Vander Jagt	Y	Y	Y	Y	Y
10 Albosta	Y	N	Y	Y	Y
11 Davis	Y	N	Y	Y	Y
12 Bonior	Y	N	N	Y	Y
13 Crockett	Y	N	N	Y	?
14 Hertel	Y	N	N	Y	?
15 Ford	Y	N	Y	?	Y
16 Dingell	Y	N	Y	Y	Y
17 Brodhead	Y	N	Y	Y	?
18 Blanchard	?	?	?	?	?
19 Broomfield	N	Y	N	Y	Y
MINNESOTA					
1 Erdahl	N	N	Y	N	Y
2 Hagedorn	N	N	Y	N	Y
3 Frenzel	N	Y	N	N	Y
4 Vento	Y	N	Y	Y	Y
5 Sabo	Y	N	N	Y	?
6 Weber	N	Y	N	N	N
7 Stangeland	Y	Y	Y	Y	N
8 Oberstar	Y	N	Y	Y	Y
MISSISSIPPI					
1 Whitten	Y	N	Y	Y	Y
2 Bowen	?	?	?	?	?
3 Montgomery	Y	N	Y	Y	Y
4 Dowdy	Y	N	Y	Y	Y
5 Lott	Y	Y	Y	Y	Y
MISSOURI					
1 Clay	Y	N	Y	N	N
2 Young	Y	N	Y	Y	Y
3 Gephardt	Y	N	N	Y	Y
4 Skelton	Y	Y	Y	Y	Y
5 Bolling	?	N	?	?	?
6 Coleman	Y	Y	Y	Y	Y
7 Taylor	N	Y	N	Y	Y
8 Bailey	N	Y	N	Y	Y
9 Volkmer	Y	N	N	Y	Y
10 Emerson	N	Y	N	Y	N
MONTANA					
1 Williams	?	N	N	?	?
2 Marlenee	Y	Y	N	Y	Y
NEBRASKA					
1 Bereuter	N	N	N	Y	Y
2 Daub	N	Y	Y	Y	Y
3 Smith	Y	Y	Y	Y	Y
NEVADA					
AL Santini	Y	N	Y	Y	Y
NEW HAMPSHIRE					
1 D'Amours	Y	N	Y	Y	Y
2 Gregg	N	Y	N	Y	Y
NEW JERSEY					
1 Florio	Y	N	Y	Y	Y
2 Hughes	Y	N	N	Y	Y
3 Howard	Y	N	Y	Y	Y
4 Smith	Y	Y	Y	Y	Y
5 Fenwick	Y	Y	N	Y	Y
6 Forsythe	?	?	?	?	?
7 Roukema	Y	Y	Y	Y	Y
8 Roe	Y	N	Y	Y	Y
9 Hollenbeck	Y	N	Y	Y	Y
10 Rodino	Y	N	N	Y	Y
11 Minish	Y	N	Y	Y	Y
12 Rinaldo	Y	N	Y	Y	Y
13 Courter	Y	N	Y	Y	Y
14 Guarini	Y	N	Y	Y	Y
15 Dwyer	Y	N	Y	Y	Y
NEW MEXICO					
1 Lujan	Y	Y	Y	Y	Y
2 Skeen	Y	Y	Y	Y	Y
NEW YORK					
1 Carney	Y	Y	Y	Y	Y
2 Downey	Y	N	N	Y	?
3 Carman	Y	Y	N	Y	Y
4 Lent	Y	Y	N	Y	Y
5 McGrath	Y	Y	N	Y	Y
6 LeBoutillier	Y	Y	N	Y	Y
7 Addabbo	?	?	?	?	?
8 Rosenthal	Y	N	Y	Y	?
9 Ferraro	Y	N	Y	Y	Y
10 Biaggi	Y	N	Y	Y	Y
11 Scheuer	Y	N	Y	Y	Y
12 Chisholm	?	?	?	?	?
13 Solarz	Y	N	Y	Y	Y
14 Vacancy					
15 Zeferetti	Y	N	Y	Y	?
16 Schumer	Y	N	Y	Y	Y
17 Molinari	N	Y	Y	Y	Y
18 Green	N	Y	N	Y	Y
19 Rangel	Y	N	N	Y	Y
20 Weiss	?	?	?	?	?
21 Garcia	?	?	?	?	?
22 Bingham	Y	P	Y	Y	Y
23 Peyser	Y	N	Y	Y	Y
24 Ottinger	Y	Y	Y	Y	Y
25 Fish	N	Y	N	Y	Y
26 Gilman	N	Y	N	Y	Y
27 McHugh	Y	N	Y	?	?
28 Stratton	?	?	?	?	?
29 Solomon	N	Y	N	Y	Y
30 Martin	N	Y	N	Y	Y
31 Mitchell	Y	Y	Y	Y	Y
32 Wortley	N	Y	Y	Y	Y
33 Lee	N	Y	Y	+	?
34 Horton	?	Y	N	Y	?
35 Conable	Y	N	Y	Y	Y
36 LaFalce	N	Y	Y	Y	Y
37 Nowak	N	Y	Y	Y	Y
38 Kemp	Y	Y	Y	Y	Y
39 Lundine	N	N	Y	Y	Y
NORTH CAROLINA					
1 Jones	Y	Y	Y	Y	Y
2 Fountain	Y	N	N	Y	Y
3 Whitley	Y	N	Y	Y	Y
4 Andrews	Y	N	Y	Y	Y
5 Neal	Y	N	Y	Y	Y
6 Johnston	?	Y	N	Y	Y
7 Rose	Y	N	Y	Y	?
8 Hefner	Y	N	Y	Y	Y
9 Martin	Y	Y	N	?	Y
10 Broyhill	Y	Y	Y	Y	Y
11 Hendon	N	Y	N	Y	Y
NORTH DAKOTA					
AL Dorgan	Y	N	Y	Y	Y
OHIO					
1 Gradison	N	Y	Y	Y	Y
2 Luken	Y	N	Y	Y	Y
3 Hall	Y	N	Y	Y	?
4 Oxley	Y	Y	N	Y	Y
5 Latta	Y	Y	N	Y	Y
6 McEwen	N	Y	Y	Y	Y
7 Brown	?	?	?	?	?
8 Kindness	N	Y	N	Y	Y
9 Weber	Y	Y	N	Y	Y
10 Miller	Y	Y	Y	Y	Y
11 Stanton	?	?	?	?	?
12 Shamansky	Y	N	Y	Y	Y
13 Pease	Y	N	N	Y	Y
14 Seiberling	Y	N	Y	?	Y
15 Wylie	N	Y	N	Y	Y
16 Regula	Y	Y	Y	Y	Y
17 Ashbrook	N	Y	N	Y	N
18 Applegate	Y	N	Y	Y	?
19 Williams	Y	N	Y	Y	Y
20 Oakar	Y	Y	N	Y	Y
21 Stokes	Y	N	Y	Y	Y
22 Eckart	N	N	N	Y	Y
23 Mottl	Y	N	N	Y	Y
OKLAHOMA					
1 Jones	Y	N	Y	Y	Y
2 Synar	Y	N	Y	?	?
3 Watkins	Y	N	Y	Y	Y
4 McCurdy	Y	N	N	Y	Y
5 Edwards	N	Y	N	Y	Y
6 English	Y	N	N	Y	Y
OREGON					
1 AuCoin	Y	N	N	Y	Y
2 Smith	N	Y	N	Y	Y
3 Wyden	Y	N	Y	Y	Y
4 Weaver	Y	N	N	?	Y
PENNSYLVANIA					
1 Foglietta	Y	N	Y	Y	Y
2 Gray	Y	N	N	Y	Y
3 Smith	Y	N	Y	?	Y
4 Dougherty	Y	N	Y	Y	Y
5 Schulze	N	N	N	Y	Y
6 Yatron	Y	N	Y	Y	Y
7 Edgar	N	Y	N	Y	Y
8 Coyne, J.	N	Y	N	Y	Y
9 Shuster	N	Y	N	Y	Y
10 McDade	Y	Y	Y	Y	Y
11 Nelligan	Y	Y	Y	Y	Y
12 Murtha	Y	N	Y	Y	?
13 Coughlin	N	Y	N	Y	Y
14 Coyne, W.	Y	N	Y	Y	Y
15 Ritter	Y	Y	Y	Y	Y
16 Walker	N	Y	N	Y	N
17 Ertel	?	?	?	?	?
18 Walgren	Y	Y	Y	Y	Y
19 Goodling	N	Y	N	Y	Y
20 Gaydos	Y	N	Y	Y	Y
21 Bailey	Y	N	Y	Y	Y
22 Murphy	Y	N	Y	Y	Y
23 Clinger	Y	Y	Y	Y	Y
24 Marks	Y	Y	Y	?	?
25 Atkinson	Y	Y	N	Y	Y
RHODE ISLAND					
1 St Germain	Y	N	Y	Y	Y
2 Schneider	-	Y	Y	Y	Y
SOUTH CAROLINA					
1 Hartnett	N	Y	N	Y	Y
2 Spence	Y	Y	Y	Y	Y
3 Derrick	Y	Y	Y	Y	Y
4 Campbell	Y	Y	Y	Y	Y
5 Holland	Y	N	Y	Y	Y
6 Napier	Y	Y	Y	Y	Y
SOUTH DAKOTA					
1 Daschle	Y	N	Y	Y	Y
2 Roberts	Y	Y	Y	Y	Y
TENNESSEE					
1 Quillen	Y	Y	Y	Y	Y
2 Duncan	Y	N	Y	Y	Y
3 Bouquard	Y	N	Y	Y	Y
4 Gore	Y	N	Y	Y	Y
5 Boner	Y	N	Y	Y	Y
6 Beard	Y	Y	Y	Y	Y
7 Jones	Y	N	Y	Y	Y
8 Ford	Y	N	N	Y	Y
TEXAS					
1 Hall, S.	Y	N	N	Y	Y
2 Wilson	Y	N	Y	Y	Y
3 Collins	?	?	?	?	?
4 Hall, R.	Y	N	N	Y	Y
5 Mattox	?	?	?	?	?
6 Gramm	N	Y	N	Y	Y
7 Archer	N	N	N	Y	Y
8 Fields	Y	Y	N	Y	Y
9 Brooks	Y	N	Y	Y	Y
10 Pickle	N	Y	N	Y	Y
11 Leath	Y	N	Y	Y	Y
12 Wright	Y	N	Y	Y	Y
13 Hightower	Y	N	Y	Y	Y
14 Patman	Y	N	Y	Y	Y
15 de la Garza	Y	N	Y	Y	Y
16 White	Y	N	Y	Y	Y
17 Stenholm	N	N	N	Y	Y
18 Leland	Y	N	N	Y	Y
19 Hance	Y	N	Y	Y	Y
20 Gonzalez	Y	N	Y	Y	Y
21 Loeffler	Y	Y	Y	Y	Y
22 Paul	N	Y	N	Y	Y
23 Kazen	Y	N	Y	Y	Y
24 Frost	Y	N	Y	Y	Y
UTAH					
1 Hansen	Y	Y	N	Y	Y
2 Marriott	Y	Y	Y	Y	Y
VERMONT					
AL Jeffords	N	Y	N	?	Y
VIRGINIA					
1 Trible	Y	Y	Y	Y	Y
2 Whitehurst	Y	Y	Y	Y	Y
3 Bliley	Y	Y	Y	Y	Y
4 Daniel, R.	Y	Y	Y	Y	Y
5 Daniel, D.	Y	N	N	Y	?
6 Butler	Y	Y	Y	Y	Y
7 Robinson	Y	Y	Y	Y	Y
8 Parris	Y	Y	Y	Y	Y
9 Wampler	N	Y	Y	Y	Y
10 Wolf	N	Y	Y	Y	Y
WASHINGTON					
1 Pritchard	N	Y	N	Y	Y
2 Swift	Y	N	Y	Y	Y
3 Bonker	Y	N	Y	Y	Y
4 Morrison	Y	Y	N	Y	Y
5 Foley	Y	N	Y	Y	Y
6 Dicks	Y	N	Y	Y	?
7 Lowry	N	N	N	Y	Y
WEST VIRGINIA					
1 Mollohan	Y	N	Y	Y	Y
2 Benedict	?	?	?	?	?
3 Staton	?	?	?	Y	Y
4 Rahall	N	N	N	Y	?
WISCONSIN					
1 Aspin	Y	N	Y	Y	Y
2 Kastenmeier	Y	N	N	Y	Y
3 Gunderson	N	Y	N	Y	Y
4 Zablocki	Y	N	Y	Y	Y
5 Reuss	Y	N	Y	?	Y
6 Petri	N	Y	N	Y	Y
7 Obey	N	N	N	Y	Y
8 Roth	N	Y	N	Y	Y
9 Sensenbrenner	N	Y	N	Y	Y
WYOMING					
AL Cheney	Y	Y	Y	Y	Y

Southern states - Ala., Ark., Fla., Ga., Ky., La., Miss., N.C., Okla., S.C., Tenn., Texas, Va.

339. Procedural Motion. Bliley, R-Va., motion to approve the House *Journal* of Wednesday, Sept. 22. Motion agreed to 332-32: R 147-19; D 185-13 (ND 119-12, SD 66-1), Sept. 23, 1982.

340. HR 5447. Futures Trading Act of 1982. Adoption of the rule (H Res 566) providing for House floor consideration of the bill to authorize funds for the Commodity Futures Trading Commission through Sept. 30, 1986, to affirm a jurisdictional agreement between the commission and the Securities and Exchange Commission, and to make other changes in commodities law. Adopted 387-0: R 175-0; D 212-0 (ND 143-0, SD 69-0), Sept. 23, 1982.

341. HR 6156. Securities and Exchange Commission Jurisdiction. Adoption of the rule (H Res 565) providing for House floor consideration of the bill to revise federal securities laws to affirm a jurisdictional agreement between the Securities and Exchange Commission and the Commodity Futures Trading Commission. Adopted 387-0: R 171-0; D 216-0 (ND 146-0, SD 70-0), Sept. 23, 1982.

342. HR 5447. Futures Trading Act of 1982. Conable, R-N.Y., amendment to provide for fees on futures and options transactions, and to authorize the Commodity Futures Trading Commission to reduce or suspend the fees in certain circumstances. Rejected 170-216: R 99-78; D 71-138 (ND 66-74, SD 5-64), Sept. 23, 1982. A "yea" was a vote supporting the president's position.

343. HR 5447. Futures Trading Act of 1982. Passage of the bill to authorize funds as needed for the Commodity Futures Trading Commission through Sept. 30, 1986, to affirm a jurisdictional agreement between the commission and the Securities and Exchange Commission, and to make other changes in commodities law. Passed 319-59: R 124-50; D 195-9 (ND 131-5, SD 64-4), Sept. 23, 1982. A "nay" was a vote supporting the president's position.

344. HR 5540. Defense Industrial Base Revitalization Act. Blanchard, D-Mich., motion that the House resolve itself into the Committee of the Whole for consideration of the bill to authorize a total of $6.75 billion in economic and educational aid to improve defense-related industries. Motion agreed to 298-51: R 118-47; D 180-4 (ND 119-1, SD 61-3), Sept. 23, 1982.

345. HR 5540. Defense Industrial Base Revitalization Act. Erlenborn, R-Ill., amendment to strike the provision extending the wage requirements of the Davis-Bacon Act to programs established by the bill. Rejected 162-189: R 126-37; D 36-152 (ND 3-119, SD 33-33), Sept. 23, 1982.

346. HR 5540. Defense Industrial Base Revitalization Act. McCollum, R-Fla., amendment to prohibit loans or loan guarantees under the bill if the Treasury Department determined that they would lead to higher interest rates or harm the thrift industry. Adopted 173-154: R 135-16; D 38-138 (ND 8-108, SD 30-30), Sept. 23, 1982.

KEY

Y Voted for (yea).
\# Paired for.
\+ Announced for.
N Voted against (nay).
X Paired against.
- Announced against.
P Voted "present".
C Voted "present" to avoid possible conflict of interest.
? Did not vote or otherwise make a position known.

Democrats   *Republicans*

	339	340	341	342	343	344	345	346
ALABAMA								
1 *Edwards*	Y	Y	?	Y	Y	Y	Y	Y
2 *Dickinson*	N	?	Y	Y	N	N	?	?
3 Nichols	Y	Y	Y	N	Y	Y	N	N
4 Bevill	Y	Y	Y	N	Y	Y	N	N
5 Flippo	Y	Y	Y	N	Y	Y	N	N
6 *Smith*	Y	Y	Y	N	N	Y	Y	Y
7 Shelby	Y	Y	Y	N	Y	N	Y	N
ALASKA								
AL *Young*	Y	Y	Y	N	Y	N	N	Y
ARIZONA								
1 *Rhodes*	?	?	?	?	?	?	?	?
2 Udall	Y	Y	Y	Y	?	Y	N	N
3 Stump	Y	Y	Y	Y	N	N	Y	Y
4 *Rudd*	Y	Y	Y	Y	N	N	Y	Y
ARKANSAS								
1 Alexander	Y	Y	Y	N	Y	N	Y	N
2 *Bethune*	Y	Y	Y	N	Y	N	Y	Y
3 *Hammerschmidt*	Y	Y	Y	N	Y	N	Y	Y
4 Anthony	Y	Y	Y	N	Y	Y	Y	Y
CALIFORNIA								
1 *Chappie*	Y	Y	Y	N	Y	Y	Y	Y
2 *Clausen*	Y	Y	Y	Y	Y	Y	N	Y
3 Matsui	Y	Y	N	Y	Y	N	N	N
4 Fazio	Y	Y	N	Y	N	Y	N	N
5 Burton, J.	?	?	?	?	?	?	?	?
6 Burton, P.	?	?	?	?	?	?	X	?
7 Miller	Y	Y	Y	Y	Y	Y	N	N
8 Dellums	Y	Y	Y	N	Y	N	N	N
9 Stark	?	Y	Y	?	Y	?	N	N
10 Edwards	Y	Y	Y	Y	Y	Y	N	N
11 Lantos	Y	Y	Y	N	Y	N	N	N
12 *McCloskey*	?	Y	Y	Y	N	?	Y	?
13 Mineta	Y	Y	Y	N	Y	N	N	N
14 *Shumway*	Y	Y	Y	N	N	Y	N	Y
15 Coelho	Y	Y	Y	N	?	?	?	?
16 Panetta	Y	Y	Y	N	Y	Y	N	N
17 *Pashayan*	Y	Y	Y	N	Y	Y	N	Y
18 *Thomas*	Y	Y	Y	N	Y	Y	Y	Y
19 *Lagomarsino*	Y	Y	Y	Y	N	Y	Y	Y
20 *Goldwater*	?	?	Y	Y	Y	?	Y	Y
21 *Fiedler*	?	Y	Y	Y	Y	Y	Y	Y
22 *Moorhead*	Y	Y	Y	N	Y	Y	Y	Y
23 Beilenson	Y	Y	Y	Y	Y	?	?	?
24 Waxman	Y	Y	Y	Y	Y	Y	N	N
25 Roybal	Y	Y	Y	N	Y	N	N	N
26 *Rousselot*	?	?	?	?	?	?	?	?
27 *Dornan*	Y	Y	Y	?	N	Y	Y	Y
28 Dixon	?	Y	Y	Y	Y	Y	N	?
29 Hawkins	N	Y	Y	Y	Y	Y	N	?
30 Martinez	Y	Y	Y	N	Y	Y	N	N
31 Dymally	Y	Y	Y	N	Y	Y	N	N
32 Anderson	Y	Y	Y	Y	Y	?	N	N
33 *Grisham*	Y	Y	Y	Y	?	?	?	?
34 Lungren	Y	Y	Y	N	N	N	Y	Y
35 *Dreier*	Y	Y	Y	N	N	N	?	?
36 Brown	Y	Y	Y	N	Y	Y	?	?
37 *Lewis*	Y	Y	Y	N	Y	Y	Y	Y
38 Patterson	Y	Y	Y	N	Y	Y	N	N
39 *Dannemeyer*	Y	Y	Y	N	?	Y	Y	Y
40 *Badham*	?	?	?	?	?	?	?	?
41 *Lowery*	Y	Y	Y	N	Y	Y	Y	Y
42 *Hunter*	Y	Y	Y	N	Y	Y	Y	Y
43 *Burgener*	Y	Y	Y	?	?	?	#	?
COLORADO								
1 Schroeder	N	Y	Y	N	Y	N	Y	?
2 Wirth	Y	Y	Y	N	Y	?	N	N
3 Kogovsek	Y	Y	Y	N	Y	Y	N	N
4 *Brown*	N	Y	Y	N	N	N	N	Y

	339	340	341	342	343	344	345	346
5 *Kramer*	Y	Y	Y	N	N	Y	Y	Y
CONNECTICUT								
1 Kennelly	Y	Y	Y	N	Y	Y	N	N
2 Gejdenson	N	Y	Y	Y	Y	Y	N	N
3 *DeNardis*	Y	Y	?	Y	Y	?	N	Y
4 *McKinney*	?	Y	Y	Y	Y	Y	N	N
5 Ratchford	Y	Y	Y	N	?	?	?	?
6 Moffett	?	?	?	?	?	?	?	?
DELAWARE								
AL *Evans*	Y	Y	Y	N	Y	Y	Y	Y
FLORIDA								
1 Hutto	Y	Y	Y	N	Y	Y	Y	Y
2 Fuqua	Y	Y	Y	N	Y	Y	N	Y
3 Bennett	Y	Y	Y	Y	Y	Y	N	Y
4 Chappell	?	?	?	?	?	?	?	?
5 *McCollum*	Y	Y	Y	N	N	N	Y	Y
6 *Young*	Y	Y	Y	N	Y	N	Y	Y
7 Gibbons	Y	Y	Y	Y	?	Y	?	?
8 Ireland	?	?	?	?	?	?	?	?
9 Nelson	Y	Y	Y	N	Y	Y	N	N
10 *Bafalis*	?	?	?	?	?	?	?	?
11 Mica	Y	Y	Y	N	Y	Y	N	N
12 *Shaw*	Y	Y	Y	N	N	Y	N	Y
13 Lehman	Y	Y	Y	?	?	?	?	?
14 Pepper	Y	Y	Y	N	Y	Y	N	N
15 Fascell	?	?	?	?	?	?	?	?
GEORGIA								
1 Ginn	Y	Y	Y	N	Y	Y	N	N
2 Hatcher	Y	Y	Y	N	Y	Y	N	N
3 Brinkley	Y	Y	Y	N	Y	Y	N	N
4 Levitas	Y	Y	Y	Y	Y	Y	N	Y
5 Fowler	?	?	N	Y	Y	N	Y	N
6 *Gingrich*	?	?	Y	Y	N	Y	Y	Y
7 McDonald	Y	Y	N	N	N	Y	Y	Y
8 Evans	?	?	?	?	?	?	?	?
9 Jenkins	Y	Y	N	N	Y	Y	Y	Y
10 Barnard	Y	Y	Y	?	?	?	?	?
HAWAII								
1 Heftel	Y	Y	Y	N	?	?	?	?
2 Akaka	Y	Y	Y	N	Y	N	N	N
IDAHO								
1 *Craig*	Y	Y	Y	N	Y	N	?	?
2 *Hansen*	Y	Y	Y	N	N	N	Y	Y
ILLINOIS								
1 Washington	N	Y	Y	N	Y	Y	N	N
2 Savage	?	?	?	?	?	?	?	?
3 Russo	Y	Y	Y	N	Y	Y	N	N
4 *Derwinski*	N	Y	Y	Y	?	?	?	?
5 Fary	Y	Y	Y	N	Y	Y	N	N
6 *Hyde*	?	Y	Y	N	Y	Y	Y	Y
7 Collins	Y	Y	Y	?	?	?	?	?
8 Rostenkowski	Y	Y	Y	N	Y	Y	N	N
9 Yates	Y	Y	Y	?	?	?	?	?
10 *Porter*	Y	Y	Y	N	Y	N	?	?
11 Annunzio	Y	Y	Y	N	Y	Y	N	N
12 *Crane, P.*	Y	Y	N	Y	N	N	Y	Y
13 *McClory*	Y	Y	Y	Y	Y	Y	Y	Y
14 *Erlenborn*	Y	Y	Y	N	Y	Y	Y	Y
15 *Corcoran*	Y	Y	N	Y	Y	Y	Y	Y
16 *Martin*	Y	Y	Y	N	Y	Y	Y	Y
17 *O'Brien*	Y	Y	Y	?	?	?	?	?
18 *Michel*	Y	Y	Y	N	Y	Y	N	N
19 *Railsback*	Y	Y	Y	N	Y	Y	Y	?
20 *Findley*	Y	Y	Y	N	N	Y	N	N
21 *Madigan*	Y	Y	Y	N	Y	Y	Y	Y
22 *Crane, D.*	Y	Y	Y	N	Y	Y	Y	Y
23 Price	Y	Y	Y	N	Y	Y	N	N
24 Simon	Y	Y	Y	N	Y	Y	N	?
INDIANA								
1 Vacancy								
2 Fithian	?	?	?	?	?	?	?	?
3 *Hiler*	N	Y	Y	N	N	N	Y	Y
4 *Coats*	N	Y	Y	N	N	Y	Y	Y
5 Hillis	Y	Y	Y	N	Y	N	N	Y
6 Evans	Y	Y	Y	N	Y	Y	N	N
7 *Myers*	Y	Y	Y	N	Y	Y	N	Y
8 *Deckard*	?	?	?	?	Y	Y	Y	?
9 Hamilton	Y	Y	Y	Y	Y	Y	N	Y
10 Sharp	Y	Y	Y	Y	Y	Y	N	Y
11 Jacobs	N	Y	Y	N	Y	N	Y	Y
IOWA								
1 *Leach*	Y	Y	Y	Y	Y	Y	Y	Y
2 *Tauke*	Y	Y	Y	N	Y	N	Y	Y
3 *Evans*	N	Y	Y	Y	Y	Y	Y	Y
4 Smith	Y	Y	Y	N	Y	N	N	N
5 Harkin	N	Y	Y	N	Y	N	N	N
6 Bedell	Y	Y	Y	Y	Y	N	N	N

Corresponding to Congressional Record Votes 362, 363, 364, 365, 366, 367, 368, 369

	339	340	341	342	343	344	345	346
KANSAS								
1 ***Roberts***	Y	Y	Y	N	Y	Y	Y	Y
2 ***Jeffries***	Y	Y	Y	N	N	N	Y	Y
3 ***Winn***	Y	Y	Y	N	Y	Y	Y	Y
4 Glickman	Y	Y	Y	N	Y	Y	N	Y
5 ***Whittaker***	Y	Y	Y	Y	Y	Y	Y	Y
KENTUCKY								
1 Hubbard	Y	Y	Y	N	N	Y	N	N
2 Natcher	Y	Y	Y	N	Y	Y	N	N
3 Mazzoli	Y	Y	Y	N	Y	Y	N	Y
4 ***Snyder***	Y	Y	Y	Y	Y	N	Y	Y
5 ***Rogers***	Y	Y	Y	Y	Y	Y	Y	Y
6 ***Hopkins***	Y	Y	Y	N	Y	Y	Y	Y
7 Perkins	Y	Y	Y	N	Y	Y	N	N
LOUISIANA								
1 ***Livingston***	Y	Y	Y	Y	N	Y	Y	Y
2 Boggs	Y	Y	Y	N	Y	Y	N	N
3 Tauzin	Y	Y	Y	N	Y	Y	N	Y
4 Roemer	N	Y	Y	Y	N	Y	Y	Y
5 Huckaby	Y	Y	Y	N	Y	?	Y	N
6 ***Moore***	Y	Y	Y	N	Y	Y	Y	Y
7 Breaux	?	?	Y	N	Y	Y	N	N
8 Long	Y	Y	Y	N	Y	Y	N	N
MAINE								
1 ***Emery***	Y	Y	?	N	Y	?	#	?
2 ***Snowe***	Y	Y	Y	N	Y	Y	Y	Y
MARYLAND								
1 Dyson	Y	Y	Y	N	Y	Y	N	N
2 Long	Y	Y	Y	Y	Y	Y	Y	N
3 Mikulski	Y	Y	Y	Y	Y	Y	N	N
4 ***Holt***	Y	Y	Y	Y	Y	Y	Y	?
5 Hoyer	Y	Y	Y	N	Y	Y	N	?
6 Byron	?	Y	Y	N	Y	Y	Y	?
7 Mitchell	N	?	Y	N	Y	Y	N	N
8 Barnes	Y	Y	Y	Y	Y	Y	N	N
MASSACHUSETTS								
1 ***Conte***	Y	Y	Y	Y	N	Y	N	N
2 Boland	Y	Y	Y	Y	Y	?	?	?
3 Early	Y	Y	Y	Y	Y	?	?	?
4 Frank	Y	Y	Y	Y	Y	?	?	?
5 Shannon	Y	Y	Y	N	Y	?	?	?
6 Mavroules	Y	Y	Y	N	Y	Y	N	N
7 Markey	N	Y	Y	Y	Y	Y	?	?
8 O'Neill								
9 Moakley	Y	Y	Y	Y	Y	Y	N	N
10 ***Heckler***	?	Y	Y	Y	Y	Y	N	Y
11 Donnelly	?	Y	Y	Y	Y	Y	N	N
12 Studds	Y	Y	Y	Y	Y	Y	N	N
MICHIGAN								
1 Conyers	?	?	?	?	?	?	?	?
2 ***Pursell***	Y	Y	?	Y	Y	Y	N	Y
3 Wolpe	Y	Y	Y	Y	Y	Y	N	N
4 ***Siljander***	Y	Y	Y	N	Y	N	Y	Y
5 ***Sawyer***	Y	Y	Y	N	Y	Y	N	Y
6 ***Dunn***	Y	Y	Y	Y	Y	Y	Y	Y
7 Kildee	Y	Y	Y	Y	Y	Y	N	N
8 Traxler	Y	Y	Y	N	Y	Y	N	N
9 ***Vander Jagt***	Y	Y	Y	N	Y	Y	Y	Y
10 Albosta	Y	Y	Y	N	Y	Y	N	N
11 ***Davis***	Y	Y	Y	N	Y	Y	N	N
12 Bonior	Y	Y	Y	N	Y	?	N	N
13 Crockett	?	Y	Y	Y	Y	?	N	N
14 Hertel	Y	Y	Y	N	Y	Y	N	N
15 Ford	?	?	Y	?	Y	Y	N	N
16 Dingell	Y	Y	Y	?	Y	Y	N	N
17 Brodhead	Y	Y	Y	Y	Y	Y	N	N
18 Blanchard	Y	Y	Y	N	Y	Y	N	N
19 ***Broomfield***	Y	Y	Y	Y	N	Y	Y	?
MINNESOTA								
1 ***Erdahl***	Y	Y	Y	N	Y	Y	Y	Y
2 ***Hagedorn***	Y	Y	Y	N	Y	Y	Y	Y
3 ***Frenzel***	Y	Y	Y	N	N	Y	Y	Y
4 Vento	Y	Y	Y	Y	Y	Y	N	N
5 Sabo	N	Y	Y	Y	Y	Y	N	N
6 ***Weber***	N	Y	Y	N	Y	Y	Y	Y
7 ***Stangeland***	Y	Y	Y	N	Y	Y	Y	Y
8 Oberstar	P	Y	Y	Y	Y	Y	N	N
MISSISSIPPI								
1 Whitten	Y	Y	Y	N	Y	Y	Y	?
2 Bowen	?	Y	Y	Y	Y	Y	Y	N
3 Montgomery	Y	Y	Y	N	Y	Y	Y	Y
4 Dowdy	Y	Y	Y	N	Y	Y	N	Y
5 ***Lott***	Y	Y	Y	Y	Y	Y	?	?
MISSOURI								
1 Clay	N	Y	Y	Y	Y	Y	N	N
2 Young	Y	Y	Y	N	?	?	?	?
3 Gephardt	Y	Y	Y	N	Y	Y	N	N
4 Skelton	Y	Y	Y	?	?	?	?	?
5 Bolling	?	?	Y	Y	Y	?	?	?
6 ***Coleman***	Y	Y	Y	N	Y	Y	Y	Y
7 ***Taylor***	Y	Y	Y	Y	Y	Y	?	?
8 ***Bailey***	N	Y	Y	N	Y	Y	Y	Y
9 Volkmer	Y	Y	Y	N	Y	Y	N	Y
10 ***Emerson***	N	Y	Y	N	Y	Y	Y	Y
MONTANA								
1 Williams	?	Y	Y	N	Y	?	N	N
2 ***Marlenee***	Y	Y	Y	N	Y	Y	Y	Y
NEBRASKA								
1 ***Bereuter***	Y	Y	Y	Y	Y	Y	Y	N
2 ***Daub***	Y	Y	Y	Y	Y	N	Y	Y
3 ***Smith***	Y	Y	Y	Y	Y	Y	Y	Y
NEVADA								
AL Santini	Y	Y	?	N	Y	Y	?	N
NEW HAMPSHIRE								
1 D'Amours	Y	Y	Y	Y	Y	Y	N	N
2 ***Gregg***	Y	Y	Y	N	Y	N	Y	Y
NEW JERSEY								
1 Florio	Y	Y	Y	Y	Y	Y	N	N
2 Hughes	Y	Y	Y	Y	Y	Y	N	N
3 Howard	Y	Y	Y	N	Y	Y	N	N
4 ***Smith***	Y	Y	Y	Y	Y	Y	N	Y
5 ***Fenwick***	?	Y	Y	Y	N	Y	Y	Y
6 ***Forsythe***	?	?	?	?	?	?	X	?
7 ***Roukema***	Y	Y	Y	Y	N	Y	N	Y
8 Roe	Y	Y	Y	N	Y	Y	N	N
9 ***Hollenbeck***	Y	Y	Y	Y	Y	N	N	?
10 Rodino	Y	Y	Y	Y	Y	Y	N	?
11 Minish	Y	Y	Y	Y	Y	Y	N	N
12 ***Rinaldo***	Y	Y	Y	Y	Y	Y	N	N
13 ***Courter***	Y	Y	Y	Y	N	N	N	Y
14 Guarini	Y	Y	Y	N	Y	Y	N	N
15 Dwyer	Y	Y	Y	Y	Y	Y	N	N
NEW MEXICO								
1 ***Lujan***	Y	Y	Y	Y	Y	N	Y	Y
2 ***Skeen***	Y	Y	Y	N	Y	Y	Y	Y
NEW YORK								
1 ***Carney***	Y	Y	Y	Y	Y	Y	?	Y
2 Downey	Y	Y	Y	N	Y	Y	N	N
3 ***Carman***	?	Y	Y	Y	N	Y	Y	Y
4 ***Lent***	Y	Y	Y	N	Y	Y	N	Y
5 ***McGrath***	Y	Y	Y	N	Y	N	N	Y
6 ***LeBoutillier***	Y	Y	Y	N	Y	N	N	Y
7 Addabbo	?	?	?	?	?	?	X	?
8 Rosenthal	?	Y	Y	Y	Y	Y	?	?
9 Ferraro	Y	Y	Y	N	Y	Y	N	N
10 Biaggi	Y	Y	Y	N	Y	?	?	?
11 Scheuer	?	?	?	Y	Y	Y	N	N
12 Chisholm	?	?	?	?	?	?	?	?
13 Solarz	Y	Y	Y	Y	?	?	?	?
14 Vacancy								
15 Zeferetti	?	?	?	?	?	?	X	?
16 Schumer	Y	Y	Y	Y	Y	Y	N	N
17 ***Molinari***	Y	Y	Y	N	Y	Y	Y	Y
18 ***Green***	Y	Y	Y	Y	N	Y	N	N
19 Rangel	Y	Y	Y	N	Y	?	?	?
20 Weiss	?	?	?	?	?	?	?	?
21 Garcia	?	?	?	?	?	?	?	?
22 Bingham	?	Y	Y	Y	Y	Y	N	N
23 Peyser	Y	Y	Y	Y	N	Y	N	N
24 Ottinger	P	Y	Y	Y	Y	P	N	N
25 ***Fish***	Y	Y	Y	?	Y	Y	N	N
26 ***Gilman***	Y	Y	Y	Y	N	Y	N	N
27 McHugh	Y	Y	Y	N	Y	Y	N	Y
28 Stratton	?	?	?	?	?	?	?	?
29 ***Solomon***	Y	Y	Y	Y	N	Y	Y	Y
30 ***Martin***	Y	Y	Y	Y	N	Y	Y	Y
31 ***Mitchell***	Y	Y	Y	Y	Y	Y	Y	?
32 ***Wortley***	?	?	?	?	?	?	?	?
33 ***Lee***	?	?	?	?	?	?	?	?
34 ***Horton***	Y	Y	Y	Y	Y	Y	N	?
35 ***Conable***	Y	Y	Y	Y	N	N	Y	?
36 LaFalce	Y	Y	Y	?	?	?	?	?
37 Nowak	Y	Y	Y	Y	Y	Y	N	N
38 ***Kemp***	Y	Y	Y	N	Y	N	?	Y
39 Lundine	Y	Y	Y	Y	Y	Y	N	?
NORTH CAROLINA								
1 Jones	Y	Y	Y	N	Y	Y	Y	Y
2 Fountain	?	Y	Y	N	Y	Y	Y	Y
3 Whitley	Y	Y	Y	N	Y	Y	Y	Y
4 Andrews	Y	Y	Y	N	Y	Y	Y	Y
5 Neal	Y	Y	Y	N	Y	Y	?	?
6 ***Johnston***	N	Y	Y	Y	N	N	Y	?
7 Rose	?	?	?	?	?	?	?	?
8 Hefner	Y	Y	Y	N	Y	Y	Y	Y
9 ***Martin***	Y	Y	Y	Y	Y	N	Y	Y
10 ***Broyhill***	Y	Y	Y	Y	Y	Y	Y	Y
11 ***Hendon***	Y	Y	Y	N	Y	Y	Y	Y
NORTH DAKOTA								
AL Dorgan	Y	Y	Y	N	Y	Y	N	N
OHIO								
1 ***Gradison***	Y	Y	Y	Y	Y	N	Y	Y
2 Luken	N	Y	Y	N	Y	?	?	?
3 Hall	Y	Y	Y	Y	Y	Y	N	N
4 ***Oxley***	Y	Y	Y	Y	Y	Y	Y	Y
5 ***Latta***	Y	Y	Y	Y	Y	Y	Y	Y
6 ***McEwen***	Y	Y	Y	Y	Y	Y	Y	?
7 ***Brown***	?	?	?	?	?	?	?	?
8 ***Kindness***	Y	Y	Y	Y	Y	N	Y	Y
9 ***Weber***	Y	Y	Y	Y	Y	Y	Y	Y
10 ***Miller***	N	Y	Y	Y	Y	Y	Y	Y
11 ***Stanton***	?	?	?	Y	Y	?	?	?
12 Shamansky	Y	Y	Y	Y	Y	Y	N	N
13 Pease	Y	Y	Y	Y	Y	Y	N	N
14 Seiberling	?	Y	Y	Y	Y	Y	N	N
15 ***Wylie***	Y	Y	Y	N	Y	Y	N	N
16 ***Regula***	Y	Y	Y	Y	Y	Y	N	Y
17 ***Ashbrook***	Y	Y	Y	Y	N	N	Y	Y
18 Applegate	?	Y	Y	N	Y	?	N	Y
19 ***Williams***	Y	Y	Y	Y	Y	Y	N	N
20 Oakar	Y	Y	Y	N	Y	Y	N	N
21 Stokes	Y	Y	Y	Y	Y	Y	N	N
22 Eckart	Y	Y	Y	N	Y	Y	N	N
23 Mottl	Y	Y	Y	N	N	Y	N	N
OKLAHOMA								
1 Jones	Y	Y	Y	N	Y	Y	N	?
2 Synar	Y	Y	Y	N	Y	Y	?	?
3 Watkins	Y	Y	Y	N	Y	Y	Y	Y
4 McCurdy	Y	Y	Y	N	?	?	?	?
5 ***Edwards***	N	Y	Y	N	Y	Y	Y	Y
6 English	Y	Y	Y	N	Y	Y	Y	Y
OREGON								
1 AuCoin	Y	Y	Y	N	Y	Y	N	N
2 ***Smith***	N	Y	Y	Y	N	N	Y	Y
3 Wyden	Y	Y	Y	N	Y	Y	N	N
4 Weaver	Y	Y	Y	Y	Y	Y	N	N
PENNSYLVANIA								
1 Foglietta	Y	Y	Y	Y	Y	Y	N	N
2 Gray	Y	Y	Y	N	?	?	?	?
3 Smith	Y	Y	Y	?	?	?	?	?
4 ***Dougherty***	?	Y	Y	N	Y	Y	N	N
5 ***Schulze***	Y	Y	Y	N	Y	Y	?	?
6 Yatron	Y	Y	Y	N	Y	Y	N	N
7 Edgar	?	?	Y	Y	Y	Y	N	N
8 ***Coyne, J.***	Y	Y	Y	Y	N	?	N	Y
9 ***Shuster***	Y	Y	Y	Y	N	Y	Y	Y
10 ***McDade***	Y	Y	Y	Y	Y	Y	N	N
11 ***Nelligan***	Y	Y	Y	Y	N	Y	N	Y
12 Murtha	Y	Y	Y	N	Y	Y	N	N
13 ***Coughlin***	N	Y	Y	Y	?	?	Y	Y
14 Coyne, W.	Y	Y	Y	Y	Y	Y	N	N
15 ***Ritter***	?	Y	Y	Y	N	Y	N	Y
16 ***Walker***	N	Y	Y	Y	N	N	Y	Y
17 Ertel	?	?	?	?	?	?	?	?
18 Walgren	Y	Y	Y	Y	Y	Y	N	N
19 ***Goodling***	N	Y	Y	Y	Y	N	Y	Y
20 Gaydos	Y	Y	Y	N	Y	Y	N	N
21 Bailey	Y	Y	Y	N	Y	Y	N	N
22 Murphy	N	Y	Y	Y	Y	?	N	N
23 ***Clinger***	Y	Y	Y	Y	N	Y	N	N
24 ***Marks***	?	?	?	Y	Y	Y	?	?
25 ***Atkinson***	Y	Y	Y	Y	N	Y	N	Y
RHODE ISLAND								
1 St Germain	Y	Y	Y	Y	Y	Y	N	N
2 ***Schneider***	Y	Y	Y	Y	Y	Y	N	N
SOUTH CAROLINA								
1 ***Hartnett***	N	Y	Y	Y	N	?	Y	Y
2 ***Spence***	Y	Y	Y	Y	Y	Y	Y	Y
3 Derrick	Y	Y	Y	N	Y	Y	Y	N
4 ***Campbell***	Y	Y	Y	N	Y	Y	Y	Y
5 Holland	?	Y	Y	N	Y	Y	N	?
6 ***Napier***	Y	Y	Y	?	?	?	?	?
SOUTH DAKOTA								
1 Daschle	Y	Y	Y	N	Y	Y	N	N
2 ***Roberts***	Y	Y	Y	N	Y	Y	Y	Y
TENNESSEE								
1 ***Quillen***	Y	Y	Y	N	Y	Y	N	Y
2 ***Duncan***	Y	Y	Y	N	Y	Y	Y	Y
3 Bouquard	Y	Y	Y	N	Y	Y	N	Y
4 Gore	Y	?	Y	N	Y	Y	N	N
5 Boner	Y	?	?	?	?	?	?	?
6 ***Beard***	?	?	?	?	?	?	#	?
7 Jones	Y	Y	Y	N	Y	Y	N	N
8 Ford	Y	Y	Y	N	Y	Y	N	N
TEXAS								
1 Hall, S.	Y	Y	Y	N	Y	Y	Y	Y
2 Wilson	?	Y	Y	N	Y	Y	N	?
3 ***Collins***	?	?	?	?	?	?	?	?
4 Hall, R.	Y	Y	Y	N	Y	N	Y	Y
5 Mattox	?	?	?	?	?	?	?	?
6 Gramm	Y	Y	Y	Y	N	N	Y	Y
7 ***Archer***	Y	Y	Y	N	Y	N	Y	Y
8 ***Fields***	N	Y	Y	Y	N	Y	Y	Y
9 Brooks	Y	Y	Y	N	Y	Y	N	?
10 Pickle	Y	Y	Y	N	Y	Y	N	N
11 Leath	Y	Y	Y	N	Y	Y	Y	Y
12 Wright	Y	Y	?	N	Y	Y	N	N
13 Hightower	Y	Y	Y	N	Y	Y	Y	N
14 Patman	Y	Y	Y	N	Y	Y	Y	N
15 de la Garza	Y	Y	Y	N	Y	Y	N	N
16 White	Y	Y	Y	N	Y	Y	Y	Y
17 Stenholm	Y	Y	Y	N	Y	Y	Y	Y
18 Leland	Y	Y	Y	N	Y	Y	N	N
19 Hance	Y	Y	Y	?	?	?	?	?
20 Gonzalez	Y	Y	Y	N	Y	Y	N	N
21 ***Loeffler***	Y	Y	Y	N	Y	Y	Y	Y
22 ***Paul***	Y	Y	Y	N	N	N	Y	Y
23 Kazen	Y	Y	Y	N	Y	Y	Y	Y
24 Frost	Y	Y	Y	N	Y	?	N	N
UTAH								
1 ***Hansen***	Y	Y	Y	Y	N	N	Y	Y
2 ***Marriott***	Y	Y	Y	N	Y	Y	Y	Y
VERMONT								
AL ***Jeffords***	Y	Y	Y	N	Y	Y	N	N
VIRGINIA								
1 ***Trible***	?	?	?	N	Y	Y	Y	?
2 ***Whitehurst***	Y	Y	Y	N	Y	Y	Y	?
3 ***Bliley***	Y	Y	Y	Y	Y	Y	Y	Y
4 ***Daniel, R.***	Y	Y	Y	N	Y	N	Y	Y
5 Daniel, D.	Y	Y	Y	N	Y	?	Y	Y
6 ***Butler***	N	Y	Y	Y	N	Y	Y	Y
7 ***Robinson***	Y	Y	Y	N	Y	N	Y	Y
8 ***Parris***	Y	Y	?	N	Y	Y	Y	Y
9 ***Wampler***	Y	Y	Y	N	Y	Y	Y	Y
10 ***Wolf***	Y	Y	Y	N	Y	Y	Y	Y
WASHINGTON								
1 ***Pritchard***	Y	Y	Y	Y	Y	Y	Y	Y
2 Swift	Y	Y	Y	N	N	Y	N	N
3 Bonker	Y	Y	Y	N	Y	Y	N	N
4 ***Morrison***	Y	Y	Y	N	Y	Y	Y	Y
5 Foley	Y	Y	Y	N	Y	Y	N	N
6 Dicks	Y	Y	Y	N	Y	Y	N	N
7 Lowry	Y	Y	Y	Y	Y	Y	N	N
WEST VIRGINIA								
1 Mollohan	Y	Y	Y	N	Y	Y	N	N
2 ***Benedict***	Y	Y	Y	N	?	?	?	?
3 ***Staton***	Y	Y	Y	Y	N	Y	N	Y
4 Rahall	Y	Y	Y	N	Y	Y	N	N
WISCONSIN								
1 Aspin	Y	Y	Y	N	Y	Y	N	N
2 Kastenmeier	Y	Y	Y	Y	Y	Y	N	N
3 ***Gunderson***	Y	Y	Y	N	Y	Y	Y	Y
4 Zablocki	Y	Y	Y	N	Y	Y	N	N
5 Reuss	Y	Y	Y	N	Y	Y	N	?
6 ***Petri***	Y	Y	Y	?	?	Y	Y	Y
7 Obey	P	Y	Y	Y	Y	Y	N	N
8 ***Roth***	Y	Y	Y	Y	Y	Y	Y	Y
9 ***Sensenbrenner***	Y	Y	Y	N	Y	N	Y	Y
WYOMING								
AL ***Cheney***	?	Y	?	Y	N	?	#	?

Southern states - Ala., Ark., Fla., Ga., Ky., La., Miss., N.C., Okla., S.C., Tenn., Texas, Va.

347. H Res 581. House of Representatives Historian. Adoption of the resolution to establish an office of Historian for the House of Representatives. Rejected 132-180: R 19-125; D 113-55 (ND 76-34, SD 37-21), Sept. 24, 1982.

348. HR 6173. Health Planning Grants. Passage of the bill to repeal the federal health planning program and to authorize $65.6 million in fiscal 1983-84 for grants to state health planning and certificate-of-need programs. Passed 302-14: R 137-11; D 165-3 (ND 112-1, SD 53-2), Sept. 24, 1982.

349. HR 4863. Recovery of Damages by Foreign Seamen. Biaggi, D-N.Y., motion to suspend the rules and pass the bill to limit maritime suits by foreign seamen while engaged in certain activities related to energy resources exploration, development or production in the coastal waters adjacent to a foreign nation. Motion rejected 224-182: R 150-28; D 74-154 (ND 18-134, SD 56-20), Sept. 28, 1982. A two-thirds majority of those present and voting (272 in this case) is required for passage under suspension of the rules.

350. HR 3252. Coastal Barrier Resources Act. Breaux, D-La., motion to suspend the rules and pass the bill to ban federal aid that would encourage development on specified undeveloped coastal barrier islands. Motion agreed to 399-4: R 175-1; D 224-3 (ND 152-0, SD 72-3), Sept. 28, 1982. A two-thirds majority of those present and voting (269 in this case) is required for passage under suspension of the rules. A "yea" was a vote supporting the president's position.

351. HR 5949. Cable Copyright Bill. Kastenmeier, D-Wis., motion to suspend the rules and pass the bill to clarify the rights of cable television operators to retransmit copyrighted material broadcast by non-cable stations. Motion agreed to 347-53: R 133-40; D 214-13 (ND 143-9, SD 71-4), Sept. 28, 1982. A two-thirds majority of those present and voting (268 in this case) is required for passage under suspension of the rules.

352. H Con Res 409. Massacre of Palestinians in Lebanon. Zablocki, D-Wis., motion to suspend the rules and adopt the concurrent resolution deploring recent events in Lebanon, including the massacre of several hundred Palestinian civilians in refugee camps and the assassination of President-elect Bashir Gemayel. Motion agreed to 401-1: R 174-1; D 227-0 (ND 152-0, SD 75-0), Sept. 28, 1982. A two-thirds majority of those present and voting (268 in this case) is required for adoption under suspension of the rules.

353. HR 5162. National Park System Protection and Resources Management Act. Seiberling, D-Ohio, motion to suspend the rules and pass the bill to require a biennial State of the Parks Report and establish a comprehensive planning system to protect National Park System units from internal and external threats. Motion agreed to 319-84: R 116-63; D 203-21 (ND 148-2, SD 55-19), Sept. 29, 1982. A two-thirds majority of those present and voting (269 in this case) is required for passage under suspension of the rules. A "nay" was a vote supporting the president's position.

354. HR 6838. Soviet Economic Sanctions. Broomfield, R-Mich., motion to recommit the bill to the Foreign Affairs Committee with instructions to insert an amendment repealing economic sanctions against the Soviet Union 90 days after enactment of the bill, provided that during that period the president certified to Congress that the Soviet Union was not using forced labor on certain construction projects. The original bill would have immediately repealed economic sanctions against the Soviet Union. Motion agreed to 206-203: R 124-57; D 82-146 (ND 41-111, SD 41-35), Sept. 29, 1982. A "yea" was a vote supporting the president's position.

KEY

Y	Voted for (yea).
#	Paired for.
+	Announced for.
N	Voted against (nay).
X	Paired against.
-	Announced against.
P	Voted "present".
C	Voted "present" to avoid possible conflict of interest.
?	Did not vote or otherwise make a position known.

Democrats **Republicans**

	347	348	349	350	351	352	353	354
ALABAMA								
1 *Edwards*	Y	Y	Y	Y	Y	Y	Y	Y
2 Dickinson	N	Y	Y	Y	Y	Y	Y	N
3 Nichols	Y	Y	Y	Y	Y	Y	Y	Y
4 Bevill	Y	Y	N	Y	Y	Y	Y	Y
5 Flippo	Y	Y	N	Y	Y	Y	Y	Y
6 *Smith*	N	Y	Y	N	Y	Y	Y	Y
7 Shelby	N	Y	Y	Y	Y	Y	Y	Y
ALASKA								
AL *Young*	N	Y	Y	N	Y	Y	N	Y
ARIZONA								
1 *Rhodes*	?	?	Y	Y	?	?	N	Y
2 Udall	?	?	Y	Y	N	Y	N	Y
3 *Stump*	?	?	Y	Y	N	Y	N	Y
4 *Rudd*	N	Y	Y	Y	N	Y	N	Y
ARKANSAS								
1 Alexander	Y	?	Y	Y	Y	Y	Y	N
2 *Bethune*	N	Y	Y	Y	Y	Y	Y	Y
3 *Hammerschmidt*	N	Y	Y	Y	Y	Y	Y	Y
4 Anthony	N	Y	Y	Y	Y	Y	Y	N
CALIFORNIA								
1 *Chappie*	N	Y	Y	Y	Y	Y	Y	N
2 *Clausen*	N	Y	Y	Y	Y	Y	Y	Y
3 Matsui	Y	Y	N	Y	Y	Y	Y	N
4 Fazio	Y	Y	N	Y	Y	Y	Y	N
5 Burton, J.	?	?	?	?	?	?	?	?
6 Burton, P.	?	?	N	Y	Y	Y	Y	N
7 Miller	?	Y	N	Y	Y	Y	Y	N
8 Dellums	Y	N	Y	N	Y	Y	Y	N
9 Stark	Y	Y	N	Y	N	Y	Y	N
10 Edwards	Y	Y	N	Y	Y	Y	Y	N
11 Lantos	?	?	?	?	?	?	Y	N
12 *McCloskey*	N	Y	Y	Y	?	Y	Y	N
13 Mineta	Y	Y	N	Y	Y	Y	Y	N
14 *Shumway*	N	Y	Y	N	Y	N	N	Y
15 Coelho	?	?	Y	Y	Y	Y	Y	N
16 Panetta	Y	Y	N	Y	N	Y	Y	N
17 *Pashayan*	N	Y	Y	Y	Y	Y	Y	Y
18 *Thomas*	N	Y	Y	Y	Y	Y	N	N
19 *Lagomarsino*	N	Y	Y	Y	Y	Y	N	Y
20 *Goldwater*	?	?	Y	N	Y	N	N	Y
21 *Fiedler*	N	Y	Y	Y	Y	Y	Y	Y
22 *Moorhead*	N	Y	Y	Y	Y	Y	Y	Y
23 Beilenson	?	?	N	Y	Y	Y	Y	N
24 Waxman	Y	N	Y	Y	Y	Y	Y	Y
25 Roybal	Y	N	N	Y	N	Y	Y	N
26 *Rousselot*	?	?	Y	N	Y	N	N	Y
27 *Dornan*	?	?	?	?	?	?	N	Y
28 Dixon	Y	N	N	Y	Y	Y	Y	N
29 Hawkins	Y	?	N	Y	Y	Y	Y	N
30 Martinez	N	N	N	N	N	Y	Y	N
31 Dymally	Y	Y	N	Y	Y	Y	Y	Y
32 Anderson	N	Y	N	Y	Y	Y	Y	Y
33 *Grisham*	?	?	Y	N	Y	N	N	Y
34 Lungren	?	?	Y	Y	N	Y	N	Y
35 *Dreier*	?	?	Y	Y	N	Y	N	Y
36 Brown	?	?	N	Y	Y	Y	Y	N
37 *Lewis*	N	Y	?	?	?	?	Y	Y
38 Patterson	N	Y	N	Y	Y	Y	Y	N
39 *Dannemeyer*	?	N	Y	N	Y	N	N	Y
40 *Badham*	?	?	Y	Y	Y	N	N	Y
41 *Lowery*	N	Y	Y	Y	N	Y	N	Y
42 *Hunter*	N	Y	N	Y	Y	Y	Y	Y
43 *Burgener*	?	?	Y	Y	Y	Y	N	Y
COLORADO								
1 Schroeder	N	N	Y	N	Y	Y	Y	N
2 Wirth	?	?	N	Y	Y	Y	Y	N
3 Kogovsek	N	Y	N	Y	N	Y	Y	N
4 *Brown*	N	Y	Y	Y	Y	Y	N	Y

	347	348	349	350	351	352	353	354
5 *Kramer*	N	N	Y	Y	Y	Y	Y	Y
CONNECTICUT								
1 Kennelly	Y	Y	N	Y	Y	Y	Y	Y
2 Gejdenson	Y	N	Y	Y	Y	Y	Y	N
3 *DeNardis*	?	?	N	Y	Y	Y	Y	N
4 *McKinney*	Y	Y	Y	Y	Y	Y	Y	N
5 Ratchford	?	?	N	Y	Y	Y	Y	N
6 Moffett	?	?	?	?	?	?	?	?
DELAWARE								
AL *Evans*	N	Y	N	Y	Y	Y	Y	Y
FLORIDA								
1 Hutto	Y	Y	Y	Y	Y	Y	Y	Y
2 Fuqua	N	Y	Y	Y	Y	Y	Y	Y
3 Bennett	N	Y	Y	Y	Y	Y	Y	Y
4 Chappell	?	?	?	?	?	?	?	?
5 *McCollum*	N	Y	Y	Y	Y	Y	Y	Y
6 *Young*	N	Y	?	?	?	?	?	?
7 Gibbons	N	Y	N	Y	Y	Y	Y	N
8 Ireland	?	?	Y	Y	Y	Y	Y	Y
9 Nelson	Y	Y	Y	Y	Y	Y	Y	Y
10 *Bafalis*	?	?	?	?	?	?	?	?
11 Mica	N	Y	Y	Y	Y	Y	Y	Y
12 *Shaw*	N	Y	Y	Y	Y	Y	Y	Y
13 Lehman	?	?	N	Y	Y	Y	Y	N
14 Pepper	Y	Y	Y	Y	Y	Y	?	Y
15 Fascell	?	?	N	Y	Y	Y	Y	N
GEORGIA								
1 Ginn	Y	Y	Y	Y	Y	Y	Y	Y
2 Hatcher	?	?	Y	Y	Y	Y	Y	Y
3 Brinkley	Y	Y	Y	N	Y	Y	Y	Y
4 Levitas	Y	Y	Y	Y	Y	Y	Y	Y
5 Fowler	Y	Y	Y	Y	Y	Y	Y	N
6 *Gingrich*	Y	Y	Y	N	Y	Y	Y	Y
7 McDonald	N	N	N	N	Y	N	Y	N
8 Evans	Y	Y	Y	Y	Y	Y	Y	Y
9 Jenkins	?	?	?	?	?	?	Y	Y
10 Barnard	?	?	Y	Y	Y	Y	Y	N
HAWAII								
1 Heftel	?	?	Y	Y	Y	?	Y	N
2 Akaka	Y	N	Y	Y	Y	Y	Y	N
IDAHO								
1 *Craig*	?	?	Y	Y	N	Y	N	Y
2 Hansen	Y	Y	Y	N	Y	Y	Y	Y
ILLINOIS								
1 Washington	?	?	N	Y	Y	Y	Y	N
2 Savage	?	?	N	Y	Y	Y	?	N
3 Russo	Y	Y	N	Y	Y	Y	Y	N
4 *Derwinski*	N	Y	Y	N	Y	Y	Y	Y
5 Fary	Y	Y	Y	Y	Y	Y	Y	Y
6 *Hyde*	Y	Y	Y	Y	N	Y	N	Y
7 Collins	Y	N	Y	Y	Y	Y	Y	N
8 Rostenkowski	Y	Y	N	Y	Y	Y	Y	N
9 Yates	Y	N	N	Y	Y	Y	Y	N
10 *Porter*	Y	Y	Y	Y	Y	Y	Y	N
11 Annunzio	Y	N	Y	Y	Y	Y	Y	Y
12 Crane, P.	N	N	N	N	N	Y	N	Y
13 *McClory*	N	N	N	N	Y	N	N	Y
14 *Erlenborn*	?	?	Y	Y	N	Y	N	Y
15 *Corcoran*	N	Y	Y	Y	Y	Y	Y	Y
16 *Martin*	N	Y	Y	Y	Y	Y	N	N
17 O'Brien	?	?	Y	Y	Y	Y	?	X
18 *Michel*	?	?	Y	Y	Y	Y	N	Y
19 Railsback	N	Y	Y	Y	Y	Y	Y	N
20 *Findley*	N	Y	Y	Y	Y	Y	Y	N
21 Madigan	Y	Y	Y	Y	Y	Y	Y	N
22 Crane, D.	N	N	N	N	Y	N	N	Y
23 Price	Y	N	Y	Y	Y	Y	Y	N
24 Simon	?	?	N	Y	Y	Y	Y	N
INDIANA								
1 Vacancy								
2 Fithian	?	?	N	Y	Y	Y	Y	N
3 *Hiler*	N	Y	Y	Y	Y	Y	N	Y
4 *Coats*	N	Y	Y	N	Y	N	N	Y
5 Hillis	N	Y	N	N	Y	N	N	Y
6 Evans	?	?	N	Y	Y	Y	Y	N
7 *Myers*	N	Y	Y	Y	Y	N	N	Y
8 *Deckard*	N	Y	Y	Y	Y	Y	N	Y
9 Hamilton	Y	Y	N	Y	Y	Y	Y	N
10 Sharp	Y	N	Y	Y	Y	Y	Y	N
11 Jacobs	N	Y	N	Y	Y	Y	Y	N
IOWA								
1 Leach	N	Y	N	Y	Y	Y	Y	N
2 Tauke	N	Y	Y	Y	Y	Y	Y	N
3 Evans	N	Y	N	Y	Y	Y	Y	N
4 Smith	N	Y	Y	Y	Y	Y	Y	N
5 Harkin	N	Y	N	Y	Y	Y	Y	N
6 Bedell	?	?	N	Y	Y	Y	Y	N

ND - Northern Democrats   SD - Southern Democrats

Corresponding to Congressional Record Votes 370, 371, 372, 373, 374, 375, 376, 378

	347	348	349	350	351	352	353	354
KANSAS								
1 ***Roberts***	?	?	Y	Y	Y	Y	Y	N
2 ***Jeffries***	N	Y	Y	Y	N	Y	N	Y
3 ***Winn***	N	Y	Y	Y	Y	Y	Y	Y
4 Glickman	N	Y	Y	Y	Y	Y	Y	N
5 ***Whittaker***	?	?	Y	Y	Y	Y	Y	Y
KENTUCKY								
1 Hubbard	N	Y	Y	Y	Y	Y	N	Y
2 Natcher	Y	Y	N	Y	Y	Y	Y	N
3 Mazzoli	N	Y	N	Y	Y	Y	Y	N
4 ***Snyder***	N	Y	Y	Y	Y	Y	Y	Y
5 ***Rogers***	N	Y	Y	Y	Y	Y	N	Y
6 ***Hopkins***	?	?	Y	Y	Y	Y	Y	Y
7 Perkins	Y	Y	N	Y	Y	Y	Y	N
LOUISIANA								
1 ***Livingston***	Y	N	Y	Y	Y	Y	N	Y
2 Boggs	Y	Y	Y	Y	Y	Y	Y	N
3 Tauzin	N	Y	Y	Y	Y	Y	N	N
4 Roemer	N	Y	Y	Y	N	Y	N	N
5 Huckaby	N	Y	Y	Y	Y	Y	Y	N
6 ***Moore***	?	?	Y	Y	P	Y	N	N
7 Breaux	Y	?	Y	Y	Y	Y	N	N
8 Long	Y	Y	Y	Y	Y	Y	Y	Y
MAINE								
1 ***Emery***	?	?	Y	Y	Y	Y	Y	Y
2 ***Snowe***	N	Y	Y	Y	Y	Y	Y	N
MARYLAND								
1 Dyson	Y	Y	N	Y	Y	Y	Y	Y
2 Long	N	Y	Y	Y	Y	Y	Y	Y
3 Mikulski	Y	Y	N	Y	Y	Y	Y	N
4 ***Holt***	Y	Y	Y	Y	Y	Y	N	Y
5 Hoyer	Y	Y	N	Y	Y	Y	Y	N
6 Byron	Y	Y	Y	Y	Y	Y	Y	Y
7 Mitchell	?	Y	N	Y	Y	Y	Y	N
8 Barnes	Y	Y	N	Y	Y	Y	Y	N
MASSACHUSETTS								
1 ***Conte***	N	Y	N	Y	Y	Y	Y	N
2 Boland	?	?	N	Y	Y	Y	Y	N
3 Early	?	?	N	Y	Y	Y	Y	Y
4 Frank	N	Y	N	Y	N	Y	Y	Y
5 Shannon	?	?	N	Y	N	Y	Y	N
6 Mavroules	Y	Y	N	Y	Y	Y	Y	Y
7 Markey	Y	Y	N	Y	Y	Y	Y	N
8 O'Neill								
9 Moakley	Y	Y	N	Y	Y	Y	Y	N
10 ***Heckler***	N	Y	N	Y	Y	Y	Y	Y
11 Donnelly	Y	Y	N	Y	Y	Y	Y	Y
12 Studds	Y	Y	N	Y	Y	Y	Y	N
MICHIGAN								
1 Conyers	?	?	N	Y	Y	Y	Y	Y
2 ***Pursell***	?	?	Y	Y	Y	Y	Y	N
3 Wolpe	N	Y	N	Y	Y	Y	Y	N
4 ***Siljander***	N	Y	Y	Y	Y	Y	Y	Y
5 ***Sawyer***	N	Y	N	Y	N	Y	Y	Y
6 ***Dunn***	N	Y	Y	Y	Y	Y	Y	N
7 Kildee	N	Y	N	Y	Y	Y	Y	N
8 Traxler	N	Y	N	Y	Y	Y	Y	N
9 ***Vander Jagt***	N	Y	Y	Y	N	Y	Y	Y
10 Albosta	N	Y	N	Y	Y	Y	Y	N
11 ***Davis***	N	Y	Y	Y	Y	Y	Y	Y
12 Bonior	Y	Y	N	Y	Y	Y	Y	Y
13 Crockett	?	Y	N	Y	Y	Y	Y	N
14 Hertel	?	?	N	Y	Y	Y	Y	N
15 Ford	?	?	N	Y	Y	Y	Y	N
16 Dingell	Y	Y	N	Y	Y	Y	Y	N
17 Brodhead	?	?	Y	Y	Y	Y	Y	N
18 Blanchard	?	?	?	?	?	?	?	?
19 ***Broomfield***	N	Y	N	Y	Y	Y	Y	Y
MINNESOTA								
1 ***Erdahl***	N	Y	Y	Y	Y	Y	Y	N
2 ***Hagedorn***	N	N	Y	Y	Y	Y	Y	Y
3 ***Frenzel***	N	Y	Y	Y	Y	Y	Y	N
4 Vento	Y	Y	N	Y	Y	Y	Y	N
5 Sabo	Y	Y	N	Y	Y	Y	Y	N
6 ***Weber***	N	Y	Y	Y	N	Y	Y	N
7 ***Stangeland***	N	Y	Y	Y	N	Y	Y	N
8 Oberstar	Y	Y	N	Y	Y	Y	Y	N
MISSISSIPPI								
1 Whitten	Y	Y	N	Y	Y	Y	Y	N
2 Bowen	Y	Y	Y	Y	Y	Y	Y	N
3 Montgomery	Y	Y	Y	Y	Y	Y	N	Y
4 Dowdy	?	?	Y	Y	Y	Y	Y	N
5 ***Lott***	?	?	Y	Y	Y	Y	N	Y
MISSOURI								
1 Clay	Y	Y	N	Y	Y	Y	?	?
2 Young	?	?	N	Y	Y	Y	Y	N
3 Gephardt	Y	Y	N	Y	Y	Y	Y	N

	347	348	349	350	351	352	353	354
4 Skelton	?	?	N	Y	Y	Y	?	?
5 Bolling	Y	?	N	?	?	?	?	N
6 ***Coleman***	N	Y	?	?	?	?	Y	Y
7 ***Taylor***	?	?	?	?	?	?	Y	N
8 ***Bailey***	?	?	?	?	?	?	N	N
9 Volkmer	N	Y	N	Y	Y	Y	Y	N
10 ***Emerson***	N	Y	Y	Y	Y	Y	N	N
MONTANA								
1 Williams	?	?	N	Y	Y	Y	Y	N
2 ***Marlenee***	?	Y	Y	Y	Y	Y	N	N
NEBRASKA								
1 ***Bereuter***	N	Y	Y	Y	Y	Y	Y	Y
2 ***Daub***	N	Y	Y	Y	Y	Y	Y	Y
3 ***Smith***	N	Y	Y	Y	Y	Y	N	N
NEVADA								
AL Santini	?	?	N	Y	Y	Y	?	?
NEW HAMPSHIRE								
1 D'Amours	N	Y	N	Y	Y	Y	Y	Y
2 ***Gregg***	N	Y	Y	Y	Y	Y	Y	Y
NEW JERSEY								
1 Florio	?	?	N	Y	Y	Y	Y	N
2 Hughes	Y	Y	Y	Y	Y	Y	Y	Y
3 Howard	Y	Y	N	Y	Y	Y	Y	N
4 ***Smith***	Y	Y	Y	Y	Y	Y	Y	Y
5 ***Fenwick***	N	Y	Y	?	?	?	?	N
6 ***Forsythe***	?	?	?	?	?	?	?	#
7 ***Roukema***	-	+	Y	Y	Y	Y	Y	N
8 Roe	Y	Y	N	Y	Y	Y	Y	N
9 ***Hollenbeck***	Y	Y	N	Y	Y	Y	Y	N
10 Rodino	?	Y	N	Y	Y	Y	Y	N
11 Minish	?	Y	N	Y	Y	Y	Y	Y
12 ***Rinaldo***	N	Y	N	Y	Y	Y	Y	Y
13 ***Courter***	N	Y	Y	Y	Y	Y	Y	Y
14 Guarini	N	Y	N	Y	Y	Y	Y	N
15 Dwyer	Y	Y	N	Y	Y	Y	Y	N
NEW MEXICO								
1 ***Lujan***	Y	Y	Y	Y	N	Y	Y	Y
2 ***Skeen***	N	Y	Y	Y	N	Y	N	Y
NEW YORK								
1 ***Carney***	N	Y	Y	Y	N	Y	Y	Y
2 Downey	Y	Y	N	Y	Y	Y	Y	N
3 ***Carman***	N	Y	Y	Y	Y	Y	Y	Y
4 ***Lent***	N	Y	Y	Y	Y	?	Y	Y
5 ***McGrath***	N	Y	Y	Y	Y	Y	Y	Y
6 ***LeBoutillier***	N	Y	Y	Y	Y	Y	Y	?
7 Addabbo	?	?	N	Y	Y	Y	Y	Y
8 Rosenthal	Y	Y	?	?	?	?	Y	N
9 Ferraro	Y	Y	N	Y	Y	Y	Y	N
10 Biaggi	?	?	Y	Y	Y	Y	Y	Y
11 Scheuer	Y	Y	Y	Y	Y	Y	Y	?
12 Chisholm	?	?	Y	Y	Y	Y	Y	N
13 Solarz	Y	Y	N	Y	Y	Y	Y	N
14 Vacancy								
15 Zeferetti	?	?	N	Y	Y	Y	Y	Y
16 Schumer	Y	Y	N	Y	Y	Y	Y	N
17 ***Molinari***	N	Y	Y	Y	Y	Y	Y	Y
18 ***Green***	Y	Y	N	Y	Y	Y	Y	Y
19 Rangel	?	?	N	Y	Y	Y	Y	N
20 Weiss	?	?	?	?	?	?	?	?
21 Garcia	?	?	N	Y	N	Y	Y	N
22 Bingham	?	?	N	Y	Y	Y	Y	N
23 Peyser	Y	Y	N	Y	Y	Y	Y	Y
24 Ottinger	N	Y	N	Y	Y	Y	Y	Y
25 ***Fish***	N	Y	N	Y	Y	Y	Y	N
26 ***Gilman***	N	Y	N	Y	Y	Y	Y	Y
27 McHugh	Y	Y	N	Y	Y	Y	Y	N
28 Stratton	N	Y	Y	Y	Y	Y	Y	N
29 ***Solomon***	N	Y	Y	Y	Y	Y	N	Y
30 ***Martin***	N	Y	Y	Y	Y	Y	Y	Y
31 ***Mitchell***	?	?	N	Y	Y	Y	Y	Y
32 ***Wortley***	N	Y	N	?	Y	Y	Y	Y
33 ***Lee***	?	?	Y	Y	N	Y	Y	Y
34 ***Horton***	N	Y	Y	Y	Y	Y	Y	N
35 ***Conable***	?	?	Y	Y	N	Y	N	N
36 LaFalce	Y	Y	N	Y	Y	Y	Y	N
37 Nowak	Y	Y	N	Y	Y	Y	Y	Y
38 ***Kemp***	Y	Y	?	?	?	?	Y	Y
39 Lundine	Y	Y	N	Y	Y	Y	Y	N
NORTH CAROLINA								
1 Jones	Y	Y	Y	Y	?	Y	Y	N
2 Fountain	Y	+	Y	Y	Y	Y	N	Y
3 Whitley	Y	Y	Y	Y	Y	Y	Y	Y
4 Andrews	Y	Y	Y	Y	Y	Y	Y	Y
5 Neal	N	Y	Y	?	Y	Y	Y	Y
6 ***Johnston***	N	N	Y	Y	Y	Y	N	Y
7 Rose	?	?	N	Y	Y	Y	Y	N
8 Hefner	?	?	Y	Y	Y	Y	Y	Y

	347	348	349	350	351	352	353	354
9 ***Martin***	N	Y	Y	Y	Y	Y	N	Y
10 ***Broyhill***	N	Y	Y	Y	Y	Y	N	Y
11 ***Hendon***	N	?	Y	Y	N	Y	N	Y
NORTH DAKOTA								
AL Dorgan	N	Y	Y	Y	Y	Y	Y	N
OHIO								
1 ***Gradison***	N	N	Y	Y	N	Y	Y	N
2 Luken	N	Y	N	Y	Y	Y	Y	N
3 Hall	Y	Y	N	Y	Y	Y	Y	N
4 ***Oxley***	?	?	Y	Y	Y	Y	N	N
5 ***Latta***	N	Y	Y	Y	Y	Y	Y	Y
6 ***McEwen***	?	?	Y	Y	N	Y	Y	Y
7 ***Brown***	?	?	?	?	?	?	?	?
8 ***Kindness***	N	Y	N	Y	Y	Y	Y	Y
9 ***Weber***	N	Y	Y	Y	Y	Y	Y	N
10 ***Miller***	N	Y	Y	Y	Y	Y	Y	Y
11 ***Stanton***	?	?	?	?	?	?	?	N
12 Shamansky	N	Y	?	?	Y	Y	Y	N
13 Pease	N	Y	N	Y	Y	Y	Y	N
14 Seiberling	N	Y	N	Y	Y	Y	Y	N
15 ***Wylie***	N	Y	N	Y	N	Y	Y	?
16 ***Regula***	N	Y	N	Y	N	Y	Y	Y
17 ***Ashbrook***	N	N	Y	Y	N	Y	N	Y
18 Applegate	N	Y	N	Y	Y	Y	Y	Y
19 ***Williams***	Y	Y	N	Y	Y	Y	Y	N
20 Oakar	Y	Y	N	Y	Y	Y	Y	Y
21 Stokes	Y	Y	N	Y	Y	Y	Y	N
22 Eckart	Y	Y	N	Y	Y	Y	Y	N
23 Mottl	Y	Y	N	Y	Y	Y	Y	Y
OKLAHOMA								
1 Jones	N	Y	Y	Y	Y	Y	Y	N
2 Synar	?	?	Y	Y	Y	Y	Y	N
3 Watkins	?	?	Y	Y	Y	Y	N	Y
4 McCurdy	?	?	Y	Y	Y	Y	N	N
5 ***Edwards***	N	Y	Y	Y	Y	Y	N	Y
6 English	N	Y	Y	Y	Y	Y	N	Y
OREGON								
1 AuCoin	Y	Y	Y	Y	Y	Y	Y	N
2 ***Smith***	N	Y	Y	Y	N	Y	N	Y
3 Wyden	?	?	Y	Y	Y	Y	Y	N
4 Weaver	?	?	N	Y	Y	Y	Y	N
PENNSYLVANIA								
1 Foglietta	N	Y	N	Y	Y	Y	Y	Y
2 Gray	?	?	N	Y	Y	Y	Y	N
3 Smith	?	?	N	Y	Y	Y	Y	Y
4 ***Dougherty***	?	?	N	Y	Y	Y	Y	Y
5 ***Schulze***	?	?	Y	Y	N	Y	N	?
6 Yatron	N	Y	N	Y	Y	Y	Y	Y
7 Edgar	Y	Y	N	Y	Y	Y	Y	N
8 ***Coyne, J.***	N	Y	Y	Y	Y	Y	Y	Y
9 ***Shuster***	N	Y	Y	Y	Y	Y	Y	Y
10 ***McDade***	N	Y	Y	Y	Y	Y	Y	N
11 ***Nelligan***	N	Y	N	Y	Y	Y	Y	Y
12 Murtha	Y	Y	N	Y	Y	Y	Y	Y
13 ***Coughlin***	N	Y	Y	Y	Y	Y	Y	Y
14 Coyne, W.	?	?	N	Y	Y	Y	Y	N
15 ***Ritter***	N	Y	Y	Y	Y	Y	Y	Y
16 ***Walker***	N	Y	Y	Y	Y	Y	N	Y
17 Ertel	?	?	?	?	?	?	?	?
18 Walgren	N	N	N	Y	Y	Y	Y	N
19 ***Goodling***	?	?	Y	Y	N	Y	N	N
20 Gaydos	N	Y	N	Y	Y	Y	Y	Y
21 Bailey	Y	Y	N	Y	Y	Y	Y	Y
22 Murphy	N	Y	N	Y	Y	Y	Y	Y
23 ***Clinger***	N	Y	Y	Y	Y	Y	Y	N
24 ***Marks***	?	Y	Y	Y	Y	Y	?	?
25 ***Atkinson***	Y	?	N	Y	Y	Y	Y	Y
RHODE ISLAND								
1 St Germain	Y	Y	P	Y	Y	Y	Y	N
2 ***Schneider***	N	Y	N	Y	Y	Y	Y	N
SOUTH CAROLINA								
1 ***Hartnett***	N	?	Y	Y	Y	Y	N	Y
2 ***Spence***	Y	Y	Y	Y	Y	Y	Y	Y
3 Derrick	?	+	Y	Y	Y	Y	Y	N
4 ***Campbell***	?	Y	Y	Y	Y	Y	Y	Y
5 Holland	Y	Y	N	Y	Y	Y	?	Y
6 ***Napier***	?	?	Y	Y	Y	Y	Y	Y
SOUTH DAKOTA								
1 Daschle	Y	Y	Y	Y	Y	Y	Y	N
2 ***Roberts***	?	?	Y	Y	N	Y	N	N
TENNESSEE								
1 ***Quillen***	Y	Y	Y	Y	Y	Y	N	Y
2 ***Duncan***	Y	Y	Y	Y	Y	Y	Y	Y
3 Bouquard	?	?	N	Y	Y	Y	Y	N
4 Gore	Y	Y	Y	Y	Y	Y	Y	N
5 Boner	?	?	N	Y	Y	Y	Y	Y
6 ***Beard***	?	?	?	?	?	?	?	?

	347	348	349	350	351	352	353	354
7 Jones	N	Y	Y	Y	Y	Y	Y	N
8 Ford	Y	Y	N	Y	Y	Y	Y	N
TEXAS								
1 Hall, S.	Y	Y	N	N	Y	Y	Y	Y
2 Wilson	Y	Y	Y	Y	Y	Y	Y	Y
3 ***Collins***	?	?	?	?	?	?	?	?
4 Hall, R.	N	Y	Y	Y	Y	Y	N	N
5 Mattox	?	?	?	?	?	?	?	?
6 Gramm	N	N	Y	Y	Y	Y	N	Y
7 ***Archer***	N	Y	Y	Y	Y	Y	N	N
8 ***Fields***	?	?	Y	Y	Y	Y	N	Y
9 Brooks	Y	Y	Y	N	Y	Y	Y	N
10 Pickle	N	Y	Y	Y	Y	Y	Y	N
11 Leath	Y	Y	Y	Y	Y	Y	N	Y
12 Wright	?	?	Y	Y	Y	Y	Y	N
13 Hightower	Y	Y	Y	Y	Y	Y	N	N
14 Patman	Y	Y	Y	N	N	Y	N	Y
15 de la Garza	Y	Y	Y	Y	Y	Y	?	Y
16 White	Y	Y	N	Y	Y	Y	?	Y
17 Stenholm	N	Y	Y	Y	Y	Y	N	Y
18 Leland	?	?	N	Y	Y	Y	Y	N
19 Hance	?	?	Y	Y	Y	Y	N	Y
20 Gonzalez	Y	Y	N	Y	Y	Y	Y	Y
21 ***Loeffler***	N	Y	Y	Y	Y	Y	N	Y
22 ***Paul***	N	N	Y	Y	N	N	N	N
23 Kazen	N	Y	Y	Y	Y	Y	N	Y
24 Frost	?	?	N	Y	Y	Y	Y	N
UTAH								
1 ***Hansen***	?	?	Y	Y	Y	Y	N	Y
2 ***Marriott***	N	Y	Y	Y	Y	Y	N	Y
VERMONT								
AL ***Jeffords***	N	Y	Y	Y	N	Y	Y	N
VIRGINIA								
1 ***Trible***	N	Y	Y	Y	Y	Y	?	Y
2 ***Whitehurst***	?	?	Y	Y	Y	Y	Y	Y
3 ***Bliley***	N	Y	Y	Y	Y	Y	?	Y
4 ***Daniel, R.***	N	Y	Y	Y	Y	Y	Y	Y
5 Daniel, D.	Y	Y	Y	Y	Y	Y	Y	?
6 ***Butler***	N	Y	Y	Y	N	Y	Y	Y
7 ***Robinson***	N	Y	Y	Y	Y	Y	?	Y
8 ***Parris***	N	Y	Y	Y	P	Y	Y	Y
9 ***Wampler***	Y	Y	Y	Y	Y	Y	Y	Y
10 ***Wolf***	N	Y	Y	Y	Y	Y	Y	Y
WASHINGTON								
1 ***Pritchard***	Y	Y	Y	Y	Y	Y	Y	N
2 Swift	N	Y	N	Y	Y	Y	Y	N
3 Bonker	N	Y	N	Y	Y	Y	Y	N
4 ***Morrison***	N	Y	Y	Y	Y	Y	N	Y
5 Foley	Y	Y	N	Y	Y	Y	Y	N
6 Dicks	Y	Y	N	Y	Y	Y	Y	N
7 Lowry	Y	Y	N	Y	Y	Y	Y	N
WEST VIRGINIA								
1 Mollohan	N	Y	N	Y	Y	Y	Y	Y
2 ***Benedict***	?	Y	?	?	?	?	N	N
3 ***Staton***	N	Y	Y	Y	Y	Y	N	Y
4 Rahall	Y	Y	N	Y	Y	+	Y	Y
WISCONSIN								
1 Aspin	?	?	N	Y	Y	Y	Y	N
2 Kastenmeier	Y	Y	N	Y	Y	Y	Y	N
3 ***Gunderson***	N	Y	N	Y	Y	Y	Y	N
4 Zablocki	Y	Y	N	Y	Y	Y	Y	N
5 Reuss	Y	Y	N	Y	Y	Y	Y	N
6 ***Petri***	N	Y	Y	Y	Y	Y	N	Y
7 Obey	Y	Y	N	Y	Y	Y	Y	N
8 ***Roth***	N	Y	Y	Y	Y	Y	?	Y
9 ***Sensenbrenner***	N	Y	Y	Y	Y	Y	Y	Y
WYOMING								
AL ***Cheney***	N	Y	Y	Y	Y	Y	N	Y

Southern states - Ala., Ark., Fla., Ga., Ky., La., Miss., N.C., Okla., S.C., Tenn., Texas, Va.

355. HR 6838. Soviet Economic Sanctions. Passage of the bill to repeal economic sanctions against the Soviet Union 90 days after enactment of the bill, provided that the president certified to Congress that the Soviet Union was not using forced labor on certain construction projects. Passed 209-197: R 66-113; D 143-84 (ND 108-44, SD 35-40), Sept. 29, 1982.

356. HR 5543. Ocean and Coastal Resources Management and Development Fund. Passage of the bill to set aside up to $300 million in federal revenues from offshore oil and gas leasing to fund state coastal resource management programs. Passed 260-134: R 65-113; D 195-21 (ND 138-7, SD 57-14), Sept. 29, 1982. A "nay" was a vote supporting the president's position.

357. HR 6457. Health Research Extension. Waxman, D-Calif., motion that the House resolve itself into the Committee of the Whole for consideration of the bill to authorize $6.6 billion for fiscal years 1983-85 for the National Cancer and Heart-Lung-Blood Institutes and for research on certain other diseases; to explicitly authorize the existing National Institutes of Health, and to create a National Institute of Arthritis and Musculoskeletal Diseases. Motion agreed to 365-12: R 162-9; D 203-3 (ND 135-1, SD 68-2), Sept. 30, 1982.

358. HR 6457. Health Research Extension. Dannemeyer, R-Calif., amendment to the Broyhill, R-N.C., substitute, to prohibit the use of National Institutes of Health funds for research or experimentation on human fetuses while they are alive unless the research directly benefited the affected fetus. Adopted 260-140: R 156-23; D 104-117 (ND 55-92, SD 49-25), Sept. 30, 1982. (The Broyhill substitute subsequently was defeated (see vote 359, below)).

359. HR 6457. Health Research Extension. Broyhill, R-N.C., substitute to authorize $5 billion in fiscal 1983-85 for the National Cancer and Heart-Lung-Blood Institutes and for research on certain other diseases, and to create a National Institute of Arthritis and Musculoskeletal Diseases. Rejected 130-275: R 120-60; D 10-215 (ND 3-147, SD 7-68), Sept. 30, 1982. A "yea" was a vote supporting the president's position. (HR 6467 subsequently was passed by voice vote.)

KEY

Y	Voted for (yea).
#	Paired for.
+	Announced for.
N	Voted against (nay).
X	Paired against.
-	Announced against.
P	Voted "present".
C	Voted "present" to avoid possible conflict of interest.
?	Did not vote or otherwise make a position known.

Democrats   *Republicans*

	355	356	357	358	359
ALABAMA					
1 Edwards	N	Y	Y	Y	Y
2 Dickinson	N	N	Y	Y	Y
3 Nichols	N	?	Y	Y	N
4 Bevill	N	Y	Y	Y	N
5 Flippo	N	Y	Y	N	N
6 Smith	N	N	Y	Y	Y
7 Shelby	N	N	Y	Y	N
ALASKA					
AL Young	N	N	?	Y	Y
ARIZONA					
1 Rhodes	N	N	Y	Y	N
2 Udall	Y	Y	Y	N	N
3 Stump	N	N	Y	Y	Y
4 Rudd	N	N	Y	Y	Y
ARKANSAS					
1 Alexander	Y	Y	Y	N	N
2 Bethune	N	N	Y	Y	Y
3 Hammerschmidt	N	N	Y	Y	N
4 Anthony	N	Y	Y	N	N
CALIFORNIA					
1 Chappie	N	N	Y	Y	Y
2 Clausen	N	Y	Y	Y	Y
3 Matsui	Y	Y	Y	N	N
4 Fazio	Y	Y	Y	N	N
5 Burton, J.	?	?	?	?	?
6 Burton, P.	Y	Y	Y	N	N
7 Miller	Y	Y	Y	N	N
8 Dellums	Y	Y	Y	N	N
9 Stark	Y	Y	Y	N	N
10 Edwards	Y	Y	Y	N	N
11 Lantos	Y	Y	Y	N	N
12 McCloskey	Y	N	?	?	?
13 Mineta	Y	Y	Y	N	N
14 Shumway	N	N	Y	Y	Y
15 Coelho	Y	Y	Y	Y	Y
16 Panetta	Y	Y	Y	N	N
17 Pashayan	Y	N	Y	Y	Y
18 Thomas	N	N	Y	Y	Y
19 Lagomarsino	N	Y	Y	Y	Y
20 Goldwater	?	Y	?	Y	Y
21 Fiedler	N	Y	Y	Y	Y
22 Moorhead	N	N	Y	Y	Y
23 Beilenson	Y	Y	Y	N	N
24 Waxman	N	Y	Y	N	N
25 Roybal	Y	Y	Y	N	N
26 Rousselot	N	N	N	Y	Y
27 Dornan	N	N	Y	Y	Y
28 Dixon	Y	Y	Y	N	N
29 Hawkins	Y	Y	Y	N	N
30 Martinez	Y	Y	Y	N	N
31 Dymally	Y	Y	Y	N	N
32 Anderson	N	Y	Y	Y	N
33 Grisham	N	N	Y	Y	Y
34 Lungren	N	N	Y	Y	Y
35 Dreier	N	N	N	Y	Y
36 Brown	Y	Y	Y	N	N
37 Lewis	N	N	Y	Y	Y
38 Patterson	Y	Y	Y	N	N
39 Dannemeyer	Y	N	Y	Y	Y
40 Badham	Y	N	Y	Y	Y
41 Lowery	Y	Y	?	Y	Y
42 Hunter	N	N	Y	Y	Y
43 Burgener	N	N	Y	Y	Y
COLORADO					
1 Schroeder	Y	Y	Y	N	N
2 Wirth	N	Y	?	N	N
3 Kogovsek	Y	N	Y	N	N
4 Brown	N	N	Y	Y	Y

	355	356	357	358	359
5 Kramer	N	N	Y	Y	Y
CONNECTICUT					
1 Kennelly	N	Y	Y	N	N
2 Gejdenson	Y	Y	Y	N	N
3 DeNardis	Y	Y	?	N	N
4 McKinney	N	Y	Y	N	N
5 Ratchford	Y	Y	Y	N	N
6 Moffett	?	?	?	?	?
DELAWARE					
AL Evans	Y	Y	Y	Y	N
FLORIDA					
1 Hutto	N	Y	P	Y	N
2 Fuqua	N	Y	Y	Y	N
3 Bennett	N	Y	Y	Y	N
4 Chappell	?	?	?	?	?
5 McCollum	N	N	Y	Y	Y
6 Young	?	?	?	?	?
7 Gibbons	Y	Y	Y	N	N
8 Ireland	N	N	?	Y	Y
9 Nelson	N	Y	Y	Y	N
10 Bafalis	?	?	?	?	?
11 Mica	Y	Y	Y	N	N
12 Shaw	N	N	Y	Y	Y
13 Lehman	N	Y	Y	N	N
14 Pepper	Y	Y	Y	N	N
15 Fascell	N	Y	Y	?	?
GEORGIA					
1 Ginn	N	Y	Y	N	N
2 Hatcher	N	Y	Y	N	N
3 Brinkley	Y	Y	Y	N	N
4 Levitas	N	Y	Y	N	N
5 Fowler	Y	Y	Y	N	N
6 Gingrich	N	Y	Y	Y	Y
7 McDonald	N	N	N	Y	Y
8 Evans	N	Y	Y	Y	N
9 Jenkins	N	Y	Y	N	N
10 Barnard	N	Y	Y	Y	N
HAWAII					
1 Heftel	N	Y	Y	N	N
2 Akaka	Y	Y	Y	N	N
IDAHO					
1 Craig	N	N	N	Y	Y
2 Hansen	N	N	Y	Y	Y
ILLINOIS					
1 Washington	Y	Y	Y	N	N
2 Savage	Y	Y	?	?	?
3 Russo	Y	?	Y	Y	N
4 Derwinski	N	N	Y	Y	Y
5 Fary	N	Y	Y	N	N
6 Hyde	N	N	Y	Y	Y
7 Collins	Y	Y	Y	N	N
8 Rostenkowski	Y	Y	Y	N	N
9 Yates	Y	?	Y	N	N
10 Porter	Y	N	Y	Y	N
11 Annunzio	Y	Y	Y	N	N
12 Crane, P.	N	N	Y	Y	Y
13 McClory	Y	Y	Y	Y	Y
14 Erlenborn	N	N	Y	Y	Y
15 Corcoran	N	N	Y	Y	Y
16 Martin	Y	N	Y	N	N
17 O'Brien	?	?	Y	Y	N
18 Michel	Y	N	Y	Y	Y
19 Railsback	Y	N	Y	?	?
20 Findley	Y	N	Y	N	N
21 Madigan	Y	N	Y	Y	Y
22 Crane, D.	N	N	Y	Y	Y
23 Price	Y	Y	Y	Y	Y
24 Simon	Y	Y	Y	N	N
INDIANA					
1 Vacancy					
2 Fithian	Y	Y	Y	Y	N
3 Hiler	N	N	Y	Y	Y
4 Coats	Y	N	Y	Y	Y
5 Hillis	Y	N	Y	Y	N
6 Evans	Y	Y	Y	Y	N
7 Myers	Y	N	Y	Y	N
8 Deckard	Y	N	Y	Y	N
9 Hamilton	Y	Y	Y	N	N
10 Sharp	Y	Y	Y	Y	N
11 Jacobs	Y	Y	Y	N	N
IOWA					
1 Leach	Y	N	Y	Y	Y
2 Tauke	Y	N	Y	Y	Y
3 Evans	Y	N	Y	N	N
4 Smith	Y	N	Y	N	N
5 Harkin	Y	Y	Y	N	N
6 Bedell	Y	Y	?	N	Y

ND - Northern Democrats   SD - Southern Democrats

KANSAS	355	356	357	358	359
1 Roberts	Y	N	Y	Y	Y
2 Jeffries	N	N	Y	Y	Y
3 Winn	Y	N	Y	N	Y
4 Glickman	Y	N	Y	N	N
5 Whittaker	Y	N	Y	N	Y
KENTUCKY					
1 Hubbard	N	N	Y	Y	N
2 Natcher	N	Y	Y	Y	N
3 Mazzoli	N	Y	Y	Y	N
4 Snyder	N	N	Y	Y	Y
5 Rogers	N	N	Y	Y	Y
6 Hopkins	N	N	Y	Y	Y
7 Perkins	N	N	Y	Y	N
LOUISIANA					
1 Livingston	N	Y	Y	Y	N
2 Boggs	Y	Y	Y	Y	N
3 Tauzin	Y	?	Y	Y	N
4 Roemer	Y	Y	N	Y	N
5 Huckaby	Y	Y	Y	Y	N
6 Moore	Y	N	Y	Y	Y
7 Breaux	Y	Y	Y	Y	N
8 Long	N	Y	?	N	N
MAINE					
1 Emery	N	Y	Y	Y	Y
2 Snowe	Y	Y	Y	N	Y
MARYLAND					
1 Dyson	N	Y	Y	Y	N
2 Long	Y	Y	Y	N	N
3 Mikulski	N	Y	Y	N	N
4 Holt	N	Y	Y	Y	Y
5 Hoyer	Y	Y	Y	N	N
6 Byron	N	Y	Y	Y	N
7 Mitchell	Y	Y	Y	Y	N
8 Barnes	Y	Y	Y	N	N
MASSACHUSETTS					
1 Conte	N	Y	Y	Y	N
2 Boland	Y	Y	Y	Y	N
3 Early	Y	Y	?	N	N
4 Frank	N	Y	Y	Y	N
5 Shannon	Y	Y	Y	Y	N
6 Mavroules	N	Y	Y	Y	N
7 Markey	Y	Y	Y	Y	N
8 O'Neill					
9 Moakley	Y	Y	Y	Y	N
10 Heckler	Y	?	Y	Y	N
11 Donnelly	Y	Y	Y	Y	N
12 Studds	Y	Y	Y	N	N
MICHIGAN					
1 Conyers	N	Y	Y	N	?
2 Pursell	Y	N	N	N	N
3 Wolpe	Y	Y	Y	N	N
4 Siljander	N	Y	Y	Y	Y
5 Sawyer	N	N	Y	Y	Y
6 Dunn	Y	Y	Y	N	N
7 Kildee	Y	Y	Y	N	N
8 Traxler	Y	Y	?	Y	N
9 Vander Jagt	N	Y	Y	?	?
10 Albosta	Y	Y	Y	Y	N
11 Davis	Y	Y	Y	Y	N
12 Bonior	Y	Y	Y	N	N
13 Crockett	Y	Y	?	N	N
14 Hertel	Y	Y	Y	Y	N
15 Ford	Y	Y	?	N	N
16 Dingell	Y	Y	Y	Y	N
17 Brodhead	Y	Y	Y	?	N
18 Blanchard	?	?	?	?	?
19 Broomfield	Y	Y	Y	Y	N
MINNESOTA					
1 Erdahl	Y	Y	Y	Y	N
2 Hagedorn	Y	N	Y	Y	Y
3 Frenzel	Y	N	Y	N	Y
4 Vento	Y	N	Y	Y	N
5 Sabo	Y	Y	Y	N	N
6 Weber	Y	Y	Y	Y	Y
7 Stangeland	Y	N	Y	Y	Y
8 Oberstar	Y	Y	Y	Y	N
MISSISSIPPI					
1 Whitten	N	Y	Y	Y	N
2 Bowen	Y	Y	Y	Y	N
3 Montgomery	N	Y	Y	Y	Y
4 Dowdy	Y	?	Y	Y	N
5 Lott	N	Y	Y	Y	Y
MISSOURI					
1 Clay	?	?	N	N	N
2 Young	Y	Y	Y	Y	N
3 Gephardt	N	Y	?	Y	N

	355	356	357	358	359
4 Skelton	N	Y	Y	Y	Y
5 Bolling	?	Y	?	?	?
6 Coleman	N	N	Y	Y	Y
7 Taylor	N	N	Y	Y	Y
8 Bailey	Y	N	N	Y	Y
9 Volkmer	Y	N	Y	Y	N
10 Emerson	Y	N	?	Y	Y
MONTANA					
1 Williams	Y	?	Y	N	N
2 Marlenee	N	N	Y	Y	Y
NEBRASKA					
1 Bereuter	N	N	Y	Y	Y
2 Daub	N	N	Y	Y	Y
3 Smith	Y	N	Y	Y	Y
NEVADA					
AL Santini	?	?	Y	Y	N
NEW HAMPSHIRE					
1 D'Amours	N	Y	Y	Y	N
2 Gregg	N	Y	Y	Y	Y
NEW JERSEY					
1 Florio	N	Y	Y	N	N
2 Hughes	N	Y	Y	N	N
3 Howard	N	Y	Y	N	N
4 Smith	N	Y	Y	Y	N
5 Fenwick	Y	Y	Y	N	N
6 Forsythe	?	?	?	?	?
7 Roukema	N	Y	Y	N	Y
8 Roe	N	Y	Y	N	N
9 Hollenbeck	Y	Y	Y	N	N
10 Rodino	N	Y	Y	N	N
11 Minish	N	Y	Y	N	N
12 Rinaldo	N	Y	Y	N	N
13 Courter	Y	?	Y	Y	N
14 Guarini	N	Y	N	N	N
15 Dwyer	N	Y	Y	N	N
NEW MEXICO					
1 Lujan	N	N	Y	Y	Y
2 Skeen	N	N	Y	Y	Y
NEW YORK					
1 Carney	N	Y	Y	Y	Y
2 Downey	Y	Y	Y	N	N
3 Carman	N	N	Y	?	Y
4 Lent	N	Y	Y	N	N
5 McGrath	N	Y	Y	N	N
6 LeBoutillier	?	?	?	Y	N
7 Addabbo	N	Y	Y	N	N
8 Rosenthal	N	?	?	N	N
9 Ferraro	N	Y	Y	N	N
10 Biaggi	N	Y	Y	N	N
11 Scheuer	N	Y	Y	N	N
12 Chisholm	Y	?	?	?	?
13 Solarz	Y	Y	Y	N	N
14 Vacancy					
15 Zeferetti	N	Y	Y	Y	N
16 Schumer	Y	Y	Y	N	N
17 Molinari	N	Y	Y	N	N
18 Green	Y	Y	Y	N	N
19 Rangel	Y	Y	?	N	N
20 Weiss	?	?	?	?	?
21 Garcia	Y	Y	Y	?	N
22 Bingham	Y	Y	Y	N	N
23 Peyser	Y	Y	Y	N	N
24 Ottinger	Y	Y	P	N	N
25 Fish	Y	Y	Y	Y	N
26 Gilman	N	Y	Y	N	N
27 McHugh	Y	Y	Y	N	N
28 Stratton	Y	Y	Y	Y	N
29 Solomon	Y	Y	Y	Y	Y
30 Martin	N	Y	Y	N	N
31 Mitchell	Y	Y	Y	Y	N
32 Wortley	N	N	Y	Y	Y
33 Lee	N	?	Y	Y	Y
34 Horton	N	Y	Y	Y	N
35 Conable	Y	N	Y	N	Y
36 LaFalce	Y	Y	?	N	N
37 Nowak	N	Y	Y	N	N
38 Kemp	N	N	Y	Y	Y
39 Lundine	Y	Y	Y	N	N
NORTH CAROLINA					
1 Jones	Y	Y	Y	N	N
2 Fountain	Y	Y	Y	Y	Y
3 Whitley	N	Y	Y	N	N
4 Andrews	Y	Y	Y	N	N
5 Neal	Y	Y	Y	Y	N
6 Johnston	N	N	N	Y	N
7 Rose	Y	Y	Y	N	N
8 Hefner	N	Y	Y	Y	N

	355	356	357	358	359
9 Martin	N	N	Y	Y	Y
10 Broyhill	N	N	Y	Y	Y
11 Hendon	N	N	Y	Y	N
NORTH DAKOTA					
AL Dorgan	Y	Y	Y	Y	N
OHIO					
1 Gradison	N	N	Y	Y	Y
2 Luken	Y	Y	Y	Y	Y
3 Hall	Y	Y	Y	?	N
4 Oxley	Y	N	Y	Y	Y
5 Latta	N	N	Y	Y	Y
6 McEwen	N	?	Y	Y	Y
7 Brown	?	?	?	?	?
8 Kindness	N	N	N	Y	Y
9 Weber	N	Y	Y	N	Y
10 Miller	N	N	Y	Y	Y
11 Stanton	Y	N	?	Y	Y
12 Shamansky	Y	Y	Y	Y	N
13 Pease	Y	Y	Y	N	N
14 Seiberling	Y	Y	Y	Y	N
15 Wylie	?	?	Y	Y	N
16 Regula	Y	N	Y	Y	N
17 Ashbrook	N	N	N	Y	Y
18 Applegate	N	Y	?	Y	N
19 Williams	Y	Y	Y	Y	N
20 Oakar	N	Y	Y	Y	N
21 Stokes	Y	?	Y	Y	N
22 Eckart	Y	Y	Y	Y	N
23 Mottl	N	Y	Y	Y	N
OKLAHOMA					
1 Jones	N	N	Y	N	N
2 Synar	Y	Y	Y	N	N
3 Watkins	?	N	Y	Y	N
4 McCurdy	Y	?	Y	Y	N
5 Edwards	N	N	?	?	?
6 English	Y	N	Y	Y	N
OREGON					
1 AuCoin	Y	Y	Y	N	N
2 Smith	N	N	Y	Y	Y
3 Wyden	Y	Y	Y	N	N
4 Weaver	Y	Y	Y	N	N
PENNSYLVANIA					
1 Foglietta	N	Y	Y	Y	N
2 Gray	Y	Y	Y	Y	N
3 Smith	Y	Y	Y	Y	N
4 Dougherty	N	Y	?	Y	N
5 Schulze	?	N	Y	Y	Y
6 Yatron	N	?	Y	Y	N
7 Edgar	?	?	Y	N	N
8 Coyne, J.	Y	Y	Y	Y	N
9 Shuster	Y	N	Y	Y	Y
10 McDade	Y	Y	Y	Y	N
11 Nelligan	N	N	Y	Y	N
12 Murtha	N	Y	Y	Y	N
13 Coughlin	Y	Y	Y	Y	N
14 Coyne, W.	N	Y	Y	Y	N
15 Ritter	N	N	Y	Y	Y
16 Walker	Y	N	N	Y	Y
17 Ertel	?	?	?	?	?
18 Walgren	Y	Y	Y	Y	N
19 Goodling	Y	N	Y	Y	N
20 Gaydos	N	Y	Y	Y	N
21 Bailey	N	Y	Y	Y	N
22 Murphy	N	Y	Y	Y	N
23 Clinger	Y	N	Y	Y	N
24 Marks	?	?	?	N	N
25 Atkinson	N	Y	Y	Y	N
RHODE ISLAND					
1 St Germain	Y	Y	Y	Y	N
2 Schneider	Y	Y	Y	N	N
SOUTH CAROLINA					
1 Hartnett	N	Y	?	Y	Y
2 Spence	N	Y	Y	Y	Y
3 Derrick	Y	Y	Y	Y	N
4 Campbell	N	Y	Y	Y	Y
5 Holland	N	Y	?	N	N
6 Napier	Y	Y	Y	Y	N
SOUTH DAKOTA					
1 Daschle	Y	Y	Y	N	N
2 Roberts	Y	N	Y	Y	Y
TENNESSEE					
1 Quillen	N	N	Y	Y	N
2 Duncan	N	N	Y	Y	Y
3 Bouquard	Y	Y	?	Y	N
4 Gore	Y	Y	Y	Y	N
5 Boner	N	Y	Y	Y	N
6 Beard	?	?	?	?	?

	355	356	357	358	359
7 Jones	Y	Y	Y	N	N
8 Ford	Y	?	Y	N	N
TEXAS					
1 Hall, S.	N	Y	Y	Y	N
2 Wilson	N	N	Y	N	N
3 Collins	?	?	?	?	?
4 Hall, R.	Y	Y	Y	Y	N
5 Mattox	?	?	?	?	?
6 Gramm	N	N	Y	Y	Y
7 Archer	Y	N	?	Y	Y
8 Fields	N	N	Y	Y	Y
9 Brooks	N	Y	Y	N	N
10 Pickle	N	Y	Y	Y	N
11 Leath	N	Y	Y	Y	N
12 Wright	Y	Y	Y	Y	N
13 Hightower	N	Y	Y	Y	N
14 Patman	N	Y	Y	Y	N
15 de la Garza	N	Y	Y	Y	N
16 White	N	N	Y	Y	N
17 Stenholm	Y	N	Y	Y	Y
18 Leland	Y	Y	Y	Y	N
19 Hance	N	Y	Y	Y	N
20 Gonzalez	Y	Y	Y	Y	N
21 Loeffler	N	N	Y	Y	Y
22 Paul	N	Y	Y	Y	N
23 Kazen	Y	Y	Y	Y	N
24 Frost	Y	Y	Y	Y	N
UTAH					
1 Hansen	N	N	Y	Y	Y
2 Marriott	N	N	Y	Y	N
VERMONT					
AL Jeffords	Y	N	Y	N	N
VIRGINIA					
1 Trible	N	?	Y	Y	Y
2 Whitehurst	N	Y	Y	?	Y
3 Bliley	N	Y	Y	Y	Y
4 Daniel, R.	N	Y	Y	Y	Y
5 Daniel, D.	?	?	?	?	?
6 Butler	N	N	N	N	Y
7 Robinson	N	Y	Y	Y	N
8 Parris	N	Y	Y	N	N
9 Wampler	N	N	?	?	Y
10 Wolf	N	Y	Y	Y	N
WASHINGTON					
1 Pritchard	Y	Y	Y	N	N
2 Swift	Y	Y	Y	N	N
3 Bonker	Y	Y	?	Y	N
4 Morrison	N	Y	Y	Y	N
5 Foley	Y	Y	Y	N	N
6 Dicks	Y	Y	Y	N	N
7 Lowry	Y	Y	Y	Y	N
WEST VIRGINIA					
1 Mollohan	N	Y	Y	N	N
2 Benedict	Y	N	Y	Y	Y
3 Staton	N	N	Y	Y	Y
4 Rahall	N	N	?	N	N
WISCONSIN					
1 Aspin	Y	?	?	?	?
2 Kastenmeier	N	Y	Y	N	N
3 Gunderson	N	N	Y	Y	Y
4 Zablocki	Y	Y	Y	Y	N
5 Reuss	Y	Y	Y	N	N
6 Petri	N	Y	Y	N	N
7 Obey	Y	Y	Y	?	N
8 Roth	Y	Y	Y	Y	N
9 Sensenbrenner	Y	Y	Y	Y	Y
WYOMING					
AL Cheney	N	N	Y	Y	Y

Southern states - Ala., Ark., Fla., Ga., Ky., La., Miss., N.C., Okla., S.C., Tenn., Texas, Va.

KEY

Y Voted for (yea).
\# Paired for.
+ Announced for.
N Voted against (nay).
X Paired against.
- Announced against.
P Voted "present".
C Voted "present" to avoid possible conflict of interest.
? Did not vote or otherwise make a position known.

Democrats   *Republicans*

360. HR 3809. Nuclear Waste Policy Act. Udall, D-Ariz., motion that the House resolve itself into the Committee of the Whole for consideration of the bill to establish a federal program for the interim storage and eventual permanent disposal of highly radioactive nuclear waste. Motion agreed to 370-1: R 165-0; D 205-1 (ND 136-1, SD 69-0), Sept. 30, 1982.

361. Procedural Motion. Walker, R-Pa., motion to approve the House *Journal* of Thursday, Sept. 30. Motion agreed to 331-26: R 150-15; D 181-11 (ND 116-10, SD 65-1), Oct. 1, 1982.

362. H J Res 350. Balanced Budget Constitutional Amendment. Alexander, D-Ark., substitute to require the president to submit a balanced budget to Congress each year and to require Congress to adopt a balanced budget unless a majority of Congress declares a "national emergency," in which case deficit spending would be allowed. Rejected 77-346: R 0-187; D 77-159 (ND 52-107, SD 25-52), Oct. 1, 1982.

363. H J Res 350. Balanced Budget Constitutional Amendment. Passage of the joint resolution to propose an amendment to the Constitution to require Congress to adopt a balanced federal budget every year, except in time of war, unless a three-fifths majority of Congress agreed to deficit spending. Rejected 236-187: R 167-20; D 69-167 (ND 12-147, SD 57-20), Oct. 1, 1982. A two-thirds majority of those present and voting (282 in this case) of both houses is required for passage of a joint resolution proposing an amendment to the Constitution. A "yea" was a vote supporting the president's position.

	360	361	362	363
ALABAMA				
1 *Edwards*	Y	Y	N	Y
2 *Dickinson*	?	N	N	Y
3 Nichols	Y	Y	N	Y
4 Bevill	Y	Y	Y	Y
5 Flippo	Y	Y	Y	Y
6 *Smith*	Y	Y	N	Y
7 Shelby	Y	?	N	Y
ALASKA				
AL *Young*	Y	?	N	Y
ARIZONA				
1 *Rhodes*	Y	Y	N	N
2 Udall	Y	Y	Y	N
3 *Stump*	Y	Y	N	Y
4 *Rudd*	Y	Y	N	Y
ARKANSAS				
1 Alexander	Y	Y	Y	N
2 *Bethune*	Y	Y	N	N
3 *Hammerschmidt*	Y	Y	N	Y
4 Anthony	Y	Y	Y	Y
CALIFORNIA				
1 *Chappie*	Y	Y	N	Y
2 *Clausen*	Y	?	N	Y
3 Matsui	Y	Y	N	N
4 Fazio	Y	Y	N	N
5 Burton, J.	?	?	N	N
6 Burton, P.	Y	Y	N	N
7 Miller	Y	Y	N	N
8 Dellums	Y	Y	N	N
9 Stark	Y	?	N	N
10 Edwards	Y	Y	N	N
11 Lantos	Y	Y	N	N
12 *McCloskey*	?	?	?	?
13 Mineta	Y	?	N	N
14 *Shumway*	Y	Y	N	Y
15 Coelho	Y	Y	N	Y
16 Panetta	Y	Y	Y	N
17 *Pashayan*	Y	Y	N	Y
18 *Thomas*	Y	Y	N	Y
19 *Lagomarsino*	Y	Y	N	Y
20 *Goldwater*	?	?	?	?
21 *Fiedler*	Y	Y	N	Y
22 *Moorhead*	Y	Y	N	Y
23 Beilenson	Y	?	N	N
24 Waxman	Y	?	N	N
25 Roybal	Y	Y	N	N
26 *Rousselot*	Y	Y	N	Y
27 *Dornan*	Y	?	N	Y
28 Dixon	Y	?	N	N
29 Hawkins	Y	Y	N	N
30 Martinez	Y	?	Y	N
31 Dymally	Y	Y	N	N
32 Anderson	Y	Y	Y	Y
33 *Grisham*	Y	?	N	Y
34 *Lungren*	Y	Y	N	Y
35 *Dreier*	Y	N	N	Y
36 Brown	Y	?	Y	N
37 *Lewis*	Y	?	N	Y
38 Patterson	Y	Y	N	Y
39 *Dannemeyer*	Y	Y	N	Y
40 *Badham*	Y	?	?	#
41 *Lowery*	Y	Y	N	Y
42 *Hunter*	Y	Y	N	Y
43 *Burgener*	Y	Y	N	Y
COLORADO				
1 Schroeder	P	N	Y	N
2 Wirth	Y	Y	N	N
3 Kogovsek	Y	Y	N	N
4 *Brown*	Y	N	N	Y

	360	361	362	363
5 *Kramer*	Y	Y	N	Y
CONNECTICUT				
1 Kennelly	Y	Y	N	N
2 Gejdenson	Y	N	N	N
3 *DeNardis*	Y	?	N	N
4 *McKinney*	?	?	N	N
5 Ratchford	Y	Y	N	N
6 Moffett	?	?	N	N
DELAWARE				
AL *Evans*	Y	Y	N	Y
FLORIDA				
1 Hutto	P	P	N	Y
2 Fuqua	Y	Y	N	Y
3 Bennett	Y	Y	N	Y
4 Chappell	?	?	?	#
5 *McCollum*	Y	Y	N	Y
6 *Young*	?	?	N	Y
7 Gibbons	Y	?	Y	Y
8 Ireland	?	Y	N	Y
9 Nelson	Y	Y	N	Y
10 *Bafalis*	?	?	N	Y
11 Mica	Y	?	Y	Y
12 *Shaw*	Y	Y	N	Y
13 Lehman	Y	Y	N	N
14 Pepper	Y	Y	N	N
15 Fascell	?	?	N	N
GEORGIA				
1 Ginn	Y	Y	N	Y
2 Hatcher	Y	Y	N	Y
3 Brinkley	Y	Y	N	Y
4 Levitas	Y	Y	N	Y
5 Fowler	Y	Y	Y	N
6 *Gingrich*	Y	N	N	Y
7 McDonald	Y	Y	N	Y
8 Evans	?	?	N	Y
9 Jenkins	Y	Y	N	Y
10 Barnard	Y	Y	N	Y
HAWAII				
1 Heftel	Y	?	Y	N
2 Akaka	Y	Y	N	N
IDAHO				
1 *Craig*	Y	Y	N	Y
2 *Hansen*	Y	Y	N	Y
ILLINOIS				
1 Washington	Y	?	N	N
2 Savage	Y	?	N	N
3 Russo	Y	Y	N	N
4 *Derwinski*	?	Y	N	Y
5 Fary	Y	Y	N	N
6 *Hyde*	Y	Y	N	Y
7 Collins	Y	Y	N	N
8 Rostenkowski	Y	Y	N	N
9 Yates	Y	N	N	N
10 *Porter*	Y	Y	N	Y
11 Annunzio	Y	Y	N	N
12 *Crane, P.*	Y	Y	N	Y
13 *McClory*	Y	Y	N	Y
14 *Erlenborn*	Y	Y	N	Y
15 *Corcoran*	Y	Y	N	Y
16 *Martin*	Y	Y	N	Y
17 *O'Brien*	Y	Y	N	Y
18 *Michel*	Y	Y	N	Y
19 *Railsback*	Y	Y	N	Y
20 *Findley*	Y	Y	N	Y
21 *Madigan*	Y	Y	N	Y
22 *Crane, D.*	Y	Y	N	Y
23 Price	Y	Y	N	N
24 Simon	Y	Y	Y	Y
INDIANA				
1 Vacancy				
2 Fithian	?	?	Y	N
3 *Hiler*	Y	Y	N	Y
4 *Coats*	Y	Y	N	Y
5 *Hillis*	Y	Y	N	Y
6 Evans	Y	Y	Y	N
7 *Myers*	Y	Y	N	Y
8 *Deckard*	Y	Y	N	Y
9 Hamilton	Y	Y	Y	N
10 Sharp	Y	Y	N	N
11 Jacobs	Y	N	N	Y
IOWA				
1 *Leach*	Y	Y	N	Y
2 *Tauke*	Y	Y	N	Y
3 *Evans*	Y	N	N	Y
4 *Smith*	Y	Y	N	N
5 Harkin	Y	N	Y	N
6 Bedell	Y	Y	Y	N

ND - Northern Democrats   SD - Southern Democrats

	360 361 362 363		360 361 362 363		360 361 362 363		360 361 362 363
KANSAS		4 Skelton	Y Y Y Y	9 *Martin*	Y Y N Y	7 Jones	Y Y Y Y
1 *Roberts*	Y Y N Y	5 Bolling	? Y N N	10 *Broyhill*	Y Y N Y	8 Ford	Y ? N N
2 *Jeffries*	Y Y N Y	6 Coleman	Y Y N Y	11 *Hendon*	? Y N Y	**TEXAS**	
3 *Winn*	Y Y N Y	7 Taylor	Y Y N Y	**NORTH DAKOTA**		1 Hall, S.	Y Y N Y
4 Glickman	Y Y Y N	8 *Bailey*	Y Y N Y	AL Dorgan	N N Y N	2 Wilson	Y Y N Y
5 *Whittaker*	Y Y N Y	9 Volkmer	Y Y Y Y	**OHIO**		3 *Collins*	? ? N Y
KENTUCKY		10 Emerson	Y N N Y	1 *Gradison*	Y Y N Y	4 Hall, R.	Y Y N Y
1 Hubbard	Y Y N Y	**MONTANA**		2 Luken	Y Y N N	5 Mattox	? ? Y N
2 Natcher	Y Y Y Y	1 Williams	? ? N N	3 Hall	? Y N N	6 *Gramm*	Y Y N Y
3 Mazzoli	Y Y N N	2 *Marlenee*	Y Y N Y	4 *Oxley*	Y Y N Y	7 *Archer*	Y Y N Y
4 *Snyder*	Y Y N Y	**NEBRASKA**		5 *Latta*	Y Y N Y	8 *Fields*	? N N Y
5 *Rogers*	Y Y N Y	1 *Bereuter*	Y Y N Y	6 *McEwen*	Y Y N Y	9 Brooks	Y Y N N
6 *Hopkins*	Y Y N Y	2 *Daub*	Y Y N Y	7 *Brown*	? ? N Y	10 Pickle	Y Y N Y
7 Perkins	Y Y Y N	3 *Smith*	Y Y N Y	8 *Kindness*	Y Y N Y	11 Leath	Y Y N Y
LOUISIANA		**NEVADA**		9 *Weber*	Y Y N Y	12 Wright	Y Y Y N
1 *Livingston*	Y Y N Y	AL Santini	Y ? N Y	10 *Miller*	Y N N Y	13 Hightower	Y Y N Y
2 Boggs	Y ? N N	**NEW HAMPSHIRE**		11 *Stanton*	Y Y N Y	14 Patman	Y Y N Y
3 Tauzin	Y Y N Y	1 D'Amours	Y Y Y N	12 Shamansky	Y Y Y N	15 de la Garza	Y Y Y Y
4 Roemer	Y N N Y	2 *Gregg*	Y Y N Y	13 Pease	Y Y N N	16 White	Y Y N Y
5 Huckaby	Y Y N Y	**NEW JERSEY**		14 Seiberling	Y Y N N	17 Stenholm	Y Y N Y
6 *Moore*	Y Y N Y	1 Florio	? Y N N	15 *Wylie*	Y Y N Y	18 Leland	Y Y N N
7 Breaux	Y ? N Y	2 Hughes	Y Y N N	16 *Regula*	Y Y N Y	19 Hance	Y Y N Y
8 Long	Y Y Y N	3 Howard	Y Y N N	17 *Ashbrook*	Y Y N Y	20 Gonzalez	Y Y Y N
MAINE		4 Smith	Y Y N Y	18 Applegate	Y ? Y Y	21 *Loeffler*	Y Y N Y
1 *Emery*	? Y N Y	5 *Fenwick*	? P N Y	19 *Williams*	Y Y N Y	22 *Paul*	Y ? N Y
2 *Snowe*	Y Y N Y	6 *Forsythe*	? ? ? ?	20 Oakar	Y Y N Y	23 Kazen	Y Y N Y
MARYLAND		7 *Roukema*	? Y N N	21 Stokes	Y Y N N	24 Frost	? Y Y N
1 Dyson	Y Y Y Y	8 Roe	Y P Y N	22 Eckart	Y Y Y Y	**UTAH**	
2 Long	Y Y Y N	9 *Hollenbeck*	? Y N N	23 Mottl	Y Y Y Y	1 *Hansen*	Y Y N Y
3 Mikulski	Y Y N N	10 Rodino	Y Y N N	**OKLAHOMA**		2 *Marriott*	Y Y N Y
4 *Holt*	Y Y N Y	11 Minish	Y Y Y N	1 Jones	Y Y N N	**VERMONT**	
5 Hoyer	Y Y N N	12 *Rinaldo*	Y Y N N	2 Synar	Y Y Y N	AL *Jeffords*	Y Y N N
6 Byron	Y Y N Y	13 *Courter*	Y Y N Y	3 Watkins	Y Y Y Y	**VIRGINIA**	
7 Mitchell	Y N N N	14 Guarini	Y Y - X	4 McCurdy	Y Y N Y	1 *Trible*	Y ? N Y
8 Barnes	Y Y N N	15 Dwyer	Y Y N N	5 *Edwards*	? ? ? ?	2 *Whitehurst*	? ? N Y
MASSACHUSETTS		**NEW MEXICO**		6 English	Y Y N Y	3 Bliley	Y Y N Y
1 *Conte*	Y Y N N	1 *Lujan*	Y Y N Y	**OREGON**		4 *Daniel, R.*	Y Y N Y
2 Boland	Y Y N N	2 *Skeen*	Y Y N Y	1 AuCoin	Y Y N N	5 Daniel, D.	? ? ? ?
3 Early	Y ? N N	**NEW YORK**		2 *Smith*	Y Y N Y	6 *Butler*	Y N N Y
4 Frank	Y ? N N	1 *Carney*	? ? N Y	3 Wyden	Y Y N N	7 *Robinson*	Y Y N Y
5 Shannon	Y Y N N	2 Downey	Y Y N N	4 Weaver	Y Y N N	8 *Parris*	Y Y N Y
6 Mavroules	? Y N N	3 *Carman*	Y Y N Y	**PENNSYLVANIA**		9 *Wampler*	Y Y N Y
7 Markey	Y Y N N	4 *Lent*	Y Y N Y	1 Foglietta	Y Y N N	10 *Wolf*	Y Y N Y
8 O'Neill		5 *McGrath*	Y Y N Y	2 Gray	? ? N N	**WASHINGTON**	
9 *Moakley*	Y Y N N	6 *LeBoutillier*	Y Y N Y	3 Smith	? Y N N	1 *Pritchard*	Y Y N N
10 *Heckler*	Y Y N N	7 Addabbo	Y ? N N	4 *Dougherty*	? Y N N	2 Swift	Y Y N N
11 Donnelly	Y Y N N	8 Rosenthal	Y ? N N	5 *Schulze*	Y Y N Y	3 Bonker	Y Y Y N
12 Studds	Y Y N N	9 Ferraro	Y ? N N	6 Yatron	Y Y N Y	4 *Morrison*	Y ? N Y
MICHIGAN		10 Biaggi	Y Y N N	7 Edgar	Y Y N N	5 Foley	? Y Y N
1 Conyers	Y Y N N	11 Scheuer	Y Y Y N	8 *Coyne, J.*	Y Y N Y	6 Dicks	Y Y Y N
2 *Pursell*	? ? N Y	12 Chisholm	? ? N N	9 *Shuster*	Y Y N Y	7 Lowry	Y Y N N
3 Wolpe	Y Y N N	13 Solarz	Y ? N N	10 *McDade*	Y Y N N	**WEST VIRGINIA**	
4 *Siljander*	Y ? N Y	14 Vacancy		11 *Nelligan*	Y Y N N	1 Mollohan	Y Y Y N
5 *Sawyer*	Y Y N Y	15 Zeferetti	Y Y N N	12 Murtha	Y Y N N	2 *Benedict*	Y Y N Y
6 *Dunn*	Y Y N Y	16 Schumer	Y Y N N	13 Coughlin	Y N N Y	3 *Staton*	Y Y N Y
7 Kildee	Y Y N N	17 Molinari	Y N N Y	14 Coyne, W.	Y Y N N	4 Rahall	Y Y N N
8 Traxler	Y Y Y N	18 *Green*	Y Y N N	15 *Ritter*	Y Y N Y	**WISCONSIN**	
9 *Vander Jagt*	Y Y Y Y	19 Rangel	Y Y N N	16 *Walker*	Y N N Y	1 Aspin	? Y Y N
10 Albosta	Y Y N Y	20 Weiss	? ? N N	17 Ertel	? ? Y Y	2 Kastenmeier	Y Y N N
11 *Davis*	Y Y N Y	21 Garcia	Y ? N N	18 Walgren	Y Y N Y	3 *Gunderson*	Y Y N Y
12 Bonior	Y Y Y N	22 Bingham	Y Y N N	19 *Goodling*	? N N Y	4 Zablocki	Y Y Y N
13 Crockett	? Y N N	23 Peyser	? Y N N	20 Gaydos	? Y Y N	5 Reuss	Y Y N N
14 Hertel	Y ? N N	24 Ottinger	P P N N	21 Bailey	Y Y N N	6 *Petri*	Y Y N Y
15 Ford	Y ? N N	25 *Fish*	Y Y N Y	22 Murphy	Y N N N	7 Obey	Y Y N N
16 Dingell	Y Y N N	26 Gilman	Y Y N N	23 Clinger	Y Y N Y	8 *Roth*	Y Y N Y
17 Brodhead	Y Y Y N	27 McHugh	? Y N N	24 *Marks*	? ? N N	9 *Sensenbrenner*	Y Y N Y
18 Blanchard	? ? ? ?	28 Stratton	? ? N N	25 Atkinson	Y ? N Y	**WYOMING**	
19 *Broomfield*	Y N N Y	29 Solomon	Y Y N Y	**RHODE ISLAND**		AL *Cheney*	Y Y N Y
MINNESOTA		30 *Martin*	Y Y N Y	1 St Germain	Y Y N N		
1 *Erdahl*	Y Y N Y	31 *Mitchell*	Y Y N Y	2 *Schneider*	Y Y N N		
2 *Hagedorn*	Y Y N Y	32 *Wortley*	? Y N Y	**SOUTH CAROLINA**			
3 *Frenzel*	Y Y N Y	33 *Lee*	? Y N Y	1 *Hartnett*	Y Y N Y		
4 Vento	Y Y N N	34 Horton	Y Y N Y	2 *Spence*	Y Y N Y		
5 Sabo	Y N N N	35 *Conable*	Y Y N Y	3 Derrick	Y Y N Y		
6 *Weber*	Y Y N Y	36 LaFalce	Y ? Y N	4 *Campbell*	Y Y N Y		
7 *Stangeland*	Y Y N Y	37 Nowak	Y Y N N	5 Holland	Y Y N N		
8 Oberstar	Y ? N N	38 *Kemp*	Y Y N N	6 *Napier*	Y Y N Y		
MISSISSIPPI		39 Lundine	Y Y N N	**SOUTH DAKOTA**			
I Whitten	? Y Y Y	**NORTH CAROLINA**		1 Daschle	Y Y N N		
2 Bowen	Y Y Y Y	1 Jones	Y ? Y Y	2 *Roberts*	? Y N Y		
3 Montgomery	Y Y N Y	2 Fountain	Y Y N Y	**TENNESSEE**			
4 Dowdy	Y Y N Y	3 Whitley	Y Y N Y	1 *Quillen*	Y Y N Y		
5 *Lott*	Y Y N Y	4 Andrews	Y Y N Y	2 *Duncan*	Y Y N Y		
MISSOURI		5 Neal	Y Y N Y	3 Bouquard	Y Y N Y		
1 Clay	Y N N N	6 *Johnston*	Y N N Y	4 Gore	Y Y N N		
2 Young	? Y Y N	7 kose	? Y Y Y	5 Boner	Y Y Y Y		
3 Gephardt	Y Y Y N	8 Hefner	Y Y N Y	6 *Beard*	? ? N Y		

Southern states - Ala., Ark., Fla., Ga., Ky., La., Miss., N.C., Okla., S.C., Tenn., Texas, Va.

KEY

Y Voted for (yea).
Paired for.
+ Announced for.
N Voted against (nay).
X Paired against.
- Announced against.
P Voted "present".
C Voted "present" to avoid possible conflict of interest.
? Did not vote or otherwise make a position known.

Democrats   *Republicans*

364. H J Res 599. Continuing Appropriations, Fiscal 1983. Adoption of the conference report on the joint resolution to provide temporary funding, through Dec. 17, 1982, for government agencies whose regular fiscal 1983 appropriations bills had not been enacted by Oct. 1. Adopted 290-123: R 125-60; D 165-63 (ND 104-47, SD 61-16), Oct. 1, 1982.

365. H J Res 599. Continuing Appropriations, Fiscal 1983. Ford, D-Mich., motion that the House concur in a Senate amendment to increase the salaries of air traffic controllers 6.6 percent annually, with an amendment that would permit the administration to rehire former air traffic controllers. Motion rejected 128-267: R 8-173; D 120-94 (ND 110-33, SD 10-61), Oct. 1, 1982.

366. HR 5890. NASA Authorization. Adoption of the conference report on the bill to authorize $6,772,900,000 in fiscal 1983 for the National Aeronautics and Space Administration. Adopted 284-83: R 113-62; D 171-21 (ND 112-16, SD 59-5), Oct. 1, 1982.

367. HR 6267. Net Worth Guarantee Act. Adoption of the rule (H Res 603) providing for House floor consideration of the conference report on the bill to strengthen the financial stability of the savings and loan industry and expand the powers of both savings and loan institutions and commercial banks. Adopted 294-59: R 151-18; D 143-41 (ND 103-18, SD 40-23), Oct. 1, 1982. (The conference report subsequently was adopted by voice vote, clearing the bill for the president.)

368. S 2036. Job Training. Adoption of the conference report on the bill to establish a new program, replacing the expired Comprehensive Employment and Training Act, of grants to states and local governments for providing skill training and other employment-related assistance to economically disadvantaged youths and adults. Adopted (and thus cleared for the president) 339-12: R 159-9; D 180-3 (ND 122-1, SD 58-2), Oct. 1, 1982. A "yea" was a vote supporting the president's position.

	364	365	366	367	368
ALABAMA					
1 *Edwards*	Y	N	?	Y	Y
2 *Dickinson*	?	X	?	?	?
3 Nichols	Y	?	?	?	Y
4 Bevill	Y	N	Y	Y	Y
5 Flippo	Y	N	Y	?	?
6 *Smith*	Y	N	N	Y	Y
7 Shelby	N	N	Y	Y	Y
ALASKA					
AL *Young*	Y	N	Y	Y	Y
ARIZONA					
1 *Rhodes*	Y	N	Y	Y	Y
2 Udall	Y	Y	Y	Y	Y
3 Stump	N	N	N	Y	N
4 *Rudd*	Y	N	?	?	?
ARKANSAS					
1 Alexander	Y	N	Y	N	Y
2 *Bethune*	Y	N	Y	N	Y
3 *Hammerschmidt*	Y	N	Y	N	Y
4 Anthony	Y	N	Y	Y	Y
CALIFORNIA					
1 *Chappie*	N	N	Y	Y	Y
2 *Clausen*	Y	N	Y	Y	Y
3 Matsui	N	Y	Y	N	Y
4 Fazio	Y	?	?	?	?
5 Burton, J.	N	Y	?	?	?
6 Burton, P.	N	Y	Y	N	?
7 Miller	N	Y	?	Y	Y
8 Dellums	N	Y	N	N	Y
9 Stark	N	Y	N	Y	Y
10 Edwards	Y	Y	Y	Y	Y
11 Lantos	Y	Y	?	?	?
12 *McCloskey*	?	?	?	?	?
13 Mineta	Y	N	Y	Y	Y
14 *Shumway*	N	N	N	Y	Y
15 Coelho	Y	N	Y	Y	Y
16 Panetta	N	Y	Y	Y	Y
17 *Pashayan*	Y	?	N	N	Y
18 *Thomas*	N	N	Y	Y	Y
19 *Lagomarsino*	Y	N	Y	Y	Y
20 *Goldwater*	?	?	?	?	?
21 *Fiedler*	Y	N	Y	Y	Y
22 *Moorhead*	N	N	Y	Y	Y
23 Beilenson	?	?	?	?	?
24 Waxman	Y	Y	Y	?	Y
25 Roybal	Y	Y	N	Y	Y
26 *Rousselot*	N	N	?	?	?
27 *Dornan*	N	N	Y	Y	Y
28 Dixon	Y	Y	Y	?	Y
29 Hawkins	Y	N	Y	Y	Y
30 Martinez	?	?	?	?	?
31 Dymally	Y	N	Y	Y	Y
32 Anderson	N	N	Y	Y	Y
33 *Grisham*	N	N	N	Y	Y
34 *Lungren*	N	N	N	Y	Y
35 *Dreier*	N	N	N	Y	Y
36 Brown	Y	Y	Y	Y	Y
37 *Lewis*	N	N	N	Y	Y
38 Patterson	Y	Y	Y	Y	?
39 *Dannemeyer*	N	N	N	Y	Y
40 *Badham*	?	X	?	?	?
41 *Lowery*	Y	N	Y	Y	Y
42 *Hunter*	N	N	Y	Y	Y
43 *Burgener*	Y	N	?	?	Y
COLORADO					
1 Schroeder	N	P	Y	N	Y
2 Wirth	Y	Y	Y	N	Y
3 Kogovsek	Y	Y	Y	N	Y
4 *Brown*	N	N	N	N	N

	364	365	366	367	368
5 *Kramer*	Y	N	Y	?	Y
CONNECTICUT					
1 Kennelly	Y	Y	Y	Y	Y
2 Gejdenson	Y	Y	Y	Y	Y
3 *DeNardis*	Y	Y	Y	Y	Y
4 *McKinney*	Y	?	Y	Y	Y
5 Ratchford	Y	Y	Y	Y	Y
6 Moffett	Y	#	?	?	?
DELAWARE					
AL *Evans*	Y	N	Y	Y	Y
FLORIDA					
1 Hutto	Y	N	Y	Y	Y
2 Fuqua	Y	N	?	?	?
3 Bennett	N	N	Y	Y	Y
4 Chappell	Y	?	?	?	?
5 *McCollum*	N	N	Y	Y	Y
6 *Young*	Y	N	?	?	?
7 Gibbons	N	N	Y	Y	Y
8 Ireland	Y	N	?	?	?
9 Nelson	Y	N	Y	Y	Y
10 *Bafalis*	Y	N	Y	Y	Y
11 Mica	Y	N	Y	Y	Y
12 *Shaw*	Y	N	Y	Y	Y
13 Lehman	Y	Y	?	Y	Y
14 Pepper	Y	Y	Y	Y	Y
15 Fascell	Y	Y	Y	Y	Y
GEORGIA					
1 Ginn	Y	N	Y	?	?
2 Hatcher	Y	N	Y	Y	Y
3 Brinkley	Y	N	Y	Y	Y
4 Levitas	Y	N	Y	Y	Y
5 Fowler	Y	N	Y	?	?
6 *Gingrich*	Y	N	Y	Y	Y
7 McDonald	N	N	N	N	N
8 Evans	N	N	Y	Y	Y
9 Jenkins	Y	N	Y	?	?
10 Barnard	Y	N	Y	Y	Y
HAWAII					
1 Heftel	Y	Y	?	Y	Y
2 Akaka	Y	Y	Y	Y	Y
IDAHO					
1 *Craig*	Y	N	N	Y	Y
2 *Hansen*	Y	N	N	Y	Y
ILLINOIS					
1 Washington	N	Y	Y	N	Y
2 Savage	N	Y	?	Y	Y
3 Russo	N	N	N	Y	Y
4 *Derwinski*	Y	N	Y	Y	Y
5 Fary	Y	Y	Y	Y	Y
6 *Hyde*	N	N	Y	Y	Y
7 Collins	N	Y	Y	Y	Y
8 Rostenkowski	Y	N	Y	Y	Y
9 Yates	Y	Y	?	?	?
10 *Porter*	N	N	Y	Y	Y
11 Annunzio	Y	Y	Y	Y	Y
12 *Crane, P.*	N	N	N	N	N
13 *McClory*	Y	N	Y	N	Y
14 *Erlenborn*	Y	N	Y	Y	Y
15 *Corcoran*	Y	N	Y	Y	Y
16 *Martin*	Y	N	Y	Y	Y
17 *O'Brien*	Y	N	Y	Y	Y
18 *Michel*	Y	N	N	Y	Y
19 *Railsback*	Y	N	Y	?	?
20 *Findley*	Y	N	Y	Y	Y
21 *Madigan*	Y	N	N	Y	Y
22 *Crane, D.*	N	N	N	N	N
23 Price	Y	Y	Y	Y	Y
24 Simon	Y	N	N	Y	Y
INDIANA					
1 Vacancy					
2 Fithian	Y	Y	Y	Y	Y
3 *Hiler*	N	N	N	Y	Y
4 *Coats*	N	N	N	Y	Y
5 *Hillis*	Y	N	N	Y	Y
6 Evans	Y	Y	Y	Y	Y
7 *Myers*	Y	N	N	Y	Y
8 *Deckard*	Y	N	Y	?	Y
9 Hamilton	N	N	Y	?	?
10 Sharp	N	Y	Y	Y	Y
11 Jacobs	Y	Y	N	N	Y
IOWA					
1 *Leach*	Y	N	Y	Y	Y
2 *Tauke*	N	N	N	Y	Y
3 *Evans*	Y	N	Y	Y	Y
4 Smith	Y	Y	Y	Y	Y
5 Harkin	N	N	Y	Y	Y
6 Bedell	N	Y	Y	Y	Y

ND - Northern Democrats   SD - Southern Democrats

	364	365	366	367	368
KANSAS					
1 *Roberts*	Y	N	N	Y	Y
2 *Jeffries*	N	N	N	N	N
3 *Winn*	Y	N	Y	Y	Y
4 Glickman	N	N	N	Y	Y
5 *Whittaker*	Y	N	N	Y	Y
KENTUCKY					
1 Hubbard	N	N	?	N	Y
2 Natcher	Y	N	Y	Y	Y
3 Mazzoli	Y	N	Y	Y	Y
4 *Snyder*	N	N	N	Y	Y
5 Rogers	Y	N	Y	Y	Y
6 Hopkins	Y	N	Y	Y	Y
7 Perkins	Y	N	Y	N	Y
LOUISIANA					
1 *Livingston*	Y	N	Y	Y	Y
2 Boggs	Y	N	Y	N	Y
3 Tauzin	Y	N	Y	N	Y
4 Roemer	Y	N	Y	Y	Y
5 Huckaby	Y	N	Y	Y	Y
6 *Moore*	Y	N	Y	N	Y
7 Breaux	Y	N	Y	Y	Y
8 Long	Y	N	Y	Y	Y
MAINE					
1 *Emery*	Y	N	Y	Y	?
2 *Snowe*	Y	N	Y	Y	Y
MARYLAND					
1 Dyson	Y	Y	Y	Y	Y
2 Long	Y	Y	Y	Y	Y
3 Mikulski	Y	Y	Y	Y	Y
4 *Holt*	Y	N	Y	N	Y
5 Hoyer	Y	Y	Y	Y	Y
6 Byron	Y	N	Y	N	Y
7 Mitchell	Y	Y	?	Y	Y
8 Barnes	Y	Y	Y	Y	Y
MASSACHUSETTS					
1 *Conte*	Y	N	Y	?	?
2 Boland	Y	N	?	?	?
3 Early	Y	Y	Y	Y	Y
4 Frank	N	Y	Y	Y	Y
5 Shannon	Y	Y	Y	Y	Y
6 Mavroules	Y	Y	Y	Y	Y
7 Markey	Y	Y	Y	N	Y
8 O'Neill					
9 Moakley	Y	Y	Y	Y	Y
10 *Heckler*	Y	Y	Y	Y	Y
11 Donnelly	Y	Y	Y	Y	Y
12 Studds	N	Y	Y	Y	Y
MICHIGAN					
1 Conyers	N	Y	?	?	?
2 *Pursell*	Y	N	N	?	?
3 Wolpe	N	Y	Y	Y	Y
4 *Siljander*	N	N	N	Y	Y
5 *Sawyer*	N	N	Y	Y	Y
6 *Dunn*	Y	N	N	Y	Y
7 Kildee	N	Y	Y	Y	Y
8 Traxler	?	?	?	?	?
9 *Vander Jagt*	Y	N	Y	?	?
10 Albosta	Y	Y	Y	?	?
11 *Davis*	Y	N	Y	?	?
12 Bonior	N	Y	Y	Y	Y
13 Crockett	Y	Y	Y	?	?
14 Hertel	N	Y	Y	Y	Y
15 Ford	Y	Y	?	?	?
16 Dingell	Y	Y	Y	N	Y
17 Brodhead	Y	Y	Y	Y	Y
18 Blanchard	?	?	?	?	?
19 *Broomfield*	N	N	Y	Y	Y
MINNESOTA					
1 *Erdahl*	Y	N	N	Y	Y
2 *Hagedorn*	Y	Y	N	Y	Y
3 *Frenzel*	N	N	N	Y	Y
4 Vento	N	Y	Y	Y	Y
5 Sabo	N	Y	Y	Y	Y
6 *Weber*	N	N	N	Y	Y
7 *Stangeland*	Y	N	N	Y	Y
8 Oberstar	N	Y	N	Y	Y
MISSISSIPPI					
1 Whitten	Y	Y	Y	Y	?
2 Bowen	Y	N	Y	Y	Y
3 Montgomery	Y	N	Y	Y	Y
4 Dowdy	Y	?	?	?	?
5 *Lott*	Y	N	Y	Y	Y
MISSOURI					
1 Clay	N	Y	Y	N	Y
2 Young	Y	Y	Y	Y	Y
3 Gephardt	N	Y	Y	Y	Y

	364	365	366	367	368
4 Skelton	N	N	?	?	?
5 Bolling	Y	Y	Y	?	?
6 Coleman	Y	N	Y	Y	Y
7 Taylor	Y	N	Y	Y	Y
8 Bailey	N	N	N	Y	Y
9 Volkmer	N	N	?	?	?
10 *Emerson*	N	N	N	Y	Y
MONTANA					
1 Williams	Y	Y	Y	?	Y
2 *Marlenee*	Y	N	Y	Y	Y
NEBRASKA					
1 *Bereuter*	N	N	N	Y	Y
2 *Daub*	N	N	N	Y	Y
3 *Smith*	Y	N	N	Y	Y
NEVADA					
AL Santini	Y	N	Y	Y	Y
NEW HAMPSHIRE					
1 D'Amours	?	?	?	?	?
2 *Gregg*	N	N	N	Y	Y
NEW JERSEY					
1 Florio	Y	N	Y	Y	Y
2 Hughes	N	?	?	Y	Y
3 Howard	Y	N	Y	Y	Y
4 *Smith*	Y	N	Y	Y	Y
5 *Fenwick*	Y	N	Y	Y	Y
6 *Forsythe*	?	?	?	?	?
7 *Roukema*	Y	N	Y	Y	Y
8 Roe	Y	?	?	?	?
9 *Hollenbeck*	Y	Y	Y	Y	Y
10 Rodino	Y	Y	?	?	?
11 Minish	Y	N	Y	Y	Y
12 *Rinaldo*	Y	Y	Y	Y	Y
13 *Courter*	Y	N	Y	Y	Y
14 Guarini	?	#	Y	Y	Y
15 Dwyer	Y	Y	Y	Y	Y
NEW MEXICO					
1 *Lujan*	Y	N	Y	Y	Y
2 *Skeen*	Y	N	Y	Y	Y
NEW YORK					
1 *Carney*	N	N	N	Y	Y
2 Downey	Y	Y	Y	Y	Y
3 *Carman*	N	N	N	Y	Y
4 *Lent*	Y	N	Y	Y	Y
5 McGrath	N	N	Y	Y	Y
6 *LeBoutillier*	N	N	N	Y	Y
7 Addabbo	Y	Y	Y	?	?
8 Rosenthal	Y	Y	?	?	?
9 Ferraro	Y	?	?	?	?
10 Biaggi	Y	Y	N	Y	Y
11 Scheuer	Y	Y	Y	Y	Y
12 Chisholm	?	?	?	?	?
13 Solarz	Y	Y	Y	Y	Y
14 Vacancy					
15 Zeferetti	Y	N	Y	?	?
16 Schumer	Y	Y	N	Y	Y
17 *Molinari*	Y	N	Y	Y	Y
18 *Green*	Y	N	Y	Y	Y
19 Rangel	Y	Y	Y	Y	Y
20 Weiss	?	?	?	?	?
21 Garcia	Y	Y	Y	Y	Y
22 Bingham	Y	Y	Y	Y	Y
23 Peyser	Y	Y	Y	Y	Y
24 Ottinger	Y	Y	N	Y	?
25 *Fish*	Y	N	Y	?	?
26 Gilman	Y	Y	Y	Y	Y
27 McHugh	Y	Y	Y	Y	Y
28 Stratton	Y	N	Y	Y	Y
29 *Solomon*	N	N	N	Y	Y
30 *Martin*	Y	N	Y	Y	Y
31 Mitchell	Y	N	Y	Y	Y
32 *Wortley*	Y	N	Y	Y	Y
33 Lee	N	N	?	N	Y
34 Horton	N	N	?	?	?
35 *Conable*	N	N	N	Y	Y
36 LaFalce	Y	Y	Y	Y	Y
37 Nowak	Y	Y	Y	Y	Y
38 *Kemp*	Y	N	Y	Y	Y
39 Lundine	Y	Y	Y	Y	Y
NORTH CAROLINA					
1 Jones	Y	N	Y	?	?
2 Fountain	Y	N	Y	Y	Y
3 Whitley	?	?	?	?	?
4 Andrews	Y	N	?	Y	Y
5 Neal	N	N	Y	Y	Y
6 *Johnston*	N	N	N	N	Y
7 Rose	Y	N	?	Y	Y
8 Hefner	Y	N	?	?	?

	364	365	366	367	368
9 *Martin*	N	N	N	Y	Y
10 *Broyhill*	N	N	N	Y	Y
11 *Hendon*	Y	N	Y	Y	Y
NORTH DAKOTA					
AL Dorgan	+	N	Y	N	Y
OHIO					
1 *Gradison*	Y	N	Y	Y	Y
2 Luken	Y	Y	Y	Y	?
3 Hall	Y	?	?	Y	Y
4 *Oxley*	Y	N	N	Y	Y
5 *Latta*	N	N	N	N	Y
6 *McEwen*	Y	?	?	?	?
7 *Brown*	Y	N	Y	Y	Y
8 *Kindness*	N	N	N	Y	Y
9 *Weber*	Y	N	Y	Y	Y
10 *Miller*	Y	N	Y	Y	Y
11 *Stanton*	Y	N	Y	Y	?
12 Shamansky	Y	N	Y	Y	Y
13 Pease	Y	Y	Y	N	Y
14 Seiberling	Y	Y	Y	Y	Y
15 *Wylie*	Y	N	Y	Y	Y
16 *Regula*	Y	N	Y	Y	Y
17 *Ashbrook*	N	N	N	N	N
18 Applegate	Y	Y	Y	?	?
19 *Williams*	Y	N	Y	Y	Y
20 Oakar	N	Y	Y	Y	Y
21 Stokes	Y	Y	Y	Y	Y
22 Eckart	N	Y	Y	Y	Y
23 Mottl	N	N	?	?	?
OKLAHOMA					
1 Jones	N	N	N	Y	Y
2 Synar	Y	Y	Y	Y	Y
3 Watkins	Y	N	Y	N	Y
4 McCurdy	Y	N	Y	Y	Y
5 *Edwards*	?	?	?	?	?
6 English	N	N	Y	N	Y
OREGON					
1 AuCoin	N	Y	Y	Y	Y
2 *Smith*	N	N	N	Y	N
3 Wyden	N	N	Y	Y	Y
4 Weaver	N	Y	N	Y	Y
PENNSYLVANIA					
1 Foglietta	Y	N	Y	N	Y
2 Gray	N	?	Y	Y	Y
3 Smith	Y	N	?	?	?
4 *Dougherty*	Y	N	Y	?	?
5 *Schulze*	N	N	Y	Y	Y
6 Yatron	Y	N	Y	Y	Y
7 Edgar	N	N	Y	Y	Y
8 *Coyne, J.*	N	N	N	Y	Y
9 *Shuster*	N	N	N	Y	Y
10 *McDade*	Y	N	?	Y	Y
11 *Nelligan*	Y	N	Y	Y	Y
12 Murtha	Y	Y	Y	Y	Y
13 *Coughlin*	Y	N	N	Y	Y
14 Coyne, W.	Y	Y	Y	Y	Y
15 *Ritter*	Y	N	Y	Y	Y
16 *Walker*	N	N	Y	Y	Y
17 Ertel	?	?	?	?	?
18 Walgren	Y	?	Y	Y	Y
19 *Goodling*	N	N	N	Y	Y
20 Gaydos	Y	Y	Y	Y	Y
21 Bailey	Y	Y	Y	Y	Y
22 Murphy	N	Y	N	Y	Y
23 *Clinger*	Y	N	Y	Y	Y
24 *Marks*	Y	?	Y	Y	Y
25 *Atkinson*	Y	N	Y	Y	Y
RHODE ISLAND					
1 St Germain	Y	N	Y	Y	Y
2 *Schneider*	Y	Y	Y	Y	Y
SOUTH CAROLINA					
1 *Hartnett*	Y	N	Y	Y	Y
2 *Spence*	Y	N	Y	Y	Y
3 Derrick	Y	N	Y	Y	Y
4 *Campbell*	Y	N	Y	Y	Y
5 Holland	Y	N	Y	Y	Y
6 *Napier*	Y	N	Y	Y	Y
SOUTH DAKOTA					
1 Daschle	Y	Y	Y	Y	?
2 *Roberts*	Y	N	Y	N	Y
TENNESSEE					
1 *Quillen*	Y	N	Y	Y	Y
2 *Duncan*	Y	N	Y	Y	Y
3 Bouquard	Y	N	Y	Y	Y
4 Gore	Y	N	Y	Y	Y
5 Boner	Y	?	?	?	?
6 *Beard*	Y	N	Y	Y	Y

	364	365	366	367	368
7 Jones	Y	N	Y	Y	Y
8 Ford	Y	?	Y	Y	?
TEXAS					
1 Hall, S.	Y	N	Y	N	Y
2 Wilson	Y	N	Y	N	Y
3 *Collins*	N	N	?	?	?
4 Hall, R.	Y	N	Y	N	Y
5 Mattox	Y	?	Y	N	Y
6 *Gramm*	N	N	N	N	N
7 *Archer*	N	N	Y	N	N
8 *Fields*	Y	N	Y	N	Y
9 Brooks	Y	Y	Y	Y	Y
10 Pickle	N	Y	Y	N	Y
11 Leath	Y	N	N	N	Y
12 Wright	Y	N	Y	N	Y
13 Hightower	Y	N	?	?	?
14 Patman	N	N	Y	N	Y
15 de la Garza	Y	N	Y	N	Y
16 White	Y	N	Y	N	Y
17 Stenholm	N	N	N	N	Y
18 Leland	N	Y	Y	Y	Y
19 Hance	N	N	?	?	?
20 Gonzalez	Y	Y	Y	Y	Y
21 *Loeffler*	Y	N	N	N	Y
22 *Paul*	N	N	N	N	N
23 Kazen	Y	N	Y	N	Y
24 Frost	Y	Y	Y	N	Y
UTAH					
1 *Hansen*	?	?	?	?	?
2 *Marriott*	Y	N	Y	Y	Y
VERMONT					
AL *Jeffords*	Y	Y	Y	Y	Y
VIRGINIA					
1 *Trible*	Y	N	Y	Y	Y
2 *Whitehurst*	Y	N	Y	Y	Y
3 *Bliley*	Y	N	Y	Y	Y
4 *Daniel, R.*	Y	N	Y	Y	Y
5 *Daniel, D.*	?	?	?	?	?
6 *Butler*	N	N	Y	Y	Y
7 *Robinson*	Y	N	Y	Y	Y
8 *Parris*	Y	N	Y	Y	Y
9 *Wampler*	Y	N	Y	Y	Y
10 *Wolf*	Y	N	Y	Y	Y
WASHINGTON					
1 *Pritchard*	N	N	Y	Y	Y
2 Swift	Y	Y	Y	Y	Y
3 Bonker	Y	Y	Y	Y	Y
4 *Morrison*	Y	N	Y	Y	Y
5 Foley	Y	Y	Y	Y	Y
6 Dicks	Y	Y	Y	Y	Y
7 Lowry	N	Y	Y	Y	Y
WEST VIRGINIA					
1 Mollohan	Y	N	?	?	?
2 *Benedict*	Y	N	Y	Y	Y
3 *Staton*	Y	N	Y	Y	Y
4 Rahall	N	Y	Y	N	Y
WISCONSIN					
1 Aspin	Y	N	?	?	?
2 Kastenmeier	N	Y	Y	Y	Y
3 *Gunderson*	Y	N	N	Y	Y
4 Zablocki	Y	N	Y	Y	Y
5 Reuss	N	Y	?	?	?
6 *Petri*	N	N	Y	Y	Y
7 Obey	Y	N	Y	Y	Y
8 *Roth*	Y	N	N	Y	Y
9 *Sensenbrenner*	N	N	N	Y	Y
WYOMING					
AL *Cheney*	Y	N	N	Y	Y

Southern states - Ala., Ark., Fla., Ga., Ky., La., Miss., N.C., Okla., S.C., Tenn., Texas, Va.

369. HR 3809. Nuclear Waste Policy Act. Udall, D-Ariz., motion that the House resolve itself into the Committee of the Whole for consideration of the bill to establish a federal program for the interim storage and eventual permanent disposal of highly radioactive nuclear waste. Motion agreed to 333-4: R 145-0; D 188-4 (ND 123-4, SD 65-0), Nov. 29, 1982.

370. HR 3809. Nuclear Waste Policy Act. Lujan, R-N.M., amendment to reduce the power of the states to veto the location of an interim storage facility for spent nuclear fuel within their borders by requiring a vote by one house of Congress to sustain a state veto, rather than letting the veto stand unless overruled by both houses of Congress, as provided in the bill. Rejected 181-194: R 126-36; D 55-158 (ND 24-123, SD 31-35), Nov. 29, 1982.

371. HR 3809. Nuclear Waste Policy Act. Lott, R-Miss., amendment to prohibit the location of a permanent nuclear waste repository at a site adjacent to an area one mile by one mile with a population of 1,000 or more. Rejected 81-296: R 65-99; D 16-197 (ND 7-139, SD 9-58), Nov. 29, 1982.

372. HR 3809. Nuclear Waste Policy Act. Broyhill, R-N.C., amendment to reduce the power of states to veto the location of a permanent nuclear waste repository within their borders by requiring a vote by one house of Congress to sustain a state veto, rather than letting the veto stand unless overruled by both houses of Congress, as provided in the bill. Adopted 190-184: R 133-34; D 57-150 (ND 21-117, SD 36-33), Nov. 29, 1982.

373. HR 3809. Nuclear Waste Policy Act. Lundine, D-N.Y., amendment to eliminate from the bill the provisions authorizing the creation of federal interim storage for spent fuel from nuclear utilities. Rejected 84-308: R 15-160; D 69-148 (ND 63-84, SD 6-64), Nov. 30, 1982.

374. HR 3809. Nuclear Waste Policy Act. Wirth, D-Colo., amendment to require that guidelines for the location of a permanent nuclear waste repository provide for the disqualification of any site if the repository's surface facility would be in a highly populated area. Rejected 109-293: R 8-173; D 101-120 (ND 91-58, SD 10-62), Nov. 30, 1982.

375. HR 7158. Treasury, Postal Service, General Government Appropriations, Fiscal 1983. Miller, R-Ohio, motion to recommit the bill to the Appropriations Committee with instructions to report it back with an amendment cutting 2 percent from non-mandatory spending. Motion agreed to 193-172: R 151-13; D 42-159 (ND 20-114, SD 22-45), Nov. 30, 1982.

376. HR 7158. Treasury, Postal Service, General Government Appropriations, Fiscal 1983. Passage of the bill to appropriate $10,680,236,100 for the Treasury Department, Postal Service, executive offices and several independent agencies in fiscal 1983. Passed 269-98: R 84-82; D 185-16 (ND 127-6, SD 58-10), Nov. 30, 1982. The president had requested $10,487,814,000.

KEY

Y Voted for (yea).
\# Paired for.
\+ Announced for.
N Voted against (nay).
X Paired against.
\- Announced against.
P Voted ''present''.
C Voted ''present'' to avoid possible conflict of interest.
? Did not vote or otherwise make a position known.

Democrats *Republicans*

	369	370	371	372	373	374	375	376
ALABAMA								
1 *Edwards*	Y	Y	Y	Y	N	N	Y	N
2 *Dickinson*	Y	Y	N	?	N	N	?	?
3 Nichols	Y	Y	Y	Y	N	N	Y	Y
4 Bevill	Y	N	N	N	N	N	N	Y
5 Flippo	Y	N	N	N	N	N	N	Y
6 Smith	Y	Y	N	N	N	N	N	Y
7 Shelby	Y	Y	N	Y	N	N	Y	N
ALASKA								
AL *Young*	Y	Y	?	N	N	N	Y	Y
ARIZONA								
1 *Rhodes*	Y	Y	N	Y	N	N	?	?
2 Udall	Y	N	N	N	N	N	?	?
3 *Stump*	Y	Y	Y	Y	N	N	Y	N
4 *Rudd*	Y	Y	Y	Y	N	N	Y	Y
ARKANSAS								
1 Alexander	Y	N	N	N	N	N	N	Y
2 *Bethune*	Y	Y	N	N	N	N	Y	?
3 *Hammerschmidt*	Y	Y	N	Y	N	Y	N	Y
4 Anthony	?	?	?	?	?	N	N	Y
CALIFORNIA								
1 *Chappie*	Y	Y	N	N	N	N	Y	N
2 *Clausen*	Y	Y	N	N	N	N	Y	Y
3 Matsui	Y	N	N	N	N	Y	N	Y
4 Fazio	Y	N	N	N	N	N	N	Y
5 Burton, J.	N	N	N	N	Y	Y	N	?
6 Burton, P.	Y	N	N	N	Y	Y	N	Y
7 Miller	Y	N	N	N	?	?	?	?
8 Dellums	Y	N	N	N	Y	Y	Y	Y
9 Stark	Y	N	?	?	Y	Y	N	Y
10 Edwards	?	N	N	N	Y	Y	N	Y
11 Lantos	Y	N	N	N	?	?	?	
12 McCloskey	?	?	?	?	N	Y	?	?
13 Mineta	Y	N	N	N	N	Y	N	Y
14 *Shumway*	Y	Y	Y	Y	N	N	Y	N
15 Coelho	Y	N	N	?	N	Y	?	?
16 Panetta	Y	N	N	N	N	N	Y	?
17 *Pashayan*	Y	Y	N	N	N	N	Y	N
18 *Thomas*	Y	Y	N	Y	N	N	Y	N
19 *Lagomarsino*	Y	Y	N	N	N	N	Y	N
20 *Goldwater*	?	?	?	Y	N	?	?	
21 *Fiedler*	Y	Y	N	N	N	Y	N	Y
22 *Moorhead*	Y	Y	N	Y	N	N	Y	N
23 Beilenson	Y	N	N	N	Y	Y	N	Y
24 Waxman	Y	N	N	Y	N	Y	N	Y
25 Roybal	Y	N	N	N	Y	Y	N	Y
26 *Rousselot*	Y	Y	Y	Y	?	?	?	?
27 *Dornan*	Y	Y	N	N	Y	N	Y	N
28 Dixon	Y	N	N	N	N	N	N	Y
29 Hawkins	?	N	N	N	?	?	N	Y
30 Martinez	?	N	N	N	N	N	N	Y
31 Dymally	?	?	?	N	Y	Y	N	Y
32 Anderson	Y	N	Y	N	N	N	N	Y
33 *Grisham*	Y	?	?	N	N	Y	N	N
34 *Lungren*	Y	Y	N	N	N	N	Y	N
35 *Dreier*	Y	Y	Y	N	N	N	Y	N
36 Brown	Y	N	N	N	N	Y	N	Y
37 *Lewis*	?	Y	Y	N	N	N	Y	N
38 Patterson	Y	N	N	N	N	N	N	Y
39 *Dannemeyer*	Y	Y	N	N	Y	N	N	N
40 *Badham*	Y	Y	Y	N	N	N	Y	N
41 *Lowery*	Y	Y	N	N	Y	N	N	Y
42 *Hunter*	Y	Y	N	N	Y	N	Y	N
43 *Burgener*	?	?	?	?	N	?	?	?
COLORADO								
1 Schroeder	Y	N	N	N	N	?	Y	?
2 Wirth	Y	N	N	N	Y	N	Y	N
3 Kogovsek	?	?	?	?	N	Y	N	Y
4 *Brown*	Y	Y	N	Y	N	N	Y	N

	369	370	371	372	373	374	375	376
5 *Kramer*	Y	Y	N	Y	N	N	Y	N
CONNECTICUT								
1 Kennelly	Y	Y	N	Y	N	Y	N	Y
2 Gejdenson	Y	Y	N	Y	Y	Y	N	Y
3 *DeNardis*	?	N	?	N	?	Y	Y	Y
4 *McKinney*	?	Y	N	Y	?	N	?	Y
5 Ratchford	Y	N	N	N	N	N	Y	Y
6 Moffett	?	?	?	?	?	?	?	?
DELAWARE								
AL *Evans*	?	?	?	?	N	N	?	Y
FLORIDA								
1 Hutto	Y	Y	Y	Y	N	N	Y	Y
2 Fuqua	Y	Y	N	Y	N	Y	Y	Y
3 Bennett	Y	Y	N	Y	N	Y	Y	Y
4 Chappell	?	?	?	Y	N	N	N	Y
5 *McCollum*	Y	Y	N	N	Y	N	N	Y
6 *Young*	Y	?	?	?	N	N	Y	N
7 Gibbons	Y	N	N	N	N	N	N	Y
8 Ireland	?	?	?	?	Y	N	N	Y
9 Nelson	Y	N	N	N	N	N	#	Y
10 *Bafalis*	?	?	?	Y	N	N	Y	Y
11 Mica	Y	N	N	Y	N	Y	Y	Y
12 *Shaw*	Y	N	N	N	N	N	Y	Y
13 Lehman	?	?	?	?	?	?	?	?
14 Pepper	Y	N	N	N	N	N	N	Y
15 Fascell	Y	Y	N	Y	N	Y	N	Y
GEORGIA								
1 Ginn	Y	Y	?	Y	N	N	N	Y
2 Hatcher	Y	Y	N	Y	N	N	N	Y
3 Brinkley	Y	Y	N	Y	N	N	Y	N
4 Levitas	?	?	?	?	?	?	?	?
5 Fowler	?	?	?	?	?	?	?	?
6 *Gingrich*	Y	Y	N	Y	?	?	?	?
7 McDonald	Y	Y	N	N	N	N	Y	Y
8 Evans	Y	?	?	Y	?	?	?	?
9 Jenkins	Y	N	N	Y	N	N	N	Y
10 Barnard	Y	Y	N	N	N	N	N	Y
HAWAII								
1 Heftel	?	?	?	?	Y	Y	Y	N
2 Akaka	?	?	?	?	N	N	N	Y
IDAHO								
1 *Craig*	Y	N	N	Y	N	N	Y	N
2 *Hansen*	Y	N	N	Y	N	N	Y	N
ILLINOIS								
1 Washington	?	?	?	?	#	?	?	?
2 Savage	N	N	N	N	N	Y	N	Y
3 Russo	Y	N	N	N	N	N	N	Y
4 *Derwinski*	Y	?	?	?	N	N	?	?
5 Fary	Y	N	N	N	N	N	N	Y
6 *Hyde*	Y	N	N	N	N	N	N	Y
7 Collins	Y	N	?	N	Y	Y	N	Y
8 Rostenkowski	Y	N	N	N	N	N	N	Y
9 Yates	?	?	?	?	?	?	?	?
10 *Porter*	?	Y	N	Y	N	N	+	+
11 Annunzio	Y	N	N	N	N	N	N	Y
12 *Crane, P.*	Y	Y	Y	Y	N	N	Y	N
13 *McClory*	Y	Y	N	Y	N	N	Y	Y
14 *Erlenborn*	Y	Y	N	Y	N	N	N	Y
15 *Corcoran*	Y	N	N	N	N	N	Y	Y
16 *Martin*	Y	N	Y	N	Y	N	Y	N
17 *O'Brien*	?	?	?	?	N	N	Y	Y
18 *Michel*	?	Y	N	Y	N	N	N	Y
19 *Railsback*	?	Y	N	Y	N	N	?	?
20 *Findley*	Y	Y	N	N	Y	N	?	?
21 *Madigan*	Y	Y	Y	N	N	?	?	?
22 *Crane, D.*	?	?	?	?	N	N	Y	N
23 Price	Y	N	N	N	N	N	N	Y
24 Simon	Y	N	N	N	Y	N	N	Y
INDIANA								
1 Hall*	Y	Y	N	?	N	Y	N	Y
2 Fithian	Y	N	N	N	N	N	N	Y
3 *Hiler*	?	?	?	?	N	N	Y	N
4 *Coats*	Y	Y	N	Y	N	N	Y	Y
5 *Hillis*	Y	Y	N	N	Y	N	Y	N
6 Evans	Y	N	N	N	N	N	Y	Y
7 *Myers*	Y	Y	N	N	N	N	Y	N
8 *Deckard*	?	?	?	?	Y	Y	Y	Y
9 Hamilton	Y	Y	N	N	N	Y	N	Y
10 Sharp	Y	N	N	Y	N	Y	Y	Y
11 Jacobs	N	N	N	N	N	N	Y	N
IOWA								
1 *Leach*	?	?	?	?	N	N	Y	Y
2 *Tauke*	?	?	N	Y	N	N	Y	N
3 Evans	Y	Y	Y	Y	?	N	Y	N
4 Smith	Y	N	N	N	N	N	N	Y
5 Harkin	Y	N	N	N	N	Y	Y	Y
6 Bedell	Y	N	N	N	Y	Y	Y	Y

ND - Northern Democrats   SD - Southern Democrats

Corresponding to Congressional Record Votes 393, 394, 395, 396, 398, 399, 400, 401

	369	370	371	372	373	374	375	376
KANSAS								
1 **Roberts**	Y	Y	N	Y	N	N	Y	Y
2 **Jeffries**	Y	Y	N	Y	N	N	Y	N
3 **Winn**	Y	Y	N	Y	N	N	Y	Y
4 Glickman	Y	N	N	N	N	Y	Y	Y
5 **Whittaker**	Y	Y	N	Y	N	N	?	?
KENTUCKY								
1 Hubbard	Y	Y	N	Y	N	N	Y	N
2 Natcher	Y	N	N	Y	N	N	N	Y
3 Mazzoli	Y	N	N	N	N	N	N	Y
4 **Snyder**	Y	Y	N	Y	N	N	Y	Y
5 **Rogers**	Y	Y	Y	Y	N	N	Y	Y
6 **Hopkins**	Y	Y	N	Y	N	N	Y	Y
7 Perkins	Y	N	N	Y	N	N	N	Y
LOUISIANA								
1 **Livingston**	?	N	N	N	N	N	Y	N
2 Boggs	?	N	N	N	N	Y	N	Y
3 Tauzin	Y	N	N	N	N	Y	Y	N
4 Roemer	Y	N	N	N	Y	N	Y	N
5 Huckaby	Y	N	N	N	Y	Y	Y	Y
6 **Moore**	Y	N	N	N	N	Y	Y	N
7 Breaux	Y	N	Y	N	?	?	?	?
8 Long	Y	N	N	N	N	N	N	N
MAINE								
1 **Emery**	?	?	?	?	?	?	?	?
2 **Snowe**	?	N	N	N	N	N	Y	Y
MARYLAND								
1 Dyson	Y	N	N	N	N	N	N	Y
2 Long	?	N	N	N	N	Y	N	Y
3 Mikulski	Y	N	N	N	N	Y	N	Y
4 **Holt**	Y	Y	N	Y	N	N	N	N
5 Hoyer	Y	N	N	N	N	N	N	Y
6 Byron	Y	Y	N	Y	N	N	N	Y
7 Mitchell	N	N	N	N	Y	Y	N	Y
8 Barnes	Y	N	N	N	N	N	N	Y
MASSACHUSETTS								
1 **Conte**	Y	N	N	N	N	N	Y	Y
2 Boland	Y	N	N	N	N	N	N	Y
3 Early	Y	N	N	N	N	N	N	Y
4 Frank	Y	N	N	N	N	Y	N	Y
5 Shannon	Y	N	N	N	Y	Y	N	Y
6 Mavroules	Y	N	N	N	Y	?	N	Y
7 Markey	Y	N	N	N	Y	Y	?	?
8 O'Neill								
9 Moakley	Y	N	N	N	Y	Y	N	Y
10 **Heckler**	?	N	N	Y	?	Y	?	?
11 Donnelly	Y	N	N	N	N	?	N	Y
12 Studds	Y	N	N	N	Y	Y	N	Y
MICHIGAN								
1 Conyers	N	N	N	N	Y	Y	N	Y
2 **Pursell**	?	?	?	?	?	?	?	?
3 Wolpe	Y	N	N	N	Y	Y	N	Y
4 **Siljander**	?	?	Y	Y	N	N	Y	N
5 **Sawyer**	Y	Y	N	Y	N	N	Y	Y
6 **Dunn**	Y	Y	N	Y	N	N	Y	Y
7 Kildee	Y	N	N	N	N	Y	N	Y
8 Traxler	?	N	N	N	?	N	N	Y
9 **Vander Jagt**	Y	Y	N	Y	N	N	Y	Y
10 Albosta	Y	N	N	N	N	N	?	?
11 **Davis**	?	?	?	?	N	N	N	Y
12 Bonior	Y	N	N	N	N	Y	N	Y
13 Crockett	?	N	N	N	Y	Y	N	Y
14 Hertel	?	N	N	N	?	?	?	?
15 Ford	Y	N	N	N	N	N	?	?
16 Dingell	Y	N	N	N	N	N	N	Y
17 Brodhead	Y	N	N	N	Y	Y	N	Y
18 Blanchard	?	?	?	?	?	?	?	?
19 **Broomfield**	Y	Y	N	Y	N	N	?	?
MINNESOTA								
1 **Erdahl**	Y	Y	N	Y	N	N	Y	Y
2 **Hagedorn**	?	?	?	Y	N	N	Y	N
3 **Frenzel**	Y	Y	N	Y	N	N	Y	N
4 Vento	Y	N	N	N	Y	Y	N	Y
5 Sabo	Y	N	N	N	N	Y	N	Y
6 **Weber**	Y	N	Y	N	Y	N	Y	N
7 **Stangeland**	?	Y	Y	Y	N	N	Y	N
8 Oberstar	Y	N	N	N	Y	Y	N	Y
MISSISSIPPI								
1 Whitten	Y	N	Y	N	N	N	N	Y
2 Bowen	Y	N	Y	N	N	N	N	Y
3 Montgomery	?	N	Y	N	N	N	?	?
4 Dowdy	Y	N	Y	N	N	N	N	Y
5 **Lott**	Y	N	Y	N	N	N	Y	N
MISSOURI								
1 Clay	Y	N	N	?	Y	Y	N	Y
2 Young	Y	Y	N	Y	N	N	Y	Y
3 Gephardt	?	?	?	?	N	N	?	?

	369	370	371	372	373	374	375	376
4 Skelton	Y	N	N	Y	N	N	?	?
5 Bolling	?	?	?	?	?	?	?	?
6 **Coleman**	Y	Y	N	Y	N	N	Y	N
7 **Taylor**	Y	Y	Y	Y	N	N	Y	Y
8 **Bailey**	Y	Y	Y	Y	N	N	Y	N
9 Volkmer	Y	N	N	Y	N	Y	Y	Y
10 **Emerson**	Y	Y	Y	Y	N	N	Y	Y
MONTANA								
1 Williams	Y	N	N	N	Y	Y	N	Y
2 **Marlenee**	Y	N	Y	N	N	N	Y	N
NEBRASKA								
1 **Bereuter**	Y	N	Y	Y	N	N	Y	Y
2 **Daub**	Y	Y	Y	Y	N	N	Y	Y
3 **Smith**	Y	Y	Y	Y	N	N	Y	Y
NEVADA								
AL Santini	?	N	N	N	N	N	Y	Y
NEW HAMPSHIRE								
1 D'Amours	Y	Y	N	Y	N	N	N	Y
2 **Gregg**	Y	Y	Y	Y	Y	N	Y	N
NEW JERSEY								
1 Florio	Y	N	N	N	N	Y	N	Y
2 Hughes	Y	N	N	N	N	N	N	Y
3 Howard	Y	N	N	N	Y	Y	N	Y
4 **Smith**	?	?	?	?	N	N	N	Y
5 **Fenwick**	Y	Y	N	N	N	N	Y	N
6 **Forsythe**	?	?	N	Y	N	N	?	?
7 **Roukema**	Y	Y	N	Y	N	N	Y	Y
8 Roe	?	Y	N	N	Y	N	X	?
9 **Hollenbeck**	?	Y	N	Y	?	?	?	?
10 Rodino	Y	N	N	N	Y	Y	N	Y
11 Minish	Y	N	N	N	Y	Y	N	Y
12 **Rinaldo**	Y	Y	N	Y	N	N	N	Y
13 **Courter**	Y	N	N	Y	N	N	Y	N
14 Guarini	Y	N	N	?	N	Y	N	Y
15 Dwyer	Y	N	N	N	N	Y	N	Y
NEW MEXICO								
1 **Lujan**	Y	Y	N	N	N	N	Y	N
2 **Skeen**	Y	Y	N	Y	N	N	Y	Y
NEW YORK								
1 **Carney**	Y	Y	N	Y	N	N	?	Y
2 Downey	Y	N	N	N	Y	Y	?	?
3 **Carman**	Y	Y	N	Y	N	N	Y	N
4 **Lent**	Y	Y	N	Y	N	N	Y	Y
5 **McGrath**	Y	Y	N	Y	Y	N	Y	Y
6 **LeBoutillier**	Y	Y	N	Y	?	N	Y	Y
7 Addabbo	Y	N	N	N	Y	Y	N	Y
8 Rosenthal	?	N	N	N	Y	Y	?	?
9 Ferraro	Y	N	N	-	Y	Y	N	Y
10 Biaggi	Y	N	N	N	Y	N	N	Y
11 Scheuer	Y	Y	N	N	Y	N	N	Y
12 Chisholm	?	?	?	?	?	?	N	Y
13 Solarz	Y	N	N	N	Y	Y	N	Y
14 Vacancy								
15 Zeferetti	Y	N	N	N	?	N	N	Y
16 Schumer	Y	N	N	N	Y	Y	N	Y
17 **Molinari**	Y	Y	Y	Y	Y	N	Y	Y
18 **Green**	Y	N	N	N	N	N	N	Y
19 Rangel	?	?	?	?	Y	Y	N	Y
20 Weiss	Y	N	N	N	Y	Y	N	Y
21 Garcia	Y	N	N	?	Y	Y	?	?
22 Bingham	?	Y	N	N	Y	Y	?	?
23 Peyser	Y	N	N	N	N	Y	?	Y
24 Ottinger	Y	N	N	N	N	Y	?	Y
25 **Fish**	Y	N	N	N	?	?	Y	Y
26 **Gilman**	Y	N	N	N	Y	Y	N	Y
27 McHugh	?	N	N	N	Y	Y	N	Y
28 Stratton	Y	Y	N	Y	N	N	N	Y
29 **Solomon**	Y	Y	Y	Y	N	N	Y	N
30 **Martin**	Y	Y	N	Y	N	N	Y	N
31 **Mitchell**	?	?	?	?	N	N	N	Y
32 **Wortley**	Y	Y	Y	Y	N	N	Y	Y
33 **Lee**	?	?	?	?	?	N	Y	N
34 **Horton**	Y	Y	N	N	N	?	Y	Y
35 **Conable**	Y	Y	N	Y	N	N	Y	N
36 LaFalce	Y	N	N	N	Y	Y	N	Y
37 Nowak	?	N	N	N	Y	Y	N	Y
38 **Kemp**	?	N	N	Y	?	N	Y	N
39 Lundine	Y	N	N	N	Y	Y	Y	Y
NORTH CAROLINA								
1 Jones	?	?	?	?	N	N	N	Y
2 Fountain	Y	?	N	Y	N	N	Y	Y
3 Whitley	Y	Y	N	N	N	N	Y	Y
4 Andrews	Y	Y	N	?	N	N	Y	?
5 Neal	Y	N	N	N	N	N	N	Y
6 **Johnston**	Y	Y	Y	Y	N	N	?	?
7 Rose	Y	N	N	N	?	N	N	Y
8 Hefner	Y	N	N	N	N	N	N	Y

	369	370	371	372	373	374	375	376
9 **Martin**	Y	Y	Y	Y	N	N	Y	N
10 **Broyhill**	Y	Y	Y	Y	N	N	Y	N
11 **Hendon**	Y	Y	Y	Y	N	N	Y	Y
NORTH DAKOTA								
AL Dorgan	Y	N	N	N	N	Y	N	Y
OHIO								
1 **Gradison**	Y	Y	N	Y	N	N	Y	N
2 Luken	Y	N	N	N	N	N	?	?
3 Hall	?	?	?	?	N	N	N	Y
4 **Oxley**	Y	Y	Y	Y	N	N	Y	N
5 **Latta**	Y	Y	Y	Y	N	N	Y	N
6 **McEwen**	Y	Y	Y	Y	N	N	Y	Y
7 **Brown**	?	Y	N	Y	N	N	Y	N
8 **Kindness**	Y	Y	Y	N	?	N	Y	N
9 **Weber**	Y	Y	N	Y	N	N	Y	Y
10 **Miller**	Y	Y	Y	N	N	N	Y	N
11 **Stanton**	?	?	?	?	N	?	?	?
12 Shamansky	Y	N	N	N	N	Y	N	Y
13 Pease	Y	Y	N	Y	N	Y	N	Y
14 Seiberling	Y	N	N	N	?	N	?	?
15 **Wylie**	Y	Y	N	Y	N	N	Y	Y
16 **Regula**	Y	Y	N	Y	N	N	Y	Y
17 **Ashbrook**	?	?	?	?	?	N	Y	N
18 Applegate	Y	N	Y	N	N	Y	Y	Y
19 **Williams**	Y	Y	N	Y	N	N	N	Y
20 Oakar	Y	N	Y	Y	Y	N	N	Y
21 Stokes	Y	N	N	N	Y	Y	N	Y
22 Eckart	Y	N	Y	N	Y	N	N	Y
23 Mottl	Y	Y	Y	N	Y	N	Y	N
OKLAHOMA								
1 Jones	?	?	?	?	N	N	Y	Y
2 Synar	Y	Y	N	Y	N	Y	N	Y
3 Watkins	Y	N	N	N	N	N	N	Y
4 McCurdy	Y	N	N	N	N	N	N	Y
5 **Edwards**	?	Y	Y	Y	N	N	Y	Y
6 English	Y	N	N	N	N	N	Y	Y
OREGON								
1 AuCoin	Y	N	N	N	Y	Y	N	N
2 **Smith**	Y	Y	Y	N	N	N	Y	N
3 Wyden	Y	N	N	N	N	Y	N	Y
4 Weaver	Y	N	N	N	Y	Y	Y	N
PENNSYLVANIA								
1 Foglietta	Y	N	N	N	N	Y	N	Y
2 Gray	?	N	N	Y	Y	Y	?	?
3 Smith	?	?	?	?	N	?	N	Y
4 **Dougherty**	?	?	?	?	N	N	N	Y
5 **Schulze**	Y	Y	N	Y	N	N	Y	N
6 Yatron	Y	N	N	N	N	N	N	Y
7 Edgar	Y	N	N	N	Y	Y	N	Y
8 **Coyne, J.**	?	Y	Y	Y	N	N	Y	Y
9 **Shuster**	?	?	?	?	?	?	?	?
10 **McDade**	Y	N	Y	Y	N	N	Y	Y
11 **Nelligan**	Y	N	Y	Y	N	N	?	?
12 Murtha	Y	N	N	Y	N	N	N	Y
13 **Coughlin**	Y	N	N	N	N	Y	Y	Y
14 Coyne, W.	?	N	N	N	N	N	N	Y
15 **Ritter**	?	Y	N	Y	N	N	Y	N
16 **Walker**	Y	Y	Y	Y	N	N	Y	N
17 Ertel	Y	N	N	?	N	N	?	?
18 Walgren	Y	N	N	N	N	Y	Y	Y
19 **Goodling**	Y	N	Y	Y	N	N	Y	N
20 Gaydos	?	N	N	N	N	N	N	Y
21 Bailey	Y	Y	N	Y	N	N	N	Y
22 Murphy	Y	Y	N	N	N	N	N	N
23 **Clinger**	Y	Y	N	Y	Y	N	Y	Y
24 **Marks**	?	?	?	Y	?	?	N	Y
25 **Atkinson**	?	Y	Y	Y	N	N	Y	Y
RHODE ISLAND								
1 St Germain	?	N	N	N	N	N	N	Y
2 **Schneider**	?	N	Y	N	Y	Y	N	Y
SOUTH CAROLINA								
1 **Hartnett**	Y	Y	Y	Y	Y	N	Y	N
2 **Spence**	?	N	Y	Y	Y	N	Y	Y
3 Derrick	Y	Y	N	N	Y	N	N	Y
4 **Campbell**	?	Y	Y	Y	Y	N	Y	Y
5 Holland	?	?	?	?	N	N	?	?
6 **Napier**	?	Y	Y	Y	Y	N	Y	Y
SOUTH DAKOTA								
1 Daschle	?	?	?	?	N	N	Y	Y
2 **Roberts**	Y	Y	Y	Y	N	N	Y	N
TENNESSEE								
1 **Quillen**	Y	Y	Y	Y	N	N	Y	Y
2 **Duncan**	Y	Y	N	Y	N	N	Y	Y
3 Bouquard	Y	Y	N	Y	N	N	N	Y
4 Gore	Y	N	N	N	Y	Y	N	Y
5 Boner	Y	N	N	N	N	N	N	Y
6 **Beard**	Y	Y	Y	N	N	N	Y	Y

	369	370	371	372	373	374	375	376
7 Jones	?	?	?	?	N	N	N	Y
8 Ford	Y	N	N	N	Y	Y	N	Y
TEXAS								
1 Hall, S.	Y	N	Y	N	N	N	Y	N
2 Wilson	?	Y	N	Y	N	N	N	Y
3 **Collins**	Y	Y	Y	Y	N	N	Y	N
4 Hall, R.	Y	N	N	N	N	N	Y	Y
5 Mattox	Y	N	N	N	N	N	N	Y
6 Gramm	Y	Y	Y	Y	N	N	Y	N
7 **Archer**	Y	Y	Y	Y	N	N	Y	N
8 **Fields**	Y	N	Y	N	N	N	Y	N
9 Brooks	Y	Y	N	Y	N	N	N	Y
10 Pickle	Y	Y	N	Y	N	N	N	Y
11 Leath	Y	Y	N	Y	N	N	Y	N
12 Wright	Y	Y	N	Y	N	N	?	Y
13 Hightower	Y	N	N	N	N	N	N	Y
14 Patman	?	?	N	Y	N	N	N	Y
15 de la Garza	Y	Y	N	Y	?	?	?	?
16 White	Y	Y	N	Y	N	N	Y	Y
17 Stenholm	Y	Y	N	Y	?	?	?	?
18 Leland	Y	N	N	N	Y	Y	N	Y
19 Hance	Y	N	N	N	N	N	N	N
20 Gonzalez	Y	N	N	N	N	N	N	Y
21 **Loeffler**	Y	Y	Y	Y	N	N	Y	N
22 **Paul**	Y	N	N	N	Y	N	Y	N
23 Kazen	Y	Y	N	Y	N	N	N	Y
24 Frost	Y	Y	N	Y	N	Y	N	Y
UTAH								
1 **Hansen**	Y	N	N	N	N	N	Y	N
2 **Marriott**	Y	N	N	N	N	N	Y	Y
VERMONT								
AL **Jeffords**	?	?	?	?	N	N	Y	N
VIRGINIA								
1 **Trible**	Y	Y	N	?	N	N	Y	Y
2 **Whitehurst**	Y	Y	N	Y	N	N	Y	Y
3 **Bliley**	Y	Y	N	Y	N	N	Y	Y
4 **Daniel, R.**	Y	Y	Y	Y	N	N	Y	N
5 Daniel, D.	Y	Y	N	Y	N	N	Y	Y
6 **Butler**	Y	Y	N	Y	N	N	Y	Y
7 **Robinson**	Y	Y	N	Y	N	N	Y	Y
8 **Parris**	Y	Y	Y	Y	N	N	N	Y
9 **Wampler**	Y	Y	Y	Y	N	N	Y	Y
10 **Wolf**	Y	Y	N	Y	N	N	N	Y
WASHINGTON								
1 **Pritchard**	Y	?	?	N	N	N	Y	Y
2 Swift	Y	N	N	N	N	Y	N	Y
3 Bonker	Y	N	N	N	?	N	N	?
4 **Morrison**	Y	Y	Y	N	N	N	Y	N
5 Foley	Y	N	N	N	N	N	N	Y
6 Dicks	?	N	N	N	N	N	N	Y
7 Lowry	Y	N	N	N	Y	Y	N	Y
WEST VIRGINIA								
1 Mollohan	Y	Y	Y	Y	X	N	N	Y
2 **Benedict**	Y	Y	N	Y	N	N	Y	N
3 **Staton**	Y	N	Y	N	N	N	?	?
4 Rahall	Y	Y	N	N	N	N	N	Y
WISCONSIN								
1 Aspin	Y	N	N	N	N	Y	Y	Y
2 Kastenmeier	Y	N	N	N	Y	Y	N	Y
3 **Gunderson**	Y	N	N	N	N	N	Y	Y
4 Zablocki	Y	N	N	N	N	N	Y	Y
5 Reuss	Y	N	N	N	Y	Y	?	?
6 **Petri**	Y	N	Y	N	N	N	?	?
7 Obey	?	N	N	N	Y	Y	N	Y
8 **Roth**	Y	N	N	N	N	N	Y	Y
9 **Sensenbrenner**	Y	N	Y	N	N	N	Y	N
WYOMING								
AL **Cheney**	Y	Y	N	Y	N	N	Y	N

**Rep. Katie Hall, D-Ind., was sworn in Nov. 29, 1982. The first vote for which she was eligible was CQ vote 369.*

Southern states - Ala., Ark., Fla., Ga., Ky., La., Miss., N.C., Okla., S.C., Tenn., Texas, Va.

377. HR 7205. Labor-Health and Human Services-Education Appropriations, Fiscal 1983. Passage of the bill to provide $85,390,630,000 for the Departments of Labor, Health and Human Services and Education and related agencies for fiscal 1983. Passed 330-70: R 115-62; D 215-8 (ND 148-2, SD 67-6), Dec. 1, 1982. The president had requested $80,036,943,000.

378. HR 6995. Federal Trade Commission (FTC) Authorization. Broyhill, R-N.C., substitute for the Luken, D-Ohio, amendment, to provide that anti-competitive practices by professionals that are required and supervised by states cannot be challenged under federal antitrust law. Rejected 195-208: R 55-125; D 140-83 (ND 123-28, SD 17-55), Dec. 1, 1982. A "yea" was a vote supporting the president's position. (The Luken amendment to exempt professionals from FTC jurisdiction until Congress specifically grants that authority subsequently was adopted *(see vote 379, below).)*

379. HR 6995. Federal Trade Commission (FTC) Authorization. Luken, D-Ohio, amendment to exempt professionals from FTC jurisdiction until Congress specifically grants that authority. Adopted 245-155: R 151-27; D 94-128 (ND 36-115, SD 58-13), Dec. 1, 1982. A "nay" was a vote supporting the president's position.

380. HR 6995. Federal Trade Commission (FTC) Authorization. Dannemeyer, R-Calif., amendment to reduce FTC authorizations to $60.8 million for fiscal 1983; $55.1 million, 1984; $54.6 million, 1985; from the bill's levels of $66 million, $70.7 million and $75.7 million. Adopted 241-158: R 167-11; D 74-147 (ND 22-126, SD 52-21), Dec. 1, 1982.

381. HR 3809. Nuclear Waste Policy Act. Udall, D-Ariz., motion that the House resolve itself into the Committee of the Whole for further consideration of the bill to establish a federal program for the interim storage and eventual permanent disposal of highly radioactive nuclear waste. Motion agreed to 345-6: R 158-2; D 187-4 (ND 126-3, SD 61-1), Dec. 2, 1982.

382. HR 3809. Nuclear Waste Policy Act. Markey, D-Mass., amendment to increase federal reimbursement of states or Indian tribes for costs resulting from the placement of a nuclear waste storage test or evaluation facility in that state or reservation. Payments would be 90 percent for states, 100 percent for Indian tribes, rather than 75 percent as in the bill. Rejected 72-321: R 4-170; D 68-151 (ND 63-84, SD 5-67), Dec. 2, 1982.

383. HR 3809. Nuclear Waste Policy Act. Markey, D-Mass., amendment to include storage of military nuclear waste under the provisions of the act. Rejected 105-281: R 5-170; D 100-111 (ND 90-54, SD 10-57), Dec. 2, 1982.

384. HR 3809. Nuclear Waste Policy Act. Broyhill, R-N.C., amendment to reduce the power of states to veto the location of a permanent nuclear waste repository within their borders by requiring a vote by one house of Congress to sustain a state veto, rather than letting the veto stand unless overruled by both houses of Congress, as provided in the bill. Adopted 213-179: R 140-35; D 73-144 (ND 29-115, SD 44-29), Dec. 2, 1982. (This amendment previously had been adopted in the Committee of the Whole *(see vote 372, p. 112-H).)*

KEY

Y	Voted for (yea).
#	Paired for.
+	Announced for.
N	Voted against (nay).
X	Paired against.
-	Announced against.
P	Voted "present".
C	Voted "present" to avoid possible conflict of interest.
?	Did not vote or otherwise make a position known.

Democrats   *Republicans*

	377	378	379	380	381	382	383	384
ALABAMA								
1 *Edwards*	Y	N	Y	Y	Y	N	N	Y
2 *Dickinson*	Y	?	?	?	Y	N	N	Y
3 Nichols	Y	N	Y	Y	?	N	N	Y
4 Bevill	Y	Y	Y	Y	Y	N	N	Y
5 Flippo	Y	N	Y	Y	Y	N	N	Y
6 *Smith*	Y	N	Y	Y	Y	N	N	Y
7 Shelby	N	N	Y	Y	Y	N	N	Y
ALASKA								
AL *Young*	Y	N	Y	N	Y	N	N	N
ARIZONA								
1 *Rhodes*	?	Y	Y	?	Y	N	N	Y
2 Udall	?	?	?	?	Y	N	N	N
3 *Stump*	N	N	Y	Y	Y	N	N	Y
4 *Rudd*	Y	N	Y	Y	Y	N	N	Y
ARKANSAS								
1 Alexander	Y	N	Y	N	Y	N	N	Y
2 *Bethune*	Y	N	Y	?	?	N	N	Y
3 *Hammerschmidt*	Y	N	Y	Y	Y	N	N	Y
4 Anthony	Y	N	Y	Y	Y	N	?	Y
CALIFORNIA								
1 *Chappie*	N	N	Y	Y	Y	N	N	Y
2 *Clausen*	Y	N	Y	Y	Y	N	N	Y
3 Matsui	?	N	N	N	Y	N	Y	N
4 Fazio	Y	N	Y	N	Y	N	Y	N
5 Burton, J.	Y	Y	N	N	?	?	Y	N
6 Burton, P.	?	Y	N	N	?	?	?	?
7 Miller	Y	Y	N	Y	N	Y	N	Y
8 Dellums	Y	Y	N	N	?	Y	Y	N
9 Stark	Y	Y	N	N	Y	Y	Y	N
10 Edwards	Y	Y	N	Y	N	Y	Y	N
11 Lantos	Y	N	Y	N	Y	N	N	N
12 *McCloskey*	?	?	?	?	?	?	?	?
13 Mineta	Y	N	Y	N	Y	N	N	Y
14 Shumway	N	N	Y	Y	Y	N	N	Y
15 Coelho	Y	N	Y	N	Y	Y	N	Y
16 Panetta	Y	N	Y	N	Y	N	Y	Y
17 *Pashayan*	N	N	Y	Y	Y	N	N	Y
18 *Thomas*	N	N	Y	Y	Y	N	N	Y
19 *Lagomarsino*	N	N	Y	Y	Y	N	N	Y
20 *Goldwater*	?	?	?	?	?	?	N	Y
21 *Fiedler*	Y	N	Y	Y	Y	N	N	Y
22 *Moorhead*	N	N	Y	Y	Y	N	N	Y
23 Beilenson	Y	Y	N	N	Y	Y	Y	N
24 Waxman	Y	Y	N	N	Y	Y	Y	N
25 Roybal	Y	N	Y	N	Y	N	N	N
26 *Rousselot*	?	?	?	?	?	?	?	?
27 *Dornan*	N	N	Y	Y	Y	N	N	Y
28 Dixon	Y	Y	N	N	Y	Y	?	?
29 Hawkins	Y	Y	N	N	N	Y	Y	?
30 Martinez	?	?	?	?	?	?	?	?
31 Dymally	Y	Y	N	Y	?	?	?	?
32 Anderson	Y	Y	N	Y	Y	N	Y	?
33 *Grisham*	N	N	Y	Y	Y	N	N	Y
34 *Lungren*	N	N	Y	Y	Y	N	N	Y
35 *Dreier*	N	N	Y	Y	Y	N	N	Y
36 Brown	Y	Y	N	N	Y	N	N	N
37 *Lewis*	N	N	Y	Y	Y	N	N	Y
38 Patterson	Y	Y	Y	Y	?	?	?	?
39 *Dannemeyer*	N	N	Y	Y	Y	N	N	Y
40 *Badham*	N	N	Y	Y	Y	N	N	Y
41 *Lowery*	N	N	Y	Y	Y	N	N	Y
42 *Hunter*	N	N	Y	Y	Y	N	N	Y
43 *Burgener*	?	?	?	?	Y	N	N	Y
COLORADO								
1 Schroeder	Y	Y	N	Y	Y	Y	Y	N
2 Wirth	Y	N	N	Y	N	Y	Y	N
3 Kogovsek	Y	Y	N	Y	Y	Y	N	N
4 *Brown*	N	N	Y	Y	Y	N	N	Y

	377	378	379	380	381	382	383	384
5 *Kramer*	N	N	Y	Y	Y	N	N	Y
CONNECTICUT								
1 Kennelly	Y	N	Y	N	Y	Y	N	Y
2 Gejdenson	Y	Y	N	N	Y	Y	N	Y
3 *DeNardis*	Y	Y	Y	?	?	?	N	?
4 *McKinney*	Y	Y	Y	Y	?	?	Y	?
5 Ratchford	Y	Y	N	N	Y	N	Y	N
6 Moffett	?	?	?	?	?	?	?	?
DELAWARE								
AL *Evans*	Y	Y	Y	Y	?	N	?	Y
FLORIDA								
1 Hutto	Y	N	Y	Y	Y	N	N	Y
2 Fuqua	Y	N	Y	N	Y	N	N	Y
3 Bennett	Y	Y	Y	Y	Y	N	N	Y
4 Chappell	Y	N	Y	Y	Y	N	N	?
5 *McCollum*	N	N	Y	Y	Y	N	N	Y
6 *Young*	Y	N	Y	Y	Y	N	N	Y
7 Gibbons	Y	Y	N	N	?	N	Y	Y
8 Ireland	Y	Y	Y	Y	?	?	?	Y
9 Nelson	Y	N	Y	N	Y	N	N	N
10 *Bafalis*	Y	N	Y	Y	Y	N	N	?
11 Mica	Y	Y	?	N	Y	N	Y	Y
12 *Shaw*	N	N	Y	Y	Y	N	N	Y
13 Lehman	?	?	?	?	?	?	?	?
14 Pepper	Y	N	Y	N	N	Y	N	Y
15 Fascell	Y	N	N	Y	N	Y	Y	Y
GEORGIA								
1 Ginn	Y	N	Y	Y	Y	N	N	Y
2 Hatcher	Y	N	Y	Y	Y	N	N	Y
3 Brinkley	Y	N	Y	Y	Y	N	N	Y
4 Levitas	Y	N	N	N	Y	N	Y	Y
5 Fowler	?	N	N	N	Y	N	Y	Y
6 *Gingrich*	Y	N	Y	?	?	?	?	?
7 McDonald	X	N	Y	Y	?	?	N	?
8 Evans	Y	?	?	?	?	Y	?	Y
9 Jenkins	Y	N	Y	Y	Y	?	?	Y
10 Barnard	Y	N	Y	Y	Y	N	N	Y
HAWAII								
1 Heftel	Y	Y	Y	Y	Y	N	N	N
2 Akaka	Y	N	Y	N	Y	N	N	N
IDAHO								
1 *Craig*	N	N	Y	Y	N	N	N	Y
2 *Hansen*	N	N	Y	?	?	N	N	?
ILLINOIS								
1 Washington	?	?	?	?	Y	Y	Y	N
2 Savage	Y	Y	N	N	?	?	?	N
3 Russo	Y	Y	N	N	N	N	N	N
4 *Derwinski*	N	Y	?	Y	N	N	?	?
5 Fary	Y	N	N	N	Y	N	N	N
6 *Hyde*	Y	N	Y	N	N	Y	N	Y
7 Collins	Y	N	N	Y	Y	?	?	Y
8 Rostenkowski	Y	N	Y	N	Y	N	N	Y
9 Yates	Y	Y	N	X	Y	Y	Y	N
10 *Porter*	+	-	+	+	+	-	-	+
11 Annunzio	Y	N	Y	N	Y	N	N	Y
12 *Crane, P.*	N	N	Y	?	?	N	Y	Y
13 *McClory*	Y	Y	Y	Y	Y	N	N	Y
14 *Erlenborn*	Y	N	Y	N	Y	N	N	Y
15 *Corcoran*	Y	N	Y	N	Y	N	N	Y
16 *Martin*	?	Y	N	Y	N	Y	N	Y
17 *O'Brien*	Y	N	Y	N	Y	N	N	Y
18 *Michel*	Y	N	Y	N	Y	N	N	Y
19 *Railsback*	Y	Y	N	Y	?	N	N	Y
20 *Findley*	Y	Y	Y	N	Y	?	?	Y
21 *Madigan*	Y	N	Y	N	Y	N	N	Y
22 *Crane, D.*	N	N	Y	Y	Y	N	N	Y
23 Price	Y	N	N	Y	N	N	N	Y
24 Simon	Y	Y	N	N	Y	Y	?	N
INDIANA								
1 Hall	Y	Y	N	N	?	N	N	N
2 Fithian	?	Y	N	Y	N	Y	N	Y
3 *Hiler*	Y	N	Y	Y	Y	N	N	Y
4 *Coats*	Y	N	Y	Y	Y	N	N	Y
5 *Hillis*	Y	N	Y	N	Y	N	N	Y
6 Evans	Y	N	Y	Y	Y	N	N	?
7 *Myers*	Y	N	Y	N	Y	N	N	Y
8 *Deckard*	Y	?	?	Y	?	?	Y	N
9 Hamilton	Y	Y	Y	Y	Y	N	N	Y
10 Sharp	Y	N	Y	N	Y	N	N	Y
11 Jacobs	Y	Y	N	N	Y	N	Y	N
IOWA								
1 *Leach*	Y	Y	N	N	Y	N	N	N
2 *Tauke*	N	N	Y	Y	Y	N	N	Y
3 *Evans*	Y	N	Y	N	Y	N	N	Y
4 *Smith*	Y	N	Y	N	Y	N	N	Y
5 Harkin	Y	N	N	N	N	N	N	N
6 Bedell	Y	Y	N	Y	N	Y	N	Y

ND - Northern Democrats   SD - Southern Democrats

	377	378	379	380	381	382	383	384
KANSAS								
1 *Roberts*	Y	N	Y	Y	Y	N	N	Y
2 *Jeffries*	N	N	Y	Y	?	N	N	Y
3 *Winn*	Y	N	Y	Y	Y	N	N	Y
4 Glickman	Y	Y	N	N	Y	N	N	N
5 *Whittaker*	Y	N	Y	Y	Y	N	N	Y
KENTUCKY								
1 Hubbard	N	N	Y	Y	Y	N	N	Y
2 Natcher	Y	N	Y	N	Y	N	N	Y
3 Mazzoli	Y	Y	N	N	Y	N	Y	N
4 *Snyder*	Y	N	Y	Y	Y	N	N	Y
5 *Rogers*	Y	N	Y	Y	Y	N	N	Y
6 *Hopkins*	Y	Y	Y	Y	Y	N	N	Y
7 Perkins	Y	N	Y	N	Y	N	N	N
LOUISIANA								
1 *Livingston*	Y	Y	Y	Y	Y	N	N	N
2 Boggs	Y	N	Y	Y	Y	N	Y	N
3 Tauzin	Y	N	Y	Y	Y	Y	N	N
4 Roemer	N	Y	N	Y	N	N	N	N
5 Huckaby	Y	N	Y	Y	Y	Y	N	N
6 *Moore*	Y	N	Y	Y	Y	N	N	N
7 Breaux	#	?	?	#	?	?	?	?
8 Long	Y	Y	Y	Y	Y	Y	?	N
MAINE								
1 *Emery*	Y	N	Y	Y	Y	N	N	Y
2 *Snowe*	Y	Y	N	Y	Y	N	N	Y
MARYLAND								
1 Dyson	Y	N	Y	Y	Y	N	N	N
2 Long	Y	Y	N	N	Y	N	Y	N
3 Mikulski	Y	Y	N	N	Y	Y	Y	N
4 *Holt*	N	N	Y	Y	Y	N	N	Y
5 Hoyer	Y	N	Y	N	Y	N	Y	N
6 Byron	Y	N	Y	Y	?	N	N	Y
7 Mitchell	Y	Y	N	N	Y	Y	?	N
8 Barnes	Y	N	N	N	Y	N	Y	N
MASSACHUSETTS								
1 *Conte*	Y	Y	N	Y	Y	N	N	N
2 Boland	Y	Y	N	N	Y	N	N	N
3 Early	Y	Y	N	N	Y	N	Y	N
4 Frank	Y	Y	?	?	Y	Y	Y	N
5 Shannon	Y	Y	N	N	Y	N	Y	N
6 Mavroules	Y	Y	N	N	Y	Y	N	N
7 Markey	?	Y	N	N	Y	Y	Y	N
8 O'Neill								
9 Moakley	Y	Y	N	N	Y	Y	Y	N
10 *Heckler*	Y	?	?	Y	?	?	?	?
11 Donnelly	Y	Y	N	N	Y	Y	Y	N
12 Studds	Y	Y	N	N	Y	Y	Y	N
MICHIGAN								
1 Conyers	Y	Y	N	N	Y	Y	Y	N
2 *Pursell*	Y	Y	N	Y	Y	N	N	Y
3 Wolpe	Y	Y	N	N	Y	N	Y	N
4 *Siljander*	N	N	Y	Y	Y	N	N	Y
5 *Sawyer*	Y	N	Y	Y	Y	N	N	Y
6 *Dunn*	Y	N	Y	Y	Y	N	N	Y
7 Kildee	Y	Y	N	N	Y	Y	Y	N
8 Traxler	Y	Y	N	N	Y	N	Y	?
9 *Vander Jagt*	Y	N	Y	Y	?	N	N	Y
10 Albosta	?	N	Y	N	Y	N	N	N
11 *Davis*	Y	N	Y	N	Y	Y	N	?
12 Bonior	Y	Y	N	N	Y	Y	Y	N
13 Crockett	Y	Y	N	N	Y	Y	Y	N
14 Hertel	Y	Y	N	?	?	N	Y	N
15 Ford	Y	Y	N	N	Y	N	Y	N
16 Dingell	Y	Y	N	N	Y	N	N	N
17 Brodhead	Y	Y	N	N	Y	Y	Y	N
18 Blanchard	?	?	?	?	?	?	?	?
19 *Broomfield*	Y	N	Y	Y	Y	N	N	Y
MINNESOTA								
1 *Erdahl*	Y	Y	N	Y	Y	N	N	Y
2 *Hagedorn*	N	N	Y	Y	Y	N	N	Y
3 *Frenzel*	N	N	Y	Y	Y	N	N	Y
4 Vento	Y	Y	N	N	?	Y	Y	N
5 Sabo	Y	Y	N	N	Y	N	Y	N
6 *Weber*	?	N	Y	Y	Y	N	N	N
7 *Stangeland*	Y	N	Y	Y	Y	N	N	Y
8 Oberstar	Y	Y	N	N	Y	Y	Y	N
MISSISSIPPI								
1 Whitten	Y	N	Y	N	Y	N	Y	N
2 Bowen	Y	?	?	Y	Y	N	N	N
3 Montgomery	Y	N	Y	Y	Y	N	N	N
4 Dowdy	Y	N	Y	Y	Y	N	N	N
5 *Lott*	N	N	Y	Y	?	N	N	N
MISSOURI								
1 Clay	Y	Y	N	N	?	Y	Y	N
2 Young	Y	N	Y	N	Y	N	N	Y
3 Gephardt	Y	Y	N	N	Y	N	N	Y

	377	378	379	380	381	382	383	384
4 Skelton	Y	N	Y	Y	Y	N	N	N
5 Bolling	?	?	?	?	?	?	?	?
6 *Coleman*	Y	N	Y	Y	Y	N	N	Y
7 *Taylor*	N	N	Y	Y	Y	N	N	Y
8 *Bailey*	N	N	Y	Y	Y	N	N	Y
9 Volkmer	Y	N	Y	N	Y	N	N	Y
10 *Emerson*	Y	N	Y	Y	Y	N	N	Y
MONTANA								
1 Williams	Y	Y	N	N	?	Y	Y	N
2 *Marlenee*	Y	N	Y	Y	Y	N	N	N
NEBRASKA								
1 *Bereuter*	Y	Y	N	Y	Y	N	N	Y
2 *Daub*	Y	N	Y	Y	Y	N	N	Y
3 *Smith*	Y	N	Y	Y	Y	N	N	Y
NEVADA								
AL Santini	Y	N	Y	Y	?	Y	Y	N
NEW HAMPSHIRE								
1 D'Amours	Y	+	-	Y	Y	N	N	Y
2 *Gregg*	N	N	Y	Y	Y	N	N	Y
NEW JERSEY								
1 Florio	Y	Y	N	N	Y	N	Y	N
2 Hughes	Y	Y	Y	N	Y	N	N	N
3 Howard	?	Y	N	N	Y	Y	Y	N
4 *Smith*	Y	Y	N	Y	Y	N	N	Y
5 *Fenwick*	Y	Y	N	N	Y	N	N	N
6 *Forsythe*	N	N	Y	Y	Y	N	N	Y
7 *Roukema*	Y	Y	Y	Y	Y	N	N	Y
8 Roe	Y	Y	Y	N	Y	N	Y	Y
9 *Hollenbeck*	Y	Y	N	N	?	N	N	Y
10 Rodino	Y	Y	N	N	Y	N	Y	N
11 Minish	Y	Y	N	N	Y	N	Y	N
12 *Rinaldo*	Y	Y	N	N	Y	N	N	Y
13 *Courter*	Y	N	Y	Y	Y	N	N	Y
14 Guarini	Y	N	Y	N	Y	N	Y	Y
15 Dwyer	Y	Y	Y	N	Y	N	Y	N
NEW MEXICO								
1 *Lujan*	Y	N	Y	Y	Y	N	N	N
2 *Skeen*	Y	N	Y	Y	Y	N	N	Y
NEW YORK								
1 *Carney*	N	N	Y	Y	Y	N	N	Y
2 Downey	Y	Y	N	N	Y	Y	Y	N
3 *Carman*	N	N	Y	Y	?	N	N	Y
4 *Lent*	Y	Y	N	N	Y	N	N	Y
5 *McGrath*	Y	Y	N	Y	Y	N	N	Y
6 *LeBoutillier*	Y	N	Y	Y	Y	N	N	Y
7 Addabbo	Y	Y	Y	N	Y	N	Y	N
8 Rosenthal	Y	Y	N	N	?	Y	Y	N
9 Ferraro	Y	Y	N	N	Y	N	N	N
10 Biaggi	Y	Y	N	N	Y	N	Y	N
11 Scheuer	Y	Y	N	N	Y	N	Y	N
12 Chisholm	Y	Y	N	?	?	?	?	?
13 Solarz	Y	Y	?	?	Y	Y	Y	N
14 Vacancy								
15 Zeferetti	Y	Y	N	?	Y	N	N	Y
16 Schumer	Y	Y	N	N	Y	Y	Y	N
17 *Molinari*	Y	N	Y	Y	Y	N	?	N
18 *Green*	Y	Y	N	N	Y	N	N	N
19 Rangel	Y	Y	N	N	Y	Y	Y	Y
20 Weiss	Y	Y	N	N	Y	Y	Y	N
21 Garcia	Y	Y	N	N	?	Y	Y	N
22 Bingham	Y	Y	N	N	?	Y	Y	N
23 Peyser	Y	Y	N	N	Y	N	N	N
24 Ottinger	Y	Y	N	N	Y	N	N	N
25 *Fish*	Y	Y	N	Y	Y	N	N	N
26 *Gilman*	Y	Y	N	N	Y	N	N	N
27 McHugh	Y	Y	N	N	Y	N	Y	N
28 Stratton	Y	N	Y	Y	Y	N	N	Y
29 *Solomon*	N	Y	?	Y	Y	N	N	Y
30 *Martin*	Y	?	?	?	?	?	N	Y
31 *Mitchell*	Y	N	Y	Y	N	N	N	N
32 *Wortley*	Y	Y	N	Y	?	N	N	Y
33 *Lee*	?	N	Y	Y	?	N	?	?
34 *Horton*	Y	Y	N	Y	Y	N	N	Y
35 *Conable*	N	Y	Y	Y	Y	N	N	Y
36 LaFalce	Y	Y	N	N	Y	N	?	?
37 Nowak	Y	Y	N	N	Y	Y	Y	N
38 *Kemp*	N	N	Y	Y	Y	N	N	Y
39 Lundine	Y	Y	N	N	Y	N	Y	N
NORTH CAROLINA								
1 Jones	Y	N	Y	Y	?	N	N	Y
2 Fountain	+	N	Y	Y	?	?	N	N
3 Whitley	Y	N	Y	Y	Y	N	N	Y
4 Andrews	Y	N	Y	Y	Y	N	N	Y
5 Neal	Y	?	?	?	Y	N	N	N
6 *Johnston*	N	Y	Y	Y	?	N	?	Y
7 Rose	Y	N	Y	Y	Y	N	N	Y
8 Hefner	Y	N	Y	Y	Y	N	N	Y

	377	378	379	380	381	382	383	384
9 *Martin*	N	N	Y	Y	Y	N	N	Y
10 *Broyhill*	N	Y	N	N	Y	N	N	Y
11 *Hendon*	Y	N	Y	Y	Y	N	N	Y
NORTH DAKOTA								
AL Dorgan	Y	Y	N	N	Y	Y	Y	N
OHIO								
1 *Gradison*	Y	Y	N	Y	Y	N	N	Y
2 Luken	Y	N	Y	N	Y	N	N	N
3 Hall	Y	N	Y	Y	Y	?	N	Y
4 *Oxley*	Y	Y	Y	Y	?	N	N	Y
5 *Latta*	N	N	Y	Y	Y	N	N	Y
6 *McEwen*	Y	N	Y	Y	Y	N	N	Y
7 *Brown*	Y	Y	Y	Y	Y	N	N	Y
8 *Kindness*	N	N	Y	Y	Y	N	?	Y
9 *Weber*	Y	N	Y	Y	Y	N	N	Y
10 *Miller*	N	Y	Y	Y	Y	N	N	N
11 *Stanton*	?	?	?	?	?	?	?	?
12 Shamansky	Y	Y	N	N	Y	Y	Y	N
13 Pease	Y	Y	N	N	Y	N	Y	Y
14 Seiberling	Y	Y	N	N	Y	Y	Y	N
15 *Wylie*	Y	N	Y	Y	Y	N	N	Y
16 *Regula*	Y	Y	Y	Y	Y	N	N	N
17 *Ashbrook*	N	N	Y	Y	Y	N	N	Y
18 Applegate	Y	?	Y	Y	?	N	N	N
19 *Williams*	?	Y	Y	Y	Y	Y	N	Y
20 Oakar	Y	Y	N	N	Y	N	Y	N
21 Stokes	Y	Y	N	N	Y	Y	Y	N
22 Eckart	Y	Y	N	N	Y	N	Y	N
23 Mottl	Y	Y	N	N	Y	N	Y	N
OKLAHOMA								
1 Jones	Y	?	?	?	?	N	N	N
2 Synar	Y	Y	N	N	Y	N	Y	Y
3 Watkins	Y	N	Y	Y	?	N	N	N
4 McCurdy	Y	N	Y	Y	?	N	N	N
5 *Edwards*	N	N	Y	Y	Y	N	N	Y
6 English	Y	N	Y	Y	Y	N	N	N
OREGON								
1 AuCoin	N	Y	N	N	Y	Y	Y	N
2 *Smith*	N	N	Y	Y	Y	N	N	Y
3 Wyden	Y	Y	N	N	Y	Y	Y	N
4 Weaver	Y	Y	N	N	Y	Y	Y	N
PENNSYLVANIA								
1 Foglietta	Y	Y	N	N	Y	N	Y	N
2 Gray	Y	Y	N	N	Y	Y	N	Y
3 Smith	?	?	?	?	?	N	N	N
4 *Dougherty*	Y	Y	Y	Y	?	N	N	Y
5 *Schulze*	N	Y	Y	Y	Y	N	N	Y
6 Yatron	Y	N	Y	Y	Y	N	N	Y
7 Edgar	Y	Y	N	N	?	?	?	?
8 *Coyne, J.*	Y	N	Y	Y	Y	N	?	?
9 *Shuster*	?	?	?	?	?	?	?	?
10 *McDade*	Y	Y	Y	Y	Y	N	N	Y
11 *Nelligan*	Y	N	Y	Y	Y	N	N	Y
12 Murtha	Y	N	Y	Y	Y	N	N	Y
13 *Coughlin*	Y	Y	N	Y	Y	N	N	N
14 Coyne, W.	Y	Y	N	N	Y	Y	Y	N
15 *Ritter*	Y	Y	Y	Y	Y	N	N	Y
16 *Walker*	N	N	Y	Y	Y	N	N	Y
17 Ertel	Y	?	N	Y	?	?	N	Y
18 Walgren	Y	Y	N	N	Y	Y	Y	N
19 *Goodling*	Y	Y	Y	Y	N	?	N	Y
20 Gaydos	Y	Y	Y	Y	?	N	N	Y
21 Bailey	Y	Y	N	N	?	N	N	Y
22 Murphy	Y	?	Y	?	?	N	Y	Y
23 *Clinger*	Y	Y	Y	Y	Y	N	N	Y
24 *Marks*	?	?	?	?	?	?	?	Y
25 *Atkinson*	Y	N	Y	Y	Y	?	?	?
RHODE ISLAND								
1 St Germain	Y	Y	N	N	?	?	?	?
2 *Schneider*	Y	Y	N	Y	Y	N	N	N
SOUTH CAROLINA								
1 *Hartnett*	N	N	Y	Y	Y	N	N	Y
2 *Spence*	N	N	Y	Y	Y	N	N	Y
3 Derrick	Y	N	Y	Y	Y	N	N	N
4 *Campbell*	Y	N	Y	Y	Y	N	N	Y
5 Holland	Y	N	Y	Y	Y	N	?	Y
6 *Napier*	Y	N	Y	Y	Y	N	N	Y
SOUTH DAKOTA								
1 Daschle	Y	Y	N	N	?	?	?	?
2 *Roberts*	?	N	Y	Y	Y	N	N	Y
TENNESSEE								
1 *Quillen*	Y	N	Y	Y	Y	N	N	Y
2 *Duncan*	Y	N	Y	Y	Y	N	N	Y
3 Bouquard	Y	N	Y	Y	Y	N	N	Y
4 Gore	Y	Y	N	N	Y	N	N	N
5 Boner	Y	Y	Y	Y	Y	N	N	Y
6 *Beard*	Y	Y	Y	Y	Y	N	N	Y

	377	378	379	380	381	382	383	384
7 Jones	Y	Y	Y	Y	Y	N	N	Y
8 Ford	Y	Y	N	Y	?	N	N	N
TEXAS								
1 Hall, S.	Y	N	Y	Y	Y	N	N	N
2 Wilson	Y	N	Y	Y	Y	N	?	?
3 *Collins*	N	N	Y	Y	Y	N	N	Y
4 Hall, R.	Y	N	Y	Y	Y	N	N	N
5 Mattox	Y	Y	Y	N	Y	N	Y	Y
6 Gramm	N	Y	N	Y	Y	N	N	Y
7 *Archer*	N	N	Y	Y	Y	N	N	Y
8 *Fields*	N	N	Y	Y	Y	N	N	N
9 Brooks	Y	N	Y	N	?	N	N	Y
10 Pickle	Y	N	Y	Y	Y	N	N	Y
11 Leath	Y	N	Y	Y	Y	N	N	Y
12 Wright	Y	N	Y	N	?	?	N	Y
13 Hightower	Y	N	Y	Y	Y	N	N	N
14 Patman	Y	N	Y	Y	Y	N	N	N
15 de la Garza	?	?	?	?	?	?	?	?
16 White	Y	N	Y	Y	Y	N	N	Y
17 Stenholm	N	N	Y	Y	Y	N	N	Y
18 Leland	Y	Y	N	N	Y	Y	?	N
19 Hance	N	N	Y	Y	Y	N	?	?
20 Gonzalez	Y	N	N	N	Y	N	N	N
21 *Loeffler*	N	N	Y	Y	Y	N	N	Y
22 *Paul*	N	N	Y	Y	Y	N	N	N
23 Kazen	Y	N	Y	Y	Y	N	N	Y
24 Frost	Y	N	Y	N	Y	N	N	Y
UTAH								
1 *Hansen*	?	N	Y	Y	Y	?	N	N
2 *Marriott*	Y	N	Y	Y	Y	N	N	N
VERMONT								
AL *Jeffords*	Y	Y	N	Y	Y	Y	Y	N
VIRGINIA								
1 *Trible*	Y	N	Y	Y	Y	N	N	Y
2 *Whitehurst*	Y	N	Y	Y	Y	N	N	Y
3 *Bliley*	Y	N	Y	Y	Y	N	N	Y
4 *Daniel, R.*	N	N	Y	Y	Y	N	N	Y
5 Daniel, D.	Y	N	Y	Y	?	N	N	Y
6 *Butler*	Y	Y	Y	Y	?	N	N	Y
7 *Robinson*	Y	N	Y	Y	Y	N	N	Y
8 *Parris*	Y	N	Y	N	Y	N	N	Y
9 *Wampler*	Y	N	Y	Y	Y	N	N	Y
10 *Wolf*	Y	N	Y	Y	Y	N	N	Y
WASHINGTON								
1 *Pritchard*	Y	N	Y	Y	Y	N	N	N
2 Swift	Y	Y	N	N	Y	Y	N	N
3 Bonker	Y	Y	N	N	Y	N	Y	N
4 *Morrison*	Y	Y	Y	Y	Y	Y	N	N
5 Foley	Y	Y	Y	N	?	Y	N	N
6 Dicks	Y	Y	N	N	Y	Y	Y	N
7 Lowry	Y	N	N	N	N	Y	Y	N
WEST VIRGINIA								
1 Mollohan	Y	N	?	N	?	N	N	?
2 *Benedict*	Y	N	Y	Y	?	N	N	Y
3 *Staton*	N	N	Y	Y	Y	N	N	N
4 Rahall	Y	N	Y	Y	?	N	N	Y
WISCONSIN								
1 Aspin	Y	Y	N	N	Y	Y	Y	N
2 Kastenmeier	Y	Y	N	N	Y	Y	Y	N
3 *Gunderson*	Y	N	Y	Y	Y	N	N	N
4 Zablocki	Y	Y	N	N	Y	N	N	N
5 Reuss	Y	Y	N	N	Y	N	Y	N
6 *Petri*	Y	Y	Y	Y	Y	N	N	N
7 Obey	Y	Y	N	N	Y	Y	Y	N
8 *Roth*	Y	N	Y	Y	Y	N	N	N
9 *Sensenbrenner*	N	N	Y	Y	Y	N	Y	N
WYOMING								
AL *Cheney*	N	N	Y	Y	?	N	N	Y

Southern states - Ala., Ark., Fla., Ga., Ky., La., Miss., N.C., Okla., S.C., Tenn., Texas, Va.

385. HR 2330. Nuclear Regulatory Commission Authorization. Frenzel, R-Minn., motion to eliminate a provision requiring the president to make a comprehensive study of the domestic uranium industry and imposing a moratorium on new contracts for uranium imports if such imports exceeded 37.5 percent of total U.S. demand for two consecutive years. Motion agreed to 241-148: R 127-45; D 114-103 (ND 81-64, SD 33-39), Dec. 2, 1982. A "yea" was a vote supporting the president's position.

386. HR 2330. Nuclear Regulatory Commission Authorization. Stratton, D-N.Y., motion to eliminate provisions prohibiting the use of burned fuel from civilian nuclear power plants for the production of nuclear weapons; limiting the authority of the Department of Energy to withhold certain unclassified information, and changing the schedule for issuing regulations concerning the cleanup of uranium tailings. Motion rejected 107-281: R 73-102; D 34-179 (ND 8-133, SD 26-46), Dec. 2, 1982.

387. HR 7356. Interior Appropriations, Fiscal 1983. Adoption of the rule (H Res 616) providing for House floor consideration of the bill to appropriate funds in fiscal 1983 for the Interior Department, Forest Service, certain Energy Department programs and related agencies. Adopted 293-29: R 123-26; D 170-3 (ND 110-1, SD 60-2), Dec. 3, 1982.

388. HR 7356. Interior Appropriations, Fiscal 1983. Passage of the bill to appropriate $7,386,522,000 in fiscal 1983 for the Interior Department, Forest Service, certain Energy Department programs and related agencies. Passed 275-73: R 97-63; D 178-10 (ND 120-2, SD 58-8), Dec. 3, 1982. The president had requested $6,576,960,000.

389. HR 6211. Transportation Assistance Act of 1982. Adoption of the rule (H Res 620) providing for House floor consideration of the bill to authorize funds for highway and mass transit programs for fiscal 1983-1986 and to increase gasoline and other highway taxes. Adopted 197-194: R 59-114; D 138-80 (ND 112-34, SD 26-46), Dec. 6, 1982.

390. HR 6211. Transportation Assistance Act of 1982. Conte, R-Mass., amendment to ensure that funds for highway and mass transit projects substituted for planned Interstate Highway segments are subject to the appropriations process. Rejected 96-305: R 52-127; D 44-178 (ND 32-118, SD 12-60), Dec. 6, 1982.

391. HR 6211. Transportation Assistance Act of 1982. Stenholm, D-Texas, amendment to waive Davis-Bacon Act wage requirements for federally funded transportation projects. Rejected 174-223: R 138-41; D 36-182 (ND 3-143, SD 33-39), Dec. 6, 1982.

392. HR 6211. Transportation Assistance Act of 1982. Roemer, D-La., amendment to apply Davis-Bacon Act wage requirements for federally funded highway projects to "initial" highway construction. Rejected 191-194: R 147-22; D 44-172 (ND 4-140, SD 40-32), Dec. 6, 1982.

KEY

Y Voted for (yea).
\# Paired for.
+ Announced for.
N Voted against (nay).
X Paired against.
- Announced against.
P Voted "present".
C Voted "present" to avoid possible conflict of interest.
? Did not vote or otherwise make a position known.

Democrats   *Republicans*

	385	386	387	388	389	390	391	392
ALABAMA								
1 Edwards	Y	Y	Y	Y	Y	Y	Y	Y
2 *Dickinson*	Y	N	Y	Y	N	N	?	Y
3 Nichols	N	Y	Y	?	N	N	N	Y
4 Bevill	N	Y	Y	Y	?	?	?	?
5 Flippo	N	Y	?	?	Y	N	N	N
6 *Smith*	Y	N	N	N	N	Y	Y	Y
7 Shelby	N	N	Y	N	N	N	N	N
ALASKA								
AL *Young*	?	N	?	Y	N	N	N	N
ARIZONA								
1 *Rhodes*	N	N	?	Y	Y	?	?	?
2 Udall	N	N	Y	Y	Y	N	N	N
3 *Stump*	N	Y	N	N	N	N	Y	Y
4 *Rudd*	N	Y	Y	N	Y	Y	Y	Y
ARKANSAS								
1 Alexander	?	N	Y	Y	?	?	?	?
2 *Bethune*	Y	N	N	Y	N	Y	N	N
3 *Hammerschmidt*	Y	Y	Y	N	N	N	Y	Y
4 Anthony	Y	N	Y	Y	Y	N	Y	Y
CALIFORNIA								
1 *Chappie*	N	N	Y	N	N	N	Y	Y
2 *Clausen*	Y	N	Y	Y	Y	N	N	Y
3 Matsui	N	N	Y	Y	Y	N	N	N
4 Fazio	Y	N	?	Y	Y	Y	N	N
5 Burton, J.	Y	N	Y	Y	Y	N	N	N
6 Burton, P.	?	?	?	?	Y	N	N	N
7 Miller	N	N	Y	Y	Y	N	N	N
8 Dellums	Y	N	Y	Y	Y	N	N	N
9 Stark	Y	N	?	Y	Y	N	N	N
10 Edwards	Y	N	Y	Y	Y	N	N	N
11 Lantos	Y	N	Y	?	?	?	?	?
12 *McCloskey*	?	?	?	?	?	?	?	?
13 Mineta	N	N	Y	Y	Y	N	N	N
14 *Shumway*	Y	Y	Y	N	N	N	Y	Y
15 Coelho	N	?	Y	Y	Y	N	N	N
16 Panetta	Y	N	Y	Y	Y	N	N	N
17 *Pashayan*	Y	Y	Y	Y	Y	N	N	N
18 *Thomas*	Y	N	Y	N	Y	N	N	N
19 *Lagomarsino*	Y	N	Y	N	Y	N	Y	Y
20 *Goldwater*	?	Y	?	N	N	?	Y	?
21 *Fiedler*	Y	N	Y	N	Y	Y	Y	Y
22 *Moorhead*	N	N	Y	N	N	N	Y	Y
23 Beilenson	Y	N	Y	Y	Y	N	N	N
24 Waxman	Y	N	?	Y	Y	N	N	N
25 Roybal	?	?	?	?	Y	Y	N	N
26 *Rousselot*	?	?	?	Y	Y	Y	Y	Y
27 *Dornan*	Y	Y	Y	N	Y	N	Y	Y
28 Dixon	?	?	?	?	Y	Y	N	N
29 Hawkins	N	N	?	Y	Y	Y	N	N
30 Martinez	?	?	?	?	Y	Y	N	N
31 Dymally	?	?	?	?	Y	Y	N	N
32 Anderson	N	N	Y	Y	Y	N	N	N
33 *Grisham*	Y	Y	?	N	Y	N	Y	Y
34 *Lungren*	Y	N	N	Y	N	Y	N	Y
35 *Dreier*	Y	Y	N	N	N	Y	N	Y
36 Brown	Y	N	Y	Y	Y	N	N	N
37 *Lewis*	Y	Y	Y	N	Y	N	Y	Y
38 *Patterson*	?	?	?	?	?	?	?	?
39 *Dannemeyer*	Y	N	N	N	N	N	N	Y
40 *Badham*	?	?	?	?	N	N	Y	?
41 *Lowery*	Y	N	Y	N	N	Y	N	Y
42 *Hunter*	N	Y	Y	Y	Y	N	Y	Y
43 *Burgener*	Y	?	Y	Y	Y	Y	Y	?
COLORADO								
1 Schroeder	N	N	Y	Y	N	N	N	N
2 Wirth	N	N	Y	Y	Y	N	N	N
3 Kogovsek	N	N	Y	Y	Y	N	N	N
4 *Brown*	Y	N	Y	N	N	N	N	N

	385	386	387	388	389	390	391	392
5 *Kramer*	N	Y	Y	N	N	N	Y	Y
CONNECTICUT								
1 Kennelly	N	N	Y	Y	N	N	N	N
2 Gejdenson	Y	N	Y	Y	N	N	N	N
3 *DeNardis*	?	N	?	?	?	Y	N	N
4 *McKinney*	Y	N	Y	N	N	N	N	N
5 Ratchford	Y	N	Y	Y	Y	Y	N	N
6 Moffett	?	?	?	?	Y	Y	N	N
DELAWARE								
AL *Evans*	Y	N	Y	Y	Y	?	Y	Y
FLORIDA								
1 Hutto	Y	Y	Y	N	N	N	Y	Y
2 Fuqua	N	N	Y	?	N	N	Y	Y
3 Bennett	Y	Y	Y	Y	N	N	Y	Y
4 Chappell	?	Y	Y	N	N	Y	N	Y
5 *McCollum*	Y	N	N	N	N	N	Y	Y
6 *Young*	Y	?	Y	N	Y	N	Y	Y
7 Gibbons	Y	N	Y	Y	N	N	N	N
8 Ireland	Y	?	?	Y	N	?	N	?
9 Nelson	Y	N	Y	Y	N	Y	N	N
10 *Bafalis*	?	Y	Y	Y	?	?	?	?
11 Mica	Y	N	Y	Y	Y	N	N	N
12 *Shaw*	Y	N	Y	N	N	N	Y	Y
13 Lehman	?	?	?	?	Y	?	?	?
14 Pepper	N	N	Y	Y	Y	N	N	N
15 Fascell	N	N	Y	Y	?	?	?	?
GEORGIA								
1 Ginn	N	Y	Y	?	N	N	N	N
2 Hatcher	N	N	?	N	N	N	N	N
3 Brinkley	Y	Y	Y	Y	N	N	N	N
4 Levitas	Y	N	Y	Y	N	Y	N	N
5 Fowler	Y	N	Y	Y	Y	N	N	N
6 *Gingrich*	?	?	?	?	Y	N	Y	Y
7 McDonald	Y	Y	N	N	N	Y	Y	Y
8 Evans	N	N	Y	Y	N	Y	N	Y
9 Jenkins	Y	N	Y	Y	N	Y	N	Y
10 Barnard	N	Y	Y	N	N	N	Y	Y
HAWAII								
1 Heftel	N	N	Y	?	N	N	?	Y
2 Akaka	N	N	Y	Y	N	N	N	N
IDAHO								
1 *Craig*	N	N	?	Y	N	Y	N	N
2 *Hansen*	N	N	Y	N	N	N	Y	Y
ILLINOIS								
1 Washington	Y	N	?	?	?	N	N	N
2 Savage	?	N	?	?	N	N	N	N
3 Russo	Y	N	Y	Y	Y	N	N	N
4 *Derwinski*	Y	Y	Y	Y	Y	N	N	N
5 Fary	N	Y	Y	Y	N	N	N	N
6 *Hyde*	Y	N	Y	N	N	N	Y	Y
7 Collins	N	N	?	Y	N	N	N	N
8 Rostenkowski	Y	N	Y	Y	Y	N	N	N
9 Yates	N	N	Y	Y	Y	?	N	N
10 *Porter*	-	-	+	+	N	Y	Y	N
11 Annunzio	Y	Y	Y	Y	N	N	N	N
12 *Crane, P.*	?	?	?	?	N	N	Y	Y
13 *McClory*	Y	Y	Y	Y	N	Y	N	Y
14 *Erlenborn*	Y	?	Y	?	Y	Y	Y	Y
15 *Corcoran*	Y	N	?	Y	Y	N	N	N
16 *Martin*	Y	N	?	?	N	N	N	N
17 *O'Brien*	Y	Y	?	?	Y	Y	N	Y
18 *Michel*	Y	N	?	N	Y	N	N	N
19 *Railsback*	Y	N	Y	Y	N	?	Y	?
20 *Findley*	Y	N	Y	Y	N	Y	N	Y
21 *Madigan*	Y	N	?	Y	Y	N	N	N
22 *Crane, D.*	Y	Y	N	N	N	N	Y	Y
23 Price	Y	Y	Y	Y	N	N	N	N
24 Simon	N	N	Y	Y	N	N	N	N
INDIANA								
1 Hall	Y	N	Y	Y	Y	N	N	N
2 Fithian	N	N	Y	Y	Y	N	N	N
3 *Hiler*	Y	N	?	N	Y	Y	Y	Y
4 *Coats*	Y	N	Y	N	N	N	Y	Y
5 *Hillis*	N	Y	Y	Y	N	N	Y	Y
6 Evans	N	N	?	?	?	N	N	N
7 *Myers*	Y	Y	?	?	N	Y	Y	Y
8 *Deckard*	?	N	?	Y	?	?	Y	?
9 Hamilton	Y	N	Y	Y	N	N	N	N
10 Sharp	Y	N	Y	Y	N	N	N	N
11 Jacobs	Y	N	Y	N	N	N	N	N
IOWA								
1 *Leach*	Y	N	Y	Y	N	Y	N	Y
2 *Tauke*	Y	N	Y	Y	N	N	N	Y
3 *Evans*	Y	N	Y	N	N	N	Y	Y
4 Smith	Y	N	Y	Y	Y	N	N	N
5 Harkin	Y	N	Y	Y	N	N	N	N
6 Bedell	Y	N	Y	Y	N	N	N	Y

ND - Northern Democrats   SD - Southern Democrats

	385	386	387	388	389	390	391	392
KANSAS								
1 ***Roberts***	Y	N	N	N	N	Y	Y	Y
2 ***Jeffries***	Y	Y	N	N	N	N	Y	Y
3 ***Winn***	Y	Y	Y	N	?	N	Y	Y
4 Glickman	Y	N	Y	Y	N	N	N	N
5 ***Whittaker***	Y	N	Y	N	N	Y	Y	Y
KENTUCKY								
1 Hubbard	N	N	Y	N	N	N	N	N
2 Natcher	N	N	Y	Y	Y	N	N	N
3 Mazzoli	N	N	Y	Y	Y	?	N	N
4 ***Snyder***	N	N	?	?	Y	N	Y	Y
5 ***Rogers***	N	N	Y	Y	N	N	Y	Y
6 ***Hopkins***	N	N	Y	N	N	N	Y	Y
7 Perkins	N	N	Y	Y	N	Y	N	N
LOUISIANA								
1 ***Livingston***	N	N	Y	Y	N	Y	Y	Y
2 Boggs	N	N	Y	Y	Y	?	N	N
3 Tauzin	Y	N	Y	N	N	N	N	N
4 Roemer	Y	N	N	N	N	N	N	Y
5 Huckaby	Y	?	Y	Y	N	N	Y	Y
6 ***Moore***	Y	N	Y	N	N	N	Y	Y
7 Breaux	N	N	Y	Y	Y	N	N	N
8 Long	N	N	?	Y	Y	N	N	N
MAINE								
1 ***Emery***	N	N	Y	Y	?	Y	Y	?
2 ***Snowe***	N	N	Y	Y	N	Y	Y	Y
MARYLAND								
1 Dyson	Y	N	Y	Y	Y	N	N	N
2 Long	N	N	Y	Y	Y	Y	Y	Y
3 Mikulski	Y	N	?	Y	Y	N	N	N
4 ***Holt***	N	Y	Y	N	N	N	Y	Y
5 Hoyer	N	N	?	Y	Y	N	N	N
6 Byron	N	Y	Y	Y	?	N	Y	Y
7 Mitchell	N	N	Y	Y	Y	N	N	N
8 Barnes	Y	N	Y	Y	?	?	?	?
MASSACHUSETTS								
1 ***Conte***	Y	N	Y	Y	?	Y	N	N
2 Boland	N	N	?	?	Y	Y	N	N
3 Early	Y	N	?	?	Y	Y	N	N
4 Frank	Y	N	Y	Y	Y	Y	N	N
5 Shannon	Y	N	Y	Y	Y	Y	N	N
6 Mavroules	Y	Y	Y	Y	Y	Y	N	N
7 Markey	Y	N	Y	Y	Y	Y	N	N
8 O'Neill								
9 Moakley	Y	N	Y	Y	Y	Y	N	N
10 ***Heckler***	?	?	?	?	Y	Y	N	N
11 Donnelly	Y	N	?	N	Y	Y	N	N
12 Studds	Y	N	Y	Y	N	Y	N	N
MICHIGAN								
1 Conyers	N	N	?	?	N	N	?	?
2 ***Pursell***	N	N	Y	Y	N	Y	Y	Y
3 Wolpe	Y	N	Y	Y	Y	N	N	N
4 ***Siljander***	Y	Y	Y	N	N	N	Y	Y
5 ***Sawyer***	Y	Y	Y	Y	N	Y	Y	Y
6 ***Dunn***	Y	N	Y	?	?	N	Y	Y
7 Kildee	Y	N	Y	Y	Y	N	N	N
8 Traxler	Y	N	Y	?	Y	Y	N	N
9 ***Vander Jagt***	Y	N	Y	Y	N	Y	Y	Y
10 Albosta	Y	N	Y	Y	N	N	N	N
11 ***Davis***	?	Y	N	Y	N	N	N	N
12 Bonior	Y	N	Y	Y	Y	Y	N	N
13 Crockett	Y	N	?	Y	Y	N	N	N
14 Hertel	Y	N	Y	Y	Y	Y	N	N
15 Ford	N	N	?	?	Y	N	N	N
16 Dingell	N	?	Y	?	Y	N	N	N
17 Brodhead	Y	N	?	?	Y	N	N	N
18 Blanchard	?	?	?	?	?	?	?	?
19 ***Broomfield***	Y	Y	Y	?	N	N	Y	Y
MINNESOTA								
1 ***Erdahl***	Y	N	?	Y	N	N	Y	Y
2 ***Hagedorn***	Y	Y	Y	N	N	N	Y	Y
3 ***Frenzel***	Y	N	N	N	N	N	Y	Y
4 Vento	N	N	Y	Y	Y	N	N	N
5 Sabo	N	N	Y	Y	Y	Y	N	N
6 ***Weber***	Y	N	Y	N	N	N	Y	Y
7 ***Stangeland***	Y	Y	Y	N	N	N	Y	Y
8 Oberstar	Y	N	Y	Y	N	N	N	N
MISSISSIPPI								
1 Whitten	N	Y	Y	Y	Y	Y	N	N
2 Bowen	Y	N	Y	Y	Y	N	N	N
3 Montgomery	Y	Y	Y	Y	Y	N	Y	Y
4 Dowdy	N	N	?	?	Y	N	N	N
5 ***Lott***	Y	Y	Y	N	Y	N	Y	Y
MISSOURI								
1 Clay	N	N	?	Y	Y	N	N	N
2 Young	Y	N	Y	Y	Y	N	N	N
3 Gephardt	Y	N	?	Y	Y	N	N	N
4 Skelton	Y	N	Y	Y	?	?	?	?
5 Bolling	?	?	?	?	Y	?	?	?
6 ***Coleman***	Y	N	Y	Y	N	N	Y	Y
7 ***Taylor***	N	Y	Y	Y	?	?	Y	?
8 ***Bailey***	N	N	N	N	N	N	Y	Y
9 Volkmer	Y	?	?	?	N	N	N	N
10 ***Emerson***	Y	N	N	Y	N	N	Y	Y
MONTANA								
1 Williams	N	N	Y	Y	N	N	N	N
2 ***Marlenee***	Y	Y	Y	Y	?	?	?	Y
NEBRASKA								
1 ***Bereuter***	Y	N	Y	Y	N	N	Y	Y
2 ***Daub***	Y	N	Y	Y	N	Y	Y	Y
3 ***Smith***	Y	N	Y	Y	N	Y	Y	Y
NEVADA								
AL Santini	N	Y	?	Y	?	?	?	?
NEW HAMPSHIRE								
1 D'Amours	Y	N	Y	Y	Y	N	N	N
2 ***Gregg***	Y	N	Y	Y	Y	N	Y	Y
NEW JERSEY								
1 Florio	Y	N	?	?	?	?	?	?
2 Hughes	N	N	Y	Y	N	N	N	N
3 Howard	N	N	Y	Y	Y	N	N	N
4 ***Smith***	Y	N	Y	Y	Y	N	N	N
5 ***Fenwick***	Y	N	Y	Y	Y	Y	Y	Y
6 ***Forsythe***	Y	?	Y	N	Y	N	+	+
7 ***Roukema***	Y	N	Y	Y	N	N	Y	Y
8 Roe	N	N	Y	Y	N	N	N	N
9 ***Hollenbeck***	N	N	Y	Y	Y	?	N	?
10 Rodino	N	N	Y	Y	Y	N	N	N
11 Minish	N	N	Y	Y	Y	N	N	N
12 ***Rinaldo***	Y	N	?	Y	Y	N	N	N
13 ***Courter***	Y	N	Y	Y	N	N	N	N
14 Guarini	Y	N	Y	Y	Y	N	N	N
15 Dwyer	Y	N	?	?	Y	N	N	N
NEW MEXICO								
1 ***Lujan***	N	N	Y	Y	N	N	Y	Y
2 ***Skeen***	N	N	?	Y	N	Y	Y	Y
NEW YORK								
1 ***Carney***	N	Y	?	N	?	N	Y	Y
2 Downey	Y	N	Y	Y	Y	N	N	N
3 ***Carman***	Y	Y	Y	N	Y	N	N	Y
4 ***Lent***	Y	N	Y	?	Y	N	N	N
5 ***McGrath***	Y	N	Y	Y	Y	N	N	N
6 ***LeBoutillier***	N	Y	Y	Y	?	N	N	Y
7 Addabbo	N	N	?	?	Y	Y	N	N
8 Rosenthal	N	N	?	Y	Y	N	N	N
9 Ferraro	N	N	Y	Y	Y	?	N	N
10 Biaggi	Y	N	?	?	Y	N	N	N
11 Scheuer	N	N	Y	Y	Y	N	N	N
12 Chisholm	?	?	?	Y	?	?	?	?
13 Solarz	N	N	Y	Y	Y	N	N	N
14 Vacancy								
15 Zeferetti	N	?	?	?	?	Y	N	N
16 Schumer	Y	N	Y	Y	Y	N	N	N
17 ***Molinari***	Y	Y	Y	Y	?	N	Y	Y
18 ***Green***	Y	N	Y	Y	Y	Y	N	Y
19 Rangel	Y	N	?	?	Y	N	N	N
20 Weiss	Y	N	Y	Y	N	N	N	N
21 Garcia	Y	N	?	?	Y	N	N	N
22 Bingham	Y	N	Y	Y	Y	N	N	N
23 Peyser	Y	N	Y	Y	Y	N	N	N
24 Ottinger	N	N	Y	Y	N	N	N	N
25 ***Fish***	Y	N	Y	Y	Y	N	N	N
26 ***Gilman***	Y	N	Y	Y	N	Y	N	N
27 McHugh	N	N	Y	Y	Y	Y	N	N
28 Stratton	Y	Y	Y	Y	Y	N	N	N
29 ***Solomon***	Y	Y	N	N	N	N	Y	Y
30 ***Martin***	N	Y	Y	Y	N	N	Y	Y
31 ***Mitchell***	N	Y	?	?	N	N	N	N
32 ***Wortley***	Y	Y	Y	Y	Y	N	Y	Y
33 ***Lee***	?	?	N	N	N	N	?	?
34 ***Horton***	Y	Y	N	Y	N	Y	N	N
35 ***Conable***	Y	N	Y	N	Y	N	Y	Y
36 LaFalce	?	?	?	?	N	N	?	?
37 Nowak	N	?	?	?	N	N	N	N
38 ***Kemp***	?	Y	?	N	N	Y	?	Y
39 Lundine	Y	N	Y	?	N	Y	N	N
NORTH CAROLINA								
1 Jones	Y	N	Y	Y	Y	N	Y	Y
2 Fountain	?	Y	?	Y	N	Y	Y	Y
3 Whitley	N	Y	Y	Y	N	N	Y	Y
4 Andrews	N	N	Y	Y	N	N	Y	Y
5 Neal	Y	N	Y	Y	N	N	Y	Y
6 ***Johnston***	Y	N	Y	N	Y	Y	Y	Y
7 Rose	N	N	?	Y	Y	N	Y	Y
8 Hefner	N	N	Y	Y	N	N	Y	Y
9 ***Martin***	Y	Y	Y	N	N	N	Y	Y
10 ***Broyhill***	N	N	Y	Y	N	Y	Y	Y
11 ***Hendon***	N	Y	Y	Y	?	N	Y	Y
NORTH DAKOTA								
AL Dorgan	Y	N	Y	Y	Y	N	N	N
OHIO								
1 ***Gradison***	Y	Y	Y	?	Y	N	N	Y
2 Luken	N	N	Y	Y	Y	N	N	N
3 Hall	Y	N	Y	Y	Y	N	N	N
4 ***Oxley***	Y	Y	Y	N	N	N	Y	Y
5 ***Latta***	Y	Y	?	?	Y	Y	Y	Y
6 ***McEwen***	N	Y	N	N	N	N	Y	Y
7 ***Brown***	Y	N	Y	N	Y	N	Y	Y
8 ***Kindness***	Y	Y	N	N	N	N	Y	?
9 ***Weber***	Y	Y	Y	N	N	N	N	Y
10 ***Miller***	Y	Y	N	Y	N	Y	Y	Y
11 ***Stanton***	?	?	?	?	?	?	?	?
12 Shamansky	Y	N	Y	Y	Y	N	N	N
13 Pease	Y	N	Y	Y	Y	N	N	N
14 Seiberling	N	N	?	Y	N	N	N	N
15 ***Wylie***	Y	N	Y	Y	Y	N	Y	Y
16 ***Regula***	N	N	Y	Y	N	Y	Y	Y
17 ***Ashbrook***	Y	Y	N	N	N	N	Y	Y
18 Applegate	N	N	?	?	Y	N	N	N
19 ***Williams***	?	N	Y	Y	N	N	N	N
20 Oakar	N	N	Y	Y	Y	Y	N	N
21 Stokes	N	N	Y	Y	Y	N	N	N
22 Eckart	N	N	Y	Y	Y	Y	N	N
23 Mottl	Y	?	?	?	?	?	?	?
OKLAHOMA								
1 Jones	Y	N	Y	Y	N	Y	N	N
2 Synar	N	N	Y	Y	N	Y	N	N
3 Watkins	N	N	Y	Y	Y	Y	Y	Y
4 McCurdy	N	?	?	?	N	Y	Y	Y
5 ***Edwards***	N	N	Y	Y	N	Y	Y	Y
6 English	N	N	Y	Y	N	Y	Y	Y
OREGON								
1 AuCoin	Y	N	Y	Y	Y	Y	N	N
2 ***Smith***	Y	N	N	?	N	N	Y	Y
3 Wyden	Y	N	Y	Y	Y	N	N	N
4 Weaver	N	N	Y	Y	N	Y	N	N
PENNSYLVANIA								
1 Foglietta	Y	N	Y	Y	Y	N	N	N
2 Gray	N	N	Y	Y	Y	Y	N	N
3 Smith	N	N	?	?	Y	N	N	N
4 ***Dougherty***	Y	Y	?	Y	Y	N	N	N
5 ***Schulze***	N	Y	Y	Y	Y	N	N	Y
6 Yatron	N	N	?	?	N	N	N	N
7 Edgar	?	?	Y	Y	Y	N	N	N
8 ***Coyne, J.***	?	?	?	?	?	N	N	Y
9 ***Shuster***	?	?	?	?	Y	N	Y	?
10 ***McDade***	Y	N	Y	Y	Y	Y	N	N
11 ***Nelligan***	N	Y	Y	Y	Y	N	N	Y
12 Murtha	N	N	Y	Y	Y	N	N	N
13 ***Coughlin***	Y	N	Y	Y	Y	Y	Y	Y
14 Coyne, W.	Y	N	Y	Y	Y	N	N	N
15 ***Ritter***	Y	N	Y	N	N	N	N	Y
16 ***Walker***	N	N	N	N	N	Y	Y	Y
17 Ertel	N	N	?	?	N	N	N	N
18 Walgren	Y	N	?	Y	Y	N	N	N
19 ***Goodling***	N	N	?	?	N	Y	Y	Y
20 Gaydos	N	N	Y	Y	Y	N	N	N
21 Bailey	N	N	Y	Y	Y	N	N	N
22 Murphy	N	N	?	?	N	N	N	N
23 ***Clinger***	Y	N	Y	Y	Y	N	N	Y
24 ***Marks***	?	?	?	?	?	?	?	?
25 ***Atkinson***	Y	Y	?	N	?	N	N	Y
RHODE ISLAND								
1 St Germain	?	?	?	?	Y	N	N	N
2 ***Schneider***	Y	N	Y	Y	N	N	N	?
SOUTH CAROLINA								
1 ***Hartnett***	Y	Y	?	?	N	N	Y	Y
2 ***Spence***	Y	Y	Y	Y	N	N	Y	Y
3 Derrick	Y	N	Y	Y	Y	N	Y	Y
4 ***Campbell***	Y	Y	?	Y	N	?	?	?
5 Holland	Y	N	Y	Y	N	N	Y	Y
6 ***Napier***	Y	Y	Y	Y	N	N	Y	Y
SOUTH DAKOTA								
1 Daschle	?	?	Y	Y	N	N	N	N
2 ***Roberts***	N	Y	Y	N	N	Y	Y	?
TENNESSEE								
1 ***Quillen***	N	N	?	?	N	N	N	N
2 ***Duncan***	N	N	Y	Y	N	N	Y	Y
3 Bouquard	N	Y	Y	?	N	N	N	N
4 Gore	Y	N	Y	Y	N	N	N	N
5 Boner	N	N	Y	Y	N	N	N	N
6 ***Beard***	N	?	?	?	N	N	Y	?
7 Jones	N	N	Y	Y	N	N	N	N
8 Ford	Y	N	?	Y	N	N	N	N
TEXAS								
1 Hall, S.	N	N	Y	N	N	N	?	?
2 Wilson	N	Y	?	Y	N	Y	N	N
3 ***Collins***	Y	Y	Y	N	N	Y	Y	Y
4 Hall, R.	N	N	Y	Y	N	N	Y	Y
5 Mattox	Y	N	?	?	?	?	?	?
6 Gramm	Y	Y	Y	N	N	N	Y	Y
7 ***Archer***	Y	Y	N	N	Y	N	Y	Y
8 ***Fields***	Y	Y	Y	N	Y	N	Y	Y
9 Brooks	Y	N	Y	Y	Y	N	N	N
10 Pickle	Y	Y	Y	Y	Y	N	N	Y
11 Leath	Y	Y	Y	N	N	N	Y	Y
12 Wright	N	N	Y	Y	Y	N	N	N
13 Hightower	N	Y	?	?	N	Y	Y	Y
14 Patman	Y	Y	Y	Y	N	Y	N	N
15 de la Garza	?	?	?	?	N	N	N	Y
16 White	N	Y	Y	Y	N	N	Y	Y
17 Stenholm	Y	Y	?	?	N	N	Y	Y
18 Leland	Y	N	Y	Y	?	N	N	N
19 Hance	?	?	?	?	?	N	Y	Y
20 Gonzalez	N	Y	Y	Y	N	N	N	N
21 ***Loeffler***	Y	Y	Y	Y	N	Y	Y	Y
22 ***Paul***	Y	?	?	?	N	Y	Y	Y
23 Kazen	N	Y	Y	Y	N	N	N	Y
24 Frost	?	?	?	Y	Y	N	N	N
UTAH								
1 ***Hansen***	N	N	?	?	N	N	Y	Y
2 ***Marriott***	N	N	Y	Y	N	N	Y	Y
VERMONT								
AL ***Jeffords***	Y	N	Y	Y	N	N	N	Y
VIRGINIA								
1 ***Trible***	Y	Y	Y	?	N	N	Y	Y
2 ***Whitehurst***	Y	Y	Y	Y	Y	N	Y	Y
3 ***Bliley***	Y	N	N	Y	N	N	Y	Y
4 ***Daniel, R.***	Y	Y	Y	N	Y	N	Y	?
5 Daniel, D.	Y	Y	Y	Y	N	N	Y	Y
6 ***Butler***	Y	Y	N	Y	N	N	Y	Y
7 ***Robinson***	Y	Y	Y	Y	N	Y	Y	Y
8 ***Parris***	Y	Y	Y	Y	Y	?	?	?
9 ***Wampler***	N	Y	Y	Y	N	N	Y	Y
10 ***Wolf***	Y	N	Y	Y	N	N	Y	Y
WASHINGTON								
1 ***Pritchard***	Y	N	Y	Y	Y	N	Y	Y
2 Swift	Y	N	Y	Y	N	N	N	N
3 Bonker	Y	N	Y	Y	-	-	-	-
4 ***Morrison***	N	N	Y	Y	N	N	Y	Y
5 Foley	?	N	Y	Y	Y	N	N	N
6 Dicks	Y	N	Y	Y	Y	Y	N	N
7 Lowry	Y	N	Y	Y	Y	N	N	N
WEST VIRGINIA								
1 Mollohan	?	?	?	?	Y	N	?	?
2 ***Benedict***	Y	N	Y	N	N	N	Y	Y
3 ***Staton***	Y	N	Y	N	Y	N	Y	Y
4 Rahall	N	N	Y	Y	N	N	N	?
WISCONSIN								
1 Aspin	N	N	Y	Y	N	N	N	N
2 Kastenmeier	Y	N	Y	Y	N	N	?	N
3 ***Gunderson***	Y	N	Y	Y	N	N	Y	Y
4 Zablocki	Y	N	Y	Y	Y	N	N	N
5 Reuss	Y	N	Y	Y	Y	N	N	N
6 ***Petri***	Y	N	Y	Y	N	Y	N	Y
7 Obey	Y	N	Y	Y	N	Y	N	N
8 ***Roth***	N	N	Y	Y	N	Y	Y	Y
9 ***Sensenbrenner***	Y	N	N	N	N	N	Y	Y
WYOMING								
AL ***Cheney***	N	Y	Y	N	N	Y	Y	Y

Southern states - Ala., Ark., Fla., Ga., Ky., La., Miss., N.C., Okla., S.C., Tenn., Texas, Va.

KEY

Y Voted for (yea).
Paired for.
+ Announced for.
N Voted against (nay).
X Paired against.
- Announced against.
P Voted "present".
C Voted "present" to avoid possible conflict of interest.
? Did not vote or otherwise make a position known.

Democrats   *Republicans*

393. HR 6211. Transportation Assistance Act of 1982. Weiss, D-N.Y., amendment to delete provisions directing the secretary to make certain discretionary funds available to complete high cost Interstate segments. Rejected 21-329: R 2-151; D 19-178 (ND 18-110, SD 1-68), Dec. 6, 1982.

394. HR 6211. Transportation Assistance Act of 1982. Walker, R-Pa., amendment to prevent Davis-Bacon Act wage provisions from limiting legitimate job opportunities for any individual. Rejected 149-217: R 123-40; D 26-177 (ND 2-132, SD 24-45), Dec. 6, 1982.

395. HR 6211. Transportation Assistance Act of 1982. Rostenkowski, D-Ill., amendment to increase the 4-cents-a-gallon fuel tax to 9-cents-a-gallon, increase heavy-truck levies and make other changes in highway taxes. Adopted 236-169: R 96-87; D 140-82 (ND 110-39, SD 30-43), in the session which began Dec. 6, 1982. A "yea" was a vote supporting the president's position.

396. HR 6211. Transportation Assistance Act of 1982. Passage of the bill to authorize $71.3 billion for fiscal 1983-1986 for highway and transit programs and to increase gasoline and other highway taxes. Passed 262-143: R 103-80; D 159-63 (ND 124-25, SD 35-38), in the session which began Dec. 6, 1982.

397. Procedural Motion. Walker, R-Pa., motion to approve the House *Journal* of Monday, Dec. 6. Motion agreed to 314-35: R 138-20; D 176-15 (ND 118-12, SD 58-3), Dec. 7, 1982.

398. HR 7355. Department of Defense Appropriations, Fiscal 1983. Addabbo, D-N.Y., amendment to delete $988 million for procurement of five MX missiles. Adopted 245-176: R 50-138; D 195-38 (ND 151-7, SD 44-31), Dec. 7, 1982. A "nay" was a vote supporting the president's position.

399. HR 7355. Department of Defense Appropriations, Fiscal 1983. Boland, D-Mass., substitute for the Harkin, D-Iowa, amendment, to bar the use of funds in the bill by the Central Intelligence Agency or Defense Department to extend military assistance to any non-governmental organization for the purpose of overthrowing the government of Nicaragua or for provoking a military exchange between Nicaragua and Honduras. Adopted 411-0: R 181-0; D 230-0 (ND 155-0, SD 75-0), Dec. 8, 1982. The Harkin amendment, as amended, subsequently was adopted by voice vote. (The original Harkin amendment would have barred the use of funds in the bill to extend military assistance to any non-governmental organization for its military activities in or against Nicaragua.)

400. HR 7355. Department of Defense Appropriations, Fiscal 1983. Passage of the bill to appropriate $230,330,492,000 for military programs of the Department of Defense in fiscal 1983. Passed 346-68: R 175-10; D 171-58 (ND 97-57, SD 74-1), Dec. 8, 1982. The president had requested $249,612,409,000.

	393	394	395	396	397	398	399	400
ALABAMA								
1 Edwards	?	Y	Y	Y	Y	N	Y	Y
2 Dickinson	N	Y	N	N	N	N	Y	Y
3 Nichols	N	Y	N	N	?	N	Y	Y
4 Bevill	?	?	X	X	Y	N	Y	Y
5 Flippo	N	N	Y	Y	Y	N	Y	Y
6 Smith	N	Y	N	N	Y	N	Y	Y
7 Shelby	N	N	N	N	Y	N	Y	Y
ALASKA								
AL Young	?	?	N	N	N	N	Y	Y
ARIZONA								
1 Rhodes	?	?	?	?	?	N	Y	Y
2 Udall	N	N	Y	Y	Y	Y	Y	Y
3 Stump	N	Y	N	N	N	N	Y	Y
4 Rudd	N	Y	N	N	Y	N	Y	Y
ARKANSAS								
1 Alexander	?	?	?	?	?	?	?	?
2 Bethune	N	Y	N	N	Y	N	?	?
3 Hammerschmidt	N	Y	N	Y	N	Y	Y	Y
4 Anthony	N	N	Y	Y	Y	Y	Y	Y
CALIFORNIA								
1 Chappie	N	Y	N	N	Y	N	Y	Y
2 Clausen	N	N	Y	Y	Y	N	Y	Y
3 Matsui	N	N	Y	Y	Y	Y	Y	Y
4 Fazio	N	N	Y	Y	Y	Y	Y	Y
5 Burton, J.	Y	N	N	Y	N	Y	Y	N
6 Burton, P.	Y	Y	N	Y	Y	Y	Y	N
7 Miller	N	N	Y	Y	Y	Y	Y	N
8 Dellums	?	N	N	Y	Y	Y	Y	N
9 Stark	N	?	Y	Y	Y	Y	Y	N
10 Edwards	Y	N	Y	Y	Y	Y	Y	N
11 Lantos	?	?	#	#	?	Y	Y	Y
12 McCloskey	?	?	?	?	?	Y	Y	Y
13 Mineta	N	N	Y	Y	Y	Y	Y	N
14 Shumway	N	Y	N	N	Y	N	Y	Y
15 Coelho	?	?	Y	Y	Y	Y	Y	N
16 Panetta	N	N	N	Y	Y	Y	Y	N
17 Pashayan	N	N	Y	Y	?	N	Y	Y
18 Thomas	N	Y	Y	N	Y	N	Y	Y
19 Lagomarsino	N	Y	N	N	Y	N	Y	Y
20 Goldwater	N	?	?	?	Y	N	?	Y
21 Fiedler	N	Y	N	N	N	N	Y	Y
22 Moorhead	N	Y	N	N	Y	N	Y	Y
23 Beilenson	Y	N	Y	Y	Y	Y	Y	N
24 Waxman	N	N	Y	Y	Y	Y	Y	N
25 Roybal	N	N	N	N	Y	N	Y	Y
26 Rousselot	N	Y	Y	N	?	N	Y	Y
27 Dornan	N	Y	N	Y	N	Y	Y	Y
28 Dixon	N	N	Y	Y	Y	Y	Y	Y
29 Hawkins	N	N	N	Y	N	Y	Y	Y
30 Martinez	N	N	Y	Y	Y	Y	Y	Y
31 Dymally	N	N	Y	Y	Y	Y	Y	Y
32 Anderson	N	N	Y	Y	Y	Y	Y	Y
33 Grisham	?	?	Y	Y	?	N	Y	Y
34 Lungren	N	Y	Y	N	Y	N	Y	Y
35 Dreier	N	Y	N	N	N	N	Y	Y
36 Brown	N	N	Y	Y	Y	Y	Y	Y
37 Lewis	N	N	Y	Y	Y	Y	Y	Y
38 Patterson	?	?	?	?	?	Y	Y	Y
39 Dannemeyer	N	Y	N	N	N	N	Y	Y
40 Badham	?	?	Y	Y	N	N	Y	Y
41 Lowery	?	?	Y	Y	Y	N	Y	Y
42 Hunter	N	Y	Y	N	Y	N	Y	Y
43 Burgener	?	?	Y	Y	Y	N	Y	Y
COLORADO								
1 Schroeder	N	N	Y	Y	N	Y	Y	N
2 Wirth	N	N	Y	Y	Y	Y	Y	N
3 Kogovsek	N	N	Y	Y	Y	Y	Y	Y
4 Brown	N	Y	N	N	N	N	Y	N

	393	394	395	396	397	398	399	400
5 Kramer	N	Y	Y	Y	Y	N	Y	Y
CONNECTICUT								
1 Kennelly	N	N	Y	Y	Y	Y	Y	Y
2 Gejdenson	N	N	N	Y	N	Y	Y	Y
3 DeNardis	?	N	Y	Y	?	Y	Y	Y
4 McKinney	N	N	Y	Y	?	Y	Y	N
5 Ratchford	N	N	Y	Y	Y	Y	Y	Y
6 Moffett	N	?	Y	Y	N	Y	Y	N
DELAWARE								
AL Evans	N	Y	Y	Y	?	N	?	?
FLORIDA								
1 Hutto	N	Y	Y	Y	Y	Y	Y	Y
2 Fuqua	N	?	N	N	Y	Y	Y	Y
3 Bennett	N	N	Y	Y	Y	Y	Y	Y
4 Chappell	N	N	N	N	?	N	Y	Y
5 McCollum	N	Y	Y	N	N	N	Y	Y
6 Young	N	Y	N	Y	N	Y	N	Y
7 Gibbons	N	Y	Y	Y	Y	Y	Y	Y
8 Ireland	?	?	Y	Y	?	N	?	?
9 Nelson	N	N	Y	Y	Y	N	Y	Y
10 Bafalis	?	?	?	?	?	?	?	?
11 Mica	N	N	Y	Y	Y	Y	Y	Y
12 Shaw	N	Y	Y	Y	Y	N	Y	Y
13 Lehman	?	?	?	?	?	Y	Y	Y
14 Pepper	N	N	Y	Y	Y	Y	Y	Y
15 Fascell	?	?	?	?	?	Y	Y	Y
GEORGIA								
1 Ginn	?	N	N	N	?	N	Y	Y
2 Hatcher	N	N	N	Y	Y	Y	Y	Y
3 Brinkley	N	N	N	Y	Y	Y	Y	Y
4 Levitas	N	N	N	Y	Y	Y	Y	Y
5 Fowler	N	Y	Y	Y	Y	Y	Y	Y
6 Gingrich	?	Y	Y	Y	N	Y	Y	Y
7 McDonald	N	Y	N	N	N	N	Y	Y
8 Evans	?	?	?	?	?	N	Y	Y
9 Jenkins	N	Y	N	N	Y	Y	Y	Y
10 Barnard	N	Y	Y	Y	?	Y	Y	Y
HAWAII								
1 Heftel	N	N	Y	Y	?	Y	Y	Y
2 Akaka	N	N	N	N	Y	Y	Y	Y
IDAHO								
1 Craig	N	Y	N	N	Y	N	Y	Y
2 Hansen	N	Y	N	N	?	N	Y	Y
ILLINOIS								
1 Washington	N	N	N	Y	?	Y	Y	N
2 Savage	N	N	N	Y	?	Y	Y	N
3 Russo	N	N	Y	Y	Y	Y	Y	N
4 Derwinski	N	N	Y	Y	Y	N	Y	N
5 Fary	N	N	Y	Y	Y	Y	Y	N
6 Hyde	N	Y	N	N	Y	N	Y	Y
7 Collins	N	N	Y	Y	?	Y	Y	N
8 Rostenkowski	N	N	Y	Y	Y	Y	Y	N
9 Yates	?	N	Y	Y	N	Y	Y	N
10 Porter	N	Y	Y	Y	?	N	Y	N
11 Annunzio	N	N	Y	Y	Y	Y	Y	N
12 Crane, P.	N	Y	N	N	Y	N	Y	Y
13 McClory	?	?	Y	Y	Y	N	Y	Y
14 Erlenborn	N	Y	Y	N	Y	N	Y	Y
15 Corcoran	N	Y	Y	Y	Y	N	Y	Y
16 Martin	N	Y	Y	Y	Y	N	Y	Y
17 O'Brien	?	?	Y	Y	Y	Y	Y	N
18 Michel	N	N	Y	Y	Y	N	Y	N
19 Railsback	?	?	Y	Y	Y	N	Y	Y
20 Findley	N	N	Y	Y	Y	N	Y	N
21 Madigan	?	N	Y	Y	Y	N	Y	Y
22 Crane, D.	N	Y	N	N	N	N	Y	N
23 Price	N	N	Y	Y	Y	Y	Y	N
24 Simon	N	N	Y	Y	?	Y	Y	N
INDIANA								
1 Hall	N	N	Y	Y	Y	Y	Y	N
2 Fithian	N	N	Y	Y	Y	Y	Y	Y
3 Hiler	N	Y	Y	Y	Y	N	Y	Y
4 Coats	N	Y	Y	Y	Y	N	Y	Y
5 Hillis	N	Y	N	Y	Y	N	Y	Y
6 Evans	?	?	Y	Y	Y	Y	Y	Y
7 Myers	N	Y	N	N	?	N	Y	Y
8 Deckard	?	?	?	?	Y	Y	Y	?
9 Hamilton	N	N	Y	Y	Y	Y	Y	Y
10 Sharp	N	N	Y	Y	Y	Y	Y	Y
11 Jacobs	N	N	Y	N	Y	Y	Y	Y
IOWA								
1 Leach	N	Y	N	Y	?	Y	Y	N
2 Tauke	Y	Y	Y	Y	Y	Y	Y	N
3 Evans	Y	Y	N	Y	N	Y	Y	N
4 Smith	Y	N	Y	Y	Y	Y	Y	Y
5 Harkin	Y	N	N	Y	N	Y	Y	N
6 Bedell	Y	N	Y	Y	Y	Y	Y	N

ND - Northern Democrats   SD - Southern Democrats

	393	394	395	396	397	398	399	400
KANSAS								
1 ***Roberts***	N	Y	N	N	N	Y	Y	Y
2 ***Jeffries***	N	Y	N	N	Y	N	Y	Y
3 ***Winn***	N	Y	N	N	Y	N	Y	Y
4 Glickman	Y	N	Y	N	Y	Y	Y	Y
5 ***Whittaker***	N	Y	N	N	Y	Y	Y	Y
KENTUCKY								
1 Hubbard	N	N	N	N	Y	Y	Y	Y
2 Natcher	N	N	Y	Y	Y	Y	Y	Y
3 Mazzoli	N	N	N	Y	Y	Y	Y	Y
4 ***Snyder***	N	Y	Y	Y	Y	Y	Y	Y
5 ***Rogers***	N	Y	N	N	N	N	Y	Y
6 ***Hopkins***	N	Y	N	N	Y	Y	Y	Y
7 Perkins	N	N	N	N	Y	Y	Y	Y
LOUISIANA								
1 ***Livingston***	N	Y	N	N	Y	N	Y	Y
2 Boggs	N	N	N	Y	Y	Y	Y	Y
3 Tauzin	N	N	N	N	Y	N	Y	Y
4 Roemer	N	Y	N	Y	N	Y	Y	Y
5 Huckaby	N	Y	Y	N	Y	Y	Y	Y
6 ***Moore***	N	Y	N	N	Y	N	Y	Y
7 Breaux	N	N	Y	Y	Y	N	Y	Y
8 Long	N	N	N	Y	Y	Y	Y	Y
MAINE								
1 ***Emery***	?	?	N	N	?	N	Y	Y
2 ***Snowe***	N	N	N	N	Y	Y	Y	Y
MARYLAND								
1 Dyson	N	N	N	Y	Y	Y	Y	Y
2 Long	N	N	N	N	?	Y	Y	Y
3 Mikulski	N	N	Y	Y	Y	Y	Y	Y
4 ***Holt***	N	Y	N	N	N	N	Y	Y
5 Hoyer	N	N	Y	Y	Y	Y	Y	Y
6 Byron	N	Y	N	N	Y	Y	Y	Y
7 Mitchell	N	N	Y	Y	N	Y	Y	N
8 Barnes	?	?	?	?	?	Y	Y	Y
MASSACHUSETTS								
1 ***Conte***	N	N	Y	Y	?	Y	Y	Y
2 Boland	N	N	Y	Y	Y	Y	Y	Y
3 Early	N	?	N	N	Y	Y	Y	N
4 Frank	N	N	Y	Y	Y	Y	Y	N
5 Shannon	N	?	Y	Y	Y	Y	Y	N
6 Mavroules	N	?	Y	Y	?	Y	Y	Y
7 Markey	N	N	Y	Y	Y	Y	Y	N
8 O'Neill								
9 Moakley	N	N	Y	Y	Y	Y	Y	Y
10 ***Heckler***	N	?	Y	Y	?	?	?	Y
11 Donnelly	?	?	Y	Y	Y	Y	Y	N
12 Studds	Y	N	N	N	Y	Y	Y	N
MICHIGAN								
1 Conyers	?	?	?	?	?	Y	Y	N
2 ***Pursell***	N	Y	Y	Y	?	Y	Y	Y
3 Wolpe	Y	N	Y	Y	Y	Y	Y	N
4 ***Siljander***	N	Y	N	N	Y	N	Y	Y
5 ***Sawyer***	N	Y	N	N	Y	N	Y	Y
6 ***Dunn***	N	Y	Y	Y	Y	N	Y	Y
7 Kildee	N	N	Y	Y	Y	Y	Y	N
8 Traxler	N	N	Y	Y	Y	Y	Y	Y
9 ***Vander Jagt***	N	Y	Y	Y	Y	N	Y	Y
10 Albosta	N	N	Y	Y	Y	Y	Y	Y
11 ***Davis***	N	N	N	N	Y	N	Y	Y
12 Bonior	?	N	N	N	Y	Y	Y	N
13 Crockett	Y	N	Y	Y	?	Y	Y	N
14 Hertel	?	N	N	N	Y	Y	Y	Y
15 Ford	?	N	Y	Y	?	Y	Y	Y
16 Dingell	N	N	Y	Y	?	Y	Y	Y
17 Brodhead	?	N	Y	Y	Y	Y	Y	N
18 Blanchard	?	?	?	?	?	?	?	?
19 ***Broomfield***	?	Y	Y	Y	Y	N	Y	Y
MINNESOTA								
1 ***Erdahl***	N	Y	Y	Y	Y	Y	Y	Y
2 ***Hagedorn***	N	Y	Y	Y	Y	N	Y	Y
3 ***Frenzel***	N	Y	Y	Y	Y	Y	Y	Y
4 Vento	N	N	Y	Y	Y	Y	Y	N
5 Sabo	N	N	Y	Y	N	Y	Y	N
6 ***Weber***	N	Y	Y	Y	Y	Y	Y	Y
7 ***Stangeland***	?	Y	N	N	Y	N	Y	Y
8 Oberstar	N	N	Y	Y	Y	Y	Y	N
MISSISSIPPI								
1 Whitten	N	N	N	N	Y	Y	Y	Y
2 Bowen	N	N	Y	Y	Y	N	Y	Y
3 Montgomery	N	Y	Y	Y	?	N	Y	Y
4 Dowdy	N	N	Y	Y	Y	Y	Y	Y
5 ***Lott***	N	Y	Y	Y	Y	N	Y	Y
MISSOURI								
1 Clay	?	N	Y	Y	?	Y	Y	N
2 Young	N	N	Y	Y	?	Y	Y	Y
3 Gephardt	N	N	Y	Y	?	Y	Y	Y

	393	394	395	396	397	398	399	400
4 Skelton	?	?	?	?	?	?	?	?
5 Bolling	?	?	?	?	?	?	?	?
6 ***Coleman***	N	Y	N	N	Y	N	Y	Y
7 ***Taylor***	?	Y	N	N	Y	N	Y	Y
8 ***Bailey***	N	Y	N	Y	N	N	Y	Y
9 Volkmer	N	N	N	Y	Y	Y	Y	Y
10 ***Emerson***	N	Y	N	N	N	N	Y	Y
MONTANA								
1 Williams	N	N	N	N	?	Y	Y	Y
2 ***Marlenee***	N	Y	N	N	Y	N	Y	Y
NEBRASKA								
1 ***Bereuter***	N	Y	Y	Y	Y	N	Y	Y
2 ***Daub***	N	Y	Y	Y	Y	N	Y	Y
3 ***Smith***	N	Y	Y	Y	Y	Y	Y	Y
NEVADA								
AL Santini	?	?	?	?	?	?	Y	Y
NEW HAMPSHIRE								
1 D'Amours	N	N	Y	Y	Y	Y	Y	Y
2 ***Gregg***	N	Y	Y	Y	Y	Y	Y	Y
NEW JERSEY								
1 Florio	?	?	N	N	Y	Y	Y	Y
2 Hughes	N	N	N	N	Y	Y	Y	Y
3 Howard	N	N	Y	Y	Y	Y	Y	Y
4 ***Smith***	N	N	Y	Y	Y	Y	Y	Y
5 ***Fenwick***	N	Y	Y	Y	Y	Y	Y	Y
6 ***Forsythe***	?	?	?	?	N	Y	Y	N
7 ***Roukema***	N	N	Y	Y	Y	Y	Y	Y
8 Roe	N	N	N	Y	Y	Y	Y	Y
9 ***Hollenbeck***	?	N	Y	Y	Y	Y	Y	N
10 Rodino	N	N	Y	Y	Y	Y	Y	N
11 Minish	N	N	N	N	Y	Y	Y	Y
12 ***Rinaldo***	N	N	N	N	?	Y	Y	Y
13 ***Courter***	N	N	N	N	Y	N	Y	Y
14 Guarini	N	N	Y	Y	Y	Y	Y	Y
15 Dwyer	N	N	N	Y	Y	Y	Y	Y
NEW MEXICO								
1 ***Lujan***	N	Y	N	Y	Y	N	Y	Y
2 ***Skeen***	N	Y	Y	N	Y	N	Y	Y
NEW YORK								
1 ***Carney***	N	Y	Y	Y	Y	N	Y	Y
2 Downey	N	?	Y	Y	Y	Y	Y	Y
3 ***Carman***	N	Y	Y	Y	Y	N	Y	Y
4 ***Lent***	N	N	Y	Y	Y	Y	Y	Y
5 ***McGrath***	N	N	Y	Y	Y	Y	Y	Y
6 ***LeBoutillier***	?	?	Y	Y	?	N	Y	Y
7 Addabbo	N	N	Y	Y	Y	Y	Y	Y
8 Rosenthal	Y	N	#	#	?	Y	Y	N
9 Ferraro	Y	N	Y	Y	Y	Y	Y	Y
10 Biaggi	N	N	Y	Y	Y	Y	Y	Y
11 Scheuer	N	N	Y	Y	Y	Y	Y	Y
12 Chisholm	?	?	?	?	?	Y	Y	N
13 Solarz	N	N	Y	Y	Y	Y	Y	Y
14 Vacancy								
15 Zeferetti	N	N	Y	Y	?	Y	Y	Y
16 Schumer	Y	N	Y	Y	Y	Y	Y	Y
17 ***Molinari***	N	Y	Y	Y	Y	N	Y	Y
18 ***Green***	N	N	Y	Y	Y	Y	Y	N
19 Rangel	Y	N	Y	Y	Y	Y	Y	N
20 Weiss	Y	N	Y	Y	Y	Y	Y	N
21 Garcia	N	N	Y	Y	Y	Y	Y	N
22 Bingham	?	N	Y	Y	Y	Y	Y	N
23 Peyser	N	N	Y	Y	Y	Y	Y	N
24 Ottinger	Y	N	N	N	?	Y	Y	N
25 ***Fish***	?	N	Y	Y	Y	N	Y	Y
26 ***Gilman***	N	N	N	Y	Y	N	Y	Y
27 McHugh	N	N	Y	Y	Y	Y	Y	Y
28 Stratton	N	N	Y	Y	Y	N	Y	+
29 ***Solomon***	N	Y	N	N	N	N	Y	Y
30 ***Martin***	N	N	N	N	Y	N	Y	Y
31 ***Mitchell***	N	N	N	Y	Y	N	Y	Y
32 ***Wortley***	N	Y	Y	Y	Y	N	Y	Y
33 ***Lee***	?	N	Y	Y	?	N	Y	Y
34 ***Horton***	N	N	N	N	?	Y	Y	Y
35 ***Conable***	N	Y	Y	Y	Y	N	Y	Y
36 LaFalce	?	N	Y	Y	Y	Y	Y	Y
37 Nowak	N	N	N	Y	Y	Y	?	?
38 ***Kemp***	N	N	N	N	?	N	Y	Y
39 Lundine	?	?	N	N	Y	Y	Y	Y
NORTH CAROLINA								
1 Jones	N	N	Y	Y	Y	Y	Y	Y
2 Fountain	N	Y	N	N	N	N	Y	Y
3 Whitley	N	Y	N	N	Y	N	Y	Y
4 Andrews	N	Y	N	N	Y	Y	Y	Y
5 Neal	N	Y	N	N	Y	Y	Y	Y
6 ***Johnston***	N	Y	N	N	?	N	Y	Y
7 Rose	?	N	N	N	Y	Y	Y	Y
8 Hefner	N	Y	N	N	Y	?	Y	Y

	393	394	395	396	397	398	399	400
9 ***Martin***	?	Y	N	N	Y	N	Y	Y
10 ***Broyhill***	N	Y	N	N	Y	N	Y	Y
11 ***Hendon***	N	Y	Y	Y	Y	N	Y	Y
NORTH DAKOTA								
AL Dorgan	N	N	Y	Y	Y	Y	Y	Y
OHIO								
1 ***Gradison***	N	N	Y	Y	Y	Y	Y	Y
2 Luken	N	N	Y	Y	Y	Y	?	?
3 Hall	?	?	N	N	?	Y	Y	Y
4 ***Oxley***	N	Y	N	N	?	N	Y	Y
5 ***Latta***	N	Y	Y	Y	Y	N	Y	Y
6 ***McEwen***	N	Y	N	Y	Y	N	Y	Y
7 ***Brown***	N	Y	Y	Y	Y	N	?	?
8 ***Kindness***	N	Y	N	N	Y	N	Y	Y
9 ***Weber***	N	Y	Y	Y	?	N	Y	Y
10 ***Miller***	N	Y	N	N	N	N	Y	N
11 ***Stanton***	?	?	?	?	?	N	Y	Y
12 Shamansky	N	N	Y	Y	Y	Y	Y	Y
13 Pease	N	N	Y	Y	Y	Y	Y	Y
14 Seiberling	Y	N	N	Y	Y	Y	Y	N
15 ***Wylie***	N	N	Y	Y	Y	N	Y	?
16 ***Regula***	?	?	Y	Y	Y	N	Y	Y
17 ***Ashbrook***	N	Y	N	N	?	N	Y	Y
18 Applegate	?	N	N	Y	?	Y	Y	Y
19 ***Williams***	N	N	N	Y	Y	Y	Y	Y
20 Oakar	N	N	Y	Y	Y	Y	Y	Y
21 Stokes	?	N	Y	Y	Y	Y	Y	N
22 Eckart	N	N	Y	N	Y	Y	Y	Y
23 Mottl	?	?	X	X	Y	N	Y	Y
OKLAHOMA								
1 Jones	N	N	Y	N	Y	Y	Y	Y
2 Synar	N	N	N	N	Y	Y	Y	Y
3 Watkins	N	N	N	N	Y	Y	Y	Y
4 McCurdy	N	N	Y	N	Y	Y	Y	Y
5 ***Edwards***	N	Y	N	N	Y	N	Y	Y
6 English	N	Y	N	N	Y	Y	Y	Y
OREGON								
1 AuCoin	N	N	N	N	Y	Y	Y	N
2 ***Smith***	N	Y	N	N	N	Y	Y	Y
3 Wyden	N	N	Y	Y	Y	Y	Y	N
4 Weaver	N	?	N	N	Y	Y	Y	N
PENNSYLVANIA								
1 Foglietta	N	N	Y	Y	Y	Y	Y	Y
2 Gray	?	N	Y	Y	Y	Y	Y	N
3 Smith	N	?	Y	Y	Y	Y	?	?
4 ***Dougherty***	N	N	Y	Y	?	?	Y	Y
5 ***Schulze***	N	Y	Y	Y	Y	N	Y	Y
6 Yatron	N	N	N	N	Y	Y	Y	Y
7 Edgar	N	N	Y	Y	Y	Y	Y	N
8 ***Coyne, J.***	?	?	Y	Y	Y	N	Y	Y
9 ***Shuster***	?	?	?	?	?	?	?	?
10 ***McDade***	N	N	Y	Y	Y	Y	Y	Y
11 ***Nelligan***	N	N	Y	Y	Y	N	Y	Y
12 Murtha	N	N	Y	Y	Y	N	Y	Y
13 ***Coughlin***	N	Y	Y	Y	N	Y	Y	Y
14 Coyne, W.	N	N	Y	Y	Y	Y	Y	Y
15 ***Ritter***	N	Y	N	N	?	N	Y	Y
16 ***Walker***	N	Y	N	N	N	N	Y	Y
17 Ertel	N	N	Y	Y	Y	Y	Y	Y
18 Walgren	N	N	Y	Y	Y	Y	Y	Y
19 ***Goodling***	N	Y	Y	Y	N	Y	Y	Y
20 Gaydos	N	N	N	N	?	Y	Y	Y
21 Bailey	N	N	Y	Y	Y	N	Y	Y
22 Murphy	N	?	N	N	?	Y	?	?
23 ***Clinger***	N	N	Y	Y	Y	N	Y	Y
24 ***Marks***	?	?	?	?	?	Y	?	Y
25 ***Atkinson***	N	N	Y	Y	?	N	Y	Y
RHODE ISLAND								
1 St Germain	N	N	Y	Y	N	Y	Y	Y
2 ***Schneider***	?	?	Y	Y	Y	Y	Y	Y
SOUTH CAROLINA								
1 ***Hartnett***	N	Y	N	N	N	N	Y	Y
2 ***Spence***	N	Y	N	N	Y	N	Y	Y
3 Derrick	N	N	Y	Y	?	Y	Y	Y
4 ***Campbell***	?	?	N	N	Y	N	Y	Y
5 Holland	N	N	N	N	?	Y	Y	Y
6 ***Napier***	N	Y	Y	Y	Y	N	Y	Y
SOUTH DAKOTA								
1 Daschle	?	N	N	N	Y	Y	Y	Y
2 ***Roberts***	?	Y	N	N	Y	N	Y	Y
TENNESSEE								
1 ***Quillen***	N	Y	N	Y	Y	N	Y	Y
2 ***Duncan***	N	N	N	N	Y	N	Y	Y
3 Bouquard	N	?	N	N	Y	Y	Y	Y
4 Gore	N	N	N	N	Y	Y	Y	Y
5 Boner	N	N	N	N	Y	Y	Y	Y
6 ***Beard***	?	?	N	N	Y	N	?	Y

	393	394	395	396	397	398	399	400
7 Jones	N	N	N	N	Y	Y	Y	Y
8 Ford	Y	N	N	Y	Y	Y	Y	Y
TEXAS								
1 Hall, S.	N	Y	N	N	?	N	Y	Y
2 Wilson	N	?	Y	Y	Y	N	Y	Y
3 ***Collins***	N	Y	N	N	Y	N	Y	Y
4 Hall, R.	N	N	N	N	?	N	Y	Y
5 Mattox	?	?	?	?	?	?	?	?
6 Gramm	N	Y	N	N	Y	N	Y	Y
7 ***Archer***	N	Y	N	N	?	N	Y	Y
8 ***Fields***	N	Y	N	N	?	N	Y	Y
9 Brooks	N	N	Y	Y	Y	Y	Y	Y
10 Pickle	N	N	Y	Y	?	Y	Y	Y
11 Leath	N	Y	N	N	Y	N	Y	Y
12 Wright	N	N	Y	Y	Y	Y	Y	Y
13 Hightower	N	Y	Y	Y	Y	N	Y	Y
14 Patman	N	N	Y	Y	Y	N	Y	Y
15 de la Garza	?	N	N	N	Y	N	Y	Y
16 White	N	Y	N	N	Y	N	Y	Y
17 Stenholm	N	Y	N	N	Y	N	Y	Y
18 Leland	N	N	Y	Y	?	Y	Y	N
19 Hance	N	Y	Y	Y	Y	N	Y	Y
20 Gonzalez	N	N	N	N	Y	Y	Y	Y
21 ***Loeffler***	N	Y	N	N	Y	N	Y	Y
22 ***Paul***	N	Y	N	N	Y	Y	Y	N
23 Kazen	N	N	N	N	Y	N	Y	Y
24 Frost	N	N	Y	Y	Y	Y	Y	Y
UTAH								
1 ***Hansen***	N	Y	N	N	Y	N	?	Y
2 ***Marriott***	N	Y	N	N	Y	N	Y	Y
VERMONT								
AL ***Jeffords***	N	N	Y	Y	Y	Y	Y	Y
VIRGINIA								
1 ***Trible***	N	Y	Y	Y	Y	N	Y	Y
2 ***Whitehurst***	N	Y	Y	Y	Y	N	Y	Y
3 ***Bliley***	N	Y	Y	Y	Y	N	Y	Y
4 ***Daniel, R.***	?	?	N	N	Y	N	Y	Y
5 Daniel, D.	N	Y	N	N	N	N	Y	Y
6 ***Butler***	?	?	Y	Y	N	N	Y	Y
7 ***Robinson***	N	Y	N	N	Y	N	Y	Y
8 ***Parris***	?	?	N	N	Y	N	Y	Y
9 ***Wampler***	N	Y	N	N	Y	N	Y	Y
10 ***Wolf***	N	Y	Y	Y	Y	N	Y	Y
WASHINGTON								
1 ***Pritchard***	?	?	Y	Y	Y	Y	Y	Y
2 Swift	N	N	Y	Y	Y	Y	Y	Y
3 Bonker	-	-	+	+	Y	Y	Y	Y
4 ***Morrison***	N	Y	Y	Y	Y	N	Y	Y
5 Foley	?	N	Y	Y	Y	Y	Y	Y
6 Dicks	N	N	Y	Y	?	Y	Y	Y
7 Lowry	N	N	Y	Y	Y	Y	Y	N
WEST VIRGINIA								
1 Mollohan	?	?	?	?	Y	N	Y	Y
2 ***Benedict***	N	Y	Y	Y	?	N	Y	Y
3 ***Staton***	N	Y	Y	Y	Y	N	Y	Y
4 Rahall	N	N	Y	Y	Y	Y	Y	N
WISCONSIN								
1 Aspin	N	N	Y	Y	Y	Y	Y	Y
2 Kastenmeier	?	?	Y	Y	Y	Y	Y	N
3 ***Gunderson***	N	N	N	Y	Y	Y	Y	Y
4 Zablocki	N	N	Y	Y	Y	Y	Y	Y
5 Reuss	N	N	N	Y	Y	Y	Y	N
6 ***Petri***	N	N	Y	Y	Y	Y	Y	Y
7 Obey	?	N	Y	Y	Y	Y	Y	N
8 ***Roth***	N	Y	N	N	Y	N	Y	Y
9 ***Sensenbrenner***	N	Y	N	N	Y	Y	Y	Y
WYOMING								
AL ***Cheney***	N	Y	N	N	Y	N	Y	Y

Southern states - Ala., Ark., Fla., Ga., Ky., La., Miss., N.C., Okla., S.C., Tenn., Texas, Va.

KEY

Y Voted for (yea).
Paired for.
+ Announced for.
N Voted against (nay).
X Paired against.
- Announced against.
P Voted "present".
C Voted "present" to avoid possible conflict of interest.
? Did not vote or otherwise make a position known.

Democrats *Republicans*

401. Procedural Motion. Dannemeyer, R-Calif., motion to approve the House *Journal* of Wednesday, Dec. 8. Motion agreed to 340-18: R 147-8; D 193-10 (ND 125-9, SD 68-1), Dec. 9, 1982.

402. HR 6957. State, Justice, Commerce Appropriations, Fiscal 1983. Collins, R-Texas, amendment to bar use of any Justice Department funds in the bill to bring any sort of action to require "directly or indirectly" busing beyond a school nearest a pupil's home, except for special education for the handicapped. Adopted 243-153: R 149-26; D 94-127 (ND 41-109, SD 53-18), Dec. 9, 1982.

403. HR 6957. State, Justice, Commerce Appropriations, Fiscal 1983. Sensenbrenner, R-Wis., amendment to reduce the Legal Services Corporation appropriation from $241 million to $100 million. Rejected 121-269: R 98-74; D 23-195 (ND 3-146, SD 20-49), Dec. 9, 1982.

404. HR 6957. State, Justice, Commerce Appropriations, Fiscal 1983. Smith, D-Iowa, motion to conclude debate on the bill and amendments by 8 p.m. Dec. 9. Motion agreed to 205-132: R 21-124; D 184-8 (ND 123-2, SD 61-6), Dec. 9, 1982.

405. HR 6957. State, Justice, Commerce Appropriations, Fiscal 1983. Frenzel, R-Minn., motion that the Committee of the Whole House rise and report the bill back to the House with a recommendation to strike the enacting clause, which would kill the bill. Motion rejected 32-299: R 31-112; D 1-187 (ND 0-125, SD 1-62), Dec. 9, 1982.

406. HR 6957. State, Justice, Commerce Appropriations, Fiscal 1983. Passage of the bill to appropriate $9,004,628,000 in fiscal 1983 for the State, Justice and Commerce departments, the judiciary and related agencies. Passed 234-125: R 54-104; D 180-21 (ND 129-6, SD 51-15), Dec. 9, 1982. The president had requested $8,670,794,000.

407. HR 5133. Automobile Domestic Content Requirements. Adoption of the rule (H Res 622) providing for House floor consideration of the bill to require auto manufacturers to use specific levels of American-generated "domestic content" in vehicles sold in the United States. Adopted 191-120: R 34-97; D 157-23 (ND 117-4, SD 40-19), Dec. 9, 1982.

	401	402	403	404	405	406	407
ALABAMA							
1 *Edwards*	Y	Y	Y	?	?	N	?
2 *Dickinson*	N	Y	Y	N	N	N	?
3 Nichols	?	Y	Y	Y	N	Y	?
4 Bevill	Y	Y	Y	N	Y	N	Y
5 Flippo	Y	Y	N	Y	N	Y	Y
6 *Smith*	Y	Y	Y	N	?	N	Y
7 Shelby	Y	Y	Y	Y	N	N	Y
ALASKA							
AL *Young*	Y	?	N	?	?	Y	N
ARIZONA							
1 *Rhodes*	Y	Y	?	?	?	?	?
2 Udall	Y	N	N	Y	N	Y	?
3 *Stump*	Y	Y	N	N	N	N	N
4 *Rudd*	Y	Y	Y	N	N	N	N
ARKANSAS							
1 Alexander	?	?	?	?	?	?	?
2 *Bethune*	?	?	N	N	N	N	N
3 *Hammerschmidt*	Y	Y	N	N	N	Y	N
4 Anthony	Y	Y	N	Y	N	?	Y
CALIFORNIA							
1 *Chappie*	?	?	?	?	?	X	X
2 *Clausen*	Y	Y	?	N	N	Y	N
3 Matsui	Y	N	N	Y	N	Y	Y
4 Fazio	Y	N	Y	N	Y	Y	Y
5 Burton, J.	?	N	N	?	Y	?	Y
6 Burton, P.	Y	N	N	Y	?	?	Y
7 Miller	N	N	?	?	?	?	Y
8 Dellums	Y	N	N	?	Y	?	Y
9 Stark	Y	N	N	?	?	Y	Y
10 Edwards	Y	N	N	N	N	Y	Y
11 Lantos	Y	N	N	Y	N	Y	Y
12 *McCloskey*	?	N	N	N	Y	N	N
13 Mineta	Y	N	N	Y	N	Y	Y
14 *Shumway*	Y	Y	N	N	N	N	N
15 Coelho	Y	N	?	Y	N	Y	Y
16 Panetta	Y	N	N	Y	N	Y	Y
17 *Pashayan*	Y	Y	N	N	N	N	N
18 *Thomas*	Y	?	?	?	?	?	X
19 *Lagomarsino*	Y	Y	Y	N	Y	N	N
20 *Goldwater*	?	Y	?	?	Y	N	N
21 *Fiedler*	Y	Y	Y	N	N	Y	N
22 *Moorhead*	Y	Y	Y	Y	N	N	N
23 Beilenson	Y	N	N	Y	N	Y	Y
24 Waxman	Y	N	Y	?	?	?	?
25 Roybal	Y	N	?	Y	N	Y	Y
26 *Rousselot*	Y	Y	N	N	N	N	N
27 *Dornan*	?	Y	N	N	N	N	N
28 Dixon	Y	N	N	Y	?	?	Y
29 Hawkins	?	N	N	?	?	#	#
30 Martinez	Y	Y	N	Y	N	N	N
31 Dymally	?	N	N	Y	N	Y	Y
32 Anderson	Y	Y	N	N	N	N	N
33 Grisham	?	Y	Y	?	?	N	Y
34 *Lungren*	Y	Y	Y	N	Y	N	N
35 *Dreier*	Y	Y	Y	N	N	N	N
36 Brown	Y	N	N	Y	N	Y	?
37 *Lewis*	Y	N	N	N	N	Y	N
38 Patterson	Y	N	N	Y	N	Y	?
39 *Dannemeyer*	Y	Y	Y	N	N	N	N
40 *Badham*	Y	Y	Y	?	?	?	X
41 *Lowery*	Y	Y	Y	N	N	N	N
42 *Hunter*	?	?	?	?	?	X	X
43 *Burgener*	Y	Y	Y	?	?	?	?
COLORADO							
1 Schroeder	N	N	N	Y	N	N	Y
2 Wirth	Y	N	N	Y	N	Y	Y
3 Kogovsek	Y	N	N	Y	N	Y	Y
4 *Brown*	Y	Y	Y	N	N	N	N

	401	402	403	404	405	406	407
5 *Kramer*	Y	Y	Y	N	N	N	?
CONNECTICUT							
1 Kennelly	Y	N	N	Y	N	Y	Y
2 Gejdenson	N	N	N	Y	N	Y	Y
3 *DeNardis*	?	N	N	?	?	?	?
4 *McKinney*	?	N	N	?	?	?	?
5 Ratchford	Y	N	N	Y	N	Y	Y
6 Moffett	?	N	N	?	?	?	Y
DELAWARE							
AL *Evans*	Y	Y	N	N	N	Y	?
FLORIDA							
1 Hutto	Y	Y	Y	N	Y	N	?
2 Fuqua	Y	Y	N	N	N	Y	N
3 Bennett	Y	Y	N	Y	N	Y	N
4 Chappell	Y	Y	N	Y	N	Y	?
5 *McCollum*	Y	Y	Y	N	N	N	N
6 *Young*	Y	Y	Y	N	Y	N	N
7 Gibbons	Y	Y	N	N	?	Y	N
8 *Ireland*	Y	Y	Y	N	?	?	?
9 Nelson	Y	Y	N	Y	N	Y	N
10 *Bafalis*	?	?	?	?	?	?	?
11 Mica	Y	Y	N	Y	N	Y	N
12 *Shaw*	Y	Y	Y	N	N	N	N
13 Lehman	?	?	?	?	?	?	?
14 Pepper	Y	N	N	Y	N	Y	Y
15 Fascell	?	N	N	?	?	?	?
GEORGIA							
1 Ginn	Y	Y	N	Y	N	Y	Y
2 Hatcher	Y	Y	N	Y	N	Y	Y
3 Brinkley	Y	Y	N	Y	N	Y	Y
4 Levitas	Y	Y	N	Y	N	Y	N
5 Fowler	Y	N	?	?	?	?	?
6 *Gingrich*	Y	Y	Y	N	?	N	Y
7 McDonald	Y	Y	Y	N	Y	N	N
8 Evans	?	?	?	?	?	Y	Y
9 Jenkins	Y	Y	Y	?	Y	Y	Y
10 Barnard	Y	Y	Y	Y	N	Y	N
HAWAII							
1 Heftel	Y	Y	N	Y	N	Y	Y
2 Akaka	Y	N	N	Y	N	Y	Y
IDAHO							
1 *Craig*	Y	Y	?	?	?	#	X
2 *Hansen*	?	Y	Y	N	N	N	N
ILLINOIS							
1 Washington	N	N	N	Y	N	Y	?
2 Savage	?	N	N	?	N	Y	?
3 Russo	Y	Y	N	?	?	?	?
4 *Derwinski*	?	?	Y	N	N	Y	?
5 Fary	Y	N	Y	N	Y	Y	Y
6 *Hyde*	Y	N	N	N	N	N	N
7 Collins	Y	N	N	Y	N	Y	Y
8 Rostenkowski	Y	N	?	?	?	?	?
9 Yates	N	N	N	Y	N	Y	Y
10 *Porter*	Y	Y	N	N	N	Y	?
11 Annunzio	Y	N	N	Y	N	Y	?
12 *Crane, P.*	Y	?	?	?	?	?	?
13 *McClory*	?	N	N	N	Y	N	N
14 *Erlenborn*	N	N	?	?	?	?	?
15 *Corcoran*	Y	Y	N	N	N	N	N
16 *Martin*	Y	?	?	?	?	?	?
17 *O'Brien*	Y	Y	N	N	N	+	?
18 *Michel*	Y	Y	N	N	N	N	N
19 *Railsback*	Y	N	N	?	?	?	?
20 *Findley*	N	N	N	?	?	?	?
21 *Madigan*	Y	Y	?	N	Y	N	N
22 *Crane, D.*	Y	Y	Y	N	Y	N	N
23 Price	Y	N	N	Y	N	Y	?
24 Simon	?	?	X	?	?	#	?
INDIANA							
1 Hall	Y	N	N	Y	N	Y	Y
2 Fithian	?	N	N	Y	N	Y	Y
3 *Hiler*	Y	Y	Y	N	N	N	N
4 *Coats*	Y	Y	Y	N	N	N	N
5 *Hillis*	Y	Y	Y	N	Y	N	Y
6 Evans	Y	N	Y	N	?	?	Y
7 *Myers*	Y	Y	Y	N	N	N	N
8 *Deckard*	?	Y	N	?	?	?	?
9 Hamilton	Y	Y	N	Y	N	Y	Y
10 Sharp	Y	Y	Y	N	?	Y	Y
11 Jacobs	N	N	N	Y	?	Y	Y
IOWA							
1 *Leach*	Y	N	N	Y	?	Y	Y
2 *Tauke*	Y	N	N	N	N	N	N
3 Evans	N	N	N	N	N	N	N
4 Smith	Y	N	N	Y	N	Y	Y
5 Harkin	N	N	N	Y	N	N	Y
6 Bedell	Y	N	N	Y	N	Y	Y

ND - Northern Democrats SD - Southern Democrats

Corresponding to Congressional Record Votes 426, 427, 428, 429, 430, 431, 432

	401	402	403	404	405	406	407
KANSAS							
1 ***Roberts***	Y	Y	Y	Y	Y	N	N
2 ***Jeffries***	?	Y	Y	N	N	N	N
3 ***Winn***	Y	Y	Y	Y	N	N	N
4 Glickman	Y	Y	N	Y	?	Y	Y
5 ***Whittaker***	Y	Y	Y	?	?	?	?
KENTUCKY							
1 Hubbard	Y	Y	N	Y	N	N	Y
2 Natcher	Y	Y	N	Y	N	Y	Y
3 Mazzoli	Y	N	N	Y	N	Y	Y
4 ***Snyder***	Y	Y	Y	Y	N	Y	Y
5 ***Rogers***	Y	Y	Y	N	N	Y	Y
6 ***Hopkins***	Y	Y	N	N	N	N	Y
7 Perkins	Y	N	N	Y	N	Y	Y
LOUISIANA							
1 ***Livingston***	Y	Y	Y	Y	Y	Y	N
2 Boggs	Y	Y	N	Y	N	Y	Y
3 Tauzin	Y	Y	N	N	N	N	Y
4 Roemer	N	Y	N	N	N	N	Y
5 Huckaby	Y	?	?	?	?	?	?
6 ***Moore***	Y	Y	N	N	N	N	Y
7 Breaux	Y	Y	Y	Y	N	Y	Y
8 Long	Y	Y	N	Y	N	Y	Y
MAINE							
1 ***Emery***	?	N	N	?	?	?	?
2 ***Snowe***	Y	?	N	N	N	Y	N
MARYLAND							
1 Dyson	Y	Y	N	Y	N	Y	Y
2 Long	?	N	N	Y	N	Y	?
3 Mikulski	Y	N	N	Y	N	Y	Y
4 ***Holt***	N	Y	Y	N	N	N	N
5 Hoyer	Y	N	N	Y	N	Y	Y
6 Byron	Y	Y	Y	Y	N	Y	Y
7 Mitchell	?	N	N	Y	N	Y	Y
8 Barnes	Y	N	N	Y	N	Y	Y
MASSACHUSETTS							
1 ***Conte***	?	N	N	Y	N	Y	Y
2 Boland	Y	Y	N	Y	N	?	Y
3 Early	Y	Y	N	Y	N	Y	Y
4 Frank	Y	N	N	Y	N	Y	Y
5 Shannon	Y	N	N	?	N	Y	Y
6 Mavroules	?	?	?	?	?	?	?
7 Markey	N	N	N	Y	?	?	?
8 O'Neill							
9 Moakley	Y	Y	N	Y	N	Y	Y
10 ***Heckler***	?	?	?	?	?	?	?
11 Donnelly	Y	Y	N	Y	N	N	N
12 Studds	Y	N	N	Y	N	Y	Y
MICHIGAN							
1 Conyers	?	N	N	?	?	Y	?
2 ***Pursell***	Y	Y	N	?	Y	N	?
3 Wolpe	Y	N	N	Y	N	Y	Y
4 ***Siljander***	Y	Y	Y	?	N	N	N
5 ***Sawyer***	Y	Y	N	Y	N	Y	N
6 ***Dunn***	Y	Y	N	Y	N	Y	?
7 Kildee	Y	N	N	Y	N	Y	Y
8 Traxler	Y	Y	?	Y	N	Y	Y
9 ***Vander Jagt***	Y	Y	N	?	?	?	?
10 Albosta	Y	Y	N	Y	N	Y	Y
11 ***Davis***	Y	Y	N	Y	N	Y	Y
12 Bonior	Y	Y	N	Y	N	Y	Y
13 Crockett	?	N	N	Y	N	Y	Y
14 Hertel	Y	Y	N	?	N	Y	Y
15 Ford	Y	N	N	Y	N	Y	Y
16 Dingell	?	N	N	Y	N	Y	Y
17 Brodhead	Y	N	N	Y	?	?	?
18 Blanchard	?	?	?	?	?	?	?
19 ***Broomfield***	?	Y	Y	?	Y	N	Y
MINNESOTA							
1 ***Erdahl***	Y	N	N	N	N	N	N
2 ***Hagedorn***	Y	Y	?	?	?	X	?
3 ***Frenzel***	Y	N	N	N	N	N	N
4 Vento	Y	N	N	Y	N	Y	Y
5 Sabo	N	N	N	Y	N	Y	Y
6 ***Weber***	Y	Y	Y	N	Y	N	?
7 ***Stangeland***	Y	Y	Y	?	Y	N	N
8 Oberstar	Y	N	N	Y	N	Y	Y
MISSISSIPPI							
1 Whitten	Y	Y	?	Y	N	N	Y
2 Bowen	Y	Y	N	Y	N	Y	N
3 Montgomery	Y	Y	Y	Y	N	Y	#
4 Dowdy	Y	Y	N	Y	N	Y	Y
5 ***Lott***	Y	Y	Y	N	N	N	N
MISSOURI							
1 Clay	?	N	N	Y	N	Y	Y
2 Young	Y	Y	N	Y	N	Y	Y
3 Gephardt	Y	Y	N	Y	N	Y	Y
4 Skelton	?	?	?	?	?	?	?
5 Bolling	?	?	?	?	?	?	?
6 ***Coleman***	Y	Y	N	N	N	Y	N
7 ***Taylor***	Y	Y	Y	Y	N	N	N
8 ***Bailey***	Y	Y	Y	N	Y	N	N
9 Volkmer	Y	Y	N	Y	N	Y	Y
10 ***Emerson***	N	Y	Y	N	N	N	N
MONTANA							
1 Williams	?	N	N	Y	N	Y	Y
2 ***Marlenee***	Y	Y	Y	Y	Y	N	?
NEBRASKA							
1 ***Bereuter***	Y	N	N	N	Y	N	N
2 ***Daub***	Y	Y	Y	N	N	N	N
3 ***Smith***	Y	Y	Y	Y	N	Y	N
NEVADA							
AL Santini	Y	Y	Y	?	N	Y	Y
NEW HAMPSHIRE							
1 D'Amours	?	Y	N	Y	N	Y	Y
2 ***Gregg***	Y	Y	Y	N	N	N	N
NEW JERSEY							
1 Florio	Y	N	N	Y	N	Y	Y
2 Hughes	Y	N	N	Y	N	Y	Y
3 Howard	Y	N	N	Y	N	Y	Y
4 ***Smith***	Y	Y	N	N	N	Y	Y
5 ***Fenwick***	Y	Y	N	N	N	Y	N
6 ***Forsythe***	?	Y	N	?	?	?	?
7 ***Roukema***	Y	Y	N	N	N	Y	N
8 Roe	Y	Y	N	Y	N	Y	?
9 ***Hollenbeck***	Y	N	?	?	?	Y	N
10 Rodino	Y	N	N	Y	N	Y	Y
11 Minish	Y	?	N	Y	N	Y	Y
12 ***Rinaldo***	Y	Y	N	N	N	Y	Y
13 ***Courter***	Y	Y	N	Y	N	N	Y
14 Guarini	Y	N	N	Y	N	Y	Y
15 Dwyer	Y	N	N	Y	N	Y	Y
NEW MEXICO							
1 ***Lujan***	Y	Y	N	Y	?	N	N
2 ***Skeen***	Y	Y	N	N	N	N	N
NEW YORK							
1 ***Carney***	Y	Y	Y	?	?	?	?
2 Downey	Y	N	N	?	N	Y	Y
3 ***Carman***	Y	Y	Y	N	N	N	N
4 ***Lent***	Y	Y	N	N	N	Y	N
5 ***McGrath***	Y	Y	N	N	N	N	N
6 ***LeBoutillier***	?	Y	Y	N	N	Y	N
7 Addabbo	Y	N	N	?	N	Y	?
8 Rosenthal	?	N	N	Y	?	?	?
9 Ferraro	Y	Y	N	Y	N	Y	Y
10 Biaggi	Y	?	?	?	?	?	?
11 Scheuer	Y	N	N	Y	N	Y	Y
12 Chisholm	?	N	N	?	?	?	#
13 Solarz	Y	N	N	Y	N	Y	Y
14 Vacancy							
15 Zeferetti	?	?	?	?	?	?	?
16 Schumer	Y	N	N	Y	N	Y	Y
17 ***Molinari***	Y	Y	N	N	N	Y	N
18 ***Green***	Y	N	?	?	?	?	?
19 Rangel	Y	N	N	?	N	Y	Y
20 Weiss	Y	N	?	?	?	?	?
21 Garcia	Y	N	?	?	?	#	#
22 Bingham	?	?	?	?	?	?	?
23 Peyser	Y	N	N	Y	?	Y	Y
24 Ottinger	?	N	N	Y	N	Y	Y
25 ***Fish***	Y	N	N	Y	N	Y	Y
26 ***Gilman***	Y	N	N	N	N	Y	Y
27 McHugh	Y	N	N	Y	N	Y	Y
28 Stratton	Y	N	N	Y	N	Y	Y
29 ***Solomon***	N	Y	Y	N	Y	N	Y
30 ***Martin***	?	Y	Y	N	N	N	Y
31 ***Mitchell***	Y	Y	N	?	?	?	?
32 ***Wortley***	Y	Y	Y	N	N	N	Y
33 ***Lee***	?	Y	Y	Y	N	N	?
34 ***Horton***	Y	N	N	Y	N	Y	Y
35 ***Conable***	Y	N	N	N	N	N	N
36 LaFalce	Y	N	N	Y	?	Y	#
37 Nowak	Y	N	N	Y	N	Y	Y
38 ***Kemp***	?	N	N	N	?	N	N
39 Lundine	?	N	N	Y	N	Y	?
NORTH CAROLINA							
1 Jones	Y	N	N	Y	N	Y	?
2 Fountain	Y	Y	?	?	N	N	Y
3 Whitley	Y	N	N	Y	N	Y	Y
4 Andrews	Y	N	N	Y	N	Y	?
5 Neal	?	Y	N	N	?	Y	N
6 ***Johnston***	?	?	Y	?	?	?	?
7 Rose	Y	N	N	?	N	Y	?
8 Hefner	Y	N	N	Y	N	Y	N
9 ***Martin***	Y	Y	N	N	?	N	?
10 ***Broyhill***	Y	Y	N	N	N	N	N
11 ***Hendon***	Y	Y	Y	?	N	N	?
NORTH DAKOTA							
AL Dorgan	Y	N	N	Y	N	Y	Y
OHIO							
1 ***Gradison***	Y	Y	N	Y	N	N	?
2 Luken	Y	Y	N	Y	N	?	Y
3 Hall	Y	Y	N	?	N	Y	Y
4 ***Oxley***	?	Y	Y	N	N	N	N
5 ***Latta***	Y	Y	Y	N	N	N	Y
6 ***McEwen***	Y	Y	Y	?	N	N	Y
7 ***Brown***	?	Y	Y	N	N	N	Y
8 ***Kindness***	Y	Y	N	N	N	N	Y
9 ***Weber***	Y	Y	N	N	N	Y	N
10 ***Miller***	N	Y	Y	N	N	N	Y
11 ***Stanton***	?	?	?	?	?	?	?
12 Shamansky	Y	N	N	Y	N	Y	Y
13 Pease	Y	N	N	Y	N	Y	Y
14 Seiberling	Y	N	N	Y	N	Y	?
15 ***Wylie***	Y	Y	N	N	?	?	?
16 ***Regula***	Y	Y	N	N	N	Y	Y
17 ***Ashbrook***	Y	Y	Y	N	N	N	N
18 Applegate	Y	Y	N	?	N	N	?
19 ***Williams***	Y	Y	?	?	?	?	?
20 Oakar	Y	Y	N	Y	N	Y	Y
21 Stokes	Y	N	N	Y	N	Y	Y
22 Eckart	Y	?	N	Y	N	Y	Y
23 Mottl	Y	Y	N	Y	N	?	?
OKLAHOMA							
1 Jones	Y	Y	N	Y	N	N	N
2 Synar	Y	N	N	Y	N	Y	Y
3 Watkins	Y	Y	N	Y	N	Y	Y
4 McCurdy	Y	Y	N	Y	N	N	Y
5 ***Edwards***	Y	Y	Y	N	Y	N	?
6 English	Y	Y	N	Y	N	N	Y
OREGON							
1 AuCoin	Y	N	N	Y	N	Y	Y
2 ***Smith***	Y	Y	Y	N	N	N	N
3 Wyden	Y	N	N	Y	N	Y	Y
4 Weaver	Y	N	N	Y	N	N	Y
PENNSYLVANIA							
1 Foglietta	Y	N	N	Y	N	Y	Y
2 Gray	Y	N	N	?	N	Y	Y
3 Smith	?	N	N	Y	?	Y	?
4 ***Dougherty***	?	?	Y	Y	?	Y	Y
5 ***Schulze***	Y	Y	N	Y	Y	N	Y
6 Yatron	Y	Y	N	Y	N	Y	?
7 Edgar	Y	N	N	Y	N	Y	Y
8 ***Coyne, J.***	Y	Y	Y	N	N	N	?
9 ***Shuster***	?	?	?	?	?	?	?
10 ***McDade***	Y	Y	N	N	N	Y	Y
11 ***Nelligan***	Y	Y	Y	?	?	?	?
12 Murtha	Y	Y	N	Y	N	Y	Y
13 ***Coughlin***	Y	Y	N	N	N	Y	Y
14 Coyne, W.	Y	N	N	Y	N	Y	?
15 ***Ritter***	Y	Y	Y	N	N	N	Y
16 ***Walker***	N	Y	Y	N	N	N	N
17 Ertel	Y	?	N	Y	N	?	Y
18 Walgren	Y	Y	N	Y	N	Y	Y
19 ***Goodling***	N	Y	N	N	N	Y	Y
20 Gaydos	Y	Y	N	Y	?	Y	Y
21 Bailey	Y	N	N	Y	N	Y	Y
22 Murphy	Y	Y	N	Y	N	Y	Y
23 ***Clinger***	Y	Y	N	N	Y	Y	+
24 ***Marks***	?	?	?	?	?	?	?
25 ***Atkinson***	?	Y	Y	N	N	N	N
RHODE ISLAND							
1 St Germain	Y	N	N	Y	N	Y	Y
2 ***Schneider***	?	N	N	N	N	Y	Y
SOUTH CAROLINA							
1 ***Hartnett***	Y	Y	Y	N	Y	N	N
2 ***Spence***	Y	Y	Y	N	Y	N	N
3 Derrick	Y	N	Y	Y	N	Y	Y
4 ***Campbell***	Y	Y	Y	N	N	Y	N
5 Holland	?	Y	N	?	?	?	N
6 ***Napier***	Y	Y	Y	N	N	Y	?
SOUTH DAKOTA							
1 Daschle	Y	N	N	Y	N	Y	?
2 ***Roberts***	?	Y	Y	?	?	N	?
TENNESSEE							
1 ***Quillen***	Y	Y	N	?	N	Y	N
2 ***Duncan***	?	?	?	?	?	?	?
3 Bouquard	Y	Y	N	Y	N	Y	?
4 Gore	Y	N	N	Y	N	Y	N
5 Boner	Y	Y	N	Y	?	Y	Y
6 ***Beard***	?	Y	Y	?	?	N	?
7 Jones	Y	Y	N	Y	N	Y	Y
8 Ford	Y	N	N	Y	N	Y	Y
TEXAS							
1 Hall, S.	Y	Y	Y	Y	N	N	Y
2 Wilson	Y	Y	Y	Y	?	?	Y
3 ***Collins***	Y	Y	Y	N	Y	N	N
4 Hall, R.	Y	Y	Y	Y	N	N	Y
5 Mattox	?	?	?	?	?	#	?
6 Gramm	?	?	#	?	?	X	?
7 ***Archer***	Y	Y	Y	N	Y	N	N
8 ***Fields***	Y	Y	Y	N	Y	N	N
9 Brooks	Y	Y	N	Y	N	Y	Y
10 Pickle	Y	Y	N	N	N	Y	?
11 Leath	Y	Y	Y	Y	N	N	N
12 Wright	Y	?	N	Y	N	Y	Y
13 Hightower	Y	Y	Y	Y	N	Y	Y
14 Patman	Y	Y	Y	Y	N	Y	N
15 de la Garza	Y	N	N	Y	N	Y	N
16 White	?	?	?	?	?	?	?
17 Stenholm	Y	Y	Y	Y	?	?	?
18 Leland	Y	N	N	Y	N	Y	Y
19 Hance	Y	Y	Y	Y	N	N	Y
20 Gonzalez	Y	N	N	Y	N	Y	Y
21 ***Loeffler***	Y	Y	Y	N	N	N	N
22 ***Paul***	Y	Y	Y	N	Y	N	N
23 Kazen	Y	Y	N	Y	N	Y	N
24 Frost	Y	N	N	Y	N	Y	Y
UTAH							
1 ***Hansen***	Y	Y	Y	N	N	N	N
2 ***Marriott***	Y	Y	N	N	N	N	N
VERMONT							
AL ***Jeffords***	Y	N	N	N	N	Y	?
VIRGINIA							
1 ***Trible***	Y	Y	N	N	N	N	?
2 ***Whitehurst***	Y	Y	N	N	N	N	N
3 ***Bliley***	Y	Y	Y	N	N	N	N
4 ***Daniel, R.***	Y	Y	Y	N	N	N	N
5 Daniel, D.	Y	Y	Y	Y	N	N	N
6 ***Butler***	?	Y	N	N	?	Y	N
7 ***Robinson***	Y	Y	Y	N	N	N	N
8 ***Parris***	Y	Y	Y	N	N	Y	?
9 ***Wampler***	Y	Y	Y	N	N	Y	N
10 ***Wolf***	Y	Y	Y	N	N	Y	N
WASHINGTON							
1 ***Pritchard***	Y	N	?	?	?	Y	N
2 Swift	Y	N	N	?	N	Y	Y
3 Bonker	Y	Y	N	Y	?	Y	Y
4 ***Morrison***	Y	Y	N	N	N	Y	N
5 Foley	Y	?	N	Y	N	Y	N
6 Dicks	Y	N	N	Y	N	Y	Y
7 Lowry	?	N	N	?	?	?	Y
WEST VIRGINIA							
1 Mollohan	?	Y	N	Y	N	Y	Y
2 ***Benedict***	Y	?	N	N	Y	N	N
3 ***Staton***	Y	Y	Y	N	N	N	Y
4 Rahall	Y	N	N	Y	N	Y	Y
WISCONSIN							
1 Aspin	Y	N	N	?	N	Y	Y
2 Kastenmeier	Y	N	N	Y	N	Y	Y
3 ***Gunderson***	Y	Y	N	N	N	N	N
4 Zablocki	Y	Y	N	Y	N	Y	Y
5 Reuss	Y	N	N	?	?	?	?
6 ***Petri***	Y	Y	Y	N	N	N	N
7 Obey	Y	N	N	Y	N	Y	Y
8 ***Roth***	Y	Y	N	N	N	Y	?
9 ***Sensenbrenner***	Y	Y	Y	N	N	N	N
WYOMING							
AL ***Cheney***	Y	Y	Y	?	Y	X	?

Southern states - Ala., Ark., Fla., Ga., Ky., La., Miss., N.C., Okla., S.C., Tenn., Texas, Va.

408. Procedural Motion. Oxley, R-Ohio, motion to approve the House *Journal* of Thursday, Dec. 9. Motion agreed to 282-26: R 120-18; D 162-8 (ND 103-7, SD 59-1), Dec. 10, 1982.

409. HR 5133. Automobile Domestic Content Requirements. Stratton, D-N.Y., amendment to permit the secretary of transportation to adjust domestic content requirements if the adjustments would prevent the closing of, or encourage the construction of, foreign automobile plants in the United States. Rejected 11-331: R 8-137; D 3-194 (ND 1-135, SD 2-59), Dec. 10, 1982.

410. S 2355. Telecommunications for the Disabled. Wirth, D-Colo., motion to suspend the rules and pass the bill to require that coin-operated and emergency telephones be usable by persons with hearing aids. Motion agreed to 365-14: R 158-10; D 207-4 (ND 144-1, SD 63-3), Dec. 13, 1982. A two-thirds majority of those present and voting (253 in this case) is required for passage under suspension of the rules.

411. H J Res 429. State Commissions on Teacher Excellence. Simon, D-Ill., motion to suspend the rules and pass the joint resolution calling on states to establish commissions to study the quality of teaching in the schools. Motion rejected 225-153: R 29-139; D 196-14 (ND 141-3, SD 55-11), Dec. 13, 1982. A two-thirds majority of those present and voting (252 in this case) is required for passage under suspension of the rules.

412. HR 4281. Critical Materials Act. Glickman, D-Kan., motion to suspend the rules and pass the bill to establish a Council on Critical Materials, within the Office of the President, to coordinate federal policies aimed at ensuring a safe, stable supply of essential minerals and other products. Motion rejected 215-164: R 40-129; D 175-35 (ND 131-13, SD 44-22), Dec. 13, 1982. A two-thirds majority of those present and voting (253 in this case) is required for passage under suspension of the rules.

413. HR 7044. Mail Order Consumer Protection. Ford, D-Mich., motion to suspend the rules and pass the bill to strengthen the authority of the U.S. Postal Service to crack down on mail fraud. Motion agreed to 320-61: R 125-44; D 195-17 (ND 136-9, SD 59-8), Dec. 13, 1982. A two-thirds majority of those present and voting (255 in this case) is required for passage under suspension of the rules.

414. S 2059. Ethics in Government Act of 1982. Hall, D-Texas, motion to suspend the rules and pass the bill to revise and extend for five years a law allowing for the appointment of an independent counsel to investigate matters involving high government and political party campaign officials. Motion agreed to 347-37: R 137-34; D 210-3 (ND 144-1, SD 66-2), Dec. 13, 1982. A two-thirds majority of those present and voting (256 in this case) is required for passage under suspension of the rules.

415. S 1621. Southern Nevada Water Project. Kazen, D-Texas, motion to suspend the rules and pass the bill to authorize $1.5 million for federal purchase, on a non-reimbursable basis, of certain new parts for pumping stations of the southern Nevada water project. Motion rejected 67-315: R 15-156; D 52-159 (ND 33-110, SD 19-49), Dec. 13, 1982. A two-thirds majority of those present and voting (255 in this case) is required for passage under suspension of the rules.

KEY

Y Voted for (yea).
\# Paired for.
\+ Announced for.
N Voted against (nay).
X Paired against.
\- Announced against.
P Voted "present".
C Voted "present" to avoid possible conflict of interest.
? Did not vote or otherwise make a position known.

Democrats **Republicans**

	408	409	410	411	412	413	414	415
ALABAMA								
1 *Edwards*	?	?	Y	N	N	Y	Y	N
2 *Dickinson*	N	N	?	?	?	Y	Y	N
3 Nichols	Y	Y	Y	N	Y	Y	Y	N
4 Bevill	Y	N	Y	Y	Y	Y	Y	N
5 Flippo	Y	?	Y	Y	Y	Y	Y	N
6 *Smith*	?	N	Y	N	N	N	Y	N
7 Shelby	?	N	Y	Y	Y	Y	Y	N
ALASKA								
AL *Young*	N	N	Y	N	Y	Y	N	Y
ARIZONA								
1 *Rhodes*	?	?	?	?	?	?	?	?
2 Udall	?	N	Y	Y	Y	Y	Y	?
3 *Stump*	Y	N	N	N	N	N	N	Y
4 *Rudd*	?	?	N	N	Y	Y	Y	Y
ARKANSAS								
1 Alexander	?	?	Y	Y	Y	Y	Y	N
2 *Bethune*	?	N	Y	N	Y	Y	Y	N
3 *Hammerschmidt*	Y	N	Y	N	Y	Y	Y	N
4 Anthony	Y	N	Y	Y	Y	Y	Y	N
CALIFORNIA								
1 *Chappie*	?	?	?	?	?	?	?	?
2 *Clausen*	Y	N	Y	N	Y	Y	Y	N
3 Matsui	Y	N	Y	Y	Y	Y	Y	N
4 Fazio	Y	N	Y	Y	Y	Y	Y	N
5 Burton, J.	?	?	Y	Y	Y	Y	Y	N
6 Burton, P.	?	N	Y	Y	Y	Y	Y	Y
7 Miller	Y	N	Y	Y	N	Y	Y	N
8 Dellums	?	N	Y	Y	Y	Y	Y	N
9 Stark	?	N	Y	Y	Y	Y	Y	N
10 Edwards	Y	N	Y	Y	N	Y	Y	N
11 Lantos	Y	N	Y	Y	Y	Y	Y	N
12 *McCloskey*	Y	Y	Y	Y	N	Y	Y	N
13 Mineta	Y	N	Y	Y	Y	Y	Y	N
14 *Shumway*	Y	N	N	N	N	N	N	N
15 Coelho	?	N	Y	Y	Y	Y	Y	N
16 Panetta	Y	N	Y	Y	Y	Y	Y	N
17 *Pashayan*	Y	N	Y	N	N	Y	Y	Y
18 *Thomas*	Y	?	?	?	?	?	?	?
19 *Lagomarsino*	Y	N	Y	N	N	Y	Y	N
20 *Goldwater*	?	?	?	?	?	?	?	?
21 *Fiedler*	Y	N	Y	N	Y	Y	Y	N
22 *Moorhead*	Y	N	?	?	?	?	?	?
23 Beilenson	?	N	?	?	?	?	?	?
24 Waxman	Y	?	Y	Y	Y	Y	Y	N
25 Roybal	Y	N	Y	Y	Y	Y	Y	N
26 *Rousselot*	Y	N	Y	N	Y	N	Y	N
27 *Dornan*	Y	N	N	N	N	Y	Y	N
28 Dixon	?	N	Y	Y	Y	Y	Y	N
29 Hawkins	N	N	Y	Y	Y	Y	Y	N
30 Martinez	Y	N	?	?	?	?	?	?
31 Dymally	Y	N	Y	Y	Y	Y	Y	Y
32 Anderson	Y	N	Y	Y	Y	Y	Y	Y
33 Grisham	Y	?	Y	N	Y	Y	Y	N
34 *Lungren*	Y	?	?	?	?	?	?	?
35 *Dreier*	N	N	Y	N	N	N	N	N
36 Brown	Y	N	Y	Y	Y	Y	Y	N
37 *Lewis*	?	N	Y	N	N	Y	Y	Y
38 Patterson	Y	N	Y	Y	Y	Y	Y	N
39 *Dannemeyer*	N	N	N	N	N	N	N	N
40 *Badham*	Y	N	N	N	N	N	N	Y
41 *Lowery*	?	N	?	N	N	Y	Y	N
42 *Hunter*	?	?	Y	N	Y	Y	Y	N
43 *Burgener*	Y	?	?	N	N	Y	Y	N
COLORADO								
1 Schroeder	N	N	N	N	Y	Y	Y	N
2 Wirth	Y	N	Y	Y	Y	Y	Y	Y
3 Kogovsek	Y	N	Y	Y	Y	Y	Y	Y
4 Brown	Y	Y	Y	N	N	N	Y	N

	408	409	410	411	412	413	414	415
5 *Kramer*	Y	N	Y	N	N	N	Y	N
CONNECTICUT								
1 Kennelly	Y	N	Y	Y	Y	Y	Y	N
2 Gejdenson	N	N	Y	Y	Y	Y	Y	N
3 *DeNardis*	?	?	Y	Y	Y	Y	Y	N
4 *McKinney*	?	?	Y	Y	Y	Y	Y	N
5 Ratchford	Y	N	Y	Y	Y	Y	Y	N
6 Moffett	?	N	?	?	?	?	?	?
DELAWARE								
AL *Evans*	?	?	?	?	?	?	?	?
FLORIDA								
1 Hutto	Y	N	Y	Y	Y	Y	Y	N
2 Fuqua	Y	N	Y	Y	Y	Y	Y	N
3 Bennett	Y	N	Y	Y	Y	Y	Y	N
4 Chappell	?	?	?	?	?	?	?	?
5 *McCollum*	?	?	Y	N	N	Y	N	N
6 *Young*	?	N	Y	N	N	Y	N	N
7 Gibbons	?	N	Y	Y	Y	Y	Y	N
8 Ireland	?	?	?	?	?	?	?	?
9 Nelson	?	N	Y	Y	Y	Y	Y	N
10 *Bafalis*	?	?	Y	N	Y	Y	Y	N
11 Mica	Y	N	Y	Y	Y	Y	Y	N
12 *Shaw*	Y	N	Y	N	N	Y	N	N
13 Lehman	?	?	?	?	?	?	?	?
14 Pepper	?	Y	Y	Y	Y	Y	Y	N
15 Fascell	?	N	?	?	?	?	?	?
GEORGIA								
1 Ginn	Y	N	Y	Y	Y	Y	Y	Y
2 Hatcher	Y	?	?	?	?	?	?	?
3 Brinkley	Y	N	Y	Y	Y	Y	Y	N
4 Levitas	Y	N	Y	Y	Y	Y	Y	N
5 Fowler	?	?	?	?	?	?	?	?
6 *Gingrich*	Y	N	Y	N	N	N	N	N
7 McDonald	Y	N	N	N	N	N	N	N
8 Evans	?	?	?	?	?	N	Y	Y
9 Jenkins	Y	?	?	?	?	?	?	?
10 Barnard	Y	N	Y	Y	Y	N	Y	N
HAWAII								
1 Heftel	?	N	Y	Y	Y	Y	Y	N
2 Akaka	Y	N	Y	Y	Y	Y	Y	N
IDAHO								
1 *Craig*	?	?	Y	N	Y	N	N	N
2 *Hansen*	?	N	Y	N	Y	N	N	N
ILLINOIS								
1 Washington	?	?	?	?	?	?	?	?
2 Savage	?	?	?	?	?	?	?	?
3 Russo	Y	N	Y	Y	Y	Y	Y	N
4 *Derwinski*	N	Y	N	Y	N	N	N	N
5 Fary	Y	N	Y	Y	Y	Y	Y	N
6 *Hyde*	Y	N	Y	N	Y	Y	Y	N
7 Collins	Y	N	Y	Y	Y	Y	Y	N
8 Rostenkowski	?	?	Y	Y	Y	Y	Y	N
9 Yates	Y	N	Y	Y	Y	Y	Y	N
10 *Porter*	Y	N	Y	N	N	Y	Y	N
11 Annunzio	Y	N	Y	Y	Y	Y	Y	N
12 *Crane, P.*	?	?	N	N	N	N	N	N
13 *McClory*	?	?	Y	N	N	N	N	N
14 *Erlenborn*	Y	N	Y	N	Y	Y	Y	N
15 *Corcoran*	+	-	Y	N	Y	Y	Y	N
16 *Martin*	Y	N	Y	N	N	N	Y	N
17 O'Brien	Y	N	Y	Y	Y	N	N	Y
18 *Michel*	Y	N	Y	N	N	N	Y	N
19 *Railsback*	Y	?	?	?	?	?	?	?
20 *Findley*	Y	N	Y	Y	Y	Y	Y	N
21 Madigan	?	N	Y	Y	Y	Y	Y	N
22 *Crane, D.*	Y	?	N	N	N	N	N	N
23 Price	Y	N	Y	Y	Y	Y	Y	N
24 Simon	Y	?	Y	Y	Y	Y	Y	Y
INDIANA								
1 Hall	Y	N	Y	Y	Y	Y	Y	N
2 Fithian	Y	N	Y	Y	N	Y	Y	N
3 *Hiler*	Y	N	N	N	N	N	N	N
4 *Coats*	Y	N	Y	N	N	N	Y	N
5 *Hillis*	Y	N	N	N	Y	N	Y	N
6 Evans	?	?	Y	N	Y	Y	Y	?
7 *Myers*	Y	N	Y	N	N	Y	Y	N
8 *Deckard*	?	?	Y	Y	Y	Y	Y	N
9 Hamilton	Y	?	Y	Y	Y	Y	Y	N
10 Sharp	Y	N	Y	Y	Y	Y	Y	N
11 Jacobs	N	N	Y	N	Y	N	Y	N
IOWA								
1 *Leach*	Y	N	Y	Y	Y	Y	Y	N
2 *Tauke*	Y	N	Y	Y	Y	Y	Y	N
3 *Evans*	N	N	Y	N	Y	Y	Y	N
4 Smith	Y	N	Y	Y	Y	Y	Y	N
5 Harkin	?	?	Y	?	Y	Y	Y	N
6 Bedell	Y	N	Y	Y	Y	Y	Y	Y

ND - Northern Democrats   SD - Southern Democrats

	408	409	410	411	412	413	414	415
KANSAS								
1 ***Roberts***	N	N	Y	N	N	Y	Y	N
2 ***Jeffries***	?	N	Y	N	N	N	N	N
3 ***Winn***	Y	N	Y	N	N	Y	Y	N
4 Glickman	Y	N	Y	Y	Y	N	Y	N
5 ***Whittaker***	Y	N	Y	N	N	Y	Y	N
KENTUCKY								
1 Hubbard	Y	N	Y	Y	N	Y	Y	N
2 Natcher	Y	N	Y	Y	Y	Y	Y	N
3 Mazzoli	Y	N	Y	Y	N	Y	Y	N
4 ***Snyder***	Y	N	Y	Y	N	Y	Y	N
5 ***Rogers***	Y	N	Y	N	N	Y	Y	N
6 ***Hopkins***	Y	N	Y	N	N	Y	Y	N
7 Perkins	Y	N	Y	Y	Y	Y	Y	N
LOUISIANA								
1 ***Livingston***	?	N	Y	N	N	Y	N	N
2 Boggs	Y	N	Y	Y	?	Y	Y	N
3 Tauzin	Y	N	Y	Y	N	Y	Y	N
4 Roemer	N	N	Y	Y	N	N	Y	N
5 Huckaby	?	N	Y	Y	N	Y	Y	Y
6 ***Moore***	Y	N	Y	N	N	Y	Y	N
7 Breaux	Y	N	Y	N	N	Y	Y	Y
8 Long	Y	N	Y	Y	Y	Y	Y	N
MAINE								
1 ***Emery***	Y	N	?	?	?	?	?	?
2 ***Snowe***	Y	N	Y	Y	Y	Y	Y	N
MARYLAND								
1 Dyson	?	N	Y	Y	Y	Y	Y	Y
2 Long	?	N	Y	Y	Y	Y	Y	N
3 Mikulski	Y	N	Y	Y	Y	Y	Y	N
4 ***Holt***	Y	N	Y	N	N	Y	Y	N
5 Hoyer	Y	N	Y	Y	Y	Y	Y	N
6 Byron	?	N	Y	Y	N	Y	Y	N
7 Mitchell	?	N	Y	Y	Y	Y	Y	N
8 Barnes	Y	N	Y	Y	Y	Y	Y	N
MASSACHUSETTS								
1 ***Conte***	Y	N	Y	Y	Y	Y	Y	N
2 Boland	Y	?	Y	Y	Y	Y	Y	N
3 Early	Y	?	Y	Y	Y	Y	Y	N
4 Frank	Y	N	Y	Y	Y	Y	Y	N
5 Shannon	Y	N	Y	Y	Y	N	Y	N
6 Mavroules	?	?	?	?	?	?	?	?
7 Markey	?	N	Y	Y	Y	Y	Y	N
8 O'Neill								
9 Moakley	Y	N	?	?	?	?	?	?
10 ***Heckler***	?	?	Y	N	?	?	?	N
11 Donnelly	Y	N	Y	Y	Y	Y	Y	Y
12 Studds	Y	N	Y	Y	N	Y	Y	N
MICHIGAN								
1 Conyers	?	N	?	?	?	?	?	?
2 ***Pursell***	?	?	?	?	?	?	N	N
3 Wolpe	Y	N	Y	Y	Y	Y	Y	N
4 ***Siljander***	Y	?	Y	N	N	N	Y	N
5 ***Sawyer***	Y	N	Y	N	N	Y	Y	N
6 ***Dunn***	Y	N	Y	N	Y	Y	Y	N
7 Kildee	Y	N	Y	Y	Y	Y	Y	N
8 Traxler	?	N	Y	Y	Y	Y	Y	N
9 ***Vander Jagt***	?	?	Y	N	N	N	Y	N
10 Albosta	Y	N	?	?	?	?	?	?
11 ***Davis***	Y	N	Y	Y	Y	Y	Y	Y
12 Bonior	Y	N	Y	Y	Y	Y	Y	N
13 Crockett	?	N	?	?	?	?	?	?
14 Hertel	?	N	Y	Y	Y	Y	Y	N
15 Ford	Y	N	Y	Y	Y	Y	Y	Y
16 Dingell	Y	N	Y	Y	Y	Y	Y	Y
17 Brodhead	Y	N	Y	Y	Y	Y	Y	N
18 Blanchard	?	?	?	?	?	?	?	?
19 ***Broomfield***	Y	N	Y	N	N	Y	Y	N
MINNESOTA								
1 ***Erdahl***	Y	N	Y	Y	N	Y	Y	N
2 ***Hagedorn***	Y	N	Y	N	N	Y	Y	Y
3 ***Frenzel***	Y	N	Y	N	N	Y	Y	N
4 Vento	Y	N	Y	Y	Y	Y	Y	N
5 Sabo	N	N	Y	Y	Y	Y	Y	N
6 ***Weber***	Y	N	Y	N	N	N	Y	N
7 ***Stangeland***	?	N	Y	N	N	Y	Y	N
8 Oberstar	Y	N	Y	Y	Y	Y	Y	N
MISSISSIPPI								
1 Whitten	Y	N	Y	N	N	Y	Y	N
2 Bowen	Y	N	Y	Y	N	Y	Y	N
3 Montgomery	Y	N	Y	Y	N	Y	Y	N
4 Dowdy	Y	N	Y	Y	Y	Y	Y	N
5 ***Lott***	?	N	Y	N	N	Y	N	N
MISSOURI								
1 Clay	N	N	Y	Y	Y	Y	Y	N
2 Young	Y	N	Y	Y	Y	Y	Y	N
3 Gephardt	Y	N	Y	Y	Y	Y	Y	N

	408	409	410	411	412	413	414	415
4 Skelton	Y	N	Y	Y	Y	Y	Y	Y
5 Bolling	?	?	?	?	?	?	?	?
6 ***Coleman***	?	N	Y	N	Y	Y	Y	N
7 ***Taylor***	Y	N	Y	N	N	Y	Y	N
8 ***Bailey***	N	N	Y	N	N	N	N	N
9 Volkmer	Y	N	Y	Y	Y	Y	Y	N
10 ***Emerson***	?	N	Y	N	N	Y	Y	N
MONTANA								
1 Williams	?	N	Y	Y	Y	Y	Y	Y
2 ***Marlenee***	Y	N	Y	N	Y	N	Y	Y
NEBRASKA								
1 ***Bereuter***	Y	N	Y	N	Y	Y	Y	Y
2 ***Daub***	Y	N	Y	N	N	Y	Y	N
3 ***Smith***	Y	N	Y	N	N	Y	Y	Y
NEVADA								
AL Santini	?	N	Y	Y	Y	Y	Y	Y
NEW HAMPSHIRE								
1 D'Amours	Y	N	Y	Y	Y	Y	Y	N
2 ***Gregg***	N	N	Y	N	N	N	Y	N
NEW JERSEY								
1 Florio	Y	N	Y	Y	Y	N	Y	N
2 Hughes	Y	N	Y	Y	Y	Y	Y	N
3 Howard	Y	N	Y	Y	Y	Y	Y	N
4 ***Smith***	Y	N	Y	Y	N	Y	Y	N
5 ***Fenwick***	Y	N	Y	N	N	Y	Y	N
6 ***Forsythe***	N	?	Y	N	N	Y	N	N
7 ***Roukema***	?	N	Y	N	Y	Y	Y	N
8 Roe	?	N	Y	Y	Y	Y	Y	Y
9 ***Hollenbeck***	?	N	Y	Y	Y	Y	Y	N
10 Rodino	Y	N	Y	Y	Y	Y	Y	N
11 Minish	Y	N	Y	Y	Y	Y	Y	N
12 ***Rinaldo***	?	N	Y	Y	Y	Y	Y	N
13 ***Courter***	Y	N	Y	N	N	Y	Y	N
14 Guarini	Y	N	Y	Y	?	Y	Y	N
15 Dwyer	Y	N	Y	Y	Y	Y	Y	N
NEW MEXICO								
1 ***Lujan***	Y	N	Y	N	Y	Y	Y	Y
2 ***Skeen***	Y	N	Y	Y	Y	Y	Y	N
NEW YORK								
1 ***Carney***	?	?	?	?	?	?	?	?
2 Downey	Y	N	Y	Y	Y	Y	Y	N
3 ***Carman***	Y	?	Y	N	N	N	Y	N
4 ***Lent***	?	N	?	?	?	?	?	?
5 ***McGrath***	Y	N	Y	N	N	Y	Y	N
6 ***LeBoutillier***	Y	N	Y	N	N	N	Y	N
7 Addabbo	Y	?	Y	Y	Y	Y	Y	N
8 Rosenthal	Y	N	?	?	?	?	?	?
9 Ferraro	Y	N	Y	Y	Y	Y	Y	N
10 Biaggi	?	?	Y	Y	Y	Y	Y	N
11 Scheuer	Y	N	Y	Y	Y	Y	Y	N
12 Chisholm	?	?	?	?	?	?	?	?
13 Solarz	Y	N	Y	Y	Y	Y	Y	N
14 Vacancy								
15 Zeferetti	?	?	Y	Y	Y	Y	Y	N
16 Schumer	Y	N	Y	Y	Y	Y	Y	N
17 ***Molinari***	Y	N	Y	N	N	Y	Y	N
18 ***Green***	Y	N	?	?	?	?	?	?
19 Rangel	Y	N	Y	Y	Y	Y	Y	N
20 Weiss	?	?	Y	Y	Y	Y	Y	N
21 Garcia	?	?	Y	Y	Y	Y	Y	N
22 Bingham	?	?	Y	Y	Y	Y	Y	Y
23 Peyser	Y	N	Y	Y	N	Y	Y	N
24 Ottinger	P	N	Y	Y	Y	N	Y	N
25 ***Fish***	Y	N	Y	N	Y	Y	Y	N
26 ***Gilman***	Y	N	Y	Y	Y	Y	Y	N
27 McHugh	Y	N	Y	Y	Y	Y	Y	N
28 Stratton	Y	Y	Y	N	N	N	Y	N
29 ***Solomon***	N	?	Y	N	N	Y	Y	N
30 ***Martin***	Y	?	Y	N	N	Y	Y	N
31 ***Mitchell***	?	?	?	?	?	?	?	?
32 ***Wortley***	Y	Y	Y	N	N	Y	Y	N
33 ***Lee***	?	?	Y	N	N	Y	Y	N
34 ***Horton***	Y	N	Y	Y	N	Y	Y	N
35 ***Conable***	Y	N	Y	N	N	Y	Y	N
36 LaFalce	?	N	Y	Y	Y	Y	Y	N
37 Nowak	Y	N	Y	Y	Y	Y	Y	N
38 ***Kemp***	?	?	Y	N	N	N	Y	N
39 Lundine	Y	N	Y	Y	Y	Y	Y	N
NORTH CAROLINA								
1 Jones	Y	?	Y	Y	Y	Y	Y	Y
2 Fountain	Y	N	Y	N	N	Y	Y	N
3 Whitley	Y	?	Y	Y	N	Y	Y	N
4 Andrews	Y	N	Y	Y	Y	Y	Y	N
5 Neal	?	N	?	?	?	?	?	?
6 ***Johnston***	?	Y	N	N	N	N	N	N
7 Rose	?	?	Y	Y	Y	Y	Y	N
8 Hefner	Y	N	Y	Y	Y	Y	Y	N

	408	409	410	411	412	413	414	415
9 ***Martin***	Y	N	?	?	?	?	?	?
10 ***Broyhill***	Y	N	Y	N	N	Y	Y	N
11 ***Hendon***	Y	N	Y	N	N	Y	Y	N
NORTH DAKOTA								
AL Dorgan	Y	N	Y	Y	Y	Y	Y	N
OHIO								
1 ***Gradison***	Y	N	Y	N	N	Y	Y	N
2 Luken	N	N	Y	Y	Y	Y	Y	N
3 Hall	Y	N	Y	Y	Y	Y	Y	N
4 ***Oxley***	N	N	Y	?	N	N	N	N
5 ***Latta***	Y	N	Y	N	N	Y	Y	N
6 ***McEwen***	Y	N	Y	N	Y	N	Y	N
7 ***Brown***	Y	N	Y	N	N	Y	N	N
8 ***Kindness***	Y	N	Y	N	N	N	N	N
9 ***Weber***	Y	N	Y	N	N	Y	Y	N
10 ***Miller***	N	N	Y	N	N	N	Y	N
11 ***Stanton***	?	?	?	?	?	?	?	?
12 Shamansky	Y	N	Y	Y	Y	Y	Y	N
13 Pease	Y	N	Y	Y	Y	Y	Y	N
14 Seiberling	?	N	Y	Y	Y	N	Y	Y
15 ***Wylie***	?	?	Y	N	N	Y	Y	N
16 ***Regula***	Y	N	Y	N	N	Y	Y	N
17 ***Ashbrook***	Y	N	Y	N	N	N	N	N
18 Applegate	?	N	Y	N	Y	Y	Y	Y
19 ***Williams***	?	N	Y	Y	Y	Y	Y	N
20 Oakar	Y	N	Y	Y	N	Y	Y	N
21 Stokes	Y	N	Y	Y	Y	Y	Y	N
22 Eckart	Y	N	Y	Y	Y	Y	Y	N
23 Mottl	?	?	Y	Y	Y	Y	Y	N
OKLAHOMA								
1 Jones	Y	N	Y	Y	N	Y	Y	N
2 Synar	Y	N	Y	Y	Y	Y	Y	N
3 Watkins	Y	N	Y	Y	N	Y	Y	N
4 McCurdy	Y	N	Y	Y	Y	Y	Y	N
5 ***Edwards***	Y	N	Y	N	N	Y	Y	N
6 English	Y	N	Y	Y	N	Y	Y	N
OREGON								
1 AuCoin	?	N	Y	Y	Y	Y	Y	Y
2 ***Smith***	Y	N	Y	N	N	N	N	N
3 Wyden	Y	N	Y	Y	Y	Y	Y	N
4 Weaver	Y	N	Y	Y	Y	Y	Y	Y
PENNSYLVANIA								
1 Foglietta	Y	N	Y	Y	Y	Y	Y	N
2 Gray	Y	N	Y	Y	Y	Y	Y	N
3 Smith	?	?	?	?	?	?	?	?
4 ***Dougherty***	?	?	?	?	?	?	?	?
5 ***Schulze***	Y	?	Y	N	N	Y	Y	N
6 Yatron	Y	N	Y	Y	Y	Y	Y	N
7 Edgar	?	N	Y	Y	Y	Y	Y	N
8 ***Coyne, J.***	Y	N	Y	N	N	Y	Y	N
9 ***Shuster***	?	?	?	?	?	?	?	?
10 ***McDade***	Y	N	Y	N	Y	Y	Y	N
11 ***Nelligan***	?	?	Y	Y	N	Y	Y	N
12 Murtha	Y	N	Y	Y	Y	Y	Y	N
13 ***Coughlin***	N	N	Y	N	N	Y	Y	N
14 Coyne, W.	Y	N	Y	Y	Y	Y	Y	N
15 ***Ritter***	Y	Y	Y	N	Y	Y	Y	N
16 ***Walker***	N	?	Y	N	N	Y	Y	N
17 Ertel	Y	N	?	?	?	?	?	?
18 Walgren	?	N	Y	Y	Y	Y	Y	N
19 ***Goodling***	N	N	Y	N	Y	Y	Y	N
20 Gaydos	?	?	Y	Y	Y	Y	Y	N
21 Bailey	Y	N	Y	Y	Y	Y	Y	Y
22 Murphy	Y	N	Y	Y	Y	Y	N	Y
23 ***Clinger***	Y	N	Y	Y	Y	Y	Y	N
24 ***Marks***	?	N	Y	N	N	Y	Y	Y
25 ***Atkinson***	Y	?	?	?	?	?	?	?
RHODE ISLAND								
1 St Germain	P	?	Y	Y	Y	Y	Y	?
2 ***Schneider***	Y	N	Y	Y	Y	Y	Y	N
SOUTH CAROLINA								
1 ***Hartnett***	Y	N	?	?	?	?	?	?
2 ***Spence***	Y	N	Y	N	N	Y	Y	N
3 Derrick	?	N	Y	Y	Y	Y	Y	N
4 ***Campbell***	Y	N	Y	N	N	Y	Y	N
5 Holland	Y	?	?	?	?	?	?	?
6 ***Napier***	?	Y	Y	N	N	Y	Y	N
SOUTH DAKOTA								
1 Daschle	?	N	Y	Y	Y	Y	Y	Y
2 ***Roberts***	?	?	Y	N	N	Y	N	N
TENNESSEE								
1 ***Quillen***	Y	?	Y	N	N	N	Y	N
2 ***Duncan***	?	?	Y	N	Y	Y	Y	N
3 Bouquard	Y	N	Y	Y	Y	Y	Y	Y
4 Gore	Y	N	Y	Y	Y	N	Y	N
5 Boner	Y	N	Y	Y	Y	Y	Y	Y
6 ***Beard***	?	N	Y	N	N	N	Y	N

	408	409	410	411	412	413	414	415
7 Jones	Y	N	Y	Y	Y	Y	Y	Y
8 Ford	Y	N	Y	Y	Y	Y	Y	Y
TEXAS								
1 Hall, S.	Y	N	Y	N	N	Y	Y	Y
2 Wilson	Y	N	?	?	Y	Y	N	N
3 ***Collins***	Y	N	N	N	N	N	N	N
4 Hall, R.	Y	N	N	N	Y	Y	Y	N
5 Mattox	?	?	Y	Y	Y	Y	Y	N
6 Gramm	?	?	Y	N	N	N	Y	N
7 ***Archer***	Y	N	Y	N	N	N	Y	N
8 ***Fields***	Y	N	Y	N	N	N	Y	N
9 Brooks	Y	N	?	?	?	?	?	?
10 Pickle	Y	N	Y	Y	Y	Y	Y	N
11 Leath	Y	N	Y	N	N	N	Y	N
12 Wright	Y	N	Y	Y	Y	Y	Y	Y
13 Hightower	Y	?	Y	N	N	Y	Y	Y
14 Patman	Y	N	Y	Y	Y	Y	Y	N
15 de la Garza	Y	N	Y	Y	Y	Y	Y	Y
16 White	?	?	Y	Y	Y	Y	Y	Y
17 Stenholm	?	?	Y	N	N	Y	Y	N
18 Leland	Y	N	Y	Y	Y	Y	Y	Y
19 Hance	Y	N	Y	Y	Y	N	Y	N
20 Gonzalez	Y	N	Y	Y	Y	P	Y	Y
21 ***Loeffler***	Y	N	Y	N	N	N	Y	N
22 ***Paul***	Y	N	N	N	N	N	N	N
23 Kazen	Y	N	Y	Y	Y	Y	Y	Y
24 Frost	Y	N	?	?	?	?	?	?
UTAH								
1 ***Hansen***	N	N	Y	N	N	N	Y	Y
2 ***Marriott***	Y	N	?	?	Y	Y	Y	N
VERMONT								
AL ***Jeffords***	?	?	Y	Y	N	Y	Y	N
VIRGINIA								
1 ***Trible***	?	N	Y	N	N	Y	Y	N
2 ***Whitehurst***	Y	?	Y	N	N	Y	Y	N
3 ***Bliley***	Y	N	-	-	-	-	-	-
4 ***Daniel, R.***	Y	N	Y	N	N	Y	Y	N
5 Daniel, D.	Y	N	N	N	N	Y	Y	N
6 ***Butler***	N	N	N	N	N	N	N	N
7 ***Robinson***	Y	N	N	N	N	Y	Y	N
8 ***Parris***	Y	N	Y	N	N	Y	Y	N
9 ***Wampler***	Y	N	Y	N	N	Y	Y	N
10 ***Wolf***	Y	N	Y	N	Y	Y	Y	N
WASHINGTON								
1 ***Pritchard***	Y	N	Y	Y	N	Y	Y	N
2 Swift	Y	N	Y	Y	Y	N	Y	N
3 Bonker	P	N	Y	Y	Y	Y	Y	Y
4 ***Morrison***	Y	N	Y	N	N	Y	Y	N
5 Foley	Y	N	Y	Y	Y	Y	Y	Y
6 Dicks	Y	N	Y	Y	Y	Y	Y	N
7 Lowry	Y	N	Y	Y	Y	Y	Y	N
WEST VIRGINIA								
1 Mollohan	?	N	Y	Y	Y	Y	Y	N
2 ***Benedict***	?	N	Y	N	N	Y	N	N
3 ***Staton***	Y	N	Y	N	Y	N	N	N
4 Rahall	?	N	Y	Y	Y	Y	Y	Y
WISCONSIN								
1 Aspin	Y	N	?	?	?	?	?	?
2 Kastenmeier	Y	N	Y	Y	Y	Y	Y	Y
3 ***Gunderson***	Y	N	Y	N	N	Y	Y	N
4 Zablocki	Y	N	Y	Y	Y	Y	Y	N
5 Reuss	?	?	Y	Y	Y	Y	Y	N
6 ***Petri***	Y	N	Y	Y	N	Y	Y	N
7 Obey	Y	N	Y	Y	Y	Y	Y	Y
8 ***Roth***	Y	N	Y	N	N	Y	Y	N
9 ***Sensenbrenner***	Y	N	Y	N	N	Y	Y	N
WYOMING								
AL ***Cheney***	Y	N	Y	N	N	Y	N	N

Southern states - Ala., Ark., Fla., Ga., Ky., La., Miss., N.C., Okla., S.C., Tenn., Texas, Va.

KEY

Y Voted for (yea).
\# Paired for.
\+ Announced for.
N Voted against (nay).
X Paired against.
− Announced against.
P Voted "present".
C Voted "present" to avoid possible conflict of interest.
? Did not vote or otherwise make a position known.

Democrats   *Republicans*

---

416. HR 3191. North American Convention Tax. Stark, D-Calif., motion to suspend the rules and pass the bill to allow certain tax deductions for business conventions held on North American cruise ships. Motion rejected 219-164: R 67-103; D 152-61 (ND 106-39, SD 46-22), Dec. 13, 1982. A two-thirds majority of those present and voting (256 in this case) is required for passage under suspension of the rules.

417. H J Res 553. Indian Tribes Legal Claims. Udall, D-Ariz., motion to suspend the rules and pass the joint resolution to extend the time limit for American Indian tribes to bring legal damage suits in cases arising prior to 1966. Motion rejected 228-153: R 47-123; D 181-30 (ND 130-13, SD 51-17), Dec. 13, 1982. A two-thirds majority of those present and voting (254 in this case) is required for passage under suspension of the rules.

418. H J Res 631. Continuing Appropriations, Fiscal 1983. Adoption of the rule (H Res 626) providing for House floor consideration of the joint resolution to provide temporary funding for various government agencies and to provide $5.4 billion for jobs programs. Adopted 223-163: R 35-137; D 188-26 (ND 134-13, SD 54-13), Dec. 14, 1982.

419. H J Res 631. Continuing Appropriations, Fiscal 1983. Simon, D-Ill., amendment to require that at least 50 percent of Agency for International Development bilateral assistance funds be used to finance projects that benefit those living in absolute poverty. Adopted 227-184: R 48-136; D 179-48 (ND 133-20, SD 46-28), Dec. 14, 1982. A "nay" was a vote supporting the president's position.

420. H J Res 631. Continuing Appropriations, Fiscal 1983/Pay Raise. Fazio, D-Calif., amendment to increase pay for members of Congress by 15 percent, to $69,800, and to provide pay increases of varying percentages for senior-level federal officials and employees. Adopted 303-109: R 106-78; D 197-31 (ND 133-20, SD 64-11), Dec. 14, 1982.

421. H J Res 631. Continuing Appropriations, Fiscal 1983/Pay Raise. Traxler, D-Mich., amendment to retain the existing cap on salaries of members of Congress at $60,662.50 a year. Rejected 208-208: R 121-65; D 87-143 (ND 46-109, SD 41-34), Dec. 14, 1982.

422. H J Res 631. Continuing Appropriations, Fiscal 1983/Clinch River. Coughlin, R-Pa., amendment to bar use of funds provided by the joint resolution for research and development, design or construction of the Clinch River breeder reactor. Adopted 217-196: R 80-102; D 137-94 (ND 121-33, SD 16-61), Dec. 14, 1982. A "nay" was a vote supporting the president's position.

423. H J Res 631. Continuing Appropriations, Fiscal 1983. Bonior, D-Mich., amendment to bar use of funds in the resolution for construction of the O'Neill irrigation unit in Nebraska. Adopted 245-144: R 89-79; D 156-65 (ND 126-21, SD 30-44), Dec. 14, 1982.

	416	417	418	419	420	421	422	423
ALABAMA								
1 *Edwards*	Y	Y	N	N	Y	Y	N	N
2 *Dickinson*	N	N	N	Y	N	Y	N	N
3 Nichols	Y	Y	?	N	Y	Y	N	N
4 Bevill	Y	Y	Y	N	Y	Y	N	N
5 Flippo	Y	Y	Y	N	Y	Y	N	N
6 *Smith*	N	N	N	N	Y	Y	N	N
7 Shelby	N	N	N	N	N	Y	N	N
ALASKA								
AL *Young*	Y	Y	N	N	?	N	N	N
ARIZONA								
1 *Rhodes*	?	?	N	N	Y	N	?	?
2 Udall	Y	Y	Y	Y	Y	N	Y	Y
3 *Stump*	N	N	Y	N	Y	Y	N	N
4 *Rudd*	N	N	N	N	N	Y	N	N
ARKANSAS								
1 Alexander	Y	Y	Y	Y	Y	N	N	N
2 *Bethune*	N	N	N	N	Y	Y	N	N
3 *Hammerschmidt*	N	N	N	Y	Y	Y	N	N
4 Anthony	Y	N	?	Y	Y	N	N	Y
CALIFORNIA								
1 *Chappie*	?	?	?	?	?	?	?	?
2 *Clausen*	Y	Y	N	N	N	Y	N	N
3 Matsui	Y	Y	Y	Y	Y	Y	N	Y
4 Fazio	Y	Y	Y	N	Y	N	Y	Y
5 Burton, J.	Y	Y	?	?	?	?	?	?
6 Burton, P.	Y	Y	Y	Y	Y	N	Y	?
7 Miller	Y	Y	Y	Y	Y	N	Y	Y
8 Dellums	Y	Y	Y	Y	Y	N	Y	Y
9 Stark	Y	N	Y	Y	N	Y	N	?
10 Edwards	Y	Y	Y	Y	Y	N	Y	Y
11 Lantos	Y	Y	Y	Y	N	Y	N	Y
12 *McCloskey*	Y	Y	N	Y	Y	N	Y	Y
13 Mineta	Y	Y	Y	Y	Y	N	Y	Y
14 *Shumway*	N	N	N	N	N	Y	Y	Y
15 Coelho	Y	Y	Y	Y	Y	N	Y	Y
16 Panetta	Y	Y	Y	Y	Y	Y	Y	Y
17 Pashayan	Y	Y	Y	N	Y	Y	N	?
18 Thomas	N	N	N	Y	N	Y	N	Y
19 *Lagomarsino*	N	Y	N	N	N	Y	N	Y
20 *Goldwater*	?	?	?	?	Y	?	N	?
21 *Fiedler*	N	Y	Y	N	Y	N	N	Y
22 *Moorhead*	?	?	N	Y	N	Y	N	Y
23 Beilenson	?	?	?	#	?	?	?	?
24 Waxman	N	Y	Y	Y	Y	Y	Y	Y
25 Roybal	Y	Y	Y	Y	Y	N	Y	Y
26 *Rousselot*	Y	N	N	Y	N	N	N	N
27 *Dornan*	N	N	N	N	N	Y	N	N
28 Dixon	Y	Y	Y	N	Y	N	Y	?
29 Hawkins	Y	Y	Y	Y	Y	N	Y	Y
30 Martinez	?	?	?	?	?	?	?	N
31 Dymally	Y	Y	?	Y	Y	N	Y	Y
32 Anderson	Y	Y	Y	Y	N	Y	N	Y
33 Grisham	N	N	Y	N	N	Y	N	Y
34 *Lungren*	?	?	N	N	Y	N	Y	Y
35 *Dreier*	Y	N	N	N	N	Y	N	Y
36 Brown	Y	Y	#	Y	Y	N	Y	Y
37 *Lewis*	N	N	Y	N	Y	N	N	N
38 Patterson	N	Y	Y	Y	Y	Y	N	Y
39 *Dannemeyer*	N	N	N	N	N	Y	N	N
40 *Badham*	Y	N	N	N	Y	N	N	N
41 *Lowery*	N	N	N	N	Y	N	N	N
42 *Hunter*	N	N	?	Y	N	Y	N	Y
43 *Burgener*	N	Y	N	N	Y	N	N	N
COLORADO								
1 Schroeder	Y	Y	N	Y	N	Y	Y	Y
2 Wirth	N	Y	Y	Y	N	Y	Y	Y
3 Kogovsek	Y	Y	Y	Y	Y	Y	Y	N
4 *Brown*	N	N	N	Y	N	Y	N	Y

	416	417	418	419	420	421	422	423
5 *Kramer*	N	Y	N	N	N	Y	Y	N
CONNECTICUT								
1 Kennelly	Y	Y	Y	Y	Y	N	Y	Y
2 Gejdenson	Y	Y	Y	Y	Y	N	Y	Y
3 *DeNardis*	Y	Y	?	Y	N	Y	?	?
4 *McKinney*	N	Y	Y	N	Y	N	Y	Y
5 Ratchford	Y	Y	Y	Y	Y	N	Y	Y
6 Moffett	?	?	?	Y	N	Y	Y	Y
DELAWARE								
AL *Evans*	?	?	?	N	Y	N	Y	Y
FLORIDA								
1 Hutto	Y	N	N	Y	N	N	N	Y
2 Fuqua	Y	N	Y	Y	Y	Y	N	Y
3 Bennett	Y	Y	Y	Y	Y	Y	N	N
4 Chappell	?	?	?	N	Y	N	N	N
5 *McCollum*	N	N	N	N	Y	Y	N	N
6 *Young*	N	N	N	N	Y	Y	N	N
7 Gibbons	Y	Y	Y	N	Y	N	N	N
8 Ireland	?	?	?	N	N	Y	N	?
9 Nelson	Y	Y	Y	N	Y	N	Y	?
10 *Bafalis*	Y	N	N	N	N	N	N	N
11 Mica	Y	Y	Y	N	Y	N	N	N
12 *Shaw*	N	N	N	N	Y	Y	Y	Y
13 Lehman	?	?	?	?	?	?	?	?
14 Pepper	Y	Y	Y	Y	Y	N	N	N
15 Fascell	?	?	Y	N	N	Y	Y	Y
GEORGIA								
1 Ginn	N	Y	N	N	Y	N	N	Y
2 Hatcher	?	?	Y	N	N	Y	N	N
3 Brinkley	Y	Y	Y	Y	Y	N	N	Y
4 Levitas	N	Y	N	Y	N	Y	N	Y
5 Fowler	?	?	Y	N	Y	N	Y	Y
6 *Gingrich*	N	N	?	Y	Y	Y	Y	Y
7 McDonald	Y	N	N	N	N	N	N	N
8 Evans	Y	N	Y	N	?	?	?	?
9 Jenkins	?	?	N	Y	N	Y	Y	Y
10 Barnard	N	N	Y	N	N	Y	N	N
HAWAII								
1 Heftel	Y	N	Y	N	Y	N	N	Y
2 Akaka	Y	Y	Y	Y	Y	N	N	N
IDAHO								
1 *Craig*	N	N	N	N	Y	N	Y	N
2 *Hansen*	N	N	N	N	Y	Y	N	N
ILLINOIS								
1 Washington	?	?	Y	Y	Y	?	Y	Y
2 Savage	?	?	?	Y	Y	N	Y	Y
3 Russo	Y	Y	Y	Y	Y	N	Y	Y
4 *Derwinski*	?	?	?	Y	N	Y	Y	Y
5 Fary	Y	Y	Y	X	?	?	?	?
6 *Hyde*	Y	N	N	N	Y	N	N	Y
7 Collins	Y	Y	Y	Y	Y	N	Y	Y
8 Rostenkowski	Y	Y	Y	Y	Y	N	Y	Y
9 Yates	N	Y	Y	Y	Y	N	Y	Y
10 *Porter*	N	N	N	Y	N	Y	N	Y
11 Annunzio	Y	Y	Y	Y	Y	N	Y	Y
12 *Crane, P.*	Y	N	N	N	N	Y	N	Y
13 *McClory*	N	Y	Y	N	Y	N	N	Y
14 *Erlenborn*	Y	N	Y	N	Y	N	N	Y
15 *Corcoran*	N	N	N	N	Y	N	N	Y
16 *Martin*	N	N	N	Y	N	Y	N	Y
17 *O'Brien*	N	Y	N	Y	N	Y	N	?
18 *Michel*	N	N	Y	N	N	Y	N	N
19 *Railsback*	?	?	?	?	?	?	?	?
20 Findley	N	N	N	N	Y	N	Y	Y
21 Madigan	N	?	Y	Y	N	Y	N	N
22 *Crane, D.*	Y	N	N	N	Y	Y	N	N
23 Price	Y	Y	Y	N	Y	N	N	?
24 Simon	Y	Y	Y	Y	Y	N	Y	Y
INDIANA								
1 Hall	Y	Y	Y	Y	Y	N	Y	N
2 Fithian	Y	N	?	Y	Y	N	?	N
3 *Hiler*	N	Y	N	N	Y	Y	Y	Y
4 *Coats*	N	Y	N	N	Y	Y	Y	Y
5 *Hillis*	Y	N	N	Y	Y	N	N	Y
6 Evans	Y	Y	?	Y	N	N	Y	Y
7 *Myers*	N	Y	N	N	Y	N	N	N
8 *Deckard*	N	Y	?	N	Y	Y	?	?
9 Hamilton	N	Y	N	Y	N	Y	Y	Y
10 Sharp	N	Y	N	Y	N	Y	Y	Y
11 Jacobs	N	Y	?	Y	N	Y	Y	Y
IOWA								
1 *Leach*	N	Y	N	Y	N	Y	Y	?
2 *Tauke*	N	N	N	Y	N	Y	Y	Y
3 *Evans*	N	Y	N	Y	N	N	Y	Y
4 *Smith*	N	Y	Y	Y	N	N	N	N
5 Harkin	N	Y	Y	N	Y	N	Y	Y
6 Bedell	N	Y	Y	Y	N	Y	Y	Y

ND - Northern Democrats   SD - Southern Democrats

Corresponding to Congressional Record Votes 441, 442, 443, 444, 445, 446, 447, 448

	416	417	418	419	420	421	422	423
KANSAS								
1 ***Roberts***	N	N	N	Y	Y	Y	N	N
2 ***Jeffries***	Y	N	N	N	N	Y	Y	Y
3 ***Winn***	N	N	N	N	Y	N	N	?
4 Glickman	N	Y	N	Y	Y	Y	Y	Y
5 ***Whittaker***	N	N	N	Y	Y	Y	Y	N
KENTUCKY								
1 Hubbard	Y	N	N	Y	Y	Y	N	N
2 Natcher	Y	Y	Y	Y	N	Y	N	N
3 Mazzoli	N	Y	Y	N	Y	N	N	N
4 ***Snyder***	Y	N	Y	N	N	Y	Y	N
5 ***Rogers***	N	N	Y	N	N	Y	Y	N
6 ***Hopkins***	N	N	N	N	N	Y	Y	N
7 Perkins	Y	Y	Y	Y	Y	Y	N	N
LOUISIANA								
1 ***Livingston***	Y	N	Y	N	Y	N	N	N
2 Boggs	Y	Y	Y	Y	Y	N	N	N
3 Tauzin	Y	Y	Y	Y	Y	Y	N	Y
4 Roemer	N	Y	Y	N	Y	Y	Y	Y
5 Huckaby	N	N	Y	Y	Y	Y	Y	Y
6 ***Moore***	Y	N	N	N	N	Y	Y	Y
7 Breaux	Y	Y	Y	N	Y	N	N	N
8 Long	Y	Y	Y	Y	Y	N	N	N
MAINE								
1 ***Emery***	?	?	N	Y	Y	Y	Y	Y
2 ***Snowe***	N	N	X	Y	Y	Y	Y	N
MARYLAND								
1 Dyson	Y	Y	Y	N	N	Y	N	N
2 Long	Y	Y	Y	Y	Y	Y	Y	Y
3 Mikulski	Y	Y	Y	Y	Y	Y	Y	Y
4 ***Holt***	Y	N	N	?	N	N	N	N
5 Hoyer	Y	Y	Y	Y	Y	N	Y	Y
6 Byron	N	N	Y	N	N	Y	Y	Y
7 Mitchell	Y	Y	Y	Y	N	Y	Y	Y
8 Barnes	Y	Y	Y	Y	Y	N	Y	Y
MASSACHUSETTS								
1 ***Conte***	Y	N	Y	Y	Y	N	Y	Y
2 Boland	Y	Y	Y	N	Y	Y	Y	Y
3 Early	Y	Y	N	Y	Y	N	Y	Y
4 Frank	Y	Y	Y	Y	Y	Y	Y	Y
5 Shannon	N	Y	Y	Y	Y	N	Y	Y
6 Mavroules	?	?	Y	Y	Y	N	Y	Y
7 Markey	Y	Y	Y	Y	Y	N	Y	Y
8 O'Neill						N		
9 Moakley	?	?	Y	Y	Y	N	Y	Y
10 ***Heckler***	Y	Y	?	Y	Y	N	Y	N
11 Donnelly	Y	Y	Y	Y	Y	N	Y	N
12 Studds	Y	Y	Y	Y	Y	N	Y	Y
MICHIGAN								
1 Conyers	?	?	Y	Y	Y	N	Y	?
2 ***Pursell***	?	Y	N	Y	N	Y	Y	N
3 Wolpe	N	Y	Y	Y	Y	Y	Y	Y
4 ***Siljander***	Y	Y	N	N	N	Y	N	Y
5 ***Sawyer***	Y	N	Y	N	N	Y	Y	Y
6 ***Dunn***	N	N	N	N	Y	Y	Y	Y
7 Kildee	N	Y	Y	Y	Y	Y	Y	Y
8 Traxler	Y	Y	Y	Y	Y	Y	Y	Y
9 ***Vander Jagt***	Y	N	Y	N	Y	Y	Y	Y
10 Albosta	?	?	?	?	?	Y	Y	N
11 ***Davis***	Y	Y	N	Y	N	Y	N	N
12 Bonior	Y	Y	Y	Y	Y	Y	Y	Y
13 Crockett	?	?	?	Y	Y	N	Y	Y
14 Hertel	Y	?	Y	Y	Y	Y	Y	Y
15 Ford	Y	Y	Y	Y	Y	N	Y	Y
16 Dingell	Y	N	Y	Y	N	Y	Y	Y
17 Brodhead	N	Y	?	Y	Y	N	Y	Y
18 Blanchard	?	?	?	?	?	?	?	?
19 ***Broomfield***	N	N	N	N	?	N	Y	N
MINNESOTA								
1 ***Erdahl***	N	Y	Y	N	Y	Y	?	Y
2 ***Hagedorn***	Y	N	?	?	?	?	?	?
3 ***Frenzel***	N	N	N	Y	Y	N	Y	Y
4 Vento	Y	Y	Y	Y	Y	N	Y	Y
5 Sabo	N	Y	Y	Y	Y	N	Y	Y
6 ***Weber***	N	Y	Y	N	Y	Y	Y	Y
7 ***Stangeland***	Y	N	N	N	Y	Y	N	N
8 Oberstar	Y	Y	Y	Y	Y	N	Y	Y
MISSISSIPPI								
1 Whitten	Y	Y	Y	Y	N	N	N	N
2 Bowen	N	Y	Y	N	Y	N	N	N
3 Montgomery	N	N	?	?	?	?	N	N
4 Dowdy	Y	Y	Y	Y	Y	N	N	N
5 ***Lott***	Y	N	Y	N	Y	N	Y	N
MISSOURI								
1 Clay	Y	Y	Y	Y	Y	N	Y	Y
2 Young	Y	Y	Y	Y	Y	N	N	N
3 Gephardt	Y	Y	Y	N	Y	Y	Y	Y

	416	417	418	419	420	421	422	423
4 Skelton	N	N	N	N	Y	N	N	N
5 Bolling	?	?	Y	Y	?	N	?	?
6 ***Coleman***	N	Y	N	N	Y	N	N	N
7 ***Taylor***	N	N	N	Y	Y	Y	N	N
8 ***Bailey***	N	N	N	N	N	Y	Y	Y
9 Volkmer	N	Y	N	Y	N	Y	Y	Y
10 ***Emerson***	N	N	N	N	Y	Y	N	N
MONTANA								
1 Williams	Y	Y	Y	Y	Y	N	Y	Y
2 ***Marlenee***	Y	N	N	N	Y	N	N	N
NEBRASKA								
1 ***Bereuter***	N	Y	Y	N	Y	Y	N	Y
2 ***Daub***	N	N	N	Y	N	Y	N	N
3 ***Smith***	N	N	N	N	N	Y	N	N
NEVADA								
AL Santini	N	Y	Y	Y	N	Y	N	Y
NEW HAMPSHIRE								
1 D'Amours	N	Y	Y	Y	N	Y	Y	Y
2 ***Gregg***	N	Y	Y	N	N	Y	Y	N
NEW JERSEY								
1 Florio	Y	Y	Y	Y	N	N	Y	Y
2 Hughes	N	Y	N	Y	Y	Y	Y	Y
3 Howard	Y	Y	Y	Y	Y	N	Y	Y
4 ***Smith***	Y	Y	N	Y	N	Y	Y	Y
5 ***Fenwick***	Y	N	N	Y	Y	N	Y	Y
6 ***Forsythe***	N	N	N	N	Y	N	N	Y
7 ***Roukema***	N	N	N	N	N	Y	N	Y
8 Roe	Y	Y	Y	Y	Y	N	N	?
9 ***Hollenbeck***	Y	N	Y	Y	?	N	N	?
10 Rodino	Y	Y	Y	Y	Y	N	Y	Y
11 Minish	Y	Y	Y	Y	Y	N	Y	Y
12 ***Rinaldo***	Y	Y	Y	Y	N	Y	N	Y
13 ***Courter***	N	N	N	N	Y	Y	Y	Y
14 Guarini	Y	N	Y	Y	Y	N	Y	Y
15 Dwyer	Y	Y	Y	Y	Y	N	N	Y
NEW MEXICO								
1 ***Lujan***	N	Y	N	N	N	Y	N	N
2 ***Skeen***	N	Y	N	N	N	Y	N	N
NEW YORK								
1 ***Carney***	?	?	?	N	Y	N	N	N
2 Downey	Y	Y	Y	Y	Y	N	Y	Y
3 ***Carman***	N	N	N	N	Y	N	Y	Y
4 ***Lent***	?	?	N	N	Y	N	Y	N
5 ***McGrath***	N	N	N	N	Y	N	Y	Y
6 ***LeBoutillier***	N	N	N	N	N	Y	Y	Y
7 Addabbo	Y	Y	Y	Y	Y	N	Y	N
8 Rosenthal	?	?	?	?	?	?	Y	Y
9 Ferraro	Y	Y	Y	Y	Y	N	Y	Y
10 Biaggi	Y	Y	Y	Y	Y	N	N	Y
11 Scheuer	Y	Y	Y	Y	Y	N	Y	Y
12 Chisholm	?	?	Y	?	Y	N	Y	?
13 Solarz	Y	Y	Y	Y	Y	N	Y	Y
14 Vacancy								
15 Zeferetti	Y	Y	Y	?	Y	N	N	?
16 Schumer	Y	Y	Y	Y	Y	N	Y	Y
17 ***Molinari***	N	Y	Y	N	Y	N	Y	Y
18 ***Green***	?	?	Y	Y	Y	N	Y	Y
19 Rangel	Y	Y	Y	Y	Y	N	Y	Y
20 Weiss	N	Y	Y	Y	Y	N	Y	Y
21 Garcia	Y	Y	Y	Y	Y	N	Y	Y
22 Bingham	Y	Y	Y	N	Y	N	Y	Y
23 Peyser	Y	Y	Y	Y	Y	N	Y	Y
24 Ottinger	N	Y	Y	Y	Y	N	Y	Y
25 ***Fish***	Y	Y	Y	Y	Y	N	Y	Y
26 ***Gilman***	Y	Y	N	Y	N	Y	Y	Y
27 McHugh	N	Y	Y	N	Y	N	Y	Y
28 Stratton	N	N	Y	Y	Y	N	N	Y
29 ***Solomon***	N	N	N	N	Y	Y	N	Y
30 ***Martin***	N	N	N	N	Y	Y	Y	Y
31 ***Mitchell***	?	?	N	N	N	Y	Y	?
32 ***Wortley***	Y	N	N	N	Y	Y	Y	Y
33 ***Lee***	N	N	?	N	Y	N	Y	Y
34 ***Horton***	N	N	Y	Y	N	Y	N	Y
35 ***Conable***	N	Y	Y	N	Y	Y	N	Y
36 LaFalce	Y	Y	Y	Y	Y	N	Y	?
37 Nowak	Y	Y	Y	Y	Y	N	Y	Y
38 ***Kemp***	Y	Y	N	N	Y	N	Y	?
39 Lundine	Y	Y	Y	Y	Y	N	Y	Y
NORTH CAROLINA								
1 Jones	Y	N	Y	Y	Y	N	N	N
2 Fountain	Y	Y	Y	N	Y	N	N	N
3 Whitley	Y	N	Y	Y	Y	Y	N	N
4 Andrews	Y	Y	Y	Y	Y	Y	N	N
5 Neal	?	?	?	Y	Y	Y	Y	Y
6 ***Johnston***	Y	N	N	N	N	N	?	?
7 Rose	Y	Y	Y	Y	Y	Y	N	N
8 Hefner	Y	Y	Y	Y	Y	Y	N	Y

	416	417	418	419	420	421	422	423
9 ***Martin***	?	?	N	Y	Y	N	N	N
10 ***Broyhill***	N	N	N	Y	N	Y	N	Y
11 ***Hendon***	N	N	?	N	N	Y	N	N
NORTH DAKOTA								
AL Dorgan	N	Y	N	Y	Y	Y	N	N
OHIO								
1 ***Gradison***	N	N	N	N	N	Y	Y	Y
2 Luken	Y	Y	Y	Y	Y	N	N	Y
3 Hall	Y	Y	Y	Y	Y	N	Y	Y
4 ***Oxley***	N	Y	N	N	N	Y	N	?
5 ***Latta***	N	N	Y	N	Y	Y	N	N
6 ***McEwen***	N	N	N	N	N	Y	N	N
7 ***Brown***	Y	N	N	N	Y	Y	N	N
8 ***Kindness***	N	N	N	N	N	Y	N	?
9 ***Weber***	N	N	N	N	N	Y	Y	Y
10 ***Miller***	N	N	N	N	Y	Y	N	N
11 ***Stanton***	?	?	N	N	Y	N	N	?
12 Shamansky	Y	Y	Y	Y	Y	Y	Y	Y
13 Pease	N	Y	Y	Y	Y	Y	Y	Y
14 Seiberling	Y	Y	Y	Y	Y	N	Y	Y
15 ***Wylie***	N	N	N	N	N	Y	Y	N
16 ***Regula***	N	N	N	N	N	Y	N	N
17 ***Ashbrook***	Y	N	N	N	N	N	N	Y
18 Applegate	Y	Y	Y	Y	Y	Y	Y	Y
19 ***Williams***	Y	Y	N	N	Y	Y	N	N
20 Oakar	Y	Y	Y	Y	Y	Y	Y	N
21 Stokes	Y	Y	Y	Y	Y	N	Y	Y
22 Eckart	N	Y	Y	Y	Y	Y	Y	Y
23 Mottl	N	N	N	Y	N	Y	N	Y
OKLAHOMA								
1 Jones	Y	Y	N	Y	Y	Y	N	Y
2 Synar	Y	Y	Y	Y	Y	Y	Y	Y
3 Watkins	N	Y	Y	Y	Y	Y	N	N
4 McCurdy	N	Y	Y	Y	Y	Y	Y	Y
5 ***Edwards***	N	Y	N	N	Y	Y	Y	N
6 English	N	Y	Y	Y	Y	Y	N	Y
OREGON								
1 AuCoin	Y	Y	Y	Y	Y	Y	?	Y
2 ***Smith***	N	N	N	N	N	Y	N	N
3 Wyden	N	Y	Y	Y	Y	Y	Y	Y
4 Weaver	N	Y	Y	Y	Y	?	Y	Y
PENNSYLVANIA								
1 Foglietta	Y	Y	Y	Y	Y	N	Y	Y
2 Gray	Y	Y	Y	Y	Y	N	Y	Y
3 Smith	?	?	Y	N	Y	N	N	?
4 ***Dougherty***	?	?	?	?	Y	N	?	Y
5 ***Schulze***	Y	N	?	?	?	?	?	?
6 Yatron	Y	Y	N	N	N	N	Y	Y
7 Edgar	N	Y	Y	Y	Y	N	Y	?
8 ***Coyne, J.***	N	Y	N	Y	Y	Y	Y	N
9 ***Shuster***	?	?	?	?	?	?	?	?
10 ***McDade***	N	N	Y	Y	Y	N	Y	Y
11 ***Nelligan***	Y	Y	N	N	N	Y	N	Y
12 Murtha	Y	?	Y	Y	Y	N	N	Y
13 ***Coughlin***	N	N	Y	N	Y	N	Y	Y
14 Coyne, W.	Y	Y	Y	Y	Y	N	N	N
15 ***Ritter***	N	N	N	N	Y	Y	Y	Y
16 ***Walker***	N	N	N	Y	Y	Y	Y	Y
17 Ertel	?	?	Y	Y	Y	N	Y	Y
18 Walgren	N	Y	Y	Y	N	Y	Y	Y
19 ***Goodling***	N	N	N	N	N	N	Y	N
20 Gaydos	Y	Y	N	Y	N	Y	N	N
21 Bailey	Y	Y	Y	N	Y	N	N	N
22 Murphy	Y	Y	Y	Y	Y	N	N	Y
23 ***Clinger***	N	N	Y	Y	Y	Y	Y	Y
24 ***Marks***	Y	N	?	N	Y	N	N	?
25 ***Atkinson***	?	?	N	N	N	Y	N	Y
RHODE ISLAND								
1 St Germain	N	Y	Y	Y	Y	N	Y	Y
2 ***Schneider***	Y	Y	Y	Y	Y	Y	Y	Y
SOUTH CAROLINA								
1 ***Hartnett***	?	?	N	N	Y	N	N	Y
2 ***Spence***	Y	N	N	N	Y	Y	N	N
3 Derrick	N	Y	?	Y	Y	N	Y	Y
4 ***Campbell***	N	N	N	N	Y	N	N	Y
5 Holland	?	?	?	?	Y	N	N	?
6 ***Napier***	Y	N	N	N	Y	N	N	N
SOUTH DAKOTA								
1 Daschle	Y	Y	Y	Y	Y	Y	Y	Y
2 ***Roberts***	Y	N	N	N	Y	Y	N	N
TENNESSEE								
1 ***Quillen***	Y	N	N	Y	Y	Y	N	N
2 ***Duncan***	Y	N	N	N	Y	Y	N	N
3 Bouquard	N	Y	N	Y	N	Y	N	N
4 Gore	N	Y	Y	Y	Y	Y	N	N
5 Boner	Y	Y	Y	Y	Y	Y	N	N
6 ***Beard***	Y	N	N	N	Y	Y	?	?

	416	417	418	419	420	421	422	423
7 Jones	N	Y	Y	Y	Y	Y	N	N
8 Ford	Y	Y	Y	Y	Y	N	N	Y
TEXAS								
1 Hall, S.	N	Y	Y	Y	Y	Y	N	N
2 Wilson	Y	Y	?	?	?	?	N	N
3 ***Collins***	N	N	N	N	N	Y	Y	Y
4 Hall, R.	N	Y	Y	Y	Y	Y	N	Y
5 Mattox	Y	Y	Y	Y	Y	N	Y	?
6 Gramm	N	N	N	N	Y	Y	Y	Y
7 ***Archer***	Y	N	N	N	N	Y	N	Y
8 ***Fields***	Y	N	N	N	N	Y	N	Y
9 Brooks	?	?	Y	Y	Y	N	N	N
10 Pickle	Y	Y	N	Y	N	Y	N	N
11 Leath	N	N	?	N	Y	N	N	N
12 Wright	Y	Y	Y	Y	Y	N	N	N
13 Hightower	N	Y	N	Y	Y	Y	N	N
14 Patman	Y	N	N	Y	N	Y	N	N
15 de la Garza	Y	Y	Y	N	Y	Y	Y	N
16 White	Y	Y	Y	N	Y	N	N	N
17 Stenholm	N	N	N	N	Y	Y	N	N
18 Leland	Y	Y	Y	Y	Y	N	Y	Y
19 Hance	Y	Y	Y	N	Y	Y	N	Y
20 Gonzalez	Y	Y	Y	Y	Y	N	N	Y
21 ***Loeffler***	N	N	N	N	Y	Y	N	N
22 ***Paul***	Y	N	N	N	N	Y	Y	Y
23 Kazen	Y	Y	Y	Y	Y	Y	N	N
24 Frost	?	?	?	?	Y	N	Y	Y
UTAH								
1 ***Hansen***	N	N	N	N	N	Y	N	N
2 ***Marriott***	N	N	Y	Y	N	Y	N	N
VERMONT								
AL ***Jeffords***	N	N	N	Y	Y	N	Y	?
VIRGINIA								
1 ***Trible***	Y	N	N	N	Y	N	Y	Y
2 ***Whitehurst***	Y	N	N	N	Y	N	Y	Y
3 ***Bliley***	-	-	N	N	Y	N	N	Y
4 ***Daniel, R.***	Y	N	N	N	Y	N	N	Y
5 Daniel, D.	Y	N	N	N	Y	N	N	N
6 ***Butler***	N	N	N	N	Y	N	N	N
7 ***Robinson***	Y	N	N	N	Y	N	N	N
8 ***Parris***	Y	N	N	N	N	Y	N	N
9 ***Wampler***	Y	N	N	N	Y	N	N	N
10 ***Wolf***	Y	N	N	N	Y	N	Y	Y
WASHINGTON								
1 ***Pritchard***	Y	Y	N	N	Y	N	Y	Y
2 Swift	Y	N	Y	Y	Y	N	Y	Y
3 Bonker	Y	Y	Y	Y	Y	N	Y	Y
4 ***Morrison***	Y	N	N	N	Y	Y	N	N
5 Foley	Y	N	Y	Y	Y	N	N	N
6 Dicks	Y	N	Y	Y	Y	N	Y	Y
7 Lowry	Y	Y	Y	Y	Y	N	Y	Y
WEST VIRGINIA								
1 Mollohan	Y	Y	Y	Y	Y	N	N	N
2 ***Benedict***	N	N	Y	N	N	Y	N	N
3 ***Staton***	N	N	N	Y	Y	N	N	N
4 Rahall	Y	Y	Y	Y	Y	N	Y	N
WISCONSIN								
1 Aspin	?	?	Y	N	Y	Y	Y	Y
2 Kastenmeier	N	Y	Y	Y	Y	N	Y	Y
3 ***Gunderson***	N	N	Y	Y	Y	Y	Y	Y
4 Zablocki	Y	Y	Y	N	Y	N	N	N
5 Reuss	N	Y	Y	Y	Y	N	Y	Y
6 ***Petri***	N	N	N	Y	N	Y	Y	Y
7 Obey	N	Y	N	N	Y	N	Y	Y
8 ***Roth***	Y	Y	N	N	N	Y	N	Y
9 ***Sensenbrenner***	N	N	N	N	Y	Y	Y	Y
WYOMING								
AL ***Cheney***	Y	N	?	N	Y	Y	N	N

Southern states - Ala., Ark., Fla., Ga., Ky., La., Miss., N.C., Okla., S.C., Tenn., Texas, Va.

424. H J Res 631. Continuing Appropriations, Fiscal 1983. Conte, R-Mass., amendment to bar use of funds in the resolution for the Garrison Diversion water project in North Dakota. Adopted 252-152: R 126-50; D 126-102 (ND 109-44, SD 17-58), Dec. 14, 1982.

425. H J Res 631. Continuing Appropriations, Fiscal 1983/Jobs. Conte, R-Mass., motion to recommit the joint resolution to the Appropriations Committee with instructions to delete jobs program funding (Title II) and add $44 million in funding for Radio Liberty. Motion rejected 191-215: R 171-7; D 20-208 (ND 2-150, SD 18-58), Dec. 14, 1982. A "yea" was a vote supporting the president's position.

426. H J Res 631. Continuing Appropriations, Fiscal 1983. Passage of the joint resolution to provide continued funding, through March 15, 1983, for government agencies whose regular fiscal 1983 appropriations bills had not been enacted, and to provide $5.4 billion for jobs programs. Passed 204-200: R 13-164; D 191-36 (ND 136-15, SD 55-21), Dec. 14, 1982.

427. Procedural Motion. Smith, R-Ore., motion to adjourn. By adjourning, Smith hoped to block House consideration of the bill (HR 7340) to designate certain land in Oregon as part of the National Forest System. Motion rejected 122-202: R 121-33; D 1-169 (ND 1-108, SD 0-61), Dec. 14, 1982. (HR 7340 subsequently was rejected by the House under suspension of the rules (see vote 429, below).)

428. Procedural Motion. Smith, R-Ore., motion to approve the House *Journal* of Tuesday, Dec. 14. Motion agreed to 270-57: R 110-44; D 160-13 (ND 105-8, SD 55-5), Dec. 15, 1982.

429. HR 7340. Oregon Wilderness Act. Seiberling, D-Ohio, motion to suspend the rules and pass the bill to designate as federally protected wilderness 1,006,000 acres of Oregon national forest land and to designate another 112,000 acres for further wilderness study. Motion rejected 247-141: R 45-131; D 202-10 (ND 140-1, SD 62-9), Dec. 15, 1982. A two-thirds majority of those present and voting (259 in this case) is required for passage under suspension of the rules.

430. S 1965. Paddy Creek Wilderness Act. Seiberling, D-Ohio, motion to suspend the rules and pass the bill to designate as federally protected wilderness some 6,888 acres in the Mark Twain National Forest in Missouri. Motion rejected 250-143: R 43-131; D 207-12 (ND 140-6, SD 67-6), Dec. 15, 1982. A two-thirds majority of those present and voting (262 in this case) is required for passage under suspension of the rules.

431. HR 7072. Agriculture Appropriations, Fiscal 1983. Adoption of the conference report on the bill to appropriate $31,733,548,000 in fiscal 1983 for the Agriculture Department, the Food and Drug Administration and the Commodity Futures Trading Commission. Adopted 324-73: R 119-56; D 205-17 (ND 137-12, SD 68-5), Dec. 15, 1982. The president had requested $31,833,247,000.

KEY

- Y Voted for (yea).
- # Paired for.
- + Announced for.
- N Voted against (nay).
- X Paired against.
- - Announced against.
- P Voted "present".
- C Voted "present" to avoid possible conflict of interest.
- ? Did not vote or otherwise make a position known.

Democrats   *Republicans*

	424	425	426	427	428	429	430	431
ALABAMA								
1 *Edwards*	N	Y	N	Y	?	N	N	Y
2 *Dickinson*	N	Y	N	N	N	N	N	Y
3 Nichols	N	Y	N	N	Y	Y	N	Y
4 Bevill	N	N	Y	N	Y	Y	Y	Y
5 Flippo	N	N	Y	?	Y	Y	Y	Y
6 *Smith*	N	Y	N	?	N	?	N	N
7 Shelby	N	N	N	N	Y	N	N	Y
ALASKA								
AL *Young*	N	Y	N	Y	N	N	N	Y
ARIZONA								
1 *Rhodes*	?	?	?	?	Y	N	N	?
2 Udall	Y	N	Y	N	Y	Y	Y	Y
3 *Stump*	N	Y	N	Y	N	N	N	N
4 *Rudd*	N	Y	N	N	N	N	N	N
ARKANSAS								
1 Alexander	N	N	Y	N	?	Y	Y	Y
2 *Bethune*	N	Y	N	Y	Y	?	?	?
3 *Hammerschmidt*	N	Y	N	?	Y	N	N	Y
4 Anthony	N	N	Y	N	?	?	?	?
CALIFORNIA								
1 *Chappie*	?	#	X	?	Y	N	N	Y
2 *Clausen*	N	Y	N	?	?	N	N	Y
3 Matsui	N	N	Y	N	Y	Y	Y	Y
4 Fazio	N	N	Y	N	Y	Y	Y	Y
5 Burton, J.	?	X	#	?	?	?	?	?
6 Burton, P.	N	N	?	N	Y	Y	Y	?
7 Miller	Y	N	Y	N	Y	?	Y	Y
8 Dellums	Y	N	Y	N	Y	Y	Y	Y
9 Stark	Y	N	Y	?	?	?	?	?
10 Edwards	Y	N	?	Y	Y	Y	Y	Y
11 Lantos	N	N	Y	?	Y	Y	Y	Y
12 *McCloskey*	N	Y	N	N	?	Y	N	?
13 Mineta	N	N	Y	N	Y	Y	Y	Y
14 *Shumway*	Y	Y	N	Y	N	N	N	N
15 Coelho	N	N	Y	N	?	Y	Y	Y
16 Panetta	N	N	Y	N	Y	Y	Y	Y
17 *Pashayan*	N	Y	N	Y	N	N	N	Y
18 *Thomas*	?	#	X	?	Y	N	N	Y
19 *Lagomarsino*	Y	Y	N	Y	N	N	N	N
20 *Goldwater*	?	?	?	?	?	?	?	?
21 *Fiedler*	Y	Y	N	Y	N	N	N	Y
22 *Moorhead*	Y	Y	N	Y	N	N	N	N
23 Beilenson	?	?	?	?	?	?	?	Y
24 Waxman	Y	N	Y	N	?	Y	Y	Y
25 Roybal	Y	N	Y	N	Y	Y	Y	Y
26 *Rousselot*	Y	Y	N	Y	N	N	N	?
27 *Dornan*	Y	Y	N	Y	N	N	N	N
28 Dixon	N	N	Y	N	Y	Y	Y	Y
29 Hawkins	N	N	Y	?	N	Y	Y	Y
30 Martinez	Y	N	Y	N	?	Y	Y	Y
31 Dymally	N	N	Y	N	Y	?	Y	Y
32 Anderson	Y	N	N	N	Y	Y	Y	N
33 *Grisham*	Y	Y	N	Y	?	N	N	N
34 *Lungren*	Y	Y	N	Y	N	N	N	N
35 *Dreier*	Y	Y	N	Y	N	N	N	N
36 Brown	Y	N	Y	N	Y	Y	Y	Y
37 *Lewis*	?	Y	N	Y	N	N	N	Y
38 Patterson	Y	N	Y	N	Y	Y	Y	Y
39 *Dannemeyer*	Y	Y	N	Y	N	N	N	N
40 *Badham*	Y	Y	?	?	Y	N	N	N
41 *Lowery*	Y	Y	N	Y	N	Y	N	Y
42 *Hunter*	N	Y	N	Y	Y	N	N	N
43 *Burgener*	N	Y	N	?	?	Y	N	Y
COLORADO								
1 Schroeder	?	?	N	?	N	Y	Y	N
2 Wirth	Y	N	N	?	?	?	?	Y
3 Kogovsek	N	N	N	N	Y	Y	Y	Y
4 *Brown*	Y	Y	N	Y	N	N	N	N

	424	425	426	427	428	429	430	431
5 *Kramer*	N	Y	N	Y	?	N	N	Y
CONNECTICUT								
1 Kennelly	Y	N	Y	N	Y	Y	Y	Y
2 Gejdenson	Y	N	Y	N	N	Y	Y	Y
3 *DeNardis*	?	?	?	?	?	?	?	Y
4 *McKinney*	?	Y	N	N	?	Y	N	Y
5 Ratchford	N	N	Y	Y	Y	Y	Y	Y
6 Moffett	?	?	?	?	Y	Y	Y	Y
DELAWARE								
AL *Evans*	?	?	?	?	?	?	?	Y
FLORIDA								
1 Hutto	N	N	Y	N	Y	Y	Y	Y
2 Fuqua	Y	N	Y	?	Y	Y	Y	Y
3 Bennett	N	N	N	N	N	Y	Y	N
4 Chappell	N	N	Y	N	Y	Y	Y	Y
5 *McCollum*	Y	N	Y	N	Y	N	N	N
6 *Young*	Y	Y	N	Y	Y	Y	Y	N
7 Gibbons	N	N	Y	N	?	Y	Y	Y
8 *Ireland*	Y	Y	N	N	?	?	?	?
9 Nelson	N	N	Y	N	Y	Y	Y	Y
10 *Bafalis*	Y	Y	N	?	N	Y	Y	Y
11 Mica	N	N	Y	N	Y	Y	Y	Y
12 *Shaw*	Y	Y	N	Y	N	N	N	N
13 Lehman	?	?	?	?	?	?	?	Y
14 Pepper	N	N	Y	N	Y	Y	Y	Y
15 Fascell	Y	N	Y	?	?	?	?	Y
GEORGIA								
1 Ginn	N	N	Y	N	?	Y	Y	Y
2 Hatcher	N	N	N	N	Y	Y	Y	Y
3 Brinkley	Y	N	Y	N	Y	Y	Y	Y
4 Levitas	N	Y	N	N	Y	Y	Y	Y
5 Fowler	Y	Y	N	Y	Y	Y	Y	Y
6 *Gingrich*	Y	Y	N	Y	N	N	N	N
7 *McDonald*	Y	Y	N	Y	N	N	N	N
8 Evans	?	?	?	?	?	?	?	Y
9 Jenkins	Y	Y	N	Y	Y	Y	Y	Y
10 Barnard	N	N	Y	N	Y	Y	Y	Y
HAWAII								
1 Heftel	N	N	Y	?	?	Y	Y	Y
2 Akaka	N	N	Y	N	Y	Y	Y	Y
IDAHO								
1 *Craig*	Y	Y	N	Y	N	N	N	Y
2 *Hansen*	N	Y	N	Y	N	N	N	Y
ILLINOIS								
1 Washington	Y	N	Y	?	Y	Y	Y	Y
2 Savage	Y	N	Y	?	?	?	?	?
3 Russo	Y	N	Y	N	Y	Y	Y	N
4 *Derwinski*	Y	Y	Y	N	N	N	N	Y
5 Fary	?	X	#	?	?	?	?	Y
6 *Hyde*	Y	Y	N	Y	N	N	N	Y
7 Collins	Y	N	Y	?	Y	Y	Y	Y
8 Rostenkowski	Y	N	Y	N	Y	Y	Y	Y
9 Yates	Y	N	Y	?	?	?	?	Y
10 *Porter*	Y	N	Y	N	Y	N	N	Y
11 Annunzio	Y	N	Y	N	Y	Y	Y	Y
12 *Crane, P.*	Y	Y	N	N	N	N	N	N
13 *McClory*	Y	Y	N	P	N	N	Y	
14 *Erlenborn*	Y	N	Y	N	N	Y	N	Y
15 *Corcoran*	Y	Y	N	Y	N	N	Y	Y
16 *Martin*	Y	Y	N	Y	N	N	Y	N
17 O'Brien	N	Y	N	?	N	Y	N	Y
18 *Michel*	Y	Y	N	?	N	N	Y	Y
19 *Railsback*	?	?	?	?	?	?	?	?
20 *Findley*	Y	Y	N	Y	N	N	N	Y
21 *Madigan*	Y	Y	?	?	?	?	?	Y
22 *Crane, D.*	Y	Y	N	Y	N	N	N	N
23 Price	Y	N	Y	N	Y	Y	Y	Y
24 Simon	N	N	Y	Y	Y	Y	Y	
INDIANA								
1 Hall	Y	N	Y	N	Y	Y	Y	Y
2 Fithian	Y	N	Y	N	Y	Y	Y	Y
3 *Hiler*	Y	Y	N	Y	N	N	N	Y
4 *Coats*	Y	Y	N	Y	N	N	N	Y
5 *Hillis*	Y	Y	N	Y	N	N	N	Y
6 Evans	Y	N	Y	N	Y	Y	Y	Y
7 *Myers*	N	Y	N	N	Y	Y	Y	Y
8 *Deckard*	Y	Y	N	?	?	?	?	Y
9 Hamilton	Y	N	N	N	Y	Y	Y	Y
10 Sharp	Y	N	Y	N	Y	Y	Y	Y
11 Jacobs	Y	N	N	?	N	N	N	N
IOWA								
1 *Leach*	Y	Y	N	N	Y	Y	Y	Y
2 *Tauke*	Y	Y	N	Y	Y	Y	+	+
3 *Evans*	N	Y	N	Y	N	Y	Y	Y
4 Smith	N	N	Y	N	Y	Y	Y	Y
5 Harkin	N	Y	N	Y	Y	Y	Y	Y
6 Bedell	Y	N	Y	N	Y	Y	Y	Y

ND · Northern Democrats   SD · Southern Democrats

Corresponding to Congressional Record Votes 449, 450, 451, 452, 453, 454, 455, 456

	424	425	426	427	428	429	430	431
KANSAS								
1 ***Roberts***	N	Y	N	Y	Y	N	N	Y
2 ***Jeffries***	Y	Y	N	Y	Y	N	N	N
3 ***Winn***	N	Y	N	?	Y	N	N	Y
4 Glickman	N	N	N	N	?	Y	Y	Y
5 ***Whittaker***	N	Y	N	Y	N	N	N	Y
KENTUCKY								
1 Hubbard	N	Y	N	N	Y	Y	Y	Y
2 Natcher	N	N	Y	N	Y	Y	Y	Y
3 Mazzoli	N	N	Y	?	?	Y	Y	Y
4 ***Snyder***	Y	Y	N	N	N	N	N	Y
5 ***Rogers***	N	Y	N	Y	N	N	N	Y
6 ***Hopkins***	N	Y	N	Y	N	N	N	Y
7 Perkins	N	N	Y	N	Y	Y	Y	Y
LOUISIANA								
1 ***Livingston***	Y	Y	N	Y	Y	N	N	N
2 Boggs	N	N	Y	N	?	Y	Y	Y
3 Tauzin	Y	Y	N	N	Y	Y	Y	Y
4 Roemer	Y	Y	N	N	N	Y	Y	N
5 Huckaby	Y	Y	Y	N	Y	?	Y	Y
6 ***Moore***	Y	Y	N	Y	Y	N	Y	Y
7 Breaux	Y	N	Y	N	?	Y	Y	Y
8 Long	N	N	Y	?	Y	Y	Y	Y
MAINE								
1 ***Emery***	Y	Y	N	N	?	Y	Y	Y
2 ***Snowe***	Y	Y	N	Y	Y	Y	N	Y
MARYLAND								
1 Dyson	N	N	N	N	?	?	Y	Y
2 Long	Y	N	Y	?	?	Y	Y	Y
3 Mikulski	Y	N	Y	N	?	?	?	Y
4 ***Holt***	Y	Y	N	N	?	?	?	?
5 Hoyer	Y	N	Y	N	Y	Y	Y	Y
6 Byron	Y	N	N	N	Y	Y	N	Y
7 Mitchell	Y	N	Y	?	?	Y	Y	?
8 Barnes	Y	N	Y	N	Y	Y	Y	Y
MASSACHUSETTS								
1 ***Conte***	Y	Y	N	?	Y	Y	Y	Y
2 Boland	Y	N	Y	N	Y	Y	Y	Y
3 Early	Y	N	Y	N	Y	Y	Y	Y
4 Frank	Y	N	Y	N	Y	Y	Y	N
5 Shannon	Y	N	Y	N	Y	Y	Y	Y
6 Mavroules	Y	N	Y	N	Y	Y	Y	Y
7 Markey	Y	N	Y	N	Y	Y	Y	Y
8 O'Neill								
9 Moakley	Y	N	Y	N	Y	Y	Y	Y
10 ***Heckler***	?	?	?	?	?	Y	Y	Y
11 Donnelly	N	N	Y	N	?	Y	N	Y
12 Studds	Y	N	Y	N	Y	Y	Y	Y
MICHIGAN								
1 Conyers	Y	N	Y	?	Y	Y	Y	Y
2 ***Pursell***	Y	Y	N	N	?	Y	?	Y
3 Wolpe	Y	N	Y	N	Y	Y	Y	Y
4 ***Siljander***	Y	Y	N	Y	Y	N	N	Y
5 ***Sawyer***	Y	Y	N	Y	Y	Y	Y	Y
6 ***Dunn***	Y	Y	N	?	?	N	N	Y
7 Kildee	Y	N	Y	N	Y	Y	Y	Y
8 Traxler	N	N	Y	N	Y	Y	Y	Y
9 ***Vander Jagt***	Y	Y	?	?	?	N	Y	Y
10 Albosta	N	N	Y	N	Y	Y	Y	Y
11 ***Davis***	Y	N	N	Y	?	N	N	Y
12 Bonior	Y	N	Y	?	?	Y	Y	Y
13 Crockett	Y	N	Y	?	?	?	?	Y
14 Hertel	Y	N	Y	N	?	?	Y	Y
15 Ford	Y	N	Y	N	?	?	?	?
16 Dingell	Y	N	Y	N	Y	Y	Y	Y
17 Brodhead	Y	N	Y	?	Y	Y	Y	Y
18 Blanchard	?	?	?	?	?	?	?	?
19 ***Broomfield***	Y	Y	Y	?	Y	N	N	Y
MINNESOTA								
1 ***Erdahl***	Y	Y	N	N	Y	Y	N	Y
2 ***Hagedorn***	?	?	?	?	?	?	?	?
3 ***Frenzel***	Y	Y	N	Y	Y	N	N	N
4 Vento	Y	N	Y	N	?	Y	Y	Y
5 Sabo	Y	N	Y	?	N	Y	Y	Y
6 ***Weber***	Y	Y	N	Y	N	N	Y	Y
7 ***Stangeland***	N	Y	N	Y	Y	N	N	Y
8 Oberstar	Y	N	Y	N	Y	Y	Y	Y
MISSISSIPPI								
1 Whitten	N	N	Y	N	Y	Y	Y	Y
2 Bowen	N	N	Y	N	Y	Y	Y	Y
3 Montgomery	N	Y	N	N	Y	N	Y	Y
4 Dowdy	N	N	Y	N	Y	N	Y	Y
5 ***Lott***	N	Y	N	Y	Y	N	N	Y
MISSOURI								
1 Clay	Y	N	Y	?	?	Y	Y	Y
2 Young	N	N	Y	?	Y	Y	Y	Y
3 Gephardt	N	N	Y	?	?	?	Y	Y
4 Skelton	N	N	Y	N	Y	Y	Y	Y
5 Bolling	?	?	?	?	?	?	Y	?
6 ***Coleman***	Y	Y	N	Y	Y	N	Y	Y
7 ***Taylor***	N	Y	N	N	Y	N	N	Y
8 ***Bailey***	Y	Y	N	Y	N	N	N	N
9 Volkmer	N	N	N	N	Y	Y	Y	Y
10 ***Emerson***	N	Y	N	Y	N	N	N	Y
MONTANA								
1 Williams	N	N	Y	?	?	Y	Y	Y
2 ***Marlenee***	Y	Y	N	Y	N	N	N	Y
NEBRASKA								
1 ***Bereuter***	N	Y	N	Y	Y	N	Y	Y
2 ***Daub***	N	Y	N	Y	N	N	N	Y
3 ***Smith***	N	Y	N	Y	Y	N	N	Y
NEVADA								
AL Santini	N	?	?	?	?	?	?	Y
NEW HAMPSHIRE								
1 D'Amours	Y	N	Y	N	Y	Y	Y	Y
2 ***Gregg***	Y	Y	N	Y	Y	N	Y	N
NEW JERSEY								
1 Florio	Y	N	Y	N	Y	Y	Y	Y
2 Hughes	Y	N	Y	N	Y	Y	Y	N
3 Howard	Y	N	Y	N	Y	Y	Y	Y
4 ***Smith***	Y	N	Y	Y	Y	Y	Y	Y
5 ***Fenwick***	Y	Y	N	Y	Y	Y	Y	Y
6 ***Forsythe***	Y	Y	N	?	?	Y	N	Y
7 ***Roukema***	Y	Y	N	Y	Y	Y	Y	N
8 Roe	Y	N	Y	?	Y	Y	Y	Y
9 ***Hollenbeck***	?	?	?	?	?	?	?	Y
10 Rodino	Y	N	Y	N	Y	Y	Y	Y
11 Minish	Y	N	Y	N	?	Y	Y	N
12 ***Rinaldo***	Y	N	Y	N	Y	Y	Y	Y
13 ***Courter***	Y	Y	N	Y	Y	Y	Y	Y
14 Guarini	Y	N	Y	N	Y	Y	Y	Y
15 Dwyer	N	N	Y	?	Y	Y	Y	Y
NEW MEXICO								
1 ***Lujan***	N	Y	N	Y	Y	N	N	Y
2 ***Skeen***	N	Y	N	Y	Y	N	N	Y
NEW YORK								
1 ***Carney***	N	Y	N	Y	Y	N	N	Y
2 Downey	Y	N	Y	?	Y	Y	Y	Y
3 ***Carman***	Y	Y	N	Y	Y	N	N	N
4 ***Lent***	Y	Y	N	Y	Y	N	?	Y
5 ***McGrath***	Y	Y	N	Y	N	N	N	N
6 ***LeBoutillier***	Y	Y	N	Y	N	N	N	N
7 Addabbo	Y	N	Y	?	?	Y	Y	Y
8 Rosenthal	N	N	Y	N	?	?	?	?
9 Ferraro	Y	N	Y	N	Y	Y	Y	Y
10 Biaggi	Y	N	Y	?	Y	Y	Y	Y
11 Scheuer	Y	N	Y	?	Y	Y	Y	Y
12 Chisholm	Y	N	Y	?	?	?	?	Y
13 Solarz	Y	N	Y	N	Y	Y	Y	Y
14 Vacancy								
15 Zeferetti	Y	N	Y	?	?	?	?	?
16 Schumer	Y	N	Y	N	Y	Y	Y	Y
17 ***Molinari***	Y	Y	N	Y	Y	N	N	Y
18 ***Green***	Y	Y	N	Y	Y	Y	Y	Y
19 Rangel	Y	N	Y	N	Y	Y	Y	Y
20 Weiss	N	N	Y	N	?	Y	Y	Y
21 Garcia	Y	N	Y	?	?	Y	Y	Y
22 Bingham	Y	?	?	?	Y	Y	Y	?
23 Peyser	Y	N	Y	?	Y	Y	Y	Y
24 Ottinger	Y	N	Y	N	P	Y	Y	N
25 ***Fish***	Y	Y	N	N	Y	Y	N	Y
26 ***Gilman***	Y	Y	Y	N	Y	Y	Y	Y
27 McHugh	Y	N	Y	?	Y	Y	Y	Y
28 Stratton	Y	N	Y	N	Y	Y	N	Y
29 ***Solomon***	Y	Y	N	Y	N	N	N	Y
30 ***Martin***	Y	Y	N	Y	Y	N	N	Y
31 ***Mitchell***	Y	Y	N	N	Y	Y	Y	Y
32 ***Wortley***	Y	Y	N	Y	Y	N	N	N
33 ***Lee***	Y	Y	N	Y	?	?	?	?
34 ***Horton***	Y	Y	N	N	Y	N	N	N
35 ***Conable***	Y	Y	N	Y	Y	Y	Y	N
36 LaFalce	?	N	Y	N	Y	Y	N	Y
37 Nowak	N	N	Y	?	Y	Y	Y	Y
38 ***Kemp***	Y	Y	N	Y	?	N	Y	N
39 Lundine	N	N	Y	?	Y	Y	Y	Y
NORTH CAROLINA								
1 Jones	N	N	Y	?	?	Y	Y	Y
2 Fountain	N	Y	Y	N	?	N	Y	Y
3 Whitley	N	N	N	N	Y	Y	Y	Y
4 Andrews	N	N	Y	N	Y	Y	Y	Y
5 Neal	Y	N	Y	N	?	?	?	Y
6 ***Johnston***	?	Y	N	?	?	N	N	N
7 Rose	N	N	Y	?	?	Y	Y	Y
8 Hefner	N	N	Y	N	Y	Y	Y	Y
9 ***Martin***	Y	Y	N	Y	?	N	N	N
10 ***Broyhill***	Y	Y	N	N	Y	N	N	N
11 ***Hendon***	N	Y	N	Y	N	N	N	Y
NORTH DAKOTA								
AL Dorgan	N	N	Y	N	Y	Y	Y	N
OHIO								
1 ***Gradison***	Y	Y	N	Y	Y	Y	Y	N
2 Luken	N	N	Y	N	Y	Y	Y	Y
3 Hall	Y	N	Y	?	?	Y	Y	Y
4 ***Oxley***	N	Y	N	?	N	N	N	Y
5 ***Latta***	Y	Y	N	N	N	N	N	Y
6 ***McEwen***	N	Y	N	?	Y	Y	Y	N
7 ***Brown***	Y	Y	N	Y	Y	N	N	Y
8 ***Kindness***	N	?	N	?	Y	N	N	Y
9 ***Weber***	Y	Y	N	?	Y	N	N	Y
10 ***Miller***	Y	Y	N	Y	N	Y	Y	N
11 ***Stanton***	Y	Y	N	?	?	Y	Y	Y
12 Shamansky	Y	N	Y	N	Y	Y	Y	Y
13 Pease	Y	N	Y	N	Y	Y	Y	Y
14 Seiberling	Y	N	Y	N	Y	Y	Y	Y
15 ***Wylie***	Y	Y	N	N	Y	N	Y	Y
16 ***Regula***	N	Y	N	Y	Y	Y	Y	Y
17 ***Ashbrook***	Y	Y	N	Y	Y	N	N	N
18 Applegate	N	N	N	?	?	Y	Y	Y
19 ***Williams***	Y	N	Y	?	Y	N	N	Y
20 Oakar	Y	N	Y	N	Y	Y	Y	Y
21 Stokes	Y	N	Y	N	Y	Y	Y	Y
22 Eckart	N	N	Y	N	Y	Y	Y	Y
23 Mottl	Y	N	N	N	Y	Y	Y	N
OKLAHOMA								
1 Jones	N	N	Y	N	Y	Y	Y	N
2 Synar	Y	Y	N	N	Y	Y	Y	Y
3 Watkins	N	N	Y	N	Y	Y	Y	Y
4 McCurdy	N	Y	Y	N	Y	Y	Y	Y
5 ***Edwards***	Y	Y	N	Y	N	N	N	Y
6 English	N	Y	N	N	Y	Y	Y	Y
OREGON								
1 AuCoin	Y	N	Y	N	Y	Y	Y	Y
2 ***Smith***	N	Y	N	Y	N	N	N	N
3 Wyden	Y	N	Y	N	Y	Y	Y	Y
4 Weaver	Y	N	Y	N	Y	Y	Y	N
PENNSYLVANIA								
1 Foglietta	Y	N	Y	N	Y	Y	Y	Y
2 Gray	Y	N	Y	N	Y	Y	Y	Y
3 Smith	?	?	?	?	?	?	?	Y
4 ***Dougherty***	Y	N	Y	Y	Y	N	N	Y
5 ***Schulze***	?	?	?	?	?	?	?	?
6 Yatron	Y	N	N	N	Y	Y	Y	Y
7 Edgar	Y	N	Y	N	N	Y	Y	Y
8 ***Coyne, J.***	Y	Y	N	Y	Y	N	N	N
9 ***Shuster***	?	?	?	?	?	?	?	?
10 ***McDade***	Y	N	Y	Y	Y	Y	N	Y
11 ***Nelligan***	Y	Y	N	Y	N	N	N	Y
12 Murtha	Y	N	Y	N	Y	Y	Y	Y
13 ***Coughlin***	Y	Y	N	N	N	Y	Y	Y
14 Coyne, W.	N	N	Y	N	Y	Y	Y	Y
15 ***Ritter***	Y	Y	N	Y	Y	Y	N	N
16 ***Walker***	Y	Y	N	Y	N	N	N	N
17 Ertel	N	N	Y	?	?	?	Y	Y
18 Walgren	Y	N	Y	N	Y	Y	Y	Y
19 ***Goodling***	Y	Y	N	Y	N	N	Y	Y
20 Gaydos	Y	N	Y	N	?	Y	Y	Y
21 Bailey	Y	N	Y	N	?	Y	Y	Y
22 Murphy	Y	N	Y	N	?	Y	Y	Y
23 ***Clinger***	Y	Y	N	Y	N	N	Y	N
24 ***Marks***	?	N	Y	?	?	?	?	?
25 ***Atkinson***	Y	Y	N	Y	N	Y	N	N
RHODE ISLAND								
1 St Germain	Y	N	Y	?	P	Y	Y	Y
2 ***Schneider***	Y	Y	Y	Y	Y	Y	Y	Y
SOUTH CAROLINA								
1 ***Hartnett***	Y	Y	N	Y	Y	N	N	Y
2 ***Spence***	Y	Y	N	N	Y	N	N	Y
3 Derrick	Y	N	Y	?	Y	Y	Y	?
4 ***Campbell***	Y	Y	N	Y	Y	N	N	Y
5 Holland	N	N	Y	?	Y	Y	Y	?
6 ***Napier***	N	Y	N	Y	Y	N	N	Y
SOUTH DAKOTA								
1 Daschle	Y	Y	N	N	Y	Y	Y	Y
2 ***Roberts***	N	Y	N	?	?	N	N	?
TENNESSEE								
1 ***Quillen***	N	Y	N	N	Y	N	N	Y
2 ***Duncan***	Y	Y	N	Y	Y	N	Y	Y
3 Bouquard	N	N	N	?	N	Y	Y	Y
4 Gore	N	N	Y	N	Y	Y	Y	Y
5 Boner	N	N	Y	N	Y	Y	Y	Y
6 ***Beard***	?	?	?	?	?	?	?	?
7 Jones	N	N	Y	N	Y	Y	Y	Y
8 Ford	?	N	Y	?	?	Y	Y	Y
TEXAS								
1 Hall, S.	N	N	N	N	Y	Y	Y	Y
2 Wilson	?	?	?	?	?	?	?	Y
3 ***Collins***	Y	Y	N	Y	Y	N	N	N
4 Hall, R.	N	N	N	N	Y	N	N	Y
5 Mattox	Y	N	Y	?	?	Y	Y	Y
6 Gramm	Y	Y	N	N	N	N	N	N
7 ***Archer***	Y	Y	N	Y	Y	N	N	N
8 ***Fields***	Y	Y	N	Y	N	N	N	N
9 Brooks	N	N	Y	?	Y	Y	Y	Y
10 Pickle	N	N	Y	N	Y	Y	Y	Y
11 Leath	N	N	Y	N	Y	Y	Y	Y
12 Wright	N	N	Y	N	Y	Y	Y	Y
13 Hightower	N	N	N	N	Y	Y	Y	Y
14 Patman	N	N	Y	N	N	Y	Y	Y
15 de la Garza	N	N	Y	N	Y	Y	Y	Y
16 White	N	N	Y	?	Y	Y	Y	Y
17 Stenholm	N	Y	N	N	N	Y	Y	Y
18 Leland	N	N	Y	?	Y	Y	Y	Y
19 Hance	N	N	Y	N	Y	Y	Y	Y
20 Gonzalez	N	N	Y	N	Y	Y	Y	Y
21 ***Loeffler***	Y	Y	N	Y	N	N	N	Y
22 ***Paul***	Y	Y	N	Y	Y	N	N	N
23 Kazen	N	N	Y	N	Y	Y	Y	Y
24 Frost	N	N	Y	N	?	Y	Y	Y
UTAH								
1 ***Hansen***	N	Y	N	Y	N	N	N	N
2 ***Marriott***	N	Y	N	N	Y	N	N	?
VERMONT								
AL ***Jeffords***	Y	Y	Y	N	Y	Y	Y	Y
VIRGINIA								
1 ***Trible***	Y	Y	N	N	Y	N	N	Y
2 ***Whitehurst***	Y	Y	N	Y	Y	N	N	Y
3 ***Bliley***	Y	Y	N	Y	Y	N	N	Y
4 ***Daniel, R.***	Y	Y	N	Y	Y	N	N	Y
5 Daniel, D.	Y	Y	N	N	Y	N	N	Y
6 ***Butler***	Y	Y	N	Y	N	N	N	?
7 ***Robinson***	N	Y	N	Y	Y	N	N	Y
8 ***Parris***	Y	Y	N	N	Y	N	N	Y
9 ***Wampler***	N	Y	N	N	Y	N	N	Y
10 ***Wolf***	Y	Y	N	Y	Y	N	N	Y
WASHINGTON								
1 ***Pritchard***	Y	Y	N	Y	?	Y	Y	Y
2 Swift	Y	N	Y	N	Y	Y	Y	Y
3 Bonker	Y	N	Y	?	?	Y	Y	Y
4 ***Morrison***	N	Y	N	Y	Y	Y	N	Y
5 Foley	N	N	Y	N	Y	Y	Y	Y
6 Dicks	N	N	Y	N	Y	Y	Y	Y
7 Lowry	N	N	Y	N	N	Y	Y	Y
WEST VIRGINIA								
1 Mollohan	N	N	Y	N	Y	Y	Y	?
2 ***Benedict***	N	Y	N	Y	Y	N	N	N
3 ***Staton***	Y	Y	N	Y	Y	N	N	Y
4 Rahall	N	N	Y	N	?	Y	Y	Y
WISCONSIN								
1 Aspin	Y	N	Y	N	Y	Y	Y	Y
2 Kastenmeier	Y	N	Y	N	Y	Y	Y	Y
3 ***Gunderson***	Y	Y	N	Y	Y	N	N	Y
4 Zablocki	Y	N	Y	N	Y	Y	Y	Y
5 Reuss	Y	N	Y	?	Y	Y	Y	Y
6 ***Petri***	N	Y	N	N	Y	Y	Y	N
7 Obey	Y	N	Y	N	Y	Y	Y	Y
8 ***Roth***	N	Y	N	Y	Y	N	Y	N
9 ***Sensenbrenner***	Y	Y	N	Y	N	Y	Y	N
WYOMING								
AL ***Cheney***	N	Y	N	Y	Y	N	N	N

Southern states - Ala., Ark., Fla., Ga., Ky., La., Miss., N.C., Okla., S.C., Tenn., Texas, Va.

432. HR 5133. Automobile Domestic Content Requirements. Dannemeyer, R-Calif., amendment to rename the bill the "Smoot-Hawley Trade Barriers Act of 1982," and state that its purpose is "to reduce competition in the automobile industry, protect jobs in one industry to the detriment of jobs in other industries, and to increase the price of automobiles to consumers." Rejected 92-301: R 88-80; D 4-221 (ND 1-154, SD 3-67), Dec. 15, 1982.

433. HR 5133. Automobile Domestic Content Requirements. Schumer, D-N.Y., amendment to eliminate penalties for Japanese automakers who fail to meet domestic content requirements if Japan's trade surplus falls by specified percentages over the next four years. Rejected 88-310: R 43-129; D 45-181 (ND 19-131, SD 26-50), Dec. 15, 1982.

434. HR 5133. Automobile Domestic Content Requirements. Fenwick, R-N.J., amendment to stipulate that the provisions of the bill do not supersede the requirements of international treaties, conventions or agreements on tariffs and trade. Adopted 195-194: R 137-32; D 58-162 (ND 20-128, SD 38-34), Dec. 15, 1982.

435. HR 5133. Automobile Domestic Content Requirements. Passage of the bill to require automakers to use set percentages of U.S. labor and parts in automobiles they sell in the United States. Passed 215-188: R 44-130; D 171-58 (ND 132-20, SD 39-38), Dec. 15, 1982. A "nay" was a vote supporting the president's position.

436. HR 3191. North American Convention Tax. Adoption of the rule (H Res 630) providing for House floor consideration of the bill to allow certain tax deductions for business conventions held on North American cruise ships. Adopted 236-146: R 52-121; D 184-25 (ND 121-16, SD 63-9), Dec. 16, 1982.

437. S 1965. Paddy Creek Wilderness Act. Adoption of the rule (H Res 631) providing for House floor consideration of the bill to designate 6,888 acres in the Mark Twain National Forest, Missouri, as the Paddy Creek Wilderness Area. Adopted 217-179: R 11-165; D 206-14 (ND 145-2, SD 61-12), Dec. 16, 1982.

438. S 1964. Irish Wilderness Act. Adoption of the rule (H Res 628) providing for House floor consideration of the bill to designate 17,562 acres in the Mark Twain National Forest, Missouri, as the Irish Wilderness. Rejected 186-191: R 2-162; D 184-29 (ND 135-8, SD 49-21), Dec. 16, 1982.

439. HR 7357. Immigration Reform and Control Act of 1982. Adoption of the rule (H Res 623) providing for House consideration of the bill to revise immigration law by providing for sanctions against employers who knowingly hire illegal aliens; granting legal status to undocumented aliens already in the United States; broadening an existing temporary worker program; and revising current procedures for handling asylum, deportation and exclusion cases. Adopted 257-137: R 96-72; D 161-65 (ND 114-43, SD 47-22), Dec. 16, 1982.

KEY

Y Voted for (yea).
Paired for.
+ Announced for.
N Voted against (nay).
X Paired against.
- Announced against.
P Voted "present".
C Voted "present" to avoid possible conflict of interest.
? Did not vote or otherwise make a position known.

Democrats   *Republicans*

	432	433	434	435	436	437	438	439
ALABAMA								
1 *Edwards*	N	N	Y	N	?	N	N	Y
2 *Dickinson*	N	N	Y	N	N	?	?	?
3 Nichols	N	N	Y	Y	Y	Y	Y	Y
4 Bevill	N	N	N	Y	Y	Y	Y	Y
5 Flippo	N	N	N	Y	Y	Y	Y	Y
6 *Smith*	N	Y	Y	N	N	N	N	?
7 Shelby	?	N	N	Y	N	N	N	Y
ALASKA								
AL *Young*	Y	N	N	?	Y	N	N	?
ARIZONA								
1 *Rhodes*	N	Y	?	?	N	N	N	Y
2 Udall	N	N	?	Y	Y	Y	Y	Y
3 *Stump*	Y	N	Y	N	N	N	N	N
4 *Rudd*	Y	N	Y	N	N	N	N	N
ARKANSAS								
1 Alexander	N	Y	?	#	?	?	?	?
2 *Bethune*	Y	Y	Y	N	N	N	N	N
3 *Hammerschmidt*	Y	Y	Y	N	N	N	N	N
4 Anthony	?	N	Y	N	Y	N	Y	N
CALIFORNIA								
1 *Chappie*	Y	N	Y	N	N	N	N	N
2 *Clausen*	Y	N	Y	X	Y	N	N	Y
3 Matsui	N	N	N	Y	Y	Y	Y	N
4 Fazio	N	N	Y	Y	Y	Y	Y	Y
5 Burton, J.	?	?	?	#	?	?	?	N
6 Burton, P.	N	?	N	Y	Y	Y	N	Y
7 Miller	N	N	N	Y	Y	Y	Y	Y
8 Dellums	N	N	N	?	Y	N	Y	Y
9 Stark	N	N	N	Y	Y	Y	?	N
10 Edwards	N	N	N	Y	Y	Y	Y	Y
11 Lantos	N	N	N	Y	Y	Y	Y	Y
12 *McCloskey*	?	N	N	N	Y	N	?	?
13 Mineta	N	N	N	Y	Y	Y	Y	Y
14 *Shumway*	Y	N	Y	N	N	N	N	N
15 Coelho	N	N	N	Y	Y	Y	Y	N
16 Panetta	N	Y	N	Y	Y	Y	N	Y
17 *Pashayan*	Y	N	Y	N	N	N	N	N
18 *Thomas*	Y	N	Y	N	N	N	N	Y
19 *Lagomarsino*	Y	N	Y	N	N	N	N	N
20 *Goldwater*	?	?	?	?	?	?	?	Y
21 *Fiedler*	Y	N	Y	N	N	N	N	Y
22 *Moorhead*	Y	N	Y	N	N	N	N	N
23 Beilenson	N	N	N	N	?	Y	Y	Y
24 Waxman	N	?	N	N	Y	Y	Y	Y
25 Roybal	N	N	N	Y	Y	Y	Y	Y
26 *Rousselot*	Y	N	?	N	Y	N	N	Y
27 *Dornan*	Y	N	Y	N	N	N	N	N
28 Dixon	N	N	N	Y	?	Y	Y	N
29 Hawkins	N	N	N	Y	Y	Y	Y	Y
30 Martinez	N	N	N	Y	Y	Y	Y	N
31 Dymally	N	N	Y	?	?	?	?	Y
32 Anderson	N	N	Y	N	Y	Y	Y	Y
33 Grisham	?	N	Y	N	N	?	?	?
34 Lungren	Y	N	Y	N	N	N	N	Y
35 *Dreier*	Y	N	Y	N	N	N	N	Y
36 Brown	N	N	N	?	Y	Y	Y	N
37 Lewis	Y	N	Y	N	N	N	N	N
38 Patterson	N	N	N	Y	Y	Y	Y	N
39 *Dannemeyer*	Y	N	Y	N	N	N	N	N
40 *Badham*	Y	N	Y	X	N	N	N	N
41 Lowery	Y	Y	Y	N	N	N	N	Y
42 Hunter	Y	?	N	Y	N	N	N	N
43 *Burgener*	N	N	Y	N	N	N	?	Y
COLORADO								
1 Schroeder	N	N	N	?	Y	Y	Y	N
2 Wirth	N	N	N	Y	Y	Y	Y	N
3 Kogovsek	N	N	N	Y	?	Y	Y	Y
4 *Brown*	N	Y	Y	N	N	N	N	Y

	432	433	434	435	436	437	438	439
5 *Kramer*	N	Y	Y	N	N	N	N	Y
CONNECTICUT								
1 Kennelly	N	N	N	Y	Y	Y	Y	Y
2 Gejdenson	N	N	N	Y	Y	Y	?	Y
3 *DeNardis*	?	N	Y	N	Y	Y	Y	Y
4 *McKinney*	?	Y	Y	Y	Y	N	?	Y
5 Ratchford	N	N	N	Y	Y	Y	Y	Y
6 Moffett	N	N	Y	?	?	?	?	Y
DELAWARE								
AL *Evans*	?	?	Y	N	?	?	?	N
FLORIDA								
1 Hutto	N	N	Y	N	Y	Y	Y	Y
2 Fuqua	N	N	N	N	Y	Y	Y	Y
3 Bennett	N	N	Y	N	Y	Y	Y	Y
4 Chappell	N	N	Y	N	Y	Y	Y	Y
5 *McCollum*	Y	N	N	N	N	N	N	Y
6 *Young*	Y	N	N	N	N	N	N	Y
7 Gibbons	Y	N	N	Y	Y	Y	Y	Y
8 Ireland	?	Y	?	N	?	Y	N	?
9 Nelson	N	Y	Y	N	Y	Y	Y	Y
10 *Bafalis*	Y	N	N	N	N	N	N	?
11 Mica	N	N	N	Y	Y	Y	Y	Y
12 *Shaw*	N	N	N	N	N	N	N	Y
13 Lehman	?	?	?	?	?	?	?	?
14 Pepper	N	N	N	Y	Y	Y	Y	Y
15 Fascell	?	?	?	Y	?	?	?	?
GEORGIA								
1 Ginn	?	Y	N	Y	Y	Y	Y	Y
2 Hatcher	N	N	N	Y	Y	Y	Y	Y
3 Brinkley	N	N	Y	N	Y	Y	Y	Y
4 Levitas	Y	Y	Y	N	Y	Y	N	Y
5 Fowler	N	Y	N	Y	Y	Y	N	Y
6 *Gingrich*	N	N	Y	N	N	?	N	?
7 McDonald	Y	Y	Y	N	N	N	N	N
8 Evans	?	?	?	N	Y	Y	Y	N
9 Jenkins	N	Y	Y	N	Y	N	Y	N
10 Barnard	N	N	Y	N	Y	Y	Y	Y
HAWAII								
1 Heftel	N	N	N	Y	Y	Y	Y	Y
2 Akaka	N	N	N	Y	Y	Y	Y	Y
IDAHO								
1 *Craig*	Y	N	Y	N	N	N	N	N
2 *Hansen*	Y	N	Y	N	N	N	N	N
ILLINOIS								
1 Washington	N	N	N	Y	N	Y	N	Y
2 Savage	N	N	N	Y	?	?	?	?
3 Russo	N	N	N	Y	Y	Y	Y	Y
4 *Derwinski*	N	N	?	N	N	N	N	Y
5 Fary	N	N	N	Y	Y	Y	Y	Y
6 *Hyde*	Y	N	N	N	N	N	N	Y
7 Collins	N	N	N	Y	N	?	Y	?
8 Rostenkowski	N	N	N	Y	Y	Y	Y	Y
9 Yates	?	?	?	N	Y	Y	Y	Y
10 *Porter*	N	N	Y	N	N	N	N	Y
11 Annunzio	N	N	N	Y	Y	Y	Y	Y
12 *Crane, P.*	Y	N	Y	N	N	N	N	N
13 *McClory*	Y	N	N	N	N	N	N	Y
14 *Erlenborn*	Y	N	Y	N	N	N	N	N
15 *Corcoran*	Y	N	Y	N	N	N	N	Y
16 *Martin*	N	Y	N	Y	N	N	N	Y
17 *O'Brien*	N	Y	N	N	N	N	N	Y
18 *Michel*	Y	?	Y	N	N	N	N	?
19 *Railsback*	?	?	?	Y	N	N	?	Y
20 *Findley*	N	?	Y	N	N	N	N	?
21 *Madigan*	N	N	Y	N	N	N	N	?
22 *Crane, D.*	Y	N	Y	N	N	N	N	N
23 Price	N	N	N	Y	Y	Y	Y	Y
24 Simon	N	Y	Y	Y	Y	Y	Y	Y
INDIANA								
1 Hall	N	N	N	Y	Y	Y	Y	Y
2 Fithian	N	N	N	Y	Y	Y	Y	Y
3 *Hiler*	Y	N	Y	N	N	N	N	N
4 *Coats*	Y	Y	Y	N	N	N	N	N
5 Hillis	N	N	N	Y	N	N	N	N
6 Evans	N	?	N	Y	Y	Y	Y	N
7 *Myers*	Y	N	N	N	N	N	N	N
8 *Deckard*	?	Y	N	?	?	?	?	Y
9 Hamilton	N	N	Y	N	Y	Y	Y	Y
10 Sharp	N	N	N	Y	N	Y	Y	Y
11 Jacobs	N	N	N	Y	N	N	N	N
IOWA								
1 *Leach*	N	Y	Y	Y	N	Y	N	Y
2 *Tauke*	-	+	+	X	-	+	-	+
3 *Evans*	Y	Y	Y	N	N	N	N	Y
4 *Smith*	N	Y	Y	N	N	N	N	Y
5 Harkin	N	Y	Y	?	?	?	?	Y
6 Bedell	N	Y	Y	N	N	Y	Y	Y

Corresponding to Congressional Record Votes 457, 458, 459, 460, 462, 463, 464, 465

	432	433	434	435	436	437	438	439
KANSAS								
1 ***Roberts***	Y	N	Y	N	N	N	N	N
2 ***Jeffries***	Y	N	Y	N	N	N	N	Y
3 ***Winn***	Y	Y	Y	N	N	N	N	Y
4 Glickman	N	Y	N	N	Y	Y	Y	Y
5 ***Whittaker***	Y	N	Y	N	N	N	N	N
KENTUCKY								
1 Hubbard	N	Y	N	Y	Y	?	?	?
2 Natcher	N	N	Y	Y	Y	Y	Y	Y
3 Mazzoli	N	N	Y	Y	Y	Y	Y	Y
4 ***Snyder***	N	N	N	Y	Y	N	N	Y
5 ***Rogers***	N	N	N	Y	N	N	N	Y
6 ***Hopkins***	N	N	N	Y	N	N	N	Y
7 Perkins	N	N	N	Y	N	Y	Y	Y
LOUISIANA								
1 ***Livingston***	Y	Y	Y	N	Y	N	N	Y
2 Boggs	N	Y	?	Y	Y	Y	Y	Y
3 Tauzin	N	Y	Y	Y	Y	N	N	Y
4 Roemer	N	Y	Y	Y	N	N	N	Y
5 Huckaby	N	N	Y	N	N	Y	Y	N
6 ***Moore***	Y	N	Y	N	N	N	N	N
7 Breaux	N	Y	Y	N	Y	N	N	Y
8 Long	N	N	N	Y	Y	Y	Y	Y
MAINE								
1 ***Emery***	?	?	?	?	?	?	?	?
2 ***Snowe***	N	N	Y	N	N	N	N	N
MARYLAND								
1 Dyson	N	N	N	Y	Y	Y	Y	Y
2 Long	N	N	N	Y	Y	Y	Y	N
3 Mikulski	N	N	N	Y	Y	Y	Y	Y
4 ***Holt***	?	N	Y	N	N	N	N	N
5 Hoyer	N	N	N	Y	Y	Y	Y	Y
6 Byron	N	N	N	N	?	Y	?	Y
7 Mitchell	N	N	N	Y	Y	Y	Y	N
8 Barnes	N	N	Y	Y	Y	Y	Y	Y
MASSACHUSETTS								
1 ***Conte***	N	N	N	Y	N	Y	N	Y
2 Boland	N	N	N	Y	Y	Y	Y	Y
3 Early	N	N	N	Y	Y	Y	Y	Y
4 Frank	N	N	N	Y	Y	Y	?	Y
5 Shannon	N	N	N	Y	N	Y	Y	Y
6 Mavroules	N	N	N	Y	Y	Y	N	Y
7 Markey	N	N	N	Y	?	Y	Y	Y
8 O'Neill								
9 Moakley	N	N	N	Y	Y	Y	Y	Y
10 ***Heckler***	N	Y	Y	?	Y	N	N	?
11 Donnelly	N	Y	Y	N	Y	Y	Y	Y
12 Studds	N	N	N	Y	Y	Y	Y	Y
MICHIGAN								
1 Conyers	N	N	N	Y	Y	Y	Y	N
2 ***Pursell***	?	?	?	?	?	N	?	?
3 Wolpe	N	N	N	Y	Y	Y	Y	Y
4 ***Siljander***	N	N	Y	Y	Y	N	N	N
5 ***Sawyer***	N	Y	Y	N	Y	N	N	Y
6 ***Dunn***	N	N	N	Y	N	N	N	N
7 Kildee	N	N	N	Y	Y	Y	Y	N
8 Traxler	N	?	N	Y	Y	Y	Y	Y
9 ***Vander Jagt***	Y	N	Y	N	Y	N	?	Y
10 Albosta	N	N	N	Y	Y	Y	Y	Y
11 ***Davis***	N	N	N	Y	Y	Y	N	Y
12 Bonior	N	N	N	Y	Y	Y	Y	Y
13 Crockett	N	N	N	Y	Y	Y	Y	N
14 Hertel	N	N	N	Y	Y	Y	Y	Y
15 Ford	N	N	N	Y	Y	Y	Y	Y
16 Dingell	N	N	N	Y	?	Y	Y	Y
17 Brodhead	N	N	N	Y	N	Y	Y	Y
18 Blanchard	?	?	?	#	?	?	?	?
19 ***Broomfield***	N	N	N	Y	N	N	N	N
MINNESOTA								
1 ***Erdahl***	?	N	Y	N	N	N	N	Y
2 ***Hagedorn***	?	?	?	?	?	?	?	?
3 ***Frenzel***	Y	N	Y	N	N	N	N	Y
4 Vento	N	N	N	Y	N	Y	Y	Y
5 Sabo	N	Y	N	Y	Y	Y	Y	Y
6 ***Weber***	Y	N	Y	N	N	N	N	Y
7 ***Stangeland***	Y	N	?	N	Y	N	N	N
8 Oberstar	N	N	N	Y	Y	Y	Y	Y
MISSISSIPPI								
1 Whitten	N	N	Y	Y	Y	Y	N	N
2 Bowen	N	N	Y	N	Y	Y	Y	Y
3 Montgomery	N	N	Y	N	Y	Y	N	N
4 Dowdy	N	N	N	Y	Y	Y	?	N
5 ***Lott***	N	N	Y	N	N	N	N	Y
MISSOURI								
1 Clay	N	N	N	Y	Y	Y	Y	N
2 Young	N	N	?	Y	Y	Y	Y	Y
3 Gephardt	N	N	N	Y	Y	Y	Y	Y
4 Skelton	N	N	N	Y	Y	Y	Y	Y
5 Bolling	?	?	?	?	Y	Y	?	Y
6 ***Coleman***	N	N	Y	Y	N	N	N	N
7 ***Taylor***	N	Y	N	N	N	N	N	Y
8 ***Bailey***	Y	N	Y	N	N	N	N	N
9 Volkmer	N	N	N	Y	Y	Y	Y	Y
10 ***Emerson***	?	Y	Y	N	N	N	N	N
MONTANA								
1 Williams	N	N	N	Y	?	?	Y	Y
2 ***Marlenee***	Y	N	Y	N	N	N	N	N
NEBRASKA								
1 ***Bereuter***	Y	Y	Y	N	N	N	N	Y
2 ***Daub***	Y	Y	Y	N	N	N	N	N
3 ***Smith***	Y	Y	Y	N	N	N	N	N
NEVADA								
AL Santini	N	N	N	N	?	?	N	N
NEW HAMPSHIRE								
1 D'Amours	N	N	?	?	Y	Y	Y	Y
2 ***Gregg***	Y	N	Y	N	N	N	N	N
NEW JERSEY								
1 Florio	N	N	N	Y	Y	Y	Y	Y
2 Hughes	N	N	N	Y	Y	Y	Y	Y
3 Howard	N	N	N	Y	Y	Y	Y	Y
4 ***Smith***	N	N	N	Y	Y	Y	N	Y
5 ***Fenwick***	N	N	Y	N	N	N	N	Y
6 ***Forsythe***	?	?	?	?	N	N	N	Y
7 ***Roukema***	N	N	Y	N	N	N	N	Y
8 Roe	N	N	N	Y	Y	Y	N	Y
9 ***Hollenbeck***	N	?	?	Y	?	N	?	Y
10 Rodino	N	N	N	Y	Y	Y	Y	Y
11 Minish	N	N	N	Y	Y	Y	Y	Y
12 ***Rinaldo***	N	N	N	Y	Y	Y	N	Y
13 ***Courter***	N	N	Y	N	Y	N	N	Y
14 Guarini	N	N	N	Y	Y	Y	Y	Y
15 Dwyer	N	N	N	Y	Y	Y	Y	Y
NEW MEXICO								
1 ***Lujan***	Y	N	Y	N	N	N	N	N
2 ***Skeen***	N	N	Y	N	N	N	N	N
NEW YORK								
1 ***Carney***	P	N	Y	N	Y	N	N	Y
2 Downey	N	N	N	Y	Y	Y	Y	Y
3 ***Carman***	N	N	Y	N	N	N	N	N
4 ***Lent***	Y	Y	Y	N	Y	N	N	N
5 ***McGrath***	Y	Y	Y	N	N	N	Y	N
6 ***LeBoutillier***	Y	?	?	?	?	?	?	?
7 Addabbo	N	N	?	Y	Y	Y	Y	Y
8 Rosenthal	?	N	N	Y	?	?	Y	Y
9 Ferraro	N	N	N	Y	Y	Y	Y	Y
10 Biaggi	N	Y	N	Y	Y	Y	Y	Y
11 Scheuer	N	N	Y	Y	Y	Y	Y	Y
12 Chisholm	N	?	?	Y	?	Y	?	N
13 Solarz	N	N	N	Y	Y	Y	Y	Y
14 Vacancy								
15 Zeferetti	N	N	?	?	Y	Y	Y	Y
16 Schumer	N	Y	N	Y	Y	Y	Y	Y
17 ***Molinari***	Y	N	Y	N	N	N	N	N
18 ***Green***	Y	Y	Y	N	Y	Y	N	Y
19 Rangel	N	N	N	Y	?	Y	Y	N
20 Weiss	N	N	N	Y	Y	Y	Y	N
21 Garcia	N	N	N	Y	Y	Y	Y	N
22 Bingham	P	Y	Y	N	Y	Y	Y	Y
23 Peyser	N	N	N	Y	Y	Y	Y	Y
24 Ottinger	N	N	N	Y	Y	Y	Y	Y
25 ***Fish***	?	N	N	Y	Y	Y	N	Y
26 ***Gilman***	N	N	N	Y	Y	Y	N	Y
27 McHugh	N	N	Y	N	Y	Y	Y	Y
28 Stratton	N	N	N	Y	Y	Y	Y	Y
29 ***Solomon***	N	N	Y	Y	N	N	N	N
30 ***Martin***	?	N	Y	N	N	N	N	N
31 ***Mitchell***	N	N	Y	N	N	N	N	Y
32 ***Wortley***	N	N	N	Y	Y	N	N	N
33 ***Lee***	?	N	?	Y	?	N	?	?
34 ***Horton***	N	N	N	Y	N	N	N	?
35 ***Conable***	Y	N	Y	N	N	N	N	Y
36 LaFalce	N	N	N	Y	Y	Y	Y	Y
37 Nowak	N	N	N	Y	Y	Y	Y	N
38 ***Kemp***	Y	?	Y	N	Y	?	N	Y
39 Lundine	P	Y	N	Y	Y	Y	?	Y
NORTH CAROLINA								
1 Jones	N	N	N	Y	Y	Y	N	Y
2 Fountain	N	N	Y	N	Y	N	N	N
3 Whitley	N	N	N	N	Y	Y	Y	Y
4 Andrews	N	N	N	N	Y	Y	Y	N
5 Neal	N	Y	Y	N	?	?	?	?
6 ***Johnston***	Y	N	Y	N	?	N	?	N
7 Rose	N	Y	N	Y	Y	Y	Y	Y
8 Hefner	N	N	N	N	Y	Y	Y	N
9 ***Martin***	Y	?	Y	N	Y	N	N	Y
10 ***Broyhill***	N	N	Y	N	N	N	N	Y
11 ***Hendon***	Y	N	Y	N	N	N	N	N
NORTH DAKOTA								
AL Dorgan	N	Y	N	Y	Y	Y	Y	Y
OHIO								
1 ***Gradison***	Y	N	Y	N	N	N	N	N
2 Luken	N	N	N	Y	Y	Y	Y	Y
3 Hall	N	N	N	Y	Y	Y	Y	Y
4 ***Oxley***	N	N	Y	N	N	N	N	Y
5 ***Latta***	N	N	N	Y	N	N	N	N
6 ***McEwen***	N	N	N	Y	Y	N	N	N
7 ***Brown***	N	Y	?	?	N	N	N	Y
8 ***Kindness***	N	Y	Y	Y	N	N	N	N
9 ***Weber***	Y	Y	Y	N	N	N	?	Y
10 ***Miller***	N	Y	N	Y	Y	Y	N	Y
11 ***Stanton***	Y	N	Y	N	?	?	N	?
12 Shamansky	N	N	N	Y	Y	?	?	Y
13 Pease	N	N	N	Y	N	Y	Y	N
14 Seiberling	N	N	?	Y	?	Y	Y	Y
15 ***Wylie***	N	N	Y	Y	N	N	N	Y
16 ***Regula***	N	N	N	Y	N	N	N	Y
17 ***Ashbrook***	Y	N	Y	N	Y	N	N	N
18 Applegate	N	N	N	Y	Y	Y	Y	Y
19 ***Williams***	N	N	N	Y	N	N	?	Y
20 Oakar	N	N	N	Y	Y	Y	Y	N
21 Stokes	N	?	?	#	Y	Y	Y	N
22 Eckart	N	N	N	Y	N	Y	Y	Y
23 Mottl	N	Y	N	Y	Y	Y	N	N
OKLAHOMA								
1 Jones	N	N	Y	N	Y	Y	Y	Y
2 Synar	N	N	Y	N	Y	Y	Y	Y
3 Watkins	N	Y	N	Y	Y	Y	Y	Y
4 McCurdy	N	Y	Y	Y	Y	Y	Y	Y
5 ***Edwards***	N	N	Y	N	N	N	N	N
6 English	N	Y	N	Y	N	Y	Y	Y
OREGON								
1 AuCoin	N	N	N	N	?	?	Y	N
2 ***Smith***	Y	Y	Y	N	N	N	N	Y
3 Wyden	N	N	Y	N	Y	Y	Y	Y
4 Weaver	N	N	N	Y	?	Y	Y	N
PENNSYLVANIA								
1 Foglietta	N	Y	N	Y	Y	Y	Y	Y
2 Gray	N	N	N	Y	Y	Y	Y	N
3 Smith	N	?	?	Y	?	?	?	?
4 ***Dougherty***	?	N	N	Y	?	N	N	?
5 ***Schulze***	?	?	?	?	?	?	?	?
6 Yatron	N	N	N	Y	Y	Y	Y	Y
7 Edgar	N	N	N	Y	Y	Y	Y	Y
8 ***Coyne, J.***	N	Y	?	?	N	N	N	Y
9 ***Shuster***	?	?	?	?	?	?	?	?
10 ***McDade***	N	N	N	Y	Y	N	N	Y
11 ***Nelligan***	N	N	N	Y	Y	N	N	N
12 Murtha	N	N	N	Y	Y	Y	Y	Y
13 ***Coughlin***	N	N	Y	Y	N	N	N	Y
14 Coyne, W.	N	N	N	Y	Y	Y	Y	Y
15 ***Ritter***	N	Y	N	Y	N	N	N	N
16 ***Walker***	Y	Y	Y	N	N	N	N	N
17 Ertel	N	?	N	Y	?	?	?	Y
18 Walgren	N	N	N	Y	Y	Y	Y	N
19 ***Goodling***	N	N	N	Y	N	N	N	?
20 Gaydos	N	N	N	Y	Y	Y	N	Y
21 Bailey	N	N	N	Y	Y	Y	Y	Y
22 Murphy	N	N	N	Y	Y	Y	?	Y
23 ***Clinger***	N	N	Y	N	N	N	N	Y
24 ***Marks***	N	N	?	Y	?	?	?	?
25 ***Atkinson***	Y	Y	Y	N	Y	N	N	N
RHODE ISLAND								
1 St Germain	N	N	N	Y	Y	Y	N	Y
2 ***Schneider***	N	N	Y	Y	Y	Y	Y	Y
SOUTH CAROLINA								
1 ***Hartnett***	N	Y	?	N	Y	N	N	N
2 ***Spence***	N	N	Y	N	Y	N	N	Y
3 Derrick	N	N	N	N	Y	Y	Y	Y
4 ***Campbell***	N	N	Y	N	N	N	N	Y
5 Holland	?	N	?	N	?	?	?	?
6 ***Napier***	N	N	Y	N	Y	N	?	Y
SOUTH DAKOTA								
1 Daschle	N	Y	?	?	Y	Y	Y	Y
2 ***Roberts***	Y	Y	?	N	N	N	N	N
TENNESSEE								
1 ***Quillen***	Y	N	Y	N	Y	N	N	Y
2 ***Duncan***	N	N	Y	N	Y	N	N	N
3 Bouquard	?	Y	N	N	Y	Y	N	N
4 Gore	N	N	N	N	Y	Y	Y	Y
5 Boner	N	N	N	Y	Y	Y	?	Y
6 ***Beard***	?	?	?	X	?	?	?	?
7 Jones	N	N	N	Y	Y	Y	Y	Y
8 Ford	N	N	N	Y	?	Y	Y	Y
TEXAS								
1 Hall, S.	N	Y	Y	Y	Y	Y	Y	Y
2 Wilson	N	N	N	Y	Y	N	?	?
3 ***Collins***	Y	Y	Y	N	N	N	N	N
4 Hall, R.	N	N	N	Y	Y	N	N	N
5 Mattox	N	N	N	Y	Y	Y	Y	?
6 Gramm	Y	Y	Y	N	N	N	N	N
7 ***Archer***	Y	N	Y	N	Y	N	N	N
8 ***Fields***	Y	N	Y	N	Y	N	N	N
9 Brooks	N	N	N	Y	Y	Y	Y	N
10 Pickle	N	N	Y	N	Y	Y	Y	Y
11 Leath	N	N	Y	N	Y	Y	N	N
12 Wright	N	N	N	Y	Y	Y	Y	Y
13 Hightower	N	Y	Y	N	N	Y	N	N
14 Patman	N	Y	Y	N	Y	Y	Y	N
15 de la Garza	N	Y	Y	N	Y	Y	Y	N
16 White	N	N	Y	N	Y	Y	N	Y
17 Stenholm	N	Y	Y	N	N	N	N	N
18 Leland	N	N	N	Y	Y	Y	Y	N
19 Hance	N	N	Y	N	Y	Y	Y	N
20 Gonzalez	N	N	N	Y	Y	Y	Y	N
21 ***Loeffler***	Y	Y	Y	N	Y	N	N	N
22 ***Paul***	Y	N	Y	N	N	N	N	N
23 Kazen	N	Y	Y	N	Y	Y	Y	N
24 Frost	N	N	N	Y	Y	Y	Y	Y
UTAH								
1 ***Hansen***	N	N	Y	N	N	N	N	Y
2 ***Marriott***	N	N	Y	N	N	N	N	N
VERMONT								
AL ***Jeffords***	N	?	Y	N	N	N	N	Y
VIRGINIA								
1 ***Trible***	N	N	Y	N	Y	N	N	Y
2 ***Whitehurst***	N	N	Y	N	Y	N	N	N
3 ***Bliley***	Y	Y	Y	N	N	N	N	Y
4 ***Daniel, R.***	Y	N	Y	N	Y	N	N	N
5 Daniel, D.	N	N	Y	N	Y	N	N	Y
6 ***Butler***	Y	N	Y	N	N	N	N	Y
7 ***Robinson***	Y	N	Y	N	N	N	N	Y
8 ***Parris***	N	N	Y	N	Y	N	N	Y
9 ***Wampler***	N	?	Y	N	Y	N	?	N
10 ***Wolf***	Y	N	Y	N	Y	N	N	Y
WASHINGTON								
1 ***Pritchard***	Y	N	Y	N	Y	N	N	Y
2 Swift	N	N	N	Y	Y	Y	Y	Y
3 Bonker	N	N	Y	N	Y	?	?	Y
4 ***Morrison***	Y	Y	Y	N	Y	N	N	N
5 Foley	N	N	Y	N	Y	Y	Y	Y
6 Dicks	N	Y	Y	Y	Y	Y	Y	Y
7 Lowry	N	N	Y	N	Y	Y	Y	Y
WEST VIRGINIA								
1 Mollohan	N	N	N	Y	Y	Y	?	Y
2 ***Benedict***	N	Y	Y	N	N	N	N	Y
3 ***Staton***	N	N	Y	N	N	N	N	N
4 Rahall	N	N	N	Y	?	Y	Y	Y
WISCONSIN								
1 Aspin	N	N	N	Y	?	Y	Y	Y
2 Kastenmeier	N	N	Y	Y	Y	Y	Y	Y
3 ***Gunderson***	N	N	Y	N	N	N	N	Y
4 Zablocki	N	N	N	Y	Y	Y	Y	Y
5 Reuss	N	N	N	N	Y	Y	Y	Y
6 ***Petri***	Y	N	Y	N	N	N	N	N
7 Obey	N	Y	Y	Y	Y	Y	Y	Y
8 ***Roth***	N	Y	Y	Y	N	N	N	Y
9 ***Sensenbrenner***	Y	N	Y	N	N	N	N	N
WYOMING								
AL ***Cheney***	Y	N	Y	N	N	N	N	Y

Southern states - Ala., Ark., Fla., Ga., Ky., La., Miss., N.C., Okla., S.C., Tenn., Texas, Va.

440. HR 3191. North American Convention Tax. Stark, D-Calif., motion that the House resolve itself into the Committee of the Whole for consideration of the bill to allow certain business tax deductions for conventions held on North American cruise ships. Motion agreed to 326-26: R 128-24; D 198-2 (ND 130-2, SD 68-0), Dec. 16, 1982.

441. HR 3191. North American Convention Tax. Passage of the bill to allow certain business tax deductions for conventions held on North American cruise ships. Passed 227-172: R 69-105; D 158-67 (ND 110-43, SD 48-24), Dec. 16, 1982.

442. S 1965. Paddy Creek Wilderness Act. Passage of the bill to designate 6,888 acres in the Mark Twain National Forest, Missouri, as the Paddy Creek Wilderness Area. Passed 367-23: R 151-19; D 216-4 (ND 150-1, SD 66-3), Dec. 16, 1982.

443. HR 7019. Transportation Appropriations, Fiscal 1983. Sabo, D-Minn., motion that the House recede from its disagreement to the Senate amendment to cancel the St. Lawrence Seaway's federal debt for original construction costs. Motion agreed to 298-77: R 111-47; D 187-30 (ND 135-12, SD 52-18), Dec. 16, 1982.

444. H Res 632. Contempt of Congress Proceedings Against Anne M. Gorsuch. Adoption of the resolution to cite Environmental Protection Agency Administrator Anne M. Gorsuch for contempt of Congress for refusing to furnish certain documents under subpoena to the House Public Works and Transportation Subcommittee on Investigations and Oversight. Adopted 259-105: R 55-101; D 204-4 (ND 145-2, SD 59-2), Dec. 16, 1982.

445. HR 7357. Immigration Reform and Control Act of 1982. Rodino, D-N.J., motion that the House resolve itself into the Committee of the Whole for consideration of the bill to revise immigration law by providing for sanctions against employers who knowingly hire illegal aliens; granting legal status to undocumented aliens already in the United States; broadening an existing temporary worker program; and revising current procedures for handling asylum, deportation and exclusion cases. Motion agreed to 212-65: R 83-48; D 129-17 (ND 87-9, SD 42-8), Dec. 16, 1982.

446. HR 7397. Caribbean Basin Initiative. De Lugo, D-Virgin Islands, amendment to put a quota on duty-free rum from Caribbean nations allowed to enter the United States. Rejected 171-226: R 24-150; D 147-76 (ND 108-43, SD 39-33), Dec. 17, 1982.

447. HR 7397. Caribbean Basin Initiative. Passage of the bill to provide duty-free entry into the United States of certain products from most Caribbean nations and to allow tax deductions for the expenses of conventions held in the Caribbean. Passed 260-142: R 162-15; D 98-127 (ND 50-99, SD 48-28), Dec. 17, 1982. A "yea" was a vote supporting the president's position.

KEY

Y Voted for (yea).
\# Paired for.
\+ Announced for.
N Voted against (nay).
X Paired against.
\- Announced against.
P Voted "present".
C Voted "present" to avoid possible conflict of interest.
? Did not vote or otherwise make a position known.

Democrats **Republicans**

Member	440	441	442	443	444	445	446	447
ALABAMA								
1 Edwards	?	Y	Y	Y	?	?	N	Y
2 Dickinson	Y	N	Y	N	N	N	N	Y
3 Nichols	Y	Y	Y	Y	?	?	Y	N
4 Bevill	Y	Y	Y	Y	Y	Y	Y	N
5 Flippo	Y	Y	Y	Y	#	?	N	Y
6 Smith	Y	Y	Y	N	N	N	N	Y
7 Shelby	Y	N	N	N	Y	?	Y	N
ALASKA								
AL Young	N	Y	N	?	?	?	?	Y
ARIZONA								
1 Rhodes	Y	N	Y	?	?	?	?	?
2 Udall	?	Y	Y	Y	Y	?	Y	Y
3 Stump	Y	N	N	N	N	N	N	Y
4 Rudd	Y	N	Y	N	N	Y	N	?
ARKANSAS								
1 Alexander	?	?	?	?	?	?	Y	N
2 Bethune	Y	Y	Y	Y	N	Y	Y	Y
3 Hammerschmidt	Y	Y	Y	Y	N	Y	Y	Y
4 Anthony	Y	Y	Y	Y	Y	?	N	Y
CALIFORNIA								
1 Chappie	Y	N	Y	N	Y	N	N	Y
2 Clausen	Y	Y	Y	Y	N	Y	Y	Y
3 Matsui	?	Y	Y	Y	Y	N	N	N
4 Fazio	Y	Y	Y	Y	Y	Y	N	N
5 Burton, J.	?	Y	Y	Y	Y	?	Y	N
6 Burton, P.	Y	Y	Y	N	N	Y	N	N
7 Miller	?	Y	Y	Y	Y	Y	Y	N
8 Dellums	Y	?	Y	Y	Y	Y	Y	N
9 Stark	Y	Y	?	Y	N	Y	N	N
10 Edwards	Y	Y	Y	Y	Y	N	N	N
11 Lantos	Y	Y	Y	Y	?	?	Y	N
12 McCloskey	?	Y	Y	Y	Y	N	Y	Y
13 Mineta	Y	Y	Y	Y	Y	Y	Y	N
14 Shumway	Y	Y	N	N	N	?	N	Y
15 Coelho	Y	Y	Y	Y	Y	Y	Y	N
16 Panetta	Y	Y	Y	N	Y	N	N	N
17 Pashayan	Y	N	Y	N	N	N	N	N
18 Thomas	Y	N	Y	?	?	?	N	Y
19 Lagomarsino	Y	N	Y	N	N	Y	N	Y
20 Goldwater	?	?	Y	?	?	?	?	?
21 Fiedler	?	N	Y	N	N	N	N	Y
22 Moorhead	Y	N	N	N	N	N	N	Y
23 Beilenson	Y	Y	Y	Y	Y	Y	N	Y
24 Waxman	?	N	?	?	Y	Y	Y	N
25 Roybal	Y	Y	Y	Y	Y	N	Y	N
26 Rousselot	?	?	?	?	?	?	?	?
27 Dornan	Y	Y	Y	N	N	Y	N	Y
28 Dixon	Y	Y	Y	Y	Y	?	Y	N
29 Hawkins	?	Y	Y	Y	?	?	Y	N
30 Martinez	Y	Y	Y	Y	Y	Y	N	N
31 Dymally	?	?	?	?	?	?	?	?
32 Anderson	Y	Y	Y	N	Y	Y	Y	N
33 Grisham	?	Y	N	Y	N	N	Y	N
34 Lungren	Y	Y	Y	N	N	Y	N	Y
35 Dreier	Y	N	N	N	N	N	N	Y
36 Brown	Y	Y	Y	Y	?	Y	N	Y
37 Lewis	Y	N	Y	Y	?	?	N	Y
38 Patterson	Y	Y	Y	Y	Y	Y	N	Y
39 Dannemeyer	N	N	N	N	N	N	N	Y
40 Badham	Y	Y	Y	N	X	?	N	Y
41 Lowery	Y	N	Y	N	Y	N	N	Y
42 Hunter	Y	N	Y	N	Y	N	N	Y
43 Burgener	?	N	Y	N	X	?	N	Y
COLORADO								
1 Schroeder	Y	N	Y	N	N	?	Y	N
2 Wirth	Y	N	Y	N	Y	Y	N	Y
3 Kogovsek	Y	N	Y	Y	Y	Y	Y	N
4 Brown	Y	N	Y	N	N	Y	N	Y
5 Kramer	N	N	Y	N	N	Y	N	Y
CONNECTICUT								
1 Kennelly	Y	N	Y	Y	Y	Y	N	Y
2 Gejdenson	Y	Y	Y	Y	Y	?	Y	Y
3 DeNardis	?	Y	Y	?	Y	Y	Y	?
4 McKinney	Y	Y	?	?	Y	Y	N	Y
5 Ratchford	Y	Y	Y	Y	Y	Y	?	?
6 Moffett	?	N	Y	?	?	?	?	?
DELAWARE								
AL Evans	?	Y	?	Y	?	?	N	Y
FLORIDA								
1 Hutto	Y	Y	Y	Y	Y	?	N	Y
2 Fuqua	Y	Y	Y	Y	#	?	?	?
3 Bennett	Y	Y	Y	Y	Y	Y	Y	Y
4 Chappell	?	Y	Y	Y	Y	?	N	Y
5 McCollum	Y	N	Y	Y	Y	N	N	Y
6 Young	?	N	Y	Y	N	N	N	Y
7 Gibbons	Y	Y	Y	Y	Y	Y	N	Y
8 Ireland	?	Y	?	?	Y	?	N	Y
9 Nelson	Y	?	Y	Y	Y	?	N	Y
10 Bafalis	Y	?	Y	?	N	Y	N	Y
11 Mica	Y	Y	Y	Y	Y	Y	?	Y
12 Shaw	Y	N	Y	N	N	?	N	Y
13 Lehman	?	?	?	?	?	?	?	?
14 Pepper	Y	N	Y	Y	Y	Y	N	Y
15 Fascell	?	?	?	?	?	?	?	Y
GEORGIA								
1 Ginn	Y	Y	Y	Y	Y	Y	Y	Y
2 Hatcher	Y	N	Y	Y	?	?	N	Y
3 Brinkley	Y	Y	Y	Y	Y	?	N	Y
4 Levitas	Y	N	Y	N	Y	Y	N	Y
5 Fowler	Y	Y	Y	?	?	Y	N	Y
6 Gingrich	Y	N	Y	N	N	Y	N	Y
7 McDonald	Y	N	N	N	N	N	N	N
8 Evans	Y	Y	Y	?	?	?	?	Y
9 Jenkins	Y	N	N	Y	N	Y	Y	Y
10 Barnard	Y	Y	Y	N	Y	Y	Y	Y
HAWAII								
1 Heftel	Y	Y	?	N	Y	Y	Y	N
2 Akaka	?	Y	Y	Y	Y	?	Y	N
IDAHO								
1 Craig	N	N	N	N	X	?	N	Y
2 Hansen	N	N	N	N	N	N	N	Y
ILLINOIS								
1 Washington	Y	N	Y	Y	Y	?	Y	N
2 Savage	?	?	?	Y	Y	?	Y	N
3 Russo	Y	Y	Y	Y	Y	Y	Y	N
4 Derwinski	N	N	Y	N	Y	N	N	Y
5 Fary	Y	Y	Y	Y	Y	?	Y	N
6 Hyde	?	Y	Y	Y	Y	Y	Y	N
7 Collins	Y	N	Y	Y	Y	Y	Y	N
8 Rostenkowski	Y	Y	Y	Y	Y	Y	Y	N
9 Yates	Y	N	Y	Y	Y	Y	N	N
10 Porter	Y	N	Y	Y	Y	Y	Y	N
11 Annunzio	Y	Y	Y	Y	Y	Y	Y	N
12 Crane, P.	Y	N	Y	N	N	N	N	Y
13 McClory	Y	Y	Y	N	Y	N	N	Y
14 Erlenborn	Y	Y	Y	N	N	Y	N	Y
15 Corcoran	Y	N	Y	N	Y	N	N	Y
16 Martin	Y	N	Y	Y	Y	Y	N	Y
17 O'Brien	Y	N	Y	?	N	Y	N	Y
18 Michel	Y	N	Y	N	Y	N	N	Y
19 Railsback	Y	N	Y	?	?	N	Y	Y
20 Findley	?	N	Y	N	Y	Y	?	?
21 Madigan	Y	N	Y	N	Y	N	N	Y
22 Crane, D.	Y	N	N	Y	N	N	N	Y
23 Price	Y	Y	Y	Y	Y	Y	Y	N
24 Simon	Y	Y	Y	Y	Y	Y	Y	Y
INDIANA								
1 Hall	Y	Y	Y	Y	Y	Y	Y	N
2 Fithian	Y	Y	Y	Y	Y	Y	Y	N
3 Hiler	Y	N	Y	N	N	N	N	Y
4 Coats	Y	N	Y	N	Y	?	N	Y
5 Hillis	Y	Y	Y	N	Y	Y	N	Y
6 Evans	Y	N	Y	Y	Y	N	N	Y
7 Myers	Y	N	Y	N	Y	N	Y	N
8 Deckard	?	?	?	?	Y	?	?	Y
9 Hamilton	Y	N	Y	Y	Y	Y	N	Y
10 Sharp	N	N	Y	Y	Y	Y	Y	N
11 Jacobs	?	N	Y	?	?	?	N	Y
IOWA								
1 Leach	?	N	Y	N	Y	?	N	Y
2 Tauke	+	.	+	.	.	Y	Y	N
3 Evans	N	N	N	N	N	Y	N	Y
4 Smith	N	N	Y	N	Y	N	N	Y
5 Harkin	Y	N	Y	N	Y	Y	N	N
6 Bedell	Y	N	Y	N	Y	Y	Y	Y

ND - Northern Democrats   SD - Southern Democrats

Corresponding to Congressional Record Votes 466, 467, 468, 469, 471, 472, 475, 476

	440	441	442	443	444	445	446	447
KANSAS								
1 ***Roberts***	Y	N	Y	Y	N	N	N	Y
2 ***Jeffries***	Y	Y	N	N	X	?	N	Y
3 ***Winn***	Y	N	Y	Y	N	Y	?	#
4 Glickman	Y	N	Y	N	Y	Y	N	N
5 ***Whittaker***	Y	N	Y	N	Y	Y	N	Y
KENTUCKY								
1 Hubbard	?	?	?	?	?	?	N	Y
2 Natcher	Y	Y	Y	Y	Y	Y	N	N
3 Mazzoli	Y	N	Y	Y	Y	Y	N	Y
4 ***Snyder***	Y	Y	Y	N	?	?	Y	N
5 ***Rogers***	Y	N	Y	Y	N	N	Y	N
6 ***Hopkins***	Y	N	Y	Y	Y	N	Y	N
7 Perkins	Y	N	Y	Y	Y	Y	N	N
LOUISIANA								
1 ***Livingston***	Y	Y	Y	Y	Y	Y	N	Y
2 Boggs	Y	Y	?	Y	Y	Y	N	Y
3 Tauzin	Y	Y	Y	Y	Y	Y	N	Y
4 Roemer	Y	N	Y	Y	Y	Y	Y	Y
5 Huckaby	?	N	Y	Y	?	?	Y	Y
6 ***Moore***	Y	Y	Y	N	Y	Y	N	Y
7 Breaux	Y	Y	Y	Y	Y	?	Y	Y
8 Long	Y	Y	Y	Y	Y	?	Y	N
MAINE								
1 ***Emery***	?	Y	Y	Y	N	?	Y	Y
2 ***Snowe***	Y	N	Y	Y	Y	Y	N	Y
MARYLAND								
1 Dyson	Y	Y	Y	Y	Y	Y	Y	N
2 Long	Y	Y	Y	Y	?	?	N	Y
3 Mikulski	Y	Y	Y	Y	Y	Y	Y	N
4 ***Holt***	?	?	?	?	?	?	Y	Y
5 Hoyer	Y	Y	Y	Y	Y	Y	Y	Y
6 Byron	Y	N	Y	Y	Y	?	N	Y
7 Mitchell	?	Y	Y	Y	Y	Y	?	N
8 Barnes	Y	Y	Y	Y	Y	?	N	Y
MASSACHUSETTS								
1 ***Conte***	Y	N	Y	Y	Y	Y	N	Y
2 Boland	Y	Y	Y	Y	Y	Y	Y	N
3 Early	Y	Y	Y	N	Y	Y	Y	N
4 Frank	Y	N	Y	N	?	?	Y	N
5 Shannon	Y	N	Y	Y	Y	Y	Y	N
6 Mavroules	Y	Y	Y	Y	Y	?	Y	N
7 Markey	Y	?	Y	Y	Y	Y	Y	N
8 O'Neill								
9 Moakley	Y	Y	Y	Y	Y	Y	Y	N
10 ***Heckler***	?	?	Y	Y	?	?	N	Y
11 Donnelly	Y	Y	Y	Y	Y	Y	Y	N
12 Studds	Y	Y	Y	Y	Y	Y	N	Y
MICHIGAN								
1 Conyers	Y	Y	Y	Y	Y	N	Y	N
2 ***Pursell***	Y	?	Y	Y	?	?	N	Y
3 Wolpe	Y	N	Y	Y	Y	Y	N	N
4 ***Siljander***	Y	Y	Y	Y	N	Y	N	Y
5 ***Sawyer***	Y	Y	Y	Y	N	Y	N	Y
6 ***Dunn***	Y	N	?	Y	N	?	N	N
7 Kildee	Y	N	Y	Y	Y	Y	Y	N
8 Traxler	Y	Y	Y	Y	Y	Y	Y	N
9 ***Vander Jagt***	Y	Y	Y	Y	?	?	N	Y
10 Albosta	Y	Y	Y	Y	Y	?	Y	N
11 ***Davis***	?	Y	Y	Y	Y	Y	Y	N
12 Bonior	?	Y	Y	Y	Y	?	N	N
13 Crockett	?	N	Y	Y	Y	?	Y	N
14 Hertel	Y	Y	Y	Y	Y	?	Y	N
15 Ford	Y	?	Y	Y	Y	Y	Y	N
16 Dingell	Y	Y	Y	Y	Y	Y	Y	N
17 Brodhead	?	N	Y	Y	Y	Y	N	N
18 Blanchard	?	?	?	?	?	?	?	?
19 ***Broomfield***	Y	N	Y	Y	?	?	N	Y
MINNESOTA								
1 ***Erdahl***	Y	N	Y	?	Y	N	N	Y
2 ***Hagedorn***	?	?	?	?	?	?	?	?
3 ***Frenzel***	Y	N	Y	Y	Y	N	N	Y
4 Vento	Y	N	Y	Y	Y	?	Y	N
5 Sabo	?	N	Y	Y	Y	Y	Y	Y
6 ***Weber***	Y	N	Y	Y	Y	N	N	Y
7 ***Stangeland***	Y	Y	Y	?	N	N	N	Y
8 Oberstar	Y	Y	Y	Y	Y	Y	Y	N
MISSISSIPPI								
1 Whitten	Y	Y	Y	Y	Y	Y	N	N
2 Bowen	Y	Y	Y	Y	Y	Y	Y	Y
3 Montgomery	Y	N	Y	Y	Y	Y	N	Y
4 Dowdy	Y	Y	Y	Y	Y	Y	N	N
5 ***Lott***	Y	N	Y	Y	N	N	N	Y
MISSOURI								
1 Clay	Y	Y	Y	Y	Y	?	Y	N
2 Young	Y	Y	Y	Y	Y	?	Y	N
3 Gephardt	Y	Y	Y	Y	Y	Y	N	Y
4 Skelton	Y	Y	Y	Y	Y	?	Y	N
5 Bolling	?	Y	?	?	?	?	?	?
6 ***Coleman***	N	N	Y	N	Y	?	Y	Y
7 ***Taylor***	Y	Y	Y	Y	N	Y	N	Y
8 ***Bailey***	N	N	Y	Y	N	N	N	Y
9 Volkmer	Y	N	Y	Y	Y	Y	Y	N
10 ***Emerson***	Y	Y	Y	?	N	?	N	Y
MONTANA								
1 Williams	Y	Y	Y	?	Y	?	Y	N
2 ***Marlenee***	Y	N	Y	Y	N	Y	?	N
NEBRASKA								
1 ***Bereuter***	N	N	Y	N	Y	Y	N	Y
2 ***Daub***	N	N	Y	N	N	N	N	Y
3 ***Smith***	Y	N	Y	Y	N	Y	N	Y
NEVADA								
AL Santini	Y	N	Y	?	?	?	?	?
NEW HAMPSHIRE								
1 D'Amours	Y	Y	Y	?	Y	?	Y	N
2 ***Gregg***	?	N	Y	N	N	?	N	Y
NEW JERSEY								
1 Florio	Y	Y	Y	Y	Y	?	Y	N
2 Hughes	Y	Y	Y	Y	Y	Y	Y	N
3 Howard	Y	Y	Y	Y	Y	Y	Y	N
4 ***Smith***	Y	Y	Y	Y	N	Y	N	Y
5 ***Fenwick***	N	N	Y	Y	Y	Y	N	Y
6 ***Forsythe***	N	N	?	Y	N	?	N	Y
7 ***Roukema***	Y	N	Y	Y	Y	Y	N	Y
8 Roe	Y	Y	Y	Y	Y	?	Y	Y
9 ***Hollenbeck***	Y	Y	?	?	N	?	Y	Y
10 Rodino	Y	Y	Y	Y	Y	Y	Y	N
11 Minish	Y	Y	Y	Y	Y	Y	Y	N
12 ***Rinaldo***	Y	Y	Y	Y	Y	Y	Y	N
13 ***Courter***	Y	N	Y	N	Y	Y	N	Y
14 Guarini	Y	Y	Y	Y	Y	?	Y	N
15 Dwyer	Y	Y	Y	Y	Y	?	Y	Y
NEW MEXICO								
1 ***Lujan***	N	N	Y	N	N	N	Y	Y
2 ***Skeen***	Y	N	N	Y	N	N	N	Y
NEW YORK								
1 ***Carney***	Y	Y	Y	Y	N	N	N	Y
2 Downey	?	Y	Y	Y	Y	Y	N	Y
3 ***Carman***	Y	N	?	Y	N	Y	N	Y
4 ***Lent***	Y	Y	Y	Y	N	Y	N	Y
5 ***McGrath***	Y	Y	Y	Y	N	N	N	Y
6 ***LeBoutillier***	?	?	?	?	?	?	N	Y
7 Addabbo	?	Y	Y	Y	Y	?	Y	Y
8 Rosenthal	Y	?	Y	?	?	?	Y	Y
9 Ferraro	Y	Y	Y	Y	Y	Y	Y	N
10 Biaggi	Y	Y	Y	Y	Y	Y	Y	Y
11 Scheuer	Y	Y	Y	Y	Y	Y	Y	Y
12 Chisholm	?	Y	?	?	Y	?	Y	Y
13 Solarz	Y	Y	Y	Y	Y	Y	N	Y
14 Vacancy								
15 Zeferetti	Y	Y	Y	Y	Y	?	?	?
16 Schumer	Y	Y	Y	Y	Y	Y	N	N
17 ***Molinari***	Y	N	Y	Y	Y	Y	N	Y
18 ***Green***	Y	P	Y	N	Y	Y	N	Y
19 Rangel	?	Y	Y	Y	Y	Y	Y	Y
20 Weiss	Y	Y	Y	Y	Y	Y	Y	Y
21 Garcia	?	?	?	?	?	?	Y	Y
22 Bingham	Y	N	Y	Y	Y	?	Y	Y
23 Peyser	Y	Y	Y	Y	Y	Y	Y	N
24 Ottinger	Y	N	Y	Y	Y	?	Y	Y
25 ***Fish***	Y	Y	Y	Y	Y	Y	N	Y
26 ***Gilman***	Y	Y	Y	Y	Y	Y	Y	Y
27 McHugh	?	N	Y	Y	Y	Y	Y	N
28 Stratton	Y	Y	Y	Y	Y	Y	Y	Y
29 ***Solomon***	Y	N	Y	Y	N	N	N	Y
30 ***Martin***	N	N	Y	Y	Y	?	N	Y
31 ***Mitchell***	Y	Y	Y	Y	Y	Y	N	Y
32 ***Wortley***	Y	Y	Y	Y	N	Y	N	Y
33 ***Lee***	Y	?	?	?	?	?	?	Y
34 ***Horton***	?	Y	Y	Y	?	?	?	#
35 ***Conable***	N	N	Y	Y	Y	Y	N	Y
36 LaFalce	?	Y	Y	Y	Y	Y	Y	Y
37 Nowak	Y	Y	Y	Y	Y	Y	Y	N
38 ***Kemp***	Y	Y	?	?	?	?	N	Y
39 Lundine	Y	Y	Y	Y	?	?	Y	N
NORTH CAROLINA								
1 Jones	Y	?	?	?	?	?	Y	Y
2 Fountain	Y	N	Y	N	Y	N	Y	N
3 Whitley	Y	Y	Y	N	Y	Y	Y	N
4 Andrews	Y	N	Y	N	Y	Y	N	Y
5 Neal	Y	Y	Y	N	Y	Y	Y	N
6 ***Johnston***	Y	Y	Y	?	N	N	?	?
7 Rose	Y	Y	Y	Y	?	?	Y	Y
8 Hefner	Y	N	Y	N	Y	Y	Y	N
9 ***Martin***	Y	N	Y	N	N	N	N	Y
10 ***Broyhill***	Y	N	Y	N	N	Y	N	Y
11 ***Hendon***	N	N	N	N	N	N	N	Y
NORTH DAKOTA								
AL Dorgan	Y	N	Y	Y	Y	Y	N	Y
OHIO								
1 ***Gradison***	Y	N	Y	Y	Y	?	N	Y
2 Luken	Y	Y	Y	Y	Y	?	N	?
3 Hall	Y	Y	Y	Y	Y	?	Y	N
4 ***Oxley***	?	N	Y	Y	N	?	N	Y
5 ***Latta***	N	N	Y	Y	N	N	N	Y
6 ***McEwen***	Y	N	Y	Y	N	N	N	Y
7 ***Brown***	Y	Y	Y	Y	N	N	N	Y
8 ***Kindness***	N	N	N	Y	N	?	?	Y
9 ***Weber***	Y	N	Y	Y	N	?	N	Y
10 ***Miller***	Y	N	Y	N	Y	Y	N	N
11 ***Stanton***	Y	?	?	?	?	?	?	?
12 Shamansky	Y	Y	Y	Y	Y	Y	N	N
13 Pease	N	N	Y	Y	Y	Y	Y	N
14 Seiberling	Y	N	Y	Y	Y	Y	Y	N
15 ***Wylie***	N	N	Y	Y	N	Y	N	Y
16 ***Regula***	Y	N	Y	Y	Y	Y	N	Y
17 ***Ashbrook***	Y	Y	N	N	?	?	N	Y
18 Applegate	?	Y	Y	Y	Y	Y	N	N
19 ***Williams***	?	Y	?	?	#	?	N	N
20 Oakar	Y	Y	Y	Y	Y	?	Y	N
21 Stokes	Y	Y	Y	Y	Y	Y	Y	N
22 Eckart	Y	N	Y	Y	Y	Y	Y	N
23 Mottl	Y	Y	Y	Y	Y	Y	N	N
OKLAHOMA								
1 Jones	Y	Y	Y	N	Y	Y	Y	N
2 Synar	Y	Y	Y	Y	Y	?	Y	Y
3 Watkins	Y	N	Y	N	Y	Y	Y	N
4 McCurdy	Y	N	Y	N	Y	?	N	Y
5 ***Edwards***	?	N	Y	N	Y	N	N	Y
6 English	Y	N	Y	N	Y	Y	Y	Y
OREGON								
1 AuCoin	Y	Y	Y	Y	Y	Y	Y	N
2 ***Smith***	Y	N	N	N	Y	N	N	Y
3 Wyden	Y	N	Y	Y	Y	Y	Y	N
4 Weaver	Y	Y	Y	Y	Y	?	Y	N
PENNSYLVANIA								
1 Foglietta	Y	Y	Y	Y	Y	?	Y	N
2 Gray	Y	Y	?	Y	Y	?	Y	N
3 Smith	?	?	?	?	?	?	?	?
4 ***Dougherty***	?	Y	?	?	?	?	N	Y
5 ***Schulze***	?	?	?	?	?	?	?	?
6 Yatron	Y	Y	Y	Y	Y	?	N	Y
7 Edgar	Y	N	Y	Y	Y	Y	N	N
8 ***Coyne, J.***	Y	N	Y	Y	N	N	N	Y
9 ***Shuster***	?	?	?	?	?	?	?	?
10 ***McDade***	Y	N	Y	Y	N	Y	N	Y
11 ***Nelligan***	Y	Y	Y	Y	Y	Y	N	Y
12 Murtha	Y	Y	Y	Y	Y	?	N	N
13 ***Coughlin***	Y	N	Y	Y	N	?	N	Y
14 Coyne, W.	Y	Y	Y	Y	Y	?	N	Y
15 ***Ritter***	Y	N	Y	Y	N	Y	N	Y
16 ***Walker***	?	N	Y	N	N	N	N	N
17 Ertel	Y	N	Y	Y	Y	?	Y	?
18 Walgren	Y	N	Y	Y	Y	Y	Y	N
19 ***Goodling***	?	N	Y	Y	Y	N	N	Y
20 Gaydos	Y	Y	Y	?	Y	Y	N	N
21 Bailey	Y	Y	Y	Y	Y	?	N	N
22 Murphy	?	Y	Y	Y	Y	?	Y	N
23 ***Clinger***	Y	N	Y	Y	N	Y	N	Y
24 ***Marks***	?	?	?	?	Y	?	?	?
25 ***Atkinson***	?	Y	Y	Y	N	?	Y	Y
RHODE ISLAND								
1 St Germain	Y	Y	Y	Y	Y	?	Y	N
2 ***Schneider***	?	Y	Y	?	Y	?	Y	Y
SOUTH CAROLINA								
1 ***Hartnett***	Y	Y	Y	Y	N	N	N	Y
2 ***Spence***	Y	Y	Y	Y	N	Y	N	Y
3 Derrick	Y	Y	?	?	#	?	?	N
4 ***Campbell***	Y	Y	Y	Y	?	?	N	Y
5 Holland	?	?	?	?	?	?	?	?
6 ***Napier***	Y	Y	Y	Y	N	Y	Y	N
SOUTH DAKOTA								
1 Daschle	Y	Y	Y	Y	Y	Y	Y	N
2 ***Roberts***	?	N	N	?	N	N	?	?
TENNESSEE								
1 ***Quillen***	Y	Y	Y	Y	N	Y	Y	Y
2 ***Duncan***	Y	Y	Y	Y	N	Y	Y	N
3 Bouquard	Y	Y	Y	Y	Y	Y	N	N
4 Gore	Y	Y	Y	Y	Y	Y	Y	N
5 Boner	?	Y	Y	Y	Y	?	Y	N
6 ***Beard***	?	?	?	?	?	?	N	Y
7 Jones	Y	Y	Y	Y	Y	Y	N	N
8 Ford	Y	Y	Y	Y	Y	Y	Y	N
TEXAS								
1 Hall, S.	Y	N	Y	N	Y	Y	N	Y
2 Wilson	?	Y	?	Y	Y	Y	N	Y
3 ***Collins***	Y	N	N	N	N	Y	N	Y
4 Hall, R.	Y	N	Y	N	Y	Y	N	N
5 Mattox	Y	N	Y	Y	Y	Y	N	N
6 Gramm	Y	N	N	N	N	?	N	Y
7 ***Archer***	?	Y	Y	N	?	?	N	Y
8 ***Fields***	?	Y	Y	N	N	N	N	Y
9 Brooks	Y	Y	Y	Y	Y	Y	Y	Y
10 Pickle	Y	Y	Y	Y	Y	Y	N	Y
11 Leath	Y	Y	Y	Y	?	?	N	Y
12 Wright	Y	Y	Y	Y	Y	Y	Y	Y
13 Hightower	Y	N	Y	Y	Y	Y	N	Y
14 Patman	Y	Y	Y	N	Y	N	Y	N
15 de la Garza	Y	Y	Y	Y	Y	Y	Y	Y
16 White	Y	Y	Y	Y	Y	Y	Y	Y
17 Stenholm	Y	N	Y	N	Y	N	N	Y
18 Leland	Y	Y	Y	Y	Y	N	Y	N
19 Hance	Y	Y	Y	Y	Y	Y	N	Y
20 Gonzalez	Y	N	Y	Y	Y	N	Y	N
21 ***Loeffler***	Y	N	Y	Y	N	N	N	Y
22 ***Paul***	Y	Y	N	N	Y	N	N	N
23 Kazen	Y	N	Y	Y	Y	N	Y	Y
24 Frost	?	Y	Y	Y	Y	N	N	N
UTAH								
1 ***Hansen***	Y	?	?	N	N	N	N	Y
2 ***Marriott***	Y	N	Y	Y	N	N	N	Y
VERMONT								
AL ***Jeffords***	N	N	Y	N	Y	Y	Y	Y
VIRGINIA								
1 ***Trible***	Y	Y	Y	Y	N	Y	N	Y
2 ***Whitehurst***	Y	Y	Y	Y	N	?	N	Y
3 ***Bliley***	Y	Y	Y	N	N	Y	N	Y
4 ***Daniel, R.***	Y	Y	Y	N	N	Y	N	Y
5 Daniel, D.	Y	Y	Y	Y	Y	?	N	Y
6 ***Butler***	Y	N	Y	Y	N	Y	N	Y
7 ***Robinson***	Y	Y	Y	Y	N	N	N	Y
8 ***Parris***	Y	Y	Y	Y	Y	?	N	Y
9 ***Wampler***	Y	Y	Y	Y	N	N	Y	Y
10 ***Wolf***	Y	Y	Y	Y	N	Y	N	Y
WASHINGTON								
1 ***Pritchard***	Y	Y	Y	Y	Y	Y	N	Y
2 Swift	?	Y	Y	Y	Y	?	Y	N
3 Bonker	Y	Y	Y	Y	Y	?	N	Y
4 ***Morrison***	Y	Y	Y	Y	N	N	N	Y
5 Foley	Y	Y	Y	Y	Y	Y	?	?
6 Dicks	Y	Y	Y	Y	Y	Y	N	Y
7 Lowry	Y	Y	Y	N	Y	Y	Y	N
WEST VIRGINIA								
1 Mollohan	Y	Y	?	Y	Y	?	Y	X
2 ***Benedict***	?	N	Y	?	N	Y	N	Y
3 ***Staton***	Y	N	N	?	N	Y	N	Y
4 Rahall	Y	Y	Y	Y	Y	?	?	X
WISCONSIN								
1 Aspin	Y	N	Y	Y	Y	Y	Y	Y
2 Kastenmeier	Y	N	Y	Y	Y	Y	Y	N
3 ***Gunderson***	N	N	Y	Y	Y	Y	N	Y
4 Zablocki	Y	Y	Y	Y	Y	Y	N	Y
5 Reuss	Y	N	Y	Y	Y	Y	N	Y
6 ***Petri***	N	N	Y	Y	Y	Y	N	Y
7 Obey	Y	N	Y	Y	Y	Y	Y	N
8 ***Roth***	Y	N	Y	Y	N	Y	Y	Y
9 ***Sensenbrenner***	N	N	Y	Y	Y	N	N	Y
WYOMING								
AL ***Cheney***	Y	N	Y	Y	N	Y	N	Y

Southern states - Ala., Ark., Fla., Ga., Ky., La., Miss., N.C., Okla., S.C., Tenn., Texas, Va.

448. HR 7144. District of Columbia Appropriations, Fiscal 1983. Adoption of the conference report on the bill to appropriate $524,180,100 in federal funds for the District of Columbia in fiscal 1983, and $1,998,841,900 in funds from the District's own treasury. Adopted 288-79: R 100-62; D 188-17 (ND 130-5, SD 58-12), Dec. 17, 1982. The president had requested $579,870,000 in federal funds and $2,005,949,400 in District funds.

449. HR 7144. District of Columbia Appropriations, Fiscal 1983. Walker, R-Pa., motion that the House recede from its disagreement with the Senate on the amendment to authorize the mayor of the District of Columbia to set the salary of the city administrator at a rate not to exceed the maximum established for level IV of the Federal Executive Schedule. Motion agreed to 236-122: R 67-91; D 169-31 (ND 119-14, SD 50-17), Dec. 17, 1982.

450. H Res 621. House Historian. Adoption of the resolution to create a House Office for the Bicentennial to prepare for the 200th anniversary of Congress. Authority for the office would expire in 1989. Adopted 230-97: R 64-85; D 166-12 (ND 110-5, SD 56-7), Dec. 17, 1982. (A resolution (H Res 581) to create a permanent historian previously was rejected by the House *(see vote 347, p. 104-H).)*

451. HR 7357. Immigration Reform and Control Act of 1982. Mazzoli, D-Ky., motion that the House resolve itself into the Committee of the Whole for consideration of the bill to revise immigration law by providing for sanctions against employers who knowingly hire illegal aliens; granting legal status to undocumented aliens already in the United States; broadening an existing temporary worker program; and revising current procedures for handling asylum, deportation and exclusion cases. Motion agreed to 148-113: R 56-59; D 92-54 (ND 59-29, SD 33-25), Dec. 17, 1982.

452. Procedural Motion. Sensenbrenner, R-Wis., motion to approve the House *Journal* of Friday, Dec. 17. Motion agreed to 256-38: R 104-25; D 152-13 (ND 97-10, SD 55-3), Dec. 18, 1982.

453. HR 7356. Interior Appropriations, Fiscal 1983. Adoption of the conference report on the bill to appropriate $7,500,025,000 in fiscal 1983 for the Department of Interior and certain related agencies. Adopted 282-63: R 103-46; D 179-17 (ND 125-7, SD 54-10), Dec. 18, 1982. The president had requested $6,576,960,000.

454. HR 7357. Immigration Reform and Control Act of 1982. Education and Labor Committee amendment, offered by Hawkins, D-Calif., to require employers to compile and retain job applicant data, including the names and addresses of all individuals who apply for a position in writing at least 90 days before the date on which the job is filled. Rejected 110-213: R 4-133; D 106-80 (ND 96-32, SD 10-48), Dec. 18, 1982.

455. HR 3963. Contract Services for Drug Dependent Federal Offenders Act Amendment. Sawyer, R-Mich., demand for a second on the Hughes, D-N.J., motion to suspend the rules and recede from disagreement to the Senate amendment and concur in the Senate amendment with an amendment to provide stiff new penalties for drug trafficking, a new crime aid program for states, a new federal offense to curb tampering with drugs and other consumer products, new protections for U.S. intelligence officials, federal authority to try certain repeat violators of state law, and a new Cabinet-level office to coordinate anti-drug operations. Second ordered 275-15: R 118-4; D 157-11 (ND 97-10, SD 60-1), Dec. 20, 1982. (A second is a procedural move to allow consideration of a bill prior to a vote to suspend the rules.)

KEY

Y Voted for (yea).
\# Paired for.
\+ Announced for.
N Voted against (nay).
X Paired against.
- Announced against.
P Voted "present".
C Voted "present" to avoid possible conflict of interest.
? Did not vote or otherwise make a position known.

Democrats   *Republicans*

	448	449	450	451	452	453	454	455
ALABAMA								
1 Edwards	Y	Y	Y	Y	Y	Y	N	Y
2 Dickinson	Y	N	?	N	N	Y	N	Y
3 Nichols	Y	Y	?	?	Y	Y	N	?
4 Bevill	Y	Y	Y	Y	Y	Y	?	Y
5 Flippo	Y	Y	Y	Y	Y	Y	N	Y
6 Smith	N	N	?	?	?	?	N	Y
7 Shelby	N	N	?	N	Y	N	N	Y
ALASKA								
AL Young	?	N	Y	?	?	?	?	Y
ARIZONA								
1 Rhodes	?	?	?	?	?	?	?	?
2 Udall	Y	Y	Y	?	Y	Y	Y	Y
3 Stump	N	N	N	N	N	N	N	Y
4 Rudd	?	?	?	?	?	?	?	?
ARKANSAS								
1 Alexander	Y	?	Y	Y	Y	Y	Y	Y
2 Bethune	Y	N	?	Y	Y	N	Y	?
3 Hammerschmidt	Y	N	N	N	Y	Y	N	N
4 Anthony	Y	Y	Y	Y	Y	Y	N	Y
CALIFORNIA								
1 Chappie	Y	N	N	?	Y	Y	N	?
2 Clausen	Y	?	Y	?	Y	Y	N	Y
3 Matsui	Y	Y	Y	N	Y	Y	Y	Y
4 Fazio	Y	Y	Y	N	Y	Y	Y	Y
5 Burton, J.	?	?	?	?	?	Y	Y	N
6 Burton, P.	Y	Y	Y	N	Y	Y	Y	Y
7 Miller	Y	Y	Y	Y	?	Y	Y	?
8 Dellums	Y	Y	Y	N	Y	Y	Y	Y
9 Stark	Y	?	?	?	Y	Y	Y	?
10 Edwards	Y	Y	Y	Y	Y	Y	Y	N
11 Lantos	Y	Y	?	Y	Y	Y	Y	Y
12 McCloskey	?	?	Y	?	?	Y	N	Y
13 Mineta	Y	Y	Y	?	Y	Y	Y	Y
14 Shumway	N	N	N	N	N	Y	N	Y
15 Coelho	Y	Y	Y	N	?	N	Y	Y
16 Panetta	Y	Y	Y	Y	Y	Y	Y	Y
17 Pashayan	Y	N	N	?	Y	Y	N	Y
18 Thomas	Y	Y	N	N	Y	Y	?	?
19 Lagomarsino	N	N	N	Y	Y	Y	N	Y
20 Goldwater	?	?	?	?	?	?	?	?
21 Fiedler	Y	N	Y	N	Y	Y	N	Y
22 Moorhead	N	N	Y	N	Y	Y	N	Y
23 Beilenson	Y	Y	?	Y	Y	Y	Y	Y
24 Waxman	?	?	?	?	?	?	Y	Y
25 Roybal	Y	Y	Y	N	Y	Y	Y	N
26 Rousselot	?	?	?	?	?	?	N	?
27 Dornan	N	N	Y	N	?	N	Y	?
28 Dixon	Y	Y	Y	N	?	Y	Y	?
29 Hawkins	Y	Y	Y	?	P	Y	Y	Y
30 Martinez	Y	Y	Y	N	Y	Y	Y	Y
31 Dymally	?	?	?	?	?	?	?	?
32 Anderson	Y	N	Y	N	Y	Y	Y	Y
33 Grisham	Y	N	?	?	?	?	?	?
34 Lungren	Y	Y	N	Y	Y	Y	N	Y
35 Dreier	N	N	N	Y	N	N	N	Y
36 Brown	Y	Y	Y	N	Y	Y	N	Y
37 Lewis	?	?	N	Y	N	Y	N	N
38 Patterson	Y	Y	Y	N	Y	Y	Y	Y
39 Dannemeyer	N	N	N	N	N	N	N	Y
40 Badham	Y	Y	N	N	N	N	N	Y
41 Lowery	Y	Y	Y	N	Y	Y	N	Y
42 Hunter	Y	Y	Y	N	Y	Y	N	Y
43 Burgener	Y	Y	N	?	Y	N	N	?
COLORADO								
1 Schroeder	Y	N	?	?	N	Y	Y	Y
2 Wirth	Y	Y	?	?	Y	Y	Y	Y
3 Kogovsek	Y	Y	Y	N	Y	Y	Y	Y
4 Brown	N	N	N	N	Y	N	N	Y

	448	449	450	451	452	453	454	455
5 Kramer	Y	N	N	N	Y	N	N	Y
CONNECTICUT								
1 Kennelly	Y	Y	Y	Y	Y	Y	Y	Y
2 Gejdenson	Y	Y	Y	N	Y	Y	Y	Y
3 DeNardis	?	?	Y	?	?	?	?	?
4 McKinney	Y	Y	?	?	Y	Y	?	Y
5 Ratchford	?	?	?	?	?	Y	Y	Y
6 Moffett	?	?	?	?	?	?	?	?
DELAWARE								
AL Evans	Y	Y	?	?	?	?	?	?
FLORIDA								
1 Hutto	Y	Y	Y	Y	P	Y	N	Y
2 Fuqua	?	?	?	?	?	?	?	Y
3 Bennett	Y	Y	N	Y	Y	Y	N	Y
4 Chappell	Y	Y	N	Y	?	Y	?	?
5 McCollum	N	N	N	Y	Y	Y	N	Y
6 Young	Y	N	Y	?	Y	Y	N	?
7 Gibbons	Y	Y	Y	Y	Y	Y	N	Y
8 Ireland	?	?	?	?	Y	Y	?	?
9 Nelson	Y	Y	?	Y	?	Y	Y	Y
10 Bafalis	?	?	?	?	?	Y	Y	Y
11 Mica	N	Y	N	Y	?	?	N	Y
12 Shaw	Y	Y	N	Y	Y	N	N	?
13 Lehman	?	?	?	?	?	?	?	?
14 Pepper	Y	Y	Y	?	Y	Y	Y	Y
15 Fascell	?	?	?	?	?	?	?	?
GEORGIA								
1 Ginn	?	?	Y	N	?	?	?	?
2 Hatcher	Y	Y	Y	N	Y	Y	N	Y
3 Brinkley	Y	N	Y	N	Y	Y	N	Y
4 Levitas	Y	?	Y	Y	Y	Y	N	Y
5 Fowler	Y	Y	Y	Y	Y	Y	N	Y
6 Gingrich	Y	N	Y	Y	Y	Y	N	Y
7 McDonald	N	N	N	N	Y	N	-	Y
8 Evans	?	?	?	?	?	?	?	?
9 Jenkins	Y	N	Y	Y	Y	Y	N	Y
10 Barnard	Y	N	Y	Y	Y	Y	N	Y
HAWAII								
1 Heftel	Y	Y	?	?	?	?	?	?
2 Akaka	Y	Y	Y	Y	Y	Y	Y	Y
IDAHO								
1 Craig	N	N	N	N	?	Y	N	Y
2 Hansen	N	N	N	N	N	Y	N	Y
ILLINOIS								
1 Washington	Y	Y	?	?	?	?	?	?
2 Savage	Y	Y	?	?	?	Y	?	N
3 Russo	Y	Y	Y	?	Y	N	N	Y
4 Derwinski	Y	N	N	Y	N	Y	N	Y
5 Fary	Y	Y	Y	Y	Y	Y	Y	Y
6 Hyde	Y	Y	Y	Y	P	Y	N	Y
7 Collins	#	?	?	?	?	?	?	?
8 Rostenkowski	Y	Y	?	Y	Y	Y	Y	Y
9 Yates	Y	Y	?	Y	Y	Y	?	Y
10 Porter	Y	N	Y	N	Y	Y	N	Y
11 Annunzio	Y	Y	Y	Y	Y	Y	Y	Y
12 Crane, P.	N	N	?	?	?	N	N	Y
13 McClory	Y	Y	Y	Y	Y	Y	Y	Y
14 Erlenborn	Y	Y	Y	Y	Y	N	Y	N
15 Corcoran	Y	N	Y	Y	Y	Y	Y	Y
16 Martin	Y	N	Y	Y	N	Y	N	Y
17 O'Brien	Y	Y	?	?	?	Y	N	Y
18 Michel	N	N	Y	Y	Y	N	Y	Y
19 Railsback	Y	Y	Y	Y	Y	Y	Y	?
20 Findley	?	?	?	?	?	?	?	Y
21 Madigan	Y	N	Y	Y	Y	Y	Y	Y
22 Crane, D.	?	?	N	Y	N	Y	N	?
23 Price	Y	Y	?	Y	Y	Y	Y	?
24 Simon	Y	Y	Y	Y	Y	Y	Y	?
INDIANA								
1 Hall	Y	Y	Y	N	Y	Y	Y	Y
2 Fithian	Y	Y	Y	N	Y	Y	Y	Y
3 Hiler	N	Y	N	Y	N	Y	N	Y
4 Coats	N	Y	N	?	N	N	N	Y
5 Hillis	Y	?	?	?	?	?	?	?
6 Evans	Y	Y	Y	N	Y	Y	N	Y
7 Myers	Y	N	N	N	Y	Y	N	Y
8 Deckard	Y	?	?	?	?	?	?	?
9 Hamilton	Y	N	Y	?	Y	Y	N	Y
10 Sharp	Y	N	?	Y	Y	Y	N	Y
11 Jacobs	Y	N	N	?	N	N	Y	N
IOWA								
1 Leach	Y	N	Y	?	Y	Y	N	Y
2 Tauke	Y	N	Y	Y	Y	Y	N	Y
3 Evans	Y	Y	Y	N	P	N	N	N
4 Smith	Y	Y	Y	N	N	N	N	Y
5 Harkin	Y	Y	Y	N	Y	Y	Y	Y
6 Bedell	Y	Y	Y	Y	Y	Y	N	Y

ND · Northern Democrats   SD · Southern Democrats

Corresponding to Congressional Record Votes 477, 478, 479, 480, 481, 482, 483, 484

	448	449	450	451	452	453	454	455
KANSAS								
1 ***Roberts***	?	?	N	N	?	Y	N	?
2 ***Jeffries***	?	?	?	?	?	?	?	?
3 ***Winn***	?	?	?	?	?	?	?	Y
4 Glickman	Y	Y	Y	Y	Y	Y	N	Y
5 ***Whittaker***	Y	N	N	?	Y	N	N	Y
KENTUCKY								
1 Hubbard	Y	Y	N	Y	?	Y	N	Y
2 Natcher	Y	Y	Y	Y	Y	Y	N	Y
3 Mazzoli	Y	Y	Y	Y	Y	Y	N	?
4 ***Snyder***	Y	N	N	Y	Y	Y	N	Y
5 ***Rogers***	Y	N	N	?	Y	Y	N	Y
6 ***Hopkins***	N	N	N	N	N	N	N	?
7 Perkins	Y	Y	Y	Y	Y	Y	Y	Y
LOUISIANA								
1 ***Livingston***	N	N	Y	Y	N	Y	N	?
2 Boggs	Y	Y	Y	Y	?	?	N	Y
3 Tauzin	Y	Y	?	?	Y	Y	N	Y
4 Roemer	Y	Y	Y	Y	N	Y	N	Y
5 Huckaby	Y	Y	Y	N	Y	Y	N	Y
6 ***Moore***	Y	Y	?	?	Y	N	N	Y
7 Breaux	Y	Y	Y	?	Y	Y	N	Y
8 Long	Y	Y	Y	?	Y	Y	Y	?
MAINE								
1 ***Emery***	N	?	N	?	?	Y	N	Y
2 ***Snowe***	Y	Y	N	Y	Y	Y	N	Y
MARYLAND								
1 Dyson	Y	Y	Y	Y	?	?	Y	Y
2 Long	Y	Y	?	?	Y	Y	Y	Y
3 Mikulski	Y	Y	Y	?	Y	Y	Y	Y
4 ***Holt***	Y	?	?	?	?	?	?	?
5 Hoyer	Y	Y	Y	?	Y	Y	Y	Y
6 Byron	?	N	Y	N	?	?	N	Y
7 Mitchell	Y	Y	Y	Y	?	Y	Y	?
8 Barnes	Y	Y	Y	Y	Y	Y	Y	Y
MASSACHUSETTS								
1 ***Conte***	Y	Y	Y	Y	Y	Y	N	Y
2 Boland	Y	Y	Y	?	Y	Y	?	Y
3 Early	?	Y	N	?	Y	Y	Y	Y
4 Frank	Y	Y	?	?	Y	Y	Y	Y
5 Shannon	?	Y	Y	?	Y	Y	Y	Y
6 Mavroules	Y	Y	Y	Y	Y	Y	Y	Y
7 Markey	Y	Y	?	?	Y	Y	Y	?
8 O'Neill								
9 Moakley	Y	Y	Y	?	Y	Y	Y	Y
10 ***Heckler***	Y	Y	?	N	?	?	?	?
11 Donnelly	Y	Y	Y	Y	?	?	N	Y
12 Studds	Y	Y	Y	Y	Y	Y	Y	Y
MICHIGAN								
1 Conyers	Y	Y	Y	N	?	?	Y	N
2 ***Pursell***	Y	Y	?	?	?	?	?	?
3 Wolpe	Y	Y	Y	Y	Y	Y	Y	Y
4 ***Siljander***	N	N	N	N	?	Y	N	?
5 ***Sawyer***	Y	Y	?	Y	Y	Y	N	Y
6 ***Dunn***	Y	N	N	?	N	Y	Y	Y
7 Kildee	Y	Y	Y	Y	Y	Y	Y	Y
8 Traxler	Y	Y	?	?	?	?	N	?
9 ***Vander Jagt***	Y	Y	Y	?	?	?	?	?
10 Albosta	N	Y	Y	Y	Y	Y	Y	Y
11 ***Davis***	?	?	Y	?	P	Y	Y	?
12 Bonior	Y	Y	?	?	?	?	?	?
13 Crockett	Y	Y	?	?	?	Y	Y	N
14 Hertel	Y	Y	?	?	?	Y	N	Y
15 Ford	Y	Y	Y	Y	?	?	?	Y
16 Dingell	Y	N	Y	Y	?	?	?	Y
17 Brodhead	?	Y	?	?	?	?	Y	Y
18 Blanchard	?	?	?	?	?	?	?	?
19 ***Broomfield***	Y	N	?	?	Y	N	N	?
MINNESOTA								
1 ***Erdahl***	Y	Y	N	N	Y	Y	N	Y
2 ***Hagedorn***	?	?	?	?	?	?	?	?
3 ***Frenzel***	Y	Y	N	Y	N	N	N	Y
4 Vento	Y	Y	Y	Y	Y	Y	Y	Y
5 Sabo	?	?	Y	Y	N	Y	Y	?
6 ***Weber***	N	Y	N	?	Y	N	N	?
7 ***Stangeland***	Y	Y	N	?	Y	N	N	?
8 Oberstar	Y	Y	Y	Y	P	Y	Y	Y
MISSISSIPPI								
1 Whitten	Y	N	?	?	Y	Y	?	Y
2 Bowen	Y	Y	Y	N	Y	Y	N	Y
3 Montgomery	Y	N	Y	N	Y	Y	N	Y
4 Dowdy	Y	Y	Y	Y	Y	Y	Y	Y
5 ***Lott***	N	N	Y	Y	Y	Y	N	?
MISSOURI								
1 Clay	?	?	Y	N	?	?	Y	?
2 Young	Y	Y	Y	N	Y	Y	Y	?
3 Gephardt	Y	Y	Y	?	Y	Y	?	Y

	448	449	450	451	452	453	454	455
4 Skelton	N	Y	Y	?	Y	Y	N	Y
5 Bolling	?	?	?	?	?	?	?	?
6 ***Coleman***	?	N	Y	N	Y	Y	?	?
7 ***Taylor***	Y	N	N	N	Y	Y	N	?
8 ***Bailey***	N	N	N	N	Y	N	?	Y
9 Volkmer	Y	Y	Y	Y	Y	Y	N	Y
10 ***Emerson***	N	N	N	N	N	Y	N	Y
MONTANA								
1 Williams	Y	Y	Y	?	Y	N	Y	Y
2 ***Marlenee***	N	N	N	N	Y	Y	N	?
NEBRASKA								
1 ***Bereuter***	Y	N	Y	Y	Y	Y	N	Y
2 ***Daub***	N	N	N	Y	Y	Y	N	Y
3 ***Smith***	N	N	N	N	Y	Y	N	?
NEVADA								
AL Santini	?	?	?	?	?	?	?	?
NEW HAMPSHIRE								
1 D'Amours	Y	Y	?	?	Y	Y	N	Y
2 ***Gregg***	N	Y	N	Y	Y	N	?	?
NEW JERSEY								
1 Florio	Y	Y	Y	?	Y	Y	N	Y
2 Hughes	Y	N	Y	Y	Y	Y	N	Y
3 Howard	Y	Y	Y	Y	Y	Y	Y	Y
4 ***Smith***	Y	Y	Y	N	Y	Y	N	?
5 ***Fenwick***	N	N	N	Y	?	Y	N	?
6 ***Forsythe***	Y	Y	Y	?	N	Y	?	?
7 ***Roukema***	Y	N	Y	Y	Y	Y	N	Y
8 Roe	Y	Y	?	?	?	?	Y	?
9 ***Hollenbeck***	?	?	?	?	?	?	?	Y
10 Rodino	Y	Y	Y	Y	Y	Y	Y	Y
11 Minish	Y	Y	Y	Y	Y	Y	?	Y
12 ***Rinaldo***	Y	N	N	Y	?	Y	N	Y
13 ***Courter***	Y	N	N	N	Y	Y	N	Y
14 Guarini	Y	Y	Y	Y	Y	Y	Y	Y
15 Dwyer	Y	Y	Y	Y	Y	Y	Y	Y
NEW MEXICO								
1 ***Lujan***	N	N	N	N	Y	Y	N	Y
2 ***Skeen***	N	N	N	N	?	Y	N	Y
NEW YORK								
1 ***Carney***	Y	Y	N	Y	N	Y	N	Y
2 Downey	?	?	Y	Y	Y	Y	?	?
3 ***Carman***	Y	Y	N	?	Y	N	N	Y
4 ***Lent***	Y	N	?	?	?	Y	N	Y
5 ***McGrath***	N	Y	N	Y	Y	Y	N	?
6 ***LeBoutillier***	N	N	Y	N	?	?	N	?
7 Addabbo	Y	Y	Y	?	Y	Y	Y	?
8 Rosenthal	Y	?	?	?	?	?	?	?
9 Ferraro	Y	Y	Y	?	Y	Y	?	?
10 Biaggi	Y	Y	?	?	?	?	?	?
11 Scheuer	Y	Y	Y	Y	Y	Y	Y	Y
12 Chisholm	Y	?	Y	?	?	?	Y	?
13 Solarz	Y	Y	Y	Y	Y	Y	Y	Y
14 Vacancy								
15 Zeferetti	?	?	?	?	?	?	?	?
16 Schumer	Y	Y	Y	Y	Y	Y	Y	Y
17 ***Molinari***	Y	Y	Y	N	Y	Y	N	Y
18 ***Green***	Y	Y	Y	?	Y	Y	N	?
19 Rangel	Y	?	Y	Y	Y	Y	Y	N
20 Weiss	Y	Y	Y	?	Y	Y	Y	?
21 Garcia	Y	Y	Y	N	?	Y	Y	Y
22 Bingham	Y	Y	Y	?	Y	Y	N	?
23 Peyser	Y	Y	Y	?	Y	Y	Y	?
24 Ottinger	Y	Y	Y	?	P	Y	Y	?
25 ***Fish***	Y	Y	Y	Y	Y	Y	N	?
26 ***Gilman***	Y	N	Y	Y	Y	Y	N	Y
27 McHugh	Y	Y	Y	Y	?	?	N	Y
28 Stratton	Y	Y	N	Y	Y	Y	?	Y
29 ***Solomon***	N	N	N	N	N	N	N	Y
30 ***Martin***	Y	N	N	N	?	Y	N	Y
31 ***Mitchell***	?	?	?	?	?	?	?	?
32 ***Wortley***	Y	Y	?	Y	Y	N	N	Y
33 ***Lee***	?	?	?	?	?	?	?	?
34 ***Horton***	?	?	?	?	?	?	?	?
35 ***Conable***	Y	N	Y	Y	Y	N	N	Y
36 LaFalce	Y	Y	?	?	?	?	?	Y
37 Nowak	Y	Y	Y	Y	?	?	N	Y
38 ***Kemp***	Y	Y	Y	?	Y	Y	N	Y
39 Lundine	Y	?	Y	?	?	?	Y	?
NORTH CAROLINA								
1 Jones	Y	Y	Y	?	Y	Y	Y	Y
2 Fountain	Y	Y	Y	N	?	?	N	Y
3 Whitley	Y	Y	Y	Y	Y	Y	N	Y
4 Andrews	Y	Y	Y	Y	Y	Y	?	Y
5 Neal	Y	?	Y	?	?	?	?	Y
6 ***Johnston***	X	?	?	?	N	N	?	Y
7 Rose	Y	Y	?	?	?	?	?	Y
8 Hefner	?	?	?	?	?	?	?	Y

	448	449	450	451	452	453	454	455
9 ***Martin***	N	N	N	?	?	?	?	Y
10 ***Broyhill***	N	N	Y	N	P	N	N	Y
11 ***Hendon***	N	?	?	?	?	?	?	Y
NORTH DAKOTA								
AL Dorgan	Y	Y	?	?	Y	Y	N	Y
OHIO								
1 ***Gradison***	Y	Y	N	?	Y	N	N	Y
2 Luken	?	?	?	?	?	?	?	?
3 Hall	?	?	Y	?	Y	Y	Y	?
4 ***Oxley***	?	?	?	?	?	Y	N	Y
5 ***Latta***	N	N	N	Y	N	Y	?	Y
6 ***McEwen***	N	N	Y	Y	Y	N	N	?
7 ***Brown***	Y	N	Y	?	N	Y	N	?
8 ***Kindness***	Y	Y	N	Y	Y	N	N	Y
9 ***Weber***	Y	Y	N	N	Y	Y	N	Y
10 ***Miller***	N	N	N	Y	N	N	N	Y
11 ***Stanton***	?	?	?	?	?	?	?	?
12 Shamansky	Y	Y	Y	Y	?	Y	N	?
13 Pease	Y	Y	Y	Y	?	Y	N	Y
14 Seiberling	Y	Y	Y	?	?	Y	Y	Y
15 ***Wylie***	Y	Y	Y	Y	Y	Y	N	Y
16 ***Regula***	Y	N	Y	Y	Y	Y	?	Y
17 ***Ashbrook***	N	N	?	?	Y	?	?	Y
18 Applegate	Y	Y	Y	Y	?	Y	N	Y
19 ***Williams***	Y	Y	?	?	Y	Y	?	Y
20 Oakar	Y	Y	Y	N	Y	Y	Y	?
21 Stokes	Y	Y	?	?	Y	Y	Y	Y
22 Eckart	Y	Y	Y	Y	Y	Y	Y	Y
23 Mottl	N	N	?	?	?	?	?	?
OKLAHOMA								
1 Jones	N	Y	Y	Y	Y	N	N	Y
2 Synar	Y	Y	?	?	Y	Y	N	?
3 Watkins	Y	Y	Y	Y	Y	Y	N	Y
4 McCurdy	?	?	Y	Y	Y	N	N	Y
5 ***Edwards***	N	Y	Y	N	Y	Y	N	Y
6 English	N	N	Y	N	Y	N	N	Y
OREGON								
1 AuCoin	Y	?	Y	N	?	?	Y	Y
2 ***Smith***	N	N	N	N	N	N	N	N
3 Wyden	Y	Y	Y	Y	Y	Y	N	Y
4 Weaver	N	N	Y	?	Y	Y	N	Y
PENNSYLVANIA								
1 Foglietta	Y	Y	Y	Y	Y	Y	Y	Y
2 Gray	?	Y	Y	N	Y	Y	Y	?
3 Smith	?	?	?	?	?	?	?	?
4 ***Dougherty***	Y	Y	Y	Y	?	?	?	?
5 ***Schulze***	?	?	?	?	?	?	?	?
6 Yatron	Y	N	?	?	Y	Y	N	Y
7 Edgar	Y	Y	Y	N	N	Y	Y	N
8 ***Coyne, J.***	Y	Y	?	?	?	?	?	Y
9 ***Shuster***	?	?	?	?	?	?	?	?
10 ***McDade***	Y	Y	?	?	Y	Y	?	Y
11 ***Nelligan***	Y	N	N	N	Y	?	N	?
12 Murtha	Y	Y	Y	Y	Y	Y	N	Y
13 ***Coughlin***	Y	Y	N	Y	N	Y	N	?
14 Coyne, W.	Y	Y	Y	Y	Y	Y	N	Y
15 ***Ritter***	N	N	N	?	Y	N	N	Y
16 ***Walker***	N	N	Y	N	N	N	N	Y
17 Ertel	?	?	?	?	?	?	?	?
18 Walgren	Y	Y	?	?	?	?	?	?
19 ***Goodling***	Y	N	N	N	?	N	N	?
20 Gaydos	?	N	?	Y	Y	Y	?	?
21 Bailey	?	?	Y	?	Y	Y	Y	Y
22 Murphy	Y	N	?	N	N	Y	Y	?
23 ***Clinger***	Y	N	Y	Y	Y	Y	N	Y
24 ***Marks***	?	?	?	?	?	?	?	Y
25 ***Atkinson***	?	Y	Y	?	?	Y	N	Y
RHODE ISLAND								
1 St Germain	Y	Y	Y	N	N	Y	Y	Y
2 ***Schneider***	Y	Y	Y	?	?	Y	N	Y
SOUTH CAROLINA								
1 ***Hartnett***	N	Y	N	N	N	N	N	?
2 ***Spence***	N	N	Y	N	Y	Y	N	Y
3 Derrick	Y	Y	Y	?	Y	Y	N	Y
4 ***Campbell***	N	Y	Y	N	?	Y	N	Y
5 Holland	?	?	?	?	?	?	?	?
6 ***Napier***	N	N	?	?	?	?	?	Y
SOUTH DAKOTA								
1 Daschle	Y	Y	Y	Y	Y	Y	?	Y
2 ***Roberts***	?	?	?	?	?	?	?	?
TENNESSEE								
1 ***Quillen***	N	Y	Y	N	Y	Y	?	Y
2 ***Duncan***	Y	Y	Y	N	Y	Y	N	Y
3 Bouquard	N	N	Y	N	Y	Y	N	?
4 Gore	Y	Y	Y	Y	Y	Y	N	Y
5 Boner	Y	Y	Y	Y	Y	Y	N	Y
6 ***Beard***	?	Y	?	?	?	?	?	?

	448	449	450	451	452	453	454	455
7 Jones	Y	Y	Y	N	Y	Y	Y	Y
8 Ford	Y	Y	?	N	?	?	Y	Y
TEXAS								
1 Hall, S.	N	N	N	Y	Y	N	N	Y
2 Wilson	Y	Y	Y	Y	Y	Y	N	?
3 ***Collins***	N	N	N	?	?	?	?	?
4 Hall, R.	N	N	N	Y	Y	Y	N	Y
5 Mattox	Y	Y	?	?	Y	Y	?	?
6 Gramm	N	N	N	N	N	N	N	Y
7 ***Archer***	N	N	N	N	Y	N	N	Y
8 ***Fields***	N	N	N	?	N	N	N	?
9 Brooks	Y	Y	Y	N	Y	Y	Y	Y
10 Pickle	Y	Y	Y	?	Y	Y	N	Y
11 Leath	Y	N	Y	N	Y	N	N	Y
12 Wright	Y	Y	Y	?	Y	Y	?	Y
13 Hightower	Y	Y	Y	N	Y	Y	N	Y
14 Patman	N	N	Y	N	Y	Y	N	Y
15 de la Garza	Y	Y	Y	N	Y	Y	N	?
16 White	Y	Y	Y	Y	?	?	N	Y
17 Stenholm	N	N	Y	N	N	N	N	Y
18 Leland	Y	Y	Y	N	Y	Y	Y	Y
19 Hance	N	N	Y	N	Y	N	N	Y
20 Gonzalez	Y	Y	Y	N	Y	Y	P	N
21 ***Loeffler***	N	N	N	N	Y	Y	N	Y
22 ***Paul***	N	N	N	N	Y	N	N	?
23 Kazen	Y	Y	Y	N	Y	Y	N	Y
24 Frost	Y	Y	Y	Y	?	?	?	?
UTAH								
1 ***Hansen***	N	?	Y	N	N	N	N	?
2 ***Marriott***	Y	Y	Y	N	Y	Y	N	Y
VERMONT								
AL ***Jeffords***	Y	Y	N	Y	Y	Y	Y	Y
VIRGINIA								
1 ***Trible***	Y	Y	?	?	Y	Y	?	Y
2 ***Whitehurst***	Y	N	Y	?	Y	Y	?	?
3 ***Bliley***	Y	Y	Y	N	Y	Y	N	Y
4 ***Daniel, R.***	N	N	N	Y	Y	Y	N	?
5 Daniel, D.	Y	N	Y	N	Y	Y	N	Y
6 ***Butler***	Y	N	N	Y	?	Y	?	Y
7 ***Robinson***	Y	N	Y	N	Y	Y	N	Y
8 ***Parris***	Y	Y	N	Y	Y	Y	N	Y
9 ***Wampler***	Y	N	Y	Y	Y	Y	N	Y
10 ***Wolf***	Y	Y	Y	N	Y	Y	N	Y
WASHINGTON								
1 ***Pritchard***	Y	Y	Y	?	Y	Y	N	?
2 Swift	Y	Y	Y	?	Y	Y	?	Y
3 Bonker	Y	Y	Y	?	Y	Y	N	?
4 ***Morrison***	Y	N	Y	N	Y	Y	N	Y
5 Foley	?	?	?	?	Y	Y	N	?
6 Dicks	?	?	Y	Y	Y	Y	?	Y
7 Lowry	Y	Y	Y	Y	Y	Y	Y	Y
WEST VIRGINIA								
1 Mollohan	Y	Y	Y	N	?	Y	Y	?
2 ***Benedict***	N	N	Y	N	?	Y	?	?
3 ***Staton***	N	Y	N	N	?	?	N	?
4 Rahall	?	?	Y	Y	Y	Y	Y	Y
WISCONSIN								
1 Aspin	Y	Y	?	N	N	N	N	?
2 Kastenmeier	Y	Y	Y	Y	Y	Y	Y	Y
3 ***Gunderson***	N	Y	N	Y	Y	Y	N	Y
4 Zablocki	Y	Y	Y	Y	Y	Y	Y	Y
5 Reuss	Y	Y	?	?	Y	Y	Y	?
6 ***Petri***	N	N	N	Y	N	N	N	Y
7 Obey	Y	P	Y	Y	Y	Y	Y	Y
8 ***Roth***	N	N	?	N	Y	Y	N	Y
9 ***Sensenbrenner***	N	N	N	N	Y	N	N	Y
WYOMING								
AL ***Cheney***	N	?	N	Y	Y	Y	N	Y

Southern states - Ala., Ark., Fla., Ga., Ky., La., Miss., N.C., Okla., S.C., Tenn., Texas, Va.

KEY

Y Voted for (yea).
\# Paired for.
\+ Announced for.
N Voted against (nay).
X Paired against.
- Announced against.
P Voted "present".
C Voted "present" to avoid possible conflict of interest.
? Did not vote or otherwise make a position known.

Democrats   *Republicans*

456. HR 3963. Contract Services for Drug Dependent Federal Offenders Act Amendment. Hughes, D-N.J., motion to suspend the rules and recede from disagreement to the Senate amendment and concur in the Senate amendment with an amendment to provide stiff new penalties for drug trafficking, a new crime aid program for states, a new federal offense to curb tampering with drugs and other consumer products, new protections for U.S. intelligence officials, federal authority to try certain repeat violators of state law, and a new Cabinet-level office to coordinate anti-drug operations. Motion agreed to 271-27: R 113-15; D 158-12 (ND 102-8, SD 56-4), Dec. 20, 1982. A two-thirds majority of those present and voting (199 in this case) is required to suspend the rules.

457. HR 3809. Nuclear Waste Policy Act. Adoption of the rule (H Res 636) providing for consideration of the bill to establish a federal program for the interim storage and eventual permanent disposal of highly radioactive nuclear waste and spent (burned) fuel from civilian nuclear reactors. The rule provided that the bill, as amended by the Senate, would be passed upon adoption of the rule. Adopted 256-32: R 121-6; D 135-26 (ND 81-24, SD 54-2), Dec. 20, 1982. A "yea" was a vote supporting the president's position.

458. HR 7093. Virgin Islands Tax Reduction/Disability Insurance. Adoption of the conference report on the bill to allow the Virgin Islands to reduce taxes on certain investment income earned from sources within the Virgin Islands and paid to individuals in the United States; to provide disability insurance payments and Medicare coverage to individuals appealing their termination from the disability rolls before Oct. 1, 1983, and to make other changes in the disability review process. Adopted 259-0: R 115-0; D 144-0 (ND 102-0, SD 42-0), Dec. 21, 1982.

459. HR 6211. Transportation Assistance Act of 1982. Adoption of the conference report on the bill to authorize $71.3 billion in fiscal 1983-1986 for highway construction and repairs and mass transit, and to increase gasoline and other highway taxes. Adopted 180-87: R 73-46; D 107-41 (ND 85-19, SD 22-22), Dec. 21, 1982. A "yea" was a vote supporting the president's position.

	456	457	458	459
ALABAMA				
1 *Edwards*	?	?	?	?
2 *Dickinson*	Y	?	?	?
3 Nichols	?	?	?	X
4 Bevill	Y	Y	Y	N
5 Flippo	?	?	?	?
6 *Smith*	Y	Y	N	N
7 Shelby	Y	Y	?	N
ALASKA				
AL *Young*	?	?	?	?
ARIZONA				
1 *Rhodes*	?	?	?	?
2 Udall	Y	Y	Y	Y
3 Stump	N	Y	Y	N
4 *Rudd*	?	?	?	?
ARKANSAS				
1 Alexander	Y	?	Y	Y
2 *Bethune*	?	?	?	?
3 *Hammerschmidt*	N	Y	Y	Y
4 Anthony	Y	?	Y	Y
CALIFORNIA				
1 *Chappie*	Y	Y	?	?
2 *Clausen*	Y	Y	Y	Y
3 Matsui	Y	Y	Y	Y
4 Fazio	Y	?	?	#
5 Burton, J.	N	?	Y	Y
6 Burton, P.	?	?	?	?
7 Miller	Y	?	Y	?
8 Dellums	?	N	N	Y
9 Stark	?	?	?	?
10 Edwards	Y	?	?	?
11 Lantos	?	?	?	?
12 *McCloskey*	Y	Y	Y	Y
13 Mineta	Y	Y	Y	Y
14 *Shumway*	N	Y	Y	N
15 Coelho	Y	Y	Y	Y
16 Panetta	?	?	?	X
17 *Pashayan*	Y	Y	Y	Y
18 *Thomas*	?	?	Y	Y
19 *Lagomarsino*	Y	Y	Y	N
20 *Goldwater*	?	?	?	?
21 *Fiedler*	Y	Y	Y	N
22 *Moorhead*	Y	Y	Y	N
23 Beilenson	Y	N	Y	Y
24 Waxman	?	?	Y	Y
25 Roybal	Y	N	Y	Y
26 *Rousselot*	Y	Y	Y	Y
27 *Dornan*	Y	Y	Y	N
28 Dixon	?	?	Y	Y
29 Hawkins	?	?	?	?
30 Martinez	Y	Y	?	?
31 Dymally	?	?	?	?
32 Anderson	Y	Y	Y	Y
33 Grisham	?	?	?	?
34 *Lungren*	Y	Y	?	N
35 *Dreier*	Y	Y	?	?
36 Brown	Y	Y	Y	Y
37 *Lewis*	Y	Y	?	?
38 Patterson	N	Y	?	?
39 *Dannemeyer*	N	Y	Y	N
40 *Badham*	?	Y	?	Y
41 *Lowery*	Y	?	Y	Y
42 Hunter	Y	Y	?	?
43 *Burgener*	?	?	?	?
COLORADO				
1 Schroeder	?	N	Y	N
2 Wirth	?	?	Y	Y
3 Kogovsek	Y	N	Y	Y
4 *Brown*	Y	Y	Y	Y

	456	457	458	459
5 *Kramer*	Y	Y	Y	Y
CONNECTICUT				
1 Kennelly	Y	Y	Y	Y
2 Gejdenson	Y	Y	Y	Y
3 *DeNardis*	?	?	?	?
4 *McKinney*	?	Y	Y	Y
5 Ratchford	Y	N	Y	Y
6 Moffett	?	?	?	?
DELAWARE				
AL *Evans*	?	?	?	?
FLORIDA				
1 Hutto	?	?	Y	Y
2 Fuqua	?	?	?	?
3 Bennett	Y	Y	Y	Y
4 Chappell	?	?	?	?
5 *McCollum*	Y	Y	Y	Y
6 *Young*	?	Y	Y	N
7 Gibbons	Y	Y	Y	Y
8 Ireland	?	Y	?	?
9 Nelson	Y	?	?	?
10 *Bafalis*	?	?	?	?
11 Mica	Y	Y	?	?
12 *Shaw*	Y	Y	Y	Y
13 Lehman	?	?	?	?
14 Pepper	Y	Y	Y	Y
15 Fascell	?	?	?	?
GEORGIA				
1 Ginn	Y	?	?	?
2 Hatcher	Y	Y	?	?
3 Brinkley	Y	Y	Y	Y
4 Levitas	Y	Y	?	?
5 Fowler	Y	Y	Y	Y
6 *Gingrich*	Y	Y	Y	N
7 McDonald	N	Y	N	N
8 Evans	?	?	?	?
9 Jenkins	?	?	?	?
10 Barnard	Y	Y	?	?
HAWAII				
1 Heftel	?	Y	?	?
2 Akaka	Y	Y	Y	N
IDAHO				
1 *Craig*	Y	Y	Y	N
2 *Hansen*	N	Y	Y	N
ILLINOIS				
1 Washington	?	?	?	?
2 Savage	N	?	Y	Y
3 Russo	?	?	?	?
4 *Derwinski*	Y	Y	Y	Y
5 Fary	Y	Y	Y	Y
6 *Hyde*	Y	Y	?	?
7 Collins	Y	?	Y	Y
8 Rostenkowski	Y	Y	Y	Y
9 Yates	?	?	Y	Y
10 *Porter*	Y	Y	Y	Y
11 Annunzio	Y	?	?	?
12 *Crane, P.*	Y	Y	Y	N
13 *McClory*	?	?	?	?
14 *Erlenborn*	Y	?	Y	Y
15 *Corcoran*	Y	Y	+	Y
16 *Martin*	?	Y	Y	Y
17 *O'Brien*	Y	Y	Y	Y
18 *Michel*	Y	Y	Y	Y
19 *Railsback*	?	?	?	?
20 *Findley*	Y	Y	Y	Y
21 *Madigan*	Y	Y	Y	Y
22 *Crane, D.*	Y	?	?	?
23 Price	Y	N	?	?
24 Simon	?	?	?	#
INDIANA				
1 Hall	N	Y	Y	Y
2 Fithian	Y	?	Y	Y
3 *Hiler*	Y	Y	Y	Y
4 *Coats*	Y	Y	Y	Y
5 *Hillis*	?	?	?	?
6 Evans	?	?	?	?
7 *Myers*	N	N	Y	X
8 *Deckard*	Y	N	Y	Y
9 Hamilton	Y	Y	Y	Y
10 Sharp	Y	Y	Y	Y
11 Jacobs	?	Y	Y	Y
IOWA				
1 *Leach*	Y	Y	Y	Y
2 *Tauke*	Y	Y	Y	Y
3 *Evans*	Y	Y	Y	Y
4 Smith	Y	?	?	?
5 Harkin	Y	?	?	?
6 Bedell	Y	Y	Y	Y

ND - Northern Democrats   SD - Southern Democrats

	456	457	458	459
KANSAS				
1 Roberts	Y	Y	Y	N
2 Jeffries	?	?	?	?
3 Winn	Y	Y	?	?
4 Glickman	Y	Y	Y	N
5 Whittaker	Y	Y	Y	N
KENTUCKY				
1 Hubbard	Y	Y	Y	N
2 Natcher	Y	Y	Y	Y
3 Mazzoli	Y	Y	Y	N
4 Snyder	Y	Y	Y	Y
5 Rogers	?	Y	?	?
6 Hopkins	?	?	?	?
7 Perkins	Y	Y	?	?
LOUISIANA				
1 Livingston	?	?	?	?
2 Boggs	?	Y	Y	Y
3 Tauzin	Y	Y	Y	N
4 Roemer	Y	Y	Y	Y
5 Huckaby	Y	Y	Y	N
6 Moore	Y	Y	Y	N
7 Breaux	Y	Y	Y	Y
8 Long	?	?	?	?
MAINE				
1 Emery	Y	Y	?	N
2 Snowe	Y	Y	Y	N
MARYLAND				
1 Dyson	Y	Y	Y	Y
2 Long	Y	Y	Y	Y
3 Mikulski	Y	N	Y	Y
4 Holt	?	?	Y	N
5 Hoyer	Y	Y	Y	Y
6 Byron	Y	Y	Y	N
7 Mitchell	?	N	Y	Y
8 Barnes	?	Y	Y	Y
MASSACHUSETTS				
1 Conte	Y	Y	Y	#
2 Boland	Y	Y	?	?
3 Early	Y	?	?	?
4 Frank	Y	N	?	?
5 Shannon	Y	?	Y	Y
6 Mavroules	Y	Y	Y	Y
7 Markey	Y	N	Y	Y
8 O'Neill				
9 Moakley	Y	Y	Y	Y
10 Heckler	?	?	Y	Y
11 Donnelly	Y	Y	Y	Y
12 Studds	Y	Y	Y	N
MICHIGAN				
1 Conyers	N	N	Y	N
2 Pursell	?	?	?	?
3 Wolpe	Y	Y	?	?
4 Siljander	Y	Y	?	?
5 Sawyer	Y	Y	?	?
6 Dunn	?	?	?	?
7 Kildee	Y	N	Y	Y
8 Traxler	?	?	?	?
9 Vander Jagt	Y	Y	Y	Y
10 Albosta	Y	Y	?	?
11 Davis	?	N	Y	N
12 Bonior	?	?	?	N
13 Crockett	Y	?	Y	Y
14 Hertel	Y	?	?	?
15 Ford	?	Y	Y	Y
16 Dingell	Y	Y	Y	Y
17 Brodhead	Y	Y	Y	Y
18 Blanchard	?	?	?	?
19 Broomfield	?	?	?	?
MINNESOTA				
1 Erdahl	Y	Y	Y	Y
2 Hagedorn	?	Y	Y	Y
3 Frenzel	Y	Y	Y	Y
4 Vento	Y	Y	Y	Y
5 Sabo	Y	Y	Y	Y
6 Weber	Y	Y	Y	N
7 Stangeland	?	Y	?	?
8 Oberstar	Y	Y	Y	Y
MISSISSIPPI				
1 Whitten	Y	?	Y	N
2 Bowen	Y	Y	Y	Y
3 Montgomery	Y	Y	Y	Y
4 Dowdy	?	?	?	?
5 Lott	?	?	?	?
MISSOURI				
1 Clay	?	?	Y	Y
2 Young	?	Y	Y	Y
3 Gephardt	Y	Y	Y	Y
4 Skelton	Y	Y	Y	Y
5 Bolling	?	?	?	?
6 Coleman	Y	Y	Y	N
7 Taylor	?	?	?	?
8 Bailey	N	Y	Y	Y
9 Volkmer	Y	Y	Y	N
10 Emerson	Y	Y	Y	N
MONTANA				
1 Williams	?	Y	Y	N
2 Marlenee	?	?	?	?
NEBRASKA				
1 Bereuter	Y	Y	Y	Y
2 Daub	Y	Y	Y	Y
3 Smith	Y	?	Y	Y
NEVADA				
AL Santini	?	?	?	?
NEW HAMPSHIRE				
1 D'Amours	Y	Y	Y	Y
2 Gregg	?	?	?	?
NEW JERSEY				
1 Florio	Y	Y	Y	N
2 Hughes	Y	Y	Y	N
3 Howard	Y	Y	Y	Y
4 Smith	?	Y	Y	Y
5 Fenwick	Y	Y	Y	Y
6 Forsythe	?	?	?	?
7 Roukema	Y	Y	Y	Y
8 Roe	Y	Y	Y	Y
9 Hollenbeck	?	?	Y	Y
10 Rodino	Y	Y	Y	Y
11 Minish	Y	?	?	?
12 Rinaldo	Y	Y	Y	N
13 Courter	Y	?	?	?
14 Guarini	Y	Y	Y	Y
15 Dwyer	Y	?	?	?
NEW MEXICO				
1 Lujan	Y	Y	Y	Y
2 Skeen	Y	Y	Y	Y
NEW YORK				
1 Carney	Y	Y	Y	Y
2 Downey	Y	N	Y	Y
3 Carman	Y	?	?	?
4 Lent	Y	Y	Y	Y
5 McGrath	Y	Y	?	?
6 LeBoutillier	?	?	?	?
7 Addabbo	?	?	?	?
8 Rosenthal	?	?	?	?
9 Ferraro	?	?	?	?
10 Biaggi	?	?	?	?
11 Scheuer	Y	Y	?	?
12 Chisholm	?	?	?	?
13 Solarz	Y	Y	Y	Y
14 Vacancy				
15 Zeferetti	?	Y	?	?
16 Schumer	Y	N	Y	Y
17 Molinari	Y	Y	Y	Y
18 Green	?	Y	Y	Y
19 Rangel	N	Y	Y	Y
20 Weiss	N	N	Y	Y
21 Garcia	Y	Y	Y	Y
22 Bingham	?	?	?	?
23 Peyser	Y	?	?	?
24 Ottinger	?	?	?	?
25 Fish	?	Y	?	?
26 Gilman	Y	Y	Y	Y
27 McHugh	Y	?	Y	Y
28 Stratton	Y	N	Y	Y
29 Solomon	Y	Y	Y	N
30 Martin	Y	Y	?	?
31 Mitchell	?	?	?	?
32 Wortley	Y	Y	Y	Y
33 Lee	?	?	?	?
34 Horton	Y	?	Y	N
35 Conable	Y	Y	Y	Y
36 LaFalce	Y	N	Y	?
37 Nowak	Y	Y	Y	Y
38 Kemp	Y	?	Y	N
39 Lundine	Y	Y	Y	N
NORTH CAROLINA				
1 Jones	Y	Y	?	?
2 Fountain	Y	Y	Y	N
3 Whitley	Y	Y	Y	N
4 Andrews	Y	Y	?	?
5 Neal	Y	Y	Y	N
6 Johnston	N	Y	?	?
7 Rose	Y	Y	?	?
8 Hefner	Y	Y	Y	N
9 Martin	Y	Y	?	N
10 Broyhill	N	Y	?	N
11 Hendon	Y	Y	Y	Y
NORTH DAKOTA				
AL Dorgan	Y	Y	Y	Y
OHIO				
1 Gradison	Y	?	?	Y
2 Luken	?	?	?	?
3 Hall	?	?	?	?
4 Oxley	Y	Y	?	?
5 Latta	Y	Y	?	?
6 McEwen	?	?	?	?
7 Brown	?	?	?	?
8 Kindness	Y	Y	Y	N
9 Weber	Y	Y	?	Y
10 Miller	Y	Y	Y	N
11 Stanton	?	?	?	Y
12 Shamansky	?	?	?	?
13 Pease	Y	Y	Y	Y
14 Seiberling	Y	N	Y	Y
15 Wylie	Y	Y	Y	Y
16 Regula	Y	Y	Y	Y
17 Ashbrook	N	Y	Y	N
18 Applegate	Y	Y	Y	Y
19 Williams	?	?	?	?
20 Oakar	?	Y	Y	Y
21 Stokes	Y	N	Y	Y
22 Eckart	Y	N	Y	Y
23 Mottl	?	?	?	X
OKLAHOMA				
1 Jones	N	Y	Y	N
2 Synar	Y	Y	?	?
3 Watkins	Y	Y	?	?
4 McCurdy	Y	Y	?	N
5 Edwards	N	Y	Y	N
6 English	Y	Y	Y	N
OREGON				
1 AuCoin	Y	Y	Y	N
2 Smith	?	?	?	?
3 Wyden	Y	?	Y	N
4 Weaver	Y	?	?	?
PENNSYLVANIA				
1 Foglietta	?	N	Y	Y
2 Gray	?	?	?	#
3 Smith	?	?	?	?
4 Dougherty	Y	Y	Y	Y
5 Schulze	?	?	Y	Y
6 Yatron	Y	Y	Y	Y
7 Edgar	Y	Y	Y	Y
8 Coyne, J.	Y	Y	Y	Y
9 Shuster	?	?	Y	Y
10 McDade	Y	?	?	?
11 Nelligan	?	?	?	?
12 Murtha	Y	Y	Y	Y
13 Coughlin	Y	Y	Y	Y
14 Coyne, W.	Y	Y	Y	Y
15 Ritter	Y	Y	Y	N
16 Walker	N	Y	Y	N
17 Ertel	?	?	?	?
18 Walgren	?	Y	?	?
19 Goodling	Y	Y	Y	?
20 Gaydos	Y	Y	Y	N
21 Bailey	Y	Y	Y	Y
22 Murphy	Y	?	?	?
23 Clinger	Y	Y	Y	Y
24 Marks	?	N	Y	Y
25 Atkinson	Y	Y	Y	Y
RHODE ISLAND				
1 St Germain	Y	Y	Y	Y
2 Schneider	Y	Y	Y	Y
SOUTH CAROLINA				
1 Hartnett	?	?	?	X
2 Spence	Y	Y	Y	N
3 Derrick	Y	Y	Y	Y
4 Campbell	Y	Y	Y	#
5 Holland	?	Y	?	?
6 Napier	Y	Y	Y	Y
SOUTH DAKOTA				
1 Daschle	?	N	?	N
2 Roberts	?	?	?	?
TENNESSEE				
1 Quillen	Y	Y	?	?
2 Duncan	Y	Y	Y	N
3 Bouquard	?	?	?	X
4 Gore	Y	Y	?	?
5 Boner	Y	Y	?	?
6 Beard	?	?	?	?
7 Jones	Y	Y	?	?
8 Ford	N	?	?	?
TEXAS				
1 Hall, S.	Y	Y	?	?
2 Wilson	Y	?	Y	Y
3 Collins	?	?	?	?
4 Hall, R.	Y	Y	Y	N
5 Mattox	?	?	?	?
6 Gramm	Y	Y	Y	N
7 Archer	Y	Y	Y	N
8 Fields	Y	Y	Y	N
9 Brooks	Y	Y	Y	Y
10 Pickle	Y	Y	Y	Y
11 Leath	Y	?	Y	N
12 Wright	Y	Y	Y	Y
13 Hightower	Y	Y	?	?
14 Patman	Y	Y	Y	Y
15 de la Garza	?	?	?	?
16 White	Y	Y	Y	N
17 Stenholm	Y	Y	Y	N
18 Leland	?	N	Y	Y
19 Hance	Y	N	Y	Y
20 Gonzalez	N	Y	Y	N
21 Loeffler	Y	Y	Y	N
22 Paul	N	N	?	?
23 Kazen	Y	Y	Y	N
24 Frost	?	?	?	?
UTAH				
1 Hansen	?	?	?	?
2 Marriott	?	?	?	?
VERMONT				
AL Jeffords	Y	Y	Y	Y
VIRGINIA				
1 Trible	Y	?	Y	Y
2 Whitehurst	?	?	?	?
3 Bliley	N	Y	Y	Y
4 Daniel, R.	?	?	?	?
5 Daniel, D.	Y	Y	?	?
6 Butler	Y	Y	?	?
7 Robinson	Y	?	Y	N
8 Parris	?	?	Y	N
9 Wampler	Y	Y	Y	N
10 Wolf	Y	Y	Y	Y
WASHINGTON				
1 Pritchard	Y	Y	Y	Y
2 Swift	Y	Y	Y	Y
3 Bonker	Y	?	Y	?
4 Morrison	Y	Y	?	?
5 Foley	Y	Y	Y	Y
6 Dicks	Y	Y	Y	Y
7 Lowry	Y	N	Y	Y
WEST VIRGINIA				
1 Mollohan	?	?	?	?
2 Benedict	?	?	?	?
3 Staton	?	?	Y	?
4 Rahall	Y	Y	?	#
WISCONSIN				
1 Aspin	?	?	Y	Y
2 Kastenmeier	Y	Y	Y	Y
3 Gunderson	Y	Y	Y	Y
4 Zablocki	Y	Y	Y	Y
5 Reuss	?	Y	Y	N
6 Petri	N	?	Y	Y
7 Obey	Y	Y	Y	Y
8 Roth	Y	N	Y	N
9 Sensenbrenner	N	Y	Y	N
WYOMING				
AL Cheney	Y	Y	Y	N

Southern states - Ala., Ark., Fla., Ga., Ky., La., Miss., N.C., Okla., S.C., Tenn., Texas, Va.

HOUSE ROLL-CALL VOTES

SENATE ROLL-CALL VOTES

INDEX

C_Q

INDEX

A

(continued)

Phosphate mining - 464-465
PHS. *See Public Health Service.*
Physicians - 316, 347-349 *(See also Professional Standards Review Organizations.)*
Pickle, J. J., D-Texas (10)
  Congressional voting studies - 3-C-40-C
  Nuclear freeze resolution - 117
  Roll call votes - 2-H-135-H
PIK. *See Payment-in-kind (PIK) program.*
Pilots - 332
Pipeline sanctions - 163-165, 9-C
Piper Aircraft Co. v. Reyno, Hartzell Propeller v. Reyno - 16-A
Pittman, Virgil - 375
Planned Parenthood of Kansas City v. Ashcroft - 403
Plutonium - 108-109
Plyler v. Doe, Texas v. Certain Named and Unnamed Undocumented Alien Children - 8-A
Poisons. *See Hazardous substances.*
Poland
  Loans - 208-209, 221, 230, 257
  Red Cross program - 137
  Presidential messages (text) - 6-E, 22-E-23-E
  Trading status - 163
Police and law enforcement officers. *See Federal Bureau of Investigation; Searches and seizures; Secret Service.*
Political parties. *See Democratic Party; Republican Party.)*
Politics. *See Elections and politics.*
Polk County v. Dodson - 17-A
Pollution. *(See also Air pollution; Environmental health; Environmental Protection Agency; Hazardous substances; Noise pollution; Radiation hazards; Waste disposal and treatment; Water pollution.)*
  Acid rain - 428, 430-432
  Budget - 180 (chart), 182
  Clean Air Act proposals - 425-434
  Research authorization bill - 535
  Superfund enforcement - 451, 453, 455
POMCUS sites - 82, 279, 291
Poor, assistance to. *See Welfare and social services.*
Population - 245
Pornography. *See Obscenity and pornography.*
Porter, John Edward, R-Ill. (10)
  Congressional voting studies - 3-C-40-C
  Defense authorization - 101
  Nuclear freeze resolution - 122
  Refugee resettlement - 414
  Roll call votes - 2-H-135-H
Ports and harbors - 182
Portugal
  Foreign aid - 244
  Military construction funds - 217 (chart)
Post Office. *See Postal Service, U.S.*
Postal Rate Commission - 24-A
Postal service
  Appropriations
    FY 1982 supplemental - 206, 220
    FY 1983 continuing resolution - 239, 273-276
  Budget - 180 (chart), 195
  Franking privileges, congressional - 521
  Mail fraud bill - 531-532
  Subsidies - 239, 273, 275
Postal Service, U.S. - 206
Postsecondary education. *(See also Education Department; Student aid; Vocational education.)*
  Appropriations - 252
  Budget - 181 (chart)
  Indian colleges aid - 501
  Science education - 499-500
Poverty assistance. *See Welfare and social services.*
Powell, Lewis F. Jr.
  Supreme Court background - 3-A-4-A
  Supreme Court term, 1981-1982 - 3-A-18-A

Pratt, George C. - 509
Pratt, Richard T. - 48
Prescription drug industry. *See Drug industry.*
Presidency. *See Executive branch.*
President, U.S. *See Reagan, President Ronald; Executive branch.*
Presidential messages (texts)
  Budget messages - 6-E-13-E, 19-E-21-E
  Caribbean Basin - 15-E-17-E
  Contract disputes veto - 30-E
  Copyright bill veto - 25-E
  Crime legislation - 28-E-29-E
  East-West relations - 21-E-24-E
  Economic report - 13-E-15-E
  Enterprise zones - 17-E-19-E
  Environmental Research Act veto - 30-E-31-E
  Lebanon - 29-E-30-E
  Middle East - 26-E-28-E
  Nuclear arms control - 31-E-33-E
  Petroleum allocations - 17-E
  Supplemental appropriations vetoes - 24-E-26-E
  State of the Union - 3-E-6-E
  Water rights veto - 24-E
President's Commission for the Study of Ethical Problems in Medicine. *See Commission for the Study of Ethical Problems in Medicine.*
President's Council on Environmental Quality. *See Council on Environmental Quality.*
Pressler, Larry, R-S.D.
  Appropriations - 235
  Bus industry deregulation - 338
  Congressional voting studies - 3-C-40-C
  Cuba resolution - 143
  Defense authorization - 108
  FTC used-car rule - 347
  Roll call votes - 2-S-77-S
Preventive medicine - 220, 228
Price-fixing. *See Antitrust and competition.*
Price, Melvin, D-Ill. (23)
  Congressional voting studies - 3-C-40-C
  Defense authorization - 101
  Nuclear freeze resolution - 117
  Roll call votes - 2-H-135-H
Price supports, agricultural. *See Agricultural price supports.*
Princeton University v. Schmid* - 9-A
Print media and publishing. *(See also Government Printing Office.)*
  Copyright bill veto - 380, 25-E
  Electronic publishing - 331-332
Prisons and prisoners
  Federal Prison System appropriations - 220
  Supreme Court cases - 6-A
  Surplus federal property - 400
Pritchard, Joel, R-Wash. (1)
  Appropriations - 225
  Congressional voting studies - 3-C-40-C
  Roll call votes - 2-H-135-H
Privacy protection. *See Freedom of information; Searches and seizures; Wiretapping.)*
Private and parochial schools
  Tax-exempt status - 276, 374, 397-399
  Tuition tax credits - 489-490
Private Industry Council (PIC) - 40
Professional Standards Review Organizations (PSRO) - 471, 473
Property rights, Supreme Court cases - 15-A
Proxmire, William, D-Wis.
  Appropriations - 208-209, 222-223, 235, 241
  Arms sales - 146
  Budget - 204
  Congressional tax deductions - 543
  Congressional voting studies - 3-C-40-C
  Defense authorization - 94-95
  Hart Senate Office Building - 539
  Nuclear waste disposal - 304, 307

Roll call votes - 2-S-77-S
  Water projects - 356
Pryor, David, D-Ark.
  Appropriations - 292
  Congressional voting studies - 3-C-40-C
  Defense authorization - 95
  Highway/gas tax bill - 327
  Mail fraud bill - 531
  Roll call votes - 2-S-77-S
  Tax reconciliation bill - 35
Psychological counseling. *See Mental health and illness.*
Public assistance. *See Welfare and social services.*
Public broadcasting - 205, 252, 254, 340
Public debt. *See Budget, U.S.*
Public financing of elections. *See Campaign financing.*
Public health. *See Health.*
Public Health Service - 206
Public Health Service Commissioned Corps - 206
Public housing and housing assistance. *(See also Middle-income housing assistance.)*
  Appropriations
    FY 1982 supplemental - 205, 221
    FY 1983 - 69, 232-235
  Authorization proposals - 68-70, 72
  Elderly and handicapped - 69
  Indian housing programs - 69
  Public housing modernization - 69
  Supreme Court ruling - 9-A
Public lands. *(See also Bureau of Land Management; Indian lands; National forests; Outer Continental Shelf; Parks and recreation areas; Wild and scenic rivers; Wilderness preservation areas; Wildlife and wildlife refuges.)*
  Conservation programs - 444
  Federal payments in lieu of taxes - 264
  Oil and gas leases - 177, 182, 263-264, 438-439, 461-464
  Oil and gas royalties - 446-448
  Youth conservation corps - 505-506
Public laws
  List - 3-F-15-F
  Totals (box) - 4
Public schools. *See Elementary and secondary education.*
Public service employment programs. *See Employment and training programs.*
Public utilities. *See Utilities.*
Public Works Administration (PWA) - 61 (box)
Publishing industry. *See Print media and publishing.*
Puccio, Thomas H. - 513
Puerto Rico
  Caribbean Basin Initiative - 55
  Food stamp program - 479-483
  Foreign trade - 16-E
  Nutrition assistance - 256
  Veteran health programs - 487
Pullman-Standard v. Swint, United Steelworkers v. Swint - 7-A
Pursell, Carl D. R-Mich. (2)
  Congressional voting studies - 3-C-40-C
  Roll call votes - 2-H-135-H

Q

Quadrennial Commission - 546
Quayle, Dan, R-Ind.
  Appropriations - 227, 241
  Congressional voting studies - 3-C-40-C
  Debt limit - 45
  Defense authorization - 95
  Health planning system - 497-498
  Jobs training program - 40-41
  Roll call votes - 2-S-77-S
Quillen, James H., R-Tenn. (1)
  Congressional voting studies - 3-C-40-C

Roll call votes - 2-H-135-H

R

Radiation hazards
  Nuclear bomb testing - 490-493
  Radiation compensation - 493-494
Radio
  Broadcast deregulation - 341
  Broadcast licenses - 338-339
  International communications policy - 137
  Radio Marti bill - 147-151
  Senate coverage - 540-541
Radio Free Europe - 137, 166
Radio Liberty - 137, 166
Radio Marti
  Appropriations bill - 247, 249-250
  Authorization debate - 137, 147-151
Rahall, Nick J. II, D-W.Va. (4)
  Congressional voting studies - 3-C-40-C
  Roll call votes - 2-H-135-H
Railroad Retirement Board
  Appropriations - 252
  Budget - 184, 192
Railroads. *(See also Amtrak; Conrail; Mass transit.)*
  Appropriations - 267-273
  Authorizations - 320, 346
  Highway/gas tax bill - 320
  Rail strike legislation - 335
  Safety programs - 268, 346
Railsback, Tom, R-Ill. (19)
  Congressional voting studies - 3-C-40-C
  Roll call votes - 2-H-135-H
Railway Association, U.S. (USRA) - 267, 272
Railway Labor Act of 1926 - 335
Railway Labor Executives' Association v. Gibbons - 11-A
Ralston v. Robinson - 6-A
Ramah Navajo School Board v. Bureau of Revenue of New Mexico - 16-A
Randolph, Jennings, D-W.Va.
  Clean Air Act proposals - 428-429
  Congressional voting studies - 3-C-40-C
  Economic development funds - 63
  Roll call votes - 2-S-77-S
  Senate television and radio coverage - 541
Rangel, Charles B., D-N.Y. (19)
  Congressional voting studies - 3-C-40-C
  Health care cuts - 471, 475
  Roll call votes - 2-H-135-H
Rapid Deployment Force (RDF)
  Appropriations - 213-214, 216-219, 282
  Authorization - 88-90
  Military construction funds - 104, 106
RARE II
  Leasing ban - 462-463
  Wilderness bills - 464-466
Ras Banas - 106, 213-214, 216-218
Ratchford, William R., D-Conn. (5)
  Congressional voting studies - 3-C-40-C
  Roll call votes - 2-H-135-H
Rather, Dan - 140
Reagan, President Ronald. *(See also Executive branch; Nominations and confirmations; Presidential messages.)*
  Abortion - 403-405
  Agriculture
    Commodity futures trading bill - 365
    Payment-in-kind (PIK) program - 362
  Arms control - 31-E-33-E
  Budget
    Administration plans - 175-185
    Balanced Budget Amendment - 391-394
    Texts - 4-E, 6-E-13-E, 19-E-21-E
  Commerce and consumer affairs
    Enterprise Zone program - 68, 17-E-19-E (text)
    Rail strike - 335

(continued)

(continued)

(continued)